ENCARTA® THESAURUS

ENCARTA® THESAURUS

GENERAL EDITOR
SUSAN JELLIS

BLOOMSBURY

A BLOOMSBURY REFERENCE BOOK

Created from the Bloomsbury Database of World English

First published in 2001 by
Bloomsbury Publishing Plc
38 Soho Square
London W1D 3HB

www.bloomsburymagazine.com

British Library Cataloguing in Publication Data
A CIP record for this book is available from the British Library

ISBN 0 7475 3905 7

10 9 8 7 6 5 4 3 2 1

Typeset by Selwood Systems, Midsomer Norton, Bath
Printed in the United States of America

Contents

THESAURUS DATABASE

General Editor
Susan Jellis

Thematic Section Editors
Diane Nicholls
David Hallworth

Quotations Editors
Stephen Adamson
James Randall

Project Manager
Katy McAdam

Production Editor
Nicky Thompson

COMPILERS AND EDITORS

Debra Bailey
David Barnett
Jane Bradbury
Patricia Bulhosen
Rebecca Campbell
Robert Clevenger
Dewayne Crawford
Huw Davies
Gloria George
Alice Grandison
Isabel Griffiths

Jennifer Goss Duby
Orin Hargraves
Ruth Hein
Margaret Jull Costa
Barbara Kelly
Imogen Kerr
Stanley A. Kurzban
Laura Lawrie
Jill Leatherbarrow
Wendy Lee
Heloise McGuiness

Duncan Marshall
Martha Mayou
Margaret Mullen
Michael Munro
Paula Parish
Christina Rammell
Fraser Sutherland
Katharine Turok
Donald Watt
Pamela White
Carol Zhong

Project Coordinator
Alasdair Maclean

Database Administrator
Peter Hosking

PROJECT ASSISTANTS

Max Fincher
Emma Harrison
Katherine Hill
Misty Shock
Eleanor Welsh

BLOOMSBURY REFERENCE

Publisher
Nigel Newton

Editor-in-Chief
Dr. Kathy Rooney

Dictionaries' Editor
Faye Carney

U.S. General Editor
Encarta® World English Dictionary
Anne H. Soukhanov

Production Director
Penny Edwards

Database Manager
Edmund Wright

Design Manager
Nathan Burton

Introduction

A **DICTIONARY IS AN ALPHABETICAL LIST** of words and their meanings, a thesaurus groups together words of similar or related meaning. The *Encarta® Thesaurus* has been developed specifically to help users in the twenty-first century answer two frequently asked questions: 'Which word can I use **instead** of this one?' and 'Which words **relate** to this one?'

The *Encarta Thesaurus* is the latest in a long line of language reference works which can trace their ancestry back to the pioneering work of Peter Mark Roget in the mid-nineteenth century. Roget had started collecting words and phrases of similar meaning more than 50 years before his *Thesaurus of English Words and Phrases* was published in 1852, following his retirement from a distinguished career as a scientist. As Roget's introduction spells out, his interest was in classifying words into categories, bringing together words and phrases of similar meaning, 'arranged . . . according to the ideas which they express'. The term 'Thesaurus' means treasure house or store house, indicating the linguistic richness found within its pages. Since Roget's initial publication, the thesaurus has become a staple companion to the dictionary and the book of quotations on reference shelves.

The world today demands fast and clear communication – so being able to choose quickly the best word to use in any context is an important contribution to accurate and elegant communication. The first section of the *Encarta Thesaurus* provides a fast-access alphabetical listing of over 300,000 words of similar meaning (synonyms), listed under 40,000 headings. An important aspect of Roget's original Thesaurus was the listing of words of *opposite* meaning (antonyms) close to the lists of synonyms. This useful feature has been included in the *Encarta Thesaurus,* which lists over 18,000 antonyms.

One of the most innovative aspects of Roget's original compilation was the system of categories into which he grouped the words. A completely new system of categories, reflecting the way language works at the start of the twenty-first century, forms the second section of the *Encarta Thesaurus.* There are over 1,200 themes listing over 50,000 related terms.

The *Encarta Thesaurus* was compiled by a team of experienced editors drawn from English-speaking countries around the world, many of whom also contributed to the *Encarta World English Dictionary.* Linguistic data for the *Encarta Thesaurus* was drawn from the Bloomsbury Database of World English. The compilers' brief was to write a Thesaurus which met the needs of users at the turn of a new millennium. In the days of Peter Mark Roget the intellectual focus was on ideas, concepts and abstract relationships – indeed the first section of Roget's categorization was called 'Abstract Relations'.

Today, however, the focus of language is much more concrete: we will probably need to know types of software more often than the aspects of existence which preoccupied Roget and his contemporaries. In addition, the importance today of English as an international medium of communication means that writers – whether of e-mails or novels, poems or school assignments, business plans or short stories – must strive to express themselves with accuracy and grace, choosing the word most appropriate for its context. The increasing cross-cultural awareness of language differences, accelerated by the spread of computer and Internet use, is reflected in the breadth of words included in the *Encarta Thesaurus*.

QUICK-REFERENCE SECTION

The first part of the book enables users to look up a word in alphabetical order and speedily check its most frequent possible alternatives. The compilers reflected modern usage when choosing and listing alternatives for the words. We have tried to reflect the way a word fits into the grammatical context of a sentence so that users can as often as possible simply substitute the new word into the sentence. For example, *rain* can be used as a noun (*rainfall* or *volley*) or as a verb (*pour* or *lavish*) – synonyms are listed for each of these senses.

Alternatives that are outside the neutral core of English are marked with a label, for example (*formal)* or (*informal)*, to indicate the restrictions on how they should be used.

Care is always needed when choosing an alternative for any word. Only rarely can one word be exchanged for another in all contexts. For example, *sad* and *unhappy* are similar in meaning and are often interchangeable, but it would be unusual to talk about '*an unhappy film*' or '*a sad marriage*'. In the *Encarta Thesaurus*, the lists of alternatives are broadly arranged for ease of use, with the most general alternatives near the beginning of the list, and alternatives that can only be used in more restricted contexts towards the end. Over 130 'Compare and Contrast' notes have been added to help discriminate between the meanings of closely related words. For instance, at the entry for *guide* (meaning *to show somebody the way*) the notes explain the shift in meaning between *conduct*, *direct*, *lead*, *steer* and *usher*.

Many English words have more than one sense. To reflect this, the synonym lists are divided into senses which are based on those in the *Encarta World English Dictionary*. Sometimes the lists of alternative words for different meanings are completely distinct, but sometimes they contain words which themselves have multiple meanings and therefore appear in more than one list. For example, *reasonable* means both 'rational and sensible' and 'fairly good' and appears in the list of alternatives for both these senses of *fair*.

THEMATIC SECTION

In the Thematic Section, the words are grouped according to much broader categories of meaning divided into 1,200 themes. The themes were chosen to reflect the general usage of English today, and each one is enhanced by an apt quotation from the Bloomsbury Quotations Database. The lists of words of related meaning are more extensive than those in the Quick-Reference Section, since the aim of the Thematic Section is to open up to the reader a rich network of linguistic relationship and association. The themes also include extensive sub-listings of 'parts of' large objects – for example, an aircraft or the human body – and 'types of' which list the main members of a group, such as plants or mythological creatures.

The *Encarta Thesaurus* offers the reader both a speedy synonym search in the first section, and a vivid verbal variety in the second. Peter Mark Roget came from French Huguenot stock, and his father was Pastor of the French Protestant Church in London. Today that church is in Soho Square, not far from where our editors compiled the *Encarta Thesaurus*. It is our hope that Roget himself might – from his place in lexicographic history – greet the publication of this volume as a worthy successor to his original work, and as an equally practical companion to the language of today.

How to use the Encarta® Thesaurus

This Thesaurus has a Quick-Reference Section and a Thematic Section. In the alphabetical Quick-Reference Section, you can look up a word and find synonyms for its common meanings. You will sometimes also be offered words with opposite or contrasting meaning.

first synonym indicating the meaning

number to distinguish the senses

reference to the numbered paragraph in the Thematic Section

masses 1 *n* **common people**, crowd, multitude, commonality, hoi polloi, the many, the multitude, the people, grassroots. [➡CLASS STATUS; 891] *Opposite:* elite. 2 *n* (*informal*) **lots**, loads (*informal*), tons (*informal*), heaps (*informal*), oodles (*informal*). [➡MANY, MUCH, LARGE AMOUNT; 118]

massif *n* **mountain range**, chain, sierra, ridge, line. [➡MOUNTAINS AND HILLS; 1047]

massive 1 *adj* **bulky**, heavy, solid, weighty, vast, colossal, great. [➡WEIGHT: HEAVY; 1207] *Opposite:* slight. 2 *adj* **huge**, enormous, gigantic, immense, colossal, substantial, considerable, great, vast, mammoth, giant. [➡LARGE; 1195] *Opposite:* tiny

word with opposite meaning

label indicating the normal range of use

part of speech

All words, whether they have lists of synonyms or not, have a reference to the Thematic Section and the number at which they appear.

giant-sized *adj* [➡LARGE; 1195]

reference to the Thematic Section

In the numbered Thematic Section, you can look for a theme or concept and find a wide-ranging list of broadly related words, listed alphabetically under different parts of speech.

title and number of Thematic Section

label indicating normal range of use

part of speech

1195 Large

(*adj*) airy, almighty (*informal*), astronomical (*informal*), awkward, big, bulging, bulky, capacious, cavernous, colossal, commodious, considerable, cosmic, *cumbrous*, elephantine, enormous, expansive, extensive, extra-large, fantastic, fat, full-size, galactic (*informal*), gargantuan, giant, *giant-sized*, gigantic, ginormous (*informal*), global, good-sized, grand, great, herculean, huge, hulking, humongous (*informal*), immeasurable, immense, inestimable, infinite, jumbo, king-size, large, life-size, mammoth, massive, maxi, measurable, measureless, *mega*, mighty, monolithic, monster, monstrous, monumental, mountainous, outsize, outsized, oversize, *oversized*, prodigious, queen-size, rambling, roomy, significant, sizable, spacious, spectacular, stupendous, substantial, substantive, sweeping, terrific, thumping (*informal*), thundering, tidy, titanic, tremendous, vast, voluminous, walloping (*informal*), whacking (*informal*), whopping (*informal*)

(*n*) airiness, amplitude, bulkiness, *capaciousness*, *chunkiness*, *cumbersomeness*, enormity, expansiveness, extensiveness, *immenseness*, immensity, largeness, magnitude, *ponderousness*, prodigiousness, roominess, *unwieldiness*, vastness, *voluminousness*

words in roman type have a synonym list in the Quick-Reference Section

List of Thematic Categories

Move and Function

Action: Start, Continue, and Finish

Movement and Locomotion

Creation, Production, and Emission

Change and Transformation

Contact and Impact

Obtaining, Losing, and Exchanging Possession

Using and Functioning

People and their Way of Life

Qualities and Characteristics

Emotions and States of Mind

The Written Word

Communication and Interaction

The Human Body and Bodily Functions

The Mind and Mental Processes

Philosophies, Beliefs, and Morality

Social Structures and Institutions

Work and Leisure: Lifestyles and the Home

People

Relationships with Others

The World Around Us

Living Things

The Natural Environment and The Forces of Nature

Space and the Universe

Places and Human Geography

Buildings and Structures

Technology

Energy, Fuels, and Foods

Physical Qualities of Objects

Physical Objects

Sounds

Substances

QUICK-REFERENCE SECTION

A1 (*informal*) *adj* **excellent**, first-rate, first-class, topnotch (*informal*), perfect, flawless, great, superb. [➡EXTRAORDINARY: AMAZING; 205] *Opposite:* inferior.

aardwolf *type of* **canine.** [➡CANINE; 979]

abalone *type of* **aquatic invertebrate.** [➡AQUATIC INVERTEBRATE; 1022]

abandon 1 *v* **dump**, ditch (*informal*), discard, dispose of, throw out, throw away. [➡GET RID OF SOMETHING; 452] *Opposite:* keep. 2 *v* **desert**, leave, walk out on (*informal*), forsake, leave behind, vacate. [➡RUN AWAY AND AVOID; 10] 3 *v* **end**, call off, cancel, give up, stop, halt, abort. [➡CAUSE TO STOP; 267] *Opposite:* continue. 4 *n* **recklessness**, wildness, licence, intemperance, unrestraint, uninhibitedness. [➡INSECURITY AND LOSS OF COMPOSURE; 545] *Opposite:* restraint.

abandoned 1 *adj* **discarded**, forsaken, derelict, vacant, dumped, neglected, cast off, empty. [➡UNPOPULAR AND UNWANTED; 259] 2 *adj* **empty**, deserted, derelict, vacant. [➡EMPTY; 1237] 3 *adj* **wild**, uncontrolled, unrestricted, uninhibited, unrestrained, out of control, reckless. [➡PLEASURE, EXCITEMENT, AND ELATION; 535] *Opposite:* restrained.

abandonment *n* **desertion**, leaving behind, leaving, rejection, neglect, relinquishment. [➡EMPTY; 1237]

abandon ship *v* [➡RUN AWAY AND AVOID; 10]

abase (*literary*) *v* **lower**, demean, degrade, belittle, humiliate, subjugate, denigrate. [➡UPSET, DISTRESS, AND HUMILIATE; 568] *Opposite:* respect.

abasement (*literary*) *n* **degradation**, humiliation, abnegation (*formal*), effacement, belittlement, deprecation, denigration, subjugation. [➡EMBARRASSMENT AND HUMILIATION; 543] *Opposite:* aggrandizement.

abase yourself (*literary*) *v* **grovel**, humble yourself, demean yourself, debase yourself, degrade yourself, lower yourself, efface yourself. [➡FLATTER AND FAWN; 622]

abash *v* [➡CONFUSE AND BEWILDER; 572]

abashed *adj* **embarrassed**, ashamed, mortified, disconcerted, dismayed, confused. [➡EMBARRASSMENT AND HUMILIATION; 543] *Opposite:* unabashed.

abate (*formal or literary*) *v* **decrease**, subside, grow less, decline, fade away, fall, stop, halt, end, terminate (*formal*), lessen. [➡CHANGE OF INTENSITY: LESS; 396] *Opposite:* rise.

abatement 1 *n* **reduction**, cut, drop, fall, decline, diminution, lessening, decrease. [➡LESS; 124] *Opposite:* increase. 2 *n* **deduction**, discount, cut, reduction, decrease, saving. [➡MONEY, PAYMENTS, AND CHARGES; 800] *Opposite:* increment.

abattoir *n* **slaughterhouse**, knacker's yard, shambles (*dated*). [➡INDUSTRIAL BUILDINGS; 1086]

abbey 1 *n* **religious foundation**, religious house, cloister, monastery, convent, priory. [➡PARTS OF RELIGIOUS BUILDINGS; 1085] 2 *type of* **church.** [➡RELIGIOUS BUILDINGS; 1084]

abbot *n* [➡RELIGIOUS PEOPLE; 779]

abbreviate *v* **shorten**, cut, cut short, condense, abridge, truncate, curtail, reduce. [➡CHANGE OF SIZE: SMALLER; 394] *Opposite:* lengthen.

abbreviated *adj* **shortened**, condensed, abridged, truncated, curtailed, reduced. [➡CHANGE OF SIZE: SMALLER; 394] *Opposite:* full-length.

abbreviation *n* **short form**, contraction, ellipsis, acronym, shortening, condensation, abridgment, truncation, curtailment, reduction. [➡ASPECTS OF LANGUAGE; 683]

ABC 1 *n* **alphabet**, Roman alphabet, spelling system. [➡SYMBOLS, SIGNS, AND NUMBERS; 597] 2 *n* **basics**, fundamentals, essentials, rudiments, nitty-gritty (*informal*), nuts and bolts (*informal*). [➡BASIC DETAILS; 689]

abdicate *v* **renounce**, relinquish, resign, step down, hand over, give up, abandon. [➡FOREGO AND DENY ONESELF; 450] *Opposite:* accept.

abdication *n* **resignation**, handing over, renunciation, abandonment, relinquishment. [➡FOREGO AND DENY ONESELF; 450]

abdomen 1 *part of* **torso.** [➡TORSO; 694] 2 *part of* **insect.** [➡PARTS OF AN INSECT; 1019]

abdominal *adj* **stomach**, belly, front, intestinal, gut. [➡THE DIGESTIVE TRACT; 710]

abdominals *type of* **muscle or tendon.** [➡THE MUSCLES; 719]

abduct *v* **kidnap**, make off with, seize, hold somebody against his or her will, capture, snatch (*US informal*). [➡STEAL AND ROB; 427]

abduction *n* **kidnap**, seizure, kidnapping, carrying off, capture, snatching (*US informal*). [➡CRIMES; 817]

abductor *n* **kidnapper**, hostage taker, captor, hijacker, snatcher (*US informal*). [➡CRIMINALS; 821]

abecedarian *n* [➡STUDENTS AND PUPILS; 841]

aberrant *adj* **abnormal**, unusual, deviant, anomalous, peculiar, uncharacteristic, irregular, atypical, eccentric, odd. [➡BIZARRE AND PECULIAR; 258] *Opposite:* normal.

aberration *n* **deviation**, abnormality, anomaly, irregularity, peculiarity, eccentricity, oddness, unusualness. [➡MISTAKES; 251]

abet 1 *v* **assist**, help, support, aid, back, back up. [➡HELP; 294] *Opposite:* hinder. 2 *v* **encourage**, urge, connive, put up to, incite. [➡MAKE POSSIBLE; 276] *Opposite:* deter.

abhor (*formal*) *v* **detest**, hate, loathe, dislike, despise, be repulsed, be revolted. [➡DISLIKE AND HATE; 578] *Opposite:* adore.

abhorrence *n* **hatred**, loathing, detestation, disgust, repugnance, revulsion, abomination (*literary*), aversion. [➡IRRITATION AND ANGER; 542] *Opposite:* adoration.

See Compare and Contrast at **dislike**.

abhorrent (*formal*) *adj* **repugnant**, objectionable, repulsive, detestable, hateful, distasteful, disgusting. [➡DISGUSTING AND REPULSIVE; 231] *Opposite:* desirable.

abide 1 *v* (*archaic*) **dwell** (*literary*), live, lodge (*dated*), have your home, stay. [➡INHABIT; 20] 2 *v* **put up with**, stand for, stand, bear, stomach, take, tolerate, accept. [➡TOLERATE AND ENDURE; 767] 3 *v* (*archaic*) **withstand**, endure, survive, resist, bear, weather, tolerate. [➡CONTINUE TO EXIST; 17]

abide by *v* **obey**, follow, keep to, conform to, stick to, adhere to, accept. [➡OBEY AND ABIDE BY; 302] *Opposite:* defy.

abiding *adj* **enduring**, remaining, surviving, long-lasting, unshakable, steadfast, permanent. [➡PERMANENCE: WITHOUT END; 94] *Opposite:* transient.

ability *n* **aptitude**, skill, proficiency, competence, capacity, capability, talent, gift, knack. [➡SKILLS, TALENTS, AND ABILITIES; 527]

Compare and Contrast: ***ability, skill, competence, aptitude, talent, capacity, capability***

CORE MEANING: THE NECESSARY SKILL, KNOWLEDGE, OR EXPERIENCE TO DO SOMETHING

ability natural and acquired skills or knowledge; ***skill*** proficiency gained through training or experience; ***competence*** ability measured against a standard; ***aptitude*** a natural tendency to do something well; ***talent*** an unusual natural ability to do something well; ***capacity*** mental or physical ability for something or to do something; ***capability*** the ability of a person or machine to do something.

a bit (*informal*) *adv* **slightly**, rather, somewhat, a little, a tad (*informal*). [➡TO A CERTAIN EXTENT; 134] *Opposite:* very.

abject 1 *adj* **hopeless**, miserable, wretched, dismal, horrible, gloomy, utter. [➡ABSOLUTE AND ABSOLUTELY; 131] 2 *adj* **humble**, servile, meek, submissive, subservient, deferential, self-effacing. [➡LEVELS OF FORMALITY; 523]

abjection 1 *n* **wretchedness**, misery, desolation, despair, despondence, distress, gloom, unhappiness, abjectness, hopelessness. [➡SADNESS, DISTRESS, AND DESPAIR; 540] *Opposite:* cheerfulness. 2 *n* **humility**, humbleness, subservience, deference, servility, meekness, submissiveness. [➡LEVELS OF FORMALITY; 523] *Opposite:* confidence.

abjectly 1 *adv* **wretchedly**, miserably, desolately, despairingly, despondently, gloomily, unhappily, hopelessly, dismally. [➡SADNESS, DISTRESS, AND DESPAIR; 540] *Opposite:* cheerfully. 2 *adv* **humbly**, submissively, subserviently, deferentially, self-effacingly, meekly. [➡LEVELS OF FORMALITY; 523] *Opposite:* confidently.

abjuration *n* **renunciation**, rejection, disavowal (*formal*), denial, repudiation, abnegation (*formal*), refrainment, avoidance, abstention. [➡FOREGO AND DENY ONESELF; 450] *Opposite:* affirmation.

abjure 1 *v* **renounce**, reject, repudiate, abnegate (*formal*), deny, disavow (*formal*). [➡DENY AND REJECT; 645] 2 *v* (*literary*) **abstain**, forswear, refrain, reject, deny yourself, shun, give up, refuse. [➡FOREGO AND DENY ONESELF; 450]

ablaze *adj* **on fire**, blazing, burning, in flames, alight, afire, aflame. [➡FIRE, FLAMMABILITY, AND BURNING; 1164]

able 1 *adj* **capable**, competent, proficient, adept, skilled. [➡TALENTED AND SKILFUL; 528] *Opposite:* incompetent. 2 *adj* **clever**, talented, intelligent, bright, gifted. [➡POSITIVE INTELLECTUAL CHARACTERISTICS; 525] *Opposite:* incapable.

See Compare and Contrast at **intelligent**.

able-bodied *adj* **healthy**, fit, well, active, strong, vigorous. [➡FIT AND STRONG; 737] *Opposite:* weak.

ablutions (*formal or humorous*) *n* **washing**, bathing, cleansing, wash, clean up, wash and brush up. [➡CLEAN AND POLISH; 404]

ably *adv* **capably**, well, skilfully, competently, with ease, proficiently, adeptly, easily. [➡TALENTED AND SKILFUL; 528] *Opposite:* incompetently.

abnegate (*formal*) *v* **renounce**, reject, deny, repudiate, abjure, give up, shun, refrain, abstain, disavow (*formal*), forswear (*archaic or literary*). [➡FOREGO AND DENY ONESELF; 450] *Opposite:* accept.

abnegation (*formal*) *n* **rejection**, renunciation, repudiation, denial, abstention, refrainment, avoidance, disavowal (*formal*). [➡FOREGO AND DENY ONESELF; 450]

abnormal *adj* **irregular**, nonstandard, uncharacteristic, atypical, anomalous, unusual, strange, odd, peculiar, deviant, aberrant, malformed. [➡BIZARRE AND PECULIAR; 258] *Opposite:* normal.

abnormality 1 *n* **defect**, deformity, irregularity, malformation, malfunction, fault. [➡FAULTS, FLAWS, AND WEAKNESSES; 252] 2 *n* **irregularity**, aberration, anomaly, deviation, oddity, idiosyncrasy. [➡FAULTS, FLAWS, AND WEAKNESSES; 252]

aboard 1 *adv* **on board**, on the ship, on the bus, on the train, on the plane. [➡LACK OF ACTIVITY; 343] 2 *adv* (*informal*) **involved**, participating, on the team, with us, on our side, on the books, with. [➡PRESENT AND AVAILABLE; 11] 3 *prep* **on to**, on, in to, inside. [➡RELATIVE LOCATION; 162]

abode (*literary*) *n* **house**, dwelling (*formal*), home, residence, place, lodgings (*dated*). [➡ACCOMMODATION; 855]

abolish *v* **put an end to**, eliminate, close down, bring to an end, stop, do away with, eradicate, get rid of, obliterate, end. [➡ABOLISH AND ANNUL; 453] *Opposite:* establish.

abolition *n* **elimination**, ending, closing down, eradication, closure, obliteration. [➡END; 54] *Opposite:* establishment.

abolitionist *n* **opponent**, objector, protester, eradicator, adversary, enemy, foe (*literary*). [➡UNCOOPERATIVE OR REBELLIOUS PERSON; 567] *Opposite:* supporter.

A-bomb *n* **atom bomb**, neutron bomb, nuclear missile, nuclear warhead, nuclear weapon, bomb. [➡EXPLOSIVES; 1154]

abominable *adj* **dreadful**, repulsive, offensive, detestable, monstrous, terrible, awful, horrible, vile, horrendous, repugnant, atrocious, revulsive. [➡DISGUSTING AND REPULSIVE; 231]

Abominable Snowman *n* **yeti**, bigfoot, sasquatch. [➡MYTHICAL BEINGS; 790]

abominate (*formal*) *v* **hate**, loathe, detest, abhor (*formal*), despise, dislike, disapprove. [➡DISLIKE AND HATE; 578] *Opposite:* love.

abomination 1 *n* **outrage**, disgrace, scandal, eyesore, atrocity, horror. [➡NUISANCES; 254] 2 *n* (*literary*) **hatred**, dislike, repugnance, loathing, revulsion, abhorrence, detestation, disgust. [➡DISLIKE AND HATE; 578] *Opposite:* love.

aboriginal *adj* **indigenous**, original, native, autochthonous, local. [➡COUNTRIES AND REGIONS; 1066]

See Compare and Contrast at **native**.

abort *v* **terminate** (*formal*), end, abandon, call off, call a halt, cancel, stop midstream, break off, halt, stop, quit. [➡CAUSE TO STOP; 267]

abortive *adj* **unsuccessful**, failed, fruitless, unproductive, futile, bungled (*informal*). [➡UNSUCCESSFUL AND UNPROMISING; 76] *Opposite:* successful.

abound 1 *v* **thrive**, flourish, prosper, proliferate, overflow, swarm, be plentiful, be abundant. [➡PROSPER AND ABOUND; 16] 2 *v* **brim**, overflow, throng, teem, be rich in, be abundant in. [➡PROSPER AND ABOUND; 16]

abounding *adj* **many**, varied, multifarious, plenteous (*literary*), plentiful, abundant, fruitful. [➡MANY, MUCH, LARGE AMOUNT; 117] *Opposite:* scarce.

about 1 *prep* **concerning**, regarding, in relation to, on the subject of, on, with reference to, as regards, apropos (*formal*), vis-à-vis, re. [➡EXPRESSIONS OF REFERENCE; 63] 2 *adv* **approximately**, roughly, in the region of, around, almost, nearly, approaching, not far off, of the order of, going on for, nigh on, roughly speaking, more or less, something like, just about, on the order of (*US*). [➡APPROXIMATELY; 133] 3 *adv* **around**, close, nearby, near. [➡PRESENT AND AVAILABLE; 11]

about-face (*US*) 1 *n* **turnaround**, U-turn, reversal, shift, transformation, about-turn, sea change, change of heart, change of tack, volte-face. [➡DECISIVE MOMENTS; 44] 2 *n* **turn**, U-turn, 180° turn, revolution. [➡CHANGE DIRECTION OF MOTION; 345]

about to *prep* **ready to**, on the verge of, on the point of, just going to, set to, all set to, on the brink of. [➡FUTURE; 86]

about to happen *adv* [➡ABOUT TO HAPPEN; 33]

about-turn 1 *n* **turnaround**, U-turn, reversal, shift, transformation, change of tack, sea change, change of heart, volte-face, about-face (*US*). [➡DECISIVE MOMENTS; 44] 2 *n* **turn**, U-turn, 180° turn, revolution. [➡CHANGE DIRECTION OF MOTION; 345]

above 1 *prep* **more than**, greater than, higher than, beyond, exceeding. [➡MORE AND EXCESS; 122] *Opposite:* below. 2 *prep* **on top of**, over, higher than, atop (*literary*). [➡RELATIVE LOCATION; 162] *Opposite:* below.

above all *adv* **especially**, in particular, primarily, principally, most of all. [➡MAINLY AND PRIMARILY; 138]

above average *adj* [➡GOOD, WELL, BETTER; 184]

aboveboard 1 *adj* **open**, fair, honest, forthright, straightforward, legal, on the level (*informal*), lawful, kosher (*informal*), correct, legitimate, regular. [➡MORALLY GOOD; 775] *Opposite:* shady. 2 *adv* **openly**, fairly, honestly, legally, lawfully. [➡LEGAL; 815] *Opposite:* illegally.

above criticism *adj* [➡MORALLY GOOD; 775]

abovementioned *adj* **aforementioned** (*formal*), aforesaid (*formal*), said. [➡EXPRESSIONS OF REFERENCE; 63]

above reproach *adj* **blameless**, irreproachable, unimpeachable, honest, decent, virtuous, upright, honourable. [➡HONEST AND RELIABLE; 503] *Opposite:* dishonourable.

above suspicion *adj* **honest**, decent, irreproachable, unimpeachable, innocent, reliable, trustworthy, dependable. [➡HONEST AND RELIABLE; 503] *Opposite:* dubious.

abracadabra *interj* **hocus-pocus**, open sesame, hey presto (*informal*), voilà. [➡THE SUPERNATURAL; 788]

abrade *v* **graze**, scrape, roughen, chafe, grind down, grind, scratch, scuff, rub, rasp. [➡WORSEN APPEARANCE; 383] *Opposite:* smooth.

abrasion *n* **scrape**, scratch, scuff, graze. [➡CONDITIONS AFFECTING THE SKIN; 722]

abrasive 1 *adj* **rough**, coarse, harsh, rasping, scratchy, grainy. [➡PHYSICAL TEXTURE; 1221] *Opposite:* smooth. 2 *adj* **rude**, sharp, harsh, brusque, argumentative, aggressive, unfriendly, gruff, severe. [➡RUDE AND HOSTILE; 626] *Opposite:* gentle.

abrasively *adv* **harshly**, roughly, brusquely, aggressively, insensitively, unfeelingly. [➡RUDE AND HOSTILE; 626] *Opposite:* gently.

abrasiveness *n* **harshness**, roughness, brusqueness, aggressiveness, insensitivity, unfeelingness. [➡BAD MANNERS AND SOCIAL SKILLS; 522] *Opposite:* gentleness.

abreast 1 *adv* **side by side**, alongside, shoulder to shoulder, beside, level, next to. [➡RELATIVE LOCATION; 162] 2 *adj* **well-informed**, in touch, up-to-date, up on, up with, in on, au fait, au courant. [➡KNOWLEDGE AND WISDOM; 559]

abridge *v* **shorten**, edit, condense, abbreviate, reduce, curtail, slash. [➡CHANGE OF SIZE: SMALLER; 394] *Opposite:* expand.

abridged *adj* **shortened**, edited, condensed, reduced, abbreviated. [➡CHANGE OF SIZE: SMALLER; 394] *Opposite:* complete.

abridgement *see* **abridgment**.

abridgment *n* **synopsis**, digest, condensation, précis, abstract, summary, brief. [➡SUMMARIES, OUTLINES, AND EXCERPTS; 589]

abroad *adv* **overseas**, away, out of the country. [➡COUNTRIES AND REGIONS; 1066]

abrogate (*formal*) *v* **repeal**, revoke, rescind, retract, annul, abolish, nullify, do away with. [➡ABOLISH AND ANNUL; 453]

See Compare and Contrast at **nullify.**

abrogation (*formal*) *n* **retraction**, repeal, annulment, abolition, rescindment, revocation, nullification. [➡END; 54]

abrupt 1 *adj* **sudden**, unexpected, unforeseen, rapid, hasty, immediate, quick, rushed. [➡HAPPENING QUICKLY; 104] *Opposite:* gradual. 2 *adj* **curt**, short, brusque, terse, rude, gruff, snappy, snappish, sharp. [➡BAD-TEMPERED AND HUMOURLESS; 627] *Opposite:* polite.

abruptness 1 *n* **suddenness**, unexpectedness, rapidity, hastiness, quickness. [➡SPEED; 102] *Opposite:* slowness. 2 *n* **brusqueness**, shortness, terseness, sharpness, rudeness, gruffness, snappiness. [➡UNINTERESTED AND DETACHED; 630] *Opposite:* politeness.

abscess *n* **boil**, pustule, swelling, eruption, blister, carbuncle, sore, inflammation. [➡CONDITIONS AFFECTING THE SKIN; 722]

abscond *v* **run away**, escape, break out, make off, flee, run off. [➡RUN AWAY AND AVOID; 10]

absconder *n* **deserter**, runaway, escapee, fugitive, truant, absentee. [➡RUNAWAYS AND ABSENTEES; 9]

absence 1 *n* **nonappearance**, absenteeism, time off. [➡ABSENT AND UNAVAILABLE; 7] *Opposite:* presence. 2 *n* **lack**, nonexistence, deficiency, want, dearth, privation. [➡ABSENT AND UNAVAILABLE; 7] *Opposite:* surplus.

absent 1 *adj* **missing**, gone, out, away. [➡ABSENT AND UNAVAILABLE; 7] *Opposite:* present. 2 *adj* **inattentive**, absent-minded, far away, preoccupied, vague. [➡NEUTRALITY AND INDIFFERENCE; 554] *Opposite:* alert. 3 *adj* **lacking**, deficient, nonexistent, in short supply. [➡ABSENT AND UNAVAILABLE; 7] *Opposite:* present.

absentee *n* **truant**, defaulter, runaway, absconder. [➡RUNAWAYS AND ABSENTEES; 9]

absenteeism *n* **absence**, skiving (*informal*), nonattendance, nonappearance, bunking off (*informal*), truancy. [➡WORK-RELATED ACTIVITIES; 834]

absently *adv* **inattentively**, vaguely, dreamily, distractedly, abstractedly, absent-mindedly. [➡NEUTRALITY AND INDIFFERENCE; 554] *Opposite:* attentively.

absent-minded *adj* **forgetful**, distracted, scatterbrained, preoccupied, vague, scatty (*informal*), daydreaming, dreamy, inattentive, abstracted, idle. [➡NEGATIVE INTELLECTUAL CHARACTERISTICS; 526] *Opposite:* attentive.

absent-mindedness *n* **forgetfulness**, vagueness, dreaminess, inattentiveness, scattiness (*informal*), distraction, abstraction, idleness. [➡NEGATIVE INTELLECTUAL CHARACTERISTICS; 526] *Opposite:* concentration.

absent without leave *adj* [➡ABSENT AND UNAVAILABLE; 7]

absent yourself *v* **excuse yourself**, send your apologies, stay away. [➡ABSENT ONESELF; 8] *Opposite:* attend.

absolute 1 *adj* **total**, complete, utter, unqualified, out-and-out, outright, entire. [➡WHOLENESS AND COMPLETENESS; 199] 2 *adj* **unconditional**, unlimited, supreme, unmodified, unadulterated, pure, perfect, unquestionable, unequivocal, unbounded. [➡ABSOLUTE AND ABSOLUTELY; 131] *Opposite:* provisional. 3 *adj* **conclusive**, resolved, firm, fixed, definite, unmovable, final, unchangeable, certain. [➡CERTAIN; 175] *Opposite:* unconfirmed. 4 *n* **given**, rule, principle, truth, fundamental. [➡TRUE AND REAL; 172]

absolution *n* **forgiveness**, pardon, release, freedom, liberty. [➡RELIGIONS AND RELIGIOUS PRACTICES; 778]

absolutism *n* **totalitarianism**, despotism, dictatorship, tyranny, autocracy, authoritarianism. [➡STYLES AND SYSTEMS OF GOVERNMENT; 806]

absolve *v* **pardon**, forgive, clear, release, free, liberate, remit, excuse. [➡FORGET, FORGIVE, AND ACCEPT; 749] *Opposite:* punish.

absorb 1 *v* **soak up**, attract, take in, take up, suck up, sop up. [➡FILL; 407] *Opposite:* exude. 2 *v* **understand**, learn, grasp, admit, take in, recognize, realize. [➡UNDERSTAND AND GRASP; 760] 3 *v* **engross**, fascinate, engage, captivate, grip, enthral, rivet (*informal*). [➡APPEAL TO AND AROUSE INTEREST; 576] *Opposite:* bore.

absorbed *adj* **engrossed**, wrapped up, fascinated, captivated, riveted (*informal*), immersed, rapt, engaged, enthralled, gripped, interested. [➡PENSIVENESS AND INTEREST; 539] *Opposite:* detached.

absorbency *n* **porosity**, sponginess, permeability, penetrability, perviousness. [➡FLUID AND NON-SOLID; 1212]

absorbent *adj* **porous**, spongy, permeable, penetrable, pervious. [➡FLUID AND NON-SOLID; 1212]

absorbing *adj* **fascinating**, engrossing, captivating, gripping, riveting (*informal*), enthralling, spellbinding, interesting, engaging. [➡INTERESTING AND MEANINGFUL; 191] *Opposite:* boring.

absorption 1 *n* **preoccupation**, fascination, interest, captivation, engagement, immersion, raptness, concentration, enthralment, engrossment. [➡ATTENTION AND ATTENTIVENESS; 764] 2 *n* **amalgamation**, incorporation, assimilation, combination, inclusion. [➡COMBINE AND MIX; 401] *Opposite:* rejection.

absorptive *adj* [➡FLUID AND NON-SOLID; 1212]

absorptivity *n* [➡FLUID AND NON-SOLID; 1212]

abstain 1 *v* **desist**, refrain, withdraw, withhold, go without, give up, curb. [➡NOT DO AND REFUSE TO DO; 275] *Opposite:* indulge. 2 *v* **sit on the fence**, stay neutral, not take sides. [➡ELECTIONS AND SUFFRAGE; 807] *Opposite:* vote.

abstainer 1 *n* **refrainer**, avoider, shunner, teetotaller, withholder. [➡ASCETIC PEOPLE; 883] 2 *n* **nonvoter**, hedger, fence sitter. [➡ELECTIONS AND SUFFRAGE; 807]

abstemious *adj* **self-denying**, self-disciplined, moderate, ascetic, sober, temperate, teetotal. [➡ABSTEMIOUSNESS AND SELF-DENIAL; 882] *Opposite:* unrestrained.

abstemiousness *n* **sobriety**, self-denial, moderation, temperance, self-discipline, asceticism, judiciousness. [➡ABSTEMIOUSNESS AND SELF-DENIAL; 882] *Opposite:* excess.

abstention *n* **nonparticipation**, abstaining, refraining, holding back. [➡ELECTIONS AND SUFFRAGE; 807]

abstinence *n* **self-denial**, self-restraint, self-discipline, moderation, asceticism. [➡ABSTEMIOUSNESS AND SELF-DENIAL; 882] *Opposite:* indulgence.

abstinent *adj* **ascetic**, abstemious, sober, temperate, teetotal, dry. [➡ABSTEMIOUSNESS AND SELF-DENIAL; 882] *Opposite:* indulgent.

abstract 1 *adj* **nonconcrete**, intellectual, mental, immaterial, intangible, nonfigurative, nonrepresentational. [➡ARTISTIC MOVEMENTS AND STYLES; 899] *Opposite:* concrete. 2 *adj* **theoretical**, conceptual, conjectural, hypothetical, speculative, academic. [➡FALSE AND UNREAL; 174] *Opposite:* practical. 3 *n* **summary**, extract, précis, synopsis, abridgment, short version. [➡SUMMARIES, OUTLINES, AND EXCERPTS; 589] 4 *v* **conceptualize**, theorize, hypothesize, intellectualize. [➡DEVELOP THEORIES AND REASON; 745] 5 *v* **summarize**, condense, shorten, précis, abridge, synopsize. [➡CHANGE OF SIZE: SMALLER; 394] *Opposite:* expand. 6 *v* **extract**, take out, select, remove, separate, isolate. [➡EXTRACT AND SEVER; 342]

abstracted *adj* **inattentive**, preoccupied, vague, distant, distracted, absent-minded. [➡NEUTRALITY AND INDIFFERENCE; 554] *Opposite:* alert.

abstractedness *n* **preoccupation**, inattentiveness, inattention, pensiveness, distractedness, vagueness, dreaminess. [➡NOT PAY ATTENTION; 765] *Opposite:* alertness.

abstract expressionism *type of* **20th-century art movement**. [➡ARTISTIC MOVEMENTS AND STYLES; 899]

abstraction 1 *n* **pensiveness**, preoccupation, dreaminess, vagueness, daydreaming, woolgathering. [➡NOT PAY ATTENTION; 765] *Opposite:* concentration. 2 *n* **concept**, idea, thought, notion, construct, generalization, intellection (*formal*), perception. [➡IDEA AND THOUGHT; 771] *Opposite:* fact. 3 *n* **removal**, extraction, withdrawal, deduction. [➡REMOVE SOMETHING; 339] *Opposite:* inclusion.

abstractly *adv* **theoretically**, conceptually, hypothetically, in theory. [➡UNCERTAIN; 176] *Opposite:* practically.

abstruse *adj* **obscure**, perplexing, puzzling, complex, profound, mysterious, rarefied, technical, highbrow, recondite, difficult. [➡DIFFICULTY AND COMPLEXITY; 243] *Opposite:* simple.

See Compare and Contrast at **obscure**.

abstrusely *adv* **obscurely**, unclearly, unintelligibly, incomprehensibly, puzzlingly, perplexingly, mysteriously, profoundly. [➡SECRET AND UNKNOWN; 180] *Opposite:* clearly.

abstruseness *n* **complexity**, obscurity, difficulty, profundity, mysteriousness, perplexity. [➡DIFFICULTY AND COMPLEXITY; 243] *Opposite:* simplicity.

absurd 1 *adj* **ridiculous**, silly, strange, illogical, irrational, bizarre, incongruous, ludicrous, farcical. [➡BIZARRE AND PECULIAR; 258] *Opposite:* reasonable. 2 *adj* **meaningless**, pointless, futile, empty, purposeless, hollow. [➡REDUNDANT AND USELESS; 241]

absurdity 1 *n* **farce**, joke, nonsense, incongruity. [➡BIZARRE AND PECULIAR; 258] 2 *n* **illogicality**, irrationality, silliness, ludicrousness, ridiculousness, meaninglessness, incongruity, farcicality, preposterousness. [➡BIZARRE AND PECULIAR; 258] *Opposite:* logic.

absurdly *adv* **ridiculously**, farcically, nonsensically, ludicrously, incongruously, preposterously, oddly. [➡BIZARRE AND PECULIAR; 258] *Opposite:* reasonably.

absurdness 1 *n* **ludicrousness**, ridiculousness, preposterousness, irrationality, incongruity, illogicality, farcicality, silliness. [➡BIZARRE AND PECULIAR; 258] *Opposite:* reasonableness. 2 *n* **meaninglessness**, pointlessness, futility, emptiness, purposelessness, hollowness. [➡REDUNDANT AND USELESS; 241]

abundance *n* **profusion**, plenty, richness, wealth, copiousness, lavishness. [➡MANY, MUCH, LARGE AMOUNT; 117] *Opposite:* scarcity.

abundant *adj* **plentiful**, copious, rich, profuse, ample, lavish. [➡MANY, MUCH, LARGE AMOUNT; 117] *Opposite:* scarce.

a bundle of laughs *n* **good fun**, laugh (*informal*), a barrel of monkeys, gas (*informal*), a barrel of laughs, riot (*informal*), a lot of fun. [➡FUNNY AND AMUSING; 217]

abuse 1 *n* **mistreatment**, cruelty, ill-treatment, violence, maltreatment, neglect, exploitation. [➡UNKIND ACTION OR BEHAVIOUR; 297] 2 *n* **misuse**, exploitation, manipulation, taking advantage, mishandling, misapplication. [➡MISUSE AND ABUSE; 472] 3 *n* **insults**, verbal abuse, swearing, name-calling, foul language, invective (*formal*). [➡INSULTS, ABUSE, AND SWEARING; 659] 4 *v* **exploit**, take advantage, misuse, manipulate. [➡MISUSE AND ABUSE; 472] 5 *v* **treat badly**, ill-treat, mistreat, maltreat, molest, be violent towards, batter, hurt, harm, injure. [➡WOUND A PERSON OR ANIMAL; 384] *Opposite:* look after. 6 *v* **insult**, swear, shout abuse, hurl abuse, shout insults, call names, use foul language. [➡INSULTS, ABUSE, AND SWEARING; 659] *Opposite:* compliment.

See Compare and Contrast at **misuse**.

abused *adj* **ill-treated**, physically abused, battered, badly treated, injured, harmed, mistreated, maltreated, neglected, molested. [➡IN TROUBLE AND DISADVANTAGED; 73] *Opposite:* looked after.

abusive 1 *adj* **rude**, insulting, unmannerly, foul, offensive, obnoxious. [➡RUDE AND HOSTILE; 626] *Opposite:* polite. 2 *adj* **violent**, cruel, vicious, sadistic, rough. [➡MORALLY BAD; 776] *Opposite:* gentle.

abusiveness *n* **rudeness**, unpleasantness, impoliteness, nastiness, vulgarity, offensiveness. [➡UNKIND ACTION OR BEHAVIOUR; 297]

abut *v* **be next to**, adjoin, border, be adjacent to, touch, lie alongside, bound, neighbour. [➡EXIST IN CLOSE PROXIMITY; 21]

abutment *n* **support**, buttress, prop, strut, brace, bulwark. [➡SUPPORTS AND BASES; 1254]

abutting *adj* **adjoining**, next to, bordering, adjacent to, against, neighbouring. [➡CLOSENESS; 160]

abuzz *adj* **alive**, throbbing, humming, pulsating, busy, lively. [➡ENERGY AND ENTHUSIASM; 497] *Opposite:* still.

abysmal *adj* **terrible**, awful, dreadful, horrible, appalling, bad. [➡BAD AND BADLY; 224] *Opposite:* superb.

abyss *n* **gulf**, chasm, gorge, hole, void, depth. [➡HOLES, GAPS, AND FORKS; 1251]

acacia *type of* **deciduous tree.** [➡DECIDUOUS TREES; 1028]

academe (*formal*) *n* [➡EDUCATIONAL INSTITUTIONS; 813]

academia *n* **academic world**, academic circles, academe (*formal*), university, university circles, ivory tower, the academy (*US*), college circles (*US*). [➡EDUCATIONAL INSTITUTIONS; 813]

academic 1 *adj* **educational**, school, college, university, scholastic. [➡EDUCATION; 838] 2 *adj* **studious**, intellectual, scholarly, bookish, literary, learned. [➡KNOWLEDGE AND WISDOM; 559] 3 *adj* **theoretical**, speculative, abstract, moot, hypothetical. [➡FALSE AND UNREAL; 174] *Opposite:* practical. 4 *n* **lecturer**, researcher, instructor, college lecturer, teacher, professor, scholar, tutor, don. [➡EDUCATORS; 840]

academic circles *n* [➡EDUCATIONAL INSTITUTIONS; 813]

academic world *n* [➡EDUCATIONAL INSTITUTIONS; 813]

academy *n* **school**, college, conservatory, conservatoire, arts school, private school, military institute (*US*). [➡EDUCATIONAL INSTITUTIONS; 813]

a cappella *type of* **musical term.** [➡MUSICAL TERMS; 912]

a case in point *n* **working example**, instance, case, paradigm, illustration, living proof, proof positive. [➡EVIDENCE AND PROOF; 69]

accede 1 *v* **agree**, assent, consent, comply, grant, allow. [➡AGREE; 646] *Opposite:* reject. 2 *v* **come into**, inherit, succeed, take over, enter upon, attain, ascend. [➡GET; 421]

accelerate *v* **go faster**, speed up, increase speed, gather speed, pick up the pace, pick up speed, hurry, hasten, step up, quicken, rush, fast-track. [➡CHANGE OF SPEED: MORE; 397] *Opposite:* slow down.

accelerated *adj* **speeded up**, faster, quicker, quickened up, hurried up, enhanced, augmented, fast-tracked, speeded, hastened. [➡MOVING QUICKLY; 103] *Opposite:* slowed down.

acceleration 1 *n* **increase of rate**, increase of velocity, spurt, burst of speed. [➡SPEED; 102] *Opposite:* deceleration. 2 *n* **speeding up**, stepping up, hastening, hurrying, quickening, rushing. [➡CHANGE OF SPEED: MORE; 397] *Opposite:* deceleration.

accelerator *part of* **controls.** [➡VEHICLES; 1144]

accelerator card *type of* **hardware.** [➡COMPUTERS AND COMPUTING; 1126]

accent 1 *n* **pronunciation**, inflection, intonation, tone of voice, enunciation, drawl, twang, brogue, burr. [➡THE SPOKEN WORD; 672] 2 *n* **emphasis**, stress, beat, accentuation, inflection, prominence. [➡MOST IMPORTANT THING; 198] 3 *type of* **diacritic.** [➡ASPECTS OF LANGUAGE; 683] 4 *v* **emphasize**, stress, accentuate, put stress on, give weight to, give prominence to, highlight, heighten, put the accent on, draw attention to. [➡CLAIM, INSIST, AND EMPHASIZE; 615]

accentuate *v* **emphasize**, highlight, put emphasis on, stress, draw attention to, bring out, put the accent on, heighten, make a feature of, give prominence to, give weight to. [➡CLAIM, INSIST, AND EMPHASIZE; 615] *Opposite:* play down.

accentuation 1 *n* **prominence**, highlighting, attention, notice, emphasis, stress. [➡IMPORTANCE AND SIGNIFICANCE; 193] 2 *n* **accent**, rhythm, stress, inflection, beat, emphasis. [➡ASPECTS OF LANGUAGE; 683]

accept 1 *v* **receive**, take, agree to take, admit. [➡ACCEPT POSSESSION; 451] *Opposite:* refuse. 2 *v* **consent**, agree, say yes, say you will, give a positive response, assent, accede. [➡APPROVE AND CONFIRM; 647] *Opposite:* turn down. 3 *v* **put up with**, endure, tolerate, bow, take, resign yourself. [➡TOLERATE AND ENDURE; 767] 4 *v* **believe**, recognize, agree, admit, acknowledge, understand, allow (*formal*). [➡UNDERSTAND AND GRASP; 760] *Opposite:* deny. 5 *v* **take on**, undertake, acknowledge, assume, bear, shoulder. [➡AGREE; 646] *Opposite:* reject.

acceptability *n* **suitability**, adequacy, appropriateness, tolerability. [➡ACCEPTABLE AND PASSABLE; 220]

acceptable 1 *adj* **satisfactory**, suitable, good enough, adequate, up to standard, tolerable, appropriate, okay (*informal*), all right. [➡ACCEPTABLE AND PASSABLE; 220] *Opposite:* unacceptable. 2 *adj* **welcome**, pleasing, gratifying, agreeable, enjoyable. [➡ACCEPTABLE AND PASSABLE; 220] *Opposite:* annoying.

acceptably *adv* **well enough**, adequately, sufficiently well, suitably, tolerably, passably, reasonably. [➡ACCEPTABLE AND PASSABLE; 220] *Opposite:* unreasonably.

acceptance 1 *n* **agreement**, assent, acquiescence, concurrence, accession, favourable reception. [➡AGREE; 646] *Opposite:* refusal. 2 *n* **receipt**, taking, getting, reception, receiving. [➡ACCEPT POSSESSION; 451] *Opposite:* rejection. 3 *n* **belief**, acknowledgment, credence, currency, agreement, approval. [➡AGREE; 646] 4 *n* **recognition**, approval, tolerance, acknowledgment, toleration. [➡FORGET, FORGIVE, AND ACCEPT; 749] *Opposite:* disapproval.

accepted *adj* **conventional**, established, customary, acknowledged, usual, traditional, time-honoured, received, expected, normal. [➡ORDINARINESS; 245] *Opposite:* unconventional.

accepting *adj* **tolerant**, compliant, patient, long-suffering, uncomplaining, accommodating, acquiescent. [➡THE WILL AND WILLINGNESS; 564]

access 1 *n* **way in**, entrance, entry, approach, gate, door. [➡DOORS AND ACCESS POINTS; 1100] 2 *n* **right of entry**, admission, right to use, admittance, entrée, contact. [➡PERMIT AND ALLOW; 670] 3 *v* **get into**, gain access to, retrieve, call up, log on, read, open. [➡COMPUTERS AND COMPUTING; 1126]

accessibility *n* **convenience**, user-friendliness, openness, availability, approachability, ease of access, ease of understanding, ease of use. [➡USEFULNESS; 200]

accessible 1 *adj* **nearby**, available, reachable, easily reached, handy, to hand, at hand, within reach, open, manageable. [➡USEFULNESS; 200] *Opposite:* inaccessible. 2 *adj* **comprehensible**, understandable, user-friendly, easy to use, clear, straightforward, simple. [➡EASE AND SIMPLICITY; 201] *Opposite:* obscure. 3 *adj* **approachable**, affable, genial, friendly, welcoming. [➡FRIENDLINESS AND SOCIABILITY; 495] *Opposite:* unapproachable.

accessibly 1 *adv* **conveniently**, handily, suitably, helpfully, usefully. [➡USEFULNESS; 200] *Opposite:* inconveniently. 2 *adv* **clearly**, simply, understandably, comprehensibly, straightforwardly, helpfully. [➡EASE AND SIMPLICITY; 201] *Opposite:* obscurely.

accession 1 *n* **attainment**, succession, taking over, taking office, appointment. [➡BEGINNING; 53] 2 *n* **agreement**, consent, concurrence, accord, assent, compliance. [➡AGREE; 646]

accessorize *v* **ornament**, decorate, beautify, trim, embellish, garnish, adorn. [➡DRESS, WEAR, AND UNDRESS; 868]

accessory 1 *n* **addition**, decoration, fixture, fitment, attachment, adjunct, auxiliary, add-on, extra, trimming, accompaniment, adornment, embellishment. [➡ORNAMENTS AND DECORATIONS; 1247] 2 *n* **accomplice**, partner, partner in crime, assistant, abettor, co-conspirator, collaborator. [➡CRIMINALS; 821]

accessory

◆ *types of accessory*
bandanna, belt, bootlace, bow tie, braces, cravat, cummerbund, dicky (*informal*), dicky bow (*informal*), earmuffs, glove, handkerchief, hat, jewellery, mitt, mitten, muff, muffler, neckerchief (*US*), necktie (*US*), pashmina, sash, scarf, shawl, stole, suspenders (*US*), tie, veil, wrap

access profile *n* [➡E-COMMERCE; 1128]

access road *type of* **minor road.** [➡ROADS; 1105]

access strip *type of* **minor road.** [➡ROADS; 1105]

accident 1 *n* **chance**, coincidence, fortune, fate. [➡CHANCE, COINCIDENCE, AND ACCIDENT; 787] *Opposite:* design. 2 *n* **crash**, collision, bump, smash, smash-up, pile-up (*informal*), shunt (*informal*). [➡TRAFFIC ACCIDENTS; 256] 3 *n* **mishap**, misfortune, calamity, catastrophe, disaster, industrial accident, upset, mistake. [➡DISASTERS; 253]

accidental *adj* **unintentional**, unintended, inadvertent, chance, unplanned, fortuitous. [➡CHANCE, COINCIDENCE, AND ACCIDENT; 787] *Opposite:* deliberate.

accidentally *adv* **by chance**, by accident, by mistake, unintentionally, inadvertently, fortuitously, by coincidence, out of the blue. [➡UNINTENTIONAL AND ACCIDENTAL; 282] *Opposite:* on purpose.

accident-prone *adj* **ill-fated**, unfortunate, unlucky, ill-starred (*formal*), doomed, disaster-prone. [➡BAD LUCK AND UNLUCKY; 785]

acclaim 1 *v* **praise**, sing the praises of, give approval, hail, commend, applaud, cheer. [➡PRAISE AND ENCOURAGE; 648] *Opposite:* criticize. 2 *n* **approval**, praise, commendation, acclamation, approbation, applause, compliments. [➡PRAISE AND ENCOURAGE; 648] *Opposite:* disapproval.

acclaimed *adj* **praised**, admired, commended, celebrated, applauded. [➡EXTRAORDINARY: AMAZING; 205]

acclamation 1 *n* **acclaim**, praise, commendation, approbation, approval. [➡PRAISE AND ENCOURAGE; 648] 2 *n* **applause**, clapping, cheering, ovation, roar, cheers. [➡APPLAUSE; 653] *Opposite:* jeering.

acclimate *v* **get used to**, become accustomed, accustom, adapt, adjust, familiarize, acclimatize. [➡CHANGE; 373]

acclimatization *n* **adaptation**, getting used to, becoming accustomed, adjustment, accommodation, familiarization. [➡CHANGE; 373]

acclimatize *v* **get used to**, become accustomed, accustom, adapt, adjust, familiarize. [➡CHANGE; 373]

acclimatize yourself *v* [➡CHANGE OF MOOD AND COMPOSURE; 581]

accolade *n* **tribute**, honour, compliment, palm, award, praise, rave review (*informal*). [➡REWARDS AND AWARDS; 440]

accommodate 1 *v* **house**, lodge, put up, billet, quarter, provide lodgings, provide accommodation. [➡TAKE CARE OF AND SPOIL; 301] 2 *v* **contain**, have room for, hold, seat, have capacity for, be big enough for. [➡HOLD AND CONTAIN; 456] 3 *v* **get used to**, adapt, adjust, become accustomed to, familiarize, acclimatize, acclimate. [➡CHANGE; 373] 4 *v* **assist**, help, oblige, be of service, find ways to help. [➡HELP; 294]

accommodating *adj* **helpful**, willing, obliging, compliant, cooperative, accepting, long-suffering. [➡THE WILL AND WILLINGNESS; 564] *Opposite:* uncooperative.

accommodation 1 *n* **lodging**, housing, room, space, place, accommodations (*US*). [➡ACCOMMODATION; 855] 2 *n* **adjustment**, adaptation, alteration, change, modification. [➡CHANGE; 373]

accommodation address *n* [➡ACCOMMODATION; 855]

accommodations (*US*) *n* **housing**, lodging, room, space, place, accommodation. [➡ACCOMMODATION; 855]

accompanied by *adv* **along with**, together with, with, in the company of, in consort with (*archaic or formal*). [➡RELATED; 143]

accompaniment *n* **supplement**, accessory, garnish, adjunct, complement, addition, auxiliary, trimming, side dish. [➡PHYSICAL OBJECTS; 1242]

accompanist *n* **pianist**, instrumentalist, musician, player. [➡MUSICIANS AND SINGERS; 908]

accompany 1 *v* **escort**, go with, go together with, go along with, attend, convoy. [➡ACCOMPANY AND FOLLOW; 338] 2 *v* **go together with**, come with, be an adjunct to, supplement, complement, be associated with, be tied in with. [➡RECIPROCITY AND INTERDEPENDENCE; 148]

accompanying *adj* **supplementary**, associated, complementary, additional, add-on. [➡MORE AND EXCESS; 122]

accomplice *n* **partner in crime**, assistant, accessory, collaborator, co-conspirator, partner, abettor. [➡CRIMINALS; 821]

accomplish *v* **achieve**, complete, do, finish, get done, bring about, carry out, realize, pull off (*informal*), attain. [➡CARRY OUT AN ACTION; 270]

Compare and Contrast: ***accomplish, achieve, attain, realize, carry out, pull off***

CORE MEANING: TO BRING SOMETHING TO A SUCCESSFUL CONCLUSION

accomplish succeed in doing something; ***achieve*** succeed in something, usually with effort; ***attain*** reach a specific objective; ***realize*** to fulfil a specific vision or plan; ***carry out*** perform or accomplish a task or activity; ***pull off*** (*informal*) accomplish something, despite difficulties.

accomplished *adj* **talented**, skilful, gifted, skilled, proficient, expert, consummate, able, adept, capable. [➡TALENTED AND SKILFUL; 528]

accomplishment 1 *n* **completion**, execution, carrying out, finishing, realization, achievement, attainment. [➡CARRY OUT AN ACTION; 270] 2 *n* **feat**, achievement, triumph, success, deed, exploit. [➡SUCCESS; 82] 3 *n* **talent**, skill, ability, expertise, capability, endowment. [➡SKILLS, TALENTS, AND ABILITIES; 527]

accord 1 *v* **render** (*formal*), give, confer (*formal*), bestow (*formal*), afford (*formal*), allow, permit. [➡GIVE AND PROVIDE; 431] 2 *v* **agree**, concur, fit, match, correspond, be in harmony with. [➡HARMONY; 156] *Opposite:* clash. 3 *n* **agreement**, treaty, settlement, pact, deal. [➡OFFICIAL DOCUMENTS; 587] 4 *n* **consensus**, harmony, concurrence, unity, agreement, solidarity. [➡HARMONY; 156]

accordingly 1 *adv* **appropriately**, suitably, correspondingly, fittingly. [➡APPROPRIATE, SUITABLE, ADVISABLE; 185] *Opposite:* inappropriately. 2 *adv* **so**, for that reason, therefore, hence (*formal*), as a result, in consequence (*formal*), consequently (*formal*), thus (*formal*). [➡CAUSATION; 169]

according to 1 *prep* **as said by**, as stated by, on the word of. [➡EXPRESSIONS OF REFERENCE; 63] 2 *prep* **consistent with**, along with, in line with, in keeping with, in relation to, in proportion to, in accordance with, as per. [➡HARMONY; 156] *Opposite:* counter to.

according to plan *adv* **as intended**, as proposed, as organized, as arranged, as suggested, swimmingly, perfectly, flawlessly. [➡CORRECT; 183]

accordion *type of* **keyboard**. [➡MUSICAL INSTRUMENTS; 910]

accost *v* **approach**, stop, confront, buttonhole (*informal*), detain, hound. [➡INITIATE AND ESTABLISH COMMUNICATION; 681]

account 1 *n* **report**, description, story, relation, narrative. [➡EXPLAIN AND CLARIFY; 611] 2 *n* **explanation**, version, interpretation, justification, reason, excuse. [➡EXPLAIN AND CLARIFY; 611] 3 *n* **bank account**, cheque account, current account, deposit account, savings account, checking account (*US*). [➡ACCOUNTING, BANKING, AND BUDGETING; 799] 4 *n* **arrangement**, credit, tally, balance, bill, tab (*US informal*). [➡RECEIPTS AND INVOICES; 592]

accountability *n* **answerability**, responsibility, liability, culpability. [➡RESPONSIBILITY; 171]

accountable *adj* **answerable**, responsible, liable, held responsible, blamed. [➡RESPONSIBILITY; 171]

accountant *n* **bookkeeper**, auditor, chartered accountant, certified accountant, cost accountant. [➡PEOPLE INVOLVED IN FINANCE; 804]

account for 1 *v* **explain**, justify, give an explanation for, give a reason for, answer for. [➡EXPLAIN AND CLARIFY; 611] 2 *v* **comprise**, make up, total, represent, constitute, form. [➡AMOUNT TO AND EQUAL; 70]

account holder *n* [➡ACCOUNTING, BANKING, AND BUDGETING; 799]

accounting *adj* [➡FINANCE AND ECONOMICS; 797]

accounts *n* **books**, balance sheet, financial statement. [➡ACCOUNTING, BANKING, AND BUDGETING; 799]

accounts clerk *n* [➡PEOPLE INVOLVED IN FINANCE; 804]

accoutrement *n* **accessory**, trapping, trimming, appurtenance (*formal*), tool of the trade, equipment. [➡PHYSICAL OBJECTS; 1242]

accoutrements *n* [➡ORNAMENTS AND DECORATIONS; 1247]

accredit *v* **recognize**, sanction, endorse, authorize, certify, certificate, approve. [➡APPROVE AND CONFIRM; 647]

accreditation *n* **authorization**, endorsement, approval, certification, sanction, recognition, qualification. [➡APPROVE AND CONFIRM; 647]

accredited *adj* **credited**, attributed, qualified, endorsed, ascribed (*formal*), official, recognized, certified, approved. [➡APPROPRIATE, SUITABLE, ADVISABLE; 185] *Opposite:* unofficial.

accretion 1 *n* **accumulation**, buildup, increase, enlargement, addition, growth, amassment, agglomeration. [➡CHANGE OF SIZE: BIGGER; 393] *Opposite:* erosion. 2 *n* **deposit**, layer, mass, lump, bump, growth, addition, pile. [➡MANY, MUCH, LARGE AMOUNT; 117]

accrual *n* **accumulation**, increase, buildup, accretion, addition, growth, enlargement. [➡CHANGE OF SIZE: BIGGER; 393] *Opposite:* loss.

accrue *v* **accumulate**, ensue, grow, mount up, build up, amass, increase, add, enlarge. [➡CHANGE OF SIZE: BIGGER; 393] *Opposite:* dwindle.

accumulate *v* **build up**, mount up, accrue, amass, collect, gather, hoard, add, store, pile up, assemble, stockpile. [➡GET; 421] *Opposite:* disperse.

See Compare and Contrast at **collect**.

accumulation 1 *n* **buildup**, accretion, accrual, gathering, growth, addition, increase, enlargement, amassing. [➡CHANGE OF SIZE: BIGGER; 393] 2 *n* **collection**, stock, store, hoard, deposit, heap. [➡COLLECTIONS AND MIXTURES OF THINGS; 1243]

accumulative 1 *adj* **acquisitive**, hoarding, materialistic, covetous, grasping, avaricious. [➡FINANCIALLY MEAN AND GRASPING; 520] 2 *adj* **incremental**, increasing, rising, growing, mounting, amassing, piling up, progressive, gradual, cumulative. [➡CHANGE OF SIZE: BIGGER; 393]

accumulator 1 *n* **bet**, wager, flutter (*informal*), stake, gamble, money. [➡GAMBLE AND TAKE RISKS; 467] **2** *n* **collector**, saver, amasser, magpie (*informal*), squirrel (*informal*). [➡PEOPLE WHO COLLECT THINGS; 455] **3** *type of* **software.** [➡COMPUTERS AND COMPUTING; 1126]

accuracy *n* **correctness**, accurateness, exactness, precision, truth, truthfulness, exactitude. [➡EXACT; 204] *Opposite:* inaccuracy.

accurate *adj* **precise**, correct, exact, true, truthful, perfect. [➡EXACT; 204] *Opposite:* inaccurate.

accursed (*archaic or literary*) **1** *adj* **doomed**, ill-fated, fated, ill-starred (*formal*), damned, cursed, under a curse. [➡BAD LUCK AND UNLUCKY; 785] *Opposite:* blessed. **2** *adj* **awful**, horrible, terrible, appalling, hateful, detestable, vile, foul. [➡EMOTIONALLY UNPLEASANT AND UPSETTING; 228]

accusation *n* **allegation**, indictment, claim, complaint, charge, denunciation. [➡CRITICISMS AND ANGRY OUTBURSTS; 50]

accusatorial (*formal*) **1** *adj* **critical**, judgmental, condemnatory, accusing, reproachful, reproving, fault-finding, harsh, severe, accusatory (*formal*). [➡ACCUSATORY AND DISAPPROVING; 635] **2** *adj* **adversarial**, confrontational, argumentative, combative, antagonistic. [➡ACCUSATORY AND DISAPPROVING; 635] *Opposite:* amicable.

accusatorially (*formal*) *adv* [➡ACCUSATORY AND DISAPPROVING; 635]

accusatory (*formal*) *adj* [➡ACCUSATORY AND DISAPPROVING; 635]

accuse *v* **blame**, lay blame on, indict, point the finger, allege, fault, reproach, censure, charge, denunciate (*formal*), inculpate (*formal*). [➡ACCUSE, BLAME, AND CRITICIZE; 642]

accuser **1** *n* **challenger**, confronter, criticizer, opponent, faultfinder, complainant. [➡ENEMIES AND TORMENTORS; 969] **2** *n* **indicter**, litigant, petitioner, appellant, complainant, prosecutor (*US*). [➡PEOPLE IN LAW COURTS; 820] **3** *n* **informer**, telltale, talebearer, whistle-blower, sneak, grass (*slang*), supergrass (*informal*), nark (*slang*), tattletale (*US*). [➡INTERFERING PEOPLE AND TELLTALES; 950]

accusing *adj* **reproachful**, condemning, reproving, critical, condemnatory, accusatory (*formal*), accusatorial (*formal*). [➡ACCUSATORY AND DISAPPROVING; 635]

accustom *v* **get to know**, get used to, acclimatize, acclimate, become accustomed to, familiarize, adjust, adapt, acquaint, inure. [➡LEARN AND DISCOVER; 763]

accustomed **1** *adj* **familiar**, familiarized, habituated (*formal*), inured, adapted, comfortable. [➡CALMNESS, CONFIDENCE, AND COMPOSURE; 537] *Opposite:* unaccustomed. **2** *adj* **usual**, habitual, regular, familiar, customary, favourite. [➡ORDINARINESS; 245] *Opposite:* unusual.

accustomed to *adj* **in the habit of**, given to, used to, at home, prone to. [➡KNOWLEDGE AND WISDOM; 559]

accustom yourself *v* [➡CHANGE OF MOOD AND COMPOSURE; 581]

ace **1** *n* **champion**, top player (*informal*), star, expert, winner, victor. [➡TALENTED OR INTELLIGENT PERSON; 529] **2** *v* (*US slang*) **pass with flying colours**, do well, sail through, get an A on (*US*), max (*US slang*). [➡SUCCEED AND WIN; 79] *Opposite:* fail. **3** *adj* (*informal*) **first-rate**, top, world-class, wonderful, super (*informal*), excellent, brilliant, champion, star, leading, topnotch (*informal*) [➡EXTRAORDINARY: AMAZING; 205]. *Opposite:* lousy (*informal*).

acerbic *adj* **cutting**, bitter, caustic, acid, sour, mordant, barbed, biting, critical, harsh, pointed, sarcastic. [➡RUDE AND HOSTILE; 626] *Opposite:* mild.

acerbity *n* **sharpness**, bitterness, sourness, acidity, acrimony, mordancy, pointedness, causticity, causticness. [➡RUDE AND HOSTILE; 626]

acetate *type of* **plastic.** [➡PLASTICS; 1133]

acetylene *type of* **gas.** [➡GASES; 1274]

ache **1** *v* (*formal*) **long**, desire, yearn, want, wish, burn, hanker, pine, crave, hunger. [➡DESIRE AND WANT; 580] **2** *v* **hurt**, throb, be painful, sting, smart, be killing. [➡PAIN AND OTHER PHYSICAL SENSATIONS; 734] **3** *n* **pain**, throbbing, aching, twinge, headache, stomachache, backache. [➡PAIN AND OTHER PHYSICAL SENSATIONS; 734]

achene *n* [➡PARTS OF TREES AND PLANTS; 1026]

achievable *adj* **attainable**, realizable, possible, reachable, doable, practicable, feasible, viable, realistic. [➡POSSIBLE AND PROBABLE; 178] *Opposite:* unrealistic.

achieve *v* **attain**, realize, accomplish, reach, complete, do, carry out, pull off (*informal*), succeed, triumph. [➡SUCCEED AND WIN; 79] *Opposite:* fail.

See Compare and Contrast at **accomplish.**

achievement *n* **attainment**, accomplishment, success, feat, triumph, realization. [➡SUCCESS; 82] *Opposite:* failure.

achiever *n* **high-flier**, go-getter (*informal*), doer, self-starter, success. [➡TALENTED OR INTELLIGENT PERSON; 529] *Opposite:* loser.

Achilles heel *n* **weakness**, flaw, failing, weak point, chink in somebody's armour, weak spot. [➡FAULTS, FLAWS, AND WEAKNESSES; 252]

Achilles tendon *type of* **muscle or tendon.** [➡THE MUSCLES; 719]

aching **1** *adj* **painful**, sore, tender, throbbing, sensitive, hurting, stinging, achy. [➡PAIN AND OTHER PHYSICAL SENSATIONS; 734] **2** *n* **ache**, pain, painful feeling, throbbing, throb, twinge, sore spot, sting. [➡PAIN AND OTHER PHYSICAL SENSATIONS; 734] **3** *n* (*formal*) **longing**, desire, yearning, pining, itch, craving, hunger, hankering. [➡DESIRE AND WANT; 580]

achy *adj* **aching**, painful, hurting, sore, tender, sensitive. [➡PAIN AND OTHER PHYSICAL SENSATIONS; 734]

acid **1** *adj* **acidic**, tart, sour, bitter, sharp. [➡TASTE; 704] *Opposite:* sweet. **2** *adj* **cutting**, biting, caustic, acerbic, mordant, barbed, harsh, critical. [➡RUDE AND HOSTILE; 626] *Opposite:* mild.

acidic *adj* **acid**, tart, sour, bitter, sharp. [➡TASTE; 704] *Opposite:* sweet.

acidity *n* **sourness**, sharpness, tartness, bitterness. [➡TASTE; 704] *Opposite:* sweetness.

acidly *adv* **sharply**, cuttingly, tartly, sourly, acerbically, bitterly, bitingly, caustically. [➡RUDE AND HOSTILE; 626] *Opposite:* sweetly.

acid stomach *n* [➡DISORDERS OF THE DIGESTIVE SYSTEM; 714]

acid test *n* **litmus test**, touchstone, trial, indicator, confirmation. [➡EVIDENCE AND PROOF; 69]

acknowledge 1 *v* **admit**, recognize, allow (*formal*), accept, concede, grant, confess, own up, fess up (*US informal*). [➡AGREE; 646] *Opposite:* deny. 2 *v* **greet**, salute, wave, nod, hail. [➡GESTURES AND GESTICULATION; 654] *Opposite:* ignore. 3 *v* **reply**, answer, respond, react, return, rejoin (*formal*). [➡REPLY AND ANSWER; 669] *Opposite:* ignore.

acknowledged *adj* **recognized**, approved, known, accredited, accepted, agreed. [➡KNOWN AND FAMOUS; 182] *Opposite:* denied.

acknowledgment 1 *n* **greeting**, salutation, nod, wave, salute. [➡GREETINGS, FAREWELLS, AND SALUTATIONS; 660] 2 *n* **response**, reply, reaction, answer, rejoinder (*formal*), retort. [➡REPLY AND ANSWER; 669] 3 *n* **recognition**, acceptance, admission, confession, appreciation, tribute. [➡AGREE; 646]

acme *n* **peak**, summit, top, zenith, pinnacle, culmination, apex, apogee. [➡INTERMEDIATE STAGES; 55] *Opposite:* nadir.

acned *adj* [➡COMPLEXION; 481]

acolyte 1 *n* **attendant**, assistant, aide, helper. [➡BOSSES AND MANAGEMENT; 965] 2 *n* **follower**, devotee, disciple, adherent, supporter, admirer, enthusiast. [➡DEVOTEES AND ADDICTED PEOPLE; 557]

acorn *type of* **nut**. [➡NUTS; 1184]

acoustic *adj* **audio**, aural, auditory, audile, sound. [➡ACOUSTICS; 1137]

acoustics *n* **audibility**, auditory range, sound quality. [➡ACOUSTICS; 1137]

acquaint *v* **make aware**, inform, let know, let in on, apprise (*formal*), make familiar with, explain, notify, tell, run by, familiarize. [➡INFORM AND ANNOUNCE; 612] *Opposite:* keep from.

acquaintance 1 *n* **associate**, friend, contact, colleague, consociate (*formal*), confrère (*formal*). [➡FRIENDS; 963] *Opposite:* stranger. 2 *n* **knowledge**, familiarity, understanding, awareness, conversance. [➡KNOWLEDGE AND WISDOM; 559] *Opposite:* ignorance. 3 *n* **relationship**, contact, association, friendship, relations. [➡RELATIONSHIP TO ANOTHER; 973]

acquaintanceship 1 *n* **social circle**, circle, friendship group, company, acquaintance. [➡FRIENDS AND ACQUAINTANCES; 936] 2 *n* **knowledge**, familiarity, awareness, understanding, grasp, appreciation, acquaintance. [➡KNOWLEDGE AND WISDOM; 559] *Opposite:* unfamiliarity.

acquainted *adj* [➡RELATIONSHIP TO ANOTHER; 973]

acquiesce *v* **agree**, comply, accept, consent, assent, give in, submit, go along with, yield, concede, concur, accede. [➡AGREE; 646] *Opposite:* resist.

See Compare and Contrast at **agree.**

acquiescence *n* **agreement**, consent, compliance, submission, acceptance, assent. [➡AGREE; 646] *Opposite:* resistance.

acquiescent *adj* **agreeable**, compliant, yielding, accepting, submissive, consenting, willing. [➡THE WILL AND WILLINGNESS; 564] *Opposite:* resistant.

acquire 1 *v* **obtain**, get, get hold of, get your hands on, gain, attain, buy, purchase, come by, procure, secure, pick up. [➡GET; 421] *Opposite:* lose. 2 *v* **develop**, learn, pick up, take up, assimilate. [➡LEARN AND DISCOVER; 763] *Opposite:* drop.

See Compare and Contrast at **get.**

acquisition 1 *n* **gaining**, attainment, achievement, getting hold of, purchase, procurement, acquirement. [➡FIND; 464] *Opposite:* loss. 2 *n* **purchase**, possession, asset, gain. [➡PURCHASE; 423]

acquisitive *adj* **greedy**, covetous, grasping, avaricious, materialistic. [➡FINANCIALLY MEAN AND GRASPING; 520] *Opposite:* generous.

acquisitiveness *n* **greed**, hoarding, avarice, covetousness, materialism. [➡FINANCIALLY MEAN AND GRASPING; 520] *Opposite:* generosity.

acquit *v* **find not guilty**, clear, set free, free, release, exonerate. [➡TRIAL, PUNISHMENT, AND LEGAL OUTCOMES; 819] *Opposite:* convict.

acquittal *n* **release**, discharge, freeing, clearing, exoneration. [➡TRIAL, PUNISHMENT, AND LEGAL OUTCOMES; 819] *Opposite:* conviction.

acquit yourself *v* **conduct yourself**, act, behave, perform, work, comport yourself (*formal*). [➡CARRY OUT AN ACTION; 270]

acreage *n* **land**, estate, property, domain, acres. [➡SIZE AND DIMENSIONS; 1191]

acres 1 *n* **land**, estate, domain, property, acreage. [➡SIZE AND DIMENSIONS; 1191] 2 *n* (*informal*) **expanse**, stretch, tracts, swathes, masses (*informal*), lots. [➡MANY, MUCH, LARGE AMOUNT; 117]

acrid 1 *adj* **pungent**, harsh, unpleasant, choking, bitter, sour, tart. [➡TASTE; 704] *Opposite:* pleasant. 2 *adj* **sharp**, cutting, caustic, bitter, vitriolic, mordant, trenchant, acerbic. [➡RUDE AND HOSTILE; 626]

acridly *adv* **bitterly**, pungently, unpleasantly, sharply, sourly, acerbically, acidly. [➡TASTE; 704]

acrimonious *adj* **spiteful**, rancorous, discordant, hostile, unfriendly, harsh. [➡RUDE AND HOSTILE; 626] *Opposite:* amicable.

acrimony *n* **bitterness**, spite, rancour, animosity, hostility, unfriendliness, ill will, bad blood, bad feeling. [➡ANTAGONISM; 553] *Opposite:* harmony.

acrobat *n* **tumbler**, trapeze artist, circus performer, gymnast, funambulist, entertainer. [➡PEOPLE IN SPORTS AND LEISURE; 876]

acrobatic *adj* **gymnastic**, athletic, lithe, supple, flexible. [➡AGILITY OF THE BODY; 477]

acrobatics 1 *n* **gymnastics**, aerobics, physical exercises, callisthenics. [➡HOBBIES, GAMES, AND SPORTS; 875] 2 *n* **agility**, skill, dexterity, nimbleness, quickness, gymnastics, virtuosity. [➡SKILLS, TALENTS, AND ABILITIES; 527]

acronym *n* **abbreviation**, short form, shortening, contraction, condensation. [➡ASPECTS OF LANGUAGE; 683]

acrophobia *type of* **phobia**. [➡FEARS AND PHOBIAS; 555]

across *adv* **crossways**, crosswise, transversely, athwart, diagonally, from corner to corner. [➡ORIENTATION AND ALIGNMENT; 1222]

across-the-board *adj* **comprehensive**, sweeping, all-embracing, wide-ranging, far-reaching, universal, extensive, wholesale. [➡ALL; 126]

acrostic *type of* **wordplay**. [➡JOKES AND TEASING; 675]

acrylic *type of* **synthetic fabric**. [➡FABRICS; 1131]

act 1 *n* **action**, deed, doing, undertaking, exploit, performance, achievement, accomplishment, feat. [➡ACTIONS OR UNDERTAKINGS; 260] 2 *n* **performance**, entertainment, turn, piece, item. [➡PERFORMANCES AND SHOWS; 42] 3 *n* **pretence**, show, sham, put-on (*informal*), con, feint, ploy, play-acting, hamming. [➡DECEPTION AND LIES; 661] 4 *n* **law**, piece of legislation, statute, decree, enactment, measure, bill. [➡THE LAW AND LEGAL AUTHORITY; 814] 5 *v* **take action**, take steps, proceed, be active, perform, operate, work, get down to, get on, get going, do your stuff. [➡CARRY OUT AN ACTION; 270] 6 *v* **behave**, conduct yourself, comport yourself (*formal*), acquit yourself, perform. [➡CARRY OUT AN ACTION; 270] 7 *v* **pretend**, put on an act, put it on, play, fake, feign, play-act (*informal*), ham it up. [➡PRETEND AND MIMIC; 60] 8 *v* **replace**, represent, act on behalf of, appear on behalf of, speak for. [➡REPRESENT SOMETHING OR SOMEBODY; 59] 9 *v* **function**, work, take effect, produce a result, produce an effect, do its stuff. [➡FUNCTION SUCCESSFULLY; 470] 10 *v* **perform**, act out, be in, appear, play, represent, enact, portray. [➡THE PERFORMING ARTS; 904]

act for *v* [➡REPRESENT SOMETHING OR SOMEBODY; 59]

acting 1 *n* **drama**, the theatre, amateur dramatics, performing, the stage, performing arts. [➡THE PERFORMING ARTS; 904] 2 *adj* **temporary**, substitute, stand-in, interim. [➡REPRESENTATIVE; 66] *Opposite:* permanent.

action 1 *n* **act**, deed, exploit, achievement, accomplishment, feat, stroke. [➡ACTIONS OR UNDERTAKINGS; 260] *Opposite:* inaction. 2 *n* **lawsuit**, suit, proceedings, charge, case. [➡TRIAL, PUNISHMENT, AND LEGAL OUTCOMES; 819] 3 *n* **battle**, fighting, combat, conflict, engagement, encounter, clash, skirmish, dogfight, raid, war, warfare. [➡AGGRESSIVE EVENT; 39]

actionable *adj* **illegal**, criminal, unlawful, tortious. [➡ILLEGAL; 816] *Opposite:* legal.

actioner (*informal*) *n* [➡FILM; 901]

action movie *n* [➡FILM; 901]

action-packed *adj* **exciting**, thrilling, gripping, enthralling, suspenseful, dynamic, vigorous, fast-moving, energetic. [➡EMOTIONALLY PLEASANT; 188] *Opposite:* dull.

activate *v* **make active**, set in motion, set off, turn on, trigger, start, get going, stimulate, galvanize, initiate, motivate, actuate (*formal*). [➡CAUSE TO START; 266] *Opposite:* stop.

activation *n* **start**, beginning, initiation, instigation, stimulation, motivation, galvanization, triggering. [➡BEGINNING; 53]

active 1 *adj* **lively**, vigorous, energetic, full of life, on the go, full of zip (*informal*), dynamic. [➡ENERGY AND ENTHUSIASM; 497] *Opposite:* inactive. 2 *adj* **in force**, functioning, effective, in action, operating, operational, functional, working. [➡HAPPENING AND IN PROGRESS; 32] 3 *adj* **working**, practising, involved, committed, enthusiastic, keen. [➡EMPLOYMENT STATUS; 831] *Opposite:* half-hearted.

actively *adv* **vigorously**, aggressively, energetically, enthusiastically, dynamically, keenly. [➡WITH ENTHUSIASM; 287] *Opposite:* half-heartedly.

activeness *n* **activity**, liveliness, animation, energy, vitality, vigour. [➡ENERGY AND ENTHUSIASM; 497] *Opposite:* passiveness.

activism *n* **direct action**, political action, social action, involvement, engagement, crusading, politicking, do-gooding (*informal*). [➡GOVERNMENT POLICIES; 810]

activist *n* **campaigner**, protester, objector, militant, advocate. [➡UNCOOPERATIVE OR REBELLIOUS PERSON; 567]

activity 1 *n* **pursuit**, interest, hobby, occupation, leisure interest, endeavour, pastime. [➡LEISURE AND RECREATION; 874] 2 *n* **action**, movement, motion, bustle, commotion, goings-on (*informal*). [➡ACTIONS OR UNDERTAKINGS; 260] *Opposite:* inactivity.

act of contrition *n* [➡RELIGIOUS CONCEPTS; 777]

act on 1 *v* **follow up on**, tackle, start in on, take action. [➡START AN ACTION; 261] 2 *v* **have an effect on**, work, affect, perform. [➡CHANGE; 373]

act on behalf of *v* [➡REPRESENT SOMETHING OR SOMEBODY; 59]

actor 1 *n* **performer**, artist, thespian, artiste, player. [➡PERFORMERS; 905] 2 *type of* **entertainer**. [➡WORKERS IN ENTERTAINMENT AND MEDIA; 873]

act out 1 *v* **enact**, perform, portray, act, play, represent, dramatize. [➡THE PERFORMING ARTS; 904] 2 *v* **work out**, work through, exorcize, express, purge, expel. [➡GET RID OF SOMETHING; 452]

actress *n* **performer**, artist, thespian, artiste, player. [➡PERFORMERS; 905]

actual *adj* **real**, genuine, authentic, concrete, tangible, definite. [➡TRUE AND REAL; 172]

actuality 1 *n* **fact**, certainty, reality, practicality, actual fact, real fact. [➡TRUE AND REAL; 172] 2 *n* **real life**, the real world, here and now, reality. [➡PRESENT; 85]

actualize *v* [➡CAUSE TO HAPPEN; 31]

actually *adv* **in fact**, really, in point of fact, in reality, truly, essentially. [➡WORDS AND PHRASES EMPHASIZING THE TRUTH OF A MATTER; 173]

actuary *n* [➡PEOPLE INVOLVED IN FINANCE; 804]

actuate (*formal*) *v* **activate**, put into action, motivate, set in motion, trigger, start, get going, stimulate. [➡CAUSE TO START; 266]

act up *v* **cause trouble**, play up, be difficult, misbehave, malfunction, go wrong, be on the blink (*informal*). [➡FAIL OR CEASE TO FUNCTION; 471] *Opposite:* behave.

acuity *n* **keenness**, acuteness, sharpness, alertness, awareness. [➡POSITIVE INTELLECTUAL CHARACTERISTICS; 525]

acumen *n* **insight**, shrewdness, penetration, judgment, wisdom, expertise, intelligence, perspicacity, perspicuity. [➡SKILLS, TALENTS, AND ABILITIES; 527]

acupressure *n* [➡HEALING; 731]

a cut above *adj* **superior**, better, finer, first-class, first-rate, high class, outstanding. [➡SUPERIORITY; 153]

acute 1 *adj* **severe**, serious, critical, grave, important, desperate, dire. [➡IMPORTANT; 195] *Opposite:* moderate. 2 *adj* **perceptive**, shrewd, intelligent, keen, sharp, astute, perspicacious. [➡POSITIVE INTELLECTUAL CHARACTERISTICS; 525] 3 *adj* **sharp**, sensitive, keen, heightened, finely tuned, discriminating, delicate. [➡STRENGTH; 202] *Opposite:* dull. 4 *adj* **intense**, violent, strong, excruciating, piercing, stabbing. [➡STRENGTH; 202] *Opposite:* mild. 5 *type of* **diacritic**. [➡ASPECTS OF LANGUAGE; 683]

acutely *adv* **very**, intensely, highly, deeply, extremely, terribly, severely. [➡TO A GREAT EXTENT; 130] *Opposite:* slightly.

acuteness 1 *n* **intensity**, severity, gravity, seriousness. [➡DIFFICULTY AND COMPLEXITY; 243] 2 *n* **sharpness**, keenness, sensitivity, perceptiveness. [➡POSITIVE INTELLECTUAL CHARACTERISTICS; 525] *Opposite:* dullness.

ad *n* **advertisement**, advert (*informal*), public notice, commercial, poster, flier, announcement, hoarding, trailer, personal ad, classified ad, want ad (*US informal*). [➡ADVERTISING AND PUBLICITY; 605]

adage *n* **saying**, saw, proverb, maxim, axiom, motto. [➡THE ORAL TRADITION; 678]

adagio *type of* **musical term**. [➡MUSICAL TERMS; 912]

adamant *adj* **obstinate**, obdurate, unyielding, unbending, inflexible, unwavering, immovable, resolute, steadfast, stubborn, fixed, resistant. [➡CALMNESS, CONFIDENCE, AND COMPOSURE; 537] *Opposite:* amenable.

adapt 1 *v* **change**, alter, modify, adjust, vary, revise, amend, bend, fit, rework. [➡CHANGE; 373] *Opposite:* leave. 2 *v* **become accustomed**, familiarize, get a feel for, get used to, acclimatize, acclimate, find your feet, settle in, adjust. [➡CHANGE OF MOOD AND COMPOSURE; 581]

adaptability *n* **flexibility**, adaptableness, malleability, compliance. [➡USEFULNESS; 200] *Opposite:* inflexibility.

adaptable *adj* **flexible**, malleable, pliable, adjustable, compliant, easygoing. [➡USEFULNESS; 200] *Opposite:* inflexible.

adaptation 1 *n* **alteration**, adjustment, acclimatization, modification, change. [➡CHANGE; 373] 2 *n* **version**, edition, revision, reworking, variation. [➡ARTWORKS; 898]

adapter *n* **electric plug**, connector, converter, device. [➡PARTS OF MACHINES AND TOOLS; 1117]

add 1 *v* **put in**, insert, adjoin, append, affix, attach, include. [➡FASTEN, LINK, AND JOIN; 409] *Opposite:* delete. 2 *v* **add up**, add together, tot up, total, combine, tally, tally up, count up, count. [➡ASSESS QUANTITY; 758] *Opposite:* subtract. 3 *v* **enhance**, complement, improve, augment (*formal*), increase, supplement, swell, enlarge, intensify. [➡IMPROVE SOMETHING; 375] *Opposite:* detract.

added *adj* **additional**, extra, supplementary, further, other, auxiliary, new, more. [➡MORE AND EXCESS; 122]

added extras *n* [➡MORE AND EXCESS; 122]

addendum *n* **addition**, supplement, appendix, postscript, PS, codicil (*formal*), add-on, rider, afterthought. [➡PARTS OF BOOKS AND DOCUMENTS; 594]

adder 1 *type of* **computer**. [➡COMPUTERS AND COMPUTING; 1126] 2 *type of* **poisonous snake**. [➡SNAKE; 995]

addict *n* **devotee**, fan, aficionado, fanatic, buff, enthusiast, follower, aficionada. [➡DEVOTEES AND ADDICTED PEOPLE; 557]

addicted *adj* [➡UNDER THE INFLUENCE OF DRUGS OR ALCOHOL; 742]

addiction *n* **habit**, compulsion, dependence, need, obsession, craving. [➡FADS, FETISHES, AND IDOLATRY; 556]

addition 1 *n* **adding**, adding up, adding together, totalling, totting up, calculation, count, accumulation, tallying, tally. [➡ASSESS QUANTITY; 758] 2 *n* **supplement**, add-on, appendage, addendum, adjunct, extra, additive, surcharge. [➡MORE AND EXCESS; 122]

additional *adj* **extra**, added, supplementary, other, further, bonus, surplus, superfluous. [➡MORE AND EXCESS; 122]

additionally *adv* **as well**, in addition, moreover, furthermore, also. [➡EXPRESSIONS INTRODUCING EXTRA INFORMATION; 137]

additive *n* **preservative**, stabilizer, improver, chemical, colourant. [➡ADDITIVES; 1171]

addled 1 *adj* **confused**, muddled, bewildered, befuddled, perplexed, bemused, addlebrained (*archaic*), addlepated (*dated informal*). [➡CONFUSION, ANXIETY, AND WORRY; 541] *Opposite:* clear. 2 *adj* **spoiled**, rotten, decayed, off, putrid, unwholesome, rancid, fetid. [➡IN BAD REPAIR; 1233] *Opposite:* fresh.

addlepated (*archaic*) *adj* **confused**, muddled, addlebrained (*dated informal*), bewildered, befuddled, perplexed, bemused. [➡CONFUSION, ANXIETY, AND WORRY; 541] *Opposite:* clear.

add-on 1 *n* **attachment**, addendum, adjunct, appendage, supplement, frill, extra, addition. [➡MORE AND EXCESS; 122] 2 *adj* **supplementary**, accompanying, additional, extra, optional, auxiliary. [➡MORE AND EXCESS; 122] *Opposite:* essential.

address 1 *n* **speech**, talk, discourse, lecture, report, statement. [➡NEUTRAL ONE-WAY COMMUNICATION; 49] 2 *v* **direct**, deliver, dispatch, refer, forward. [➡DESPATCH AND SEND; 334] 3 *v* **speak**, lecture, talk, give a lecture, give a talk, make a speech. [➡INSTRUCT AND TEACH; 610] 4 *v* **tackle**, deal with, take in hand, attend, concentrate, focus, adopt. [➡ATTEMPT AN ACTION; 262] *Opposite:* ignore.

adduce (*formal*) *v* **offer**, present, put forward, bring forward, give, cite. [➡SUGGEST, HINT, AND COMMENT; 613]

add up 1 *v* **add**, add together, tot up, total, combine, tally up, tally, count, count up, tote up (*US informal*). [➡ASSESS QUANTITY; 758] *Opposite:* subtract. **2** *v* **make sense**, hang together, be consistent, ring true, come together. [➡MEAN SOMETHING; 61]

add up to *v* **come to**, number, total, amount to, mount up to, equal. [➡AMOUNT TO AND EQUAL; 70]

adenoidal *adj* **nasal**, thick, muffled, indistinct. [➡LOUD OR UNPLEASANT SOUNDS; 1265]

adenoids *part of* **mouth.** [➡THE MOUTH; 703]

adept *adj* **skilful**, skilled, expert, proficient, adroit, practised, dexterous. [➡TALENTED AND SKILFUL; 528] *Opposite:* inept.

adeptness *n* **expertise**, proficiency, skill, adroitness, aptitude, dexterity. [➡SKILLS, TALENTS, AND ABILITIES; 527]

adequacy **1** *n* **sufficiency**, ampleness, abundance. [➡ENOUGH AND SUFFICIENT; 129] *Opposite:* insufficiency. **2** *n* **competence**, capability, suitability, tolerability, appropriateness, acceptability. [➡ACCEPTABLE AND PASSABLE; 220] *Opposite:* inadequacy.

adequate **1** *adj* **sufficient**, ample, enough, plenty. [➡ENOUGH AND SUFFICIENT; 129] *Opposite:* insufficient. **2** *adj* **passable**, satisfactory, tolerable, acceptable, suitable. [➡ACCEPTABLE AND PASSABLE; 220] *Opposite:* inadequate.

See Compare and Contrast at **enough**.

adequately *adv* **sufficiently**, passably, tolerably, effectively, satisfactorily, amply. [➡ACCEPTABLE AND PASSABLE; 220] *Opposite:* inadequately.

adhere **1** *v* **stick to**, follow, keep to, stand by, abide by, obey, observe. [➡OBEY AND ABIDE BY; 302] *Opposite:* abandon. **2** *v* **stick**, stick on, hold fast, hold, hold on, stay, remain, cling. [➡CONTACT: HOLD; 412]

adherence *n* **devotion**, obedience, observance, loyalty, faithfulness. [➡THE WILL AND WILLINGNESS; 564] *Opposite:* disobedience.

adherent *n* **supporter**, believer, devotee, advocate, fanatic, enthusiast, aficionado, member, zealot, follower, buff, aficionada. [➡DEVOTEES AND ADDICTED PEOPLE; 557] *Opposite:* opponent.

adhesion *n* **union**, sticking power, hold, grip, linkage, connection. [➡CONNECTION; 144] *Opposite:* separation.

adhesive *n* **glue**, paste, gum, epoxy resin. [➡ADHESIVES; 1270]

ad hoc *adj* **unplanned**, informal, impromptu, improvised, off-the-cuff, unprepared, extemporized, makeshift. [➡UNINTENTIONAL AND ACCIDENTAL; 282] *Opposite:* planned.

adieu **1** *interj* **goodbye**, farewell (*literary*), bye-bye (*informal*), so long (*informal*), au revoir, auf Wiedersehen, ciao (*informal*), adios (*informal*), see you later (*informal*). [➡GREETINGS, FAREWELLS, AND SALUTATIONS; 660] *Opposite:* hello. **2** *n* **farewell**, goodbye, leave-taking (*literary*), sendoff, valediction (*formal*), parting, commencement address. [➡END; 54]

a dime a dozen (*US*) *adj* **commonplace**, worthless, two a penny, ten a penny, ordinary, run of the mill. [➡ORDINARINESS; 245] *Opposite:* unique.

ad infinitum *adv* **endlessly**, for ever, ceaselessly, repeatedly, infinitely, without end, with no sign of stopping, with no end in sight, on and on. [➡PERMANENCE: WITHOUT END; 94]

adios (*informal*) *interj* **goodbye**, so long (*informal*), bye-bye (*informal*), see you later (*informal*), ciao (*informal*), farewell (*literary*), adieu, au revoir, auf Wiedersehen. [➡GREETINGS, FAREWELLS, AND SALUTATIONS; 660] *Opposite:* hello.

Adirondack chair (*US*) *type of* **seating.** [➡FURNITURE; 858]

adjacent *adj* **neighbouring**, nearby, bordering, next, next door, flanking, close. [➡CLOSENESS; 160] *Opposite:* distant.

adjective *type of* **word class.** [➡ASPECTS OF LANGUAGE; 683]

adjoin *v* **connect**, link up, attach, affix, be close to, be next to, border. [➡EXIST IN CLOSE PROXIMITY; 21]

adjoining *adj* **contiguous** (*formal*), touching, attached, connecting. [➡CLOSENESS; 160] *Opposite:* detached.

adjourn **1** *v* **suspend**, defer, delay, postpone, put off, shelve, hold back, interrupt, recess. [➡DELAY ACTION OR OCCURRENCE; 279] **2** *v* (*informal*) **stop**, end, finish, break off, call it a day, call a halt. [➡STOP ACTING; 265]

adjournment *n* **suspension**, postponement, deferment, recess, break, interruption, delay. [➡DELAY ACTION OR OCCURRENCE; 279]

adjudge **1** *v* **judge**, find, regard as, deem (*formal*), consider, decide, believe to be. [➡ASSESS QUALITY; 756] **2** *v* **pronounce**, rule, announce, declare, adjudicate, sentence, charge, decide. [➡TRIAL, PUNISHMENT, AND LEGAL OUTCOMES; 819]

adjudicate *v* **arbitrate**, sit in judgment, pass judgment, referee, umpire, decide, judge, settle, resolve, adjudge. [➡ASSESS QUALITY; 756]

adjudication **1** *n* **judgment**, arbitration, mediation, negotiation, intercession. [➡TRIAL, PUNISHMENT, AND LEGAL OUTCOMES; 819] **2** *n* **settlement**, decision, judgment, decree, resolution, verdict. [➡TRIAL, PUNISHMENT, AND LEGAL OUTCOMES; 819]

adjudicator *n* **judge**, arbitrator, referee, umpire, mediator, negotiator. [➡ADVISERS, JUDGES, AND ARBITERS; 971]

adjunct **1** *n* **addition**, attachment, add-on, appendage, accessory, extra, optional extra. [➡PHYSICAL OBJECTS; 1242] **2** *n* **assistant**, aide, aide-de-camp, secretary, helper, personal assistant. [➡SUBORDINATES AND ASSISTANTS; 966] **3** *type of* **grammatical term.** [➡ASPECTS OF LANGUAGE; 683]

adjure **1** *v* **command**, order, direct (*formal*), instruct, charge, demand, insist. [➡REQUEST AND DEMAND; 664] **2** *v* **appeal**, plead, beg, request, petition, call, importune (*formal*), entreat (*formal*). [➡REQUEST AND DEMAND; 664]

adjust *v* **regulate**, alter, fiddle with, correct, fine-tune, change, bend, amend, modify, tweak (*informal*), adapt, vary. [➡CHANGE; 373]

adjustable *adj* **adaptable**, modifiable, changeable, variable, regulating, amendable, bendable, flexible, alterable. [➡USEFULNESS; 200] *Opposite:* fixed.

adjustment *n* **change**, alteration, modification, tuning, fine-tuning, regulation, correction, amendment, variation. [➡CHANGE; 373]

adjutant *n* **assistant**, aide, aide-de-camp, secretary, personal assistant, helper. [➡MILITARY PERSONNEL; 828]

ad-lib 1 *v* **improvise**, do off the cuff, extemporize, make up on the spot, do cold, invent, wing it (*informal*), make up. [➡UTTER AND PRONOUNCE; 609] 2 *adj* **off-the-cuff**, unplanned, informal, impromptu, improvised, makeshift, spontaneous, extemporized, ad hoc, unrehearsed, unprepared, made-up. [➡UNINTENTIONAL AND ACCIDENTAL; 282] *Opposite:* rehearsed.

admin *n* [➡WORK-RELATED ACTIVITIES; 834]

administer 1 *v* **manage**, direct, run, order, control, oversee, govern, be in charge of. [➡BE IN CHARGE; 271] 2 *v* **dispense**, give out, hand out, deal out, dole out (*informal*), mete out, process. [➡DISPENSE, RATION, AND DISTRIBUTE; 435]

administrate *v* **control**, run, manage, direct, rule, govern, oversee, supervise, be in charge of. [➡BE IN CHARGE; 271]

administration 1 *n* **management**, direction, running, government, supervision, organization, admin, paperwork. [➡WORK-RELATED ACTIVITIES; 834] 2 *n* **government**, executive, management, organization, presidency. [➡LEGISLATIVE BODIES AND LEGISLATION; 809] 3 *n* **dispensation**, meting out, giving out, handing out, dealing out, doling out (*informal*), processing. [➡DISPENSE, RATION, AND DISTRIBUTE; 435]

administrative *adj* **managerial**, directorial, organizational, clerical, secretarial, executive, governmental. [➡TYPES OF WORK; 835]

administrator *n* **manager**, superintendent, commissioner, overseer, officer, bureaucrat, supervisor, proprietor, governor, official, executive, director. [➡POLITICAL OFFICES AND POLITICIANS; 808]

admirable *adj* **estimable**, commendable, venerable, good, splendid, worthy, marvellous, excellent. [➡ADMIRABLE AND COMMENDABLE; 186] *Opposite:* unworthy.

admiration *n* **respect**, esteem, approbation, regard, approval, appreciation, veneration, wonder, awe. [➡LOVE, RESPECT, AND GOODWILL; 550] *Opposite:* disapproval.

See Compare and Contrast at **regard**.

admire *v* **regard**, esteem, approve, think highly of, respect, venerate, like, be in awe of, appreciate, marvel at. [➡LIKE, LOVE, VALUE, AND ENJOY; 579] *Opposite:* disapprove.

admired *adj* **respected**, venerated, esteemed, well-regarded, revered, well-liked, appreciated, prized. [➡POPULAR AND WANTED; 221] *Opposite:* despised.

admirer *n* **fan**, devotee, follower, lover, aficionado, enthusiast, fanatic, aficionada. [➡SUPPORTERS, PROTECTORS, AND COMPATRIOTS; 970]

admiring *adj* **appreciative**, approving, complimentary, flattering, favourable, deferential, positive, sympathetic, pleased. [➡APPRECIATION AND GRATITUDE; 536] *Opposite:* disapproving.

admissibility *n* **acceptability**, tolerability, permissibility. [➡ACCEPTABLE AND PASSABLE; 220]

admissible *adj* **allowable**, permissible, acceptable, tolerable. [➡ACCEPTABLE AND PASSABLE; 220] *Opposite:* inadmissible.

admission 1 *n* **admittance**, entrance, right of entry, access, permission, entry. [➡PERMIT AND ALLOW; 670] *Opposite:* exclusion. 2 *n* **entrance fee**, entry fee, fee, charge, price, ticket price. [➡EXPENDITURE; 424] 3 *n* **confession**, declaration, profession, divulgence, disclosure, acknowledgment, statement. [➡ADMIT AND CONFESS; 616] *Opposite:* denial.

admit 1 *v* **confess**, come clean (*informal*), make a clean breast, acknowledge, own up, disclose, declare, state, concede, fess up (*US informal*). [➡ADMIT AND CONFESS; 616] *Opposite:* deny. 2 *v* **let in**, allow in, give access, permit, let pass, welcome. [➡PERMIT AND ALLOW; 670] *Opposite:* bar.

admit defeat *v* **pull out**, withdraw, stop, throw in the towel (*informal*), call it a day, back out, back down, give in, cave in, backpedal, climb down, give way, surrender, submit, capitulate, lay down your arms, give up. [➡FORGET, FORGIVE, AND ACCEPT; 749] *Opposite:* persevere.

admittance *n* **admission**, entry, access, right of entry, entrance, permission. [➡PERMIT AND ALLOW; 670] *Opposite:* exclusion.

admittedly *adv* **certainly**, definitely, indeed, undeniably, undoubtedly, really. [➡CERTAIN; 175]

admixture *n* [➡COLLECTIONS AND MIXTURES OF THINGS; 1243]

admonish *v* **reprove**, caution, warn, reprimand, rebuke, reproach, tell off (*informal*), scold, chide (*literary*), chew out (*US informal*). [➡ACCUSE, BLAME, AND CRITICIZE; 642] *Opposite:* praise.

admonishment *n* **reprimand**, rebuke, reproach, caution, talking-to (*informal*), ticking-off (*informal*), dressing-down, telling-off (*informal*), reproof, scolding, admonition. [➡CRITICISMS AND ANGRY OUTBURSTS; 50] *Opposite:* approval.

admonition *n* **caution**, warning, reprimand, rebuke, reproach, scolding, talking-to (*informal*), telling-off (*informal*), dressing-down, ticking-off (*informal*), admonishment. [➡CRITICISMS AND ANGRY OUTBURSTS; 50] *Opposite:* approval.

admonitory 1 *adj* **reproving**, reproachful, rebuking, condemnatory, critical, disapproving. [➡ACCUSATORY AND DISAPPROVING; 635] *Opposite:* approving. 2 *adj* **advisory**, cautionary, warning, deterrent, instructive, counselling, advice-giving. [➡ADVISE AND WARN; 614]

ad nauseam *adv* **on and on**, for ever, endlessly, interminably, ad infinitum. [➡PERMANENCE: WITHOUT END; 94]

ado *n* **bustle**, kerfuffle (*informal*), activity, commotion, bother, excitement, upheaval, to-do (*informal*), carry-on (*informal*), trouble, hoo-hah (*slang*), ruckus. [➡CHAOS AND UPROAR; 51]

adobe *n* [➡BUILDING MATERIALS; 1076]

adolescence *n* **teens**, youth, puberty, teenage years. [➡BABYHOOD, CHILDHOOD, AND ADOLESCENCE; 917]

adolescent 1 *n* **teenager**, youth, youngster, juvenile, minor. [➡CHILD OR YOUTH; 945] **2** *adj* **teenage**, young, youthful, juvenile, teen (*informal*), pubescent, pubertal. [➡BABYHOOD, CHILDHOOD, AND ADOLESCENCE; 917]

adopt *v* **take on**, accept, assume, approve, take up, agree, espouse, implement, embrace. [➡ACCEPT POSSESSION; 451] *Opposite:* reject.

adoption *n* **acceptance**, implementation, espousal, taking on, embracing, approval, agreement, taking up, assumption. [➡APPROVE AND CONFIRM; 647] *Opposite:* rejection.

adoptive *adj* **legal**, step. [➡RELATIONSHIP TO ANOTHER; 973] *Opposite:* natural.

adoptive parent *n* [➡OLDER GENERATION RELATIVES; 959]

adorable *adj* **lovely**, gorgeous, delightful, lovable, delectable, endearing, charming, sweet, attractive, beautiful, wonderful. [➡BEAUTY AND ATTRACTIVENESS; 190] *Opposite:* detestable.

adoration **1** *n* **esteem**, high regard, respect, admiration, adulation, worship, love. [➡LOVE, RESPECT, AND GOODWILL; 550] *Opposite:* hatred. **2** *n* **worship**, reverence, idolization, glorification, exaltation (*formal*), veneration, honour, devotion. [➡RELIGIONS AND RELIGIOUS PRACTICES; 778]

adore **1** *v* **love**, esteem, respect, admire, worship, adulate. [➡LIKE, LOVE, VALUE, AND ENJOY; 579] *Opposite:* hate. **2** *v* **worship**, revere, idolize, glorify, exalt (*formal*), venerate, honour. [➡RELIGIONS AND RELIGIOUS PRACTICES; 778] **3** *v* (*informal*) **like**, be mad about, be keen on, be crazy about (*informal*), be stuck on (*informal*). [➡LIKE, LOVE, VALUE, AND ENJOY; 579]

adored *adj* **revered**, venerated, worshipped, idolized, cherished, much-loved, esteemed, admired. [➡POPULAR AND WANTED; 221] *Opposite:* hated.

adoring *adj* **affectionate**, loving, doting, admiring, indulgent, tender, warm. [➡APPRECIATION AND GRATITUDE; 536] *Opposite:* cold.

adorn *v* **decorate**, embellish, ornament, beautify, prettify, gild, titivate, garnish, enhance. [➡DECORATE, ADORN, AND APPLY COATINGS; 406] *Opposite:* strip.

adornment *n* **decoration**, embellishment, ornamentation, beautification, prettification, gilding, trimming, titivation, enhancement, garnish. [➡IMPROVE APPEARANCE; 380]

adrift **1** *adj* **drifting**, floating, loose, free. [➡AIMLESS AND ERRANT MOTION; 344] *Opposite:* stationary. **2** *adv* **aimless**, wandering, drifting, at a loose end, lost, purposeless, floating, directionless, in limbo. [➡AIMLESS AND ERRANT MOTION; 344] *Opposite:* focused.

adroit *adj* **skilful**, nimble, practised, able, dexterous, adept, competent, accomplished, skilled. [➡TALENTED AND SKILFUL; 528] *Opposite:* clumsy.

adroitness *n* **skilfulness**, nimbleness, ability, dexterity, cleverness, competence, adeptness, capability. [➡SKILLS, TALENTS, AND ABILITIES; 527] *Opposite:* clumsiness.

a drop in the bucket (*US*) *n* [➡FEW, LITTLE, SMALL AMOUNT; 119]

a drop in the ocean *n* [➡FEW, LITTLE, SMALL AMOUNT; 119]

adulate *v* **flatter**, put on a pedestal, elevate, praise, adore, lionize, worship, revere. [➡PRAISE AND ENCOURAGE; 648] *Opposite:* disparage.

adulation *n* **adoration**, praise, worship, hero worship, exaltation (*formal*), respect, admiration, reverence, idolization, glorification. [➡LOVE, RESPECT, AND GOODWILL; 550] *Opposite:* disparagement.

adulatory *adj* **praising**, flattering, fawning, sycophantic, obsequious, toadying. [➡EXPRESSING RESPECT AND APPROVAL; 638] *Opposite:* disparaging.

adult **1** *adj* **mature**, fully developed, grown-up, grown, fully-grown. [➡ADULTHOOD; 918] *Opposite:* immature. **2** *n* **grown-up**, grown person. [➡PERSON; 931] *Opposite:* child.

adulterate *v* **contaminate**, taint, make impure, spoil, pollute, infect, ruin. [➡DIRTY AND CONTAMINATE; 405] *Opposite:* purify.

adulteration *n* **contamination**, debasement, pollution, tarnishing, sullying (*literary*), corruption, infection. [➡DIRTY AND CONTAMINATE; 405] *Opposite:* purification.

adulterer *n* [➡VILLAINS AND THUGS; 947]

adulterous *adj* [➡MORALLY BAD; 776]

adultery *n* [➡MORALLY BAD; 776]

adulthood *n* **maturity**, parenthood, middle age, old age, later life, majority. [➡ADULTHOOD; 918] *Opposite:* childhood.

advance **1** *v* **go forward**, move forward, move ahead, press forward, move on, proceed, press on, progress, go ahead. [➡PROCEED AND GO; 306] *Opposite:* retreat. **2** *v* **improve**, enhance, take forward, increase, expand, progress, further, build up. [➡IMPROVE SOMETHING; 375] *Opposite:* regress. **3** *n* **development**, improvement, spread, progress, expansion, encroachment, innovation, enhancement, increase. [➡PROGRESS AND ADVANCEMENT; 214] *Opposite:* decline. **4** *n* **loan**, early payment, fee, money up front. [➡ACCOUNTING, BANKING, AND BUDGETING; 799]

advanced **1** *adj* **higher**, developed, sophisticated, complex, difficult. [➡SUPERIORITY; 153] *Opposite:* basic. **2** *adj* **later**, far along, well along, far ahead, well ahead, future. [➡FUTURE; 86] *Opposite:* earlier. **3** *adj* **progressive**, forward-thinking, unconventional, cutting-edge, innovative, forward-looking, radical. [➡POSITIVELY COMPLEX OR COMPLICATED; 218] *Opposite:* traditional.

advancement *n* **progression**, progress, development, improvement, spread, expansion, encroachment, innovation, increase. [➡PROGRESS AND ADVANCEMENT; 214] *Opposite:* decline.

advantage *n* **benefit**, gain, lead, plus (*informal*), pro, improvement, help. [➡SOURCE OF HAPPINESS, PLEASURE, OR IMPROVEMENT; 210] *Opposite:* disadvantage.

advantageous *adj* **beneficial**, helpful, useful, to your advantage, valuable, gainful, profitable, expedient, strategic. [➡USEFULNESS; 200] *Opposite:* disadvantageous.

advent *n* **arrival**, start, beginning, coming on, dawn, initiation, introduction. [➡BEGINNING; 53] *Opposite:* departure.

adventure *n* **escapade**, exploit, quest, venture, exploration, undertaking, voyage. [➡EVENTS AND OCCURRENCES; 35]

adventure movie *n* [➡FILM; 901]

adventure playground *n* [➡URBAN OUTDOOR SPACES; 1071]

adventurer 1 *n* **explorer**, traveller, voyager, buccaneer, swashbuckler, fortune hunter. [➡TRAVEL: TRAVELLERS AND WALKERS; 320] 2 *n* **entrepreneur**, investor, speculator, trailblazer, pioneer, opportunist. [➡BUSINESS PEOPLE; 794]

adventuresome *adj* **risk-taking**, carefree, daring, thrill-seeking, exciting, venturesome (*formal*), adventurous, bold, audacious, brave, exploratory, courageous. [➡COURAGE; 499] *Opposite:* unadventurous.

adventurous *adj* **daring**, bold, audacious, brave, exploratory, courageous, exciting, seeking, carefree, risk-taking, thrill-seeking, venturesome (*formal*), adventuresome. [➡COURAGE; 499] *Opposite:* unadventurous.

adverb *type of* **word class**. [➡ASPECTS OF LANGUAGE; 683]

adversarial *adj* **confrontational**, argumentative, combative, antagonistic, accusatorial (*formal*), oppositional. [➡AGGRESSIVE AND BELLIGERENT; 519] *Opposite:* cooperative.

adversary *n* **opponent**, challenger, rival, enemy, foe (*literary*), antagonist, opposition. [➡ENEMIES AND TORMENTORS; 969] *Opposite:* supporter.

adverse 1 *adj* **opposing**, contrary, hostile, adversative, antagonistic, adversarial, confrontational, argumentative, oppositional. [➡DISHARMONY; 157] *Opposite:* cooperative. 2 *adj* **unfavourable**, unpleasant, poor, difficult, unhelpful, undesirable, unsympathetic, harmful. [➡DANGEROUS; 237] *Opposite:* favourable.

adversely *adv* **unfavourably**, harmfully, badly, unpleasantly, poorly, unhelpfully, undesirably, unsympathetically, negatively. [➡DANGEROUS; 237] *Opposite:* favourably.

adversity *n* **hardship**, difficulty, danger, misfortune, harsh conditions, hard times. [➡DIFFICULT SITUATIONS; 72] *Opposite:* privilege.

advert (*informal*) *n* **advertisement**, ad, public notice, announcement, poster, billboard, hoarding, commercial, flier, personal ad, classified ad, trailer, want ad (*US informal*). [➡ADVERTISING AND PUBLICITY; 605]

advertise 1 *v* **promote**, publicize, market, present, push, puff. [➡ADVERTISING AND PUBLICITY; 605] 2 *v* **announce**, broadcast, make known, make public, spread about, shout from the rooftops, spread abroad, shout out, publicize. [➡INFORM AND ANNOUNCE; 612] *Opposite:* keep under wraps.

advertisement *n* **ad**, advert (*informal*), announcement, poster, billboard, hoarding, commercial, personal ad, classified ad, public notice, flier, trailer, want ad (*US informal*). [➡ADVERTISING AND PUBLICITY; 605]

advertiser *n* **publicist**, promoter, backer, supporter, advocate, seller. [➡BUSINESS PEOPLE; 794]

advertising *n* **publicity**, promotion, marketing, publicizing, public relations, PR. [➡ADVERTISING AND PUBLICITY; 605]

advice 1 *n* **recommendation**, suggestion, guidance, opinion, counsel (*formal or literary*). [➡ADVICE; 690] *Opposite:* warning. 2 *n* **information**, guidance, instruction, assistance, intelligence, news. [➡BASIC DETAILS; 689]

advisability *n* **wisdom**, prudence, sense, desirability, suitability. [➡APPROPRIATE, SUITABLE, ADVISABLE; 185] *Opposite:* foolishness.

advisable *adj* **sensible**, wise, prudent, worthwhile, desirable, suitable, logical, sagacious (*formal*), judicious. [➡APPROPRIATE, SUITABLE, ADVISABLE; 185] *Opposite:* unwise.

advise 1 *v* **recommend**, direct, guide, instruct, warn, counsel (*formal or literary*), opine (*formal*). [➡ADVISE AND WARN; 614] 2 *v* **inform**, let know, make aware, notify, instruct, tell. [➡INFORM AND ANNOUNCE; 612]

See Compare and Contrast at **recommend**.

advisedly *adv* **deliberately**, carefully, purposefully, on purpose, with intent, intentionally, purposely. [➡INTENTIONAL AND DELIBERATE; 280] *Opposite:* carelessly.

adviser *n* **consultant**, counsellor, advice-giver, guru. [➡ADVISERS, JUDGES, AND ARBITERS; 971]

advisory *adj* **advice-giving**, consultative, counselling, review. [➡ADVISE AND WARN; 614]

advocacy *n* **support**, encouragement, backing, sponsorship, promotion, activism. [➡APPROVE AND CONFIRM; 647] *Opposite:* opposition.

advocate 1 *v* **support**, encourage, back, promote, be in favour of, sponsor. [➡APPROVE AND CONFIRM; 647] *Opposite:* discourage. 2 *n* **supporter**, backer, promoter, believer, activist, campaigner, sponsor. [➡DEVOTEES AND ADDICTED PEOPLE; 557] *Opposite:* opponent.

See Compare and Contrast at **recommend**.

aegis *n* **auspices**, sponsorship, guidance, protection, support, tutelage. [➡RESPONSIBILITY; 171]

aeon *n* **ages** (*informal*), long time, eternity, years, donkey's years (*informal*), forever (*informal*), yonks (*slang*). [➡LONG PERIOD OF TIME; 92] *Opposite:* moment.

aeons *n* [➡LONG PERIOD OF TIME; 92]

aerate *v* **ventilate**, let breathe, expose, freshen. [➡CLEAN AND POLISH; 404] *Opposite:* close up.

aeration *n* **ventilation**, airing, freshening. [➡HEATING, REFRIGERATION, AND VENTILATION; 1141]

aerial 1 *adj* **midair**, airborne, above ground, in-flight, floating. [➡GENERAL LOCATIONS; 159] *Opposite:* terrestrial. 2 *type of* **telecommunications equipment**. [➡TELECOMMUNICATIONS; 1129]

aerobatics *n* **stunts**, manoeuvres, aerial tricks. [➡HOBBIES, GAMES, AND SPORTS; 875]

aerobics *n* **exercises**, keep fit, callisthenics, workout. [➡HOBBIES, GAMES, AND SPORTS; 875]

aerodrome *n* **airfield**, airport, landing strip, landing field, airstrip, air base, airdrome (*US*). [➡AIRWAYS; 1108]

aerodynamic *adj* **sleek**, smooth, slick, sweptback, clean, flowing. [➡ROUNDED SHAPE; 1217]

aerofoil *part of* **external structure.** [➡EXTERNAL PARTS OF A VEHICLE; 1146]

aerogram *n* **air letter**, airmail letter, aerogramme. [➡LETTERS AND WRITTEN MESSAGES; 585]

aerogramme *see* **aerogram.**

aeronaut *n* [➡DRIVERS; 1152]

aeroplane *n* **aircraft**, plane, airplane (*US*). [➡AIRCRAFT; 1147]

aerosol *n* **spray can**, spray, atomizer, mister. [➡CONTAINERS, RECEPTACLES, AND PACKAGING; 1244]

aerospace *n* **atmosphere**, upper atmosphere, space, troposphere, stratosphere, mesosphere, thermosphere, exosphere. [➡THE EARTH'S ATMOSPHERE; 1040]

aesthete *n* **art lover**, aesthetician, connoisseur, cognoscente. [➡PLEASURE-SEEKERS AND HEDONISTS; 886]

aesthetic *adj* **artistic**, visual, appealing, beautiful. [➡ARTISTIC MOVEMENTS AND STYLES; 899]

afar (*literary*) *adv* **far afield**, in the distance, far away, far and wide, far-off, far. [➡DISTANCE; 161] *Opposite:* nearby.

a few *pron* **a small number**, some, one or two, not many, handful, hardly any. [➡FEW, LITTLE, SMALL AMOUNT; 119] *Opposite:* many.

affability *n* **friendliness**, sociability, cordiality, joviality, gregariousness, pleasantness, warmth. [➡FRIENDLINESS AND SOCIABILITY; 495] *Opposite:* unfriendliness.

affable *adj* **genial**, pleasant, friendly, sociable, jovial, gregarious, cordial, warm, easygoing. [➡FRIENDLINESS AND SOCIABILITY; 495] *Opposite:* unfriendly.

affair *n* **matter**, issue, concern, business, situation, event, thing. [➡SITUATIONS; 71]

affairs *n* **business**, matters, dealings, activities, concerns, undertakings. [➡ACTIONS OR UNDERTAKINGS; 260]

affect 1 *v* **influence**, involve, shape, concern, change, modify, alter. [➡CHANGE; 373] 2 *v* **touch**, move, disturb, mark, distress, upset, shake. [➡UPSET, DISTRESS, AND HUMILIATE; 568] 3 *v* **assume**, put on, imitate, fake, adopt, pretend. [➡PRETEND AND MIMIC; 60]

affectation 1 *n* **showing off**, pretension, exaggeration, artifice (*formal*), artificiality, affectedness, pretentiousness. [➡AFFECTATION, SELF-SATISFACTION, AND SNOBBISHNESS; 508] *Opposite:* naturalness. 2 *n* **mannerism**, way, quirk, show, trait, habit, characteristic. [➡TEMPERAMENT AND BEHAVIOUR; 493]

affected *adj* **pretentious**, artificial, exaggerated, la-di-da (*informal*), unnatural, posh (*informal*), precious. [➡AFFECTATION, SELF-SATISFACTION, AND SNOBBISHNESS; 508] *Opposite:* natural.

affectedness *n* **exaggeration**, pretension, artifice (*formal*), artificiality, affectation, showing off. [➡AFFECTATION, SELF-SATISFACTION, AND SNOBBISHNESS; 508] *Opposite:* naturalness.

affecting *adj* **moving**, touching, upsetting, distressing, disturbing, heartrending, heartwarming, affective. [➡EMOTIONALLY UNPLEASANT AND UPSETTING; 228]

affection *n* **liking**, fondness, warmth, friendliness, care, regard. [➡LOVE, RESPECT, AND GOODWILL; 550] *Opposite:* dislike.

See Compare and Contrast at **love**.

affectionate *adj* **loving**, demonstrative, warm, friendly, kind, caring. [➡FRIENDLINESS AND SOCIABILITY; 495] *Opposite:* cold.

affective *adj* **emotional**, sentimental, moving, touching, affecting, disturbing. [➡EMOTIONALLY UNPLEASANT AND UPSETTING; 228]

affenpinscher *type of* **small dog.** [➡DOG; 980]

affidavit *n* **sworn statement**, official declaration, affirmation, confirmation, proclamation, confession, document, legal instrument. [➡OFFICIAL DOCUMENTS; 587]

affiliate 1 *v* **link**, connect, join, associate, belong to, conglomerate. [➡CREATING CONNECTIONS; 145] 2 *n* **associate**, partner, colleague, member. [➡SUBORDINATES AND ASSISTANTS; 966]

affiliated *adj* [➡RELATED; 143]

affiliation *n* **association**, relationship, connection, attachment, membership, link. [➡CONNECTION; 144]

affinity 1 *n* **empathy**, sympathy, fellow feeling, attraction, kinship, like-mindedness. [➡LOVE, RESPECT, AND GOODWILL; 550] *Opposite:* indifference. 2 *n* **similarity**, resemblance, likeness, correspondence. [➡SIMILARITY; 149] *Opposite:* difference.

affirm 1 *v* **support**, confirm, encourage, sustain, uphold. [➡APPROVE AND CONFIRM; 647] 2 *v* **assert**, insist, avow (*formal*), establish, state, verify, announce, pronounce, acknowledge. [➡CLAIM, INSIST, AND EMPHASIZE; 615]

affirmation *n* **assertion**, confirmation, pronouncement, avowal (*formal*), declaration, announcement, statement, verification. [➡INFORM AND ANNOUNCE; 612] *Opposite:* denial.

affirmative *adj* **assenting**, positive, confirmatory, agreeing, favourable. [➡EXPRESSING RESPECT AND APPROVAL; 638] *Opposite:* negative.

affix 1 *v* **attach**, fix, fasten, stick, pin, glue. [➡FASTEN, LINK, AND JOIN; 409] *Opposite:* remove. 2 *type of* **grammatical term.** [➡ASPECTS OF LANGUAGE; 683]

afflict *v* **trouble**, bother, affect, worry, distress, vex, upset. [➡UPSET, DISTRESS, AND HUMILIATE; 568]

afflicted *adj* **distressed**, aggrieved, stricken, plagued, tormented, hurt, suffering. [➡SADNESS, DISTRESS, AND DESPAIR; 540]

affliction 1 *n* **suffering**, difficulty, burden, problem, hardship, pain, trouble, misery, misfortune. [➡NUISANCES; 254] 2 *n* **illness**, sickness, disease, condition, disorder, complaint, infirmity, weakness. [➡ILLNESSES AND DISORDERS; 733]

affluence *n* **riches**, prosperity, comfortable circumstances, material comfort, privileged circumstances, wealth. [➡WEALTH AND WEALTHY; 891] *Opposite:* poverty.

affluent *adj* **rich**, wealthy, well-off, well-to-do, prosperous, comfortable, well-heeled (*informal*), born with a silver spoon in your mouth. [➡WEALTH AND WEALTHY; 891] *Opposite:* poor.

afford 1 *v* **pay for**, have the funds for, manage to pay for, find the money for, come up with the money for, meet the expense of. [➡PURCHASE; 423] 2 *v* (*formal*) **give**, offer, present, allow, provide. [➡GIVE AND PROVIDE; 431]

affordable *adj* **reasonable**, within your means, inexpensive, cheap. [➡CHEAP AND INEXPENSIVE; 222] *Opposite:* expensive.

afforest *v* **reforest**. [➡GROW AND CULTIVATE; 352] *Opposite:* deforest.

affray *n* **scuffle**, fight, brawl, disturbance, commotion, tussle, donnybrook. [➡AGGRESSIVE EVENT; 39] *Opposite:* agreement.

affront 1 *n* **insult**, injury, slur, slight, outrage. [➡INSULTS, ABUSE, AND SWEARING; 659] *Opposite:* compliment. 2 *v* **offend**, insult, upset, outrage, slight, disrespect. [➡INSULTS, ABUSE, AND SWEARING; 659] *Opposite:* compliment.

affronted *adj* **insulted**, injured, slighted, disrespected, upset, in a huff (*informal*), outraged. [➡SADNESS, DISTRESS, AND DESPAIR; 540] *Opposite:* pleased.

Afghan hound *type of* **large dog**. [➡DOG; 980]

aficionada *n* **devotee**, enthusiast, adherent, fanatic, fan, addict, admirer, buff. [➡DEVOTEES AND ADDICTED PEOPLE; 557]

aficionado *n* **devotee**, enthusiast, adherent, fanatic, fan, addict, admirer, buff. [➡DEVOTEES AND ADDICTED PEOPLE; 557]

afire 1 *adj* **burning**, in flames, on fire, aflame, ablaze. [➡FIRE, FLAMMABILITY, AND BURNING; 1164] *Opposite:* extinguished. 2 *adj* **fired up**, excited, passionate, enthusiastic, avid, aflame, eager. [➡PLEASURE, EXCITEMENT, AND ELATION; 535] *Opposite:* apathetic.

aflame 1 *adj* **on fire**, burning, in flames, afire, ablaze. [➡FIRE, FLAMMABILITY, AND BURNING; 1164] *Opposite:* extinguished. 2 *adj* **ablaze**, enthusiastic, passionate, fired, fired up, excited, afire, eager. [➡PLEASURE, EXCITEMENT, AND ELATION; 535] *Opposite:* apathetic.

afloat *adj* **flooded**, awash, inundated, under water, submerged, swilling. [➡WET; 1239] *Opposite:* dry.

aflutter *adv* **agitated**, excited, trembling, aquiver, keyed up (*informal*), nervous. [➡PLEASURE, EXCITEMENT, AND ELATION; 535] *Opposite:* calm.

afoot *adj* **happening**, going on, occurring, taking place, up, in the works, stirring, in the wind. [➡HAPPENING AND IN PROGRESS; 32]

aforementioned (*formal*) *adj* **above-mentioned**, aforesaid (*formal*), said. [➡EXPRESSIONS OF REFERENCE; 63]

aforesaid (*formal*) *adj* **aforementioned** (*formal*), above-mentioned, said. [➡EXPRESSIONS OF REFERENCE; 63]

afraid *adj* **frightened**, fearful, terrified, petrified, scared, anxious. [➡FEAR AND PANIC; 544] *Opposite:* unafraid.

afresh *adv* **anew**, again, once again, once more, over, another time. [➡AGAIN; 109]

African violet *type of* **perennial flower**. [➡FLOWERS; 1032]

Afro *type of* **hairstyle**. [➡HAIR STYLES AND HAIR PIECES; 489]

after 1 *prep* **later than**, past, gone. [➡AFTER, LAST, AND FOLLOWING; 166] *Opposite:* before. 2 *prep* **behind**, following, to the rear of, next to. [➡RELATIVE LOCATION; 162] *Opposite:* ahead of. 3 *prep* **in pursuit of**, in search of, in quest of, following, on the trail of, on the heels of. [➡DESIRE AND WANT; 580] 4 *prep* **regarding**, considering, taking into account, with, bearing in mind, taking into consideration. [➡RELATED; 143] 5 *prep* **following**, subsequent to. [➡AFTER, LAST, AND FOLLOWING; 166] *Opposite:* before. 6 *prep* **in the manner of**, in imitation of, in the style of, similar to, like, in the same way as, à la. [➡SIMILARITY; 149] 7 *adv* **afterwards**, subsequently, later, next. [➡AFTER, LAST, AND FOLLOWING; 166] *Opposite:* before. 8 *conj* **when**, once, as soon as. [➡AFTER, LAST, AND FOLLOWING; 166] *Opposite:* before.

after all *adv* **on balance**, finally, in the end, in spite of everything, nevertheless, in any case, all together, taken together. [➡ALTHOUGH, NEVERTHELESS, AND DESPITE; 170]

aftercare 1 *n* **post-operative care**, post-hospital care, home care, rehabilitation, recovery programme, rehab (*US informal*). [➡HEALING; 731] 2 *n* **support**, assistance, help, upkeep, maintenance, post sales service, aftersales service. [➡BUSINESS ACTIVITIES AND PHENOMENA; 795]

aftereffect *n* **repercussion**, reverberation, aftermath, aftershock, final outcome, end result, byproduct, side effect, consequence, effect, result, outcome. [➡RESULTS AND OUTCOMES; 83] *Opposite:* precursor.

afterglow *n* **warmth**, glow, serenity, exhilaration, feel-good factor. [➡PLEASURE, EXCITEMENT, AND ELATION; 535]

afterlife *n* **next world**, life after death, eternal life, spirit world, hereafter (*formal*), sweet hereafter (*formal*), happy hunting ground. [➡RELIGIOUS CONCEPTS; 777]

aftermath *n* **result**, consequences, outcome, upshot, repercussion, aftereffects, aftershock, reverberation, end result. [➡RESULTS AND OUTCOMES; 83]

afternoon *n* **after lunch**, p.m., early afternoon, mid-afternoon, late afternoon, early evening. [➡TIMES OF DAY; 87] *Opposite:* morning.

afters (*informal*) *n* **dessert**, pudding, sweet, pud (*informal*), sweet course, dessert course. [➡MEALS AND PARTS OF MEALS; 1168]

aftershave *n* [➡PERSONAL HYGIENE; 492]

aftershock *n* [➡RESULTS AND OUTCOMES; 83]

aftertaste *n* [➡TASTE; 704]

after that *adv* **next**, afterwards, later, subsequently, then. [➡AFTER, LAST, AND FOLLOWING; 166]

afterthought *n* **addition**, postscript, extra, addendum, reflection, second thought, reconsideration. [➡IDEA AND THOUGHT; 771]

afterwards *adv* **later**, after that, subsequently, then, next. [➡AFTER, LAST, AND FOLLOWING; 166] *Opposite:* before.

again *adv* **once more**, another time, yet again, over, over again, all over again, for a second time, once again. [➡AGAIN; 109]

again and again *adv* **repeatedly**, many times, over and over, time and again, persistently, over and over again, continually, continuously. [➡AGAIN; 109] *Opposite:* once.

against 1 *prep* **in opposition to**, not in favour, anti (*informal*), hostile, critical, opposed, versus. [➡UNWILLINGNESS AND STUBBORNNESS; 565] 2 *prep* **next to**, alongside, beside, touching, adjacent to, aligned with. [➡CLOSENESS; 160] 3 *prep* **in contradiction of**, contrary to, counter to, in contrast to, compared to. [➡OPPOSITE; 158]

against the law *adj* [➡ILLEGAL; 816]

agape (*literary*) 1 *adj* **wide open**, open, ajar. [➡ORIENTATION AND ALIGNMENT; 1222] 2 *adj* **astonished**, amazed, open-mouthed, agog, surprised, shocked. [➡PLEASURE, EXCITEMENT, AND ELATION; 535] *Opposite:* unaffected.

agate *type of* **gemstone**. [➡PRECIOUS STONES; 1277]

age 1 *n* **time of life**, stage, phase, stage of development, oldness. [➡THE STAGES OF LIFE; 916] 2 *n* **era**, period, time, times, epoch. [➡EPOCHS AND ERAS; 89] 3 *v* **mature**, grow older, grow up, get on, advance in years. [➡CHANGE; 373]

aged *adj* **old**, elderly, matured, ripened, hoary, venerable, ancient. [➡OLD AGE; 919] *Opposite:* young.

age group *n* **generation**, cohort, age range, age bracket, contemporaries. [➡GROUPS OF PEOPLE; 935]

ageless 1 *adj* **youthful**, fresh, unfading, unspoiled. [➡NEW, MODERN; 167] 2 *adj* **timeless**, endless, perpetual, everlasting, infinite, unending. [➡PERMANENCE: WITHOUT END; 94]

agency 1 *n* **organization**, outfit (*informal*), bureau, society, charity, group. [➡INSTITUTIONS; 791] 2 *n* **activity**, action, work, intervention, help, support, assistance. [➡CAUSATION; 169]

agenda *n* **programme**, schedule, plan, outline, memo, schema, itinerary. [➡LISTS AND SCHEDULES; 588]

agent 1 *n* **go-between**, manager, negotiator, mediator, representative, proxy. [➡REPRESENTATIVES AND PATRONS; 968] 2 *n* **cause**, means, driving force, instrument, vehicle, driver. [➡CAUSATION; 169]

agent provocateur *n* [➡THE POLICE, ARREST, AND PRE-TRIAL PROCEEDINGS; 818]

age-old *adj* **ancient**, old, long-standing, venerable, hoary. [➡OLD, OLD-FASHIONED; 168] *Opposite:* recent.

ages (*informal*) *n* **forever** (*informal*), eternity, days, aeon, weeks, months, years, centuries (*informal*), yonks (*slang*), donkey's years (*informal*). [➡LONG PERIOD OF TIME; 92] *Opposite:* moment.

agglomeration *n* **accumulation**, mass, collection, cluster, group. [➡COLLECTIONS AND MIXTURES OF THINGS; 1243]

agglutinate *v* **adhere**, stick, clump, join, cling, cohere (*formal*). [➡COMBINE AND MIX; 401] *Opposite:* separate.

agglutination *n* **accretion**, cohesion, adhesion, clumping, joining. [➡COMBINE AND MIX; 401]

aggrandize 1 *v* **increase**, upgrade, expand, enlarge, develop, grow. [➡CHANGE OF SIZE: BIGGER; 393] *Opposite:* downgrade. 2 *v* (*formal*) **exaggerate**, overstate, puff up, build up, magnify, overvalue, glorify, make much of, boast, brag, boost. [➡BOAST; 617] *Opposite:* belittle.

aggrandizement 1 *n* **enhancement**, enlargement, expansion, amelioration, improvement, upgrading, development, growth. [➡CHANGE OF SIZE: BIGGER; 393] *Opposite:* deterioration. 2 *n* **empowerment**, enrichment, promotion, magnification, inflation, amplification. [➡CHANGE OF SIZE: BIGGER; 393] *Opposite:* deflation. 3 *n* (*formal*) **exaggeration**, overstatement, puffery (*informal*), braggadocio, glorification, embellishment, boasting. [➡BOAST; 617] *Opposite:* understatement.

aggravate 1 *v* (*informal*) **annoy**, irritate, exasperate, provoke, make angry, pester, get on somebody's nerves, frustrate, vex. [➡ANGER AND ANNOY; 570] *Opposite:* soothe. 2 *v* **worsen**, exacerbate, exaggerate, heighten, intensify, magnify, fan the flames of, augment (*formal*). [➡WORSEN SOMETHING; 381] *Opposite:* alleviate.

aggravated 1 *adj* **serious**, worse, intensified, heightened. [➡BAD AND BADLY; 224] *Opposite:* alleviated. 2 *adj* (*informal*) **annoyed**, angry, upset, worked up (*informal*), wound up (*informal*), put out, irritated, riled (*informal*), bothered, exasperated, frustrated, vexed. [➡IRRITATION AND ANGER; 542] *Opposite:* peaceful.

aggravated burglary *n* [➡CRIMES; 817]

aggravating *adj* **annoying**, irritating, infuriating, maddening, exasperating, provoking, grating, vexing. [➡IRRITATING; 229] *Opposite:* pleasing.

aggravation 1 *n* (*informal*) **bother**, trouble, hassle (*informal*), difficulty, irritation, aggro (*slang*). [➡IRRITATION AND ANGER; 542] 2 *n* **worsening**, exacerbation, intensification, magnification, augmentation. [➡CHANGE OF INTENSITY: MORE; 395] *Opposite:* alleviation.

aggregate 1 *adj* (*formal*) **collective**, total, combined, cumulative, amassed, summative, comprehensive. [➡ALL; 126] 2 *n* (*formal*) **total**, collection, mass, sum, whole, combination, group. [➡COLLECTIONS AND MIXTURES OF THINGS; 1243] 3 *v* **combine**, amass, gather, collect, accumulate, sum up, total, group. [➡COMBINE AND MIX; 401] *Opposite:* separate.

aggregation *n* **combination**, accumulation, collection, accretion, mass, clump, group, total, cluster, sum, bunch, load. [➡COLLECTIONS AND MIXTURES OF THINGS; 1243]

aggression 1 *n* **attack**, assault, invasion, onslaught, offensive, raid. [➡AGGRESSIVE EVENT; 39] *Opposite:* defence. 2 *n* **violence**, hostility, anger, belligerence, antagonism, bellicosity. [➡UNKIND ACTION OR BEHAVIOUR; 297] *Opposite:* friendliness.

aggressive 1 *adj* **violent**, hostile, destructive, belligerent, antagonistic, bellicose. [➡MORALLY BAD; 776] *Opposite:* peaceful. 2 *adj* **forceful**, insistent, assertive, hard-hitting, uncompromising, determined, hardline. [➡STRENGTH; 202] *Opposite:* mild.

aggressiveness 1 *n* **violence**, belligerence, bellicosity, ferociousness, antagonism, hostility. [➡AGGRESSIVE AND BELLIGERENT; 519] *Opposite:* friendliness. 2 *n* **fierceness**, insistence, forcefulness, determination, assertiveness. [➡UNKIND ACTION OR BEHAVIOUR; 297] *Opposite:* mildness.

aggressor *n* **attacker**, invader, assailant, provoker, antagonist, belligerent, fighter. [➡ENEMIES AND TORMENTORS; 969] *Opposite:* defender.

aggrieve (*formal*) *v* **distress**, upset, hurt, injure, pain, wound, irritate, annoy. [➡UPSET, DISTRESS, AND HUMILIATE; 568]

aggrieved 1 *adj* **hurt**, angry, upset, distressed, put out, pained, wounded, hard done by, injured. [➡SADNESS, DISTRESS, AND DESPAIR; 540] 2 *adj* **wronged**, mistreated, persecuted, maltreated, victimized, offended, ill-treated. [➡IN TROUBLE AND DISADVANTAGED; 73]

aggro (*slang*) 1 *n* **aggression**, belligerence, antagonism, hostility, violence. [➡EMOTIONALLY UNPLEASANT AND UPSETTING; 228] 2 *n* **difficulty**, hassle (*informal*), aggravation (*informal*), trouble, bother, irritation. [➡NUISANCES; 254]

aghast *adj* **horrified**, amazed, shocked, horror-struck, astonished, stunned, astounded, appalled. [➡SURPRISE, SHOCK, AND AMAZEMENT; 546] *Opposite:* unaffected.

agile 1 *adj* **nimble**, supple, lithe, sprightly, alert, responsive, swift, active, dexterous, lively. [➡MOVING QUICKLY; 103] *Opposite:* clumsy. 2 *adj* **quick-thinking**, alert, clear-headed, bright. [➡POSITIVE INTELLECTUAL CHARACTERISTICS; 525] *Opposite:* dull.

agilely *adv* **nimbly**, quickly, swiftly, neatly, smoothly, alertly, actively, dexterously. [➡MOVING QUICKLY; 103] *Opposite:* clumsily.

agility *n* **nimbleness**, suppleness, quickness, dexterity, liveliness, alertness, sprightliness, swiftness, responsiveness. [➡AGILITY OF THE BODY; 477] *Opposite:* clumsiness.

agitate 1 *v* **disturb**, stir up, trouble, excite, rouse, work up, disconcert. [➡CONFUSE AND BEWILDER; 572] *Opposite:* calm. 2 *v* **campaign**, stir up opinion, protest, advocate, raise a fuss, demonstrate. [➡PROTEST AND EXPRESS DISAPPROVAL; 643] 3 *v* **stir**, whisk, toss, shake up, disturb, mix up, move about, shake, mix, beat, move around. [➡MOVE SOMETHING ON THE SPOT; 337]

agitated *adj* **restless**, disturbed, disconcerted, frantic, twitchy (*informal*), tense, troubled, stressed, unquiet, distressed, unsettled, anxious, worked up (*informal*), excited, nervous. [➡CONFUSION, ANXIETY, AND WORRY; 541] *Opposite:* calm.

agitation 1 *n* **anxiety**, worry, nervousness, tension, distress, excitement. [➡CONFUSION, ANXIETY, AND WORRY; 541] *Opposite:* calm. 2 *n* **campaigning**, activism, demonstration, protest, stir, confrontation, disturbance, shakeup. [➡DISHARMONY; 157]

agitator *n* **campaigner**, protester, dissenter, activist. [➡UNCOOPERATIVE OR REBELLIOUS PERSON; 567]

aglow *adj* **glowing**, shining, radiant, rosy, warm, bright, burning, ruddy, luminous, incandescent, agleam (*literary*). [➡FIRE, FLAMMABILITY, AND BURNING; 1164] *Opposite:* pale.

AGM *n* **annual general meeting**, annual meeting, open meeting, public meeting, meeting. [➡MEETINGS AND ASSEMBLIES; 43]

agnostic 1 *n* **doubter**, sceptic, doubting Thomas, questioner, nonbeliever. [➡PHILOSOPHICAL AND POLITICAL THINKERS; 782] *Opposite:* believer. 2 *adj* **doubting**, sceptical, uncertain, unsure, unconvinced, undecided, doubtful, dubious, hesitant. [➡UNCERTAINTY; 560] *Opposite:* believing.

agnosticism *n* **doubt**, reservation, uncertainty, dissent, distrust, mistrust, nonbelief, dubiety (*formal*), scepticism. [➡UNCERTAINTY; 560] *Opposite:* certainty.

ago *adv* **before**, previously, back, past, since, in the past. [➡PAST; 84] *Opposite:* ahead.

agog *adj* **eager**, excited, impatient, keen, avid, interested, enthusiastic, curious, agape (*literary*). [➡POSITIVE IMPATIENCE, ENTHUSIASM, AND ALERTNESS; 538] *Opposite:* uninterested.

agonize *v* **worry**, struggle, strive, vacillate, wrestle, suffer, torture yourself, torment yourself, dwell on, brood. [➡THINK AND REFLECT; 744]

agonized *adj* **anguished**, tormented, suffering, tortured, in pain, distressed, grief-stricken, angst-ridden. [➡SADNESS, DISTRESS, AND DESPAIR; 540]

agonizing *adj* **excruciating**, unbearable, painful, distressing, worrying, heartbreaking, tormenting. [➡EMOTIONALLY UNPLEASANT AND UPSETTING; 228]

agonizingly *adv* **excruciatingly**, unbearably, painfully, distressingly, worryingly, heartbreakingly. [➡TO A GREAT EXTENT; 130]

agony *n* **anguish**, pain, torture, suffering, distress, misery, woe, torment, worry, heartbreak. [➡SADNESS, DISTRESS, AND DESPAIR; 540] *Opposite:* ecstasy.

a good deal *adv* **a lot**, very much, no end, enormously, greatly, exceedingly, decidedly, lots. [➡MANY, MUCH, LARGE AMOUNT; 117]

agoraphobia *type of* **phobia**. [➡FEARS AND PHOBIAS; 555]

agrarian *adj* **agricultural**, farm, farming, land, rural. [➡AGRICULTURE AND FARMING; 1074] *Opposite:* urban.

a great deal *adv* **a lot**, very much, no end, enormously, greatly, exceedingly, decidedly, lots. [➡MANY, MUCH, LARGE AMOUNT; 117]

agree 1 *v* **concur**, be in agreement, see eye to eye, coincide, subscribe. [➡AGREE; 646] *Opposite:* differ. 2 *v* **consent**, say yes, concur, assent, acquiesce, accede, grant, permit, allow (*formal*), go along with. [➡PERMIT AND ALLOW; 670] *Opposite:* disagree. 3 *v* **decide**, reach agreement, come to an agreement, come to an understanding, settle, reach a decision, approve. [➡MAKE DECISIONS AND CHOICES; 753] *Opposite:* disagree. 4 *v* **correspond**, match, be the same, tie in, harmonize, be consistent with, supplement, complete. [➡HARMONY; 156] *Opposite:* differ.

Compare and Contrast: *agree, consent, concur, acquiesce, assent*

CORE MEANING: TO ACCEPT AN IDEA, PLAN, OR COURSE OF ACTION THAT HAS BEEN PUT FORWARD

agree to be in agreement with somebody else about a course of action; ***consent*** give formal permission for something to happen; ***concur*** agree or reach agreement independently on a specified point; ***acquiesce*** agree to or comply with something passively; ***assent*** agree to something formally.

agreeable 1 *adj* **pleasant**, pleasing, pleasurable, enjoyable, delightful, satisfying, to your liking, good, comfortable, suitable, acceptable. [➡EMOTIONALLY PLEASANT; 188]

Opposite: unpleasant. 2 *adj* **friendly**, affable, pleasant, courteous, delightful, congenial. [➡FRIENDLINESS AND SOCIABILITY; 495] *Opposite:* disagreeable. 3 *adj* **amenable**, willing, in accord, compliant, happy. [➡THE WILL AND WILLINGNESS; 564] *Opposite:* unwilling.

agreeably *adv* **pleasantly**, enjoyably, delightfully, pleasingly, pleasurably, comfortably, suitably. [➡EMOTIONALLY PLEASANT; 188] *Opposite:* unpleasantly.

agreed *adj* **decided**, settled, arranged, approved, fixed, granted, established, contracted. [➡CERTAIN; 175]

agreement 1 *n* **contract**, arrangement, covenant, treaty, promise, pact, settlement, bargain, understanding, deal, compact, bond, concord. [➡OFFICIAL DOCUMENTS; 587] 2 *n* **accord**, concord, conformity, harmony, union, concurrence, consonance (*formal*). [➡HARMONY; 156] *Opposite:* disagreement.

agribusiness *n* **farming industry**, agroindustry, agricultural business, business, commerce, farming. [➡AGRICULTURE AND FARMING; 1074]

agricultural 1 *adj* **agrarian**, farming, agronomic, farmed, cultivated. [➡AGRICULTURE AND FARMING; 1074] 2 *adj* **unindustrialized**, pastoral, rural, bucolic, undeveloped. [➡AGRICULTURE AND FARMING; 1074] *Opposite:* urban.

agricultural science *n* [➡AGRICULTURE AND FARMING; 1074]

agricultural show *n* [➡AGRICULTURE AND FARMING; 1074]

agriculture *n* **cultivation**, husbandry, crop growing, food production, agronomy, farming, agricultural science. [➡AGRICULTURE AND FARMING; 1074]

agroindustry *n* [➡AGRICULTURE AND FARMING; 1074]

agronomic *adj* [➡AGRICULTURE AND FARMING; 1074]

agronomy *n* [➡AGRICULTURE AND FARMING; 1074]

aground *adj* **beached**, ashore, stranded, stuck, grounded, high and dry. [➡LACK OF ACTIVITY; 343] *Opposite:* afloat.

ahead 1 *adv* **in front**, to the front, in the lead, in advance, further on, to the fore, at the forefront, forward, before. [➡RELATIVE LOCATION; 162] *Opposite:* behind. 2 *adv* **into the future**, in the future, to come, yet to be, forward, onward. [➡FUTURE; 86] *Opposite:* ago. 3 *adv* **early**, in advance, prematurely, up front, ahead of, beforehand. [➡PROMPTNESS: EARLY; 98] *Opposite:* late.

ahead of 1 *prep* **in front of**, before, beyond, up ahead of, in advance of, up in front of, at the head of, in store for, waiting for. [➡FUTURE; 86] *Opposite:* behind. 2 *prep* **before**, in advance of, earlier than, in front of, just before, previous to, pre-. [➡BEFORE, FIRST, AND PRECEDING; 164] *Opposite:* after.

ahead of its time *adj* **revolutionary**, radical, innovative, modern, progressive. [➡NEW, MODERN; 167] *Opposite:* behind the times.

ahead of schedule *adv* [➡PROMPTNESS: EARLY; 98]

ahead of time *adv* **early**, in advance, prematurely, up front, ahead, beforehand. [➡PROMPTNESS: EARLY; 98] *Opposite:* behind.

aid 1 *v* **help**, assist, support, abet, give support to, minister, relieve, serve, sustain, facilitate, encourage, promote. [➡HELP; 294] *Opposite:* thwart. 2 *n* **assistance**, help, support, relief, encouragement, service. [➡KIND ACTION OR BEHAVIOUR; 296]

aid agency *n* [➡CHARITY AND CHARITABLE INSTITUTIONS; 822]

aid and abet *v* **conspire**, collaborate, collude, be in cahoots with (*informal*), connive, be in league with, assist, help, plot, contrive. [➡HELP; 294]

aide *n* **assistant**, adviser, helper, supporter, aide-de-camp, personal assistant, secretary. [➡SUBORDINATES AND ASSISTANTS; 966]

See Compare and Contrast at **assistant**.

aide-de-camp *n* **assistant**, personal assistant, PA, aide, secretary, helper, administrative assistant, staffer (*informal*). [➡MILITARY PERSONNEL; 828]

aide-mémoire (*formal*) 1 *n* **summary**, outline, résumé, synopsis, digest, note. [➡SUMMARIES, OUTLINES, AND EXCERPTS; 589] 2 *n* **memory aid**, mnemonic, crib (*informal*), note, reminder, memorandum, outline, crib sheet. [➡LETTERS AND WRITTEN MESSAGES; 585]

aid organization *n* [➡CHARITY AND CHARITABLE INSTITUTIONS; 822]

aikido *type of* **combat sport**. [➡HOBBIES, GAMES, AND SPORTS; 875]

ail (*archaic or literary*) 1 *v* **trouble**, pain, distress, be wrong with, affect, afflict, be the matter with, bother, upset, worry. [➡UPSET, DISTRESS, AND HUMILIATE; 568] 2 *v* **be ill**, be sick, feel unwell, suffer, be in pain, feel pain, be weak, nauseate. [➡ILL AND SICK; 741]

aileron *part of* **aircraft**. [➡AIRCRAFT; 1147]

ailing 1 *adj* **underperforming**, failing, deteriorating, inadequate. [➡UNSUCCESSFUL AND UNPROMISING; 76] *Opposite:* thriving. 2 *adj* (*dated*) **unwell**, ill, sick, indisposed (*formal*), poorly (*informal*), unfit, laid up, under the weather, infirm, sickly. [➡ILL AND SICK; 741] *Opposite:* well.

ailment *n* **illness**, sickness, disease, disorder, complaint, weakness, condition, infirmity. [➡ILLNESSES AND DISORDERS; 733]

ailurophobia *type of* **phobia**. [➡FEARS AND PHOBIAS; 555]

aim 1 *v* **aspire**, plan, intend, try, mean, endeavour, want, seek, set your sights on, have your sights on, strive for. [➡ATTEMPT AN ACTION; 262] 2 *v* **point towards**, point, take aim, direct, mark, target, zero in, train, level. [➡MOVE SOMETHING: INTO A NEW POSITION OR OVERTURN; 331] 3 *n* **goal**, purpose, intention, object, objective, target, ambition, wish, aspiration. [➡INTENTION AND PURPOSE; 773]

aimless *adj* **pointless**, meaningless, useless, worthless, purposeless, directionless. [➡LACK OF COMMITMENT AND UNRELIABILITY; 510] *Opposite:* purposeful.

aimlessness *n* **pointlessness**, purposelessness, senselessness. [➡LACK OF COMMITMENT AND UNRELIABILITY; 510] *Opposite:* purposefulness.

air 1 *n* **atmosphere**, space, sky, heaven. [➡THE EARTH'S ATMOSPHERE; 1040] 2 *n* **appearance**, look, manner, tone, way of being, feeling, impression, aura, quality. [➡APPEARANCE AND

ATMOSPHERE; 1236] **3** *n* **tune**, melody, song. [➡MUSIC, SONGS, AND SINGING; 907] **4** *v* **declare**, express, vent, make public, proclaim, reveal, publicize, spread, circulate, tell, announce, broadcast. [➡INFORM AND ANNOUNCE; 612] *Opposite:* suppress. **5** *v* **ventilate**, aerate, expose. [➡CLEAN AND POLISH; 404]

air bladder *part of* **fish.** [➡PARTS OF A FISH; 1011]

airborne *adj* **flying**, aerial, floating, midair, in-flight, above ground, on high, aloft. [➡GENERAL LOCATIONS; 159]

airborne army *n* [➡THE ARMED FORCES; 827]

airborne operation *n* [➡WARFARE AND WAR; 830]

air brake *part of* **aircraft.** [➡AIRCRAFT; 1147]

airbrush *v* **spraypaint**, colour, blend, blend in, touch up, cover up, doctor, mask, conceal, paint, spray. [➡CREATE IMAGES; 357]

air-circulation system *n* [➡HEATING, REFRIGERATION, AND VENTILATION; 1141]

air-conditioned *adj* **cooled**, ventilated, well-ventilated, cool, chilled. [➡HEATING, REFRIGERATION, AND VENTILATION; 1141] *Opposite:* heated.

air conditioner *n* **air cooler**, air exchanger, ventilator, dehumidifier, extractor, AC (*US*). [➡HEATING, REFRIGERATION, AND VENTILATION; 1141] *Opposite:* heater.

air conditioning *n* **air-cooling system**, ventilation system, air-circulation system, air exchange system. [➡HEATING, REFRIGERATION, AND VENTILATION; 1141] *Opposite:* heating.

air cooler *type of* **cooling appliance.** [➡HEATING, REFRIGERATION, AND VENTILATION; 1141]

air-cooling system *n* [➡HEATING, REFRIGERATION, AND VENTILATION; 1141]

aircraft *n* **aeroplane**, plane, flying machine, airplane (*US*). [➡AIRCRAFT; 1147]

aircraft

◆ *types of military aircraft*
bomber, convertiplane, fighter, fighter-bomber, helicopter gunship, stealth bomber, transport, VTOL

◆ *types of civil aircraft*
airliner, airship, autogiro, biplane, blimp, dirigible, executive jet, glider, hang glider, helicopter, jet, light aircraft, light plane (*US*), microlight, monoplane, paraglider, seaplane, skiplane, STOL, zeppelin

◆ *parts of an aircraft*
aileron, air brake, autopilot, cabin, cockpit, ejection seat (*US*), ejector seat, fin, flight deck, flight recorder, fuselage, jet engine, joystick, landing gear, nose cone, nose wheel, propeller, rotor, rudder, tail, tail rotor, tailplane, turbofan, turbojet, turboprop, undercarriage, wing

aircraft carrier *type of* **military vessel.** [➡SHIPS AND BOATS; 1149]

airdrop *v* **parachute in**, airlift, send in, parachute, drop. [➡DESPATCH AND SEND; 334]

air duct *n* [➡HEATING, REFRIGERATION, AND VENTILATION; 1141]

air exchanger *type of* **cooling appliance.** [➡HEATING, REFRIGERATION, AND VENTILATION; 1141]

air exchange system *n* [➡HEATING, REFRIGERATION, AND VENTILATION; 1141]

airfare *n* **fare**, tariff, charge, ticket price, seat rate. [➡MONEY, PAYMENTS, AND CHARGES; 800]

airfield *n* **airstrip**, landing field, landing strip, aerodrome, airport, air base, airdrome (*US*). [➡AIRWAYS; 1108]

air force *n* [➡THE ARMED FORCES; 827]

airily *adv* **lightheartedly**, lightly, carelessly, casually, easily, brightly, cheerfully, gaily. [➡GOOD-TEMPERED AND HUMOROUS; 628] *Opposite:* seriously.

airiness **1** *n* **lightheartedness**, buoyancy, animation, vivacity, cheerfulness, casualness, brightness, gaiety. [➡GOOD-TEMPERED AND HUMOROUS; 628] *Opposite:* seriousness. **2** *n* **spaciousness**, openness, freshness, lightness. [➡LARGE; 1192] *Opposite:* closeness.

airing **1** *n* **ventilation**, aeration, exposure to air, drying, freshening. [➡HEATING, REFRIGERATION, AND VENTILATION; 1141] **2** *n* **outing**, trip, excursion. [➡TRAVEL: JOURNEYS AND TRIPS; 319] **3** *n* **exposure**, expression, disclosure, divulgence, ventilation, discussion. [➡NEGOTIATION AND DEBATE; 46]

airless *adj* **stuffy**, close, muggy, unventilated, oppressive, heavy, stifling. [➡PHYSICALLY UNPLEASANT; 227] *Opposite:* airy.

airlift *v* **fly**, transfer, winch, lift. [➡DESPATCH AND SEND; 334]

airline *n* **air company**, commercial airline, scheduled carrier, carrier. [➡AIRCRAFT; 1147]

airliner *type of* **civil aircraft.** [➡AIRCRAFT; 1147]

airlock **1** *n* **blockage**, obstruction, air bubble, occlusion, block, obstacle. [➡HOLES, GAPS, AND FORKS; 1251] **2** *n* **compartment**, cubicle, cell, chamber. [➡TYPES OF ROOM; 1096]

airmail *v* **post**, send, dispatch, mail (*US*). [➡DESPATCH AND SEND; 334]

air offensive *n* [➡WARFARE AND WAR; 830]

air pistol *type of* **gun.** [➡WEAPONS FOR SHOOTING; 1155]

airplane (*US*) *n* **aircraft**, plane, aeroplane. [➡AIRCRAFT; 1147]

airplay *n* **airtime**, playing time, exposure, promotion, publicity, plugging (*informal*), broadcast. [➡TELEVISION AND RADIO; 607]

airport *n* **airfield**, aerodrome, airstrip, landing field, landing strip, airdrome (*US*). [➡AIRWAYS; 1108]

airpower *n* **air strength**, airborne army, air force, air defence. [➡THE ARMED FORCES; 827]

air raid *n* **aerial attack**, aerial bombardment, air attack, bombing, air strike, air offensive, attack, raid, offensive. [➡AGGRESSIVE EVENT; 39]

air rifle *type of* **gun.** [➡WEAPONS FOR SHOOTING; 1155]

air sac *part of* **respiratory system.** [➡RESPIRATORY ORGANS; 716]

airship *n* **dirigible**, zeppelin, blimp, aircraft. [➡AIRCRAFT; 1147]

airshow *n* **aerobatics**, stunts, show, exhibition, fly-past. [➡PERFORMANCES AND SHOWS; 42]

airsick *adj* **travel sick**, nauseous, queasy, sick, ill. [➡ILL AND SICK; 741]

airsickness *n* **travel sickness**, nausea, queasiness, sickness, motion sickness. [➡ILL AND SICK; 741]

airspace *n* **territory**, skies, boundaries, limits, flight exclusion zone, no-fly-zone. [➡AIRWAYS; 1108]

air strike *n* **aerial attack**, aerial bombardment, bombing, air raid, air offensive, attack, raid, offensive. [➡AGGRESSIVE EVENT; 39]

airstrip *n* **runway**, landing strip, strip, landing field, airfield. [➡AIRWAYS; 1108]

airtight 1 *adj* **sealed**, hermetically sealed, hermetic, impermeable. [➡IN GOOD REPAIR; 1231] 2 *adj* **sound**, strong, unquestionable, unassailable, watertight, flawless. [➡CERTAIN; 175] *Opposite:* vulnerable.

airwaves *n* **radio waves**, frequencies, frequency bands, radio frequencies, broadcasting frequencies, radio signals. [➡TELEVISION AND RADIO; 607]

airway 1 *n* **air route**, air corridor, flight lane, air lane, route, flight path. [➡AIRWAYS; 1108] 2 *n* **airline**, air transport company, air network. [➡AIRWAYS; 1108] 3 *part of* **respiratory system**. [➡RESPIRATORY ORGANS; 716]

airworthiness *n* **safety**, soundness, reliability, working order. [➡SAFE AND SAFETY; 192]

airworthy *adj* **flyable**, flightworthy, in working order, in good order, safe, sound, reliable. [➡SAFE AND SAFETY; 192]

airy 1 *adj* **roomy**, ventilated, fresh, light, open, spacious. [➡LARGE; 1192] *Opposite:* stuffy. 2 *adj* **unconcerned**, nonchalant, casual, light, carefree, lighthearted, buoyant, vivacious, blithe (*literary*), cheerful. [➡GOOD-TEMPERED AND HUMOROUS; 628] *Opposite:* serious.

airy-fairy (*informal*) *adj* **vague**, unfocused, fanciful, unrealistic, impractical. [➡VAGUENESS; 244] *Opposite:* practical.

aisle *n* **passageway**, gangway, walkway, passage, corridor, lane. [➡DOORS AND ACCESS POINTS; 1100]

ajar *adj* **half closed**, open, agape (*literary*). [➡ORIENTATION AND ALIGNMENT; 1222]

a.k.a. *adv* **also known as**, better known as, otherwise known as, known to you and me as, alias, or. [➡WRITTEN CONVENTIONS; 600]

akin *adj* **similar**, of the same kind, parallel, like, analogous, alike, affiliated. [➡SIMILARITY; 149] *Opposite:* unlike.

alabaster *type of* **stone**. [➡STONES, ROCKS, AND BOULDERS; 1057]

alacritous *adj* [➡HAPPENING QUICKLY; 104]

alacrity *n* **promptness**, quickness, rapidity, speed, readiness, swiftness, keenness, zeal, eagerness. [➡SPEED; 102] *Opposite:* sluggishness.

alarm 1 *n* **fear**, apprehension, terror, fright, panic, unease, anxiety, distress, agitation, dread. [➡FEAR AND PANIC; 544] 2 *n* **alarm bell**, bell, warning, distress signal, siren, danger signal. [➡SIGNPOSTS, SIGNALS, AND BILLBOARDS; 596] 3 *type of* **clock**. [➡CLOCKS AND TIMERS; 1125] 4 *v* **frighten**, terrify, panic, distress, startle, scare, worry, upset, shock. [➡FRIGHTEN AND SHOCK; 569] *Opposite:* calm.

alarm bell *n* [➡SIGNALLING; 1139]

alarm clock *type of* **clock**. [➡CLOCKS AND TIMERS; 1125]

alarmed *adj* **worried**, upset, distressed, shocked, frightened, startled, terrified, panicked, scared. [➡CONFUSION, ANXIETY, AND WORRY; 541] *Opposite:* untroubled.

alarming *adj* **disturbing**, upsetting, frightening, distressing, shocking, startling, disquieting, worrying, terrifying. [➡FRIGHTENING; 232] *Opposite:* soothing.

alarmist 1 *n* **pessimist**, doom merchant, doomster (*informal*), doomsayer. [➡GRUMPY AND NEGATIVE PEOPLE; 953] 2 *adj* **pessimistic**, doom-laden, gloomy, panicky, exaggerated, over-the-top (*informal*), hysterical. [➡EMOTIONALLY UNPLEASANT AND UPSETTING; 228] *Opposite:* down-to-earth.

alas *adv* **unfortunately**, sadly, regrettably, unhappily, unluckily, more's the pity (*informal*), as luck would have it. [➡EXPRESSIONS OF REGRET; 548]

albatross 1 *n* **millstone**, shackle, encumbrance, burden, impediment, hindrance. [➡PROBLEM; 257] 2 *type of* **seabird**. [➡SEABIRD; 1002]

albeit *conj* **although**, though, even though, even if, notwithstanding (*formal*). [➡ALTHOUGH, NEVERTHELESS, AND DESPITE; 170]

album 1 *n* **book**, folder, photograph album, photo album, autograph album, stamp album, sticker album, wedding album, baby book, scrapbook. [➡BOOKS AND BOOKLETS; 591] 2 *n* **record**, LP, CD, tape, cassette, compilation, collection. [➡RECORDINGS AND PLAYERS; 911]

albumen *n* **egg white**, white, white of egg. [➡FOOD COMPONENTS; 1187]

alchemy *n* **pseudoscience**, experimentation, transformation. [➡CHANGE; 373]

alcoholic *adj* **intoxicating** (*formal*), inebriating, fermented, distilled, strong, boozy (*slang*), hard, vinous, spirituous (*formal*). [➡DRINKS; 1186] *Opposite:* nonalcoholic.

alcove *n* **recess**, niche, bay, cubicle, nook. [➡ALCOVES, CUBICLES, AND COMPARTMENTS; 1095]

al dente *adj* [➡STATE OF PREPARED FOOD; 1170]

alder *type of* **deciduous tree**. [➡DECIDUOUS TREES; 1028]

alert 1 *adj* **attentive**, watchful, prepared, aware, vigilant, ready, observant, on the alert, on the ball (*informal*). [➡POSITIVE IMPATIENCE, ENTHUSIASM, AND ALERTNESS; 538] *Opposite:* unprepared. 2 *n* **warning**, signal, alarm, siren, red alert, heads-up (*US*). [➡SIGNPOSTS, SIGNALS, AND BILLBOARDS; 596] 3 *v* **warn**, forewarn, notify, draw somebody's attention to, tell, inform. [➡ADVISE AND WARN; 614]

alertness *n* **attentiveness**, watchfulness, awareness, preparedness, vigilance, readiness. [➡ENERGY AND ENTHUSIASM; 497] *Opposite:* inattentiveness.

alfalfa *type of* **salad vegetable**. [➡FRUIT AND VEGETABLES; 1175]

alfresco 1 *adv* **out of doors**, outdoors, outside, in the open air, on the lawn, on the patio. [➡GENERAL LOCATIONS; 159] *Opposite:* indoors. 2 *adj* **outdoor**, open-air, outside, patio, picnic, yard (*US*). [➡GENERAL LOCATIONS; 159] *Opposite:* indoor.

alga

◆ *types of alga*
bladder wrack, brown alga, fucus, green alga, gulfweed, Irish moss, kelp, laminaria, phytoplankton, pond scum, red alga, rockweed, sea lettuce, seaweed, sea wrack, stonewort, tangle

algebra *n* [➡MATHS; 598]

algorithm *n* **procedure**, process, system, set of rules. [➡WAYS OF DOING THINGS; 295]

alias 1 *adj* **also known as**, also called, otherwise known as, under the name of, a.k.a. [➡NAME AND DESCRIBE; 666] 2 *n* **assumed name**, pseudonym, pen name, nom de plume, stage name. [➡NAME AND DESCRIBE; 666]

alibi (*informal*) *n* **explanation**, excuse, reason, defence, account. [➡EXPLAIN AND CLARIFY; 611]

Alice band *type of* **headgear**. [➡HABERDASHERY, MILLINERY, AND LINGERIE; 867]

alien 1 *n* **extraterrestrial**, creature from outer space, space invader, Martian, intelligent life form. [➡SCIENCE FICTION; 1063] 2 *n* **foreigner**, stranger, immigrant, resident alien. [➡STRANGERS; 972] 3 *adj* **unfamiliar**, unknown, strange, outlandish, extraterrestrial. [➡SECRET AND UNKNOWN; 180]

alienate *v* **estrange**, make unfriendly, disaffect, set against, distance, push away, separate, isolate, keep apart, turn away, turn your back on. [➡REFUSING OR REJECTING RELATIONS; 975]

alienated *adj* **estranged**, disaffected, isolated, withdrawn, separate, indifferent. [➡NEUTRALITY AND INDIFFERENCE; 554] *Opposite:* involved.

alienation *n* **estrangement**, disaffection, unfriendliness, hostility, isolation, separation, dissension, division. [➡SOLITARINESS; 941] *Opposite:* closeness.

alien craft *n* [➡SCIENCE FICTION; 1063]

alight 1 *v* **get off**, get out, descend, dismount. [➡GO DOWNWARDS; 308] 2 *v* **land**, perch, rest, stop, settle. [➡ARRIVE BY TRANSPORT; 14] 3 *adj* **burning**, on fire, in flames, blazing, ablaze, flaming. [➡FIRE, FLAMMABILITY, AND BURNING; 1164]

align 1 *v* **bring into line**, line up, make straight, make parallel, make even. [➡ARRANGE AND CREATE ORDER; 358] *Opposite:* disarrange. 2 *v* **side with**, support, ally, affiliate, associate, line up with. [➡ESTABLISHING RELATIONSHIPS WITH OTHERS; 974] *Opposite:* distance.

aligned *adj* **allied**, united, associated, affiliated, ranged. [➡RELATED; 143]

alignment 1 *n* **position**, arrangement, placement, configuration, orientation. [➡ORIENTATION AND ALIGNMENT; 1222] *Opposite:* disorder. 2 *n* **alliance**, association, coalition, grouping, affiliation, support. [➡CONNECTION; 144]

alike *adj* **similar**, comparable, the same, identical, like. [➡SIMILARITY; 149] *Opposite:* different.

alikeness *n* [➡SIMILARITY; 149]

alimentary canal *part of* **digestive tract**. [➡THE DIGESTIVE TRACT; 710]

alimony *n* **allowance**, maintenance, support, financial support, funding. [➡MONEY, PAYMENTS, AND CHARGES; 800]

alive 1 *adj* **living**, animate, breathing. [➡LIVING THINGS AND LIVING; 976] *Opposite:* dead. 2 *adj* **energetic**, busy, active, perky, vibrant, bustling, vivacious, animated, full of life. [➡ENERGY AND ENTHUSIASM; 497] *Opposite:* inactive. 3 *adj* **animated**, thriving, active, flourishing, successful, blooming, buzzing. [➡SUCCESSFUL AND PROMISING; 81] *Opposite:* quiet. 4 *adj* **full**, packed, teeming, awash, swarming, jumping (*informal*), hopping (*informal*). [➡FULL; 1238] *Opposite:* dead. 5 *adj* **aware**, sensitive, tuned in, alert, interested, homed in. [➡POSITIVE IMPATIENCE, ENTHUSIASM, AND ALERTNESS; 538] *Opposite:* unaware.

See Compare and Contrast at **living**.

alive and kicking (*informal*) *adj* **going strong**, surviving, still with us, around, energetic, all right, hale and hearty, vigorous, alive and well. [➡FIT AND STRONG; 737] *Opposite:* dead.

alive and well *adj* **safe**, all right, safe and sound, okay (*informal*), unharmed, uninjured, in good shape. [➡FINE; 738]

all 1 *adv* (*informal*) **altogether**, completely, entirely, very, wholly, totally. [➡WHOLENESS AND COMPLETENESS; 199] 2 *pron* **every one**, each and every one, every single one, each. [➡ALL; 126] *Opposite:* none. 3 *pron* **every bit**, the entire, the complete, the whole. [➡ALL; 126] *Opposite:* none.

all alone *adj* [➡SOLITARINESS; 941]

all along *adv* **from the start**, right from the start, from the very beginning, from the word go, from the beginning, from the outset, all the time, the whole time, from start to finish, right from the outset (*US*). [➡PERMANENCE: WITHOUT END; 94]

all and sundry *pron* **everyone**, everybody, one and all, every person, the whole world, every last one, each and every one. [➡ALL; 126] *Opposite:* nobody.

all-around (*US*) 1 *adj* **versatile**, multifaceted, exceptional, outstanding, talented, multitalented, all-round. [➡TALENTED AND SKILFUL; 528] 2 *adj* **all-inclusive**, grand, inclusive, sweeping, large-scale, broad, comprehensive, all-embracing, wide-ranging, extensive, complete, across-the-board. [➡WHOLENESS AND COMPLETENESS; 199] *Opposite:* restricted. 3 *adj* **on all sides**, in every direction, everywhere, in all directions. [➡GENERAL LOCATIONS; 159]

all at once 1 *adv* **at the same time**, all together, together, simultaneously, concurrently, in unison, as one. [➡CON-

CURRENT AND CONTEMPORANEOUS; 165] *Opposite:* independently. 2 *adv* **suddenly**, all of a sudden, without warning, just like that, out of the blue, in a flash, in one fell swoop, unexpectedly, abruptly. [➡HAPPENING QUICKLY; 104] *Opposite:* gradually.

all at sea *adj* [➡INSECURITY AND LOSS OF COMPOSURE; 545]

allay *v* **dispel**, alleviate, calm, assuage, relieve, put to rest. [➡CHANGE OF INTENSITY: LESS; 396] *Opposite:* stimulate.

all by yourself *adv* **without help**, on your own, by yourself, of your own accord, unaided, on your own account. [➡ACTING INDEPENDENTLY; 285] *Opposite:* jointly.

all clear *n* **go-ahead** (*informal*), all-clear signal, nod, okay (*informal*), signal, thumbs-up (*informal*), green light, permission, approval, clear coast (*US*). [➡PERMIT AND ALLOW; 670]

all-clear signal *n* [➡SIGNALLING; 1139]

all-comers *n* **everyone**, everybody, one and all, all, the general public, the public. [➡ALL; 126]

all-consuming *adj* [➡STRENGTH; 202]

all ears (*informal*) *adj* [➡PENSIVENESS AND INTEREST; 539]

allegation *n* **claim**, accusation, assertion, contention, charge. [➡CLAIM, INSIST, AND EMPHASIZE; 615]

allege *v* **claim**, assert, contend, charge, declare. [➡CLAIM, INSIST, AND EMPHASIZE; 615]

alleged *adj* **supposed**, unproven, suspected, so-called, assumed, apparent, purported (*formal*). [➡UNCERTAIN; 176] *Opposite:* confirmed.

allegiance *n* **loyalty**, commitment, adherence, faithfulness, duty, fidelity. [➡CONNECTION; 144] *Opposite:* disloyalty.

allegorical *adj* **metaphorical**, symbolic, emblematic, figurative, allegoric, metaphoric, fictional. [➡FALSE AND UNREAL; 174] *Opposite:* literal.

allegory *n* **parable**, fable, metaphor, symbol, extended metaphor, tale, story. [➡THE ORAL TRADITION; 678]

allegro *type of* **musical term.** [➡MUSICAL TERMS; 912]

all-embracing *adj* **comprehensive**, complete, extensive, catholic, wide-ranging, across-the-board, broad, all-encompassing, all-inclusive, sweeping, large-scale, grand, inclusive, all-round, all-around (*US*). [➡WHOLENESS AND COMPLETENESS; 199] *Opposite:* narrow.

all-encompassing *adj* **all-inclusive**, grand, inclusive, sweeping, large-scale, broad, comprehensive, all-embracing, wide-ranging, extensive, complete, across-the-board, all-round, all-around (*US*). [➡WHOLENESS AND COMPLETENESS; 199] *Opposite:* restricted.

allergic *adj* **sensitive**, affected, sensitized, hypersensitive, averse (*formal*). [➡SICKNESS; 730]

allergy 1 *n* **reaction**, allergic reaction, sensitivity, hypersensitivity. [➡ILLNESSES AND DISORDERS; 733] 2 *n* (*informal*) **aversion**, dislike, antipathy, distaste, hate, hatred. [➡DISLIKE AND HATE; 578]

alleviate *v* **ease**, lessen, assuage, improve, lighten, relieve. [➡CHANGE OF INTENSITY: LESS; 396] *Opposite:* aggravate.

alleviation *n* **mitigation**, lessening, improvement, easing, assuagement, relief. [➡CHANGE OF INTENSITY: LESS; 396] *Opposite:* aggravation.

alley *type of* **minor road.** [➡ROADS; 1105]

alleyway *type of* **minor road.** [➡ROADS; 1105]

all fingers and thumbs *adj* [➡AGILITY OF THE BODY; 477]

all for *prep* **in favour of**, pro, for, in support of. [➡LIKE, LOVE, VALUE, AND ENJOY; 579]

alliance 1 *n* **coalition**, grouping, association, union, cooperation, agreement, treaty, pact, deal. [➡GROUPS WITH A COMMON INTEREST; 938] 2 *n* **relationship**, partnership, bond, link, tie. [➡CONNECTION; 144]

allied 1 *adj* **joined**, united, combined, amalgamated, aligned, partnered. [➡RELATED; 143] 2 *adj* **related**, associated, connected, akin, linked, similar. [➡RELATED; 143] *Opposite:* unrelated.

alligator *type of* **reptile.** [➡REPTILES; 994]

all-important *adj* [➡MOST IMPORTANT AND MAIN; 194]

all in 1 *adj* **total**, inclusive, overall, global, all-inclusive. [➡ALL; 126] 2 *adj* **exhausted**, weary, dead beat (*informal*), whacked (*informal*), tired, tired out, worn out, bushed (*informal*). [➡TIRED, ASLEEP, AND UNCONSCIOUS; 739] *Opposite:* fresh.

all in all *adv* **all things considered**, on the whole, in general, generally speaking, when all is said and done, overall, taking everything into account. [➡SUMMARIZING EXPRESSIONS; 623]

all-inclusive *adj* **comprehensive**, grand, complete, broad, all-embracing, all-encompassing, wide-ranging, all in. [➡WHOLENESS AND COMPLETENESS; 199] *Opposite:* incomplete.

all in the mind *adj* [➡FALSE AND UNREAL; 174]

alliteration *n* **assonance**, consonance, sound repetition, sound pattern, resonance, echo. [➡ASPECTS OF LANGUAGE; 683]

alliterative *adj* **repetitive**, echoing, assonant, poetic. [➡ASPECTS OF LANGUAGE; 683]

all-knowing *adj* [➡KNOWLEDGE AND WISDOM; 559]

allocate *v* **assign**, allot, apportion, distribute, deal, share out, give, hand out, earmark, divide up, share. [➡DISPENSE, RATION, AND DISTRIBUTE; 435]

allocation 1 *n* **distribution**, provision, sharing out, apportionment, division, sharing. [➡DISPENSE, RATION, AND DISTRIBUTE; 435] 2 *n* **share**, portion, allotment, allowance. [➡AMOUNT AND QUANTITY; 112]

all of a flutter *adj* [➡PLEASURE, EXCITEMENT, AND ELATION; 535]

all of a sudden *adv* **suddenly**, out of the blue, in a flash, in one fell swoop, on the spur of the moment, unexpectedly, abruptly, without warning, spontaneously, out of nowhere, all at once. [➡HAPPENING QUICKLY; 104] *Opposite:* gradually.

all-or-nothing *adj* **win-or-lose**, uncompromising,

winner-take-all, rigid, zero-sum, unyielding, high-stake, inflexible, unrelenting, tenacious, dogged. [➡ALL; 126] *Opposite:* flexible.

allosaurus *type of* **dinosaur**. [➡DINOSAUR; 996]

allot *v* **assign**, designate, allocate, earmark, apportion, set aside, give, ration, allow. [➡DISPENSE, RATION, AND DISTRIBUTE; 435]

allotment 1 *n* **vegetable garden**, vegetable patch, plot. [➡GARDENS; 1073] 2 *n* **share**, portion, part, allocation, allowance, ration. [➡DISPENSE, RATION, AND DISTRIBUTE; 435]

all-out *adj* **maximum**, supreme, extreme, thoroughgoing, determined, concentrated. [➡WHOLENESS AND COMPLETENESS; 199] *Opposite:* half-hearted.

all over *adj* **finished**, ended, concluded, done with, over and done with, done, all up. [➡PAST; 84]

all over again *adv* [➡AGAIN; 109]

all over the place (*informal*) 1 *adj* **untidy**, in disorder, in disarray, in a state (*informal*), in a mess, disorganized, topsy-turvy. [➡DISORDER AND CHAOS; 246] *Opposite:* tidy. 2 *adv* **everywhere**, all over, here and there, high and low, far and wide, around, from one place to another, hither and thither, hither and yon. [➡GENERAL LOCATIONS; 159]

allow 1 *v* **let**, permit, agree, consent, tolerate, countenance (*formal*), sanction. [➡PERMIT AND ALLOW; 670] *Opposite:* forbid. 2 *v* **allocate**, set aside, make available, set a limit, allot, apportion. [➡DISPENSE, RATION, AND DISTRIBUTE; 435] 3 *v* (*formal*) **accept**, admit, acknowledge, admit as true, grant, concede. [➡ADMIT AND CONFESS; 616] *Opposite:* disallow.

allowable *adj* **permissible**, acceptable, tolerable, admissible, suitable. [➡ACCEPTABLE AND PASSABLE; 220] *Opposite:* unacceptable.

allowance *n* **payment**, grant, stipend, pocket money, pin money, budget. [➡INCOME; 461]

allowed *adj* **permitted**, allotted, authorized, approved, legitimate, accepted, recognized, sanctioned. [➡LEGAL; 815] *Opposite:* prohibited.

allow for *v* **take into account**, take into consideration, make allowance for, make allowances for, bear in mind, keep in mind, consider. [➡PAY ATTENTION; 766]

alloy 1 *n* **blend**, amalgam, compound, mixture, composite. [➡COLLECTIONS AND MIXTURES OF THINGS; 1243] 2 *n* **additive**, contaminant, adulterant, pollutant, ingredient, component. [➡MORE AND EXCESS; 122]

See Compare and Contrast at **mixture**.

all-powerful *adj* **omnipotent**, invincible, supreme, almighty. [➡STRENGTH; 202] *Opposite:* weak.

all-purpose *adj* **general purpose**, multipurpose, universal, overall, versatile, general, multiuse, flexible. [➡USEFULNESS; 200] *Opposite:* specialized.

all right 1 *adj* **satisfactory**, okay (*informal*), good, pleasing. [➡ACCEPTABLE AND PASSABLE; 220] *Opposite:* unsatisfactory. 2 *adj* **acceptable**, so-so (*informal*), fair to middling, good enough, reasonable, fair, passable, suitable, okay (*informal*). [➡ACCEPTABLE AND PASSABLE; 220] *Opposite:* unacceptable. 3 *adj* **safe and sound**, uninjured, okay (*informal*), alive and well, safe, unharmed. [➡FINE; 738] *Opposite:* damaged. 4 *interj* **yes**, okay (*informal*), sure, why not?, no problem (*informal*), of course, agreed, fair enough (*informal*), by all means. [➡EXPRESSIONS OF AGREEMENT; 649] 5 *adv* **satisfactorily**, okay (*informal*), reasonably, acceptably, passably. [➡ACCEPTABLE AND PASSABLE; 220] *Opposite:* unsatisfactorily. 6 *adv* **certainly**, positively, obviously, without a doubt. [➡EXPRESSIONS OF AGREEMENT; 649]

all-round 1 *adj* **versatile**, multifaceted, exceptional, outstanding, talented, multitalented, all-around (*US*). [➡EXTRAORDINARY: UNCOMMON; 206] 2 *adj* **all-inclusive**, grand, inclusive, sweeping, large-scale, broad, comprehensive, all-embracing, wide-ranging, extensive, complete, across-the-board. [➡WHOLENESS AND COMPLETENESS; 199] *Opposite:* restricted. 3 *adj* **on all sides**, in every direction, everywhere, in all directions. [➡GENERAL LOCATIONS; 159]

all-seeing *adj* [➡KNOWLEDGE AND WISDOM; 559]

all set *adj* **ready**, ready to go, standing by, ready and waiting, at the ready, prepared. [➡CALMNESS, CONFIDENCE, AND COMPOSURE; 537] *Opposite:* unprepared.

allspice *type of* **spice**. [➡HERBS AND SPICES; 1174]

all-star *adj* **star-studded**, celebrity, famous, prestigious, well-known, glittering, glamorous. [➡KNOWN AND FAMOUS; 182] *Opposite:* unknown.

all-terrain vehicle *type of* **car**. [➡BIKES, CARS, AND CARRIAGES; 1148]

all the rage *adj* [➡POPULAR AND WANTED; 221]

all the same *adv* **even so**, nevertheless, in spite of everything, despite everything, however, yet. [➡ALTHOUGH, NEVERTHELESS, AND DESPITE; 170]

all the time 1 *adv* **continually**, constantly, repeatedly, incessantly, permanently, endlessly. [➡PERMANENCE: WITHOUT END; 94] *Opposite:* occasionally. 2 *adv* **all along**, from the start, from the word go, from start to finish, from the outset. [➡PERMANENCE: WITHOUT END; 94]

all things considered *adv* **all in all**, on the whole, when all's said and done, altogether, at the end of the day. [➡SUMMARIZING EXPRESSIONS; 623]

all thumbs *adj* [➡AGILITY OF THE BODY; 477]

all-time *adj* **unsurpassed**, record, unprecedented, unparalleled, best, greatest. [➡EXTRAORDINARY: AMAZING; 205] *Opposite:* insignificant.

all together 1 *adv* **together**, in agreement, united, as one, unanimous, in unison, in step, en masse, en bloc, jointly, as a unit, in partnership, in cooperation, in harmony, as a group, as a body, with one voice. [➡ACTING WITH OTHERS; 286] *Opposite:* independently. 2 *adv* **simultaneously**, at the same time, all at once, together, concurrently. [➡CONCURRENT AND CONTEMPORANEOUS; 165] *Opposite:* separately.

all told *adv* **altogether**, in total, all in all, in all, overall, all included. [➡ALL; 126] *Opposite:* in part.

allude *v* **refer**, make reference, make allusion, mention, indicate, suggest, talk about, touch on, introduce, refer in passing, make a passing reference. [➡SUGGEST, HINT, AND COMMENT; 613]

allure *n* **attraction**, appeal, draw, pull (*informal*), magnetism, charm, glamour, fascination, charisma. [➡INTERESTING AND MEANINGFUL; 191]

alluring *adj* **appealing**, attractive, tempting, interesting, fascinating, enthralling, charming, glamorous, captivating, charismatic, irresistible. [➡INTERESTING AND MEANINGFUL; 191] *Opposite:* repulsive.

allusion *n* **reference**, mention, hint, suggestion, insinuation, quotation, citation. [➡SUGGEST, HINT, AND COMMENT; 613]

allusive *adj* **indirect**, oblique, hinting, referential, suggestive, indicative. [➡RETICENT AND UNFORTHCOMING; 632] *Opposite:* direct.

alluvial *adj* **sedimentary**, silty, deposited, muddy, sandy, grainy. [➡EROSION PRODUCTS AND SOIL; 1058]

all-weather *adj* **year-round**, all-season, rain-or-shine, all-purpose, four-season. [➡PERMANENCE: WITHOUT END; 94]

ally 1 *v* **associate**, join, affiliate, align, connect, link. [➡ESTABLISHING RELATIONSHIPS WITH OTHERS; 974] 2 *n* **friend**, helper, supporter, assistant, partner, confederate, associate. [➡FRIENDS; 963] *Opposite:* enemy.

alma mater *n* **old school**, college, university, school, institution. [➡EDUCATIONAL INSTITUTIONS; 813]

almanac *n* **directory**, calendar, yearbook, handbook, manual, encyclopedia, reference book. [➡RECORDS; 586]

almighty 1 *adj* **omnipotent**, invincible, all-powerful, supreme, omnipresent. [➡STRENGTH; 202] 2 *adj* (*informal*) **enormous**, massive, huge, immense, gigantic, colossal, great, serious, terrible, terrific (*informal*), frightful. [➡LARGE; 1192]

almond *type of* **nut**. [➡NUTS; 1184]

almost *adv* **nearly**, not quite, just about, virtually, practically, more or less. [➡TO A CERTAIN EXTENT; 134] *Opposite:* exactly.

alms *n* **charity**, donation, contribution, gift, offering, handout, assistance, money. [➡GIFTS; 439]

aloft *adv* **in the air**, in flight, airborne, on the wing, high up, upwards. [➡GENERAL LOCATIONS; 159] *Opposite:* below.

alone 1 *adv* **unaccompanied**, by yourself, on your own, single-handedly, unaided, without help, solo. [➡ACTING INDEPENDENTLY; 285] 2 *adj* **lonely**, lonesome (*US*), abandoned, deserted, isolated, forlorn, solitary. [➡SOLITARINESS; 941]

along *prep* **next to**, beside, by the side of, alongside, by, adjacent to, near. [➡CLOSENESS; 160]

alongside *prep* **next to**, beside, at the side of, along, flanking, near. [➡CLOSENESS; 160]

along with *prep* **with**, together with, in company with, in conjunction with, as well as. [➡ALSO; 136]

aloof 1 *adj* **remote**, standoffish, proud, reserved, indifferent, snooty (*informal*), distant, detached, unfriendly, cold, unapproachable, lofty. [➡UNFRIENDLINESS AND UNSOCIABILITY; 505] *Opposite:* friendly. 2 *adj* **separate**, remote, distant, set apart, away, independent. [➡SOLITARINESS; 941] *Opposite:* close.

aloofly 1 *adv* **standoffishly**, reservedly, indifferently, remotely, distantly, detachedly, coldly, unapproachably, proudly, snootily (*informal*), loftily. [➡UNINTERESTED AND DETACHED; 630] 2 *adv* **separately**, remotely, distantly, independently. [➡SOLITARINESS; 941] *Opposite:* closely.

aloofness 1 *n* **unfriendliness**, coldness, detachment, remoteness, reserve, standoffishness, indifference, distance, unapproachability, proudness, snootiness (*informal*), loftiness. [➡UNFRIENDLINESS AND UNSOCIABILITY; 505] *Opposite:* friendliness. 2 *n* **distance**, remoteness, separateness, independence. [➡SOLITARINESS; 941] *Opposite:* closeness.

a lot 1 *adv* **a great deal**, lots, a whole heap (*informal*), very much, masses (*informal*), a good deal, enormously, greatly. [➡MANY, MUCH, LARGE AMOUNT; 117] 2 *pron* **plenty**, many, a large number, loads (*informal*), tons (*informal*), heaps (*informal*). [➡MANY, MUCH, LARGE AMOUNT; 117] *Opposite:* a few.

aloud 1 *adv* **audibly**, out loud, distinctly, noticeably, clearly, verbally. [➡PERCEPTIBLE; 25] *Opposite:* silently. 2 *adv* **loudly**, noisily, riotously, blusteringly, boisterously, clamorously. [➡LOUD OR UNPLEASANT SOUNDS; 1265] *Opposite:* quietly.

alp *n* [➡MOUNTAINS AND HILLS; 1044]

alpaca 1 *type of* **large mammal**. [➡LARGE MAMMAL; 986] 2 *type of* **fabric from animals**. [➡FABRICS; 1131]

alpha *adj* **important**, dominant, chief, primary, leading, first. [➡FUNDAMENTAL; 196]

alphabet *n* **ABC**, writing system, script, character set, letters, symbols. [➡SYMBOLS, SIGNS, AND NUMBERS; 597]

alphabet

◆ *types of alphabet*
Arabic, Braille, Cyrillic, Greek, Hebrew, hieroglyphics, phonetic alphabet, Roman alphabet, runic

alphabetic *adj* **arranged**, alphabetical, in order, listed, in a list, sequential, consecutive, serial. [➡SYMBOLS, SIGNS, AND NUMBERS; 597]

alphabetical *see* **alphabetic**.

alpine *adj* **mountainous**, mountain, high-altitude, hilly, high. [➡MOUNTAINS AND HILLS; 1044]

alpinism *n* [➡HOBBIES, GAMES, AND SPORTS; 875]

alpinist *n* [➡PEOPLE IN SPORTS AND LEISURE; 876]

already *adv* **by now**, previously, before now, even now, by this time, now, at present. [➡PRESENT; 85]

alright *see* **all right**.

Alsatian *type of* **large dog**. [➡DOG; 980]

also 1 *adv* **in addition**, and, what's more, moreover, furthermore, besides, additionally, plus (*informal*). [➡ALSO; 136] 2 *adv* **too**, as well, likewise, similarly, correspondingly. [➡ALSO; 136]

also-ran *n* **loser**, failure, no-hoper (*informal*), flop (*informal*), dud (*informal*). [➡FAILURE; 77] *Opposite:* winner.

altar *n* **table**, bench, slab, stand, platform, dais. [➡PARTS OF RELIGIOUS BUILDINGS; 1085]

alter *v* **change**, modify, adjust, vary, amend, revise, rework, correct, convert, shift. [➡CHANGE; 373] *Opposite:* maintain.

See Compare and Contrast at **change**.

alteration *n* **modification**, adjustment, change, variation, amendment, revision, shift, adaptation, correction. [➡CHANGE; 373]

altercate *v* **argue**, quarrel, disagree, dispute, squabble, row. [➡ARGUE AND FIGHT – TWO-WAY; 644]

altercation *n* **argument**, quarrel, disagreement, dispute, exchange, squabble, clash, difference of opinion, confrontation, row, fight. [➡ARGUMENT; 47]

alter ego *n* **double**, shadow, doppelgänger, twin, clone, stand-in. [➡SUPPORTERS, PROTECTORS, AND COMPATRIOTS; 970]

alternate 1 *v* **interchange**, swap (*informal*), rotate, exchange, intersperse, substitute. [➡CHANGE ONE THING FOR ANOTHER; 399] 2 *v* **fluctuate**, vary, swing, oscillate, vacillate, move between. [➡CHANGE; 373] 3 *adj* **every other**, alternating, every second. [➡FINITENESS, VARIABILITY, AND TRANSIENCE; 96] 4 *adj* **alternative**, substitute, different, another, other, replacement. [➡DIFFERENCE; 150] *Opposite:* same. 5 *n* (*US*) **substitute**, stand-in, alternative, fill-in, sub (*informal*), replacement, surrogate. [➡SUBSTITUTES AND STAND-INS; 400]

alternately *adv* **off and on**, in turn, by turns, one after the other, interchangeably, consecutively. [➡FINITENESS, VARIABILITY, AND TRANSIENCE; 96]

alternation *n* **change**, interchange, repetition, rotation, fluctuation, vacillation, oscillation, swing. [➡CHANGE; 373]

alternative 1 *n* **replacement**, substitute, substitution, change, another possibility, another course of action. [➡WAYS OF DOING THINGS; 295] 2 *n* **option**, choice, freedom of choice, discretion. [➡MAKE DECISIONS AND CHOICES; 753] 3 *adj* **other**, another, substitute, alternate, different. [➡DIFFERENCE; 150] 4 *adj* **unusual**, different, unconventional, out of the ordinary, marginal, unorthodox, complementary. [➡EXTRAORDINARY: UNCOMMON; 206] *Opposite:* conventional.

alternatively *adv* **on the other hand**, otherwise, instead, then again. [➡EXPRESSIONS INTRODUCING EXTRA INFORMATION; 137]

alternative therapy *n* [➡HEALING; 731]

although *conj* **though**, even though, even if, while, granting. [➡ALTHOUGH, NEVERTHELESS, AND DESPITE; 170]

altimeter *type of* **measuring device**. [➡MEASURING DEVICES; 1122]

altitude *n* **height**, elevation, height above sea level, loftiness, highness. [➡HEIGHT: HIGH; 1202]

alto *type of* **musical register**. [➡MUSICAL TERMS; 912]

altocumulus *type of* **cloud**. [➡CLOUDY AND RAINY WEATHER; 1052]

altogether 1 *adv* **in total**, all in all, all told, overall, in sum, in all. [➡ALL; 126] 2 *adv* **totally**, completely, wholly, thoroughly, entirely, fully. [➡TO A GREAT EXTENT; 130] 3 *adv* **on the whole**, when all's said and done, overall, in general, mostly, usually, generally, largely. [➡SUMMARIZING EXPRESSIONS; 623]

altostratus *type of* **cloud**. [➡CLOUDY AND RAINY WEATHER; 1052]

altruism *n* **unselfishness**, self-sacrifice, humanity, selflessness, philanthropy. [➡GENEROSITY AND KINDNESS; 496] *Opposite:* selfishness.

altruist *n* [➡PEOPLE WHO ARE APPROVED OF; 955]

altruistic *adj* **unselfish**, humane, selfless, philanthropic, noble, self-sacrificing. [➡GENEROSITY AND KINDNESS; 496] *Opposite:* selfish.

aluminium *type of* **metal**. [➡METALS; 1275]

alumna *n* **graduate**, former student, ex-student. [➡STUDENTS AND PUPILS; 841]

alumnus *n* **graduate**, former student, ex-student. [➡STUDENTS AND PUPILS; 841]

alveolus *part of* **respiratory system**. [➡RESPIRATORY ORGANS; 716]

always 1 *adv* **at all times**, continuously, all the time, continually, constantly, permanently, each time, every time. [➡PERMANENCE: WITHOUT END; 94] 2 *adv* **forever**, for all time, for eternity, until the end of time, for ever and a day, eternally. [➡PERMANENCE: WITHOUT END; 94]

a.m. *adj* **morning**, before noon, before lunch, pre-lunch. [➡TIMES OF DAY; 87] *Opposite:* p.m.

amalgam *n* **mixture**, mix, combination, blend, amalgamation, fusion. [➡COLLECTIONS AND MIXTURES OF THINGS; 1243]

See Compare and Contrast at **mixture**.

amalgamate *v* **merge**, join, combine, unite, integrate, mingle, fuse. [➡COMBINE AND MIX; 401] *Opposite:* separate.

amalgamated *adj* **combined**, merged, joined, incorporated, united, integrated, fused, mingled. [➡RELATED; 143] *Opposite:* separated.

amalgamation 1 *n* **mixture**, combination, mix, blend, fusion, compound. [➡COLLECTIONS AND MIXTURES OF THINGS; 1243] 2 *n* **merger**, union, incorporation, consolidation, unification. [➡CONNECTION; 144]

amanuensis *n* **secretary**, scribe, writer, copier, copyist, recorder, transcriber. [➡SUBORDINATES AND ASSISTANTS; 966]

amass *v* **accumulate**, collect, gather, stockpile, hoard, accrue, assemble, pile up, store up, build up. [➡GET; 421] *Opposite:* distribute.

See Compare and Contrast at **collect**.

amateur 1 *adj* **part-time**, unpaid, nonprofessional, leisure, recreational. [➡EMPLOYMENT STATUS; 831] *Opposite:* full-time. 2 *adj* **unprofessional**, shoddy, slapdash, substandard, incompetent, inexpert, unskilful, amateurish, slipshod, clumsy, crude, inept, sloppy (*informal*). [➡UNSKILLED; 530]

Opposite: skilful. **3** *n* **layperson**, nonprofessional. [➡UNSKILLED PERSON; 531] *Opposite:* professional.

amateur dramatics *n* [➡HOBBIES, GAMES, AND SPORTS; 875]

amateurish *adj* **unprofessional**, shoddy, sloppy (*informal*), slapdash, clumsy, crude, substandard, slipshod, incompetent, inexpert. [➡UNSKILLED; 530] *Opposite:* skilful.

amateurishness *n* **clumsiness**, ineptness, incompetence, unprofessionalness, sloppiness (*informal*), shoddiness, unskilfulness. [➡UNSKILLED; 530] *Opposite:* professionalism.

amateur photographer *n* [➡HOBBIES, GAMES, AND SPORTS; 875]

amaze *v* **astonish**, astound, shock, stun, startle, surprise, flabbergast (*informal*), dumbfound, stagger, take aback. [➡SURPRISE AND IMPRESS; 575]

amazed *adj* **astonished**, astounded, shocked, stunned, startled, surprised, flabbergasted (*informal*), dumbfounded, staggered, taken aback. [➡SURPRISE, SHOCK, AND AMAZEMENT; 546]

amazement *n* **astonishment**, wonder, admiration, shock, incredulity, surprise, bewilderment. [➡SURPRISE, SHOCK, AND AMAZEMENT; 546]

amazing *adj* **astonishing**, astounding, remarkable, wonderful, incredible, startling, marvellous, miraculous, surprising, mind-blowing (*informal*), mind-boggling (*informal*), staggering. [➡EXTRAORDINARY: AMAZING; 205] *Opposite:* unremarkable.

ambassador *n* **diplomat**, envoy, representative, emissary, legate. [➡REPRESENTATIVES AND PATRONS; 968]

amber *type of* **orange.** [➡COLOURS; 1223]

ambience *n* **atmosphere**, feel, setting, environment, mood, character, air, quality, tone, vibe (*slang*). [➡APPEARANCE AND ATMOSPHERE; 1236]

ambiguity *n* **vagueness**, uncertainty, haziness, doubt, indistinctness, obscurity, abstruseness, opacity, equivocality. [➡VAGUENESS; 244] *Opposite:* clarity.

ambiguous *adj* **vague**, unclear, abstruse, equivocal, uncertain, indefinite, confusing, indistinct, hazy, woolly. [➡VAGUENESS; 244] *Opposite:* clear.

ambiguousness *n* **abstruseness**, opacity, obscurity, vagueness, uncertainty, doubt, equivocality, dubiousness, confusion, indistinctness, indefiniteness. [➡VAGUENESS; 244] *Opposite:* clarity.

ambit *n* **scope**, extent, range, realm, area, field, preserve, limit. [➡DEGREE AND EXTENT; 110]

ambition **1** *n* **drive**, determination, get-up-and-go (*informal*), motivation, desire, spirit. [➡POSITIVE IMPATIENCE, ENTHUSIASM, AND ALERTNESS; 538] *Opposite:* apathy. **2** *n* **goal**, aim, objective, aspiration, dream, hope, desire, purpose. [➡FEELINGS ABOUT THE FUTURE; 534]

ambitious **1** *adj* **determined**, go-getting (*informal*), ruthless, striving, pushy (*informal*), motivated, aspiring, single-minded. [➡HARD-WORKING AND COMMITTED; 501] *Opposite:* unmotivated. **2** *adj* **grand**, impressive, bold, large-scale, elaborate, magnificent. [➡EXTRAORDINARY: AMAZING; 205] *Opposite:* small-scale.

ambitiously **1** *adv* **aspiringly**, determinedly, ruthlessly, pushily (*informal*), single-mindedly, energetically. [➡HARD-WORKING AND COMMITTED; 501] *Opposite:* unambitiously. **2** *adv* **optimistically**, overconfidently, unrealistically, idealistically, impractically, unworkably. [➡NEGATIVE INTELLECTUAL CHARACTERISTICS; 526] *Opposite:* realistically.

ambivalence *n* **uncertainty**, contradiction, unsureness, doubt, inconsistency, indecision, fluctuation, incongruity, vacillation. [➡UNCERTAINTY; 560] *Opposite:* certainty.

ambivalent *adj* **unsure**, undecided, in two minds, hesitant, uncertain, indecisive. [➡UNCERTAINTY; 560] *Opposite:* decisive.

amble *v* **stroll**, saunter, wander, mosey (*informal*), mooch (*slang*), promenade (*formal*), walk. [➡MOVE SLOWLY; 315]

ambulance *type of* **public service vehicle.** [➡VEHICLES; 1144]

ambush **1** *n* **trap**, surprise attack, ambuscade (*literary*), ensnarement. [➡SUDDEN EVENT; 52] **2** *v* **trap**, ensnare, lie in wait, take by surprise, waylay, ambuscade (*literary*). [➡INITIATE AND ESTABLISH COMMUNICATION; 681]

ameliorate (*formal*) *v* **better**, perfect, amend, upgrade, enrich, improve, enhance. [➡IMPROVE SOMETHING; 375] *Opposite:* deteriorate.

amelioration *n* **improvement**, enhancement, betterment (*formal*), enrichment, upgrading, amendment. [➡IMPROVE SOMETHING; 375] *Opposite:* deterioration.

amen (*informal*) *interj* **I agree**, you said it!, you bet! (*informal*), I'll say, yes, indeed, agreed. [➡EXPRESSIONS OF AGREEMENT; 649]

amenability *n* **acquiescence**, docility, willingness, responsiveness, pliability, cooperation, flexibility. [➡THE WILL AND WILLINGNESS; 564] *Opposite:* stubbornness.

amenable *adj* **agreeable**, open, acquiescent, willing, docile, responsive, pliable, cooperative, flexible. [➡THE WILL AND WILLINGNESS; 564] *Opposite:* stubborn.

amend *v* **alter**, adjust, modify, revise, change, improve, correct. [➡CORRECT AND PUT RIGHT; 378] *Opposite:* maintain.

amendable *adj* [➡THE WILL AND WILLINGNESS; 564]

amendment *n* **alteration**, adjustment, modification, revision, change, improvement, correction. [➡CHANGE; 373]

amends *n* **compensation**, recompense, replacement, restitution, return, substitution. [➡TREAT; 211]

amenity **1** *n* **facility**, convenience, comfort, service, feature, nicety, creature comfort. [➡PHYSICAL OBJECTS; 1242] **2** *n* **pleasantness**, attractiveness, niceness, agreeableness, affability, goodness. [➡PHYSICALLY PLEASANT; 187] *Opposite:* discomfort.

American football *type of* **ball game.** [➡HOBBIES, GAMES, AND SPORTS; 875]

amethyst **1** *type of* **gemstone.** [➡PRECIOUS STONES; 1277] **2** *type of* **purple.** [➡COLOURS; 1223]

amiability *n* **friendliness**, amicability, sociability, cordiality, agreeableness, good nature, good humour, kindness, geniality, affability. [➡FRIENDLINESS AND SOCIABILITY; 495] *Opposite:* unfriendliness.

amiable *adj* **friendly**, sociable, agreeable, affable, kind, likable, good-natured, good-humoured, amicable, genial, cordial. [➡FRIENDLINESS AND SOCIABILITY; 495] *Opposite:* unfriendly.

amicable *adj* **friendly**, good-natured, harmonious, agreeable, good-humoured, kind, polite. [➡RELATIONSHIP TO ANOTHER; 973]

amicably *adv* **good-naturedly**, cordially, harmoniously, kindly, politely, good-humouredly, agreeably, affably. [➡RELATIONSHIP TO ANOTHER; 973]

amid 1 *prep* **in the middle of**, among, in the midst of, within, in, amidst. [➡RELATIVE LOCATION; 162] 2 *prep* **accompanied by**, along with, in the course of, during, at the same time as, amidst. [➡CONCURRENT AND CONTEMPORANEOUS; 165]

amidst 1 *prep* **in the middle of**, among, in the midst of, within, in, amid. [➡RELATIVE LOCATION; 162] 2 *prep* **accompanied by**, along with, in the course of, during, at the same time as, amid. [➡CONCURRENT AND CONTEMPORANEOUS; 165]

amigo *n* [➡FRIENDS; 963]

amino acid *type of* **nutrient.** [➡FOOD COMPONENTS; 1187]

amiss 1 *adv* **incorrectly**, inappropriately, mistakenly, wrongly, erroneously, awry. [➡INCORRECT AND ERRONEOUS; 223] *Opposite:* correctly. 2 *adj* **incorrect**, inappropriate, mistaken, wrong, erroneous, awry. [➡INCORRECT AND ERRONEOUS; 223] *Opposite:* correct.

amity (*formal*) *n* **friendship**, peace, good relations, goodwill, harmony, friendliness. [➡RELATIONSHIP TO ANOTHER; 973] *Opposite:* hostility.

ammo (*informal*) *n* **ammunition**, bullets, shells, missiles, bombs, grenades. [➡WEAPONS; 1153]

ammunition *n* **bullets**, shells, missiles, bombs, grenades, ammo (*informal*). [➡WEAPONS; 1153]

amnesia *n* **loss of memory**, memory loss, forgetfulness, obliviousness, oblivion, blankness, a total blank. [➡IGNORANCE; 558]

amnesty *n* **pardon**, reprieve, forgiveness, absolution, exoneration, remission. [➡TRIAL, PUNISHMENT, AND LEGAL OUTCOMES; 819]

amoeba *type of* **microorganism.** [➡MICROORGANISMS, FUNGI, AND ALGAE; 1023]

amoebic *adj* [➡MICROORGANISMS, FUNGI, AND ALGAE; 1023]

among 1 *prep* **in the middle of**, in the midst of, amongst, amid, surrounded by, between, mid, midst. [➡RELATIVE LOCATION; 162] 2 *prep* **with**, along with, amongst, amid, together with, in the company of. [➡RELATIVE LOCATION; 162] 3 *prep* **as well as**, including, in addition to. [➡ALSO; 136]

amongst *see* **among.**

amoral *adj* **unprincipled**, unethical, dishonourable, unscrupulous, immoral. [➡MORALLY BAD; 776] *Opposite:* principled.

amorality *n* **wickedness**, sinfulness, unscrupulousness, immorality. [➡MORALLY BAD; 776] *Opposite:* morality.

amorous *adj* **ardent**, passionate, affectionate, loving, romantic, sentimental, enamoured, infatuated. [➡APPRECIATION AND GRATITUDE; 536] *Opposite:* dispassionate.

amorphous *adj* **formless**, shapeless, nebulous, vague, unstructured, fluid. [➡SHAPELESSNESS; 1218] *Opposite:* defined.

amorphousness *n* [➡SHAPELESSNESS; 1218]

amortization *n* **repayment**, paying back, payback, paying off, remuneration. [➡OWE AND DESERVE; 466]

amortize *v* **pay back**, repay, pay off, remunerate. [➡GIVE MONEY; 434]

amount *n* **quantity**, sum, total, volume, expanse, extent, aggregate. [➡AMOUNT AND QUANTITY; 112]

amount to *v* **add up to**, total, come to, make, be equal to. [➡AMOUNT TO AND EQUAL; 70]

amour-propre (*formal*) *n* [➡CALMNESS, CONFIDENCE, AND COMPOSURE; 537]

amp *type of* **audio equipment.** [➡AUDIO EQUIPMENT; 1138]

ampersand *n* **and sign**, and, symbol, character. [➡SYMBOLS, SIGNS, AND NUMBERS; 597]

amphibian 1 *type of* **amphibian.** [➡AMPHIBIANS; 1008] 2 *type of* **military vehicle.** [➡VEHICLES; 1144]

amphibian

◆ *types of amphibian*
axolotl, bullfrog, cane toad, frog, horned toad, midwife toad, natterjack toad, newt, salamander, toad, tree frog, xenopus

amphitheatre 1 *n* **stadium**, arena, auditorium, ground, showground, sports ground, ring. [➡BUILDINGS FOR PUBLIC ENTERTAINMENT; 1083] 2 *n* **lecture theatre**, auditorium, lecture hall, lecture room. [➡BUILDINGS FOR PUBLIC ENTERTAINMENT; 1083]

ample *adj* **enough**, sufficient, adequate, plenty, plentiful, abundant, full, generous, liberal, copious, bounteous (*literary*), plenteous (*literary*). [➡ENOUGH AND SUFFICIENT; 129] *Opposite:* insufficient.

See Compare and Contrast at **enough.**

amplification 1 *n* **intensification**, strengthening, magnification, augmentation, extension, increase, enlargement. [➡CHANGE OF SIZE: BIGGER; 393] *Opposite:* reduction. 2 *n* **elaboration**, clarification, development, expansion. [➡EXPLAIN AND CLARIFY; 611] *Opposite:* abbreviation.

amplifier *type of* **audio equipment.** [➡AUDIO EQUIPMENT; 1138]

amplify 1 *v* **intensify**, increase, strengthen, magnify, augment (*formal*), enlarge, swell. [➡CHANGE OF INTENSITY: MORE; 395] *Opposite:* reduce. 2 *v* **enlarge on**, go into detail, elaborate, add to, expand, clarify, develop, augment (*formal*). [➡EXPLAIN AND CLARIFY; 611] *Opposite:* abbreviate.

See Compare and Contrast at **increase**.

amplitude *n* **largeness**, scale, plenty, fullness, bounty (*literary*), breadth, generosity, bigness, profusion, large size, amount. [➡LARGE; 1192]

amply *adv* **sufficiently**, adequately, abundantly, thoroughly, fully, copiously, plentifully, liberally. [➡ENOUGH AND SUFFICIENT; 129] *Opposite:* insufficiently.

ampoule *n* **container**, vessel, bottle, flask. [➡CONTAINERS, RECEPTACLES, AND PACKAGING; 1244]

ampule *see* **ampoule**.

amputate *v* **cut off**, remove, sever, separate. [➡EXTRACT AND SEVER; 342]

amulet *n* **charm**, good luck charm, talisman, lucky charm, juju. [➡ORNAMENTS AND DECORATIONS; 1247]

amuse 1 *v* **make laugh**, make smile, charm, please, divert, distract. [➡PLEASE AND AMUSE; 573] *Opposite:* depress. 2 *v* **entertain**, keep busy, interest, absorb, engross, keep amused, fascinate. [➡APPEAL TO AND AROUSE INTEREST; 576] *Opposite:* bore.

amused *adj* **smiling**, laughing, pleased, tickled, entertained. [➡PLEASURE, EXCITEMENT, AND ELATION; 535] *Opposite:* annoyed.

amusement 1 *n* **laughter**, enjoyment, delight, fun, pleasure, glee, hilarity. [➡ENTERTAINMENT; 872] *Opposite:* sadness. 2 *n* **entertainment**, pastime, hobby, distraction, diversion, recreation, pursuit. [➡ENTERTAINMENT; 872]

amusement arcade *n* [➡BUILDINGS FOR PUBLIC ENTERTAINMENT; 1083]

amusement park *n* **funfair**, fair, theme park, amusements. [➡URBAN OUTDOOR SPACES; 1071]

amusements *n* **fun fair**, amusement arcade, amusement park, pier. [➡BUILDINGS FOR PUBLIC ENTERTAINMENT; 1083]

amusing *adj* **funny**, humorous, entertaining, comical, witty, droll, diverting, hilarious. [➡FUNNY AND AMUSING; 217]

anachronism *n* **relic**, survival, leftover, archaism, holdover. [➡OLD, OLD-FASHIONED; 168]

anachronistic *adj* **out-of-date**, dated, old-fashioned, old, obsolete, archaic, antiquated, outmoded, obsolescent, passé, outdated. [➡OLD, OLD-FASHIONED; 168] *Opposite:* contemporary.

anaconda *type of* **non-poisonous snake**. [➡SNAKE; 995]

anaemia *n* [➡THE BLOOD AND CIRCULATION; 718]

anaemic *adj* **weak**, feeble, lacklustre, insipid, pale, colourless, wishy-washy (*informal*), pallid, anodyne (*literary*), bland. [➡WEAKNESS; 242] *Opposite:* strong.

anaesthetic 1 *n* **painkiller**, local anaesthetic, general anaesthetic, sedative, analgesic. [➡REMEDIES, TREATMENTS, AND OPERATIONS; 732] 2 *adj* **painkilling**, numbing, deadening, sedating. [➡REMEDIES, TREATMENTS, AND OPERATIONS; 732]

anaesthetize *v* **deaden**, numb, sedate, freeze, put under, put out, put to sleep. [➡REMEDIES, TREATMENTS, AND OPERATIONS; 732]

anaesthetized *adj* **knocked out**, out cold, under, asleep, sedated, deadened, numb, frozen. [➡TIRED, ASLEEP, AND UNCONSCIOUS; 739]

anagram *type of* **wordplay**. [➡JOKES AND TEASING; 675]

anal fin *part of* **fish**. [➡PARTS OF A FISH; 1011]

analgesia 1 *n* **numbness**, painlessness, insensibility, insensitivity, unawareness. [➡TIRED, ASLEEP, AND UNCONSCIOUS; 739] *Opposite:* pain. 2 *n* **pain control**, pain relief, pain management, pain killing, numbing, deadening. [➡REMEDIES, TREATMENTS, AND OPERATIONS; 732]

analgesic 1 *adj* **painkilling**, palliative, pain-relieving, deadening, numbing. [➡REMEDIES, TREATMENTS, AND OPERATIONS; 732] 2 *n* **painkiller**, palliative, pain reliever, anodyne (*literary*), anaesthetic. [➡REMEDIES, TREATMENTS, AND OPERATIONS; 732]

analogous *adj* **similar**, equivalent, parallel, corresponding, comparable, like, related, akin, consonant (*formal*). [➡SIMILARITY; 149] *Opposite:* different.

analogue *n* **equivalent**, similarity, correspondent (*formal*), referent. [➡SIMILARITY; 149]

analogy *n* **similarity**, likeness, equivalence, parallel, correspondence, correlation, comparison, resemblance, consonance (*formal*), relation. [➡EQUALITY; 155] *Opposite:* contrast.

analyse *v* **examine**, study, investigate, scrutinize, evaluate, consider, question, explore, probe, dissect, inspect. [➡EXAMINE AND ASSESS; 754]

analysis 1 *n* **testing**, examination, assay, assessment. [➡EXAMINE AND ASSESS; 754] 2 *n* **examination**, study, investigation, scrutiny, breakdown, inquiry, exploration, evaluation, consideration, probe. [➡EXAMINE AND ASSESS; 754] 3 *n* **psychoanalysis**, psychiatry, psychotherapy. [➡PSYCHOLOGY AND THE MIND; 770]

analyst 1 *n* **forecaster**, predictor, political analyst, market analyst, city analyst, expert, specialist. [➡PEOPLE INVOLVED IN FINANCE; 804] 2 *n* **psychoanalyst**, psychiatrist, psychotherapist. [➡PEOPLE WHO WORK IN MEDICINE; 848]

analytic *adj* **logical**, investigative, diagnostic, systematic, critical, methodical, questioning, reasoned, analytical, rational. [➡THE NATURE OF IDEAS; 772] *Opposite:* illogical.

analytical *adj* **logical**, investigative, diagnostic, systematic, critical, methodical, questioning, analytic, reasoned, rational. [➡THE NATURE OF IDEAS; 772] *Opposite:* illogical.

anarchic 1 *adj* **revolutionary**, radical, anarchistic, rebellious, anarchical. [➡UNWILLINGNESS AND STUBBORNNESS; 565] 2 *adj* **lawless**, chaotic, disordered, disorderly, out of control, riotous. [➡DISORDER AND CHAOS; 246] *Opposite:* orderly.

anarchical *see* **anarchic**.

anarchist *n* **revolutionary**, rebel, nihilist, radical. [➡PHILOSOPHICAL AND POLITICAL THINKERS; 782]

anarchistic *adj* **revolutionary**, antigovernment,

anarchic, anarchical, rebellious. [➡REBELLIOUSNESS AND DISOBEDIENCE; 566]

anarchy *n* **disorder**, chaos, lawlessness, anarchism, revolution, mayhem (*informal*), rebellion, mobocracy (*disapproving*), ochlocracy, riot. [➡CHAOS AND UPROAR; 51] *Opposite:* order.

an arm and a leg (*informal*) *n* **fortune**, packet (*informal*), bomb (*informal*), pretty penny (*informal*), a small fortune, king's ransom. [➡LARGE AMOUNT OF MONEY; 141] *Opposite:* pittance.

anathema *n* **abhorrence**, abomination, loathing, curse, denunciation, censure. [➡NUISANCES; 254]

anathematize *v* [➡ACCUSE, BLAME, AND CRITICIZE; 642]

anatomical *adj* **functional**, structural, material, bodily, body. [➡BIOLOGICAL SCIENCES; 1037]

anatomy 1 *n* **structure**, composition, makeup, framework, frame. [➡QUALITIES AND CHARACTERISTICS; 1190] 2 *n* **analysis**, examination, investigation, review, study. [➡EXAMINE AND ASSESS; 754] 3 *type of* **bioscience**. [➡BIOLOGICAL SCIENCES; 1037]

ancestor 1 *n* **forebear**, antecedent, forefather, predecessor, progenitor. [➡THE FAMILY; 956] *Opposite:* descendant. 2 *n* **forerunner**, precursor, predecessor, progenitor, prototype, foregoer (*formal*). [➡OLDER GENERATION RELATIVES; 959] *Opposite:* successor.

ancestral *adj* **family**, familial, inherited. [➡THE FAMILY; 956]

ancestry *n* **lineage**, descent, origin, heritage, extraction, stock, pedigree, parentage, line. [➡THE FAMILY; 956]

anchor 1 *n* **newsreader**, commentator, presenter, announcer, broadcaster, journalist, anchorperson, anchorman, anchorwoman. [➡WORKERS IN ENTERTAINMENT AND MEDIA; 873] 2 *v* **fasten**, attach, fix, affix, secure, moor. [➡FASTEN, LINK, AND JOIN; 409] *Opposite:* unfasten.

anchorage *n* **port**, harbour, marina, dock, quay, wharf. [➡WATERWAYS AND SEAWAYS; 1107]

anchorite *n* **hermit**, recluse, solitary. [➡SOLITARY PEOPLE; 942]

anchorman *see* **anchorperson**.

anchorperson *n* **newsreader**, presenter, broadcaster, anchor, journalist, announcer. [➡WORKERS IN ENTERTAINMENT AND MEDIA; 873]

anchorwoman *see* **anchorperson**.

anchovy *type of* **sea fish**. [➡SEA FISH; 1009]

ancient 1 *adj* **antique**, early, earliest, olden (*archaic or literary*), prehistoric, primeval, primordial, antediluvian (*informal*), primal, ageless, age-old. [➡OLD, OLD-FASHIONED; 168] *Opposite:* modern. 2 *adj* **old-fashioned**, archaic, obsolete, outdated, antediluvian (*informal*), antiquated, prehistoric. [➡PAST; 84] *Opposite:* up-to-date.

ancient history *adj* [➡PAST; 84]

ancillary *adj* **auxiliary**, subsidiary, supplementary, additional, secondary, subordinate, adjuvant. [➡INFERIORITY; 154] *Opposite:* main.

ancillary building *n* [➡ANCILLARY BUILDINGS; 1079]

and 1 *conj* **then**, after that, next, as a consequence, afterwards. [➡CAUSATION; 169] 2 *conj* **plus** (*informal*), in addition to, as well as, with, along with, coupled with, combined with. [➡ALSO; 136] 3 *conj* **furthermore**, moreover, also, what is more, in addition, likewise. [➡ALSO; 136]

andante *type of* **musical term**. [➡MUSICAL TERMS; 912]

and/or *conj* **either-or**, one or both, either or both. [➡ALSO; 136]

androgynous *adj* [➡BUILD; 478]

android *n* **robot**, automaton, bionic person, machine, humanoid. [➡SCIENCE FICTION; 1063]

anecdotal *adj* **subjective**, circumstantial, hearsay, unreliable, untrustworthy, undependable, sketchy. [➡UNCERTAIN; 176] *Opposite:* objective.

anecdote *n* **story**, tale, yarn (*informal*), sketch, narrative, narration. [➡THE ORAL TRADITION; 678]

anemometer *type of* **measuring device**. [➡MEASURING DEVICES; 1122]

anemone *type of* **flower grown from bulb**. [➡FLOWERS FROM BULBS; 1030]

aneroid barometer *type of* **measuring device**. [➡MEASURING DEVICES; 1122]

anew *adv* **again**, afresh, once again, once more, over, new, de novo. [➡AGAIN; 109]

angel 1 *n* **seraph**, archangel, guardian angel (*informal*), cherub, messenger, spirit. [➡RELIGIOUS CONCEPTS; 777] 2 *n* **backer**, sponsor, guarantor, patron, benefactor, financier. [➡REPRESENTATIVES AND PATRONS; 968]

See Compare and Contrast at **backer**.

angelfish *type of* **flatfish**. [➡SEA FISH; 1009]

angelic *adj* **innocent**, good, pure (*literary*), beatific (*literary*), saintly, adorable, virtuous, divine, caring, kind, appealing. [➡MORALLY GOOD; 775] *Opposite:* wicked.

angelica *type of* **herb**. [➡HERBS AND SPICES; 1174]

anger 1 *n* **annoyance**, irritation, fury, rage, antagonism, resentment, ire (*literary*), wrath, dander, indignation. [➡IRRITATION AND ANGER; 542] *Opposite:* calm. 2 *v* **annoy**, irritate, infuriate, incense, enrage, madden, exasperate, rile (*informal*), aggravate (*informal*), provoke. [➡ANGER AND ANNOY; 570] *Opposite:* pacify.

Compare and Contrast: ***anger, annoyance, irritation, resentment, indignation, fury, rage, ire, wrath***

CORE MEANING: A FEELING OF STRONG DISPLEASURE IN RESPONSE TO AN ASSUMED INJURY

anger a strong feeling of grievance; ***annoyance*** mild anger and impatience; ***irritation*** impatience and exasperation; ***resentment*** aggrieved feelings caused by a sense of unfair treatment; ***indignation*** anger because something seems unfair or unreasonable; ***fury*** violent anger; ***rage*** sudden and extreme anger; ***ire*** (*literary*) strong anger; ***wrath*** strong anger, often with a desire for revenge.

angle 1 *n* **point of view**, viewpoint, approach, position, slant, perspective, outlook, direction. [➡POINT OF VIEW; 768] 2 *v* **slant**, tilt, turn, twist, slope, point, aim. [➡MOVE SOMETHING: INTO A NEW POSITION OR OVERTURN; 331] *Opposite:* level.

angle for *v* **fish for**, seek, solicit, try for, try to get. [➡OBTAIN POSSESSION BY PERSUASION; 458]

anglerfish *type of* **sea fish.** [➡SEA FISH; 1009]

angling *n* [➡HOBBIES, GAMES, AND SPORTS; 875]

angora *type of* **fabric from animals.** [➡FABRICS; 1131]

angrily *adv* **crossly**, furiously, irately, irritably, heatedly, indignantly. [➡BAD-TEMPERED AND HUMOURLESS; 627] *Opposite:* calmly.

angry *adj* **annoyed**, irritated, fuming, livid, irate, heated, gnashing your teeth, cross, furious, incensed, enraged, outraged, infuriated, ireful (*literary*), wrathful, indignant, choleric (*literary*), mad. [➡IRRITATION AND ANGER; 542] *Opposite:* calm.

angst *n* **anguish**, torment, anxiety, trouble, sorrow, worry, fear. [➡FEELINGS ABOUT THE FUTURE; 534] *Opposite:* happiness.

See Compare and Contrast at **worry.**

angst-ridden *adj* **anguished**, tormented, fearful, troubled, worried, anxious, sorrowful. [➡SADNESS, DISTRESS, AND DESPAIR; 540] *Opposite:* content.

angstrom *type of* **diacritic.** [➡ASPECTS OF LANGUAGE; 683]

anguish *n* **suffering**, torment, agony, torture, pain, distress, grief, sorrow, angst, affliction, anxiety. [➡SADNESS, DISTRESS, AND DESPAIR; 540] *Opposite:* contentment.

anguished *adj* **tormented**, suffering, agonized, tortured, painful, distressed, grief-stricken, sorrowful, angst-ridden, anxious. [➡SADNESS, DISTRESS, AND DESPAIR; 540] *Opposite:* content.

angular *adj* **bony**, rawboned, rangy, lanky, gaunt, pointed, thin, gawky (*informal*). [➡BUILD; 478] *Opposite:* rounded.

angularity *n* **boniness**, thinness, gawkiness (*informal*), ranginess, lankiness, sharpness, gauntness. [➡BUILD; 478] *Opposite:* roundness.

animal 1 *n* **creature**, being, beast, mammal, organism. [➡LIVING THINGS AND LIVING; 976] 2 *n* **monster**, beast, brute, swine. [➡VILLAINS AND THUGS; 947] 3 *adj* **physical**, bodily, visceral, instinctive, innate, intuitive, inborn, instinctual, subconscious. [➡LIVING THINGS AND LIVING; 976] *Opposite:* spiritual.

animate 1 *v* **liven up**, enliven, rouse, bring to life, stir, stimulate. [➡IMPROVE SOMETHING; 375] *Opposite:* put a damper on. 2 *adj* **living**, alive, live, breathing, flesh and blood, conscious, sentient, moving. [➡LIVING THINGS AND LIVING; 976] *Opposite:* inanimate.

See Compare and Contrast at **living.**

animated *adj* **energetic**, active, vibrant, vivacious, dynamic, full of life, enthusiastic, excited, sparkling, spirited, lively, vigorous. [➡POSITIVE IMPATIENCE, ENTHUSIASM, AND ALERTNESS; 538] *Opposite:* lifeless.

animated film *n* [➡FILM; 901]

animation 1 *n* **liveliness**, energy, vibrancy, life, vigour, vivaciousness, dynamism, enthusiasm, excitement, activity, sparkle, spirit. [➡ENERGY AND ENTHUSIASM; 497] *Opposite:* lifelessness. 2 *n* **cartoon**, moving picture, animatronics, computer graphics, simulation. [➡THE PICTORIAL ARTS; 897]

animatronics *n* [➡FILM; 901]

animosity *n* **hostility**, hatred, loathing, ill feeling, ill will, enmity, bitterness, acrimony, rancour, no love lost, dislike, antagonism, bad blood. [➡ANTAGONISM; 553] *Opposite:* goodwill.

See Compare and Contrast at **dislike.**

animus 1 *n* **hostility**, animosity, hatred, ill will, detestation, spitefulness. [➡ANTAGONISM; 553] *Opposite:* friendliness. 2 *n* **temperament**, personality, disposition, spirit, attitude. [➡TEMPERAMENT AND BEHAVIOUR; 493]

aniseed *type of* **spice.** [➡HERBS AND SPICES; 1174]

ankle *part of* **leg or foot.** [➡LEG AND FOOT; 695]

ankle-length *adj* [➡DESCRIBING CLOTHES; 869]

anklet *n* **bracelet**, chain, bangle, band. [➡JEWELLERY; 866]

ankylosaur *type of* **dinosaur.** [➡DINOSAUR; 996]

annals *n* **records**, archives, chronicles, history, accounts, registers. [➡RECORDS; 586]

anneal *v* **harden**, strengthen, toughen, galvanize, forge. [➡HARDEN, CONGEAL, DRY; 388]

annex *v* **take possession of**, seize, take over, capture, invade, take control of, appropriate, commandeer. [➡TAKE SOMETHING AWAY; 426] *Opposite:* surrender.

annexation *n* **capture**, seizure, takeover, occupation, invasion, appropriation. [➡TAKE SOMETHING AWAY; 426] *Opposite:* surrender.

annexe *n* **extension**, new building, addition, wing, ancillary building, ell. [➡ANCILLARY BUILDINGS; 1079]

annihilate 1 *v* **wipe out** (*informal*), destroy, obliterate, extinguish, eradicate, exterminate. [➡DESTRUCTION AND DEMO-

LITION; 360] *Opposite:* protect. **2** *v* (*informal*) **defeat**, rout, thrash, overwhelm, crush, beat, conquer, overpower. [➡BEAT AND DEFEAT; 80] *Opposite:* lose.

annihilation *n* **total destruction**, obliteration, extinction, eradication, extermination, wiping out (*informal*). [➡BEAT AND DEFEAT; 80] *Opposite:* protection.

anniversary *n* **birthday**, centenary, bicentenary, wedding anniversary, centennial (*US*), bicentennial (*US*) [➡CEREMONIES AND ANNIVERSARIES; 38]

annotate *v* **gloss**, add footnotes, interpret, explain, make notes on, comment on, note, mark, mark up. [➡RECORD SOMETHING; 372]

annotated *adj* **glossed**, marked, marked up. [➡WRITING; 584]

annotation *n* **footnote**, gloss, marginal note, explanation, note, comment, mark. [➡PARTS OF BOOKS AND DOCUMENTS; 594]

announce *v* **proclaim**, make known, publicize, broadcast, declare, say, pronounce, state, herald, publish, read out, post. [➡INFORM AND ANNOUNCE; 612] *Opposite:* keep secret.

announcement *n* **statement**, declaration, message, notice, proclamation, publication, broadcast, pronouncement, revelation. [➡INFORM AND ANNOUNCE; 612]

announcer *n* **presenter**, broadcaster, telecaster, reporter, newsreader, anchor. [➡WORKERS IN ENTERTAINMENT AND MEDIA; 873]

annoy *v* **irritate**, infuriate, exasperate, aggravate (*informal*), get on your nerves, drive mad (*informal*), bother, madden, anger, frustrate, displease, provoke, rile (*informal*), irk, vex, put out, cheese off (*informal*), hack off (*informal*), nark (*informal*), bug (*informal*). [➡ANGER AND ANNOY; 570] *Opposite:* please.

Compare and Contrast: ***annoy, irritate, exasperate, vex, irk***

CORE MEANING: TO CAUSE A MILD DEGREE OF ANGER IN SOMEBODY

annoy cause impatience or anger in somebody; ***irritate*** annoy somebody slightly; ***exasperate*** arouse anger or frustration in somebody; ***vex*** annoy somebody, especially causing upset or distress; ***irk*** annoy somebody by being tiresome or tedious.

annoyance *n* **irritation**, infuriation, exasperation, aggravation (*informal*), anger, frustration, displeasure, indignation. [➡IRRITATION AND ANGER; 542] *Opposite:* pleasure.

See Compare and Contrast at **anger**.

annoyed *adj* **angry**, irritated, infuriated, exasperated, aggravated, upset, wound up (*informal*), bothered, maddened, frustrated, displeased, provoked, riled (*informal*), incensed, hacked off (*informal*), cheesed off (*informal*), narked (*informal*), put out. [➡IRRITATION AND ANGER; 542] *Opposite:* pleased.

annoying *adj* **maddening**, irritating, infuriating, bothersome, exasperating, aggravating (*informal*), frustrating, trying, grating. [➡IRRITATING; 229] *Opposite:* pleasing.

annual *adj* **yearly**, twelve-monthly, once a year, once yearly, every twelve months. [➡TIMES OF YEAR; 88]

annual general meeting *n* [➡MEETINGS AND ASSEMBLIES; 43]

annuity *n* **pension**, allowance, income, grant, stipend, endowment. [➡INCOME; 461]

annul *v* **cancel**, call off, withdraw, end, terminate (*formal*), dissolve, rescind, invalidate, put an end to. [➡ABOLISH AND ANNUL; 453] *Opposite:* prolong.

See Compare and Contrast at **nullify**.

annulment *n* **cancellation**, termination (*formal*), withdrawal, dissolution, invalidation, deletion, elimination. [➡END; 54]

anode *n* **terminal**, connection, contact. [➡ELECTRONICS AND ELECTRICS; 1136]

anodyne **1** *adj* (*literary*) **soothing**, painkilling, relaxing, settling, analgesic, pain-relieving. [➡REMEDIES, TREATMENTS, AND OPERATIONS; 732] *Opposite:* stimulating. **2** *adj* **insipid**, bland, tame, neutral, inoffensive, colourless, dull, antiseptic, unexciting, anaemic. [➡BORING AND UNINTERESTING; 235] *Opposite:* exciting.

anoint *v* **smear**, daub, rub, smooth, massage, oil. [➡DECORATE, ADORN, AND APPLY COATINGS; 406]

anomalous *adj* **irregular**, uncharacteristic, strange, abnormal, inconsistent, out of the ordinary, jarring, atypical, unusual. [➡BIZARRE AND PECULIAR; 258] *Opposite:* usual.

anomaly *n* **irregularity**, incongruity, difference, variance, glitch, abnormality, inconsistency. [➡MISTAKES; 251]

anon (*archaic or literary*) *adv* **soon**, presently, shortly, later, in a while, in a moment, in two shakes of a lamb's tail. [➡FUTURE; 86] *Opposite:* now.

anonymity **1** *n* **secrecy**, obscurity, concealment, inconspicuousness, namelessness, facelessness, privacy, unrecognizability. [➡SECRET AND UNKNOWN; 180] **2** *n* **indistinctness**, blandness, insignificance, ordinariness, dullness. [➡UNIMPORTANT AND UNNECESSARY; 239] *Opposite:* distinctiveness.

anonymous **1** *adj* **nameless**, unidentified, unnamed, unsigned, unspecified, unknown, secret, mysterious, shadowy. [➡SECRET AND UNKNOWN; 180] *Opposite:* named. **2** *adj* **undistinguished**, indistinctive, ordinary, everyday, run of the mill, unexceptional, unmemorable, dull. [➡ORDINARINESS; 245] *Opposite:* distinctive.

anonymously *adv* **incognito**, namelessly, in secret, secretly, in disguise. [➡SECRET AND UNKNOWN; 180]

anorak *type of* **jacket**. [➡GARMENTS AND OUTFITS; 865]

another *adj* **one more**, additional, a new, a different, a further, extra, added, any more, alternative. [➡MORE AND EXCESS; 122]

answer **1** *n* **response**, reply, reaction, riposte, rejoinder (*formal*), retort. [➡REPLY AND ANSWER; 669] *Opposite:* question. **2** *n* **solution**, key, way out, resolution, remedy. [➡SOLUTION; 216] *Opposite:* inquiry. **3** *v* **reply**, respond, react, come back with, rejoin (*formal*), counter, retort. [➡REPLY AND ANSWER; 669]

4 *v* **solve**, satisfy, resolve, fulfil, lay to rest, meet, remedy. [➡ SOLVE AND INTERPRET; 761]

Compare and Contrast: ***answer, reply, response, rejoinder, retort, riposte***

CORE MEANING: SOMETHING SAID, WRITTEN, OR DONE IN ACKNOWLEDGMENT OF A QUESTION, REMARK, OR IN REACTION TO A SITUATION

answer acknowledgment of a question, letter, or situation; ***reply*** a spoken or written answer, or a reaction to a situation; ***response*** a spoken or written answer, or a reaction to a situation; ***rejoinder*** (*formal*) a sharp, critical, angry, or clever reply, usually spoken; ***retort*** a sharp spoken reply, often to criticism; ***riposte*** a quick or witty spoken reply.

answerability *n* [➡ RESPONSIBILITY; 171]

answerable *adj* **responsible**, accountable, liable, chargeable, subject to blame, blamable, punishable. [➡ RESPONSIBILITY; 171] *Opposite:* unaccountable.

answer back *v* **retort**, argue, counter, respond, riposte, react, fight back, come back, be rude, cheek (*informal*), talk back, contradict. [➡ REPLY AND ANSWER; 669]

answer for 1 *v* **pay for**, suffer for, be punished for, make amends for, atone (*formal*), take the rap (*slang*). [➡ VENGEANCE AND REVENGE; 686] *Opposite:* get away with. 2 *v* **be responsible for**, be accountable for, vouch for, take the responsibility for, be to blame for, be liable for. [➡ APPROVE AND CONFIRM; 647]

answering machine *type of* **telecommunications equipment.** [➡ TELECOMMUNICATIONS; 1129]

ant *n type of* **insect.** [➡ INSECTS; 1012]

ant

◆ *types of ant*
army ant, leafcutter ant, Pharaoh ant, red ant, slave ant, slave-making ant, termite, white ant

antagonism 1 *n* **resentment**, dislike, bitterness, hatred, antipathy, ill feeling, ill will, bad blood. [➡ ANTAGONISM; 553] *Opposite:* friendliness. 2 *n* **rivalry**, opposition, aggression, hostility, enmity, animosity. [➡ RELATIONSHIP TO ANOTHER; 973] *Opposite:* cooperation.

antagonist *n* **rival**, adversary, opponent, enemy, contender, competitor. [➡ ENEMIES AND TORMENTORS; 969] *Opposite:* friend.

antagonistic *adj* **aggressive**, hostile, opposed, on the warpath (*informal*), unfriendly, incompatible. [➡ IRRITATION AND ANGER; 542] *Opposite:* friendly.

antagonize *v* **provoke**, irritate, annoy, upset, get your back up, rile (*informal*), alienate. [➡ ANGER AND ANNOY; 570] *Opposite:* mollify.

ante *n* **bet**, wager, stake, payment, raise. [➡ GAMBLE AND TAKE RISKS; 467]

anteater *type of* **small mammal.** [➡ SMALL MAMMAL; 990]

antebellum *adj* **early nineteenth-century**, eighteenth-century, colonial, historical, Federalist, prewar. [➡ PAST; 84]

antecede *v* [➡ BEFORE, FIRST, AND PRECEDING; 164]

antecedence *n* [➡ BEFORE, FIRST, AND PRECEDING; 164]

antecedent *n* **precursor**, forerunner, ancestor, predecessor, forebear, originator. [➡ BEFORE, FIRST, AND PRECEDING; 164]

antecedents *n* **past history**, background, previous circumstances, qualifications, experience, past. [➡ PAST; 84]

antechamber *type of* **room in public buildings.** [➡ TYPES OF ROOM; 1096]

antedate *v* **predate**, go before, be earlier than, date from before, occur before. [➡ BEFORE, FIRST, AND PRECEDING; 164]

antediluvian 1 *adj* **prehistoric**, ancient, old, primitive, primeval, primordial. [➡ PAST; 84] *Opposite:* modern. 2 *adj* (*informal*) **antiquated**, out-of-date, obsolete, old-fashioned, archaic, outmoded, outdated. [➡ OLD, OLD-FASHIONED; 168] *Opposite:* up-to-date.

See Compare and Contrast at **old-fashioned.**

antelope *type of* **deer or antelope.** [➡ DEER AND ANTELOPE; 981]

antenatal *adj* **gynaecological**, pregnancy, pre-birth, reproductive, prenatal. [➡ REPRODUCTION AND HEREDITY; 726] *Opposite:* postnatal.

antenna 1 *n* **feeler**, projection, tentacle, probe, protuberance, whisker. [➡ PARTS OF AN INSECT; 1019] 2 (*US*) *type of* **telecommunications equipment.** [➡ TELECOMMUNICATIONS; 1129]

anteroom *type of* **room in public buildings.** [➡ TYPES OF ROOM; 1096]

anthem *n* **song of praise**, national hymn, sacred song, psalm, hymn, chorale. [➡ MUSIC, SONGS, AND SINGING; 907]

anthology *n* **collection**, compilation, album, omnibus, compendium, collected works. [➡ COLLECTIONS AND MIXTURES OF THINGS; 1243]

anthropomorphize *v* **humanize**, personify, make human, give a human face to, sentimentalize, bring alive. [➡ NAME AND DESCRIBE; 666]

anti (*informal*) *adj* **opposed**, against, antagonistic, averse (*formal*), ill-disposed, hostile, set against. [➡ UNWILLINGNESS AND STUBBORNNESS; 565] *Opposite:* pro.

antiaircraft gun *type of* **gun.** [➡ WEAPONS FOR SHOOTING; 1155]

antiballistic missile *type of* **explosive weapon.** [➡ EXPLOSIVES; 1154]

anticipate 1 *v* **do in advance**, beat somebody to it (*informal*), get ahead, forestall, do ahead, antedate. [➡ BEFORE, FIRST, AND PRECEDING; 164] 2 *v* **expect**, foresee, look forward to, await, wait for, predict, be hopeful of, think likely. [➡ PREDICT AND ANTICIPATE; 751]

anticipated *adj* **expected**, predicted, projected, estimated, awaited, foreseen. [➡ FUTURE; 86] *Opposite:* unexpected.

anticipation *n* **expectation**, expectancy, hope, eagerness, keenness, looking forward. [➡FEELINGS ABOUT THE FUTURE; 534]

anticlimax *n* **comedown** (*informal*), letdown, disappointment, damp squib (*informal*), deflation. [➡FAILURE; 77] *Opposite:* climax.

anticlockwise *adj* [➡DIRECTION OF MOTION; 346]

antics 1 *n* **clowning**, tricks, pranks, larks, frolics, capers, playfulness. [➡ACTIONS OR UNDERTAKINGS; 260] 2 *n* **behaviour**, actions, activities, tricks, conduct. [➡TEMPERAMENT AND BEHAVIOUR; 493]

antidote *n* **cure**, remedy, solution, answer, corrective, medicine. [➡SOLUTION; 216] *Opposite:* poison.

antihero *n* [➡VILLAINS AND THUGS; 947]

antineutron *type of* **elementary particle.** [➡ELEMENTARY PARTICLES; 1278]

antipasto *part of* **meal.** [➡MEALS AND PARTS OF MEALS; 1168]

antipathetic *adj* **opposed**, averse (*formal*), hostile, antagonistic, conflicting, anti (*informal*). [➡IRRITATION AND ANGER; 542] *Opposite:* sympathetic.

antipathy *n* **opposition**, aversion, hostility, antagonism, hatred, dislike, ill feeling, ill will. [➡ANTAGONISM; 553] *Opposite:* support.

See Compare and Contrast at **dislike.**

antiproton *type of* **elementary particle.** [➡ELEMENTARY PARTICLES; 1278]

antiquark *type of* **elementary particle.** [➡ELEMENTARY PARTICLES; 1278]

antiquated *adj* **out-of-date**, old-fashioned, old, obsolete, archaic, antediluvian (*informal*), outdated, outmoded. [➡OLD, OLD-FASHIONED; 168] *Opposite:* modern.

See Compare and Contrast at **old-fashioned.**

antique *adj* **old**, traditional, aged, historic, old-fashioned, vintage. [➡OLD, OLD-FASHIONED; 168] *Opposite:* new.

antiquity 1 *n* **ancient times**, the distant past, olden days, olden times, time immemorial, bygone days. [➡PAST; 84] 2 *n* **relic**, remains, archaeological find, antique, artefact. [➡ORNAMENTS AND DECORATIONS; 1247]

antiseptic 1 *adj* **sterile**, antibacterial, uncontaminated, clean, pure, disinfected, germ-killing. [➡CLEAN; 1232] *Opposite:* infected. 2 *adj* **bland**, insipid, tame, uninteresting, colourless, dull, unexciting. [➡BORING AND UNINTERESTING; 235] *Opposite:* colourful.

antisocial 1 *adj* **disruptive**, rebellious, harmful, inconsiderate, belligerent, disorderly. [➡SELFISH AND UNKIND; 506] *Opposite:* constructive. 2 *adj* **unsociable**, unfriendly, disagreeable, shy, reserved, withdrawn. [➡UNFRIENDLINESS AND UNSOCIABILITY; 505] *Opposite:* sociable.

antithesis *n* **opposite**, direct opposite, exact opposite, contrast, converse, reverse, opposition. [➡OPPOSITE; 158]

antitrade *type of* **wind.** [➡WINDY AND STORMY WEATHER; 1053]

antsy (*US informal*) *adj* [➡IRRITATION AND ANGER; 542]

anus *part of* **digestive tract.** [➡THE DIGESTIVE TRACT; 710]

anxiety *n* **nervousness**, worry, concern, unease, apprehension, disquiet, fretfulness, angst, fear. [➡CONFUSION, ANXIETY, AND WORRY; 541] *Opposite:* calmness.

See Compare and Contrast at **worry.**

anxious 1 *adj* **worried**, concerned, uneasy, apprehensive, restless, fretful, fearful, frightened, nervous. [➡CONFUSION, ANXIETY, AND WORRY; 541] *Opposite:* calm. 2 *adj* **eager**, keen, enthusiastic, concerned, impatient, itching, intent, yearning. [➡POSITIVE IMPATIENCE, ENTHUSIASM, AND ALERTNESS; 538] *Opposite:* indifferent.

anxiousness *n* [➡CONFUSION, ANXIETY, AND WORRY; 541]

any 1 *adj* **some**, one, several, a few. [➡AMOUNT AND QUANTITY; 112] *Opposite:* none. 2 *adj* **every**, each, whichever, whatever. [➡ALL; 126] 3 *adv* **at all**, in the least, slightly, a little, somewhat, to some extent. [➡TO A CERTAIN EXTENT; 134]

anybody *pron* **anyone**, any person, somebody, someone, everybody, everyone. [➡PERSON; 931] *Opposite:* nobody.

anyhow *adv* **anyway**, in any case, at any rate, nevertheless, nonetheless, besides, at least, well. [➡ALTHOUGH, NEVERTHELESS, AND DESPITE; 170]

anyone *pron* **anybody**, any person, someone, somebody, everyone, everybody. [➡PERSON; 931] *Opposite:* no one.

anyplace (*US informal*) *adv* **anywhere**, wherever, where, somewhere, everywhere, someplace (*US informal*), everyplace (*US informal*). [➡GENERAL LOCATIONS; 159]

anyway *adv* **anyhow**, at any rate, in any case, nevertheless, nonetheless, besides, at least, well. [➡ALTHOUGH, NEVERTHELESS, AND DESPITE; 170]

anywhere *adv* **wherever**, where, somewhere, everywhere, anyplace (*US informal*), everyplace (*US informal*), someplace (*US informal*). [➡GENERAL LOCATIONS; 159]

A-OK (*informal*) *adv* **excellent**, perfect, all right, just right, good, great (*informal*), fine (*informal*). [➡CORRECT; 183]

aorta *type of* **blood vessel.** [➡THE BLOOD AND CIRCULATION; 718]

apace *adv* **quickly**, rapidly, swiftly, briskly, at a rate of knots, like lightning. [➡HAPPENING QUICKLY; 104] *Opposite:* slowly.

apart *adv* **separately**, not together, at a distance, to one side, away from each other. [➡DISTANCE; 161] *Opposite:* together.

apart from 1 *prep* **aside from**, excepting (*formal*), except for, with the exception of, not counting, excluding, not including, except, besides. [➡NOT; 135] *Opposite:* including. 2 *prep* **as well as**, in addition to, on top of, besides. [➡ALSO; 136]

apartment (*US*) *type of* **apartment.** [➡RESIDENTIAL BUILDINGS; 1077]

apartment block *n* [➡RESIDENTIAL BUILDINGS; 1077]

apartment building (*US*) *n* [➡RESIDENTIAL BUILDINGS; 1077]

apartment house (*US*) *n* [➡RESIDENTIAL BUILDINGS; 1077]

apathetic *adj* **indifferent**, uninterested, listless, dispirited, droopy, unconcerned, lethargic, lazy, bored. [➡NEUTRALITY AND INDIFFERENCE; 554] *Opposite:* enthusiastic.

See Compare and Contrast at **impassive**.

apathy *n* **indifference**, unconcern, lethargy, laziness, boredom, ennui, droopiness, dispiritedness. [➡NEUTRALITY AND INDIFFERENCE; 554] *Opposite:* interest.

ape 1 *v* **imitate**, mimic, copy, reproduce, simulate, mirror, parrot. [➡PRETEND AND MIMIC; 60] 2 *type of* **primate**. [➡PRIMATE; 988]

See Compare and Contrast at **imitate**.

aperitif *part of* **meal**. [➡MEALS AND PARTS OF MEALS; 1168]

aperture *n* **opening**, hole, space, orifice (*literary*), crack, slit. [➡HOLES, GAPS, AND FORKS; 1251]

apex *n* **top**, peak, summit, climax, zenith, head, high point. [➡EXTREMITIES OF PHYSICAL OBJECTS; 1249] *Opposite:* base.

aphid *type of* **flying insect**. [➡FLYING INSECTS; 1013]

aphorism *n* **saying**, maxim, adage, cliché, saw, dictum (*formal*), precept (*formal*). [➡FIGURES OF SPEECH; 674]

apiary *n* [➡ANIMAL OR BIRD ACCOMMODATION; 1078]

apiece *adv* **each**, respectively, to each, for each, individually, separately. [➡APPORTIONMENT; 113] *Opposite:* collectively.

aplenty *adj* [➡MANY, MUCH, LARGE AMOUNT; 117]

aplomb *n* **assurance**, self-confidence, self-possession, composure, style, ease, poise. [➡CONFIDENCE AND COMPOSURE; 500] *Opposite:* awkwardness.

apocalypse *n* **disaster**, catastrophe, day of reckoning, Judgment Day, end of the world, destruction, Armageddon. [➡RELIGIOUS CONCEPTS; 777]

apocryphal *adj* **mythical**, fictional, untrue, legendary, invented, made-up, dubious. [➡FALSE AND UNREAL; 174] *Opposite:* true.

apogee *n* [➡INTERMEDIATE STAGES; 55]

apologetic *adj* **sorry**, remorseful, contrite, repentant, rueful, diffident. [➡EMBARRASSMENT AND HUMILIATION; 543] *Opposite:* unrepentant.

apologist *n* **defender**, supporter, ally, protector, champion, advocator. [➡SUPPORTERS, PROTECTORS, AND COMPATRIOTS; 970]

apologize *v* **say sorry**, make an apology, ask for forgiveness, express regret, act contrite. [➡APOLOGIZE AND RETRACT; 684]

apology 1 *n* **admission of guilt**, request for forgiveness, expression of regret, confession, act of contrition. [➡APOLOGIZE AND RETRACT; 684] 2 *n* (*humorous*) **poor substitute**, pathetic excuse, poor example, pretence, stop gap, imitation. [➡FAULTS, FLAWS, AND WEAKNESSES; 252] 3 *n* **defence**, excuse, explanation, justification. [➡APOLOGIZE AND RETRACT; 684]

apoplectic *adj* [➡IRRITATION AND ANGER; 542]

apostate *n* **renouncer**, defector, deserter, renegade. [➡UNCOOPERATIVE OR REBELLIOUS PERSON; 567]

apostle 1 *n* **advocate**, supporter, promoter, champion, proponent, believer. [➡SUPPORTERS, PROTECTORS, AND COMPATRIOTS; 970] *Opposite:* detractor. 2 *n* **disciple**, follower, missionary, messenger, devotee, adherent. [➡RELIGIOUS PEOPLE; 779] *Opposite:* leader.

apostrophe *type of* **diacritic**. [➡ASPECTS OF LANGUAGE; 683]

appal *v* **horrify**, shock, disgust, dismay, upset, sicken, outrage, scandalize, distress. [➡UPSET, DISTRESS, AND HUMILIATE; 568] *Opposite:* appeal.

appalled *adj* **horrified**, shocked, stunned, repelled, sickened, disgusted, revolted. [➡SURPRISE, SHOCK, AND AMAZEMENT; 546] *Opposite:* delighted.

appalling 1 *adj* **horrifying**, shocking, disgusting, upsetting, sickening, outrageous, scandalous, distressing. [➡EMOTIONALLY UNPLEASANT AND UPSETTING; 228] *Opposite:* appealing. 2 *adj* **awful**, terrible, dreadful, horrendous, inexcusable, unspeakable, atrocious, abysmal. [➡BAD AND BADLY; 224] *Opposite:* wonderful.

appallingly *adv* **awfully**, terribly, dreadfully, horrendously, inexcusably, unspeakably, atrociously, abysmally. [➡DISGUSTING AND REPULSIVE; 231] *Opposite:* wonderfully.

apparatus 1 *n* **device**, gadget, gear, tackle, kit, contraption, machine, tool. [➡DEVICES; 1114] 2 *n* **system**, method, mechanism, arrangement, operation, machine, machinery, organization. [➡WAYS OF DOING THINGS; 295]

apparel *n* **attire** (*formal*), clothing, clothes, garb, wear, kit, gear (*informal*). [➡CLOTHES AND ACCESSORIES; 864]

apparent 1 *adj* **obvious**, clear, evident, plain, noticeable, perceptible, visible, plain as the nose on your face. [➡PERCEPTIBLE; 25] *Opposite:* unclear. 2 *adj* **seeming**, ostensible, deceptive, superficial, specious, outward. [➡UNCERTAIN; 176] *Opposite:* actual.

apparently 1 *adv* **it seems that**, it appears that, in fact, rumour has it that, it sounds as if, according to the grapevine (*informal*), actually, evidently, obviously. [➡EXPRESSIONS OF UNCERTAINTY; 561] 2 *adv* **seemingly**, deceptively, speciously, ostensibly, outwardly, superficially. [➡UNCERTAIN; 176] *Opposite:* actually.

apparition *n* **ghost**, spirit, spectre, phantom, ghoul, vision. [➡THE SUPERNATURAL; 788]

appassionato *type of* **musical term**. [➡MUSICAL TERMS; 912]

appeal 1 *n* **plea**, petition, application, request, call, entreaty. [➡REQUEST AND DEMAND; 664] 2 *n* **charm**, attractiveness, attraction, allure, influence, draw, pull (*informal*), interest, fascination, temptation. [➡BEAUTY AND ATTRACTIVENESS; 190] *Opposite:* repulsion. 3 *v* **request**, ask, plead, urge, petition, call, entreat (*formal*). [➡REQUEST AND DEMAND; 664] 4 *v* **attract**, interest, fascinate, charm, tempt, entice, please, draw, pull (*informal*), grab (*informal*). [➡APPEAL TO AND AROUSE INTEREST; 576] *Opposite:* repel.

appealing *adj* **attractive**, tempting, interesting, pleasing, alluring, likable, engaging, charming, fascinating. [➡BEAUTY AND ATTRACTIVENESS; 190] *Opposite:* repulsive.

appear 1 *v* **come into view**, come into sight, become visible, emerge, come out, show, materialize. [➡APPEAR AND EMERGE; 3] *Opposite:* disappear. 2 *v* **happen**, occur, be found, exist, surface, emerge, arrive on the scene, grow, begin. [➡GRADUALLY COME INTO EXISTENCE; 1] 3 *v* **seem**, look, look as if, give the impression, give the idea, look like. [➡SEEM TO BE SOMETHING; 58] 4 *v* **perform**, be seen, act, play, take part in, play a part. [➡PARTICIPATE; 293] 5 *v* **turn up**, show, be seen, arrive, roll up, arrive on the scene. [➡ARRIVE; 12]

appearance 1 *n* **emergence**, development, arrival, growth, beginning, advent. [➡BEGINNING; 53] *Opposite:* disappearance. 2 *n* **look**, form, exterior, manifestation, outer shell, façade, outward show. [➡APPEARANCE AND ATMOSPHERE; 1236] 3 *n* **arrival**, entrance, advent, attendance, presence. [➡ARRIVAL; 13]

appease 1 *v* **mollify**, conciliate, pacify, placate, soothe, settle, quieten down, calm down, accede to somebody's demands. [➡SOOTHE AND CALM; 574] *Opposite:* provoke. 2 *v* **satisfy**, assuage, attenuate, calm, soothe, ease. [➡SOOTHE AND CALM; 574] *Opposite:* intensify.

appeasement *n* **conciliation**, pacification, accession, mollification, placation, concession. [➡APOLOGIZE AND RETRACT; 684] *Opposite:* provocation.

appeaser *n* **conciliator**, pacifier, gratifier, mollifier. [➡ADVISERS, JUDGES, AND ARBITERS; 971]

appellant *n* [➡TRIAL, PUNISHMENT, AND LEGAL OUTCOMES; 819]

appellation (*formal*) *n* **name**, designation, title, style, tag, nickname. [➡NAME AND DESCRIBE; 666]

append *v* **add**, add on, tag on, attach, affix, join. [➡FASTEN, LINK, AND JOIN; 409] *Opposite:* detach.

appendage 1 *n* **addition**, attachment, adjunct, add-on, accessory, extra, supplement. [➡PHYSICAL OBJECTS; 1242] 2 *n* **extremity**, feeler, limb, member, projection, tentacle, flipper. [➡TORSO; 694]

appendix 1 *n* **adjunct**, add-on, supplement, PS, appendage, addition. [➡PARTS OF BOOKS AND DOCUMENTS; 594] 2 *part of* **digestive tract**. [➡THE DIGESTIVE TRACT; 710]

appertain (*formal*) *v* **relate**, belong, be associated with, be relevant to, have a bearing on, connect to. [➡BE ABOUT SOMETHING; 62]

appetite 1 *n* **hunger**, craving, taste, need to eat, desire for food, hungriness. [➡EAT AND NOT EAT; 711] 2 *n* **desire**, taste, enthusiasm, eagerness, keenness, inclination, hunger, passion, craving, wish. [➡DESIRE AND WANT; 580] *Opposite:* aversion.

appetizer 1 *n* **taster**, sample, introduction, sneak preview, taste, foretaste, example. [➡INDICATIONS, SIGNS, AND WARNINGS; 68] 2 *part of* **meal**. [➡MEALS AND PARTS OF MEALS; 1168]

appetizing 1 *adj* **delicious**, tasty, mouthwatering, enticing, tempting, scrumptious (*informal*). [➡TASTE; 704] *Opposite:* revolting. 2 *adj* **tempting**, appealing, inviting, attractive, desirable, enticing. [➡INTERESTING AND MEANINGFUL; 191] *Opposite:* unappealing.

applaud 1 *v* **clap**, give a round of applause, give a standing ovation, show your appreciation, congratulate, put your hands together. [➡APPLAUSE; 653] *Opposite:* boo. 2 *v* **approve**, support, admire, celebrate, congratulate, praise. [➡PRAISE AND ENCOURAGE; 648] *Opposite:* disapprove.

applause 1 *n* **clapping**, round of applause, ovation, hand, handclapping, show of appreciation. [➡APPLAUSE; 653] *Opposite:* jeering. 2 *n* **praise**, appreciation, approval, approbation, support, commendation. [➡PRAISE AND ENCOURAGE; 648] *Opposite:* condemnation.

apple *type of* **fruit**. [➡FRUIT AND VEGETABLES; 1175]

apple green *type of* **green**. [➡COLOURS; 1223]

apple sauce *type of* **seasonings, sauces, and dips**. [➡SEASONINGS AND SAUCES; 1173]

appliance 1 *n* **application**, use, employment, utilization, purpose, usage. [➡USE; 468] 2 *n* **domestic appliance**, labour-saving device, electrical equipment, machine, device. [➡HOUSEHOLD APPLIANCES; 1116]

appliance

◆ *types of appliance*
blender, coffeemaker, cooker, dishwasher, dryer, furnace, grill, hob, iron, microwave, microwave oven, minibar, percolator, range, rotisserie, smoke alarm, smoke detector, spin-dryer, stove, television, toaster, tumble dryer, washing machine

applicable *adj* **appropriate**, valid, related, pertinent, relevant, germane (*formal*). [➡CORRECT; 183] *Opposite:* unrelated.

applicant *n* **candidate**, interviewee, claimant, hopeful, aspirant, contender, entrant. [➡WORKER; 836]

See Compare and Contrast at **candidate**.

application 1 *n* **request**, claim, submission, bid, tender, presentation, solicitation. [➡REQUEST AND DEMAND; 664] 2 *n* **use**, function, purpose, relevance, appliance, usage. [➡USE; 468] 3 *n* **diligence**, concentration, hard work, effort, attention, single-mindedness, devotion. [➡HARD-WORKING AND COMMITTED; 501] *Opposite:* negligence. 4 *type of* **software**. [➡COMPUTERS AND COMPUTING; 1126]

applied *adj* **practical**, functional, useful, everyday, pragmatic, realistic. [➡USEFULNESS; 200] *Opposite:* theoretical.

appliqué *type of* **handicraft**. [➡CRAFTS AND CARVING; 356]

apply 1 *v* **submit an application**, request, ask, go in, put in, make a claim. [➡REQUEST AND DEMAND; 664] 2 *v* **use**, operate, put into operation, employ, utilize, direct, harness. [➡USE; 468] 3 *v* **be relevant**, relate, be appropriate, be valid, pertain, affect, concern. [➡BE ABOUT SOMETHING; 62] 4 *v* **put on**, rub on, spread over, smear, spread on, rub in. [➡DECORATE, ADORN, AND APPLY COATINGS; 406] *Opposite:* remove.

apply yourself *v* **devote yourself**, work hard, concentrate, direct your efforts towards, attend to, apply your mind, pay attention to. [➡PAY ATTENTION; 766] *Opposite:* neglect.

appoint 1 *v* **employ**, sign up, hire, assign, take on, engage, retain. [➡CONFER STATUS; 459] *Opposite:* dismiss. 2 *v* (*formal*) **select**, choose, settle on, agree, pick, decide on, fix, arrange, allot. [➡MAKE DECISIONS AND CHOICES; 753] *Opposite:* reject.

appointed *adj* **chosen**, selected, agreed, fixed, prearranged, allotted. [➡BEFORE, FIRST, AND PRECEDING; 164]

appointment 1 *n* **meeting**, date, scheduled time, engagement, rendezvous, prior arrangement, slot. [➡MEETINGS AND ASSEMBLIES; 43] 2 *n* **selection**, choice, employment, choosing, nomination, promotion. [➡WORK-RELATED ACTIVITIES; 834] 3 *n* **job**, position, opening, office, place, assignment, post. [➡JOB; 833]

apportion *v* **allocate**, allot, dole out (*informal*), assign, dish out (*informal*), divide up, distribute, dispense. [➡DISPENSE, RATION, AND DISTRIBUTE; 435]

apposite *adj* **appropriate**, apt, pertinent, relevant, suitable, to the point. [➡APPROPRIATE, SUITABLE, ADVISABLE; 185] *Opposite:* inappropriate.

appositeness *n* [➡APPROPRIATE, SUITABLE, ADVISABLE; 185]

appraisal *n* **assessment**, evaluation, judgment, review, consideration. [➡SCORES AND EVALUATIONS; 599]

appraise *v* **assess**, evaluate, judge, review, consider, weigh up, value. [➡EXAMINE AND ASSESS; 754]

appreciable *adj* **considerable**, substantial, significant, noticeable, palpable, visible. [➡MANY, MUCH, LARGE AMOUNT; 117] *Opposite:* insignificant.

appreciably *adv* **substantially**, significantly, noticeably, palpably, visibly, considerably. [➡MANY, MUCH, LARGE AMOUNT; 117] *Opposite:* insignificantly.

appreciate 1 *v* **be grateful for**, be thankful for, be glad about, be pleased about, value, welcome. [➡LIKE, LOVE, VALUE, AND ENJOY; 579] 2 *v* **understand**, realize, be aware, recognize the value of, grasp, be conscious of. [➡UNDERSTAND AND GRASP; 760] 3 *v* **increase in value**, go up in price, rise, escalate, raise the value of, gain, grow. [➡ACCOUNTING, BANKING, AND BUDGETING; 799] *Opposite:* depreciate.

appreciation 1 *n* **thanks**, gratitude, indebtedness, gratefulness, obligation, thankfulness. [➡APPRECIATION AND GRATITUDE; 536] 2 *n* **approval**, admiration, positive reception, enjoyment, pleasure. [➡APPRECIATION AND GRATITUDE; 536] *Opposite:* disapproval. 3 *n* **understanding**, grasp, comprehension, handle, awareness, judgment. [➡UNDERSTAND AND GRASP; 760] 4 *n* **rise**, increase, escalation, growth, inflation, gain. [➡CHANGE OF SIZE: BIGGER; 393] *Opposite:* depreciation.

appreciative 1 *adj* **grateful**, thankful, indebted, obliged, beholden, in debt. [➡APPRECIATION AND GRATITUDE; 536] *Opposite:* ungrateful. 2 *adj* **approving**, enthusiastic, admiring, positive, favourable, supportive. [➡ENTHUSIASTIC AND INQUISITIVE; 629] *Opposite:* disapproving.

appreciatively *adv* **approvingly**, enthusiastically, admiringly, positively, favourably, supportively. [➡EXPRESSING RESPECT AND APPROVAL; 638] *Opposite:* disapprovingly.

apprehend *v* **catch**, arrest, detain, take in for questioning, take into custody, capture, pick up (*informal*), stop. [➡THE POLICE, ARREST, AND PRE-TRIAL PROCEEDINGS; 818] *Opposite:* release.

apprehension 1 *n* **anxiety**, uneasiness, worry, trepidation, nervousness, fear, hesitation, dread, fearfulness, angst, misgiving, alarm, disquiet, foreboding, apprehensiveness. [➡FEELINGS ABOUT THE FUTURE; 534] *Opposite:* confidence. 2 *n* **capture**, arrest, detention, seizure, taking, imprisonment. [➡TAKE SOMETHING AWAY; 426] *Opposite:* discharge.

apprehensive *adj* **uneasy**, worried, nervous, fearful, hesitant, frightened, concerned, angst-ridden, anxious. [➡CONFUSION, ANXIETY, AND WORRY; 541] *Opposite:* confident.

apprehensiveness *n* **fearfulness**, fear, anxiety, trepidation, apprehension, disquiet, foreboding, alarm, dread, hesitation, angst, misgiving. [➡INSECURITY AND LOSS OF COMPOSURE; 545] *Opposite:* confidence.

apprentice *n* **trainee**, learner, beginner, novice, student, intern (*US*). [➡UNSKILLED PERSON; 531] *Opposite:* expert.

See Compare and Contrast at **beginner**.

apprenticeship *n* **traineeship**, training, education, preparation, internship (*US*). [➡LESSONS, COURSE WORK, AND EXAMINATIONS; 842]

apprise (*formal*) *v* [➡INFORM AND ANNOUNCE; 612]

approach 1 *v* **move towards**, come up to, come near, draw near, come within reach of, come close to, loom, advance. [➡PROCEED AND GO; 306] *Opposite:* retreat. 2 *v* **speak to**, talk to, get in touch with, contact, make contact with, sound out, waylay, accost, buttonhole (*informal*). [➡INITIATE AND ESTABLISH COMMUNICATION; 681] 3 *v* **set about**, tackle, deal with, handle, manage, attempt, consider. [➡START AN ACTION; 261] 4 *v* **approximate**, come close to, be similar to, come near to, move towards, verge on. [➡SEEM TO BE SOMETHING; 58] 5 *n* **method**, line of attack, tactic, line, slant, style, attitude, methodology. [➡WAYS OF DOING THINGS; 295]

approachability 1 *n* **friendliness**, accessibility, openness, affability, cordiality, availability. [➡FRIENDLINESS AND SOCIABILITY; 495] *Opposite:* aloofness. 2 *n* **user-friendliness**, accessibility, availability, ease of use, usability, usefulness, practicality, helpfulness. [➡USEFULNESS; 200] *Opposite:* inaccessibility.

approachable 1 *adj* **friendly**, amicable, sociable, open, open-minded, amenable, welcoming, available, accessible. [➡FRIENDLINESS AND SOCIABILITY; 495] *Opposite:* forbidding. 2 *adj* **user-friendly**, accessible, usable, useful, helpful, practical. [➡USEFULNESS; 200] *Opposite:* inaccessible.

approaching *adj* **imminent**, impending, pending, future, forthcoming, upcoming (*US*), oncoming, potential. [➡FUTURE; 86]

approbation *n* **approval**, consent, praise, admiration, esteem, commendation, regard. [➡PRAISE AND ENCOURAGE; 648] *Opposite:* disapproval.

approbatory *adj* [➡EXPRESSING RESPECT AND APPROVAL; 638]

appropriate 1 *adj* **suitable**, fitting, apt, apposite, right, correct, applicable. [➡APPROPRIATE, SUITABLE, ADVISABLE; 185] *Oppo-*

site: inappropriate. **2** *v* **take,** take over, misappropriate, seize, assume, arrogate (*formal*), usurp, adopt. [➡TAKE SOMETHING AWAY; 426]

appropriateness *n* **suitability,** correctness, aptness, appositeness, relevance, pertinence, fitness. [➡APPROPRIATE, SUITABLE, ADVISABLE; 185]

appropriation *n* **seizure,** assumption, arrogation (*formal*), annexation, adoption. [➡TAKE SOMETHING AWAY; 426]

approval 1 *n* **appreciation,** admiration, liking, praise, esteem, approbation. [➡LIKE, LOVE, VALUE, AND ENJOY; 579] **2** *n* **endorsement,** support, sanction, consent, agreement, authorization, say-so (*informal*). [➡APPROVE AND CONFIRM; 647]

approve 1 *v* **favour,** like, support, agree, accept, commend, esteem, admire. [➡APPROVE AND CONFIRM; 647] *Opposite:* disapprove. **2** *v* **grant,** consent, sanction, allow, pass, authorize, ratify, certify, OK (*informal*), endorse. [➡PERMIT AND ALLOW; 670] *Opposite:* reject.

approved *adj* **accepted,** permitted, official, agreed, appropriate, correct, sanctioned, ratified. [➡APPROPRIATE, SUITABLE, ADVISABLE; 185]

approving *adj* **positive,** favourable, appreciative, sympathetic, complimentary, admiring. [➡APPRECIATION AND GRATITUDE; 536] *Opposite:* disapproving.

approvingly *adv* **positively,** favourably, appreciatively, sympathetically, admiringly. [➡EXPRESSING RESPECT AND APPROVAL; 638] *Opposite:* disapprovingly.

approximate *adj* **estimated,** rough, loose, near, inexact, imprecise, ballpark (*US informal*). [➡APPROXIMATELY; 133] *Opposite:* exact.

approximation *n* **estimate,** guess, calculation, guesstimate (*informal*). [➡ASSESS QUANTITY; 758]

appurtenance (*formal*) *n* [➡MORE AND EXCESS; 122]

apricot 1 *type of* **orange.** [➡COLOURS; 1223] **2** *type of* **fruit.** [➡FRUIT AND VEGETABLES; 1175]

apron *n* **bib,** pinny (*informal*), smock, pinafore, overall. [➡GARMENTS AND OUTFITS; 865]

apropos (*formal*) **1** *prep* **regarding,** concerning, about, on the subject of, in relation to, in connection with. [➡EXPRESSIONS OF REFERENCE; 63] **2** *adj* **right,** appropriate, fitting, suitable, seemly, correct. [➡APPROPRIATE, SUITABLE, ADVISABLE; 185]

apse *n* [➡PARTS OF RELIGIOUS BUILDINGS; 1085]

apt 1 *adj* **appropriate,** suitable, fitting, apposite, pertinent, right, proper, apropos (*formal*). [➡APPROPRIATE, SUITABLE, ADVISABLE; 185] *Opposite:* inappropriate. **2** *adj* **quick,** capable, competent, able, skilled, ready. [➡TALENTED AND SKILFUL; 528] *Opposite:* inept.

aptitude *n* **ability,** skill, talent, gift, capacity, fitness, propensity (*formal*). [➡SKILLS, TALENTS, AND ABILITIES; 527] *Opposite:* inability.

> *See Compare and Contrast at* **ability, talent.**

aptly *adv* **appropriately,** fittingly, suitably, rightly, pertinently, appositely, properly. [➡APPROPRIATE, SUITABLE, ADVISABLE; 185] *Opposite:* inappropriately.

apt to *adj* **prone,** likely, given to, inclined, tending, disposed. [➡THE WILL AND WILLINGNESS; 564]

aquamarine 1 *type of* **gemstone.** [➡PRECIOUS STONES; 1277] **2** *type of* **green.** [➡COLOURS; 1223]

aquarium *type of* **pen or cage.** [➡ANIMAL OR BIRD ACCOMMODATION; 1078]

Aquarius *type of* **star sign.** [➡FATE, DESTINY, AND ASTROLOGY; 783]

aquatic *adj* **water,** marine, sea, river. [➡THE SEAS, OCEANS, AND SHORES; 1041]

aqueduct 1 *n* **channel,** conduit, canal, watercourse, culvert, pipe. [➡WATERCOURSES; 1110] **2** *type of* **bridge.** [➡BRIDGES, TUNNELS, CROSSINGS, AND JUNCTIONS; 1111]

aquilegia *type of* **perennial flower.** [➡FLOWERS; 1032]

aquiline *adj* [➡ANGULAR SHAPE; 1216]

aquiver *adj* [➡INSECURITY AND LOSS OF COMPOSURE; 545]

Arabian horse *type of* **horse.** [➡HORSE; 985]

Arabic *type of* **alphabet.** [➡SYMBOLS, SIGNS, AND NUMBERS; 597]

> **arachnid**
>
> ◆ *types of arachnid*
> black widow, daddy longlegs (*US*), funnel-web spider, mite, money spider, scorpion, spider, tarantula, trapdoor spider, wolf spider

arachnophobia *type of* **phobia.** [➡FEARS AND PHOBIAS; 555]

arbiter 1 *n* **arbitrator,** mediator, intermediary, negotiator, go-between, peacemaker, referee, conciliator, judge. [➡ADVISERS, JUDGES, AND ARBITERS; 971] **2** *n* **authority,** influence, role model, leader, example, trendsetter, style guru. [➡DEVOTEES AND ADDICTED PEOPLE; 557]

arbitrary *adj* **random,** chance, subjective, uninformed, illogical, capricious, indiscriminate, haphazard. [➡UNINTENTIONAL AND ACCIDENTAL; 282] *Opposite:* systematic.

arbitrate *v* **judge,** adjudicate, pass judgment, decide, settle, sort out, mediate, referee, intercede, determine, adjudge, assess. [➡ASSESS QUALITY; 756]

arbitration *n* **adjudication,** negotiation, mediation, settlement, intercession. [➡NEGOTIATION AND DEBATE; 46]

arbitrator *n* **judge,** arbiter, mediator, go-between, intermediary, conciliator, negotiator, peacemaker, referee, umpire. [➡PEOPLE IN SPORTS AND LEISURE; 876]

arbour *n* **bower,** retreat, nook, gazebo, dell (*literary*). [➡GARDENS; 1073]

arc *n* **curve,** arch, semicircle, sweep, bow, bend, curvature. [➡ROUNDED SHAPE; 1217]

arcade 1 *n* **colonnade,** cloister, loggia, gallery, walkway, portico, pergola, passageway. [➡ANCILLARY BUILDINGS; 1079] **2** *n*

precinct, shopping centre, shopping arcade, shopping mall (*US*). [➡RETAIL OUTLETS; 1082]

arcadia *n* [➡NON-EXISTENT PLACE; 1065]

arcane *adj* **mysterious**, secret, esoteric, deep, hidden, unfathomable, unknowable, obscure, impenetrable, inscrutable. [➡SECRET AND UNKNOWN; 180]

See Compare and Contrast at **obscure**.

arch 1 *n* **arc**, curve, semicircle, bend, bow, sweep, curvature. [➡ROUNDED SHAPE; 1217] 2 *n* **archway**, doorway, portico. [➡DOORS AND ACCESS POINTS; 1100] 3 *v* **curve**, bend, bow, arc. [➡CHANGE OF SHAPE; 386] *Opposite:* hollow. 4 *adj* **playful**, mischievous, roguish, knowing, cunning, coy. [➡DECEITFUL; 514]

archaic *adj* **old**, ancient, dated, outdated, out-of-date, antiquated, old-fashioned, outmoded, prehistoric, behind the times, antediluvian (*informal*). [➡OLD, OLD-FASHIONED; 168] *Opposite:* modern.

See Compare and Contrast at **old-fashioned**.

archangel *n* [➡RELIGIOUS CONCEPTS; 777]

archbishop *n* [➡RELIGIOUS PEOPLE; 779]

archbishopric *n* [➡RELIGIOUS PEOPLE; 779]

arch bridge *type of* **bridge**. [➡BRIDGES, TUNNELS, CROSSINGS, AND JUNCTIONS; 1111]

arched *adj* **curved**, rounded, round, high, bowed, bent, vaulted, domed, semicircular, hemispherical. [➡ROUNDED SHAPE; 1217]

archenemy *n* **opponent**, enemy, rival, challenger, nemesis (*literary*), foe (*literary*). [➡ENEMIES AND TORMENTORS; 969] *Opposite:* ally.

archetypal *adj* **typical**, model, representative, standard, archetypical, classic, exemplary, conventional, prototypical. [➡REPRESENTATIVE; 66] *Opposite:* unconventional.

archetype *n* **model**, epitome, prototype, original, classic. [➡PERFECT EXAMPLES AND EMBODIMENTS; 67]

archetypical *adj* **typical**, model, representative, standard, archetypal, classic, exemplary, conventional, prototypical. [➡REPRESENTATIVE; 66] *Opposite:* unconventional.

archipelago *n* [➡THE CONTINENTS AND ISLANDS; 1048]

architect 1 *n* **designer**, draughtsman, draughtswoman, draughtsperson, planner, engineer, builder. [➡DESIGNERS, CREATORS AND INSTIGATORS; 348] 2 *n* **originator**, inventor, founder, creator, engineer, prime mover, builder. [➡DESIGNERS, CREATORS, AND INSTIGATORS; 348]

architectural *adj* [➡BUILDING AND ARCHITECTURE; 1075]

architecture *n* **design**, planning, building, construction. [➡BUILDING AND ARCHITECTURE; 1075]

architecture

◆ *types of 20th-century architecture*
art deco, Bauhaus, brutalist, Federation, moderne, modernist, postmodern

◆ *types of pre-20th-century architecture*
art nouveau, Baroque, Byzantine, cinquecento, classical, colonial, Corinthian, Decorated, Doric, Elizabethan, Empire, Georgian, Gothic, Gothic revival, Ionic, Moorish, neoclassical, Norman, Palladian, perpendicular, Renaissance, rococo, Romanesque, Tudor, Victorian

archive *n* **record**, file, documentation, document, annal (*dated*), library, collection. [➡RECORDS; 586]

archly *adv* **playfully**, mischievously, roguishly, knowingly, cunningly, coyly. [➡DECEITFUL; 514]

archness *n* **playfulness**, mischievousness (*formal*), roguishness, cunning, coyness. [➡DECEITFUL; 514]

archway *n* **arch**, arcade, pergola, portico, doorway, cloister. [➡DOORS AND ACCESS POINTS; 1100]

arc lamp *type of* **light**. [➡LIGHT; 1163]

arctic (*informal*) *adj* **freezing**, cold, chilly, wintry, frozen, icy, frosty, subzero, glacial, frigid. [➡COLD WEATHER; 1051] *Opposite:* tropical.

ardent *adj* **passionate**, enthusiastic, keen, fervent, zealous, eager, devoted, dedicated, committed, fiery, fervid. [➡ENERGY AND ENTHUSIASM; 497] *Opposite:* dispassionate.

ardently *adv* **passionately**, enthusiastically, keenly, fervently, zealously, eagerly, fervidly. [➡ENTHUSIASTIC AND INQUISITIVE; 629] *Opposite:* dispassionately.

ardour *n* **passion**, love, enthusiasm, zeal, fervour, eagerness, devotion, dedication, commitment. [➡LOVE, RESPECT, AND GOODWILL; 550] *Opposite:* indifference.

arduous *adj* **difficult**, hard, laborious, gruelling, demanding, strenuous, onerous, tiring, toilsome, taxing, operose (*formal*). [➡DIFFICULTY AND COMPLEXITY; 243] *Opposite:* easy.

See Compare and Contrast at **hard**.

arduously *adv* **laboriously**, onerously, strenuously, gruellingly, tiringly, with difficulty. [➡PHYSICALLY UNPLEASANT; 227] *Opposite:* easily.

arduousness *n* **difficulty**, laboriousness, strenuousness, onerousness, rigorousness. [➡DIFFICULTY AND COMPLEXITY; 243] *Opposite:* ease.

area 1 *n* **part**, zone, extent, expanse, range, space, capacity, region, band, belt, stretch. [➡AREA AND RANGE; 111] 2 *n* **neighbourhood**, locale, vicinity, part, quarter, spot, region, corner, district. [➡PLACE; 1064] 3 *n* **subject**, topic, field, question, matter, sphere, theme. [➡SUBJECT AREA; 769]

area of expertise *n* [➡SUBJECT AREA; 769]

arena *n* **stadium**, ground, showground, sports ground, pitch, field, ring, amphitheatre, dome. [➡URBAN OUTDOOR SPACES; 1071]

argon *type of* **gas.** [➡GASES; 1274]

argot *n* **jargon**, slang, idiom, speech, dialect, patois, vernacular. [➡THE SPOKEN WORD; 672]

arguable *adj* **debatable**, open to question, questionable, doubtful, dubious, uncertain, far from certain, disputable. [➡UNCERTAIN; 176] *Opposite:* certain.

arguably *adv* **debatably**, questionably, perhaps, possibly, maybe, doubtfully, disputably. [➡POSSIBLE AND PROBABLE; 178] *Opposite:* certainly.

argue 1 *v* **quarrel**, dispute, fight, disagree, bicker, squabble, fall out. [➡ARGUE AND FIGHT – TWO-WAY; 644] *Opposite:* make friends. 2 *v* **make a case**, contend, claim, say, maintain, reason, debate, dispute, discuss, go over, thrash out, explore, hash out (*US*). [➡CLAIM, INSIST, AND EMPHASIZE; 615]

argument 1 *n* **quarrel**, fight, disagreement, dispute, row, spat, squabble, barney (*informal*). [➡ARGUMENT; 47] 2 *n* **case**, line of reasoning, reason, contention, claim. [➡POINT OF VIEW; 768]

argumentative *adj* **quarrelsome**, confrontational, contrary, belligerent, aggressive, challenging, stroppy (*informal*), awkward. [➡DIFFICULT TO PLEASE; 516] *Opposite:* peaceable.

argumentativeness *n* [➡DIFFICULT TO PLEASE; 516]

aria *type of* **vocal music.** [➡MUSIC, SONGS, AND SINGING; 907]

arid 1 *adj* **dry**, parched, bone dry, baked, waterless, scorched, infertile, barren, sere (*archaic or literary*). [➡DRY; 1241] *Opposite:* humid. 2 *adj* **boring**, dull, uninteresting, dry, sterile, uninspired, unexciting, tepid, unimaginative. [➡BORING AND UNINTERESTING; 235] *Opposite:* exciting.

See Compare and Contrast at **dry.**

aridity *n* **dryness**, waterlessness, drought, infertility, barrenness. [➡DRY; 1241] *Opposite:* humidity.

aridness *n* **dryness**, parchedness, desiccation, dehydration, scorchedness. [➡DRY; 1241] *Opposite:* wetness.

Aries *type of* **star sign.** [➡FATE, DESTINY, AND ASTROLOGY; 783]

arise 1 *v* **happen**, occur, take place, come up, crop up (*informal*), come to pass (*archaic or literary*), begin, start, appear, surface, commence (*formal*). [➡HAPPEN; 27] 2 *v* **result from**, be the result of, arise from, arise out of, be caused by, stem from, come from, evolve. [➡GRADUALLY COME INTO EXISTENCE; 1] 3 *v* (*archaic or literary*) **get up**, stand up, rise, get to your feet, ascend. [➡GO UPWARDS; 307] *Opposite:* sit down. 4 *v* (*archaic or literary*) **get out of bed**, get up, rise. [➡GO UPWARDS; 307] *Opposite:* retire.

aristocracy *n* **nobility**, upper classes, peers of the realm, landed gentry, lords and ladies, upper crust (*informal*), gentry. [➡CLASS STATUS; 889] *Opposite:* lower class.

aristocrat *n* **noble**, lord, lady, peer, grandee, nob (*informal*), toff (*informal*). [➡CLASS STATUS; 889]

aristocrat

◆ *types of aristocrat*
baron, baroness, baronet, count, countess, crown prince, duchess, duke, earl, king, knight, maharajah, maharani, marchioness, marquess, prince, princess, queen, viscount, viscountess

aristocratic 1 *adj* **noble**, titled, patrician, upper-class, blue-blooded, highborn (*literary*). [➡CLASS STATUS; 889] *Opposite:* lower-class. 2 *adj* **refined**, well-bred, patrician, noble. [➡CLASS STATUS; 889] *Opposite:* lowly.

arithmetic *n* [➡MATHS; 598]

arithmetical *adj* [➡MATHS; 598]

arithmetic mean *n* [➡MATHS; 598]

arm 1 *n* **limb**, appendage, member. [➡ARM AND HAND; 696] 2 *n* **support**, armrest, rest. [➡FURNITURE; 858] 3 *n* **division**, wing, branch, subdivision, offshoot, limb. [➡SUBDIVISIONS AND OFFSHOOTS; 1252] 4 *v* **equip**, furnish (*formal*), provide, supply, prepare, ready. [➡EQUIP AND SUPPLY; 436] *Opposite:* disarm.

arm

◆ *parts of an arm or hand*
ball, cuticle, elbow, finger, fingernail, fingerprint, fingertip, fist, forearm, forefinger, hand, hangnail, heel, index finger, knuckle, little finger, middle finger, palm, pinkie (*informal*), ring finger, thumb, thumbnail, wrist

armada *n* **fleet**, flotilla, navy, squadron, task force. [➡GROUPS OF VEHICLES; 1151]

armadillo *type of* **small mammal.** [➡SMALL MAMMAL; 990]

Armageddon *n* **apocalypse**, disaster, destruction, day of reckoning, end of the world, Judgment Day. [➡RELIGIOUS CONCEPTS; 777]

armament *n* **arming**, mobilization, rearmament, deployment, buildup, preparation, disarmament. [➡WARFARE AND WAR; 830]

armaments *n* **arms**, weapons, weaponry, guns, missiles, artillery, munitions. [➡WEAPONS; 1153]

armature *n* [➡PARTS OF MACHINES AND TOOLS; 1117]

armchair *type of* **seating.** [➡FURNITURE; 858]

armed *adj* **equipped**, fortified, prepared. [➡MILITARY; 829] *Opposite:* unarmed.

armed forces *n* **military**, forces, services, army, militia, air force, navy, defence force. [➡THE ARMED FORCES; 827]

armed robbery *n* [➡CRIMES; 817]

armed services *n* [➡THE ARMED FORCES; 827]

armhole *n* **opening**, slit, hole. [➡HOLES, GAPS, AND FORKS; 1251]

armistice *n* **truce**, peace agreement, settlement, ceasefire, resolution. [➡HARMONY; 156]

armlet *type of* **jewellery.** [➡JEWELLERY; 866]

armoire *type of* **cabinet.** [➡FURNITURE; 858]

armour 1 *n* **bulletproof vest**, flak jacket, breastplate, panoply, chain mail, suit of armour, body armour, mail, coat of mail. [➡GARMENTS AND OUTFITS; 865] 2 *n* **protection**, reinforcement, defence, covering, cover, armature, shell, shield. [➡COVERS AND COATINGS; 1245]

armoured *adj* **arsenal**, reinforced, steel-clad, armour-plated, strengthened, bulletproof, protected, secure, covered. [➡STRENGTH; 202] *Opposite:* unprotected.

armoured car *type of* **military vehicle.** [➡VEHICLES; 1144]

armour-plated *adj* **reinforced**, steel-clad, armoured, strengthened, bulletproof, protected, secure, covered. [➡STRENGTH; 202] *Opposite:* unprotected.

armoury 1 *n* **arms depot**, magazine, ordnance depot, munitions store, weapon store, missile silo, gunroom. [➡STORES AND STORAGE BUILDINGS; 1087] 2 *n* **stock**, source, supply, resource. [➡COLLECTIONS AND MIXTURES OF THINGS; 1243]

armpit *part of* **torso.** [➡TORSO; 694]

armrest *n* **support**, arm, rest. [➡FURNITURE; 858]

arms *n* **weapons**, weaponry, armaments, guns, missiles, artillery, munitions. [➡WEAPONS; 1153]

arms depot *type of* **storage space.** [➡STORES AND STORAGE BUILDINGS; 1087]

arms reduction *n* [➡WARFARE AND WAR; 830]

army 1 *n* **military**, armed forces, defence force, militia, territorial army, soldiers. [➡THE ARMED FORCES; 827] 2 *n* **crowd**, throng, mass, host, multitude, legion, band. [➡GROUPS OF PEOPLE; 935]

army ant *type of* **ant.** [➡ANTS; 1014]

army cadet *n* [➡MILITARY PERSONNEL; 828]

army camp *n* [➡WARFARE AND WAR; 830]

army chaplain *n* [➡RELIGIOUS PEOPLE; 779]

A-road *type of* **major road.** [➡ROADS; 1105]

aroma *n* **smell**, perfume, fragrance, scent, odour, bouquet, whiff (*informal*), tang. [➡SMELL AND SMELLING; 706]

See Compare and Contrast at **smell.**

aromatic *adj* **perfumed**, fragrant, sweet-smelling, scented, pungent, musky. [➡SMELL AND SMELLING; 706] *Opposite:* odourless.

around 1 *prep* **about**, all round, surrounding, covering, over, all around. [➡RELATIVE LOCATION; 162] 2 *prep* **close to**, near, in the vicinity, in the neighbourhood, in the environs, round. [➡CLOSENESS; 160] 3 *prep* **all over**, throughout, here and there, about, round, across. [➡RELATIVE LOCATION; 162] 4 *prep* **approximately**, about, in the region of, just about, roughly, more or less, in the order of, give or take, almost, nearly, going on for, roughly speaking, going on (*US*). [➡APPROXIMATELY; 133] 5 *adv* **in**, here, round, about, present, available. [➡PRESENT AND AVAILABLE; 11] 6 *adv* **from one place to another**, from place to place, about, all over the place (*informal*), everywhere. [➡GENERAL LOCATIONS; 159] 7 *adv* **roundabouts**, roundabout, round here, near here, nearby, about, round, in the area, in the vicinity. [➡CLOSENESS; 160]

around the clock *adv* **continuously**, nonstop, permanently, full-time, constantly, all day long, every hour in the day. [➡PERMANENCE: WITHOUT END; 94] *Opposite:* sporadically.

around-the-clock *adj* [➡PERMANENCE: WITHOUT END; 94]

arousal *n* **stimulation**, provocation, awakening, encouragement, excitement, urging. [➡PLEASURE, EXCITEMENT, AND ELATION; 535]

arouse *v* **stimulate**, provoke, awaken, produce, stir, stir up, rouse. [➡APPEAL TO AND AROUSE INTEREST; 576] *Opposite:* dampen.

aroused *adj* [➡PLEASURE, EXCITEMENT, AND ELATION; 535]

arpeggio *type of* **musical term.** [➡MUSICAL TERMS; 912]

arraign *v* **accuse**, impeach, prosecute, have up (*informal*), bring before the court. [➡TRIAL, PUNISHMENT, AND LEGAL OUTCOMES; 819]

arraignment *n* **charge**, prosecution, legal process, legal action, indictment, impeachment, summons, inculpation (*formal*), citation. [➡TRIAL, PUNISHMENT, AND LEGAL OUTCOMES; 819] *Opposite:* exculpation (*formal*).

arrange 1 *v* **organize**, set up, coordinate, fix, fix up, make plans for, plan, orchestrate. [➡CAUSE TO HAPPEN; 31] 2 *v* **position**, put in order, place, assemble, put together, organize, display, lay out, dispose (*formal*), pose, array (*formal*). [➡POSITION SOMETHING; 326] *Opposite:* disarrange.

arranged *adj* **decided**, agreed, set, settled, organized, prescribed, prepared, ready. [➡CERTAIN; 175]

arrangement 1 *n* **preparation**, plan, procedure, prearrangement, planning, making ready. [➡WAYS OF DOING THINGS; 295] 2 *n* **agreement**, understanding, bargain, pact, deal. [➡RECIPROCITY AND INTERDEPENDENCE; 148] 3 *n* **display**, array, composition, layout, assembly, collection, grouping. [➡COLLECTIONS AND MIXTURES OF THINGS; 1243]

arrant *adj* **complete**, total, outright, unmitigated, utter, extreme, out-and-out, straight-out (*US informal*). [➡ABSOLUTE AND ABSOLUTELY; 131]

arras *n* [➡SOFT FURNISHINGS, LINEN, AND DRAPERY; 860]

array 1 *n* **collection**, selection, display, range, arrangement, assortment, grouping. [➡COLLECTIONS AND MIXTURES OF THINGS; 1243] 2 *n* **dress**, clothing, attire (*formal*), regalia, finery, garb, apparel. [➡CLOTHES AND ACCESSORIES; 864] 3 *v* (*formal*) **arrange**, display, organize, set out, exhibit, group, put in order, order, range, dispose (*formal*), lay out. [➡ARRANGE AND CREATE ORDER; 358] 4 *v* (*literary*) **clothe**, dress, attire (*formal*), deck out, drape, bedeck (*literary*). [➡DECORATE, ADORN, AND APPLY COATINGS; 406]

arrears *n* **amount overdue**, amount outstanding, debts, sum unpaid. [➡OWE AND DESERVE; 466] *Opposite:* credit.

arrest 1 *v* **take into custody**, seize, capture, detain, catch, hold, apprehend, take in for questioning, stop. [➡THE POLICE, ARREST, AND PRE-TRIAL PROCEEDINGS; 818] *Opposite:* release. 2 *v* (*formal*) **halt**, stop, block, prevent, obstruct, impede, bring to an end, hinder, stem, check. [➡CAUSE TO STOP; 267] *Opposite:* start. 3 *v* (*formal*) **attract**, engage, catch, hold, fix, grab (*informal*). [➡APPEAL TO AND AROUSE INTEREST; 576] 4 *n* **capture**, seizure, detention, apprehension, custody. [➡THE POLICE, ARREST, AND PRE-TRIAL PROCEEDINGS; 818] *Opposite:* release.

arresting *adj* **impressive**, eye-catching, stunning, striking, interesting, fascinating, attractive, noticeable, attention-grabbing. [➡BEAUTY AND ATTRACTIVENESS; 190] *Opposite:* uninteresting.

arrière-pensée (*formal*) *n* [➡IDEA AND THOUGHT; 771]

arrival *n* **influx**, entrance, onset, coming, advent, appearance. [➡ARRIVAL; 13] *Opposite:* departure.

arrive 1 *v* **reach**, turn up, get there, land, disembark, pull in, appear, enter. [➡ARRIVE; 12] *Opposite:* depart. 2 *v* **work out**, reach, come to, attain, thrash out, decide on, hash out (*US*). [➡MAKE DECISIONS AND CHOICES; 753] 3 *v* **succeed**, be successful, make it (*informal*), gain recognition, make your mark. [➡SUCCEED AND WIN; 79]

arriviste (*disapproving*) *n* [➡SELF-IMPORTANT AND SELF-SEEKING PEOPLE; 949]

arrogance *n* **conceit**, haughtiness, egotism, pride, overconfidence, superciliousness, self-importance, condescension. [➡MORALLY BAD; 776] *Opposite:* humility.

arrogant *adj* **conceited**, haughty, egotistic, bigheaded (*informal*), superior, proud, overconfident, supercilious, self-important. [➡POMPOUS, LOUD, AND OVER-CONFIDENT; 636] *Opposite:* humble.

See Compare and Contrast at **proud**.

arrogate (*formal*) *v* **claim**, lay claim to, appropriate, misappropriate, assume, take over, demand, annex [➡TAKE SOMETHING AWAY; 426] *Opposite:* cede (*formal*).

arrogation (*formal*) *n* **appropriation**, misappropriation, assumption, takeover, annexation, seizure. [➡TAKE SOMETHING AWAY; 426]

arrow 1 *n* **projectile**, missile, dart, barb, shaft, bolt. [➡PROJECTILES; 1158] 2 *n* **symbol**, sign, pointer, marker, indicator, cursor, signpost, road sign. [➡SYMBOLS, SIGNS, AND NUMBERS; 597] 3 *type of* **projectile**. [➡WEAPONS FOR SHOOTING; 1155]

arrowhead *n* **point**, tip, barb. [➡PROJECTILES; 1158]

arrowroot *n* **thickener**, starch, stiffener. [➡SEASONINGS AND SAUCES; 1173]

arsenal 1 *n* **weapon store**, munitions store, magazine, armoury. [➡STORES AND STORAGE BUILDINGS; 1087] 2 *n* **store**, battery, fund, cache, collection, stash (*informal*), resource. [➡COLLECTIONS AND MIXTURES OF THINGS; 1243]

arsenic *type of* **mineral**. [➡MINERALS; 1276]

arson *n* **fire raising**, incendiarism (*formal*), pyromania, burning, incineration, ignition, firebombing, torching (*slang*). [➡CRIMES; 817]

arsonist *n* **fire raiser**, pyromaniac, burner, firebomber, incendiary (*formal*), firebug (*slang*), torcher (*slang*). [➡CRIMINALS; 821]

art 1 *n* **painting**, drawing, fine art, graphic arts, sculpture. [➡THE PICTORIAL ARTS; 897] 2 *n* **skill**, talent, knack, ability, virtuosity. [➡SKILLS, TALENTS, AND ABILITIES; 527]

art

◆ *types of 20th-century art movement*
abstract expressionism, art deco, conceptual art, constructivism, cubism, Dada, expressionism, Fauvism, futurism, minimalism, modernism, op art, photorealism, pop art, postmodernism, socialist realism, surrealism, vorticism

◆ *types of pre-20th-century art movement*
art nouveau, Arts and Crafts, Baroque, classicism, impressionism, Mannerism, pointillism, post-impressionism, Pre-Raphaelitism, realism, Renaissance, Romanticism, symbolism

art deco 1 *type of* **20th-century art movement**. [➡ARTISTIC MOVEMENTS AND STYLES; 899] 2 *type of* **20th-century architecture**. [➡BUILDING AND ARCHITECTURE; 1075]

artefact *n* **object**, objet d'art, manufactured object, article, manufactured article, work of art, item, piece, thing, product, relic, archaeological find. [➡PHYSICAL OBJECTS; 1242]

arterial *adj* **major**, main, trunk, principal, through. [➡COMMUNICATION NETWORKS; 1104] *Opposite:* side.

artery 1 *n* **route**, road, line, channel, pathway, main line, conduit, major road, trunk road, highway (*US*). [➡ROADS; 1105] 2 *type of* **blood vessel**. [➡THE BLOOD AND CIRCULATION; 718]

artful *adj* **crafty**, devious, sly, deceitful, cunning, wily, sneaky. [➡DECEITFUL; 514] *Opposite:* open.

artfulness *n* **craftiness**, deviousness, slyness, cleverness, deceitfulness, cunning, wiles, sneakiness, artifice (*formal*). [➡DECEITFUL; 514] *Opposite:* straightforwardness.

art-house *adj* **highbrow**, intellectual, sophisticated, esoteric, specialist, avant-garde, trendy (*informal*) [➡LEVEL OF EDUCATION AND SOPHISTICATION; 894]. *Opposite:* lowbrow (*disapproving*).

arthritic *adj* **stiff**, swollen, aching, sore, painful, inflamed. [➡THE BONES AND JOINTS; 720]

arthritis *n* **stiffness**, swelling, ache, pain, soreness, inflammation. [➡THE BONES AND JOINTS; 720]

artichoke *type of* **vegetable**. [➡FRUIT AND VEGETABLES; 1175]

article 1 *n* **piece of writing**, editorial, piece, item, commentary, critique, exposé. [➡ANALYTICAL NONFICTION WRITING; 593] 2 *n* **object**, item, piece, thing, artefact. [➡PHYSICAL OBJECTS; 1242] 3 *n* **clause**, term, stipulation, condition, regulation, paragraph, section. [➡SUMMARIES, OUTLINES, AND EXCERPTS; 589] 4 *type of* **word class**. [➡ASPECTS OF LANGUAGE; 683]

articles *n* **training**, traineeship, apprenticeship, pupillage (*formal*), tutelage, course, qualifications. [➡LESSONS, COURSE WORK, AND EXAMINATIONS; 842]

articulacy *n* **self-expression**, expressiveness, eloquence, fluency, articulateness, coherence, clarity, lucidity. [➡ELOQUENT, TALKATIVE, AND LONG-WINDED; 633]

articulate 1 *adj* **eloquent**, clear, coherent, fluent, lucid, expressive, communicative. [➡ELOQUENT, TALKATIVE, AND LONG-WINDED; 633] *Opposite:* inarticulate. 2 *v* **speak about**, express, put into words, convey, verbalize, communicate, formulate. [➡UTTER AND PRONOUNCE; 609] *Opposite:* keep secret. 3 *v* **enunciate**, pronounce, speak clearly, speak, say, utter. [➡UTTER AND PRONOUNCE; 609] *Opposite:* mumble.

articulated 1 *adj* **modular**, jointed, coupled, linked, connected, interconnected. [➡FASTEN, LINK, AND JOIN; 409] *Opposite:* rigid. 2 *adj* **spoken**, voiced, uttered, expressed, pronounced, enunciated, said, verbalized, put into words, communicated. [➡THE SPOKEN WORD; 672] *Opposite:* unspoken.

articulated lorry *type of* **commercial or industrial vehicle**. [➡VEHICLES; 1144]

articulateness *n* **eloquence**, expressiveness, fluency, self-expression, coherence, clarity, lucidity, articulacy. [➡ELOQUENT, TALKATIVE, AND LONG-WINDED; 633]

articulation 1 *n* **enunciation**, pronunciation, speech, diction, delivery, voicing, vocalization. [➡THE SPOKEN WORD; 672] 2 *n* **expression**, verbalization, communication, formulation. [➡THE SPOKEN WORD; 672]

artifact *see* **artefact**.

artifice (*formal*) 1 *n* **pretence**, ploy, trick, lie, sleight of hand, ruse. [➡DECEPTION AND LIES; 661] 2 *n* **deception**, deceit, cunning, trickery, artfulness, wiles, craft. [➡DECEPTION AND LIES; 661]

artificial 1 *adj* **false**, fake, mock, reproduction, synthetic, simulated, imitation, man-made. [➡FALSE AND UNREAL; 174] *Opposite:* natural. 2 *adj* **insincere**, false, put-on, pretend, unnatural, contrived, feigned, hollow. [➡FALSE AND UNREAL; 174] *Opposite:* sincere.

artificial insemination *n* [➡REPRODUCTION AND HEREDITY; 726]

artificiality *n* **insincerity**, disingenuousness, affectedness, affectation, phoniness, inauthenticity, play-acting, pretentiousness, pretension. [➡AFFECTATION, SELF-SATISFACTION, AND SNOBBISHNESS; 508] *Opposite:* sincerity.

artillery *n* **weaponry**, arms, guns, armaments, weapons, missiles, cannons, howitzers. [➡WEAPONS; 1153]

artilleryman *n* [➡MILITARY PERSONNEL; 828]

artisan *n* **craftsperson**, craft worker, artist, skilled worker, artificer (*dated*), crafts worker (*US*), handicrafts worker (*US*). [➡ARTISTS; 900]

artist 1 *n* **painter**, illustrator, drawer, sketcher, cartoonist, sculptor. [➡ARTISTS; 900] 2 *n* **performer**, artiste, singer, actor, musician, dancer, comedian. [➡MUSICIANS AND SINGERS; 908]

artiste *n* **performer**, entertainer, artist, singer, actor, musician, dancer, comedian. [➡MUSICIANS AND SINGERS; 908]

artistic *adj* **creative**, imaginative, inventive, arty (*informal disapproving*). [➡ARTISTIC MOVEMENTS AND STYLES; 899]

artistry *n* **creativity**, originality, artistic ability, imagination, invention, ability, skill, talent, skilfulness, inventiveness. [➡SKILLS, TALENTS, AND ABILITIES; 527]

artless *adj* **simple**, guileless, natural, unworldly, ingenuous, open, innocent, sincere, naive, unsophisticated, uncontrived, pure (*literary*), childlike. [➡NATURALNESS; 498] *Opposite:* disingenuous.

artlessness *n* **guilelessness**, naturalness, innocence, unaffectedness, inexperience, unpretentiousness, ingenuousness, genuineness, naivety, sincerity, unworldliness, openness, spontaneity. [➡NATURALNESS; 498] *Opposite:* disingenuousness.

art nouveau 1 *type of* **pre-20th-century art movement**. [➡ARTISTIC MOVEMENTS AND STYLES; 899] 2 *type of* **pre-20th-century architecture**. [➡BUILDING AND ARCHITECTURE; 1075]

Arts and Crafts *type of* **pre-20th-century art movement**. [➡ARTISTIC MOVEMENTS AND STYLES; 899]

artwork 1 *n* **work of art**, creation, representation, reproduction, oeuvre (*formal*), painting, drawing, sculpture, sketch, print, collage, mural. [➡ARTWORKS; 898] 2 *n* **illustrations**, pictures, photographs, diagrams, plates, drawings, graphics. [➡ARTWORKS; 898]

arty-crafty 1 *adj* (*informal disapproving*) **overdecorative**, fanciful, pretentious, chintzy (*informal disapproving*), quaint. [➡IN POOR TASTE; 230] 2 *adj* (*informal*) **rustic**, homespun, homemade, traditional, artistic, quaint. [➡ARTISTIC MOVEMENTS AND STYLES; 899] *Opposite:* sophisticated.

as 1 *conj* **while**, when, during, whilst. [➡CONCURRENT AND CONTEMPORANEOUS; 165] 2 *conj* **because**, since, seeing that, being as, considering that, inasmuch as. [➡CAUSATION; 169]

as a matter of fact *adv* **actually**, in consequence (*formal*), in fact, really, in point of fact, to tell the truth. [➡WORDS AND PHRASES EMPHASIZING THE TRUTH OF A MATTER; 173]

as a result *adv* **consequently** (*formal*), accordingly, thus (*formal*), so, therefore. [➡RESULTS AND OUTCOMES; 83]

as a result of *prep* **because of**, by, through, by means of, on account of, due to, thanks to, owing to, by dint of. [➡CAUSATION; 169]

as a rule *adv* **usually**, in general, most of the time, generally, normally, as often as not, nine times out of ten. [➡USUALLY; 108] *Opposite:* exceptionally.

asbestos *type of* **mineral**. [➡MINERALS; 1276]

ascend 1 *v* **rise**, climb, soar, go up, come up, arise (*archaic or literary*). [➡GO UPWARDS; 307] *Opposite:* descend. 2 *v* **climb**, go up, come up, mount, scale, get up, move upward. [➡GO UPWARDS; 307] *Opposite:* descend.

ascendancy *n* **dominance**, domination, predominance, pre-eminence, power, upper hand, control, hegemony (*formal*). [➡SUPERIORITY; 153] *Opposite:* subordination.

ascendant 1 *adj* (*literary*) **rising**, dominant, ascending, prevailing, mounting, overriding, climbing, upward, soaring, moving up, uprising, spiralling. [➡DIRECTION OF MOTION; 346] *Opposite:* descendent. 2 *adj* **dominant**, controlling, governing, ruling, influential, main, principal, leading, chief, foremost, major, superior, supreme. [➡MOST IMPORTANT AND MAIN; 194] *Opposite:* subordinate.

ascendency *see* **ascendancy.**

ascension (*formal*) *n* **rise**, ascent, climb, mounting, scaling, moving up, surmounting, travelling up. [➡GO UPWARDS; 307] *Opposite:* descent.

ascent 1 *n* **climb**, rise, ascension (*formal*), mounting, scaling. [➡GO UPWARDS; 307] *Opposite:* descent. 2 *n* **gradient**, slope, incline, rake, angle, elevation. [➡MOUNTAINS AND HILLS; 1044]

ascertain (*formal*) *v* **determine**, discover, find out, learn, make certain. [➡LEARN AND DISCOVER; 763]

ascetic 1 *n* **abstainer**, celibate, puritan, penitent. [➡ASCETIC PEOPLE; 883] *Opposite:* hedonist. 2 *adj* **austere**, abstinent, frugal, abstemious, Spartan, severe. [➡ABSTEMIOUSNESS AND SELF-DENIAL; 882] *Opposite:* hedonistic.

asceticism *n* **austerity**, self-discipline, abstemiousness, self-denial, self-restraint, abstinence, frugality, plainness, simplicity, severity, starkness, strictness. [➡ABSTEMIOUSNESS AND SELF-DENIAL; 882] *Opposite:* hedonism.

ascribe (*formal*) 1 *v* **assign**, credit, attribute, accredit, chalk up, give credit. [➡GIVE AND PROVIDE; 431] 2 *v* **put down to**, attribute, blame on, lay at the door of, charge, impute. [➡CREATING CONNECTIONS; 145]

aseptic *adj* **clean**, sterile, pure, sterilized, uninfected, hygienic, uncontaminated, disinfected, germ-free, antiseptic, disease-free, purified, sanitized. [➡CLEAN; 1232] *Opposite:* septic.

asexual 1 *adj* **genderless**, androgynous, neutral, sexless. [➡GENDER IDENTITY AND SEXUALITY; 932] 2 *adj* **vegetative**, somatic, parthenogenetic, nonsexual. [➡REPRODUCTION AND HEREDITY; 726]

as far as *conj* **to the extent that**, to the degree that, so far as, insofar as (*formal*), as much as, as concerns. [➡EXPRESSIONS OF REFERENCE; 63]

as far as I'm concerned *adv* [➡EXPRESSIONS OF OPINION; 624]

as good as 1 *prep* **equal to**, equivalent to, the same as, on a par with, comparable with, tantamount to. [➡EQUALITY; 155] 2 *adv* **almost**, nearly, practically, virtually, effectively, more or less, to all intents and purposes. [➡TO A CERTAIN EXTENT; 134]

ash 1 *n* **residue**, cinders, slag, embers, powder, dust. [➡PRODUCTS OF FIRE; 1165] 2 *type of* **deciduous tree.** [➡DECIDUOUS TREES; 1028] 3 *type of* **grey.** [➡COLOURS; 1223]

ashamed 1 *adj* **embarrassed**, mortified, humiliated, abashed, humbled, chagrined. [➡EMBARRASSMENT AND HUMILIATION; 543] *Opposite:* proud. 2 *adj* **regretful**, reluctant, unwilling, uncomfortable, restrained, reserved, deterred. [➡EMBARRASSMENT AND HUMILIATION; 543]

ashen *adj* **pallid**, wan, ashy, pasty, white as a sheet, drained of colour, grey, greyish, pale. [➡COMPLEXION; 481] *Opposite:* rosy.

ashes *n* **ruins**, remains, vestiges, remnants, fragments, debris. [➡FAILURE; 77]

ashore *adv* **aground**, onto land, onto dry land, on shore. [➡DIRECTION OF MOTION; 346]

ashy *adj* **pallid**, wan, pasty, white as a sheet, drained of colour, grey, ashen, pale. [➡COMPLEXION; 481] *Opposite:* rosy.

aside 1 *adv* **sideways**, away, to the side, sidewise, to the left, on the side, to the right, to one side, apart, out of the way. [➡DIRECTION OF MOTION; 346] 2 *adv* **notwithstanding** (*formal*), regardless, however, anyway, anyhow. [➡ALTHOUGH, NEVERTHELESS, AND DESPITE; 170] 3 *adv* **in reserve**, separately, away, to one side, up your sleeve. [➡UNRELATEDNESS AND SEPARATENESS; 147] 4 *n* **digression**, departure, tangent, interposition, parenthesis, excursion, excursus (*formal*). [➡MEANINGLESS SPEECH OR WRITING; 677] 5 *n* **whisper**, mumbled comment, remark, undertone, by-play, soliloquy. [➡NEUTRAL ONE-WAY COMMUNICATION; 49]

aside from 1 *prep* **as well as**, in addition to, on top of, besides, over and beyond, above and beyond. [➡ALSO; 136] 2 *prep* **barring**, excluding, except, except for, excepting (*formal*), with the exception of, apart from, besides, other than, despite, outside of, saving (*literary*). [➡NOT; 135] *Opposite:* including.

asinine *adj* **silly**, foolish, unintelligent. [➡NEGATIVE INTELLECTUAL CHARACTERISTICS; 526] *Opposite:* intelligent.

as it were (*formal*) *adv* **so to speak**, in a manner of speaking, sort of (*informal*), as you might say, so to say, as it seems. [➡SUMMARIZING EXPRESSIONS; 623]

ask 1 *v* **request**, inquire, solicit, question, query, probe, examine, test, catechize. [➡REQUEST AND DEMAND; 664] *Opposite:* answer. 2 *v* **invite**, ask over, have over, summon, request, bid (*archaic*). [➡ESTABLISHING RELATIONSHIPS WITH OTHERS; 974] 3 *v* **count on**, expect, demand, look for, require, call for, solicit. [➡REQUEST AND DEMAND; 664]

askance *adv* **doubtfully**, suspiciously, sideways, dubiously, distrustfully, sceptically, mistrustfully. [➡UNCERTAINTY; 560] *Opposite:* trustingly.

askew *adv* **crookedly**, awry, out of kilter, out of line (*informal*), off centre, skewwhiff (*informal*), cockeyed. [➡ORIENTATION AND ALIGNMENT; 1222] *Opposite:* straight.

ask for *v* **request**, provoke, solicit, inspire, demand, incite, petition for, induce, beg for, bring on, plead, bring to pass, sue (*formal*). [➡REQUEST AND DEMAND; 664] *Opposite:* refuse.

asking price *n* **price**, selling price, starting price, marked price. [➡EXPENDITURE; 424]

ask out *v* [➡INITIATE AND ESTABLISH COMMUNICATION; 681]

aslant 1 *adv* **obliquely**, at an angle, on a slope, diagonally, slantingly, sideways, crookedly, crossways, crosswise. [➡ORIENTATION AND ALIGNMENT; 1222] *Opposite:* straight. 2 *adj* **slanting**, slant, slantwise, oblique, diagonal, sloping, aslope, angled. [➡ORIENTATION AND ALIGNMENT; 1222]

asleep 1 *adj* **sleeping**, slumbering, dead to the world, snoozing (*informal*), napping, having forty winks (*informal*), sound asleep, fast asleep. [➡TIRED, ASLEEP, AND UNCONSCIOUS; 739] *Opposite:* awake. 2 *adj* **numb**, dead, benumbed, without feeling, insensible, lifeless. [➡TIRED, ASLEEP, AND UNCONSCIOUS; 739]

as long as *conj* **providing**, on condition that, given that, provided that, if, with the proviso that, with the understanding that, on the assumption that, supposing that, since, because. [➡CAUSATION; 169]

as of (*formal*) *prep* **from**, after, on or after, beginning, starting, commencing (*formal*), since. [➡AFTER, LAST, AND FOLLOWING; 166]

as one *adv* **simultaneously**, together, in concert, en masse, with one accord (*formal*), with one voice, in unison. [➡ACTING WITH OTHERS; 286] *Opposite:* separately.

asp *type of* **poisonous snake**. [➡SNAKE; 995]

asparagus *type of* **vegetable**. [➡FRUIT AND VEGETABLES; 1175]

aspect 1 *n* **feature**, facet, characteristic, part, piece, phase, side, trait, property, quality, attribute. [➡QUALITIES AND CHARACTERISTICS; 1190] 2 *n* **position**, outlook, side, standpoint, viewpoint, view. [➡POINT OF VIEW; 768] 3 *n* **appearance**, look, quality, bearing, air, countenance, mien (*literary*), facial expression, expression, demeanour. [➡APPEARANCE AND ATMOSPHERE; 1236]

aspen *type of* **deciduous tree**. [➡DECIDUOUS TREES; 1028]

as per *prep* **according to**, in accordance with, following, consistent with, in keeping with, in line with. [➡EXPRESSIONS OF REFERENCE; 63] *Opposite:* counter.

asperity (*formal*) *n* **severity**, brusqueness, gruffness, harshness, sharpness, astringency, sternness, stringency. [➡BAD-TEMPERED AND HUMOURLESS; 627] *Opposite:* affability.

aspersion *n* **slander**, slur, calumny (*formal*), slight, smear, accusation, criticism, disparagement, defamation, vilification, denunciation. [➡INSULTS, ABUSE, AND SWEARING; 659] *Opposite:* praise.

asphalt 1 *n* **tar**, Tarmac, bitumen, blacktop (*US*). [➡COVERS AND COATINGS; 1245] 2 *type of* **mineral**. [➡MINERALS; 1276]

asphyxia *n* **suffocation**, choking, lack of oxygen, oxygen deprivation, unconsciousness, blockage. [➡BREATHE AND NOT BREATHE; 717]

asphyxiate *v* **suffocate**, smother, choke, stifle, strangulate, throttle. [➡KILL; 923] *Opposite:* breathe.

asphyxiation *n* **suffocation**, choking, smothering, stifling, throttling, strangling, gassing. [➡CAUSES OF DEATH; 921] *Opposite:* breathing.

aspic *n* **jelly**, gel, mousseline. [➡SEASONINGS AND SAUCES; 1173]

aspidistra *type of* **foliage plant**. [➡FOLIAGE PLANTS; 1035]

aspirant *n* **candidate**, contender, applicant, job seeker, job hunter, office seeker, hopeful, postulant (*formal*). [➡WORKER; 836]

See Compare and Contrast at **candidate**.

aspirate 1 *v* **pronounce**, enunciate, articulate, sound, voice, say. [➡UTTER AND PRONOUNCE; 609] 2 *v* **remove**, extract, suck out, draw out, take out, suction. [➡EXTRACT AND SEVER; 342] *Opposite:* inject.

aspiration *n* **ambition**, goal, objective, aim, end, target, hope, desire, want, wish. [➡FEELINGS ABOUT THE FUTURE; 534]

aspirational *adj* **ambitious**, self-improving, aspiring, hopeful, eager, go-getting (*informal*), thrusting, motivated, materialistic. [➡HARD-WORKING AND COMMITTED; 501] *Opposite:* unambitious.

aspire *v* **seek**, aim, hope, desire, want, wish. [➡DESIRE AND WANT; 580]

aspiring *adj* **wishful**, hopeful, aspirant, would-be, ambitious, wannabe (*informal disapproving*). [➡DESIRE AND WANT; 580]

as regards *prep* **with regard to**, regarding, concerning, with reference to, as to, vis-à-vis, re, in respect of. [➡EXPRESSIONS OF REFERENCE; 63]

ass *type of* **farm animal**. [➡FARM ANIMAL; 982]

assail 1 *v* **attack**, assault, set about, lay into, beset, raid, storm, charge, rush, blitz. [➡PHYSICAL ATTACK AND PUNISHMENT; 416] *Opposite:* defend. 2 *v* **criticize**, attack, lay into, berate, revile, vituperate, abuse. [➡ACCUSE, BLAME, AND CRITICIZE; 642] *Opposite:* praise.

assailant *n* **attacker**, mugger, accoster, assaulter, aggressor, goon (*US*). [➡ENEMIES AND TORMENTORS; 969]

assassin *n* **killer**, murderer, hired gun (*slang*), hit man (*slang*), slayer (*formal or literary*), cutthroat, dispatcher. [➡CRIMINALS; 821]

assassinate *v* **kill**, murder, slay (*formal or literary*), shoot, gun down (*informal*), snuff out (*informal*), kill in cold blood, eliminate, liquidate, wipe out (*slang*). [➡KILL; 923]

See Compare and Contrast at **kill**.

assassination *n* **foul play**, murder, killing, shooting, elimination, slaying, homicide, manslaughter. [➡CAUSES OF DEATH; 921]

assault 1 *n* **attack**, beating, stabbing, mugging, battering, pasting (*informal*). [➡UNKIND ACTION OR BEHAVIOUR; 297] *Opposite:* defence. 2 *n* **offensive**, attack, onslaught, incursion, storming, blitz, raid, charge. [➡AGGRESSIVE EVENT; 39] *Opposite:* retreat. 3 *v* **attack**, mug, beat up (*informal*), set about, assail, lay into, jump (*informal*), strike, hit. [➡PHYSICAL ATTACK AND PUNISHMENT; 416] *Opposite:* defend.

assay 1 *v* **examine**, assess, analyse, evaluate, test, try, prove, inspect, scrutinize. [➡EXAMINE AND ASSESS; 754] 2 *v* (*literary*) **attempt**, try, essay (*formal*), give a go (*informal*), take a stab at (*informal*), take a shot at, undertake, endeavour. [➡ATTEMPT AN ACTION; 262]

assegai *type of* **projectile**. [➡PROJECTILES; 1158]

assemblage 1 *n* **accumulation**, grouping, assembly, collection, meeting, gathering, congregation. [➡COLLECTIONS AND MIXTURES OF THINGS; 1243] 2 *n* **crowd**, throng, assembly, group, mass, body, collection. [➡AUDIENCES AND ATTENDEES; 937]

assemble 1 *v* **bring together**, collect, pull together, draw together, accumulate, amass, gather, lump together. [➡COMBINE AND MIX; 401] *Opposite:* disband. 2 *v* **muster**, collect, meet, come together, convene, congregate, rally, marshal, gather. [➡GET CLOSER TOGETHER; 311] 3 *v* **put together**, build, fit together, make, compile, connect, manufacture, construct, set up, throw together (*informal*). [➡BUILD; 353] *Opposite:* take apart.

See Compare and Contrast at **collect**.

assembly 1 *n* **gathering**, coming together, meeting, association, assemblage, congregation, congress. [➡MEETINGS AND ASSEMBLIES; 43] 2 *n* **meeting**, get-together (*informal*), congress, assemblage, gathering, muster, rally. [➡MEETINGS AND ASSEMBLIES; 43] 3 *n* **legislative body**, legislature, council, government, representatives, community, congregation, conclave. [➡LEGISLATIVE BODIES AND LEGISLATION; 809] 4 *n* **construction**, building, compilation, putting together, fabrication. [➡BUILDING AND ARCHITECTURE; 1075] *Opposite:* destruction.

assembly hall *n* [➡BUILDINGS FOR PUBLIC ENTERTAINMENT; 1083]

assembly plant *type of* **factory**. [➡INDUSTRIAL BUILDINGS; 1086]

assembly point *n* **meeting point**, meeting place, rendezvous, rallying point, muster station. [➡PUBLIC BUILDINGS AND MEETING PLACES; 1080]

assembly room *n* [➡BUILDINGS FOR PUBLIC ENTERTAINMENT; 1083]

assent 1 *v* **agree**, acquiesce, concur, go along with, subscribe to, approve, consent, grant, allow. [➡AGREE; 646] *Opposite:* disagree. 2 *n* **agreement**, acquiescence, concurrence, nod, acceptance, approval, approbation, sanction, consent. [➡AGREE; 646] *Opposite:* disagreement.

See Compare and Contrast at **agree**.

assert 1 *v* **declare**, state, insist on, avow (*formal*), proclaim, emphasize, stress, affirm, aver (*formal*), claim, allege, contend. [➡CLAIM, INSIST, AND EMPHASIZE; 615] *Opposite:* deny. 2 *v* **stand up for**, profess, defend, maintain, uphold, support, champion, insist on. [➡CLAIM, INSIST, AND EMPHASIZE; 615] *Opposite:* renounce.

assertion *n* **declaration**, statement, proclamation, claim, avowal (*formal*), allegation, contention, affirmation. [➡CLAIM, INSIST, AND EMPHASIZE; 615] *Opposite:* denial.

assertive *adj* **self-confident**, self-assured, confident, firm, forceful, emphatic, insistent, positive, decided, forward, pushy (*informal*), aggressive. [➡CONFIDENCE AND COMPOSURE; 500] *Opposite:* timid.

assertively *adv* **insistently**, forcefully, aggressively, vigorously, emphatically, strongly, energetically. [➡ENTHUSIASTIC AND INQUISITIVE; 629] *Opposite:* submissively.

assertiveness *n* **confidence**, forcefulness, insistence, decisiveness, boldness, firmness, aggressiveness. [➡CONFIDENCE AND COMPOSURE; 500] *Opposite:* timidity.

assess 1 *v* **measure**, calculate, evaluate, judge, weigh, weigh up, consider, gauge. [➡EXAMINE AND ASSESS; 754] 2 *v* **tax**, review, charge, levy, evaluate, value, fine, rate. [➡ASSESS QUANTITY; 758]

assessment 1 *n* **evaluation**, appraisal, estimation, measurement, judgment, review, consideration, opinion. [➡POINT OF VIEW; 768] 2 *n* **valuation**, calculation, taxation. [➡ACCOUNTING, BANKING, AND BUDGETING; 799] 3 *n* **duty**, charge, impost, debt, bill. [➡ACCOUNTING, BANKING, AND BUDGETING; 799]

assessor *n* **evaluator**, appraiser, judge, taxer, inspector, revenuer (*US informal*). [➡ADVISERS, JUDGES, AND ARBITERS; 971]

asset 1 *n* **advantage**, strength, benefit, plus (*informal*), plus point, positive feature, quality, skill, talent, ability, qualification, power, endowment, boon, blessing, resource. [➡SOURCE OF HAPPINESS, PLEASURE, OR IMPROVEMENT; 210] *Opposite:* drawback. 2 *n* **possession**, property, resource, holding. [➡POSSESSIONS; 462]

assets *n* **possessions**, property, resources, material goods, worldly goods, wherewithal, belongings, effects (*formal*), wealth, chattels, money, estate. [➡FINANCIAL ASSETS; 463] *Opposite:* liabilities.

asset-stripping *n* **profit taking**, profitmaking, selling off, buying and selling, trading, trafficking, profiteering, wheeling and dealing. [➡BUSINESS ACTIVITIES AND PHENOMENA; 795]

assiduity *n* **diligence**, care, attention, application, industriousness, industry (*formal or literary*), perseverance, sedulousness (*literary*), sedulity (*literary*), conscientiousness, assiduousness. [➡HARD-WORKING AND COMMITTED; 501] *Opposite:* carelessness.

assiduous *adj* **diligent**, persevering, industrious, tireless, sedulous (*literary*), painstaking, conscientious, thorough, meticulous. [➡HARD-WORKING AND COMMITTED; 501] *Opposite:* lazy.

See Compare and Contrast at **careful**.

assiduousness *n* **diligence**, persistence, industriousness, attentiveness, tirelessness, sedulousness (*literary*), indefatigability. [➡HARD-WORKING AND COMMITTED; 501] *Opposite:* laziness.

assign 1 *v* **allocate**, allot, give, dispense, disperse, dole out (*informal*), consign, hand over, apportion, ascribe (*formal*). [➡DISPENSE, RATION, AND DISTRIBUTE; 435] 2 *v* **appoint**, designate, delegate, send, transfer, detail. [➡CONFER STATUS; 459]

assignation *n* **meeting**, tryst, rendezvous, get-together (*informal*), appointment, date. [➡MEETINGS AND ASSEMBLIES; 43]

assignment 1 *n* **task**, job, project, duty, obligation, mission. [➡JOB; 833] 2 *n* **appointment**, duty, position, role, job, responsibilities. [➡JOB; 833] 3 *n* **transfer**, handing over, consignment, allocation, delegation, designation. [➡DISPENSE, RATION, AND DISTRIBUTE; 435]

assimilate 1 *v* **integrate**, adapt, adjust, blend in, fit in, conform, go native (*humorous*), espouse, embrace. [➡COMBINE AND MIX; 401] 2 *v* **incorporate**, take in, digest, absorb, understand, learn. [➡LEARN AND DISCOVER; 763] *Opposite:* reject.

assimilation 1 *n* **integration**, adjustment, acclimatization, accommodation, adaptation. [➡CHANGE; 373] 2 *n* **absorption**, incorporation, digestion, ingestion, inculcation. [➡COMBINE AND MIX; 401]

assist 1 *v* **help**, aid, help out, lend a hand, give a hand, support, back, abet. [➡HELP; 294] *Opposite:* hinder. 2 *n* (*US*) **contribution**, backing, promotion, support, assistance, succour (*literary*). [➡KIND ACTION OR BEHAVIOUR; 296] *Opposite:* hindrance.

assistance *n* **help**, aid, support, backing, succour

(*literary*), assist (*US*). [➡KIND ACTION OR BEHAVIOUR; 296] *Opposite:* hindrance.

assistant 1 *n* **helper**, supporter, aide, PA, subordinate, junior, personal assistant, deputy, aide-de-camp. [➡SUBORDINATES AND ASSISTANTS; 966] 2 *adj* **associate**, subordinate, secondary, junior, sub-, vice-. [➡INFERIORITY; 154]

Compare and Contrast: ***assistant, helper, deputy, aide***

CORE MEANING: SOMEBODY WHO HELPS ANOTHER PERSON IN CARRYING OUT A TASK

assistant somebody who works to somebody else's instructions, often in a paid capacity; ***helper*** an informal, often voluntary, role; ***deputy*** an officially designated chief assistant authorized to act on a superior's behalf; ***aide*** an assistant in military, political, or commercial contexts.

assisted *adj* **aided**, helped, abetted, supported, sponsored. [➡ACTING WITH OTHERS; 286] *Opposite:* unassisted.

assize (*US*) *n* **inquest**, court case, hearing, inquiry, examination. [➡TRIAL, PUNISHMENT, AND LEGAL OUTCOMES; 819]

assizes *n* **court session**, judicial proceedings, court sitting, circuit court. [➡TRIAL, PUNISHMENT, AND LEGAL OUTCOMES; 819]

associate 1 *v* **connect**, relate, link, correlate, bracket, combine, couple. [➡CREATING CONNECTIONS; 145] *Opposite:* separate. 2 *v* **mix**, socialize, spend time with, frequent, see, be involved with, assort. [➡ESTABLISHING RELATIONSHIPS WITH OTHERS; 974] *Opposite:* avoid. 3 *v* **unite**, combine, join together, group together, join, conjoin (*formal*), yoke, amalgamate. [➡CREATING CONNECTIONS; 145] *Opposite:* disband. 4 *n* **partner**, colleague, business partner, fellow worker, coworker, accomplice, confederate. [➡COLLEAGUES AND EQUALS; 967] 5 *n* **companion**, comrade, acquaintance, friend, ally, fellow (*dated*), crony (*disapproving*), confrère (*formal*). [➡FRIENDS; 963] 6 *adj* **subordinate**, secondary, junior, assistant, sub-, vice-. [➡RELATED; 143]

associated *adj* **related**, allied, linked, connected, accompanying, concomitant, supplementary, attendant. [➡RELATED; 143]

association 1 *n* **organization**, union, alliance, society, company, group, fraternity (*US*), sorority (*US*). [➡CLUBS AND SOCIETIES; 939] 2 *n* **friendship**, relationship, connection, fellowship, involvement. [➡RELATIONSHIP TO ANOTHER; 973] 3 *n* **connotation**, overtone, suggestion, memory, reminder, link. [➡MEANING; 691]

assonance *n* **repetition**, recurrence, duplication, iteration, alliteration, echoing, rhyme, similarity. [➡ASPECTS OF LANGUAGE; 683] *Opposite:* dissonance.

assonant *adj* [➡SOFT OR PLEASANT SOUNDS; 1264]

as soon as *conj* **once**, the moment, the instant, the minute, immediately, when, after. [➡AFTER, LAST, AND FOLLOWING; 166]

assort *v* **classify**, separate, sort out, group, divide, categorize, class, arrange, methodize. [➡ARRANGE AND CREATE ORDER; 358] *Opposite:* disarrange.

assorted *adj* **mixed**, various, miscellaneous, varied, multifarious. [➡DIFFERENCE; 150]

assortment *n* **variety**, collection, range, mixture, mixed bag, hotchpotch, group. [➡COLLECTIONS AND MIXTURES OF THINGS; 1243]

assort with *v* **associate**, mix with, socialize with, frequent, see, spend time with. [➡ESTABLISHING RELATIONSHIPS WITH OTHERS; 974]

assuage *v* **moderate**, ease, soften, lessen, appease, satisfy, mitigate, alleviate, quiet, allay, temper, pacify, conciliate, placate. [➡CHANGE OF INTENSITY: LESS; 396] *Opposite:* inflame.

assume 1 *v* **take for granted**, suppose, presume, presuppose, think, guess, imagine, believe. [➡DEVELOP THEORIES AND REASON; 745] 2 *v* **take up**, take responsibility, take on, take upon yourself, shoulder, undertake, accept, adopt, don (*formal*). [➡ACCEPT POSSESSION; 451] 3 *v* **feign**, affect, fake, simulate, put on, act, pretend, sham, bluff. [➡PRETEND AND MIMIC; 60]

See Compare and Contrast at **deduce**.

assumed 1 *adj* **expected**, presumed, supposed, rumoured, implicit, anticipated. [➡UNCERTAIN; 176] 2 *adj* **false**, artificial, fake, phoney, bogus, feigned, untrue. [➡FALSE AND UNREAL; 174]

assumed name *n* **alias**, pseudonym, pen name, nom de plume, stage name, false identity. [➡NAME AND DESCRIBE; 666]

assuming *adj* **presumptuous**, pretentious, arrogant, haughty, high and mighty, supercilious. [➡POMPOUS, LOUD, AND OVER-CONFIDENT; 636] *Opposite:* humble.

assumption *n* **supposition**, statement, postulation, hypothesis, guess, theory, conjecture, notion, belief, idea. [➡IDEA AND THOUGHT; 771]

assurance 1 *n* **pledge**, declaration, word, guarantee, oath, promise, reassurance, assertion, warrant. [➡PROMISE AND ASSURE; 685] 2 *n* **self-confidence**, self-possession, self-reliance, confidence, poise, self-assurance, aplomb, composure. [➡CONFIDENCE AND COMPOSURE; 500] *Opposite:* timidity.

assure 1 *v* **promise**, guarantee, give surety, pledge, swear, declare, reassure, convince. [➡PROMISE AND ASSURE; 685] 2 *v* **make certain**, ensure, guarantee, nail down, know for certain, substantiate, verify, secure. [➡MAKE POSSIBLE; 276]

assured 1 *adj* **certain**, guaranteed, sure, confident, solid. [➡CERTAIN; 175] *Opposite:* uncertain. 2 *adj* **confident**, self-confident, self-assured, self-possessed, poised, cool. [➡CONFIDENCE AND COMPOSURE; 500] *Opposite:* diffident.

aster *type of* **annual flower**. [➡FLOWERS; 1032]

asterisk 1 *n* **symbol**, sign, mark, character, star, reference mark. [➡SYMBOLS, SIGNS, AND NUMBERS; 597] 2 *type of* **punctuation mark**. [➡ASPECTS OF LANGUAGE; 683] 3 *v* **mark**, identify, label, indicate, specify, star. [➡NAME AND DESCRIBE; 666]

astern 1 *adv* **behind**, aft, at the back, at the rear, abaft, forward, in back of (*US*), back of (*US*). [➡RELATIVE LOCATION; 162] 2 *adv* **to the rear**, backwards, in reverse. [➡DIRECTION OF MOTION; 346] *Opposite:* ahead.

asteroid *type of* **heavenly body**. [➡CELESTIAL BODIES; 1060]

as the crow flies *adv* [➡DIRECTION OF MOTION; 346]

astir 1 *adj* **awake**, out of bed, up, up and about, aroused, roused, awakened. [➡WIDE AWAKE AND CONSCIOUS; 736] *Opposite:* asleep. 2 *adj* **active**, alive, moving, stirring, live, busy. [➡HAPPENING AND IN PROGRESS; 32] *Opposite:* inactive.

as to *prep* **with regard to**, as regards, regarding, concerning, in respect of, with reference to, vis-à-vis, re. [➡EXPRESSIONS OF REFERENCE; 63]

astonish *v* **surprise**, amaze, astound, dumbfound, flabbergast (*informal*), overwhelm, daze, render speechless, take your breath away, knock for six (*informal*), shock. [➡SURPRISE AND IMPRESS; 575]

astonished *adj* **surprised**, amazed, astounded, dumbfounded, flabbergasted (*informal*), incredulous, overwhelmed, dazed, speechless, knocked for six (*informal*), bewildered, shocked, gobsmacked (*slang*). [➡SURPRISE, SHOCK, AND AMAZEMENT; 546]

astonishing *adj* **amazing**, surprising, astounding, shocking, bewildering, beyond belief. [➡EXTRAORDINARY: AMAZING; 205] *Opposite:* predictable.

astonishment *n* **surprise**, amazement, wonder, bewilderment, shock. [➡SURPRISE, SHOCK, AND AMAZEMENT; 546]

astound *v* **amaze**, astonish, surprise, shock, dumbfound, flabbergast (*informal*), overwhelm, daze, render speechless, take your breath away, knock for six (*informal*). [➡SURPRISE AND IMPRESS; 575]

astounded *adj* **astonished**, surprised, amazed, stunned, dazed, confused, flabbergasted (*informal*), speechless, thunderstruck, aghast, horrified, knocked for six (*informal*), gobsmacked (*slang*). [➡SURPRISE, SHOCK, AND AMAZEMENT; 546]

astounding *adj* **amazing**, astonishing, surprising, shocking, beyond belief. [➡EXTRAORDINARY: AMAZING; 205] *Opposite:* unsurprising.

astrakhan *type of* **fabric from animals**. [➡FABRICS; 1131]

astral 1 *adj* **stellar**, sidereal, astronomical, astrophysical, cosmological, celestial, starry, stellular. [➡THE SOLAR SYSTEM AND ASTRONOMY; 1059] 2 *adj* **immaterial**, spiritual, psychical, otherworldly, incorporeal (*formal*), transcendent, ethereal, bodiless, metaphysical. [➡FATE, DESTINY, AND ASTROLOGY; 783] *Opposite:* material.

astray *adv* **off course**, lost, off track, off target, off beam, amiss, afield, awry. [➡AIMLESS AND ERRANT MOTION; 344]

astride *prep* **on both sides of**, spanning, straddling, across. [➡RELATIVE LOCATION; 162]

astringency *n* **acerbity**, acidity, causticity, mordancy, sharpness, bite, sting, harshness, severity. [➡HONEST AND OPEN; 631] *Opposite:* blandness.

astringent *adj* **harsh**, severe, biting, caustic, acerbic, mordant, cutting. [➡RUDE AND HOSTILE; 626] *Opposite:* bland.

astrologer *n* **fortune-teller**, seer, soothsayer, prophet, forecaster, astrologist. [➡FATE, DESTINY, AND ASTROLOGY; 783]

astrological *adj* **zodiacal**, horoscopic, fortune-telling, prophetic, forecasting, soothsaying, stargazing. [➡FATE, DESTINY, AND ASTROLOGY; 783]

astrologist *n* [➡FATE, DESTINY, AND ASTROLOGY; 783]

astrology *n* **fortune-telling**, clairvoyance, soothsaying, forecasting, prediction, prophecy. [➡FATE, DESTINY, AND ASTROLOGY; 783]

astronaut *n* **space traveller**, space pilot, cosmonaut, rocket pilot, spaceman, spacewoman, rocketeer. [➡SPACE TRAVEL AND EXPLORATION; 1061]

astronomer *n* **stargazer**, starwatcher, radio astronomer, astrophysicist, space scientist. [➡THE SOLAR SYSTEM AND ASTRONOMY; 1059]

astronomical 1 *adj* **astral**, planetary, cosmological, astrophysical, lunar, stellar, solar, cosmic. [➡THE SOLAR SYSTEM AND ASTRONOMY; 1059] 2 *adj* (*informal*) **exorbitant**, excessive, sky-high, through the ceiling, huge, enormous, vast, immense, prodigious. [➡TOO MUCH; 118] *Opposite:* affordable.

astronomically (*informal*) *adv* **exorbitantly**, exceedingly, excessively, inordinately, extremely, exceptionally, hugely, immensely, prodigiously, vastly. [➡TO A GREAT EXTENT; 130]

astronomical telescope *type of* **optical instrument**. [➡OPTICAL INSTRUMENTS; 1123]

astronomy *n* **stargazing**, starwatching, radio astronomy, astrophysics, space science. [➡THE SOLAR SYSTEM AND ASTRONOMY; 1059]

astute *adj* **shrewd**, smart, perceptive, judicious, incisive, wise, intelligent, clever, perspicacious. [➡POSITIVE INTELLECTUAL CHARACTERISTICS; 525] *Opposite:* stupid.

astuteness *n* **shrewdness**, good judgment, smartness, intelligence, wisdom, sharpness, cleverness, perspicacity. [➡POSITIVE INTELLECTUAL CHARACTERISTICS; 525] *Opposite:* stupidity.

asunder (*formal*) *adv* **apart**, open, in pieces, in bits, in halves, in two, in twain (*archaic or literary*). [➡DIRECTION OF MOTION; 346] *Opposite:* together.

as well *adv* **too**, also, additionally, in addition, on top. [➡ALSO; 136]

as well as *conj* **in addition to**, on top of, over and above, plus (*informal*), with, and. [➡ALSO; 136]

as yet *adv* **at this time**, at present, up to now, so far, up to the present moment, yet. [➡BEFORE, FIRST, AND PRECEDING; 164]

asylum 1 *n* **refuge**, haven, safe haven, sanctuary, shelter, place of safety, safe house, retreat. [➡SAFE BUILDINGS OR PLACES; 1092] 2 *n* **protection**, refuge, sanctuary, shelter, safety. [➡SAFE AND SAFETY; 192]

asymmetric *adj* **unequal**, uneven, irregular, lopsided, disproportionate, distorted, unbalanced. [➡ORIENTATION AND ALIGNMENT; 1222] *Opposite:* symmetrical.

asymmetrical *see* **asymmetric**.

asymmetry *n* **irregularity**, lopsidedness, unevenness, disproportionateness. [➡ORIENTATION AND ALIGNMENT; 1222] *Opposite:* symmetry.

at a complete loss *adj* [➡INSECURITY AND LOSS OF COMPOSURE; 545]

at a disadvantage *adj* **in a weak position**, disadvantaged, vulnerable, hampered, hindered, held back. [➡IN TROUBLE AND DISADVANTAGED; 73] *Opposite:* at an advantage.

at a lick (*informal*) *adv* **at high speed**, quickly, fast, lickety-split (*informal*), like lightning, like the wind, at a rate of knots. [➡MOVING QUICKLY; 103] *Opposite:* slowly.

at a loose end *adj* [➡INSECURITY AND LOSS OF COMPOSURE; 545]

at a loss *adj* **stuck**, perplexed, stumped, confused, puzzled, beaten, defeated, uncertain. [➡IGNORANCE; 558]

at an advantage *adj* **in a strong position**, with the upper hand. [➡STRENGTH; 202] *Opposite:* at a disadvantage.

at an angle *adv* [➡ORIENTATION AND ALIGNMENT; 1222]

at any rate *adv* **in any case**, anyway, anyhow, in any event, at least. [➡SUMMARIZING EXPRESSIONS; 623]

at a rate of knots *adv* **at high speed**, lickety-split (*informal*), fast, quickly, like lightning, like the wind, at a lick (*informal*). [➡MOVING QUICKLY; 103] *Opposite:* slowly.

at a standstill *adv* **at a halt**, immobile, stationary, still, becalmed, motionless. [➡LACK OF ACTIVITY; 343] *Opposite:* on the move.

atavistic *adj* **primitive**, primeval, primal, ancient, ancestral, archaic. [➡OLD, OLD-FASHIONED; 168] *Opposite:* modern.

at death's door *adj* **ill**, dying, sinking, slipping away, fading, declining. [➡UNFIT AND WEAK; 740] *Opposite:* alive and kicking (*informal*).

at ease *adj* **comfortable**, relaxed, easy, calm, composed, unperturbed, happy. [➡CALMNESS, CONFIDENCE, AND COMPOSURE; 537] *Opposite:* tense.

atelier *type of* **room in the home**. [➡TYPES OF ROOM; 1096]

at every turn *adv* **continually**, all the time, constantly, repeatedly. [➡PERMANENCE: WITHOUT END; 94] *Opposite:* occasionally.

at fault *adj* **in the wrong**, to blame, guilty, wrong, responsible, mistaken, misguided, incorrect. [➡INCORRECT AND ERRONEOUS; 223] *Opposite:* in the right.

at first *adv* **in the beginning**, at the start, originally, initially, at the outset, in the early days. [➡BEFORE, FIRST, AND PRECEDING; 164]

at first glance *adv* **at first sight**, on the face of it, superficially, on the surface, ostensibly, apparently. [➡UNCERTAIN; 176]

at first sight *adv* **at first glance**, on the face of it, superficially, on the surface, ostensibly, apparently. [➡UNCERTAIN; 176]

at hand 1 *adv* **nearby**, just round the corner, within reach, near, close by, handy, accessible, in sight. [➡CLOSENESS; 160] *Opposite:* distant. 2 *adj* **imminent**, approaching, impending, on the way, coming, just round the corner, near, close, about to happen, in sight. [➡FUTURE; 86] *Opposite:* far-off.

at heart *adv* **basically**, fundamentally, essentially, in fact, actually, truly, really, in reality, in essence. [➡FUNDAMENTAL; 196] *Opposite:* superficially.

atheism *n* **unbelief**, doubt, freethinking, humanism, nonbelief, incredulity, agnosticism, disbelief, godlessness, scepticism. [➡PHILOSOPHIES AND BELIEFS; 781] *Opposite:* belief.

atheist *n* **unbeliever**, doubter, sceptic, nonbeliever, agnostic, freethinker, disbeliever, humanist. [➡PHILOSOPHICAL AND POLITICAL THINKERS; 782] *Opposite:* believer.

atheistic *adj* **unbelieving**, nonbelieving, disbelieving, incredulous, irreligious, godless, ungodly, agnostic, sceptical, doubting, freethinking, humanistic. [➡PHILOSOPHIES AND BELIEFS; 781] *Opposite:* believing.

athlete *n* **sportsperson**, contestant, participant, competitor, team member, player. [➡PEOPLE IN SPORTS AND LEISURE; 876]

athletic *adj* **fit**, sporty, healthy, in good shape, physical, agile, nimble, lithe, muscular, vigorous, energetic, strong, powerful, active. [➡AGILITY OF THE BODY; 477] *Opposite:* unfit.

athleticism *n* **litheness**, suppleness, flexibility, power, activeness, muscularity, powerfulness, strength, vigour. [➡AGILITY OF THE BODY; 477] *Opposite:* clumsiness.

athletics *n* **sports**, track-and-field events, games, exercises, PE, races, sports events, training, sporting contests, sports competitions, physical education, sports activities. [➡HOBBIES, GAMES, AND SPORTS; 875]

at home 1 *adj* **comfortable**, at ease, relaxed, easy, comfy (*informal*). [➡CALMNESS, CONFIDENCE, AND COMPOSURE; 537] *Opposite:* uncomfortable. 2 *adj* **accustomed**, used to, familiar, confident, sure, competent, capable, proficient, skilled, experienced, knowledgeable, in control. [➡KNOWLEDGE AND WISDOM; 559] *Opposite:* ill at ease.

athwart *adv* [➡ORIENTATION AND ALIGNMENT; 1222]

at issue *adj* **under consideration**, under discussion, under debate, in question, in the balance, in doubt, to be decided, at stake. [➡IMPORTANT; 195]

at large 1 *adj* **in general**, on the whole, overall, as a whole, all together. [➡ALL; 126] 2 *adj* **free**, at liberty, unconfined, on the loose, out. [➡FREEDOM AND LIBERTY; 209] *Opposite:* confined.

atlas *n* **book of maps**, diagrams, charts, plans, drawings, graphics. [➡BOOKS AND BOOKLETS; 591]

at last *adv* **eventually**, finally, ultimately, in the end, at length. [➡AFTER, LAST, AND FOLLOWING; 166] *Opposite:* immediately.

at least 1 *adv* **as a minimum**, no less than, at best. [➡ALTHOUGH, NEVERTHELESS, AND DESPITE; 170] 2 *adv* **at any rate**, in any case, however, nonetheless, nevertheless. [➡SUMMARIZING EXPRESSIONS; 623]

at leisure *adj* **free**, at liberty, at ease, at rest, left to your own devices, unoccupied. [➡FREEDOM AND LIBERTY; 209] *Opposite:* busy.

at length 1 *adv* (*formal*) **long-windedly**, in detail, in depth, verbosely, wordily, prolixly, ramblingly. [➡INARTICU-

LATE, RAMBLING, AND AWKWARD; 634] *Opposite:* in brief. 2 *adv* **eventually**, at last, at long last, finally, in the end. [➡AFTER, LAST, AND FOLLOWING; 166] *Opposite:* immediately.

at liberty 1 *adj* **free**, at large, on the loose, released, unconfined, out, unrestricted, unconstrained. [➡FREEDOM AND LIBERTY; 209] *Opposite:* imprisoned. 2 *adj* **at leisure**, free, permitted. [➡FREEDOM AND LIBERTY; 209]

at loggerheads *adj* **at odds**, at variance, fighting, quarrelling, at daggers drawn, at each other's throats, in conflict. [➡DISHARMONY; 157]

at long last *adv* **finally**, in the end, ultimately, at last, at length, eventually. [➡AFTER, LAST, AND FOLLOWING; 166]

ATM (*US*) *n* **cash dispenser**, cash machine, cashpoint, hole-in-the-wall, automated teller machine. [➡ACCOUNTING, BANKING, AND BUDGETING; 799]

atmosphere 1 *n* **air**, sky, heaven, ether (*literary*), exosphere, ionosphere, mesosphere, ozonosphere, stratosphere, thermosphere, troposphere. [➡THE EARTH'S ATMOSPHERE; 1040] 2 *n* **ambience**, impression, feeling, feel, mood, tone, environment, surroundings, character. [➡APPEARANCE AND ATMOSPHERE; 1236]

atmospheric *adj* **impressive**, distinctive, moody, special, full of character, full of atmosphere. [➡EMOTIONALLY PLEASANT; 188]

atmospherics *n* **interference**, disturbance, static, snow, hissing, crackling. [➡ACOUSTICS; 1137]

at no cost *adj* **free**, free of charge, gratis, for nothing, for free, on the house. [➡GIFTS; 439]

at odds 1 *adj* **in conflict**, at loggerheads, at variance, arguing, quarrelling, in opposition, in contention. [➡DISHARMONY; 157] *Opposite:* in agreement. 2 *adj* **contradictory**, incompatible, conflicting, inconsistent, in disagreement, at variance, in conflict, out of sync (*informal*). [➡DISHARMONY; 157] *Opposite:* consistent.

atoll *n* **island**, coral reef, coral island, isle, islet, coral isle, key, cay. [➡THE CONTINENTS AND ISLANDS; 1048]

atom *n* **particle**, bit, tiny part, iota, jot, molecule, fragment, grain, glimmer. [➡SMALL PIECE; 127]

atom bomb *type of* **explosive weapon**. [➡EXPLOSIVES; 1154]

atomic 1 *adj* **nuclear**, thermonuclear, fissionable. [➡ENERGY SOURCES; 1161] 2 *adj* **microscopic**, submicroscopic, minute, infinitesimal, minuscule, tiny, miniature. [➡SMALL; 1194] *Opposite:* gigantic.

atomic bomb (*US*) *type of* **explosive weapon**. [➡EXPLOSIVES; 1154]

atomizer *n* **spray**, spray can, vaporizer, aerosol. [➡CONTAINERS, RECEPTACLES, AND PACKAGING; 1244]

atonal *adj* **twelve-note**, twelve-tone, discordant, dissonant, inharmonious, unharmonious, cacophonous. [➡LOUD OR UNPLEASANT SOUNDS; 1265]

atonality *n* **twelve-note scale**, twelve-tone scale, serialism, discordance, dissonance, disharmony, lack of harmony, cacophony. [➡LOUD OR UNPLEASANT SOUNDS; 1265] *Opposite:* tonality.

at once 1 *adv* **immediately**, straightaway, right away, right now, now, without further ado, without delay, promptly, in that instant, instantly, this instant. [➡PRESENT; 85] *Opposite:* later. 2 *adv* **simultaneously**, at the same time, in unison, in chorus, together, all together, at one go, coincidentally. [➡CONCURRENT AND CONTEMPORANEOUS; 165] *Opposite:* separately.

atone (*formal*) *v* **compensate**, make up, make amends, redress, apologize, say sorry, do penance, expiate, recompense. [➡APOLOGIZE AND RETRACT; 684]

at one fell swoop *adv* **at one go**, at the same time, at once, all together, simultaneously. [➡CONCURRENT AND CONTEMPORANEOUS; 165] *Opposite:* gradually.

at one go *adv* **together**, at once, at one fell swoop. [➡CONCURRENT AND CONTEMPORANEOUS; 165] *Opposite:* gradually.

atonement *n* **compensation**, amends, penitence, penance, punishment, expiation, apology, reparation, recompense. [➡APOLOGIZE AND RETRACT; 684]

at one time *adv* **in the past**, formerly, once, once upon a time, long ago, time was. [➡PAST; 84] *Opposite:* at present.

at one with *adj* [➡HARMONY; 156]

atop (*literary*) *prep* **on**, upon, on the top of, over, higher than, on the crest of, above. [➡RELATIVE LOCATION; 162]. *Opposite:* beneath (*formal*).

at peace 1 *adj* **calm**, contented, relaxed, at ease, peaceful, comfortable. [➡CALMNESS, CONFIDENCE, AND COMPOSURE; 537] 2 *adj* **dead**, at rest, no longer with us, deceased (*formal*), passed away, departed (*formal or literary*). [➡DEAD AND DYING; 925]

at present *adv* **now**, right now, just now, presently, at the present time, at the moment, at this time, at this moment in time, at this point in time, currently, today, nowadays. [➡PRESENT; 85] *Opposite:* then.

at random *adv* **haphazardly**, randomly, aimlessly, at the dictates of chance, unselectively. [➡DISORDER AND CHAOS; 246] *Opposite:* systematically.

at rest 1 *adj* **dead**, no longer with us, deceased (*formal*), passed away, departed (*formal or literary*), at peace. [➡DEAD AND DYING; 925] 2 *adj* **stationary**, not working, inactive, immobile, still, not moving. [➡LACK OF ACTIVITY; 343] *Opposite:* active. 3 *adj* **at ease**, at peace, free from worry, free from anxiety, reassured, comforted, relaxed. [➡CALMNESS, CONFIDENCE, AND COMPOSURE; 537] *Opposite:* uneasy.

at right angles *adv* [➡ORIENTATION AND ALIGNMENT; 1222]

at risk 1 *adj* **vulnerable**, susceptible, exposed, helpless, defenceless. [➡IN DANGER; 238] *Opposite:* safe. 2 *adj* **endangered**, imperilled (*formal*), dying, vulnerable, threatened. [➡IN DANGER; 238] *Opposite:* protected. 3 *adv* **at stake**, at issue, to be won or lost, riding on it, in the balance. [➡IN DANGER; 238]

atrium *n* **hall**, foyer, entrance hall, entrance, vestibule, reception area, porch, lobby, court, patio, concourse. [➡DOORS AND ACCESS POINTS; 1100]

atrocious *adj* **terrible**, brutal, appalling, vicious, fearful, wicked, dreadful, evil, awful, cruel, frightful, vile, dire, horrible, horrific, horrendous, hideous, ghastly. [➡BAD AND BADLY; 224] *Opposite:* wonderful.

atrociously 1 *adv* **terribly**, badly, unspeakably, appallingly, fearfully, evilly, dreadfully, awfully, frightfully, horribly, horrifically, horrendously, hideously. [➡BAD AND BADLY; 224] *Opposite:* wonderfully. 2 *adv* **brutally**, viciously, wickedly, cruelly. [➡DISGUSTING AND REPULSIVE; 231]

atrociousness *n* **fearfulness**, dreadfulness, viciousness, awfulness, wickedness, badness, frightfulness, hideousness. [➡DISGUSTING AND REPULSIVE; 231]

atrocity 1 *n* **act of violence**, massacre, killing, outrage, brutality, barbarism, evil, murder, crime. [➡UNKIND ACTION OR BEHAVIOUR; 297] 2 *n* **violence**, cruelty, viciousness, barbarity. [➡UNKIND ACTION OR BEHAVIOUR; 297]

atrophy *v* **waste away**, waste, wither, weaken, shrivel, degenerate, deteriorate. [➡GET WORSE; 382]

at sea *adj* **lost**, bewildered, confused, puzzled, baffled, mystified, bemused, disorientated, not following. [➡CONFUSION, ANXIETY, AND WORRY; 541]

at somebody's expense *adv* **to make somebody look silly**, to make somebody look foolish, to show somebody up. [➡JOKES AND TEASING; 675]

at speed *adv* **hurriedly**, hastily, in a hurry, rapidly, swiftly, speedily, quickly, in a rush. [➡HAPPENING QUICKLY; 104] *Opposite:* slowly.

at stake *adj* **in the balance**, at risk, in danger, in jeopardy, up for grabs (*informal*), at issue, to be won or lost, riding on it. [➡IN DANGER; 238]

attach 1 *v* **fasten**, join, connect, fix, put together, add, affix, append, stick, glue, screw, nail, clip. [➡FASTEN, LINK, AND JOIN; 409] *Opposite:* detach. 2 *v* **ascribe** (*formal*), assign, award, confer (*formal*), attribute, accord, bestow (*formal*). [➡GIVE AND PROVIDE; 431]

attaché *n* **diplomat**, public servant, civil servant, representative, envoy, ambassador, cultural attaché, military attaché. [➡POLITICAL OFFICES AND POLITICIANS; 808]

attaché case *type of* **baggage**. [➡CONTAINERS, RECEPTACLES, AND PACKAGING; 1244]

attached 1 *adj* (*informal*) **emotionally involved**, devoted, fond of, close, friendly, involved, committed. [➡RELATIONSHIP TO ANOTHER; 973] *Opposite:* uninvolved. 2 *adj* **enclosed**, accompanying, supporting, supplementary. [➡PRESENT AND AVAILABLE; 11]

attachment 1 *n* **add-on**, accessory, extra, addition, supplement. [➡PARTS OF MACHINES AND TOOLS; 1117] 2 *n* **bond**, affection, connection, regard, friendship, liking, fondness, tenderness, warmth, love. [➡LOVE, RESPECT, AND GOODWILL; 550]

attack 1 *v* **harm**, assault, harass, bother, molest, assail, hit, strike, beat, hurt, damage. [➡PHYSICAL ATTACK AND PUNISHMENT; 416] *Opposite:* defend. 2 *v* **criticize**, argue, confront, pounce on, disagree, lay into, take on, start on (*informal*), start in (*US*). [➡ACCUSE, BLAME, AND CRITICIZE; 642] *Opposite:* support. 3 *v* **infect**, occur, strike, hit, strike down, affect. [➡HAPPEN TO SOMEBODY; 30] 4 *v* **set to**, deal with, tackle, start on (*informal*), pile in, turn to. [➡START AN ACTION; 261] 5 *n* **bout**, dose, spell, occurrence, outbreak, spasm. [➡SUDDEN EVENT; 52] 6 *n* **violence**, assault, confrontation, act of violence, incident, strike, hit, raid, commencement of hostilities. [➡UNKIND ACTION OR BEHAVIOUR; 297] *Opposite:* defence. 7 *n* **criticism**, condemnation, argument, disagreement. [➡CRITICISMS AND ANGRY OUTBURSTS; 50] *Opposite:* praise.

attacker *n* **assailant**, aggressor, invader, enemy, foe (*literary*). [➡UNCOOPERATIVE OR REBELLIOUS PERSON; 567] *Opposite:* defender.

attack somebody's dignity *v* **insult**, call names, abuse, give offence, offend, hurl insults. [➡INSULTS, ABUSE, AND SWEARING; 659]

attain *v* **reach**, achieve, accomplish, conquer, manage, make, arrive at, realize. [➡SUCCEED AND WIN; 79] *Opposite:* fall short.

See Compare and Contrast at **accomplish**.

attainable *adj* **within reach**, possible, achievable, realistic, reasonable, manageable. [➡POSSIBLE AND PROBABLE; 178] *Opposite:* unattainable.

attainment 1 *n* **achievement**, accomplishment, realization, fulfilment, completion, execution. [➡SUCCESS; 82] *Opposite:* failure. 2 *n* **skill**, ability, talent, achievement, accomplishment, success. [➡SKILLS, TALENTS, AND ABILITIES; 527]

attar *n* **essence**, extract, essential oil, distillate, perfume, scented oil. [➡PERSONAL HYGIENE; 492]

attempt 1 *v* **endeavour**, make an effort, try, bid, make an attempt, have a go (*informal*), have a shot, have a stab (*informal*), have a crack (*informal*), struggle. [➡ATTEMPT AN ACTION; 262] *Opposite:* fail. 2 *n* **effort**, try, go, shot, bid, endeavour, stab (*informal*), crack (*informal*). [➡ATTEMPT AN ACTION; 262]

See Compare and Contrast at **try**.

attend 1 *v* **be present**, go to, be there, grace with your presence, join, appear, show up (*informal*). [➡ARRIVE; 12] *Opposite:* miss. 2 *v* **listen**, concentrate, focus, keep your mind on, pay attention, think about, apply your mind. [➡PAY ATTENTION; 766] *Opposite:* ignore.

attendance 1 *n* **presence**, attending, appearance, being present. [➡PRESENT AND AVAILABLE; 11] 2 *n* **turnout**, audience, number present, gate, crowd. [➡AUDIENCES AND ATTENDEES; 937]

attendant 1 *adj* **associated**, linked, related, connected, consequent, resultant. [➡RELATED; 143] 2 *n* **assistant**, helper, aide, guide, employee. [➡SUBORDINATES AND ASSISTANTS; 966] 3 *n* **escort**, usher, bridesmaid, groomsman, pageboy. [➡SUBORDINATES AND ASSISTANTS; 966]

attend to *v* **deal with**, see to, tackle, turn your attention to, address, take care of, look after. [➡CARRY OUT AN ACTION; 270] *Opposite:* ignore.

attention 1 *n* **notice**, concentration, thought, awareness, consideration, mind, interest. [➡ATTENTION AND ATTENTIVENESS; 764] *Opposite:* inattention. 2 *n* **care**, courtesy, consideration, kindness, devotion, helpfulness, thoughtfulness, responsiveness, attentiveness. [➡KIND ACTION OR BEHAVIOUR; 296] *Opposite:* neglect.

attention-grabbing *adj* **eye-catching**, conspicuous, arresting, noticeable, striking, flamboyant. [➡PERCEPTIBLE; 25]

attention-seeker *n* [➡SELF-IMPORTANT AND SELF-SEEKING PEOPLE; 949]

attention to detail *n* **meticulousness**, thoroughness, care, carefulness, exactness, consecutiveness, assiduousness. [➡EXACT; 204]

attentive 1 *adj* **considerate**, responsive, helpful, caring, thoughtful, dutiful, conscientious, kind, courteous, assiduous. [➡GENEROSITY AND KINDNESS; 496] *Opposite:* inconsiderate. 2 *adj* **paying attention**, listening carefully, concentrating, observant, focused, attending, alert, all ears (*informal*), intent, rapt. [➡PENSIVENESS AND INTEREST; 539] *Opposite:* inattentive.

attentiveness 1 *n* **care**, courtesy, thoughtfulness, consideration, kindness, devotion, helpfulness, responsiveness, attention. [➡GOOD MANNERS AND SOCIAL SKILLS; 521] *Opposite:* neglect. 2 *n* **concentration**, attention, focus, alertness. [➡ATTENTION AND ATTENTIVENESS; 764] *Opposite:* inattention.

attenuate *v* **reduce**, decrease, lessen, diminish, dilute, water down, take the edge off, temper, offset, mitigate, assuage, soothe, calm, lighten, thin, rarefy, weaken. [➡CHANGE OF INTENSITY: LESS; 396] *Opposite:* intensify.

attenuation *n* **reduction**, decrease, lessening, diminution, dilution, watering down, taking the edge off, tempering, offsetting, mitigation, lightening, thinning, rarefication, assuagement, weakening. [➡CHANGE OF INTENSITY: LESS; 396] *Opposite:* intensification.

attest *v* **show**, bear out, prove, confirm, corroborate, verify. [➡APPROVE AND CONFIRM; 647] *Opposite:* refute.

attestation *n* **confirmation**, substantiation, verification, corroboration, testimony, proof. [➡APOLOGIZE AND RETRACT; 684] *Opposite:* refutation.

at that moment *adv* **just then**, then, at that point, at that time, at that point in time, at that juncture, at that moment in time. [➡CONCURRENT AND CONTEMPORANEOUS; 165]

at the appointed time *adv* **promptly**, punctually, on time, at the right time, on the dot, at the appointed hour. [➡PROMPTNESS: ON TIME; 99] *Opposite:* late.

at the double *adv* **fast**, quickly, at once, immediately, right away, straightaway, without delay, speedily, swiftly, rapidly. [➡MOVING QUICKLY; 103] *Opposite:* slowly.

at the end of the day *adv* **when all's said and done**, basically, ultimately, in the end, all things considered, on balance, finally. [➡SUMMARIZING EXPRESSIONS; 623]

at the heart of *adv* **central to**, integral to, fundamental to, at the core of, at the centre of. [➡FUNDAMENTAL; 196]

at the moment *adv* **now**, currently, at present, at the present time, at this point in time, at this moment in time, right now, just now, presently, today, nowadays. [➡PRESENT; 85]

at the outset *adv* **at first**, initially, originally, in the beginning, to begin with, at the start. [➡BEFORE, FIRST, AND PRECEDING; 164]

at the present time *adv* **now**, at present, at the moment, nowadays, currently, for the moment, just now, right now, at this moment in time. [➡PRESENT; 85]

at the ready *adj* **prepared**, in readiness, ready, set, geared up, about to, to hand, at hand, open, out, up. [➡PRESENT AND AVAILABLE; 11] *Opposite:* unprepared.

at the rear *adv* **behind**, at the back, to the rear, following, coming behind, coming after, in back (*US*). [➡RELATIVE LOCATION; 162] *Opposite:* in front.

at the same time *adv* **together**, all at once, simultaneously, all together, in unison, in chorus, at one fell swoop, at one go. [➡CONCURRENT AND CONTEMPORANEOUS; 165]

at the side of *prep* **beside**, next to, alongside, with, adjacent to, next door to, by. [➡CLOSENESS; 160]

at the start *adv* **in the beginning**, at first, initially, originally, at the outset, to begin with, to start with. [➡BEFORE, FIRST, AND PRECEDING; 164]

at this moment *adv* [➡PRESENT; 85]

at this moment in time *adv* **now**, at present, at the moment, at this point in time, at this time, at the present time, currently, just now, right now. [➡PRESENT; 85]

at this point *adv* [➡PRESENT; 85]

at this point in time *adv* [➡PRESENT; 85]

at this time *adv* **at the moment**, at present, now, at this moment in time, at this point in time, at the present time, currently, just now, right now. [➡PRESENT; 85]

attic *n* **loft**, garret, roof space, upper floor. [➡TYPES OF ROOM; 1096]

at times *adv* **sometimes**, from time to time, on occasion, once in a while, now and then, now and again, every so often, every now and then, periodically, every now and again, occasionally. [➡NEVER AND INFREQUENCY; 97] *Opposite:* rarely.

attire (*formal*) *n* **clothing**, dress, clothes, outfit, garments, apparel, wear, garb, costume, wardrobe. [➡CLOTHES AND ACCESSORIES; 864]

attired (*formal*) *adj* [➡DRESS, WEAR, AND UNDRESS; 868]

attitude 1 *n* **view**, opinion, viewpoint, point of view, feeling, thought, mind. [➡POINT OF VIEW; 768] 2 *n* **posture**, pose, position, bearing, stance, carriage (*formal*). [➡TEMPERAMENT AND BEHAVIOUR; 493] 3 *n* (*informal*) **boldness**, brashness, arrogance, insolence, defiance, assertiveness. [➡BAD MANNERS AND SOCIAL SKILLS; 522]

attorney (*US*) *n* **lawyer**, barrister, counsel, advocate, legal representative, solicitor, attorney at law (*US*), prosecutor (*US*), criminal lawyer (*US*), district attorney (*US*), public defender (*US*). [➡PEOPLE IN LAW COURTS; 820]

attorney at law (*US*) *n* [➡PEOPLE IN LAW COURTS; 820]

attract 1 *v* **draw**, bring together, pull, exert a pull on.

[➡GET; 421] *Opposite:* repel. **2** *v* **entice**, appeal, fascinate, charm, interest, draw, invite. [➡APPEAL TO AND AROUSE INTEREST; 576] *Opposite:* put off.

attraction *n* **magnetism**, lure, pull (*informal*), desirability, hold, charm, fascination, allure, temptation, draw, attractiveness. [➡ENERGY GENERAL; 1160] *Opposite:* repulsion.

attractive **1** *adj* **appealing**, alluring, charming, pleasing, inviting, eye-catching, lovely. [➡BEAUTY AND ATTRACTIVENESS; 190] *Opposite:* unattractive. **2** *adj* **good-looking**, beautiful, handsome, lovely, pretty, nice-looking, stunning. [➡PEOPLE'S PHYSICAL APPEARANCE; 476] *Opposite:* ugly.

See Compare and Contrast at **good-looking**.

attractively *adv* **nicely**, delightfully, charmingly, appealingly, prettily, beautifully, pleasantly. [➡PHYSICALLY PLEASANT; 187] *Opposite:* unattractively.

attractiveness **1** *n* **good looks**, pleasant appearance, magnetism, charisma, charm, beauty, prettiness. [➡PEOPLE'S PHYSICAL APPEARANCE; 476] *Opposite:* ugliness. **2** *n* **pull** (*informal*), draw, appeal, lure, allure, charm, attraction, desirability, fascination. [➡BEAUTY AND ATTRACTIVENESS; 190] *Opposite:* repulsiveness.

attribute *n* **quality**, characteristic, trait, property, feature, point, aspect, element. [➡QUALITIES AND CHARACTERISTICS; 1190]

attribution *n* **ascription** (*formal*), credit, acknowledgment, designation. [➡CONNECTION; 144]

attributive **1** *adj* **prenominal**, preceding, modifying, qualifying. [➡ASPECTS OF LANGUAGE; 683] **2** *type of* **grammatical term**. [➡ASPECTS OF LANGUAGE; 683]

attrition *n* **abrasion**, erosion, slow destruction. [➡EROSION AND WEATHERING; 1055]

attune *v* **adjust**, accustom, adapt, accommodate, acclimate, acclimatize, become used to, grow accustomed to. [➡CHANGE OF MOOD AND COMPOSURE; 581]

at variance *adj* **in conflict**, at odds, in disagreement, conflicting, contradictory, incompatible, inconsistent, out of sync (*informal*). [➡DISHARMONY; 157] *Opposite:* consistent.

at your leisure *adv* **at your convenience**, in your own time, at your own pace, when you feel like it, in a leisurely way, slowly, at a relaxed pace, unhurriedly, taking your time. [➡HAPPENING SLOWLY; 106] *Opposite:* immediately.

at your own pace *adv* **at your own speed**, at your convenience, at your leisure, unhurriedly, when it suits you, without hurry. [➡HAPPENING SLOWLY; 106] *Opposite:* immediately.

atypical *adj* **different**, unusual, uncommon, strange, odd, abnormal, weird, peculiar. [➡BIZARRE AND PECULIAR; 258] *Opposite:* typical.

aubergine **1** *type of* **purple**. [➡COLOURS; 1223] **2** *type of* **vegetable**. [➡FRUIT AND VEGETABLES; 1175]

auburn *type of* **brown**. [➡COLOURS; 1223]

au courant *adj* [➡KNOWLEDGE AND WISDOM; 559]

auction *n* **sale**, mart, Dutch auction, silent auction. [➡SALES AND SHOWS; 444]

audacious **1** *adj* **daring**, bold, brave, fearless, courageous, risky, foolhardy. [➡COURAGE; 499] *Opposite:* pusillanimous (*formal*). **2** *adj* **impudent**, bold, disrespectful, cheeky, overconfident. [➡RUDE AND HOSTILE; 626]

audaciously *adv* **daringly**, bravely, boldly, fearlessly, courageously. [➡COURAGE; 499] *Opposite:* pusillanimously (*formal*).

audaciousness *n* **daring**, boldness, courage, bravery, fearlessness, nerve, pluck, mettle, bottle (*informal*), courageousness, guts (*slang*). [➡COURAGE; 499]. *Opposite:* pusillanimity (*formal*).

audacity **1** *n* **boldness**, daring, courage, bravery, fearlessness, courageousness, nerve, pluck, mettle, bottle (*informal*), guts (*slang*). [➡COURAGE; 499]. *Opposite:* pusillanimity (*formal*). **2** *n* **impudence**, disrespect, boldness, cheek (*informal*), rudeness, discourtesy. [➡BAD MANNERS AND SOCIAL SKILLS; 522] *Opposite:* courtesy.

audibility *n* **loudness**, noise, distinctness, discernibility, perceptibility, decibel level, acoustics, clarity. [➡PERCEPTIBLE; 25] *Opposite:* inaudibility.

audible *adj* **perceptible**, clear, distinct, noticeable, loud. [➡PERCEPTIBLE; 25] *Opposite:* inaudible.

audience **1** *n* **spectators**, viewers, addressees, listeners, onlookers, watchers, hearers. [➡AUDIENCES AND ATTENDEES; 937] **2** *n* **meeting**, interview, consultation, appointment, hearing. [➡MEETINGS AND ASSEMBLIES; 43]

audio *adj* **acoustic**, auditory, aural, audial. [➡HEAR; 708]

audio

◆ *types of audio equipment*
amp, amplifier, boom box (*US*), cassette recorder, CD player, compact disc player, gramophone (*dated*), hi-fi, horn, jukebox, megaphone, PA, personal stereo, phonograph (*US*), preamplifier, radio, radio set, record player, sound system, stereo, stereo system, tape deck, tape player, tape recorder, transistor, tuner, wireless (*dated*)

◆ *parts of audio equipment*
audiotape, cartridge, cassette, CD, compact disc, DVD, earphone, earphones, earpiece, handset, headphones, headpiece, headset, loudspeaker, microphone, record, speaker, stylus, tone arm, turntable

audiotape *part of* **audio equipment**. [➡AUDIO EQUIPMENT; 1138]

audiovisual *adj* **video**, filmed, film, cinematic, cinematographic, movie (*US*). [➡THE PERFORMING ARTS; 904]

audit **1** *n* **review**, check, inspection, examination, assessment, appraisal, stocktaking, inventory. [➡EXAMINE AND ASSESS; 754] **2** *v* **review**, inspect, examine, assess, appraise, take stock. [➡EXAMINE AND ASSESS; 754]

audition **1** *n* **test**, tryout, trial, interview. [➡PREPARATORY

EVENT; 57] 2 *v* **try out**, test, hear, interview. [➡EXAMINE AND ASSESS; 754]

auditor 1 *n* **examiner**, accountant, assessor, checker. [➡PEOPLE INVOLVED IN FINANCE; 804] 2 *n* (*formal*) **listener**, hearer, eavesdropper. [➡LISTEN AND LISTENERS; 709]

auditorium *n* **hall**, theatre, amphitheatre, lecture hall. [➡BUILDINGS FOR PUBLIC ENTERTAINMENT; 1083]

auditory *adj* **aural**, hearing, audio, acoustic. [➡HEAR; 708]

au fait *adj* [➡KNOWLEDGE AND WISDOM; 559]

auf Wiedersehen *interj* [➡GREETINGS, FAREWELLS, AND SALUTATIONS; 660]

augment (*formal*) *v* **increase**, enlarge, expand, extend, amplify, strengthen, boost, intensify. [➡CHANGE OF INTENSITY: MORE; 395] *Opposite:* diminish.

See Compare and Contrast at **increase**.

augmentation *n* **increase**, growth, rise, expansion, intensification, amplification, escalation, enlargement. [➡CHANGE OF INTENSITY: MORE; 395] *Opposite:* decrease.

augur *v* **foretell**, predict, portend, promise, prophesy, prognosticate, indicate, point to. [➡MEAN SOMETHING; 61]

augury 1 *n* **divination**, prediction, prophecy, forecasting, prognostication. [➡THE SUPERNATURAL; 788] 2 *n* **portent**, omen, auspice, indication, prediction, sign, prophecy, forewarning, forecast. [➡INDICATIONS, SIGNS, AND WARNINGS; 68]

august (*formal*) *adj* **imposing**, impressive, grand, majestic, dignified, stately, noble, eminent. [➡CLASS STATUS; 889] *Opposite:* humble.

auk *type of* **seabird**. [➡SEABIRD; 1002]

aunt *type of* **older relative**. [➡OLDER GENERATION RELATIVES; 959]

aura *n* **air**, atmosphere, force, appearance, quality, glow. [➡APPEARANCE AND ATMOSPHERE; 1236]

aural *adj* **auditory**, hearing, acoustic, audio. [➡HEAR; 708]

au revoir *interj* [➡GREETINGS, FAREWELLS, AND SALUTATIONS; 660]

auricle *n* [➡THE EAR; 707]

auspice *n* **omen**, portent, augury, sign, indication, token, prediction. [➡INDICATIONS, SIGNS, AND WARNINGS; 68]

auspices *n* **sponsorship**, patronage, backing, support, help, umbrella. [➡RESPONSIBILITY; 171]

auspicious *adj* **favourable**, fortunate, promising, propitious, lucky, opportune, providential. [➡SUCCESSFUL AND PROMISING; 81] *Opposite:* inauspicious.

austere 1 *adj* **stark**, severe, simple, basic, sparse, Spartan, harsh. [➡PLAIN; 233] *Opposite:* comfortable. 2 *adj* **serious**, grim, severe, unsmiling, harsh, ascetic, rigid, sombre. [➡RUDE AND HOSTILE; 626] *Opposite:* gentle. 3 *adj* **plain**, bare, simple, clean, undecorated, unembellished, unadorned. [➡EASE AND SIMPLICITY; 201] *Opposite:* ornate.

austerity 1 *n* **severity**, strictness, sternness, graveness, soberness, sombreness, asceticism, seriousness, rigour. [➡UNFRIENDLINESS AND UNSOCIABILITY; 505] *Opposite:* levity. 2 *n* **self-denial**, shortage, scarcity, economy. [➡TOO FEW, TOO LITTLE; 120] *Opposite:* plenty. 3 *n* **plainness**, starkness, bareness, simplicity, cleanness. [➡PLAIN; 233] *Opposite:* opulence.

Australian Rules *type of* **ball game**. [➡HOBBIES, GAMES, AND SPORTS; 875]

autarchy *n* **autocracy**, absolute power, absolutism, despotism, tyranny, dictatorship. [➡STYLES AND SYSTEMS OF GOVERNMENT; 806] *Opposite:* democracy.

authentic 1 *adj* **genuine**, original, authenticated, valid. [➡TRUE AND REAL; 172] *Opposite:* fake. 2 *adj* **true**, reliable, dependable, trustworthy, faithful, accurate, genuine. [➡TRUE AND REAL; 172] *Opposite:* false.

authenticate *v* **validate**, confirm, verify, substantiate, endorse, check. [➡APPROVE AND CONFIRM; 647]

authentication *n* **verification**, confirmation, substantiation, validation, certification, endorsement. [➡CERTAIN; 175]

authenticity *n* **genuineness**, legitimacy, validity, reality, truth, truthfulness. [➡TRUE AND REAL; 172]

author 1 *n* **writer**, novelist, playwright, dramatist, poet, journalist, essayist. [➡WRITERS AND STYLES; 914] 2 *n* **creator**, originator, inventor, source. [➡DESIGNERS, CREATORS, AND INSTIGATORS; 348]

authoritarian *adj* **strict**, demanding, totalitarian, despotic, absolute, dictatorial, tyrannical, autocratic. [➡BOSSY AND OVERBEARING; 517] *Opposite:* liberal.

authoritarianism *n* **totalitarianism**, dictatorship, oppression, absolutism, tyranny, despotism, autocracy. [➡STYLES AND SYSTEMS OF GOVERNMENT; 806] *Opposite:* democracy.

authoritative 1 *adj* **reliable**, trustworthy, dependable, respected, convincing, solid. [➡HONEST AND RELIABLE; 503] *Opposite:* unreliable. 2 *adj* **commanding**, imposing, firm, confident, convincing, respected, influential. [➡STRENGTH; 202] *Opposite:* weak.

authoritatively *adv* **with authority**, confidently, firmly, commandingly, convincingly. [➡STRENGTH; 202]

authoritativeness 1 *n* **reliability**, trustworthiness, dependability, validity, credibility, solidity. [➡STRENGTH; 202] *Opposite:* unreliability. 2 *n* **authority**, command, standing, position, weight, influence, clout (*informal*). [➡CONFIDENCE AND COMPOSURE; 500]

authority 1 *n* **power**, right, ability, influence, weight, clout (*informal*), say-so (*informal*). [➡STRENGTH; 202] 2 *n* **agency**, group, government department, board, corporation. [➡INSTITUTIONS; 791] 3 *n* **confidence**, conviction, knowledge, experience. [➡CERTAINTY; 562] 4 *n* **citation**, source, evidence. [➡EVIDENCE AND PROOF; 69] 5 *n* **expert**, specialist, consultant, buff, expert witness. [➡TALENTED OR INTELLIGENT PERSON; 529]

authority figure *n* **mentor**, person of influence, leader, role model, example, guide, influence, idol, parent, boss. [➡IMPORTANT OR FAMOUS PEOPLE; 893]

authorization *n* **approval**, consent, endorsement, leave (*formal*), sanction, agreement, permission. [➡PERMIT AND ALLOW; 670]

authorize *v* **approve**, allow, sanction, permit, give permission, okay (*informal*), consent, empower. [➡PERMIT AND ALLOW; 670] *Opposite:* forbid.

authorized *adj* **official**, lawful, legal, sanctioned, approved, ratified, accredited, certified. [➡LEGAL; 815] *Opposite:* unauthorized.

authorship 1 *n* **writing**, composition, invention, production, output, generation. [➡CREATION; 347] 2 *n* **origin**, source, provenance, derivation, genesis, background. [➡BEGINNING; 53]

auto (*informal*) *n* [➡BIKES, CARS, AND CARRIAGES; 1148]

autobiographer *n* [➡WRITERS AND STYLES; 914]

autobiographical *adj* **nonfictional**, factual, first-person, real-life, true to life, narrative, historical, documentary. [➡TRUE AND REAL; 172] *Opposite:* biographical.

autobiography *n* **memoirs**, life story, life history. [➡FICTION AND DRAMA; 913]

autocracy *n* **dictatorship**, monocracy, despotism, tyranny, absolutism, authoritarianism, totalitarianism. [➡STYLES AND SYSTEMS OF GOVERNMENT; 806] *Opposite:* democracy.

autocrat *n* **dictator**, absolute ruler, tyrant, despot. [➡VILLAINS AND THUGS; 947]

autocratic 1 *adj* **despotic**, tyrannical, repressive, oppressive, monocratic. [➡STYLES AND SYSTEMS OF GOVERNMENT; 806] *Opposite:* democratic. 2 *adj* **dictatorial**, domineering, bossy, overbearing, imperious, tyrannical. [➡BOSSY AND OVERBEARING; 517]

autofocus *part of* **photographic equipment**. [➡PHOTOGRAPHY AND PHOTOGRAPHIC EQUIPMENT; 1121]

autogamy *n* [➡REPRODUCTION AND HEREDITY; 726]

autogiro *type of* **civil aircraft**. [➡AIRCRAFT; 1147]

autograph *n* **signature**, name, inscription, dedication. [➡NAME AND DESCRIBE; 666]

automated *adj* **automatic**, mechanical, programmed, preset, mechanized. [➡MACHINERY; 1113] *Opposite:* manual.

automatic 1 *adj* **mechanized**, automated, mechanical, programmed, preset. [➡MACHINERY; 1113] *Opposite:* manual. 2 *adj* **involuntary**, reflex, unconscious, instinctive, programmed, unthinking, mindless, spontaneous, impulsive. [➡AUTOMATIC AND INSTINCTIVE; 281] *Opposite:* voluntary. 3 *adj* **routine**, habitual, mechanical, regular, repeated, inevitable, usual, robotic, robot-like. [➡AUTOMATIC AND INSTINCTIVE; 281] *Opposite:* spontaneous. 4 *type of* **gun**. [➡WEAPONS FOR SHOOTING; 1155]

automation *n* **mechanization**, computerization, robotics. [➡MACHINERY; 1113]

automaton *n* **robot**, android, mechanism, machine. [➡MACHINES AND MACHINE PARTS; 1115]

automobile *n* [➡BIKES, CARS, AND CARRIAGES; 1148]

autonomous *adj* **self-governing**, sovereign, free, independent, separate. [➡STYLES AND SYSTEMS OF GOVERNMENT; 806] *Opposite:* dependent.

autonomy *n* **independence**, self-government, self-rule, sovereignty. [➡STYLES AND SYSTEMS OF GOVERNMENT; 806] *Opposite:* dependence.

autopilot *part of* **aircraft**. [➡AIRCRAFT; 1147]

autopsy *n* **postmortem**, dissection, analysis, debriefing, examination. [➡BURIAL AND PREPARATION FOR BURIAL; 929]

autosuggestion *n* **self-suggestion**, self-hypnosis, autohypnosis, power of suggestion, self-deception, self-delusion. [➡PSYCHOLOGY AND THE MIND; 770]

autumn 1 *n* **season**, harvest time, equinox, Indian summer, fall (*US*). [➡TIMES OF YEAR; 88] 2 *n* **end**, conclusion, close, culmination, decline. [➡END; 54] *Opposite:* beginning.

autumnal *adj* **seasonal**, equinoctial. [➡TIMES OF YEAR; 88] *Opposite:* spring.

auxiliary *adj* **supplementary**, secondary, support, supporting, assisting, ancillary, back up. [➡MORE AND EXCESS; 122] *Opposite:* main.

avail *n* **benefit**, advantage, reward, gain, purpose, aim, profit. [➡RESULTS AND OUTCOMES; 83]

availability *n* **obtainability**, handiness, convenience, readiness, accessibility, disposal. [➡PRESENT AND AVAILABLE; 11] *Opposite:* unavailability.

available *adj* **obtainable**, accessible, on hand, to be had, existing, offered, vacant. [➡PRESENT AND AVAILABLE; 11] *Opposite:* unavailable.

avail yourself *v* **make use of**, use, benefit from, take, help yourself to. [➡MAKE GOOD USE OF SOMETHING; 474]

avalanche 1 *n* **snow slip**, fall, slide. [➡EROSION AND WEATHERING; 1055] 2 *n* **quantity**, increase, mass, inundation (*formal*), flood, shower, storm. [➡MANY, MUCH, LARGE AMOUNT; 117]

avant-garde *adj* **new**, modern, experimental, unconventional, innovative, advanced. [➡NEW, MODERN; 167] *Opposite:* traditional.

avarice *n* **greed**, greediness, materialism, covetousness, acquisitiveness, avariciousness, cupidity (*formal*), desire, avidity. [➡MORALLY BAD; 776] *Opposite:* generosity.

avaricious *adj* **greedy**, rapacious, grasping, acquisitive, covetous, materialistic. [➡MORALLY BAD; 776] *Opposite:* generous.

avariciousness *n* **greed**, avarice, greediness, covetousness, acquisitiveness, rapaciousness, materialism. [➡MORALLY BAD; 776] *Opposite:* generosity.

avenge *v* **retaliate**, punish, even the score, take vengeance, get even, hit back, get back at, redress, revenge. [➡VENGEANCE AND REVENGE; 686]

avenger *n* **punisher**, retaliator, nemesis (*literary*). [➡ENEMIES AND TORMENTORS; 969]

avenue 1 *n* **opportunity**, possibility, way, chance, opening. [➡WAYS OF DOING THINGS; 295] 2 *type of* **major road**. [➡ROADS; 1105]

aver (*formal*) *v* **avow** (*formal*), state, claim, declare, assert, affirm, maintain, profess, swear. [➡CLAIM, INSIST, AND EMPHASIZE; 615] *Opposite:* refute.

average 1 *n* **mean**, arithmetic mean, mode, median, norm. [➡ENOUGH AND SUFFICIENT; 129] 2 *adj* **regular**, normal, usual, typical, middling, mediocre, run-of-the-mill, common, ordinary. [➡ORDINARINESS; 245] *Opposite:* extraordinary. 3 *v* **be around**, be in the region of, be more or less, be close to. [➡AMOUNT TO AND EQUAL; 70]

average down *v* **round down**, level down, bring down, lower, decrease. [➡CHANGE OF SIZE: SMALLER; 394]

averagely 1 *adv* **on average**, normally, typically, standardly, commonly, usually. [➡USUALLY; 108] *Opposite:* exceptionally. 2 *adv* **passably**, tolerably, adequately, unspectacularly, indifferently, mediocrely, middlingly. [➡ACCEPTABLE AND PASSABLE; 220] *Opposite:* exceptionally.

average out *v* **equalize**, level out, balance out, even out. [➡ARRANGE AND CREATE ORDER; 358]

average up *v* **round up**, level up, bring up, raise, increase. [➡CHANGE OF SIZE: BIGGER; 393]

averse (*formal*) *adj* **opposed**, antagonistic, loath, unenthusiastic, ill-disposed, unfavourable, antipathetic, hostile, disinclined, unwilling, reluctant, hesitant, anti (*informal*). [➡UNWILLINGNESS AND STUBBORNNESS; 565] *Opposite:* favourable.

See Compare and Contrast at **unwilling**.

aversion *n* **dislike**, hatred, loathing, repugnance, distaste, hate, antipathy, abhorrence, detestation, repulsion, disgust. [➡IRRITATION AND ANGER; 542] *Opposite:* liking.

See Compare and Contrast at **dislike**.

avert 1 *v* **prevent**, stop, ward off, avoid, forestall, deter, forfend, obviate. [➡AVOID, PREVENT, LIMIT, AND CONTROL; 278] 2 *v* **turn away**, turn from, turn aside, divert, deflect, veer. [➡CHANGE DIRECTION OF MOTION; 345]

aviary *n* **birdcage**, coop, chicken coop, chicken run, hen house, dovecote, pigeon loft. [➡ANIMAL OR BIRD ACCOMMODATION; 1078]

aviation *n* **flying**, flight, aeronautics, air travel. [➡AIRWAYS; 1108]

aviator *n* **pilot**, flier, aeronaut, copilot. [➡DRIVERS; 1152]

avid *adj* **keen**, enthusiastic, passionate, eager, devoted, ardent, fervent. [➡DESIRE AND WANT; 580] *Opposite:* indifferent.

avidity *n* **greed**, eagerness, voracity, covetousness, greediness, desire. [➡ENVY AND JEALOUSY; 549] *Opposite:* indifference.

avidly *adv* **keenly**, enthusiastically, passionately, eagerly, devotedly, ardently, fervently. [➡WITH ENTHUSIASM; 287] *Opposite:* indifferently.

avocado 1 *type of* **fruit**. [➡FRUIT AND VEGETABLES; 1175] 2 *type of* **green**. [➡COLOURS; 1223]

avocation (*formal*) 1 *n* **occupation**, job, vocation, calling, profession, pursuit, employment, line, career. [➡PROFESSIONS; 845] 2 *n* **hobby**, pastime, diversion, amusement, sport, whimsy, distraction. [➡LEISURE AND RECREATION; 874]

avocet *type of* **seabird**. [➡SEABIRD; 1002]

avoid 1 *v* **keep away**, stay away from, shun, steer clear, let alone, pass up. [➡AVOID OR ESCAPE CONTACT; 419] 2 *v* **evade**, circumvent, get round, get out of, dodge, duck, sidestep, elude, escape, shun, eschew. [➡NOT PAY ATTENTION; 765] *Opposite:* face. 3 *v* **prevent**, forestall, preclude (*formal*), avert. [➡AVOID, PREVENT, LIMIT, AND CONTROL; 278] *Opposite:* promote.

avoidable *adj* **preventable**, unnecessary, needless, stoppable. [➡UNIMPORTANT AND UNNECESSARY; 239] *Opposite:* inevitable.

avoidance 1 *n* **evasion**, escaping, evading, dodging, circumvention. [➡NOT PAY ATTENTION; 765] 2 *n* **prevention**, anticipation, averting, forestalling, annulment, stopping. [➡AVOID, PREVENT, LIMIT, AND CONTROL; 278] *Opposite:* promotion. 3 *n* **eschewal**, abstention, refraining, refrainment, holding off. [➡FOREGO AND DENY ONESELF; 450] *Opposite:* indulgence.

avow (*formal*) *v* **affirm**, state, declare, acknowledge, admit, maintain, aver (*formal*), assert, depose. [➡CLAIM, INSIST, AND EMPHASIZE; 615] *Opposite:* deny.

avowal (*formal*) *n* **affirmation**, statement, confirmation, declaration, acknowledgment, admission, confession, profession. [➡ADMIT AND CONFESS; 616] *Opposite:* denial.

avowed (*formal*) *adj* **affirmed**, stated, confirmed, declared, acknowledged, admitted, self-confessed, asserted. [➡KNOWN AND FAMOUS; 182] *Opposite:* unspoken.

avowedly (*formal*) *adv* **admittedly**, by your own admission, openly, self-confessedly, frankly. [➡HONEST AND OPEN; 631]

avuncular *adj* **kindly**, kind, kind-hearted, benign, friendly, genial, indulgent, helpful, good-humoured. [➡GOOD-TEMPERED AND HUMOROUS; 628] *Opposite:* unkindly.

await 1 *v* **lie in wait for**, wait on, expect, look forward to, look out for, anticipate. [➡PREDICT AND ANTICIPATE; 751] 2 *v* **lie ahead**, be in store, be to come, loom, near, be approaching, draw near. [➡ABOUT TO HAPPEN; 33]

awaited *adj* **anticipated**, expected, presumed, waited for. [➡FUTURE; 86] *Opposite:* unexpected.

awake *adj* **wide-awake**, conscious, wakeful, up, up and about, stirring, aware, alert, roused, aroused. [➡WIDE AWAKE AND CONSCIOUS; 736] *Opposite:* asleep.

awaken 1 *v* **wake**, wake up, rouse, get up, stir. [➡WAKE AND REGAIN CONSCIOUSNESS; 725] 2 *v* **rouse**, arouse, set off, stir, promote, stimulate, initiate. [➡CAUSE TO START; 266] *Opposite:* suppress.

awakening 1 *adj* **developing**, growing, emerging, arising (*archaic or literary*), emergent, new. [➡ABOUT TO HAPPEN; 33] 2 *n* **arousal**, wakening, emergence, stirring. [➡BEGINNING; 53] 3 *n* **awareness**, attention, recognition, realization, revival. [➡KNOWLEDGE AND WISDOM; 559]

award 1 *n* **prize**, honour, reward, gift, grant, decoration, medal, accolade. [➡REWARDS AND AWARDS; 440] 2 *n* **verdict**, decision, determination, judgment, settlement. [➡TRIAL, PUNISHMENT, AND LEGAL OUTCOMES; 819] 3 *v* **give**, bestow (*formal*), present, grant, confer (*formal*), endow. [➡REWARD; 437]

aware 1 *adj* **conscious**, alert, mindful, cognizant (*formal*), attentive, awake, responsive, sensible (*formal*). [➡WIDE AWAKE AND CONSCIOUS; 736] *Opposite:* unaware. 2 *adj* **knowledgeable**, interested, concerned, informed, experienced, discerning, perceptive. [➡KNOWLEDGE AND WISDOM; 559] *Opposite:* ignorant.

Compare and Contrast: ***aware, conscious, mindful, cognizant, sensible***

CORE MEANING: HAVING KNOWLEDGE OF THE EXISTENCE OF SOMETHING

aware knowing something either intellectually or intuitively; ***conscious*** keenly aware of something and regarding it as important; ***mindful*** actively attentive, or deliberately keeping something in mind; ***cognizant*** (*formal*) having special knowledge about something; ***sensible*** (*formal*) keenly aware of something.

awareness 1 *n* **consciousness**, mindfulness, cognizance (*formal*), alertness, responsiveness, attentiveness, sentience. [➡WIDE AWAKE AND CONSCIOUS; 736] *Opposite:* ignorance. 2 *n* **knowledge**, understanding, grasp, appreciation, familiarity, recognition, perception, discernment. [➡KNOWLEDGE AND WISDOM; 559] *Opposite:* ignorance.

awash 1 *adj* **soaked**, flooded, drenched, waterlogged, saturated, sopping, brimming. [➡WET; 1239] *Opposite:* dry. 2 *adj* **oversupplied**, full of, overflowing, packed, crammed, inundated, overprovided, overstocked. [➡FULL; 1238] *Opposite:* lacking.

away *adj* **absent**, gone, left, missing, not here. [➡ABSENT AND UNAVAILABLE; 7] *Opposite:* present.

away day *n* [➡TRAVEL: JOURNEYS AND TRIPS; 319]

awe 1 *n* **wonder**, admiration, respect, amazement, surprise, wonderment, astonishment, reverence, esteem, veneration, worship. [➡SURPRISE, SHOCK, AND AMAZEMENT; 546] 2 *n* **fear**, terror, dread, fright, trepidation, fearfulness. [➡FEAR AND PANIC; 544]

awe-inspiring *adj* **overwhelming**, grand, breathtaking, splendid, tremendous, remarkable, amazing, awesome, fearsome, astounding, humbling, impressive. [➡EXTRAORDINARY: AMAZING; 205]

awesome *adj* **overwhelming**, grand, breathtaking, splendid, tremendous, remarkable, amazing, awe-inspiring, fearsome, astounding, humbling. [➡EXTRAORDINARY: AMAZING; 205]

awesomely *adv* **impressively**, awe-inspiringly, overwhelmingly, fearsomely, formidably, strikingly, amazingly, astonishingly, tremendously, devastatingly, overpoweringly. [➡EXTRAORDINARY: AMAZING; 205]

awestricken *adj* **impressed**, enthralled, overwhelmed, rapt, captivated, mesmerized, fascinated, stunned, spellbound, awestruck. [➡SURPRISE, SHOCK, AND AMAZEMENT; 546] *Opposite:* unimpressed.

awestruck *adj* **impressed**, overwhelmed, stunned, enthralled, rapt, captivated, mesmerized, fascinated, spellbound, awestricken. [➡SURPRISE, SHOCK, AND AMAZEMENT; 546] *Opposite:* unimpressed.

awful *adj* **dreadful**, terrible, appalling, unpleasant, horrible, poor, horrific, shocking. [➡BAD AND BADLY; 224]

awfully 1 *adv* **extremely**, very, really, terrifically, terribly, dreadfully. [➡TO A GREAT EXTENT; 130] 2 *adv* **badly**, unpleasantly, dreadfully, terribly, appallingly, horrifically, horribly, shockingly. [➡BAD AND BADLY; 224] *Opposite:* well.

awfulness *n* **dreadfulness**, horror, misery, unpleasantness, terribleness, horridness, direness. [➡FAULTS, FLAWS, AND WEAKNESSES; 252]

awhile (*literary*) *adv* **a little**, for a moment, a moment or two, a short time, for a while, for a time, some time, a bit (*informal*), a little bit. [➡FUTURE; 86]

a whole new ball game (*slang*) *n* **something else entirely**, another thing altogether, quite another matter, a different kettle of fish, a horse of a different color (*US*). [➡DIFFERENCE; 150]

awkward 1 *adj* **embarrassing**, tricky, problematic, difficult, thorny, complex. [➡DIFFICULTY AND COMPLEXITY; 243] *Opposite:* straightforward. 2 *adj* **uncooperative**, difficult, stubborn, obstinate, stroppy (*informal*), obdurate. [➡REBELLIOUSNESS AND DISOBEDIENCE; 566] *Opposite:* cooperative. 3 *adj* **unwieldy**, cumbersome, bulky. [➡LARGE; 1192] *Opposite:* compact. 4 *adj* **clumsy**, inelegant, graceless, gawky (*informal*), uncoordinated, ungainly. [➡AGILITY OF THE BODY; 477] *Opposite:* graceful. 5 *adj* **uncomfortable**, embarrassed, out of your depth, tongue-tied, self-conscious, discomfited (*formal*), gauche, inept, discomforted, ill at ease, uneasy. [➡INSECURITY AND LOSS OF COMPOSURE; 545] *Opposite:* comfortable.

awkwardly 1 *adv* **uncomfortably**, uneasily, with embarrassment, self-consciously, gauchely, ineptly. [➡INSECURITY AND LOSS OF COMPOSURE; 545] *Opposite:* comfortably. 2 *adv* **clumsily**, inelegantly, gracelessly, gawkily (*informal*), cumbersomely. [➡AGILITY OF THE BODY; 477] *Opposite:* easily.

awkwardness 1 *n* **discomfort**, unease, embarrassment, discomfiture (*formal*), uneasiness, self-consciousness, gaucheness. [➡INSECURITY AND LOSS OF COMPOSURE; 545] *Opposite:* ease. 2 *n* **clumsiness**, ineptness, inelegance, gracelessness, gawkiness (*informal*), ungainliness. [➡AGILITY OF THE BODY; 477] *Opposite:* ease.

awl *type of* **carpentry tool**. [➡HAND TOOLS; 1118]

awning *n* **canopy**, sunshade, sun shelter, blind. [➡COVERS AND COATINGS; 1245]

AWOL *adj* **absent without leave**, absent, missing, deserting, wanted, truant, absconding, disappeared, gone. [➡ABSENT AND UNAVAILABLE; 7] *Opposite:* present.

awry 1 *adj* **crooked**, askew, skewed, off beam, out of kilter, twisted, out of true, off-centre, cockeyed, aslant, skewwhiff (*informal*). [➡ORIENTATION AND ALIGNMENT; 1222] *Opposite:* straight. 2 *adj* **amiss**, wrong, muddled, incorrect, astray, inappropriate, not as it should be. [➡INCORRECT AND ERRONEOUS; 223] *Opposite:* all right.

axe 1 *v* (*informal*) **dismiss**, fire (*informal*), discharge (*formal*), put an end to, make redundant, sack (*informal*), give the sack (*informal*), let go, lay off, can (*US slang*). [➡REVOKE STATUS; 460] *Opposite:* employ. 2 *v* **cut**, cut back, scale down, slim down, downsize, decimate, chop (*informal*).

[➡BUSINESS ACTIVITIES AND PHENOMENA; 795] **3** *type of* **cutting tool.** [➡CUTTING TOOLS; 1119]

axiom *n* **maxim**, adage, saying, saw, proverb, truism. [➡FIGURES OF SPEECH; 674]

axiomatic *adj* **self-evident**, goes without saying, obvious, manifest, clear, accepted. [➡CERTAIN; 175]

axis *n* **alliance**, partnership, bloc, league, federation, affiliation, alignment. [➡CONNECTION; 144]

axle *part of* **external structure.** [➡EXTERNAL PARTS OF A VEHICLE; 1146]

axolotl *type of* **amphibian.** [➡AMPHIBIANS; 1008]

aye (*regional*) *interj* **yes**, yeah (*informal*), indeed, absolutely, right (*informal*), yea (*archaic*). [➡EXPRESSIONS OF AGREEMENT; 649] *Opposite:* no.

aye-aye *type of* **primate.** [➡PRIMATE; 988]

azalea *type of* **shrub or bush.** [➡BUSHES AND SHRUBS; 1027]

azure *type of* **blue.** [➡COLOURS; 1223]

B

B2B *adv* [➡E-COMMERCE; 1128]

B2C *adv* [➡E-COMMERCE; 1128]

baa *type of* **animal sound.** [➡SOUNDS MADE BY ANIMALS; 1260]

babble 1 *v* **gabble**, mutter, prattle, blather (*informal*), gab (*informal*), chatter. [➡WITTER AND BABBLE; 618] 2 *n* **hum**, buzz, hubbub, drone, murmur, sound. [➡SOUNDS MADE BY PEOPLE; 1261]

babe 1 *n* (*slang*) **darling**, sugar (*informal*), sweetheart, love, lover, baby (*slang*), honey (*US informal*). [➡ENDEARMENTS; 657] 2 *n* (*literary or archaic*) **baby**, infant, little one, tot (*informal*), child, kid (*informal*), newborn, babe in arms. [➡CHILD OR YOUTH; 945]

babe in arms *n* [➡CHILD OR YOUTH; 945]

baboon *type of* **primate.** [➡PRIMATE; 988]

baby 1 *n* **infant**, child, newborn, babe in arms, tot (*informal*), little one, kid (*informal*), babe (*literary or archaic*). [➡CHILD OR YOUTH; 945] 2 *n* (*slang*) **darling**, sugar (*informal*), sweetheart, love, lover, babe (*slang*), honey (*US informal*). [➡ENDEARMENTS; 657] 3 *v* **pamper**, coddle, mollycoddle, cosset, overprotect, spoil, indulge, make much of, fuss over. [➡TAKE CARE OF AND SPOIL; 301]

baby-faced *adj* **youthful**, boyish, girlish, childlike, wide-eyed, cute, innocent. [➡FACIAL CHARACTERISTICS; 482] *Opposite:* wizened.

baby grand *type of* **keyboard.** [➡MUSICAL INSTRUMENTS; 910]

babyhood *n* **infancy**, childhood, early years, youth. [➡BABYHOOD, CHILDHOOD AND ADOLESCENCE; 917]

babyish *adj* **childish**, infantile, immature, puerile, adolescent, naive. [➡NEGATIVE INTELLECTUAL CHARACTERISTICS; 526] *Opposite:* mature.

babysit *v* **look after**, child mind, protect, watch, mind, tend, take care of, sit. [➡TAKE CARE OF AND SPOIL; 301]

babysitter *n* **child minder**, minder, carer, sitter. [➡PEOPLE WHO GUARD AND PROTECT; 846]

baby tooth *type of* **tooth.** [➡THE MOUTH; 703]

babywear *n* [➡GARMENTS AND OUTFITS; 865]

bachelor *n* **unmarried man**, single man, unattached man, eligible male, confirmed bachelor. [➡MARITAL STATUS; 890]

back 1 *n* **backbone**, spine, spinal column, vertebral column, vertebrae. [➡THE BONES AND JOINTS; 720] 2 *part of* **torso.** [➡TORSO; 694] 3 *adv* **behind**, to the rear, backwards, rearward. [➡DIRECTION OF MOTION; 346] *Opposite:* forwards. 4 *v* **go backwards**, reverse, move backwards, recede, back up. [➡GO BACKWARDS; 310] *Opposite:* proceed.

backache *n* **back pain**, back trouble, bad back, lumbago, sciatica, slipped disc. [➡PAIN AND OTHER PHYSICAL SENSATIONS; 734]

back and forth *adv* **backwards and forwards**, from side to side, to and fro, hither and thither. [➡DIRECTION OF MOTION; 346]

back-and-forth *adj* [➡DIRECTION OF MOTION; 346]

back away *v* **recoil**, shrink, draw back, shy away, back off, withdraw, pull back, move away, retreat, backpedal. [➡GO BACKWARDS; 310] *Opposite:* stay.

backbiter *n* [➡GRUMPY AND NEGATIVE PEOPLE; 953]

backbiting *n* **unkind remarks**, infighting, viciousness, spitefulness, backstabbing, badmouthing (*slang*). [➡INSULTS, ABUSE, AND SWEARING; 659]

backbone 1 *n* **spine**, spinal column, vertebral column, back, vertebrae. [➡THE BONES AND JOINTS; 720] 2 *n* **mainstay**, support, prop, spine, pillar, strength. [➡CENTRAL PARTS OF PHYSICAL OBJECTS; 1250] 3 *n* **moral fibre**, strength of character, stamina, fortitude, courage, grit, determination, resilience, self-discipline, guts (*slang*). [➡COURAGE; 499]

backbreaking *adj* **strenuous**, arduous, gruelling, exhausting, taxing, wearisome, laborious, hard. [➡PHYSICALLY UNPLEASANT; 227] *Opposite:* easy.

backchat (*informal*) *n* **rudeness**, impudence, impertinence, disrespect, mouth (*informal*), attitude (*informal*), cheek (*informal*), cheekiness (*informal*), sauce (*informal*), lip (*slang*), sauciness, sassiness (*US*). [➡BAD MANNERS AND SOCIAL SKILLS; 522] *Opposite:* respect.

backcloth *n* **backdrop**, scenery, set, stage set, background, scene, reredos. [➡IN THE THEATRE; 906]

backcomb *v* **brush**, comb, tease, style, coif (*formal*), coax, ruffle. [➡CHANGE OF SHAPE; 386]

backcombed *adj* [➡DESCRIBING HAIR; 487]

back country (*US*) *n* **wilderness**, wilds, backwoods, rough country, sticks (*informal*). [➡REMOTE PLACES; 1046]

backdate *v* **predate**, date, validate, sign, stamp. [➡NAME AND DESCRIBE; 666]

back down *v* **withdraw**, concede defeat, accept defeat, yield, admit defeat, admit you were wrong, backpedal, take back, back off, eat humble pie, give in, climb down, pull out, back out. [➡APOLOGIZE AND RETRACT; 684] *Opposite:* stand your ground.

backdrop 1 *n* **backcloth**, scenery, set, stage set, background, scene. [➡IN THE THEATRE; 906] 2 *n* **background**, setting, milieu (*formal*), environment, framework, locale, conditions, surroundings, circumstances. [➡SITUATIONS; 71]

backer *n* **sponsor**, supporter, patron, promoter, benefactor, financier, champion, angel, guarantor. [➡REPRESENTATIVES AND PATRONS; 968]

Compare and Contrast: ***backer, angel, guarantor, patron, sponsor***

CORE MEANING: SOMEBODY WHO PROVIDES FINANCIAL SUPPORT

backer somebody who gives moral or financial support; ***angel*** a person who provides financial support for an enterprise, for example a theatrical venture; ***guarantor*** somebody who gives a legal undertaking to be responsible for somebody else's debts or obligations; ***patron*** a person who gives financial or moral support to a person, institution, or charity, especially in the arts; ***sponsor*** a person or organization that contributes money to help fund an event, usually in return for publicity, or gives money to a person taking part in fundraising.

backfire *v* **go wrong**, boomerang, miscarry, fail, flop (*informal*), not go as planned, rebound, bomb (*informal*). [➡FAIL OR BE UNSUCCESSFUL; 75]

background 1 *n* **upbringing**, circumstances, personal history, family, experience, social class, education, training, credentials, qualifications. [➡STATUS; 888] 2 *n* **backdrop**, setting, milieu (*formal*), environment, surroundings, conditions, locale, set, circumstances. [➡SITUATIONS; 71]

backhanded *adj* **indirect**, doubtful, oblique, insincere, snide, sneaky. [➡RUDE AND HOSTILE; 626]

backhander (*informal*) *n* **bribe**, rake-off (*informal*), kickback, sweetener (*informal*), incentive, payment, carrot, favour. [➡BRIBES; 441]

backing *n* **support**, help, assistance, sponsorship, patronage, aid, backup, funding, finance, money, grant, subsidy. [➡SOURCE OF HAPPINESS, PLEASURE, OR IMPROVEMENT; 210]

backlash *n* **reaction**, repercussion, counterattack, criticism, hostile response. [➡RESULTS AND OUTCOMES; 83]

backlog *n* **accumulation**, buildup, excess, surfeit, logjam, bottleneck. [➡MORE AND EXCESS; 122]

back off 1 *v* **retreat**, pull back, move away, go backwards, recoil, shrink, draw back, shy away, withdraw, back away. [➡GO BACKWARDS; 310] *Opposite:* advance. 2 *v* **yield**, withdraw, admit you were wrong, backpedal, take back, back down, eat humble pie, give in, climb down. [➡APOLOGIZE AND RETRACT; 684] *Opposite:* insist.

back out *v* **pull out**, withdraw, renege, go back on, cancel, change your mind, beg off, drop out, call off, cry off (*informal*), fink out (*US slang*). [➡NOT DO AND REFUSE TO DO; 275] *Opposite:* continue.

backpack 1 *n* **rucksack**, knapsack, pack, bag, haversack. [➡CONTAINERS, RECEPTACLES, AND PACKAGING; 1244] 2 *v* [➡TRAVEL: WAYS OF TRAVELLING; 321]

backpacker *n* **traveller**, hiker, walker, tourist, hitchhiker. [➡TRAVEL: TRAVELLERS AND WALKERS; 320]

back pain *n* **backache**, lumbago, back trouble, bad back, sciatica, slipped disc. [➡ILLNESSES AND DISORDERS; 733]

backpedal *v* **backtrack**, back down, shift ground, go back on your word, recant, retreat, do an about-turn, back off. [➡APOLOGIZE AND RETRACT; 684]

backroom *adj* **unobtrusive**, clandestine, secret, private, secretive, hush-hush (*informal*). [➡SECRET AND UNKNOWN; 180] *Opposite:* public.

back seat *type of* **internal feature**. [➡VEHICLES; 1144]

backside (*informal*) *n* **buttocks**, rump, behind, bottom, rear (*informal*), bum (*informal*), rear end (*US informal*). [➡TORSO; 694]

backslash *type of* **punctuation mark**. [➡ASPECTS OF LANGUAGE; 683]

backslide *v* **relapse**, go back to your old ways, lapse, revert, regress, slip back. [➡GET WORSE; 382]

backslider *n* **recidivist**, defaulter, transgressor, apostate, deserter, repeater (*US*). [➡LAZY OR UNSUCCESSFUL PEOPLE; 948]

backspace *type of* **hardware**. [➡COMPUTERS AND COMPUTING; 1126]

backstage *adv* **offstage**, behind the scenes, in the wings, in private, in secret. [➡SECRET AND UNKNOWN; 180]

backstreet *n* **alley**, back alley, lane, side street. [➡ROADS; 1105] *Opposite:* thoroughfare.

back talk (*US*) *n* **rudeness**, cheek (*informal*), cheekiness (*informal*), sauce (*informal*), sauciness, backchat (*informal*), impudence, impertinence, disrespect, lip (*slang*), mouth (*informal*), attitude (*informal*), sassiness (*US*). [➡BAD MANNERS AND SOCIAL SKILLS; 522] *Opposite:* respect.

back-to-back *adj* **consecutive**, end-to-end, nonstop, continuous, uninterrupted, following. [➡AFTER, LAST, AND FOLLOWING; 166]

back to front 1 *adv* **the wrong way round**, in reverse, inversely, contrariwise, inside out, backwards. [➡ORIENTATION AND ALIGNMENT; 1222] 2 *adv* **thoroughly**, inside out, like the back of your hand, intimately, from A to Z. [➡WHOLENESS AND COMPLETENESS; 199]

backtrack 1 *v* **retrace your steps**, go back over the same ground, turn back, begin again. [➡GO BACKWARDS; 310] 2 *v* **backpedal**, go into reverse, do a volte-face, do an about-turn, do a U-turn, back down, back off, change your mind, do an about-face (*US*). [➡APOLOGIZE AND RETRACT; 684]

back up 1 *v* **corroborate**, substantiate, authenticate, vouch for, reinforce, second, support. [➡APPROVE AND CONFIRM; 647] *Opposite:* contradict. 2 *v* **copy**, duplicate, make a backup, keep a backup, keep a copy. [➡COPY AND DUPLICATE; 403] 3 *v* **move backwards**, reverse, go backwards, recede. [➡GO BACKWARDS; 310] *Opposite:* advance.

backup 1 *n* **support**, encouragement, help, moral support, assistance, backing. [➡KIND ACTION OR BEHAVIOUR; 296] 2 *n* **stand-by**, reserve, substitute, reinforcement, help. [➡MORE AND EXCESS; 122] 3 *n* **copy**, duplicate, replica, substitute, fill-in, surrogate, alternate (*US*). [➡COPIES AND REPLICAS; 152] 4 *n* (*US*) **holdup**, stoppage, gridlock, tailback, snarl-up, snarl (*US*), tie-up (*US*). [➡TRAVEL: TRAFFIC PROBLEMS AND HOLDUPS; 324]

backward 1 *adj* **rearward**, to the rear, towards the back. [➡DIRECTION OF MOTION; 346] *Opposite:* forward. 2 *adj* **retrograde**, regressive, recessive. [➡DIRECTION OF MOTION; 346] *Opposite:* progressive. **3** *adj* **shy**, diffident, hesitant, reluctant, timid, bashful, retiring. [➡RETICENT AND UNFORTHCOMING; 632] *Opposite:* confident.

backward-looking *adj* **retrospective**, nostalgic, retrograde, traditional, conservative. [➡THE NATURE OF IDEAS; 772] *Opposite:* forward-looking.

backwards **1** *adv* **towards the back**, back, rearward, towards the rear. [➡DIRECTION OF MOTION; 346] **2** *adv* **the wrong way**, in reverse, back to front, the wrong way round. [➡ORIENTATION AND ALIGNMENT; 1222] *Opposite:* forwards.

backwards and forwards *adv* **back and forth**, to and fro, up and down, hither and thither, from side to side. [➡DIRECTION OF MOTION; 346]

backwater *n* **backwoods**, the back of beyond, the middle of nowhere, sticks (*informal*), boondocks (*US informal*). [➡REMOTE PLACES; 1046]

backwoods **1** *n* **wilderness**, wilds, rough country, back country (*US*). [➡REMOTE PLACES; 1046] **2** *n* **the middle of nowhere**, the back of beyond, backwater, sticks (*informal*), boondocks (*US informal*). [➡REMOTE PLACES; 1046]

back yard *n* **courtyard**, patio, yard, terrace, porch, veranda, deck (*US*). [➡GARDENS; 1073]

bacon *type of* **processed meat**. [➡TYPES AND CUTS OF MEAT; 1176]

bacterial *adj* **microbial**, bacteriological, infective, infectious, contagious, microscopic. [➡MICROORGANISMS, FUNGI, AND ALGAE; 1023]

bacteriological *adj* **microbiological**, biological, bacterial, pathological. [➡BIOLOGICAL SCIENCES; 1037]

bacteriology *type of* **bioscience**. [➡BIOLOGICAL SCIENCES; 1037]

bacteriophage *type of* **microorganism**. [➡MICROORGANISMS, FUNGI, AND ALGAE; 1023]

bacterium *type of* **microorganism**. [➡MICROORGANISMS, FUNGI, AND ALGAE; 1023]

bactrian camel *type of* **large mammal**. [➡LARGE MAMMAL; 986]

bad **1** *adj* **poor**, inferior, deficient, flawed, faulty, defective, substandard, imperfect, abysmal. [➡BAD AND BADLY; 224] *Opposite:* good. **2** *adj* **evil**, wicked, corrupt, immoral, depraved, debauched, unscrupulous, ruthless, merciless, cruel, base, shameless. [➡MORALLY BAD; 776] *Opposite:* good. **3** *adj* **naughty**, disobedient, troublesome, wayward, mischievous, unmanageable, unruly, wilful, criminal, delinquent. [➡REBELLIOUSNESS AND DISOBEDIENCE; 566] *Opposite:* good. **4** *adj* **unhealthy**, damaging, injurious, ruinous, dangerous, prejudicial, harmful. [➡DANGEROUS; 237] *Opposite:* good. **5** *adj* **rotten**, off, decayed, decaying, decomposing, putrid, mouldy, sour, stale, rancid. [➡DECAYING OR INFESTED; 1235] *Opposite:* fresh. **6** *adj* **regretful**, penitent, remorseful, ashamed, apologetic, contrite, guilty, repentant, uneasy, sad. [➡SADNESS, DISTRESS, AND DESPAIR; 540] *Opposite:* good. **7** *adj* **awful**, terrible, dreadful, appalling, shocking, ghastly, horrific, unpleasant. [➡BAD AND BADLY; 224] *Opposite:* good. **8** *adj* **adverse**, difficult, unhappy, testing, unpleasant, distressing, harsh, austere. [➡BAD AND BADLY; 224] *Opposite:* good. **9** *adj* **serious**, severe, grave, critical, life-threatening, acute. [➡DANGEROUS; 237] *Opposite:* slight.

Compare and Contrast: ***bad, criminal, delinquent, mischievous, naughty***

CORE MEANING: INDICATING WRONGDOING

bad applies to a whole range of wrongdoing from the most trivial to the most immoral or evil; ***criminal*** punishable as a crime; ***delinquent*** antisocial or unlawful, or (*formal*) neglecting a duty, commitment or responsibility; ***mischievous*** playfully naughty or troublesome, or (*formal*) causing or meant to cause serious trouble, damage, or hurt; ***naughty*** badly behaved or disobedient, or (*humorous*) mildly indecent or sinful.

bad blood *n* **bad feeling**, ill feeling, bitterness, acrimony, antagonism, animosity, spite, spitefulness, rancour. [➡ANTAGONISM; 553] *Opposite:* affection.

baddie (*informal*) *n* **bad character**, rogue, villain, scoundrel, outlaw, crook (*informal*), criminal, lawbreaker, evildoer, wrongdoer. [➡VILLAINS AND THUGS; 947] *Opposite:* hero.

bad feeling *n* **spite**, rancour, spitefulness, bad blood, bitterness, acrimony, antagonism, animosity, ill feeling. [➡ANTAGONISM; 553] *Opposite:* affection.

badge **1** *n* **brooch**, pin, clasp, button (*US*). [➡JEWELLERY; 866] **2** *n* **insignia**, emblem, symbol, mark, device, coat of arms. [➡SYMBOLS, SIGNS, AND NUMBERS; 597]

badger **1** *v* **pester**, press, hassle (*informal*), harass, plague, harry, go on at (*informal*). [➡COMPLAIN AND NAG; 687] **2** *type of* **small mammal**. [➡SMALL MAMMAL; 990]

bad guy *n* [➡VILLAINS AND THUGS; 947]

bad habit *n* **weakness**, failing, flaw, character defect, vice, foible. [➡FAULTS, FLAWS, AND WEAKNESSES; 252] *Opposite:* virtue.

badinage *n* [➡INFORMAL COMMUNICATION; 45]

badlands *n* [➡REMOTE PLACES; 1046]

bad language *n* **swearing**, swearwords, vulgar language, profanities, coarse language, vulgarity, obscenities. [➡INSULTS, ABUSE, AND SWEARING; 659]

bad luck *n* **misfortune**, hard luck, ill luck, unluckiness, ill fortune. [➡BAD LUCK AND UNLUCKY; 785] *Opposite:* luck.

badly **1** *adv* **poorly**, deficiently, faultily, defectively, imperfectly, shoddily, roughly, inadequately. [➡BAD AND BADLY; 224] *Opposite:* well. **2** *adv* **seriously**, severely, gravely, critically, desperately, acutely. [➡CRITICALLY AND SERIOUSLY; 132] *Opposite:* slightly. **3** *adv* **naughtily**, disobediently, troublesomely, waywardly, mischievously, unmanageably, wilfully, rudely, improperly. [➡BAD MANNERS AND SOCIAL SKILLS; 522]

badly behaved *adj* **naughty**, disobedient, mischievous, unruly, unmanageable, wayward. [➡BAD MANNERS AND SOCIAL SKILLS; 522]

badly off *adj* **poor**, strapped (*informal*), struggling, lacking, wanting, unfortunate, ill-supplied, ill-furnished. [➡POVERTY AND POOR; 892] *Opposite:* well-off.

badly timed *adj* **ill-timed**, inopportune, mistimed, untimely, unseasonable, inconvenient. [➡PROMPTNESS: BADLY TIMED; 101] *Opposite:* well-timed.

bad-mannered *adj* **rude**, ill-mannered, impolite, charmless, discourteous, unmannerly, ill-bred, coarse, uncouth, boorish. [➡BAD MANNERS AND SOCIAL SKILLS; 522] *Opposite:* well-mannered.

bad manners *n* **rudeness**, impoliteness, incivility, discourtesy, discourteousness, impertinence, insolence. [➡BAD MANNERS AND SOCIAL SKILLS; 522] *Opposite:* courtesy.

badminton *type of* **court game**. [➡HOBBIES, GAMES, AND SPORTS; 875]

bad mood *n* **bad humour**, sulk, huff, bad temper, temper, mood. [➡IRRITATION AND ANGER; 542]

badmouth (*slang*) *v* **criticize**, disparage, run down, belittle, defame, slur, slight, backstab. [➡INSULTS, ABUSE, AND SWEARING; 659] *Opposite:* praise.

badness *n* **evilness**, wickedness, immorality, evil, depravity, unscrupulousness, ruthlessness, mercilessness, cruelty. [➡MORALLY BAD; 776] *Opposite:* goodness.

bad taste *n* **tastelessness**, vulgarity, showiness, crassness, crudeness, cheapness, tackiness (*informal*). [➡IN POOR TASTE; 230] *Opposite:* good taste.

bad temper *n* **spleen**, irritability, petulance, sulkiness, ill temper, bad mood, mood. [➡IRRITATION AND ANGER; 542]

bad-tempered *adj* **cross**, ill-tempered, ill-humoured, irascible, short-tempered, irritable, surly, crabby, grumpy, grouchy (*informal*), testy (*informal*), cranky (*US informal*). [➡IRRITATION AND ANGER; 542] *Opposite:* good-tempered.

bad-temperedness *n* [➡DIFFICULT TO PLEASE; 516]

baffle *v* **confuse**, perplex, puzzle, flummox (*informal*), stump, nonplus, mystify, confound, bewilder, bemuse, befuddle, bamboozle (*informal*). [➡CONFUSE AND BEWILDER; 572]

baffled *adj* **puzzled**, perplexed, mystified, lost, stumped, at sea, confounded, confused, bewildered, bemused, nonplussed, flummoxed (*informal*), bamboozled (*informal*). [➡CONFUSION, ANXIETY, AND WORRY; 541]

bafflement *n* **bewilderment**, perplexity, confusion, puzzlement, bemusement, befuddlement. [➡CONFUSION, ANXIETY, AND WORRY; 541] *Opposite:* understanding.

baffling *adj* **puzzling**, perplexing, mystifying, confusing, bewildering, mysterious, strange, unexplained, inexplicable. [➡BIZARRE AND PECULIAR; 258] *Opposite:* obvious.

bag **1** *n* **container**, receptacle, sack, paper bag, plastic bag. [➡CONTAINERS, RECEPTACLES, AND PACKAGING; 1244] **2** *v* **take possession**, grab, occupy, reserve, keep, claim. [➡GET; 421] **3** *v* **catch**, shoot, snare, take, capture, seize. [➡GET; 421]

bag

◆ *types of bag*
bum bag, carrier, carrier bag, clutch bag, fanny pack (*US*), handbag, mailbag, nosebag, pocketbook, postbag, pouch, purse, reticule, satchel, shopper, shopping bag, shopping basket, shoulder bag, sporran, tote bag

bag and baggage *adv* **lock, stock and barrel**, entirely, completely, totally, in its entirety, root and branch. [➡ALL; 126]

bagatelle (*formal*) *n* **trifle**, trifling sum, nothing, drop in the ocean, thing of no importance, detail, minor detail, drop in the bucket (*US*). [➡SMALL AMOUNT OF MONEY; 142]

bagel *type of* **roll or bun**. [➡BREAD, FLOUR, AND BREAD PRODUCTS; 1178]

baggage *n* **luggage**, gear (*informal*), bags, suitcases, cases, belongings, personal belongings. [➡POSSESSIONS; 462]

baggage

◆ *types of baggage*
attaché case, backpack, briefcase, carryall (*US*), carrycase, case, duffel bag, haversack, holdall, kitbag, knapsack, luggage, overnight bag, pack, portmanteau, rucksack, suitcase, travel case, valise, vanity case, weekend bag

bagginess *n* **looseness**, formlessness, shapelessness, roominess, floppiness, droopiness, slackness. [➡SHAPELESSNESS; 1218] *Opposite:* tightness.

baggy *adj* **loose**, loose-fitting, slack, shapeless, saggy, flowing. [➡SHAPELESSNESS; 1218] *Opposite:* tight.

bagpipes *type of* **wind instrument**. [➡MUSICAL INSTRUMENTS; 910]

bags *n* **luggage**, baggage, gear (*informal*), belongings, personal belongings. [➡POSSESSIONS; 462]

bag-snatcher *n* [➡CRIMINALS; 821]

bags of (*informal*) *n* **lots**, loads (*informal*), heaps (*informal*), oodles (*informal*), plenty, masses (*informal*). [➡MANY, MUCH, LARGE AMOUNT; 117]

baguette *type of* **bread**. [➡BREAD, FLOUR, AND BREAD PRODUCTS; 1178]

bail *n* **security**, surety, payment, financial guarantee, bond. [➡TRIAL, PUNISHMENT, AND LEGAL OUTCOMES; 819]

Bailey bridge *type of* **bridge**. [➡BRIDGES, TUNNELS, CROSSINGS, AND JUNCTIONS; 1111]

bailiff **1** *n* **steward**, agent, factor, estate manager, overseer, land agent. [➡PEOPLE WHO GUARD AND PROTECT; 846] **2** *n* **sheriff's officer**, law officer, legal officer, dispossessor, evictor. [➡PEOPLE IN LAW COURTS; 820]

bailiwick *n* [➡SUBJECT AREA; 769]

bail out **1** *v* **stand surety**, obtain somebody's release, put up bail, post security (*US*). [➡TRIAL, PUNISHMENT, AND LEGAL OUTCOMES; 819] **2** *v* **escape**, run away, desert, flee, evacuate, abandon, duck out, drop out. [➡RUN AWAY AND AVOID; 10] *Opposite:* stick out. **3** *v* **help**, rescue, save, assist, aid, come to somebody's aid. [➡HELP; 294]

bait **1** *n* **lure**, attraction, enticement, temptation, inducement, draw, pull (*informal*), carrot. [➡TREAT; 211] **2** *v* **entice**, lure, tempt, attract, draw, pull (*informal*). [➡APPEAL TO AND AROUSE INTEREST; 576] **3** *v* **taunt**, tease, torment, harass, provoke, goad, rag (*dated*), razz (*US informal*). [➡JOKES AND TEASING; 675]

baize *type of* **fabric from animals**. [➡FABRICS; 1131]

bake **1** *v* **cook**, heat, harden, dry out. [➡HARDEN, CONGEAL, DRY;

388] 2 *v* (*informal*) **swelter**, overheat, scorch, burn, roast, boil (*informal*). [➡CHANGE OF TEMPERATURE; 387] *Opposite:* freeze.

bakery *type of* **food outlet.** [➡RETAIL OUTLETS; 1082]

baking *adj* **sweltering**, boiling, blazing, scorching (*informal*), burning, roasting (*informal*), blistering. [➡HOT WEATHER; 1050] *Opposite:* freezing.

baking dish *n* [➡TABLEWARE, CUTLERY, AND KITCHENWARE; 861]

baking sheet (*US*) *n* [➡TABLEWARE, CUTLERY, AND KITCHENWARE; 861]

baking tray *n* [➡TABLEWARE, CUTLERY, AND KITCHENWARE; 861]

baksheesh *n* **bribe**, handout, tip, gift, token, backhander (*informal*), kickback, bung (*slang*). [➡BRIBES; 441]

balaclava *type of* **headgear.** [➡HABERDASHERY, MILLINERY, AND LINGERIE; 867]

balalaika *type of* **stringed instrument.** [➡MUSICAL INSTRUMENTS; 910]

balance 1 *n* **equilibrium**, poise, sense of balance, stability, steadiness. [➡HARMONY; 156] *Opposite:* unsteadiness. 2 *n* **weighing machine**, weighing scales, set of scales, weighing scale (*US*). [➡MEASURING DEVICES; 1122] 3 *n* **remainder**, surplus, rest, what's left, residue. [➡REMAINDER AND REMAINDERS; 123] 4 *v* **equalize**, square, settle, even out, offset, even up, balance out. [➡ASSESS QUANTITY; 758] *Opposite:* weight. 5 *v* **maintain equilibrium**, stay poised, keep upright, keep steady, poise, stabilize, steady, keep in place, hold steady. [➡LACK OF ACTIVITY; 343] *Opposite:* wobble. 6 *v* **assess**, weigh up, weigh, consider, compare, evaluate, calculate. [➡EXAMINE AND ASSESS; 754]

balanced 1 *adj* **fair**, impartial, unbiased, unprejudiced, disinterested, objective, reasonable, neutral, evenhanded. [➡MORALLY GOOD; 775] *Opposite:* biased. 2 *adj* **stable**, composed, well-adjusted, together (*informal*), sensible, sane, poised, secure. [➡CONFIDENCE AND COMPOSURE; 500] *Opposite:* unbalanced.

balance out *v* **even out**, offset, compensate, make up, redress the balance, even up, equalize. [➡EQUALITY; 155] *Opposite:* weight.

balcony 1 *n* **veranda**, terrace, loggia, lanai, gallery. [➡STAGES, PLATFORMS, AND RAISED AREAS; 1097] 2 *n* **circle**, upper circle, gallery, upper tier, the gods (*informal*). [➡STAIRS AND STOREYS; 1101] 3 *part of* **building.** [➡PARTS OF A BUILDING; 1094]

bald 1 *adj* **hairless**, balding, receding, thin on top, baldheaded. [➡BALDNESS AND BALDING; 488] *Opposite:* hirsute. 2 *adj* **bare**, worn, threadbare, smooth, patchy. [➡PHYSICAL TEXTURE; 1221] 3 *adj* **plain**, bold, blunt, frank, direct, straightforward, unadorned, simple. [➡HONEST AND OPEN; 631] *Opposite:* florid.

bald as a coot *adj* [➡BALDNESS AND BALDING; 488]

bald eagle *type of* **bird of prey.** [➡BIRD OF PREY; 998]

balderdash *n* **baloney** (*informal*), claptrap (*informal*), rubbish, nonsense, tripe (*informal*), garbage, twaddle (*informal*), drivel, hogwash (*informal*), bunkum (*informal*). [➡MEANINGLESS SPEECH OR WRITING; 677]

bald-faced (*US*) *adj* **bold**, barefaced, brazen, shameless, unabashed, brash, blatant, sheer, outright, flagrant. [➡HONEST AND OPEN; 631] *Opposite:* meek.

baldheaded *adj* **bald**, hairless, balding, receding, thin on top. [➡BALDNESS AND BALDING; 488] *Opposite:* hirsute.

balding *adj* **bald**, baldheaded, hairless, receding, thin on top. [➡BALDNESS AND BALDING; 488] *Opposite:* hirsute.

baldly *adv* **bluntly**, plainly, flatly, frankly, directly, straightforwardly, simply. [➡HONEST AND OPEN; 631]

baldness 1 *n* **hairlessness**, hair loss, baldheadedness, lack of hair. [➡BALDNESS AND BALDING; 488] *Opposite:* hairiness. 2 *n* **bluntness**, plainness, frankness, directness, straightforwardness. [➡HONEST AND OPEN; 631]

bale *n* **bundle**, package, pack, roll, block. [➡AMOUNT OF SOLID OR SEMI-SOLID; 115]

baleful *adj* **threatening**, menacing, malevolent, sinister, malignant, vindictive, spiteful. [➡DANGEROUS; 237] *Opposite:* benevolent.

balk *see* **baulk.**

ball 1 *n* **sphere**, orb, globe, globule, droplet, pellet, spheroid, bead, marble. [➡ROUNDED SHAPE; 1217] 2 *type of* **sports equipment.** [➡SPORTS EQUIPMENT; 879] 3 *part of* **arm or hand.** [➡ARM AND HAND; 696]

ballad *n* **poem**, song, narrative, folk song, traditional song, epic poem. [➡MUSIC, SONGS, AND SINGING; 907]

ballast *n* **weight**, bulk, makeweight, stabilizer, balance, counterweight, counterbalance. [➡WEIGHT: HEAVY; 1204]

ball bearing *part of* **engine.** [➡PARTS OF AN ENGINE; 1143]

ball cock *n* **regulator**, controller, control, device. [➡FITTINGS; 859]

ballet *type of* **dance.** [➡DANCE; 903]

ballet shoe *type of* **shoe.** [➡FOOTWEAR; 871]

ball game *n* **sport**, football, soccer, rugby, tennis, cricket, rounders, basketball, baseball, hockey. [➡HOBBIES, GAMES, AND SPORTS; 875]

ballgown *type of* **dress.** [➡GARMENTS AND OUTFITS; 865]

ballistic *adj* **airborne**, air-to-air, surface-to-air, flying. [➡DIRECTION OF MOTION; 346]

ballistic missile *type of* **explosive weapon.** [➡EXPLOSIVES; 1154]

balloon 1 *n* **hot-air balloon**, helium balloon, inflatable, dirigible. [➡AIRCRAFT; 1147] 2 *v* **swell**, distend, inflate, expand, puff out, blow up, bloat. [➡CHANGE OF SIZE: BIGGER; 393] *Opposite:* deflate.

ballot 1 *n* **vote**, secret ballot, poll, election, survey, opinion poll. [➡ELECTIONS AND SUFFRAGE; 807] 2 *v* **canvass**, consult, survey, poll, assess opinion, arrange a vote. [➡ASK PEOPLE QUESTIONS; 667]

ballpark 1 *n* (*US*) **stadium**, playing field, field, ground, pitch. [➡URBAN OUTDOOR SPACES; 1071] 2 *adj* (*US informal*) **approximate**, rough, estimated, inexact, imprecise, vague. [➡APPROXIMATELY; 133] *Opposite:* exact.

ballpark figure (*informal*) *n* [➡GUESS; 755]

ballpoint *type of* **pen.** [➡WRITING AND DRAWING IMPLEMENTS, AND MEDIA; 602]

ballroom *type of* **room in public buildings.** [➡TYPES OF ROOM; 1096]

ballyhoo *n* **uproar**, to-do (*informal*), racket (*informal*), hullabaloo, kerfuffle (*informal*), commotion, ruckus, shemozzle (*dated informal*). [➡CHAOS AND UPROAR; 51]

balm 1 *n* **ointment**, unguent, salve, oil, cream. [➡LOTIONS, PASTES, AND GELS; 1271] 2 *n* **comfort**, relief, solace, consolation, palliative, tranquillizer. [➡TREAT; 211]

balminess *n* [➡HOT WEATHER; 1050]

balmy *adj* **mild**, clement, pleasant, temperate, gentle, soft. [➡HOT WEATHER; 1050] *Opposite:* wintry.

baloney (*informal*) *n* **tripe** (*informal*), drivel, balderdash, nonsense, rubbish, twaddle (*informal*), claptrap (*informal*), bunkum (*informal*), hogwash (*informal*), garbage. [➡MEANINGLESS SPEECH OR WRITING; 677]

baluster *n* **post**, support, leg, upright, pole, stick. [➡STICKS, POLES, AND WEDGES; 1253]

balustrade *n* **railing**, handrail, guardrail, rail, banister, barrier, bar. [➡STICKS, POLES, AND WEDGES; 1253]

bamboo *type of* **grass.** [➡GRASS; 1031]

bamboozle (*informal*) 1 *v* **cheat**, deceive, con, trick, hoodwink, take in, swindle, dupe, fool. [➡DECEPTION AND LIES; 661] 2 *v* **confuse**, bewilder, puzzle, bemuse, perplex, muddle, baffle, flummox (*informal*). [➡CONFUSE AND BEWILDER; 572]

bamboozled (*informal*) *adj* [➡CONFUSION, ANXIETY, AND WORRY; 541]

ban 1 *v* **forbid**, outlaw, prohibit, veto, bar, proscribe, disallow, interdict. [➡REFUSE PERMISSION AND NOT ALLOW; 671] *Opposite:* allow. 2 *n* **prohibition**, veto, bar, injunction, court order, embargo, sanction, interdict. [➡THE LAW AND LEGAL AUTHORITY; 814]

banal *adj* **commonplace**, hackneyed, prosaic, predictable, ordinary, dull, boring, clichéd, trivial, facile. [➡BORING AND UNINTERESTING; 235] *Opposite:* original.

banality *n* **triteness**, predictability, ordinariness, dullness, triviality, facileness. [➡ORDINARINESS; 245] *Opposite:* originality.

banana *type of* **fruit.** [➡FRUIT AND VEGETABLES; 1175]

band 1 *n* **group**, combo, ensemble. [➡MUSICIANS AND SINGERS; 908] 2 *n* **gang**, crew (*informal*), posse (*slang*), crowd, mob, group. [➡GROUPS OF PEOPLE; 935] 3 *n* **stripe**, strip, belt, stretch, range. [➡AREA AND RANGE; 111]

band

◆ *types of band*
big band, brass band, chamber orchestra, choir, chorale, chorus, dance band, duo, ensemble, jazz band, octet, orchestra, pipe band, pop group, quartet, quintet, septet, sextet, sinfonietta, steel band, string band, string quartet, symphony orchestra, trio

bandage 1 *n* **dressing**, binding, strapping, compress. [➡COVERS AND COATINGS; 1245] 2 *v* **dress**, bind, tie up, cover, bind up, strap up, swathe. [➡DECORATE, ADORN, AND APPLY COATINGS; 406]

bandanna *n* **scarf**, neckerchief, headscarf, headsquare, kerchief. [➡HABERDASHERY, MILLINERY, AND LINGERIE; 867]

B & B (*informal*) *type of* **hotel.** [➡HOTELS, RESTAURANTS, AND CLUBS; 1081]

bandeau *type of* **headgear.** [➡HABERDASHERY, MILLINERY, AND LINGERIE; 867]

bandicoot *type of* **marsupial.** [➡MARSUPIAL; 992]

bandit *n* **outlaw**, crook (*informal*), robber, thief, thug, gangster, brigand (*literary*). [➡CRIMINALS; 821]

banditry *n* **lawlessness**, violence, crime, armed robbery, robbery, thieving. [➡CRIMES; 817]

bandstand *n* **platform**, pavilion, stand, shelter, podium, dais, open-air stage. [➡BUILDINGS FOR PUBLIC ENTERTAINMENT; 1083]

band together *v* **join up**, unite, associate, get together, combine, club together, amalgamate. [➡GET CLOSER TOGETHER; 311]

bandwagon *n* **movement**, cause, trend, craze, fashion, lobby. [➡FADS, FETISHES, AND IDOLATRY; 556]

bandwidth *n* [➡ACOUSTICS; 1137]

bandy 1 *v* **exchange**, toss around, throw around, mention, debate, discuss, cite. [➡TWO-WAY COMMUNICATION; 608] 2 *adj* **outward-curving**, bowed, bent, warped, convex, curvy. [➡ROUNDED SHAPE; 1217] *Opposite:* straight.

bandy-legged *adj* **bandy**, bent, bowlegged. [➡BUILD; 478]

bandy words with *v* **argue**, dispute, bicker, wrangle, spar, have it out. [➡ARGUE AND FIGHT – TWO-WAY; 644]

bane *n* **nuisance**, curse, blight, bother, irritation, annoyance, pest (*informal*), misery. [➡NUISANCES; 254] *Opposite:* blessing.

bang 1 *n* **report**, explosion, boom, crash, knock, thud, thump, crack. [➡IMPACT SOUNDS; 1259] 2 *n* **knock**, hit, bump, blow, thump, whack. [➡PHYSICAL ATTACK AND PUNISHMENT; 416] 3 *v* **hit**, knock, bash (*informal*), thump, hammer, pound, batter, whack, thud, slam, smash, crash. [➡CONTACT: IMPACT; 414] 4 *v* **bump**, knock, jolt, hit, collide, crash. [➡CONTACT: IMPACT; 414]

banger 1 *n* (*informal*) **wreck**, rattletrap (*informal*), heap (*slang*), jalopy (*dated informal*), beater (*US informal*). [➡BIKES, CARS, AND CARRIAGES; 1148] 2 *type of* **firework.** [➡EXPLOSIVES; 1154]

bang into *v* **bump into**, knock, hit, collide with, crash against, smash into, go slap into (*informal*), shunt (*informal*). [➡CONTACT: IMPACT; 414]

bangle *type of* **jewellery.** [➡JEWELLERY; 866]

bang on (*informal*) 1 *adj* **dead right**, spot-on (*informal*), exactly right, just right, on the mark, on the button, perfect, on target. [➡EXACT; 204] 2 *v* **go on**, harp on, keep on, dwell on, labour the point, overstress, blather (*informal*), ramble, blether (*informal*), blither (*informal*). [➡CLAIM, INSIST, AND EMPHASIZE; 615]

bangs (*US*) *type of* **hairstyle.** [➡HAIR STYLES AND HAIR PIECES; 489]

banish 1 *v* **expel**, send away, exile, deport, evict, drive out, throw out, cast out (*formal*), eject. [➡EJECT AND EXCLUDE; 341] 2 *v* **get rid of**, remove, dismiss, eliminate, discard, do away with, drive out. [➡GET RID OF SOMETHING; 452]

banishment *n* **expulsion**, exile, deportation, eviction, exclusion, transportation. [➡EJECT AND EXCLUDE; 341]

banister *n* **handrail**, balustrade, guardrail, bar, rail, railing, barrier. [➡STAIRS AND STOREYS; 1101]

banjo *type of* **stringed instrument.** [➡MUSICAL INSTRUMENTS; 910]

bank 1 *n* **set**, row, tier, series, group, array, panel. [➡COLLECTIONS AND MIXTURES OF THINGS; 1243] 2 *n* **store**, depository, reservoir, stock, collection, pool, cache, stockpile, reserve, hoard. [➡COLLECTIONS AND MIXTURES OF THINGS; 1243] 3 *n* **side**, edge, margin, embankment, border, shore. [➡BARRIERS; 1112] 4 *n* **pile**, heap, mound, stack, mass. [➡MANY, MUCH, LARGE AMOUNT; 117] 5 *v* **deposit**, pay in, put in. [➡GIVE MONEY; 434] *Opposite:* withdraw. 6 *v* **have an account**, save, deposit, invest. [➡ACCOUNTING, BANKING, AND BUDGETING; 799] 7 *v* **heap**, pile, mound, stack, mass, amass. [➡STORE AND KEEP; 454] *Opposite:* disperse. 8 *v* **tilt**, pitch, turn, lean, veer, incline, slope. [➡TAKE UP A NEW POSITION; 313] *Opposite:* level off.

bank account *n* **account**, current account, deposit account, loan account, joint account, savings account, checking account (*US*). [➡ACCOUNTING, BANKING, AND BUDGETING; 799]

banker *n* **bank manager**, investment banker, merchant banker, banking executive, financier. [➡PEOPLE INVOLVED IN FINANCE; 804]

banking *n* **investment**, lending, finance, funding, backing, financial transactions. [➡ACCOUNTING, BANKING, AND BUDGETING; 799]

banknote *n* **note**, dollar bill, paper money, folding money (*informal*), bill (*US*), Federal Reserve note (*US*). [➡CURRENCIES; 798] *Opposite:* coin.

bank on *v* **count on**, depend on, rely on, trust, have confidence in, be sure of. [➡LIKE, LOVE, VALUE AND ENJOY; 579] *Opposite:* doubt.

bankroll (*informal*) *v* **finance**, fund, back, pay, sponsor, invest, subsidize. [➡GIVE MONEY; 434]

bankrupt 1 *adj* **broke** (*informal*), insolvent, penniless, ruined, bust (*informal*), cleaned out (*informal*), cleared out (*slang*). [➡POVERTY AND POOR; 892] *Opposite:* solvent. 2 *v* **ruin**, destroy, liquidate, clear out (*slang*), clean out (*informal*), bleed dry (*informal*), impoverish, make destitute. [➡TAKE SOMETHING AWAY; 426]

bankruptcy *n* **insolvency**, ruin, liquidation, economic failure, impoverishment. [➡ACCOUNTING, BANKING, AND BUDGETING; 799]

banned 1 *adj* **barred**, disqualified, debarred, excluded, expelled. [➡REFUSE PERMISSION AND NOT ALLOW; 671] *Opposite:* admitted. 2 *adj* **forbidden**, proscribed, prohibited, illegal, illicit, controlled, restricted. [➡ILLEGAL; 816] *Opposite:* permitted.

banner 1 *n* **sign**, poster, flag, placard, streamer, hanging. [➡SIGNPOSTS, SIGNALS AND BILLBOARDS; 596] 2 *adj* (*US*) **excellent**, exceptional, notable, outstanding, marvellous, tremendous, good. *Opposite:* lousy. (*informal*). [➡EXTRAORDINARY: UNCOMMON; 206]

banquet 1 *n* **feast**, dinner, meal, formal meal, ceremonial meal, slap-up meal (*informal*), blowout (*slang*). [➡PARTIES, DANCES, AND CELEBRATIONS; 37] 2 *type of* **meal.** [➡MEALS AND PARTS OF MEALS; 1168]

banshee *n* **spirit**, supernatural being, ghost, ghoul, spectre, phantom. [➡THE SUPERNATURAL; 788]

bantam *type of* **fowl.** [➡FOOD BIRD; 999]

banter 1 *n* **teasing**, mockery, joking, repartee, wit, chitchat (*informal*). [➡JOKES AND TEASING; 675] 2 *v* **tease**, mock, joke, poke fun at, make fun of, have a joke with, rag (*dated*), razz (*US informal*). [➡JOKES AND TEASING; 675]

baobab *type of* **deciduous tree.** [➡DECIDUOUS TREES; 1028]

bap *type of* **roll or bun.** [➡BREAD, FLOUR, AND BREAD PRODUCTS; 1178]

baptism *n* **initiation**, introduction, debut, beginning, induction, rite, ceremony. [➡BEGINNING; 53]

baptismal *adj* **christening**, naming, ceremonial, ritual, sacramental, initiatory, initiation. [➡RELIGIOUS CONCEPTS; 777]

baptize *v* **christen**, bless, immerse, sprinkle, initiate, induct, receive. [➡RELIGIONS AND RELIGIOUS PRACTICES; 778]

bar 1 *n* **rod**, pole, stick, staff, shaft, rail. [➡STICKS, POLES, AND WEDGES; 1253] 2 *n* **block**, slab, piece, ingot. [➡AMOUNT OF SOLID OR SEMI-SOLID; 115] 3 *n* **obstruction**, hindrance, block, barrier, impediment, restriction. [➡PROBLEM; 257] 4 *n* **hostelry**, drinking place, watering hole (*informal*). [➡HOTELS, RESTAURANTS, AND CLUBS; 1081] 5 *v* **secure**, fasten, bolt, lock, barricade. [➡BAR AND OBSTRUCT ACCESS; 411] 6 *v* **obstruct**, close off, hinder, get in the way, block, impede. [➡MAKE IMPOSSIBLE; 277] 7 *v* **ban**, exclude, keep out, debar, prohibit, forbid, stop, restrain, prevent, restrict. [➡REFUSE PERMISSION AND NOT ALLOW; 671] *Opposite:* admit. 8 *prep* **excluding**, save, except, with the exception of, apart from, but. [➡NOT; 135]

bar

◆ *types of bar or club*
bodega, casino, club, country club, joint (*slang*), local (*informal*), nightclub, nightspot, pub, roadhouse (*dated*), saloon, shebeen, speakeasy, tavern (*archaic*), wine bar

barb 1 *n* **point**, hook, tip, spur, spike, spine. [➡ANGULAR SHAPE; 1216] 2 *n* **gibe**, insult, dig, taunt, cutting remark, sting. [➡JOKES AND TEASING; 675]

barbaric *adj* **cruel**, brutal, vicious, ferocious, fierce, barbarous. [➡MORALLY BAD; 776] *Opposite:* gentle.

barbarism *n* **cruelty**, brutality, savagery, viciousness, ferociousness, bloodthirstiness, barbarousness. [➡MORALLY BAD; 776] *Opposite:* gentleness.

barbarity 1 *n* **cruelty**, brutality, savagery, viciousness, ferociousness, bloodthirstiness, barbarousness, barbarism. [➡MORALLY BAD; 776] *Opposite:* gentleness. 2 *n* **atrocity**, cruelty, outrage, assault, abuse, misdeed (*formal*). [➡UNKIND ACTION OR BEHAVIOUR; 297]

barbarous *adj* **cruel**, brutal, vicious, ferocious, fierce, barbaric. [➡MORALLY BAD; 776] *Opposite:* gentle.

Barbary ape *type of* **primate**. [➡PRIMATE; 988]

barbecue 1 *v* **grill**, sear, flame, chargrill, cook on a spit, roast, broil (*US*). [➡COOKING AND FOOD PREPARATION; 354] 2 *type of* **meal**. [➡MEALS AND PARTS OF MEALS; 1168]

barbecued *adj* [➡STATE OF PREPARED FOOD; 1170]

barbecue sauce *type of* **seasonings, sauces, and dips**. [➡SEASONINGS AND SAUCES; 1173]

barbed 1 *adj* **pointed**, hooked, spiky, spiny, thorny, prickly. [➡PHYSICAL TEXTURE; 1221] 2 *adj* **snide**, pointed, cutting, unkind, hurtful, acid, acerbic, taunting, cruel, sarcastic. [➡RUDE AND HOSTILE; 626]

barber *n* **gents' hairdresser**, hairdresser, hair stylist, stylist, gents' hair stylist, coiffeur (*formal*), men's hair stylist (*US*). [➡HAIR STYLISTS; 851]

barbican *n* **tower**, keep, stronghold, turret, fortification. [➡PARTS OF FORTRESSES; 1090]

bard (*literary or humorous*) *n* **poet**, versifier, composer, wordsmith, songster, minstrel, writer. [➡WRITERS AND STYLES; 914]

bare 1 *adj* **naked**, nude, exposed, uncovered, undressed, unclothed, stripped. [➡DRESS, WEAR, AND UNDRESS; 868] *Opposite:* covered. 2 *adj* **empty**, vacant, blank, clean, clear, cleared, unfurnished, unoccupied. [➡EMPTY; 1237] *Opposite:* full. 3 *adj* **stark**, barren, austere, severe, hard, inhospitable, hostile. [➡PLAIN; 233] *Opposite:* lush. 4 *adj* **simple**, unadorned, plain, basic, unembellished, undecorated. [➡EASE AND SIMPLICITY; 201] *Opposite:* ornate. 5 *adj* **mere**, scant, meagre, measly (*informal*). [➡TOO FEW, TOO LITTLE; 120] 6 *v* **expose**, reveal, display, show, uncover, disclose. [➡CAUSE TO APPEAR; 5] *Opposite:* cover.

See Compare and Contrast at **naked**.

barefaced *adj* **brazen**, blatant, unashamed, obvious, unabashed, outright, flagrant, bald-faced (*US*). [➡HONEST AND OPEN; 631]

barefaced lie *n* [➡DECEPTION AND LIES; 661]

barefoot *adj* **unshod**, shoeless, barefooted. [➡DRESS, WEAR, AND UNDRESS; 868]

barely *adv* **hardly**, scarcely, only just, just about. [➡TO A CERTAIN EXTENT; 134] *Opposite:* easily.

bareness *n* **emptiness**, nakedness, starkness, austerity, plainness, baldness. [➡PLAIN; 233]

barf (*US informal*) 1 *v* **vomit**, spew, regurgitate, sick up (*informal*), throw up (*informal*), bring up, hurl (*slang*). [➡VOMIT AND BELCH; 713] 2 *n* [➡VOMIT AND BELCH; 713]

bargain 1 *n* **good deal**, good buy, steal (*informal*), snip (*informal*), giveaway (*informal*). [➡ECONOMICAL AND RESOURCEFUL; 208] 2 *n* **deal**, agreement, accord, arrangement, pact, covenant. [➡HARMONY; 156] 3 *v* **haggle**, barter, negotiate, make a deal, trade, wheel and deal, broker. [➡OBTAIN POSSESSION BY PERSUASION; 458] 4 *adj* **cheap**, low, reduced, inexpensive, rock-bottom, bargain-basement, giveaway (*informal*). [➡CHEAP AND INEXPENSIVE; 222]

bargain-basement *adj* **cheap**, cut-price, low-priced, reduced-price, bargain, rock-bottom, sale, cut-rate (*US*). [➡CHEAP AND INEXPENSIVE; 222]

bargain for *v* **expect**, count on, take into account, depend on, reckon with, anticipate, allow (*formal*), make allowance for, make provision for, provide, bargain on. [➡PREDICT AND ANTICIPATE; 751]

bargain on *v* **expect**, count on, take into account, depend on, reckon with, anticipate, allow (*formal*), make allowance for, make provision for, provide for, bargain for. [➡PREDICT AND ANTICIPATE; 751]

barge 1 *v* **rush**, push, elbow, burst, surge, shove, charge. [➡CONTACT: IMPACT; 414] 2 *type of* **motor vessel**. [➡SHIPS AND BOATS; 1149]

barge in 1 *v* **walk in**, storm in, push in, rush in, breeze in, intrude. [➡ARRIVE; 12] 2 *v* **interrupt**, butt in, cut in, break in, interject. [➡INTERRUPT AND BUTT IN; 620]

barge into *v* **bump into**, collide with, clash with, smash into, bash into (*informal*), knock into, go slap into (*informal*). [➡CONTACT: IMPACT; 414]

barista *n* [➡DOMESTIC AND KITCHEN WORKERS; 850]

baritone *type of* **musical register**. [➡MUSICAL TERMS; 912]

bark 1 *v* **howl**, yap, growl, yowl, snarl. [➡SOUND EMISSION BY ANIMALS OR BIRDS; 365] 2 *type of* **animal sound**. [➡SOUNDS MADE BY ANIMALS; 1260] 3 *n type of* **parts of trees and plants**. [➡PARTS OF TREES AND PLANTS; 1026] 4 *see* **barque**.

barley *type of* **cereal**. [➡CEREAL FOODS; 1177]

barmy (*informal*) *adj* **irrational**, crazy (*informal*), silly, batty (*informal*), crackers (*informal*), bonkers (*informal*), potty (*informal*), out of your mind, not in your right mind. [➡ECCENTRICITY AND IRRATIONALITY; 563] *Opposite:* rational.

barn 1 *n* **outbuilding**, outhouse, shed, cowshed, byre (*regional*), store, storehouse. [➡ANCILLARY BUILDINGS; 1079] 2 *type of* **storage space**. [➡STORES AND STORAGE BUILDINGS; 1087]

barnacle *type of* **aquatic invertebrate**. [➡AQUATIC INVERTEBRATE; 1022]

barnacle goose *type of* **freshwater bird**. [➡FRESHWATER BIRD; 1000]

barney (*informal*) *n* **argument**, spat, row, quarrel, tiff. [➡ARGUMENT; 47]

barn owl *type of* **owl**. [➡OWL; 1001]

barnyard *n* **farmyard**, yard, court, forecourt. [➡THE COUNTRYSIDE AND OUTDOOR SPACES; 1070]

barograph *type of* **measuring device**. [➡MEASURING DEVICES; 1122]

barometer *n* **weatherglass**, indicator, gauge, aneroid barometer, barograph, guide, statoscope. [➡MEASURING DEVICES; 1122]

barometric *adj* **atmospheric**, air, meteorological. [➡WEATHER AND CLIMATE; 1049]

baron 1 *n* **tycoon**, magnate, mogul, industrialist, captain of industry, boss, robber baron (*US*). [➡IMPORTANT OR FAMOUS PEOPLE; 893] **2** *type of* **aristocrat.** [➡RULERS AND ARISTOCRACY; 823]

baroness *type of* **aristocrat.** [➡RULERS AND ARISTOCRACY; 823]

baronet *type of* **aristocrat.** [➡RULERS AND ARISTOCRACY; 823]

baronial *adj* **grand**, impressive, opulent, stately, imposing, sumptuous. [➡EXPENSIVE AND LUXURIOUS; 219] *Opposite:* humble.

Baroque **1** *type of* **pre-20th-century architecture.** [➡BUILDING AND ARCHITECTURE; 1075] **2** *type of* **classical music.** [➡MUSIC, SONGS, AND SINGING; 907] **3** *type of* **pre-20th-century art movement.** [➡ARTISTIC MOVEMENTS AND STYLES; 899]

baroque **1** *adj* **ornate**, ornamental, decorative, elaborate, exaggerated, rococo. [➡ARTISTIC MOVEMENTS AND STYLES; 899] *Opposite:* plain. **2** *adj* **flamboyant**, exaggerated, over-the-top (*informal*), overdone. [➡IN POOR TASTE; 230] *Opposite:* restrained.

barouche *type of* **wagon or carriage.** [➡VEHICLES; 1144]

barque *type of* **sailing vessel.** [➡SHIPS AND BOATS; 1149]

barrack (*informal*) *v* **heckle**, shout, interrupt, jeer. [➡ACCUSE, BLAME, AND CRITICIZE; 642]

barracks *n* **quarters**, garrison, station, billet. [➡RESIDENTIAL BUILDINGS; 1077]

barracuda *type of* **tropical sea fish.** [➡SEA FISH; 1009]

barrage **1** *n* **bombardment**, salvo, volley, fusillade. [➡SUDDEN EVENT; 52] **2** *n* **onslaught**, outpouring, hail, storm, flood, salvo. [➡SUDDEN EVENT; 52] *Opposite:* trickle. **3** *n* **dam**, dike, bank, embankment. [➡BARRIERS; 1112]

barred **1** *adj* **striped**, banded, lined, stripy, streaked, streaky. [➡DESCRIBING PATTERNS; 1226] **2** *adj* **grilled**, meshed, fenced, secure, solid, fastened. [➡FASTEN, LINK, AND JOIN; 409] **3** *adj* **banned**, excluded, disqualified, debarred, not allowed, forbidden. [➡REFUSE PERMISSION AND NOT ALLOW; 671] *Opposite:* admitted.

barrel *n* **tub**, cask, vat, butt, water butt, container, rain barrel (*US*). [➡CONTAINERS, RECEPTACLES, AND PACKAGING; 1244]

barrel-chested *adj* [➡BUILD; 478]

barren **1** *adj* **desolate**, bleak, inhospitable, stark, harsh, austere, bare, empty, deserted, lonely, windswept. [➡IN BAD REPAIR; 1233] **2** *adj* **infertile**, unproductive, sterile, unfruitful. [➡REPRODUCTION AND HEREDITY; 726] *Opposite:* fertile.

barrenness **1** *n* **emptiness**, bleakness, bareness, loneliness, inhospitableness, harshness, starkness, desolation, austereness. [➡IN BAD REPAIR; 1233] **2** *n* **infertility**, sterility, unfruitfulness, unproductiveness. [➡REPRODUCTION AND HEREDITY; 726] *Opposite:* fertility.

barricade **1** *n* **blockade**, barrier, cordon, obstruction, fortification. [➡BARRIERS; 1112] **2** *v* **secure**, obstruct, bar, fortify, block, blockade, lock up. [➡IMPROVE STRENGTH AND DURABILITY; 379]

barrier **1** *n* **obstacle**, difficulty, stumbling block, sticking point, impediment, hindrance, obstruction. [➡PROBLEM; 257] **2** *n* **fence**, wall, barricade, blockade, block, obstacle, obstruction. [➡BARRIERS; 1112]

barring *prep* **except for**, without, excluding, apart from. [➡NOT; 135]

barrister *n* **lawyer**, attorney, counsellor, advocate, defender. [➡PEOPLE IN LAW COURTS; 820]

barrow **1** *n* **cart**, handcart, pushcart, stall, fruit stall. [➡BIKES, CARS, AND CARRIAGES; 1148] **2** *n* **wheelbarrow**, trolley, push-cart, transporter, trailer, truck, cart. [➡BIKES, CARS, AND CARRIAGES; 1148] **3** *n* **burial mound**, mound, tumulus, long barrow, tomb, hill, swell, grave mound. [➡BURIAL PLACES AND ACCESSORIES; 930]

barter *v* **exchange**, trade, switch, swap (*informal*), negotiate, bargain, haggle. [➡PURCHASE; 423]

baryon *type of* **elementary particle.** [➡ELEMENTARY PARTICLES; 1278]

basalt *type of* **stone.** [➡STONES, ROCKS, AND BOULDERS; 1057]

bascule bridge *type of* **bridge.** [➡BRIDGES, TUNNELS, CROSSINGS, AND JUNCTIONS; 1111]

base **1** *n* **foundation**, support, stand, pedestal, rest, pier. [➡SUPPORTS AND BASES; 1254] **2** *n* **source**, origin, heart, starting point, root, centre. [➡BEGINNING; 53] **3** *n* **headquarters**, centre, main office, seat, station. [➡PLACE OF EMPLOYMENT; 832] **4** *v* **found**, ground, build, create, construct, centre. [➡INSTITUTE AND INAUGURATE; 349] **5** *adj* **dishonourable**, sordid, disreputable, squalid, immoral, ignoble. [➡MORALLY BAD; 776]

See Compare and Contrast at **mean.**

baseball *type of* **ball game.** [➡HOBBIES, GAMES, AND SPORTS; 875]

baseball cap *type of* **headgear.** [➡HABERDASHERY, MILLINERY, AND LINGERIE; 867]

baseball player *n* [➡PEOPLE IN SPORTS AND LEISURE; 876]

baseless *adj* **unfounded**, untrue, unjustified, unsubstantiated, groundless, unsupported, without foundation, without merit. [➡UNCERTAIN; 176] *Opposite:* well-founded.

baseline **1** *n* **starting point**, point of departure, reference point, reference line, starting position, zero. [➡BEGINNING; 53] **2** *n* **standard**, model, criterion, starting point, quality check. [➡PERFECT EXAMPLES AND EMBODIMENTS; 67] **3** *n* **reference**, control, check, set of data, set of values, set of results. [➡BASIC DETAILS; 689] **4** *n* **boundary**, boundary line, line, periphery, white line, limit. [➡EXTREMITIES OF PHYSICAL OBJECTS; 1249]

basement *n* **cellar**, vault, crypt, lower ground floor. [➡STAIRS AND STOREYS; 1101] *Opposite:* attic.

baseness *n* **wickedness**, sordidness, vileness, immorality, ignobility, corruptness. [➡MORALLY BAD; 776] *Opposite:* nobility.

basenji *type of* **small dog.** [➡DOG; 980]

bash **1** *v* (*informal*) **thump**, punch, smash, whack, sock (*informal*), belt (*informal*), clobber (*informal*), clout, wallop (*informal*), knock about (*informal*), cream (*US informal*). [➡PHYSICAL ATTACK AND PUNISHMENT; 416] **2** *v* (*informal*) **criticize**, condemn, find fault with, attack, put down (*informal*), knock, abuse. [➡ACCUSE, BLAME, AND CRITICIZE; 642] **3** *n* (*informal*) **punch**, hit, blow, thump, knock, smash, whack, wallop (*informal*), belt (*informal*), clout, sock (*informal*). [➡ PHYSICAL ATTACK AND PUNISHMENT; 416] **4** *n* (*informal*) **dent**, bump, smash, knock, prang (*informal*). [➡ CONTACT: IMPACT; 414] **5** *n* **party**, do (*informal*), celebration, shindig (*informal*), get-together (*informal*), dance, ball, gala. [➡ PARTIES, DANCES, AND CELEBRATIONS; 37] **6** *n* (*informal*) **attempt**, try, go, stab (*informal*), whirl (*informal*). [➡ ATTEMPT AN ACTION; 262]

bashful *adj* **shy**, timid, reserved, retiring, self-conscious, withdrawn, modest, blushing, reticent, diffident, timorous, coy. [➡ RETICENT AND UNFORTHCOMING; 632] *Opposite:* bold.

bashfulness *n* **shyness**, modesty, self-consciousness, quietness, coyness, timidity, reserve, reticence, diffidence. [➡ RETICENT AND UNFORTHCOMING; 632] *Opposite:* boldness.

basic **1** *adj* **essential**, central, key, principal, main, vital, critical, fundamental, most (most important), important. [➡ FUNDAMENTAL; 196] **2** *adj* **rudimentary**, straightforward, elementary, undeveloped, uncomplicated, plain. [➡ EASE AND SIMPLICITY; 201]

basics *n* **fundamentals**, essentials, nitty-gritty (*informal*), nuts and bolts (*informal*), necessities. [➡ BASIC DETAILS; 689]

basil *type of* **herb**. [➡ HERBS AND SPICES; 1174]

basilica *type of* **church**. [➡ RELIGIOUS BUILDINGS; 1084]

basilisk *type of* **reptile**. [➡ REPTILES; 994]

basin **1** *n* **sink**, hand basin, washbasin, washbowl. [➡ FITTINGS; 859] **2** *n* **bowl**, mixing bowl, dish. [➡ CONTAINERS, RECEPTACLES, AND PACKAGING; 1244]

basis *n* **foundation**, base, root, source, starting point, beginning, core. [➡ BEGINNING; 53]

bask **1** *v* **laze around**, lie, recline, lounge, stretch out, spread out. [➡ LACK OF ACTIVITY; 343] **2** *v* **enjoy**, savour, relish, soak up, luxuriate, delight in, wallow. [➡ LIKE, LOVE, VALUE AND ENJOY; 579]

basket *n* **carrier**, bag, hamper, picnic basket, linen basket, wicker basket, shopping basket. [➡ CONTAINERS, RECEPTACLES, AND PACKAGING; 1244]

basketball *type of* **ball game**. [➡ HOBBIES, GAMES, AND SPORTS; 875]

basque *type of* **upper body underwear**. [➡ HABERDASHERY, MILLINERY, AND LINGERIE; 867]

bas-relief *n* **moulding**, relief, basso-relievo, panelling, carving, decoration, sculpture. [➡ SCULPTURE; 902]

bass **1** *adj* **deep**, deep-toned, low-voiced, low-pitched. [➡ SOFT OR PLEASANT SOUNDS; 1264] **2** *type of* **musical register**. [➡ MUSIC, SONGS, AND SINGING; 907] **3** *type of* **freshwater fish**. [➡ FRESHWATER FISH; 1010]

bass drum *type of* **percussion instrument**. [➡ MUSICAL INSTRUMENTS; 910]

basset *type of* **small dog**. [➡ DOG; 980]

bass guitar *type of* **stringed instrument**. [➡ MUSICAL INSTRUMENTS; 910]

bassinet *type of* **bed**. [➡ FURNITURE; 858]

bassoon *type of* **wind instrument**. [➡ MUSICAL INSTRUMENTS; 910]

baste **1** *v* **moisten**, drizzle, grease, cover, saturate, daub. [➡ COOKING AND FOOD PREPARATION; 354] **2** *v* **clobber** (*informal*), thrash, bash (*informal*), beat up (*informal*), thump, wallop (*informal*). [➡ PHYSICAL ATTACK AND PUNISHMENT; 416] **3** *v* **sew**, stitch, tack, hem, seam. [➡ CRAFTS AND CARVING; 356]

bastion **1** *n* **stronghold**, fortification, mainstay, support. [➡ FORTRESSES AND FORTIFICATIONS; 1089] **2** *n* **defender**, upholder, supporter. [➡ PERFECT EXAMPLES AND EMBODIMENTS; 67]

bat **1** *n* **racket**, paddle, willow, club. [➡ SPORTS EQUIPMENT; 879] **2** *n* **flying mammal**, chiropteran (*technical*). [➡ FLYING MAMMAL; 986]. **3** *v* **flutter**, wink, flicker, flap, blink. [➡ MOVE SOMETHING ON THE SPOT; 337]

bat

◆ *types of flying mammal*
flying fox, flying squirrel, fruit bat, pipistrelle, vampire bat

batch *n* **lot**, consignment, group, set, bunch, collection. [➡ COLLECTIONS AND MIXTURES OF THINGS; 1243]

bath **1** *n* **bathtub**, tub, hip bath. [➡ FITTINGS; 859] **2** *n* **immersion**, soak, steam bath, bubble bath, bed bath, mud bath, sponge bath (*US*). [➡ CLEAN AND POLISH; 404] **3** *n* **tank**, basin, reservoir, container. [➡ CONTAINERS, RECEPTACLES, AND PACKAGING; 1244] **4** *v* **soak**, immerse yourself, have a bath, take a bath, wash, bathe (*US*). [➡ CLEAN AND POLISH; 404]

bathe **1** *v* **swim**, go for a dip, paddle. [➡ HOBBIES, GAMES, AND SPORTS; 875] **2** *v* **immerse**, dip, soak, rinse, dunk, submerge, flood, inundate. [➡ SOFTEN, LIQUEFY, DAMPEN; 389]

bather *n* **swimmer**, skinny-dipper (*informal*), diver, snorkeller, paddler. [➡ PEOPLE IN SPORTS AND LEISURE; 876]

bathetic *adj* [➡ BIZARRE AND PECULIAR; 258]

bathing costume (*dated*) *type of* **sportswear**. [➡ GARMENTS AND OUTFITS; 865]

bathing suit (*US*) *type of* **sportswear**. [➡ GARMENTS AND OUTFITS; 865]

bathing trunks *type of* **sportswear**. [➡ GARMENTS AND OUTFITS; 865]

bathos *n* **anticlimax**, letdown, comedown (*informal*). [➡ FAILURE; 77]

bathrobe (*US*) *type of* **sleepwear**. [➡ GARMENTS AND OUTFITS; 865]

bathroom *type of* **room in the home**. [➡ TYPES OF ROOM; 1096]

baths **1** *n* **bathhouse**, Turkish bath, steam bath, sauna, Russian bath (*US*). [➡ BUILDINGS FOR PUBLIC ENTERTAINMENT; 1083] **2** *n* **swimming pool**, bath, pool, swimming baths. [➡ BUILDINGS FOR PUBLIC ENTERTAINMENT; 1083]

bathtub *type of* **plumbing fittings**. [➡ FITTINGS; 859]

baton **1** *n* **stick**, rod, wand, cane, pointer. [➡ STICKS, POLES, AND WEDGES; 1253] **2** *type of* **club**. [➡ BLUNT INSTRUMENTS AND WHIPS; 1157]

batsman *n* **batter**, hitter, cricketer. [➡ PEOPLE IN SPORTS AND LEISURE; 876]

battalion *n* **throng**, crowd, mass, multitude, horde, host. [➡ MANY, MUCH, LARGE AMOUNT; 117]

batten *v* **fasten**, fix, close, secure, batten down, lock up. [➡BAR AND OBSTRUCT ACCESS; 411] *Opposite:* open.

batter 1 *v* **pound**, hammer (*informal*), bang, thump, thrash, hit. [➡CONTACT: IMPACT; 414] 2 *v* **assault**, maim, brutalize, attack, abuse, injure, maltreat, beat. [➡WOUND A PERSON OR ANIMAL; 384]

battercake (*US*) *type of* **pancake**. [➡CAKES, BISCUITS, AND DESSERTS; 1180]

battered 1 *adj* **maltreated**, assaulted, abused, beaten, injured. [➡INJURED; 743] 2 *adj* **tattered**, tatty, decrepit, worn out, weather-beaten, beat-up (*informal*), damaged, knocked around (*informal*). [➡IN BAD REPAIR; 1233] *Opposite:* pristine.

battering *n* **pounding**, buffeting, hammering, beating, lashing, pummelling. [➡PHYSICAL ATTACK AND PUNISHMENT; 416]

battery 1 *n* **series**, set, sequence, succession, run, string, array. [➡COLLECTIONS AND MIXTURES OF THINGS; 1243] 2 *n* [➡ENERGY STORAGE AND GENERATION; 1162]

battle 1 *n* **fight**, clash, encounter, skirmish, engagement, combat, scuffle, mêlée, conflict, confrontation, fracas, fray, action. [➡AGGRESSIVE EVENT; 39] 2 *n* **struggle**, crusade, fight, war, campaign, drive, wrangle. [➡AGGRESSIVE EVENT; 39] 3 *v* **fight**, go to war, attack, come to blows, engage, join battle. [➡WARFARE AND WAR; 830] 4 *v* **struggle**, wrestle, contend, fight, strive, try. [➡COMPETE, CONTEND, AND COMBAT; 304]

See Compare and Contrast at **fight**.

battleaxe *n* **axe**, hatchet, tomahawk, halberd. [➡SWORDS AND KNIVES; 1156]

battle cruiser *type of* **military vessel**. [➡SHIPS AND BOATS; 1149]

battle cry *n* **whoop**, war cry, yell, shout, cry, rallying cry, cheer. [➡SOUNDS MADE BY PEOPLE; 1261]

battledress *n* **soldier's uniform**, army uniform, uniform, fatigues, khakis, camouflage. [➡GARMENTS AND OUTFITS; 865]

battlefield *n* **battleground**, combat zone, arena, theatre of war, front line, field, trenches. [➡WARFARE AND WAR; 830]

battleground *n* **battlefield**, combat zone, arena, theatre of war, front line, field, trenches. [➡WARFARE AND WAR; 830]

battlements *n* **ramparts**, fortifications, walls, parapet, bulwark, stockade. [➡PARTS OF FORTRESSES; 1090]

battler *n* [➡PEOPLE WHO ARE APPROVED OF; 955]

battleship *type of* **military vessel**. [➡SHIPS AND BOATS; 1149]

battleship grey *type of* **grey**. [➡COLOURS; 1223]

batty (*informal*) *adj* **crazy** (*informal*), eccentric, round the bend (*informal*), round the twist (*slang*), barmy (*informal*), potty (*informal*), crackers (*informal*), bonkers (*informal*). [➡ECCENTRICITY AND IRRATIONALITY; 563] *Opposite:* rational.

bauble *n* **trinket**, trifle, gewgaw, decoration, ornament. [➡ORNAMENTS AND DECORATIONS; 1247]

Bauhaus *type of* **20th-century architecture**. [➡BUILDING AND ARCHITECTURE; 1075]

baulk 1 *v* **recoil**, draw back, hesitate, pull back. [➡HESITATE; 273] *Opposite:* leap at. 2 *v* **stop short**, pull up short, rein in. [➡NOT DO AND REFUSE TO DO; 275]

bauxite *type of* **mineral**. [➡MINERALS; 1276]

bawdy *adj* [➡MORALLY BAD; 776]

bawl 1 *v* **shout**, yell, roar, holler (*informal*), shriek, screech. [➡SOUND EMISSION BY PEOPLE; 364] *Opposite:* whisper. 2 *v* (*informal*) **cry**, howl, wail, sob, weep, blubber (*informal*), blub (*informal*). [➡CRYING; 651] 3 *type of* **human sound**. [➡SOUNDS MADE BY PEOPLE; 1261]

bawl out (*informal*) *v* **tell off** (*informal*), give a talking-to, haul over the coals, read the riot act, take to task, scold, tick off (*informal*), rap on/over the knuckles (*informal*), tear off a strip, rake over the coals (*US*), chew out (*US informal*), rap across the knuckles (*US*). [➡ACCUSE, BLAME, AND CRITICIZE; 642]

bay 1 *n* **inlet**, cove, natural harbour, haven (*literary*), anchorage. [➡THE SEAS, OCEANS, AND SHORES; 1041] 2 *n* **compartment**, alcove, cubicle, recess, loading bay. [➡ALCOVES, CUBICLES, AND COMPARTMENTS; 1095] 3 *n* **bark**, woof, yap, yelp, howl, cry, wail. [➡SOUNDS MADE BY ANIMALS; 1260] 4 *type of* **brown**. [➡COLOURS; 1223] 5 *v* **woof**, bark, yap, yelp, howl, cry, wail. [➡SOUND EMISSION BY ANIMALS OR BIRDS; 365]

bay for *v* **demand**, insist on, be out for, cry for, shout for, yell for, howl for. [➡REQUEST AND DEMAND; 664]

bay leaf *type of* **herb**. [➡HERBS AND SPICES; 1174]

bayonet 1 *n* **blade**, knife, dagger, lance, spike. [➡SWORDS AND KNIVES; 1156] 2 *v* **stab**, spear, impale, spike, knife, run through (*literary*). [➡STAB; 417]

bayou (*US*) *n* **marsh**, marshland, bog, wetlands, everglade (*US*). [➡RIVERS, LAKES, AND STREAMS; 1042]

bay window *type of* **window**. [➡WINDOWS; 1099]

bazaar 1 *n* **market**, marketplace, souk, open market, flea market. [➡URBAN OUTDOOR SPACES; 1071] 2 *type of* **retail outlet**. [➡RETAIL OUTLETS; 1082]

bazooka *type of* **gun**. [➡WEAPONS FOR SHOOTING; 1155]

be 1 *v* **exist**, live, have being, be present, coexist, subsist. [➡EXIST; 15] 2 *v* **take place**, happen, occur, transpire, come about, ensue, befall (*archaic or literary*), come to pass (*archaic or literary*). [➡HAPPEN; 27] 3 *v* **be situated**, be located, remain, be there, be present, stand, stay. [➡EXIST IN A PLACE; 19]

be a bundle of nerves (*informal*) *v* **be on edge**, be nervous, be uptight (*informal*), be highly strung, be like a cat on a hot tin roof, be like a coiled spring, be high strung (*US*). [➡BE CONCERNED AND CARE; 582] *Opposite:* relax.

be accepted *v* **integrate**, assimilate, become one of, join, belong, pass muster, blend in, pass, get in. [➡ESTABLISHING RELATIONSHIPS WITH OTHERS; 974]

beach *n* **seashore**, seaside, coast, shore, coastline, shoreline, sand, strand. [➡THE SEAS, OCEANS, AND SHORES; 1041]

beach ball *type of* **toy**. [➡TOYS; 880]

beachcomber *n* **scavenger**, forager, explorer, collector, hoarder. [➡PEOPLE WHO COLLECT THINGS; 455]

beached *adj* **stranded**, aground, stuck, high and dry, run aground, shipwrecked, marooned. [➡LACK OF ACTIVITY; 343] *Opposite:* afloat.

beach grass *type of* **grass.** [➡GRASS; 1031]

beachhead *n* **lodgment**, foothold, base, strategic position, position, foot in the door. [➡ADVANTAGE; 213]

beachwear *n* **swimwear**, swimsuit, bikini, leisurewear, swimming costume, swimming trunks, bathing costume (*dated*), shorts, holiday wear, summer clothes, bathing suit (*US*). [➡GARMENTS AND OUTFITS; 865]

beacon 1 *n* **signal**, sign, alarm, warning, flare, warning light. [➡SIGNPOSTS, SIGNALS AND BILLBOARDS; 596] 2 *n* **bonfire**, fire, flare. [➡FIRE, FLAMMABILITY, AND BURNING; 1164] 3 *n* (*literary*) **inspiration**, guiding light, encouragement, example, shining example, ideal, symbol of hope. [➡PERFECT EXAMPLES AND EMBODIMENTS; 67]

be acquainted with *v* **have knowledge of**, know about, be familiar with, be aware of, be informed of, be on familiar terms with. [➡KNOWLEDGE AND WISDOM; 559]

bead *n* **drop**, droplet, drip, blob, globule. [➡AMOUNT OF LIQUID; 114]

beaded 1 *adj* **decorated**, ornate, bead-trimmed, bejewelled (*literary*), encrusted, sequined, bedizened (*literary*). [➡DECORATE, ADORN, AND APPLY COATINGS; 406] 2 *adj* **covered**, dripping, sparkling, moist, soaked, drenched, wet. [➡MOIST; 1240]

beading *n* **edging**, border, trim, detail, moulding, ornamentation. [➡ORNAMENTS AND DECORATIONS; 1247]

be adjoining *v* **abut**, border, border on, be alongside, be next door to, neighbour, adjoin. [➡EXIST IN CLOSE PROXIMITY; 21]

beads *type of* **necklace.** [➡JEWELLERY; 866]

beady 1 *adj* **small**, round, shiny, bright, shining, twinkling. [➡SMALL; 1194] *Opposite:* wide. 2 *adj* **beaded**, decorated, ornate, bead-trimmed, bejewelled (*literary*), sequined. [➡DECORATE, ADORN, AND APPLY COATINGS; 406] 3 *adj* (*informal*) **watchful**, unblinking, piercing, attentive, bright, fixed. [➡FACIAL CHARACTERISTICS; 482]

be afraid *v* **be scared**, be frightened, be fearful, be nervous, be terrified, be apprehensive, be anxious. [➡FEARS AND PHOBIAS; 555]

be after *v* **want**, wish for, desire, try to get, look for, seek, need, aim for. [➡DESIRE AND WANT; 580]

be against *v* **oppose**, be opposed, object, disapprove, protest, be in opposition to, dislike, be an adversary of. [➡PROTEST AND EXPRESS DISAPPROVAL; 643]

beagle *type of* **small dog.** [➡DOG; 980]

beak *part of* **bird.** [➡PARTS OF A BIRD; 1006]

beaked *adj* **hooked**, aquiline, Roman. [➡ANGULAR SHAPE; 1216]

beaker *n* **cup**, glass, mug, paper cup, plastic cup, tumbler. [➡CONTAINERS, RECEPTACLES, AND PACKAGING; 1244]

be alive *v* **live**, exist, be living, survive, be alive and kicking, be alive and well. [➡EXIST; 15]

be alive with *v* **be crawling with**, swarm with, seethe with, teem with, ooze, emanate (*formal*), abound in. [➡PROSPER AND ABOUND; 16]

beam 1 *n* **girder**, rafter, joist, RSJ, timber, shaft, plank, bar. [➡BUILDING MATERIALS; 1076] 2 *n* **ray**, shaft of light, sunbeam, stream of light. [➡LIGHT; 1163] 3 *n* **smile**, grin, wide smile, big smile. [➡FACIAL EXPRESSION; 652] *Opposite:* scowl. 4 *v* **smile**, grin, look happy. [➡FACIAL EXPRESSION; 652] *Opposite:* scowl. 5 *v* **shine**, radiate, emit, send out, glow, gleam, flash, glimmer. [➡LIGHT EMISSION; 369]

beam bridge *type of* **bridge.** [➡BRIDGES, TUNNELS, CROSSINGS, AND JUNCTIONS; 1111]

beaming *adj* **smiling**, cheery, cheerful, sunny, genial, bright, warm, grinning. [➡FACIAL EXPRESSION; 652] *Opposite:* scowling.

bean *type of* **pulse.** [➡BEANS AND PULSES; 1188]

beanbag *n* **cushion**, floor cushion, pouf, seat, sag bag. [➡SOFT FURNISHINGS, LINEN, AND DRAPERY; 860]

be anchored in *v* **be based on**, be rooted in, be founded on, be grounded in. [➡BE ABOUT SOMETHING; 62]

beanfeast (*dated informal*) *n* [➡PARTIES, DANCES, AND CELEBRATIONS; 37]

be angry *v* **seethe**, fume, boil, rage, go berserk, lose control, lose your temper, have a fit (*informal*), go off the deep end, see red (*informal*), hit the roof, gnash your teeth. [➡GIVING VENT TO EMOTIONS; 680]

beanpole *n* **support**, stick, pole, post, cane, trellis. [➡STICKS, POLES, AND WEDGES; 1253]

bean sprout *type of* **salad vegetable.** [➡FRUIT AND VEGETABLES; 1175]

be appropriate *v* **be suitable**, be relevant, apply, be fitting, be apt, be applicable. [➡APPROPRIATE, SUITABLE, ADVISABLE; 185]

bear 1 *type of* **large mammal.** [➡LARGE MAMMAL; 986] 2 *v* **tolerate**, stand, put up with, stomach, accept, allow, swallow, abide, endure, suffer, go through. [➡TOLERATE AND ENDURE; 767] 3 *v* **support**, take, stand, sustain, hold, withstand. [➡HOLD AND CONTAIN; 456] 4 *v* **assume**, accept, shoulder, carry, take, take on, have. [➡ACCEPT POSSESSION; 451] *Opposite:* discard. 5 *v* **show**, display, exhibit, present, evince, manifest. [➡POSSESS; 445] 6 *v* **carry**, convey, bring, take, transport, move. [➡MOVE SOMETHING TO ANOTHER LOCATION; 325] 7 *v* **produce**, develop, yield, give birth, bring forth, create, bring about, bring into being, generate. [➡ENGENDER; 351]

bearable *adj* **manageable**, tolerable, endurable, acceptable, sufferable, supportable (*literary*). [➡ACCEPTABLE AND PASSABLE; 220] *Opposite:* unbearable.

bear a grudge *v* [➡DISLIKE AND HATE; 578]

beard 1 *n* **facial hair**, whiskers, goatee, bush, stubble. [➡FACIAL HAIR; 490] 2 *v* **challenge**, confront, accost, stand up to, face up to, oppose. [➡ACCUSE, BLAME, AND CRITICIZE; 642]

bearded *adj* **unshaven**, hirsute, hairy, whiskery, bewhiskered, bristly. [➡FACIAL HAIR; 490] *Opposite:* clean-shaven.

bearded dragon *type of* **reptile.** [➡REPTILES; 994]

beardless *adj* [➡FACIAL HAIR; 490]

bear down on 1 *v* **advance on**, close in on, converge on, march on, charge, draw near, approach, accost. [➡GET CLOSER TOGETHER; 311] *Opposite:* retreat. 2 *v* **push down**, press down, thrust, press, lean on, depress. [➡CONTACT: EXERT PRESSURE; 415]

bearer 1 *n* **carrier**, bringer, deliverer, conveyor, transporter, porter. [➡MESSENGERS AND COURIERS; 852] 2 *n* **holder**, possessor, owner, keeper, custodian, guardian. [➡OWNERS; 447]

bear false witness *v* [➡DECEPTION AND LIES; 661]

bear fruit *v* **succeed**, be successful, show results, produce results, pay off, work out, turn out well. [➡SUCCEED AND WIN; 79] *Opposite:* fail.

bear hug *n* **embrace**, cuddle, hug, clinch, squeeze. [➡PHYSICAL CONTACT AS COMMUNICATION; 656]

bearing 1 *n* **influence**, effect, impact, connection, relevance, sway. [➡IMPORTANCE AND SIGNIFICANCE; 193] 2 *n* **manner**, behaviour, attitude, comportment (*formal*), deportment (*formal*), demeanour, posture. [➡TEMPERAMENT AND BEHAVIOUR; 493] 3 *n* **compass reading**, direction, course, orientation, point of reference. [➡NAVIGATION; 1140]

bear in mind *v* **remember**, keep in mind, think of, consider, take into consideration, take into account, recall, recollect. [➡REMEMBER; 747] *Opposite:* forget.

bear out *v* **support**, verify, prove, substantiate, corroborate, uphold, validate, back up. [➡APPROVE AND CONFIRM; 647] *Opposite:* undermine.

bearskin 1 *type of* **fabric from animals.** [➡FABRICS; 1131] 2 *type of* **headgear.** [➡HABERDASHERY, MILLINERY, AND LINGERIE; 867]

bear the brunt *v* **receive the impact**, take the strain, receive the full force, bear the burden, bear the responsibility, be in the front line, stand fast, endure, tolerate. [➡TOLERATE AND ENDURE; 767]

bear up *v* **hold up**, hold out, cope, manage, get along, get by, survive. [➡CONTINUE TO EXIST; 17] *Opposite:* give in.

bear with *v* **be patient**, put up with, make allowance for, show forbearance, bear, stand, tolerate, accept, endure, forbear (*formal*). [➡TOLERATE AND ENDURE; 767]

be a sign of *v* **indicate**, reflect, herald, mark, signify, symbolize, be indicative of, portend, anticipate. [➡MEAN SOMETHING; 61]

beast 1 *n* **creature**, animal, being, living thing, quadruped. [➡LIVING THINGS AND LIVING; 976] 2 *n* **monster**, fiend, brute (*literary*), ogre, animal. [➡VILLAINS AND THUGS; 947]

beastly (*dated informal*) *adj* **horrid**, horrible, terrible, awful, foul, rotten, nasty, revolting, vile, dreadful, ghastly, appalling, objectionable, unpleasant. [➡BEASTLY AND BRUTISH; 511] *Opposite:* lovely.

be a success *v* **succeed**, be successful, do well, make it (*informal*), arrive, work out, be a winner, be a smash hit, score high marks, make out. [➡SUCCEED AND WIN; 79] *Opposite:* fail.

be a symbol of *v* **symbolize**, represent, stand for, embody, personify, epitomize, be a figurehead. [➡REPRESENT SOMETHING OR SOMEBODY; 59]

beat 1 *v* **defeat**, overcome, overwhelm, hammer (*informal*), thrash, trounce, outdo, outclass, get the better of, triumph over, wipe the floor with (*informal*), slaughter (*slang*), cream (*US informal*). [➡BEAT AND DEFEAT; 80] 2 *v* **hit**, strike, bang, hammer, thump, pound, punch, tap. [➡CONTACT: IMPACT; 414] 3 *v* **throb**, palpitate, thump, pound, pulsate, drum, thud, knock. [➡EMIT SOUNDS THROUGH IMPACT AND ABRASION; 366] 4 *v* **whisk**, whip, blend, mix, combine, stir, purée. [➡COOKING AND FOOD PREPARATION; 354] 5 *v* **surpass**, break, smash, do better than, go one better than, better, best, top, outstrip, outdo, outshine, outdistance, outperform, outrun. [➡BEAT AND DEFEAT; 80] 6 *n* **stroke**, blow, hit, bang, thump, knock, tap. [➡CONTACT: IMPACT; 414] 7 *n* **rhythm**, pulse, pulsation, throb, thump, drumming, stress. [➡IMPACT SOUNDS; 1259] 8 *adj* (*informal*) **tired**, tired out, worn out, weary, exhausted, dog-tired (*informal*), had it (*informal*), fit to drop (*informal*), ready to drop. [➡TIRED, ASLEEP AND UNCONSCIOUS; 739] *Opposite:* fresh.

See Compare and Contrast at **defeat.**

beat a hasty retreat *v* [➡RUN AWAY AND AVOID; 10]

beaten 1 *adj* **compressed**, packed down, trodden, flattened, crushed, trampled, compacted. [➡DENSITY AND CONSISTENCY; 1206] 2 *adj* **defeated**, conquered, crushed, vanquished. [➡BEATEN AND DEFEATED; 78]

beaten-up *adj* **scruffy**, battered, tatty, tattered, worn out, old, dilapidated, decrepit, shabby, weather-beaten. [➡IN BAD REPAIR; 1233] *Opposite:* pristine.

beater 1 *n* **whisk**, blade, attachment, paddle, stick. [➡TABLEWARE, CUTLERY, AND KITCHENWARE; 861] 2 *n* (*US informal*) **jalopy** (*dated informal*), rattletrap (*informal*), banger (*informal*), heap (*slang*), wreck. [➡BIKES, CARS, AND CARRIAGES; 1148]

beatific (*literary*) *adj* **blissful**, radiant, sublime, heavenly, serene, saintly, ecstatic. [➡FACIAL EXPRESSION; 652]

beatification *n* **sanctification**, canonization, sainting, elevation, blessing, consecration. [➡RELIGIONS AND RELIGIOUS PRACTICES; 778]

beatify *v* **sanctify**, bless, consecrate, canonize, saint. [➡CONFER STATUS; 459]

beating 1 *n* **thrashing**, whipping, thumping, pounding, hiding (*informal*), walloping (*informal*). [➡AGGRESSIVE EVENT; 39] 2 *n* **defeat**, setback, pasting (*informal*), thrashing, trouncing, hammering (*informal*). [➡BEAT AND DEFEAT; 80]

beat it (*informal*) *v* **clear off** (*informal*), go away, leave, be off, head off, retreat, depart, vamoose (*US slang*). [➡RUN AWAY AND AVOID; 10] *Opposite:* stay.

be at odds *v* **disagree**, be at loggerheads, be in disagreement, be fighting, be quarrelling, be at daggers drawn, be at each other's throats, be in conflict. [➡DISHARMONY; 157]

be attracted *v* **fall for**, fancy (*informal*), fall in love with, be smitten (*literary or humorous*), be infatuated with, have a crush on (*informal*), take to. [➡LIKE, LOVE, VALUE AND ENJOY; 579]

beat up (*informal*) *v* **attack**, assault, batter, mug, injure, hit, strike. [➡ PHYSICAL ATTACK AND PUNISHMENT; 416]

beat-up (*informal*) *adj* **battered**, tattered, tatty, dilapidated, decrepit, shabby, scruffy, worn out, weather-beaten, old, seen better days, ratty (*US informal*). [➡ IN BAD REPAIR; 1233] *Opposite:* pristine.

be at variance *v* **contradict**, be at odds, disagree with, be in opposition to, be in conflict. [➡ DISHARMONY; 157]

beau 1 *n* (*dated*) **boyfriend**, suitor (*formal*), admirer, steady (*informal*), swain (*literary*), lover, gallant (*archaic*), squire (*dated*). [➡ SEXUAL AND ROMANTIC RELATIONSHIPS; 964] 2 *n* (*archaic*) **fop**, peacock, swell (*dated informal*), dandy (*informal*), popinjay (*dated*), poseur. [➡ MALE PERSON; 934]

beau monde *n* [➡ RICH PEOPLE; 895]

beaut (*US informal*) *n* **smasher** (*informal*), beauty, stunner (*informal*), peach (*informal*), nice one, stonker (*slang*), knockout (*informal*). [➡ AMAZING THING; 212]

beauteous (*literary*) *adj* **lovely**, beautiful, gorgeous, exquisite, elegant, attractive, handsome. [➡ BEAUTY AND ATTRACTIVENESS; 190] *Opposite:* ugly.

beautification *n* **enhancement**, sprucing up, prettification, redecoration, embellishment, improvement, transformation, titivation, revamping, remodelling. [➡ IMPROVE APPEARANCE; 380]

beautiful 1 *adj* **good-looking**, lovely, gorgeous, stunning, striking, fine-looking, attractive, handsome, pretty. [➡ PEOPLE'S PHYSICAL APPEARANCE; 476] *Opposite:* ugly. 2 *adj* **lovely**, picturesque, scenic, delightful, charming, wonderful, exquisite, pleasing, superb, magnificent. [➡ BEAUTY AND ATTRACTIVENESS; 190] *Opposite:* unattractive.

See Compare and Contrast at **good-looking**.

beautifully 1 *adv* **attractively**, gorgeously, stunningly, handsomely, prettily, charmingly, exquisitely, strikingly. [➡ BEAUTY AND ATTRACTIVENESS; 190] *Opposite:* unattractively. 2 *adv* **wonderfully**, delightfully, brilliantly, superbly, magnificently, excellently, marvellously, skilfully. [➡ CORRECT; 183] *Opposite:* poorly.

beautiful people *n* [➡ RICH PEOPLE; 895]

beautify *v* **prettify**, smarten, enhance, remodel, spruce up, embellish, revamp, doll up (*informal*), redecorate, give a facelift, titivate. [➡ IMPROVE APPEARANCE; 380]

beauty 1 *n* **loveliness**, attractiveness, good looks, prettiness, exquisiteness, gorgeousness, splendour, magnificence. [➡ BEAUTY AND ATTRACTIVENESS; 190] *Opposite:* unattractiveness. 2 *n* **advantage**, attraction, benefit, plus (*informal*), upside. [➡ SOURCE OF HAPPINESS, PLEASURE, OR IMPROVEMENT; 210] *Opposite:* drawback.

beauty parlour *n* **beauty salon**, salon, beautician's, hair salon. [➡ RETAIL OUTLETS; 1082]

beauty product *n* [➡ MAKEUP AND BEAUTY PRODUCTS; 491]

beaver 1 *v* (*informal*) **work**, labour, toil, plug away (*informal*), exert yourself, keep at, persevere, persist. [➡ CONTINUE AN ACTION; 263] *Opposite:* laze around. 2 *type of* **rodent**. [➡ RODENT; 989]

be aware of *v* **appreciate**, understand, be familiar with, be acquainted with, be informed about, have knowledge of, be up-to-date with, be abreast of, know, sense, feel, notice. [➡ PAY ATTENTION; 766]

be blunt *v* **speak plainly**, lay it on the line (*informal*), call a spade a spade, be to the point, shoot from the hip (*slang*), be candid, be honest, be direct, be up-front (*informal*), be frank, be straightforward. [➡ EXPLAIN AND CLARIFY; 611]

bebop *type of* **popular music**. [➡ MUSIC, SONGS, AND SINGING; 907]

be bothered *v* **be alarmed**, be anxious, worry, be apprehensive, be concerned, be nervous. [➡ BE CONCERNED AND CARE; 582]

be burning to *v* **be dying to**, be desperate to, be yearning to, be eager to, be keen to, want madly to, be aching to. [➡ DESIRE AND WANT; 580]

becalmed *adj* **stuck**, at a standstill, stationary, at a halt, marooned, stranded, in the doldrums. [➡ LACK OF ACTIVITY; 343] *Opposite:* on the move.

be carried away *v* **be overcome**, be moved, be overwhelmed, be enraptured (*formal*), be transported, be over the moon, be swept off your feet, be caught up. [➡ CHANGE OF MOOD AND COMPOSURE; 581]

because *conj* **since**, as, for. [➡ CAUSATION; 169]

be caused by *v* **result from**, arise from, arise out of, be an effect of, follow from, stem from, develop out of. [➡ CAUSATION; 169]

because of *prep* **owing to**, on account of, as a consequence of, due to, as a result of. [➡ CAUSATION; 169] *Opposite:* despite.

béchamel sauce *type of* **seasonings, sauces, and dips**. [➡ SEASONINGS AND SAUCES; 1173]

beck *n* **brook**, stream, rivulet, burn. [➡ RIVERS, LAKES, AND STREAMS; 1042]

beckon *v* **signal**, sign, summon, gesture, indicate, motion. [➡ GESTURES AND GESTICULATION; 654] *Opposite:* dismiss.

be close to *v* **border on**, verge on, come close to, approach, be similar to, be almost, approximate. [➡ SEEM TO BE SOMETHING; 58]

become 1 *v* **turn out to be**, turn into, develop, convert, grow into, come to be. [➡ GRADUALLY COME INTO EXISTENCE; 1] 2 *v* **suit**, befit, flatter, enhance, show off, show to advantage. [➡ IMPROVE SOMETHING; 375]

become acquainted *v* **meet**, meet for the first time, be introduced to, make somebody's acquaintance, get to know. [➡ ESTABLISHING RELATIONSHIPS WITH OTHERS; 974]

become aware of *v* **notice**, detect, discern, make out, sense, perceive, observe. [➡ LEARN AND DISCOVER; 763] *Opposite:* miss.

become of *v* **happen to**, befall (*archaic or literary*), come somebody's way. [➡ HAPPEN TO SOMEBODY; 30]

becoming 1 *adj* **flattering**, attractive, fetching, charming, pretty, pleasant. [➡BEAUTY AND ATTRACTIVENESS; 190] *Opposite:* unattractive. 2 *adj* **suitable**, appropriate, apt, fitting, befitting, in keeping, right, seemly. [➡APPROPRIATE, SUITABLE, ADVISABLE; 185] *Opposite:* inappropriate.

be compatible 1 *v* **get on with**, get on well with, be well-suited, be like-minded, be in harmony with, be attuned to, relate well to, have affinities with, get along with (*US*). [➡HARMONY; 156] *Opposite:* clash. 2 *v* **be reconcilable**, be consistent with, be in keeping with, be in line with, match, coincide, corroborate, tally. [➡HARMONY; 156] *Opposite:* contradict.

be concerned *v* **worry**, be anxious, be perturbed, be bothered, be troubled, care, sweat (*informal*). [➡BE CONCERNED AND CARE; 582]

be consistent with *v* **tally**, coincide with, match, bear out, corroborate, be in sync with (*informal*). [➡EQUALITY; 155] *Opposite:* contradict.

be crazy about (*informal*) *v* **adore**, love, be besotted with, be nuts about (*slang*), be passionate about, fall for, be all over, be mad about. [➡LIKE, LOVE, VALUE AND ENJOY; 579] *Opposite:* hate.

bed 1 *n* **plot**, flowerbed, patch, border. [➡GARDENS; 1073] 2 *n* **layer**, band, base, stratum (*formal*), strip, seam. [➡COVERS AND COATINGS; 1245] 3 *n* **bottom**, floor, base, seabed, riverbed. [➡EXTREMITIES OF PHYSICAL OBJECTS; 1249]

bed

◆ *types of bed*
bassinet, berth, bunk, bunk bed, camp bed, carrycot, cot, couchette, cradle, crib (*US*), day bed, divan, double bed, four-poster, futon, hammock, king-size bed, Moses basket, Murphy bed (*US*), queen-size bed, single bed, sofa bed, studio couch, trundle bed, twin bed, water bed

bed and board *n* [➡ACCOMMODATION; 855]

bed and breakfast *type of* **hotel**. [➡HOTELS, RESTAURANTS, AND CLUBS; 1081]

bedazzle *v* [➡CONFUSE AND BEWILDER; 572]

bedazzled (*literary*) *adj* **bewildered**, dazed, bemused, amazed, confused, stunned, stupefied, impressed. [➡APPRECIATION AND GRATITUDE; 536] *Opposite:* unimpressed.

bedbug *type of* **parasitic insect**. [➡PARASITES; 1017]

bedchamber (*archaic or literary*) *type of* **room in the home**. [➡TYPES OF ROOM; 1096]

bedclothes *n* **bedcovers**, bedding, bed linen, sheet, blanket, eiderdown, duvet, quilt, comforter (*US*). [➡SOFT FURNISHINGS, LINEN, AND DRAPERY; 860]

bedcovers *n* **bed linen**, bedclothes, bedding, sheet, blanket, eiderdown, duvet, quilt, comforter (*US*), counterpane (*dated*), throw, coverlet. [➡SOFT FURNISHINGS, LINEN, AND DRAPERY; 860]

bedding *n* **bedclothes**, bedcovers, bed linen, sheet, blanket, eiderdown, duvet, quilt, comforter (*US*), covers. [➡SOFT FURNISHINGS, LINEN, AND DRAPERY; 860]

bedeck (*literary*) *v* **decorate**, festoon, adorn, ornament, deck (*literary*), deck out, garland, bejewel (*literary*), bedizen (*literary*). [➡DECORATE, ADORN, AND APPLY COATINGS; 406] *Opposite:* strip.

bedecked (*literary*) *adj* **decorated**, festooned, adorned, ornamented, decked out, decked (*literary*), bejewelled (*literary*), garlanded, bedizened (*literary*). [➡DECORATE, ADORN, AND APPLY COATINGS; 406] *Opposite:* stripped.

bedevil *v* [➡ANGER AND ANNOY; 570]

bedhead *n* **headboard**, rail, bedrail, bed end, bedpost. [➡FURNITURE; 858]

bedlam *n* **chaos**, mayhem (*informal*), pandemonium, confusion, anarchy, disorder, disarray, turmoil, commotion, uproar. [➡CHAOS AND UPROAR; 51] *Opposite:* order.

bed linen *n* **bedding**, bedclothes, bedcovers, sheet, blanket, pillowcase, covers. [➡SOFT FURNISHINGS, LINEN, AND DRAPERY; 860]

bed of roses *n* [➡PLEASANT SITUATIONS; 74]

bedpan *n* **chamber pot**, pot (*informal*), potty (*informal*), commode, receptacle. [➡CONTAINERS, RECEPTACLES, AND PACKAGING; 1244]

bedraggled *adj* **unkempt**, dishevelled, untidy, messy, scruffy, grubby, in a state (*informal*). [➡BADLY GROOMED; 484] *Opposite:* neat.

bedridden *adj* **confined to bed**, flat on your back, laid up, incapacitated, disabled, out of action. [➡UNFIT AND WEAK; 740] *Opposite:* up and about.

bedrock 1 *n* **rock layer**, substratum, solid rock, base, foundation. [➡SUPPORTS AND BASES; 1254] 2 *n* **basis**, base, core, heart, root, foundation, anchor. [➡MOST IMPORTANT THING; 198]

bedroom *n* **sleeping quarters**, dorm (*informal*), dormitory, boudoir, bedchamber (*archaic or literary*), chamber (*archaic or literary*), room. [➡TYPES OF ROOM; 1096]

bedside lamp *n* [➡LIGHTING; 862]

bedside manner *n* **rapport**, style, approach, relationship, comportment (*formal*), behaviour, conduct. [➡TEMPERAMENT AND BEHAVIOUR; 493]

bedside table *type of* **table**. [➡FURNITURE; 858]

bedsit *n* **flat**, studio flat, bedsitter, bedsitting room, studio apartment, studio, room, apartment (*US*). [➡RESIDENTIAL BUILDINGS; 1077]

bedsitter *n type of* **apartment**. [➡RESIDENTIAL BUILDINGS; 1077]

bedsitting room *type of* **apartment**. [➡RESIDENTIAL BUILDINGS; 1077]

bedsore *n* **ulcer**, pressure sore, decubitus ulcer (*technical*), ulceration, sore, bruise. [➡CONDITIONS AFFECTING THE SKIN; 722]

bedspread *n* **coverlet**, cover, quilt, throw, eiderdown, counterpane (*dated*), spread, comforter (*US*). [➡SOFT FURNISHINGS, LINEN, AND DRAPERY; 860]

bedstead *n* **bedframe**, frame, base, pallet, bed. [➡FURNITURE; 858]

bedtime *n* **time to retire**, time to turn in (*informal*), time for bed, time to hit the hay (*informal*), time to hit the sack (*informal*), sleep time. [➡TIMES OF DAY; 87]

bee *type of* **flying insect**. [➡FLYING INSECTS; 1013]

beech *type of* **deciduous tree**. [➡DECIDUOUS TREES; 1028]

beef 1 *type of* **meat**. [➡TYPES AND CUTS OF MEAT; 1176] 2 *n* (*slang*) **complaint**, grumble, moan (*informal*), bellyache (*informal*), grouse (*informal*), gripe (*informal*), whinge (*informal*). [➡COMPLAIN AND NAG; 687] 3 *v* (*slang*) **complain**, grumble, moan (*informal*), bellyache (*informal*), grouse (*informal*), gripe (*informal*), whinge (*informal*), carp, chunter (*informal*), whine. [➡COMPLAIN AND NAG; 687] *Opposite:* praise.

beefiness *n* **muscularity**, sturdiness, burliness, brawniness, stockiness, bulkiness. [➡MUSCLES AND MUSCULATURE; 480]

beefsteak fungus *type of* **fungus**. [➡MICROORGANISMS, FUNGI, AND ALGAE; 1023]

beef up (*informal*) *v* **strengthen**, improve, enhance, boost, reinforce, upgrade, build up. [➡IMPROVE STRENGTH AND DURABILITY; 379] *Opposite:* weaken.

beefy *adj* **muscular**, strapping (*informal*), brawny, heavy, hefty, burly, sturdy, well built, powerfully built, big, thickset. [➡MUSCLES AND MUSCULATURE; 480] *Opposite:* puny.

beehive 1 *n* **apiary**, hive, skep. [➡ANIMAL OR BIRD ACCOMMODATION; 1078] 2 *type of* **hairstyle**. [➡HAIR STYLES AND HAIR PIECES; 489]

beep 1 *n* **peep**, toot, parp, bleep, beep-beep, honk, hoot. [➡RINGING AND TOOTING SOUNDS; 1258] 2 *v* **toot**, peep, parp, bleep, beep-beep, honk, hoot. [➡EMIT CONTINUOUS SOUNDS; 367] 3 *type of* **continuous sound**. [➡CONTINUOUS SOUNDS; 1257]

beeper (*informal*) *n* **pager**, bleeper, monitor. [➡TELECOMMUNICATIONS; 1129]

beer belly (*slang*) *n* [➡EXTRA WEIGHT; 479]

beer gut (*slang*) *n* [➡EXTRA WEIGHT; 479]

beermat *n* **coaster**, mat, rest, bar cloth. [➡COVERS AND COATINGS; 1245]

beet *n* **sugar beet**, beetroot, chard, Swiss chard, mangelwurzel. [➡FRUIT AND VEGETABLES; 1175]

beetle 1 (*informal*) *v* **hurry**, scurry, scuttle, scoot (*informal*), scud, dart. [➡MOVE FAST; 314] 2 *type of* **insect**. [➡INSECTS; 1012]

beetle

◆ *types of beetle*
cockroach, Colorado beetle, Colorado potato beetle (*US*), deathwatch beetle, dung beetle, flea beetle, Japanese beetle, ladybird, ladybug (*US*), rhinoceros beetle, roach (*informal*), scarab, stag beetle, water beetle, weevil

beetroot *type of* **root vegetable**. [➡FRUIT AND VEGETABLES; 1175]

befall (*archaic or literary*) *v* **happen**, occur, take place, come about, transpire, come to pass (*archaic or literary*), ensue. [➡HAPPEN TO SOMEBODY; 30]

befit *v* **suit**, become, be fitting, be suitable for, be appropriate, be right. [➡APPROPRIATE, SUITABLE, ADVISABLE; 185]

befitting *adj* **becoming**, suitable, appropriate, apt, fitting, in keeping, right, seemly. [➡APPROPRIATE, SUITABLE, ADVISABLE; 185] *Opposite:* unsuitable.

before 1 *prep* **in front of**, facing, ahead of, afore (*regional*). [➡RELATIVE LOCATION; 162] *Opposite:* behind. 2 *prep* **previous to**, earlier than, sooner than, prior to, ahead of, by, afore (*regional*). [➡BEFORE, FIRST, AND PRECEDING; 164] *Opposite:* after. 3 *adv* **beforehand**, previously, earlier, in advance, in the past, already, formerly, afore (*regional*). [➡BEFORE, FIRST, AND PRECEDING; 164] *Opposite:* afterwards.

beforehand *adv* **earlier**, in advance, before, early, ahead of time. [➡PROMPTNESS: EARLY; 98] *Opposite:* late.

before long *adv* **soon**, in a short time, in a little while, shortly, after a short time, after a while, by and by (*literary*). [➡FUTURE; 86]

before now *adv* **by now**, already, before this time, in the past, previously, before. [➡BEFORE, FIRST, AND PRECEDING; 164]

befriend *v* **make friends with**, take care of, look after, help, assist, support. [➡ESTABLISHING RELATIONSHIPS WITH OTHERS; 974] *Opposite:* shun.

befuddle *v* **confuse**, muddle, mix up, bewilder, baffle, puzzle, stupefy, perplex, stump, flummox (*informal*), nonplus, confound. [➡CONFUSE AND BEWILDER; 572] *Opposite:* enlighten.

befuddled *adj* **confused**, muddled, baffled, puzzled, perplexed, stumped, flummoxed (*informal*), nonplussed. [➡CONFUSION, ANXIETY, AND WORRY; 541] *Opposite:* clear.

befuddlement *n* **confusion**, perplexity, bewilderment, bafflement, puzzlement. [➡CONFUSION, ANXIETY, AND WORRY; 541] *Opposite:* clarity.

beg *v* **ask for**, request, plead, solicit, implore (*formal*), supplicate (*formal*), beseech (*literary*), entreat (*formal*). [➡REQUEST AND DEMAND; 664]

beget *v* **cause**, bring about, precipitate, create, bring, produce, result in, lead to. [➡CAUSE TO HAPPEN; 31]

beg forgiveness *v* [➡APOLOGIZE AND RETRACT; 684]

beggar 1 *n* **mendicant**, scrounger (*informal*), homeless person, vagabond, vagrant, tramp, street dweller, panhandler (*US*), bum (*informal*). [➡POOR PEOPLE; 896] 2 *v* **defy**, be beyond, confound, surpass, exceed, defeat. [➡BEAT AND DEFEAT; 80]

begin 1 *v* **start**, start on, commence (*formal*), start in on, set in motion, set in train, embark on. [➡START AN ACTION; 261] *Opposite:* finish. 2 *v* **bring into being**, instigate, initiate, inaugurate, activate, create, set off, set up, come into being, arise, start off, originate. [➡CAUSE TO START; 266] 3 *v* **start the ball rolling**, get down to, get to, get underway, set off, kick off (*informal*), open, start, commence (*formal*), launch. [➡START AN ACTION; 261] *Opposite:* end.

beginner *n* **novice**, learner, trainee, apprentice,

student, pupil, tyro, greenhorn. [➡UNSKILLED PERSON; 531] *Opposite:* old hand.

Compare and Contrast: ***beginner, apprentice, greenhorn, novice, trainee, tyro***

CORE MEANING: A PERSON WHO HAS NOT ACQUIRED THE NECESSARY EXPERIENCE OR SKILLS TO DO SOMETHING

beginner somebody who has just started to learn or do something; ***apprentice*** somebody who is being taught the skills of a trade over an agreed period of time by somebody fully trained; ***greenhorn*** somebody who lacks experience and may be naïve or gullible; ***novice*** somebody with no previous experience or skill in the activity undertaken; ***trainee*** somebody who is being trained to do a job; ***tyro*** somebody who is raw and inexperienced.

beginning *n* **start**, commencement (*formal*), opening, launch, establishment, creation, inauguration, initiation, activation, introduction, instigation. [➡BEGINNING; 53] *Opposite:* end.

beg off *v* [➡NOT DO AND REFUSE TO DO; 275]

begonia *type of* **perennial flower.** [➡FLOWERS FROM BULBS; 1030]

begrime (*literary*) *v* [➡DIRTY AND CONTAMINATE; 405]

begrimed (*literary*) *adj* [➡DIRTY; 1234]

begrudge *v* **resent**, envy, be envious, be jealous, be resentful, grudge. [➡DISLIKE AND HATE; 578]

begrudging *adj* [➡REBELLIOUSNESS AND DISOBEDIENCE; 566]

beg to differ *v* [➡DENY AND REJECT; 645]

beguile *v* **entice**, lure, charm, captivate, mesmerize, hypnotize, fascinate, enthral, put under a spell, appeal to, attract. [➡APPEAL TO AND AROUSE INTEREST; 576]

beguiled *adj* [➡PENSIVENESS AND INTEREST; 539]

beguilement *n* [➡ATTENTION AND ATTENTIVENESS; 764]

beguiling *adj* **enticing**, charming, mesmeric, fascinating, captivating, enthralling, appealing, attractive, charismatic, mesmerizing. [➡BEAUTY AND ATTRACTIVENESS; 190]

behave 1 *v* **act**, perform, conduct yourself, deport yourself, comport yourself (*formal*), work, run. [➡CARRY OUT AN ACTION; 270] 2 *v* **be good**, obey the rules, do the right thing, toe the line, keep out of mischief, mind your p's and q's. [➡OBEY AND ABIDE BY; 302] *Opposite:* misbehave.

behaviour *n* **performance**, actions, deeds, activities, manners, conduct, comportment (*formal*). [➡TEMPERAMENT AND BEHAVIOUR; 493]

behavioural *adj* **social**, interactive, communication, communicative, negotiating, developmental, behaviour. [➡PSYCHOLOGY AND THE MIND; 770]

behead *v* **decapitate**, guillotine, execute, put to death, cut off somebody's head, top (*slang*), kill. [➡KILL; 923]

behemoth *n* [➡BIG THINGS; 1193]

behest (*formal*) *n* **request**, order, command, bidding, directive, call. [➡REQUEST AND DEMAND; 664]

behind 1 *prep* **following**, after, in the wake of, at the back of, at the rear of. [➡RELATIVE LOCATION; 162] 2 *adv* **at the back**, at the rear, after, following, last, in the rear (*US*). [➡RELATIVE LOCATION; 162] *Opposite:* in front. 3 *adj* **behindhand**, late, overdue, behind schedule, in arrears. [➡PROMPTNESS: LATE; 100] *Opposite:* ahead of time.

behind closed doors *adv* **privately**, in private, in secret, secretly, confidentially, in secrecy. [➡SECRET AND UNKNOWN; 180] *Opposite:* openly.

behindhand *adj* **late**, behind, behind schedule, overdue, slow, in arrears. [➡PROMPTNESS: LATE; 100] *Opposite:* early.

behind schedule *adj* **behind**, late, slow, delayed, overdue, behindhand. [➡PROMPTNESS: LATE; 100] *Opposite:* early.

behind the scenes *adv* **out of sight**, surreptitiously, unobtrusively, unnoticed, in the background, quietly. [➡SECRET AND UNKNOWN; 180] *Opposite:* openly.

behind the times *adj* **old-fashioned**, dated, unfashionable, out-of-date, outmoded, old, old hat (*informal*), outdated. [➡OLD, OLD-FASHIONED; 168]

behind your back *adv* **without your knowledge**, furtively, surreptitiously, on the sly, slyly, secretively, sneakily. [➡SECRET AND UNKNOWN; 180] *Opposite:* openly.

behold (*archaic or literary*) *v* **look at**, look on, see, observe, witness, feast your eyes on. [➡LOOKING AND LOOKS; 701]

beholden *adj* **obliged**, grateful, in somebody's debt, indebted, obligated, bound. [➡RELATIONSHIP TO ANOTHER; 973]

behove (*formal*) *v* **be somebody's duty**, be somebody's bounden duty, fall to somebody, befit, be incumbent upon somebody (*formal*), be appropriate for, be fitting for. [➡APPROPRIATE, SUITABLE, ADVISABLE; 185]

beige *type of* **colour.** [➡COLOURS; 1223]

beige

◆ *types of beige*
buff, butterscotch, café au lait, camel, coffee, dun, ecru, fawn, flesh colour, honey, oatmeal

be in charge of *v* **control**, run, manage, head, lead, direct, operate, oversee, supervise, preside. [➡BE IN CHARGE; 271]

be in contact with *v* **be in touch with**, communicate, have dealings with, correspond, interact with. [➡INITIATE AND ESTABLISH COMMUNICATION; 681] *Opposite:* ignore.

being 1 *n* **existence**, life, actuality, presence, animation. [➡THE STAGES OF LIFE; 916] *Opposite:* nothingness. 2 *n* **self**, soul, mind, essence, spirit, core, heart, nature, personality, consciousness. [➡PSYCHOLOGY AND THE MIND; 770] 3 *n* **life form**, organism, creature, living being, human being, person, individual, mortal. [➡LIVING THINGS AND LIVING; 976]

belabour 1 *v* **overemphasize**, overdo, overstate, labour, stress, harp on, hammer home. [➡CLAIM, INSIST, AND EMPHASIZE;

615] 2 *v* (*literary or humorous*) **hit**, thrash, whip, cudgel, bludgeon, beat. [➡PHYSICAL ATTACK AND PUNISHMENT; 416]

belated *adj* **late**, delayed, postponed, deferred, tardy, overdue. [➡PROMPTNESS: LATE; 100] *Opposite:* timely.

belatedness *n* [➡PROMPTNESS: LATE; 100]

belch 1 *v* **bring up wind**, burp, hiccup, eruct (*technical*), posset, gulp. [➡VOMIT AND BELCH; 713] 2 *n* **burp**, hiccup, eructation (*technical*). [➡VOMIT AND BELCH; 713]

beleaguer 1 *v* **harass**, annoy, pester, plague, badger, hound, vex, hassle (*informal*), worry, stress. [➡UPSET, DISTRESS, AND HUMILIATE; 568] 2 *v* **besiege**, surround, lay siege to, threaten, menace. [➡EXIST IN CLOSE PROXIMITY; 21]

beleaguered *adj* **stressed**, under pressure, harassed, fraught, careworn, struggling, besieged, under attack, long-suffering. [➡SADNESS, DISTRESS, AND DESPAIR; 540] *Opposite:* carefree.

belfry *n* **bell tower**, campanile, tower, spire, steeple. [➡TOWERS; 1098]

belie *v* **contradict**, disprove, give the lie to, call into question, deny, oppose. [➡DISHARMONY; 157] *Opposite:* confirm.

belief 1 *n* **faith**, conviction, principle, creed, idea. [➡POINT OF VIEW; 768] 2 *n* **confidence**, trust, certainty, credence, acceptance. [➡CERTAINTY; 562] *Opposite:* distrust.

belief system *n* [➡POINT OF VIEW; 768]

believability *n* **credibility**, plausibility, acceptability, trustworthiness, authenticity. [➡TRUE AND REAL; 172]

believable *adj* **credible**, authentic, realistic, plausible, convincing, acceptable, true to life. [➡POSSIBLE AND PROBABLE; 178] *Opposite:* unbelievable.

believe 1 *v* **trust**, have faith in, be certain of, have confidence in, accept as true, rely on. [➡CERTAINTY; 562] *Opposite:* disbelieve. 2 *v* **consider**, think, suppose, deem (*formal*), judge, imagine. [➡HAVE AN OPINION OF SOMETHING; 757] *Opposite:* doubt.

believer *n* **supporter**, advocate, fan, devotee, follower, disciple. [➡RELIGIOUS PEOPLE; 779] *Opposite:* sceptic.

belittle *v* **disparage**, demean, decry (*formal*), deride, put down (*informal*), depreciate, rubbish (*informal*). [➡UPSET, DISTRESS, AND HUMILIATE; 568] *Opposite:* praise.

belittlement *n* **depreciation**, disparagement, playing down, marginalization, disdain. [➡INSULTS, ABUSE, AND SWEARING; 659] *Opposite:* praise.

belittling *adj* **demeaning**, disparaging, depreciating, condescending, patronizing, sneering, derisive. [➡MOCKING AND DISMISSIVE; 637] *Opposite:* supportive.

bell 1 *n* **hand bell**, church bell, ship's bell, sleigh bell, school bell, alarm bell. [➡SIGNALLING; 1139] 2 *n* (*informal*) **call**, ring, buzz (*informal*), tinkle (*informal*), phone call, telephone call. [➡TELEPHONE COMMUNICATION; 48] 3 *n* **buzzer**, doorbell, chime, alarm, alarm bell. [➡SIGNALLING; 1139]

bell-bottom trousers *type of* **trousers**. [➡GARMENTS AND OUTFITS; 865]

bellicose *adj* **belligerent**, aggressive, warlike, pugnacious, combative, confrontational, argumentative, quarrelsome. [➡AGGRESSIVE AND BELLIGERENT; 519] *Opposite:* compliant.

bellicosity *n* [➡AGGRESSIVE AND BELLIGERENT; 519]

belligerence *n* **hostility**, pugnaciousness, bellicosity, warlike nature, aggression, ferociousness, violence, antagonism, argumentativeness. [➡AGGRESSIVE AND BELLIGERENT; 519]

belligerency *see* **belligerence**.

belligerent *adj* **aggressive**, argumentative, quarrelsome, loudmouthed (*informal*), confrontational, pugnacious, spoiling for a fight, cantankerous, stroppy (*informal*). [➡AGGRESSIVE AND BELLIGERENT; 519] *Opposite:* cooperative.

belligerently *adv* **aggressively**, pugnaciously, bellicosely, antagonistically, ferociously, violently, argumentatively. [➡RUDE AND HOSTILE; 626] *Opposite:* cooperatively.

bellow 1 *v* **shout**, roar, yell, bawl, holler (*informal*), thunder. [➡GIVING VENT TO EMOTIONS; 680] *Opposite:* whisper. 2 *n* **roar**, shout, yell, bawl, holler (*informal*). [➡SOUNDS MADE BY PEOPLE; 1261] *Opposite:* whisper.

bellows *type of* **general tool**. [➡HAND TOOLS; 1118]

bell-shaped *adj* [➡ROUNDED SHAPE; 1217]

bell tower *n* [➡TOWERS; 1098]

belly *n* (*informal*) **stomach**, abdomen, tummy (*informal*), middle, gut (*slang disapproving*). [➡TORSO; 694]

bellyache (*informal*) 1 *n* **upset stomach**, stomach ache, stomach pains, tummy ache (*informal*). [➡DISORDERS OF THE DIGESTIVE SYSTEM; 714] 2 *n* **complaint**, moan (*informal*), grumble, grouse (*informal*), gripe (*informal*), whinge (*informal*), beef (*slang*). [➡COMPLAIN AND NAG; 687] 3 *v* **complain**, moan (*informal*), grumble, grouse (*informal*), gripe (*informal*), whinge (*informal*), carp, chunter (*informal*), beef (*slang*), whine. [➡COMPLAIN AND NAG; 687]

bellybutton (*informal*) *n* **navel**, tummy button (*informal*), umbilicus (*technical*). [➡TORSO; 694]

belly dance *type of* **dance**. [➡DANCE; 903]

belly flop *n* **fall**, flop, crash, dive. [➡FAILURE; 77]

belly laugh *n* **guffaw**, laugh, chortle, horselaugh, hoot, cry of mirth. [➡LAUGHTER; 650]

belong *v* **fit in**, fit, go, have its place, be in the right place, feel right, be appropriate. [➡HARMONY; 156]

belongings *n* **possessions**, property, things, stuff, bits and pieces (*informal*), bits and bobs (*informal*), luggage, baggage, effects (*formal*), personal effects. [➡POSSESSIONS; 462]

beloved *adj* **much-loved**, dearly loved, adored, favourite, darling, treasured, dear, cherished. [➡POPULAR AND WANTED; 221] *Opposite:* despised.

below 1 *prep* **less than**, under, beneath (*formal*), not more than. [➡LESS; 124] 2 *adv* **underneath**, under, beneath (*formal*), lower, inferior to. [➡INFERIORITY; 154] *Opposite:* above.

3 *adv* **under**, underneath, beneath (*formal*), lower than, further down. [➡RELATIVE LOCATION; 162] *Opposite:* above.

below average *adj* [➡INAPPROPRIATE AND UNSUITABLE; 225]

below par 1 *adj* (*informal*) **poorly** (*informal*), unwell, under the weather, not yourself, not a hundred percent, out of sorts, run-down, ill. [➡UNFIT AND WEAK; 740] *Opposite:* healthy. 2 *adj* **unsatisfactory**, unacceptable, second-rate, poor, disappointing, not up to scratch (*informal*), inadequate. [➡ORDINARINESS; 245] *Opposite:* satisfactory. 3 *adj* (*informal*) **poor**, below average, substandard, inferior, not up to scratch (*informal*), weak. [➡INAPPROPRIATE AND UNSUITABLE; 225] *Opposite:* superior.

below standard *adj* [➡INAPPROPRIATE AND UNSUITABLE; 225]

belt 1 *n* **girdle**, tie, sash, cummerbund, strap, drawstring, binding, restraint. [➡FASTENERS, LINKS, AND NETWORKS; 1246] 2 *n* **band**, ring, strip, ribbon, line, stretch, stripe. [➡AMOUNT OF SOLID OR SEMI-SOLID; 115] 3 *v* (*informal*) **hit**, thump, thrash, beat, strike, smash, smack, punch. [➡PHYSICAL ATTACK AND PUNISHMENT; 416] 4 *v* **fasten**, buckle, secure, attach, belt up. [➡FASTEN, LINK, AND JOIN; 409] *Opposite:* undo. 5 *v* (*informal*) **dash**, rush, speed, hurry, race. [➡MOVE FAST; 314] *Opposite:* dawdle. 6 *type of* **accessory**. [➡HABERDASHERY, MILLINERY, AND LINGERIE; 867]

belt up 1 *v* (*slang*) **be quiet**, shut up, keep quiet, shut it (*informal*), quieten down, put a sock in it (*slang*). [➡WITHHOLD INFORMATION; 688] 2 *v* **fasten your belt**, secure your belt, put on your belt, buckle up. [➡FASTEN, LINK, AND JOIN; 409]

beltway (*US*) *type of* **major road**. [➡ROADS; 1105]

bemoan *v* **lament**, bewail (*formal*), regret, mourn, complain, moan (*informal*), grumble. [➡COMPLAIN AND NAG; 687] *Opposite:* applaud.

bemuse *v* **confuse**, daze, puzzle, perplex, stun, overwhelm, muddle. [➡CONFUSE AND BEWILDER; 572]

bemused *adj* **confused**, puzzled, mystified, bewildered, perplexed, baffled. [➡CONFUSION, ANXIETY, AND WORRY; 541] *Opposite:* clear-headed.

bemusement *n* [➡SURPRISE, SHOCK, AND AMAZEMENT; 546]

bemusing *adj* [➡DIFFICULTY AND COMPLEXITY; 243]

bench 1 *n* **seat**, form, pew, stall. [➡FURNITURE; 858] 2 *n* **worktable**, counter, work surface, worktop, workbench. [➡FURNITURE; 858]

benchmark *n* **standard**, yardstick, level, target, point of reference. [➡PERFECT EXAMPLES AND EMBODIMENTS; 67]

bend 1 *v* **stoop**, bow, bend over, lean down, lean over, incline your body. [➡ASSUME A POSITION; 318] *Opposite:* straighten up. 2 *v* **turn**, bow, twist, crook, change direction, bear. [➡CHANGE OF SHAPE; 386] *Opposite:* straighten. 3 *n* **curve**, turn, crook, twist, curvature, bow, corner. [➡ROUNDED SHAPE; 1217]

bendability *n* [➡MALLEABLE AND ELASTIC; 1211]

bendable *adj* **bendy**, flexible, pliant, pliable, malleable, plastic, supple. [➡MALLEABLE AND ELASTIC; 1211] *Opposite:* inflexible.

bendiness *n* [➡MALLEABLE AND ELASTIC; 1211]

bend over backwards *v* **do all you can**, put yourself out, pull out all the stops, do your utmost, go all out, make a supreme effort, give your all, try your best. [➡HARD WORK OR EFFORT; 299]

bendy *adj* **flexible**, malleable, plastic, supple, bendable. [➡MALLEABLE AND ELASTIC; 1211] *Opposite:* stiff.

beneath (*formal*) 1 *prep* **under**, underneath, below, lower than, less than. [➡RELATIVE LOCATION; 162] *Opposite:* over. 2 *adv* **underneath**, under, below, lower, less. [➡RELATIVE LOCATION; 162] *Opposite:* above.

benediction *n* **approval**, sanction, blessing. [➡SOURCE OF HAPPINESS, PLEASURE, OR IMPROVEMENT; 210]. *Opposite:* malediction (*formal*).

benefactor *n* **sponsor**, patron, supporter, backer. [➡REPRESENTATIVES AND PATRONS; 968]

beneficence *n* **generosity**, charity, benevolence, big-heartedness, magnanimity, kindness, goodness. [➡GENEROSITY AND KINDNESS; 496] *Opposite:* stinginess.

beneficent 1 *adj* **charitable**, altruistic, generous, benevolent, humanitarian, philanthropic. [➡GENEROSITY AND KINDNESS; 496] *Opposite:* self-seeking. 2 *adj* **beneficial**, helpful, useful, advantageous, valuable, favourable. [➡USEFULNESS; 200]. *Opposite:* deleterious (*formal*).

beneficial *adj* **helpful**, useful, valuable, advantageous, positive, favourable, of assistance, of use, constructive. [➡USEFULNESS; 200] *Opposite:* detrimental.

beneficiary *n* **recipient**, receiver, heir, payee, legatee. [➡OWNERS; 447] *Opposite:* benefactor.

benefit 1 *n* **advantage**, profit, help, assistance, use, value. [➡SOURCE OF HAPPINESS, PLEASURE, OR IMPROVEMENT; 210] *Opposite:* detriment. 2 *n* **subsidy**, allowance, payment, grant. [➡SOCIAL WELFARE; 812] 3 *n* **fundraiser**, charity performance, charity event. [➡PARTIES, DANCES, AND CELEBRATIONS; 37] 4 *v* **help**, promote, profit, do good to, advance, further, aid. [➡IMPROVE SOMETHING; 375] *Opposite:* harm.

benefit from *v* **profit from**, enjoy, use, gain from, take advantage of. [➡GET; 421]

benevolence *n* **kindness**, compassion, generosity, munificence, goodwill, altruism, magnanimity. [➡KIND ACTION OR BEHAVIOUR; 296] *Opposite:* malevolence.

benevolent *adj* **kind**, caring, compassionate, generous, giving, kindly, benign, munificent, altruistic. [➡GENEROSITY AND KINDNESS; 496] *Opposite:* malevolent.

benighted *adj* **ignorant**, unenlightened, unfortunate, disadvantaged. [➡NEGATIVE INTELLECTUAL CHARACTERISTICS; 526] *Opposite:* enlightened.

benign *adj* **kind**, benevolent, caring, kindly, gentle, nonthreatening, compassionate. [➡GENEROSITY AND KINDNESS; 496] *Opposite:* malignant.

benignity *n* **kindliness**, gentleness, benevolence, compassion, warm-heartedness. [➡GENEROSITY AND KINDNESS; 496] *Opposite:* malice.

be no more *v* **cease to exist**, disappear, die off, die out, peter out, vanish, become extinct, fade away. [➡CEASE TO EXIST; 22] *Opposite:* come into being.

bent 1 *adj* **twisted**, curved, bowed, crooked, turned. [➡ROUNDED SHAPE; 1217] *Opposite:* straight. 2 *adj* **determined**, set, fixed, resolved, decided, focused. [➡DESIRE AND WANT; 580] 3 *adj* (*slang*) **criminal**, crooked (*informal*), dishonest, corrupt. [➡DECEITFUL; 514] *Opposite:* honest. 4 *n* **inclination**, gift, talent, flair. [➡SKILLS, TALENTS, AND ABILITIES; 527]

See Compare and Contrast at **talent**.

be on course *v* **be set to**, be heading for, be on target for, be on track, be on the right track, be on route to, be headed for, be in line for. [➡ABOUT TO HAPPEN; 33]

be partial to *v* **favour**, like, prefer, fancy (*informal*), be biased towards, have a soft spot for. [➡LIKE, LOVE, VALUE, AND ENJOY; 579]. *Opposite:* disfavour (*formal*).

bequeath *v* **leave**, give, bestow (*formal*), confer on (*formal*), donate, hand down, will, hand on. [➡BEQUEATH AND BEQUESTS; 433]

bequest *n* **inheritance**, legacy, gift, donation, settlement, endowment. [➡BEQUEATH AND BEQUESTS; 433]

berate *v* **rebuke**, tell off (*informal*), shout at, harangue, criticize, scold, reprimand. [➡ACCUSE, BLAME, AND CRITICIZE; 642] *Opposite:* praise.

bereaved *adj* **mourning**, in mourning, grieving, orphaned, bereft, widowed. [➡DEATH AND BEREAVEMENT; 927]

bereavement *n* **loss**, grief, sorrow, mourning, death. [➡DEATH AND BEREAVEMENT; 927]

bereft 1 *adj* **deprived**, bereaved, mourning, in mourning, grieving, orphaned, widowed. [➡DEATH AND BEREAVEMENT; 927] 2 *adj* **empty**, starved, devoid, deprived, stripped, without, lacking. [➡LACK OF POSSESSION; 446] *Opposite:* overwhelmed.

beret *type of* **headgear**. [➡HABERDASHERY, MILLINERY, AND LINGERIE; 867]

Bermuda shorts *type of* **trousers**. [➡GARMENTS AND OUTFITS; 865]

berry

◆ *types of berry*
bilberry, blackberry, blackcurrant, blueberry, boysenberry, cranberry, currant, elderberry, gooseberry, huckleberry, juniper, loganberry, mulberry, raspberry, redcurrant, rowan, whortleberry

berserk *adj* **crazy** (*informal*), mad, out of control, wild, bonkers (*informal*), bananas (*informal*), off your rocker (*informal*), off the deep end, out to lunch (*slang*), round the bend (*informal*). [➡ECCENTRICITY AND IRRATIONALITY; 563] *Opposite:* rational.

berth 1 *n* **mooring**, dock, landing place, mooring place, wharf, quay. [➡WATERWAYS AND SEAWAYS; 1107] 2 *v* **dock**, moor, tie up, come in, land, disembark. [➡ARRIVE BY TRANSPORT; 14] *Opposite:* put out. 3 *type of* **bed**. [➡FURNITURE; 858]

beryl *type of* **gemstone**. [➡PRECIOUS STONES; 1277]

beseech (*literary*) *v* **implore** (*formal*), beg, request, ask, entreat (*formal*), plead, press, demand. [➡REQUEST AND DEMAND; 664]

beseeching (*literary*) *adj* **imploring** (*formal*), pleading, begging, suppliant (*formal*), supplicatory (*formal*), earnest, persuasive. [➡REQUEST AND DEMAND; 664] *Opposite:* diffident.

beset 1 *adj* **affected**, plagued, tormented, overwhelmed, overcome, harassed, surrounded, full of. [➡CONFUSION, ANXIETY, AND WORRY; 541] *Opposite:* free. 2 *v* **harass**, annoy, hamper, trouble, overwhelm, affect, weigh down, assail. [➡HAPPEN TO SOMEBODY; 30] *Opposite:* support. 3 *v* (*formal*) **surround**, attack, overcome, overwhelm, assail, harass, hamper. [➡UPSET, DISTRESS, AND HUMILIATE; 568]

beside *prep* **next to**, at the side of, alongside, by, near, nearby, close, adjacent, adjoining, contiguous (*formal*). [➡RELATIVE LOCATION; 162]

besides 1 *adv* **as well**, in addition, also, above and beyond, too. [➡ALSO; 136] 2 *adv* **moreover**, what's more, further, more to the point, anyway, furthermore. [➡EXPRESSIONS INTRODUCING EXTRA INFORMATION; 137]

beside the point *adj* **irrelevant**, unimportant, superfluous, immaterial, extraneous, inconsequential, insignificant, of no consequence. [➡UNIMPORTANT AND UNNECESSARY; 239] *Opposite:* central.

beside yourself 1 *adj* **upset**, distressed, frantic, worried sick, distraught, hysterical, excited, agitated, in a state (*informal*). [➡SADNESS, DISTRESS, AND DESPAIR; 540] *Opposite:* composed. 2 *adj* **angry**, furious, enraged, wild, livid, ranting, raving. [➡IRRITATION AND ANGER; 542] *Opposite:* calm.

besiege *v* **surround**, siege, lay siege to, encircle, blockade, overwhelm. [➡EXIST IN CLOSE PROXIMITY; 21] *Opposite:* defend.

besieged *adj* **overwhelmed**, snowed under, inundated, beleaguered, weighed down, plagued, beset (*formal*). [➡SADNESS, DISTRESS, AND DESPAIR; 540]

besmear *v* [➡DIRTY AND CONTAMINATE; 405]

besmirch *v* **sully**, defame, tarnish, damage, slander, drag in the mud. [➡ACCUSE, BLAME, AND CRITICIZE; 642] *Opposite:* praise.

besmirched *adj* [➡DIRTY; 1234]

besotted *adj* **infatuated**, smitten (*humorous or literary*), love-struck, head over heels in love, fanatical, obsessed. [➡APPRECIATION AND GRATITUDE; 536] *Opposite:* repelled.

bespatter *v* [➡DIRTY AND CONTAMINATE; 405]

bespeak *v* **signify**, signal, indicate, convey, reveal, show, suggest, imply. [➡MEAN SOMETHING; 61]

be spoiling for *v* **look for**, expect, anticipate, itch, be bent on, be out for. [➡DESIRE AND WANT; 580]

bespoke *adj* **custom-made**, tailor-made, made to measure, customized, custom-built, commissioned, tailored. [➡DESCRIBING CLOTHES; 869] *Opposite:* ready-to-wear.

best 1 *adj* **top**, finest, greatest, unsurpassed, paramount, pre-eminent, superlative, Grade A, first class. [➡GOOD, WELL,

BETTER; 184] *Opposite:* worst. **2** *v* **outdo**, overcome, top, surpass, defeat. [➡BEAT AND DEFEAT; 80]

best bib and tucker (*informal*) *n* [➡GARMENTS AND OUTFITS; 865]

best-case scenario *n* [➡SITUATIONS; 71]

best clothes *n* [➡GARMENTS AND OUTFITS; 865]

best end *type of* **cut**. [➡TYPES AND CUTS OF MEAT; 1176]

best friend *n* [➡FRIENDS; 963]

bestial *adj* **inhuman**, foul, degrading, cruel, brutish, base, boorish, sordid, repulsive. [➡MORALLY BAD; 776] *Opposite:* humane.

bestiality *n* **cruelty**, inhumanity, savagery, brutality, depravity, wickedness. [➡MORALLY BAD; 776] *Opposite:* humanity.

bestir yourself (*formal*) *v* **motivate yourself**, stir yourself, busy yourself, rouse yourself, get off your backside (*informal*), be up and doing. [➡START AN ACTION; 261]

best man *n* **chief attendant**, attendant, groomsman. [➡SUPPORTERS, PROTECTORS, AND COMPATRIOTS; 970]

best mate *n* [➡FRIENDS; 963]

bestow (*formal*) *v* **give**, confer (*formal*), bequeath, donate, grant, present, impart. [➡GIVE AND PROVIDE; 431] *Opposite:* withdraw.

See Compare and Contrast at **give**.

bestride *v* **straddle**, span, sit astride, stand astride, be astride. [➡ASSUME A POSITION; 318]

bestseller *n* **record-breaker**, hit, smash, success, blockbuster (*informal*), winner, moneymaker, money-spinner (*informal*), runaway success, roaring success, big hit, smash hit, chart-topper. [➡ADVANTAGE; 213]. *Opposite:* flop (*informal*).

bestselling *adj* **successful**, popular, blockbusting, hit, chart-topping, record-breaking. [➡SUCCESSFUL AND PROMISING; 81]

best togs (*informal*) *n* [➡GARMENTS AND OUTFITS; 865]

be sure of *v* **count on**, depend on, rely on, depend upon, trust, rely upon, have confidence in, be certain about. [➡LIKE, LOVE, VALUE AND ENJOY; 579] *Opposite:* doubt.

bet **1** *v* **gamble**, stake, wager, put money on, lay a wager, back, risk, play, have a flutter (*informal*). [➡GAMBLE AND TAKE RISKS; 467] **2** *v* (*informal*) **think**, expect, anticipate, consider, believe, suppose. [➡PREDICT AND ANTICIPATE; 751] **3** *n* **wager**, gamble, stake, flutter (*informal*), play. [➡GAMBLE AND TAKE RISKS; 467]

bete noir (*literary*) *n* [➡PROBLEM; 257]

be that as it may *adv* **nevertheless**, nonetheless, despite that, even so, just the same, all the same, at the same time. [➡ALTHOUGH, NEVERTHELESS, AND DESPITE; 170]

be there *v* **be present**, be in attendance, turn up, stay, remain, attend. [➡EXIST IN A PLACE; 19]

be there for *v* **stand by**, support, help, care for, take care of, look after. [➡TAKE CARE OF AND SPOIL; 301] *Opposite:* abandon.

be through with *v* **finish**, complete, conclude, do, finish off, tie up, finish up. [➡COMPLETE AN ACTION; 264] *Opposite:* start.

betoken (*literary*) *v* [➡REPRESENT SOMETHING OR SOMEBODY; 59]

betray **1** *v* **be disloyal**, give up, hand over, grass (*slang*), inform on, let down. [➡BETRAY CONFIDENCES AND GOSSIP; 619] *Opposite:* stand by. **2** *v* **disclose**, leak, tell, give away, reveal, let slip, let drop, let the cat out of the bag. [➡BETRAY CONFIDENCES AND GOSSIP; 619]

betrayal *n* **disloyalty**, unfaithfulness, duplicity, infidelity, treachery, perfidy (*literary*). [➡UNKIND ACTION OR BEHAVIOUR; 297] *Opposite:* loyalty.

betrothal (*formal*) *n* **engagement**, troth (*archaic*), promise, pact, compact. [➡CEREMONIES AND ANNIVERSARIES; 38]

betrothed (*formal*) *n* **fiancé**, fiancée, husband-to-be, wife-to-be, girlfriend, boyfriend, intended (*dated or humorous*). [➡RELATIVES BY MARRIAGE; 960]

better **1** *adj* **improved**, enhanced, superior. [➡GOOD, WELL, BETTER; 184] *Opposite:* worse. **2** *adj* **healthier**, improved, well, recovering, in good health, restored, on the mend. [➡HEALING; 731] *Opposite:* worse. **3** *v* (*formal*) **improve on**, top, outdo, outshine, surpass, exceed. [➡BEAT AND DEFEAT; 80] **4** *v* (*formal*) **enhance**, improve, change for the better, advance, ameliorate (*formal*), progress. [➡IMPROVE SOMETHING; 375] *Opposite:* worsen.

betterment (*formal*) *n* **furtherance**, improvement, advancement, benefit, progress, upward mobility. [➡PROGRESS AND ADVANCEMENT; 214] *Opposite:* deterioration.

better-off *adj* **rich**, wealthy, affluent, comfortable, well-heeled (*informal*), prosperous. [➡WEALTH AND WEALTHY; 891] *Opposite:* poor.

bettong *type of* **marsupial**. [➡MARSUPIAL; 992]

between **1** *prep* **flanked by**, sandwiched between, stuck between, amid, among, in the middle of. [➡RELATIVE LOCATION; 162] **2** *prep* **connecting**, linking, joining, involving, concerning, relating. [➡RELATIVE LOCATION; 162]

between a rock and a hard place *adj* [➡IN TROUBLE AND DISADVANTAGED; 73]

between ourselves **1** *adj* **private**, quiet, hush-hush (*informal*), under wraps (*informal*), secret, discreet. [➡SECRET AND UNKNOWN; 180] *Opposite:* public. **2** *adv* **entre nous**, between you and me, off the record, confidentially. [➡EXPRESSIONS OF OPINION; 624]

between you and me *adv* [➡EXPRESSIONS OF OPINION; 624]

between you, me, and the bedpost (*US*) *adv* [➡EXPRESSIONS OF OPINION; 624]

between you, me, and the gatepost *adv* [➡EXPRESSIONS OF OPINION; 624]

bevelled *adj* **oblique**, chamfered, slanting, bias-cut, sloping. [➡ORIENTATION AND ALIGNMENT; 1222]

beverage (*formal*) *n* **drink**, hot drink, cold drink, brew (*informal*), liquid refreshment, cuppa (*informal*), pick-me-up (*informal*). [➡DRINKS; 1186]

bevvy (*slang*) *n* [➡DRINKS; 1186]

bevy 1 *type of* **flock.** [➡GROUP OF BIRDS; 1007] 2 *type of* **herd.** [➡GROUP OF ANIMALS; 993]

bewail (*formal*) *v* **lament**, bemoan, complain, regret, moan (*informal*), grumble, grieve, deplore. [➡COMPLAIN AND NAG; 687] *Opposite:* applaud.

beware *v* **be careful**, be cautious, be wary, look out, watch out, take heed, think twice. [➡PAY ATTENTION; 766]

bewhiskered *adj* [➡FACIAL HAIR; 490]

bewilder *v* **confuse**, puzzle, baffle, perplex, confound, bamboozle (*informal*), mystify, nonplus, stump, bemuse, daze, disconcert, disorientate, disorient. [➡CONFUSE AND BEWILDER; 572]

bewildered *adj* **confused**, puzzled, dazed, bemused, befuddled, taken aback, disorientated, disconcerted, panicky, baffled. [➡CONFUSION, ANXIETY, AND WORRY; 541] *Opposite:* clear-headed.

bewildering *adj* **confusing**, puzzling, baffling, mystifying, incomprehensible, perplexing, disorientating, disconcerting. [➡DIFFICULTY AND COMPLEXITY; 243] *Opposite:* clear.

bewilderment *n* **confusion**, incomprehension, bafflement, puzzlement, perplexity, panic, disorientation. [➡CONFUSION, ANXIETY, AND WORRY; 541] *Opposite:* clarity.

bewitch *v* [➡APPEAL TO AND AROUSE INTEREST; 576]

bewitched *adj* [➡APPRECIATION AND GRATITUDE; 536]

bewitching *adj* [➡BEAUTY AND ATTRACTIVENESS; 190]

beyond *prep* **further than**, past, away from, clear of, ahead of, outside. [➡RELATIVE LOCATION; 162]

beyond a doubt *adv* [➡CERTAIN; 175]

beyond a shadow of a doubt *adv* [➡CERTAIN; 175]

beyond doubt *adv* [➡CERTAIN; 175]

beyond question *adv* [➡CERTAIN; 175]

beyond repair *adj* [➡IN BAD REPAIR; 1233]

beyond the pale *adj* **unacceptable**, too much, over-the-top (*informal*), inexcusable, indefensible, unjustifiable, intolerable, excessive, unreasonable, a bit much. [➡UNACCEPTABLE AND UNFORGIVEABLE; 226] *Opposite:* acceptable.

B film *n* [➡FILM; 901]

bhangra *type of* **popular music.** [➡MUSIC, SONGS, AND SINGING; 907]

biannual *adj* **twice-yearly**, twice-a-year, six-monthly, semiannual. [➡TIMES OF YEAR; 88]

bias *n* **prejudice**, partiality, preference, unfairness, predisposition, preconception, favouritism. [➡PREJUDICE; 551] *Opposite:* impartiality.

bias-cut *adj* [➡DESCRIBING CLOTHES; 869]

biased *adj* **prejudiced**, unfair, partial, influenced, predisposed, subjective, jaundiced. [➡THE NATURE OF IDEAS; 772] *Opposite:* unbiased.

biathlon *type of* **winter sport.** [➡HOBBIES, GAMES, AND SPORTS; 875]

biblical *adj* **scriptural**, holy, bible, sacred, theological, canonical. [➡RELIGIOUS CONCEPTS; 777]

bibliography *n* **list**, index, appendix, checklist, catalogue, directory, reading list, book list, list of references. [➡LISTS AND SCHEDULES; 588]

bibliophile *n* [➡DEVOTEES AND ADDICTED PEOPLE; 557]

bicameral *adj* **two-tier**, two-house, dual, bilateral, bipartite, dualistic. [➡STYLES AND SYSTEMS OF GOVERNMENT; 806]

bicentenary *n* **200th anniversary**, 200th birthday, anniversary, bicentennial (*US*). [➡CEREMONIES AND ANNIVERSARIES; 38]

bicentennial (*US*) *n* **200th anniversary**, 200th birthday, anniversary, bicentenary. [➡CEREMONIES AND ANNIVERSARIES; 38]

biceps *type of* **muscle or tendon.** [➡THE MUSCLES; 719]

bicker *v* **argue**, dispute, quarrel, debate, squabble, wrangle. [➡ARGUE AND FIGHT – TWO-WAY; 644] *Opposite:* agree.

bicycle *n* **bike** (*informal*), cycle, push-bike (*dated informal*). [➡BIKES, CARS, AND CARRIAGES; 1148]

bid 1 *v* **tender**, offer, propose, submit, proffer. [➡SUGGEST, HINT, AND COMMENT; 613] 2 *v* **try**, attempt, undertake, endeavour, seek, strive, make a move. [➡ATTEMPT AN ACTION; 262] 3 *v* (*archaic*) **order**, enjoin (*formal*), call on, command, direct, tell, request. [➡REQUEST AND DEMAND; 664] 4 *n* **offer**, proposal, proposition, tender, submission. [➡REQUEST AND DEMAND; 664] 5 *n* **attempt**, try, effort, undertaking, endeavour, move. [➡ATTEMPT AN ACTION; 262]

biddable *adj* **compliant**, acquiescent, docile, obedient, amenable, pliant, pliable [➡THE WILL AND WILLINGNESS; 564]. *Opposite:* intractable (*formal*).

bidder *n* **buyer**, auction-goer, collector, dealer, purchaser, customer. [➡BUSINESS PEOPLE; 794]

bidding *n* **request**, command, order, will, behest (*formal*), call. [➡REQUEST AND DEMAND; 664]

bidet *type of* **plumbing fittings.** [➡FITTINGS; 859]

bide your time *v* **wait**, be patient, wait and see, play the waiting game, hold back, hold off, cool your heels (*informal*), twiddle your thumbs. [➡SHIRK AND DELAY; 274]

biennial *adj* **two-yearly**, regular, periodic. [➡TIMES OF YEAR; 88]

bier *n* **stand**, rest, base, pedestal, table, platform. [➡SUPPORTS AND BASES; 1254]

biff (*informal*) *v* **hit**, punch, wallop (*informal*), thump, knock, clout (*informal*), clobber (*informal*), belt (*informal*), clock (*slang*). [➡PHYSICAL ATTACK AND PUNISHMENT; 416]

bifocals *type of* **glasses.** [➡GLASSES AND SPECTACLES; 1124]

bifurcate *v* **divide**, branch, split, fork, diverge, separate. [➡SEPARATE AND DIVIDE; 402] *Opposite:* converge.

bifurcation *n* **fork**, junction, split, divergence, branching, division. [➡HOLES, GAPS, AND FORKS; 1251] *Opposite:* convergence.

big 1 *adj* **large**, giant, immense, vast, great, gigantic, great big, huge, enormous, whopping (*informal*), full-size, life-size. [➡LARGE; 1192] *Opposite:* small. **2** *adj* **spacious**, capacious, roomy, large, deep. [➡LARGE; 1192] *Opposite:* cramped. **3** *adj* **significant**, considerable, substantial, sizable, large, important, good. [➡IMPORTANT; 195] *Opposite:* insignificant. **4** *adj* **extensive**, vast, immense, wide, great, broad. [➡WIDTH: WIDE; 1198] *Opposite:* narrow. **5** *adj* **older**, elder, grown-up, adult, mature, of age. [➡ADULTHOOD; 918] *Opposite:* little. **6** *adj* **bulky**, large, cumbersome, massive, outsize, hulking. [➡LARGE; 1192] *Opposite:* petite. **7** *adj* **tall**, high, lofty, towering, soaring. [➡HEIGHT: HIGH; 1202] *Opposite:* short.

bigamist *n* **polygamist**, two-timer (*informal*), adulterer, lawbreaker, criminal. [➡CRIMINALS; 821]

bigamous *adj* **polygamous**, two-timing (*informal*), adulterous, criminal, illegal. [➡ILLEGAL; 816] *Opposite:* monogamous.

bigamy *n* **polygamy**, two-timing (*informal*), adultery. [➡CRIMES; 817] *Opposite:* monogamy.

big band *type of* **band**. [➡MUSICIANS AND SINGERS; 908]

big business *n* **trade**, commerce, industry, business sector, business world, private sector. [➡BUSINESS; 792]

big cat *type of* **cat**. [➡FELINE; 983]

big cheese (*slang*) *n* **bigwig** (*informal*), big shot (*informal*), big wheel (*informal*), VIP, key player, major player. [➡IMPORTANT OR FAMOUS PEOPLE; 893] *Opposite:* nobody.

big deal (*informal*) *n* **major concern**, serious issue, matter of life and death, federal case (*US*). [➡MOST IMPORTANT THING; 198]

Bigfoot *n* [➡MYTHICAL BEINGS; 790]

biggie (*informal*) **1** *n* **big one**, giant, whopper (*informal*), colossus, monster, stonker (*slang*). [➡BIG THINGS; 1193] **2** *n* **big name**, big shot (*informal*), bigwig (*informal*), big wheel (*informal*), big cheese (*slang*), VIP, star, celebrity. [➡IMPORTANT OR FAMOUS PEOPLE; 893] *Opposite:* nobody.

big hair (*informal*) *type of* **hairstyle**. [➡HAIR STYLES AND HAIR PIECES; 489]

bighead (*informal*) *n* **show-off** (*informal*), boaster, bragger, smart aleck (*informal*), clever clogs (*informal*), know-all (*informal*). [➡SELF-IMPORTANT AND SELF-SEEKING PEOPLE; 949]

bigheaded (*informal*) *adj* **conceited**, egotistical, arrogant, vain, self-centred, pompous, pretentious, immodest, full of yourself, swollen-headed, boastful, cocky (*informal*), too big for your breeches (*informal*), too big for your boots (*informal*), high and mighty. [➡POMPOUS, LOUD, AND OVER-CONFIDENT; 636] *Opposite:* modest.

big-hearted *adj* **kind**, good-natured, supportive, helpful, kindly, kind-hearted, philanthropic, charitable, benevolent, beneficent. [➡GENEROSITY AND KINDNESS; 496] *Opposite:* mean-spirited.

bight *n* [➡THE SEAS, OCEANS, AND SHORES; 1041]

bigmouth (*informal*) **1** *n* **blabbermouth** (*informal*), telltale, gossip, gossipmonger, tattler, tattletale (*US informal*). [➡INTERFERING PEOPLE AND TELLTALES; 950] **2** *n* **boaster**, bragger, know-all (*informal*), braggart, blowhard (*US*). [➡SELF-IMPORTANT AND SELF-SEEKING PEOPLE; 949]

big name *n* **famous name**, celebrity, star, superstar, VIP, public figure. [➡IMPORTANT OR FAMOUS PEOPLE; 893] *Opposite:* unknown.

bigot *n* **extremist**, diehard, dogmatist, chauvinist, hypocrite, racist. [➡GRUMPY AND NEGATIVE PEOPLE; 953]

bigoted *adj* **prejudiced**, dogmatic, opinionated, intolerant, narrow-minded, chauvinistic, biased. [➡NEGATIVE INTELLECTUAL CHARACTERISTICS; 526] *Opposite:* open-minded.

bigotry *n* **prejudice**, intolerance, bias, narrow-mindedness, chauvinism, racism. [➡MORALLY BAD; 776] *Opposite:* open-mindedness.

big shot (*informal*) *n* **bigwig** (*informal*), key player, major player, VIP, big wheel (*informal*), big cheese (*slang*). [➡IMPORTANT OR FAMOUS PEOPLE; 893] *Opposite:* nobody.

big time (*slang*) *adv* **greatly**, massively (*informal*), a great deal, on a grand scale, in a big way, to a great extent. [➡TO A GREAT EXTENT; 130]

big toe *part of* **leg or foot**. [➡LEG AND FOOT; 695]

bigwig (*informal*) *n* **big shot** (*informal*), VIP, big wheel (*informal*), big cheese (*slang*), major player, key player. [➡IMPORTANT OR FAMOUS PEOPLE; 893] *Opposite:* nobody.

bijou (*humorous*) *adj* **compact**, tiny, cramped, small, poky (*informal*). [➡SMALL; 1194] *Opposite:* spacious.

bike (*informal*) *n* **bicycle**, cycle, push-bike (*dated*), motorbike). [➡BIKES, CARS, AND CARRIAGES; 1148]

bike

◆ *parts of a bike*
brake, chain, crossbar, derailleur, fender (*US*), handlebars, mudguard, pedal, reflector, seat, spoke, tyre, wheel

◆ *types of bike*
bicycle, boneshaker, cycle, dirt bike, exercise bike, moped, motor scooter, motorbike, motorcycle, mountain bike, penny-farthing, push-bike (*dated informal*), racing bike, rickshaw, scooter, scrambler, tandem, tandem bicycle (*US*), ten-speed, three-wheeler, trail bike, tricycle, unicycle

biker *n* **motorcyclist**, scrambler, racer, rider. [➡TRAVEL: TRAVELLERS AND WALKERS; 320]

bikini *n* **swimsuit**, two-piece, bathing costume (*dated*), swimming costume, bathing suit (*US*). [➡GARMENTS AND OUTFITS; 865]

bilateral *adj* **two-sided**, two-pronged, joint, mutual, consensual. [➡ACTING WITH OTHERS; 286] *Opposite:* unilateral.

bilberry *type of* **berry**. [➡FRUIT AND VEGETABLES; 1175]

bilby *type of* **marsupial**. [➡MARSUPIAL; 992]

bile (*literary*) *n* **bitterness**, irritability, ire (*literary*), vitriol, spleen, sourness, temper, wrath, anger. [➡IRRITATION AND ANGER; 542] *Opposite:* sweetness.

bile duct *part of* **digestive tract.** [➡THE DIGESTIVE TRACT; 710]

bilge 1 *n* **hull**, keel, base, bottom. [➡PARTS OF A SHIP OR BOAT; 1150] 2 *n* **hold**, tank, interior, recesses, bowels, bottom. [➡PARTS OF A SHIP OR BOAT; 1150] 3 *n* **sludge**, mud, bilge water, silt, effluent, swill, sewage. [➡UNPLEASANT AND DIRTY SUBSTANCES; 1267] 4 *n* (*informal*) **bunkum** (*informal*), nonsense, rubbish, trash, twaddle (*informal*), claptrap (*informal*), drivel, balderdash. [➡MEANINGLESS SPEECH OR WRITING; 677]

bilingual *adj* **fluent**, multilingual, polyglot. [➡TALENTED AND SKILFUL; 528]

bilious *adj* **nauseous**, sickly, queasy, sick, green around the gills (*informal*), ill, off-colour, unwell, not a hundred percent, under the weather, below par (*informal*), ailing (*dated*). [➡ILL AND SICK; 741]

bilk (*informal*) *v* **cheat**, trick, deceive, con, swindle, defraud, bamboozle (*informal*), take advantage of, dupe. [➡DECEPTION AND LIES; 661]

bill 1 *n* **invoice**, statement, demand, receipt, damage (*informal*), tab (*US informal*), check (*US*). [➡RECEIPTS AND INVOICES; 592] 2 *n* **amount**, total, sum, fee, price, debt. [➡EXPENDITURE; 424] 3 *n* **proposal**, measure, document, petition, proposition, law. [➡TRIAL, PUNISHMENT, AND LEGAL OUTCOMES; 819] 4 *n* **beak**, mouth, mandible. [➡PARTS OF A BIRD; 1006] 5 *n* (*US*) **poster**, flyer, notice, advertisement, leaflet, handbill, placard. [➡ADVERTISING AND PUBLICITY; 605] 6 *v* **charge**, invoice, debit, send the bill to. [➡SELL; 442] 7 *v* (*US*) **promote**, portray, publicize, hype, advertise, present, introduce, put forward. [➡ADVERTISING AND PUBLICITY; 605]

billboard *n* **sign**, hoarding, poster, advertisement, panel, display. [➡SIGNPOSTS, SIGNALS AND BILLBOARDS; 596]

billet 1 *n* **accommodation**, lodgings (*dated*), quarters, boarding house, guest house, digs (*dated informal*). [➡ACCOMMODATION; 855] 2 *v* **accommodate**, quarter, house, station, shelter, board, put up. [➡TAKE CARE OF AND SPOIL; 301]

billet-doux (*literary*) *n* **love letter**, letter, missive, note, valentine. [➡LETTERS AND WRITTEN MESSAGES; 585]

billfold (*US*) *n* **wallet**, purse, pocketbook. [➡CONTAINERS, RECEPTACLES, AND PACKAGING; 1244]

billhook *type of* **cutting tool.** [➡CUTTING TOOLS; 1119]

billiards *type of* **target ball game.** [➡HOBBIES, GAMES, AND SPORTS; 875]

billionaire *n* **multimillionaire**, magnate, tycoon, fat cat (*slang*), moneybags (*informal*). [➡RICH PEOPLE; 895]

billionth *n* **tiny part**, morsel, particle, modicum, touch, portion, fraction. [➡FEW, LITTLE, SMALL AMOUNT; 119]

billow 1 *v* **catch the wind**, swell, bulge, balloon, fill, mushroom, inflate. [➡CHANGE OF SIZE: BIGGER; 393] *Opposite:* sag. 2 *v* **roll upwards**, waft, rise, curl, flow. [➡GO UPWARDS; 307] *Opposite:* fall. 3 *n* **puff**, cloud, swell, swirl, rush, wave, surge. [➡AMOUNT OF GAS; 116]

billycan *n* **cooking pot**, pail, pan, pot, tin, container, billy. [➡CONTAINERS, RECEPTACLES, AND PACKAGING; 1244]

billy club (*US*) *type of* **club.** [➡BLUNT INSTRUMENTS AND WHIPS; 1157]

billy goat *type of* **male animal.** [➡MALE OR FEMALE ANIMAL; 978]

bin 1 *n* **rubbish bin**, wastepaper basket, waste bin, dustbin, litter bin, trash can (*US*), garbage can (*US*), wastebasket (*US*). [➡CONTAINERS, RECEPTACLES, AND PACKAGING; 1244] 2 *n* **storage bin**, basket, container, silo, holder, box, tub, case, vat. [➡CONTAINERS, RECEPTACLES, AND PACKAGING; 1244] 3 *v* **throw away**, throw out, discard, chuck out (*informal*), dispose of, ditch (*informal*), jettison. [➡GET RID OF SOMETHING; 452] *Opposite:* keep.

binary *adj* **two**, dual, twice, double, twofold, dualistic. [➡MATHS; 598]

bind 1 *v* **attach**, connect, join, combine, unite, tie, fasten, fix, truss, rope. [➡FASTEN, LINK, AND JOIN; 409] *Opposite:* undo. 2 *v* **oblige**, force, require, compel, coerce, constrain. [➡CAUSE OR COMPEL TO ACT; 272] 3 *n* **quandary**, tight situation, predicament, dilemma, muddle, fix (*informal*), impasse, hole (*informal*), jam (*informal*), pickle (*informal*). [➡DIFFICULT SITUATIONS; 72] 4 *n* **nuisance**, drag, bore, pain (*informal*), hassle (*informal*), annoyance. [➡NUISANCES; 254]

binder 1 *n* **folder**, file, ring binder, looseleaf folder. [➡CONTAINERS, RECEPTACLES, AND PACKAGING; 1244] 2 *n* (*US*) **promise**, pledge, vow, obligation, assurance, guarantee, warrant, commitment. [➡PROMISE AND ASSURE; 685]

binding 1 *n* **tie**, band, attachment, fastening, truss. [➡FASTENERS, LINKS, AND NETWORKS; 1246] 2 *n* **edging**, cover, trim, stitching, strip. [➡FASTENERS, LINKS, AND NETWORKS; 1246] 3 *adj* **compulsory**, obligatory, required, requisite (*formal*), necessary, mandatory. [➡NECESSARY AND ESSENTIAL; 197] *Opposite:* voluntary.

bindweed *type of* **weed.** [➡WEEDS AND THISTLES; 1034]

binge 1 *n* **spree**, splurge (*informal*), orgy, bender (*slang*), rampage, blast (*US slang*). [➡EVENTS AND OCCURRENCES; 35] 2 *v* **overdo**, indulge, overindulge, gorge, go on a bender (*slang*), splurge (*informal*). [➡OVERDO SOMETHING; 291]

bingo *n* [➡HOBBIES, GAMES, AND SPORTS; 875]

binoculars *n* **opera glasses**, field glasses, eyeglasses (*US formal*). [➡OPTICAL INSTRUMENTS; 1123]

biochemical *adj* **chemical**, biological, living, organic, natural. [➡BIOLOGICAL SCIENCES; 1037]

biochemistry *type of* **bioscience.** [➡BIOLOGICAL SCIENCES; 1037]

biodegradable *adj* **recyclable**, decomposable, ecological, environmental, green, ecofriendly. [➡ECONOMICAL AND RESOURCEFUL; 208]

biogas *n* [➡GASES; 1274]

biographer *n* **writer**, author, historian, profiler, researcher. [➡WRITERS AND STYLES; 914]

biographical *adj* **factual**, nonfiction, true, fact-based, realistic, authentic, historical, real. [➡TRUE AND REAL; 172]

biography *n* **life story**, life history, profile, memoir, life, account, autobiography. [➡FICTION AND DRAMA; 913]

biological 1 *adj* **organic**, life, living, natural, biotic. [➡BIOLOGICAL SCIENCES; 1037] 2 *adj* **natal**, birth, natural, genetic, true. [➡THE FAMILY; 956] *Opposite:* adoptive.

biological parent [➡OLDER GENERATION RELATIVES; 959]

biologist [➡BIOLOGICAL SCIENCES; 1037]

biology *type of* **bioscience.** [➡BIOLOGICAL SCIENCES; 1037]

bionic *adj* **electronic**, automatic, robotic, semirobotic, electromechanical. [➡MACHINERY; 1113]

biopic *n* **film**, movie, biography, documentary, life story, life history, life. [➡FILM; 901]

biopsy *n* **cell removal**, operation, surgery, culture, tissue removal. [➡REMEDIES, TREATMENTS AND OPERATIONS; 732]

biorhythm *n* **cycle**, change, cyclical change, rhythm. [➡CHANGE; 373]

biosatellite *type of* **spacecraft.** [➡SPACE VEHICLES; 1062]

bioscience

◆ *types of bioscience*
anatomy, bacteriology, biochemistry, biology, botany, ecology, genetics, microbiology, molecular biology, physiology, zoology

biosphere *n* **environment**, planet, earth, land, sea, atmosphere. [➡NATURE AND THE ENVIRONMENT; 1038]

bipartisan *adj* **two-party**, dual-party, cross-party, bilateral, bipartite. [➡STYLES AND SYSTEMS OF GOVERNMENT; 806]

bipartite *adj* **two-part**, divided, split, mutual, shared, in common, common. [➡APPORTIONMENT; 113]

biped *n* **two-legged animal**, human, primate, humanoid. [➡LIVING THINGS AND LIVING; 976]

biplane *type of* **civil aircraft.** [➡AIRCRAFT; 1147]

birch 1 *n* **cane**, rod, stick, switch, whip. [➡BLUNT INSTRUMENTS AND WHIPS; 1157] **2** *v* **whip**, flog, punish, strike, thrash, lash, flay, wallop (*informal*), beat. [➡WHIP AND CLUB; 418] **3** *type of* **deciduous tree.** [➡DECIDUOUS TREES; 1028]

bird

◆ *parts of a bird*
beak, bill, carina, cockscomb, comb, crest, crop, down, feather, gizzard, gorge, plumage, plume, quill, ruff, tail, talon, web, wing, wingtip, wishbone

◆ *types of common bird*
blue jay, bluetit, camp robber (*US regional*), cardinal, chaffinch, chickadee, cuckoo, dove, finch, house martin, jay, martin, nuthatch, pigeon, robin, sparrow, starling, swallow, swift, tit, turtledove, woodpecker, wren

◆ *types of pet bird*
budgerigar, canary, cockatoo, homing pigeon, lovebird, macaw, parakeet, parrot

◆ *types of flightless bird*
dodo, emu, kiwi, ostrich, peacock, penguin

◆ *types of scavenger*
buzzard (*US*), condor, crow, jackdaw, lammergeier, magpie, marabou, raven, rook, vulture

birdbath *n* **basin**, bowl, receptacle. [➡CONTAINERS, RECEPTACLES, AND PACKAGING; 1244]

birdbrained (*informal*) *adj* **silly**, foolish, stupid, dopey, daft (*informal*), asinine, witless, scatterbrained. [➡NEGATIVE INTELLECTUAL CHARACTERISTICS; 526] *Opposite:* sensible.

birdcage *n* **cage**, coop, pen, aviary, enclosure, henhouse, pigeon loft. [➡ANIMAL OR BIRD ACCOMMODATION; 1078]

birdlike *adj* **dainty**, petite, small-boned, delicate, slight. [➡BUILD; 478] *Opposite:* heavyset.

bird of prey

◆ *types of bird of prey*
bald eagle, buteo (*US*), buzzard, eagle, falcon, golden eagle, hawk, kestrel, kite, osprey, peregrine falcon, sea eagle, sparrowhawk

birdseed *n* **seed**, grain, mixture, feed, chicken feed. [➡ANIMAL FEED; 1167]

birdsong *n* **call**, cry, song, trill, whistle, piping, tweet. [➡SOUNDS MADE BY BIRDS; 1262]

birdwatcher *n* **ornithologist**, bird lover, twitcher, birder (*US*). [➡PEOPLE IN SPORTS AND LEISURE; 876]

biretta *type of* **headgear.** [➡HABERDASHERY, MILLINERY, AND LINGERIE; 867]

birth 1 *n* **delivery**, labour, confinement (*dated*), childbirth, parturition (*formal*), nativity. [➡REPRODUCTION AND HEREDITY; 726] *Opposite:* death. **2** *n* **beginning**, origin, dawn, naissance, start, founding (*dated*), commencement (*formal*), onset, outset, formation. [➡BEGINNING; 53]. *Opposite:* demise (*formal*). **3** *adj* **natal**, natural, true, biological, genetic. [➡REPRODUCTION AND HEREDITY; 726] *Opposite:* adoptive.

birthdate *n* **birthday**, anniversary, date of birth. [➡TIMES OF YEAR; 88]

birthday *n* **date of birth**, birthdate, anniversary. [➡TIMES OF YEAR; 88]

birthmark *n* **mark**, stain, discoloration, blemish, strawberry mark, naevus, patch, mole. [➡CONDITIONS AFFECTING THE SKIN; 722]

birthplace *n* **origin**, source, home, hometown, place of birth, native land, homeland. [➡BEGINNING; 53]

birthright *n* **inheritance**, legacy, bequest, heritage, patrimony, due, entitlement. [➡BEQUEATH AND BEQUESTS; 433]

birth sign *n* [➡FATE, DESTINY, AND ASTROLOGY; 783]

biscuit *n* [➡CAKES, BISCUITS, AND DESSERTS; 1180]

biscuit tin *type of* **container.** [➡CONTAINERS, RECEPTACLES, AND PACKAGING; 1244]

bise *type of* **wind.** [➡WINDY AND STORMY WEATHER; 1053]

bisect *v* **cut in half**, intersect, divide, cut across, sever, cross, break in two, split, cleave, dissect, part, dichotomize (*formal*). [➡TEAR, BREAK, AND CUT; 361] *Opposite:* join.

bisection *n* **cutting in two**, halving, splitting, dissection, division, parting. [➡SEPARATE AND DIVIDE; 402] *Opposite:* union.

bishop *n* [➡RELIGIOUS PEOPLE; 779]

bishopric *n* [➡RELIGIOUS PEOPLE; 779]

bison *type of* **large mammal.** [➡LARGE MAMMAL; 986]

bisque *type of* **soup.** [➡SOUP; 1185]

bistro *type of* **eating place.** [➡HOTELS, RESTAURANTS, AND CLUBS; 1081]

bit 1 *n* **small piece**, tad (*informal*), morsel, crumb, fragment, speck, smidgen (*informal*), spot, trace, scrap, drop. [➡SMALL PIECE; 127] 2 *n* **minute**, while, moment, jiffy (*informal*), jiff. [➡SHORT PERIOD OF TIME; 93]

bit by bit *adv* **little by little**, slowly, by degrees, gradually, in stages, step by step. [➡HAPPENING SLOWLY; 106] *Opposite:* suddenly.

bitch 1 *v* (*slang*) **be spiteful**, be malicious about, be nasty, slander, malign, moan (*informal*). [➡ACCUSE, BLAME, AND CRITICIZE; 642] *Opposite:* compliment. 2 *v* (*US slang*) **complain**, grumble, carp, gripe (*informal*), moan (*informal*), grouse (*informal*), beef (*slang*), bellyache (*informal*), whine, fuss, squawk (*informal*). [➡COMPLAIN AND NAG; 687] 3 *type of* **female animal.** [➡MALE OR FEMALE ANIMAL; 978]

bitchily (*slang*) *adv* **maliciously**, unpleasantly, nastily, spitefully, cattily, venomously, shrewishly, cruelly, meanly, hatefully, viciously. [➡RUDE AND HOSTILE; 626] *Opposite:* kindly.

bitchiness (*slang*) *n* **maliciousness**, unpleasantness, nastiness, spitefulness, cattiness, venom, shrewishness, hatefulness, meanness, viciousness. [➡AGGRESSIVE AND BELLIGERENT; 519] *Opposite:* kindness.

bitchy (*slang*) *adj* **catty**, malicious, unpleasant, cruel, nasty, spiteful, venomous, shrewish, hateful, vicious, mean. [➡BEASTLY AND BRUTISH; 511] *Opposite:* kind.

bite 1 *v* **sink your teeth into**, nibble, gnaw, bite off, bite into, chomp (*informal*), masticate. [➡EAT AND NOT EAT; 711] 2 *v* **wound**, nip, snap, attack, maul, sink your teeth into. [➡PHYSICAL ATTACK AND PUNISHMENT; 416] 3 *v* **hurt**, sting, feel painful, nip, prick, smart. [➡PAIN AND OTHER PHYSICAL SENSATIONS; 734] 4 *n* **sharp taste**, spiciness, tartness, piquancy, tang, kick, smack. [➡TASTE; 704] 5 *n* **taste**, mouthful, nibble, chew, piece, morsel, taster, bit. [➡SMALL PIECE; 127] 6 *n* **wound**, sting, puncture, bite mark. [➡CONDITIONS AFFECTING THE SKIN; 722]

bite off more than you can chew *v* [➡OVERDO SOMETHING; 291]

bite the bullet *v* **grasp the nettle**, take the bull by the horns, go for it (*slang*), face up to. [➡PREPARE FOR ACTION; 290] *Opposite:* avoid.

bite the dust (*informal*) 1 *v* **fall down**, fall flat, take a fall, tumble, tumble down, come clattering down. [➡GO DOWNWARDS; 308] 2 *v* **die**, pass away, expire (*formal or literary*), give up the ghost (*literary*), breathe your last (*literary*). [➡DIE; 922] 3 *v* **fail**, go under, die a death, be unsuccessful, go bankrupt, go broke. [➡FAIL OR BE UNSUCCESSFUL; 75] *Opposite:* succeed.

biting 1 *adj* **cold**, freezing, piercing, cutting, stinging, frigid, raw, icy, arctic (*informal*), glacial. [➡COLD WEATHER; 1051] *Opposite:* hot. 2 *adj* **sarcastic**, acerbic, mordant, satirical, cruel, scornful, derisive, mocking, wounding. [➡RUDE AND HOSTILE; 626] *Opposite:* sympathetic.

bitingly *adv* **acidly**, acerbically, tartly, woundingly, cruelly, sarcastically, mordantly. [➡RUDE AND HOSTILE; 626] *Opposite:* sympathetically.

bit map *type of* **software.** [➡COMPUTERS AND COMPUTING; 1126]

bits and bobs (*informal*) 1 *n* **belongings**, things, stuff, gear (*informal*), personal possessions, clobber (*informal*), effects (*formal*), chattels. [➡POSSESSIONS; 462] 2 *n* **odds and ends**, bits and pieces (*informal*), bric-a-brac, knick-knacks, leftovers, scraps, stuff. [➡COLLECTIONS AND MIXTURES OF THINGS; 1243]

bits and pieces (*informal*) 1 *n* **belongings**, things, bits and bobs (*informal*), odds and ends, stuff, personal possessions, gear (*informal*), clobber (*informal*). [➡POSSESSIONS; 462] 2 *n* **knick-knacks**, leftovers, scraps, odds and ends, stuff, bric-a-brac, bits and bobs (*informal*). [➡COLLECTIONS AND MIXTURES OF THINGS; 1243]

bitter 1 *adj* **sour**, acid, acidic, tart, astringent, vinegary, pungent, harsh, acrid. [➡TASTE; 704] *Opposite:* sweet. 2 *adj* **resentful**, embittered, sulky, cheated, angry, hard done by, cynical, indignant. [➡IRRITATION AND ANGER; 542] *Opposite:* glad. 3 *adj* **unpleasant**, acrimonious, nasty, vicious, hostile, harsh. [➡RUDE AND HOSTILE; 626] *Opposite:* pleasant. 4 *adj* **hostile**, nasty, vicious, rancorous, virulent, vehement. [➡IRRITATION AND ANGER; 542] 5 *adj* **cold**, freezing, icy, biting, raw, polar, sharp, piercing, cutting, stinging, glacial, arctic (*informal*). [➡COLD WEATHER; 1051] *Opposite:* hot.

bitterly 1 *adv* **resentfully**, acrimoniously, sulkily, sullenly, cynically, angrily, indignantly. [➡RUDE AND HOSTILE; 626] *Opposite:* gladly. 2 *adv* **severely**, excessively, intensely, inordinately, desperately, terribly, penetratingly. [➡CRITICALLY AND SERIOUSLY; 132] *Opposite:* slightly.

bittern *type of* **freshwater bird.** [➡FRESHWATER BIRD; 1000]

bitterness 1 *n* **resentment**, acrimony, unpleasantness, sullenness, anger, animosity, hostility, cynicism, indignation. [➡FEELINGS ABOUT THE PAST; 533] *Opposite:* pleasure. 2 *n* **sourness**, acidity, sour taste, bitter taste, sharpness, tartness. [➡TASTE; 704] *Opposite:* sweetness.

bittersweet *adj* **poignant**, nostalgic, affecting, touching, sentimental, with a sting in the tail. [➡EMOTIONALLY UNPLEASANT AND UPSETTING; 228]

bitty 1 *adj* **disjointed**, fragmented, scrappy, fragmentary, disconnected, sketchy. [➡UNFINISHEDNESS; 240] *Opposite:* cohesive. 2 *adj* (*US informal*) **itsy-bitsy** (*informal*), tiny, teeny (*informal*), teeny-weeny (*informal*), teensy-weensy (*informal*). [➡SMALL; 1194]

bitumen *n* **tar**, asphalt, Tarmac, blacktop (*US*). [➡BUILDING MATERIALS; 1076]

bivalve *type of* **aquatic invertebrate.** [➡AQUATIC INVERTEBRATE; 1022]

bivouac 1 *n* **shelter**, awning, tent, camp, encampment, temporary camp, mountaineering camp, military camp. [➡HUMAN SETTLEMENTS; 1069] 2 *v* **camp**, set up camp, pitch a tent. [➡HOBBIES, GAMES, AND SPORTS; 875]

biweekly *adv* **once every two weeks**, every fortnight, once a fortnight, twice a month. [➡TIMES OF YEAR; 88]

bizarre *adj* **strange**, curious, inexplicable, out of the ordinary, unusual, weird, peculiar, odd, uncanny, wacky (*informal*), fantastic, off the wall. [➡BIZARRE AND PECULIAR; 258] *Opposite:* ordinary.

bizarreness *n* [➡BIZARRE AND PECULIAR; 258]

blab (*informal*) *v* **tell tales**, gossip, spread rumours, tattle, leak, snitch (*slang*), tell, tell on, talk out of turn. [➡BETRAY CONFIDENCES AND GOSSIP; 619]

blabber *v* **chatter**, babble, waffle (*informal*), chat, rabbit on (*informal*), go on, drivel, blather (*informal*), yammer (*informal*), jabber. [➡WITTER AND BABBLE; 618]

blabbermouth (*informal*) *n* **bigmouth** (*informal*), gossip, chatterbox (*informal*), telltale, chatterer, sneak, tattletale (*US informal*). [➡INTERFERING PEOPLE AND TELLTALES; 950]

black 1 *adj* **dark**, gloomy, obscure, dusky, murky, dim, shadowy. [➡DESCRIBING LIGHT; 1227] *Opposite:* light. 2 *type of* **colour**. [➡COLOURS; 1223]

black

◆ *types of black*
blue-black, coal black, ebony, inky, jet black, pitch-black, raven, sable

black-and-blue *adj* **bruised**, aching, hurt, injured, battered, beaten. [➡INJURED; 743]

black-and-white *adj* **clear-cut**, straightforward, unambiguous, categorical, unequivocal, uncompromising. [➡EASE AND SIMPLICITY; 201] *Opposite:* ambiguous.

black as night *adj* [➡DESCRIBING LIGHT; 1227]

blackball *v* **exclude**, ban, keep out, debar, snub, shun, ostracize, boycott, blacklist, give the cold shoulder. [➡REFUSING OR REJECTING RELATIONS; 975] *Opposite:* welcome.

black bean *type of* **pulse**. [➡BEANS AND PULSES; 1188]

blackberry *type of* **berry**. [➡FRUIT AND VEGETABLES; 1175]

blackbird *type of* **songbird**. [➡SONGBIRD; 1003]

blackboard *n* **writing board**, board, slate, chalkboard (*US*), whiteboard. [➡WRITING AND DRAWING IMPLEMENTS, AND MEDIA; 602]

black bread *type of* **bread**. [➡BREAD, FLOUR, AND BREAD PRODUCTS; 1178]

black cab *type of* **commercial or industrial vehicle**. [➡VEHICLES; 1144]

blackcurrant *type of* **berry**. [➡FRUIT AND VEGETABLES; 1175]

blacken 1 *v* **darken**, make black, dirty, begrime (*literary*), turn black, besmirch, sully (*literary*). [➡CHANGE OF COLOUR; 392] *Opposite:* lighten. 2 *v* **slander**, libel, defame, vilify, malign, besmirch, denigrate, sully (*literary*), slur, speak ill of, asperse (*formal*). [➡PROTEST AND EXPRESS DISAPPROVAL; 643] *Opposite:* praise.

black-eyed bean *type of* **pulse**. [➡BEANS AND PULSES; 1188]

black-eyed pea (*US*) *type of* **pulse**. [➡BEANS AND PULSES; 1188]

black fly *type of* **flying insect**. [➡FLYING INSECTS; 1013]

blackguard *n* **scoundrel**, rascal, rogue, villain, wretch (*formal*), rotter (*informal dated*), cad (*dated*). [➡VILLAINS AND THUGS; 947]

blackhead *n* **blocked pore**, spot, pimple, zit (*slang*), blemish. [➡CONDITIONS AFFECTING THE SKIN; 722]

black hole *type of* **star or star system**. [➡CELESTIAL BODIES; 1060]

blackjack (*US*) *type of* **club**. [➡BLUNT INSTRUMENTS AND WHIPS; 1157]

blacklist *v* **ban**, debar, bar, exclude, shut out, boycott, preclude (*formal*), prohibit, outlaw. [➡REVOKE STATUS; 460]

black look *n* [➡FACIAL EXPRESSION; 652]

blackly 1 *adv* **angrily**, menacingly, threateningly, belligerently, aggressively, resentfully, furiously, sullenly. [➡RUDE AND HOSTILE; 626] *Opposite:* happily. 2 *adv* **hopelessly**, gloomily, lugubriously, dismally, dolefully, mournfully, sadly, sombrely, depressingly. [➡BAD-TEMPERED AND HUMOURLESS; 627] *Opposite:* sunnily.

black magic *n* [➡THE SUPERNATURAL; 788]

blackmail 1 *n* **extortion**, intimidation, bribery, corruption, extraction, protection, coercion, threat. [➡CRIMES; 817] 2 *v* **extort**, extract, exact, bribe, force, coerce, compel, threaten. [➡CAUSE OR COMPEL TO ACT; 272]

blackmailer *n* **extortionist**, coercer, criminal, crook (*informal*). [➡CRIMINALS; 821]

blackness 1 *n* **darkness**, duskiness, dimness, shadow, gloom, dusk, murkiness, night. [➡DESCRIBING LIGHT; 1227] *Opposite:* light. 2 *n* **hopelessness**, despondency, gloominess, depression, dolefulness, gloom, mournfulness, lugubriousness, sombreness, melancholy, pessimism. [➡SADNESS, DISTRESS, AND DESPAIR; 540] *Opposite:* optimism. 3 *n* **anger**, fury, temper, aggression, belligerence, resentment, menace, sullenness, hostility. [➡IRRITATION AND ANGER; 542] *Opposite:* cheerfulness.

blackout 1 *n* **fainting fit**, seizure, loss of consciousness, collapse. [➡ILLNESSES AND DISORDERS; 733] 2 *n* **power cut**, shutdown, power failure, brownout (*US*). [➡SUDDEN EVENT; 52] 3 *n* **embargo**, veto, clampdown, suppression, prohibition, curfew. [➡REFUSE PERMISSION AND NOT ALLOW; 671]

black out *v* **faint**, pass out, lose consciousness, collapse, become unconscious, fall in a faint, swoon. [➡FALL ILL, TREAT, AND RECOVER; 729] *Opposite:* come to.

black pepper *type of* **spice**. [➡HERBS AND SPICES; 1174]

blacksnake *type of* **non-poisonous snake**. [➡SNAKE; 995]

black-tie *adj* **formal**, dressy, posh (*informal*), ceremonial. [➡DESCRIBING CLOTHES; 869] *Opposite:* casual.

black tie *n* [➡GARMENTS AND OUTFITS; 865]

blacktop (*US*) *n* **asphalt**, tar, bitumen, Tarmac. [➡COVERS AND COATINGS; 1245]

black widow *type of* **arachnid**. [➡ARACHNIDS; 1018]

bladder *part of* **digestive tract**. [➡THE DIGESTIVE TRACT; 710]

bladder wrack *type of* **alga.** [➡MICROORGANISMS, FUNGI, AND ALGAE; 1023]

blade 1 *n* **cutting edge**, knife-edge, edge, razor blade, knife blade. [➡EXTREMITIES OF PHYSICAL OBJECTS; 1249] 2 *n* **vane**, fin, flat, propeller, sail, oar. [➡PARTS OF A SHIP OR BOAT; 1150]

blame 1 *v* **hold responsible**, censure, accuse, point the finger at, hold accountable, attribute, impugn (*formal*), impute [➡CREATING CONNECTIONS; 145]. *Opposite:* exculpate (*formal*). 2 *v* **criticize**, reproach, condemn, think badly of, upbraid, reprimand, reprehend, denunciate (*formal*). [➡ACCUSE, BLAME, AND CRITICIZE; 642] *Opposite:* commend. 3 *n* **responsibility**, guilt, culpability, fault, blameworthiness, liability, denunciation. [➡MORALLY BAD; 776] *Opposite:* commendation.

blameless *adj* **innocent**, virtuous, righteous, faultless, irreproachable, spotless, guiltless, scrupulous, inculpable (*formal*), unblemished, untarnished, clean (*slang*), above suspicion. [➡MORALLY GOOD; 775] *Opposite:* guilty.

blameworthy *adj* **responsible**, guilty, culpable, at fault, chargeable, to blame, blamable. [➡MORALLY BAD; 776] *Opposite:* innocent.

blanch *v* **go pale**, grow pale, lighten, bleach, blench. [➡CHANGE OF COLOUR; 392] *Opposite:* blush.

blancmange *type of* **dessert.** [➡CAKES, BISCUITS, AND DESSERTS; 1180]

bland 1 *adj* **insipid**, weak, tasteless, mild, plain, flat, flavourless, wishy-washy (*informal*). [➡TASTE; 704] *Opposite:* tasty. 2 *adj* **featureless**, ordinary, dull, lacklustre, boring, flat, nondescript, unappealing, mediocre, unremarkable, vapid, banal. [➡BORING AND UNINTERESTING; 235] *Opposite:* exciting.

blandish (*formal*) *v* [➡FLATTER AND FAWN; 622]

blandishment *n* **flattery**, cajolery, praise, sweet talk (*informal*), fawning, soft words, blarney (*informal*), smooth talk. [➡INGRATIATING; 639]

blandness 1 *n* **tastelessness**, weakness, insipidness, mildness, plainness, dullness, flatness. [➡TASTE; 704] *Opposite:* tastiness. 2 *n* **dullness**, banality, flatness, triteness, insipidness, vapidness. [➡BORING AND UNINTERESTING; 235]

blank 1 *adj* **empty**, vacant, bare, clean, clear, plain, void. [➡EMPTY; 1237] *Opposite:* full. 2 *adj* **outright**, complete, total, absolute, unqualified, unmitigated, utter, downright, straight-out (*US informal*). [➡ABSOLUTE AND ABSOLUTELY; 131] *Opposite:* partial. 3 *adj* **uncomprehending**, impassive, vacant, empty, bemused, perplexed, unexpressive. [➡FACIAL EXPRESSION; 652] *Opposite:* knowing. 4 *n* **space**, void, gap, empty space, break. [➡HOLES, GAPS, AND FORKS; 1251]

blanket 1 *n* **coverlet**, cover, covering, over-blanket, bedspread, electric blanket. [➡COVERS AND COATINGS; 1245] 2 *adj* **comprehensive**, extensive, complete, total, wholesale, unlimited, absolute, unmitigated, straight-out (*US informal*). [➡WHOLENESS AND COMPLETENESS; 199] *Opposite:* partial. 3 *v* **cover**, obscure, encase, drape, carpet, swathe, overspread, overlay. [➡CAUSE TO DISAPPEAR; 6] *Opposite:* uncover.

blankly *adv* **impassively**, vacantly, uncomprehendingly, perplexedly, uninterestedly, expressionlessly. [➡FACIAL EXPRESSION; 652] *Opposite:* animatedly.

blankness 1 *n* **emptiness**, void, vacancy, bareness, barrenness, vacuum, nothingness, vacuity (*formal*). [➡EMPTY; 1237] 2 *n* **expressionlessness**, vacancy, indifference, emotionlessness, vacuousness. [➡UNINTERESTED AND DETACHED; 630] *Opposite:* animation. 3 *n* **bewilderment**, confusion, obliviousness, incomprehension, lack of understanding. [➡CONFUSION, ANXIETY, AND WORRY; 541] *Opposite:* acuity.

blank out *v* **block out**, blot out, suppress, wipe out, erase, deny, refuse. [➡NOT PAY ATTENTION; 765] *Opposite:* acknowledge.

blare *v* **ring out**, make a racket, blast (*informal*), boom, resound, shout, shriek. [➡EMIT CONTINUOUS SOUNDS; 367]

blare out *v* **ring out**, make a racket, blast out, resound, boom out. [➡EMIT CONTINUOUS SOUNDS; 367] *Opposite:* quieten.

blaring *adj* **deafening**, earsplitting, cacophonous, raucous, booming, shrieking, rowdy. [➡LOUD OR UNPLEASANT SOUNDS; 1265] *Opposite:* quiet.

blarney (*informal*) *n* **nonsense**, smooth talk, charm, drivel, flattery, bunk (*slang*), claptrap (*informal*), cobblers (*slang*). [➡INGRATIATING; 639]

blasé *adj* **nonchalant**, laid back, cool, relaxed, unmoved, unconcerned, carefree, offhand. [➡NEUTRALITY AND INDIFFERENCE; 554] *Opposite:* concerned.

blaspheme *v* **curse**, swear, cuss (*informal*), eff and blind (*slang*), issue oaths, use foul language. [➡INSULTS, ABUSE, AND SWEARING; 659]

blasphemer *n* **swearer**, curser, foul mouth. [➡RELIGIOUS CONCEPTS; 777]

blasphemous *adj* **profane**, sacrilegious, irreligious, offensive, improper, irreverent, impious, ungodly. [➡RELIGIOUS CONCEPTS; 777] *Opposite:* pious.

blasphemy 1 *n* **profanity**, sacrilege, wickedness, irreverence, violation, desecration. [➡RELIGIOUS CONCEPTS; 777] *Opposite:* piety. 2 *n* **oath**, curse, profanity, imprecation (*formal*), execration (*literary or formal*), swearword, cuss (*informal*), cussword (*US informal*). [➡INSULTS, ABUSE, AND SWEARING; 659]

blast 1 *n* **explosion**, detonation, discharge (*formal*), flash, flare, gust, boom. [➡SUDDEN EVENT; 52] 2 *v* (*informal*) **blare**, resound, boom, make a racket, ring out. [➡EMIT CONTINUOUS SOUNDS; 367] 3 *v* **blow up**, explode, detonate, shoot, demolish, discharge (*formal*), blow away (*US slang*). [➡DESTRUCTION AND DEMOLITION; 360] 4 *v* (*informal*) **criticize**, attack, have a go at (*informal*), lambaste, vilify, castigate (*formal*), carpet (*informal*), censure. [➡ACCUSE, BLAME, AND CRITICIZE; 642] 5 *v* **damage**, blight, disfigure, burn, blister, scar, sear, scorch. [➡WORSEN APPEARANCE; 383]

See Compare and Contrast at **criticize**.

blast off *v* **take off**, lift off, launch. [➡THROW SOMETHING; 335]

blastoff *n* **launch**, takeoff, liftoff. [➡BEGINNING; 53] *Opposite:* touchdown.

blast out *v* **blare out**, ring out, make a racket, blare, boom, resound, thud. [➡EMIT CONTINUOUS SOUNDS; 367]

blatancy *n* **obviousness**, conspicuousness, ostentation, flagrancy, overtness, barefacedness, shamelessness, brazenness. [➡PERCEPTIBLE; 25] *Opposite:* subtlety.

blatant *adj* **obvious**, unconcealed, barefaced, unashamed, deliberate, flagrant, transparent, patent, manifest, palpable, brazen. [➡INTENTIONAL AND DELIBERATE; 280] *Opposite:* furtive.

blather (*informal*) 1 *v* **chatter**, go on, babble, blabber, jabber, ramble on, prate, prattle, drivel, waffle (*informal*), yammer (*informal*). [➡WITTER AND BABBLE; 618] 2 *n* **drivel**, twaddle (*informal*), prattle, chatter, babble, blabber, gossip. [➡MEANINGLESS SPEECH OR WRITING; 677]

blaze 1 *v* **burn**, be on fire, burst into flames, rage, glow, shine, radiate, flash, flame, flare, illuminate. [➡FIRE, FLAMMABILITY, AND BURNING; 1164] 2 *n* **fire**, inferno, conflagration, combustion. [➡FIRE, FLAMMABILITY, AND BURNING; 1164] 3 *n* **glare**, glow, flash, brightness, intensity, illumination, incandescence. [➡DESCRIBING LIGHT; 1227] 4 *v* **break new ground**, lead the way, be the first, light the way, set an example, instigate, initiate, pioneer. [➡START AN ACTION; 261]

See Compare and Contrast at **fire**.

blaze a trail *v* [➡CAUSE TO HAPPEN; 31]

blazer *type of* **jacket**. [➡GARMENTS AND OUTFITS; 865]

blazing 1 *adj* **intense**, raging, mighty, heated, furious, tremendous, violent, vehement, fierce. [➡STRENGTH; 202] 2 *adj* **burning**, glowing, shining, radiating, scorching (*informal*), blistering, baking, roaring, searing, glaring. [➡FIRE, FLAMMABILITY, AND BURNING; 1164]

blazon *v* **splash**, emblazon, display. [➡DECORATE, ADORN, AND APPLY COATINGS; 406]

bleach *v* **lighten**, peroxide, blanch, blench, whiten, decolorize. [➡CHANGE OF COLOUR; 392]

bleached *adj* **lightened**, faded, sun-bleached, washed-out, blanched, whitened. [➡DESCRIBING COLOURS; 1225]

bleachers (*US*) *n* **benches**, stand seats, seating, seats. [➡FURNITURE; 858]

bleak 1 *adj* **hopeless**, unpromising, gloomy, doubtful, futile, grim. [➡DANGEROUS; 237] *Opposite:* promising. 2 *adj* **unwelcoming**, austere, miserable, drab, dreary, depressing, desolate, uninviting, lonely, isolated, dismal. [➡PLAIN; 233] *Opposite:* friendly. 3 *adj* **cold**, harsh, wintry, cheerless, miserable, bitter, chilling, biting. [➡COLD WEATHER; 1051] *Opposite:* warm. 4 *adj* **forlorn**, miserable, dejected, disheartened, downhearted, hopeless, sorrowful, sad, despairing, despondent, dour, depressing, funereal. [➡SADNESS, DISTRESS, AND DESPAIR; 540] *Opposite:* cheerful.

bleakly *adv* **forlornly**, dismally, hopelessly, drearily, despondently, cheerlessly, miserably, austerely, dejectedly, drably, sorrowfully, desolately, sadly, despairingly. [➡SADNESS, DISTRESS, AND DESPAIR; 540] *Opposite:* cheerfully.

bleakness 1 *n* **hopelessness**, despondency, sorrow, misery, sadness, dejection, despair. [➡FEELINGS ABOUT THE FUTURE; 534] *Opposite:* hopefulness. 2 *n* **cheerlessness**, drabness, austerity, harshness, bareness, loneliness, isolation, desolation, dreariness. [➡PLAIN; 233] *Opposite:* cheerfulness.

blearily *adv* **fuzzily**, hazily, groggily, sleepily, drowsily, vaguely. [➡TIRED, ASLEEP AND UNCONSCIOUS; 739] *Opposite:* clearly.

bleary *adj* **hazy**, watery, unfocused, fuzzy, blurry, groggy, sleepy, shadowy. [➡SEE; 700] *Opposite:* clear.

bleary-eyed *adj* **sleepy**, tired, half-awake, dozy, groggy, heavy-lidded, drowsy, slumberous, torpid. [➡TIRED, ASLEEP AND UNCONSCIOUS; 739]

bleat *v* **whinge** (*informal*), moan (*informal*), whine, complain, nag, bellyache (*informal*), gripe (*informal*), fuss, squawk (*informal*), yammer (*informal*). [➡COMPLAIN AND NAG; 687]

bleed 1 *v* **lose blood**, haemorrhage, shed blood. [➡THE BLOOD AND CIRCULATION; 718] 2 *v* (*informal*) **exploit**, drain, wring, milk (*informal*), fleece (*informal*), deplete, suck the life out of. [➡USE UP AND WASTE; 475] *Opposite:* conserve. 3 *n* **blood loss**, haemorrhage, nosebleed. [➡THE BLOOD AND CIRCULATION; 718]

bleed dry (*informal*) *v* **drain**, suck dry, deplete, fleece (*informal*), bring to its knees, exploit, suck the life out of. [➡USE UP AND WASTE; 475] *Opposite:* replenish.

bleeding *n* **blood loss**, haemorrhage, flow of blood, flow. [➡THE BLOOD AND CIRCULATION; 718]

bleep 1 *n* **beep**, tone, sound, noise. [➡RINGING AND TOOTING SOUNDS; 1258] 2 *v* **call**, page, alert, signal, contact, summon, get (*informal*). [➡TELEPHONE AND PAGE; 682] 3 *type of* **continuous sound**. [➡CONTINUOUS SOUNDS; 1257]

bleeper *n* **pager**, beeper (*informal*), monitor. [➡TELECOMMUNICATIONS; 1129]

blemish 1 *n* **mark**, defect, imperfection, flaw, fault, stain, spot, blotch, discoloration, fleck, disfigurement, wart. [➡FAULTS, FLAWS, AND WEAKNESSES; 252] 2 *v* **damage**, tarnish, spoil, ruin, stain, injure, discolour, mar, vitiate. [➡WORSEN APPEARANCE; 383] *Opposite:* restore.

See Compare and Contrast at **flaw**.

blemished *adj* **marked**, stained, imperfect, flawed, tarnished, mottled, flecked, marred, scarred, discoloured. [➡IN BAD REPAIR; 1233] *Opposite:* unblemished.

blench 1 *v* **draw back**, hesitate, falter, recoil, flinch, shrink back, quail. [➡HESITATE; 273] 2 *v* **go pale**, grow pale, lighten, blanch, whiten, drain of colour. [➡CHANGE OF COLOUR; 392] *Opposite:* redden.

blend 1 *v* **mix**, merge, combine, bring together, unify, intermingle, mingle, amalgamate, meld. [➡COMBINE AND MIX; 401] *Opposite:* separate. 2 *n* **mixture**, merger, combination, intermingling, balance, assortment, amalgam, composite, fusion. [➡COLLECTIONS AND MIXTURES OF THINGS; 1243]

See Compare and Contrast at **mixture**.

blender 1 *n* **mixer**, food processor, liquidizer. [➡HOUSEHOLD APPLIANCES; 1116] 2 *type of* **utensil**. [➡TABLEWARE, CUTLERY, AND KITCHENWARE; 861]

bless 1 *v* **sanctify**, consecrate, exalt (*formal*), hallow, extol, laud. [➡RELIGIONS AND RELIGIOUS PRACTICES; 778] *Opposite:* curse. 2 *v* **approve**, sanction, support, endorse, back, commend. [➡APPROVE AND CONFIRM; 647]. *Opposite:* decry (*formal*).

blessed 1 *adj* **holy**, sacred, sanctified, hallowed, consecrated, set apart. [➡RELIGIOUS CONCEPTS; 777] *Opposite:* profane. 2 *adj* **welcome**, providential, lucky, fortunate, pleasant, happy. [➡EMOTIONALLY PLEASANT; 188] *Opposite:* unfortunate.

blessing 1 *n* **consecration**, sanctification, benediction, dedication. [➡RELIGIONS AND RELIGIOUS PRACTICES; 778] 2 *n* **approval**, sanction, permission, go-ahead (*informal*), consent, approbation. [➡APPROVE AND CONFIRM; 647] *Opposite:* veto. 3 *n* **lucky thing**, good thing, miracle, piece of good fortune, stroke of luck, boon, godsend. [➡SOURCE OF HAPPINESS, PLEASURE, OR IMPROVEMENT; 210] *Opposite:* disaster.

blether (*informal*) 1 *v* **chatter**, go on, babble, jabber, ramble, prattle, twitter, talk rubbish, rattle on, rabbit (*informal*), waffle (*informal*), natter (*informal*), witter (*informal*). [➡WITTER AND BABBLE; 618] 2 *n* **drivel**, twaddle (*informal*), prattle, chatter, gibberish, gobbledegook (*informal disapproving*), gossip, wittering (*informal*), chit-chat (*informal*), muttering, waffle (*informal*). [➡MEANINGLESS SPEECH OR WRITING; 677]

blight 1 *n* **disfigurement**, stain, scar, blot, affliction, disease. [➡FAULTS, FLAWS, AND WEAKNESSES; 252] 2 *v* **ruin**, disfigure, stain, scar, impair, damage, blast, afflict. [➡WORSEN APPEARANCE; 383]

blimp *type of* **civil aircraft**. [➡AIRCRAFT; 1147]

blimpish *adj* **bigoted**, narrow-minded, prejudiced, intolerant, dogmatic, inflexible, rigid. [➡DIFFICULT TO PLEASE; 516] *Opposite:* tolerant.

blind 1 *adj* **sightless**, unsighted, unseeing, eyeless, visionless. [➡SEE; 700] *Opposite:* sighted. 2 *n* **screen**, window shade, canopy, visor, venetian blind, roller blind, shade (*US*). [➡COVERS AND COATINGS; 1245]

blind alley *n* **dead end**, cul-de-sac, impasse. [➡ROADS; 1105]

blind date *n* **rendezvous**, date, meeting, assignation, appointment. [➡MEETINGS AND ASSEMBLIES; 43]

blindfold *n* **bandage**, cloth, covering, scarf, band. [➡COVERS AND COATINGS; 1245]

blinding 1 *adj* **glaring**, dazzling, bright, bedazzling, strong. [➡DESCRIBING LIGHT; 1227] *Opposite:* soft. 2 *adj* (*informal*) **striking**, extraordinary, outstanding, arresting, amazing, fantastic, superb. [➡EXTRAORDINARY: AMAZING; 205] *Opposite:* ordinary.

blindly 1 *adv* **sightlessly**, unseeingly, dimly. [➡SEE; 700] 2 *adv* **without thinking**, thoughtlessly, instinctively, carelessly, recklessly, uncritically, irrationally, indiscriminately, impetuously, heedlessly. [➡NEGATIVE INTELLECTUAL CHARACTERISTICS; 526] *Opposite:* thoughtfully.

blindness 1 *n* **sightlessness**, loss of sight, impaired vision. [➡SEE; 700] *Opposite:* sight. 2 *n* **thoughtlessness**, carelessness, recklessness, rashness, impetuousness, heedlessness. [➡NEGATIVE INTELLECTUAL CHARACTERISTICS; 526] *Opposite:* carefulness.

blind spot *n* **weakness**, failing, failure, fault, flaw, block. [➡FAULTS, FLAWS, AND WEAKNESSES; 252] *Opposite:* strength.

blini *type of* **pancake**. [➡CAKES, BISCUITS, AND DESSERTS; 1180]

blink 1 *v* **wink**, bat an eyelid, flutter an eyelid, flicker an eyelid. [➡LOOKING AND LOOKS; 701] 2 *v* **flash**, wink, flicker, twinkle, signal, glisten, shine, shimmer, glimmer. [➡LIGHT EMISSION; 369]

blinker *type of* **external feature**. [➡VEHICLES; 1144]

blinkered *adj* **inward-looking**, insular, narrow-minded, narrow, limited. [➡NEGATIVE INTELLECTUAL CHARACTERISTICS; 526]

blinkeredness *n* **insularity**, narrow-mindedness, narrowness. [➡NEGATIVE INTELLECTUAL CHARACTERISTICS; 526]

blink of an eye *n* [➡SHORT PERIOD OF TIME; 93]

blintz *type of* **pancake**. [➡CAKES, BISCUITS, AND DESSERTS; 1180]

blip *n* **problem**, glitch, error, failure, breakdown, malfunction, fault, bug (*informal*), gremlin (*informal*). [➡FAULTS, FLAWS, AND WEAKNESSES; 252]

bliss *n* **ecstasy**, heaven, paradise, enjoyment, happiness, delight, pleasure, harmony, blessedness. [➡PLEASURE, EXCITEMENT, AND ELATION; 535] *Opposite:* misery.

blissful *adj* **heavenly**, wonderful, delightful, idyllic, perfect, peaceful, pleasurable, enjoyable, harmonious, joyful, ecstatic, beatific (*literary*). [➡EMOTIONALLY PLEASANT; 188] *Opposite:* miserable.

blissfully *adv* **supremely**, wonderfully, ecstatically, delightfully, happily, blessedly, idyllically, joyfully, beatifically (*literary*). [➡PLEASURE, EXCITEMENT, AND ELATION; 535] *Opposite:* miserably.

blister 1 *n* **sore**, swelling, eruption, burn, blood blister. [➡CONDITIONS AFFECTING THE SKIN; 722] 2 *v* **swell up**, erupt, bubble, break out, suppurate. [➡EXCRETION AND EXCRETA; 723]

blistering *adj* **sweltering**, scorching (*informal*), baking, roasting (*informal*), blazing, burning, searing, intense, severe. [➡HOT WEATHER; 1050]

blithe 1 *adj* (*literary*) **carefree**, cheerful, happy, merry, happy-go-lucky, easygoing, amiable, lighthearted. [➡CHEERFULNESS OF OUTLOOK; 504] *Opposite:* anxious. 2 *adj* **casual**, unconcerned, indifferent, unthinking, uncaring, thoughtless, careless. [➡NEUTRALITY AND INDIFFERENCE; 554] *Opposite:* thoughtful.

blithely 1 *adv* (*literary*) **merrily**, cheerfully, happily, gaily, amiably, lightheartedly, merrily, lightly, without a care in the world. [➡GOOD-TEMPERED AND HUMOROUS; 628] *Opposite:* anxiously. 2 *adv* **casually**, carelessly, unthinkingly, indifferently, thoughtlessly, unconcernedly. [➡NEUTRALITY AND INDIFFERENCE; 554] *Opposite:* thoughtfully.

blitheness (*literary*) *n* [➡CHEERFULNESS OF OUTLOOK; 504]

blither (*informal*) *v* [➡WITTER AND BABBLE; 618]

blithering (*informal*) *adj* **stupid**, total, complete, absolute, utter, downright, out-and-out, outright. [➡ABSOLUTE AND ABSOLUTELY; 131]

blitz 1 *n* **bombardment**, blitzkrieg, saturation bombing, onslaught, offensive, barrage, salvo, cannonade. [➡WARFARE AND WAR; 830] 2 *n* (*informal*) **onslaught**, attack, crackdown, concerted effort, clear-out, cleanup, tidy-up. [➡SUDDEN EVENT; 52] 3 *v* (*informal*) **crack down** (*informal*), concentrate on, focus on, come down on, fall on, hit, lower the boom (*US* *informal*). [➡CARRY OUT AN ACTION; 270] 4 *v* **bombard**, bomb, blast, barrage, hit, target, strafe, saturate, overwhelm, attack, assault. [➡WARFARE AND WAR; 830] 5 *v* (*informal*) **clean**, clean up, tidy, whip round, clear away, clear up. [➡ARRANGE AND CREATE ORDER; 358]

blitzed (*informal*) *adj* [➡UNDER THE INFLUENCE OF DRUGS OR ALCOHOL; 742]

blitzkrieg *n* [➡WARFARE AND WAR; 830]

blizzard *n* **snowstorm**, whiteout, storm. [➡COLD WEATHER; 1051]

bloat *v* **swell**, inflate, blow up, expand, distend, swell up, puff up, dilate, balloon. [➡CHANGE OF SIZE: BIGGER; 393] *Opposite:* contract.

bloated *adj* **swollen**, distended, stuffed (*informal*), overstuffed, full, overfed, blown up, puffy, ballooned, dilated. [➡ILL AND SICK; 741]

blob 1 *n* **splotch**, globule, spot, splash, dash, dribble, drop, bead, dot, daub, splodge. [➡AMOUNT OF SOLID OR SEMI-SOLID; 115] 2 *v* **splotch**, dot, dab, daub, smudge, splodge. [➡DECORATE, ADORN, AND APPLY COATINGS; 406]

bloc *n* **alliance**, coalition, union, federation, league, syndicate, confederacy, partnership. [➡TERRITORIES AND GROUPS OF NATIONS; 1067]

block 1 *n* **chunk**, hunk, lump, slab, wedge, tablet, mass, cake. [➡LARGE PIECE; 128] 2 *n* **building**, apartment block, block of flats. [➡RESIDENTIAL BUILDINGS; 1077] 3 *n* **wing**, extension, unit, module, part. [➡LARGE PIECE; 128] 4 *n* **cellblock**, toilet block, shower block, tower block. [➡BUILDING MATERIALS; 1076] 5 *n* **expanse**, section, sector, zone, band, stretch, region. [➡LARGE PIECE; 128] 6 *v* **obstruct**, impede, hinder, jam, prevent, oppose, stop, blockade, bar, deter, frustrate, thwart, hamper, hold back. [➡MAKE IMPOSSIBLE; 277] *Opposite:* encourage.

See Compare and Contrast at **hinder**.

blockade 1 *n* **barrier**, barricade, obstruction, line of defence, cordon. [➡BARRIERS; 1112] 2 *v* **deny access**, lay siege to, obstruct, defend, block, guard, shut in, impede, deter. [➡MAKE IMPOSSIBLE; 277]

blockage *n* **obstruction**, impasse, jam, snarl-up, logjam, obstacle, stumbling block, snarl (*US*). [➡PROBLEM; 257]

blockbuster (*informal*) *n* **runaway success**, hit, smash hit, epic, chartbuster, bestseller [➡SUCCESS; 82]. *Opposite:* flop (*informal*).

blockbusting *adj* **successful**, earthshattering, epic, outstanding, popular, chartbusting, record-breaking, sensational, earthshaking. [➡SUCCESSFUL AND PROMISING; 81]

blocked *adj* **congested**, impassable, choked up, jammed, gridlocked, bunged up (*informal*), choked, unnavigable, obstructed, clogged. [➡FULL; 1238] *Opposite:* clear.

blocking *adj* **obstructive**, delaying, stalling, hindering, spoiling, filibustering. [➡REBELLIOUSNESS AND DISOBEDIENCE; 566] *Opposite:* cooperative.

block off 1 *v* **close off**, block, close, cordon off, isolate, barricade, impede, dam, clog. [➡BAR AND OBSTRUCT ACCESS; 411] *Opposite:* free. 2 *v* **obstruct**, obscure, hide, mask, cover, block out, screen, shroud. [➡CAUSE TO DISAPPEAR; 6] *Opposite:* reveal.

block of flats *n* [➡RESIDENTIAL BUILDINGS; 1077]

block out *v* **blank out**, blot out, suppress, wipe out, erase, deny, forget, repress, censor. [➡NOT PAY ATTENTION; 765] *Opposite:* confront.

block up *v* **jam**, fill, stop, obstruct, choke, clog up, impede. [➡FILL; 407] *Opposite:* free.

bloke (*informal*) *n* **man**, fella (*informal*), fellow, guy (*informal*), lad (*informal*), gent (*dated informal*). [➡MALE PERSON; 934]

blond *adj* **fair-haired**, pale, light-coloured, flaxen, golden, straw-coloured. [➡HAIR COLOUR; 486] *Opposite:* dark.

blonde *see* **blond**.

blood 1 *n* **gore**, body fluid, plasma, lifeblood. [➡THE BLOOD AND CIRCULATION; 718] 2 *n* **family**, relations, kinship, kin, relatives, kindred, folk, clan, household. [➡THE FAMILY; 956] 3 *n* **lineage**, ancestry, extraction, heritage, stock, pedigree, genealogy, descent, origin, background. [➡STATUS; 888]

bloodbath *n* **massacre**, slaughter, atrocity, scene of carnage. [➡AGGRESSIVE EVENT; 39]

blood blister *n* [➡CONDITIONS AFFECTING THE SKIN; 722]

blood brother *n* **best friend**, friend, mate, ally, supporter, amigo. [➡FRIENDS; 963] *Opposite:* enemy.

bloodcurdling *adj* **terrifying**, frightening, hair-raising, chilling, spine-tingling, spine-chilling, horrific, macabre, scary (*informal*). [➡FRIGHTENING; 232] *Opposite:* comforting.

bloodhound *type of* **large dog**. [➡DOG; 980]

bloodless 1 *adj* **nonviolent**, peaceful, nonaggressive, orderly, controlled, pacific. [➡PEACEFULNESS AND GENTLENESS; 215] *Opposite:* violent. 2 *adj* **pale**, anaemic, white, pallid, wan, ashen, sallow, pasty, sickly, peaky, white as a sheet, peaked (*US*). [➡COMPLEXION; 481]

bloodletting *n* **quarrel**, fight, dispute, argument, fracas, disagreement, altercation, melee. [➡CHAOS AND UPROAR; 51]

bloodline *n* **descent**, heritage, lineage, ancestry, background, pedigree, family, history, origin, extraction, stock, genealogy. [➡STATUS; 888]

blood lust *n* **bloodthirstiness**, hatred, cruelty, inhumanity, revenge, passion, savagery. [➡UNKIND ACTION OR BEHAVIOUR; 297]

blood money *n* **compensation**, money, recompense, retribution, atonement, reparation, redress, restitution. [➡MONEY, PAYMENTS, AND CHARGES; 800]

blood red *type of* **red**. [➡COLOURS; 1223]

blood relation *n* [➡THE FAMILY; 956]

blood relative *n* [➡THE FAMILY; 956]

bloodshed *n* **carnage**, killing, violence, slaughter, murder, massacre, mayhem (*informal*), butchery. [➡CAUSES OF DEATH; 921]

bloodshot *adj* **red**, inflamed, sore, pink. [➡SEE; 700] *Opposite:* clear.

bloodstone *type of* **gemstone**. [➡PRECIOUS STONES; 1277]

bloodstream *n* **flow**, circulation, blood, arteries, veins, capillaries. [➡THE BLOOD AND CIRCULATION; 718]

bloodsucker *n* **parasite**, leech, tick, mosquito, vampire. [➡PARASITES; 1017]

bloodsucking *adj* **parasitical**, leechlike, vampiric, vampirish. [➡FINANCIALLY MEAN AND GRASPING; 520]

blood, sweat, and tears *n* [➡HARD WORK OR EFFORT; 299]

bloodthirstiness *n* **ferociousness**, viciousness, cruelty, barbarism, brutality, barbarity, savagery. [➡MORALLY BAD; 776]

bloodthirsty *adj* **cruel**, gory, murderous, ferocious, vicious, horrible. [➡MORALLY BAD; 776] *Opposite:* kind.

blood vessel

◆ *types of blood vessel*
aorta, artery, capillary, jugular vein, vein, venule

bloody *adj* **gory**, blood-spattered, bleeding, wounded, injured, bloodstained. [➡INJURED; 743]

bloody-minded (*informal*) *adj* **uncooperative**, obstructive, stubborn, pigheaded, contrary, strong-willed, obstinate, determined. [➡UNWILLINGNESS AND STUBBORNNESS; 565] *Opposite:* cooperative.

bloody-mindedness (*informal*) *n* **lack of cooperation**, obstructiveness, stubbornness, obstinacy, pigheadedness, contrariness, determination. [➡UNWILLINGNESS AND STUBBORNNESS; 565] *Opposite:* cooperation.

bloom **1** *n* (*literary*) **flower**, flower head, blossom, bud. [➡PARTS OF TREES AND PLANTS; 1026] **2** *n* **coloration**, tinge, tint, shadow, flush, blush. [➡DESCRIBING COLOURS; 1225] *Opposite:* pallor. **3** *v* **blossom**, flower, come into flower, come into bud. [➡GROW AND CULTIVATE; 352] *Opposite:* wither. **4** *v* (*literary*) **thrive**, prosper, blossom, flourish, do well, mature, develop, grow. [➡PROSPER AND ABOUND; 16] *Opposite:* struggle. **5** *v* (*literary*) **be a picture of health**, glow, be radiant, thrive, flourish, blossom. [➡PROSPER AND ABOUND; 16]

bloomer (*informal humorous*) *n* **error**, blunder, mistake, gaffe, faux pas (*literary*), slip, howler (*informal*), Freudian slip, blooper (*US informal humorous*). [➡MISTAKES; 251]

bloomers (*dated*) *type of* **lower body underwear**. [➡HABERDASHERY, MILLINERY, AND LINGERIE; 867]

blooming **1** *adj* **flourishing**, thriving, budding, up-and-coming, promising, prospering. [➡SUCCESSFUL AND PROMISING; 81] *Opposite:* struggling. **2** *adj* **blossoming**, flowering, budding, in flower, in bloom. [➡VEGETATION; 1025]

blooper (*US informal humorous*) *n* [➡MISTAKES; 251]

blossom **1** *n* **flower**, flower head, bloom, bud. [➡PARTS OF TREES AND PLANTS; 1026] **2** *v* **bloom**, flower, bud, come into flower, come into bud. [➡GROW AND CULTIVATE; 352] *Opposite:* wither. **3** *v* **flourish**, thrive, grow, bloom, prosper, do well. [➡SUCCEED AND WIN; 79] *Opposite:* struggle. **4** *v* **develop**, grow, come out of your shell, come out of yourself, blossom out, spread your wings. [➡PROSPER AND ABOUND; 16]

blossoming *adj* **developing**, growing, prospering, maturing, thriving, burgeoning, blooming. [➡SUCCESSFUL AND PROMISING; 81]

blossom out *v* **develop**, grow, come out of your shell, come out of yourself, blossom, spread your wings. [➡PROSPER AND ABOUND; 16]

blot **1** *n* **spot**, blemish, splodge, stain, mark, imperfection, discoloration, stigma, blotch, speck, fleck, splotch (*US*). [➡FAULTS, FLAWS, AND WEAKNESSES; 252] **2** *v* **stain**, tarnish, spoil, ruin, disfigure, mark, impair, discolour, fleck, speckle. [➡WORSEN APPEARANCE; 383]

blotch *n* **blot**, mark, blemish, spot, splodge, stain, imperfection, splotch (*US*). [➡FAULTS, FLAWS, AND WEAKNESSES; 252]

blotchy *adj* **mottled**, blemished, marked, spotty, spotted, dappled, discoloured, freckled, reddened, red. [➡COMPLEXION; 481] *Opposite:* plain.

blot on the landscape *n* **scar**, eyesore, blemish, disfigurement, monstrosity, disgrace. [➡UGLINESS AND UNATTRACTIVENESS; 234]

blot out **1** *v* **conceal**, hide, cover, eclipse, block, shadow, obscure. [➡CAUSE TO DISAPPEAR; 6] *Opposite:* reveal. **2** *v* **blank out**, block out, forget, erase, put out of your mind, wipe out. [➡NOT PAY ATTENTION; 765] *Opposite:* recall.

blotter (*US*) *n* **logbook**, notebook, log, record, journal, diary. [➡WRITING AND DRAWING IMPLEMENTS, AND MEDIA; 602]

blouse *type of* **top**. [➡GARMENTS AND OUTFITS; 865]

blouson *type of* **jacket**. [➡GARMENTS AND OUTFITS; 865]

blow **1** *v* **whoosh**, gust, waft, puff, bluster, rage. [➡WINDY AND STORMY WEATHER; 1053] **2** *v* **move**, propel, drive, carry, waft, whoosh. [➡THROW SOMETHING; 335] **3** *v* (*slang*) **squander**, fritter away, waste, throw away. [➡USE UP AND WASTE; 475] **4** *n* **knock**, crack, jolt, swipe, strike, hit, bash (*informal*), thump, whack, wallop (*informal*), clout. [➡CONTACT: IMPACT; 414] **5** *n* **setback**, upset, disappointment, knock-back (*informal*), disappointment, shock, kick in the teeth, misfortune, body blow. [➡DISASTERS; 253] *Opposite:* boost.

blow a fuse (*informal*) *v* [➡GIVING VENT TO EMOTIONS; 680]

blow a gasket (*informal*) *v* [➡GIVING VENT TO EMOTIONS; 680]

blow away **1** *v* (*slang*) **shoot**, gun down (*informal*), kill, execute, murder, waste (*slang*). [➡KILL; 923] **2** *v* **distribute**, disperse, scatter, dispel, spread. [➡THROW SOMETHING; 335] **3** *v* (*US slang*) **defeat**, beat, get the better of, hammer (*informal*), trounce, thrash, cream (*US informal*). [➡BEAT AND DEFEAT; 80] **4** *v* (*US slang*) **overwhelm**, overcome, affect, shake, psych out (*informal*), blow your mind (*informal*), psych (*US*). [➡SURPRISE AND IMPRESS; 575]

blow-by-blow *adj* **thorough**, step by step, detailed, full, complete, in-depth, minute, precise. [➡WHOLENESS AND COMPLETENESS; 199] *Opposite:* sketchy.

blower **1** *n* (*dated informal*) **phone**, telephone, mobile, line, dog and bone (*slang*). [➡TELECOMMUNICATIONS; 1129] **2** *n* (*US informal*) **boaster**, show-off (*informal*), bigmouth (*informal*), loudmouth (*informal*), windbag (*informal*), egotist. [➡SELF-IMPORTANT AND SELF-SEEKING PEOPLE; 949]

blowhard (*US*) *n* [➡SELF-IMPORTANT AND SELF-SEEKING PEOPLE; 949]

blowlamp *see* **blowtorch**.

blown-up 1 *adj* **air-filled**, inflated, hard, rigid, pumped-up. [➡RIGID AND HARD; 1210] *Opposite:* deflated. 2 *adj* **distended**, swollen, bloated, enlarged, puffed-up, puffy. [➡FULL; 1238] *Opposite:* sagging. 3 *adj* **overdone**, exaggerated, over-the-top (*informal*), attention-grabbing, hyped, puffed-up, larger-than-life. [➡BIZARRE AND PECULIAR; 258] *Opposite:* understated. 4 *adj* **bombed**, wrecked, burned-out, ruined, demolished. [➡IN BAD REPAIR; 1233]

blow off (*US slang*) *v* **ignore**, slough off, dismiss, pay no attention to, make light of, neglect, avoid, shun. [➡NOT PAY ATTENTION; 765] *Opposite:* notice.

blow out *v* **extinguish**, put out, snuff out, douse, dampen. [➡CAUSE TO STOP; 267] *Opposite:* ignite.

blowout (*slang*) 1 *n* **puncture**, flat tyre, flat (*informal*). [➡TRAFFIC ACCIDENTS; 256] 2 *n* **walkover** (*informal*), doddle (*informal*), cinch (*informal*), certainty, sure thing (*informal*), piece of cake (*informal*). [➡EASY WORK; 300] 3 *n* **binge**, feast, pig out (*informal*), nosh-up (*informal*), bean-feast (*dated informal*). [➡MEALS AND PARTS OF MEALS; 1168]

blow somebody's cover *v* [➡BETRAY CONFIDENCES AND GOSSIP; 619]

blow the gaff (*slang*) *v* [➡BETRAY CONFIDENCES AND GOSSIP; 619]

blow the whistle *v* **inform**, report, turn in, expose, sneak, snitch (*slang*), tell on, grass up (*slang*), squeal (*slang disapproving*). [➡BETRAY CONFIDENCES AND GOSSIP; 619]

blowtorch *type of* **general tool**. [➡HAND TOOLS; 1118]

blow up 1 *v* **destroy**, explode, detonate, blast, demolish, flatten. [➡DESTRUCTION AND DEMOLITION; 360] 2 *v* **inflate**, pump up, fill, puff up, swell, fill out, balloon, distend, expand. [➡CHANGE OF SIZE: BIGGER; 393] *Opposite:* deflate. 3 *v* **enlarge**, magnify, expand, increase, make larger. [➡CHANGE OF SIZE: BIGGER; 393] *Opposite:* reduce. 4 *v* (*informal*) **lose your temper**, go mad, explode, blow your top (*informal*), fly off the handle (*informal*), be furious, hit the roof, lose your rag (*slang*), flare up, rage, storm, blow a fuse (*informal*), blow a gasket (*informal*), go ballistic (*slang*), lose it (*informal*), flip your lid (*slang*), lose your cool. [➡GIVING VENT TO EMOTIONS; 680] 5 *v* (*informal*) **exaggerate**, overstress, embellish, embroider, make a mountain out of a molehill, inflate, lay on, amplify, overstate, dramatize. [➡CLAIM, INSIST, AND EMPHASIZE; 615] *Opposite:* play down.

blowup *n* **enlargement**, magnification. [➡ARTWORKS; 898] *Opposite:* reduction.

blowy (*informal*) *adj* **windy**, breezy, blustery, gusty, squally, bracing, turbulent. [➡WINDY AND STORMY WEATHER; 1053] *Opposite:* calm.

blow your own trumpet (*informal*) *v* **brag**, boast, fly your own kite, crow, show off, sing your own praises, swank (*informal*), blow your own horn (*US*). [➡BOAST; 617] *Opposite:* deprecate.

blow your top (*informal*) *v* **flare up**, fly off the handle (*informal*), hit the roof, lose your temper, fly into a rage, explode, erupt, blow up (*informal*), go mad, blow a fuse (*informal*), blow a gasket (*informal*), rage, storm, go ballistic (*slang*). [➡GIVING VENT TO EMOTIONS; 680] *Opposite:* calm down.

blowzy 1 *adj* (*disapproving*) **ruddy**, red-faced, rubicund, coarse complexioned. [➡COMPLEXION; 481] 2 *adj* **unkempt**, bedraggled, messy, tousled, dishevelled. [➡BADLY GROOMED; 484] *Opposite:* smart.

blub (*informal*) *v* **sob**, weep, cry, snivel, whimper, blubber (*informal*), bawl (*informal*), burst into tears, break down. [➡CRYING; 651]

blubber (*informal*) *v* **sob**, weep, cry, snivel, whimper, blub (*informal*), bawl (*informal*), burst into tears, break down. [➡CRYING; 651]

blubbering (*informal*) *n* [➡CRYING; 651]

bludgeon 1 *v* **beat**, bash (*informal*), hit, slam, strike, batter, hammer. [➡WHIP AND CLUB; 418] 2 *v* **cajole**, coerce, compel, bully, bulldoze, steamroller, intimidate. [➡CAUSE OR COMPEL TO ACT; 272] 3 *type of* **club**. [➡BLUNT INSTRUMENTS AND WHIPS; 1157]

blue 1 *adj* (*informal*) **depressed**, down, sad, fed up (*informal*), low, dejected, melancholy, desolate, wretched, unhappy, downcast. [➡SADNESS, DISTRESS, AND DESPAIR; 540] *Opposite:* happy. 2 *type of* **colour**. [➡COLOURS; 1223]

blue

◆ *types of blue*
azure, cobalt blue, cornflower blue, cyan, electric blue, ice blue, indigo, lapis lazuli, midnight blue, navy blue, peacock blue, powder blue, Prussian blue, royal blue, sapphire, saxe blue, sky blue, slate blue, steel blue, turquoise, ultramarine

bluebell *type of* **flower grown from bulb**. [➡FLOWERS FROM BULBS; 1030]

blueberry *type of* **berry**. [➡FRUIT AND VEGETABLES; 1175]

bluebird *type of* **songbird**. [➡SONGBIRD; 1003]

blue-black *type of* **black**. [➡COLOURS; 1223]

blue-blooded *adj* **aristocratic**, noble, highborn (*literary*), high-class, well-bred, refined. [➡CLASS STATUS; 889] *Opposite:* common.

bluebottle *type of* **flying insect**. [➡FLYING INSECTS; 1013]

blue-chip *adj* **top-class**, first-class, topnotch (*informal*), first-rate, top-grade, number one (*informal*). [➡GOOD, WELL, BETTER; 184] *Opposite:* second-rate.

blue-collar *adj* **manual**, proletarian, working class. [➡TYPES OF WORK; 835] *Opposite:* white-collar.

blue-collar worker *n* [➡FARMERS, GARDENERS, AND MANUAL WORKERS; 849]

blue-eyed boy (*informal*) *n* [➡PEOPLE WHO ARE APPROVED OF; 955]

bluegrass *type of* **grass**. [➡GRASS; 1031]

blue jay *type of* **common bird**. [➡BIRD; 997]

blueprint *n* **plan**, drawing, design, proposal, outline, draft, scheme. [➡OFFICIAL DOCUMENTS; 587]

blues 1 *n* (*informal*) **sadness**, melancholy, dejection, depression, despair, unhappiness, despondency, pessimism, doldrums. [➡SADNESS, DISTRESS, AND DESPAIR; 540] *Opposite:* happiness. 2 *type of* **popular music**. [➡MUSIC, SONGS, AND SINGING; 907]

bluetit *type of* **common bird**. [➡BIRD; 997]

blue whale *type of* **whale**. [➡WHALE; 991]

bluff 1 *v* **trick**, con, fake, lie, pretend, deceive, pass off, blag (*informal*), scam (*slang*). [➡DECEPTION AND LIES; 661] 2 *n* **sham**, trick, con, pretence, fake, lie, deceit, ruse. [➡DECEPTION AND LIES; 661] 3 *n* **cliff**, headland, hillside, hill, mound, height. [➡MOUNTAINS AND HILLS; 1044] 4 *adj* **plain-spoken**, cheery, loud, hearty, forthright, no-nonsense, outspoken, direct, blunt. [➡HONEST AND OPEN; 631]

bluffness *n* **cheeriness**, heartiness, directness, bluntness, plain-spokenness, outspokenness, candidness. [➡HONEST AND OPEN; 631]

blunder 1 *n* **faux pas** (*literary*), mistake, gaffe, error, slip-up (*informal*), mix-up, bloomer (*informal humorous*), howler (*informal*), clanger (*informal*), bungle (*informal*), misstep, blooper (*US informal humorous*). [➡MISTAKES; 251] 2 *v* **make a mistake**, get it wrong, slip up (*informal*), err, goof (*informal*), foul up (*informal*), mess up (*informal*). [➡MESS UP AND MAKE MISTAKES; 473] 3 *v* **stumble**, stagger, lurch, flounder, trip, careen. [➡AIMLESS AND ERRANT MOTION; 344]

See Compare and Contrast at **mistake**.

blunderbuss *type of* **gun**. [➡WEAPONS FOR SHOOTING; 1155]

blunder in *v* [➡ARRIVE; 12]

blundering *adj* **ham-handed** (*informal*), clumsy, careless, ham-fisted (*informal*), awkward, lumbering, ungainly. [➡DESCRIBING BODY MOVEMENTS; 289] *Opposite:* dexterous.

blunt 1 *adj* **dull**, rounded, dulled, blunted, unsharpened. [➡ROUNDED SHAPE; 1217] *Opposite:* sharp. 2 *adj* **uncompromising**, straightforward, direct, frank, honest, candid, straight-talking, no-nonsense, forthright, bluff. [➡HONEST AND OPEN; 631] *Opposite:* indirect. 3 *v* **dampen**, dull, put a damper on, take the edge off, diminish, soothe, moderate, lessen. [➡CHANGE OF INTENSITY: LESS; 396] *Opposite:* heighten.

bluntly *adv* **frankly**, straightforwardly, honestly, directly, candidly, openly, uncompromisingly. [➡HONEST AND OPEN; 631] *Opposite:* indirectly.

bluntness *n* **candour**, frankness, directness, straightforwardness, honesty. [➡HONEST AND OPEN; 631] *Opposite:* mendacity.

blur 1 *v* **distort**, muddle, obscure, cloud, make indistinct, hide, conceal, confuse. [➡CAUSE TO DISAPPEAR; 6] *Opposite:* clarify. 2 *n* **blob**, smudge, smear, blot, blotch. [➡FAULTS, FLAWS, AND WEAKNESSES; 252] 3 *n* **distortion**, fuzziness, haze, impression, shape, shadow, haziness, cloudiness. [➡VAGUENESS; 244] 4 *v* **smudge**, smear, distort, mist, fog. [➡CHANGE OF SHAPE; 386] *Opposite:* clear.

blurb (*slang*) *n* **description**, info (*informal*), write-up, details, notes, bumf (*informal*), gloss. [➡SUMMARIES, OUTLINES, AND EXCERPTS; 589]

blurred *adj* **blurry**, indistinct, unclear, hazy, distorted, fuzzy, imprecise, faint, vague. [➡VAGUENESS; 244] *Opposite:* distinct.

blurry *adj* **fuzzy**, blurred, dim, shadowy, indistinct, unclear, hazy. [➡VAGUENESS; 244] *Opposite:* clear.

blurt *v* **exclaim**, cry, utter, come out with, announce, burst out, let drop, let slip, ejaculate (*literary*). [➡BETRAY CONFIDENCES AND GOSSIP; 619]

blush 1 *v* **go red**, flush, colour, go red in the face, redden. [➡FACIAL EXPRESSION; 652] *Opposite:* blanch. 2 *n* (*US*) **rouge** (*dated*), makeup, cosmetic, blusher. [➡MAKEUP AND BEAUTY PRODUCTS; 491]

blusher *n* **rouge** (*dated*), makeup, cosmetic, blush (*US*). [➡MAKEUP AND BEAUTY PRODUCTS; 491]

blushing *adj* **embarrassed**, self-conscious, red-faced, flushed, coy, shy, timid, modest. [➡RETICENT AND UNFORTHCOMING; 632] *Opposite:* bold.

bluster 1 *v* **harangue**, threaten, bully, protest, rant, bristle, bridle, complain. [➡PROTEST AND EXPRESS DISAPPROVAL; 643] 2 *v* **blow**, gust, rage, puff, waft. [➡WINDY AND STORMY WEATHER; 1053]

blustery *adj* **windy**, gusty, stormy, squally, breezy, blowy (*informal*). [➡WINDY AND STORMY WEATHER; 1053] *Opposite:* still.

B movie *n* **supporting film**, short, supporting movie, B picture, B film, trailer, support. [➡FILM; 901]

BO (*informal*) *n* **body odour**, smell, sweatiness, rankness, reek, perspiration, stench. [➡SMELL AND SMELLING; 706]

boa *type of* **non-poisonous snake**. [➡SNAKE; 995]

boa constrictor *type of* **non-poisonous snake**. [➡SNAKE; 995]

boar 1 *type of* **male animal**. [➡MALE OR FEMALE ANIMAL; 978] 2 *type of* **large mammal**. [➡LARGE MAMMAL; 986]

board 1 *n* **plank**, slat, floorboard, timber, beam. [➡BUILDING MATERIALS; 1076] 2 *n* **panel**, sheet, boarding. [➡BUILDING MATERIALS; 1076] 3 *n* **food**, meal, sustenance, nourishment, rations, refreshment. [➡ACCOMMODATION; 855] 4 *v* **embark**, enter, go on board, go aboard, go into, get on. [➡TRAVEL: WAYS OF TRAVELLING; 321] *Opposite:* disembark. 5 *v* **lodge** (*dated*), stay, live, room, be accommodated. [➡INHABIT; 20]

boarder *n* **lodger**, paying guest, resident, tenant, occupant, occupier. [➡INHABITANT; 857]

boarding house *type of* **hotel**. [➡HOTELS, RESTAURANTS, AND CLUBS; 1081]

boarding school *type of* **school**. [➡EDUCATIONAL INSTITUTIONS; 813]

boardroom *type of* **room in a public building**. [➡TYPES OF ROOM; 1096]

board up *v* **close**, shutter, secure, cover up. [➡BAR AND OBSTRUCT ACCESS; 411]

boardwalk *n* **walkway**, footpath, path, causeway. [➡PATHWAYS; 1109]

boast 1 *v* **brag**, show off, crow, swank (*informal*), fly your own kite, blow your own trumpet (*informal*), sing your own praises, blow your own horn (*US*). [➡BOAST; 617] 2 *v* **have**, possess, pride yourself on, lay claim to, feature, display, enjoy. [➡POSSESS; 445] 3 *n* **claim**, assertion, brag, avowal (*formal*), vaunt, pretension. [➡BOAST; 617]

boaster *n* [➡SELF-IMPORTANT AND SELF-SEEKING PEOPLE; 949]

boastful *adj* **arrogant**, proud, conceited, full of yourself, bragging, immodest, vain, self-important, self-satisfied, overweening, complacent, bigheaded (*informal*). [➡POMPOUS, LOUD, AND OVER-CONFIDENT; 636] *Opposite:* modest.

boastfulness *n* **immodesty**, arrogance, conceit, self-importance, showing off, bragging, boasting, self-aggrandizement. [➡POMPOUS, LOUD, AND OVER-CONFIDENT; 636] *Opposite:* modesty.

boasting 1 *n* **boastfulness**, bragging, showing off, arrogance, self-aggrandizement, conceit, immodesty, self-importance. [➡BOAST; 617] *Opposite:* modesty. 2 *adj* **boastful**, cocky (*informal*), arrogant, self-important, conceited, swaggering. [➡POMPOUS, LOUD, AND OVER-CONFIDENT; 636] *Opposite:* modest.

boat *n* **craft**, ship, vessel, dinghy, yacht. [➡SHIPS AND BOATS; 1149]

Compare and Contrast: ***boat., craft, dinghy, ship, vessel, yacht, dinghy***

CORE MEANING: A KIND OF FLOATING STRUCTURE USED TO TRANSPORT PEOPLE AND GOODS OVER WATER

boat any water-going structure, whether for commercial or leisure use, but specifically used to describe a small, open floating structure which is propelled by oars, sails or a portable engine.; ***craft*** a general designation but not restricted as to size; ***dinghy*** a small boat, especially one that is towed behind or carried on a larger boat; ***ship*** usually restricted to a large floating structure used for commercial purposes; ***vessel*** a ship or large boat; ***yacht*** any relatively small sailing or powered craft used for leisure purposes.

boater *type of* **hat**. [➡HABERDASHERY, MILLINERY, AND LINGERIE; 867]

boat hook *n* [➡PARTS OF A SHIP OR BOAT; 1150]

bob 1 *v* **move up and down**, nod, dip, bobble, jog. [➡BOUNCE, UNDULATE, AND VIBRATE; 309] 2 *type of* **hairstyle**. [➡HAIR STYLES AND HAIR PIECES; 489] 3 *v* **curtsy**, bow, nod, duck, genuflect. [➡GESTURES AND GESTICULATION; 654]

bobbin *n* **reel**, spindle, spool, cylinder, roll, drum. [➡CONTAINERS, RECEPTACLES, AND PACKAGING; 1244]

bobble 1 *n* **ball**, pompom, tassel. [➡ORNAMENTS AND DECORATIONS; 1247] 2 *v* **move up and down**, nod, bob, jog, dip. [➡BOUNCE, UNDULATE, AND VIBRATE; 309]

bobble hat *type of* **headgear**. [➡HABERDASHERY, MILLINERY, AND LINGERIE; 867]

bobbly *adj* **bumpy**, lumpy, rough, knobbly, textured, coarse. [➡PHYSICAL TEXTURE; 1221] *Opposite:* smooth.

bobby (*dated informal*) *n* **police officer**, constable, cop (*slang*). [➡THE POLICE, ARREST, AND PRE-TRIAL PROCEEDINGS; 818]

bobcat *type of* **cat**. [➡FELINE; 983]

bobsled (*US*) 1 *n* **toboggan**, sledge, bobsleigh, sled (*US*). [➡VEHICLES; 1144] 2 *type of* **winter sport**. [➡HOBBIES, GAMES, AND SPORTS; 875]

bobsleigh 1 *n* **toboggan**, sledge, sled (*US*), bobsled (*US*). [➡VEHICLES; 1144] 2 *type of* **winter sport**. [➡HOBBIES, GAMES, AND SPORTS; 875]

Bob's your uncle (*informal*) *interj* **hey presto** (*informal*), there you have it, there you are, what do you know, before you know it, voilà. [➡SUMMARIZING EXPRESSIONS; 623]

bod (*slang*) *n* **person**, character, individual, human being, man, woman. [➡PERSON; 931]

bode *v* **augur**, portend, promise, divine, betoken (*literary*), prefigure. [➡MEAN SOMETHING; 61]

bodega 1 *type of* **bar or club**. [➡HOTELS, RESTAURANTS, AND CLUBS; 1081] 2 (*US*) *type of* **food outlet**. [➡RETAIL OUTLETS; 1082]

bodge (*informal*) *v* **botch**, spoil, damage, do badly, bungle (*informal*), ruin, make a hash (*informal*), butcher (*informal*). [➡MESS UP AND MAKE MISTAKES; 473]

bodice *type of* **top**. [➡GARMENTS AND OUTFITS; 865]

bodily *adj* **physical**, corporal, corporeal, fleshly, human, biological. [➡LIVING THINGS AND LIVING; 976] *Opposite:* spiritual.

body 1 *n* **form**, figure, frame, physique, build, bulk. [➡CENTRAL PARTS OF PHYSICAL OBJECTS; 1250] 2 *n* **corpse**, dead body, cadaver, remains, carcass, stiff (*slang*), deceased (*formal*). [➡DEAD PERSON; 926] 3 *n* **organization**, group, association, federation, society, party. [➡INSTITUTIONS; 791] 4 *n* **quantity**, corpus, amount, mass, area, reservoir, supply. [➡COLLECTIONS AND MIXTURES OF THINGS; 1243] 5 *n* **bulk**, main part, essence, majority, mass, better part, lion's share. [➡BODY; 692] 6 *type of* **upper body underwear**. [➡HABERDASHERY, MILLINERY, AND LINGERIE; 867]

body blow *n* **setback**, blow, disappointment, upset, shock, letdown, kick in the teeth, trauma, upheaval. [➡DISASTERS; 253]

body builder *n* **athlete**, weightlifter, gymnast. [➡PEOPLE IN SPORTS AND LEISURE; 876]

body fluid *n* **saliva**, blood, urine, sweat, semen, tears, lymph, synovia. [➡EXCRETION AND EXCRETA; 723]

bodyguard *n* **guard**, security officer, minder (*informal*), attendant, guardian, protection officer. [➡PEOPLE WHO GUARD AND PROTECT; 846]

body-hugging *adj* [➡DESCRIBING CLOTHES; 869]

body language *n* **mannerisms**, stance, facial expression, movements, motion, physical response, gesture, bearing, behaviour. [➡GESTURES AND GESTICULATION; 654]

body mist *n* [➡PERSONAL HYGIENE; 492]

body odour *n* [➡SMELL AND SMELLING; 706]

body spray *n* [➡PERSONAL HYGIENE; 492]

body stocking *type of* **upper body underwear**. [➡HABERDASHERY, MILLINERY, AND LINGERIE; 867]

bodysuit *type of* **upper body underwear**. [➡HABERDASHERY, MILLINERY, AND LINGERIE; 867]

body warmer *type of* **top**. [➡GARMENTS AND OUTFITS; 865]

bodywork *part of* **external structure**. [➡EXTERNAL PARTS OF A VEHICLE; 1146]

boffin (*informal*) *n* **scientist**, expert, genius, researcher, inventor, professor. [➡TALENTED OR INTELLIGENT PERSON; 529]

bog *n* **swamp**, quagmire, marsh, fen, fenland, marshland. [➡WETLANDS; 1043]

bog down (*informal*) *v* [➡GIVE TOO MUCH; 438]

bogey *n* **bogeyman**, monster, creature, beast, monstrosity, booger (*US informal*). [➡MYTHICAL BEINGS; 790]

bogged down (*informal*) *adj* **caught up**, delayed, stalled, slowed down, held up, overinvolved, hindered, mired, stuck. [➡CONFUSION, ANXIETY, AND WORRY; 541] *Opposite:* freed up.

boggle (*informal*) *v* **confuse**, baffle, perplex, astonish, overwhelm, throw, stun, disorientate, disorient. [➡CONFUSE AND BEWILDER; 572]

boggy *adj* **marshy**, swampy, muddy, watery, wet, sloppy, soggy, sodden. [➡WET; 1239] *Opposite:* parched.

bog-standard (*informal*) *adj* **basic**, standard, ordinary, simple, unadorned, plain. [➡ORDINARINESS; 245] *Opposite:* superior.

bogus *adj* **false**, fake, counterfeit, phoney, trick, hoax, sham, spurious, mock. [➡FALSE AND UNREAL; 174] *Opposite:* genuine.

bohemian 1 *n* **free spirit**, freethinker, nonconformist, hippie, New Age traveller. [➡PLEASURE-SEEKERS AND HEDONISTS; 886] 2 *adj* **unconventional**, nonconformist, alternative, laid-back (*informal*), carefree, relaxed, avant-garde. [➡PLEASURE-SEEKING AND EXCESS; 885] *Opposite:* conformist.

boil 1 *v* **simmer**, bubble, poach, cook, stew, heat. [➡COOKING AND FOOD PREPARATION; 354] 2 *v* **rage**, fume, seethe, be angry, be irate, be infuriated. [➡GIVING VENT TO EMOTIONS; 680] 3 *v* (*informal*) **overheat**, swelter, stew, roast (*informal*), bake, burn. [➡PAIN AND OTHER PHYSICAL SENSATIONS; 734] 4 *n* **ulcer**, sore, spot, swelling, abscess, cyst. [➡CONDITIONS AFFECTING THE SKIN; 722]

boil down to (*informal*) *v* **amount to**, come down to, end up as, add up to, wind up as. [➡AMOUNT TO AND EQUAL; 70]

boiler *type of* **heating appliance**. [➡HEATING, REFRIGERATION, AND VENTILATION; 1141]

boiler suit *n* **overalls**, coveralls, protective clothing, dungarees. [➡GARMENTS AND OUTFITS; 865]

boiling *adj* **hot**, sweltering, scorching (*informal*), roasting (*informal*), baking, steaming, torrid, blistering, searing, scalding, broiling. [➡HOT WEATHER; 1050] *Opposite:* freezing.

boiling hot *adj* [➡HOT WEATHER; 1050]

boiling point *n* **crisis point**, danger level, flashpoint, high point, peak. [➡DECISIVE MOMENTS; 44]

boil over *v* **overflow**, erupt, bubble up, overheat, spill over, explode. [➡CHANGE OF TEMPERATURE; 387]

boil with rage *v* [➡GIVING VENT TO EMOTIONS; 680]

boisterous *adj* **energetic**, active, animated, rowdy, unruly, noisy, overexcited, over-the-top (*informal*). [➡ENERGY AND ENTHUSIASM; 497] *Opposite:* placid.

boisterously *adv* **energetically**, exuberantly, wildly, rowdily, noisily, raucously. [➡ENTHUSIASTIC AND INQUISITIVE; 629] *Opposite:* placidly.

boisterousness 1 *n* **unruliness**, overexcitement, roughness, riotousness, rowdiness, disruptiveness, liveliness, noisiness, loudness, exuberance, rumbustiousness, animation. [➡CHAOS AND UPROAR; 51] *Opposite:* placidity. 2 *n* **wildness**, turbulence, roughness, storminess. [➡WINDY AND STORMY WEATHER; 1053] *Opposite:* calmness. 3 *n* **horseplay**, rough and tumble, high spirits, exuberance, high jinks (*informal*), joshing (*informal*). [➡JOKES AND TEASING; 675]

bold 1 *adj* **brave**, daring, courageous, intrepid (*literary or humorous*), audacious, gallant (*literary*), valiant, unflinching. [➡COURAGE; 499] *Opposite:* cowardly. 2 *adj* **confident**, forward, brash, self-assured, impudent, bold-faced, cheeky, not backwards in coming forwards, nervy (*US informal*). [➡CONFIDENCE AND COMPOSURE; 500] *Opposite:* timid. 3 *adj* **black**, heavy, boldface. [➡PRINTING; 601] *Opposite:* light.

bold as brass *adj* [➡CONFIDENCE AND COMPOSURE; 500]

bold-faced *adj* **impudent**, cheeky, brash, unconcerned, flagrant, bold as brass, nervy (*US informal*). [➡POMPOUS, LOUD, AND OVER-CONFIDENT; 636] *Opposite:* unassuming.

boldly 1 *adv* **bravely**, courageously, daringly, intrepidly (*literary or humorous*), audaciously, gallantly (*literary*), fearlessly, unflinchingly, valiantly. [➡COURAGE; 499] *Opposite:* cautiously. 2 *adv* **confidently**, brashly, cheekily (*informal*), brazenly, shamelessly, impudently. [➡CONFIDENCE AND COMPOSURE; 500] *Opposite:* timidly.

boldness 1 *n* **courage**, daring, audacity, bravery, bravado, valour. [➡COURAGE; 499] *Opposite:* cowardice. 2 *n* **confidence**, self-assurance, brashness, nerve, cheek (*informal*), audaciousness, impudence, chutzpah (*informal*). [➡CONFIDENCE AND COMPOSURE; 500] *Opposite:* timidity.

bole *n* **trunk**, stem, stalk. [➡PARTS OF TREES AND PLANTS; 1026]

bolero *type of* **top**. [➡GARMENTS AND OUTFITS; 865]

boletus *type of* **fungus**. [➡MICROORGANISMS, FUNGI, AND ALGAE; 1023]

bolide *type of* **heavenly body**. [➡CELESTIAL BODIES; 1060]

bollard *n* **post**, marker, pillar, stake, pole, cone. [➡STICKS, POLES, AND WEDGES; 1253]

bologna (*US*) *type of* **processed meat**. [➡TYPES AND CUTS OF MEAT; 1176]

bolshevik (*informal*) *n* **red** (*informal disapproving*), communist, leftie (*informal*), socialist, bolshie (*informal dated*). [➡PHILOSOPHICAL AND POLITICAL THINKERS; 782]

bolshie 1 *n* (*informal dated*) **red** (*informal disapproving*), communist, leftie (*informal*), socialist, bolshevik (*informal*). [➡PHILOSOPHICAL AND POLITICAL THINKERS; 782] 2 *adj* (*informal*) **stroppy** (*informal*), difficult, belligerent, quarrelsome, argumentative, tetchy (*informal*), crabby, grouchy (*informal*). [➡ DIFFICULT TO PLEASE; 516]

bolshiness (*informal*) *n* [➡ UNWILLINGNESS AND STUBBORNNESS; 565]

bolster *v* **boost**, strengthen, reinforce, encourage, shore up, support, augment (*formal*), sustain. [➡ CHANGE OF INTENSITY: MORE; 395] *Opposite:* undermine.

bolt 1 *n* **bar**, pin, rod, screw. [➡ FASTENERS, LINKS, AND NETWORKS; 1246] **2** *type of* **projectile**. [➡ PROJECTILES; 1158] **3** *v* **fasten**, secure, lock, lock up, attach, anchor. [➡ FASTEN, LINK, AND JOIN; 409] *Opposite:* unlock. **4** *v* **run off**, scram (*informal*), make a dash for it, scarper (*slang*), take off (*informal*), run, make a run for it, disappear, escape. [➡ RUN AWAY AND AVOID; 10] **5** *v* **gulp**, wolf, gobble, guzzle (*informal*), scoff (*informal*), devour, down, scarf down (*US slang*). [➡ EAT AND NOT EAT; 711] *Opposite:* nibble.

bolt from the blue *n* **surprise**, shock, bombshell (*informal*), jolt, blow, upset. [➡ SUDDEN EVENT; 52]

bolthole *n* **hideaway**, refuge, sanctuary, den, place of safety, private space. [➡ SAFE BUILDINGS OR PLACES; 1092]

bolt upright *adv* [➡ ORIENTATION AND ALIGNMENT; 1222]

bomb 1 *type of* **explosive weapon**. [➡ EXPLOSIVES; 1154] **2** *n* (*informal*) **fortune**, bundle (*informal*), pile (*informal*), an arm and a leg (*informal*), loads (*informal*). [➡ LARGE AMOUNT OF MONEY; 141] **3** *n* (*US informal*) **failure**, letdown, catastrophe, fiasco, disaster, botch (*informal*), miscarriage (*formal*), flop (*informal*), washout (*informal*). [➡ DISASTERS; 253] *Opposite:* success. **4** *v* **bombard**, shell, blast, barrage, blitz, explode, attack, assault. [➡ WARFARE AND WAR; 830] **5** *v* (*informal*) **fail**, flop, fall flat, sink without trace, disappoint, flounder. [➡ FAIL OR BE UNSUCCESSFUL; 75] *Opposite:* succeed.

bombard 1 *v* **bomb**, shell, open fire on, blast, barrage, blitz, attack, assault. [➡ DESTRUCTION AND DEMOLITION; 360] **2** *v* **assail**, shower, flood, inundate, overrun, overwhelm. [➡ GIVE TOO MUCH; 438]

bombardier *n* [➡ MILITARY PERSONNEL; 828]

bombardment 1 *n* **attack**, offensive, assault, salvo, bombing, shelling. [➡ AGGRESSIVE EVENT; 39] **2** *n* **barrage**, flood, onslaught, blitz, volley, hail, shower. [➡ SUDDEN EVENT; 52]

bombast *n* **pomposity**, pretentiousness, verboseness, affectation, grandiloquence, long-windedness. [➡ MEANINGLESS SPEECH OR WRITING; 677] *Opposite:* simplicity.

bombastic *adj* **pompous**, pretentious, verbose, long-winded, grandiloquent, affected. [➡ POMPOUS, LOUD, AND OVER-CONFIDENT; 636] *Opposite:* simple.

bombed (*slang*) *adj* [➡ UNDER THE INFLUENCE OF DRUGS OR ALCOHOL; 742]

bomber *type of* **military aircraft**. [➡ AIRCRAFT; 1147]

bomber jacket *type of* **jacket**. [➡ GARMENTS AND OUTFITS; 865]

bombshell (*informal*) *n* **shock**, surprise, bolt from the blue, blow, upset, disaster. [➡ SUDDEN EVENT; 52]

bomb site *n* **area of devastation**, crater, ruins, battlefield. [➡ URBAN OUTDOOR SPACES; 1071]

bona fide *adj* **genuine**, authentic, true, real, valid, aboveboard, legitimate, legal, authenticated, certified. [➡ TRUE AND REAL; 172] *Opposite:* bogus.

bonanza *n* **jackpot**, pot of gold, gold mine, prize, wealth, windfall, crock of gold (*US*). [➡ TREAT; 211]

bonbon *type of* **confectionery**. [➡ CONFECTIONERY; 1181]

bonce (*informal*) *n* **head**, nut (*informal*), noddle (*dated informal*), skull, cranium, brains. [➡ HEAD; 693]

bond 1 *n* **tie**, link, connection, union, attachment, relationship, friendship, acquaintance. [➡ CONNECTION; 144] **2** *n* **promise**, pledge, oath, word. [➡ PROMISE AND ASSURE; 685] **3** *v* **adhere**, stick, glue, fix, join, bind, attach, cement, link, affix. [➡ FASTEN, LINK, AND JOIN; 409] **4** *v* **connect**, get on, hit it off (*informal*), relate, become attached, get along (*US*). [➡ ESTABLISHING RELATIONSHIPS WITH OTHERS; 974] *Opposite:* clash.

bondage *n* **slavery**, captivity, oppression, servitude, repression, suppression. [➡ CAPTIVITY AND LOSS OF FREEDOM; 249] *Opposite:* freedom.

bonded *adj* **fused together**, fused, stuck, glued, attached, merged, united, joined, welded. [➡ CLOSENESS; 160] *Opposite:* split.

bonding *n* **attachment**, closeness, tie, connection, love, affection, relationship. [➡ CONNECTION; 144]

bone

◆ *types of bone*
backbone, breastbone, cheekbone, coccyx, collarbone, cranium, femur, fibula, humerus, jawbone, kneecap, long bone, patella, pelvis, radius, rib, shoulder blade, skull, spinal column, spine, sternum, tibia, ulna, vertebra

bone china *type of* **pottery**. [➡ POTTERY; 1134]

bone dry *adj* **parched**, dry as a bone, arid, scorched, seared, baked. [➡ DRY; 1241]

bone idle *adj* **lazy**, indolent, idle, slothful (*formal*), lethargic, inactive. [➡ LIFELESS, LAZY, AND UNENTHUSIASTIC; 507] *Opposite:* diligent.

bone of contention *n* **disagreement**, sticking point, difficulty, problem, obstacle, hurdle, dispute, difference. [➡ NUISANCES; 254]

boner (*informal*) *n* [➡ MISTAKES; 251]

boneshaker *n* (*informal*) **jalopy** (*dated informal*), banger (*informal*), wreck, rattletrap (*informal*), heap (*slang*). [➡ BIKES, CARS, AND CARRIAGES; 1148]

bone up (*informal*) *v* **find out about**, gen up (*informal*), swot up (*informal*), research, look into, study, mug up (*informal*). [➡ STUDYING; 844]

bonfire *n* **fire**, conflagration, blaze, beacon. [➡ FIRE, FLAMMABILITY, AND BURNING; 1164]

bong *n* **bang**, blow, thud, crash, knock, clang, dong, bonk (*informal*). [➡ IMPACT SOUNDS; 1259]

bongo drums *type of* **percussion instrument**. [➡ MUSICAL INSTRUMENTS; 910]

bonhomie *n* **friendliness**, sociability, affability, geniality, amenability, kindliness. [➡FRIENDLINESS AND SOCIABILITY; 495]

boniness *n* [➡BUILD; 478]

bonk (*informal*) 1 *v* **hit**, bang, knock, tap, slap, thump, punch. [➡CONTACT: IMPACT; 414] 2 *n* **knock**, blow, slap, bang, tap, thud. [➡IMPACT SOUNDS; 1259]

bonkers (*informal*) *adj* **irrational**, crazy (*informal*), off the deep end, silly, berserk. [➡ECCENTRICITY AND IRRATIONALITY; 563] *Opposite:* rational.

bon mot *n* **witticism**, quip, joke, epigram, clever remark, pun. [➡JOKES AND TEASING; 675]

bonne bouche *n* [➡MEALS AND PARTS OF MEALS; 1168]

bonnet 1 *type of* **hat**. [➡HABERDASHERY, MILLINERY, AND LINGERIE; 867] 2 *part of* **external structure**. [➡EXTERNAL PARTS OF A VEHICLE; 1146]

bonnet monkey *type of* **primate**. [➡PRIMATE; 988]

bonny *adj* **good-looking**, lovely, pretty, handsome, attractive, appealing, healthy. [➡PEOPLE'S PHYSICAL APPEARANCE; 476] *Opposite:* unattractive.

bonsai *n* [➡FOLIAGE PLANTS; 1035]

bonus 1 *n* **extra**, plus (*informal*), addition, advantage, windfall. [➡MORE AND EXCESS; 122] 2 *n* **gratuity**, handout, dividend, pay supplement. [➡REWARDS AND AWARDS; 440]

bon vivant (*literary*) *n* **pleasure-seeker**, lotus-eater, gourmet, epicure, gourmand, foodie (*informal*). [➡PLEASURE-SEEKERS AND HEDONISTS; 886] *Opposite:* ascetic.

bon viveur (*literary*) *n* [➡PLEASURE-SEEKERS AND HEDONISTS; 886]

bon voyage *interj* [➡GREETINGS, FAREWELLS, AND SALUTATIONS; 660]

bony *adj* **skinny**, scrawny, lanky, lean, thin, emaciated, skeletal, gaunt, underweight, skin and bones. [➡BUILD; 478] *Opposite:* plump.

boo 1 *n* **catcall**, jeer, hoot. [➡UNFAVOURABLE NON-VERBAL RESPONSES; 655] *Opposite:* cheer. 2 *type of* **human sound**. [➡SOUNDS MADE BY PEOPLE; 1261] 3 *v* **jeer**, hoot, catcall, hiss, barrack (*informal*). [➡UNFAVOURABLE NON-VERBAL RESPONSES; 655] *Opposite:* applaud.

boob (*informal*) 1 *n* **blunder**, mistake, error, gaffe, slip-up (*informal*), cockup (*informal*), botch-up (*informal*), snafu (*informal*), bungle (*informal*), faux pas (*literary*). [➡MISTAKES; 251] 2 *n* **fool**, chump (*dated informal*), mug (*slang*), sucker (*informal*), fall guy (*slang*), dupe. *Opposite:* sage. (*literary*). [➡LAZY OR UNSUCCESSFUL PEOPLE; 948] 3 *v* **make a mistake**, get it wrong, slip up (*informal*), err, foul up (*informal*), mess up (*informal*). [➡MESS UP AND MAKE MISTAKES; 473]

boo-boo (*informal*) *n* **blunder**, mistake, error, gaffe, slip-up (*informal*), cockup (*informal*), botch-up (*informal*), snafu (*informal*), bungle (*informal*), faux pas (*literary*). [➡MISTAKES; 251]

boob tube 1 (*slang*) *type of* **top**. [➡GARMENTS AND OUTFITS; 865] 2 *n* (*US informal*) **television**, telly, TV (*informal*), box (*slang*), small screen (*informal*), goggle-box (*dated informal*), tube (*US*). [➡TELEVISION AND RADIO; 607]

booby trap 1 *n* **snare**, trap, setup (*informal*), trick, ruse, con, ambush. [➡DECEPTION AND LIES; 661] 2 *n* **bomb**, tripwire, mine, explosive device. [➡EXPLOSIVES; 1154]

boodle (*slang*) *n* [➡LARGE AMOUNT OF MONEY; 141]

boogie 1 *v* (*informal*) **dance**, bop (*informal*), jig, caper, jive, party (*informal*). [➡FIDGET AND FROLIC; 312] 2 *n* **jig**, jive, party (*informal*). [➡FIDGET AND FROLIC; 312]

book 1 *n* **volume**, tome, manuscript, paperback, hardback, hardcover. [➡BOOKS AND BOOKLETS; 591] 2 *v* **reserve**, order, engage, put your name down for, sign up. [➡PURCHASE; 423]

bookable *adj* [➡ILLEGAL; 816]

bookcase *type of* **cabinet**. [➡FURNITURE; 858]

book in *v* **check in**, register, sign in, enlist, enrol. [➡ARRIVE; 12] *Opposite:* leave.

booking *n* **reservation**, hold, option, deposit. [➡BUSINESS ACTIVITIES AND PHENOMENA; 795]

bookish *adj* **studious**, serious, academic, scholarly, well-informed, erudite, learned, pedantic. [➡KNOWLEDGE AND WISDOM; 559]

bookishness *n* **studiousness**, erudition, scholarliness, learning, learnedness. [➡LEVEL OF EDUCATION AND SOPHISTICATION; 894]

bookkeeper *n* [➡PEOPLE INVOLVED IN FINANCE; 804]

booklet *n* **brochure**, pamphlet, leaflet, flier. [➡BOOKS AND BOOKLETS; 591]

book lover *n* [➡DEVOTEES AND ADDICTED PEOPLE; 557]

books *n* **records**, accounts, balance sheet, profit and loss, files, paperwork. [➡RECORDS; 586]

bookshelf *n* **shelf**, ledge, stand, rack, bookstand, bookrest. [➡FURNITURE; 858]

bookshop *type of* **retail outlet**. [➡RETAIL OUTLETS; 1082]

bookworm (*informal*) *n* **avid reader**, book lover, bibliophile. [➡PEOPLE IN SPORTS AND LEISURE; 876]

boom 1 *v* **roar**, rumble, thunder, bellow, resound, reverberate, sound. [➡EMIT CONTINUOUS SOUNDS; 367] 2 *v* **grow**, soar, rocket, increase, rise, expand, explode, surge, gain. [➡PROSPER AND ABOUND; 16] *Opposite:* collapse. 3 *n* **bang**, roar, rumble, report, detonation, explosion, shot, blast. [➡CONTINUOUS SOUNDS; 1257] 4 *n* **growth**, increase, rise, expansion, development, escalation, explosion, surge. [➡SUDDEN EVENT; 52] *Opposite:* collapse. 5 *adj* **prosperous**, flourishing, affluent, successful, thriving. [➡SUCCESSFUL AND PROMISING; 81] 6 *n* **pole**, arm, bracket, beam. [➡STICKS, POLES, AND WEDGES; 1253] 7 *part of* **sailing vessel**. [➡PARTS OF A SHIP OR BOAT; 1150]

boom box (*US*) *type of* **audio equipment**. [➡AUDIO EQUIPMENT; 1138]

boomerang 1 *v* **rebound**, bounce back, return, ricochet, come back. [➡CHANGE DIRECTION OF MOTION; 345] 2 *type of* **projectile**. [➡PROJECTILES; 1158]

booming 1 *adj* **thriving**, prosperous, wealthy, flourishing, successful, growing, on the up and up. [➡SUCCESSFUL AND PROMISING; 81] *Opposite:* failing. 2 *adj* **thunderous**, roaring, resounding, resonant, sonorous, loud. [➡LOUD OR UNPLEASANT SOUNDS; 1265] *Opposite:* quiet.

boon *n* **advantage**, benefit, bonus, help, godsend, windfall, gain. [➡SOURCE OF HAPPINESS, PLEASURE, OR IMPROVEMENT; 210] *Opposite:* disadvantage.

boon companion *n* [➡FRIENDS; 963]

boondocks (*US informal*) *n* **backwater**, sticks (*informal*), back of beyond, country, provinces, middle of nowhere. [➡REMOTE PLACES; 1046]

boor *n* **yob** (*informal*), loudmouth (*informal*), yobbo (*informal*), churl. [➡VILLAINS AND THUGS; 947]

boorish *adj* **rude**, ill-mannered, impolite, coarse, rough, loutish, uncouth, crude, ignorant, churlish, base. [➡RUDE AND HOSTILE; 626] *Opposite:* well-mannered.

boorishness *n* **crudeness**, loutishness, uncouthness, incivility, rudeness, insensitivity, bad manners, crassness, vulgarity. [➡BAD MANNERS AND SOCIAL SKILLS; 522] *Opposite:* courteousness.

boost 1 *v* **increase**, improve, enhance, make better, further, advance, heighten. [➡CHANGE OF SIZE: BIGGER; 393] *Opposite:* reduce. 2 *v* **encourage**, support, lift, uplift, give a boost to, give a lift, inspire, raise, build up, motivate. [➡IMPROVE STRENGTH AND DURABILITY; 379] *Opposite:* discourage. 3 *n* **improvement**, increase, enhancement, lift, helping hand, pep talk (*informal*), shot in the arm. [➡TREAT; 211] *Opposite:* blow.

booster 1 *n* **injection**, inoculation, vaccination, jab (*informal*), shot (*informal*), immunization. [➡REMEDIES, TREATMENTS AND OPERATIONS; 732] 2 *n* (*US*) **promoter**, supporter, fan, advocate, admirer, idolizer, rooter, groupie (*informal*). [➡DEVOTEES AND ADDICTED PEOPLE; 557]

booster rocket *part of* **spacecraft**. [➡SPACE VEHICLES; 1062]

booster seat *type of* **internal feature**. [➡VEHICLES; 1144]

boost up 1 *v* **increase**, improve, enhance, boost, augment (*formal*), add to. [➡CHANGE OF SIZE: BIGGER; 393] *Opposite:* reduce. 2 *v* **encourage**, support, lift, uplift, give a boost to, give a lift, inspire, rally, motivate, build up. [➡IMPROVE STRENGTH AND DURABILITY; 379] *Opposite:* discourage.

boot 1 *type of* **boot**. [➡FOOTWEAR; 871] 2 *part of* **external structure**. [➡EXTERNAL PARTS OF A VEHICLE; 1146]

bootee *type of* **boot**. [➡FOOTWEAR; 871]

booth 1 *n* **cubicle**, stand, closet, compartment, sukkah, tabernacle. [➡ALCOVES, CUBICLES, AND COMPARTMENTS; 1095] 2 *type of* **outbuilding**. [➡ANCILLARY BUILDINGS; 1079]

bootlace *n* **shoelace**, cord, lace, strap, tie. [➡HABERDASHERY, MILLINERY, AND LINGERIE; 867]

bootleg *adj* **illegal**, pirate, stolen, illicit, unlicensed, plagiarized. [➡ILLEGAL; 816] *Opposite:* legal.

bootless *adj* **useless**, scant, feeble, inadequate, unsuccessful, unprofitable. [➡REDUNDANT AND USELESS; 241] *Opposite:* successful.

bootlicker (*informal disapproving*) *n* [➡SUPERFICIAL OR INSINCERE PEOPLE; 951]

boot out (*informal*) *v* **dismiss**, kick out (*informal*), get rid of, give somebody the push (*informal*), give somebody the boot (*informal*), give the heave-ho (*informal*), fire (*informal*), sack (*informal*), give the elbow (*informal*), eject, evict, can (*US slang*). [➡EJECT AND EXCLUDE; 341] *Opposite:* appoint.

booty *n* **loot**, spoils, plunder, ill-gotten gains, valuables, pickings, proceeds, treasure, swag (*slang*). [➡PROCEEDS OF CRIME; 428]

bop (*informal*) 1 *v* **dance**, boogie (*informal*), jig, caper, jive, party (*informal*). [➡FIDGET AND FROLIC; 312] 2 *n* **jig**, dance, boogie (*informal*), jive. [➡DANCE; 903] 3 *n* **disco**, dance, rave (*slang*), party, ball. [➡PARTIES, DANCES, AND CELEBRATIONS; 37] 4 *v* **hit**, bash (*informal*), bang, knock, tap, thump, punch, bonk (*informal*). [➡PHYSICAL ATTACK AND PUNISHMENT; 416]

border 1 *n* **frontier**, borderline, boundary, state line (*US*). [➡GEOGRAPHICAL BORDERS AND BOUNDARIES; 1068] 2 *n* **edge**, limit, boundary, margin, rim, edging, frame, perimeter, periphery, circumference. [➡EXTREMITIES OF PHYSICAL OBJECTS; 1249] *Opposite:* centre. 3 *n* **flowerbed**, bed, shrub border, herbaceous border. [➡GARDENS; 1073] 4 *v* **be next to**, touch, be bounded by, border on, run alongside, be adjacent to, adjoin, abut, conjoin (*formal*), fringe, skirt. [➡EXIST IN CLOSE PROXIMITY; 21]

bordering *adj* **adjoining**, neighbouring, adjacent, next door, nearby, contiguous (*formal*). [➡CLOSENESS; 160]

bordering on *adj* **verging on**, tantamount to, close to, on the brink of, on the verge of, approaching, on the threshold of. [➡ABOUT TO HAPPEN; 33]

borderland *n* **boundary**, edge, frontier, limits, border, fringe, margin, outer edge, outer limits, outer fringe (*US*). [➡GEOGRAPHICAL BORDERS AND BOUNDARIES; 1068] *Opposite:* heartland.

borderline 1 *n* **frontier**, boundary, border, state line (*US*). [➡GEOGRAPHICAL BORDERS AND BOUNDARIES; 1068] 2 *adj* **marginal**, disputed, uncertain, doubtful, unclear, dubious, undecided, in doubt, up in the air. [➡UNCERTAIN; 176] *Opposite:* clear-cut.

border on 1 *v* **approach**, be close to, resemble, be similar to. [➡EXIST IN CLOSE PROXIMITY; 21] 2 *v* **be next to**, touch, be bounded by, border, adjoin, be adjacent to, fringe, skirt, abut, conjoin (*formal*). [➡EXIST IN CLOSE PROXIMITY; 21]

bore 1 *v* **turn off** (*informal*), weary, irk, bore to death, bore to tears, bore stiff, bore rigid, tire. [➡BORE AND FAIL TO INTEREST; 571] *Opposite:* interest. 2 *v* **penetrate**, pierce, make a hole in, gouge. [➡TEAR, BREAK, AND CUT; 361]

bored *adj* **uninterested**, fed up (*informal*), tired, bored rigid, bored stiff, bored to death, bored to tears, jaded. [➡NEUTRALITY AND INDIFFERENCE; 554] *Opposite:* fascinated.

boredom *n* **tedium**, monotony, dullness, tediousness, ennui, world-weariness. [➡BORING AND UNINTERESTING; 235] *Opposite:* interest.

bored rigid *adj* [➡NEUTRALITY AND INDIFFERENCE; 554]

bored stiff *adj* [➡NEUTRALITY AND INDIFFERENCE; 554]

bored to death *adj* [➡NEUTRALITY AND INDIFFERENCE; 554]

bored to tears *adj* [➡NEUTRALITY AND INDIFFERENCE; 554]

borehole *n* **well**, hole, shaft. [➡HOLES, GAPS, AND FORKS; 1251]

bore rigid *v* [➡BORE AND FAIL TO INTEREST; 571]

bore stiff *v* [➡BORE AND FAIL TO INTEREST; 571]

bore to death *v* [➡BORE AND FAIL TO INTEREST; 571]

bore to tears *v* [➡BORE AND FAIL TO INTEREST; 571]

boring *adj* **uninteresting**, tedious, dull, dreary, mind-numbing, tiresome, lacklustre, unexciting, monotonous, repetitive, wearisome, humdrum, uninspiring. [➡BORING AND UNINTERESTING; 235] *Opposite:* exciting.

Compare and Contrast: ***boring, dull, monotonous, tedious, uninteresting***

CORE MEANING: LACKING IN INTEREST, STIMULATION, OR VARIETY

boring lacking in interest or causing a loss of attention; ***dull*** arousing no interest or excitement; ***monotonous*** repetitious and unvaried; ***tedious*** boring and lasting for too long; ***uninteresting*** not having qualities that arouse positive response.

born *adj* **instinctive**, congenital, innate, intuitive, natural, untaught, native. [➡TALENTED AND SKILFUL; 528] *Opposite:* trained.

born-again *adj* **reinvigorated**, reborn, enthusiastic, avid, fervid, passionate, revitalized, zealous. [➡APPRECIATION AND GRATITUDE; 536]

born with a silver spoon in your mouth *adj* [➡WEALTH AND WEALTHY; 891]

borough *n* **area**, district, municipality, division, township (*US*). [➡HUMAN SETTLEMENTS; 1069]

borrow **1** *v* **use**, make use of, have access to, scrounge (*informal*), sponge. [➡LEND, LEASE, AND BORROW; 429] *Opposite:* lend. **2** *v* **copy**, plagiarize, derive, pirate, steal, appropriate. [➡STEAL AND ROB; 427]

borscht *type of* **soup**. [➡SOUP; 1185]

borstal *n* **detention centre**, youth custody centre, prison, reformatory, jail, bail hostel, reform school. [➡BUILDINGS FOR CONFINING PEOPLE; 1093]

borzoi *type of* **large dog**. [➡DOG; 980]

bosom **1** *adj* (*informal*) **close**, best, dearest, special, firm, dear, inseparable. [➡RELATIONSHIP TO ANOTHER; 973] *Opposite:* distant. **2** *n* (*literary*) **heart**, arms, centre, midst, embrace, security, haven. [➡CENTRAL PARTS OF PHYSICAL OBJECTS; 1250] **3** *part of* **torso**. [➡TORSO; 694]

bosom buddy (*US*) *n* [➡FRIENDS; 963]

bosom friend *n* [➡FRIENDS; 963]

boson *type of* **elementary particle**. [➡ELEMENTARY PARTICLES; 1278]

boss **1** *n* **manager**, supervisor, chief, person in charge, superior, commander. [➡BOSSES AND MANAGEMENT; 965] *Opposite:* subordinate. **2** *v* **give orders**, tell what to do, boss about, boss around, order around, command, bully. [➡CAUSE OR COMPEL TO ACT; 272] *Opposite:* obey.

boss about *v* **give orders**, tell what to do, order about, order around, boss, boss around, command, bully. [➡CAUSE OR COMPEL TO ACT; 272] *Opposite:* obey.

bossa nova *type of* **dance**. [➡DANCE; 903]

boss around *v* **give orders**, tell what to do, order about, order around, boss, boss about, command, bully. [➡CAUSE OR COMPEL TO ACT; 272] *Opposite:* obey.

bossily *adv* **imperiously**, dictatorially, domineeringly, officiously, authoritatively, high-handedly, persuasively, overbearingly. [➡BOSSY AND OVERBEARING; 517] *Opposite:* meekly.

bossiness *n* **imperiousness**, officiousness, high-handedness, authoritarianism, overbearingness. [➡BOSSY AND OVERBEARING; 517] *Opposite:* meekness.

bossy *adj* **domineering**, officious, dominant, dictatorial, interfering, interventionist, overbearing, authoritarian, authoritative. [➡BOSSY AND OVERBEARING; 517] *Opposite:* meek.

Boston rocker *type of* **seating**. [➡FURNITURE; 858]

botanic *see* **botanical**.

botanical *adj* **botanic**, vegetal, plant. [➡BIOLOGICAL SCIENCES; 1037]

botanical garden *n* [➡GARDENS; 1073]

botany *type of* **bioscience**. [➡BIOLOGICAL SCIENCES; 1037]

botch **1** *n* (*informal*) **fiasco**, failure, disaster, flop (*informal*), cockup (*informal*). [➡MISTAKES; 251] **2** *v* **spoil**, damage, do something badly, make a botch of (*informal*), make a mess of, bodge (*informal*), fail, foul up (*informal*), mess up (*informal*). [➡MESS UP AND MAKE MISTAKES; 473] *Opposite:* correct.

botched *adj* **failed**, substandard, poor, messed up (*informal*), ruined, inferior, bungled (*informal*), slipshod, spoiled. [➡UNSUCCESSFUL AND UNPROMISING; 76] *Opposite:* first-rate.

botch up *v* [➡MESS UP AND MAKE MISTAKES; 473]

botfly *type of* **parasitic insect**. [➡PARASITES; 1017]

bother **1** *v* **make an effort**, take the trouble, put yourself out, go to the trouble of. [➡ATTEMPT AN ACTION; 262] **2** *v* **worry**, trouble, disturb, upset, unsettle, annoy, perturb, fret, disconcert, irk, bug (*informal*). [➡UPSET, DISTRESS, AND HUMILIATE; 568] **3** *v* **interrupt**, disturb, distract, trouble, pester, hassle (*informal*). [➡ANGER AND ANNOY; 570] **4** *n* **trouble**, difficulty, problem, nuisance, inconvenience, worry, anxiety, hassle (*informal*), vexation, thorny problem. [➡NUISANCES; 254]

Compare and Contrast: ***bother, annoy, bug, disturb, irk, trouble, worry***

CORE MEANING: TO INTERFERE WITH SOMEBODY'S COMPOSURE

bother to make somebody feel worried, anxious, or upset, or to disturb or interrupt somebody; ***annoy*** to irritate or harrass somebody; ***bug*** (*informal*) to cause persistent trouble and annoyance; ***disturb*** to interrupt or distract somebody in the process of doing something, or to upset somebody's peace of mind; ***irk*** to annoy somebody slightly, especially by being tedious; ***trouble*** to cause distress or inconvenience; ***worry*** to cause anxiety in somebody.

bothered *adj* **worried**, concerned, troubled, upset, hot and bothered, disturbed, perturbed, nervous, tense. [➡CONFUSION, ANXIETY, AND WORRY; 541] *Opposite:* untroubled.

bothersome *adj* **troublesome**, inconvenient, worrisome, niggling, incommodious (*formal*), difficult, vexing, annoying. [➡IRRITATING; 229]

bothy *n* **hut**, cottage, cabin, house, shelter, shed, croft. [➡RESIDENTIAL BUILDINGS; 1077]

bo tree *type of* **evergreen tree.** [➡EVERGREEN AND CONIFEROUS TREES; 1029]

bottle 1 *n* **flask**, jug, carafe, flagon, decanter, magnum, thermos, canteen. [➡CONTAINERS, RECEPTACLES, AND PACKAGING; 1244] 2 *n* (*informal*) **courage**, bravery, nerve, guts (*slang*), spirit, spine, backbone, front. [➡COURAGE; 499]

bottle green *type of* **green.** [➡COLOURS; 1223]

bottleneck *n* **block**, blockage, restricted access, holdup, traffic jam, jam, logjam. [➡TRAVEL: TRAFFIC PROBLEMS AND HOLDUPS; 324]

bottle opener *type of* **utensil.** [➡TABLEWARE, CUTLERY, AND KITCHENWARE; 861]

bottle out (*informal*) *v* **withdraw**, fail, refuse to do, lose courage, chicken out (*slang*), fall at the first fence. [➡NOT DO AND REFUSE TO DO; 275]

bottle up *v* **contain**, repress, suppress, keep in check, control, curb. [➡WITHHOLD INFORMATION; 688]

bottom 1 *n* **base**, bed, foot, floor, substructure, foundation. [➡EXTREMITIES OF PHYSICAL OBJECTS; 1249] *Opposite:* top. 2 *n* **end**, far end, foot, extremity, limit. [➡EXTREMITIES OF PHYSICAL OBJECTS; 1249] *Opposite:* top. 3 *n* **underside**, underneath, bottom side, underbelly. [➡EXTREMITIES OF PHYSICAL OBJECTS; 1249] *Opposite:* top. 4 *adj* **lowest**, bottommost, nethermost (*formal*), lowermost. [➡RELATIVE LOCATION; 162] *Opposite:* top. 5 *part of* **torso.** [➡TORSO; 694]

bottomless *adj* **unlimited**, unrestricted, endless, limitless, unending, infinite, never-ending, boundless. [➡DEPTH: DEEP; 1200] *Opposite:* restricted.

bottom line *n* **outcome**, end result, end product, upshot, main thing, sine qua non. [➡RESULTS AND OUTCOMES; 83]

bottommost *adj* **lowest**, last, bottom, final. [➡RELATIVE LOCATION; 162] *Opposite:* topmost.

botulinum *type of* **microorganism.** [➡MICROORGANISMS, FUNGI, AND ALGAE; 1023]

boudoir *n* **bedroom**, dressing room, chamber (*archaic or literary*), bedchamber (*archaic or literary*). [➡TYPES OF ROOM; 1096]

bouffant 1 *adj* **backcombed**, fluffy, full, puffed up, voluminous, teased. [➡DESCRIBING HAIR; 487] 2 *type of* **hairstyle.** [➡HAIR STYLES AND HAIR PIECES; 489]

bougainvillea *type of* **climber.** [➡CLIMBERS; 1033]

bough *n* **branch**, limb, spur. [➡PARTS OF TREES AND PLANTS; 1026]

bouillabaisse *type of* **soup.** [➡SOUP; 1185]

bouillon *type of* **soup.** [➡SOUP; 1185]

boulder *n* **rock**, stone, sarsen. [➡STONES, ROCKS, AND BOULDERS; 1057]

boules *type of* **target ball game.** [➡HOBBIES, GAMES, AND SPORTS; 875]

boulevard *type of* **major road.** [➡ROADS; 1105]

bounce 1 *v* **rebound**, spring back, bound, spring up, recoil. [➡BOUNCE, UNDULATE, AND VIBRATE; 309] 2 *v* **spring**, jump, bound, bob, bobble. [➡BOUNCE, UNDULATE, AND VIBRATE; 309]

bounce back *v* **recover**, improve, get better, pull through, pick up (*informal*), perk up, recuperate. [➡GET BETTER; 376]

bounciness 1 *n* **liveliness**, spirit, vivacity, friskiness, playfulness, verve, energy. [➡ENERGY AND ENTHUSIASM; 497] *Opposite:* lethargy. 2 *n* **elasticity**, springiness, resistance, pliability, give. [➡MALLEABLE AND ELASTIC; 1211] *Opposite:* firmness.

bouncy 1 *adj* **effervescent**, energetic, full of beans (*informal*), playful, lively, vivacious, animated. [➡ENERGY AND ENTHUSIASM; 497] *Opposite:* lethargic. 2 *adj* **springy**, elastic, pliable. [➡MALLEABLE AND ELASTIC; 1211] *Opposite:* firm.

bound 1 *adj* **certain**, sure, guaranteed, destined, assured, inevitable, unavoidable. [➡CERTAIN; 175] *Opposite:* unlikely. 2 *adj* **obliged**, compelled, forced, obligated, duty-bound, required, constrained. [➡RESPONSIBILITY; 171] *Opposite:* free. 3 *n* **jump**, leap, spring, bounce, hop, vault, hurdle. [➡BOUNCE, UNDULATE, AND VIBRATE; 309] 4 *v* **border**, border on, be next to, be contiguous to, touch, be adjacent to, be bounded by, adjoin, abut, conjoin (*formal*), fringe, skirt. [➡EXIST IN CLOSE PROXIMITY; 21]

boundary *n* **border**, frontier, borderline, edge, limit, margin, periphery, state line (*US*). [➡EXTREMITIES OF PHYSICAL OBJECTS; 1249]

bounded 1 *adj* **surrounded**, bordered, delimited (*formal*), enclosed, encircled. [➡CAPTIVITY AND LOSS OF FREEDOM; 249] 2 *adj* **restricted**, circumscribed (*formal*), hemmed in, limited, constrained, confined. [➡CAPTIVITY AND LOSS OF FREEDOM; 249] *Opposite:* free.

boundless *adj* **unlimited**, endless, limitless, infinite, ceaseless, never-ending, illimitable (*formal*), vast, without end, interminable, bottomless. [➡PERMANENCE: WITHOUT END; 94] *Opposite:* restricted.

bounds *n* **limits**, boundaries, confines, restrictions, constraints, restraints. [➡EXTREMITIES OF PHYSICAL OBJECTS; 1249]

bounteous (*literary*) 1 *adj* **generous**, giving, charitable, munificent, openhanded, magnanimous. [➡GENEROSITY AND KINDNESS; 496] *Opposite:* tightfisted. 2 *adj* **abundant**, plentiful, ample, plenteous (*literary*), profuse, copious. [➡MANY, MUCH, LARGE AMOUNT; 117] *Opposite:* scarce.

bountiful (*literary*) 1 *adj* **generous**, giving, munificent, openhanded, magnanimous. [➡GENEROSITY AND KINDNESS; 496] *Opposite:* tightfisted. 2 *adj* **plentiful**, generous, abundant, copious, profuse, ample, numerous, unstinting, plenteous (*literary*). [➡MANY, MUCH, LARGE AMOUNT; 117] *Opposite:* scarce.

See Compare and Contrast at **generous.**

bounty 1 *n* **reward**, price, prize, payment, gift. [➡REWARDS AND AWARDS; 440] 2 *n* (*literary*) **abundance**, plenty, plenteousness (*literary*), glut. [➡MANY, MUCH, LARGE AMOUNT; 117] *Opposite:* scarcity.

bouquet 1 *n* **bunch**, spray, posy. [➡COLLECTIONS AND MIXTURES OF THINGS; 1243] 2 *n* **smell**, aroma, scent, fragrance, perfume. [➡SMELL AND SMELLING; 706]

See Compare and Contrast at **smell.**

bourgeois 1 *adj* **middle-class**, conventional, conformist, unadventurous, staid, predictable. [➡CLASS STATUS; 889] 2 *n* **conservative**, traditionalist, stick-in-the-mud (*informal*), conformist, reactionary, conventional person. [➡CLASS STATUS; 889]

bout *n* **short period**, short time, session, spell, attack, fit, stretch, stint. [➡SHORT PERIOD OF TIME; 93]

boutique *type of* **retail outlet.** [➡RETAIL OUTLETS; 1082]

boutique hotel *n type of* **hotel.** [➡HOTELS, RESTAURANTS, AND CLUBS; 1081]

bouzouki *type of* **stringed instrument.** [➡MUSICAL INSTRUMENTS; 910]

bovine (*literary*) *adj* **stupid**, slow, unintelligent, dim, dense, dull. [➡NEGATIVE INTELLECTUAL CHARACTERISTICS; 526]

bow 1 *n* **arc**, curve, arch, sweep, bend, kink. [➡ROUNDED SHAPE; 1217] 2 *n* **bob**, bend, curtsy, obeisance (*formal*). [➡GESTURES AND GESTICULATION; 654] 3 *part of* **ship or boat.** [➡PARTS OF A SHIP OR BOAT; 1150] 4 *types of* **bow.** [➡WEAPONS FOR SHOOTING; 1155] 5 *v* **bend**, bend over, lower, stoop, lean, curtsy, genuflect, bob, duck, nod. [➡GESTURES AND GESTICULATION; 654] *Opposite:* straighten up. 6 *v* **distort**, deform, arch, droop, sag. [➡CHANGE OF SHAPE; 386] *Opposite:* straighten.

bow

◆ *types of bow*
crossbow, Cupid's bow, longbow

bow and scrape *v* [➡GESTURES AND GESTICULATION; 654]

bowdlerize *v* **censor**, edit, abridge, clean up, expurgate, amend. [➡WITHHOLD INFORMATION; 688]

bowed *adj* **curved**, bent, deformed, convex, hooked, arched, stooped, hunched. [➡ROUNDED SHAPE; 1217] *Opposite:* straight.

bowel *part of* **digestive tract.** [➡THE DIGESTIVE TRACT; 710]

bowels *n* **guts**, entrails, innards (*informal*), insides (*informal*). [➡THE DIGESTIVE TRACT; 710]

bower *n* **arbour**, retreat, grove, copse, den, hideaway, nook, dell (*literary*). [➡GARDENS; 1073]

bowie knife *type of* **sword or knife.** [➡SWORDS AND KNIVES; 1156]

bowing and scraping *n* [➡GESTURES AND GESTICULATION; 654]

bowl 1 *n* **container**, vessel, dish, basin, mixing bowl, pudding basin, washbasin. [➡TABLEWARE, CUTLERY, AND KITCHENWARE; 861] 2 *n* **hollow**, depression, basin, vale (*literary*), valley. [➡GEOLOGICAL FEATURES; 1056] 3 *n* **ball**, wood, boule. [➡SPORTS EQUIPMENT; 879] 4 *n* (*US*) **stadium**, arena, amphitheatre, venue, ballpark (*US*). [➡BUILDINGS FOR PUBLIC ENTERTAINMENT; 1083] 5 *v* **careen**, career, roll along, travel, speed, traverse. [➡MOVE FAST; 314] 6 *v* **roll**, pitch, throw, lob, hurl, cast, toss, fling, chuck (*informal*). [➡THROW SOMETHING; 335]

bowled over *adj* **astonished**, surprised, speechless, taken aback, thunderstruck, flabbergasted (*informal*), amazed, dumbfounded, staggered, gobsmacked (*slang*). [➡SURPRISE, SHOCK, AND AMAZEMENT; 546]

bowlegged *adj* **bandy-legged**, bandy, bent. [➡BUILD; 478]

bowler hat *type of* **hat.** [➡HABERDASHERY, MILLINERY, AND LINGERIE; 867]

bowling *type of* **target ball game.** [➡HOBBIES, GAMES, AND SPORTS; 875]

bowl over 1 *v* **astonish**, amaze, delight, overwhelm, knock for six (*informal*), take by surprise. [➡SURPRISE AND IMPRESS; 575] 2 *v* **knock down**, knock over, scatter, upturn, overturn. [➡MOVE SOMETHING: INTO A NEW POSITION OR OVERTURN; 331]

bowls *type of* **target ball game.** [➡HOBBIES, GAMES, AND SPORTS; 875]

bow out *v* [➡NOT DO AND REFUSE TO DO; 275]

bowsprit *part of* **sailing vessel.** [➡PARTS OF A SHIP OR BOAT; 1150]

bow tie *n* **tie**, cravat, dicky bow (*informal*), dicky (*informal*), necktie (*US*). [➡HABERDASHERY, MILLINERY, AND LINGERIE; 867]

bow to *v* **accept**, yield, resign yourself to, recognize, acknowledge, give in to, submit, succumb to, acquiesce, give way to. [➡FORGET, FORGIVE, AND ACCEPT; 749] *Opposite:* reject.

box 1 *n* **container**, case, chest, packet, carton, package, strongbox, punnet. [➡CONTAINERS, RECEPTACLES, AND PACKAGING; 1244] 2 *n* **rectangle**, square, frame, tick box, check box. [➡ANGULAR SHAPE; 1216] 3 *n* **cubicle**, stall, booth, compartment, enclosure. [➡ALCOVES, CUBICLES, AND COMPARTMENTS; 1095] 4 *n* (*slang*) **television**, telly, TV (*informal*), small screen (*informal*), gogglebox (*dated informal*), tube (*US*). [➡TELEVISION AND RADIO; 607] 5 *v* **fight**, spar, punch, hit, thump, land a punch. [➡PHYSICAL ATTACK AND PUNISHMENT; 416]

box camera *type of* **photographic equipment.** [➡PHOTOGRAPHY AND PHOTOGRAPHIC EQUIPMENT; 1121]

boxer 1 *n* [➡PEOPLE IN SPORTS AND LEISURE; 876] 2 *type of* **large dog.** [➡DOG; 980]

boxer shorts *type of* **lower body underwear.** [➡HABERDASHERY, MILLINERY, AND LINGERIE; 867]

box in *v* **enclose**, surround, contain, shut in, trap, hem in. [➡EXIST IN CLOSE PROXIMITY; 21]

boxing *type of* **combat sport.** [➡HOBBIES, GAMES, AND SPORTS; 875]

boxroom *n* **cubbyhole**, spare room, attic, storeroom, glory hole (*informal*), loft, closet (*US*). [➡TYPES OF ROOM; 1096]

boy *n* **young man**, lad, schoolboy, son, youngster, child, teenager, youth. [➡MALE PERSON; 934]

boycott *v* **refuse**, stay away from, impose sanctions, embargo, shun, proscribe, prohibit, reject. [➡AVOID, PREVENT, LIMIT, AND CONTROL; 278]

boyfriend *n* **male friend**, steady (*informal*), date, escort, suitor (*formal*), fiancé, mate, partner, beau (*dated*). [➡SEXUAL AND ROMANTIC RELATIONSHIPS; 964]

boyhood *n* **childhood**, youth, early years. [➡BABYHOOD, CHILDHOOD AND ADOLESCENCE; 917]

boyish *adj* **youthful**, adolescent, childlike, fresh-faced, young. [➡PEOPLE'S PHYSICAL APPEARANCE; 476]

boysenberry *type of* **berry.** [➡FRUIT AND VEGETABLES; 1175]

boy wonder *n* [➡TALENTED OR INTELLIGENT PERSON; 529]

B picture *n* [➡FILM; 901]

bra *type of* **upper body underwear.** [➡HABERDASHERY, MILLINERY, AND LINGERIE; 867]

brace *n* **support**, strut, prop, stay, bracket, buttress. [➡SUPPORTS AND BASES; 1254]

bracelet *type of* **jewellery.** [➡JEWELLERY; 866]

braces *type of* **accessory.** [➡HABERDASHERY, MILLINERY, AND LINGERIE; 867]

brace yourself *v* **prepare yourself**, ready yourself, make preparations, get ready for, prime yourself, get ready, steel yourself. [➡PREPARE FOR ACTION; 290]

brachiosaurus *type of* **dinosaur.** [➡DINOSAUR; 996]

bracing *adj* **invigorating**, stimulating, brisk, healthy, cold, refreshing, revitalizing, restorative, fortifying. [➡PHYSICALLY PLEASANT; 187] *Opposite:* soporific.

bracket 1 *n* **support**, strut, prop, stay, brace. [➡SUPPORTS AND BASES; 1254] 2 *n* **group**, set, range, cohort, band, collection, category, grade, sort, kind. [➡VARIETY, TYPE, KIND; 146] 3 *type of* **punctuation mark.** [➡ASPECTS OF LANGUAGE; 683] 4 *v* **connect**, link, join, relate, associate, group. [➡CREATING CONNECTIONS; 145] *Opposite:* separate.

bracket fungus *type of* **fungus.** [➡MICROORGANISMS, FUNGI, AND ALGAE; 1023]

brackish *adj* **salty**, saline, salted, briny, salt. [➡TASTE; 704] *Opposite:* fresh.

bradawl *type of* **carpentry tool.** [➡HAND TOOLS; 1118]

brag *v* **boast**, blow your own trumpet (*informal*), crow, show off, swagger, swank (*informal*), talk big, blow your own horn (*US*). [➡BOAST; 617] *Opposite:* underplay.

braggadocio *n* [➡BOAST; 617]

braggart *n* **boaster**, show-off (*informal*), bigmouth (*informal*), loudmouth (*informal*), windbag (*informal*), egotist. [➡SELF-IMPORTANT AND SELF-SEEKING PEOPLE; 949]

bragger *n* [➡SELF-IMPORTANT AND SELF-SEEKING PEOPLE; 949]

bragging 1 *n* **boasting**, boastfulness, showing off, arrogance, self-aggrandizement, hot air (*informal*). [➡BOAST; 617] *Opposite:* modesty. 2 *adj* **boastful**, cocky (*informal*), arrogant, self-important, conceited, swaggering. [➡POMPOUS, LOUD, AND OVER-CONFIDENT; 636] *Opposite:* modest.

braid 1 *v* **plait**, interweave, interlace, intertwine, weave, thread, entwine. [➡CRAFTS AND CARVING; 356] *Opposite:* unravel. 2 *v* **decorate**, trim, edge, fringe, bind. [➡DECORATE, ADORN, AND APPLY COATINGS; 406] *Opposite:* strip.

braids *type of* **hairstyle.** [➡HAIR STYLES AND HAIR PIECES; 489]

Braille *type of* **alphabet.** [➡SYMBOLS, SIGNS, AND NUMBERS; 597]

brain 1 *n* **intelligence**, mind, intellect, head, wits, common sense, understanding. [➡DESCRIBING SOMEBODY'S INTELLECT; 524] 2 *n* (*informal*) **egghead** (*informal*), mastermind, intellectual, genius, intellect, prodigy. [➡TALENTED OR INTELLIGENT PERSON; 529]

brainbox *n* [➡TALENTED OR INTELLIGENT PERSON; 529]

brainchild *n* **idea**, invention, creation, innovation, breakthrough, discovery. [➡IDEA AND THOUGHT; 771]

brainless *adj* **foolish**, stupid, mindless, unintelligent, silly, senseless, obtuse, daft (*informal*). [➡NEGATIVE INTELLECTUAL CHARACTERISTICS; 526] *Opposite:* sensible.

brainpower *n* **intellect**, brains, capacity, ability, intellectual capacity, mental ability, understanding, grasp, IQ, intelligence. [➡DESCRIBING SOMEBODY'S INTELLECT; 524]

brains *n* **intelligence**, common sense, wits, intellect, brainpower, mental ability. [➡DESCRIBING SOMEBODY'S INTELLECT; 524] *Opposite:* ignorance.

brainstorm 1 *n* **aberration**, fit, turn, disturbance, upset, attack. [➡IDEA AND THOUGHT; 771] 2 *n* (*US informal*) **bright idea**, inspiration, idea, breakthrough, brain wave, innovation. [➡IDEA AND THOUGHT; 771] 3 *v* **think**, suggest, come up with, devise, dream up, free-associate. [➡TWO-WAY COMMUNICATION; 608]

brainteaser *n* **problem**, puzzle, riddle, challenge, conundrum, mystery. [➡JOKES AND TEASING; 675]

brainwash *v* **persuade**, indoctrinate, condition, convince, programme, mould, talk into. [➡INSTRUCT AND TEACH; 610]

brain wave (*informal*) *n* **bright idea**, inspiration, idea, breakthrough, innovation, brainstorm (*US informal*). [➡IDEA AND THOUGHT; 771]

brainy (*informal*) *adj* **intelligent**, clever, bright, quick, academic, intellectual, sharp, alert, brilliant, gifted, quick-witted, able. [➡POSITIVE INTELLECTUAL CHARACTERISTICS; 525] *Opposite:* unintelligent.

braise *v* **cook**, stew, casserole, boil, steam, simmer, poach. [➡ COOKING AND FOOD PREPARATION; 354]

braised *adj* [➡ STATE OF PREPARED FOOD; 1170]

brake 1 *n* **restraint**, constraint, curb, control, limitation, damper, deterrent, discouragement. [➡ PROBLEM; 257] *Opposite:* incentive. 2 *v* **decelerate**, slow down, reduce speed, put on the brakes, lose speed, slam on the brakes, slow, slow up, ease up, let up. [➡ CHANGE OF SPEED: LESS; 398] *Opposite:* accelerate. 3 *type of* **controls.** [➡ VEHICLES; 1144] 4 *part of* **bike** (*informal*). [➡ BIKES, CARS, AND CARRIAGES; 1148]

brake light *type of* **external feature.** [➡ VEHICLES; 1144]

bramble *type of* **shrub or bush.** [➡ BUSHES AND SHRUBS; 1027]

bran *n* **fibre**, dietary fibre, cellulose, roughage, bulk. [➡ FOOD COMPONENTS; 1187]

branch 1 *n* **bough**, limb, stem, twig. [➡ PARTS OF TREES AND PLANTS; 1026] 2 *n* **local office**, division, area office, subdivision, outlet, office. [➡ PLACE OF EMPLOYMENT; 832] *Opposite:* headquarters. 3 *n* **division**, department, offshoot, wing, arm, subdivision. [➡ SUBDIVISIONS AND OFFSHOOTS; 1252] 4 *n* **area**, field, topic, domain, sphere, aspect, side. [➡ SUBJECT AREA; 769] 5 *n* **turning**, turn-off, arm, tributary, fork, sideroad, turn. [➡ HOLES, GAPS, AND FORKS; 1251] 6 *v* **split**, fork, divide, diverge, separate, branch off, bifurcate. [➡ SEPARATE AND DIVIDE; 402] *Opposite:* converge.

branch off *v* **fork**, turn off, leave, divide, split, diverge, separate. [➡ SEPARATE AND DIVIDE; 402] *Opposite:* merge.

branch out *v* **diversify**, diverge, take a new direction, broaden, expand, separate from, split off. [➡ SEPARATE AND DIVIDE; 402] *Opposite:* consolidate.

brand 1 *n* **make**, product, brand name, variety, kind, sort, trade name, trademark, marque. [➡ NAME AND DESCRIBE; 666] 2 *n* **type**, kind, sort, style, variety, class. [➡ VARIETY, TYPE, KIND; 146] 3 *n* **identifying mark**, mark, marker, identification, label, stamp. [➡ SYMBOLS, SIGNS, AND NUMBERS; 597] 4 *v* **mark**, imprint, stamp, label. [➡ CREATE IMAGES; 357] 5 *v* **call**, classify, label, name, describe, class, categorize. [➡ NAME AND DESCRIBE; 666]

brandish *v* **wield**, wave, flourish, handle, ply, flaunt, show off, display. [➡ MOVE SOMETHING ON THE SPOT; 337] *Opposite:* conceal.

brand name *n* **trade name**, brand, label, make, trademark, registered trademark, marque, service mark. [➡ NAME AND DESCRIBE; 666]

brand-new *adj* **new**, unused, pristine, fresh, mint, untouched, spanking new. [➡ NEW, MODERN; 167] *Opposite:* old.

brash 1 *adj* **aggressive**, arrogant, pushy (*informal*), self-confident, brazen, presumptuous, bold, forceful, impudent. [➡ POMPOUS, LOUD, AND OVER-CONFIDENT; 636] *Opposite:* self-effacing. 2 *adj* **loud**, garish, vulgar, gaudy, bright, tasteless, trashy. [➡ IN POOR TASTE; 230] *Opposite:* muted. 3 *adj* (*US*) **hasty**, impetuous, rash, foolhardy, slapdash, hurried, impatient. [➡ INCAUTIOUS AND CARELESS; 284] *Opposite:* measured.

brashly *adv* **brazenly**, forcefully, insolently, assertively, rudely, obnoxiously, boldly, impudently. [➡ POMPOUS, LOUD, AND OVER-CONFIDENT; 636] *Opposite:* shyly.

brashness *n* **boldness**, brazenness, forcefulness, insolence, assertiveness, rudeness, impudence, presumptuousness. [➡ POMPOUS, LOUD, AND OVER-CONFIDENT; 636] *Opposite:* shyness.

brass 1 *n* (*informal*) **nerve**, cheek (*informal*), impudence, self-assurance, self-confidence, gall, boldness, assertiveness, chutzpah (*informal*). [➡ BOSSY AND OVERBEARING; 517] *Opposite:* bashfulness. 2 *type of* **metal.** [➡ METALS; 1275]

brass band *type of* **band.** [➡ MUSICIANS AND SINGERS; 908]

brasserie *type of* **eating place.** [➡ HOTELS, RESTAURANTS, AND CLUBS; 1081]

brassica *type of* **vegetable.** [➡ FRUIT AND VEGETABLES; 1175]

brass tacks *n* **basics**, essentials, fundamentals, nuts and bolts (*informal*), bare essentials, nitty-gritty (*informal*). [➡ BASIC DETAILS; 689]

brassy 1 *adj* **harsh**, loud, metallic, strident, grating, high-pitched. [➡ LOUD OR UNPLEASANT SOUNDS; 1265] *Opposite:* soft. 2 *adj* **brazen**, strident, overbearing, brash, arrogant, forceful. [➡ POMPOUS, LOUD, AND OVER-CONFIDENT; 636] *Opposite:* self-effacing.

brat *n* **little monster**, horror (*informal*), spoiled brat, terror (*informal*), holy terror (*informal*), imp. [➡ MISCHIEVOUS OR BADLY-BEHAVED CHILD; 946] *Opposite:* cherub.

brattish *adj* [➡ AGGRESSIVE AND BELLIGERENT; 519]

bratty *adj* **obnoxious**, spoiled, demanding, overindulged, selfish, troublesome, ill-mannered. [➡ AGGRESSIVE AND BELLIGERENT; 519] *Opposite:* well-behaved.

bravado *n* **audacity**, boldness, daring, bluster, boasting, show, swagger. [➡ CALMNESS, CONFIDENCE, AND COMPOSURE; 537] *Opposite:* cowardice.

brave 1 *adj* **courageous**, valiant, heroic, bold, daring, fearless, plucky. [➡ COURAGE; 499] *Opposite:* cowardly. 2 *v* **defy**, face, stand up to, confront, take on, bear, endure, suffer. [➡ TOLERATE AND ENDURE; 767] *Opposite:* shrink.

brave out *v* **suffer**, face, bear, endure, tough it out (*informal*), stay the course, sit out, grin and bear it (*informal*), put up with. [➡ TOLERATE AND ENDURE; 767] *Opposite:* give up.

bravery *n* **courage**, courageousness, valour, gallantry, daring, heroism, guts (*slang*), nerve, fearlessness, boldness, pluckiness, pluck. [➡ COURAGE; 499] *Opposite:* cowardice.

See Compare and Contrast at **courage**.

bravo *interj* [➡ COMPLIMENTS; 658]

bravura 1 *n* **boldness**, daring, spirit, nerve, guts (*slang*), chutzpah (*informal*). [➡ COURAGE; 499] *Opposite:* timidity. 2 *adj* **brilliant**, magnificent, exceptional, dazzling, outstanding, superlative, virtuoso. [➡ EXTRAORDINARY: UNCOMMON; 206] *Opposite:* nondescript.

brawl 1 *n* **scuffle**, fight, punch-up, clash, affray, scrap (*informal*), fracas. [➡ AGGRESSIVE EVENT; 39] 2 *v* **fight**, scuffle, tussle, wrestle, clash, scrap. [➡ COMPETE, CONTEND, AND COMBAT; 304]

brawn 1 *n* **strength**, muscle, brute force, power, burliness, muscularity. [➡ MUSCLES AND MUSCULATURE; 480] *Opposite:* weakness. 2 *n* [➡ THE MUSCLES; 719]

brawniness *n* [➡BUILD; 478]

brawny *adj* **muscular**, strong, powerfully built, strapping (*informal*), hefty, burly, beefy. [➡MUSCLES AND MUSCULATURE; 480] *Opposite:* scrawny.

bray 1 *n* **neigh**, whinny, cry, call, sound. [➡SOUNDS MADE BY ANIMALS; 1260] 2 *v* **whinny**, neigh, cry, call. [➡SOUND EMISSION BY ANIMALS OR BIRDS; 365] 3 *v* **grate**, rasp, bark, bellow, snort, cackle, shriek, screech. [➡SOUND EMISSION BY PEOPLE; 364] *Opposite:* murmur.

braying *adj* **harsh**, loud, strident, jarring, grating, raucous. [➡LOUD OR UNPLEASANT SOUNDS; 1265] *Opposite:* soft.

brazen *adj* **bold**, barefaced, shameless, brash, unabashed, unashamed, blatant, audacious, forward, bald-faced (*US*). [➡POMPOUS, LOUD, AND OVER-CONFIDENT; 636] *Opposite:* discreet.

brazenly *adv* **shamelessly**, barefacedly, openly, blatantly, audaciously, brashly, impudently, bald-facedly (*US*). [➡BAD MANNERS AND SOCIAL SKILLS; 522] *Opposite:* discreetly.

brazenness *n* **shamelessness**, boldness, barefacedness, flagrancy, impudence, defiance, bald-facedness (*US*). [➡POMPOUS, LOUD, AND OVER-CONFIDENT; 636] *Opposite:* discretion.

brazen out *v* **face down**, stand your ground, face out, hold your own, stay the course, stick to your guns. [➡CONTINUE AN ACTION; 263] *Opposite:* cave in.

brazier *n* **stove**, barbecue, fire, open fire. [➡FIRE, FLAMMABILITY, AND BURNING; 1164]

brazil nut *type of* **nut**. [➡NUTS; 1184]

breach 1 *v* **get through**, break through, break, rupture, penetrate, open, crack open. [➡MOVE PAST, INTO OR THROUGH SOMETHING; 332] *Opposite:* block. 2 *v* **break**, violate, contravene, infringe, flout, disobey. [➡DISOBEY; 303] *Opposite:* honour. 3 *n* **opening**, break, hole, crack, fissure, rupture. [➡HOLES, GAPS, AND FORKS; 1251] *Opposite:* obstacle. 4 *n* **violation**, contravention, infringement, defiance, betrayal, breaking. [➡BAD BEHAVIOUR OR ACTION; 255] *Opposite:* compliance. 5 *n* **rift**, separation, division, rupture, estrangement, drifting apart. [➡DISHARMONY; 157] *Opposite:* reconciliation.

breach of the peace *n* **public disturbance**, public nuisance, nuisance, riot, fracas, commotion, ruckus, disorderly conduct, uproar. [➡CRIMES; 817] *Opposite:* order.

bread 1 *n* **food**, daily bread, sustenance, nourishment, rations, diet, means of survival. [➡FOOD; 1166] 2 *n* (*dated slang*) **cash**, dosh (*slang*), dough (*slang*), lolly (*informal*), funds, finance, bucks (*US informal*). [➡MONEY; 140]

bread

◆ *types of bread*
baguette, black bread, brown bread, chapati, ciabatta, corn bread (*US*), cottage loaf, crouton, focaccia, matzo, nan, pitta, poppadom, pumpernickel, puri, roti, rye bread, soda bread, toast, tortilla, white bread

◆ *types of roll or bun*
bagel, bap, bun, croissant, crumpet, English muffin (*US*), muffin, roll

bread and butter 1 *n* **livelihood**, living, income, maintenance, upkeep, support, means of support, means. [➡INCOME; 461] 2 *n* **mainstay**, lifeblood, backbone, basis, core. [➡MOST IMPORTANT THING; 198]

bread-and-butter *adj* **basic**, primary, fundamental, essential, important, key, central, everyday, main. [➡FUNDAMENTAL; 196] *Opposite:* superfluous.

bread knife *type of* **knife**. [➡CUTTING TOOLS; 1119]

breadth 1 *n* **width**, span, wideness, extent, size, girth. [➡WIDTH: WIDE; 1198] *Opposite:* depth. 2 *n* **extensiveness**, extent, range, scope, span, coverage, scale. [➡DEGREE AND EXTENT; 110] *Opposite:* narrowness. 3 *n* **latitude**, room, freedom, space, leeway, tolerance, broad-mindedness. [➡FREEDOM AND LIBERTY; 209] *Opposite:* restriction.

breadthways 1 *adj* **sideways**, side-to-side, breadthwise (*US*). [➡ORIENTATION AND ALIGNMENT; 1222] 2 *adv* **across**, from side to side, widthways, breadthwise (*US*), widthwise (*US*). [➡ORIENTATION AND ALIGNMENT; 1222]

breadthwise (*US*) 1 *adj* **breadthways**, sideways, side-to-side. [➡ORIENTATION AND ALIGNMENT; 1222] 2 *adv* **across**, from side to side, breadthways, widthways, widthwise (*US*). [➡ORIENTATION AND ALIGNMENT; 1222]

breadwinner *n* **wage earner**, worker, employee. [➡WORKER; 836] *Opposite:* dependant.

break 1 *v* **smash**, fracture, rupture, shatter, split, crack, sever. [➡TEAR, BREAK, AND CUT; 361] *Opposite:* mend. 2 *v* **break down**, stop working, fail, collapse, crash, bite the dust (*informal*), go kaput (*informal*), go down. [➡FAIL OR CEASE TO FUNCTION; 471] 3 *v* **infringe**, violate, contravene, breach, disobey, be in breach of, fall foul of, disregard. [➡DISOBEY; 303] *Opposite:* uphold. 4 *v* **stop**, end, interrupt, disturb, break into, cut into. [➡CAUSE TO STOP; 267] 5 *v* **take a break**, break into, have a break, rest, stop, take a breather (*informal*), put your feet up, take it easy, relax, take five (*informal*), have time out. [➡STOP ACTING; 265] 6 *v* **beat**, surpass, exceed, top, better, crack. [➡BEAT AND DEFEAT; 80] 7 *v* **destroy**, shatter, crush, overwhelm, defeat, rout. [➡BEAT AND DEFEAT; 80] 8 *v* **become known**, make public, become public, disclose, get round, get out, be revealed, leak out. [➡APPEAR AND EMERGE; 3] 9 *v* **decipher**, crack, decode, solve, unravel, unscramble. [➡SOLVE AND INTERPRET; 761] 10 *n* **disruption**, breakdown, discontinuity, interruption, pause, halt, cessation, opportunity, opening, occasion. [➡PAUSES AND PHASES; 56] 11 *n* (*informal*) **chance**, opportunity, opening, occasion, leg up, way in, start. [➡SOURCE OF HAPPINESS, PLEASURE, OR IMPROVEMENT; 210] 12 *n* **rest**, respite, breather (*informal*), coffee break, pause, lunch break, tea break, sit-down (*informal*). [➡PERIOD OF REST; 91] 13 *n* **holiday**, time off, weekend break, trip, vacation, weekend trip (*US*). [➡PERIOD OF REST; 91] 14 *n* **interruption**, pause, space, disruption, halt, stop. [➡PAUSES AND PHASES; 56]

breakable *adj* **fragile**, delicate, brittle, frail, flimsy. [➡FRAGILE; 1208] *Opposite:* sturdy.

breakage *n* **breaking**, smashing, cracking, rupture, splintering, fracture, damage. [➡TEAR, BREAK, AND CUT; 361] *Opposite:* mending.

break away *v* **secede**, separate, become independent, split, disaffiliate, gain autonomy, divide off. [➡SEPARATE AND DIVIDE; 402] *Opposite:* join.

breakaway 1 *n* **separation**, rupture, severance, splitting up, breakup, parting. [➡END; 54] *Opposite:* fusion. 2 *adj* **separate**, splinter, independent, autonomous, alternative, unconnected, nonaligned. [➡UNRELATEDNESS AND SEPARATENESS; 147] *Opposite:* mainstream.

break down 1 *v* **stop working**, break, fail, go down, crash, go kaput (*informal*), go wrong, stop. [➡FAIL OR CEASE TO FUNCTION; 471] 2 *v* **lose control**, cry, be overcome, collapse, lose it (*informal*), burst into tears. [➡GIVING VENT TO EMOTIONS; 680] 3 *v* **overcome**, defeat, destroy, knock down, smash down, wear down, work away at. [➡BEAT AND DEFEAT; 80] *Opposite:* build. 4 *v* **analyse**, separate, dissect, break up, split, go through with a fine-tooth comb. [➡EXAMINE AND ASSESS; 754] 5 *v* **divide**, classify, categorize, split, separate, group. [➡SEPARATE AND DIVIDE; 402] *Opposite:* lump. 6 *v* **decompose**, decay, putrefy, disintegrate, moulder. [➡WORSEN SOMETHING; 381]

breakdown 1 *n* **failure**, collapse, cessation, halt, interruption, break. [➡FAILURE; 77] 2 *n* **analysis**, rundown, classification, dissection, summary, itemization. [➡EXAMINE AND ASSESS; 754]

break down and cry *v* [➡GIVING VENT TO EMOTIONS; 680]

breakdown lorry *type of* **commercial or industrial vehicle.** [➡VEHICLES; 1144]

breaker *n* **wave**, roller, whitecap, white horse. [➡THE SEAS, OCEANS, AND SHORES; 1041]

breakfast *type of* **meal.** [➡MEALS AND PARTS OF MEALS; 1168]

breakfast cereal *n* [➡CEREAL FOODS; 1177]

break free *v* **escape**, break away, cut loose (*informal*), break with, separate, get away, break out, disentangle yourself. [➡AVOID OR ESCAPE CONTACT; 419]

breakfront *type of* **cabinet.** [➡FURNITURE; 858]

break in 1 *v* **tame**, train, discipline, domesticate, house-train, school, housebreak (*US*). [➡INSTRUCT AND TEACH; 610] 2 *v* **force an entry**, break into, burgle, break and enter, force the lock, break down the door, get in, burglarize (*US*). [➡STEAL AND ROB; 427] 3 *v* **interrupt**, butt in, interject, interpose, cut in, cut off. [➡INTERRUPT AND BUTT IN; 620]

break-in *n* **forced entry**, burglary, robbery, crime, felony, incident. [➡CRIMES; 817]

breaking *n* **contravention**, infringement, violation, breach, transgression, flouting. [➡CRIMES; 817] *Opposite:* observance.

breaking and entering *n* [➡CRIMES; 817]

breaking point *n* **verge of collapse**, limit, threshold, snapping point, crisis, breakpoint, edge, brink. [➡DECISIVE MOMENTS; 44]

break into 1 *v* **break in**, force an entry, burgle, break and enter, break down the door, force the lock, get in, burglarize (*US*). [➡MOVE PAST, INTO OR THROUGH SOMETHING; 332] 2 *v* **begin**, burst into, launch into, start on (*informal*), embark on, burst out. [➡SUDDENLY COME INTO EXISTENCE; 2] *Opposite:* break off.

breakneck *adj* **quick**, speedy, hurried, hasty, rapid, swift, fast. [➡HAPPENING QUICKLY; 104] *Opposite:* slow.

break new ground *v* **be the first**, blaze a trail, lead the way, be in the vanguard, set a trend, set an example. [➡START AN ACTION; 261]

break of day *n* **daybreak**, sunrise, daylight, first light, dawn, crack of dawn, cockcrow (*archaic or literary*), morning, sunup (*US*). [➡TIMES OF DAY; 87] *Opposite:* sundown.

break off 1 *v* **detach**, come off, snap off, come away, separate, break away. [➡SEPARATE AND DIVIDE; 402] *Opposite:* attach. 2 *v* **end**, terminate (*formal*), stop, cease, finish, halt, pause, falter. [➡STOP ACTING; 265] *Opposite:* begin.

breakoff *n* **discontinuation**, ending, interruption, suspension, stopping, pause. [➡PAUSES AND PHASES; 56] *Opposite:* continuation.

break open *v* **open**, divide, come apart, burst, shatter, part, crack, split, prise, pry (*US*). [➡SEPARATE AND DIVIDE; 402]

break out 1 *v* **begin**, start, erupt, burst into, embark on, burst out, explode. [➡SUDDENLY COME INTO EXISTENCE; 2] *Opposite:* end. 2 *v* **escape**, break loose, cut loose (*informal*), burst out, break free, emerge, come out, get out. [➡RUN AWAY AND AVOID; 10]

breakout *n* **escape**, getaway, flight, running away, running off, escaping, absconding. [➡END; 54]

break the ice *v* **get to know**, make friends, get acquainted, introduce yourself, set the ball rolling, make the first move. [➡INITIATE AND ESTABLISH COMMUNICATION; 681]

break through *v* **burst through**, penetrate, come through, breach, wear down, break down, batter down, destroy, infiltrate. [➡MOVE PAST, INTO OR THROUGH SOMETHING; 332]

breakthrough *n* **advance**, step forward, leap forward, new idea, innovation, revolution, invention, discovery, development. [➡PROGRESS AND ADVANCEMENT; 214]

break up 1 *v* **divide**, fragment, disintegrate, crumble, fall apart, fall to pieces, fall to bits. [➡TEAR, BREAK, AND CUT; 361] *Opposite:* fuse. 2 *v* **disperse**, separate, split up, keep apart, divide up, tear apart, break down, cut up, section. [➡SEPARATE AND DIVIDE; 402] *Opposite:* unite. 3 *v* **separate**, tell somebody it's over, split up, ditch (*informal*), dump (*informal*), end, finish. [➡REFUSING OR REJECTING RELATIONS; 975]

breakup 1 *n* **disintegration**, fragmentation, division, crumbling, destruction, collapse. [➡TEAR, BREAK, AND CUT; 361] *Opposite:* merger. 2 *n* **ending**, end, splitting up, finish, separation, divorce. [➡END; 54]

breakwater *n* **offshore barrier**, mole, sea wall, harbour wall, causeway, pier. [➡WATERWAYS AND SEAWAYS; 1107]

break with *v* **separate**, split, leave, part company, escape, pull away, secede. [➡REFUSING OR REJECTING RELATIONS; 975] *Opposite:* associate.

bream *type of* **freshwater fish.** [➡FRESHWATER FISH; 1010]

breast 1 *part of* **torso.** [➡TORSO; 694] 2 *type of* **cut.** [➡TYPES AND CUTS OF MEAT; 1176]

breastbone *type of* **bone.** [➡THE BONES AND JOINTS; 720]

breath 1 *n* **gasp**, sigh, pant, inhalation, exhalation.

[➡ BREATHE AND NOT BREATHE; 717] **2** *n* **puff**, waft, current, draught, gush, rush. [➡ AMOUNT OF GAS; 116]

breathe *v* **respire**, take breaths, inhale, exhale, suck in air, take in air, breathe in, breathe out, blow, puff. [➡ BREATHE AND NOT BREATHE; 717]

breathe new life into *v* **revitalize**, reinvigorate, revive, resurrect, rejuvenate, boost. [➡ IMPROVE STRENGTH AND DURABILITY; 379]

breather (*informal*) *n* **rest**, break, respite, breathing space, pause. [➡ PERIOD OF REST; 91]

breathe your last (*literary*) *v* **die**, expire, go to meet your maker, pass away, pass on, depart this life (*formal*), give up the ghost (*literary*). [➡ DIE; 922]

breath freshener *n* [➡ PERSONAL HYGIENE; 492]

breathing **1** *n* **inhalation**, exhalation, panting, gasping, puffing, blowing. [➡ BREATHE AND NOT BREATHE; 717] **2** *adj* **living**, alive, conscious, sentient, aware. [➡ LIVING THINGS AND LIVING; 976]

breathing space *n* **respite**, relief, space, recovery time, rest, breather (*informal*), pause, breathing room. [➡ PAUSES AND PHASES; 56]

breathless *adj* **out of breath**, panting, gasping, puffing, winded, wheezing. [➡ ILL AND SICK; 741]

breathlessly *adv* **eagerly**, excitedly, with bated breath, on tenterhooks, anxiously, nervously. [➡ POSITIVE IMPATIENCE, ENTHUSIASM, AND ALERTNESS; 538] *Opposite:* nonchalantly.

breathlessness *n* **panting**, gasping, breathing difficulty, rapid breathing, shallow breathing. [➡ BREATHE AND NOT BREATHE; 717]

breathtaking *adj* **out of this world**, wonderful, magnificent, spectacular, incredible, awesome, awe-inspiring, amazing, stunning, astounding, mind-blowing (*informal*). [➡ EXTRAORDINARY: AMAZING; 205] *Opposite:* banal.

breathy *adj* **wheezy**, hissing, gasping, panting, husky. [➡ BREATHE AND NOT BREATHE; 717]

breeches *type of* **trousers**. [➡ GARMENTS AND OUTFITS; 865]

breed **1** *n* **type**, strain, class, kind, variety, sort. [➡ VARIETY, TYPE, KIND; 146] **2** *v* **reproduce**, have babies, propagate, procreate, multiply. [➡ ENGENDER; 351] **3** *v* **raise**, rear, bring up, farm, produce, keep. [➡ ENGENDER; 351] **4** *v* **cause**, create, generate, bring about, produce, give rise to, trigger. [➡ CREATION; 347]

breeding *n* **upbringing**, education, background, social standing, refinement, good manners, manners. [➡ STATUS; 888]

breeding ground *n* **environment**, conditions, source, medium, place, situation. [➡ BEGINNING; 53]

breeze **1** *n* **wind**, gust, gentle wind, light wind, waft, zephyr, puff of air, draught. [➡ WINDY AND STORMY WEATHER; 1053] **2** *n* (*informal*) **cinch** (*informal*), piece of cake (*informal*), doddle (*informal*), child's play, walkover (*informal*), waltz (*informal*), doss (*slang*), walkaway (*US informal*). [➡ EASY WORK; 300]

breeze block *n* [➡ BUILDING MATERIALS; 1076]

breeze in *v* [➡ ARRIVE; 12]

breezily *adv* **brightly**, cheerfully, cheerily, happily, merrily, easily, lightheartedly, flippantly. [➡ GOOD-TEMPERED AND HUMOROUS; 628] *Opposite:* seriously.

breeziness *n* **lightheartedness**, cheerfulness, brightness, cheeriness, flippancy, offhandedness. [➡ CHEERFULNESS OF OUTLOOK; 504] *Opposite:* seriousness.

breezy **1** *adj* **blustery**, gusty, windy, blowy (*informal*), brisk, windswept. [➡ WINDY AND STORMY WEATHER; 1053] *Opposite:* still. **2** *adj* **cheerful**, cheery, jolly, lighthearted, offhand. [➡ CHEERFULNESS OF OUTLOOK; 504] *Opposite:* serious.

breviary *n* **missal**, prayer book, hymnal, book of psalms. [➡ RELIGIOUS OBJECTS; 780]

brevity **1** *n* **shortness**, briefness, quickness, swiftness, transience. [➡ FINITENESS, VARIABILITY, AND TRANSIENCE; 96] *Opposite:* length. **2** *n* **conciseness**, succinctness, concision, pithiness, terseness, curtness. [➡ SUCCINCT AND TO-THE-POINT; 641] *Opposite:* long-windedness.

brew **1** *n* (*informal*) **drink**, beverage (*formal*), potion, infusion, cocktail, swill. [➡ DRINKS; 1186] **2** *v* **prepare**, make, infuse, steep, ferment, concoct, distil. [➡ COOKING AND FOOD PREPARATION; 354] **3** *v* **develop**, loom, threaten, grow, blow up, gather force. [➡ ABOUT TO HAPPEN; 33] **4** *n* **mixture**, mix, blend, combination, concoction, cocktail. [➡ COLLECTIONS AND MIXTURES OF THINGS; 1243]

brewery *type of* **factory**. [➡ INDUSTRIAL BUILDINGS; 1086]

briar *type of* **shrub or bush**. [➡ BUSHES AND SHRUBS; 1027]

bribe **1** *v* **induce**, corrupt, entice, suborn, persuade, win over, buy off, pay off (*informal*). [➡ CAUSE OR COMPEL TO ACT; 272] **2** *n* **inducement**, backhander (*informal*), enticement, carrot, sweetener (*informal*), kickback, payoff (*informal*), bung (*slang*). [➡ BRIBES; 441]

bribery *n* **corruption**, inducement, enticement, subornation. [➡ CRIMES; 817]

bric-a-brac *n* **knick-knacks**, bits and pieces (*informal*), curios, ornaments, junk (*informal*), stuff, jumble. [➡ RUBBISH AND USELESS OBJECTS; 1248]

brick **1** *n* [➡ BUILDING MATERIALS; 1076] **2** *n* **block**, slab, ingot, lump, piece, tablet, cake. [➡ AMOUNT OF SOLID OR SEMI-SOLID; 115]

brickbat **1** *n* **insult**, criticism, insinuation, suggestion, comment. [➡ INSULTS, ABUSE, AND SWEARING; 659] **2** *type of* **projectile**. [➡ PROJECTILES; 1158]

brick red *type of* **red**. [➡ COLOURS; 1223]

bricks and mortar *n* [➡ BUILDING MATERIALS; 1076]

bricks-and-mortar *adj* [➡ E-COMMERCE; 1128]

brickwork *n* **fabric**, structure, bricks and mortar, masonry, stonework. [➡ BUILDING MATERIALS; 1076]

bridal *adj* **wedding**, nuptial, marriage, ceremonial, honeymoon, celebratory. [➡ CEREMONIES AND ANNIVERSARIES; 38]

bride *n* **wife**, wife-to-be, newlywed, spouse, intended (*dated or humorous*), partner, fiancée. [➡ RELATIVES BY MARRIAGE; 960]

bride and groom *n* [➡RELATIVES BY MARRIAGE; 960]

bridegroom *n* **husband**, husband-to-be, newlywed, spouse, intended (*dated or humorous*), partner, fiancé. [➡RELATIVES BY MARRIAGE; 960]

bridesmaid *n* **maid of honour**, attendant, matron of honour, flower girl. [➡SUPPORTERS, PROTECTORS, AND COMPATRIOTS; 970]

bridge 1 *n* **bond**, tie, link, connection, conduit, association, channel, passage, join. [➡CONNECTION; 144] 2 *part of* **ship or boat.** [➡PARTS OF A SHIP OR BOAT; 1150] 3 *v* **link**, connect, join, span, tie together, associate. [➡FASTEN, LINK, AND JOIN; 409]

bridge

◆ *types of bridge*
aqueduct, arch bridge, Bailey bridge, bascule bridge, beam bridge, cable-stayed bridge, cantilever bridge, drawbridge, flyover, footbridge, gangplank, humpback bridge, overpass, pontoon bridge, suspension bridge, swing bridge, viaduct, walkway

bridgehead *n* **foothold**, position, stepping stone, jumping-off point, vantage point, front line, foot in the door. [➡BEGINNING; 53]

bridle 1 *v* **bristle**, get angry, become annoyed, become indignant, prickle, get your hackles up. [➡GIVING VENT TO EMOTIONS; 680] 2 *v* **curb**, restrain, control, rein in, keep in check, arrest, contain. [➡AVOID, PREVENT, LIMIT, AND CONTROL; 278] *Opposite:* let loose.

bridle path *n* **bridleway**, ride, path, track, trail, horse trail (*US*). [➡PATHWAYS; 1109]

bridleway *n* [➡PATHWAYS; 1109]

Brie *type of* **soft cheese.** [➡DAIRY PRODUCTS AND CHEESES; 1182]

brief 1 *adj* **short-lived**, transitory, fleeting, ephemeral, short-term, momentary, passing. [➡HAPPENING QUICKLY; 104] *Opposite:* lasting. 2 *adj* **short**, concise, succinct, to the point, pithy, epigrammatic. [➡SUCCINCT AND TO-THE-POINT; 641] *Opposite:* lengthy. 3 *n* (*informal*) **legal representative**, lawyer, barrister, QC, attorney. [➡PEOPLE IN LAW COURTS; 820] 4 *n* **synopsis**, summary, digest, abstract, outline. [➡SUMMARIES, OUTLINES, AND EXCERPTS; 589] 5 *n* **briefing**, instructions, guidelines, preparation, orders, ground rules. [➡BASIC DETAILS; 689] 6 *n* **task**, remit, mission, mandate, assignment, duties. [➡WORK IN GENERAL; 298] 7 *v* **inform**, tell, give instructions, prepare, instruct, direct, fill in, update. [➡INFORM AND ANNOUNCE; 612]

briefcase *n* **document case**, attaché case, case, portfolio, music case, folder, carrycase, bag. [➡CONTAINERS, RECEPTACLES, AND PACKAGING; 1244]

briefing *n* **meeting**, conference, seminar, press conference, updating, session, update, consultation. [➡MEETINGS AND ASSEMBLIES; 43]

briefs *type of* **lower body underwear.** [➡HABERDASHERY, MILLINERY, AND LINGERIE; 867]

brier *see* **briar.**

brig *type of* **sailing vessel.** [➡SHIPS AND BOATS; 1149]

brigade *n* **group**, team, crew, contingent, gang, unit. [➡GROUPS WITH A COMMON INTEREST; 938]

brigadier *n* [➡MILITARY PERSONNEL; 828]

brigand (*literary*) *n* **lawbreaker**, bandit, thief, robber, thug, felon, gangster, outlaw. [➡CRIMINALS; 821]

brigantine *type of* **sailing vessel.** [➡SHIPS AND BOATS; 1149]

bright 1 *adj* **brilliant**, vivid, intense, dazzling, light, clear. [➡DESCRIBING LIGHT; 1227] *Opposite:* dark. 2 *adj* **intelligent**, brainy (*informal*), quick, sharp-witted, clever, smart. [➡POSITIVE INTELLECTUAL CHARACTERISTICS; 525] *Opposite:* unintelligent. 3 *adj* **cheerful**, happy, lively, optimistic, positive, upbeat (*informal*), sunny, perky. [➡CHEERFULNESS OF OUTLOOK; 504] *Opposite:* gloomy.

See Compare and Contrast at **intelligent.**

brighten 1 *v* **feel better**, brighten up, look up, perk up, cheer up, snap out of it. [➡CHANGE OF MOOD AND COMPOSURE; 581] 2 *v* **make brighter**, lighten, make lighter, brighten up, illuminate, open up. [➡CHANGE OF COLOUR; 392] *Opposite:* darken. 3 *v* **improve**, make better, enhance, animate, revivify, vivify, revitalize, add to, cheer up, liven up, jazz up (*informal*). [➡IMPROVE SOMETHING; 375]

brighten up *v* **raise the spirits**, make brighter, brighten, lighten, make lighter, perk up, animate, come to life, revitalize, cheer up, jazz up (*informal*). [➡ENCOURAGE; 577] *Opposite:* cast down.

bright-eyed and bushy-tailed *adj* [➡CHEERFULNESS OF OUTLOOK; 504]

brightly 1 *adv* **luminously**, lustrously, radiantly, glossily, glowingly, blazingly, brilliantly, intensely, vibrantly, fiercely, dazzlingly. [➡DESCRIBING LIGHT; 1227] *Opposite:* dully. 2 *adv* **sunnily**, perkily, cheerfully, cheerily, optimistically, happily, enthusiastically. [➡GOOD-TEMPERED AND HUMOROUS; 628] *Opposite:* gloomily.

brightness 1 *n* **illumination**, glare, intensity, brilliance, vividness, clarity, lustre, glow. [➡DESCRIBING LIGHT; 1227] *Opposite:* dullness. 2 *n* **sunniness**, high spirits, cheerfulness, optimism, cheeriness, good humour, enthusiasm, happiness. [➡PLEASURE, EXCITEMENT, AND ELATION; 535] *Opposite:* gloominess.

bright spark (*informal*) *n* [➡TALENTED OR INTELLIGENT PERSON; 529]

brilliance 1 *n* **brightness**, brilliancy, intensity, vividness, luminosity, radiance, lustre, shine. [➡DESCRIBING LIGHT; 1227] *Opposite:* dullness. 2 *n* **cleverness**, wisdom, smartness, braininess (*informal*), genius, talent, skill, virtuosity, ability, intelligence, smarts (*US informal*). [➡POSITIVE INTELLECTUAL CHARACTERISTICS; 525] *Opposite:* stupidity.

brilliancy *see* **brilliance.**

brilliant 1 *adj* **luminous**, radiant, dazzling, sparkling, gleaming, shining, bright. [➡DESCRIBING LIGHT; 1227] *Opposite:* dull. 2 *adj* **vivid**, bright, clear, intense, dazzling. [➡DESCRIBING COLOURS; 1225] *Opposite:* faded. 3 *adj* **talented**, virtuoso, inspired, skilful, gifted, exceptional, accomplished. [➡TALENTED AND SKILFUL; 528] *Opposite:* mediocre. 4 *adj* (*informal*)

wonderful, marvellous, superb, excellent, magnificent, splendid, great. [➡EXTRAORDINARY: AMAZING; 205] *Opposite:* awful.

brilliantly 1 *adv* **dazzlingly**, brightly, luminously, radiantly, intensely, vividly, fiercely. [➡DESCRIBING LIGHT; 1227] *Opposite:* dully. 2 *adv* **ably**, giftedly, skilfully, exceptionally, consummately, adeptly. [➡TALENTED AND SKILFUL; 528] *Opposite:* ineptly. 3 *adv* **marvellously**, wonderfully, excellently, superbly, magnificently, splendidly. [➡EXTRAORDINARY: AMAZING; 205] *Opposite:* terribly.

brim 1 *n* **ridge**, edge, top, rim, lip. [➡EXTREMITIES OF PHYSICAL OBJECTS; 1249] 2 *part of* **garment**. [➡PARTS OF A GARMENT; 870]

brimful *adj* **full to the top**, full, filled up, filled to the brim, overfull, overfilled, overflowing, spilling over. [➡FULL; 1238] *Opposite:* empty.

brimming *adj* **bursting**, teeming, overflowing, packed, filled, crammed. [➡FULL; 1238]

brine *n* **saline**, salt water, sea water. [➡LIQUIDS; 1268]

bring 1 *v* **take along**, carry, fetch, convey, transport, take, get, pass. [➡MOVE SOMETHING TO ANOTHER LOCATION; 325] *Opposite:* take away. 2 *v* **cause**, bring about, produce, lead to, result in, end in, make happen, create, beget, be the cause of, generate, effect (*formal*). [➡CAUSE TO HAPPEN; 31] 3 *v* **command**, market for, earn, produce, make, bring in, fetch, sell for, give. [➡GET MONEY OR REWARD; 422]

bring about *v* **generate**, cause, produce, result in, end in, lead to, make happen, create, bring, beget, effect (*formal*). [➡CAUSE TO HAPPEN; 31] *Opposite:* prevent.

bring alive *v* **awaken**, bring to life, make real, animate, enliven, give life to, flesh out, breathe life into. [➡IMPROVE SOMETHING; 375]

bring back 1 *v* **evoke**, recall, bring to mind, summon up, reawaken, stir up, rekindle, renew, revive. [➡REMIND; 748] 2 *v* **return**, replace, restore, reinstate, recapture, revive. [➡MOVE SOMETHING TO ANOTHER LOCATION; 325]

bring down 1 *v* **overthrow**, topple, depose, defeat, dethrone, seize power, humble. [➡BEAT AND DEFEAT; 80] *Opposite:* elect. 2 *v* **fell**, floor, topple, demolish, knock over, knock down, knock the wind out of, deck (*informal*). [➡MOVE SOMETHING: INTO A NEW POSITION OR OVERTURN; 331] *Opposite:* raise.

bring down a peg *v* [➡UPSET, DISTRESS, AND HUMILIATE; 568]

bring down to earth *v* [➡UPSET, DISTRESS, AND HUMILIATE; 568]

bring forth 1 *v* **deliver**, bear, give birth to, produce, yield, breed. [➡ENGENDER; 351] 2 *v* **yield**, bear, produce, give, generate, give rise to. [➡CREATION; 347]

bring forward 1 *v* **speed**, advance, reschedule, move forward, change, move forwards. [➡CAUSE TO HAPPEN; 31] *Opposite:* delay. 2 *v* **put on the table**, produce, present, offer, bring out, reveal, propose. [➡SUGGEST, HINT, AND COMMENT; 613] *Opposite:* withdraw.

bring home *v* **make clear**, clarify, illustrate, illuminate, underline, emphasize. [➡EXPLAIN AND CLARIFY; 611]

bring home the bacon (*informal*) 1 *v* **be successful**, bring off, come up with the goods, come through, keep your end of the bargain, see it through, make good your promise, deliver. [➡SUCCEED AND WIN; 79] *Opposite:* fail. 2 *v* **provide**, keep a roof over your head, put food on the table, keep the wolf from the door, keep clothes on your back, make a living, earn your keep, feed your family. [➡GET MONEY OR REWARD; 422]

bring in 1 *v* **introduce**, set up, establish, launch, start, phase in. [➡CAUSE TO START; 266] *Opposite:* end. 2 *v* **recoup**, acquire, earn, make, take home, get paid. [➡GET MONEY OR REWARD; 422]

bring into being *v* **create**, establish, found, institute, set up, engender, start up, get underway. [➡INSTITUTE AND INAUGURATE; 349] *Opposite:* destroy.

bring into disrepute *v* [➡UPSET, DISTRESS, AND HUMILIATE; 568]

bring into line *v* **standardize**, coordinate, synchronize, make uniform, harmonize, systematize, correct, discipline. [➡ARRANGE AND CREATE ORDER; 358]

bring off *v* **succeed**, carry off, pull off (*informal*), achieve, accomplish, engineer, make work. [➡CARRY OUT AN ACTION; 270] *Opposite:* fail.

bring on *v* **cause**, create, produce, make, start, set off. [➡CAUSE TO START; 266]

bring out 1 *v* **highlight**, spotlight, show up, reveal, bring to the surface, elicit, draw out. [➡CAUSE TO APPEAR; 5] *Opposite:* suppress. 2 *v* **introduce**, produce, release, put on sale, launch, present, start, sell. [➡SELL; 442] *Opposite:* withdraw.

bring round 1 *v* **sway**, reason, get round, convince, persuade, win over, get on your side, induce, cajole. [➡SOOTHE AND CALM; 574] *Opposite:* deter. 2 *v* **bring to**, rouse, awaken, wake up, revive, resuscitate, get going. [➡WAKE AND REGAIN CONSCIOUSNESS; 725] *Opposite:* knock out.

bring shame on *v* [➡UPSET, DISTRESS, AND HUMILIATE; 568]

bring to *v* **bring round**, rouse, awaken, wake up, revive, resuscitate. [➡WAKE AND REGAIN CONSCIOUSNESS; 725] *Opposite:* knock out.

bring to a close *v* **put a stop to**, end, halt, discontinue, run down, call a halt, bring to an end, finish, wrap up (*informal*), stop, conclude, complete, close, wind up. [➡CAUSE TO STOP; 267] *Opposite:* start.

bring to a halt *v* [➡CAUSE TO STOP; 267]

bring to an end *v* **wrap up** (*informal*), wind up (*informal*), conclude, bring to a close, put a stop to, end, stop, halt, complete, finish, call a halt, discontinue, run down. [➡CAUSE TO STOP; 267] *Opposite:* start.

bring to a standstill *v* [➡CAUSE TO STOP; 267]

bring to completion *v* [➡COMPLETE AN ACTION; 264]

bring to fruition *v* [➡CAUSE TO HAPPEN; 31]

bring together 1 *v* **combine**, mix, mix together, blend, pool, concentrate, focus. [➡COMBINE AND MIX; 401] *Opposite:* separate. 2 *v* **gather**, amass, rally, compile, glean, round up, collate, collect, pull together, assemble. [➡ARRANGE AND CREATE ORDER; 358] *Opposite:* distribute. 3 *v* **reconcile**, integrate, unite, unify, link, join, connect, coordinate, organize. [➡CREATING CONNECTIONS; 145]

bring to life *v* **make real**, animate, bring alive, anthropomorphize, give life to, awaken, breathe life into. [➡IMPROVE SOMETHING; 375]

bring to light *v* **expose**, unearth, disclose, uncover, publicize, reveal. [➡CAUSE TO APPEAR; 5] *Opposite:* hide.

bring to mind *v* **summon up**, reawaken, rekindle, stir up, bring back, recall, think of, evoke, call to mind, recollect, think back to, conjure up. [➡REMIND; 748]

bring to pass *v* [➡CAUSE TO HAPPEN; 31]

bring up 1 *v* **mention**, broach, raise, suggest, introduce, talk about, discuss. [➡SUGGEST, HINT, AND COMMENT; 613] *Opposite:* gloss over. 2 *v* **raise**, rear, care for, nurture, look after, educate. [➡TAKE CARE OF AND SPOIL; 301] 3 *v* **vomit**, expel, spew, regurgitate, disgorge, discharge. [➡VOMIT AND BELCH; 713]

bring up-to-date *v* **inform**, give the lowdown, look after, put in the picture, update, give the latest, fill in, keep posted, keep informed, let know. [➡INFORM AND ANNOUNCE; 612] *Opposite:* keep in the dark.

brink 1 *n* **verge**, threshold, edge, point, precipice. [➡BEGINNING; 53] 2 *n* **edge**, rim, lip, brim, border, periphery. [➡EXTREMITIES OF PHYSICAL OBJECTS; 1249] *Opposite:* centre.

brinkmanship *n* **strategy**, tactics, politics, bluff, bluffing, bluster, politicking, manoeuvring. [➡DECEPTION AND LIES; 661]

briny 1 *adj* **salty**, salt, saline, salted, brackish. [➡TASTE; 704] 2 *n* **sea**, ocean, deep, drink (*informal*). [➡THE SEAS, OCEANS, AND SHORES; 1041]

briquette *n* **block**, lump, brick, piece, cake. [➡AMOUNT OF SOLID OR SEMI-SOLID; 115]

brisk 1 *adj* **energetic**, fast, quick, rapid, hurried, vigorous. [➡MOVING QUICKLY; 103] *Opposite:* slow. 2 *adj* **abrupt**, curt, impatient, brusque, hurried, no-nonsense, sharp. [➡BAD-TEMPERED AND HUMOURLESS; 627] *Opposite:* measured. 3 *adj* **refreshing**, cool, cold, parky (*informal*), invigorating, stimulating, bracing, sharp, zesty, fresh, reviving. [➡PHYSICALLY PLEASANT; 187] *Opposite:* warm.

brisket *type of* **cut**. [➡TYPES AND CUTS OF MEAT; 1176]

briskly *adv* **energetically**, quickly, rapidly, fast, smartly, hurriedly, vigorously, efficiently. [➡MOVING QUICKLY; 103] *Opposite:* slowly.

briskness 1 *n* **speed**, rapidity, vigour, efficiency, urgency, alacrity. [➡SPEED; 102] *Opposite:* tardiness. 2 *n* **abruptness**, coldness, reserve, brusqueness, curtness, sharpness, impatience. [➡BAD-TEMPERED AND HUMOURLESS; 627] *Opposite:* patience.

bristle 1 *n* **stubble**, hackle, hair, spine, spike, quill. [➡FACIAL HAIR; 490] 2 *v* **stiffen**, become erect, stand up, rise, prickle, stand on end, stick out, poke out. [➡GO UPWARDS; 307] 3 *v* **recoil**, resent, get your hackles up, object, bridle, get angry, become annoyed, become indignant, prickle, take umbrage. [➡GIVING VENT TO EMOTIONS; 680] 4 *v* **brim**, be full, teem, overflow, be thick with, be packed with. [➡PROSPER AND ABOUND; 16]

bristly *adj* **spiky**, coarse, wiry, stubbly, sharp, rough. [➡PHYSICAL TEXTURE; 1221] *Opposite:* smooth.

brittle *adj* **hard**, stiff, inelastic, fragile, breakable, weak, frail, delicate. [➡FRAGILE; 1208] *Opposite:* robust.

brittleness *n* **hardness**, stiffness, fragility, weakness, frailty, delicacy, daintiness, delicate state. [➡FRAGILE; 1208] *Opposite:* robustness.

broach *v* **propose**, present, submit, mention, raise, bring up, introduce, approach, try out. [➡SUGGEST, HINT, AND COMMENT; 613]

B-road *type of* **minor road**. [➡ROADS; 1105]

broad 1 *adj* **spacious**, wide, large, big, extensive, expansive, open. [➡WIDTH: WIDE; 1198] *Opposite:* narrow. 2 *adj* **comprehensive**, extensive, wide, far-reaching, wide-ranging, expansive, open, all-encompassing, general. [➡WHOLENESS AND COMPLETENESS; 199] *Opposite:* restricted. 3 *adj* **inexact**, rough, general, approximate, sketchy, hazy, imprecise. [➡APPROXIMATELY; 133] *Opposite:* precise. 4 *adj* **visible**, obvious, plain, clear, patent, transparent, unsubtle. [➡PERCEPTIBLE; 25] *Opposite:* subtle. 5 *adj* **distinctive**, distinct, thick, heavy, strong, marked, pronounced. [➡THE SPOKEN WORD; 672] *Opposite:* slight. 6 *n* **lake**, expanse of water, stretch of water, body of water, mere (*archaic or literary*). [➡RIVERS, LAKES, AND STREAMS; 1042]

broad bean *type of* **pulse**. [➡BEANS AND PULSES; 1188]

broadcast 1 *v* **transmit**, air, show, televise, screen, put out, relay, rerun. [➡TELEVISION AND RADIO; 607] 2 *v* **air**, spread, disseminate, publicize, make known, advertise, announce, shout. [➡INFORM AND ANNOUNCE; 612] 3 *v* **scatter**, sow, distribute, disseminate, strew, cast. [➡SPREAD AND SCATTER; 333] 4 *n* **transmission**, programme, show, airing, newscast, rerun, recording. [➡TELEVISION AND RADIO; 607]

broadcast

◆ *types of broadcast*

news flash, newscast, newsreel, soap (*informal*), travelogue, chat show, commercial, concert, current affairs, distance learning, docudrama, documentary, drama, game show, infomercial, call-in (*US*), infotainment, news, phone-in, play, sitcom (*informal*), soap opera, sport, sportscast, talk show (*US*), telethon

See Compare and Contrast at **scatter**.

broadcaster *n* **presenter**, anchor, announcer, journalist, newsreader. [➡WORKERS IN ENTERTAINMENT AND MEDIA; 873]

broaden *v* **widen**, extend, increase, make wider, become wider, thicken, expand, enlarge, stretch. [➡CHANGE OF SIZE: BIGGER; 393] *Opposite:* narrow.

broadly *adv* **approximately**, sketchily, generally, largely, roughly, mostly. [➡USUALLY; 108]

broadly-based *adj* **wide**, broad, wide-ranging, extensive, sweeping, general, comprehensive. [➡WHOLENESS AND COMPLETENESS; 199]

broad-minded *adj* **tolerant**, progressive, liberal, permissive, open-minded, forward-thinking, non-judgmental, free thinking, unprejudiced, open. [➡POSITIVE INTELLECTUAL CHARACTERISTICS; 525] *Opposite:* narrow-minded.

broad-mindedness *n* **liberality**, open-mindedness, tolerance, progressiveness, permissiveness, openness, free thought. [➡POSITIVE INTELLECTUAL CHARACTERISTICS; 525] *Opposite:* narrow-mindedness.

broadness 1 *n* **width**, breadth, wideness. [➡WIDTH: WIDE; 1198] 2 *n* **scope**, breadth, span, range, extensiveness, extent. [➡WHOLENESS AND COMPLETENESS; 199]

broadsheet *n* **paper**, newspaper, quality newspaper, serious newspaper, heavyweight (*informal*). [➡NEWSPAPERS; 606]

broadside *n* **attack**, diatribe, tirade, onslaught, volley, assault. [➡CRITICISMS AND ANGRY OUTBURSTS; 50]

broadsword *type of* **sword or knife**. [➡SWORDS AND KNIVES; 1156]

brocade *type of* **fabric from animals**. [➡FABRICS; 1131]

broccoli *type of* **vegetable**. [➡FRUIT AND VEGETABLES; 1175]

brochure *n* **booklet**, catalogue, leaflet, pamphlet, information sheet, flier. [➡BOOKS AND BOOKLETS; 591]

brogue 1 *n* **accent**, burr, drawl. [➡ASPECTS OF LANGUAGE; 683] 2 *type of* **shoe**. [➡FOOTWEAR; 871]

broil 1 *v* **swelter**, burn, roast, bake, boil, cook. [➡COOKING AND FOOD PREPARATION; 354] *Opposite:* freeze. 2 *v* (*US*) **grill**, barbecue, roast, cook. [➡COOKING AND FOOD PREPARATION; 354] 3 *v* (*US archaic*) **fight**, brawl, clash, tussle, scuffle, scrap. [➡COMPETE, CONTEND, AND COMBAT; 304] 4 *n* (*US archaic*) **brawl**, fight, riot, tussle, scuffle, clash, scrap, uproar, fracas, tumult. [➡AGGRESSIVE EVENT; 39]

broiled (*US*) *adj* [➡STATE OF PREPARED FOOD; 1170]

broiler *type of* **fowl**. [➡FOOD BIRD; 999]

broke (*informal*) *adj* **bankrupt**, penniless, poor, in the red, overdrawn, bust (*informal*), insolvent, in debt, poverty-stricken, destitute, ruined. [➡POVERTY AND POOR; 892] *Opposite:* wealthy.

broken 1 *adj* **wrecked**, fragmented, shattered, cracked, smashed, damaged, ruined, destroyed. [➡IN BAD REPAIR; 1233] *Opposite:* intact. 2 *adj* **inoperative**, malfunctioning, faulty, defective, out of order, broken-down, bust (*informal*), kaput (*informal*), conked-out (*informal*), worn-out, wrecked, had it (*informal*), busted (*US informal*). [➡IN BAD REPAIR; 1233] *Opposite:* working. 3 *adj* **beaten**, licked, defeated, dejected, crushed, dispirited, without hope. [➡SADNESS, DISTRESS, AND DESPAIR; 540] *Opposite:* triumphant.

broken-down 1 *adj* **conked-out** (*informal*), inoperative, malfunctioning, not working, broken, out of order, faulty, damaged, defective. [➡IN BAD REPAIR; 1233] *Opposite:* working. 2 *adj* **in poor condition**, dilapidated, run-down, falling apart, ramshackle, worn-out. [➡IN BAD REPAIR; 1233]

brokenhearted *adj* **sad**, grief-stricken, disappointed, desolate, despairing, lovesick, upset, wretched, unhappy, miserable, depressed, crushed, despondent, melancholy, heartbroken, sorrowful, dejected. [➡SADNESS, DISTRESS, AND DESPAIR; 540] *Opposite:* overjoyed.

broker *n* **trader**, agent, dealer, negotiator, stockbroker. [➡PEOPLE INVOLVED IN FINANCE; 804]

brolly (*informal*) *n* [➡COVERS AND COATINGS; 1245]

bronchial *adj* **respiratory**, tubercular, tracheal, lung, chest, thoracic, pleural. [➡RESPIRATORY ORGANS; 716]

bronchial tube *part of* **respiratory system**. [➡RESPIRATORY ORGANS; 716]

bronchiole *part of* **respiratory system**. [➡RESPIRATORY ORGANS; 716]

bronchus *part of* **respiratory system**. [➡RESPIRATORY ORGANS; 716]

bronco *type of* **horse**. [➡HORSE; 985]

brontosaurus *type of* **dinosaur**. [➡DINOSAUR; 996]

Bronx cheer (*US informal*) *n* [➡UNFAVOURABLE NON-VERBAL RESPONSES; 655]

bronze 1 *n* **sculpture**, figure, statue, statuette, effigy, bust, head, model, figurine. [➡SCULPTURE; 902] 2 *type of* **brown**. [➡COLOURS; 1223] 3 *type of* **metal**. [➡METALS; 1275]

bronzed *adj* **tanned**, brown, suntanned, golden-brown, coppery. [➡COMPLEXION; 481]

brooch *n* **pin**, badge, ornament, trinket, accessory. [➡JEWELLERY; 866]

brood 1 *n* **young**, clutch, litter, issue, family, flock. [➡GROUP OF BIRDS; 1007] 2 *n* **children**, kids (*informal*), offspring, family, progeny. [➡YOUNGER GENERATION RELATIVES; 958] 3 *v* **ruminate**, worry, mope, dwell on, fret, agonize. [➡THINK AND REFLECT; 744]

broodily *adv* **thoughtfully**, pensively, meditatively, fretfully, sullenly, morosely, glumly, moodily. [➡SADNESS, DISTRESS, AND DESPAIR; 540] *Opposite:* cheerfully.

broodiness *n* **pensiveness**, glumness, fretfulness, sullenness, moroseness, meditativeness, moodiness. [➡SADNESS, DISTRESS, AND DESPAIR; 540]

brooding *adj* **ominous**, menacing, threatening, gloomy, heavy (*slang*), dark. [➡DANGEROUS; 237]

broodingly *adv* **glumly**, fretfully, sullenly, morosely, moodily, pensively, deep in thought, meditatively, musingly. [➡PENSIVENESS AND INTEREST; 539] *Opposite:* cheerfully.

brood mare *type of* **horse**. [➡HORSE; 985]

broody 1 *adj* **sullen**, thoughtful, pensive, moody, glum, gloomy. [➡SADNESS, DISTRESS, AND DESPAIR; 540] *Opposite:* cheerful. 2 *adj* **maternal**, motherly, tender, caring. [➡APPRECIATION AND GRATITUDE; 536]

brook 1 *n* **stream**, beck, rivulet, river, creek (*US*), burn. [➡RIVERS, LAKES, AND STREAMS; 1042] 2 *v* (*formal*) **tolerate**, allow, accept, put up with, countenance (*formal*), suffer, sanction. [➡TOLERATE AND ENDURE; 767]

broom 1 *n* **brush**, besom, sweeper. [➡HAND TOOLS; 1118] 2 *type of* **shrub or bush**. [➡BUSHES AND SHRUBS; 1027]

broomstick *n* **handle**, broom handle, pole, stick, stave, staff. [➡STICKS, POLES, AND WEDGES; 1253]

broth *type of* **soup**. [➡SOUP; 1185]

brother 1 *n* **comrade**, member, colleague, associate.

[➡FRIENDS; 963] 2 *type of* **same generation relative.** [➡SAME GENERATION RELATIVES; 957]

brotherhood 1 *n* **comradeship**, friendship, companionship, unity, loyalty, camaraderie. [➡RELATIONSHIP TO ANOTHER; 973] 2 *n* **association**, society, union, guild, organization, group. [➡INSTITUTIONS; 791]

brother-in-law *type of* **in-law.** [➡RELATIVES BY MARRIAGE; 960]

brotherly *adj* **companionable**, fraternal, affectionate, kind, friendly, cordial, sympathetic. [➡FRIENDLINESS AND SOCIABILITY; 495]

brougham *type of* **wagon or carriage.** [➡VEHICLES; 1144]

brouhaha (*formal*) *n* **commotion**, ruckus, brawl, free-for-all (*informal*), rumpus, melee, confusion, to-do (*informal*), uproar. [➡CHAOS AND UPROAR; 51]

brow 1 *n* **summit**, top, crest, ridge, peak, crown. [➡EXTREMITIES OF PHYSICAL OBJECTS; 1249] 2 *part of* **face.** [➡HEAD; 693]

browbeat *v* **intimidate**, badger, bully, dragoon, nag, twist somebody's arm (*informal*), push, pester, threaten, force, coerce. [➡COMPLAIN AND NAG; 687] *Opposite:* persuade.

browbeaten *adj* **downtrodden**, oppressed, intimidated, bullied, subjugated, cowed, broken, demoralized, frightened, scared. [➡CONFUSION, ANXIETY, AND WORRY; 541] *Opposite:* resistant.

brown 1 *adj* **tanned**, sunburnt, bronzed. [➡COMPLEXION; 481] 2 *v* **fry**, grill, sear, toast, char, burn. [➡COOKING AND FOOD PREPARATION; 354] 3 *type of* **colour.** [➡COLOURS; 1223]

brown

◆ *types of brown*
auburn, bay, bronze, burnt sienna, burnt umber, caramel, chestnut, chocolate, copper, hazel, henna, khaki, liver, mahogany, mocha, mousy, nut-brown, roan, russet, sorrel, tan, tawny, umber, walnut

brown alga *type of* **alga.** [➡MICROORGANISMS, FUNGI, AND ALGAE; 1023]

brown bread *type of* **bread.** [➡BREAD, FLOUR, AND BREAD PRODUCTS; 1178]

brown dwarf *type of* **star or star system.** [➡CELESTIAL BODIES; 1060]

browned-off (*dated slang*) *adj* **annoyed**, fed up (*informal*), irritated, discouraged, miffed (*informal*). [➡SADNESS, DISTRESS, AND DESPAIR; 540]

brownfield site *n* [➡URBAN OUTDOOR SPACES; 1071]

brownie *type of* **cake.** [➡CAKES, BISCUITS, AND DESSERTS; 1180]

brown sauce *type of* **seasonings, sauces, and dips.** [➡SEASONINGS AND SAUCES; 1173]

brownstone (*US*) *type of* **house.** [➡RESIDENTIAL BUILDINGS; 1077]

browse *v* **glance**, cruise, look, look through, leaf through, surf, peruse. [➡LOOKING AND LOOKS; 701]

browser *type of* **software.** [➡COMPUTERS AND COMPUTING; 1126]

bruise 1 *n* **contusion** (*technical*), discoloration, black eye, shiner (*informal*), welt, bump. [➡CONDITIONS AFFECTING THE SKIN; 722] 2 *v* **hurt**, damage, bash (*informal*), mark, injure, discolour. [➡WORSEN APPEARANCE; 383]

bruised 1 *adj* **injured**, hurt, sore, black-and-blue, damaged, aching, battered, painful, discoloured. [➡INJURED; 743] *Opposite:* unhurt. 2 *adj* **wounded**, upset, hurt, offended, battered, affected, crushed. [➡SADNESS, DISTRESS, AND DESPAIR; 540] *Opposite:* unaffected.

bruiser (*informal*) *n* **muscleman**, bodyguard, bouncer, tough, toughie (*informal*), heavy (*slang*), heavyweight. [➡VILLAINS AND THUGS; 947]

brume (*literary*) *n* [➡CLOUDY AND RAINY WEATHER; 1052]

brunch *type of* **meal.** [➡MEALS AND PARTS OF MEALS; 1168]

brunette *adj* **dark**, brown, chestnut, auburn. [➡HAIR COLOUR; 486] *Opposite:* blonde.

brunt *n* **effect**, force, impact, burden, substance. [➡RESULTS AND OUTCOMES; 83]

brush 1 *n* **broom**, besom, sweeper. [➡HAND TOOLS; 1118] 2 *n* **contact**, touch, stroke, graze, sweep, scrape. [➡CONTACT: TOUCH; 413] 3 *n* **encounter**, meeting, confrontation, skirmish, disagreement, argument, clash, run-in (*informal*). [➡ARGUMENT; 47] 4 *v* **scrub**, clear, coat, groom, sweep, clean, polish. [➡CLEAN AND POLISH; 404] 5 *v* **touch**, graze, scrape, sweep, stroke, skim, contact. [➡CONTACT: TOUCH; 413]

brush against *v* [➡CONTACT: TOUCH; 413]

brushed *adj* **fleecy**, fluffy, downy, furry, soft, woolly. [➡PHYSICAL TEXTURE; 1221]

brush fire *n* [➡FIRE, FLAMMABILITY, AND BURNING; 1164]

brush off *v* **dismiss**, rebuff, snub, reject, give the cold shoulder to, ignore. [➡REFUSING OR REJECTING RELATIONS; 975]

brushoff (*informal*) *n* **turndown**, rebuff, snub, rejection, the elbow (*informal*), cold shoulder. [➡UNKIND ACTION OR BEHAVIOUR; 297]

brush up *v* **reread**, refresh, renew, revise, review, go over. [➡IMPROVE SOMETHING; 375]

brushwood *n* **firewood**, twigs, branches, undergrowth, kindling. [➡VEGETATION; 1025]

brusque *adj* **abrupt**, curt, offhand, rough, brisk, gruff, harsh, terse, short. [➡BAD-TEMPERED AND HUMOURLESS; 627] *Opposite:* gentle.

brusqueness *n* **roughness**, asperity (*formal*), terseness, abruptness, offhandedness, lack of warmth, unfriendliness. [➡UNINTERESTED AND DETACHED; 630] *Opposite:* gentleness.

Brussels sprout *type of* **vegetable.** [➡FRUIT AND VEGETABLES; 1175]

brutal 1 *adj* **ruthless**, cruel, vicious, fierce, pitiless, heartless, inhuman, inhumane, violent, ferocious. [➡MORALLY BAD; 776] *Opposite:* humane. 2 *adj* **harsh**, severe, rough, callous, insensitive, unfeeling, unkind, terrible. [➡SELFISH AND UNKIND; 506] *Opposite:* kind.

brutalist *type of* **20th-century architecture.** [➡BUILDING AND ARCHITECTURE; 1075]

brutality *n* **cruelty**, viciousness, violence, rough treatment, harshness, ruthlessness, callousness, inhumaneness. [➡UNKIND ACTION OR BEHAVIOUR; 297] *Opposite:* gentleness.

brutalize 1 *v* **coarsen**, harden, dehumanize, desensitize. [➡UPSET, DISTRESS, AND HUMILIATE; 568] *Opposite:* humanize. 2 *v* **abuse**, assault, maltreat, ill-treat. [➡WOUND A PERSON OR ANIMAL; 384]

brute 1 *n* **bully**, thug, beast, swine, monster. [➡VILLAINS AND THUGS; 947] 2 *n* (*literary*) **animal**, beast, creature, monster. [➡LIVING THINGS AND LIVING; 976]

brutish 1 *adj* **animal**, wild, violent, bestial. [➡BEASTLY AND BRUTISH; 511] 2 *adj* **cruel**, ruthless, insensitive, pitiless, harsh, unfeeling, inhuman, inhumane. [➡SELFISH AND UNKIND; 506] *Opposite:* humane. 3 *adj* **loutish**, boorish, rough, unrefined, uncivilized, coarse, crude, hooligan (*informal*). [➡RUDE AND HOSTILE; 626] *Opposite:* civilized.

brutishly *adv* **cruelly**, harshly, unfeelingly, insensitively, callously, ruthlessly, inhumanly, inhumanely. [➡SELFISH AND UNKIND; 506] *Opposite:* humanely.

brutishness *n* **cruelty**, harshness, unkindness, unfeelingness, insensitivity, callousness. [➡SELFISH AND UNKIND; 506] *Opposite:* humanity.

bryony *type of* **climber.** [➡CLIMBERS; 1033]

BtoB *adv* [➡E-COMMERCE; 1128]

bubble *v* **fizz**, effervesce, boil, simmer. [➡FROTH AND EFFERVESCE; 390]

bubblegum *type of* **confectionery.** [➡CONFECTIONERY; 1181]

bubbliness *n* [➡CHEERFULNESS OF OUTLOOK; 504]

bubbly 1 *adj* **effervescent**, foamy, sparkling, fizzy, fizzing, carbonated. [➡PHYSICAL TEXTURE; 1221] *Opposite:* still. 2 *adj* **cheerful**, lively, sparkling, vivacious, bouncy, animated, full of life. [➡CHEERFULNESS OF OUTLOOK; 504] *Opposite:* sad.

buccaneer *n* **pirate**, adventurer, swashbuckler. [➡VILLAINS AND THUGS; 947]

buck 1 *v* **jump**, rear, kick, kick out (*informal*), bound, spring. [➡BOUNCE, UNDULATE, AND VIBRATE; 309] 2 *v* **resist**, oppose, fly in the face of, go against, challenge, beat. [➡HESITATE; 273] 3 *n* (*informal*) **responsibility**, blame, liability, culpability, fault, guilt. [➡RESPONSIBILITY; 171] 4 *n* (*US informal*) **dollar**, money, cash, dough (*slang*). [➡CURRENCIES; 798] 5 *type of* **male animal.** [➡MALE OR FEMALE ANIMAL; 978] 6 *adj* (*US*) **lowly**, lowest, low-grade. [➡INFERIORITY; 154]

bucket 1 *n* **pail**, container, vessel. [➡CONTAINERS, RECEPTACLES, AND PACKAGING; 1244] 2 *v* (*informal*) **pour**, pour with rain, pour down, teem, come down in torrents, chuck down (*informal*), rain cats and dogs (*informal*). [➡CLOUDY AND RAINY WEATHER; 1052]

bucket down (*informal*) *v* [➡CLOUDY AND RAINY WEATHER; 1052]

bucketing (*informal*) *adj* [➡CLOUDY AND RAINY WEATHER; 1052]

buckets (*informal*) *n* **loads** (*informal*), lots, tons (*informal*), heaps (*informal*), stacks (*informal*), piles (*informal*), masses (*informal*), scores. [➡MANY, MUCH, LARGE AMOUNT; 117]

bucket seat *type of* **seating.** [➡FURNITURE; 858]

buckle 1 *n* **clasp**, clip, fastener, catch, fastening, hasp. [➡FASTENERS, LINKS, AND NETWORKS; 1246] 2 *part of* **garment.** [➡PARTS OF A GARMENT; 870] 3 *v* **fasten**, clip, clasp, secure, close, do up. [➡FASTEN, LINK, AND JOIN; 409] *Opposite:* undo. 4 *v* **collapse**, crumple, cave in, bulge, fold, warp, bend. [➡CHANGE OF SHAPE; 386] *Opposite:* straighten.

buckle down (*informal*) *v* **knuckle down** (*informal*), get on with, put your shoulder to the wheel, set to, get down to. [➡START AN ACTION; 261]

buckshee (*informal*) 1 *adj* **free**, complimentary, gratis, on the house. [➡CHEAP AND INEXPENSIVE; 222] 2 *adv* **free of charge**, free, gratis, for nothing, without paying, on the house. [➡CHEAP AND INEXPENSIVE; 222]

buckshot *type of* **projectile.** [➡PROJECTILES; 1158]

buckskin *type of* **leather.** [➡FABRICS; 1131]

bucktooth (*informal*) *type of* **tooth.** [➡THE MOUTH; 703]

buck up 1 *v* (*informal*) **cheer up**, liven up, revive, cheer, raise your spirits, hearten. [➡CHANGE OF MOOD AND COMPOSURE; 581] 2 *v* **improve**, get better, look up, pick up (*informal*), take off (*informal*), get going. [➡GET BETTER; 376] 3 *v* (*informal dated*) **hurry up**, get a move on (*informal*), get your skates on (*informal*), shift (*informal*), look lively, get cracking (*informal*). [➡START AN ACTION; 261]

bucolic *adj* **rural**, pastoral, rustic, country, countrified. [➡THE COUNTRYSIDE AND OUTDOOR SPACES; 1070] *Opposite:* urban.

bud 1 *n* **sprout**, blossom, shoot, outgrowth. [➡PARTS OF TREES AND PLANTS; 1026] 2 *v* **blossom**, flower, grow, bloom, open out, flourish. [➡GROW AND CULTIVATE; 352]

budding *adj* **promising**, potential, up-and-coming, nascent, burgeoning. [➡SUCCESSFUL AND PROMISING; 81]

buddy (*US informal*) *n* **friend**, mate, pal (*informal*), playmate, soul mate, companion, partner. [➡FRIENDS; 963]

budge *v* **move**, shift, dislodge, nudge, push, shove. [➡MOVE SOMETHING TO ANOTHER LOCATION; 325]

budgerigar *type of* **pet bird.** [➡BIRD; 997]

budget 1 *n* **financial plan**, financial statement, accounts, finances, funds, resources. [➡ACCOUNTING, BANKING, AND BUDGETING; 799] 2 *adj* **cheap**, economical, inexpensive, reasonable, low-priced, modest. [➡CHEAP AND INEXPENSIVE; 222] *Opposite:* expensive. 3 *v* **plan**, account, make financial arrangements, make provisions, cost. [➡DISPENSE, RATION, AND DISTRIBUTE; 435]

budgetary *adj* **financial**, economic, fiscal, commercial, monetary. [➡FINANCE AND ECONOMICS; 797]

bud vase *n* [➡CONTAINERS, RECEPTACLES, AND PACKAGING; 1244]

buff 1 *v* **polish**, rub, rub up, burnish, shine, clean, put a shine on. [➡CLEAN AND POLISH; 404] 2 *type of* **beige.** [➡COLOURS; 1223] 3 *n* **fan**, enthusiast, admirer, expert, connoisseur, aficionado, aficionada. [➡TALENTED OR INTELLIGENT PERSON; 529] 4 *adj* (*US informal*) **muscular**, fit, healthy, toned, hard. [➡FIT AND STRONG; 737]

buffalo 1 *type of* **large mammal.** [➡LARGE MAMMAL; 986] 2 *v* (*informal*) **intimidate**, coerce, threaten, inhibit, bully, browbeat, frighten, cow. [➡CAUSE OR COMPEL TO ACT; 272] **3** *v* (*US informal*) **confuse**, baffle, deceive, hoodwink, bewilder, dupe, bamboozle (*informal*). [➡CONFUSE AND BEWILDER; 572]

buffer **1** *n* **shock absorber**, bumper, cushion, barrier, shield, safeguard, defence, bulwark. [➡COVERS AND COATINGS; 1245] **2** *type of* **software**. [➡COMPUTERS AND COMPUTING; 1126] **3** *v* **cushion**, shield, safeguard, defend, protect. [➡IMPROVE STRENGTH AND DURABILITY; 379]

buffet **1** *v* **rock**, pound, batter, bang, knock, strike, pummel. [➡CONTACT: IMPACT; 414] **2** *type of* **meal**. [➡MEALS AND PARTS OF MEALS; 1168]

buffeting *n* **battering**, pounding, knocking, beating, pummelling, bashing (*informal*). [➡PHYSICAL ATTACK AND PUNISHMENT; 416]

buffoon *n* **clown**, joker, comedian, fool, wag (*dated*). [➡LAZY OR UNSUCCESSFUL PEOPLE; 948]

buffoonery *n* **horseplay**, clowning, fooling around, tomfoolery (*informal*), frivolity. [➡JOKES AND TEASING; 675]

bug **1** *n* **insect**, fly, creepy-crawly (*informal*), pest, creature. [➡INSECTS; 1012] **2** *n* (*informal*) **germ**, microbe, virus, bacterium, infection, microorganism. [➡MICROORGANISMS, FUNGI, AND ALGAE; 1023] **3** *n* (*informal*) **fault**, error, mistake, problem, gremlin (*informal*). [➡FAULTS, FLAWS, AND WEAKNESSES; 252] **4** *n* (*informal*) **listening device**, hidden microphone, surveillance device, wiretap. [➡TELECOMMUNICATIONS; 1129] **5** *v* (*informal*) **annoy**, irritate, infuriate, bother, madden, irk, get (*informal*). [➡ANGER AND ANNOY; 570] **6** *v* **tap**, listen in on, keep under surveillance, spy on. [➡LISTEN AND LISTENERS; 709]

See Compare and Contrast at **bother**.

bugaboo *n* **bogeyman**, bugbear, monster, gremlin (*informal*). [➡MYTHICAL BEINGS; 790]

bugbear *n* **worry**, problem, concern, bother, annoyance, nuisance. [➡PROBLEM; 257]

bug-eyed (*informal*) *adj* **popeyed**, exophthalmic (*technical*), staring, big-eyed, wide-eyed, agog. [➡FACIAL EXPRESSION; 652]

buggy **1** *n* **cart**, vehicle, truck, transporter. [➡BIKES, CARS, AND CARRIAGES; 1148] **2** *n* **pushchair**, pram, perambulator (*formal*), stroller (*US*), baby carriage (*US*). [➡BIKES, CARS, AND CARRIAGES; 1148] **3** *type of* **wagon or carriage**. [➡VEHICLES; 1144]

bugle **1** *v* **announce**, sound off, herald, trumpet. [➡INFORM AND ANNOUNCE; 612] **2** *type of* **brass instrument**. [➡MUSICAL INSTRUMENTS; 910]

build **1** *v* **construct**, put up, erect, make, put together, manufacture, assemble, fabricate. [➡BUILD; 353] **2** *v* **put together**, create, make, join, assemble, foster, encourage, build up. [➡CREATION; 347] **3** *n* **shape**, size, figure, body, physique, form, dimensions. [➡SHAPE; 1215]

build in *v* **incorporate**, include, integrate, add in. [➡COMBINE AND MIX; 401] *Opposite:* exclude.

building *n* **structure**, construction, edifice, erection (*formal*). [➡BUILDING AND ARCHITECTURE; 1075]

building

◆ *parts of a building*
balcony, buttress, ceiling, chimney, colonnade, doorway, elevator (*US*), escalator, exterior, façade, fire escape, frame, frontage, gable, guttering, landing, lift, paternoster, porch, roof, smokestack (*US*), staircase, stairs, stairway, stairwell, veranda, vestibule, wall, window, wing

building blocks **1** *n* [➡BASIC DETAILS; 689] **2** *type of* **toy**. [➡TOYS; 880]

building society *n* [➡ACCOUNTING, BANKING, AND BUDGETING; 799]

build up **1** *v* **increase**, rise, develop, expand, enlarge, accumulate, amass, stock up. [➡CHANGE OF SIZE: BIGGER; 393] *Opposite:* fall off. **2** *v* **boost**, bolster, pump up, inspire, encourage. [➡ENCOURAGE; 577] *Opposite:* discourage.

buildup **1** *n* **accumulation**, backlog, accrual, collection, stockpile, logjam. [➡AMOUNT AND QUANTITY; 112] **2** *n* **hype**, publicity, puff, praise, flattery. [➡ADVERTISING AND PUBLICITY; 605]

built-in **1** *adj* **integral**, fitted, fixed, en suite, in-built, incorporated, integrated. [➡RELATIVE LOCATION; 162] **2** *adj* **natural**, inherent, innate, intrinsic, ingrained, acquired. [➡HUMAN SETTLEMENTS; 1069]

built-up *adj* **urbanized**, urban, developed, residential, industrial. [➡HUMAN SETTLEMENTS; 1069]

bulb **1** *n* **corm**, rhizome, tuber, storage organ, underground part. [➡PARTS OF TREES AND PLANTS; 1026] **2** *type of* **rounded shape**. [➡ROUNDED SHAPE; 1217]

bulb

◆ *types of flowers grown from bulbs*
anemone, bluebell, crocus, cyclamen, daffodil, dahlia, freesia, gladiolus, hyacinth, iris, jonquil, lily, narcissus, snowdrop, tulip

bulbous *adj* **rounded**, spherical, bulging, globular, swollen. [➡ROUNDED SHAPE; 1217]

bulge **1** *v* **stick out**, protrude, expand, be full to bursting, swell, be swollen, puff out, puff up. [➡CHANGE OF SHAPE; 386] **2** *n* **protuberance**, swell, swelling, knot, lump, hump, knob, prominence, projection. [➡EXTREMITIES OF PHYSICAL OBJECTS; 1249]

bulging **1** *adj* **protruding**, protuberant, distended, swollen, swelling, bloated, expanded, extended, projecting. [➡LARGE; 1192] *Opposite:* concave. **2** *adj* (*informal*) **full**, overfull, overfilled, stuffed (*informal*), overstuffed, crammed, full to bursting. [➡FULL; 1238] *Opposite:* flat.

bulk **1** *n* **size**, mass, volume, immensity, vastness, bulkiness, massiveness, largeness. [➡SIZE AND DIMENSIONS; 1191] **2** *n* **form**, body, weight, mass, hulk. [➡SHAPE; 1215] **3** *n* **greater part**, main part, largest part, majority, substance, almost all, lion's share, chief part, best part. [➡MAJORITY; 139]

bulkhead *n* **partition**, wall, dividing wall, screen, divider. [➡WALLS AND PARTITIONS; 1103]

bulkiness **1** *n* **unwieldiness**, awkwardness, ungainliness, cumbersomeness, ponderousness. [➡LARGE; 1192] **2** *n* **large size**, largeness, weight, bulk, mass, thickness. [➡LARGE; 1192] *Opposite:* compactness.

bulk large *v* **be prominent**, figure prominently, loom large, dominate, be important, stand out. [➡MOST IMPORTANT AND MAIN; 194]

bulk mail (*US*) *n* [➡ADVERTISING AND PUBLICITY; 605]

bulk up (*informal*) *v* **build up**, increase, pad out, gain weight, gain muscle. [➡CHANGE OF SIZE: BIGGER; 393]

bulky **1** *adj* **unwieldy**, cumbersome, awkward, ungainly, ponderous, unmanageable. [➡LARGE; 1192] *Opposite:* manageable. **2** *adj* **large**, huge, immense, massive, colossal, hulking. [➡LARGE; 1192] *Opposite:* compact.

bull **1** *n* **papal decree**, decree, official statement, encyclical, instruction, edict, proclamation. [➡RELIGIOUS CONCEPTS; 777] **2** *type of* **male animal**. [➡MALE OR FEMALE ANIMAL; 978]

bulldog *type of* **large dog**. [➡DOG; 980]

bulldoze **1** *v* **flatten**, raze, level, demolish, clear. [➡DESTRUCTION AND DEMOLITION; 360] **2** *v* (*informal*) **coerce**, bully, bludgeon, browbeat, push, railroad (*informal*), steamroller. [➡CAUSE OR COMPEL TO ACT; 272]

bulldozer *type of* **commercial or industrial vehicle**. [➡VEHICLES; 1144]

bullet *type of* **projectile**. [➡PROJECTILES; 1158]

bulletin **1** *n* **news report**, update, news item, news summary, press release, news flash. [➡TELEVISION AND RADIO; 607] **2** *n* **official statement**, communiqué, statement, announcement, press release, dispatch, notice, report. [➡BASIC DETAILS; 689] **3** *n* **periodical**, journal, newsletter, newspaper, publication. [➡NEWSPAPERS; 606]

bulletproof **1** *adj* **toughened**, armoured, protective, reinforced, shatterproof. [➡RIGID AND HARD; 1210] **2** *adj* (*informal*) **invulnerable**, secure, invincible, unassailable, untouchable, above criticism. [➡SAFE AND SAFETY; 192] *Opposite:* vulnerable.

bulletproof glass *type of* **glass**. [➡GLASS; 1135]

bullfrog *type of* **amphibian**. [➡AMPHIBIANS; 1008]

bullheaded (*informal*) *adj* **obstinate**, headstrong, stubborn, wilful, intransigent, uncooperative, obdurate, self-willed. [➡UNWILLINGNESS AND STUBBORNNESS; 565]

bullheadedness (*informal*) *n* **obstinacy**, stubbornness, wilfulness, intransigence, self-will, obduracy. [➡REBELLIOUSNESS AND DISOBEDIENCE; 566]

bullion *n* **gold**, gold bars, gold ingots. [➡FINANCIAL ASSETS; 463]

bullish **1** *adj* **muscular**, strong, hulking, brawny. [➡MUSCLES AND MUSCULATURE; 480] **2** *adj* (*informal*) **optimistic**, upbeat (*informal*), confident, buoyant, cheerful, chipper (*informal*), enthusiastic. [➡CALMNESS, CONFIDENCE, AND COMPOSURE; 537] *Opposite:* pessimistic.

bullishly (*informal*) *adv* **confidently**, optimistically, buoyantly, positively, cheerfully, hopefully, self-confidently, self-assuredly. [➡CALMNESS, CONFIDENCE, AND COMPOSURE; 537] *Opposite:* diffidently.

bullishness (*informal*) *n* **confidence**, optimism, buoyancy, hopefulness, self-confidence, self-assuredness. [➡FEELINGS ABOUT THE FUTURE; 534] *Opposite:* diffidence.

bullnecked *adj* **stocky**, bullish, brawny, beefy, muscular, thickset. [➡MUSCLES AND MUSCULATURE; 480]

bullock **1** *type of* **young animal**. [➡YOUNG ANIMAL; 977] **2** *type of* **male animal**. [➡MALE OR FEMALE ANIMAL; 978]

bullring *n* **arena**, ring, stadium, amphitheatre, sports stadium. [➡BUILDINGS FOR PUBLIC ENTERTAINMENT; 1083]

bull's eye *n* **target**, centre, mark, middle, middle point. [➡CENTRAL PARTS OF PHYSICAL OBJECTS; 1250]

bull terrier *type of* **small dog**. [➡DOG; 980]

bully **1** *n* **tormenter**, aggressor, persecutor, tyrant, oppressor, intimidator. [➡VILLAINS AND THUGS; 947] **2** *v* **intimidate**, terrorize, persecute, torment, frighten, oppress, browbeat, harass. [➡FRIGHTEN AND SHOCK; 569]

bullyboy **1** *n* **thug**, bully, heavy (*slang*), hooligan (*informal*), yob (*informal*), oppressor, harasser. [➡VILLAINS AND THUGS; 947] **2** *adj* **aggressive**, intimidating, bullying, rough, threatening, strong-arm (*informal*), menacing. [➡FRIGHTENING; 232]

bullying *n* **intimidation**, mistreatment, oppression, harassment, victimization, maltreatment, hounding. [➡UNKIND ACTION OR BEHAVIOUR; 297]

bully-off *n* **start of play**, start, kickoff, beginning, commencement (*formal*). [➡SPORTS TERMS; 877]

bulrush *type of* **grass**. [➡GRASS; 1031]

bulwark **1** *n* **fortification**, embankment, earthwork, barricade, rampart, wall. [➡BARRIERS; 1112] **2** *n* **safeguard**, protection, defence, buttress, buffer, barrier. [➡SAFE AND SAFETY; 192]

bum bag *type of* **handbag**. [➡CONTAINERS, RECEPTACLES, AND PACKAGING; 1244]

bumble **1** *v* **mumble**, murmur, hesitate, mutter, stutter, burble (*informal*). [➡WITTER AND BABBLE; 618] **2** *v* **stumble**, lumber, hesitate, blunder, stagger, lurch, shamble. [➡WALK UNSTEADILY; 316]

bumblebee *type of* **flying insect**. [➡FLYING INSECTS; 1013]

bumbler *n* [➡LAZY OR UNSUCCESSFUL PEOPLE; 948]

bumbling (*informal*) *adj* **awkward**, clumsy, blundering, lumbering, ungainly, inept, shambling. [➡DESCRIBING BODY MOVEMENTS; 289] *Opposite:* graceful.

bumf (*informal*) *n* **documents**, leaflets, pamphlets, brochures, papers, forms, official papers, booklets. [➡BOOKS AND BOOKLETS; 591]

bummer (*slang*) *n* **annoyance**, nuisance, pest (*informal*), downer (*informal*), comedown (*informal*), disappointment, letdown, discouragement. [➡NUISANCES; 254]

bump **1** *v* **hit**, knock, bang, strike, wallop (*informal*), bash (*informal*). [➡CONTACT: IMPACT; 414] **2** *v* **jolt**, bounce, jounce, jar, jerk, bound, spring. [➡CONTACT: IMPACT; 414] **3** *n* **knock**, collision, smash, accident, crash, shunt (*informal*). [➡CONTACT:

IMPACT; 414] 4 *v* **collide**, slam into, crash into, knock, smash into. [➡CONTACT: IMPACT; 414] 5 *n* **swelling**, lump, contusion (*technical*), bruise, bulge. [➡CONDITIONS AFFECTING THE SKIN; 722] 6 *n* **thud**, thump, bang, crash, blow, smash. [➡IMPACT SOUNDS; 1259]

bumper 1 *adj* **plentiful**, plenteous (*literary*), profuse, copious, extra-large, jumbo, mammoth, mega, super (*informal*). [➡MANY, MUCH, LARGE AMOUNT; 117] *Opposite:* meagre. 2 *type of* **external feature**. [➡VEHICLES; 1144]

bumpiness *n* **unevenness**, roughness, lumpiness. [➡PHYSICAL TEXTURE; 1221] *Opposite:* smoothness.

bump into 1 *v* **collide**, slam into, crash into, knock into, smash into. [➡CONTACT: IMPACT; 414] 2 *v* **meet by chance**, run into, happen upon, happen on, meet, come across. [➡EXPERIENCE AND ENCOUNTER; 583]

bumpkin (*informal*) *n* [➡LEVEL OF EDUCATION AND SOPHISTICATION; 894]

bump off (*slang*) *v* **kill**, murder, do in (*informal*), do away with (*informal*), get rid of, assassinate, waste (*slang*). [➡KILL; 923]

bumptious *adj* **full of yourself**, pleased with yourself, self-satisfied, self-important, smug, conceited, arrogant, overbearing, brash, prideful. [➡POMPOUS, LOUD, AND OVER-CONFIDENT; 636] *Opposite:* modest.

bumptiousness *n* **self-importance**, conceitedness, arrogance, pompousness, pushiness (*informal*), brashness, presumptuousness. [➡POMPOUS, LOUD, AND OVER-CONFIDENT; 636] *Opposite:* modesty.

bump up (*informal*) *v* **increase**, put up, boost, augment (*formal*), enhance, add to, inflate. [➡CHANGE OF SIZE: BIGGER; 393] *Opposite:* decrease.

bumpy 1 *adj* **uneven**, rough, rutted, potholed. [➡PHYSICAL TEXTURE; 1221] *Opposite:* smooth. 2 *adj* **uncomfortable**, rough, bouncy, jarring, jerky. [➡PHYSICALLY UNPLEASANT; 227] *Opposite:* smooth.

bun 1 *type of* **roll or bun**. [➡BREAD, FLOUR, AND BREAD PRODUCTS; 1178] 2 *type of* **hairstyle**. [➡HAIR STYLES AND HAIR PIECES; 489]

bunch 1 *n* **group**, set, lot, mixture, collection, assembly, cluster, clump. [➡COLLECTIONS AND MIXTURES OF THINGS; 1243] 2 *n* (*informal*) **gang**, gathering, team, crew (*informal*), set, group. [➡GROUPS OF PEOPLE; 935] 3 *n* **bouquet**, posy, spray, corsage. [➡COLLECTIONS AND MIXTURES OF THINGS; 1243] 4 *v* **crowd together**, huddle, form a group, gather, cluster. [➡GET CLOSER TOGETHER; 311] *Opposite:* disperse.

bunches *type of* **hairstyle**. [➡HAIR STYLES AND HAIR PIECES; 489]

bundle 1 *n* **package**, pack, parcel, packet, bale, wad, roll. [➡COLLECTIONS AND MIXTURES OF THINGS; 1243] 2 *n* (*slang*) **fortune**, packet (*informal*), mint (*informal*), bomb (*informal*), big money, king's ransom. [➡LARGE AMOUNT OF MONEY; 141] 3 *v* (*informal*) **hustle**, hurry, rush, push, shove. [➡MOVE FAST; 314]

bundle up 1 *v* **package**, pack, wrap, parcel, parcel up, tie up. [➡FASTEN, LINK, AND JOIN; 409] 2 *v* (*informal*) **dress warmly**, wrap up, wrap up warmly. [➡DRESS, WEAR, AND UNDRESS; 868]

bung 1 *n* **stopper**, plug, cork. [➡COVERS AND COATINGS; 1245] 2 *n* (*slang*) **bribe**, payoff (*informal*), backhander (*informal*), kickback, sweetener (*informal*), inducement. [➡BRIBES; 441] 3 *v* (*informal*) **throw**, toss, fling, lob, pass. [➡THROW SOMETHING; 335]

bungalow *type of* **house**. [➡RESIDENTIAL BUILDINGS; 1077]

bungle (*informal*) *v* **botch**, bodge (*informal*), mismanage, ruin, do badly, mess up (*informal*), make a mess of, make a hash of (*informal*), make a dog's dinner of, spoil. [➡MESS UP AND MAKE MISTAKES; 473] *Opposite:* succeed.

bungler (*informal*) *n* **blunderer**, incompetent, bumbler, botcher, muddler. [➡UNSKILLED PERSON; 531]

bungling (*informal*) *adj* **clumsy**, unskilful, incompetent, inept, blundering, maladroit (*formal*), ham-fisted (*informal*), useless, gauche, amateurish, ham-handed (*informal*). [➡UNSKILLED; 530] *Opposite:* competent.

bung up (*informal*) *v* **stop up**, block, close, clog, caulk, clog up, obstruct. [➡FILL; 407] *Opposite:* open.

bunion *n* **swelling**, lump, enlargement, distension, bulge, bump, growth. [➡CONDITIONS AFFECTING THE SKIN; 722]

bunk 1 *n* **bed**, single bed, berth, couchette, bunk bed. [➡FURNITURE; 858] 2 *n* (*slang*) **bunkum** (*informal*), nonsense, humbug, claptrap (*informal*), twaddle (*informal*), rubbish, hot air (*informal*), codswallop (*informal*), hogwash (*informal*), drivel, gibberish, hooey (*informal*), garbage, hokum (*US informal disapproving*). [➡MEANINGLESS SPEECH OR WRITING; 677]

bunk bed *type of* **bed**. [➡FURNITURE; 858]

bunker 1 *n* **bin**, chest, container, box, store, coal bunker, coalbin (*US*). [➡CONTAINERS, RECEPTACLES, AND PACKAGING; 1244] 2 *n* **underground shelter**, shelter, dugout, foxhole, ditch, trench. [➡SAFE BUILDINGS OR PLACES; 1092] 3 *type of* **storage space**. [➡STORES AND STORAGE BUILDINGS; 1087]

bunk off (*informal*) *v* [➡RUN AWAY AND AVOID; 10]

bunkum (*informal*) *n* **nonsense**, humbug, claptrap (*informal*), twaddle (*informal*), bunk (*slang*), rubbish, hot air (*informal*), codswallop (*informal*), hogwash (*informal*), drivel, gibberish, hooey (*informal*), garbage, hokum (*US informal disapproving*). [➡MEANINGLESS SPEECH OR WRITING; 677]

bunting *n* **streamers**, decorations, flags, paper chains, ticker tape, ribbons, garlands. [➡ORNAMENTS AND DECORATIONS; 1247]

bunya *type of* **evergreen tree**. [➡EVERGREEN AND CONIFEROUS TREES; 1029]

buoy 1 *n* **marker**, float, signal. [➡SIGNPOSTS, SIGNALS AND BILLBOARDS; 596] 2 *v* **keep afloat**, hold up, sustain, maintain, prop up, keep up, buoy up. [➡CAUSE TO CONTINUE; 268]

buoyancy 1 *n* **lightness**, weightlessness. [➡WEIGHT: LIGHT; 1205] *Opposite:* heaviness. 2 *n* **resilience**, resistance, flexibility, toughness. [➡CHEERFULNESS OF OUTLOOK; 504] 3 *n* **optimism**, cheerfulness, good spirits, enthusiasm, jauntiness, lightheartedness. [➡POSITIVE IMPATIENCE, ENTHUSIASM, AND ALERTNESS; 538] *Opposite:* moroseness.

buoyant 1 *adj* **floating**, afloat, light. [➡WEIGHT: LIGHT; 1205] 2 *adj* **resilient**, resistant, flexible, tough. [➡STRENGTH; 202] 3 *adj* **cheerful**, upbeat (*informal*), optimistic, happy, jaunty, carefree, lighthearted. [➡PLEASURE, EXCITEMENT, AND ELATION; 535] *Opposite:* morose.

buoyantly *adv* **cheerfully**, brightly, happily, optimistically, positively, confidently, hopefully. [➡PLEASURE, EXCITEMENT, AND ELATION; 535] *Opposite:* morosely.

buoy up *v* **cheer**, uplift, encourage, boost, lift, sustain. [➡ENCOURAGE; 577] *Opposite:* depress.

burble 1 *v* **bubble**, ripple, babble, splash, plash (*literary*), murmur. [➡EMIT CONTINUOUS SOUNDS; 367] 2 *v* (*informal*) **gush**, babble, ramble, go on about, prattle, waffle (*informal*). [➡WITTER AND BABBLE; 618] 3 *type of* **continuous sound**. [➡CONTINUOUS SOUNDS; 1257]

burden 1 *n* **load**, weight, cargo. [➡AMOUNT AND QUANTITY; 112] 2 *n* **problem**, drain, encumbrance, affliction, liability, weight, worry, tax, inconvenience, millstone, responsibility, duty, onus, obligation. [➡NUISANCES; 254] 3 *v* **lumber** (*informal*), weigh down, saddle, encumber, trouble, yoke, inconvenience, load. [➡GIVE TOO MUCH; 438]

See Compare and Contrast at **subject**.

burdened *adj* **loaded**, fraught, weighed down, laden, held back, troubled, hampered. [➡SADNESS, DISTRESS, AND DESPAIR; 540]

burdensome *adj* **onerous**, heavy, taxing, troublesome, arduous, oppressive, difficult, worrying. [➡IRRITATING; 229]

burdock *type of* **weed**. [➡WEEDS AND THISTLES; 1034]

bureau 1 *n* **government department**, agency, office, department, unit, section. [➡LEGISLATIVE BODIES AND LEGISLATION; 809] 2 *n* **writing desk**, desk, writing table, escritoire. [➡FURNITURE; 858] 3 *n* (*US*) **chest of drawers**, dresser, chest. [➡FURNITURE; 858]

bureaucracy 1 *n* **administration**, government, civil service, officialdom (*informal*), establishment, organization, system of government. [➡STYLES AND SYSTEMS OF GOVERNMENT; 806] 2 *n* **official procedure**, red tape (*informal*), rules and regulations, formalities, paperwork. [➡WAYS OF DOING THINGS; 295]

bureaucrat *n* **official**, public servant, civil servant, administrator, office holder. [➡POLITICAL OFFICES AND POLITICIANS; 808]

bureaucratic 1 *adj* **administrative**, official, governmental, civil service, organizational. [➡STYLES AND SYSTEMS OF GOVERNMENT; 806] 2 *adj* **rigid**, inflexible, unbending, officious, involved, complex. [➡DIFFICULTY AND COMPLEXITY; 243]

burgeon (*literary*) 1 *v* **mushroom**, multiply, prosper, proliferate, flourish, grow rapidly. [➡PROSPER AND ABOUND; 16] *Opposite:* dwindle. 2 *v* **bud**, bloom, blossom, flower. [➡SUCCEED AND WIN; 79]

burgeoning 1 *adj* **growing**, mushrooming, increasing, escalating, expanding, flourishing. [➡CHANGE OF SIZE: BIGGER; 393] *Opposite:* dwindling. 2 *adj* **budding**, promising, up-and-coming, nascent. [➡SUCCESSFUL AND PROMISING; 81] *Opposite:* fading.

burger *type of* **processed meat**. [➡TYPES AND CUTS OF MEAT; 1176]

burgher *n* **citizen**, resident, inhabitant, denizen, voter, taxpayer. [➡INHABITANT; 857]

burglar *n* **thief**, robber, intruder, cat burglar, criminal, housebreaker (*US*). [➡CRIMINALS; 821]

burglarize (*US*) *v* **rob**, burgle, steal, break into, break and enter, raid. [➡STEAL AND ROB; 427]

burglary 1 *n* **theft**, breaking and entering, robbery, aggravated burglary, stealing, larceny (*dated*). [➡CRIMES; 817] 2 *n* **break-in**, theft, robbery, crime, housebreak (*US*). [➡CRIMES; 817]

See Compare and Contrast at **theft**.

burgle *v* **rob**, thieve, break in, loot, steal from, burglarize (*US*). [➡STEAL AND ROB; 427]

burgundy *type of* **red**. [➡COLOURS; 1223]

burial *n* **interment** (*formal*), committal, entombment, funeral. [➡BURIAL AND PREPARATION FOR BURIAL; 929]

burial chamber *n* **sepulchre**, tomb, mausoleum, vault, resting place, grave. [➡MONUMENTS; 1091]

burial ground *n* **cemetery**, graveyard, churchyard, last resting place, necropolis, burial place, God's Acre (*literary*). [➡BURIAL PLACES AND ACCESSORIES; 930]

burial place *n* **cemetery**, graveyard, burial ground, necropolis, churchyard, God's Acre (*literary*), mausoleum, last resting place, tomb, crypt. [➡BURIAL PLACES AND ACCESSORIES; 930]

buried 1 *adj* **underground**, concealed, hidden, covered, dug in, secreted. [➡ORIENTATION AND ALIGNMENT; 1222] *Opposite:* dug up. 2 *adj* **suppressed**, hidden, covered up, repressed, forgotten, concealed, submerged, dormant. [➡SECRET AND UNKNOWN; 180] *Opposite:* exposed.

burlap *type of* **fibre**. [➡FABRICS; 1131]

burlesque 1 *n* **parody**, caricature, travesty, sendup (*informal*), lampoon, skit, imitation, distortion, satire, mockery. [➡JOKES AND TEASING; 675] 2 *n* (*US*) **variety show**, vaudeville, revue, extravaganza, spectacular, floor show, cabaret. [➡PERFORMANCES AND SHOWS; 42] 3 *v* **send up** (*informal*), spoof, mock, take off (*informal*), make fun of, lampoon, caricature, satirize, parody. [➡JOKES AND TEASING; 675]

burliness *n* **brawniness**, heftiness, broad shoulders, muscularity, robustness, beefiness. [➡BUILD; 478] *Opposite:* slimness.

burly *adj* **brawny**, hefty, broad-shouldered, husky, muscular, strong, robust, beefy. [➡BUILD; 478] *Opposite:* slight.

Burmese cat *type of* **cat**. [➡FELINE; 983]

burn 1 *v* **blaze**, be ablaze, flame, smoulder, glow. [➡FIRE, FLAMMABILITY, AND BURNING; 1164] 2 *v* **burn up**, burn down, burn away, gut, reduce to ashes, burn to a crisp, char, incinerate. [➡FIRE, FLAMMABILITY, AND BURNING; 1164] 3 *v* **scorch**, singe, sear, char, scald, blister. [➡FIRE, FLAMMABILITY, AND BURNING; 1164] 4 *v* **use up**, use, expend, consume. [➡USE UP AND WASTE; 475] 5 *v* **go red**, flush, blush, redden, colour, glow. [➡CHANGE OF COLOUR; 392] 6 *v* **tingle**, sting, hurt, prickle, be on fire. [➡PAIN AND OTHER PHYSICAL SENSATIONS; 734] 7 *v* **corrode**, eat away, eat into, etch. [➡DELETE AND ERASE; 340] 8 *v* **glow**, shine, twinkle, flare, glimmer. [➡LIGHT EMISSION; 369] 9 *v* (*informal*) **race**, hurtle, tear, speed, scorch, zoom, go full tilt. [➡MOVE FAST; 314] *Opposite:* dawdle. **10** *n* **injury**, blister, scald, scorch. [➡CONDITIONS AFFECTING THE SKIN; 722] **11** *n* **stream**, brook, rivulet, beck. [➡RIVERS, LAKES, AND STREAMS; 1042]

burn down *v* **incinerate**, go up in flames, burn to the ground, burn to a crisp, torch (*slang*), reduce to ashes. [➡FIRE, FLAMMABILITY, AND BURNING; 1164]

burned-out **1** *adj* **gutted**, destroyed, reduced to ashes, burnt down, burnt up, incinerated, torched (*slang*). [➡IN BAD REPAIR; 1233] **2** *adj* **exhausted**, stressed out (*informal*), worn out, tired out, drained, unwell, in poor health. [➡TIRED, ASLEEP AND UNCONSCIOUS; 739]

burner *n* **gas ring**, ring, heat, flame, gas jet, Bunsen burner, jet. [➡FIRE, FLAMMABILITY, AND BURNING; 1164]

burning **1** *adj* **red-hot**, piping hot, scorching (*informal*), boiling hot, fiery hot, sweltering, fiery, boiling, hot. [➡TEMPERATURE: HOT; 1228] *Opposite:* cold. **2** *adj* **on fire**, ablaze, blazing, flaming, smouldering, fiery. [➡FIRE, FLAMMABILITY, AND BURNING; 1164] *Opposite:* extinguished. **3** *adj* **strong**, ardent, fervent, all-consuming, passionate, intense, fiery. [➡STRENGTH; 202] *Opposite:* weak. **4** *adj* **important**, vital, crucial, urgent, significant, major. [➡IMPORTANT; 195] *Opposite:* routine. **5** *adj* **smarting**, stinging, tingly, prickly, painful. [➡PAIN AND OTHER PHYSICAL SENSATIONS; 734] **6** *adj* **feverish**, febrile, flushed, hot, red, overheated, fevered. [➡ILL AND SICK; 741] *Opposite:* cool.

burning hot *adj* [➡TEMPERATURE: HOT; 1228]

burning up *adj* **hot**, overheated, feverish, burning hot, burning, fevered, sweltering, flushed. [➡ILL AND SICK; 741] *Opposite:* cold.

burnish *v* **polish**, shine, buff, rub up, rub, clean, put a shine on. [➡CLEAN AND POLISH; 404]

burn out (*informal*) *v* **exhaust**, break down, wear out, tire, fatigue, flag, run down. [➡OVERDO SOMETHING; 291]

burnout *n* **exhaustion**, stress, tension, weariness, poor health, fatigue, breakdown. [➡ILL AND SICK; 741]

burnt *adj* **overcooked**, well-done, cooked, seared, singed, scorched, scalded, blistered, charbroiled, charred, burnt to a crisp. [➡STATE OF PREPARED FOOD; 1170] *Opposite:* rare.

burn the candle at both ends *v* **overdo things**, wear yourself out, do too much, exhaust yourself, burn the midnight oil. [➡HARD WORK OR EFFORT; 299]

burn the midnight oil *v* **work late**, stay up, work day and night, work overtime, burn the candle at both ends, toil, keep your nose to the grindstone. [➡HARD WORK OR EFFORT; 299] *Opposite:* slack.

burnt-out **1** *adj* **gutted**, destroyed, reduced to ashes, burnt down, burnt up, incinerated, torched (*slang*). [➡IN BAD REPAIR; 1233] **2** *adj* **exhausted**, stressed out (*informal*), worn out, tired out, drained, unwell, in poor health. [➡UNFIT AND WEAK; 740]

burnt sienna *type of* **brown**. [➡COLOURS; 1223]

burnt to a crisp *adj* [➡STATE OF PREPARED FOOD; 1170]

burnt umber *type of* **brown**. [➡COLOURS; 1223]

burn up **1** *v* **incinerate**, burn, burn down, reduce to ashes, burn to a crisp, go up in flames, burn to the ground. [➡FIRE, FLAMMABILITY, AND BURNING; 1164] **2** *v* (*US informal*) **annoy**, irritate, vex, anger, obsess, eat up (*informal*), consume, eat away at. [➡UPSET, DISTRESS, AND HUMILIATE; 568] *Opposite:* please.

burn your boats *v* **pass the point of no return**, burn your bridges, cross the Rubicon, nail your colours to the mast. [➡MAKE DECISIONS AND CHOICES; 753]

burn your bridges *v* **pass the point of no return**, burn your boats, cross the Rubicon, nail your colours to the mast. [➡MAKE DECISIONS AND CHOICES; 753]

burp **1** *n* [➡VOMIT AND BELCH; 713] **2** *v* [➡VOMIT AND BELCH; 713]

burr **1** *n* **seed husk**, pod, pericarp, seed pod. [➡PARTS OF TREES AND PLANTS; 1026] **2** *n* **accent**, pronunciation, twang, drawl, brogue, enunciation, intonation, inflection, stress, accentuation, emphasis, tone of voice. [➡ASPECTS OF LANGUAGE; 683]

burrow **1** *n* **hole**, warren, den, lair, hideaway, tunnel, earth, sett. [➡ANIMAL OR BIRD ACCOMMODATION; 1078] **2** *v* **dig**, tunnel, excavate, channel, dig out, delve (*archaic*), grub, hollow out. [➡SEEK POSSESSION AND SEARCH; 457] **3** *v* **search**, dig, investigate, delve, scrabble, grope, ferret around, rummage, forage. [➡SEEK POSSESSION AND SEARCH; 457] **4** *v* **nestle**, snuggle, cuddle, nuzzle, cozy up (*US*). [➡GET CLOSER TOGETHER; 311]

bursary *n* **scholarship**, grant, award, fund, stipend, exhibition. [➡INCOME; 461]

burst **1** *v* **rupture**, split open, disintegrate, break open, fracture, rip open, come apart, explode. [➡DESTRUCTION AND DEMOLITION; 360] **2** *v* **erupt**, spout, gush, rush, break out, surge, explode. [➡MOVE FAST; 314] *Opposite:* trickle. **3** *n* **spurt**, eruption, gust, torrent, rupture, surge, rush. [➡SUDDEN EVENT; 52] *Opposite:* trickle.

bursting **1** *adj* **full**, overflowing, teeming, bursting at the seams, full to bursting, jam-packed (*informal*), packed, stuffed (*informal*), abounding, brimming with, full of, abounding in, loaded with, filled with. [➡FULL; 1238] *Opposite:* empty. **2** *adj* (*informal*) **eager**, desperate, keen, dying, longing, excited, thrilled. [➡POSITIVE IMPATIENCE, ENTHUSIASM, AND ALERTNESS; 538] *Opposite:* unwilling.

bursting at the seams *adj* **crowded**, full, crammed, stuffed (*informal*), packed, jam-packed (*informal*), seething, at full capacity, teeming, full to bursting, fit to bust, bulging. [➡FULL; 1238]

burst in on **1** *v* **interrupt**, intrude upon, intrude on, come upon, disturb, disrupt. [➡INTERRUPT AND BUTT IN; 620] **2** *v* **surprise**, take by surprise, catch unawares, take unawares, catch in the act, catch red-handed, catch in flagrante. [➡ARRIVE; 12]

burst into flames *v* [➡FIRE, FLAMMABILITY, AND BURNING; 1164]

burst into tears *v* **break down**, dissolve in tears, break down and cry, burst out crying, lose control, be overcome, lose it (*informal*), start sobbing, start weeping. [➡CRYING; 651] *Opposite:* laugh.

burst out **1** *v* **start**, begin, commence (*formal*), burst into, break into, break out. [➡SUDDENLY COME INTO EXISTENCE; 2] **2** *v*

exclaim, shout, cry, call out, say, yell, blurt out. [➡BETRAY CONFIDENCES AND GOSSIP; 619] *Opposite:* whisper.

burst out crying *v* [➡GIVING VENT TO EMOTIONS; 680]

bury 1 *v* **inter** (*formal*), put in the ground, lay to rest, entomb, put six feet under. [➡BURIAL AND PREPARATION FOR BURIAL; 929] *Opposite:* exhume. 2 *v* **hide**, conceal, cover, put out of sight, submerge, secrete. [➡CAUSE TO DISAPPEAR; 6] *Opposite:* expose.

bury the hatchet *v* **make up**, make peace, be reconciled, kiss and make up, fall upon each other's necks, resolve differences. [➡FORGET, FORGIVE, AND ACCEPT; 749] *Opposite:* fight.

bus 1 *type of* **public service vehicle** [➡VEHICLES; 1144] 2 *type of* **software.** [➡COMPUTERS AND COMPUTING; 1126] 3 *part of* **spacecraft.** [➡SPACE VEHICLES; 1062] 4 *v* **transport**, carry, take, convey, move, travel, journey. [➡TRAVEL: WAYS OF TRAVELLING; 321]

busby *n* **bearskin**, helmet, headgear, beret, balaclava. [➡HABERDASHERY, MILLINERY, AND LINGERIE; 867]

bush 1 *n* **shrub**, plant, flowering shrub, hedging plant. [➡BUSHES AND SHRUBS; 1027] 2 *n* **scrubland**, wilds, outback, savanna, scrub. [➡DESERTS AND PLAINS; 1045]

bushed (*informal*) *adj* **exhausted**, tired, worn-out, done in (*informal*), whacked (*informal*), dead beat (*informal*), dog-tired (*informal*), dead on your feet, all in, wiped out (*slang*). [➡TIRED, ASLEEP AND UNCONSCIOUS; 739] *Opposite:* refreshed.

bushes *n* **undergrowth**, scrub, shrubbery, greenery, underbrush (*US*). [➡VEGETATION; 1025]

bushwhack (*US informal*) *v* **ambush**, lie in wait for, hold up, surprise, attack. [➡COMPETE, CONTEND, AND COMBAT; 304]

bushy *adj* **luxuriant**, abundant, profuse, shaggy, thick, hairy, unkempt, wild. [➡DESCRIBING HAIR; 487] *Opposite:* sparse.

busily *adv* **actively**, energetically, briskly, industriously, vigorously, enthusiastically, feverishly. [➡WITH ENTHUSIASM; 287] *Opposite:* lazily.

business 1 *n* **commerce**, trade, industry, selling, production, big business, dealing. [➡BUSINESS; 792] 2 *n* **company**, corporation, conglomerate, establishment, partnership, firm, multinational, transnational, enterprise, venture, concern, organization. [➡BUSINESS ENTERPRISES AND RELATED BODIES; 793] 3 *n* **custom**, trade, dealings, transactions, sales. [➡BUSINESS ACTIVITIES AND PHENOMENA; 795] 4 *n* **concern**, affair, problem, responsibility, interest, sphere. [➡SUBJECT AREA; 769] 5 *n* **matter**, affair, issue, situation, event, thing, to-do (*informal*). [➡EVENTS AND OCCURRENCES; 35] 6 *adj* **commercial**, occupational, corporate, professional. [➡BUSINESS; 792] *Opposite:* private.

businesslike 1 *adj* **efficient**, practical, professional, competent, systematic, methodical, organized, thorough, ordered, well-organized. [➡HARD-WORKING AND COMMITTED; 501] *Opposite:* unprofessional. 2 *adj* **unemotional**, objective, professional, detached, uninvolved, impersonal. [➡NEUTRALITY AND INDIFFERENCE; 554] *Opposite:* emotional.

business meeting *n* [➡MEETINGS AND ASSEMBLIES; 43]

business park *type of* **industrial site.** [➡INDUSTRIAL BUILDINGS; 1086]

businessperson *n* **business executive**, executive, executive director, director, manager, entrepreneur. [➡BUSINESS PEOPLE; 794]

business suit *type of* **suit.** [➡GARMENTS AND OUTFITS; 865]

busk *v* **entertain**, perform, sing, play. [➡ENTERTAINMENT; 872]

busker *n* **street entertainer**, street musician, entertainer, performer, musician, singer, street performer. [➡WORKERS IN ENTERTAINMENT AND MEDIA; 873]

busload *n* [➡MANY, MUCH, LARGE AMOUNT; 117]

bust 1 *n* **sculpture**, torso, statue, figure, model. [➡SCULPTURE; 902] 2 *part of* **torso.** [➡TORSO; 694] 3 *n* (*slang*) **raid**, police raid, arrest, seizure, search. [➡THE POLICE, ARREST, AND PRE-TRIAL PROCEEDINGS; 818] 4 *v* (*informal*) **break**, smash, shatter, burst, fracture, rupture, damage. [➡TEAR, BREAK, AND CUT; 361] *Opposite:* mend. 5 *v* (*slang*) **arrest**, capture, take prisoner, apprehend, take into custody, seize, detain, nick (*slang*), catch, stop, take downtown (*US*). [➡THE POLICE, ARREST, AND PRE-TRIAL PROCEEDINGS; 818] 6 *adj* (*informal*) **not working**, out of order, broken, ruined, had it (*informal*), kaput (*informal*), out of action, smashed, busted (*US informal*). [➡IN BAD REPAIR; 1233]

busted (*US informal*) *adj* **broken**, bust (*informal*), kaput (*informal*), out of action, out of order, not working, smashed. [➡IN BAD REPAIR; 1233] *Opposite:* fixed.

bustle 1 *v* **busy yourself**, be on the go, be busy, hurry, rush around, rush, hustle. [➡MOVE FAST; 314] 2 *n* **activity**, movement, stir, hustle and bustle, commotion, flurry, hubbub. [➡CHAOS AND UPROAR; 51] *Opposite:* calm.

bustling *adj* **busy**, active, full of go, full of life, hurried, full of commotion. [➡EMOTIONALLY PLEASANT; 188] *Opposite:* still.

bust-up (*informal*) *n* **argument**, disagreement, fight, split. [➡ARGUMENT; 47]

bust up (*informal*) *v* **split up**, break up, separate, part, break apart, trash (*informal*). [➡REFUSING OR REJECTING RELATIONS; 975] *Opposite:* mend.

busy 1 *adj* **active**, on the go, hard-working, hard at it, diligent, industrious, in demand, occupied, harried. [➡HARD-WORKING AND COMMITTED; 501] *Opposite:* idle. 2 *adj* **full**, full of activity, demanding, hard, tiring, hectic, eventful. [➡DIFFICULTY AND COMPLEXITY; 243] *Opposite:* empty. 3 *adj* **engaged**, occupied, unavailable, taken. [➡ABSENT AND UNAVAILABLE; 7] *Opposite:* free.

busybody (*informal*) *n* **interferer**, nosy parker (*informal*), bigmouth (*informal*), chatterer, meddler, stirrer (*informal*), nuisance, pest (*informal*), gossip, nosy person (*US*). [➡INTERFERING PEOPLE AND TELLTALES; 950]

but 1 *prep* **however**, although, nevertheless, on the contrary. [➡NOT; 135] 2 *prep* **other than**, except, excluding, bar, save for. [➡NOT; 135] 3 *n* (*informal*) **objection**, proviso, provision, rider, condition, if. [➡PROBLEM; 257]

butane *type of* **gas.** [➡GASES; 1274]

butch *adj* **masculine**, tough, strong, muscular, beefy, strapping (*informal*). [➡BUILD; 478]

butcher 1 *n* **killer**, murderer, slaughterer, slayer (*formal or literary*), exterminator. [➡PEOPLE WHO KILL; 924] 2 *v* **slaughter**, murder, kill, exterminate, massacre, assassinate, slay (*formal or literary*). [➡KILL; 923] 3 *v* (*informal*) **botch**, ruin, make a mess of, make a hash of (*informal*), spoil, bungle (*informal*), bodge (*informal*). [➡MESS UP AND MAKE MISTAKES; 473]

butcher's *type of* **food outlet**. [➡RETAIL OUTLETS; 1082]

butcher's knife *type of* **knife**. [➡CUTTING TOOLS; 1119]

butchery *n* **slaughter**, carnage, bloodshed, killing. [➡CAUSES OF DEATH; 921]

buteo (*US*) *type of* **bird of prey**. [➡BIRD OF PREY; 998]

butler *type of* **servant**. [➡DOMESTIC AND KITCHEN WORKERS; 850]

butt 1 *v* **ram**, hit, bump, strike, knock against (*informal*), run into, push. [➡CONTACT: IMPACT; 414] 2 *n* **object**, target, victim, objective, mark, goal. [➡INTENTION AND PURPOSE; 773] 3 *n* **handle**, stock, grip. [➡EXTREMITIES OF PHYSICAL OBJECTS; 1249] 4 *n* **end**, stub, stump, base, nub end. [➡EXTREMITIES OF PHYSICAL OBJECTS; 1249] 5 *n* **barrel**, tub, drum, cask, container, keg. [➡CONTAINERS, RECEPTACLES, AND PACKAGING; 1244]

butte *n* **hill**, foothill, rise, mount, bluff, height. [➡MOUNTAINS AND HILLS; 1044]

butter *type of* **cooking fat and oil**. [➡FATS AND OILS; 1172]

butter bean *type of* **pulse**. [➡BEANS AND PULSES; 1188]

buttercup *type of* **perennial flower**. [➡FLOWERS; 1032]

butterfingered (*informal*) *adj* [➡AGILITY OF THE BODY; 477]

butterflies (*informal*) *n* **nervousness**, nerves (*informal*), excitement, anxiety, tenseness, apprehension. [➡FEAR AND PANIC; 544] *Opposite:* confidence.

butterfly *n type of* **flying insect**. [➡FLYING INSECTS; 1013]

butterfly

◆ *types of butterfly*
cabbage white, Camberwell beauty, emperor butterfly, monarch butterfly, mourning cloak (*US*), painted lady, peacock butterfly, red admiral, swallowtail, cabbage butterfly (*US*), tiger swallowtail, tortoiseshell

butter knife *type of* **cutlery**. [➡TABLEWARE, CUTLERY, AND KITCHENWARE; 861]

butterscotch 1 *type of* **confectionery**. [➡CONFECTIONERY; 1181] 2 *type of* **beige**. [➡COLOURS; 1223]

butter up (*informal*) *v* **sweet-talk** (*informal*), suck up (*informal*), get on the right side of, soft-soap (*informal*), flatter, curry favour. [➡FLATTER AND FAWN; 622] *Opposite:* insult.

but then again *adv* **but**, but then, then again, nonetheless, nevertheless, then, on the other hand. [➡ALTHOUGH, NEVERTHELESS, AND DESPITE; 170]

butt in 1 *v* **interrupt**, break in, cut in, stick your oar in, interfere, interject, stick your nose in. [➡INTERRUPT AND BUTT IN; 620] *Opposite:* mind your own business. 2 *v* **squeeze in**, barge in, shove in, jump the queue, queue-jump, jump the line (*US*), skip the line (*US*). [➡ARRIVE; 12]

buttock *part of* **torso**. [➡TORSO; 694]

button 1 *part of* **garment**. [➡PARTS OF A GARMENT; 870] 2 *n* **push button**, switch, knob, key. [➡PARTS OF MACHINES AND TOOLS; 1117] 3 *n* (*US*) **badge**, pin, brooch. [➡ORNAMENTS AND DECORATIONS; 1247] 4 *v* **fasten**, do up, close. [➡FASTEN, LINK, AND JOIN; 409] *Opposite:* undo.

buttoned-down (*US informal*) *adj* **conservative**, traditional, stuffy, formal, strait-laced, old-fashioned, conventional, strict, narrow-minded. [➡RETICENT AND UNFORTHCOMING; 632] *Opposite:* easygoing.

buttonhole 1 (*informal*) *part of* **garment**. [➡PARTS OF A GARMENT; 870] 2 *n* **flower**, spray, carnation, corsage, boutonniere (*US formal*). [➡ORNAMENTS AND DECORATIONS; 1247] 3 *v* (*informal*) **accost**, waylay, corner, grab, confront, intercept, ambush. [➡INITIATE AND ESTABLISH COMMUNICATION; 681]

button-nosed *adj* [➡FACIAL CHARACTERISTICS; 482]

button up (*informal*) *v* **be quiet**, shut up (*informal*), keep quiet, keep mum (*informal*), be silent, say nothing, stop talking. *Opposite:* blather. (*informal*). [➡WITHHOLD INFORMATION; 688]

buttress 1 *n* **support**, prop, reinforcement, flying buttress, structure. [➡PARTS OF A BUILDING; 1094] 2 *v* **strengthen**, support, prop, prop up, reinforce, shore up, hold up. [➡IMPROVE STRENGTH AND DURABILITY; 379]

butty (*informal*) *n* **sandwich**, sarnie (*informal*), baguette, roll, bagel, wrap, tortilla. [➡PREPARED DISHES; 1169]

buxom (*humorous*) *adj* **plump**, rounded, ample, curvaceous, curvy, shapely, well-rounded, well-padded. [➡BUILD; 478]

buy 1 *v* **pay for**, purchase, acquire, procure, obtain, get, splash out on. [➡PURCHASE; 423] *Opposite:* sell. 2 *v* (*US informal*) **accept**, believe, swallow (*informal*), fall for, credit, subscribe. [➡APPROVE AND CONFIRM; 647] *Opposite:* disbelieve. 3 *n* **purchase**, acquisition, good buy, bad buy, good deal, bad deal, bargain. [➡PURCHASE; 423]

buyer *n* **purchaser**, consumer, shopper, bargain hunter, customer. [➡PURCHASER; 425] *Opposite:* seller.

buy off *v* **bribe**, pay hush money to, induce, corrupt, pay off (*informal*), suborn. [➡CAUSE OR COMPEL TO ACT; 272]

buy out *v* **acquire**, take over, purchase, take control. [➡PURCHASE; 423]

buyout *n* **takeover**, merger, acquisition, purchase. [➡BUSINESS ACTIVITIES AND PHENOMENA; 795]

buzz 1 *n* **noise**, hum, drone, murmur, hubbub. [➡CONTINUOUS SOUNDS; 1257] *Opposite:* silence. 2 *n* (*informal*) **telephone call**, ring, phone call, bell (*informal*), tinkle, call. [➡TELEPHONE COMMUNICATION; 48] 3 *n* (*informal*) **thrill**, high, kick, lift, jolt [➡AMAZING THING; 212]. *Opposite:* downer (*informal*). 4 *n* (*informal*) **gossip**, talk, word, rumour, whisper, information, news, word of mouth. [➡GOSSIP; 679] 5 *v* **hum**, drone, murmur, whine, whirr, hiss. [➡EMIT CONTINUOUS SOUNDS; 367]

buzzard *type of* **bird of prey**. [➡BIRD OF PREY; 998]

buzz cut (*US*) *type of* **hairstyle**. [➡HAIR STYLES AND HAIR PIECES; 489]

buzzer *n* **signal**, bell, beeper (*informal*), bleeper. [➡SIGNALLING; 1139]

buzzing *adj* **busy**, bustling, vibrant, full of life, lively, active, humming. [➡FULL; 1238] *Opposite:* still.

buzz off (*informal*) *v* [➡RUN AWAY AND AVOID; 10]

buzzword (*informal*) *n* **slogan**, catchword, saying, byword, catch phrase, axiom. [➡FIGURES OF SPEECH; 674]

by **1** *prep* **with**, near, next to, beside. [➡RELATIVE LOCATION; 162] **2** *prep* **through**, via, in, by means of, as a result of. [➡RELATED; 143] **3** *prep* **not later than**, before, sooner than. [➡BEFORE, FIRST, AND PRECEDING; 164]

by accident *adv* **unintentionally**, inadvertently, accidentally, fortuitously, coincidentally, by luck, by chance, by a quirk of fate. [➡UNINTENTIONAL AND ACCIDENTAL; 282] *Opposite:* on purpose.

by a hair's-breadth *adv* **hardly**, by a fraction, by a whisker, by a nose, by the skin of your teeth, barely. [➡TO A CERTAIN EXTENT; 134] *Opposite:* easily.

by all accounts *adv* **seemingly**, according to what is being said, apparently, it appears that, the word is that. [➡EXPRESSIONS OF UNCERTAINTY; 561]

by all means *adv* **certainly**, of course, please do. [➡EXPRESSIONS OF AGREEMENT; 649]

by and by (*literary*) *adv* **before long**, eventually, in a short time, in time, in a while, presently, after a while. [➡FUTURE; 86] *Opposite:* immediately.

by and large *adv* **generally**, as a rule, normally, usually, in general, on the whole. [➡USUALLY; 108] *Opposite:* specifically.

by chance *adv* **accidentally**, by accident, unintentionally, inadvertently, coincidentally, unexpectedly, by luck, fortuitously, by coincidence, by a quirk of fate. [➡CHANCE, COINCIDENCE, AND ACCIDENT; 787] *Opposite:* on purpose.

by choice *adv* **by preference**, voluntarily, willingly, of your own free will, eagerly, freely, readily. [➡THE WILL AND WILLINGNESS; 564] *Opposite:* unwillingly.

by coincidence *adv* **by chance**, by a fluke, by a quirk of fate, as luck would have it, coincidentally, unintentionally, accidentally. [➡CHANCE, COINCIDENCE, AND ACCIDENT; 787] *Opposite:* by design.

by degrees *adv* **little by little**, bit by bit, gradually, slowly, a little at a time, progressively, piecemeal, purposefully, with intent. [➡HAPPENING SLOWLY; 106] *Opposite:* at once.

by design *adv* **intentionally**, knowingly, on purpose, purposely, deliberately. [➡INTENTIONAL AND DELIBERATE; 280] *Opposite:* by coincidence.

by dint of *adv* **by means of**, by use of, using, as a result of, because of. [➡WAYS OF DOING THINGS; 295]

bye (*informal*) *interj* **goodbye**, bye-bye (*informal*), cheerio (*informal*), ciao (*informal*), see you (*informal*), so long (*informal*), see you later (*informal*), au revoir, adios (*informal*), ta-ta (*informal*). [➡GREETINGS, FAREWELLS, AND SALUTATIONS; 660] *Opposite:* hello.

bye-bye (*informal*) *see* **bye**

bye-byes (*babytalk*) *n* **sleep**, bed, land of nod (*informal humorous*), beddy-bye (*babytalk*). [➡SLEEP AND DREAM; 724]

bye for now (*informal*) *interj* [➡GREETINGS, FAREWELLS, AND SALUTATIONS; 660]

by-election *n* **election**, general election, local election, poll, ballot. [➡ELECTIONS AND SUFFRAGE; 807]

by far *adv* **considerably**, by a long way, by a long chalk, much, easily, undoubtedly, certainly, without a doubt, beyond a doubt. [➡TO A GREAT EXTENT; 130]

bygone *adj* **past**, former, previous, departed (*formal or literary*), long-gone, olden (*archaic or literary*). [➡PAST; 84] *Opposite:* future.

bygone days *n* [➡PAST; 84]

by heart *adv* **by rote**, from memory, off by heart, off pat, backwards. [➡KNOWLEDGE AND WISDOM; 559]

by hook or by crook *adv* **one way or another**, somehow or other, no matter how, no matter what, no matter what it takes. [➡EXPRESSIONS OF AGREEMENT; 649]

by itself *adv* **of its own accord**, automatically, independently, without help. [➡AUTOMATIC AND INSTINCTIVE; 281]

bylaw *n* **regulation**, rule, ruling, statute, guideline, law. [➡THE LAW AND LEGAL AUTHORITY; 814]

byline *n* **acknowledgement**, credit, heading, strap line. [➡NEWSPAPERS; 606]

by means of *adv* **by**, through, via, using, by way of, by dint of. [➡WAYS OF DOING THINGS; 295]

by mistake *adv* **accidentally**, mistakenly, inadvertently, wrongly, incorrectly, unintentionally, by accident, unexpectedly. [➡UNINTENTIONAL AND ACCIDENTAL; 282] *Opposite:* on purpose.

by nature *adv* **characteristically**, naturally, innately, instinctively, normally, inherently. [➡TRUE AND REAL; 172]

by no means *adv* **not at all**, in no way, not the least bit, not in the slightest, absolutely not. [➡NOT; 135] *Opposite:* absolutely.

bypass **1** *v* **go around**, avoid, get round, find a way round, sidestep, evade, circumvent, detour, skirt. [➡AVOID OR ESCAPE CONTACT; 419] **2** *type of* **major road.** [➡ROADS; 1105]

byproduct *n* **side effect**, spin-off, consequence, result, derivative, offshoot. [➡RESULTS AND OUTCOMES; 83]

byre (*regional*) *n* **cowshed**, shed, barn, milking parlour, stable, outhouse, outbuilding, cow barn (*US*). [➡ANCILLARY BUILDINGS; 1079]

by rights *adv* **in all fairness**, properly, to be fair, if justice were done, correctly, officially, legally. [➡MORALLY GOOD; 775]

byroad *type of* **minor road.** [➡ROADS; 1105]

by rote *adv* **by heart**, off pat, off by heart, from memory. [➡KNOWLEDGE AND WISDOM; 559]

bystander *n* **onlooker**, passer-by, witness, eyewitness, spectator, looker-on. [➡LOOKERS AND SPECTATORS; 702] *Opposite:* participant.

by the way *adv* **incidentally**, parenthetically, in passing, apropos (*formal*), by the by. [➡EXPRESSIONS INTRODUCING EXTRA INFORMATION; 137]

byway *type of* **minor road.** [➡ROADS; 1105]

by way of 1 *adv* **as**, by means of, in place of, as per. [➡REPRESENTATIVE; 66] 2 *adv* **via**, by, through, past. [➡DIRECTION OF MOTION; 346]

byword 1 *n* **embodiment**, perfect example, epitome, shining example. [➡PERFECT EXAMPLES AND EMBODIMENTS; 67] 2 *n* **catch phrase**, proverb, axiom, buzzword (*informal*), slogan, saying. [➡FIGURES OF SPEECH; 674]

by yourself *adv* **on your own**, alone, without help, unaided, single-handed, all by yourself. [➡ACTING INDEPENDENTLY; 285]

Byzantine *type of* **pre-20th-century architecture.** [➡BUILDING AND ARCHITECTURE; 1075]

byzantine 1 *adj* **complex**, intricate, tortuous, convoluted, complicated. [➡DIFFICULTY AND COMPLEXITY; 243] *Opposite:* straightforward. 2 *adj* **devious**, scheming, underhand, deceitful, secretive, plotting, dishonest, calculating. [➡DECEITFUL; 514] *Opposite:* honest.

C

cab 1 *n* **taxi**, taxicab, black cab, hackney cab, hackney carriage, minicab, private hire car, yellow cab (*US*), hack (*US*). [➡VEHICLES; 1144] 2 *n* **cabin**, compartment, cockpit. [➡INTERNAL PARTS OF A VEHICLE; 1145]

cabal 1 *n* **faction**, section, unit, group, sect, clique, cell, league, caucus, ring, gang, band. [➡GROUPS WITH A COMMON INTEREST; 938] 2 *n* **plot**, scheme, conspiracy, artifice (*formal*), connivance, collusion. [➡DECEPTION AND LIES; 661]

cabana (*US*) *n* **bathhouse**, shelter, changing room, change room (*US*). [➡RESIDENTIAL BUILDINGS; 1077]

cabaret 1 *n* **show**, floor show, live entertainment, burlesque. [➡PERFORMANCES AND SHOWS; 42] 2 *n* **nightclub**, club, bar, nightspot. [➡BUILDINGS FOR PUBLIC ENTERTAINMENT; 1083]

cabbage *type of* **vegetable**. [➡FRUIT AND VEGETABLES; 1175]

cabbage butterfly (*US*) *type of* **butterfly**. [➡MOTHS AND BUTTERFLIES; 1015]

cabbage white *type of* **butterfly**. [➡MOTHS AND BUTTERFLIES; 1015]

caber *n* **log**, beam, pole, stick. [➡STICKS, POLES, AND WEDGES; 1253]

cabin 1 *n* **hut**, log cabin, cottage, bungalow, chalet, lodge. [➡RESIDENTIAL BUILDINGS; 1077] 2 *n* **compartment**, cubicle, berth, cab. [➡ALCOVES, CUBICLES, AND COMPARTMENTS; 1095] 3 *part of* **ship or boat**. [➡PARTS OF A SHIP OR BOAT; 1150] 4 *part of* **spacecraft**. [➡SPACE VEHICLES; 1062] 5 *part of* **train**. [➡RAILWAYS; 1106] 6 *part of* **aircraft**. [➡SPACE VEHICLES; 1062]

cabin cruiser *type of* **motor vessel**. [➡SHIPS AND BOATS; 1149]

cabinet

◆ *types of cabinet*
armoire, bookcase, breakfront, bureau, cassone, chest of drawers, china closet, closet, cocktail cabinet, commode, credenza, cupboard, display cabinet, display case, dresser, drinks cabinet, highboy (*US*), lowboy, press, secretary, sideboard, tallboy, wardrobe, whatnot

cabinetmaking *n* [➡CRAFTS AND CARVING; 356]

cable *type of* **telecommunications equipment**. [➡TELECOMMUNICATIONS; 1129]

cable car *type of* **rail vehicle**. [➡RAILWAYS; 1106]

cablegram *n* [➡LETTERS AND WRITTEN MESSAGES; 585]

cable railroad (*US*) *type of* **railway**. [➡RAILWAYS; 1106]

cable railway *type of* **railway**. [➡RAILWAYS; 1106]

cable-stayed bridge *type of* **bridge**. [➡BRIDGES, TUNNELS, CROSSINGS, AND JUNCTIONS; 1111]

caboodle (*informal*) *n* **lot**, whole lot, entirety, totality, integrality, ensemble, the whole kit and caboodle (*informal*), the whole enchilada (*US slang*). [➡ALL; 126]

caboose (*US*) 1 *n* **car**, carriage, wagon, guard's van. [➡BIKES, CARS, AND CARRIAGES; 1148] 2 *part of* **train**. [➡RAILWAYS; 1106]

cache 1 *n* **hoard**, store, accumulation, reserve, collection. [➡COLLECTIONS AND MIXTURES OF THINGS; 1243] 2 *type of* **software**. [➡COMPUTERS AND COMPUTING; 1126] 3 *v* **hide**, hoard, store, secrete, reserve, accumulate, collect. [➡STORE AND KEEP; 454] *Opposite:* discard.

cachet *n* **status**, prestige, distinction, respect, reputation, standing, importance, class, snob value, snob appeal (*US*). [➡STATUS; 888]

cack-handed (*informal*) *adj* **clumsy**, awkward, gauche, maladroit (*formal*), ham-handed (*informal*), ham-fisted (*informal*), uncoordinated, inept, bungling (*informal*). [➡UNSKILLED; 530] *Opposite:* dexterous.

cackle *v* **laugh**, hoot, screech, crow, guffaw, chortle. [➡LAUGHTER; 650]

cacophonous *adj* **discordant**, unmusical, unmelodious, dissonant, inharmonious, jarring, harsh, strident, grating, loud, noisy. [➡LOUD OR UNPLEASANT SOUNDS; 1265] *Opposite:* melodious.

cacophony *n* **discord**, discordance, dissonance, disharmony, unmusicality, harshness, unmelodiousness, stridency, loudness, noise. [➡CHAOS AND UPROAR; 51] *Opposite:* melodiousness.

cad (*dated*) *n* **rogue**, scoundrel, rake, rascal, scallywag (*dated informal*), blackguard. [➡VILLAINS AND THUGS; 947] *Opposite:* gentleman.

CAD *n* **computer-aided design**, computer graphics, graphics, product design, drafting. [➡ARTWORKS; 898]

cadaver *n* **corpse**, dead body, remains, body. [➡DEAD PERSON; 926]

cadaverous 1 *adj* **bony**, skeletal, emaciated, wasted, gaunt, thin. [➡BUILD; 478] *Opposite:* healthy. 2 *adj* (*literary*) **pale**, pallid, wan, ashen, ghastly (*literary*). [➡COMPLEXION; 481] *Opposite:* rosy. 3 *adj* (*formal or literary*) **corpselike**, deathly, deathlike, skeletal, spectral, macabre. [➡UNFIT AND WEAK; 740]

caddie 1 *n* **assistant**, porter, carrier, transporter. [➡PEOPLE IN SPORTS AND LEISURE; 876] 2 *v* **transport**, assist, carry. [➡PUSH, PULL, SLIDE; 336]

caddish *adj* **dishonourable**, ungallant, rascally, rakish, ungentlemanly. [➡BAD MANNERS AND SOCIAL SKILLS; 522] *Opposite:* gallant.

caddy *n* **container**, tin, box, receptacle, carton, casket, coffer, chest, tea caddy. [➡CONTAINERS, RECEPTACLES, AND PACKAGING; 1244]

cadence 1 *n* **tempo**, rhythm, pace, pulse, stroke, beat. [➡SPEED; 102] 2 *n* **lilt**, intonation, accent, modulation, inflection, tone. [➡THE SPOKEN WORD; 672]

cadenza *n* **solo passage**, improvisation, solo, unaccompanied passage, showpiece, run of notes, roulade, riff. [➡MUSICAL TERMS; 912]

cadet *n* **trainee**, police cadet, army cadet, sea cadet, plebe (*US*). [➡STUDENTS AND PUPILS; 841]

cadge (*informal*) *v* [➡OBTAIN POSSESSION BY PERSUASION; 458]

cadger (*informal*) *n* **scrounger** (*informal*), moocher (*informal*), sponger (*informal*), borrower, ligger (*informal*), freeloader (*informal*), beggar. [➡LAZY OR UNSUCCESSFUL PEOPLE; 948]

cadre 1 *n* **squad**, corps, unit, team, band, company, crew, force, troop, nucleus. [➡GROUPS OF PEOPLE; 935] 2 *n* **faction**, group, core, hard core, band, set, bloc, clique. [➡GROUPS WITH A COMMON INTEREST; 938]

caecum *part of* **digestive tract**. [➡THE DIGESTIVE TRACT; 710]

caerphilly *type of* **hard cheese**. [➡DAIRY PRODUCTS AND CHEESES; 1182]

café *type of* **eating place**. [➡HOTELS, RESTAURANTS, AND CLUBS; 1081]

café au lait 1 *type of* **coffee**. [➡DRINKS; 1186] 2 *type of* **beige**. [➡COLOURS; 1223]

café noir *type of* **coffee**. [➡DRINKS; 1186]

café society *n* [➡RICH PEOPLE; 895]

cafeteria *type of* **eating place**. [➡HOTELS, RESTAURANTS, AND CLUBS; 1081]

caffè latte *type of* **coffee**. [➡DRINKS; 1186]

cage 1 *n* **enclosure**, coop, pen, birdcage, crate. [➡ANIMAL OR BIRD ACCOMMODATION; 1078] 2 *v* **confine**, enclose, pen, coop up, impound, shut in, fence in, lock in, hem in. [➡CAPTIVITY AND LOSS OF FREEDOM; 249] *Opposite:* release.

cage

◆ *types of pen or cage*
apiary, aquarium, aviary, beehive, birdcage, chicken coop, chicken run, coop, corral (*US*), cowshed, doghouse (*US*), dovecote, henhouse, hutch, kennel, piggery, pigsty, pound, stable, stall, sty

caged *adj* **captive**, detained, confined, imprisoned, incarcerated (*formal*), jailed, behind bars, in prison, locked up, interned, put away (*informal*), trapped, inside (*informal*), shut in, constricted, restrained. [➡CAPTIVITY AND LOSS OF FREEDOM; 249] *Opposite:* free.

cagey (*informal*) *adj* **wary**, guarded, cautious, careful, reticent, evasive, secretive, chary. [➡INSECURITY AND LOSS OF COMPOSURE; 545] *Opposite:* reckless.

cagily (*informal*) *adv* **warily**, guardedly, cautiously, carefully, reticently, evasively, secretively. [➡INSECURITY AND LOSS OF COMPOSURE; 545] *Opposite:* recklessly.

caginess (*informal*) *n* **wariness**, caution, reticence, evasiveness, chariness, shrewdness, cautiousness. [➡INSECURITY AND LOSS OF COMPOSURE; 545] *Opposite:* recklessness.

cagoule *n* **waterproof jacket**, cag (*informal*), anorak, windcheater, parka, raincoat, mac (*informal*), mackintosh (*dated*). [➡GARMENTS AND OUTFITS; 865]

cairn 1 *n* **landmark**, marker, waymark, signpost, direction post, milestone. [➡SIGNPOSTS, SIGNALS AND BILLBOARDS; 596] 2 *n* **memorial**, monument, barrow, tomb, tombstone, gravestone, tablet, slab. [➡MONUMENTS; 1091]

cajole *v* **coax**, persuade, wheedle, entice, sweet-talk (*informal*), inveigle, flatter. [➡CAUSE OR COMPEL TO ACT; 272] *Opposite:* compel.

cajolery *n* [➡INGRATIATING; 639]

cake 1 *n* **gateau**, pastry, fancy. [➡CAKES, BISCUITS, AND DESSERTS; 1180] 2 *n* **bar**, block, slab, lump, tablet, cube, loaf. [➡AMOUNT OF SOLID OR SEMI-SOLID; 115] 3 *v* **cover**, coat, encrust, congeal, coagulate. [➡DECORATE, ADORN, AND APPLY COATINGS; 406]

cake

◆ *types of cake*
brownie, carrot cake, cheesecake, Christmas cake, coffee cake, cupcake, Danish pastry, devil's food cake, doughnut, éclair, flapjack, fruitcake, gateau, gingerbread, jelly roll (*US*), macaroon, Madeira cake, madeleine, mince pie, muffin, seedcake, sponge cake, Swiss roll, turnover, wedding cake

caked *adj* **covered**, coated, encrusted, layered. [➡FULL; 1238]

cakehole (*slang*) *n* [➡THE MOUTH; 703]

cake slice *type of* **cutlery**. [➡TABLEWARE, CUTLERY, AND KITCHENWARE; 861]

cakewalk (*informal*) *n* **child's play**, kid's stuff, cinch (*informal*), piece of cake (*informal*), doddle (*informal*), easy victory, runaway victory, pushover (*informal*), walkover (*informal*). [➡EASY WORK; 300]

calamitous *adj* **disastrous**, dreadful, catastrophic, ruinous, tragic, cataclysmic, devastating, appalling, shattering, earth-shattering, frightful, terrible, dire. [➡EMOTIONALLY UNPLEASANT AND UPSETTING; 228] *Opposite:* beneficial.

calamity *n* **disaster**, catastrophe, mishap, misfortune, tragedy, blow. [➡DISASTERS; 253]

calcified *adj* [➡RIGID AND HARD; 1210]

calcify *v* **harden**, set, solidify, fossilize, turn into stone, petrify. [➡HARDEN, CONGEAL, DRY; 388] *Opposite:* soften.

calculable *adj* **predictable**, anticipated, expected, foreseeable, likely, knowable. [➡POSSIBLE AND PROBABLE; 178] *Opposite:* unpredictable.

calculate *v* **work out**, compute, analyse, estimate, weigh up, gauge, determine, reckon, evaluate, assess. [➡ASSESS QUANTITY; 758]

calculated *adj* **intended**, designed, planned, considered, premeditated, deliberate. [➡INTENTIONAL AND DELIBERATE; 280] *Opposite:* spontaneous.

calculating *adj* **scheming**, manipulative, devious, shrewd, conniving, cunning. [➡DECEITFUL; 514] *Opposite:* candid.

calculatingly *adv* **intentionally**, deliberately, knowingly, shrewdly, purposefully, deviously, cunningly. [➡INTENTIONAL AND DELIBERATE; 280] *Opposite:* candidly.

calculation 1 *n* **computation**, estimate, reckoning, sum, result, answer. [➡MATHS; 598] 2 *n* **control**, cunning, scheming, intention, design, shrewdness, deviousness. [➡INTENTION AND PURPOSE; 773] *Opposite:* candidness.

calculator *type of* **computer.** [➡COMPUTERS AND COMPUTING; 1126]

calculus *n* [➡MATHS; 598]

calendar *n* **diary**, schedule, year planner, timetable, agenda, datebook (*US*). [➡LISTS AND SCHEDULES; 588]

calendar month *type of* **time period.** [➡TIMES OF YEAR; 88]

calf 1 *type of* **young animal.** [➡YOUNG ANIMAL; 977] 2 *type of* **leather.** [➡FABRICS; 1131] 3 *part of* **leg or foot.** [➡LEG AND FOOT; 695]

calfskin *type of* **leather.** [➡FABRICS; 1131]

calibrate *v* **standardize**, adjust, regulate, attune, bring into line, rectify. [➡CORRECT AND PUT RIGHT; 378]

calibration 1 *n* **standardization**, correction, adjustment, tuning, setting, regulation. [➡CHANGE; 373] 2 *n* **graduation**, gradation, mark, measurement, degree, point. [➡SCORES AND EVALUATIONS; 599]

calibre 1 *n* **quality**, ability, capacity, talent, competence, capability, standard, level, stature. [➡SKILLS, TALENTS, AND ABILITIES; 527] 2 *n* **size**, bore, diameter, gauge, measure, magnitude, dimension. [➡SIZE AND DIMENSIONS; 1191]

calico *type of* **fabric from plants.** [➡FABRICS; 1131]

call 1 *v* **name**, describe, identify, entitle, label, term, dub, christen, baptize. [➡NAME AND DESCRIBE; 666] 2 *v* **shout**, cry out, scream, yell, call out, exclaim, cry. [➡UTTER AND PRONOUNCE; 609] 3 *v* **request**, summon, call on, invite, beckon, appeal, ask. [➡REQUEST AND DEMAND; 664] 4 *v* **phone**, give a call, telephone, call up, phone up, ring, give a bell (*informal*), give a buzz (*informal*). [➡TELEPHONE AND PAGE; 682] 5 *v* **visit**, call on, pay a visit, drop in, stop off, pop in (*informal*), go to see, stop by, call by, come round, call in, look up, look in, come around (*US*). [➡INITIATE AND ESTABLISH COMMUNICATION; 681] 6 *v* **arrange**, convene, set up, organize, assemble, gather, summon. [➡CAUSE TO HAPPEN; 31] 7 *n* **noise**, shout, cry, sound. [➡SOUNDS MADE BY PEOPLE; 1261] 8 *n* **song**, cry, birdsong. [➡SOUNDS MADE BY BIRDS; 1262] 9 *n* **phone call**, telephone call, buzz (*informal*), bell (*informal*), ring. [➡TELEPHONE COMMUNICATION; 48] 10 *n* **visit**, stop, halt. [➡ARRIVAL; 13] 11 *n* **demand**, request, plea, appeal, bid, invitation. [➡REQUEST AND DEMAND; 664] 12 *n* **judgment**, verdict, decision, assessment, ruling, say. [➡TRIAL, PUNISHMENT, AND LEGAL OUTCOMES; 819]

call a halt *v* **end**, stop, halt, bring to an end, terminate (*formal*), close, call it a day, finish, give up, break off, quit, call off. [➡CAUSE TO STOP; 267] *Opposite:* start up.

call a spade a spade *v* **be direct**, speak plainly, be blunt, speak your mind, lay it on the line (*informal*). [➡NAME AND DESCRIBE; 666] *Opposite:* prevaricate.

call attention to *v* **make known**, draw attention to, expose, publicize, highlight, point out. [➡CAUSE TO APPEAR; 5] *Opposite:* conceal.

call by *v* **visit**, stop by, come round, drop in, pop in (*informal*), call in, come by, stop off, look in, come around (*US*). [➡INITIATE AND ESTABLISH COMMUNICATION; 681]

call down 1 *v* **invoke**, invite, request, appeal, pray, imprecate (*formal*). [➡REQUEST AND DEMAND; 664] 2 *v* **cause**, provoke, instigate, generate, produce. [➡CAUSE TO HAPPEN; 31] 3 *v* (*US*) **reprimand**, rebuke, reproach, chide (*literary*), admonish, scold, denounce. [➡ACCUSE, BLAME, AND CRITICIZE; 642] *Opposite:* praise.

caller *n* **visitor**, guest, friend. [➡FRIENDS; 963]

call for 1 *v* **order**, demand, claim, clamour, request, ask. [➡REQUEST AND DEMAND; 664] 2 *v* **need**, require, justify, necessitate, cry out for, order, be in need of, demand, claim. [➡REQUEST AND DEMAND; 664]

call forth *v* [➡CAUSE TO HAPPEN; 31]

calligraphy *n* **handwriting**, hand, writing, script, print, lettering. [➡WRITING; 584]

call in 1 *v* **phone**, ring, telephone, give a call, phone up, give a buzz (*informal*), give a ring, give a bell (*informal*). [➡TELEPHONE AND PAGE; 682] 2 *v* **visit**, pop in (*informal*), drop in, drop by, come by, come round, stop by, call by, look in, stop off, come around (*US*). [➡ARRIVE; 12] 3 *v* **recall**, call back, pull in, take off the market. [➡REGAIN POSSESSION; 430] 4 *v* **summon**, invite in, call for, send for, bring in, have in. [➡CAUSE OR COMPEL TO ACT; 272]

call-in (*US*) *type of* **broadcast.** [➡TELEVISION AND RADIO; 607]

calling *n* **vocation**, profession, occupation, business, work, mission. [➡PROFESSIONS; 845]

call into question *v* **query**, question, dispute, challenge, doubt, contest. [➡QUESTION THINGS; 752] *Opposite:* accept.

callipers *type of* **measuring device.** [➡MEASURING DEVICES; 1122]

callisthenics *n* **exercise system**, keep fit, exercises, aerobics, step aerobics, isometrics, stretching, training, working-out, gymnastics. [➡HOBBIES, GAMES, AND SPORTS; 875]

call it a day *v* **stop**, finish, end, give up, break off, quit, call a halt, call off, bring to an end, halt. [➡STOP ACTING; 265] *Opposite:* start up.

call it quits (*informal*) *v* [➡STOP ACTING; 265]

call names *v* **insult**, abuse, hurl insults at, taunt, bait, rib (*informal*), laugh at, jeer at, mock, tease. [➡INSULTS, ABUSE, AND SWEARING; 659] *Opposite:* compliment.

call off *v* **cancel**, stop, abandon, suspend, shelve, break off, halt. [➡CAUSE TO STOP; 267]

call on 1 *v* **ask**, request, appeal to, urge, entreat (*formal*), implore (*formal*), bid (*archaic*), beg, invite. [➡REQUEST AND DEMAND; 664] 2 *v* **visit**, drop in on, go to see, look up, look in on, call in on. [➡INITIATE AND ESTABLISH COMMUNICATION; 681]

callous *adj* **heartless**, unfeeling, cold-hearted, hard-hearted, uncaring, insensitive, unsympathetic, cold, cruel, pitiless, hard, thick-skinned. [➡SELFISH AND UNKIND; 506] *Opposite:* warm-hearted.

calloused *adj* **hard**, hardened, hard-skinned, rough, rough-skinned, tough-skinned, horny. [➡CONDITIONS AFFECTING THE SKIN; 722] *Opposite:* soft.

callousness *n* **heartlessness**, insensitivity, cruelty, coldness, cold-heartedness, hardheartedness, pitilessness. [➡SELFISH AND UNKIND; 506] *Opposite:* warm-heartedness.

call out 1 *v* **summon**, call for, get, phone up, page. [➡INITIATE AND ESTABLISH COMMUNICATION; 681] 2 *v* **shout out**, exclaim, call, yell, make a noise, holler (*informal*), cry out. [➡UTTER AND PRONOUNCE; 609]

call out for *v* **demand**, clamour, be in dire need of, require, request, beg, cry out, need, necessitate, justify, claim. [➡REQUEST AND DEMAND; 664]

callow *adj* **inexperienced**, immature, naïve, adolescent, green, raw, youthful. [➡UNSKILLED; 530] *Opposite:* mature.

callowness *n* [➡NEGATIVE INTELLECTUAL CHARACTERISTICS; 526]

call together *v* **summon**, convene, hold, gather, collect, round up, muster, assemble. [➡COMBINE AND MIX; 401] *Opposite:* disperse.

call to mind *v* **evoke**, recall, recollect, suggest, call up, stir up memories of, invoke, remind. [➡REMIND; 748] *Opposite:* forget.

call-up *n* **conscription**, mobilization, recruitment, enlistment, muster, call-to-arms, levy, national service, draft (*US*). [➡WARFARE AND WAR; 830] *Opposite:* demobilization.

call up *v* **phone**, give a ring, call, telephone, phone up, ring, give a bell (*informal*), give a buzz (*informal*). [➡TELEPHONE AND PAGE; 682]

call upon 1 *v* **ask**, request, appeal to, urge, entreat (*formal*), implore (*formal*), bid (*archaic*), beg, invite. [➡REQUEST AND DEMAND; 664] 2 *v* **make demands on**, summon up, use, call for, demand, require. [➡REQUEST AND DEMAND; 664]

callus *n* **hard skin**, corn, bump, lump, nodule. [➡CONDITIONS AFFECTING THE SKIN; 722]

calm 1 *adj* **tranquil**, peaceful, still, cool, composed, unruffled, serene, relaxed, quiet. [➡CALMNESS, CONFIDENCE, AND COMPOSURE; 537] *Opposite:* agitated. 2 *n* **peace**, tranquillity, quietness, stillness, calmness, coolness, composure, serenity. [➡CALMNESS, CONFIDENCE, AND COMPOSURE; 537] *Opposite:* turbulence. 3 *v* **pacify**, calm down, quieten, quieten down, soothe, settle down, appease, subside. [➡SOOTHE AND CALM; 574] *Opposite:* excite.

calmative *adj* **calming**, soothing, pacifying, quietening, relaxing, sedative, palliative, comforting, tranquillizing, quieting (*US*). [➡EMOTIONALLY PLEASANT; 188] *Opposite:* disturbing.

calm down *v* **settle down**, relax, soothe, quieten, quieten down, pacify. [➡CHANGE OF MOOD AND COMPOSURE; 581] *Opposite:* agitate.

calming *adj* **soothing**, reassuring, comforting, restful, sedative, relaxing, calmative, palliative, quietening, quieting (*US*). [➡CALMING; 189] *Opposite:* disturbing.

calmness *n* **serenity**, tranquillity, quietness, stillness, peace, coolness, calm, composure. [➡CALMNESS, CONFIDENCE, AND COMPOSURE; 537] *Opposite:* restlessness.

calumny (*formal*) *n* **slander**, defamation, denigration, libel, lies, misrepresentation, lie, slur, smear. [➡INSULTS, ABUSE, AND SWEARING; 659]

calve *v* **give birth**, drop, reproduce, produce. [➡REPRODUCTION AND HEREDITY; 726]

calypso *type of* **popular music**. [➡MUSIC, SONGS, AND SINGING; 907]

cam *part of* **engine**. [➡PARTS OF AN ENGINE; 1143]

camaraderie *n* **friendship**, amity (*formal*), companionship, solidarity, company, comradeship. [➡RELATIONSHIP TO ANOTHER; 973] *Opposite:* enmity.

Camberwell beauty *type of* **butterfly**. [➡MOTHS AND BUTTERFLIES; 1015]

camcorder *type of* **video equipment**. [➡PHOTOGRAPHY AND PHOTOGRAPHIC EQUIPMENT; 1121]

camel 1 *type of* **large mammal**. [➡LARGE MAMMAL; 986] 2 *type of* **beige**. [➡COLOURS; 1223]

camelback (*US*) *adj* **arched**, humped, curved, rounded. [➡ROUNDED SHAPE; 1217] *Opposite:* flat.

camel hair *type of* **fabric from animals**. [➡FABRICS; 1131]

camellia *type of* **shrub or bush**. [➡BUSHES AND SHRUBS; 1027]

Camembert *type of* **soft cheese**. [➡DAIRY PRODUCTS AND CHEESES; 1182]

cameo 1 *n* **character part**, cameo role, appearance, role, part, walk-on. [➡IN THE THEATRE; 906] 2 *type of* **jewellery**. [➡JEWELLERY; 866]

camera *type of* **photographic equipment**. [➡PHOTOGRAPHY AND PHOTOGRAPHIC EQUIPMENT; 1121]

camera-shy *adj* **reclusive**, retiring, reserved, private, aloof, shy. [➡RETICENT AND UNFORTHCOMING; 632] *Opposite:* extrovert.

camiknickers *type of* **lower body underwear**. [➡HABERDASHERY, MILLINERY, AND LINGERIE; 867]

camisole *type of* **upper body underwear**. [➡HABERDASHERY, MILLINERY, AND LINGERIE; 867]

camomile *type of* **herb**. [➡HERBS AND SPICES; 1174]

camouflage 1 *n* **concealment**, disguise, smoke screen, cover-up, façade. [➡COVERS AND COATINGS; 1245] 2 *v* **disguise**, mask, hide, conceal, obscure. [➡CAUSE TO DISAPPEAR; 6]

camp 1 *n* **site**, campsite, encampment, base camp, holiday camp, campground (*US*). [➡HUMAN SETTLEMENTS; 1069] 2 *n* **group**, faction, followers, clique, supporters, cohorts. [➡GROUPS WITH A COMMON INTEREST; 938] 3 *v* **go camping**, camp out, sleep out. [➡HOBBIES, GAMES, AND SPORTS; 875]

campaign 1 *n* **movement**, crusade, operation, drive, fight, battle, war, promotion. [➡HARD WORK OR EFFORT; 299] 2 *v* **fight**, work, push, struggle, battle. [➡COMPETE, CONTEND, AND COMBAT;

304] 3 *v* **electioneer**, canvass, drum up support, solicit votes, stump, crusade, run. [➡ELECTIONS AND SUFFRAGE; 807]

campaigner *n* **activist**, crusader, fighter, supporter, champion, promoter. [➡DEVOTEES AND ADDICTED PEOPLE; 557]

campanile *n* [➡TOWERS; 1098]

camp bed *type of* **bed.** [➡FURNITURE; 858]

camper 1 *n* **holidaymaker**, vacationer (*US*), vacationist (*US*). [➡PEOPLE IN SPORTS AND LEISURE; 876] 2 *type of* **leisure vehicle.** [➡VEHICLES; 1144]

camper van *type of* **leisure vehicle.** [➡VEHICLES; 1144]

campground (*US*) *n* **encampment**, camping area, campsite (*UK*). [➡THE COUNTRYSIDE AND OUTDOOR SPACES; 1070]

camping area *n* [➡THE COUNTRYSIDE AND OUTDOOR SPACES; 1070]

camp robber (*US regional*) *type of* **common bird.** [➡BIRD; 997]

campsite (*UK*) 1 *n* **encampment**, camping area, campground (*US*). [➡THE COUNTRYSIDE AND OUTDOOR SPACES; 1070] 2 *n* (*US*) **area**, pitch, site, place. [➡THE COUNTRYSIDE AND OUTDOOR SPACES; 1070]

campus *n* **grounds**, precincts, site, property, estate. [➡URBAN OUTDOOR SPACES; 1071]

camshaft *part of* **engine.** [➡PARTS OF AN ENGINE; 1143]

can 1 *v* (*US slang*) **dismiss**, fire (*informal*), sack (*informal*), discharge (*formal*), give notice, let go, lay off, terminate (*US*). [➡REVOKE STATUS; 460] *Opposite:* hire. 2 *type of* **container.** [➡CONTAINERS, RECEPTACLES, AND PACKAGING; 1244]

Canada goose *type of* **freshwater bird.** [➡FRESHWATER BIRD; 1000]

canal 1 *n* **waterway**, channel, seaway. [➡WATERWAYS AND SEAWAYS; 1107] 2 *n* **duct**, tube, passage, vessel. [➡WATERCOURSES; 1110]

canal boat *type of* **motor vessel.** [➡SHIPS AND BOATS; 1149]

canalize (*formal*) *v* **direct**, channel, funnel, guide, convey, conduct, lead, focus, concentrate. [➡MOVE SOMETHING TO ANOTHER LOCATION; 325] *Opposite:* diffuse.

canapé *part of* **meal.** [➡MEALS AND PARTS OF MEALS; 1168]

canard (*literary*) *n* [➡JOKES AND TEASING; 675]

canary *type of* **pet bird.** [➡BIRD; 997]

canary yellow *type of* **yellow.** [➡COLOURS; 1223]

cancan *type of* **dance.** [➡DANCE; 903]

cancel 1 *v* **call off**, stop, abandon, withdraw, scratch. [➡CAUSE TO STOP; 267] 2 *v* **annul**, revoke, terminate (*formal*), stop, rescind, repeal. [➡ABOLISH AND ANNUL; 453]

cancelled *adj* [➡NOT HAPPENING; 34]

cancel out *v* **negate** (*formal*), efface, nullify, undo, contradict, neutralize, work against. [➡MAKE IMPOSSIBLE; 277]

cancer 1 *n* **growth**, tumour, malignancy, disease, melanoma, sarcoma. [➡ILLNESSES AND DISORDERS; 733] 2 *n* **evil**, blight, scourge, canker, pest (*informal*), plague, menace, corruption, disease, bane. [➡NUISANCES; 254]

Cancer *type of* **star sign.** [➡FATE, DESTINY, AND ASTROLOGY; 783]

cancerous 1 *adj* **tumorous**, malignant, carcinomatous, carcinogenic, oncogenic, diseased. [➡SICKNESS; 730] *Opposite:* benign. 2 *adj* **harmful**, pernicious, malign, malignant, noxious, damaging, deleterious (*formal*), destructive, cankerous. [➡DANGEROUS; 237] *Opposite:* beneficent.

candelabrum *n* **candleholder**, candlestick, chandelier, lamp holder, lamp, light fitting. [➡LIGHTING; 862]

candid *adj* **honest**, frank, open, truthful, sincere, blunt, straight, outspoken, forthright, straightforward, upfront. [➡HONEST AND OPEN; 631] *Opposite:* guarded.

candida *type of* **microorganism.** [➡MICROORGANISMS, FUNGI, AND ALGAE; 1023]

candidacy *n* **application**, contention, entry, submission, candidature, standing. [➡ELECTIONS AND SUFFRAGE; 807]

candidate *n* **applicant**, contender, entrant, runner, aspirant, nominee, contestant. [➡COMPETITORS; 41]

Compare and Contrast: ***candidate, contender, contestant, aspirant, applicant, entrant, runner***

CORE MEANING: SOMEBODY WHO IS SEEKING TO BE CHOSEN FOR SOMETHING OR TO WIN SOMETHING

candidate somebody who is being considered for a job, grant, or prize, standing for election, or taking part in an examination; ***contender*** a competitior, especially somebody who has a good chance of winning; ***contestant*** somebody who takes part in a contest or competitive event; ***aspirant*** somebody aspiring to distinction or advancement; ***applicant*** somebody who has formally applied to be a candidate for something; ***entrant*** somebody who enters an examination or contest; ***runner*** a candidate in an election.

candidness *n* **honesty**, frankness, openness, truthfulness, bluntness, straightforwardness, outspokenness, candour. [➡HONEST AND OPEN; 631]

candied *adj* **crystallized**, glacé, preserved, sugar-coated, sugared, iced, glazed. [➡STATE OF PREPARED FOOD; 1170]

candle *n* **taper**, nightlight, rush light, rush candle, rush, wax light, torch, tallow candle, birthday candle, cake candle. [➡LIGHTING; 862]

candlelight *n* **dim light**, soft light, low light, glow, glimmer, flicker, glim. [➡LIGHT; 1163]

candlelit *adj* **dimly lit**, softly lit, low-lit. [➡DESCRIBING LIGHT; 1227]

candlestick *n* **candleholder**, candelabrum, chandelier, sconce. [➡LIGHTING; 862]

can-do (*informal*) *adj* **positive**, willing, go-getting (*informal*), upbeat (*informal*), confident, ambitious, eager, keen. [➡CONFIDENCE AND COMPOSURE; 500] *Opposite:* diffident.

candour *n* **frankness**, forthrightness, directness, candidness, outspokenness, bluntness, honesty. [➡HONEST AND OPEN; 631]

candy (*US*) *type of* **confectionery.** [➡CONFECTIONERY; 1181]

candy apple (*US*) *type of* **confectionery on a stick.** [➡CONFECTIONERY; 1181]

candyfloss *type of* **confectionery on a stick.** [➡CONFECTIONERY; 1181]

candy store (*US*) *type of* **food outlet.** [➡RETAIL OUTLETS; 1082]

candy-striped *adj* **striped**, stripy, pink-and-white striped. [➡DESCRIBING PATTERNS; 1226]

cane 1 *n* **bamboo**, wicker, rattan. [➡PLANT MATERIALS; 1132] 2 *n* **stick**, walking stick, staff. [➡STICKS, POLES, AND WEDGES; 1253] 3 *v* **beat**, thrash, strike, hit, punish. [➡WHIP AND CLUB; 418]

cane toad *type of* **amphibian.** [➡AMPHIBIANS; 1008]

canine 1 *adj* **doggy**, doglike, doggish. [➡DOG; 980] 2 *n* (*humorous*) **dog**, pooch (*informal*), mongrel, bow-wow (*babytalk*), cur, hound. [➡DOG; 980] 3 *type of* **tooth.** [➡THE MOUTH; 703]

canine

◆ *types of canine*
aardwolf, coyote, dingo, dog, fox, hyena, jackal, wolf

canister *n* **container**, can, tin, flask, cylinder. [➡CONTAINERS, RECEPTACLES, AND PACKAGING; 1244]

canker *n* **evil**, cancer, scourge, blight, pest (*informal*), plague, menace, bane, corruption, disease, malignancy. [➡NUISANCES; 254]

canned 1 *adj* **tinned**, preserved, conserved. [➡STATE OF PREPARED FOOD; 1170] *Opposite:* fresh. 2 *adj* **prerecorded**, recorded, taped, reproduced, artificial, synthetic, nonspontaneous. [➡FALSE AND UNREAL; 174] *Opposite:* live.

cannelloni *type of* **pasta.** [➡PASTA; 1179]

cannery *type of* **factory.** [➡INDUSTRIAL BUILDINGS; 1086]

canniness *n* [➡POSITIVE INTELLECTUAL CHARACTERISTICS; 525]

cannon *type of* **gun.** [➡WEAPONS FOR SHOOTING; 1155]

cannonade *n* **barrage**, bombardment, hail, onslaught, pounding, volley. [➡SUDDEN EVENT; 52]

cannonball *n* **projectile**, missile, ball, stone, grapeshot, shot, chain shot, shell. [➡PROJECTILES; 1158]

canny *adj* **shrewd**, clever, astute, smart, careful, cunning, sly, wily, crafty. [➡POSITIVE INTELLECTUAL CHARACTERISTICS; 525]

canoe *type of* **small vessel.** [➡SHIPS AND BOATS; 1149]

canola oil *type of* **cooking fat and oil.** [➡FATS AND OILS; 1172]

canonical *adj* **official**, recognized, acknowledged, established, undisputed, undoubted, unquestioned, uncontested, canonic. [➡TRUE AND REAL; 172] *Opposite:* apocryphal.

canonization 1 *n* **making into a saint**, beatification, sanctification, consecration, hallowing, blessing. [➡RELIGIONS AND RELIGIOUS PRACTICES; 778] 2 *n* **idolization**, glorification, adoration, worship, adulation, veneration. [➡FADS, FETISHES, AND IDOLATRY; 556]

canonize 1 *v* **make into a saint**, beatify, sanctify, consecrate, hallow, bless. [➡CONFER STATUS; 459] 2 *v* **idolize**, glorify, adore, worship, venerate, revere. [➡LIKE, LOVE, VALUE AND ENJOY; 579]

canoodle (*informal*) *v* **smooch** (*informal*), carry on, neck (*dated*), kiss and cuddle, pet, snog (*slang*), make out (*US slang*). [➡PHYSICAL CONTACT AS COMMUNICATION; 656]

can opener *type of* **utensil.** [➡TABLEWARE, CUTLERY, AND KITCHENWARE; 861]

canopy 1 *n* **awning**, cover, covering, shelter, blind, shade, sunshade. [➡COVERS AND COATINGS; 1245] 2 *n* **top**, crown, roof, covering, cover. [➡PARTS OF TREES AND PLANTS; 1026]

cant 1 *n* **clichés**, platitudes, banalities, commonplaces, triteness, corniness. [➡MEANINGLESS SPEECH OR WRITING; 677] 2 *n* **hypocrisy**, insincerity, false piety, humbug, lip service, tokenism. [➡DECEPTION AND LIES; 661] *Opposite:* sincerity. 3 *n* **jargon**, lingo (*informal*), slang, argot, patois, vernacular, blather (*informal*). [➡MEANINGLESS SPEECH OR WRITING; 677]

cantankerous *adj* [➡DIFFICULT TO PLEASE; 516]

cantankerousness *n* [➡DIFFICULT TO PLEASE; 516]

cantata *type of* **vocal music.** [➡MUSIC, SONGS, AND SINGING; 907]

canteen *type of* **eating place.** [➡HOTELS, RESTAURANTS, AND CLUBS; 1081]

canter 1 *n* **trot**, run, gallop, jog, sprint. [➡PROCEED AND GO; 306] 2 *v* **run**, gallop, trot, jog, sprint. [➡MOVE FAST; 314]

canticle *type of* **vocal music.** [➡MUSIC, SONGS, AND SINGING; 907]

cantilever *n* **beam**, plank, girder. [➡BUILDING MATERIALS; 1076]

cantilever bridge *type of* **bridge.** [➡BRIDGES, TUNNELS, CROSSINGS, AND JUNCTIONS; 1111]

canto *n* **stanza**, verse, strophe, section, division, segment, part. [➡POETRY AND VERSE; 915]

canton *n* **region**, district, area, borough, constituency, parish, province. [➡COUNTRIES AND REGIONS; 1066]

canvas 1 *n* **painting**, oil painting, picture, old master, work of art, image, work, piece, opus. [➡ARTWORKS; 898] 2 *n* **background**, backdrop, setting, context, scene, panorama, overview. [➡SITUATIONS; 71] 3 *type of* **fabric from plants.** [➡FABRICS; 1131]

canvasback *type of* **freshwater bird.** [➡FRESHWATER BIRD; 1000]

canvass 1 *v* **campaign**, electioneer, drum up support, solicit votes, stump, crusade, appeal. [➡ELECTIONS AND SUFFRAGE; 807] 2 *v* **test**, research, investigate, survey, poll, ballot, circularize. [➡QUESTION THINGS; 752]

canvasser 1 *n* **campaigner**, supporter, party worker. [➡DEVOTEES AND ADDICTED PEOPLE; 557] 2 *n* **researcher**, investigator, examiner, pollster. [➡QUESTIONERS; 668]

canyon *n* **ravine**, gully, gorge, chasm, rift, gulch (*US*), coulee (*US*). [➡GEOLOGICAL FEATURES; 1056]

cap 1 *n* **cover**, lid, top, stopper, plug. [➡COVERS AND COATINGS; 1245] 2 *n* **limit**, restraint, control, restriction, check, ceiling, threshold. [➡EXTREMITIES OF PHYSICAL OBJECTS; 1249] 3 *v* **cover**, top, stop, plug, overlay. [➡DECORATE, ADORN, AND APPLY COATINGS; 406] **4** *v* **surpass**, top, improve, better, outdo, outshine, excel. [➡BEAT AND DEFEAT; 80] **5** *v* **limit**, regulate, control, restrain, restrict, check. [➡CHANGE OF SIZE: SMALLER; 394] **6** *type of* **headgear**. [➡HABERDASHERY, MILLINERY, AND LINGERIE; 867]

capability *n* **ability**, capacity, competence, skill, resources, wherewithal. [➡SKILLS, TALENTS, AND ABILITIES; 527]

See Compare and Contrast at **ability**.

capable **1** *adj* **accomplished**, talented, skilled, gifted, clever, adept, efficient. [➡TALENTED AND SKILFUL; 528] *Opposite:* inept. **2** *adj* **able**, competent, proficient, efficient, qualified, adept. [➡TALENTED AND SKILFUL; 528] *Opposite:* incapable.

capably *adv* **competently**, proficiently, adeptly, ably, efficiently. [➡TALENTED AND SKILFUL; 528] *Opposite:* ineptly.

capacious *adj* **roomy**, spacious, large, ample, big, voluminous, commodious, extensive, vast, sizable. [➡LARGE; 1192] *Opposite:* cramped.

capaciousness *n* [➡LARGE; 1192]

capacity **1** *n* **ability**, capability, skill, talent, aptitude. [➡SKILLS, TALENTS, AND ABILITIES; 527] **2** *n* **volume**, space, room, size, dimensions. [➡SIZE AND DIMENSIONS; 1191] **3** *n* **role**, position, responsibility, function, office. [➡JOB; 833]

See Compare and Contrast at **ability**.

cape **1** *type of* **overcoat**. [➡GARMENTS AND OUTFITS; 865] **2** *n* **promontory**, peninsula, headland, outcrop, point. [➡THE SEAS, OCEANS, AND SHORES; 1041]

Cape Cod (*US*) *type of* **house**. [➡RESIDENTIAL BUILDINGS; 1077]

capellini *type of* **pasta**. [➡PASTA; 1179]

caper **1** *n* **escapade**, adventure, jaunt, lark, antics, jape (*archaic*). [➡EVENTS AND OCCURRENCES; 35] **2** *v* **frolic**, cavort, jump, leap, dance, prance, gambol, play around, play about. [➡FIDGET AND FROLIC; 312]

capillary *type of* **blood vessel**. [➡THE BLOOD AND CIRCULATION; 718]

cap in hand *adv* **humbly**, meekly, deferentially, submissively, subserviently, abjectly, on bended knee. [➡EXPRESSING RESPECT AND APPROVAL; 638] *Opposite:* boldly.

capital **1** *n* **assets**, resources, funds, wealth, money, principal, investment. [➡FINANCIAL ASSETS; 463] **2** *n* **centre**, headquarters, hub. [➡HUMAN SETTLEMENTS; 1069]

capitalist **1** *n* **entrepreneur**, financier, industrialist, businessperson, investor. [➡BUSINESS PEOPLE; 794] **2** *adj* **entrepreneurial**, industrial, consumerist, consumer, commercial. [➡STYLES AND SYSTEMS OF GOVERNMENT; 806]

capitalize *v* **benefit from**, profit from, exploit, take advantage of, make the most of, get the most out of. [➡MAKE GOOD USE OF SOMETHING; 474]

capitalize on *v* **make the most of**, maximize, take advantage of, use, utilize, build on, exploit. [➡MAKE GOOD USE OF SOMETHING; 474]

capital punishment *n* [➡TRIAL, PUNISHMENT, AND LEGAL OUTCOMES; 819]

capitation **1** *n* **tax**, poll tax, levy, toll, duty. [➡TAX AND TAXATION; 802] **2** *n* **fee**, charge, payment, amount. [➡MONEY, PAYMENTS, AND CHARGES; 800]

capitulate *v* **surrender**, submit, yield, succumb, give way, give in, give up. [➡NOT DO AND REFUSE TO DO; 275] *Opposite:* resist.

See Compare and Contrast at **yield**.

capitulation *n* **surrender**, submission, defeat, retreat. [➡FAILURE; 77] *Opposite:* resistance.

capon *type of* **male or female bird**. [➡MALE OR FEMALE BIRD; 1005]

cappelletti *type of* **pasta**. [➡PASTA; 1179]

cappuccino *type of* **coffee**. [➡DRINKS; 1186]

capriccio *type of* **instrumental music**. [➡MUSIC, SONGS, AND SINGING; 907]

capriccioso *type of* **musical term**. [➡MUSICAL TERMS; 912]

caprice *n* **whim**, impulse, quirk, fancy, fad, notion. [➡IDEA AND THOUGHT; 771]

capricious *adj* **unpredictable**, changeable, variable, impulsive, whimsical, unreliable, fickle, erratic, wayward, flighty. [➡LACK OF COMMITMENT AND UNRELIABILITY; 510] *Opposite:* predictable.

capriciously *adv* **impulsively**, on impulse, unpredictably, changeably, on a whim, without rhyme or reason, as the mood takes you, quixotically, as the fancy takes you, at your own sweet will. [➡UNINTENTIONAL AND ACCIDENTAL; 282] *Opposite:* predictably.

capriciousness *n* **unpredictability**, changeability, variability, whimsicality, impulsiveness, unreliability, waywardness, fickleness. [➡LACK OF COMMITMENT AND UNRELIABILITY; 510] *Opposite:* predictability.

Capricorn *type of* **star sign**. [➡FATE, DESTINY, AND ASTROLOGY; 783]

capri pants *type of* **trousers**. [➡GARMENTS AND OUTFITS; 865]

capsicum *type of* **salad vegetable**. [➡FRUIT AND VEGETABLES; 1175]

capsize *v* **overturn**, turn over, roll over, keel over, turn turtle. [➡MOVE SOMETHING: INTO A NEW POSITION OR OVERTURN; 331] *Opposite:* right.

capstan *part of* **ship or boat**. [➡PARTS OF A SHIP OR BOAT; 1150]

capsule **1** *n* **pod**, container, case, casing, shell. [➡CONTAINERS, RECEPTACLES, AND PACKAGING; 1244] **2** *n* **pill**, tablet, lozenge. [➡REMEDIES, TREATMENTS AND OPERATIONS; 732]

captain **1** *n* **head**, skipper, leader, chief, boss, commander, team leader. [➡IMPORTANT OR FAMOUS PEOPLE; 893] **2** *v* **lead**, skipper, manage, take charge, head, control. [➡BE IN CHARGE; 271]

captain of industry *n* [➡BUSINESS PEOPLE; 794]

caption *n* **slogan**, subtitle, title, description, legend, heading, header, footer. [➡PARTS OF BOOKS AND DOCUMENTS; 594]

captious 1 *adj* **critical**, pedantic, trivial, petty, nit-picking, hairsplitting, pettifogging, negative, unfair, unjust. [➡DIFFICULT TO PLEASE; 516] *Opposite:* compliant. 2 *adj* **confusing**, misleading, devious, bewildering, disingenuous, malicious, entrapping. [➡DECEITFUL; 514] *Opposite:* clear.

captivate *v* **attract**, charm, enchant, fascinate, entrance, draw. [➡APPEAL TO AND AROUSE INTEREST; 576] *Opposite:* repel.

captivated *adj* **enchanted**, fascinated, charmed, entranced, spellbound, enthralled, mesmerized, transfixed, riveted (*informal*), stunned, impressed. [➡APPRECIATION AND GRATITUDE; 536] *Opposite:* repulsed.

captivating *adj* **charming**, attractive, appealing, fascinating, charismatic, enchanting, entrancing. [➡BEAUTY AND ATTRACTIVENESS; 190] *Opposite:* uninteresting.

captive 1 *n* **prisoner**, detainee, internee, prisoner of war, hostage. [➡CAPTIVES AND PRISONERS; 250] *Opposite:* escapee. 2 *adj* **imprisoned**, in prison, incarcerated (*formal*), locked up, enslaved, confined, caged. [➡CAPTIVITY AND LOSS OF FREEDOM; 249] *Opposite:* free. 3 *adj* **attentive**, intent, fascinated, spellbound, rapt, ensnared, trapped. [➡PENSIVENESS AND INTEREST; 539]

captivity *n* **imprisonment**, custody, detention, incarceration (*formal*), confinement, internment. [➡CAPTIVITY AND LOSS OF FREEDOM; 249] *Opposite:* freedom.

captor *n* **abductor**, imprisoner, kidnapper, hostage taker, jailer, hijacker. [➡CRIMINALS; 821] *Opposite:* liberator.

capture 1 *v* **take**, seize, apprehend, arrest, pick up, catch, bag, net. [➡TAKE SOMETHING AWAY; 426] *Opposite:* release. 2 *v* **imprison**, detain, arrest, incarcerate (*formal*), confine, take into custody, jail. [➡CAPTIVITY AND LOSS OF FREEDOM; 249] *Opposite:* liberate. 3 *v* **encapsulate**, summarize, sum up, portray, describe, depict, denote. [➡REPRESENT SOMETHING OR SOMEBODY; 59] 4 *v* **secure**, attain, gain, acquire, obtain, gain control, win. [➡GET; 421] *Opposite:* lose. 5 *v* **catch**, seize, get (*informal*), grab hold of, trap, ensnare, net. [➡CONTACT: HOLD; 412] 6 *n* **imprisonment**, detention, arrest, seizure, apprehension, incarceration (*formal*), internment. [➡CAPTIVITY AND LOSS OF FREEDOM; 249] *Opposite:* release.

capture your imagination *v* **fascinate**, excite, inspire, interest, enchant, entrance, enrapture (*formal*). [➡APPEAL TO AND AROUSE INTEREST; 576]

capuchin *type of* **primate**. [➡PRIMATE; 988]

capybara *type of* **rodent**. [➡RODENT; 989]

car 1 *n* **motor** (*dated or informal*), automobile, wheels (*slang*), auto (*US*). [➡BIKES, CARS, AND CARRIAGES; 1148] 2 *n* **railway carriage**, cabin, carriage, coach, compartment, wagon, sleeper, flatcar, Pullman. [➡RAILWAYS; 1106]

car

◆ *types of car*
all-terrain vehicle, banger (*informal*), beater (*US informal*), compact, convertible, coupé, dragster, estate car, four-by-four, hatchback, hot rod (*slang*), limo, limousine, minivan, people carrier, racing car, runabout, saloon, sedan (*US*), sports car, station wagon (*US*), stock car, subcompact (*US*), three-wheeler

carafe *n* **flask**, decanter, bottle. [➡TABLEWARE, CUTLERY, AND KITCHENWARE; 861]

caramel 1 *type of* **confectionery**. [➡CONFECTIONERY; 1181] 2 *type of* **brown**. [➡COLOURS; 1223]

caramelize *v* **burn**, heat, scorch, brown, broil (*US*). [➡COOKING AND FOOD PREPARATION; 354]

carapace *n* **case**, shell, covering, sheath, outside, exterior. [➡COVERS AND COATINGS; 1245]

caravan 1 *n* **convoy**, group, procession, parade, motorcade, column, line, cavalcade. [➡GROUPS OF VEHICLES; 1151] 2 *type of* **leisure vehicle**. [➡VEHICLES; 1144]

caraway *type of* **herb**. [➡HERBS AND SPICES; 1174]

caraway seed *type of* **spice**. [➡HERBS AND SPICES; 1174]

carbine *type of* **gun**. [➡WEAPONS FOR SHOOTING; 1155]

carbohydrate *n* **biological compound**, simple carbohydrate, complex carbohydrate, starch, sugar, cellulose. [➡FOOD COMPONENTS; 1187]

carbon *type of* **mineral**. [➡MINERALS; 1276]

carbon copy *n* **replica**, duplicate, copy, facsimile, exact likeness, reproduction. [➡REPRESENTATIONS AND GENERAL EXAMPLES; 65] *Opposite:* original.

car boot sale *n* [➡SALES AND SHOWS; 444]

carbuncle *n* **spot**, blemish, boil, pustule, abscess, sore. [➡CONDITIONS AFFECTING THE SKIN; 722]

carcass *n* **corpse**, remains, cadaver, body, skeleton, shell. [➡THE BONES AND JOINTS; 720]

carcinogenic *adj* **cancer-causing**, oncogenic, hazardous, toxic, poisonous, dangerous, noxious, unsafe. [➡DANGEROUS; 237]

carcinomatous *adj* [➡SICKNESS; 730]

card 1 *n* **greetings card**, birthday card, anniversary card, postcard, picture postcard. [➡LETTERS AND WRITTEN MESSAGES; 585] 2 *n* **pass**, identification card, membership card, business card, calling card. [➡OFFICIAL DOCUMENTS; 587]

cardamom *type of* **spice**. [➡HERBS AND SPICES; 1174]

cardboard 1 *n* **board**, paper, card, packaging, packing, wrapping. [➡COVERS AND COATINGS; 1245] 2 *adj* **insubstantial**, unconvincing, phoney, plastic, wooden, flat, two-dimensional. [➡FALSE AND UNREAL; 174] *Opposite:* substantial.

cardboard box *type of* **container**. [➡CONTAINERS, RECEPTACLES, AND PACKAGING; 1244]

card-carrying *adj* **official**, paid-up, bona fide, listed, genuine, authentic, committed. [➡TRUE AND REAL; 172]

cardiac *adj* [➡THE BLOOD AND CIRCULATION; 718]

cardigan *type of* **sweater or cardigan**. [➡GARMENTS AND OUTFITS; 865]

cardinal 1 *adj* **basic**, fundamental, key, prime, serious, important, chief, principal, essential, central, core.

[➡IMPORTANT; 195] *Opposite:* secondary. **2** *type of* **common bird.** [➡BIRD; 997]

cardiovascular *adj* **circulatory**, cardiac, vascular, heart, blood. [➡THE BLOOD AND CIRCULATION; 718]

cardsharp *n* **cheat**, gambler, con artist (*slang*), pro, hustler, swindler. [➡PEOPLE WHO DECEIVE; 662]

cardsharping *n* **cheating**, tricking, swindling, gambling, hustling. [➡GAMBLE AND TAKE RISKS; 467]

card table *type of* **table.** [➡FURNITURE; 858]

care 1 *v* **be concerned**, be interested, feel a concern, take an interest. [➡BE CONCERNED AND CARE; 582] *Opposite:* disregard. **2** *v* **feel affection**, love, like, have a soft spot for, cherish, be fond of. [➡LIKE, LOVE, VALUE AND ENJOY; 579] *Opposite:* dislike. **3** *v* **look after**, tend, supervise, oversee, see to, attend to. [➡TAKE CARE OF AND SPOIL; 301] *Opposite:* ignore. **4** *v* (*formal*) **want**, like, favour, appreciate, enjoy. [➡LIKE, LOVE, VALUE AND ENJOY; 579] *Opposite:* dislike. **5** *n* **upkeep**, maintenance, repair, overhaul, attention. [➡KIND ACTION OR BEHAVIOUR; 296] **6** *n* **attention**, caution, precaution, carefulness, watchfulness, alertness. [➡EXACT; 204] **7** *n* **worry**, concern, anxiety, trouble, unease, stress. [➡CONFUSION, ANXIETY, AND WORRY; 541] **8** *n* **treatment**, provision, support, attention. [➡KIND ACTION OR BEHAVIOUR; 296] **9** *n* **oversight** (*formal*), supervision, guardianship, protection, custody. [➡RESPONSIBILITY; 171]

See Compare and Contrast at **worry.**

careen *v* [➡AIMLESS AND ERRANT MOTION; 344]

career 1 *n* **vocation**, job, occupation, profession, calling, livelihood, line of business. [➡PROFESSIONS; 845] **2** *v* **rush**, race, hurry, dash, hurtle, tear. [➡MOVE FAST; 314]

career into *v* [➡CONTACT: IMPACT; 414]

careerism *n* **determination**, single-mindedness, motivation, commitment, drive, professionalism. [➡HARD-WORKING AND COMMITTED; 501]

careerist 1 *n* **professional**, go-getter (*informal*), achiever, high flier. [➡PEOPLE WHO ARE APPROVED OF; 955] **2** *adj* **single-minded**, determined, motivated, focused, professional. [➡HARD-WORKING AND COMMITTED; 501]

care for *v* [➡TAKE CARE OF AND SPOIL; 301]

carefree *adj* **untroubled**, happy-go-lucky, cheery, relaxed, cheerful, blithe (*literary*), lighthearted. [➡CALMNESS, CONFIDENCE, AND COMPOSURE; 537] *Opposite:* troubled.

carefreeness *n* **lightheartedness**, cheerfulness, cheeriness, happiness, jollity, buoyancy, breeziness, nonchalance, insouciance. [➡CALMNESS, CONFIDENCE, AND COMPOSURE; 537] *Opposite:* anxiety.

careful 1 *adj* **cautious**, wary, vigilant, watchful, alert, suspicious, chary, circumspect, cagey, guarded. [➡CAUTIOUS AND CAREFUL; 283] *Opposite:* reckless. **2** *adj* **thorough**, meticulous, painstaking, particular, precise, conscientious, fastidious, assiduous, scrupulous, punctilious, finicky, fussy. [➡CAUTIOUS AND CAREFUL; 283] *Opposite:* imprecise. **3** *adj* **prudent**, sensible, judicious, cautious, well thought-out, shrewd, wise. [➡THE NATURE OF IDEAS; 772] *Opposite:* foolish. **4** *adj* **protective**, sympathetic, sensitive, gentle, tender, caring. [➡GENEROSITY AND KINDNESS; 496] *Opposite:* rough.

Compare and Contrast: ***careful, conscientious, scrupulous, thorough, meticulous, painstaking, assiduous, punctilious, finicky, fussy***

CORE MEANING: EXERCISING CARE AND ATTENTION IN DOING SOMETHING

careful a wide-ranging term, suggesting attention to detail and implying cautiousness in avoiding errors or inaccuracies; ***conscientious*** showing great care, attention, and industriousness in carrying out a task; ***scrupulous*** having or showing careful regard for what is morally right; ***thorough*** extremely careful and accurate; ***meticulous*** extremely careful and precise; ***painstaking*** involving or showing great care and attention to detail; ***assiduous*** undeviating in effort and care; ***punctilious*** very careful about the conventions of correct behaviour and etiquette; ***finicky*** concentrating too much on unimportant details; ***fussy*** tending to worry over details or trivial things.

carefulness 1 *n* **caution**, care, suspicion, wariness, watchfulness, alertness, chariness, circumspection. [➡POSITIVE INTELLECTUAL CHARACTERISTICS; 525] *Opposite:* recklessness. **2** *n* **attention to detail**, thoroughness, precision, care, meticulousness, conscientiousness, assiduousness. [➡HARD-WORKING AND COMMITTED; 501] *Opposite:* carelessness. **3** *n* (*informal*) **prudence**, caution, judiciousness, wisdom, judgment, common sense, care, sense. [➡POSITIVE INTELLECTUAL CHARACTERISTICS; 525] *Opposite:* foolishness.

caregiver (*US*) *n* [➡SUPPORTERS, PROTECTORS, AND COMPATRIOTS; 970]

careless 1 *adj* **slapdash**, happy-go-lucky, casual, slipshod, sloppy, hasty, inaccurate, lackadaisical, lax. [➡INCAUTIOUS AND CARELESS; 284] *Opposite:* careful. **2** *adj* **uncaring**, thoughtless, offhand, inconsiderate, unthinking, unconcerned, insensitive, unsympathetic, casual, cavalier, irresponsible, rash, reckless, negligent, heedless. [➡NEUTRALITY AND INDIFFERENCE; 554] *Opposite:* considerate.

carelessly 1 *adv* **sloppily**, hastily, inaccurately, imprecisely, haphazardly, casually. [➡NEUTRALITY AND INDIFFERENCE; 554] *Opposite:* carefully. **2** *adv* **uncaringly**, offhandedly, inconsiderately, unthinkingly, unsympathetically, insensitively, thoughtlessly, casually. [➡INCAUTIOUS AND CARELESS; 284] *Opposite:* considerately.

carelessness *n* **sloppiness**, inattentiveness, inaccuracy, imprecision, negligence, inattention. [➡VAGUENESS; 244] *Opposite:* care.

carer *n* [➡ADOPTION, FOSTERING, AND EXTENDED FAMILY; 962]

caress 1 *v* **stroke**, touch, pat, embrace, cuddle, hug. [➡CONTACT: TOUCH; 413] **2** *n* **touch**, stroke, pat, embrace, hug, cuddle. [➡PHYSICAL CONTACT AS COMMUNICATION; 656]

caretaker 1 *n* **concierge**, warden, porter, custodian, janitor. [➡PEOPLE WHO GUARD AND PROTECT; 846] **2** *n* (*US*) **caregiver**, attendant, nurse, carer, minder. [➡ADOPTION, FOSTERING, AND EXTENDED FAMILY; 962]

careworn *adj* **haggard**, drawn, beleaguered, worried, burdened, weighed down, oppressed, exhausted, worn-out. [➡SADNESS, DISTRESS, AND DESPAIR; 540] *Opposite:* carefree.

cargo *n* **load**, freight, consignment, shipment, goods, payload. [➡TRANSPORTATION, TRANSPORTERS, AND CARGOS; 323]

caribou *type of* **deer or antelope**. [➡DEER AND ANTELOPE; 981]

caricature 1 *n* **cartoon**, picture, drawing, sketch. [➡ART-WORKS; 898] 2 *n* **travesty**, misrepresentation, false impression, distortion, falsification, exaggeration, skit, sendup (*informal*). [➡JOKES AND TEASING; 675]

caricaturist *n* **artist**, cartoonist, humorist, satirist. [➡ARTISTS; 900]

carina *part of* **bird**. [➡PARTS OF A BIRD; 1006]

caring *adj* **kind**, thoughtful, gentle, helpful, considerate, compassionate, concerned, loving, affectionate, sensitive, attentive. [➡GENEROSITY AND KINDNESS; 496] *Opposite:* uncaring.

carjack *v* [➡STEAL AND ROB; 427]

carjacker *n* [➡CRIMINALS; 821]

carjacking *n* [➡CRIMES; 817]

carmine *type of* **red**. [➡COLOURS; 1223]

carnage *n* **killing**, bloodshed, slaughter, massacre, bloodbath, butchery. [➡CAUSES OF DEATH; 921]

carnal (*formal*) *adj* [➡MORALLY BAD; 776]

carnality (*formal*) *n* [➡MORALLY BAD; 776]

carnation 1 *type of* **perennial flower**. [➡FLOWERS; 1032] 2 *type of* **red**. [➡COLOURS; 1223]

carnelian *type of* **gemstone**. [➡PRECIOUS STONES; 1277]

carnival 1 *n* **festival**, celebration, street party, fair, fete, parade, pageant, cavalcade, Mardi Gras. [➡PARTIES, DANCES, AND CELEBRATIONS; 37] 2 *n* (*US*) **fairground**, sideshow, midway, amusement park, travelling fair, funfair, fair. [➡URBAN OUTDOOR SPACES; 1071]

carnivore *n* **flesh-eater**, meat-eater, predator, scavenger, omnivore, insectivore, fish-eater, raptor. [➡EATERS, GOURMETS, AND DIETARY CHOICES; 715]

carnivorous *adj* **flesh-eating**, meat-eating, predatory, scavenging, insectivorous, fish-eating. [➡EATERS, GOURMETS, AND DIETARY CHOICES; 715]

carob *type of* **evergreen tree**. [➡EVERGREEN AND CONIFEROUS TREES; 1029]

carol *n* **song**, hymn, chant, chorus. [➡MUSIC, SONGS, AND SINGING; 907]

carousal (*literary*) *n* **party**, celebration, binge, bender (*slang*), spree. [➡PARTIES, DANCES, AND CELEBRATIONS; 37]

carouse (*literary*) *v* **drink**, get drunk, party (*informal*), raise the roof, go on the town, paint the town red (*informal*), revel, celebrate. [➡LEISURE AND RECREATION; 874]

carousel 1 *n* **merry-go-round**, roundabout, ride. [➡ENTERTAINMENT; 872] 2 *n* **container**, cassette, cartridge, drum, magazine, holder, rack, receptacle. [➡CONTAINERS, RECEPTACLES, AND PACKAGING; 1244]

carouser (*literary*) *n* [➡PLEASURE-SEEKERS AND HEDONISTS; 886]

carousing (*literary*) *n* **festivities**, partying, revels, revelry, celebrations. [➡PARTIES, DANCES, AND CELEBRATIONS; 37]

carp 1 *v* **complain**, moan (*informal*), grumble, find fault, grouse (*informal*), knock (*slang*), nag, go on, gripe (*informal*), criticize, crab, whine, object. [➡COMPLAIN AND NAG; 687] 2 *type of* **freshwater fish**. [➡FRESHWATER FISH; 1010]

See Compare and Contrast at **complain**.

carpentry *n* **joinery**, woodwork, turning, carving, cabinetmaking. [➡CRAFTS AND CARVING; 356]

carper *n* [➡GRUMPY AND NEGATIVE PEOPLE; 953]

carpet 1 *n* **rug**, mat, runner, fitted carpet, carpet tiles, carpeting, floor covering, flooring. [➡SOFT FURNISHINGS, LINEN, AND DRAPERY; 860] 2 *n* **covering**, layer, blanket, mass, spread, cover. [➡COVERS AND COATINGS; 1245] 3 *v* (*literary*) **cover**, swathe, coat, overlay, strew, spread. [➡DECORATE, ADORN, AND APPLY COATINGS; 406] 4 *v* (*informal*) **reprimand**, tell off, rebuke, blast (*informal*), criticize, castigate (*formal*), chew out (*US informal*). [➡ACCUSE, BLAME, AND CRITICIZE; 642]

carpeting *n* **floor covering**, flooring, matting, carpet tiles. [➡SOFT FURNISHINGS, LINEN, AND DRAPERY; 860]

carping 1 *adj* **critical**, nitpicking, complaining, dissatisfied, discontented, disapproving, disparaging. [➡ACCUSATORY AND DISAPPROVING; 635] 2 *n* **complaining**, moaning (*informal*), nitpicking, faultfinding, grousing (*informal*), dissatisfaction, griping (*informal*), whining, criticism. [➡COMPLAIN AND NAG; 687]

carport *n* **garage**, lean-to, shelter, porch, parking space. [➡ANCILLARY BUILDINGS; 1079]

carriage 1 *n* **horse-drawn carriage**, coach, horse and carriage. [➡BIKES, CARS, AND CARRIAGES; 1148] 2 *n* (*formal*) **bearing**, posture, deportment (*formal*), air, presence, poise, pose, stance, comportment (*formal*), attitude, gait. [➡TEMPERAMENT AND BEHAVIOUR; 493] 3 *n* **transport**, delivery, carrying, haulage, conveyance, shipment. [➡TRANSPORTATION, TRANSPORTERS, AND CARGOS; 323] 4 *part of* **train**. [➡RAILWAYS; 1106] 5 *type of* **wagon or carriage**. [➡VEHICLES; 1144]

carriageway *n* **traffic lane**, roadway, road, thoroughfare, side of the road. [➡ROADS; 1105]

carried *adj* **approved**, accepted, passed, agreed, supported, voted for. [➡CERTAIN; 175] *Opposite:* rejected.

carried away *adj* [➡PLEASURE, EXCITEMENT, AND ELATION; 535]

carrier 1 *n* **transporter**, haulier, delivery service, carter, shipper, mover, exporter, importer, shipping agent, transferrer. [➡TRANSPORTATION, TRANSPORTERS, AND CARGOS; 323] 2 *n* **shopping bag**, carrier bag, shopper. [➡CONTAINERS, RECEPTACLES, AND PACKAGING; 1244]

carrier bag *type of* **bag**. [➡CONTAINERS, RECEPTACLES, AND PACKAGING; 1244]

carrion *n* **flesh**, meat, tissue, muscle, sinew, guts. [➡DEAD PERSON; 926]

carrot 1 *n* **incentive**, inducement, bribe, bait, lure, sugared pill, encouragement, sweetener (*informal*), persuasion, bung (*slang*), candy (*US*). [➡BRIBES; 441] 2 *type of* **root vegetable**. [➡FRUIT AND VEGETABLES; 1175]

carrot cake *type of* **cake**. [➡CAKES, BISCUITS, AND DESSERTS; 1180]

carroty *adj* **orange**, red, ginger, auburn. [➡HAIR COLOUR; 486]

carry 1 *v* **take**, bear, hold, support, clutch, sustain. [➡MOVE SOMETHING TO ANOTHER LOCATION; 325] 2 *v* **transmit**, transport, convey, transfer, bring, lug, cart, move, pass on, conduct, pass, relay. [➡MOVE SOMETHING TO ANOTHER LOCATION; 325] 3 *v* **contain**, include, involve, incorporate, hold, have. [➡HOLD AND CONTAIN; 456] 4 *v* **have in stock**, stock, store, keep, supply, have available. [➡STORE AND KEEP; 454] 5 *v* **approve**, accept, pass, agree, vote for, support. [➡APPROVE AND CONFIRM; 647]

carryall (*US*) *type of* **baggage**. [➡CONTAINERS, RECEPTACLES, AND PACKAGING; 1244]

carrycase *type of* **baggage**. [➡CONTAINERS, RECEPTACLES, AND PACKAGING; 1244]

carrycot *type of* **bed**. [➡FURNITURE; 858]

carrying *adj* **loud**, resonant, resounding, booming, ringing, stentorian. [➡LOUD OR UNPLEASANT SOUNDS; 1265] *Opposite:* quiet.

carrying-on (*informal*) *n* **goings-on** (*informal*), doings (*informal*), pranks, high jinks (*informal*). [➡BAD BEHAVIOUR OR ACTION; 255]

carry off 1 *v* **take away**, take off, remove, steal, abduct, carry away, cart off. [➡REMOVE SOMETHING; 339] *Opposite:* bring back. 2 *v* **succeed**, manage, accomplish, pull off (*informal*), achieve, do. [➡SUCCEED AND WIN; 79] *Opposite:* fail.

carry-on (*informal*) *n* **fuss**, commotion, to-do (*informal*), hullabaloo, palaver, bother. [➡CHAOS AND UPROAR; 51]

carry on 1 *v* **continue**, keep, keep on, keep at, go on, persist, keep going, be persistent, persevere. [➡CONTINUE AN ACTION; 263] *Opposite:* stop. 2 *v* **complain**, moan (*informal*), grumble, carp, witter (*informal*), nag, go on. [➡COMPLAIN AND NAG; 687]

carry out *v* **do**, perform, complete, achieve, succeed, accomplish, fulfil, discharge (*formal*), execute, realize, pull off (*informal*). [➡CARRY OUT AN ACTION; 270] *Opposite:* neglect.

See Compare and Contrast at **perform**.

carryout *n* **takeaway**, fast food, takeout (*US*). [➡MEALS AND PARTS OF MEALS; 1168]

carry over *v* **postpone**, defer, leave, reschedule, put back, adjourn [➡DELAY ACTION OR OCCURRENCE; 279] *Opposite:* expedite (*formal*).

carryover *n* **leftover**, legacy, inheritance, residue, remnant, remainder, surplus. [➡REMAINDER AND REMAINDERS; 123]

carry the can (*informal*) *v* **take the blame**, accept responsibility, accept the blame, shoulder the blame, be the scapegoat, be the fall guy (*informal*), take the rap (*slang*), incur blame, catch it (*informal*). [➡FORGET, FORGIVE, AND ACCEPT; 749]

carsick *adj* **sick**, nauseous, ill, poorly (*informal*), unwell. [➡ILL AND SICK; 741]

cart 1 *n* **farm cart**, wagon, dray, tumbril, wain. [➡BIKES, CARS, AND CARRIAGES; 1148] 2 *n* **handcart**, pushcart, barrow, trolley. [➡BIKES, CARS, AND CARRIAGES; 1148] 3 *v* **carry**, lug, heave, haul, drag, draw. [➡MOVE SOMETHING TO ANOTHER LOCATION; 325]

carte blanche *n* **free hand**, free rein, blank cheque, complete freedom, full authority, complete discretion. [➡FREEDOM AND LIBERTY; 209]

cartel *n* **interest group**, lobby, alliance, association, union, league. [➡GROUPS WITH A COMMON INTEREST; 938]

car theft *n* [➡CRIMES; 817]

car thief *n* [➡CRIMINALS; 821]

carthorse *type of* **horse**. [➡HORSE; 985]

cartilage *n* [➡THE BONES AND JOINTS; 720]

cart off *v* **remove**, drag off, take away, haul off, carry off, carry away. [➡REMOVE SOMETHING; 339]

carton *n* **box**, cardboard box, container, pack, sachet. [➡CONTAINERS, RECEPTACLES, AND PACKAGING; 1244]

cartoon 1 *n* **animation**, animated film, movie. [➡FILM; 901] 2 *n* **drawing**, caricature, picture, comic strip. [➡ARTWORKS; 898]

cartoonist *n* **artist**, animator, caricaturist, satirist, humorist. [➡ARTISTS; 900]

cartridge 1 *n* **container**, holder, casing, unit, cassette. [➡CONTAINERS, RECEPTACLES, AND PACKAGING; 1244] 2 *part of* **audio equipment**. [➡AUDIO EQUIPMENT; 1138]

cart track *type of* **minor road**. [➡ROADS; 1105]

cartwheel 1 *n* **somersault**, turn, handspring, vault, forward roll, flip, tumble, flip flop. [➡FIDGET AND FROLIC; 312] 2 *v* **turn**, somersault, handspring, go head over heels, roll, flip, flip over, turn over, vault, tumble, flip-flop. [➡FIDGET AND FROLIC; 312]

carve 1 *v* **engrave**, inscribe, etch, cut, notch, score, scribe. [➡CRAFTS AND CARVING; 356] 2 *v* **slice**, pare, cut in slices, whittle, cut up, cut, shape, fashion, sculpt. [➡TEAR, BREAK, AND CUT; 361]

carve out *v* **create**, make, establish, build, set up, lay down, construct. [➡INSTITUTE AND INAUGURATE; 349]

carver *type of* **seating**. [➡FURNITURE; 858]

carve-up *n* **division**, allocation, distribution, partitioning, share-out, splitting up. [➡DISPENSE, RATION, AND DISTRIBUTE; 435]

carve up (*informal*) *v* **divide**, allocate, share out, apportion, distribute, allot, split up, partition. [➡DISPENSE, RATION, AND DISTRIBUTE; 435]

carving 1 *n* **artefact**, model, statue, statuette, figure, figurine, bas-relief, frieze. [➡ARTWORKS; 898] 2 *n* **cutting**, engraving, etching, sculpting, fashioning, shaping, slicing. [➡CRAFTS AND CARVING; 356]

carving knife 1 *type of* **cutlery.** [➡TABLEWARE, CUTLERY, AND KITCHENWARE; 861] 2 *type of* **knife.** [➡CUTTING TOOLS; 1119]

Casanova *n* **philanderer** (*dated disapproving*), libertine, Don Juan, Lothario (*literary*), gigolo, Romeo, ladies' man, lover, seducer, adulterer, satyr, stud. [➡PLEASURE-SEEKERS AND HEDONISTS; 886]

cascade 1 *n* **waterfall**, chute, cataract, force, falls, torrent. [➡RIVERS, LAKES, AND STREAMS; 1042] 2 *v* **flow**, pour, fall, drop, gush, spill, surge, tumble. [➡GO DOWNWARDS; 308]

case 1 *n* **circumstance**, situation, instance, event, occasion, incident. [➡SITUATIONS; 71] 2 *n* **instance**, item, example, illustration, paradigm, a case in point. [➡EVIDENCE AND PROOF; 69] 3 *n* **job**, project, commission, assignment, task, problem, issue. [➡WORK IN GENERAL; 298] 4 *n* **court case**, legal action, lawsuit, suit, indictment, litigation. [➡TRIAL, PUNISHMENT, AND LEGAL OUTCOMES; 819] 5 *n* **argument**, reason, defence, justification, rationale, basis. [➡CAUSATION; 169] 6 *n* **container**, holder, box, casing, cover, folder, crate, pencil case, glasses case. [➡CONTAINERS, RECEPTACLES, AND PACKAGING; 1244] 7 *n* **suitcase**, overnight case, weekend case, briefcase, attaché case, carrycase, travel case. [➡CONTAINERS, RECEPTACLES, AND PACKAGING; 1244]

casebook *n* **record**, log, diary, journal, notebook. [➡BOOKS AND BOOKLETS; 591]

case-hardened *adj* **unsympathetic**, unfeeling, hard, hardened, toughened, tough, hard-boiled (*informal*), hardhearted, hard-bitten, hard-nosed (*informal*), cynical, callous, insensitive. [➡NEGATIVE OF OUTLOOK; 515] *Opposite:* sensitive.

case in point *n* [➡PERFECT EXAMPLES AND EMBODIMENTS; 67]

casement *type of* **window.** [➡WINDOWS; 1099]

casern *n* [➡RESIDENTIAL BUILDINGS; 1077]

cash *n* **money**, hard cash, ready money, coins, currency, notes, petty cash. [➡MONEY; 140]

cashew *type of* **nut.** [➡NUTS; 1184]

cashier 1 *n* **treasurer**, banker, bursar. [➡PEOPLE INVOLVED IN FINANCE; 804] 2 *n* **bank clerk**, clerk, teller, official, assistant. [➡PEOPLE INVOLVED IN FINANCE; 804] 3 *v* **dismiss**, expel, drum out, boot out (*informal*), kick out (*informal*), court martial. [➡REVOKE STATUS; 460]

cash in *v* **redeem**, trade in, sell, realize, bank. [➡SELL; 442]

cash-in-hand *adv* **in cash**, cash, no questions asked, unofficially, off the record. [➡TYPES OF WORK; 835]

cash in on *v* **take advantage**, benefit, do well from, exploit, make the most of, profit, ride on the coat-tails. [➡MAKE GOOD USE OF SOMETHING; 474]

cashmere *type of* **fabric from animals.** [➡FABRICS; 1131]

cashpoint *n* **cash dispenser**, cash machine, hole-in-the-wall (*informal*), till, ATM. [➡ACCOUNTING, BANKING, AND BUDGETING; 799]

casing *n* **covering**, case, outside, exterior, skin, sleeve, sheath, shell, carapace. [➡COVERS AND COATINGS; 1245]

casino 1 *n* **gaming club**, gambling den, nightclub, gaming house. [➡BUILDINGS FOR PUBLIC ENTERTAINMENT; 1083] 2 *type of* **bar or club.** [➡HOTELS, RESTAURANTS, AND CLUBS; 1081]

cask *n* **barrel**, tub, drum, butt, vat, container. [➡CONTAINERS, RECEPTACLES, AND PACKAGING; 1244]

casket 1 *type of* **container.** [➡CONTAINERS, RECEPTACLES, AND PACKAGING; 1244] 2 *n* (*US*) **coffin**, sarcophagus, cist, box. [➡BURIAL PLACES AND ACCESSORIES; 930]

Cassandra *n* [➡GRUMPY AND NEGATIVE PEOPLE; 953]

cassava *type of* **root vegetable.** [➡FRUIT AND VEGETABLES; 1175]

casserole 1 *n* **cooking pot**, deep dish, covered dish, oven dish, crockpot (*US*). [➡PREPARED DISHES; 1169] 2 *v* **braise**, stew, simmer, slow cook. [➡COOKING AND FOOD PREPARATION; 354]

cassette 1 *n* **cartridge**, tape, videotape. [➡RECORDINGS AND PLAYERS; 911] 2 *n* **case**, cartridge, holder, container, cover. [➡CONTAINERS, RECEPTACLES, AND PACKAGING; 1244] 3 *part of* **audio equipment.** [➡AUDIO EQUIPMENT; 1138]

cassette recorder *type of* **audio equipment.** [➡AUDIO EQUIPMENT; 1138]

cassone *type of* **cabinet.** [➡FURNITURE; 858]

cassoulet *type of* **cooked dish.** [➡PREPARED DISHES; 1169]

cast 1 *v* **throw**, hurl, chuck (*informal*), fling, toss, pitch, lob. [➡THROW SOMETHING; 335] 2 *v* **produce**, generate, create, give rise to, engender, breed. [➡ENGENDER; 351] 3 *v* **mould**, form, shape, model. [➡MANUFACTURE; 350] 4 *n* **company**, troupe, dramatis personae, actors, players, performers. [➡PERFORMERS; 905]

See Compare and Contrast at **throw.**

cast about *v* [➡SEEK POSSESSION AND SEARCH; 457]

castanet *type of* **percussion instrument.** [➡MUSICAL INSTRUMENTS; 910]

cast an eye over *v* [➡LOOKING AND LOOKS; 701]

cast around *v* [➡SEEK POSSESSION AND SEARCH; 457]

cast a shadow over *v* **spoil**, hang over, darken, loom over, eclipse, chill, threaten, dampen. [➡WORSEN SOMETHING; 381] *Opposite:* brighten.

cast aside *v* **get rid of**, put aside, throw away, toss aside, forget, ignore, dismiss, take no notice of, spurn, reject, abandon. [➡GET RID OF SOMETHING; 452] *Opposite:* keep.

cast away *v* **give up**, throw away, throw up (*informal*), cast off, discard, jettison. [➡GET RID OF SOMETHING; 452] *Opposite:* keep.

castaway *n* **shipwrecked person**, survivor, exile. [➡SOLITARY PEOPLE; 942]

cast down *v* **discourage**, dishearten, deject (*archaic*), depress, demoralize, disparage, make unhappy. [➡UPSET, DISTRESS, AND HUMILIATE; 568] *Opposite:* cheer up.

caste *n* **class**, social group, standing, background, social order, kind, status. [➡CLASS STATUS; 889]

castigate (*formal*) *v* **criticize**, reprimand, tell off (*informal*), chastise (*formal*), scold, rebuke, haul over the coals, censure, blast (*informal*). [➡ACCUSE, BLAME, AND CRITICIZE; 642] *Opposite:* praise.

See Compare and Contrast at **criticize**.

castigation (*formal*) *n* **criticism**, rebuke, reprimand, telling-off (*informal*), ticking-off (*informal*), scolding, chastisement (*formal*). [➡CRITICISMS AND ANGRY OUTBURSTS; 50] *Opposite:* praise.

castigatory (*formal*) *adj* [➡ACCUSATORY AND DISAPPROVING; 635]

casting 1 *n* **forming**, manufacture, moulding. [➡CREATION; 347] 2 *n* **object**, artefact, cast, moulding. [➡REPRESENTATIONS AND GENERAL EXAMPLES; 65] 3 *n* **audition**, selection, screen test, interview, test, tryout. [➡PREPARATORY EVENT; 57]

cast-iron *adj* **guaranteed**, definite, firm, sure, watertight, unimpeachable, unshakable. [➡CERTAIN; 175] *Opposite:* dubious.

castle *n* **fortress**, fort, citadel, stronghold, bastion, palace, chateau. [➡FORTRESSES AND FORTIFICATIONS; 1089]

castles in Spain *n* [➡NONEXISTENT THINGS; 23]

castles in the air *n* **flight of fancy**, castles in Spain, fancy, dream, fantasy, notion, pipe dream, castles in the sky (*US*). [➡NONEXISTENT THINGS; 23] *Opposite:* reality.

castles in the sky (*US*) *n* [➡NONEXISTENT THINGS; 23]

castoff 1 *n* **reject**, discard, hand-me-down, throwaway. [➡RUBBISH AND USELESS OBJECTS; 1248] *Opposite:* purchase. 2 *adj* **discarded**, rejected, unwanted, old, second-hand, redundant, abandoned. [➡UNPOPULAR AND UNWANTED; 259] *Opposite:* new.

cast off *v* **discard**, get rid of, reject, dispose of, abandon, ditch (*informal*). [➡GET RID OF SOMETHING; 452]

castoffs *n* [➡GARMENTS AND OUTFITS; 865]

cast out (*formal*) *v* **throw out**, evict, boot out (*informal*), oust, eject, reject, sack (*informal*), remove, dispossess (*archaic or formal*), exile, banish, expel, exclude. [➡GET RID OF SOMETHING; 452] *Opposite:* install.

castrate *v* [➡STERILIZE; 727]

castration *n* [➡STERILIZE; 727]

casual 1 *adj* **unpremeditated**, unplanned, chance, unintentional, unintended, unexpected, off-the-cuff, spontaneous. [➡CHANCE, COINCIDENCE, AND ACCIDENT; 787] *Opposite:* premeditated. 2 *adj* **seasonal**, informal, temporary, occasional, periodic. [➡NEVER AND INFREQUENCY; 97] *Opposite:* permanent. 3 *adj* **informal**, nonchalant, relaxed, laid-back (*informal*), calm, cool, unconcerned, insouciant. [➡UNINTERESTED AND DETACHED; 630] *Opposite:* formal. 4 *adj* **indifferent**, careless, offhand, blasé, cavalier, slapdash, heedless. [➡NEUTRALITY AND INDIFFERENCE; 554] *Opposite:* careful.

casual clothes *n* [➡GARMENTS AND OUTFITS; 865]

casually 1 *adv* **informally**, nonchalantly, calmly, coolly, unconcernedly, insouciantly. [➡UNINTERESTED AND DETACHED; 630] *Opposite:* formally. 2 *adv* **carelessly**, offhandedly, indifferently, unceremoniously, heedlessly, cavalierly. [➡NEUTRALITY AND INDIFFERENCE; 554] *Opposite:* carefully.

casualness 1 *n* **informality**, nonchalance, calmness, coolness, insouciance, unconcern. [➡NEUTRALITY AND INDIFFERENCE; 554] *Opposite:* formality. 2 *n* **indifference**, undependability, carelessness, negligence, disregard, heedlessness, inattention. [➡LACK OF COMMITMENT AND UNRELIABILITY; 510] *Opposite:* care.

casuals *n* [➡GARMENTS AND OUTFITS; 865]

casualty *n* **injured person**, wounded person, dead person, fatality, loss. [➡DEAD PERSON; 926]

casual wear *n* [➡GARMENTS AND OUTFITS; 865]

casual work *n* [➡TYPES OF WORK; 835]

casual worker *n* [➡WORKER; 836]

casuistry *n* **sophistry**, unsound reasoning, subtlety, twisting the facts, justification, vindication, excuse. [➡INTENTION AND PURPOSE; 773]

cat 1 *n* **feline**, moggy, kitten, mouser, tom, tabby, tom cat. [➡FELINE; 983] 2 *n* (*US dated slang*) **man**, dude (*US slang*), guy (*informal*), bloke (*informal*), fella (*informal*), fellow (*dated*), boy, kid (*informal*). [➡MALE PERSON; 934]

cat

◆ *types of cat*
big cat, bobcat, Burmese cat, cheetah, jaguar, leopard, lion, lynx, Manx cat, mountain lion (*US*), ocelot, panther, Persian cat, puma, Siamese cat, tabby, tiger, tortoiseshell, wildcat

cataclysm *n* **catastrophe**, disaster, upheaval, calamity, debacle, tragedy. [➡DISASTERS; 253]

cataclysmic *adj* **catastrophic**, disastrous, calamitous, dreadful, tragic, earth-shattering, devastating. [➡DANGEROUS; 237]

catacomb 1 *n* **underground cemetery**, crypt, vault, tomb, mausoleum, sepulchre, burial chamber, necropolis, burial ground. [➡BURIAL PLACES AND ACCESSORIES; 930] 2 *n* **tunnel network**, underground passage, warren, tunnel, labyrinth, maze, cave, cavern. [➡BRIDGES, TUNNELS, CROSSINGS, AND JUNCTIONS; 1111]

catalepsy *n* [➡TIRED, ASLEEP AND UNCONSCIOUS; 739]

cataleptic *adj* [➡TIRED, ASLEEP AND UNCONSCIOUS; 739]

catalogue 1 *n* **list**, directory, index, file, register, log, record. [➡LISTS AND SCHEDULES; 588] 2 *n* **set**, collection, list, litany, series, string, sequence, succession, parade. [➡COLLECTIONS AND MIXTURES OF THINGS; 1243] 3 *v* **classify**, assemble, compile, arrange, categorize, record, sort, quantify, itemize. [➡ARRANGE AND CREATE ORDER; 358] 4 *v* **enter**, record, insert, include, document, register, log. [➡RECORD SOMETHING; 372] 5 *v* **itemize**, list, enumerate, document, detail, set out, record, make a list. [➡RECORD SOMETHING; 372]

cataloguing *n* **classification**, categorization, logging, sorting, taking down, arrangement. [➡ARRANGE AND CREATE ORDER; 358]

catalyst *n* **promoter**, facilitator, stimulus, spur, incentive, goad, spark. [➡BEGINNING; 53]

catamaran *type of* **sailing vessel**. [➡SHIPS AND BOATS; 1149]

cat-and-mouse *adj* **cruel**, sadistic, heartless, merciless, callous, exploitative. [➡MORALLY BAD; 776]

catapult *v* **hurtle**, shoot, throw, project, propel, toss, fling, sling, hurl. [➡DESPATCH AND SEND; 334]

cataract *n* **waterfall**, cascade, falls, chute, torrent, flume. [➡RIVERS, LAKES, AND STREAMS; 1042]

catarrh *n* **mucus**, phlegm, discharge. [➡EXCRETION AND EXCRETA; 723]

catastrophe *n* **disaster**, calamity, upheaval, devastation, ruin, misfortune, tragedy, cataclysm. [➡DISASTERS; 253] *Opposite:* good fortune.

catastrophic *adj* **disastrous**, shattering, calamitous, appalling, terrible, ruinous, tragic, devastating, cataclysmic. [➡BAD AND BADLY; 224] *Opposite:* fortunate.

catatonic 1 *adj* **inert**, rigid, unresponsive, withdrawn, impassive, introspective. [➡NEUTRALITY AND INDIFFERENCE; 554] 2 *adj* (*informal*) **unconscious**, asleep, comatose, inert, stupefied, incapable. [➡TIRED, ASLEEP AND UNCONSCIOUS; 739]

catboat *type of* **sailing vessel**. [➡SHIPS AND BOATS; 1149]

cat burglar *n* [➡CRIMINALS; 821]

catcall 1 *n* **jeer**, hiss, boo, whistle, shout, taunt, insult, mockery. [➡SOUNDS MADE BY PEOPLE; 1261] 2 *v* **taunt**, jeer, hiss, boo, shout, whistle. [➡UNFAVOURABLE NON-VERBAL RESPONSES; 655]

catch 1 *v* **hold**, hold on to, gather, grasp, receive. [➡CONTACT: HOLD; 412] 2 *v* **grasp**, grab, hold, take, clutch, seize, grab hold of. [➡GET; 421] *Opposite:* drop. 3 *v* **snare**, ensnare, entrap, hook, capture, net. [➡GET; 421] 4 *v* **capture**, arrest, apprehend, take prisoner, detain, seize, take captive, take hostage. [➡CAPTIVITY AND LOSS OF FREEDOM; 249] *Opposite:* release. 5 *v* **contract**, become infected with, fall victim to, pick up, go down with, fall prey to. [➡FALL ILL, TREAT, AND RECOVER; 729] 6 *v* **find**, discover, surprise, spot, notice, see. [➡FIND; 464] 7 *v* **hear**, perceive, notice, become aware of, grasp, understand. [➡HEAR; 708] 8 *v* **hit**, strike, knock, bump, bump into, crash into. [➡CONTACT: IMPACT; 414] 9 *v* **stick**, get trapped in, snag, cling, entangle, snarl, tangle. [➡FASTEN, LINK, AND JOIN; 409] *Opposite:* free. 10 *n* **fastening**, fastener, clasp, hook, latch, clip. [➡FASTENERS, LINKS, AND NETWORKS; 1246] 11 *n* (*informal*) **snag**, drawback, problem, difficulty, hitch, obstacle, impediment. [➡PROBLEM; 257]

catch-22 *n* **predicament**, no-win situation, dilemma. [➡DIFFICULT SITUATIONS; 72]

catch a glimpse of *v* **spot**, notice, spy, glimpse, catch sight of, catch, see. [➡SEE; 700]

catchall *adj* **general**, universal, all-encompassing, wide-ranging, blanket, comprehensive, complete. [➡WHOLENESS AND COMPLETENESS; 199]

catch fire *v* [➡FIRE, FLAMMABILITY, AND BURNING; 1164]

catch hold of *v* [➡CONTACT: HOLD; 412]

catching *adj* **infectious**, contagious, communicable, transmittable, easily spread. [➡SICKNESS; 730]

catch light *v* [➡FIRE, FLAMMABILITY, AND BURNING; 1164]

catch napping *v* **surprise**, catch out, catch on the hop, catch somebody with their pants down, catch somebody with their trousers down, take by surprise, catch in the act, catch red-handed, catch unawares, catch somebody off their guard. [➡ARRIVE; 12]

catch on (*informal*) 1 *v* **become popular**, take off (*informal*), rise in popularity, become fashionable, work, be in fashion. [➡SUCCEED AND WIN; 79] *Opposite:* flop. 2 *v* **understand**, get the message (*informal*), get the picture (*informal*), be with you, follow you, comprehend, grasp, get your drift. [➡UNDERSTAND AND GRASP; 760] *Opposite:* misunderstand.

catch out (*informal*) *v* **trip up**, wrong-foot, trick, discover, expose, trip, find out, catch. [➡LEARN AND DISCOVER; 763]

catch phrase *n* **catchword**, motto, slogan, tag. [➡THE SPOKEN WORD; 672]

catch sight of *v* **spot**, glimpse, catch a glimpse of, get a view of, see, notice, perceive. [➡SEE; 700] *Opposite:* miss.

catch some z's (*US informal*) *v* [➡SLEEP AND DREAM; 724]

catch unawares *v* **surprise**, startle, creep up on, give somebody a shock, ambush, pounce on, catch napping. [➡SURPRISE AND IMPRESS; 575]

catch up *v* **draw near**, draw level, get closer to, become equal, pull alongside, draw alongside, come up to, catch up with, overtake. [➡ACCOMPANY AND FOLLOW; 338] *Opposite:* fall behind.

catchword *n* **catch phrase**, byword, motto, watchword, slogan, tag. [➡THE SPOKEN WORD; 672]

catchy *adj* **memorable**, attractive, likable, beguiling, haunting, appealing, popular, captivating. [➡INTERESTING AND MEANINGFUL; 191] *Opposite:* forgettable.

catechesis *n* [➡RELIGIOUS PEOPLE; 779]

catechism 1 *n* **religious instruction**, religious education, religious teaching. [➡RELIGIOUS CONCEPTS; 777] 2 *n* **dogma**, party line, mantra, article of faith, tenet (*formal*), propaganda, creed. [➡RELIGIONS AND RELIGIOUS PRACTICES; 778] 3 *n* **examination**, questioning, interrogation, dialectic. [➡ASK PEOPLE QUESTIONS; 667]

catechize *v* [➡RELIGIONS AND RELIGIOUS PRACTICES; 778]

categorical *adj* **definite**, clear-cut, uncompromising, unconditional, unqualified, resounding, firm. [➡CERTAIN; 175] *Opposite:* tentative.

categorization 1 *n* **classification**, cataloguing, labelling, tagging, grouping, sorting. [➡ARRANGE AND CREATE ORDER; 358] 2 *n* **category**, class, group, set, grouping, division, classification. [➡COLLECTIONS AND MIXTURES OF THINGS; 1243]

categorize *v* **classify**, sort out, catalogue, label, tag, group, pigeonhole, compartmentalize. [➡ARRANGE AND CREATE ORDER; 358]

category *n* **class**, sort, grouping, type, kind, set, classification, group. [➡VARIETY, TYPE, KIND; 146]

See Compare and Contrast at **type**.

cater *v* **provide**, supply, outfit, furnish (*formal*), accommodate, gratify, satisfy, make provision, tailor, serve. [➡EQUIP AND SUPPLY; 436]

cater-cornered (*US*) *adv* [➡ORIENTATION AND ALIGNMENT; 1222]

caterpillar *type of* **insect stages of development**. [➡INSECT STAGES; 1020]

caterwaul 1 *v* **howl**, yowl, wail, squall, squeal, shriek, cry. [➡SOUND EMISSION BY ANIMALS OR BIRDS; 365] 2 *n* **yowl**, howl, wail, squall, squeal, shriek, cry. [➡SOUNDS MADE BY ANIMALS; 1260]

catfish *type of* **freshwater fish**. [➡FRESHWATER FISH; 1010]

catgut *n* **cord**, line, thread, string, filament. [➡TEXTILES AND THREADS; 1130]

catharsis *n* **release**, purification, cleansing, purging, purgation, liberation, freeing up. [➡FREEDOM AND LIBERTY; 209]

cathartic 1 *adj* **purifying**, cleansing, liberating, releasing, intense, emotional. [➡CALMING; 189] 2 *adj* **purgative** (*formal*), therapeutic, excretory, expulsive. [➡EMOTIONALLY PLEASANT; 188]

cathedral *type of* **church**. [➡RELIGIOUS BUILDINGS; 1084]

Catherine wheel *type of* **firework**. [➡EXPLOSIVES; 1154]

catheter *n* **tube**, line, drip, drain, feed, pipe. [➡WATERCOURSES; 1110]

catholic *adj* **wide-ranging**, broad, wide-reaching, all-embracing, extensive, varied. [➡DIFFERENCE; 150] *Opposite:* narrow.

catkin *n* **flower**, tassel, ament. [➡PARTS OF TREES AND PLANTS; 1026]

catnap 1 *n* **snooze** (*informal*), nap, doze, forty winks (*informal*), rest, siesta, power nap, sleep. [➡SLEEP AND DREAM; 724] 2 *v* **nap**, nod off, snooze (*informal*), catch forty winks (*informal*), doze, sleep, drop off (*informal*). [➡SLEEP AND DREAM; 724]

cat-o'-nine-tails *n* **whip**, scourge, lash, birch. [➡BLUNT INSTRUMENTS AND WHIPS; 1157]

catsuit *type of* **suit**. [➡GARMENTS AND OUTFITS; 865]

cattiness *n* **spitefulness**, nastiness, meanness, maliciousness, malevolence, viciousness, unkindness. [➡BAD MANNERS AND SOCIAL SKILLS; 522] *Opposite:* kindness.

cattle *n* **cows**, oxen, bulls, bullocks, steers, heifers, calves, beef, livestock. [➡FARM ANIMAL; 982]

cattle thief *n* [➡CRIMINALS; 821]

catty *adj* **spiteful**, nasty, venomous, mean, malicious, malevolent, vicious, unkind. [➡RUDE AND HOSTILE; 626] *Opposite:* nice.

catty-cornered (*US*) *adv* [➡ORIENTATION AND ALIGNMENT; 1222]

catwalk 1 *n* **stage**, walkway, runway, ramp, gangplank. [➡STAGES, PLATFORMS, AND RAISED AREAS; 1097] 2 *n* **bridge**, footbridge, walkway. [➡BRIDGES, TUNNELS, CROSSINGS, AND JUNCTIONS; 1111]

caucus 1 *n* **conclave**, assembly, committee, conference, convention, group. [➡MEETINGS AND ASSEMBLIES; 43] 2 *n* **faction**, bloc, alliance, league, union, interest group. [➡GROUPS WITH A COMMON INTEREST; 938]

caught up 1 *adj* **engrossed**, absorbed, captivated, enthralled, involved, occupied, abstracted, preoccupied. [➡PENSIVENESS AND INTEREST; 539] *Opposite:* indifferent. 2 *adj* **involved**, embroiled, implicated, engaged, connected, mixed up, entangled, drawn in. [➡RELATED; 143] *Opposite:* uninvolved.

cauldron *n* **pan**, container, cooking pot, pot, vat. [➡CONTAINERS, RECEPTACLES, AND PACKAGING; 1244]

cauliflower *type of* **vegetable**. [➡FRUIT AND VEGETABLES; 1175]

caulk *v* **seal**, waterproof, fill, block, plug, line. [➡DECORATE, ADORN, AND APPLY COATINGS; 406]

causal *adj* **fundamental**, underlying, contributory, contributing, connecting, pivotal, instrumental, causative. [➡CAUSATION; 169]

causality *n* **cause and effect**, connection, interconnection, connectedness, causation, causativeness, fate, destiny, karma. [➡CONNECTION; 144]

causation *n* **action**, connection, interconnection, relationship, causality, causativeness. [➡CAUSATION; 169]

causative *adj* **causal**, instrumental, contributing, contributory, connective, relevant, two-way. [➡RELATED; 143]

cause 1 *n* **reason**, grounds, source, root, origin, basis, foundation. [➡CAUSATION; 169] *Opposite:* effect. 2 *v* **make happen**, bring about, produce, set off, instigate, trigger, trigger off, begin, initiate, effect. [➡CAUSE TO HAPPEN; 31] *Opposite:* impede.

cause offence *v* **be offensive**, shock, hurt somebody's feelings, offend, put somebody's nose out of joint, antagonize, irritate. [➡UPSET, DISTRESS, AND HUMILIATE; 568]

causeway *n* **walkway**, ramp, boardwalk, path, road, dike, land bridge. [➡BRIDGES, TUNNELS, CROSSINGS, AND JUNCTIONS; 1111]

caustic 1 *adj* **corrosive**, acid, acidic, corroding, burning. [➡PHYSICAL TEXTURE; 1221] 2 *adj* **sarcastic**, scathing, mordant, astringent, cutting, biting, acerbic, acid, razor-sharp, unkind. [➡RUDE AND HOSTILE; 626] *Opposite:* gentle.

See Compare and Contrast at **sarcastic**.

cauterize *v* **seal**, close, burn, sear, treat. [➡FASTEN, LINK, AND JOIN; 409]

caution 1 *n* **carefulness**, thoughtfulness, attentiveness, attention, risk avoidance, care, restraint, cautiousness. [➡POSITIVE INTELLECTUAL CHARACTERISTICS; 525] 2 *n* **warning**, alert, notification, ultimatum, caveat. [➡ADVICE; 690] 3 *v* **warn**, alert, notify, signal, give notice, advise, admonish. [➡ADVISE AND WARN; 614]

cautionary *adj* **warning**, deterrent, admonitory, advisory, instructive. [➡ADVISE AND WARN; 614]

cautious *adj* **careful**, watchful, thoughtful, alert, vigilant, guarded, wary, restrained, precautious, circumspect, chary, prudent, cagey (*informal*). [➡CAUTIOUS AND CAREFUL; 283] *Opposite:* reckless.

Compare and Contrast: ***cautious, careful, chary, circumspect, prudent, vigilant, wary, guarded, cagey***

CORE MEANING: ATTENTIVE TO RISK OR DANGER

cautious aware of potential risk and behaving accordingly; ***careful*** taking reasonable care to avoid risks; ***chary*** cautiously reluctant to act; ***circumspect*** taking into consideration all possible circumstances and consequences before acting; ***prudent*** showing good judgment or shrewdness; ***vigilant*** alert and conscious of possible dangers; ***wary*** showing watchfulness or suspicion; ***guarded*** reluctant to share information with others; ***cagey*** (*informal*) secretive and guarded.

cautiousness *n* **caution**, carefulness, thoughtfulness, attentiveness, wariness, care, restraint, prudence. [➡POSITIVE INTELLECTUAL CHARACTERISTICS; 525] *Opposite:* recklessness.

cavalcade *n* **procession**, parade, column, line, convoy, caravan. [➡PERFORMANCES AND SHOWS; 42]

cavalier *adj* **careless**, offhand, inconsiderate, high-handed, arrogant, haughty, casual, rude. [➡LACK OF COMMITMENT AND UNRELIABILITY; 510] *Opposite:* polite.

cavalry *n* **mounted troops**, horse regiment, horse soldiers. [➡THE ARMED FORCES; 827]

cave *n* **cavern**, grotto, hollow, pothole, fissure, cavity. [➡GEOLOGICAL FEATURES; 1056]

caveat *n* **warning**, caution, admonition, qualification, stipulation, requirement, limitation, proviso. [➡ADVICE; 690]

cave in 1 *v* **collapse**, subside, fall in, fall down, topple, crash, tumble down. [➡CHANGE OF SHAPE; 386] 2 *v* **yield**, give in, surrender, give, admit defeat, concede. [➡FORGET, FORGIVE, AND ACCEPT; 749] *Opposite:* withstand.

cave-in 1 *n* **collapse**, fall, drop, slide, demolition. [➡DISASTERS; 253] 2 *n* **capitulation**, yielding, collapse, surrender, concession, withdrawal, about-turn, U-turn, about-face (*US*). [➡DECISIVE MOMENTS; 44]

caveman (*informal*) *n* **brute**, animal, gorilla, boor, ape, pig, barbarian. [➡VILLAINS AND THUGS; 947]

caver *n* [➡PEOPLE IN SPORTS AND LEISURE; 876]

cavern *n* **cave**, grotto, pothole, hollow, cavity, fissure. [➡GEOLOGICAL FEATURES; 1056]

cavernous 1 *adj* **vast**, spacious, deep, yawning, gaping, roomy, commodious. [➡LARGE; 1192] *Opposite:* cramped. 2 *adj* **hollow**, echoing, resounding, sounding, resonant, reverberating, sonorous. [➡EMPTY; 1237]

caviar *n* **roe**, eggs, spawn, ova. [➡SEA FOOD; 1189]

cavil *v* **quibble**, split hairs, be picky, complain, carp, object. [➡ARGUE AND FIGHT – TWO-WAY; 644] *Opposite:* accept.

cavity *n* **hole**, space, hollow, crater, void, crack, opening, nook, fissure, cleft. [➡HOLES, GAPS, AND FORKS; 1251]

cavort *v* **frolic**, prance, caper, gambol, romp, dance, horse around, horse about. [➡FIDGET AND FROLIC; 312]

caw 1 *v* **call**, cry, croak, squawk. [➡SOUND EMISSION BY ANIMALS OR BIRDS; 365] 2 *n* **cry**, call, croak, croaking, squawk, squawking. [➡SOUNDS MADE BY BIRDS; 1262]

cayenne pepper *type of* **spice**. [➡HERBS AND SPICES; 1174]

cayman *type of* **reptile**. [➡REPTILES; 994]

CB *n* **radio**, shortwave radio, citizens' band, telecommunication, walkie-talkie. [➡TELEVISION AND RADIO; 607]

CD *part of* **audio equipment**. [➡AUDIO EQUIPMENT; 1138]

CD player 1 *n* **stereo**, personal stereo, hi-fi, CD, sound system, boom box (*US*). [➡RECORDINGS AND PLAYERS; 911] 2 *type of* **audio equipment**. [➡AUDIO EQUIPMENT; 1138]

CD-ROM *type of* **hardware**. [➡COMPUTERS AND COMPUTING; 1126]

cease *v* **stop**, finish, end, come to an end, come to a close, die away, die down, close down, conclude, terminate (*formal*). [➡STOP ACTING; 265] *Opposite:* start.

ceasefire *n* **truce**, armistice, cessation of hostilities, end of hostilities, break in fighting, negotiating period. [➡PAUSES AND PHASES; 56]

ceaseless *adj* **unending**, continual, constant, incessant, perpetual, never-ending, eternal, interminable, continuous, endless. [➡PERMANENCE: WITHOUT END; 94] *Opposite:* sporadic.

ceaselessness *n* [➡PERMANENCE: WITHOUT END; 94]

cease to exist *v* [➡CEASE TO EXIST; 22]

cease trading *v* **go out of business**, go bust, shut down, go bankrupt, close, fold. [➡FAIL OR BE UNSUCCESSFUL; 75]

cedar *type of* **evergreen tree**. [➡EVERGREEN AND CONIFEROUS TREES; 1029]

cede (*formal*) *v* **yield**, concede, give up, give way, let go, surrender, relinquish, abandon. [➡FORGET, FORGIVE, AND ACCEPT; 749] *Opposite:* resist.

cedilla *type of* **diacritic**. [➡ASPECTS OF LANGUAGE; 683]

ceilidh *n* **dance**, barn dance, singsong, party, celebration, sing-along (*US*). [➡PARTIES, DANCES, AND CELEBRATIONS; 37]

ceiling 1 *n* **limit**, threshold, cutoff point, cap, check, constraint, control. [➡MAJORITY; 139] 2 *n* [➡ROOFS, ROOF PARTS, AND CEILINGS; 1102]

ceiling rose *type of* **general fittings**. [➡FITTINGS; 859]

celeb (*informal*) *n* [➡IMPORTANT OR FAMOUS PEOPLE; 893]

celebrate 1 *v* **enjoy yourself**, have fun, have a good time, make merry, revel, push the boat out (*informal*), party (*informal*), rejoice (*literary*). [➡LEISURE AND RECREATION; 874] *Opposite:* lament. 2 *v* **commemorate**, observe, mark, keep, remember, honour. [➡REMEMBER; 747] 3 *v* **praise**, acclaim, commend, applaud, hail, sing the praises. [➡PRAISE AND ENCOURAGE; 648]

celebrated *adj* **famous**, renowned, eminent, distinguished, illustrious, notable, great, feted, admired. [➡KNOWN AND FAMOUS; 182] *Opposite:* unknown.

celebration 1 *n* **festivity**, party, festival, gala, fete, jamboree, revel. [➡PARTIES, DANCES, AND CELEBRATIONS; 37] 2 *n* **commemoration**, remembrance, observance, salutation, memorial, salute. [➡CEREMONIES AND ANNIVERSARIES; 38]

celebratory *adj* **festive**, triumphant, special, congratulatory, commemorative. [➡PARTIES, DANCES, AND CELEBRATIONS; 37]

celebrity 1 *n* **superstar**, star, personality, name, figure, celeb (*informal*), personage (*formal*), big shot (*informal*), household name, public figure, luminary, icon. [➡RICH PEOPLE; 895] *Opposite:* nobody. 2 *n* **fame**, renown, notoriety, superstardom, prominence, stardom, recognition, acclaim, popularity. [➡KNOWN AND FAMOUS; 182] *Opposite:* obscurity.

celerity (*formal*) *n* **speed**, rapidity, swiftness, alacrity, haste, briskness, hurry, speediness. [➡SPEED; 102] *Opposite:* slowness.

celery *type of* **salad vegetable.** [➡FRUIT AND VEGETABLES; 1175]

celesta *type of* **keyboard.** [➡MUSICAL INSTRUMENTS; 910]

celestial 1 *adj* **heavenly**, holy, spiritual, godly, otherworldly, saintly. [➡RELIGIOUS CONCEPTS; 777] 2 *adj* **cosmic**, astronomic, planetary, galactic, solar, lunar, extraterrestrial, space. [➡THE SOLAR SYSTEM AND ASTRONOMY; 1059]

celibate *n* [➡ASCETIC PEOPLE; 883]

cell 1 *n* **lockup**, prison cell, jail cell. [➡BUILDINGS FOR CONFINING PEOPLE; 1093] 2 *n* **group**, sect, faction, cabal, caucus, offshoot. [➡GROUPS WITH A COMMON INTEREST; 938] 3 *type of* **room in public buildings.** [➡TYPES OF ROOM; 1096]

cellar *type of* **storage space.** [➡STORES AND STORAGE BUILDINGS; 1087]

cellist *n* **musician**, instrumentalist, player, soloist. [➡MUSICIANS AND SINGERS; 908]

cello *type of* **stringed instrument.** [➡MUSICAL INSTRUMENTS; 910]

cellphone *type of* **telecommunications equipment.** [➡TELECOMMUNICATIONS; 1129]

cellular phone *type of* **telecommunications equipment.** [➡TELECOMMUNICATIONS; 1129]

cellulite *n* **fat**, fatty deposits, orange-peel skin, lumpiness, dimpling. [➡CONDITIONS AFFECTING THE SKIN; 722]

celluloid *type of* **plastic.** [➡PLASTICS; 1133]

cement 1 *n* [➡BUILDING MATERIALS; 1076] 2 *n* **glue**, adhesive, paste, epoxy resin. [➡ADHESIVES; 1270] 3 *v* **join**, stick, fix, glue, fasten together. [➡FASTEN, LINK, AND JOIN; 409] *Opposite:* separate. 4 *v* **strengthen**, reinforce, make stronger, prop up, fortify, buttress. [➡IMPROVE STRENGTH AND DURABILITY; 379] *Opposite:* undermine.

cemetery *n* **graveyard**, burial ground, churchyard, garden of remembrance, boneyard (*informal*), mausoleum. [➡BURIAL AND PREPARATION FOR BURIAL; 929]

cenotaph *n* **war memorial**, monument, memorial. [➡MONUMENTS; 1091]

censor 1 *v* **edit**, cut, remove, expurgate, bowdlerize, amend, blue-pencil. [➡WITHHOLD INFORMATION; 688] 2 *v* **stifle**, gag, repress, suppress, control. [➡WITHHOLD INFORMATION; 688]

censored *adj* **cut**, expurgated, bowdlerized, changed, amended, blue-pencilled. [➡SECRET AND UNKNOWN; 180] *Opposite:* complete.

censorious *adj* **disapproving**, critical, severe, stern, hypercritical, overcritical, contemptuous. [➡ACCUSATORY AND DISAPPROVING; 635] *Opposite:* approving.

censoriousness *n* [➡ANTAGONISM; 553]

censorship *n* **restriction**, control, cutting, editing, bowdlerization, expurgation, suppression. [➡WITHHOLD INFORMATION; 688]

censure 1 *n* **criticism**, disapproval, condemnation, denunciation, deprecation, scorn, contempt. [➡ANTAGONISM; 553] *Opposite:* approval. 2 *v* **criticize**, fault, reprimand, condemn, slate, knock (*slang*), reproach, scorn, denounce. [➡PROTEST AND EXPRESS DISAPPROVAL; 643] *Opposite:* praise.

See Compare and Contrast at **criticize, disapprove.**

census 1 *n* **population count**, survey, poll, registration. [➡ELECTIONS AND SUFFRAGE; 807] 2 *n* **survey**, count, poll, tally, register, information gathering, fact finding. [➡ELECTIONS AND SUFFRAGE; 807]

centaur *type of* **mythological creature.** [➡MYTHICAL CREATURES; 1036]

centenary *n* **anniversary**, birthday, centennial (*US*). [➡CEREMONIES AND ANNIVERSARIES; 38]

centennial (*US*) *n* **anniversary**, birthday, centenary. [➡CEREMONIES AND ANNIVERSARIES; 38]

centipede *type of* **land invertebrate.** [➡LAND INVERTEBRATE; 1021]

central 1 *adj* **middle**, mid, inner, innermost. [➡CENTRAL PARTS OF PHYSICAL OBJECTS; 1250] *Opposite:* outer. 2 *adj* **vital**, dominant, essential, fundamental, chief, most important, crucial, principal, significant, main, predominant, key, pivotal, focal. [➡IMPORTANT; 195] *Opposite:* unimportant.

central heating *n* [➡HEATING, REFRIGERATION, AND VENTILATION; 1141]

centralism *n* **control**, concentration, monopolism, authoritarianism, centralization. [➡STYLES AND SYSTEMS OF GOVERNMENT; 806]

centrality *n* **importance**, significance, criticality, supremacy, uniqueness, consequence (*formal*), import. [➡IMPORTANCE AND SIGNIFICANCE; 193] *Opposite:* irrelevance.

centralization *n* **unification**, integration, concentration, control, domination, monopolization, centralism. [➡GOVERNMENT POLICIES; 810] *Opposite:* decentralization.

centralize *v* **unify**, consolidate, integrate, compact, concentrate, collect, merge. [➡COMBINE AND MIX; 401] *Opposite:* decentralize.

central processing unit *type of* **hardware.** [➡COMPUTERS AND COMPUTING; 1126]

centre 1 *n* **midpoint**, middle, halfway point, focus, focal point, epicentre, bull's eye. [➡CENTRAL PARTS OF PHYSICAL OBJECTS; 1250] *Opposite:* edge. 2 *n* **filling**, inside, middle, core, layer, kernel, heart, interior. [➡CENTRAL PARTS OF PHYSICAL OBJECTS; 1250] *Opposite:* coating. 3 *n* **heart**, city centre, downtown (*US*). [➡HUMAN SETTLEMENTS; 1069] 4 *n* **complex**, facility, development, building. [➡PUBLIC BUILDINGS AND MEETING PLACES; 1080] 5 *n* **focus**, heart, core, bottom, root, nub. [➡CENTRAL PARTS OF PHYSICAL OBJECTS; 1250] *Opposite:* periphery. 6 *n* **cluster**, concentration, focus, magnet, hotbed, breeding ground, birthplace. [➡CENTRAL PARTS OF PHYSICAL OBJECTS; 1250] 7 *n* **middle ground**, consensus, majority, middle course, happy medium, middle England, centre ground, middle America (*US*). [➡STYLES AND SYSTEMS OF GOVERNMENT; 806] *Opposite:* extreme. 8 *n* **axis**, pivot, pivotal point, fulcrum. [➡CENTRAL PARTS OF PHYSICAL OBJECTS; 1250] 9 *v* **align**, position, arrange, balance, adjust, place. [➡POSITION SOMETHING; 326] 10 *v* **focus on**, turn on, concentrate on, home in on, revolve around, get to grips with, relate to, address, involve, target, examine, deal with. [➡BE ABOUT SOMETHING; 62] *Opposite:* ignore.

centrepiece *n* **centre of attention**, focus, key feature, flagship, jewel in the crown, heart, core, linchpin, cornerstone, foundation, pride and joy. [➡MOST IMPORTANT THING; 198]

centre stage *adv* **to the fore**, at the fore, to the front, at the front, at the centre of attention, in the limelight, into the limelight. [➡FUNDAMENTAL; 196]

centrist *adj* **middle-of-the-road**, moderate, mainstream, reasonable, uncontroversial, safe. [➡STYLES AND SYSTEMS OF GOVERNMENT; 806] *Opposite:* extreme.

centuries old *adj* [➡OLD, OLD-FASHIONED; 168]

century *n* **period**, era, time, span, epoch. [➡EPOCHS AND ERAS; 89]

CEO *n* **chief executive officer**, boss, chief, head, manager, number one (*informal*), chief executive, managing director, MD. [➡BUSINESS PEOPLE; 794]

cep *type of* **fungus**. [➡MICROORGANISMS, FUNGI, AND ALGAE; 1023]

ceramic 1 *adj* **earthenware**, clay, pottery, terracotta, ironstone china, ironstone, stoneware, porcelain. [➡POTTERY; 1134] 2 *type of* **pottery**. [➡POTTERY; 1134]

cereal *n* **breakfast cereal**, porridge, grits (*US*). [➡CEREAL FOODS; 1177]

cereal

◆ *types of cereal*
barley, corn (*US*), maize, millet, oat, rice, rye, sorghum, wheat

cerebral *adj* **intellectual**, rational, brainy (*informal*), highbrow, logical, analytical. [➡THE NATURE OF IDEAS; 772] *Opposite:* intuitive.

ceremonial 1 *adj* **ritual**, traditional, ritualistic, formal, official, grand, state. [➡CEREMONIES AND ANNIVERSARIES; 38] *Opposite:* informal. 2 *n* **rite**, ritual, ceremony, pomp, pageantry, formality. [➡CEREMONIES AND ANNIVERSARIES; 38]

ceremonial dress *n* [➡GARMENTS AND OUTFITS; 865]

ceremonious *adj* **formal**, solemn, dignified, grand, majestic, regal, imperious, pompous. [➡LEVELS OF FORMALITY; 523] *Opposite:* informal.

ceremony *n* **rite**, ritual, formality, formal procedure, service, observance, ceremonial. [➡CEREMONIES AND ANNIVERSARIES; 38]

cerise *type of* **pink**. [➡COLOURS; 1223]

cert (*informal*) *n* **certainty**, foregone conclusion, dead cert (*informal*), cast-iron certainty, fait accompli, safe bet, inevitability. [➡CERTAIN; 175]

certain 1 *adj* **sure**, convinced, positive, confident, firm, definite, assured. [➡CERTAINTY; 562] *Opposite:* unsure. 2 *adj* **some**, a number of, a few, several, selected, a selection of, a variety of. [➡AMOUNT AND QUANTITY; 112] *Opposite:* all. 3 *adj* **evident**, dependable, undeniable, guaranteed, clear, certified, assured, accurate, reliable. [➡CERTAIN; 175] *Opposite:* uncertain. 4 *adj* **particular**, specific, individual, precise, specified, one. [➡EXACT; 204]

certainly 1 *adv* **surely**, positively, definitely, without doubt, undoubtedly, unquestionably. [➡CERTAINTY; 562] *Opposite:* possibly. 2 *adv* **indeed**, absolutely, definitely, of course, sure, indubitably (*formal*), emphatically. [➡CERTAIN; 175]

certainty 1 *n* **foregone conclusion**, safe bet, cert (*informal*), cast-iron certainty, inevitability. [➡CERTAIN; 175] 2 *n* **confidence**, conviction, faith, belief, assurance, firmness, sureness, certitude. [➡CERTAINTY; 562] *Opposite:* uncertainty.

certifiable *adj* [➡TRUE AND REAL; 172]

certificate *n* **document**, licence, diploma, credential, documentation, record, permit. [➡OFFICIAL DOCUMENTS; 587]

certification *n* **guarantee**, warranty, documentation, authorization, accreditation, endorsement. [➡OFFICIAL DOCUMENTS; 587]

certified *adj* **official**, licensed, approved, authorized, accredited, professional, expert, qualified. [➡QUALIFICATIONS; 843]

certify *v* **confirm**, state, verify, endorse, attest, declare. [➡APPROVE AND CONFIRM; 647]

certitude *n* **conviction**, certainty, sureness, assurance, confidence, belief, faith. [➡CERTAINTY; 562]

cessation *n* **end**, termination, close, stop, ending, pause, interruption. [➡END; 54] *Opposite:* start.

cesspit *n* **tank**, pit, sewer, drain, gutter, cesspool. [➡WATERCOURSES; 1110]

cha-cha *type of* **dance**. [➡DANCE; 903]

chafe 1 *v* **rub**, scrape, irritate, scratch, abrade, wear down. [➡WORSEN APPEARANCE; 383] 2 *v* **annoy**, bother, provoke, vex, irritate, aggravate (*informal*). [➡ANGER AND ANNOY; 570]

chaff 1 *v* **tease**, mock, josh (*informal*), make fun of, pull somebody's leg (*informal*). [➡JOKES AND TEASING; 675] 2 *n* **joking**, banter, repartee, teasing. [➡JOKES AND TEASING; 675]

chaffinch *type of* **common bird**. [➡BIRD; 997]

chagrin *n* **humiliation**, mortification, vexation, irritation, disappointment, embarrassment, sorrow, annoyance. [➡ EMBARRASSMENT AND HUMILIATION; 543]

chagrined *adj* [➡ SADNESS, DISTRESS, AND DESPAIR; 540]

chain 1 *n* **cable**, hawser, restraint, shackle, manacle. [➡ FASTENERS, LINKS, AND NETWORKS; 1246] 2 *n* **group**, string, franchise, series. [➡ BUSINESS ENTERPRISES AND RELATED BODIES; 793] 3 *n* **sequence**, series, string, succession, procession. [➡ CHAIN OF EVENTS; 163] 4 *v* **bind**, manacle, shackle, lock up, restrain, immobilize, chain up. [➡ FASTEN, LINK, AND JOIN; 409] 5 *type of* **necklace**. [➡ JEWELLERY; 866] 6 *part of* **bike**. [➡ BIKES, CARS, AND CARRIAGES; 1148]

chain reaction *n* **series of events**, train of events, knock-on effect, domino effect. [➡ EVENTS AND OCCURRENCES; 35]

chain store *type of* **retail outlet**. [➡ RETAIL OUTLETS; 1082]

chair 1 *n* **chairperson**, presiding officer, president, head, leader. [➡ BUSINESS PEOPLE; 794] 2 *v* **preside**, take the chair, lead, direct, oversee, manage. [➡ BE IN CHARGE; 271] 3 *type of* **seating**. [➡ FURNITURE; 858]

chair lift *type of* **leisure vehicle**. [➡ VEHICLES; 1144]

chairperson *n* **presiding officer**, president, chair, head, leader. [➡ BUSINESS PEOPLE; 794]

chaise longue *type of* **seating**. [➡ FURNITURE; 858]

chalcedony *type of* **gemstone**. [➡ PRECIOUS STONES; 1277]

chalet *type of* **house**. [➡ RESIDENTIAL BUILDINGS; 1077]

chalice (*literary*) *n* **cup**, goblet, vessel. [➡ CONTAINERS, RECEPTACLES, AND PACKAGING; 1244]

chalk 1 *v* **write**, draw, mark, doodle, scribble, sketch. [➡ CREATE IMAGES; 357] 2 *type of* **stone**. [➡ STONES, ROCKS, AND BOULDERS; 1057]

chalkboard (*US*) *n* [➡ WRITING AND DRAWING IMPLEMENTS, AND MEDIA; 602]

chalk up *v* **score**, mark up, rack up (*informal*), gain, win, obtain, get, collect, accumulate. [➡ GET MONEY OR REWARD; 422]

chalky 1 *adj* **crumbly**, dry, powdery, fine, dusty, soft. [➡ PHYSICAL TEXTURE; 1221] 2 *adj* **white**, pale, pallid, ghostly, deathly, ashen, anaemic. [➡ COMPLEXION; 481]

challenge 1 *v* **dare**, defy, throw down the gauntlet, test. [➡ GAMBLE AND TAKE RISKS; 467] 2 *v* **confront**, defy, brave, face up to. [➡ ACCUSE, BLAME, AND CRITICIZE; 642] 3 *v* **dispute**, contest, object to, question, argue, oppose. [➡ DENY AND REJECT; 645] 4 *n* **test**, trial, task, contest, encounter. [➡ NON-AGGRESSIVE/SPORTING EVENT; 40]

challenger *n* **contestant**, contender, competitor, opponent, pretender, rival. [➡ COMPETITORS; 41]

challenging 1 *adj* **demanding**, taxing, testing, difficult, tough, exigent (*formal*), trying, tricky. [➡ POSITIVELY COMPLEX OR COMPLICATED; 218] *Opposite:* easy. 2 *adj* **stimulating**, thought-provoking, interesting, inspiring, exciting, puzzling, perplexing. [➡ INTERESTING AND MEANINGFUL; 191] *Opposite:* routine. 3 *adj* **defiant**, disobedient, rebellious, insolent, impudent, bold. [➡ REBELLIOUSNESS AND DISOBEDIENCE; 566] *Opposite:* compliant.

chamber 1 *n* **hall**, assembly room, meeting room, boardroom, legislative chamber, judicial chamber. [➡ TYPES OF ROOM; 1096] 2 *n* **cavity**, hollow, compartment, space, slot. [➡ HOLES, GAPS, AND FORKS; 1251]

chamberlain *n* **official**, attendant, courtier, servant, manager, supervisor, administrator. [➡ ADMINISTRATIVE OFFICERS; 811]

chambermaid *type of* **servant**. [➡ DOMESTIC AND KITCHEN WORKERS; 850]

chamber music *type of* **classical music**. [➡ MUSIC, SONGS, AND SINGING; 907]

chamber orchestra *type of* **band**. [➡ MUSICIANS AND SINGERS; 908]

chamber pot *n* [➡ CONTAINERS, RECEPTACLES, AND PACKAGING; 1244]

chameleon 1 *n* **changeable person**, butterfly, trimmer, dilettante. [➡ SUPERFICIAL OR INSINCERE PEOPLE; 951] 2 *type of* **reptile**. [➡ REPTILES; 994]

chamois 1 *type of* **leather**. [➡ FABRICS; 1131] 2 *type of* **deer or antelope**. [➡ DEER AND ANTELOPE; 981]

champ 1 *v* **chew**, munch, chomp (*informal*), grind, masticate. [➡ EAT AND NOT EAT; 711] 2 *n* (*informal*) **champion**, winner, victor, title holder. [➡ COMPETITORS; 41]

champagne *type of* **yellow**. [➡ COLOURS; 1223]

champing at the bit *adj* [➡ DESIRE AND WANT; 580]

champion 1 *n* **winner**, champ (*informal*), victor, title holder. [➡ COMPETITORS; 41] 2 *n* **defender**, supporter, backer, campaigner, advocate, guardian. [➡ DEVOTEES AND ADDICTED PEOPLE; 557] 3 *v* **defend**, support, back, campaign, fight for, advocate, side with, stand up for. [➡ APPROVE AND CONFIRM; 647]

championship *n* **finals**, contest, challenge, title fight, battle, competition, tournament. [➡ NON-AGGRESSIVE/SPORTING EVENT; 40]

chance 1 *n* **possibility**, probability, likelihood, opening, opportunity, option, prospect, occasion. [➡ POSSIBLE AND PROBABLE; 178] 2 *n* **gamble**, risk, hazard, venture, stake. [➡ GAMBLE AND TAKE RISKS; 467] 3 *n* **luck**, fate, fortune, destiny, good fortune. [➡ CHANCE, COINCIDENCE, AND ACCIDENT; 787] 4 *v* **risk**, hazard, gamble, try, attempt, venture. [➡ GAMBLE AND TAKE RISKS; 467] 5 *adj* **accidental**, coincidental, casual, fortuitous, unintended, unplanned. [➡ CHANCE, COINCIDENCE, AND ACCIDENT; 787] *Opposite:* planned.

chancel *n* [➡ PARTS OF RELIGIOUS BUILDINGS; 1085]

chancellor *n* **president**, leader, head of state, premier, prime minister, head of government. [➡ POLITICAL OFFICES AND POLITICIANS; 808]

chance meeting *n* [➡ CHANCE EVENT; 36]

chance occurrence *n* [➡ CHANCE EVENT; 36]

chance on *v* **stumble on**, happen on, strike on, hit on, come across, run into, find. [➡ FIND; 464]

chancy *adj* **risky**, dicey (*informal*), dodgy (*informal*), hazardous, dangerous, perilous, uncertain, precarious, unreliable. [➡ DANGEROUS; 237] *Opposite:* safe.

chandelier *type of* **light.** [➡LIGHT; 1163]

change 1 *n* **alteration**, modification, variation, transformation, revolution, conversion, adjustment, amendment, difference. [➡CHANGE; 373] 2 *n* **coins**, cash, loose change. [➡MONEY; 140] 3 *v* **alter**, modify, vary, shift, revolutionize, adjust, amend. [➡CHANGE; 373] 4 *v* **exchange**, swap (*informal*), replace, substitute, change over, trade, switch, convert, transform, transmute. [➡EXCHANGE AND INTERCHANGE; 449]

> **Compare and Contrast:** ***change, alter, modify, convert, vary, shift, transform, transmute***
>
> CORE MEANING: TO MAKE OR BECOME DIFFERENT
>
> ***change*** to make or become different in any way; ***alter*** to change, especially to change an aspect of something; ***modify*** to make minor changes or alterations, especially in order to improve something; ***convert*** to change something from one form or function to another; ***vary*** to change within a range of possibilities, or in connection with something else, with a suggestion of instability; ***shift*** to change from one position or direction to another; ***transform*** to make a radical change into a different form; ***transmute*** to change into another form, used especially in technical contexts.

changeability 1 *n* **unpredictability**, unsettledness, variableness, variability, irregularity, instability. [➡FINITENESS, VARIABILITY, AND TRANSIENCE; 96] *Opposite:* constancy. 2 *n* **indecisiveness**, fickleness, unpredictability, flightiness, volatility, instability, untrustworthiness, unreliability, changeableness. [➡LACK OF COMMITMENT AND UNRELIABILITY; 510] *Opposite:* constancy.

changeable *adj* **variable**, unsettled, unpredictable, unreliable, unstable, unfixed, irregular, undependable, erratic, inconsistent, inconstant. [➡FINITENESS, VARIABILITY, AND TRANSIENCE; 96] *Opposite:* constant.

change course *v* [➡CHANGE DIRECTION OF MOTION; 345]

changed *adj* **altered**, different, transformed, reformed, rehabilitated, improved, new. [➡CHANGE; 373] *Opposite:* unchanged.

change direction 1 *v* **veer off**, swerve, turn, bend, curve round. [➡CHANGE DIRECTION OF MOTION; 345] 2 *v* **start afresh**, change course, change tack, rethink, remodel, turn over a new leaf, have second thoughts. [➡MAKE DECISIONS AND CHOICES; 753]

change for the better 1 *v* **improve**, get better, look up, pick up (*informal*), progress. [➡IMPROVE SOMETHING; 375] *Opposite:* deteriorate. 2 *n* **improvement**, progress, development, turn-up, upswing. [➡SOURCE OF HAPPINESS, PLEASURE, OR IMPROVEMENT; 210] *Opposite:* deterioration.

changeless *adj* **unchanging**, consistent, fixed, immutable, permanent, everlasting, eternal, unalterable. [➡PERMANENCE: WITHOUT CHANGE; 95] *Opposite:* changing.

changelessness *n* [➡PERMANENCE: WITHOUT CHANGE; 95]

change of heart *n* **about-turn**, volte-face, second thoughts, rethink, change of attitude, change of opinion, U-turn, about-face (*US*). [➡DECISIVE MOMENTS; 44]

change over *v* **switch**, swap (*informal*), substitute, convert, transfer, change round, exchange. [➡CHANGE ONE THING FOR ANOTHER; 399]

changeover *n* **move**, reversal, conversion, swap (*informal*), alteration, substitution. [➡CHANGE ONE THING FOR ANOTHER; 399]

change round 1 *v* **alter**, modify, amend, adjust, jiggle around, juggle. [➡CHANGE; 373] *Opposite:* leave alone. 2 *v* **reorganize**, move around, rethink, alter, change, juggle around, tamper with. [➡POSITION SOMETHING; 326] *Opposite:* leave alone. 3 *v* **swap** (*informal*), exchange, substitute, change, change over, reverse, replace, switch. [➡EXCHANGE AND INTERCHANGE; 449]

change your mind *v* **have second thoughts**, come round, relent, back out, pull out, go back on, do an about-turn, do a U-turn, do an about-face (*US*), come around (*US*). [➡MAKE DECISIONS AND CHOICES; 753]

changing *adj* **altering**, varying, shifting, moving, fluctuating, mutable. [➡FINITENESS, VARIABILITY, AND TRANSIENCE; 96] *Opposite:* changeless.

changing room *type of* **room in the home.** [➡TYPES OF ROOM; 1096]

channel 1 *n* **canal**, conduit, waterway, strait, passage. [➡WATERWAYS AND SEAWAYS; 1107] 2 *n* **ditch**, dike, groove, drain, trench, duct. [➡WATERCOURSES; 1110] 3 *n* **means**, outlet, conduit, path, way, avenue, route. [➡WAYS OF DOING THINGS; 295] 4 *n* **station**, network, frequency. [➡TELEVISION AND RADIO; 607] 5 *v* **direct**, control, feed, conduct, route. [➡MOVE SOMETHING TO ANOTHER LOCATION; 325]

chant 1 *n* **song**, hymn, mantra, tune, carol, psalm. [➡MUSIC, SONGS, AND SINGING; 907] 2 *v* **sing**, recite, intone (*formal*), repeat, vocalize. [➡MUSIC, SONGS, AND SINGING; 907]

chanterelle *type of* **fungus.** [➡MICROORGANISMS, FUNGI, AND ALGAE; 1023]

chanteuse *n* [➡MUSICIANS AND SINGERS; 908]

chanting *n* [➡MUSIC, SONGS, AND SINGING; 907]

chantry *n* [➡PARTS OF RELIGIOUS BUILDINGS; 1085]

chaos *n* **disorder**, confusion, bedlam, anarchy, pandemonium, commotion, disarray, turmoil, madness, unruliness. [➡DISORDER AND CHAOS; 246] *Opposite:* order.

chaotic *adj* **disordered**, muddled, confused, messy, untidy, hectic, frenzied, unruly, anarchic, tumultuous. [➡DISORDER AND CHAOS; 246] *Opposite:* orderly.

chap (*informal*) *n* **guy** (*informal*), lad (*informal*), fellow (*dated*), gentleman, man, character, person, dude (*US slang*). [➡MALE PERSON; 934]

chapati *type of* **bread.** [➡BREAD, FLOUR, AND BREAD PRODUCTS; 1178]

chapel *n* **sanctuary**, oratory, chantry, side chapel, side altar. [➡RELIGIOUS BUILDINGS; 1084]

chaperon 1 *n* [➡SUPPORTERS, PROTECTORS, AND COMPATRIOTS; 970] 2 *see* **chaperone.**

chaperone 1 *n* **supervisor**, attendant, overseer, governess, escort, guardian, warden, companion, duenna. [➡SUPPORTERS, PROTECTORS, AND COMPATRIOTS; 970] 2 *v* **supervise**, oversee, escort, watch, look after, conduct, attend, guard, safeguard, accompany, shepherd. [➡TAKE CARE OF AND SPOIL; 301]

chaplain *n* **minister**, vicar, priest, pastor, school chaplain, rabbi, prison chaplain, army chaplain, air force chaplain. [➡RELIGIOUS PEOPLE; 779]

chaplet *type of* **headgear**. [➡HABERDASHERY, MILLINERY, AND LINGERIE; 867]

chapter 1 *n* **section**, part, subdivision, division, segment, unit. [➡PARTS OF BOOKS AND DOCUMENTS; 594] 2 *n* **period**, episode, stage, phase, interval, era, clause. [➡PERIOD OF TIME; 90]

char 1 *v* **burn**, singe, scorch, carbonize, sear, cauterize. [➡FIRE, FLAMMABILITY, AND BURNING; 1164] 2 *n* **domestic**, help, cleaner. [➡DOMESTIC AND KITCHEN WORKERS; 850]

charabanc *type of* **public service vehicle**. [➡VEHICLES; 1144]

character 1 *n* **nature**, quality, temperament, personality, disposition, spirit, makeup. [➡TEMPERAMENT AND BEHAVIOUR; 493] 2 *n* **charm**, appeal, atmosphere, attractiveness, charisma. [➡BEAUTY AND ATTRACTIVENESS; 190] 3 *n* **integrity**, strength, uprightness, rectitude, honour, moral fibre. [➡MORALLY GOOD; 775] 4 *n* **eccentric**, personality, oddity, original. [➡ECCENTRICITY AND IRRATIONALITY; 563] 5 *n* **person**, individual, creature, sort, type, fellow, chap (*informal*). [➡PERSON; 931]

character assassination *n* **defamation**, slander, libel, affront, verbal abuse, verbal assault, public humiliation, attack. [➡INSULTS, ABUSE, AND SWEARING; 659]

character-building *adj* **challenging**, demanding, instructive, educative, empowering, trying. [➡USEFULNESS; 200]

characterful *adj* **individual**, distinctive, strong, upright, inspiring, honourable. [➡MORALLY GOOD; 775]

characteristic 1 *n* **trait**, feature, quality, attribute, point, property. [➡QUALITIES AND CHARACTERISTICS; 1190] 2 *adj* **typical**, distinguishing, distinctive, individual, representative, specific, normal. [➡REPRESENTATIVE; 66] *Opposite:* uncharacteristic.

characteristically *adv* **typically**, usually, normally, naturally, routinely, symptomatically, habitually. [➡USUALLY; 108] *Opposite:* unusually.

characterization *n* **description**, classification, account, portrayal, depiction, report, representation. [➡REPRESENTATIONS AND GENERAL EXAMPLES; 65]

characterize 1 *v* **describe**, portray, illustrate, depict, brand, stamp. [➡NAME AND DESCRIBE; 666] 2 *v* **typify**, set apart, distinguish, differentiate, exemplify, indicate. [➡REPRESENT SOMETHING OR SOMEBODY; 59]

characterless *adj* **bland**, dull, soulless, uninteresting, insipid, nondescript, uninspired, tepid. [➡BORING AND UNINTERESTING; 235] *Opposite:* interesting.

characterlessness *n* [➡BORING AND UNINTERESTING; 235]

charade *n* **pretence**, farce, sham, fake, travesty, imitation, simulation, make-believe. [➡DECEPTION AND LIES; 661]

charbroiled (*US*) *adj* [➡STATE OF PREPARED FOOD; 1170]

charcoal grey *type of* **grey**. [➡COLOURS; 1223]

charge 1 *v* **accuse**, indict, allege, arraign, incriminate, lay the blame on, blame. [➡ACCUSE, BLAME, AND CRITICIZE; 642] *Opposite:* absolve. 2 *v* **attack**, rush, storm, assault, assail, launch an attack. [➡MOVE FAST; 314] *Opposite:* retreat. 3 *v* **rush**, dash, hurtle, stampede, hurry, race. [➡MOVE FAST; 314] 4 *n* **cost**, price, expense, rate, amount, fee, payment. [➡EXPENDITURE; 424] 5 *n* **custody**, care, responsibility, control, trust, safekeeping, burden, duty, concern. [➡RESPONSIBILITY; 171] 6 *n* **accusation**, indictment, allegation, arraignment, imputation. [➡THE POLICE, ARREST, AND PRE-TRIAL PROCEEDINGS; 818] 7 *n* **assault**, attack, advance, offensive, onslaught, push. [➡WARFARE AND WAR; 830] 8 *n* **order**, command, direction, instruction, exhortation (*formal*), injunction. [➡REQUEST AND DEMAND; 664]

chargeable 1 *adj* **punishable**, criminal, serious, indictable, imputable, actionable. [➡ILLEGAL; 816] 2 *adj* **taxable**, liable to tax, declarable, dutiable. [➡TAX AND TAXATION; 802]

charged *adj* **emotional**, exciting, electric, thrilling, stimulating. [➡INTERESTING AND MEANINGFUL; 191] *Opposite:* calm.

charger *type of* **horse**. [➡HORSE; 985]

chargrill *v* [➡COOKING AND FOOD PREPARATION; 354]

chariness *n* [➡INSECURITY AND LOSS OF COMPOSURE; 545]

chariot *type of* **wagon or carriage**. [➡VEHICLES; 1144]

charisma *n* **charm**, personality, appeal, magnetism, allure, captivation, attractiveness. [➡INTERESTING AND MEANINGFUL; 191]

charismatic *adj* **magnetic**, compelling, alluring, fascinating, captivating, charming, appealing. [➡INTERESTING AND MEANINGFUL; 191]

charitable 1 *adj* **generous**, giving, benevolent, altruistic, helpful, liberal, bountiful (*literary*), openhanded. [➡GENEROSITY AND KINDNESS; 496] *Opposite:* uncharitable. 2 *adj* **considerate**, understanding, accepting, sympathetic, tolerant, gracious, lenient, indulgent. [➡FRIENDLINESS AND SOCIABILITY; 495] *Opposite:* unforgiving.

charitable foundation *n* [➡CHARITY AND CHARITABLE INSTITUTIONS; 822]

charitable organization *n* [➡CHARITY AND CHARITABLE INSTITUTIONS; 822]

charitable trust *n* [➡CHARITY AND CHARITABLE INSTITUTIONS; 822]

charity 1 *n* **aid**, contributions, gifts, donations, help, assistance, offerings, handouts, alms. [➡KIND ACTION OR BEHAVIOUR; 296] 2 *n* **aid organization**, charitable trust, charitable foundation, aid agency. [➡CHARITY AND CHARITABLE INSTITUTIONS; 822] 3 *n* **kindness**, tolerance, humanity, compassion, generosity, altruism, goodwill, benevolence, sympathy, understanding, consideration. [➡KIND ACTION OR BEHAVIOUR; 296] *Opposite:* unkindness.

charity appeal *n* [➡PERFORMANCES AND SHOWS; 42]

charity event *n* [➡PERFORMANCES AND SHOWS; 42]

charity performance *n* [➡PERFORMANCES AND SHOWS; 42]

charlatan *n* **fake**, fraud, swindler, quack, counterfeit, pretender, con artist (*slang*), sham, impostor. [➡ PEOPLE WHO DECEIVE; 662]

charlatanism *n* [➡ DECEPTION AND LIES; 661]

Charleston *type of* **dance.** [➡ DANCE; 903]

charm 1 *n* **attraction**, appeal, allure, charisma, magic, fascination, magnetism, lure. [➡ BEAUTY AND ATTRACTIVENESS; 190] 2 *n* **ornament**, keepsake, trinket, talisman, amulet, memento, accessory, lucky piece. [➡ ORNAMENTS AND DECORATIONS; 1247] 3 *v* **captivate**, enchant, beguile, hypnotize, mesmerize, enthral, win over, fascinate, entrance, enrapture (*formal*). [➡ APPEAL TO AND AROUSE INTEREST; 576] 4 *type of* **jewellery.** [➡ JEWELLERY; 866]

charmed 1 *adj* **lucky**, fortunate, enchanted, magical, fairy-tale, protected. [➡ LUCK; 784] *Opposite:* unlucky. 2 *adj* **delighted**, pleased, enchanted, thrilled, glad, happy. [➡ APPRECIATION AND GRATITUDE; 536]

charmer *n* **smooth talker**, enchanter, smoothie (*informal*), fascinator, smooth operator, ladies' man, Romeo, Lothario (*literary*), Casanova, flirt, coquette (*literary*), siren. [➡ SUPERFICIAL OR INSINCERE PEOPLE; 951]

charming *adj* **delightful**, amiable, attractive, appealing, pleasant, polite, charismatic, fascinating, enchanting, persuasive, captivating, alluring, enthralling, entrancing. [➡ BEAUTY AND ATTRACTIVENESS; 190] *Opposite:* unattractive.

charmless *adj* **unattractive**, unappealing, uninteresting, unsympathetic, unprepossessing, ugly, unpleasant. [➡ SELFISH AND UNKIND; 506] *Opposite:* charming.

charnel house *n* [➡ BURIAL PLACES AND ACCESSORIES; 930]

chart 1 *n* **diagram**, plan, graph, table, graphic representation, visual aid, map. [➡ DRAWINGS, CHARTS AND TABLES; 595] 2 *v* **register**, record, project, plot, chronicle, log, follow, map, outline. [➡ RECORD SOMETHING; 372]

charter 1 *n* **contract**, deed, agreement, licence, grant, approval, commission. [➡ OFFICIAL DOCUMENTS; 587] 2 *v* **rent**, lease, hire, take on, commission, let. [➡ PURCHASE; 423]

See Compare and Contrast at **hire.**

chartered accountant *n* [➡ PEOPLE INVOLVED IN FINANCE; 804]

chartered surveyor *n* [➡ SURVEYORS, EXAMINERS, AND JUDGES; 853]

chartreuse *type of* **green.** [➡ COLOURS; 1223]

chary *adj* **wary**, cautious, suspicious, guarded, cagey, careful, circumspect. [➡ INSECURITY AND LOSS OF COMPOSURE; 545] *Opposite:* reckless.

See Compare and Contrast at **cautious.**

chase 1 *v* **pursue**, run after, hunt, hound, follow, trail, track, look for, search for, go after, go in pursuit of, tail. [➡ ACCOMPANY AND FOLLOW; 338] 2 *v* **race**, dash, rush, career, hurtle, hurry. [➡ MOVE FAST; 314] 3 *n* **pursuit**, hunt, hunting. [➡ SEEK POSSESSION AND SEARCH; 457]

See Compare and Contrast at **follow.**

chaser *n* **pursuer**, follower, hunter, shadow, tail, trailer. [➡ ENEMIES AND TORMENTORS; 969]

chasm *n* **crater**, gulf, gap, abyss, gorge, rift, crevasse, break, cleft, ravine, split, void, arroyo (*US*), gulch (*US*). [➡ HOLES, GAPS, AND FORKS; 1251]

chassis *part of* **external structure.** [➡ EXTERNAL PARTS OF A VEHICLE; 1146]

chaste *adj* **innocent**, uncorrupted, virtuous, unblemished, unsullied, spotless, faithful, pure (*literary*). [➡ MORALLY GOOD; 775] *Opposite:* impure.

chasten 1 *v* **subdue**, suppress, restrain, tame, humble, subjugate. [➡ UPSET, DISTRESS, AND HUMILIATE; 568] 2 *v* **punish**, reprimand, discipline, censure, chastise (*formal*), correct, castigate (*formal*). [➡ ACCUSE, BLAME, AND CRITICIZE; 642]

chasteness *n* **pureness**, innocence, purity, virtuousness, faithfulness. [➡ MORALLY GOOD; 775] *Opposite:* immorality.

chastise (*formal*) *v* **reprimand**, tell off (*informal*), discipline, censure, punish, rebuke, reprove, penalize, correct, castigate (*formal*), upbraid, scold, chasten. [➡ ACCUSE, BLAME, AND CRITICIZE; 642] *Opposite:* praise.

chastisement (*formal*) *n* **reprimand**, discipline, punishment, rebuke, scolding, telling-off (*informal*), correction, censure, penalty. [➡ CRITICISMS AND ANGRY OUTBURSTS; 50] *Opposite:* praise.

chastity *n* [➡ MORALLY GOOD; 775]

chat 1 *v* **talk**, converse, gossip, dialogue, chitchat (*informal*), natter (*informal*), yak (*informal*), chinwag (*informal*), jaw (*slang*), chew the fat (*slang*), shoot the breeze (*US slang*). [➡ TWO-WAY COMMUNICATION; 608] 2 *n* **conversation**, one-to-one, heart-to-heart, tête-à-tête, talk, dialogue, exchange, discussion, chinwag (*informal*), natter (*informal*). [➡ INFORMAL COMMUNICATION; 45]

chateau *type of* **house.** [➡ RESIDENTIAL BUILDINGS; 1077]

Chateaubriand *type of* **steak.** [➡ TYPES AND CUTS OF MEAT; 1176]

chat show *type of* **broadcast.** [➡ TELEVISION AND RADIO; 607]

chattels *n* **possessions**, belongings, things, stuff, gear (*informal*), personal property, material, holdings. [➡ POSSESSIONS; 462]

chatter 1 *v* **babble**, rattle on, talk nineteen to the dozen, prattle, rant, gossip, go on. [➡ WITTER AND BABBLE; 618] 2 *n* **talk**, gossip, chat, conversation. [➡ INFORMAL COMMUNICATION; 45]

chatterbox (*informal*) *n* **blabbermouth** (*informal*), gabber (*informal*), gossip, chinwagger (*informal*), windbag (*informal*), chatterer, talker, tattler. [➡ INTERFERING PEOPLE AND TELLTALES; 950]

chatterer *n* **talker**, chatterbox (*informal*), chinwagger (*informal*), windbag (*informal*), gossip, tattler. [➡ INTERFERING PEOPLE AND TELLTALES; 950]

chattering classes *n* [➡ CLASS STATUS; 889]

chattily *adv* [➡ ELOQUENT, TALKATIVE AND LONG-WINDED; 633]

chattiness *n* [➡ ELOQUENT, TALKATIVE AND LONG-WINDED; 633]

chatty 1 *adj* **talkative**, garrulous, loquacious (*formal*), forthcoming, gossipy, friendly. [➡ELOQUENT, TALKATIVE AND LONG-WINDED; 633] *Opposite:* quiet. 2 *adj* **informal**, friendly, personal, casual, relaxed. [➡LEVELS OF FORMALITY; 523] *Opposite:* formal.

See Compare and Contrast at **talkative.**

chat up (*informal*) *v* **flirt**, lead on, pick up (*informal*), make eyes at, hit on (*US slang*). [➡ESTABLISHING RELATIONSHIPS WITH OTHERS; 974]

chauffeur *n* **driver**, motorist, valet. [➡DRIVERS; 1152]

chauvinism *n* **bigotry**, sexism, prejudice, narrow-mindedness, dogmatism, machismo, jingoism. [➡PREJUDICE; 551]

chauvinist *n* **bigot**, sexist, homophobe, jingoist, xenophobe. [➡SELF-IMPORTANT AND SELF-SEEKING PEOPLE; 949]

chauvinistic *adj* **bigoted**, prejudiced, opinionated, dogmatic, narrow-minded, homophobic, xenophobic, jingoistic. [➡NEGATIVE INTELLECTUAL CHARACTERISTICS; 526]

cheap 1 *adj* **inexpensive**, economy, low-priced, economical, discounted, low-cost, cut-price, on sale, for a song, reduced, bargain, bargain-basement, cut-rate (*US*). [➡CHEAP AND INEXPENSIVE; 222] *Opposite:* expensive. 2 *adj* **shoddy**, inferior, second-rate, substandard, common, tawdry. [➡ORDINARINESS; 245] *Opposite:* superior. 3 *adj* **contemptible**, despicable, shameful, low, base, scurvy. [➡IN POOR TASTE; 230] *Opposite:* admirable. 4 *adj* **stingy** (*informal*), tightfisted, close-fisted (*informal*), miserly, mean, penny-pinching (*informal*), parsimonious. [➡FINANCIALLY MEAN AND GRASPING; 520] *Opposite:* generous.

cheap and nasty *adj* [➡CHEAP AND INEXPENSIVE; 222]

cheapen *v* **denigrate**, demean, belittle, lower, degrade, devalue, depreciate, undervalue. [➡WORSEN SOMETHING; 381] *Opposite:* elevate.

cheaply *adv* **inexpensively**, economically, reasonably, modestly, competitively, on the cheap (*informal*). [➡CHEAP AND INEXPENSIVE; 222] *Opposite:* expensively.

cheapness 1 *n* **tawdriness**, inferiority, shoddiness, tackiness (*informal*). [➡IN POOR TASTE; 230] *Opposite:* tastefulness. 2 *n* **stinginess**, tightfistedness, miserliness, meanness, parsimony, close-fistedness (*informal*). [➡FINANCIALLY MEAN AND GRASPING; 520] *Opposite:* generosity.

cheapo (*informal*) *adj* [➡CHEAP AND INEXPENSIVE; 222]

cheapskate (*informal*) *n* **miser**, skinflint, scrooge (*informal*), killjoy. [➡FINANCIALLY MEAN PEOPLE; 952]

cheat 1 *v* **deceive**, trick, con, swindle, defraud, bamboozle (*informal*), bilk (*informal*), rogue, dupe. [➡FALSIFY AND CHEAT; 177] 2 *n* **double-dealer**, cheater, charlatan, con artist (*slang*), con man (*informal*), double-crosser, trickster, fraudster. [➡PEOPLE WHO DECEIVE; 662]

cheating 1 *adj* **duplicitous**, double-dealing, dishonest, unprincipled, deceitful, underhand, false. [➡DECEITFUL; 514] *Opposite:* honest. 2 *n* **dishonesty**, deceit, deception, duplicity, chicanery, double-dealing, fiddling (*informal*), misappropriation, fraud, embezzlement. [➡DECEPTION AND LIES; 661]

check 1 *v* **test**, test out, prove, try, try out, examine. [➡EXAMINE AND ASSESS; 754] 2 *v* **make sure**, ensure, verify, confirm, certify, establish. [➡APPROVE AND CONFIRM; 647] 3 *v* **limit**, hold in, stop, impede, hold up, hold back, delay, restrain, inhibit, repress, constrain, withhold, curb [➡AVOID, PREVENT, LIMIT, AND CONTROL; 278] *Opposite:* expedite (*formal*). 4 *n* **inspection**, examination, test, assessment, trial, safety test, safety check, safety inspection, investigation. [➡EXAMINE AND ASSESS; 754] 5 *n* **safeguard**, curb, restraint, buttress, catch, rein. [➡AVOID, PREVENT, LIMIT, AND CONTROL; 278] 6 *n* (*US*) **bill**, invoice, damage (*informal*), score, tab (*US informal*). [➡RECEIPTS AND INVOICES; 592]

checked *adj* **check**, patterned, crisscross, plaid, squared, chequered. [➡DESCRIBING PATTERNS; 1226]

checker 1 *n* **inspector**, examiner, assessor, regulator, overseer, supervisor. [➡SURVEYORS, EXAMINERS, AND JUDGES; 853] 2 (*US*) *type of* **game piece**. [➡GAMES PIECES; 878]

check in *v* **register**, sign in, sign up, sign on, enrol. [➡ARRIVE; 12]

check-in *n* **registration desk**, registration, reception desk, reception area, reception, desk. [➡DOORS AND ACCESS POINTS; 1100]

checklist *n* **list**, specification, spec, agenda, worksheet. [➡LISTS AND SCHEDULES; 588]

checkmate *n* **check**, mate, end, ending, victory, defeat. [➡SUCCESS; 82] *Opposite:* stalemate.

check out 1 *v* **leave**, depart, vacate, sign out, exit. [➡ABSENT ONESELF; 8] 2 *v* **inspect**, investigate, look into, explore, examine, scrutinize, research, take a look at, have a look at. [➡EXAMINE AND ASSESS; 754]

check over *v* **look over**, reread, go through, go over, examine, edit, give the once-over (*informal*). [➡EXAMINE AND ASSESS; 754]

checkpoint *n* **barrier**, turnpike, frontier, border, spot check, frontier post. [➡BARRIERS; 1112]

checkup *n* **examination**, medical, lookover (*informal*), inspection, once-over (*informal*), health check, survey, doctor's visit, review, scan, looking over (*US*). [➡REMEDIES, TREATMENTS AND OPERATIONS; 732]

check up on *v* **keep an eye on**, check on, spy on, nose around (*informal*), watch, monitor. [➡EXAMINE AND ASSESS; 754] *Opposite:* ignore.

cheddar *type of* **hard cheese**. [➡DAIRY PRODUCTS AND CHEESES; 1182]

cheek 1 *n* (*informal*) **nerve**, gall, impertinence, brashness, chutzpah (*informal*), effrontery, rudeness, brass, impudence, audacity, boldness. [➡BAD MANNERS AND SOCIAL SKILLS; 522] *Opposite:* humility. 2 *part of* **face**. [➡HEAD; 693]

cheekbone *type of* **bone**. [➡THE BONES AND JOINTS; 720]

cheek by jowl *adv* **side by side**, on top of one another, close together, together, close, in each other's pockets. [➡CLOSENESS; 160]

cheekily *adv* **audaciously**, boldly, defiantly, irreverently, insolently, impertinently (*formal*), disrespectfully, brazenly, impudently, sassily (*US*). [➡RUDE AND HOSTILE; 626] *Opposite:* respectfully.

cheekiness *n* **impudence**, disrespect, effrontery, insolence, irreverence, brazenness, audacity, sassiness (*US*). [➡BAD MANNERS AND SOCIAL SKILLS; 522] *Opposite:* respect.

cheek-to-cheek *adv* **close**, close up, close together, together, intimately. [➡CLOSENESS; 160]

cheeky *adj* **rude**, bold, mischievous, disrespectful, pert, insolent, naughty, brazen, defiant, impudent, impertinent (*formal*), sassy (*US*). [➡BAD MANNERS AND SOCIAL SKILLS; 522] *Opposite:* respectful.

cheep 1 *v* **chirp**, peep, tweet, twitter, sing. [➡SOUND EMISSION BY ANIMALS OR BIRDS; 365] **2** *type of* **bird sound**. [➡SOUNDS MADE BY BIRDS; 1262]

cheeping *n* **chirping**, tweeting, peeping, twittering, singing. [➡SOUNDS MADE BY BIRDS; 1262]

cheer 1 *n* **cheerfulness**, optimism, merriment, joyfulness, liveliness, good spirits. [➡PLEASURE, EXCITEMENT, AND ELATION; 535] *Opposite:* gloom. **2** *v* **applaud**, shout, root for, hail, praise. [➡PRAISE AND ENCOURAGE; 648] *Opposite:* boo.

cheerful *adj* **happy**, cheery, jolly, smiling, joyful, merry, jovial, sunny, in good spirits, chirpy (*informal*), jaunty, gleeful, optimistic. [➡PLEASURE, EXCITEMENT, AND ELATION; 535] *Opposite:* sad.

cheerfully 1 *adv* **happily**, optimistically, merrily, joyfully, gleefully, with good cheer, sunnily, chirpily (*informal*), jauntily. [➡PLEASURE, EXCITEMENT, AND ELATION; 535] *Opposite:* sadly. **2** *adv* **gladly**, willingly, readily, with pleasure. [➡THE WILL AND WILLINGNESS; 564] *Opposite:* grudgingly.

cheerfulness *n* **happiness**, joyfulness, cheer, cheeriness, jollity, merriment, exuberance, optimism, joviality, vivaciousness, chirpiness (*informal*), jauntiness. [➡PLEASURE, EXCITEMENT, AND ELATION; 535] *Opposite:* sadness.

cheeriness *n* **cheerfulness**, happiness, joyfulness, liveliness, joviality, chirpiness (*informal*), jauntiness, gloominess. [➡PLEASURE, EXCITEMENT, AND ELATION; 535]

cheering *adj* **heartening**, encouraging, positive, uplifting, promising, hopeful. [➡EMOTIONALLY PLEASANT; 188] *Opposite:* discouraging.

cheerio (*informal*) *interj* **goodbye**, bye (*informal*), bye bye (*informal*), see you (*informal*), bye for now (*informal*), ta-ta (*informal*), cheers (*informal*), be seeing you, au revoir. [➡GREETINGS, FAREWELLS, AND SALUTATIONS; 660]

cheerleader *n* **performer**, supporter, cheerer. [➡PEOPLE IN SPORTS AND LEISURE; 876]

cheerless *adj* **gloomy**, depressing, dismal, miserable, sad, unhappy, sombre, sullen, dour, morose, drab. [➡EMOTIONALLY UNPLEASANT AND UPSETTING; 228] *Opposite:* bright.

cheerlessness *n* **bleakness**, dreariness, gloominess, soullessness, wintriness, dinginess, sombreness, dismalness, sullenness, dourness, moroseness, drabness. [➡EMOTIONALLY UNPLEASANT AND UPSETTING; 228] *Opposite:* brightness.

cheer on *v* **encourage**, root, support, laud, egg on. [➡PRAISE AND ENCOURAGE; 648] *Opposite:* discourage.

cheers 1 *interj* **thanks**, thank you, thanks a lot, nice one. [➡GREETINGS, FAREWELLS, AND SALUTATIONS; 660] **2** *interj* **goodbye**, bye (*informal*), bye bye (*informal*), ta-ta (*informal*), cheerio (*informal*), bye for now (*informal*), be seeing you, au revoir. [➡GREETINGS, FAREWELLS, AND SALUTATIONS; 660]

cheer up *v* **perk up**, brighten, brighten up, liven, enliven. [➡PLEASE AND AMUSE; 573] *Opposite:* depress.

cheery *adj* **happy**, jolly, joyful, smiling, cheerful, merry, bright and breezy, jovial, chirpy (*informal*), jaunty, radiant. [➡PLEASURE, EXCITEMENT, AND ELATION; 535] *Opposite:* gloomy.

cheese

◆ *types of soft cheese*
Brie, Camembert, chèvre, cottage cheese, cream cheese, curd, Danish blue, Dolcelatte, feta, Gorgonzola, mascarpone, mozzarella, ricotta, Roquefort

◆ *types of hard cheese*
caerphilly, cheddar, Cheshire, Edam, Emmental, Emmenthaler (*US*), Gouda, Gruyère, haloumi, Monterey Jack, Parmesan, pecorino, Stilton, Wensleydale

cheesecake *type of* **cake**. [➡CAKES, BISCUITS, AND DESSERTS; 1180]

cheesecloth *type of* **fabric from plants**. [➡FABRICS; 1131]

cheesed off (*informal*) *adj* **annoyed**, miffed (*informal*), browned off (*dated slang*), fed up (*informal*), cross, angry, vexed, perturbed, irritated, frustrated, teed off (*US informal*). [➡SADNESS, DISTRESS, AND DESPAIR; 540]

cheese off (*informal*) *v* [➡ANGER AND ANNOY; 570]

cheeseparing 1 *adj* **mean**, miserly, stingy (*informal*), mean-spirited, avaricious, miserable, tightfisted, closefisted (*informal*), cheap (*US*). [➡FINANCIALLY MEAN AND GRASPING; 520] *Opposite:* generous. **2** *n* **meanness**, miserliness, stinginess, mean-spiritedness, avarice, cheapness, tightfistedness, close-fistedness (*informal*). [➡FINANCIALLY MEAN AND GRASPING; 520] *Opposite:* generosity.

cheesy 1 *adj* [➡SMELL AND SMELLING; 706] **2** *adj* (*informal*) **tacky** (*informal*), unpleasant, cheap, tasteless, tawdry. [➡IN POOR TASTE; 230] *Opposite:* stylish.

cheetah *type of* **cat**. [➡FELINE; 983]

chef *n* [➡DOMESTIC AND KITCHEN WORKERS; 850]

chemical *n* **substance**, element, compound. [➡SUBSTANCES; 1266]

chemise *type of* **upper body underwear**. [➡HABERDASHERY, MILLINERY, AND LINGERIE; 867]

chemist *type of* **retail outlet**. [➡RETAIL OUTLETS; 1082]

chemistry *n* **interaction**, attraction, understanding, empathy, sympathy, harmony, vibes (*slang*), nonverbal communication. [➡COMMUNICATION; 603]

chenille *type of* **fabric from animals**. [➡FABRICS; 1131]

cheongsam *type of* **dress**. [➡GARMENTS AND OUTFITS; 865]

cheque *n* **payment**, form, order, draft, authorization, instruction. [➡MANUALS AND INSTRUCTIONS; 590]

chequered 1 *adj* **check**, checked, squared, patterned, crisscross, plaid. [➡DESCRIBING PATTERNS; 1226] 2 *adj* **uneven**, inconsistent, up-and-down, variable, changeable, volatile, unpredictable, irregular, patchy. [➡FINITENESS, VARIABILITY, AND TRANSIENCE; 96] *Opposite:* even.

cherish *v* **treasure**, appreciate, relish, take pleasure in, esteem, revere, value, prize, apprize (*formal*). [➡LIKE, LOVE, VALUE AND ENJOY; 579] *Opposite:* neglect.

cherished *adj* **valued**, precious, beloved, unforgettable, memorable, esteemed, appreciated, treasured, prized. [➡POPULAR AND WANTED; 221] *Opposite:* neglected.

cherry *type of* **fruit**. [➡FRUIT AND VEGETABLES; 1175]

cherry bomb (*US*) *type of* **firework**. [➡EXPLOSIVES; 1154]

cherry-pick *v* **select**, choose, pick, pick and choose, help yourself, opt, single out, pick out. [➡MAKE DECISIONS AND CHOICES; 753]

cherry red *type of* **red**. [➡COLOURS; 1223]

cherub *n* **angel**, cupid, amoretto, putto. [➡RELIGIOUS CONCEPTS; 777]

cherubic 1 *adj* **holy**, divine, spiritual, saintly, blessed, godly, supernatural, ethereal, seraphic. [➡RELIGIOUS CONCEPTS; 777] 2 *adj* **angelic**, cute, innocent, attractive, lovable, adorable. [➡PEOPLE'S PHYSICAL APPEARANCE; 476]

chervil *type of* **herb**. [➡HERBS AND SPICES; 1174]

Cheshire *type of* **hard cheese**. [➡DAIRY PRODUCTS AND CHEESES; 1182]

chessman (*US*) *type of* **game piece**. [➡GAMES PIECES; 878]

chesspiece *type of* **game piece**. [➡GAMES PIECES; 878]

chest 1 *n* **upper body**, torso, rib cage, ribs, trunk. [➡TORSO; 694] 2 *type of* **container**. [➡CONTAINERS, RECEPTACLES, AND PACKAGING; 1244]

chesterfield *n* [➡FURNITURE; 858]

chestiness *n* [➡BREATHE AND NOT BREATHE; 717]

chestnut 1 *n* (*informal*) **joke**, tired joke, anecdote, old favourite (*informal*), cliché. [➡JOKES AND TEASING; 675] 2 *type of* **nut**. [➡NUTS; 1184] 3 *type of* **brown**. [➡COLOURS; 1223] 4 *type of* **deciduous tree**. [➡DECIDUOUS TREES; 1028]

chestnut-haired *adj* [➡HAIR COLOUR; 486]

chest of drawers *type of* **cabinet**. [➡FURNITURE; 858]

chesty *adj* **wheezy**, rasping, phlegmy, congested. [➡LOUD OR UNPLEASANT SOUNDS; 1265]

chèvre *type of* **soft cheese**. [➡DAIRY PRODUCTS AND CHEESES; 1182]

chevron *n* **V-shape**, V, stripe, badge, insignia, rank. [➡SYMBOLS, SIGNS, AND NUMBERS; 597]

chevrotain *type of* **deer or antelope**. [➡DEER AND ANTELOPE; 981]

chew 1 *v* **masticate**, chew up, gnaw, grind, crush, chomp (*informal*), squash, champ, munch. [➡EAT AND NOT EAT; 711] 2 *n* (*US*) **portion**, plug, wad. [➡AMOUNT OF SOLID OR SEMI-SOLID; 115]

chewing gum *type of* **confectionery**. [➡CONFECTIONERY; 1181]

chew on *v* [➡THINK AND REFLECT; 744]

chew out (*US informal*) *v* **scold**, tell off (*informal*), bawl out (*informal*), reproach, reprimand, take to task. [➡ACCUSE, BLAME, AND CRITICIZE; 642]

chew over *v* **meditate**, ponder, think about, ruminate, consider, mull over, deliberate, contemplate, perpend (*archaic*), weigh, muse, reflect. [➡THINK AND REFLECT; 744]

chew the cud *v* [➡THINK AND REFLECT; 744]

chew the fat (*slang*) *v* **chat**, converse, chinwag (*informal*), chatter, gossip, natter (*informal*). [➡TWO-WAY COMMUNICATION; 608]

chew up 1 *v* **damage**, crush, rip up, injure, destroy, mangle. [➡DESTRUCTION AND DEMOLITION; 360] 2 *v* **chew**, chomp (*informal*), grind, masticate, champ, munch, consume. [➡EAT AND NOT EAT; 711]

chewy *adj* **rubbery**, stringy, fibrous, gristly, leathery. [➡STATE OF PREPARED FOOD; 1170] *Opposite:* tender.

chic 1 *adj* **stylish**, fashionable, well-dressed, attractive, smart, elegant, well-groomed, modish, well turned-out, dashing, classy (*informal*), swanky (*informal*), well put together (*US*), tony (*US informal*). [➡WELL GROOMED; 483] *Opposite:* unfashionable. 2 *n* **style**, elegance, panache, stylishness, modishness, classiness (*informal*). [➡WELL GROOMED; 483]

chicanery *n* **deception**, trickery, verbiage, talk, nonsense, flimflam (*slang*), waffle (*informal*), hot air (*informal*), underhandedness, double-dealing, smoke and mirrors (*US*). [➡MEANINGLESS SPEECH OR WRITING; 677]

chichi (*disapproving*) *adj* **contrived**, recherché, self-conscious, pretentious, affected, over-the-top (*informal*), OTT (*informal*), too much, uncool (*slang*). [➡AFFECTATION, SELF-SATISFACTION, AND SNOBBISHNESS; 508]

chick *type of* **young bird**. [➡YOUNG BIRD; 1004]

chickadee *type of* **common bird**. [➡BIRD; 997]

chicken 1 *adj* (*informal*) **cowardly**, frightened, scared, reluctant, fearful, apprehensive, jumpy, afraid, lily-livered (*literary*), hesitant, craven (*literary*), faint-hearted, gutless. [➡COWARDICE AND WEAKNESS OF WILL; 509] *Opposite:* brave. 2 *type of* **fowl**. [➡FOOD BIRD; 999] 3 *type of* **meat**. [➡TYPES AND CUTS OF MEAT; 1176]

See Compare and Contrast at **cowardly**.

chicken coop *type of* **pen or cage**. [➡ANIMAL OR BIRD ACCOMMODATION; 1078]

chicken feed (*informal*) *n* **small change**, next to nothing, small beer (*informal*), small potatoes (*informal*), chump change (*US slang*). [➡SMALL AMOUNT OF MONEY; 142]

chicken out (*slang*) *v* **back out**, drop out, think better of something, give up, withdraw, renege, cop out (*slang*), lose your nerve, bottle out (*informal*). [➡NOT DO AND REFUSE TO DO; 275]

chicken run *type of* **pen or cage**. [➡ANIMAL OR BIRD ACCOMMODATION; 1078]

chickpea *type of* **pulse.** [➡BEANS AND PULSES; 1188]

chickweed *type of* **weed.** [➡WEEDS AND THISTLES; 1034]

chicory *type of* **salad vegetable.** [➡FRUIT AND VEGETABLES; 1175]

chide (*literary*) *v* **reproach**, scold, reprimand, rebuke, blame, take to task, nag, harass, tell off (*informal*), reprove. [➡ACCUSE, BLAME, AND CRITICIZE; 642] *Opposite:* praise.

chief 1 *n* **ruler**, head, boss, captain, commander, supremo (*informal*), leader, superior. [➡BOSSES AND MANAGEMENT; 965] 2 *adj* **principal**, main, topmost, leading, foremost, paramount, primary, dominant, first, highest. [➡MOST IMPORTANT AND MAIN; 194]

chief executive *n* **CEO**, boss, leader, president. [➡BUSINESS PEOPLE; 794]

chiefly *adv* **primarily**, mainly, essentially, mostly, predominantly, in the main, largely, for the most part, principally, above all, first and foremost. [➡MAINLY AND PRIMARILY; 138]

chieftain *n* **tribal chief**, ruler, chief, overlord, lord. [➡BOSSES AND MANAGEMENT; 965]

chieftainship *n* **leadership**, command, authority, rank, status, position. [➡STATUS; 888]

chiffon *type of* **synthetic fabric.** [➡FABRICS; 1131]

chignon *type of* **hairstyle.** [➡HAIR STYLES AND HAIR PIECES; 489]

chigoe *type of* **parasitic insect.** [➡PARASITES; 1017]

chihuahua *type of* **small dog.** [➡DOG; 980]

chilblain *n* **swelling**, inflammation, blister. [➡CONDITIONS AFFECTING THE SKIN; 722]

child 1 *n* **youngster**, kid (*informal*), young person, teenager, teen (*informal*), adolescent, youth, juvenile, nipper (*informal*). [➡CHILD OR YOUTH; 945] 2 *n* **offspring**, descendant, spawn, son, daughter. [➡YOUNGER GENERATION RELATIVES; 958] 3 *n* **baby**, infant, newborn, toddler, nursling, suckling, neonate, preschooler (*US*). [➡CHILD OR YOUTH; 945] 4 *n* **result**, product, outcome, creation. [➡RESULTS AND OUTCOMES; 83]

See Compare and Contrast at **youth**.

childbearing *n* **reproduction**, pregnancy, gestation, childbirth, motherhood. [➡REPRODUCTION AND HEREDITY; 726]

childbirth *n* **giving birth**, delivery, labour, contractions, childbearing. [➡REPRODUCTION AND HEREDITY; 726]

childhood *n* **babyhood**, infancy, youth, upbringing, infanthood, nonage, early years. [➡BABYHOOD, CHILDHOOD AND ADOLESCENCE; 917] *Opposite:* adulthood.

childish 1 *adj* **childlike**, juvenile, innocent, ingenuous. [➡NEGATIVE INTELLECTUAL CHARACTERISTICS; 526] 2 *adj* **immature**, irresponsible, silly, self-indulgent, foolish, babyish, infantile, juvenile. [➡BAD MANNERS AND SOCIAL SKILLS; 522] *Opposite:* mature.

childishness *n* **immaturity**, silliness, irresponsibility, pettiness. [➡BAD MANNERS AND SOCIAL SKILLS; 522] *Opposite:* maturity.

childlike *adj* **innocent**, pure (*literary*), naive, candid, uncomplicated, unsophisticated, trusting, simple, childish, ingenuous. [➡NEGATIVE INTELLECTUAL CHARACTERISTICS; 526] *Opposite:* jaded.

childproof *adj* **safe**, tamper-proof, secure. [➡SAFE AND SAFETY; 192]

child seat *type of* **internal.** [➡INTERNAL PARTS OF A VEHICLE; 1145]

child's play *n* **piece of cake** (*informal*), picnic (*informal*), doddle (*informal*), walkover (*informal*), pushover (*informal*). [➡EASY WORK; 300]

chill 1 *n* **coldness**, coolness, low temperature, chilliness, nippiness, frostiness, nip. [➡COLD WEATHER; 1051] *Opposite:* warmth. 2 *n* **sudden fear**, anxiety, apprehension, wariness, shudder. [➡FEAR AND PANIC; 544] 3 *n* **gloom**, depression, pall, shadow. [➡NUISANCES; 254] 4 *n* **unfriendliness**, aloofness, detachment, coolness, coldness, remoteness, indifference, chilliness. [➡ANTAGONISM; 553] *Opposite:* warmth. 5 *adj* **biting**, freezing, wintry, nippy, chilly. [➡COLD WEATHER; 1051] 6 *adj* **remote**, uninvolved, aloof, indifferent, chilly, cold, icy. [➡NEUTRALITY AND INDIFFERENCE; 554] *Opposite:* warm. 7 *v* (*slang*) **chill out** (*slang*), relax, loosen up, rest, take it easy, have a break, put your feet up, lie down, calm down, be calm. [➡STOP ACTING; 265] 8 *v* **cool**, freeze, make colder, put on ice, refrigerate. [➡CHANGE OF TEMPERATURE; 387] *Opposite:* warm. 9 *v* **discourage**, depress, deter, dispirit, cast a shadow, frighten. [➡UPSET, DISTRESS, AND HUMILIATE; 568] *Opposite:* encourage.

chilled 1 *adj* **ice-cold**, freezing, frozen, refrigerated, cooled, iced. [➡TEMPERATURE: COLD; 1230] *Opposite:* hot. 2 *adj* (*slang*) **laid-back** (*informal*), cool, relaxed, unflustered, calm. [➡CALMNESS, CONFIDENCE, AND COMPOSURE; 537] *Opposite:* agitated.

chilled out (*slang*) *adj* [➡CALMNESS, CONFIDENCE, AND COMPOSURE; 537]

chilli *type of* **spice.** [➡HERBS AND SPICES; 1174]

chilliness 1 *n* **coolness**, coldness, nip, frostiness, nippiness, low temperature, chill. [➡COLD WEATHER; 1051] *Opposite:* warmth. 2 *n* **unfriendliness**, aloofness, stiffness, detachment, formality, coldness, reserve, chill. [➡ANTAGONISM; 553] *Opposite:* friendliness.

chilling *adj* **frightening**, scary (*informal*), alarming, unsettling, distressing, terrifying, disturbing, unnerving, nerve-racking. [➡FRIGHTENING; 232] *Opposite:* reassuring.

chilli sauce *type of* **seasonings, sauces, and dips.** [➡SEASONINGS AND SAUCES; 1173]

chill out (*slang*) 1 *v* **calm down**, take it easy, stop worrying, lighten up (*informal*). [➡CHANGE OF MOOD AND COMPOSURE; 581] 2 *v* **relax**, loosen up, rest, kick back (*informal*), unwind. [➡CHANGE OF MOOD AND COMPOSURE; 581]

chilly 1 *adj* **cold**, cool, nippy, chill, frosty, icy. [➡COLD WEATHER; 1051] *Opposite:* warm. 2 *adj* **frigid**, formal, supercilious, aloof, detached, frosty, icy, reserved, cold, unfriendly. [➡UNFRIENDLINESS AND UNSOCIABILITY; 505] *Opposite:* warm.

chime 1 *n* **clang**, ding, ding-dong, sound, peal. [➡RINGING AND TOOTING SOUNDS; 1258] 2 *v* **strike**, peal, ring, sound, ring out, toll. [➡EMIT RINGING AND TOOTING SOUNDS; 368]

chime in 1 *v* **butt in**, interrupt, interject, voice your opinion, speak up, have your say, pipe up, chip in (*informal*), put your two cents in (*US*). [➡INTERRUPT AND BUTT IN; 620] **2** *v* **agree**, be compatible, be consistent, be in line, be in agreement, be in accord. [➡HARMONY; 156] *Opposite:* contradict.

chimera *n* **fantasy**, fancy, whimsy, illusion, figment, daydream. [➡NONEXISTENT THINGS; 23]

Chimera *type of* **mythological creature.** [➡MYTHICAL CREATURES; 1036]

chimerical *adj* [➡FALSE AND UNREAL; 174]

chimes *n* **bells**, glockenspiel, carillon. [➡MUSICAL INSTRUMENTS; 910]

chimney *part of* **building.** [➡PARTS OF A BUILDING; 1094]

chimneypiece *type of* **general fittings.** [➡FITTINGS; 859]

chimp *type of* **primate.** [➡PRIMATE; 988]

chimpanzee *type of* **primate.** [➡PRIMATE; 988]

chin *part of* **face.** [➡HEAD; 693]

china **1** *n* **tableware**, dishes, plates, cups, saucers, serving plates, platters. [➡TABLEWARE, CUTLERY, AND KITCHENWARE; 861] **2** *n* **figurines**, collectibles, porcelain, breakables, china doll. [➡POTTERY; 1134]

china closet *type of* **cabinet.** [➡FURNITURE; 858]

chinchilla *type of* **rodent.** [➡RODENT; 989]

chink **1** *n* **narrow opening**, crack, crevice, slit, opening, fissure. [➡HOLES, GAPS, AND FORKS; 1251] **2** *type of* **ringing sound.** [➡RINGING AND TOOTING SOUNDS; 1258]

chink in somebody's armour *n* **weak spot**, weakness, Achilles heel, flaw, failing, defect. [➡FAULTS, FLAWS, AND WEAKNESSES; 252]

chinook *type of* **wind.** [➡WINDY AND STORMY WEATHER; 1053]

chinos *type of* **trousers.** [➡GARMENTS AND OUTFITS; 865]

chintz *type of* **fabric from plants.** [➡FABRICS; 1131]

chintzy **1** *adj* (*informal disapproving*) **fussy**, quaint, cottagey, overelaborate, twee, pretty-pretty (*informal*). [➡IN POOR TASTE; 230] **2** *adj* (*US*) **tightfisted**, stingy (*informal*), miserly, penny-pinching (*informal*), parsimonious, mean, ungenerous, cheap (*US*). [➡FINANCIALLY MEAN AND GRASPING; 520] *Opposite:* generous. **3** *adj* (*US*) **trashy**, cheap, tacky (*informal*), inferior, shoddy, gaudy, showy, tawdry. [➡IN POOR TASTE; 230] *Opposite:* superior.

chinwag **1** *n* (*informal*) **chat**, natter (*informal*), gossip, talk, conversation, chitchat (*informal*). [➡INFORMAL COMMUNICATION; 45] **2** *v* (*US*) **chatter**, talk, chat, gab (*informal*), natter (*informal*), gossip, converse, chitchat (*informal*). [➡TWO-WAY COMMUNICATION; 608]

chip **1** *n* **piece**, bit, crumb, flake, chunk, morsel. [➡SMALL PIECE; 127] **2** *n* **mark**, damage, imperfection, flaw, blemish. [➡FAULTS, FLAWS, AND WEAKNESSES; 252] **3** *n* **token**, counter, marker, playing piece, poker chip. [➡GAMES PIECES; 878] **4** *v* **break off**, fragment, hew, flake, pare, whittle, chisel. [➡TEAR, BREAK, AND CUT; 361] **5** *v* **damage**, disfigure, mark, blemish, notch. [➡WORSEN APPEARANCE; 383] **6** *type of* **hardware.** [➡COMPUTERS AND COMPUTING; 1126] **7** *type of* **processed potato.** [➡FRUIT AND VEGETABLES; 1175]

chip away at *v* **weaken**, wear away, eat into, erode, diminish. [➡WORSEN SOMETHING; 381]

chipboard *n* [➡BUILDING MATERIALS; 1076]

chip in (*informal*) **1** *v* **contribute**, help, participate, collaborate, take part, partake, share the expense, go shares in, stump up. [➡GIVE MONEY; 434] **2** *v* **chime in**, butt in, interject, voice your opinion, say what you think, speak up, pipe up, have your say, put in your two cents worth (*US*). [➡INTERRUPT AND BUTT IN; 620]

chipmunk *type of* **rodent.** [➡RODENT; 989]

chip off the old block (*informal*) *n* **spitting image** (*informal*), younger version, mirror image, clone, living image, replica. [➡COPIES AND REPLICAS; 152]

chipped *adj* [➡IN BAD REPAIR; 1233]

chipper (*informal*) **1** *adj* **cheerful**, high-spirited, lively, exuberant, good-humoured, bright, chirpy (*informal*), sprightly, energetic, frisky, animated, perky, upbeat (*informal*). [➡PLEASURE, EXCITEMENT, AND ELATION; 535] *Opposite:* glum. **2** *adj* **smartly dressed**, well-dressed, neat, trim, smart, dapper. [➡WELL GROOMED; 483] *Opposite:* scruffy.

chipping *n* **chip**, piece, fragment, bit, shaving, shard, chippings. [➡SMALL PIECE; 127]

chippings *n* **stones**, pebbles, gravel, shingle. [➡SMALL PIECE; 127]

chip shop *type of* **food outlet.** [➡RETAIL OUTLETS; 1082]

chirp *type of* **bird sound.** [➡SOUNDS MADE BY BIRDS; 1262]

chirpiness (*informal*) *n* [➡CHEERFULNESS OF OUTLOOK; 504]

chirpy (*informal*) *adj* **lively**, vivacious, alert, bright, effervescent, cheery, chipper (*informal*), cheerful, happy, high-spirited, in good spirits. [➡PLEASURE, EXCITEMENT, AND ELATION; 535] *Opposite:* gloomy.

chirrup *type of* **bird sound.** [➡SOUNDS MADE BY BIRDS; 1262]

chisel *type of* **cutting tool.** [➡CUTTING TOOLS; 1119]

chit (*dated*) *n* **receipt**, bill, tally, account, tab (*US informal*). [➡RECEIPTS AND INVOICES; 592]

chitchat (*informal*) **1** *v* **talk**, discuss, have a tête-à-tête, gossip, babble, chatter, have a chat, natter (*informal*). [➡TWO-WAY COMMUNICATION; 608] **2** *n* **chatter**, gossip, chat, natter (*informal*), chinwag (*informal*), conversation, talk, gab (*informal*). [➡INFORMAL COMMUNICATION; 45]

chivalrous **1** *adj* **courteous**, mannerly, gracious, polite, well-mannered, attentive, considerate. [➡GOOD MANNERS AND SOCIAL SKILLS; 521] *Opposite:* discourteous. **2** *adj* **gallant**, courtly, brave, valiant, loyal, magnanimous, noble. [➡GOOD MANNERS AND SOCIAL SKILLS; 521] *Opposite:* cowardly.

chivalry **1** *n* **courtesy**, courteousness, politeness, attentiveness, gentility, good manners, kindness, consideration, civility. [➡GOOD MANNERS AND SOCIAL SKILLS; 521] *Opposite:* discourteousness. **2** *n* **gallantry**, courtliness, loyalty, courage, bravery, magnanimity, valour, nobility. [➡GOOD MANNERS AND SOCIAL SKILLS; 521] *Opposite:* cowardice.

chive *type of* **herb**. [➡HERBS AND SPICES; 1174]

chivvy *v* **urge**, pester, harass, badger, hassle (*informal*), pressure, push. [➡CAUSE OR COMPEL TO ACT; 272] *Opposite:* discourage.

chlorine *type of* **gas**. [➡GASES; 1274]

chock 1 *n* **wedge**, block, doorstop, chuck. [➡STICKS, POLES, AND WEDGES; 1253] 2 *v* **brace**, steady, fix, block, stop. [➡FASTEN, LINK, AND JOIN; 409] *Opposite:* release.

chock-a-block (*informal*) *adj* **jam-packed** (*informal*), crowded, jammed, packed, chock-full (*informal*), wall-to-wall (*informal*), teeming, crammed, full, bursting, heaving, packed out (*informal*), brimful. [➡FULL; 1238]

chock-full (*informal*) *adj* **packed**, jammed, crammed, full, full up, crowded, jam-packed (*informal*), chock-a-block (*informal*), wall-to-wall (*informal*), bursting, heaving, filled, teeming, packed out (*informal*), brimful. [➡FULL; 1238] *Opposite:* empty.

chocolate 1 *type of* **brown**. [➡COLOURS; 1223] 2 *type of* **confectionery**. [➡CONFECTIONERY; 1181]

chocolate-box *adj* **pretty**, pretty-pretty (*informal*), romanticized, twee, picturesque, soft-focus, attractive, sentimental. [➡IN POOR TASTE; 230]

choice 1 *n* **selection**, choosing, pick, election, adoption. [➡MAKE DECISIONS AND CHOICES; 753] 2 *n* **range**, selection, variety, set, group. [➡COLLECTIONS AND MIXTURES OF THINGS; 1243] 3 *adj* **excellent**, high-quality, optimal, special, prime, best, select. [➡SUPERIORITY; 153]

choir *type of* **band**. [➡MUSICIANS AND SINGERS; 908]

choke 1 *v* **strangle**, throttle, stifle, suffocate, garrotte. [➡KILL; 923] 2 *v* **obstruct**, clog, block, stop up, congest, plug, dam, fill, fill up, gag, halt [➡FILL; 407] *Opposite:* free up (*informal*). 3 *v* **fill with emotion**, freeze up, weep, well up, become teary-eyed (*US*). [➡GIVING VENT TO EMOTIONS; 680] 4 *type of* **controls**. [➡VEHICLES; 1144]

choke back *v* **suppress**, hold back, fight back, stifle, repress, stop. [➡WITHHOLD INFORMATION; 688] *Opposite:* let out.

choked 1 *adj* [➡FULL; 1238] 2 *adj* (*informal*) **upset**, emotional, overcome, dismayed, disappointed, unhappy. [➡SADNESS, DISTRESS, AND DESPAIR; 540]

choked up 1 *adj* [➡FULL; 1238] 2 *adj* (*US informal*) [➡SADNESS, DISTRESS, AND DESPAIR; 540]

choker *type of* **necklace**. [➡JEWELLERY; 866]

choler (*archaic or literary*) *n* [➡IRRITATION AND ANGER; 542]

choleric (*literary*) *adj* [➡IRRITATION AND ANGER; 542]

cholesterol *n* **fat**, saturated fat, saturated fatty acid, fatty acid, lipid, dietary fat. [➡FOOD COMPONENTS; 1187]

chomp (*informal*) *v* **chew**, munch, crunch, eat, masticate, gnaw, bite on, grind. [➡EAT AND NOT EAT; 711]

choose 1 *v* **select**, pick, take, pick out, point out, indicate, elect, vote for, decide on, go for (*informal*), cherry-pick (*disapproving*), plump for. [➡MAKE DECISIONS AND CHOICES; 753] *Opposite:* reject. 2 *v* **decide**, want, prefer, desire, wish, opt. [➡MAKE DECISIONS AND CHOICES; 753]

choose up (*US*) *v* **select team members**, choose sides, pick sides. [➡MAKE DECISIONS AND CHOICES; 753]

choosiness *n* [➡DIFFICULT TO PLEASE; 516]

choosy (*informal*) *adj* **particular**, hard to please, fussy, picky, fastidious, demanding, selective, finicky, pernickety (*informal*), faddy. [➡DIFFICULT TO PLEASE; 516] *Opposite:* indifferent.

chop 1 *v* **cut up**, chop up, slice, hack, axe, lop, hew, sever, slash, split, fell. [➡TEAR, BREAK, AND CUT; 361] 2 *type of* **cut**. [➡TYPES AND CUTS OF MEAT; 1176]

chop-chop (*informal*) *interj* **quickly**, immediately, right away, fast, right now, at once, without delay, with no delay, at the double. [➡HAPPENING QUICKLY; 104]

chop down *v* **shorten**, decrease, cut back, cut down, deliver a blow to, dispense with, lop off. [➡CHANGE OF SIZE: SMALLER; 394]

chopper 1 *n* (*slang*) *type of* **tooth**. [➡THE MOUTH; 703] 2 *type of* **cutting tool**. [➡CUTTING TOOLS; 1119]

choppy *adj* **uneven**, broken up, variable, shifting, changing, irregular, jerky, rough. [➡WINDY AND STORMY WEATHER; 1053] *Opposite:* smooth.

chops (*informal*) *n* **jaw**, mouth, gob (*slang disapproving*). [➡HEAD; 693]

chopstick *type of* **cutlery**. [➡TABLEWARE, CUTLERY, AND KITCHENWARE; 861]

chop suey *type of* **cooked dish**. [➡PREPARED DISHES; 1169]

chop up *v* **cut up**, chop, cut into pieces, mill, slice, cube, dice, mince, grind. [➡TEAR, BREAK, AND CUT; 361]

choral *adj* **vocal**, harmonic, sung. [➡MUSICAL TERMS; 912]

chorale 1 *type of* **band**. [➡MUSICIANS AND SINGERS; 908] 2 *type of* **vocal music**. [➡MUSIC, SONGS, AND SINGING; 907]

chord *n* **harmony**, triad, arpeggio, major chord, minor chord. [➡NOTES AND CHORDS; 909]

chore 1 *n* **task**, job, errand, odd job, assignment, responsibility, duty. [➡WORK IN GENERAL; 298] 2 *n* **routine**, bore, hard work, imposition, inconvenience. [➡NUISANCES; 254]

choreograph 1 *v* **create**, compose, design, arrange, put together, devise. [➡ARRANGE AND CREATE ORDER; 358] 2 *v* **manoeuvre**, plan, direct, strategize, manage, manipulate, stage-manage, organize. [➡MAKE POSSIBLE; 276]

choreography 1 *n* **composition**, dance routine, step design, step sequence, step arrangement, dance composition. [➡DANCE; 903] 2 *n* **manoeuvring**, direction, management, manipulation, strategy, planning, stage management. [➡WAYS OF DOING THINGS; 295]

chorister *n* **singer**, musician, treble. [➡MUSICIANS AND SINGERS; 908]

chortle 1 *n* **laugh**, chuckle, gurgle, giggle, snigger, cackle, snicker (*US*). [➡SOUNDS MADE BY PEOPLE; 1261] 2 *v* **chuckle**, laugh, gurgle, giggle, snigger, cackle, snicker (*US*). [➡LAUGHTER; 650]

chorus 1 *n* **refrain**, chorus line, response, repeat, repetition, reprise. [➡MUSIC, SONGS, AND SINGING; 907] 2 *v* **speak at once**, speak together, speak in unison. [➡TWO-WAY COMMUNICATION; 608] 3 *type of* **band**. [➡MUSICIANS AND SINGERS; 908]

chosen *adj* **selected**, select, elect, preferred, special. [➡SUPERIORITY; 153]

choux pastry *n* [➡BREAD, FLOUR, AND BREAD PRODUCTS; 1178]

chow 1 *n* (*slang*) **food**, grub (*informal*), nosh (*informal*), eats (*slang*), tucker (*informal*), victuals, vittles (*archaic*), chuck (*US regional*). [➡FOOD; 1166] 2 *type of* **small dog**. [➡DOG; 980]

chowder *type of* **soup**. [➡SOUP; 1185]

chow down (*US informal*) *v* **eat**, dine, eat heartily, gulp, gobble, wolf, nosh (*informal*). [➡EAT AND NOT EAT; 711]

chow mein *type of* **cooked dish**. [➡PREPARED DISHES; 1169]

christen 1 *v* **baptize**, name, bless, sanctify. [➡RELIGIONS AND RELIGIOUS PRACTICES; 778] 2 *v* **name**, nickname, call, dub, label, style (*formal*). [➡NAME AND DESCRIBE; 666] 3 *v* (*informal*) **launch**, inaugurate, debut. [➡CAUSE TO START; 266]

christening 1 *n* **baptism**, ceremony, rite, naming. [➡RELIGIONS AND RELIGIOUS PRACTICES; 778] 2 *n* **launch**, first use, inauguration, debut. [➡BEGINNING; 53]

Christian name *n* **first name**, forename, given name, personal name, praenomen, name, middle name. [➡NAME AND DESCRIBE; 666]

Christmas cake *type of* **cake**. [➡CAKES, BISCUITS, AND DESSERTS; 1180]

chrome yellow *type of* **yellow**. [➡COLOURS; 1223]

chromium *type of* **metal**. [➡METALS; 1275]

chromosome *n* **genetic material**, DNA, RNA. [➡REPRODUCTION AND HEREDITY; 726]

chronic 1 *adj* **long-lasting**, lingering, continuing, enduring, lasting, prolonged, protracted. [➡PERMANENCE: WITHOUT END; 94] *Opposite:* fleeting. 2 *adj* **habitual**, persistent, ingrained, compulsive, inveterate, established, confirmed, longstanding. [➡PERMANENCE: WITHOUT END; 94] *Opposite:* occasional.

chronicle 1 *n* **record**, history, account, annals, journal, narrative, story. [➡RECORDS; 586] 2 *v* **report**, record, recount, relate, narrate, keep track of, make note of, set down, register, write down. [➡RECORD SOMETHING; 372]

chronological *adj* **sequential**, consecutive, linear. [➡CHAIN OF EVENTS; 163]

chronology 1 *n* **sequence of events**, order of events, time line, timetable, table of events, things as they happened. [➡CHAIN OF EVENTS; 163] 2 *n* **account**, record, chronicle, narrative, history, annals, list. [➡LISTS AND SCHEDULES; 588]

chronometer *n* [➡CLOCKS AND TIMERS; 1125]

chrysalis *type of* **insect stages of development**. [➡INSECT STAGES; 1020]

chrysanthemum *type of* **perennial flower**. [➡FLOWERS; 1032]

chrysoprase *type of* **gemstone**. [➡PRECIOUS STONES; 1277]

chubbiness *n* **plumpness**, roundness, fleshiness, stoutness, fatness, obesity. [➡BUILD; 478] *Opposite:* slenderness.

chubby *adj* **plump**, rotund, round, fleshy, stout, fat, obese, overweight. [➡BUILD; 478] *Opposite:* slender.

chuck 1 *v* (*informal*) **throw**, hurl, toss, fling, pitch, lob. [➡THROW SOMETHING; 335] 2 *v* (*informal*) **get rid of**, throw out, throw away, dispose of, discard. [➡GET RID OF SOMETHING; 452] *Opposite:* keep. 3 *v* (*informal*) **quit**, resign, walk off, leave, walk out, throw in the towel (*informal*), give up. [➡STOP ACTING; 265] 4 *v* **tap**, pat lightly, pat, tickle. [➡PHYSICAL CONTACT AS COMMUNICATION; 656] 5 *n* **chock**, wedge, block, clamp. [➡AMOUNT OF SOLID OR SEMI-SOLID; 115] 6 *n* (*US regional*) **food**, provisions, provender (*literary or humorous*), grub (*informal*). [➡FOOD; 1166] 7 *type of* **cut**. [➡TYPES AND CUTS OF MEAT; 1176]

See Compare and Contrast at **throw**.

chuck down (*informal*) *v* **rain hard**, pour, rain cats and dogs (*informal*), bucket (*informal*), teem, come down in torrents, pour down. [➡CLOUDY AND RAINY WEATHER; 1052] *Opposite:* drizzle.

chuck in (*informal*) *v* **call it quits** (*informal*), pack it in, throw in the towel (*informal*), stop, give in, give up, concede defeat. [➡STOP ACTING; 265]

chuckle 1 *v* **laugh**, laugh to yourself, chortle, laugh inwardly, giggle, snigger, gurgle, snicker. [➡LAUGHTER; 650] 2 *n* **laughter**, chortle, inward laughter, giggle, snigger, gurgle, snicker (*US*). [➡SOUNDS MADE BY PEOPLE; 1261]

chuck out (*informal*) *v* [➡GET RID OF SOMETHING; 452]

chuffed (*informal*) *adj* **pleased**, content, satisfied, happy, delighted, thrilled, gratified. [➡APPRECIATION AND GRATITUDE; 536]

chug 1 *v* (*informal*) **continue**, keep going, plug away (*informal*), keep at it, persist. [➡CONTINUE AN ACTION; 263] *Opposite:* stop. 2 *v* (*US slang*) **guzzle** (*informal*), gulp, gulp down, swig (*informal*). [➡EAT AND NOT EAT; 711] 3 *type of* **continuous sound**. [➡CONTINUOUS SOUNDS; 1257]

chugalug (*US informal*) *v* [➡DRINK; 712]

chum (*informal*) *n* **friend**, associate, acquaintance, mate, pal (*informal*), companion, buddy (*US informal*). [➡FRIENDS; 963] *Opposite:* stranger.

chumminess (*informal*) *n* **friendliness**, sociability, closeness, intimacy, matiness, friendship. [➡RELATIONSHIP TO ANOTHER; 973]

chummy (*informal*) *adj* **friendly**, sociable, congenial, matey, close, intimate, inseparable. [➡FRIENDLINESS AND SOCIABILITY; 495]

chump *type of* **cut**. [➡TYPES AND CUTS OF MEAT; 1176]

chunk *n* **piece**, hunk, mass, lump, portion, amount. [➡LARGE PIECE; 128]

chunkiness 1 *n (informal)* [➡BUILD; 478] 2 *n* [➡LARGE; 1192]

chunky 1 *adj* **lumpy**, bumpy, coarse, rough. [➡PHYSICAL TEXTURE; 1221] *Opposite:* smooth. 2 *adj* **solid**, heavy, hefty, weighty, substantial, strong. [➡WEIGHT: HEAVY; 1204] *Opposite:* lightweight. 3 *adj (informal)* **stocky**, stout, fat, chubby, plump, hefty, thickset, heavy. [➡BUILD; 478] *Opposite:* slender.

chunter *(informal) n* [➡COMPLAIN AND NAG; 687]

church *type of* **place of worship.** [➡RELIGIOUS BUILDINGS; 1084]

church

◆ *types of church*
abbey, basilica, cathedral, chapel, meeting house, minster, tabernacle

churchgoer *n* **worshipper**, congregant, communicant. [➡RELIGIOUS PEOPLE; 779]

churchyard *n* **graveyard**, burial ground, cemetery, boneyard *(informal)*, necropolis. [➡BURIAL PLACES AND ACCESSORIES; 930]

churlish 1 *adj* **rude**, boorish, coarse, truculent, crass, ill-bred, bad-mannered, impolite. [➡BAD MANNERS AND SOCIAL SKILLS; 522] *Opposite:* polite. 2 *adj* **ill-natured**, irritable, unpleasant, grumpy, sullen, surly. [➡BAD-TEMPERED AND HUMOURLESS; 627] *Opposite:* pleasant.

churlishly *adv* [➡BAD MANNERS AND SOCIAL SKILLS; 522]

churlishness *n* [➡DIFFICULT TO PLEASE; 516]

churn *v* **mix**, roil, agitate, shake, whip, toss, stir up, stir, blend. [➡COMBINE AND MIX; 401]

churn out *v* **mass-produce**, manufacture, turn out, issue. [➡MANUFACTURE; 350]

chute 1 *n* **shaft**, tube, channel, sluice, raceway, spillway, slide, trough. [➡WATERCOURSES; 1110] 2 *n* **waterfall**, cascade, force, cataract, descent, drop, rapids. [➡RIVERS, LAKES, AND STREAMS; 1042]

chutney *type of* **pickle.** [➡SEASONINGS AND SAUCES; 1173]

chutzpah *(informal) n* **gall**, cheek *(informal)*, boldness, nerve, impudence, fearlessness, effrontery, audacity, brass neck *(informal)*. [➡BAD MANNERS AND SOCIAL SKILLS; 522]

CIA *n* **security service**, intelligence service, federal bureau, counterintelligence service, spy organization, intelligence-gathering organization. [➡LEGISLATIVE BODIES AND LEGISLATION; 809]

ciabatta *type of* **bread.** [➡BREAD, FLOUR, AND BREAD PRODUCTS; 1178]

ciao *(informal) interj* **hello**, hi *(informal)*, goodbye, so long *(informal)*, see you later *(informal)*. [➡GREETINGS, FAREWELLS, AND SALUTATIONS; 660]

cicada *type of* **flying insect.** [➡FLYING INSECTS; 1013]

cilantro *(US) type of* **herb.** [➡HERBS AND SPICES; 1174]

ciliate *type of* **microorganism.** [➡MICROORGANISMS, FUNGI, AND ALGAE; 1023]

C in C *n* **commander in chief**, field marshal, generalissimo, commander, leader, chief of staff, president. [➡BUSINESS PEOPLE; 794]

cinch 1 *n (informal)* **piece of cake** *(informal)*, breeze *(informal)*, walk in the park *(informal)*, doddle *(informal)*, child's play, nothing, gift *(informal)*, snap *(US)*. [➡EASY WORK; 300] 2 *n (informal)* **sure bet**, certainty, dead certainty, sure thing *(informal)*. [➡CERTAIN; 175] 3 *n* **girth**, restraint, belt, strap. [➡FASTENERS, LINKS, AND NETWORKS; 1246] 4 *v* **bind**, restrain, gird *(literary)*, fix, tighten. [➡FASTEN, LINK, AND JOIN; 409] 5 *v (dated informal)* **guarantee**, assure, insure, settle, make certain. [➡APPROVE AND CONFIRM; 647]

cinder block *(US) n* [➡BUILDING MATERIALS; 1076]

cinders *n* **embers**, ashes, residue, coals. [➡PRODUCTS OF FIRE; 1165]

cine camera *type of* **photographic equipment.** [➡PHOTOGRAPHY AND PHOTOGRAPHIC EQUIPMENT; 1121]

cinema 1 *n* **movies**, films *(informal)*, pictures *(informal dated)*, motion pictures, film. [➡FILM; 901] 2 *n* [➡BUILDINGS FOR PUBLIC ENTERTAINMENT; 1083]

cinematic *adj* **filmic**, photographic, movielike, filmmaking, moviemaking. [➡THE PERFORMING ARTS; 904]

cinematography *n* **photography**, shooting, film making, picture making, movie making, camera work. [➡FILM; 901]

cinnabar moth *type of* **moth.** [➡MOTHS AND BUTTERFLIES; 1015]

cinnamon *type of* **spice.** [➡HERBS AND SPICES; 1174]

cinquecento *type of* **pre-20th-century architecture.** [➡BUILDING AND ARCHITECTURE; 1075]

cipher 1 *n* **code**, secret message, symbols, cryptograph, encryption, cryptogram. [➡SYMBOLS, SIGNS, AND NUMBERS; 597] 2 *n* **nobody**, nonentity, nothing, zero. [➡NONE; 121]

circa *prep* **approximately**, about, around, roughly, round about, on or about. [➡APPROXIMATELY; 133] *Opposite:* exactly.

circadian *adj* **daily**, 24-hour, 24-hourly, diurnal, quotidian *(formal)*, day by day, day-to-day, everyday. [➡TIMES OF DAY; 87]

circle 1 *n* **ring**, loop, round, sphere, disk, ball. [➡ROUNDED SHAPE; 1217] 2 *n* **group**, gang, set, clique, crowd. [➡FRIENDS AND ACQUAINTANCES; 936] 3 *v* **go around**, orbit, fly around, fly in a circle, circumnavigate *(formal)*, revolve. [➡PROCEED AND GO; 306] 4 *v* **encircle**, surround, ring, enclose, bound, contain. [➡EXIST IN CLOSE PROXIMITY; 21]

circlet *n* **band**, coronet, tiara, diadem, crown, wreath. [➡ROUNDED SHAPE; 1217]

circuit 1 *n* **route**, track, trail, path. [➡ROADS; 1105] 2 *n* **tour**, trip, journey, route. [➡TRAVEL: JOURNEYS AND TRIPS; 319]

circuitous *adj* **indirect**, winding, convoluted, meandering, roundabout, twisting, lengthy, tortuous, devious. [➡INARTICULATE, RAMBLING, AND AWKWARD; 634] *Opposite:* direct.

circuitously 1 *adv* **indirectly**, tortuously, in a roundabout way, obliquely, meanderingly, windingly, twistingly. [➡DIRECTION OF MOTION; 346] *Opposite:* directly. 2 *adv* **complicatedly**, convolutedly, discursively, tangentially, long-windedly. [➡INARTICULATE, RAMBLING, AND AWKWARD; 634] *Opposite:* straightforwardly.

circuitry *n* **electrical system**, electrical structure, electric circuit, circuit board, motherboard, printed circuit, integrated circuit. [➡PARTS OF MACHINES AND TOOLS; 1117]

circular 1 *adj* **spherical**, rounded, globular, round. [➡ROUNDED SHAPE; 1217] 2 *n* **leaflet**, flier, pamphlet, advertisement, handbill, handout, tract, brochure. [➡ADVERTISING AND PUBLICITY; 605]

circularity *n* **indirectness**, circuitousness, obliqueness, roundaboutness, convolutedness, tortuousness, complexity. [➡INARTICULATE, RAMBLING, AND AWKWARD; 634] *Opposite:* directness.

circulate 1 *v* **flow**, move, travel, pass. [➡PROCEED AND GO; 306] 2 *v* **pass around**, distribute, hand out, give out, send out, spread, issue, disseminate, make known. [➡INFORM AND ANNOUNCE; 612] *Opposite:* conceal. 3 *v* (*informal*) **mingle**, socialize, mix, meet people, be sociable, party (*informal*). [➡ESTABLISHING RELATIONSHIPS WITH OTHERS; 974]

circulation 1 *n* **flow**, movement, passage, motion, rotation. [➡SELF-PROPULSION; 305] 2 *n* **exchange**, flow, transmission, spread, dissemination. [➡SELF-PROPULSION; 305] 3 *n* **distribution**, readership, sales. [➡NEWSPAPERS; 606]

circumference *n* **perimeter**, boundary, bounds, limits, edge, border, fringe. [➡EXTREMITIES OF PHYSICAL OBJECTS; 1249] *Opposite:* middle.

circumflex *type of* **diacritic**. [➡ASPECTS OF LANGUAGE; 683]

circumlocution *n* **periphrasis**, indirectness, roundaboutness, convolutedness, obliqueness, circuitousness. [➡INARTICULATE, RAMBLING, AND AWKWARD; 634] *Opposite:* directness.

circumlocutory *adj* **periphrastic**, indirect, meandering, roundabout, circuitous, convoluted, oblique, tortuous. [➡INARTICULATE, RAMBLING, AND AWKWARD; 634] *Opposite:* direct.

circumnavigate (*formal*) *v* **sail round**, orbit, circle, travel around, go around, travel round, fly round, sail around. [➡TRAVEL: WAYS OF TRAVELLING; 321]

circumscribe (*formal*) *v* **limit**, restrict, define, demarcate, mark out, confine, delineate (*formal*). [➡AVOID, PREVENT, LIMIT, AND CONTROL; 278]

circumscription (*formal*) *n* **restriction**, limit, limitation, constraint, restraint, curb. [➡REFUSE PERMISSION AND NOT ALLOW; 671] *Opposite:* freedom.

circumspect *adj* **cautious**, prudent, careful, guarded, wary, judicious, chary, cagey (*informal*). [➡INSECURITY AND LOSS OF COMPOSURE; 545] *Opposite:* reckless.

See Compare and Contrast at **cautious**.

circumspection *n* **care**, carefulness, caution, cautiousness, judiciousness, caginess (*informal*), guardedness, wariness, chariness, prudence. [➡INSECURITY AND LOSS OF COMPOSURE; 545] *Opposite:* recklessness.

circumstance 1 *n* **condition**, situation, state of affairs, status quo, context. [➡SITUATIONS; 71] 2 *n* (*formal*) **event**, occurrence, incident, instance, happening, episode, case. [➡EVENTS AND OCCURRENCES; 35]

circumstantial *adj* **incidental**, contingent, indirect, inferred, conditional, anecdotal, secondary. [➡UNCERTAIN; 176] *Opposite:* concrete.

circumvent *v* **avoid**, get round, evade, skirt, dodge, sidestep, bypass, get out of, outwit, thwart, elude. [➡NOT PAY ATTENTION; 765]

circumvention *n* **avoidance**, evasion, escape, sidestepping, dodging, bypassing, eluding. [➡NOT PAY ATTENTION; 765]

circus 1 *n* [➡BUILDINGS FOR PUBLIC ENTERTAINMENT; 1083] 2 *n* (*informal*) **show**, festival, spectacle, extravaganza, event, revel. [➡PERFORMANCES AND SHOWS; 42]

cirque *n* **corrie**, cwm, combe, hollow, valley, glaciated valley. [➡GEOLOGICAL FEATURES; 1056]

cirrocumulus *type of* **cloud**. [➡CLOUDY AND RAINY WEATHER; 1052]

cirrus *type of* **cloud**. [➡CLOUDY AND RAINY WEATHER; 1052]

cistern *n* **water tank**, storage tank, tank, reservoir, container, boiler, underground tank, hot water tank. [➡CONTAINERS, RECEPTACLES, AND PACKAGING; 1244]

citadel *n* **fortress**, stronghold, bastion, fort, castle, refuge, sanctuary. [➡FORTRESSES AND FORTIFICATIONS; 1089]

citation *n* **quote**, quotation, mention, reference, excerpt, extract, illustration. [➡SUMMARIES, OUTLINES, AND EXCERPTS; 589]

cite (*formal*) *v* **quote**, mention, refer to, allude to. [➡RECITE, REPEAT, AND NARRATE; 621]

citified (*disapproving*) *adj* **oversophisticated**, sophisticated, slick, suave, urbane, cosmopolitan. [➡LEVEL OF EDUCATION AND SOPHISTICATION; 894] *Opposite:* countrified.

citizen *n* **inhabitant**, resident, national, legal resident, voter, naturalized citizen, native. [➡INHABITANT; 857]

citizenry (*formal*) *n* **people**, population, community, public, electorate, voters, populace, general public. [➡GROUPS IN SOCIETY; 940]

citizenship 1 *n* **nationality**, residency, right of abode. [➡STATUS; 888] 2 *n* **social responsibility**, public spirit, social conscience. [➡MORALLY GOOD; 775]

citrine *type of* **yellow**. [➡COLOURS; 1223]

citron *type of* **yellow**. [➡COLOURS; 1223]

citrus

◆ *types of citrus*
clementine, grapefruit, lemon, lime, mandarin, orange, pomelo, satsuma, tangerine

city 1 *n* **metropolis**, municipality, conurbation, capital, town. [➡HUMAN SETTLEMENTS; 1069] 2 *adj* **urban**, metropolitan, town, municipal. [➡HUMAN SETTLEMENTS; 1069]

Compare and Contrast: ***city, conurbation, metropolis, town, municipality***

CORE MEANING: AN URBAN AREA WHERE A LARGE NUMBER OF PEOPLE LIVE

city originally a town having a cathedral or having such a status conferred on it by the Crown; in the United States, a large municipal centre governed under a charter granted by the state; in Canada, a large municipal unit incorporated by the provincial government, but now used generally for any large urban area; ***conurbation*** an urban region formed or enlarged by the merging of adjacent cities and towns through expansion or development; ***metropolis*** a large or important city, sometimes the capital of a country, state, or region; ***town*** a populated area smaller than a city and larger than a village; ***municipality*** a city, town, or area with some degree of self-government.

city dweller *n* [➡INHABITANT; 857]

civic *adj* **public**, municipal, local, community, town, city, civil. [➡HUMAN SETTLEMENTS; 1069] *Opposite:* private.

civil 1 *adj* **public**, political, municipal, civic, civilian, domestic, interior. [➡BELONGING OR RELATING TO PEOPLE; 943] **2** *adj* **courteous**, polite, respectful, well-mannered, accommodating, obliging, gracious, considerate, amicable. [➡GOOD MANNERS AND SOCIAL SKILLS; 521] *Opposite:* rude.

civilian *n* **noncombatant**, private citizen, citizen, member of the public, neutral. [➡PERSON; 931]

civilian clothes *n* [➡GARMENTS AND OUTFITS; 865]

civility *n* **politeness**, courtesy, good manners, courteousness, respect, graciousness, consideration. [➡GOOD MANNERS AND SOCIAL SKILLS; 521] *Opposite:* rudeness.

civilization 1 *n* **society**, nation, culture, empire, polity. [➡GROUPS IN SOCIETY; 940] **2** *n* **development**, evolution, progress, cultivation, refinement, sophistication, advancement. [➡LEVEL OF EDUCATION AND SOPHISTICATION; 894]

civilize *v* **enlighten**, educate, cultivate, improve, advance, develop, refine, humanize. [➡IMPROVE SOMETHING; 375]

civilized *adj* **cultured**, educated, refined, enlightened, polite, elegant, urbane. [➡GOOD MANNERS AND SOCIAL SKILLS; 521] *Opposite:* barbarous.

civilizing *adj* **humanizing**, taming, educating, cultivating, refining, enlightening. [➡MORALLY GOOD; 775]

civil liberties *n* **privileges**, freedoms, rights, human rights, civil rights, constitutional rights. [➡THE LAW AND LEGAL AUTHORITY; 814]

civilly *adv* **politely**, respectfully, courteously, amicably, considerately, graciously. [➡GOOD MANNERS AND SOCIAL SKILLS; 521] *Opposite:* rudely.

civil rights *n* **human rights**, rights, constitutional rights, civil liberties, privileges, freedoms. [➡THE LAW AND LEGAL AUTHORITY; 814]

civil servant *n* **public servant**, government employee, bureaucrat, official, administrator. [➡ADMINISTRATIVE OFFICERS; 811]

civvies *n* [➡GARMENTS AND OUTFITS; 865]

clack *v* **snap**, click, clap, bang, rap, smack, clatter. [➡EMIT SOUNDS THROUGH IMPACT AND ABRASION; 366]

clad *adj* **dressed**, clothed, covered, attired (*formal*), arrayed (*literary*). [➡DRESS, WEAR, AND UNDRESS; 868]

cladding *n* **covering**, layer, facing, casing, shell, shield. [➡COVERS AND COATINGS; 1245]

claim 1 *v* **maintain**, assert, say, state, declare, argue, allege, aver (*formal*), profess. [➡CLAIM, INSIST, AND EMPHASIZE; 615] **2** *v* **ask for**, call for, demand, apply for, request, appeal, sue. [➡REQUEST AND DEMAND; 664] *Opposite:* deny. **3** *v* **receive**, obtain, take, pick up, retrieve, collect. [➡GET MONEY OR REWARD; 422] **4** *n* **assertion**, statement, accusation, declaration, allegation, contention. [➡CLAIM, INSIST, AND EMPHASIZE; 615] **5** *n* **demand**, request, application, petition, call. [➡REQUEST AND DEMAND; 664] **6** *n* **right**, entitlement, prerogative, privilege, due, title. [➡POSSESS; 445]

claimant *n* **applicant**, plaintiff, pretender, petitioner, appellant, supplicant (*formal*), suitor. [➡PEOPLE WHO MAKE REQUESTS; 665]

clairvoyance *n* **psychic power**, telepathy, prophecy, fortune telling, palm reading, astrology, soothsaying, augury, second sight, extrasensory perception, ESP, sixth sense, divining. [➡THE SUPERNATURAL; 788]

clairvoyant 1 *n* **psychic**, mystic, spiritualist, telepathist, diviner, seer, mind reader, medium. [➡PEOPLE WITH SUPERNATURAL POWERS; 789] **2** *adj* **intuitive**, psychic, telepathic, second-sighted, perceptive, farsighted. [➡THE SUPERNATURAL; 788]

clam *type of* **aquatic invertebrate.** [➡AQUATIC INVERTEBRATE; 1022]

clambake *type of* **meal.** [➡MEALS AND PARTS OF MEALS; 1168]

clamber *v* **climb**, scramble, crawl, scale. [➡GO UPWARDS; 307]

clamminess 1 *n* **dampness**, wetness, moistness, dankness, sliminess. [➡PHYSICAL TEXTURE; 1221] *Opposite:* dryness. **2** *n* **humidity**, mugginess, closeness, heat, airlessness, stuffiness, dampness, stickiness, moistness. [➡CLOUDY AND RAINY WEATHER; 1052] *Opposite:* dryness.

clammy 1 *adj* **damp**, slimy, wet, moist, dank. [➡MOIST; 1240] *Opposite:* dry. **2** *adj* **humid**, muggy, close, sticky, sweaty. [➡HOT WEATHER; 1050] *Opposite:* dry.

clamorous *adj* **noisy**, vociferous, loud, rowdy, boisterous, deafening, riotous, raucous. [➡LOUD OR UNPLEASANT SOUNDS; 1265] *Opposite:* tranquil.

clamour 1 *v* **shout**, scream, yell, cry, screech, bellow, bawl, holler (*informal*). [➡SOUND EMISSION BY PEOPLE; 364] *Opposite:* whisper. **2** *n* **appeal**, demand, call, request, cry, outcry. [➡REQUEST AND DEMAND; 664] **3** *n* **uproar**, hullabaloo, din, commotion, racket (*informal*), noise, shouting, agitation, outcry, hubbub. [➡CHAOS AND UPROAR; 51] **4** *v* **demand**, insist, appeal, cry out, bay, call out. [➡REQUEST AND DEMAND; 664]

clamp *v* **fasten**, hold, compress, fix, brace, clinch, close, make fast. [➡FASTEN, LINK, AND JOIN; 409]

clamp down *v* **shut down**, crack down (*informal*), take tough action, come down on, restrict, limit, curb. [➡AVOID, PREVENT, LIMIT, AND CONTROL; 278] *Opposite:* relent.

clampdown *n* **crackdown**, restriction, curb, suppression, embargo, shutdown, squelching (*US slang*). [➡END; 54]

clam up (*informal*) *v* **stop talking**, choke, refuse to speak, dry up (*informal*), remain silent, be unforthcoming, be unwilling to talk, withhold information, shut up (*informal*). [➡WITHHOLD INFORMATION; 688]

clan 1 *n* **tribe**, family, relations, relatives, kinfolk, kin. [➡THE FAMILY; 956] 2 *n* (*informal*) **clique**, fraternity, band, coterie, set, circle, in-group. [➡FRIENDS AND ACQUAINTANCES; 936]

clandestine *adj* **secret**, underground, covert, concealed, stealthy, furtive, undercover, surreptitious, illegal. [➡SECRET AND UNKNOWN; 180] *Opposite:* open.

See Compare and Contrast at **secret**.

clang 1 *v* **clank**, sound, toll, reverberate, resound, clink, chime, jingle, jangle. [➡EMIT SOUNDS THROUGH IMPACT AND ABRASION; 366] 2 *n* **clash**, clank, ring, bang, clink, jangle, ding-dong, knell, clangour. [➡IMPACT SOUNDS; 1259] 3 *type of* **ringing sound**. [➡RINGING AND TOOTING SOUNDS; 1258]

clanger (*informal*) *n* **blunder**, mistake, error, slip-up (*informal*), boob (*informal*), boo-boo (*informal*), howler (*informal*), faux pas (*literary*), blooper (*US informal humorous*). [➡MISTAKES; 251]

clanging *adj* [➡LOUD OR UNPLEASANT SOUNDS; 1265]

clank 1 *n* **clang**, clink, clatter, clash, bang, crash, jangle, clangour. [➡IMPACT SOUNDS; 1259] 2 *type of* **ringing sound**. [➡RINGING AND TOOTING SOUNDS; 1258]

clannish *adj* **cliquey**, cliquish, unfriendly, unsociable, aloof, exclusive, exclusionary, insular, narrow, parochial. [➡UNFRIENDLINESS AND UNSOCIABILITY; 505] *Opposite:* open.

clap 1 *v* **applaud**, give a standing ovation, put your hands together, give a round of applause, acclaim, cheer. [➡APPLAUSE; 653] *Opposite:* boo. 2 *n* **slap**, pat, tap, thrust, thwack, wallop (*informal*). [➡IMPACT SOUNDS; 1259]

clapboard *n* [➡BUILDING MATERIALS; 1076]

clapped-out (*informal*) *adj* **worn out**, dilapidated, rundown, decrepit, falling apart, shabby, battered, rickety, tatty. [➡IN BAD REPAIR; 1233]

clapping *n* **applause**, appreciation, ovation, acclamation, acclaim, support. [➡APPLAUSE; 653] *Opposite:* jeering.

claptrap (*informal*) *n* **nonsense**, humbug, drivel, hogwash (*informal*), twaddle (*informal*), rubbish, rot (*informal*), bunkum (*informal*). [➡MEANINGLESS SPEECH OR WRITING; 677] *Opposite:* sense.

claret *type of* **red**. [➡COLOURS; 1223]

clarification *n* **explanation**, amplification, illumination, clearing up, explaining, elucidation (*formal*), interpretation. [➡EXPLAIN AND CLARIFY; 611] *Opposite:* obfuscation.

clarify 1 *v* **elucidate** (*formal*), make clear, explain, clear up, illuminate, spell out, simplify, shed light on. [➡EXPLAIN AND CLARIFY; 611] *Opposite:* confuse. 2 *v* **refine**, purify, cleanse, filter, process. [➡CLEAN AND POLISH; 404] *Opposite:* cloud.

clarinet *type of* **wind instrument**. [➡MUSICAL INSTRUMENTS; 910]

clarity *n* **clearness**, lucidity, simplicity, precision, intelligibility, transparency. [➡CONCISE AND CLEAR; 203] *Opposite:* ambiguity.

clash 1 *v* **fight**, conflict, disagree, quarrel, collide, come to blows, be at odds, spar, argue, row. [➡ARGUE AND FIGHT – TWO-WAY; 644] *Opposite:* agree. 2 *v* **clank**, clang, clatter, crash, bang. [➡EMIT SOUNDS THROUGH IMPACT AND ABRASION; 366] 3 *v* **conflict**, mismatch, jar, contravene. [➡DISHARMONY; 157] *Opposite:* match. 4 *n* **clatter**, clang, clank, crash, bang, smash, jar, rattle. [➡IMPACT SOUNDS; 1259] 5 *n* **battle**, conflict, disagreement, collision, quarrel, argument, row, brush, fight, skirmish. [➡ARGUMENT; 47] *Opposite:* agreement.

See Compare and Contrast at **fight**.

clashing *adj* **inharmonious**, conflicting, jarring, incompatible, nonmatching, mismatched. [➡DIFFERENCE; 150] *Opposite:* compatible.

clasp 1 *v* **grasp**, hold, clutch, embrace, hug, clinch, grip, fasten. [➡CONTACT: HOLD; 412] *Opposite:* release. 2 *n* **fastener**, hook, catch, hook and eye, popper, press stud, fastening, clip. [➡FASTENERS, LINKS, AND NETWORKS; 1246]

class 1 *n* **group**, set, tutorial group, tutor group, course group. [➡STUDENTS AND PUPILS; 841] 2 *n* **lesson**, period, session, lecture, seminar, course, tutorial, discussion. [➡LESSONS, COURSE WORK, AND EXAMINATIONS; 842] 3 *n* **refinement**, sophistication, elegance, style, flair, panache, taste, chic. [➡GOOD MANNERS AND SOCIAL SKILLS; 521] *Opposite:* tackiness (*informal*). 4 *n* **division**, category, rank, order, group, grade, caste, status, genre, classification. [➡VARIETY, TYPE, KIND; 146] 5 *v* **categorize**, classify, rank, assign, group, grade, brand, arrange, pigeonhole. [➡ARRANGE AND CREATE ORDER; 358]

See Compare and Contrast at **type**.

class-conscious *adj* **snobbish**, classist, elitist, toffee-nosed (*informal*), stuck-up (*informal*). [➡NEGATIVE INTELLECTUAL CHARACTERISTICS; 526] *Opposite:* egalitarian.

classic 1 *adj* **timeless**, immortal, unforgettable, memorable, abiding, lasting, ageless. [➡PERMANENCE: WITHOUT END; 94] 2 *adj* **definitive**, typical, characteristic, standard, model, usual, common, archetypal, traditional. [➡REPRESENTATIVE; 66] *Opposite:* atypical. 3 *adj* **simple**, stylish, elegant, chic, understated, restrained. [➡EASE AND SIMPLICITY; 201] 4 *n* **masterpiece**, landmark, benchmark, model, masterwork, prototype. [➡PERFECT EXAMPLES AND EMBODIMENTS; 67]

classical 1 *adj* **traditional**, conventional, orthodox, usual, typical, established, old. [➡REPRESENTATIVE; 66] *Opposite:* modern. 2 *type of* **pre-20th-century architecture**. [➡BUILDING AND ARCHITECTURE; 1075]

classicism *type of* **pre-20th-century art movement**. [➡ARTISTIC MOVEMENTS AND STYLES; 899]

classification 1 *n* **organization**, cataloguing, arrangement, sorting, ordering, grouping, taxonomy, categorization. [➡VARIETY, TYPE, KIND; 146] 2 *n* **category**, class, group, grouping, set, division. [➡COLLECTIONS AND MIXTURES OF THINGS; 1243]

classified *adj* **secret**, confidential, top secret, hush-hush (*informal*), off the record. [➡SECRET AND UNKNOWN; 180] *Opposite:* open.

classify *v* **categorize**, order, organize, pigeonhole, catalogue, grade, class, arrange, group, rank, brand. [➡ARRANGE AND CREATE ORDER; 358]

classiness (*informal*) *n* **refinement**, sophistication, elegance, stylishness, class, exclusiveness, exclusivity, urbanity, chic. [➡GOOD MANNERS AND SOCIAL SKILLS; 521] *Opposite:* tackiness (*informal*).

classless *adj* **egalitarian**, equal, open, free, unrestricted. [➡FREEDOM AND LIBERTY; 209] *Opposite:* class-conscious.

classmate *n* **fellow student**, fellow pupil, contemporary, peer. [➡STUDENTS AND PUPILS; 841]

classroom 1 *n* **schoolroom**, teaching space, seminar room, tutorial room, lecture theatre, lecture hall, laboratory, language laboratory. [➡EDUCATIONAL INSTITUTIONS; 813] 2 *type of* **room in public buildings.** [➡TYPES OF ROOM; 1096]

classy (*informal*) *adj* **refined**, sophisticated, elegant, stylish, chic, fashionable, tasteful, exclusive, upmarket. [➡LEVEL OF EDUCATION AND SOPHISTICATION; 894] *Opposite:* tacky (*informal*).

clatter 1 *v* **rattle**, bang, clang, smash, clank, jangle, clash. [➡EMIT SOUNDS THROUGH IMPACT AND ABRASION; 366] 2 *n* **clang**, rattle, bang, jangle, clank, clash, racket (*informal*). [➡IMPACT SOUNDS; 1259]

clause 1 *n* **section**, article, part, division, passage, item. [➡SUMMARIES, OUTLINES, AND EXCERPTS; 589] 2 *type of* **grammatical term.** [➡ASPECTS OF LANGUAGE; 683]

claustrophobia *type of* **phobia.** [➡FEARS AND PHOBIAS; 555]

claustrophobic *adj* **enclosed**, confining, oppressive, suffocating, stifling, restricting, restricted, shut in. [➡PHYSICALLY UNPLEASANT; 227]

clavichord *type of* **keyboard.** [➡MUSICAL INSTRUMENTS; 910]

claw 1 *v* **scrape**, scratch, scrabble, tear, graze, pierce. [➡CONTACT: TOUCH; 413] 2 *n* **talon**, nail, hook. [➡ARM AND HAND; 696]

claw back *v* **recover**, regain, recoup, retrieve. [➡REGAIN POSSESSION; 430] *Opposite:* lose.

clay 1 *n* **soil**, earth, dirt, mud. [➡EROSION PRODUCTS AND SOIL; 1058] 2 *type of* **mineral.** [➡MINERALS; 1276]

claymore *type of* **sword or knife.** [➡SWORDS AND KNIVES; 1156]

clean 1 *adj* **spotless**, dirt-free, unsoiled, fresh, sparkling, hygienic, sanitary, uncontaminated, unpolluted, sterile. [➡CLEAN; 1232] *Opposite:* dirty. 2 *adj* **pure**, wholesome, untainted, unadulterated, unpolluted. [➡MORALLY GOOD; 775] *Opposite:* impure. 3 *adj* **tidy**, neat, orderly, shipshape, immaculate, spick-and-span. [➡ORDER AND ORGANISATION; 207] *Opposite:* slovenly. 4 *v* **scrub**, scour, wipe, cleanse, dust, vacuum, launder, mop, polish. [➡CLEAN AND POLISH; 404] *Opposite:* soil.

clean as a new pin *adj* [➡CLEAN; 1232]

clean-cut *adj* **neat**, well-groomed, tidy, smart, well turned-out, presentable, sharp. [➡WELL GROOMED; 483] *Opposite:* untidy.

cleaned out (*informal*) *adj* **ruined**, penniless, out of cash, bankrupt, finished. [➡POVERTY AND POOR; 892]

cleaner 1 *n* **domestic**, home help, help, char, domestic worker (*US*). [➡DOMESTIC AND KITCHEN WORKERS; 850] 2 *n* **cleaning product**, detergent, stain remover, cleanser, soap, disinfectant, antiseptic, bleach, antibacterial cleaner, washing-up liquid, washing powder. [➡CLEANING AGENTS; 863]

cleaning *n* **housework**, spring-cleaning, scrubbing, dusting, washing, vacuuming. [➡CLEAN AND POLISH; 404]

cleanliness *n* **hygiene**, sanitation, purity, spotlessness. [➡CLEAN; 1232] *Opposite:* uncleanliness.

clean-living *adj* [➡ABSTEMIOUSNESS AND SELF-DENIAL; 882]

cleanly *adv* **easily**, efficiently, effectively, neatly, simply, quickly. [➡MOVING QUICKLY; 103]

cleanness *n* **purity**, freshness, simplicity, clearness, neatness, order. [➡CLEAN; 1232] *Opposite:* impurity.

clean out 1 *v* (*informal*) **bankrupt**, impoverish, bleed dry (*informal*), reduce, drain, make somebody broke, make somebody skint (*informal*). [➡TAKE SOMETHING AWAY; 426] 2 *v* **unclog**, flush, clear, clean, wash out, clean off, unblock. [➡EMPTY AND UNLOAD; 408] *Opposite:* block up.

cleanse *v* **rinse**, clean, rinse out, bathe, purify. [➡CLEAN AND POLISH; 404] *Opposite:* soil.

cleanser 1 *n* **cleaner**, cleaning product, detergent, stain remover, soap, disinfectant, antiseptic. [➡CLEANING AGENTS; 863] 2 *n* **make-up remover**, cleansing cream, lotion, cream, cold cream, face wash. [➡MAKEUP AND BEAUTY PRODUCTS; 491]

clean-shaven *adj* **shaved**, smooth, smooth-shaven, hairless. [➡FACIAL HAIR; 490] *Opposite:* bearded.

cleansing *n* **cleaning**, washing, scrubbing, bathing, rinsing, flushing, disinfection, sanitization, purification. [➡CLEAN AND POLISH; 404]

cleanup *n* **crackdown**, onslaught, attack, offensive, clampdown, elimination. [➡END; 54]

clean up 1 *v* **smarten**, spruce up, tart up (*informal*), tidy up, sanitize, clear up, mop up, blitz (*informal*). [➡CLEAN AND POLISH; 404] 2 *v* **wipe out**, eradicate, eliminate, get rid of, do away with. [➡GET RID OF SOMETHING; 452] 3 *v* (*slang*) **make a mint** (*informal*), make a fortune, hit the jackpot, be laughing all the way to the bank, make a pile (*informal*). [➡GET MONEY OR REWARD; 422]

clear 1 *adj* **transparent**, translucent, see-through, sheer, filmy, limpid, pellucid (*literary*). [➡VISUAL TEXTURE; 1220] *Opposite:* opaque. 2 *adj* **strong**, rich, pure, vibrant. [➡STRENGTH; 202] *Opposite:* indistinct. 3 *adj* **unblemished**, perfect, pure, flawless, faultless. [➡COMPLEXION; 481] 4 *adj* **well-defined**, sharp, distinct, clear-cut. [➡PERCEPTIBLE; 25] *Opposite:* indistinct. 5 *adj* **ringing**, pure, pleasant, resounding. [➡SOFT OR PLEASANT SOUNDS; 1264] *Opposite:* muffled. 6 *adj* **sure**, positive, obvious, evident, certain. [➡CERTAIN; 175] *Opposite:* unclear. 7 *adj* **obvious**, apparent, understandable, comprehensible, lucid, patent, plain, unambiguous, unmistakable, evident, apprehensible. [➡CONCISE AND CLEAR; 203] *Opposite:* unclear. **8** *adj* **unobstructed**, empty, free, open, unencumbered, unhampered. [➡EMPTY; 1237] *Opposite:* blocked. **9** *adj* **cloudless**, bright, sunny, fine, fair, sunshiny, unclouded. [➡HOT WEATHER; 1050] *Opposite:* cloudy. **10** *v* **tidy**, clear out, empty, straighten, clean up, tidy up. [➡ARRANGE AND CREATE ORDER; 358] **11** *v* **free**, vindicate, exonerate, absolve, acquit, release, discharge, exculpate (*formal*). [➡FREEDOM AND LIBERTY; 209] **12** *v* **evaporate**, dissipate, disperse, disappear, dispel. [➡DISAPPEAR; 4] *Opposite:* form. **13** *v* **unblock**, free, unclutter, unclog, empty. [➡EMPTY AND UNLOAD; 408] *Opposite:* block. **14** *v* (*informal*) **net**, earn, gain, take home, make, bring in. [➡GET MONEY OR REWARD; 422] *Opposite:* lose.

clearance *n* **permission**, authorization, go-ahead (*informal*), consent, approval, okay (*informal*), green light, allowance, sanction. [➡PERMIT AND ALLOW; 670] *Opposite:* prohibition.

clear-cut *adj* **precise**, unambiguous, definite, clear, straightforward, specific, easy. [➡CONCISE AND CLEAR; 203] *Opposite:* ambiguous.

clear-headed *adj* **lucid**, alert, coherent, perceptive, decisive, logical, realistic, sensible. [➡POSITIVE INTELLECTUAL CHARACTERISTICS; 525] *Opposite:* muddled.

clearing *n* **glade**, clearance, dell (*literary*). [➡THE COUNTRYSIDE AND OUTDOOR SPACES; 1070]

clearly *adv* **obviously**, evidently, undoubtedly, plainly, visibly, unmistakably, noticeably, openly, lucidly, distinctly, patently, unambiguously, without a doubt. [➡CERTAIN; 175] *Opposite:* ambiguously.

clearness **1** *n* **translucency**, transparency, flawlessness, luminousness. [➡VISUAL TEXTURE; 1220] *Opposite:* opacity. **2** *n* **directness**, unambiguousness, clarity, lucidity, comprehensibility, plainness. [➡CONCISE AND CLEAR; 203] *Opposite:* vagueness. **3** *n* **emptiness**, cleanness, unclutteredness, uncrowdedness, freshness. [➡EMPTY; 1237] *Opposite:* clutter.

clear off (*informal*) *v* **go away**, push off (*informal*), shove off (*informal*), beat it (*informal*), leave, depart, get going, head off, be off. [➡RUN AWAY AND AVOID; 10] *Opposite:* stay.

clear-out *n* **clean-out**, throw-out, tidy, spring clean, tidy-up. [➡ARRANGE AND CREATE ORDER; 358]

clear out **1** *v* **leave**, depart, get going, head off, be off, push off (*informal*). [➡ABSENT ONESELF; 8] **2** *v* **empty**, clear, clean out (*informal*), clean up, turn out, throw out, chuck out (*informal*). [➡EMPTY AND UNLOAD; 408]

clear-sighted *adj* **perceptive**, insightful, percipient, realistic, sensible, practical, wise, clear-eyed, discerning. [➡POSITIVE INTELLECTUAL CHARACTERISTICS; 525] *Opposite:* confused.

clear-thinking *adj* [➡POSITIVE INTELLECTUAL CHARACTERISTICS; 525]

clear up **1** *v* **tidy up**, straighten, clear, clean up, tidy, put away, arrange. [➡ARRANGE AND CREATE ORDER; 358] **2** *v* **resolve**, solve, clarify, explain, settle, sort out, get to the bottom of, illuminate, decipher. [➡EXPLAIN AND CLARIFY; 611] *Opposite:* complicate.

clearway *type of* **major road.** [➡ROADS; 1105]

clearwing *type of* **moth.** [➡MOTHS AND BUTTERFLIES; 1015]

cleave **1** *v* **slice**, cut, slash, smite (*archaic or literary*), hew, chop, sever, split, sunder (*literary*). [➡TEAR, BREAK, AND CUT; 361] *Opposite:* join. **2** *v* (*literary*) **stick**, hold on, stick to like glue, cling, conjoin (*formal*), link, embrace. [➡CONTACT: HOLD; 412] *Opposite:* separate.

cleaver *type of* **knife.** [➡CUTTING TOOLS; 1119]

cleft *n* **fissure**, crevice, crack, gap, split, break, chimney. [➡HOLES, GAPS, AND FORKS; 1251]

clematis *type of* **climber.** [➡CLIMBERS; 1033]

clemency *n* **mercy**, leniency, forgiveness, pity, compassion, kindness, moderation. [➡MORALLY GOOD; 775] *Opposite:* heartlessness.

clement *adj* **mild**, moderate, temperate, balmy, pleasant, warm, gentle. [➡HOT WEATHER; 1050] *Opposite:* inclement.

clementine *type of* **citrus.** [➡FRUIT AND VEGETABLES; 1175]

clench *v* **compress**, grit, tighten, clasp, scrunch, clamp. [➡CONTACT: EXERT PRESSURE; 415] *Opposite:* relax.

clergy *n* **priesthood**, ministry, ordained priests, clerics. [➡RELIGIOUS PEOPLE; 779] *Opposite:* laity.

clergyman *n* [➡RELIGIOUS PEOPLE; 779]

clergywoman *n* [➡RELIGIOUS PEOPLE; 779]

cleric *n* **priest**, minister, ecclesiastic. [➡RELIGIOUS PEOPLE; 779]

clerical **1** *adj* **secretarial**, office, bookkeeping, accounting. [➡TYPES OF WORK; 835] **2** *adj* **religious**, ecclesiastical, church, priestly (*formal or literary*). [➡RELIGIOUS CONCEPTS; 777]

clerical worker *n* [➡OFFICE WORKERS; 847]

clerk **1** *n* **office worker**, counter clerk, bank clerk, accounts clerk, worker, assistant. [➡OFFICE WORKERS; 847] **2** *n* **administrator**, official, recorder, clerk to the council, clerk to the governors. [➡OFFICE WORKERS; 847]

clever **1** *adj* **bright**, intelligent, smart, knowledgeable, intellectual, quick, brainy (*informal*), on the ball (*informal*), alert. [➡POSITIVE INTELLECTUAL CHARACTERISTICS; 525] *Opposite:* foolish. **2** *adj* **ingenious**, shrewd, astute, adroit, crafty, wily, cunning, knowing. [➡POSITIVE INTELLECTUAL CHARACTERISTICS; 525] *Opposite:* inept. **3** *adj* **glib**, smart, slick, pert, flippant, superficial, pat. [➡UNINTERESTED AND DETACHED; 630] **4** *adj* **skilful**, talented, quick, adroit, gifted, dexterous, adept, able. [➡TALENTED AND SKILFUL; 528] *Opposite:* clumsy. **5** *adj* **useful**, handy, convenient, effective, ingenious, nifty (*informal*), neat. [➡USEFULNESS; 200] *Opposite:* useless.

See Compare and Contrast at **intelligent.**

clever clogs (*informal*) *n* [➡TALENTED OR INTELLIGENT PERSON; 529]

clever Dick (*informal*) *n* [➡TALENTED OR INTELLIGENT PERSON; 529]

cleverly *adv* **ingeniously**, shrewdly, smartly, skilfully, expertly. [➡POSITIVE INTELLECTUAL CHARACTERISTICS; 525] *Opposite:* ineptly.

cleverness *n* **skill**, ingenuity, quickness, shrewdness, talent, expertise, adeptness, dexterity, smartness, intelligence. [➡ POSITIVE INTELLECTUAL CHARACTERISTICS; 525] *Opposite:* ineptness.

cliché *n* **chestnut** (*informal*), truism, formula, line, platitude, prosaism, saying, saw. [➡ FIGURES OF SPEECH; 674]

clichéd *adj* **corny**, hackneyed, passé, old, naff (*informal*), stereotypical, unoriginal, timeworn, dull, overused, lifeless, trite, unimaginative. [➡ BORING AND UNINTERESTING; 235] *Opposite:* original.

cliché-ridden *adj* [➡ BORING AND UNINTERESTING; 235]

click 1 *n* **clack**, tick, snap, clunk. [➡ IMPACT SOUNDS; 1259] 2 *v* **snap**, tick, clack, clunk. [➡ EMIT SOUNDS THROUGH IMPACT AND ABRASION; 366] 3 *v* (*informal*) **make sense**, sink in, become clear, fall into place. [➡ UNDERSTAND AND GRASP; 760] 4 *v* (*informal*) **get on**, hit it off (*informal*), be on the same wavelength, connect, relate to. [➡ ESTABLISHING RELATIONSHIPS WITH OTHERS; 974] *Opposite:* clash.

click rate *n* [➡ THE INTERNET; 1127]

clicks-and-mortar *adj* [➡ E-COMMERCE; 1128]

client *n* **customer**, shopper, consumer, user, buyer, purchaser, patron, punter (*informal*), regular. [➡ BUSINESS ACTIVITIES AND PHENOMENA; 795]

clientele *n* **customers**, clients, regulars, patrons, punters (*informal*), custom, consumers, trade, business, following. [➡ BUSINESS ACTIVITIES AND PHENOMENA; 795]

cliff *n* **precipice**, rock face, face, crag, overhang, bluff. [➡ MOUNTAINS AND HILLS; 1044]

cliffhanger *n* [➡ DECISIVE MOMENTS; 44]

climate 1 *n* **weather**, temperature, environment, microclimate, macroclimate, climatic zone. [➡ WEATHER AND CLIMATE; 1049] 2 *n* **atmosphere**, situation, ambience, surroundings, environment, conditions, feeling, mood, sense. [➡ SITUATIONS; 71]

climatic *adj* [➡ WEATHER AND CLIMATE; 1049]

climatology *n* [➡ WEATHER AND CLIMATE; 1049]

climax *n* **peak**, high point, pinnacle, culmination, height, highlight, apex, acme, summit, apogee. [➡ DECISIVE MOMENTS; 44]

climb 1 *v* **scale**, go up, move up, mount, ascend, clamber, scramble, scrabble. [➡ GO UPWARDS; 307] *Opposite:* descend. 2 *v* **rise**, soar, go up, rocket, escalate, shoot up, increase. [➡ CHANGE OF SIZE: BIGGER; 393] *Opposite:* descend. 3 *n* **ascent**, scramble. [➡ GO UPWARDS; 307] *Opposite:* descent. 4 *n* **increase**, rise, soar, hike. [➡ CHANGE OF INTENSITY: MORE; 395]

climb down 1 *v* **descend**, go down, get down, come down, dismount. [➡ GO DOWNWARDS; 308] *Opposite:* ascend. 2 *v* **back down**, retreat, make concessions, give way, eat your words (*informal*), eat humble pie, eat crow (*US informal*). [➡ APOLOGIZE AND RETRACT; 684] *Opposite:* stand your ground.

climb-down *n* **change of mind**, concession, U-turn, shift, retreat, change of heart. [➡ DECISIVE MOMENTS; 44]

climber 1 *n* **mountaineer**, rock climber, hiker, walker, rambler, backpacker. [➡ PEOPLE IN SPORTS AND LEISURE; 876] 2 *n* **trailer**, creeper, vine. [➡ CLIMBERS; 1033]

climber

◆ *types of climber*
bougainvillea, bryony, clematis, convolvulus, grapevine, honeysuckle, ivy, jasmine, kudzu, liana, morning glory, passionflower, poison ivy, rattan, sarsaparilla, Virginia creeper, wisteria, woodbine

climbing *n* **mountaineering**, hiking, hillwalking, alpinism, rock climbing, artificial climbing, free climbing, bouldering, mountain climbing. [➡ HOBBIES, GAMES, AND SPORTS; 875]

clime (*literary*) *n* **climate**, weather, zone, region, place, country. [➡ WEATHER AND CLIMATE; 1049]

clinch 1 *v* **settle**, seal, wrap up (*informal*), close, tie up, decide, finalize, determine, resolve. [➡ APPROVE AND CONFIRM; 647] 2 *v* **embrace**, hug, hold, bear hug, cuddle, squeeze. [➡ CONTACT: HOLD; 412]

cling 1 *v* **clutch**, grasp, hug, hang on, hold, embrace. [➡ CONTACT: HOLD; 412] *Opposite:* let go. 2 *v* **adhere**, grip, stick, hug, fit tightly, hang, cohere (*formal*), cleave (*literary*). [➡ EXIST IN A PLACE; 19] 3 *v* **retain**, maintain, hold to, keep to. [➡ STORE AND KEEP; 454] *Opposite:* give up. 4 *v* **latch onto**, be dependent on, depend on, hang on, attach. [➡ DESIRE AND WANT; 580]

clingy 1 *adj* (*informal*) **clinging**, figure-hugging, tight-fitting, snug, close-fitting. [➡ DESCRIBING CLOTHES; 869] *Opposite:* baggy. 2 *adj* **dependent**, insecure, anxious, clinging. [➡ UNCERTAINTY; 560] *Opposite:* independent.

clinic 1 *n* **hospital**, health centre, surgery, consulting room, private clinic, treatment centre, doctor's office (*US*). [➡ HOSPITALS AND CLINICS; 826] 2 *n* **workshop**, seminar, class, meeting, practicum (*US*). [➡ MEETINGS AND ASSEMBLIES; 43]

clinical 1 *adj* **scientific**, medical, experimental, quantifiable, proven. [➡ THE NATURE OF IDEAS; 772] 2 *adj* **detached**, disinterested, dispassionate, scientific, cold, distant, uninvolved, objective, unemotional. [➡ NEUTRALITY AND INDIFFERENCE; 554] *Opposite:* personal.

clinician *n* [➡ PEOPLE WHO WORK IN MEDICINE; 848]

clink 1 *v* **clank**, jingle, tinkle, chink, jangle. [➡ EMIT SOUNDS THROUGH IMPACT AND ABRASION; 366] 2 *n* **chink**, clank, jingle, jangle, tinkle. [➡ RINGING AND TOOTING SOUNDS; 1258] 3 *n* (*dated slang*) [➡ BUILDINGS FOR CONFINING PEOPLE; 1093]

clinker *n* [➡ PRODUCTS OF FIRE; 1165]

clip 1 *v* **cut**, trim, shorten, shear, cut off, prune, crop, pare, shave. [➡ TEAR, BREAK, AND CUT; 361] 2 *n* **excerpt**, passage, extract, quotation, quote, piece, sound bite. [➡ SUMMARIES, OUTLINES, AND EXCERPTS; 589] 3 *n* **fastener**, pin, staple, paperclip, clasp, slide. [➡ FASTENERS, LINKS, AND NETWORKS; 1246] 4 *v* **fasten**, attach, pin, staple, secure, fix. [➡ FASTEN, LINK, AND JOIN; 409] *Opposite:* undo.

clip-clop *type of* **impact sound**. [➡ IMPACT SOUNDS; 1259]

clip-on *adj* **attachable**, fasten-on, hook-on, separable, removable, separate. [➡ FASTEN, LINK, AND JOIN; 409]

clipped 1 *adj* **trimmed**, neat, cut back, tidy, cut, pared, sheared, cropped, shaved. [➡DESCRIBING HAIR; 487] 2 *adj* **distinct**, short, brusque, concise, curt, abrupt, terse. [➡SUCCINCT AND TO-THE-POINT; 641]

clipper *type of* **historical vessel**. [➡SHIPS AND BOATS; 1149]

clippers *type of* **cutting tool**. [➡CUTTING TOOLS; 1119]

clipping *n* **cutting**, extract, excerpt, article, feature, piece. [➡SUMMARIES, OUTLINES, AND EXCERPTS; 589]

clippings *n* **trimmings**, parings, ends, offcuts, pieces. [➡REMAINDER AND REMAINDERS; 123]

clique *n* **group**, in-group, faction, set, gang, elite, coterie, circle, clan (*informal*), fraternity. [➡FRIENDS AND ACQUAINTANCES; 936]

cliquey *adj* **cliquish**, exclusive, clannish, unfriendly, unsociable, aloof, insular, selective, superior, limited, restricted, privileged, elite, exclusionary. [➡UNFRIENDLINESS AND UNSOCIABILITY; 505] *Opposite:* open.

cloak 1 *n* (*literary*) **screen**, cover, shroud, veil, façade, pretence. [➡COVERS AND COATINGS; 1245] 2 *v* **cover**, hide, conceal, shroud, veil, envelop, wrap, swathe, mask, camouflage. [➡CAUSE TO DISAPPEAR; 6] *Opposite:* reveal. 3 *type of* **overcoat**. [➡GARMENTS AND OUTFITS; 865]

cloak-and-dagger *adj* **secret**, hush-hush (*informal*), clandestine, undercover, covert, mysterious. [➡SECRET AND UNKNOWN; 180] *Opposite:* aboveboard.

cloaked *adj* [➡IMPERCEPTIBLE; 26]

cloakroom *n* **lavatory**, toilet, loo, WC, powder room, rest room, restroom (*US*). [➡TYPES OF ROOM; 1096]

clobber (*informal*) 1 *v* **hit**, bash (*informal*), thump, beat, strike, drub, punch, clock (*slang*), belt (*informal*). [➡PHYSICAL ATTACK AND PUNISHMENT; 416] 2 *n* **stuff**, gear (*informal*), tackle, things, belongings, possessions. [➡POSSESSIONS; 462] 3 *n* **clothes**, gear (*informal*), outfit, clothing, threads (*US slang*). [➡CLOTHES AND ACCESSORIES; 864]

cloche 1 *n* **cover**, cold frame, protection. [➡COVERS AND COATINGS; 1245] 2 *type of* **hat**. [➡HABERDASHERY, MILLINERY, AND LINGERIE; 867]

clock 1 *n* **timepiece**, timer, chronometer. [➡CLOCKS AND TIMERS; 1125] 2 *n* **regulator**, timer, device, control, meter, dial. [➡PARTS OF MACHINES AND TOOLS; 1117] 3 *v* (*slang*) **hit**, wallop (*informal*), bash (*informal*), biff (*informal*), belt (*informal*), clobber (*informal*). [➡PHYSICAL ATTACK AND PUNISHMENT; 416] 4 *type of* **measuring device**. [➡MEASURING DEVICES; 1122]

clock

◆ *types of clock*
alarm, alarm clock, clock radio, cuckoo clock, grandfather clock, hourglass, longcase clock, pocket watch, stopwatch, sundial, watch, wristwatch

clock radio *type of* **clock**. [➡CLOCKS AND TIMERS; 1125]

clock up *v* **achieve**, reach, score, attain, accomplish, record, rack up (*informal*), total, chalk up. [➡GET; 421]

clockwise *adj* [➡DIRECTION OF MOTION; 346]

clockwork 1 *n* **mechanism**, device, machinery. [➡PARTS OF MACHINES AND TOOLS; 1117] 2 *n* **regularity**, preciseness, accuracy, flawlessness, smoothness, efficiency. [➡EXACT; 204]

clod *n* **lump**, clump, chunk, wad, hunk, glob (*informal*). [➡AMOUNT OF SOLID OR SEMI-SOLID; 115]

clog 1 *v* **block**, clog up, stop up, choke, obstruct, congest, jam, fill up, clutter up. [➡FILL; 407] *Opposite:* unblock. 2 *type of* **shoe**. [➡FOOTWEAR; 871]

clogged *adj* [➡FULL; 1238]

clogged up *adj* [➡FULL; 1238]

clog up *v* **block**, jam, obstruct, congest, stop up, choke, fill up, clutter up, clog. [➡FILL; 407] *Opposite:* unblock.

cloister 1 *n* **quadrangle**, colonnade, arcade, portico, walkway, gallery. [➡PARTS OF RELIGIOUS BUILDINGS; 1085] 2 *n* **monastery**, abbey, friary, convent, nunnery. [➡RELIGIOUS BUILDINGS; 1084] 3 *v* **seclude**, shelter, retreat, withdraw, closet, withdraw from the world, confine, sequester (*formal*), shut away. [➡CAUSE TO DISAPPEAR; 6]

cloistered *adj* **secluded**, sheltered, confined, protected, sequestered (*formal*), insulated, isolated. [➡SOLITARINESS; 941] *Opposite:* accessible.

clomp *v* **clump**, stomp, stamp, thump, bang, galumph (*informal*), clunk, plod. [➡PROCEED AND GO; 306] *Opposite:* tiptoe.

clone 1 *n* **replica**, duplicate, genetic copy, twin, double, copy, carbon copy, emulation. [➡COPIES AND REPLICAS; 152] 2 *v* **duplicate**, copy, make a replica, replicate, emulate, reproduce, re-create. [➡COPY AND DUPLICATE; 403]

See Compare and Contrast at **copy**.

clonk *v* **knock**, bump, crash into, thump, bang, clunk, clink, thud. [➡EMIT SOUNDS THROUGH IMPACT AND ABRASION; 366]

clop *type of* **impact sound**. [➡IMPACT SOUNDS; 1259]

close 1 *adj* **near**, nearby, close by, adjacent, handy, local, on your doorstep, within walking distance, close at hand, neighbouring. [➡CLOSENESS; 160] *Opposite:* distant. 2 *adj* **intimate**, familiar, chummy (*informal*), dear, devoted, loving, attached, friendly, warm. [➡FRIENDLINESS AND SOCIABILITY; 495] *Opposite:* distant. 3 *adj* **careful**, rigorous, particular, keen, meticulous, minute, tight, firm, secure. [➡EXACT; 204] *Opposite:* lax. 4 *adj* **compact**, tight, concentrated, dense, packed, solid, cramped, confined, compressed. [➡DENSITY AND CONSISTENCY; 1206] *Opposite:* loose. 5 *adj* **similar**, faithful, precise, exact, literal, strict, accurate, near, strong, pronounced, marked, definite, firm. [➡SIMILARITY; 149] 6 *adj* **silent**, mum (*informal*), secretive, taciturn, uncommunicative, quiet. [➡RETICENT AND UNFORTHCOMING; 632] *Opposite:* open. 7 *adj* **oppressive**, muggy, airless, sultry, heavy, sticky, sweltering, uncomfortable, humid. [➡HOT WEATHER; 1050] *Opposite:* fresh. 8 *adj* **stingy** (*informal*), miserly, tight, tightfisted, penny-pinching (*informal*), grudging, close-fisted (*informal*), mean, ungenerous, parsimonious (*formal*), niggardly. [➡FINANCIALLY MEAN AND GRASPING; 520] *Opposite:* generous. 9 *v* **shut**, lock, seal, close up, slam, put up the shutters, secure, bolt. [➡FASTEN, LINK, AND JOIN; 409] *Opposite:* open. 10 *v* **come together**, meet, join, unite, gather, fuse, link, connect, couple. [➡GET CLOSER TOGETHER; 311] 11 *v* **shut down**, close down, shut up shop, go out of business, stop trading, go into liquidation, go bust, discontinue, fold, collapse. [➡STOP ACTING; 265] *Opposite:* open. **12** *v* **block**, bar, plug, obstruct, seal off, blockade. [➡FASTEN, LINK, AND JOIN; 409] *Opposite:* unblock. **13** *v* **conclude**, end, finish, complete, be over, bring to a close, draw to a close, wrap up (*informal*), culminate, terminate (*formal*), wind up, discontinue. [➡COMPLETE AN ACTION; 264] *Opposite:* start. **14** *n* **end**, conclusion, finale, completion, finish, ending, cessation, denouement (*formal*), wind-up. [➡END; 54] *Opposite:* start.

close at hand *adj* **nearby**, near, round the corner, on hand, around, close by, within spitting distance (*informal*), just a stone's throw away, adjacent, handy, local. [➡CLOSENESS; 160]

close by *adj* **nearby**, near, round the corner, on hand, close at hand, around, within spitting distance (*informal*), just a stone's throw away, adjacent, handy, local. [➡CLOSENESS; 160]

close call *n* **close thing**, close shave, near thing (*informal*), near miss, narrow escape, lucky escape, narrow squeak. [➡SUCCESS; 82]

close-cropped *adj* **short**, close-cut, trimmed, close-trimmed. [➡DESCRIBING HAIR; 487]

closed **1** *adj* **shut**, locked, bolted, padlocked, fastened, barred, sealed, secure. [➡FASTEN, LINK, AND JOIN; 409] *Opposite:* open. **2** *adj* **impassable**, inaccessible, blocked, obstructed, impenetrable, unnavigable. [➡FASTEN, LINK, AND JOIN; 409] *Opposite:* open. **3** *adj* **settled**, concluded, terminated, decided, ended, over. [➡FINITENESS, VARIABILITY, AND TRANSIENCE; 96] *Opposite:* unfinished. **4** *adj* **narrow-minded**, closed-minded, prejudiced, bigoted, intolerant. [➡NEGATIVE INTELLECTUAL CHARACTERISTICS; 526] *Opposite:* open. **5** *adj* **exclusive**, restricted, private, limited, cliquish, cliquey, clannish, elite. [➡UNFRIENDLINESS AND UNSOCIABILITY; 505] *Opposite:* open.

closed book *n* **mystery**, puzzle, enigma, conundrum, riddle. [➡SECRETS AND MYSTERIES; 181]

closed-minded (*US*) *adj* **narrow-minded**, intolerant, prejudiced, bigoted, closed. [➡NEGATIVE INTELLECTUAL CHARACTERISTICS; 526] *Opposite:* open-minded.

closed-mindedness *n* [➡NEGATIVE INTELLECTUAL CHARACTERISTICS; 526]

close down **1** *v* **end**, shut down, pull the plug on, close, wrap up (*informal*), conclude, finish, wind down, bring to an end, complete, terminate (*formal*). [➡CAUSE TO STOP; 267] *Opposite:* start. **2** *v* **shut**, go out of business, cease trading, come to an end, wind down, shut up. [➡STOP ACTING; 265] *Opposite:* open.

closedown *n* **closure**, closing down, shutting, shutting down, closing, winding up. [➡END; 54]

close-fisted (*informal*) *adj* **mean**, miserly, tight, stingy (*informal*), niggardly, penny-pinching (*informal*), parsimonious, mingy (*informal*), grudging, ungenerous, tightfisted. [➡FINANCIALLY MEAN AND GRASPING; 520] *Opposite:* generous.

close-fitting *adj* **body-hugging**, clingy (*informal*), tight-fitting, figure-hugging, clinging, well-fitting, tight, fitted, skintight, snug, constricting. [➡DESCRIBING CLOTHES; 869] *Opposite:* baggy.

close friend *n* [➡FRIENDS; 963]

close in *v* **draw near**, bear down on, move in, approach, creep up, converge. [➡ARRIVE; 12] *Opposite:* move away.

close-knit *adj* **close**, supportive, strong, caring, cohesive, interdependent. [➡RELATIONSHIP TO ANOTHER; 973] *Opposite:* loose.

close-lipped *adj* **reticent**, closemouthed, tight-lipped, silent, reserved, buttoned up (*informal*). [➡RETICENT AND UNFORTHCOMING; 632] *Opposite:* forthcoming.

closely **1** *adv* **carefully**, thoroughly, faithfully, meticulously, to the letter, strictly, watchfully, narrowly, diligently, attentively, intently. [➡EXACT; 204] *Opposite:* casually. **2** *adv* **densely**, compactly, tightly, thickly. [➡CLOSENESS; 160] *Opposite:* loosely. **3** *adv* **intimately**, personally, directly, strongly, very much. [➡CLOSENESS; 160] *Opposite:* distantly.

closemouthed *adj* **reticent**, tight-lipped, close-lipped, silent, reserved, buttoned up (*informal*). [➡RETICENT AND UNFORTHCOMING; 632] *Opposite:* forthcoming.

closeness **1** *n* **nearness**, proximity, contact, convenience, imminence. [➡CLOSENESS; 160] *Opposite:* distance. **2** *n* **intimacy**, familiarity, friendship, nearness, understanding, confidence, chumminess (*informal*), lovingness, attachment. [➡RELATIONSHIP TO ANOTHER; 973] *Opposite:* distance. **3** *n* **airlessness**, stuffiness, mugginess, sultriness, oppressiveness, heaviness. [➡HOT WEATHER; 1050] *Opposite:* freshness.

close on *adv* **nearly**, close to, almost, near enough, not far off. [➡TO A CERTAIN EXTENT; 134]

close relative *n* [➡THE FAMILY; 956]

close-run *adj* **near**, close, closely contested, neck and neck, hard-fought. [➡CLOSENESS; 160]

close shave *n* **near thing** (*informal*), close call, near miss, narrow squeak, narrow escape, lucky escape. [➡DIFFICULT SITUATIONS; 72]

closet **1** *v* **cloister**, sequester (*formal*), seclude, confine, shut up, lock up. [➡CAUSE TO DISAPPEAR; 6] **2** *adj* **secret**, private, clandestine, undeclared, unprofessed, unrevealed. [➡SECRET AND UNKNOWN; 180] *Opposite:* open. **3** *type of* **cabinet.** [➡FURNITURE; 858] **4** (*US*) *type of* **room in the home.** [➡TYPES OF ROOM; 1096]

close thing *n* **narrow escape**, close shave, close call, near thing (*informal*), near miss, narrow squeak, lucky escape. [➡RESULTS AND OUTCOMES; 83]

close to **1** *prep* **on the brink of**, on the point of, near to, about to, considering, getting ready to. [➡FUTURE; 86] **2** *prep* **like**, similar to, resembling, akin to, bordering on, not unlike. [➡SIMILARITY; 149] **3** *adv* **nearly**, close on, almost, near enough, not far off. [➡TO A CERTAIN EXTENT; 134]

close to tears *adj* [➡SADNESS, DISTRESS, AND DESPAIR; 540]

close-up *n* **detail**, zoom, camera shot, shot, photo, photograph, picture. [➡ARTWORKS; 898]

close up **1** *v* **shut**, close, lock, lock up, secure, bolt, seal. [➡FASTEN, LINK, AND JOIN; 409] *Opposite:* open. **2** *v* **huddle together**, squeeze up, squash up, bunch up, move up, move together. [➡GET CLOSER TOGETHER; 311]

close your eyes to *v* **ignore**, overlook, disregard, turn a blind eye to, pay no attention to, take no heed of, pay no heed to, let pass, take no notice of, condone. [➡NOT PAY ATTENTION; 765] *Opposite:* notice.

closing *adj* **final**, concluding, last, finishing, ultimate, dying, terminating, winding up, departing. [➡AFTER, LAST, AND FOLLOWING; 166] *Opposite:* opening.

closing stages *n* **last part**, final stages, conclusion, end, finale, closure. [➡END; 54]

closure 1 *n* **end**, conclusion, finish, closing, shutting, shutting down, termination, ending, cessation. [➡END; 54] *Opposite:* opening. 2 *n* **finality**, resolution, conclusiveness, definiteness, stoppage, stop, cloture (*US*). [➡END; 54]

clot 1 *n* **mass**, lump, accumulation, globule, blob, gob (*slang*), glob (*informal*). [➡AMOUNT OF SOLID OR SEMI-SOLID; 115] 2 *v* **coagulate**, coalesce, thicken, congeal, set, form clots, solidify. [➡HARDEN, CONGEAL, DRY; 388]

cloth 1 *n* **material**, fabric, textile, stuff, yard goods, dry goods (*US*). [➡TEXTILES AND THREADS; 1130] 2 *n* **rag**, duster, tablecloth, handkerchief, napkin. [➡SOFT FURNISHINGS, LINEN, AND DRAPERY; 860]

cloth cap *type of* **headgear**. [➡HABERDASHERY, MILLINERY, AND LINGERIE; 867]

clothe *v* **dress**, fit out, attire (*formal*), cover, array (*literary*), garb, cloak, don (*formal*). [➡DRESS, WEAR, AND UNDRESS; 868] *Opposite:* undress.

clothes *n* **clothing**, garments, attire (*formal*), dress, outfit, apparel, fashion, wardrobe, wear. [➡CLOTHES AND ACCESSORIES; 864]

clothes moth *type of* **moth**. [➡MOTHS AND BUTTERFLIES; 1015]

clothing *n* **clothes**, garments, apparel, dress, wardrobe, fashion, wear, outfit, attire (*formal*). [➡CLOTHES AND ACCESSORIES; 864]

cloud 1 *n* **mist**, fog, haze, bank of cloud. [➡CLOUDY AND RAINY WEATHER; 1052] 2 *v* **veil**, blur, obscure, shadow, make unclear, overshadow, confuse, darken, dim. [➡CAUSE TO DISAPPEAR; 6] *Opposite:* clarify.

> **cloud**
>
> ◆ *types of cloud*
> altocumulus, altostratus, cirrocumulus, cirrus, cumulonimbus, cumulus, funnel cloud, mare's-tail, nimbus, rain cloud, storm cloud, stratocumulus, stratus, thundercloud, thunderhead (*US*)

cloudburst *n* **rainstorm**, downpour, deluge, flood, shower. [➡CLOUDY AND RAINY WEATHER; 1052]

cloud-cuckoo-land *n* **dream world**, fantasy world, land of make-believe, dreamland, pipe dream, fantasy. [➡NON-EXISTENT PLACE; 1065]

clouded 1 *adj* **troubled**, anxious, concerned, worried, apprehensive, disquieted (*archaic or literary*). [➡CONFUSION, ANXIETY, AND WORRY; 541] *Opposite:* untroubled. 2 *adj* **opaque**, cloudy, murky, misty, hazy, muddy. [➡DESCRIBING LIGHT; 1227] *Opposite:* clear.

cloudiness 1 *n* **muddiness**, murkiness, muckiness (*informal*), dirtiness, mistiness, opacity. [➡VISUAL TEXTURE; 1220] *Opposite:* transparency. 2 *n* **vagueness**, confusion, ambiguousness, uncertainness, imprecision, obfuscation. [➡VAGUENESS; 244] *Opposite:* clarity. 3 *n* **darkness**, gloominess, dullness, greyness. [➡CLOUDY AND RAINY WEATHER; 1052] *Opposite:* brightness.

cloudless *adj* **clear**, blue, sunny, bright, brilliant, sunshiny. [➡HOT WEATHER; 1050] *Opposite:* cloudy.

cloud nine *n* [➡PLEASANT SITUATIONS; 74]

cloud over *v* [➡CLOUDY AND RAINY WEATHER; 1052]

cloudy 1 *adj* **overcast**, grey, gloomy, dull, hazy, leaden. [➡CLOUDY AND RAINY WEATHER; 1052] *Opposite:* bright. 2 *adj* **murky**, muddy, opaque, milky, churned up, unstrained. [➡VISUAL TEXTURE; 1220] *Opposite:* transparent. 3 *adj* **uncertain**, unclear, vague, confused, imprecise, indistinct, ambiguous, hazy. [➡VAGUENESS; 244] *Opposite:* clear.

clout 1 *n* (*informal*) **influence**, power, pull (*informal*), authority, weight, sway, effectiveness. [➡SKILLS, TALENTS, AND ABILITIES; 527] 2 *n* **thump**, wallop (*informal*), whack, smack, blow, cuff. [➡PHYSICAL ATTACK AND PUNISHMENT; 416] 3 *v* **hit**, strike, thump, bash (*informal*), wallop (*informal*), smack, slap, whack. [➡PHYSICAL ATTACK AND PUNISHMENT; 416]

clove 1 *n* **piece**, segment, section, portion, fragment, wedge. [➡AMOUNT OF SOLID OR SEMI-SOLID; 115] 2 *type of* **spice**. [➡HERBS AND SPICES; 1174]

clover *n* [➡PLEASANT SITUATIONS; 74]

cloverleaf *n* **junction**, intersection, crossroads, crossing, highway interchange (*US*), traffic circle (*US*), rotary (*US*). [➡BRIDGES, TUNNELS, CROSSINGS, AND JUNCTIONS; 1111]

clown 1 *n* (*informal*) [➡JOKERS AND TEASES; 676] 2 *v* **mess about** (*informal*), clown around, fool around, horse around, play the fool, lark about, be silly, play for laughs, joke, jest (*literary*). [➡JOKES AND TEASING; 675] 3 *type of* **entertainer**. [➡WORKERS IN ENTERTAINMENT AND MEDIA; 873]

clown around *v* [➡JOKES AND TEASING; 675]

clowning *n* **joking**, buffoonery, tomfoolery (*informal*), horseplay, playing around, fooling around, comedy, jesting (*literary*). [➡JOKES AND TEASING; 675] *Opposite:* seriousness.

cloy *v* **nauseate**, sicken, be too much, satiate, pall, glut, sate. [➡GIVE TOO MUCH; 438]

cloying 1 *adj* **syrupy**, sticky, sickly, sugary, saccharine. [➡TASTE; 704] 2 *adj* **sentimental**, nauseating, sickly-sweet, sickening, heavy, mawkish. [➡EMOTIONALLY UNPLEASANT AND UPSETTING; 228]

club 1 *n* **association**, society, guild, organization, union, alliance, fellowship, group, league. [➡CLUBS AND SOCIETIES; 939] 2 *n* **weapon**, blunt instrument, stick. [➡BLUNT INSTRUMENTS AND WHIPS; 1157] 3 *n* **nightclub**, disco, discotheque, casino, private club, country club. [➡HOTELS, RESTAURANTS, AND CLUBS; 1081] 4 *v* **batter**, hit, bludgeon, bash (*informal*), bang, strike, smash, beat, slug, cudgel. [➡WHIP AND CLUB; 418] 5 *type of* **sports equipment.** [➡SPORTS EQUIPMENT; 879]

club

◆ *types of club*
baton, billy club (*US*), blackjack, bludgeon, cosh, cudgel, mace, nightstick (*US*), shillelagh, truncheon

club sandwich *n* [➡PREPARED DISHES; 1169]

cluck 1 *v* **cackle**, squawk, clack, make a commotion. [➡SOUND EMISSION BY ANIMALS OR BIRDS; 365] 2 *v* **fuss**, coo, chuckle, tut, flap (*informal*). [➡GIVING VENT TO EMOTIONS; 680] 3 *type of* **bird sound.** [➡SOUNDS MADE BY BIRDS; 1262]

clue *n* **sign**, hint, evidence, inkling, suspicion, trace, indication, intimation, pointer, cue. [➡ADVICE; 690]

clued in (*US*) *adj* [➡KNOWLEDGE AND WISDOM; 559]

clued-up (*informal*) *adj* **well-informed**, knowledgeable, au fait, on the ball (*informal*), competent, in the know. *Opposite:* clueless. (*informal*). [➡KNOWLEDGE AND WISDOM; 559]

clueless (*informal*) *adj* **naive**, inexperienced, impractical, incompetent, ignorant, ill-informed, green, oblivious. [➡IGNORANCE; 558] *Opposite:* well-informed.

cluelessness (*informal*) *n* [➡IGNORANCE; 558]

clump 1 *n* **bunch**, cluster, mass, tuft, thicket, batch, bundle. [➡COLLECTIONS AND MIXTURES OF THINGS; 1243] 2 *v* **clomp**, plod, stomp, clatter, tramp, stamp, clunk. [➡EMIT SOUNDS THROUGH IMPACT AND ABRASION; 366]

clumpy *adj* **ungainly**, awkward, cumbersome, unwieldy, chunky, bulky, inelegant, heavy. [➡WEIGHT: HEAVY; 1204] *Opposite:* dainty.

clumsiness *n* **awkwardness**, ungainliness, ineptness, gaucheness, gaucherie, inelegance. [➡AGILITY OF THE BODY; 477] *Opposite:* gracefulness.

clumsy *adj* **awkward**, inept, ungainly, maladroit (*formal*), gauche, all thumbs, ham-fisted (*informal*), lumbering, gawky (*informal*), inelegant, blundering, bungling (*informal*), heavy-handed. [➡DESCRIBING BODY MOVEMENTS; 289] *Opposite:* graceful.

clunk *type of* **impact sound.** [➡IMPACT SOUNDS; 1259]

clunky *adj* **chunky**, heavy, solid, bulky, awkward, unwieldy, clumpy. [➡WEIGHT: HEAVY; 1204]

cluster 1 *n* **bunch**, group, collection, band, gathering, constellation, knot, mass, bundle. [➡COLLECTIONS AND MIXTURES OF THINGS; 1243] 2 *v* **gather**, come together, bunch, group, collect, huddle, crowd, bundle (*informal*), assemble, round up. [➡GET CLOSER TOGETHER; 311] *Opposite:* disperse.

clutch 1 *v* **grasp**, hold, grab, grip, hang on, clasp, seize, catch, grapple, clench. [➡CONTACT: HOLD; 412] 2 *n* [➡CONTACT: HOLD; 412] 3 *type of* **controls.** [➡VEHICLES; 1144] 4 *type of* **flock.** [➡GROUP OF BIRDS; 1007]

clutch bag *type of* **handbag**, *type of* **purse.** [➡CONTAINERS, RECEPTACLES, AND PACKAGING; 1244]

clutter 1 *n* **mess**, litter, disorder, confusion, untidiness, muddle, chaos. [➡DISORDER AND CHAOS; 246] *Opposite:* order. 2 *v* **encumber**, litter, strew, fill, cover, mess up (*informal*), muddle, disarrange. [➡FILL; 407] *Opposite:* free.

cluttered *adj* **untidy**, messy, disorderly, muddled, slovenly, mixed-up (*informal*), disarranged. [➡DISORDER AND CHAOS; 246] *Opposite:* orderly.

clutter up *v* [➡CREATE DISORDER AND CAUSE CHAOS; 359]

coach 1 *n* **trainer**, teacher, instructor, tutor. [➡EDUCATORS; 840] 2 *v* **teach**, train, prepare, instruct, tutor, drill, educate, school. [➡INSTRUCT AND TEACH; 610] 3 *type of* **wagon or carriage.** [➡VEHICLES; 1144] 4 *part of* **train.** [➡RAILWAYS; 1106] 5 *type of* **public service vehicle.** [➡VEHICLES; 1144]

See Compare and Contrast at **teach.**

coaching *n* **training**, education, schooling, teaching, tutoring, instruction, preparation, drilling. [➡TEACHING; 839]

coachload *n* **busload**, group, party, crowd, horde, mass, flock, herd. [➡MANY, MUCH, LARGE AMOUNT; 117]

coachwork *n* **bodywork**, exterior, outside, paintwork. [➡EXTERNAL PARTS OF A VEHICLE; 1146]

coagulate *v* **clot**, congeal, thicken, coalesce, set, gel, jell, cake. [➡HARDEN, CONGEAL, DRY; 388] *Opposite:* thin.

coagulated *adj* [➡DENSITY AND CONSISTENCY; 1206]

coagulation 1 *n* **clotting**, thickening, setting, congealing, gelling, jelling, caking, coalescence. [➡HARDEN, CONGEAL, DRY; 388] 2 *n* **clot**, lump, glob (*informal*), gob (*slang*), ball, mass, cake. [➡AMOUNT OF SOLID OR SEMI-SOLID; 115]

coal *type of* **mineral.** [➡MINERALS; 1276]

coal black *type of* **black.** [➡COLOURS; 1223]

coalesce *v* **merge**, unite, combine, amalgamate, come together, band together, join, conjoin (*formal*), cleave (*literary*), blend, mingle, fuse, meld. [➡COMBINE AND MIX; 401] *Opposite:* separate.

coalescence *n* **union**, combination, amalgamation, meld, merger, merging, coming together, banding together, joining, conjoining (*formal*), cleaving (*literary*), mingling, blending, fusing, melding. [➡COMBINE AND MIX; 401] *Opposite:* separation.

coalfield *n* **coalmine**, seam, mine, pit, colliery, mine workings, excavation. [➡INDUSTRIAL BUILDINGS; 1086]

coal gas *type of* **gas.** [➡GASES; 1274]

coalition *n* **alliance**, union, partnership, combination, league, association, federation, merger, confederacy, confederation. [➡GROUPS WITH A COMMON INTEREST; 938]

coalmine *n* **colliery**, mine, pit, coalface, quarry, coalfield, mine workings, excavation. [➡HOLES, GAPS, AND FORKS; 1251]

coarse 1 *adj* **rough**, bristly, uneven, abrasive, stiff, grainy, granular, harsh, thick, crude. [➡PHYSICAL TEXTURE; 1221] *Opposite:* smooth. 2 *adj* **indelicate**, tasteless, vulgar, uncouth, crude, rude, uncivil, smutty (*informal*), foul-mouthed, loutish, boorish, bad-mannered, crass, gross, obscene. [➡RUDE AND HOSTILE; 626] *Opposite:* polite. 3 *adj* **unre-**

fined, crude, untreated, organic, unprocessed, raw. [➡RAW AND NATURAL; 1213] *Opposite:* refined.

coarsely 1 *adv* **roughly**, thickly, crudely, unevenly, harshly. [➡PHYSICAL TEXTURE; 1221] *Opposite:* finely. 2 *adv* **indelicately**, tastelessly, vulgarly, crudely, rudely, loutishly, uncivilly, boorishly, brashly, uncouthly, smuttily (*informal*), crassly, grossly, obscenely. [➡RUDE AND HOSTILE; 626] *Opposite:* politely.

coarsen *v* **roughen**, harden, toughen, season, stiffen, thicken. [➡HARDEN, CONGEAL, DRY; 388] *Opposite:* soften.

coarseness 1 *n* **roughness**, thickness, unevenness, stiffness, crudeness, abrasiveness, graininess, granularity, harshness. [➡PHYSICAL TEXTURE; 1221] *Opposite:* smoothness. 2 *n* **indelicateness**, tastelessness, vulgarity, uncouthness, smuttiness (*informal*), crassness, grossness, obscenity, rudeness, incivility, crudeness, bad manners, boorishness, loutishness. [➡BAD MANNERS AND SOCIAL SKILLS; 522] *Opposite:* politeness.

coast 1 *n* **shore**, shoreline, coastline, beach, seashore, seaside, bank, strand, seaboard. [➡THE SEAS, OCEANS, AND SHORES; 1041] *Opposite:* interior. 2 *v* **glide**, cruise, drift, sail, freewheel, breeze, slide. [➡MOVE SLOWLY; 315] *Opposite:* struggle.

coastal *adj* **seaside**, littoral, sea, beach, shore, shoreline, coastline. [➡THE SEAS, OCEANS, AND SHORES; 1041]

coaster *type of* **motor vessel**. [➡SHIPS AND BOATS; 1149]

coastline *n* **shoreline**, seashore, coast, shore, seaboard, seaside, beach, strand. [➡THE SEAS, OCEANS, AND SHORES; 1041] *Opposite:* interior.

coast-to-coast *adj* **comprehensive**, extensive, complete, umbrella, blanket, nationwide. [➡WHOLENESS AND COMPLETENESS; 199]

coat 1 *n* **fur**, wool, fleece, hide, skin, hair, pelt. [➡COVERS AND COATINGS; 1245] 2 *n* **covering**, coating, layer, veneer, glaze, undercoat, crust, cake, overlay, varnish. [➡COVERS AND COATINGS; 1245] 3 *v* **cover**, paint, smother, dip, smear, spread, conceal, hide, spread over, varnish. [➡DECORATE, ADORN, AND APPLY COATINGS; 406]

coat

◆ *types of jacket*
anorak, blazer, blouson, bomber jacket, dinner jacket, DJ, flak jacket, fleece, jacket, Nehru jacket, reefer (*US*), reefer jacket, smoking jacket, sports jacket, tail coat, tails, tux (*US informal*), *tuxedo* (*US*), *waterproof jacket, windcheater*

◆ *types of overcoat*
cagoule, cape, cloak, duffel coat, frock coat, gabardine, greatcoat, mac (*informal*), mackintosh (*dated*), overcoat, parka, poncho, raincoat, topcoat

coated *adj* **covered**, caked, glazed, treated, layered, dusted, smeared, crusted, plastered, painted, overlaid, encrusted. [➡DECORATE, ADORN, AND APPLY COATINGS; 406]

coating *n* **covering**, veneer, varnish, glaze, layer, coat, undercoat, crust, cake, overlay. [➡COVERS AND COATINGS; 1245]

coat of arms *n* **crest**, emblem, badge, logo, design, shield. [➡SYMBOLS, SIGNS, AND NUMBERS; 597]

coatrack *n* **rack**, hooks, coat stand. [➡FURNITURE; 858]

coat stand *n* **hat stand**, coat tree (*US*), coatrack. [➡FURNITURE; 858]

coat-tail *part of* **garment**. [➡PARTS OF A GARMENT; 870]

coauthor *n* [➡SUPPORTERS, PROTECTORS, AND COMPATRIOTS; 970]

coax *v* **wheedle**, persuade, sweet-talk (*informal*), cajole, win over, charm, entice, twist somebody's arm (*informal*), inveigle, lure, tempt. [➡CAUSE OR COMPEL TO ACT; 272]

cob 1 *type of* **male or female bird**. [➡MALE OR FEMALE BIRD; 1005] 2 *type of* **horse**. [➡HORSE; 985] 3 *type of* **nut**. [➡NUTS; 1184]

cobalt blue *type of* **blue**. [➡COLOURS; 1223]

cobble 1 *n* **cobblestone**, paving stone, sett, stone, flagstone, flag. [➡STONES, ROCKS, AND BOULDERS; 1057] 2 *v* **mend**, repair, patch, patch up, stitch, put back together. [➡REPAIR AND MEND; 377]

cobbled *adj* **paved**, cobblestoned, flagged. [➡PHYSICAL TEXTURE; 1221]

cobbler *type of* **dessert**. [➡CAKES, BISCUITS, AND DESSERTS; 1180]

cobblestone *n* **cobble**, paving stone, sett, stone, flagstone, flag. [➡STONES, ROCKS, AND BOULDERS; 1057]

cobble together *v* **improvise**, rig, knock together (*informal*), concoct, whip up (*informal*), contrive, devise, invent, fix up. [➡CREATION; 347]

cobnut *type of* **nut**. [➡NUTS; 1184]

cobra *type of* **poisonous snake**. [➡SNAKE; 995]

cobwebs *n* **sluggishness**, tiredness, torpor, lethargy, listlessness. [➡UNPLEASANT AND DIRTY SUBSTANCES; 1267] *Opposite:* liveliness.

coccus *type of* **microorganism**. [➡MICROORGANISMS, FUNGI, AND ALGAE; 1023]

coccyx *type of* **bone**. [➡THE BONES AND JOINTS; 720]

cochineal *n* **colouring**, food dye, dye, food additive, additive. [➡DYES AND COLOURANTS; 1269]

cock 1 *v* **tilt**, lift, slant, angle, incline, elevate. [➡MOVE SOMETHING: INTO A NEW POSITION OR OVERTURN; 331] *Opposite:* lower. 2 *type of* **male or female bird**. [➡MALE OR FEMALE BIRD; 1005]

cock-a-doodle-doo *n* **crowing**, crow, cry, call. [➡SOUNDS MADE BY BIRDS; 1262]

cock-a-hoop *adj* **elated**, delighted, thrilled, overjoyed, jubilant, over the moon, chuffed (*informal*), ecstatic, excited, pleased, happy, exhilarated, euphoric, exultant. [➡PLEASURE, EXCITEMENT, AND ELATION; 535] *Opposite:* dejected.

cock-a-leekie *type of* **soup**. [➡SOUP; 1185]

cock-and-bull story *n* [➡DECEPTION AND LIES; 661]

cockatoo *type of* **pet bird**. [➡BIRD; 997]

cockcrow (*archaic or literary*) *n* **dawn**, sunrise,

morning, daybreak, morn (*literary*), the crack of dawn, first light, sunup (*US*). [➡TIMES OF DAY; 87] *Opposite:* sunset.

cockerel *type of* **male or female bird.** [➡MALE OR FEMALE BIRD; 1005]

cockeyed 1 *adj* (*informal*) **foolish**, absurd, madcap, ridiculous, silly, crazy (*informal*), outlandish, barmy (*informal*), potty (*informal*), wacky (*informal*). [➡BIZARRE AND PECULIAR; 258] *Opposite:* sensible. 2 *adj* **misaligned**, crooked, askew, awry, uneven, out of kilter, off beam, off-centre, skewwhiff (*informal*), off the beam (*US*). [➡ORIENTATION AND ALIGNMENT; 1222] *Opposite:* straight.

cockiness *n* [➡POMPOUS, LOUD, AND OVER-CONFIDENT; 636]

cockle *type of* **aquatic invertebrate.** [➡AQUATIC INVERTEBRATE; 1022]

cockpit 1 *n* **arena**, battleground, fight arena, boxing ring, floor, ring, theatre, field. [➡ALCOVES, CUBICLES, AND COMPARTMENTS; 1095] 2 *part of* **aircraft.** [➡AIRCRAFT; 1147]

cockroach *type of* **beetle.** [➡BEETLES AND WEEVILS; 1016]

cockscomb *part of* **bird.** [➡PARTS OF A BIRD; 1006]

cocksure *adj* **cocky** (*informal*), arrogant, conceited, confident, overconfident, self-assured, self-confident, cavalier, supercilious, showy, pompous, smug. [➡POMPOUS, LOUD, AND OVER-CONFIDENT; 636] *Opposite:* modest.

cocksureness *n* [➡POMPOUS, LOUD, AND OVER-CONFIDENT; 636]

cocktail *n* **concoction**, mixture, brew, blend, combination, mélange (*literary or formal*), mix. [➡COLLECTIONS AND MIXTURES OF THINGS; 1243]

cocktail cabinet *type of* **cabinet.** [➡FURNITURE; 858]

cocktail party *n* [➡PARTIES, DANCES, AND CELEBRATIONS; 37]

cocktail snacks *n* [➡PREPARED DISHES; 1169]

cockup (*informal*) *n* **blunder**, mess-up (*informal*), mess, mistake, error, slip-up (*informal*), blooper (*US informal humorous*). [➡MISTAKES; 251]

cocky (*informal*) *adj* **smug**, arrogant, boastful, brash, self-assured, self-confident, swaggering, conceited, self-satisfied, overconfident. [➡POMPOUS, LOUD, AND OVER-CONFIDENT; 636] *Opposite:* modest.

co-conspirator *n* **collaborator**, partner in crime, accomplice, partner, associate, abettor, accessory. [➡SUPPORTERS, PROTECTORS, AND COMPATRIOTS; 970]

coconut *type of* **nut.** [➡NUTS; 1184]

coconut matting *type of* **fibre.** [➡PLANT MATERIALS; 1132]

cocoon 1 *n* **sheath**, covering, shell, case, bubble, layer, nest, coat. [➡COVERS AND COATINGS; 1245] 2 *v* **wrap**, cover, envelop, insulate, protect, cushion, isolate, shelter, cosset. [➡TAKE CARE OF AND SPOIL; 301] *Opposite:* expose.

cocotte *n* [➡TABLEWARE, CUTLERY, AND KITCHENWARE; 861]

cod *type of* **sea fish.** [➡SEA FISH; 1009]

coda 1 *n* **conclusion**, ending, end, close, finale, finish, tail end. [➡END; 54] *Opposite:* introduction. 2 *n* **addendum**, postscript, addition, afterthought, adjunct, appendix. [➡PARTS OF BOOKS AND DOCUMENTS; 594]

coddle *v* **pamper**, mollycoddle, indulge, baby, overprotect, cosset, fuss, spoil, cocoon. [➡TAKE CARE OF AND SPOIL; 301]

code 1 *n* **cipher**, cryptogram, encryption, cryptograph, enigma, puzzle. [➡SYMBOLS, SIGNS, AND NUMBERS; 597] 2 *n* **program**, programming, data, instructions, language, information. [➡SYMBOLS, SIGNS, AND NUMBERS; 597] 3 *n* **system**, policy, convention, regulations, rules, laws, protocol, canon, procedure. [➡WAYS OF DOING THINGS; 295]

code-named *adj* **alias**, known as, dubbed, identified, named, called, designated, a.k.a.. [➡NAME AND DESCRIBE; 666]

code of behaviour *n* [➡WAYS OF DOING THINGS; 295]

code of conduct *n* **agreement**, rules, guidelines, regulations, protocol, procedure, convention, principle. [➡WAYS OF DOING THINGS; 295]

code of practice *n* **regulations**, rules, guidelines, principles, protocol, procedure, convention. [➡WAYS OF DOING THINGS; 295]

codependent *adj* [➡RELATIONSHIP TO ANOTHER; 973]

codex *n* **manuscript**, scroll, papyrus, palimpsest, parchment, text, book, volume, collection. [➡BOOKS AND BOOKLETS; 591]

codger (*informal*) *n* **man**, bloke (*informal*), fellow, chap (*informal*), guy (*informal*). [➡MALE PERSON; 934]

codicil (*formal*) *n* **appendix**, supplement, addition, rider, add-on, adjunct, extra. [➡PARTS OF BOOKS AND DOCUMENTS; 594]

codification *n* **systematization**, organization, categorization, classification, collation, arrangement, methodization. [➡ARRANGE AND CREATE ORDER; 358]

codify *v* **organize**, collect, collate, gather together, arrange, order, classify, categorize, array (*formal*), methodize, systemize. [➡ARRANGE AND CREATE ORDER; 358]

codswallop (*informal*) *n* **nonsense**, rubbish, drivel, claptrap (*informal*), twaddle (*informal*), bunkum (*informal*), tosh (*dated informal*), baloney (*informal*), tripe (*informal*). [➡MEANINGLESS SPEECH OR WRITING; 677]

coefficient *n* **number**, constant, factor, amount, quantity, measurement, figure. [➡MATHS; 598]

coerce *v* **force**, press, pressure, strong-arm (*informal*), twist somebody's arm (*informal*), force somebody's hand, compel, bully, intimidate, drive, put the arm on (*US informal*). [➡CAUSE OR COMPEL TO ACT; 272] *Opposite:* persuade.

coercion *n* **pressure**, compulsion, force, intimidation, strong-arming (*informal*), bullying, duress, strong arm tactics. [➡MORALLY BAD; 776] *Opposite:* persuasion.

coercive *adj* **forced**, forcible, intimidating, bullying, strong-arm (*informal*), strong, powerful, tough. [➡PHYSICALLY UNPLEASANT; 227] *Opposite:* gentle.

coexist 1 *v* **live**, exist, cohabit (*formal*), live together, coincide, co-occur, concur. [➡EXIST WITH OTHERS; 18] 2 *v* **harmonize**, synchronize, collaborate, cooperate, reconcile, cohabit (*formal*), live and let live, coevolve. [➡HARMONY; 156]

coexistence 1 *n* **living**, existence, cohabitation (*formal*), living together, synchronicity, co-occurrence, concomitance, simultaneity, concurrence, coincidence, contemporaneity, synchronism. [➡CONCURRENT AND CONTEMPORANEOUS; 165] 2 *n* **harmony**, accord, cohabitation (*formal*), harmonization, coevolution, synchronization, reconciliation, cooperation, collaboration. [➡HARMONY; 156]

coexistent *adj* **concurrent**, simultaneous, contemporaneous, coincident, concomitant, synchronous. [➡CONCURRENT AND CONTEMPORANEOUS; 165]

coextensive *adj* **coincident**, equivalent, equal, parallel, corresponding, comparable, conterminous (*formal*), coterminous (*formal*). [➡CONCURRENT AND CONTEMPORANEOUS; 165]

coffee *type of* **beige**. [➡COLOURS; 1223]

coffee

◆ *types of coffee*
café au lait, café noir, caffè latte, cappuccino, decaf, espresso, Greek coffee, Irish coffee, latte, mocha, Turkish coffee

coffee bar *type of* **eating place**. [➡HOTELS, RESTAURANTS, AND CLUBS; 1081]

coffee break *n* **breather** (*informal*), time off, break, rest, time out. [➡PERIOD OF REST; 91]

coffee cake *type of* **cake**. [➡CAKES, BISCUITS, AND DESSERTS; 1180]

coffeemaker *n* **percolator**, espresso machine, coffeepot, filter, drip pot (*US*). [➡HOUSEHOLD APPLIANCES; 1116]

coffee shop *type of* **eating place**. [➡HOTELS, RESTAURANTS, AND CLUBS; 1081]

coffee table *type of* **table**. [➡FURNITURE; 858]

coffer *n* **strongbox**, chest, casket, treasure chest, safe, treasury. [➡CONTAINERS, RECEPTACLES, AND PACKAGING; 1244]

coffers *n* **funds**, reserves, assets, capital, resources, money, treasury. [➡FINANCIAL ASSETS; 463]

coffin *n* **box**, sarcophagus, cist, casket (*US*). [➡BURIAL PLACES AND ACCESSORIES; 930]

cog 1 *n* **component**, part, gear, mechanism, cogwheel, wheel, gearwheel, flywheel, sprocket-wheel. [➡PARTS OF MACHINES AND TOOLS; 1117] 2 *part of* **engine**. [➡PARTS OF AN ENGINE; 1143]

cogency (*formal*) *n* **power**, strength, intensity, vigour, dynamism, influence, force, weight, persuasiveness. [➡THE NATURE OF IDEAS; 772]

cogent *adj* **forceful**, convincing, persuasive, clear, lucid, strong, logical, rational, coherent, sound. [➡THE NATURE OF IDEAS; 772] *Opposite:* unconvincing.

See Compare and Contrast at **valid**.

cogently *adv* **clearly**, lucidly, convincingly, persuasively, forcefully, coherently, soundly, strongly, logically, sensibly, rationally. [➡CONCISE AND CLEAR; 203] *Opposite:* unconvincingly.

cogitate (*formal*) *v* **think**, consider, reflect, deliberate, ponder, ruminate, muse, meditate. [➡THINK AND REFLECT; 744]

cogitation (*formal*) *n* **thought**, consideration, deliberation (*formal*), rumination, musing, reflection, meditation, pondering. [➡THINK AND REFLECT; 744]

cognate *adj* **similar**, alike, related, kindred, equivalent, associated. [➡RELATED; 143] *Opposite:* different.

cognition *n* **thought**, reasoning, understanding, perception, reason, intellect, awareness, cognizance (*formal*), intuition. [➡PSYCHOLOGY AND THE MIND; 770]

cognitive *adj* **reasoning**, mental, intellectual, cerebral, perceptive, rational, thinking, thought. [➡PSYCHOLOGY AND THE MIND; 770]

cognizance (*formal*) *n* **knowledge**, awareness, grasp, perception, understanding, acquaintance, appreciation. [➡KNOWLEDGE AND WISDOM; 559] *Opposite:* ignorance.

cognizant (*formal*) *adj* **knowing**, aware, conscious, acquainted, familiar, sensible (*formal*), mindful. [➡KNOWLEDGE AND WISDOM; 559] *Opposite:* ignorant.

See Compare and Contrast at **aware**.

cognomen (*formal*) *n* [➡NAME AND DESCRIBE; 666]

cognoscente *n* [➡LEVEL OF EDUCATION AND SOPHISTICATION; 894]

cognoscenti *n* **literati** (*formal*), connoisseurs, experts, specialists, authorities, pundits. [➡LEVEL OF EDUCATION AND SOPHISTICATION; 894]

cogwheel 1 *n* **cog**, wheel, gearwheel, gear, flywheel. [➡PARTS OF MACHINES AND TOOLS; 1117] 2 *part of* **engine**. [➡PARTS OF AN ENGINE; 1143]

cohabit (*formal*) *v* **live together**, live in sin (*dated or humorous*), shack up (*informal disapproving*), share. [➡EXIST WITH OTHERS; 18]

cohabitation (*formal*) *n* **living together**, living in sin (*dated or humorous*), sharing. [➡MARITAL STATUS; 890]

cohabitee *n* [➡SEXUAL AND ROMANTIC RELATIONSHIPS; 964]

cohere (*formal*) 1 *v* **adhere**, bind, stick, join together, gel (*informal*), jell, stick together. [➡COMBINE AND MIX; 401] 2 *v* **conform**, match, tally, correspond, hang together, follow. [➡HARMONY; 156] *Opposite:* disagree.

coherence *n* **consistency**, unity, rationality, logic, lucidity, reason, soundness. [➡ORDER AND ORGANISATION; 207] *Opposite:* inconsistency.

coherent 1 *adj* **consistent**, logical, sound, reasoned, reasonable, rational. [➡THE NATURE OF IDEAS; 772] *Opposite:* inconsistent. 2 *adj* **intelligible**, clear, comprehensible, articulate, lucid, rational. [➡THE NATURE OF IDEAS; 772] *Opposite:* unintelligible.

cohesion *n* **sticking together**, unity, consistency, solidity, organization, pulling together, interconnection, interrelation. [➡HARMONY; 156] *Opposite:* disintegration.

cohesive *adj* **unified**, consistent, solid, interconnected, organized, interrelated. [➡HARMONY; 156] *Opposite:* fragmented.

cohort 1 *n* **unit**, troop, regiment, legion, army, group. [➡GROUPS OF PEOPLE; 935] 2 *n* (*US disapproving*) **supporter**, accomplice, associate, partner, ally, follower, crony (*disapproving*). [➡FRIENDS; 963]

coiffeur (*formal*) *n* [➡HAIR STYLISTS; 851]

coiffeuse (*formal*) *n* [➡HAIR STYLISTS; 851]

coiffure (*formal*) 1 *n* **hairstyle**, haircut, hairdo (*informal*). [➡HAIR STYLES AND HAIR PIECES; 489] 2 *v* **style**, arrange, dress, coif (*formal*), cut. [➡IMPROVE APPEARANCE; 380]

coil 1 *n* **loop**, curl, spiral, twist, twirl, helix. [➡ROUNDED SHAPE; 1217] 2 *v* **wind**, convolute, twine, curl, loop, spiral, twist, twirl. [➡POSITION SOMETHING: AROUND SOMETHING; 328] 3 *part of* **engine**. [➡PARTS OF AN ENGINE; 1143]

coiled *adj* **wound**, looped, twisted, helical, spiral, convoluted, twisting, curled. [➡ROUNDED SHAPE; 1217] *Opposite:* straight.

coin 1 *n* **currency**, money, coinage, denomination, change. [➡MONEY; 140] 2 *v* **invent**, think up, make up, create, devise. [➡INSTITUTE AND INAUGURATE; 349]

coinage *n* [➡ASPECTS OF LANGUAGE; 683]

coincide *v* **accord**, agree, match, correspond, concur, overlap. [➡HARMONY; 156] *Opposite:* differ.

coincidence 1 *n* **accident**, chance, luck, fluke (*informal*), twist of fate, quirk, happenstance. [➡CHANCE EVENT; 36] 2 *n* (*formal*) **concurrence**, correspondence, correlation, agreement, relationship, link. [➡CONNECTION; 144]

coincidental 1 *adj* **accidental**, chance, unplanned, spontaneous, unexpected, unpredicted, uncalculated, unintentional, fluky (*informal*). [➡CHANCE, COINCIDENCE, AND ACCIDENT; 787] *Opposite:* intentional. 2 *adj* **concurrent**, corresponding, simultaneous, correlated, related, linked. [➡RELATED; 143] *Opposite:* separate.

coincidentally *adv* **accidentally**, by accident, by chance, unpredictably, unexpectedly, uncalculatedly, spontaneously, unintentionally, luckily, fortunately. [➡CHANCE, COINCIDENCE, AND ACCIDENT; 787] *Opposite:* intentionally.

coir *type of* **fibre**. [➡PLANT MATERIALS; 1132]

coke *type of* **mineral**. [➡MINERALS; 1276]

col *n* **pass**, saddle, gap, dip, passage, defile. [➡GEOLOGICAL FEATURES; 1056]

cola *type of* **evergreen tree**. [➡EVERGREEN AND CONIFEROUS TREES; 1029]

cola nut *type of* **nut**. [➡NUTS; 1184]

cold 1 *adj* **chilly**, freezing, icy, frosty, bitter, wintry, frozen, arctic (*informal*). [➡TEMPERATURE: COLD; 1230] *Opposite:* hot. 2 *adj* **emotionless**, taciturn, unfriendly, unemotional, unsympathetic, unkind, icy, stony, callous, uncaring, impersonal, hardhearted, aloof, distant, unfeeling, indifferent, formal, cool, remote, detached, frosty. [➡UNFRIENDLINESS AND UNSOCIABILITY; 505] *Opposite:* friendly. 3 *n* **coldness**, chill, chilliness, frost, iciness, wintriness, winter. [➡TEMPERATURE: COLD; 1230] *Opposite:* heat. 4 *n* **common cold**, head cold, flu, influenza, chill. [➡ILLNESSES AND DISORDERS; 733]

cold-blooded *adj* **pitiless**, hardhearted, cold, callous, cruel, premeditated, unemotional, unfeeling, ruthless, heartless, uncaring, merciless, remorseless, cold-hearted. [➡SELFISH AND UNKIND; 506] *Opposite:* compassionate.

cold-bloodedly *adv* **pitilessly**, coldly, hardheartedly, callously, cruelly, premeditatedly, unemotionally, unfeelingly, ruthlessly, heartlessly, uncaringly, mercilessly, remorselessly, cold-heartedly. [➡RUDE AND HOSTILE; 626] *Opposite:* compassionately.

cold-bloodedness *n* **pitilessness**, coldness, hardheartedness, callousness, cruelty, emotionlessness, unfeelingness, ruthlessness, heartlessness, mercilessness, remorselessness, cold-heartedness. [➡BAD MANNERS AND SOCIAL SKILLS; 522] *Opposite:* compassion.

cold front *n* [➡COLD WEATHER; 1051]

cold-hearted *adj* **cold-blooded**, cruel, callous, ruthless, unfeeling, uncaring, hardhearted, hard, impenetrable, remorseless, unsympathetic, cold. [➡SELFISH AND UNKIND; 506] *Opposite:* compassionate.

cold-heartedness *n* **cold-bloodedness**, cruelty, callousness, ruthlessness, unfeelingness, uncaringness, hardheartedness, hardness, impenetrability, remorselessness. [➡BAD MANNERS AND SOCIAL SKILLS; 522] *Opposite:* compassion.

coldly *adv* **emotionlessly**, taciturnly, aloofly, distantly, unfeelingly, indifferently, formally, coolly, frostily, unemotionally, unsympathetically, unkindly, icily, stonily, callously, frigidly, uncaringly, impersonally, hardheartedly. [➡UNINTERESTED AND DETACHED; 630] *Opposite:* warmly.

coldness 1 *n* **cold**, chilliness, frostiness, iciness, wintriness. [➡TEMPERATURE: COLD; 1230] *Opposite:* warmness. 2 *n* **emotionlessness**, taciturnity, unfriendliness, aloofness, distantness, unfeelingness, indifference, coolness, remoteness, frostiness, unkindness, iciness, stoniness, callousness, impersonality, hardheartedness, cold-heartedness, formality. [➡NEUTRALITY AND INDIFFERENCE; 554] *Opposite:* friendliness.

cold shoulder *n* **rebuff**, rejection, snub, slight, brushoff (*informal*), slap in the face (*informal*), putdown (*informal*). [➡UNKIND ACTION OR BEHAVIOUR; 297] *Opposite:* welcome.

cold snap *n* **freeze**, frost, iciness, wintriness, cold spell. [➡COLD WEATHER; 1051]

cold spell *n* [➡COLD WEATHER; 1051]

coleslaw *type of* **salad vegetable**. [➡FRUIT AND VEGETABLES; 1175]

coleus *type of* **foliage plant**. [➡FOLIAGE PLANTS; 1035]

coley *type of* **sea fish**. [➡SEA FISH; 1009]

colic *n* **stomachache**, bellyache (*informal*), cramp, indigestion, stitch, pain, tummy ache (*informal*). [➡DISORDERS OF THE DIGESTIVE SYSTEM; 714]

collaborate *v* **work together**, join forces, team up, work in partnership, pool resources, act as a team, cooperate. [➡HELP; 294]

collaboration *n* **cooperation**, teamwork, partnership, association, alliance, relationship. [➡RECIPROCITY AND INTERDEPENDENCE; 148]

collaborative *adj* **cooperative**, concerted, collective, joint, combined, shared, two-way, common, united, mutual. [➡ACTING WITH OTHERS; 286]

collaborator 1 *n* **colleague**, coworker, partner, team-mate, associate, ally. [➡COLLEAGUES AND EQUALS; 967] 2 *n* **traitor**, turncoat, spy, agent, double agent, grass (*slang*). [➡PEOPLE WHO DECEIVE; 662]

collage *n* **collection**, combination, assortment, hotchpotch, medley, mixture. [➡COLLECTIONS AND MIXTURES OF THINGS; 1243]

collapse 1 *v* **fall down**, cave in, give way, crumple, subside, disintegrate. [➡CEASE TO EXIST; 22] 2 *v* **fail**, end, fold, break down, dissolve, flop. [➡FAIL OR BE UNSUCCESSFUL; 75] 3 *v* **fold**, disassemble, fold up, put away, minimize, shut down. [➡CHANGE OF SHAPE; 386] 4 *n* **failure**, ruin, downfall, breakdown, flop, fall, end, folding, bankruptcy. [➡FAILURE; 77] 5 *n* **illness**, breakdown, attack, crisis, crack-up (*informal*). [➡ILLNESSES AND DISORDERS; 733]

collapsible *adj* **folding**, foldup, stacking, foldaway, portable, inflatable, knockdown. [➡CHANGE OF SHAPE; 386]

collar 1 *v* (*slang*) **catch**, corner, get hold of, grab, seize, nab (*informal*), arrest, get a hold of (*US*). [➡GET; 421] 2 *part of* **garment**. [➡PARTS OF A GARMENT; 870] 3 *type of* **necklace**. [➡JEWELLERY; 866]

collarbone *type of* **bone**. [➡THE BONES AND JOINTS; 720]

collard greens (*US*) *type of* **vegetable**. [➡FRUIT AND VEGETABLES; 1175]

collate *v* **order**, organize, collect, gather, assemble, check, compare, arrange, classify, codify, systematize. [➡ARRANGE AND CREATE ORDER; 358]

collateral *n* **security**, surety, warranty, guarantee, insurance, indemnity. [➡INSURANCE; 801]

collation 1 *n* **ordering**, organization, collection, gathering, assembling, checking, comparison, arrangement, classification, codification, systematization. [➡ARRANGE AND CREATE ORDER; 358] 2 *n* **meal**, repast (*literary*), spread (*informal*), snack, buffet, refreshment. [➡MEALS AND PARTS OF MEALS; 1168]

colleague *n* **coworker**, associate, assistant, partner, collaborator, team-mate. [➡COLLEAGUES AND EQUALS; 967]

collect 1 *v* **gather**, amass, assemble, accumulate, bring together, pull together. [➡COMBINE AND MIX; 401] *Opposite:* disperse. 2 *v* **store**, hoard, amass, stockpile, accumulate, treasure, save. [➡STORE AND KEEP; 454]

Compare and Contrast: ***collect, accumulate, gather, amass, assemble, stockpile, hoard***

CORE MEANING: TO BRING DISPERSED THINGS TOGETHER

collect to bring things together, or to make a collection of similar things as a hobby; ***accumulate*** to obtain things over a period of time; ***gather*** to bring together things from various locations; ***amass*** to obtain a large amount of things over an extended period; ***assemble*** to bring things together in an orderly way; ***stockpile*** to collect and store in large amounts for future use; ***hoard*** to collect and store in large amounts, often secretly.

collected *adj* **calm**, composed, poised, placid, together (*informal*), serene, unruffled, cool. [➡CALMNESS, CONFIDENCE, AND COMPOSURE; 537] *Opposite:* flustered.

collection 1 *n* **group**, gathering, assortment, assembly, assemblage, pool, throng. [➡COLLECTIONS AND MIXTURES OF THINGS; 1243] 2 *n* **compendium**, compilation, set, corpus, anthology, collectanea, album. [➡COLLECTIONS AND MIXTURES OF THINGS; 1243]

collective 1 *adj* **shared**, cooperative, communal, joint, united, combined, mutual, group. [➡BELONGING OR RELATING TO PEOPLE; 943] *Opposite:* individual. 2 *n* **cooperative**, co-op (*informal*), colony, kibbutz, commune, farm, enclave. [➡GROUPS WITH A COMMON INTEREST; 938]

collectively *adv* **en masse**, cooperatively, communally, jointly, together, mutually. [➡ACTING WITH OTHERS; 286] *Opposite:* individually.

collectivism *n* **communism**, socialism, syndicalism, anarcho-syndicalism, Marxism, Leninism, Maoism, communalism, Stalinism. [➡STYLES AND SYSTEMS OF GOVERNMENT; 806]

collectivist *adj* **communist**, socialist, syndicalist, anarcho-syndicalist, Marxist, Leninist, Maoist, communalist, Stalinist. [➡STYLES AND SYSTEMS OF GOVERNMENT; 806]

collector *n* **gatherer**, amasser, gleaner, hoarder, accumulator. [➡PEOPLE WHO COLLECT THINGS; 455]

college *n* **school**, university, academy, seminary, institution. [➡EDUCATIONAL INSTITUTIONS; 813]

college of further education *n* [➡EDUCATIONAL INSTITUTIONS; 813]

collegial 1 *adj* **shared**, reciprocal, mutual, interconnected, community, uncompetitive. [➡BELONGING OR RELATING TO PEOPLE; 943] 2 *adj* **collegiate**, scholastic, academic, educational, institutional. [➡EDUCATION; 838]

collegiate *adj* **academic**, university, scholastic, educational, institutional, collegial. [➡LEVEL OF EDUCATION AND SOPHISTICATION; 894]

collide *v* **hit**, strike, crash, bump, bump into, run into, run over, ram, go into, plough into, rear-end (*US*). [➡CONTACT: IMPACT; 414]

collie *type of* **large dog**. [➡DOG; 980]

colliery *n* **coalmine**, shaft, seam, pit, mine, coalface, excavation, quarry. [➡INDUSTRIAL BUILDINGS; 1086]

collision 1 *n* **crash**, smash, accident, impact, pile-up (*informal*), rear-ender (*US*), fender-bender (*US informal*). [➡TRAFFIC ACCIDENTS; 256] 2 *n* **clash**, conflict, confrontation, disagreement, difficulty, overlap. [➡ARGUMENT; 47]

collocation *n* [➡ASPECTS OF LANGUAGE; 683]

colloquial *adj* **informal**, idiomatic, conversational, everyday, spoken, slang. [➡COMMUNICATIVE STYLE; 625] *Opposite:* formal.

colloquialism *n* **idiom**, popular expression, common term, vulgarism. [➡FIGURES OF SPEECH; 674]

colloquium *n* **seminar**, symposium, discussion, conference, debate, workshop, class, meeting, round table. [➡MEETINGS AND ASSEMBLIES; 43]

colloquy (*formal*) *n* **discussion**, meeting, conference, seminar, conversation, debate. [➡MEETINGS AND ASSEMBLIES; 43]

collude *v* **conspire**, plot, scheme, be in cahoots (*informal*), plan, get together, join together, connive, machinate. [➡DEVELOP THEORIES AND REASON; 745]

collusion *n* **conspiracy**, complicity, involvement, agreement, knowledge, consent, approval. [➡RELATIONSHIP TO ANOTHER; 973]

colobus *type of* **primate**. [➡PRIMATE; 988]

cologne *n* **fragrance**, perfume, toilet water, scent, aftershave, eau de toilette. [➡PERSONAL HYGIENE; 492]

colon *part of* **digestive tract**, *type of* **punctuation mark**. [➡THE DIGESTIVE TRACT; 710]

colonel *n* [➡MILITARY PERSONNEL; 828]

colonial 1 *adj* **foreign**, overseas, expatriate. [➡STYLES AND SYSTEMS OF GOVERNMENT; 806] 2 *n* **expatriate**, expat (*informal*), settler, emigrant, émigré, migrant, colonist, colonialist, colonizer. [➡STYLES AND SYSTEMS OF GOVERNMENT; 806] 3 *type of* **pre-20th-century architecture**. [➡BUILDING AND ARCHITECTURE; 1075]

colonialism *n* **expansionism**, colonization, imperialism, interventionism. [➡STYLES AND SYSTEMS OF GOVERNMENT; 806]

colonialist *adj* **expansionist**, imperialist, interventionist, colonial, colonist, colonizer. [➡STYLES AND SYSTEMS OF GOVERNMENT; 806]

colonist *n* **settler**, immigrant, pioneer, migrant, explorer, planter (*archaic*), colonial, colonizer, conqueror, invader. [➡PEOPLE LIVING AWAY FROM HOME; 887] *Opposite:* native.

colonization *n* **settlement**, establishment, foundation, occupation, annexation. [➡STYLES AND SYSTEMS OF GOVERNMENT; 806]

colonize *v* **settle**, people, inhabit, take over, take possession of, lay claim to. [➡EXIST WITH OTHERS; 18]

colonizer *n* **settler**, immigrant, colonist, explorer, conqueror, invader, pioneer, colonialist, colonial, planter (*archaic*), migrant. [➡PEOPLE LIVING AWAY FROM HOME; 887]

colonnade 1 *n* **arcade**, walkway, portico, porch, loggia. [➡ANCILLARY BUILDINGS; 1079] 2 *part of* **building**. [➡PARTS OF A BUILDING; 1094]

colony 1 *n* **settlement**, outpost, dependency, protectorate, satellite. [➡TERRITORIES AND GROUPS OF NATIONS; 1067] 2 *n* **gathering**, group, collection, cluster, association, society. [➡GROUPS OF PEOPLE; 935] 3 *type of* **herd**. [➡GROUP OF ANIMALS; 993]

Colorado beetle *type of* **beetle**. [➡BEETLES AND WEEVILS; 1016]

Colorado potato beetle (*US*) *type of* **beetle**. [➡BEETLES AND WEEVILS; 1016]

coloration *n* **pattern**, colouring, colour, pigmentation, shade, tint, tinge, flush. [➡DESCRIBING COLOURS; 1225]

coloratura *type of* **vocal music**. [➡MUSIC, SONGS, AND SINGING; 907]

colossal *adj* **huge**, massive, immense, gigantic, enormous, vast, titanic, oversize. [➡LARGE; 1192] *Opposite:* tiny.

colossus *n* **giant**, titan, leviathan, behemoth, goliath, hulk. [➡BIG THINGS; 1193]

colour 1 *n* **hue**, tint, shade, dye, paint, pigment. [➡DYES AND COLOURANTS; 1269] 2 *v* **tint**, dye, paint, shade, wash. [➡CHANGE OF COLOUR; 392] *Opposite:* bleach. 3 *v* **blush**, go red, flush, redden. [➡FACIAL EXPRESSION; 652] *Opposite:* blanch. 4 *v* **affect**, influence, modify, alter, tint, slant, incline. [➡CHANGE; 373]

colour

◆ *types of colour*
beige, black, blue, brown, green, grey, orange, pink, purple, red, white, yellow

colourant *n* **dye**, hair dye, hair colour, pigment, stain, tint, colour, rinse, bleach, henna, peroxide. [➡DYES AND COLOURANTS; 1269]

colouration *see* **coloration**.

coloured *adj* **tinted**, dyed, painted, highlighted, stained, bleached. [➡DESCRIBING COLOURS; 1225]

colourful 1 *adj* **bright**, multicoloured, rich, vivid, vibrant, lively, gaudy, multihued. [➡DESCRIBING COLOURS; 1225] *Opposite:* dull. 2 *adj* **interesting**, vibrant, full of character, flamboyant, imaginative, intriguing, unusual, lively, exciting. [➡INTERESTING AND MEANINGFUL; 191] *Opposite:* uninteresting.

colouring *n* **complexion**, skin tone, skin colour, ruddiness, pallor, tan. [➡COMPLEXION; 481]

colourless 1 *adj* **neutral**, monochrome, pale, pallid, dull, drab. [➡DESCRIBING COLOURS; 1225] *Opposite:* colourful. 2 *adj* **dull**, drab, dreary, monotonous, uninteresting, prosaic, uneventful. [➡BORING AND UNINTERESTING; 235] *Opposite:* interesting.

colours *n* **flag**, standard, ensign, insignia. [➡SYMBOLS, SIGNS, AND NUMBERS; 597]

colt *type of* **young animal**. [➡YOUNG ANIMAL; 977]

columbine *type of* **perennial flower**. [➡FLOWERS; 1032]

column 1 *n* **pillar**, post, support, pilaster, stake, pole, pier, buttress, underpinning. [➡STICKS, POLES, AND WEDGES; 1253] 2 *n* **line**, file, string, procession, queue, cavalcade, convoy. [➡AREA AND RANGE; 111] 3 *n* **article**, feature, editorial, piece, contribution, paragraph. [➡NEWSPAPERS; 606]

columnist *n* **writer**, journalist, newspaper columnist, magazine columnist, correspondent, contributor, essayist. [➡WORKERS IN ENTERTAINMENT AND MEDIA; 873]

coma *n* **unconsciousness**, blackout, stupor, oblivion. [➡TIRED, ASLEEP AND UNCONSCIOUS; 739]

comatose 1 *adj* **unconscious**, passed out, out for the count (*informal*), blacked out. [➡TIRED, ASLEEP AND UNCONSCIOUS; 739] 2 *adj* (*informal*) **exhausted**, tired, spent, out for the count (*informal*), used up, passed out, down for the count (*US*). [➡TIRED, ASLEEP AND UNCONSCIOUS; 739] *Opposite:* energetic.

comb 1 *v* **untangle**, unsnarl, disentangle, get knots out of, run through. [➡ARRANGE AND CREATE ORDER; 358] 2 *v* **search**, examine, scrutinize, explore, rake, go over, scour. [➡SEEK POSSESSION AND SEARCH; 457] 3 *type of* **cosmetic tool**, *part of* **bird**. [➡PARTS OF A BIRD; 1006]

combat 1 *n* **battle**, fight, war, contest, struggle, fighting, warfare, conflict. [➡AGGRESSIVE EVENT; 39] 2 *v* **fight**, battle, oppose, contest, contend, struggle. [➡COMPETE, CONTEND, AND COMBAT; 304] 3 *v* **resist**, prevent, reduce, stop, tackle, fight back. [➡MAKE IMPOSSIBLE; 277]

combatant *n* **fighter**, soldier, enemy, warrior, participant, opponent, competitor. [➡UNCOOPERATIVE OR REBELLIOUS PERSON; 567]

combative *adj* **argumentative**, antagonistic, aggressive, belligerent, confrontational, bellicose, contentious. [➡IRRITATION AND ANGER; 542] *Opposite:* peaceable.

combat officer *n* [➡MILITARY PERSONNEL; 828]

combat zone *n* **battleground**, battlefield, frontline, theatre of war, war zone, trench. [➡WARFARE AND WAR; 830]

combination 1 *n* **mixture**, grouping, blend, amalgamation, recipe, mishmash. [➡COLLECTIONS AND MIXTURES OF THINGS; 1243] 2 *n* **arrangement**, permutation, code, pattern, order, sequence. [➡SYMBOLS, SIGNS, AND NUMBERS; 597]

See Compare and Contrast at **mixture**.

combine 1 *v* **unite**, join, merge, coalesce, mingle, come together, conjoin (*formal*), link, relate. [➡COMBINE AND MIX; 401] *Opposite:* divide. 2 *v* **mix**, blend, intermix, amalgamate, bring together, mingle, commingle (*literary*), fuse. [➡COMBINE AND MIX; 401] *Opposite:* separate. 3 *n* **syndicate**, cartel, bloc, trust, association, chain, conglomerate. [➡BUSINESS ENTERPRISES AND RELATED BODIES; 793] 4 *n* **harvester**, thresher, reaper. [➡BIKES, CARS, AND CARRIAGES; 1148]

combined *adj* **joint**, mutual, shared, collective, united, pooled. [➡ACTING WITH OTHERS; 286] *Opposite:* individual.

combine harvester *type of* **commercial or industrial vehicle**. [➡VEHICLES; 1144]

combustible *adj* **flammable**, inflammable, explosive, burnable, ignitable. [➡FIRE, FLAMMABILITY, AND BURNING; 1164]

combustion *n* **ignition**, fire, burning, incineration. [➡ENERGY GENERAL; 1160]

come 1 *v* **approach**, move towards, draw closer, get nearer, come up to. [➡PROCEED AND GO; 306] *Opposite:* leave. 2 *v* **arrive**, appear, turn up, get here, roll up, show your face. [➡ARRIVE; 12] *Opposite:* go. 3 *v* **happen**, occur, take place, fall, befall (*archaic or literary*). [➡HAPPEN; 27] 4 *v* **reach**, extend, stretch, go, touch. [➡EXIST IN A PLACE; 19] 5 *v* **originate**, hail from, derive, come from, arise, emanate. [➡GRADUALLY COME INTO EXISTENCE; 1]

come about *v* **happen**, occur, take place, come to pass (*archaic or literary*), transpire, fall out. [➡HAPPEN; 27]

come across 1 *v* **come by**, stumble across, meet, find, stumble upon, encounter, happen upon, come upon, fall upon, strike, get, obtain, acquire, luck into (*US*). [➡FIND; 464] *Opposite:* lose. 2 *v* **look**, impress, appear, seem, strike, give an impression. [➡SEEM TO BE SOMETHING; 58]

come alive *v* **bloom**, thrive, blossom, take off, enliven, brighten up, cheer up, liven. [➡GET BETTER; 376]

come along 1 *v* **appear**, arrive, turn up, show up (*informal*), occur, materialize. [➡ARRIVE; 12] *Opposite:* disappear. 2 *v* **progress**, make headway, proceed, advance, unfold, open up. [➡GET BETTER; 376] 3 *v* **accompany**, chaperon, escort, tag along, follow, attend, keep company. [➡ACCOMPANY AND FOLLOW; 338]

come apart *v* **tear**, fall apart, break, shatter, collapse, disintegrate. [➡TEAR, BREAK, AND CUT; 361]

come at *v* **rush**, fly, jump (*informal*), leap, pounce, attack, threaten, fly at, leap at. [➡MOVE FAST; 314]

come back 1 *v* **return**, reappear, flood back, rush back, revive. [➡ARRIVE; 12] *Opposite:* go away. 2 *v* (*US*) **reply**, answer, retort, respond, talk back, riposte, answer back, react, reciprocate. [➡REPLY AND ANSWER; 669]

comeback 1 *n* **retaliation**, reply, retort, response, rejoinder (*formal*), riposte, answer, witticism. [➡REPLY AND ANSWER; 669] 2 *n* **return**, revival, reinstatement, rebirth, regeneration, renewal, success story. [➡PROGRESS AND ADVANCEMENT; 214]

come between *v* **interfere**, set against, meddle, alienate, disaffect, separate, divide, estrange, pull apart. [➡SEPARATE AND DIVIDE; 402] *Opposite:* unite.

come by *v* **happen upon**, come upon, fall upon, stumble upon, come across, obtain, acquire, get, find, encounter, luck into (*US*). [➡GET; 421] *Opposite:* lose.

come clean (*informal*) *v* **bare**, reveal, confess, own up, tell the truth, make a clean breast of it, put your hand up to something, tell all. [➡ADMIT AND CONFESS; 616] *Opposite:* keep secret.

comedian *n* **humorist**, comic, stand-up, clown, wit, joker, jester, funny man. [➡WORKERS IN ENTERTAINMENT AND MEDIA; 873]

come down 1 *v* **decrease**, drop, go down, dip, plunge, plummet. [➡GO DOWNWARDS; 308] *Opposite:* go up. 2 *v* **lose status**, suffer reverses, know misfortune, have a run of bad luck, have a change of fortune. [➡FAIL OR BE UNSUCCESSFUL; 75]

comedown (*informal*) *n* **disillusionment**, blow, disappointment, letdown, downer (*slang*), reality check (*US informal*). [➡FAILURE; 77] *Opposite:* boost.

come down in favour of *v* [➡APPROVE AND CONFIRM; 647]

come down in sheets (*informal*) *v* [➡CLOUDY AND RAINY WEATHER; 1052]

come down in torrents *v* [➡CLOUDY AND RAINY WEATHER; 1052]

come down on *v* **tell off** (*informal*), take to task, pick on, scapegoat, come down on like a ton of bricks (*informal*), be hard on, scold, punish, chastise (*formal*), criticize, yell at, rebuke, reprimand, tear off a strip, have a go at (*informal*), chew out (*US informal*). [➡ACCUSE, BLAME, AND CRITICIZE; 642]

come down on like a ton of bricks (*informal*) *v* [➡ACCUSE, BLAME, AND CRITICIZE; 642]

come down on the side of *v* **support**, come down in favour of, favour, back, endorse, side. [➡MAKE DECISIONS AND CHOICES; 753] *Opposite:* oppose.

come down to *v* **signify**, amount to, mean, boil down to (*informal*), hinge on. [➡AMOUNT TO AND EQUAL; 70]

come down with *v* **contract**, sicken, incubate, take to your bed, catch, get, succumb. [➡FALL ILL, TREAT, AND RECOVER; 729] *Opposite:* fight off.

comedy *n* **funniness**, joking, amusement, entertainment, humour, wit, jesting (*literary*), pleasantry, slapstick, farce, clowning. [➡ENTERTAINMENT; 872] *Opposite:* tragedy.

come first 1 *v* **head**, top, be at the top of, be at the head of, be in the lead, win, triumph. [➡SUCCEED AND WIN; 79] *Opposite:* lose. 2 *v* **be your priority**, be your main concern, be the most important thing, be paramount, be the only thing that matters. [➡MOST IMPORTANT AND MAIN; 194]

come forward *v* **volunteer**, offer, put up your hand, present yourself, emerge, materialize, surface, appear. [➡AGREE; 646] *Opposite:* hold back.

come from 1 *v* **descend**, derive, issue, emanate, originate, emerge. [➡CAUSATION; 169] 2 *v* **originate from**, be from, hail from, live in, grew up in, have roots in. [➡EXIST IN A PLACE; 19]

come in 1 *v* **finish**, cross the line, be placed, finish up, end up. [➡COMPLETE AN ACTION; 264] 2 *v* **land**, berth, enter, arrive, pull in, touch down, dock. [➡ARRIVE BY TRANSPORT; 14] *Opposite:* depart.

come into *v* **inherit**, receive, be left, be bequeathed. [➡GET MONEY OR REWARD; 422]

come into being *v* **come about**, begin life, develop, take form, take shape. [➡GRADUALLY COME INTO EXISTENCE; 1]

come into bud *v* **blossom**, flower, burgeon (*literary*), bud, come to life. [➡GROW AND CULTIVATE; 352]

come into contact 1 *v* **meet**, encounter, experience, come across, have dealings with. [➡EXPERIENCE AND ENCOUNTER; 583] 2 *v* **touch**, brush against, be contaminated by, be infected by, meet, strike, come across. [➡CONTACT: TOUCH; 413]

come into flower *v* **blossom**, bloom, come into bud, flower, come to life. [➡GROW AND CULTIVATE; 352]

come into sight *v* **appear**, emerge, come into view, heave into view (*literary*), become visible. [➡APPEAR AND EMERGE; 3] *Opposite:* disappear.

comeliness (*archaic or literary*) *n* [➡PEOPLE'S PHYSICAL APPEARANCE; 476]

comely (*archaic or literary*) *adj* [➡PEOPLE'S PHYSICAL APPEARANCE; 476]

come off (*informal*) *v* **happen**, occur, take place, come about, succeed, work. [➡SUCCEED AND WIN; 79] *Opposite:* fail.

come on *v* **start**, begin, kick in (*informal*), go on, self-start, occur. [➡SUDDENLY COME INTO EXISTENCE; 2] *Opposite:* stop.

come out *v* **emerge**, materialize, appear, surface, come to light, leak out. [➡APPEAR AND EMERGE; 3]

come out of 1 *v* **originate**, grow, develop, arise, have roots in, be rooted in, come from. [➡GRADUALLY COME INTO EXISTENCE; 1] 2 *v* **survive**, live through, escape, endure, come through, get through. [➡TOLERATE AND ENDURE; 767]

come out on top *v* [➡SUCCEED AND WIN; 79]

come out with *v* **utter**, confess, admit, make known, blurt, broadcast. [➡ADMIT AND CONFESS; 616] *Opposite:* conceal.

come over 1 *v* **visit**, stop by, drop round, pop round (*informal*), pop in (*informal*), drop in, come round, call, call by, swing by (*US*). [➡INITIATE AND ESTABLISH COMMUNICATION; 681] 2 *v* **affect**, engulf, flow over, sweep over. [➡HAPPEN TO SOMEBODY; 30]

come round 1 *v* **visit**, stop by, pop in (*informal*), pop round (*informal*), call, call by, come by, come over, drop in, swing by (*US*). [➡ARRIVE; 12] 2 *v* **regain consciousness**, come to, revive, wake up, awaken, come to life. [➡WAKE AND REGAIN CONSCIOUSNESS; 725] *Opposite:* black out. 3 *v* **agree**, consent, comply, acquiesce, yield, compromise, change your mind, see eye to eye. [➡FORGET, FORGIVE, AND ACCEPT; 749]

comestible (*formal*) *adj* [➡FOOD; 1166]

comestibles (*formal*) *n* [➡FOOD; 1166]

comet *type of* **heavenly body**. [➡CELESTIAL BODIES; 1060]

come through *v* **survive**, endure, last, make it (*informal*), prevail, get through. [➡CONTINUE TO EXIST; 17]

come to 1 *v* **regain consciousness**, come round, awaken, wake up, revive, come to life, come around (*US*). [➡WAKE AND REGAIN CONSCIOUSNESS; 725] *Opposite:* black out. 2 *v* **tally**, amount to, total, add up to, equal, make. [➡AMOUNT TO AND EQUAL; 70]

come to a close *v* **end**, finish, conclude, come to an end, stop, terminate (*formal*), draw to a close. [➡STOP ACTING; 265] *Opposite:* begin.

come to a decision *v* **make up your mind**, reach a verdict, decide, make a choice, reach an agreement. [➡MAKE DECISIONS AND CHOICES; 753] *Opposite:* prevaricate.

come to a halt *v* **stop**, come to rest, come to a stop, shut down, stop in your tracks, stop dead, cease. [➡STOP ACTING; 265] *Opposite:* continue.

come to an end *v* **finish**, end, conclude, stop, cease, run out, run your term, fizzle out. [➡STOP ACTING; 265] *Opposite:* continue.

come to a standstill *v* **come to a halt**, stop dead, shut down, come to a stop, come to rest, stop in your tracks, cease. [➡STOP ACTING; 265] *Opposite:* continue.

come to blows *v* **fight**, exchange blows, start fighting, raise your fists, go for each other, have a fight. [➡COMPETE, CONTEND, AND COMBAT; 304]

come together 1 *v* **meet**, rendezvous, converge, gather together, congregate, assemble, group, rally, huddle, crowd together, get together. [➡GET CLOSER TOGETHER; 311] *Opposite:* disperse. 2 *v* **combine**, mingle, mix, unite, join together, join forces, team up, collaborate, cohere (*formal*), gel (*informal*). [➡GET CLOSER TOGETHER; 311] *Opposite:* separate.

come to grief *v* **fall flat**, go up in smoke, come to a bad end, collapse, fizzle, go on the rocks (*informal*), fail, fall short, come to a sticky end (*informal*), founder. [➡FAIL OR BE UNSUCCESSFUL; 75] *Opposite:* succeed.

come to grips with *v* **cope**, deal, manage, handle, tackle, come to terms with, accept, face up to, face, bite the bullet, confront. [➡CARRY OUT AN ACTION; 270]

come to life *v* **awaken**, come to, revive, regenerate, breathe, bloom, blossom, bud, regain consciousness, come round, come alive, perk up, come around (*US*). [➡WAKE AND REGAIN CONSCIOUSNESS; 725] *Opposite:* flag.

come to light *v* **leak out**, surface, emerge, come out, arise, be revealed, become public. [➡APPEAR AND EMERGE; 3]

come to naught (*archaic or literary*) *v* [➡FAIL OR BE UNSUCCESSFUL; 75]

come to nothing *v* **end in failure**, fail, end in tears, go down the tube (*informal*), come to naught (*archaic or literary*), fall to pieces, fall through, founder, collapse, go wrong. [➡FAIL OR BE UNSUCCESSFUL; 75] *Opposite:* succeed.

come to pass (*archaic or literary*) *v* **happen**, occur, come about, turn out, take place, transpire, end up, work out, finish up. [➡HAPPEN; 27]

come to rest *v* **pause**, stop, come to a halt, come to a standstill, halt, land, settle. [➡STOP ACTING; 265]

come to terms with *v* **come to grips with**, resolve, bite the bullet, handle, accept, deal with, cope, face, manage, face up to, confront. [➡FORGET, FORGIVE, AND ACCEPT; 749]

come up *v* **arise**, rise, crop up (*informal*), turn up, happen, occur, come about. [➡SUDDENLY COME INTO EXISTENCE; 2]

come up against *v* [➡EXPERIENCE AND ENCOUNTER; 583]

come up for air *v* **take a break**, relax, take a breather (*informal*), take five (*informal*), break off, rest. [➡STOP ACTING; 265] *Opposite:* continue.

come upon *v* **happen upon**, fall upon, come across, encounter, meet, stumble upon, find, bump into, chance upon, turn up. [➡FIND; 464]

comeuppance (*informal*) *n* **retaliation**, due, punishment, just deserts, reward, what you deserve, what's coming to you. [➡RESULTS AND OUTCOMES; 83]

come up to *v* **fill the bill**, match, meet, equal, satisfy, reach, fulfil. [➡EQUALITY; 155]

come up with *v* **discover**, create, produce, supply, find, get hold of, procure, get your hands on, furnish (*formal*). [➡GIVE AND PROVIDE; 431]

come what may *adv* **anyhow**, no matter what, regardless, anyway, whatever happens, nevertheless, in any case. [➡ALTHOUGH, NEVERTHELESS, AND DESPITE; 170]

comfort 1 *n* **wellbeing**, ease, luxury, cosiness, relief, security, relaxation, contentment. [➡TREAT; 211] *Opposite:* discomfort. 2 *n* **consolation**, reassurance, relief, cheer, solace, succour (*literary*), a sight for sore eyes. [➡TREAT; 211] *Opposite:* distress. 3 *v* **cheer**, cheer up, encourage, gladden, hearten, bolster. [➡SOOTHE AND CALM; 574] *Opposite:* depress. 4 *v* **pacify**, soothe, console, reassure, calm, relieve, ease, placate. [➡SOOTHE AND CALM; 574] *Opposite:* upset.

comfortable 1 *adj* **relaxed**, at ease, contented, happy, easy, calm. [➡CALMNESS, CONFIDENCE, AND COMPOSURE; 537] *Opposite:* on edge. 2 *adj* **comfy** (*informal*), snug, cosy, relaxing, restful, secure. [➡PHYSICALLY PLEASANT; 187] *Opposite:* uncomfortable. 3 *adj* **well-off**, well-heeled (*informal*), well-to-do, rich, wealthy, affluent. [➡WEALTH AND WEALTHY; 891] *Opposite:* poor.

comfortably *adv* **at ease**, restfully, contentedly, happily, securely, easily. [➡CALMNESS, CONFIDENCE, AND COMPOSURE; 537] *Opposite:* uncomfortably.

comforted *adj* **consoled**, supported, reassured, solaced, cheered, gladdened. [➡CALMNESS, CONFIDENCE, AND COMPOSURE; 537] *Opposite:* distressed.

comforter 1 *n* **consoler**, reliever, comfort, ray of sunshine. [➡TREAT; 211] 2 *n* (*US*) **quilt**, eiderdown, duvet, continental quilt. [➡SOFT FURNISHINGS, LINEN, AND DRAPERY; 860]

comforting *adj* **heartening**, bolstering, uplifting, reassuring, cheering, soothing, encouraging, calming, consoling, kindly, kind. [➡EMOTIONALLY PLEASANT; 188] *Opposite:* upsetting.

comfy (*informal*) *adj* **comfortable**, secure, snug, cosy, relaxing, restful. [➡PHYSICALLY PLEASANT; 187] *Opposite:* uncomfortable.

comic 1 *adj* **amusing**, funny, humorous, droll, sidesplitting, hilarious, rib-tickling (*informal*), laughable, comical. [➡FUNNY AND AMUSING; 217] *Opposite:* tragic. 2 *n* **joker**, jester, comedian, stand-up, clown, wit, funny man, humorist. [➡WORKERS IN ENTERTAINMENT AND MEDIA; 873] 3 *n* **comic book**, magazine, funny book, funny paper, comic strip, graphic novel. [➡NEWSPAPERS; 606]

See Compare and Contrast at **funny**.

comical *adj* **amusing**, funny, humorous, droll, hilarious, sidesplitting, rib-tickling (*informal*), laughable, comic. [➡FUNNY AND AMUSING; 217] *Opposite:* tragic.

See Compare and Contrast at **funny**.

comicality *n* [➡FUNNY AND AMUSING; 217]

comicalness *n* [➡FUNNY AND AMUSING; 217]

comic opera *type of* **classical music.** [➡MUSIC, SONGS, AND SINGING; 907]

comics *n* **funnies**, comic books, comic strips, cartoons, cartoon strips, caricatures. [➡NEWSPAPERS; 606]

coming 1 *adj* **forthcoming**, pending, impending, approaching, imminent, near-term, future, next, upcoming (*US*). [➡FUTURE; 86] *Opposite:* past. 2 *n* **emergence**, launch, arrival, appearance, approach, entrance, advent. [➡ARRIVAL; 13] *Opposite:* departure.

comings and goings *n* [➡EVENTS AND OCCURRENCES; 35]

coming up *adj* **imminent**, impending, forthcoming, about to happen, on the cards (*informal*), pending, in the offing, on the agenda, on the horizon, upcoming (*US*). [➡FUTURE; 86]

comma *type of* **punctuation mark.** [➡ASPECTS OF LANGUAGE; 683]

command 1 *n* **order**, directive, commandment, demand, charge, instruction, mandate, decree. [➡REQUEST AND DEMAND; 664] 2 *n* **knowledge**, facility, knack, grasp, expertise, understanding, appreciation. [➡KNOWLEDGE AND WISDOM; 559] 3 *n* **authority**, control, rule, domination, power, sway, dominion. [➡STRENGTH; 202] 4 *v* **order**, direct, demand, charge, instruct, decree. [➡REQUEST AND DEMAND; 664] *Opposite:* obey. 5 *v* **control**, dominate, rule, lead, be in charge, direct. [➡CAUSE OR COMPEL TO ACT; 272]

commandant *n* **superior**, chief, commander, chief officer, commanding officer, commander in chief. [➡MILITARY PERSONNEL; 828]

commandeer *v* **seize**, requisition, hijack, take, grab, appropriate, confiscate, capture, annex. [➡TAKE SOMETHING AWAY; 426] *Opposite:* request.

commandeering *n* **appropriation**, acquisition, confiscation, seizure, takeover, capture, hijacking, annexing, taking. [➡TAKE SOMETHING AWAY; 426]

commander *n* **superior**, chief, commandant, chief officer, commanding officer, commander in chief. [➡MILITARY PERSONNEL; 828]

commanding *adj* **impressive**, forceful, strong, powerful, imposing, authoritative, unassailable, imperious, masterful. [➡STRENGTH; 202] *Opposite:* weak.

commandingly *adv* **authoritatively**, impressively, imperiously, masterfully, majestically, regally, augustly (*formal*), grandly, strikingly. [➡ELOQUENT, TALKATIVE AND LONG-WINDED; 633] *Opposite:* timidly.

command module *part of* **spacecraft.** [➡SPACE VEHICLES; 1062]

commando *n* [➡MILITARY PERSONNEL; 828]

commemorate *v* **honour**, remember, celebrate, observe, venerate, memorialize. [➡REMEMBER; 747] *Opposite:* ignore.

commemoration *n* **memorial**, tribute, honour, remembrance, service, commemorative (*US*). [➡CEREMONIES AND ANNIVERSARIES; 38]

commemorative 1 *adj* **memorial**, in memory, honouring, dedicatory, celebratory. [➡CEREMONIES AND ANNIVERSARIES; 38] 2 *n* (*US*) **remembrance**, memorial, tribute, commemoration. [➡CEREMONIES AND ANNIVERSARIES; 38]

commence (*formal*) *v* **begin**, start, originate, inaugurate, instigate, initiate, launch, embark. *Opposite:* terminate. (*formal*). [➡START AN ACTION; 261]

commencement 1 *n* (*formal*) **beginning**, start, origination, inauguration, instigation, initiation, commencing (*formal*), dawn, dawning, onset, opening, startup. [➡BEGINNING; 53] *Opposite:* end. 2 *n* (*US formal*) **graduation**, graduation day, graduation ceremony. [➡LESSONS, COURSE WORK, AND EXAMINATIONS; 842]

commend 1 *v* **praise**, speak well of, acclaim, extol, laud, mention, applaud. [➡PRAISE AND ENCOURAGE; 648] *Opposite:* denigrate. 2 *v* **entrust**, convey, hand over, consign, commit, give. [➡GIVE AND PROVIDE; 431] *Opposite:* keep.

commendable *adj* **praiseworthy**, admirable, worthy, creditable, laudable, estimable. [➡ADMIRABLE AND COMMENDABLE; 186] *Opposite:* lamentable.

commendation 1 *n* **praise**, approval, recommendation, acclamation, approbation. [➡APPROVE AND CONFIRM; 647] *Opposite:* criticism. 2 *n* **award**, citation, certificate, honour, special mention, honourable mention, medal, prize. [➡REWARDS AND AWARDS; 440]

commensurate (*formal*) *adj* **equal**, proportionate, corresponding, appropriate, adequate, matching. [➡EQUALITY; 155] *Opposite:* disproportionate.

comment 1 *n* **remark**, observation, statement, aside, reference, mention, note, dictum (*formal*), good word. [➡SUGGEST, HINT, AND COMMENT; 613] 2 *n* **judgment**, observation, criticism, analysis, critique. [➡SUGGEST, HINT, AND COMMENT; 613] 3 *n* **explanation**, interpretation, clarification, expansion, commentary, interpolation, note, annotation. [➡SUGGEST, HINT, AND COMMENT; 613] 4 *v* **observe**, remark, mention, state, note, point out. [➡SUGGEST, HINT, AND COMMENT; 613]

commentary 1 *n* **comment**, explanation, observation, note, annotation, clarification, interpretation. [➡SUGGEST, HINT, AND COMMENT; 613] 2 *n* **review**, essay, report, treatise, thesis, analysis. [➡ANALYTICAL NONFICTION WRITING; 593]

commentate *v* **describe**, explain, report, analyse, review, expound, pontificate, discuss, interpret. [➡SUGGEST, HINT, AND COMMENT; 613]

commentator *n* **critic**, observer, reporter, analyst, reviewer, pundit, interpreter. [➡WORKERS IN ENTERTAINMENT AND MEDIA; 873]

commerce *n* **trade**, business, market, export, import, buying, selling, exchange, retail, wholesale. [➡BUSINESS; 792]

commercial 1 *adj* **business**, business-related, trade, industrial, mercantile, for-profit. [➡BUSINESS; 792] *Opposite:* charitable. 2 *adj* **profitable**, saleable, marketable, viable, moneymaking, profitmaking. [➡BUSINESS; 792] 3 *n* **advertisement**, ad, infomercial, advert (*informal*), trailer. [➡ADVER-

TISING AND PUBLICITY; 605] 4 *type of* **broadcast.** [➡TELEVISION AND RADIO; 607]

commingle (*literary*) *v* [➡COMBINE AND MIX; 401]

comminute *v* [➡HARDEN, CONGEAL, DRY; 388]

commis chef *n* [➡DOMESTIC AND KITCHEN WORKERS; 850]

commiserate *v* **sympathize**, pity, empathize, show compassion, offer condolences, console. [➡GIVING VENT TO EMOTIONS; 680]

commiseration *n* [➡COMPASSION AND FORGIVENESS; 552]

commiserations *interj* **bad luck**, never mind, better luck next time, hard luck, sorry. [➡EXPRESSIONS OF REGRET; 548] *Opposite:* congratulations.

commission 1 *n* **payment**, fee, cut (*informal*), costs, percentage, expenses. [➡INCOME; 461] 2 *n* **task**, assignment, duty, job, charge, mission. [➡JOB; 833] 3 *n* **committee**, authority, agency, administration, board, group, working group. [➡GROUPS WITH A COMMON INTEREST; 938] 4 *n* **authority**, power, responsibility, position, appointment. [➡WORK IN GENERAL; 298] 5 *n* **formal order**, command, directive, instruction, charge, contract, assignment, warrant. [➡REQUEST AND DEMAND; 664] 6 *v* **assign**, appoint, authorize, contract, order, hire. [➡CONFER STATUS; 459]

commissioner *n* **official**, officer, representative, administrator. [➡POLITICAL OFFICES AND POLITICIANS; 808]

commit 1 *v* **obligate**, pledge, bind, promise, oblige, require, constrain, compel. [➡PROMISE AND ASSURE; 685] 2 *v* **earmark**, designate, dedicate, reserve, devote, pledge. [➡PROMISE AND ASSURE; 685] 3 *v* **do**, perform, execute, carry out, perpetrate, cause. [➡CARRY OUT AN ACTION; 270] 4 *v* **entrust**, give, consign, place, hand over, assign, commend, confide, turn over. [➡GIVE AND PROVIDE; 431]

commit hara-kiri *v* [➡DIE; 922]

commitment 1 *n* **promise**, pledge, vow, obligation, assurance, word, guarantee, warrant, binder (*US*). [➡PROMISE AND ASSURE; 685] 2 *n* **dedication**, loyalty, devotion, steadfastness, allegiance, faithfulness, staunchness. [➡HARD-WORKING AND COMMITTED; 501] *Opposite:* indifference. 3 *n* **obligation**, duty, responsibility, liability, charge. [➡WORK IN GENERAL; 298]

commit suicide *v* [➡DIE; 922]

commit suttee *v* [➡DIE; 922]

committed *adj* **devoted**, dedicated, loyal, staunch, steadfast, unswerving, faithful, dyed-in-the-wool. [➡HARD-WORKING AND COMMITTED; 501] *Opposite:* uncommitted.

committee *n* **group**, board, team, commission, working group, agency. [➡GROUPS OF PEOPLE; 935]

commit to memory *v* [➡REMEMBER; 747]

commode *type of* **cabinet.** [➡FURNITURE; 858]

commodious *adj* **spacious**, roomy, capacious, sizable, ample. [➡LARGE; 1192] *Opposite:* cramped.

commodity *n* **product**, service, goods, article of trade. [➡BUSINESS PRODUCTS; 796]

common 1 *adj* **shared**, mutual, joint, public, for all, communal, collective, conjoint, corporate. [➡BELONGING OR RELATING TO PEOPLE; 943] *Opposite:* individual. 2 *adj* **everyday**, usual, customary, familiar, normal, nothing special, ordinary, commonplace, conventional, unexceptional, regular, popular. [➡ORDINARINESS; 245] *Opposite:* extraordinary. 3 *adj* **widespread**, frequent, general, universal, familiar, regular, generic, commonplace. [➡ORDINARINESS; 245] *Opposite:* rare. 4 *adj* **vulgar**, coarse, ill-mannered, rough, low-class, unrefined. [➡LEVEL OF EDUCATION AND SOPHISTICATION; 894] *Opposite:* refined. 5 *n* **green**, park, open space, playing field, playground, recreational area, recreation ground. [➡THE COUNTRYSIDE AND OUTDOOR SPACES; 1070]

common denominator *n* **shared quality**, shared belief, commonality, universal, universality. [➡CONNECTION; 144]

commoner *n* [➡CLASS STATUS; 889]

commonly *adv* **usually**, normally, frequently, generally, regularly, universally, ordinarily. [➡USUALLY; 108] *Opposite:* unusually.

commonness *n* **ordinariness**, normalness, frequency, prevalence, regularity. [➡ORDINARINESS; 245]

common or garden *adj* [➡ORDINARINESS; 245]

commonplace 1 *adj* **ordinary**, everyday, usual, routine, common, conventional, normal, familiar, unexceptional. [➡ORDINARINESS; 245] *Opposite:* extraordinary. 2 *adj* **dull**, pedestrian, hackneyed, obvious, stale, unoriginal, trite, tired, uninteresting, humdrum. [➡BORING AND UNINTERESTING; 235] *Opposite:* original.

commonplaceness *n* [➡ORDINARINESS; 245]

commons *type of* **eating place.** [➡HOTELS, RESTAURANTS, AND CLUBS; 1081]

common sense *n* **good judgment**, horse sense (*informal*), good sense, practicality, realism, nous (*informal*), knowledge, judgment, reasonableness. [➡POSITIVE INTELLECTUAL CHARACTERISTICS; 525]

commonsense *adj* [➡THE NATURE OF IDEAS; 772]

commonsensical *adj* [➡THE NATURE OF IDEAS; 772]

commonwealth *n* **nation**, people, nationality, state, country, kingdom, republic. [➡TERRITORIES AND GROUPS OF NATIONS; 1067]

commotion *n* **ruckus**, tumult, uproar, turmoil, hubbub, disorder, upheaval, hullabaloo, fuss, din, stir, disturbance, furore, to-do (*informal*). [➡CHAOS AND UPROAR; 51] *Opposite:* peace.

communal *adj* **shared**, public, collective, joint, mutual. [➡BELONGING OR RELATING TO PEOPLE; 943] *Opposite:* individual.

communally *adv* **mutually**, jointly, collectively, together, publicly. [➡RECIPROCITY AND INTERDEPENDENCE; 148] *Opposite:* individually.

commune 1 *n* **community**, collective, collective farm, kibbutz, cooperative. [➡HUMAN SETTLEMENTS; 1069] 2 *v* **communicate**, converse, empathize, feel, connect, be in touch with. [➡INITIATE AND ESTABLISH COMMUNICATION; 681]

communicable *adj* **infectious**, catching, transmissible, contagious, transmittable. [➡SICKNESS; 730]

communicant *n* [➡RELIGIOUS PEOPLE; 779]

communicate 1 *v* **converse**, talk, speak, commune, be in touch, correspond, write, be in contact. [➡TWO-WAY COMMUNICATION; 608] 2 *v* **convey**, share, impart, transmit, reveal, put out, publicize. [➡INFORM AND ANNOUNCE; 612] 3 *v* **connect**, interconnect, lead into, link, join, transfer. [➡EXIST IN CLOSE PROXIMITY; 21]

communication 1 *n* **contact**, interaction, consultation, transfer, exchange, transmission. [➡COMMUNICATION; 603] 2 *n* **message**, communiqué, announcement, statement, letter, email, phone call, fax. [➡COMMUNICATION; 603]

communications 1 *n* **infrastructure**, public services, transportation, transport network, water supply, power supply. [➡COMMUNICATION NETWORKS; 1104] 2 *n* **telecommunications**, broadcasting, postal system, data lines, network. [➡COMMUNICATION; 603]

communicative *adj* **talkative**, open, forthcoming, outgoing, unrestrained, chatty, expansive. [➡ELOQUENT, TALKATIVE AND LONG-WINDED; 633] *Opposite:* restrained.

communion *n* **unity**, spiritual union, empathy, closeness, relationship, intimacy. [➡CONNECTION; 144]

communiqué *n* **announcement**, statement, communication, press release, bulletin, report, dispatch, message. [➡LETTERS AND WRITTEN MESSAGES; 585]

communism *n* **collectivism**, socialism, communalism, Marxism, Leninism, Trotskyism, Maoism. [➡PHILOSOPHIES AND BELIEFS; 781]

communist *n* **socialist**, collectivist, communalist, Marxist, Trotskyist, Maoist, red (*informal disapproving*). [➡PHILOSOPHICAL AND POLITICAL THINKERS; 782] *Opposite:* capitalist.

community 1 *n* **neighbourhood**, area, village, hamlet, commune. [➡HUMAN SETTLEMENTS; 1069] 2 *n* **kinship**, unity, identity, cooperation, spirit, convergence, similarity. [➡SIMILARITY; 149] *Opposite:* isolation. 3 *n* **society**, public, people, population, group. [➡GROUPS IN SOCIETY; 940]

commute 1 *v* **travel**, go back and forth, shuttle. [➡TRAVEL: WAYS OF TRAVELLING; 321] 2 *v* **convert**, alter, exchange, transform, substitute, change, transmute, metamorphose. [➡CHANGE ONE THING FOR ANOTHER; 399]

commuter *n* [➡WORKER; 836]

compact 1 *adj* **dense**, solid, packed in, packed together, compressed, compacted, condensed, squashed, squeezed, close. [➡DENSITY AND CONSISTENCY; 1206] *Opposite:* loose. 2 *adj* **small**, neat, trim, tiny, miniature, pocket-sized, reduced, efficient. [➡SMALL; 1194] *Opposite:* large. 3 *v* **compress**, pack, squeeze, squash, tamp, press, condense. [➡CHANGE OF SIZE: SMALLER; 394] *Opposite:* loosen. 4 *type of* **car**. [➡BIKES, CARS, AND CARRIAGES; 1148] 5 *n* **contract**, pact, agreement, deal, treaty. [➡PROMISE AND ASSURE; 685]

compact disc *part of* **audio equipment**. [➡AUDIO EQUIPMENT; 1138]

compact disc player *type of* **audio equipment**. [➡AUDIO EQUIPMENT; 1138]

compactly *adv* **efficiently**, neatly, trimly, closely, densely. [➡DENSITY AND CONSISTENCY; 1206] *Opposite:* loosely.

compactness 1 *n* **density**, solidity, compression, firmness. [➡DENSITY AND CONSISTENCY; 1206] *Opposite:* looseness. 2 *n* **smallness**, neatness, trimness, tininess, miniaturization. [➡ORDER AND ORGANISATION; 207] *Opposite:* largeness.

companion 1 *n* **friend**, mate, buddy (*US informal*), chum (*informal*), acquaintance, confidant, colleague. [➡FRIENDS; 963] 2 *n* **escort**, attendant, fellow traveller. [➡FRIENDS; 963]

companionability *n* [➡FRIENDLINESS AND SOCIABILITY; 495]

companionable *adj* **friendly**, sociable, close, intimate, chummy (*informal*), pally (*informal*). [➡FRIENDLINESS AND SOCIABILITY; 495] *Opposite:* frosty.

companionship *n* **company**, friendship, camaraderie, comradeship, esprit de corps. [➡RELATIONSHIP TO ANOTHER; 973] *Opposite:* enmity.

company 1 *n* **business**, corporation, firm, concern, enterprise, establishment, house, syndicate. [➡BUSINESS ENTERPRISES AND RELATED BODIES; 793] 2 *n* **companionship**, friendship, camaraderie, comradeship, esprit de corps. [➡RELATIONSHIP TO ANOTHER; 973] *Opposite:* isolation. 3 *n* **group**, crowd, circle, set, party, coterie, gathering, band, assembly, congregation. [➡FRIENDS AND ACQUAINTANCES; 936] *Opposite:* individual. 4 *n* **visitors**, guests, friends, companions, invitees. [➡FRIENDS; 963] 5 *n* **theatre company**, troupe, theatre group, ballet, touring company, concert party, band, corps, troop. [➡PERFORMERS; 905]

comparable *adj* **similar**, analogous, akin, equal, equivalent, as good as, like. [➡SIMILARITY; 149] *Opposite:* dissimilar.

comparative *adj* **relative**, reasonable, fair. [➡TO A CERTAIN EXTENT; 134] *Opposite:* absolute.

compare 1 *v* **evaluate**, contrast, assess, measure up, match up to, weigh against, put side by side, balance, judge. [➡EXAMINE AND ASSESS; 754] 2 *v* **liken**, associate, link, relate, equate. [➡CREATING CONNECTIONS; 145] 3 *v* **equal**, match, measure up, parallel, compete, rival, stand the test, stand the pace. [➡SUCCEED AND WIN; 79]

compare notes *v* **exchange information**, tell, relate, share, pass on, swap opinions, trade. [➡TWO-WAY COMMUNICATION; 608]

comparison 1 *n* **contrast**, judgment, assessment, evaluation, appraisal. [➡EXAMINE AND ASSESS; 754] 2 *n* **association**, link, relationship, similarity, likeness, resemblance, difference, divergence, contrast, affinity, analogy, semblance, parallel. [➡CONNECTION; 144]

compartment 1 *n* **cubicle**, booth, partition, box, stall. [➡ALCOVES, CUBICLES, AND COMPARTMENTS; 1095] 2 *part of* **train**. [➡RAILWAYS; 1106]

compass 1 *n* **scope**, range, area, extent, breadth, remit. [➡SIZE AND DIMENSIONS; 1191] 2 *type of* **measuring device**. [➡MEASURING DEVICES; 1122]

compassion *n* **sympathy**, empathy, concern, kindness, consideration, care, kind-heartedness, benevolence. [➡COMPASSION AND FORGIVENESS; 552] *Opposite:* coldness.

compassionate *adj* **sympathetic**, empathetic, feeling, concerned, kind, kindly, kind-hearted, considerate, caring, gentle, benevolent. [➡GENEROSITY AND KINDNESS; 496] *Opposite:* unfeeling.

compassionless *adj* [➡UNFRIENDLINESS AND UNSOCIABILITY; 505]

compatible 1 *adj* **well-matched**, like-minded, well-suited, companionable, friendly, attuned, harmonious. [➡HARMONY; 156] *Opposite:* incompatible. 2 *adj* **matching**, fitting, consistent, corresponding, harmonizing, congruent (*formal*). [➡HARMONY; 156] *Opposite:* incompatible.

compatriot *n* **national**, fellow citizen, countryman, countrywoman. [➡SUPPORTERS, PROTECTORS, AND COMPATRIOTS; 970] *Opposite:* foreigner.

compel *v* **force**, induce, require, coerce, oblige, make, twist somebody's arm (*informal*), lean on (*informal*), constrain. [➡CAUSE OR COMPEL TO ACT; 272]

compelling 1 *adj* **convincing**, persuasive, gripping, captivating, fascinating, enthralling, absorbing, exciting. [➡INTERESTING AND MEANINGFUL; 191] *Opposite:* unconvincing. 2 *adj* **forceful**, powerful, urgent, undeniable, insistent, involuntary, compulsive. [➡STRENGTH; 202]

compendium *n* [➡COLLECTIONS AND MIXTURES OF THINGS; 1243]

compensate 1 *v* **recompense**, reimburse, pay off, pay compensation, pay damages, pay costs, give back, pay, reward. [➡REWARD; 437] 2 *v* **balance**, counterweigh, counteract, counterbalance, offset, make up for. [➡CORRECT AND PUT RIGHT; 378]

compensation 1 *n* **recompense**, return, reward, reimbursement, payment, damages, costs, reparation. [➡REWARDS AND AWARDS; 440] 2 *n* **advantage**, reward, recompense, return, benefit, plus (*informal*). [➡TREAT; 211]

compete 1 *v* **contest**, contend, vie, strive, participate, take part, enter, play. [➡COMPETE, CONTEND, AND COMBAT; 304] 2 *v* **compare**, equal, measure up, rival, match, parallel, stand the test, stand the pace. [➡SUCCEED AND WIN; 79]

competence *n* **capability**, ability, skill, fitness, aptitude, proficiency, competency, know-how (*informal*), experience, expertise. [➡SKILLS, TALENTS, AND ABILITIES; 527] *Opposite:* ineptitude.

See Compare and Contrast at **ability**.

competent *adj* **able**, capable, skilled, proficient, adept, expert, fit, knowledgeable, experienced. [➡TALENTED AND SKILFUL; 528] *Opposite:* inept.

competition 1 *n* **rivalry**, opposition, antagonism, war, struggle. [➡NON-AGGRESSIVE/SPORTING EVENT; 40] *Opposite:* cooperation. 2 *n* **contest**, match, race, struggle, battle. [➡NON-AGGRESSIVE/SPORTING EVENT; 40]

competitive 1 *adj* **spirited**, aggressive, bloodthirsty, ready for action, driven, gung ho (*informal*), cutthroat. [➡BOSSY AND OVERBEARING; 517] *Opposite:* passive. 2 *adj* **reasonable**, modest, good, inexpensive, cheap, viable. [➡CHEAP AND INEXPENSIVE; 222] *Opposite:* expensive.

competitor *n* **contestant**, participant, entrant, player, opponent, challenger, contender, rival, sportsperson. [➡COMPETITORS; 41]

compilation 1 *n* **gathering**, compiling, collecting, assembling, composing, collation, drawing together, bringing together, accumulation. [➡ARRANGE AND CREATE ORDER; 358] *Opposite:* dispersal. 2 *n* **collection**, set, anthology, assemblage, edition. [➡COLLECTIONS AND MIXTURES OF THINGS; 1243]

compile 1 *v* **amass**, accumulate, collect, bring together, assemble, gather, pile up, hoard. [➡STORE AND KEEP; 454] *Opposite:* disperse. 2 *v* **list**, compose, set down, register, record, put together. [➡RECORD SOMETHING; 372]

complacency *n* **satisfaction**, smugness, self-satisfaction, contentment, gratification, self-righteousness (*disapproving*). [➡CALMNESS, CONFIDENCE, AND COMPOSURE; 537] *Opposite:* anxiety.

complacent *adj* **satisfied**, self-satisfied, smug, content, contented, self-righteous (*disapproving*). [➡NEUTRALITY AND INDIFFERENCE; 554] *Opposite:* anxious.

complain *v* **protest**, criticize, grumble, whine, whinge (*informal*), carp, find fault, nitpick, nag, moan (*informal*), murmur, object, knock (*slang*), grouse, gripe (*informal*). [➡COMPLAIN AND NAG; 687] *Opposite:* praise.

Compare and Contrast: ***complain, object, protest, grumble, grouse, carp, gripe, whine, nag***

CORE MEANING: TO INDICATE DISSATISFACTION WITH SOMETHING

complain to express unhappiness about a situation; ***object*** to be opposed to something, or express opposition to it; ***protest*** to express strong disapproval or disagreement; ***grumble*** to disagree in a discontented way, possibly repeatedly or continually; ***grouse*** to complain regularly and continually, often in a way that is not constructive; ***carp*** to keep complaining or finding fault, especially about unimportant things; ***gripe*** (*informal*) to complain continually and irritatingly; ***whine*** to complain in an unreasonable, repeated, or irritating way; ***nag*** to find fault with somebody regularly and repeatedly.

complainer *n* **whiner**, objector, protester, moaner (*informal*), grumbler, faultfinder, nitpicker, carper, knocker (*informal*), whinger (*informal*). [➡GRUMPY AND NEGATIVE PEOPLE; 953]

complaint 1 *n* **grievance**, criticism, protest, grumble, whinge (*informal*), moan (*informal*), objection. [➡COMPLAIN AND NAG; 687] *Opposite:* praise. 2 *n* **illness**, condition, ailment, disorder. [➡SICKNESS; 730]

complaisant *adj* [➡THE WILL AND WILLINGNESS; 564]

complement 1 *n* **accompaniment**, foil, match, balance, counterpart, supplement, pair. [➡HARMONY; 156] 2 *n* **quota**, set, allowance, quantity, number, amount. [➡AMOUNT AND QUANTITY; 112] 3 *v* **complete**, add, supplement, round out, make up for, perfect, accompany. [➡CHANGE OF SIZE: BIGGER; 393] *Opposite:* detract. 4 *v* **balance**, set off, harmonize, match, be a foil for. [➡HARMONY; 156] *Opposite:* clash.

complementary *adj* **balancing**, opposite, matching, corresponding. [➡HARMONY; 156] *Opposite:* clashing.

complete 1 *adj* **whole**, comprehensive, wide-ranging, broad, ample, widespread, far-reaching, thorough, all-embracing, all-inclusive, overall, extensive, full. [➡WHOLE-

NESS AND COMPLETENESS; 199] *Opposite:* partial. **2** *adj* **finished**, completed, concluded, accomplished, fulfilled, done. [➡WHOLENESS AND COMPLETENESS; 199] *Opposite:* unfinished. **3** *adj* **absolute**, extreme, utter, great, downright, perfect, total, entire. [➡ABSOLUTE AND ABSOLUTELY; 131] **4** *v* **finish**, finalize, conclude, end, bring to an end, put the last touches to, put the finishing touches to. [➡COMPLETE AN ACTION; 264] *Opposite:* start. **5** *v* **accomplish**, achieve, fulfil, carry out, realize, perfect. [➡COMPLETE AN ACTION; 264]

completed *adj* **finished**, accomplished, finalized, done, complete, concluded, over, over and done with, ended. [➡WHOLENESS AND COMPLETENESS; 199] *Opposite:* unfinished.

completely *adv* **totally**, wholly, entirely, fully, finally, utterly, absolutely, downright, from top to bottom, from tip to toe. [➡WHOLENESS AND COMPLETENESS; 199] *Opposite:* partially.

completeness *n* **wholeness**, fullness, extensiveness, comprehensiveness, inclusiveness, broadness. [➡WHOLENESS AND COMPLETENESS; 199] *Opposite:* partiality.

completion *n* **conclusion**, close, achievement, accomplishment, end, finishing point. [➡END; 54] *Opposite:* start.

complex **1** *adj* **complicated**, difficult, convoluted, involved, dense, byzantine, thorny. [➡DIFFICULTY AND COMPLEXITY; 243] *Opposite:* simple. **2** *adj* **multifaceted**, compound, composite, multipart, intricate, multifarious. [➡POSITIVELY COMPLEX OR COMPLICATED; 218] *Opposite:* simple. **3** *n* (*informal*) **hang-up** (*informal*), fixation, psychosis, neurosis (*dated*), phobia, obsession, obsession. [➡PSYCHOLOGY AND THE MIND; 770] **4** *n* **development**, centre, campus, facility, multiplex. [➡BUILDING AND ARCHITECTURE; 1075]

complexion **1** *n* **skin**, face, appearance, features. [➡COMPLEXION; 481] **2** *n* **nature**, character, cast, tone, aspect. [➡APPEARANCE AND ATMOSPHERE; 1236]

complexity *n* **difficulty**, intricacy, complication, involvedness, density, convolution. [➡DIFFICULTY AND COMPLEXITY; 243] *Opposite:* simplicity.

compliance **1** *n* **obedience**, acquiescence, agreement, submission, amenability, amenableness, passivity. [➡THE WILL AND WILLINGNESS; 564] *Opposite:* defiance. **2** *n* **conformity**, observance, accordance, fulfilment. [➡HARMONY; 156] *Opposite:* noncompliance.

compliant **1** *adj* **acquiescent**, obedient, biddable, yielding, amenable, accommodating. [➡THE WILL AND WILLINGNESS; 564] *Opposite:* defiant. **2** *adj* **conforming**, in compliance, compatible. [➡HARMONY; 156] *Opposite:* noncompliant.

compliantly *adv* **acquiescently**, passively, amenably, submissively, obediently, accommodatingly. [➡THE WILL AND WILLINGNESS; 564] *Opposite:* defiantly.

complicate *v* **make difficulties**, set hurdles, thwart, confound, confuse, muddle, muddy, obscure, obfuscate. [➡CREATE DISORDER AND CAUSE CHAOS; 359] *Opposite:* simplify.

complicated *adj* **complex**, difficult, intricate, byzantine, thorny, dense, convoluted, problematical, full of twists and turns, problematic. [➡DIFFICULTY AND COMPLEXITY; 243] *Opposite:* simple.

complication *n* **difficulty**, snag, problem, impediment, obstacle, hurdle, barrier. [➡PROBLEM; 257] *Opposite:* solution.

complicity *n* **involvement**, collusion, collaboration, connivance, participation, support. [➡RECIPROCITY AND INTERDEPENDENCE; 148] *Opposite:* detachment.

compliment **1** *n* **praise**, commendation, tribute, encomium (*formal*), accolade, approval, kudos. [➡PRAISE AND ENCOURAGE; 648] *Opposite:* criticism. **2** *v* **flatter**, praise, admire, congratulate, approve, pay tribute to, butter up (*informal*). [➡PRAISE AND ENCOURAGE; 648] *Opposite:* criticize.

complimentary **1** *adj* **flattering**, admiring, kind, gracious, civil, approving. [➡EXPRESSING RESPECT AND APPROVAL; 638] *Opposite:* critical. **2** *adj* **free**, gratis, courtesy, on the house, free of charge. [➡GIFTS; 439] *Opposite:* full price.

comply *v* **obey**, fulfil, observe, conform, abide by, submit. [➡OBEY AND ABIDE BY; 302] *Opposite:* disobey.

component *n* **constituent**, module, section, factor, element, piece, part, cog. [➡QUALITIES AND CHARACTERISTICS; 1190] *Opposite:* whole.

comportment (*formal*) *n* **behaviour**, conduct, bearing, deportment (*formal*), carriage (*formal*), manner, style, manners, attitude, demeanour. [➡TEMPERAMENT AND BEHAVIOUR; 493]

compose **1** *v* **make up**, comprise, constitute, combine, unite. [➡COMBINE AND MIX; 401] **2** *v* **arrange**, order, set out, dispose (*formal*), marshal, organize, put together. [➡ARRANGE AND CREATE ORDER; 358] *Opposite:* disturb. **3** *v* **create**, invent, make up, make, compile, write. [➡INSTITUTE AND INAUGURATE; 349]

composed *adj* **calm**, collected, self-possessed, serene, unruffled, poised, tranquil. [➡CALMNESS, CONFIDENCE, AND COMPOSURE; 537] *Opposite:* flustered.

composer *n* **creator**, originator, musician, writer, author. [➡MUSICIANS AND SINGERS; 908]

compose yourself *v* **calm yourself**, control yourself, calm down, get a grip on yourself (*informal*), get your act together (*informal*), chill out (*slang*), get a hold of yourself, settle down, relax, unwind. [➡CHANGE OF MOOD AND COMPOSURE; 581] *Opposite:* panic.

composite **1** *adj* **compound**, complex, multiple, multipart, multifactorial, multifarious. [➡DIFFERENCE; 150] *Opposite:* simple. **2** *n* **amalgam**, mixture, complex, compound, fusion, synthesis, combination, aggregate, amalgamation. [➡COLLECTIONS AND MIXTURES OF THINGS; 1243]

composition **1** *n* **constitution**, makeup, structure, components, constituents, parts. [➡APPEARANCE AND ATMOSPHERE; 1236] **2** *n* **work of art**, creation, work, opus, masterpiece, piece. [➡ARTWORKS; 898] **3** *n* **arrangement**, configuration, conformation, structure, alignment. [➡QUALITIES AND CHARACTERISTICS; 1190]

compos mentis *adj* [➡POSITIVE INTELLECTUAL CHARACTERISTICS; 525]

composure *n* **equanimity**, calm, serenity, self-possession, tranquillity, self-control, poise, calmness. [➡CALMNESS, CONFIDENCE, AND COMPOSURE; 537] *Opposite:* agitation.

compote *type of* **preserve**. [➡SUGAR AND PRESERVES; 1183]

compound **1** *n* **mix**, mixture, complex, amalgam, composite, combination. [➡COLLECTIONS AND MIXTURES OF THINGS; 1243] **2** *adj* **multiple**, complex, composite, multifaceted, multifarious, multipart, multifactorial. [➡POSITIVELY COMPLEX OR COMPLICATED; 218] *Opposite:* simple.

See Compare and Contrast at **mixture**.

comprehend 1 *v* **understand**, know, realize, grasp, get (*informal*), twig (*informal*), figure out, have a handle on, follow. [➡UNDERSTAND AND GRASP; 760] 2 *v* (*formal*) **include**, incorporate, bring in, add in, involve. [➡HOLD AND CONTAIN; 456]

comprehensible *adj* **understandable**, clear, logical, plain, coherent, intelligible, lucid, graspable. [➡CONCISE AND CLEAR; 203] *Opposite:* unintelligible.

comprehensibly *adv* **intelligibly**, understandably, coherently, clearly, plainly, lucidly, logically, articulately, distinctly. [➡THE NATURE OF IDEAS; 772] *Opposite:* unintelligibly.

comprehension *n* **understanding**, grasp, knowledge, command, conception, ability. [➡KNOWLEDGE AND WISDOM; 559]

comprehensive 1 *adj* **complete**, inclusive, full, all-inclusive, wide-ranging, broad, ample, widespread, far-reaching, across-the-board, thorough, all-embracing. [➡WHOLENESS AND COMPLETENESS; 199] *Opposite:* incomplete. 2 *type of* **school**. [➡EDUCATIONAL INSTITUTIONS; 813]

comprehensiveness *n* **inclusiveness**, completeness, all-inclusiveness, exhaustiveness, generality, extensiveness, fullness, breadth, depth. [➡WHOLENESS AND COMPLETENESS; 199]

compress 1 *v* **squeeze**, condense, pack together, squash, constrict, compact, tamp. [➡CHANGE OF SIZE: SMALLER; 394] *Opposite:* expand. 2 *n* **pad**, wad, cold compress, ice pack, wrapping, poultice. [➡COVERS AND COATINGS; 1245]

comprise *v* **include**, encompass, contain, cover, consist of, embrace. [➡POSSESS; 445] *Opposite:* exclude.

compromise 1 *n* **agreement**, settlement, arrangement, bargain, concession, deal. [➡SOLUTION; 216] 2 *v* **cooperate**, bargain, negotiate, meet halfway, find the middle ground, give in, concede. [➡HARMONY; 156] *Opposite:* confront.

compulsion 1 *n* **urge**, impulse, desire, craving, force, need. [➡FEELINGS ABOUT THE FUTURE; 534] 2 *n* **coercion**, force, pressure, obligation, duress. [➡CAPTIVITY AND LOSS OF FREEDOM; 249]

compulsive 1 *adj* **obsessive**, neurotic (*informal*), habitual, uncontrollable, irrational, driven. [➡PSYCHOLOGY AND THE MIND; 770] *Opposite:* rational. 2 *adj* **gripping**, compelling, mesmerizing, attention-grabbing, exciting, thrilling, interesting. [➡INTERESTING AND MEANINGFUL; 191] *Opposite:* boring.

compulsory *adj* **required**, obligatory, necessary, enforced, essential, unavoidable. [➡NECESSARY AND ESSENTIAL; 197] *Opposite:* optional.

compunction *n* **regret**, scruple, reluctance, qualm, second thoughts, guilt, hesitation, shame. [➡FEELINGS ABOUT THE PAST; 533]

computation *n* **calculation**, reckoning, totalling, addition, subtraction, multiplication, division. [➡MATHS; 598] *Opposite:* estimation.

compute *v* **calculate**, work out, total, add, subtract, multiply, divide. [➡ASSESS QUANTITY; 758] *Opposite:* estimate.

computer

◆ *types of computer*
adder, calculator, hand-held computer, laptop, mainframe, microcomputer, minicomputer, notebook, palmtop, PC, personal computer, personal organizer, supercomputer, tablet computer, workstation

◆ *types of software*
accumulator, application, bit map, browser, buffer, bus, cache, computer-aided design, cursor, database, directory, emoticon, firmware, interface, macro, memory, pixel, program, RAM, readout, ROM, simulator, smiley, spell checker, spreadsheet, subdirectory, virus, wallpaper, window, word processor

◆ *types of hardware*
accelerator card, backspace, CD-ROM, central processing unit, chip, console, disk, disk drive, diskette, DVD, floppy disk, hard disk, integrated circuit, joystick, keyboard, microchip, microprocessor, modem, monitor, motherboard, mouse, numeric keypad, port, printed circuit, printer, processor, scanner, screen, server, sound card, space-bar, terminal, touch screen, VDT, VDU, video display terminal, visual display unit

computer-aided design *n* [➡COMPUTERS AND COMPUTING; 1126]

computer graphics *n* [➡COMPUTERS AND COMPUTING; 1126]

computer modelling *n* [➡COMPUTERS AND COMPUTING; 1126]

computer processing *n* [➡COMPUTERS AND COMPUTING; 1126]

computer program *n* [➡COMPUTERS AND COMPUTING; 1126]

computer programmer *n* [➡COMPUTERS AND COMPUTING; 1126]

computer science *n* [➡COMPUTERS AND COMPUTING; 1126]

computer scientist *n* [➡COMPUTERS AND COMPUTING; 1126]

computer technology *n* [➡COMPUTERS AND COMPUTING; 1126]

comrade *n* **friend**, chum (*informal*), buddy (*US informal*), pal (*informal*), mate, companion. [➡FRIENDS; 963] *Opposite:* enemy.

comradely *adj* [➡FRIENDLINESS AND SOCIABILITY; 495]

comradeship *n* [➡RELATIONSHIP TO ANOTHER; 973]

con 1 *v* **swindle**, defraud, rip off (*informal*), cheat, trick, do (*informal*). [➡STEAL AND ROB; 427] 2 *v* (*informal*) **deceive**, hoodwink, trick, mislead, dupe, pull a fast one (*slang*), inveigle, sweet-talk (*informal*), entrap, take in, lure. [➡DECEPTION AND LIES; 661] 3 *n* **confidence trick**, fraud, scam (*slang*), rip-off (*informal*), ploy, confidence game (*US*). [➡DECEPTION AND LIES; 661] 4 *n* **negative**, disadvantage, minus, objection. [➡PROBLEM; 257] *Opposite:* pro. 5 *n* (*slang*) **convict**, prisoner, jailbird (*slang*), old lag (*slang*). [➡CAPTIVES AND PRISONERS; 250]

con artist (*slang*) *n* **trickster**, cheat, swindler, shark (*informal*), con man (*informal*), fraud. [➡PEOPLE WHO DECEIVE; 662]

con brio *type of* **musical term.** [➡MUSICAL TERMS; 912]

concave *adj* **curved in**, dished, hollow. [➡ROUNDED SHAPE; 1217] *Opposite:* convex.

conceal 1 *v* **hide**, cover, cover up, secrete, screen, obscure, mask, disguise, camouflage. [➡CAUSE TO DISAPPEAR; 6] *Opposite:* reveal. 2 *v* **suppress**, keep quiet, keep under wraps, sit on, censor, cover up, hold back, disguise. [➡WITHHOLD INFORMATION; 688] *Opposite:* divulge.

concealed 1 *adj* **hidden**, covered, buried, obscured, masked. [➡IMPERCEPTIBLE; 26] *Opposite:* visible. 2 *adj* **secret**, cloaked, masked, veiled, disguised, camouflaged, hidden away. [➡SECRET AND UNKNOWN; 180] *Opposite:* open.

concealment *n* **cover-up**, disguise, camouflage, suppression. [➡SECRET AND UNKNOWN; 180] *Opposite:* revelation.

concede 1 *v* **allow** (*formal*), acknowledge, grant, admit, accept, own (*formal*). [➡FORGET, FORGIVE, AND ACCEPT; 749] *Opposite:* deny. 2 *v* **yield**, give in, give up, compromise, forfeit. [➡FORGET, FORGIVE, AND ACCEPT; 749] *Opposite:* stand firm.

conceit *n* **self-importance**, pride, vanity, smugness, arrogance, superiority, self-satisfaction, snobbery, bigheadedness (*informal*), narcissism. [➡AFFECTATION, SELF-SATISFACTION, AND SNOBBISHNESS; 508] *Opposite:* modesty.

conceited *adj* **self-important**, proud, vain, smug, arrogant, high and mighty, superior, stuck-up (*informal*), self-satisfied, snobbish, bigheaded (*informal*), narcissistic. [➡POMPOUS, LOUD, AND OVER-CONFIDENT; 636] *Opposite:* modest.

See Compare and Contrast at **proud.**

conceitedness *n* [➡AFFECTATION, SELF-SATISFACTION, AND SNOBBISHNESS; 508]

conceivable *adj* **imaginable**, believable, possible, plausible, likely, feasible, credible. [➡POSSIBLE AND PROBABLE; 178] *Opposite:* implausible.

conceive 1 *v* **imagine**, envisage, visualize, envision, think up, picture. [➡DREAM, IMAGINE, AND FANTASIZE; 750] 2 *v* **create**, think up, dream up, make up, elaborate, form, invent, formulate, devise. [➡INSTITUTE AND INAUGURATE; 349] 3 *v* **consider**, regard, think of, look on, perceive, apprehend, comprehend. [➡DEVELOP THEORIES AND REASON; 745]

concentrate 1 *v* **think**, focus, ponder, muse, deliberate, contemplate, give attention to. [➡THINK AND REFLECT; 744] *Opposite:* daydream. 2 *v* **converge**, come together, assemble, collect, cluster, mass. [➡GET CLOSER TOGETHER; 311] *Opposite:* disperse. 3 *v* **thicken**, strengthen, purify, distil. [➡HARDEN, CONGEAL, DRY; 388] *Opposite:* dilute. 4 *n* **distillate**, essence, quintessence. [➡SOLIDS; 1273]

concentrated 1 *adj* **strong**, thick, condensed, reduced. [➡NOT IN A NATURAL STATE; 1214] *Opposite:* diluted. 2 *adj* **focused**, intense, concerted, rigorous, strenuous, determined, resolute. [➡STRENGTH; 202] *Opposite:* half-hearted.

concentration 1 *n* **attentiveness**, attention, absorption, awareness, focus, application. [➡ATTENTION AND ATTENTIVENESS; 764] *Opposite:* distraction. 2 *n* **strength**, intensity. [➡DENSITY AND CONSISTENCY; 1206] *Opposite:* dilution.

concept *n* **idea**, notion, thought, impression, perception, conception, theory, model, hypothesis, view, belief. [➡IDEA AND THOUGHT; 771]

conception 1 *n* **comprehension**, understanding, grasp, command. [➡UNDERSTAND AND GRASP; 760] 2 *n* **idea**, notion, concept, thought, impression, perception, theory, model, hypothesis, view, belief. [➡IDEA AND THOUGHT; 771] 3 *n* **beginning**, start, outset, origin, commencement (*formal*), formation. [➡BEGINNING; 53]

conceptual art *type of* **20th-century art movement.** [➡ARTISTIC MOVEMENTS AND STYLES; 899]

concern 1 *v* **worry**, trouble, disturb, bother, upset, alarm, disquiet (*archaic or literary*). [➡UPSET, DISTRESS, AND HUMILIATE; 568] *Opposite:* reassure. 2 *v* **relate**, affect, be about, have to do with, be connected with. [➡BE ABOUT SOMETHING; 62] 3 *n* **anxiety**, worry, fear, apprehension, distress, alarm, unease, disquiet, trepidation, fretfulness, nervousness, uneasiness. [➡CONFUSION, ANXIETY, AND WORRY; 541] *Opposite:* reassurance. 4 *n* **interest**, business, point, item, affair, matter, involvement. [➡SUBJECT AREA; 769] 5 *n* **company**, firm, business, enterprise, establishment, outfit (*informal*), house. [➡BUSINESS ENTERPRISES AND RELATED BODIES; 793]

concerned *adj* **worried**, afraid, disturbed, alarmed, fretful, apprehensive, uneasy, upset, nervous, anxious. [➡CONFUSION, ANXIETY, AND WORRY; 541] *Opposite:* carefree.

concerning *prep* **about**, relating to, regarding, with reference to, as to, in relation to, pertaining to, re, with regard to, as regards, in connection with, vis-à-vis. [➡EXPRESSIONS OF REFERENCE; 63]

concert 1 *n* **recital**, performance, show, gig (*informal*). [➡PERFORMANCES AND SHOWS; 42] 2 *type of* **broadcast.** [➡TELEVISION AND RADIO; 607]

concerted 1 *adj* **combined**, collaborative, joint, mutual. [➡ACTING WITH OTHERS; 286] *Opposite:* solitary. 2 *adj* **concentrated**, intensive, rigorous, strenuous, determined, resolute. [➡STRENGTH; 202] *Opposite:* half-hearted.

concerted effort *n* [➡HARD WORK OR EFFORT; 299]

concert hall *n* [➡BUILDINGS FOR PUBLIC ENTERTAINMENT; 1083]

concertina *type of* **keyboard.** [➡MUSICAL INSTRUMENTS; 910]

concerto *type of* **instrumental music.** [➡MUSIC, SONGS, AND SINGING; 907]

concession 1 *n* **privilege**, allowance, dispensation, indulgence, acknowledgment, recognition, consideration. [➡KIND ACTION OR BEHAVIOUR; 296] 2 *n* **reduction**, discount, allowance, markdown, decrease. [➡EXPENDITURE; 424] 3 *n* **yielding**, surrendering, granting, giving way, conceding, compromise. [➡GIFTS; 439] 4 *n* (*US*) **franchise**, business, enterprise, concern, refreshment stand. [➡BUSINESS ENTERPRISES AND RELATED BODIES; 793]

conch *type of* **aquatic invertebrate.** [➡AQUATIC INVERTEBRATE; 1022]

conchiglie *type of* **pasta.** [➡PASTA; 1179]

concierge 1 *n* **caretaker**, janitor, doorman, doorkeeper, gatekeeper, warden, porter, custodian. [➡PEOPLE WHO GUARD AND PROTECT; 846] 2 *n* (*US*) **helper**, porter, agent, intermediary, booker, assistant. [➡SUBORDINATES AND ASSISTANTS; 966]

conciliate *v* **reconcile**, appease, placate, pacify, make peace, mollify, soothe, resolve. [➡APOLOGIZE AND RETRACT; 684] *Opposite:* provoke.

conciliation *n* **reconciliation**, appeasement, pacification, reunion, mollification, resolution. [➡HARMONY; 156] *Opposite:* provocation.

conciliator *n* **peacemaker**, mediator, intermediary, arbitrator, arbiter, go-between, negotiator, referee, appeaser. [➡ADVISERS, JUDGES, AND ARBITERS; 971] *Opposite:* troublemaker.

conciliatory *adj* **appeasing**, peacemaking, pacifying, assuaging, mollifying. [➡CALMING; 189] *Opposite:* provocative.

concise *adj* **brief**, short, to the point, succinct, summarizing, terse, short and sweet, crisp, curt, abridged. [➡SUCCINCT AND TO-THE-POINT; 641] *Opposite:* verbose.

conciseness *n* **succinctness**, concision, terseness, brevity, shortness, curtness. [➡SUCCINCT AND TO-THE-POINT; 641] *Opposite:* wordiness.

concision *n* **succinctness**, conciseness, terseness, brevity, shortness, curtness. [➡SUCCINCT AND TO-THE-POINT; 641] *Opposite:* wordiness.

conclave *n* **meeting**, assembly, council, congress, gathering, caucus. [➡MEETINGS AND ASSEMBLIES; 43]

conclude 1 *v* **deduce**, assume, presume, decide, reckon, construe, suppose, infer, work out, figure out. [➡MAKE DECISIONS AND CHOICES; 753] *Opposite:* speculate. 2 *v* **end**, close, finish, terminate (*formal*), finish off, wrap up (*informal*), halt, call a halt. [➡COMPLETE AN ACTION; 264] *Opposite:* start. 3 *v* **settle**, complete, close, clinch, arrange, achieve, accomplish, bring about, determine, resolve. [➡APPROVE AND CONFIRM; 647]

See Compare and Contrast at **deduce**.

concluded *adj* **decided**, settled, determined, resolved, clinched, established. [➡WHOLENESS AND COMPLETENESS; 199] *Opposite:* unresolved.

concluding *adj* **closing**, final, last, ultimate, ending. [➡AFTER, LAST, AND FOLLOWING; 166] *Opposite:* opening.

conclusion 1 *n* **deduction**, assumption, inference, supposition, decision. [➡IDEA AND THOUGHT; 771] 2 *n* **end**, close, finish, termination, wind-up, finale, ending, closing, wrap-up (*US*). [➡END; 54] *Opposite:* start.

conclusive *adj* **decisive**, beyond question, definite, convincing, irrefutable, sure, certain, final, categorical. [➡CERTAIN; 175] *Opposite:* unconvincing.

concoct 1 *v* **prepare**, cook, make, put together, rustle up (*informal*), mix up, stir up, create, produce. [➡MEAL PREPARATION; 355] 2 *v* **make up**, create, devise, invent, dream up, fabricate, think up, put together, cook up (*informal*), formulate, conceive. [➡DREAM, IMAGINE, AND FANTASIZE; 750]

concoction 1 *n* **mixture**, brew, blend, potion, drink. [➡COLLECTIONS AND MIXTURES OF THINGS; 1243] 2 *n* **invention**, creation, fabrication, fantasy, fiction. [➡NONEXISTENT THINGS; 23]

concomitance *n* **accompaniment**, coexistence, conjunction, combination, association, connection. [➡CONNECTION; 144] *Opposite:* independence.

concomitant 1 *adj* **simultaneous**, parallel, concurrent, coexistent, contemporaneous. [➡CONCURRENT AND CONTEMPORANEOUS; 165] *Opposite:* independent. 2 *adj* **attendant**, associated, connected, affiliated, related. [➡RELATED; 143] *Opposite:* unrelated.

concord 1 *n* **agreement**, harmony, unity, accord, peace, accordance, friendship. [➡HARMONY; 156] *Opposite:* conflict. 2 *n* **treaty**, pact, agreement, settlement, compact. [➡OFFICIAL DOCUMENTS; 587]

concourse 1 *n* **open space**, public space, forecourt, courtyard, square, mall, hall, space. [➡URBAN OUTDOOR SPACES; 1071] 2 *n* **crowd**, throng, horde, multitude, mass. [➡AUDIENCES AND ATTENDEES; 937] 3 *n* **gathering**, assembly, meeting, rally, muster. [➡MEETINGS AND ASSEMBLIES; 43]

concrete 1 *n* [➡BUILDING MATERIALS; 1076] 2 *adj* **tangible**, existing, actual, material, solid, physical, real. [➡TRUE AND REAL; 172] *Opposite:* insubstantial. 3 *adj* **specific**, particular, distinct, certain, definite. [➡CONCISE AND CLEAR; 203] *Opposite:* indeterminate.

concubine *n* [➡SEXUAL AND ROMANTIC RELATIONSHIPS; 964]

concur 1 *v* **agree**, harmonize, be in accord, correspond, coincide, see eye to eye, be together. [➡AGREE; 646] *Opposite:* conflict. 2 *v* **assent**, go along with, agree to, acquiesce, accept, consent. [➡PERMIT AND ALLOW; 670] *Opposite:* resist. 3 *v* **coincide**, synchronize, fall together, coexist. [➡EXIST WITH OTHERS; 18] *Opposite:* diverge.

See Compare and Contrast at **agree**.

concurrence 1 *n* **agreement**, accord, harmony, consensus, correspondence, coincidence, togetherness. [➡HARMONY; 156] *Opposite:* conflict. 2 *n* **simultaneity**, coexistence, concomitance, coincidence, synchronism, accompaniment. [➡CONCURRENT AND CONTEMPORANEOUS; 165]

concurrent *adj* **simultaneous**, synchronized, parallel, coexisting, contemporaneous, concomitant, contemporary. [➡CONCURRENT AND CONTEMPORANEOUS; 165] *Opposite:* separate.

condemn 1 *v* **censure**, denounce, criticize, attack, revile, slam (*informal*), pan (*informal*), disparage. [➡PROTEST AND EXPRESS DISAPPROVAL; 643] *Opposite:* commend. 2 *v* **rebuke**, reprove, reprimand, reproach, blame, criticize. [➡ACCUSE, BLAME, AND CRITICIZE; 642] *Opposite:* commend. 3 *v* **convict**, sentence, find guilty, doom, judge. [➡TRIAL, PUNISHMENT, AND LEGAL OUTCOMES; 819] *Opposite:* absolve.

See Compare and Contrast at **criticize**.

condemnation 1 *n* **censure**, disapproval, blame, denunciation, criticism, attack. [➡CRITICISMS AND ANGRY OUTBURSTS; 50] *Opposite:* commendation. 2 *n* **conviction**, sentence, judgment. [➡TRIAL, PUNISHMENT, AND LEGAL OUTCOMES; 819] *Opposite:* absolution.

condemnatory *adj* **disapproving**, critical, disparaging, reproving, denouncing, judgmental. [➡ACCUSATORY AND DISAPPROVING; 635] *Opposite:* complimentary.

condensation 1 *n* **wetness**, dampness, damp, humidity, water, mist, droplets. [➡MOIST; 1240] 2 *n* **concentration**, compression, reduction. [➡DENSITY AND CONSISTENCY; 1206] 3 *n* **abbreviation**, shortening, abridgment, summarization, cutting. [➡SUMMARIES, OUTLINES, AND EXCERPTS; 589] *Opposite:* expansion.

condense 1 *v* **concentrate**, compress, compact, squeeze, pack into, consolidate. [➡CHANGE OF SIZE: SMALLER; 394] *Opposite:* expand. 2 *v* **abbreviate**, shorten, abridge, shrink, summarize, reduce, cut down, précis, edit, contract. [➡CHANGE OF SIZE: SMALLER; 394] *Opposite:* expand.

condensed 1 *adj* **shortened**, reduced, summarized, edited, abbreviated, cut, abridged, compressed, précised, abstracted. [➡CHANGE OF SIZE: SMALLER; 394] *Opposite:* expanded. 2 *adj* **concentrated**, thickened, reduced, evaporated, thick, dense. [➡NOT IN A NATURAL STATE; 1214] *Opposite:* diluted.

condescend 1 *v* **patronize**, humiliate, talk down, look down on, disdain. [➡INSULTS, ABUSE, AND SWEARING; 659] *Opposite:* respect. 2 *v* **deign**, lower yourself, stoop, humble, demean, lower. [➡PERMIT AND ALLOW; 670]

condescending *adj* **patronizing**, disdainful, superior, haughty, pompous, arrogant, lofty, supercilious, snooty (*informal*), snobbish, contemptuous. [➡POMPOUS, LOUD, AND OVERCONFIDENT; 636] *Opposite:* deferential.

condescendingly *adv* **patronizingly**, pompously, superciliously, loftily, disdainfully, haughtily, arrogantly, snootily (*informal*), snobbishly, contemptuously. [➡RUDE AND HOSTILE; 626] *Opposite:* deferentially.

condescension *n* **disdain**, arrogance, superciliousness, aloofness, haughtiness, snobbery, pomposity, snootiness (*informal*), contempt. [➡ANTAGONISM; 553] *Opposite:* deference.

condiment *n* [➡SEASONINGS AND SAUCES; 1173]

condition 1 *n* **state**, form, order, repair, fitness. [➡STATE; 1207] 2 *n* **stipulation**, clause, proviso, provision, requirement, prerequisite, specification, term, restriction, precondition, rider. [➡NECESSARY AND ESSENTIAL; 197] 3 *n* **disorder**, illness, complaint, ailment. [➡SICKNESS; 730] 4 *v* **acclimatize**, get used to, prepare, train, get ready, shape up. [➡CHANGE; 373]

conditional 1 *adj* **provisional**, restricted, restrictive, qualified, uncertain, unconfirmed. [➡RECIPROCITY AND INTERDEPENDENCE; 148] *Opposite:* unrestricted. 2 *type of* **grammatical term**. [➡ASPECTS OF LANGUAGE; 683]

conditioned *adj* **trained**, broken in, habituated (*formal*), inured, hardened, accustomed. [➡KNOWLEDGE AND WISDOM; 559] *Opposite:* untrained.

conditioning *n* **training**, breaking in, taming, habituation (*formal*). [➡PSYCHOLOGY AND THE MIND; 770]

conditions *n* **circumstances**, situation, surroundings, setting, environment, state of affairs. [➡SITUATIONS; 71]

condo (*US informal*) *n* [➡RESIDENTIAL BUILDINGS; 1077]

condolence *n* **sympathy**, commiseration, pity, comfort, concern. [➡COMPASSION AND FORGIVENESS; 552]

condolences *n* [➡GREETINGS, FAREWELLS, AND SALUTATIONS; 660]

condominium (*US*) *n* **house**, apartment block, condo (*US informal*), cooperative, co-op (*informal*), apartment house (*US*). [➡RESIDENTIAL BUILDINGS; 1077]

condone *v* **overlook**, excuse, disregard, forgive, ignore, pardon, tolerate, make allowances for. [➡NOT PAY ATTENTION; 765] *Opposite:* oppose.

condor *type of* **scavenger**. [➡BIRD; 997]

conducive *adj* **favourable**, helpful, contributing to, encouraging, advantageous, beneficial. [➡EMOTIONALLY PLEASANT; 188]

conduct 1 *v* **manage**, run, control, direct, organize, handle, operate, oversee, supervise. [➡BE IN CHARGE; 271] 2 *v* **lead**, show, direct, steer, accompany, pilot, shepherd, guide, usher. [➡ACCOMPANY AND FOLLOW; 338] 3 *n* **behaviour**, demeanour, ways, manner, comportment (*formal*), deportment (*formal*), bearing, mien (*literary*). [➡TEMPERAMENT AND BEHAVIOUR; 493] 4 *n* **management**, handling, organization, administration, running, controlling, oversight, care, charge, supervision, superintendence. [➡WAYS OF DOING THINGS; 295]

See Compare and Contrast at **guide**.

conduction *n* **transmission**, transference, transfer, conveyance, passage. [➡MOVE SOMETHING TO ANOTHER LOCATION; 325]

conduct yourself *v* **behave**, act, acquit yourself, comport yourself (*formal*), behave yourself, carry yourself. [➡CARRY OUT AN ACTION; 270]

conduit *n* **channel**, canal, duct, tube, pipe, ditch, drain, outlet, watercourse. [➡WATERCOURSES; 1110]

cone *type of* **rounded shape**. [➡ROUNDED SHAPE; 1217]

Conestoga wagon *type of* **wagon or carriage**. [➡VEHICLES; 1144]

confab (*informal*) *n* [➡INFORMAL COMMUNICATION; 45]

confectionery **sweetie** (*informal*). [➡CONFECTIONERY; 1181]

confectionery

◆ *types of confectionery*
bubblegum, bonbon, butterscotch, candy (*US*), caramel, chewing gum, chocolate, fondant, fudge, gobstopper, gum, gumdrop, jawbreaker (*US*), jellybean, liquorice, marshmallow, marzipan, nougat, peppermint, praline, sweet, sweetie (*informal*), sweetmeat (*archaic*), taffy (*US*), toffee, truffle

◆ *types of confectionery on a stick*
candy apple (*US*), candyfloss, cotton candy (*US*), lollipop, lolly (*informal*), toffee apple

confederacy *n* **union**, league, association, alliance, grouping, confederation, coalition, federation, partnership. [➡GROUPS WITH A COMMON INTEREST; 938]

confederate 1 *n* **partner**, associate, ally, colleague, sidekick (*informal*), accomplice, co-conspirator. [➡SUPPORTERS, PROTECTORS, AND COMPATRIOTS; 970] *Opposite:* rival. 2 *adj* **allied**, united, joined, associated, affiliated. [➡RELATED; 143] *Opposite:*

rival. **3** *v* **ally**, unite, join, affiliate, associate, link. [➡CREATING CONNECTIONS; 145] *Opposite:* disconnect.

confederation *n* **association**, league, union, coalition, confederacy, federation, alliance, partnership, grouping. [➡GROUPS WITH A COMMON INTEREST; 938]

confer **1** *v* (*formal*) **award**, bestow (*formal*), present, grant, give. [➡REWARD; 437] *Opposite:* withhold. **2** *v* **discuss**, consider, talk over, go over, thrash out, hash over (*US*). [➡TWO-WAY COMMUNICATION; 608]

See Compare and Contrast at **give**.

conference **1** *n* **session**, meeting, consultation, discussion, talks. [➡MEETINGS AND ASSEMBLIES; 43] **2** *n* **symposium**, seminar, convention, forum, meeting, congress, summit. [➡MEETINGS AND ASSEMBLIES; 43] **3** *n* **league**, association, alliance, union, federation. [➡AUDIENCES AND ATTENDEES; 937]

confess **1** *v* **admit**, own up, come clean (*informal*), acknowledge, make a clean breast. [➡ADMIT AND CONFESS; 616] *Opposite:* deny. **2** *v* **declare**, profess, affirm, assert, make known, acknowledge. [➡ADMIT AND CONFESS; 616] *Opposite:* repress.

confession **1** *n* **admission**, concession, revelation, acknowledgment. [➡ADMIT AND CONFESS; 616] *Opposite:* denial. **2** *n* **declaration**, affirmation, profession, assertion, statement, acknowledgment. [➡ADMIT AND CONFESS; 616]

confidant *n* **friend**, soul mate, alter ego, sister, brother, amigo, intimate, sounding board, best friend. [➡FRIENDS; 963]

confidante *n* [➡FRIENDS; 963]

confide *v* **unburden**, disclose, reveal, divulge, tell, pass on, share a confidence, make known, confess, open your heart. [➡BETRAY CONFIDENCES AND GOSSIP; 619] *Opposite:* withhold.

confidence **1** *n* **sureness**, self-assurance, self-confidence, poise, assurance, self-reliance, buoyancy, coolness. [➡CONFIDENCE AND COMPOSURE; 500] *Opposite:* timidity. **2** *n* **assurance**, certainty, conviction, belief, faith, trust, support, loyalty. [➡CALMNESS, CONFIDENCE, AND COMPOSURE; 537] *Opposite:* doubt. **3** *n* **secret**, intimacy, classified information. [➡SECRETS AND MYSTERIES; 181]

confidence game (*US*) *n* [➡DECEPTION AND LIES; 661]

confidence trick *n* [➡DECEPTION AND LIES; 661]

confidence trickster *n* [➡PEOPLE WHO DECEIVE; 662]

confident **1** *adj* **self-assured**, poised, self-confident, self-possessed, assured, assertive, self-reliant, buoyant, cool. [➡CONFIDENCE AND COMPOSURE; 500] *Opposite:* timid. **2** *adj* **definite**, sure, certain, positive, convinced, secure. [➡CERTAINTY; 562] *Opposite:* unsure.

confidential **1** *adj* **private**, secret, classified, censored, off the record, hush-hush (*informal*), restricted. [➡SECRET AND UNKNOWN; 180] *Opposite:* unrestricted. **2** *adj* **sound**, stable, trusted, trustworthy, reliable, dependable, faithful. [➡HONEST AND RELIABLE; 503] *Opposite:* untrustworthy. **3** *adj* **intimate**, private, close, personal. [➡RELATIONSHIP TO ANOTHER; 973]

confidentially *adv* **behind the scenes**, privately, in secret, just between you and me, behind closed doors, in confidence, off the record. [➡SECRET AND UNKNOWN; 180] *Opposite:* openly.

configuration *n* **shape**, outline, formation, conformation, arrangement, alignment, structure. [➡SHAPE; 1215]

configure *v* **arrange**, design, set up, construct, align, shape. [➡ARRANGE AND CREATE ORDER; 358]

confine **1** *v* **restrain**, restrict, limit, narrow, keep, curb. [➡REFUSE PERMISSION AND NOT ALLOW; 671] *Opposite:* unleash. **2** *v* **detain**, sequester (*formal*), quarantine, imprison, jail, lock up, impound, shut in, incarcerate (*formal*), keep. [➡CAPTIVITY AND LOSS OF FREEDOM; 249] *Opposite:* release.

confined **1** *adj* **limited**, narrowed, kept, restricted, cramped, curbed, restrained. [➡CAPTIVITY AND LOSS OF FREEDOM; 249] *Opposite:* open. **2** *adj* **constricted**, small, cramped, enclosed, poky (*informal*). [➡SMALL; 1194] *Opposite:* open.

confinement **1** *n* (*dated*) **labour**, childbirth, giving birth. [➡REPRODUCTION AND HEREDITY; 726] **2** *n* **imprisonment**, quarantine, incarceration (*formal*), internment, detention, captivity. [➡CAPTIVITY AND LOSS OF FREEDOM; 249] *Opposite:* freedom. **3** *n* **limitation**, scope, restriction, restraint, limit, bounds, boundary. [➡CAPTIVITY AND LOSS OF FREEDOM; 249]

confines *n* **limits**, boundaries, borders, limitations, margins, precincts, restrictions. [➡EXTREMITIES OF PHYSICAL OBJECTS; 1249]

confirm **1** *v* **corroborate**, verify, substantiate, bear out, prove, authenticate, validate, back up. [➡APPROVE AND CONFIRM; 647] *Opposite:* refute. **2** *v* **settle**, check, authorize, approve, sanction, endorse, ratify. [➡APPROVE AND CONFIRM; 647] **3** *v* (*formal*) **strengthen**, firm up, fortify, reinforce, deepen, enhance. [➡IMPROVE STRENGTH AND DURABILITY; 379] *Opposite:* undermine.

confirmation **1** *n* **corroboration**, verification, substantiation, authentication, evidence, affirmation. [➡EVIDENCE AND PROOF; 69] **2** *n* **validation**, authorization, approval, sanction, endorsement, ratification. [➡PERMIT AND ALLOW; 670]

confirmed *adj* **long-established**, established, dyed-in-the-wool, inveterate, deep-rooted, complete, definite, incorrigible, set, fixed, longtime. [➡UNWILLINGNESS AND STUBBORNNESS; 565]

confiscate *v* **take away**, remove, sequester, seize, impound, appropriate, commandeer, repossess. [➡TAKE SOMETHING AWAY; 426] *Opposite:* restore.

confiscation *n* **seizure**, repossession, appropriation, removal, sequestration, impounding. [➡TAKE SOMETHING AWAY; 426] *Opposite:* return.

conflagration *n* **fire**, blaze, inferno, forest fire, brush fire, bushfire. [➡FIRE, FLAMMABILITY, AND BURNING; 1164]

See Compare and Contrast at **fire**.

conflate *v* [➡COMBINE AND MIX; 401]

conflation *n* [➡COLLECTIONS AND MIXTURES OF THINGS; 1243]

conflict **1** *n* **battle**, fight, war, struggle, encounter, skirmish, clash, engagement. [➡AGGRESSIVE EVENT; 39] *Opposite:* peace. 2 *n* **opposition**, disagreement, clash, divergence, difference, argument, variance, quarrel, inconsistency, discord, contradiction, dispute, tension, fracas. [➡ARGUMENT; 47] *Opposite:* concord. 3 *v* **disagree**, oppose, clash, dispute, be at odds, be incompatible, differ, diverge. [➡DISHARMONY; 157] *Opposite:* concur. 4 *v* **fight**, quarrel, struggle, argue, scrap. [➡ACCUSE, BLAME, AND CRITICIZE; 642] *Opposite:* agree.

See Compare and Contrast at **fight**.

conflicting *adj* **contradictory**, incompatible, at odds, inconsistent, differing, disagreeing. [➡DISHARMONY; 157] *Opposite:* consistent.

confluence *n* **meeting**, convergence, union, joining together, coming together, flowing together. [➡CONNECTION; 144] *Opposite:* divergence.

conform 1 *v* **fit in**, imitate, follow, toe the line, obey, adapt, follow the crowd, play the game, kowtow. [➡OBEY AND ABIDE BY; 302] *Opposite:* rebel. 2 *v* **agree**, match, correspond, fit, coincide, match up, measure up. [➡HARMONY; 156] *Opposite:* contradict.

conformism *n* **conventionality**, toeing the line, conformity, orthodoxy, traditionalism, compliance. [➡THE WILL AND WILLINGNESS; 564] *Opposite:* dissidence.

conformist 1 *n* **yes man**, traditionalist, follower, sheep. [➡LAZY OR UNSUCCESSFUL PEOPLE; 948] *Opposite:* rebel. 2 *adj* **conventional**, traditional, orthodox, obedient, unadventurous, unquestioning. [➡CONSERVATIVE AND UNADVENTUROUS; 518] *Opposite:* rebellious.

conformity 1 *n* **toeing the line**, playing the game, conformism, conventionality, traditionalism, orthodoxy. [➡ORDINARINESS; 245] *Opposite:* rebellion. 2 *n* **agreement**, compliance, consistency, correspondence, accord, obedience, submission. [➡HARMONY; 156] *Opposite:* divergence.

confound 1 *v* **confuse**, muddle, mix up, mistake, misperceive. [➡CONFUSE AND BEWILDER; 572] *Opposite:* distinguish. 2 *v* **stun**, amaze, puzzle, mystify, confuse, bewilder, baffle, perplex, floor. [➡CONFUSE AND BEWILDER; 572]

confounded 1 *adj* (*informal*) **annoying**, irritating, blasted (*informal*), darned (*informal*), flaming (*informal*), wretched, pesky (*US informal*). [➡BAD AND BADLY; 224] 2 *adj* **confused**, perplexed, mystified, baffled, puzzled, bewildered. [➡CONFUSION, ANXIETY, AND WORRY; 541]

confrère (*formal*) *n* [➡FRIENDS; 963]

confront 1 *v* **challenge**, oppose, antagonize, provoke, meet, threaten, defy. [➡ACCUSE, BLAME, AND CRITICIZE; 642] 2 *v* **encounter**, handle, tackle, face up to, meet, face, deal with, brazen out. [➡COMPETE, CONTEND, AND COMBAT; 304]

confrontation 1 *n* **opposition**, argument, disagreement, quarrel, altercation, war of words, conflict, row. [➡ARGUMENT; 47] *Opposite:* consensus. 2 *n* **hostility**, war, battle, fight, clash, skirmish, conflict. [➡AGGRESSIVE EVENT; 39]

confrontational *adj* **argumentative**, quarrelsome, hostile, challenging, aggressive, provocative, militant, combative, truculent, belligerent. [➡IRRITATION AND ANGER; 542] *Opposite:* amicable.

confuse 1 *v* **puzzle**, perplex, baffle, mystify, bewilder, bamboozle (*informal*), confound. [➡CONFUSE AND BEWILDER; 572] *Opposite:* enlighten. 2 *v* **cloud**, muddy the waters, complicate, blur, muddy, obscure. [➡CREATE DISORDER AND CAUSE CHAOS; 359] *Opposite:* clarify. 3 *v* **muddle**, misperceive, mix up, mistake, confound. [➡COMBINE AND MIX; 401] *Opposite:* distinguish.

confused 1 *adj* **puzzled**, perplexed, baffled, mystified, bewildered, bemused, befuddled. [➡CONFUSION, ANXIETY, AND WORRY; 541] *Opposite:* enlightened. 2 *adj* **disordered**, disorderly, muddled, mixed up, in disarray, jumbled, disorganized, chaotic, tangled. [➡DISORDER AND CHAOS; 246] *Opposite:* orderly.

confusing *adj* **unclear**, puzzling, perplexing, baffling, mystifying, bewildering, befuddling. [➡DIFFICULTY AND COMPLEXITY; 243] *Opposite:* clear.

confusion 1 *n* **bewilderment**, perplexity, puzzlement, mystification, uncertainty, misunderstanding. [➡CONFUSION, ANXIETY, AND WORRY; 541] *Opposite:* understanding. 2 *n* **misperception**, misunderstanding, mix-up, muddle, mistake, slip-up (*informal*). [➡MISTAKES; 251] *Opposite:* clarity. 3 *n* **disorder**, chaos, turmoil, upheaval, commotion, muddle, mayhem (*informal*). [➡DISORDER AND CHAOS; 246] *Opposite:* order. 4 *n* **embarrassment**, awkwardness, disorientation, uncertainty, self-consciousness. [➡EMBARRASSMENT AND HUMILIATION; 543] *Opposite:* confidence.

conga drum *type of* **percussion instrument**. [➡MUSICAL INSTRUMENTS; 910]

con game (*US informal*) *n* [➡DECEPTION AND LIES; 661]

congeal *v* **set**, clot, coagulate, thicken, solidify, harden, gel. [➡HARDEN, CONGEAL, DRY; 388] *Opposite:* liquefy.

congealed *adj* [➡DENSITY AND CONSISTENCY; 1206]

congenial *adj* **agreeable**, friendly, affable, amiable, pleasant, genial, good-natured, hospitable. [➡FRIENDLINESS AND SOCIABILITY; 495] *Opposite:* hostile.

congeniality *n* [➡HARMONY; 156]

congenital 1 *adj* **inherited**, hereditary, inborn, inbred, genetic, natural, organic, innate. [➡REPRODUCTION AND HEREDITY; 726] *Opposite:* acquired. 2 *adj* **ingrained**, frequent, established, long-established, habitual, inveterate, incorrigible. [➡FREQUENT AND OFTEN; 107]

congest *v* **clog**, overfill, overcrowd, block, jam, crowd, pack, choke, obstruct. [➡FILL; 407] *Opposite:* clear.

congested 1 *adj* **overfilled**, jammed, choked, mobbed (*informal*), clogged, blocked, crowded, overcrowded, jam-packed (*informal*), packed, crammed. [➡FULL; 1238] *Opposite:* empty. 2 *adj* **obstructed**, clogged, mucous, stuffy, filled, blocked. [➡FULL; 1238] *Opposite:* clear.

congestion 1 *n* **overcrowding**, bottleneck, cramming, jamming, blocking, crowding, mobbing. [➡FULL; 1238] *Opposite:* emptiness. 2 *n* **blockage**, clogging, obstruction. [➡PROBLEM; 257]

conglomerate 1 *n* **parent company**, corporation, multinational, company, firm, business. [➡BUSINESS ENTERPRISES AND RELATED BODIES; 793] 2 *type of* **stone**. [➡STONES, ROCKS, AND BOULDERS; 1057]

conglomeration 1 *n* **composite**, accumulation, mass,

collection, assembly, gathering. [➡COLLECTIONS AND MIXTURES OF THINGS; 1243] 2 *n* **assortment**, potpourri, hotchpotch, collection, accumulation, miscellany. [➡COLLECTIONS AND MIXTURES OF THINGS; 1243]

congratulate *v* **commend**, acknowledge, toast, pat on the back, cheer, applaud, praise. [➡PRAISE AND ENCOURAGE; 648] *Opposite:* denigrate.

congratulations *interj* **cheers** (*informal*), compliments, felicitations (*formal*), greetings, hats off, well done. [➡COMPLIMENTS; 658] *Opposite:* commiserations.

congregate *v* **gather**, assemble, collect, meet, mass, flock, come together. [➡GET CLOSER TOGETHER; 311] *Opposite:* disperse.

congregation 1 *n* **worshippers**, churchgoers, audience, parishioners, flock. [➡RELIGIOUS PEOPLE; 779] 2 *n* **gathering**, crowd, throng, host, mass, assembly, audience. [➡AUDIENCES AND ATTENDEES; 937]

congress *n* **assembly**, council, conference, meeting, convention. [➡MEETINGS AND ASSEMBLIES; 43]

congressperson *n* **Representative**, senator, legislator, lawmaker, deputy. [➡POLITICAL OFFICES AND POLITICIANS; 808]

congruent (*formal*) *adj* **corresponding**, consistent, matching, compatible, similar, harmonious, harmonizing. [➡HARMONY; 156] *Opposite:* disparate.

conjectural *adj* [➡FALSE AND UNREAL; 174]

conjecture 1 *n* **guesswork**, estimation, guess, surmise, inference, speculation, assumption, supposition. [➡GUESS; 755] 2 *v* **estimate**, imagine, guess, speculate, infer, assume, suppose. [➡GUESS; 755]

conjoin (*formal*) *v* [➡FASTEN, LINK, AND JOIN; 409]

conjugal *adj* **marital**, matrimonial, married, wedded, connubial (*formal*). [➡MARRIED STATE; 961] *Opposite:* unmarried.

conjugation *type of* **grammatical term**. [➡ASPECTS OF LANGUAGE; 683]

conjunction 1 *n* **combination**, aggregation, unification, coincidence, concurrence, juxtaposition, union, combining. [➡CONNECTION; 144] 2 *type of* **word class**. [➡ASPECTS OF LANGUAGE; 683]

conjure 1 *v* **raise**, summon, call up, invoke, conjure up. [➡CAUSE TO APPEAR; 5] 2 *v* **mesmerize**, charm, trick, voodoo, spellbind. [➡HOBBIES, GAMES, AND SPORTS; 875]

conjurer *type of* **entertainer**. [➡WORKERS IN ENTERTAINMENT AND MEDIA; 873]

conjure up 1 *v* **evoke**, create, recall, call up. [➡REMIND; 748] 2 *v* **raise**, conjure, summon, call up, invoke. [➡CAUSE TO APPEAR; 5]

conjuror *see* **conjurer**.

conk (*slang*) *n* [➡THE NOSE; 705]

conked-out (*informal*) *adj* [➡TIRED, ASLEEP AND UNCONSCIOUS; 739]

conk out (*informal*) 1 *v* **fail**, break, wear out, malfunction, stall, break down, pack up (*informal*), die, fade. [➡FAIL OR CEASE TO FUNCTION; 471] *Opposite:* kick in (*informal*). 2 *v* **collapse**, pass out, doze off, drop off (*informal*), nod off, fall asleep. [➡SLEEP AND DREAM; 724] *Opposite:* wake up.

con man (*informal*) *n* [➡PEOPLE WHO DECEIVE; 662]

connect 1 *v* **attach**, join, link, fix, tie, unite, bond, hook up (*informal*), link up. [➡FASTEN, LINK, AND JOIN; 409] *Opposite:* disconnect. 2 *v* **associate**, relate, link, tie, link up. [➡CREATING CONNECTIONS; 145] *Opposite:* separate. 3 *v* **get along**, get on, click (*informal*), hook up (*informal*), hit it off (*informal*), bond. [➡ESTABLISHING RELATIONSHIPS WITH OTHERS; 974]

connected 1 *adj* **joined**, attached, fixed, united, tied, coupled, together. [➡CLOSENESS; 160] *Opposite:* separate. 2 *adj* **linked**, associated, related, allied, coupled. [➡RELATED; 143] *Opposite:* unrelated.

connection 1 *n* **joining**, fitting together, assembly, linking, piecing together, construction. [➡FASTEN, LINK, AND JOIN; 409] 2 *n* **bond**, tie, union, link, join, fixture, joint. [➡CONNECTION; 144] 3 *n* **context**, association, relationship, correlation, relation, link. [➡CONNECTION; 144]

connections 1 *n* **influence**, network, associates, acquaintances, links, friends, contacts. [➡SUPPORTERS, PROTECTORS, AND COMPATRIOTS; 970] 2 *n* **relations**, relatives, associations, links, family. [➡THE FAMILY; 956]

connive *v* **plot**, scheme, co-conspire, conspire, plan, hatch, cook up (*informal*). [➡CAUSE TO HAPPEN; 31]

conniver *n* **manipulator**, schemer, plotter, intriguer, planner, conspirator, manoeuvrer, deceiver. [➡PEOPLE WHO DECEIVE; 662]

conniving *adj* **devious**, scheming, conspiratorial, sly, crafty, deceitful. [➡DECEITFUL; 514] *Opposite:* ingenuous.

connoisseur *n* **specialist**, authority, expert, enthusiast, aficionado, aficionada, buff. [➡TALENTED OR INTELLIGENT PERSON; 529]

connotation *n* **implication**, association, suggestion, meaning, undertone, subtext, overtone, inference, reference, nuance. [➡MEANING; 691]

connote *v* **mean**, signify, suggest, purport (*formal*), intimate, imply, indicate, betoken (*literary*), signal. [➡MEAN SOMETHING; 61]

connubial (*formal*) *adj* **nuptial**, marital, matrimonial, wedded, conjugal, married. [➡MARRIED STATE; 961] *Opposite:* unmarried.

conquer 1 *v* **seize**, take, take over, take control, capture, dominate. [➡BEAT AND DEFEAT; 80] *Opposite:* surrender. 2 *v* **defeat**, beat, overpower, overthrow, subjugate, vanquish, confound. [➡BEAT AND DEFEAT; 80] *Opposite:* lose. 3 *v* **overcome**, surmount, get the better of, triumph over, master, defeat. [➡BEAT AND DEFEAT; 80] *Opposite:* give in.

See Compare and Contrast at **defeat**.

conquered *adj* [➡BEATEN AND DEFEATED; 78]

conqueror *n* **defeater**, vanquisher, subjugator, captor, victor. [➡ENEMIES AND TORMENTORS; 969] *Opposite:* vanquished.

conquest 1 *n* **defeat**, subjugation, downfall, beating, overthrow, takeover, rout, invasion, occupation, capture, acquisition, annexation. [➡BEAT AND DEFEAT; 80] *Opposite:* surrender. **2** *n* **victory**, success, triumph, win. [➡SUCCESS; 82] *Opposite:* defeat.

conscience *n* **scruples**, principles, ethics, integrity, sense of right and wrong, morality. [➡MORAL CONCEPTS; 774]

conscience-stricken *adj* [➡SADNESS, DISTRESS, AND DESPAIR; 540]

conscientious **1** *adj* **careful**, thorough, meticulous, painstaking, reliable, diligent, hard-working, assiduous, punctilious, scrupulous, industrious, attentive, dependable. [➡HARD-WORKING AND COMMITTED; 501] *Opposite:* careless. **2** *adj* **dutiful**, responsible, honourable, upright, upstanding, honest. [➡HONEST AND RELIABLE; 503] *Opposite:* dishonest.

See Compare and Contrast at **careful**.

conscientiousness *n* **scrupulousness**, thoroughness, assiduousness, meticulousness, carefulness, care, industriousness, diligence, reliability, attentiveness, dependability, punctiliousness. [➡HONEST AND RELIABLE; 503] *Opposite:* carelessness.

conscious **1** *adj* **awake**, wide awake, sleepless, insomniac. [➡WIDE AWAKE AND CONSCIOUS; 736] *Opposite:* unconscious. **2** *adj* **aware**, mindful, cognizant (*formal*), sentient, sensible. [➡KNOWLEDGE AND WISDOM; 559] *Opposite:* unaware. **3** *adj* **deliberate**, intentional, premeditated, on purpose, wilful, determined, considered. [➡INTENTIONAL AND DELIBERATE; 280] *Opposite:* unintentional.

See Compare and Contrast at **aware**.

consciously *adv* **deliberately**, intentionally, knowingly, determinedly, wilfully, on purpose. [➡INTENTIONAL AND DELIBERATE; 280] *Opposite:* unintentionally.

consciousness *n* **awareness**, realization, notice, perception, mindfulness, cognizance (*formal*). [➡KNOWLEDGE AND WISDOM; 559] *Opposite:* unconsciousness.

conscript **1** *v* **call up**, recruit, enlist, enrol, draft (*US*). [➡WARFARE AND WAR; 830] **2** *n* **recruit**, novice, rookie (*US informal*), draftee (*US*). [➡MILITARY PERSONNEL; 828]

conscription *n* **recruitment**, call-up, mobilization, enlistment, enrolment, draft (*US*). [➡WARFARE AND WAR; 830]

consecrate *v* **sanctify**, bless, set apart, hallow, dedicate, devote. [➡RELIGIONS AND RELIGIOUS PRACTICES; 778] *Opposite:* desecrate.

consecrated *adj* **hallowed**, sanctified, sacred, holy, blessed, sacrosanct. [➡RELIGIOUS CONCEPTS; 777] *Opposite:* desecrated.

consecration *n* **sanctification**, dedication, blessing, hallowing. [➡RELIGIOUS CONCEPTS; 777] *Opposite:* desecration.

consecutive *adj* **successive**, uninterrupted, following, repeated, serial, sequential, succeeding, next. [➡AFTER, LAST, AND FOLLOWING; 166] *Opposite:* alternate.

consensus *n* **agreement**, accord, harmony, compromise, consent, unanimity. [➡HARMONY; 156] *Opposite:* disagreement.

consent **1** *v* **permit**, allow, approve, accept, sanction, endorse, okay (*informal*). [➡PERMIT AND ALLOW; 670] *Opposite:* forbid. **2** *v* **agree**, comply, assent, acquiesce, accede, concur, subscribe. [➡AGREE; 646] *Opposite:* refuse. **3** *n* **permission**, approval, say-so (*informal*), assent, blessing, sanction, authority, okay (*informal*), go-ahead (*informal*), agreement, acquiescence, concurrence, allowance, sufferance, compliance. [➡PERMIT AND ALLOW; 670] *Opposite:* refusal. **4** *n* **agreement**, accord, consensus, harmony. [➡PERMIT AND ALLOW; 670]

See Compare and Contrast at **agree**.

consequence **1** *n* **result**, effect, outcome, end result, corollary, aftereffect, aftermath, upshot. [➡RESULTS AND OUTCOMES; 83] **2** *n* (*formal*) **importance**, significance, value, moment (*formal*), concern, import, magnitude. [➡IMPORTANCE AND SIGNIFICANCE; 193]

consequent *adj* **resulting**, resultant, consequential, following, subsequent, ensuing. [➡AFTER, LAST, AND FOLLOWING; 166]

consequential **1** *adj* **resulting**, resultant, consequent, following, subsequent, ensuing. [➡AFTER, LAST, AND FOLLOWING; 166] **2** *adj* **important**, significant, momentous, far-reaching, substantial, major. [➡IMPORTANT; 195] *Opposite:* inconsequential.

consequently (*formal*) *adv* **as a result**, so, thus (*formal*), therefore, subsequently, accordingly. [➡CAUSATION; 169]

conservation *n* **preservation**, upkeep, maintenance, protection, management, safeguarding, saving. [➡PREVENT CONTACT OR ATTACK; 420] *Opposite:* destruction.

conservative **1** *adj* **traditional**, middle-of-the-road, conventional, conformist, unadventurous, old-fashioned, traditionalist, old-school. [➡CONSERVATIVE AND UNADVENTUROUS; 518] *Opposite:* avant-garde. **2** *adj* **cautious**, moderate, careful. [➡ECONOMICAL AND RESOURCEFUL; 208] *Opposite:* speculative. **3** *n* **traditionalist**, conformist, fundamentalist, purist. [➡UNCOOPERATIVE OR REBELLIOUS PERSON; 567] *Opposite:* progressive.

conservatoire *n* [➡EDUCATIONAL INSTITUTIONS; 813]

conservatory **1** *n* **greenhouse**, glasshouse, hothouse. [➡ANCILLARY BUILDINGS; 1079] **2** *n* **school of the arts**, music school, art school, school of dance, conservatoire. [➡EDUCATIONAL INSTITUTIONS; 813]

conserve **1** *v* **preserve**, save, keep, protect, safeguard, take care of, support, maintain, sustain. [➡STORE AND KEEP; 454] *Opposite:* destroy. **2** *v* **store**, save, keep, go easy on (*informal*), be careful with. [➡STORE AND KEEP; 454] *Opposite:* expend. **3** *n* **jam**, marmalade, preserve. [➡SUGAR AND PRESERVES; 1183]

consider **1** *v* **think through**, mull over, chew over, reflect, deliberate, contemplate, take into account, ponder, weigh up, study, cogitate (*formal*), ruminate. [➡THINK AND REFLECT; 744] **2** *v* **judge**, deem (*formal*), believe, think, regard as. [➡HAVE AN OPINION OF SOMETHING; 757] **3** *v* **respect**, bear in mind, care about, take into consideration, count. [➡PAY ATTENTION; 766] *Opposite:* disregard.

considerable *adj* **substantial**, significant, large, extensive, sizable, great, huge. [➡LARGE; 1192] *Opposite:* insignificant.

considerably *adv* **significantly**, much, noticeably, by far, greatly, substantially, extensively, sizably, largely. [➡TO A GREAT EXTENT; 130] *Opposite:* slightly.

considerate *adj* **thoughtful**, kind, understanding, caring, selfless, attentive, sympathetic, respectful, solicitous, mindful. [➡GENEROSITY AND KINDNESS; 496] *Opposite:* inconsiderate.

consideration 1 *n* **thought**, deliberation (*formal*), reflection, contemplation, attention. [➡IDEA AND THOUGHT; 771] 2 *n* **respect**, concern, thoughtfulness, kindness, selflessness, sympathy, sensitivity, understanding, care, courtesy, considerateness. [➡GENEROSITY AND KINDNESS; 496] *Opposite:* thoughtlessness. 3 *n* **matter**, factor, point, issue, fact, item. [➡SUBJECT AREA; 769] 4 *n* **regard**, esteem, importance, significance, consequence (*formal*), weight, substance. [➡IMPORTANCE AND SIGNIFICANCE; 193]

considered *adj* **careful**, measured, well-thought-out, painstaking. [➡THE NATURE OF IDEAS; 772] *Opposite:* rash.

considering *prep* **bearing in mind**, allowing for, in view of, taking into account. [➡EXPRESSIONS OF REFERENCE; 63] *Opposite:* excluding.

consign 1 *v* **entrust**, commit, hand over, give. [➡DISPENSE, RATION, AND DISTRIBUTE; 435] 2 *v* **relegate**, pack off (*informal*), dispatch, condemn, get rid of, dispose of. [➡GET RID OF SOMETHING; 452] 3 *v* **deliver**, transfer, send, send off, dispatch, remit, hand over, ship. [➡DESPATCH AND SEND; 334]

consignment *n* **batch**, delivery, shipment, load, package, quantity. [➡TRANSPORTATION, TRANSPORTERS, AND CARGOS; 323]

consist 1 *v* **reside**, lie, be based on, depend on, be defined by. [➡AMOUNT TO AND EQUAL; 70] 2 *v* **contain**, be made up of, be made of, entail, involve, comprise. [➡POSSESS; 445]

consistency 1 *n* **constancy**, steadiness, reliability, uniformity, evenness, stability, regularity, dependability. [➡PERMANENCE: WITHOUT CHANGE; 95] *Opposite:* inconsistency. 2 *n* **texture**, thickness, runniness, feel, makeup. [➡DENSITY AND CONSISTENCY; 1206]

consistent 1 *adj* **coherent**, uniform, harmonious, even. [➡HARMONY; 156] *Opposite:* contradictory. 2 *adj* **reliable**, steady, dependable, constant, unswerving, unfailing, regular, stable. [➡PERMANENCE: WITHOUT CHANGE; 95] *Opposite:* inconsistent.

consistently 1 *adv* **time after time**, time and again, again and again, every time, constantly, without fail, over and over, always. [➡PERMANENCE: WITHOUT CHANGE; 95] *Opposite:* erratically. 2 *adv* **reliably**, steadily, dependably, constantly, unswervingly, unfailingly, regularly. [➡PERMANENCE: WITHOUT END; 94] *Opposite:* inconsistently.

consolation *n* **comfort**, solace, relief, support. [➡TREAT; 211] *Opposite:* grief.

consolatory *adj* [➡CALMING; 189]

console 1 *v* **comfort**, cheer up, soothe, calm, relieve, support, solace. [➡SOOTHE AND CALM; 574] *Opposite:* depress. 2 *type of* **hardware**. [➡COMPUTERS AND COMPUTING; 1126] 3 *type of* **table**. [➡FURNITURE; 858]

consolidate 1 *v* **combine**, unite, join, fuse, merge, associate, amalgamate. [➡COMBINE AND MIX; 401] *Opposite:* split up. 2 *v* **strengthen**, firm up, establish, confirm, enhance. [➡IMPROVE STRENGTH AND DURABILITY; 379] *Opposite:* weaken.

consolidation 1 *n* **alliance**, merging, union, link, association, amalgamation, partnership, joining. [➡CONNECTION; 144] *Opposite:* split. 2 *n* **strengthening**, firming, establishment, solidification, firming up. [➡IMPROVE STRENGTH AND DURABILITY; 379] *Opposite:* weakening.

consoling *adj* [➡GENEROSITY AND KINDNESS; 496]

consommé *type of* **soup**. [➡SOUP; 1185]

consonant (*formal*) *adj* **in agreement with**, at one with, consistent with, compatible with, in harmony with. [➡HARMONY; 156] *Opposite:* incompatible.

consort 1 *n* (*formal*) **companion**, partner, associate, spouse, wife, husband. [➡RELATIVES BY MARRIAGE; 960] 2 *n* **ensemble**, group, orchestra, band. [➡MUSICIANS AND SINGERS; 908]

consortium *n* **group**, grouping, association, conglomerate, syndicate, confederation. [➡BUSINESS ENTERPRISES AND RELATED BODIES; 793]

consort with (*formal*) *v* **associate with**, hang out (*informal*), accompany, mix, mingle, hang around. [➡ESTABLISHING RELATIONSHIPS WITH OTHERS; 974]

conspicuous 1 *adj* **visible**, noticeable, obvious, exposed, on show, in the limelight. [➡PERCEPTIBLE; 25] *Opposite:* inconspicuous. 2 *adj* **eye-catching**, striking, prominent, outstanding, notable, marked, noticeable, obvious, evident, patent, plain, clear. [➡PERCEPTIBLE; 25] *Opposite:* unremarkable.

conspicuously *adv* **noticeably**, obviously, clearly, evidently, visibly. [➡PERCEPTIBLE; 25] *Opposite:* inconspicuously.

conspicuousness *n* [➡PERCEPTIBLE; 25]

conspiracy *n* **plot**, scheme, plan, intrigue, collusion, machination, sedition, treachery. [➡BAD BEHAVIOUR OR ACTION; 255]

conspirator *n* **schemer**, plotter, conniver, collaborator, accomplice. [➡PEOPLE WHO DECEIVE; 662]

conspire 1 *v* **plot**, connive, plan, work against. [➡PREDICT AND ANTICIPATE; 751] 2 *v* **combine**, work together, unite, collaborate, collude, contrive, devise, machinate. [➡DEVELOP THEORIES AND REASON; 745]

constable *n* [➡THE POLICE, ARREST, AND PRE-TRIAL PROCEEDINGS; 818]

constabulary *n* [➡THE POLICE, ARREST, AND PRE-TRIAL PROCEEDINGS; 818]

constancy 1 *n* **faithfulness**, loyalty, fidelity, dependability, reliability, devotion. [➡HARD-WORKING AND COMMITTED; 501] *Opposite:* unfaithfulness. 2 *n* **steadiness**, firmness, consistency, steadfastness, endurance, single-mindedness. [➡PERMANENCE: WITHOUT CHANGE; 95] *Opposite:* inconsistency.

constant 1 *adj* **continuous**, endless, relentless, continual, persistent, perpetual, unbroken, unceasing, ceaseless, unremitting, incessant. [➡PERMANENCE: WITHOUT END; 94] *Opposite:*

intermittent. 2 *adj* **frequent**, persistent, recurrent, incessant, recurring, continual. [➡FREQUENT AND OFTEN; 107] *Opposite:* occasional. 3 *adj* **steady**, stable, even, invariable, unvarying, regular, uniform, unchanging. [➡PERMANENCE: WITHOUT CHANGE; 95] *Opposite:* irregular. 4 *adj* **faithful**, loyal, trustworthy, devoted, allegiant, staunch, steadfast. [➡HARD-WORKING AND COMMITTED; 501] *Opposite:* disloyal.

constantly *adv* **continually**, continuously, always, regularly, frequently, persistently, relentlessly, incessantly, endlessly, ceaselessly, perpetually, forever, repetitively. [➡PERMANENCE: WITHOUT END; 94] *Opposite:* intermittently.

constellation 1 *n type of* **star or star system**. [➡CELESTIAL BODIES; 1060] 2 *n* **group**, gathering, collection, assemblage, pattern, arrangement. [➡COLLECTIONS AND MIXTURES OF THINGS; 1243]

consternation *n* **dismay**, disquiet, alarm, anxiety, worry, dread, trepidation, bewilderment. [➡SADNESS, DISTRESS, AND DESPAIR; 540] *Opposite:* composure.

constituency 1 *n* **area**, borough, ward, region. [➡HUMAN SETTLEMENTS; 1069] 2 *n* **electorate**, voters, population, public, community, citizenry (*formal*). [➡GROUPS IN SOCIETY; 940]

constituent 1 *n* **voter**, citizen, resident. [➡INHABITANT; 857] 2 *n* **ingredient**, element, component, part. [➡PHYSICAL OBJECTS; 1242] 3 *adj* **basic**, essential, integral, component, fundamental, principal. [➡FUNDAMENTAL; 196]

constitute 1 *v* **amount to**, represent, add up to, signify, total, equal. [➡AMOUNT TO AND EQUAL; 70] *Opposite:* fall short of. 2 *v* **comprise**, make up, form, compose, represent. [➡POSSESS; 445] 3 *v* (*formal*) **set up**, establish, found, create, institute, start, organize. [➡INSTITUTE AND INAUGURATE; 349] *Opposite:* disband.

constitution 1 *n* **charter**, bill, instrument of government, statute. [➡LEGISLATIVE BODIES AND LEGISLATION; 809] 2 *n* **health**, makeup, disposition, nature, condition. [➡PHYSICAL STATES; 735] 3 *n* **establishment**, creation, formation, organization, foundation. [➡BEGINNING; 53] 4 *n* **composition**, structure, makeup, components, constituents, parts. [➡QUALITIES AND CHARACTERISTICS; 1190]

constitutional *adj* **legitimate**, legal, lawful, statutory. [➡LEGAL; 815] *Opposite:* unconstitutional.

constrain 1 *v* **oblige**, compel, pressure, make, coerce, force. [➡CAUSE OR COMPEL TO ACT; 272] 2 *v* **limit**, restrain, hold back, confine, restrict, constrict, hamper, hinder, inhibit, check. [➡AVOID, PREVENT, LIMIT, AND CONTROL; 278]

constrained *adj* **forced**, unnatural, inhibited, controlled, embarrassed, guarded, self-conscious, reserved. [➡CAPTIVITY AND LOSS OF FREEDOM; 249] *Opposite:* natural.

constraint *n* **restriction**, limitation, restraint, constriction, limit, control. [➡CAPTIVITY AND LOSS OF FREEDOM; 249] *Opposite:* freedom.

constrict 1 *v* **tighten**, narrow, contract, compress, shrink, squeeze. [➡CONTACT: EXERT PRESSURE; 415] *Opposite:* loosen. 2 *v* **limit**, restrict, constrain, narrow, control, restrain, inhibit. [➡CAPTIVITY AND LOSS OF FREEDOM; 249] *Opposite:* extend.

constricted *adj* **limited**, restricted, restrained, bound, confined, held, trapped, straitened. [➡CAPTIVITY AND LOSS OF FREEDOM; 249] *Opposite:* free.

constriction 1 *n* **tightening**, contraction, narrowing, compression, shrinking. [➡CHANGE OF SIZE: SMALLER; 394] *Opposite:* loosening. 2 *n* **restriction**, constraint, limitation, limit, condition, check. [➡CAPTIVITY AND LOSS OF FREEDOM; 249]

construct 1 *v* **build**, make, create, put up, erect, raise, assemble, fabricate, fashion, form. [➡BUILD; 353] *Opposite:* knock down. 2 *v* **compose**, put together, create, structure, piece together. [➡CREATION; 347] *Opposite:* take apart. 3 *n* **concept**, hypothesis, theory, paradigm, idea. [➡IDEA AND THOUGHT; 771]

construction 1 *n* **creation**, assembly, manufacture, production, erection, formation, composition. [➡CREATION; 347] *Opposite:* destruction. 2 *n* **building**, edifice, structure, creation, erection. [➡BUILDING AND ARCHITECTURE; 1075] 3 *n* **interpretation**, understanding, comprehension, meaning, spin (*slang*), explanation. [➡IDEA AND THOUGHT; 771]

constructive *adj* **positive**, helpful, productive, useful, beneficial, practical, fruitful, profitable. [➡CHEERFULNESS OF OUTLOOK; 504] *Opposite:* unhelpful.

constructively *adv* **usefully**, beneficially, helpfully, fruitfully, positively, profitably, practically, productively. [➡USEFULNESS; 200] *Opposite:* unhelpfully.

constructivism *type of* **20th-century art movement**. [➡ARTISTIC MOVEMENTS AND STYLES; 899]

construe *v* **interpret**, take, read, see, understand. [➡UNDERSTAND AND GRASP; 760]

consul *n* **diplomat**, ambassador, representative, emissary, envoy. [➡POLITICAL OFFICES AND POLITICIANS; 808]

consult 1 *v* **ask**, check, discuss, talk to, confer, see, sound out. [➡ASK PEOPLE QUESTIONS; 667] 2 *v* **refer**, look up, turn to, check, access. [➡EXAMINE AND ASSESS; 754]

consultant *n* **adviser**, mentor, counsellor, expert, specialist, professional, authority. [➡BOSSES AND MANAGEMENT; 965]

consultation *n* **discussion**, talk, session, meeting, conference, soundings. [➡NEGOTIATION AND DEBATE; 46]

consume 1 *v* **eat**, drink, devour, put away (*informal*), munch, chomp (*informal*), guzzle (*informal*), feed on, ingest. [➡EAT AND NOT EAT; 711] 2 *v* **use**, use up, expend, spend, utilize, exhaust, get through. [➡USE UP AND WASTE; 475] *Opposite:* conserve. 3 *v* **destroy**, annihilate, burn up, incinerate, burn down, raze, devour. [➡DESTRUCTION AND DEMOLITION; 360]

consumer *n* **buyer**, purchaser, shopper, customer, user, end user, punter (*informal*). [➡PURCHASER; 425]

consummate 1 *v* **complete**, carry out, achieve, accomplish, conclude, effectuate. [➡COMPLETE AN ACTION; 264] 2 *adj* **skilled**, skilful, expert, accomplished, talented, competent. [➡TALENTED AND SKILFUL; 528] *Opposite:* inept. 3 *adj* **perfect**, excellent, complete, ideal, flawless, supreme. [➡EXTRAORDINARY: AMAZING; 205] *Opposite:* imperfect. 4 *adj* **utter**, out-and-out, total, complete, absolute, unmitigated, chronic, errant, unredeemed. [➡ABSOLUTE AND ABSOLUTELY; 131]

consumption 1 *n* **depletion**, use, expenditure, utilization, spending, using up, burning up. [➡USE UP AND WASTE; 475] *Opposite:* conservation. 2 *n* **ingesting**, feasting, feeding, eating, drinking, intake, ingestion. [➡EAT AND NOT EAT; 711]

contact 1 *n* **interaction**, communication, dealings, connection, exchange, commerce, touching base (*US*). [➡COMMUNICATION; 603] 2 *n* **advocate**, reference, acquaintance, connection, friend, link, associate. [➡SUPPORTERS, PROTECTORS, AND COMPATRIOTS; 970] 3 *v* **get in touch**, make contact, drop a line, communicate, write, telephone, call, phone, ring up, e-mail, touch base. [➡INITIATE AND ESTABLISH COMMUNICATION; 681]

contagious *adj* **transmissible**, transmittable, spreadable, infectious, catching, communicable. [➡SICKNESS; 730]

contain 1 *v* **cover**, take in, comprise, encompass, comprehend (*formal*), hold, have, enclose, surround, include. [➡HOLD AND CONTAIN; 456] *Opposite:* exclude. 2 *v* **check**, control, restrain, hold back, inhibit, suppress, repress. [➡AVOID, PREVENT, LIMIT, AND CONTROL; 278] *Opposite:* unleash. 3 *v* **limit**, control, keep in check, delimit (*formal*), restrict, confine. [➡CAPTIVITY AND LOSS OF FREEDOM; 249]

contained *adj* **limited**, controlled, delimited (*formal*), checked, confined, restricted, kept in check. [➡CAPTIVITY AND LOSS OF FREEDOM; 249] *Opposite:* unbounded.

container

◆ *types of container*
barrel, billycan, biscuit tin, box, caddy, can, cardboard box, carton, cartridge, case, cask, casket, chest, cover, crate, creel, cylinder, drawer, drum, hamper, holder, jam jar, jar, jerry can, keg, pencil case, pigeonhole, pillbox, pot, punnet, storage bin, storage tank, tea caddy, trunk

contaminate *v* **soil**, pollute, foul, taint, infect, sully, dirty. [➡DIRTY AND CONTAMINATE; 405] *Opposite:* purify.

contaminated *adj* **dirty**, dirtied, filthy, soiled, polluted, unclean, adulterated, diseased, spoiled, ruined, tainted, stained, infected, infested, fouled, corrupted, unhealthy, unsanitary, unhygienic, noxious, poisonous, poisoned, impure. [➡DIRTY; 1234] *Opposite:* pure.

contamination *n* **pollution**, adulteration, corruption, infection, uncleanness, impurity. [➡DIRTY AND CONTAMINATE; 405] *Opposite:* decontamination.

contemplate 1 *v* **look**, gaze, stare, watch, examine, observe, survey, scrutinize. [➡LOOKING AND LOOKS; 701] 2 *v* **weigh**, muse, deliberate, consider, think, mull over, reflect, study, ponder. [➡THINK AND REFLECT; 744] 3 *v* **anticipate**, expect, plan, think of, consider, intend, envisage, envision. [➡PREDICT AND ANTICIPATE; 751] 4 *v* **meditate**, muse, imagine, envisage, envision, think, picture, consider, deliberate, study. [➡DREAM, IMAGINE, AND FANTASIZE; 750]

contemplation 1 *n* **inspection**, observation, survey, review, scrutiny, examination. [➡LOOKING AND LOOKS; 701] 2 *n* **thought**, meditation, consideration, deliberation (*formal*), study, reflection. [➡THINK AND REFLECT; 744]

contemplative *adj* **thoughtful**, meditative, deep in thought, lost in thought, absorbed, pensive, reflective, introspective, musing, brooding. [➡PENSIVENESS AND INTEREST; 539] *Opposite:* unthinking.

contemporaneity *n* [➡CONCURRENT AND CONTEMPORANEOUS; 165]

contemporaneous *adj* **concurrent**, coexistent, concomitant, contemporary, simultaneous, synchronous. [➡CONCURRENT AND CONTEMPORANEOUS; 165]

contemporaneousness *n* [➡CONCURRENT AND CONTEMPORANEOUS; 165]

contemporaries *n* [➡CONCURRENT AND CONTEMPORANEOUS; 165]

contemporarily *adv* [➡CONCURRENT AND CONTEMPORANEOUS; 165]

contemporary 1 *adj* **current**, modern, up-to-date, present-day, existing, present, ongoing. [➡PRESENT; 85] *Opposite:* old. 2 *n* **peer**, colleague, classmate. [➡COLLEAGUES AND EQUALS; 967] *Opposite:* senior.

contempt *n* **disdain**, dislike, disrespect, disapproval, scorn, hatred, derision, condescension. [➡ANTAGONISM; 553] *Opposite:* admiration.

contemptibility *n* [➡UNACCEPTABLE AND UNFORGIVEABLE; 226]

contemptible *adj* **despicable**, disgraceful, shameful, detestable, distasteful, disreputable, loathsome. [➡UNACCEPTABLE AND UNFORGIVEABLE; 226] *Opposite:* laudable.

contemptibleness *n* [➡UNACCEPTABLE AND UNFORGIVEABLE; 226]

contemptibly *adv* **despicably**, shamefully, disgracefully, dishonourably, detestably, shabbily, unworthily, meanly, loathsomely, vilely, badly, dreadfully, shockingly, appallingly. [➡MORALLY BAD; 776] *Opposite:* laudably.

contemptuous *adj* **scornful**, derisive, condescending, disdainful, disapproving, sneering, disrespectful, supercilious. [➡POMPOUS, LOUD, AND OVER-CONFIDENT; 636] *Opposite:* admiring.

contemptuously *adv* **scornfully**, sneeringly, disdainfully, disapprovingly, derisively, condescendingly, disrespectfully. [➡RUDE AND HOSTILE; 626] *Opposite:* admiringly.

contemptuousness *n* **scornfulness**, disrespect, scorn, disdain, derision, contempt, condescension, disdainfulness. [➡BAD MANNERS AND SOCIAL SKILLS; 522] *Opposite:* admiration.

contend 1 *v* **argue**, assert, insist, maintain, state, declare. [➡CLAIM, INSIST, AND EMPHASIZE; 615] 2 *v* **compete**, vie, challenge, run, put yourself forward, nominate yourself. [➡COMPETE, CONTEND, AND COMBAT; 304] 3 *v* **struggle**, resist, oppose, deal with, put up with, cope. [➡COMPETE, CONTEND, AND COMBAT; 304]

contender *n* **candidate**, nominee, competitor, contestant, challenger, runner, entrant. [➡COMPETITORS; 41]

See Compare and Contrast at **candidate**.

contend with *v* [➡EXPERIENCE AND ENCOUNTER; 583]

content 1 *n* **substance**, matter, subject matter, gist, contents, subject. [➡BASIC DETAILS; 689] 2 *adj* **gratified**, happy, satisfied, contented, pleased, comfortable, at ease, relaxed. [➡PLEASURE, EXCITEMENT, AND ELATION; 535] *Opposite:* unhappy. 3 *v* **gladden**, soothe, satisfy, please, make happy, gratify, comfort. [➡PLEASE AND AMUSE; 573] *Opposite:* dissatisfy.

contented *adj* **happy**, satisfied, pleased, content, comfortable, at ease, relaxed, gratified. [➡PLEASURE, EXCITEMENT, AND ELATION; 535] *Opposite:* unhappy.

contention 1 *n* **assertion**, position, argument, opinion, belief, claim. [➡POINT OF VIEW; 768] 2 *n* **argument**, disagreement, dispute, disputation (*formal*), debate, conflict, controversy, strife. [➡CRITICISMS AND ANGRY OUTBURSTS; 50] *Opposite:* harmony.

contentious 1 *adj* **controversial**, polemical, provocative, critical, disputatious (*formal*). [➡UNCERTAIN; 176] *Opposite:* uncontroversial. 2 *adj* **argumentative**, combative, quarrelsome, antagonistic, prickly (*informal*), touchy, naysaying, belligerent, hot-blooded. [➡AGGRESSIVE AND BELLIGERENT; 519] *Opposite:* easygoing.

contentment *n* **serenity**, gladness, satisfaction, happiness, pleasure, gratification, ease. [➡APPRECIATION AND GRATITUDE; 536] *Opposite:* discontent.

contest 1 *n* **competition**, tournament, challenge, race, match, gala, fight, game. [➡NON-AGGRESSIVE/SPORTING EVENT; 40] 2 *v* **challenge**, dispute, question, oppose, query, argue. [➡DENY AND REJECT; 645] *Opposite:* accept.

contestant *n* **competitor**, contender, participant, participator, challenger, entrant, runner, opponent, rival. [➡COMPETITORS; 41]

See Compare and Contrast at **candidate**.

context *n* **setting**, background, circumstances, situation, framework, milieu (*formal*), perspective, environment. [➡SITUATIONS; 71]

contextual *adj* **background**, related, circumstantial. [➡RELATED; 143]

contiguity (*formal*) *n* [➡CLOSENESS; 160]

contiguous (*formal*) *adj* [➡CLOSENESS; 160]

continent *n* **landmass**, mainland, land. [➡THE CONTINENTS AND ISLANDS; 1048]

continental quilt *n* [➡SOFT FURNISHINGS, LINEN, AND DRAPERY; 860]

contingency *n* **eventuality**, possibility, likelihood, exigency, emergency, incident. [➡CHANCE EVENT; 36]

contingent 1 *adj* **depending**, liable, dependent, reliant, conditional, subject, provisional. [➡RECIPROCITY AND INTERDEPENDENCE; 148] 2 *n* **commission**, legation, committee, party, group, deputation, delegation. [➡GROUPS OF PEOPLE; 935]

continual *adj* **repeated**, frequent, recurrent, incessant, constant, persistent, repetitive. [➡PERMANENCE: WITHOUT END; 94] *Opposite:* intermittent.

continuance *n* **extension**, protraction, extending, protracting, perpetuation, endurance, continuation, persistence, maintenance, prolongation. [➡PERMANENCE: WITHOUT END; 94] *Opposite:* halting.

continuation 1 *n* **continuance**, extension, drawing out, persistence, maintenance, furtherance, prolongation, perpetuation, protraction. [➡PERMANENCE: WITHOUT END; 94] *Opposite:* halting. 2 *n* **addition**, sequel, instalment, extension, carry over, follow-up, furtherance, follow-on, spin-off. [➡PERMANENCE: WITHOUT END; 94]

continue 1 *v* **prolong**, maintain, carry on. [➡CAUSE TO CONTINUE; 268] *Opposite:* stop. 2 *v* **last**, endure, linger, remain, stay. [➡CONTINUE TO EXIST; 17] *Opposite:* end. 3 *v* **renew**, restart, revive, regenerate, resume. [➡CONTINUE AN ACTION; 263]

continuing *adj* **ongoing**, current, enduring, remaining, unending, lasting, permanent, persistent, steady, constant, perpetual. [➡PERMANENCE: WITHOUT END; 94] *Opposite:* finished.

continuity *n* **steadiness**, endurance, continuousness, permanence, stability. [➡PERMANENCE: WITHOUT CHANGE; 95] *Opposite:* interruption.

continuous *adj* **incessant**, unceasing, nonstop, unremitting, constant, unbroken, uninterrupted, endless. [➡PERMANENCE: WITHOUT END; 94] *Opposite:* intermittent.

continuousness *n* [➡PERMANENCE: WITHOUT END; 94]

continuum *n* [➡PERMANENCE: WITHOUT END; 94]

contort *v* **grimace**, distort, twist, screw, warp, deform. [➡CHANGE OF SHAPE; 386]

contour *n* **outline**, delineation, silhouette, relief, curve, line, shape. [➡SHAPE; 1215]

contra *prep* [➡FOREIGN WORDS AND PHRASES; 673]

contraband *n* [➡PROCEEDS OF CRIME; 428]

contract 1 *n* **agreement**, bond, indenture, pact, convention, deal, treaty. [➡OFFICIAL DOCUMENTS; 587] 2 *v* **diminish**, grow smaller, shrink, tighten, narrow, shrivel, wither. [➡CHANGE OF SIZE: SMALLER; 394] *Opposite:* expand. 3 *v* **incubate**, catch, go down, become infected with, get, develop, come down with. [➡FALL ILL, TREAT, AND RECOVER; 729] *Opposite:* fight off. 4 *v* **sign**, commission, sign up, commit, engage, hire, employ. [➡CONFER STATUS; 459]

contraction 1 *n* **reduction**, shrinkage, tightening, narrowing, retrenchment, shrivelling, withering. [➡CHANGE OF SIZE: SMALLER; 394] *Opposite:* expansion. 2 *n* **tightening**, jerking, cramp, spasm, tic, convulsion. [➡PAIN AND OTHER PHYSICAL SENSATIONS; 734] 3 *n* **shortening**, merging, combining, abbreviation, ellipsis, reduction. [➡ASPECTS OF LANGUAGE; 683]

contractor *n* **servicer**, worker, independent, outworker, freelancer, supplier. [➡BUSINESS PEOPLE; 794]

contract out *v* **delegate**, offer, subcontract, outsource, farm, farm out, lease. [➡DISPENSE, RATION, AND DISTRIBUTE; 435]

contradict 1 *v* **deny**, reverse, gainsay (*formal*), oppose, challenge, dispute, controvert (*formal*), refute, negate (*formal*). [➡DENY AND REJECT; 645] *Opposite:* confirm. 2 *v* **disprove**, cancel, refute, dispute, undermine, cancel out. [➡DISHARMONY; 157] *Opposite:* support.

contradiction 1 *n* **illogicality**, flaw, inconsistency, incongruity, ambiguity, paradox, conflict. [➡DISHARMONY; 157] 2 *n* **denial**, disputation (*formal*), disagreement, challenge, negation, opposition, refutation. [➡DENY AND REJECT; 645] *Opposite:* confirmation.

contradictory *adj* **inconsistent**, self-contradictory, contrary, opposing, clashing, conflicting, at odds, differing, incongruous, ambiguous, paradoxical. [➡DISHARMONY; 157] *Opposite:* consistent.

contraption *n* **gadget**, machine, device, apparatus, contrivance, mechanism. [➡DEVICES; 1114]

contrarily *adv* **disobediently**, rebelliously, stubbornly, wilfully, defiantly, obstinately, uncooperatively, perversely. [➡UNWILLINGNESS AND STUBBORNNESS; 565] *Opposite:* cooperatively.

contrariness *n* **disobedience**, uncooperativeness, perversity, rebelliousness, wilfulness, defiance, obstinacy, stubbornness. [➡UNWILLINGNESS AND STUBBORNNESS; 565] *Opposite:* cooperation.

contrary 1 *adj* **conflicting**, opposing, different, differing, divergent, dissimilar, antagonistic, disagreeing. [➡DISHARMONY; 157] *Opposite:* similar. 2 *adj* **disobedient**, rebellious, obstinate, uncooperative, defiant, difficult, perverse, stubborn, wilful. [➡UNWILLINGNESS AND STUBBORNNESS; 565] *Opposite:* cooperative. 3 *n* **opposite**, inverse, other side of the coin, converse, reverse, antithesis. [➡OPPOSITE; 158]

contrast 1 *n* **difference**, dissimilarity, distinction, disparity, gap, divergence. [➡DIFFERENCE; 150] *Opposite:* similarity. 2 *v* **compare**, juxtapose, analogize, weigh, distinguish, differentiate, discriminate. [➡EXAMINE AND ASSESS; 754] 3 *v* **stand out**, stick out like a sore thumb, differ, diverge, conflict, disagree. [➡DIFFERENCE; 150] *Opposite:* agree.

contrasting *adj* **conflicting**, opposing, complementary, different, distinct, divergent, dissimilar, antagonistic. [➡DIFFERENCE; 150] *Opposite:* similar.

contravene *v* **break**, flout, breach, disobey, disregard, infringe, violate. [➡DISOBEY; 303] *Opposite:* observe.

contravention *n* **breaking**, flouting, breach, infringement, disobeying, violation. [➡BAD BEHAVIOUR OR ACTION; 255] *Opposite:* observance.

contretemps (*formal*) *n* [➡ARGUMENT; 47]

contribute 1 *v* **donate**, pay, underwrite, subsidize, back, fund, add, give, supply, provide, sponsor. [➡GIVE AND PROVIDE; 431] 2 *v* **weigh in**, have a say, chip in (*informal*), add, throw in, say, interject, interpose. [➡INTERRUPT AND BUTT IN; 620] 3 *v* **cause**, further, influence, impact, participate, promote, aid, support. [➡PARTICIPATE; 293]

contribution 1 *n* **donation**, gift, giving, payment, subsidy, backing, supply, provision. [➡GIFTS; 439] 2 *n* **influence**, input, role, involvement, say, impact, aid, support. [➡ACTIONS OR UNDERTAKINGS; 260]

contributor *n* **donor**, funder, sponsor, giver, supplier, provider, backer. [➡SUPPORTERS, PROTECTORS, AND COMPATRIOTS; 970]

contributory *adj* **related**, influential, causal, causative, contributing, instrumental, responsible. [➡CAUSATION; 169]

con trick (*informal*) *n* [➡DECEPTION AND LIES; 661]

contrite *adj* **sorry**, repentant, remorseful, regretful, apologetic, penitent, ashamed. [➡EMBARRASSMENT AND HUMILIATION; 543] *Opposite:* impenitent.

contriteness *n* [➡SADNESS, DISTRESS, AND DESPAIR; 540]

contrition *n* **remorse**, repentance, penitence, regret, sorrow, apology, shame. [➡FEELINGS ABOUT THE PAST; 533] *Opposite:* impenitence.

contrivance 1 *n* **gadget**, thingamajig (*informal*), device, apparatus, machine, contraption. [➡DEVICES; 1114] 2 *n* **plot**, setup (*informal*), plan, machination, means, device. [➡WAYS OF DOING THINGS; 295]

contrive *v* **design**, lay out, engineer, arrange, plan, manufacture, plot, machinate, cook up (*informal*). [➡CAUSE TO HAPPEN; 31]

contrived *adj* **forced**, artificial, unnatural, manufactured, fixed, false, affected, unspontaneous. [➡FALSE AND UNREAL; 174] *Opposite:* genuine.

control 1 *v* **operate**, work, run, use, utilize, manipulate, manoeuvre. [➡USE; 468] 2 *v* **restrain**, limit, restrict, hold back, rein in, contain. [➡AVOID, PREVENT, LIMIT, AND CONTROL; 278] 3 *v* **manage**, command, supervise, run, direct, organize. [➡BE IN CHARGE; 271] 4 *v* **rule**, manipulate, influence, dominate, oppress, have a hold over, hold sway over, dictate. [➡BE IN CHARGE; 271] 5 *v* **oversee**, monitor, regulate, inspect, limit, restrict. [➡EXAMINE AND ASSESS; 754] 6 *n* **switch**, regulator, controller, governor, circuit breaker, rheostat, resistor, mechanism, device. [➡ELECTRONICS AND ELECTRICS; 1136] 7 *n* **power**, jurisdiction, rule, domination, hegemony (*formal*), management, direction, running. [➡RESPONSIBILITY; 171] 8 *n* **skill**, manipulation, influence, handling, expertise, skilfulness. [➡SKILLS, TALENTS, AND ABILITIES; 527] 9 *n* **limit**, limitation, constraint, restriction, restraint, regulation, check, curb. [➡CAPTIVITY AND LOSS OF FREEDOM; 249]

controllable *adj* **manageable**, governable, untroublesome, easy to deal with, well-behaved, well-disciplined, well-regulated. [➡THE WILL AND WILLINGNESS; 564] *Opposite:* uncontrollable.

controlled 1 *adj* **skilful**, measured, precise, meticulous, exact, well-ordered, organized, orderly, ordered, coordinated, structured, restrained, disciplined. [➡INTENTIONAL AND DELIBERATE; 280] *Opposite:* slapdash. 2 *adj* **regulated**, delimited (*formal*), structured, planned, measured. [➡ORDER AND ORGANISATION; 207] *Opposite:* free. 3 *adj* **contained**, unflappable, under control, constrained, self-controlled, self-possessed, composed, calm, cool, unemotional, limited, restricted; in check, tamed, reserved, restrained, deliberate, disciplined, moderate, guarded, inhibited. [➡CONFIDENCE AND COMPOSURE; 500] *Opposite:* unconstrained.

controller 1 *n* **supervisor**, manager, organizer, regulator, director, checker. [➡BOSSES AND MANAGEMENT; 965] 2 *n* **regulator**, switch, control, device, governor, rheostat. [➡ELECTRONICS AND ELECTRICS; 1136]

control panel *n* **instrument panel**, console, dashboard, dash, instrumentation. [➡PARTS OF MACHINES AND TOOLS; 1117]

controls *n* **instrument panel**, wheel, helm. [➡PARTS OF MACHINES AND TOOLS; 1117]

controversial *adj* **contentious**, provocative, debated, debatable, divisive, hot, notorious, scandalous, heated, polemic. [➡UNCERTAIN; 176]

controversy *n* **disagreement**, argument, debate, storm, hullabaloo, dispute, polemic. [➡ARGUMENT; 47] *Opposite:* agreement.

contumely (*archaic or literary*) *n* [➡CRITICISMS AND ANGRY OUTBURSTS; 50]

conundrum *n* **puzzle**, mystery, challenge, problem, riddle, enigma. [➡SECRETS AND MYSTERIES; 181]

See Compare and Contrast at **problem**.

conurbation *n* **urban area**, built-up area, urban sprawl, city, metropolis, municipality. [➡HUMAN SETTLEMENTS; 1069]

See Compare and Contrast at **city**.

convalesce *v* **improve**, recover, recuperate, get better, rally, pull through, rest. [➡FALL ILL, TREAT, AND RECOVER; 729] *Opposite:* deteriorate.

convalescence *n* **recuperation**, recovery, restoration, rehabilitation, improvement, getting better. [➡HEALING; 731] *Opposite:* deterioration.

convalescent *adj* **convalescing**, recovering, recuperating, improving, getting better, mending, on the mend. [➡HEALING; 731] *Opposite:* deteriorating.

convene *v* **call together**, assemble, summon, set up, organize, arrange, call up, convoke. [➡CAUSE TO HAPPEN; 31] *Opposite:* disband.

convenience *n* **suitability**, expediency, ease, handiness, opportuneness, accessibility, closeness, nearness. [➡USEFULNESS; 200] *Opposite:* inconvenience.

convenience store *(US) type of* **retail outlet**. [➡RETAIL OUTLETS; 1082]

convenient 1 *adj* **suitable**, expedient, opportune, fitting, appropriate, useful. [➡APPROPRIATE, SUITABLE, ADVISABLE; 185] *Opposite:* inconvenient. 2 *adj* **handy**, close at hand, adjacent, near, close, nearby, accessible. [➡USEFULNESS; 200] *Opposite:* out-of-the-way.

conveniently *adv* **suitably**, expediently, handily, opportunely, accessibly, fittingly, appropriately, usefully. [➡USEFULNESS; 200] *Opposite:* inconveniently.

convent *n* [➡RELIGIOUS BUILDINGS; 1084]

convention 1 *n* **gathering**, meeting, conference, reunion, get-together *(informal)*, caucus. [➡MEETINGS AND ASSEMBLIES; 43] 2 *n* **agreement**, pact, resolution, contract, settlement, treaty, concord, bond, covenant. [➡OFFICIAL DOCUMENTS; 587] 3 *n* **rule**, principle, custom, precept *(formal)*, practice, habit. [➡WAYS OF DOING THINGS; 295]

conventional 1 *adj* **conservative**, conformist, straight *(slang)*, predictable, unadventurous, orthodox, unoriginal. [➡CONSERVATIVE AND UNADVENTUROUS; 518] *Opposite:* adventurous. 2 *adj* **usual**, established, standard, normal, regular, typical, traditional, common. [➡ORDINARINESS; 245] *Opposite:* unusual.

conventionality *n* **conformism**, conservatism, orthodoxy, predictability. [➡APPROPRIATE, SUITABLE, ADVISABLE; 185] *Opposite:* unconventionality.

conventionally 1 *adv* **conservatively**, unadventurously, predictably, orthodoxly, unoriginally. [➡ORDINARINESS; 245] *Opposite:* adventurously. 2 *adv* **usually**, typically, traditionally, commonly, normally, regularly. [➡USUALLY; 108] *Opposite:* unusually.

converge *v* **meet**, join, touch, unite, congregate, come together. [➡FASTEN, LINK, AND JOIN; 409] *Opposite:* diverge.

convergence *n* **meeting**, junction, union, coming together, conjunction, merging. [➡CONNECTION; 144] *Opposite:* divergence.

conversance *n* [➡KNOWLEDGE AND WISDOM; 559]

conversant *adj* **familiar**, up-to-date, au fait, acquainted, aware, knowledgeable. [➡KNOWLEDGE AND WISDOM; 559] *Opposite:* unfamiliar.

conversation *n* **talk**, chat, discussion, tête-à-tête, dialogue, exchange, colloquy *(formal)*, natter *(informal)*. [➡INFORMAL COMMUNICATION; 45]

conversational 1 *adj* **informal**, chatty, relaxed, casual, familiar, intimate. [➡ELOQUENT, TALKATIVE AND LONG-WINDED; 633] *Opposite:* formal. 2 *adj* **colloquial**, spoken, everyday, vernacular, informal, ordinary. [➡COMMUNICATIVE STYLE; 625] *Opposite:* technical.

conversationalist *n* **talker**, communicator, speaker, chatterbox *(informal)*, raconteur, gossip. [➡SPEAKERS AND ORATORS; 604]

converse 1 *v* **talk**, speak, communicate, chat, natter *(informal)*, discuss. [➡TWO-WAY COMMUNICATION; 608] 2 *n* **contrary**, opposite, reverse, inverse, antithesis, other side of the coin. [➡OPPOSITE; 158] *Opposite:* same. 3 *adj* **opposite**, contrary, opposing, reverse, inverse, adverse, antithetical *(formal)*, antipodal, counter. [➡OPPOSITE; 158] *Opposite:* same.

conversely *adv* **on the other hand**, equally, on the contrary, in opposition, contrariwise. [➡OPPOSITE; 158]

conversion 1 *n* **change**, adaptation, alteration, translation, renovation, transformation, transfiguration. [➡CHANGE; 373] 2 *n* **switch**, change, changeover, transfer, move, transition. [➡CHANGE ONE THING FOR ANOTHER; 399]

convert 1 *v* **change**, adapt, alter, renovate, transform, transfigure, transmute. [➡CHANGE; 373] 2 *v* **switch**, change, change over, transfer, go over, exchange. [➡CHANGE ONE THING FOR ANOTHER; 399] 3 *v* **win over**, bring round, talk round, convince, induce, talk into, persuade. [➡INSTRUCT AND TEACH; 610]

See Compare and Contrast at **change**.

convertible 1 *adj* **adaptable**, exchangeable, alterable, translatable, changeable, transformable. [➡USEFULNESS; 200] 2 *type of* **car**. [➡BIKES, CARS, AND CARRIAGES; 1148]

convertiplane *type of* **military aircraft**. [➡AIRCRAFT; 1147]

convex *adj* **curved**, curving, arched, rounded, bowed, U-shaped. [➡ROUNDED SHAPE; 1217] *Opposite:* concave.

convey 1 *v* **take**, carry, transport, bear, send, transfer, deliver. [➡DESPATCH AND SEND; 334] 2 *v* **communicate**, express, suggest, put across, get across, mean. [➡MEAN SOMETHING; 61]

conveyance *n* **transportation**, transport, carriage, transference, transmission, passage, delivery. [➡TRANSPORTATION, TRANSPORTERS, AND CARGOS; 323]

convict 1 *v* **find guilty**, sentence, imprison, condemn, put away *(informal)*, send down *(slang)*. [➡TRIAL, PUNISHMENT,

AND LEGAL OUTCOMES; 819] *Opposite:* acquit. 2 *n* **criminal**, old lag (*slang*), offender, prisoner, villain (*slang*), felon, lawbreaker. [➡CAPTIVES AND PRISONERS; 250]

conviction 1 *n* **certainty**, certitude, confidence, assurance, sincerity, passion, fervour. [➡CERTAINTY; 562] *Opposite:* doubt. 2 *n* **belief**, opinion, principle, faith, persuasion, view. [➡POINT OF VIEW; 768] 3 *n* **sentence**, verdict, condemnation, imprisonment. [➡TRIAL, PUNISHMENT, AND LEGAL OUTCOMES; 819] *Opposite:* acquittal.

convince *v* **persuade**, prove, sway, influence, convert, win over, satisfy, assure, induce, talk into. [➡INSTRUCT AND TEACH; 610]

convinced 1 *adj* **persuaded**, influenced, swayed, won over, converted, induced. [➡CALMNESS, CONFIDENCE, AND COMPOSURE; 537] *Opposite:* doubtful. 2 *adj* **certain**, sure, positive, persuaded, confident, satisfied. [➡CERTAINTY; 562] *Opposite:* unsure. 3 *adj* **committed**, strong, firm, staunch, wholehearted, earnest. [➡CALMNESS, CONFIDENCE, AND COMPOSURE; 537]

convincing 1 *adj* **persuasive**, believable, credible, realistic, true-to-life, compelling, forceful, influential, strong. [➡TRUE AND REAL; 172] *Opposite:* unconvincing. 2 *adj* **undoubted**, substantial, resounding, considerable, conclusive, definite. [➡WHOLENESS AND COMPLETENESS; 199] *Opposite:* doubtful.

See Compare and Contrast at **valid**.

convincingly *adv* **persuasively**, credibly, believably, realistically, influentially, forcefully, compellingly, strongly. [➡TRUE AND REAL; 172] *Opposite:* unconvincingly.

convivial *adj* **pleasant**, welcoming, warm, friendly, hospitable, genial, social, cordial, companionable. [➡FRIENDLINESS AND SOCIABILITY; 495] *Opposite:* unfriendly.

conviviality *n* **pleasantness**, welcome, warmth, friendliness, hospitality, geniality, cordiality, companionableness. [➡FRIENDLINESS AND SOCIABILITY; 495] *Opposite:* unfriendliness.

convivially *adv* [➡GOOD-TEMPERED AND HUMOROUS; 628]

convoluted *adj* **intricate**, complex, complicated, long-winded, elaborate, difficult, tortuous, drawn-out, long-drawn-out. [➡DIFFICULTY AND COMPLEXITY; 243] *Opposite:* straightforward.

convolvulus *type of* **climber**. [➡CLIMBERS; 1033]

convoy 1 *n* **group**, band, party, fleet, line, file, procession. [➡GROUPS OF PEOPLE; 935] 2 *n* **motorcade**, cavalcade, caravan, flotilla, fleet. [➡GROUPS OF VEHICLES; 1151]

convulse *v* **shake**, jerk, tremble, shudder, quiver, agitate, judder. [➡PHYSICAL REACTIONS; 317]

convulsion *n* **seizure**, fit, spasm, paroxysm, tremor, shaking. [➡PAIN AND OTHER PHYSICAL SENSATIONS; 734]

convulsive *adj* **jerky**, sudden, abrupt, violent, uncontrollable, irregular. [➡DESCRIBING BODY MOVEMENTS; 289]

coo *type of* **bird sound**. [➡SOUNDS MADE BY BIRDS; 1262]

co-occur *v* [➡EXIST WITH OTHERS; 18]

cook 1 *v* **heat**, boil, prepare, fry, roast, bake, steam, grill, barbecue, scramble, braise, poach, microwave, sauté, stir-fry, casserole, broil (*US*). [➡COOKING AND FOOD PREPARATION; 354] 2 *n* **chef**, cordon bleu, sous-chef, commis chef. [➡DOMESTIC AND KITCHEN WORKERS; 850]

cooked *adj* **heated**, baked, prepared, roasted, microwaved, boiled, grilled, stewed, steamed, fried, sautéed, stir-fried, barbecued, braised, casseroled, scrambled, poached, broiled (*US*). [➡STATE OF PREPARED FOOD; 1170] *Opposite:* raw.

cooker *type of* **appliance**. [➡HOUSEHOLD APPLIANCES; 1116]

cookery *n* [➡COOKING AND FOOD PREPARATION; 354]

cookie 1 *n* (*US*) [➡CAKES, BISCUITS, AND DESSERTS; 1180] 2 *n* (*informal*) **person**, character, individual, sort (*informal*), type (*informal*), dude (*US slang*). [➡PERSON; 931] 3 *n* [➡THE INTERNET; 1127]

cooking *n* **cookery**, cuisine, catering, home economics. [➡COOKING AND FOOD PREPARATION; 354]

cookout (*US*) *type of* **meal**. [➡MEALS AND PARTS OF MEALS; 1168]

cook the books (*slang*) *v* **embezzle**, cheat, misappropriate, peculate (*formal*). [➡FALSIFY AND CHEAT; 177]

cook up 1 *v* **prepare**, throw together (*informal*), rustle up (*informal*), fix (*informal*), concoct, make. [➡MEAL PREPARATION; 355] 2 *v* (*informal*) **invent**, think up, concoct, devise, plan, plot, contrive. [➡DEVELOP THEORIES AND REASON; 745]

cool 1 *adj* **cold**, chilly, chill, nippy, fresh, arctic (*informal*), frigid, frosty. [➡COLD WEATHER; 1051] *Opposite:* warm. 2 *adj* (*slang*) **wonderful**, fantastic, magnificent, excellent, terrific, groovy (*dated slang*), good. [➡EXTRAORDINARY: AMAZING; 205] *Opposite:* awful. 3 *adj* **calm**, unruffled, nonchalant, casual, imperturbable, unflappable, level-headed, equable, dispassionate, unemotional, tranquil, serene, composed, collected, placid. [➡CALMNESS, CONFIDENCE, AND COMPOSURE; 537] *Opposite:* excited. 4 *adj* **unfriendly**, unenthusiastic, offhand, icy, distant, detached, cold, chilly, frosty, frigid, muted, aloof, unsociable, impersonal, inhospitable. [➡RUDE AND HOSTILE; 626] *Opposite:* friendly. 5 *adj* **fashionable**, sophisticated, stylish, trendy (*informal*), hip (*slang*), with-it (*dated informal*), groovy (*dated slang*), nifty (*informal*). [➡NEW, MODERN; 167] *Opposite:* unfashionable. 6 *v* **make cold**, freshen, refrigerate, cool off, cool down. [➡CHANGE OF TEMPERATURE; 387] *Opposite:* warm. 7 *v* **wane**, dampen down, dampen, cool off, decrease, abate (*formal or literary*). [➡CHANGE OF INTENSITY: LESS; 396] *Opposite:* increase.

cool bag *n* **chiller**, cooler (*US*), cool box. [➡CONTAINERS, RECEPTACLES, AND PACKAGING; 1244]

cool box *n* **cool bag**, chiller, cooler (*US*). [➡CONTAINERS, RECEPTACLES, AND PACKAGING; 1244]

cool down 1 *v* **turn cold**, cool, chill (*slang*), freshen. [➡CHANGE OF TEMPERATURE; 387] *Opposite:* warm up. 2 *v* **calm down**, compose yourself, settle down, simmer down, cool off (*informal*), back off. [➡CHANGE OF MOOD AND COMPOSURE; 581] *Opposite:* flare up.

cooler *n* **chiller**, cool box, cool bag. [➡HEATING, REFRIGERATION, AND VENTILATION; 1141]

cooler

◆ *types of cooling appliance*
air conditioner, air cooler, air exchanger, deepfreeze, freezer, fridge, fridge-freezers, icebox (*US*), refrigerator

coolly 1 *adv* **calmly**, casually, nonchalantly, equably, imperturbably, dispassionately, unflappably, unemotionally, collectedly, evenly, placidly, serenely, tranquilly, sedately. [➡CALMNESS, CONFIDENCE, AND COMPOSURE; 537] *Opposite:* excitedly. 2 *adv* **unenthusiastically**, coldly, impersonally, distantly, unsociably, inhospitably, frostily, icily, frigidly, aloofly. [➡UNINTERESTED AND DETACHED; 630] *Opposite:* enthusiastically.

coolness 1 *n* **cold**, coldness, chill, chilliness, freshness, rawness, nippiness, nip, iciness, frostiness. [➡COLD WEATHER; 1051] *Opposite:* warmth. 2 *n* **calmness**, level-headedness, detachment, aloofness, distance, equanimity, tranquillity, calm, peace, serenity, composure, poise, assurance, self-assurance, self-possession, imperturbability, unflappability. [➡CALMNESS, CONFIDENCE, AND COMPOSURE; 537] *Opposite:* nervousness. 3 *n* **unfriendliness**, chill, chilliness, reserve, hostility, inhospitality, unsociability, coldness, iciness. [➡BAD MANNERS AND SOCIAL SKILLS; 522] *Opposite:* friendliness.

cool off 1 *v* **turn cold**, cool, chill (*slang*), freshen. [➡CHANGE OF TEMPERATURE; 387] *Opposite:* warm up. 2 *v* (*informal*) **calm down**, compose yourself, settle down, simmer down, cool down. [➡CHANGE OF MOOD AND COMPOSURE; 581] *Opposite:* flare up.

co-op 1 *n* (*informal*) **cooperative**, collective, mutual society, friendly society. [➡BUSINESS ENTERPRISES AND RELATED BODIES; 793] 2 *n* (*US informal*) **block of flats**, flats, apartment block, condominium (*US*), apartment house (*US*), apartment building (*US*). [➡RESIDENTIAL BUILDINGS; 1077]

coop *n* **pen**, cage, run, enclosure, hutch, hut, house. [➡ANIMAL OR BIRD ACCOMMODATION; 1078]

cooperate 1 *v* **collaborate**, work together, unite, liaise, band, conjoin (*formal*), join forces. [➡ESTABLISHING RELATIONSHIPS WITH OTHERS; 974] *Opposite:* compete. 2 *v* **oblige**, accommodate, help, aid, assist, play the game. [➡HELP; 294] *Opposite:* hinder.

cooperation *n* **collaboration**, assistance, help, support, teamwork, aid. [➡RECIPROCITY AND INTERDEPENDENCE; 148] *Opposite:* hindrance.

cooperative 1 *adj* **obliging**, helpful, supportive, accommodating, willing, compliant, complaisant. [➡THE WILL AND WILLINGNESS; 564] *Opposite:* difficult. 2 *adj* **joint**, two-way, mutual, shared, collaborative, common, communal, united. [➡BELONGING OR RELATING TO PEOPLE; 943] 3 *n* **collective**, company, co-op (*informal*), organization, association, enterprise. [➡PLACE OF EMPLOYMENT; 832]

cooperatively 1 *adv* **helpfully**, obligingly, accommodatingly, supportively, willingly, compliantly, complaisantly. [➡THE WILL AND WILLINGNESS; 564] *Opposite:* unhelpfully. 2 *adv* **together**, jointly, communally, in common, unitedly, in unison, in concert. [➡ACTING WITH OTHERS; 286] *Opposite:* alone.

cooperativeness *n* [➡THE WILL AND WILLINGNESS; 564]

co-opt *v* **appoint**, designate, choose, bring on board, draft, invite, nominate. [➡CONFER STATUS; 459] *Opposite:* exclude.

coop up *v* **cage**, enclose, pen, house, imprison, shut up, confine. [➡CAPTIVITY AND LOSS OF FREEDOM; 249] *Opposite:* let out.

coordinate *v* **organize**, direct, manage, synchronize, harmonize, bring together, match. [➡ARRANGE AND CREATE ORDER; 358]

coordinates *n* [➡GARMENTS AND OUTFITS; 865]

coordination 1 *n* **organization**, direction, management, harmonization, synchronization, bringing together, matching. [➡ARRANGE AND CREATE ORDER; 358] *Opposite:* disorganization. 2 *n* **dexterity**, skill, adroitness, proficiency, expertise, facility. [➡SKILLS, TALENTS, AND ABILITIES; 527] *Opposite:* clumsiness.

coot *type of* **freshwater bird.** [➡BIRD; 997]

cope *v* **manage**, handle, deal with, survive, hack it (*informal*), get by, muddle through. [➡CONTINUE TO EXIST; 17] *Opposite:* fail.

copied *adj* **imitated**, imitative, counterfeit, mock, imitation, phony, sham, derivative, fake, artificial, bogus, derived, unoriginal, plagiarized, plagiaristic, forged. [➡FALSE AND UNREAL; 174] *Opposite:* original.

copious *adj* **abundant**, plentiful, profuse, bountiful (*literary*), many, numerous, ample, bounteous (*literary*), liberal. [➡MANY, MUCH, LARGE AMOUNT; 117] *Opposite:* scant.

cop-out (*slang*) *n* **excuse**, way round, dodge, evasion, escape, subterfuge. [➡NOT PAY ATTENTION; 765]

cop out (*slang*) *v* **back out**, get out, evade, avoid, withdraw, shirk, dodge. [➡NOT PAY ATTENTION; 765]

copper 1 *type of* **metal.** [➡METALS; 1275] 2 *type of* **brown.** [➡COLOURS; 1223]

copperhead *type of* **poisonous snake.** [➡SNAKE; 995]

coppice *n* **wood**, copse, thicket, grove, covert. [➡WOODS, FORESTS, AND JUNGLES; 1047]

copse *n* **wood**, coppice, thicket, grove, covert. [➡WOODS, FORESTS, AND JUNGLES; 1047]

copy 1 *n* **reproduction**, duplicate, replica, facsimile, print, carbon copy, photocopy, fake, counterfeit, imitation, model. [➡REPRESENTATIONS AND GENERAL EXAMPLES; 65] *Opposite:* original. 2 *n* **item**, book, disk, version, publication. [➡COPIES AND REPLICAS; 152] 3 *n* **text**, words, manuscript, typescript. [➡WRITING; 584] 4 *v* **reproduce**, duplicate, clone, fake, counterfeit, replicate, photocopy, re-create. [➡COPY AND DUPLICATE; 403] 5 *v* **imitate**, mimic, emulate, ape, simulate, impersonate, mime, mock. [➡PRETEND AND MIMIC; 60] *Opposite:* originate.

Compare and Contrast: ***copy, reproduce, duplicate, clone, replicate, re-create***

CORE MEANING: TO MAKE SOMETHING THAT RESEMBLES SOMETHING ELSE TO A GREATER OR LESSER DEGREE

copy to make another identical version of something; ***reproduce*** to make a copy by technical means; ***duplicate*** to copy something two or more times; ***clone*** to make a near or exact copy, especially of a piece of equipment or an organism; ***replicate*** to copy something repeatedly and exactly; ***re-create*** to make something that appears to be the same as something that no longer exists, or that exists in a different place.

coquettish (*literary*) *adj* [➡ FLIRTATIOUS; 640]

coral 1 *type of* **aquatic invertebrate.** [➡ AQUATIC INVERTEBRATE; 1022] 2 *type of* **pink.** [➡ COLOURS; 1223]

coral snake *type of* **poisonous snake.** [➡ SNAKE; 995]

cor anglais *type of* **wind instrument.** [➡ MUSICAL INSTRUMENTS; 910]

cord *n* **string**, twine, rope, cable, flex, thread, lead. [➡ FASTENERS, LINKS, AND NETWORKS; 1246]

cordial 1 *adj* **pleasant**, affable, genial, friendly, affectionate, warm, amiable, jovial, convivial. [➡ FRIENDLINESS AND SOCIABILITY; 495] *Opposite:* unfriendly. 2 *n* [➡ DRINKS; 1186]

cordiality *n* **pleasantness**, geniality, affability, friendliness, affectionateness, warmth, conviviality, jovialness, amiability. [➡ FRIENDLINESS AND SOCIABILITY; 495] *Opposite:* unfriendliness.

cordless *adj* **battery**, battery-operated, freestyle, mobile. [➡ DESCRIBING TECHNOLOGY; 1159]

cordon *n* **barrier**, barricade, obstruction, obstacle, line, chain. [➡ BARRIERS; 1112]

cordon off *v* **close**, bar, isolate, block off, barricade, rope. [➡ SEPARATE AND DIVIDE; 402] *Opposite:* open.

cords *type of* **trousers.** [➡ GARMENTS AND OUTFITS; 865]

corduroy *type of* **fabric from plants.** [➡ FABRICS; 1131]

core 1 *n* **centre**, heart, hub, nucleus, middle, interior, mainstay, focal point, basis, crux, meat, substance, midpoint. [➡ MOST IMPORTANT THING; 198] 2 *n* **essence**, spirit, soul, heart, gist, centre. [➡ CENTRAL PARTS OF PHYSICAL OBJECTS; 1250] 3 *n* **sample**, plug, extract. [➡ PERFECT EXAMPLES AND EMBODIMENTS; 67] 4 *adj* **essential**, central, fundamental, main, principal, basic, primary, staple, underlying. [➡ MOST IMPORTANT AND MAIN; 194] *Opposite:* peripheral.

corgi *type of* **small dog.** [➡ DOG; 980]

coriander 1 *type of* **spice.** [➡ HERBS AND SPICES; 1174] 2 *type of* **herb.** [➡ HERBS AND SPICES; 1174]

Corinthian *type of* **pre-20th-century architecture.** [➡ BUILDING AND ARCHITECTURE; 1075]

corker (*dated informal*) *n* [➡ AMAZING THING; 212]

corkscrew *type of* **utensil.** [➡ TABLEWARE, CUTLERY, AND KITCHENWARE; 861]

cormorant *type of* **seabird.** [➡ SEABIRD; 1002]

corn (*US*) *type of* **cereal.** [➡ CEREAL FOODS; 1177]

corn bread (*US*) *type of* **bread.** [➡ BREAD, FLOUR, AND BREAD PRODUCTS; 1178]

cornea *n* [➡ THE EYE; 699]

corner 1 *n* **angle**, crook, bend. [➡ ANGULAR SHAPE; 1216] 2 *n* **bend**, turn, turning, curve, junction. [➡ BRIDGES, TUNNELS, CROSSINGS, AND JUNCTIONS; 1111] *Opposite:* straight. 3 *n* **place**, spot, area, location, locality, position. [➡ PLACE; 1064] 4 *v* **pin down**, surround, restrict, confront, detain, waylay, accost. [➡ ACCUSE, BLAME, AND CRITICIZE; 642]

corner shop *n* [➡ RETAIL OUTLETS; 1082]

cornerstone *n* **foundation stone**, keystone, foundation, basis. [➡ BUILDING MATERIALS; 1076]

corner the market *v* **dominate**, monopolize, control, command, predominate, prevail. [➡ POSSESS; 445]

cornet *type of* **brass instrument.** [➡ MUSICAL INSTRUMENTS; 910]

cornflour *type of* **flour.** [➡ BREAD, FLOUR, AND BREAD PRODUCTS; 1178]

cornflower blue *type of* **blue.** [➡ COLOURS; 1223]

cornice *n* [➡ ROOFS, ROOF PARTS, AND CEILINGS; 1102]

cornichon *type of* **pickle.** [➡ SEASONINGS AND SAUCES; 1173]

Cornish pasty *n* [➡ BREAD, FLOUR, AND BREAD PRODUCTS; 1178]

cornmeal *type of* **flour.** [➡ BREAD, FLOUR, AND BREAD PRODUCTS; 1178]

corn oil *type of* **cooking fat and oil.** [➡ FATS AND OILS; 1172]

cornrow *type of* **hairstyle.** [➡ HAIR STYLES AND HAIR PIECES; 489]

cornstarch (*US*) *type of* **flour.** [➡ BREAD, FLOUR, AND BREAD PRODUCTS; 1178]

corn syrup (*US*) *n* [➡ SUGAR AND PRESERVES; 1183]

cornucopia *n* **abundance**, profusion, wealth, copiousness, bounty (*literary*), excess. [➡ MANY, MUCH, LARGE AMOUNT; 117] *Opposite:* dearth.

corny *adj* **unsophisticated**, trite, banal, clichéd, hackneyed, unoriginal, old, well-worn, overworked. [➡ BORING AND UNINTERESTING; 235] *Opposite:* original.

corollary *n* **consequence**, result, effect, outcome, upshot, repercussion. [➡ RESULTS AND OUTCOMES; 83]

coronet *n* **crown**, tiara, diadem, circlet, wreath. [➡ JEWELLERY; 866]

corporate 1 *adj* **business**, company, commercial, trade. [➡ BUSINESS; 792] 2 *adj* **communal**, shared, group, community, mutual, joint. [➡ BELONGING OR RELATING TO PEOPLE; 943] *Opposite:* individual.

corporation *n* **company**, business, firm, establishment, concern, organization, house, conglomerate, group. [➡ BUSINESS ENTERPRISES AND RELATED BODIES; 793]

corps 1 *n* **force**, troop, group, company, band, outfit (*informal*). [➡ GROUPS OF PEOPLE; 935] 2 *n* **group**, body, company, organization, league, service. [➡ THE ARMED FORCES; 827]

corpse *n* **dead body**, cadaver, carcass, stiff (*slang*). [➡DEAD PERSON; 926]

corpulence (*formal or literary*) *n* [➡BUILD; 478]

corpulent (*formal or literary*) *adj* **obese**, fat, fleshy, rotund, plump, podgy, pudgy (*informal*). [➡BUILD; 478] *Opposite:* slim.

corral (*US*) *type of* **pen or cage**. [➡ANIMAL OR BIRD ACCOMMODATION; 1078]

correct 1 *v* **rectify**, fix, put right, sort out, mark, amend, emend. [➡CORRECT AND PUT RIGHT; 378] 2 *v* **modify**, amend, alter, adjust, revise, improve. [➡IMPROVE SOMETHING; 375] 3 *adj* **precise**, right, accurate, exact, truthful, spot-on (*informal*), true. [➡EXACT; 204] *Opposite:* inaccurate. 4 *adj* **appropriate**, suitable, proper, acceptable, approved, accepted, standard. [➡CORRECT; 183] *Opposite:* incorrect.

correction *n* **alteration**, improvement, rectification, modification, amendment, adjustment, tweak. [➡IMPROVE SOMETHING; 375]

correctly 1 *adv* **precisely**, right, accurately, rightly, perfectly, exactly. [➡CORRECT; 183] *Opposite:* inaccurately. 2 *adv* **appropriately**, suitably, properly, acceptably, fittingly, decorously. [➡APPROPRIATE, SUITABLE, ADVISABLE; 185] *Opposite:* incorrectly.

correctness 1 *n* **precision**, rightness, truth, accuracy, exactness, perfection. [➡EXACT; 204] *Opposite:* inaccuracy. 2 *n* **appropriateness**, suitability, acceptability, fittingness, uprightness, rectitude, conventionality. [➡APPROPRIATE, SUITABLE, ADVISABLE; 185] *Opposite:* incorrectness.

correlate *v* **relate**, associate, compare, link, draw a parallel, connect. [➡CREATING CONNECTIONS; 145] *Opposite:* dissociate.

correlation *n* **association**, connection, relationship, link, parallel, correspondence. [➡CONNECTION; 144]

correspond 1 *v* **agree**, resemble, parallel, link, match, match up, relate, tally. [➡CREATING CONNECTIONS; 145] *Opposite:* conflict. 2 *v* **communicate**, keep in touch, write, drop a line, fax, e-mail. [➡INITIATE AND ESTABLISH COMMUNICATION; 681]

correspondence 1 *n* **letters**, mail, communication, messages, memos, faxes, e-mail, notes. [➡COMMUNICATION; 603] 2 *n* **agreement**, similarity, resemblance, association, connection, match, equivalence, correlation, conformity. [➡CONNECTION; 144] *Opposite:* clash.

correspondent 1 *n* **communicator**, letter writer, writer, pen friend, pen pal. [➡SUPPORTERS, PROTECTORS, AND COMPATRIOTS; 970] 2 *n* **foreign correspondent**, newspaperman, newspaperwoman, columnist, reporter, journalist, stringer, contributor, author, writer. [➡WORKERS IN ENTERTAINMENT AND MEDIA; 873]

corresponding *adj* **consistent**, conforming, agreeing, matching, equivalent, parallel, analogous. [➡HARMONY; 156]

corridor 1 *n* **passage**, passageway, hall, hallway, walkway. [➡DOORS AND ACCESS POINTS; 1100] 2 *n* **strip**, access strip, air corridor, flight path. [➡AREA AND RANGE; 111]

corrie *n* [➡GEOLOGICAL FEATURES; 1056]

corroborate *v* **verify**, validate, document, support, agree, substantiate, back up, uphold. [➡APPROVE AND CONFIRM; 647] *Opposite:* contradict.

corrode *v* **rust**, disintegrate, destroy, decompose, decay, crumble, flake, wear away, oxidize, eat away. [➡GO BAD AND CORRODE; 391]

corroded *adj* **rusty**, rusted, tarnished, blemished, oxidized, stained, marked, discoloured. [➡DECAYING OR INFESTED; 1235] *Opposite:* pristine.

corrosion *n* **erosion**, weathering, decay, rust, deterioration, decomposition, oxidization. [➡GO BAD AND CORRODE; 391]

corrosive 1 *adj* **harsh**, scarring, eroding, destructive, acidic, caustic, acid. [➡PHYSICAL TEXTURE; 1221] *Opposite:* gentle. 2 *adj* **sarcastic**, undermining, harsh, bitter, biting, caustic, mordant, acerbic, cutting. [➡RUDE AND HOSTILE; 626] *Opposite:* kind.

corrugated *adj* **crenellated**, ridged, ribbed, grooved, wavy, uneven. [➡PHYSICAL TEXTURE; 1221] *Opposite:* smooth.

corrupt 1 *adj* **immoral**, unethical, dishonest, crooked (*informal*), shady, fraudulent. [➡MORALLY BAD; 776] *Opposite:* honest. 2 *v* **debase**, degrade, taint, pervert, warp, spoil, contaminate, alter, damage, distort, harm. [➡MISUSE AND ABUSE; 472]

corrupted *adj* **debased**, degraded, sullied, despoiled, spoiled, besmirched, soiled, stained, contaminated, tainted, fouled, polluted, tarnished, ruined, infected, dirtied. [➡IN BAD REPAIR; 1233] *Opposite:* pure (*literary*).

corruption 1 *n* **dishonesty**, exploitation, bribery, sleaze, fraud, venality. [➡MORALLY BAD; 776] *Opposite:* honesty. 2 *n* **depravity**, perversion (*disapproving*), immorality, harm, debasement, degeneracy, vice. [➡CRIMES; 817]

corruptness *n* [➡MORALLY BAD; 776]

corsage *n* **bouquet**, spray, flowers, arrangement, buttonhole, boutonniere (*formal*). [➡ORNAMENTS AND DECORATIONS; 1247]

corset *type of* **lower body underwear**. [➡HABERDASHERY, MILLINERY, AND LINGERIE; 867]

cosh 1 *v* **hit**, bludgeon, club, strike. [➡WHIP AND CLUB; 418] 2 *type of* **club**. [➡BLUNT INSTRUMENTS AND WHIPS; 1157]

cosily 1 *adv* **snugly**, warmly, pleasantly, comfortably, invitingly, appealingly. [➡PHYSICALLY PLEASANT; 187] *Opposite:* bleakly. 2 *adv* **familiarly**, intimately, closely, warmly, lovingly. [➡EMOTIONALLY PLEASANT; 188] *Opposite:* coldly.

cosmetic 1 *n* **lipstick**, blush, foundation, eye shadow, eyeliner, nail polish, rouge (*dated*), grease paint, makeup, powder, mascara, blusher. [➡MAKEUP AND BEAUTY PRODUCTS; 491] 2 *adj* **superficial**, skin-deep, surface, ornamental, decorative, aesthetic. [➡SECRET AND UNKNOWN; 180] *Opposite:* in-depth.

cosmic 1 *adj* **intergalactic**, interplanetary, interstellar, galactic, planetary, space, extraterrestrial, celestial. [➡THE SOLAR SYSTEM AND ASTRONOMY; 1059] *Opposite:* terrestrial. 2 *adj* **universal**, vast, enormous, huge, immense, global. [➡LARGE; 1192] *Opposite:* tiny.

cosmonaut *n* [➡SPACE TRAVEL AND EXPLORATION; 1061]

cosmopolitan *adj* **multicultural**, multiethnic, pluralistic, diverse, international, multinational, broad-based. [➡POSITIVELY COMPLEX OR COMPLICATED; 218] *Opposite:* provincial (*disapproving*).

cosmos *n* **universe**, space, outer space, ether, heaven. [➡THE SOLAR SYSTEM AND ASTRONOMY; 1059]

cosset *v* **shelter**, protect, spoil, mollycoddle, coddle, indulge, pamper. [➡TAKE CARE OF AND SPOIL; 301] *Opposite:* neglect.

cost 1 *n* **price**, charge, rate, fee, price tag, asking price, total. [➡EXPENDITURE; 424] 2 *n* **budget**, amount, outlay, expenditure, expense, outgoings. [➡EXPENDITURE; 424] 3 *n* **effort**, suffering, detriment, loss, expense, sacrifice, damage (*informal*), harm. [➡NUISANCES; 254]

co-star 1 *n* **star**, film star, actor, lead, movie star (*US*). [➡PERFORMERS; 905] 2 *v* **perform**, collaborate, entertain, star, appear, act. [➡THE PERFORMING ARTS; 904] 3 *v* **feature**, showcase, spotlight, star. [➡THE PERFORMING ARTS; 904] 4 *type of* **entertainer**. [➡WORKERS IN ENTERTAINMENT AND MEDIA; 873]

cost-cutting *n* **saving**, cutbacks, economizing, cutting back, belt tightening, thrift, thriftiness, frugality, downsizing. [➡ACCOUNTING, BANKING, AND BUDGETING; 799]

cost-effective *adj* **lucrative**, moneymaking, profitable, gainful, economical, commercial, worthwhile. [➡ECONOMICAL AND RESOURCEFUL; 208] *Opposite:* uneconomical.

cost-effectiveness *n* [➡ECONOMICAL AND RESOURCEFUL; 208]

costly 1 *adj* **expensive**, overpriced, inflated, high, pricey (*informal*), exorbitant. [➡EXPENSIVE AND OVERPRICED; 248] *Opposite:* inexpensive. 2 *adj* **luxurious**, precious, valuable, lavish, rich, sumptuous. [➡EXPENSIVE AND LUXURIOUS; 219] *Opposite:* basic. 3 *adj* **damaging**, harmful, detrimental, sacrificial. [➡DANGEROUS; 237]

costs *n* **price**, charges, budget, expenses, outlay, expenditure, overheads. [➡EXPENDITURE; 424]

costume *n* **clothes**, clothing, getup (*informal*), regalia, dress, outfit, attire (*formal*), gear (*informal*), uniform. [➡CLOTHES AND ACCESSORIES; 864]

costume drama *n* **play**, spectacle, drama, historical drama, period piece. [➡THE PERFORMING ARTS; 904]

cosy 1 *adj* **snug**, warm, pleasant, comfortable, comfy (*informal*), inviting, appealing, welcoming. [➡PHYSICALLY PLEASANT; 187] *Opposite:* inhospitable. 2 *adj* **familiar**, friendly, intimate, close, warm, loving. [➡EMOTIONALLY PLEASANT; 188] *Opposite:* cold.

cosy up *v* **ingratiate yourself**, curry favour with, make overtures, pander, insinuate, worm your way in. [➡ESTABLISHING RELATIONSHIPS WITH OTHERS; 974] *Opposite:* distance.

cot *type of* **bed**. [➡FURNITURE; 858]

coterie *n* [➡FRIENDS AND ACQUAINTANCES; 936]

cottage *type of* **house**. [➡RESIDENTIAL BUILDINGS; 1077]

cottage cheese *type of* **soft cheese**. [➡DAIRY PRODUCTS AND CHEESES; 1182]

cottage loaf *type of* **bread**. [➡BREAD, FLOUR, AND BREAD PRODUCTS; 1178]

cotton *type of* **fabric from plants**. [➡FABRICS; 1131]

cotton candy (*US*) *type of* **confectionery on a stick**. [➡CONFECTIONERY; 1181]

cotton on (*informal*) *v* **comprehend**, understand, follow, grasp, realize, catch on (*informal*). [➡UNDERSTAND AND GRASP; 760]

cotylosaur *type of* **dinosaur**. [➡DINOSAUR; 996]

couch 1 *n* **sofa**, settee, divan, chaise longue, chesterfield, love seat. [➡FURNITURE; 858] 2 *v* **express**, phrase, put, dress up, word, formulate. [➡NAME AND DESCRIBE; 666]

couchette *type of* **bed**. [➡FURNITURE; 858]

couch grass *type of* **grass**. [➡GRASS; 1031]

cough up (*informal*) *v* **fork out** (*informal*), fork up (*informal*), give, pay, pay up, shell out (*informal*), fork over (*US informal*). [➡GIVE MONEY; 434]

coulis *type of* **seasonings, sauces, and dips**. [➡SEASONINGS AND SAUCES; 1173]

council *n* **assembly**, meeting, board, congress, body, convention, association. [➡ADMINISTRATIVE OFFICERS; 811]

counsel 1 *n* (*formal or literary*) **advice**, guidance, direction, warning, guidelines, suggestions. [➡ADVICE; 690] 2 *v* **support**, advise, help, guide, aid, lend a listening ear. [➡ADVISE AND WARN; 614] 3 *v* (*formal or literary*) **advise**, recommend, advocate, encourage, direct, suggest, instruct, warn. [➡ADVISE AND WARN; 614]

See Compare and Contrast at **recommend**.

counselling *n* **therapy**, psychotherapy, psychoanalysis, analysis, treatment. [➡PSYCHOLOGY AND THE MIND; 770]

counsellor *n* **therapist**, psychotherapist, psychoanalyst, analyst, social worker. [➡ADVISERS, JUDGES, AND ARBITERS; 971]

count 1 *v* **add up**, total, calculate, number crunch (*slang*), tot up, tally, reckon, count up. [➡ASSESS QUANTITY; 758] 2 *v* **consider**, regard, view, deem (*formal*), hold, esteem. [➡DEVELOP THEORIES AND REASON; 745] 3 *v* **make your mark**, weigh, amount to, matter, be important, make a difference, signify. [➡MEAN SOMETHING; 61] 4 *n* **calculation**, computation, reckoning, number crunching (*slang*). [➡SCORES AND EVALUATIONS; 599] 5 *n* **total**, sum total, sum, amount, tally. [➡AMOUNT AND QUANTITY; 112] 6 *type of* **aristocrat**. [➡RULERS AND ARISTOCRACY; 823]

count against *v* **weigh against**, detract, diminish, hurt, backfire, reverse, militate against, counter, oppose. [➡MAKE IMPOSSIBLE; 277] *Opposite:* help.

countenance 1 *n* **expression**, face, features, mien (*literary*), visage (*literary*). [➡HEAD; 693] 2 *v* (*formal*) **tolerate**, stand for, put up with, allow, approve, stomach. [➡TOLERATE AND ENDURE; 767]

counter 1 *type of* **game piece**. [➡GAMES PIECES; 878] 2 *v* **contradict**, dispute, refute, oppose, answer, defy. [➡DISHARMONY; 157] 3 *v* **counteract**, offset, respond, frustrate, thwart, neutralize. [➡MAKE IMPOSSIBLE; 277] 4 *n* [➡MEASURING DEVICES; 1122]

counteract *v* **counter**, offset, respond, frustrate, thwart, neutralize, stabilize, lessen, reduce. [➡MAKE IMPOSSIBLE; 277]

counterattack *n* **attack**, revenge, counteroffensive, retaliation, defence, response, reaction. [➡AGGRESSIVE EVENT; 39]

counterbalance *v* **tip the scales**, offset, balance, correct, compensate. [➡ARRANGE AND CREATE ORDER; 358]

counterclockwise (*US*) *adj* [➡DIRECTION OF MOTION; 346]

counterfeit 1 *adj* **fake**, forged, phoney, bogus, sham, imitation. [➡FALSE AND UNREAL; 174] *Opposite:* genuine. 2 *v* **forge**, fake, copy, fabricate, imitate, simulate. [➡FALSIFY AND CHEAT; 177] 3 *n* **forgery**, copy, fake, imitation, reproduction. [➡REPRESENTATIONS AND GENERAL EXAMPLES; 65] *Opposite:* original.

counterfeited *adj* [➡FALSE AND UNREAL; 174]

counterfeiter *n* **forger**, criminal, fraudster, imitator, faker. [➡CRIMINALS; 821]

countermand *v* **cancel**, revoke, stop, reverse, annul, retract, go against. [➡APOLOGIZE AND RETRACT; 684]

counterpart *n* **opposite number**, equal, equivalent, colleague. [➡COLLEAGUES AND EQUALS; 967]

counter-revolutionary 1 *n* **rebel**, insurgent, insurrectionist, anarchist, radical. [➡UNCOOPERATIVE OR REBELLIOUS PERSON; 567] 2 *adj* **anti-revolutionary**, moderate, democratic, pacifist. [➡STYLES AND SYSTEMS OF GOVERNMENT; 806] *Opposite:* revolutionary.

countertenor *type of* **musical register**. [➡MUSICAL TERMS; 912]

counter to *prep* **against the grain**, against, contrary, in opposition to, at odds with. [➡OPPOSITE; 158]

countess *type of* **aristocrat**. [➡RULERS AND ARISTOCRACY; 823]

countless *adj* **uncountable**, innumerable, myriad, limitless, immeasurable, incalculable, numerous. [➡MANY, MUCH, LARGE AMOUNT; 117] *Opposite:* few.

count on *v* **depend on**, be sure of, rely on, trust, bank on, count upon. [➡LIKE, LOVE, VALUE AND ENJOY; 579]

count out *v* **exclude**, weed out, leave out, omit, disregard. [➡EJECT AND EXCLUDE; 341] *Opposite:* include.

countrified 1 *adj* **unspoiled**, rural, rustic. [➡THE COUNTRYSIDE AND OUTDOOR SPACES; 1070] *Opposite:* urban. 2 *adj* **unsophisticated**, unpolished, unfashionable, simple, rough, ordinary. [➡LEVEL OF EDUCATION AND SOPHISTICATION; 894] *Opposite:* urbane.

country 1 *n* **republic**, state, nation, realm, kingdom, fatherland, motherland, nation state. [➡COUNTRIES AND REGIONS; 1066] 2 *n* **farmland**, woodland, grazing, pastures, wilderness, countryside. [➡THE COUNTRYSIDE AND OUTDOOR SPACES; 1070] *Opposite:* town. 3 *n* **people**, inhabitants, residents, nation, population, voters, populace, citizenry (*formal*). [➡GROUPS IN SOCIETY; 940] 4 *type of* **popular music**. [➡MUSIC, SONGS, AND SINGING; 907]

country club *type of* **bar or club**. [➡HOTELS, RESTAURANTS, AND CLUBS; 1081]

country house *type of* **house**. [➡RESIDENTIAL BUILDINGS; 1077]

countryman *n* **compatriot**, national, citizen, inhabitant, native. [➡SUPPORTERS, PROTECTORS, AND COMPATRIOTS; 970]

countryside *n* [➡THE COUNTRYSIDE AND OUTDOOR SPACES; 1070]

countrywoman *n* **compatriot**, national, citizen, inhabitant, native. [➡SUPPORTERS, PROTECTORS, AND COMPATRIOTS; 970]

count up *v* **total**, add up, count, calculate, tot up, tally, reckon. [➡ASSESS QUANTITY; 758]

county *n* **region**, section, province, district, shire, canton. [➡COUNTRIES AND REGIONS; 1066]

county show *n* [➡PERFORMANCES AND SHOWS; 42]

coup 1 *n* **coup d'état**, overthrow, revolution, rebellion, takeover, upheaval. [➡AGGRESSIVE EVENT; 39] 2 *n* **feather in somebody's cap**, achievement, accomplishment, triumph, feat, success. [➡SUCCESS; 82]

coup de grâce *n* [➡END; 54]

coup d'état *n* **overthrow**, coup, revolution, rebellion, takeover, upheaval. [➡AGGRESSIVE EVENT; 39]

coupé *type of* **car**. [➡BIKES, CARS, AND CARRIAGES; 1148]

couple 1 *n* **twosome**, pair, duo. [➡GROUPS OF PEOPLE; 935] 2 *v* **combine**, link, join, connect, pair, team, fasten. [➡FASTEN, LINK, AND JOIN; 409] *Opposite:* separate.

coupled with *prep* **together with**, in addition to, on top of, as well as, besides. [➡ALSO; 136]

couplet *n* **verse**, distich, stanza, unit, rhyme. [➡POETRY AND VERSE; 915]

coupling 1 *n* **link**, join, connection, connector, coupler. [➡FASTENERS, LINKS, AND NETWORKS; 1246] 2 *n* **combination**, juxtaposition, pairing, blend, mixture. [➡CONNECTION; 144]

coupon *n* **voucher**, ticket, token, slip, form. [➡RECEIPTS AND INVOICES; 592]

courage *n* **bravery**, nerve, pluck, valour, daring, audacity, mettle, resolution, fearlessness, guts (*slang*). [➡CALMNESS, CONFIDENCE, AND COMPOSURE; 537] *Opposite:* cowardice.

Compare and Contrast: ***courage, bravery, fearlessness, nerve, guts, pluck, mettle***

CORE MEANING: PERSONAL RESOLUTENESS IN THE FACE OF DANGER OR DIFFICULTIES

courage the ability to show resoluteness and determination, whether physical, mental, or moral, against a wide range of difficulties or dangers; ***bravery*** extreme lack of fear; ***fearlessness*** resoluteness in the face of dangers or challenges; ***nerve*** coolness, steadiness, and self-assurance; ***guts*** (*slang*) strength of character and boldness; ***pluck*** resolution and willingness to continue struggling against the odds; ***mettle*** spirited determination.

courageous *adj* **brave**, daring, bold, gutsy (*informal*), spirited, plucky, audacious, dauntless (*literary*), fearless, intrepid (*literary or humorous*). [➡COURAGE; 499] *Opposite:* cowardly.

courageousness *n* [➡COURAGE; 499]

courgette *type of* **vegetable**. [➡FRUIT AND VEGETABLES; 1175]

courier 1 *n* **messenger**, carrier, biker, dispatch rider.

[➡MESSENGERS AND COURIERS; 852] **2** *n* **holiday rep**, rep, agent, guide. [➡TRAVEL: SIGHT-SEEING AND TOURISM; 322]

course **1** *n* **sequence**, progression, development, passage, path, way, progress. [➡DIRECTION OF MOTION; 346] **2** *n* **direction**, route, path, track, road, way. [➡DIRECTION OF MOTION; 346] **3** *n* **option**, choice, possibility, route, avenue, strategy, alternative, plan, procedure, policy, enterprise. [➡WAYS OF DOING THINGS; 295] **4** *n* **lesson**, class, programme, module, curriculum, lecture series. [➡LESSONS, COURSE WORK, AND EXAMINATIONS; 842] **5** *v* **flow**, pour, run, gush, stream, surge. [➡PROCEED AND GO; 306] *Opposite:* trickle.

course of action *n* **strategy**, course, policy, plan, method, procedure, system, formula, route, mission, enterprise, undertaking, choice, option, alternative, modus operandi, avenue. [➡WAYS OF DOING THINGS; 295]

coursework *n* **assignments**, homework, project, prep (*informal*). [➡LESSONS, COURSE WORK, AND EXAMINATIONS; 842]

court **1** *n* **law court**, court of law, high court, crown court, magistrate's court, Federal Court, Supreme Court. [➡TRIAL, PUNISHMENT, AND LEGAL OUTCOMES; 819] **2** *n* **courtyard**, square, yard, quad (*informal*), patio, piazza, close, enclosure. [➡URBAN OUTDOOR SPACES; 1071] **3** *v* (*dated*) **date**, go out, see, pay court to (*dated*). [➡ESTABLISHING RELATIONSHIPS WITH OTHERS; 974] **4** *v* **woo**, curry favour with, cosy up, pander to, flatter, ingratiate. [➡FLATTER AND FAWN; 622] *Opposite:* shun. **5** *v* **risk**, invite, encourage, incite, attract, ask for, tempt. [➡INITIATE AND ESTABLISH COMMUNICATION; 681] *Opposite:* shun.

court case *n* **lawsuit**, suit, case, hearing, indictment, prosecution, complaint, litigation, action, proceedings. [➡TRIAL, PUNISHMENT, AND LEGAL OUTCOMES; 819]

courteous *adj* **polite**, well-mannered, considerate, chivalrous, civil, genteel, gallant. [➡GOOD MANNERS AND SOCIAL SKILLS; 521] *Opposite:* rude.

courteousness *n* **politeness**, good manners, courtesy, consideration, civility, manners, gallantry, gentility. [➡GOOD MANNERS AND SOCIAL SKILLS; 521] *Opposite:* rudeness.

courtesy *n* **politeness**, good manners, courteousness, consideration, civility, manners, gallantry, gentility. [➡GOOD MANNERS AND SOCIAL SKILLS; 521] *Opposite:* rudeness.

courthouse *n* **court**, law court, court of law, high court, crown court, magistrate's court, Federal Court, Supreme Court. [➡TRIAL, PUNISHMENT, AND LEGAL OUTCOMES; 819]

courtier *n* **flatterer**, sycophant, self-seeker, toady, creep (*informal*), climber, crawler (*informal*), hanger-on, leech. [➡SUPERFICIAL OR INSINCERE PEOPLE; 951]

courtly *adj* **courteous**, chivalrous, polite, civil, refined, genteel. [➡GOOD MANNERS AND SOCIAL SKILLS; 521] *Opposite:* rude.

court order *n* **legal ruling**, order, sanction, interdict, veto, ban, bar, prohibition, injunction, proscription (*formal*), restriction, embargo, summons, gagging order, exclusion order, ruling, restraining order (*US*). [➡TRIAL, PUNISHMENT, AND LEGAL OUTCOMES; 819]

courtship *n* **wooing**, dating, engagement. [➡SEXUAL AND ROMANTIC RELATIONSHIPS; 964]

court shoe *type of* **shoe**. [➡FOOTWEAR; 871]

courtyard *n* **patio**, yard, square, quad (*informal*), court, enclosure, piazza, close. [➡URBAN OUTDOOR SPACES; 1071]

couscous *type of* **cooked dish**. [➡PREPARED DISHES; 1169]

cousin **1** *n* **friend**, companion, colleague, partner, counterpart. [➡SUPPORTERS, PROTECTORS, AND COMPATRIOTS; 970] **2** *type of* **same generation relative**. [➡SAME GENERATION RELATIVES; 957]

cove *n* **bay**, inlet, harbour. [➡THE SEAS, OCEANS, AND SHORES; 1041]

covenant *n* **agreement**, contract, treaty, promise, pledge, bond, pact. [➡OFFICIAL DOCUMENTS; 587]

cover **1** *v* **conceal**, hide, cover up, obscure, disguise, mask, bury, ensconce. [➡CAUSE TO DISAPPEAR; 6] *Opposite:* expose. **2** *v* **protect**, shield, guard, shelter, defend, safeguard, screen, fend. [➡PREVENT CONTACT OR ATTACK; 420] **3** *v* **wrap**, coat, cover up, envelop, swathe, overlay, enfold, shroud. [➡DECORATE, ADORN, AND APPLY COATINGS; 406] *Opposite:* reveal. **4** *v* **deal with**, include, comprise, embrace, take in, contain, report. [➡BE ABOUT SOMETHING; 62] **5** *v* **travel**, cross, traverse, pass through, go through. [➡TRAVEL: WAYS OF TRAVELLING; 321] **6** *n* **covering**, wrapping, jacket, shell, case, top, lid. [➡COVERS AND COATINGS; 1245] **7** *n* **shelter**, concealment, protection, hiding place, refuge, asylum. [➡COVERS AND COATINGS; 1245] **8** *type of* **container**. [➡CONTAINERS, RECEPTACLES, AND PACKAGING; 1244]

coverage *n* **attention**, treatment, reporting, exposure, handling, analysis, reportage. [➡NEWSPAPERS; 606]

coveralls *n* [➡GARMENTS AND OUTFITS; 865]

covered *adj* **enclosed**, roofed, sheltered, protected, shielded. [➡CAPTIVITY AND LOSS OF FREEDOM; 249] *Opposite:* exposed.

covered market *type of* **retail outlet**. [➡RETAIL OUTLETS; 1082]

covered wagon *type of* **wagon or carriage**. [➡VEHICLES; 1144]

covering *n* **cover**, casing, top, lid, layer, wrapper, shell, jacket. [➡COVERS AND COATINGS; 1245]

coverlet *n* **bedspread**, cover, counterpane (*dated*), throw, bedcover. [➡SOFT FURNISHINGS, LINEN, AND DRAPERY; 860]

covert **1** *adj* **secret**, clandestine, underground, concealed, hidden, furtive, undercover, surreptitious, veiled, hush-hush (*informal*). [➡SECRET AND UNKNOWN; 180] *Opposite:* open. **2** *n* **copse**, wood, thicket, coppice, undergrowth. [➡WOODS, FORESTS, AND JUNGLES; 1047]

See Compare and Contrast at **secret**.

covertness *n* **secrecy**, stealth, concealment, surreptitiousness, clandestineness, underhandedness, furtiveness. [➡SECRET AND UNKNOWN; 180] *Opposite:* openness.

cover-up *n* **whitewash** (*informal*), conspiracy, plot, scheme, smoke screen. [➡WITHHOLD INFORMATION; 688]

cover up **1** *v* **conceal**, hide, obscure, mask, disguise, bury. [➡CAUSE TO DISAPPEAR; 6] *Opposite:* expose. **2** *v* **suppress**, keep under wraps, keep secret, paper over, hide, conceal, hush up (*informal*). [➡WITHHOLD INFORMATION; 688] *Opposite:* divulge.

covet *v* **want**, long for, yearn for, crave, hanker after, desire, wish for. [➡DESIRE AND WANT; 580]

See Compare and Contrast at **want**.

coveted *adj* **sought-after**, longed for, wanted, fashionable, desired, desirable, popular, in demand. [➡POPULAR AND WANTED; 221] *Opposite:* scorned.

covetous *adj* **envious**, jealous, desirous (*formal*), greedy, avaricious, acquisitive. [➡ENVY AND JEALOUSY; 549] *Opposite:* generous.

covetousness *n* **envy**, enviousness, jealousy, cupidity (*formal*), avarice, avariciousness, greed, greediness, acquisitiveness, graspingness. [➡MORALLY BAD; 776] *Opposite:* generosity.

covey *type of* **flock**. [➡GROUP OF BIRDS; 1007]

coving *n* [➡ROOFS, ROOF PARTS, AND CEILINGS; 1102]

cow 1 *type of* **farm animal**. [➡FARM ANIMAL; 982] 2 *type of* **female animal**. [➡MALE OR FEMALE ANIMAL; 978] 3 *v* **intimidate**, scare, frighten, bully, overawe, browbeat. [➡FRIGHTEN AND SHOCK; 569]

coward *n* **chicken** (*informal*), quitter (*informal*), weakling, deserter, runaway, scaredy-cat (*informal*), fraidy-cat (*US informal*). [➡LAZY OR UNSUCCESSFUL PEOPLE; 948]

cowardice *n* **weakness**, fearfulness, spinelessness, fear, timidity, faint-heartedness, pusillanimity (*formal*), cravenness (*literary*). [➡COWARDICE AND WEAKNESS OF WILL; 509] *Opposite:* courage.

cowardliness *n* [➡COWARDICE AND WEAKNESS OF WILL; 509]

cowardly *adj* **gutless**, spineless, weak, craven (*literary*), faint-hearted, lily-livered (*literary*), pusillanimous (*formal*), chicken (*informal*). [➡COWARDICE AND WEAKNESS OF WILL; 509] *Opposite:* brave.

Compare and Contrast: ***cowardly, faint-hearted, spineless, gutless, pusillanimous, craven, chicken***

CORE MEANING: LACKING IN COURAGE

cowardly lacking in courage, or caused by a lack of courage; ***faint-hearted*** timid and lacking in resolve; ***spineless*** seriously lacking willpower or strength of character; ***gutless*** seriously lacking in courage and determination; ***pusillanimous*** (*formal*) showing an extreme and contemptible degree of cowardice; ***craven*** showing a contemptible degree of cowardice and weakness of will; ***chicken*** (*informal*, often used by children and young people) cowardly.

cowboy 1 *n* (*informal*) **fly-by-night**, crook (*informal*), dodgy operator. [➡VILLAINS AND THUGS; 947] 2 *n* **cowhand**, cowman, herdsman, stockman, rancher. [➡FARMERS, GARDENERS, AND MANUAL WORKERS; 849]

cowboy boot *type of* **boot**. [➡FOOTWEAR; 871]

cowboy film *n* [➡FILM; 901]

cowboy hat *type of* **hat**. [➡HABERDASHERY, MILLINERY, AND LINGERIE; 867]

cowed *adj* **intimidated**, browbeaten, scared, frightened, submissive. [➡FEAR AND PANIC; 544] *Opposite:* defiant.

cower *v* **shrink**, cringe, tremble, recoil, shy away. [➡PHYSICAL REACTIONS; 317] *Opposite:* stand your ground.

cowl *n* **hood**, cover, cloak, top. [➡HABERDASHERY, MILLINERY, AND LINGERIE; 867]

cowlick *type of* **hairstyle**. [➡HAIR STYLES AND HAIR PIECES; 489]

coworker *n* **colleague**, fellow worker, collaborator, associate, workmate, workfellow. [➡COLLEAGUES AND EQUALS; 967]

cowshed 1 *n* **barn**, stable, byre (*regional*), pen, stockyard, corral (*US*). [➡ANCILLARY BUILDINGS; 1079] 2 *type of* **pen or cage**. [➡ANIMAL OR BIRD ACCOMMODATION; 1078]

cowslip *type of* **perennial flower**. [➡FLOWERS; 1032]

cox *v* **steer**, direct, pilot, navigate. [➡TRAVEL: WAYS OF TRAVELLING; 321]

coxswain *v* **steer**, direct, pilot, navigate. [➡TRAVEL: WAYS OF TRAVELLING; 321]

coy 1 *adj* **coquettish** (*literary*), teasing, playful, engaging, provocative. [➡FLIRTATIOUS; 640] 2 *adj* **shy**, bashful, timid, modest, reserved, demure. [➡RETICENT AND UNFORTHCOMING; 632] *Opposite:* brazen.

coyote *type of* **canine**. [➡CANINE; 979]

coypu *type of* **rodent**. [➡RODENT; 989]

crab *type of* **crustacean**. [➡AQUATIC INVERTEBRATE; 1022]

crabbed *adj* **grouchy** (*informal*), bad-tempered, crabby, grumpy, irritable, out of sorts, touchy, testy (*informal*), short-tempered, surly, cantankerous, snappy, sullen, petulant, cross, tetchy (*informal*), cranky (*US informal*). [➡IRRITATION AND ANGER; 542] *Opposite:* easygoing.

crabbiness *n* **bad-temperedness**, bad temper, irritability, grumpiness, grouchiness (*informal*), cantankerousness, snappiness, testiness (*informal*), touchiness, petulance, crossness, sullenness, tetchiness (*informal*), crankiness (*US informal*). [➡IRRITATION AND ANGER; 542] *Opposite:* equanimity.

crabby *adj* **grumpy**, bad-tempered, short-tempered, tetchy (*informal*), irritable, snappy, surly, cross, grouchy (*informal*), testy (*informal*), sullen, sulky, touchy, cantankerous, crabbed, cranky (*US informal*). [➡IRRITATION AND ANGER; 542] *Opposite:* easygoing.

crab grass *type of* **grass**. [➡GRASS; 1031]

crab louse *type of* **parasitic insect**. [➡PARASITES; 1017]

crack 1 *v* **break**, fracture, split, splinter, snap, rupture, chink, fissure, disintegrate. [➡TEAR, BREAK, AND CUT; 361] 2 *v* **break down**, crack up (*informal*), go to pieces, lose control, collapse. [➡FAIL OR CEASE TO FUNCTION; 471] 3 *v* **bash** (*informal*), bang, bump, hit, whack, wallop (*informal*). [➡CONTACT: IMPACT; 414] 4 *v* (*informal*) **solve**, work out, figure out, fathom, decipher, decode, decrypt, break. [➡SOLVE AND INTERPRET; 761] 5 *n* **fissure**, flaw, break, fracture, chink, fault, crevice, gap, rift, cleft, crevasse. [➡HOLES, GAPS, AND FORKS; 1251] 6 *n* (*informal*) **blow**, crash, bang, snap, pop, clap. [➡IMPACT SOUNDS; 1259] 7 *n* **weakness**, flaw, fault, imperfection, defect. [➡FAULTS, FLAWS, AND WEAKNESSES; 252] 8 *n* (*informal*) **gibe**, quip, dig, joke, aside, remark, gag (*informal*), jape (*archaic*), jest (*literary*), wisecrack (*informal*). [➡JOKES AND TEASING; 675]

crack a joke *v* **make a joke**, quip, joke, jest (*literary*). [➡JOKES AND TEASING; 675]

crackbrained *adj* **eccentric**, irrational, crazy (*informal*), foolish, stupid, daft (*informal*). [➡BIZARRE AND PECULIAR; 258] *Opposite:* rational.

crack down (*informal*) *v* **clamp down**, tighten up on, come down on, get tough. [➡REFUSE PERMISSION AND NOT ALLOW; 671]

cracked 1 *adj* **fractured**, broken, split, splintered, cleft, fissured. [➡IN BAD REPAIR; 1233] *Opposite:* intact. 2 *adj* (*informal*) **irrational**, eccentric, crazy (*informal*), crazed, crackbrained, foolish, stupid, daft (*informal*). [➡ECCENTRICITY AND IRRATIONALITY; 563] *Opposite:* rational.

cracker (*informal*) *n* [➡AMAZING THING; 212]

crackers (*informal*) *adj* [➡ECCENTRICITY AND IRRATIONALITY; 563]

cracking (*informal*) 1 *adj* **fast**, furious, rapid, swift, outrageous. [➡HAPPENING QUICKLY; 104] *Opposite:* slow. 2 *adj* **excellent**, brilliant, great (*informal*), fantastic, fabulous, super (*informal*), marvellous. [➡EXTRAORDINARY: AMAZING; 205] *Opposite:* terrible. 3 *adv* **very**, extremely, especially, terribly, exceedingly, outrageously. [➡TO A GREAT EXTENT; 130]

crackle 1 *v* **crunch**, snap, pop, sizzle, crack, scrunch. [➡EMIT SOUNDS THROUGH IMPACT AND ABRASION; 366] 2 *n* **crack**, snap, pop, sizzle, crunch, scrunch. [➡CONTINUOUS SOUNDS; 1257]

crack of dawn *n* **daybreak**, dawn, daylight, sunrise, cockcrow (*archaic or literary*), first light, morning, sunup (*US*). [➡TIMES OF DAY; 87] *Opposite:* dusk.

crackpot (*informal*) *adj* **impractical**, unrealistic, eccentric, wild, crazy (*informal*), outlandish. [➡THE NATURE OF IDEAS; 772] *Opposite:* realistic.

crack-up (*informal*) 1 *n* **breakdown**, collapse, crisis. [➡END; 54] 2 *n* **crash**, accident, wreck, smash, collision. [➡TRAFFIC ACCIDENTS; 256]

crack up (*informal*) 1 *v* **break down**, crack (*informal*), go to pieces, lose control, collapse. [➡FAIL OR CEASE TO FUNCTION; 471] 2 *v* **break up**, crease up (*informal*), laugh, guffaw, giggle, titter. [➡PLEASE AND AMUSE; 573]

cradle 1 *n* **support**, frame, structure, framework, underpinning, foundation. [➡CONTAINERS, RECEPTACLES, AND PACKAGING; 1244] 2 *v* **hold**, embrace, support, cuddle, clasp, rock. [➡CONTACT: HOLD; 412] *Opposite:* drop. 3 *type of* **bed**. [➡FURNITURE; 858]

craft 1 *n* **skill**, dexterity, expertise, ability, craftsmanship, technique, artistry. [➡SKILLS, TALENTS, AND ABILITIES; 527] 2 *n* **trade**, profession, art, job, calling, métier. [➡PROFESSIONS; 845] 3 *n* **vehicle**, vessel, boat, aircraft, spacecraft. [➡SHIPS AND BOATS; 1149] 4 *n* **cunning**, deceit, slyness, wiliness, shrewdness, guile, sneakiness, deviousness, underhandedness. [➡DECEITFUL; 514] *Opposite:* ingenuousness. 5 *v* **make**, fashion, create, manufacture, construct, shape, hew, produce. [➡MANUFACTURE; 350]

craftiness *n* **cunning**, slyness, shrewdness, wiliness, guile, underhandedness, deceit, deviousness, sneakiness. [➡DECEITFUL; 514] *Opposite:* forthrightness.

craftsmanship *n* **skill**, artistry, workmanship, expertise, technique, ability, dexterity, craft. [➡SKILLS, TALENTS, AND ABILITIES; 527]

crafty *adj* **cunning**, sneaky, sly, shrewd, devious, astute, wily, deceitful, underhand. [➡DECEITFUL; 514] *Opposite:* forthright.

crag *n* **cliff**, rock face, precipice, peak, scarp, mountain, escarpment, bluff. [➡MOUNTAINS AND HILLS; 1044]

craggy 1 *adj* **rocky**, stony, rough, rugged, uneven, steep. [➡ORIENTATION AND ALIGNMENT; 1222] *Opposite:* even. 2 *adj* **lined**, rugged, wrinkled, wrinkly, weathered, weather-beaten, rough-hewn. [➡FACIAL CHARACTERISTICS; 482] *Opposite:* smooth.

cram 1 *v* **stuff**, pack, fill up, ram, shove, force. [➡FILL; 407] *Opposite:* remove. 2 *v* (*informal*) **study**, revise, review, swot (*informal*), go over, swot up (*informal*), memorize, mug up (*informal*), peruse, gen up (*informal*), learn. [➡STUDYING; 844] *Opposite:* forget.

crammed *adj* **full**, stuffed (*informal*), packed, filled, jam-packed (*informal*), full up, crowded, cramped. [➡FULL; 1238] *Opposite:* empty.

cramp 1 *n* **spasm**, pain, contraction, shooting pain, twinge, convulsion. [➡PAIN AND OTHER PHYSICAL SENSATIONS; 734] 2 *v* **restrict**, hamper, limit, constrict, constrain, hold back. [➡AVOID, PREVENT, LIMIT, AND CONTROL; 278]

cramped *adj* **overcrowded**, confined, restricted, close, poky (*informal*), small. [➡SMALL; 1194] *Opposite:* spacious.

cranberry *type of* **berry**. [➡FRUIT AND VEGETABLES; 1175]

crane 1 *n* **hoist**, derrick, winch, gantry. [➡MACHINES AND MACHINE PARTS; 1115] 2 *type of* **freshwater bird**. [➡FRESHWATER BIRD; 1000]

crane fly *type of* **flying insect**. [➡FLYING INSECTS; 1013]

cranium *type of* **bone**. [➡THE BONES AND JOINTS; 720]

crank 1 *n* (*informal*) **eccentric**, original, character, maverick. [➡GRUMPY AND NEGATIVE PEOPLE; 953] 2 *v* **turn**, reel, wind, activate, move. [➡MOVE SOMETHING ON THE SPOT; 337] 3 *part of* **engine**. [➡PARTS OF AN ENGINE; 1143]

crankiness 1 *n* (*informal*) **eccentricity**, nonconformity, originality, idiosyncrasy, quirkiness, bizarreness. [➡BIZARRE AND PECULIAR; 258] 2 *n* (*US informal*) **crabbiness**, irritability, grouchiness (*informal*), touchiness, crossness, peevishness, cantankerousness. [➡IRRITATION AND ANGER; 542] *Opposite:* affability.

crankshaft *part of* **engine**. [➡PARTS OF AN ENGINE; 1143]

crank up *v* **start**, turn on, wind up, activate, get going. [➡CAUSE TO START; 266] *Opposite:* turn off.

cranky 1 *adj* (*informal*) **eccentric**, quirky, idiosyncratic, bizarre, strange, weird, original. [➡BIZARRE AND PECULIAR; 258] *Opposite:* ordinary. 2 *adj* (*US informal*) **bad-tempered**, irritable, ratty (*informal*), crabby, cantankerous, grouchy (*informal*), touchy, cross, peevish, ornery (*US informal*). [➡IRRITATION AND ANGER; 542] *Opposite:* good-humoured.

cranny *n* **crevice**, crack, fissure, chink, cleft, split, hole, opening. [➡HOLES, GAPS, AND FORKS; 1251]

crappie *type of* **freshwater fish.** [➡FRESHWATER FISH; 1010]

crash 1 *n* **collision**, accident, smash, pile-up (*informal*), smash-up. [➡TRAFFIC ACCIDENTS; 256] 2 *n* **failure**, breakdown, collapse, shutdown. [➡FAILURE; 77] 3 *n* **bang**, smash, din, clatter, clang, boom, crack, thump, thud, wallop (*informal*), crunch, racket (*informal*). [➡IMPACT SOUNDS; 1259] 4 *n* **bankruptcy**, failure, collapse, liquidation. [➡ACCOUNTING, BANKING, AND BUDGETING; 799] 5 *v* **collide**, run into, smash into, bump into, hurtle, hit. [➡CONTACT: IMPACT; 414] 6 *v* **break down**, collapse, fizzle, fail. [➡FAIL OR CEASE TO FUNCTION; 471] 7 *v* **boom**, bang, thunder, clash, clatter, roar, rumble, resound. [➡EMIT SOUNDS THROUGH IMPACT AND ABRASION; 366] 8 *v* **go under**, fold, collapse, fail. [➡ACCOUNTING, BANKING, AND BUDGETING; 799] *Opposite:* thrive.

crash course *n* **training**, orientation, workshop, induction. [➡LESSONS, COURSE WORK, AND EXAMINATIONS; 842]

crash helmet *type of* **headgear.** [➡HABERDASHERY, MILLINERY, AND LINGERIE; 867]

crash-land *v* **collide**, crash, fall, smash, come down, land, ditch (*informal*). [➡GO DOWNWARDS; 308]

crass *adj* **insensitive**, tactless, thoughtless, vulgar, obnoxious, gross, asinine. [➡BAD MANNERS AND SOCIAL SKILLS; 522] *Opposite:* sensitive.

crassness *n* **insensitivity**, vulgarity, tactlessness, obnoxiousness, grossness, asininity, thoughtlessness. [➡BAD MANNERS AND SOCIAL SKILLS; 522] *Opposite:* sensitivity.

crate *type of* **container.** [➡CONTAINERS, RECEPTACLES, AND PACKAGING; 1244]

crater *n* **pit**, depression, hole, cavity, hollow. [➡GEOLOGICAL FEATURES; 1056] *Opposite:* mound.

cravat *type of* **accessory.** [➡HABERDASHERY, MILLINERY, AND LINGERIE; 867]

crave 1 *v* **desire**, long for, need, want, yearn for, require, hanker after, hunger after, pine for, thirst for. [➡DESIRE AND WANT; 580] *Opposite:* dislike. 2 *v* (*archaic*) **ask**, beg, pray, request, sue (*formal*), implore (*formal*), entreat (*formal*), beseech (*literary*). [➡REQUEST AND DEMAND; 664] *Opposite:* reject.

See Compare and Contrast at **want.**

craven (*literary*) *adj* **cowardly**, gutless, spineless, weak, lily-livered (*literary*), timorous, fearful, pusillanimous (*formal*). [➡COWARDICE AND WEAKNESS OF WILL; 509] *Opposite:* bold.

See Compare and Contrast at **cowardly.**

cravenness (*literary*) *n* [➡COWARDICE AND WEAKNESS OF WILL; 509]

craving *n* **longing**, desire, passion, hunger, thirst, yearning, hankering, yen, appetite. [➡DESIRE AND WANT; 580] *Opposite:* dislike.

crawl 1 *v* **creep**, edge, inch, wriggle, slither, snake, grovel, clamber, scramble. [➡MOVE SLOWLY; 315] 2 *v* **skulk**, scuttle, creep, sneak, slink, move at a snail's pace. [➡MOVE SLOWLY; 315] 3 *v* (*informal*) **suck up** (*informal*), ingratiate yourself, flatter, butter up (*informal*), grovel. [➡FLATTER AND FAWN; 622] *Opposite:* alienate. 4 *v* **apologize**, eat humble pie, grovel, humiliate yourself, prostrate yourself, eat crow (*US informal*). [➡APOLOGIZE AND RETRACT; 684]

crayfish *type of* **crustacean.** [➡AQUATIC INVERTEBRATE; 1022]

craze *n* **fad**, trend, fashion, enthusiasm, rage, obsession, vogue. [➡FADS, FETISHES, AND IDOLATRY; 556]

crazed *adj* **irrational**, distraught, overwrought, demented (*informal*), wild, crazy (*informal*), cracked (*informal*), inflamed, excited, fevered. [➡IRRITATION AND ANGER; 542] *Opposite:* rational.

crazily (*informal*) *adv* **foolishly**, stupidly, unwisely, mindlessly, senselessly, irrationally. [➡ECCENTRICITY AND IRRATIONALITY; 563] *Opposite:* sensibly.

craziness (*informal*) *n* **foolishness**, stupidity, folly, idiocy, madness. [➡ECCENTRICITY AND IRRATIONALITY; 563] *Opposite:* reasonableness.

crazy (*informal*) 1 *adj* **foolish**, unwise, silly, daft (*informal*), senseless, irrational, wild, cracked (*informal*), stupid, outrageous, outlandish, ridiculous, bizarre, peculiar, weird, eccentric, odd, zany. [➡ECCENTRICITY AND IRRATIONALITY; 563] *Opposite:* sensible. 2 *adj* **fond**, keen, passionate, enthusiastic, devoted, avid. [➡APPRECIATION AND GRATITUDE; 536] *Opposite:* lukewarm.

creak 1 *v* **squeak**, screech, scrape, groan, rasp. [➡EMIT SOUNDS THROUGH IMPACT AND ABRASION; 366] 2 *n* **screech**, squeak, scrape, groan, rasp. [➡CONTINUOUS SOUNDS; 1257]

creaky 1 *adj* **squeaky**, rusty, grating, rasping. [➡LOUD OR UNPLEASANT SOUNDS; 1265] 2 *adj* (*informal*) **stiff**, rigid, inflexible, firm. [➡IN BAD REPAIR; 1233] *Opposite:* supple.

cream 1 *n* **ointment**, salve, balm, unguent, emulsion. [➡LOTIONS, PASTES, AND GELS; 1271] 2 *n* **best**, elite, finest, pick of the bunch. [➡SUPERIORITY; 153] *Opposite:* dregs. 3 *v* **blend**, soften, mash, emulsify, combine. [➡COOKING AND FOOD PREPARATION; 354] 4 *v* (*US informal*) **defeat**, thrash, hammer (*informal*), clobber (*informal*), demolish (*informal*). [➡BEAT AND DEFEAT; 80] 5 *type of* **white.** [➡COLOURS; 1223]

cream cheese *type of* **soft cheese.** [➡DAIRY PRODUCTS AND CHEESES; 1182]

cream off *v* **skim off**, cherry-pick (*disapproving*), hand-pick, select, choose, pick out. [➡MAKE DECISIONS AND CHOICES; 753] *Opposite:* reject.

crease 1 *n* **pleat**, fold, tuck, gather. [➡CHANGE OF SHAPE; 386] 2 *n* **crinkle**, crumple, wrinkle, rumple, pucker. [➡CHANGE OF SHAPE; 386] 3 *n* **furrow**, wrinkle, line, groove, crow's foot. [➡FACIAL CHARACTERISTICS; 482] 4 *v* **fold**, pleat, tuck, gather. [➡CHANGE OF SHAPE; 386] 5 *v* **crumple**, wrinkle, scrunch, crinkle, rumple, pucker. [➡CHANGE OF SHAPE; 386] *Opposite:* smooth.

creased *adj* **wrinkled**, wrinkly, crinkled, crinkly, lined, crumpled, rumpled, puckered, furrowed, rutted, wizened. [➡IN BAD REPAIR; 1233] *Opposite:* smooth.

crease up (*informal*) *v* **amuse**, crack up (*informal*), break up, have somebody in hysterics, tickle pink, tickle. [➡PLEASE AND AMUSE; 573]

create 1 *v* **make**, produce, generate, fashion, form, craft, build, construct. [➡MANUFACTURE; 350] *Opposite:* destroy. 2 *v* **invent**, design, originate, initiate, give rise to, coin, conceive. [➡CREATION; 347] **3** *v* **establish**, set up, found, start, get going. [➡INSTITUTE AND INAUGURATE; 349] **4** *v* (*informal*) **make a fuss**, kick up a fuss, kick up a rumpus, complain, cry. [➡GIVING VENT TO EMOTIONS; 680]

See Compare and Contrast at **make**.

creation **1** *n* **formation**, making, conception, construction, manufacture, design, establishment. [➡CREATION; 347] *Opposite:* destruction. **2** *n* **nature**, cosmos, universe, life, world. [➡NATURE AND THE ENVIRONMENT; 1038] **3** *n* **invention**, handiwork, fabrication, innovation, concept, conception. [➡BEGINNING; 53]

creative *adj* **original**, imaginative, inspired, artistic, inventive, resourceful, ingenious, innovative, productive. [➡POSITIVE INTELLECTUAL CHARACTERISTICS; 525] *Opposite:* unimaginative.

creativeness *n* **creativity**, imagination, inspiration, vision, innovativeness, imaginativeness, originality, inventiveness, ingenuity, resourcefulness. [➡POSITIVE INTELLECTUAL CHARACTERISTICS; 525]

creativity *n* **originality**, imagination, inspiration, ingenuity, inventiveness, resourcefulness, creativeness, vision, innovation. [➡POSITIVE INTELLECTUAL CHARACTERISTICS; 525]

creator *n* **maker**, inventor, originator, architect, designer, author, initiator. [➡DESIGNERS, CREATORS AND INSTIGATORS; 348] *Opposite:* destroyer.

creature **1** *n* **being**, living being, person, man, woman, human being, individual, mortal. [➡PERSON; 931] **2** *n* **animal**, beast, organism, insect. [➡LIVING THINGS AND LIVING; 976]

crèche **1** *n* **playgroup**, kindergarten, playschool, nursery. [➡EDUCATIONAL INSTITUTIONS; 813] **2** *n* **Nativity**, crib, display, scene, tableau, spectacle, exhibit. [➡RELIGIOUS OBJECTS; 780]

credence *n* **credibility**, authority, weight, belief, confidence, acceptance. [➡TRUE AND REAL; 172]

credential *n* **qualification**, diploma, recommendation, testimonial, certificate. [➡QUALIFICATIONS; 843]

credentials *n* **identification**, authorization, ID, permit, pass, badge. [➡OFFICIAL DOCUMENTS; 587]

credenza *type of* **cabinet**. [➡FURNITURE; 858]

credibility *n* **trustworthiness**, reliability, integrity, authority, standing, sincerity, believability. [➡TRUE AND REAL; 172]

credible **1** *adj* **believable**, convincing, plausible, likely, probable, realistic. [➡POSSIBLE AND PROBABLE; 178] *Opposite:* unbelievable. **2** *adj* **trustworthy**, reliable, sincere, dependable, sound, tried. [➡TRUE AND REAL; 172] *Opposite:* unreliable.

credibly *adv* **believably**, realistically, convincingly, plausibly, reliably. [➡POSSIBLE AND PROBABLE; 178] *Opposite:* unconvincingly.

credit **1** *n* **praise**, recognition, thanks, acclaim, glory, acknowledgment, tribute. [➡PRAISE AND ENCOURAGE; 648] *Opposite:* blame. **2** *n* **repute** (*formal*), standing, position, status, esteem, prestige, honour, character. [➡STATUS; 888] **3** *n* **belief**, confidence, trust, faith. [➡CALMNESS, CONFIDENCE, AND COMPOSURE; 537] *Opposite:* disbelief. **4** *v* **believe**, accept, trust, have faith in, have confidence in, rely on. [➡APPROVE AND CONFIRM; 647] *Opposite:* disbelieve. **5** *v* **acknowledge**, recognize, acclaim, pay tribute, praise, attribute. [➡PRAISE AND ENCOURAGE; 648]

creditable *adj* **admirable**, praiseworthy, good, worthy, laudable, commendable, honourable, respectable. [➡ADMIRABLE AND COMMENDABLE; 186] *Opposite:* poor.

credo *n* **creed**, doctrine, ideology, principle, view, belief, stand, stance, philosophy, dogma. [➡RELIGIOUS CONCEPTS; 777]

credulity *n* **gullibility**, naivety, innocence, trust, imprudence. [➡NEGATIVE INTELLECTUAL CHARACTERISTICS; 526] *Opposite:* shrewdness.

credulous *adj* **gullible**, naive, trusting, imprudent (*formal*), unsuspecting, innocent, uncritical. [➡NEGATIVE INTELLECTUAL CHARACTERISTICS; 526] *Opposite:* shrewd.

credulousness *n* [➡NEGATIVE INTELLECTUAL CHARACTERISTICS; 526]

creed *n* **faith**, dogma, doctrine, credo, belief, article of faith, principle. [➡RELIGIONS AND RELIGIOUS PRACTICES; 778]

creek **1** *n* **cove**, bay, inlet, gulf. [➡THE SEAS, OCEANS, AND SHORES; 1041] **2** *n* (*US*) **stream**, rivulet, brook, arroyo (*US*). [➡RIVERS, LAKES, AND STREAMS; 1042]

creel *type of* **container**. [➡CONTAINERS, RECEPTACLES, AND PACKAGING; 1244]

creep **1** *v* **tiptoe**, skulk, steal, sneak, slink, sidle. [➡MOVE SLOWLY; 315] **2** *v* **crawl**, slither, inch, edge, worm, snake. [➡MOVE SLOWLY; 315] **3** *v* (*informal*) **grovel**, crawl, fawn, toady, flatter. [➡FLATTER AND FAWN; 622] **4** *n* (*informal*) **flatterer**, toady, sycophant, bootlicker (*informal disapproving*), crawler (*informal*). [➡LAZY OR UNSUCCESSFUL PEOPLE; 948]

creeper *n* **climber**, trailer, vine, liana. [➡CLIMBERS; 1033]

creepiness (*informal*) *n* **eeriness**, scariness, weirdness, uncanniness, strangeness, spookiness (*informal*). [➡FRIGHTENING; 232]

creep up on *v* **sneak up on**, surprise, stalk, take by surprise. [➡ACCOMPANY AND FOLLOW; 338]

creepy (*informal*) *adj* **eerie**, scary (*informal*), disturbing, spine-chilling, uncanny, weird, strange, hair-raising, unnerving, unsettling, spooky (*informal*). [➡FRIGHTENING; 232]

creepy-crawly (*informal*) *n* **insect**, bug, beetle, centipede, millipede, caterpillar. [➡INSECTS; 1012]

cremate *v* **incinerate**, burn, consume, immolate (*formal*). [➡FIRE, FLAMMABILITY, AND BURNING; 1164]

cremation *n* **burning**, incineration, immolation (*formal*). [➡BURIAL AND PREPARATION FOR BURIAL; 929]

crème brûlée *type of* **dessert**. [➡CAKES, BISCUITS, AND DESSERTS; 1180]

crème caramel *type of* **dessert**. [➡CAKES, BISCUITS, AND DESSERTS; 1180]

crème de la crème *n* [➡PERFECT EXAMPLES AND EMBODIMENTS; 67]

crenellated *adj* **fortified**, notched, indented. [➡DIFFICULTY AND COMPLEXITY; 243]

crêpe 1 *type of* **synthetic fabric.** [➡FABRICS; 1131] 2 *type of* **pancake.** [➡CAKES, BISCUITS, AND DESSERTS; 1180]

crêpe de Chine *type of* **fabric from animals.** [➡FABRICS; 1131]

crepuscular (*literary*) *adj* [➡DESCRIBING LIGHT; 1227]

crescendo 1 *n* **increase**, upsurge, swelling, buildup, climax, loudening. [➡CHANGE OF INTENSITY: MORE; 395] 2 *type of* **musical term.** [➡MUSICAL TERMS; 912]

crescent 1 *adj* **semicircular**, hemispherical, falcate, curved, arced. [➡ROUNDED SHAPE; 1217] 2 *type of* **rounded shape.** [➡ROUNDED SHAPE; 1217]

cress *type of* **salad vegetable.** [➡FRUIT AND VEGETABLES; 1175]

crest 1 *n* **top**, peak, summit, crown, apex, pinnacle, roof, ridge. [➡EXTREMITIES OF PHYSICAL OBJECTS; 1249] *Opposite:* base. 2 *n* **tuft**, topknot, growth, cockscomb, comb. [➡PARTS OF A BIRD; 1006] 3 *n* **coat of arms**, emblem, symbol, heraldry. [➡SYMBOLS, SIGNS, AND NUMBERS; 597]

crestfallen *adj* **downcast**, dejected, disappointed, deflated, down, depressed, sad, disconsolate, discouraged. [➡SADNESS, DISTRESS, AND DESPAIR; 540] *Opposite:* cheerful.

crevasse *n* **fissure**, cleft, crack, split, fracture, bergschrund. [➡GEOLOGICAL FEATURES; 1056]

crevice *n* **crack**, fissure, chink, split, cleft, fracture, cranny, opening. [➡HOLES, GAPS, AND FORKS; 1251]

crew 1 *n* **team**, squad, staff, troop, company. [➡THE WORK FORCE; 837] 2 *n* (*informal*) **group**, gang, bunch (*informal*), party, circle, crowd, band, assembly. [➡GROUPS OF PEOPLE; 935]

crew cut *type of* **hairstyle.** [➡HAIR STYLES AND HAIR PIECES; 489]

crew neck *type of* **sweater or cardigan.** [➡GARMENTS AND OUTFITS; 865]

crib 1 *v* (*informal*) **cheat**, copy, plagiarize, steal, borrow, pilfer. [➡FALSIFY AND CHEAT; 177] 2 *type of* **bed.** [➡FURNITURE; 858]

crick 1 *n* **pain**, strain, discomfort, cramp, spasm. [➡PAIN AND OTHER PHYSICAL SENSATIONS; 734] 2 *v* **strain**, hurt, pull, cramp, wrench, rick, kink. [➡PAIN AND OTHER PHYSICAL SENSATIONS; 734]

cricket *type of* **ball game.** [➡HOBBIES, GAMES, AND SPORTS; 875]

cricketer *n* [➡PEOPLE IN SPORTS AND LEISURE; 876]

crime 1 *n* **offence**, misdeed (*formal*), felony, misdemeanour, transgression, violation, illegality, infringement. [➡CRIMES; 817] 2 *n* **corruption**, wrongdoing, misconduct, lawbreaking, delinquency, criminality. [➡CRIMES; 817] 3 *n* **wrong**, sin, fault, transgression. [➡MORALLY BAD; 776]

crime novel *n* [➡FICTION AND DRAMA; 913]

criminal 1 *n* **offender**, convict, prisoner, felon, lawbreaker, delinquent, villain (*slang*). [➡CRIMINALS; 821] 2 *adj* **illegal**, wrong, against the law, illicit, unlawful, felonious, lawless, illegitimate. [➡ILLEGAL; 816] *Opposite:* legal. 3 *adj* **scandalous**, excessive, iniquitous, senseless, outrageous, wicked, disgraceful, sinful, immoral. [➡MORALLY BAD; 776]

See Compare and Contrast at **bad.**

criminality *n* **delinquency**, misconduct, wrongdoing, corruption, lawbreaking. [➡CRIMES; 817] *Opposite:* honesty.

criminalization 1 *n* **outlawing**, banning, proscription (*formal*), interdiction, illegalization (*US*). [➡THE LAW AND LEGAL AUTHORITY; 814] *Opposite:* legalization. 2 *n* **corruption**, delinquency, marginalization, alienation, deterioration. [➡TRIAL, PUNISHMENT, AND LEGAL OUTCOMES; 819] *Opposite:* rehabilitation.

criminalize 1 *v* **outlaw**, ban, forbid, proscribe, interdict. [➡REFUSE PERMISSION AND NOT ALLOW; 671] *Opposite:* legalize. 2 *v* **corrupt**, marginalize, deprave, pervert. [➡TRIAL, PUNISHMENT, AND LEGAL OUTCOMES; 819] *Opposite:* rehabilitate.

criminal lawyer (*US*) *n* [➡PEOPLE IN LAW COURTS; 820]

criminally *adv* **illegally**, unlawfully, lawlessly, illegitimately, feloniously. [➡ILLEGAL; 816] *Opposite:* legally.

criminal world *n* [➡CRIMINALS; 821]

crimp 1 *v* **fold**, crumple, crinkle, press, rumple, scrunch. [➡CHANGE OF SHAPE; 386] 2 *v* **pleat**, gather, fold, concertina, ruche, goffer. [➡CHANGE OF SHAPE; 386] *Opposite:* smooth. 3 *v* **interfere**, hamper, hinder, constrain, curb, keep in check. [➡AVOID, PREVENT, LIMIT, AND CONTROL; 278]

crimped *adj* [➡DESCRIBING HAIR; 487]

crimson *type of* **red.** [➡COLOURS; 1223]

cringe 1 *v* **recoil**, wince, flinch, shrink, shy away, cower, quail. [➡PHYSICAL REACTIONS; 317] 2 *v* **squirm**, blush, wince, suffer embarrassment. [➡PHYSICAL REACTIONS; 317]

cringe-making (*informal*) *adj* [➡IN POOR TASTE; 230]

crinkle 1 *v* **crumple**, crease, rumple, wrinkle, ruffle, scrunch. [➡CHANGE OF SHAPE; 386] *Opposite:* straighten out. 2 *n* **wrinkle**, fold, crease, line, pucker, wave, corrugation. [➡CHANGE OF SHAPE; 386]

crinkled *adj* **creased**, lined, wrinkled, crumpled, rumpled, puckered, corrugated. [➡PHYSICAL TEXTURE; 1221] *Opposite:* straight.

crinkly *adj* **wrinkled**, creased, furrowed, wavy, puckered. [➡IN BAD REPAIR; 1233] *Opposite:* smooth.

crinoline *type of* **lower body underwear.** [➡HABERDASHERY, MILLINERY, AND LINGERIE; 867]

crippling *adj* [➡PHYSICALLY UNPLEASANT; 227]

crisis 1 *n* **disaster**, catastrophe, emergency, calamity, predicament, crunch. [➡DISASTERS; 253] 2 *n* **turning point**, head, watershed, defining moment. [➡DECISIVE MOMENTS; 44]

crisis point *n* [➡DECISIVE MOMENTS; 44]

crisp 1 *adj* **crunchy**, brittle, hard, crusty, crispy, crumbly, al dente. [➡PHYSICAL TEXTURE; 1221] *Opposite:* soggy. 2 *adj* **snappy**, brusque, terse, curt, sharp, blunt, gruff, short, brief, snappish. [➡UNINTERESTED AND DETACHED; 630] 3 *adj* **cold**, cool, fresh, frosty, chilly, bracing, invigorating, brisk. [➡COLD WEATHER; 1051] *Opposite:* warm. 4 *adj* **incisive**, decisive, confident, businesslike, efficient, competent. [➡CONFIDENCE AND COMPOSURE; 500] *Opposite:* hesitant. 5 *type of*

processed potato. [➡FRUIT AND VEGETABLES; 1175] 6 (*US*) *type of* **dessert.** [➡CAKES, BISCUITS, AND DESSERTS; 1180]

crispy *adj* **crunchy**, brittle, hard, crusty, crisp. [➡PHYSICAL TEXTURE; 1221] *Opposite:* soggy.

crisscross 1 *n* **lattice**, network, grid. [➡FASTENERS, LINKS, AND NETWORKS; 1246] 2 *v* **cross**, traverse, intersect, overlap, crossover, go across, cut across. [➡MOVE PAST, INTO OR THROUGH SOMETHING; 332]

criterion *n* **standard**, principle, measure, norm, condition, benchmark, gauge, yardstick. [➡WAYS OF DOING THINGS; 295]

critic 1 *n* **reviewer**, columnist, commentator, reporter, journalist. [➡WORKERS IN ENTERTAINMENT AND MEDIA; 873] 2 *n* **evaluator**, appraiser, judge, commentator. [➡SURVEYORS, EXAMINERS, AND JUDGES; 853] 3 *n* **detractor**, opponent, enemy, censor, criticizer, faultfinder, knocker (*informal*), decrier (*formal*), denigrator. [➡ENEMIES AND TORMENTORS; 969] *Opposite:* supporter.

critical 1 *adj* **unfavourable**, disparaging, disapproving, nitpicking, judgmental, unsympathetic, derogatory, faultfinding, censorious. [➡ACCUSATORY AND DISAPPROVING; 635] *Opposite:* favourable. 2 *adj* **analytical**, judicious, diagnostic, serious, detailed, searching. [➡THE NATURE OF IDEAS; 772] 3 *adj* **significant**, decisive, vital, important, essential, crucial, key, indispensable. [➡IMPORTANT; 195] *Opposite:* insignificant. 4 *adj* **dangerous**, serious, grave, life-threatening, perilous, precarious, acute, dire, desperate. [➡DANGEROUS; 237] *Opposite:* stable.

critically 1 *adv* **disapprovingly**, unsympathetically, judgmentally, disparagingly, censoriously, unfavourably. [➡RUDE AND HOSTILE; 626] *Opposite:* favourably. 2 *adv* **analytically**, judiciously, diagnostically, searchingly, seriously. [➡POSITIVE INTELLECTUAL CHARACTERISTICS; 525] 3 *adv* **significantly**, decisively, vitally, importantly, essentially, crucially, indispensably. [➡IMPORTANT; 195] *Opposite:* insignificantly. 4 *adv* **seriously**, gravely, dangerously, perilously, precariously, acutely, desperately. [➡CRITICALLY AND SERIOUSLY; 132]

criticism 1 *n* **censure**, disapproval, reproach, disparagement, condemnation, denigration, blame, denunciation. [➡CRITICISMS AND ANGRY OUTBURSTS; 50] *Opposite:* praise. 2 *n* **analysis**, appreciation, assessment, evaluation, critique, comment, review, report. [➡EXAMINE AND ASSESS; 754]

criticize 1 *v* **assess**, analyse, evaluate, appraise, critique. [➡EXAMINE AND ASSESS; 754] 2 *v* **disapprove**, censure, disparage, slate, pan (*informal*), carp, complain, pass judgment on, find fault with, pick holes in, condemn, maul, blast (*informal*), decry (*formal*), lash, nitpick, castigate (*formal*). [➡ACCUSE, BLAME, AND CRITICIZE; 642] *Opposite:* praise.

Compare and Contrast: *criticize, censure, castigate, blast, condemn, find fault with, pick holes in, nitpick*

CORE MEANING: TO EXPRESS DISAPPROVAL OR DISSATISFACTION WITH SOMEBODY OR SOMETHING

criticize to point out faults; ***censure*** to make a formal, often public or official statement of disapproval; ***castigate (formal)*** to criticize or rebuke severely; ***blast*** (*informal*) to criticize severely; ***condemn*** to give an unfavourable judgment on somebody or something; ***find fault with*** to criticize, often unfairly; ***pick holes in*** to look for and find mistakes, particularly in an argument; ***nitpick*** to find fault, often unjustifiably, with insignificant details.

critique 1 *n* **analysis**, assessment, evaluation, account, review, criticism, appraisal. [➡ANALYTICAL NONFICTION WRITING; 593] 2 *v* **assess**, evaluate, criticize, comment, review, appraise. [➡EXAMINE AND ASSESS; 754]

croak 1 *n* **cry**, caw, rasp, squawk. [➡SOUNDS MADE BY ANIMALS; 1260] 2 *v* **call**, cry, squawk, caw, rasp. [➡SOUND EMISSION BY ANIMALS OR BIRDS; 365] 3 *v* **rasp**, grate, gutturalize, growl. [➡SOUND EMISSION BY PEOPLE; 364] 4 *v* (*slang*) [➡DIE; 922] 5 *v* (*informal*) **grumble**, mutter, complain, moan, grouse (*informal*), whinge (*informal*). [➡COMPLAIN AND NAG; 687]

croaky *adj* [➡LOUD OR UNPLEASANT SOUNDS; 1265]

crochet *type of* **handicraft.** [➡CRAFTS AND CARVING; 356]

crockery *n* **tableware**, china, earthenware, plates, dishes. [➡TABLEWARE, CUTLERY, AND KITCHENWARE; 861]

crocodile *type of* **reptile.** [➡REPTILES; 994]

crocus *type of* **flower grown from bulb.** [➡FLOWERS FROM BULBS; 1030]

croft *n* [➡AGRICULTURE AND FARMING; 1074]

crofter *n* [➡INHABITANT; 857]

croissant *type of* **roll or bun.** [➡BREAD, FLOUR, AND BREAD PRODUCTS; 1178]

crony (*disapproving*) *n* **associate**, ally, sidekick (*informal*), supporter, accomplice, co-conspirator, cohort (*US disapproving*). [➡SUPPORTERS, PROTECTORS, AND COMPATRIOTS; 970]

crook 1 *n* (*informal*) **criminal**, offender, villain (*slang*), felon, robber, lawbreaker, outlaw, convict, jailbird (*slang*), malefactor (*formal*). [➡CRIMINALS; 821] 2 *n* **staff**, rod, stick, crosier. [➡STICKS, POLES, AND WEDGES; 1253]

crooked 1 *adj* **bent**, curved, warped, twisted, kinked, circuitous, indirect, roundabout, meandering, serpentine, winding. [➡ORIENTATION AND ALIGNMENT; 1222] *Opposite:* straight. 2 *adj* **uneven**, jagged, zigzag, oblique. [➡ORIENTATION AND ALIGNMENT; 1222] *Opposite:* straight. 3 *adj* (*informal*) **dishonest**, criminal, corrupt, fraudulent, illegal, shady, questionable, underhand, unlawful, devious, unscrupulous, deceitful. [➡DECEITFUL; 514] *Opposite:* honest.

crookedly 1 *adv* **indirectly**, askance, aslant, obliquely. [➡ORIENTATION AND ALIGNMENT; 1222] 2 *adv* (*informal*) **illegally**, dishonestly, corruptly, fraudulently, shadily, underhandedly, deceitfully, deviously, unscrupulously. [➡DECEITFUL; 514] *Opposite:* honestly.

crookedness *n* **dishonesty**, shadiness, corruption, illegality, fraudulence, deviousness, deceitfulness, unscrupulousness. [➡DECEITFUL; 514] *Opposite:* honesty.

croon *v* **sing**, serenade, murmur, hum, warble. [➡SOUND EMISSION BY PEOPLE; 364]

crop 1 *n* **harvest**, yield, produce. [➡COLLECTIONS AND MIXTURES OF THINGS; 1243] 2 *v* **collect**, harvest, gather, pick, bring in, reap, garner, ingather. [➡GROW AND CULTIVATE; 352] 3 *v* **cut**, shorten, clip, trim, shear, curtail, pare, shave. [➡EXTRACT AND SEVER; 342] 4 *type of* **hairstyle**, *part of* **bird.** [➡PARTS OF A BIRD; 1006]

cropped *adj* [➡DESCRIBING HAIR; 487]

crop up (*informal*) *v* **appear**, happen, turn up, arise, emerge, occur. [➡SUDDENLY COME INTO EXISTENCE; 2]

croquet *type of* **target ball game.** [➡ HOBBIES, GAMES, AND SPORTS; 875]

croquette *type of* **processed potato.** [➡ FRUIT AND VEGETABLES; 1175]

crosier *n* **staff,** rod, stick, crook. [➡ STICKS, POLES, AND WEDGES; 1253]

cross 1 *n* **symbol,** mark, sign. [➡ SYMBOLS, SIGNS, AND NUMBERS; 597] 2 *n* **Celtic cross,** Greek cross, Latin cross, Maltese cross, St. Andrew's cross, St. George's cross, cross of Lorraine, St. Anthony's cross, tau cross. [➡ RELIGIOUS OBJECTS; 780] 3 *v* **traverse,** go across, crisscross, cut across, span, intersect, overlap, cross over. [➡ MOVE PAST, INTO OR THROUGH SOMETHING; 332] 4 *v* **thwart,** frustrate, impede, oppose, obstruct, resist, annoy, foil, vie, circumvent. [➡ ANGER AND ANNOY; 570] *Opposite:* assist. 5 *adj* **irritated,** angry, irritable, annoyed, snappy, fractious, out of sorts, cantankerous, bad-tempered, cranky (*US informal*). [➡ IRRITATION AND ANGER; 542] 6 *type of* **angular shape.** [➡ ANGULAR SHAPE; 1216]

crossbar *part of* **bike** (*informal*). [➡ BIKES, CARS, AND CARRIAGES; 1148]

crossbow *type of* **bow.** [➡ WEAPONS FOR SHOOTING; 1155]

crossbreed *v* **hybridize,** cross, mongrelize. [➡ COMBINE AND MIX; 401]

crosscheck 1 *v* **validate,** substantiate, double-check, document, verify. [➡ EXAMINE AND ASSESS; 754] 2 *n* **validation,** substantiation, double-checking, documentation, verification. [➡ EXAMINE AND ASSESS; 754]

cross-country 1 *adj* **off-road,** rough, outdoor. [➡ THE COUNTRYSIDE AND OUTDOOR SPACES; 1070] 2 *type of* **track and field.** [➡ HOBBIES, GAMES, AND SPORTS; 875]

cross-country skiing *type of* **winter sport.** [➡ HOBBIES, GAMES, AND SPORTS; 875]

cross-cultural *adj* **multicultural,** multiethnic, cosmopolitan. [➡ LEVEL OF EDUCATION AND SOPHISTICATION; 894]

cross-examination *n* **questioning,** re-examination, interrogation, cross-questioning, probe, review, double-checking, investigation. [➡ TRIAL, PUNISHMENT, AND LEGAL OUTCOMES; 819]

cross-examine *v* **question,** interrogate, grill (*informal*), quiz, probe, review, investigate, re-examine, double-check, bombard, give the third degree (*informal*). [➡ ASK PEOPLE QUESTIONS; 667]

cross-fertilization 1 *n* **pollination,** fertilization, cross-pollination. [➡ COMBINE AND MIX; 401] 2 *n* **exchange,** interchange, interaction, synthesis, sharing. [➡ EXCHANGE AND INTERCHANGE; 449]

cross-fertilize 1 *v* **fertilize,** pollinate, cross-pollinate. [➡ EXCHANGE AND INTERCHANGE; 449] 2 *v* **exchange,** interchange, interact, synthesize, share, exchange ideas. [➡ TWO-WAY COMMUNICATION; 608]

crossfire *n* **clash,** disagreement, conflict, antagonism, fireworks (*informal*), barrage, clash of opinions. [➡ ARGUMENT; 47]

crossing 1 *n* **journey,** adventure, trip, voyage, passage. [➡ TRAVEL: JOURNEYS AND TRIPS; 319] 2 *n* **intersection,** junction, overpass, flyover, level crossing, crossroads, border point, grade crossing (*US*). [➡ BRIDGES, TUNNELS, CROSSINGS, AND JUNCTIONS; 1111]

crossly *adv* **grumpily,** angrily, snappily, impatiently, irately, irritably, furiously. [➡ BAD-TEMPERED AND HUMOURLESS; 627] *Opposite:* good-naturedly.

cross out *v* **score out,** score through, strike out, strike through, scrub (*informal*), scrub out (*informal*), rub out, wipe out, edit out, delete, erase, obliterate, scrap, remove, cut, cancel, cancel out. [➡ DELETE AND ERASE; 340]

crosspatch (*dated informal*) *n* **grouch** (*informal*), grump (*informal*), misery (*informal*), malcontent, pain, curmudgeon. [➡ GRUMPY AND NEGATIVE PEOPLE; 953]

cross-purposes *n* **disagreement,** disparity, variance, contrast, frustration, misunderstanding. [➡ MISUNDERSTAND AND FAIL TO GRASP; 762]

cross-question *v* **cross-examine,** re-examine, interrogate, question, review, probe, investigate, double-check, quiz, grill (*informal*), bombard, give the third degree (*informal*). [➡ TRIAL, PUNISHMENT, AND LEGAL OUTCOMES; 819]

cross-questioning *n* **cross-examination,** re-examination, interrogation, review, double-checking, investigation, probing, questioning, third degree (*informal*). [➡ TRIAL, PUNISHMENT, AND LEGAL OUTCOMES; 819]

cross-reference *n* **citation,** reference, documentation, source, note. [➡ PARTS OF BOOKS AND DOCUMENTS; 594]

crossroads 1 *n* **junction,** intersection, crossing, roundabout, crossway (*US*), traffic circle (*US*). [➡ BRIDGES, TUNNELS, CROSSINGS, AND JUNCTIONS; 1111] 2 *n* **landmark,** juncture (*formal*), decision, turning point, moment of truth, crisis, crunch. [➡ DECISIVE MOMENTS; 44]

cross section 1 *n* **view,** section, slice, layer, plane, stratum (*formal*). [➡ AREA AND RANGE; 111] 2 *n* **sample,** example, range, representation. [➡ REPRESENTATIONS AND GENERAL EXAMPLES; 65]

cross swords *v* **clash,** argue, disagree, do battle, fight, conflict, butt heads (*US*). [➡ ARGUE AND FIGHT – TWO-WAY; 644] *Opposite:* agree.

crossways *adv* [➡ ORIENTATION AND ALIGNMENT; 1222]

crosswise *adv* **crossways,** sideways, diagonally, across, corner to corner, on the cross, obliquely, catty-cornered (*US*), kitty-cornered (*US*), cater-cornered (*US*). [➡ ORIENTATION AND ALIGNMENT; 1222]

crossword *n* **acrostic,** mind-bender, game, puzzle. [➡ HOBBIES, GAMES, AND SPORTS; 875]

crotchetiness (*informal*) *n* [➡ DIFFICULT TO PLEASE; 516]

crotchety (*informal*) *adj* **grumpy,** bad-tempered, irritable, difficult, cantankerous, crusty, crabby, touchy, tetchy (*informal*), surly, short-tempered, cranky (*US informal*). [➡ IRRITATION AND ANGER; 542] *Opposite:* good-humoured.

crouch *v* **squat,** bend, hunker, stoop, duck, bow. [➡ ASSUME A POSITION; 318]

croup *part of* **horse.** [➡ HORSE; 985]

crouton *type of* **bread.** [➡ BREAD, FLOUR, AND BREAD PRODUCTS; 1178]

crow 1 *v* **caw,** cry, call, squawk, screech. [➡ SOUND EMISSION BY ANIMALS OR BIRDS; 365] 2 *v* **gloat,** boast, brag, show off, swagger, swank (*informal*), blow your own trumpet (*informal*), blow your own horn (*US*). [➡BOAST; 617] 3 *type of* **scavenger**. [➡BIRD; 997]

crowbar *type of* **general tool**. [➡HAND TOOLS; 1118]

crowd 1 *n* **troop**, throng, mass, multitude, swarm, horde, mob, host, pack, assembly, gathering, press, crush. [➡GROUPS OF PEOPLE; 935] 2 *n* **group**, set, gang, circle, clique. [➡GROUPS WITH A COMMON INTEREST; 938] 3 *v* **throng**, flock, herd, assemble, gather, mass, congregate, swarm. [➡GET CLOSER TOGETHER; 311] 4 *v* **jam-pack** (*informal*), overcrowd, pack, cram, pile (*informal*), squeeze, squash, jam. [➡FILL; 407]

crowded *adj* **overcrowded**, packed, full, jam-packed (*informal*), teeming, swarming, busy, congested. [➡FULL; 1238] *Opposite:* deserted.

crown 1 *n* **circlet**, coronet, tiara, diadem. [➡JEWELLERY; 866] 2 *n* **trophy**, prize, garland, laurels, honour, award. [➡REWARDS AND AWARDS; 440] 3 *n* **top**, peak, summit, pinnacle, head, crest, brow. [➡EXTREMITIES OF PHYSICAL OBJECTS; 1249] 4 *v* **cap**, top, round off, complete, finish off, put the finishing touch to. [➡COMPLETE AN ACTION; 264] 5 *part of* **head**. [➡HEAD; 693]

crown prince *type of* **aristocrat**. [➡RULERS AND ARISTOCRACY; 823]

crow's foot *n* [➡FACIAL CHARACTERISTICS; 482]

crow's nest *part of* **ship or boat**. [➡PARTS OF A SHIP OR BOAT; 1150]

crucial *adj* **vital**, critical, central, decisive, key, essential, fundamental, important, necessary, imperative. [➡IMPORTANT; 195] *Opposite:* trivial.

crucible 1 *n* **container**, pot, receptacle, vat, kettle, vessel, cauldron. [➡CONTAINERS, RECEPTACLES, AND PACKAGING; 1244] 2 *n* **ordeal**, trial, test, burden, affliction, predicament. [➡DIFFICULT SITUATIONS; 72]

crucifixion 1 *n* **execution**, killing, punishment. [➡CAUSES OF DEATH; 921] 2 *n* **ordeal**, victimization, torment, agony, suffering, misery, torture, persecution. [➡DIFFICULT SITUATIONS; 72]

crucify 1 *v* **execute**, kill, hang, punish. [➡KILL; 923] 2 *v* **torment**, victimize, torture, mistreat, oppress, persecute. [➡UPSET, DISTRESS, AND HUMILIATE; 568]

crud 1 *n* (*slang*) **filth**, scum, muck (*informal*), grime, slime, sludge, dirt. [➡UNPLEASANT AND DIRTY SUBSTANCES; 1267] 2 *n* (*informal*) **nonsense**, gibberish, malarkey (*informal*), twaddle (*informal*), bunkum (*informal*). [➡MEANINGLESS SPEECH OR WRITING; 677]

cruddy (*slang*) *adj* **filthy**, scummy, mucky (*informal*), grimy, slimy, sludgy. [➡DIRTY; 1234] *Opposite:* spotless.

crude 1 *adj* **raw**, unrefined, unprocessed. [➡RAW AND NATURAL; 1213] *Opposite:* refined. 2 *adj* **approximate**, rough, inaccurate, inexact, loose, sketchy. [➡APPROXIMATELY; 133] *Opposite:* accurate. 3 *adj* **unpolished**, basic, simple, rudimentary, makeshift, unsophisticated, rough, unfinished, unskilful. [➡UNFINISHEDNESS; 240] *Opposite:* sophisticated. 4 *adj* **obscene**, indecent, rude, coarse, vulgar, offensive, foul-mouthed, uncouth, indelicate, smutty (*informal*), boorish, unrefined, earthy. [➡RUDE AND HOSTILE; 626] *Opposite:* delicate.

crudely 1 *adv* **approximately**, roughly, inaccurately, inexactly, loosely, sketchily. [➡APPROXIMATELY; 133] *Opposite:* accurately. 2 *adv* **clumsily**, coarsely, sloppily (*informal*), messily, unskilfully, inexpertly, roughly. [➡UNFINISHEDNESS; 240] *Opposite:* skilfully. 3 *adv* **vulgarly**, obscenely, indecently, disgustingly, profanely (*formal*), sordidly, coarsely, earthily, uncouthly, boorishly, tastelessly, offensively, indelicately, smuttily (*informal*). [➡RUDE AND HOSTILE; 626] *Opposite:* delicately.

crudeness 1 *n* **primitiveness**, roughness, rawness, coarseness, simplicity, rusticity. [➡UNFINISHEDNESS; 240] *Opposite:* sophistication. 2 *n* **rudeness**, crudity, coarseness, vulgarity, offensiveness, uncouthness, indelicacy, smuttiness (*informal*), earthiness. [➡BAD MANNERS AND SOCIAL SKILLS; 522] *Opposite:* delicacy.

crudity 1 *n* **rudeness**, crudeness, coarseness, vulgarity, offensiveness, smuttiness (*informal*). [➡BAD MANNERS AND SOCIAL SKILLS; 522] *Opposite:* delicacy. 2 *n* **roughness**, coarseness, rawness, simplicity, rusticity, primitiveness. [➡LEVEL OF EDUCATION AND SOPHISTICATION; 894] *Opposite:* sophistication.

cruel 1 *adj* **unkind**, merciless, nasty, pitiless, brutal, malicious, spiteful, vindictive, heartless, ruthless, harsh, vicious, callous, mean. [➡SELFISH AND UNKIND; 506] *Opposite:* kind. 2 *adj* **painful**, punishing, harsh, hard, forbidding, unpleasant. [➡EMOTIONALLY UNPLEASANT AND UPSETTING; 228] *Opposite:* pleasant.

cruelly *adv* **unkindly**, nastily, brutally, maliciously, viciously, harshly, callously, heartlessly, pitilessly, ruthlessly, meanly, mercilessly. [➡SELFISH AND UNKIND; 506] *Opposite:* kindly.

cruelty *n* **unkindness**, nastiness, brutality, malice, spite, spitefulness, vindictiveness, mercilessness, viciousness, ruthlessness, callousness, heartlessness, harshness, meanness. [➡UNKIND ACTION OR BEHAVIOUR; 297] *Opposite:* kindness.

cruise 1 *v* **voyage**, sail, journey, travel, boat, set sail, tour. [➡TRAVEL: WAYS OF TRAVELLING; 321] 2 *v* **coast**, skim, spin, travel, glide, drift, proceed. [➡MOVE FAST; 314] 3 *n* **voyage**, vacation, trip, journey, tour. [➡TRAVEL: JOURNEYS AND TRIPS; 319]

cruiser *type of* **military vessel**. [➡SHIPS AND BOATS; 1149]

crumb *n* **morsel**, scrap, titbit, bit, speck, spot, fragment, iota. [➡SMALL PIECE; 127]

crumble 1 *v* **smash**, beat, crush, grind, powder, pound. [➡TEAR, BREAK, AND CUT; 361] 2 *v* **dissolve**, disintegrate, deteriorate, fall apart, fall down, collapse, cave in. [➡TEAR, BREAK, AND CUT; 361] 3 *type of* **dessert**. [➡CAKES, BISCUITS, AND DESSERTS; 1180]

crumbling *adj* **disintegrating**, decomposing, decaying, putrefying, caving in, peeling, collapsing, breaking up, falling in, falling apart, on its last legs, in bad condition, falling to pieces, in ruins, rundown, rickety, crumbly, dilapidated, rotting, rotten, ramshackle, fragile, subsiding, derelict, mouldering. [➡DECAYING OR INFESTED; 1235] *Opposite:* solid.

crumbly *adj* **brittle**, powdery, flaky, friable, crumbling, fragile. [➡FRAGILE; 1208] *Opposite:* solid.

crumhorn *type of* **wind instrument**. [➡MUSICAL INSTRUMENTS; 910]

crummy (*informal*) 1 *adj* **inferior**, shoddy, tacky (*informal*), shabby, worthless, poor-quality, cheap, trashy, rubbishy, lousy (*informal*), terrible. [➡IN BAD REPAIR; 1233] *Opposite:* superior. 2 *adj* **unwell**, sick, ill, sickly, miserable, under the weather, poorly (*informal*), off-colour, lousy (*informal*), terrible, below par (*informal*), under par (*informal*). [➡UNFIT AND WEAK; 740] *Opposite:* healthy.

crumpet *type of* **roll or bun.** [➡BREAD, FLOUR, AND BREAD PRODUCTS; 1178]

crumple *v* **crease**, crinkle, rumple, crush, screw, wrinkle, scrunch, pucker. [➡CHANGE OF SHAPE; 386] *Opposite:* smooth.

crumpled *adj* **creased**, wrinkled, wrinkly, crinkly, lined, puckered, crinkled, rumpled, crushed. [➡IN BAD REPAIR; 1233] *Opposite:* smooth.

crunch 1 *v* **chomp** (*informal*), munch, chew, champ. [➡EAT AND NOT EAT; 711] **2** *n* **crisis**, moment of truth, critical situation, crux, critical point, decisive moment, head. [➡DECISIVE MOMENTS; 44]

crunchy *adj* **crispy**, crisp, brittle, crusty. [➡PHYSICAL TEXTURE; 1221] *Opposite:* soggy.

crusade 1 *n* **cause**, campaign, movement, battle, fight, war, struggle, action. [➡NON-AGGRESSIVE/SPORTING EVENT; 40] **2** *v* **campaign**, struggle, battle, apply yourself, exert yourself, put your back into. [➡COMPETE, CONTEND, AND COMBAT; 304]

crusader *n* **campaigner**, supporter, advocate, champion, activist. [➡DEVOTEES AND ADDICTED PEOPLE; 557]

crush 1 *v* **squash**, squeeze, compress, press, mash, pound. [➡CHANGE OF SHAPE; 386] **2** *v* **quell**, suppress, put down, quash, subdue, overcome, conquer. [➡BEAT AND DEFEAT; 80] *Opposite:* resist. **3** *v* **defeat**, rout, slaughter (*slang*), massacre, trounce, overwhelm, cream (*US informal*). [➡BEAT AND DEFEAT; 80] **4** *v* **humiliate**, devastate, mortify, put down, abash, chagrin. [➡UPSET, DISTRESS, AND HUMILIATE; 568] **5** *n* (*informal*) **infatuation**, passion, affection, fondness, liking, love. [➡LOVE, RESPECT, AND GOODWILL; 550] *Opposite:* dislike. **6** *n* **press**, squash, squeeze, crowd, throng. [➡GROUPS OF PEOPLE; 935]

See Compare and Contrast at **love**.

crushed *adj* **crumpled**, creased, wrinkled, crinkly, crinkled, rumpled, wrinkly. [➡IN BAD REPAIR; 1233] *Opposite:* smooth.

crushing *adj* **devastating**, overwhelming, severe, humiliating, serious, grave. [➡EMOTIONALLY UNPLEASANT AND UPSETTING; 228] *Opposite:* mild.

crushingly *adv* **triumphantly**, exultantly, superciliously, haughtily, contemptuously, disdainfully. [➡TO A GREAT EXTENT; 130]

crust *n* **coating**, outside, outer layer, shell, top, skin, scab, covering, casing, layer, film. [➡COVERS AND COATINGS; 1245]

crustacean *type of* **aquatic invertebrate.** [➡AQUATIC INVERTEBRATE; 1022]

crusted *adj* **encrusted**, caked, coated, covered, thick, encased. [➡DECORATE, ADORN, AND APPLY COATINGS; 406]

crusty 1 *adj* **crispy**, crisp, hard, brittle, crunchy. [➡PHYSICAL TEXTURE; 1221] *Opposite:* soft. **2** *adj* **grumpy**, bad-tempered, irritable, cantankerous, crotchety (*informal*), peevish, grouchy (*informal*), crabby, surly, tetchy (*informal*), cranky (*US informal*). [➡BAD-TEMPERED AND HUMOURLESS; 627] *Opposite:* good-humoured.

crutch 1 *n* **stick**, support, prop, walking aid, staff, rest. [➡STICKS, POLES, AND WEDGES; 1253] **2** *n* **prop**, support, aid, help, buttress, support system. [➡TREAT; 211]

crux *n* **root**, bottom, heart, core, nub, nitty-gritty (*informal*), bottom line. [➡MOST IMPORTANT THING; 198]

cry 1 *v* **weep**, sob, blub (*informal*), blubber (*informal*), snivel, whimper, shed tears, howl, wail, bawl (*informal*), cry your eyes out. [➡CRYING; 651] *Opposite:* laugh. **2** *v* **shout**, exclaim, shout out, call, call out, yell, scream, shriek, yelp, roar, bellow, holler (*informal*). [➡SOUND EMISSION BY PEOPLE; 364] *Opposite:* whisper. **3** *n* **call**, shout, exclamation, yell, scream, shriek, yelp, bellow, holler (*informal*). [➡SOUNDS MADE BY PEOPLE; 1261] *Opposite:* whisper.

crying 1 *adj* **in tears**, tearful, weepy (*informal*), lachrymose (*literary*), teary, sobbing, weeping, bawling (*informal*), howling, blubbering (*informal*), wailing, blubbing (*informal*), snivelling. [➡SADNESS, DISTRESS, AND DESPAIR; 540] **2** *adj* **desperate**, deplorable, awful, horrible, terrible, dreadful, lousy (*informal*). [➡EMOTIONALLY UNPLEASANT AND UPSETTING; 228]

cry off (*informal*) *v* [➡NOT DO AND REFUSE TO DO; 275]

cry out 1 *v* **shout out**, shout, cry, call, call out, yell, roar, scream, howl, exclaim, holler (*informal*). [➡GIVING VENT TO EMOTIONS; 680] *Opposite:* whisper. **2** *v* **need**, be in need of, require, demand, call for, ask for, lack. [➡REQUEST AND DEMAND; 664]

crypt *n* **vault**, tomb, catacomb, sepulchre, burial chamber, cellar, basement, undercroft. [➡PARTS OF RELIGIOUS BUILDINGS; 1085]

cryptic *adj* **mysterious**, enigmatic, puzzling, obscure, ambiguous, hidden, secret. [➡SECRET AND UNKNOWN; 180] *Opposite:* straightforward.

See Compare and Contrast at **obscure**.

crystal 1 *n* **mineral**, rock crystal, quartz. [➡PRECIOUS STONES; 1277] **2** *type of* **glass.** [➡GLASS; 1135]

crystal clear 1 *adj* **clean**, sparkling, limpid, transparent, crystalline, translucent. [➡CLEAN; 1232] *Opposite:* muddy. **2** *adj* **obvious**, clear, clear as day, clear-cut, distinct, sharp, intelligible, explicit, well-defined, unambiguous, lucid, plain, understood, understandable, comprehensible. [➡CONCISE AND CLEAR; 203] *Opposite:* opaque.

crystalline 1 *adj* **crystal-like**, glassy, sparkling. [➡VISUAL TEXTURE; 1220] **2** *adj* **clear**, transparent, crystal clear, limpid, translucent. [➡VISUAL TEXTURE; 1220] *Opposite:* opaque.

crystallization *n* **manifestation**, representation, outward expression, illustration, summation, final product, mature expression. [➡PERFECT EXAMPLES AND EMBODIMENTS; 67]

crystallize *v* **form**, gel (*informal*), take shape, fall into place, come together, shape up, set, grow, mature, resolve itself, sort itself out, develop, manifest. [➡GRADUALLY COME INTO EXISTENCE; 1] *Opposite:* disintegrate.

cry your eyes out *v* [➡CRYING; 651]

cub 1 *n* **novice**, beginner, learner, apprentice, trainee, fledgling, stripling, tenderfoot (*informal*), rookie (*US informal*). [➡UNSKILLED PERSON; 531] *Opposite:* old hand. 2 *type of* **young animal**. [➡YOUNG ANIMAL; 977]

cubbyhole *n* **compartment**, nook, cranny, pigeonhole, cupboard, closet, storeroom, niche, cubicle. [➡ALCOVES, CUBICLES, AND COMPARTMENTS; 1095]

cube *type of* **angular shape**. [➡ANGULAR SHAPE; 1216]

cubicle *n* **compartment**, booth, partition, stall, workspace. [➡ALCOVES, CUBICLES, AND COMPARTMENTS; 1095]

cubism *type of* **20th-century art movement**. [➡ARTISTIC MOVEMENTS AND STYLES; 899]

cubist *adj* **abstract**, geometric, modern. [➡ARTISTIC MOVEMENTS AND STYLES; 899]

cuckoo 1 *adj* (*informal*) **eccentric**, strange, weird, unusual, bizarre, unconventional. [➡BIZARRE AND PECULIAR; 258] *Opposite:* ordinary. 2 *type of* **common bird**. [➡BIRD; 997]

cuckoo clock *type of* **clock**. [➡CLOCKS AND TIMERS; 1125]

cucumber *type of* **salad vegetable**. [➡FRUIT AND VEGETABLES; 1175]

cuddle 1 *v* **hug**, embrace, clasp, hold, nuzzle, cling to, fondle, snuggle, nestle, huddle, curl up, draw close, cosy up. [➡PHYSICAL CONTACT AS COMMUNICATION; 656] 2 *n* **embrace**, hug, clasp, hold, clinch. [➡PHYSICAL CONTACT AS COMMUNICATION; 656]

cuddle up *v* [➡GET CLOSER TOGETHER; 311]

cuddly *adj* **soft**, lovable, fluffy, warm, endearing, appealing, huggable, embraceable. [➡PHYSICAL TEXTURE; 1221]

cudgel 1 *v* **hit**, bludgeon, whack, pound, bash (*informal*), batter, club, thrash, beat. [➡WHIP AND CLUB; 418] 2 *type of* **club**. [➡BLUNT INSTRUMENTS AND WHIPS; 1157]

cue 1 *n* **signal**, prompt, sign, indication, reminder, nod, hint, clue, key. [➡INDICATIONS, SIGNS, AND WARNINGS; 68] 2 *v* **prompt**, signal, show, indicate, remind, nod. [➡GESTURES AND GESTICULATION; 654]

cuff 1 *n* (*slang*) **handcuff**, manacle, shackle, restraint, fetter, bracelet (*slang*), irons. [➡FASTENERS, LINKS, AND NETWORKS; 1246] 2 *v* **buffet**, slap, strike, hit, rap, box somebody's ears. [➡PHYSICAL ATTACK AND PUNISHMENT; 416] 3 *part of* **garment**. [➡PARTS OF A GARMENT; 870]

cuff link *type of* **jewellery**. [➡JEWELLERY; 866]

cuisine *n* **food**, fare, cooking, gastronomy, cookery. [➡FOOD; 1166]

cul-de-sac *n* **dead end**, no through road, impasse, blind alley. [➡ROADS; 1105]

culinary *adj* **cooking**, gastronomic, cookery, food. [➡FOOD; 1166]

cull 1 *v* **discard**, reject, remove, scrap, get rid of, cast off. [➡GET RID OF SOMETHING; 452] *Opposite:* retain. 2 *v* **pick**, select, choose, gather, harvest, collect, amass, garner, glean, sift, winnow. [➡GET; 421] 3 *n* **reject**, scrap, discard, castoff, second. [➡RUBBISH AND USELESS OBJECTS; 1248]

culminate *v* **end**, conclude, finish, terminate (*formal*), climax, close, cap, crown. [➡STOP ACTING; 265] *Opposite:* start.

culmination *n* **conclusion**, finale, peak, height, zenith, result, end, termination, climax, apex, apogee, consummation. [➡END; 54]

culottes *type of* **trousers**. [➡GARMENTS AND OUTFITS; 865]

culpability *n* **blameworthiness**, liability, blame, guilt, fault, accountability, responsibility, answerability. [➡MORALLY BAD; 776] *Opposite:* innocence.

culpable *adj* **guilty**, in the wrong, to blame, blameworthy, responsible, liable, at fault. [➡MORALLY BAD; 776] *Opposite:* innocent.

culprit *n* **offender**, criminal, guilty party, perpetrator, wrongdoer, felon, lawbreaker, malefactor (*formal*). [➡CRIMINALS; 821]

cult 1 *n* **sect**, religious group, faction, party. [➡RELIGIOUS PEOPLE; 779] 2 *n* **fad**, craze, trend, adoration, veneration, worship. [➡FADS, FETISHES, AND IDOLATRY; 556] 3 *adj* **trendy** (*informal*), alternative, offbeat, out of the ordinary, unusual. [➡BIZARRE AND PECULIAR; 258] *Opposite:* mainstream.

cultivate 1 *v* **farm**, grow, plant, plough, tend. [➡GROW AND CULTIVATE; 352] 2 *v* **promote**, encourage, nurture, work on, foster, support, help, develop, improve, enrich. [➡MAKE POSSIBLE; 276] *Opposite:* neglect.

cultivated *adj* **refined**, educated, cultured, sophisticated, urbane, civilized. [➡LEVEL OF EDUCATION AND SOPHISTICATION; 894] *Opposite:* uncouth.

cultivation 1 *n* **farming**, agriculture, husbandry, crop growing, agronomy, gardening, tilling. [➡GROW AND CULTIVATE; 352] 2 *n* **development**, promotion, encouragement, nurturing, fostering. [➡PROGRESS AND ADVANCEMENT; 214] *Opposite:* neglect. 3 *n* **refinement**, education, culture, sophistication, urbanity, civilization. [➡LEVEL OF EDUCATION AND SOPHISTICATION; 894] *Opposite:* uncouthness.

cultivator *n* **grower**, farmer, gardener, planter, agronomist, tiller. [➡FARMERS, GARDENERS, AND MANUAL WORKERS; 849]

cultural 1 *adj* **national**, social, ethnic, folk, traditional, racial. [➡BELONGING OR RELATING TO PEOPLE; 943] 2 *adj* **educational**, edifying, enlightening, enriching, civilizing, artistic, literary, intellectual. [➡INTERESTING AND MEANINGFUL; 191]

culturally 1 *adv* **socially**, ethnically, in cultural terms, customarily, traditionally. [➡BELONGING OR RELATING TO PEOPLE; 943] 2 *adv* **artistically**, aesthetically, creatively. [➡LEVEL OF EDUCATION AND SOPHISTICATION; 894]

culture 1 *n* **civilization**, society, mores, traditions, customs, way of life, background, ethnicity. [➡GROUPS IN SOCIETY; 940] 2 *n* **ethos**, philosophy, values, principles, beliefs. [➡PHILOSOPHIES AND BELIEFS; 781] 3 *n* **sophistication**, refinement, urbanity, civilization, cultivation, polish, taste, discernment, discrimination. [➡LEVEL OF EDUCATION AND SOPHISTICATION; 894] *Opposite:* uncouthness. 4 *n* **art, music, and literature**, arts, humanities, fine art, visual art. [➡LEVEL OF EDUCATION AND SOPHISTICATION; 894]

cultured *adj* **refined**, well-educated, learned, educated, erudite, cultivated, urbane, civilized. [➡LEVEL OF EDUCATION AND SOPHISTICATION; 894] *Opposite:* uncouth.

culvert *n* **duct**, channel, conduit, tunnel, main, sewer, drain, watercourse, ditch, gutter. [➡WATERCOURSES; 1110]

cum (*informal*) *prep* **with**, together with, along with, in combination with, also used as, functioning as. [➡ALSO; 136]

cumbersome *adj* **unwieldy**, awkward, weighty, bulky, clumsy, burdensome, cumbrous (*archaic or literary*), ungainly, heavy. [➡WEIGHT: HEAVY; 1204] *Opposite:* manageable.

cumbersomeness *n* [➡LARGE; 1192]

cumbrous (*archaic or literary*) *adj* [➡LARGE; 1192]

cumin *type of* **spice**. [➡HERBS AND SPICES; 1174]

cummerbund *type of* **accessory**. [➡HABERDASHERY, MILLINERY, AND LINGERIE; 867]

cumulative *adj* **increasing**, snowballing, swelling, accumulative, growing, aggregate, collective, amassed. [➡RELATED; 143] *Opposite:* diminishing.

cumulonimbus *type of* **cloud**. [➡CLOUDY AND RAINY WEATHER; 1052]

cumulus *type of* **cloud**. [➡CLOUDY AND RAINY WEATHER; 1052]

cunning 1 *adj* **sly**, wily, crafty, sneaky, shrewd, canny, guileful, scheming, foxy, astute, Machiavellian, calculating. [➡DECEITFUL; 514] *Opposite:* guileless. 2 *adj* **ingenious**, inventive, resourceful, creative, innovative, clever, artful. [➡POSITIVE INTELLECTUAL CHARACTERISTICS; 525] 3 *n* **slyness**, wiliness, craftiness, sneakiness, shrewdness, astuteness, canniness, guile, artifice (*formal*), foxiness. [➡DECEITFUL; 514] *Opposite:* guilelessness. 4 *n* **skill**, cleverness, ingenuity, creativity, dexterity, adroitness, ability, inventiveness, resourcefulness, expertise, art, craft, deftness. [➡SKILLS, TALENTS, AND ABILITIES; 527]

cup 1 *n* **mug**, beaker, demitasse, teacup. [➡TABLEWARE, CUTLERY, AND KITCHENWARE; 861] 2 *n* **trophy**, chalice, goblet, prize. [➡REWARDS AND AWARDS; 440]

cupboard *type of* **cabinet**. [➡FURNITURE; 858]

cupcake *type of* **cake**. [➡CAKES, BISCUITS, AND DESSERTS; 1180]

cupidity (*formal*) *n* **greed**, avarice, covetousness, materialism, rapacity, acquisitiveness, greediness, avariciousness, avidity. [➡MORALLY BAD; 776] *Opposite:* generosity.

Cupid's bow *type of* **bow**. [➡WEAPONS FOR SHOOTING; 1155]

cupola *n* **dome**, vault, roof, ceiling. [➡ROOFS, ROOF PARTS, AND CEILINGS; 1102]

cur *n* **mongrel**, dog, hound, mutt (*slang*). [➡DOG; 980] *Opposite:* purebred.

curable *adj* **treatable**, remediable, correctable, mendable, repairable, fixable, improvable. [➡HEALING; 731] *Opposite:* incurable.

curative *adj* **healing**, remedial, restorative, therapeutic, medicinal, health-giving, healthful, beneficial, salutary. [➡HEALING; 731] *Opposite:* injurious.

curator *n* **warden**, custodian, keeper, steward, guardian, overseer, superintendent, supervisor. [➡PEOPLE WHO GUARD AND PROTECT; 846]

curb 1 *n* **control**, limit, restriction, restraint, check. [➡CAPTIVITY AND LOSS OF FREEDOM; 249] 2 *v* **restrain**, control, limit, hold back, rein in, curtail, cut back. [➡AVOID, PREVENT, LIMIT, AND CONTROL; 278] *Opposite:* promote.

curd *type of* **soft cheese**. [➡DAIRY PRODUCTS AND CHEESES; 1182]

curdle 1 *v* **coagulate**, clot, thicken, congeal, gel. [➡HARDEN, CONGEAL, DRY; 388] *Opposite:* separate. 2 *v* (*informal*) **go sour**, go bad, go off, turn, sour, spoil, ferment. [➡GO BAD AND CORRODE; 391]

cure 1 *v* **heal**, treat, make well, restore to health, alleviate. [➡FALL ILL, TREAT, AND RECOVER; 729] *Opposite:* exacerbate. 2 *n* **treatment**, therapy, medicine, medication, remedy, antidote. [➡HEALING; 731] 3 *v* **preserve**, smoke, dry, salt, pickle. [➡COOKING AND FOOD PREPARATION; 354]

cure-all *n* **panacea**, universal remedy, magic potion, antidote, elixir, remedy, cure, answer, solution, nostrum. [➡SOLUTION; 216]

curfew *n* **restriction**, time limit, deadline, limitation, regulation, control. [➡END; 54]

curio *n* **trinket**, antique, curiosity, souvenir, knick-knack, bric-a-brac, novelty, gewgaw, novelty item. [➡ORNAMENTS AND DECORATIONS; 1247]

curiosity 1 *n* **inquisitiveness**, interest, nosiness (*informal*), prying, snooping (*informal*). [➡ATTENTION AND ATTENTIVENESS; 764] *Opposite:* apathy. 2 *n* **oddity**, rarity, novelty, curio, strange thing, marvel, wonder, phenomenon. [➡EXTRAORDINARY: UNCOMMON; 206]

curious 1 *adj* **inquisitive**, inquiring, interested, questioning, probing, nosy (*informal*), prying, snooping (*informal*). [➡PENSIVENESS AND INTEREST; 539] *Opposite:* apathetic. 2 *adj* **peculiar**, odd, strange, unusual, intriguing, remarkable, bizarre, weird. [➡BIZARRE AND PECULIAR; 258] *Opposite:* ordinary.

curiousness *n* [➡BIZARRE AND PECULIAR; 258]

curl 1 *v* **twist**, coil, bend, wind, wave, crimp. [➡POSITION SOMETHING: AROUND SOMETHING; 328] 2 *v* **swirl**, spiral, twirl, twist, curve, coil. [➡POSITION SOMETHING: AROUND SOMETHING; 328] 3 *n* **coil**, twist, whorl. [➡ROUNDED SHAPE; 1217] 4 *n* **ringlet**, wave, lock. [➡HAIR; 485]

curling *type of* **winter sport**. [➡HOBBIES, GAMES, AND SPORTS; 875]

curl up *v* **double up**, crouch, hug your knees, roll into a ball, go into the foetal position, coil, bend. [➡ASSUME A POSITION; 318] *Opposite:* straighten.

curly *adj* **wavy**, coiled, twisted, frizzy, crimped, curling, kinky, corkscrew. [➡ROUNDED SHAPE; 1217] *Opposite:* straight.

curmudgeon *n* **grouch** (*informal*), grump (*informal*), misery (*informal*), malcontent, pain (*informal*), crosspatch (*dated informal*). [➡FINANCIALLY MEAN PEOPLE; 952]

curmudgeonly *adj* **bad-tempered**, crabby, cantankerous, grouchy (*informal*), grumpy, grumbly, testy (*informal*), tetchy (*informal*), irascible, peevish, moody, irritable, cranky (*US informal*). [➡NEGATIVE OF OUTLOOK; 515] *Opposite:* pleasant.

currant *type of* **berry.** [➡FRUIT AND VEGETABLES; 1175]

currency 1 *n* **money**, legal tender, coinage, coins, exchange, notes, cash, bills, paper money. [➡CURRENCIES; 798] 2 *n* **prevalence**, frequency, vogue, commonness, popularity, circulation, acceptance, predominance. [➡PRESENT AND AVAILABLE; 11]

current 1 *adj* **present**, existing, in progress, recent, up-to-date, contemporary, present-day, modern. [➡PRESENT; 85] *Opposite:* dated. 2 *n* **flow**, stream, undercurrent, tide, flux. [➡RIVERS, LAKES, AND STREAMS; 1042]

current affairs *type of* **broadcast.** [➡TELEVISION AND RADIO; 607]

curriculum *n* **course**, prospectus, programme, syllabus, core curriculum, national curriculum. [➡LESSONS, COURSE WORK, AND EXAMINATIONS; 842]

curriculum vitae *n* [➡SUMMARIES, OUTLINES, AND EXCERPTS; 589]

curried *adj* [➡STATE OF PREPARED FOOD; 1170]

curry *type of* **cooked dish.** [➡PREPARED DISHES; 1169]

curry favour *v* **ingratiate yourself**, cosy up, get in with, play up to, smarm (*informal*), crawl (*informal*), grovel, get in good with (*US*). [➡ESTABLISHING RELATIONSHIPS WITH OTHERS; 974]

curse 1 *n* **swearword**, oath, expletive, blasphemy, profanity, obscenity. [➡INSULTS, ABUSE, AND SWEARING; 659] 2 *n* **jinx**, spell, magic, whammy (*informal*), setback, blow, anathema, execration (*literary or formal*). [➡NUISANCES; 254] *Opposite:* blessing. 3 *n* **scourge**, plague, bane, misfortune, trouble, torment, ordeal, affliction, trial, tribulation. [➡NUISANCES; 254] 4 *v* **swear**, blaspheme, damn, eff and blind (*slang*), use bad language, cuss (*informal*). [➡INSULTS, ABUSE, AND SWEARING; 659] 5 *v* **plague**, afflict, trouble, blight, torment, scourge, burden. [➡HAPPEN TO SOMEBODY; 30]

cursed 1 *adj* **damned**, afflicted, banned, anathematized, blighted. [➡IRRITATING; 229] *Opposite:* blessed. 2 *adj* (*informal*) **annoying**, irritating, bothersome, vexatious, perturbing, trying, cussed (*informal*), execrable, damnable, abominable. [➡UNACCEPTABLE AND UNFORGIVABLE; 226]

cursor *n* **pointer**, arrow, marker, indicator. [➡COMPUTERS AND COMPUTING; 1126]

cursory *adj* **superficial**, hasty, brief, passing, quick, rapid, perfunctory, hurried, fleeting, desultory. [➡HAPPENING QUICKLY; 104] *Opposite:* thorough.

curt *adj* **abrupt**, brisk, brusque, rude, brief, terse, offhand, snappy, blunt, summary, peremptory, short, snippy (*informal*). [➡BAD-TEMPERED AND HUMOURLESS; 627] *Opposite:* civil.

curtail *v* **limit**, restrain, restrict, hold back, cut back, curb, rein in, shorten, inhibit, decrease, clip, pare down, trim, cut short. [➡AVOID, PREVENT, LIMIT, AND CONTROL; 278] *Opposite:* extend.

curtailment *n* **limitation**, restriction, curb, shortening, reduction, decrease, cut. [➡AVOID, PREVENT, LIMIT, AND CONTROL; 278] *Opposite:* extension.

curtain *n* **drape**, blind, screen, shutter, shade. [➡SOFT FURNISHINGS, LINEN, AND DRAPERY; 860]

curtness *n* **brusqueness**, abruptness, shortness, briskness, snappiness, peremptoriness, snippiness (*informal*), rudeness, terseness, bluntness. [➡SUCCINCT AND TO-THE-POINT; 641] *Opposite:* civility.

curtsy 1 *v* **genuflect**, bow, bob, kneel, stoop, greet. [➡GESTURES AND GESTICULATION; 654] 2 *n* **bow**, genuflection, obeisance (*formal*), bob. [➡GESTURES AND GESTICULATION; 654]

curvaceous *adj* **curvy**, rounded, curved, shapely, voluptuous. [➡BUILD; 478]

curvature *n* **curving**, bend, twist, warp, arc, curve, arch. [➡ROUNDED SHAPE; 1217]

curve 1 *n* **arc**, bend, bow, arch, camber, curvature, turn. [➡ROUNDED SHAPE; 1217] 2 *v* **bend**, bow, curl, coil, twist, turn, hook, arch. [➡CHANGE OF SHAPE; 386] *Opposite:* straighten.

curved *adj* **bent**, bowed, curled, coiled, rounded, arched, warped, hooked, curvilinear. [➡ROUNDED SHAPE; 1217] *Opposite:* straight.

curvilinear *adj* [➡ROUNDED SHAPE; 1217]

curviness *n* [➡ROUNDED SHAPE; 1217]

curving 1 *adj* **curved**, curvy, bending, sinuous, snaking, winding, meandering, curvilinear, undulating. [➡ROUNDED SHAPE; 1217] *Opposite:* straight. 2 *adj* **bent**, warped, twisted, bowed, crooked, distorted, hooked, coiled, arched. [➡ROUNDED SHAPE; 1217] *Opposite:* straight.

curvy *adj* **wavy**, rounded, curved, curvilinear, curvaceous. [➡ROUNDED SHAPE; 1217] *Opposite:* straight.

cushion 1 *n* **pillow**, bolster, pad, headrest, beanbag, hassock. [➡SOFT FURNISHINGS, LINEN, AND DRAPERY; 860] 2 *v* **protect**, shield, guard, support, bolster, pad. [➡PREVENT CONTACT OR ATTACK; 420] *Opposite:* expose. 3 *v* **mitigate**, moderate, lessen, stifle, soften, suppress, dampen, muffle. [➡CHANGE OF INTENSITY: LESS; 396] *Opposite:* exacerbate.

cushy (*informal*) *adj* **easy**, jammy (*informal*), comfortable, undemanding, cosy, agreeable, pleasant. [➡EASE AND SIMPLICITY; 201] *Opposite:* difficult.

cushy number *n* [➡EASY WORK; 300]

cusp 1 *n* **point**, tip, nib, end. [➡EXTREMITIES OF PHYSICAL OBJECTS; 1249] 2 *n* **crossover**, border, limit, edge, verge, boundary. [➡EXTREMITIES OF PHYSICAL OBJECTS; 1249]

cuspid *type of* **tooth.** [➡THE MOUTH; 703]

cuss (*informal*) *v* **swear**, curse, blaspheme, profane, use bad language, damn. [➡INSULTS, ABUSE, AND SWEARING; 659]

cussed (*informal*) *adj* **annoying**, irritating, uncooperative, obstinate, stubborn, perverse. [➡UNWILLINGNESS AND STUBBORNNESS; 565] *Opposite:* cooperative.

cussedness (*informal*) *n* **pigheadedness**, stubbornness, obstinacy, wilfulness, perversity. [➡REBELLIOUSNESS AND DISOBEDIENCE; 566] *Opposite:* cooperation.

custard *type of* **dessert.** [➡CAKES, BISCUITS, AND DESSERTS; 1180]

custodial 1 *adj* **prison**, jail, secure, penal, residential. [➡CAPTIVITY AND LOSS OF FREEDOM; 249] 2 *adj* **protective**, safeguarding, safekeeping, sheltered, supervisory. [➡SAFE AND SAFETY; 192]

custodian 1 *n* **guardian**, curator, keeper, defender, upholder, protector, overseer, warden. [➡SUPPORTERS, PROTECTORS, AND COMPATRIOTS; 970] 2 *n* **caretaker**, janitor, concierge, warden, night watchman. [➡PEOPLE WHO GUARD AND PROTECT; 846]

custody 1 *n* **detention**, arrest, confinement, imprisonment, incarceration (*formal*). [➡CAPTIVITY AND LOSS OF FREEDOM; 249] *Opposite:* liberty. 2 *n* **protection**, keeping, safekeeping, care, charge, guardianship, supervision, trusteeship, watch. [➡RESPONSIBILITY; 171]

custom 1 *n* **tradition**, practice, convention, institution, ritual, habit, norm, routine. [➡WAYS OF DOING THINGS; 295] *Opposite:* novelty. 2 *n* **habit**, practice, routine, pattern, way. [➡WAYS OF DOING THINGS; 295] 3 *n* **trade**, business, patronage, clientele, market, client base. [➡BUSINESS ACTIVITIES AND PHENOMENA; 795]

See Compare and Contrast at **habit**.

customarily *adv* **usually**, normally, habitually, regularly, routinely, as a matter of course, as a rule, typically, ordinarily. [➡USUALLY; 108] *Opposite:* unusually.

customary 1 *adj* **usual**, normal, habitual, expected, routine, regular, accustomed, ordinary, everyday. [➡ORDINARINESS; 245] *Opposite:* exceptional. 2 *adj* **traditional**, conventional, time-honoured, established, long-established, general. [➡PERMANENCE: WITHOUT END; 94] *Opposite:* unconventional. 3 *adj* **typical**, characteristic, usual, habitual, normal, wonted (*formal*). [➡ORDINARINESS; 245] *Opposite:* uncharacteristic.

See Compare and Contrast at **usual**.

custom-built *adj* **specially made**, commissioned, custom-made, bespoke, customized, personalized, made-to-order (*US*). [➡EXTRAORDINARY: UNCOMMON; 206] *Opposite:* off-the-peg.

customer *n* **client**, buyer, purchaser, patron, punter (*informal*), shopper, consumer, habitué. [➡PURCHASER; 425]

customize *v* **modify**, tailor, adapt, alter, make to order, make specially, convert. [➡CHANGE; 373]

customized *adj* **modified**, tailored, adapted, personalized, custom-made, specially made, commissioned, custom-built, made-to-order (*US*). [➡EXTRAORDINARY: UNCOMMON; 206] *Opposite:* mass-produced.

custom-made *adj* **specially made**, commissioned, custom-built, bespoke, customized, personalized, made-to-order (*US*). [➡EXTRAORDINARY: UNCOMMON; 206] *Opposite:* mass-produced.

customs *n* **tax**, duty, levy, impost, toll, payment. [➡ADMINISTRATIVE OFFICERS; 811]

cut 1 *v* **chop**, slice, carve, saw, hack, slash, sever, cube, mince. [➡TEAR, BREAK, AND CUT; 361] *Opposite:* join. 2 *v* **pierce**, score, nick, incise, engrave, scratch, carve, lacerate, gash, slit. [➡TEAR, BREAK, AND CUT; 361] *Opposite:* seal. 3 *v* **reduce**, decrease, limit, curtail, cut down, cut back, restrict, diminish. [➡CHANGE OF SIZE: SMALLER; 394] *Opposite:* increase. 4 *v* **edit**, shorten, censor, condense, chop, prune, slash, remove, expurgate, excise, abridge, abbreviate, reduce. [➡DELETE AND ERASE; 340] *Opposite:* restore. 5 *v* **stop**, discontinue, bring to an end, bring to a halt, finish, cut off, disconnect, withdraw, withhold. [➡CAUSE TO STOP; 267] *Opposite:* continue. 6 *n* **scratch**, wound, slash, graze, incision, nick, puncture. [➡HOLES, GAPS, AND FORKS; 1251] 7 *n* **reduction**, decrease, cutback, decline, drop, fall. [➡CHANGE OF SIZE: SMALLER; 394] *Opposite:* increase. 8 *n* (*informal*) **share**, commission, percentage, rake-off (*informal*), kickback. [➡MEASURABLE PORTION; 125]

cut-and-dried 1 *adj* **decided**, finished, settled, fixed, agreed, sorted out, done and dusted. [➡WHOLENESS AND COMPLETENESS; 199] *Opposite:* undecided. 2 *adj* **predictable**, obvious, anticipated, expected, foreseen, plain, plain as the nose on your face, clear, plain as a pikestaff, plodding, trite, hackneyed. [➡PERCEPTIBLE; 25] *Opposite:* unexpected.

cut back *v* **reduce**, curtail, curb, decrease, restrain, hold back, rein in, cut down, contract, retrench. [➡CHANGE OF SIZE: SMALLER; 394] *Opposite:* develop.

cutback *n* **reduction**, cut, decrease, decline, drop, falloff, phasedown, downturn. [➡LESS; 124]

cut dead *v* [➡REFUSING OR REJECTING RELATIONS; 975]

cut down 1 *v* **reduce**, decrease, cut back, ease up on, rein back, contract, abate (*formal or literary*), shorten. [➡CHANGE OF SIZE: SMALLER; 394] *Opposite:* increase. 2 *v* **fell**, chop down, bring down, hack down, lop, clear. [➡TEAR, BREAK, AND CUT; 361] 3 *v* (*informal*) **kill**, strike down, slaughter, mow down, assassinate, slay (*formal or literary*). [➡KILL; 923]

cute 1 *adj* **attractive**, pretty, delightful, charming, appealing, endearing, adorable, sweet, darling, lovable. [➡PEOPLE'S PHYSICAL APPEARANCE; 476] *Opposite:* ugly. 2 *adj* **shrewd**, cunning, smart, sharp, quick, quick-witted. [➡POSITIVE INTELLECTUAL CHARACTERISTICS; 525]

cuteness 1 *n* **adorability**, lovability, attractiveness, appeal, charm, delightfulness, beauty, prettiness, loveliness, handsomeness, looks, comeliness (*archaic or literary*). [➡BEAUTY AND ATTRACTIVENESS; 190] *Opposite:* ugliness. 2 *n* **shrewdness**, cunning, smartness, sharpness, quickness, wiliness. [➡POSITIVE INTELLECTUAL CHARACTERISTICS; 525]

cutesy *adj* **mawkish**, saccharine, sugary, twee, chocolate-box, kitsch, tacky (*informal*), precious. [➡IN POOR TASTE; 230] *Opposite:* austere.

cut glass *type of* **glass**. [➡GLASS; 1135]

cut-glass *adj* **upper-class**, plummy, posh (*informal*), public-school, county (*informal*). [➡CLASS STATUS; 889] *Opposite:* broad.

cuticle *part of* **arm or hand**. [➡ARM AND HAND; 696]

cut in *v* **interrupt**, break in, butt in, interject, move in, interpose, interpolate. [➡INTERRUPT AND BUTT IN; 620]

cutlass *type of* **sword or knife**. [➡SWORDS AND KNIVES; 1156]

cutlery *n* **knives and forks**, tableware, silverware, silver, fighting irons, silver plate, flatware (*US*), flat silver (*US*). [➡TABLEWARE, CUTLERY, AND KITCHENWARE; 861]

cutlery

◆ *types of cutlery*
butter knife, cake slice, carving knife, chopstick, dessertspoon, fish knife, fork, knife, pastry fork, pastry slice, serving spoon, soupspoon, spoon, steak knife, tablespoon, teaspoon

cutlet *type of* **cut.** [➡TYPES AND CUTS OF MEAT; 1176]

cut loose (*informal*) *v* **get free**, get away, escape, make a break, break away, break free, break loose, burst out, get out, disentangle yourself. [➡RUN AWAY AND AVOID; 10]

cut off 1 *v* **remove**, sever, amputate, excise, detach, take off. [➡EXTRACT AND SEVER; 342] *Opposite:* reconnect. 2 *v* **stop**, disconnect, discontinue, bring to an end, halt, bring to a halt, withdraw, finish, withhold. [➡CAUSE TO STOP; 267] *Opposite:* restore. 3 *v* **isolate**, separate, keep apart, strand, detach, maroon. [➡UNFASTEN AND UNDO; 410] *Opposite:* connect. 4 *v* **interrupt**, stop, cut short, cut in, butt in, break in. [➡INTERRUPT AND BUTT IN; 620]

cutoff 1 *n* **limit**, end point, end date, deadline, expiry, finish, point of no return. [➡END; 54] *Opposite:* start. 2 *n* **stoppage**, end, finish, halt, freeze, break, termination, severance, breakdown, failure. [➡END; 54] *Opposite:* continuation.

cut out 1 *v* **remove**, take away, excise, extract, take out, delete. [➡EXTRACT AND SEVER; 342] *Opposite:* put in. 2 *v* **give up**, stop, renounce, forgo, do without, quit. [➡FORGO AND DENY ONESELF; 450] 3 *v* **exclude**, ignore, overlook, isolate, marginalize, eliminate, snub, cut dead. [➡NOT PAY ATTENTION; 765] *Opposite:* include.

cutout 1 *n* **shape**, template, stencil, outline, silhouette. [➡SHAPE; 1215] 2 *n* **safety device**, circuit breaker, safety switch, trip switch, kill switch (*US*). [➡PARTS OF MACHINES AND TOOLS; 1117]

cut out for *adj* **suited**, suitable, designed, destined, right, appropriate, qualified. [➡APPROPRIATE, SUITABLE, ADVISABLE; 185]

cut-price *adj* **reduced**, cheap, bargain, budget, discount, sale, inexpensive, cut-rate (*US*). [➡CHEAP AND INEXPENSIVE; 222]

cut-rate (*US*) *adj* [➡CHEAP AND INEXPENSIVE; 222]

cut short *v* **break off**, discontinue, call a halt, suspend, terminate (*formal*), stop in full flow, stop, interrupt. [➡CAUSE TO STOP; 267]

cutter 1 *type of* **military vessel.** [➡SHIPS AND BOATS; 1149] 2 *type of* **cutting tool.** [➡CUTTING TOOLS; 1119]

cutter

◆ *types of cutting tool*
axe, billhook, chisel, chopper, clippers, hatchet, hoe, knife, machete, pickaxe, plough, razor blade, scissors, scythe, secateurs, shears, sickle

cutthroat *adj* **merciless**, pitiless, ruthless, unsparing, fierce, aggressive, cruel, callous, competitive. [➡SELFISH AND UNKIND; 506] *Opposite:* merciful.

cutting 1 *adj* **hurtful**, wounding, unkind, acerbic, critical, spiteful, harsh, callous, heartless, sharp, caustic, stinging, abrasive. [➡RUDE AND HOSTILE; 626] *Opposite:* kind. 2 *adj* **cold**, biting, icy, sharp, keen, penetrating, piercing, harsh. [➡COLD WEATHER; 1051] *Opposite:* mild. 3 *n* **sprig**, offshoot, scion. [➡PARTS OF TREES AND PLANTS; 1026] 4 *type of* **part of trees and plants.** [➡PLANTS AND TREES; 1024]

cutting edge 1 *n* **vanguard**, van, forefront, edge, leading edge, lead, sharp end, frontier, top, limit, uncharted territory, fore (*literary*), front line, front, avant-garde. [➡NEW, MODERN; 167] *Opposite:* rearguard. 2 *n* **sharp edge**, razor edge, knife edge, serrated edge, blade, razor blade, knife blade. [➡EXTREMITIES OF PHYSICAL OBJECTS; 1249]

cutting-edge *adj* **leading-edge**, front-line, pioneering, trailblazing, radical, innovative, brand-new, forward-looking, progressive, revolutionary, unconventional, avant-garde. [➡NEW, MODERN; 167] *Opposite:* old-fashioned.

cuttingly *adv* **harshly**, abrasively, hurtfully, sharply, severely, caustically, tartly, acerbically, acidly, mordantly, bitingly. [➡RUDE AND HOSTILE; 626] *Opposite:* kindly.

cuttlefish *type of* **aquatic invertebrate.** [➡AQUATIC INVERTEBRATE; 1022]

cut up 1 *v* **chop**, mince, slice, chop up, dice, shred, cube. [➡TEAR, BREAK, AND CUT; 361] 2 *adj* (*informal*) **distressed**, upset, affected, distraught, heartbroken, miserable. [➡SADNESS, DISTRESS, AND DESPAIR; 540] *Opposite:* happy.

cutup (*US informal*) *n* **joker**, wisecracker (*informal*), smart aleck (*informal*), comic, comedian, prankster, wise guy (*US informal*). [➡JOKERS AND TEASES; 676]

CV *n* **curriculum vitae**, qualifications, employment record, résumé, vita. [➡SUMMARIES, OUTLINES, AND EXCERPTS; 589]

cwm *n* [➡GEOLOGICAL FEATURES; 1056]

cyan *type of* **blue.** [➡COLOURS; 1223]

cybermall *n* [➡E-COMMERCE; 1128]

cybermarketing *n* [➡E-COMMERCE; 1128]

cybermediary *n* [➡E-COMMERCE; 1128]

cybernetics *n* **artificial intelligence**, information technology, AI, IT. [➡COMPUTERS AND COMPUTING; 1126]

cyberspace *n* **virtual reality**, Internet, World Wide Web, information superhighway, data superhighway, infobahn. [➡THE INTERNET; 1127]

cyclamen *type of* **flower grown from bulb.** [➡FLOWERS FROM BULBS; 1030]

cycle 1 *n* **series**, sequence, set, round, rotation, succession, phase, progression, run. [➡CHAIN OF EVENTS; 163] 2 *type of* **bike** (*informal*). [➡BIKES, CARS, AND CARRIAGES; 1148]

cyclic *see* **cyclical.**

cyclical *adj* **recurring**, returning, repeated, cyclical, recurrent. [➡FREQUENT AND OFTEN; 107] *Opposite:* unique.

cyclone *n* **storm**, windstorm, hurricane, typhoon, tornado, tempest, whirlwind, tropical storm. [➡WINDY AND STORMY WEATHER; 1053]

cygnet *type of* **young bird.** [➡YOUNG BIRD; 1004]

cylinder 1 *n* **tube**, roll, pipe, chamber, piston. [➡ROUNDED SHAPE; 1217] 2 *n* **container**, drum, canister, tank, bottle. [➡CONTAINERS, RECEPTACLES, AND PACKAGING; 1244] 3 *part of* **engine.** [➡PARTS OF AN ENGINE; 1143]

cylindrical *adj* **tubular**, tube-shaped, cylinder-shaped, rod-shaped, rodlike. [➡ROUNDED SHAPE; 1217]

cymbal *type of* **percussion instrument.** [➡MUSICAL INSTRUMENTS; 910]

cynic *n* **sceptic**, doubter, detractor, disparager, misanthropist, pessimist, scoffer. [➡GRUMPY AND NEGATIVE PEOPLE; 953]

cynical 1 *adj* **sceptical**, distrustful, suspicious, disparaging, negative, detracting, pessimistic, misanthropic, scoffing, sardonic. [➡NEGATIVE OF OUTLOOK; 515] *Opposite:* naive. 2 *adj* **sarcastic**, mocking, scornful, sardonic, sneering, derisive, contemptuous, scathing. [➡MOCKING AND DISMISSIVE; 637] *Opposite:* respectful.

cynically 1 *adv* **sceptically**, pessimistically, negatively, distrustfully, suspiciously, disparagingly. [➡MOCKING AND DISMISSIVE; 637] *Opposite:* naively. 2 *adv* **sarcastically**, scornfully, sneeringly, sardonically, scathingly, contemptuously. [➡RUDE AND HOSTILE; 626] *Opposite:* respectfully.

cynicism *n* **scepticism**, sarcasm, distrust, doubt, scorn, suspicion, pessimism, disparagement, contempt. [➡CALMNESS, CONFIDENCE, AND COMPOSURE; 537] *Opposite:* naivety.

cypress *type of* **evergreen tree.** [➡EVERGREEN AND CONIFEROUS TREES; 1029]

Cyrillic *type of* **alphabet.** [➡SYMBOLS, SIGNS, AND NUMBERS; 597]

cyst *n* **swelling**, lump, polyp, nodule, growth, ganglion, tumour, sac, blister, wen. [➡ILLNESSES AND DISORDERS; 733]

czar *n* [➡IMPORTANT OR FAMOUS PEOPLE; 893]

D

dab 1 *v* **pat**, wipe, apply, touch, tap, daub. [➡DECORATE, ADORN, AND APPLY COATINGS; 406] 2 *n* **bit**, blob, spot, dash, drop, pat, smidgeon (*informal*), daub. [➡AMOUNT OF LIQUID; 114]

dabble 1 *v* **experiment**, try your hand, dip into, play at, have a go at (*informal*), potter, fiddle, toy with. [➡PARTICIPATE; 293] 2 *v* **dip**, paddle, splash, immerse. [➡FIDGET AND FROLIC; 312]

dab hand (*informal*) *n* **expert**, specialist, authority, whiz (*informal*), ace (*informal*). [➡TALENTED OR INTELLIGENT PERSON; 529]

dachshund *type of* **small dog**. [➡DOG; 980]

dad (*informal*) *n* **father**, pop (*informal*), papa (*informal dated*), pa (*informal*), daddy (*informal*). [➡OLDER GENERATION RELATIVES; 959]

Dada *type of* **20th-century art movement**. [➡ARTISTIC MOVEMENTS AND STYLES; 899]

daddy *see* **dad**.

daddy longlegs 1 *type of* **flying insect**. [➡FLYING INSECTS; 1013] 2 (*US*) *type of* **arachnid**. [➡ARACHNIDS; 1018]

dado 1 *n* **panel**, moulding, frieze, feature. [➡ROOFS, ROOF PARTS, AND CEILINGS; 1102] 2 *type of* **general fittings**. [➡FITTINGS; 859]

dado rail *n* [➡ROOFS, ROOF PARTS, AND CEILINGS; 1102]

daemon 1 *n* **demigod**, supernatural being, spirit. [➡MYTHICAL BEINGS; 790] 2 *n* **guardian spirit**, inspiration, guiding force, inner spirit, muse. [➡PSYCHOLOGY AND THE MIND; 770]

daffodil *type of* **flower grown from bulb**. [➡FLOWERS FROM BULBS; 1030]

daffy (*informal*) *adj* **silly**, wacky (*informal*), dippy, daft (*informal*), giddy (*dated*). [➡NEGATIVE INTELLECTUAL CHARACTERISTICS; 526] *Opposite:* sensible.

daft (*informal*) *adj* **silly**, foolish, dippy, eccentric, daffy (*informal*). [➡FUNNY AND AMUSING; 217] *Opposite:* sensible.

daftness (*informal*) *n* **silliness**, foolishness, thoughtlessness, eccentricity, dimness. [➡NEGATIVE INTELLECTUAL CHARACTERISTICS; 526] *Opposite:* good sense.

dagger *type of* **sword or knife**. [➡SWORDS AND KNIVES; 1156]

dahlia *type of* **flower grown from bulb**. [➡FLOWERS FROM BULBS; 1030]

daily 1 *adv* **every day**, each day, on a daily basis, day by day, day after day. [➡FREQUENT AND OFTEN; 107] 2 *adj* **everyday**, day-to-day, regular, diurnal, quotidian (*formal*), circadian, per diem. [➡TIMES OF DAY; 87]

daintiness *n* **delicacy**, elegance, gracefulness, refinement, prettiness, neatness, exquisiteness, deftness. [➡WELL GROOMED; 483] *Opposite:* clumsiness.

dainty *adj* **pretty**, delicate, graceful, refined, exquisite, elegant, petite, neat, deft. [➡DESCRIBING BODY MOVEMENTS; 289] *Opposite:* clumsy.

dais *n* **platform**, podium, pulpit, stage, stand. [➡STAGES, PLATFORMS, AND RAISED AREAS; 1097]

daisy *type of* **perennial flower**. [➡FLOWERS; 1032]

dale *n* **valley**, glen, dene, vale (*literary*). [➡GEOLOGICAL FEATURES; 1056] *Opposite:* hill.

dalliance (*literary*) *n* **flirtation**, romance, relationship, liaison, involvement, coquetry (*literary*). [➡SEXUAL AND ROMANTIC RELATIONSHIPS; 964]

dally *v* **linger**, hang about, dawdle, loiter, hang around, waste time, dilly-dally, fritter away. [➡SHIRK AND DELAY; 274] *Opposite:* hurry.

dalmatian *type of* **large dog**. [➡DOG; 980]

dam 1 *n* **barrier**, barrage, weir, wall, boom, block, obstruction. [➡BARRIERS; 1112] 2 *v* **block**, block up, stem, hold back, control, inhibit, blockade, hinder, obstruct, impede, restrict. [➡AVOID, PREVENT, LIMIT, AND CONTROL; 278] 3 *type of* **female animal**. [➡MALE OR FEMALE ANIMAL; 978]

damage 1 *n* **injury**, harm, hurt, impairment, destruction, mutilation, loss. [➡FAULTS, FLAWS, AND WEAKNESSES; 252] *Opposite:* reparation. 2 *n* (*informal*) **cost**, price, bill, total, amount. [➡EXPENDITURE; 424] 3 *v* **injure**, harm, spoil, hurt, smash up, break, scratch, dent, wound, mar, ravage. [➡DESTRUCTION AND DEMOLITION; 360] *Opposite:* repair.

See Compare and Contrast at **harm**.

damaged *adj* **injured**, hurt, spoiled, dented, scratched, smashed, broken, impaired, marred, beat-up (*informal*). [➡IN BAD REPAIR; 1233] *Opposite:* pristine.

damages *n* **compensation**, costs, reparation, reimbursement, recompense. [➡MONEY, PAYMENTS, AND CHARGES; 800]

damaging *adj* **harmful**, destructive, negative, detrimental, hurtful, injurious. [➡DANGEROUS; 237] *Opposite:* harmless.

damask *type of* **red**. [➡COLOURS; 1223]

damning *adj* **critical**, pejorative (*formal*), negative, disapproving, unfavourable, condemning, incriminatory. [➡ACCUSATORY AND DISAPPROVING; 635] *Opposite:* complimentary.

damp 1 *adj* **dank**, moist, humid, soggy, clammy, wet, wettish. [➡MOIST; 1240] *Opposite:* dry. 2 *adj* **half-hearted**, indifferent, insipid, unenthusiastic, weak. [➡NEUTRALITY AND INDIFFERENCE; 554] *Opposite:* enthusiastic. 3 *n* **moisture**, dampness, humidity, clamminess, wetness, dankness. [➡MOIST; 1240] *Opposite:* dryness. 4 *v* **check**, curb, restrain, hinder, hamper, inhibit, stifle. [➡MAKE IMPOSSIBLE; 277] *Opposite:*

encourage. 5 *v* **dampen**, moisten, humidify, wet. [➡SOFTEN, LIQUEFY, DAMPEN; 389] *Opposite:* dry out.

See Compare and Contrast at **wet.**

damp down *v* **dampen**, diminish, check, dull, curb, reduce, stifle, restrain, inhibit. [➡CHANGE OF INTENSITY: LESS; 396] *Opposite:* increase.

dampen 1 *v* **damp**, moisten, humidify, wet. [➡SOFTEN, LIQUEFY, DAMPEN; 389] *Opposite:* dry out. 2 *v* **damp down**, reduce, diminish, check, dull, inhibit, stifle. [➡CHANGE OF INTENSITY: LESS; 396] *Opposite:* increase.

damper 1 *n* **discouragement**, inhibition, hindrance, impediment, obstruction, curb, obstacle, check, restraint. [➡PROBLEM; 257] *Opposite:* spur. 2 *n* **mute**, silencer, softener, muffler (*US*). [➡ACOUSTICS; 1137] 3 *n* **regulator**, stopper, control, controller. [➡PARTS OF MACHINES AND TOOLS; 1117]

damply *adv* **indifferently**, half-heartedly, insipidly, wetly, unenthusiastically, weakly. [➡NEUTRALITY AND INDIFFERENCE; 554] *Opposite:* enthusiastically.

dampness *n* **humidity**, moisture, moistness, clamminess, wetness, damp, sogginess. [➡MOIST; 1240] *Opposite:* dryness.

damp squib (*informal*) *n* [➡DISASTERS; 253]

damsel (*archaic or literary*) *n* [➡FEMALE PERSON; 933]

damson *type of* **fruit.** [➡FRUIT AND VEGETABLES; 1175]

dance 1 *v* **bop** (*informal*), boogie (*informal*), twirl, pirouette, sway, turn. [➡FIDGET AND FROLIC; 312] 2 *v* **gambol**, prance, skip, caper, frolic, hop, jump, leap, cavort, wiggle. [➡FIDGET AND FROLIC; 312] 3 *n* **ball**, disco, hop (*dated informal*), rave (*slang*). [➡PARTIES, DANCES, AND CELEBRATIONS; 37]

dance

◆ *types of dance*
ballet, belly dance, bop (*informal*), bossa nova, cancan, cha-cha, Charleston, fandango, flamenco, foxtrot, jig, jitterbug, jive, line dancing, mambo, minuet, polka, quadrille, quickstep, rumba, salsa, samba, square dance, tango, tap dance, waltz

dance band *type of* **band.** [➡MUSICIANS AND SINGERS; 908]

dancer *type of* **entertainer.** [➡WORKERS IN ENTERTAINMENT AND MEDIA; 873]

dandelion *type of* **weed.** [➡WEEDS AND THISTLES; 1034]

dandified *adj* **dressed up**, dressed to kill, overdressed, fashionable, natty, dapper, modish, foppish. [➡WELL GROOMED; 483] *Opposite:* scruffy.

dandle 1 *v* **jiggle**, jog, bounce, dance, rock, shake. [➡MOVE SOMETHING ON THE SPOT; 337] 2 *v* **pet**, stroke, caress, fondle, pamper, rub, cuddle, nuzzle. [➡PHYSICAL CONTACT AS COMMUNICATION; 656]

dandruff *n* **scurf**, scale, skin flake. [➡CONDITIONS AFFECTING THE SKIN; 722]

dandy 1 *adj* (*US informal*) **great** (*informal*), excellent, cool (*slang*), groovy (*dated slang*), fine, superb, swell (*US dated informal*). [➡GOOD, WELL, BETTER; 184] *Opposite:* bad. 2 *n* (*dated*) **fop**, clotheshorse, beau (*archaic*), coxcomb (*archaic*), fashion plate, dude (*US slang*). [➡MALE PERSON; 934]

dandyish (*dated*) *adj* [➡WELL GROOMED; 483]

danger 1 *n* **hazard**, risk, peril, threat, menace, jeopardy, endangerment, vulnerability. [➡DANGER; 236] *Opposite:* safety. 2 *n* **chance**, possibility, likelihood, risk. [➡POSSIBLE AND PROBABLE; 178]

dangerous 1 *adj* **unsafe**, hazardous, risky, dodgy (*informal*), treacherous, perilous, precarious, chancy, daring, threatening. [➡DANGEROUS; 237] *Opposite:* safe. 2 *adj* **grave**, serious, critical, grievous, alarming. [➡DANGEROUS; 237] *Opposite:* safe.

dangerously 1 *adv* **hazardously**, treacherously, perilously, precariously, riskily, uncertainly. [➡DANGEROUS; 237] *Opposite:* safely. 2 *adv* **seriously**, severely, gravely, critically, grievously, alarmingly. [➡CRITICALLY AND SERIOUSLY; 132] *Opposite:* slightly.

dangerousness *n* [➡DANGER; 236]

dangle *v* **hang**, hang down, swing, sway, suspend, droop, sag, draggle. [➡GO DOWNWARDS; 308] *Opposite:* stick up.

dangling *adj* [➡ORIENTATION AND ALIGNMENT; 1222]

Danish blue *type of* **soft cheese.** [➡DAIRY PRODUCTS AND CHEESES; 1182]

Danish pastry *type of* **cake.** [➡CAKES, BISCUITS, AND DESSERTS; 1180]

dank *adj* **damp**, moist, chilly, clammy, humid, soggy, wet, fusty. [➡MOIST; 1240] *Opposite:* warm.

See Compare and Contrast at **wet.**

dankness *n* **wetness**, dampness, moistness, humidity, clamminess, chilliness, fustiness, sogginess. [➡MOIST; 1240] *Opposite:* warmth.

dapper *adj* **neat**, elegant, smart, trim, well-dressed, well turned-out, tidy, spruce, well-groomed, debonair, modish, sporty, stylish. [➡WELL GROOMED; 483] *Opposite:* scruffy.

dappled *adj* **speckled**, spotted, mottled, stippled, piebald, flecked, variegated. [➡DESCRIBING PATTERNS; 1226]

dare 1 *v* **venture**, risk, gamble, face up to, have the courage, have the guts, have the nerve. [➡ATTEMPT AN ACTION; 262] 2 *v* **challenge**, defy, taunt, provoke, goad, urge. [➡GAMBLE AND TAKE RISKS; 467] 3 *v* **presume**, venture, have the audacity, be so bold, take the liberty, have the cheek, have the nerve. [➡CARRY OUT AN ACTION; 270] 4 *n* **taunt**, challenge, provocation, ultimatum, goad, spur, stimulus. [➡NON-AGGRESSIVE/SPORTING EVENT; 40]

daredevil 1 *n* **risk-taker**, madcap, hothead, show-off (*informal*). [➡SELF-IMPORTANT AND SELF-SEEKING PEOPLE; 949] *Opposite:* stick-in-the-mud (*informal*). 2 *adj* **reckless**, rash, madcap, hotheaded, intrepid (*literary or humorous*), bold, foolhardy, fearless, wild, adventurous, risk-taking. [➡COURAGE; 499] *Opposite:* staid.

daresay *v* **guess**, suppose, expect, assume, admit, acknowledge. [➡QUESTION THINGS; 752] *Opposite:* deny.

daring 1 *adj* **bold**, brave, audacious, courageous, enterprising, intrepid (*literary or humorous*), heroic, adventurous, valiant, gallant (*literary*), dauntless (*literary*), plucky. [➡COURAGE; 499] *Opposite:* cowardly. 2 *adj* **dangerous**, risky, unsafe, hazardous, dodgy (*informal*), treacherous, perilous. [➡DANGEROUS; 237] *Opposite:* safe. 3 *n* **bravery**, bottle (*informal*), nerve, boldness, audacity, courage, heroism, adventurousness, valour, intrepidity. [➡COURAGE; 499] *Opposite:* cowardice.

daringly *adv* **boldly**, bravely, audaciously, courageously, heroically, valiantly, adventurously. [➡COURAGE; 499] *Opposite:* timidly.

dark 1 *adj* **dim**, shady, shadowy, murky, gloomy, dusky, black, obscure, opaque. [➡DESCRIBING LIGHT; 1227] *Opposite:* bright. 2 *adj* **black**, brunette, brown, chestnut, sable. [➡HAIR COLOUR; 486] *Opposite:* fair. 3 *adj* **gloomy**, depressing, bleak, sad, unhappy, cheerless, dreary, dismal, joyless, sombre. [➡EMOTIONALLY UNPLEASANT AND UPSETTING; 228] *Opposite:* cheery. 4 *adj* **sinister**, mysterious, spooky (*informal*), threatening, evil, nefarious, wicked, nasty. [➡DANGEROUS; 237] *Opposite:* good. 5 *n* **darkness**, dusk, gloom, dimness, shadows, obscurity, blackness, night, nighttime. [➡DESCRIBING LIGHT; 1227] *Opposite:* light.

darken *v* **blacken**, dim, deepen, cast a shadow, grow dim, grow dark, cloud over, obscure. [➡CHANGE OF COLOUR; 392] *Opposite:* brighten.

dark glasses *n* **sunglasses**, sunspecs (*informal*), shades (*informal*). [➡GLASSES AND SPECTACLES; 1124]

darkly 1 *adv* **threateningly**, sinisterly, forebodingly, menacingly, warningly, ominously, enigmatically, with intent. [➡RETICENT AND UNFORTHCOMING; 632] *Opposite:* cheerily. 2 *adv* **gloomily**, bleakly, dismally, forbiddingly, depressingly, cheerlessly, joylessly, sombrely. [➡BAD-TEMPERED AND HUMOURLESS; 627] *Opposite:* brightly.

darkness *n* **dark**, night, dusk, gloom, dimness, shadows, obscurity, blackness, nightfall, nighttime. [➡TIMES OF DAY; 87] *Opposite:* light.

darkroom *type of* **photographic equipment**. [➡PHOTOGRAPHY AND PHOTOGRAPHIC EQUIPMENT; 1121]

dark star *type of* **star or star system**. [➡CELESTIAL BODIES; 1060]

darling 1 *n* **sweetheart**, dear, love, dearest, beloved, pet, honey (*US informal*). [➡ENDEARMENTS; 657] 2 *n* **favourite**, firm favourite, pet, blue-eyed boy (*informal*), the apple of somebody's eye, fair-haired boy (*US*). [➡PEOPLE WHO ARE APPROVED OF; 955] 3 *adj* **wonderful**, gorgeous, lovely, adorable, dear, cute, charming, precious, sweet. [➡BEAUTY AND ATTRACTIVENESS; 190] *Opposite:* horrible.

darn *v* **sew**, stitch, repair, mend, sew up. [➡CRAFTS AND CARVING; 356] *Opposite:* tear.

dart 1 *n* **arrow**, barb, shaft, missile, projectile. [➡PROJECTILES; 1158] 2 *v* **dash**, scurry, nip (*informal*), whiz, rush, run, zip (*informal*), scoot (*informal*), zoom, shoot (*informal*), sprint, tear. [➡MOVE FAST; 314] *Opposite:* saunter.

dash 1 *n* **sprint**, rush, run, race, surge. [➡PROCEED AND GO; 306] 2 *n* **trace**, splash, drop, smidge (*informal*), smidgen (*informal*), pinch, soupçon, touch, bit. [➡AMOUNT OF LIQUID; 114] *Opposite:* dollop (*informal*). 3 *n* **verve**, vigour, spirit, flair, panache, élan (*literary*) [➡ENERGY AND ENTHUSIASM; 497]. 4 *type of* **punctuation mark** [➡ASPECTS OF LANGUAGE; 683]. 5 *v* **rush**, hurry, hasten, tear, race, run, dart, scurry, sprint, bolt, zip (*informal*). [➡MOVE FAST; 314] *Opposite:* amble. 6 *v* (*formal*) **knock**, throw, hurl, slam, fling, sling. [➡THROW SOMETHING; 335] 7 *v* (*formal*) **smash**, break, shatter, crash, splinter. [➡TEAR, BREAK, AND CUT; 361] 8 *v* **shatter**, ruin, crush, blight, destroy, spoil. [➡MAKE IMPOSSIBLE; 277] *Opposite:* bolster. 9 *v* **frustrate**, confound, foil, shatter, discourage, disappoint, crush, thwart, destroy. [➡MAKE IMPOSSIBLE; 277] *Opposite:* encourage.

dashboard *type of* **internal feature**. [➡INTERNAL PARTS OF A VEHICLE; 1145]

dashing 1 *adj* (*dated*) **spirited**, confident, jaunty, flamboyant, bold, dynamic, adventurous, daring, gallant (*literary*), swashbuckling. [➡COURAGE; 499] *Opposite:* staid. 2 *adj* **elegant**, stylish, chic, debonair, fashionable, smart, showy, striking. [➡WELL GROOMED; 483] *Opposite:* dowdy.

dashingly *adv* **adventurously**, dynamically, confidently, boldly, gallantly (*literary*), spiritedly, jauntily, self-confidently, flamboyantly. [➡COURAGE; 499]

dastardly *adj* **low**, shameful, dishonourable, mean, reprehensible, ignoble, immoral, sneaky, cowardly, base, despicable. [➡MORALLY BAD; 776] *Opposite:* honourable.

data *n* **information**, statistics, facts, figures, numbers, records, documents, files. [➡BASIC DETAILS; 689]

database *n* **data bank**, store, folder, list, archive, catalogue, record. [➡COMPUTERS AND COMPUTING; 1126]

data processing *n* **information retrieval**, data handling, number-crunching (*slang*). [➡COMPUTERS AND COMPUTING; 1126]

date 1 *n* **day**, day of the week, year, time. [➡TIMES OF YEAR; 88] 2 *n* **time**, point in time, period, era, day, epoch, age. [➡TIMES OF DAY; 87] 3 *n* **meeting**, rendezvous, appointment, blind date, engagement, assignation, tryst, get-together (*informal*). [➡MEETINGS AND ASSEMBLIES; 43] 4 *type of* **fruit**. [➡FRUIT AND VEGETABLES; 1175]

dated *adj* **old-fashioned**, old, behind the times, square (*slang dated*), unfashionable, passé, outmoded, out, old hat (*informal*), out-of-date. [➡OLD, OLD-FASHIONED; 168] *Opposite:* up-to-date.

dateline *n* **heading**, subheading, subhead, identification. [➡PARTS OF BOOKS AND DOCUMENTS; 594]

datum *n* [➡BASIC DETAILS; 689]

daub 1 *v* **smear**, spread, slap, spatter, slop, splatter, apply, cover, paint. [➡DECORATE, ADORN, AND APPLY COATINGS; 406] 2 *n* **blot**, blotch, spot, splotch, stain. [➡AMOUNT OF SOLID OR SEMI-SOLID; 115]

daughter *type of* **younger relative**. [➡YOUNGER GENERATION RELATIVES; 958]

daughter-in-law *type of* **in-law**. [➡RELATIVES BY MARRIAGE; 960]

daunt *v* **put off**, deter, discourage, intimidate, scare, frighten, overwhelm, dishearten, overawe, unnerve, unman, dismay, faze, subdue. [➡FRIGHTEN AND SHOCK; 569] *Opposite:* encourage.

daunted *adj* [➡INSECURITY AND LOSS OF COMPOSURE; 545]

daunting *adj* **intimidating**, unnerving, discouraging, scary (*informal*), frightening, overwhelming, formidable, disheartening, demoralizing, dismaying, fazing. [➡FRIGHTENING; 232] *Opposite:* heartening.

dauntless (*literary*) *adj* **resolute**, determined, confident, intrepid (*literary or humorous*), fearless, bold, undaunted, valiant, indomitable, heroic, daring, stouthearted. [➡COURAGE; 499] *Opposite:* timid.

dauntlessness (*literary*) *n* [➡COURAGE; 499]

davenport (*US*) *type of* **table**. [➡FURNITURE; 858]

dawdle 1 *v* **loiter**, delay, linger, plod, lag, fall behind, dally, tarry. [➡MOVE SLOWLY; 315] *Opposite:* hurry. 2 *v* **waste time**, hang around, hang about, dally, linger, delay, dilly-dally, loiter, shilly-shally, plod, lag behind, kill time, fritter away, procrastinate. [➡DELAY ACTION OR OCCURRENCE; 279] *Opposite:* hurry.

dawdler 1 *n* **straggler**, stroller, moocher (*slang*), wanderer, laggard, slowcoach (*informal*), foot-dragger (*informal*), dallier, dilly-dallier, slowpoke (*US informal*). [➡LAZY OR UNSUCCESSFUL PEOPLE; 948] *Opposite:* leader. 2 *n* **idler**, lazybones (*informal*), slacker, shirker, timewaster, shilly-shallier, lollygagger (*US dated*), goldbricker (*US informal*). [➡LAZY OR UNSUCCESSFUL PEOPLE; 948]

dawdling 1 *n* **dilly-dallying**, shilly-shallying, delaying, tarrying, loitering, dragging your feet, lagging behind, lingering, stalling. [➡DELAY ACTION OR OCCURRENCE; 279] *Opposite:* haste. 2 *adj* **slow**, sluggish, measured, leisurely, casual, deliberate, unhurried. [➡MOVING SLOWLY; 105] *Opposite:* hasty.

dawn 1 *n* **sunrise**, crack of dawn, daybreak, first light, daylight, morning, cockcrow (*archaic or literary*), sunup (*US*). [➡TIMES OF DAY; 87] *Opposite:* dusk. 2 *n* **beginning**, start, birth, emergence, dawning, origin, commencement (*formal*), genesis, advent, inception (*formal*). [➡BEGINNING; 53] *Opposite:* end. 3 *v* **begin**, start, be born, emerge, originate, commence (*formal*), appear. [➡SUDDENLY COME INTO EXISTENCE; 2] *Opposite:* end. 4 *v* **occur**, cross your mind, register with, strike, become clear to, become apparent to. [➡UNDERSTAND AND GRASP; 760]

day 1 *n* **daylight hours**, daylight, daytime, sunlight hours. [➡TIMES OF DAY; 87] *Opposite:* night. 2 *n* **date**, day of the week, calendar day. [➡TIMES OF YEAR; 88] 3 *n* **time**, era, period, generation, epoch, date, age. [➡TIMES OF YEAR; 88]

day after day *adv* **day in day out**, relentlessly, continually, constantly, without respite, persistently, ceaselessly, regularly. [➡PERMANENCE: WITHOUT END; 94] *Opposite:* intermittently.

day bed *type of* **bed**. [➡FURNITURE; 858]

daybreak *n* **dawn**, crack of dawn, first light, daylight, morning, sunrise, sunup (*US*). [➡TIMES OF DAY; 87] *Opposite:* dusk.

day by day *adv* **gradually**, slowly, little by little, bit by bit, step by step, progressively, steadily. [➡HAPPENING SLOWLY; 106] *Opposite:* all at once.

daydream 1 *n* **reverie**, fantasy, musing, contemplation, dream, fancy, pipe dream. [➡DREAM, IMAGINE, AND FANTASIZE; 750] 2 *v* **dream**, have your head in the clouds, be miles away, be inattentive, fantasize, muse, be lost in thought, woolgather, stare into space, contemplate, stargaze, imagine. [➡DREAM, IMAGINE, AND FANTASIZE; 750] *Opposite:* concentrate.

daydreamer *n* **idealist**, dreamer, fantasist, visionary, woolgatherer. [➡LAZY OR UNSUCCESSFUL PEOPLE; 948]

daydreaming 1 *n* **reverie**, woolgathering, pensiveness, dreaminess, inattention, inattentiveness, negligence, preoccupation, distraction. [➡DREAM, IMAGINE, AND FANTASIZE; 750] *Opposite:* concentration. 2 *adj* **fantasizing**, imagining, dreaming, dreamy, woolgathering, pensive, inattentive, negligent, preoccupied, distracted, in a world of your own, wandering, lost in thought, distant, unmindful. [➡PENSIVENESS AND INTEREST; 539] *Opposite:* concentrating.

day in day out *adv* [➡PERMANENCE: WITHOUT END; 94]

daylight 1 *n* **day**, daytime, sunshine, light of day, hours of daylight. [➡LIGHT; 1163] *Opposite:* nighttime. 2 *n* **dawn**, crack of dawn, sunrise, daybreak, first light, morning, cockcrow (*archaic or literary*), sunup (*US*). [➡TIMES OF DAY; 87] *Opposite:* dusk.

day off *n* [➡PERIOD OF REST; 91]

Day of Judgment *n* [➡RELIGIOUS CONCEPTS; 777]

day out *n* **outing**, away day, trip, spree, jaunt, tour, visit, day trip, break, excursion, journey, day away. [➡TRAVEL: JOURNEYS AND TRIPS; 319]

day room *n* **lounge**, recreation room, seating area, reception room, sitting room. [➡TYPES OF ROOM; 1096]

days gone by *n* **former times**, earlier times, previous times, days of old, olden days, yesteryear, past. [➡PAST; 84] *Opposite:* future.

daytime *n* **day**, daylight, hours of daylight, morning, afternoon. [➡TIMES OF DAY; 87] *Opposite:* nighttime.

day-to-day *adj* **everyday**, commonplace, daily, routine, usual, habitual, regular, customary. [➡ORDINARINESS; 245] *Opposite:* unusual.

day trip *n* **excursion**, outing, day out, trip, visit, jaunt, tour. [➡TRAVEL: JOURNEYS AND TRIPS; 319]

day tripper *n* **tourist**, traveller, tripper (*informal*), sightseer, holidaymaker, vacationer (*US*). [➡TRAVEL: TRAVELLERS AND WALKERS; 320]

daze 1 *n* **confusion**, stupor, shock, bewilderment, bemusement, bafflement, astonishment, surprise. [➡CONFUSION, ANXIETY, AND WORRY; 541] 2 *v* **stun**, shock, astonish, astound, surprise, bemuse, confound, bewilder, baffle, stupefy, stagger, confuse. [➡CONFUSE AND BEWILDER; 572]

dazed *adj* **confused**, stunned, shocked, astonished, astounded, surprised, bemused, overcome, bewildered, stupefied, confounded, baffled. [➡CONFUSION, ANXIETY, AND WORRY; 541] *Opposite:* alert.

dazzle 1 *v* **bedazzle**, blind, daze, confuse, overwhelm. [➡ CONFUSE AND BEWILDER; 572] 2 *v* **amaze**, astonish, astound, impress, overwhelm, stun, awe, dumbfound, hypnotize, take somebody's breath away, bowl over, overpower. [➡ SURPRISE AND IMPRESS; 575] *Opposite:* bore. 3 *n* **glare**, brightness, reflection, blaze, brilliance. [➡ DESCRIBING LIGHT; 1227]

dazzling 1 *adj* **stunning**, amazing, astounding, incredible, alluring, glittering, glittery, impressive, awing, overpowering. [➡ EXTRAORDINARY: AMAZING; 205] *Opposite:* unimpressive. 2 *adj* **bright**, glaring, glittering, blazing, luminous, fierce, intense. [➡ DESCRIBING LIGHT; 1227] *Opposite:* dull.

deactivate *v* **neutralize**, disable, switch off, turn off, disengage. [➡ CAUSE TO STOP; 267] *Opposite:* activate.

dead 1 *adj* **deceased** (*formal*), lifeless, passed on, late, defunct, gone (*informal*), departed (*formal or literary*). [➡ DEAD AND DYING; 925] *Opposite:* alive. 2 *adj* **numb**, benumbed, stiff, insensitive, frozen, unresponsive. [➡ TIRED, ASLEEP AND UNCONSCIOUS; 739] *Opposite:* sensitive. 3 *adj* **boring**, quiet, dull, uninteresting, deadly, flat. [➡ BORING AND UNINTERESTING; 235] *Opposite:* exciting. 4 *adj* **finished**, obsolete, over, ended, empty, exhausted, done with, extinct. [➡ REDUNDANT AND USELESS; 241] *Opposite:* current. 5 *adj* **silent**, blank, quiet, down, inactive, inert, extinct. [➡ LACK OF ACTIVITY; 343] *Opposite:* live.

Compare and Contrast: ***dead, deceased, departed, late, lifeless, defunct, extinct***

CORE MEANING: NO LONGER LIVING, FUNCTIONING, OR IN EXISTENCE

dead the most general term, used of organisms that are no longer alive, physical objects that no longer function or exist, and abstract entities that are no longer valid or relevant; ***deceased*** (*formal*, restricted to people, especially in legal or other technical contexts, or as a euphemism) no longer living; ***departed*** (*formal or literary*, restricted to people) dead; ***late*** (restricted to people) having died recently or within living memory; ***lifeless*** not living, or apparently not living; ***defunct*** (used of machines or systems) no longer operative, valid, or functional; ***extinct*** no longer in existence, or no longer active.

dead as a dodo *adj* [➡ DEAD AND DYING; 925]

dead as a doornail *adj* [➡ DEAD AND DYING; 925]

dead beat (*informal*) *adj* **spent**, bushed (*informal*), exhausted, shattered, worn-out, tired, weary, tired out, all in. [➡ TIRED, ASLEEP AND UNCONSCIOUS; 739] *Opposite:* fresh.

deadbeat (*slang*) *n* **loafer**, idler, waster, ne'er-do-well (*dated*), layabout, skiver (*informal*). [➡ LAZY OR UNSUCCESSFUL PEOPLE; 948]

deaden *v* **soften**, dull, muffle, dampen, mute, stifle. [➡ CHANGE OF INTENSITY: LESS; 396] *Opposite:* amplify.

dead end 1 *n* **cul-de-sac**, blind alley, impasse, no through road, roadblock. [➡ EXTREMITIES OF PHYSICAL OBJECTS; 1249] 2 *n* **block**, stalemate, standstill, impasse, deadlock, end of the road. [➡ PROBLEM; 257] 3 *type of* **minor road.** [➡ ROADS; 1105]

deadened *adj* **desensitized**, unfeeling, insensitive, insensible, numb, frozen, anaesthetized. [➡ TIRED, ASLEEP AND UNCONSCIOUS; 739] *Opposite:* sensitive.

deadhead *v* **take away**, cut off, remove. [➡ EXTRACT AND SEVER; 342]

dead heat *n* **draw**, tie, photo finish, drawn game, stalemate, deuce. [➡ RESULTS AND OUTCOMES; 83]

deadline *n* **time limit**, limit, goal, aim, target, cutoff date, closing date. [➡ END; 54] *Opposite:* extension.

deadlock *n* **impasse**, stalemate, gridlock, standstill, logjam, block, end of the road. [➡ DIFFICULT SITUATIONS; 72]

deadly 1 *adj* **lethal**, fatal, terminal, mortal, poisonous, noxious, toxic. [➡ DEADLY; 928] *Opposite:* harmless. 2 *adj* (*informal*) **boring**, tedious, tiresome, dull, dead, uninteresting. [➡ BORING AND UNINTERESTING; 235] *Opposite:* interesting. 3 *adj* **extreme**, implacable (*formal*), mortal, sworn, absolute, irreconcilable. [➡ DANGEROUS; 237] 4 *adv* **completely**, absolutely, extremely, very, perfectly, wholly, terribly. [➡ CRITICALLY AND SERIOUSLY; 132] *Opposite:* slightly.

Compare and Contrast: ***deadly, fatal, mortal, lethal, terminal***

CORE MEANING: CAUSING DEATH

deadly likely or designed to cause death; ***fatal*** describes accidents or illnesses that result in death; ***mortal*** causing, continuing until, or relating to, death; ***lethal*** certain to or intended to cause death; ***terminal*** describes illnesses that cause death.

deadpan *adj* **unsmiling**, straight-faced, poker-faced, expressionless, blank, po-faced. [➡ FACIAL EXPRESSION; 652] *Opposite:* expressive.

dead ringer (*informal*) *n* **double**, spitting image (*informal*), lookalike (*informal*), doppelgänger, image. [➡ COPIES AND REPLICAS; 152] *Opposite:* opposite.

dead to the world *adj* **asleep**, fast asleep, sound asleep, sleeping, sleeping like a baby, snoozing (*informal*), slumbering, napping. [➡ TIRED, ASLEEP AND UNCONSCIOUS; 739] *Opposite:* awake.

deaf 1 *adj* **hearing-impaired**, deafened, tone-deaf. [➡ HEAR; 708] *Opposite:* hearing. 2 *adj* **unresponsive**, indifferent, oblivious, heedless, unmoved, unaffected. [➡ NEUTRALITY AND INDIFFERENCE; 554] *Opposite:* mindful.

deafening *adj* **loud**, earsplitting, ear-piercing, booming, thunderous, resounding. [➡ LOUD OR UNPLEASANT SOUNDS; 1265] *Opposite:* quiet.

deal 1 *n* **transaction**, contract, agreement, arrangement, pact, treaty, covenant, compact. [➡ EXCHANGE AND INTERCHANGE; 449] 2 *v* **distribute**, share out, dole out (*informal*), give out, allocate, apportion, dispense. [➡ DISPENSE, RATION, AND DISTRIBUTE; 435] *Opposite:* receive. 3 *v* **trade**, do business, exchange, sell, transact business, hawk. [➡ SELL; 442] *Opposite:* buy.

dealer *n* **trader**, merchant, seller, broker, supplier, wholesaler. [➡ PEOPLE INVOLVED IN FINANCE; 804]

dealership 1 *n* **charter**, authorization, agreement, right, licence, franchise. [➡ BUSINESS ENTERPRISES AND RELATED BODIES; 793] 2 *n* **premises**, showroom, offices, workplace, workshop, site, place of business. [➡ PLACE OF EMPLOYMENT; 832]

dealings *n* **transactions**, contact, communication, business, connections, relations. [➡COMMUNICATION; 603]

deal out *v* **give out**, issue, distribute, mete out, dish out (*informal*), administer, dispense, allocate, assign, dole out (*informal*). [➡DISPENSE, RATION, AND DISTRIBUTE; 435] *Opposite:* collect.

deal with *v* **cope**, manage, handle, see to, take care of, sort out, take in hand, contend. [➡CARRY OUT AN ACTION; 270]

dear 1 *adj* **beloved**, cherished, prized, valued, precious, loved. [➡POPULAR AND WANTED; 221] *Opposite:* hated. 2 *adj* **expensive**, pricey (*informal*), costly, extortionate, valuable, exorbitant. [➡EXPENSIVE AND OVERPRICED; 248] *Opposite:* cheap. 3 *n* **darling**, sweetheart, dearest, beloved, pet, love. [➡ENDEARMENTS; 657]

dearest *n* **love**, sweetheart, pet, sugar (*informal*), precious, sweetie (*informal*), honey (*US informal*). [➡ENDEARMENTS; 657]

dearie (*informal*) *n* **love**, sweetheart, pet, sugar (*informal*), precious, sweetie (*informal*), honey (*US informal*), [➡ENDEARMENTS; 657]

dearly *adv* **greatly**, extremely, exceedingly, profoundly, sincerely, deeply. [➡TO A GREAT EXTENT; 130]

dearth *n* **lack**, shortage, scarcity, drought, famine, want, deficiency, absence, need. [➡TOO FEW, TOO LITTLE; 120] *Opposite:* glut.

See Compare and Contrast at **lack**.

death 1 *n* **demise** (*formal*), passing, decease (*formal*), expiry (*formal or literary*), bereavement, loss. [➡DEATH AND BEREAVEMENT; 927] *Opposite:* birth. 2 *n* **fatality**, casualty, mortality (*archaic*), loss of life, killing, murder. [➡DEAD PERSON; 926] *Opposite:* birth. 3 *n* **end**, fall, downfall, ruin, demise (*formal*), collapse, overthrow. [➡END; 54] *Opposite:* beginning.

deathblow *n* **death knell**, body blow, final blow, last straw, last nail in the coffin, end, destruction. [➡END; 54]

death cap *type of* **fungus**. [➡MICROORGANISMS, FUNGI, AND ALGAE; 1023]

death knell *n* **finish**, end point, end of the road, point of no return, final blow, last straw, last nail in the coffin, body blow, death warrant, deathblow. [➡END; 54]

deathless *adj* **eternal**, timeless, immortal, everlasting, undying, perpetual, ceaseless. [➡PERMANENCE: WITHOUT END; 94] *Opposite:* mortal.

deathlike *adj* **skeletal**, gaunt, ashen, ghastly (*literary*), spectral, pallid, corpselike, deathly, cadaverous (*formal or literary*). [➡COMPLEXION; 481]

deathly 1 *adj* **deadly**, deathlike, tomblike, ghastly (*literary*), deep, stony. [➡EMOTIONALLY UNPLEASANT AND UPSETTING; 228] 2 *adv* **extremely**, intensely, deadly, intensively, absolutely, totally. [➡CRITICALLY AND SERIOUSLY; 132] *Opposite:* slightly.

death mask *n* **effigy**, cast, head, model, sculpture, mould. [➡SCULPTURE; 902]

death rattle *n* **gurgle**, rattle, rasp, wheeze, croak, gasp. [➡SOUNDS MADE BY PEOPLE; 1261]

death's head moth *type of* **moth**. [➡MOTHS AND BUTTERFLIES; 1015]

death toll *n* **fatalities**, death rate, mortality rate, fatality rate, loss of life, mortality. [➡DEAD PERSON; 926]

deathtrap (*informal*) *n* **safety risk**, hazard, minefield, pitfall, health hazard, firetrap, threat to life and limb. [➡PROBLEM; 257]

death warrant *n* **death knell**, end, finish, end point, end of the road, point of no return, final blow, last straw, last nail in the coffin. [➡END; 54]

deathwatch beetle *type of* **beetle**. [➡BEETLES AND WEEVILS; 1016]

debacle *n* **disaster**, catastrophe, fiasco, shambles, tragedy, calamity, misfortune, farce. [➡DISASTERS; 253] *Opposite:* success.

debar *v* **exclude**, expel, bar, ban, prohibit, veto, refuse. [➡REFUSE PERMISSION AND NOT ALLOW; 671] *Opposite:* admit.

debark *v* **disembark**, alight, go ashore, land, get off, arrive. [➡ARRIVE BY TRANSPORT; 14] *Opposite:* embark.

debarkation *n* **disembarkation**, alighting, going ashore, landing, getting off, arrival. [➡ARRIVAL; 13]

debase 1 *v* **degrade**, defile (*formal*), impair, adulterate, sully, corrupt, taint, tarnish, soil. [➡WORSEN SOMETHING; 381] *Opposite:* purify. 2 *v* **humiliate**, demean, degrade, shame, humble, disgrace, lower, dishonour. [➡UPSET, DISTRESS, AND HUMILIATE; 568] *Opposite:* glorify.

debasement 1 *n* **ruination**, adulteration, corruption, defilement, tarnishing, sullying. [➡WORSEN SOMETHING; 381] *Opposite:* purification. 2 *n* **humiliation**, degradation, disgrace, shame, disparagement, ignominy, dishonour. [➡EMBARRASSMENT AND HUMILIATION; 543] *Opposite:* glorification.

debatable *adj* **arguable**, dubious, controversial, doubtful, contentious, unsettled, undecided, questionable, disputable, undetermined. [➡UNCERTAIN; 176] *Opposite:* settled.

debatably *adv* **arguably**, disputably, questionably, dubiously, doubtfully, maybe, uncertainly, possibly, perhaps. [➡POSSIBLE AND PROBABLE; 178] *Opposite:* indisputably.

debate 1 *v* **discuss**, argue, dispute, deliberate, contest, question. [➡TWO-WAY COMMUNICATION; 608] *Opposite:* conclude. 2 *v* **ponder**, wonder, deliberate, weigh up, consider, contemplate, meditate, think over. [➡QUESTION THINGS; 752] *Opposite:* decide. 3 *n* **discussion**, argument, dispute, deliberation (*formal*), examination, consideration. [➡NEGOTIATION AND DEBATE; 46] *Opposite:* conclusion.

debater *n* **speaker**, orator, public speaker, disputant, arguer. [➡SPEAKERS AND ORATORS; 604]

debauched *adj* **decadent**, dissolute, degenerate, dissipated, immoral, self-indulgent. [➡MORALLY BAD; 776] *Opposite:* moral.

debauchee (*formal*) *n* [➡PLEASURE-SEEKERS AND HEDONISTS; 886]

debauchery *n* **decadence**, dissoluteness, immorality, self-indulgence. [➡MORALLY BAD; 776] *Opposite:* morality.

debilitate *v* **weaken**, incapacitate, enervate, drain, hamper, encumber, hinder. [➡AVOID, PREVENT, LIMIT, AND CONTROL; 278] *Opposite:* fortify.

debilitated *adj* **weakened**, incapacitated, enervated, drained, hampered, encumbered, hindered. [➡UNFIT AND WEAK; 740] *Opposite:* fortified.

See Compare and Contrast at **weak**.

debilitating *adj* **weakening**, incapacitating, enervating, draining, devastating, sapping. [➡PHYSICALLY UNPLEASANT; 227] *Opposite:* refreshing.

debility *n* **weakness**, incapacity, frailty, encumbrance, ineffectiveness, enfeeblement, enervation. [➡FAULTS, FLAWS, AND WEAKNESSES; 252] *Opposite:* strength.

debit 1 *n* **withdrawal**, subtraction, deduction, debt, charge, record, bill. [➡ACCOUNTING, BANKING, AND BUDGETING; 799] *Opposite:* credit. **2** *v* **deduct**, take out, withdraw, subtract, charge, record. [➡GET MONEY OR REWARD; 422] *Opposite:* credit.

debonair *adj* **suave**, elegant, refined, charming, well-groomed, urbane, cultured, dashing, cultivated. [➡WELL GROOMED; 483] *Opposite:* graceless.

debouch *v* **emerge**, move out, spread out, exit, come out, issue. [➡EMIT AND EMANATE; 362] *Opposite:* confine.

debrief *v* **question**, interrogate, interview, examine, quiz, probe. [➡ASK PEOPLE QUESTIONS; 667]

debriefing *n* **interrogation**, questioning, interview, examination, probing, quizzing, sounding out. [➡ASK PEOPLE QUESTIONS; 667] *Opposite:* briefing.

debris *n* **wreckage**, remains, fragments, rubble, waste, flotsam and jetsam, garbage (*US*), trash (*US*). [➡RUBBISH AND USELESS OBJECTS; 1248]

debt 1 *n* **arrears**, liability, debit, balance, balance due, bill. [➡OWE AND DESERVE; 466] *Opposite:* credit. **2** *n* **obligation**, duty, responsibility, dues, liability, commitment. [➡RESPONSIBILITY; 171]

debtor *n* **borrower**, mortgagor, insolvent, defaulter, pledger, nonpayer. [➡PEOPLE INVOLVED IN FINANCE; 804]

debug *v* **clear up**, correct, sort out, repair, fix, restore, mend, service. [➡REPAIR AND MEND; 377] *Opposite:* corrupt.

debunk *v* **expose**, show up, deflate, demystify, discredit, set straight, throw light on, lay bare. [➡DENY AND REJECT; 645] *Opposite:* perpetuate.

debut *n* **entrance**, introduction, unveiling, presentation, inauguration, coming out. [➡BEGINNING; 53] *Opposite:* retirement.

decade 1 *n* **period**, era, time, epoch. [➡EPOCHS AND ERAS; 89] **2** *type of* **time period**. [➡TIMES OF YEAR; 88]

decadence *n* **corruption**, debauchery, depravity, dissolution, self-indulgence, profligacy, dissipation, excess. [➡MORALLY BAD; 776] *Opposite:* decency.

decadent *adj* **debauched**, corrupt, depraved, dissolute, degenerate, immoral, licentious (*formal*), profligate, self-indulgent. [➡PLEASURE-SEEKING AND EXCESS; 885] *Opposite:* innocent.

decadently *adv* **dissolutely**, degenerately, immorally, profligately, licentiously (*formal*), self-indulgently. [➡PLEASURE-SEEKING AND EXCESS; 885] *Opposite:* innocently.

decaf *type of* **coffee**. [➡DRINKS; 1186]

decamp *v* **run away**, run off, escape, flee, abscond, leave, retreat, desert, do a bunk (*informal*), flit. [➡RUN AWAY AND AVOID; 10] *Opposite:* stay.

decant *v* **pour**, pour out, transfer, empty, empty out, draw off. [➡EMPTY AND UNLOAD; 408] *Opposite:* fill.

decanter *n* **carafe**, flask, vessel, bottle, pitcher, container. [➡TABLEWARE, CUTLERY, AND KITCHENWARE; 861]

decapitate *v* **behead**, guillotine, execute, amputate, truncate, kill. [➡KILL; 923]

decapitation *n* **beheading**, amputation, killing, guillotining, execution. [➡CAUSES OF DEATH; 921]

decathlon *type of* **track and field**. [➡HOBBIES, GAMES, AND SPORTS; 875]

decay 1 *v* **decompose**, rot, fester, perish, crumble, putrefy, corrode, waste away, go mouldy, moulder. [➡GO BAD AND CORRODE; 391] **2** *v* **decline**, degenerate, deteriorate, fall off, dwindle, wane. [➡CEASE TO EXIST; 22] *Opposite:* flourish. **3** *n* **deterioration**, decline, degeneration, falling-off, falloff, dwindling, waning. [➡END; 54] *Opposite:* growth. **4** *n* **decomposition**, rot, rotting, putrefaction, corrosion, mould. [➡WORSEN SOMETHING; 381]

decayed *adj* **decomposed**, rotten, rotting, putrefied, perished, corroded, mouldy. [➡DECAYING OR INFESTED; 1235] *Opposite:* fresh.

decaying *adj* **decomposing**, rotting, rotten, putrefying, crumbling, mouldy, mouldering. [➡DECAYING OR INFESTED; 1235] *Opposite:* fresh.

decease (*formal*) *n* **death**, passing, demise (*formal*), departure, release, expiry (*formal or literary*). [➡DEATH AND BEREAVEMENT; 927] *Opposite:* birth.

deceased (*formal*) 1 *n* **corpse**, cadaver, body, decedent (*formal*), departed (*formal or literary*). [➡DEAD PERSON; 926] **2** *adj* **dead**, late, departed (*formal or literary*), lifeless, defunct, extinct. [➡DEAD AND DYING; 925] *Opposite:* alive.

See Compare and Contrast at **dead**.

deceit *n* **dishonesty**, treachery, deceitfulness, deception, trickery, sham, cheating, duplicity, falseness, guile, fraud, pretence. [➡DECEPTION AND LIES; 661] *Opposite:* honesty.

deceitful *adj* **dishonest**, deceiving, fraudulent, untrustworthy, cunning, lying, devious, cheating, faithless. [➡DECEITFUL; 514] *Opposite:* honest.

deceitfully *adv* **dishonestly**, cunningly, fraudulently, deviously, treacherously, craftily, by deceit, faithlessly. [➡FALSE AND UNREAL; 174] *Opposite:* honestly.

deceitfulness *n* **dishonesty**, deceit, treachery, lies, falseness, fraudulence, untrustworthiness, faithlessness. [➡DECEITFUL; 514] *Opposite:* honesty.

deceive 1 *v* **mislead**, betray, trick, take in, lie to, swindle, double-cross, con, misinform, cheat, hoodwink, defraud, dupe, delude. [➡DECEPTION AND LIES; 661] 2 *v* **cheat**, two-time, cuckold (*archaic*), betray, step out (*informal*), play away (*informal*). [➡DECEPTION AND LIES; 661]

deceiver *n* **liar**, fraud, swindler, con artist (*slang*), cheat, fraudster. [➡PEOPLE WHO DECEIVE; 662]

deceiving *adj* **misleading**, lying, cheating, devious, deceptive, unreliable, dishonest, illusory, fraudulent, fallacious, faithless, specious, cunning, plausible, glib, false, pretending, insincere, untrustworthy. [➡DECEITFUL; 514] *Opposite:* honest.

decelerate *v* **slow down**, slow, slow up, brake, lose speed, reduce speed, lose pace. [➡CHANGE OF SPEED: LESS; 398] *Opposite:* accelerate.

deceleration *n* **slowing down**, slowing up, slowing, braking, checking, retardation. [➡CHANGE OF SPEED: LESS; 398] *Opposite:* acceleration.

decency 1 *n* **politeness**, decorum, decorousness, civility, courtesy, politesse, correctness, dignity. [➡GOOD MANNERS AND SOCIAL SKILLS; 521] *Opposite:* incivility. 2 *n* **modesty**, respectability, uprightness, integrity, wholesomeness, propriety, righteousness, morality, honesty. [➡MORALLY GOOD; 775] *Opposite:* decadence.

decent 1 *adj* **moral**, honest, virtuous, pure (*literary*), wholesome, demure, modest, honourable. [➡MORALLY GOOD; 775] *Opposite:* decadent. 2 *adj* **good**, right, proper, correct, suitable, appropriate, fitting. [➡APPROPRIATE, SUITABLE, ADVISABLE; 185] *Opposite:* inappropriate. 3 *adj* **reasonable**, respectable, adequate, sizable, generous, ample, moderate, passable, sufficient. [➡ACCEPTABLE AND PASSABLE; 220] *Opposite:* inadequate. 4 *adj* (*informal*) **dressed**, clothed, clad, attired (*formal*), garbed, covered. [➡DRESS, WEAR, AND UNDRESS; 868] *Opposite:* undressed. 5 *adj* **respectable**, upright, polite, civilized, well-mannered, well-brought-up, courteous, considerate. [➡GOOD MANNERS AND SOCIAL SKILLS; 521]

decently 1 *adv* **morally**, respectably, demurely, properly, virtuously, righteously. [➡MORALLY GOOD; 775] *Opposite:* improperly. 2 *adv* **politely**, decorously, graciously, civilly, affably, courteously, correctly. [➡GOOD MANNERS AND SOCIAL SKILLS; 521] *Opposite:* rudely.

decentralization *n* **devolution**, subsidiarity, regionalization, delegation, reorganization. [➡STYLES AND SYSTEMS OF GOVERNMENT; 806] *Opposite:* centralization.

decentralize *v* **devolve**, regionalize, reorganize, disperse, distribute, spread out. [➡SEPARATE AND DIVIDE; 402] *Opposite:* centralize.

deception 1 *n* **dishonesty**, duplicity, deceptiveness, deceit, cheating, trickery. [➡DECEPTION AND LIES; 661] *Opposite:* truthfulness. 2 *n* **trick**, ruse, sham, fraud, con, pretext. [➡DECEPTION AND LIES; 661]

deceptive *adj* **misleading**, illusory, deceiving, dishonest, false, unreliable, illusive, pretended, disingenuous, devious, deceitful, fraudulent, phoney, spurious, specious. [➡FALSE AND UNREAL; 174] *Opposite:* reliable.

deceptiveness *n* **falseness**, falsity, disingenuousness, deviousness, spuriousness, speciousness, deceitfulness, fraudulence, phoniness, unreliableness, unreliability, inaccurateness, inaccuracy, illusoriness, unrepresentativeness. [➡FALSE AND UNREAL; 174] *Opposite:* reliability.

decide 1 *v* **make a decision**, choose, come to a decision, make your mind up, settle on, fix on, agree, resolve, adopt, elect, go for (*informal*), select, plump for, pick, take, opt. [➡MAKE DECISIONS AND CHOICES; 753] *Opposite:* prevaricate. 2 *v* **settle**, determine, conclude, resolve, decree, rule. [➡MAKE DECISIONS AND CHOICES; 753] *Opposite:* put off.

decided 1 *adj* **obvious**, definite, absolute, categorical, unquestionable, unambiguous, unequivocal, certain, distinct, particular, clear-cut, unmistakable, indisputable. [➡CERTAIN; 175] *Opposite:* unclear. 2 *adj* **determined**, resolute, decisive, firm, sure, certain, unfaltering, unwavering, definite, unhesitating, emphatic. [➡CERTAINTY; 562] *Opposite:* hesitant.

decidedly *adv* **categorically**, definitely, absolutely, distinctly, particularly, unquestionably, unambiguously, unequivocally, emphatically, undoubtedly, obviously, unmistakably. [➡ABSOLUTE AND ABSOLUTELY; 131] *Opposite:* possibly.

decider *n* **game**, match, contest, trial, play-off, shoot-out, tiebreaker, tie-break. [➡DECISIVE MOMENTS; 44]

deciding *adj* **determining**, decisive, conclusive, key, pivotal, significant, critical, crucial. [➡MOST IMPORTANT AND MAIN; 194] *Opposite:* insignificant.

deciduous tree

◆ *types of deciduous tree*
acacia, alder, ash, aspen, baobab, beech, birch, chestnut, elm, ginkgo, hickory, horse chestnut, laburnum, lime, maple, mesquite, mimosa, oak, plane tree, poplar, rowan, sassafras, silver birch, sycamore, teak, willow

decimal *n* **number**, fraction, unit. [➡SYMBOLS, SIGNS, AND NUMBERS; 597]

decimate *v* **devastate**, destroy, annihilate, ruin, cut a swath through, slaughter, lay waste, demolish, cut down. [➡DESTRUCTION AND DEMOLITION; 360]

decimation *n* **devastation**, destruction, slaughter, annihilation, ruin, demolition, obliteration. [➡CAUSES OF DEATH; 921]

decipher *v* **decode**, decrypt, interpret, translate, make out, work out, read, crack, make sense of, puzzle out, untangle. [➡SOLVE AND INTERPRET; 761] *Opposite:* encode.

decipherable *adj* **readable**, legible, intelligible, comprehensible, understandable, fathomable, identifiable, soluble, solvable, resolvable, clear. [➡CONCISE AND CLEAR; 203] *Opposite:* unintelligible.

decision 1 *n* **choice**, result, conclusion, verdict, pronouncement, judgment, resolution, assessment, evaluation, ruling, finding, outcome, decree. [➡MAKE DECISIONS AND CHOICES; 753] 2 *n* **determination**, resolve, firmness, willpower, strength of mind, strength of will, certitude, surety, resolution, decisiveness. [➡CERTAINTY; 562] *Opposite:* indecision.

decisive 1 *adj* **conclusive**, pivotal, key, critical, significant, crucial, vital, influential, important, convincing, final, definitive, authoritative. [➡IMPORTANT; 195] *Opposite:* insignificant. 2 *adj* **strong-minded**, resolute, determined, certain, clear-sighted, focused, positive, earnest, purposeful, definite, firm. [➡CERTAINTY; 562] *Opposite:* uncertain.

decisively 1 *adv* **conclusively**, authoritatively, once and for all, finally, definitively. [➡IMPORTANT; 195] 2 *adv* **resolutely**, determinedly, assertively, unfalteringly, unwaveringly, positively, definitely, firmly. [➡INTENTIONAL AND DELIBERATE; 280] *Opposite:* uncertainly.

decisiveness *n* **resoluteness**, determination, conclusiveness, authoritativeness, positiveness, purposefulness, firmness, certainty, definiteness. [➡CERTAINTY; 562] *Opposite:* indecisiveness.

deck 1 *n* **level**, floor, surface, area, sun deck, car deck, top deck. [➡PARTS OF A SHIP OR BOAT; 1150] 2 *v* (*literary*) **adorn**, decorate, bedeck (*literary*), hang, cover, wreathe, dress, clothe, garb. [➡DRESS, WEAR, AND UNDRESS; 868] *Opposite:* strip. 3 *v* (*informal*) **hit**, knock down, knock over, floor, thump, punch, strike. [➡PHYSICAL ATTACK AND PUNISHMENT; 416]

deck chair *type of* **seating**. [➡FURNITURE; 858]

deck hand *n* **sailor**, rating, seaman. [➡TRAVEL: TRAVELLERS AND WALKERS; 320]

declaim *v* **orate** (*formal*), hold forth, pronounce, proclaim, declare, utter, sermonize, pontificate, trumpet, state, assert, deliver. [➡INSTRUCT AND TEACH; 610] *Opposite:* mutter.

declamatory *adj* **dramatic**, formal, oratorical, rhetorical, theatrical, pompous, melodramatic, booming, arresting. [➡ELOQUENT, TALKATIVE AND LONG-WINDED; 633] *Opposite:* low-key.

declaration *n* **statement**, announcement, assertion, speech, pronouncement, avowal (*formal*), affirmation, testimony, deposition. [➡NEUTRAL ONE-WAY COMMUNICATION; 49]

declare *v* **announce**, state, speak out, assert, affirm, pronounce, proclaim. [➡INFORM AND ANNOUNCE; 612]

declassification *n* **release**, publication, open access, derestriction, delimitation (*formal*), decontrol. [➡INFORM AND ANNOUNCE; 612] *Opposite:* restriction.

declassify *v* **release**, publish, derestrict, open up, bring out, make public. [➡INFORM AND ANNOUNCE; 612] *Opposite:* classify.

decline 1 *v* **refuse**, turn down, reject, pass up, beg off, eschew, spurn, take a rain check (*US informal*). [➡FORGO AND DENY ONESELF; 450] *Opposite:* accept. 2 *v* **weaken**, fail, deteriorate, degenerate, fall off, decay, wane, drop, wilt, go to seed, flag, sink, worsen. [➡DISAPPEAR; 4] *Opposite:* improve. 3 *n* **deterioration**, falling-off, falloff, decay, drop, fall, degeneration, regression, decrease. [➡FAILURE; 77] *Opposite:* improvement.

declining *adj* **deteriorating**, decreasing, lessening, falling, diminishing, weakening, waning, abating (*formal or literary*), failing, fading, flagging, dwindling, disappearing, vanishing, worsening, sinking. [➡CEASE TO EXIST; 22] *Opposite:* improving.

decode *v* **decipher**, make out, make sense of, interpret, translate, decrypt, work out, crack, puzzle out. [➡SOLVE AND INTERPRET; 761] *Opposite:* encode.

decoder *n* **cryptographer**, decipherer, interpreter, translator. [➡PEOPLE WHO WORK WITH LANGUAGE AND CODE; 854]

décolletage *part of* **garment**. [➡PARTS OF A GARMENT; 870]

décolleté *adj* **low-necked**, low-cut, plunging, low, revealing. [➡DESCRIBING CLOTHES; 869]

decommission *v* **retire**, mothball, withdraw, take out, neutralize, discharge. [➡REVOKE STATUS; 460] *Opposite:* introduce.

decompose *v* **rot**, decay, crumble, go mouldy, fester, putrefy, moulder, go off, spoil. [➡GO BAD AND CORRODE; 391]

decomposed *adj* **rotten**, disintegrated, decayed, perished, putrid, putrefied, fetid, spoiled, mouldy, moldy (*US*). [➡DECAYING OR INFESTED; 1235] *Opposite:* fresh.

decomposing *adj* **rotting**, disintegrating, decaying, perishing, putrid, putrefying, fetid, crumbling, spoiling, festering, mouldering, mouldy, sour, stale, off, going bad, going off, rancid, rank (*literary*), infected, diseased, bad. [➡DECAYING OR INFESTED; 1235] *Opposite:* fresh.

decomposition *n* **decay**, rottenness, putrefaction, breakdown, disintegration, corrosion, fetidness, mouldiness, putridness, rot. [➡GO BAD AND CORRODE; 391] *Opposite:* soundness.

deconstruct *v* **critique**, criticize, decompose, review, take apart (*informal*), analyse. [➡EXAMINE AND ASSESS; 754]

decontaminate *v* **cleanse**, clean up, clean, purify, disinfect, fumigate, neutralize. [➡CLEAN AND POLISH; 404] *Opposite:* contaminate.

decontrol *v* **deregulate**, delimit (*formal*), free, set free, loosen. [➡FREEDOM AND LIBERTY; 209] *Opposite:* control.

decor *n* **decoration**, furnishings, colour scheme, interior decoration, scheme, design, style, ornamentation. [➡ORNAMENTS AND DECORATIONS; 1247]

decorate 1 *v* **beautify**, adorn, ornament, embellish, trim, garnish, deck (*literary*), bedeck (*literary*), wreathe, garland, enhance, array (*literary*), festoon. [➡DECORATE, ADORN, AND APPLY COATINGS; 406] *Opposite:* strip. 2 *v* **paint**, smarten up, do up, do over (*slang*), spruce, fix up. [➡IMPROVE APPEARANCE; 380] 3 *v* **honour**, award, garland, recognize, acknowledge. [➡CONFER STATUS; 459]

decorated *adj* **ornamented**, ornate, adorned, decked (*literary*), bedecked (*literary*), festooned, draped, wreathed, encircled, edged, inset, picked out, sequined, veneered, carved, beaded, etched, framed, tinted, painted, dyed, enamelled, swathed, garlanded, trimmed, encrusted, sewn, bead-trimmed, inscribed, bordered, bejewelled (*literary*), patterned, incised, stitched. [➡DECORATE, ADORN, AND APPLY COATINGS; 406] *Opposite:* plain.

Decorated *type of* **pre-20th-century architecture**. [➡BUILDING AND ARCHITECTURE; 1075]

decoration 1 *n* **feature**, festoon, beading, border, carving, garland, sequin, wreath. [➡ORNAMENTS AND DECORATIONS;

1247] **2** *n* **beautification**, adornment, ornament, ornamentation, embellishment, trimming. [➡IMPROVE APPEARANCE; 380] **3** *n* **honour**, medal, award, gong (*slang*), sash, ribbon, emblem. [➡REWARDS AND AWARDS; 440]

decorative *adj* **ornamental**, pretty, attractive, pleasing to the eye, enhancing, ornate, embellished. [➡BEAUTY AND ATTRACTIVENESS; 190] *Opposite:* ugly.

decorous *adj* **well-mannered**, well-behaved, good, correct, modest, demure, sedate, seemly, proper, appropriate, respectable, restrained, suitable. [➡GOOD MANNERS AND SOCIAL SKILLS; 521] *Opposite:* improper.

decorousness *n* [➡GOOD MANNERS AND SOCIAL SKILLS; 521]

decorum *n* **dignity**, propriety, sedateness, good behaviour, modesty, appropriateness, correctness, demureness, politesse, restraint, politeness, tact, gentility. [➡GOOD MANNERS AND SOCIAL SKILLS; 521] *Opposite:* abandon.

decoy **1** *n* **lure**, trap, snare, trick, distraction, bait, red herring, inducement, smoke screen. [➡REPRESENTATIONS AND GENERAL EXAMPLES; 65] **2** *v* **entice**, lure, lead astray, distract, entrap, ensnare, bait, allure. [➡DECEPTION AND LIES; 661]

decrease **1** *v* **reduce**, cut, diminish, cut down, contract, shrink. [➡CHANGE OF SIZE: SMALLER; 394] *Opposite:* increase. **2** *v* **diminish**, decline, dwindle, drop off (*informal*), subside, lessen, fall. [➡DISAPPEAR; 4] **3** *n* **reduction**, cut, diminution, lessening, decline, shrinkage, drop, fall, loss, cutback. [➡CHANGE OF SIZE: SMALLER; 394] *Opposite:* increase.

decreasing *adj* **diminishing**, declining, reducing, dwindling, shrinking, lessening, falling, subsiding. [➡CHANGE OF SIZE: SMALLER; 394] *Opposite:* increasing.

decree **1** *n* **ruling**, verdict, announcement, pronouncement, declaration, judgment, diktat, order, law, command, proclamation, statute. [➡REQUEST AND DEMAND; 664] *Opposite:* request. **2** *v* **command**, rule, pronounce, announce, dictate, declare, direct (*formal*), order, lay down the law, authorize, proclaim. [➡REQUEST AND DEMAND; 664] *Opposite:* persuade.

decrepit **1** *adj* **dilapidated**, crumbling, decaying, falling to pieces, falling apart, on its last legs, broken-down, battered, rickety. [➡IN BAD REPAIR; 1233] *Opposite:* pristine. **2** *adj* (*archaic or humorous*) **old**, feeble, frail, weak, infirm. [➡UNFIT AND WEAK; 740] *Opposite:* vigorous.

See Compare and Contrast at **weak**.

decrepitude **1** *n* **decay**, dilapidation, ruin, shabbiness. [➡IN BAD REPAIR; 1233] *Opposite:* soundness. **2** *n* **infirmity**, frailty, feebleness, weakness, debility, decline. [➡UNFIT AND WEAK; 740]

decrescendo (*US*) *type of* **musical term**. [➡MUSICAL TERMS; 912]

decriminalization *n* **legalization**, acceptance, allowance, toleration, sanction. [➡TRIAL, PUNISHMENT, AND LEGAL OUTCOMES; 819] *Opposite:* criminalization.

decriminalize *v* **make legal**, legalize, authorize, sanction, permit, accept, allow, tolerate. [➡PERMIT AND ALLOW; 670] *Opposite:* outlaw.

See Compare and Contrast at **legal**.

decry (*formal*) *v* **criticize**, complain, belittle, disparage, deprecate, run down, denounce, rail, condemn. [➡PROTEST AND EXPRESS DISAPPROVAL; 643] *Opposite:* praise.

dedicate **1** *v* **give**, commit, devote, consecrate, bestow (*formal*), pledge, donate, offer. [➡GIVE AND PROVIDE; 431] **2** *v* **reserve**, devote, set aside, earmark, give over to. [➡GIVE AND PROVIDE; 431]

dedicated *adj* **committed**, devoted, steadfast, loyal, faithful, enthusiastic, keen, staunch, stalwart, out-and-out. [➡HARD-WORKING AND COMMITTED; 501] *Opposite:* uncommitted.

dedicatedly *adv* **wholeheartedly**, loyally, steadfastly, devotedly, enthusiastically, unreservedly, faithfully, stalwartly, staunchly. [➡HARD-WORKING AND COMMITTED; 501] *Opposite:* half-heartedly.

dedication *n* **devotion**, commitment, enthusiasm, keenness, perseverance, allegiance, ardour, loyalty, staunchness, devotedness. [➡ENERGY AND ENTHUSIASM; 497]

deduce **1** *v* **conclude**, judge, deem (*formal*), suppose, reckon, gather. [➡HAVE AN OPINION OF SOMETHING; 757] **2** *v* **infer**, assume, presume, reason, construe, figure out, work out, realize, comprehend, understand. [➡DEVELOP THEORIES AND REASON; 745]

Compare and Contrast: *deduce, infer, assume, reason, conclude, work out, figure out*

CORE MEANING: TO REACH A LOGICAL CONCLUSION ON THE BASIS OF INFORMATION

deduce to reach a conclusion using available knowledge; ***infer*** to draw a conclusion from specific circumstances or evidence; ***assume*** to take a premise or information as true without checking or confirming; ***reason*** to consider information and use it to reach a conclusion in a logical way; ***conclude*** to form an opinion or make a judgment after much consideration; ***work out*** to find a solution or explanation by careful thought or reasoning; ***figure out*** to find a solution or reach a conclusion by careful thought or reasoning.

deduct *v* **subtract**, take away, take, remove, abstract, withhold, decrease by. [➡REMOVE SOMETHING; 339] *Opposite:* add.

deduction **1** *n* **inference**, assumption, conclusion, presumption, judgment, reasoning, supposition, interpretation, analysis. [➡IDEA AND THOUGHT; 771] **2** *n* **subtraction**, removal, withdrawal, abstraction, contribution, payment. [➡REMOVE SOMETHING; 339] *Opposite:* addition.

deductive *adj* **logical**, inferential, reasonable, empirical, rational. [➡THE NATURE OF IDEAS; 772] *Opposite:* illogical.

deed **1** *n* **action**, feat, act, endeavour, exploit, accomplishment, achievement, effort. [➡ACTIONS OR UNDERTAKINGS; 260] **2** *n* **document**, title deed, title, charter, record, certificate, lease, voucher. [➡OFFICIAL DOCUMENTS; 587]

deem (*formal*) *v* **think**, believe, consider, estimate, suppose, reason, judge, reckon, regard, hold, view. [➡HAVE AN OPINION OF SOMETHING; 757]

deep 1 *adj* **bottomless**, profound, unfathomable, subterranean, cavernous, yawning, abysmal. [➡DEPTH: DEEP; 1200] *Opposite:* shallow. 2 *adj* **deep-seated**, innate, inherent, entrenched, subconscious, deep-rooted, hidden. [➡THE NATURE OF IDEAS; 772] *Opposite:* superficial. 3 *adj* **low**, rumbling, booming, sonorous, resonant, rich. [➡SOFT OR PLEASANT SOUNDS; 1264] *Opposite:* shrill. 4 *adj* **intense**, profound, concentrated, immersed, absorbed. [➡STRENGTH; 202] *Opposite:* superficial. 5 *adj* **profound**, unfathomable, multifaceted, multilayered, mysterious, meaningful. [➡INTERESTING AND MEANINGFUL; 191] *Opposite:* facile. 6 *adj* **hidden**, secret, arcane, mysterious, silent, untold, inscrutable. [➡SECRET AND UNKNOWN; 180] *Opposite:* open.

deepen 1 *v* **dig out**, excavate, hollow out, scoop out, extend, expand. [➡CHANGE OF INTENSITY: MORE; 395] *Opposite:* fill in. 2 *v* **intensify**, extend, expand, concentrate, accumulate, increase, develop, grow, heighten, strengthen. [➡CHANGE OF INTENSITY: LESS; 396] *Opposite:* weaken.

deepfreeze *type of* **cooling appliance**. [➡HEATING, REFRIGERATION, AND VENTILATION; 1141]

deep in thought *adj* **contemplative**, thoughtful, pensive, lost in thought, mulling things over, miles away. [➡PENSIVENESS AND INTEREST; 539]

deeply *adv* **intensely**, extremely, profoundly, severely, acutely, genuinely, totally, sincerely, truly, greatly, entirely. [➡TO A GREAT EXTENT; 130] *Opposite:* mildly.

deepness 1 *n* **depth**, profundity, profoundness, bottomlessness, fathomlessness. [➡DEPTH: DEEP; 1200] 2 *n* **lowness**, resonance, sonority, low pitch. [➡SOFT OR PLEASANT SOUNDS; 1264]

deep-rooted *adj* **innate**, deep-seated, inherent, entrenched, established, subconscious. [➡STRENGTH; 202] *Opposite:* superficial.

deep-sea *adj* **marine**, oceanic, ocean. [➡THE SEAS, OCEANS, AND SHORES; 1041]

deep-seated *adj* **innate**, deep-rooted, inherent, entrenched, subconscious, ingrained. [➡THE NATURE OF IDEAS; 772] *Opposite:* superficial.

deer

◆ *types of deer or antelope*
antelope, caribou, chamois, chevrotain, dik-dik, elk, gazelle, gnu, impala, moose, okapi, reindeer, springbok, Thomson's gazelle

deer fly *type of* **flying insect**. [➡FLYING INSECTS; 1013]

deerstalker *type of* **hat**. [➡HABERDASHERY, MILLINERY, AND LINGERIE; 867]

deer tick *type of* **parasitic insect**. [➡PARASITES; 1017]

de-escalate *v* **scale down**, reduce, decrease, slow, damp down, check, diminish, curb, step down, scale back (*US*). [➡CHANGE OF INTENSITY: LESS; 396] *Opposite:* escalate.

de-escalation *n* **reduction**, stepping down, scaling down, cutback, decrease, phasedown. [➡CHANGE OF INTENSITY: LESS; 396] *Opposite:* escalation.

deface *v* **spoil**, ruin, mar, disfigure, mutilate, vandalize, impair, damage, injure. [➡WORSEN APPEARANCE; 383] *Opposite:* renovate.

defacement *n* **disfigurement**, mutilation, vandalism, destruction, damage, injury. [➡BAD BEHAVIOUR OR ACTION; 255] *Opposite:* restoration.

de facto 1 *adv* **in effect**, to all intents and purposes, in reality, actually, effectively, in fact. [➡FOREIGN WORDS AND PHRASES; 673] 2 *adj* **actual**, genuine, effective, existing, real. [➡TRUE AND REAL; 172]

defamation *n* **insult**, offence, slander, libel, slur, smear, denigration, vilification, calumny (*formal*), character assassination. [➡INSULTS, ABUSE, AND SWEARING; 659] *Opposite:* praise.

defamatory *adj* **insulting**, offensive, slanderous, libellous, derogatory, disparaging, deprecating. [➡ACCUSATORY AND DISAPPROVING; 635] *Opposite:* complimentary.

defame *v* **insult**, slander, libel, denigrate, deprecate, disparage, offend, vilify. [➡INSULTS, ABUSE, AND SWEARING; 659] *Opposite:* praise.

See Compare and Contrast at **malign**.

default 1 *n* **evasion**, avoidance, nonpayment, defaulting, nonattendance, nonappearance. [➡OWE AND DESERVE; 466] 2 *v* **fail to pay**, evade, dodge, shirk, duck, duck out, let lapse. [➡OWE AND DESERVE; 466] *Opposite:* pay.

defaulter *n* **nonpayer**, debtor, cheat, dodger (*informal*), shirker, absentee. [➡PEOPLE INVOLVED IN FINANCE; 804]

defeat 1 *n* **overthrow**, conquest, downfall, rout. [➡BEAT AND DEFEAT; 80] *Opposite:* victory. 2 *n* **loss**, reverse, setback, thrashing, beating, rout, whitewash (*informal*), trouncing, hiding (*informal*). [➡BEAT AND DEFEAT; 80] *Opposite:* victory. 3 *v* **beat**, overcome, overpower, overwhelm, conquer, crush, rout, trounce, whitewash, thrash, vanquish, triumph over, cream (*US informal*). [➡BEAT AND DEFEAT; 80] *Opposite:* lose. 4 *v* **baffle**, confound, foil, frustrate, thwart, bamboozle (*informal*), stump. [➡CONFUSE AND BEWILDER; 572]

Compare and Contrast: ***defeat, beat, conquer, vanquish, overcome, triumph over, thrash, trounce***

CORE MEANING: TO WIN A VICTORY

defeat to win a victory over an enemy or competitor, or to cause failure; ***beat*** to defeat somebody in a contest, or to overcome a difficulty; ***conquer*** to defeat decisively in battle, or to overcome a difficulty; ***vanquish*** to defeat decisively in battle or competition; ***overcome*** to win or succeed after a struggle; ***triumph over*** to succeed against an adversary or against difficult odds; ***thrash*** to gain an easy decisive victory in a sporting contest; ***trounce*** to defeat an opponent convincingly.

defeated *adj* **beaten**, overcome, overpowered, overwhelmed, conquered, crushed, routed, whitewashed, trounced, vanquished, subjugated. [➡BEATEN AND DEFEATED; 78] *Opposite:* victorious.

defeatism *n* **pessimism**, resignation, despondency,

despair, negativity, spinelessness, fatalism. [➡FEELINGS ABOUT THE FUTURE; 534] *Opposite:* resilience.

defeatist 1 *adj* **pessimistic**, negative, fatalistic, resigned, despondent, despairing, spineless. [➡NEGATIVE OF OUTLOOK; 515] *Opposite:* optimistic. 2 *n* **pessimist**, quitter (*informal*), loser, fatalist, doomsayer, doom-monger, Cassandra. [➡LAZY OR UNSUCCESSFUL PEOPLE; 948] *Opposite:* optimist.

defecate (*formal or technical*) *v* **excrete**, eliminate waste, empty the bowels, have a bowel movement, evacuate, expel. [➡EXCRETION AND EXCRETA; 723]

defecation *n* **excretion**, evacuation, elimination. [➡EXCRETION AND EXCRETA; 723]

defect 1 *n* **flaw**, fault, imperfection, blemish, shortcoming, failing, deficiency, weakness. [➡FAULTS, FLAWS, AND WEAKNESSES; 252] 2 *v* **desert**, change sides, abscond, go over, turn traitor, decamp. [➡RUN AWAY AND AVOID; 10]

See Compare and Contrast at **flaw.**

defective *adj* **faulty**, imperfect, flawed, substandard, malfunctioning, out of order, not working, on the blink (*informal*), unreliable. [➡IN BAD REPAIR; 1233] *Opposite:* perfect.

defectiveness *n* **faultiness**, failure, inadequacy, unreliability, imperfection, malfunction. [➡REDUNDANT AND USELESS; 241]

defector *n* **traitor**, turncoat, renegade, convert, rebel, apostate. [➡UNCOOPERATIVE OR REBELLIOUS PERSON; 567] *Opposite:* loyalist.

defence 1 *n* **protection**, resistance, guard, security, cover, shield. [➡SAFE AND SAFETY; 192] *Opposite:* attack. 2 *n* **justification**, argument, vindication, plea, apology, excuse, alibi (*informal*). [➡TRIAL, PUNISHMENT, AND LEGAL OUTCOMES; 819] *Opposite:* accusation.

defence force *n* **army**, armed forces, armed services, task force, fighters, national guard. [➡THE ARMED FORCES; 827]

defenceless *adj* **unprotected**, unarmed, exposed, unguarded, vulnerable, helpless, wide open, weak, frail, powerless. [➡IN DANGER; 238] *Opposite:* protected.

defencelessness *n* **vulnerability**, helplessness, powerlessness, weakness, frailty. [➡DANGER; 236] *Opposite:* strength.

defences 1 *n* **resistance**, immunity, protection, shield, safeguard, resilience. [➡STRENGTH; 202] 2 *n* **fortifications**, ramparts, battlements, earthworks, emplacements, lines, barricades. [➡FORTRESSES AND FORTIFICATIONS; 1089]

defend 1 *v* **protect**, guard, shield, look after, preserve, secure. [➡PREVENT CONTACT OR ATTACK; 420] *Opposite:* attack. 2 *v* **support**, stand up for, stick up for, stand for, represent, uphold, endorse, back, champion. [➡APPROVE AND CONFIRM; 647] *Opposite:* oppose.

See Compare and Contrast at **safeguard.**

defendant *n* **perpetrator**, offender, respondent, suspect, culprit. [➡PEOPLE IN LAW COURTS; 820] *Opposite:* accuser.

defender 1 *n* **protector**, guard, warden, guardian, escort, bodyguard. [➡PEOPLE WHO GUARD AND PROTECT; 846] *Opposite:* attacker. 2 *n* **supporter**, champion, advocate, sponsor, upholder, backer. [➡DEVOTEES AND ADDICTED PEOPLE; 557] *Opposite:* opponent.

defensible 1 *adj* **defendable**, impregnable, unassailable, invulnerable, secure, strong. [➡STRENGTH; 202] *Opposite:* vulnerable. 2 *adj* **justifiable**, valid, cast-iron, secure, rock-solid, sound. [➡ACCEPTABLE AND PASSABLE; 220] *Opposite:* indefensible.

defensibly *adv* **excusably**, justifiably, explicably, forgivably, understandably, pardonably. [➡ACCEPTABLE AND PASSABLE; 220] *Opposite:* unjustifiably.

defensive 1 *adj* **self-justifying**, self-protective, apologetic, distrustful, wary, cautious. [➡INSECURITY AND LOSS OF COMPOSURE; 545] *Opposite:* aggressive. 2 *adj* **protective**, protecting, defending, shielding, fortified, armoured. [➡STRENGTH; 202]

defensively *adv* **sensitively**, oversensitively, protectively, warily, cautiously, apologetically. [➡INSECURITY AND LOSS OF COMPOSURE; 545] *Opposite:* aggressively.

defer 1 *v* **put off**, reschedule, put back, adjourn, suspend. [➡DELAY ACTION OR OCCURRENCE; 279] *Opposite:* bring forward. 2 *v* **bow to**, submit, be deferential, accede, comply, accept, concede, give way. [➡AGREE; 646]

deference *n* **respect**, esteem, regard, reverence, admiration, awe, obsequiousness, submissiveness. [➡LOVE, RESPECT, AND GOODWILL; 550] *Opposite:* disrespect.

deferential *adj* **respectful**, admiring, reverent, polite, obsequious, courteous, submissive. [➡EXPRESSING RESPECT AND APPROVAL; 638] *Opposite:* disrespectful.

deferment *n* **adjournment**, suspension, postponement, delay, stay, deferral, rain check (*US informal*). [➡DELAY ACTION OR OCCURRENCE; 279]

deferral *n* **postponement**, adjournment, delay, stay, deferment, rain check (*US informal*). [➡PAUSES AND PHASES; 56]

defiance *n* **insubordination**, disobedience, insolence, rebelliousness, boldness, cheek (*informal*), cheekiness (*informal*), noncooperation. [➡REBELLIOUSNESS AND DISOBEDIENCE; 566] *Opposite:* compliance.

defiant *adj* **disobedient**, insolent, insubordinate, rebellious, bold, cheeky. [➡REBELLIOUSNESS AND DISOBEDIENCE; 566] *Opposite:* compliant.

deficiency 1 *n* **lack**, shortage, absence, deficit, dearth, insufficiency, paucity, scarcity. [➡TOO FEW, TOO LITTLE; 120] *Opposite:* excess. 2 *n* **inadequacy**, defect, flaw, fault, imperfection, shortcoming, failing, weakness. [➡FAULTS, FLAWS, AND WEAKNESSES; 252]

See Compare and Contrast at **lack.**

deficient 1 *adj* **lacking**, poor, underprovided, undersupplied, short, incomplete, wanting, scarce. [➡LACK OF POSSESSION; 446] *Opposite:* abundant. 2 *adj* **inadequate**, flawed, faulty, unsatisfactory, defective, poor, shoddy, imperfect, not up to scratch (*informal*). [➡INAPPROPRIATE AND UNSUITABLE; 225] *Opposite:* perfect.

deficiently *adv* **inadequately**, defectively, faultily, incorrectly, wrongly, imperfectly, weakly, poorly, shoddily. [➡ INAPPROPRIATE AND UNSUITABLE; 225] *Opposite:* perfectly.

deficit *n* **shortfall**, shortage, arrears, discrepancy, debit, scarcity, insufficiency, dearth. [➡ TOO FEW, TOO LITTLE; 120] *Opposite:* surplus.

See Compare and Contrast at **lack.**

defile 1 *v* (*formal*) **corrupt**, taint, besmirch, sully, spoil, tarnish, pollute, ruin, degrade, contaminate. [➡ WORSEN SOMETHING; 381] *Opposite:* enhance. 2 *v* (*formal*) **dishonour**, desecrate, sully, violate, debase. [➡ RELIGIONS AND RELIGIOUS PRACTICES; 778] *Opposite:* respect. 3 *n* **pass**, valley, gorge, gap. [➡ GEOLOGICAL FEATURES; 1056]

defiled (*formal*) 1 *adj* **corrupted**, tainted, besmirched, sullied, tarnished, spoiled, polluted, ruined, degraded, contaminated. [➡ DIRTY; 1234] *Opposite:* untarnished. 2 *adj* **dishonoured**, desecrated, sullied, spoiled, violated, debased. [➡ MORALLY BAD; 776] *Opposite:* pure.

define 1 *v* **describe**, outline, express, state, explain, term. [➡ NAME AND DESCRIBE; 666] 2 *v* **characterize**, classify, identify, distinguish, specify, label. [➡ NAME AND DESCRIBE; 666] 3 *v* **delineate** (*formal*), mark out, outline, delimit (*formal*), demarcate, circumscribe (*formal*), mark. [➡ NAME AND DESCRIBE; 666]

defined *adj* **clear**, distinct, definite, well-defined, sharp, demarcated. [➡ CONCISE AND CLEAR; 203] *Opposite:* indistinct.

defining moment *n* **turning point**, landmark, watershed, crossroads, moment of truth, crisis, crunch. [➡ DECISIVE MOMENTS; 44]

definite 1 *adj* **exact**, specific, explicit, clear-cut, unambiguous, distinct, crystal clear. [➡ EXACT; 204] *Opposite:* vague. 2 *adj* **obvious**, recognized, significant, unquestionable, unmistakable, important, well-defined, noteworthy. [➡ IMPORTANT; 195] *Opposite:* dubious. 3 *adj* **fixed**, settled, positive, assured, known, stated. [➡ CERTAIN; 175] *Opposite:* indefinite. 4 *adj* **sure**, certain, positive, fixed, final, confident. [➡ CERTAINTY; 562] *Opposite:* uncertain.

definite article *type of* **word class.** [➡ ASPECTS OF LANGUAGE; 683]

definitely *adv* **certainly**, absolutely, positively, unquestionably, without doubt, beyond doubt, undeniably, categorically. [➡ CERTAIN; 175] *Opposite:* perhaps.

definiteness *n* **certainty**, assurance, assuredness, conviction, finality, confidence, determination. [➡ CERTAIN; 175] *Opposite:* uncertainty.

definition 1 *n* **meaning**, description, explanation, classification, characterization, designation, delineation (*formal*), demarcation. [➡ NAME AND DESCRIBE; 666] 2 *n* **clarity**, sharpness, distinctness, focus, clearness, exactness. [➡ EXACT; 204] *Opposite:* haziness.

definitive 1 *adj* **conclusive**, final, decisive, ultimate, absolute, complete. [➡ ABSOLUTE AND ABSOLUTELY; 131] *Opposite:* tentative. 2 *adj* **authoritative**, conclusive, perfect, best, classic, state-of-the-art, standard. [➡ EXTRAORDINARY: AMAZING; 205]

definitively *adv* **finally**, ultimately, once and for all, conclusively, absolutely. [➡ ABSOLUTE AND ABSOLUTELY; 131] *Opposite:* temporarily.

deflate 1 *v* **let the air out**, go down, let down, collapse, shrink, puncture. [➡ EMPTY AND UNLOAD; 408] *Opposite:* inflate. 2 *v* **belittle**, put down (*informal*), squash, quash, snub, humiliate, destroy, take the wind out of somebody's sails. [➡ UPSET, DISTRESS, AND HUMILIATE; 568] *Opposite:* boost. 3 *v* **devalue**, depress, decrease, reduce, lower. [➡ CHANGE OF SIZE: SMALLER; 394]

deflated 1 *adj* **subdued**, put down (*informal*), humiliated, flattened, humbled, dispirited, disappointed. [➡ SADNESS, DISTRESS, AND DESPAIR; 540] *Opposite:* exhilarated. 2 *adj* **emptied**, flattened, shrunk, collapsed, let down, punctured, squashed. [➡ IN BAD REPAIR; 1233] *Opposite:* inflated.

deflation *n* **depression**, devaluation, depreciation, reduction, decrease, lowering. [➡ MARKET FORCES; 803] *Opposite:* inflation.

deflect 1 *v* **bounce**, glance, ricochet, rebound, bend, swerve, refract. [➡ CHANGE DIRECTION OF MOTION; 345] 2 *v* **turn aside**, ward off, repel, redirect, sidetrack, avert, prevent, draw away. [➡ PREVENT CONTACT OR ATTACK; 420] *Opposite:* attract.

deflection *n* **refraction**, ricochet, rebound, glance, bend, swerve. [➡ CHANGE DIRECTION OF MOTION; 345]

deforest *v* **log**, denude, strip, desolate, devastate, lay waste. [➡ DESTRUCTION AND DEMOLITION; 360]

deform *v* **distort**, bend, warp, buckle, bow, twist. [➡ CHANGE OF SHAPE; 386]

deformation *n* **distortion**, twist, buckle, bend, warp. [➡ CHANGE OF SHAPE; 386]

deformed 1 *adj* **misshapen**, distorted, bent, warped, malformed, mutilated, buckled, bowed, twisted, shrunken, contorted, crooked. [➡ ORIENTATION AND ALIGNMENT; 1222] 2 *adj* **abnormal**, corrupted, perverted, spoilt, ruined, damaged. [➡ IN BAD REPAIR; 1233]

deformity *n* **disfigurement**, malformation, distortion, abnormality, misshapenness, irregularity. [➡ ORIENTATION AND ALIGNMENT; 1222]

defraud *v* **deceive**, swindle, cheat, fleece (*informal*), trick, take advantage of, con, dupe, rip off (*informal*). [➡ STEAL AND ROB; 427]

defray (*formal*) *v* **pay**, cover, meet, contribute, finance, bear the cost of. [➡ GIVE MONEY; 434]

defrock *v* **unfrock**, excommunicate, disqualify, drum out, expel, demote, dismiss. [➡ REVOKE STATUS; 460]

defrost *v* **melt**, thaw, thaw out, de-ice, unfreeze. [➡ SOFTEN, LIQUEFY, DAMPEN; 389] *Opposite:* freeze.

deft *adj* **skilful**, adroit, nifty (*informal*), neat, nimble, dexterous, precise, adept. [➡ TALENTED AND SKILFUL; 528] *Opposite:* clumsy.

deftness *n* **skill**, dexterity, precision, swiftness, neatness, niftiness (*informal*), adroitness. [➡ SKILLS, TALENTS, AND ABILITIES; 527] *Opposite:* clumsiness.

defunct 1 *adj* **obsolete**, invalid, redundant, outdated, out-of-date. [➡PAST; 84] *Opposite:* current. **2** *adj* **dead**, deceased (*formal*), departed (*formal or literary*), expired, extinct, gone (*informal*). [➡DEAD AND DYING; 925] *Opposite:* alive.

See Compare and Contrast at **dead**.

defuse *v* **resolve**, calm, soothe, smooth out, neutralize, rescue, save, recover, mollify, cool, placate. [➡IMPROVE SOMETHING; 375] *Opposite:* aggravate.

defy *v* **challenge**, confront, disobey, rebel, resist, dare, flout, disregard, treat with contempt. [➡DISOBEY; 303] *Opposite:* obey.

degeneracy *n* **depravity**, wickedness, corruption, dissoluteness, decadence, wantonness, immorality. [➡MORALLY BAD; 776] *Opposite:* morality.

degenerate **1** *v* **deteriorate**, collapse, relapse, worsen, reduce, sink, slip, fall. [➡GET WORSE; 382] *Opposite:* improve. **2** *adj* **debased**, decadent, immoral, debauched, corrupt, perverted, wicked. [➡MORALLY BAD; 776] *Opposite:* moral.

degeneration *n* **deterioration**, collapse, disintegration, falling apart, worsening, relapse. [➡WORSEN SOMETHING; 381] *Opposite:* regeneration.

degenerative *adj* **wasting**, worsening, deteriorating, progressive. [➡WORSEN SOMETHING; 381]

degradation **1** *n* **humiliation**, disgrace, shame, mortification, misery, obloquy (*formal or literary*), infamy. [➡EMBARRASSMENT AND HUMILIATION; 543] **2** *n* **squalor**, filth, dilapidation, deprivation, poverty, ruin. [➡IN BAD REPAIR; 1233]

degrade **1** *v* **humiliate**, shame, disgrace, mortify, demean, debase, corrupt, vitiate. *Opposite:* exalt. (*formal*). [➡UPSET, DISTRESS, AND HUMILIATE; 568] **2** *v* **damage**, destroy, reduce, cut down, worsen, lower, vitiate. [➡DESTRUCTION AND DEMOLITION; 360] *Opposite:* upgrade. **3** *v* **decay**, decompose, disintegrate, break down, rot, perish. [➡GO BAD AND CORRODE; 391]

degrading *adj* **humiliating**, debasing, demeaning, undignified, corrupting, mortifying, shameful, unbecoming. [➡EMOTIONALLY UNPLEASANT AND UPSETTING; 228] *Opposite:* dignified.

degree **1** *n* **extent**, quantity, intensity, level, amount. [➡DEGREE AND EXTENT; 110] **2** *n* **grade**, gradation, mark, notch, step, unit, point. [➡DEGREE AND EXTENT; 110]

dehumanize *v* **desensitize**, brutalize, degrade, debase. [➡WOUND A PERSON OR ANIMAL; 384] *Opposite:* humanize.

dehydrate *v* **dry out**, dry up, become dry, desiccate, parch. [➡HARDEN, CONGEAL, DRY; 388]

dehydrated *adj* **dry**, dried out, arid, parched, desiccated, shrivelled, dried up, thirsty. [➡DRY; 1241]

See Compare and Contrast at **dry**.

dehydration *n* **dryness**, drying out, drying up, desiccation, thirst. [➡ILL AND SICK; 741]

de-ice *v* **unfreeze**, melt, thaw. [➡SOFTEN, LIQUEFY, DAMPEN; 389] *Opposite:* ice up.

deification (*formal*) *n* **exaltation** (*formal*), elevation, veneration, adoration, beatification. [➡PRAISE AND ENCOURAGE; 648]

deify *v* **idolize**, worship, exalt (*formal*), glorify, adore, venerate, beatify. [➡LIKE, LOVE, VALUE AND ENJOY; 579]

deign *v* **condescend**, lower yourself, stoop, consent, agree, force yourself, demean yourself. [➡AGREE; 646]

deity *n* **divinity**, god, goddess, divine being, immortal. [➡RELIGIOUS CONCEPTS; 777]

dejected *adj* **sad**, disappointed, unhappy, miserable, depressed, disconsolate, gloomy, crestfallen, down in the mouth (*informal*), dismal, doleful, glum. [➡SADNESS, DISTRESS, AND DESPAIR; 540] *Opposite:* cheerful.

dejection *n* **sadness**, unhappiness, misery, gloom, depression, glumness, gloominess. [➡SADNESS, DISTRESS, AND DESPAIR; 540] *Opposite:* cheerfulness.

dekko (*informal*) *n* **look**, shufti (*informal*), glance, peek, gander (*informal*). [➡LOOKING AND LOOKS; 701]

delay **1** *v* **postpone**, put off, suspend, adjourn, defer, reschedule, shelve, put back, table (*US*). [➡DELAY ACTION OR OCCURRENCE; 279] *Opposite:* bring forward. **2** *v* **procrastinate**, hesitate, linger, dawdle, pause, prolong, lag, wait, loiter. [➡MOVE SLOWLY; 315] *Opposite:* hurry up. **3** *v* **slow down**, slow up, hold up, set back, obstruct, impede, hinder. [➡DELAY ACTION OR OCCURRENCE; 279] *Opposite:* speed up. **4** *n* **postponement**, interruption, stay, suspension, adjournment, deferral, deferment. [➡DELAY ACTION OR OCCURRENCE; 279] **5** *n* **interval**, wait, pause, break, lull, lag, holdup, stoppage, setback. [➡PROBLEM; 257]

delayed *adj* **late**, behind, behind schedule, overdue, tardy, deferred, put off, put back, held up, hindered, caught up, stuck, postponed, pushed back (*US*). [➡PROMPTNESS: LATE; 100] *Opposite:* early.

delectable **1** *adj* **delicious**, tasty, mouthwatering, scrumptious (*informal*), appetizing, luscious, enjoyable, palatable. [➡TASTE; 704] *Opposite:* tasteless. **2** *adj* **delightful**, charming, adorable, appealing, heavenly, lovely, attractive. [➡BEAUTY AND ATTRACTIVENESS; 190] *Opposite:* unappealing.

delectably **1** *adv* **deliciously**, appetizingly, mouthwateringly, scrumptiously (*informal*), tastily. [➡TASTE; 704] **2** *adv* **delightfully**, attractively, beautifully, adorably, charmingly, gorgeously. [➡BEAUTY AND ATTRACTIVENESS; 190]

delectation (*formal*) *n* **enjoyment**, delight, pleasure, appreciation, entertainment, amusement. [➡PLEASURE, EXCITEMENT, AND ELATION; 535]

delegate **1** *n* **representative**, agent, envoy, ambassador, deputy, emissary. [➡REPRESENTATIVES AND PATRONS; 968] **2** *v* **hand over**, farm out, pass on, give, assign, allocate, allot, entrust. [➡DISPENSE, RATION, AND DISTRIBUTE; 435] *Opposite:* retain. **3** *v* **designate**, assign, appoint, allocate, depute (*formal*), deputize, order. [➡DISPENSE, RATION, AND DISTRIBUTE; 435]

delegation **1** *n* **commission**, deputation, mission, lobby. [➡GROUPS WITH A COMMON INTEREST; 938] **2** *n* **allocation**, handing over, assignment, giving out, passing on, entrustment. [➡DISPENSE, RATION, AND DISTRIBUTE; 435] *Opposite:* retention.

delete *v* **erase**, remove, rub out, strike out, cross out, obliterate, cancel, score, scrub (*informal*), scrap, scratch, expunge. [➡DELETE AND ERASE; 340] *Opposite:* insert.

deleterious (*formal*) *adj* **damaging**, harmful, injurious, destructive, adverse, detrimental, negative. [➡DANGEROUS; 237] *Opposite:* beneficial.

deletion *n* **removal**, obliteration, erasure, loss, omission, crossing out, scoring, cutting. [➡REMOVE SOMETHING; 339] *Opposite:* addition.

delft *type of* **pottery**. [➡POTTERY; 1134]

deli *type of* **food outlet**. [➡RETAIL OUTLETS; 1082]

deliberate 1 *adj* **intentional**, purposeful, premeditated, conscious, calculated, planned. [➡INTENTIONAL AND DELIBERATE; 280] *Opposite:* accidental. 2 *adj* **careful**, thoughtful, slow, cautious, unhurried, measured, considered, methodical, wary, meditative. [➡CAUTIOUS AND CAREFUL; 283] *Opposite:* hasty. 3 *v* **think**, reflect, consider, mull over, weigh up, ponder, think about. [➡THINK AND REFLECT; 744]

deliberately 1 *adv* **intentionally**, on purpose, purposely, with intent, consciously, calculatingly, by design, knowingly, purposefully. [➡INTENTIONAL AND DELIBERATE; 280] *Opposite:* accidentally. 2 *adv* **thoughtfully**, carefully, slowly, cautiously, methodically, unhurriedly, warily. [➡CAUTIOUS AND CAREFUL; 283] *Opposite:* hastily.

deliberation 1 *n* **discussion**, debate, negotiation, planning, pondering, thought, consideration. [➡NEGOTIATION AND DEBATE; 46] 2 *n* (*formal*) **reflection**, thought, consideration, care, forethought, premeditation, calculation. [➡THINK AND REFLECT; 744] *Opposite:* impulsiveness.

deliberations (*formal*) *n* [➡MEETINGS AND ASSEMBLIES; 43]

deliberative (*formal*) *adj* **considered**, premeditated, planned, calculated, thought through, purposeful, intentional. [➡THE NATURE OF IDEAS; 772] *Opposite:* casual.

delicacy 1 *n* **titbit**, treat, luxury, dainty, fancy. [➡MEALS AND PARTS OF MEALS; 1168] 2 *n* **sensitivity**, tact, diplomacy, consideration, care, thoughtfulness, feeling, sympathy. [➡GOOD MANNERS AND SOCIAL SKILLS; 521] *Opposite:* insensitivity. 3 *n* **refinement**, fastidiousness, subtlety, elegance, fineness, polish. [➡GOOD MANNERS AND SOCIAL SKILLS; 521] *Opposite:* vulgarity. 4 *n* **gracefulness**, attractiveness, elegance, charm, grace, fluidity, smoothness. [➡BEAUTY AND ATTRACTIVENESS; 190] *Opposite:* awkwardness. 5 *n* **fragility**, flimsiness, slenderness, frailty, weakness, daintiness. [➡WEAKNESS; 242] *Opposite:* sturdiness. 6 *n* **precision**, skill, care, deftness, adroitness, dexterity, fineness, accuracy, sensitivity. [➡EXACT; 204] *Opposite:* inaccuracy.

delicate 1 *adj* **fragile**, frail, weak, slight, flimsy, insubstantial. [➡WEAKNESS; 242] *Opposite:* robust. 2 *adj* **subtle**, faint, slight, gentle, mild, pale, soft, elusive, tantalizing. [➡IMPERCEPTIBLE; 26] *Opposite:* overpowering. 3 *adj* **fine**, precise, detailed, accurate, skilled. [➡EXACT; 204] *Opposite:* rough. 4 *adj* **refined**, graceful, elegant, dainty, nice, attractive. [➡BEAUTY AND ATTRACTIVENESS; 190] *Opposite:* inelegant. 5 *adj* **difficult**, tricky, complicated, sensitive, awkward, sticky, uncomfortable. [➡DIFFICULTY AND COMPLEXITY; 243] *Opposite:* straightforward. 6 *adj* **sensitive**, refined, thoughtful, considerate, sympathetic, tactful, diplomatic. [➡GOOD MANNERS AND SOCIAL SKILLS; 521] *Opposite:* tactless.

See Compare and Contrast at **fragile**.

delicately 1 *adv* **finely**, carefully, precisely, skilfully, dexterously, deftly, adroitly. [➡EXACT; 204] *Opposite:* clumsily. 2 *adv* **faintly**, subtly, slightly, elusively, softly, mildly. [➡IMPERCEPTIBLE; 26] *Opposite:* intensely. 3 *adv* **gracefully**, elegantly, daintily, nicely, attractively, with refinement, pleasantly. [➡BEAUTY AND ATTRACTIVENESS; 190] *Opposite:* inelegantly. 4 *adv* **tactfully**, diplomatically, sensitively, carefully, thoughtfully, sympathetically. [➡GOOD MANNERS AND SOCIAL SKILLS; 521] *Opposite:* tactlessly.

delicateness *n* **fragility**, fragileness, frailty, vulnerability, feebleness, weakness, thinness, delicacy, frailness. [➡WEAKNESS; 242] *Opposite:* robustness.

delicatessen *type of* **food outlet**. [➡RETAIL OUTLETS; 1082]

delicious 1 *adj* **tasty**, appetizing, scrumptious (*informal*), yummy, luscious, delectable, mouthwatering. [➡TASTE; 704] *Opposite:* tasteless. 2 *adj* **delightful**, lovely, wonderful, pleasant, enjoyable, appealing, enchanting, charming, delectable. [➡EMOTIONALLY PLEASANT; 188] *Opposite:* unpleasant.

deliciousness 1 *n* **delectableness**, palatability, lusciousness, sweetness, tastiness, scrumptiousness (*informal*). [➡TASTE; 704] *Opposite:* tastelessness. 2 *n* **delightfulness**, charm, sweetness, attractiveness, pleasantness, appeal. [➡EMOTIONALLY PLEASANT; 188] *Opposite:* unpleasantness.

delight 1 *n* **joy**, enjoyment, pleasure, happiness, glee, gladness, enchantment, amusement, satisfaction. [➡PLEASURE, EXCITEMENT, AND ELATION; 535] *Opposite:* displeasure. 2 *v* **please**, charm, amuse, thrill, gratify, make happy, enchant. [➡PLEASE AND AMUSE; 573] *Opposite:* disappoint. 3 *v* **take pleasure in**, appreciate, revel in, relish, enjoy, savour, bask in. [➡LIKE, LOVE, VALUE AND ENJOY; 579] *Opposite:* dislike.

delighted *adj* **pleased**, happy, charmed, enchanted, thrilled, elated, overjoyed, over the moon. [➡PLEASURE, EXCITEMENT, AND ELATION; 535] *Opposite:* unhappy.

delightful *adj* **pleasant**, charming, lovely, wonderful, enjoyable, amusing, agreeable, enchanting, pleasing. [➡EMOTIONALLY PLEASANT; 188] *Opposite:* unpleasant.

delightfulness *n* [➡EMOTIONALLY PLEASANT; 188]

delimit (*formal*) *v* **set the limits**, demarcate, define, restrict, delineate (*formal*), mark out, bound. [➡SEPARATE AND DIVIDE; 402]

delimitation (*formal*) *n* **demarcation**, definition, marking out, limitation, restriction, allocation, delineation (*formal*). [➡AVOID, PREVENT, LIMIT, AND CONTROL; 278]

delineate 1 *v* (*formal*) **define**, describe, explain, portray, present, set out. [➡NAME AND DESCRIBE; 666] 2 *v* **outline**, delimit (*formal*), mark out, demarcate, define, allocate, set. [➡NAME AND DESCRIBE; 666]

delineation 1 *n* (*formal*) **description**, definition, explanation, setting down. [➡EXPLAIN AND CLARIFY; 611] 2 *n* **demarcation**, delimitation (*formal*), definition, allocation, marking out, outlining. [➡NAME AND DESCRIBE; 666]

delinquency 1 *n* **criminal behaviour**, crime, felony, lawbreaking, misbehaviour, wrongdoing. [➡BAD BEHAVIOUR OR ACTION; 255] *Opposite:* uprightness. 2 *n* (*formal*) **negligence**, carelessness, recklessness, failure, irresponsibility, dereliction. [➡MORALLY BAD; 776] *Opposite:* carefulness.

delinquent 1 *n* **crook** (*informal*), criminal, guilty party, felon, lawbreaker, wrongdoer. [➡CRIMINALS; 821] 2 *adj* **criminal**, aberrant, antisocial, offending, felonious, wrong, bad. [➡MORALLY BAD; 776] *Opposite:* law-abiding. 3 *adj* (*formal*) **negligent**, careless, reckless, irresponsible, neglectful, failing. [➡LACK OF COMMITMENT AND UNRELIABILITY; 510] *Opposite:* dutiful.

See Compare and Contrast at **bad**.

deliquesce *v* [➡SOFTEN, LIQUEFY, DAMPEN; 389]

delirious 1 *adj* **feverish**, fevered, hot, hallucinating, rambling, restless, confused. [➡ILL AND SICK; 741] *Opposite:* rational. 2 *adj* **elated**, ecstatic, transported, on cloud nine (*informal*), in seventh heaven, over the moon, beside yourself, excited, emotional, high. [➡PLEASURE, EXCITEMENT, AND ELATION; 535] *Opposite:* dejected.

delirium 1 *n* **fever**, hallucination, restlessness, confusion, frenzy, disorientation. [➡ILL AND SICK; 741] *Opposite:* clarity. 2 *n* **ecstasy**, elation, fervour, euphoria, excitement, happiness. [➡PLEASURE, EXCITEMENT, AND ELATION; 535] *Opposite:* dejection.

delish (*slang*) *adj* [➡TASTE; 704]

deliver 1 *v* **carry**, bring, transport, distribute, send, convey, supply, provide. [➡MOVE SOMETHING TO ANOTHER LOCATION; 325] *Opposite:* take away. 2 *v* **produce**, provide, supply, dispense, serve, give, present, furnish (*formal*). [➡EQUIP AND SUPPLY; 436] 3 *v* (*literary*) **set free**, release, rescue, save, liberate, free. [➡FREEDOM AND LIBERTY; 209] *Opposite:* capture. 4 *v* **hand over**, give up, surrender, transfer, relinquish, cede (*formal*), consign. [➡GIVE AND PROVIDE; 431] *Opposite:* keep.

deliverance (*formal*) *n* **rescue**, release, liberation, relief, escape, freedom, delivery. [➡FREEDOM AND LIBERTY; 209] *Opposite:* capture.

delivery 1 *n* **distribution**, transfer, transport, sending, conveyance, carriage, provision, supply. [➡TRANSPORTATION, TRANSPORTERS, AND CARGOS; 323] 2 *n* **manner of speaking**, approach, manner, technique. [➡TEMPERAMENT AND BEHAVIOUR; 493] 3 *n* **rescue**, release, liberation, relief, escape, freedom, deliverance (*formal*). [➡FREEDOM AND LIBERTY; 209] *Opposite:* capture.

dell (*literary*) *n* **small valley**, glade, hollow, clearing, basin, dip, dene. [➡THE COUNTRYSIDE AND OUTDOOR SPACES; 1070]

delphinium *type of* **perennial flower**. [➡FLOWERS; 1032]

delta *n* **estuary**, outlet, mouth, channel. [➡THE SEAS, OCEANS, AND SHORES; 1041]

deltoid *adj* [➡ANGULAR SHAPE; 1216]

delude *v* **deceive**, take in, cheat, mislead, con, fool, trick, dupe, hoodwink, pull the wool over somebody's eyes. [➡DECEPTION AND LIES; 661]

deluded *adj* **mistaken**, deceived, misled, duped, conned, tricked, fooled, gullible. [➡NEGATIVE INTELLECTUAL CHARACTERISTICS; 526]

deluge 1 *n* **torrent**, downpour, cloudburst, rainstorm, monsoon. [➡CLOUDY AND RAINY WEATHER; 1052] 2 *n* **flood**, inundation (*formal*), torrent, overflow, surge, cascade. [➡MANY, MUCH, LARGE AMOUNT; 117] *Opposite:* drought. 3 *v* **overwhelm**, overload, overrun, swamp, bury, shower, bombard, engulf, snow under, saturate, inundate. [➡GIVE TOO MUCH; 438] 4 *v* **inundate**, flood, swamp, drown, soak, drench, saturate. [➡SOFTEN, LIQUEFY, DAMPEN; 389] *Opposite:* dry up.

delusion 1 *n* **illusion**, hallucination, vision, mirage, figment of the imagination, fantasy, apparition, image. [➡NONEXISTENT THINGS; 23] *Opposite:* reality. 2 *n* **misunderstanding**, misapprehension, misbelief, false impression, misconception, mistake, aberration. [➡MISUNDERSTAND AND FAIL TO GRASP; 762]

delusive *adj* **deceptive**, chimerical, misleading, specious, illusory, imaginary, vain. [➡FALSE AND UNREAL; 174] *Opposite:* genuine.

deluxe *adj* **sumptuous**, luxurious, luxury, exclusive, plush (*informal*), select, expensive. [➡EXPENSIVE AND LUXURIOUS; 219] *Opposite:* cheap.

delve 1 *v* **look into**, investigate, research, probe, dig, explore, examine, inquire. [➡EXAMINE AND ASSESS; 754] 2 *v* (*archaic*) **dig**, burrow, tunnel, scrabble, scratch, root, rootle. [➡SEEK POSSESSION AND SEARCH; 457] 3 *n* **rummage**, hunt, dig, search, dive, plunge, dip into, reach. [➡SEEK POSSESSION AND SEARCH; 457]

demagogic *adj* **rabble-rousing**, inflammatory, manipulative, declamatory, stirring, emotional. [➡ELOQUENT, TALKATIVE AND LONG-WINDED; 633]

demagogical *see* **demagogic**.

demagogue *n* **firebrand**, agitator, manipulator, crowd pleaser, haranguer, orator, tub-thumper (*informal*). [➡UNCOOPERATIVE OR REBELLIOUS PERSON; 567]

demand 1 *n* **request**, call, claim, petition, mandate, ultimatum, plea. [➡REQUEST AND DEMAND; 664] *Opposite:* response. 2 *n* **requirement**, need, pressure, exigency, claim, necessity. [➡NECESSARY AND ESSENTIAL; 197] 3 *v* **insist**, command, order, require, stipulate, exact, claim. [➡REQUEST AND DEMAND; 664] *Opposite:* request. 4 *v* **ask**, inquire, question, query, want, challenge, plead. [➡REQUEST AND DEMAND; 664] *Opposite:* answer. 5 *v* **require**, need, want, call for, necessitate, command, claim, press for. [➡NEED AND REQUIRE; 465]

demanding 1 *adj* **difficult**, hard, challenging, tough, severe, serious, trying, arduous, stressful, taxing, exacting, time-consuming. [➡DIFFICULTY AND COMPLEXITY; 243] *Opposite:* easy. 2 *adj* **insistent**, self-centred, persistent, dissatisfied, discontented, needy. [➡DIFFICULT TO PLEASE; 516] *Opposite:* satisfied.

demarcate 1 *v* **define**, mark out, delineate, draw, fix, establish, determine, delimit (*formal*). [➡SEPARATE AND DIVIDE; 402] 2 *v* **separate**, distinguish, differentiate, isolate, discriminate, segregate. [➡SEPARATE AND DIVIDE; 402] *Opposite:* unite.

demarcation *n* **separation**, differentiation, distinction, discrimination, segregation, isolation. [➡SEPARATE AND DIVIDE; 402] *Opposite:* unity.

dematerialize *v* [➡CEASE TO EXIST; 22]

demean *v* **degrade**, debase, humiliate, put down (*informal*), disgrace, humble, lower. [➡UPSET, DISTRESS, AND HUMILIATE; 568] *Opposite:* uplift.

demeanour *n* **manner**, conduct, behaviour, character, deportment (*formal*), performance, appearance, bearing, attitude, image, expression, air, mien (*literary*). [➡TEMPERAMENT AND BEHAVIOUR; 493]

demean yourself *v* **lower yourself**, swallow your pride, stoop low, go down on your knees, abase yourself (*literary*). [➡CHANGE OF MOOD AND COMPOSURE; 581]

demented (*informal*) *adj* **irrational**, unreasonable, wild, crazy (*informal*), frenzied, frantic, uncontrolled, manic (*informal*). [➡ECCENTRICITY AND IRRATIONALITY; 563] *Opposite:* rational.

demerger *n* **separation**, split, break, breakup, divergence, dissolution, division, partition. [➡END; 54] *Opposite:* merger.

demerit *n* **disadvantage**, failing, shortcoming, drawback, fault, imperfection. [➡FAULTS, FLAWS, AND WEAKNESSES; 252] *Opposite:* merit.

demesne (*formal*) *n* [➡REALMS AND RULES; 824]

demijohn *n* **bottle**, flagon, magnum, jeroboam, rehoboam, Methuselah. [➡CONTAINERS, RECEPTACLES, AND PACKAGING; 1244]

demise (*formal*) **1** *n* **death**, decease (*formal*), passing, departure, expiry (*formal or literary*), expiration (*literary*). [➡DEATH AND BEREAVEMENT; 927] *Opposite:* birth. **2** *n* **end**, termination, finish, failure, ruin, downfall. [➡END; 54] *Opposite:* creation.

demo (*informal*) **1** *n* **protest**, demonstration, protest march, march, protest rally, rally, parade. [➡MEETINGS AND ASSEMBLIES; 43] **2** *n* **sample**, showpiece, example, specimen, demonstrator, demo tape. [➡REPRESENTATIONS AND GENERAL EXAMPLES; 65] **3** *n* **demonstration**, presentation, display, show, exhibition, exposition. [➡SALES AND SHOWS; 444]

demob (*informal*) **1** *v* **demobilize**, disband, discharge, dismiss, release, retire. [➡FREEDOM AND LIBERTY; 209] *Opposite:* mobilize. **2** *n* **demobilization**, disbandment, discharge, release, dismissal, retirement. [➡FREEDOM AND LIBERTY; 209]

demobilization *n* **discharge**, release, disbandment, dismissal, retirement, demob (*informal*). [➡FREEDOM AND LIBERTY; 209] *Opposite:* mobilization.

demobilize *v* **discharge**, demob (*informal*), dismiss, disband, release, retire. [➡FREEDOM AND LIBERTY; 209] *Opposite:* mobilize.

democracy **1** *n* **social equality**, equality, egalitarianism, classlessness, consensus, fairness. [➡STYLES AND SYSTEMS OF GOVERNMENT; 806] *Opposite:* inequality. **2** *n* **democratic system**, democratic state, democratic organization, representative form of government, republic, parliamentary government. [➡STYLES AND SYSTEMS OF GOVERNMENT; 806] *Opposite:* dictatorship.

democrat *n* **egalitarian**, populist, republican, social democrat, constitutionalist, moderate. [➡POLITICAL OFFICES AND POLITICIANS; 808] *Opposite:* totalitarian.

democratic **1** *adj* **self-governing**, self-ruled, independent, autonomous, elected, representative. [➡STYLES AND SYSTEMS OF GOVERNMENT; 806] *Opposite:* autocratic. **2** *adj* **egalitarian**, free, classless, equal, open, unrestricted, uncensored. [➡EQUALITY; 155] *Opposite:* repressive.

demolish **1** *v* **knock down**, tear down, pull down, bulldoze, blow up, flatten, destroy, raze. [➡DESTRUCTION AND DEMOLITION; 360] *Opposite:* build. **2** *v* **destroy**, ruin, flatten, smash, wreck, ravage. [➡DESTRUCTION AND DEMOLITION; 360] *Opposite:* preserve. **3** *v* (*informal*) **beat**, annihilate, defeat, rout, thrash, trounce. [➡BEAT AND DEFEAT; 80] **4** *v* (*informal*) **disprove**, tear to pieces, dismantle, take apart (*informal*), undermine. [➡GET RID OF SOMETHING; 452] *Opposite:* support. **5** *v* (*informal*) **devour**, gobble, eat up (*informal*), eat, consume, scoff (*informal*), wolf. [➡EAT AND NOT EAT; 711] *Opposite:* nibble.

demolished *adj* [➡IN BAD REPAIR; 1233]

demolition *n* **destruction**, pulling down, knocking down, annihilation, devastation, flattening. [➡DESTRUCTION AND DEMOLITION; 360] *Opposite:* construction.

demon **1** *n* **fiend**, evil spirit, devil, monster. [➡THE SUPERNATURAL; 788] *Opposite:* angel. **2** *n* **fear**, anxiety, terror, torment, trouble, worry. [➡PROBLEM; 257] **3** *n* (*informal*) **expert**, whiz (*informal*), genius, fiend, wizard (*informal*), ace (*informal*). [➡TALENTED OR INTELLIGENT PERSON; 529]

demonstrable **1** *adj* **obvious**, palpable, patent, evident, noticeable, perceptible, discernible, apparent, clear. [➡PERCEPTIBLE; 25] *Opposite:* imperceptible. **2** *adj* **provable**, verifiable, self-evident, confirmable, comprehensible, certain, sure, definite. [➡CERTAIN; 175] *Opposite:* doubtful.

demonstrably *adv* **obviously**, palpably, patently, evidently, noticeably, perceptibly, discernibly, apparently, clearly. [➡PERCEPTIBLE; 25] *Opposite:* imperceptibly.

demonstrate **1** *v* **explain**, expound, display, operate, instruct, show, show off, put something through its paces. [➡EXPLAIN AND CLARIFY; 611] **2** *v* **prove**, validate, establish, reveal, make evident, make plain, determine, exhibit, show. [➡CAUSE TO APPEAR; 5] **3** *v* **protest**, march, rally, lobby, support, parade. [➡PROTEST AND EXPRESS DISAPPROVAL; 643]

demonstration **1** *n* **presentation**, display, illustration, explanation, exposition, show. [➡PERFORMANCES AND SHOWS; 42] **2** *n* **proof**, evidence, validation, establishment, revelation, determination. [➡EVIDENCE AND PROOF; 69] **3** *n* **protest**, demo (*informal*), protest march, march, protest rally, rally, parade, sit-in, sit-down. [➡MEETINGS AND ASSEMBLIES; 43]

demonstrative *adj* **affectionate**, warm, loving, friendly, emotional, effusive, open, expressive. [➡FRIENDLINESS AND SOCIABILITY; 495] *Opposite:* reserved.

demonstratively *adv* **affectionately**, warmly, lovingly, emotionally, effusively, openly, expressively. [➡HONEST AND OPEN; 631] *Opposite:* reservedly.

demonstrator **1** *n* **protester**, supporter, activist, campaigner, lobbyist, marcher. [➡UNCOOPERATIVE OR REBELLIOUS PERSON; 567] **2** *n* **presenter**, instructor, tutor, teacher, trainer, expounder. [➡EDUCATORS; 840]

demoralization *n* **discouragement**, deflation, undermining, depression, dejection, disheartenment. [➡SADNESS, DISTRESS, AND DESPAIR; 540] *Opposite:* encouragement.

demoralize *v* **dishearten**, undermine, dispirit, deflate, discourage, depress, deject (*archaic*). [➡UPSET, DISTRESS, AND HUMILIATE; 568] *Opposite:* encourage.

demoralized *adj* **disheartened**, dispirited, downhearted, discouraged, deflated, depressed, dejected. [➡SADNESS, DISTRESS, AND DESPAIR; 540] *Opposite:* optimistic.

demoralizing *adj* **disheartening**, discouraging, depressing, dispiriting, crushing, disturbing, distressing, upsetting, off-putting, unsettling, intimidating. [➡EMOTIONALLY UNPLEASANT AND UPSETTING; 228] *Opposite:* encouraging.

demote *v* **downgrade**, relegate, move down, devalue, reduce, reduce to the ranks, lower, humble. [➡REVOKE STATUS; 460] *Opposite:* promote.

demotion *n* **relegation**, downgrading, devaluation, reduction, lowering. [➡REVOKE STATUS; 460] *Opposite:* promotion.

demotivate *v* **discourage**, demoralize, dishearten, dispirit, deter, put off, daunt, dissuade. [➡UPSET, DISTRESS, AND HUMILIATE; 568] *Opposite:* motivate.

demotivation *n* **demoralization**, discouragement, disheartenment, deterrence, putting off, dissuasion. [➡NEUTRALITY AND INDIFFERENCE; 554] *Opposite:* motivation.

demur *v* **object**, protest, raise objections, baulk, express doubts, doubt, be reluctant, jib. [➡PROTEST AND EXPRESS DISAPPROVAL; 643] *Opposite:* agree.

See Compare and Contrast at **object**.

demure 1 *adj* **modest**, sedate, decorous, reserved, shy, retiring, diffident, bashful. [➡GOOD MANNERS AND SOCIAL SKILLS; 521] *Opposite:* bold. 2 *adj* **prim**, coy, prudish, strait-laced. [➡EXCESSIVE SENSITIVITY; 512] *Opposite:* pert.

demurely 1 *adv* **modestly**, sedately, decorously, reservedly, shyly, retiringly, diffidently, bashfully. [➡GOOD MANNERS AND SOCIAL SKILLS; 521] *Opposite:* boldly. 2 *adv* **primly**, coyly, prudishly. [➡RETICENT AND UNFORTHCOMING; 632] *Opposite:* pertly.

demureness *n* [➡GOOD MANNERS AND SOCIAL SKILLS; 521]

demystification *n* **clarification**, explanation, elucidation (*formal*), interpretation, revelation, decipherment, translation. [➡EXPLAIN AND CLARIFY; 611] *Opposite:* obfuscation.

demystify *v* **clarify**, explain, elucidate (*formal*), interpret, reveal, decipher, translate. [➡EXPLAIN AND CLARIFY; 611] *Opposite:* obscure.

den *type of* **room in the home**. [➡TYPES OF ROOM; 1096]

den

◆ *types of den or nest*
burrow, drey, earth, eyrie, form, hole, lair, lodge, nest, sett, tunnel, warren

denationalization *n* [➡SOCIAL, POLITICAL, AND ECONOMIC CHANGE; 374]

denationalize *v* [➡SOCIAL, POLITICAL, AND ECONOMIC CHANGE; 374]

denial 1 *n* **disavowal** (*formal*), refutation, rejection, rebuttal, contradiction, defiance, denunciation, dissent, repudiation. [➡DENY AND REJECT; 645] *Opposite:* confirmation. 2 *n* **refusal**, deprivation, withholding, begrudging, turning down, rejection. [➡REFUSE PERMISSION AND NOT ALLOW; 671]

denigrate 1 *v* **defame**, slander, libel, abuse, stigmatize, insult. [➡INSULTS, ABUSE, AND SWEARING; 659] *Opposite:* praise. 2 *v* **disparage**, vilify, pour scorn on, put down (*informal*), degrade, belittle, malign, depreciate. [➡ACCUSE, BLAME, AND CRITICIZE; 642] *Opposite:* glorify.

denigration 1 *n* **defamation**, slander, libel, abuse, stigmatization. [➡INSULTS, ABUSE, AND SWEARING; 659] *Opposite:* commendation. 2 *n* **disparagement**, vilification, scorn, depreciation, belittling, belittlement. [➡CRITICISMS AND ANGRY OUTBURSTS; 50] *Opposite:* glorification.

denim *type of* **fabric from plants**. [➡FABRICS; 1131]

denizen *n* **inhabitant**, resident, citizen, occupant, native, dweller (*literary*), tenant. [➡INHABITANT; 857]

denotation *n* **meaning**, import, sense, signification, significance, substance. [➡MEANING; 691] *Opposite:* connotation.

denote 1 *v* **mean**, signify, stand for, represent, symbolize, designate. [➡MEAN SOMETHING; 61] *Opposite:* connote. 2 *v* **refer to**, allude to, imply, convey, express, designate. [➡MEAN SOMETHING; 61]

denouement (*formal*) *n* **ending**, end, finale, conclusion, termination, finish. [➡END; 54] *Opposite:* opening.

denounce 1 *v* **criticize**, censure, deplore, deprecate, condemn, decry (*formal*). [➡PROTEST AND EXPRESS DISAPPROVAL; 643] *Opposite:* support. 2 *v* **accuse**, point the finger at, blame, charge, inform, betray. [➡ACCUSE, BLAME, AND CRITICIZE; 642]

See Compare and Contrast at **disapprove**.

de novo *adv* [➡AGAIN; 109]

dense 1 *adj* **crowded**, packed, jam-packed (*informal*), packed in, full, thick (*informal insult*). [➡FULL; 1238] *Opposite:* sparse. 2 *adj* **thick** (*informal insult*), solid, impenetrable, compressed, condensed, compact, opaque, dark, deep, intense, even. [➡DENSITY AND CONSISTENCY; 1206] *Opposite:* transparent. 3 *adj* **complicated**, complex, difficult, obscure, deep, opaque, involved, impenetrable, heavy-going. [➡DIFFICULTY AND COMPLEXITY; 243] *Opposite:* clear.

denseness 1 *n* **crowdedness**, crowding, tightness, impenetrability, closeness, density. [➡DENSITY AND CONSISTENCY; 1206] *Opposite:* roominess. 2 *n* **thickness**, opacity, solidity, impenetrability, darkness, compression, depth, intensity, heaviness, evenness. [➡DENSITY AND CONSISTENCY; 1206] *Opposite:* transparency. 3 *n* **complexity**, difficulty, complication, obscurity, opacity, impenetrability. [➡DIFFICULTY AND COMPLEXITY; 243] *Opposite:* clarity.

density *n* **thickness**, compactness, mass, concentration, bulk, solidity, concreteness. [➡DENSITY AND CONSISTENCY; 1206]

dent 1 *v* **knock**, hit, bump, bang, indent, damage, dint. [➡WORSEN APPEARANCE; 383] 2 *v* **damage**, hurt, undermine, diminish, lessen, reduce. [➡CHANGE OF SIZE: SMALLER; 394] 3 *n* **hollow**, indentation, depression, dimple, cavity, impression, dip, indent. [➡HOLES, GAPS, AND FORKS; 1251] *Opposite:* lump. 4 *n* (*informal*) **blow**, knock, shock, setback, reversal. [➡PROBLEM; 257] *Opposite:* boost. 5 *n* (*informal*) **reduction**, hole, cut, dip, decrease, dint. [➡CHANGE OF SIZE: SMALLER; 394]

denture 1 *part of* **mouth**. [➡THE MOUTH; 703] 2 *type of* **tooth**. [➡THE MOUTH; 703]

denude *v* **strip**, uncover, bare, remove, shed, discard. [➡REMOVE SOMETHING; 339] *Opposite:* cover.

denunciate (*formal*) *v* **condemn**, criticize, accuse, censure, reprove, admonish, rebuke. [➡PROTEST AND EXPRESS DISAPPROVAL; 643] *Opposite:* commend.

denunciation *n* **condemnation**, criticism, accusation, censure, reproof, admonition, scolding, rebuke. [➡CRITICISMS AND ANGRY OUTBURSTS; 50] *Opposite:* commendation.

Denver boot (*US*) *n* [➡FASTENERS, LINKS, AND NETWORKS; 1246]

deny 1 *v* **repudiate**, refute, reject, contradict, disagree, negate (*formal*). [➡DENY AND REJECT; 645] *Opposite:* agree. 2 *v* **refuse**, disallow, block, forbid, prevent, stand in the way. [➡REFUSE PERMISSION AND NOT ALLOW; 671] *Opposite:* permit. 3 *v* **forgo**, renounce, disavow (*formal*), reject, disown, abjure (*literary*), forswear (*archaic or literary*), give up, turn down, decline, repudiate. [➡FORGO AND DENY ONESELF; 450]

deodorant *n* **roll-on**, deodorizer, spray, cream, lotion. [➡PERSONAL HYGIENE; 492]

deodorize *v* **freshen**, scent, refresh, perfume, aromatize, fragrance. [➡CLEAN AND POLISH; 404]

depart 1 *v* **start out**, set out, move off, set off, set forth (*literary*), leave, proceed, advance, go forward, sally. [➡ABSENT ONESELF; 8] *Opposite:* return. 2 *v* **deviate**, diverge, differ, vary, change, digress, meander, stray. [➡CHANGE DIRECTION OF MOTION; 345] *Opposite:* stick to. 3 *v* **pull out**, leave, go away, quit (*archaic*), make tracks (*informal*), disappear, be off, head off. [➡ABSENT ONESELF; 8] *Opposite:* arrive. 4 *v* (*formal*) **die**, pass on, pass away, expire, perish (*literary*), depart this life (*formal*), succumb, decease (*formal*). [➡DIE; 922]

departed (*formal or literary*) *adj* **dead**, deceased (*formal*), late, defunct, lamented, lifeless. [➡DEAD AND DYING; 925] *Opposite:* living.

See Compare and Contrast at **dead**.

departing *n* **leaving**, going away, withdrawal, leave-taking (*literary*), departure, retreat, parting. [➡END; 54] *Opposite:* arriving.

department 1 *n* **subdivision**, division, branch, sector, section, constituent part. [➡SUBDIVISIONS AND OFFSHOOTS; 1252] 2 *n* (*informal*) **responsibility**, area, speciality, realm, sphere, field. [➡SUBJECT AREA; 769]

department store *type of* **retail outlet**. [➡RETAIL OUTLETS; 1082]

depart this life (*formal*) *v* [➡DIE; 922]

departure 1 *n* **leaving**, going away, parting, exit, exodus, withdrawal, retreat, leave-taking (*literary*). [➡END; 54] *Opposite:* arrival. 2 *n* **change**, deviation, divergence, digression, variation, difference, novelty. [➡WAYS OF DOING THINGS; 295] 3 *n* **venture**, project, enterprise, endeavour, undertaking, course of action. [➡ACTIONS OR UNDERTAKINGS; 260]

depend *v* **be contingent**, hinge on, rest on, be subject to, hang on, be governed by, be determined by, be influenced by. [➡RECIPROCITY AND INTERDEPENDENCE; 148]

dependability *n* **reliability**, steadiness, trustworthiness, loyalty, fidelity, steadfastness, constancy, soundness, staunchness. [➡HONEST AND RELIABLE; 503] *Opposite:* unreliability.

dependable *adj* **reliable**, trustworthy, loyal, faithful, steady, responsible, steadfast, trusty, staunch. [➡HONEST AND RELIABLE; 503] *Opposite:* unreliable.

dependant *type of* **younger relative**. [➡YOUNGER GENERATION RELATIVES; 958]

dependence 1 *n* **reliance**, trust, confidence, belief, hope, faith. [➡RECIPROCITY AND INTERDEPENDENCE; 148] *Opposite:* independence. 2 *n* **need**, requirement, necessity, want. [➡DESIRE AND WANT; 580] 3 *n* **addiction**, dependency, reliance, need, craving, habit, enslavement. [➡UNDER THE INFLUENCE OF DRUGS OR ALCOHOL; 742]

dependency 1 *n* **territory**, colony, dependent state, dependent territory, adjunct. [➡COUNTRIES AND REGIONS; 1066] 2 *n* **dependence**, need, reliance, addiction, habit, craving, enslavement. [➡RELATIONSHIP TO ANOTHER; 973]

dependent 1 *adj* **needy**, reliant, helpless, supported. [➡POVERTY AND POOR; 892] *Opposite:* independent. 2 *adj* **reliant on**, in need of, at the mercy of, hooked on (*slang*). [➡DESIRE AND WANT; 580] *Opposite:* independent. 3 *adj* **contingent**, conditional, determined, subject, related. [➡RECIPROCITY AND INTERDEPENDENCE; 148] *Opposite:* independent.

depend on 1 *v* **need**, require, rely on, be dependent on, lean on, look to. [➡RECIPROCITY AND INTERDEPENDENCE; 148] 2 *v* **rely on**, count on, trust, be sure of, be certain of. [➡LIKE, LOVE, VALUE AND ENJOY; 579] *Opposite:* mistrust.

depict *v* **portray**, show, represent, describe, illustrate, paint, give a picture of. [➡REPRESENT SOMETHING OR SOMEBODY; 59]

depiction *n* **representation**, portrayal, description, illustration, delineation, drawing, picture. [➡REPRESENTATIONS AND GENERAL EXAMPLES; 65]

deplete *v* **use up**, eat up (*informal*), drain, exhaust, diminish, lessen, run down. [➡USE UP AND WASTE; 475] *Opposite:* increase.

depletion *n* **reduction**, exhaustion, diminution, lessening, running down, weakening. [➡CHANGE OF SIZE: SMALLER; 394] *Opposite:* restoration.

deplorable 1 *adj* **disgraceful**, terrible, awful, appalling, unacceptable, dreadful, shocking, unpardonable, unforgivable, shameful. [➡BAD AND BADLY; 224] *Opposite:* praiseworthy. 2 *adj* **pitiful**, lamentable, execrable, woeful, appalling, shameful, pathetic, wretched. [➡EMOTIONALLY UNPLEASANT AND UPSETTING; 228]

deplorably *adv* **disgracefully**, appallingly, unpardonably, unforgivably, execrably, shockingly, shamefully, unacceptably. [➡BAD AND BADLY; 224] *Opposite:* excellently.

deplore 1 *v* **censure**, condemn, criticize, abhor (*formal*), deprecate, disapprove. [➡PROTEST AND EXPRESS DISAPPROVAL; 643] *Opposite:* praise. 2 *v* **lament**, bewail (*formal*), bemoan, regret, be sorry, rue. [➡COMPLAIN AND NAG; 687]

See Compare and Contrast at **disapprove**.

deploy 1 *v* **position**, arrange, set up, set out, install, array (*literary*), organize. [➡POSITION SOMETHING; 326] 2 *v* **use**, employ, implement, utilize, adopt. [➡USE; 468]

deployment 1 *n* **placement**, disposition, positioning, distribution, arrangement, organization, setting out. [➡MOVE SOMETHING TO ANOTHER LOCATION; 325] 2 *n* **utilization**, employment, implementation. [➡USE; 468]

depoliticize *v* **humanize**, personalize, socialize, neutralize. [➡SOCIAL, POLITICAL, AND ECONOMIC CHANGE; 374] *Opposite:* politicize.

depopulate *v* **clear**, relocate, remove, clear out, evacuate. [➡EMPTY AND UNLOAD; 408] *Opposite:* populate.

depopulation *n* **clearance**, relocation, removal, evacuation, abandonment. [➡SOCIAL, POLITICAL, AND ECONOMIC CHANGE; 374] *Opposite:* settlement.

deport *v* **expel**, extradite, banish, exile, transport, expatriate. [➡EJECT AND EXCLUDE; 341]

deportation *n* **exile**, banishment, extradition, expatriation, expulsion, transportation. [➡EJECT AND EXCLUDE; 341]

deportee *n* **exile**, outcast, expatriate, expat (*informal*). [➡PEOPLE LIVING AWAY FROM HOME; 887]

deportment (*formal*) *n* **carriage** (*formal*), manner, gait, attitude, posture, demeanour, bearing, behaviour. [➡TEMPERAMENT AND BEHAVIOUR; 493]

depose *v* **overthrow**, oust, topple, throw out, remove, unseat. [➡REVOKE STATUS; 460] *Opposite:* install.

deposit 1 *v* **put**, put down, set down, leave, place, drop, dump. [➡POSITION SOMETHING; 326] *Opposite:* remove. 2 *v* **accumulate**, lay down, leave behind, build up, pile up, add to. [➡POSITION SOMETHING; 326] 3 *v* **pay in**, credit, put in, bank, consign, add. [➡GIVE MONEY; 434] *Opposite:* withdraw. 4 *n* **credit**, payment, sum. [➡MONEY, PAYMENTS, AND CHARGES; 800] *Opposite:* withdrawal. 5 *n* **security**, guarantee, pledge, surety. [➡INSURANCE; 801] 6 *n* **sediment**, residue, accretion, layer, accumulation, buildup. [➡SOLIDS; 1273]

deposition 1 *n* **statement**, testimony, admission, sworn testimony, confession. [➡TRIAL, PUNISHMENT, AND LEGAL OUTCOMES; 819] 2 *n* **removal**, unseating, installation, overthrow, ousting. [➡REVOKE STATUS; 460] 3 *n* **accumulation**, accretion, sedimentation, silting, buildup. [➡REMAINDER AND REMAINDERS; 123]

depositor *n* **saver**, investor, account holder, creditor. [➡PEOPLE INVOLVED IN FINANCE; 804]

depository *type of* **storage space**. [➡STORES AND STORAGE BUILDINGS; 1087]

depot 1 *n* **yard**, maintenance yard, goods yard, garage, workshop, siding. [➡INDUSTRIAL BUILDINGS; 1086] 2 *n* (*US*) **railroad station**, bus station, terminus. [➡PUBLIC BUILDINGS AND MEETING PLACES; 1080] 3 *type of* **storage space**. [➡STORES AND STORAGE BUILDINGS; 1087]

deprave *v* **lead astray**, corrupt, debauch (*formal*), degrade, ruin, debase. [➡WORSEN SOMETHING; 381]

depraved *adj* **debauched**, immoral, corrupt, evil, wicked, degenerate, decadent, dissolute, wanton. [➡MORALLY BAD; 776] *Opposite:* righteous.

depravity *n* **debauchery**, immorality, corruption, wickedness, evil, decadence, dissoluteness, degeneracy, wantonness, vice. [➡MORALLY BAD; 776] *Opposite:* righteousness.

deprecate *v* **condemn**, censure, denigrate, denounce, deplore, criticize, disapprove, decry (*formal*), belittle. [➡PROTEST AND EXPRESS DISAPPROVAL; 643] *Opposite:* approve.

deprecating *adj* **condemnatory**, disapproving, derogatory, pejorative (*formal*), deprecatory. [➡ACCUSATORY AND DISAPPROVING; 635] *Opposite:* approving.

deprecation *n* **disapproval**, denigration, condemnation, censure, criticism. [➡CRITICISMS AND ANGRY OUTBURSTS; 50] *Opposite:* praise.

deprecatory 1 *adj* **disapproving**, derogatory, critical, denigrating, pejorative (*formal*), condemnatory. [➡ACCUSATORY AND DISAPPROVING; 635] *Opposite:* approving. 2 *adj* **apologetic**, sorry, repentant, contrite, remorseful. [➡EMBARRASSMENT AND HUMILIATION; 543] *Opposite:* unrepentant.

depreciate 1 *v* **lessen**, devalue, deflate, decline, downgrade. [➡CHANGE OF INTENSITY: LESS; 396] *Opposite:* appreciate. 2 *v* **denigrate**, belittle, disparage, run down, criticize, dis (*slang*). [➡ACCUSE, BLAME, AND CRITICIZE; 642] *Opposite:* commend.

depreciation *n* **devaluation**, reduction, decrease, decline, downgrading, fall, drop. [➡CHANGE OF INTENSITY: LESS; 396] *Opposite:* rise.

depreciatory *adj* **belittling**, deprecatory, critical, denigrating, pejorative (*formal*), derogatory, disapproving. [➡ACCUSATORY AND DISAPPROVING; 635] *Opposite:* complimentary.

depredation *n* **plunder**, destruction, pillage, despoliation, attack, sack. [➡DESTRUCTION AND DEMOLITION; 360]

depress 1 *v* **sadden**, dishearten, discourage, dispirit, demoralize. [➡UPSET, DISTRESS, AND HUMILIATE; 568] *Opposite:* cheer up. 2 *v* **press down**, push down, press, push, lower, move downwards. [➡MOVE SOMETHING: DOWNWARDS; 330] *Opposite:* release.

depressant 1 *n* **tranquillizer**, sedative, downer (*slang*), drug, narcotic. [➡REMEDIES, TREATMENTS AND OPERATIONS; 732] 2 *adj* **sedative**, tranquillizing, sedating, calming, narcotic. [➡REMEDIES, TREATMENTS AND OPERATIONS; 732]

depressed 1 *adj* **unhappy**, blue (*informal*), miserable, down in the dumps (*informal*), dejected, low, disheartened, sad, down, glum, despondent. [➡SADNESS, DISTRESS, AND DESPAIR; 540] *Opposite:* happy. 2 *adj* **rundown**, deprived, poor, underprivileged, neglected, derelict. [➡POVERTY AND POOR; 892] *Opposite:* affluent.

depressing *adj* **sad**, miserable, disheartening, discouraging, gloomy, dismal, disappointing. [➡EMOTIONALLY UNPLEASANT AND UPSETTING; 228] *Opposite:* cheering.

depression 1 *n* **downheartedness**, unhappiness, despair, sadness, gloominess, misery, hopelessness, melancholy, dejection. [➡SADNESS, DISTRESS, AND DESPAIR; 540] *Opposite:* happiness. 2 *n* **slump**, recession, decline, downturn, slide, poverty. [➡MARKET FORCES; 803] *Opposite:* recovery. **3** *n* **hollow**, dip, dent, impression, dimple, indent. [➡HOLES, GAPS, AND FORKS; 1251] *Opposite:* hump.

depressive *adj* **gloomy**, depressing, cheerless, miserable, bleak, grim. [➡EMOTIONALLY UNPLEASANT AND UPSETTING; 228] *Opposite:* cheerful.

deprivation *n* **lack**, deficiency, scarcity, denial, withdrawal, removal, dispossession, deficit, poverty. [➡POVERTY AND POOR; 892] *Opposite:* plenty.

See Compare and Contrast at **poverty**.

deprive *v* **divest**, rob, deny, take away, remove, withdraw, dispossess (*archaic or formal*). [➡TAKE SOMETHING AWAY; 426] *Opposite:* provide.

deprived *adj* **disadvantaged**, underprivileged, poor, destitute, depressed, rundown, dispossessed. [➡POVERTY AND POOR; 892] *Opposite:* privileged.

deprived of *adj* **without**, lacking, wanting, short of, starved of, shorn of. [➡LACK OF POSSESSION; 446]

depth **1** *n* **deepness**, profundity, distance. [➡DEPTH: DEEP; 1200] **2** *n* **intensity**, strength, power, vigour, concentration, extent. [➡STRENGTH; 202] *Opposite:* weakness. **3** *n* **complexity**, profundity, seriousness, gravity, wisdom, penetration, deepness. [➡DIFFICULTY AND COMPLEXITY; 243] *Opposite:* flippancy.

depth charge *type of* **explosive weapon**. [➡EXPLOSIVES; 1154]

deputation *n* **delegation**, commission, mission, lobby group. [➡GROUPS WITH A COMMON INTEREST; 938]

depute *v* **delegate**, hand over, relinquish, allot, transfer, pass on. [➡CHANGE ONE THING FOR ANOTHER; 399]

deputize *v* **stand in**, represent, fill in, act, replace, substitute, sub (*informal*). [➡REPRESENT SOMETHING OR SOMEBODY; 59]

deputy *n* **second-in-command**, assistant, agent, delegate, representative. [➡SUBORDINATES AND ASSISTANTS; 966]

See Compare and Contrast at **assistant**.

derail *v* **disrupt**, upset, wreck, ruin, spoil, overturn, unsettle, disorganize, interfere, dislocate, disturb, derange, disorder. [➡MAKE IMPOSSIBLE; 277]

derailleur *part of* **bike** (*informal*). [➡BIKES, CARS, AND CARRIAGES; 1148]

derange **1** *v* **distress**, unsettle, upset, disorder, shake, shock. [➡UPSET, DISTRESS, AND HUMILIATE; 568] **2** *v* **upset**, disrupt, wreck, disturb, spoil, unsettle, disorganize, dislocate, interfere, derail, disorder. [➡CREATE DISORDER AND CAUSE CHAOS; 359]

deranged *adj* [➡ECCENTRICITY AND IRRATIONALITY; 563]

derangement **1** *n* **imbalance**, irrationality, madness, instability. [➡ECCENTRICITY AND IRRATIONALITY; 563] *Opposite:* sanity. **2** *n* **disorder**, confusion, muddle, upset, disorganization, mess. [➡DISORDER AND CHAOS; 246] *Opposite:* order.

derby **1** *n* **contest**, race, match, clash, sporting event. [➡NON-AGGRESSIVE/SPORTING EVENT; 40] **2** (*US*) *type of* **hat**. [➡HABERDASHERY, MILLINERY, AND LINGERIE; 867]

deregulate *v* **free**, relax, liberalize, decontrol, derestrict, release. [➡FREEDOM AND LIBERTY; 209] *Opposite:* regulate.

derelict *adj* **dilapidated**, in ruins, rundown, ruined, neglected, abandoned, deserted. [➡IN BAD REPAIR; 1233]

dereliction **1** *n* **neglect**, negligence, disregard, recklessness, carelessness, delinquency. [➡BAD BEHAVIOUR OR ACTION; 255] *Opposite:* regard. **2** *n* **abandonment**, desertion, neglect, dilapidation, default, relinquishment. [➡IN BAD REPAIR; 1233]

deride *v* **ridicule**, scoff, put down (*informal*), disparage, mock, scorn, disdain, knock (*slang*). [➡PROTEST AND EXPRESS DISAPPROVAL; 643] *Opposite:* admire.

See Compare and Contrast at **ridicule**.

de rigueur (*formal*) *adj* [➡NECESSARY AND ESSENTIAL; 197]

derision *n* **disparagement**, scorn, disdain, mockery, ridicule, contempt, disrespect, contumely (*archaic or literary*). [➡JOKES AND TEASING; 675] *Opposite:* admiration.

derisive *adj* **mocking**, scathing, sarcastic, irreverent, contemptuous, scornful, disdainful, cynical, sardonic. [➡MOCKING AND DISMISSIVE; 637] *Opposite:* admiring.

derisively *adv* **mockingly**, scathingly, sarcastically, irreverently, contemptuously, scornfully, disdainfully, cynically, sardonically. [➡RUDE AND HOSTILE; 626] *Opposite:* admiringly.

derisory *adj* **pitiful**, laughable, insulting, ridiculous, contemptible, mean, pathetic (*informal*), inadequate. [➡UNIMPORTANT AND UNNECESSARY; 239] *Opposite:* generous.

derivation *n* **origin**, root, source, beginning, seed, cradle, descent. [➡BEGINNING; 53]

See Compare and Contrast at **origin**.

derivative **1** *adj* **unoriginal**, imitative, plagiaristic, copied, derived. [➡SIMILARITY; 149] *Opposite:* original. **2** *n* **offshoot**, byproduct, result, end product, spin-off. [➡RESULTS AND OUTCOMES; 83]

derive **1** *v* **get**, gain, obtain, draw, receive, take. [➡GET; 421] **2** *v* **originate**, stem, spring, arise, descend, come from, grow, draw on. [➡GRADUALLY COME INTO EXISTENCE; 1]

dermal *adj* [➡THE SKIN; 721]

dermatological *adj* [➡THE SKIN; 721]

dermis *n* [➡THE SKIN; 721]

derogatory *adj* **pejorative** (*formal*), disparaging, critical, insulting, offensive, deprecating, belittling. [➡ACCUSATORY AND DISAPPROVING; 635] *Opposite:* complimentary.

derrick **1** *n* **crane**, hoist, winch, elevator, lift. [➡MACHINES AND MACHINE PARTS; 1115] **2** *n* **wellhead**, rig, gantry, oil platform, frame, support. [➡SUPPORTS AND BASES; 1254]

derring-do (*literary*) *n* **boldness**, bravery, courage, guts (*slang*), daring, bravado. [➡COURAGE; 499] *Opposite:* cowardice.

desalinate *v* **purify**, desalt, detoxify, distil, refine, sweeten. [➡CLEAN AND POLISH; 404]

desalination *n* **purification**, detoxification, distillation, salt removal. [➡CLEAN AND POLISH; 404]

descale *v* **clean out** (*informal*), scrape, scour, flush, clean. [➡CLEAN AND POLISH; 404]

descant *n* **harmony**, part, line, tune, air, melody. [➡MUSIC, SONGS, AND SINGING; 907]

descend 1 *v* **go down**, move down, come down, slide down, fall down, tumble down. [➡GO DOWNWARDS; 308] *Opposite:* ascend. 2 *v* **slope**, incline, fall away, go downhill, drop away, run down. [➡GO DOWNWARDS; 308] *Opposite:* ascend. 3 *v* **derive**, originate, come from, stem, spring. [➡GRADUALLY COME INTO EXISTENCE; 1] 4 *v* **lower yourself**, stoop, sink, resort, fall, decline. [➡GET WORSE; 382] *Opposite:* rise. 5 *v* **arrive**, drop in, appear, turn up, show up. [➡ARRIVE; 12] *Opposite:* leave. 6 *v* **fall**, fall on, affect, come over, come upon, hit, pervade, prevail. [➡HAPPEN TO SOMEBODY; 30]

descendant *n* **successor**, offspring, progeny, child, heir, inheritor. [➡THE FAMILY; 956] *Opposite:* ancestor.

descendent *adj* **descending**, down, downward, plunging, sinking, sliding, downhill. [➡DIRECTION OF MOTION; 346] *Opposite:* ascendant (*literary*).

descent 1 *n* **fall**, drop, dive, tumble, plunge, crash. [➡GO DOWNWARDS; 308] *Opposite:* ascent. 2 *n* **decline**, deterioration, depreciation, degeneration, drop, plunge, tumble, downward spiral. [➡FAILURE; 77] *Opposite:* improvement. 3 *n* **ancestry**, parentage, lineage, origin, succession, pedigree, background. [➡THE FAMILY; 956]

describe 1 *v* **explain**, portray, depict, illustrate, express, communicate. [➡EXPLAIN AND CLARIFY; 611] 2 *v* **label**, refer to, define, designate, pronounce, call, term, style (*formal*). [➡NAME AND DESCRIBE; 666]

description 1 *n* **account**, report, explanation, portrayal, picture, narrative, depiction. [➡NAME AND DESCRIBE; 666] 2 *n* **type**, sort, kind, class, variety, category. [➡VARIETY, TYPE, KIND; 146]

descriptive 1 *adj* **explanatory**, illustrative, narrative, informative, factual. [➡EXPLAIN AND CLARIFY; 611] *Opposite:* imaginative. 2 *adj* **evocative**, expressive, vivid, graphic, eloquent, colourful, imaginative. [➡ELOQUENT, TALKATIVE AND LONG-WINDED; 633]

descry (*literary*) *v* [➡SEE; 700]

desecrate *v* **defile**, vandalize, insult, violate, outrage, lay waste to, commit sacrilege against, damage, blaspheme. [➡WORSEN SOMETHING; 381] *Opposite:* consecrate.

desecration *n* **violation**, defilement, vandalism, sacrilege, despoliation, ruin, damage. [➡BAD BEHAVIOUR OR ACTION; 255] *Opposite:* consecration.

deseed *v* **pit**, stone, core. [➡COOKING AND FOOD PREPARATION; 354]

desegregate *v* **integrate**, unify, unite, bring together, merge, reconcile, reunite. [➡COMBINE AND MIX; 401] *Opposite:* segregate.

desegregation *n* **integration**, unification, reunion, reconciliation, merging. [➡COMBINE AND MIX; 401] *Opposite:* segregation.

deselect *v* **reject**, abandon, discard, cast off, dump (*informal*), ditch (*informal*), remove. [➡GET RID OF SOMETHING; 452] *Opposite:* select.

desensitize *v* **numb**, deaden, dull, soothe, pacify, lull. [➡SOOTHE AND CALM; 574] *Opposite:* sensitize.

desert 1 *n* **wasteland**, wilderness, barren region, arid region, waste. [➡DESERTS AND PLAINS; 1045] 2 *v* **abscond**, leave, go AWOL, jump ship, take off (*informal*), go missing, do a bunk (*informal*), scarper (*slang*). [➡RUN AWAY AND AVOID; 10] *Opposite:* stay. 3 *v* **abandon**, leave high and dry, leave, walk out on (*informal*), forsake, discard, dump (*informal*), ditch (*informal*). [➡REFUSING OR REJECTING RELATIONS; 975] *Opposite:* support. 4 *n* **reward**, return, recompense, wages, just reward, punishment, comeuppance (*informal*). [➡REWARDS AND AWARDS; 440]

deserted 1 *adj* **empty**, abandoned, isolated, uninhabited, forsaken, desolate, derelict. [➡EMPTY; 1237] *Opposite:* inhabited. 2 *adj* **abandoned**, discarded, forsaken, ditched (*informal*), solitary, cast off. [➡SOLITARINESS; 941]

deserter *n* **absconder**, runaway, fugitive, defector, traitor, renegade, apostate, AWOL. [➡RUNAWAYS AND ABSENTEES; 9]

desertion *n* **absconding**, abandonment, running away, disappearance, departure, leaving. [➡END; 54]

deserve *v* **merit**, be worthy, earn, warrant, justify, rate, ask for. [➡OWE AND DESERVE; 466]

deservedly *adv* **justly**, rightly, justifiably, reasonably, properly, with good reason. [➡MORALLY GOOD; 775] *Opposite:* unreasonably.

deserving *adj* **worthy**, commendable, admirable, praiseworthy, justified, justifiable, eligible. [➡ADMIRABLE AND COMMENDABLE; 186] *Opposite:* unworthy.

desiccate *v* **dry up**, wither, dry out, dehydrate, parch, dry, shrivel, shrink. [➡HARDEN, CONGEAL, DRY; 388]

desiccated *adj* **dry**, dried, dried out, shrivelled, dehydrated, shrunken. [➡DRY; 1241] *Opposite:* moist.

See Compare and Contrast at **dry**.

desiccation *n* **dryness**, dehydration, withering, shrivelling, drying. [➡DRY; 1241]

design 1 *v* **create**, invent, conceive, originate, fabricate, draw up, construct. [➡CREATION; 347] 2 *v* **plan**, intend, aim, devise, propose, suggest. [➡PREDICT AND ANTICIPATE; 751] 3 *n* **project**, scheme, enterprise, plan, strategy, proposal, policy. [➡WAYS OF DOING THINGS; 295] 4 *n* **drawing**, blueprint, plan, sketch, outline, model, layout. [➡DRAWINGS, CHARTS AND TABLES; 595] 5 *n* **pattern**, motif, figure, shape, device, outline. [➡PATTERNS; 1224] 6 *n* **intention**, purpose, scheme, plan, object, aim, end, point, target, goal, will. [➡INTENTION AND PURPOSE; 773]

designate 1 *v* **call**, label, title, entitle, term, style (*formal*), describe, define, refer to. [➡NAME AND DESCRIBE; 666] 2 *v* **assign**, select, choose, delegate, allocate, elect, appoint, authorize. [➡CONFER STATUS; 459] 3 *v* **specify**, point out, indicate, choose, select, allocate. [➡MAKE DECISIONS AND CHOICES; 753] 4 *adj* **in waiting**, elect, to be. [➡FUTURE; 86]

designation *n* **title**, description, term, label, alias, nickname. [➡NAME AND DESCRIBE; 666]

designedly *adv* **intentionally**, on purpose, purposely, deliberately, purposefully, wilfully, by design. [➡INTENTIONAL AND DELIBERATE; 280] *Opposite:* accidentally.

designer 1 *n* **creator**, inventor, originator, engineer, stylist, artist, graphic designer. [➡DESIGNERS, CREATORS AND INSTIGATORS; 348] 2 *adj* **fashionable**, stylish, chic, expensive, trendy (*informal*), exclusive, upmarket, upscale (*US*). [➡DESCRIBING CLOTHES; 869] *Opposite:* mass-produced.

designing *adj* **scheming**, conniving, deceitful, wily, manipulative, crafty. [➡DECEITFUL; 514] *Opposite:* ingenuous.

desirability 1 *n* **appeal**, attractiveness, attraction, allure, prestige, cachet, popularity. [➡BEAUTY AND ATTRACTIVENESS; 190] 2 *n* **appropriateness**, aptness, rightness, suitability, advantage. [➡APPROPRIATE, SUITABLE, ADVISABLE; 185]

desirable 1 *adj* **wanted**, needed, necessary, required, looked-for, desired, anticipated, appropriate, suitable, right, advantageous. [➡POPULAR AND WANTED; 221] *Opposite:* undesirable. 2 *adj* **attractive**, pleasing, enviable, pleasant, popular, sought after. [➡POPULAR AND WANTED; 221] *Opposite:* undesirable.

desirably *adv* **advantageously**, appropriately, suitably, enviably, pleasantly, pleasingly, popularly. [➡POPULAR AND WANTED; 221]

desire 1 *v* **want**, wish for, long for, covet, crave, yearn for. [➡DESIRE AND WANT; 580] 2 *v* (*formal*) **request**, ask, require, appeal, implore (*formal*), entreat (*formal*), beg. [➡REQUEST AND DEMAND; 664] 3 *n* **wish**, want, longing, craving, yearning, need, aspiration, plea, request, appeal, entreaty, petition. [➡DESIRE AND WANT; 580]

See Compare and Contrast at **want**.

desired *adj* **wanted**, anticipated, sought after, looked-for, favourite, chosen, preferred. [➡POPULAR AND WANTED; 221] *Opposite:* unwanted.

desirous (*formal*) *adj* **eager**, hopeful, wishing for, longing for, hoping for, wanting. [➡POSITIVE IMPATIENCE, ENTHUSIASM, AND ALERTNESS; 538]

desirously (*formal*) *adv* [➡POSITIVE IMPATIENCE, ENTHUSIASM, AND ALERTNESS; 538]

desirousness (*formal*) *n* [➡DESIRE AND WANT; 580]

desist *v* **cease**, stop, discontinue, give up, end, abstain. [➡STOP ACTING; 265] *Opposite:* continue.

desk *type of* **table**. [➡FURNITURE; 858]

desk lamp *n* [➡LIGHTING; 862]

desolate 1 *adj* **deserted**, isolated, bleak, abandoned, forsaken, uninhabited, wild, barren. [➡IN BAD REPAIR; 1233] *Opposite:* populous. 2 *adj* **unhappy**, forlorn, miserable, depressed, inconsolable, wretched, dejected, despondent, mournful, sad. [➡SADNESS, DISTRESS, AND DESPAIR; 540] *Opposite:* happy. 3 *adj* **depressing**, gloomy, dismal, austere, forbidding, unwelcoming, grim, bleak. [➡EMOTIONALLY UNPLEASANT AND UPSETTING; 228] *Opposite:* cheerful.

desolately *adv* **unhappily**, sadly, mournfully, miserably, inconsolably, wretchedly, dejectedly, despondently. [➡SADNESS, DISTRESS, AND DESPAIR; 540] *Opposite:* happily.

desolation 1 *n* **barrenness**, isolation, bleakness, emptiness, dereliction, devastation. [➡EMPTY; 1237] 2 *n* **unhappiness**, misery, despair, anguish, sadness, wretchedness, despondency. [➡SADNESS, DISTRESS, AND DESPAIR; 540] *Opposite:* happiness.

despair 1 *n* **misery**, desolation, hopelessness, anguish, gloom, depression, despondency, dejection. [➡SADNESS, DISTRESS, AND DESPAIR; 540] *Opposite:* joy. 2 *v* **lose hope**, give up hope, have no hope, see no light at the end of the tunnel, lose heart, give up on, sink, plumb the depths. [➡CHANGE OF MOOD AND COMPOSURE; 581] *Opposite:* hope.

despairing *adj* **hopeless**, desolate, miserable, pained, despondent, desperate, weary, depressed, long-suffering, inconsolable, bleak. [➡SADNESS, DISTRESS, AND DESPAIR; 540] *Opposite:* hopeful.

desperado (*literary*) *n* **criminal**, outlaw, gangster, bandit, villain, renegade, baddie (*informal*). [➡VILLAINS AND THUGS; 947]

desperate 1 *adj* **frantic**, anxious, worried, distressed, distracted, at the end of your tether, despairing, fraught. [➡CONFUSION, ANXIETY, AND WORRY; 541] *Opposite:* calm. 2 *adj* **reckless**, careless, rash, impulsive, dangerous, violent, risky, drastic. [➡INCAUTIOUS AND CARELESS; 284] *Opposite:* safe. 3 *adj* **serious**, grave, extreme, critical, threatening, acute. [➡DANGEROUS; 237] *Opposite:* harmless. 4 *adj* **eager**, dying, raring, bursting, impatient, determined, in urgent need. [➡POSITIVE IMPATIENCE, ENTHUSIASM, AND ALERTNESS; 538] *Opposite:* loath. 5 *adj* **hopeless**, wretched, irredeemable, deplorable, dreadful. [➡SADNESS, DISTRESS, AND DESPAIR; 540] *Opposite:* hopeful.

desperately 1 *adv* **frantically**, anxiously, frenziedly, hastily, distractedly, distraughtly, worriedly. [➡SADNESS, DISTRESS, AND DESPAIR; 540] *Opposite:* calmly. 2 *adv* **very much**, badly, to a great extent, dreadfully, urgently. [➡TO A GREAT EXTENT; 130] *Opposite:* hardly.

desperation 1 *n* **anxiety**, worry, fear, distraction, nervousness, harassment. [➡CONFUSION, ANXIETY, AND WORRY; 541] *Opposite:* calmness. 2 *n* **hopelessness**, despair, despondency, misery, anguish, desolation. [➡SADNESS, DISTRESS, AND DESPAIR; 540] *Opposite:* hopefulness.

despicable *adj* **appalling**, dreadful, contemptible, wicked, shameful, disgraceful, vile, loathsome. [➡BAD AND BADLY; 224] *Opposite:* admirable.

despise *v* **loathe**, scorn, look down on, hate, spurn, deride, feel contempt. [➡DISLIKE AND HATE; 578] *Opposite:* admire.

despised *adj* **hated**, reviled, loathed, shunned, scorned, derided. [➡UNPOPULAR AND UNWANTED; 259] *Opposite:* beloved.

despite *prep* **in spite of**, regardless of, notwithstanding (*formal*), in the face of, even with, even though, although. [➡ALTHOUGH, NEVERTHELESS, AND DESPITE; 170]

despoil *v* **rob**, plunder, sack, pillage, loot, rifle, ransack. [➡STEAL AND ROB; 427]

despoilment *n* **despoliation**, vandalism, defacement, destruction, desecration, defilement. [➡DESTRUCTION AND DEMOLITION; 360]

despoliation *n* **plundering**, pillage, sack, theft, robbery, appropriation. [➡CRIMES; 817]

despondency *n* **hopelessness**, sadness, misery, dejection, depression, unhappiness, gloom, cheerlessness, joylessness, discouragement. [➡SADNESS, DISTRESS, AND DESPAIR; 540] *Opposite:* cheerfulness.

despondent *adj* **hopeless**, low, dejected, despairing, downhearted, downcast, unhappy, sad, pessimistic, miserable, glum, discouraged. [➡SADNESS, DISTRESS, AND DESPAIR; 540] *Opposite:* cheerful.

despot *n* **dictator**, tyrant, autocrat, oppressor, authoritarian, disciplinarian, martinet. [➡VILLAINS AND THUGS; 947]

despotic *adj* **tyrannical**, dictatorial, autocratic, authoritarian, repressive, absolute, high-handed, domineering. [➡BOSSY AND OVERBEARING; 517] *Opposite:* democratic.

despotism *n* **tyranny**, dictatorship, absolutism, autocracy, authoritarianism, repression. [➡MORALLY BAD; 776] *Opposite:* democracy.

dessert *n* **sweet**, pudding, pud (*informal*), afters (*informal*). [➡MEALS AND PARTS OF MEALS; 1168]

dessert

◆ *types of dessert*
blancmange, cobbler, crème brûlée, crème caramel, crisp (*US*), crumble, custard, flan, fruit salad, ice cream, jelly, junket, meringue, mousse, pie, pudding, sorbet, soufflé, sundae, syllabub, tart

dessertspoon *type of* **cutlery**. [➡TABLEWARE, CUTLERY, AND KITCHENWARE; 861]

dessertspoonful *n* [➡AMOUNT AND QUANTITY; 112]

destabilization *n* **weakening**, subversion, undermining, disruption, dislocation. [➡WORSEN SOMETHING; 381]

destabilize *v* **undermine**, subvert, weaken, threaten, disrupt, dislocate, strike at the foundations, knock off balance. [➡WORSEN SOMETHING; 381] *Opposite:* strengthen.

destination 1 *n* **journey's end**, terminus, last stop, end point. [➡END; 54] *Opposite:* starting point. 2 *n* **end**, purpose, target, aim, goal, objective, intention. [➡INTENTION AND PURPOSE; 773]

destined *adj* **intended**, meant, ordained (*formal*), fated, designed, certain, predestined, preordained. [➡FATE, DESTINY, AND ASTROLOGY; 783]

destiny 1 *n* **fate**, fortune, lot, luck, providence, future. [➡FATE, DESTINY, AND ASTROLOGY; 783] 2 *n* **purpose**, vocation, intention, call, calling. [➡INTENTION AND PURPOSE; 773]

destitute *adj* **poor**, penniless, impoverished, insolvent, needy, deprived, indigent (*formal*). [➡POVERTY AND POOR; 892] *Opposite:* solvent.

destitution *n* **poverty**, penury, hardship, need, insolvency, deprivation, impoverishment, want, privation, indigence (*formal*), misery. [➡POVERTY AND POOR; 892] *Opposite:* prosperity.

See Compare and Contrast at **poverty**.

destroy 1 *v* **obliterate**, wipe out (*informal*), annihilate, demolish, devastate, tear down, raze. [➡DESTRUCTION AND DEMOLITION; 360] *Opposite:* build. 2 *v* **ruin**, damage, break, break up, spoil, wreck. [➡DESTRUCTION AND DEMOLITION; 360] *Opposite:* conserve. 3 *v* **abolish**, put an end to, end, finish (*informal*), extinguish, terminate (*formal*), do away with, rescind. [➡CAUSE TO STOP; 267] *Opposite:* sustain. 4 *v* **defeat**, crush, wipe out (*informal*), subdue, demolish, annihilate (*informal*), overcome, overthrow. [➡BEAT AND DEFEAT; 80]

destroyed *adj* **demolished**, devastated, ruined, wrecked, smashed, damaged, shattered, wiped out (*slang*), in shreds, in pieces. [➡IN BAD REPAIR; 1233] *Opposite:* intact.

destroyer 1 *n* **destructive force**, natural disaster, cause of death, killer, slayer (*formal or literary*), demolisher. [➡DISASTERS; 253] *Opposite:* creator. 2 *type of* **military vessel**. [➡SHIPS AND BOATS; 1149]

destroying angel *type of* **fungus**. [➡MICROORGANISMS, FUNGI, AND ALGAE; 1023]

destruction *n* **obliteration**, annihilation, devastation, demolition, ruin, damage. [➡DESTRUCTION AND DEMOLITION; 360] *Opposite:* construction.

destructive 1 *adj* **damaging**, devastating, harmful, detrimental, injurious. [➡DANGEROUS; 237] 2 *adj* **unhelpful**, critical, negative, damaging, disparaging, harsh, caustic, vicious, hurtful. [➡RUDE AND HOSTILE; 626] *Opposite:* constructive.

destructiveness 1 *n* **harmfulness**, power, force, violence, ferocity, roughness. [➡DANGER; 236] 2 *n* **criticism**, negativity, harshness, viciousness, hurtfulness, unhelpfulness. [➡AGGRESSIVE AND BELLIGERENT; 519] *Opposite:* helpfulness.

desultorily *adv* **casually**, haphazardly, randomly, erratically, aimlessly, indiscriminately. [➡DISORDER AND CHAOS; 246] *Opposite:* methodically.

desultory *adj* **aimless**, casual, random, unfocused, haphazard, erratic, indiscriminate. [➡DISORDER AND CHAOS; 246] *Opposite:* methodical.

detach *v* **separate**, remove, disengage, disconnect, isolate, cut off, unfasten. [➡UNFASTEN AND UNDO; 410] *Opposite:* attach.

detachable *adj* **removable**, separable, clip-on, hook-on, attachable, separate. [➡UNRELATEDNESS AND SEPARATENESS; 147] *Opposite:* fixed.

detached 1 *adj* **separate**, disconnected, standing apart, apart, removed, separated, isolated. [➡UNRELATEDNESS AND SEPARATENESS; 147] *Opposite:* connected. 2 *adj* **aloof**, indifferent, unemotional, unbiased, uninvolved, disinterested, distant, impassive, impersonal. [➡NEUTRALITY AND INDIFFERENCE; 554] *Opposite:* involved.

detached house *type of* **house**. [➡RESIDENTIAL BUILDINGS; 1077]

detachment 1 *n* **aloofness**, remoteness, indifference, impassiveness, distance, coldness. [➡NEUTRALITY AND INDIFFERENCE; 554] *Opposite:* involvement. 2 *n* **objectivity**, disinterest, disinterestedness, impartiality, fairness, unbiasedness, dispassion. [➡POSITIVE INTELLECTUAL CHARACTERISTICS; 525] 3 *n* **disconnection**, separation, disengagement, disentanglement, extrication, uncoupling, severance. [➡SEPARATE AND DIVIDE; 402] *Opposite:* connection. 4 *n* **group**, unit, task force, detail, party, posse (*informal*). [➡MILITARY PERSONNEL; 828]

detail 1 *n* **part**, feature, aspect, point, element, fact, factor, facet. [➡QUALITIES AND CHARACTERISTICS; 1190] 2 *n* **group**, unit, task force, detachment, party, posse (*informal*). [➡MILITARY PERSONNEL; 828] 3 *v* **list**, specify, describe, itemize, particularize, note, notify. [➡EXPLAIN AND CLARIFY; 611] 4 *v* **assign**, delegate, allocate, conscript, designate, order. [➡CAUSE OR COMPEL TO ACT; 272]

detailed *adj* **full**, thorough, comprehensive, complete, exhaustive, meticulous, in depth. [➡WHOLENESS AND COMPLETENESS; 199] *Opposite:* sketchy.

details *n* **particulars**, facts, information, minutiae, niceties, fine points, specifics. [➡BASIC DETAILS; 689]

detain 1 *v* **delay**, hold up, keep, keep back, impede, slow up, hinder. [➡DELAY ACTION OR OCCURRENCE; 279] *Opposite:* let go. 2 *v* **arrest**, hold, keep in custody, capture, confine, control, restrain. [➡THE POLICE, ARREST, AND PRE-TRIAL PROCEEDINGS; 818] *Opposite:* release.

detained *adj* **in custody**, in detention, under arrest, inside (*informal*), behind bars, in prison, imprisoned, incarcerated (*formal*), locked up, held, interned, apprehended, captive, arrested, seized, caged, trapped, shut in, constricted, restrained, confined, jailed, put away (*informal*). [➡CAPTIVITY AND LOSS OF FREEDOM; 249] *Opposite:* at liberty.

detainee *n* **prisoner**, captive, internee, hostage, convict. [➡CAPTIVES AND PRISONERS; 250]

detect *v* **notice**, sense, become aware of, perceive, spot, distinguish, identify, discover. [➡USING THE SENSES; 698]

detectable *adj* **obvious**, visible, noticeable, measurable, demonstrable, evident. [➡PERCEPTIBLE; 25] *Opposite:* undetectable.

detection *n* **discovery**, uncovering, finding, recognition, exposure, revealing. [➡FIND; 464] *Opposite:* concealment.

detective *n* **investigator**, private detective, plainclothes officer, private eye (*informal*), dick (*US dated slang*), gumshoe (*US informal*). [➡THE POLICE, ARREST, AND PRE-TRIAL PROCEEDINGS; 818]

detective novel *n* [➡FICTION AND DRAMA; 913]

detective story *n* [➡FICTION AND DRAMA; 913]

detector *n* **sensor**, indicator, gauge, finder. [➡PARTS OF MACHINES AND TOOLS; 1117]

détente *n* **rapprochement** (*formal*), agreement, cooperation, compromise, accommodation, truce. [➡HARMONY; 156] *Opposite:* hostility.

detention *n* **custody**, imprisonment, confinement, arrest, incarceration (*formal*), locking up. [➡CAPTIVITY AND LOSS OF FREEDOM; 249] *Opposite:* release.

deter *v* **discourage**, put off, daunt, dissuade, prevent, frighten. [➡UPSET, DISTRESS, AND HUMILIATE; 568] *Opposite:* encourage.

detergent *n* **cleaner**, cleansing agent, cleanser, shampoo, washing-up liquid, soap, laundry detergent (*US*), dishwashing liquid (*US*). [➡CLEANING AGENTS; 863]

deteriorate *v* **get worse**, worsen, decline, depreciate, go downhill, weaken, wane, fail, fade. [➡GET WORSE; 382] *Opposite:* improve.

deteriorated *adj* [➡DECAYING OR INFESTED; 1235]

deteriorating *adj* **worsening**, getting worse, falling, fading, waning, failing. [➡WORSEN SOMETHING; 381] *Opposite:* improving.

deterioration *n* **worsening**, decline, weakening, drop, descent, depreciation. [➡WORSEN SOMETHING; 381] *Opposite:* improvement.

determinant *n* **cause**, determining factor, factor, element, basis, contributing factor. [➡MOST IMPORTANT THING; 198]

determination *n* **strength of mind**, willpower, resolve, purpose, fortitude, grit, strength of character. [➡STRENGTH OF WILL; 502] *Opposite:* weakness.

determine 1 *v* **decide**, settle, conclude, resolve, agree, finalize. [➡MAKE DECISIONS AND CHOICES; 753] 2 *v* **find out**, verify, ascertain (*formal*), clarify, uncover, establish. [➡LEARN AND DISCOVER; 763] 3 *v* **influence**, affect, shape, mould, form. [➡CREATION; 347] 4 *v* **control**, regulate, govern, fix, limit, define. [➡CAUSE TO HAPPEN; 31]

determined *adj* **strong-minded**, resolute, gritty, single-minded, unwavering, firm, dogged, indomitable, untiring, heroic. [➡STRENGTH OF WILL; 502] *Opposite:* irresolute.

determiner *type of* **word class**. [➡ASPECTS OF LANGUAGE; 683]

determining *adj* **decisive**, causal, defining, influential, shaping, responsible. [➡MOST IMPORTANT AND MAIN; 194] *Opposite:* irrelevant.

deterrence *n* **discouragement**, dissuasion, pre-emption, prevention, restriction, limitation. [➡PROBLEM; 257] *Opposite:* encouragement.

deterrent 1 *adj* **warning**, preventive, restrictive, restraining, limiting, constraining. [➡AVOID, PREVENT, LIMIT, AND CONTROL; 278] *Opposite:* encouraging. 2 *n* **restraint**, disincentive, rein, curb, limit, constraint, limitation. [➡AVOID, PREVENT, LIMIT, AND CONTROL; 278] *Opposite:* incitement.

detest *v* **hate**, loathe, despise, abhor (*formal*), abominate (*formal*), dislike. [➡DISLIKE AND HATE; 578] *Opposite:* love.

detestable *adj* **hateful**, despicable, repugnant, vile, revolting, abominable, abhorrent (*formal*), loathsome. [➡EMOTIONALLY UNPLEASANT AND UPSETTING; 228] *Opposite:* lovable.

detestation *n* **hatred**, hate, abhorrence, loathing, dislike, abomination (*literary*). [➡IRRITATION AND ANGER; 542] *Opposite:* adoration.

detested *adj* [➡UNPOPULAR AND UNWANTED; 259]

dethrone *v* **depose**, oust, unseat, overthrow, overwhelm, triumph, defeat, remove. [➡REVOKE STATUS; 460] *Opposite:* install.

detonate *v* **explode**, blow up, set off, ignite, spark off, discharge (*formal*). [➡CAUSE TO START; 266]

detonation *n* **explosion**, blast, ignition, discharge (*formal*), report, bang. [➡SUDDEN EVENT; 52]

detour *n* **deviation**, diversion, roundabout route, alternative route, long way round, indirect route, bypass, long way around (*US*). [➡TRAVEL: JOURNEYS AND TRIPS; 319]

detoxication *see* **detoxification.**

detoxification *n* **cleansing**, decontamination, depollution, purification, reclamation, cleaning, clearing. [➡CLEAN AND POLISH; 404] *Opposite:* contamination.

detoxify *v* **cleanse**, purify, clear, clean, depollute, decontaminate, reclaim. [➡CLEAN AND POLISH; 404] *Opposite:* contaminate.

detract *v* **take away from**, diminish, lessen, reduce, weaken, undermine. [➡WORSEN SOMETHING; 381] *Opposite:* bolster.

detraction 1 *n* (*formal*) **slander**, abuse, disparagement, aspersion, denigration, calumny (*formal*). [➡INSULTS, ABUSE, AND SWEARING; 659] *Opposite:* praise. 2 *n* **lessening**, reduction, subtraction, taking away, deduction, diminution. [➡CHANGE OF SIZE: SMALLER; 394] *Opposite:* addition.

detractor *n* **critic**, disparager, decrier (*formal*), knocker (*informal*), cynic, heckler, attacker. [➡GRUMPY AND NEGATIVE PEOPLE; 953] *Opposite:* supporter.

detriment *n* **disadvantage**, loss, harm, damage, injury, impairment. [➡PROBLEM; 257] *Opposite:* advantage.

detrimental *adj* **harmful**, damaging, disadvantageous, unfavourable, negative, injurious. [➡DANGEROUS; 237] *Opposite:* beneficial.

detritus *n* **debris**, litter, waste, trash, rubbish, flotsam and jetsam, leftovers, scraps, garbage (*US*). [➡RUBBISH AND USELESS OBJECTS; 1248]

de trop *adj* [➡TOO MUCH; 118]

deuce *n* **tie**, draw, even-steven (*informal*), level pegging. [➡SPORTS TERMS; 877]

devaluation *n* **deflation**, depreciation, reduction, depression, devaluing, weakening. [➡MARKET FORCES; 803] *Opposite:* appreciation.

devalue *v* **diminish**, lessen, undervalue, bring down, cheapen, revalue, devaluate, degrade, debase, reduce. [➡CHANGE OF INTENSITY: LESS; 396] *Opposite:* overvalue.

devastate 1 *v* **destroy**, demolish, ravage, wreck, ruin, spoil. [➡DESTRUCTION AND DEMOLITION; 360] *Opposite:* preserve. 2 *v* **overwhelm**, overcome, shock, distress, upset, shatter, confound, destroy. [➡UPSET, DISTRESS, AND HUMILIATE; 568] *Opposite:* comfort.

devastated *adj* **overwhelmed**, overcome, shattered, confounded, shocked, distressed, upset, distraught. [➡SADNESS, DISTRESS, AND DESPAIR; 540] *Opposite:* comforted.

devastating 1 *adj* **destructive**, harmful, damaging, ruinous, injurious, dreadful. [➡DANGEROUS; 237] 2 *adj* **overwhelming**, shocking, upsetting, disturbing, distressing, shattering, demoralizing. [➡EMOTIONALLY UNPLEASANT AND UPSETTING; 228] *Opposite:* comforting.

devastatingly *adv* **terribly**, dreadfully, overwhelmingly, extraordinarily, hugely, extremely, very. [➡EXTRAORDINARY: AMAZING; 205]

devastation *n* **destruction**, damage, ruin, desolation, waste, wreckage. [➡DESTRUCTION AND DEMOLITION; 360] *Opposite:* preservation.

develop 1 *v* **grow**, mature, progress, advance, change, improve, ripen. [➡CHANGE; 373] 2 *v* **arise**, result, happen, stem, come, come into being. [➡GRADUALLY COME INTO EXISTENCE; 1] 3 *v* **acquire**, pick up, foster, create, breed, get, obtain. [➡GET; 421] 4 *v* **expand**, enlarge, extend, increase, widen, build up, work up. [➡CHANGE OF SIZE: BIGGER; 393] *Opposite:* contract. 5 *v* **work out**, flesh out, expound, fill in, explain, elaborate, enlarge, amplify. [➡EXPLAIN AND CLARIFY; 611] *Opposite:* outline. 6 *v* **build on**, exploit, utilize, build. [➡MAKE GOOD USE OF SOMETHING; 474] 7 *v* **improve**, do up, renovate, refurbish, remodel, upgrade. [➡MANUFACTURE; 350]

developed *adj* **technologically advanced**, industrialized, advanced, established, settled. [➡WEALTH AND WEALTHY; 891] *Opposite:* developing.

developer 1 *n* **designer**, creator, inventor, brains, maker, originator. [➡DESIGNERS, CREATORS AND INSTIGATORS; 348] 2 *n* **buyer**, property developer, land developer, contractor, speculator. [➡BUSINESS PEOPLE; 794] 3 *type of* **photographic equipment.** [➡PHOTOGRAPHY AND PHOTOGRAPHIC EQUIPMENT; 1121]

developing *adj* **emerging**, emergent, evolving. [➡ABOUT TO HAPPEN; 33] *Opposite:* developed.

development 1 *n* **event**, happening, occurrence, change, incident, stage. [➡EVENTS AND OCCURRENCES; 35] 2 *n* **growth**, expansion, progress, advance, change, increase, enlargement, improvement, elaboration. [➡PROGRESS AND ADVANCEMENT; 214] *Opposite:* stasis. 3 *n* **enhancement**, expansion, advancement, training, education, extension. [➡TEACHING; 839]

developmental 1 *adj* **developing**, growing, evolving, changing, progressive. [➡HAPPENING AND IN PROGRESS; 32] *Opposite:* static. 2 *adj* **age-related**, age-linked, growth-related, hormonal, child-development. [➡REPRODUCTION AND HEREDITY; 726]

deviance *n* **nonconformity**, unconventionality, eccentricity, unorthodoxy, aberration, abnormality, deviation, deviancy. [➡DIFFERENCE; 150] *Opposite:* conformity.

deviant *adj* **different**, divergent, nonstandard, aberrant, irregular, out of the ordinary, unusual, unexpected. [➡DIFFERENCE; 150] *Opposite:* standard.

deviate 1 *v* **differ**, depart, diverge, stray, digress. [➡CHANGE DIRECTION OF MOTION; 345] *Opposite:* conform. 2 *v* **diverge**, move away, stray, depart, swerve, turn aside, turn from, turn off. [➡CHANGE DIRECTION OF MOTION; 345] *Opposite:* keep to.

deviation 1 *n* **difference**, departure, change, divergence, variation, digression. [➡CHANGE DIRECTION OF MOTION; 345] 2 *n*

nonconformity, unconventionality, eccentricity, unorthodoxy, aberration, abnormality, deviance, deviancy. [➡DIFFERENCE; 150]

device 1 *n* **machine**, tool, piece of equipment, mechanism, apparatus, appliance, gadget, contrivance, contraption. [➡DEVICES; 1114] 2 *n* **expedient**, manoeuvre, stratagem, ruse, dodge, trick, means, ploy, scheme, method, way, plan. [➡WAYS OF DOING THINGS; 295] 3 *n* **design**, emblem, logo, badge, crest, symbol. [➡SYMBOLS, SIGNS, AND NUMBERS; 597]

devil *n* [➡VILLAINS AND THUGS; 947]

devil's food cake *type of* **cake**. [➡CAKES, BISCUITS, AND DESSERTS; 1180]

devious 1 *adj* **deceitful**, tricky, scheming, designing, wily, underhand, conniving, Machiavellian, sneaky, cunning, crafty, sly. [➡DECEITFUL; 514] *Opposite:* straightforward. 2 *adj* **circuitous**, oblique, meandering, tortuous, winding, roundabout. [➡DIRECTION OF MOTION; 346] *Opposite:* direct.

deviously *adv* **deceitfully**, sneakily, cunningly, artfully, subtly, cleverly. [➡DECEITFUL; 514] *Opposite:* straightforwardly.

deviousness *n* **guile**, cunning, artfulness, deceitfulness, untrustworthiness, shadiness, underhandedness. [➡DECEITFUL; 514] *Opposite:* straightforwardness.

devise *v* **think up**, plan, work out, invent, create, formulate, set up, concoct, conceive, contrive. [➡INSTITUTE AND INAUGURATE; 349]

devoid *adj* **empty**, barren, without, bereft, lacking, wanting. [➡LACK OF POSSESSION; 446] *Opposite:* full.

devolution *n* **decentralization**, delegation, transference, transfer, federalization. [➡STYLES AND SYSTEMS OF GOVERNMENT; 806] *Opposite:* centralization.

devolve *v* **transfer**, decentralize, give to, hand to, pass to, delegate, entrust. [➡GIVE AND PROVIDE; 431] *Opposite:* centralize.

devote *v* **dedicate**, give, offer, apply, bestow (*formal*), assign, allocate, allot. [➡GIVE AND PROVIDE; 431]

devoted 1 *adj* **committed**, loving, caring, affectionate, kind, fond, attentive, supportive, dedicated, dutiful. [➡GENEROSITY AND KINDNESS; 496] *Opposite:* uncaring. 2 *adj* **dedicated**, loyal, dutiful, faithful, staunch, constant, committed. [➡HARD-WORKING AND COMMITTED; 501] *Opposite:* uncommitted. 3 *adj* **keen**, enthusiastic, dedicated, ardent, fervent, zealous, fanatical. [➡ENERGY AND ENTHUSIASM; 497] *Opposite:* unenthusiastic.

devotedly 1 *adv* **lovingly**, caringly, affectionately, kindly, fondly, attentively, supportively. [➡GENEROSITY AND KINDNESS; 496] *Opposite:* uncaringly. 2 *adv* **loyally**, faithfully, dutifully, staunchly, consistently, unfailingly. [➡HARD-WORKING AND COMMITTED; 501] *Opposite:* unreliably. 3 *adv* **keenly**, enthusiastically, ardently, fervently, fanatically, zealously. [➡APPRECIATION AND GRATITUDE; 536] *Opposite:* unenthusiastically.

devotee 1 *n* **fan**, follower, supporter, aficionado, enthusiast, aficionada. [➡DEVOTEES AND ADDICTED PEOPLE; 557] 2 *n* **disciple**, follower, believer, votary. [➡DEVOTEES AND ADDICTED PEOPLE; 557]

devotion 1 *n* **commitment**, attachment, love, fondness, affection, adoration. [➡APPRECIATION AND GRATITUDE; 536] *Opposite:* dislike. 2 *n* **dedication**, care, attentiveness, support, loyalty, fidelity, constancy, commitment, steadfastness. [➡LOVE, RESPECT, AND GOODWILL; 550] *Opposite:* neglect. 3 *n* **enthusiasm**, admiration, zeal, keenness, fervour. [➡ENERGY AND ENTHUSIASM; 497] *Opposite:* apathy. 4 *n* (*formal*) **piety**, devoutness, religious zeal, religious fervour, religious observance, dedication, consecration, commitment. [➡MORALLY GOOD; 775] *Opposite:* impiety.

devotional *adj* **religious**, worshipful, worshipping, prayerful, holy, sacred, ceremonial, ritual. [➡RELIGIONS AND RELIGIOUS PRACTICES; 778]

devotions *n* **prayers**, holy rites, observances, supplications (*formal*). [➡RELIGIONS AND RELIGIOUS PRACTICES; 778]

devour 1 *v* **consume**, demolish, dispose of, gulp, scoff (*informal*), wolf, gobble. [➡EAT AND NOT EAT; 711] 2 *v* (*literary*) **overwhelm**, overcome, engulf, consume, destroy, use up, obsess. [➡UPSET, DISTRESS, AND HUMILIATE; 568]

devout 1 *adj* **religious**, pious, spiritual, devoted, dedicated, committed, staunch. [➡RELIGIOUS CONCEPTS; 777] *Opposite:* uncommitted. 2 *adj* (*formal*) **sincere**, heartfelt, deep, earnest, fervent, serious. [➡TRUE AND REAL; 172] *Opposite:* insincere.

devoutly 1 *adv* **religiously**, piously, spiritually, devotedly, staunchly. [➡RELIGIOUS CONCEPTS; 777] 2 *adv* (*formal*) **sincerely**, earnestly, fervently, deeply, seriously. [➡TO A GREAT EXTENT; 130] *Opposite:* insincerely.

devoutness *n* **piety**, spirituality, religious fervour, religious zeal, piousness. [➡RELIGIOUS CONCEPTS; 777] *Opposite:* impiety.

dew *n* **droplets**, precipitation, condensation, dewdrops. [➡MOIST; 1240]

dewdrop *n* **bead of moisture**, droplet, drop, drip. [➡AMOUNT OF LIQUID; 114]

dewy *adj* **wet**, dew-covered, heavy with dew, damp, moist. [➡MOIST; 1240] *Opposite:* dry.

dewy-eyed *adj* **innocent**, naive, trusting, inexperienced, unrealistic, idealistic, sentimental, soppy (*informal*). [➡NEGATIVE INTELLECTUAL CHARACTERISTICS; 526] *Opposite:* down-to-earth.

dexterity 1 *n* **deftness**, skill, adroitness, handiness, legerdemain, agility, nimbleness, dexterousness. [➡SKILLS, TALENTS, AND ABILITIES; 527] *Opposite:* clumsiness. 2 *n* **ingenuity**, acuity, sharpness, quickness, resourcefulness, quick-wittedness, ability. [➡POSITIVE INTELLECTUAL CHARACTERISTICS; 525] *Opposite:* ineptitude.

dexterous 1 *adj* **deft**, adroit, handy, nimble-fingered, nimble, agile, expert. [➡TALENTED AND SKILFUL; 528] *Opposite:* clumsy. 2 *adj* **quick-witted**, sharp, acute, resourceful, clever, ingenious, able, adept, efficient, skilful. [➡POSITIVE INTELLECTUAL CHARACTERISTICS; 525] *Opposite:* inept.

dexterousness *n* [➡SKILLS, TALENTS, AND ABILITIES; 527]

dextrose *type of* **nutrient.** [➡FOOD COMPONENTS; 1187]

dextrous *see* **dexterous.**

dhow *type of* **sailing vessel.** [➡SHIPS AND BOATS; 1149]

diacritic *n* [➡ASPECTS OF LANGUAGE; 683]

diacritic

◆ *types of diacritic*
accent, acute, apostrophe, cedilla, circumflex, diaeresis, grave, háček, tilde, umlaut

diadem *n* **crown**, tiara, circlet, coronet, wreath, headband, headdress. [➡JEWELLERY; 866]

diaeresis *type of* **diacritic.** [➡ASPECTS OF LANGUAGE; 683]

diagnose *v* **make a diagnosis**, identify, analyse, spot, detect, make out, establish. [➡MAKE DECISIONS AND CHOICES; 753]

diagnosis *n* **identification**, analysis, judgment, finding, verdict, opinion, conclusion. [➡POINT OF VIEW; 768]

diagnostic *adj* **analytic**, analytical, indicative, investigative, problem-solving, pinpointing. [➡EXAMINE AND ASSESS; 754]

diagonal *adj* **slanting**, oblique, sloping, crossways, crosswise, transverse. [➡ORIENTATION AND ALIGNMENT; 1222]

diagram *n* **drawing**, figure, illustration, plan, map, chart, table, graph, scheme, schema. [➡DRAWINGS, CHARTS AND TABLES; 595]

diagrammatic *adj* **graphic**, illustrative, pictorial, visual, drawn. [➡REPRESENTATIVE; 66] *Opposite:* verbal.

dial 1 *n* **face**, gauge, indicator, disc, control panel, clock face. [➡PARTS OF MACHINES AND TOOLS; 1117] 2 *n* **knob**, handle, control, button. [➡PARTS OF MACHINES AND TOOLS; 1117] 3 *v* **call**, telephone, phone, phone up, ring, call up, ring up. [➡TELEPHONE AND PAGE; 682]

dialect *n* **vernacular**, language, parlance, tongue, idiom, talk. [➡ASPECTS OF LANGUAGE; 683]

dialectic 1 *n* **tension**, conflict, interaction, clash, opposition, contention. [➡ARGUMENT; 47] *Opposite:* harmony. 2 *n* **discussion**, debate, disputation (*formal*), investigation, examination, analysis. [➡EXAMINE AND ASSESS; 754]

dialogue 1 *n* **discussion**, exchange of ideas, channel of communication, discourse, interchange, information flow, negotiation. [➡NEGOTIATION AND DEBATE; 46] 2 *n* (*formal*) **conversation**, interview, chat, discussion, discourse, talk. [➡INFORMAL COMMUNICATION; 45]

diamanté 1 *adj* **glittery**, sparkly, glittering, sparkling, diamantine, rhinestone. [➡BEAUTY AND ATTRACTIVENESS; 190] *Opposite:* dull. 2 *n* **rhinestones**, paste, strass. [➡PRECIOUS STONES; 1277]

diameter *n* **width**, thickness, breadth, length, distance, span. [➡WIDTH: WIDE; 1198]

diametrically *adv* **absolutely**, completely, utterly, totally, entirely, wholly. [➡ABSOLUTE AND ABSOLUTELY; 131] *Opposite:* partially.

diamond 1 *n* **rhombus**, parallelogram, lozenge, equilateral. [➡ANGULAR SHAPE; 1216] 2 *type of* **gemstone.** [➡PRECIOUS STONES; 1277]

diamondback *type of* **poisonous snake.** [➡SNAKE; 995]

diaphanous *adj* **transparent**, delicate, gauzy, see-through, sheer, gossamer, filmy, thin. [➡VISUAL TEXTURE; 1220] *Opposite:* opaque.

diaphragm 1 *type of* **muscle or tendon.** [➡THE MUSCLES; 719] 2 *part of* **photographic equipment.** [➡PHOTOGRAPHY AND PHOTOGRAPHIC EQUIPMENT; 1121]

diarist *n* **memoirist**, writer, autobiographer, author, chronicler, memoir writer. [➡WRITERS AND STYLES; 914]

diary 1 *n* **appointment book**, personal organizer, year planner, calendar, schedule. [➡LISTS AND SCHEDULES; 588] 2 *n* **journal**, record, log, chronicle, memoir, account. [➡RECORDS; 586]

diaspora *n* **dispersion**, scattering, movement, displacement, migration, spread. [➡SEPARATE AND DIVIDE; 402] *Opposite:* concentration.

diatribe *n* **criticism**, attack, tirade, invective (*formal*), denunciation, harangue, rant, discourse. [➡CRITICISMS AND ANGRY OUTBURSTS; 50]

dice 1 *v* **cube**, cut up, chop, cut into cubes. [➡TEAR, BREAK, AND CUT; 361] 2 *v* **gamble**, risk, stake, bet, wager, venture, hazard, chance. [➡GAMBLE AND TAKE RISKS; 467]

dice with death *v* **face danger**, sail close to the wind, play a dangerous game, cut it fine, play Russian roulette, court disaster, run a risk, take a risk. [➡GAMBLE AND TAKE RISKS; 467]

dicey (*informal*) *adj* **risky**, dangerous, hazardous, chancy, uncertain, unpredictable, dubious. [➡DANGEROUS; 237] *Opposite:* safe.

dichotomy *n* **contrast**, opposition, irreconcilable difference, contradiction, gulf, separation, clash. [➡DIFFERENCE; 150] *Opposite:* harmony.

dicker (*informal*) *v* **bargain**, haggle, argue, trade, wrangle, exchange. [➡ARGUE AND FIGHT – TWO-WAY; 644]

dicky (*informal*) *type of* **accessory.** [➡HABERDASHERY, MILLINERY, AND LINGERIE; 867]

dicky bow (*informal*) *type of* **accessory.** [➡HABERDASHERY, MILLINERY, AND LINGERIE; 867]

dictate 1 *v* **speak**, say, say aloud, read out, read aloud, utter, verbalize. [➡RECITE, REPEAT, AND NARRATE; 621] 2 *v* **order**, state, command, decree, ordain (*formal*), lay down, prescribe, impose. [➡REQUEST AND DEMAND; 664] 3 *v* **control**, determine, have a bearing on, influence, shape, affect, direct (*formal*). [➡CAUSE TO HAPPEN; 31] 4 *n* **principle**, rule, standard, precept (*formal*), tenet (*formal*). [➡IDEA AND THOUGHT; 771] 5 *n* **command**, order, decree, prescription, injunction, directive, diktat, edict, pronouncement. [➡REQUEST AND DEMAND; 664]

dictation *n* **transcription**, notation, transcript. [➡WRITING; 584]

dictator *n* **tyrant**, ruler, despot, autocrat, authoritarian, totalitarian. [➡VILLAINS AND THUGS; 947] *Opposite:* democrat.

dictatorial *adj* **tyrannical**, despotic, autocratic, authoritarian, overbearing, domineering, arrogant, imperious, officious, high-handed, heavy-handed, bossy, dogmatic. [➡BOSSY AND OVERBEARING; 517] *Opposite:* democratic.

dictatorship 1 *n* **regime**, government, rule, era, reign, leadership, junta, reign of terror. [➡STYLES AND SYSTEMS OF GOVERNMENT; 806] 2 *n* **despotism**, autocracy, totalitarianism, authoritarianism, tyranny, repression, absolute rule, one-party rule. [➡STYLES AND SYSTEMS OF GOVERNMENT; 806] *Opposite:* democracy.

diction 1 *n* **pronunciation**, enunciation, articulation, delivery, elocution, projection, speech, accent. [➡ASPECTS OF LANGUAGE; 683] 2 *n* **wording**, language, expression, phraseology, phrasing, style, choice of words. [➡ASPECTS OF LANGUAGE; 683]

dictionary *n* **lexicon**, vocabulary, glossary, phrase book, word list, thesaurus. [➡LISTS AND SCHEDULES; 588]

dictum (*formal*) *n* **pronouncement**, dictate, saying, statement, maxim, motto, aphorism, truism. [➡THE ORAL TRADITION; 678]

dicynodont *type of* **dinosaur**. [➡DINOSAUR; 996]

didactic *adj* **educational**, instructive, informative, edifying, teaching, improving, moralizing, moralistic, moral. [➡INTERESTING AND MEANINGFUL; 191]

didgeridoo *type of* **wind instrument**. [➡MUSICAL INSTRUMENTS; 910]

die 1 *v* **expire**, pass away, pass on, depart this life (*formal*), decease (*formal*), perish (*literary*), give up the ghost (*literary*), kick the bucket (*slang*), croak (*slang*). [➡DIE; 922] *Opposite:* live. 2 *v* **pack up** (*informal*), stop, pack in (*informal*), give out, conk out (*informal*), go dead, break down, fail, go down, crash. [➡FAIL OR CEASE TO FUNCTION; 471] *Opposite:* start.

die a death *v* [➡CEASE TO EXIST; 22]

die away *v* **fade**, fade away, dwindle, fizzle, ebb, wane, diminish, dip, drop, decline, recede, peter out. [➡CEASE TO EXIST; 22] *Opposite:* revive.

die down *v* **subside**, decrease, lessen, diminish, decline, recede, abate (*formal or literary*). [➡CHANGE OF INTENSITY: LESS; 396] *Opposite:* revive.

diehard 1 *adj* **intransigent**, reactionary, conservative, traditionalist, dyed-in-the-wool, fogyish, conformist, stick-in-the-mud (*informal*). [➡UNWILLINGNESS AND STUBBORNNESS; 565] *Opposite:* progressive. 2 *n* **reactionary**, intransigent (*formal*), conservative, traditionalist, fogy, conformist, stick-in-the-mud (*informal*), member of the old guard, member of the old school. [➡UNCOOPERATIVE OR REBELLIOUS PERSON; 567] *Opposite:* progressive.

die of *v* **succumb**, fall victim to, surrender, yield, submit, capitulate. [➡DIE; 922] *Opposite:* survive.

die off *v* **die out**, become extinct, perish (*literary*), expire, pass away, pass on, disappear, vanish. [➡CEASE TO EXIST; 22] *Opposite:* survive.

die out *v* **become extinct**, disappear, vanish, perish (*literary*), die off, pass away, pass on, expire. [➡CEASE TO EXIST; 22] *Opposite:* survive.

diet 1 *n* **food**, fare, nourishment, nutrition, regime, regimen. [➡FOOD; 1166] 2 *n* **regime**, intake, supply, regimen, stock, quantity. [➡AMOUNT AND QUANTITY; 112] 3 *v* **slim**, starve, fast, cut back, cut down, abstain, reduce (*US*), slenderize (*US dated*). [➡EAT AND NOT EAT; 711] *Opposite:* binge. 4 *n* **parliament**, legislature, assembly, council, congress, senate. [➡LEGISLATIVE BODIES AND LEGISLATION; 809]

dietary *adj* **nutritional**, dietetic, eating, alimentary, alimental, nutritive. [➡FOOD; 1166]

dieter *n* **slimmer**, weightwatcher, faster, starver, abstainer. [➡EATERS, GOURMETS, AND DIETARY CHOICES; 715]

differ 1 *v* **be different**, be unlike, be at variance, vary, fluctuate, change, diverge, contrast. [➡DIFFERENCE; 150] *Opposite:* match. 2 *v* **disagree**, argue, quarrel, fall out, wrangle, be at odds, be at variance, clash. [➡ARGUE AND FIGHT - TWO-WAY; 644] *Opposite:* agree.

difference 1 *n* **dissimilarity**, disparity, distinction, differentiation, divergence, variation, variance, contrast, diversity, discrepancy. [➡DIFFERENCE; 150] *Opposite:* similarity. 2 *n* **change**, alteration, variance, modification, transformation, metamorphosis. [➡DIFFERENCE; 150] *Opposite:* consistency. 3 *n* **argument**, dispute, disagreement, quarrel, contretemps (*formal*), tiff, spat, barney (*informal*). [➡ARGUMENT; 47]

difference of opinion *n* [➡ARGUMENT; 47]

different 1 *adj* **dissimilar**, diverse, unlike, unalike, poles apart, as like as chalk and cheese, changed, altered, not the same. [➡DIFFERENCE; 150] *Opposite:* similar. 2 *adj* **distinct**, separate, discrete, another. [➡DIFFERENCE; 150] *Opposite:* same. 3 *adj* **unusual**, special, singular, distinctive, atypical, out of the ordinary, uncommon, unique. [➡EXTRAORDINARY: UNCOMMON; 206] *Opposite:* run-of-the-mill.

differential *n* **difference**, discrepancy, disparity, gap, variance, distinction. [➡SPEED; 102]

differentiate *v* **distinguish**, discriminate, tell apart, set apart, discern, separate, segregate, single out. [➡EXAMINE AND ASSESS; 754] *Opposite:* confuse.

differentiation 1 *n* **distinction**, discrimination, delineation, demarcation, separation. [➡DIFFERENCE; 150] *Opposite:* assimilation. 2 *n* **difference**, diversity, variation, distinction, discrepancy, disparity. [➡DIFFERENCE; 150] *Opposite:* similarity.

differently *adv* **in a different way**, another way, in your own way, otherwise, inversely, contrarily. [➡DIFFERENCE; 150] *Opposite:* similarly.

differing *adj* **opposing**, contradictory, contrary, divergent, different, opposite, conflicting, clashing. [➡DISHARMONY; 157] *Opposite:* similar.

difficult 1 *adj* **hard**, tricky, complicated, knotty, thorny, complex, intricate. [➡DIFFICULTY AND COMPLEXITY; 243] *Opposite:* easy. 2 *adj* **problematic**, hard, tough, trying, grim, challenging, demanding, testing, arduous, tiring, strenuous, gruelling. [➡PHYSICALLY UNPLEASANT; 227] *Opposite:* simple. 3 *adj*

incomprehensible, unintelligible, impenetrable, involved, complicated, complex, intricate, abstruse, obscure. [➡DIFFICULTY AND COMPLEXITY; 243] *Opposite:* simple. **4** *adj* **obstinate**, stubborn, recalcitrant, intractable, fractious, unmanageable, awkward. [➡UNWILLINGNESS AND STUBBORNNESS; 565] *Opposite:* amenable.

See Compare and Contrast at **hard**.

difficulty 1 *n* **complexity**, complicatedness, intricacy, adversity, complication, trickiness. [➡DIFFICULTY AND COMPLEXITY; 243] **2** *n* **problem**, snag, obstacle, impediment, stumbling block, hurdle. [➡PROBLEM; 257] **3** *n* **trouble**, effort, struggle, exertion, strain, sweat, striving, toil. [➡HARD WORK OR EFFORT; 299] *Opposite:* ease.

diffidence *n* **shyness**, hesitancy, reserve, timidity, reticence, quietness. [➡RETICENT AND UNFORTHCOMING; 632] *Opposite:* brashness.

diffident *adj* **shy**, hesitant, insecure, timid, reticent, reserved, retiring, unobtrusive, self-effacing, quiet. [➡RETICENT AND UNFORTHCOMING; 632] *Opposite:* brash.

diffract *v* **bend**, deflect, curve, divert, spread, diffuse. [➡SPREAD AND SCATTER; 333]

diffraction *n* **deflection**, bending, curving, diversion, spreading, diffusion. [➡CHANGE DIRECTION OF MOTION; 345]

diffuse 1 *v* **disperse**, spread, disseminate, distribute, circulate, scatter, strew. [➡DISPENSE, RATION, AND DISTRIBUTE; 435] *Opposite:* concentrate. **2** *adj* **dispersed**, spread, disseminated, distributed, circulated, scattered, strewn. [➡ORIENTATION AND ALIGNMENT; 1222] *Opposite:* concentrated. **3** *adj* **wordy**, verbose, prolix, long-winded, drawn-out, long-drawn-out, turgid, rambling. [➡INARTICULATE, RAMBLING, AND AWKWARD; 634] *Opposite:* concise.

See Compare and Contrast at **wordy**.

diffusely *adv* **wordily**, verbosely, prolixly, long-windedly, turgidly, ramblingly. [➡INARTICULATE, RAMBLING, AND AWKWARD; 634] *Opposite:* concisely.

diffusion *n* **dispersal**, dispersion, dissemination, distribution, circulation, transmission, flow. [➡DISPENSE, RATION, AND DISTRIBUTE; 435] *Opposite:* concentration.

dig 1 *v* **break up**, plough, turn, hoe, till, rake. [➡TEAR, BREAK, AND CUT; 361] **2** *v* **excavate**, tunnel, hollow out, burrow, mine, quarry. [➡USE TOOLS AND MACHINERY; 469] **3** *v* **prod**, nudge, push, shove, jab, poke. [➡CONTACT: TOUCH; 413] **4** *n* **poke**, prod, nudge, push, shove, jab. [➡CONTACT: TOUCH; 413] **5** *n* **gibe**, taunt, jeer, crack, insult, slur, remark. [➡JOKES AND TEASING; 675] *Opposite:* compliment.

digest 1 *v* **process**, assimilate, absorb, break down, consume, eat. [➡EAT AND NOT EAT; 711] **2** *v* **assimilate**, absorb, take in, take on board, grasp, process. [➡UNDERSTAND AND GRASP; 760] *Opposite:* ignore. **3** *n* **abridgment**, résumé, summary, condensation, abstract, précis. [➡SUMMARIES, OUTLINES, AND EXCERPTS; 589] **4** *n* **publication**, journal, magazine, periodical, book, tome, volume. [➡BOOKS AND BOOKLETS; 591]

digestible *adj* **edible**, palatable, eatable, consumable, comestible (*formal*), esculent (*formal*). [➡FOOD; 1166] *Opposite:* indigestible.

digestion *n* **assimilation**, ingestion, absorption, incorporation, breakdown, consumption. [➡EAT AND NOT EAT; 711]

digestive *adj* **peptic**, gastric, intestinal, gastrointestinal, duodenal, excretory. [➡EAT AND NOT EAT; 711]

digestive tract

◆ *parts of a digestive tract*
alimentary canal, anus, appendix, bile duct, bladder, bowel, caecum, colon, duodenum, gallbladder, gullet, gut, intestine, kidney, large intestine, liver, oesophagus, pancreas, rectum, small intestine, spleen, stomach, throat

digger 1 *n* **miner**, excavator, gravedigger, gold digger, prospector, archaeologist. [➡FARMERS, GARDENERS, AND MANUAL WORKERS; 849] **2** *n* **excavator**, bulldozer, earthmover, crawler, backhoe, shovel. [➡BIKES, CARS, AND CARRIAGES; 1148] **3** *type of* **commercial or industrial vehicle**. [➡VEHICLES; 1144]

diggings *n* **excavation**, mine, quarry, pit, dig. [➡HOLES, GAPS, AND FORKS; 1251]

dig into 1 *v* **stick into**, push into, sink into, stab, prod, jab. [➡CONTACT: TOUCH; 413] **2** *v* **examine**, look at, delve into, investigate, go into, probe, research. [➡EXAMINE AND ASSESS; 754] *Opposite:* ignore.

dig in your heels *v* **stand firm**, hold your ground, stand your ground, hold out, resist, persist, stick it out, be stubborn. [➡NOT DO AND REFUSE TO DO; 275] *Opposite:* give in.

digit *n* **number**, numeral, figure, cipher, character, symbol. [➡SYMBOLS, SIGNS, AND NUMBERS; 597]

digital *adj* **numerical**, numerary, numeral, alphanumeric, cardinal, ordinal, arithmetical. [➡MATHS; 598]

digital cash *n* [➡E-COMMERCE; 1128]

digital signature *n* [➡E-COMMERCE; 1128]

dignified *adj* **distinguished**, honourable, decorous, exalted (*formal*), stately, noble, gracious, imposing, grand, venerable, regal, majestic, self-respecting, proper, respectable. [➡CONFIDENCE AND COMPOSURE; 500] *Opposite:* undignified.

dignify *v* **distinguish**, exalt (*formal*), honour, grace, glorify, venerate. [➡CONFER STATUS; 459] *Opposite:* degrade.

dignitary *n* **notable**, VIP, personage (*formal*), bigwig (*informal*), worthy, celebrity, luminary, public figure. [➡IMPORTANT OR FAMOUS PEOPLE; 893] *Opposite:* nobody.

dignity 1 *n* **self-respect**, self-esteem, pride, self-possession, self-worth. [➡CONFIDENCE AND COMPOSURE; 500] *Opposite:* ignominy. **2** *n* **formality**, gravity, solemnity, grandeur, decorum, stateliness, majesty, poise, composure. [➡GOOD MANNERS AND SOCIAL SKILLS; 521] *Opposite:* informality. **3** *n* **worthiness**, worth, nobility, nobleness, goodness, excellence, respectability, propriety, seemliness. [➡MORALLY GOOD; 775] *Opposite:* unworthiness.

dig out 1 *v* **uncover**, excavate, dig up, unearth, expose, extricate, remove. [➡FIND; 464] *Opposite:* bury. **2** *v* (*informal*) **retrieve**, find, discover, locate, reveal, bring to light, dredge up. [➡FIND; 464]

digress *v* **deviate**, depart, wander, go off at a tangent, stray, ramble, divagate (*literary*). [➡WITTER AND BABBLE; 618] *Opposite:* focus.

digression *n* **deviation**, departure, aside, parenthesis, detour, excursion, foray. [➡DIFFERENCE; 150] *Opposite:* focus.

digs (*dated informal*) *n* **lodgings** (*dated*), lodging, accommodation, rooms, quarters, home, accommodations (*US*). [➡ACCOMMODATION; 855]

dig up **1** *v* **unearth**, excavate, disinter, exhume, expose, uncover. [➡CAUSE TO APPEAR; 5] *Opposite:* bury. **2** *v* (*informal*) **bring to light**, dredge up, expose, reveal, find, discover. [➡FIND; 464] *Opposite:* hide.

dik-dik *type of* **deer or antelope**. [➡DEER AND ANTELOPE; 981]

diktat *n* **command**, decree, edict, dictate, order, instruction. [➡REQUEST AND DEMAND; 664]

dilapidated *adj* **decrepit**, rundown, derelict, ramshackle, on its last legs, the worse for wear, tumbledown, broken-down, ruined, destroyed, wrecked, shabby, beat-up (*informal*). [➡IN BAD REPAIR; 1233] *Opposite:* pristine.

dilapidation *n* **disrepair**, dereliction, decrepitude, decay, ruin, destruction, collapse, shabbiness. [➡IN BAD REPAIR; 1233]

dilate **1** *v* **expand**, widen, open, enlarge, increase, stretch, distend, amplify. [➡CHANGE OF SIZE: BIGGER; 393] *Opposite:* contract. **2** *v* **amplify**, expatiate, expand, dwell on, expound, elucidate (*formal*), elaborate. [➡EXPLAIN AND CLARIFY; 611] *Opposite:* abbreviate.

dilation *n* **expansion**, opening, enlargement, increase, distension, stretching. [➡EXPLAIN AND CLARIFY; 611] *Opposite:* contraction.

dilatory *adj* **slow**, tardy, remiss, behindhand, slack, problem, negligent, lazy, lagging, dragging, flagging, laggard, slow-paced, slow-going. [➡MOVING SLOWLY; 105] *Opposite:* prompt.

dilemma *n* **quandary**, tight spot, catch-22, predicament, impasse, problem, catch. [➡PROBLEM; 257]

dilettante *n* **amateur**, dabbler, abecedarian, neophyte, novice. [➡UNSKILLED PERSON; 531] *Opposite:* expert.

diligence *n* **assiduousness**, meticulousness, conscientiousness, thoroughness, attentiveness, carefulness, persistence, industry (*formal or literary*). [➡HARD-WORKING AND COMMITTED; 501] *Opposite:* carelessness.

diligent *adj* **industrious**, assiduous, painstaking, meticulous, conscientious, thorough, attentive, careful, persistent. [➡HARD-WORKING AND COMMITTED; 501] *Opposite:* lazy.

dill *type of* **herb**. [➡HERBS AND SPICES; 1174]

dilly (*US slang*) *n* [➡AMAZING THING; 212]

dilly-dally *v* **dawdle**, dally, delay, shilly-shally, drag your heels, waste time. [➡SHIRK AND DELAY; 274] *Opposite:* hurry.

dilly-dallying *n* [➡DELAY ACTION OR OCCURRENCE; 279]

dilute **1** *v* **thin**, weaken, water down, adulterate. [➡CHANGE OF INTENSITY: LESS; 396] *Opposite:* concentrate. **2** *v* **reduce**, attenuate, temper, mitigate, water down, take the edge off, offset. [➡CHANGE OF INTENSITY: LESS; 396] *Opposite:* increase. **3** *adj* **weak**, watered down, thinned, watery, insipid, diluted. [➡FLUID AND NON-SOLID; 1212] *Opposite:* concentrated.

diluted *adj* **weak**, watered down, thinned, watery, dilute. [➡FLUID AND NON-SOLID; 1212] *Opposite:* concentrated.

dilution **1** *n* **thinning**, weakening, watering down, watering. [➡CHANGE OF INTENSITY: LESS; 396] **2** *n* **reduction**, attenuation, enfeeblement, erosion, weakening. [➡CHANGE OF INTENSITY: LESS; 396] *Opposite:* strengthening. **3** *n* **concentration**, strength, intensity, potency. [➡DEGREE AND EXTENT; 110]

dim **1** *adj* **badly lit**, murky, gloomy, shadowy, dusky, dark. [➡DESCRIBING LIGHT; 1227] *Opposite:* bright. **2** *adj* **soft**, faint, muted, weak, diffuse, dull. [➡DESCRIBING LIGHT; 1227] *Opposite:* strong. **3** *adj* **indistinct**, vague, blurred, blurry, hazy, faint, unclear, shadowy, subdued. [➡VAGUENESS; 244] *Opposite:* clear. **4** *v* **turn down**, lower, darken, reduce. [➡CHANGE OF INTENSITY: LESS; 396] *Opposite:* turn up.

dimension **1** *n* **measurement**, length, height, width, breadth. [➡SIZE AND DIMENSIONS; 1191] **2** *n* **aspect**, element, facet, feature, factor, component. [➡QUALITIES AND CHARACTERISTICS; 1190]

dimensions *n* **size**, scope, extent, magnitude, proportions. [➡SIZE AND DIMENSIONS; 1191]

dime store (*US*) *type of* **retail outlet**. [➡RETAIL OUTLETS; 1082]

diminish **1** *v* **reduce**, lessen, make smaller, weaken, moderate, contract. [➡CHANGE OF INTENSITY: LESS; 396] *Opposite:* increase. **2** *v* **shrink**, ebb, fade, fade away, fade out, peter out, taper. [➡CEASE TO EXIST; 22] *Opposite:* grow.

diminishing *adj* **lessening**, fading, waning, weakening, falling, shrinking. [➡CEASE TO EXIST; 22] *Opposite:* increasing.

diminuendo *type of* **musical term**. [➡MUSIC, SONGS, AND SINGING; 907]

diminution *n* **decrease**, reduction, lessening, attenuation, shrinking, dwindling, contraction. [➡CHANGE OF INTENSITY: LESS; 396] *Opposite:* growth.

diminutive *adj* **small**, little, tiny, minuscule, miniature, minute, pocket-size, pint-size (*informal*). [➡SMALL; 1194] *Opposite:* huge.

dimly **1** *adv* **softly**, faintly, mutedly, weakly, diffusely. [➡DESCRIBING LIGHT; 1227] *Opposite:* brightly. **2** *adv* **indistinctly**, vaguely, hazily, faintly, obscurely, blurrily, unclearly. [➡VAGUENESS; 244] *Opposite:* clearly.

dimmer *n* **light switch**, dimmer switch, brightness control, regulator, rheostat. [➡PARTS OF MACHINES AND TOOLS; 1117]

dimness **1** *n* **softness**, faintness, weakness, diffuseness, dullness. [➡DESCRIBING LIGHT; 1227] *Opposite:* brightness. **2** *n* **murkiness**, gloom, gloominess, shadowiness, duskiness, darkness. [➡DESCRIBING LIGHT; 1227] *Opposite:* brightness. **3** *n* **indistinctness**, vagueness, blurriness, haziness, faintness, shadowiness. [➡VAGUENESS; 244] *Opposite:* clearness.

dimple *n* **hollow**, depression, pit, indentation, dent, dint. [➡ FACIAL CHARACTERISTICS; 482] *Opposite:* bump.

dimpled 1 *adj* **dimply**, cleft, indented, dented, chubby, plump. [➡ FACIAL CHARACTERISTICS; 482] *Opposite:* smooth. 2 *adj* **textured**, indented, dented, pocked, pockmarked, pitted, orange-peel, uneven. [➡ FACIAL CHARACTERISTICS; 482] *Opposite:* smooth.

din 1 *n* **noise**, hubbub, rumpus, racket (*informal*), hullabaloo, commotion, disturbance, pandemonium, tumult. [➡ CHAOS AND UPROAR; 51] 2 *v* **drum into**, hammer, inculcate, instil, impress. [➡ CLAIM, INSIST, AND EMPHASIZE; 615]

dine *v* **eat**, feast, banquet, consume, ingest, partake. [➡ EAT AND NOT EAT; 711]

diner 1 *n* **patron**, customer, guest. [➡ EATERS, GOURMETS, AND DIETARY CHOICES; 715] 2 (*US*) *type of* **eating place**. [➡ RETAIL OUTLETS; 1082]

ding 1 *n* **ringing**, ring, dong, ding-dong, ding-a-ling, ting-a-ling, tinkle. [➡ RINGING AND TOOTING SOUNDS; 1258] 2 *v* **ring**, tinkle, dong. [➡ EMIT RINGING AND TOOTING SOUNDS; 368] *Opposite:* ding-dong. 3 *n* (*US informal*) **dent**, indentation, dint, hollow, dimple, pit, mark. [➡ HOLES, GAPS, AND FORKS; 1251]

ding-a-ling *type of* **ringing sound**. [➡ RINGING AND TOOTING SOUNDS; 1258]

ding-dong 1 *n* (*informal*) **argument**, spat, row, quarrel, tiff, barney (*informal*). [➡ ARGUMENT; 47] 2 *type of* **ringing sound**. [➡ RINGING AND TOOTING SOUNDS; 1258]

dinge *n* **filth**, grime, mess, muck (*informal*), grunge (*informal*), dirt. [➡ UNPLEASANT AND DIRTY SUBSTANCES; 1267] *Opposite:* cleanliness.

dinghy *type of* **small vessel**. [➡ SHIPS AND BOATS; 1149]

dinginess 1 *n* **dirtiness**, discoloration, griminess, dullness, dreariness, grubbiness. [➡ DIRTY; 1234] *Opposite:* brightness. 2 *n* **shabbiness**, drabness, squalidness, cheerlessness, seediness. [➡ IN BAD REPAIR; 1233] *Opposite:* neatness.

dingo *type of* **canine**. [➡ CANINE; 979]

dingy 1 *adj* **dirty**, grimy, soiled, grubby, begrimed (*literary*), besmirched (*literary*), dull. [➡ DIRTY; 1234] *Opposite:* clean. 2 *adj* **shabby**, drab, squalid, tatty, worn, cheerless, seedy, poor. [➡ IN BAD REPAIR; 1233] *Opposite:* bright.

dining car (*US*) *part of* **train**. [➡ RAILWAYS; 1106]

dining hall *type of* **room in a public building**. [➡ TYPES OF ROOM; 1096]

dining room *type of* **room in the home**. [➡ TYPES OF ROOM; 1096]

dining table *type of* **table**. [➡ FURNITURE; 858]

dinky (*informal*) *adj* **small**, compact, neat, natty, cute. [➡ SMALL; 1194] *Opposite:* hefty.

dinner *type of* **meal**. [➡ MEALS AND PARTS OF MEALS; 1168]

dinner jacket *type of* **jacket**. [➡ GARMENTS AND OUTFITS; 865]

dinner service *n* [➡ TABLEWARE, CUTLERY, AND KITCHENWARE; 861]

dinnertime *n* **mealtime**, suppertime, lunchtime, teatime. [➡ TIMES OF DAY; 87]

dinosaur *n* **relic**, fossil, has-been (*informal*), vestige, leftover, hangover. [➡ REMAINDER AND REMAINDERS; 123]

dinosaur

◆ *types of dinosaur*
allosaurus, ankylosaur, brachiosaurus, brontosaurus, cotylosaur, dicynodont, diplodocus, hadrosaur, ichthyosaur, iguanodon, megalosaur, mosasaur, pelycosaur, plesiosaur, pteranodon, pterodactyl, pterosaur, stegosaur, titanosaur, triceratops, tyrannosaur

dint 1 *n* **indent**, dent, indentation, depression, hollow, pit, mark. [➡ HOLES, GAPS, AND FORKS; 1251] 2 *v* **dent**, damage, mark, spoil, blemish. [➡ TEAR, BREAK, AND CUT; 361]

dip 1 *v* **plunge**, immerse, dunk, douse, bathe, wet, wash, rinse, submerge, duck, submerse. [➡ SOFTEN, LIQUEFY, DAMPEN; 389] 2 *v* **drop**, drop down, descend, decline, sink, fall, fall away, drop away, plummet. [➡ GO DOWNWARDS; 308] *Opposite:* rise. 3 *v* **slope**, incline, slant, descend, fall away, drop away, recede, veer. [➡ GO DOWNWARDS; 308] *Opposite:* level. 4 *n* **swim**, plunge, bathe. [➡ HOBBIES, GAMES, AND SPORTS; 875] 5 *n* **fall**, decline, drop, depression, falling off, slump, downturn, plunge. [➡ LESS; 124] *Opposite:* rise. 6 *n* **hollow**, depression, incline, slope, rise and fall, concavity, sinkage. [➡ HOLES, GAPS, AND FORKS; 1251]

diphthong *type of* **grammatical term**. [➡ ASPECTS OF LANGUAGE; 683]

dip into *v* **skim**, flick through, flip through, glance, browse, look through, cast an eye over. [➡ READ; 759] *Opposite:* study.

diplodocus *type of* **dinosaur**. [➡ DINOSAUR; 996]

diploma *n* **certificate**, qualification, credential. [➡ QUALIFICATIONS; 843]

diplomacy 1 *n* **international relations**, mediation, negotiation, peacekeeping. [➡ GOVERNMENT POLICIES; 810] 2 *n* **tact**, skill, subtlety, discretion, savoir-faire, address. [➡ GOOD MANNERS AND SOCIAL SKILLS; 521] *Opposite:* tactlessness.

diplomat 1 *n* **civil servant**, envoy, representative, attaché, ambassador, consul, legate, cultural attaché, military attaché, public servant. [➡ ADMINISTRATIVE OFFICERS; 811] 2 *n* **tactician**, peacekeeper, negotiator, mediator, go-between, PR expert, moderator. [➡ POLITICAL OFFICES AND POLITICIANS; 808]

diplomatic 1 *adj* **political**, ambassadorial, consular, embassy. [➡ STYLES AND SYSTEMS OF GOVERNMENT; 806] 2 *adj* **tactful**, subtle, suave, discreet, sensitive, cautious, politic, wily. [➡ GOOD MANNERS AND SOCIAL SKILLS; 521] *Opposite:* tactless.

dipper *n* **ladle**, scoop, spoon. [➡ SPOONS, SCOOPS, AND SHOVELS; 1120]

dippy *adj* [➡ ECCENTRICITY AND IRRATIONALITY; 563]

dipstick *type of* **measuring device**. [➡ MEASURING DEVICES; 1122]

dire *adj* **terrible**, awful, dreadful, calamitous, horrible, ominous, dismal, grim, disastrous, frightful, appalling. [➡ UNACCEPTABLE AND UNFORGIVABLE; 226] *Opposite:* wonderful.

direct 1 *v* **manage**, control, regulate, rule, oversee, supervise, preside, produce. [➡BE IN CHARGE; 271] 2 *v* (*formal*) **order**, give orders, instruct, give instructions, command, charge, dictate, tell. [➡REQUEST AND DEMAND; 664] *Opposite:* request. 3 *v* **aim**, point, turn, target, train, level, focus, address. [➡POSITION SOMETHING; 326] 4 *v* **show the way**, guide, lead, put on the right track, point in the right direction, point, give directions, steer. [➡ACCOMPANY AND FOLLOW; 338] 5 *adj* **straight**, shortest, through, unswerving, undeviating, nonstop, uninterrupted, express. [➡DIRECTION OF MOTION; 346] *Opposite:* circuitous. 6 *adj* **straightforward**, honest, open, candid, frank, sincere, plain-spoken, outspoken, up-front (*informal*), blunt. [➡HONEST AND OPEN; 631] *Opposite:* devious. 7 *adj* **precise**, exact, absolute, complete, unequivocal, immediate, close. [➡EXACT; 204] *Opposite:* vague. 8 *adv* **directly**, straight, nonstop, right, in a straight line, as the crow flies. [➡DIRECTION OF MOTION; 346] *Opposite:* indirectly.

See Compare and Contrast at **guide**.

direction 1 *n* **management**, control, government, guidance, leadership, administration, command, supervision. [➡BUSINESS; 792] 2 *n* **way**, course, track, route, path, bearing, road. [➡DIRECTION OF MOTION; 346] 3 *n* **trend**, course, route, focus, aim, target, objective, tendency. [➡INTENTION AND PURPOSE; 773]

directional *adj* **manoeuvring**, steering, turning, reversing, guiding, indicator. [➡DIRECTION OF MOTION; 346]

directions *n* **instructions**, information, orders, guidelines, commands, tips. [➡ADVICE; 690]

directive *n* **order**, command, instruction, direction, edict, demand. [➡REQUEST AND DEMAND; 664]

directly 1 *adv* **in a straight line**, straight, right, unswervingly, nonstop, as the crow flies. [➡DIRECTION OF MOTION; 346] *Opposite:* indirectly. 2 *adv* **completely**, diametrically, absolutely, wholly, unequivocally, in every respect. [➡ABSOLUTE AND ABSOLUTELY; 131] 3 *adv* **openly**, honestly, frankly, straightforwardly, truthfully, candidly, sincerely, bluntly, clearly, exactly, precisely, unambiguously. [➡HONEST AND OPEN; 631] *Opposite:* ambiguously. 4 *adv* (*formal*) **immediately**, quickly, at once, promptly, without delay, speedily, soon, right away. [➡HAPPENING QUICKLY; 104]

direct mail *n* **promotional mailing**, mail shot, circular, junk mail, unsolicited mail, mailing, advertising. [➡ADVERTISING AND PUBLICITY; 605]

directness *n* **honesty**, openness, straightforwardness, truthfulness, sincerity, frankness, bluntness. [➡HONEST AND OPEN; 631] *Opposite:* deviousness.

director *n* **manager**, leader, executive, boss, administrator, principal, chief. [➡BUSINESS PEOPLE; 794]

directorate *n* **board of directors**, executive, executive board, executive committee, board, board of controllers, board of executives. [➡BUSINESS PEOPLE; 794]

director-general *n* **president**, head, director, chairperson, chief executive, chief administrator, executive director. [➡BUSINESS PEOPLE; 794]

directorship *n* **director's post**, management post, executive post, managerial position, presidency. [➡BUSINESS PEOPLE; 794]

directory *type of* **software**. [➡COMPUTERS AND COMPUTING; 1126]

dirge *n* **elegy**, requiem, funeral hymn, lament, chant, song. [➡RELIGIONS AND RELIGIOUS PRACTICES; 778]

dirigible *type of* **civil aircraft**. [➡AIRCRAFT; 1147]

dirk *type of* **sword or knife**. [➡SWORDS AND KNIVES; 1156]

dirndl *type of* **skirt**. [➡GARMENTS AND OUTFITS; 865]

dirt 1 *n* **grime**, filth, mud, dust, muck (*informal*). [➡UNPLEASANT AND DIRTY SUBSTANCES; 1267] 2 *n* **soil**, earth, clay, loam, mud. [➡EROSION PRODUCTS AND SOIL; 1058] 3 *n* **gossip**, scandal, filth, smut, lowdown (*informal*), scuttlebutt (*US slang*). [➡GOSSIP; 679]

dirt-cheap (*informal*) 1 *adj* **cheap**, reduced, cut-price, bargain, inexpensive, discounted, cut-rate (*US*). [➡CHEAP AND INEXPENSIVE; 222] *Opposite:* dear. 2 *adv* **cheaply**, on the cheap (*informal*), at a knockdown price, at bargain-basement prices, for a song, for next to nothing, on sale. [➡CHEAP AND INEXPENSIVE; 222]

dirt-free *adj* [➡CLEAN; 1232]

dirtied *adj* [➡DIRTY; 1234]

dirtiness *n* **griminess**, filthiness, messiness, muddiness, grubbiness, pollution. [➡DIRTY; 1234] *Opposite:* cleanliness.

dirt track *type of* **minor road**. [➡ROADS; 1105]

dirty 1 *adj* **unclean**, filthy, grimy, soiled, grubby, muddy, polluted, foul, sullied (*literary*), squalid. [➡DIRTY; 1234] *Opposite:* clean. 2 *adj* **dishonest**, illegal, corrupt, unfair, crooked (*informal*), immoral, fraudulent, unscrupulous. [➡MORALLY BAD; 776] *Opposite:* honest. 3 *adj* **dull**, muted, muddy, cloudy, murky. [➡DESCRIBING COLOURS; 1225] *Opposite:* clear. 4 *v* **soil**, stain, sully (*literary*), pollute, defile (*formal*), foul. [➡DIRTY AND CONTAMINATE; 405] *Opposite:* clean.

Compare and Contrast: ***dirty, filthy, grubby, grimy, soiled, squalid, unclean***

CORE MEANING: NOT CLEAN

dirty stained or marked with dirt; ***filthy*** extremely or disgustingly dirty; ***grubby*** slightly dirty; ***grimy*** heavily ingrained with accumulated dirt; ***soiled*** stained or marked, especially during normal use; ***squalid*** insanitary and unpleasant; ***unclean*** dirty or impure, especially in moral or religious contexts.

dirty look *n* [➡FACIAL EXPRESSION; 652]

dirty tricks *n* **unfair tactics**, foul play, jiggery-pokery (*informal*), deviousness, dishonesty, trickery. [➡DECEPTION AND LIES; 661]

dirty word *n* **swear word**, expletive, four-letter word, cussword (*US informal*). [➡INSULTS, ABUSE, AND SWEARING; 659]

dis (*slang*) 1 *v* **insult**, affront, disrespect, belittle, disparage, denigrate, lessen, put down (*informal*). [➡INSULTS, ABUSE, AND SWEARING; 659] *Opposite:* compliment. 2 *v* **criticize**, attack, denigrate, maul, savage, find fault with, trash (*informal*). [➡ACCUSE, BLAME, AND CRITICIZE; 642] *Opposite:* support.

disability *n* **incapacity**, infirmity, frailty, debility, ill health. [➡ILLNESSES AND DISORDERS; 733]

disable *v* **incapacitate**, restrict, inactivate, deactivate, put out of action, spike (*informal*), knock out. [➡CAUSE TO STOP; 267]

disablement *n* **impairment**, incapacitation, deactivation, spiking (*informal*). [➡ILLNESSES AND DISORDERS; 733]

disabuse *v* **persuade out of**, disillusion, enlighten, set straight, shatter somebody's illusions, correct, deprive. [➡INFORM AND ANNOUNCE; 612]

disadvantage *n* **difficulty**, drawback, shortcoming, weakness, hindrance, handicap, detriment, minus, demerit, inconvenience. [➡FAULTS, FLAWS, AND WEAKNESSES; 252] *Opposite:* advantage.

disadvantaged *adj* **deprived**, underprivileged, needy, destitute, poor, in need, lacking, badly off. [➡POVERTY AND POOR; 892] *Opposite:* privileged.

disadvantageous *adj* **detrimental**, damaging, hurtful, harmful, injurious, prejudicial, inconvenient, troublesome, unhelpful. [➡DANGEROUS; 237] *Opposite:* advantageous.

disadvantageously *adv* **detrimentally**, harmfully, hurtfully, inconveniently, injuriously, prejudicially, unhelpfully. [➡DANGEROUS; 237] *Opposite:* desirably.

disaffect *v* **estrange**, disillusion, disenchant, dissatisfy, alienate, disgruntle, turn off (*informal*). [➡UPSET, DISTRESS, AND HUMILIATE; 568]

disaffected *adj* **disillusioned**, dissatisfied, disgruntled, cynical, alienated, estranged, apathetic. [➡NEUTRALITY AND INDIFFERENCE; 554] *Opposite:* enthusiastic.

disaffection *n* **disillusionment**, alienation, estrangement, dissatisfaction, cynicism, apathy. [➡NEUTRALITY AND INDIFFERENCE; 554] *Opposite:* enthusiasm.

disagree 1 *v* **demur**, differ, take issue with, agree to differ, be at odds. [➡PROTEST AND EXPRESS DISAPPROVAL; 643] *Opposite:* agree. 2 *v* **differ**, vary, diverge, conflict, oppose, deviate, be dissimilar, contradict. [➡DIFFERENCE; 150] *Opposite:* agree. 3 *v* **argue**, quarrel, wrangle, dispute, bicker, clash, fall out, row, fight. [➡ARGUE AND FIGHT - TWO-WAY; 644] *Opposite:* agree.

Compare and Contrast: ***disagree, differ, argue, dispute, take issue with, contradict, agree to differ, be at odds***

CORE MEANING: TO HAVE OR EXPRESS A DIFFERENCE OF OPINION WITH SOMEBODY

disagree to have or put forward a different view or opinion from somebody; ***differ*** to have different opinions about something; ***argue*** to express disagreement with somebody, especially continuously or angrily; ***dispute*** to have a heated argument; ***take issue with*** to disagree strongly with somebody or something; ***contradict*** to argue against the truth or correctness of somebody's statement or claim; ***agree to differ*** to stop arguing and accept that the opposing viewpoints are irreconcilable; ***be at odds*** to be in disagreement, especially over a period of time or about a particular issue.

disagreeable 1 *adj* **displeasing**, distasteful, offensive, nasty, unpleasant, dislikable, horrible. [➡EMOTIONALLY UNPLEASANT AND UPSETTING; 228] *Opposite:* agreeable. 2 *adj* **bad-tempered**, unfriendly, unhelpful, difficult, contrary, rude, surly, brusque, crabby, quarrelsome. [➡AGGRESSIVE AND BELLIGERENT; 519] *Opposite:* pleasant.

disagreement 1 *n* **dispute**, difference of opinion, quarrel, argument, misunderstanding, discord, conflict, wrangle, dissent, clash, falling-out. [➡ARGUMENT; 47] *Opposite:* agreement. 2 *n* **difference**, divergence, incongruity, discrepancy, dissimilarity, disparity, variance, deviation. [➡DIFFERENCE; 150] *Opposite:* agreement.

disallow 1 *v* (*formal*) **reject**, refuse, deny, throw, negate (*formal*), disapprove, turn down. [➡REFUSE PERMISSION AND NOT ALLOW; 671] *Opposite:* pass. 2 *v* **cancel**, prohibit, forbid, veto, bar, ban, outlaw, overrule, preclude (*formal*), exclude. [➡REFUSE PERMISSION AND NOT ALLOW; 671] *Opposite:* allow.

disallowed *adj* **rejected**, forbidden, banned, excluded, vetoed, prohibited, precluded (*formal*), overruled. [➡REFUSE PERMISSION AND NOT ALLOW; 671] *Opposite:* allowed.

disappear 1 *v* **vanish**, fade, fade away, go, evaporate, dissolve, melt, wane, withdraw, ebb, depart, flee, recede, dematerialize, dissipate. [➡DISAPPEAR; 4] *Opposite:* appear. 2 *v* **cease to exist**, die out, die off, expire, pass away, perish (*formal*), vanish. [➡CEASE TO EXIST; 22] *Opposite:* appear.

disappearance *n* **vanishing**, evaporation, fading, loss, desertion, withdrawal, departure. [➡END; 54] *Opposite:* appearance.

disappearing *adj* **vanishing**, waning, endangered, threatened, dying. [➡IN DANGER; 238]

disappoint *v* **let down**, disillusion, fail, dissatisfy, dishearten, upset, thwart, frustrate, sadden, disenchant. [➡UPSET, DISTRESS, AND HUMILIATE; 568] *Opposite:* please.

disappointed *adj* **let down**, dissatisfied, disillusioned, upset, saddened, thwarted, disenchanted, frustrated. [➡SADNESS, DISTRESS, AND DESPAIR; 540] *Opposite:* satisfied.

disappointing *adj* **unsatisfactory**, unacceptable, second-rate, poor, below par, not up to scratch (*informal*), inadequate. [➡BAD AND BADLY; 224] *Opposite:* satisfactory.

disappointment 1 *n* **dissatisfaction**, displeasure, distress, discontent, disenchantment, disillusionment, frustration, regret. [➡SADNESS, DISTRESS, AND DESPAIR; 540] *Opposite:* satisfaction. 2 *n* **setback**, failure, frustration, defeat, drawback, hindrance, inconvenience. [➡NUISANCES; 254]

disapprobation (*formal*) *n* **disfavour**, condemnation, disapproval, dislike, displeasure, censure, discontentment, dissatisfaction. [➡ANTAGONISM; 553] *Opposite:* approval.

disapproval *n* **condemnation**, displeasure, dissatisfaction, censure, discontentment, disapprobation (*formal*). [➡IRRITATION AND ANGER; 542] *Opposite:* approval.

disapprove 1 *v* **condemn**, censure, criticize, dislike, object, frown on, reject, not hold with, have a problem with, deplore, denounce. [➡DISLIKE AND HATE; 578] *Opposite:* approve. 2 *v* (*formal*) **reject**, refuse, veto, turn down, negate (*formal*), deny, throw out. [➡PROTEST AND EXPRESS DISAPPROVAL; 643] *Opposite:* approve.

Compare and Contrast: ***disapprove, frown on, object, criticize, condemn, deplore, denounce, censure***

CORE MEANING: TO HAVE AN UNFAVOURABLE OPINION OF SOMETHING OR SOMEBODY

disapprove to judge somebody or something negatively based on personal standards; ***frown on*** to dislike or disapprove of something; ***object*** to be opposed to something, or express opposition; ***criticize*** to point out flaws or faults; ***condemn*** to give an unfavourable judgment on somebody or something; ***deplore*** to disapprove of something strongly; ***denounce*** to criticize or condemn publicly and harshly; ***censure*** to make a formal, often public or official, statement of disapproval.

disapproving *adj* **critical**, judgmental, negative, censorious, stern, harsh. [➡ACCUSATORY AND DISAPPROVING; 635] *Opposite:* approving.

disarm 1 *v* **deactivate**, defuse, make safe, neutralize. [➡MAKE IMPOSSIBLE; 277] *Opposite:* arm. 2 *v* **win over**, charm, enchant, beguile, win the affection of, put off guard, captivate. [➡PLEASE AND AMUSE; 573] *Opposite:* annoy.

disarmament *n* **arms reduction**, nuclear disarmament, unilateral disarmament, decommissioning, demilitarization, demobilization, demob (*informal*). [➡WARFARE AND WAR; 830]

disarming *adj* **charming**, enchanting, attractive, appealing, captivating, winning, beguiling. [➡EMOTIONALLY PLEASANT; 188] *Opposite:* cold.

disarrange *v* **disorder**, mess up (*informal*), disturb, jumble, dishevel, mix up. [➡CREATE DISORDER AND CAUSE CHAOS; 359] *Opposite:* order.

disarranged *adj* **disordered**, untidy, rumpled, messy, jumbled, dishevelled, mixed up. [➡DISORDER AND CHAOS; 246]

disarray 1 *n* **confusion**, dismay, panic, alarm, hysteria, frenzy, disorder. [➡DISORDER AND CHAOS; 246] *Opposite:* order. 2 *n* **mess**, disorder, chaos, confusion, untidiness, shambles, clutter, jumble, tangle. [➡DISORDER AND CHAOS; 246] *Opposite:* order.

disassemble *v* **take apart**, take to bits, undo, take down, take to pieces, strip. [➡UNFASTEN AND UNDO; 410] *Opposite:* assemble.

disassociate 1 *v* **dissociate**, separate, split, set apart, disentangle, isolate, withdraw. [➡SEPARATE AND DIVIDE; 402] *Opposite:* associate. 2 *v* **distance**, detach, set apart, dissociate, draw back, disconnect, extricate. [➡SEPARATE AND DIVIDE; 402] *Opposite:* implicate.

disaster 1 *n* **tragedy**, ruin, adversity, catastrophe, calamity, cataclysm, misadventure, mischance, misfortune. [➡DISASTERS; 253] 2 *n* (*informal*) **failure**, debacle, fiasco, shambles, farce, mess, catastrophe, calamity, blow. [➡FAILURE; 77] *Opposite:* success.

disastrous 1 *adj* **calamitous**, catastrophic, tragic, terrible, devastating, dreadful. [➡UNSUCCESSFUL AND UNPROMISING; 76] 2 *adj* **unsuccessful**, unfortunate, luckless, doomed, unlucky, grievous, ill-starred (*formal*). [➡UNSUCCESSFUL AND UNPROMISING; 76] *Opposite:* successful.

disavow (*formal*) *v* **disown**, deny, renounce, reject, recant, refute, forswear (*archaic or literary*), give up. [➡DENY AND REJECT; 645]

disavowal (*formal*) *n* **repudiation**, denial, negation, renunciation, abjuration, refutation, recantation, rejection, forswearing (*archaic or literary*). *Opposite:* avowal. (*formal*). [➡DENY AND REJECT; 645]

disband *v* **break up**, split up, scatter, separate, part, disperse, split. [➡SEPARATE AND DIVIDE; 402]

disbar *v* **expel**, throw out, dismiss, banish, discharge (*formal*), exclude, remove. [➡REFUSE PERMISSION AND NOT ALLOW; 671]

disbarment *n* **expulsion**, dismissal, banishment, discharge (*formal*), exclusion, removal. [➡REFUSE PERMISSION AND NOT ALLOW; 671]

disbelief *n* **incredulity**, doubt, distrust, mistrust, suspicion. [➡UNCERTAINTY; 560]

disbelieve *v* **distrust**, doubt, mistrust, suspect, be suspicious of, question, have no faith in. [➡UNCERTAINTY; 560] *Opposite:* believe.

disbeliever *n* **doubter**, agnostic, atheist, nonbeliever, sceptic. [➡UNCERTAINTY; 560] *Opposite:* believer.

disbelieving *adj* **unconvinced**, incredulous, suspicious, doubtful, distrustful, sceptical. [➡UNCERTAINTY; 560] *Opposite:* believing.

disburden (*archaic*) *v* [➡ADMIT AND CONFESS; 616]

disburse *v* **pay out**, pay, spend, expend, lay out, give out, distribute. [➡DISPENSE, RATION, AND DISTRIBUTE; 435]

disbursement *n* **payment**, expenditure, expense, costs, distribution, pay out. [➡EXPENDITURE; 424]

discard *v* **throw away**, abandon, dispose of, remove, get rid of, reject, thrust aside, cast off, shed, dispense with. [➡GET RID OF SOMETHING; 452] *Opposite:* keep.

discarded *adj* **cast off**, thrown away, thrown out, rejected, dispensed with, tossed out, waste, superfluous, unwanted. [➡UNPOPULAR AND UNWANTED; 259] *Opposite:* kept.

disc camera *type of* **photographic equipment**. [➡PHOTOGRAPHY AND PHOTOGRAPHIC EQUIPMENT; 1121]

discern 1 *v* **make out**, notice, see, perceive, discover, observe, catch sight of, glimpse, detect, spot. [➡LOOKING AND LOOKS; 701] *Opposite:* miss. 2 *v* **understand**, perceive, distinguish, fathom, be aware of, detect. [➡UNDERSTAND AND GRASP; 760] *Opposite:* miss. 3 *v* **distinguish**, tell the difference, separate, discriminate, differentiate, determine, detect, recognize, know by sight. [➡KNOWLEDGE AND WISDOM; 559]

discernible *adj* **visible**, apparent, obvious, perceptible, noticeable, distinct, palpable, evident, marked. [➡PERCEPTIBLE; 25]

discerning *adj* **discriminating**, sharp, astute, judicious, sensitive, shrewd, selective. [➡POSITIVE INTELLECTUAL CHARACTERISTICS; 525] *Opposite:* indiscriminate.

discernment *n* **judgment**, acumen, discrimination, perspicacity, taste, shrewdness, sensitivity, selectivity. [➡POSITIVE INTELLECTUAL CHARACTERISTICS; 525]

discharge 1 *v* **emit**, send out, excrete, expel, ooze, leak, exude. [➡LIQUID EMISSION; 371] 2 *v* **free**, release, set free, emancipate, liberate, loose. [➡FREEDOM AND LIBERTY; 209] 3 *v* **dismiss**, sack (*informal*), relieve of duty, send away, fire, bounce, terminate (*US*), can (*US slang*). [➡REVOKE STATUS; 460] 4 *v* (*formal*) **pay off**, clear, settle, satisfy, liquidate, square, quit (*archaic*). [➡MONEY, PAYMENTS, AND CHARGES; 800] 5 *n* **emission**, flow, secretion, excretion, seepage, pus. [➡EMIT AND EMANATE; 362] 6 *n* **release**, liberation, emancipation, expulsion, ejection. [➡FREEDOM AND LIBERTY; 209]

See Compare and Contrast at **perform**.

disciple *n* **follower**, believer, supporter, devotee, partisan, adherent, student, pupil, scholar, learner. [➡SUPPORTERS, PROTECTORS, AND COMPATRIOTS; 970]

disciplinarian *n* **tyrant**, martinet, despot, authoritarian, stickler. [➡VILLAINS AND THUGS; 947]

disciplinary *adj* **punitive**, corrective, penal, penalizing. [➡TRIAL, PUNISHMENT, AND LEGAL OUTCOMES; 819]

discipline 1 *n* **punishment**, correction, chastisement (*formal*), castigation (*formal*). [➡TRIAL, PUNISHMENT, AND LEGAL OUTCOMES; 819] *Opposite:* persuasion. 2 *n* **regulation**, order, control, restraint, authority, obedience. [➡ORDER AND ORGANISATION; 207] *Opposite:* chaos. 3 *n* **self-control**, self-restraint, restraint, control, regulation, strictness, mastery, continence. [➡STRENGTH OF WILL; 502] 4 *n* **subject**, branch of learning, field. [➡LESSONS, COURSE WORK, AND EXAMINATIONS; 842] 5 *v* **punish**, chastise (*formal*), correct, castigate (*formal*), chasten. [➡TRIAL, PUNISHMENT, AND LEGAL OUTCOMES; 819] 6 *v* **instruct**, educate, exercise, drill, prepare, train, regulate, teach, school. [➡INSTRUCT AND TEACH; 610]

disciplined *adj* **controlled**, self-controlled, orderly, well-ordered, methodical, meticulous, restrained, systematic, well-organized, ordered. [➡ORDER AND ORGANISATION; 207] *Opposite:* undisciplined.

disclaim *v* **deny**, disown, renounce, reject, repudiate, refute, turn your back on. [➡DENY AND REJECT; 645]

disclaimer 1 *n* **rider**, proviso, qualification, provision, condition, stipulation, requirement, criterion, clause, specification, prerequisite. [➡NECESSARY AND ESSENTIAL; 197] 2 *n* **repudiation**, denial, renunciation, negation, dissassociation. [➡DENY AND REJECT; 645]

disclose *v* **reveal**, unveil, divulge, make known, relate, release. [➡INFORM AND ANNOUNCE; 612] *Opposite:* conceal.

disclosure *n* **revelation**, exposé, discovery, leak, confession, admission, release. [➡ADMIT AND CONFESS; 616]

discoloration *n* **staining**, stain, tint, mark, streak, bloom, yellowing, bruising. [➡DESCRIBING COLOURS; 1225]

discolour *v* **fade**, stain, colour, darken, tarnish, dull, dye, bruise, scorch. [➡CHANGE OF COLOUR; 392]

discoloured *adj* **stained**, dirty, tarnished, faded, streaked, yellowed, bruised. [➡DESCRIBING COLOURS; 1225]

discombobulate (*informal*) *v* [➡CONFUSE AND BEWILDER; 572]

discomfit (*formal*) *v* **embarrass**, unsettle, disconcert, distress, discompose (*formal*), rattle, fluster, unnerve, make uncomfortable, make self-conscious, throw (*informal*), discombobulate (*informal*), perturb, take aback, put off his or her stride. [➡CONFUSE AND BEWILDER; 572] *Opposite:* relax.

discomfited (*formal*) *adj* [➡INSECURITY AND LOSS OF COMPOSURE; 545]

discomfiting (*formal*) *adj* **disconcerting**, embarrassing, unsettling, disturbing, distressing, upsetting, nerve-racking, off-putting. [➡EMOTIONALLY UNPLEASANT AND UPSETTING; 228] *Opposite:* reassuring.

discomfiture (*formal*) *n* **embarrassment**, awkwardness, confusion, unease, disconcertment, discomposure, uneasiness. [➡EMBARRASSMENT AND HUMILIATION; 543]

discomfort 1 *n* **ache**, pain, soreness, tenderness, irritation. [➡PAIN AND OTHER PHYSICAL SENSATIONS; 734] 2 *n* **uneasiness**, worry, distress, anxiety, embarrassment, awkwardness. [➡EMBARRASSMENT AND HUMILIATION; 543]

discomposure *n* **agitation**, upset, uneasiness, embarrassment, discomfort, dismay, confusion. [➡EMBARRASSMENT AND HUMILIATION; 543]

disconcert *v* **unsettle**, perturb, discompose (*formal*), discomfit (*formal*), rattle, fluster, unnerve, discombobulate (*informal*), throw (*informal*), take aback. [➡CONFUSE AND BEWILDER; 572] *Opposite:* relax.

disconcerted *adj* **unsettled**, thrown off balance, confused, flustered, taken aback, perturbed, thrown (*informal*). [➡CONFUSION, ANXIETY, AND WORRY; 541] *Opposite:* calm.

disconcerting *adj* **disturbing**, alarming, confusing, perplexing, bewildering, upsetting, distressing, perturbing, unnerving. [➡EMOTIONALLY UNPLEASANT AND UPSETTING; 228] *Opposite:* soothing.

disconnect *v* **cut off**, detach, separate, divide, disengage, sever. [➡UNFASTEN AND UNDO; 410] *Opposite:* connect.

disconnected *adj* **detached**, severed, disengaged, separated, divided. [➡UNFASTEN AND UNDO; 410] *Opposite:* attached.

disconnection 1 *n* **stoppage**, interruption, cessation, cutting off, discontinuation, withdrawal, suspension. [➡END; 54] *Opposite:* connection. 2 *n* **separation**, severance, decoupling, disengagement, break, detachment. [➡END; 54] *Opposite:* connection.

disconsolate *adj* **unhappy**, dejected, gloomy, melancholy, sad, discontent, unsatisfied, miserable. [➡SADNESS, DISTRESS, AND DESPAIR; 540] *Opposite:* content.

discontent *n* **dissatisfaction**, unhappiness, displeasure, disgruntlement, sadness, gloominess. [➡SADNESS, DISTRESS, AND DESPAIR; 540] *Opposite:* contentment.

discontented *adj* **dissatisfied**, unhappy, disgruntled, malcontent, displeased, grumbling, grumpy, sullen, resentful. [➡SADNESS, DISTRESS, AND DESPAIR; 540] *Opposite:* contented.

discontentment *n* **dissatisfaction**, discontent, displeasure, unhappiness, irritation, annoyance. [➡SADNESS, DISTRESS, AND DESPAIR; 540] *Opposite:* contentment.

discontinuation *n* **cessation**, termination, suspension, withdrawal, stoppage, interruption. [➡END; 54] *Opposite:* continuation.

discontinue *v* **stop**, cease, halt, end, suspend, break off, terminate (*formal*), withdraw. [➡CAUSE TO STOP; 267] *Opposite:* continue.

discontinued *adj* **obsolete**, finished, superseded, out-of-date, withdrawn, dropped, unobtainable. [➡ABSENT AND UNAVAILABLE; 7]

discontinuity *n* **break**, gap, cutoff, cutout, disjointedness, incoherence. [➡FINITENESS, VARIABILITY, AND TRANSIENCE; 96] *Opposite:* continuity.

discontinuous *adj* **intermittent**, sporadic, broken, irregular, disjointed, spasmodic, uneven. [➡FINITENESS, VARIABILITY, AND TRANSIENCE; 96] *Opposite:* continuous.

discord 1 *n* **disagreement**, conflict, dispute, argument, friction, dissension. [➡DISHARMONY; 157] *Opposite:* accord. 2 *n* **dissonance**, cacophony, disharmony, inharmoniousness, discordance. [➡LOUD OR UNPLEASANT SOUNDS; 1265] *Opposite:* harmony.

discordant 1 *adj* **disagreeing**, conflicting, frictional, dissenting, disputatious (*formal*), acrimonious. [➡DISHARMONY; 157] 2 *adj* **dissonant**, jarring, harsh, inharmonious, cacophonous, shrill, unmusical. [➡LOUD OR UNPLEASANT SOUNDS; 1265] *Opposite:* harmonious.

discount 1 *n* **reduction**, money off, markdown, price cut, cut rate, concession, deduction, rebate. [➡MONEY, PAYMENTS, AND CHARGES; 800] 2 *v* **disregard**, overlook, ignore, disbelieve, pass over, write off (*informal*), omit, slight. [➡NOT PAY ATTENTION; 765] *Opposite:* accept. 3 *v* **reduce**, mark down, lower, take off, deduct, subtract. [➡MONEY, PAYMENTS, AND CHARGES; 800] *Opposite:* put up.

discounted *adj* **reduced**, on offer, cut-price, sale, on special offer, cheap, promotional, bargain-basement, on sale, cut-rate (*US*), on special (*US*). [➡CHEAP AND INEXPENSIVE; 222]

discourage 1 *v* **dissuade**, oppose, hinder, inhibit, prevent, stop, suppress. [➡MAKE IMPOSSIBLE; 277] *Opposite:* encourage. 2 *v* **dispirit**, dishearten, cast down, depress, deject (*archaic*), dismay, disappoint. [➡UPSET, DISTRESS, AND HUMILIATE; 568] *Opposite:* cheer.

discouraged *adj* **disheartened**, dispirited, downcast, depressed, dejected, low, melancholy, hopeless, gloomy, unenthusiastic. [➡SADNESS, DISTRESS, AND DESPAIR; 540] *Opposite:* positive.

discouragement 1 *n* **disappointment**, dismay, despair, depression, low spirits, melancholy, pessimism, gloominess, worry. [➡SADNESS, DISTRESS, AND DESPAIR; 540] *Opposite:* hopefulness. 2 *n* **dissuasion**, caution, warning, opposition, deterrence. [➡ADVICE; 690] *Opposite:* encouragement. 3 *n* **deterrent**, hindrance, obstacle, impediment, damper, restraint. [➡PROBLEM; 257] *Opposite:* incentive.

discouraging *adj* **disheartening**, depressing, dispiriting, gloomy, unpromising, inauspicious, ominous, unfavourable. [➡EMOTIONALLY UNPLEASANT AND UPSETTING; 228] *Opposite:* encouraging.

discourse 1 *n* **dissertation**, treatise, homily, sermon, address, speech. [➡NEUTRAL ONE-WAY COMMUNICATION; 49] 2 *n* **dialogue**, conversation, discussion, communication, speech, talk, chat. [➡INFORMAL COMMUNICATION; 45] 3 *v* (*formal*) **converse**, debate, compare notes, have a word, have a discussion, discuss, negotiate, confer, reason, deliberate, consult, parley. [➡TWO-WAY COMMUNICATION; 608]

discourteous *adj* **rude**, ill-mannered, impolite, insolent, uncivil, unmannerly, disrespectful. [➡BAD MANNERS AND SOCIAL SKILLS; 522] *Opposite:* polite.

discourteousness *n* **impoliteness**, rudeness, disrespect, unmannerliness, incivility, uncouthness, impertinence, impudence, insolence. [➡BAD MANNERS AND SOCIAL SKILLS; 522] *Opposite:* politeness.

discourtesy *n* **rudeness**, impoliteness, disrespect, incivility, insolence. [➡BAD MANNERS AND SOCIAL SKILLS; 522] *Opposite:* politeness.

discover 1 *v* **find out**, learn, determine, notice, realize, see, ascertain (*formal*), discern. [➡LEARN AND DISCOVER; 763] 2 *v* **come across**, find, turn up, uncover, unearth, dig up, locate, detect, encounter. [➡FIND; 464]

discoverer *n* **inventor**, originator, pioneer, innovator, creator, architect. [➡DESIGNERS, CREATORS AND INSTIGATORS; 348]

discovery 1 *n* **find**, innovation, breakthrough, invention, finding. [➡CREATION; 347] 2 *n* **detection**, finding, unearthing, sighting, encounter, location. [➡FIND; 464]

discredit 1 *v* **slur**, demean, smear, insult, humiliate, disgrace. [➡INSULTS, ABUSE, AND SWEARING; 659] 2 *v* **question**, doubt, disbelieve, query, suspect, dispute. [➡QUESTION THINGS; 752]

discreditable *adj* **shameful**, disreputable, ignominious, disgraceful, reprehensible, appalling, wrong. [➡UNACCEPTABLE AND UNFORGIVABLE; 226]

discreditably *adv* **disreputably**, shamefully, disgracefully, ignominiously, reprehensibly, appallingly. [➡MORALLY BAD; 776]

discreet 1 *adj* **tactful**, prudent, circumspect, cautious, careful, diplomatic, judicious. [➡GOOD MANNERS AND SOCIAL SKILLS; 521] *Opposite:* tactless. 2 *adj* **inconspicuous**, subtle, unnoticeable, unobtrusive, understated, tasteful, restrained, modest. [➡IMPERCEPTIBLE; 26] *Opposite:* obvious.

discrepancy *n* **inconsistency**, difference, incongruity, divergence, disagreement. [➡DIFFERENCE; 150] *Opposite:* correspondence.

discrete *adj* **separate**, distinct, disconnected, detached, isolated, unconnected. [➡UNRELATEDNESS AND SEPARATENESS; 147]

discretion 1 *n* **carefulness**, prudence, caution, canniness, maturity, responsibility, moderation, foresight, judgment, diplomacy, tact, acumen, discrimination. [➡CONFIDENCE AND COMPOSURE; 500] 2 *n* **freedom of choice**, will, pleasure, option, choice, decision. [➡MAKE DECISIONS AND CHOICES; 753]

discretionary *adj* **optional**, flexible, open, unrestricted. [➡POSSIBLE AND PROBABLE; 178] *Opposite:* mandatory.

discriminate *v* **distinguish**, tell apart, differentiate, separate, categorize, classify. [➡UNDERSTAND AND GRASP; 760]

discriminating *adj* **discerning**, sharp, astute, selective, judicious, tasteful, cultivated, refined. [➡POSITIVE INTELLECTUAL CHARACTERISTICS; 525]

discrimination 1 *n* **bias**, prejudice, unfairness, inequity, bigotry, intolerance. [➡PREJUDICE; 551] 2 *n* **taste**, judgment, good taste, discernment, insight, acumen, perception, refinement, percipience. [➡POSITIVE INTELLECTUAL CHARACTERISTICS; 525] 3 *n* **distinction**, difference, differential, contrast. [➡DIFFERENCE; 150]

discriminatory *adj* **biased**, prejudiced, unfair, bigoted, inequitable, intolerant. [➡MORALLY BAD; 776]

discursive *adj* **broad**, lengthy, conversational, expansive, informal, free, loose, rambling, musing, roundabout. [➡ELOQUENT, TALKATIVE AND LONG-WINDED; 633] *Opposite:* concise.

discursiveness *n* **informality**, breadth, expansiveness, freeness, roundaboutness. [➡ELOQUENT, TALKATIVE AND LONG-WINDED; 633] *Opposite:* concision.

discus 1 *type of* **sports equipment**. [➡SPORTS EQUIPMENT; 879] 2 *type of* **track and field**. [➡HOBBIES, GAMES, AND SPORTS; 875]

discuss *v* **talk over**, deliberate, debate, converse, confer, thrash out, chew over, discourse (*formal*), kick around (*informal*), chat, hash out (*US*). [➡TWO-WAY COMMUNICATION; 608]

discussion *n* **conversation**, debate, argument, dialogue, chat, talk, confab (*informal*). [➡INFORMAL COMMUNICATION; 45]

discussion group *n* **class**, seminar, tutorial, round table, committee, working party. [➡LESSONS, COURSE WORK, AND EXAMINATIONS; 842]

disdain 1 *n* **scorn**, contempt, derision, condescension, disparagement, disregard, aloofness. [➡DISLIKE AND HATE; 578] *Opposite:* respect. 2 *v* **despise**, scorn, spurn, hold in contempt, disparage, turn your nose up at. [➡DISLIKE AND HATE; 578] *Opposite:* respect.

disdainful *adj* **sneering**, scornful, derisive, condescending, aloof, contemptuous, mocking. [➡MOCKING AND DISMISSIVE; 637] *Opposite:* respectful.

disease *n* **illness**, sickness, ailment, infection, syndrome, malady, bug (*informal*), virus, disorder, complaint. [➡SICKNESS; 730] *Opposite:* health.

diseased *adj* **unhealthy**, unwell, sickly, ailing (*dated*), ill, poorly (*informal*), sick. [➡ILL AND SICK; 741] *Opposite:* healthy.

disease-ridden *adj* [➡ILL AND SICK; 741]

disembark *v* **come ashore**, go ashore, land, get off, arrive in port, debark. [➡ARRIVE BY TRANSPORT; 14] *Opposite:* embark.

disembarkation *n* **arrival**, alighting, debarkation, landing, getting off. [➡ARRIVAL; 13]

disembodied *adj* **incorporeal** (*formal*), ghostly, spiritual, intangible, ethereal, immaterial. [➡IMPERCEPTIBLE; 26] *Opposite:* tangible.

disembowel *v* **eviscerate**, gut, fillet, exenterate. [➡WOUND A PERSON OR ANIMAL; 384]

disenchant *v* [➡UPSET, DISTRESS, AND HUMILIATE; 568]

disenchanted *adj* **disillusioned**, disappointed, dissatisfied, crestfallen, embittered, let down, unhappy. [➡SADNESS, DISTRESS, AND DESPAIR; 540] *Opposite:* idealistic.

disenchantment *n* **disillusionment**, disappointment, dissatisfaction, embitterment, bitterness, world-weariness, unhappiness. [➡SADNESS, DISTRESS, AND DESPAIR; 540] *Opposite:* idealism.

disenfranchise *v* **marginalize**, exclude, alienate, subjugate, disqualify. [➡REVOKE STATUS; 460] *Opposite:* enfranchise.

disenfranchisement *n* **marginalization**, exclusion, alienation, subjugation, disqualification. [➡REVOKE STATUS; 460] *Opposite:* enfranchisement.

disengage *v* **undo**, unfasten, unlock, untie, uncouple, free, extricate, separate. [➡UNFASTEN AND UNDO; 410] *Opposite:* fasten.

disengagement 1 *n* **withdrawal**, disentanglement, detachment, disconnection, extrication, breaking away, break. [➡END; 54] *Opposite:* engagement. 2 *n* **release**, uncoupling, separation, extrication, withdrawal, disentanglement. [➡END; 54] *Opposite:* attachment.

disentangle *v* **unravel**, unscramble, untie, separate, straighten out, sort out, extricate, untangle. [➡ARRANGE AND CREATE ORDER; 358] *Opposite:* entangle.

disequilibrium *n* **imbalance**, instability, uncertainty, flux, volatility. [➡UNCERTAIN; 176] *Opposite:* equilibrium.

disestablish *v* **reform**, repudiate, renounce, re-evaluate, disclaim. [➡SOCIAL, POLITICAL, AND ECONOMIC CHANGE; 374] *Opposite:* establish.

disfavour 1 *n* **disrepute**, unpopularity, discredit, disgrace, obscurity, disapproval. [➡DIFFICULT SITUATIONS; 72] *Opposite:* favour. 2 *n* **distaste**, disdain, disapproval, disapprobation (*formal*), displeasure, scorn. [➡DISLIKE AND HATE; 578] *Opposite:* favour.

disfigure *v* **mutilate**, scar, deface, mar, spoil, harm, damage, blemish. [➡WOUND A PERSON OR ANIMAL; 384] *Opposite:* enhance.

disfigured *adj* [➡IN BAD REPAIR; 1233]

disfigurement *n* **scar**, mutilation, defacement, deformity, blemish, defect, mark, blotch. [➡WOUND A PERSON OR ANIMAL; 384] *Opposite:* enhancement.

disgorge *v* **expel**, eject, empty, pour out, spew, erupt. [➡LIQUID EMISSION; 371] *Opposite:* retain.

disgrace 1 *n* **shame**, discredit, scandal, ignominy, humiliation, degradation, dishonour. [➡DIFFICULT SITUATIONS; 72] 2 *v* **bring shame on**, discredit, bring into disrepute, shame, degrade, tarnish, stain, humiliate. [➡UPSET, DISTRESS, AND HUMILIATE; 568]

disgraced *adj* **discredited**, shamed, condemned, humiliated, fallen, shunned. [➡IN TROUBLE AND DISADVANTAGED; 73] *Opposite:* popular.

disgraceful *adj* **shameful**, shocking, outrageous, scandalous, discreditable, reprehensible, appalling, dreadful. [➡UNACCEPTABLE AND UNFORGIVABLE; 226]

disgruntle *v* **displease**, irritate, anger, annoy, dissatisfy, peeve (*informal*). [➡ANGER AND ANNOY; 570] *Opposite:* satisfy.

disgruntled *adj* **discontented**, dissatisfied, resentful, displeased, unhappy, irritated, angry, sullen, annoyed, peeved (*informal*), put out. [➡IRRITATION AND ANGER; 542] *Opposite:* contented.

disguise 1 *v* **cover up**, hide, conceal, mask, masquerade, veil, camouflage, cloak. [➡CAUSE TO DISAPPEAR; 6] *Opposite:* reveal. 2 *n* **mask**, costume, camouflage, masquerade, cover, cloak, front, veneer, concealment. [➡CLOTHES AND ACCESSORIES; 864]

disguised *adj* **camouflaged**, masked, masquerading, cloaked, veiled, hidden, concealed. [➡IMPERCEPTIBLE; 26] *Opposite:* overt.

disgust 1 *n* **revulsion**, repugnance, abhorrence, repulsion, antipathy, aversion, loathing, hatred. [➡DISLIKE AND HATE; 578] *Opposite:* attraction. 2 *v* **sicken**, repulse, revolt, repel, shock, turn your stomach, nauseate. [➡FRIGHTEN AND SHOCK; 569] *Opposite:* please.

See Compare and Contrast at **dislike**.

disgusted *adj* **sickened**, revolted, repulsed, repelled, offended, appalled. [➡SADNESS, DISTRESS, AND DESPAIR; 540] *Opposite:* charmed.

disgusting *adj* **revolting**, repulsive, sickening, ghastly, filthy, sordid, horrible, nauseating, repellent. [➡DISGUSTING AND REPULSIVE; 231] *Opposite:* attractive.

dish 1 *n* **plate**, bowl, saucer. [➡TABLEWARE, CUTLERY, AND KITCHENWARE; 861] 2 *n* **food item**, course, recipe. [➡PREPARED DISHES; 1169]

dish

◆ *types of cooked dish*
casserole, cassoulet, chop suey, chow mein, couscous, curry, fish cake, fondue, fricassee, fry-up, goulash, gruel, Irish stew, kedgeree, mixed grill, nasi goreng, paella, pilaf (*US*), pilau, pizza, ragout, ratatouille, risotto, stir-fry

disharmonious *adj* **conflicting**, discordant, tense, uneasy, bitter, resentful, at odds. [➡DISHARMONY; 157] *Opposite:* harmonious.

disharmony *n* **conflict**, disagreement, tension, unrest, bitterness, resentment. [➡DISHARMONY; 157] *Opposite:* harmony.

dishcloth *n* **washing-up cloth**, kitchen cloth, towel, drying-up cloth, dishrag (*US*). [➡SOFT FURNISHINGS, LINEN, AND DRAPERY; 860]

dishearten *v* **discourage**, depress, sadden, cast down, dismay, bring down, deject (*archaic*), dampen, disappoint. [➡UPSET, DISTRESS, AND HUMILIATE; 568] *Opposite:* buoy up.

disheartened *adj* **discouraged**, depressed, saddened, dismayed, dejected, disconsolate, downcast, dispirited, crestfallen, low. [➡SADNESS, DISTRESS, AND DESPAIR; 540] *Opposite:* encouraged.

disheartening *adj* **intimidating**, off-putting, daunting, dispiriting, depressing, demoralizing, discouragingly, dismaying. [➡EMOTIONALLY UNPLEASANT AND UPSETTING; 228] *Opposite:* encouraging.

dishevelled *adj* **unkempt**, wild and woolly, tousled, ruffled, untidy, scruffy, unruly. [➡BADLY GROOMED; 484] *Opposite:* well-groomed.

dishonest *adj* **lying**, deceitful, false, untruthful, fraudulent, corrupt, unfair, insincere, mendacious, underhand, misleading. [➡DECEITFUL; 514] *Opposite:* honest.

dishonesty *n* **deceit**, deceitfulness, fraudulence, lying, untruthfulness, corruption, treachery, duplicity, cheating, trickery. [➡DECEPTION AND LIES; 661] *Opposite:* honesty.

dishonour 1 *n* **disgrace**, shame, discredit, ignominy, disrepute, infamy. [➡DIFFICULT SITUATIONS; 72] *Opposite:* honour. 2 *v* **disgrace**, shame, discredit, defame, bring into disrepute, bring shame on. [➡UPSET, DISTRESS, AND HUMILIATE; 568] *Opposite:* honour.

dishonourable *adj* **disgraceful**, disreputable, discreditable, shameful, ignominious, ignoble. [➡MORALLY BAD; 776] *Opposite:* honourable.

dish out (*informal*) *v* **distribute**, parcel out, dole out (*informal*), allot, hand out, deal out, mete out. [➡DISPENSE, RATION, AND DISTRIBUTE; 435]

dish the dirt (*informal*) *v* [➡BETRAY CONFIDENCES AND GOSSIP; 619]

dishwasher *type of* **appliance**. [➡HOUSEHOLD APPLIANCES; 1116]

dishy (*informal*) *adj* **good-looking**, attractive, handsome, gorgeous, pretty, nice-looking, hunky (*informal*). [➡PEOPLE'S PHYSICAL APPEARANCE; 476] *Opposite:* ugly.

disillusion *v* **disenchant**, bring down to earth, disappoint, let down, dishearten, dissatisfy. [➡UPSET, DISTRESS, AND HUMILIATE; 568] *Opposite:* inspire.

disillusioned *adj* **disenchanted**, disappointed, disheartened, cynical. [➡SADNESS, DISTRESS, AND DESPAIR; 540] *Opposite:* starry-eyed.

disillusionment *n* **disenchantment**, disappointment, cynicism, letdown, discouragement. [➡SADNESS, DISTRESS, AND DESPAIR; 540] *Opposite:* gratification.

disincentive *n* **deterrent**, discouragement, hindrance, impediment, encumbrance. [➡PROBLEM; 257] *Opposite:* incentive.

disinclination *n* **reluctance**, unwillingness, opposition, hesitation, aversion. [➡UNWILLINGNESS AND STUBBORNNESS; 565] *Opposite:* inclination.

disincline *v* **put off**, deter, discourage, dissuade, prevent. [➡BORE AND FAIL TO INTEREST; 571] *Opposite:* encourage.

disinclined *adj* **reluctant**, unwilling, averse (*formal*), opposed, unenthusiastic, loath, hesitant. [➡UNWILLINGNESS AND STUBBORNNESS; 565] *Opposite:* inclined.

See Compare and Contrast at **unwilling**.

disinfect *v* **sterilize**, sanitize, purify, fumigate, cleanse, clean thoroughly, clean, decontaminate. [➡CLEAN AND POLISH; 404] *Opposite:* contaminate.

disinfectant *n* **antiseptic**, sanitizer, sterilizer, purifier. [➡CLEANING AGENTS; 863]

disinfected *adj* [➡CLEAN; 1232]

disinformation *n* **deception**, falsehood, propaganda, half-truth, misinformation, untruth. [➡DECEPTION AND LIES; 661] *Opposite:* truth.

disingenuous *adj* **dishonest**, insincere, untruthful, deceitful, hypocritical, misleading, duplicitous. [➡DECEITFUL; 514] *Opposite:* honest.

disingenuousness *n* **dishonesty**, insincerity, untruthfulness, deceit, hypocrisy, duplicity, duplicitousness. [➡DECEITFUL; 514] *Opposite:* honesty.

disinherit *v* **cut off**, disown, leave penniless, dispossess (*archaic or formal*), cut out, divest, deprive. [➡REVOKE STATUS; 460] *Opposite:* bequeath.

disintegrate *v* **crumble**, fragment, break, collapse, split, breakdown, degenerate. [➡CEASE TO EXIST; 22] *Opposite:* combine.

disintegration *n* **breakdown**, breakup, collapse, fragmentation, crumbling, dissolution, degeneration. [➡END; 54]

disinter 1 *v* **exhume**, dig up, unearth. [➡BURIAL AND PREPARATION FOR BURIAL; 929] *Opposite:* bury. 2 *v* (*formal*) **uncover**, unearth, bring to light, expose, reveal, disclose, divulge, unveil. [➡CAUSE TO APPEAR; 5] *Opposite:* cover up.

disinterest *n* **indifference**, unconcern, apathy, disregard, heedlessness, listlessness, insouciance. [➡NEUTRALITY AND INDIFFERENCE; 554] *Opposite:* interest.

disinterested *adj* **fair-minded**, unbiased, impartial, without prejudice, neutral, objective. [➡POSITIVE INTELLECTUAL CHARACTERISTICS; 525] *Opposite:* biased.

disinterestedness *n* **impartiality**, objectivity, fair-mindedness, neutrality, distance. [➡POSITIVE INTELLECTUAL CHARACTERISTICS; 525] *Opposite:* bias.

disinterment 1 *n* **exhumation**, digging up, unearthing, exposure. *Opposite:* interment. (*formal*). [➡BURIAL AND PREPARATION FOR BURIAL; 929] 2 *n* (*formal*) **exposure**, unearthing, discovery, revelation, uncovering, disclosure. [➡INFORM AND ANNOUNCE; 612] *Opposite:* concealment.

disjoint 1 *v* **split**, separate, come apart, sever, divide, disconnect, dismember. [➡UNFASTEN AND UNDO; 410] *Opposite:* join. 2 *v* **dislocate**, dislodge, move, relocate, separate. [➡SEPARATE AND DIVIDE; 402] *Opposite:* retain.

disjointed *adj* **rambling**, fragmented, incoherent, disorganized, disorderly, jumpy, jerky, unconnected. [➡INARTICULATE, RAMBLING, AND AWKWARD; 634] *Opposite:* coherent.

disjointedness *n* **disjunction**, disjuncture, incoherence, dislocation, disconnection, disconnectedness. [➡UNRELATEDNESS AND SEPARATENESS; 147] *Opposite:* coherence.

disk *type of* **hardware**. [➡COMPUTERS AND COMPUTING; 1126]

disk drive *type of* **hardware**. [➡COMPUTERS AND COMPUTING; 1126]

diskette *type of* **hardware**. [➡COMPUTERS AND COMPUTING; 1126]

dislikable *adj* **disagreeable**, unpleasant, offensive, repugnant, horrible, obnoxious. [➡DISGUSTING AND REPULSIVE; 231] *Opposite:* likable.

dislike 1 *v* **hate**, abhor (*formal*), detest, loathe, frown on, disapprove. [➡DISLIKE AND HATE; 578] *Opposite:* like. 2 *n* **aversion**, hatred, hate, loathing, abhorrence, pet hate, bete noir (*literary*), displeasure, disinclination, distaste, disgust, repugnance, antipathy, animosity, revulsion. [➡DISLIKE AND HATE; 578] *Opposite:* liking.

Compare and Contrast: *dislike, distaste, hatred, hate, disgust, loathing, repugnance, abhorrence, animosity, antipathy, aversion, revulsion*

CORE MEANING: NOT LIKING SOMEBODY OR SOMETHING

dislike a feeling or attitude of disapproval; ***distaste*** mild dislike, mainly of behaviour and activities; ***hatred or hate*** intense dislike or hostility; ***disgust*** a feeling of horrified and sickened disapproval; ***loathing*** intense dislike; ***repugnance*** strong disgust, mainly of behaviour and activities; ***abhorrence*** a feeling of aversion or intense disapproval, mainly of behaviour and activities; ***animosity*** a feeling of hostility and resentment; ***antipathy*** a deep-seated dislike or hostility; ***aversion*** a strong feeling of dislike; ***revulsion*** a sudden violent feeling of disgust.

dislocate 1 *v* **put out of place**, displace, put out of joint, disjoint, dislodge, disarticulate. [➡UNFASTEN AND UNDO; 410] *Opposite:* replace. 2 *v* **disrupt**, interrupt, disturb, upset, disorder, perturb. [➡CREATE DISORDER AND CAUSE CHAOS; 359] *Opposite:* restore.

dislocation 1 *n* **displacement**, disarticulation, dislodgment. [➡MOVE SOMETHING TO ANOTHER LOCATION; 325] 2 *n* **disruption**, interruption, disturbance, disorder, upset, confusion. [➡DISORDER AND CHAOS; 246]

dislodge *v* **remove**, get out, extricate, free, displace, dislocate. [➡FREEDOM AND LIBERTY; 209] *Opposite:* wedge.

disloyal *adj* **unfaithful**, treacherous, untrue, false, fickle, untrustworthy, perfidious (*literary*), faithless. [➡LACK OF COMMITMENT AND UNRELIABILITY; 510] *Opposite:* loyal.

disloyalty *n* **unfaithfulness**, treachery, falseness, infidelity, betrayal, fickleness, untrustworthiness, perfidy (*literary*). [➡LACK OF COMMITMENT AND UNRELIABILITY; 510] *Opposite:* loyalty.

dismal *adj* **miserable**, gloomy, depressing, dreary, dull, murky, bleak, drab, grim, cheerless. [➡EMOTIONALLY UNPLEASANT AND UPSETTING; 228] *Opposite:* bright.

dismantle *v* [➡UNFASTEN AND UNDO; 410]

dismay 1 *v* **disappoint**, shock, sadden, depress, perturb, discourage. [➡UPSET, DISTRESS, AND HUMILIATE; 568] *Opposite:* comfort. 2 *n* **disappointment**, shock, consternation, apprehension, panic, alarm, sadness, depression. [➡SADNESS, DISTRESS, AND DESPAIR; 540] *Opposite:* comfort.

dismayed *adj* **discouraged**, disheartened, demoralized, downcast, fed up (*informal*), depressed, intimidated, perturbed, distressed. [➡SADNESS, DISTRESS, AND DESPAIR; 540] *Opposite:* heartened.

dismember *v* **tear limb from limb**, cut into pieces, cut up, dissect, tear apart, mutilate, disarticulate, disjoint. [➡WOUND A PERSON OR ANIMAL; 384]

dismemberment *n* **taking apart**, mutilation, division, maiming, splitting off, disintegration. [➡WOUND A PERSON OR ANIMAL; 384]

dismiss 1 *v* **give notice**, discharge, sack (*informal*), fire (*informal*), let go, lay off, can (*US slang*), terminate (*US*). [➡REVOKE STATUS; 460] *Opposite:* detain. 2 *v* **send away**, allow to go, release, send home. [➡REVOKE STATUS; 460] 3 *v* **reject**, set aside, think no more of, write off (*informal*), put out of your mind, shelve, disdain, scorn. [➡NOT PAY ATTENTION; 765] *Opposite:* dwell on.

dismissal *n* **removal**, sack (*informal*), notice, discharge, firing (*informal*), release. [➡REVOKE STATUS; 460] *Opposite:* appointment.

dismissive *adj* **flippant**, indifferent, unconcerned, trivializing, contemptuous, glib, facetious, airy, frivolous. [➡MOCKING AND DISMISSIVE; 637] *Opposite:* attentive.

dismount *v* **get down**, get off, alight, descend. [➡GO DOWNWARDS; 308] *Opposite:* mount.

disobedience *n* **defiance**, noncompliance, breaking the rules, insubordination, waywardness, naughtiness, rebellion. [➡REBELLIOUSNESS AND DISOBEDIENCE; 566] *Opposite:* obedience.

disobedient *adj* **defiant**, noncompliant, rebellious, insubordinate, badly behaved, naughty, wayward. [➡REBELLIOUSNESS AND DISOBEDIENCE; 566] *Opposite:* obedient.

disobey *v* **defy**, refuse to comply, break the rules, contravene, violate, go against, flout, challenge. [➡DISOBEY; 303]

disobliging *adj* **unhelpful**, uncooperative, unaccommodating, rude, unfriendly, discourteous. [➡REBELLIOUSNESS AND DISOBEDIENCE; 566] *Opposite:* obliging.

disorder 1 *n* **chaos**, disarray, confusion, mess, muddle, turmoil, anarchy, mayhem (*informal*), bedlam, unrest. [➡DISORDER AND CHAOS; 246] *Opposite:* order. 2 *n* **complaint**, illness, sickness, ailment, syndrome, malady, condition. [➡SICKNESS; 730]

disordered *adj* **chaotic**, messy, muddled, topsy-turvy, higgledy-piggledy, anarchic, tangled, disorderly, jumbled. [➡DISORDER AND CHAOS; 246] *Opposite:* well-ordered.

disorderliness *n* **confusion**, messiness, muddle, chaos, disarray, disarrangement, disorder, disruption. [➡DISORDER AND CHAOS; 246] *Opposite:* orderliness.

disorderly 1 *adj* **unruly**, riotous, uncontrollable, rebellious, wild, unmanageable, rowdy, boisterous, undisciplined. [➡REBELLIOUSNESS AND DISOBEDIENCE; 566] *Opposite:* orderly. 2 *adj* **muddled**, jumbled, confused, messy, unsystematic, disorganized, higgledy-piggledy, topsy-turvy, anarchic, disordered, chaotic. [➡DISORDER AND CHAOS; 246]

disorderly conduct *n* [➡CRIMES; 817]

disorganization *n* **inefficiency**, ineptitude, ineffectiveness, incompetence, disorder, inadequacy. [➡UNSKILLED; 530] *Opposite:* organization.

disorganize *v* **muddle**, mix up, mess up (*informal*), confuse, jumble, dislocate, disorder, upset. [➡CREATE DISORDER AND CAUSE CHAOS; 359] *Opposite:* organize.

disorganized *adj* **muddled**, jumbled, confused, messy, unsystematic, higgledy-piggledy, topsy-turvy, disordered, chaotic, incoherent, disjointed, anarchic, disorderly. [➡DISORDER AND CHAOS; 246] *Opposite:* organized.

disorient *v* **confuse**, perplex, throw (*informal*), fox, befuddle, fuddle, puzzle, mystify, baffle, bewilder, flummox (*informal*), stupefy, nonplus, confound, bamboozle (*informal*), disorientate. [➡CONFUSE AND BEWILDER; 572] *Opposite:* orient.

disorientate *v* **confuse**, perplex, throw (*informal*), fox, befuddle, fuddle, puzzle, mystify, baffle, bewilder, flummox (*informal*), stupefy, nonplus, bamboozle (*informal*), confound, disorient. [➡CONFUSE AND BEWILDER; 572] *Opposite:* orientate.

disorientated *adj* [➡CONFUSION, ANXIETY, AND WORRY; 541]

disorientation *n* **puzzlement**, bafflement, stupefaction, bewilderment, confusion, uncertainty, incomprehension, perplexity, panic. [➡CONFUSION, ANXIETY, AND WORRY; 541]

disown *v* **renounce**, reject, wash your hands of, turn your back on, disclaim, deny, repudiate. [➡FORGO AND DENY ONESELF; 450] *Opposite:* acknowledge.

disparage *v* **belittle**, laugh at, mock, ridicule, pour scorn on, sneer, criticize, vilify, denigrate, run down, deride, scorn. [➡ACCUSE, BLAME, AND CRITICIZE; 642] *Opposite:* praise.

disparagement *n* **belittling**, mocking, ridicule, criticism, derision, scorn, vilification, denigration. [➡CRITICISMS AND ANGRY OUTBURSTS; 50] *Opposite:* praise.

disparaging *adj* **critical**, unfavourable, disapproving, censorious, unsympathetic, judgmental, scornful, approving. [➡ACCUSATORY AND DISAPPROVING; 635]

disparate *adj* **dissimilar**, unlike, unequal, different, incongruent, unrelated, contrasting, distinct. [➡DIFFERENCE; 150] *Opposite:* similar.

disparity *n* **difference**, inequality, discrepancy, disproportion, gap, inconsistency, incongruence. [➡DIFFERENCE; 150] *Opposite:* parity.

dispassion *n* **aloofness**, coolness, calmness, impassivity, serenity, detachment, objectivity. [➡NEUTRALITY AND INDIFFERENCE; 554] *Opposite:* enthusiasm.

dispassionate *adj* **calm**, composed, unflustered, unemotional, detached, cool, aloof, objective, impassive, serene. [➡NEUTRALITY AND INDIFFERENCE; 554] *Opposite:* fiery.

dispassionately *adv* **impassively**, objectively, disinterestedly, without bias, serenely, unflappably, unemotionally, undemonstratively, imperturbably, evenly, calmly, coolly, equably, neutrally, remotely, distantly, aloofly. [➡UNINTERESTED AND DETACHED; 630] *Opposite:* emotionally.

dispatch 1 *v* **send off**, send out, post, mail, ship, transmit, forward, remit. [➡DESPATCH AND SEND; 334] *Opposite:* keep. 2 *v* **kill**, murder, assassinate, put to death, slay (*formal or literary*), slaughter, destroy. [➡KILL; 923] 3 *n* **message**, communication, notice, letter, report. [➡LETTERS AND WRITTEN MESSAGES; 585]

dispatch rider *n* **courier**, messenger, deliverer. [➡MESSENGERS AND COURIERS; 852]

dispel *v* **dismiss**, chase away, drive out, disperse, scatter, dissipate, oust. [➡GET RID OF SOMETHING; 452] *Opposite:* attract.

dispensable *adj* **expendable**, superfluous, unessential, unnecessary, replaceable, surplus to requirements. [➡REDUNDANT AND USELESS; 241] *Opposite:* indispensable.

dispensary *n* **chemist's**, pharmacy, drugstore (*US*). [➡RETAIL OUTLETS; 1082]

dispensation *n* **indulgence**, allowance, special consideration, privilege, exemption, release. [➡FREEDOM AND LIBERTY; 209]

dispense *v* **give out**, hand out, distribute, dole out (*informal*), allot, mete out, bestow (*formal*), dish out (*informal*). [➡DISPENSE, RATION, AND DISTRIBUTE; 435] *Opposite:* withhold.

dispenser *n* **distributor**, slot machine, machine, vending machine. [➡MACHINES AND MACHINE PARTS; 1115]

dispense with *v* [➡GET RID OF SOMETHING; 452]

dispersal *n* **dispersion**, spreading, scattering, diffusion, distribution, thinning out, diaspora. [➡MOVE SOMETHING TO ANOTHER LOCATION; 325] *Opposite:* concentration.

disperse *v* **scatter**, go away, disband, break up, dissolve, separate, diffuse, melt away, disappear. [➡ABSENT ONESELF; 8] *Opposite:* concentrate.

dispersion *n* **dispersal**, spreading, scattering, diffusion, distribution, thinning out. [➡MOVE SOMETHING TO ANOTHER LOCATION; 325] *Opposite:* concentration.

dispirit *v* **dishearten**, discourage, dampen, depress, dismay, cast down, deject (*archaic*). [➡UPSET, DISTRESS, AND HUMILIATE; 568] *Opposite:* rouse.

dispirited *adj* **disheartened**, discouraged, dejected, depressed, downhearted, low, disconsolate, dismayed, crestfallen, demoralized. [➡SADNESS, DISTRESS, AND DESPAIR; 540] *Opposite:* cheerful.

dispiriting *adj* **disheartening**, depressing, demoralizing, upsetting, saddening. [➡EMOTIONALLY UNPLEASANT AND UPSETTING; 228] *Opposite:* uplifting.

displace 1 *v* **move**, relocate, shift, transfer, put out of place, dislocate, dislodge. [➡MOVE SOMETHING TO ANOTHER LOCATION; 325] *Opposite:* restore. 2 *v* **oust**, supplant, replace, supersede, succeed, depose. [➡REVOKE STATUS; 460] *Opposite:* restore.

displacement *n* **movement**, dislocation, dislodgment, shift, supplanting, translation, transposition. [➡MOVE SOMETHING TO ANOTHER LOCATION; 325]

display 1 *v* **show**, exhibit, put on show, present, put on view, demonstrate, expose, reveal. [➡CAUSE TO APPEAR; 5] *Opposite:* conceal. 2 *v* **flaunt**, parade, show off, strut, pose, flash (*informal*), brandish. [➡CAUSE TO APPEAR; 5] *Opposite:* conceal. 3 *n* **show**, exhibition, presentation, demonstration, parade, spectacle, ceremony, pageant. [➡PERFORMANCES AND SHOWS; 42]

display cabinet *type of* **cabinet**. [➡FURNITURE; 858]

display case *type of* **cabinet**. [➡FURNITURE; 858]

displease *v* **anger**, annoy, irritate, upset, put out, offend, dissatisfy, irk, peeve (*informal*). [➡ANGER AND ANNOY; 570] *Opposite:* please.

displeased *adj* **annoyed**, dissatisfied, put out, irked, unhappy, irritated, peeved (*informal*), upset. [➡IRRITATION AND ANGER; 542] *Opposite:* pleased.

displeasing *adj* [➡INAPPROPRIATE AND UNSUITABLE; 225]

displeasure *n* **anger**, annoyance, irritation, disapproval, discontentment, discontent, unhappiness. [➡IRRITATION AND ANGER; 542] *Opposite:* pleasure.

disport (*archaic or humorous*) *v* **show off**, pose, swagger, strut, flaunt, display. [➡CAUSE TO APPEAR; 5]

disposable *adj* **throwaway**, one-use, nonrefundable. [➡FINITENESS, VARIABILITY, AND TRANSIENCE; 96] *Opposite:* reusable.

disposal *n* **removal**, discarding, clearance, dumping, throwing away. [➡REMOVE SOMETHING; 339] *Opposite:* retention.

dispose 1 *v* **incline**, influence, persuade, prompt, predispose (*formal*), encourage. [➡ENCOURAGE; 577] 2 *v* (*formal*) **position**, place, set out, arrange, set, marshal, array (*formal*). [➡POSITION SOMETHING; 326] 3 *v* **settle**, resolve, fix, decide, determine, rule. [➡MAKE DECISIONS AND CHOICES; 753]

disposed *adj* **willing**, likely, liable, inclined, of a mind, feeling like, predisposed, ready, prepared. [➡THE WILL AND WILLINGNESS; 564] *Opposite:* unwilling.

dispose of 1 *v* **throw away**, throw out, dispense with, discard, get rid of, bin, jettison, axe (*informal*), scrap, dump, ditch (*informal*), chuck (*informal*), get shot of (*informal*). [➡GET RID OF SOMETHING; 452] *Opposite:* keep. 2 *v* **transfer**, pass on, divest yourself of, relieve yourself of, sell. [➡GET RID OF SOMETHING; 452] *Opposite:* keep. 3 *v* (*formal*) **attend to**, determine, settle, sort out, sort, eliminate, mop up. [➡CARRY OUT AN ACTION; 270] 4 *v* **kill**, murder, execute, assassinate, dispatch, do away with (*informal*). [➡KILL; 923] 5 *v* (*formal*) **consume**, demolish, get through, devour, use up, finish off, finish up. [➡USE UP AND WASTE; 475]

disposition *n* **nature**, character, temperament, temper, outlook, mood, personality. [➡TEMPERAMENT AND BEHAVIOUR; 493]

dispossess (*archaic or formal*) *v* **deprive**, divest, strip, rob, disinherit, take away. [➡TAKE SOMETHING AWAY; 426]

dispossessed *adj* **evicted**, expelled, ejected, cast out (*formal*), turned out, driven out, homeless. [➡NOMADIC AND ROOTLESS LIFESTYLES; 884]

dispossession *n* **deprivation**, denial, withdrawal, removal. [➡TOO FEW, TOO LITTLE; 120]

disproportion *n* **imbalance**, discrepancy, disparity, inequality, inconsistency, inequity. [➡DIFFERENCE; 150] *Opposite:* equality.

disproportionate *adj* **uneven**, unequal, lopsided, inconsistent, top-heavy, unbalanced, disparate. [➡DIFFERENCE; 150] *Opposite:* corresponding.

disproportionately *adv* **excessively**, unduly, unreasonably, extremely, too, overly. [➡TOO MUCH; 118] *Opposite:* slightly.

disprove *v* **refute**, invalidate, contradict, negate (*formal*), controvert (*formal*), challenge. [➡DENY AND REJECT; 645] *Opposite:* prove.

disputable *adj* **arguable**, debatable, moot, questionable, uncertain, doubtful. [➡UNCERTAIN; 176] *Opposite:* incontrovertible.

disputation (*formal*) *n* **argument**, strife, conflict, debate, disagreement, contention, controversy. [➡ARGUMENT; 47] *Opposite:* agreement.

disputatious (*formal*) *adj* **argumentative**, quarrelsome, awkward, difficult, contrary, perverse, fractious, troublesome, hostile, disputative (*formal*). [➡DIFFICULT TO PLEASE; 516] *Opposite:* conciliatory.

disputatiously (*formal*) *adv* **argumentatively**, quarrelsomely, awkwardly, contrarily, perversely, fractiously, troublesomely, hostilely. [➡RUDE AND HOSTILE; 626] *Opposite:* agreeably.

disputatiousness (*formal*) *n* **argumentativeness**, quarrelsomeness, awkwardness, contrariness, fractiousness, troublesomeness. [➡DIFFICULT TO PLEASE; 516] *Opposite:* agreement.

disputative (*formal*) *adj* **argumentative**, quarrelsome, awkward, difficult, contrary, perverse, fractious, troublesome, hostile, disputatious (*formal*). [➡DIFFICULT TO PLEASE; 516] *Opposite:* conciliatory.

dispute **1** *v* **argue**, debate, discuss, quarrel, wrangle, disagree. [➡ARGUE AND FIGHT – TWO-WAY; 644] *Opposite:* agree. **2** *v* **challenge**, question, contest, impugn (*formal*), query, doubt. [➡QUESTION THINGS; 752] *Opposite:* accept. **3** *n* **argument**, disagreement, quarrel, difference, clash, row. [➡ARGUMENT; 47] *Opposite:* agreement.

disqualification *n* **ineligibility**, banning, barring, disentitlement, debarment, exclusion, prohibition. [➡REFUSE PERMISSION AND NOT ALLOW; 671] *Opposite:* entitlement.

disqualified *adj* **ineligible**, banned, barred, debarred, prohibited, excluded. [➡REFUSE PERMISSION AND NOT ALLOW; 671] *Opposite:* eligible.

disqualify *v* **ban**, bar, debar, prohibit, exclude, eliminate, except (*formal*), rule out. [➡REFUSE PERMISSION AND NOT ALLOW; 671] *Opposite:* allow.

disquiet **1** *n* **unrest**, uneasiness, concern, worry, anxiety, foreboding, alarm. [➡INSECURITY AND LOSS OF COMPOSURE; 545] *Opposite:* calmness. **2** *v* (*archaic or literary*) **worry**, disturb, upset, disconcert, perturb, unsettle, bother, fluster. [➡UPSET, DISTRESS, AND HUMILIATE; 568]

disquieted (*archaic or literary*) *adj* [➡INSECURITY AND LOSS OF COMPOSURE; 545]

disquieting *adj* **worrying**, disturbing, alarming, unsettling, troubling, distressing. [➡EMOTIONALLY UNPLEASANT AND UPSETTING; 228] *Opposite:* reassuring.

disquisition (*formal*) *n* **essay**, tract, discussion, address, speech, debate. [➡NEUTRAL ONE-WAY COMMUNICATION; 49]

disquisitional (*formal*) *adj* **verbose**, wordy, long-winded, rambling, digressive. [➡INARTICULATE, RAMBLING, AND AWKWARD; 634] *Opposite:* concise.

disregard **1** *v* **ignore**, take no notice of, turn a blind eye to, discount, pay no attention to, forget. [➡NOT PAY ATTENTION; 765] *Opposite:* heed. **2** *n* **disrespect**, indifference, contempt, disdain, neglect. [➡NEUTRALITY AND INDIFFERENCE; 554] *Opposite:* regard.

disregarded **1** *adj* **ignored**, omitted, overlooked, unheeded, unnoticed, marginalized, unsung. [➡UNPOPULAR AND UNWANTED; 259] *Opposite:* noticed. **2** *adj* **snubbed**, slighted, dishonoured, disparaged, ridiculed. [➡IN TROUBLE AND DISADVANTAGED; 73] *Opposite:* respected.

disrepair *n* **poor shape**, bad shape, bad condition, poor order, disorder, shabbiness. [➡IN BAD REPAIR; 1233]

disreputable *adj* **notorious**, infamous, scandalous, disgraceful, seedy. [➡MORALLY BAD; 776] *Opposite:* reputable.

disrepute *n* **disgrace**, ill repute, disrespect, disregard, discredit, opprobrium, shame, dishonour. [➡DIFFICULT SITUATIONS; 72]

disrespect **1** *n* **disregard**, contempt, insolence, impertinence, impudence. [➡ANTAGONISM; 553] *Opposite:* respect. **2** *v* **insult**, affront, belittle, disparage, denigrate, put down (*informal*), dis (*slang*). [➡PROTEST AND EXPRESS DISAPPROVAL; 643] *Opposite:* respect.

disrespectable *adj* **dishonourable**, frowned on, disreputable, unpopular, infamous, notorious. [➡MORALLY BAD; 776] *Opposite:* respectable.

disrespectful *adj* **rude**, impolite, bad-mannered, discourteous, insolent, impertinent (*formal*), ill-mannered. [➡BAD MANNERS AND SOCIAL SKILLS; 522] *Opposite:* respectful.

disrobe (*formal*) *v* **strip**, undress, divest (*formal or humorous*), unclothe, uncover. [➡DRESS, WEAR, AND UNDRESS; 868] *Opposite:* dress.

disrupt *v* **disturb**, upset, interrupt, dislocate, disorder, mess up (*informal*), unsettle. [➡CREATE DISORDER AND CAUSE CHAOS; 359]

disruption *n* **disturbance**, commotion, trouble, interruption, distraction, interference, disorder. [➡PROBLEM; 257]

disruptive *adj* **troublesome**, troublemaking, unruly, disorderly, unsettling, upsetting, disrupting, disturbing, distracting. [➡IRRITATING; 229]

disruptively *adv* **noisily**, rudely, raucously, wildly, boisterously, rowdily, obtrusively. [➡POMPOUS, LOUD, AND OVER-CONFIDENT; 636] *Opposite:* unobtrusively.

disruptiveness *n* **unruliness**, rowdiness, disorderliness, indiscipline, naughtiness. [➡REBELLIOUSNESS AND DISOBEDIENCE; 566]

diss *see* **dis.**

dissatisfaction *n* **displeasure**, discontent, disappointment, unhappiness, frustration. [➡IRRITATION AND ANGER; 542] *Opposite:* satisfaction.

dissatisfied *adj* **disgruntled**, displeased, discontented, disappointed, unhappy, frustrated, fed up (*informal*). [➡IRRITATION AND ANGER; 542] *Opposite:* satisfied.

dissatisfy *v* **disgruntle**, displease, disappoint, put out, peeve (*informal*), frustrate. [➡ANGER AND ANNOY; 570] *Opposite:* satisfy.

dissect 1 *v* **cut up**, cut apart, divide, dismember, slice up, separate, dichotomize (*formal*), dissever (*formal*). [➡TEAR, BREAK, AND CUT; 361] 2 *v* **scrutinize**, break down, examine, study, explore, analyse, anatomize. [➡EXAMINE AND ASSESS; 754]

dissection 1 *n* **cutting up**, partition, division, separation, segmentation, splitting up, dismemberment. [➡TEAR, BREAK, AND CUT; 361] 2 *n* **examination**, analysis, investigation, scrutiny, observation, going-over (*informal*). [➡EXAMINE AND ASSESS; 754]

dissemble 1 *v* **pretend**, mislead, act, put on an act, play-act (*informal*), dissimulate (*formal*), feign. [➡DECEPTION AND LIES; 661] 2 *v* (*formal*) **disguise**, conceal, hide, suppress, mask, cloak, veil, camouflage, obscure, dissimulate (*formal*). [➡WITHHOLD INFORMATION; 688] *Opposite:* disclose.

dissembler (*formal*) *n* [➡PEOPLE WHO DECEIVE; 662]

disseminate *v* **distribute**, broadcast, circulate, spread, publicize, publish, propagate. [➡INFORM AND ANNOUNCE; 612]

See Compare and Contrast at **scatter.**

dissemination *n* **distribution**, broadcasting, diffusion, propagation, spreading, giving out. [➡INFORM AND ANNOUNCE; 612]

dissension *n* **opposition**, disagreement, dissent, discord, rebellion, conflict. [➡DISHARMONY; 157] *Opposite:* consent.

dissent 1 *v* **disagree**, oppose, rebel, dispute, differ, divide, vary. [➡PROTEST AND EXPRESS DISAPPROVAL; 643] *Opposite:* agree. 2 *n* **opposition**, disagreement, dissension, discord, rebellion, conflict, difference. [➡DISHARMONY; 157] *Opposite:* consent.

dissenter *n* **rebel**, dissident, nonconformist, insurgent, mutineer, malcontent, revolutionist. [➡UNCOOPERATIVE OR REBELLIOUS PERSON; 567]

dissertation *n* **thesis**, paper, study, critique, essay, exposition, tract. [➡ANALYTICAL NONFICTION WRITING; 593]

disservice *n* **damage**, harm, wrong, injury, difficulty. [➡NUISANCES; 254] *Opposite:* service.

dissever (*formal*) *v* [➡SEPARATE AND DIVIDE; 402]

dissidence *n* **disagreement**, unorthodoxy, nonconformity, independence, rebellion, resistance. [➡REBELLIOUSNESS AND DISOBEDIENCE; 566] *Opposite:* conformism.

dissident 1 *n* **dissenter**, rebel, nonconformist, protester, insurgent, mutineer, revolutionist, malcontent. [➡UNCOOPERATIVE OR REBELLIOUS PERSON; 567] *Opposite:* conformist. 2 *adj* **rebel**, rebellious, dissenting, unorthodox, nonconforming, nonconformist. [➡REBELLIOUSNESS AND DISOBEDIENCE; 566] *Opposite:* conformist.

dissimilar *adj* **unlike**, different, far from, unrelated, disparate, divergent, unalike, contradictory. [➡DIFFERENCE; 150] *Opposite:* similar.

dissimilarity *n* **difference**, variation, distinction, contrast, divergence, unlikeness. [➡DIFFERENCE; 150] *Opposite:* similarity.

dissimulate (*formal*) *v* **disguise**, conceal, hide, suppress, mask, cloak, veil, camouflage, obscure, dissemble (*formal*). [➡CAUSE TO DISAPPEAR; 6] *Opposite:* disclose.

dissimulation (*formal*) *n* **concealment**, suppression, disguise, camouflage, dishonesty, subterfuge. [➡DECEPTION AND LIES; 661] *Opposite:* disclosure.

dissipate 1 *v* **dispel**, disperse, dissolve, scatter, drive away, disintegrate. [➡SPREAD AND SCATTER; 333] 2 *v* **squander**, waste, fritter away, throw away, blow (*slang*). [➡GIVE MONEY; 434]

dissipated *adj* **dissolute**, degenerate, debauched, self-indulgent, immoral, intemperate. [➡PLEASURE-SEEKING AND EXCESS; 885] *Opposite:* upright.

dissipation *n* **debauchery**, indulgence, rakishness, overindulgence, degeneracy, intemperance. [➡PLEASURE-SEEKING AND EXCESS; 885] *Opposite:* uprightness.

dissociate *v* **distance**, detach, divorce, separate, disconnect, disassociate. [➡SEPARATE AND DIVIDE; 402] *Opposite:* associate.

dissociation *n* **detachment**, separation, disconnection, severance, alienation, division. [➡SEPARATE AND DIVIDE; 402] *Opposite:* association.

dissolute *adj* **degenerate**, depraved, immoral, debauched, self-indulgent, dissipated. [➡PLEASURE-SEEKING AND EXCESS; 885] *Opposite:* upright.

dissoluteness *n* **decadence**, overindulgence, licentiousness (*formal*), extravagance, self-indulgence, degeneracy, recklessness, wastefulness, profligacy, dissipation, depravity. [➡PLEASURE-SEEKING AND EXCESS; 885] *Opposite:* temperance.

dissolution *n* **closure**, disbanding, termination, ending, suspension, conclusion. [➡END; 54] *Opposite:* inauguration.

dissolve 1 *v* **melt**, soften, liquefy, thaw, run. [➡SOFTEN, LIQUEFY, DAMPEN; 389] *Opposite:* solidify. 2 *v* **disband**, close, break up, suspend, end, disperse, adjourn. [➡CAUSE TO STOP; 267] *Opposite:* inaugurate. 3 *v* **disappear**, dissipate, dispel, disperse, melt away, evaporate, vanish. [➡CEASE TO EXIST; 22] *Opposite:* appear.

dissonance *n* **discord**, disagreement, dissension, conflict, difference, difference of opinion. [➡DISHARMONY; 157] *Opposite:* harmony.

dissonant *adj* **discordant**, unmusical, harsh, inharmonious, cacophonous, jarring. [➡LOUD OR UNPLEASANT SOUNDS; 1265] *Opposite:* harmonious.

dissuade *v* **deter**, put off, discourage, advise against, persuade against, talk out of. [➡ADVISE AND WARN; 614] *Opposite:* persuade.

dissuasion *n* **discouragement**, deterrence, persuasion, opposition, warning. [➡ADVISE AND WARN; 614] *Opposite:* encouragement.

dissuasive *adj* **discouraging**, opposing, inhibitive, hindering. [➡ADVISE AND WARN; 614] *Opposite:* encouraging.

distance 1 *n* **coldness**, aloofness, detachment, reserve, remoteness. [➡UNINTERESTED AND DETACHED; 630] *Opposite:* warmth. 2 *n* **space**, expanse, void, vastness, gap. [➡DISTANCE; 161] *Opposite:* closeness. 3 *v* **dissociate**, move away, detach, separate, avoid. [➡NOT PAY ATTENTION; 765] *Opposite:* associate.

distance learning *type of* **broadcast**. [➡TELEVISION AND RADIO; 607]

distant 1 *adj* **faraway**, remote, far-off, far-flung, outlying, far, isolated, secluded. [➡DISTANCE; 161] *Opposite:* near. 2 *adj* **vague**, faint, indistinct, hazy, obscure. [➡VAGUENESS; 244] *Opposite:* clear. 3 *adj* **aloof**, cold, unfriendly, detached, reserved, unsociable, cool, withdrawn. [➡UNINTERESTED AND DETACHED; 630] *Opposite:* warm.

distantly 1 *adv* **vaguely**, faintly, indistinctly, abstractedly, far, remotely. [➡VAGUENESS; 244] *Opposite:* clearly. 2 *adv* **coldly**, coolly, aloofly, reservedly, unsociably. [➡UNINTERESTED AND DETACHED; 630] *Opposite:* warmly.

distaste *n* **aversion**, dislike, revulsion, disgust, disfavour. [➡DISLIKE AND HATE; 578] *Opposite:* love.

See Compare and Contrast at **dislike**.

distasteful *adj* **repugnant**, offensive, disgusting, repulsive, objectionable, revolting, obnoxious, odious. [➡DISGUSTING AND REPULSIVE; 231] *Opposite:* pleasant.

distastefulness *n* **unpleasantness**, offensiveness, nastiness, unattractiveness, hideousness, repulsiveness. [➡DISGUSTING AND REPULSIVE; 231] *Opposite:* pleasantness.

distend *v* **swell**, bloat, balloon, inflate, swell up, expand, increase, enlarge. [➡CHANGE OF SIZE: BIGGER; 393] *Opposite:* deflate.

distended *adj* **swollen**, bloated, inflated, enlarged, expanded. [➡CHANGE OF SIZE: BIGGER; 393]

distension *n* **swelling**, swollenness, tightness, expansion, enlargement. [➡CHANGE OF SIZE: BIGGER; 393] *Opposite:* dilation.

distil 1 *v* **purify**, refine, condense, extract, concentrate, clean. [➡CLEAN AND POLISH; 404] *Opposite:* dilute. 2 *v* **extract**, garner, glean, cull, collect, gather, obtain. [➡GET; 421] *Opposite:* expand.

distillate *n* **essence**, tincture, concentrate, extract, distillation. [➡LIQUIDS; 1268]

distillation 1 *n* **concentration**, condensation, refinement, purification, extraction, decontamination. [➡CLEAN AND POLISH; 404] *Opposite:* dilution. 2 *n* **essence**, epitome, embodiment, summation, condensation, image, concentration, concentrate. [➡PERFECT EXAMPLES AND EMBODIMENTS; 67] 3 *n* **distillate**, tincture, extract, concentrate. [➡LIQUIDS; 1268] *Opposite:* solution.

distillery *type of* **factory**. [➡INDUSTRIAL BUILDINGS; 1086]

distinct 1 *adj* **separate**, different, dissimilar, discrete, diverse, divergent, distinctive, individual. [➡DIFFERENCE; 150] *Opposite:* indistinct. 2 *adj* **clear**, definite, well-defined, noticeable, marked, apparent, conspicuous, manifest, patent, plain, evident. [➡PERCEPTIBLE; 25] *Opposite:* unclear.

distinction 1 *n* **difference**, division, dissimilarity, discrepancy, otherness. [➡DIFFERENCE; 150] *Opposite:* similarity. 2 *n* **feature**, characteristic, idiosyncrasy, peculiarity, trait, particularity, individualism. [➡PERSONAL ECCENTRICITIES; 494] 3 *n* **merit**, excellence, note, worth, accolade, award, decoration, honour. [➡REWARDS AND AWARDS; 440] *Opposite:* disgrace.

distinctive *adj* **characteristic**, idiosyncratic, distinguishing, individual, typical, unique, distinct. [➡REPRESENTATIVE; 66] *Opposite:* common.

distinctively *adv* **characteristically**, idiosyncratically, peculiarly, individually, typically, uniquely, particularly, specifically. [➡UNRELATEDNESS AND SEPARATENESS; 147]

distinctiveness *n* **uniqueness**, individuality, particularity, individualism, singularity. [➡UNRELATEDNESS AND SEPARATENESS; 147] *Opposite:* sameness.

distinctly *adv* **definitely**, clearly, noticeably, markedly, particularly, specifically, conspicuously, manifestly, patently, plainly. [➡PERCEPTIBLE; 25] *Opposite:* vaguely.

distinctness *n* [➡PERCEPTIBLE; 25]

distinguish 1 *v* **differentiate**, tell apart, tell between, discriminate, decide, extricate, separate. [➡EXAMINE AND ASSESS; 754] 2 *v* **make out**, discern, see, recognize, perceive, pick out, notice, observe. [➡LOOKING AND LOOKS; 701] 3 *v* **set apart**, single out, characterize, mark, classify, individualize, singularize (*formal*). [➡SEPARATE AND DIVIDE; 402]

distinguishability *n* [➡PERCEPTIBLE; 25]

distinguishable 1 *adj* **different**, unique, distinct, special, divergent, discrete. [➡DIFFERENCE; 150] 2 *adj* **discernible**, obvious, noticeable, clear, evident, apparent. [➡PERCEPTIBLE; 25] *Opposite:* indistinguishable.

distinguished *adj* **illustrious**, eminent, famous, famed, well-known, renowned, great, prominent, celebrated, notable. [➡LEVEL OF EDUCATION AND SOPHISTICATION; 894] *Opposite:* undistinguished.

distinguishing *adj* **unique**, individual, personal, distinctive, characteristic, peculiar. [➡EXTRAORDINARY: UNCOMMON; 206] *Opposite:* typical.

distort 1 *v* **misrepresent**, interfere with, twist, alter, garble, change, falsify, mislead. [➡CHANGE; 373] 2 *v* **deform**, disfigure, twist, warp, alter, bend. [➡CHANGE OF SHAPE; 386] *Opposite:* straighten.

distorted 1 *adj* **one-sided**, slanted, partial, inaccurate, partisan, misleading, biased, unfair. [➡FALSE AND UNREAL; 174] *Opposite:* accurate. 2 *adj* **twisted**, malformed, warped, bent, contorted, deformed, misshapen. [➡IN BAD REPAIR; 1233] *Opposite:* straight. 3 *adj* **unrecognizable**, grotesque, unnatural, monstrous, bizarre. [➡UGLINESS AND UNATTRACTIVENESS; 234]

distortion 1 *n* **bend**, buckle, twist, deformation, warp, disfigurement. [➡CHANGE OF SHAPE; 386] 2 *n* **misrepresentation**, alteration, lie, falsehood, falsification, spin (*slang*), bias. [➡ DECEPTION AND LIES; 661]

distract 1 *v* **sidetrack**, divert, confuse, addle, befuddle, disturb. [➡ CONFUSE AND BEWILDER; 572] 2 *v* **entertain**, amuse, divert, absorb, engross, engage. [➡ PLEASE AND AMUSE; 573]

distracted 1 *adj* **unfocused**, abstracted, preoccupied, sidetracked, diverted, confused, dreamy, inattentive, vague, absent-minded, distrait (*literary*). [➡ NEUTRALITY AND INDIFFERENCE; 554] *Opposite:* attentive. 2 *adj* **troubled**, agitated, anxious, perplexed, confused, upset, twitchy (*informal*). [➡ CONFUSION, ANXIETY, AND WORRY; 541] *Opposite:* assured.

distractedly 1 *adv* **vaguely**, abstractedly, dreamily, absent-mindedly, absently. [➡ INCAUTIOUS AND CARELESS; 284] *Opposite:* attentively. 2 *adv* **anxiously**, frantically, agitatedly, twitchily, worriedly. [➡ CONFUSION, ANXIETY, AND WORRY; 541] *Opposite:* calmly.

distracting *adj* **off-putting**, disturbing, diverting, disrupting. [➡ IRRITATING; 229]

distraction 1 *n* **interruption**, disruption, commotion, disturbance, interference. [➡ DISORDER AND CHAOS; 246] 2 *n* **diversion**, entertainment, hobby, pastime, leisure activity, amusement, recreation. [➡ LEISURE AND RECREATION; 874] 3 *n* **agitation**, anxiety, bewilderment, confusion, desperation, trouble, upset. [➡ CONFUSION, ANXIETY, AND WORRY; 541]

distrait (*literary*) *adj* **inattentive**, distracted, unmindful, dreamy, vague, preoccupied, absent-minded, woolgathering. [➡ NEUTRALITY AND INDIFFERENCE; 554] *Opposite:* alert.

distraught *adj* **distressed**, beside yourself, out of your mind, hysterical, upset, troubled, worried, flustered, agitated, disturbed, distrait (*archaic*), panic-stricken. [➡ CONFUSION, ANXIETY, AND WORRY; 541] *Opposite:* calm.

distress 1 *n* **suffering**, pain, sorrow, anguish, agony, grief, misery, ache, pang, concern, worry, angst. [➡ SADNESS, DISTRESS, AND DESPAIR; 540] *Opposite:* peace. 2 *n* **trouble**, danger, rigour, difficulty, misfortune, hardship, trial. [➡ DIFFICULT SITUATIONS; 72] 3 *v* **upset**, disturb, trouble, bother, afflict, torment, stress, worry. [➡ UPSET, DISTRESS, AND HUMILIATE; 568] *Opposite:* soothe.

distressed 1 *adj* **upset**, distraught, troubled, concerned, worried, anxious, distrait (*archaic*), unhappy, bothered. [➡ SADNESS, DISTRESS, AND DESPAIR; 540] *Opposite:* content. 2 *adj* **in pain**, suffering, anguished, tormented, miserable, aching. [➡ SADNESS, DISTRESS, AND DESPAIR; 540]

distressing *adj* **upsetting**, worrying, difficult, stressful, painful, sad. [➡ EMOTIONALLY UNPLEASANT AND UPSETTING; 228]

distress signal *n* **call for help**, cry for help, alarm bell, alarm, call, cry, alert, SOS. [➡ SOUNDS MADE BY PEOPLE; 1261]

distribute 1 *v* **deal out**, hand out, dole out (*informal*), share out, allocate, give out, issue, dispense, allot, dish out (*informal*), mete out. [➡ DISPENSE, RATION, AND DISTRIBUTE; 435] 2 *v* **deliver**, supply, circulate, spread out, spread, disperse, disseminate, scatter. [➡ DISPENSE, RATION, AND DISTRIBUTE; 435]

See Compare and Contrast at **scatter**.

distributer *see* **distributor**.

distribution 1 *n* **sharing**, allocation, giving out, division, allotment. [➡ DISPENSE, RATION, AND DISTRIBUTE; 435] 2 *n* **delivery**, supply, circulation, spreading, dispersal, dissemination, scattering. [➡ DISPENSE, RATION, AND DISTRIBUTE; 435] 3 *n* **spreading**, dispersal, dissemination, scattering. [➡ MOVE SOMETHING TO ANOTHER LOCATION; 325]

distributor *n* **supplier**, provider, purveyor (*formal*), wholesaler, broker, trader, merchant, distributer. [➡ BUSINESS PEOPLE; 794]

district *n* **region**, area, locality, quarter, borough, ward, constituency. [➡ COUNTRIES AND REGIONS; 1066]

district attorney (*US*) *n* [➡ PEOPLE IN LAW COURTS; 820]

distrust 1 *n* **suspicion**, disbelief, doubt, misgiving, cynicism, mistrust, wariness, chariness. [➡ UNCERTAINTY; 560] *Opposite:* trust. 2 *v* **disbelieve**, doubt, be suspicious of, mistrust, suspect. [➡ QUESTION THINGS; 752] *Opposite:* trust.

distrustful *adj* **suspicious**, doubting, wary, nervous, disbelieving, cynical, mistrustful, chary. [➡ UNCERTAINTY; 560] *Opposite:* trusting.

disturb 1 *v* **interrupt**, distract, bother, disrupt, annoy, get in the way, intrude. [➡ ANGER AND ANNOY; 570] 2 *v* **upset**, worry, bother, concern, perturb, agitate, scare, alarm, frighten, trouble. [➡ UPSET, DISTRESS, AND HUMILIATE; 568] 3 *v* **move**, transfer, shift, dislocate, remove. [➡ MOVE SOMETHING TO ANOTHER LOCATION; 325] 4 *v* **spoil**, mess up (*informal*), unsettle, upset, meddle, tamper, jumble, muddle. [➡ CREATE DISORDER AND CAUSE CHAOS; 359]

See Compare and Contrast at **bother**.

disturbance 1 *n* **trouble**, commotion, riot, uproar, fracas, disorder, disruption, ruckus. [➡ CHAOS AND UPROAR; 51] 2 *n* **annoyance**, interruption, intrusion, bother, disruption, irritation, distraction. [➡ NUISANCES; 254]

disturbed 1 *adj* **troubled**, bothered, concerned, worried, distressed, anxious, uneasy, upset, agitated, distraught. [➡ CONFUSION, ANXIETY, AND WORRY; 541] *Opposite:* unconcerned. 2 *adj* **unstable**, troubled, traumatized, unbalanced, unhinged, messed up (*informal*). [➡ ECCENTRICITY AND IRRATIONALITY; 563] *Opposite:* stable.

disturbing *adj* **worrying**, troubling, alarming, upsetting, distressing, disquieting, disconcerting, unsettling, ominous, unnerving. [➡ EMOTIONALLY UNPLEASANT AND UPSETTING; 228] *Opposite:* reassuring.

disunite *v* **split**, divide, separate, undo, dissolve, break, sever. [➡ UNFASTEN AND UNDO; 410] *Opposite:* unite.

disunity *n* **disagreement**, discord, divergence, dissent, conflict, dispute, division. [➡ DISHARMONY; 157] *Opposite:* unity.

disuse *n* **neglect**, abandonment, unemployment, dereliction. [➡ IN BAD REPAIR; 1233] *Opposite:* use.

disused *adj* **empty**, abandoned, neglected, derelict, deserted. [➡ IN BAD REPAIR; 1233] *Opposite:* occupied.

ditch 1 *n* **channel**, trench, dike, drain, waterway, conduit, gully, trough. [➡ WATERCOURSES; 1110] 2 *v* (*informal*) **dump** (*informal*), scrap, get rid of, chuck (*informal*), drop, give somebody the boot (*informal*), split up with, discard, throw out, leave. [➡REFUSING OR REJECTING RELATIONS; 975]

dither *v* **hesitate**, dally, dawdle, waste time, vacillate, waver, shilly-shally. [➡HESITATE; 273]

ditherer *n* **vacillator**, dawdler, waverer, hesitater. [➡LAZY OR UNSUCCESSFUL PEOPLE; 948]

dithering *n* **indecisiveness**, indecision, hesitation, irresolution, wavering, hesitancy, shilly-shallying, uncertainty, faltering, vacillation. [➡UNCERTAINTY; 560] *Opposite:* decisiveness.

ditsy (*US informal*) *adj* **empty-headed**, forgetful, absent-minded, scatterbrained, dizzy (*informal*), vague, woolly-headed, unreliable, eccentric, frivolous. [➡LACK OF COMMITMENT AND UNRELIABILITY; 510]

ditty *n* **song**, poem, rhyme, limerick, nursery rhyme, ode. [➡MUSIC, SONGS, AND SINGING; 907]

diurnal 1 *adj* **day**, daytime, daylight. [➡TIMES OF DAY; 87] *Opposite:* nocturnal. 2 *adj* **daily**, 24-hour, 24-hourly, circadian, quotidian (*formal*). [➡TIMES OF DAY; 87]

diva *n* **prima donna**, singer, chanteuse, soprano. [➡MUSICIANS AND SINGERS; 908]

divan *n* **settee**, couch, sofa. [➡FURNITURE; 858]

dive 1 *v* **jump**, leap, drop, lunge, submerge. [➡GO DOWNWARDS; 308] *Opposite:* surface. 2 *v* **plummet**, plunge, fall, nose-dive, crash, free-fall, go down, decrease. [➡CHANGE OF INTENSITY: LESS; 396] *Opposite:* shoot up. 3 *n* **lunge**, leap, drop, jump. [➡GO DOWNWARDS; 308] 4 *n* **plunge**, fall, nose dive, crash, free-fall, descent, plummet, decrease. [➡CHANGE OF INTENSITY: LESS; 396] 5 *n* (*informal*) **dump** (*informal*), bar, joint (*slang*), hangout (*informal*), honky-tonk (*US slang*), saloon (*US*). [➡BUILDINGS FOR PUBLIC ENTERTAINMENT; 1083]

diver 1 *n* **swimmer**, deep-sea diver, snorkeller, frogman, scuba diver, aquanaut. [➡PEOPLE IN SPORTS AND LEISURE; 876] 2 *type of* **freshwater bird.** [➡FRESHWATER BIRD; 1000]

diverge 1 *v* **deviate**, move away, wander, depart, swerve, separate. [➡SEPARATE AND DIVIDE; 402] *Opposite:* converge. 2 *v* **differ**, disagree, vary, conflict. [➡PROTEST AND EXPRESS DISAPPROVAL; 643] *Opposite:* concur. 3 *v* **digress**, ramble, stray, deviate. [➡WITTER AND BABBLE; 618]

divergence 1 *n* **deviation**, departure, discrepancy, disagreement, separation. [➡DIFFERENCE; 150] *Opposite:* convergence. 2 *n* **difference**, difference of opinion, disagreement, variance, conflict, nonconformity. [➡DIFFERENCE; 150] *Opposite:* agreement.

divergent *adj* **different**, differing, deviating, conflicting, contradictory, opposing, opposite, contrary. [➡DIFFERENCE; 150] *Opposite:* similar.

divers (*formal*) *adj* **various**, miscellaneous, assorted, sundry, several, distinct, disparate, different. [➡DIFFERENCE; 150] *Opposite:* similar.

diverse 1 *adj* **varied**, miscellaneous, assorted, sundry. [➡DIFFERENCE; 150] 2 *adj* **different**, dissimilar, unlike, distinct, separate, opposite, disparate. [➡DIFFERENCE; 150] *Opposite:* similar.

diversely *adv* **varyingly**, variously, distinctly, separately, dissimilarly, differently, peculiarly, inconsistently, disparately. [➡DIFFERENCE; 150] *Opposite:* similarly.

diversification *n* **change**, divergence, variation, modification, broadening, branching out, expansion. [➡CHANGE; 373] *Opposite:* specialization.

diversify *v* **branch out**, expand, spread, broaden your horizons, vary, differentiate. [➡CHANGE; 373] *Opposite:* specialize.

diversion 1 *n* **distraction**, entertainment, pastime, hobby, leisure activity, amusement, recreation. [➡LEISURE AND RECREATION; 874] 2 *n* **change**, alteration, departure, digression, deviation. [➡CHANGE; 373]

diversionary *adj* **distracting**, diverting, misleading, deflecting, deceptive. [➡FALSE AND UNREAL; 174]

diversity *n* **variety**, assortment, multiplicity, range, mixture. [➡COLLECTIONS AND MIXTURES OF THINGS; 1243] *Opposite:* uniformity.

divert 1 *v* **redirect**, deflect, reroute, switch. [➡CHANGE DIRECTION OF MOTION; 345] 2 *v* **distract**, sidetrack, turn away, avert, deter, dissuade. [➡APPEAL TO AND AROUSE INTEREST; 576] *Opposite:* focus. 3 *v* **entertain**, amuse, please, delight, gladden, regale, recreate. [➡PLEASE AND AMUSE; 573]

divest *v* **strip**, rid, dissociate, separate, part from, deny, deprive, rob. [➡TAKE SOMETHING AWAY; 426] *Opposite:* give.

divide 1 *v* **split**, separate, partition, segregate, break up, carve up (*informal*), part. [➡SEPARATE AND DIVIDE; 402] *Opposite:* join. 2 *v* **share**, share out, divide up, deal out, distribute, allocate, apportion, allot, split, divvy (*informal*), dole out (*informal*). [➡DISPENSE, RATION, AND DISTRIBUTE; 435] 3 *v* **cause a rift**, split up, break up, split, come between, differ, dissent, rive (*literary*). [➡UNFASTEN AND UNDO; 410] *Opposite:* unite. 4 *n* **gulf**, rift, division, split, gap, boundary. [➡HOLES, GAPS, AND FORKS; 1251]

divided highway (*US*) *type of* **major road.** [➡ROADS; 1105]

dividend *n* **bonus**, extra, payment, share, surplus, disbursement. [➡MONEY, PAYMENTS, AND CHARGES; 800]

divider *n* **partition**, separator, screen. [➡WALLS AND PARTITIONS; 1103]

dividers *type of* **measuring device.** [➡MEASURING DEVICES; 1122]

dividing line *n* **distinction**, margin, borderline, border, watershed, divider. [➡GEOGRAPHICAL BORDERS AND BOUNDARIES; 1068]

divination *n* **prophecy**, prediction, forecast, foretelling, insight, premonition, second sight. [➡PREDICT AND ANTICIPATE; 751]

divine 1 *adj* **heavenly**, celestial, godly, deific (*formal*), godlike. [➡RELIGIOUS CONCEPTS; 777] *Opposite:* earthly. 2 *adj* (*informal or humorous*) **great**, exquisite, delightful, lovely, pleasing, heavenly, cool (*slang*). [➡EMOTIONALLY PLEASANT; 188] 3 *v* **discover**, guess, presume, deduce, discern, perceive. [➡UNDERSTAND AND GRASP; 760]

divine intervention *n* [➡RELIGIOUS CONCEPTS; 777]

divinely (*informal*) *adv* **exquisitely**, beautifully, delightfully, well, pleasingly, attractively. [➡EMOTIONALLY PLEASANT; 188]

divinity *n* **religion**, theology, religious studies, spirituality, mysticism. [➡LESSONS, COURSE WORK, AND EXAMINATIONS; 842]

divisible *adj* **isolatable**, detachable, separable, dividable. [➡UNRELATEDNESS AND SEPARATENESS; 147] *Opposite:* inseparable.

division 1 *n* **separation**, splitting up, partition, dissection, detachment, disunion. [➡SEPARATE AND DIVIDE; 402] *Opposite:* union. 2 *n* **sharing out**, distribution, allotment, allocation, apportionment, sharing. [➡DISPENSE, RATION, AND DISTRIBUTE; 435] 3 *n* **split**, rift, disagreement, discord, break, schism, rupture, gulf, divide, disharmony, dissonance. [➡DISHARMONY; 157] *Opposite:* unity. 4 *n* **boundary**, partition, border, dividing line, demarcation. [➡GEOGRAPHICAL BORDERS AND BOUNDARIES; 1068] 5 *n* **category**, classification, type, class, grouping, group. [➡VARIETY, TYPE, KIND; 146] 6 *n* **department**, section, group, branch, sector. [➡SUBDIVISIONS AND OFFSHOOTS; 1252]

divisive *adj* **discordant**, troublesome, disruptive, conflict-ridden, contentious, acrimonious. [➡DISHARMONY; 157]

divisiveness *n* **disruptiveness**, dissension, disagreement, discord, disunity, acrimony, schism. [➡DISHARMONY; 157]

divorce 1 *n* **separation**, split, break up, split-up, annulment. [➡END; 54] *Opposite:* marriage. 2 *v* **dissociate**, disconnect, separate, distance, detach, break up, split up, break apart. [➡SEPARATE AND DIVIDE; 402] *Opposite:* associate.

divorced *adj* **separated**, removed, unconnected, split, detached, broken up. [➡MARITAL STATUS; 890] *Opposite:* together.

divot *n* **turf**, sod, clump, clod, piece, lump. [➡AMOUNT OF SOLID OR SEMI-SOLID; 115]

divulge *v* **reveal**, tell, make known, disclose, let drop, give away, let slip. [➡BETRAY CONFIDENCES AND GOSSIP; 619]

divvy (*informal*) *v* **divide up**, divide, share out, deal out, distribute, allocate, split, apportion, allot, dole out (*informal*). [➡DISPENSE, RATION, AND DISTRIBUTE; 435]

divvy up (*informal*) *v* [➡SEPARATE AND DIVIDE; 402]

dizzily *adv* **giddily** (*dated*), dazedly, woozily, lightheadedly, shakily, unsteadily, groggily. [➡UNFIT AND WEAK; 740] *Opposite:* steadily.

dizziness *n* **faintness**, giddiness, wooziness, vertigo, shakiness, lightheadedness, unsteadiness. [➡UNFIT AND WEAK; 740]

dizzy 1 *adj* (*informal*) **frivolous**, flippant, silly, giddy (*dated*), lighthearted, perky, frolicsome, playful. [➡LACK OF COMMITMENT AND UNRELIABILITY; 510] 2 *adj* **faint**, giddy, wobbly (*informal*), woozy, shaky, lightheaded, dazed, vertiginous, unsteady. [➡UNFIT AND WEAK; 740]

DJ 1 *n* **dinner jacket**, tuxedo, tux (*informal*), black tie. [➡GARMENTS AND OUTFITS; 865] 2 *n* **disc jockey**, deejay (*informal*), MC, radio presenter, broadcaster, jock (*informal*). [➡WORKERS IN ENTERTAINMENT AND MEDIA; 873]

do 1 *v* (*informal*) **cheat**, trick, con, swindle, defraud, bamboozle (*informal*). [➡DECEPTION AND LIES; 661] 2 *v* **perform**, accomplish, act, carry out, complete, achieve, make, execute, get something done. [➡CARRY OUT AN ACTION; 270] 3 *v* **see to**, fix, prepare, sort out, look after, make sure of, organize, ensure. [➡ATTEMPT AN ACTION; 262] 4 *v* **solve**, work out, resolve, figure out, puzzle out. [➡DEVELOP THEORIES AND REASON; 745] 5 *n* (*informal*) **reception**, party, function, drinks party, cocktail party, gathering, get-together (*informal*), soirée (*formal*). [➡PARTIES, DANCES, AND CELEBRATIONS; 37]

See Compare and Contrast at **perform.**

doable *adj* **achievable**, possible, workable, feasible, attainable. [➡POSSIBLE AND PROBABLE; 178] *Opposite:* impossible.

do a bunk (*informal*) *v* **disappear**, vanish, bolt, scoot (*informal*), run away, split (*slang*), skedaddle (*slang*), vamoose (*US slang*). [➡RUN AWAY AND AVOID; 10] *Opposite:* hang around.

do a moonlight flit *v* [➡RUN AWAY AND AVOID; 10]

do a runner *v* [➡RUN AWAY AND AVOID; 10]

do a U-turn *v* [➡CHANGE DIRECTION OF MOTION; 345]

do away with 1 *v* **abolish**, dispense with, remove, dispose of, get rid of, eradicate. [➡ABOLISH AND ANNUL; 453] *Opposite:* retain. 2 *v* (*informal*) **kill**, murder, finish off (*informal*), blow away (*slang*), do in (*informal*), assassinate. [➡KILL; 923]

do battle *v* [➡COMPETE, CONTEND, AND COMBAT; 304]

Doberman pinscher *type of* **large dog.** [➡DOG; 980]

docile *adj* **quiet**, passive, unassuming, compliant, submissive, tame, meek, obedient, biddable, pliable. [➡THE WILL AND WILLINGNESS; 564] *Opposite:* wild.

docility *n* **quietness**, submissiveness, meekness, tameness, gentleness, obedience, compliance. [➡THE WILL AND WILLINGNESS; 564] *Opposite:* fierceness.

dock 1 *n* **berth**, mooring, anchorage, wharf, quay, marina, waterfront, port. [➡WATERWAYS AND SEAWAYS; 1107] 2 *v* **come in**, tie up, land, berth, moor. [➡ARRIVE BY TRANSPORT; 14] 3 *v* **cut**, cut off, crop, stop, reduce, curtail, deduct. [➡TAKE SOMETHING AWAY; 426] *Opposite:* increase. 4 *type of* **weed.** [➡WEEDS AND THISTLES; 1034] 5 (*US*) *type of* **industrial site.** [➡INDUSTRIAL BUILDINGS; 1086]

docket 1 *n* **tag**, sticker, label, marker, ticket, receipt, invoice, note, chit (*dated*), tab (*US informal*). [➡RECEIPTS AND INVOICES; 592] 2 *v* **label**, tag, identify, disclose, declare. [➡NAME AND DESCRIBE; 666] 3 *n* **agenda**, programme, schedule, calendar, timetable, card, bill, slate, roster. [➡RECORDS; 586]

dockside *n* **wharf**, jetty, dock, quayside, quay, landing stage, pier, waterfront, wharfage, harbour, port. [➡WATERWAYS AND SEAWAYS; 1107]

dockyard 1 *n* **shipyard**, boatyard, dry dock. [➡WATERWAYS AND SEAWAYS; 1107] 2 *type of* **industrial site.** [➡INDUSTRIAL BUILDINGS; 1086]

doctor 1 *n* **medic** (*informal*), consultant, registrar, clinician, medical practitioner, specialist, surgeon, GP, general practitioner, family doctor, physician. [➡PEOPLE WHO WORK IN MEDICINE; 848] 2 *n* **academic**, scholar, expert, specialist, Doctor of Philosophy, PhD. [➡QUALIFICATIONS; 843] 3 *v* **treat**, care for, look after, cure, heal, minister to. [➡TAKE CARE OF AND SPOIL; 301] 4 *v* **amend**, modify, adjust, meddle with, rework, tamper with, falsify, change, alter, fix (*US babytalk*). [➡CHANGE; 373]

doctorate *n* **higher degree**, research degree, university degree, PhD, Doctor of Philosophy. [➡QUALIFICATIONS; 843]

doctrinaire *adj* **rigid**, inflexible, stern, strict, unbending, dogmatic. [➡NEGATIVE INTELLECTUAL CHARACTERISTICS; 526] *Opposite:* liberal.

doctrine *n* **policy**, principle, set of guidelines, canon, dogma, rule, guideline, creed, code. [➡WAYS OF DOING THINGS; 295]

docudrama *type of* **broadcast**. [➡TELEVISION AND RADIO; 607]

document 1 *n* **text**, file, article, essay, paper, manuscript, deed, certificate, record. [➡WRITING; 584] 2 *v* **record**, keep a record, detail, write down, provide evidence, give proof, verify, authenticate, support. [➡RECORD SOMETHING; 372]

documentary *type of* **broadcast**. [➡TELEVISION AND RADIO; 607]

documentation *n* **certification**, papers, credentials, documents, citations, records. [➡OFFICIAL DOCUMENTS; 587]

document case *type of* **baggage**. [➡CONTAINERS, RECEPTACLES, AND PACKAGING; 1244]

dodder 1 *v* **tremble**, shake, waver, quake, quiver, judder, shudder. [➡PHYSICAL REACTIONS; 317] 2 *v* **totter**, reel, teeter, stagger, wobble, sway, waver, lurch, weave. [➡WALK UNSTEADILY; 316] *Opposite:* stride.

doddering *adj* **tottering**, reeling, teetering, staggering, wobbling, shaking, swaying, wavering, rocking, lurching, weaving. [➡DESCRIBING BODY MOVEMENTS; 289]

doddery *adj* **shaky**, unsteady, tottery, feeble, frail, weak. [➡UNFIT AND WEAK; 740] *Opposite:* steady.

doddle (*informal*) *n* **piece of cake** (*informal*), cinch (*informal*), pushover (*informal*), child's play, nothing, gift (*informal*), breeze (*informal*), snap (*US*). [➡EASY WORK; 300] *Opposite:* challenge.

dodecahedron *type of* **angular shape**. [➡ANGULAR SHAPE; 1216]

dodge 1 *v* **move**, cut, duck, move away, avoid, sidestep. [➡AVOID OR ESCAPE CONTACT; 419] 2 *v* **avoid**, evade, shirk, elude, get out of. [➡NOT PAY ATTENTION; 765]

dodgy (*informal*) 1 *adj* **dishonest**, suspect, unreliable, untrustworthy, doubtful, dubious. [➡UNCERTAIN; 176] *Opposite:* reliable. 2 *adj* **risky**, dangerous, hazardous, unsafe, chancy, precarious, perilous. [➡DANGEROUS; 237] *Opposite:* safe.

dodo *type of* **flightless bird**. [➡BIRD; 997]

do down (*informal*) *v* **disparage**, smear, knock (*informal*), belittle, deride, pour scorn on, denigrate. [➡PROTEST AND EXPRESS DISAPPROVAL; 643]

doe *type of* **female animal**. [➡MALE OR FEMALE ANIMAL; 978]

doer *n* **go-getter** (*informal*), live wire (*informal*), achiever, dynamo. [➡PEOPLE WHO ARE APPROVED OF; 955]

doff *v* **take off**, lift, tip, tilt, remove, peel off, shed, discard. *Opposite:* don. (*formal*). [➡DRESS, WEAR, AND UNDRESS; 868]

dog 1 *n* **canine**, pooch (*informal*), mongrel, mutt (*slang*), hound, bitch, pup, puppy. [➡DOG; 980] 2 *v* **follow**, pursue, chase, trail, track, stalk, hunt. [➡ACCOMPANY AND FOLLOW; 338] 3 *v* **bother**, beleaguer, harass, vex, plague, afflict, pester, hassle (*informal*), badger, hound, trouble. [➡COMPLAIN AND NAG; 687] 4 *type of* **male animal**. [➡MALE OR FEMALE ANIMAL; 978] 5 *type of* **canine**. [➡CANINE; 979]

> **dog**
>
> ◆ *types of small dog*
> affenpinscher, basenji, basset, beagle, bull terrier, chihuahua, chow, corgi, dachshund, foxhound, Pekingese, poodle, pug, spaniel, terrier, whippet
>
> ◆ *types of large dog*
> Afghan hound, Alsatian, bloodhound, borzoi, boxer, bulldog, collie, dalmatian, Doberman pinscher, German shepherd (*US*), greyhound, guide dog, husky, Labrador, mastiff, retriever, Rottweiler, Saint Bernard, setter, sheepdog, wolfhound

dog days *n* [➡TIMES OF YEAR; 88]

dog-eared *adj* **damaged**, tattered, battered, well-read, worn, well-thumbed. [➡IN BAD REPAIR; 1233]

dogfight *n* **fight**, conflict, combat, encounter, raid, clash, engagement, battle, fracas, fray, scrap (*informal*), skirmish. [➡AGGRESSIVE EVENT; 39]

dogfish *type of* **sea fish**. [➡SEA FISH; 1009]

dogged *adj* **determined**, single-minded, unwavering, indefatigable, steadfast, resolute, stubborn, persistent, relentless. [➡UNWILLINGNESS AND STUBBORNNESS; 565] *Opposite:* half-hearted.

doggedness *n* **perseverance**, persistence, single-mindedness, tenacity, resolve, steadfastness, staying power, determination, indefatigability. [➡UNWILLINGNESS AND STUBBORNNESS; 565] *Opposite:* apathy.

doggerel 1 *n* **verse**, poetry, rhyme, limerick, ditty. [➡FICTION AND DRAMA; 913] 2 *n* **gibberish**, nonsense, twaddle (*informal*), prattle, baloney (*informal*), rubbish, garbage. [➡MEANINGLESS SPEECH OR WRITING; 677]

doggy *adj* [➡DOG; 980]

doghouse (*US*) *type of* **pen or cage**. [➡ANIMAL OR BIRD ACCOMMODATION; 1078]

dog in the manger *n* [➡GRUMPY AND NEGATIVE PEOPLE; 953]

dogleg 1 *n* **sharp bend**, angle, corner, curve, bend, turn, hairpin bend. [➡ANGULAR SHAPE; 1216] 2 *v* **bend**, turn, curve, swerve. [➡CHANGE DIRECTION OF MOTION; 345]

dogma *n* **creed**, doctrine, philosophy, canon, belief, view, tenets (*formal*), code. [➡IDEA AND THOUGHT; 771]

dogmatic *adj* **rigid**, inflexible, unbending, strict, intransigent, narrow, doctrinaire, fixed. [➡NEGATIVE INTELLECTUAL CHARACTERISTICS; 526] *Opposite:* flexible.

dogmatism *n* **intransigence**, inflexibility, strictness, presumption, arrogance, rigidity, firmness. [➡NEGATIVE INTELLECTUAL CHARACTERISTICS; 526] *Opposite:* openness.

dog of war *n* [➡MILITARY PERSONNEL; 828]

do-gooder (*informal*) *n* [➡INTERFERING PEOPLE AND TELLTALES; 950]

dogsbody (*informal*) *n* [➡WORKER; 836]

dogsled *type of* **leisure vehicle.** [➡VEHICLES; 1144]

dog-tired (*informal*) *adj* **exhausted**, worn out, shattered, tired, done in (*informal*), all in, whacked (*informal*), tired out, fatigued. [➡TIRED, ASLEEP AND UNCONSCIOUS; 739] *Opposite:* fresh.

doily *n* [➡ORNAMENTS AND DECORATIONS; 1247]

do in (*informal*) *v* **kill**, murder, finish off (*informal*), blow away (*slang*), do away with (*informal*), assassinate. [➡KILL; 923]

doings (*informal*) *n* **activities**, actions, events, happenings, goings-on (*informal*), deeds, comings and goings, accomplishments, undertakings. [➡ACTIONS OR UNDERTAKINGS; 260]

Dolcelatte *type of* **soft cheese.** [➡DAIRY PRODUCTS AND CHEESES; 1182]

doldrums 1 *n* **stagnation**, sluggishness, boredom, lethargy, lassitude. [➡SADNESS, DISTRESS, AND DESPAIR; 540] *Opposite:* energy. 2 *n* **gloominess**, melancholy, dejection, despondency, pessimism, blues (*informal*), misery, gloom, glumness, sadness, unhappiness. [➡SADNESS, DISTRESS, AND DESPAIR; 540] *Opposite:* cheerfulness.

doleful *adj* **unhappy**, miserable, sad, woeful, dejected, mournful, down in the dumps (*informal*), down, downcast, forlorn, gloomy, glum, despondent. [➡SADNESS, DISTRESS, AND DESPAIR; 540] *Opposite:* cheerful.

dolefulness *n* **sadness**, unhappiness, misery, mournfulness, woefulness, dejectedness, gloom, despondency, cheerlessness. [➡SADNESS, DISTRESS, AND DESPAIR; 540] *Opposite:* cheerfulness.

dole out (*informal*) *v* **share out**, dispense, distribute, allocate, allot, deal out, divide up, apportion, serve, give out, dish out (*informal*), issue, deal. [➡DISPENSE, RATION, AND DISTRIBUTE; 435] *Opposite:* hoard.

doll *n* **toy**, figurine, figure, dolly (*babytalk*), model, puppet. [➡TOYS; 880]

dollar *n* **buck** (*informal*), big one, dollar bill, greenback (*US slang*). [➡CURRENCIES; 798]

dollop (*informal*) *n* **blob**, spoonful, spoon, squirt, drop. [➡AMOUNT OF SOLID OR SEMI-SOLID; 115]

doll's house *type of* **toy.** [➡TOYS; 880]

doll up (*informal*) *v* **dress up**, smarten up, spruce up, titivate, smarten, glam up. [➡DRESS, WEAR, AND UNDRESS; 868] *Opposite:* tone down.

dolly (*babytalk*) *n* **figurine**, toy, model, figure, puppet, plaything. [➡TOYS; 880]

dolmen *n* **megalith**, obelisk, trilithon, monument, standing stone. [➡ANCIENT MANMADE STRUCTURES; 1088]

dolphin *type of* **marine mammal.** [➡MARINE MAMMAL; 987]

domain *n* **area**, field, sphere, sphere of influence, province, realm, dominion, territory, purview. [➡PLACE; 1064]

dome 1 *n* **vault**, cupola, roof, ceiling. [➡ROOFS, ROOF PARTS, AND CEILINGS; 1102] 2 *type of* **rounded shape.** [➡ROUNDED SHAPE; 1217]

domed *adj* **vaulted**, hemispherical, rounded, round. [➡ROUNDED SHAPE; 1217]

domestic 1 *adj* **home**, family, house, household, familial, marital, conjugal, married, matrimonial. [➡ACCOMMODATION; 855] *Opposite:* public. 2 *adj* **national**, local, internal, inland, native, home. [➡COUNTRIES AND REGIONS; 1066] *Opposite:* international.

domesticate *v* **tame**, break, bring under control, control, housetrain, train, housebreak (*US*). [➡INSTRUCT AND TEACH; 610]

domesticated *adj* **tame**, pet, trained, tamed, housetrained, farm, housebroken (*US*). [➡GOOD MANNERS AND SOCIAL SKILLS; 521] *Opposite:* wild.

domestication *n* **taming**, training, housetraining, subjugation, housebreaking (*US*). [➡EDUCATORS; 840]

domesticity *n* **home life**, family life, home comforts, married life, creature comforts. [➡PLEASANT SITUATIONS; 74]

domicile (*formal*) *n* **home**, residence, house, flat, quarters, dwelling (*formal*), abode (*literary*), apartment (*US*). [➡ACCOMMODATION; 855]

domiciliary *adj* [➡ACCOMMODATION; 855]

dominance *n* **supremacy**, ascendancy, domination, governance (*formal*), power, authority, control. [➡STRENGTH; 202] *Opposite:* weakness.

dominant 1 *adj* **domineering**, bossy, overbearing, officious, authoritarian, assertive, forceful. [➡BOSSY AND OVERBEARING; 517] *Opposite:* weak. 2 *adj* **leading**, main, central, foremost, prevailing, governing, principal, major, chief, ascendant, influential. [➡MOST IMPORTANT AND MAIN; 194] *Opposite:* minor.

dominate 1 *v* **control**, rule, lead, govern, direct, dictate, take over. [➡CAUSE OR COMPEL TO ACT; 272] 2 *v* **overlook**, overshadow, tower above, tower over, dwarf. [➡EXIST IN CLOSE PROXIMITY; 21]

domination *n* **power**, control, command, authority, dominion, dominance, supremacy, ascendancy, government, rule. [➡STRENGTH; 202]

domineering *adj* **bossy**, dominant, overbearing, officious, authoritarian, forceful, dictatorial, assertive. [➡BOSSY AND OVERBEARING; 517] *Opposite:* meek.

dominion 1 *n* **power**, authority, control, command, sayso (*informal*), domination, dominance. [➡STRENGTH; 202] 2 *n* **territory**, colony, province, region, protectorate, state, domain. [➡PLACE; 1064]

domino *type of* **game piece.** [➡GAMES PIECES; 878]

don 1 *n* **university teacher**, lecturer, fellow, academic, tutor. [➡EDUCATORS; 840] 2 *v* (*formal*) **put on**, throw on, get into, pull on, dress in, slip on. [➡DRESS, WEAR, AND UNDRESS; 868] *Opposite:* take off.

donate *v* **give**, contribute, bestow (*formal*), bequeath, provide, offer. [➡GIVE AND PROVIDE; 431]

See Compare and Contrast at **give**.

donation *n* **gift**, contribution, payment, bequest, endowment, bestowment (*formal*). [➡GIFTS; 439]

done *adj* **complete**, completed, ended, finished, through, ready, prepared, made. [➡WHOLENESS AND COMPLETENESS; 199]

done and dusted *adj* [➡WHOLENESS AND COMPLETENESS; 199]

done for (*informal*) **1** *adj* **finished**, in serious trouble, in deep trouble, in hot water, in dire straits. [➡IN TROUBLE AND DISADVANTAGED; 73] **2** *adj* **exhausted**, tired, worn out, shattered, dog-tired (*informal*), whacked (*informal*), tired out, fatigued. [➡TIRED, ASLEEP AND UNCONSCIOUS; 739] *Opposite:* fresh.

done in (*informal*) *adj* [➡TIRED, ASLEEP AND UNCONSCIOUS; 739]

Don Juan *n* [➡PLEASURE-SEEKERS AND HEDONISTS; 886]

donkey *type of* **farm animal**. [➡FARM ANIMAL; 982]

donkey's years (*informal*) *n* **years**, aeons, yonks (*slang*), for ever, ages (*informal*). [➡LONG PERIOD OF TIME; 92]

donkeywork (*informal*) **1** *n* **hard work**, heavy labour, hard graft. [➡HARD WORK OR EFFORT; 299] **2** *n* **groundwork**, preparatory, work, legwork (*informal*), preparation, research. [➡HARD WORK OR EFFORT; 299]

donnish *adj* **academic**, bookish, dry, serious, intellectual, scholarly, erudite, pedantic, learned. [➡LEVEL OF EDUCATION AND SOPHISTICATION; 894]

donnybrook *n* [➡CHAOS AND UPROAR; 51]

donor *n* **giver**, contributor, benefactor, patron, supporter, subscriber. [➡REPRESENTATIVES AND PATRONS; 968]

Don Quixote *n* [➡PLEASURE-SEEKERS AND HEDONISTS; 886]

doodad (*US informal*) *n* [➡PHYSICAL OBJECTS; 1242]

doodah (*informal*) *n* [➡PHYSICAL OBJECTS; 1242]

doodle **1** *v* **draw**, sketch, scribble, squiggle. [➡CREATE IMAGES; 357] **2** *n* **drawing**, sketch, scribble, picture, squiggle. [➡ARTWORKS; 898]

doofer (*slang*) *n* [➡PHYSICAL OBJECTS; 1242]

doohickey (*US informal*) *n* **thingamajig** (*informal*), gadget, widget (*humorous*), thingy (*informal*), thingummy (*informal*), whatchamacallit, whatsit (*informal*), doodah (*informal*), doofer (*slang*), doodad (*US informal*). [➡PHYSICAL OBJECTS; 1242]

doom **1** *n* **fate**, destiny, lot, kismet, portion (*literary*). [➡FATE, DESTINY, AND ASTROLOGY; 783] **2** *n* **disaster**, trouble, end, death, tragedy, ruin, catastrophe, misfortune, calamity. [➡DISASTERS; 253]

doomed **1** *adj* **fated**, destined, damned, condemned, predestined. [➡FATE, DESTINY, AND ASTROLOGY; 783] **2** *adj* **hopeless**, disaster-prone, ruined, lost, damned, done for (*informal*), ill-fated, unlucky. [➡IN TROUBLE AND DISADVANTAGED; 73]

doom-laden *adj* **gloomy**, pessimistic, dismal, depressing, despairing, hopeless, full of despair, doomy (*informal*). *Opposite:* upbeat. (*informal*). [➡SADNESS, DISTRESS, AND DESPAIR; 540]

doomsday *n* **end of the world**, end of time, Last Judgment, Judgment Day, Day of Judgment, day of reckoning, Armageddon. [➡RELIGIOUS CONCEPTS; 777]

doomy (*informal*) **1** *adj* **pessimistic**, despairing, gloomy, glum, melancholy. [➡INSECURITY AND LOSS OF COMPOSURE; 545] *Opposite:* cheery. **2** *adj* **ominous**, threatening, portentous, worrying, troubling. [➡FRIGHTENING; 232] *Opposite:* hopeful.

door *n* **entrance**, gate, entry, exit, access, flap, ingress (*formal*), egress (*formal*). [➡DOORS AND ACCESS POINTS; 1100]

doorplate *n* **name plate**, sign, plaque, house sign, plate. [➡DOORS AND ACCESS POINTS; 1100]

doorstep *n* **entrance**, threshold, access, doorway, front doorstep, step. [➡DOORS AND ACCESS POINTS; 1100]

doorway **1** *n* **entrance**, door, front entrance, entry, front door, entranceway, entryway (*US*). [➡DOORS AND ACCESS POINTS; 1100] **2** *part of* **building**. [➡PARTS OF A BUILDING; 1094]

do out of (*informal*) *v* [➡TAKE SOMETHING AWAY; 426]

doozy (*US slang*) *n* [➡AMAZING THING; 212]

dopey *adj* [➡NEGATIVE INTELLECTUAL CHARACTERISTICS; 526]

doppelgänger *n* **double**, mirror image, lookalike (*informal*), spitting image (*informal*), shadow, spit (*informal*), twin, clone, alter ego. [➡COPIES AND REPLICAS; 152]

Doric *type of* **pre-20th-century architecture**. [➡BUILDING AND ARCHITECTURE; 1075]

dorm (*informal*) *n* **hall of residence**, student house, dormitory, hall, residence, frat house (*US*). [➡RESIDENTIAL BUILDINGS; 1077]

dormant **1** *adj* **inactive**, asleep, sleeping, quiescent, quiet. [➡LACK OF ACTIVITY; 343] *Opposite:* active. **2** *adj* **latent**, undeveloped, hidden, unexpressed. [➡TIRED, ASLEEP AND UNCONSCIOUS; 739]

dormer window *type of* **window**. [➡WINDOWS; 1099]

dormitory **1** *n* **hall of residence**, student house, hall, dorm (*informal*), residence, frat house (*US*). [➡RESIDENTIAL BUILDINGS; 1077] **2** *type of* **room in public buildings**. [➡TYPES OF ROOM; 1096]

dormouse *type of* **rodent**. [➡RODENT; 989]

dorsal fin *part of* **fish**. [➡PARTS OF A FISH; 1011]

dory *type of* **small vessel**. [➡SHIPS AND BOATS; 1149]

dosage *n* **amount**, quantity, dose, measure, prescription. [➡AMOUNT AND QUANTITY; 112]

dose **1** *n* **amount**, quantity, dosage, measure, prescription. [➡AMOUNT AND QUANTITY; 112] **2** *n* (*informal*) **bout**, spell, period, attack, experience. [➡SHORT PERIOD OF TIME; 93] **3** *v* **treat**, give medicine to, dose up, medicate. [➡TAKE CARE OF AND SPOIL; 301]

dosh (*slang*) *n* [➡MONEY; 140]

doss **1** *v* (*slang*) **crash** (*informal*), bed down, sleep, kip (*informal*), lie down. [➡SLEEP AND DREAM; 724] **2** *n* **sleep**, snooze (*informal*), nap, forty winks (*informal*), catnap, siesta. [➡SLEEP AND DREAM; 724] **3** *n* (*slang*) **cinch** (*informal*), piece of cake (*informal*), doddle (*informal*), walkover (*informal*), waltz (*informal*), child's play, snap (*US*), walkaway (*US informal*). [➡EASY WORK; 300]

dosser (*slang*) *n* **homeless person**, tramp, hobo, vagrant, vagabond. [➡NOMADIC AND ROOTLESS LIFESTYLES; 884]

dosshouse (*slang*) *n* **hostel**, lodging house (*dated*), shelter, night shelter, flophouse (*US informal*). [➡RESIDENTIAL BUILDINGS; 1077]

dossier *n* **file**, record, report, folder, profile, database. [➡RECORDS; 586]

dot **1** *n* **spot**, point, mark, blotch, speck, particle. [➡AMOUNT OF LIQUID; 114] **2** *v* **speckle**, sprinkle, pepper, fleck, spot, mark. [➡DISPENSE, RATION, AND DISTRIBUTE; 435]

doting *adj* **fond**, loving, devoted, affectionate, adoring, caring. [➡APPRECIATION AND GRATITUDE; 536]

dotted *adj* **scattered**, sprinkled, spotted, speckled, spread, strewn. [➡GENERAL LOCATIONS; 159]

dotty **1** *adj* **unconventional**, odd, eccentric, idiosyncratic, strange, bizarre. [➡BIZARRE AND PECULIAR; 258] *Opposite:* normal. **2** *adj* **absurd**, impractical, illogical, foolish, nonsensical. [➡NEGATIVE INTELLECTUAL CHARACTERISTICS; 526] *Opposite:* practical. **3** *adj* (*informal*) **crazy** (*informal*), mad, fond, besotted, doting, infatuated, smitten (*humorous or literary*). [➡APPRECIATION AND GRATITUDE; 536]

double **1** *adj* **dual**, binary, twofold, duple, twin, paired. [➡APPORTIONMENT; 113] **2** *adv* **twice**, twofold, twice over, two times. [➡APPORTIONMENT; 113] **3** *n* **duo**, pair, duet, couple. [➡GROUPS OF PEOPLE; 935] **4** *n* **lookalike** (*informal*), doppelgänger, clone, alter ego, twin, spitting image (*informal*), stand-in, duplicate, match. [➡COPIES AND REPLICAS; 152] **5** *v* **increase twofold**, double up, amplify, magnify, expand, augment (*formal*), multiply. [➡CHANGE OF INTENSITY: MORE; 395] *Opposite:* lessen. **6** *v* **bend**, fold, double up, bend over, fold up. [➡CHANGE OF SHAPE; 386]

double act *n* **pair**, twosome, duo, two-hander, couple. [➡WORKERS IN ENTERTAINMENT AND MEDIA; 873]

double agent *n* **spy**, mole, infiltrator, plant (*informal*), inside agent, secret agent. [➡INTERFERING PEOPLE AND TELLTALES; 950]

double back *v* [➡CHANGE DIRECTION OF MOTION; 345]

double bass *type of* **stringed instrument**. [➡MUSICAL INSTRUMENTS; 910]

double bed *type of* **bed**. [➡FURNITURE; 858]

double-book *v* **overbook**, overfill, overextend, overstretch. [➡OVERDO SOMETHING; 291]

double check *n* **second check**, reassessment, check, verification. [➡EXAMINE AND ASSESS; 754]

double-check *v* **make sure**, ensure, reassure yourself, check, verify, insure. [➡EXAMINE AND ASSESS; 754]

double-cross **1** *v* **betray**, con, stab in the back (*informal*), let down, cheat, sell out, swindle, deceive, dupe. [➡DECEPTION AND LIES; 661] **2** *n* **betrayal**, stab in the back (*informal*), deception, swindle, trick, con. [➡DECEPTION AND LIES; 661]

double-crosser *n* **swindler**, cheat, trickster, liar, rat (*slang*), fraudster, double-dealer. [➡PEOPLE WHO DECEIVE; 662]

double-dealer *n* **swindler**, liar, cheat, rat (*slang*), fraudster, trickster, double-crosser. [➡PEOPLE WHO DECEIVE; 662]

double-dealing **1** *n* **duplicity**, betrayal, deceit, cheating, treachery, deception. [➡DECEPTION AND LIES; 661] *Opposite:* honesty. **2** *adj* **duplicitous**, deceitful, double-faced, cheating, swindling, two-faced, dishonest, false, treacherous, double-crossing. [➡DECEITFUL; 514] *Opposite:* honest.

double Dutch (*informal*) *n* **rubbish**, gibberish, mumbo jumbo (*informal*), gabble, nonsense, twaddle (*informal*), garbage. [➡MEANINGLESS SPEECH OR WRITING; 677]

double-edged *adj* **ambiguous**, two-edged, disingenuous, ironic, sly. [➡VAGUENESS; 244] *Opposite:* ingenuous.

double-faced *adj* **insincere**, deceitful, dishonest, two-faced, false, double-crossing, double-dealing, duplicitous, treacherous. [➡DECEITFUL; 514] *Opposite:* honest.

double-jointed *adj* **flexible**, supple, agile, lithe. [➡AGILITY OF THE BODY; 477]

double-quick (*informal*) **1** *adj* **rapid**, swift, speedy, prompt, instant, fast, quick. [➡HAPPENING QUICKLY; 104] *Opposite:* slow. **2** *adv* **rapidly**, swiftly, speedily, promptly, quickly, instantly, fast. [➡HAPPENING QUICKLY; 104] *Opposite:* slowly.

doublespeak *n* [➡DECEPTION AND LIES; 661]

double talk **1** *n* **hogwash** (*informal*), gibberish, nonsense, rubbish, malarkey (*informal*), twaddle (*informal*), trash, garbage. [➡MEANINGLESS SPEECH OR WRITING; 677] **2** *n* **sophistry**, doublespeak, deceit, jargon, smoke and mirrors (*US*). [➡DECEPTION AND LIES; 661]

double up *v* **bend**, fold, double, bend over, fold up. [➡CHANGE OF SHAPE; 386]

doubt **1** *v* **disbelieve**, mistrust, suspect, have reservations, have doubts, distrust, question, query. [➡UNCERTAINTY; 560] *Opposite:* believe. **2** *n* **hesitation**, uncertainty, reservation, misgiving, distrust, disbelief, qualm, suspicion. [➡UNCERTAINTY; 560] *Opposite:* certainty.

See Compare and Contrast at **doubtful**.

doubter *n* **nonbeliever**, cynic, doubting Thomas, agnostic, pessimist, sceptic. [➡UNCERTAINTY; 560] *Opposite:* believer.

doubtful **1** *adj* **unsure**, uncertain, hesitant, undecided, disbelieving, cynical, unconvinced, distrustful, sceptical, in doubt. [➡UNCERTAINTY; 560] *Opposite:* certain. **2** *adj* **unlikely**, unpromising, uncertain, insecure, shaky, in doubt, improbable. [➡IMPOSSIBLE AND IMPROBABLE; 179] *Opposite:* probable. **3** *adj* **unreliable**, dubious, suspect, questionable, untrustworthy, shady, fishy (*informal*), suspicious. [➡UNCERTAIN; 176] *Opposite:* reliable.

Compare and Contrast: ***doubtful, uncertain, unsure, in doubt, dubious, sceptical***

CORE MEANING: FEELING DOUBT OR UNCERTAINTY

doubtful undecided or feeling hesitant; ***uncertain or unsure*** lacking certainty or confidence; ***in doubt*** still undecided and liable to change; ***dubious*** doubtful and, often, suspicious; ***sceptical*** questioning the truth or likelihood of something.

doubtfully *adv* **uncertainly**, hesitantly, distrustfully, doubtingly, suspiciously, apprehensively. [➡UNCERTAINTY; 560] *Opposite:* confidently.

doubtfulness 1 *n* **uncertainty**, hesitancy, indecision, doubt, distrust, suspicion, apprehension. [➡UNCERTAINTY; 560] *Opposite:* certainty. 2 *n* **unlikelihood**, improbability, chance in a million, slim chance. [➡IMPOSSIBLE AND IMPROBABLE; 179] *Opposite:* likelihood.

doubting *adj* **hesitant**, doubtful, distrustful, suspicious, unbelieving. [➡UNCERTAINTY; 560] *Opposite:* trusting.

doubtless *adv* **no doubt**, without a doubt, probably, almost certainly, without question, beyond question, beyond a shadow of a doubt, undoubtedly. [➡CERTAIN; 175] *Opposite:* possibly.

dough (*slang*) *n* **cash**, currency, bread (*dated slang*), money, chips, greenbacks (*US slang*). [➡MONEY; 140]

doughnut *type of* **cake**. [➡CAKES, BISCUITS, AND DESSERTS; 1180]

doughty (*literary*) *adj* **brave**, determined, tough, spirited, feisty (*informal*), indomitable, hardy, intrepid (*literary or humorous*), formidable. [➡COURAGE; 499] *Opposite:* feeble.

dour 1 *adj* **severe**, unfriendly, sour, stern, hard-faced, grim, harsh. [➡FACIAL EXPRESSION; 652] *Opposite:* kindly. 2 *adj* **determined**, stubborn, set, purposeful, resolute, resolved. [➡UNWILLINGNESS AND STUBBORNNESS; 565] *Opposite:* indecisive.

dourly 1 *adv* **severely**, sourly, sternly, dryly, grimly, harshly. [➡BAD-TEMPERED AND HUMOURLESS; 627] *Opposite:* kindly. 2 *adv* **determinedly**, stubbornly, purposefully, resolutely. [➡UNWILLINGNESS AND STUBBORNNESS; 565] *Opposite:* indecisively.

dourness 1 *n* **severity**, unfriendliness, sourness, sternness, grimness. [➡UNFRIENDLINESS AND UNSOCIABILITY; 505] *Opposite:* kindness. 2 *n* **determination**, stubbornness, purpose, drive, resoluteness, resolve. [➡UNWILLINGNESS AND STUBBORNNESS; 565] *Opposite:* indecision.

douse 1 *v* **drench**, soak, wet, souse, cover, saturate, sop, drown, immerse. [➡SOFTEN, LIQUEFY, DAMPEN; 389] 2 *v* **quench**, extinguish, put out, smother, snuff. [➡CHANGE OF INTENSITY: LESS; 396]

dove *type of* **common bird**. [➡BIRD; 997]

dovecote *type of* **pen or cage**. [➡ANIMAL OR BIRD ACCOMMODATION; 1078]

dove grey *type of* **grey**. [➡COLOURS; 1223]

dovetail *v* **fit together**, slot in, join together, come together, unite. [➡FASTEN, LINK, AND JOIN; 409] *Opposite:* separate.

dowdily *adv* **plainly**, frumpily, drably, unfashionably, drearily. [➡BADLY GROOMED; 484] *Opposite:* fashionably.

dowdiness *n* **drabness**, plainness, dullness, dreariness, frumpiness. [➡BADLY GROOMED; 484]

dowdy *adj* **plain**, frumpy, drab, unfashionable, dreary. [➡BADLY GROOMED; 484] *Opposite:* fashionable.

dowel *n* **rod**, pin, peg. [➡FASTENERS, LINKS, AND NETWORKS; 1246]

do without *v* **abstain**, deny yourself, go without, keep off, forgo. [➡FORGO AND DENY ONESELF; 450]

down 1 *prep* **along**, through, the length of. [➡DIRECTION OF MOTION; 346] 2 *adj* **listed**, nominated, scheduled, timetabled, tabled. [➡PRESENT AND AVAILABLE; 11] 3 *adj* **depressed**, unhappy, miserable, down in the dumps (*informal*), dejected, downhearted, downcast, despondent, sad, low, blue (*informal*). [➡SADNESS, DISTRESS, AND DESPAIR; 540] *Opposite:* happy. 4 *adj* **out of action**, inoperative, not working, out of order. [➡IN BAD REPAIR; 1233] *Opposite:* working. 5 *adj* **behind**, losing, short. [➡IN TROUBLE AND DISADVANTAGED; 73] *Opposite:* winning. 6 *v* **put down**, lay down, throw down, set down, lay aside, put aside. [➡MOVE SOMETHING: DOWNWARDS; 330] *Opposite:* pick up. 7 *v* **knock down**, floor, overpower, overcome, defeat, bring down. [➡BEAT AND DEFEAT; 80] 8 *v* **consume**, eat, drink, knock back (*informal*), put away (*informal*), guzzle (*informal*), gulp down, swallow. [➡EAT AND NOT EAT; 711] 9 *part of* **bird**. [➡PARTS OF A BIRD; 1006]

down-and-out *adj* **destitute**, penniless, broke (*informal*), homeless, on the skids (*slang*), on the streets [➡POVERTY AND POOR; 892]. *Opposite:* well-heeled (*informal*).

down-at-heel *adj* [➡POVERTY AND POOR; 892]

downbeat 1 *adj* **pessimistic**, gloomy, dark, bleak, negative, depressing. *Opposite:* upbeat. (*informal*). [➡INSECURITY AND LOSS OF COMPOSURE; 545] 2 *adj* (*informal*) **casual**, informal, relaxed, unpretentious, laid-back (*informal*), downhome (*US informal*). [➡CALMING; 189]

downcast *adj* **sad**, pessimistic, dejected, depressed, down, disappointed, discouraged, disheartened, unhappy, downhearted, dismayed. [➡SADNESS, DISTRESS, AND DESPAIR; 540] *Opposite:* cheerful.

downer (*informal*) *n* **disappointment**, shame, pity, letdown, comedown (*informal*), bummer (*slang*), discouragement. [➡NUISANCES; 254]

downfall *n* **failure**, ruin, fall, end, demise (*formal*). [➡FAILURE; 77] *Opposite:* success.

downgrade *v* **demote**, reduce, lower, relegate. [➡REVOKE STATUS; 460] *Opposite:* upgrade.

downhearted *adj* **sad**, pessimistic, dejected, disappointed, depressed, down, upset, in low spirits, unhappy, disheartened, downcast, discouraged, dismayed. [➡SADNESS, DISTRESS, AND DESPAIR; 540] *Opposite:* cheerful.

downhill 1 *adj* **easy**, simple, effortless, plain sailing, straightforward. [➡EASE AND SIMPLICITY; 201] *Opposite:* uphill. 2 *type of* **winter sport**. [➡HOBBIES, GAMES, AND SPORTS; 875]

downhome (*US informal*) *adj* [➡ORDINARINESS; 245]

downiness *n* **softness**, fluffiness, fleeciness. [➡PHYSICAL TEXTURE; 1221]

down in the dumps *adj* **miserable**, unhappy, gloomy, depressed, down in the mouth (*informal*), low, dejected, downhearted, downcast, sad, despondent, blue (*informal*). [➡SADNESS, DISTRESS, AND DESPAIR; 540] *Opposite:* happy.

down in the mouth (*informal*) *adj* [➡SADNESS, DISTRESS, AND DESPAIR; 540]

download *v* **transfer**, copy, move, take. [➡COPY AND DUPLICATE; 403]

downmarket *adj* **low quality**, inferior, cheap, low cost, second-rate, mediocre, shoddy, tacky (*informal*), shabby. [➡ORDINARINESS; 245] *Opposite:* upmarket.

down payment *n* **payment**, instalment, deposit, disbursement. [➡MONEY, PAYMENTS, AND CHARGES; 800]

downplay *v* **tone down**, moderate, restrain, soften, modulate, give a lower profile, talk down. [➡CHANGE OF INTENSITY: LESS; 396] *Opposite:* highlight.

downpour *n* **heavy shower**, deluge, rainstorm, cloudburst, torrent, monsoon, inundation (*formal*). [➡CLOUDY AND RAINY WEATHER; 1052]

downright *adv* **positively**, undeniably, unquestionably, undoubtedly, totally. [➡ABSOLUTE AND ABSOLUTELY; 131] *Opposite:* questionably.

downriver *adv* [➡DIRECTION OF MOTION; 346]

downside *n* **negative aspect**, shortcoming, weakness, snag, stumbling block, pitfall, problem. [➡NUISANCES; 254] *Opposite:* advantage.

downsize *v* **slim down**, cut back, economize, rationalize, trim, reduce. [➡BUSINESS ACTIVITIES AND PHENOMENA; 795] *Opposite:* expand.

downstairs *adv* **below**, down the stairs, down, down below. [➡GENERAL LOCATIONS; 159]

downswing *n* **fall**, slump, decline, dip, downturn, recession. [➡MARKET FORCES; 803] *Opposite:* upswing.

downtime *n* **stoppage**, lost time, idle time, interruption. [➡PERIOD OF REST; 91]

down-to-earth *adj* **practical**, realistic, sensible, matter-of-fact, pragmatic, no-nonsense. [➡POSITIVE INTELLECTUAL CHARACTERISTICS; 525] *Opposite:* fanciful.

downtrodden *adj* **browbeaten**, subjugated, broken, oppressed, demoralized, beaten, defeated. [➡SADNESS, DISTRESS, AND DESPAIR; 540]

downturn *n* **slump**, recession, dip, decline, depression, downward spiral. [➡MARKET FORCES; 803] *Opposite:* upturn.

downward *adj* **descending**, down, downhill, sliding, descendent, plunging, sinking. [➡DIRECTION OF MOTION; 346] *Opposite:* upward.

downwards *adv* [➡DIRECTION OF MOTION; 346]

downy *adj* **silky**, soft, velvety, furry, feathery, fluffy. [➡PHYSICAL TEXTURE; 1221] *Opposite:* rough.

dowry *n* **wedding gift**, present, grant, settlement, portion, payment, money. [➡GIFTS; 439]

doyen *n* **leading figure**, senior member, leading light, notable, leader. [➡IMPORTANT OR FAMOUS PEOPLE; 893]

doyenne *n* **leading figure**, senior member, leading light, notable, leader. [➡IMPORTANT OR FAMOUS PEOPLE; 893]

do your homework (*informal*) *v* **prepare**, research, plan, find out. [➡EXAMINE AND ASSESS; 754]

doze 1 *v* **snooze** (*informal*), nap, sleep, slumber, kip (*informal*). [➡SLEEP AND DREAM; 724] **2** *n* **nap**, snooze (*informal*), slumber, sleep, kip (*informal*). [➡SLEEP AND DREAM; 724]

dozens (*informal*) *n* **lots**, loads (*informal*), masses (*informal*), tons (*informal*), oodles (*informal*), heaps (*informal*). [➡MANY, MUCH, LARGE AMOUNT; 117]

doze off *v* **fall asleep**, go to sleep, drop off (*informal*), nod off, nod, drift off. [➡SLEEP AND DREAM; 724] *Opposite:* wake up.

dozily *adv* **sleepily**, tiredly, lethargically, sluggishly, drowsily. [➡TIRED, ASLEEP AND UNCONSCIOUS; 739] *Opposite:* alertly.

doziness *n* **sleepiness**, tiredness, lethargy, sluggishness, drowsiness. [➡TIRED, ASLEEP AND UNCONSCIOUS; 739] *Opposite:* alertness.

dozy 1 *adj* **sleepy**, drowsy, tired, dozing, nodding, lethargic. [➡TIRED, ASLEEP AND UNCONSCIOUS; 739] *Opposite:* alert. **2** *adj* **silly**, foolish, dreamy, daffy (*informal*), scatterbrained, ditsy (*US informal*). [➡NEGATIVE INTELLECTUAL CHARACTERISTICS; 526]

drab 1 *adj* **gloomy**, sombre, dull, grey, dingy, dowdy, dreary, cheerless, plain. [➡PLAIN; 233] *Opposite:* bright. **2** *adj* **uninteresting**, unexciting, monotonous, boring, dreary, dull. [➡BORING AND UNINTERESTING; 235] *Opposite:* interesting.

drably *adv* **sombrely**, gloomily, greyly, drearily, dingily, cheerlessly. [➡BORING AND UNINTERESTING; 235] *Opposite:* brightly.

drabness *n* **dullness**, plainness, dowdiness, dreariness, dinginess, cheerlessness, gloominess. [➡BORING AND UNINTERESTING; 235]

draconian *adj* **harsh**, severe, strict, strong, austere, ruthless. [➡STRENGTH; 202] *Opposite:* mild.

draft 1 *n* **outline**, sketch, summary, plan, rough copy, version. [➡REPRESENTATIONS AND GENERAL EXAMPLES; 65] **2** *v* **draw up**, prepare, sketch out, outline, write, plan, design, compose, rough out. [➡CREATE IMAGES; 357]

drag 1 *v* **pull**, haul, draw, heave, lug, tug, tow, trail, draggle. [➡PUSH, PULL, SLIDE; 336] **2** *v* **dawdle**, lag, crawl, creep, loiter, linger. [➡MOVE SLOWLY; 315] *Opposite:* fly. **3** *n* (*informal*) [➡NUISANCES; 254]

See Compare and Contrast at **pull**.

dragging *adj* **slow**, tedious, tiresome, wearisome, uninteresting, boring. [➡BORING AND UNINTERESTING; 235] *Opposite:* interesting.

draggy (*informal*) 1 *adj* **sluggish**, slow, slow-moving, foot-dragging (*informal*), snail-paced, logy (*US*), slow as molasses (*US*). [➡HAPPENING SLOWLY; 106] *Opposite:* lively. **2** *adj*

tiresome, tedious, dragging, wearisome, uninteresting, boring. [➡BORING AND UNINTERESTING; 235] *Opposite:* interesting.

drag in *v* **bring in**, involve, allude to, mention, implicate, suck in. [➡SUGGEST, HINT, AND COMMENT; 613] *Opposite:* exclude.

dragnet 1 *n* **net**, mesh, trawl net, game net, trap, snare. [➡CONTAINERS, RECEPTACLES, AND PACKAGING; 1244] 2 *n* **search**, hunt, pursuit, tracking operation, quest. [➡SEEK POSSESSION AND SEARCH; 457]

dragon *type of* **mythological creature**. [➡MYTHICAL CREATURES; 1036]

dragonfly *type of* **flying insect**. [➡FLYING INSECTS; 1013]

dragoon *v* **coerce**, press, bully, intimidate, browbeat, harass, force, compel. [➡CAUSE OR COMPEL TO ACT; 272]

drag out *v* **extend**, prolong, draw out, lengthen, stretch, protract, spin out. [➡CONTINUE AN ACTION; 263] *Opposite:* cut short.

dragster *type of* **car**. [➡BIKES, CARS, AND CARRIAGES; 1148]

drag up *v* **rake up** (*informal*), return to, bring up, dredge up, revive, mention. [➡SUGGEST, HINT, AND COMMENT; 613]

drag your feet *v* **hold back**, hang back, drag your heels, take your time, stall, lag, procrastinate, play for time. [➡SHIRK AND DELAY; 274]

drain 1 *v* **use up**, exhaust, consume, deplete, bleed (*informal*), sap. [➡USE UP AND WASTE; 475] *Opposite:* replenish. 2 *n* **sewer**, ditch, channel, culvert, conduit. [➡WATERCOURSES; 1110]

drained *adj* **exhausted**, weak, weary, tired, worn out, shattered, sapped, all in. [➡TIRED, ASLEEP AND UNCONSCIOUS; 739] *Opposite:* energetic.

drainer *type of* **utensil**. [➡TABLEWARE, CUTLERY, AND KITCHENWARE; 861]

draining *adj* **exhausting**, trying, wearing, tiring, gruelling, taxing, enervating, fatiguing. [➡PHYSICALLY UNPLEASANT; 227]

drake *type of* **male or female bird**. [➡MALE OR FEMALE BIRD; 1005]

dram *n* [➡DRINKS; 1186]

drama 1 *n* **play**, stage show, performance, production, spectacle, tragedy, comedy. [➡FICTION AND DRAMA; 913] 2 *n* **excitement**, commotion, fuss, performance, to-do (*informal*), song and dance (*informal*), crisis, scene. [➡DISASTERS; 253] 3 *type of* **broadcast**. [➡TELEVISION AND RADIO; 607]

dramatic *adj* **affected**, melodramatic, theatrical, histrionic, studied, intense, vivid. [➡AFFECTATION, SELF-SATISFACTION, AND SNOBBISHNESS; 508] *Opposite:* natural.

dramatically 1 *adv* **melodramatically**, intensely, vividly, histrionically, theatrically, affectedly. [➡AFFECTATION, SELF-SATISFACTION, AND SNOBBISHNESS; 508] *Opposite:* naturally. 2 *adv* **radically**, noticeably, severely, considerably, spectacularly, significantly, markedly. [➡ABSOLUTE AND ABSOLUTELY; 131] *Opposite:* modestly.

dramatics *n* **histrionics**, hysterics, excitement, commotion, fuss, drama. [➡AFFECTATION, SELF-SATISFACTION, AND SNOBBISHNESS; 508]

dramatis personae *n* [➡PERFORMERS; 905]

dramatist *n* **playwright**, writer, author, scriptwriter. [➡WRITERS AND STYLES; 914]

dramatization *n* **staging**, performance, production, adaptation. [➡FICTION AND DRAMA; 913]

dramatize *v* **exaggerate**, sensationalize, play up, embellish, lay on, overstate, blow up (*informal*). [➡OVERDO SOMETHING; 291] *Opposite:* play down.

dramaturgy *n* [➡THE PERFORMING ARTS; 904]

drape *v* **swathe**, dress, wrap, cover, clothe, adorn, decorate, arrange, array (*literary*). [➡DECORATE, ADORN, AND APPLY COATINGS; 406]

drapery *n* **curtains**, hangings, drapes, swags. [➡SOFT FURNISHINGS, LINEN, AND DRAPERY; 860]

drastic *adj* **radical**, severe, extreme, dire, sweeping, far-reaching, harsh, strong, desperate. [➡ABSOLUTE AND ABSOLUTELY; 131] *Opposite:* modest.

draught 1 *n* **current**, flow, waft, breeze, breath. [➡WINDY AND STORMY WEATHER; 1053] 2 *n* (*dated*) **medicine**, concoction, mixture, brew, tonic. [➡DRINK; 712] 3 *type of* **game piece**. [➡GAMES PIECES; 878]

draw 1 *v* **sketch**, illustrate, copy, depict, describe, represent, portray, pencil, crayon. [➡CREATE IMAGES; 357] 2 *v* **pull**, drag, haul, move, tow, tug, lug, heave. [➡PUSH, PULL, SLIDE; 336] *Opposite:* shove. 3 *v* **pull out**, extract, withdraw, take out, unsheathe. [➡CAUSE TO APPEAR; 5] *Opposite:* put away. 4 *v* **get**, obtain, extract, derive, gain, take, elicit. [➡GET; 421] 5 *v* **attract**, pull, lure, appeal, entice, bring in, captivate, charm. [➡APPEAL TO AND AROUSE INTEREST; 576] 6 *v* **finish equal**, tie, equal, square, even. [➡EQUALITY; 155] 7 *n* **dead heat**, tie, stalemate, deadlock, standoff, photo finish. [➡RESULTS AND OUTCOMES; 83] 8 *n* **attraction**, magnet, crowd puller, inducement, lure, enticement, pull, allurement, appeal. [➡TREAT; 211]

See Compare and Contrast at **pull**.

draw a veil over *v* **hush up** (*informal*), conceal, keep quiet about, keep mum about (*informal*), ignore, forget. [➡WITHHOLD INFORMATION; 688] *Opposite:* expose.

drawback *n* **disadvantage**, problem, downside, negative, weakness, shortcoming, hitch, snag, obstacle, minus, stumbling block. [➡NUISANCES; 254] *Opposite:* advantage.

draw back *v* **move away**, draw away, withdraw, retreat, recoil, fall back, drop out. [➡GO BACKWARDS; 310] *Opposite:* approach.

drawbridge *type of* **bridge**. [➡BRIDGES, TUNNELS, CROSSINGS, AND JUNCTIONS; 1111]

drawer *type of* **container**. [➡CONTAINERS, RECEPTACLES, AND PACKAGING; 1244]

drawers *type of* **lower body underwear**. [➡HABERDASHERY, MILLINERY, AND LINGERIE; 867]

draw in *v* **involve**, implicate, engage, ensnare, hook. [➡APPEAL TO AND AROUSE INTEREST; 576]

drawing *n* **sketch**, picture, illustration, diagram, portrayal, depiction, cartoon, representation, doodle, outline. [➡DRAWINGS, CHARTS AND TABLES; 595]

drawing room *type of* **room in the home.** [➡TYPES OF ROOM; 1096]

drawl *n* **pronunciation**, intonation, inflection, enunciation, twang, brogue, burr. [➡ASPECTS OF LANGUAGE; 683]

drawn *adj* **haggard**, strained, pinched, tired, wan, drained, careworn, tense, fraught. [➡FACIAL EXPRESSION; 652] *Opposite:* relaxed.

draw near *v* **approach**, get closer, come nearer, come up, creep up, move in on, converge. [➡ARRIVE; 12] *Opposite:* move away.

drawn-out *adj* **protracted**, lengthy, long, convoluted, interminable, dragging, lingering. [➡HAPPENING SLOWLY; 106] *Opposite:* swift.

draw off *v* **pour**, siphon off, pull, drain off, suck up, abstract, pump, tap. [➡EJECT AND EXCLUDE; 341]

draw on *v* **use**, employ, be inspired by, resort to, fall back on, bring into play, utilize, exploit, make use of, rely on. [➡USE; 468]

draw out *v* **prolong**, extend, make last, lengthen, stretch, protract, drag out, spin out. [➡CAUSE TO CONTINUE; 268] *Opposite:* cut short.

drawstring 1 *n* **tie**, string, lace, belt. [➡FASTENERS, LINKS, AND NETWORKS; 1246] 2 *part of* **garment.** [➡PARTS OF A GARMENT; 870]

draw up *v* **draft**, put together, assemble, prepare, write, set down, sketch out, outline. [➡CREATE IMAGES; 357]

dray *n* **wagon**, cart, low-loader, transporter, lorry, truck. [➡BIKES, CARS, AND CARRIAGES; 1148]

dread 1 *v* **fear**, be afraid of, be terrified of, be frightened of, be worried about, be anxious about, shrink from. [➡DISLIKE AND HATE; 578] *Opposite:* look forward to. 2 *n* **terror**, fear, trepidation, anxiety, dismay, alarm, fright, horror. [➡FEAR AND PANIC; 544] *Opposite:* confidence.

dreadful *adj* **terrible**, awful, horrible, frightful, alarming, shocking, appalling, outrageous, vile, ghastly. [➡DISGUSTING AND REPULSIVE; 231] *Opposite:* lovely.

dreadfully *adv* **terribly**, awfully, really, extremely, very, truly, appallingly, outrageously. [➡TO A GREAT EXTENT; 130]

dreadfulness *n* **awfulness**, horror, misery, ghastliness, gruesomeness, atrociousness, vileness, hideousness. [➡DISGUSTING AND REPULSIVE; 231]

dreadlocks *type of* **hairstyle.** [➡HAIR STYLES AND HAIR PIECES; 489]

dream 1 *n* **vision**, daydream, reverie, nightmare, hallucination, delusion, trance, fantasy. [➡NONEXISTENT THINGS; 23] *Opposite:* reality. 2 *n* **aspiration**, wish, goal, hope, ambition, desire, pipe dream, castle in Spain, castle in the air. [➡DESIRE AND WANT; 580] 3 *n* **delight**, joy, pleasure, marvel, ideal. [➡AMAZING THING; 212] *Opposite:* nightmare. 4 *v* **fantasize**, visualize, imagine, fancy, daydream, envisage, think. [➡DREAM, IMAGINE, AND FANTASIZE; 750]

dreamer *n* **visionary**, idealist, romantic, fantasist. [➡LAZY OR UNSUCCESSFUL PEOPLE; 948] *Opposite:* realist.

dreamily *adv* **vaguely**, distantly, distractedly, languorously, abstractedly, pensively, absent-mindedly. [➡NEUTRALITY AND INDIFFERENCE; 554]

dreaminess 1 *n* **pensiveness**, abstraction, vagueness, wistfulness, languor, absent-mindedness. [➡NOT PAY ATTENTION; 765] 2 *n* **perfection**, beauty, exquisiteness, loveliness, gorgeousness. [➡BEAUTY AND ATTRACTIVENESS; 190]

dreamland *n* **paradise**, heaven, nirvana, fairyland, fantasy world, never-never land, cloudland, land of make-believe, dream world, la-la land (*US*). [➡NON-EXISTENT PLACE; 1065] *Opposite:* real world.

dreamlike *adj* **unreal**, fantastic, surreal, weird, bizarre, otherworldly, illusory, trancelike. [➡FALSE AND UNREAL; 174] *Opposite:* real.

dream up *v* **concoct**, think up, invent, imagine, come up with, cook up (*informal*), devise. [➡DREAM, IMAGINE, AND FANTASIZE; 750]

dream world *n* **fantasy world**, land of make-believe, storyland, fairyland, never-never land, cloudland, dreamland. [➡NON-EXISTENT PLACE; 1065] *Opposite:* real world.

dreamy 1 *adj* **pensive**, vague, faraway, wistful, preoccupied, distracted, inattentive, distrait (*literary*). [➡NEUTRALITY AND INDIFFERENCE; 554] *Opposite:* alert. 2 *adj* **wonderful**, beautiful, superb, out of this world, terrific (*informal*), fantastic. [➡EXTRAORDINARY: AMAZING; 205] *Opposite:* ordinary.

drearily *adv* **dully**, monotonously, boringly, tediously, uninterestingly, routinely. [➡BORING AND UNINTERESTING; 235] *Opposite:* interestingly.

dreariness 1 *n* **dullness**, monotony, tedium, boredom, routine. [➡BORING AND UNINTERESTING; 235] *Opposite:* excitement. 2 *n* **bleakness**, misery, cheerlessness, grimness, gloominess, drabness. [➡EMOTIONALLY UNPLEASANT AND UPSETTING; 228] *Opposite:* cheerfulness.

dreary 1 *adj* **dull**, boring, monotonous, tedious, lifeless, unexciting, routine. [➡BORING AND UNINTERESTING; 235] *Opposite:* interesting. 2 *adj* **bleak**, cheerless, dismal, miserable, grim, desolate, depressing, drab, gloomy. [➡SADNESS, DISTRESS, AND DESPAIR; 540] *Opposite:* cheerful.

dredge *v* **search**, scour, comb, ransack, rummage, dig up. [➡SEEK POSSESSION AND SEARCH; 457]

dredger *type of* **motor vessel.** [➡SHIPS AND BOATS; 1149]

dredge up *v* **unearth**, dig up, drag up, rake up (*informal*), bring up, uncover. [➡CAUSE TO APPEAR; 5] *Opposite:* bury.

dregs 1 *n* (*literary*) **relics**, remains, vestiges, remainder, remnants, residue, leftovers. [➡REMAINDER AND REMAINDERS; 123] 2 *n* **remains**, residue, sediment, silt, lees, deposit, waste, grounds. [➡UNPLEASANT AND DIRTY SUBSTANCES; 1267]

drench *v* **soak**, wet, saturate, douse, steep, flood, inundate. [➡SOFTEN, LIQUEFY, DAMPEN; 389] *Opposite:* dry out.

drenched *adj* **soaked**, sodden, wet, inundated, saturated, soaked to the skin, dripping wet, sopping, sopping wet. [➡WET; 1239] *Opposite:* dry.

Dresden china *type of* **pottery.** [➡POTTERY; 1134]

dress 1 *v* **wear**, put on, dress up, clothe, slip into, don (*formal*), array (*literary*), attire (*formal*). [➡DRESS, WEAR, AND UNDRESS; 868] *Opposite:* undress. 2 *v* **adorn**, decorate, bedeck (*literary*), deck out, ornament, trim. [➡DECORATE, ADORN, AND APPLY COATINGS; 406] 3 *n* **clothing**, clothes, costume, garb, gear (*informal*), wear, outfit. [➡CLOTHES AND ACCESSORIES; 864]

dress

◆ *types of dress*
ballgown, cheongsam, evening dress, evening gown (*US*), frock, gown, gymslip, jumper (*US*), kaftan, kimono, muumuu, pinafore, robe, sari, sheath, shift, shirtdress, sundress, wedding dress

dress circle *n* [➡IN THE THEATRE; 906]

dress down *v* **scold**, reprimand, tell off (*informal*), lecture, rebuke, censure, chew out (*US informal*). [➡ACCUSE, BLAME, AND CRITICIZE; 642] *Opposite:* praise.

dressed *adj* **turned out**, kitted out, robed, garbed, outfitted. [➡DRESS, WEAR, AND UNDRESS; 868] *Opposite:* undressed.

dresser *type of* **cabinet**. [➡FURNITURE; 858]

dressing 1 *n* **bandage**, covering, gauze. [➡COVERS AND COATINGS; 1245] 2 *type of* **seasonings, sauces, and dips**. [➡SEASONINGS AND SAUCES; 1173]

dressing gown *n* **housecoat**, negligée, wrap, peignoir, robe. [➡GARMENTS AND OUTFITS; 865]

dressing room *type of* **room in public buildings**. [➡TYPES OF ROOM; 1096]

dressing table *type of* **table**. [➡FURNITURE; 858]

dressmaking *n* **couture**, tailoring, sewing. [➡CRAFTS AND CARVING; 356]

dress rehearsal *n* **practice**, run through, trial, dummy run, rehearsal, preparation, dry run, tryout (*US*). [➡PREPARATORY EVENT; 57]

dress sense *n* **flair**, stylishness, fashion sense, panache, chic, elegance. [➡WELL GROOMED; 483]

dress suit *type of* **suit**. [➡GARMENTS AND OUTFITS; 865]

dress uniform *n* [➡GARMENTS AND OUTFITS; 865]

dress up *v* **disguise**, revamp, embellish, decorate, titivate, do up, doll up (*informal*). [➡DECORATE, ADORN, AND APPLY COATINGS; 406]

dressy *adj* **elegant**, fashionable, stylish, chic, classy (*informal*), swish (*informal*). [➡DESCRIBING CLOTHES; 869] *Opposite:* sloppy.

drey *type of* **den or nest**. [➡ANIMAL OR BIRD ACCOMMODATION; 1078]

dribble 1 *v* **drool**, salivate, slobber, slaver, drivel. [➡EXCRETION AND EXCRETA; 723] 2 *v* **trickle**, ooze, drip, seep, leak, drop. [➡LIQUID EMISSION; 371] *Opposite:* gush.

dried *adj* **dehydrated**, dried out, dried up, desiccated, dry. [➡DRY; 1241]

drift 1 *v* **float**, flow, glide, coast, waft, wander, go with the flow. [➡MOVE SLOWLY; 315] 2 *n* **gist**, meaning, point, sense, idea, implication, theme. [➡MEANING; 691]

drifter *n* **wanderer**, tramp, vagabond, rolling stone, vagrant. [➡NOMADIC AND ROOTLESS LIFESTYLES; 884]

drifting *adj* **wandering**, nomadic, homeless, itinerant, travelling, migratory, rootless, migrant, peripatetic. [➡NOMADIC AND ROOTLESS LIFESTYLES; 884] *Opposite:* settled.

driftwood *n* **flotsam**, jetsam, wreckage, refuse, waste, trash (*US*). [➡RUBBISH AND USELESS OBJECTS; 1248]

drill 1 *n* **practice**, exercise, discipline, training, instruction, preparation. [➡PREPARATORY EVENT; 57] 2 *v* **bore**, make a hole, pierce, puncture, penetrate. [➡TEAR, BREAK, AND CUT; 361] 3 *v* **train**, coach, school, discipline, instruct, teach. [➡INSTRUCT AND TEACH; 610] 4 *type of* **fabric from plants**. [➡FABRICS; 1131] 5 *type of* **carpentry tool**. [➡HAND TOOLS; 1118]

See Compare and Contrast at **teach**.

drily *adv* **ironically**, humorously, wittily, subtly, wryly. [➡GOOD-TEMPERED AND HUMOROUS; 628]

drink 1 *v* **swallow**, imbibe (*formal or humorous*), down, sip, gulp, slurp, swig (*informal*), knock back (*informal*), glug (*informal*), lap up. [➡DRINK; 712] 2 *n* **beverage** (*formal*), thirst-quencher, swill, pick-me-up (*informal*), hot drink, cold drink. [➡DRINKS; 1186] 3 *n* **alcoholic drink**, cocktail, beer, nip, tipple (*informal*), snifter (*informal*). [➡DRINKS; 1186] 4 *n* **mouthful**, taste, gulp, swallow, swig (*informal*), slurp (*informal*), sip, glug (*informal*), swill. [➡DRINK; 712]

drinkable *adj* **fit to drink**, safe to drink, filtered, potable. [➡CLEAN; 1232]

drinking fountain *n* **water spout**, jet, tap, faucet (*US*). [➡FITTINGS; 859]

drinks cabinet *type of* **cabinet**. [➡FURNITURE; 858]

drinks party *n* [➡PARTIES, DANCES, AND CELEBRATIONS; 37]

drip 1 *v* **dribble**, trickle, drop, leak, seep, ooze. [➡LIQUID EMISSION; 371] *Opposite:* gush. 2 *n* **drop**, trickle, dribble, leak. [➡AMOUNT OF LIQUID; 114] *Opposite:* stream.

drip-dry *adj* **noniron**, wash-and-wear, crease-resistant. [➡DESCRIBING CLOTHES; 869]

dripping 1 *adj* **wet**, soaked, drenched, sodden, saturated, sopping, sopping wet, soaked to the skin, wet through. [➡WET; 1239] *Opposite:* dry. 2 *type of* **cooking fat and oil**. [➡FATS AND OILS; 1172]

dripping wet *adj* [➡WET; 1239]

drive 1 *v* **steer**, handle, guide, direct, operate, pilot, lead. [➡TRAVEL: WAYS OF TRAVELLING; 321] 2 *v* **take**, run, chauffeur, transport. [➡ACCOMPANY AND FOLLOW; 338] 3 *v* **power**, run, cause to move, set in motion. [➡USE TOOLS AND MACHINERY; 469] 4 *v* **force**, make, coerce, constrain, impel, compel, oblige. [➡CAUSE OR COMPEL TO ACT; 272] 5 *v* **push**, propel, urge, goad, send, hurl, shove, thrust. [➡PUSH, PULL, SLIDE; 336] 6 *v* **hammer**, push, force, plunge, sink, thrust, pound. [➡MOVE PAST, INTO OR THROUGH SOMETHING; 332] 7 *n* **energy**, determination, ambition, initiative, get-up-and-go (*informal*), motivation, effort, enterprise, push, vitality. [➡ENERGY AND ENTHUSIASM; 497] *Opposite:* lethargy. 8 *n*

urge, desire, need, instinct, passion. [➡POSITIVE IMPATIENCE, ENTHUSIASM, AND ALERTNESS; 538] **9** *n* **campaign**, crusade, push, fundraiser, appeal. [➡NON-AGGRESSIVE/SPORTING EVENT; 40]

drive insane *v* [➡CONFUSE AND BEWILDER; 572]

drivel *n* **nonsense**, bunkum (*informal*), hogwash (*informal*), malarkey (*informal*), balderdash, twaddle (*informal*), gibberish, bunk (*slang*), hokum (*US informal disapproving*). [➡MEANINGLESS SPEECH OR WRITING; 677]

drive mad (*informal*) *v* [➡CONFUSE AND BEWILDER; 572]

driven *adj* **ambitious**, determined, obsessed, motivated, compelled, energetic. [➡HARD-WORKING AND COMMITTED; 501] *Opposite:* apathetic.

driver *n* **chauffeur**, motorist, valet, teamster (*US*). [➡DRIVERS; 1152]

drive round the bend *v* [➡CONFUSE AND BEWILDER; 572]

driver's seat (*US*) *type of* **internal feature.** [➡INTERNAL PARTS OF A VEHICLE; 1145]

drive-through *type of* **food outlet.** [➡RETAIL OUTLETS; 1082]

drive up the wall (*informal*) *v* **exasperate**, infuriate, make your blood boil, enrage, irritate, irk, drive mad (*informal*), annoy. [➡ANGER AND ANNOY; 570]

driving **1** *adj* **heavy**, pouring, lashing. [➡CLOUDY AND RAINY WEATHER; 1052] *Opposite:* light. **2** *adj* **powerful**, dynamic, energetic, motivating, forceful, compelling, influential, major. [➡STRENGTH; 202]

driving rain *n* [➡CLOUDY AND RAINY WEATHER; 1052]

driving seat *type of* **internal feature.** [➡INTERNAL PARTS OF A VEHICLE; 1145]

drizzle **1** *n* **light rain**, trickle, shower, sprinkle (*US*). [➡CLOUDY AND RAINY WEATHER; 1052] *Opposite:* downpour. **2** *v* **rain**, spit, spot, shower, sprinkle, trickle, dribble, drip, drop. [➡CLOUDY AND RAINY WEATHER; 1052] *Opposite:* pour.

drizzling *adj* [➡CLOUDY AND RAINY WEATHER; 1052]

drizzly *adj* **damp**, wet, rainy, misty. [➡CLOUDY AND RAINY WEATHER; 1052]

drogue parachute *part of* **spacecraft.** [➡SPACE VEHICLES; 1062]

droll *adj* **amusing**, funny, comic, witty, humorous, comical, entertaining, quaint, absurd. [➡FUNNY AND AMUSING; 217] *Opposite:* dull.

See Compare and Contrast at **funny.**

drollness *n* [➡FUNNY AND AMUSING; 217]

drolly *adv* **amusingly**, comically, humorously, wittily, absurdly, entertainingly. [➡FUNNY AND AMUSING; 217]

dromedary *type of* **large mammal.** [➡LARGE MAMMAL; 986]

drone **1** *v* **hum**, buzz, whine, whirr, murmur. [➡EMIT CONTINUOUS SOUNDS; 367] **2** *n* **buzz**, hum, whine, murmur, whirr. [➡CONTINUOUS SOUNDS; 1257]

drone on *v* [➡WITTER AND BABBLE; 618]

drool *v* **dribble**, salivate, slobber, slaver, drivel. [➡EXCRETION AND EXCRETA; 723]

droop **1** *v* **sag**, wilt, bow, hang down, flop, sink, slouch. [➡TAKE UP A NEW POSITION; 313] **2** *v* **tire**, tire out, wear out, flag, wilt, fade, slump, subside. [➡GET WORSE; 382] *Opposite:* perk up.

droopiness **1** *n* **tiredness**, fatigue, weariness, exhaustion, apathy. [➡TIRED, ASLEEP AND UNCONSCIOUS; 739] *Opposite:* freshness. **2** *n* **floppiness**, limpness, lifelessness, slackness, bagginess, flaccidity. [➡MALLEABLE AND ELASTIC; 1211] *Opposite:* stiffness.

droopy **1** *adj* **tired**, tired out, worn out, fatigued, weary, exhausted. [➡TIRED, ASLEEP AND UNCONSCIOUS; 739] *Opposite:* fresh. **2** *adj* **hanging**, floppy, limp, dangling, sagging, lifeless, flaccid, slack, baggy. [➡MALLEABLE AND ELASTIC; 1211] *Opposite:* upright.

drop **1** *v* **fall**, go down, plunge, plummet, crash, jump down, dive, slump, decline. [➡GO DOWNWARDS; 308] *Opposite:* rise. **2** *v* **let fall**, let go, release, throw down. [➡MOVE SOMETHING: DOWNWARDS; 330] **3** *v* **drip**, trickle, ooze, seep, dribble. [➡LIQUID EMISSION; 371] *Opposite:* pour. **4** *v* **abandon**, stop, shelve, give up, discontinue, cut, leave out, ditch (*informal*), dump, cut out. [➡STOP ACTING; 265] *Opposite:* maintain. **5** *n* **descent**, fall, plunge, decline, dip, declivity. [➡GO DOWNWARDS; 308] *Opposite:* ascent. **6** *n* **droplet**, drip, bead, globule, dewdrop, drib. [➡AMOUNT OF LIQUID; 114] **7** *n* **reduction**, decrease, decline, fall, cut, deterioration, falling off, slump, sag, downswing. [➡LESS; 124] *Opposite:* increase.

drop a line *v* **write**, get in touch, correspond, contact, send a letter, send a note. [➡INITIATE AND ESTABLISH COMMUNICATION; 681]

drop back *v* **fall behind**, fall back, drop behind, slow down, lag behind, straggle. [➡MOVE SLOWLY; 315]

drop behind *v* **fall back**, fall behind, drop back, slow down, lag behind, straggle. [➡MOVE SLOWLY; 315]

drop in *v* **call**, call by, call in, come round, drop by, drop over, look in, stop by, visit, come around (*US*). [➡ARRIVE; 12]

droplet *n* **drop**, drip, bead, dewdrop, globule, drib. [➡AMOUNT OF LIQUID; 114]

drop off (*informal*) **1** *v* **go to sleep**, nod off, fall asleep, doze off, drift off, drowse, snooze (*informal*). [➡SLEEP AND DREAM; 724] **2** *v* **deliver**, unload, deposit, leave. [➡DISPENSE, RATION, AND DISTRIBUTE; 435] *Opposite:* pick up.

drop out *v* **leave**, give up, quit, withdraw, stop, abandon. [➡STOP ACTING; 265] *Opposite:* carry on.

dropper *n* **dispenser**, measurer, tube, glass dropper, eye dropper, ear dropper. [➡MEASURING DEVICES; 1122]

droppings *n* **dung**, muck, stools, faeces, excreta (*technical*), manure. [➡EXCRETION AND EXCRETA; 723]

drop scone *type of* **pancake.** [➡CAKES, BISCUITS, AND DESSERTS; 1180]

dross *n* **rubbish**, trash, garbage, scum, waste, junk (*informal*). [➡RUBBISH AND USELESS OBJECTS; 1248]

drought *n* **lack**, dearth, deficiency, scarcity, famine. [➡TOO FEW, TOO LITTLE; 120] *Opposite:* abundance.

drove 1 *n* **throng**, horde, crowd, gaggle, multitude, group. [➡GROUPS OF PEOPLE; 935] *Opposite:* trickle. **2** *type of* **herd.** [➡GROUP OF ANIMALS; 993]

droves *n* **multitudes**, hordes, crowds, scores, masses (*informal*), flocks. [➡MANY, MUCH, LARGE AMOUNT; 117]

drown 1 *v* **go down**, go under, sink, die. [➡DIE; 922] *Opposite:* float. **2** *v* **drench**, overwater, soak, swamp, saturate, flood, submerge, engulf, inundate. [➡SOFTEN, LIQUEFY, DAMPEN; 389] *Opposite:* dry. **3** *v* **cover**, mask, obscure, hide, overlie, overwhelm, drown out. [➡CAUSE TO DISAPPEAR; 6] *Opposite:* amplify.

drowse *v* **snooze** (*informal*), be sleepy, doze, nap, have a nap, have forty winks (*informal*), catnap, sleep, nod off, slumber. [➡SLEEP AND DREAM; 724] *Opposite:* wake.

drowsiness *n* **sleepiness**, lethargy, stupor, tiredness. [➡TIRED, ASLEEP AND UNCONSCIOUS; 739] *Opposite:* wakefulness.

drowsy *adj* **sleepy**, tired, dozy, snoozing (*informal*), lethargic, somnolent, nodding. [➡TIRED, ASLEEP AND UNCONSCIOUS; 739] *Opposite:* awake.

drub *v* **beat**, pound, hammer (*informal*), thrash, whip (*informal*), defeat, lick (*informal*). [➡BEAT AND DEFEAT; 80]

drubbing *n* **beating**, thrashing, hammering (*informal*), pasting (*informal*), licking (*informal*). [➡BEAT AND DEFEAT; 80]

drudge 1 *n* **worker**, skivvy (*informal*), menial (*formal*). [➡WORKER; 836] *Opposite:* drone. **2** *v* **work**, toil, labour, skivvy (*informal*), graft (*informal*), grind, plod, slog. [➡HARD WORK OR EFFORT; 299]

drudgery *n* **labour**, toil, work, graft (*informal*), chore, grind, slog. [➡HARD WORK OR EFFORT; 299]

See Compare and Contrast at **work.**

drug *n* **medication**, medicine, painkiller. [➡REMEDIES, TREATMENTS AND OPERATIONS; 732]

druggist (*US*) *type of* **retail outlet.** [➡RETAIL OUTLETS; 1082]

drug squad *n* [➡THE POLICE, ARREST, AND PRE-TRIAL PROCEEDINGS; 818]

drugstore (*US*) *type of* **retail outlet.** [➡RETAIL OUTLETS; 1082]

druid *n* [➡RELIGIOUS PEOPLE; 779]

drum 1 *n* **barrel**, cask, cylinder, container. [➡CONTAINERS, RECEPTACLES, AND PACKAGING; 1244] **2** *v* **play the drums**, pulsate, throb, tap, thump. [➡EMIT SOUNDS THROUGH IMPACT AND ABRASION; 366] **3** *type of* **percussion instrument.** [➡MUSICAL INSTRUMENTS; 910]

drum and bass *type of* **popular music.** [➡MUSIC, SONGS, AND SINGING; 907]

drum in *v* **impress**, instil, drive into, teach, din in, inculcate, repeat. [➡INSTRUCT AND TEACH; 610]

drum into *see* **drum in.**

drummer *n* **percussionist**, drum player, timpanist, rhythmist, instrumentalist. [➡MUSICIANS AND SINGERS; 908]

drumming *n* **thudding**, pounding, beating, hammering, tapping, throbbing. [➡IMPACT SOUNDS; 1259]

drum roll *n* **roll of drums**, tattoo, rattle, paradiddle, rumble, crescendo, buildup. [➡IMPACT SOUNDS; 1259]

drumstick 1 *n* **stick**, wire brush, mallet, beater, baton. [➡STICKS, POLES, AND WEDGES; 1253] **2** *type of* **cut.** [➡TYPES AND CUTS OF MEAT; 1176]

drum up *v* **gather**, stimulate, rally, foster, encourage, whip up, arouse, mobilize, stir up, create. [➡GET; 421] *Opposite:* suppress.

drunk *adj* **inebriated** (*formal*), intoxicated (*formal*), plastered (*informal*), smashed (*informal*), bombed (*slang*), stewed (*slang*), tanked (*slang*), tanked-up (*slang*), sloshed (*slang*), soused (*slang*), under the influence (*informal*), liquored up (*US informal*), loaded (*US slang*), crocked (*US slang*). [➡UNDER THE INFLUENCE OF DRUGS OR ALCOHOL; 742] *Opposite:* sober.

drunkard *n* [➡PLEASURE-SEEKERS AND HEDONISTS; 886]

druthers (*informal*) *n* **preference**, free choice, first choice, fancy, cup of tea. [➡APPRECIATION AND GRATITUDE; 536]

dry 1 *adj* **dehydrated**, dried out, dried up, arid, waterless, desiccated, dry as a bone, parched, shrivelled, sere (*literary*). [➡DRY; 1241] *Opposite:* wet. **2** *adj* **thirsty**, dehydrated, parched, in need of a drink, gasping. [➡DRINK; 712] **3** *adj* **deadpan**, wry, ironic, understated, laconic, deprecating, matter-of-fact, sarcastic, sardonic, emotionless. [➡MOCKING AND DISMISSIVE; 637] **4** *adj* **uninteresting**, dull, tedious, boring, monotonous, dreary, unexciting, uninspired. [➡BORING AND UNINTERESTING; 235] *Opposite:* interesting. **5** *adj* **teetotal**, abstinent, abstemious, temperate, anti-alcohol, alcohol-free. [➡ABSTEMIOUSNESS AND SELF-DENIAL; 882] **6** *v* **make dry**, rub, rub down, towel, wipe, soak up, mop up. [➡HARDEN, CONGEAL, DRY; 388] *Opposite:* wet. **7** *v* **desiccate**, become dry, dry out, dry up, dehydrate, parch, wither. [➡HARDEN, CONGEAL, DRY; 388] *Opposite:* swell.

Compare and Contrast: ***dry, dehydrated, desiccated, arid, parched, shrivelled***

CORE MEANING: LACKING MOISTURE

dry having little or no moisture; ***dehydrated*** experiencing fluid loss, or preserved by drying; ***desiccated*** (used of products, especially food) free from moisture, or preserved by drying; ***arid*** (used of land) dry from lack of rain; ***parched*** dry from excessive heat or lack of rain; ***shrivelled*** dry, shrunken, and wrinkled.

dryad *n* **wood nymph**, fairy, naiad, pixie, nymph, elf, sprite. [➡MYTHICAL BEINGS; 790]

dry as a bone *adj* [➡DRY; 1241]

dry-clean *v* **clean**, launder, wash, valet. [➡CLEAN AND POLISH; 404]

dryer *n* **drying device**, hair dryer, tumble dryer, clothes dryer, clothes horse, hand dryer. [➡HOUSEHOLD APPLIANCES; 1116]

dry-eyed *adj* **unemotional**, impassive, expressionless, unmoved, stoical, stoic. [➡NEUTRALITY AND INDIFFERENCE; 554] *Opposite:* tearful.

dry land *n* **solid ground**, shore, beach, terra firma. [➡THE SEAS, OCEANS, AND SHORES; 1041] *Opposite:* sea.

dryness 1 *n* **aridness**, aridity, waterlessness, dehydration, drought, desiccation, parchedness. [➡DRY; 1241] *Opposite:* wetness. 2 *n* **wryness**, irony, understatement, matter-of-factness, sarcasm. [➡MOCKING AND DISMISSIVE; 637]

dry out 1 *v* **air**, dry, dry off, tumble dry, tumble, hang out to dry. [➡HARDEN, CONGEAL, DRY; 388] 2 *v* **shrivel up**, curl up, dry up, wither, become dehydrated. [➡HARDEN, CONGEAL, DRY; 388]

dry run *n* **rehearsal**, run-through, dummy run, trial run, trial, practice, tryout (*US*). [➡PREPARATORY EVENT; 57]

dry up 1 *v* **desiccate**, become dry, dry out, dry, dehydrate, parch, wither, shrink. [➡HARDEN, CONGEAL, DRY; 388] *Opposite:* swell. 2 *v* (*informal*) **falter**, lose the thread, stop midstream, forget your lines, come to a halt, finish, stop dead, shut up, stop talking, hesitate. [➡HESITATE; 273] *Opposite:* continue. 3 *v* **fail**, run out, be used up, come to an end, disappear, stop. [➡DISAPPEAR; 4] *Opposite:* continue.

dual *adj* **double**, twin, twofold. [➡APPORTIONMENT; 113]

dual carriageway *type of* **major road**. [➡ROADS; 1105]

dualism *n* **symmetry**, contrast, dichotomy, opposition, polarity, differentiation, duality. [➡DIFFERENCE; 150]

duality *n* **dichotomy**, division, dyad, contrast, opposition, complement, dualism. [➡DIFFERENCE; 150]

dub 1 *v* **call**, nickname, christen, hail as, label, style (*formal*). [➡NAME AND DESCRIBE; 666] 2 *type of* **popular music**. [➡MUSIC, SONGS, AND SINGING; 907]

dubbin *n* **polish**, wax, blacking, dressing, waterproofing, weatherproofing. [➡COVERS AND COATINGS; 1245]

dubiety (*formal*) *n* **doubtfulness**, doubt, dubiousness, uncertainty, hesitancy, suspicion. [➡UNCERTAIN; 176] *Opposite:* certitude.

dubious 1 *adj* **doubtful**, uncertain, unsure, undecided, unconvinced, in doubt, questioning, hesitant, suspicious, sceptical. [➡UNCERTAINTY; 560] *Opposite:* certain. 2 *adj* **suspect**, untrustworthy, fishy (*informal*), questionable, shady, unsavoury. [➡MORALLY BAD; 776] *Opposite:* trustworthy. 3 *adj* **ambiguous**, doubtful, debatable, uncertain, questionable, imprecise, vague. [➡UNCERTAIN; 176] *Opposite:* unambiguous.

See Compare and Contrast at **doubtful**.

dubiously *adv* **doubtfully**, uncertainly, unsurely, questioningly, hesitantly, suspiciously. [➡UNCERTAINTY; 560] *Opposite:* certainly.

dubiousness 1 *n* **doubt**, doubtfulness, uncertainty, hesitancy, suspicion, incertitude. [➡UNCERTAINTY; 560] *Opposite:* certainty. 2 *n* **fallibility**, unreliability, improbability, ambiguity, vagueness, flimsiness, shakiness. [➡UNCERTAIN; 176] *Opposite:* reliability.

duchess *type of* **aristocrat**. [➡RULERS AND ARISTOCRACY; 823]

duchy *n* **dukedom**, estate, territory, barony, principality, region. [➡REALMS AND RULES; 824]

duck 1 *n* **water bird**, waterfowl, diver. [➡FRESHWATER BIRD; 1000] 2 *type of* **meat**. [➡TYPES AND CUTS OF MEAT; 1176] 3 *type of* **fowl**. [➡FOOD BIRD; 999] 4 *type of* **male or female bird**. [➡MALE OR FEMALE BIRD; 1005] 5 *v* **stoop**, bend, bow, bob, nod, dip, lower, drop. [➡ASSUME A POSITION; 318] *Opposite:* straighten. 6 *v* **avoid**, evade, dodge, sidestep, circumvent, elude, escape. [➡NOT DO AND REFUSE TO DO; 275] *Opposite:* confront.

duckboard *n* **walkway**, boardwalk, path, planking, catwalk, gangplank. [➡PATHWAYS; 1109]

duckling *type of* **young bird**. [➡YOUNG BIRD; 1004]

duck out *v* **back out**, pull out, drop out, withdraw, get out, renege, avoid. [➡NOT DO AND REFUSE TO DO; 275]

ducks (*regional informal*) *n* **dear**, ducky (*dated informal*), chuck (*regional*), love (*informal*), lovey (*informal*), dearie (*informal*). [➡ENDEARMENTS; 657]

ducky (*dated informal*) *n* [➡ENDEARMENTS; 657]

duct *n* **channel**, canal, pipe, tube, vessel, conduit. [➡WATERCOURSES; 1110]

ductile *adj* **pliable**, malleable, elastic, pliant, plastic, flexible. [➡MALLEABLE AND ELASTIC; 1211]

See Compare and Contrast at **pliable**.

dud (*informal*) 1 *n* **failure**, flop (*informal*), fiasco, damp squib (*informal*), washout (*informal*), letdown, disappointment. [➡FAILURE; 77] *Opposite:* success. 2 *adj* **useless**, worthless, ineffective, broken, no good, duff (*informal*). [➡REDUNDANT AND USELESS; 241] *Opposite:* usable.

dude (*US slang*) 1 *n* **man**, boy, guy (*informal*), chap (*informal*), fella (*informal*), gentleman, bloke (*informal*), fellow (*dated*). [➡MALE PERSON; 934] 2 *n* **dandy** (*informal*), fop, swell (*dated informal*), hipster (*dated informal*), fashion victim. [➡MALE PERSON; 934]

duds (*informal*) *n* [➡CLOTHES AND ACCESSORIES; 864]

due 1 *adj* **expected**, scheduled, appointed, anticipated, looked-for, awaited. [➡FUTURE; 86] 2 *adj* **appropriate**, fitting, suitable, proper, right and proper, correct. [➡APPROPRIATE, SUITABLE, ADVISABLE; 185] *Opposite:* undue. 3 *adj* **owing**, unpaid, outstanding, payable, owed, in arrears. [➡OWE AND DESERVE; 466] *Opposite:* paid. 4 *adv* **directly**, exactly, direct, dead, straight, precisely. [➡DIRECTION OF MOTION; 346] *Opposite:* indirectly.

duel 1 *n* **contest**, fight, battle, gunfight, combat, clash. [➡AGGRESSIVE EVENT; 39] 2 *v* **fight**, clash, battle, contest, struggle, conflict. [➡COMPETE, CONTEND, AND COMBAT; 304]

duellist *n* **fighter**, combatant, opponent, gunfighter, contender, dueller. [➡COMPETITORS; 41]

dues *n* **fees**, subscription, payment, charge, levy, toll. [➡TAX AND TAXATION; 802]

duet *n* **duo**, double act, twosome, couple, pair, double. [➡GROUPS OF PEOPLE; 935]

due to *prep* **because of**, owing to, by reason of, as a result of, attributable to, thanks to, down to. [➡EXPRESSIONS OF REFERENCE; 63]

duff (*informal*) *adj* **useless**, inferior, broken, faulty, rotten, bad, lousy (*informal*). [➡IN BAD REPAIR; 1233] *Opposite:* excellent.

duffel bag *type of* **baggage**. [➡CONTAINERS, RECEPTACLES, AND PACKAGING; 1244]

duffel coat *type of* **overcoat**. [➡GARMENTS AND OUTFITS; 865]

dugong *type of* **marine mammal**. [➡MARINE MAMMAL; 987]

dugout *n* **bunker**, trench, foxhole, ditch, hollow, pit. [➡HOLES, GAPS, AND FORKS; 1251]

duke *type of* **aristocrat**. [➡RULERS AND ARISTOCRACY; 823]

dulcet *adj* **melodious**, melodic, honeyed, soothing, pleasant, soft. [➡SOFT OR PLEASANT SOUNDS; 1264] *Opposite:* harsh.

dull 1 *adj* **stupid**, obtuse, plodding, sluggish, unintelligent. [➡NEGATIVE INTELLECTUAL CHARACTERISTICS; 526] *Opposite:* bright. 2 *adj* **boring**, uninteresting, tedious, monotonous, dreary, dry, deadly (*informal*), unexciting, mind-numbing, lifeless, lacklustre. [➡BORING AND UNINTERESTING; 235] *Opposite:* interesting. 3 *adj* **cloudy**, overcast, gloomy, leaden, dismal, grey. [➡CLOUDY AND RAINY WEATHER; 1052] *Opposite:* bright. 4 *adj* **dark**, dim, muted, faded, lacklustre, insipid. [➡DESCRIBING COLOURS; 1225] *Opposite:* bright. 5 *v* **deaden**, dampen, stultify, cloud, blunt, reduce, blur, muffle, allay, assuage. [➡CHANGE OF INTENSITY: LESS; 396] *Opposite:* accentuate.

See Compare and Contrast at **boring**.

dullness 1 *n* **tediousness**, tedium, monotony, dreariness, dryness, lifelessness, flatness, insipidness, unimaginativeness. [➡BORING AND UNINTERESTING; 235] *Opposite:* liveliness. 2 *n* **cloudiness**, gloom, half-light, gloominess, leadenness, greyness. [➡CLOUDY AND RAINY WEATHER; 1052] *Opposite:* brightness. 3 *n* **darkness**, dimness, drabness, dowdiness, dinginess, murkiness. [➡DESCRIBING COLOURS; 1225] *Opposite:* brightness.

dull-witted *adj* [➡NEGATIVE INTELLECTUAL CHARACTERISTICS; 526]

dully 1 *adv* **boringly**, uninterestingly, drearily, tediously, monotonously, mind-numbingly. [➡BORING AND UNINTERESTING; 235] *Opposite:* interestingly. 2 *adv* **dimly**, faintly, weakly, feebly, insipidly, wanly. [➡DESCRIBING COLOURS; 1225] *Opposite:* brightly. 3 *adv* **bleakly**, monotonously, drearily, dismally, listlessly, lifelessly. [➡UNINTERESTED AND DETACHED; 630] *Opposite:* brightly. 4 *adv* **unintelligently**, stupidly, dimly, obtusely, sluggishly. [➡NEGATIVE INTELLECTUAL CHARACTERISTICS; 526] *Opposite:* intelligently.

duly *adv* **accordingly**, suitably, fittingly, appropriately, properly, correctly. [➡RESULTS AND OUTCOMES; 83] *Opposite:* unduly.

dumb *adj* [➡ABSENCE OF SOUND; 1256]

dumbfound *v* **astonish**, amaze, astound, surprise, stagger, flabbergast (*informal*), confound, stun. [➡CONFUSE AND BEWILDER; 572]

dumbfounded *adj* **astonished**, amazed, astounded, thunderstruck, staggered, surprised, stunned, flabbergasted (*informal*). [➡SURPRISE, SHOCK, AND AMAZEMENT; 546] *Opposite:* nonplussed.

dumbstruck *adj* [➡SURPRISE, SHOCK, AND AMAZEMENT; 546]

dumdum bullet *type of* **projectile**. [➡PROJECTILES; 1158]

dummy 1 *n* **mannequin**, model, lay figure, figure, form. [➡REPRESENTATIONS AND GENERAL EXAMPLES; 65] 2 *n* **copy**, replica, imitation, fake, mock-up, duplicate. [➡COPIES AND REPLICAS; 152] *Opposite:* original. 3 *adj* **imitation**, fake, mock, pretend, replica, false, bogus. [➡FALSE AND UNREAL; 174] *Opposite:* original.

dummy run *n* **rehearsal**, run-through, dry run, trial run, trial, practice, tryout (*US*). [➡PREPARATORY EVENT; 57]

dump 1 *v* (*informal*) **abandon**, walk out on (*informal*), discard, chuck (*informal*), leave, desert, finish with (*informal*). [➡REFUSING OR REJECTING RELATIONS; 975] *Opposite:* stay. 2 *v* **put**, leave, abandon, tip, throw, unload, deposit, chuck (*informal*), plunk, plonk. [➡GET RID OF SOMETHING; 452] 3 *n* **landfill**, junkyard, scrapyard, rubbish dump, tip, scrapheap, garbage dump (*US*). [➡STORES AND STORAGE BUILDINGS; 1087] 4 *v* **get rid of**, abandon, leave, ditch (*informal*), dispose of, discard. [➡GET RID OF SOMETHING; 452] *Opposite:* keep. 5 *n* (*informal*) **hole** (*informal*), tip, eyesore, mess, pigsty, monstrosity, hovel, pigpen (*US*). [➡UNDESIRABLE ACCOMMODATION; 856]

dumper *n* **tipper**, fly-tipper, litter lout (*informal disapproving*), litterer, litterbug (*informal*). [➡DIRTY AND SLOVENLY PEOPLE; 954]

dumper truck *type of* **commercial or industrial vehicle**. [➡VEHICLES; 1144]

dumpiness *n* [➡BUILD; 478]

dump on *v* [➡GIVE TOO MUCH; 438]

dump truck (*US*) *type of* **commercial or industrial vehicle**. [➡VEHICLES; 1144]

dun *type of* **beige**. [➡COLOURS; 1223]

dune *n* **bank**, sandbank, hill, mound, ridge, hump. [➡THE SEAS, OCEANS, AND SHORES; 1041]

dune buggy *type of* **leisure vehicle**. [➡VEHICLES; 1144]

dung *n* **manure**, droppings, slurry, muck, fertilizer, excrement. [➡UNPLEASANT AND DIRTY SUBSTANCES; 1267]

dungarees *type of* **trousers**. [➡GARMENTS AND OUTFITS; 865]

dung beetle *type of* **beetle**. [➡BEETLES AND WEEVILS; 1016]

dungeon *n* **prison**, cell, jail, vault, oubliette, chamber. [➡BUILDINGS FOR CONFINING PEOPLE; 1093]

dunk *v* **dip**, submerge, immerse, soak, steep, plunge, put in. [➡MOVE SOMETHING: DOWNWARDS; 330]

duo 1 *n* **pair**, twosome, couple, double act, two of a kind, duet. [➡GROUPS OF PEOPLE; 935] 2 *type of* **band**. [➡MUSICIANS AND SINGERS; 908]

duodenum *part of* **digestive tract**. [➡THE DIGESTIVE TRACT; 710]

dupe 1 *v* **fool**, trick, deceive, con, take in, cheat, hoodwink, swindle, pull the wool over somebody's eyes. [➡DECEPTION AND LIES; 661] 2 *n* **sucker** (*informal*), victim, target, fool, mug (*slang*), fall guy (*slang*). [➡VICTIMS OF DECEIT; 663]

duple *adj* [➡ APPORTIONMENT; 113]

duplex (*US*) *type of* **apartment.** [➡ RESIDENTIAL BUILDINGS; 1077]

duplicate 1 *v* **copy**, replicate, photocopy, reproduce, make two of, clone. [➡ COPY AND DUPLICATE; 403] 2 *v* **repeat**, replicate, reproduce, copy, do again, redo, double. [➡ COPY AND DUPLICATE; 403] 3 *n* **copy**, replacement, photocopy, spare, carbon copy, reproduction, replica, facsimile. [➡ COPIES AND REPLICAS; 152] *Opposite:* original. 4 *adj* **identical**, matching, replica, replacement, spare. [➡ SAMENESS; 151] *Opposite:* original.

See Compare and Contrast at **copy.**

duplication 1 *n* **repetition**, replication, doubling, copying, photocopying, reduplication. [➡ SAMENESS; 151] 2 *n* **replica**, duplicate, copy, print, facsimile, carbon copy, photocopy. [➡ COPIES AND REPLICAS; 152] *Opposite:* original.

duplicitous *adj* **double-dealing**, two-faced, tricky, deceitful, dishonest, disloyal, unfaithful, treacherous, fraudulent, misleading, deceptive. [➡ DECEITFUL; 514] *Opposite:* honest.

duplicitousness *n* [➡ DECEITFUL; 514]

duplicity *n* **deceit**, deception, dishonesty, disloyalty, unfaithfulness, treachery, fraudulence, betrayal, deceitfulness. [➡ DECEPTION AND LIES; 661] *Opposite:* honesty.

durability *n* **toughness**, sturdiness, strength, robustness, resilience, stability, permanence, hardiness, endurance, indestructibility. [➡ DURABLE; 1209] *Opposite:* flimsiness.

durable *adj* **tough**, hard-wearing, sturdy, strong, robust, long-lasting, resilient, heavy-duty, stable, enduring, permanent, hardy, indestructible. [➡ DURABLE; 1209] *Opposite:* flimsy.

duration *n* **length**, extent, period, time, interval, spell. [➡ PERIOD OF TIME; 90]

duress *n* **pressure**, force, threat, coercion, compulsion, constraint. [➡ CAPTIVITY AND LOSS OF FREEDOM; 249] *Opposite:* persuasion.

during *prep* **throughout**, through, in, in the course of. [➡ CONCURRENT AND CONTEMPORANEOUS; 165]

dusk *n* **twilight**, sunset, nightfall, sundown, evening, even (*literary*), eventide (*literary*). [➡ TIMES OF DAY; 87] *Opposite:* dawn.

dusky *adj* **shadowy**, dark, darkish, dim, hazy, grey, greyish. [➡ DESCRIBING COLOURS; 1225] *Opposite:* bright.

dust 1 *n* **powder**, dirt, sand, earth, soil, filth, grime. [➡ UNPLEASANT AND DIRTY SUBSTANCES; 1267] 2 *v* **clean**, clean up, wipe, wipe down, wipe up, brush. [➡ CLEAN AND POLISH; 404] 3 *v* **sprinkle**, brush, cover, scatter, sift, dredge. [➡ DECORATE, ADORN, AND APPLY COATINGS; 406]

dustbin *n* **bin**, litter bin, wheelie bin, wastepaper bin, rubbish bin, garbage can (*US*), trash can (*US*), wastebasket (*US*). [➡ CONTAINERS, RECEPTACLES, AND PACKAGING; 1244]

dust bowl *n* **desert**, waste, wasteland, wilderness. [➡ DESERTS AND PLAINS; 1045]

dustcart *type of* **public service vehicle.** [➡ VEHICLES; 1144]

dust cloth (*US*) *n* **duster**, cloth, rag. [➡ SOFT FURNISHINGS, LINEN, AND DRAPERY; 860]

duster *n* **cloth**, rag, feather duster, dust cloth (*US*). [➡ SOFT FURNISHINGS, LINEN, AND DRAPERY; 860]

dust jacket *n* **cover**, jacket, outer, dust cover, paper cover, outer cover, wrapper. [➡ COVERS AND COATINGS; 1245]

dustpan *n* **pan**, scoop, shovel, receptacle, container, collector, box. [➡ CONTAINERS, RECEPTACLES, AND PACKAGING; 1244]

dustsheet *n* **dust cover**, cover, sheet, throw, cloth, drop cloth (*US*). [➡ COVERS AND COATINGS; 1245]

dusty *adj* **dirty**, grimy, filthy, sandy, grubby, sooty. [➡ DIRTY; 1234] *Opposite:* clean.

dutiful *adj* **obedient**, well-behaved, compliant, loyal, devoted, respectful. [➡ HARD-WORKING AND COMMITTED; 501] *Opposite:* disobedient.

duty 1 *n* **responsibility**, obligation, onus, burden, calling, liability. [➡ RESPONSIBILITY; 171] 2 *n* **job**, task, function, responsibility, obligation, undertaking. [➡ JOB; 833] 3 *n* **tax**, payment, levy, due, impost, toll. [➡ TAX AND TAXATION; 802]

duty-bound *adj* **constrained**, compelled, obliged, forced, obligated, required. [➡ RESPONSIBILITY; 171]

duty-free 1 *adj* (*informal*) **tax-free**, tax-exempt, untaxed, nontaxable, nontaxed. [➡ TAX AND TAXATION; 802] 2 *type of* **retail outlet.** [➡ RETAIL OUTLETS; 1082]

duvet *n* **quilt**, eiderdown, coverlet, comforter (*US*). [➡ SOFT FURNISHINGS, LINEN, AND DRAPERY; 860]

DVD 1 *type of* **video equipment.** [➡ PHOTOGRAPHY AND PHOTOGRAPHIC EQUIPMENT; 1121] 2 *part of* **audio equipment.** [➡ AUDIO EQUIPMENT; 1138] 3 *type of* **hardware.** [➡ COMPUTERS AND COMPUTING; 1126]

dwarf star *type of* **star or star system.** [➡ CELESTIAL BODIES; 1060]

dwell (*literary*) *v* **reside**, live, lodge (*dated*), have your home, stay, abide (*archaic*), inhabit. [➡ INHABIT; 20] *Opposite:* leave.

dweller *n* **inhabitant**, resident, occupant, occupier, tenant. [➡ INHABITANT; 857]

dwelling (*formal*) *n* **house**, home, abode (*literary*), residence, private house, private residence, place of abode, lodging, flat, apartment (*US*). [➡ ACCOMMODATION; 855]

dwell on *v* **think about**, ponder, brood over, mull over, go on about, turn over, keep talking about, linger on, keep thinking about, wallow in, linger upon, spend too much time thinking about. [➡ THINK AND REFLECT; 744] *Opposite:* forget.

dwindle *v* **decrease**, decline, diminish, fall off, drop, drop off (*informal*), lessen, shrink, fade, fade away, disappear. [➡ DISAPPEAR; 4] *Opposite:* increase.

dwindling *adj* **declining**, decreasing, diminishing, deteriorating, falling. [➡ CEASE TO EXIST; 22] *Opposite:* burgeoning.

dye 1 *v* **colour**, stain, tint, change the colour of. [➡ CHANGE

OF COLOUR; 392] **2** *n* **colouring**, colour, stain, pigment. [➡DESCRIBING COLOURS; 1225] **3** *n* **hair dye**, colour, tint, rinse, peroxide, bleach, henna. [➡DYES AND COLOURANTS; 1269]

dyed-in-the-wool *adj* **long-established**, confirmed, committed, dedicated, incorrigible, diehard. [➡CONSERVATIVE AND UNADVENTUROUS; 518]

dying **1** *adj* **last**, final, ultimate, closing, ending. [➡AFTER, LAST, AND FOLLOWING; 166] **2** *adj* **disappearing**, failing, fading, vanishing, becoming extinct, on its last legs. [➡CEASE TO EXIST; 22] *Opposite:* thriving.

dying to *adj* **desperate to**, eager to, longing to, bursting to, impatient to, raring to, keen to. [➡DESIRE AND WANT; 580]

dyke **1** *n* **embankment**, dam, barrier, bank, wall, fortification, sea wall, barrage. [➡BARRIERS; 1112] **2** *n* **ditch**, watercourse, channel, drain, conduit, gutter. [➡WATERCOURSES; 1110]

dynamic *adj* **active**, go-ahead (*informal*), self-motivated, energetic, vibrant, forceful, full of life, vigorous. [➡ENERGY AND ENTHUSIASM; 497] *Opposite:* lethargic.

dynamics **1** *n* **changing aspects**, subtleties, forces at work, dynamic forces, underlying forces, undercurrents. [➡BASIC DETAILS; 689] **2** *n* **louds and softs**, dynamic range, changes in volume, crescendos, diminuendos, dynamic contrast. [➡CHANGE; 373]

dynamism *n* **vitality**, vigour, zing (*informal*), zip (*informal*), energy, drive, enthusiasm. [➡ENERGY AND ENTHUSIASM; 497] *Opposite:* lethargy.

dynamite **1** *v* **blow up**, blast, explode, detonate, wreck, destroy. [➡DESTRUCTION AND DEMOLITION; 360] **2** *type of* **explosive material**. [➡EXPLOSIVES; 1154]

dynamo **1** *n* **electric generator**, generator, motor, turbine. [➡ENERGY STORAGE AND GENERATION; 1162] **2** *n* (*informal*) **live wire** (*informal*), go-getter (*informal*), live one (*informal*), extrovert. [➡PEOPLE WHO ARE APPROVED OF; 955]

dynastic *adj* **hereditary**, successional, imperial, sovereign, ruling. [➡THE FAMILY; 956]

dynasty **1** *n* **reign**, rule, empire, period, era. [➡REALMS AND RULES; 824] **2** *n* **family**, house, line. [➡THE FAMILY; 956]

dyspepsia (*technical*) *n* **indigestion**, heartburn, acid stomach, upset stomach, unsettled stomach, digestive disorder, stomachache. [➡DISORDERS OF THE DIGESTIVE SYSTEM; 714]

dyspeptic *adj* [➡PAIN AND OTHER PHYSICAL SENSATIONS; 734]

dysphemism **1** *n* **offensiveness**, rudeness, vulgarity, obscenity, ribaldry, indecency. [➡INSULTS, ABUSE, AND SWEARING; 659] *Opposite:* euphemism. **2** *n* **obscenity**, swear word, expletive, oath, profanity, four-letter word. [➡INSULTS, ABUSE, AND SWEARING; 659] *Opposite:* euphemism.

dysphemistic *adj* **vulgar**, lewd, offensive, obscene, rude, ribald. [➡INSULTS, ABUSE, AND SWEARING; 659] *Opposite:* euphemistic.

each 1 *pron* **every one**, each one, all, both. [➡ALL; 126] 2 *adj* **every**, all, both, every single. [➡ALL; 126]

eager *adj* **keen**, enthusiastic, excited, raring to go, ready, willing, impatient, fervent, zealous. [➡DESIRE AND WANT; 580] *Opposite:* unenthusiastic.

eagerly *adv* **keenly**, enthusiastically, excitedly, readily, willingly, impatiently, fervently, zealously. [➡WITH ENTHUSIASM; 287] *Opposite:* unenthusiastically.

eagerness *n* **keenness**, enthusiasm, excitement, readiness, willingness, zeal, impatience, fervour. [➡POSITIVE IMPATIENCE, ENTHUSIASM, AND ALERTNESS; 538] *Opposite:* apathy.

eagle *type of* **bird of prey**. [➡BIRD OF PREY; 998]

eagle-eyed *adj* **observant**, hawk-eyed, sharp-sighted, sharp-eyed, alert, not missing much, attentive, quick, on the ball (*informal*). [➡POSITIVE INTELLECTUAL CHARACTERISTICS; 525] *Opposite:* unobservant.

eaglet *type of* **young bird**. [➡YOUNG BIRD; 1004]

ear 1 *n* **external ear**, outer ear, shell-like (*informal humorous*), auricle, earlobe, earhole, lobe, lug (*informal*). [➡THE EAR; 707] 2 *n* **ability**, sensitivity, talent, knack, facility, feel. [➡SKILLS, TALENTS, AND ABILITIES; 527] 3 *n* **attention**, hearing, heed, regard. [➡THE SENSES; 697] 4 *part of* **head**. [➡HEAD; 693]

eardrop *type of* **jewellery**. [➡JEWELLERY; 866]

eardrum *n* **membrane**, drum, tympanum (*technical*), tympanic membrane (*technical*). [➡THE EAR; 707]

earful (*informal*) *n* **scolding**, talking-to (*informal*), ticking-off (*informal*), telling-off (*informal*), lecture, piece of your mind, reprimand. [➡CRITICISMS AND ANGRY OUTBURSTS; 50]

earl *type of* **aristocrat**. [➡RULERS AND ARISTOCRACY; 823]

earlier 1 *adv* **before**, in advance, previously, formerly, beforehand, ahead, at an earlier time. [➡BEFORE, FIRST, AND PRECEDING; 164] *Opposite:* later. 2 *adj* **previous**, former, past, prior. [➡BEFORE, FIRST, AND PRECEDING; 164] *Opposite:* later.

earliest *adj* **first**, initial, original. [➡BEFORE, FIRST, AND PRECEDING; 164] *Opposite:* latest.

earlobe *n* [➡THE EAR; 707]

early 1 *adv* **early on**, at the beginning, before time, in advance, ahead of schedule, beforehand, prematurely. [➡PROMPTNESS: EARLY; 98] *Opposite:* late. 2 *adv* **soon**, promptly, without delay, now, as soon as possible. [➡PROMPTNESS: EARLY; 98] *Opposite:* later. 3 *adj* **initial**, first, primary, premature. [➡PROMPTNESS: EARLY; 98] *Opposite:* later. 4 *adj* **timely**, prompt, quick, speedy, immediate, hasty. [➡BEFORE, FIRST, AND PRECEDING; 164] *Opposite:* tardy.

early music *type of* **classical music**. [➡MUSIC, SONGS, AND SINGING; 907]

early years *n* **babyhood**, infancy, childhood, youth, formative years. [➡BABYHOOD, CHILDHOOD AND ADOLESCENCE; 917] *Opposite:* adulthood.

earmark *v* **allocate**, assign, allot, set aside, put aside, put by, put to one side, mark down, tag, save, reserve, keep. [➡DISPENSE, RATION, AND DISTRIBUTE; 435]

earmuffs *type of* **accessory**. [➡HABERDASHERY, MILLINERY, AND LINGERIE; 867]

earn 1 *v* **make**, be paid, take home, receive, get, bring in, produce, gross, net, clear (*informal*). [➡GET MONEY OR REWARD; 422] 2 *v* **deserve**, work for, win, warrant, merit, be worthy of, secure, gain. [➡OWE AND DESERVE; 466]

earnest 1 *adj* **serious**, solemn, grave, sober, intense, deep. [➡BAD-TEMPERED AND HUMOURLESS; 627] *Opposite:* frivolous. 2 *adj* **sincere**, heartfelt, deep, intense, strong. [➡TRUE AND REAL; 172] *Opposite:* superficial.

earnestly *adv* **sincerely**, seriously, solemnly, intensely, deeply, strongly. [➡BAD-TEMPERED AND HUMOURLESS; 627]

earnestness *n* **sincerity**, seriousness, solemnity, intensity, feeling, depth. [➡BAD-TEMPERED AND HUMOURLESS; 627]

earnings 1 *n* **pay**, salary, wages, income, take-home pay, pay cheque, pay packet, pay envelope (*US*). [➡INCOME; 461] 2 *n* **profit**, revenue, gain, return, dividend, interest, yield, balance. [➡INCOME; 461]

earphone *n* **earpiece**, phone, receiver, stereo phone, stereo headphone, headphone. [➡AUDIO EQUIPMENT; 1138]

earpiece *n* **earphone**, headset, headphones. [➡AUDIO EQUIPMENT; 1138]

earring *n type of* **jewellery**. [➡JEWELLERY; 866]

earshot *n* **hearing range**, range, hearing distance, hearing. [➡CLOSENESS; 160]

earsplitting *adj* **loud**, piercing, shrill, deafening, noisy, thunderous. [➡LOUD OR UNPLEASANT SOUNDS; 1265] *Opposite:* quiet.

earth 1 *n* **soil**, ground, dirt, mud, terrain, gravel. [➡THE EARTH; 1039] 2 *type of* **den or nest**. [➡ANIMAL OR BIRD ACCOMMODATION; 1078]

Earth *n* **world**, globe, planet. [➡CELESTIAL BODIES; 1060]

earthenware *type of* **pottery**. [➡POTTERY; 1134]

earthling *n* **human being**, human, earthly being, intelligent life-form, human life-form, homo sapiens. [➡SCIENCE FICTION; 1063] *Opposite:* extraterrestrial.

earthly 1 *adj* **worldly**, material, mortal, secular, everyday, human. [➡THE EARTH; 1039] *Opposite:* heavenly. 2 *adj* **possible**, imaginable, conceivable. [➡POSSIBLE AND PROBABLE; 178]

earthmover *n* **bulldozer**, power shovel, excavator, steam shovel, front-end loader (*US*). [➡BIKES, CARS, AND CARRIAGES; 1148]

earthquake *n* **tremor**, quake (*informal*), trembling, shaking, upheaval, volcanic activity, seismic activity. [➡VOLCANOES AND EARTHQUAKES; 1054]

earthshaking *adj* **momentous**, earthshattering, tremendous, remarkable, stunning, devastating. [➡IMPORTANT; 195] *Opposite:* trivial.

earthshattering *adj* **earthshaking**, momentous, tremendous, remarkable, stunning, devastating. [➡IMPORTANT; 195] *Opposite:* trivial.

earthwards *adv* **towards the earth**, towards the ground, downwards, down, in a nose-dive, earthbound. [➡DIRECTION OF MOTION; 346] *Opposite:* skyward.

earthwork *n* **fortification**, rampart, bulwark, barrier. [➡FORTRESSES AND FORTIFICATIONS; 1089]

earthworm *type of* **land invertebrate.** [➡LAND INVERTEBRATE; 1021]

earthy 1 *adj* **unpretentious**, down-to-earth, no-nonsense, simple, unsophisticated, basic, practical. [➡LEVEL OF EDUCATION AND SOPHISTICATION; 894] *Opposite:* refined. 2 *adj* **vulgar**, crude, raunchy (*informal*), gross, bawdy, rude, dirty, coarse, rough. [➡MORALLY BAD; 776]

earwig (*humorous*) *v* [➡LISTEN AND LISTENERS; 709]

ease 1 *n* **effortlessness**, easiness, simplicity, straightforwardness, facility. [➡EASE AND SIMPLICITY; 201] *Opposite:* difficulty. 2 *n* **comfort**, luxury, affluence. [➡PLEASANT SITUATIONS; 74] *Opposite:* hardship. 3 *v* **relieve**, alleviate, reduce, lessen, improve, make better, take pressure off. [➡CORRECT AND PUT RIGHT; 378] *Opposite:* worsen. 4 *v* **slide**, slip, edge, push gently, draw out, manoeuvre, work. [➡PUSH, PULL, SLIDE; 336] 5 *v* **make easier**, facilitate, help, aid, assist, smooth, improve, relieve. [➡MAKE POSSIBLE; 276] *Opposite:* hinder.

easel *n* **stand**, frame, tripod, support, mount. [➡WRITING AND DRAWING IMPLEMENTS, AND MEDIA; 602]

ease up *v* **relax**, slow down, take five (*informal*), slacken off, calm down, ease off. [➡CHANGE OF MOOD AND COMPOSURE; 581]

easily 1 *adv* **with no trouble**, without difficulty, without problems, effortlessly, simply, straightforwardly. [➡EASE AND SIMPLICITY; 201] 2 *adv* **without doubt**, by far, by a long shot, by a long way, by a long chalk, definitely, certainly, undoubtedly, clearly. [➡CERTAIN; 175]

Eastertide (*literary*) *n* [➡TIMES OF YEAR; 88]

Eastertime *n* [➡TIMES OF YEAR; 88]

easy 1 *adj* **simple**, trouble-free, straightforward, effortless, uncomplicated, undemanding, unproblematic, painless. [➡EASE AND SIMPLICITY; 201] *Opposite:* difficult. 2 *adj* **informal**, relaxed, laid-back (*informal*), calm, cool, tranquil, stress-free, at ease, easygoing. [➡EMOTIONALLY PLEASANT; 188] *Opposite:* tense. 3 *adj* **comfortable**, affluent, luxurious, undemanding, leisurely. [➡PHYSICALLY PLEASANT; 187] *Opposite:* hard.

Compare and Contrast: ***easy, simple, straightforward, uncomplicated***

CORE MEANING: NOT DIFFICULT TO DO OR ACHIEVE

easy not requiring much effort to do, achieve or understand something; ***simple*** not complicated to do, understand, or work out; ***straightforward*** not complicated or difficult to carry out, or hard to understand; ***uncomplicated*** not difficult to work out or master.

easy chair *type of* **seating.** [➡FURNITURE; 858]

easygoing *adj* **relaxed**, laid-back (*informal*), tolerant, even-tempered, calm, blasé, unconcerned, carefree, mellow. [➡FRIENDLINESS AND SOCIABILITY; 495] *Opposite:* anxious.

easy on the ear *adj* [➡SOFT OR PLEASANT SOUNDS; 1264]

easy-peasy (*informal*) *adj* **simple**, easy, straightforward, effortless. [➡EASE AND SIMPLICITY; 201] *Opposite:* difficult.

easy ride *n* [➡EASY WORK; 300]

easy street *n* [➡PLEASANT SITUATIONS; 74]

eat 1 *v* **consume**, have, gobble, scoff (*informal*), wolf, munch, chomp (*informal*), devour, bolt, gorge, swallow. [➡EAT AND NOT EAT; 711] 2 *v* **have a meal**, dine, lunch, breakfast. [➡EAT AND NOT EAT; 711] 3 *v* (*slang*) **bother**, annoy, trouble, worry, plague, vex. [➡UPSET, DISTRESS, AND HUMILIATE; 568]

eat away *v* **erode**, corrode, eat into, wear away, wear down, grind down, rot, whittle away. [➡CHANGE OF INTENSITY: LESS; 396]

eat crow (*US informal*) *v* **apologize**, retract, say sorry, eat your words (*informal*), take it all back. [➡APOLOGIZE AND RETRACT; 684] *Opposite:* stand firm.

eater *n* **guzzler** (*informal*), consumer, feeder, diner, devourer. [➡EATERS, GOURMETS, AND DIETARY CHOICES; 715] *Opposite:* abstainer.

eatery (*informal*) *n* **restaurant**, self-service restaurant, cafeteria, bistro, eating place, café, brasserie, wine bar, diner (*US*). [➡HOTELS, RESTAURANTS, AND CLUBS; 1081]

eat humble pie *v* [➡APOLOGIZE AND RETRACT; 684]

eating place *see* **eatery.**

eat into 1 *v* **use up**, eat up, gobble up, reduce, consume, make inroads into, guzzle (*informal*). [➡USE UP AND WASTE; 475] 2 *v* **corrode**, rust, pockmark, attack, destroy, eat away, wear away. [➡WORSEN SOMETHING; 381]

eats (*slang*) *n* **food**, nosh (*informal*), grub (*informal*), provisions, tucker (*informal*), chuck (*US regional*). [➡FOOD; 1166]

eat up 1 *v* **consume**, guzzle (*informal*), scoff (*informal*), down, gobble. [➡USE UP AND WASTE; 475] 2 *v* **absorb**, obsess, take over, consume, dominate, possess. [➡APPEAL TO AND AROUSE INTEREST; 576] 3 *v* (*informal*) **lap up**, love, applaud, rave about, enthuse about. [➡PRAISE AND ENCOURAGE; 648] *Opposite:* hate.

eat your heart out (*informal*) *v* **brood**, dwell on, grieve, pine. [➡BE CONCERNED AND CARE; 582]

eat your words (*informal*) *v* **apologize**, retract, say sorry, eat humble pie, take it all back, eat crow (*US informal*). [➡APOLOGIZE AND RETRACT; 684] *Opposite:* stand firm.

eau de cologne *n* **perfume**, fragrance, scent, toilet water, eau de toilette. [➡PERSONAL HYGIENE; 492]

eau de toilette *n* [➡PERSONAL HYGIENE; 492]

eaves *n* [➡ROOFS, ROOF PARTS, AND CEILINGS; 1102]

eavesdrop *v* **listen in**, overhear, snoop (*informal*), spy, pry, nose round. [➡LISTEN AND LISTENERS; 709]

eavesdropper *n* **listener**, nosy parker (*informal*), spy, observer. [➡LISTEN AND LISTENERS; 709]

ebb 1 *v* **recede**, go out, flow away, retreat, subside. [➡GO BACKWARDS; 310] *Opposite:* come in. 2 *v* **fade**, diminish, recede, fail, disappear, abate (*formal or literary*), decline. [➡DISAPPEAR; 4] *Opposite:* surge. 3 *n* **receding tide**, ebb tide, outgoing tide. [➡THE SEAS, OCEANS, AND SHORES; 1041] *Opposite:* flow.

ebb and flow 1 *n* **shift**, fluctuation, vacillation, variation, flux, variability. [➡CHANGE; 373] 2 *v* **fluctuate**, vacillate, vary. [➡CHANGE; 373]

ebony *type of* **black**. [➡COLOURS; 1223]

ebullience *n* **joviality**, enthusiasm, liveliness, happiness, cheerfulness, bounciness, jolliness, brightness. [➡ENERGY AND ENTHUSIASM; 497] *Opposite:* lugubriousness.

ebullient *adj* **jovial**, enthusiastic, lively, happy, bouncy, cheerful, bright, jolly. [➡ENERGY AND ENTHUSIASM; 497] *Opposite:* lugubrious.

ebulliently *adv* [➡ENTHUSIASTIC AND INQUISITIVE; 629]

e-business *n* [➡E-COMMERCE; 1128]

eccentric 1 *adj* **odd**, unconventional, unusual, peculiar, strange, weird, bizarre. [➡BIZARRE AND PECULIAR; 258] *Opposite:* conventional. 2 *n* **oddity**, character, original, case (*informal*). [➡ECCENTRICITY AND IRRATIONALITY; 563]

eccentricity 1 *n* **oddness**, unconventionality, peculiarity, strangeness, weirdness, bizarreness. [➡TEMPERAMENT AND BEHAVIOUR; 493] *Opposite:* conventionality. 2 *n* **quirk**, peculiarity, foible, idiosyncrasy, oddity, irregularity. [➡PERSONAL ECCENTRICITIES; 494]

ecclesiastic *n* **clergyman**, clergywoman, priest, cleric, minister. [➡RELIGIOUS PEOPLE; 779]

ecclesiastical *adj* **church**, clerical, religious, priestly (*formal or literary*), apostolic, papal. [➡RELIGIONS AND RELIGIOUS PRACTICES; 778] *Opposite:* secular.

echelon *n* **level**, rank, stratum (*formal*), tier, class. [➡STATUS; 888]

echo 1 *n* **reverberation**, resonance, repeat, boom, ricochet. [➡SOUNDS; 1255] 2 *v* **reverberate**, resonate, resound, boom, rebound, ricochet, come back, bounce back. [➡EMIT CONTINUOUS SOUNDS; 367] 3 *v* **repeat**, reiterate, copy, parrot, confirm, endorse, reaffirm. [➡RECITE, REPEAT, AND NARRATE; 621]

echoing *adj* **resounding**, reverberating, ringing, resonant, resonating. [➡LOUD OR UNPLEASANT SOUNDS; 1265]

éclair *type of* **cake**. [➡CAKES, BISCUITS, AND DESSERTS; 1180]

eclectic *adj* **heterogeneous**, varied, wide-ranging, extensive, diverse, catholic. [➡DIFFERENCE; 150] *Opposite:* narrow.

eclecticism *n* **extensiveness**, range, diversity, scope, variety, heterogeneity. [➡DIFFERENCE; 150]

eclipse 1 *v* **hide**, conceal, obscure, cover, darken. [➡CAUSE TO DISAPPEAR; 6] 2 *v* **outdo**, overshadow, outshine, surpass, overwhelm, overpower. [➡BEAT AND DEFEAT; 80]

ecofriendly *adj* **biodegradable**, green, environmentally friendly, sustainable. [➡ECONOMICAL AND RESOURCEFUL; 208]

E. coli *type of* **microorganism**. [➡MICROORGANISMS, FUNGI, AND ALGAE; 1023]

ecological *adj* **environmental**, natural, biological, organic. [➡BIOLOGICAL SCIENCES; 1037]

ecologist *n* **environmentalist**, biologist, natural scientist, naturalist, conservationist. [➡PHILOSOPHICAL AND POLITICAL THINKERS; 782]

ecology *type of* **bioscience**. [➡BIOLOGICAL SCIENCES; 1037]

e-commerce *n* [➡E-COMMERCE; 1128]

economic 1 *adj* **financial**, monetary, fiscal, pecuniary, commercial. [➡FINANCE AND ECONOMICS; 797] 2 *adj* **profitable**, cost-effective, moneymaking, lucrative, money-spinning (*informal*), efficient. [➡ECONOMICAL AND RESOURCEFUL; 208] *Opposite:* uneconomic.

economical 1 *adj* **frugal**, parsimonious, thrifty, careful, sparing, cautious. [➡FINANCIALLY MEAN AND GRASPING; 520] *Opposite:* wasteful. 2 *adj* **inexpensive**, cheap, cost-effective, reasonable, efficient. [➡ECONOMICAL AND RESOURCEFUL; 208] *Opposite:* expensive.

economize *v* **cut back**, cut down, save, scrimp and save, tighten your belt, be careful, rein in. [➡FORGO AND DENY ONESELF; 450] *Opposite:* spend.

economy 1 *n* **frugality**, thrift, cost-cutting, saving, parsimony, financial prudence. [➡FINANCIALLY MEAN AND GRASPING; 520] *Opposite:* extravagance. 2 *n* **saving**, cutback, reduction, scaling-down. [➡ECONOMICAL AND RESOURCEFUL; 208] 3 *adj* **cheap**, budget, reduced, family, low-cost, bargain. [➡CHEAP AND INEXPENSIVE; 222] *Opposite:* expensive.

ecosystem *n* **bionetwork**, biome, biota, ecology, environment, flora and fauna. [➡NATURE AND THE ENVIRONMENT; 1038]

ecru *type of* **beige**. [➡COLOURS; 1223]

ecstasy 1 *n* **joy**, delight, elation, bliss, rapture, happiness, seventh heaven, thrill, excitement, pleasure. [➡PLEASURE, EXCITEMENT, AND ELATION; 535] *Opposite:* misery. 2 *n* **trance**, high, frenzy, state (*informal*), stupor. [➡PLEASURE, EXCITEMENT, AND ELATION; 535]

ecstatic 1 *adj* **overjoyed**, delighted, thrilled, elated, blissful, rapturous, in raptures, euphoric, in seventh heaven, on cloud nine (*informal*), jubilant, over the moon, joyful, joyous, gleeful, happy. [➡PLEASURE, EXCITEMENT, AND ELATION; 535] *Opposite:* miserable. 2 *adj* **elated**, high, overexcited, frenzied, in a frenzy, excited. [➡PLEASURE, EXCITEMENT, AND ELATION; 535] *Opposite:* calm.

Edam *type of* **hard cheese**. [➡DAIRY PRODUCTS AND CHEESES; 1182]

eddy *n* **whirlpool**, swirl, vortex, whirl, maelstrom, current. [➡RIVERS, LAKES, AND STREAMS; 1042]

edge 1 *n* **border**, rim, boundary, perimeter, periphery, side, limit, verge, edging, frame, circumference, lip, bank. [➡EXTREMITIES OF PHYSICAL OBJECTS; 1249] 2 *n* **brink**, verge, threshold, point. [➡EXTREMITIES OF PHYSICAL OBJECTS; 1249] 3 *n* **sharpness**, bitterness, acidity, harshness, venom. [➡LOUD OR UNPLEASANT SOUNDS; 1265] 4 *n* **advantage**, upper hand, superiority, control, authority, power. [➡SUPERIORITY; 153] 5 *v* **approach**, skirt, sidle, pick your way, creep, tiptoe. [➡MOVE SLOWLY; 315] 6 *v* **border**, frame, trim, fringe, enclose, decorate, flank, encircle, girdle. [➡EXIST IN CLOSE PROXIMITY; 21]

edgeways *adv* **sideways**, side-on, crossways, across, laterally, on its side, obliquely, edgewise (*US*). [➡ORIENTATION AND ALIGNMENT; 1222]

edgily *adv* **tensely**, uneasily, nervously, agitatedly, anxiously, twitchily, jumpily, impatiently, restlessly, irritably. [➡POSITIVE IMPATIENCE, ENTHUSIASM, AND ALERTNESS; 538] *Opposite:* calmly.

edginess *n* [➡INSECURITY AND LOSS OF COMPOSURE; 545]

edging *n* **border**, trim, fringe, hem, frill, decoration, margin, surround, edge. [➡EXTREMITIES OF PHYSICAL OBJECTS; 1249]

edgy *adj* **nervous**, on edge, anxious, jumpy, jittery, oversensitive, tense, stressed, uneasy, like a cat on a hot tin roof, like a cat on hot bricks, touchy, irritable, moody, prickly (*informal*), tetchy (*informal*), agitated, restless. [➡POSITIVE IMPATIENCE, ENTHUSIASM, AND ALERTNESS; 538] *Opposite:* relaxed.

edible *adj* **comestible** (*formal*), eatable, fit for human consumption, palatable, appetizing. [➡FOOD; 1166] *Opposite:* poisonous.

edict *n* **proclamation**, announcement, pronouncement, decree, statute, act, diktat, order, command, ruling, statement, declaration, law. [➡OFFICIAL DOCUMENTS; 587]

edification *n* **improvement**, education, enlightenment, instruction, elevation. [➡TEACHING; 839] *Opposite:* obfuscation.

edifice 1 *n* **building**, construction, pile, structure, mansion. [➡BUILDING AND ARCHITECTURE; 1075] 2 *n* **organization**, network, structure, association, group, society, order. [➡GROUPS IN SOCIETY; 940]

edify *v* **enlighten**, inform, educate, instruct, improve, teach. [➡INSTRUCT AND TEACH; 610] *Opposite:* obfuscate.

edifying *adj* **educational**, informative, illuminating, instructive, scholastic, enlightening. [➡INTERESTING AND MEANINGFUL; 191]

edit 1 *v* **rewrite**, revise, amend, rework, correct, check over, alter, tidy up, rearrange, rehash, improve, change. [➡CORRECT AND PUT RIGHT; 378] 2 *v* **oversee**, run, manage, be in charge of, direct, control. [➡BE IN CHARGE; 271]

edited 1 *adj* **amended**, corrected, revised, rewritten, modified. [➡CHANGE; 373] *Opposite:* unedited. 2 *adj* **abridged**, concise, shorter, summarized, truncated. [➡CHANGE OF SIZE: SMALLER; 394] *Opposite:* complete.

edition *n* **version**, publication, copy, issue, impression, printing, imprint. [➡BOOKS AND BOOKLETS; 591]

editor 1 *n* **publishing supervisor**, publishing manager, editor in chief, managing editor, executive editor. [➡WORKERS IN ENTERTAINMENT AND MEDIA; 873] 2 *n* **subeditor**, copy editor, corrector, checker, cutter, copyreader (*US*), line editor (*US*). [➡WORKERS IN ENTERTAINMENT AND MEDIA; 873]

editorial *n* **leader**, editorial column, viewpoint, perspective, essay, commentary, exposition, article. [➡NEWSPAPERS; 606]

editorialize *v* **expound**, opine (*formal*), pontificate, spout, preach, sermonize. [➡INFORM AND ANNOUNCE; 612]

edit out *v* **delete**, remove, cut, omit, cut back, leave out, miss out, chop. [➡DELETE AND ERASE; 340]

educate *v* **teach**, instruct, edify, tutor, train, coach, inform, school. [➡INSTRUCT AND TEACH; 610]

See Compare and Contrast at **teach**.

educated 1 *adj* **well-informed**, well-read, learned, erudite, knowledgeable, scholarly. [➡LEVEL OF EDUCATION AND SOPHISTICATION; 894] *Opposite:* uneducated. 2 *adj* **cultured**, cultivated, tasteful, sophisticated, refined, accomplished, polished. [➡LEVEL OF EDUCATION AND SOPHISTICATION; 894] *Opposite:* boorish.

educated guess *n* **guess**, estimation, estimate, guesstimate (*informal*), approximation, postulate, opinion. [➡GUESS; 755]

education *n* **teaching**, learning, schooling, tutoring, instruction, edification, training, tutelage. [➡TEACHING; 839]

educational *adj* **instructive**, enlightening, didactic, edifying, informative, scholastic. [➡INTERESTING AND MEANINGFUL; 191]

educationalist *n* [➡EDUCATORS; 840]

educator *n* **coach**, teacher, instructor, lecturer, professor, educationalist, mentor, tutor, guru. [➡EDUCATORS; 840]

eel *type of* **sea fish**. [➡SEA FISH; 1009]

eerie *adj* **unnerving**, spooky (*informal*), creepy (*informal*), uncanny, weird, strange, peculiar, unnatural, supernatural, ghostly, ghostlike, paranormal, spine-chilling, disconcerting, sinister, scary (*informal*). [➡BIZARRE AND PECULIAR; 258] *Opposite:* normal.

eerily *adv* **creepily** (*informal*), spookily (*informal*), disconcertingly, unnervingly, strangely, weirdly, uncannily. [➡BIZARRE AND PECULIAR; 258]

eeriness *n* [➡FRIGHTENING; 232]

efface *v* **wipe out** (*informal*), obliterate, eradicate, destroy, wear away, rub out, rub away, smooth away, erode, delete, cancel out. [➡DELETE AND ERASE; 340]

eff and blind (*slang*) *v* [➡INSULTS, ABUSE, AND SWEARING; 659]

effect 1 *n* **result**, consequence, outcome, upshot, end product, conclusion. [➡RESULTS AND OUTCOMES; 83] 2 *n* **influence**, weight, force, power, validity, clout (*informal*). [➡APPEARANCE AND ATMOSPHERE; 1236] 3 *n* **impression**, meaning, sense, impact, purpose, drift. [➡MEANING; 691] 4 *v* (*formal*) **achieve**, carry out, produce, bring about, realize, perform, accomplish, create, make. [➡CAUSE TO HAPPEN; 31]

effective 1 *adj* **effectual** (*formal*), efficacious (*formal*), successful, efficient, useful, helpful, valuable, fruitful. [➡USEFULNESS; 200] *Opposite:* ineffective. 2 *adj* **real**, actual, in effect, active, operative, current. [➡TRUE AND REAL; 172] *Opposite:* nominal. 3 *adj* **operational**, operative, in force, in operation, in effect, with effect, applicable. [➡HAPPENING AND IN PROGRESS; 32] *Opposite:* inoperative.

Compare and Contrast: ***effective, efficient, effectual, efficacious***

CORE MEANING: PRODUCING A RESULT

effective causing the desired or intended result; ***efficient*** capable of achieving the desired result with the minimum use of resources, time, and effort; ***effectual*** (*formal*) potentially successful in producing a desired or intended result; ***efficacious*** (*formal*) having the power to achieve the desired result, especially an improvement in somebody's physical condition.

effectively 1 *adv* **efficiently**, successfully, well, effectually (*formal*), excellently, meritoriously (*formal*), commendably. [➡USEFULNESS; 200] *Opposite:* ineffectively. 2 *adv* **in effect**, in fact, actually, really, essentially, to all intents and purposes, realistically. [➡TRUE AND REAL; 172] *Opposite:* nominally.

effectiveness *n* **efficiency**, efficacy, success, use, usefulness, helpfulness, value. [➡USEFULNESS; 200] *Opposite:* ineffectiveness.

effects (*formal*) *n* **belongings**, property, personal property, possessions, things, paraphernalia. [➡POSSESSIONS; 462]

effectual (*formal*) *adj* **effective**, efficacious (*formal*), worthwhile, successful, helpful, fruitful, useful. [➡USEFULNESS; 200] *Opposite:* ineffectual.

effervesce *v* **hiss**, fizz, bubble, sparkle, froth, foam. [➡FROTH AND EFFERVESCE; 390]

effervescence 1 *n* **fizz**, bubbles, sparkle, froth, foam, fizziness, frothiness, foaminess, bubbliness. [➡FROTH; 1272] 2 *n* **vivacity**, vibrancy, vitality, animation, sparkle, liveliness, joie de vivre, enthusiasm, bubbliness. [➡ENERGY AND ENTHUSIASM; 497] *Opposite:* languor.

effervescent 1 *adj* **gassy** (*informal*), fizzy, sparkling, bubbly, aerated, bubbling. [➡VISUAL TEXTURE; 1220] *Opposite:* still. 2 *adj* **lively**, vibrant, bubbly, bouncy, sparkling, vivacious, animated. [➡ENERGY AND ENTHUSIASM; 497] *Opposite:* dull.

efficacious (*formal*) *adj* **effective**, efficient, effectual (*formal*), successful, useful, worthwhile, valuable. [➡USEFULNESS; 200] *Opposite:* ineffective.

efficacy *n* **effectiveness**, efficiency, usefulness, worth, value, ability. [➡USEFULNESS; 200] *Opposite:* ineffectiveness.

efficiency *n* **competence**, efficacy, effectiveness, productivity, proficiency, adeptness. [➡HARD-WORKING AND COMMITTED; 501] *Opposite:* inefficiency.

efficiency apartment (*US*) *type of* **apartment**. [➡RESIDENTIAL BUILDINGS; 1077]

efficient 1 *adj* **well-organized**, effectual (*formal*), effective, competent, capable, able, professional, proficient, resourceful. [➡HARD-WORKING AND COMMITTED; 501] *Opposite:* ineffective. 2 *adj* **inexpensive**, timesaving, labour-saving, economical, cost-effective. [➡ECONOMICAL AND RESOURCEFUL; 208] *Opposite:* wasteful.

effigy *n* **image**, statue, figure, figurine, dummy, carving, representation, likeness. [➡REPRESENTATIONS AND GENERAL EXAMPLES; 65]

effluence *n* [➡UNPLEASANT AND DIRTY SUBSTANCES; 1267]

effluent *n* **waste**, sewage, bilge water, seepage, runoff, overflow, emission, discharge. [➡UNPLEASANT AND DIRTY SUBSTANCES; 1267]

effort 1 *n* **exertion**, energy, determination, force, strength, power, sweat, struggle, work, industry (*formal or literary*), labour. [➡HARD WORK OR EFFORT; 299] *Opposite:* ease. 2 *n* **attempt**, try, endeavour, go, stab (*informal*), crack (*informal*), shot. [➡ATTEMPT AN ACTION; 262]

effortless *adj* **easy**, natural, unforced, graceful, unproblematic, uncomplicated, painless. [➡EASE AND SIMPLICITY; 201] *Opposite:* strenuous.

effortlessness *n* **ease**, naturalness, smoothness, simplicity, facility, confidence, grace. [➡EASE AND SIMPLICITY; 201] *Opposite:* difficulty.

effrontery *n* **impudence**, nerve, cheek (*informal*), cheekiness (*informal*), boldness, arrogance, chutzpah (*informal*), brashness, shamelessness. [➡BAD MANNERS AND SOCIAL SKILLS; 522]

effusion *n* **outpouring**, gush, rush, expression, declaration, proclamation, pouring, outflow, discharge. [➡THE SPOKEN WORD; 672]

effusive *adj* **gushing**, demonstrative, fulsome, vociferous, extravagant, unreserved, ebullient, gushy, lavish, unrestrained, profuse, expansive. [➡ELOQUENT, TALKATIVE AND LONG-WINDED; 633] *Opposite:* reserved.

effusively *adv* **fulsomely**, vociferously, unrestrainedly, demonstratively, profusely, lavishly, gushingly, extravagantly, ebulliently, gushily, expansively. [➡ENTHUSIASTIC AND INQUISITIVE; 629] *Opposite:* reservedly.

e.g. *adv* **for example**, for instance, say, let's say, perhaps, maybe. [➡WRITTEN CONVENTIONS; 600]

egalitarian *adj* **equal**, classless, free, democratic, equal opportunities. [➡EQUALITY; 155]

egg 1 *n* **reproductive cell**, ovum, egg cell, ovule. [➡EGGS AND SPAWN; 728] 2 *v* **urge**, incite, spur, encourage, push, egg on, pressure, drive. [➡CAUSE OR COMPEL TO ACT; 272] *Opposite:* dissuade.

egghead (*informal*) *n* **brainbox**, boffin (*informal*), intellectual, brain (*informal*), bookworm (*informal*). [➡LEVEL OF EDUCATION AND SOPHISTICATION; 894]

egg on *v* **encourage**, urge, push, incite, spur, egg, pressure, drive. [➡CAUSE OR COMPEL TO ACT; 272] *Opposite:* dissuade.

eggplant (*US*) *type of* **vegetable.** [➡FRUIT AND VEGETABLES; 1175]

eggshell 1 *n* **protective covering**, shell, case, casing, covering. [➡COVERS AND COATINGS; 1245] 2 *type of* **white.** [➡COLOURS; 1223]

egg timer *type of* **clock.** [➡CLOCKS AND TIMERS; 1125]

ego *n* **personality**, character, self, self-image, self-worth, self-esteem, individuality. [➡PSYCHOLOGY AND THE MIND; 770]

egocentric *adj* **selfish**, egoistical, conceited, vain, self-centred, egotistic, egoistic, insensitive, inconsiderate, self-absorbed, self-obsessed, narcissistic. [➡SELFISH AND UNKIND; 506]

egocentricity *n* [➡SELFISH AND UNKIND; 506]

egocentrism *n* [➡SELFISH AND UNKIND; 506]

egoism *n* **conceit**, vanity, self-importance, selfishness, self-centredness, egotism, arrogance, self-absorption, narcissism. [➡SELFISH AND UNKIND; 506]

egoist *n* **egotist**, egomaniac, narcissist, individualist, self-seeker, self-publicist, self-aggrandizer, boaster, show-off (*informal*). [➡SELF-IMPORTANT AND SELF-SEEKING PEOPLE; 949]

egoistic *adj* **selfish**, egotistic, conceited, vain, self-centred, egocentric, self-seeking, insensitive, inconsiderate, self-absorbed, self-obsessed. [➡SELFISH AND UNKIND; 506] *Opposite:* altruistic.

egoistical *adj* [➡SELFISH AND UNKIND; 506]

egomaniac *n* **egotist**, egoist, narcissist, self-publicist, self-aggrandizer, individualist, boaster, show-off (*informal*). [➡SELF-IMPORTANT AND SELF-SEEKING PEOPLE; 949]

egotism *n* **egoism**, self-centredness, selfishness, conceit, vanity, arrogance, self-importance, self-absorption, narcissism. [➡SELFISH AND UNKIND; 506] *Opposite:* altruism.

egotist *n* **egoist**, egomaniac, narcissist, self-seeker, individualist, self-publicist, self-aggrandizer, boaster, show-off (*informal*). [➡SELF-IMPORTANT AND SELF-SEEKING PEOPLE; 949]

egotistic *adj* [➡SELFISH AND UNKIND; 506]

egotistical *adj* [➡SELFISH AND UNKIND; 506]

egret *type of* **freshwater bird.** [➡FRESHWATER BIRD; 1000]

eiderdown *n* **quilt**, continental quilt, duvet, bedcover, bedspread, comforter (*US*). [➡SOFT FURNISHINGS, LINEN, AND DRAPERY; 860]

either 1 *adj* **whichever**, any, both, each. [➡ALSO; 136] 2 *adj* **each**, both, one or the other, either one. [➡ALSO; 136]

ejaculate (*literary*) *v* **exclaim**, cry, cry out, shout, utter, voice. [➡BETRAY CONFIDENCES AND GOSSIP; 619]

eject 1 *v* **discharge** (*formal*), expel, cast out (*formal*), emit, get rid of, spew, spout, disgorge. [➡EJECT AND EXCLUDE; 341] 2 *v* **expel**, banish, drive out, throw out, remove, oust, evict, force out. [➡GET RID OF SOMETHING; 452]

ejection seat (*US*) *part of* **aircraft.** [➡AIRCRAFT; 1147]

ejector seat *part of* **aircraft.** [➡AIRCRAFT; 1147]

eke out 1 *v* **make something last**, spin out, make a little go a long way, draw out, use sparingly, drag out, make something go further, stretch. [➡CAUSE TO CONTINUE; 268] *Opposite:* squander. 2 *v* **supplement**, complement, add to, pad out, make up, increase, extend, stretch out. [➡CHANGE OF INTENSITY: MORE; 395] *Opposite:* diminish. 3 *v* **scrape**, scratch, scrape together, scratch out, make, earn, scrimp, manage, get by. [➡CAUSE TO CONTINUE; 268]

elaborate 1 *adj* **complex**, complicated, intricate, detailed, involved, convoluted, sophisticated. [➡DIFFICULTY AND COMPLEXITY; 243] *Opposite:* straightforward. 2 *adj* **intricate**, sumptuous, extravagant, ornate, decorative, rich, elegant, ostentatious, baroque. [➡POSITIVELY COMPLEX OR COMPLICATED; 218] *Opposite:* simple. 3 *v* **expound**, expand, enlarge, go into detail, explain, go on, particularize. [➡EXPLAIN AND CLARIFY; 611] *Opposite:* condense. 4 *v* **complicate**, work up, build on, develop, detail. [➡CHANGE; 373] *Opposite:* simplify.

elaborately *adv* **decoratively**, sumptuously, intricately, ornately, richly, extravagantly, fussily, ostentatiously (*disapproving*). [➡POSITIVELY COMPLEX OR COMPLICATED; 218] *Opposite:* simply.

elaborateness *n* [➡DIFFICULTY AND COMPLEXITY; 243]

elaboration *n* **amplification**, embellishment, explanation, expansion. [➡EXPLAIN AND CLARIFY; 611]

élan (*literary*) *n* **panache**, verve, vivacity, flair, brio (*literary*), dash, style. [➡ENERGY AND ENTHUSIASM; 497] *Opposite:* mediocrity.

elapse *v* **pass**, pass by, intervene, slip away, go by, lapse. [➡HAPPEN; 27]

elastic 1 *adj* **stretchy**, expandable, flexible, supple, resilient, springy. [➡MALLEABLE AND ELASTIC; 1211] *Opposite:* rigid. 2 *adj* **flexible**, adaptable, changeable, variable, mutable, supple, pliant, pliable. [➡USEFULNESS; 200] *Opposite:* inflexible.

See Compare and Contrast at **pliable.**

elasticated *adj* **stretchy**, elastic, expanding, expandable, stretchable, elasticized (*US*). [➡MALLEABLE AND ELASTIC; 1211] *Opposite:* rigid.

elate *v* **exhilarate**, thrill, excite, exalt (*formal*), lift, uplift. [➡PLEASE AND AMUSE; 573] *Opposite:* dishearten.

elated *adj* **ecstatic**, overjoyed, thrilled, delighted, euphoric, jubilant, excited, in seventh heaven, on cloud nine (*informal*), over the moon (*informal*), high. [➡PLEASURE, EXCITEMENT, AND ELATION; 535] *Opposite:* disheartened.

elation *n* **ecstasy**, delight, euphoria, jubilation, excitement, exultation, joy, rapture, glee. [➡PLEASURE, EXCITEMENT, AND ELATION; 535] *Opposite:* despair.

elbow 1 *v* **prod**, jostle, nudge, shove, dig, poke, bump, push. [➡CONTACT: IMPACT; 414] 2 *part of* **arm or hand.** [➡ARM AND HAND; 696]

elbowroom 1 *n* **space**, room, room to spare, room to manoeuvre. [➡AREA AND RANGE; 111] 2 *n* **scope**, freedom, leeway, room to manoeuvre, choice, free rein. [➡FREEDOM AND LIBERTY; 209]

elder 1 *n* **leader**, head, chief. [➡BOSSES AND MANAGEMENT; 965] 2 *type of* **shrub or bush**. [➡BUSHES AND SHRUBS; 1027] 3 *see* **elderberry**.

elderberry *type of* **berry**. [➡FRUIT AND VEGETABLES; 1175]

elderly *adj* **aging**, old, aged, mature, of advanced years, senior. [➡OLD AGE; 919] *Opposite:* young.

eldest *adj* **oldest**, first-born, first, primogenital. [➡BEFORE, FIRST, AND PRECEDING; 164]

El Dorado *n* [➡NON-EXISTENT PLACE; 1065]

elect 1 *v* **vote for**, return, vote into office, pick, select, choose. [➡CONFER STATUS; 459] 2 *v* **choose**, opt for, decide on, select, nominate, pick out. [➡MAKE DECISIONS AND CHOICES; 753] 3 *adj* **designate**, future, chosen, selected. [➡FUTURE; 86]

elected *adj* **chosen**, designated, selected, voted, nominated, adopted, picked out. [➡ELECTIONS AND SUFFRAGE; 807]

election 1 *n* **vote**, voting, poll, balloting. [➡ELECTIONS AND SUFFRAGE; 807] 2 *n* **selection**, choice, appointment, designation. [➡ELECTIONS AND SUFFRAGE; 807]

electioneer *v* **campaign**, canvass, run, stump (*US informal*). [➡ELECTIONS AND SUFFRAGE; 807]

elective 1 *adj* **voting**, chosen by election, filled by election, passed by vote. [➡ELECTIONS AND SUFFRAGE; 807] *Opposite:* appointed. 2 *adj* **optional**, voluntary, noncompulsory, free, selective, discretionary. [➡FREEDOM AND LIBERTY; 209] *Opposite:* compulsory.

elector *n* **voter**, member of the electorate, voting member, constituent. [➡ELECTIONS AND SUFFRAGE; 807]

electoral *adj* **democratic**, voting, election, polling, balloting. [➡ELECTIONS AND SUFFRAGE; 807]

electorate *n* **people**, voters, voting public, constituency. [➡ELECTIONS AND SUFFRAGE; 807]

electric 1 *adj* **electrical**, electronic, electrically powered, mains powered, battery operated, plug-in, rechargeable, power-driven. [➡ENERGY SOURCES; 1161] 2 *adj* **absorbing**, charged, exciting, thrilling, emotional, stimulating, electrifying, captivating, stirring. [➡INTERESTING AND MEANINGFUL; 191] *Opposite:* dull.

electrical *see* **electric**.

electric blanket *n* [➡SOFT FURNISHINGS, LINEN, AND DRAPERY; 860]

electric blue *type of* **blue**. [➡COLOURS; 1223]

electric fire *type of* **heating appliance**. [➡HEATING, REFRIGERATION, AND VENTILATION; 1141]

electric guitar *type of* **stringed instrument**. [➡MUSICAL INSTRUMENTS; 910]

electricity *n* **current**, voltage, power, energy, electrical energy. [➡ENERGY SOURCES; 1161]

electrified 1 *adj* **electric**, electrically powered, wired-up, connected. [➡ELECTRONICS AND ELECTRICS; 1136] 2 *adj* **excited**, captivated, thrilled, transfixed, awestruck, amazed, astounded, charged, stimulated. [➡SURPRISE, SHOCK, AND AMAZEMENT; 546] *Opposite:* indifferent.

electrify *v* **captivate**, transfix, thrill, excite, exhilarate, astonish, amaze, surprise, shock, stun, stimulate, charge. [➡APPEAL TO AND AROUSE INTEREST; 576]

electrifying *adj* **exciting**, stirring, thrilling, captivating, stimulating, emotional, moving. [➡EMOTIONALLY PLEASANT; 188] *Opposite:* dull.

electrifyingly *adv* **captivatingly**, excitingly, stirringly, thrillingly, emotionally, movingly. [➡INTERESTING AND MEANINGFUL; 191] *Opposite:* dully.

electrode *n* **conductor**, rod, anode, cathode, probe. [➡ELECTRONICS AND ELECTRICS; 1136]

electron *type of* **elementary particle**. [➡ELEMENTARY PARTICLES; 1278]

electronic 1 *adj* **electric**, microelectronic, electrical, automated, automatic, synthesized. [➡ELECTRONICS AND ELECTRICS; 1136] 2 *adj* **computerized**, high-tech, on-screen, online, computer, automatic. [➡COMPUTERS AND COMPUTING; 1126]

electronic cash *n* [➡E-COMMERCE; 1128]

electronics *n* **microchip technology**, microelectronics, computer electronics, integrated circuit technology, semiconductor technology, electronic engineering. [➡ELECTRONICS AND ELECTRICS; 1136]

electronic signature *n* [➡E-COMMERCE; 1128]

electron microscope *type of* **optical instrument**. [➡OPTICAL INSTRUMENTS; 1123]

elegance *n* **grace**, style, sophistication, chic, class, taste, refinement, stylishness, modishness, smartness, classiness (*informal*). [➡WELL GROOMED; 483] *Opposite:* inelegance.

elegant *adj* **sophisticated**, stylish, graceful, chic, well-designed, well-dressed, smart, neat, classy (*informal*), tasteful, refined. [➡WELL GROOMED; 483] *Opposite:* inelegant.

elegiac (*formal*) *adj* **mournful**, sad, melancholic, plaintive, nostalgic. [➡EMOTIONALLY PLEASANT; 188] *Opposite:* cheerful.

elegy *n* **funeral song**, dirge, requiem, poem, speech, composition. [➡MUSIC, SONGS, AND SINGING; 907]

element 1 *n* **component**, part, section, division, portion, group, constituent. [➡AMOUNT AND QUANTITY; 112] 2 *n* **hint**, amount, quantity, touch, bit, degree. [➡FEW, LITTLE, SMALL AMOUNT; 119] 3 *n* **factor**, cause, feature, component, ingredient, aspect. [➡QUALITIES AND CHARACTERISTICS; 1190] 4 *n* **habitat**, environment, milieu (*formal*), medium, domain, sphere. [➡PLACE; 1064]

elemental *adj* **rudimentary**, basic, fundamental, essential, primary. [➡FUNDAMENTAL; 196]

elementary *adj* **basic**, simple, straightforward, uncomplicated, plain, fundamental, rudimentary, easy. [➡EASE AND SIMPLICITY; 201]

elementary particle

◆ *types of elementary particle*
antineutron, antiproton, antiquark, baryon, boson, electron, fermion, hadron, kaon, lepton, meson, muon, neutrino, neutron, photon, pion, positron, proton, quark, tauon

elementary school (*US*) *type of* **school.** [➡EDUCATIONAL INSTITUTIONS; 813]

elements *n* **rudiments**, basics, fundamentals, essentials, foundations, origins, features. [➡BASIC DETAILS; 689]

elephant *type of* **large mammal.** [➡LARGE MAMMAL; 986]

elephantine 1 *adj* **ponderous**, lumbering, clumsy, slow, heavy, ungainly, awkward. [➡AGILITY OF THE BODY; 477] *Opposite:* dainty. 2 *adj* **huge**, enormous, colossal, gigantic, massive, great. [➡LARGE; 1192] *Opposite:* minute.

elevate 1 *v* **lift**, lift up, raise, uplift, hoist, upraise. [➡MOVE SOMETHING: UPWARDS; 329] *Opposite:* lower. 2 *v* **promote**, raise, advance, move up, further, exalt, improve. [➡CONFER STATUS; 459] *Opposite:* demote.

See Compare and Contrast at **raise.**

elevated 1 *adj* **pre-eminent**, eminent, important, prominent, high, grand, superior, lofty. [➡IMPORTANT; 195] *Opposite:* lowly. 2 *adj* **raised**, raised up, high, higher. [➡HEIGHT: HIGH; 1202]

elevation 1 *n* **height**, altitude, rise. [➡HEIGHT: HIGH; 1202] *Opposite:* depth. 2 *n* **promotion**, rise, advancement, boost. [➡CONFER STATUS; 459] *Opposite:* demotion.

elevator (*US*) 1 *n* [➡STAIRS AND STOREYS; 1101] 2 *n* **storage plant**, silo, grain elevator (*US*). [➡STORES AND STORAGE BUILDINGS; 1087]

elevenses *n* **snack**, morning snack, mid-morning snack, nibble, bite. [➡MEALS AND PARTS OF MEALS; 1168]

eleventh hour *n* [➡PROMPTNESS: LATE; 100]

eleventh-hour *adj* **ultimate**, last-minute, last-ditch, final. [➡PROMPTNESS: LATE; 100]

elf *n* **pixie**, imp, sprite, fairy, gnome, goblin, brownie, Puck. [➡MYTHICAL BEINGS; 790]

elfin *adj* **sylphlike**, petite, dainty, tiny, waiflike, fragile. [➡BUILD; 478]

elicit 1 *v* **provoke**, cause, produce, bring about, occasion, prompt, stimulate. [➡CAUSE TO HAPPEN; 31] 2 *v* **draw out**, draw, bring out, extract, obtain, bring forth, educe (*formal*). [➡OBTAIN POSSESSION BY PERSUASION; 458] *Opposite:* repress.

eligibility *n* **suitability**, aptness, entitlement, appropriateness, fitness, worthiness, admissibility. [➡APPROPRIATE, SUITABLE, ADVISABLE; 185] *Opposite:* unsuitability.

eligible 1 *adj* **qualified**, entitled, suitable, fit, appropriate, adequate, worthy, authorized. [➡APPROPRIATE, SUITABLE, ADVISABLE; 185] *Opposite:* ineligible. 2 *adj* **single**, unmarried, unattached, available. [➡MARITAL STATUS; 890]

eliminate 1 *v* **remove**, eradicate, abolish, get rid of, do away with, reject, disregard, throw out, exclude, jettison. [➡GET RID OF SOMETHING; 452] *Opposite:* retain. 2 *v* **destroy**, kill, exterminate, liquidate, wipe out (*informal*), waste (*slang*). [➡KILL; 923] *Opposite:* preserve. 3 *v* (*technical*) **defecate**, urinate, excrete, expel, pass, purge. [➡EXCRETION AND EXCRETA; 723]

elimination *n* **removal**, abolition, exclusion, rejection, eradication, dismissal. [➡REMOVE SOMETHING; 339] *Opposite:* preservation.

elision *n* [➡ASPECTS OF LANGUAGE; 683]

elite 1 *n* **best**, cream, cream of the crop, elect, crème de la crème, chosen, select few. [➡LEVEL OF EDUCATION AND SOPHISTICATION; 894] 2 *adj* **choice**, best, select, leading, top, exclusive. [➡EXTRAORDINARY: AMAZING; 205] *Opposite:* run-of-the-mill.

elitism *n* **exclusiveness**, exclusivity, superiority, selectivity, selectiveness, snobbery. [➡PREJUDICE; 551]

elitist *adj* **exclusive**, discriminatory, selective, superior, snooty (*informal*), snobbish, highbrow. [➡UNFRIENDLINESS AND UNSOCIABILITY; 505] *Opposite:* egalitarian.

elixir 1 *n* **medicine**, tincture, solution, tonic, preparation, mixture. [➡REMEDIES, TREATMENTS AND OPERATIONS; 732] 2 *n* **potion**, draught (*dated*), restorative, tonic, pick-me-up (*informal*). [➡DRINKS; 1186]

Elizabethan *type of* **pre-20th-century architecture.** [➡BUILDING AND ARCHITECTURE; 1075]

elk *type of* **deer or antelope.** [➡DEER AND ANTELOPE; 981]

ellipsis *n* **abbreviation**, contraction, elision, truncation, abridgment, compression. [➡ASPECTS OF LANGUAGE; 683]

elliptical 1 *adj* **oval**, ovoid, ovate, elongated. [➡ROUNDED SHAPE; 1217] 2 *adj* **concise**, succinct, cryptic, indirect, oblique, ambiguous, obscure. [➡INARTICULATE, RAMBLING, AND AWKWARD; 634] *Opposite:* verbose.

elm *type of* **deciduous tree.** [➡DECIDUOUS TREES; 1028]

elocution *n* **diction**, articulation, pronunciation, enunciation, delivery, vocalization. [➡ASPECTS OF LANGUAGE; 683]

elongate *v* **lengthen**, draw out, extend, stretch. [➡CHANGE OF SIZE: BIGGER; 393] *Opposite:* shorten.

elongated *adj* **lengthened**, stretched out, extended, drawn-out. [➡LENGTH: LONG; 1196] *Opposite:* shortened.

elope *v* **run away**, run off, escape, decamp, abscond, flee, desert, bolt. [➡RUN AWAY AND AVOID; 10] *Opposite:* return.

elopement *n* **flight**, escape, desertion, decampment, truancy, departure. [➡END; 54]

eloquence *n* **expressiveness**, articulateness, articulacy, persuasiveness, expression, fluency. [➡ELOQUENT, TALKATIVE AND LONG-WINDED; 633] *Opposite:* inarticulacy.

eloquent *adj* **expressive**, fluent, articulate, persuasive, stirring, powerful, moving. [➡ELOQUENT, TALKATIVE AND LONG-WINDED; 633] *Opposite:* inarticulate.

else 1 *adj* **different**, new, other, experimental. [➡DIFFERENCE; 150] 2 *adv* **as well**, besides, in addition, other, more, further. [➡MORE AND EXCESS; 122] 3 *adv* **other**, otherwise, differently, different, new. [➡DIFFERENCE; 150]

elucidate (*formal*) *v* **explain**, clarify, explicate, expound, illuminate, interpret, spell out. [➡EXPLAIN AND CLARIFY; 611] *Opposite:* confuse.

elucidation *n* **clarification**, illumination, exposition, explanation, explication, interpretation. [➡EXPLAIN AND CLARIFY; 611] *Opposite:* obfuscation.

elude 1 *v* **escape**, flee, evade, get away, dodge, avoid, give somebody the slip. [➡AVOID OR ESCAPE CONTACT; 419] 2 *v* **baffle**, confound, foil, puzzle, stump, thwart. [➡CONFUSE AND BEWILDER; 572]

elusive *adj* **indefinable**, subtle, intangible, vague, indescribable, abstract, mysterious, obscure, tenuous. [➡SECRET AND UNKNOWN; 180] *Opposite:* obvious.

elusiveness *n* **indefinability**, subtlety, intangibility, vagueness, tenuousness, obscurity. [➡RETICENT AND UNFORTHCOMING; 632] *Opposite:* accessibility.

emaciated *adj* **thin**, wasted, withered, shrunken, gaunt, pinched, skinny, scrawny, lean, scraggy. [➡BUILD; 478] *Opposite:* plump.

See Compare and Contrast at **thin**.

emaciation *n* **thinness**, skinniness, gauntness, scrawniness, scragginess, leanness. [➡BUILD; 478] *Opposite:* plumpness.

e-mail 1 *n* **electronic post**, communication, correspondence, electronic message. [➡LETTERS AND WRITTEN MESSAGES; 585] 2 *v* **send**, send by e-mail, dispatch, forward, transmit, mail. [➡DESPATCH AND SEND; 334] 3 *type of* **telecommunications equipment**. [➡TELECOMMUNICATIONS; 1129]

e-mail *n* [➡LETTERS AND WRITTEN MESSAGES; 585]

e-mall *n* [➡E-COMMERCE; 1128]

emanate 1 *v* **originate**, come, stem, spring, derive, start, arise, proceed. [➡GRADUALLY COME INTO EXISTENCE; 1] 2 *v* (*formal*) **radiate**, emit, give off, give out, send out, ooze. [➡EMIT AND EMANATE; 362] *Opposite:* absorb.

emancipate *v* **liberate**, set free, free, release, unshackle, unfetter, let go, untie. [➡FREEDOM AND LIBERTY; 209] *Opposite:* enslave.

emancipated *adj* [➡FREEDOM AND LIBERTY; 209]

emancipation *n* **liberation**, freedom, deliverance (*formal*), manumission (*formal*), release. [➡FREEDOM AND LIBERTY; 209]

emasculate (*formal*) *v* **weaken**, enfeeble, undermine, enervate, unnerve. [➡UPSET, DISTRESS, AND HUMILIATE; 568] *Opposite:* empower.

emasculated *adj* **ineffectual**, powerless, helpless, impotent, weak. [➡COWARDICE AND WEAKNESS OF WILL; 509] *Opposite:* strong.

embalm *v* **mummify**, conserve, preserve, fix, keep, protect. [➡BURIAL AND PREPARATION FOR BURIAL; 929]

embankment *n* **ridge**, bank, mound, defences, dam, levee. [➡BARRIERS; 1112]

embargo 1 *n* **ban**, restriction, prohibition, restraint, block, stoppage, impediment, bar. [➡LEGISLATIVE BODIES AND LEGISLATION; 809] *Opposite:* permission. 2 *v* **forbid**, prohibit, ban, stop, restrict, block, impede, bar. [➡MAKE IMPOSSIBLE; 277] *Opposite:* permit. 3 *v* **confiscate**, sequestrate, seize, take away, expropriate, snatch. [➡TAKE SOMETHING AWAY; 426]

embark *v* **board**, get on, go aboard. [➡TRAVEL: WAYS OF TRAVELLING; 321] *Opposite:* disembark.

embark on *v* **begin**, start, engage in, attempt, tackle, initiate, enter into, undertake, set about. [➡START AN ACTION; 261] *Opposite:* complete.

embarrass *v* **humiliate**, mortify, shame, disconcert, discomfit (*formal*), show up. [➡UPSET, DISTRESS, AND HUMILIATE; 568] *Opposite:* honour.

embarrassed *adj* **uncomfortable**, self-conscious, ill at ease, nervous, ashamed, mortified, humiliated. [➡EMBARRASSMENT AND HUMILIATION; 543] *Opposite:* proud.

embarrassing *adj* **awkward**, uncomfortable, uneasy, disconcerting, trying, excruciating, humiliating, distressing. [➡EMOTIONALLY UNPLEASANT AND UPSETTING; 228] *Opposite:* enjoyable.

embarrassment *n* **discomfiture** (*formal*), awkwardness, blushing, humiliation, mortification, shame. [➡EMBARRASSMENT AND HUMILIATION; 543] *Opposite:* pride.

embassy *n* **consulate**, legation, mission, delegation, deputation. [➡ADMINISTRATIVE OFFICERS; 811]

embed *v* **implant**, set in, insert, drive in, push in, surround, entrench. [➡POSITION SOMETHING: BETWEEN, BESIDE, OR INSIDE SOMETHING; 327]

embellish 1 *v* **decorate**, adorn, embroider, beautify, ornament. [➡IMPROVE APPEARANCE; 380] *Opposite:* denude. 2 *v* **exaggerate**, elaborate, overdo, aggrandize, enhance, enlarge, embroider. [➡BOAST; 617] *Opposite:* simplify.

embellishment 1 *n* **decoration**, adornment, ornamentation, embroidery, beautification, trimming. [➡ORNAMENTS AND DECORATIONS; 1247] 2 *n* **exaggeration**, elaboration, aggrandizement, enhancement, enlargement, embroidery. [➡BOAST; 617] *Opposite:* understatement.

ember *n* **cinder**, ash, coal. [➡PRODUCTS OF FIRE; 1165]

embezzle *v* **misappropriate**, misuse, appropriate, steal, cheat, pilfer, skim (*informal*). [➡STEAL AND ROB; 427]

See Compare and Contrast at **steal**.

embezzlement *n* **misappropriation**, misuse, appropriation, theft, larceny (*dated*), pilfering, fraud. [➡CRIMES; 817]

embezzler *n* **swindler**, con man (*informal*), fraud, thief, larcenist, fraudster, pilferer. [➡CRIMINALS; 821]

embitter *v* **disillusion**, poison, sour, estrange, alienate. [➡UPSET, DISTRESS, AND HUMILIATE; 568]

embittered *adj* **disillusioned**, bitter, resentful, sour, disaffected, cynical, estranged. [➡IRRITATION AND ANGER; 542] *Opposite:* mellow.

emblazon 1 *v* **decorate**, adorn, embellish, ornament, illustrate, inscribe, embroider. [➡DECORATE, ADORN, AND APPLY COATINGS; 406] 2 *v* (*literary*) **extol**, celebrate, glorify, praise, honour, publicize. [➡PRAISE AND ENCOURAGE; 648]

emblem *n* **symbol**, crest, logo, sign, badge, motif, device, insignia. [➡SYMBOLS, SIGNS, AND NUMBERS; 597]

emblematic *adj* **symbolic**, representative, characteristic, illustrative, exemplary, emblematical. [➡REPRESENTATIVE; 66]

emblematical *adj* **symbolic**, representative, characteristic, illustrative, exemplary, emblematic. [➡REPRESENTATIVE; 66]

embodiment *n* **personification**, example, quintessence, incarnation, epitome, expression. [➡PERFECT EXAMPLES AND EMBODIMENTS; 67]

embody *v* **exemplify**, symbolize, represent, personify, express, stand for. [➡REPRESENT SOMETHING OR SOMEBODY; 59]

embolden *v* **encourage**, hearten, buoy up, bolster, reassure, inspire, support. [➡ENCOURAGE; 577] *Opposite:* discourage.

emboss *v* **stamp**, chase, tool, engrave, mark, decorate. [➡CREATE IMAGES; 357]

embrace 1 *v* **hug**, hold, enfold, cuddle, clasp, squeeze. [➡PHYSICAL CONTACT AS COMMUNICATION; 656] 2 *v* **accept**, welcome, adopt, take up, support, take on. [➡ACCEPT POSSESSION; 451] *Opposite:* reject. 3 *v* **comprise**, contain, include, incorporate, involve, encompass. [➡HOLD AND CONTAIN; 456] *Opposite:* exclude. 4 *n* **hold**, hug, cuddle, clinch, clasp, squeeze, encirclement. [➡PHYSICAL CONTACT AS COMMUNICATION; 656]

embroider 1 *v* **sew**, stitch, cross-stitch, trim, decorate, adorn. [➡CRAFTS AND CARVING; 356] 2 *v* **elaborate**, embellish, exaggerate, overstate, inflate, blow up. [➡CLAIM, INSIST, AND EMPHASIZE; 615]

embroidery *type of* **handicraft**. [➡CRAFTS AND CARVING; 356]

embroil *v* **involve**, entangle, enmesh, ensnare, entrap, catch. [➡COMBINE AND MIX; 401]

embryo *n* **beginning**, rudiment, germ, kernel, seed, nucleus, basis. [➡BEGINNING; 53]

embryonic *adj* **developing**, emergent, nascent, primary, early, budding. [➡FUTURE; 86] *Opposite:* advanced.

emcee (*informal*) 1 *n* **MC**, master of ceremonies, compere, host, presenter. [➡WORKERS IN ENTERTAINMENT AND MEDIA; 873] 2 *v* **compere**, host, present, introduce. [➡MAKE POSSIBLE; 276]

emend *v* **alter**, correct, amend, revise, rewrite, edit. [➡CORRECT AND PUT RIGHT; 378]

emerald *type of* **gemstone**. [➡PRECIOUS STONES; 1277]

emerald green *type of* **green**. [➡COLOURS; 1223]

emerge 1 *v* **come out**, appear, materialize, come into view, come into sight, surface, crop up (*informal*). [➡APPEAR AND EMERGE; 3] *Opposite:* disappear. 2 *v* **come to light**, transpire, leak out. [➡APPEAR AND EMERGE; 3] 3 *v* **arise**, appear, occur, develop, begin. [➡GRADUALLY COME INTO EXISTENCE; 1]

emergence *n* **appearance**, rise, advent, arrival, development, occurrence, beginning. [➡BEGINNING; 53] *Opposite:* decline.

emergency 1 *n* **crisis**, disaster, tragedy, danger, trauma, predicament, difficulty. [➡DIFFICULT SITUATIONS; 72] 2 *adj* **spare**, extra, backup, alternative, reserve, substitute. [➡MORE AND EXCESS; 122]

emergent *adj* **developing**, up-and-coming, embryonic, growing, nascent, budding, promising. [➡FUTURE; 86] *Opposite:* obsolescent.

emery board *type of* **cosmetic tool**. [➡HAND TOOLS; 1118]

emigrant *n* **expatriate**, migrant, immigrant, settler, exile. [➡PEOPLE LIVING AWAY FROM HOME; 887] *Opposite:* native.

emigrate *v* **trek**, migrate, travel, move away, leave, relocate, evacuate. [➡TRAVEL: WAYS OF TRAVELLING; 321] *Opposite:* return.

emigration *n* **migration**, expatriation, exile, relocation, exodus, flight, evacuation. [➡TRAVEL: JOURNEYS AND TRIPS; 319] *Opposite:* return.

émigré *n* [➡PEOPLE LIVING AWAY FROM HOME; 887]

eminence *n* **distinction**, renown, reputation, fame, importance, prominence. [➡CLASS STATUS; 889] *Opposite:* anonymity.

eminent *adj* **well-known**, renowned, important, distinguished, famous, celebrated, prominent, outstanding. [➡KNOWN AND FAMOUS; 182] *Opposite:* unknown.

eminently *adv* **very**, highly, extremely, exceedingly, exceptionally, signally. [➡TO A GREAT EXTENT; 130]

emir *n* **ruler**, commander, prince, leader, governor. [➡RULERS AND ARISTOCRACY; 823]

emirate *n* **country**, state, nation, land, territory, region. [➡COUNTRIES AND REGIONS; 1066]

emissary *n* **representative**, envoy, ambassador, messenger, agent, delegate. [➡REPRESENTATIVES AND PATRONS; 968]

emission *n* **release**, production, discharge, emanation, secretion, radiation. [➡EMIT AND EMANATE; 362] *Opposite:* absorption.

emit *v* **produce**, release, give off, give out, send out, discharge, emanate (*formal*), secrete, radiate. [➡EMIT AND EMANATE; 362] *Opposite:* absorb.

Emmental *type of* **hard cheese**. [➡DAIRY PRODUCTS AND CHEESES; 1182]

Emmenthaler (*US*) *type of* **hard cheese**. [➡DAIRY PRODUCTS AND CHEESES; 1182]

emollient 1 *adj* **soothing**, palliative, placatory, calmative, calming. [➡CALMING; 189] *Opposite:* disruptive. 2 *n* **balm**, lotion, moisturizer, ointment, salve, cream. [➡REMEDIES, TREATMENTS AND OPERATIONS; 732] *Opposite:* irritant.

emolument (*formal or humorous*) *n* **payment**, remuneration, reward, fee, compensation, benefit. [➡INCOME; 461]

See Compare and Contrast at **wage**.

emoticon 1 *n* [➡SYMBOLS, SIGNS, AND NUMBERS; 597] 2 *type of* **software.** [➡COMPUTERS AND COMPUTING; 1126]

emotion *n* **feeling**, sentiment, reaction, passion, excitement, sensation. [➡FEELINGS; 532]

emotional 1 *adj* **moving**, touching, poignant, affecting, exciting, weepy (*informal*). [➡EMOTIONALLY PLEASANT; 188] 2 *adj* **expressive**, open, demonstrative, emotive, sensitive, responsive, passionate. [➡ELOQUENT, TALKATIVE AND LONG-WINDED; 633] *Opposite:* impassive.

emotionally *adv* **expressively**, passionately, fervently, ardently, warmly, enthusiastically. [➡ENTHUSIASTIC AND INQUISITIVE; 629] *Opposite:* coldly.

emotionless *adj* **impassive**, blank, unemotional, detached, cold, unaffected. [➡NEUTRALITY AND INDIFFERENCE; 554] *Opposite:* emotional.

emotive *adj* **sensitive**, controversial, emotional, poignant, affecting, moving, impassioned, touching. [➡EMOTIONALLY PLEASANT; 188]

empathize *v* **identify with**, understand, sympathize, commiserate, relate to, feel for. [➡BE CONCERNED AND CARE; 582] *Opposite:* dismiss.

empathy *n* **understanding**, sympathy, compassion, responsiveness, identification, fellow feeling. [➡COMPASSION AND FORGIVENESS; 552] *Opposite:* indifference.

emperor *n* **ruler**, tsar, sovereign, king, head of state, monarch. [➡RULERS AND ARISTOCRACY; 823] *Opposite:* subject.

emperor butterfly *type of* **butterfly.** [➡MOTHS AND BUTTERFLIES; 1015]

emperor moth *type of* **moth.** [➡MOTHS AND BUTTERFLIES; 1015]

emphasis *n* **stress**, importance, weight, accent, prominence. [➡IMPORTANCE AND SIGNIFICANCE; 193]

emphasize *v* **highlight**, stress, accentuate, call attention to, underline, underscore, point up, point out. [➡CLAIM, INSIST, AND EMPHASIZE; 615] *Opposite:* understate.

emphatic 1 *adj* **forceful**, categorical, vigorous, definite, unequivocal, insistent. [➡ENTHUSIASTIC AND INQUISITIVE; 629] *Opposite:* hesitant. 2 *adj* **resounding**, absolute, ringing, clear, evident, obvious, glaring. [➡STRENGTH; 202] *Opposite:* ambiguous.

empire *n* **territory**, realm, kingdom, domain. [➡TERRITORIES AND GROUPS OF NATIONS; 1067]

Empire *type of* **pre-20th-century architecture.** [➡BUILDING AND ARCHITECTURE; 1075]

empirical *adj* **experiential**, experimental, observed, pragmatic, practical, realistic, firsthand. [➡TRUE AND REAL; 172] *Opposite:* theoretical.

empiricism *n* **pragmatism**, experimentation, observation, practicality. [➡PHILOSOPHIES AND BELIEFS; 781]

empiricist *n* **pragmatist**, observer, experimenter, realist, researcher, scientist. [➡PHILOSOPHICAL AND POLITICAL THINKERS; 782] *Opposite:* theorist.

employ 1 *v* **pay**, retain, use, hire, take on, engage, commission. [➡WORK-RELATED ACTIVITIES; 834] *Opposite:* dismiss. 2 *v* **use**, utilize, make use of, occupy, spend, put to use, devote, keep busy, exercise. [➡USE; 468] *Opposite:* waste. 3 *n* **employment**, service, pay, hire, engagement, occupation, work. [➡WORK-RELATED ACTIVITIES; 834] *Opposite:* unemployment.

See Compare and Contrast at **use.**

employed *adj* **working**, in a job, in employment, in work, engaged, in use, active, busy, hired, on duty, at work, labouring. [➡EMPLOYMENT STATUS; 831] *Opposite:* unemployed.

employee *n* **worker**, operative, servant, wage earner, member, underling, hand. [➡BOSSES AND MANAGEMENT; 965] *Opposite:* employer.

employer *n* **boss**, company, manager, owner, proprietor, firm, business, establishment, organization, outfit (*informal*). [➡BOSSES AND MANAGEMENT; 965] *Opposite:* employee.

employment *n* **service**, pay, hire, engagement, occupation, work, employ (*archaic*). [➡WORK-RELATED ACTIVITIES; 834] *Opposite:* unemployment.

emporium (*formal or humorous*) *n* **store**, retail store, department store, warehouse, bazaar, market, Aladdin's cave, corner shop, general store (*US*). [➡RETAIL OUTLETS; 1082]

empower 1 *v* **authorize**, allow, sanction, permit, vest, invest, endow, enable. [➡PERMIT AND ALLOW; 670] *Opposite:* forbid. 2 *v* **inspire**, embolden, encourage, galvanize, rouse, energize. [➡IMPROVE STRENGTH AND DURABILITY; 379] *Opposite:* discourage.

empowerment 1 *n* **authorization**, enablement, enabling, permission, leave (*formal*), consent. [➡PERMIT AND ALLOW; 670] *Opposite:* embargo. 2 *n* **liberation**, enfranchisement, emancipation, inspiration, encouragement, confidence-building, equality. [➡FREEDOM AND LIBERTY; 209]

empress *n* **ruler**, tsaritsa, tsarina, sovereign, queen, head of state, monarch. [➡RULERS AND ARISTOCRACY; 823] *Opposite:* subject.

emptiness 1 *n* **bareness**, barrenness, blankness, desolation, hollowness, sparseness, vacuum, vacancy, vacuity (*formal*), void. [➡EMPTY; 1237] *Opposite:* fullness. 2 *n* **meaninglessness**, worthlessness, purposelessness, hollowness, futility, aimlessness, pointlessness. [➡REDUNDANT AND USELESS; 241] *Opposite:* purpose.

empty 1 *adj* **unfilled**, bare, blank, vacant, hollow, void, unoccupied, uninhabited. [➡EMPTY; 1237] *Opposite:* full. 2 *adj* **meaningless**, purposeless, pointless, barren, hollow, futile, aimless, worthless. [➡REDUNDANT AND USELESS; 241] *Opposite:* meaningful. 3 *v* **drain**, clear, pour out, discharge, clear out, evacuate, exhaust, void. [➡EMPTY AND UNLOAD; 408] *Opposite:* fill.

See Compare and Contrast at **vacant, vain.**

empty-handed *adj* **unsuccessful**, frustrated, thwarted, unrewarded, defeated, lacking, wanting. [➡LACK OF POSSESSION; 446] *Opposite:* successful.

empty-headed *adj* **stupid**, silly, vacuous, frivolous, inane, foolish. [➡NEGATIVE INTELLECTUAL CHARACTERISTICS; 526] *Opposite:* intelligent.

emu *type of* **flightless bird.** [➡BIRD; 997]

emulate **1** *v* **imitate**, follow, copy, mimic, ape, model yourself on, pattern yourself after. [➡PRETEND AND MIMIC; 60] **2** *v* **compete with**, vie with, contend with, rival, outdo, match. [➡BEAT AND DEFEAT; 80]

See Compare and Contrast at **imitate**.

emulation *n* **imitation**, competition, rivalry, mimicry, simulation, impersonation, aping, copying, echoing. [➡REPRESENTATIONS AND GENERAL EXAMPLES; 65] *Opposite:* originality.

emulsify *v* **blend**, combine, beat together, stir together, mix, shake up, cream. [➡COMBINE AND MIX; 401] *Opposite:* separate.

emulsion *n* **suspension**, blend, mixture, cream, mix, combination. [➡COLLECTIONS AND MIXTURES OF THINGS; 1243]

enable *v* **allow**, permit, make possible, empower, qualify, aid, assist, support, facilitate, authorize. [➡MAKE POSSIBLE; 276] *Opposite:* prevent.

enact **1** *v* **perform**, act out, play, portray, represent, present. [➡THE PERFORMING ARTS; 904] **2** *v* **pass**, ratify, endorse, decree, sanction, ordain (*formal*), legislate, authorize, proclaim. [➡APPROVE AND CONFIRM; 647] *Opposite:* reject.

enactment **1** *n* **performance**, performing, acting out, portrayal, representation, presentation, acting, depiction, play-acting. [➡PERFORMANCES AND SHOWS; 42] **2** *n* **passing**, ratification, ratifying, endorsement, sanctioning, authorization, legislation. [➡APPROVE AND CONFIRM; 647]

enamel **1** *n* **coating**, varnish, veneer, glaze, lacquer, surface, top layer, gloss. [➡COVERS AND COATINGS; 1245] **2** *v* **coat**, paint, cover, protect, dip, glaze. [➡DECORATE, ADORN, AND APPLY COATINGS; 406] **3** *type of* **pottery.** [➡POTTERY; 1134]

enamoured *adj* **fond**, in love, smitten (*humorous or literary*), charmed, taken with, captivated, besotted, infatuated, loving, hooked (*slang*), amorous, sold on, attracted, mad on, keen on, bewitched, entranced. [➡APPRECIATION AND GRATITUDE; 536] *Opposite:* repelled.

en bloc *adv* **all together**, all at once, en masse, as one, collectively, as a whole, as a group. [➡ALL; 126] *Opposite:* separately.

encamp *v* **set up camp**, set up, install, base, settle, position, place. [➡INHABIT; 20]

encampment *n* **camp**, military camp, campsite, base camp, army camp, bivouac, advance camp, campground (*US*). [➡HUMAN SETTLEMENTS; 1069]

encapsulate *v* **sum up**, summarize, put in a nutshell, condense, capture, compress. [➡EXPLAIN AND CLARIFY; 611] *Opposite:* expand.

encase *v* **cover**, enclose, sheathe, coat, wrap, swathe. [➡CAUSE TO DISAPPEAR; 6] *Opposite:* uncover.

encased *adj* **covered**, enclosed, sheathed, coated, wrapped, swathed. [➡CAPTIVITY AND LOSS OF FREEDOM; 249] *Opposite:* uncovered.

enchant *v* **charm**, captivate, fascinate, enthral, enrapture (*formal*), entrance, bewitch, hypnotize, mesmerize, beguile. [➡APPEAL TO AND AROUSE INTEREST; 576] *Opposite:* disgust.

enchanted *adj* **charmed**, enthralled, captivated, delighted, enraptured (*formal*), entranced, bewitched, hypnotized, mesmerized, beguiled. [➡APPRECIATION AND GRATITUDE; 536] *Opposite:* disgusted.

enchanting *adj* **charming**, captivating, enthralling, delightful, entrancing, fascinating, bewitching, hypnotizing, mesmerizing, beguiling. [➡BEAUTY AND ATTRACTIVENESS; 190] *Opposite:* disgusting.

enchantingly *adv* **charmingly**, captivatingly, appealingly, mesmerizingly, beguilingly, enthrallingly, fascinatingly, beautifully, delightfully, entrancingly, bewitchingly. [➡EMOTIONALLY PLEASANT; 188] *Opposite:* disgustingly.

enchantment *n* **charm**, attraction, delight, fascination, allure, magic. [➡PLEASURE, EXCITEMENT, AND ELATION; 535]

encircle *v* **surround**, enclose, ring, circle, enfold, hem in, girdle (*literary*), circumscribe, encompass. [➡EXIST IN CLOSE PROXIMITY; 21]

enclave **1** *n* **region**, reserve, territory, commune, area, district, ghetto. [➡TERRITORIES AND GROUPS OF NATIONS; 1067] **2** *n* **group**, community, class, clan (*informal*), clique. [➡GROUPS WITH A COMMON INTEREST; 938]

enclose **1** *v* **surround**, hem in, encircle, enfold, ring, circle, encompass. [➡EXIST IN CLOSE PROXIMITY; 21] **2** *v* **wall**, fence, hedge, pen, seal off, cordon off, confine. [➡BAR AND OBSTRUCT ACCESS; 411] **3** *v* **include**, put in, attach, insert, add, append. [➡HOLD AND CONTAIN; 456] *Opposite:* leave out.

enclosed *adj* **surrounded**, bounded, hemmed in, fenced, walled, encircled, sealed off, cordoned off. [➡CAPTIVITY AND LOSS OF FREEDOM; 249] *Opposite:* open.

enclosure **1** *n* **field**, arena, stockade, pen, paddock, compound, corral (*US*). [➡THE COUNTRYSIDE AND OUTDOOR SPACES; 1070] **2** *n* **inclusion**, attachment, insertion, addition, insert, appendix. [➡PARTS OF BOOKS AND DOCUMENTS; 594]

encode *v* **encrypt**, code, put into code, scramble, convert, translate, express in code. [➡CAUSE TO DISAPPEAR; 6] *Opposite:* decode.

encomium (*formal*) *n* [➡PRAISE AND ENCOURAGE; 648]

encompass *v* **include**, cover, take in, incorporate, involve, comprehend (*formal*), embrace, contain, comprise, embody, hold. [➡POSSESS; 445] *Opposite:* exclude.

encore *n* **repeat**, extra, impromptu item, curtain call, reprise, return, repetition. [➡REPETITION; 29]

encounter **1** *v* **meet**, come across, bump into, run into, come upon, stumble upon, chance upon. [➡INITIATE AND ESTABLISH COMMUNICATION; 681] **2** *v* **face**, confront, contend with, grapple with, combat, do battle with, clash with. [➡EXPERIENCE AND ENCOUNTER; 583] *Opposite:* avoid. **3** *n* **meeting**, chance meeting, happenstance. [➡CHANCE EVENT; 36]

encourage 1 *v* **inspire**, hearten, cheer, raise your spirits, buoy up, reassure, boost, embolden. [➡ENCOURAGE; 577] *Opposite:* discourage. 2 *v* **support**, egg on, urge, animate, incite, inspire. [➡PRAISE AND ENCOURAGE; 648] *Opposite:* discourage. 3 *v* **foster**, assist, help, aid, nurture. [➡MAKE POSSIBLE; 276] *Opposite:* stifle.

encouragement *n* **support**, backup, help, reassurance, inspiration, praise, cheer, backing, reinforcement, boost, lift. [➡SOURCE OF HAPPINESS, PLEASURE, OR IMPROVEMENT; 210] *Opposite:* discouragement.

encouraging *adj* **hopeful**, heartening, cheering, reassuring, promising, inspiring, positive, boosting, uplifting. [➡EMOTIONALLY PLEASANT; 188] *Opposite:* discouraging.

encroach *v* **intrude**, impinge (*formal*), infringe, invade, trespass, make inroads into, eat into, violate. [➡GET CLOSER TOGETHER; 311] *Opposite:* respect.

encroachment *n* **infringement**, violation, advance, intrusion, invasion, impingement (*formal*). [➡BAD BEHAVIOUR OR ACTION; 255]

encrusted *adj* **covered**, coated, thick, crusted, caked, enveloped. [➡FULL; 1238] *Opposite:* bare.

encrypt *v* **encode**, code, put into code, scramble, translate, express in code, convert. [➡THE INTERNET; 1127] *Opposite:* decode.

encryption *n* [➡THE INTERNET; 1127]

encumber *v* **burden**, hinder, hamper, impede, get in the way, weigh down, load, saddle with, tax, inconvenience, handicap. [➡AVOID, PREVENT, LIMIT, AND CONTROL; 278] *Opposite:* unburden.

encumbrance *n* **burden**, hindrance, nuisance, impediment, handicap, tax, strain, inconvenience. [➡NUISANCES; 254] *Opposite:* help.

encyclopaedia *see* **encyclopedia**.

encyclopedia *n* **reference work**, compendium, compilation, fact file, information database, data bank, almanac. [➡BOOKS AND BOOKLETS; 591]

encyclopedic *adj* **comprehensive**, full, complete, in-depth, thorough, wide-ranging, all-encompassing, exhaustive, universal, broad. [➡WHOLENESS AND COMPLETENESS; 199] *Opposite:* narrow.

end 1 *n* **finish**, conclusion, ending, closing stages, last part, culmination, termination, close, expiration, completion, finale, wind-up. [➡END; 54] *Opposite:* beginning. 2 *n* **extremity**, edge, side, tip, top, point, bottom, boundary, base, border, limit. [➡EXTREMITIES OF PHYSICAL OBJECTS; 1249] *Opposite:* middle. 3 *n* **purpose**, aim, result, reason, objective, goal, object, intention, design. [➡INTENTION AND PURPOSE; 773] 4 *n* **death**, demise (*formal*), downfall, decline, ruin, dissolution, extinction, annihilation. [➡DEATH AND BEREAVEMENT; 927] *Opposite:* birth. 5 *n* **remnant**, leftover, stub, scrap, remainder. [➡REMAINDER AND REMAINDERS; 123] *Opposite:* whole. 6 *v* **stop**, finish, conclude, close, terminate (*formal*), halt, wind down, bring to an end, put an end to, put a stop to, come to an end, end up, finish off, leave off. [➡CAUSE TO STOP; 267] *Opposite:* begin. 7 *v* **result**, finish, conclude, wind up (*informal*), culminate, end up. [➡CEASE TO EXIST; 22]

endanger *v* **put in danger**, imperil (*formal*), jeopardize, risk, compromise, threaten, expose. [➡PUT AT RISK; 385] *Opposite:* protect.

endangered *adj* **rare**, in danger of extinction, dying out, scarce, threatened, vanishing. [➡FEW, LITTLE, SMALL AMOUNT; 119] *Opposite:* common.

endear *v* **commend**, recommend, ingratiate, make appealing, insinuate. [➡ESTABLISHING RELATIONSHIPS WITH OTHERS; 974] *Opposite:* alienate.

endearing *adj* **appealing**, attractive, charming, engaging, winning, lovable. [➡BEAUTY AND ATTRACTIVENESS; 190] *Opposite:* unappealing.

endearingly *adv* **charmingly**, appealingly, ingenuously, fetchingly, sweetly, adorably. [➡EMOTIONALLY PLEASANT; 188] *Opposite:* unappealingly.

endearment *n* **kind word**, sweet nothing, compliment, blandishment, loving word, flattery, sweet talk (*informal*). [➡ENDEARMENTS; 657] *Opposite:* insult.

endeavour 1 *v* **try**, strive, attempt, make every effort, do your utmost, do your best, undertake, struggle, labour, work hard to. [➡ATTEMPT AN ACTION; 262] *Opposite:* neglect. 2 *n* **attempt**, effort, try, exertion, best shot, work, hard work, industry, striving, struggle. [➡ATTEMPT AN ACTION; 262] 3 *n* **enterprise**, undertaking, bid, venture, foray, effort, exercise, work, preoccupation, vocation, job, career. [➡ACTIONS OR UNDERTAKINGS; 260]

endemic *adj* **widespread**, prevalent, common, rife, rampant, pervasive. [➡PRESENT AND AVAILABLE; 11] *Opposite:* rare.

ending *n* **end**, finish, finale, conclusion, culmination, closing stages, wind-up, termination, completion, consummation. [➡END; 54] *Opposite:* beginning.

end it all *v* **commit suicide**, kill yourself, take your own life, do away with yourself, die by your own hand, commit hara-kiri, commit suttee. [➡DIE; 922]

endive *type of* **salad vegetable**. [➡FRUIT AND VEGETABLES; 1175]

endless 1 *adj* **boundless**, infinite, limitless, without end, interminable, never-ending, ceaseless, unending, uninterrupted, unbroken, unceasing. [➡PERMANENCE: WITHOUT END; 94] *Opposite:* finite. 2 *adj* **eternal**, continual, continuous, nonstop, perpetual, everlasting, constant, persistent. [➡PERMANENCE: WITHOUT END; 94] *Opposite:* temporary.

end on *adj* **end-to-end**, endwise, endways. [➡ORIENTATION AND ALIGNMENT; 1222]

endorse 1 *v* **sanction**, approve, ratify, recommend, countersign, authorize, validate, certify. [➡APPROVE AND CONFIRM; 647] *Opposite:* reject. 2 *v* **support**, back, advocate, favour, subscribe to, vouch for, approve, sanction, ratify. [➡APPROVE AND CONFIRM; 647] *Opposite:* denounce.

endorsed *adj* **permitted**, recognized, sanctioned, recommended, authorized, validated, certified. [➡LEGAL; 815] *Opposite:* disallowed.

endorsement 1 *n* **authorization**, commendation, confirmation, countersignature, ratification, seal of approval, testimonial, certification, validation. [➡APPROVE AND CONFIRM; 647] 2 *n* **backing**, support, advocacy, sanction, encouragement, approval, affirmation, ratification. [➡APPROVE AND CONFIRM; 647]

endow *v* **award**, donate, bestow (*formal*), give, bequeath, provide, grant. [➡REWARD; 437]

endowment 1 *n* **donation**, gift, bequest, legacy, award, grant, benefaction. [➡BEQUEATH AND BEQUESTS; 433] 2 *n* **natural gift**, talent, ability, capability, aptitude, faculty, attribute. [➡SKILLS, TALENTS, AND ABILITIES; 527]

end product *n* **outcome**, end result, result, upshot, product, consequence. [➡RESULTS AND OUTCOMES; 83]

end result *n* **outcome**, end product, result, upshot, product, consequence. [➡RESULTS AND OUTCOMES; 83]

end table *type of* **table**. [➡FURNITURE; 858]

end up *v* **finish up**, finish off, transpire, wind up (*informal*), turn out, result in, come to pass (*archaic or literary*), culminate in. [➡COMPLETE AN ACTION; 264] *Opposite:* start out.

endurable *adj* **tolerable**, manageable, bearable, passable, sufferable. [➡ACCEPTABLE AND PASSABLE; 220] *Opposite:* intolerable.

endurance 1 *n* **staying power**, strength, stamina, fortitude, resolution, durability, survival. [➡STRENGTH OF WILL; 502] *Opposite:* weakness. 2 *n* **persistence**, perseverance, tenacity, continuance, survival, duration. [➡PERMANENCE: WITHOUT END; 94]

endure 1 *v* **bear**, tolerate, undergo, put up with, go through, stomach, withstand, sustain, stand, experience, brave, suffer. [➡TOLERATE AND ENDURE; 767] *Opposite:* succumb. 2 *v* **last**, continue, go on, persist, survive, persevere, prevail, live, live on, remain. *Opposite:* perish. (*literary*). [➡CONTINUE TO EXIST; 17]

enduring *adj* **lasting**, continuing, durable, stable, long-term, persistent, permanent. [➡PERMANENCE: WITHOUT END; 94] *Opposite:* short-lived.

end user *n* **user**, purchaser, shopper, consumer, client, buyer. [➡BUSINESS ACTIVITIES AND PHENOMENA; 795] *Opposite:* producer.

endways *adv* **end on**, endways on, jutting out, end foremost, end uppermost, endwise. [➡ORIENTATION AND ALIGNMENT; 1222]

endwise *adv* **end on**, endways on, jutting out, end foremost, end uppermost, endways. [➡ORIENTATION AND ALIGNMENT; 1222]

enemy *n* **opponent**, adversary, foe (*literary*), rival, competitor, antagonist, nemesis (*literary*). [➡ENEMIES AND TORMENTORS; 969] *Opposite:* friend.

energetic 1 *adj* **lively**, active, vigorous, brisk, peppy (*informal*), full of beans (*informal*), animated, spirited, bouncy, robust, bouncing, enthusiastic. [➡ENERGY AND ENTHUSIASM; 497] *Opposite:* lethargic. 2 *adj* **strenuous**, vigorous, brisk, dynamic, challenging, arduous. [➡PHYSICALLY UNPLEASANT; 227] *Opposite:* easy.

energetically *adv* **vigorously**, actively, briskly, forcefully, dynamically, powerfully, enthusiastically. [➡WITH ENTHUSIASM; 287] *Opposite:* lethargically.

energize *v* **invigorate**, strengthen, boost, pep up (*informal*), galvanize, motivate, animate, empower, revitalize. [➡IMPROVE STRENGTH AND DURABILITY; 379] *Opposite:* enervate.

energizing *adj* **invigorating**, stimulating, enlivening, revitalizing, reviving, vitalizing, motivating, activating, animating, galvanizing, enabling. [➡PHYSICALLY PLEASANT; 187] *Opposite:* draining.

energy 1 *n* **vigour**, liveliness, get-up-and-go (*informal*), oomph, dynamism, vitality, drive, verve, vim (*informal*), élan (*literary*), go (*informal*), vivacity. [➡ENERGY AND ENTHUSIASM; 497] *Opposite:* lethargy. 2 *n* **power**, force, strength, momentum, resources. [➡ENERGY GENERAL; 1160]

enervate *v* **weaken**, debilitate, sap your strength, drain, fatigue, exhaust, undermine, weary, wear out, deplete, devitalize (*formal*), enfeeble, tire. [➡CHANGE OF INTENSITY: LESS; 396] *Opposite:* invigorate.

enervated *adj* [➡TIRED, ASLEEP AND UNCONSCIOUS; 739]

See Compare and Contrast at **weak**.

enervating *adj* **exhausting**, weakening, enfeebling, fatiguing, draining, wearying, tiring, depleting, sapping. [➡PHYSICALLY UNPLEASANT; 227] *Opposite:* invigorating.

enervation *n* [➡TIRED, ASLEEP AND UNCONSCIOUS; 739]

enfeeble *v* **weaken**, debilitate, enervate, devitalize (*formal*), deplete, exhaust, wear out, fatigue, sap, undermine, emasculate (*formal*). [➡WOUND A PERSON OR ANIMAL; 384] *Opposite:* strengthen.

enfold *v* **enclose**, surround, wrap, wrap up, envelop, enwrap, clasp, hug, swathe, embrace. [➡EXIST IN CLOSE PROXIMITY; 21]

enforce 1 *v* **apply**, carry out, impose, implement, make compulsory, administer. [➡CARRY OUT AN ACTION; 270] 2 *v* **coerce**, oblige, compel, require, insist on, urge. [➡CAUSE OR COMPEL TO ACT; 272]

enforced *adj* **compulsory**, obligatory, forced, imposed, required, prescribed. [➡CAPTIVITY AND LOSS OF FREEDOM; 249] *Opposite:* optional.

enforcement *n* **implementation**, application, execution, putting into practice, administration, prosecution. [➡CARRY OUT AN ACTION; 270]

enfranchise *v* **give somebody the vote**, empower, emancipate, liberate, naturalize. [➡ELECTIONS AND SUFFRAGE; 807] *Opposite:* disenfranchise.

enfranchisement *n* **empowerment**, naturalization, suffrage, manumission (*formal*). [➡ELECTIONS AND SUFFRAGE; 807] *Opposite:* disenfranchisement.

engage 1 *v* **involve**, occupy, engross, absorb, take part, participate. [➡APPEAL TO AND AROUSE INTEREST; 576] 2 *v* **appoint**, take on, employ, hire, contract, secure, retain. [➡WORK-RELATED ACTIVITIES; 834] *Opposite:* dismiss. 3 *v* **battle**, fight, combat, contest, encounter. [➡COMPETE, CONTEND, AND COMBAT; 304] 4 *v* **hold**, keep, absorb, charm, attract, draw. [➡PAY ATTENTION; 766] *Opposite:*

repel. **5** *v* **connect**, slot in, fit into place, interlock, join, mesh. [➡COMBINE AND MIX; 401] *Opposite:* disengage.

engaged **1** *adj* **busy**, occupied, unavailable, in use, being used, employed. [➡ABSENT AND UNAVAILABLE; 7] *Opposite:* free. **2** *adj* **betrothed** (*formal*), affianced (*formal*), spoken for, involved, promised, tied up. [➡MARITAL STATUS; 890] *Opposite:* free.

engagement **1** *n* **appointment**, meeting, rendezvous, assignation, visit, date, commitment, arrangement, tryst. [➡MEETINGS AND ASSEMBLIES; 43] **2** *n* **employment**, job, position, situation, gig (*informal*), post. [➡JOB; 833] **3** *n* **battle**, fight, encounter, conflict, action, skirmish, clash. [➡WARFARE AND WAR; 830]

See Compare and Contrast at **fight**.

engaging *adj* **attractive**, appealing, charming, winning, fetching, pleasing, likable, enchanting, disarming. [➡BEAUTY AND ATTRACTIVENESS; 190] *Opposite:* unattractive.

engender **1** *v* **produce**, cause, create, bring about, stimulate, provoke, prompt. [➡ENGENDER; 351] **2** *v* (*formal*) **beget**, give birth to, generate, propagate, spawn. [➡REPRODUCTION AND HEREDITY; 726]

engine *n* **machine**, motor, turbine, piston engine, steam engine, internal combustion engine. [➡ENGINES AND HYDRAULICS; 1142]

engine

◆ *parts of an engine*
ball bearing, cam, camshaft, cog, cogwheel, coil, crank, crankshaft, cylinder, gasket, gear, gearbox, gearing, lever, oil pan (*US*), piston, pump, radiator, seal, shaft, spark plug, starter, sump, tappet, valve

engineer *v* **bring about**, cause, contrive, wangle (*informal*), concoct, plot, fix up, plan. [➡CAUSE TO HAPPEN; 31]

engine room *part of* **ship or boat**. [➡PARTS OF A SHIP OR BOAT; 1150]

English breakfast *type of* **meal**. [➡MEALS AND PARTS OF MEALS; 1168]

English horn (*US*) *type of* **wind instrument**. [➡MUSICAL INSTRUMENTS; 910]

English muffin (*US*) *type of* **roll or bun**. [➡BREAD, FLOUR, AND BREAD PRODUCTS; 1178]

engorge *v* **swell up**, swell, puff up, expand, blow up. [➡CHANGE OF SIZE: BIGGER; 393] *Opposite:* deflate.

engorged *adj* [➡FULL; 1238]

engorgement *n* [➡FULL; 1238]

engrave *v* **etch**, score, scratch, carve, incise, cut in, inscribe. [➡CREATE IMAGES; 357]

engraving **1** *n* **etching**, lithograph, print, reproduction, woodcut, picture. [➡ARTWORKS; 898] **2** *n* **engraved design**, carving, etching, linocut, inscription, image, design. [➡ARTWORKS; 898]

engross *v* **absorb**, captivate, hold your attention, hold, engage, occupy, involve, enthral, mesmerize. [➡APPEAL TO AND AROUSE INTEREST; 576] *Opposite:* bore.

engrossed *adj* **absorbed**, captivated, enthralled, riveted (*informal*), gripped, held, immersed, occupied, engaged. [➡PENSIVENESS AND INTEREST; 539] *Opposite:* bored.

engrossing *adj* **absorbing**, captivating, enthralling, riveting (*informal*), gripping, interesting, fascinating, mesmerizing. [➡INTERESTING AND MEANINGFUL; 191] *Opposite:* uninteresting.

engulf *v* **swallow up**, overcome, overwhelm, immerse, submerge, swamp, surround, consume, whelm (*literary*). [➡EXIST IN CLOSE PROXIMITY; 21]

enhance *v* **improve**, augment (*formal*), add to, increase, boost, develop, enrich, heighten. [➡IMPROVE SOMETHING; 375] *Opposite:* impair.

enhanced *adj* **improved**, greater, heightened, boosted, higher, superior, enriched. [➡GOOD, WELL, BETTER; 184] *Opposite:* diminished.

enhancement *n* **improvement**, augmentation, development, enrichment, heightening, boost. [➡PROGRESS AND ADVANCEMENT; 214] *Opposite:* detraction.

enigma *n* **paradox**, conundrum, problem, mystery, puzzle, riddle, question, perplexity. [➡SECRETS AND MYSTERIES; 181]

See Compare and Contrast at **problem**.

enigmatic *adj* **mysterious**, inscrutable, puzzling, perplexing, unfathomable, unknowable, inexplicable. [➡SECRET AND UNKNOWN; 180] *Opposite:* straightforward.

See Compare and Contrast at **obscure**.

enjoin (*formal*) *v* **order**, command, instruct, bid (*archaic*), direct, tell, charge. [➡CAUSE OR COMPEL TO ACT; 272] *Opposite:* forbid.

enjoy **1** *v* **like**, delight in, appreciate, revel in, relish, love, adore. [➡LIKE, LOVE, VALUE AND ENJOY; 579] *Opposite:* dislike. **2** *v* **benefit from**, have, experience, be blessed with, possess, own. [➡POSSESS; 445] *Opposite:* lack.

enjoyable *adj* **pleasant**, agreeable, pleasing, entertaining, amusing, pleasurable, gratifying, fun. [➡EMOTIONALLY PLEASANT; 188] *Opposite:* boring.

enjoyment *n* **pleasure**, delight, satisfaction, gratification, fun, amusement. [➡PLEASURE, EXCITEMENT, AND ELATION; 535] *Opposite:* boredom.

enjoy yourself *v* **be amused**, be delighted, party (*informal*), whoop it up (*informal*), let yourself go, play. [➡LEISURE AND RECREATION; 874]

enlarge **1** *v* **increase**, expand, broaden, widen, extend, add to, amplify. [➡CHANGE OF SIZE: BIGGER; 393] *Opposite:* decrease. **2** *v* **detail**, elaborate, expand, amplify, flesh out, develop. [➡CHANGE OF INTENSITY: MORE; 395] *Opposite:* compress.

See Compare and Contrast at **increase**.

enlargement *n* **expansion**, extension, amplification, increase, widening, broadening, development, elaboration. [➡CHANGE OF SIZE: BIGGER; 393] *Opposite:* decrease.

enlarger *type of* **photographic equipment**. [➡PHOTOGRAPHY AND PHOTOGRAPHIC EQUIPMENT; 1121]

enlighten *v* **tell**, inform, explain to, instruct, edify, educate, clarify. [➡EXPLAIN AND CLARIFY; 611]

enlightened *adj* **rational**, progressive, freethinking, open-minded, tolerant, educated, liberal. [➡POSITIVE INTELLECTUAL CHARACTERISTICS; 525] *Opposite:* intolerant.

enlightening *adj* **informative**, instructive, edifying, helpful, educational, educative, illuminating, clarifying. [➡INTERESTING AND MEANINGFUL; 191] *Opposite:* uninformative.

enlightenment *n* **explanation**, illumination, clarification, insight, information, instruction, education. [➡KNOWLEDGE AND WISDOM; 559] *Opposite:* ignorance.

enlist **1** *v* **join**, join up, sign on, sign up, volunteer, enrol. [➡PARTICIPATE; 293] **2** *v* **recruit**, conscript, procure, solicit, count on, register, sign up. [➡GET; 421] *Opposite:* reject.

enliven *v* **liven up**, cheer up, pep up (*informal*), invigorate, wake up, cheer, brighten. [➡IMPROVE SOMETHING; 375]

en masse *adv* **all together**, as one, all at once, as a whole, as a group, en bloc, collectively. [➡ALL; 126] *Opposite:* singly.

enmesh *v* **entangle**, tangle, trap, catch, catch up, ensnare, embroil, involve. [➡CAPTIVITY AND LOSS OF FREEDOM; 249] *Opposite:* disentangle.

enmity *n* **hostility**, hate, hatred, ill will, animosity, antagonism, antipathy, rancour. [➡ANTAGONISM; 553] *Opposite:* goodwill.

ennui *n* **boredom**, languor, world-weariness, tedium, weariness, dissatisfaction. [➡NEUTRALITY AND INDIFFERENCE; 554] *Opposite:* excitement.

enormity **1** *n* **atrociousness**, horror, monstrousness, wickedness, heinousness, nefariousness, flagrancy. [➡BAD BEHAVIOUR OR ACTION; 255] *Opposite:* goodness. **2** *n* **atrocity**, abomination, outrage, evil, horror, crime. [➡BAD BEHAVIOUR OR ACTION; 255] *Opposite:* kindness. **3** *n* **size**, extent, vastness, scale, immensity, hugeness, magnitude. [➡LARGE; 1192]

enormous *adj* **huge**, vast, massive, giant, mammoth, gigantic, colossal, gargantuan, titanic, immense. [➡LARGE; 1192] *Opposite:* tiny.

enormously *adv* **extremely**, very, a lot, a great deal, hugely, immensely, vastly, colossally, massively (*informal*). [➡TO A GREAT EXTENT; 130] *Opposite:* slightly.

enough *adj* **sufficient**, adequate, ample, plenty, abundant, plentiful. [➡ENOUGH AND SUFFICIENT; 129] *Opposite:* insufficient.

Compare and Contrast: ***enough, sufficient, adequate, ample, plenty***

CORE MEANING: EQUAL IN QUANTITY TO WHAT IS NEEDED

enough as much as is needed; ***sufficient*** enough, especially for a particular purpose; ***adequate*** enough, but sometimes only just enough; ***ample*** more than enough of something; ***plenty*** enough, or more than enough, to meet requirements.

enquire *v* **ask**, find out, query, investigate, probe, search, question. [➡ASK PEOPLE QUESTIONS; 667] *Opposite:* reply.

enrage *v* **infuriate**, anger, make your blood boil, madden, incense. [➡ANGER AND ANNOY; 570] *Opposite:* calm.

enraged *adj* **furious**, infuriated, angry, beside yourself, hopping mad (*informal*), fuming, incensed. [➡IRRITATION AND ANGER; 542] *Opposite:* calm.

enrapture (*formal*) *v* **entrance**, delight, captivate, enchant, mesmerize, thrill, transport, enthral. [➡SURPRISE AND IMPRESS; 575] *Opposite:* bore.

enraptured (*formal*) *adj* [➡PLEASURE, EXCITEMENT, AND ELATION; 535]

enrich *v* **augment** (*formal*), supplement, improve, enhance, deepen, develop. [➡IMPROVE SOMETHING; 375] *Opposite:* diminish.

enrichment *n* **enhancement**, improvement, augmentation, amelioration, upgrading, development, supplementation. [➡IMPROVE SOMETHING; 375] *Opposite:* diminution.

enrol *v* **register**, sign up, put your name down, join, join up, sign on. [➡PARTICIPATE; 293]

enrolment *n* **registration**, matriculation, signing up, admission, acceptance, membership. [➡TEACHING; 839] *Opposite:* resignation.

en route *adv* **on the way**, while travelling, on the journey, on the road, heading for, in transit. [➡TRAVEL: WAYS OF TRAVELLING; 321]

ensconce (*archaic or literary*) *v* **entrench**, hide, hide away, conceal, screen, shield. [➡POSITION SOMETHING; 326] *Opposite:* expose.

ensemble **1** *n* **band**, company, troupe, group, outfit (*informal*), corps, assemblage. [➡MUSICIANS AND SINGERS; 908] **2** *n* **outfit** (*informal*), rigout, get-up (*informal*), suit, costume, coordinates. [➡CLOTHES AND ACCESSORIES; 864] **3** *n* **collection**, assembly, aggregate, set, combination, composite, amalgamation. [➡COLLECTIONS AND MIXTURES OF THINGS; 1243] **4** *adj* **collaborative**, collective, joint, group, cooperative, communal. [➡RECIPROCITY AND INTERDEPENDENCE; 148] *Opposite:* solo.

enshrine *v* **protect**, treasure, hallow, preserve, cherish. [➡LIKE, LOVE, VALUE AND ENJOY; 579]

enshroud *v* **obscure**, hide, mask, shield, cover, shroud. [➡CAUSE TO DISAPPEAR; 6] *Opposite:* expose.

ensign *n* **flag**, pennant, banner, standard, colours, emblem, badge. [➡SYMBOLS, SIGNS, AND NUMBERS; 597]

enslave *v* **subjugate**, dominate, subject, bind, yoke, enchain (*formal or literary*), enthral (*literary*). [➡CAPTIVITY AND LOSS OF FREEDOM; 249] *Opposite:* liberate.

ensnare *v* **entangle**, tangle, enmesh, catch up, catch, trap, snare, entrap. [➡CAPTIVITY AND LOSS OF FREEDOM; 249] *Opposite:* set free.

ensue 1 *v* **follow**, succeed, supervene (*formal*), follow on, result, arise. [➡HAPPEN; 27] *Opposite:* precede. 2 *v* **result**, follow, proceed, arise, derive, develop, stem. [➡GRADUALLY COME INTO EXISTENCE; 1] *Opposite:* precede.

ensuing *adj* **resultant**, subsequent, succeeding, resulting, following, later. [➡RESULTS AND OUTCOMES; 83] *Opposite:* preceding.

ensure *v* **make sure**, make certain, safeguard, guarantee, confirm, certify, warrant. [➡CAUSE TO HAPPEN; 31]

entail *v* **involve**, require, demand, need, necessitate. [➡CAUSE TO HAPPEN; 31]

entangle *v* **tangle**, snare, ensnare, catch up, enmesh, entrap, trap, catch, interweave. [➡CAPTIVITY AND LOSS OF FREEDOM; 249] *Opposite:* free.

entanglement *n* **predicament**, tangle, muddle, morass, mess, imbroglio (*formal or literary*). [➡DIFFICULT SITUATIONS; 72]

entente *n* [➡HARMONY; 156]

enter 1 *v* **go in**, go into, come in, come into, cross the threshold, pass into, pass in, move into, move in, arrive in, arrive, flow into. [➡ARRIVE; 12] *Opposite:* leave. 2 *v* **input**, insert, put in, record, type, write down, write, key in, key. [➡RECORD SOMETHING; 372] *Opposite:* delete. 3 *v* **submit**, put in, propose, hand in, state, put forward, announce. [➡SUGGEST, HINT, AND COMMENT; 613] 4 *v* **compete**, participate, take part, take up, try, contest, play. [➡COMPETE, CONTEND, AND COMBAT; 304] 5 *v* **join**, sign up, agree to, enlist, enrol, register. [➡PARTICIPATE; 293] 6 *v* **walk on**, come on, appear, make an entrance. [➡ARRIVE; 12] *Opposite:* exit.

enter into *v* **become involved in**, take part in, join in, throw yourself into, participate in, take up. [➡PARTICIPATE; 293] *Opposite:* withdraw.

enter on *v* **start**, begin, enter upon, move into, start out on, embark upon. [➡START AN ACTION; 261] *Opposite:* finish.

enterprise 1 *n* **business**, company, firm, organization, operation, establishment. [➡BUSINESS ENTERPRISES AND RELATED BODIES; 793] 2 *n* **venture**, project, activity, undertaking, endeavour, scheme. [➡ACTIONS OR UNDERTAKINGS; 260] 3 *n* **initiative**, innovativeness, creativity, inventiveness, originality, get-up-and-go (*informal*), readiness, boldness, willingness. [➡POSITIVE INTELLECTUAL CHARACTERISTICS; 525] *Opposite:* apathy.

enterprise zone *type of* **industrial site**. [➡INDUSTRIAL BUILDINGS; 1086]

enterprising *adj* **innovative**, inventive, imaginative, resourceful, adventurous, ingenious, creative, intrepid (*literary or humorous*), original, go-ahead (*informal*), bold. [➡POSITIVE INTELLECTUAL CHARACTERISTICS; 525] *Opposite:* unadventurous.

enterprisingly *adv* **inventively**, imaginatively, resourcefully, adventurously, ingeniously, creatively, intrepidly (*literary or humorous*), boldly. [➡INTENTIONAL AND DELIBERATE; 280] *Opposite:* lazily.

entertain 1 *v* **amuse**, divert, distract, regale, interest, tickle. [➡PLEASE AND AMUSE; 573] *Opposite:* bore. 2 *v* **accommodate**, wine and dine, feed, invite, regale, treat. [➡ENTERTAINMENT; 872] *Opposite:* visit. 3 *v* **consider**, think about, give thought to, contemplate, think over, ponder. [➡THINK AND REFLECT; 744] *Opposite:* reject.

entertainer *n* **performer**, artiste, artist. [➡WORKERS IN ENTERTAINMENT AND MEDIA; 873]

entertainer

◆ *types of entertainer*
actor, busker, clown, co-star, comedian, comic, conjurer, dancer, DJ, film star, impressionist, juggler, magician, mime, movie star (*US*), musician, singer, ventriloquist

entertaining *adj* **amusing**, enjoyable, diverting, pleasurable, charming, hilarious, humorous, engaging, compelling. [➡EMOTIONALLY PLEASANT; 188] *Opposite:* dull.

entertainingly *adv* **amusingly**, interestingly, humorously, engagingly, enjoyably, compellingly. [➡FUNNY AND AMUSING; 217] *Opposite:* boringly.

entertainment 1 *n* **entertaining**, performing, acting, show business, show biz (*informal*), theatre. [➡ENTERTAINMENT; 872] 2 *n* **amusement**, fun, diversion, distraction, enjoyment, recreation. [➡ENTERTAINMENT; 872] *Opposite:* boredom. 3 *n* **show**, production, concert, attraction, performance, cabaret. [➡PERFORMANCES AND SHOWS; 42]

enter upon *v* **start**, begin, enter on, move into, start out on, embark upon. [➡START AN ACTION; 261] *Opposite:* finish.

enthral *v* **captivate**, rivet (*informal*), charm, mesmerize, beguile, fascinate, enchant, engross, grip, entrance. [➡SURPRISE AND IMPRESS; 575] *Opposite:* bore.

enthralled *adj* **fascinated**, engrossed, gripped, captivated, absorbed, charmed, entranced, enchanted, beguiled. [➡PENSIVENESS AND INTEREST; 539] *Opposite:* bored.

enthralling *adj* **fascinating**, beguiling, engrossing, gripping, riveting (*informal*), captivating, absorbing, enchanting, alluring. [➡INTERESTING AND MEANINGFUL; 191] *Opposite:* boring.

enthrone (*formal*) *v* **crown**, instate, ordain, swear in, consecrate, install, inaugurate. [➡CONFER STATUS; 459] *Opposite:* dethrone.

enthuse 1 *v* **be enthusiastic**, be passionate, talk excitedly, show enthusiasm, rave, wax lyrical (*literary*), effuse (*formal*), be effusive, gush. [➡PRAISE AND ENCOURAGE; 648] 2 *v* **stimulate**, galvanize, excite, spur to action, impassion, stir up, whip up, fire. [➡APPEAL TO AND AROUSE INTEREST; 576] *Opposite:* bore.

enthused *adj* [➡PLEASURE, EXCITEMENT, AND ELATION; 535]

enthusiasm 1 *n* **eagerness**, interest, passion, gusto, zeal, zest, keenness, fervour, excitement, fire. [➡POSITIVE IMPATIENCE, ENTHUSIASM, AND ALERTNESS; 538] *Opposite:* apathy. 2 *n*

craze, interest, hobby, passion, mania, pastime, pursuit, fad, fashion, leisure pursuit. [➡FADS, FETISHES, AND IDOLATRY; 556]

enthusiast *n* **fan**, fanatic, buff, aficionado, devotee, supporter. [➡DEVOTEES AND ADDICTED PEOPLE; 557]

enthusiastic *adj* **eager**, keen, passionate, fervent, excited, wholehearted, animated, aflame, afire. [➡APPRECIATION AND GRATITUDE; 536] *Opposite:* apathetic.

enthusiastically *adv* **keenly**, eagerly, passionately, fervently, excitedly, wholeheartedly. [➡WITH ENTHUSIASM; 287] *Opposite:* apathetically.

entice *v* **lure**, tempt, induce, seduce, bribe, cajole, invite, attract. [➡APPEAL TO AND AROUSE INTEREST; 576] *Opposite:* put off.

enticement *n* **lure**, temptation, incentive, inducement, bribery, bribe, draw, attraction, invitation, bait. [➡CAUSATION; 169] *Opposite:* deterrent.

enticing *adj* **tempting**, alluring, inviting, attractive, appealing, tantalizing, desirable. [➡BEAUTY AND ATTRACTIVENESS; 190] *Opposite:* uninviting.

enticingly *adv* **temptingly**, invitingly, alluringly, appealingly, tantalizingly, desirably, mouthwateringly, attractively. [➡INTERESTING AND MEANINGFUL; 191] *Opposite:* uninvitingly.

entire 1 *adj* **whole**, complete, full, total, perfect, all-inclusive. [➡WHOLENESS AND COMPLETENESS; 199] *Opposite:* part. 2 *adj* **absolute**, complete, total, thorough, unqualified, unmitigated. [➡ABSOLUTE AND ABSOLUTELY; 131] *Opposite:* partial.

entirety *n* **sum**, whole, wholeness, totality, entireness, total, completeness, fullness. [➡WHOLENESS AND COMPLETENESS; 199]

entitle 1 *v* **enable**, allow, permit, sanction, authorize, warrant. [➡PERMIT AND ALLOW; 670] *Opposite:* debar. 2 *v* **title**, call, name, dub, label, designate. [➡NAME AND DESCRIBE; 666]

entitled 1 *adj* **permitted**, in your own right, eligible, allowed, enabled, authorized. [➡PERMIT AND ALLOW; 670] *Opposite:* barred. 2 *adj* **titled**, called, named, dubbed, labelled, designated. [➡NAME AND DESCRIBE; 666]

entitlement *n* **right**, power, prerogative, privilege, claim, title. [➡POSSESS; 445]

entity *n* **object**, thing, article, being, unit, individual. [➡PHYSICAL OBJECTS; 1242] *Opposite:* nonentity.

entourage *n* **staff**, associates, following, followers, train, backup, support. [➡FRIENDS AND ACQUAINTANCES; 936]

entrails *n* **innards** (*informal*), insides (*informal*), guts, intestines, bowels, viscera. [➡CENTRAL PARTS OF PHYSICAL OBJECTS; 1250]

entrance 1 *n* **entry**, way in, doorway, door, opening, entrance hall, foyer, lobby, access. [➡DOORS AND ACCESS POINTS; 1100] *Opposite:* exit. 2 *n* **arrival**, entry, appearance, entering, ingress (*formal*). [➡ARRIVAL; 13] *Opposite:* departure. 3 *n* **admission**, entry, ticket, pass, admittance, access. [➡PERMIT AND ALLOW; 670] 4 *v* **captivate**, engross, fascinate, charm, delight, spellbind, enthral, mesmerize, enchant, rivet (*informal*). [➡SURPRISE AND IMPRESS; 575] *Opposite:* bore.

entranced *adj* [➡PENSIVENESS AND INTEREST; 539]

entrance hall 1 *n* **lobby**, foyer, reception area, hallway, vestibule, reception. [➡DOORS AND ACCESS POINTS; 1100] 2 *type of* **room in public buildings**. [➡TYPES OF ROOM; 1096]

entrancing *adj* **captivating**, enchanting, enthralling, spellbinding, fascinating, delightful, mesmerizing, riveting (*informal*). [➡INTERESTING AND MEANINGFUL; 191] *Opposite:* boring.

entrant *n* **applicant**, contestant, candidate, participant, competitor, player, runner, contender. [➡COMPETITORS; 41]

See Compare and Contrast at **candidate**.

entrap *v* **trick**, deceive, ensnare, trap, lure, catch, capture, entangle, decoy, inveigle. [➡DECEPTION AND LIES; 661]

entrapment *n* **trap**, frame, snare, trick, frame-up (*slang*), setup (*informal*), sting (*US slang*). [➡CAPTIVITY AND LOSS OF FREEDOM; 249]

entreat (*formal*) *v* **plead**, implore (*formal*), beg, pray, beseech (*literary*), ask, request. [➡REQUEST AND DEMAND; 664] *Opposite:* demand.

entreaty *n* **appeal**, plea, petition, request, supplication (*formal*), suit. [➡REQUEST AND DEMAND; 664] *Opposite:* demand.

entrée 1 *n* **starter**, hors d'oeuvre, first course, appetizer, antipasto. [➡MEALS AND PARTS OF MEALS; 1168] 2 *n* **introduction**, induction, entrance, access, admittance. [➡BEGINNING; 53] *Opposite:* exclusion.

entrench *v* **embed**, ensconce, ingrain, root, establish, cement. [➡MOVE PAST, INTO OR THROUGH SOMETHING; 332]

entre nous (*formal*) *adv* **between ourselves**, between you and me, in confidence, confidentially, privately, between you, me, and the gatepost, secretly, surreptitiously, between you, me, and the bedpost (*US*). [➡FOREIGN WORDS AND PHRASES; 673] *Opposite:* publicly.

entrepreneur *n* **businessperson**, tycoon, magnate, impresario, industrialist, financier. [➡BUSINESS PEOPLE; 794]

entrepreneurial *adj* **business**, commercial, risk-taking, empire-building, tactical, innovative, ground-breaking. [➡BUSINESS; 792]

entresol *n* [➡STAIRS AND STOREYS; 1101]

entrust *v* **trust**, commend, delegate, assign, deliver, hand over. [➡GIVE AND PROVIDE; 431] *Opposite:* deprive.

entry 1 *n* **admission**, entrance, access, pass, ticket, admittance. [➡ARRIVAL; 13] 2 *n* **entrance**, doorway, door, ingress (*formal*), opening, access. [➡DOORS AND ACCESS POINTS; 1100] *Opposite:* exit. 3 *n* **record**, item, note, account, statement, minute. [➡RECORDS; 586] 4 *n* **application**, submission, attempt, effort, go, try. [➡REQUEST AND DEMAND; 664] *Opposite:* withdrawal.

entwine *v* **tangle**, entangle, twist, interweave, interlace, interlink. [➡FASTEN, LINK, AND JOIN; 409] *Opposite:* undo.

enumerate 1 *v* **detail**, list, spell out, itemize, name, specify, catalogue. [➡NAME AND DESCRIBE; 666] 2 *v* **count**, number, tally, compute, reckon, total. [➡ASSESS QUANTITY; 758] *Opposite:* estimate.

enunciate 1 *v* **pronounce**, articulate, voice, utter, speak, say, vocalize. [➡UTTER AND PRONOUNCE; 609] *Opposite:* mumble.

2 *v* **express**, spell out, detail, state, put forward, voice, clarify. [➡EXPLAIN AND CLARIFY; 611] *Opposite:* suppress.

enunciation 1 *n* **pronunciation**, articulation, diction, speech. [➡ASPECTS OF LANGUAGE; 683] 2 *n* **expression**, assertion, declaration, proclamation, clarification. [➡INFORM AND ANNOUNCE; 612] *Opposite:* suppression.

envelop *v* **enclose**, encircle, encase, swathe, shroud, cloak, wrap, cover, surround. [➡EXIST IN CLOSE PROXIMITY; 21] *Opposite:* unwrap.

envelope *n* **cover**, wrapper, covering, wrapping, casing, packet. [➡COVERS AND COATINGS; 1245]

enviable *adj* **desirable**, fortunate, lucky, privileged, to die for, happy. [➡POPULAR AND WANTED; 221] *Opposite:* unenviable.

envious *adj* **jealous**, green with envy, resentful, spiteful, covetous, green, grudging, begrudging. [➡ENVY AND JEALOUSY; 549]

enviousness *n* [➡ENVY AND JEALOUSY; 549]

environment 1 *n* **nature**, ecosystem, earth, world. [➡NATURE AND THE ENVIRONMENT; 1038] 2 *n* **surroundings**, setting, situation, atmosphere, milieu (*formal*), environs, location. [➡PLACE; 1064] 3 *n* **background**, upbringing, circumstances, conditions, situation, milieu (*formal*). [➡SITUATIONS; 71]

environmental *adj* **ecological**, conservation, conservational, environmentally friendly, ecofriendly, green. [➡ECONOMICAL AND RESOURCEFUL; 208]

environmentalist *n* **ecologist**, conservationist, preservationist, green. [➡PHILOSOPHICAL AND POLITICAL THINKERS; 782]

environs *n* **vicinity**, surroundings, locality, environment, neighbourhood. [➡PLACE; 1064]

envisage (*formal*) *v* **imagine**, visualize, envision, foresee, predict, see, picture. [➡PREDICT AND ANTICIPATE; 751]

envision *v* **imagine**, envisage, foresee, predict, visualize, see, picture. [➡PREDICT AND ANTICIPATE; 751]

envoy *n* **representative**, diplomat, emissary, herald, messenger, ambassador, legate. [➡REPRESENTATIVES AND PATRONS; 968]

envy 1 *n* **jealousy**, greed, bitterness, resentment, spite. [➡ENVY AND JEALOUSY; 549] *Opposite:* goodwill. 2 *v* **covet**, resent, begrudge, grudge. [➡DESIRE AND WANT; 580]

epaulette *n* **decoration**, insignia, strap, chevron. [➡ORNAMENTS AND DECORATIONS; 1247]

ephemeral *adj* **short-lived**, passing, fleeting, brief, momentary, temporary, transitory, transient, evanescent. [➡HAPPENING QUICKLY; 104] *Opposite:* lasting.

ephemerally *adv* **briefly**, fleetingly, temporarily, momentarily, transitorily, transiently, evanescently. [➡FINITENESS, VARIABILITY, AND TRANSIENCE; 96] *Opposite:* lastingly.

ephemeralness *n* **brevity**, transitoriness, transience, fleetingness, temporariness, evanescence, momentariness. [➡FINITENESS, VARIABILITY, AND TRANSIENCE; 96] *Opposite:* timelessness.

epic 1 *n* **classic**, blockbuster (*informal*), costume drama, period piece, extravaganza. [➡FICTION AND DRAMA; 913] 2 *adj* **marathon**, heroic, classic, larger-than-life, impressive, ambitious, grand. [➡EXTRAORDINARY: AMAZING; 205] *Opposite:* minuscule.

epicene *adj* [➡GENDER IDENTITY AND SEXUALITY; 932]

epicentre *n* [➡CENTRAL PARTS OF PHYSICAL OBJECTS; 1250]

epicure *n* **gourmet**, gastronome, connoisseur, epicurean, bon vivant (*literary*), foodie (*informal*). [➡EATERS, GOURMETS, AND DIETARY CHOICES; 715]

epicurean 1 *adj* **hedonistic**, decadent, pleasure-seeking, pleasure-loving, sensualist. [➡PLEASURE-SEEKING AND EXCESS; 885] *Opposite:* Spartan. 2 *adj* **gastronomic**, gourmet, connoisseur, gourmand, decadent, foodie (*informal*). [➡PLEASURE-SEEKING AND EXCESS; 885] *Opposite:* ascetic. 3 *see* **epicure**.

epicureanism *n* [➡PLEASURE-SEEKING AND EXCESS; 885]

epidemic 1 *n* **plague**, outbreak, endemic, scourge, contagion, pandemic. [➡SICKNESS; 730] 2 *n* **spate**, wave, rash, craze, increase, rise. [➡SUDDEN EVENT; 52] *Opposite:* decrease. 3 *adj* **widespread**, wide-ranging, prevalent, rampant, sweeping, rife, endemic. [➡PRESENT AND AVAILABLE; 11] *Opposite:* restricted.

See Compare and Contrast at **widespread**.

epidermis *n* **skin**, hide, flesh, cuticle, integument, layer. [➡THE SKIN; 721]

epigram *n* **witticism**, saying, axiom, ditty, rhyme, quip. [➡FIGURES OF SPEECH; 674]

epilogue *n* **conclusion**, coda, speech, monologue. [➡PARTS OF BOOKS AND DOCUMENTS; 594] *Opposite:* prologue.

episode 1 *n* **incident**, affair, chapter, event, occurrence, experience, period. [➡EVENTS AND OCCURRENCES; 35] 2 *n* **occurrence**, incidence, attack, outbreak, bout, spell. [➡EVENTS AND OCCURRENCES; 35] 3 *n* **chapter**, part, section, instalment. [➡PARTS OF BOOKS AND DOCUMENTS; 594]

episodic 1 *adj* **serialized**, discontinuous, divided. [➡NEVER AND INFREQUENCY; 97] 2 *adj* **sporadic**, intermittent, periodic, discontinuous, intervallic, occasional, irregular. [➡FINITENESS, VARIABILITY, AND TRANSIENCE; 96] *Opposite:* regular.

epistle (*formal*) *n* **letter**, missive, communication, message, communiqué, dispatch. [➡LETTERS AND WRITTEN MESSAGES; 585]

epitaph *n* **inscription**, legend, caption, epigraph. [➡BURIAL AND PREPARATION FOR BURIAL; 929]

epithet *n* **nickname**, description, appellation (*formal*), handle (*slang*), label, sobriquet, moniker (*slang*). [➡NAME AND DESCRIBE; 666]

epitome *n* **essence**, personification, embodiment, quintessence, archetype, height. [➡PERFECT EXAMPLES AND EMBODIMENTS; 67] *Opposite:* antithesis.

epitomize *v* **typify**, characterize, exemplify, personify, embody, symbolize. [➡REPRESENT SOMETHING OR SOMEBODY; 59]

epoch *n* **era**, age, time, period, date, aeon. [➡EPOCHS AND ERAS; 89]

epoch-making *adj* **historic**, crucial, important, momentous, earthshattering, pivotal, key, consequential. [➡IMPORTANT; 195] *Opposite:* insignificant.

epoxide *type of* **plastic**. [➡PLASTICS; 1133]

equable *adj* **composed**, calm, easygoing, unflappable, placid, level-headed, phlegmatic, serene, tranquil, dispassionate. [➡CONFIDENCE AND COMPOSURE; 500] *Opposite:* jumpy.

equably *adv* **calmly**, evenly, serenely, tranquilly, coolly, composedly, dispassionately, placidly, level-headedly, steadily. [➡GOOD-TEMPERED AND HUMOROUS; 628] *Opposite:* jumpily.

equal 1 *adj* **identical**, equivalent, like, alike, the same, one and the same. [➡SAMENESS; 151] *Opposite:* unequal. 2 *adj* **on a par**, even, uniform, level, on level pegging, on a plane (*US*). [➡EQUALITY; 155] *Opposite:* unequal. 3 *n* **match**, equivalent, counterpart, parallel, compeer (*formal*), peer. [➡EQUALITY; 155] 4 *v* **come to**, amount to, equate, make, correspond, total. [➡AMOUNT TO AND EQUAL; 70] 5 *v* **match**, rival, keep pace with, copy, meet, approximate. [➡EQUALITY; 155]

equality *n* **parity**, fairness, equivalence, likeness, equal opportunity, impartiality, egalitarianism. [➡EQUALITY; 155] *Opposite:* inequality.

equalize *v* **match**, level, even out, align, line up, balance. [➡EQUALITY; 155] *Opposite:* differentiate.

equally 1 *adv* **similarly**, likewise, in the same way, by the same token, alike, correspondingly, so. [➡ALSO; 136] *Opposite:* conversely. 2 *adv* **evenly**, uniformly, regularly, equivalently, alike, proportionately, correspondingly. [➡EQUALITY; 155] *Opposite:* unequally.

equal to *adj* **up to**, able to, capable of, fit for, ready for. [➡TALENTED AND SKILFUL; 528]

equanimity *n* **composure**, calmness, level-headedness, equability, self-control, poise. [➡CALMNESS, CONFIDENCE, AND COMPOSURE; 537] *Opposite:* volatility.

equate *v* **associate**, liken, link, connect, parallel, compare. [➡CREATING CONNECTIONS; 145] *Opposite:* contrast.

equation *n* **reckoning**, calculation, comparison, equivalence, equality, balance. [➡MATHS; 598]

equestrian *adj* **riding**, equine, show jumping, horse-racing, horsey, horse-riding. [➡HORSE; 985]

equidistant *adj* **halfway between**, midway between, between, in between, intermediate, middle. [➡RELATIVE LOCATION; 162]

equilateral *adj* **symmetrical**, regular, square, rectangular, triangular. [➡ANGULAR SHAPE; 1216]

equilibrium *n* **balance**, symmetry, steadiness, equipoise (*formal*), stability, evenness. [➡HARMONY; 156] *Opposite:* imbalance.

equine *adj* [➡HORSE; 985]

equinox *n* [➡TIMES OF YEAR; 88]

equip 1 *v* **provide**, furnish (*formal*), endow, fit out, set up, give. [➡EQUIP AND SUPPLY; 436] 2 *v* **prepare**, train, school, arm, kit out. [➡INSTRUCT AND TEACH; 610]

equipment *n* **tools**, apparatus, gear (*informal*), utensils, paraphernalia, kit. [➡DEVICES; 1114]

equitable (*formal*) *adj* **fair**, evenhanded, reasonable, justifiable, rightful, impartial, just, unbiased. [➡EQUALITY; 155] *Opposite:* unfair.

equity (*formal*) *n* **fairness**, evenhandedness, impartiality, justice, fair play, justness, parity. [➡EQUALITY; 155] *Opposite:* injustice.

equivalence *n* **correspondence**, sameness, likeness, similarity, equality, uniformity. [➡EQUALITY; 155] *Opposite:* difference.

equivalent 1 *adj* **equal**, corresponding, correspondent, alike, same, comparable. [➡EQUALITY; 155] *Opposite:* different. 2 *n* **counterpart**, equal, opposite number, parallel, twin, peer. [➡EQUALITY; 155]

equivocal *adj* **vague**, ambiguous, confusing, ambivalent, misleading, oblique, unclear, shifty, evasive. [➡RETICENT AND UNFORTHCOMING; 632] *Opposite:* unambiguous.

equivocate *v* **prevaricate**, vacillate, be evasive, quibble, beat about the bush, fudge (*informal*). [➡WITHHOLD INFORMATION; 688] *Opposite:* speak your mind.

equivocation *n* **vagueness**, indirectness, ambiguity, prevarication, weasel words (*informal*). [➡WITHHOLD INFORMATION; 688] *Opposite:* directness.

era *n* **age**, epoch, aeon, time, period, years, date. [➡EPOCHS AND ERAS; 89]

eradicate *v* **eliminate**, get rid of, wipe out (*informal*), destroy, exterminate, do away with, stamp out, remove. [➡GET RID OF SOMETHING; 452] *Opposite:* introduce.

eradication *n* **abolition**, purge, annihilation, extermination, obliteration, extinction. [➡END; 54] *Opposite:* introduction.

erase *v* **rub out**, remove, delete, wipe out (*informal*), expunge, obliterate. [➡DELETE AND ERASE; 340]

erasure *n* **removal**, destruction, eradication, elimination, deletion, obliteration. [➡REMOVE SOMETHING; 339]

erect 1 *v* **build**, construct, assemble, set up, raise, put up. [➡BUILD; 353] *Opposite:* demolish. 2 *v* **create**, set up, found, initiate, establish, institute. [➡INSTITUTE AND INAUGURATE; 349] 3 *adj* **straight**, upright, vertical, rigid, stiff, perpendicular. [➡ORIENTATION AND ALIGNMENT; 1222] *Opposite:* prone.

erection 1 *n* (*formal*) **building**, structure, construction. [➡BUILDING AND ARCHITECTURE; 1075] 2 *n* **building**, construction, assembly, creation, formation. [➡CREATION; 347]

eremite (*literary*) *n* [➡SOLITARY PEOPLE; 942]

erode *v* **wear away**, wear down, corrode, eat away, eat into, grind down. [➡CHANGE OF SIZE: SMALLER; 394]

eroded *adj* **weathered**, worn, weather-beaten. [➡IN BAD REPAIR; 1233]

erosion *n* **corrosion**, attrition, destruction, loss. [➡EROSION AND WEATHERING; 1055]

erotic *adj* **sexy**, sensual, stimulating, suggestive, amatory, erogenous. [➡PHYSICALLY PLEASANT; 187] *Opposite:* off-putting.

err (*formal*) *v* **go wrong**, blunder, slip up (*informal*), stumble, go astray, get something wrong. [➡MESS UP AND MAKE MISTAKES; 473]

errand *n* **task**, duty, run, chore, job, mission. [➡WORK IN GENERAL; 298]

errant *adj* **wayward**, sinful, naughty, misbehaving, delinquent, rowdy. [➡MORALLY BAD; 776] *Opposite:* well-behaved.

erratic *adj* **unpredictable**, unreliable, inconsistent, irregular, changeable, intermittent, uneven, fitful, variable. [➡FINITENESS, VARIABILITY, AND TRANSIENCE; 96] *Opposite:* consistent.

erroneous *adj* **mistaken**, flawed, wrong, specious, inaccurate, incorrect, invalid, untrue. [➡INCORRECT AND ERRONEOUS; 223] *Opposite:* correct.

error *n* **mistake**, fault, blunder, inaccuracy, miscalculation, boob (*informal*), slip, slip-up (*informal*), boo-boo (*informal*), oversight. [➡MISTAKES; 251]

See Compare and Contrast at **mistake**.

ersatz (*disapproving*) *adj* **faux**, artificial, substitute, reproduction, imitation, simulated, false, mock, synthetic. [➡FALSE AND UNREAL; 174] *Opposite:* genuine.

erstwhile *adj* **former**, previous, past, old, earlier, ex, sometime, onetime. [➡PAST; 84] *Opposite:* current.

erudite *adj* **scholarly**, knowledgeable, well-educated, well-read, cultured, learned, intellectual, bookish, literary, academic, studious. [➡LEVEL OF EDUCATION AND SOPHISTICATION; 894] *Opposite:* uneducated.

erudition *n* **knowledge**, learnedness, education, learning, culture, sophistication, scholarship. [➡KNOWLEDGE AND WISDOM; 559] *Opposite:* ignorance.

See Compare and Contrast at **knowledge**.

erupt 1 *v* **explode**, blow up, break out, flare up, go off, go bang, burst forth, vent. [➡SUDDENLY COME INTO EXISTENCE; 2] *Opposite:* subside. 2 *v* **blow your top** (*informal*), explode, lose your temper, hit the roof, blow a fuse (*informal*), fly off the handle (*informal*). [➡GIVING VENT TO EMOTIONS; 680] *Opposite:* hold back.

eruption *n* **outbreak**, outburst, explosion, upsurge, epidemic, wave, discharge, emission. [➡SUDDEN EVENT; 52]

escalate *v* **intensify**, worsen, heighten, go from bad to worse, deteriorate, spiral, increase, rocket, accelerate, grow rapidly. [➡CHANGE OF INTENSITY: MORE; 395] *Opposite:* improve.

escalating *adj* **mounting**, rising, intensifying, ever-increasing, swelling, increasing, growing, accelerating. [➡CHANGE OF INTENSITY: MORE; 395] *Opposite:* diminishing.

escalation *n* **rise**, growth, boom, increase, climb, acceleration, appreciation, intensification. [➡CHANGE OF INTENSITY: MORE; 395] *Opposite:* reduction.

escalator 1 *n* **moving staircase**, staircase, stairway, stairs. [➡STAIRS AND STOREYS; 1101] 2 *part of* **building**. [➡PARTS OF A BUILDING; 1094]

escapade *n* **adventure**, jaunt, antic, caper, spree, exploit. [➡EVENTS AND OCCURRENCES; 35]

escape 1 *v* **flee**, run away, get away, break out, run off, get out, break away from, bolt, cut and run, abscond. [➡RUN AWAY AND AVOID; 10] *Opposite:* capture. 2 *v* **leak out**, leak, drip, seep, flow, drain, discharge, issue. [➡EMIT AND EMANATE; 362] 3 *v* **avoid**, evade, dodge, elude, shake off. [➡AVOID OR ESCAPE CONTACT; 419] *Opposite:* face. 4 *n* **seepage**, leakage, leak, outflow, discharge, drip, spurt, emission. [➡PROCEED AND GO; 306] 5 *n* **flight**, getaway, break, breakout, escaping, running away, running off, exodus. [➡END; 54] 6 *n* **diversion**, distraction, pastime, leisure activity, escapism. [➡LEISURE AND RECREATION; 874]

escapee *n* **runaway**, fugitive, absconder, deserter, fleer. [➡RUNAWAYS AND ABSENTEES; 9]

escapism *n* **diversion**, distraction, entertainment, relaxation, daydreaming, avoidance, escape. [➡ENTERTAINMENT; 872]

escapist *adj* **diverting**, distracting, entertaining, relaxing, fantasy. [➡CALMING; 189] *Opposite:* realistic.

escarpment *n* **cliff**, bluff, scarp, ridge, incline, slope. [➡GEOLOGICAL FEATURES; 1056]

eschew *v* **avoid**, shun, abjure (*literary*), have nothing to do with, steer clear of, give a wide berth to, fight shy of, turn your back on, disdain, abstain from. [➡NOT DO AND REFUSE TO DO; 275] *Opposite:* embrace.

escort 1 *n* **guide**, attendant, minder, bodyguard, chaperon, aide, companion. [➡SUPPORTERS, PROTECTORS, AND COMPATRIOTS; 970] 2 *v* **accompany**, guide, usher, lead, attend, shepherd, chaperon, conduct. [➡ACCOMPANY AND FOLLOW; 338]

escritoire *type of* **table**. [➡FURNITURE; 858]

esoteric *adj* **obscure**, mysterious, abstruse, impenetrable, cryptic, arcane, secret, occult. [➡POSITIVELY COMPLEX OR COMPLICATED; 218] *Opposite:* straightforward.

ESP *n* **extra-sensory perception**, psychic powers, clairvoyance, second sight, telepathy, fortune telling, palm reading, prophecy, soothsaying, divining. [➡PREDICT AND ANTICIPATE; 751]

espadrille *type of* **shoe**. [➡FOOTWEAR; 871]

esparto *type of* **grass**. [➡GRASS; 1031]

especial *adj* **special**, unusual, exceptional, extraordinary, outstanding, remarkable, notable, marked, striking, signal. [➡EXTRAORDINARY: AMAZING; 205] *Opposite:* ordinary.

especially 1 *adv* **particularly**, in particular, specially, above all, more than ever, expressly, specifically, exclusively, mainly, chiefly, principally. [➡MAINLY AND PRIMARILY; 138] 2 *adv* **exceptionally**, remarkably, notably, markedly, outstandingly, unusually, uniquely. [➡TO A GREAT EXTENT; 130]

esplanade *type of* **minor road**. [➡ROADS; 1105]

espousal *n* **adoption**, backing, support, championship, promotion, advocacy, taking up, siding with. [➡AGREE; 646] *Opposite:* opposition.

espouse 1 *v* **take up**, adopt, support, back, advocate, promote, embrace, champion. [➡APPROVE AND CONFIRM; 647] *Opposite:* oppose. 2 *v* (*archaic*) **marry**, wed, get hitched (*informal*), tie the knot (*informal*), walk down the aisle. [➡ESTABLISHING RELATIONSHIPS WITH OTHERS; 974]

espresso *type of* **coffee**. [➡DRINKS; 1186]

espy (*formal*) *v* **notice**, spy, catch sight of, spot, sight, see, observe, discern, descry (*literary*), discover, make out. [➡SEE; 700]

essay 1 *n* **paper**, thesis, dissertation, composition, article, treatise, theme. [➡ANALYTICAL NONFICTION WRITING; 593] 2 *v* (*formal*) **try**, endeavour, strive, have a shot, have a go (*informal*), have a crack (*informal*), attempt. [➡ATTEMPT AN ACTION; 262]

essence 1 *n* **spirit**, core, heart, quintessence, crux, kernel, soul, principle, substance, lifeblood. [➡MOST IMPORTANT THING; 198] 2 *n* **concentrate**, extract, tincture, distillate, concentration, distillation. [➡PERSONAL HYGIENE; 492]

essential 1 *adj* **necessary**, vital, indispensable, important, crucial, critical, needed. [➡NECESSARY AND ESSENTIAL; 197] *Opposite:* unnecessary. 2 *adj* **fundamental**, basic, elemental, key, central, chief, main, principal, cardinal. [➡FUNDAMENTAL; 196] *Opposite:* secondary.

See Compare and Contrast at **necessary**.

essentially 1 *adv* **fundamentally**, basically, in essence, in effect, really, in actual fact, to all intents and purposes, principally. [➡SUMMARIZING EXPRESSIONS; 623] 2 *adv* **effectively**, more or less, broadly, in the main, for the most part, largely, to a large extent. [➡MAINLY AND PRIMARILY; 138]

essentials *n* **basics**, fundamentals, prerequisites, rudiments, necessities, nuts and bolts (*informal*), requisites, nitty-gritty (*informal*). [➡MOST IMPORTANT THING; 198] *Opposite:* frills.

establish 1 *v* **set up**, found, institute, start, create, begin, launch, bring about, form, inaugurate. [➡INSTITUTE AND INAUGURATE; 349] *Opposite:* close down. 2 *v* **ascertain** (*formal*), determine, find out, prove, confirm, verify, show, corroborate, authenticate. [➡LEARN AND DISCOVER; 763] *Opposite:* disprove.

established *adj* **recognized**, well-known, traditional, conventional, customary, time-honoured, proven, reputable. [➡KNOWN AND FAMOUS; 182] *Opposite:* new.

establishment 1 *n* **founding** (*dated*), formation, creation, setting up, institution, launch, establishing, instituting, bringing about. [➡BEGINNING; 53] *Opposite:* dissolution. 2 *n* **institution**, business, firm, company, concern, enterprise, corporation, outfit (*informal*), organization. [➡INSTITUTIONS; 791] 3 *n* **authorities**, powers that be, the ruling classes, the established order, the system. [➡GOVERNMENT AND POLITICS; 805]

estate 1 *n* **plantation**, land, park, lands, parkland, domain, manor, country estate. [➡THE COUNTRYSIDE AND OUTDOOR SPACES; 1070] 2 *n* **area**, zone, industrial estate, business park, commercial centre, development, housing estate. [➡HUMAN SETTLEMENTS; 1069] 3 *n* **assets**, property, holdings, worth, fortune, wealth. [➡FINANCIAL ASSETS; 463]

estate car *type of* **car**. [➡BIKES, CARS, AND CARRIAGES; 1148]

esteem 1 *v* **appreciate**, cherish, hold dear, venerate, value, respect, admire, approve, honour, prize. [➡LIKE, LOVE, VALUE AND ENJOY; 579] *Opposite:* scorn. 2 *n* **regard**, respect, admiration, high regard, reverence, approval, honour, good opinion, appreciation. [➡LOVE, RESPECT, AND GOODWILL; 550] *Opposite:* contempt.

See Compare and Contrast at **regard**.

esteemed *adj* **respected**, valued, honoured, revered, admired, well-regarded, venerated. [➡POPULAR AND WANTED; 221] *Opposite:* scorned.

estimable *adj* **admirable**, worthy, deserving, laudable, venerable, good, reputable, prized, praiseworthy. [➡ADMIRABLE AND COMMENDABLE; 186] *Opposite:* unimpressive.

estimate 1 *n* **approximation**, estimation, guess, educated guess, guesstimate (*informal*), ballpark figure (*informal*), evaluation, assessment, appraisal. [➡EXAMINE AND ASSESS; 754] 2 *v* **approximate**, guess, guesstimate (*informal*), assess, reckon, value, appraise. [➡ASSESS QUANTITY; 758] *Opposite:* calculate. 3 *n* **quote**, price, estimation, valuation, costing, assessment. [➡SCORES AND EVALUATIONS; 599] *Opposite:* cost.

estimated *adj* **projected**, assessed, valued, appraised. [➡EXAMINE AND ASSESS; 754]

estimation 1 *n* **opinion**, assessment, inference, evaluation, view, belief, judgment. [➡POINT OF VIEW; 768] *Opposite:* fact. 2 *n* **educated guess**, approximation, estimate, guesstimate (*informal*), assessment, valuation, appraisal, ballpark figure (*informal*). [➡ASSESS QUANTITY; 758]

estop (*archaic*) *v* **prevent**, stop, thwart, prohibit, halt, forbid, ward off. [➡REFUSE PERMISSION AND NOT ALLOW; 671]

estranged *adj* **alienated**, separated, apart, at odds, on bad terms. [➡RELATIONSHIP TO ANOTHER; 973]

estrangement *n* **separation**, hostility, rupture, distancing, disaffection, falling-out, discord, breakup, split, division, unfriendliness, schism, breach, alienation, disagreement, divorce, parting of the ways. [➡RELATIONSHIP TO ANOTHER; 973] *Opposite:* reconciliation.

estuary *n* **river mouth**, bay, inlet, sound, creek. [➡RIVERS, LAKES, AND STREAMS; 1042] *Opposite:* source.

e-tailing *n* [➡E-COMMERCE; 1128]

et al. *adv* **and company**, and co., and others, et cetera, and the rest. [➡WRITTEN CONVENTIONS; 600]

etc. *adv* **et cetera**, and so on, and so forth, and that (*informal*), and all that (*informal*), and the like, and the rest. [➡WRITTEN CONVENTIONS; 600; ➡FOREIGN WORDS AND PHRASES; 673]

etch *v* **engrave**, scratch, scrape, cut, incise, score, carve. [➡CREATE IMAGES; 357]

etching *n* **engraving**, drawing, print, design, impression, imprint, inscription. [➡ARTWORKS; 898]

eternal *adj* **everlasting**, undying, unending, never-ending, perpetual, endless, ceaseless, timeless, interminable, infinite, immortal. [➡PERMANENCE: WITHOUT END; 94] *Opposite:* transient.

eternal life *n* [➡RELIGIOUS CONCEPTS; 777]

eternity *n* **time without end**, perpetuity, infinity, all time, ever and a day. [➡LONG PERIOD OF TIME; 92]

ether (*literary*) *n* **air**, atmosphere, heaven, sky. [➡THE EARTH'S ATMOSPHERE; 1040]

ethereal 1 *adj* **ghostly**, otherworldly, unearthly, wraithlike, eerie. [➡VAGUENESS; 244] *Opposite:* earthly. 2 *adj* **waiflike**, frail, delicate, airy, insubstantial, light, fragile. [➡FRAGILE; 1208] *Opposite:* substantial.

ethic *n* **moral belief**, ethos, idea, principle, code, tenet (*formal*). [➡IDEA AND THOUGHT; 771]

ethical *adj* **moral**, principled, right, fair, decent, proper, fitting, virtuous, just, honourable, upright. [➡MORALLY GOOD; 775] *Opposite:* unethical.

ethics *n* **principles**, morals, beliefs, moral code, moral principles, moral values, integrity, conscience. [➡MORAL CONCEPTS; 774]

ethnic *adj* **cultural**, traditional, folkloric, racial, indigenous, national. [➡BELONGING OR RELATING TO PEOPLE; 943]

ethnicity *n* **culture**, way of life, origin, background, traditions, customs. [➡LIFESTYLE; 881]

ethos *n* **philosophy**, beliefs, principles, code, character, tenet (*formal*), attitude, spirit, moral belief. [➡MORAL CONCEPTS; 774]

etiquette *n* **manners**, good manners, protocol, custom, propriety, decorum, politeness. [➡GOOD MANNERS AND SOCIAL SKILLS; 521] *Opposite:* bad manners.

etymology *n* [➡ASPECTS OF LANGUAGE; 683]

eucalyptus *type of* **evergreen tree**. [➡EVERGREEN AND CONIFEROUS TREES; 1029]

eulogize (*formal*) *v* **praise**, extol, laud, sing the praises of, praise to the skies, exalt (*formal*), wax lyrical (*literary*), rave about, glorify, acclaim, hail. [➡PRAISE AND ENCOURAGE; 648] *Opposite:* criticize.

eulogy *n* **tribute**, acclamation, acclaim, exaltation (*formal*), praise, homage, panegyric (*formal*), encomium (*formal*). [➡PRAISE AND ENCOURAGE; 648] *Opposite:* criticism.

euphemism *n* **neutral term**, understatement, rewording, weasel word (*informal*), code word, synonym. [➡FIGURES OF SPEECH; 674] *Opposite:* dysphemism.

euphemistic *adj* **inoffensive**, polite, neutral, understated, indirect, oblique, softened, innocuous. [➡VAGUENESS; 244] *Opposite:* dysphemistic.

euphonious *adj* [➡SOFT OR PLEASANT SOUNDS; 1264]

euphoniousness *n* [➡SOFT OR PLEASANT SOUNDS; 1264]

euphonium *type of* **brass instrument**. [➡MUSICAL INSTRUMENTS; 910]

euphony *n* [➡SOFT OR PLEASANT SOUNDS; 1264]

euphoria *n* **elation**, ecstasy, jubilation, rapture, excitement, exhilaration, bliss, exultation, joy. [➡PLEASURE, EXCITEMENT, AND ELATION; 535] *Opposite:* despair.

euphoric *adj* **overjoyed**, elated, ecstatic, joyful, joyous, over the moon, enraptured (*formal*), excited, exhilarated, blissful, exultant. [➡PLEASURE, EXCITEMENT, AND ELATION; 535] *Opposite:* despairing.

evacuate 1 *v* **empty**, abandon, withdraw from, leave, vacate, relinquish, clear. [➡RUN AWAY AND AVOID; 10] *Opposite:* fill. 2 *v* **send away**, remove from, move out of, clear from. [➡EJECT AND EXCLUDE; 341] *Opposite:* bring in.

evacuation *n* **removal**, clearing, emptying, withdrawal, flight, emigration, migration, departure, retreat, exodus. [➡EJECT AND EXCLUDE; 341] *Opposite:* influx.

evacuee *n* **refugee**, émigré, emigrant, migrant. [➡PEOPLE LIVING AWAY FROM HOME; 887]

evade 1 *v* **avoid**, dodge, escape, elude, shirk, skirt, duck, sidestep. [➡NOT PAY ATTENTION; 765] 2 *v* **equivocate**, prevaricate, hedge, stonewall (*informal*), fudge (*informal*). [➡WITHHOLD INFORMATION; 688]

evaluate *v* **assess**, appraise, weigh up, gauge, estimate, calculate, weigh, value, price. [➡ASSESS QUALITY; 756]

evaluation *n* **assessment**, appraisal, estimation, calculation, valuation, estimate, costing. [➡SCORES AND EVALUATIONS; 599]

evaluator *n* **assessor**, surveyor, inspector. [➡ADVISERS, JUDGES, AND ARBITERS; 971]

evanescence *n* [➡FINITENESS, VARIABILITY, AND TRANSIENCE; 96]

evanescent *adj* **short-lived**, fleeting, momentary, ephemeral, passing, brief, transient. [➡FINITENESS, VARIABILITY, AND TRANSIENCE; 96] *Opposite:* permanent.

evangelical *adj* **enthusiastic**, fervent, eager, zealous, keen, intense. [➡RELIGIONS AND RELIGIOUS PRACTICES; 778] *Opposite:* apathetic.

evangelist *n* [➡RELIGIOUS PEOPLE; 779]

evangelize *v* [➡RELIGIONS AND RELIGIOUS PRACTICES; 778]

evaporate *v* **vanish**, fade away, fade, disappear, melt away, disperse, dissolve, vaporize. [➡DISAPPEAR; 4] *Opposite:* solidify.

evaporation *n* **vaporization**, drying up, loss, vanishing, disappearance, dehydration. [➡END; 54]

evasion 1 *n* **avoidance**, dodging, elusion, circumvention, fudging (*informal*), skirting, shirking, ducking. [➡NOT PAY ATTENTION; 765] 2 *n* **prevarication**, equivocation, hedging, stonewalling (*informal*). [➡WITHHOLD INFORMATION; 688]

evasive *adj* **elusive**, slippery, shifty, indirect, oblique, equivocal, ambiguous, vague, cagey (*informal*), misleading. [➡RETICENT AND UNFORTHCOMING; 632] *Opposite:* direct.

evasiveness *n* **indirectness**, caginess (*informal*), equivocation, shiftiness, elusiveness, ambiguousness, vagueness, slipperiness. [➡RETICENT AND UNFORTHCOMING; 632] *Opposite:* directness.

eve *n* **day before**, evening before, night before. [➡TIMES OF YEAR; 88]

even 1 *adj* **smooth**, flat, level, straight, unfluctuating, uniform. [➡PHYSICAL TEXTURE; 1221] *Opposite:* uneven. 2 *adj* **constant**, steady, uniform, unvarying, unchanging, regular. [➡PERMANENCE: WITHOUT CHANGE; 95] *Opposite:* fluctuating. 3 *adj* **equal**, similar, level, on a par, just as, on level pegging, drawn, at the same time, tied, even-steven (*informal*). [➡EQUALITY; 155] *Opposite:* unequal. 4 *n* (*literary*) **evening**, twilight, dusk, nightfall, sunset, sundown. [➡TIMES OF DAY; 87]

evenhanded *adj* **fair**, impartial, unbiased, just, equitable (*formal*), equal, balanced, dispassionate, nonpartisan, fair-minded. [➡EQUALITY; 155] *Opposite:* biased.

evenhandedly *adv* **fairly**, impartially, justly, equitably (*formal*), equally, dispassionately. [➡EQUALITY; 155] *Opposite:* unfairly.

evenhandedness *n* **fairness**, impartiality, equity (*formal*), justice, neutrality, fair-mindedness, equality. [➡EQUALITY; 155] *Opposite:* partiality.

even if *conj* **though**, albeit, although, even though. [➡ALTHOUGH, NEVERTHELESS, AND DESPITE; 170]

evening *n* **twilight**, sunset, dusk, nightfall, late afternoon, sundown, even (*literary*). [➡TIMES OF DAY; 87] *Opposite:* morning.

evening dress *n* [➡GARMENTS AND OUTFITS; 865]

evening gown (*US*) *type of* **dress**. [➡GARMENTS AND OUTFITS; 865]

even less *adv* **still less**, much less, let alone. [➡NOT; 135] *Opposite:* even more.

evenly *adv* **consistently**, equally, uniformly, steadily, equably, regularly. [➡PHYSICAL TEXTURE; 1221] *Opposite:* irregularly.

even more *adv* **still more**, all the more, yet more. [➡MAINLY AND PRIMARILY; 138] *Opposite:* even less.

evenness *n* **consistency**, sameness, symmetry, uniformity, flatness, steadiness, constancy, levelness. [➡PHYSICAL TEXTURE; 1221] *Opposite:* irregularity.

even out 1 *v* **flatten**, level, smooth, square, align. [➡ARRANGE AND CREATE ORDER; 358] 2 *v* **balance out**, balance, level out, balance up, equalize, make the same, even up, offset. [➡EQUALITY; 155] *Opposite:* unbalance.

even so *adv* **all the same**, nonetheless, be that as it may, nevertheless, yet, despite that, even if, even supposing, still. [➡ALTHOUGH, NEVERTHELESS, AND DESPITE; 170]

event *n* **occasion**, happening, occurrence, incident, affair, episode, experience. [➡EVENTS AND OCCURRENCES; 35]

even-tempered *adj* **calm**, unflappable, equable, placid, imperturbable, serene, steady. [➡CONFIDENCE AND COMPOSURE; 500] *Opposite:* temperamental.

eventful *adj* **exciting**, action-packed, lively, busy, hectic, important, momentous. [➡EMOTIONALLY PLEASANT; 188] *Opposite:* dull.

eventide (*literary*) *n* [➡TIMES OF DAY; 87]

eventual *adj* **ultimate**, final, last, ensuing, subsequent, concluding. [➡AFTER, LAST, AND FOLLOWING; 166] *Opposite:* immediate.

eventuality (*formal*) *n* **possibility**, prospect, case, contingency, outcome, result, consequence, upshot. [➡CHANCE EVENT; 36]

even up *v* **equalize**, stabilize, even out, redress the balance, balance up, square, redress. [➡ARRANGE AND CREATE ORDER; 358] *Opposite:* unbalance.

ever *adv* **always**, forever, eternally, all the time, constantly, continually, perpetually, endlessly, interminably, continuously. [➡PERMANENCE: WITHOUT END; 94] *Opposite:* never.

everglade (*US*) *n* [➡WETLANDS; 1043]

evergreen 1 *adj* **immortal**, perennial, ever popular, classic, old time favourite, timeless, ageless. [➡PERMANENCE: WITHOUT END; 94] *Opposite:* stale. 2 *n* [➡EVERGREEN AND CONIFEROUS TREES; 1029]

evergreen tree

◆ *types of evergreen tree*
bo tree, bunya, carob, cedar, cola, cypress, eucalyptus, fir, fir tree, gum tree, holly, juniper, kahikatea, kauri, larch, mahogany, mangrove, monkey puzzle, pine, redwood, sandalwood, sequoia, spruce, yew

everlasting *adj* **eternal**, endless, ceaseless, never-ending, perpetual, undying, unending, interminable, forever, continuous, permanent. [➡PERMANENCE: WITHOUT END; 94] *Opposite:* transient.

evermore (*literary*) *adv* **forever**, for all time, always, eternally. [➡PERMANENCE: WITHOUT END; 94]

ever-present *adj* **ubiquitous**, chronic, pervasive, omnipresent. [➡PRESENT AND AVAILABLE; 11]

ever so *adv* **extremely**, fantastically, very much so, exceptionally, really, incredibly, awfully, terribly, real (*US informal*). [➡TO A GREAT EXTENT; 130] *Opposite:* not at all.

every *adj* **each**, all, every single, every one. [➡ALL; 126]

everybody *n* **everyone**, all and sundry, one and all, every Tom, Dick, and Harry, every man jack, each one, each person, every person. [➡ALL; 126] *Opposite:* nobody.

everyday *adj* **ordinary**, average, normal, unremarkable, common, commonplace, daily, run-of-the-mill, routine. [➡ORDINARINESS; 245] *Opposite:* extraordinary.

every now and again *adv* [➡NEVER AND INFREQUENCY; 107]

every now and then *adv* **occasionally**, now and then, now and again, once in a while, on occasion, from time to time, every so often, off and on, on and off. [➡NEVER AND INFREQUENCY; 97] *Opposite:* constantly.

everyone *n* **everybody**, all and sundry, one and all, every Tom, Dick, and Harry, every man jack, each person, each one, every person. [➡ALL; 126] *Opposite:* no one.

every so often *adv* [➡NEVER AND INFREQUENCY; 97]

everything *n* **all**, the whole thing, the lot, the whole lot, entirety, the whole shebang (*informal*), the whole kit and caboodle (*informal*), the whole enchilada (*US slang*), the whole ball of wax (*US informal*). [➡ALL; 126] *Opposite:* nothing.

everywhere *adv* **all over**, ubiquitously, far and wide, all over the place (*informal*), the world over, universally. [➡GENERAL LOCATIONS; 159]

evict *v* **throw out**, expel, turn out, eject, remove, force out, kick out (*informal*), dislodge, put out. [➡EJECT AND EXCLUDE; 341] *Opposite:* install.

eviction *n* **removal**, expulsion, ejection, throwing out, kicking out (*informal*), exclusion, dislodgment. [➡EJECT AND EXCLUDE; 341]

evidence 1 *n* **indication**, sign, signal, mark, suggestion, proof. [➡EVIDENCE AND PROOF; 69] 2 *n* **proof**, confirmation, facts, data, substantiation, verification, support, testimony. [➡EVIDENCE AND PROOF; 69] 3 *v* **show**, demonstrate, evince, make clear, prove, verify, substantiate, corroborate, support. [➡CAUSE TO APPEAR; 5]

evident *adj* **obvious**, plain, apparent, clear, manifest, palpable, unmistakable, marked, patent, distinct. [➡CERTAIN; 175] *Opposite:* obscure.

evidently 1 *adv* **obviously**, clearly, plainly, manifestly, palpably, unmistakably, patently, markedly, distinctly. [➡PERCEPTIBLE; 25] 2 *adv* **apparently**, seemingly, as far as we know, it would seem, as far as one can tell. [➡UNCERTAIN; 176]

evil 1 *adj* **wicked**, malevolent, sinful, malicious, criminal, immoral. [➡MORALLY BAD; 776] *Opposite:* good. 2 *adj* **foul**, vile, nasty, horrible, unpleasant, revolting, disgusting, obnoxious. [➡DISGUSTING AND REPULSIVE; 231] *Opposite:* pleasant. 3 *n* **wickedness**, malevolence, sin, iniquity, vice, immorality. [➡MORALLY BAD; 776] *Opposite:* good.

evildoer *n* **malefactor** (*formal*), wrongdoer, sinner, criminal, offender, delinquent, villain. [➡VILLAINS AND THUGS; 947] *Opposite:* benefactor.

evilness *n* **wickedness**, badness, evil, immorality, sinfulness, vice. [➡MORALLY BAD; 776] *Opposite:* goodness.

evil spirit *n* [➡RELIGIOUS CONCEPTS; 777]

evince *v* **show**, display, reveal, exhibit, manifest, demonstrate, make clear. [➡CAUSE TO APPEAR; 5] *Opposite:* conceal.

eviscerate *v* [➡WOUND A PERSON OR ANIMAL; 384]

evocation *n* **recreation**, elicitation, recall, air, hint, trace, suggestion. [➡SUGGEST, HINT, AND COMMENT; 613]

evocative *adj* **reminiscent**, suggestive, redolent, haunting. [➡INTERESTING AND MEANINGFUL; 191]

evocatively *adv* **reminiscently**, hauntingly, suggestively, redolently, emotively. [➡ELOQUENT, TALKATIVE AND LONG-WINDED; 633]

evoke *v* **call to mind**, bring to mind, suggest, call up, induce, arouse, remind, stir up, conjure, educe (*formal*), draw out. [➡REMIND; 748] *Opposite:* suppress.

evolution *n* **development**, fruition, growth, progress, progression, advancement. [➡PROGRESS AND ADVANCEMENT; 214] *Opposite:* regression.

evolve *v* **develop**, grow, progress, advance, go forward, change. [➡GRADUALLY COME INTO EXISTENCE; 1] *Opposite:* regress.

ewe *type of* **female animal**. [➡MALE OR FEMALE ANIMAL; 978]

ewer *n* **jug**, pitcher, vessel, bottle, container, pot. [➡TABLEWARE, CUTLERY, AND KITCHENWARE; 861]

ex 1 *adj* **former**, sometime, onetime, erstwhile, lapsed. [➡PAST; 84] *Opposite:* future. 2 *n* (*informal*) [➡SEXUAL AND ROMANTIC RELATIONSHIPS; 964]

exacerbate *v* **make worse**, worsen, aggravate, impair, intensify. [➡WORSEN SOMETHING; 381] *Opposite:* soothe.

exact 1 *adj* **correct**, precise, accurate, strict, faithful, literal. [➡EXACT; 204] *Opposite:* approximate. 2 *adj* **careful**, meticulous, precise, particular, thorough, rigorous, strict, scrupulous. [➡POSITIVE INTELLECTUAL CHARACTERISTICS; 525] *Opposite:* careless. 3 *v* **demand**, obtain, extort, extract, wrest, pinch, take. [➡REQUEST AND DEMAND; 664]

exacting *adj* **demanding**, testing, challenging, rigorous, tough, thorough, onerous. [➡DIFFICULTY AND COMPLEXITY; 243] *Opposite:* easy.

exactitude *n* **precision**, correctness, accuracy, meticulousness, exactness, faithfulness, scrupulousness, thoroughness, rigour, closeness, literalness. [➡EXACT; 204] *Opposite:* carelessness.

exactly *adv* **precisely**, just, accurately, closely, faithfully, correctly, unerringly. [➡EXACT; 204] *Opposite:* approximately.

exactness *n* **precision**, accuracy, exactitude, correctness, meticulousness, strictness, faithfulness, thoroughness, scrupulousness. [➡EXACT; 204] *Opposite:* vagueness.

exaggerate *v* **overstress**, embellish, embroider, make a mountain out of a molehill, inflate, lay on, amplify, overstate. [➡CLAIM, INSIST, AND EMPHASIZE; 615] *Opposite:* understate.

exaggerated *adj* **overstated**, inflated, embroidered, embellished, blown up, larger-than-life, extravagant, hyperbolic. [➡BIZARRE AND PECULIAR; 258] *Opposite:* understated.

exaggeration *n* **overstatement**, hyperbole, embellishment, embroidery, overemphasis, overestimation, amplification. [➡CLAIM, INSIST, AND EMPHASIZE; 615] *Opposite:* understatement.

exalt (*formal*) 1 *v* **promote**, raise, elevate, intensify, boost, lift. [➡CHANGE OF INTENSITY: MORE; 395] 2 *v* **praise**, laud, acclaim, applaud, pay tribute to, extol, lionize, revere, sing the praises of. [➡PRAISE AND ENCOURAGE; 648] *Opposite:* disparage.

exaltation (*formal*) 1 *n* **adulation**, adoration, acclaim, acclamation, praise, applause. [➡PRAISE AND ENCOURAGE; 648] *Opposite:* condemnation. 2 *n* **excitement**, rapture, exhilaration, happiness, joy. [➡PLEASURE, EXCITEMENT, AND ELATION; 535] *Opposite:* despair.

exalted (*formal*) *adj* **high**, lofty, glorious, dignified, illustrious, high-ranking, noble, grand. [➡SUPERIORITY; 153] *Opposite:* lowly.

exam *n* **examination**, test, assessment, paper, question paper, oral exam, theory test. [➡LESSONS, COURSE WORK, AND EXAMINATIONS; 842]

examination 1 *n* **inspection**, scrutiny, checkup, investigation, going-over (*informal*), analysis, consideration, study, check. [➡EXAMINE AND ASSESS; 754] 2 *n* **test**, assessment, exam, paper, question paper, oral exam, theory test. [➡LESSONS, COURSE WORK, AND EXAMINATIONS; 842]

examine 1 *v* **look at**, inspect, scrutinize, observe, study, survey, scan. [➡LOOKING AND LOOKS; 701] 2 *v* **consider**, think about, look into, investigate, research, analyse, weigh up, appraise, sift, weigh. [➡EXAMINE AND ASSESS; 754] 3 *v* **test**, assess, grade, judge, question, survey, audit. [➡ASSESS QUALITY; 756]

examiner *n* **inspector**, auditor, surveyor, superintendent, assessor, judge, grader. [➡SURVEYORS, EXAMINERS, AND JUDGES; 853]

example 1 *n* **sample**, instance, case, case in point, specimen, illustration. [➡REPRESENTATIONS AND GENERAL EXAMPLES; 65] 2 *n* **model**, pattern, exemplar (*literary*), paradigm, standard, paragon. [➡PERFECT EXAMPLES AND EMBODIMENTS; 67]

exasperate *v* **infuriate**, madden, frustrate, drive mad (*informal*), annoy, irritate, incense, enrage, rile (*informal*), drive round the bend, wind up (*informal*), vex, irk. [➡ANGER AND ANNOY; 570] *Opposite:* placate.

See Compare and Contrast at **annoy**.

exasperated *adj* **infuriated**, maddened, frustrated, wound up (*informal*), annoyed, incensed, irritated, enraged, riled (*informal*). [➡IRRITATION AND ANGER; 542] *Opposite:* placated.

exasperating *adj* **infuriating**, maddening, frustrating, vexing, annoying, irksome, galling, tiresome, tedious. [➡IRRITATING; 229] *Opposite:* calming.

exasperation *n* **frustration**, irritation, enragement, annoyance, vexation, anger, fury, madness. [➡IRRITATION AND ANGER; 542]

excavate *v* **dig**, mine, quarry, dig out, exhume, unearth, hollow out, scoop out, dig up. [➡FIND; 464] *Opposite:* bury.

exceed *v* **go beyond**, surpass, go above, go over, top, outdo, overdo, outstrip, beat. [➡OVERDO SOMETHING; 291] *Opposite:* fall short.

exceedingly *adv* **very**, exceptionally, remarkably, extremely, extraordinarily, outstandingly, especially. [➡EXTRAORDINARY: AMAZING; 205] *Opposite:* slightly.

excel *v* **shine**, stand out, outshine, outclass, surpass, outrival, top, best, outdo, outstrip. [➡SUCCEED AND WIN; 79] *Opposite:* fall behind.

excellence *n* **fineness**, brilliance, superiority, distinction, quality, merit. [➡EXTRAORDINARY: AMAZING; 205] *Opposite:* mediocrity.

excellent *adj* **outstanding**, brilliant, exceptional, admirable, superb, tremendous, first-rate. [➡EXTRAORDINARY: AMAZING; 205] *Opposite:* poor.

except *prep* **apart from**, except for, but, excluding, with the exception of, excepting (*formal*), aside from, bar. [➡NOT; 135] *Opposite:* including.

except for *prep* [➡NOT; 135]

excepting (*formal*) *prep* **except**, apart from, except for, but, excluding, with the exception of, aside from, bar. [➡NOT; 135] *Opposite:* including.

exception *n* **exclusion**, omission, exemption, concession, allowance. [➡ABSENT AND UNAVAILABLE; 7] *Opposite:* compromise.

exceptionable (*formal*) *adj* **offensive**, obnoxious, rude, objectionable, repugnant, unpleasant, reprehensible, insufferable, intolerable, unacceptable. [➡UNACCEPTABLE AND UNFORGIVABLE; 226] *Opposite:* inoffensive.

exceptional *adj* **excellent**, brilliant, special, extraordinary, incomparable, unique, outstanding, remarkable. [➡EXTRAORDINARY: AMAZING; 205] *Opposite:* ordinary.

exceptionality *n* **rarity**, infrequency, extraordinariness, uniqueness, remarkability. [➡NEVER AND INFREQUENCY; 97] *Opposite:* normality.

excerpt *n* **extract**, passage, quote, quotation, selection, piece, citation. [➡SUMMARIES, OUTLINES, AND EXCERPTS; 589]

excess 1 *n* **surplus**, glut, overload, surfeit, overabundance, superfluity, oversufficiency, overkill, overflow. [➡TOO MUCH; 118] *Opposite:* shortage. 2 *n* **overindulgence**, intemperance, immoderation (*formal*), dissipation, inordinateness, prodigality, extravagance. [➡MORALLY BAD; 776] *Opposite:* moderation. 3 *adj* **extra**, additional, surplus, spare, superfluous, leftover. [➡MORE AND EXCESS; 122]

excesses *n* **extremes**, immoderation (*formal*), dissipation, intemperance, overindulgence, prodigality, extravagance. [➡MORALLY BAD; 776]

excessive *adj* **extreme**, too much, unnecessary, unwarranted, undue, disproportionate. [➡TOO MUCH; 118] *Opposite:* moderate.

excessively *adv* **very**, extremely, exceptionally, markedly, greatly, terribly. [➡TO A GREAT EXTENT; 130] *Opposite:* moderately.

excessiveness *n* **immoderateness** (*formal*), immoderation (*formal*), extremeness, exorbitance, extravagance. [➡TOO MUCH; 118] *Opposite:* moderation.

exchange 1 *v* **swap** (*informal*), swap over, switch, switch over, replace, trade, barter, substitute. [➡EXCHANGE AND INTERCHANGE; 449] *Opposite:* keep. 2 *n* **conversation**, argument, talk, chat, discussion, altercation, interchange, give-and-take (*informal*). [➡INFORMAL COMMUNICATION; 45] 3 *n* **trade**, swap (*informal*), switch, barter, replacement, substitute. [➡EXCHANGE AND INTERCHANGE; 449]

exchangeable *adj* **redeemable**, transferable, negotiable, commutable, interchangeable, replaceable, returnable. [➡SAMENESS; 151]

exchange blows *v* **fight**, scuffle, go for each other, trade punches, brawl, scrap, clash, spar. [➡PHYSICAL ATTACK AND PUNISHMENT; 416]

excise *v* **delete**, remove, edit, cut out, expunge, erase, expurgate, eliminate. [➡EXTRACT AND SEVER; 342] *Opposite:* insert.

excision *n* **editing**, deletion, removal, cutting out, erasure, expurgation, elimination. [➡REMOVE SOMETHING; 339] *Opposite:* insertion.

excitability *n* **nervousness**, edginess, moodiness, fieriness, quick-temperedness, emotionality, impulsiveness, volatility. [➡LACK OF COMMITMENT AND UNRELIABILITY; 510] *Opposite:* coolness.

excitable *adj* **nervous**, emotional, highly strung, edgy, impulsive, volatile, passionate, hasty. [➡EXCESSIVE SENSITIVITY; 512] *Opposite:* unflappable.

excite 1 *v* **stimulate**, enthuse, animate, motivate, enliven, electrify, thrill, rouse, arouse, energize. [➡APPEAL TO AND AROUSE INTEREST; 576] *Opposite:* bore. 2 *v* **incite**, agitate, provoke, instigate, stir up, wind up (*informal*), awaken. [➡CAUSE TO HAPPEN; 31] *Opposite:* soothe.

excited 1 *adj* **happy**, enthusiastic, eager, animated, motivated, thrilled. [➡PLEASURE, EXCITEMENT, AND ELATION; 535] *Opposite:* indifferent. 2 *adj* **agitated**, nervous, provoked, overwrought, hot and bothered, wound up (*informal*), upset, stirred up, fraught, distracted, anxious. [➡CONFUSION, ANXIETY, AND WORRY; 541] *Opposite:* calm.

excitedly *adv* **happily**, enthusiastically, eagerly, hungrily, impatiently, animatedly, breathlessly, elatedly. [➡PLEASURE, EXCITEMENT, AND ELATION; 535] *Opposite:* indifferently.

excitement 1 *n* **enthusiasm**, eagerness, anticipation, pleasure, exhilaration, enjoyment, delight, interest, elation. [➡POSITIVE IMPATIENCE, ENTHUSIASM, AND ALERTNESS; 538] *Opposite:* indifference. 2 *n* **agitation**, tension, unrest, ferment, restlessness, turmoil, flurry, flutter. [➡INSECURITY AND LOSS OF COMPOSURE; 545] *Opposite:* calm.

exciting *adj* **thrilling**, exhilarating, stirring, stimulating, electrifying, moving, rousing, sensational, breathtaking. [➡EMOTIONALLY PLEASANT; 188] *Opposite:* boring.

exclaim *v* **cry out**, cry, shout, call out, call, yell, scream, bellow. [➡SOUND EMISSION BY PEOPLE; 364] *Opposite:* whisper.

exclamation *n* **shout**, cry, yell, scream, howl, shriek, expletive, interjection, outcry. [➡SOUNDS MADE BY PEOPLE; 1261] *Opposite:* whisper.

exclamation mark *type of* **punctuation mark**. [➡ASPECTS OF LANGUAGE; 683]

exclude 1 *v* **keep out**, bar, reject, leave out, prevent, prohibit, leave out in the cold, stop, ban. [➡MAKE IMPOSSIBLE; 277] *Opposite:* welcome. 2 *v* **reject**, rule out, eliminate, discount, ignore, dismiss, disregard, omit, except (*formal*), leave out. [➡NOT PAY ATTENTION; 765] *Opposite:* include.

excluding *prep* **exclusive of**, not including, without, apart from. [➡NOT; 135] *Opposite:* including.

exclusion 1 *n* **keeping out**, barring, rejection, leaving out, prohibiting, segregation, omission. [➡EJECT AND EXCLUDE; 341] *Opposite:* welcome. 2 *n* **ban**, refusal, sanction, embargo, prohibition, bar, veto. [➡REFUSE PERMISSION AND NOT ALLOW; 671] 3 *n* **rejection**, elimination, marginalization, prohibition, veto, barring. [➡REFUSE PERMISSION AND NOT ALLOW; 671] *Opposite:* inclusion.

exclusive 1 *adj* **high-class**, elite, select, restricted, limited, private, fashionable, special. [➡EXPENSIVE AND LUXURIOUS; 219] *Opposite:* inclusive. 2 *adj* **sole**, complete, undivided, full, whole, absolute, total. [➡UNRELATEDNESS AND SEPARATENESS; 147] *Opposite:* partial.

exclusively *adv* **solely**, wholly, completely, entirely, fully, totally, utterly, absolutely, singularly, alone. [➡ABSOLUTE AND ABSOLUTELY; 131] *Opposite:* partially.

exclusiveness 1 *n* **luxury**, sophistication, refinement, superiority, stylishness, elegance, classiness (*informal*). [➡EXPENSIVE AND LUXURIOUS; 219] 2 *n* **selectiveness**, restrictedness, exclusivity, elitism, snobbery. [➡PREJUDICE; 551]

exclusive of *adj* **not including**, excluding, leaving out, without, excepting (*formal*), except for. [➡LACK OF POSSESSION; 446] *Opposite:* including.

excommunicate *v* **exclude**, bar, debar, expel, eject, throw out, remove, anathematize. [➡RELIGIONS AND RELIGIOUS PRACTICES; 778] *Opposite:* admit.

excommunication *n* **exclusion**, barring, debarring, expulsion, ejection, throwing out, removal. [➡RELIGIONS AND RELIGIOUS PRACTICES; 778] *Opposite:* admission.

excoriate 1 *v* (*formal*) **criticize**, denounce, attack, berate, upbraid, rebuke, condemn, haul over the coals, take to task, castigate (*formal*), censure. [➡ACCUSE, BLAME, AND CRITICIZE; 642] *Opposite:* commend. 2 *v* **skin**, peel, pare, strip, flay. [➡WOUND A PERSON OR ANIMAL; 384]

excoriation (*formal*) *n* [➡IRRITATION AND ANGER; 542]

excrement *n* [➡EXCRETION AND EXCRETA; 723]

excrescence *n* **monstrosity**, eyesore, blot, growth, outgrowth. [➡NUISANCES; 254]

excreta (*technical*) *n* [➡EXCRETION AND EXCRETA; 723]

excrete *v* [➡EXCRETION AND EXCRETA; 723]

excretion *n* [➡EXCRETION AND EXCRETA; 723]

excretory *adj* [➡EXCRETION AND EXCRETA; 723]

excruciating 1 *adj* **agonizing**, painful, unbearable, awful, terrible, severe, sharp, piercing, insufferable, racking, tormenting. [➡PHYSICALLY UNPLEASANT; 227] *Opposite:* pleasant. 2 *adj* **embarrassing**, tedious, stultifying, irritating, infuriating, painful, cringe-making (*informal*), toe-curling (*informal*), insufferable. [➡EMOTIONALLY UNPLEASANT AND UPSETTING; 228] *Opposite:* enthralling.

exculpate (*formal*) *v* **free**, let off, excuse, clear, release, acquit, exonerate. [➡FORGET, FORGIVE, AND ACCEPT; 749] *Opposite:* arraign.

exculpation (*formal*) *n* **acquittal**, exoneration, discharge, pardon, clearing. [➡TRIAL, PUNISHMENT, AND LEGAL OUTCOMES; 819] *Opposite:* arraignment.

excursion 1 *n* **trip**, jaunt, outing, tour, day trip, pleasure trip. [➡TRAVEL: JOURNEYS AND TRIPS; 319] 2 *n* (*formal*) **digression**, departure, detour, deviation, red herring. [➡NEUTRAL ONE-WAY COMMUNICATION; 49] 3 *n* **group**, team, party, expedition. [➡TRAVEL: JOURNEYS AND TRIPS; 319]

excusable *adj* **understandable**, forgivable, justifiable, explicable, pardonable, defensible, allowable, permissible. [➡ACCEPTABLE AND PASSABLE; 220] *Opposite:* inexcusable.

excuse 1 *v* **forgive**, pardon, let off, acquit, absolve, exculpate (*formal*), exonerate. [➡FORGET, FORGIVE, AND ACCEPT; 749] *Opposite:* blame. 2 *v* **overlook**, make allowances for, pass over, tolerate, justify, explain, bear with, defend. [➡APPROVE AND CONFIRM; 647] 3 *v* **exempt**, release, let off, free, relieve, discharge, spare, except (*formal*). [➡FREEDOM AND LIBERTY; 209] *Opposite:* oblige. 4 *n* **justification**, reason, explanation, pretext, defence, apology, plea, vindication, alibi (*informal*). [➡CAUSATION; 169]

excused *adj* **exempted**, released, exempt, let off, relieved, discharged. [➡FREEDOM AND LIBERTY; 209] *Opposite:* required.

excuse yourself *v* [➡ABSENT ONESELF; 8]

exec (*informal*) *n* [➡BUSINESS PEOPLE; 794]

execrable *adj* **awful**, appalling, disgusting, repulsive, deplorable, terrible, revolting, abominable, atrocious. [➡BAD AND BADLY; 224] *Opposite:* excellent.

execrate (*literary or formal*) *v* [➡INSULTS, ABUSE, AND SWEARING; 659]

execration (*literary or formal*) *n* [➡INSULTS, ABUSE, AND SWEARING; 659]

execute 1 *v* **carry out**, perform, implement, effect (*formal*), complete, accomplish, finish (*informal*), fulfil, achieve. [➡CARRY OUT AN ACTION; 270] *Opposite:* fail. 2 *v* **put to death**, kill, slay (*formal or literary*), murder, hang, electrocute, guillotine. [➡KILL; 923]

See Compare and Contrast at **kill, perform**.

execution 1 *n* **putting to death**, capital punishment, the death sentence, killing, slaying. [➡CAUSES OF DEATH; 921] 2 *n* **implementation**, performance, accomplishment, carrying out, completing, finishing, effecting. [➡CARRY OUT AN ACTION; 270]

executive 1 *n* **manager**, senior manager, director, administrator, official. [➡BUSINESS PEOPLE; 794] 2 *adj* **decision-making**, policymaking, managerial, management, administrative, supervisory. [➡TYPES OF WORK; 835] 3 *adj* **expensive**, exclusive, high class, superior, select, fashionable, high-status, luxurious. [➡EXTRAORDINARY: AMAZING; 205]

executive jet *type of* **civil aircraft**. [➡AIRCRAFT; 1147]

executor *n* **doer**, prime mover, initiator, originator, architect, facilitator, organizer. [➡DESIGNERS, CREATORS AND INSTIGATORS; 348]

exemplar (*literary*) *n* **ideal**, model, paradigm, example, archetype. [➡PERFECT EXAMPLES AND EMBODIMENTS; 67]

exemplary 1 *adj* **admirable**, praiseworthy, excellent, perfect, ideal, commendable. [➡ADMIRABLE AND COMMENDABLE; 186] 2 *adj* (*formal*) **model**, archetypal, textbook, typical, classic, prototypical. [➡REPRESENTATIVE; 66]

exemplification *n* [➡REPRESENTATIONS AND GENERAL EXAMPLES; 65]

exemplify *v* **demonstrate**, typify, represent, illustrate, show, epitomize, embody, characterize, personify. [➡REPRESENT SOMETHING OR SOMEBODY; 59]

exempt 1 *adj* **excused**, exempted, released, relieved, discharged, let off, excepted, off the hook (*informal*), not liable, immune, freed. [➡FREEDOM AND LIBERTY; 209] *Opposite:* required. 2 *v* **excuse**, free, let off, except (*formal*), let go, release, relieve, spare, discharge, pardon. [➡FORGET, FORGIVE, AND ACCEPT; 749] *Opposite:* oblige.

exemption *n* **exception**, immunity, release, indemnity, exclusion, freedom, discharge, absolution. [➡FREEDOM AND LIBERTY; 209] *Opposite:* obligation.

exercise 1 *n* **physical activity**, working out, training, keep fit, drill. [➡HOBBIES, GAMES, AND SPORTS; 875] *Opposite:* inactivity. 2 *n* **physical movements**, aerobics, workout, callisthenics, cardiovascular exercise, training, drills. [➡HOBBIES, GAMES, AND SPORTS; 875] 3 *n* (*formal*) **implementation**, carrying out, use, application, employment, practice. [➡USE; 468] *Opposite:* avoidance. 4 *v* **work out**, train, keep fit, do exercises, drill. [➡FIDGET AND FROLIC; 312] 5 *v* **use**, put into effect, implement, apply, employ, effect (*formal*), bring to bear, exert, carry out. [➡USE; 468] *Opposite:* avoid.

exercise bike *type of* **bike** (*informal*). [➡BIKES, CARS, AND CARRIAGES; 1148]

exercises *n* **military exercises**, manoeuvres, drills. [➡WARFARE AND WAR; 830]

exert *v* **bring to bear**, use, apply, exercise, make use of, employ, wield, utilize. [➡USE; 468]

exertion *n* **effort**, action, application, physical exertion, energy, hard work, force, toil, pains, labour. [➡HARD WORK OR EFFORT; 299]

exert yourself *v* **make an effort**, try hard, push yourself, work hard, put your all into something, work flat out, work up a sweat. [➡HARD WORK OR EFFORT; 299]

exhale *v* **breathe out**, blow out, puff out, let your breath out, respire. [➡BREATHE AND NOT BREATHE; 717] *Opposite:* inhale.

exhaust 1 *v* **tire out**, wear out, drain, fatigue, weaken, do in (*informal*), tire. [➡TIRED, ASLEEP AND UNCONSCIOUS; 739] *Opposite:* refresh. 2 *v* **use up**, use, finish (*informal*), wear out, consume, drain, deplete, sap, run through, expend, dissipate. [➡USE UP AND WASTE; 475] *Opposite:* renew.

exhausted *adj* **tired**, worn out, shattered, fatigued, dead beat (*informal*), pooped (*informal*), done in (*informal*), beat (*informal*), bushed (*informal*), dog-tired (*informal*), drained, wearied, spent, all in. [➡TIRED, ASLEEP AND UNCONSCIOUS; 739] *Opposite:* refreshed.

exhausting *adj* **tiring**, wearing, shattering, fatiguing, killing, gruelling, arduous, strenuous, wearying, draining. [➡PHYSICALLY UNPLEASANT; 227] *Opposite:* refreshing.

exhaustion *n* **tiredness**, fatigue, collapse, overtiredness, enervation. [➡TIRED, ASLEEP AND UNCONSCIOUS; 739] *Opposite:* energy.

exhaustive *adj* **thorough**, complete, comprehensive, in-depth, full, extensive, far-reaching, meticulous, all-inclusive, intensive, sweeping. [➡WHOLENESS AND COMPLETENESS; 199] *Opposite:* superficial.

exhaust pipe *type of* **external feature.** [➡VEHICLES; 1144]

exhibit 1 *v* **display**, show, unveil, put on a display, put on view, reveal, demonstrate. [➡CAUSE TO APPEAR; 5] *Opposite:* hide. 2 *v* **show off**, parade, flaunt, expose, display, demonstrate. [➡CAUSE TO APPEAR; 5] 3 *n* **exhibition**, display, show, parade, revelation, demonstration. [➡PERFORMANCES AND SHOWS; 42]

exhibition *n* **display**, show, showing, demonstration, exposition, trade fair, presentation, fair, retrospective, showcase. [➡PERFORMANCES AND SHOWS; 42]

exhibition hall *n* [➡BUILDINGS FOR PUBLIC ENTERTAINMENT; 1083]

exhibitionist *n* **show-off** (*informal*), play-actor (*informal*), attention-seeker, braggart. [➡SELF-IMPORTANT AND SELF-SEEKING PEOPLE; 949]

exhilarate *v* **excite**, elate, thrill, enliven, invigorate, lift, stimulate, hearten. [➡SURPRISE AND IMPRESS; 575] *Opposite:* bore.

exhilarated *adj* **elated**, ecstatic, euphoric, overjoyed, over the moon, delighted, inspired, exalted (*formal*), energized, excited. [➡PLEASURE, EXCITEMENT, AND ELATION; 535] *Opposite:* indifferent.

exhilarating *adj* [➡PHYSICALLY PLEASANT; 187]

exhilaration *n* **excitement**, elation, high spirits, animation, happiness, delight, joy. [➡PLEASURE, EXCITEMENT, AND ELATION; 535]

exhort *v* **urge**, press, push, pressure, insist, encourage, spur, goad, prod. [➡CAUSE OR COMPEL TO ACT; 272] *Opposite:* forbid.

exhortation (*formal*) *n* **appeal**, call, encouragement, urging, incitement, advice, counsel (*formal or literary*). [➡ADVICE; 690]

exhume *v* **dig up**, disinter, unearth, disentomb, disclose. [➡BURIAL AND PREPARATION FOR BURIAL; 929] *Opposite:* bury.

exigency (*formal*) *n* **need**, demand, requirement, emergency, necessity, pressure, constraint. [➡NECESSARY AND ESSENTIAL; 197]

exigent (*formal*) 1 *adj* **urgent**, pressing, crucial, vital, important, necessary, needful, insistent. [➡IMPORTANT; 195] *Opposite:* unimportant. 2 *adj* **demanding**, tough, testing, challenging, taxing, tricky, exacting, burdensome, difficult, arduous. [➡PHYSICALLY UNPLEASANT; 227] *Opposite:* easy.

exile 1 *n* **émigré**, tax exile, expatriate, deportee, refugee, outcast, DP. [➡PEOPLE LIVING AWAY FROM HOME; 887] 2 *n* **banishment**, deportation, expulsion, separation, ostracism, expatriation. [➡ABSENT AND UNAVAILABLE; 7] 3 *v* **banish**, send away, deport, expel, cast out (*formal*), separate, eject, oust, drive out. [➡EJECT AND EXCLUDE; 341]

exist 1 *v* **be**, be real, be present, be existent, happen, occur. [➡EXIST; 15] 2 *v* **live**, be, survive, continue living, stay alive, subsist, endure, last. [➡CONTINUE TO EXIST; 17]

existence *n* **being**, life, reality, presence, survival, actuality, animation. [➡THE STAGES OF LIFE; 916]

existent (*formal*) *adj* **existing**, current, present, extant, ongoing, in existence, surviving. [➡PRESENT AND AVAILABLE; 11]

existentialist *n* [➡PHILOSOPHICAL AND POLITICAL THINKERS; 782]

existing *adj* **present**, current, in effect, prevailing, standing, remaining, surviving. [➡PRESENT; 85]

exit 1 *n* **way out**, door, outlet, egress (*formal*). [➡DOORS AND ACCESS POINTS; 1100] *Opposite:* entrance. 2 *n* **departure**, exodus, walking out, leaving, going away, leave-taking (*literary*), withdrawal. [➡END; 54] *Opposite:* arrival. 3 *v* **go out**, leave, depart, go, take off (*informal*), walk out, withdraw, escape. [➡ABSENT ONESELF; 8] *Opposite:* enter.

exodus *n* **mass departure**, departure, migration, emigration, flight, evacuation, exit, hegira. [➡END; 54] *Opposite:* arrival.

exonerate *v* **clear**, absolve, acquit, vindicate, forgive, pardon, exculpate (*formal*), free. [➡FORGET, FORGIVE, AND ACCEPT; 749] *Opposite:* blame.

exoneration 1 *n* **pardon**, exculpation (*formal*), absolution, acquittal, vindication. [➡FORGET, FORGIVE, AND ACCEPT; 749] *Opposite:* blame. 2 *n* **release**, freeing, liberation, exemption, discharge. [➡FREEDOM AND LIBERTY; 209]

exorbitance *n* [➡TOO MUCH; 118]

exorbitant *adj* **excessive**, inflated, steep (*informal*), ridiculous, overpriced, unreasonable, extortionate, outrageous, inordinate. [➡EXPENSIVE AND OVERPRICED; 248] *Opposite:* reasonable.

exorcize *v* **get rid of**, get free of, banish, drive out, force out, expel. [➡GET RID OF SOMETHING; 452]

exosphere *n* [➡THE EARTH'S ATMOSPHERE; 1040]

exotic 1 *adj* **unusual**, out of the ordinary, striking, interesting, bizarre, mysterious, glamorous, colourful, outlandish, strange, different, exceptional. [➡EXTRAORDINARY: UNCOMMON; 206] *Opposite:* ordinary. 2 *adj* **foreign**, from abroad, tropical, alien. [➡EXTRAORDINARY: UNCOMMON; 206] *Opposite:* familiar.

expand *v* **make bigger**, get bigger, enlarge, increase, develop, swell, inflate, spread out, open out, grow, magnify, multiply. [➡CHANGE OF SIZE: BIGGER; 393] *Opposite:* contract.

See Compare and Contrast at **increase**.

expandable *adj* **stretchy**, elastic, foldup, foldout, pullout, inflatable, pliant, foldaway. [➡MALLEABLE AND ELASTIC; 1211]

expand upon *v* **enlarge on**, elaborate on, give details, embellish, amplify, develop. [➡EXPLAIN AND CLARIFY; 611]

expanse *n* **area**, breadth, stretch, span, region, spread, vastness. [➡SIZE AND DIMENSIONS; 1191]

expansion *n* **growth**, development, increase, extension, spreading out, opening out, enlargement. [➡CHANGE OF SIZE: BIGGER; 393] *Opposite:* contraction.

expansionism *n* [➡STYLES AND SYSTEMS OF GOVERNMENT; 806]

expansionist *adj* [➡STYLES AND SYSTEMS OF GOVERNMENT; 806]

expansive 1 *adj* **communicative**, generous, magnanimous, friendly, open, unreserved, unrestrained, outgoing, extroverted. [➡ELOQUENT, TALKATIVE AND LONG-WINDED; 633] *Opposite:* reserved. 2 *adj* **extensive**, spread-out, spacious, roomy, sizable, wide, sprawling, vast, capacious. [➡LARGE; 1192] *Opposite:* cramped.

expansively 1 *adv* **at length**, extensively, widely, comprehensively, broadly, lengthily, thoroughly. [➡HONEST AND OPEN; 631] *Opposite:* briefly. 2 *adv* **effusively**, lavishly, openly, generously, jovially, enthusiastically. [➡ENTHUSIASTIC AND INQUISITIVE; 629]

expansiveness 1 *n* **effusiveness**, lavishness, openness, generousness, enthusiasm, extravagance, magnanimity. [➡ENERGY AND ENTHUSIASM; 497] *Opposite:* reserve. 2 *n* **size**, large size, mass, extent, reach, scale, largeness, vastness. [➡LARGE; 1192]

expat (*informal*) *n* **expatriate**, emigrant, colonial, émigré, tax exile, deportee, refugee, exile. [➡PEOPLE LIVING AWAY FROM HOME; 887] *Opposite:* native.

expatiate *v* [➡INSTRUCT AND TEACH; 610]

expatriate *n* **émigré**, tax exile, emigrant, deportee, refugee, expat (*informal*), colonial, exile. [➡PEOPLE LIVING AWAY FROM HOME; 887] *Opposite:* native.

expect 1 *v* **wait for**, anticipate, look forward to, await, look ahead, hope for, envisage. [➡PREDICT AND ANTICIPATE; 751] 2 *v* **imagine**, suppose, guess, think, believe, assume, presume. [➡UNCERTAINTY; 560] 3 *v* **demand**, require, insist on, count on, anticipate. [➡REQUEST AND DEMAND; 664]

expectancy *n* **anticipation**, expectation, hope, suspense, bated breath, belief, prospect, probability. [➡FEELINGS ABOUT THE FUTURE; 534]

expectant 1 *adj* **eager**, hopeful, in suspense, hoping, on tenterhooks, excited, anxious, keen. [➡PLEASURE, EXCITEMENT, AND ELATION; 535] 2 *adj* **pregnant**, expecting, in the family way (*dated informal*), in the club (*slang*). [➡REPRODUCTION AND HEREDITY; 726]

expectantly *adv* **hopefully**, eagerly, excitedly, keenly, anxiously, with interest, with bated breath. [➡PLEASURE, EXCITEMENT, AND ELATION; 535]

expectation *n* **hope**, anticipation, expectancy, belief, prospect, probability, suspense, bated breath. [➡FEELINGS ABOUT THE FUTURE; 534]

expected *adj* **likely**, probable, foreseeable, predictable, awaited, anticipated. [➡FUTURE; 86] *Opposite:* surprising.

expecting *adj* **pregnant**, expectant, in the family way (*dated informal*), in the club (*slang*). [➡REPRODUCTION AND HEREDITY; 726]

expectorant *n* **cough medicine**, linctus, cough mixture, medicine, cough syrup (*US*). [➡REMEDIES, TREATMENTS, AND OPERATIONS; 732]

expediency 1 *n* **convenience**, practicality, pragmatism, usefulness, feasibility. [➡USEFULNESS; 200] 2 *n* **appropriateness**, suitability, fitness, advisability, convenience. [➡LACK OF COMMITMENT AND UNRELIABILITY; 510] *Opposite:* unsuitability.

expedient 1 *adj* **appropriate**, fitting, suitable, advisable, necessary, opportune. [➡USEFULNESS; 200] *Opposite:* inappropriate. 2 *adj* **advantageous**, convenient, practical, useful, beneficial, self-serving, politic, pragmatic. [➡APPROPRIATE, SUITABLE, ADVISABLE; 185] *Opposite:* altruistic. 3 *n* **measure**, means, method, manoeuvre, device, way. [➡WAYS OF DOING THINGS; 295]

expediently 1 *adv* **appropriately**, suitably, fittingly, correctly, necessarily, opportunely, advisably. [➡USEFULNESS; 200] *Opposite:* inappropriately. 2 *adv* **advantageously**, conveniently, practically, beneficially, pragmatically. [➡USEFULNESS; 200] *Opposite:* altruistically.

expedite (*formal*) *v* **speed up**, accelerate, hurry up, advance, further, rush. [➡MAKE POSSIBLE; 276] *Opposite:* impede.

expedition 1 *n* **journey**, excursion, voyage, trip, outing, mission, tour, trek. [➡TRAVEL: JOURNEYS AND TRIPS; 319] 2 *n* **team**, party, crew, group. [➡GROUPS WITH A COMMON INTEREST; 938]

expeditious *adj* **speedy**, prompt, quick, swift, hasty, efficient. [➡HAPPENING QUICKLY; 104] *Opposite:* slow.

expel 1 *v* **dismiss**, sack (*informal*), fire, eject, oust, banish. [➡REVOKE STATUS; 460] 2 *v* **drive out**, force out, push out, eject, flush out. [➡EJECT AND EXCLUDE; 341]

expend 1 *v* **use up**, use, consume, spend, burn up, apply, utilize. [➡USE UP AND WASTE; 475] *Opposite:* conserve. 2 *v* (*formal*) **spend**, disburse, pay out, lay out, pay. [➡GIVE MONEY; 434] *Opposite:* save.

expendable 1 *adj* **consumable**, replaceable, throwaway, disposable, usable. [➡UNPOPULAR AND UNWANTED; 259] *Opposite:* durable. 2 *adj* **dispensable**, disposable, superfluous, unessential, nonessential, inessential, unneeded. [➡UNIMPORTANT AND UNNECESSARY; 239] *Opposite:* indispensable.

expenditure *n* **spending**, outgoings, expenses, payments, outflow, costs, overheads, disbursement, outlay. [➡EXPENDITURE; 424] *Opposite:* income.

expense 1 *n* **cost**, expenditure, outlay, disbursement, outflow, payment, overhead. [➡EXPENDITURE; 424] *Opposite:* income. 2 *n* **price**, rate, figure, amount, price tag, fee, toll, premium, tariff. [➡EXPENDITURE; 424] 3 *n* **sacrifice**, cost, detriment, disadvantage, loss. [➡NUISANCES; 254]

expenses *n* **expenditure**, outgoings, outlay, incidentals, costs, overheads. [➡ACCOUNTING, BANKING, AND BUDGETING; 799] *Opposite:* income.

expensive 1 *adj* **costly**, dear, pricey (*informal*), high-priced, steep (*informal*), big-ticket (*US informal*). [➡EXPENSIVE AND OVERPRICED; 248] *Opposite:* cheap. 2 *adj* **luxurious**, classy (*informal*), posh (*informal*), exclusive, affluent, lavish. [➡EXPENSIVE AND LUXURIOUS; 219] *Opposite:* cheap.

expensively *adv* **luxuriously**, extravagantly, affluently, lavishly. [➡EXPENSIVE AND LUXURIOUS; 219] *Opposite:* cheaply.

experience 1 *n* **involvement**, knowledge, skill, practice, understanding, familiarity, know-how (*informal*), capability, proficiency. [➡KNOWLEDGE AND WISDOM; 559] **2** *n* **occurrence**, incident, encounter, event, happening. [➡EVENTS AND OCCURRENCES; 35] **3** *v* **feel**, go through, face, live through, undergo, come across, suffer. [➡EXPERIENCE AND ENCOUNTER; 583]

experienced *adj* **knowledgeable**, skilled, practised, qualified, veteran, expert, proficient, skilful. [➡KNOWLEDGE AND WISDOM; 559] *Opposite:* inexperienced.

experiment **1** *n* **trial**, test, tryout, research, experimentation. [➡EXAMINE AND ASSESS; 754] **2** *v* **test**, try out, investigate, try, trial. [➡EXAMINE AND ASSESS; 754]

experimental *adj* **new**, tentative, investigational, untried, trial. [➡EXTRAORDINARY: UNCOMMON; 206]

experimentation *n* **testing**, research, investigation, trialling. [➡EXAMINE AND ASSESS; 754]

expert **1** *n* **specialist**, authority, professional, connoisseur, doyen, whiz (*informal*). [➡TALENTED OR INTELLIGENT PERSON; 529] *Opposite:* amateur. **2** *adj* **skilled**, skilful, practised, proficient, professional, knowledgeable, adept. [➡TALENTED AND SKILFUL; 528] *Opposite:* inexperienced.

expertise *n* **skill**, knowledge, proficiency, capability, know-how (*informal*). [➡KNOWLEDGE AND WISDOM; 559]

expertness *n* **skilfulness**, dexterity, knowledge, expertise, proficiency, capability, ability, skill, experience. [➡SKILLS, TALENTS, AND ABILITIES; 527] *Opposite:* inexperience.

expiate *v* **make amends**, atone (*formal*), compensate, make up for, recompense, redress, do penance, amend, correct, put right. [➡RELIGIONS AND RELIGIOUS PRACTICES; 778]

expiation *n* [➡APOLOGIZE AND RETRACT; 684]

expiration *n* [➡END; 54]

expire **1** *v* **end**, run out, finish, terminate (*formal*), conclude, elapse, invalidate. [➡CEASE TO EXIST; 22] **2** *v* (*formal or literary*) **die**, pass away, pass on, perish (*literary*), breathe your last (*literary*), decease (*formal*). [➡DIE; 922]

expiry **1** *n* **end**, ending, running out, finish, finishing, expiration, termination. [➡END; 54] *Opposite:* beginning. **2** *n* (*formal or literary*) **death**, decease (*formal*), passing, dying, demise (*formal*). [➡DEATH AND BEREAVEMENT; 927]

explain **1** *v* **make clear**, describe, put in plain words, elucidate (*formal*), clarify, explicate, illuminate, enlighten, expound. [➡EXPLAIN AND CLARIFY; 611] **2** *v* **justify**, account for, defend, rationalize, vindicate, support. [➡APPROVE AND CONFIRM; 647]

explanation **1** *n* **reason**, justification, rationalization, vindication, account, excuse. [➡CAUSATION; 169] **2** *n* **description**, account, clarification, elucidation (*formal*), enlightenment, details. [➡EXPLAIN AND CLARIFY; 611]

explanatory *adj* **descriptive**, instructive, illustrative, illuminating, clarifying, expounding, advisory, helpful, explicatory, elucidatory (*formal*). [➡EXPLAIN AND CLARIFY; 611]

expletive *n* **swearword**, curse, oath, invective (*formal*), exclamation, obscenity, four-letter word, cussword (*US informal*). [➡INSULTS, ABUSE, AND SWEARING; 659]

explicable *adj* **explainable**, understandable, reasonable, justifiable, rational. [➡CORRECT; 183] *Opposite:* inexplicable.

explicate *v* **explain**, elucidate (*formal*), spell out, clarify, expound, illuminate, make clear, make plain. [➡EXPLAIN AND CLARIFY; 611]

explication *n* [➡EXPLAIN AND CLARIFY; 611]

explicit **1** *adj* **clear**, obvious, open, overt, plain, unambiguous, unequivocal, categorical, perspicuous. [➡CONCISE AND CLEAR; 203] *Opposite:* implicit. **2** *adj* **definite**, precise, exact, specific, unequivocal. [➡EXACT; 204] *Opposite:* vague. **3** *adj* **frank**, uninhibited, candid, open, graphic, raw. [➡HONEST AND OPEN; 631]

explicitly *adv* **clearly**, openly, obviously, overtly, plainly, unambiguously, unequivocally. [➡HONEST AND OPEN; 631] *Opposite:* implicitly.

explode **1** *v* **blow up**, go off, burst, burst out, blast, detonate, shatter. [➡DESTRUCTION AND DEMOLITION; 360] **2** *v* **get angry**, blow up (*informal*), fly into a rage, fly off the handle (*informal*), hit the ceiling, hit the roof, go ballistic (*slang*), go postal (*US informal*). [➡GIVING VENT TO EMOTIONS; 680] **3** *v* **disprove**, prove wrong, discredit, invalidate, nullify, negate (*formal*), challenge. [➡DENY AND REJECT; 645]

exploit **1** *v* **take advantage of**, abuse, misuse, ill-use, manipulate, play on. [➡MISUSE AND ABUSE; 472] **2** *v* **use**, develop, make use of, take advantage of, utilize, make the most of. [➡MAKE GOOD USE OF SOMETHING; 474] *Opposite:* waste. **3** *n* **feat**, deed, adventure, activity, heroic act, daring act, achievement. [➡ACTIONS OR UNDERTAKINGS; 260]

exploitable **1** *adj* **gullible**, credulous, innocent, vulnerable. [➡NEGATIVE INTELLECTUAL CHARACTERISTICS; 526] *Opposite:* mistrustful. **2** *adj* **usable**, utilizable, consumable, available. [➡USEFULNESS; 200]

exploitation **1** *n* **misuse**, abuse, mistreatment, taking advantage, manipulation, corruption. [➡MISUSE AND ABUSE; 472] **2** *n* **use**, utilization, development, management, operation. [➡USE; 468]

exploitative *adj* **unfair**, unequal, abusive, manipulative. [➡MORALLY BAD; 776] *Opposite:* fair.

exploration **1** *n* **examination**, investigation, survey, study, consideration, probe, search, assessment, evaluation. [➡EXAMINE AND ASSESS; 754] **2** *n* **travelling**, discovery, journeying, adventure, voyaging. [➡TRAVEL: JOURNEYS AND TRIPS; 319]

exploratory *adj* **investigative**, examining, probing, tentative, experimental, fact-finding, empirical, trial. [➡EXAMINE AND ASSESS; 754]

explore **1** *v* **travel**, discover, reconnoitre, see the sights, sightsee. [➡TRAVEL: WAYS OF TRAVELLING; 321] **2** *v* **investigate**, study, search, look at, survey, open up, go into, delve into, deal with. [➡EXAMINE AND ASSESS; 754]

explorer *n* **traveller**, voyager, surveyor, pioneer. [➡TRAVEL: TRAVELLERS AND WALKERS; 320]

explosion **1** *n* **bang**, blast, detonation, burst. [➡SUDDEN EVENT; 52] **2** *n* **outburst**, fit, flare-up (*informal*), eruption, paroxysm, burst, release. [➡CRITICISMS AND ANGRY OUTBURSTS; 50] **3** *n*

upsurge, leap, flood, outbreak, eruption, increase. [➡CHANGE OF SIZE: BIGGER; 393] *Opposite:* slump.

explosive 1 *adj* **volatile**, unstable, unpredictable, dangerous. [➡DANGEROUS; 237] *Opposite:* stable. 2 *adj* **short-tempered**, quick-tempered, hotheaded, volatile, fiery, touchy. [➡EXCESSIVE SENSITIVITY; 512] *Opposite:* placid.

explosive

◆ *types of explosive material*
dynamite, gelignite, gunpowder, napalm, nitroglycerine, plastic explosive, propellant, TNT, warhead

◆ *types of explosive weapon*
A-bomb, booby trap, antiballistic missile, atom bomb, atomic bomb (*US*), ballistic missile, bomb, depth charge, firebomb, guided missile, hand grenade, hydrogen bomb, mine, missile, Molotov cocktail, nail bomb, neutron bomb, nuclear missile, nuclear warhead, nuclear weapon, petrol bomb, smart bomb, smoke bomb, time bomb, torpedo, warhead

exponent 1 *n* **advocate**, proponent, promoter, fan, champion, backer, booster, supporter. [➡DEVOTEES AND ADDICTED PEOPLE; 557] 2 *n* **interpreter**, explainer, performer, practitioner. [➡WRITERS AND STYLES; 914]

export 1 *v* **sell abroad**, sell overseas, send abroad, send overseas, ship, trade, distribute, freight. [➡SELL; 442] *Opposite:* import. 2 *v* **spread**, transfer, carry across, pass on, disseminate, distribute. [➡DISPENSE, RATION, AND DISTRIBUTE; 435]

expose 1 *v* **open up**, reveal, uncover, bare, display, show. [➡CAUSE TO APPEAR; 5] *Opposite:* cover. 2 *v* **subject**, lay open to, put in danger, endanger, imperil (*formal*). [➡PUT AT RISK; 385] 3 *v* **blow the whistle on**, unmask, reveal, lay bare, bring to light, take the wraps off, catch out. [➡BETRAY CONFIDENCES AND GOSSIP; 619] *Opposite:* cover up.

exposé *n* **disclosure**, revelation, leak, exposure, discovery, uncovering. [➡NEWSPAPERS; 606]

exposed *adj* **unprotected**, visible, uncovered, bare, showing, out in the open, out, open, wide-open. [➡KNOWN AND FAMOUS; 182] *Opposite:* covered.

exposition 1 *n* **description**, discussion, explanation, account, elucidation (*formal*), clarification. [➡NEUTRAL ONE-WAY COMMUNICATION; 49] 2 *n* **exhibition**, fair, show, trade fair, display, demonstration, showcase. [➡PERFORMANCES AND SHOWS; 42]

expostulate *v* **disagree**, protest, object, reprove, remonstrate, admonish, complain, argue. [➡PROTEST AND EXPRESS DISAPPROVAL; 643]

See Compare and Contrast at **object**.

exposure 1 *n* **contact**, experience, introduction, acquaintance. [➡KNOWLEDGE AND WISDOM; 559] 2 *n* **revelation**, disclosure, revealing, unveiling, publicity, coverage. [➡NEWSPAPERS; 606]

exposure meter *part of* **photographic equipment**. [➡PHOTOGRAPHY AND PHOTOGRAPHIC EQUIPMENT; 1121]

expound *v* **explain**, expand on, talk about, develop, illustrate, expand, spell out, explicate. [➡EXPLAIN AND CLARIFY; 611]

express 1 *v* **state**, articulate, utter, voice, communicate, put across, convey, say, vent, broach, air. [➡UTTER AND PRONOUNCE; 609] 2 *v* **squeeze out**, extract, press out, force out. [➡EJECT AND EXCLUDE; 341] 3 *adj* **fast**, rapid, direct, nonstop, prompt. [➡HAPPENING QUICKLY; 104] *Opposite:* slow. 4 *adj* **precise**, explicit, definite, exact, specific, unambiguous. [➡EXACT; 204] *Opposite:* vague.

expression 1 *n* **look**, face, air, appearance, countenance, mien (*literary*). [➡FACIAL EXPRESSION; 652] 2 *n* **phrase**, idiom, turn of phrase, term, saying, set phrase. [➡THE SPOKEN WORD; 672] 3 *n* **communication**, manifestation, illustration, example, demonstration, representation, articulation, utterance, statement. [➡REPRESENTATIONS AND GENERAL EXAMPLES; 65] 4 *n* **extraction**, squeezing out, pressing out, forcing out. [➡REMOVE SOMETHING; 339]

expressionism *type of* **20th-century art movement**. [➡ARTISTIC MOVEMENTS AND STYLES; 899]

expressionless *adj* **straight-faced**, unresponsive, impassive, poker-faced, inexpressive, vacant, unreadable, deadpan, blank, lifeless, vacuous, unemotional. [➡FACIAL EXPRESSION; 652] *Opposite:* expressive.

expressive 1 *adj* **communicative**, sensitive, open, easy-to-read, animated, mobile, dramatic. [➡HONEST AND OPEN; 631] *Opposite:* impassive. 2 *adj* **representative**, representing, demonstrating, signifying, indicative, indicating. [➡REPRESENTATIVE; 66]

expressively *adv* **meaningfully**, dramatically, emotionally, sensitively, vividly. [➡INTERESTING AND MEANINGFUL; 191] *Opposite:* blandly.

expressivity *n* **articulacy**, eloquence, self-expression, fluency, clarity, lucidity, perspicuity, articulateness. [➡ELOQUENT, TALKATIVE AND LONG-WINDED; 633] *Opposite:* inarticulacy.

expressly *adv* **specifically**, particularly, explicitly, clearly, definitely, deliberately, unambiguously. [➡INTENTIONAL AND DELIBERATE; 280]

expressway (*US*) *type of* **major road**. [➡ROADS; 1105]

expropriate *v* **steal**, confiscate, seize, commandeer, appropriate, sequester, impound, take, annex. [➡TAKE SOMETHING AWAY; 426]

expulsion *n* **dismissal**, exclusion, throwing out, eviction, removal, ejection, discharge, kicking out (*informal*). [➡EJECT AND EXCLUDE; 341] *Opposite:* admittance.

expunge *v* **wipe out** (*informal*), obliterate, purge, erase, delete, rub out, cross out, edit out, remove, cut, censor. [➡DELETE AND ERASE; 340] *Opposite:* insert.

expurgate *v* [➡CORRECT AND PUT RIGHT; 378]

expurgated *adj* **cut down**, abridged, censored, edited, bowdlerized, cut. [➡LESS; 124]

expurgation *n* [➡CHANGE; 373]

exquisite 1 *adj* **beautiful**, gorgeous, delicate, attractive, superb, wonderful, pretty, good-looking, lovely, fine. [➡POPULAR AND WANTED; 221] *Opposite:* ugly. 2 *adj* **excellent**, perfect, delightful, flawless, wonderful, admirable. [➡ EXTRAORDINARY: AMAZING; 205] *Opposite:* flawed. 3 *adj* **discriminating**, discerning, sensitive, fastidious, refined, delicate, exacting, tasteful, perfect, elegant, impeccable. [➡ BEAUTY AND ATTRACTIVENESS; 190] 4 *adj* **intense**, touching, moving, excruciating, poignant, acute, stabbing, piercing, sharp. [➡ STRENGTH; 202] *Opposite:* dull.

exquisitely 1 *adv* **beautifully**, finely, delicately, intricately, superbly, divinely (*informal*), skilfully, wonderfully. [➡ EXTRAORDINARY: AMAZING; 205] *Opposite:* clumsily. 2 *adv* **tastefully**, perfectly, discerningly, sensitively, delicately, impeccably, elegantly, discriminatingly, fastidiously. [➡ BEAUTY AND ATTRACTIVENESS; 190]

exquisiteness *n* **beauty**, delicacy, daintiness, perfection, attractiveness, elegance, loveliness. [➡ BEAUTY AND ATTRACTIVENESS; 190] *Opposite:* ugliness.

extant *adj* **existing**, in existence, present, existent (*formal*), living, surviving. [➡ PRESENT; 85] *Opposite:* lost.

See Compare and Contrast at **living**.

extemporaneous *adj* **extemporary**, extemporal, unrehearsed, impromptu, ad-lib, spontaneous, off-the-cuff. [➡ HAPPENING QUICKLY; 104] *Opposite:* rehearsed.

extempore 1 *adj* **extemporaneous**, ad-lib, off-the-cuff, impromptu, unrehearsed, spontaneous. [➡ HAPPENING QUICKLY; 104] *Opposite:* rehearsed. 2 *adv* **extemporaneously**, ad lib, off the cuff, impromptu, spontaneously, offhand. [➡ HAPPENING QUICKLY; 104] *Opposite:* rehearsed.

extemporize *v* **ad-lib**, improvise, speak off the cuff, play it by ear, make it up as you go along, wing it (*informal*), do on the fly. [➡ UTTER AND PRONOUNCE; 609] *Opposite:* prepare.

extend 1 *v* **spread**, spread out, range, cover, encompass, outspread. [➡ EXIST IN A PLACE; 19] 2 *v* **continue**, reach, stretch, go on, run, run on, go, carry on. [➡ CONTINUE TO EXIST; 17] 3 *v* **make bigger**, expand, enlarge, make longer, lengthen, widen, broaden, pull out. [➡ CHANGE OF SIZE: BIGGER; 393] *Opposite:* curtail. 4 *v* **prolong**, stretch out, drag out, lengthen, postpone, delay, put off, spin out. [➡ CAUSE TO CONTINUE; 268] *Opposite:* cut short. 5 *v* **increase**, expand, widen, broaden, add to, develop. [➡ CHANGE OF SIZE: BIGGER; 393] *Opposite:* decrease. 6 *v* **offer**, give, hold out, proffer, tender, present. [➡ PROFFER AND HAND OVER; 432] *Opposite:* withdraw.

See Compare and Contrast at **increase**.

extended *adj* **lengthy**, protracted, long, prolonged, stretched, long-drawn-out, drawn-out. [➡ HAPPENING SLOWLY; 106] *Opposite:* cut short.

extension 1 *n* **additional room**, addition, lean-to, wing, conservatory, porch, annexe. [➡ ANCILLARY BUILDINGS; 1079] 2 *n* **extra time**, delay, postponement, leeway, allowance. [➡ PERIOD OF TIME; 90] 3 *n* **expansion**, enlargement, lengthening, broadening, increase, augmentation. [➡ CHANGE OF SIZE: BIGGER; 393] *Opposite:* contraction.

extensive 1 *adj* **big**, large, huge, vast, massive, wide, broad. [➡ LARGE; 1192] *Opposite:* restricted. 2 *adj* **wide**, widespread, wide-ranging, general, all-embracing, far-reaching, all-encompassing, broad. [➡ GENERAL LOCATIONS; 159] *Opposite:* narrow.

extensively 1 *adv* **significantly**, considerably, greatly, to a great extent, to a large extent, much, highly. [➡ TO A GREAT EXTENT; 130] *Opposite:* insignificantly. 2 *adv* **at length**, lengthily, widely, far, broadly, expansively, comprehensively. [➡ WHOLENESS AND COMPLETENESS; 199] *Opposite:* briefly.

extensiveness *n* **breadth**, comprehensiveness, fullness, richness, vastness, range, broadness. [➡ LARGE; 1192] *Opposite:* narrowness.

extent 1 *n* **size**, area, coverage, limit, boundary. [➡ SIZE AND DIMENSIONS; 1191] 2 *n* **degree**, amount, level, range, scope, magnitude. [➡ DEGREE AND EXTENT; 110]

extenuating *adj* **mitigating**, explanatory, justifying, moderating, palliative, qualifying. [➡ CAUSATION; 169]

exterior 1 *adj* **external**, outside, outdoor, peripheral, outward, outer. [➡ EXTREMITIES OF PHYSICAL OBJECTS; 1249] *Opposite:* interior. 2 *n* **outside**, façade, surface, shell. [➡ PARTS OF A BUILDING; 1094] *Opposite:* interior. 3 *n* **appearance**, look, aura, veneer, front, mien (*literary*). [➡ APPEARANCE AND ATMOSPHERE; 1236]

exterminate *v* **kill**, eliminate, annihilate, massacre, destroy, murder, eradicate, take out (*slang*), wipe out (*informal*), assassinate, decimate, liquidate, terminate (*formal*). [➡ KILL; 923]

extermination *n* **extinction**, annihilation, execution, killing, slaughter, massacre, butchery, termination. [➡ CAUSES OF DEATH; 921] *Opposite:* preservation.

external *adj* **outside**, exterior, outdoor, peripheral, outward, outer. [➡ EXTREMITIES OF PHYSICAL OBJECTS; 1249] *Opposite:* internal.

externalize *v* **express**, give voice to, utter, get off your chest, voice, convey. [➡ UTTER AND PRONOUNCE; 609] *Opposite:* internalize.

externally *adv* **outwardly**, on the outside, on the exterior, on the surface, superficially, outside, visibly. [➡ PERCEPTIBLE; 25] *Opposite:* inwardly.

extinct *adj* **nonexistent**, inexistent, died out, wiped out (*slang*), destroyed, vanished, defunct, dead. [➡ DEAD AND DYING; 925] *Opposite:* living.

See Compare and Contrast at **dead**.

extinction *n* **death**, extermination, destruction, loss, annihilation, disappearance, elimination. [➡ END; 54] *Opposite:* survival.

extinguish 1 *v* **douse**, quench, snuff, stub out, smother, switch off, turn off (*informal*), put out. [➡ CAUSE TO STOP; 267] *Opposite:* light. 2 *v* **end**, take away, destroy, snuff out, terminate (*formal*), do away with. [➡ DESTRUCTION AND DEMOLITION; 360] 3 *v* **eclipse**, overshadow, outshine, obscure, show up, surpass. [➡ CAUSE TO DISAPPEAR; 6]

extol (*formal or literary*) *v* **praise**, exalt (*formal*), commend, eulogize (*formal*), admire, worship. [➡ PRAISE AND ENCOURAGE; 648] *Opposite:* deprecate.

extort *v* **extract**, obtain under duress, obtain by threat, wrest, wring, force, screw (*informal*), squeeze. [➡STEAL AND ROB; 427]

extortion *n* **coercion**, threats, blackmail, squeezing, exaction (*formal*), force, pressure, shakedown (*US slang*). [➡CRIMES; 817]

extortionate *adj* **expensive**, exorbitant, inflated, high, overpriced, extravagant, usurious. [➡EXPENSIVE AND OVERPRICED; 248] *Opposite:* reasonable.

extra 1 *adj* **additional**, further, added, spare, second, superfluous. [➡MORE AND EXCESS; 122] *Opposite:* usual. 2 *adv* **more**, in addition, further, on top, spare, beyond, above. [➡MORE AND EXCESS; 122] 3 *adv* **especially**, particularly, ultra, exceptionally, more. [➡TO A GREAT EXTENT; 130] 4 *n* **optional extra**, addition, add-on, supplement, bonus, luxury, trimming, treat, extravagance. [➡MORE AND EXCESS; 122]

extract 1 *v* **take out**, remove, haul out, pull out, dig out, mine, dig up. [➡EXTRACT AND SEVER; 342] *Opposite:* put in. 2 *v* **obtain**, winkle out, unearth, extricate, root out, separate, isolate, get. [➡EXTRACT AND SEVER; 342] 3 *v* **extort**, force, wrest, wheedle out, wring, drag, winkle out. [➡TAKE SOMETHING AWAY; 426] 4 *n* **excerpt**, cutting, quotation, citation, abstract. [➡SUMMARIES, OUTLINES, AND EXCERPTS; 589] *Opposite:* source.

extraction 1 *n* **removal**, taking out, withdrawal, pulling out, drawing out, abstraction, mining. [➡REMOVE SOMETHING; 339] *Opposite:* insertion. 2 *n* **origin**, birth, descent, ancestry, family, lineage, line, heritage. [➡THE FAMILY; 956]

extracurricular 1 *adj* **additional**, supplementary, optional, secondary, extramural, subsidiary. [➡LESSONS, COURSE WORK, AND EXAMINATIONS; 842] *Opposite:* regular. 2 *adj* (*informal*) **extramarital**, adulterous, clandestine, illicit, improper. [➡MORALLY BAD; 776]

extradite *v* **deport**, expel, banish, transfer, repatriate, hand over, send back, return. [➡DESPATCH AND SEND; 334]

extradition *n* **repatriation**, handing over, deportation, expulsion, return, arrest. [➡EJECT AND EXCLUDE; 341]

extra-large *adj* **outsize**, outsized, giant, jumbo, oversized, mammoth, mega, super, gigantic, oversize, large size, economy size. [➡LARGE; 1192] *Opposite:* undersized.

extramarital *adj* **adulterous**, extracurricular, illicit, clandestine, improper, unlawful. [➡MORALLY BAD; 776]

extramural *adj* **external**, extracurricular, additional, optional, vocational. [➡EDUCATION; 838]

extraneous 1 *adj* **irrelevant**, unrelated, unconnected, inappropriate, beside the point, inapplicable. [➡REDUNDANT AND USELESS; 241] *Opposite:* pertinent. 2 *adj* **inessential**, unimportant, unnecessary, superfluous, peripheral, minor. [➡UNIMPORTANT AND UNNECESSARY; 239] *Opposite:* essential.

extraordinaire 1 *adj* **excellent**, extraordinary, superb, exceptional, remarkable. [➡EXTRAORDINARY: AMAZING; 205] *Opposite:* ordinary. 2 *adj* **extemporary**, extemporal, unrehearsed, impromptu, ad lib, spontaneous. [➡HAPPENING QUICKLY; 104] *Opposite:* rehearsed.

extraordinarily 1 *adv* **strangely**, oddly, unusually, bizarrely, abnormally, unexpectedly. [➡EXTRAORDINARY: UNCOMMON; 206] *Opposite:* normally. 2 *adv* **extremely**, very, unusually, particularly, amazingly, surprisingly, astonishingly. [➡TO A GREAT EXTENT; 130]

extraordinary 1 *adj* **strange**, odd, unusual, unexpected, astonishing, surprising, amazing, bizarre, weird, peculiar, uncommon. [➡EXTRAORDINARY: UNCOMMON; 206] *Opposite:* ordinary. 2 *adj* **special**, particular, exceptional, remarkable, great, wonderful. [➡EXTRAORDINARY: AMAZING; 205] *Opposite:* normal.

extrapolate *v* **infer**, generalize, induce, deduce, conclude, reason, draw conclusions. [➡SOLVE AND INTERPRET; 761]

extrasensory *adj* **telepathic**, psychic, clairvoyant, mystic, mystical, paranormal. [➡THE SUPERNATURAL; 788]

extrasensory perception *n* [➡THE SUPERNATURAL; 788]

extraterrestrial 1 *adj* **celestial**, interplanetary, Martian, alien, interstellar, otherworldly. [➡THE SOLAR SYSTEM AND ASTRONOMY; 1059] *Opposite:* terrestrial. 2 *n* **alien**, creature, creature from outer space, space invader, Martian, little green man (*humorous*). [➡SCIENCE FICTION; 1063] *Opposite:* earthling.

extravagance 1 *n* **profligacy**, overspending, wastefulness, excessiveness, lavishness, prodigality. [➡WASTEFUL AND UNECONOMICAL; 247] *Opposite:* prudence. 2 *n* **luxury**, indulgence, folly, nonessential, overindulgence, treat, extra. [➡WASTEFUL AND UNECONOMICAL; 247] *Opposite:* essential.

extravagant 1 *adj* **profligate**, wasteful, excessive, spendthrift, overgenerous, prodigal. [➡WASTEFUL AND UNECONOMICAL; 247] *Opposite:* thrifty. 2 *adj* **exaggerated**, overstated, profuse, excessive, elaborate, overdone, ornate, gaudy, showy. [➡IN POOR TASTE; 230] *Opposite:* restrained.

extravaganza *n* **show**, musical, variety performance, gala, festival, spectacular, pageant, burlesque (*US*). [➡PERFORMANCES AND SHOWS; 42]

extreme 1 *adj* **great**, tremendous, severe, intense, acute, excessive. [➡DIFFICULTY AND COMPLEXITY; 243] *Opposite:* insignificant. 2 *adj* **radical**, fanatical, immoderate (*formal*), zealous, excessive, intemperate. [➡NEGATIVE INTELLECTUAL CHARACTERISTICS; 526] *Opposite:* moderate. 3 *adj* **farthest**, furthest, outermost, ultimate, maximum, utmost. [➡DISTANCE; 161] 4 *adj* **dangerous**, life-threatening, thrilling, risky, exciting, punishing. [➡DANGEROUS; 237] *Opposite:* safe. 5 *n* **limit**, boundary, edge, end, pole, extremity, margin. [➡EXTREMITIES OF PHYSICAL OBJECTS; 1249]

extremely *adv* **very**, tremendously, enormously, awfully, really, particularly, exceptionally, exceedingly. [➡TO A GREAT EXTENT; 130] *Opposite:* somewhat.

extremism *n* **radicalism**, fanaticism, zealotry, immoderation (*formal*), activism, intemperance. [➡FADS, FETISHES, AND IDOLATRY; 556] *Opposite:* moderation.

extremist 1 *n* **radical**, fanatic, activist, revolutionary, rebel, terrorist. [➡PHILOSOPHICAL AND POLITICAL THINKERS; 782] *Opposite:* moderate. 2 *adj* **radical**, fanatical, revolutionary, rebel, terrorist, extreme, intemperate, immoderate (*formal*). [➡REBELLIOUSNESS AND DISOBEDIENCE; 566] *Opposite:* moderate.

extremity 1 *n* **edge**, limit, boundary, margin, extreme, end, fringe. [➡EXTREMITIES OF PHYSICAL OBJECTS; 1249] *Opposite:* centre. **2** *n* **limb**, hand, foot, arm, leg, appendage. [➡TORSO; 694]

extricate *v* **get out**, extract, remove, disentangle, detach, disengage, disconnect, free, rescue. [➡REMOVE SOMETHING; 339] *Opposite:* engage.

extrication *n* **disconnection**, detachment, disentanglement, disengagement, release, rescue, freeing. [➡REMOVE SOMETHING; 339] *Opposite:* engagement.

extroversion *n* **sociability**, friendliness, self-confidence, socialness, outgoingness, gregariousness. [➡FRIENDLINESS AND SOCIABILITY; 495] *Opposite:* introversion.

extrovert **1** *n* **outgoing person**, gregarious person, assertive person, live wire (*informal*), live one (*informal*), socializer, befriender. [➡PLEASURE-SEEKERS AND HEDONISTS; 886] *Opposite:* introvert. **2** *adj* **sociable**, outgoing, gregarious, extroverted, friendly, social. [➡FRIENDLINESS AND SOCIABILITY; 495] *Opposite:* introverted.

exuberance *n* **enthusiasm**, excitement, liveliness, energy, high spirits, cheerfulness. [➡CHEERFULNESS OF OUTLOOK; 504] *Opposite:* apathy.

exuberant *adj* **enthusiastic**, excited, lively, energetic, high-spirited, cheerful, boisterous, animated, vigorous, buoyant, vivacious. [➡ENERGY AND ENTHUSIASM; 497] *Opposite:* lethargic.

exude **1** *v* **radiate**, give out, give off, display, show, project, convey, emanate (*formal*), ooze. [➡EMIT AND EMANATE; 362] *Opposite:* absorb. **2** *v* **secrete**, release, ooze, leak, discharge, weep, emit. [➡LIQUID EMISSION; 371]

exult *v* **revel**, take pride, gloat, glory, triumph, wallow, rejoice (*literary*). [➡GIVING VENT TO EMOTIONS; 680] *Opposite:* lament.

exultant *adj* **jubilant**, overjoyed, triumphant, joyful, thrilled, happy, elated, proud, over the moon, gleeful, victorious, triumphalist. [➡PLEASURE, EXCITEMENT, AND ELATION; 535] *Opposite:* miserable.

exultation *n* **happiness**, triumph, joy, rejoicing, jubilation, celebration. [➡PLEASURE, EXCITEMENT, AND ELATION; 535] *Opposite:* misery.

eyas *type of* **young bird**. [➡YOUNG BIRD; 1004]

eye **1** *n* **appreciation**, sense, taste, discrimination, discernment, perceptiveness, judgment. [➡SKILLS, TALENTS, AND ABILITIES; 527] **2** *v* **look at**, stare at, gaze at, watch, observe, ogle, eyeball (*informal*), eye up. [➡LOOKING AND LOOKS; 701] **3** *part of* **face**. [➡HEAD; 693]

eyeball **1** *v* (*informal*) **stare at**, glare at, have a good look at, look at, gaze at, watch, ogle, eye up. [➡LOOKING AND LOOKS; 701] **2** *n* [➡THE EYE; 699]

eyebrow *n* [➡THE EYE; 699]

eye-catching *adj* **striking**, noticeable, attention-grabbing, startling, arresting, conspicuous, stunning, dazzling, astonishing. [➡BEAUTY AND ATTRACTIVENESS; 190] *Opposite:* unremarkable.

eyeful (*informal*) *n* **look**, view, gander (*informal*), glance, squint, dekko (*informal*), shufti (*informal*). [➡LOOKING AND LOOKS; 701]

eyeglasses (*US formal*) *type of* **glasses**. [➡GLASSES AND SPECTACLES; 1124]

eyelash *n* [➡THE EYE; 699]

eyelet *n* **hole**, grommet, eyehole, perforation, orifice (*literary*), loophole. [➡HOLES, GAPS, AND FORKS; 1251]

eyelid *n* [➡THE EYE; 699]

eyeliner *n* [➡MAKEUP AND BEAUTY PRODUCTS; 491]

eye opener *n* **revelation**, discovery, realization, surprise, shock, shocker (*informal*). [➡DECISIVE MOMENTS; 44] *Opposite:* expectation.

eye pencil *n* [➡MAKEUP AND BEAUTY PRODUCTS; 491]

eye shadow *n* [➡MAKEUP AND BEAUTY PRODUCTS; 491]

eyesight *n* **vision**, sight, sightedness, eye, view, perception, range of vision. [➡SEE; 700]

eyesore *n* **blot on the landscape**, blot, monstrosity, blemish, fright, horror (*informal*). [➡NUISANCES; 254]

eyetooth *type of* **tooth**. [➡THE MOUTH; 703]

eye up *v* [➡LOOKING AND LOOKS; 701]

eyewitness *n* **witness**, observer, bystander, onlooker, looker-on, watcher, spectator. [➡LOOKERS AND SPECTATORS; 702]

eyrie *type of* **den or nest**. [➡ANIMAL OR BIRD ACCOMMODATION; 1078]

fable *n* **tale**, legend, parable, myth, story, allegory. [➡THE ORAL TRADITION; 678]

fabled 1 *adj* **legendary**, wonderful, remarkable, extraordinary, famous, impressive, renowned, outstanding, important, epic. [➡KNOWN AND FAMOUS; 182] *Opposite:* unknown. 2 *adj* **fictitious**, mythical, imaginary, legendary, fairy-tale, fabulous, mythological, enchanted, magic, magical, storybook, make-believe. [➡FALSE AND UNREAL; 174] *Opposite:* factual.

fabric 1 *n* **cloth**, material, textile, stuff, yard goods, drapery, piece goods, dry goods (*US*). [➡TEXTILES AND THREADS; 1130] 2 *n* **structure**, foundation, framework, basics, makeup, composition, constitution, frame, organization. [➡QUALITIES AND CHARACTERISTICS; 1190] 3 *n* **brickwork**, stonework, masonry, structure, superstructure, material, facing, cladding, tiling, roofing. [➡BUILDING AND ARCHITECTURE; 1075]

fabric

◆ *types of fabric from animals*
alpaca, angora, astrakhan, baize, bearskin, brocade, camel hair, cashmere, chenille, crepe de Chine, felt, flannel, fur, gabardine, horsehair, jersey, lambswool, leather, loden, mohair, sheepskin, silk, snakeskin, taffeta, tweed, twill, wool, worsted

◆ *types of fabric from plants*
burlap, calico, canvas, cheesecloth, chintz, corduroy, cotton, denim, drill, flannelette, gauze, gingham, hessian, linen, moleskin, muslin, organdy, poplin, sacking, tarpaulin, terry, terry cloth (*US*), terry towelling, ticking, towelling, velvet, winceyette

◆ *types of synthetic fabric*
acrylic, chiffon, crêpe, fishnet, fleece, lamé, moquette, nylon, percale, polyester, PVC, rayon, sateen, satin, tulle, viscose

fabricate 1 *v* **invent**, make up, concoct, dream up, trump up, cook up (*informal*), contrive, counterfeit, fake, feign. [➡DECEPTION AND LIES; 661] 2 *v* **construct**, make, manufacture, produce, engineer, put together, formulate, assemble, devise, build, form. [➡MANUFACTURE; 350] *Opposite:* destroy.

fabricated *adj* **invented**, made-up, untrue, fictitious, fictional, false, fake, contrived, counterfeited, feigned. [➡FALSE AND UNREAL; 174] *Opposite:* genuine.

fabrication 1 *n* **untruth**, lie, invention, falsehood, cock-and-bull story, fib (*informal*), fiction. [➡DECEPTION AND LIES; 661] *Opposite:* truth. 2 *n* **construction**, manufacture, production, assembly, creation, building. [➡CREATION; 347] 3 *n* **counterfeit**, forgery, fake, imitation. [➡REPRESENTATIONS AND GENERAL EXAMPLES; 65]

See Compare and Contrast at **lie**.

fabulous *adj* **excellent**, wonderful, tremendous, magnificent, marvellous, great, remarkable, extraordinary, amazing, fantastic, outstanding. [➡EXTRAORDINARY: AMAZING; 205] *Opposite:* awful.

façade 1 *n* **frontage**, portico, fascia, front. [➡PARTS OF A BUILDING; 1094] 2 *n* **pretence**, veneer, impression, front, face, public image, mask. [➡APPEARANCE AND ATMOSPHERE; 1236]

face 1 *n* **countenance**, features, mug (*informal*), visage (*literary*), phiz (*slang*), phizog (*slang*). [➡HEAD; 693] 2 *n* (*informal*) **nerve**, gall, cheek (*informal*), boldness, audacity, pluck, impudence, effrontery, insolence. [➡BAD MANNERS AND SOCIAL SKILLS; 522] 3 *n* **expression**, look, appearance, air, aspect. [➡FACIAL EXPRESSION; 652] 4 *n* **outside**, surface, aspect, façade, wall, frontage. [➡EXTREMITIES OF PHYSICAL OBJECTS; 1249] *Opposite:* back. 5 *v* **be opposite**, be in front of, stand in front of, stand facing, look toward, look. [➡EXIST IN CLOSE PROXIMITY; 21] 6 *v* **confront**, tackle, meet, cope with, challenge, deal with, handle, play, play against, be drawn against, encounter. [➡INITIATE AND ESTABLISH COMMUNICATION; 681] *Opposite:* avoid. 7 *v* **accept**, admit, be realistic, realize, bite the bullet, come to terms with. [➡FORGET, FORGIVE, AND ACCEPT; 749] *Opposite:* deny.

face

◆ *parts of a face*
brow, cheek, chin, chops (*informal*), eye, jaw, jawline, jowl, mandible, mouth, nose

faceless *adj* **impersonal**, featureless, unidentified, anonymous, nameless, unnamed, unidentifiable, unknown, undisclosed, mysterious, unrevealed, characterless. [➡SECRET AND UNKNOWN; 180]

facelift 1 *n* **plastic surgery**, cosmetic surgery, operation, surgical operation, rhinoplasty, nose job (*informal*), lipectomy. [➡REMEDIES, TREATMENTS AND OPERATIONS; 732] 2 *n* **renovation**, modernization, refurbishment, redecoration, restoration, makeover, rehab (*US informal*). [➡IMPROVE APPEARANCE; 380]

face-off *n* **confrontation**, conflict, argument, run-in (*informal*), showdown, set-to (*informal*), challenge. [➡ARGUMENT; 47]

face pack *n* **face mask**, facial, beauty treatment, mudpack. [➡MAKEUP AND BEAUTY PRODUCTS; 491]

face powder *n* [➡MAKEUP AND BEAUTY PRODUCTS; 491]

face-saving *adj* **dignified**, diplomatic, tactical, tactful, restorative. [➡INTENTIONAL AND DELIBERATE; 280] *Opposite:* humiliating.

facet 1 *n* **aspect**, feature, part, component, factor, issue, quality, side. [➡QUALITIES AND CHARACTERISTICS; 1190] 2 *n* **surface**, face, side, plane, façade. [➡EXTREMITIES OF PHYSICAL OBJECTS; 1249]

face the music *v* **accept responsibility**, face the storm, face up to your actions, take the flak, bite the bullet, grasp the nettle, take the rap (*slang*), take the heat (*US*). [➡FORGET, FORGIVE, AND ACCEPT; 749]

facetious 1 *adj* **flippant**, silly, ill-timed, ill-judged, inappropriate, inane, glib, frivolous, foolish. [➡MOCKING AND DISMISSIVE; 637] *Opposite:* earnest. 2 *adj* **lighthearted**, playful, humorous, witty, droll, amusing, funny, comical, waggish (*dated*), jokey. [➡JOKES AND TEASING; 675] *Opposite:* serious.

See Compare and Contrast at **funny.**

facetiousness 1 *n* **flippancy**, frivolousness, inappropriateness, silliness, inanity, glibness, frivolity, foolishness. [➡GOOD-TEMPERED AND HUMOROUS; 628] *Opposite:* earnestness. 2 *n* **lightheartedness**, wittiness, wit, drollness, humorousness, funniness, comicalness, waggishness (*dated*), humour, playfulness, jokiness. [➡JOKES AND TEASING; 675] *Opposite:* seriousness.

face-to-face *adj* [➡CLOSENESS; 160]

face to face 1 *adv* **in person**, in the flesh, personally, head-on, man to man, woman to woman, person to person. [➡HONEST AND OPEN; 631] 2 *adv* **head on**, opposite, in confrontation, nose to nose, head to head. [➡CLOSENESS; 160]

face up to *v* **accept**, admit, come to terms with, realize, confront, tackle head on, bite the bullet, grasp the nettle, deal with. [➡FORGET, FORGIVE, AND ACCEPT; 749] *Opposite:* deny.

facial *n* **beauty treatment**, face mask, face pack, makeover, massage, facial scrub, mudpack. [➡MAKEUP AND BEAUTY PRODUCTS; 491]

facial expression *n* [➡FACIAL EXPRESSION; 652]

facial hair *n* [➡FACIAL HAIR; 490]

facile *adj* **superficial**, simplistic, flippant, trite, inane, glib, facetious, shallow, casual, slick, cursory. [➡BORING AND UNINTERESTING; 235] *Opposite:* profound.

facilitate *v* **make easy**, ease, make possible, enable, smooth, simplify, help, aid, assist, expedite, accelerate. [➡MAKE POSSIBLE; 276] *Opposite:* impede.

facilitation *n* **easing**, simplification, enablement, enabling, assistance, help, expedition, acceleration. [➡KIND ACTION OR BEHAVIOUR; 296] *Opposite:* obstruction.

facilitator *n* **organizer**, architect, originator, prime mover, initiator, helper, spur, expediter, catalyst, mediator, implementer, enabler, driving force. [➡DESIGNERS, CREATORS AND INSTIGATORS; 348]

facilities *n* **amenities**, services, conveniences, toilet, lavatory, bathroom, accommodations (*US*). [➡TYPES OF ROOM; 1096]

facility 1 *n* **skill**, capability, capacity, talent, flair, competence, ability, gift, aptitude, knack, proficiency, efficiency. [➡SKILLS, TALENTS, AND ABILITIES; 527] *Opposite:* inability. 2 *n* **service**, provision, resource, feature, advantage, means. [➡PHYSICAL OBJECTS; 1242]

facing *prep* **opposite**, in front of, fronting. [➡RELATIVE LOCATION; 162]

facsimile *n* **copy**, duplicate, reproduction, replica, likeness, double. [➡COPIES AND REPLICAS; 152]

fact 1 *n* **truth**, reality, actuality, verity (*formal*). [➡TRUE AND REAL; 172] *Opposite:* fiction. 2 *n* **piece of information**, detail, point, circumstance, datum, statistic, element. [➡BASIC DETAILS; 689] 3 *n* **happening**, deed, occurrence, event, act, circumstance. [➡EVENTS AND OCCURRENCES; 35]

fact-based *adj* [➡TRUE AND REAL; 172]

faction 1 *n* **section**, party, splinter group, bloc, division, group, offshoot, side, clique, circle. [➡GROUPS WITH A COMMON INTEREST; 938] 2 *n* **conflict**, division, disunity, schism, disharmony, discord, strife, sectarianism, dissension, disagreement, contention. [➡DISHARMONY; 157] *Opposite:* agreement.

factional 1 *adj* **sectarian**, dissenting, disaffected, separatist, schismatic, discordant, divisive. [➡UNWILLINGNESS AND STUBBORNNESS; 565] *Opposite:* united. 2 *adj* **dramatized**, semi-realistic, docudramatic, historical, pseudohistorical, documentary. [➡TRUE AND REAL; 172]

factious *adj* **divisive**, sectarian, schismatic, discordant, contentious, controversial. [➡DISHARMONY; 157] *Opposite:* unifying.

factitious *adj* **contrived**, artificial, simulated, affected, unnatural, insincere. [➡FALSE AND UNREAL; 174] *Opposite:* genuine.

fact of life *n* **reality**, practicality, fact, truth, actuality. [➡TRUE AND REAL; 172]

factor *n* **influence**, thing, feature, aspect, reason, cause, part, dynamic, issue, element, consideration, circumstance, component. [➡CAUSATION; 169]

factory

◆ *types of factory*
assembly plant, brewery, cannery, distillery, forge, foundry, machine shop, maquiladora, mill, mint, plant, pottery, sawmill, smithy, steelworks, sweatshop, water mill, works, workshop

factory ship *type of* **motor vessel.** [➡SHIPS AND BOATS; 1149]

factory worker *n* [➡WORKER; 836]

factotum *type of* **servant.** [➡DOMESTIC AND KITCHEN WORKERS; 850]

facts 1 *n* **truth**, evidence, reality, actuality, proof. [➡EVIDENCE AND PROOF; 69] 2 *n* **particulars**, details, specifics, essentials, data, statistics, figures. [➡BASIC DETAILS; 689]

fact sheet *n* **information sheet**, information leaflet, booklet, brochure, handout, sheet, leaflet, document. [➡MANUALS AND INSTRUCTIONS; 590]

factual 1 *adj* **objective**, hard, verifiable, bona fide, authentic, genuine, scientific, accurate, exact. [➡TRUE AND REAL; 172] *Opposite:* subjective. 2 *adj* **truthful**, accurate, realistic, honest, true-life, genuine, real, actual, faithful. [➡TRUE AND REAL; 172] *Opposite:* fictional.

factually *adv* **truthfully**, accurately, exactly, really, precisely, objectively, literally, concretely, empirically, realistically. [➡TRUE AND REAL; 172]

faculty 1 *n* **sense**, power, endowment, capability, function. [➡THE SENSES; 697] 2 *n* **ability**, facility, gift, talent, knack, aptitude, capacity, capability, genius. [➡SKILLS, TALENTS, AND ABILITIES; 527] *Opposite:* inability. 3 *n* **staff**, teaching body, teaching staff, teachers, professors. [➡EDUCATORS; 840]

fad *n* **fashion**, craze, trend, whim, vogue, cult, rage, mania. [➡FADS, FETISHES, AND IDOLATRY; 556]

faddiness *n* **fussiness**, fastidiousness, choosiness, pickiness, pernicketiness (*informal*), faddishness (*US*). [➡LACK OF COMMITMENT AND UNRELIABILITY; 510]

faddishness (*US*) *n* **fussiness**, faddiness, fastidiousness, choosiness, pickiness, pernicketiness (*informal*). [➡DIFFICULT TO PLEASE; 516]

faddy *adj* **fussy**, finicky, picky, choosy (*informal*), particular, pernickety (*informal*), faddish (*US*). [➡DIFFICULT TO PLEASE; 516]

fade 1 *v* **become paler**, lighten, become lighter, lose colour, bleach. [➡CHANGE OF INTENSITY: LESS; 396] *Opposite:* darken. 2 *v* **disappear**, weaken, die away, diminish, fade away, fade out, tail off, decline, dwindle, fail. [➡DISAPPEAR; 4] *Opposite:* grow. 3 *v* **wane**, wither, die, waste away, wilt, dwindle, evaporate, recede, droop, shrivel, languish. [➡CEASE TO EXIST; 22] *Opposite:* flourish.

fade away 1 *v* **disappear**, vanish, fade, evaporate, dwindle, diminish, fade out, peter out. [➡DISAPPEAR; 4] 2 *v* **waste away**, shrivel, wane, wither, atrophy, shrink. [➡DISAPPEAR; 4] *Opposite:* thrive.

fading *adj* **disappearing**, declining, dying, vanishing, diminishing, waning, failing, dwindling. [➡CEASE TO EXIST; 22] *Opposite:* growing.

faeces *n* [➡EXCRETION AND EXCRETA; 723]

faff about (*informal*) *v* **waver**, hesitate, vacillate, shilly-shally, mess about (*informal*), faff around. [➡HESITATE; 273]

faff around (*informal*) *v* **waver**, hesitate, vacillate, shilly-shally, mess about (*informal*), faff about. [➡HESITATE; 273]

faience *type of* **pottery**. [➡POTTERY; 1134]

fail 1 *v* **be unsuccessful**, go pear-shaped (*informal*), nosedive, bomb (*informal*), miss the mark, go belly up, flop (*informal*), fall flat, come to nothing, miscarry. [➡FAIL OR BE UNSUCCESSFUL; 75] *Opposite:* succeed. 2 *v* **flunk** (*informal*), fall short, not make the grade, not be up to scratch, fluff (*informal*). [➡FAIL OR BE UNSUCCESSFUL; 75] *Opposite:* pass. 3 *v* **stop working**, break down, pack up (*informal*), go on the blink (*informal*), crash, go down, stop, seize up, grind to a halt, die, give up, collapse. [➡FAIL OR CEASE TO FUNCTION; 471] 4 *v* **go out of business**, go bankrupt, crash, fold, go under, flop (*informal*), collapse, bomb (*informal*). [➡FAIL OR BE UNSUCCESSFUL; 75] *Opposite:* thrive. 5 *v* **let down**, disappoint, neglect, forsake, desert, betray. [➡UPSET, DISTRESS, AND HUMILIATE; 568] *Opposite:* satisfy. 6 *v* **weaken**, fade, diminish, dwindle, decline, wane, disappear. [➡DISAPPEAR; 4] *Opposite:* rally.

failed *adj* **unsuccessful**, botched, disastrous, futile, abortive, miscarried. [➡UNSUCCESSFUL AND UNPROMISING; 76] *Opposite:* successful.

failing 1 *n* **shortcoming**, flaw, weakness, weak point, fault, imperfection, deficiency, defect, weak spot. [➡FAULTS, FLAWS, AND WEAKNESSES; 252] 2 *prep* **without**, in the absence of, lacking. [➡LACK OF POSSESSION; 446] 3 *adj* **deteriorating**, worsening, weakening, fading, waning, dwindling, dying, inadequate, declining. [➡UNSUCCESSFUL AND UNPROMISING; 76] *Opposite:* strengthening.

See Compare and Contrast at **flaw**.

fail-safe *adj* **foolproof**, guaranteed, dependable, reliable, goofproof (*US informal*). [➡SAFE AND SAFETY; 192] *Opposite:* unreliable.

failure 1 *n* **disappointment**, letdown, catastrophe, fiasco, disaster, botch (*informal*), miscarriage, flop (*informal*), bomb (*US informal*). [➡FAILURE; 77] *Opposite:* success. 2 *n* **breakdown**, stoppage, malfunction, crash, collapse, seizure. [➡FAILURE; 77] 3 *n* **bankruptcy**, closure, crash, collapse, insolvency, ruin. [➡FAILURE; 77]

faint 1 *adj* **dim**, weak, faded, indistinct, feeble, unclear, shadowy, hazy, distant, muffled, soft, pale. [➡DESCRIBING COLOURS; 1225] *Opposite:* bright. 2 *adj* **dizzy**, giddy, woozy, wobbly (*informal*), unsteady, vertiginous, lightheaded. [➡ILL AND SICK; 741] 3 *adj* **slight**, diminished, muffled, soft, low, quiet. [➡SOFT OR PLEASANT SOUNDS; 1264] *Opposite:* loud. 4 *v* **pass out**, collapse, black out, fall down, lose consciousness. [➡FALL ILL, TREAT, AND RECOVER; 729] *Opposite:* come to.

faint-hearted *adj* **fearful**, apprehensive, hesitant, cowardly, shy, timorous, retiring, tentative, coy, pusillanimous (*formal*), nervous, diffident. [➡COWARDICE AND WEAKNESS OF WILL; 509] *Opposite:* bold.

See Compare and Contrast at **cowardly**.

faint-heartedness *n* [➡COWARDICE AND WEAKNESS OF WILL; 509]

faintly 1 *adv* **dimly**, weakly, slightly, indistinctly, feebly, unclearly, hazily, distantly, softly, palely, quietly. [➡DESCRIBING COLOURS; 1225] *Opposite:* brightly. 2 *adv* **slightly**, softly, barely, indistinctly, imperceptibly, quietly. [➡SOFT OR PLEASANT SOUNDS; 1264] *Opposite:* loudly.

faintness 1 *n* **dimness**, weakness, feebleness, indistinctness, haziness, paleness. [➡WEAKNESS; 242] *Opposite:* brightness. 2 *n* **slightness**, quietness, weakness, feebleness, softness. [➡SOFT OR PLEASANT SOUNDS; 1264] *Opposite:* loudness. 3 *n* **dizziness**, giddiness, wooziness, vertigo, lightheadedness, unsteadiness. [➡ILL AND SICK; 741]

fair 1 *adj* **reasonable**, just, fair-minded, open-minded, impartial, rational, evenhanded, nondiscriminatory, unbiased, objective, dispassionate, honest. [➡EQUALITY; 155] *Opposite:* biased. 2 *adj* **light**, blond, fair-haired, flaxen, tow-headed, pale. [➡HAIR COLOUR; 486] *Opposite:* dark. 3 *adj* **adequate**, passable, average, reasonable, decent, moderate, mediocre, fair to middling, ordinary, run-of-the-mill, acceptable. [➡ACCEPTABLE AND PASSABLE; 220] *Opposite:* poor. 4 *adj* **pleasing**, attractive, good-looking, lovely, pretty, beautiful. [➡PEOPLE'S PHYSICAL APPEARANCE; 476] *Opposite:* unattractive. 5 *adj* **fine** (*informal*), good, bright, sunny, clear, cloudless, pleasant. [➡HOT WEATHER; 1050] *Opposite:* inclement. **6** *n* **travelling fair**, fairground, funfair, amusement park, theme park, carnival (*US*), midway (*US*). [➡PERFORMANCES AND SHOWS; 42] **7** *n* **festival**, sale, fête, exposition, bazaar, trade fair, trade event, fayre, show, exhibition, gala. [➡SALES AND SHOWS; 444]

fair enough **1** *adj* **acceptable**, understandable, reasonable, okay (*informal*), justified, warranted. [➡ACCEPTABLE AND PASSABLE; 220] *Opposite:* unfair. **2** *interj* (*informal*) **okay** (*informal*), all right, that's fine, no problem (*informal*), fine. [➡EXPRESSIONS OF AGREEMENT; 649]

fairground *n* **fair**, funfair, theme park, amusement park, playground, park, midway (*US*), carnival (*US*). [➡URBAN OUTDOOR SPACES; 1071]

fair-haired *adj* **fair**, blond, flaxen, tow-headed. [➡HAIR COLOUR; 486] *Opposite:* dark.

fairly **1** *adv* **honestly**, justly, properly, legitimately, impartially, without favour, equally, equitably (*formal*), objectively, fair and square. [➡EQUALITY; 155] *Opposite:* unfairly. **2** *adv* **moderately**, rather, quite, reasonably, somewhat, comparatively, relatively, tolerably, passably. [➡TO A CERTAIN EXTENT; 134] **3** *adv* **completely**, positively, literally, practically, absolutely, really, accurately, fully, utterly. [➡TO A GREAT EXTENT; 130]

fair-minded *adj* **fair**, open-minded, evenhanded, nondiscriminatory, impartial, reasonable, disinterested, dispassionate, just, objective, honest. [➡POSITIVE INTELLECTUAL CHARACTERISTICS; 525] *Opposite:* prejudiced.

fairness *n* **justice**, equality, evenhandedness, impartiality, fair-mindedness, objectivity. [➡EQUALITY; 155] *Opposite:* unfairness.

fair to middling *adj* [➡ACCEPTABLE AND PASSABLE; 220]

fairy *n* **pixie**, brownie, sprite, elf, leprechaun, fay (*literary*), gremlin (*informal*), imp, genie, jinni. [➡MYTHICAL BEINGS; 790]

fairyland *n* **wonderland**, dreamland, dream world, seventh heaven, heaven, paradise, cloud nine. [➡NON-EXISTENT PLACE; 1065]

fairy lights *n* [➡LIGHTING; 862]

fairy ring champignon *type of* **fungus**. [➡MICROORGANISMS, FUNGI, AND ALGAE; 1023]

fairy story **1** *n* **myth**, fairy tale, folk tale, folk story, legend, fable, tale, story. [➡THE ORAL TRADITION; 678] **2** *n* **invention**, fabrication, lie, fib (*informal*), untruth, falsehood, fairy tale, fantasy, excuse, tall tale, tall story, fiction, cock-and-bull story, canard (*literary*). [➡DECEPTION AND LIES; 661]

fairy-tale **1** *adj* **mythical**, enchanted, magic, magical, imaginary, legendary, fabled, fabulous, make-believe. [➡FALSE AND UNREAL; 174] *Opposite:* real. **2** *adj* **fortunate**, happy, storybook, perfect, romantic, traditional, enchanting, wonderful, beautiful, magical, glamorous, fascinating, dazzling. [➡EXTRAORDINARY: AMAZING; 205] *Opposite:* unhappy. **3** *adj* **fabricated**, unbelievable, make-believe, made-up, highly coloured, incredible, mythical. [➡IMPOSSIBLE AND IMPROBABLE; 179] *Opposite:* truthful.

fairy tale **1** *n* **invention**, fabrication, lie, fib (*informal*), untruth, falsehood, fairy story, fantasy, excuse, tall tale, tall story, fiction, cock-and-bull story, canard (*literary*). [➡DECEPTION AND LIES; 661] **2** *n* **fairy story**, folk tale, folk story, myth, legend, fable, tale, story. [➡FICTION AND DRAMA; 913]

fait accompli *n* [➡WHOLENESS AND COMPLETENESS; 199]

faith **1** *n* **trust**, confidence, reliance, conviction, belief, assurance. [➡CALMNESS, CONFIDENCE, AND COMPOSURE; 537] *Opposite:* disbelief. **2** *n* **loyalty**, devotion, faithfulness, commitment, dedication, fidelity, constancy, allegiance, fealty (*archaic or literary*). [➡RELIGIOUS CONCEPTS; 777] *Opposite:* disloyalty.

faithful **1** *adj* **loyal**, devoted, trusty, trustworthy, staunch, dependable, reliable, dedicated, committed, true, constant. [➡HARD-WORKING AND COMMITTED; 501] *Opposite:* faithless. **2** *adj* **correct**, true, realistic, authentic, close, accurate, exact, true to life, truthful, believable. [➡TRUE AND REAL; 172] *Opposite:* unrealistic.

faithfully *adv* **loyally**, devotedly, trustworthily, staunchly, dependably. [➡HARD-WORKING AND COMMITTED; 501] *Opposite:* faithlessly.

faithfulness **1** *n* **loyalty**, devotion, staunchness, dependability, reliability, fidelity, constancy. [➡HONEST AND RELIABLE; 503] *Opposite:* faithlessness. **2** *n* **correctness**, closeness, realism, authenticity, accuracy, truthfulness, truth, exactness, believability, fidelity. [➡TRUE AND REAL; 172] *Opposite:* unreality.

faith healer *n* [➡PEOPLE WITH SUPERNATURAL POWERS; 789]

faithless *adj* **dishonest**, disloyal, untrustworthy, unfaithful, fickle, untrue, inconstant. [➡LACK OF COMMITMENT AND UNRELIABILITY; 510] *Opposite:* faithful.

faithlessly *adv* **dishonestly**, unfaithfully, deceitfully, disloyally, treacherously, untrustworthily. [➡MORALLY BAD; 776] *Opposite:* faithlessly.

faithlessness *n* **dishonesty**, infidelity, inconstancy, fickleness, disloyalty, unfaithfulness. [➡DIFFICULT TO PLEASE; 516] *Opposite:* faithfulness.

fake **1** *n* **imitation**, copy, replica, simulation, mock-up, facsimile, counterfeit, phoney, forgery, fraud, sham. [➡DECEPTION AND LIES; 661] *Opposite:* original. **2** *adj* **false**, bogus, sham, phoney, counterfeit, forged, replica, imitation, simulated, mock, faux, ersatz (*disapproving*), pretend. [➡FALSE AND UNREAL; 174] *Opposite:* genuine. **3** *v* **falsify**, copy, counterfeit, forge, replicate, reproduce. [➡FALSIFY AND CHEAT; 177] **4** *v* **simulate**, feign, pretend, act, dissemble, dissimulate (*formal*). [➡PRETEND AND MIMIC; 60]

faked *adj* [➡FALSE AND UNREAL; 174]

faker *n* **fraud**, fake, liar, pretender, impostor, hypocrite, phony. [➡PEOPLE WHO DECEIVE; 662]

falcon *type of* **bird of prey**. [➡BIRD OF PREY; 998]

fall **1** *v* **drop**, go down, descend, plunge, plummet. [➡GO DOWNWARDS; 308] *Opposite:* ascend. **2** *v* **tumble**, fall over, fall down, drop, trip over, go head over heels, collapse. [➡GO DOWNWARDS; 308] **3** *v* **decrease**, reduce, sink, come down. [➡CHANGE OF SIZE: SMALLER; 394] *Opposite:* increase. **4** *n* **reduction**, decrease, drop, tumble, descent, plummet, plunge, collapse. [➡CHANGE OF SIZE: SMALLER; 394] *Opposite:* increase. **5** *n* **waterfall**, rapids, cataract, cascade, white water. [➡RIVERS, LAKES, AND STREAMS; 1042] **6** *n (US)* **autumn**, harvest time, season, equinox, Indian summer. [➡TIMES OF YEAR; 88]

fall about *(informal) v* **laugh**, hoot, scream with laughter, be amused, guffaw, roar. [➡LAUGHTER; 650]

fallacious *adj* **mistaken**, erroneous, misleading, deceptive, false, wrong. [➡FALSE AND UNREAL; 174] *Opposite:* correct.

fallaciousness *n* [➡DECEPTION AND LIES; 661]

fallacy *n* **misconception**, myth, error, mistake, delusion, misjudgment. [➡GOSSIP; 679]

fall apart *v* **disintegrate**, crumble, collapse, fall to pieces, fall to bits, break up, fail. [➡TEAR, BREAK, AND CUT; 361] *Opposite:* come together.

fall asleep *v* **nod off**, drop off *(informal)*, doze off, go to sleep. [➡SLEEP AND DREAM; 724] *Opposite:* wake up.

fall away *v* [➡DISAPPEAR; 4]

fall back **1** *v* **retreat**, withdraw, draw back, run away, regroup. [➡GO BACKWARDS; 310] *Opposite:* advance. **2** *v* **drop behind**, fall behind, drop back, lag, lag behind, lose ground, hang back. [➡GO BACKWARDS; 310] *Opposite:* catch up.

fallback *n* **replacement**, contingency, alternative, stand-in, substitute, reserve, backup. [➡SOLUTION; 216]

fall back on *v* **resort to**, rely on, turn to, depend on, have recourse to. [➡MAKE DECISIONS AND CHOICES; 753]

fall behind **1** *v* **drop back**, drop behind, fall back, lag, lag behind, lose ground. [➡GO BACKWARDS; 310] *Opposite:* keep up. **2** *v* **be delayed**, be late, be in arrears, default. [➡MOVE SLOWLY; 315]

fall by the wayside *v* **come to nothing**, fold, collapse, fail, abandon, drop out. [➡FAIL OR BE UNSUCCESSFUL; 75]

fall down **1** *v* **collapse**, fall over, tumble, trip over, trip, fall. [➡GO DOWNWARDS; 308] **2** *v* **fail**, be unsuccessful, disappoint, go wrong, flop *(informal)*. [➡FAIL OR BE UNSUCCESSFUL; 75] *Opposite:* succeed.

fall flat *v* **fail**, miss the target, flop *(informal)*, bomb *(informal)*. [➡FAIL OR BE UNSUCCESSFUL; 75] *Opposite:* succeed.

fall for **1** *v* **fall in love with**, be attracted to, fancy *(informal)*, be smitten *(literary or humorous)*, be taken with, be stuck on *(informal)*, take a shine to *(informal)*, be crazy about *(informal)*. [➡LIKE, LOVE, VALUE AND ENJOY; 579] *Opposite:* go off. **2** *v* **be duped by**, be deceived by, be tricked by, be taken in by, believe, accept, swallow *(informal)*. [➡FORGET, FORGIVE, AND ACCEPT; 749] *Opposite:* see through.

fall foul of *v* **come into conflict with**, tangle with, have a brush with, come up against. [➡DISHARMONY; 157]

fall guy *(informal)* **1** *n* **dupe**, sucker *(informal)*, stooge, fool, chump *(dated informal)*, gull. [➡VICTIMS OF DECEIT; 663] **2** *n* **scapegoat**, whipping boy, sucker *(informal)*, victim, butt. [➡VICTIMS OF DECEIT; 663]

fallibility *n* **imperfection**, frailty, weakness, shortcoming, failure, failing. [➡NEGATIVE INTELLECTUAL CHARACTERISTICS; 526] *Opposite:* infallibility.

fallible *adj* **imperfect**, mortal, weak, frail, human. [➡COWARDICE AND WEAKNESS OF WILL; 509] *Opposite:* infallible.

falling *adj* **dwindling**, dropping, deteriorating, tumbling, sinking, dipping, decreasing, subsiding, diminishing, declining, lessening, plummeting. [➡CEASE TO EXIST; 22] *Opposite:* rising.

falling apart *adj* [➡IN BAD REPAIR; 1233]

falling down *adj* [➡IN BAD REPAIR; 1233]

falling-out *n* **quarrel**, fight, row, disagreement, misunderstanding, rift, split, dispute. [➡ARGUMENT; 47] *Opposite:* reconciliation.

falling star *type of* **heavenly body**. [➡CELESTIAL BODIES; 1060]

falling to pieces *adj* **dilapidated**, shabby, tatty, falling down, tumbledown, rundown. [➡IN BAD REPAIR; 1233] *Opposite:* pristine.

fall into place *v* **work out**, shape up, make sense, come together, sort itself out, take shape, become clear. [➡APPEAR AND EMERGE; 3]

fall in with **1** *v* **meet**, join, come across, bump into, run into, get to know, make the acquaintance of. [➡ESTABLISHING RELATIONSHIPS WITH OTHERS; 974] *Opposite:* avoid. **2** *v* **agree with**, accept, support, go along with, comply with. [➡AGREE; 646] *Opposite:* reject.

fall off *v* **decline**, go down, decrease, plunge, reduce, drop. [➡CHANGE OF SIZE: SMALLER; 394] *Opposite:* increase.

falloff *n* **decrease**, decline, falling off, reduction, drop, cut. [➡LESS; 124] *Opposite:* increase.

fall out *v* **quarrel**, argue, disagree, come to blows, row, have words, have a row, fight, have a fight. [➡ARGUE AND FIGHT – TWO-WAY; 644] *Opposite:* make up.

fallout *n* **consequence**, result, outcome, effect, knock-on effect, upshot. [➡RESULTS AND OUTCOMES; 83]

fall over *v* **tumble**, fall down, collapse, trip, trip over, go head over heels. [➡GO DOWNWARDS; 308]

fallow **1** *adj* **uncultivated**, unplanted, unseeded, unused, untilled. [➡EMPTY; 1237] *Opposite:* cultivated. **2** *adj* **inactive**, unproductive, idle, sterile, infertile, barren, uncreative. [➡REDUNDANT AND USELESS; 241] *Opposite:* creative.

fall prey to *v* [➡EXPERIENCE AND ENCOUNTER; 583]

fall short *v* **be deficient**, be wanting, be lacking, prove inadequate, not make the grade, not be up to snuff, not be up to scratch, fail. [➡FAIL OR BE UNSUCCESSFUL; 75] *Opposite:* succeed.

fall through *v* **fail**, go wrong, come to nothing, miscarry, misfire, not come off. [➡FAIL OR BE UNSUCCESSFUL; 75] *Opposite:* succeed.

fall to bits *v* **fall to pieces**, disintegrate, come apart, crumble, fall apart, break up. [➡TEAR, BREAK, AND CUT; 361]

fall victim to *v* [➡EXPERIENCE AND ENCOUNTER; 583]

false **1** *adj* **incorrect**, untruthful, untrue, wrong, dishonest, fabricated, deceitful, made-up, insincere, deceptive. [➡FALSE AND UNREAL; 174] *Opposite:* true. 2 *adj* **mistaken**, erroneous, fallacious, misleading, deceiving. [➡INCORRECT AND ERRONEOUS; 223] *Opposite:* correct. 3 *adj* **artificial**, bogus, sham, phoney, counterfeit, forged, copied, fake, fictitious, pretend, put-on, made-up, insincere. [➡FALSE AND UNREAL; 174] *Opposite:* real.

falsehood 1 *n* **lie**, story (*informal*), untruth, tale, fiction, invention, fib (*informal*), misrepresentation, cock-and-bull story, tall tale, fairy story, fairy tale, myth, fabrication, false report, canard (*literary*). [➡DECEPTION AND LIES; 661] 2 *n* **deception**, dishonesty, mendacity, deceit, fabrication, deceitfulness, lying. [➡DECEPTION AND LIES; 661]

See Compare and Contrast at **lie**.

false impression *n* **mistaken belief**, misconception, misreading, wrong idea, misapprehension, erroneous belief. [➡MISTAKES; 251]

falsely 1 *adv* **incorrectly**, misleadingly, deceptively, dishonestly, deceitfully, untruthfully, insincerely. [➡FALSE AND UNREAL; 174] *Opposite:* honestly. 2 *adv* **mistakenly**, wrongly, fallaciously, erroneously, deceivingly. [➡INCORRECT AND ERRONEOUS; 223] *Opposite:* rightly.

falseness 1 *n* **incorrectness**, dishonesty, deceit, deceitfulness, speciousness, insincerity. [➡DECEPTION AND LIES; 661] *Opposite:* honesty. 2 *n* **mistakenness**, erroneousness, wrongness, fallaciousness, deceptiveness, deception. [➡INCORRECT AND ERRONEOUS; 223] *Opposite:* rightness.

falsetto *type of* **musical register**. [➡MUSICAL TERMS; 912]

falsification *n* **fabrication**, distortion, forgery, fiddling (*informal*), misrepresentation, deception, alteration. [➡DECEPTION AND LIES; 661] *Opposite:* correction.

falsified *adj* **fabricated**, forged, untrue, counterfeit, false, fake, made-up, phoney, doctored. [➡FALSE AND UNREAL; 174] *Opposite:* true.

falsify *v* **fabricate**, fake, forge, rig, fix (*informal*), fiddle (*informal*), misrepresent, alter, change, doctor. [➡FALSIFY AND CHEAT; 177]

falsity *n* **falseness**, spuriousness, hollowness, inaccuracy, deceptiveness, fallaciousness, incorrectness, speciousness, untruth. [➡DECEPTION AND LIES; 661] *Opposite:* correctness.

falter 1 *v* **hesitate**, pause, waver, stammer, stutter, fumble, tail off. [➡HESITATE; 273] *Opposite:* continue. 2 *v* **fail**, weaken, fade, wane, abate (*formal or literary*), vacillate. [➡CEASE TO EXIST; 22] *Opposite:* rally. 3 *v* **stumble**, trip up, stagger, totter, sway, lurch, trip. [➡WALK UNSTEADILY; 316]

See Compare and Contrast at **hesitate**.

faltering *adj* **hesitant**, tentative, halting, timid, uncertain, broken. [➡UNCERTAINTY; 560]

falteringly *adv* **hesitantly**, timidly, insecurely, uncertainly, gingerly, haltingly. [➡INSECURITY AND LOSS OF COMPOSURE; 545] *Opposite:* confidently.

fame *n* **renown**, celebrity, reputation, distinction, recognition, eminence, prominence, notoriety, illustriousness, infamy, legend, myth. [➡KNOWN AND FAMOUS; 182] *Opposite:* obscurity.

famed *adj* **well-known**, famous, celebrated, renowned, eminent, prominent, illustrious, legendary, recognized, notorious (*archaic*), infamous. [➡KNOWN AND FAMOUS; 182] *Opposite:* unknown.

familial *adj* **family**, ancestral, household, domestic, matrimonial, marital, hereditary. [➡THE FAMILY; 956]

familiar 1 *adj* **well-known**, recognizable, common, customary, accustomed, habitual, usual, recurring, everyday, frequent, wonted (*formal*), regular. [➡KNOWN AND FAMOUS; 182] *Opposite:* unfamiliar. 2 *adj* **accustomed**, habitual, usual, recurring, everyday, typical, frequent, wonted (*formal*), time-honoured, traditional, established, regular. [➡ORDINARINESS; 245] *Opposite:* unusual. 3 *adj* **acquainted**, conversant, accustomed, used to, at home with, at ease with, au fait, aware, cognizant of (*formal*). [➡KNOWLEDGE AND WISDOM; 559] 4 *adj* **friendly**, intimate, easy, informal, personal, relaxed, close, cosy. [➡EMOTIONALLY PLEASANT; 188] *Opposite:* formal.

familiarity 1 *n* **knowledge**, understanding, acquaintance, awareness, ease, expertise, fluency, skill, experience, know-how (*informal*). [➡KNOWLEDGE AND WISDOM; 559] *Opposite:* unfamiliarity. 2 *n* **intimacy**, informality, friendship, ease, closeness, friendliness, relaxedness, casualness. [➡FRIENDLINESS AND SOCIABILITY; 495] *Opposite:* formality.

familiarization *n* **acquaintance**, getting used to, adjustment, adaptation, becoming accustomed, accommodation, habituation (*formal*). [➡KNOWLEDGE AND WISDOM; 559]

familiarize *v* **acquaint**, tell, explain, make clear, train, drill. [➡INSTRUCT AND TEACH; 610]

familiarize yourself *v* **get to know**, adapt, get used to, acclimatize yourself, acquaint yourself, accustom yourself, adjust, catch on (*informal*), pick up, become au fait. [➡LEARN AND DISCOVER; 763]

familiarly *adv* **intimately**, closely, informally, cosily, casually. [➡EMOTIONALLY PLEASANT; 188] *Opposite:* distantly.

family 1 *n* **relations**, relatives, people (*informal*), folks, children, family unit, extended family, nuclear family, clan (*informal*), nearest and dearest, loved ones, kinsfolk, kin. [➡THE FAMILY; 956] 2 *n* **lineage**, descendants, dynasty, ancestors, line, family tree, blood. [➡THE FAMILY; 956] 3 *n* **category**, genus, species, type, kind, line, breed, strain, variety, group. [➡VARIETY, TYPE, KIND; 146] 4 *adj* **domestic**, household, everyday, intimate, private. [➡THE FAMILY; 956]

family circle *n* **household**, family, family unit, ménage (*formal*), home, house. [➡THE FAMILY; 956]

family member *n* [➡THE FAMILY; 956]

family name *n* **surname**, last name, maternal name, paternal name, name, second name, patronymic, matronymic. [➡NAME AND DESCRIBE; 666]

family room *type of* **room in the home**. [➡TYPES OF ROOM; 1096]

family tree *n* **ancestry**, pedigree, genealogy, ancestors, descendants, lineage. [➡THE FAMILY; 956]

family unit *n* **family**, family circle, household, ménage (*formal*). [➡THE FAMILY; 956]

famine *n* **food shortage**, shortage, scarcity, dearth, want, starvation, deprivation. [➡FOOD; 1166] *Opposite:* abundance.

famish *v* [➡EAT AND NOT EAT; 711]

famished *adj* **hungry**, starving (*informal*), ravenous, starved (*informal*), underfed, unfed. [➡EAT AND NOT EAT; 711] *Opposite:* sated.

famous *adj* **well-known**, famed, celebrated, renowned, eminent, prominent, illustrious, legendary, recognized, notorious (*archaic*). [➡KNOWN AND FAMOUS; 182] *Opposite:* unknown.

famously 1 *adv* **notably**, memorably, eminently, prominently, distinctively, notoriously (*archaic*). [➡SUCCESSFUL AND PROMISING; 81] 2 *adv* **well**, excellently, superbly, like a house on fire, like nobody's business. [➡TO A GREAT EXTENT; 130]

fan 1 *v* **waft**, blow, cool, wave, percolate, circulate. [➡MOVE SOMETHING ON THE SPOT; 337] 2 *v* **stir up**, stimulate, provoke, increase, fuel, encourage, generate, incite, foment (*formal*), agitate. [➡CHANGE OF INTENSITY: MORE; 395] *Opposite:* defuse. 3 *n* **admirer**, enthusiast, aficionado, follower, devotee, buff, addict, fanatic, groupie (*informal*), supporter, aficionada. [➡DEVOTEES AND ADDICTED PEOPLE; 557]

fanatic 1 *n* **extremist**, zealot, radical, fundamentalist, crusader, partisan. [➡DEVOTEES AND ADDICTED PEOPLE; 557] 2 *n* **fan**, enthusiast, devotee, buff, nut (*informal*), follower, groupie (*informal*), supporter, addict, admirer, obsessive, maniac, aficionado, aficionada. [➡DEVOTEES AND ADDICTED PEOPLE; 557] 3 *adj* **fanatical**, obsessive, passionate, addicted, extreme, enthusiastic, frenzied, devoted, dedicated, fervent, fixated, zealous, keen. [➡ENERGY AND ENTHUSIASM; 497] *Opposite:* indifferent.

fanatical *adj* **fanatic**, obsessive, dedicated, fervent, fixated, zealous, enthusiastic, keen, passionate, devoted, extreme, addicted, frenzied. [➡APPRECIATION AND GRATITUDE; 536] *Opposite:* indifferent.

fanaticism *n* **extremism**, radicalism, fervour, zeal, keenness, dedication, passion, devotion. [➡FADS, FETISHES, AND IDOLATRY; 556] *Opposite:* indifference.

fanciful *adj* **imaginary**, fantastic, whimsical, unbelievable, out of this world, far-fetched, unlikely, bizarre, curious, invented. [➡IMPOSSIBLE AND IMPROBABLE; 179] *Opposite:* prosaic.

fancy 1 *adj* **elaborate**, ornate, decorative, ornamental, intricate, showy, rococo. [➡POSITIVELY COMPLEX OR COMPLICATED; 218] 2 *adj* **expensive**, upmarket, posh (*informal*), lavish, swanky (*informal*), extravagant, upscale (*US*). [➡EXPENSIVE AND LUXURIOUS; 219] *Opposite:* plain. 3 *v* (*informal*) **like**, want, be attracted to, wish for, desire. [➡LIKE, LOVE, VALUE AND ENJOY; 579] 4 *v* **imagine**, picture, think, conjure, believe, consider, visualize, interpret, assume, suppose, conceive. [➡DREAM, IMAGINE, AND FANTASIZE; 750] 5 *n* **notion**, dream, hope, desire, fantasy, daydream, castle in the air, castle in Spain, whim, illusion, reverie, vagary. [➡NONEXISTENT THINGS; 23]

fancy-free *adj* **free**, at liberty, unfettered, unconstrained, at leisure, footloose, carefree, liberated. [➡PLEASURE-SEEKING AND EXCESS; 885] *Opposite:* tied.

fandango *type of* **dance**. [➡DANCE; 903]

fanfare *n* **display**, trumpet blast, salute, elaboration, flourish, ballyhoo, pomp. [➡NOTES AND CHORDS; 909]

fang *type of* **tooth**. [➡THE MOUTH; 703]

fanlight *type of* **window**. [➡WINDOWS; 1099]

fanny pack (*US*) *type of* **handbag** (*US*), *type of* **purse** (*US*). [➡CONTAINERS, RECEPTACLES, AND PACKAGING; 1244]

fan out *v* **spread out**, separate, expand, broaden, disperse, scatter, split up. [➡SEPARATE AND DIVIDE; 402] *Opposite:* assemble.

fantasia *type of* **instrumental music**. [➡MUSIC, SONGS, AND SINGING; 907]

fantasize *v* **daydream**, imagine, dream, picture, visualize, invent, romanticize, conjure up, contrive. [➡DREAM, IMAGINE, AND FANTASIZE; 750]

fantastic 1 *adj* **excellent**, terrific (*informal*), superb, great, marvellous, fabulous, wonderful, tremendous, brilliant. [➡EXTRAORDINARY: AMAZING; 205] *Opposite:* awful. 2 *adj* **bizarre**, eccentric, imaginary, strange, fanciful, weird, whimsical, grotesque, odd, wild, crazy (*informal*). [➡IMPOSSIBLE AND IMPROBABLE; 179] *Opposite:* normal. 3 *adj* **incredible**, unbelievable, implausible, improbable, unlikely, far-fetched, out of this world, extraordinary, preposterous, absurd, bizarre, amazing, fanciful, illusory. [➡IMPOSSIBLE AND IMPROBABLE; 179] *Opposite:* plausible. 4 *adj* **enormous**, huge, great, tremendous, big, large, prodigious, extensive, extended, extravagant, extreme. [➡LARGE; 1192] *Opposite:* tiny.

fantastical *adj* [➡FALSE AND UNREAL; 174]

fantasy 1 *n* **dream**, daydream, image, fancy, hope, desire, vision, whimsy, pipe dream, illusion. [➡NONEXISTENT THINGS; 23] 2 *n* **imagination**, unreality, fancy, caprice, power of invention, imaginativeness, illusion, dream, fiction. [➡NONEXISTENT THINGS; 23] *Opposite:* reality.

fantasy world *n* [➡NON-EXISTENT PLACE; 1065]

fan the flames *v* **exacerbate**, aggravate, inflame, make worse, worsen, intensify. [➡WORSEN SOMETHING; 381] *Opposite:* calm.

far 1 *adv* **far off**, far away, far afield, far and wide, afar (*literary*), yonder (*regional*), distantly, remotely. [➡DISTANCE; 161] *Opposite:* close. 2 *adv* **much**, greatly, considerably, a lot, significantly, widely, extensively, extremely, immeasurably. [➡TO A GREAT EXTENT; 130] *Opposite:* barely. 3 *adj* **distant**, remote, far-off, faraway, far-flung, outlying, far-removed. [➡DISTANCE; 161] *Opposite:* near.

far afield *adv* **far away**, far off, far, far and wide, afar (*literary*), yonder (*regional*), distantly, remotely. [➡DISTANCE; 161] *Opposite:* close.

far and away *adv* **easily**, by far, much, considerably, greatly, significantly, extremely. [➡TO A GREAT EXTENT; 130] *Opposite:* barely.

far and wide *adv* **everywhere**, all over, far afield, afar (*literary*), throughout, all around, all round, high and low, generally, universally. [➡GENERAL LOCATIONS; 159]

faraway 1 *adj* **remote**, far-off, far-flung, outlying, distant, far. [➡DISTANCE; 161] *Opposite:* nearby. 2 *adj* **dreamy**, preoccupied, bemused, distant, in a world of your own, daydreaming, engrossed, rapt, absorbed, absent-minded. [➡NEUTRALITY AND INDIFFERENCE; 554] *Opposite:* alert.

far away *adj* [➡DISTANCE; 161]

farce *n* **shambles**, travesty, absurdity, circus, sham, mockery, charade, embarrassment, disgrace. [➡DISORDER AND CHAOS; 246]

farcical *adj* **absurd**, ridiculous, ludicrous, silly, nonsensical, preposterous, embarrassing, foolish, incompetent, risible, laughable, derisory. [➡FUNNY AND AMUSING; 217] *Opposite:* solemn.

fare 1 *n* **price**, tariff, ticket, cost, fee, entrance fee, toll, charge, tab (*US informal*). [➡EXPENDITURE; 424] 2 *n* **passenger**, customer, client, payer, rider. [➡TRAVEL: TRAVELLERS AND WALKERS; 320] 3 *n* **food**, menu, meal, dishes, provisions, cuisine, comestibles (*formal*), victuals, food and drink, regimen, board. [➡FOOD; 1166] 4 *v* **do**, get on, manage, cope, get by, proceed, progress, advance, perform, turn out, get along. [➡CONTINUE TO EXIST; 17]

farewell 1 *n* **goodbye**, sendoff, departure, exit, leaving, parting, leave-taking (*literary*), valediction (*formal*). [➡END; 54] *Opposite:* greeting. 2 *n* (*literary*) **goodbye**, bye-bye (*informal*), so long (*informal*), au revoir, adieu, auf Wiedersehen, ciao (*informal*), adios (*informal*), see you later (*informal*). [➡GREETINGS, FAREWELLS, AND SALUTATIONS; 660] *Opposite:* hello.

far-fetched *adj* **unbelievable**, fantastic, implausible, mind-boggling (*informal*), incredible, fanciful, unlikely, improbable, exaggerated, unconvincing. [➡IMPOSSIBLE AND IMPROBABLE; 179] *Opposite:* believable.

far-flung 1 *adj* **widespread**, extensive, sweeping, diffuse, wide-ranging. [➡GENERAL LOCATIONS; 159] *Opposite:* restricted. 2 *adj* **distant**, remote, far-off, faraway, outlying, extreme, far. [➡DISTANCE; 161] *Opposite:* nearby.

far from *prep* **anything but**, unlike, different from, poles apart from. [➡DIFFERENCE; 150] *Opposite:* near.

farm 1 *n* **smallholding**, cattle farm, dairy farm, sheep farm, fish farm, plantation, ranch. [➡AGRICULTURE AND FARMING; 1074] 2 *n* **farmhouse**, farmstead, homestead, grange, ranch. [➡AGRICULTURE AND FARMING; 1074] 3 *v* **cultivate**, work, till, plough, grow, plant, raise. [➡GROW AND CULTIVATE; 352]

farm

◆ *types of farm animal*
cow, donkey, goat, hog, horse, mule, ox, pig, sheep

farmer *n* **agriculturalist**, grower, rancher, crofter, smallholder, tenant farmer, sharecropper, dairy farmer, agronomist, market gardener, planter, agrarian, truck farmer (*US*). [➡FARMERS, GARDENERS, AND MANUAL WORKERS; 849]

farmers' market *type of* **food outlet**. [➡RETAIL OUTLETS; 1082]

farm hand *n* **farmworker**, labourer, seasonal worker, harvester, hired hand (*US*), ranch hand (*US*). [➡FARMERS, GARDENERS, AND MANUAL WORKERS; 849]

farmhouse *type of* **house**. [➡RESIDENTIAL BUILDINGS; 1077]

farming *n* **agribusiness**, agriculture, husbandry, cultivation, market gardening, agronomy, crop raising, ranching. [➡AGRICULTURE AND FARMING; 1074]

farmland *n* [➡AGRICULTURE AND FARMING; 1074]

farm out *v* **delegate**, subcontract, contract out, send out, hand out, assign, allocate, turn over, pass on. [➡DISPENSE, RATION, AND DISTRIBUTE; 435]

farmstead *n* **homestead**, farm, ranch, grange. [➡AGRICULTURE AND FARMING; 1074]

farmyard *n* **yard**, barnyard, cattle yard, stable yard. [➡THE COUNTRYSIDE AND OUTDOOR SPACES; 1070]

far-off *adj* **distant**, remote, far, faraway, far-flung, outlying, extreme. [➡DISTANCE; 161] *Opposite:* nearby.

far off *adv* [➡DISTANCE; 161]

far-out (*slang*) *adj* **unusual**, avant-garde, bizarre, offbeat, unconventional, ultramodern, outlandish, kinky (*informal*). [➡EXTRAORDINARY: AMAZING; 205] *Opposite:* outdated.

farrago *n* **hotchpotch**, potpourri, mishmash, medley, mixture, mix, blend, jumble, miscellany. [➡COLLECTIONS AND MIXTURES OF THINGS; 1243]

far-reaching *adj* **extensive**, sweeping, broad, across-the-board, comprehensive, influential, important, in-depth, widespread, wide-ranging. [➡WHOLENESS AND COMPLETENESS; 199] *Opposite:* limited.

farsighted *adj* **wise**, visionary, farseeing, provident, prophetic, judicious, perceptive, astute, cautious, sensible, prudent, discerning, sagacious (*formal*). [➡THE NATURE OF IDEAS; 772] *Opposite:* short-sighted.

farsightedness *n* **foresight**, providence, prescience, forethought, wisdom, sagacity, perceptiveness, judiciousness, perception, cautiousness, caution, prudence, vision. [➡POSITIVE INTELLECTUAL CHARACTERISTICS; 525] *Opposite:* short-sightedness.

farthermost *adj* [➡DISTANCE; 161]

farthest *adj* **furthest**, utmost, uttermost, outermost, furthermost, farthest away, furthest away, extreme, farthermost. [➡DISTANCE; 161]

fascinate *v* **captivate**, charm, attract, enthral, mesmerize, interest, absorb, intrigue, appeal, beguile, allure, entice, put under a spell, bewitch, enchant, spellbind, transfix, rivet (*informal*). [➡APPEAL TO AND AROUSE INTEREST; 576] *Opposite:* repel.

fascinated *adj* **captivated**, riveted (*informal*), rapt, spellbound, charmed, involved, intent, absorbed, engrossed, enthralled, gripped, immersed, mesmerized, entranced, enchanted, transfixed. [➡PENSIVENESS AND INTEREST; 539] *Opposite:* uninterested.

fascinating *adj* **captivating**, charming, attractive, enthralling, mesmerizing, interesting, absorbing, intriguing, appealing, beguiling, alluring, enticing, spellbinding, enchanting, riveting (*informal*). [➡INTERESTING AND MEANINGFUL; 191] *Opposite:* repellent.

fascination *n* **captivation**, charm, attraction, appeal, allure, lure, interest, enthralment, enchantment, beguilement, charisma, glamour. [➡PLEASURE, EXCITEMENT, AND ELATION; 535]

fashion 1 *n* **style**, way, manner, mode, method, approach, technique, custom, usage. [➡VARIETY, TYPE, KIND; 146] 2 *n* **trend**, craze, fad, vogue, mode, taste, in thing, rage. [➡FADS, FETISHES, AND IDOLATRY; 556] 3 *v* **shape**, mould, form, make, fit, alter, transform, create, frame, devise, adapt, pattern, fabricate. [➡CREATION; 347]

See Compare and Contrast at **make**.

fashionable *adj* **chic**, stylish, designer, up-to-the-minute, trendy (*informal*), in, hip (*slang*), cool, happening (*informal*), in vogue, modish, up-to-date, au courant, modern, swanky (*informal*), voguish. [➡NEW, MODERN; 167] *Opposite:* dated.

fashionably *adv* **stylishly**, trendily (*informal*), modishly, chicly, elegantly. [➡WELL GROOMED; 483]

fashion-conscious *adj* **trendy** (*informal*), chic, stylish, fashionable, elegant, modish, swanky (*informal*), voguish, up-to-the-minute, hip (*slang*), tony (*US informal*). [➡WELL GROOMED; 483] *Opposite:* outmoded.

fashion show *n* [➡PERFORMANCES AND SHOWS; 42]

fashion victim *n* [➡SELF-IMPORTANT AND SELF-SEEKING PEOPLE; 949]

fast 1 *adj* **quick**, speedy, rapid, swift, express, hasty, high-speed, prompt, immediate, expeditious, fleet, winged, brisk, flying. [➡MOVING QUICKLY; 103] *Opposite:* slow. 2 *adj* **sudden**, sharp, fleeting, momentary, short-lived, brief, abrupt, hurried, precipitous. [➡HAPPENING QUICKLY; 104] *Opposite:* long-lasting. 3 *adj* **ahead**, gaining, in advance. [➡BEFORE, FIRST, AND PRECEDING; 164] *Opposite:* slow. 4 *adj* **debauched**, wild, reckless, dissolute, profligate, wanton, loose. [➡MORALLY BAD; 776] 5 *adj* **firm**, steadfast, constant, unwavering, faithful, staunch. [➡HONEST AND RELIABLE; 503] *Opposite:* fickle. 6 *adv* **quickly**, speedily, rapidly, swiftly, promptly, without delay, at once, immediately, in a flash, like lightning, at the double, in no time, hastily, expeditiously, briskly. [➡MOVING QUICKLY; 103] *Opposite:* slowly. 7 *adv* **firmly**, firm, tightly, tight, stable, securely, fixed, steadily, tenaciously, fixedly, solidly, steady. [➡RIGID AND HARD; 1210] *Opposite:* loosely. 8 *v* **abstain**, starve yourself, go without. [➡EAT AND NOT EAT; 711] *Opposite:* feast. 9 *n* **diet**, abstention, starvation, cleansing, hunger strike, abstinence. [➡EAT AND NOT EAT; 711]

fast asleep *adj* [➡TIRED, ASLEEP AND UNCONSCIOUS; 739]

fasten 1 *v* **secure**, attach, fix, clip, clasp, affix, join, chain, tie, hook, hitch, pin, nail, connect, close. [➡FASTEN, LINK, AND JOIN; 409] *Opposite:* detach. 2 *v* **shut**, close, tie, tie up, do up, button, zip, zip up, lock, secure. [➡FASTEN, LINK, AND JOIN; 409] *Opposite:* undo.

fastener *n* **clasp**, fastening, tie, closure, popper, pin, clip, toggle, hook and eye, buckle, button, zip, press stud, catch, snap (*US*). [➡FASTENERS, LINKS, AND NETWORKS; 1246]

fastening *n* **clasp**, tie, closure, fastener, clip, buckle, catch, button, zip, press stud, popper, hook and eye, pin, hook, latch, lock, snap (*US*), gripper snap (*US*). [➡FASTENERS, LINKS, AND NETWORKS; 1246]

fast food *n* [➡PREPARED DISHES; 1169]

fastidious 1 *adj* **demanding**, fussy, finicky, faddy, picky, choosy (*informal*), pernickety (*informal*), particular, difficult, careful, painstaking, exacting, precise, meticulous, exact, thorough, assiduous. [➡DIFFICULT TO PLEASE; 516] *Opposite:* easygoing. 2 *adj* **delicate**, refined, particular, dainty, squeamish. [➡CAUTIOUS AND CAREFUL; 283] *Opposite:* slovenly.

fastidiousness 1 *n* **fussiness**, meticulousness, care, carefulness, neatness, preciseness, precision, assiduousness, conscientiousness, thoroughness, exactness. [➡HARD-WORKING AND COMMITTED; 501] *Opposite:* carelessness. 2 *n* **delicacy**, delicateness, daintiness, refinedness, squeamishness. [➡HARD-WORKING AND COMMITTED; 501] *Opposite:* crudeness.

fastlane *n* [➡ROADS; 1105]

fastness 1 *n* (*archaic or literary*) **stronghold**, fortress, castle, citadel, refuge, retreat, fort, fortification, redoubt. [➡FORTRESSES AND FORTIFICATIONS; 1089] 2 *n* **speediness**, swiftness, alacrity, speed, haste, pace, rapidity, rapidness, fleetness (*literary*). [➡SPEED; 102]

fast talker *n* [➡PEOPLE WHO DECEIVE; 662]

fast-track *v* **advance**, accelerate, forge ahead, progress, develop, go forward, further, promote, boost, move along, push forward, speed up. [➡MAKE POSSIBLE; 276]

fast track *n* **push**, boost, way forward, advancement, furthering, progress, promotion. [➡PROGRESS AND ADVANCEMENT; 214]

fat 1 *n* **oil**, lard, grease, shortening (*US*). [➡FATS AND OILS; 1172] 2 *n* **flab**, adipose tissue, padding, insulation, blubber (*informal*). [➡UNPLEASANT AND DIRTY SUBSTANCES; 1267] 3 *adj* **overweight**, plump, chubby, stout, portly, obese, heavy, tubby (*informal*), flabby (*informal*), podgy, pudgy (*informal*). [➡BUILD; 478] *Opposite:* thin. 4 *adj* **fatty**, greasy, oily, blubbery (*informal*), oleaginous. [➡PHYSICAL TEXTURE; 1221] *Opposite:* lean. 5 *adj* **thick**, hefty, sizable, chunky (*informal*), big, large, huge, enormous, wide. [➡LARGE; 1192] *Opposite:* slim. 6 *adj* **rich**, wealthy, affluent, well-off, prosperous, well-to-do. [➡WEALTH AND WEALTHY; 891] *Opposite:* poor. 7 *type of* **nutrient**. [➡FOOD COMPONENTS; 1187]

fatal 1 *adj* **deadly**, lethal, incurable, terminal, mortal, final. [➡DEADLY; 928] 2 *adj* **ruinous**, disastrous, destructive, serious, grave, critical, important, significant, momentous. [➡DANGEROUS; 237] *Opposite:* beneficial. 3 *adj* **decisive**, critical, crucial, fateful, pivotal, momentous. [➡IMPORTANT; 195] *Opposite:* unimportant.

See Compare and Contrast at **deadly**.

fatalism *n* **resignation**, passivity, acceptance, stoicism, pessimism, defeatism, despondency, despair. [➡PHILOSOPHIES AND BELIEFS; 781]

fatalistic *adj* **philosophical**, defeatist, resigned, stoic, stoical, passive. [➡SADNESS, DISTRESS, AND DESPAIR; 540]

fatality 1 *n* **death**, accident, casualty, loss, decease (*formal*). [➡DEATH AND BEREAVEMENT; 927] 2 *n* **deadliness**, fatalness, mortality (*archaic*), deathliness, lethalness, noxiousness. [➡DEAD PERSON; 926]

fatally 1 *adv* **lethally**, terminally, mortally, incurably, seriously. [➡CRITICALLY AND SERIOUSLY; 132] 2 *adv* **seriously**, ruinously, hopelessly, critically, disastrously, gravely. [➡CRITICALLY AND SERIOUSLY; 132]

fata morgana (*literary*) *n* [➡NONEXISTENT THINGS; 23]

fat cat (*slang*) *n* [➡RICH PEOPLE; 895]

fate 1 *n* **destiny**, fortune, providence, luck, doom, chance, lot. [➡FATE, DESTINY, AND ASTROLOGY; 783] 2 *n* **outcome**, consequence, result, upshot, end. [➡RESULTS AND OUTCOMES; 83]

fated *adj* **predetermined**, destined, predestined, preordained, meant, intended, inevitable, inescapable, doomed. [➡FATE, DESTINY, AND ASTROLOGY; 783]

fateful 1 *adj* **critical**, important, momentous, significant, crucial, historic. [➡IMPORTANT; 195] *Opposite:* insignificant. 2 *adj* **ominous**, unfortunate, inauspicious, unlucky, ill-fated, tragic. [➡BAD LUCK AND UNLUCKY; 785] *Opposite:* lucky.

father 1 *n* **dad** (*informal*), daddy (*informal*), pop (*informal*), pater (*dated slang or humorous*). [➡OLDER GENERATION RELATIVES; 959] 2 *n* **ancestor**, forefather, forebear, predecessor, founder, progenitor, patriarch. [➡OLDER GENERATION RELATIVES; 959] *Opposite:* descendant. 3 *n* **founder**, originator, initiator, contriver, architect, author. [➡DESIGNERS, CREATORS AND INSTIGATORS; 348] 4 *n* **priest**, vicar, minister, padre, pastor. [➡RELIGIOUS PEOPLE; 779] 5 *v* **beget**, sire, engender, procreate, get (*archaic*), spawn. [➡REPRODUCTION AND HEREDITY; 726] 6 *v* **protect**, comfort, advise, look after, nurture, take care of. [➡TAKE CARE OF AND SPOIL; 301]

Father *n* [➡RELIGIOUS PEOPLE; 779]

fatherhood *n* **paternity**, parenthood, kinship. [➡RELATIONSHIP TO ANOTHER; 973] *Opposite:* motherhood.

father-in-law *type of* **in-law**. [➡RELATIVES BY MARRIAGE; 960]

fatherland *n* **homeland**, native land, home, motherland, mother country, old country. [➡COUNTRIES AND REGIONS; 1066]

fatherliness *n* **protectiveness**, benevolence, affection, supportiveness, kindness. [➡GENEROSITY AND KINDNESS; 496]

fatherly *adj* **paternal**, protective, concerned, caring, loving, supportive, kind. [➡GENEROSITY AND KINDNESS; 496]

fathom 1 *v* **sound**, measure, plumb, gauge, probe. [➡ASSESS QUANTITY; 758] 2 *v* **comprehend**, understand, work out, figure out, grasp, think through, make out, divine. [➡UNDERSTAND AND GRASP; 760]

fathomable *adj* **comprehensible**, understandable, penetrable, graspable, intelligible, apprehensible. [➡EASE AND SIMPLICITY; 201] *Opposite:* unfathomable.

fathomless 1 *adj* **deep**, immeasurable, unfathomable, bottomless, inestimable. [➡DEPTH: DEEP; 1200] *Opposite:* shallow. 2 *adj* **incomprehensible**, immeasurable, unfathomable, obscure, incalculable, mysterious, impenetrable, profound, cryptic, deep, recondite. [➡DIFFICULTY AND COMPLEXITY; 243] *Opposite:* fathomable.

fathomlessness *n* [➡DEPTH: DEEP; 1200]

fatigue *n* **exhaustion**, tiredness, weariness, weakness, lethargy, lassitude. [➡TIRED, ASLEEP AND UNCONSCIOUS; 739] *Opposite:* energy.

fatigued *adj* **exhausted**, weary, tired, drained, worn-out, wiped out (*slang*), beat (*informal*), shattered, done in (*informal*), done for (*informal*), whacked (*informal*), pooped (*informal*). [➡TIRED, ASLEEP AND UNCONSCIOUS; 739] *Opposite:* fresh.

fatigues *type of* **trousers**. [➡GARMENTS AND OUTFITS; 865]

fatiguing *adj* [➡PHYSICALLY UNPLEASANT; 227]

fatness *n* **obesity**, plumpness, chubbiness, stoutness, portliness, heaviness, size, corpulence (*formal or literary*), tubbiness (*informal*), flabbiness (*informal*), podginess, pudginess (*informal*). [➡BUILD; 478] *Opposite:* thinness.

fatten *v* **feed up**, stuff, plump, build up, feed, fatten up. [➡CHANGE OF SIZE: BIGGER; 393] *Opposite:* starve.

fattening *adj* **calorific**, fatty, rich, greasy, oily. [➡FOOD; 1166]

fatten up *v* **feed up**, stuff, build up, feed, fatten. [➡CHANGE OF SIZE: BIGGER; 393] *Opposite:* starve.

fatty *adj* **greasy**, fat, oily, blubbery (*informal*). [➡PHYSICAL TEXTURE; 1221] *Opposite:* lean.

fatuity (*formal*) *n* **unintelligence**, complacency, silliness, stupidity, childishness, foolishness, inanity, mindlessness, pointlessness, senselessness. [➡NEGATIVE INTELLECTUAL CHARACTERISTICS; 526] *Opposite:* sensibleness.

fatuous *adj* **unintelligent**, complacent, unaware, silly, stupid, childish, pointless, meaningless, foolish, inane. [➡REDUNDANT AND USELESS; 241] *Opposite:* sensible.

fatuously *adv* **unintelligently**, complacently, foolishly, stupidly, inanely, mindlessly, pointlessly, senselessly, childishly, meaninglessly. [➡NEGATIVE INTELLECTUAL CHARACTERISTICS; 526] *Opposite:* sensibly.

fatuousness *n* **unintelligence**, complacency, silliness, foolishness, stupidity, inanity, mindlessness, pointlessness, senselessness. [➡THE NATURE OF IDEAS; 772] *Opposite:* sensibleness.

faucet (*US*) *n* **spout**, spigot, nozzle, outlet, stopcock, valve, tap. [➡FITTINGS; 859]

fault 1 *n* **responsibility**, liability, burden, culpability, accountability. [➡MORALLY BAD; 776] 2 *n* **shortcoming**, failing, weakness, defect, flaw, deficiency, drawback, foible. [➡FAULTS, FLAWS, AND WEAKNESSES; 252] *Opposite:* strength. 3 *n* **defect**, flaw, imperfection, blemish, weakness. [➡FAULTS, FLAWS, AND WEAKNESSES; 252] *Opposite:* asset. 4 *n* **mistake**, error, blunder, slip, omission, lapse, oversight, slip-up (*informal*). [➡MISTAKES; 251] 5 *v* **blame**, criticize, condemn, find fault with, question, censure. [➡ACCUSE, BLAME, AND CRITICIZE; 642] *Opposite:* praise.

See Compare and Contrast at **flaw**.

faultfinder *n* **critic**, carper, complainer, grumbler, moaner (*informal*), whinger (*informal*), grouser (*informal*), nitpicker. [➡GRUMPY AND NEGATIVE PEOPLE; 953]

faultfinding 1 *n* **criticism**, grumbling, nitpicking, whingeing (*informal*). [➡COMPLAIN AND NAG; 687] 2 *adj* **critical**, reproachful, carping, damning, unfavourable, nitpicky. [➡DIFFICULT TO PLEASE; 516] *Opposite:* uncritical.

faultily *adv* **imperfectly**, incorrectly, wrongly, defectively, deficiently, mistakenly, inadequately. [➡INCORRECT AND ERRONEOUS; 223] *Opposite:* properly.

faultless *adj* **flawless**, perfect, impeccable, immaculate, blameless, spotless, irreproachable, correct, ideal. [➡CORRECT; 183] *Opposite:* imperfect.

faultlessness *n* **flawlessness**, perfection, purity, impeccability, immaculateness, irreproachability, blamelessness, spotlessness, correctness. [➡CORRECT; 183] *Opposite:* imperfection.

fault line *n* **crack**, rift, split, fissure, fault, fracture. [➡VOLCANOES AND EARTHQUAKES; 1054]

faulty 1 *adj* **out of order**, defective, broken-down, broken, on the blink (*informal*). [➡IN BAD REPAIR; 1233] *Opposite:* perfect. 2 *adj* **flawed**, imperfect, incorrect, incoherent, contradictory, defective, deficient, confused. [➡INCORRECT AND ERRONEOUS; 223] *Opposite:* sound.

fauna *n* **animals**, creatures, wildlife, beasts. [➡LIVING THINGS AND LIVING; 976]

Fauvism *type of* **20th-century art movement**. [➡ARTISTIC MOVEMENTS AND STYLES; 899]

faux *adj* **fake**, artificial, unreal, reproduction, ersatz (*disapproving*), false. [➡FALSE AND UNREAL; 174] *Opposite:* genuine.

faux pas (*literary*) *n* **gaffe**, blunder, mistake, indiscretion, howler (*informal*), clanger (*informal*), misstep, boob (*informal*), blooper (*US informal humorous*). [➡MISTAKES; 251]

See Compare and Contrast at **mistake**.

fava bean (*US*) *type of* **pulse**. [➡BEANS AND PULSES; 1188]

favela *n* [➡UNDESIRABLE ACCOMMODATION; 856]

favour 1 *n* **good turn**, errand, kindness, courtesy, service, indulgence. [➡KIND ACTION OR BEHAVIOUR; 296] *Opposite:* disservice. 2 *n* **approval**, support, kindness, esteem, sympathy, partiality, preference. [➡SOURCE OF HAPPINESS, PLEASURE, OR IMPROVEMENT; 210] *Opposite:* disfavour. 3 *n* **gift** (*informal*), trinket, token, present, keepsake, memento. [➡GIFTS; 439] 4 *v* **prefer**, choose, support, back, approve, esteem. [➡APPROVE AND CONFIRM; 647] *Opposite:* reject. 5 *v* **help**, assist, aid, advance, promote, benefit, further, increase, encourage, facilitate. [➡MAKE POSSIBLE; 276] *Opposite:* hinder.

See Compare and Contrast at **regard**.

favourable 1 *adj* **advantageous**, auspicious, propitious, helpful, beneficial. [➡APPROPRIATE, SUITABLE, ADVISABLE; 185] *Opposite:* inauspicious. 2 *adj* **promising**, auspicious, satisfactory, fortunate, advantageous, encouraging. [➡GOOD, WELL, BETTER; 184] *Opposite:* unfavourable. 3 *adj* **approving**, positive, constructive, good, sympathetic, encouraging, complimentary, flattering, kind. [➡EXPRESSING RESPECT AND APPROVAL; 638] *Opposite:* negative.

favourably 1 *adv* **advantageously**, auspiciously, propitiously, helpfully, beneficially. [➡EMOTIONALLY PLEASANT; 188] *Opposite:* inauspiciously. 2 *adv* **promisingly**, well, happily, auspiciously, satisfactorily, fortunately, advantageously, encouragingly. [➡GOOD, WELL, BETTER; 184] *Opposite:* unfavourably. 3 *adv* **approvingly**, positively, constructively, well, sympathetically, kindly. [➡EXPRESSING RESPECT AND APPROVAL; 638] *Opposite:* negatively.

favourite 1 *n* **pet**, darling, beloved. [➡SUPPORTERS, PROTECTORS, AND COMPATRIOTS; 970] 2 *adj* **chosen**, pet, beloved, favoured. [➡POPULAR AND WANTED; 221] 3 *n* **choice**, preference, pick. [➡SOURCE OF HAPPINESS, PLEASURE, OR IMPROVEMENT; 210]

favouritism *n* **preferentialism**, preference, partiality, nepotism, bias, discrimination, prejudice. [➡PREJUDICE; 551] *Opposite:* impartiality.

fawn 1 *type of* **young animal**. [➡YOUNG ANIMAL; 977] 2 *type of* **beige**. [➡COLOURS; 1223] 3 *v* **flatter**, crawl (*informal*), butter up (*informal*), grovel, toady, kowtow. [➡FLATTER AND FAWN; 622]

fawning *adj* **flattering**, obsequious, smarmy, sycophantic, servile. [➡INGRATIATING; 639]

fax 1 *n* **facsimile**, message, document, transmission, copy. [➡LETTERS AND WRITTEN MESSAGES; 585] 2 *v* **send**, transmit, convey, communicate, telex, deliver. [➡DESPATCH AND SEND; 334] 3 *type of* **telecommunications equipment**. [➡TELECOMMUNICATIONS; 1129]

fay (*literary*) *n* [➡MYTHICAL BEINGS; 790]

fayre *n* [➡PARTIES, DANCES, AND CELEBRATIONS; 37]

faze *v* **fluster**, disconcert, disturb, put off, deter, daunt, throw (*informal*), intimidate, upset, discourage, confuse. [➡UPSET, DISTRESS, AND HUMILIATE; 568] *Opposite:* encourage.

fear 1 *n* **anxiety**, apprehension, distress, terror, dread, horror, fright, panic, alarm, trepidation. [➡FEAR AND PANIC; 544] *Opposite:* assurance. 2 *n* **worry**, concern, anxiety, terror, nightmare, phobia. [➡CONFUSION, ANXIETY, AND WORRY; 541] 3 *v* **dread**, be afraid, be scared, be apprehensive, be frightened, be anxious. [➡FEARS AND PHOBIAS; 555]

fearful 1 *adj* **frightening**, scary (*informal*), terrifying, terrible, frightful, horrific, fearsome. [➡FRIGHTENING; 232] 2 *adj* **worried**, afraid, scared, apprehensive, frightened, anxious, timid, nervous. [➡CONFUSION, ANXIETY, AND WORRY; 541] *Opposite:* fearless. 3 *adj* (*informal*) **terrible**, dreadful, appalling, awful, horrible, frightful, atrocious, dire, horrendous, abysmal, bad. [➡BAD AND BADLY; 224] *Opposite:* wonderful.

fearfully 1 *adv* **frighteningly**, scarily (*informal*), terrifyingly, terribly, frightfully, horrifically. [➡FRIGHTENING; 232] 2 *adv* **worriedly**, nervously, timidly, uneasily, apprehensively, anxiously. [➡CONFUSION, ANXIETY, AND WORRY; 541] *Opposite:* fearlessly. 3 *adv* (*informal*) **terribly**, dreadfully, awfully, horribly, frightfully, horrendously, extremely, very, intensely. [➡TO A GREAT EXTENT; 130]

fearfulness 1 *n* **scariness**, terribleness, frightfulness, horror, terror. [➡FRIGHTENING; 232] 2 *n* **worriedness**, anxiety, apprehension, awe, fear, dread, trepidation, alarm, terror, horror. [➡FEELINGS ABOUT THE FUTURE; 534] *Opposite:* bravery. 3 *n* (*informal*) **terribleness**, atrociousness, dreadfulness, awfulness, horror, frightfulness, hatefulness, horridness, severity. [➡DISGUSTING AND REPULSIVE; 231]

fearless *adj* **courageous**, brave, bold, unafraid, daring, plucky, valiant, heroic, confident, audacious, intrepid (*literary or humorous*). [➡COURAGE; 499] *Opposite:* cowardly.

fearlessness *n* **courage**, bravery, boldness, heroism, valour, audacity, daring, pluckiness, valiantness, confidence, pluck. [➡COURAGE; 499] *Opposite:* cowardice.

fearsome 1 *adj* **frightening**, formidable, terrifying, alarming, awesome, fearful, terrible. [➡FRIGHTENING; 232] 2 *adj* **impressive**, awesome, formidable, awe-inspiring, tremendous, striking. [➡EXTRAORDINARY: AMAZING; 205]

feasibility *n* **viability**, possibility, probability, likelihood, practicability, practicality, achievability. [➡POSSIBLE AND PROBABLE; 178] *Opposite:* impossibility.

feasible *adj* **viable**, possible, practicable, achievable, reasonable, realistic, practical, likely. [➡POSSIBLE AND PROBABLE; 178] *Opposite:* impossible.

feast 1 *n* **banquet**, spread (*informal*), repast (*literary*), dinner, meal, buffet, slap-up meal (*informal*). [➡MEALS AND PARTS OF MEALS; 1168] 2 *n* **delight**, treat, indulgence, pleasure, joy, enjoyment. [➡TREAT; 211] 3 *n* **celebration**, festival, holiday, feast day, holy day, saint's day. [➡PARTIES, DANCES, AND CELEBRATIONS; 37] 4 *v* **eat**, dine, indulge, partake, gobble, pig out (*informal*). [➡EAT AND NOT EAT; 711] *Opposite:* fast.

feat *n* **achievement**, accomplishment, deed, exploit, act, coup. [➡ACTIONS OR UNDERTAKINGS; 260]

feather *part of* **bird**. [➡PARTS OF A BIRD; 1006]

feathery *adj* **downy**, fluffy, soft, light, plumy, plumose. [➡PHYSICAL TEXTURE; 1221]

feature 1 *n* **facial feature**, contour, lineament (*literary*). [➡FACIAL CHARACTERISTICS; 482] 2 *n* **characteristic**, trait, mark, attribute, quality, facet, aspect, element, highlight. [➡QUALITIES AND CHARACTERISTICS; 1190] 3 *n* **article**, piece, report, item, story, column. [➡NEWSPAPERS; 606] 4 *v* **contain**, include, present, introduce, bring out, highlight, bring forward. [➡CAUSE TO APPEAR; 5] 5 *v* **perform**, star, appear, act, turn up, co-star. [➡THE PERFORMING ARTS; 904] 6 *v* **highlight**, star, include, showcase, show, co-star. [➡CAUSE TO APPEAR; 5] 7 *v* **figure**, appear, participate, take part, play a part. [➡PARTICIPATE; 293]

feature film *n* [➡FILM; 901]

featureless *adj* **dull**, drab, bland, uninspired, unremarkable, undistinguished, unimaginative. [➡PLAIN; 233] *Opposite:* distinctive.

febrile *adj* **feverish**, fevered, flushed, hot, delirious, pyretic. [➡ILL AND SICK; 741]

feckless *adj* **good-for-nothing**, useless, hopeless, spineless, feeble, weak, ineffectual, worthless, incompetent, ineffective, unreliable, irresponsible, aimless. [➡LACK OF COMMITMENT AND UNRELIABILITY; 510] *Opposite:* dynamic.

fecklessness *n* **uselessness**, hopelessness, spinelessness, feebleness, irresponsibility, aimlessness, unreliability. [➡LACK OF COMMITMENT AND UNRELIABILITY; 510] *Opposite:* dynamism.

fecund 1 *adj* **productive**, creative, prolific, industrious, fruitful, dynamic. [➡USEFULNESS; 200] 2 *adj* (*formal*) **fertile**, prolific, productive, fruitful, rich. [➡REPRODUCTION AND HEREDITY; 726] *Opposite:* infertile.

fecundity *n* **fertility**, prolificacy, productiveness, fruitfulness, richness. [➡REPRODUCTION AND HEREDITY; 726] *Opposite:* infertility.

federal *adj* **central**, centralized, national, state, civic. [➡STYLES AND SYSTEMS OF GOVERNMENT; 806] *Opposite:* regional.

federate 1 *v* **unite**, join, amalgamate, come together, merge, coalesce, associate. [➡CREATING CONNECTIONS; 145] *Opposite:* devolve. 2 *v* **associate**, unite, combine, join, confederate, amalgamate. [➡COMBINE AND MIX; 401] *Opposite:* disassociate.

federation 1 *n* **combination**, union, association, confederation, amalgamation. [➡INSTITUTIONS; 791] 2 *n* **alliance**, coalition, confederation, grouping, partnership, association, amalgamation, confederacy, group. [➡INSTITUTIONS; 791]

Federation *type of* **20th-century architecture**. [➡BUILDING AND ARCHITECTURE; 1075]

fedora *type of* **hat**. [➡HABERDASHERY, MILLINERY, AND LINGERIE; 867]

fed up (*informal*) *adj* **bored**, miserable, jaded, discontented, tired, sick and tired, annoyed, disgruntled, dissatisfied. [➡SADNESS, DISTRESS, AND DESPAIR; 540] *Opposite:* happy.

fee 1 *n* **payment**, remuneration, emolument (*formal or humorous*), salary, pay, stipend. [➡INCOME; 461] 2 *n* **charge**, subscription, toll, tariff, cost, fare, rate. [➡MONEY, PAYMENTS, AND CHARGES; 800]

See Compare and Contrast at **wage**.

feeble 1 *adj* **weak**, frail, delicate, shaky, thin, meagre. [➡UNFIT AND WEAK; 740] *Opposite:* robust. 2 *adj* **unconvincing**, pathetic (*informal*), ineffectual, poor, half-hearted, ineffective, weak. [➡WEAKNESS; 242] *Opposite:* convincing.

See Compare and Contrast at **weak**.

feeble-minded (*archaic*) *adj* **ill-considered**, incoherent, ill-defined, half-baked (*informal*), ineffectual, weak. [➡NEGATIVE INTELLECTUAL CHARACTERISTICS; 526] *Opposite:* well-thought-out.

feeble-mindedness *n* **irresolution**, indecision, ineffectuality, indecisiveness, half-heartedness, irresoluteness, hesitancy, weakness. [➡NEGATIVE INTELLECTUAL CHARACTERISTICS; 526] *Opposite:* resoluteness.

feebleness 1 *n* **weakness**, fragility, delicateness, frailty, shakiness, thinness, meagreness. [➡WEAKNESS; 242] *Opposite:* robustness. 2 *n* **ineffectuality**, weakness, half-heartedness, ineffectiveness. [➡COWARDICE AND WEAKNESS OF WILL; 509] *Opposite:* effectiveness.

feebly 1 *adv* **weakly**, frailly, delicately, shakily, thinly, meagrely. [➡WEAKNESS; 242] *Opposite:* robustly. 2 *adv* **unconvincingly**, half-heartedly, pathetically, ineffectively, ineffectually, weakly, softly. [➡UNFIT AND WEAK; 740] *Opposite:* convincingly.

feed 1 *v* **nourish**, nurse, suckle, breast-feed, serve, provide for, nurture. [➡TAKE CARE OF AND SPOIL; 301] *Opposite:* starve. 2 *v* **eat**, consume, partake, devour, swallow. [➡EAT AND NOT EAT; 711] 3 *v* **support**, sustain, nourish, nurture, encourage, maintain, strengthen, bolster. [➡IMPROVE STRENGTH AND DURABILITY; 379] 4 *n* **food**, feedstuff, fodder, provender, forage. [➡ANIMAL FEED; 1167]

feedback *n* **response**, reaction, comment, criticism, advice, pointer, opinion, view, reply. [➡REPLY AND ANSWER; 669]

feed into *v* **contribute**, provide, deliver, flow into, lead into, kick in (*US informal*). [➡EQUIP AND SUPPLY; 436] *Opposite:* draw on.

feedstuff *n* [➡ANIMAL FEED; 1167]

feel 1 *v* **touch**, finger, handle, sense, fondle, manipulate, stroke, caress. [➡USING THE SENSES; 698] 2 *v* **sense**, experience, undergo, be aware of, bear, suffer. [➡USING THE SENSES; 698] 3 *v* **think**, believe, consider, deem (*formal*), comprehend, understand, be of the opinion, know, suspect. [➡UNCERTAINTY; 560] 4 *n* **sensation**, touch, texture, impression, finish, sense, composition. [➡TEXTURE; 1219] 5 *n* **impression**, atmosphere, air, feeling, ambience, quality, aura, mood, character. [➡APPEARANCE AND ATMOSPHERE; 1236]

feeler *n* **sensor**, antenna, organ. [➡PARTS OF AN INSECT; 1019]

feel for *v* **sympathize**, feel sorry for, pity, commiserate, empathize, be moved by, understand. [➡BE CONCERNED AND CARE; 582]

feel-good *adj* **upbeat** (*informal*), optimistic, positive, happy, cheerful, satisfying, cheering, sanguine, contented. [➡EMOTIONALLY PLEASANT; 188] *Opposite:* downbeat.

feeling 1 *n* **sensation**, sense, sensitivity, touch. [➡THE SENSES; 697] *Opposite:* numbness. 2 *n* **emotion**, sentiment, mood, reaction, sense, impression, response. [➡FEELINGS; 532] 3 *n* **affection**, concern, regard, love, sympathy, attachment, sensitivity, compassion, pity, empathy. [➡COMPASSION AND FORGIVENESS; 552] *Opposite:* antipathy. 4 *n* **opinion**, view, point of view, belief, impression, consideration, attitude, sentiment. [➡POINT OF VIEW; 768] 5 *n* **air**, atmosphere, feel, ambience, mood, impression, quality, aura, character. [➡APPEARANCE AND ATMOSPHERE; 1236] 6 *n* **hunch**, instinct, suspicion, intuition, idea, gut reaction, notion, presentiment. [➡IDEA AND THOUGHT; 771]

feelingly *adv* **expressively**, passionately, emotionally, sensitively, with feeling, moodily, sympathetically, powerfully, fervently. [➡ELOQUENT, TALKATIVE AND LONG-WINDED; 633] *Opposite:* impassively.

feel like 1 *v* **want**, fancy (*informal*), desire, crave, wish, long for. [➡DESIRE AND WANT; 580] 2 *v* **seem**, appear, resemble, impress, look like. [➡SEEM TO BE SOMETHING; 58]

feel sorry for *v* **pity**, empathize, feel for, commiserate with, sympathize with, be moved by. [➡BE CONCERNED AND CARE; 582]

feign *v* **pretend**, put on, fake, simulate, make believe, invent, affect, assume, sham. [➡PRETEND AND MIMIC; 60]

feigned *adj* **put on**, artificial, insincere, pretend, fake, sham, affected, assumed. [➡FALSE AND UNREAL; 174] *Opposite:* genuine.

feint *n* **trick**, stratagem, ploy, ruse, gambit, sham, dodge, manoeuvre, artifice (*formal*), subterfuge, wile. [➡DECEPTION AND LIES; 661]

feistily (*informal*) *adv* [➡WITH ENTHUSIASM; 287]

feistiness (*informal*) *n* [➡ENERGY AND ENTHUSIASM; 497]

feisty (*informal*) *adj* **lively**, spirited, energetic, aggressive, go-getting (*informal*), hearty, gutsy (*informal*), full-blooded. [➡ENERGY AND ENTHUSIASM; 497] *Opposite:* feeble.

feldspar *type of* **mineral**. [➡MINERALS; 1276]

felicitations (*formal*) *n* **congratulations**, compliments, best wishes, blessings, greetings, salutations (*formal*). [➡GREETINGS, FAREWELLS, AND SALUTATIONS; 660]

felicitous 1 *adj* **appropriate**, apt, suitable, apposite, well-chosen, fitting, relevant, pertinent, germane (*formal*) [➡APPROPRIATE, SUITABLE, ADVISABLE; 185]. *Opposite:* inapposite (*formal*). 2 *adj* **fortunate**, lucky, fortuitous, timely, happy, blessed, joyous, propitious. [➡LUCK; 784] *Opposite:* unfortunate.

felicity 1 *n* **happiness**, contentment, joy, pleasure, luck, blessedness, timeliness, fortunateness, bliss, delight, ecstasy. [➡PLEASURE, EXCITEMENT, AND ELATION; 535] *Opposite:* unhappiness. 2 *n* **appropriateness**, aptness, suitability, appositeness, fittingness, choiceness, relevance. [➡APPROPRIATE, SUITABLE, ADVISABLE; 185] *Opposite:* inappropriateness.

feline *adj* **graceful**, slinky, subtle, elegant, sly, stealthy. [➡AGILITY OF THE BODY; 477]

fell 1 *v* **cut down**, chop down, chop, clear-fell, clear-cut. [➡MOVE SOMETHING: INTO A NEW POSITION OR OVERTURN; 331] 2 *v* **knock down**, knock out, floor, demolish (*informal*), take out (*slang*), deck. [➡MOVE SOMETHING: INTO A NEW POSITION OR OVERTURN; 331] *Opposite:* set up.

fella (*informal*) *n* [➡MALE PERSON; 934]

fellow 1 *n* (*dated*) **man**, guy (*informal*), chap (*informal*), bloke (*informal*), boy. [➡MALE PERSON; 934] 2 *n* (*dated*) **companion**, colleague, associate, partner, comrade, coworker. [➡COLLEAGUES AND EQUALS; 967] 3 *n* **member**, associate, researcher, academic. [➡COLLEAGUES AND EQUALS; 967]

fellow feeling *n* **sympathy**, empathy, support, affinity, mutuality, sensitivity, awareness. [➡COMPASSION AND FORGIVENESS; 552] *Opposite:* hostility.

fellowship 1 *n* **communion**, companionship, camaraderie, comradeship, friendship, friendliness, partnership, mutuality, cooperativeness, solidarity, sociability. [➡RELATIONSHIP TO ANOTHER; 973] *Opposite:* enmity. 2 *n* **society**, association, college, affiliation, cooperative, community, group, club, fraternity, brotherhood. [➡INSTITUTIONS; 791]

felon *n* **criminal**, murderer, offender, thief, killer, robber, outlaw, lawbreaker, delinquent. [➡CRIMINALS; 821]

felonious *adj* [➡ILLEGAL; 816]

felony *n* **crime**, offence, misdemeanour, wrongdoing, lawbreaking, delinquency. [➡CRIMES; 817]

felt *type of* **fabric from animals.** [➡FABRICS; 1131]

felt-tipped pen *type of* **pen.** [➡WRITING AND DRAWING IMPLEMENTS, AND MEDIA; 602]

felucca *type of* **sailing vessel.** [➡SHIPS AND BOATS; 1149]

female 1 *adj* **feminine**, womanly, womanlike, ladylike, girlish. [➡GENDER IDENTITY AND SEXUALITY; 932] *Opposite:* masculine. 2 *n* **woman**, lady, girl. [➡FEMALE PERSON; 933] *Opposite:* male.

feminine *adj* **female**, womanly, womanlike, ladylike, girlish. [➡GENDER IDENTITY AND SEXUALITY; 932] *Opposite:* masculine.

femininity *n* **femaleness**, feminineness, womanliness, ladylikeness, girlishness. [➡GENDER IDENTITY AND SEXUALITY; 932] *Opposite:* masculinity.

feminism *n* **women's movement**, women's liberation, women's lib (*informal disapproving*), women's rights, women's studies, radicalism. [➡PHILOSOPHIES AND BELIEFS; 781]

feminist *n* **women's libber** (*informal disapproving*), suffragette, activist, radical, campaigner. [➡PHILOSOPHICAL AND POLITICAL THINKERS; 782]

femur *type of* **bone.** [➡THE BONES AND JOINTS; 720]

fen *n* **marsh**, wetland, fenland, bog, lowland. [➡WETLANDS; 1043] *Opposite:* desert.

fence 1 *n* **barrier**, boundary, hurdle, hedge, railing, enclosure, screen, paling, trellis, palisade, rail, barricade. [➡BARRIERS; 1112] 2 *v* **enclose**, hedge, shut in, restrict, confine, surround, encompass, gird (*literary*), pen. [➡BAR AND OBSTRUCT ACCESS; 411] *Opposite:* open up. 3 *v* **evade**, parry, feint, dodge, fight off, contest. [➡COMPETE, CONTEND, AND COMBAT; 304]

fencer *n* [➡PEOPLE IN SPORTS AND LEISURE; 876]

fencing 1 *n* **fence**, railing, paling, trellis, barrier, chain-link fencing, palisade, rail. [➡BARRIERS; 1112] 2 *n* **repartee**, banter, wordplay, raillery. [➡JOKES AND TEASING; 675] 3 *type of* **combat sport.** [➡HOBBIES, GAMES, AND SPORTS; 875]

fender 1 *n* **fireguard**, fire screen, guard, screen. [➡FITTINGS; 859] 2 (*US*) *part of* **external structure.** [➡EXTERNAL PARTS OF A VEHICLE; 1146] 3 (*US*) *part of* **bike** (*informal*). [➡BIKES, CARS, AND CARRIAGES; 1148]

fender-bender (*US informal*) *n* [➡TRAFFIC ACCIDENTS; 256]

fend for *v* **look after**, take care of, provide for, manage, cope, defend, support, shift for. [➡TAKE CARE OF AND SPOIL; 301]

fend for yourself *v* **take care of yourself**, look after yourself, support yourself, manage on your own, paddle your own canoe (*informal*), go your own way, survive, get by, make ends meet, go on your own (*US*). [➡CONTINUE ...XIST; 17]

... off *v* **keep away**, repel, repulse, discourage, ward ...ect, hold off, stave off, fight off, keep off, keep ...eter, resist. [➡AVOID OR ESCAPE CONTACT; 419] *Opposite:*

...rsh, bog, fen, wetland, lowland. [➡WETLANDS; ...sert.

fennel 1 *type of* **herb.** [➡HERBS AND SPICES; 1174] 2 *type of* **vegetable.** [➡FRUIT AND VEGETABLES; 1175]

fenugreek *type of* **spice.** [➡HERBS AND SPICES; 1174]

feral *adj* **wild**, untamed, undomesticated, savage, uncontrollable, uncontrolled, regressive. [➡DANGEROUS; 237] *Opposite:* domesticated.

fer-de-lance *type of* **poisonous snake.** [➡SNAKE; 995]

ferment 1 *v* **agitate**, inflame, stir up, incite, provoke, cause. [➡CAUSE TO HAPPEN; 31] 2 *n* **uproar**, tumult, confusion, excitement, commotion, upheaval, agitation, turmoil, turbulence, mayhem (*informal*), unrest, disquiet. [➡CHAOS AND UPROAR; 51] *Opposite:* peace.

fermion *type of* **elementary particle.** [➡ELEMENTARY PARTICLES; 1278]

fern *type of* **foliage plant.** [➡FOLIAGE PLANTS; 1035]

ferocious 1 *adj* **fierce**, vicious, violent, cruel, brutal, aggressive, unruly, wild, savage, merciless, barbarous. [➡DANGEROUS; 237] *Opposite:* gentle. 2 *adj* **intense**, strong, heated, raging, extreme, unstoppable. [➡STRENGTH; 202] *Opposite:* mild.

ferociously 1 *adv* **fiercely**, viciously, cruelly, violently, brutally, wildly, savagely, mercilessly, barbarously. [➡DANGEROUS; 237] *Opposite:* gently. 2 *adv* **intensely**, heatedly, strongly, extremely, overwhelmingly, uncontrollably. [➡ENTHUSIASTIC AND INQUISITIVE; 629] *Opposite:* mildly.

ferociousness *n* **fierceness**, ferocity, viciousness, violence, brutality, aggressiveness, wildness, savagery, mercilessness, cruelty. [➡SELFISH AND UNKIND; 506] *Opposite:* gentleness.

ferocity 1 *n* **fierceness**, ferociousness, cruelty, wildness, viciousness, violence, aggressiveness, savagery, mercilessness. [➡DIFFICULTY AND COMPLEXITY; 243] *Opposite:* gentleness. 2 *n* **intensity**, strength, extremeness, severity. [➡STRENGTH; 202] *Opposite:* mildness.

ferret 1 *v* **hunt**, search, search out, rummage, dig out, flush out, delve. [➡SEEK POSSESSION AND SEARCH; 457] 2 *type of* **small mammal.** [➡SMALL MAMMAL; 990]

ferret about *v* [➡SEEK POSSESSION AND SEARCH; 457]

ferret around *v* **look for**, search out, ferret about, delve, search around, hunt around, rummage. [➡SEEK POSSESSION AND SEARCH; 457]

ferret out 1 *v* **discover**, uncover, find, reveal, unveil, discern. [➡FIND; 464] *Opposite:* conceal. 2 *v* **track down**, flush out, uncover, hunt down, catch, locate. [➡SEEK POSSESSION AND SEARCH; 457] *Opposite:* hide.

ferry 1 *v* **transport**, carry, ship, convey, transmit, pass, take, bring, bear, lug, send. [➡TRAVEL: WAYS OF TRAVELLING; 321] 2 *type of* **motor vessel.** [➡SHIPS AND BOATS; 1149]

ferryboat *type of* **motor vessel.** [➡SHIPS AND BOATS; 1149]

fertile 1 *adj* **productive**, fecund (*formal*), fruitful, prolific, generative. [➡USEFULNESS; 200] *Opposite:* infertile. 2 *adj* **lush**, productive, abundant, rich, fruitful, luxuriant, bountiful (*literary*). [➡ECONOMICAL AND RESOURCEFUL; 208] *Opposite:* barren.

fertility *n* **fruitfulness**, richness, lushness, productiveness, fecundity, abundance, luxuriance, potency. [➡USEFULNESS; 200] *Opposite:* barrenness.

fertilization 1 *n* **insemination**, impregnation, pollination, artificial insemination, donor insemination, conception, reproduction. [➡REPRODUCTION AND HEREDITY; 726] 2 *n* **fertilizer application**, manuring, composting, top dressing, enrichment, nourishment. [➡GROW AND CULTIVATE; 352]

fertilize 1 *v* **inseminate**, impregnate, pollinate. [➡REPRODUCTION AND HEREDITY; 726] 2 *v* **manure**, feed, top-dress, compost, enrich, nourish, muck (*informal*). [➡GROW AND CULTIVATE; 352] *Opposite:* exhaust.

fertilizer *n* **manure**, compost, nourishment, enricher, top dressing, peat. [➡UNPLEASANT AND DIRTY SUBSTANCES; 1267]

fervent *adj* **keen**, avid, ardent, eager, enthusiastic, passionate, zealous, fanatical, impassioned, burning, intense, vehement, heated. [➡APPRECIATION AND GRATITUDE; 536] *Opposite:* indifferent.

fervid *adj* [➡APPRECIATION AND GRATITUDE; 536]

fervour *n* **passion**, dedication, enthusiasm, eagerness, zeal, feeling, vehemence, commitment, intensity, ardour. [➡PLEASURE, EXCITEMENT, AND ELATION; 535] *Opposite:* indifference.

fescue *type of* **grass**. [➡GRASS; 1031]

fess up (*US informal*) *v* [➡ADMIT AND CONFESS; 616]

fester *v* **rankle**, irritate, aggravate (*informal*), embitter, annoy, gnaw, chafe, rile (*informal*), fret. [➡GET WORSE; 382]

festival *n* **feast day**, holiday, celebration, anniversary, birthday, jubilee, commemoration, fiesta, carnival, event, party, gala, fete, fair. [➡PARTIES, DANCES, AND CELEBRATIONS; 37]

festive *adj* **celebratory**, cheerful, joyful, merry, happy, jolly, jovial, festal, gala. [➡PARTIES, DANCES, AND CELEBRATIONS; 37] *Opposite:* sad.

festiveness *n* **merriness**, joyfulness, cheerfulness, happiness, jolliness, joviality. [➡TREAT; 211] *Opposite:* lugubriousness.

festivities *n* **revels**, revelry, celebrations, merriment, partying, carousing (*literary*). [➡PARTIES, DANCES, AND CELEBRATIONS; 37]

festivity 1 *n* **good cheer**, rejoicing, merriment, pleasure, enjoyment, happiness, cheeriness, gaiety, joy. [➡TREAT; 211] *Opposite:* sadness. 2 *n* **party**, event, do (*informal*), gala, carnival, fete, fiesta, entertainment, celebration, revelry. [➡PARTIES, DANCES, AND CELEBRATIONS; 37]

festoon 1 *n* **garland**, decoration, swag, ornament, chain, drape, streamer. [➡ORNAMENTS AND DECORATIONS; 1247] 2 *v* **decorate**, adorn, swathe, hang, drape, embellish, do up. [➡DECORATE, ADORN, AND APPLY COATINGS; 406] *Opposite:* strip.

festooned *adj* **garlanded**, wreathed, hung, decorated, draped, bedecked (*literary*), swathed, decked (*literary*). [➡DECORATE, ADORN, AND APPLY COATINGS; 406] *Opposite:* unadorned.

feta *type of* **soft cheese**. [➡DAIRY PRODUCTS AND CHEESES; 1182]

fetch 1 *v* **get**, obtain, bring, carry, bring back, retrieve, take, get a hold of (*US*). [➡GET; 421] 2 *v* **sell for**, make, raise, get, draw, realize, procure, bring, bring in. [➡GET; 421]

fetching *adj* **attractive**, eye-catching, handsome, dishy (*informal*), good-looking, stylish, appealing, becoming, captivating, enticing, alluring, beautiful, cute. [➡PEOPLE'S PHYSICAL APPEARANCE; 476] *Opposite:* unattractive.

fete *see* **fête**.

fête 1 *n* **bazaar**, celebration, event, fair, gala, fiesta, carnival, festival, jamboree. [➡SALES AND SHOWS; 444] 2 *n* **holiday**, anniversary, jubilee, centenary, feast day, commemoration, centennial (*US*). [➡PARTIES, DANCES, AND CELEBRATIONS; 37] 3 *v* **honour**, commemorate, lionize, entertain, praise, welcome, celebrate, congratulate. [➡PRAISE AND ENCOURAGE; 648]

fetid *adj* **rotten**, putrid, foul, rank (*literary*), squalid, fusty, stinking, smelly, decaying, malodorous, noisome. [➡DECAYING OR INFESTED; 1235] *Opposite:* fresh.

fetish 1 *n* **obsession**, thing (*informal*), fixation, mania, craze, engrossment, preoccupation, passion. [➡FADS, FETISHES, AND IDOLATRY; 556] *Opposite:* aversion. 2 *n* **talisman**, charm, idol, image, totem, amulet. [➡LUCKY CHARMS; 786]

fetishize *v* [➡LIKE, LOVE, VALUE AND ENJOY; 579]

fetlock *part of* **horse**. [➡HORSE; 985]

fetter 1 *n* **shackle**, bond, chain, yoke, handcuff, irons, restraint. [➡FASTENERS, LINKS, AND NETWORKS; 1246] 2 *v* **tie**, bind, chain, restrain, hamper, restrict, confine, impede, shackle. [➡CAPTIVITY AND LOSS OF FREEDOM; 249]

fettuccine *type of* **pasta**. [➡PASTA; 1179]

feud 1 *n* **dispute**, argument, row, quarrel, bad blood, grudge, disagreement, hostility, vendetta, strife. [➡ARGUMENT; 47] *Opposite:* friendship. 2 *v* **fight**, argue, dispute, quarrel, disagree, battle, clash, bicker, row. [➡COMPETE, CONTEND, AND COMBAT; 304]

feudal *adj* **out-of-date**, outdated, old-fashioned, medieval, primitive. [➡STYLES AND SYSTEMS OF GOVERNMENT; 806] *Opposite:* modern.

fever 1 *n* **temperature**, infection, disease, illness, malaise. [➡ILLNESSES AND DISORDERS; 733] 2 *n* **passion**, fervour, excitement, agitation, vehemence, enthusiasm, zeal, eagerness, fanaticism, impatience. [➡INSECURITY AND LOSS OF COMPOSURE; 545]

fevered *adj* **feverish**, agitated, restless, frenzied, excited, heated, enthusiastic, zealous, nervous, fanatical, impatient, passionate, intense. [➡POSITIVE IMPATIENCE, ENTHUSIASM, AND ALERTNESS; 538] *Opposite:* calm.

feverish *adj* **excited**, agitated, nervous, heated, intense, busy, exciting, vehement, enthusiastic, zealous, fevered, fanatical, impatient, passionate. [➡PLEASURE, EXCITEMENT, AND ELATION; 535] *Opposite:* tranquil.

few *adj* **insufficient**, a small number of, hardly any, not many, only some, a small amount of, scarce, rare, uncommon, limited, few and far between (*informal*), in short supply, thin on the ground. [➡FEW, LITTLE, SMALL AMOUNT; 119] *Opposite:* many.

few and far between (*informal*) *adj* **scarce**, infrequent, rare, sporadic, uncommon, in short supply, unusual, thin on the ground. [➡NEVER AND INFREQUENCY; 97] *Opposite:* commonplace.

fewer *adj* **less**, rarer, scarcer. [➡LESS; 124] *Opposite:* more.

fey *adj* **whimsical**, fanciful, otherworldly, unworldly, fantastical, capricious, irrational. [➡LACK OF COMMITMENT AND UNRELIABILITY; 510]

fez *type of* **headgear**. [➡HABERDASHERY, MILLINERY, AND LINGERIE; 867]

fiancé *n* **husband-to-be**, boyfriend, future husband, intended (*dated or humorous*), betrothed (*formal*), groom. [➡RELATIVES BY MARRIAGE; 960]

fiancée *n* **wife-to-be**, girlfriend, future wife, intended (*dated or humorous*), betrothed (*formal*), bride. [➡RELATIVES BY MARRIAGE; 960]

fiasco *n* **debacle**, disaster, mess, shambles, failure, flop (*informal*), cockup (*informal*), balls-up (*slang*). [➡FAILURE; 77] *Opposite:* success.

fiat 1 *n* **official sanction**, sanction, authorization, permission, agreement, approval. [➡PERMIT AND ALLOW; 670] 2 *n* **order**, command, decree, edict, instruction, directive. [➡REQUEST AND DEMAND; 664]

fib (*informal*) 1 *n* **untruth**, white lie, story (*informal*), lie, tall tale, whopper (*informal*), falsification, fabrication. [➡DECEPTION AND LIES; 661] *Opposite:* truth. 2 *v* **lie**, not tell the truth, misrepresent, tell stories, prevaricate, feign, dissemble, pull the wool over somebody's eyes, deceive, fake, pretend. [➡DECEPTION AND LIES; 661] *Opposite:* come clean (*informal*).

See Compare and Contrast at **lie**.

fibber (*informal*) *n* **liar**, storyteller (*informal*), deceiver, dissembler (*formal*), fabricator, prevaricator, perjurer, falsifier. [➡PEOPLE WHO DECEIVE; 662]

fibbing (*informal*) *n* [➡DECEPTION AND LIES; 661]

fibre 1 *n* **thread**, strand, string, filament, twine, yarn. [➡TEXTILES AND THREADS; 1130] 2 *n* **makeup**, composition, structure, character, stuff, grain. [➡QUALITIES AND CHARACTERISTICS; 1190] 3 *n* **grit**, strength, fortitude, backbone, character, integrity. [➡COURAGE; 499] *Opposite:* weakness. 4 *type of* **nutrient**. [➡FOOD COMPONENTS; 1187]

fibre

◆ *types of fibre*
cane, coconut matting, coir, fibreglass, jute, kapok, matting, raffia, ramie, rattan, sisal, straw, wicker

fibreboard *n* [➡BUILDING MATERIALS; 1076]

fibreglass *type of* **fibre**. [➡PLANT MATERIALS; 1132]

fibrous *adj* **tough**, leathery, stringy, rubbery, chewy. [➡PHYSICAL TEXTURE; 1221] *Opposite:* tender.

fibula *type of* **bone**. [➡THE BONES AND JOINTS; 720]

fickle *adj* **inconsistent**, changeable, capricious, inconstant, indecisive, vacillating, unfaithful, faithless, frivolous, unpredictable, unreliable, erratic. [➡LACK OF COMMITMENT AND UNRELIABILITY; 510] *Opposite:* constant.

fickleness *n* **inconsistency**, changeability, capriciousness, inconstancy, indecisiveness, vacillation, unfaithfulness, uncertainty, faithlessness, frivolity, unpredictability, unreliability. [➡LACK OF COMMITMENT AND UNRELIABILITY; 510] *Opposite:* constancy.

fiction 1 *n* **creative writing**, works of fiction, literature, narrative, novels, short stories. [➡FICTION AND DRAMA; 913] *Opposite:* nonfiction. 2 *n* **work of fiction**, novel, fantasy, story, short story, tale. [➡FICTION AND DRAMA; 913] 3 *n* **falsehood**, fabrication, lie, untruth, fib (*informal*), misrepresentation, deceit. [➡DECEPTION AND LIES; 661] *Opposite:* fact. 4 *n* **invention**, fantasy, imagination, nonsense, illusion, fancy, unrealism. [➡FALSE AND UNREAL; 174] *Opposite:* reality.

fictional *adj* **imaginary**, imagined, illusory, unreal, false, fantastic, fictitious, untrue. [➡FALSE AND UNREAL; 174] *Opposite:* real.

fictionalization *n* **fictional account**, fictional version, account, narrative, story, version, dramatization. [➡FICTION AND DRAMA; 913]

fictionalize *v* **dramatize**, novelize, recount, transpose, adapt. [➡RECORD SOMETHING; 372]

fictitious *adj* **untrue**, fabricated, invented, made-up, false, pretend, fictional. [➡FALSE AND UNREAL; 174] *Opposite:* factual.

fiddle 1 *type of* **stringed instrument** [➡MUSICAL INSTRUMENTS; 910] 2 *n* (*informal*) **swindle**, fraud, cheat, hoax, con, scam (*slang*), contrivance. [➡CRIMES; 817] 3 *v* **fidget**, play, play around, toy, pick at, jiggle, twiddle. [➡CHANGE; 373] *Opposite:* leave alone. 4 *v* **meddle**, tamper, interfere, mess around (*informal*), mess about (*informal*), mess, play, play around. [➡CONTACT: TOUCH; 413] *Opposite:* leave alone. 5 *v* **tinker**, manipulate, adjust, jiggle, play with, retune. [➡CHANGE; 373] *Opposite:* leave alone. 6 *v* (*informal*) **defraud**, swindle, cheat, con, diddle (*informal*), hoax, deceive. [➡STEAL AND ROB; 427] 7 *v* (*informal*) **falsify**, doctor, tamper with, manipulate, fix, cook the books (*slang*). [➡FALSIFY AND CHEAT; 177]

fiddling 1 *adj* **petty**, unimportant, trifling, piddling (*informal*), trivial, insignificant. [➡UNIMPORTANT AND UNNECESSARY; 239] *Opposite:* significant. 2 *n* (*informal*) **fraud**, deception, cheating, fixing, swindling, falsification. [➡CRIMES; 817]

fiddly (*informal*) *adj* **tricky**, awkward, difficult, complex, detailed, finicky. [➡DIFFICULTY AND COMPLEXITY; 243] *Opposite:* easy.

fidelity *n* **loyalty**, faithfulness, reliability, trustworthiness, dependability, devotion, conformity, commitment. [➡RELATIONSHIP TO ANOTHER; 973] *Opposite:* infidelity.

fidget 1 *v* **twitch**, squirm, fret, shuffle, jiggle, joggle, wriggle, move about, move around. [➡FIDGET AND FROLIC; 312] *Opposite:* freeze. 2 *v* **fiddle**, play, play around, toy, jiggle, twiddle. [➡CONTACT: TOUCH; 413] *Opposite:* leave alone.

fidgetiness *n* **twitchiness**, fretfulness, restlessness, squirminess, uneasiness, nervousness, jumpiness, agitation. [➡INSECURITY AND LOSS OF COMPOSURE; 545] *Opposite:* stillness.

fidgety *adj* **twitchy** (*informal*), fretful, restless, squirmy, uneasy, nervous, jumpy, jittery, agitated. [➡INSECURITY AND LOSS OF COMPOSURE; 545] *Opposite:* still.

field 1 *n* **meadow**, pasture, grassland, lea (*literary*), grazing. [➡THE COUNTRYSIDE AND OUTDOOR SPACES; 1070] 2 *n* **sports ground**, playing field, pitch, turf, arena, ground, park. [➡URBAN OUTDOOR SPACES; 1071] 3 *n* **subject**, area, topic, discipline, theme, province, domain, line of work, sphere. [➡SUBJECT AREA; 769] 4 *v* **catch**, retrieve, pick up, go after, fetch, return. [➡GET; 421] 5 *v* **deal with**, handle, tackle, take care of, see to, look after, take. [➡CARRY OUT AN ACTION; 270] *Opposite:* ignore.

fielder *n* **player**, cricketer, baseball player, sportsperson, outfielder, infielder. [➡PEOPLE IN SPORTS AND LEISURE; 876] *Opposite:* batter.

field glasses *type of* **optical instrument**. [➡OPTICAL INSTRUMENTS; 1123]

field hockey (*US*) *type of* **ball game**. [➡HOBBIES, GAMES, AND SPORTS; 875]

field marshal *n* [➡MILITARY PERSONNEL; 828]

field mushroom *type of* **fungus**. [➡MICROORGANISMS, FUNGI, AND ALGAE; 1023]

field test *n* **field trial**, test, trial, experiment, assay, controlled test. [➡PREPARATORY EVENT; 57]

field-test *v* **test**, try out, study, put through its paces, trial. [➡ATTEMPT AN ACTION; 262]

fieldwork *n* **research**, information-gathering, investigation, fact-finding, exploration, examination, observation. [➡LESSONS, COURSE WORK, AND EXAMINATIONS; 842]

fiend *n* **villain**, evil person, brute, beast, monster, terror, ogre. [➡VILLAINS AND THUGS; 947] *Opposite:* angel.

fiendish 1 *adj* **cruel**, evil, brutal, monstrous, villainous, malicious, malevolent, wicked, wretched, inhuman, barbarous. [➡MORALLY BAD; 776] *Opposite:* pleasant. 2 *adj* **cunning**, ingenious, clever, crafty, devilish, brilliant. [➡POSITIVE INTELLECTUAL CHARACTERISTICS; 525] 3 *adj* **impossible**, tricky, difficult, hard, perplexing, trying. [➡DIFFICULTY AND COMPLEXITY; 243] *Opposite:* straightforward.

fiendishly 1 *adv* **cruelly**, brutally, wickedly, inhumanly, maliciously, villainously, barbarously, malevolently, monstrously. [➡SELFISH AND UNKIND; 506] *Opposite:* pleasantly. 2 *adv* **extremely**, excessively, extraordinarily, incredibly, impossibly, horribly. [➡TO A GREAT EXTENT; 130]

fierce 1 *adj* **violent**, ferocious, aggressive, brutal, severe, stern, angry, vicious, furious. [➡AGGRESSIVE AND BELLIGERENT; 519] *Opposite:* gentle. 2 *adj* **intense**, violent, extreme, savage, almighty (*informal*), ferocious, wild, raging. [➡STRENGTH; 202] *Opposite:* mild. 3 *adj* **strong**, powerful, profound, deep, turbulent, passionate, defiant, ardent, intense, violent. [➡STRENGTH; 202] *Opposite:* mild.

fiercely 1 *adv* **violently**, ferociously, aggressively, brutally, severely, sternly, angrily, viciously, furiously. [➡AGGRESSIVE AND BELLIGERENT; 519] *Opposite:* gently. 2 *adv* **ferociously**, intensely, strongly, brightly, hotly, with a will. [➡STRENGTH; 202] *Opposite:* feebly. 3 *adv* **extremely**, exceedingly, very, passionately, resolutely, intensely. [➡TO A GREAT EXTENT; 130] *Opposite:* mildly.

fierceness 1 *n* **ferocity**, severity, brutality, violence, aggressiveness, sternness, anger, viciousness. [➡UNKIND ACTION OR BEHAVIOUR; 297] *Opposite:* gentleness. 2 *n* **intensity**, violence, strength, power, turbulence, aggressiveness, ferocity, savageness, wildness. [➡DIFFICULTY AND COMPLEXITY; 243] *Opposite:* mildness.

fiery 1 *adj* **burning**, scorching (*informal*), blistering, sweltering, sizzling (*informal*), blazing, flaming, hot, baking. [➡TEMPERATURE: HOT; 1228] *Opposite:* icy. 2 *adj* **fierce**, passionate, heated, angry, furious, intense, powerful, ardent, turbulent, forceful. [➡STRENGTH; 202] *Opposite:* mild.

fiesta *n* **feast**, holiday, festival, carnival, celebration, gala, fete, event. [➡PARTIES, DANCES, AND CELEBRATIONS; 37]

fife *type of* **wind instrument**. [➡MUSICAL INSTRUMENTS; 910]

fifty-fifty *adv* **half and half**, half each, two ways, equally, halfway, in two, down the middle, in equal parts. [➡EQUALITY; 155]

fig *type of* **fruit**. [➡FRUIT AND VEGETABLES; 1175]

fight 1 *v* **brawl**, box, clash, scrap, wrestle, tussle, battle, come to blows, exchange blows, struggle. [➡COMPETE, CONTEND, AND COMBAT; 304] 2 *v* **wage war**, clash, struggle, battle, skirmish, attack. [➡WARFARE AND WAR; 830] 3 *v* **dispute**, oppose, struggle, contest, wrangle, argue. [➡PROTEST AND EXPRESS DISAPPROVAL; 643] *Opposite:* accept. 4 *n* **conflict**, battle, brawl, war, clash, scrap (*informal*), combat, hostility, skirmish, engagement. [➡AGGRESSIVE EVENT; 39] 5 *n* **argument**, dispute, wrangle, clash, run-in (*informal*), ding-dong (*informal*), row. [➡ARGUMENT; 47] *Opposite:* reconciliation. 6 *n* **contest**, match, bout, competition, round, prize fight. [➡NON-AGGRESSIVE/SPORTING EVENT; 40]

Compare and Contrast: ***fight, battle, war, conflict, engagement, skirmish, clash***

CORE MEANING: A STRUGGLE BETWEEN OPPOSING ARMED FORCES

fight a physical struggle between individuals or groups, such as battalions or armies; ***battle*** a large-scale fight involving combat between armies, warships, or aircraft as part of an ongoing war or campaign; ***war*** a state of hostilities between nations, states, or factions involving the use of arms and the occurrence of a series of battles; ***conflict*** warfare between opposing forces, especially a prolonged and bitter but sporadic struggle; ***engagement*** a hostile encounter involving military forces; ***skirmish*** a brief minor fight, usually one that is part of a larger conflict; ***clash*** a short, fierce encounter, usually involving physical combat.

fight back 1 *v* **retaliate**, defend yourself, put up a fight, riposte, resist, counter, get back at. [➡PROTEST AND EXPRESS DISAPPROVAL; 643] *Opposite:* attack. 2 *v* **repress**, control, hold back, suppress, push back, repel, fight off, conceal, restrain. [➡NOT PAY ATTENTION; 765] *Opposite:* let out.

fighter 1 *n* **boxer**, wrestler, pugilist, prize fighter. [➡COMPETITORS; 41] 2 *type of* **military aircraft**. [➡AIRCRAFT; 1147]

fighter-bomber *type of* **military aircraft**. [➡AIRCRAFT; 1147]

fighting 1 *adj* **aggressive**, belligerent, pugnacious, hostile, rebellious, struggling. [➡AGGRESSIVE AND BELLIGERENT; 519]

Opposite: pacifist. **2** *n* **combat**, hostility, unrest, warfare, violence, war. [➡AGGRESSIVE EVENT; 39] *Opposite:* peace.

fighting fit *adj* [➡FIT AND STRONG; 737]

fight off *v* **fend off**, drive away, resist, repulse, repel, stave off, ward off, keep at bay, hold off. [➡PREVENT CONTACT OR ATTACK; 420] *Opposite:* attack.

fight shy of *v* [➡NOT DO AND REFUSE TO DO; 275]

figment *n* **fabrication**, creation, invention, illusion, fantasy, hallucination. [➡NONEXISTENT THINGS; 23]

figment of the imagination *n* [➡NONEXISTENT THINGS; 23]

figurative *adj* **metaphorical**, symbolic, metaphoric, allegorical, nonliteral, emblematic, abstract. [➡REPRESENTATIVE; 66] *Opposite:* literal.

figure **1** *n* **number**, numeral, character, symbol, digit. [➡SYMBOLS, SIGNS, AND NUMBERS; 597] **2** *n* **amount**, cost, sum, quantity, total, statistic. [➡AMOUNT AND QUANTITY; 112] **3** *n* **shape**, form, outline, stature, build, body. [➡SHAPE; 1215] **4** *n* **person**, personage (*formal*), dignitary, celebrity, notable, individual, character. [➡PERSON; 931] **5** *n* **diagram**, chart, picture, table, illustration, map. [➡DRAWINGS, CHARTS, AND TABLES; 595] **6** *v* **play a part**, feature, appear, be included, be incorporated, participate, fit into. [➡PARTICIPATE; 293] **7** *v* **reckon**, guess, believe, think, suppose, imagine, presume, assume, consider. [➡DEVELOP THEORIES AND REASON; 745] *Opposite:* doubt.

figurehead *n* [➡IMPORTANT OR FAMOUS PEOPLE; 893]

figure-hugging *adj* [➡DESCRIBING CLOTHES; 869]

figure of eight *type of* **rounded shape**. [➡ROUNDED SHAPE; 1217]

figure of speech *n* **expression**, metaphor, simile, symbol, idiom, image, rhetorical expression, idiomatic expression. [➡FIGURES OF SPEECH; 674]

figure out *v* **work out**, understand, discover, fathom, decipher, solve, comprehend, discern, realize, make out, deduce, infer, conclude. [➡UNDERSTAND AND GRASP; 760]

See Compare and Contrast at **deduce**.

figure skating *type of* **winter sport**. [➡HOBBIES, GAMES, AND SPORTS; 875]

figurine *n* **statuette**, figure, model, ornament, statue, sculpture. [➡SCULPTURE; 902]

filament *n* **thread**, strand, string, fibre, wire, monofilament. [➡TEXTILES AND THREADS; 1130]

filch (*informal*) *v* **steal**, rob, thieve, walk off with, snatch, pinch (*informal*), nick (*slang*), liberate (*informal*), help yourself to, lift (*informal*). [➡STEAL AND ROB; 427] *Opposite:* return.

See Compare and Contrast at **steal**.

file **1** *n* **folder**, sleeve, dossier, heading, box file, wallet, case, organizer. [➡CONTAINERS, RECEPTACLES, AND PACKAGING; 1244] **2** *n* **report**, dossier, profile, record, information, summary. [➡RECORDS; 586] **3** *n* **line**, queue, row, column, crocodile (*informal*), procession, lineup. [➡AREA AND RANGE; 111] **4** *v* **record**, categorize, put on record, keep, file away, store, organize. [➡RECORD SOMETHING; 372] **5** *v* **march**, troop, parade, snake, walk in single file, trail, funnel. [➡PROCEED AND GO; 306] **6** *v* **rub**, rasp, scrape, sand, smooth, sandpaper, chafe. [➡USE TOOLS AND MACHINERY; 469] **7** *type of* **general tool**. [➡HAND TOOLS; 1118]

filial *adj* **familial**, family, loving, devoted. [➡THE FAMILY; 956] *Opposite:* parental.

filigree *n* **tracery**, lacy pattern, lattice, latticework, lace, network, ornamentation. [➡ORNAMENTS AND DECORATIONS; 1247]

filing *n* **shaving**, particle, splinter, shard, shred, bit. [➡SMALL PIECE; 127]

fill **1** *v* **fill up**, pack, stuff, cram, jam, pile up, load. [➡FILL; 407] *Opposite:* empty. **2** *v* **pervade**, imbue, charge (*formal*), impart, permeate, saturate, soak. [➡FILL; 407] **3** *v* **plug**, block, block up, seal, bung up (*informal*), stop, stop up. [➡FILL; 407] *Opposite:* clear. **4** *v* **satisfy**, fulfil, meet, satiate, provide for, gratify, supply. [➡EQUIP AND SUPPLY; 436]

filler **1** *n* **padding**, stuffing, wadding, filling, packing. [➡CENTRAL PARTS OF PHYSICAL OBJECTS; 1250] **2** *n* **plaster**, grout, putty, caulking, pitch, oakum. [➡BUILDING MATERIALS; 1076]

fillet **1** *v* **bone**, clean, prepare, gut, scale, skin. [➡COOKING AND FOOD PREPARATION; 354] **2** *type of* **steak**. [➡TYPES AND CUTS OF MEAT; 1176]

fill in **1** *v* **complete**, fill out, write out, answer. [➡RECORD SOMETHING; 372] **2** *v* **take somebody's place**, stand in, substitute, deputize, cover, do the honours. [➡CHANGE ONE THING FOR ANOTHER; 399] **3** *v* **bring up-to-date**, put in the picture, give the latest, give the lowdown. [➡EXPLAIN AND CLARIFY; 611] **4** *v* **clog**, plug, choke, dam up, block, stop up, obstruct. [➡FILL; 407]

fill-in *n* **substitute**, stand-in, temp, replacement, temporary worker, casual worker, locum, supply teacher, alternate (*US*). [➡SUBSTITUTES AND STAND-INS; 400]

filling **1** *n* **inside**, contents, innards (*informal*), guts. [➡CENTRAL PARTS OF PHYSICAL OBJECTS; 1250] **2** *n* **stuffing**, padding, bulk, wadding, packing. [➡CENTRAL PARTS OF PHYSICAL OBJECTS; 1250] **3** *adj* **satisfying**, substantial, big, stodgy (*informal*), heavy, rich. [➡FOOD; 1166] *Opposite:* meagre.

filling station *n* **petrol station**, garage, service station, services, service area, petrol pumps, gas station (*US*), gas pumps (*US*). [➡RETAIL OUTLETS; 1082]

fillip *n* **boost**, tonic, spur, stimulus, impetus, impulse, incentive, inspiration, zest. [➡TREAT; 211] *Opposite:* knock.

fill out **1** *v* **complete**, fill in, write out, answer. [➡RECORD SOMETHING; 372] **2** *v* **put on weight**, fatten up, bulk up, grow, develop, get plump, increase, swell. [➡CHANGE OF SIZE: BIGGER; 393] *Opposite:* waste away.

fill up **1** *v* **refill**, fill, replenish, load, stock up, restock, top up. [➡FILL; 407] *Opposite:* empty. **2** *v* **satisfy**, satiate, stuff, bloat, fill. [➡FILL; 407]

filly *type of* **female animal**. [➡MALE OR FEMALE ANIMAL; 978]

film **1** *n* **picture**, flick (*informal*), big screen, silver screen, motion picture (*US formal or technical*), movie (*US*). [➡FILM; 901] **2** *n* **layer**, coat, coating, covering, sheet, skin, skim, glaze. [➡COVERS AND COATINGS; 1245] **3** *part of* **photographic equipment**. [➡PHOTOGRAPHY AND PHOTOGRAPHIC EQUIPMENT; 1121] **4** *v* record, video, tape, capture, shoot, take, image. [➡RECORD SOMETHING; 372]

film over *v* **mist over**, mist up, glaze over, steam up, cloud over, cloud up, become cloudy. [➡SOFTEN, LIQUEFY, DAMPEN; 389] *Opposite:* clear.

film star *type of* **entertainer**. [➡WORKERS IN ENTERTAINMENT AND MEDIA; 873]

filmy *adj* **light**, airy, translucent, transparent, diaphanous, hazy, floating, see-through, glossy, iridescent. [➡VISUAL TEXTURE; 1220] *Opposite:* solid.

filo pastry *n* [➡BREAD, FLOUR, AND BREAD PRODUCTS; 1178]

filter 1 *n* **sieve**, strainer, mesh, riddle, screen, sifter. [➡TABLEWARE, CUTLERY, AND KITCHENWARE; 861] 2 *part of* **photographic equipment**. [➡PHOTOGRAPHY AND PHOTOGRAPHIC EQUIPMENT; 1121] 3 *v* **sort**, sort out, separate out, stream, categorize, divide up, sift. [➡ARRANGE AND CREATE ORDER; 358] *Opposite:* mingle. 4 *v* **sift**, sieve, strain, clean, clarify, purify, riddle. [➡SEPARATE AND DIVIDE; 402] 5 *v* **seep**, ooze, trickle, penetrate, permeate, percolate, leak, dribble. [➡PROCEED AND GO; 306]

filth 1 *n* **dirt**, grime, rubbish, refuse, soil, waste, muck (*informal*), debris. [➡UNPLEASANT AND DIRTY SUBSTANCES; 1267] 2 *n* **smut**, rudeness, lewdness, immorality, obscenity, offensiveness, grubbiness, filthiness. [➡MORALLY BAD; 776]

filthiness 1 *n* **dirtiness**, griminess, dirt, muckiness (*informal*), grubbiness, foulness, messiness. [➡DIRTY; 1234] *Opposite:* cleanliness. 2 *n* **lewdness**, rudeness, immorality, smut, obscenity, grubbiness, offensiveness. [➡MORALLY BAD; 776] *Opposite:* decency.

filthy 1 *adj* **dirty**, grimy, muddy, mucky (*informal*), soiled, grubby, messy, squalid, unclean. [➡DIRTY; 1234] *Opposite:* clean. 2 *adj* **rude**, indecent, lewd, smutty (*informal*), obscene, grubby, offensive. [➡MORALLY BAD; 776] *Opposite:* decent.

See Compare and Contrast at **dirty**.

filtration *n* **percolation**, separation, purification, clarification, categorization, division. [➡SEPARATE AND DIVIDE; 402]

fin 1 *n* **appendage**, flipper, paddle, dorsal fin, organ, limb, member. [➡PARTS OF A FISH; 1011] 2 *n* **projection**, stabilizer, blade, paddle, propeller, rudder. [➡EXTERNAL PARTS OF A VEHICLE; 1146] 3 *part of* **aircraft**. [➡AIRCRAFT; 1147]

finagle (*informal*) *v* **trick**, cheat, manipulate, wangle (*informal*), engineer, wheedle, coax, persuade, foist. [➡OBTAIN POSSESSION BY PERSUASION; 458]

final 1 *adj* **last**, concluding, closing, ending, finishing, ultimate. [➡AFTER, LAST, AND FOLLOWING; 166] *Opposite:* first. 2 *adj* **conclusive**, definitive, absolute, decisive, irrevocable, ultimate. [➡CERTAIN; 175] *Opposite:* provisional. 3 *n* **round**, match, game, decider, last leg. [➡NON-AGGRESSIVE/SPORTING EVENT; 40]

finale *n* **ending**, end, climax, culmination, finish, denouement (*formal*). [➡END; 54]

finalist *n* **qualifier**, contestant, challenger, frontrunner (*informal*), runner-up, contender. [➡COMPETITORS; 41] *Opposite:* also-ran.

finality *n* **conclusiveness**, decisiveness, definiteness, inevitability, irrevocability, determination. [➡CERTAIN; 175] *Opposite:* uncertainty.

finalization *n* **completion**, conclusion, agreement, settlement, decision, confirmation. [➡END; 54]. *Opposite:* commencement (*formal*).

finalize *v* **confirm**, settle, decide, firm up, complete, tie up, conclude, wrap up (*informal*). [➡COMPLETE AN ACTION; 264] *Opposite:* start.

finally 1 *adv* **at last**, at length, at long last, ultimately, after all, in the end, at the end of the day. [➡AFTER, LAST, AND FOLLOWING; 166] *Opposite:* initially. 2 *adv* **conclusively**, completely, decisively, irrevocably, definitively, irreversibly, beyond doubt. [➡CERTAIN; 175] *Opposite:* tentatively. 3 *adv* **lastly**, in conclusion, to conclude, to finish, to end, to close, as a final point. [➡AFTER, LAST, AND FOLLOWING; 166] *Opposite:* firstly.

finance 1 *n* **money**, economics, business, investment, backing, sponsorship, funding. [➡MONEY, PAYMENTS, AND CHARGES; 800] 2 *v* **back**, invest in, pay for, fund, support, sponsor, bankroll (*informal*), put money into. [➡GIVE MONEY; 434]

finances *n* **money**, funds, assets, cash, capital, savings, investments, value, stock, shares. [➡MONEY, PAYMENTS, AND CHARGES; 800]

financial *adj* **monetary**, fiscal, economic, pecuniary, monetarist, commercial, business. [➡FINANCE AND ECONOMICS; 797]

financier *n* **banker**, investor, backer, sponsor, investment banker, merchant banker, supporter. [➡PEOPLE INVOLVED IN FINANCE; 804]

finch *type of* **common bird**. [➡BIRD; 997]

find 1 *v* **discover**, locate, come across, hit upon, unearth, uncover, stumble on, light on. [➡FIND; 464] 2 *v* **recover**, regain, get back, retrieve, discover, locate. [➡FIND; 464] *Opposite:* lose. 3 *v* **realize**, understand, get, obtain, attain, acquire, achieve, get hold of, get a hold of (*US*). [➡GET; 421] 4 *n* **discovery**, bargain, treasure trove, treasure, novelty, invention. [➡FIND; 464]

find fault *v* **criticize**, nag, nitpick, carp, get at, have a go at (*informal*), pick holes in, complain about. [➡COMPLAIN AND NAG; 687] *Opposite:* praise.

find fault with *v* [➡ACCUSE, BLAME, AND CRITICIZE; 642]

finding 1 *n* **discovery**, conclusion, result, verdict, outcome, definition. [➡RESULTS AND OUTCOMES; 83] 2 *n* **verdict**, ruling, result, sentence, decision, pronouncement, judgment. [➡TRIAL, PUNISHMENT, AND LEGAL OUTCOMES; 819]

find out 1 *v* **discover**, learn, realize, observe, note, notice, catch on (*informal*), detect, hear about, get wind of. [➡LEARN AND DISCOVER; 763] 2 *v* **catch**, expose, uncover, reveal, unmask, suss (*informal*). [➡FIND; 464]

fine 1 *adj* **light**, slight, faint, thin, tenuous, insubstantial, flimsy, gauzy, diaphanous, translucent, subtle. [➡IMPERCEPTIBLE; 26] *Opposite:* heavy. 2 *adj* (*informal*) **acceptable**, satisfactory, well, all right, okay (*informal*), good, reasonable, adequate, sufficient. [➡ACCEPTABLE AND PASSABLE; 220] *Opposite:* unsatisfactory. 3 *adj* **tiny**, minute, light, delicate, small, thin, wafer-thin, slight. [➡WIDTH: NARROW AND THIN; 1199] 4 *adj* **bright**, sunny, warm, beautiful, fair, pleasant, clear. [➡HOT WEATHER; 1050] *Opposite:* dull. 5 *adj* **delicate**, dainty, slender, refined, thin, slight, sharp, chiselled, well-honed. [➡FRAGILE; 1208] *Opposite:* coarse. 6 *adj* **outstanding**, superb, excellent, superior, exceptional, select, first-rate. [➡GOOD, WELL, BETTER; 184] *Opposite:* poor. 7 *adj* **subtle**, keen, sharp, skilled, refined, discerning, discriminating, perceptive, fastidious. [➡CONCISE AND CLEAR; 203] *Opposite:* dull. 8 *n* **penalty**, punishment, payment, forfeit, levy, charge. [➡TRIAL, PUNISHMENT, AND LEGAL OUTCOMES; 819] 9 *v* **penalize**, punish, levy, charge. [➡TRIAL, PUNISHMENT, AND LEGAL OUTCOMES; 819]

fine art *n* [➡THE PICTORIAL ARTS; 897]

finely 1 *adv* **delicately**, lightly, thinly, closely, intricately, sharply, daintily. [➡CONCISE AND CLEAR; 203] *Opposite:* coarsely. 2 *adv* **excellently**, outstandingly, exceptionally, superbly, magnificently, wonderfully, stupendously, marvellously. [➡GOOD, WELL, BETTER; 184] *Opposite:* poorly. 3 *adv* **subtly**, keenly, sharply, discerningly, discriminatingly, perceptively, fastidiously. [➡CONCISE AND CLEAR; 203]

fineness 1 *n* **excellence**, greatness, superiority, quality, distinction, superbness, refinement, calibre. [➡EXTRAORDINARY: AMAZING; 205] *Opposite:* poorness. 2 *n* **delicacy**, sheerness, thinness, narrowness, slenderness, daintiness, lightness, minuteness, flimsiness. [➡WIDTH: NARROW AND THIN; 1199] *Opposite:* coarseness.

fine points *n* [➡BASIC DETAILS; 689]

finery *n* **glad rags** (*informal*), attire (*formal*), regalia, jewellery, evening dress, morning dress, dress uniform, ceremonial dress. [➡CLOTHES AND ACCESSORIES; 864]

finesse 1 *n* **skill**, flair, grace, poise, assurance, refinement, elegance. [➡SKILLS, TALENTS, AND ABILITIES; 527] *Opposite:* clumsiness. 2 *n* **subtlety**, delicacy, diplomacy, tact, discretion, sensitivity. [➡GOOD MANNERS AND SOCIAL SKILLS; 521] *Opposite:* tactlessness.

finest *adj* **premium**, handpicked, optimum, best, supreme, deluxe, luxury. [➡SUPERIORITY; 153] *Opposite:* worst.

fine-tune *v* **modify**, adjust, tweak (*informal*), tune, polish up, perfect, hone. [➡CORRECT AND PUT RIGHT; 378]

fine-tuning *n* **adjustment**, refinement, modification, perfection, tuning, finish. [➡IMPROVE SOMETHING; 375]

finger 1 *n* **digit**, limb, member, extremity. [➡ARM AND HAND; 696] 2 *n* **portion**, slither, slice, bit, smidgen (*informal*), helping. [➡AMOUNT AND QUANTITY; 112] *Opposite:* hunk. 3 *v* **handle**, touch, feel, manipulate, toy with, fiddle with, pick up. [➡CONTACT: TOUCH; 413] 4 *v* (*slang*) **identify**, inform on, point to, pick out, name, grass on (*slang*), point out. [➡NAME AND DESCRIBE; 666]

finger food *n* [➡PREPARED DISHES; 1169]

fingernail *part of* **arm or hand**. [➡ARM AND HAND; 696]

fingerprint 1 *n* **impression**, print, mark, pattern, thumbprint, whorl. [➡ARM AND HAND; 696] 2 *n* **characteristic**, identification, evidence, pattern, diagnostic, sign. [➡EVIDENCE AND PROOF; 69]

fingertip 1 *adj* **sensitive**, delicate, fine, sensitized, accurate, probing. [➡EXACT; 204] 2 *part of* **arm or hand**. [➡ARM AND HAND; 696]

finicky *adj* **fastidious**, fussy, picky, choosy (*informal*), pernickety (*informal*), particular. [➡DIFFICULT TO PLEASE; 516] *Opposite:* sloppy.

See Compare and Contrast at **careful**.

finish 1 *v* **end**, stop, terminate (*formal*), close, cease, conclude, wrap up (*informal*), complete. [➡COMPLETE AN ACTION; 264] *Opposite:* start. 2 *v* **use up**, drain, exhaust, polish off, empty, finish off, demolish (*informal*), clean out (*informal*). [➡USE UP AND WASTE; 475] *Opposite:* stock up. 3 *v* (*informal*) **destroy**, ruin, annihilate, defeat, exhaust, deplete, overwhelm, devastate. [➡BEAT AND DEFEAT; 80] 4 *v* **polish**, buff, rub, varnish, lacquer, gild. [➡CLEAN AND POLISH; 404] 5 *n* **end**, ending, close, conclusion, completion, cessation, finale, termination. [➡END; 54] *Opposite:* start. 6 *n* **surface**, texture, appearance, quality, varnish, gloss, gilt, polish. [➡TEXTURE; 1219]

finished 1 *adj* **over**, ended, broken down, broken up, broken off, over and done with, kaput (*informal*), done. [➡WHOLENESS AND COMPLETENESS; 199] 2 *adj* **refined**, perfect, polished, elegant, professional. [➡TALENTED AND SKILFUL; 528] *Opposite:* rough. 3 *adj* **polished**, buffed, varnished, glossed, gilded, planed. [➡IN GOOD REPAIR; 1231] *Opposite:* unfinished. 4 *adj* **ruined**, wrecked, washed-up (*informal*), lost, destroyed, done for (*informal*), devastated. [➡BEATEN AND DEFEATED; 78]

finish off 1 *v* **complete**, bring to an end, wind up, wrap up (*informal*), fulfil, conclude, finalize, close. [➡COMPLETE AN ACTION; 264] *Opposite:* start up. 2 *v* **use up**, eat up, exhaust, polish off, demolish (*informal*), clean out (*informal*). [➡USE UP AND WASTE; 475] *Opposite:* stock up. 3 *v* (*informal*) **eliminate**, kill, exterminate, dispatch, dispose of, top (*slang*), polish off, put an end to, put somebody out of (his or her) misery (*humorous*). [➡KILL; 923]

finish up *v* **eat up**, consume, knock back (*informal*), scoff (*informal*), wolf, demolish (*informal*), finish off. [➡EAT AND NOT EAT; 711] *Opposite:* leave.

finite *adj* **limited**, restricted, determinate, fixed, set, predetermined, predictable. [➡FINITENESS, VARIABILITY, AND TRANSIENCE; 96] *Opposite:* infinite.

fink out (*US slang*) *v* [➡NOT DO AND REFUSE TO DO; 275]

fir *type of* **evergreen tree**. [➡EVERGREEN AND CONIFEROUS TREES; 1029]

fir cone *n* [➡PARTS OF TREES AND PLANTS; 1026]

fire 1 *n* **combustion**, conflagration, ignition. [➡FIRE, FLAMMABILITY, AND BURNING; 1164] 2 *n* **blaze**, flames, bonfire, conflagration, combustion, inferno. [➡FIRE, FLAMMABILITY, AND BURNING; 1164] 3 *n* **passion**, ardour, fervour, excitement, enthusiasm, vigour, spirit, intensity, energy. [➡INSECURITY AND LOSS OF COMPOSURE; 545] *Opposite:* apathy. 4 *v* **shoot**, set off, discharge (*formal*), detonate, trigger, launch. [➡USE TOOLS AND MACHINERY; 469] 5 *v* (*informal*) **dismiss**, sack (*informal*), give somebody the sack, throw out, give somebody their cards, give somebody the push (*informal*), get rid of, lay off, can (*US slang*), give somebody the pink slip (*US*). [➡EJECT AND EXCLUDE; 341] *Opposite:* take on. 6 *v* **excite**, arouse, inspire, enthuse, enliven, animate. [➡ENCOURAGE; 577]

Compare and Contrast: ***fire, blaze, conflagration, inferno***

CORE MEANING: REFERRING TO BURNING AND flAMES

fire the light, heat, and flames produced by burning material, produced intentionally or unintentionally; ***blaze*** a bright or large fire; ***conflagration*** a fierce destructive fire, affecting a large area and causing a lot of damage; ***inferno*** an intense, fiercely burning, destructive fire.

fire alarm *n* **bell**, siren, klaxon, buzzer, warning, alarm, signal. [➡SIGNALLING; 1139]

fire and brimstone *n* [➡RELIGIOUS CONCEPTS; 777]

firearm *n* **gun**, weapon, handgun, pistol, rifle, shotgun. [➡WEAPONS FOR SHOOTING; 1155]

fireball 1 *n* **ball lightning**, ball of fire, flash, lightning. [➡FIRE, FLAMMABILITY, AND BURNING; 1164] 2 *type of* **heavenly body**. [➡CELESTIAL BODIES; 1060]

firebomb *type of* **explosive weapon**. [➡EXPLOSIVES; 1154]

firebrand *n* **troublemaker**, agitator, hothead, stirrer (*informal*), revolutionary, demagogue. [➡UNCOOPERATIVE OR REBELLIOUS PERSON; 567]

firebreak *n* **clearing**, opening, strip, break, barrier, glade, fireguard. [➡THE COUNTRYSIDE AND OUTDOOR SPACES; 1070]

firecracker *type of* **firework**. [➡EXPLOSIVES; 1154]

fire drill *n* **fire practice**, drill, rehearsal, evacuation, exercise, practice. [➡PREPARATORY EVENT; 57]

fired up *adj* **enthused**, motivated, eager, psyched up (*informal*), passionate, on fire, enthusiastic. [➡PLEASURE, EXCITEMENT, AND ELATION; 535] *Opposite:* apathetic.

fire engine *type of* **public service vehicle**. [➡VEHICLES; 1144]

fire escape 1 *n* **stairway**, ladder, escape hatch, staircase, emergency exit, exit, way out, fire door, steps. [➡STAIRS AND STOREYS; 1101] 2 *part of* **building**. [➡PARTS OF A BUILDING; 1094]

firefly *type of* **flying insect**. [➡FLYING INSECTS; 1013]

fireguard 1 *n* **fire screen**, screen, guard, fender, frame. [➡COVERS AND COATINGS; 1245] 2 *n* **firebreak**, clearing, strip, glade, opening. [➡THE COUNTRYSIDE AND OUTDOOR SPACES; 1070]

firelight *n* **glow**, glimmer, flame, flare, blaze. [➡LIGHT; 1163]

fireplace 1 *n* **hearth**, inglenook, fire, fireside, chimney corner. [➡ALCOVES, CUBICLES, AND COMPARTMENTS; 1095] 2 *type of* **general fittings**. [➡FITTINGS; 859]

firepower *n* **weapons**, arms, guns, armaments, munitions. [➡WEAPONS; 1153]

fire practice *n* **fire drill**, drill, practice, rehearsal, evacuation, exercise. [➡WORK-RELATED ACTIVITIES; 834]

fireproof *adj* **incombustible**, nonflammable, flame-retardant, fire-retardant, fire-resistant, flame-resistant. [➡FIRE, FLAMMABILITY, AND BURNING; 1164] *Opposite:* combustible.

fireside *n* **hearth**, inglenook, fireplace, chimney corner. [➡ALCOVES, CUBICLES, AND COMPARTMENTS; 1095]

firetrap *n* **fire hazard**, deathtrap (*informal*), danger. [➡DANGER; 236]

firetruck (*US*) *type of* **public service vehicle**. [➡VEHICLES; 1144]

fire up 1 *v* **get going**, initiate, start off, set off, launch, trigger. [➡USE TOOLS AND MACHINERY; 469] 2 *v* **ignite**, fire, light, kindle, set alight, spark. [➡FIRE, FLAMMABILITY, AND BURNING; 1164] 3 *v* **enthuse**, motivate, incite, stimulate, excite, arouse, stir up, work up, set off. [➡ENCOURAGE; 577]firewood *n* **logs**, kindling, wood, fuel. [➡ENERGY SOURCES; 1161]

firework

◆ *types of firework*
banger, Catherine wheel, cherry bomb (*US*), firecracker, fizgig, girandole, pinwheel (*US*), rocket, Roman candle, sparkler, squib, torpedo (*US*)

firing *n* **gunfire**, fire, shooting, shots. [➡IMPACT SOUNDS; 1259]

firing line 1 *n* **front line**, front, battlefront, vanguard. [➡WARFARE AND WAR; 830] 2 *n* **forefront**, vanguard, lead, cutting edge, leading edge. [➡DIFFICULT SITUATIONS; 72]

firkin *n* [➡CONTAINERS, RECEPTACLES, AND PACKAGING; 1244]

firm 1 *adj* **solid**, compact, hard, rigid, dense, stiff, unyielding. [➡RIGID AND HARD; 1210] *Opposite:* soft. 2 *adj* **secure**, stable, fixed, strong, safe, steady, well-founded. [➡SAFE AND SAFETY; 192] *Opposite:* unstable. 3 *adj* **determined**, certain, definite, fixed, resolved, unchangeable, resolute, positive, concrete. [➡CERTAINTY; 562] *Opposite:* uncertain. 4 *v* **harden**, stiffen, solidify, set, press down, compress, tamp, compact. [➡HARDEN, CONGEAL, DRY; 388] *Opposite:* soften. 5 *n* **company**, business, partnership, multinational, corporation, organization, practice. [➡BUSINESS ENTERPRISES AND RELATED BODIES; 793]

firmament (*literary*) *n* **sky**, heaven, vault, azure, space, ether, expanse. [➡THE EARTH'S ATMOSPHERE; 1040]

firmly 1 *adv* **tightly**, securely, steadily, powerfully, strongly, safely, densely. [➡STRENGTH; 202] *Opposite:* loosely. 2 *adv* **resolutely**, inflexibly, determinedly, decisively, definitely, steadfastly, confidently. [➡CERTAINTY; 562] *Opposite:* irresolutely.

firmness 1 *n* **hardness**, rigidity, compactness, density, stiffness, solidity. [➡RIGID AND HARD; 1210] *Opposite:* softness. 2 *n* **stability**, steadiness, strength, safety. [➡SAFE AND SAFETY; 192] *Opposite:* instability. 3 *n* **determination**, steadfastness, resolve, resolution, decisiveness, insistence, control, rigidity. [➡HARD-WORKING AND COMMITTED; 501] *Opposite:* uncertainty.

firm up 1 *v* **settle**, conclude, tie up, confirm, establish, decide. [➡MAKE DECISIONS AND CHOICES; 753] 2 *v* **stabilize**, balance, steady, settle. [➡IMPROVE STRENGTH AND DURABILITY; 379] *Opposite:* destabilize.

firmware *type of* **software**. [➡COMPUTERS AND COMPUTING; 1126]

first 1 *adj* **primary**, initial, original, opening, earliest, foremost, former. [➡BEFORE, FIRST, AND PRECEDING; 164] *Opposite:* last. 2 *adj* **chief**, head, principal, leading, major, main, paramount. [➡MOST IMPORTANT AND MAIN; 194] *Opposite:* minor. 3 *adj* **fundamental**, basic, key, elementary, primary, essential. [➡FUNDAMENTAL; 196] *Opposite:* advanced. 4 *adv* **firstly**, initially, at the outset, in the beginning, to begin with, to start with, primarily, formerly, originally. [➡BEFORE, FIRST, AND PRECEDING; 164] *Opposite:* lastly.

first aid *n* **emergency treatment**, medical treatment, medical care, resuscitation, mouth-to-mouth, CPR, emergency medicine. [➡HEALING; 731]

first and foremost *adv* **most importantly**, primarily, above all, predominantly, firstly, in the first place. [➡MAINLY AND PRIMARILY; 138] *Opposite:* lastly.

first-born *n* [➡YOUNGER GENERATION RELATIVES; 958]

first-class *adj* **best**, superb, first-rate, unrivalled, excellent, topnotch (*informal*), outstanding, exceptional. [➡EXTRAORDINARY: AMAZING; 205] *Opposite:* poor.

firsthand 1 *adj* **direct**, actual, immediate, personal. [➡PRESENT; 85] *Opposite:* second-hand. 2 *adv* **directly**, personally, from the horse's mouth, straight. [➡BELONGING OR RELATING TO INDIVIDUALS; 944] *Opposite:* indirectly.

first light *n* **dawn**, daybreak, sunrise, daylight, morning, the crack of dawn, break of day, cockcrow (*archaic or literary*), sunup (*US*). [➡TIMES OF DAY; 87] *Opposite:* dusk.

firstly *adv* **to start with**, initially, first of all, at the outset, first, to begin with, primarily, originally. [➡BEFORE, FIRST, AND PRECEDING; 164] *Opposite:* lastly.

first name *n* **name**, Christian name, given name, moniker (*slang*). [➡NAME AND DESCRIBE; 666] *Opposite:* surname.

first principles *n* [➡BASIC DETAILS; 689]

first-rate *adj* **best**, superb, first-class, unrivalled, excellent, topnotch (*informal*), outstanding, exceptional. [➡EXTRAORDINARY: AMAZING; 205] *Opposite:* poor.

firth *n* **estuary**, inlet, fjord, sound, creek, river mouth. [➡THE SEAS, OCEANS, AND SHORES; 1041]

fir tree *type of* **evergreen tree**. [➡EVERGREEN AND CONIFEROUS TREES; 1029]

fish 1 *v* **catch fish**, angle, go fishing, trawl, cast a line, fly-fish. [➡HOBBIES, GAMES, AND SPORTS; 875] 2 *v* **search**, seek, trawl, probe, nose about (*informal*), dig around, nose around (*informal*), scout. [➡SEEK POSSESSION AND SEARCH; 457]

fish

◆ *parts of a fish*
air bladder, anal fin, dorsal fin, fin, gill, pectoral fin, pelvic fin, roe, scale, tail

fish cake *type of* **cooked dish**. [➡PREPARED DISHES; 1169]

fisheye lens *part of* **photographic equipment**. [➡PHOTOGRAPHY AND PHOTOGRAPHIC EQUIPMENT; 1121]

fish for *v* **search for**, angle for, be after, invite, hope for, look for, encourage. [➡OBTAIN POSSESSION BY PERSUASION; 458]

fishing *n* **angling**, casting, trawling, harpooning, whaling, spinning, fly-fishing. [➡HOBBIES, GAMES, AND SPORTS; 875]

fish knife *type of* **cutlery**. [➡TABLEWARE, CUTLERY, AND KITCHENWARE; 861]

fishmonger's *type of* **food outlet**. [➡RETAIL OUTLETS; 1082]

fishnet *n* **mesh**, netting, net, tulle, gauze, lace. [➡FABRICS; 1131]

fish out (*informal*) *v* **pull out**, take out, haul out, drag out, dig out, extract. [➡EXTRACT AND SEVER; 342] *Opposite:* put in.

fish owl *type of* **owl**. [➡OWL; 1001]

fishy (*informal*) *adj* **dubious**, suspicious, irregular, underhand, shady, dodgy (*informal*), shifty, devious, strange, odd, doubtful, questionable. [➡BIZARRE AND PECULIAR; 258] *Opposite:* aboveboard.

fission *n* **breaking up**, separation, splitting, division, schism, scission. [➡SEPARATE AND DIVIDE; 402] *Opposite:* fusion.

fissure *n* **crack**, split, crevice, fracture, cleft, opening, slit, break, gap. [➡HOLES, GAPS, AND FORKS; 1251]

fist 1 *n* (*informal*) **hand**, paw (*informal*), knuckle, duke (*slang*). [➡ARM AND HAND; 696] 2 *n* **fistful**, handful, bunch, wad. [➡AMOUNT OF SOLID OR SEMI-SOLID; 115]

fist fight *n* [➡AGGRESSIVE EVENT; 39]

fistful *n* **handful**, bunch, fist, wad. [➡AMOUNT OF SOLID OR SEMI-SOLID; 115]

fit 1 *v* **measure**, tailor, size, take in, take up, let out. [➡CRAFTS AND CARVING; 356] 2 *v* **match**, suit, correspond, tally. [➡EQUALITY; 155] 3 *v* **install**, put in, mount, fix, provide with, add, equip, supply. [➡EQUIP AND SUPPLY; 436] 4 *adj* **appropriate**, fitting, right, proper, acceptable, adequate, suitable, apt. [➡APPROPRIATE, SUITABLE, ADVISABLE; 185] *Opposite:* unfit. 5 *adj* **healthy**, well, fine, in fine fettle, hale and hearty, strong, robust, in shape, on top form, athletic, vigorous, buff (*US informal*). [➡FIT AND STRONG; 737] *Opposite:* unfit. 6 *n* **convulsion**, spasm, petit mal, grand mal, epileptic fit, turn, paroxysm, outburst. [➡ILLNESSES AND DISORDERS; 733]

fitful *adj* **disturbed**, sporadic, broken, restless, irregular, intermittent, erratic. [➡FINITENESS, VARIABILITY, AND TRANSIENCE; 96] *Opposite:* peaceful.

fit in 1 *v* **conform**, blend in, integrate, go well with, assimilate, get on, settle down. [➡COMBINE AND MIX; 401] 2 *v* **find time for**, squeeze in, manage, cope with, take on, incorporate. [➡CARRY OUT AN ACTION; 270]

fitness 1 *n* **health**, strength, robustness, vigour. [➡PHYSICAL STATES; 735] *Opposite:* weakness. 2 *n* **suitability**, appropriateness, aptness, qualification, capability, ability. [➡APPROPRIATE, SUITABLE, ADVISABLE; 185] *Opposite:* inappropriateness.

fitness centre *n* [➡BUILDINGS FOR PUBLIC ENTERTAINMENT; 1083]

fit out *v* **equip**, supply, furnish (*formal*), set up, kit out, fit up, refit. [➡EQUIP AND SUPPLY; 436]

fitted 1 *adj* **tailored**, close-fitting, formfitting, trim, snug. [➡DESCRIBING CLOTHES; 869] *Opposite:* baggy. 2 *adj* **built-in**, fixed, permanent, attached, incorporated. [➡RELATIVE LOCATION; 162] *Opposite:* freestanding.

fitted carpet *n* [➡SOFT FURNISHINGS, LINEN, AND DRAPERY; 860]

fitting *adj* **suitable**, appropriate, right, correct, proper, apt, decent, fit, timely, relevant. [➡APPROPRIATE, SUITABLE, ADVISABLE; 185] *Opposite:* inappropriate.

fittingness *n* **suitability**, appropriateness, rightness, correctness, properness, aptness, timeliness, relevance. [➡APPROPRIATE, SUITABLE, ADVISABLE; 185] *Opposite:* inappropriateness.

fittings *n* **accessories**, fixtures, decorations, furniture, equipment. [➡FITTINGS; 859]

fittings

◆ *types of plumbing fittings*
ball cock, basin, bath, bathtub, bidet, drinking fountain, faucet (*US*), hand basin, hot tub, nozzle, plumbing, rose, sauna, shower, sink, sitz bath, spa, spigot (*US*), spout, sprinkler, tap, toilet, tub, vanity (*US*), vanity unit, washbasin, washbowl, wash-hand basin, whirlpool (*US*), whirlpool bath

◆ *types of general fittings*
ceiling rose, chimneypiece, dado, fender, fireplace, hot tub, looking glass, mantel, mantelpiece, mirror, picture molding (*US*), picture rail, radiator, socket, wainscot, workbench, worktop

fit to drop (*informal*) *adj* [➡TIRED, ASLEEP, AND UNCONSCIOUS; 739]

fit up 1 *v* **equip**, supply, furnish (*formal*), set up, kit out, fit out, refit. [➡EQUIP AND SUPPLY; 436] 2 *v* (*slang*) **frame**, set up, stitch up (*slang*). [➡FALSIFY AND CHEAT; 177]

five o'clock shadow *n* [➡FACIAL HAIR; 490]

fiver *n* [➡CURRENCIES; 798]

fix 1 *v* **mend**, repair, correct, put to rights, patch up, renovate, sort out, resolve, renew, refurbish, overhaul, restore. [➡REPAIR AND MEND; 377] *Opposite:* break. 2 *v* (*informal*) **prepare**, make ready, get ready, rustle up (*informal*), cook, scare up (*US informal*). [➡MEAL PREPARATION; 355] 3 *v* **agree**, arrange, establish, organize, set up, schedule, set a date for, settle. [➡CAUSE TO HAPPEN; 31] *Opposite:* cancel. 4 *v* **fasten**, attach, glue, stick, secure, install, fit, position, locate, join, affix. [➡FASTEN, LINK, AND JOIN; 409] *Opposite:* detach. 5 *v* (*informal*) **rig**, fiddle (*informal*), manipulate, massage, arrange, hustle (*US slang*). [➡FALSIFY AND CHEAT; 177] 6 *n* (*informal*) **dilemma**, predicament, tight spot, quandary, corner, hole (*informal*), mess. [➡DIFFICULT SITUATIONS; 72] 7 *n* (*informal*) **solution**, answer, resolution, remedy, repair. [➡SOLUTION; 216] 8 *n* (*informal*) **setup** (*informal*), con, fraud, swindle, trick, hustle (*US slang*). [➡DECEPTION AND LIES; 661] 9 *n* (*humorous*) **dose**, shot (*informal*), injection, hit (*slang*). [➡AMOUNT AND QUANTITY; 112]

fixated *adj* **obsessed**, absorbed, stuck on (*informal*), fanatical, engrossed, hooked (*slang*), paranoid, neurotic (*informal*), passionate, single-minded, intense. [➡PENSIVENESS AND INTEREST; 539] *Opposite:* indifferent.

fixatedly *adv* **obsessively**, fanatically, intensely, single-mindedly, neurotically (*informal*), keenly, fervently, overenthusiastically, passionately. [➡NEGATIVE INTELLECTUAL CHARACTERISTICS; 526] *Opposite:* indifferently.

fixation *n* **obsession**, fascination, thing (*informal*), mania, complex (*informal*), passion, addiction, paranoia, neurosis (*dated*), preoccupation. [➡FADS, FETISHES, AND IDOLATRY; 556]

fixative 1 *n* **preservative**, preserver, spray, varnish, coating. [➡COVERS AND COATINGS; 1245] 2 *n* **glue**, adhesive, cement, paste, gum, bonder. [➡ADHESIVES; 1270]

fixed 1 *adj* **secure**, immovable, immobile, static, motionless, stationary, stable, permanent. [➡PERMANENCE: WITHOUT CHANGE; 95] *Opposite:* fluid. 2 *adj* **set**, unchanging, flat, preset, predetermined, permanent. [➡PERMANENCE: WITHOUT CHANGE; 95] *Opposite:* variable. 3 *adj* **rigid**, inflexible, hard-and-fast, cast-iron. [➡PERMANENCE: WITHOUT CHANGE; 95] *Opposite:* flexible.

fixed idea *n* [➡IDEA AND THOUGHT; 771]

fixedly *adv* **intently**, earnestly, attentively, steadily, directly. [➡PERMANENCE: WITHOUT CHANGE; 95]

fixedness *n* **secureness**, immovability, immobility, motionlessness, stability, permanence. [➡PERMANENCE: WITHOUT CHANGE; 95] *Opposite:* fluidity.

fixings 1 *n* (*US*) **ingredients**, elements, constituents, components, parts, makings. [➡PREPARED DISHES; 1169] 2 *n* (*US informal*) **trimmings**, accompaniments, accessories, dressing, extras. [➡ORNAMENTS AND DECORATIONS; 1247]

fixture 1 *n* **fitting**, feature, fixed object. [➡FITTINGS; 859] 2 *n* **match**, game, meeting, contest, clash, event. [➡NON-AGGRESSIVE/SPORTING EVENT; 40]

fix up 1 *v* **arrange**, schedule, plan, make plans for, organize, set up, settle, agree. [➡ARRANGE AND CREATE ORDER; 358] 2 *v* **repair**, renew, refurbish, renovate, redecorate, overhaul, restore, mend, correct, patch up, sort out. [➡REPAIR AND MEND; 377]

fizgig *type of* **firework**. [➡EXPLOSIVES; 1154]

fizz 1 *v* **effervesce**, sparkle, bubble, froth, foam, fizzle, hiss. [➡FROTH AND EFFERVESCE; 390] 2 *n* **effervescence**, sparkle, bubbles, froth, foam, fizzle. [➡FROTH; 1272]

fizzle 1 *v* **fizz**, hiss, sizzle, spit, sputter, buzz, bubble, effervesce. [➡EMIT CONTINUOUS SOUNDS; 367] 2 *v* **fail**, fade away, peter out, disappear, come to an end, vanish, dissolve, die out, end. [➡DISAPPEAR; 4] *Opposite:* flourish.

fizzy *adj* **effervescent**, sparkling, bubbly, carbonated, foamy, frothy. [➡VISUAL TEXTURE; 1220] *Opposite:* still.

fjord *n* **inlet**, sound, creek, firth. [➡THE SEAS, OCEANS, AND SHORES; 1041]

flab *n* **fat**, podginess, chubbiness, plumpness, corpulence (*formal or literary*), pudginess (*informal*). [➡EXTRA WEIGHT; 479]

flabbergast (*informal*) *v* **amaze**, astonish, astound, dumbfound, stun, surprise, shock, flummox (*informal*), stagger, bowl over, knock for six (*informal*). [➡CONFUSE AND BEWILDER; 572]

flabbergasted (*informal*) *adj* **amazed**, astonished, astounded, dumbfounded, stunned, surprised, shocked, flummoxed (*informal*), staggered, bowled over, gobsmacked (*slang*), knocked for six (*informal*). [➡SURPRISE, SHOCK, AND AMAZEMENT; 546]

flabbiness (*informal*) *n* **flaccidity**, looseness, softness, slackness, floppiness, limpness. [➡MUSCLES AND MUSCULATURE; 480] *Opposite:* firmness.

flabby (*informal*) *adj* **flaccid**, loose, soft, slack, saggy, floppy, limp. [➡UNFIT AND WEAK; 740] *Opposite:* firm.

flaccid *adj* **limp**, soft, flabby (*informal*), loose, drooping, sagging, lax, slack. [➡MALLEABLE AND ELASTIC; 1211] *Opposite:* firm.

flag 1 *n* **standard**, ensign, pennant, pennon, colours, banner, emblem, streamer. [➡SYMBOLS, SIGNS, AND NUMBERS; 597] 2 *v* **mark**, highlight, identify, label, signal, warn, select, indicate, signpost. [➡NAME AND DESCRIBE; 666] 3 *v* **weaken**, tire, weary, wane, fade, wilt, slump, droop, fail, pall, abate (*formal or literary*), sag, dwindle, languish, diminish, decline, ebb. [➡CEASE TO EXIST; 22] *Opposite:* rally.

flagellate 1 *v* **whip**, flog, scourge, lash, beat, thrash, punish. [➡WHIP AND CLUB; 418] 2 *type of* **microorganism**. [➡MICROORGANISMS, FUNGI, AND ALGAE; 1023]

flagellation *n* **whipping**, flogging, scourging, lashing, beating, thrashing, punishment. [➡PHYSICAL ATTACK AND PUNISHMENT; 416]

flagging *adj* **weakening**, tiring, wearying, waning, fading, wilting, slumping, drooping, failing, abating (*formal or literary*), dwindling, diminishing, declining, ebbing, palling, sagging, languishing. [➡CEASE TO EXIST; 22] *Opposite:* rallying.

flagon *n* **bottle**, carafe, flask, canteen, carboy, demijohn, container. [➡TABLEWARE, CUTLERY, AND KITCHENWARE; 861]

flagpole *n* **flagstaff**, staff, pole, mast, post. [➡STICKS, POLES, AND WEDGES; 1253]

flagrant *adj* **blatant**, scandalous, obvious, deliberate, brazen, unashamed, open, overt, patent, manifest, barefaced, shameless, immodest, glaring, bald-faced (*US*). [➡INTENTIONAL AND DELIBERATE; 280] *Opposite:* covert.

flagship 1 *n* **warship**, man-of-war, ship of the line, capital ship, battleship, dreadnought. [➡SHIPS AND BOATS; 1149] 2 *n* **star**, leader, jewel, pearl, pièce de résistance, ne plus ultra (*formal*). [➡MOST IMPORTANT THING; 198] 3 *adj* **prize**, star, lead, top, leading. [➡MOST IMPORTANT AND MAIN; 194]

flagstaff *n* **flagpole**, staff, pole, mast, post. [➡STICKS, POLES, AND WEDGES; 1253]

flagstone *n* **paving stone**, kerbstone, slab, block, cobblestone, cobble. [➡BUILDING MATERIALS; 1076]

flag-waving *n* **patriotism**, chauvinism, jingoism, nationalism, loyalism, triumphalism. [➡PREJUDICE; 551]

flail 1 *v* **thrash**, wave, whirl, flap, flounder, swing. [➡MOVE SOMETHING ON THE SPOT; 337] 2 *v* **flog**, beat, batter, hit, strike, bash (*informal*). [➡PHYSICAL ATTACK AND PUNISHMENT; 416]

flail about *v* **flounder**, writhe, struggle, squirm, stagger, stumble. [➡FIDGET AND FROLIC; 312]

flail around *v* [➡AIMLESS AND ERRANT MOTION; 344]

flair 1 *n* **talent**, skill, aptitude, feel, gift, ability, knack, bent, genius. [➡SKILLS, TALENTS, AND ABILITIES; 527] *Opposite:* ineptitude. 2 *n* **elegance**, stylishness, style, chic, panache, dash, glamour, verve, taste. [➡CONFIDENCE AND COMPOSURE; 500] *Opposite:* inelegance.

See Compare and Contrast at **talent**.

flak (*informal*) *n* **criticism**, condemnation, censure, disapproval, hassle (*informal*), aggravation (*informal*), hostility. [➡CRITICISMS AND ANGRY OUTBURSTS; 50] *Opposite:* support.

flake 1 *n* **shaving**, fleck, sliver, chip, scale, fragment, snowflake, bit, patch. [➡SMALL PIECE; 127] 2 *v* **peel**, crumble, chip, come off, scale, blister, chip off. [➡TEAR, BREAK, AND CUT; 361]

flake out (*slang*) *v* **collapse**, fall asleep, drop off (*informal*), doze off, faint, pass out. [➡SLEEP AND DREAM; 724]

flak jacket *type of* **jacket**. [➡GARMENTS AND OUTFITS; 865]

flaky *adj* **peeling**, crumbling, crumbly, chipped, scaly, blistering, blistered. [➡IN BAD REPAIR; 1233]

flaky pastry *n* [➡BREAD, FLOUR, AND BREAD PRODUCTS; 1178]

flamboyance *n* **showiness**, ostentation, flashiness, gaudiness, luridness, glitziness, colourfulness, loudness, splendour, grandiosity. [➡EXTRAORDINARY: AMAZING; 205] *Opposite:* modesty.

flamboyant *adj* **showy**, ostentatious, flashy, gaudy, lurid, glitzy, colourful, loud, outrageous, extravagant. [➡EXTRAORDINARY: AMAZING; 205] *Opposite:* understated.

flame 1 *n* **fire**, blaze, flare, spark, flicker, conflagration, flash. [➡FIRE, FLAMMABILITY, AND BURNING; 1164] 2 *type of* **orange**. [➡COLOURS; 1223] 3 *v* **burn**, blaze, light up, glow, flare, flicker, spark, burst into flames, kindle. [➡FIRE, FLAMMABILITY, AND BURNING; 1164] 4 *v* [➡THE INTERNET; 1127]

flamenco *type of* **dance**. [➡DANCE; 903]

flameproof *adj* **nonflammable**, noninflammable, incombustible, flame-retardant, fire-retardant, fire-resistant. [➡SAFE AND SAFETY; 192] *Opposite:* inflammable.

flame-retardant *adj* **nonflammable**, noninflammable, incombustible, fire-retardant, fire-resistant, flameproof, fireproof. [➡FIRE, FLAMMABILITY, AND BURNING; 1164] *Opposite:* inflammable.

flame-thrower *type of* **gun**. [➡WEAPONS FOR SHOOTING; 1155]

flaming 1 *adj* **blazing**, burning, flaring, flickering, sparking, on fire, fiery, glowing, afire, ablaze, alight. [➡FIRE, FLAMMABILITY, AND BURNING; 1164] *Opposite:* doused. 2 *adj* **intense**, angry, passionate, blazing, heated, fierce, furious, violent, stormy, ardent. [➡DIFFICULTY AND COMPLEXITY; 243] *Opposite:* calm.

flamingo *type of* **freshwater bird**. [➡FRESHWATER BIRD; 1000]

flammable *adj* **inflammable**, combustible, incendiary, igneous. [➡FIRE, FLAMMABILITY, AND BURNING; 1164] *Opposite:* fireproof.

flan 1 *n* **quiche**, tart, tartlet, pie, pastry. [➡BREAD, FLOUR, AND

BREAD PRODUCTS; 1178] 2 *type of* **dessert.** [➡ CAKES, BISCUITS, AND DESSERTS; 1180]

flange *n* [➡ FASTENERS, LINKS, AND NETWORKS; 1246]

flank 1 *n* **side**, edge, verge, margin, border, rim, wing. [➡ EXTREMITIES OF PHYSICAL OBJECTS; 1249] 2 *type of* **cut.** [➡ TYPES AND CUTS OF MEAT; 1176] 3 *part of* **horse.** [➡ HORSE; 985] 4 *v* **border**, edge, line, skirt, fringe, verge. [➡ EXIST IN CLOSE PROXIMITY; 21]

flannel 1 *v* (*informal*) **sweet-talk** (*informal*), soft-soap (*informal*), flatter, beguile, blarney (*informal*), blandish (*formal*). [➡ FLATTER AND FAWN; 622] 2 *n* (*informal*) **sweet talk** (*informal*), soft soap (*informal*), blarney (*informal*), weasel words (*informal*), flattery, blandishment (*formal*). [➡ INGRATIATING; 639] 3 *type of* **fabric from animals.** [➡ FABRICS; 1131]

flannelette *type of* **fabric from plants.** [➡ FABRICS; 1131]

flap 1 *v* (*informal*) **get into a state** (*informal*), panic, fret, dither, fluster, worry. [➡ CHANGE OF MOOD AND COMPOSURE; 581] *Opposite:* calm down. 2 *n* (*informal*) **panic**, fret, dither, state (*informal*), fluster, tizzy (*informal*). [➡ INSECURITY AND LOSS OF COMPOSURE; 545] *Opposite:* calm. 3 *n* **tab**, fold, lappet, lap, tail, tailpiece, fly, skirt, apron. [➡ EXTREMITIES OF PHYSICAL OBJECTS; 1249] 4 *n* **flutter**, wave, flail, shake, wag, beat. [➡ MOVE SOMETHING ON THE SPOT; 337]

flapjack 1 *type of* **cake.** [➡ CAKES, BISCUITS, AND DESSERTS; 1180] 2 (*US*) *type of* **pancake.** [➡ CAKES, BISCUITS, AND DESSERTS; 1180]

flare 1 *v* **burn**, blaze, flame, flicker, flash, flare up, sparkle. [➡ FIRE, FLAMMABILITY, AND BURNING; 1164] 2 *n* **flash**, blaze, flicker, flame, burst, sparkle. [➡ LIGHT; 1163]

flared *adj* **widening**, wide, spreading, broadening, flaring, full, splayed. [➡ DESCRIBING CLOTHES; 869] *Opposite:* tapered.

flare up *v* **erupt**, break out, explode, heat up, blaze, boil over, burst out. [➡ SUDDENLY COME INTO EXISTENCE; 2] *Opposite:* die down.

flare-up (*informal*) *n* **outbreak**, eruption, flash, outburst, explosion, blaze. [➡ ARGUMENT; 47] *Opposite:* subsidence.

flaring *adj* **widening**, bell-shaped, broadening, spreading, splaying. [➡ CHANGE OF SIZE: BIGGER; 393] *Opposite:* tapering.

flash 1 *v* **glint**, sparkle, twinkle, flare, flicker, glisten, gleam, glimmer. [➡ LIGHT EMISSION; 369] 2 *v* **pass quickly**, rush, speed, race, zip (*informal*), zoom, fly, dash. [➡ MOVE FAST; 314] *Opposite:* crawl. 3 *v* (*informal*) **flaunt**, show, show off, display, exhibit, flourish. [➡ CAUSE TO APPEAR; 5] 4 *n* **blaze**, spark, flare, flicker, sparkle, twinkle, burst, explosion, streak, flame. [➡ LIGHT; 1163] 5 *n* **moment**, jiffy (*informal*), instant, second, twinkling, tick (*informal*), minute, trice, wink. [➡ SHORT PERIOD OF TIME; 93] 6 *n* **news flash**, update, bulletin, announcement, report, communication. [➡ TELEVISION AND RADIO; 607] 7 *part of* **photographic equipment.** [➡ PHOTOGRAPHY AND PHOTOGRAPHIC EQUIPMENT; 1121] 8 *adj* (*informal*) **showy**, ostentatious, flashy, gaudy, loud, vulgar. [➡ IN POOR TASTE; 230] *Opposite:* understated.

flashback *n* **memory**, recurrence, remembrance, recollection, hallucination, evocation, recovered memory. [➡ MEMORY; 746]

flash flood *n* **deluge**, downpour, inundation (*formal*), cloudburst, spate, surge. [➡ CLOUDY AND RAINY WEATHER; 1052]

flashiness *n* **showiness**, ostentatiousness, ostentation, flashness (*informal*), glitziness, glitter, gaudiness, loudness, flamboyance, tawdriness, tackiness (*informal*), tastelessness. [➡ IN POOR TASTE; 230] *Opposite:* drabness.

flashlight (*US*) *n* **torch**, penlight, light, lamp, lantern, flash (*US informal*). [➡ LIGHT; 1163]

flashpoint 1 *n* **crisis**, breaking point, climax, turning point, crossroads. [➡ DECISIVE MOMENTS; 44] 2 *n* **trouble spot**, hot spot, minefield, inferno, hornet's nest, hellhole. [➡ DIFFICULT SITUATIONS; 72]

flashy *adj* **showy**, ostentatious, flash (*informal*), glitzy, gaudy, loud, flamboyant, tawdry, tacky (*informal*), tasteless. [➡ IN POOR TASTE; 230] *Opposite:* understated.

flask *n* **bottle**, flagon, carafe, hip flask, decanter, canteen, container. [➡ TABLEWARE, CUTLERY, AND KITCHENWARE; 861]

flat 1 *adj* **level**, even, smooth, plane, horizontal, flush, uniform, regular. [➡ ORIENTATION AND ALIGNMENT; 1222] *Opposite:* uneven. 2 *adj* **unexciting**, dull, monotonous, tedious, boring, dreary, lifeless, uninteresting, stale, insipid. [➡ BORING AND UNINTERESTING; 235] *Opposite:* exciting. 3 *adj* **fixed**, set, preset, invariable, nonnegotiable, predetermined. [➡ PERMANENCE: WITHOUT CHANGE; 95] *Opposite:* variable. 4 *adj* **categorical**, downright, absolute, out-and-out, emphatic, unequivocal, point-blank, total, complete, utter, unqualified, thorough, definite. [➡ ABSOLUTE AND ABSOLUTELY; 131] *Opposite:* equivocal. 5 *n* **surface**, plane, level, face, blade. [➡ EXTREMITIES OF PHYSICAL OBJECTS; 1249] 6 *n* **suite**, rooms, maisonette, studio, penthouse, bedsit, apartment (*US*). [➡ RESIDENTIAL BUILDINGS; 1077]

flat broke (*informal*) *adj* [➡ POVERTY AND POOR; 892]

flatfish *n* [➡ SEA FISH; 1009]

flatfish

◆ *types of flatfish*
angelfish, flounder, halibut, lemon sole, manta (*US*), manta ray, plaice, pompano, ray, skate, sole, stingray, turbot

flatly 1 *adv* **categorically**, flat, absolutely, unequivocally, emphatically, point-blank, totally, completely, utterly, thoroughly, definitely. [➡ WHOLENESS AND COMPLETENESS; 199] *Opposite:* equivocally. 2 *adv* **dully**, monotonously, lifelessly, blandly, tediously, impassively, unenthusiastically. [➡ BORING AND UNINTERESTING; 235] *Opposite:* animatedly.

flatmate *n* **cohabitant**, cohabitee, housemate, friend, roommate, roomie (*US informal*). [➡ SUPPORTERS, PROTECTORS, AND COMPATRIOTS; 970]

flatness 1 *n* **levelness**, evenness, smoothness, planeness, horizontalness, flushness, uniformity, regularity. [➡ PHYSICAL TEXTURE; 1221] *Opposite:* unevenness. 2 *n* **dullness**, monotony, monotonousness, tedium, boringness, dreariness, staleness, insipidness. [➡ BORING AND UNINTERESTING; 235] *Opposite:* excitement.

flatten 1 *v* **squash**, crush, level, even out, compress, roll out, smooth. [➡ CHANGE OF SHAPE; 386] 2 *v* **knock over**, knock down, fell, poleaxe, KO (*informal*), crush, floor, deck (*informal*). [➡MOVE SOMETHING: INTO A NEW POSITION OR OVERTURN; 331]

flatter *v* **compliment**, praise, sweet-talk (*informal*), cajole, butter up (*informal*), soft-soap (*informal*), adulate, blandish (*formal*), blarney (*informal*). [➡FLATTER AND FAWN; 622] *Opposite:* insult.

flatterer *n* **toady**, sycophant, fawner, creep (*informal*), crawler (*informal*), yes man, bootlicker (*informal disapproving*). [➡PEOPLE WHO DECEIVE; 662] *Opposite:* critic.

flattering 1 *adj* **obsequious**, smooth, toadyish, sycophantic. [➡INGRATIATING; 639] *Opposite:* uncomplimentary. 2 *adj* **gratifying**, pleasing, satisfying, satisfactory, cheering, pleasurable. [➡EMOTIONALLY PLEASANT; 188] *Opposite:* galling. 3 *adj* **becoming**, complimentary, kind, favourable, sympathetic, suitable. [➡BEAUTY AND ATTRACTIVENESS; 190] *Opposite:* unbecoming.

flattery *n* **sycophancy**, obsequiousness, toadyism, sweet talk (*informal*), adulation, soft soap (*informal*), fawning, blandishment (*formal*), snow job (*US slang*). [➡INGRATIATING; 639] *Opposite:* insult.

flat top *type of* **hairstyle**. [➡HAIR STYLES AND HAIR PIECES; 489]

flatulence *n* **pomposity**, pretentiousness, bombast, verbosity, grandiloquence, turgidity, gassiness. [➡BOAST; 617] *Opposite:* simplicity.

flatulent *adj* **pompous**, pretentious, bombastic, verbose, grandiloquent, turgid, gassy (*informal*). [➡INARTICULATE, RAMBLING, AND AWKWARD; 634] *Opposite:* unpretentious.

flaunt *v* **show off**, exhibit, display, parade, flourish, sport (*informal*), brandish, vaunt, boast. [➡CAUSE TO APPEAR; 5] *Opposite:* hide.

flavour 1 *n* **hint**, sense, feeling, feel, air, suggestion, touch. [➡FEW, LITTLE, SMALL AMOUNT; 119] 2 *n* **taste**, zest, tang, essence, aroma, relish, piquancy, smack, savour. [➡TASTE; 704] *Opposite:* tastelessness. 3 *n* **additive**, seasoning, extract, spice, essence, condiment, herb, flavouring. [➡ADDITIVES; 1171] 4 *v* **season**, spice, lace, salt, ginger. [➡COOKING AND FOOD PREPARATION; 354] 5 *v* **characterize**, distinguish, mark, pervade, run through, enhance, season, imbue, colour. [➡CHANGE; 373]

flavourful *adj* **tasty**, tangy, appetizing, palatable, savoury, toothsome. [➡TASTE; 704] *Opposite:* unappetizing.

flavouring *n* **flavour**, additive, seasoning, extract, spice, essence, condiment, herb. [➡ADDITIVES; 1171]

flavourless *adj* **tasteless**, bland, insipid, flat, anodyne (*literary*), watery, weak, boring. [➡TASTE; 704] *Opposite:* tasty.

flavourlessness *n* [➡TASTE; 704]

flavoursome *adj* [➡TASTE; 704]

flaw *n* **fault**, error, defect, mistake, failing, blemish, imperfection, weakness, weak spot, shortcoming. [➡FAULTS, FLAWS, AND WEAKNESSES; 252]

Compare and Contrast: *flaw, imperfection, fault, defect, failing, blemish*

CORE MEANING: SOMETHING THAT DETRACTS FROM PERFECTION

flaw an unintended mark or crack that prevents something from being totally perfect and detracts from its value, or a weakness in somebody's character, or in a plan, theory, or system; ***imperfection*** a fault that makes a person or thing less than perfect; ***fault*** something that detracts from the integrity, functioning, or perfection of a thing, or a weakness in somebody's character, usually more serious than a flaw; ***defect*** a fault in a machine, system, or plan, especially one that prevents it from functioning correctly, or a personal weakness; ***failing*** something that mars somebody or something in some way, especially an unfortunate feature of somebody's character; ***blemish*** a mark of some kind that detracts from something's appearance, especially the complexion or skin, or a feature that detracts from somebody's otherwise undamaged reputation or record.

flawed *adj* **faulty**, defective, damaged, blemished, imperfect, inconsistent, unsound, weak. [➡IN BAD REPAIR; 1233] *Opposite:* perfect.

flawless *adj* **perfect**, faultless, immaculate, impeccable, unblemished, unspoiled, spotless, pure, sound. [➡CORRECT; 183] *Opposite:* imperfect.

flawlessly *adv* **perfectly**, faultlessly, immaculately, impeccably, spotlessly, soundly, purely. [➡GOOD, WELL, BETTER; 184] *Opposite:* imperfectly.

flawlessness *n* **perfection**, faultlessness, immaculateness, impeccability, spotlessness, soundness, purity. [➡GOOD, WELL, BETTER; 184] *Opposite:* imperfection.

flaxen 1 *adj* **fair-haired**, fair, blond, blonde, golden-haired, tow-coloured. [➡HAIR COLOUR; 486] 2 *type of* **yellow**. [➡COLOURS; 1223]

flay 1 *v* **whip**, lash, thrash, flog, beat, scourge. [➡WHIP AND CLUB; 418] 2 *v* **criticize**, censure, condemn, slate, have a go at (*informal*), pillory, lambaste, blast (*informal*). [➡ACCUSE, BLAME, AND CRITICIZE; 642] *Opposite:* endorse.

flea *type of* **parasitic insect**. [➡PARASITES; 1017]

fleabag (*US informal*) *n* [➡UNDESIRABLE ACCOMMODATION; 856]

flea beetle *type of* **beetle**. [➡BEETLES AND WEEVILS; 1016]

flea market *type of* **retail outlet**. [➡RETAIL OUTLETS; 1082]

fleapit *n* **pit**, hole (*informal*), dump (*informal*), hovel, cinema, picture house (*dated*), venue. [➡BUILDINGS FOR PUBLIC ENTERTAINMENT; 1083]

fleck *n* **speck**, spot, speckle, dot, flyspeck, splash, streak, mark, freckle. [➡SMALL PIECE; 127]

flecked *adj* **marked**, speckled, dotted, streaked, splashed, freckled, spotted. [➡DESCRIBING PATTERNS; 1226]

fledgeling *see* **fledgling**.

fledgling 1 *n* **novice**, beginner, learner, tyro, neophyte, amateur, newcomer, recruit, rookie (*US informal*), freshman (*US*). [➡UNSKILLED PERSON; 531] *Opposite:* expert. **2** *type of* **young bird.** [➡YOUNG BIRD; 1004] **3** *adj* **inexperienced**, new, untried, young, inexpert, unqualified, green, raw, unseasoned. [➡UNSKILLED; 530] *Opposite:* experienced.

flee *v* **run away**, escape, fly, take flight, take off (*informal*), run off, abscond, bolt, make off. [➡RUN AWAY AND AVOID; 10]

fleece 1 *v* (*informal*) **swindle**, con, rip off (*informal*), cheat, take for a ride, defraud, hustle (*US slang*). [➡STEAL AND ROB; 427] **2** *type of* **jacket.** [➡GARMENTS AND OUTFITS; 865] **3** *type of* **synthetic fabric.** [➡FABRICS; 1131]

fleeciness *n* **woolliness**, downiness, fluffiness, furriness, fuzziness, flocculence, softness, shagginess. [➡PHYSICAL TEXTURE; 1221]

fleecy *adj* **woolly**, fluffy, flocculent, soft, shaggy, downy, furry. [➡PHYSICAL TEXTURE; 1221]

fleet *n* **navy**, flotilla, armada, convoy, task force, marine (*formal*). [➡GROUPS OF VEHICLES; 1151]

fleeting *adj* **brief**, transitory, short-lived, momentary, passing, ephemeral, evanescent, transient. [➡HAPPENING QUICKLY; 104] *Opposite:* permanent.

See Compare and Contrast at **temporary.**

fleetness (*literary*) *n* [➡SPEED; 102]

flesh 1 *n* **tissue**, soft tissue, muscle. [➡THE SKIN; 721] **2** *n* **skin**, surface, epithelium, epidermis, dermis, complexion. [➡THE SKIN; 721] **3** *n* **meat**, beef, lamb, pork, ham, chicken, turkey, fish. [➡TYPES AND CUTS OF MEAT; 1176] **4** *n* **pulp**, pulpiness, meat. [➡CENTRAL PARTS OF PHYSICAL OBJECTS; 1250] **5** *n* **relatives**, family, relations, blood relatives, kin, kinsfolk, flesh and blood, folk, lineage. [➡THE FAMILY; 956] **6** *n* **body**, flesh and blood, physicality, corporeality, corpus, soma, matter. [➡BODY; 692] **7** *n* **substance**, details, information, reality, solidness, meat, weight, matter. [➡BASIC DETAILS; 689] **8** *part of* **fruit.** [➡FRUIT AND VEGETABLES; 1175]

flesh and blood *n* [➡THE FAMILY; 956]

flesh-and-blood *adj* [➡LIVING THINGS AND LIVING; 976]

flesh colour *type of* **beige.** [➡COLOURS; 1223]

fleshiness *n* **beefiness**, stoutness, portliness, heftiness, corpulence (*formal or literary*), fatness, plumpness, chubbiness. [➡BUILD; 478]

fleshly 1 *adj* **bodily**, corporeal, physical, corporal, human, material, somatic. [➡LIVING THINGS AND LIVING; 976] *Opposite:* psychological. **2** *adj* **carnal**, bodily, erotic, animal, voluptuous, sensual, sensuous, lascivious, wanton. [➡MORALLY BAD; 776] *Opposite:* ascetic. **3** *adj* **worldly**, secular, material, human, mundane, earthly. [➡RELIGIOUS CONCEPTS; 777] *Opposite:* spiritual.

flesh out *v* **amplify**, elaborate, pad, pad out, expand, give substance to, embellish, add to, fill out, bring alive, make real, explain, expound, augment (*formal*). [➡CHANGE OF SIZE: BIGGER; 393] *Opposite:* condense.

fleshy *adj* **plump**, ample, overweight, fat, corpulent (*formal or literary*), chubby, heavy. [➡BUILD; 478] *Opposite:* slender.

flex 1 *v* **bend**, loosen up, activate, move, warm up, stretch, arch. [➡CHANGE OF SHAPE; 386] *Opposite:* straighten. **2** *v* **contract**, tense, tighten, expand, inflate, control. [➡CHANGE OF SIZE: BIGGER; 393] *Opposite:* relax.

flexibility *n* **suppleness**, litheness, elasticity, give, plasticity, springiness, tractability. [➡MALLEABLE AND ELASTIC; 1211] *Opposite:* rigidity.

flexible 1 *adj* **supple**, lithe, elastic, plastic, stretchy, bendable, bendy, springy, malleable. [➡MALLEABLE AND ELASTIC; 1211] *Opposite:* rigid. **2** *adj* **adaptable**, accommodating, variable, compliant, open, acquiescent, tractable, amenable, malleable, docile. [➡THE WILL AND WILLINGNESS; 564] *Opposite:* intractable.

flexibly 1 *adv* **lithely**, elastically, stretchily, tractably, malleably, springily. [➡MALLEABLE AND ELASTIC; 1211] *Opposite:* rigidly. **2** *adv* **compliantly**, amenably, malleably, biddably, docilely, submissively, openly, adaptably, accommodatingly. [➡THE WILL AND WILLINGNESS; 564] *Opposite:* uncooperatively.

flick 1 *v* **brush**, tap, glance, flip, graze, skim, strike, ping, touch. [➡THROW SOMETHING; 335] **2** *n* (*informal*) **film**, picture, big screen, silver screen, motion picture (*US formal or technical*), movie (*US*). [➡FILM; 901]

flicker 1 *v* **sparkle**, glimmer, flash, waver, sputter, gutter, shimmer, blink, twinkle, glint. [➡LIGHT EMISSION; 369] **2** *n* **glimmer**, spark, sparkle, twinkle, glint, flash, glance. [➡FEW, LITTLE, SMALL AMOUNT; 119] *Opposite:* beam. **3** *n* **trace**, ghost, impression, flash, glimmer, suggestion. [➡FEW, LITTLE, SMALL AMOUNT; 119]

flickering *adj* [➡DESCRIBING LIGHT; 1227]

flick knife *type of* **knife.** [➡CUTTING TOOLS; 1119]

flick through *v* **look through**, dip into, leaf through, flip through, riffle, skim, scan, browse. [➡READ; 759] *Opposite:* scrutinize.

flier 1 *n* **leaflet**, handout, advertisement, notice, insert, handbill, flysheet. [➡ADVERTISING AND PUBLICITY; 605] **2** *n* (*US informal*) **venture**, undertaking, endeavour, risk, attempt, try, effort. [➡PEOPLE IN SPORTS AND LEISURE; 876]

flight 1 *n* **trip**, journey, airlift, hop (*informal*), voyage, tour, expedition. [➡TRAVEL: JOURNEYS AND TRIPS; 319] **2** *type of* **flock.** [➡GROUP OF BIRDS; 1007] **3** *n* **escape**, departure, getaway, breakout, evasion, breakaway. [➡END; 54]

flight deck *part of* **aircraft.** [➡AIRCRAFT; 1147]

flightiness *n* **capriciousness**, changeability, giddiness (*dated*), frivolity, volatility, erraticism, waywardness, inconsistency, unreliability, irresponsibility, fickleness, whimsicality. [➡LACK OF COMMITMENT AND UNRELIABILITY; 510] *Opposite:* reliability.

flight of fancy *n* **fantasy**, pipe dream, fancy, dream, daydream, castle in the air, castle in Spain. [➡NONEXISTENT THINGS; 23]

flight recorder *part of* **aircraft.** [➡AIRCRAFT; 1147]

flighty *adj* **unreliable**, capricious, changeable, erratic, undependable, variable, inconsistent, whimsical, fickle, impulsive, wayward. [➡LACK OF COMMITMENT AND UNRELIABILITY; 510] *Opposite:* dependable.

flimflam (*slang*) *n* [➡DECEPTION AND LIES; 661]

flimsily 1 *adv* **lightly**, weakly, delicately, insubstantially, fragilely, feebly, airily. [➡WEAKNESS; 242] *Opposite:* sturdily. 2 *adv* **weakly**, unconvincingly, implausibly, inadequately, poorly, unsoundly. [➡WEAKNESS; 242] *Opposite:* strongly.

flimsiness *n* **fragility**, weakness, delicacy, frailty, feebleness, insubstantiality, ricketiness. [➡WEAKNESS; 242] *Opposite:* sturdiness.

flimsy 1 *adj* **fragile**, weak, delicate, insubstantial, slight, light, rickety, thin. [➡WEAKNESS; 242] *Opposite:* sturdy. 2 *adj* **poor**, feeble, unconvincing, inadequate, weak, unsound, implausible, tenuous. [➡UNCERTAIN; 176] *Opposite:* sound.

See Compare and Contrast at **fragile**.

flinch *v* **recoil**, start, cringe, shy away, baulk, draw back, quail, wince. [➡PHYSICAL REACTIONS; 317] *Opposite:* stand your ground.

See Compare and Contrast at **recoil**.

fling 1 *v* **throw**, toss, hurl, pitch, lob, let fly, cast, sling, chuck (*informal*). [➡THROW SOMETHING; 335] 2 *n* (*informal*) **romance**, love affair, affair, involvement, relationship. [➡RELATIONSHIP TO ANOTHER; 973]

See Compare and Contrast at **throw**.

flint *type of* **stone**. [➡STONES, ROCKS, AND BOULDERS; 1057]

flinty *adj* **stern**, unemotional, hard, inflexible, pitiless, stony, obdurate, cruel, unbending, steely, unyielding, merciless, relentless, callous, unfeeling. [➡SELFISH AND UNKIND; 506] *Opposite:* soft.

flip 1 *v* **turn over**, toss, flick, spin, overturn, reverse. [➡MOVE SOMETHING: INTO A NEW POSITION OR OVERTURN; 331] 2 *v* (*slang*) **lose your temper**, explode, see red (*informal*), go off the deep end, blow a fuse (*informal*), go berserk, blow up (*informal*), hit the roof, lose it (*informal*), go mad, lose your rag (*slang*), go ballistic (*slang*), flip your lid (*slang*), go postal (*US informal*). [➡GIVING VENT TO EMOTIONS; 680] 3 *adj* (*informal*) **flippant**, casual, joking, jokey, cheeky, dismissive, offhand, carefree, jesting (*literary*). [➡MOCKING AND DISMISSIVE; 637] *Opposite:* serious.

flip-flop 1 *n* **backward somersault**, backflip, tumble, flip, somersault, backward flip, backward handspring. [➡FIDGET AND FROLIC; 312] 2 (*informal*) *type of* **shoe**. [➡FOOTWEAR; 871]

flip over *v* **tip**, tip up, upset, upturn, flip, overturn, tumble, turn over, capsize, turn turtle, topple, cartwheel, tip over. [➡MOVE SOMETHING: INTO A NEW POSITION OR OVERTURN; 331]

flippancy *n* **levity**, facetiousness, glibness, offhandness, impertinence, frivolity, lightness, jesting (*literary*), jokiness. [➡GOOD-TEMPERED AND HUMOROUS; 628] *Opposite:* seriousness.

flippant *adj* **facetious**, offhand, glib, dismissive, frivolous, flip (*informal*), superficial, jokey, insouciant. [➡UNINTERESTED AND DETACHED; 630] *Opposite:* serious.

flip through *v* **leaf through**, browse, flick through, skim through, scan, glance at, riffle, dip into. [➡LOOKING AND LOOKS; 701]

flip your lid (*slang*) *v* **lose your temper**, explode, see red (*informal*), go off the deep end, blow a fuse (*informal*), go berserk, blow up (*informal*), hit the roof, lose it (*informal*), go mad, lose your rag (*slang*), flip (*slang*), go ballistic (*slang*), go postal (*US informal*). [➡GIVING VENT TO EMOTIONS; 680]

flirt 1 *v* **trifle**, toy, play, chat up (*informal*), philander (*disapproving*), seduce, lead on, dally. [➡DECEPTION AND LIES; 661] 2 *v* **flick**, jerk, toss, flip, propel, tip. [➡THROW SOMETHING; 335]

flirtation *n* **romance**, fling, love affair, amour (*dated*), entanglement, liaison, intimacy. [➡SEXUAL AND ROMANTIC RELATIONSHIPS; 964]

flirtatious *adj* [➡FLIRTATIOUS; 640]

flirt with *v* **consider**, toy with, entertain, think about, trifle with, mess with, dabble. [➡THINK AND REFLECT; 744]

flit *v* **fly**, flutter, dart, skim, flash, dip, swoop. [➡MOVE FAST; 314]

float 1 *v* **sail**, swim, drift, glide, tread water. [➡PUSH, PULL, SLIDE; 336] *Opposite:* sink. 2 *v* **hover**, soar, drift, glide, hang, lift. [➡PROCEED AND GO; 306] *Opposite:* drop. 3 *v* **propose**, suggest, put forward, promote, offer, present. [➡SUGGEST, HINT, AND COMMENT; 613] *Opposite:* reject.

floating *adj* **fluctuating**, detached, variable, moving, free, uncontrolled. [➡FINITENESS, VARIABILITY, AND TRANSIENCE; 96] *Opposite:* fixed.

flock 1 *v* **gather**, collect, congregate, assemble, cluster, herd, group. [➡GET CLOSER TOGETHER; 311] *Opposite:* disperse. 2 *type of* **herd**. [➡GROUP OF ANIMALS; 993]

flock

◆ *types of flock*
bevy, brood, clutch, covey, flight, gaggle, skein, swarm

floe *n* **ice floe**, iceberg, ice field, icecap, ice sheet, glacier. [➡GEOLOGICAL FEATURES; 1056]

flog 1 *v* (*informal*) **sell**, vend, get rid of, shift (*informal*), trade, peddle, retail, hawk. [➡SELL; 442] *Opposite:* buy. 2 *v* **whip**, lash, beat, thrash, scourge, whale, flay. [➡WHIP AND CLUB; 418]

flood 1 *n* **deluge**, overflow, inundation (*formal*), downpour, torrent, tidal wave. [➡CLOUDY AND RAINY WEATHER; 1052] *Opposite:* drought. 2 *n* **abundance**, glut, excess, stream, rush, surplus, outpouring, wave, surge. [➡MANY, MUCH, LARGE AMOUNT; 117] *Opposite:* shortage. 3 *v* **inundate**, submerge, overflow, swamp, saturate, drown, engulf, deluge. [➡GIVE TOO MUCH; 438] *Opposite:* ebb.

flooded *adj* **underwater**, swamped, waterlogged, inundated, drowned, submerged, engulfed, deluged. [➡WET; 1239]

floodgate *n* **head gate**, sluicegate, water gate, lock, weir, penstock, sluice. [➡WATERWAYS AND SEAWAYS; 1107]

floodlight 1 *n* **illumination**, lighting, stream, flood, searchlight, spotlight, beacon, beam. [➡LIGHT; 1163] 2 *v* **light**

up, illuminate, light, irradiate, illumine (*literary*), spotlight, beam, shine a light on. [➡LIGHT EMISSION; 369]

floodlit *adj* **illuminated**, lit up, well-lit, irradiated, illumined (*literary*), lit. [➡DESCRIBING LIGHT; 1227]

floodplain *n* **plain**, valley, delta, water meadow, fen, mudflat, marsh. [➡WETLANDS; 1043]

flood tide 1 *n* **inflow**, high tide, current. [➡THE SEAS, OCEANS, AND SHORES; 1041] 2 *n* **groundswell**, swell, surge, wave, upsurge, barrage, bombardment. [➡MANY, MUCH, LARGE AMOUNT; 117]

floor 1 *n* **storey**, level, deck (*US*). [➡STAIRS AND STOREYS; 1101] 2 *n* **bottom**, base, level, surface, flat, ground. [➡EXTREMITIES OF PHYSICAL OBJECTS; 1249] 3 *v* **astonish**, stupefy, astound, stagger, flabbergast (*informal*), confound, amaze, stun, flummox (*informal*), stump, baffle, bewilder. [➡CONFUSE AND BEWILDER; 572]

floorboards *n* [➡BUILDING MATERIALS; 1076]

floorcovering *n* [➡SOFT FURNISHINGS, LINEN, AND DRAPERY; 860]

floor cushion *n* [➡SOFT FURNISHINGS, LINEN, AND DRAPERY; 860]

flooring *n* **parquet**, floorboards, terrazzo, woodblocks, floor tiles, floor covering, carpeting. [➡BUILDING MATERIALS; 1076]

floor it (*US slang*) *v* [➡MOVE FAST; 314]

floor lamp (*US*) *n* [➡LIGHTING; 862]

floor manager *n* **supervisor**, overseer, manager, duty officer, line manager. [➡WORKERS IN ENTERTAINMENT AND MEDIA; 873]

floor plan *n* **layout**, plan, design, arrangement, allocation, disposition. [➡DRAWINGS, CHARTS, AND TABLES; 595]

floor tiles *n* [➡BUILDING MATERIALS; 1076]

flop 1 *v* **collapse**, slump, fall down, slacken, sag, droop, wilt, flag. [➡CHANGE OF SHAPE; 386] *Opposite:* stand up. 2 *v* (*informal*) **fail**, fold, close, crash, nose-dive, bomb (*informal*). [➡FAIL OR BE UNSUCCESSFUL; 75] *Opposite:* succeed. 3 *n* (*informal*) **failure**, dud (*informal*), washout (*informal*), fiasco, lemon (*informal*), dead duck (*slang*), dead loss, loser, bomb (*informal*), turkey (*US slang*). [➡FAILURE; 77] *Opposite:* hit.

flop about *v* [➡LACK OF ACTIVITY; 343]

flop around *v* [➡LACK OF ACTIVITY; 343]

flophouse (*US informal*) *n* [➡UNDESIRABLE ACCOMMODATION; 856]

floppiness *n* **droopiness**, looseness, slackness, limpness, flabbiness (*informal*), softness, sagginess. [➡MALLEABLE AND ELASTIC; 1211] *Opposite:* firmness.

floppy *adj* **limp**, droopy, lank, loose, flappy, soft, flaccid, flabby (*informal*), saggy, bendy. [➡MALLEABLE AND ELASTIC; 1211] *Opposite:* firm.

floppy disk *type of* **hardware**. [➡COMPUTERS AND COMPUTING; 1126]

flora *n* **plants**, flowers, vegetation, plant life. [➡VEGETATION; 1025]

flora and fauna *n* [➡LIVING THINGS AND LIVING; 976]

floral *adj* **flowery**, flowered, bloomy, floriated, florescent (*formal*), wreathed, flower-patterned. [➡DESCRIBING PATTERNS; 1226]

floral-patterned *adj* [➡DESCRIBING PATTERNS; 1226]

floret *n* **floweret**, bud, blossom, bloom, flower. [➡PARTS OF TREES AND PLANTS; 1026]

florid 1 *adj* **ornate**, baroque, elaborate, fancy, flowery, flamboyant, ostentatious, showy, rococo, extravagant. [➡IN POOR TASTE; 230] *Opposite:* plain. 2 *adj* **ruddy**, red, sanguine, rosy, heightened, blowzy (*disapproving*). [➡COMPLEXION; 481] *Opposite:* pallid.

flotation *n* **launch**, initiation, debut, inauguration, commencement (*formal*), introduction. [➡BUSINESS ACTIVITIES AND PHENOMENA; 795]

flotilla *n* **fleet**, armada, convoy, task force, navy. [➡GROUPS OF VEHICLES; 1151]

flotsam *n* **debris**, refuse, driftwood, jetsam, wreckage, junk (*informal*), waste. [➡RUBBISH AND USELESS OBJECTS; 1248]

flotsam and jetsam *n* [➡RUBBISH AND USELESS OBJECTS; 1248]

flounce *v* **prance**, storm, stomp, strut, swagger, bounce. [➡MOVE FAST; 314]

flounce out *v* [➡ABSENT ONESELF; 8]

flounder 1 *v* **splash**, struggle, thrash, wallow, stumble, flap, flail. [➡FIDGET AND FROLIC; 312] 2 *v* **dither**, hesitate, falter, get into difficulties, waver, dawdle, delay, struggle, get nowhere, have difficulty. [➡HESITATE; 273] 3 *type of* **flatfish**. [➡SEA FISH; 1009]

flour *v* **dust**, cover, coat, sprinkle, dredge. [➡COOKING AND FOOD PREPARATION; 354]

flour

◆ *types of flour*
cornflour, cornmeal, cornstarch (*US*), meal, plain flour, self-raising flour, self-rising flour (*US*), wheatmeal, wholemeal, whole-wheat (*US*)

flourish 1 *v* **be successful**, succeed, thrive, grow, do well, prosper, increase, boom, fare well, burgeon (*literary*), blossom. [➡PROSPER AND ABOUND; 16] *Opposite:* decline. 2 *v* **shake**, show, flaunt, display, wave, brandish, wield, swing. [➡MOVE SOMETHING ON THE SPOT; 337] 3 *n* **embellishment**, curl, curlicue, decoration, ornament. [➡ORNAMENTS AND DECORATIONS; 1247] 4 *n* **grand gesture**, display, fanfare, show, bravado, swagger. [➡GESTURES AND GESTICULATION; 654]

flourishing *adj* **doing well**, thriving, successful, booming, healthy, prosperous, in the ascendant, faring well, burgeoning, blossoming. [➡SUCCESSFUL AND PROMISING; 81] *Opposite:* declining.

floury *adj* **starchy**, crumbly, crumbling, farinaceous, floured, powdery. [➡PHYSICAL TEXTURE; 1221]

flout *v* **disobey**, break, ignore, defy, contravene, be in breach of, scorn, spurn, scoff. [➡DISOBEY; 303] *Opposite:* obey.

flow 1 *v* **run**, pour, flood, stream, gush, surge, roll. [➡PROCEED AND GO; 306] 2 *v* **spring**, arise, emerge, emanate, issue, well up. [➡GRADUALLY COME INTO EXISTENCE; 1] **3** *n* **movement**, current, stream, course, drift, tide. [➡RIVERS, LAKES, AND STREAMS; 1042]

flower **1** *n* **floret**, flower head, bud, blossom, bloom. [➡PARTS OF TREES AND PLANTS; 1026] **2** *n* **best**, pick, height, choicest, elite, cream. [➡SUPERIORITY; 153] *Opposite:* worst. **3** *v* **bloom**, bud, blossom, open, come into bloom. [➡GROW AND CULTIVATE; 352] *Opposite:* fade. **4** *v* **develop**, come to fruition, flourish, peak, blossom, thrive, mature. [➡PROSPER AND ABOUND; 16] *Opposite:* wane.

flower

◆ *types of annual flower*
aster, forget-me-not, lobelia, love-in-a-mist, marigold, nasturtium, pansy, petunia, poppy, sunflower, sweet pea

◆ *types of perennial flower*
African violet, aquilegia, begonia, buttercup, carnation, chrysanthemum, columbine (*US*), cowslip, daisy, delphinium, foxglove, fuchsia, geranium, lily of the valley, lotus, love-lies-bleeding, lupin, orchid, pelargonium, peony, pink, primrose, rose, snapdragon, violet

flowerbed *n* **plot**, garden plot, patch, border, herbaceous border, bed. [➡GARDENS; 1073]

flowered *adj* **floral**, flowery, flower-patterned, floral-patterned. [➡DESCRIBING PATTERNS; 1226]

flowering *n* **peak**, high point, acme, blossoming, pinnacle, zenith. [➡INTERMEDIATE STAGES; 55] *Opposite:* nadir.

flower-patterned *adj* [➡DESCRIBING PATTERNS; 1226]

flowerpot *n* **plant pot**, planter, tub, jardinière, urn, window box, container. [➡CONTAINERS, RECEPTACLES, AND PACKAGING; 1244]

flower show *n* [➡PERFORMANCES AND SHOWS; 42]

flowery **1** *adj* **ornate**, ornamental, baroque, embellished, florid, fancy, elaborate, extravagant. [➡POSITIVELY COMPLEX OR COMPLICATED; 218] *Opposite:* plain. **2** *adj* **floral**, flowered, flower-patterned, floriated. [➡DESCRIBING PATTERNS; 1226]

flowing *adj* **graceful**, smooth, curving, sinuous, elegant, fluid, unbroken, rolling, fluent. [➡ROUNDED SHAPE; 1217] *Opposite:* jerky.

flu *n* [➡ILLNESSES AND DISORDERS; 733]

flub (*US slang*) *v* [➡MESS UP AND MAKE MISTAKES; 473]

fluctuate *v* **vary**, alter, ebb and flow, rise and fall, come and go, swing, oscillate, vacillate, waver, sway, change. [➡CHANGE; 373]

fluctuating *adj* **changing**, changeable, shifting, mutable, unstable, inconsistent, unsettled, alterable, variable, inconstant, oscillating, varying, vacillating, wavering, swaying. [➡FINITENESS, VARIABILITY, AND TRANSIENCE; 96] *Opposite:* constant.

fluctuation *n* **variation**, vacillation, rise and fall, oscillation, flux, ebb and flow, instability, changeability, variability, wavering. [➡FINITENESS, VARIABILITY, AND TRANSIENCE; 96] *Opposite:* steadiness.

flue *n* **vent**, chimney, outlet, shaft, duct, tube, pipe, ventilation shaft. [➡ROOFS, ROOF PARTS, AND CEILINGS; 1102]

fluency *n* **effortlessness**, eloquence, articulacy, ease, facility, confidence, smoothness, glibness. [➡EASE AND SIMPLICITY; 201] *Opposite:* hesitancy.

fluent **1** *adj* **easy**, flowing, confident, assured, smooth, effortless, glib, self-assured. [➡CALMNESS, CONFIDENCE, AND COMPOSURE; 537] *Opposite:* halting. **2** *adj* **articulate**, eloquent, voluble, smooth-spoken, smooth-tongued, silver-tongued. [➡ELOQUENT, TALKATIVE, AND LONG-WINDED; 633] *Opposite:* tongue-tied.

fluently *adv* **assuredly**, easily, confidently, smoothly, effortlessly, glibly. [➡CALMNESS, CONFIDENCE, AND COMPOSURE; 537] *Opposite:* awkwardly.

fluff **1** *v* (*informal*) **do badly**, mess up (*informal*), make a mess of, botch, bungle (*informal*), ruin, spoil. [➡MESS UP AND MAKE MISTAKES; 473] **2** *v* **fluff up**, plump up, ruffle, shake, pat. [➡CHANGE OF SHAPE; 386] **3** *n* **down**, feathers, fuzz, fur, thistledown. [➡UNPLEASANT AND DIRTY SUBSTANCES; 1267]

fluffiness **1** *n* **furriness**, fuzziness, hairiness, woolliness, fleeciness, downiness. [➡PHYSICAL TEXTURE; 1221] *Opposite:* baldness. **2** *n* **lightness**, airiness, softness, flimsiness, frothiness, insubstantiality. [➡PHYSICAL TEXTURE; 1221] *Opposite:* heaviness.

fluff up *v* [➡MESS UP AND MAKE MISTAKES; 473]

fluffy **1** *adj* **fleecy**, cottony, feathery, downy, furry, fuzzy, soft. [➡PHYSICAL TEXTURE; 1221] **2** *adj* **frothy**, foamy, bubbly, soft, light. [➡PHYSICAL TEXTURE; 1221]

flugelhorn *type of* **brass instrument**. [➡MUSICAL INSTRUMENTS; 910]

fluid **1** *n* **liquid**, solution, water. [➡LIQUIDS; 1268] *Opposite:* solid. **2** *adj* **unsolidified**, runny, liquid, liquefied, molten, melted, watery. [➡FLUID AND NON-SOLID; 1212] *Opposite:* solid. **3** *adj* **effortless**, flowing, smooth, graceful, elegant, sinuous. [➡CALMNESS, CONFIDENCE, AND COMPOSURE; 537] *Opposite:* jerky. **4** *adj* **changeable**, fluctuating, unstable, adaptable, flexible, unpredictable, adjustable, shifting, indefinite. [➡FINITENESS, VARIABILITY, AND TRANSIENCE; 96] *Opposite:* constant.

fluidity **1** *n* **variability**, changeableness, changeability, flexibility, mutability, volatility, uncertainty, indefiniteness. [➡FINITENESS, VARIABILITY, AND TRANSIENCE; 96] *Opposite:* fixedness. **2** *n* **smoothness**, gracefulness, grace, agility, flexibility, plasticity. [➡EASE AND SIMPLICITY; 201] *Opposite:* jerkiness.

fluke (*informal*) *n* **stroke of luck**, accident, coincidence, lucky break, chance occurrence, chance, freak. [➡CHANCE EVENT; 36] *Opposite:* mischance.

fluky (*informal*) *adj* [➡LUCK; 784]

flummox (*informal*) *v* **confuse**, perplex, baffle, stump, bewilder, confound, flabbergast (*informal*), stagger, stun, floor, bemuse, fox, throw (*informal*), disconcert. [➡CONFUSE AND BEWILDER; 572]

flummoxed (*informal*) *adj* **confused**, perplexed, confounded, baffled, stumped, bemused, bewildered, at sea, flabbergasted (*informal*), mystified, at a loss, puzzled, thrown (*informal*), foxed, disconcerted. [➡CONFUSION, ANXIETY, AND WORRY; 541]

flunk (*informal*) *v* **fail**, bomb (*informal*), be unsuccessful, not pass, do badly [➡FAIL OR BE UNSUCCESSFUL; 75]. *Opposite:* ace (*informal*).

flunkey *see* **flunky**.

flunky 1 *n* (*informal*) **minion**, sidekick, assistant, helper, subordinate. [➡SUBORDINATES AND ASSISTANTS; 966] 2 *type of* **servant**. [➡DOMESTIC AND KITCHEN WORKERS; 850]

fluoresce *v* [➡LIGHT EMISSION; 369]

fluorescence *n* [➡DESCRIBING LIGHT; 1227]

fluorescent *adj* **glowing**, bright, shining, luminous, flaming, incandescent. [➡DESCRIBING LIGHT; 1227]

fluorescent lamp *type of* **light**. [➡LIGHT; 1163]

fluorite *type of* **mineral**. [➡MINERALS; 1276]

flurry 1 *n* **burst**, spell, outbreak, bout, flood, bustle, commotion, fuss. [➡SUDDEN EVENT; 52] 2 *n* **wind**, gust, puff, squall, shower. [➡WINDY AND STORMY WEATHER; 1053] 3 *v* **fluster**, agitate, disquiet (*archaic or literary*), disturb, disconcert, perturb, rattle. [➡UPSET, DISTRESS, AND HUMILIATE; 568] *Opposite:* soothe.

flush 1 *v* **redden**, blush, go red, colour, glow, bloom, tint. [➡CHANGE OF COLOUR; 392] *Opposite:* pale. 2 *v* **clear**, clean out (*informal*), wash out, cleanse, rinse, swill, flood. [➡CLEAN AND POLISH; 404] 3 *n* **blush**, high colour, redness, rosiness, ruddiness, bloom, tint. [➡PAIN AND OTHER PHYSICAL SENSATIONS; 734] *Opposite:* pallor. 4 *adj* (*informal*) [➡WEALTH AND WEALTHY; 891] 5 *adj* **even**, level, flat, true. [➡ORIENTATION AND ALIGNMENT; 1222] *Opposite:* uneven.

flushed *adj* **red-faced**, rosy, red, blushing, glowing, reddened. [➡COMPLEXION; 481] *Opposite:* pale.

fluster *v* **disconcert**, agitate, confuse, upset, bother, perturb, disturb, disquiet (*archaic or literary*). [➡CONFUSE AND BEWILDER; 572] *Opposite:* soothe.

flustered *adj* **het up** (*informal*), harassed, agitated, nervous, in a tizzy (*informal*), in a flap (*informal*), disconcerted, rattled, confused, ruffled, disturbed, perturbed. [➡CONFUSION, ANXIETY, AND WORRY; 541] *Opposite:* calm.

flute 1 *n* **groove**, channel, indentation, line, furrow, corrugation, pleat. [➡HOLES, GAPS, AND FORKS; 1251] *Opposite:* ridge. 2 *type of* **wind instrument**. [➡MUSICAL INSTRUMENTS; 910]

fluted *adj* **grooved**, channelled, corrugated, furrowed, lined, indented, pleated. [➡PHYSICAL TEXTURE; 1221] *Opposite:* flat.

flutter 1 *v* **beat**, flap, wave, tremble, quiver, waver, flicker, pulsate. [➡MOVE SOMETHING ON THE SPOT; 337] 2 *n* **fluster**, flap (*informal*), tizzy (*informal*), excitement, flurry, state (*informal*), agitation, confusion, perturbation, commotion. [➡INSECURITY AND LOSS OF COMPOSURE; 545] *Opposite:* composure. 3 *n* (*informal*) **bet**, wager, stake. [➡GAMBLE AND TAKE RISKS; 467]

flux *n* **fluidity**, mutability, fluctuation, instability, unrest, change. [➡CHANGE; 373] *Opposite:* stability.

fly 1 *v* **hover**, soar, wing, take wing, take off, glide, flutter, sail, take to the air, coast. [➡PROCEED AND GO; 306] 2 *v* **zoom**, tear, dash, hurry, race, get a move on (*informal*), rush. [➡MOVE FAST; 314] *Opposite:* dawdle. 3 *v* **bolt**, run away, escape, flee, take flight, take off, run off, split (*slang*), fly the coop. [➡RUN AWAY AND AVOID; 10] *Opposite:* stand your ground.

fly

◆ *types of flying insect*
aphid, bee, black fly, bluebottle, bumblebee, cicada, crane fly, daddy longlegs, deer fly, dragonfly, firefly, fruit fly, gnat, grasshopper, greenfly, hornet, horsefly, locust, mayfly, midge, mosquito, no-see-um (*US*), punkie (*US*), tsetse fly, wasp, whitefly

fly agaric *type of* **fungus**. [➡MICROORGANISMS, FUNGI, AND ALGAE; 1023]

flyaway *adj* **unmanageable**, unruly, uncontrollable, hard to handle, awkward, difficult. [➡DESCRIBING HAIR; 487] *Opposite:* manageable.

flyblown 1 *adj* **maggoty**, wormy, infested, worm-eaten, festering. [➡DECAYING OR INFESTED; 1235] 2 *adj* **dirty**, filthy, contaminated, tainted, unclean, unhealthy. [➡DIRTY; 1234] *Opposite:* clean.

fly-by-night *adj* **unscrupulous**, dubious, unreliable, shifty, questionable, shady, cowboy (*informal*), untrustworthy, undependable, crooked (*informal*). [➡LACK OF COMMITMENT AND UNRELIABILITY; 510] *Opposite:* reputable.

flycatcher *type of* **songbird**. [➡SONGBIRD; 1003]

flying 1 *adj* **hovering**, airborne, soaring, in the air, on the wing, winged. [➡GENERAL LOCATIONS; 159] 2 *adj* **rapid**, brief, speedy, hurried, short, hasty, snatched, fleeting. [➡HAPPENING QUICKLY; 104]

flying fish *type of* **tropical sea fish**. [➡SEA FISH; 1009]

flying fox *type of* **flying mammal**. [➡FLYING MAMMAL; 984]

flying saucer *n* **UFO**, spaceship, spacecraft. [➡SCIENCE FICTION; 1063]

flying squirrel *type of* **flying mammal**. [➡FLYING MAMMAL; 984]

fly in the face of *v* **challenge**, disagree with, go against, contradict, oppose, defy. [➡DISOBEY; 303] *Opposite:* conform.

fly in the ointment *n* **drawback**, complaint, impediment, snag, hitch, sticking point, obstacle. [➡PROBLEM; 257]

fly into a rage *v* **erupt**, explode, lose your temper, blow your top (*informal*), fly off the handle (*informal*), go mad, hit the roof, see red (*informal*), go wild, hit the ceiling, blow up (*informal*), go ballistic (*slang*), lose it (*informal*), lose your head, flip your lid (*slang*), lose your rag (*slang*). [➡GIVING VENT TO EMOTIONS; 680] *Opposite:* calm down.

flyleaf *n* **front page**, first page, frontispiece, page, leaf. [➡PARTS OF BOOKS AND DOCUMENTS; 594]

fly off the handle (*informal*) *v* **erupt**, explode, lose your temper, blow your top (*informal*), fly into a rage, go mad, hit the roof, see red (*informal*), go wild, hit the ceiling, blow up (*informal*), go ballistic (*slang*), lose it (*informal*), lose your head, flip your lid (*slang*), lose your rag (*slang*). [➡GIVING VENT TO EMOTIONS; 680] *Opposite:* calm down.

flyover 1 *type of* **major road.** [➡ROADS; 1105] 2 *type of* **bridge.** [➡BRIDGES, TUNNELS, CROSSINGS, AND JUNCTIONS; 1111]

flysheet *n* **flier**, handbill, handout, sheet, notice. [➡ADVERTISING AND PUBLICITY; 605]

fly the coop (*informal*) *v* **escape**, leave, run away, flee, take off (*informal*), bolt, run off. [➡RUN AWAY AND AVOID; 10] *Opposite:* remain.

foal 1 *v* **produce young**, produce offspring, breed, give birth, reproduce, drop a foal. [➡REPRODUCTION AND HEREDITY; 726] 2 *type of* **young animal.** [➡YOUNG ANIMAL; 977]

foam 1 *n* **bubbles**, froth, fizz, lather, suds. [➡FROTH; 1272] 2 *v* **froth up**, effervesce, froth, bubble, fizz, lather, boil. [➡EMIT AND EMANATE; 362]

foam at the mouth *v* **rage**, seethe, fume, boil, splutter. [➡GIVING VENT TO EMOTIONS; 680]

fob off 1 *v* **mislead**, misinform, deceive, stall, pull the wool over somebody's eyes, trick. [➡DECEPTION AND LIES; 661] 2 *v* **cheat**, con, palm off, rip off (*informal*), do (*informal*). [➡DECEPTION AND LIES; 661] 3 *v* **foist**, palm off, dump, pass on, offload, sell a pig in a poke. [➡GIVE TOO MUCH; 438]

focaccia *type of* **bread.** [➡BREAD, FLOUR, AND BREAD PRODUCTS; 1178]

focal *adj* **principal**, pivotal, central, crucial, important, main. [➡FUNDAMENTAL; 196] *Opposite:* peripheral.

focal point *n* **central point**, pivot, core, centre, focus, heart, hub. [➡CENTRAL PARTS OF PHYSICAL OBJECTS; 1250] *Opposite:* periphery.

fo'c's'le *part of* **ship or boat.** [➡PARTS OF A SHIP OR BOAT; 1150]

focus 1 *n* **emphasis**, attention, effort, concentration, motivation, single-mindedness, application. [➡ATTENTION AND ATTENTIVENESS; 764] 2 *n* **nub**, central point, core, spotlight, centre, centre of attention. [➡CENTRAL PARTS OF PHYSICAL OBJECTS; 1250] 3 *n* **focal point**, heart, hub, nucleus, meeting point, rallying point. [➡CENTRAL PARTS OF PHYSICAL OBJECTS; 1250] 4 *v* **concentrate**, direct, converge, meet, come together, bring together, fix, centre, aim. [➡COMBINE AND MIX; 401]

focused *adj* **motivated**, concentrated, fixated, attentive, absorbed, engrossed, intensive, dedicated, single-minded, determined, driven, resolute, firm, persistent, strong-minded, dogged. [➡POSITIVE INTELLECTUAL CHARACTERISTICS; 525]

fodder *n* **food**, silage, hay, feed, feedstuff, provender, forage, rations. [➡ANIMAL FEED; 1167]

foe (*literary*) *n* **adversary**, enemy, antagonist, rival, opponent. [➡ENEMIES AND TORMENTORS; 969] *Opposite:* friend.

foehn *type of* **wind.** [➡WINDY AND STORMY WEATHER; 1053]

fog 1 *n* **mist**, vapour, smog, haze, miasma, murkiness, condensation, precipitation, peasouper. [➡CLOUDY AND RAINY WEATHER; 1052] 2 *n* **muddle**, stupor, confusion, daze, haze, trance, bewilderment. [➡PAIN AND OTHER PHYSICAL SENSATIONS; 734] *Opposite:* clarity. 3 *v* **obscure**, cloud, bewilder, confuse, stupefy, muddle, fuddle, dim, perplex. [➡CONFUSE AND BEWILDER; 572] *Opposite:* sharpen.

fogginess 1 *n* **mistiness**, murkiness, haziness, cloudiness, gloom, murk, haze, darkness, precipitation, condensation. [➡CLOUDY AND RAINY WEATHER; 1052] *Opposite:* brightness. 2 *n* **obscurity**, confusion, unclearness, doubtfulness, bewilderment, perplexity. [➡CONFUSION, ANXIETY, AND WORRY; 541] *Opposite:* clarity.

foggy 1 *adj* **hazy**, misty, cloudy, murky, smoggy, dim, vaporous. [➡CLOUDY AND RAINY WEATHER; 1052] *Opposite:* clear. 2 *adj* **unclear**, vague, confused, muddled, bewildered, stupefied, fuddled. [➡VAGUENESS; 244] *Opposite:* precise.

foghorn *n* **horn**, siren, hooter, klaxon. [➡SIGNALLING; 1139]

fog light *type of* **external feature.** [➡VEHICLES; 1144]

fogy *n* [➡UNCOOPERATIVE OR REBELLIOUS PERSON; 567]

fogyish *adj* [➡REBELLIOUSNESS AND DISOBEDIENCE; 566]

foible *n* **weakness**, fault, shortcoming, quirk, idiosyncrasy, eccentricity, bad habit, imperfection. [➡PERSONAL ECCENTRICITIES; 494] *Opposite:* strength.

foil 1 *v* **stop**, throw a spanner in the works, frustrate, thwart, outwit, halt, halt in its tracks, baulk, hinder, promote, throw a monkey wrench in the works (*US informal*). [➡MAKE IMPOSSIBLE; 277] 2 *type of* **sword or knife.** [➡SWORDS AND KNIVES; 1156]

foist *v* **force upon**, inflict upon, thrust upon, impose, finagle (*informal*), palm off, pass off. [➡GIVE TOO MUCH; 438]

fold 1 *v* **double over**, bend, fold up, fold over, double, pleat, crease, crinkle, corrugate. [➡CHANGE OF SHAPE; 386] *Opposite:* straighten. 2 *v* **go out of business**, close, shut down, go bankrupt, collapse, go under, go to the wall, go bust (*informal*). [➡FAIL OR BE UNSUCCESSFUL; 75] 3 *n* **crinkle**, crease, wrinkle, pleat, doubling, folding, bend. [➡CHANGE OF SHAPE; 386]

foldaway *adj* **portable**, folding, foldup, collapsible, hinged, travelling, camping, compact. [➡CHANGE OF SHAPE; 386]

folded *adj* **doubled**, doubled over, doubled up, bent over, turned under, turned up, creased, gathered, pleated, crumpled, bent. [➡ORIENTATION AND ALIGNMENT; 1222] *Opposite:* outspread.

folding *adj* **portable**, foldup, foldaway, collapsible, hinged, travelling, compact, camping. [➡CHANGE OF SHAPE; 386]

fold up *v* **bend flat**, bend, collapse, double, fold over, fold down. [➡CHANGE OF SHAPE; 386]

foldup *adj* **portable**, folding, collapsible, foldaway, hinged, travelling, camping, compact. [➡CHANGE OF SHAPE; 386]

foliage *n* **leaves**, greenery, vegetation, undergrowth, shrubbery, plants, verdure. [➡PARTS OF TREES AND PLANTS; 1026]

foliage plant

◆ *types of foliage plant*
aspidistra, coleus, fern, moss, poinsettia, rubber plant, sansevieria, spider plant, yucca

folk 1 *adj* **traditional**, popular, common, widespread, vernacular, general, conventional, informal, unofficial. [➡OLD, OLD-FASHIONED; 168] 2 *n* **people**, folks, the people, the population, everyone, most people, the silent majority, society. [➡GROUPS IN SOCIETY; 940] **3** *type of* **popular music.** [➡MUSIC, SONGS, AND SINGING; 907]

folklore **1** *n* **myth**, legend, oral tradition, mythology, tradition, traditional beliefs, custom. [➡THE ORAL TRADITION; 678] **2** *n* **legends**, traditional stories, urban myths, folk tales, received wisdom. [➡THE ORAL TRADITION; 678]

folks **1** *n* (*informal*) **people**, folk, the people, the population, everyone, most people, the silent majority, society. [➡GROUPS IN SOCIETY; 940] **2** *n* (*informal*) **everyone**, everybody, ladies and gentlemen, boys and girls, girls and boys, guys (*informal*), you lot, you guys, friends, comrades, dearly beloved. [➡GROUPS IN SOCIETY; 940] **3** *n* **relations**, relatives, nearest and dearest, family, people (*informal*), kinfolk, kith and kin. [➡THE FAMILY; 956]

folk singer *n* **singer**, folkie, balladeer, troubadour. [➡MUSICIANS AND SINGERS; 908]

folk song *type of* **vocal music.** [➡MUSIC, SONGS, AND SINGING; 907]

folk story *n* [➡THE ORAL TRADITION; 678]

folksy **1** *adj* **simple**, unsophisticated, unpretentious, wholesome, traditional, downhome (*US informal*). [➡LEVEL OF EDUCATION AND SOPHISTICATION; 894] **2** *adj* (*US*) **friendly**, informal, relaxed, congenial, easygoing. [➡NATURALNESS; 498] *Opposite:* restrained.

folk tale *n* **tale**, story, legend, myth, ballad, fable, allegory. [➡THE ORAL TRADITION; 678]

folk tales *n* [➡THE ORAL TRADITION; 678]

follicle *n* **sac**, cavity, gland, hair follicle. [➡THE SKIN; 721]

follow **1** *v* **stalk**, tail (*informal*), pursue, chase, trail, track, tag on, tag along, hunt. [➡ACCOMPANY AND FOLLOW; 338] *Opposite:* precede. **2** *v* **monitor**, shadow, check on, trail, keep an eye on, tail (*informal*), track, chart, survey. [➡LOOKING AND LOOKS; 701] **3** *v* **come out of**, ensue, result, develop, arise. [➡HAPPEN; 27] **4** *v* **keep on**, go along, stay on, keep to, stick to. [➡ACCOMPANY AND FOLLOW; 338] **5** *v* **enjoy**, admire, support, keep up with, be keen on. [➡LIKE, LOVE, VALUE, AND ENJOY; 579] **6** *v* **obey**, abide by, keep to, respect, adhere to, stick to, go by, go along with. [➡OBEY AND ABIDE BY; 302] *Opposite:* break. **7** *v* **understand**, see, comprehend, grasp, catch on (*informal*), cotton on (*informal*), get the gist, twig (*informal*), get the idea. [➡UNDERSTAND AND GRASP; 760]

Compare and Contrast: ***follow, chase, pursue, tail, shadow, stalk, trail***

CORE MEANING: TO GO AFTER

follow to take the same route behind another person, for example by walking down the street or driving along the same road, deliberately or by chance, and not necessarily with the intention of closing the gap; ***chase*** to try to reach, catch, or overtake another person who is in front; ***pursue*** to make an effort to catch up with the person being followed; ***tail*** (*informal*) to follow somebody else secretly for purposes of surveillance; ***shadow*** to follow secretly, used especially to talk about the activities of spies and detectives; ***stalk*** to follow or try to get close to a person or hunted animal unobtrusively, especially obsessively to follow and criminally harrass a person; ***trail*** to follow tracks or traces left by a person or animal no longer in sight.

follower *n* **supporter**, fan, admirer, hanger-on, devotee, disciple, adherent. [➡SUPPORTERS, PROTECTORS, AND COMPATRIOTS; 970]

following *adj* **next**, subsequent, succeeding, ensuing, resulting. [➡AFTER, LAST, AND FOLLOWING; 166] *Opposite:* previous.

follow-on **1** *adj* **resulting**, consequent, resultant, ensuing, secondary, subsequent. [➡AFTER, LAST, AND FOLLOWING; 166] **2** *n* **side effect**, continuation, consequence, result, repercussion, carry over, spin-off, knock-on, knock-on effect. [➡EVIDENCE AND PROOF; 69]

follow through *v* **complete**, see through, bring to completion, bring to the end, finish off, finish. [➡COMPLETE AN ACTION; 264] *Opposite:* drop.

follow-up *n* **continuation**, addition, supplement, complement, development, sequel. [➡AFTER, LAST, AND FOLLOWING; 166]

folly *n* **irrationality**, foolishness, madness, stupidity, idiocy, silliness, craziness (*informal*), recklessness, foolhardiness, imprudence. [➡NEGATIVE INTELLECTUAL CHARACTERISTICS; 526] *Opposite:* prudence.

foment (*formal*) *v* **foster**, stir up, stimulate, incite, generate, provoke, drum up, increase, encourage, whip up, fan. [➡CAUSE TO HAPPEN; 31] *Opposite:* dampen.

fond *adj* **loving**, tender, affectionate, caring, warm, warm-hearted, doting. [➡GENEROSITY AND KINDNESS; 496] *Opposite:* uncaring.

fondant *type of* **confectionery.** [➡CONFECTIONERY; 1181]

fondle *v* **massage**, touch, stroke, caress, pet, pat, feel, rub. [➡CONTACT: TOUCH; 413]

fondness *n* **liking**, affection, weakness, soft spot, partiality, keenness, love, attachment. [➡LOVE, RESPECT, AND GOODWILL; 550] *Opposite:* dislike.

See Compare and Contrast at **love**.

fond of *adj* **devoted to**, taken with, attached to, keen on, partial to, soft on. [➡RELATIONSHIP TO ANOTHER; 973] *Opposite:* indifferent.

fondue *type of* **cooked dish.** [➡PREPARED DISHES; 1169]

font **1** *n* (*literary*) **source**, supply, wellspring, fount, basis, origin, well. [➡BEGINNING; 53] **2** *n* (*literary*) **fountain**, spring, water source, well, source. [➡RIVERS, LAKES, AND STREAMS; 1042] **3** *n* **typeface**, lettering, type style, type, sans serif, Arial, Garamond, Gill Sans, Times New Roman, Courier. [➡PRINTING; 601]

food **1** *n* **nourishment**, nutrition, nutriment, diet, sustenance, nutrients. [➡FOOD; 1166] **2** *n* **staple**, foodstuff, fare, provisions, groceries, grub (*informal*), victuals, rations, cuisine, fodder, chow (*slang*). [➡FOOD; 1166]

foodie (*informal*) *n* **food lover**, gourmet, bon vivant (*literary*), bon viveur (*literary*), epicure, connoisseur, epicurean, glutton, gastronome, gourmand. [➡EATERS, GOURMETS, AND DIETARY CHOICES; 715]

food lover *n* **gourmet**, epicure, connoisseur, epicurean, glutton, gastronome, gourmand, bon vivant (*literary*), bon viveur (*literary*), foodie (*informal*). [➡EATERS, GOURMETS, AND DIETARY CHOICES; 715]

food processor *type of* **utensil.** [➡TABLEWARE, CUTLERY, AND KITCHENWARE; 861]

foodstuff *n* **food**, staple, essential, ingredient, provisions, groceries, rations, fodder. [➡FOOD; 1166]

foofaraw *n* [➡CHAOS AND UPROAR; 51]

fool *v* **mislead**, trick, deceive, take in, con, dupe, pull the wool over somebody's eyes, bamboozle (*informal*), hoodwink. [➡DECEPTION AND LIES; 661]

fool about 1 *v* **clown**, act the fool, play around, muck about (*informal*), mess around (*informal*), mess about (*informal*), fool around, horse around. [➡LEISURE AND RECREATION; 874] 2 *v* **mess around** (*informal*), mess about (*informal*), muck about (*informal*), fool around, fiddle about, fiddle around (*informal*), footle (*informal*), lollygag (*dated*), idle, futz (*US informal*). [➡LACK OF ACTIVITY; 343]

fool around 1 *v* **clown**, act the fool, play around, fool about, mess about (*informal*), mess around (*informal*), muck about (*informal*), horse around. [➡LEISURE AND RECREATION; 874] 2 *v* **mess around** (*informal*), mess about (*informal*), muck about (*informal*), fiddle about, fiddle around (*informal*), lollygag (*dated*), footle (*informal*), idle, potter, futz (*US informal*). [➡LACK OF ACTIVITY; 343]

foolhardiness *n* **recklessness**, imprudence, stupidity, idiocy, foolishness, folly, silliness, madness, craziness (*informal*). [➡NEGATIVE INTELLECTUAL CHARACTERISTICS; 526] *Opposite:* prudence.

foolhardy *adj* **reckless**, rash, imprudent (*formal*), foolish, unwise, irresponsible, risky, unsafe, mad, silly, stupid. [➡FUNNY AND AMUSING; 217] *Opposite:* sensible.

foolish 1 *adj* **stupid**, silly, unwise, imprudent (*formal*), thoughtless, irrational, crazy (*informal*), rash, reckless. [➡NEGATIVE INTELLECTUAL CHARACTERISTICS; 526] *Opposite:* wise. 2 *adj* **ridiculous**, laughable, silly, derisible (*formal*). [➡FUNNY AND AMUSING; 217]

foolishly *adv* **stupidly**, unwisely, imprudently (*formal*), thoughtlessly, irrationally. [➡FUNNY AND AMUSING; 217] *Opposite:* wisely.

foolishness *n* **irrationality**, stupidity, idiocy, silliness, imprudence, thoughtlessness, folly, foolhardiness, recklessness, madness. [➡NEGATIVE INTELLECTUAL CHARACTERISTICS; 526] *Opposite:* wisdom.

foolproof *adj* **secure**, safe, infallible, fail-safe, perfect, sure-fire (*informal*), guaranteed. [➡SAFE AND SAFETY; 192] *Opposite:* risky.

foot 1 *n* **base**, bottom, end. [➡EXTREMITIES OF PHYSICAL OBJECTS; 1249] *Opposite:* top. 2 *part of* **leg or foot.** [➡LEG AND FOOT; 695]

footage *n* **film**, shots, tape, videotape, material. [➡TELEVISION AND RADIO; 607]

football 1 *n* **matter**, point, problem, issue, hot potato, bone of contention. [➡PROBLEM; 257] 2 *type of* **sports equipment.** [➡SPORTS EQUIPMENT; 879] 3 *type of* **ball game.** [➡HOBBIES, GAMES, AND SPORTS; 875]

footbridge *type of* **bridge.** [➡BRIDGES, TUNNELS, CROSSINGS, AND JUNCTIONS; 1111]

footer *n* **addendum**, title, footnote, note, text, gloss. [➡PARTS OF BOOKS AND DOCUMENTS; 594] *Opposite:* header.

footfall *n* **footstep**, step, tread, pace, sound. [➡IMPACT SOUNDS; 1259]

foothill *n* **hill**, slope, base, foot, bottom, lower reach. [➡MOUNTAINS AND HILLS; 1044] *Opposite:* summit.

foothold *n* **position**, base, purchase, grip, toehold, footing. [➡ADVANTAGE; 213]

footing 1 *n* **stability**, equilibrium, purchase, foothold, grip, balance. [➡ADVANTAGE; 213] 2 *n* **basis**, position, foundation, base, support, structure. [➡SUPPORTS AND BASES; 1254]

footle (*informal*) 1 *v* **mess about** (*informal*), fool around, fiddle around (*informal*), idle, potter, mess around (*informal*), dawdle, futz (*US informal*). [➡LACK OF ACTIVITY; 343] 2 *v* **blather** (*informal*), chatter, prattle, blabber, blab (*informal*), gab (*informal*), gas (*informal*), natter (*informal*). [➡WITTER AND BABBLE; 618] 3 *n* **bunkum** (*informal*), rubbish, nonsense, prattle, claptrap (*informal*), bunk (*slang*), poppycock (*dated informal*), blather (*informal*), balderdash. [➡MEANINGLESS SPEECH OR WRITING; 677]

footlights 1 *n* **acting**, the stage, the theatre, the limelight. [➡IN THE THEATRE; 906] 2 *type of* **light.** [➡LIGHT; 1163]

footling (*informal*) *adj* **trivial**, unimportant, insignificant, trifling, inconsequential, piddling (*informal*), piffling (*informal*). [➡UNIMPORTANT AND UNNECESSARY; 239] *Opposite:* important.

footloose *adj* **free**, unattached, uncommitted, unrestricted, single, unmarried. [➡PLEASURE-SEEKING AND EXCESS; 885]

footloose and fancy free *adj* [➡MARITAL STATUS; 890]

footman *type of* **servant.** [➡DOMESTIC AND KITCHEN WORKERS; 850]

footnote *n* **note**, annotation, cross-reference, appendix, addendum, postscript, footer. [➡PARTS OF BOOKS AND DOCUMENTS; 594]

footpad *part of* **spacecraft.** [➡SPACE VEHICLES; 1062]

footpath *n* **path**, trail, track, causeway, bridleway, towpath, walkway, boardwalk, bridle path, footway. [➡PATHWAYS; 1109]

footprint *n* **footmark**, print, imprint, impression, outline, mark, trail, track, spoor. [➡EVIDENCE AND PROOF; 69]

footrest *n* **rail**, bar, stool, footstool, foot rail, support, ottoman. [➡FURNITURE; 858]

footsore *adj* **tired**, weary, exhausted, aching, sore. [➡TIRED, ASLEEP, AND UNCONSCIOUS; 739]

footstep *n* **sound**, step, tread, pace, footfall. [➡IMPACT SOUNDS; 1259]

footstool *n* **footrest**, stool, support, ottoman. [➡FURNITURE; 858]

footway *n* **footpath**, path, trail, track, causeway, boardwalk, bridle path, walkway, bridleway, towpath. [➡PATHWAYS; 1109]

footwear

◆ *types of boot*
boot, bootee, cowboy boot, galoshes, gum boot, hiking boot, jackboot, mukluk, rubber (*US*), waders, walking boot, wellington boot

◆ *types of shoe*
ballet shoe, brogue, clog, court shoe, espadrille, flip-flop (*informal*), jelly, moccasin, mule, oxford, platform, plimsoll, pump, sandal, sandshoe, slingback, slipper, sneaker (*US*), snowshoe, stiletto heel, thong, trainer, wedge heel, wingtip (*US*), zori

footwork *n* **manoeuvring**, cunning, skill, negotiation, horse-trading, deviousness, politicking. [➡UNKIND ACTION OR BEHAVIOUR; 297]

fop *n* **dandy** (*dated*), popinjay (*dated*), peacock, narcissus, poseur, beau (*archaic*), poser (*informal disapproving*). [➡MALE PERSON; 934]

foppish *adj* **dandyish** (*dated*), vain, affected, preening, narcissistic, self-obsessed, decadent. [➡WELL GROOMED; 483]

for 1 *prep* **aimed at**, intended for, designed for, meant for, used for. [➡INTENTION AND PURPOSE; 773] 2 *prep* **in favour of**, in support of, pro. [➡LIKE, LOVE, VALUE, AND ENJOY; 579] *Opposite:* against.

forage 1 *n* **food**, feed, fodder, silage. [➡ANIMAL FEED; 1167] 2 *n* **quest**, search, hunt, exploration, foray, sortie. [➡SEEK POSSESSION AND SEARCH; 457] 3 *v* **look for**, search, seek, scavenge, rummage, hunt. [➡SEEK POSSESSION AND SEARCH; 457]

for a kickoff (*informal*) *adv* **firstly**, for a start, for starters, to begin with, first of all. [➡EXPRESSIONS INTRODUCING EXAMPLES; 64]

for all *prep* **notwithstanding** (*formal*), despite, in spite of, for all that. [➡ALTHOUGH, NEVERTHELESS, AND DESPITE; 170]

forasmuch as (*formal*) *conj* **since**, inasmuch as, whereas (*formal*), in view of the fact that, because, on account of. [➡CAUSATION; 169]

for a start *adv* [➡EXPRESSIONS INTRODUCING EXAMPLES; 64]

foray *n* **raid**, incursion, venture, sortie, expedition, attack, assault. [➡AGGRESSIVE EVENT; 39]

forbear (*formal*) *v* **refrain**, restrain yourself, abstain, hold back, withhold. [➡NOT DO AND REFUSE TO DO; 275]

forbearance (*formal*) *n* **patience**, self-control, restraint, tolerance, moderation, leniency, mercy. [➡GENEROSITY AND KINDNESS; 496] *Opposite:* impatience.

forbearing (*formal*) *adj* **patient**, long-suffering, forgiving, tolerant, lenient, merciful, moderate. [➡STRENGTH OF WILL; 502] *Opposite:* impatient.

forbid *v* **prohibit**, ban, bar, prevent, outlaw, stop, hinder, inhibit. [➡REFUSE PERMISSION AND NOT ALLOW; 671] *Opposite:* allow.

forbidden *adj* **prohibited**, banned, outlawed, illegal, illicit. [➡UNACCEPTABLE AND UNFORGIVEABLE; 226] *Opposite:* permissible.

forbidding 1 *adj* **hostile**, unfriendly, dark, grim, bleak, dismal, stern, gloomy, harsh, severe. [➡RUDE AND HOSTILE; 626] *Opposite:* welcoming. 2 *adj* **uninviting**, unpleasant, dismal, depressing, bleak, grim, off-putting, inhospitable, unwelcoming. [➡EMOTIONALLY UNPLEASANT AND UPSETTING; 228] *Opposite:* hospitable. 3 *adj* **threatening**, ominous, menacing, sinister, dangerous, alarming, frightening, ferocious, fierce, perilous, life-threatening, disturbing. [➡DANGEROUS; 237]

force 1 *n* **power**, strength, energy, might, vigour, potency, dynamism. [➡ENERGY GENERAL; 1160] *Opposite:* weakness. 2 *n* **influence**, weight, power, strength, intensity, cogency (*formal*). [➡STRENGTH; 202] 3 *v* **compel**, oblige, make, impose, coerce, constrain, drive. [➡CAUSE OR COMPEL TO ACT; 272] 4 *v* **push**, shove, break down, break open, prise, press, pry (*US*). [➡CONTACT: EXERT PRESSURE; 415]

forced 1 *adj* **strained**, unnatural, affected, put on, artificial. [➡INARTICULATE, RAMBLING, AND AWKWARD; 634] *Opposite:* natural. 2 *adj* **involuntary**, compulsory, required, obligatory, enforced, mandatory. [➡CAPTIVITY AND LOSS OF FREEDOM; 249] *Opposite:* voluntary.

force-feed 1 *v* **feed up**, fatten, fatten up, feed, nourish, sustain, keep alive. [➡GIVE TOO MUCH; 438] 2 *v* **teach**, brainwash, programme, ram down somebody's throat, cram. [➡INSTRUCT AND TEACH; 610]

forceful 1 *adj* **powerful**, vigorous, strong, dynamic, potent, influential, energetic, mighty. [➡STRENGTH; 202] *Opposite:* weak. 2 *adj* **persuasive**, convincing, compelling, valid, powerful, influential, weighty, cogent, vehement. [➡ENTHUSIASTIC AND INQUISITIVE; 629] *Opposite:* unconvincing.

forcefulness 1 *n* **strength**, power, vigour, dynamism, influence, weight, powerfulness, potency. [➡STRENGTH; 202] *Opposite:* weakness. 2 *n* **persuasiveness**, validity, cogency (*formal*), powerfulness, power, weightiness, weight. [➡STRENGTH; 202]

force out *v* **drive out**, expel, turn out, oust, evict, throw out. [➡EJECT AND EXCLUDE; 341]

forceps *type of* **medical instrument**. [➡HAND TOOLS; 1118]

forces *n* **armed forces**, military, services, army, navy, air force, marines (*formal*). [➡THE ARMED FORCES; 827]

forcible 1 *adj* **compulsory**, violent, aggressive, armed. [➡PHYSICALLY UNPLEASANT; 227] *Opposite:* peaceful. 2 *adj* **effective**, forceful, powerful, convincing, persuasive, influential, weighty. [➡STRENGTH; 202] *Opposite:* weak.

forcibly 1 *adv* **by force**, compulsorily, under duress, against your will, under protest. [➡WITHOUT ENTHUSIASM; 288] *Opposite:* peacefully. 2 *adv* **powerfully**, effectively, convincingly, persuasively, influentially. [➡STRENGTH; 202] *Opposite:* weakly.

ford 1 *n* **shallows**, crossing, passage, stepping stone. [➡BRIDGES, TUNNELS, CROSSINGS, AND JUNCTIONS; 1111] 2 *v* **cross**, traverse, negotiate, cross over, wade. [➡MOVE PAST, INTO, OR THROUGH SOMETHING; 332]

fore (*literary*) *n* **front**, forefront, forepart, bow, face, frontage, façade. [➡EXTREMITIES OF PHYSICAL OBJECTS; 1249] *Opposite:* back.

fore-and-aft sail (*US*) *part of* **sailing vessel.** [➡PARTS OF A SHIP OR BOAT; 1150]

forearm 1 *part of* **arm or hand.** [➡ARM AND HAND; 696] 2 *v* **prepare**, forewarn, tip the wink (*informal*), tip off, prime, alert, give advance notice, give advance warning, warn. [➡ADVISE AND WARN; 614]

forebear 1 *n* [➡OLDER GENERATION RELATIVES; 959] 2 *n* **ancestor**, forerunner, antecedent, predecessor, grandparent, forefather, precursor. [➡THE FAMILY; 956] *Opposite:* descendant.

foreboding 1 *n* **premonition**, presentiment, feeling, fear, intuition, feeling in the bones. [➡FEELINGS ABOUT THE FUTURE; 534] 2 *adj* **ominous**, menacing, threatening, sinister, forbidding, dark. [➡DANGEROUS; 237] *Opposite:* encouraging.

forecast 1 *v* **predict**, estimate, calculate, project, anticipate, foretell, guess, conjecture. [➡PREDICT AND ANTICIPATE; 751] 2 *n* **prediction**, estimate, guess, calculation, conjecture, projection, prognostication, prognosis, best guess. [➡PREDICT AND ANTICIPATE; 751]

forecaster *n* **predictor**, prognosticator, forward planner, conjecturer, interpreter, analyst, prophet, clairvoyant. [➡WORKERS IN ENTERTAINMENT AND MEDIA; 873]

foreclose (*formal*) *v* **exclude**, shut out, close out, ban, exile, bar. [➡MAKE IMPOSSIBLE; 277]

forecourt *n* **space**, area, courtyard, concourse, square, piazza, atrium. [➡URBAN OUTDOOR SPACES; 1071]

forefather *n* [➡OLDER GENERATION RELATIVES; 959]

forefinger *part of* **arm or hand.** [➡ARM AND HAND; 696]

forefront 1 *n* **pole position**, front, head, vanguard, lead, van, leading edge. [➡BEGINNING; 53] *Opposite:* back. 2 *n* **foreground**, forepart, front, frontage, face, façade, fore (*literary*), forecourt. [➡EXTREMITIES OF PHYSICAL OBJECTS; 1249] *Opposite:* background.

forego *v* **give up**, pass by, do without, miss out on, sacrifice, waive, relinquish, abstain from, go without, decline. [➡FOREGO AND DENY ONESELF; 450] *Opposite:* grab.

foregoing *adj* **previous**, prior, preceding, earlier, former, above-mentioned, above. [➡BEFORE, FIRST, AND PRECEDING; 164]

foregone *adj* **inevitable**, predetermined, inescapable, unavoidable, ordained (*formal*), fated, predictable. [➡CERTAIN; 175] *Opposite:* uncertain.

foreground *n* **forefront**, front, centre, centre stage, focus, focal point, fore (*literary*). [➡CENTRAL PARTS OF PHYSICAL OBJECTS; 1250] *Opposite:* background.

forehead *part of* **head.** [➡HEAD; 693]

foreign 1 *adj* **alien**, external, extraneous, imported, overseas, extraterritorial, transcontinental, distant, far-off, remote. [➡DISTANCE; 161] *Opposite:* indigenous. 2 *adj* **strange**, unfamiliar, unknown, alien, exotic, outlandish. [➡EXTRAORDINARY: UNCOMMON; 206] *Opposite:* familiar. 3 *adj* **unrelated**, extraneous, irrelevant, external, unconnected, irrelative. [➡UNRELATEDNESS AND SEPARATENESS; 147] *Opposite:* relevant.

foreigner *n* **stranger**, foreign person, alien, immigrant, newcomer, outsider, refugee, nonnational. [➡STRANGERS; 972] *Opposite:* national.

foreknowledge (*formal*) *n* **premonition**, prescience, feeling, foresight, intuition, intelligence. [➡FEELINGS ABOUT THE FUTURE; 534] *Opposite:* hindsight.

foreleg 1 *n* **front leg**, forelimb, limb, leg, appendage. [➡LEG AND FOOT; 695] 2 *part of* **horse.** [➡HORSE; 985]

foremost *adj* **chief**, leading, primary, prime, notable, principal, main, top, important. [➡SUPERIORITY; 153]

forename *n* **first name**, given name, Christian name, nickname, pet name, middle name, moniker (*slang*). [➡NAME AND DESCRIBE; 666] *Opposite:* surname.

forerunner 1 *n* **portent**, indication, omen, sign, harbinger, foreshadowing, augury, precursor. [➡INDICATIONS, SIGNS, AND WARNINGS; 68] 2 *n* **forebear**, ancestor, antecedent, precursor, predecessor, forefather, grandparent. [➡OLDER GENERATION RELATIVES; 959]

foresee *v* **foreknow** (*formal*), expect, foretell, prophesy, divine, predict, forecast, anticipate. [➡PREDICT AND ANTICIPATE; 751] *Opposite:* look back.

foreseeable 1 *adj* **predictable**, probable, likely, imaginable, conceivable, calculable, estimative, anticipatable. [➡POSSIBLE AND PROBABLE; 178] *Opposite:* unforeseeable. 2 *adj* **near**, immediate, imminent, prospective, impending, short-term. [➡FUTURE; 86] *Opposite:* far-off.

foreshadow *v* **presage**, indicate, suggest, warn of, augur, prefigure, foretell, predict. [➡MEAN SOMETHING; 61]

foreshank *type of* **cut.** [➡TYPES AND CUTS OF MEAT; 1176]

foreshore *n* **shore**, beach, mudflat, sand, shingle, rocks, tidemark, high-water mark, low-water mark. [➡THE SEAS, OCEANS, AND SHORES; 1041]

foresight 1 *n* **forethought**, prudence, farsightedness, anticipation, sagacity, precaution. [➡PREDICT AND ANTICIPATE; 751] 2 *n* **premonition**, insight, prescience, prevision (*formal or literary*), intuition, foreknowledge (*formal*), hindsight. [➡POSITIVE INTELLECTUAL CHARACTERISTICS; 525]

forest *n* **woods**, woodland, forestry, plantation, jungle, timberland. [➡WOODS, FORESTS, AND JUNGLES; 1047]

forestall 1 *v* **prevent**, preclude (*formal*), avert, obviate, hinder, thwart, block, pre-empt. [➡MAKE IMPOSSIBLE; 277] 2 *v* (*archaic*) **anticipate**, foresee, envision, expect, predict, forecast, project. [➡PREDICT AND ANTICIPATE; 751]

forest fire *n* [➡FIRE, FLAMMABILITY, AND BURNING; 1164]

forest green *type of* **green.** [➡COLOURS; 1223]

foretaste *n* **sample**, token, indication, example, taste, taster, preview, insight. [➡INDICATIONS, SIGNS, AND WARNINGS; 68] *Opposite:* recollection.

foretell (*literary*) *v* **predict**, prophesy, presage, portend, forecast, prognosticate, divine. [➡PREDICT AND ANTICIPATE; 751] *Opposite:* review.

forethought *n* **anticipation**, consideration, foresight, prudence, planning, precaution, farsightedness, prevision (*formal or literary*). [➡PREDICT AND ANTICIPATE; 751] *Opposite:* afterthought.

forever 1 *adv* (*informal*) **incessantly**, persistently, repeatedly, continually, endlessly, constantly, always, at all times, ever. [➡PERMANENCE: WITHOUT END; 94] *Opposite:* never. 2 *adv* **eternally**, for all time, evermore (*literary*), forevermore (*literary*), in perpetuity, indefinitely, ad infinitum. [➡PERMANENCE: WITHOUT END; 94] *Opposite:* momentarily.

forevermore (*literary*) *adv* **forever**, until the end of time, eternally, for all time, evermore (*literary*), in perpetuity, indefinitely, ad infinitum, forever and ever. [➡PERMANENCE: WITHOUT END; 94]

forewarn *v* **warn**, caution, alert, tip off, put on the alert, prepare, prime, tip the wink (*informal*). [➡ADVISE AND WARN; 614]

forewarning *n* **warning**, notice, notification, word of warning, signal, tip-off (*informal*). [➡ADVICE; 690]

foreword *n* **preface**, introduction, prelude, preamble, prologue, overture. [➡PARTS OF BOOKS AND DOCUMENTS; 594] *Opposite:* conclusion.

for example *adv* [➡EXPRESSIONS INTRODUCING EXAMPLES; 64]

forfeit 1 *n* **penalty**, forfeiture, loss, penalization, punishment, fine. [➡NUISANCES; 254] 2 *v* **lose**, pay for, be deprived of, pay with, be stripped of. [➡LOSE AND FORFEIT; 448] 3 *v* **surrender**, sacrifice, give up, part with, go without, forgo. [➡FORGO AND DENY ONESELF; 450]

forfeiture *n* **penalty**, forfeit, loss, penalization, punishment, fine. [➡TRIAL, PUNISHMENT, AND LEGAL OUTCOMES; 819]

forge 1 *n* **furnace**, hearth, oven. [➡FIRE, FLAMMABILITY, AND BURNING; 1164] 2 *type of* **factory**. [➡INDUSTRIAL BUILDINGS; 1086] 3 *v* **shape**, form, build, create, fashion, construct, establish, make. [➡MANUFACTURE; 350] 4 *v* **counterfeit**, fake, falsify, copy, imitate, duplicate. [➡FALSIFY AND CHEAT; 177]

forge ahead *v* **take the lead**, come to the fore, make progress, make headway, move forward, plough on, plow on (*US*). [➡SUCCEED AND WIN; 79] *Opposite:* lag.

forged *adj* **fake**, counterfeit, false, spurious, phoney, specious, unauthentic, bogus. [➡FALSE AND UNREAL; 174] *Opposite:* genuine.

forger *n* **counterfeiter**, falsifier, faker, coiner, imitator, copier, criminal, crook (*informal*). [➡CRIMINALS; 821]

forgery *n* **fake**, counterfeit, sham, phoney, imitation, falsification, copy. [➡CRIMES; 817] *Opposite:* original.

forget 1 *v* **overlook**, disremember, fail to recall, be unable to remember, be unable to call to mind, be unable to summon up, be unable to picture. [➡FORGET, FORGIVE, AND ACCEPT; 749] *Opposite:* remember. 2 *v* **stop thinking about**, put out of your mind, disregard, put behind you, turn your back on, erase from your mind, ignore, neglect, blank over. [➡NOT PAY ATTENTION; 765] *Opposite:* attend to.

See Compare and Contrast at **neglect**.

forgetful 1 *adj* **absent-minded**, inclined to forget, vague, absent, oblivious, insensible, preoccupied, scatty (*informal*), dreamy, scatterbrained. [➡NEGATIVE INTELLECTUAL CHARACTERISTICS; 526] *Opposite:* mindful. 2 *adj* **inattentive**, neglectful, negligent, wandering, careless, unfocused. [➡NEGATIVE INTELLECTUAL CHARACTERISTICS; 526] *Opposite:* attentive.

forgetfulness *n* **absent-mindedness**, amnesia, obliviousness, insensibleness, vagueness. [➡NEGATIVE INTELLECTUAL CHARACTERISTICS; 526]

forget-me-not *type of* **annual flower**. [➡FLOWERS; 1032]

forgettable *adj* **unmemorable**, unremarkable, undistinguished, mediocre, ordinary, uninteresting, boring. [➡ORDINARINESS; 245] *Opposite:* unforgettable.

forgivable *adj* **pardonable**, excusable, allowable, defensible, justifiable, understandable. [➡ACCEPTABLE AND PASSABLE; 220] *Opposite:* unforgivable.

forgive *v* **pardon**, excuse, forgive and forget, let off, absolve, exonerate. [➡FORGET, FORGIVE, AND ACCEPT; 749] *Opposite:* blame.

forgiveness 1 *n* **pardon**, absolution, amnesty, exoneration, exculpation (*formal*), reconciliation. [➡COMPASSION AND FORGIVENESS; 552] *Opposite:* blame. 2 *n* **clemency**, pity, mercy, compassion, understanding, tolerance. [➡FORGET, FORGIVE, AND ACCEPT; 749] *Opposite:* ruthlessness.

forgiving *adj* **merciful**, pardoning, lenient, forbearing (*formal*), magnanimous, sympathetic, compassionate, understanding, tolerant. [➡GENEROSITY AND KINDNESS; 496] *Opposite:* unforgiving.

forgo *v* **do without**, sacrifice, pass by, waive, relinquish, give up, abstain from, go without, decline, give a miss (*informal*), skip. [➡NOT DO AND REFUSE TO DO; 275] *Opposite:* take up.

forgotten *adj* **lost**, gone, neglected, disregarded, buried, unremembered. [➡ABSENT AND UNAVAILABLE; 7] *Opposite:* immortal.

for instance *adv* [➡EXPRESSIONS INTRODUCING EXAMPLES; 64]

fork 1 *n* **divide**, split, divergence, junction, branch, cleft, division, bifurcation. [➡SUBDIVISIONS AND OFFSHOOTS; 1252] 2 *type of* **cutlery**. [➡TABLEWARE, CUTLERY, AND KITCHENWARE; 861]

forked *adj* **split**, cleft, divided, branched, pronged, bifurcated. [➡ANGULAR SHAPE; 1216] *Opposite:* undivided.

forked lightning *n* [➡WINDY AND STORMY WEATHER; 1053]

fork out (*informal*) *v* [➡GIVE MONEY; 434]

fork over (*US informal*) *v* [➡GIVE MONEY; 434]

fork up (*informal*) *v* [➡GIVE MONEY; 434]

for life *adv* **for good**, forever, always, for keeps, permanently. [➡PERMANENCE: WITHOUT END; 94]

forlorn 1 *adj* **miserable**, sad, dejected, despondent, unhappy, hopeless, desperate. [➡SADNESS, DISTRESS, AND DESPAIR; 540] *Opposite:* cheerful. 2 *adj* **desolate**, neglected, abandoned, lonely, lost, forsaken, deserted, pitiful. [➡SOLITARINESS; 941] *Opposite:* cherished.

forlornly *adv* **miserably**, sadly, dejectedly, despondently, unhappily, hopelessly, desperately, desolately, pitifully. [➡ SADNESS, DISTRESS, AND DESPAIR; 540] *Opposite:* cheerfully.

form 1 *n* **structure**, state, condition, nature, status. [➡ STATE; 1207] 2 *n* **type**, variety, kind, mode, manner, style, way. [➡ VARIETY, TYPE, KIND; 146] 3 *n* **document**, paper, questionnaire, pro forma, blank, table, sheet. [➡ OFFICIAL DOCUMENTS; 587] 4 *n* **procedure**, method, system, arrangement, formula, custom, usage, practice, ritual. [➡ WAYS OF DOING THINGS; 295] 5 *n* **shape**, configuration, appearance, outline, look. [➡ SHAPE; 1215] 6 *type of* **den or nest.** [➡ ANIMAL OR BIRD ACCOMMODATION; 1078] 7 *v* **develop**, take shape, materialize, come into being, arise, grow. [➡ GRADUALLY COME INTO EXISTENCE; 1] 8 *v* **fashion**, shape, model, create, mould, construct, develop, produce. [➡ CREATION; 347] 9 *v* **start**, found, create, bring into being, establish, make, develop. [➡ INSTITUTE AND INAUGURATE; 349]

formal 1 *adj* **official**, proper, prescribed, recognized, strict, ceremonial, correct. [➡ LEVELS OF FORMALITY; 523] *Opposite:* informal. 2 *adj* **conventional**, reserved, stiff, prim, starched, decorous, correct, smart. [➡ LEVELS OF FORMALITY; 523] *Opposite:* relaxed.

formal attire *n* [➡ GARMENTS AND OUTFITS; 865]

formality 1 *n* **conventionalism**, reserve, stiffness, primness, correctness, decorum, smartness. [➡ LEVELS OF FORMALITY; 523] *Opposite:* informality. 2 *n* **procedure**, requirement, regulation, custom, ritual, ceremony, form, rule. [➡ WAYS OF DOING THINGS; 295]

formalization *n* **validation**, ratification, solemnization, reinforcement, celebration, enactment, sanctification. [➡ ARRANGE AND CREATE ORDER; 358]

formalize *v* **validate**, ratify, solemnize, reinforce, honour, celebrate, enact, sanctify. [➡ ARRANGE AND CREATE ORDER; 358]

formally *adv* **officially**, properly, lawfully, correctly, strictly, ceremoniously, legally. [➡ MORALLY GOOD; 775] *Opposite:* informally.

formal wear *n* [➡ GARMENTS AND OUTFITS; 865]

format 1 *n* **structure**, presentation, organization, arrangement, setup, plan, layout, design, system. [➡ SHAPE; 1215] 2 *v* **arrange**, lay out, organize, configure, set up, plan, structure, construct. [➡ ARRANGE AND CREATE ORDER; 358]

formation 1 *n* **arrangement**, configuration, shape, structure, pattern, disposition, setup, organization. [➡ QUALITIES AND CHARACTERISTICS; 1190] 2 *n* **creation**, development, construction, establishment, foundation, founding (*dated*), realization, materialization, growth. [➡ CREATION; 347]

formative *adj* **influential**, determinative, seminal, decisive, developmental, creative, foundational, constructive. [➡ FUNDAMENTAL; 196]

formative years *n* **childhood**, early life, early years, early childhood, infancy, babyhood, immaturity, adolescence, youth. [➡ BABYHOOD, CHILDHOOD, AND ADOLESCENCE; 917] *Opposite:* maturity.

former *adj* **previous**, past, ex-, earlier, prior, first, last, anterior. [➡ PAST; 84]

former times *n* [➡ PAST; 84]

formidable 1 *adj* **difficult**, tough, daunting, arduous, challenging, forbidding, terrible. [➡ DIFFICULTY AND COMPLEXITY; 243] *Opposite:* easy. 2 *adj* **alarming**, frightening, dreadful, fearsome, redoubtable, terrifying, intimidating. [➡ FRIGHTENING; 232] *Opposite:* encouraging. 3 *adj* **awe-inspiring**, impressive, remarkable, astounding, awesome, amazing, admirable. [➡ EXTRAORDINARY: AMAZING; 205] *Opposite:* uninspiring.

formidably 1 *adv* **dauntingly**, forbiddingly, horrendously, worryingly, disturbingly, fearfully, terribly, dreadfully. [➡ DIFFICULTY AND COMPLEXITY; 243] *Opposite:* wonderfully. 2 *adv* **awesomely**, impressively, compellingly, overwhelmingly, wonderfully, admirably, inspiringly, convincingly. [➡ EXTRAORDINARY: AMAZING; 205] 3 *adv* **frighteningly**, redoubtably, terrifyingly, viciously, alarmingly, dauntingly, intimidatingly, fearsomely, dreadfully, encouragingly. [➡ FRIGHTENING; 232]

formless *adj* **shapeless**, amorphous, unformed, unshaped, unstructured, indistinct, unshapen, unrecognizable. [➡ SHAPELESSNESS; 1218] *Opposite:* distinct.

formlessness *n* [➡ SHAPELESSNESS; 1218]

formula 1 *n* **method**, plan, modus operandi, recipe, prescription, procedure, rule, blueprint, formulary (*archaic or technical*), formulation, principle. [➡ WAYS OF DOING THINGS; 295] 2 *n* **cliché**, stock phrase, expression, phrase, formulation. [➡ FIGURES OF SPEECH; 674]

formulaic 1 *adj* **prescribed**, standard, rigid, fixed, set, methodic, systematic. [➡ BORING AND UNINTERESTING; 235] 2 *adj* **unoriginal**, imitative, clichéd, overused, mechanical, automatic. [➡ ORDINARINESS; 245] *Opposite:* original.

formulate 1 *v* **devise**, invent, prepare, put together, make, plan, create, originate. [➡ INSTITUTE AND INAUGURATE; 349] 2 *v* **express**, frame, put into words, verbalize, voice, articulate, communicate, convey, put across. [➡ UTTER AND PRONOUNCE; 609]

formulation 1 *n* **preparation**, design, construction, creation, invention, origination, interpretation, devising, drawing up, making. [➡ CREATION; 347] 2 *n* **expression**, articulation, verbalization, communication, presentation, conveyance, utterance. [➡ EXPLAIN AND CLARIFY; 611]

for nothing *adj* **free of charge**, for free, gratis, at no expense, cost-free, toll-free (*US*). [➡ GIFTS; 439]

for now *adv* **for the time being**, for the moment, in the interim, pro tem. [➡ PRESENT; 85] *Opposite:* always.

forsake 1 *v* **abandon**, leave, disown, quit, desert, ditch (*informal*), cast off, reject. [➡ RUN AWAY AND AVOID; 10] *Opposite:* support. 2 *v* **renounce**, relinquish, give up, turn your back on, sacrifice, abstain from. [➡ FOREGO AND DENY ONESELF; 450]

forsaken *adj* **abandoned**, cast off, ditched (*informal*), discarded, deserted, jilted, left in the lurch, rejected, disowned. [➡ SOLITARINESS; 941] *Opposite:* supported.

for sale *adj* **available**, on the market, on sale, purchasable. [➡ SELL; 442]

for sure 1 *adv* (*informal*) **certainly**, okay (*informal*), of course, naturally, definitely. [➡ CERTAIN; 175] 2 *adv* **definitely**, securely, positively, confidently, with certainty, with confidence, with assurance. [➡EXPRESSIONS OF AGREEMENT; 649] *Opposite:* tentatively.

forswear (*archaic or literary*) 1 *v* **reject**, renounce, abjure, give up, disown, dissociate from. [➡FOREGO AND DENY ONESELF; 450] *Opposite:* resort to. 2 *v* **deny**, disavow (*formal*), contradict, gainsay (*formal*), disclaim, swear, reject. [➡DENY AND REJECT; 645] *Opposite:* admit.

forsythia *type of* **shrub or bush**. [➡BUSHES AND SHRUBS; 1027]

fort *n* **fortification**, fortress, stronghold, citadel, castle, garrison, fastness. [➡FORTRESSES AND FORTIFICATIONS; 1089]

forte 1 *n* **strong point**, speciality, strong suit, gift, strength, talent. [➡SKILLS, TALENTS, AND ABILITIES; 527] *Opposite:* failing. 2 *type of* **musical term**. [➡MUSICAL TERMS; 912]

forth (*formal*) 1 *adv* **forwards**, ahead, onward. [➡DIRECTION OF MOTION; 346] *Opposite:* back. 2 *adv* **out**, into view, into the open, into the world. [➡DIRECTION OF MOTION; 346] *Opposite:* back.

forthcoming 1 *adj* **approaching**, impending, imminent, future, coming, upcoming (*US*). [➡FUTURE; 86] *Opposite:* distant. 2 *adj* **available**, ready, offered, supplied, in the offing, there. [➡PRESENT AND AVAILABLE; 11] *Opposite:* unavailable. 3 *adj* **helpful**, open, obliging, cooperative, informative, communicative. [➡THE WILL AND WILLINGNESS; 564] *Opposite:* reticent.

for the meantime *adv* **meanwhile**, in the meantime, in the interim, in the intervening time, for now, for the time being, temporarily, for the moment. [➡PRESENT; 85]

for the time being *adv* **for now**, for the moment, in the interim, pro tem. [➡PRESENT; 85]

forthright *adj* **up-front** (*informal*), straightforward, direct, frank, outspoken, plain-spoken, blunt, candid, honest. [➡HONEST AND OPEN; 631] *Opposite:* timid.

forthrightness *n* **frankness**, candour, directness, candidness, outspokenness, bluntness, honesty. [➡HONEST AND OPEN; 631] *Opposite:* timidity.

forthwith (*formal*) *adv* **immediately**, without delay, at once, directly, straightaway, instantly. [➡PRESENT; 85] *Opposite:* later.

fortification 1 *n* **defences**, ramparts, buttresses, walls, ditches, protection. [➡FORTRESSES AND FORTIFICATIONS; 1089] 2 *n* **strengthening**, defence, reinforcement, buttressing, building up. [➡IMPROVE STRENGTH AND DURABILITY; 379] *Opposite:* erosion.

fortified 1 *adj* **defended**, protected, walled, garrisoned, secured, armoured, safeguarded. [➡SAFE AND SAFETY; 192] *Opposite:* exposed. 2 *adj* **reinforced**, strengthened, hardened, buttressed, toughened, supported, braced. [➡STRENGTH; 202] *Opposite:* unsupported. 3 *adj* **encouraged**, heartened, invigorated, reinvigorated, stimulated, refreshed, exhilarated, cheered, revived. [➡CALMNESS, CONFIDENCE, AND COMPOSURE; 537] *Opposite:* drained.

fortify 1 *v* **defend**, protect, wall, garrison, secure, safeguard. [➡PREVENT CONTACT OR ATTACK; 420] *Opposite:* expose. 2 *v* **make stronger**, strengthen, reinforce, brace, support, buttress, toughen, harden. [➡IMPROVE STRENGTH AND DURABILITY; 379] *Opposite:* weaken. 3 *v* **enrich**, boost, enhance, improve, mix, lace. [➡CHANGE OF INTENSITY: MORE; 395] *Opposite:* deplete. 4 *v* **give a boost to**, revive, refresh, reinvigorate, invigorate, exhilarate, pep up (*informal*), hearten, cheer, encourage. [➡ENCOURAGE; 577] *Opposite:* drain. 5 *v* **build up**, boost, bolster, augment (*formal*), support, sustain, strengthen. [➡IMPROVE STRENGTH AND DURABILITY; 379] *Opposite:* weaken.

fortissimo *type of* **musical term**. [➡MUSICAL TERMS; 912]

fortitude *n* **strength**, courage, resilience, guts (*slang*), staying power, grit, stamina, determination, endurance. [➡COURAGE; 499] *Opposite:* weakness.

fortnight *type of* **time period**. [➡TIMES OF YEAR; 88]

fortnightly *adv* [➡TIMES OF YEAR; 88]

fortress *n* **stronghold**, fort, citadel, fortification, bastion, castle. [➡FORTRESSES AND FORTIFICATIONS; 1089]

fortuitous *adj* **accidental**, chance, casual, unexpected, unplanned, incidental. [➡CHANCE, COINCIDENCE, AND ACCIDENT; 787] *Opposite:* planned.

fortunate 1 *adj* **privileged**, lucky, blessed, jammy (*informal*), well-off, prosperous. [➡WEALTH AND WEALTHY; 891] *Opposite:* unfortunate. 2 *adj* **lucky**, providential, happy, opportune, auspicious, fortuitous. [➡LUCK; 784] *Opposite:* unfortunate.

See Compare and Contrast at **lucky**.

fortunately 1 *adv* **as luck would have it**, by chance, luckily, providentially, opportunely, auspiciously, fortuitously. [➡LUCK; 784] *Opposite:* unfortunately. 2 *adv* **happily**, luckily, mercifully, thank goodness, thank heavens. [➡EXPRESSIONS OF SURPRISE; 547] *Opposite:* unfortunately.

fortune 1 *n* **wealth**, riches, affluence, opulence, prosperity, treasure. [➡FINANCIAL ASSETS; 463] *Opposite:* poverty. 2 *n* **packet** (*informal*), bomb (*informal*), mint (*informal*), pile (*informal*), tidy sum (*informal*), an arm and a leg (*informal*). [➡LARGE AMOUNT OF MONEY; 141] *Opposite:* pittance. 3 *n* **luck**, chance, providence, accident, fate. [➡LUCK; 784] *Opposite:* design. 4 *n* **destiny**, fate, kismet, karma, future, lot. [➡FATE, DESTINY, AND ASTROLOGY; 783] *Opposite:* past.

fortune-teller *n* **clairvoyant**, seer, soothsayer, psychic, medium, astrologer, mystic. [➡PEOPLE WITH SUPERNATURAL POWERS; 789]

fortune telling *n* [➡THE SUPERNATURAL; 788]

forty winks (*informal*) *n* **nap**, doze, sleep, siesta, catnap, power nap, snooze (*informal*). [➡SLEEP AND DREAM; 724]

forum 1 *n* **opportunity**, medium, environment, setting, scene, aid. [➡SITUATIONS; 71] 2 *n* **meeting**, debate, discussion, round table, conference, assembly, council. [➡MEETINGS AND ASSEMBLIES; 43]

forward 1 *adj* **onward**, advancing, frontwards, headlong, headfirst, accelerative. [➡DIRECTION OF MOTION; 346] *Opposite:* backward. 2 *adj* **presumptuous**, self-assured, bold, familiar, cheeky, brazen, uninhibited, forthright, direct, overfriendly. [➡BAD MANNERS AND SOCIAL SKILLS; 522] *Opposite:* reticent. 3 *v* **send**, dispatch, post, send on, redirect, pass on, mail. [➡DESPATCH AND SEND; 334] 4 *v* **advance**, promote, further, progress, accelerate. [➡CAUSE TO HAPPEN; 31] *Opposite:* hold back.

forward-looking *adj* **progressive**, modern, forward-thinking, avant-garde, open-minded, revolutionary. [➡THE NATURE OF IDEAS; 772] *Opposite:* backward-looking.

forwardness *n* **boldness**, directness, brazenness, forthrightness, self-assurance, presumptuousness, cheek (*informal*), overfriendliness, informality. [➡HONEST AND OPEN; 631] *Opposite:* reticence.

forwards 1 *adv* **ahead**, frontwards, to the fore, up, onward. [➡DIRECTION OF MOTION; 346] *Opposite:* backwards. 2 *adv* **to the fore**, into view, into the open, up. [➡DIRECTION OF MOTION; 346] *Opposite:* backwards.

forward-thinking *adj* **progressive**, advanced, forward-looking, radical, avant-garde, revolutionary, cutting-edge. [➡POSITIVE INTELLECTUAL CHARACTERISTICS; 525] *Opposite:* old-fashioned.

fosse *n* [➡WATERCOURSES; 1110]

fossil *n* **relic**, remnant, vestige, remains. [➡REMAINDER AND REMAINDERS; 123]

fossilization *n* **petrification**, preservation, calcification, hardening, solidification, ossification, turning into stone. [➡HARDEN, CONGEAL, DRY; 388]

fossilize *v* **turn into stone**, petrify, solidify, harden, calcify, ossify. [➡HARDEN, CONGEAL, DRY; 388]

foster 1 *v* **look after**, care for, take in, bring up, nurture, raise, adopt. [➡TAKE CARE OF AND SPOIL; 301] 2 *v* **promote**, further, advance, cultivate, forward, encourage. [➡MAKE POSSIBLE; 276] *Opposite:* discourage. 3 *adj* **stand-in**, substitute, adoptive, temporary, short-term. [➡RELATIONSHIP TO ANOTHER; 973] *Opposite:* natural.

foster child *n* **child**, dependant, adoptee, ward. [➡ADOPTION, FOSTERING, AND EXTENDED FAMILY; 962] *Opposite:* foster parent.

foster father *n* [➡ADOPTION, FOSTERING, AND EXTENDED FAMILY; 962]

foster mother *n* [➡ADOPTION, FOSTERING, AND EXTENDED FAMILY; 962]

foster parent *n* **substitute parent**, carer, guardian, foster mother, foster father, adoptive parent. [➡ADOPTION, FOSTERING, AND EXTENDED FAMILY; 962] *Opposite:* foster child.

foul 1 *adj* **unpleasant**, disgusting, offensive, distasteful, filthy, indecent, dirty. [➡DISGUSTING AND REPULSIVE; 231] *Opposite:* pleasant. 2 *adj* **unclean**, stinking, rank (*literary*), polluted, tainted, soiled, fetid. [➡DIRTY; 1234] *Opposite:* clean. 3 *adj* (*informal*) **horrible**, rotten, unpleasant, nasty, dreadful, frightful, abominable. [➡EMOTIONALLY UNPLEASANT AND UPSETTING; 228] *Opposite:* charming. 4 *adj* **vulgar**, obscene, lewd, profane, uncouth, unwholesome, coarse, filthy, indecent. [➡MORALLY BAD; 776] *Opposite:* decent. 5 *adj* **dishonest**, shady, criminal, treacherous, dishonourable, crooked (*informal*). [➡MORALLY BAD; 776] *Opposite:* legitimate. 6 *adj* **inclement**, stormy, wet, unpleasant, rotten, dreadful, frightful. [➡PHYSICALLY UNPLEASANT; 227] *Opposite:* fair. 7 *v* **entangle**, tangle up, catch, ensnarl, snarl, ensnare. [➡CAPTIVITY AND LOSS OF FREEDOM; 249] *Opposite:* free. 8 *v* **pollute**, soil, make dirty, contaminate, sully (*literary*), defile (*formal*), taint, mess up (*informal*). [➡DIRTY AND CONTAMINATE; 405]

foully *adv* **offensively**, obscenely, abhorrently (*formal*), disgustingly, repugnantly, revoltingly, unpleasantly, grossly. [➡DISGUSTING AND REPULSIVE; 231] *Opposite:* delightfully.

foul-mouthed *adj* **blasphemous**, crude, rude, dirty, vulgar, coarse. [➡RUDE AND HOSTILE; 626] *Opposite:* polite.

foulness 1 *n* **filth**, filthiness, squalor, pollution, muck (*informal*), dirt, mire, uncleanness, muckiness (*informal*), vileness, murkiness, dirtiness, unwholesomeness. [➡DIRTY; 1234] *Opposite:* cleanness. 2 *n* **vulgarity**, obscenity, lewdness, profanity, uncouthness, unwholesomeness, coarseness, filth, indecency. [➡MORALLY BAD; 776] *Opposite:* decency.

foul play 1 *n* **deviousness**, unfairness, cheating, trickery, monkey business (*informal*), shenanigans (*informal*). [➡UNKIND ACTION OR BEHAVIOUR; 297] 2 *n* **criminal action**, treachery, dishonesty, villainy, violence, crime, treacherousness. [➡MORALLY BAD; 776] *Opposite:* honesty.

foul-smelling *adj* **smelly**, humming (*informal*), reeking, malodorous, rank (*literary*), fetid, rotten, putrid, nauseating, sour, rancid. [➡SMELL AND SMELLING; 706] *Opposite:* sweet-smelling.

foul-tasting *adj* **nasty**, disgusting, unpleasant, indigestible, revolting, nauseating, unpalatable, rancid, bitter, sour. [➡TASTE; 704]

foul up (*informal*) *v* [➡MESS UP AND MAKE MISTAKES; 473]

foul-up (*informal*) *n* **blunder**, bungle (*informal*), slip, slip-up (*informal*), mix-up, error, mistake, mishap. [➡MISTAKES; 251] *Opposite:* success.

found *v* **originate**, set up, create, start, bring into being, initiate, institute, establish. [➡INSTITUTE AND INAUGURATE; 349] *Opposite:* close.

foundation 1 *n* **basis**, grounds, substance, groundwork, underpinning, footing. [➡SUPPORTS AND BASES; 1254] 2 *n* **establishment**, institution, charity, institute, society, organization. [➡CHARITY AND CHARITABLE INSTITUTIONS; 822]

foundation garment *type of* **lower body underwear**. [➡HABERDASHERY, MILLINERY, AND LINGERIE; 867]

founder 1 *n* **creator**, originator, initiator, organizer, forefather, author. [➡DESIGNERS, CREATORS, AND INSTIGATORS; 348] 2 *v* **sink**, go down, plunge, wallow, submerge, wreck. [➡TAKE UP A NEW POSITION; 313] *Opposite:* float. 3 *v* **fail**, break down, come to nothing, fall through, miscarry, misfire, come to grief. [➡FAIL OR BE UNSUCCESSFUL; 75] *Opposite:* succeed.

foundling (*dated*) *n* **orphan**, waif, stray, ragamuffin (*dated*), urchin, outcast. [➡SOLITARY PEOPLE; 942]

foundry *type of* **factory**. [➡INDUSTRIAL BUILDINGS; 1086]

fount (*literary*) *n* **source**, fountain, well, spring, wellspring, fountainhead, origin. [➡RIVERS, LAKES, AND STREAMS; 1042]

fountain 1 *n* **cascade**, water feature, spout, jet, spring, source, spray. [➡RIVERS, LAKES, AND STREAMS; 1042] 2 *n* **source**, origin, cause, beginning, fountainhead, fount. [➡BEGINNING; 53]

fountainhead 1 *n* **spring**, source, wellspring, wellhead, fount, fountain. [➡RIVERS, LAKES, AND STREAMS; 1042] 2 *n* **source**, origin, fount, seed, nucleus. [➡BEGINNING; 53]

fountain pen *type of* **pen.** [➡WRITING AND DRAWING IMPLEMENTS, AND MEDIA; 602]

four-by-four *type of* **car.** [➡BIKES, CARS, AND CARRIAGES; 1148]

four-letter word *n* **swearword**, vulgarity, vulgarism, obscenity, expletive, oath, curse, cussword (*US informal*). [➡INSULTS, ABUSE, AND SWEARING; 659] *Opposite:* euphemism.

four-poster *type of* **bed.** [➡FURNITURE; 858]

foursome *n* **group of four**, quartet, group, ensemble. [➡GROUPS OF PEOPLE; 935]

fourth *n* **quarter**, twenty-five percent, fourth part. [➡MEASUREABLE PORTION; 125]

fowl

◆ *types of fowl*
bantam, broiler (*US*), chicken, duck, goose, grouse, guinea fowl, partridge, pheasant, pigeon, quail, turkey, waterfowl, wildfowl, woodcock

fox 1 *v* **confuse**, baffle, muddle, puzzle, perplex, flummox (*informal*), stump. [➡CONFUSE AND BEWILDER; 572] *Opposite:* enlighten. 2 *v* **deceive**, trick, bamboozle (*informal*), outwit, fool, con, hoodwink. [➡DECEPTION AND LIES; 661] *Opposite:* enlighten. 3 *type of* **canine.** [➡CANINE; 979]

foxglove *type of* **perennial flower.** [➡FLOWERS; 1032]

foxhound *type of* **small dog.** [➡DOG; 980]

foxtrot *type of* **dance.** [➡DANCE; 903]

foxy 1 *adj* **foxlike**, vulpine, canine, pungent, strong, sharp. [➡SMELL AND SMELLING; 706] 2 *adj* **sly**, cunning, crafty, sharp, wily, astute, shrewd, tricky. [➡DECEITFUL; 514] *Opposite:* naive.

foyer 1 *n* **lobby**, vestibule, reception area, hall, entrance hall, hallway. [➡DOORS AND ACCESS POINTS; 1100] 2 *type of* **room in public buildings.** [➡TYPES OF ROOM; 1096]

fracas *n* **quarrel**, row, fight, brawl, melee, argument, disturbance, scuffle. [➡CHAOS AND UPROAR; 51] *Opposite:* calm.

fraction 1 *n* **part**, portion, segment, section, division, element. [➡MEASUREABLE PORTION; 125] *Opposite:* whole. 2 *n* **little bit**, little, small part, tiny proportion, small percentage. [➡SMALL PIECE; 127]

fractional *adj* **slight**, small, tiny, minuscule, insignificant, paltry. [➡SMALL; 1194] *Opposite:* great.

fractionally *adv* **slightly**, marginally, just, a little, a fraction. [➡TO A CERTAIN EXTENT; 134] *Opposite:* greatly.

fractious *adj* **irritable**, peevish, restless, complaining, testy (*informal*), grumpy, touchy. [➡IRRITATION AND ANGER; 542] *Opposite:* even-tempered.

fracture 1 *n* **break**, breakage, crack, rupture, fissure, hairline fracture, splintering. [➡HOLES, GAPS, AND FORKS; 1251] *Opposite:* repair. 2 *v* **crack**, break, rupture, splinter, split, shatter. [➡TEAR, BREAK, AND CUT; 361] *Opposite:* mend.

fractured *adj* [➡IN BAD REPAIR; 1233]

fragile 1 *adj* **delicate**, brittle, flimsy, breakable, frail, insubstantial, frangible, friable. [➡FRAGILE; 1208] *Opposite:* sturdy. 2 *adj* **tenuous**, unstable, delicate, precarious, shaky, slight. [➡WEAKNESS; 242] *Opposite:* stable. 3 *adj* **frail**, weak, delicate, infirm, feeble, in poor health. [➡UNFIT AND WEAK; 740] *Opposite:* strong.

Compare and Contrast: ***fragile, delicate, frail, flimsy, frangible, friable***

CORE MEANING: EASILY BROKEN OR DAMAGED

fragile not having a strong structure or not made of robust materials, and therefore easily broken or damaged; ***delicate*** similar to *fragile*, used especially to talk about things that are beautiful or remarkable because of their fragility; ***frail*** easily broken or damaged, or physically weak and vulnerable to injury; ***flimsy*** too easily broken, torn, or damaged, especially used of badly or cheaply made goods, or light and insubstantial clothing; ***frangible*** capable of being broken or easily damaged; ***friable*** easily reduced to tiny particles.

fragility 1 *n* **brittleness**, flimsiness, delicateness, delicacy, breakability, friability, crumbliness, insubstantiality, instability. [➡FRAGILE; 1208] *Opposite:* solidity. 2 *n* **tenuousness**, instability, delicacy, delicateness, precariousness, shakiness. [➡DIFFICULTY AND COMPLEXITY; 243] *Opposite:* stability. 3 *n* **frailty**, weakness, feebleness, ill health, infirmity. [➡UNFIT AND WEAK; 740] *Opposite:* strength.

fragment 1 *n* **piece**, portion, bit, splinter, sliver, section, part, chip, scrap. [➡SMALL PIECE; 127] *Opposite:* whole. 2 *v* **break**, divide, break up, disintegrate, crumble, shatter, fall to pieces, split, fall apart, destroy. [➡TEAR, BREAK, AND CUT; 361] *Opposite:* fuse.

fragmentary *adj* **incomplete**, disconnected, bitty, scrappy, patchy, fragmented. [➡UNFINISHEDNESS; 240] *Opposite:* entire.

fragmentation *n* **disintegration**, destruction, shattering, breaking up, crumbling, division. [➡TEAR, BREAK, AND CUT; 361] *Opposite:* fusion.

fragmented *adj* **disjointed**, uneven, scrappy, bitty, patchy. [➡UNFINISHEDNESS; 240] *Opposite:* continuous.

fragrance 1 *n* **smell**, scent, perfume, bouquet, aroma, odour. [➡SMELL AND SMELLING; 706] 2 *n* **cologne**, scent, perfume, toilet water, eau de toilette, attar. [➡PERSONAL HYGIENE; 492]

See Compare and Contrast at **smell**.

fragranced *adj* **perfumed**, scented, sweet-smelling, fragrant. [➡SMELL AND SMELLING; 706]

fragrant *adj* **perfumed**, aromatic, scented, sweet-smelling, fragranced, odorous. [➡SMELL AND SMELLING; 706] *Opposite:* smelly.

fraidy-cat (*US informal*) *n* [➡LAZY OR UNSUCCESSFUL PEOPLE; 948]

frail 1 *adj* **weak**, infirm, delicate, feeble, puny, in poor health, fragile. [➡UNFIT AND WEAK; 740] *Opposite:* robust. 2 *adj* **flimsy**, insubstantial, fragile, delicate, spindly, brittle. [➡WEAKNESS; 242] *Opposite:* sturdy.

See Compare and Contrast at **fragile, weak.**

frailty 1 *n* **infirmity**, weakness, feebleness, fragility, puniness, ill health. [➡UNFIT AND WEAK; 740] *Opposite:* robustness. 2 *n* **shortcoming**, weakness, imperfection, failing, defect, flaw, vice. [➡FAULTS, FLAWS, AND WEAKNESSES; 252] *Opposite:* strength.

frame 1 *n* **structure**, framework, scaffold, skeleton, support, construction. [➡PARTS OF A BUILDING; 1094] 2 *n* **edge**, surround, border, mount, setting, edging. [➡EXTREMITIES OF PHYSICAL OBJECTS; 1249] *Opposite:* inner. 3 *n* **body**, form, build, physique, skeleton, structure. [➡THE BONES AND JOINTS; 720] 4 *v* **enclose**, mount, border, edge, outline, surround. [➡EXIST IN CLOSE PROXIMITY; 21] *Opposite:* inset. 5 *v* (*slang*) **trap**, entrap, set up (*informal*), trick, entice, fit up (*slang*). [➡FALSIFY AND CHEAT; 177]

frame of mind *n* **mood**, mental state, mental condition, humour, temper, disposition. [➡PSYCHOLOGY AND THE MIND; 770]

frame of reference *n* **context**, situation, standpoint, background, setting, belief system. [➡POINT OF VIEW; 768]

frame-up (*slang*) *n* **trap**, setup (*informal*), entrapment, snare, fit-up (*slang*), sting (*US slang*). [➡DECEPTION AND LIES; 661]

framework 1 *n* **structure**, frame, scaffold, skeleton, support, construction. [➡QUALITIES AND CHARACTERISTICS; 1190] 2 *n* **outline**, agenda, basis, context, background, charter, structure. [➡WAYS OF DOING THINGS; 295]

franchise 1 *n* **permit**, licence, contract, authorization, charter, agreement. [➡PERMIT AND ALLOW; 670] 2 *v* **license**, permit, contract, contract out, grant, authorize. [➡PERMIT AND ALLOW; 670]

frangible *adj* **breakable**, fragile, brittle, easily broken. [➡FRAGILE; 1208]

See Compare and Contrast at **fragile.**

frank *adj* **forthright**, free, honest, guileless, open, blunt, truthful, candid, aboveboard, outspoken. [➡HONEST AND OPEN; 631] *Opposite:* insincere.

frankfurter *n* **hot dog**, sausage, frank (*US informal*), wiener (*US*), wienerwurst (*US*). [➡TYPES AND CUTS OF MEAT; 1176]

frankness *n* **honesty**, forthrightness, openness, bluntness, truthfulness, candour, guilelessness, outspokenness. [➡HONEST AND RELIABLE; 503] *Opposite:* insincerity.

frantic 1 *adj* **panicky**, hysterical, beside yourself, desperate, agitated, wild, uptight (*informal*), worried, anxious. [➡CONFUSION, ANXIETY, AND WORRY; 541] *Opposite:* calm. 2 *adj* **frenzied**, frenetic, hectic, feverish, wild, last-minute. [➡DISORDER AND CHAOS; 246] *Opposite:* calm.

fraternal 1 *adj* **sibling**, brotherly, brother's, familial, genealogical. [➡THE FAMILY; 956] 2 *adj* **comradely**, brotherly, friendly, amicable, communal, amiable. [➡RELATIONSHIP TO ANOTHER; 973] *Opposite:* hostile.

fraternity 1 *n* **community**, clan (*informal*), network, group, world. [➡GROUPS WITH A COMMON INTEREST; 938] 2 *n* **brotherliness**, brotherhood, comradeship, mutual support, friendship, friendliness. [➡RELATIONSHIP TO ANOTHER; 973] *Opposite:* hostility. 3 *n* (*US*) **society**, clan (*informal*), guild, association, gang, group, frat (*US*). [➡STUDENTS AND PUPILS; 841]

fraternization *n* **mixing**, socializing, intercourse, mingling, partying, collaborating, involvement, relations. [➡COMMUNICATION; 603] *Opposite:* avoidance.

fraternize *v* **associate**, consort (*formal*), socialize, mix, hang out (*informal*), hobnob (*disapproving*), go around with (*informal*). [➡ESTABLISHING RELATIONSHIPS WITH OTHERS; 974] *Opposite:* avoid.

fraud 1 *n* **dishonesty**, deceit, deception, double-dealing, trickery, cheating, snake oil (*US*), smoke and mirrors (*US*). [➡DECEPTION AND LIES; 661] *Opposite:* honesty. 2 *n* **impostor**, charlatan, hoaxer, swindler, cheat, fake, sham, phoney, fraudster. [➡PEOPLE WHO DECEIVE; 662] 3 *n* **deception**, con, scheme, swindle, deceit, fake, counterfeit, scam (*slang*), racket (*informal*), imitation, sham, wooden nickel (*US*). [➡CRIMES; 817]

fraud squad *n* [➡THE POLICE, ARREST, AND PRE-TRIAL PROCEEDINGS; 818]

fraudster *n* **confidence trickster**, swindler, cheat, hoaxer, charlatan, impostor, fraud, fake, sham, phoney. [➡PEOPLE WHO DECEIVE; 662]

fraudulence *n* **deceit**, duplicity, deceitfulness, illegitimacy, dishonesty, deception, imposture (*formal*), illegality. [➡DECEPTION AND LIES; 661] *Opposite:* honesty.

fraudulent *adj* **fake**, deceitful, untrue, duplicitous, dishonest, sham, false, falsified, counterfeit, imitation, illegal. [➡FALSE AND UNREAL; 174] *Opposite:* genuine.

fraught 1 *adj* **full**, beset (*formal*), charged, filled, weighed down, laden. [➡FULL; 1238] *Opposite:* free. 2 *adj* **tense**, anxious, nervous, uptight (*informal*), troubled, apprehensive. [➡CONFUSION, ANXIETY, AND WORRY; 541] *Opposite:* calm.

fray 1 *v* **unravel**, ravel, wear, wear out, tatter, distress. [➡TEAR, BREAK, AND CUT; 361] *Opposite:* mend. 2 *n* **fight**, argument, quarrel, fracas, dispute, disagreement, affray. [➡AGGRESSIVE EVENT; 39]

frayed *adj* **threadbare**, worn, tattered, ragged, unravelled, distressed. [➡IN BAD REPAIR; 1233]

frazzled (*informal*) *adj* **exhausted**, weary, tired out, drained, stressed out (*informal*), fatigued. [➡TIRED, ASLEEP, AND UNCONSCIOUS; 739] *Opposite:* lively.

freak 1 *n* **curiosity**, rarity, oddity, one-off, aberration, anomaly. [➡MISTAKES; 251] 2 *n* **chance**, surprise, happenstance, accident, fluke (*informal*), one-off. [➡CHANCE EVENT; 36] 3 *n* (*informal*) **enthusiast**, fanatic, fiend, buff, nut (*informal*), lover. [➡DEVOTEES AND ADDICTED PEOPLE; 557]

freakish *adj* **variable**, volatile, changeable, unpredictable, inexplicable, mercurial. [➡FINITENESS, VARIABILITY, AND TRANSIENCE; 96] *Opposite:* stable.

freak out (*informal*) *v* [➡GIVING VENT TO EMOTIONS; 680]

freaky *adj* **weird**, strange, amazing, grotesque, unexpected, unusual, odd, unnatural, abnormal, bizarre, chance. [➡BIZARRE AND PECULIAR; 258] *Opposite:* commonplace.

freckle *n* **spot**, mark, patch, speckle, speck, blotch, mole. [➡COMPLEXION; 481]

freckled *adj* **speckled**, freckly, dappled, spotted, stippled, dotted, flecked. [➡DESCRIBING PATTERNS; 1226]

freckly *adj* [➡COMPLEXION; 481]

free 1 *adj* **allowed**, at liberty, permitted, able, welcome, unrestricted. [➡FREEDOM AND LIBERTY; 209] *Opposite:* restricted. **2** *adj* **liberated**, unbound, released, emancipated, freed, set free. [➡FREEDOM AND LIBERTY; 209] *Opposite:* imprisoned. **3** *adj* **unrestricted**, unregimented, unconventional, loose, unstructured, open. [➡FREEDOM AND LIBERTY; 209] *Opposite:* conventional. **4** *adj* **gratis**, free of charge, without charge, at no cost, complimentary, on the house. [➡GIFTS; 439] *Opposite:* expensive. **5** *adj* **relaxing**, off, available, unoccupied, on holiday, on vacation (*US*). [➡FREEDOM AND LIBERTY; 209] *Opposite:* working. **6** *adj* **open**, uninhibited, uncontrolled, spontaneous, honest, expansive. [➡HONEST AND OPEN; 631] *Opposite:* inhibited. **7** *v* **release**, let go, set free, liberate, emancipate, deliver (*literary*). [➡FREEDOM AND LIBERTY; 209] *Opposite:* imprison. **8** *v* **exempt**, rid, unhamper, unburden, excuse, pardon, let off. [➡FREEDOM AND LIBERTY; 209] *Opposite:* hamper.

free-and-easy *adj* **indulgent**, overindulgent, lax, overfamiliar, relaxed, laid-back (*informal*) [➡PERMIT AND ALLOW; 670]. *Opposite:* uptight (*informal*).

freebie (*informal*) *n* **free sample**, handout, giveaway (*informal*), perk, free gift, free offer, free go (*US*). [➡GIFTS; 439]

freedom 1 *n* **liberty**, autonomy, lack of restrictions, self-determination, independence, choice, free will, sovereignty. [➡FREEDOM AND LIBERTY; 209] *Opposite:* restriction. **2** *n* **looseness**, inventiveness, nonconformity. [➡REBELLIOUSNESS AND DISOBEDIENCE; 566] *Opposite:* conformity. **3** *n* **frankness**, openness, abandon, free expression, candour, ease. [➡HONEST AND OPEN; 631] *Opposite:* inhibition.

free fall 1 *n* **skydive**, jump, descent, drop, fall, dive. [➡GO DOWNWARDS; 308] **2** *n* **decline**, descent, collapse, confusion, turmoil, chaos. [➡FAILURE; 77] *Opposite:* upturn.

free-fall 1 *v* **skydive**, drop, plummet, fall, descend, jump, parachute, dive. [➡GO DOWNWARDS; 308] **2** *v* **drop**, bomb (*informal*), plummet, collapse, decline, fall apart, go pear-shaped (*informal*), self-destruct. [➡FAIL OR BE UNSUCCESSFUL; 75] *Opposite:* soar.

free-for-all (*informal*) *n* **brawl**, fight, set-to (*informal*), brouhaha (*formal*), riot, scuffle, fracas, commotion. [➡CHAOS AND UPROAR; 51]

free gift *n* **giveaway** (*informal*), freebie (*informal*), free sample, free offer. [➡GIFTS; 439]

freehand *adj* **without a pattern**, by eye, by hand, untraced, sketchy, free. [➡ARTISTIC MOVEMENTS AND STYLES; 899]

freehanded (*US*) *adj* **generous**, openhanded, liberal, unstinting, giving, bountiful (*literary*) [➡GENEROSITY AND KINDNESS; 496]. *Opposite:* stingy (*informal*).

freehold 1 *n* **tenure**, ownership, right, occupancy. [➡ACCOMMODATION; 855] **2** *n* **property**, estate, land, building, holding. [➡POSSESSIONS; 462]

freeholder *n* **property owner**, landowner, owner, holder, landlord, landholder. [➡OWNERS; 447]

freeing *n* **release**, liberation, acquittal, emancipation, freedom, deliverance (*formal*). [➡FREEDOM AND LIBERTY; 209] *Opposite:* capture.

freelance *adj* **self-employed**, temporary, irregular, casual, ad hoc. [➡EMPLOYMENT STATUS; 831] *Opposite:* permanent.

freelancer *n* [➡WORKER; 836]

freelancing *n* [➡TYPES OF WORK; 835]

freeload (*informal*) *v* **sponge**, live off others, parasitize, scrounge (*informal*), take advantage, use others. [➡TAKE SOMETHING AWAY; 426]

freeloader (*informal*) *n* **sponger** (*informal*), slacker, scrounger (*informal*), sponge, parasite, idler, hanger-on, user. [➡LAZY OR UNSUCCESSFUL PEOPLE; 948]

freely 1 *adv* **without restrictions**, at will, at liberty, easily, spontaneously, without obstruction. [➡FREEDOM AND LIBERTY; 209] **2** *adv* **liberally**, generously, unreservedly, without restraint, without stinting, to all comers. [➡FREEDOM AND LIBERTY; 209] *Opposite:* parsimoniously.

free of charge *adj* **gratis**, free, without charge, at no cost, complimentary, on the house, cost-free, toll-free (*US*). [➡GIFTS; 439]

free-range *adj* **unconfined**, happy, free, loose, at large, uncaged, unrestricted, at liberty. [➡FREEDOM AND LIBERTY; 209] *Opposite:* battery.

freesia *type of* **flower grown from bulb**. [➡FLOWERS FROM BULBS; 1030]

free spirit *n* **individualist**, nonconformist, maverick, freethinker, rebel. [➡SOLITARY PEOPLE; 942] *Opposite:* conformist.

freestanding *adj* **self-supporting**, unconnected, separate, detached, unattached, isolated. [➡UNRELATEDNESS AND SEPARATENESS; 147] *Opposite:* attached.

freethinker *n* **individualist**, free spirit, nonconformist, nonbeliever, sceptic, rationalist. [➡PHILOSOPHICAL AND POLITICAL THINKERS; 782] *Opposite:* conformist.

freethinking *adj* **independent**, open-minded, enlightened, nonconformist, liberal, unconventional, radical, individualistic, rational, tolerant. [➡POSITIVE INTELLECTUAL CHARACTERISTICS; 525] *Opposite:* conformist.

free time *n* **leisure**, leisure time, spare time, time off, recreation, rest time. [➡PERIOD OF REST; 91]

free up 1 *v* **make available**, empty, make space for, clear, liberate. [➡EMPTY AND UNLOAD; 408] *Opposite:* occupy. **2** *v* (*informal*) **loosen**, unjam, unblock, unsnarl, unclog, clear. [➡UNFASTEN AND UNDO; 410] *Opposite:* snarl.

free verse *n* [➡POETRY AND VERSE; 915]

freeway (*US*) *type of* **major road**. [➡ROADS; 1105]

freewheel 1 *v* **coast**, sail, glide, cruise, roll along.

[➡PROCEED AND GO; 306] **2** *v* **take it easy**, drift, go with the flow, cruise. [➡LACK OF ACTIVITY; 343] *Opposite:* struggle.

freewheeling (*US*) **1** *adj* **carefree**, free and easy, easy-going, unrestricted, laid-back (*informal*), self-indulgent, permissive, laissez faire. [➡CHEERFULNESS OF OUTLOOK; 504] **2** *adj* **wide-ranging**, open-ended, unstructured, unrestricted, no-holds-barred, open, undefined. [➡FREEDOM AND LIBERTY; 209] *Opposite:* methodical.

free will *n* **autonomy**, self-determination, choice, liberty, freedom, independence. [➡PHILOSOPHIES AND BELIEFS; 781] *Opposite:* dependence.

freeze **1** *v* **turn to ice**, solidify, congeal, harden, ice up, ice over. [➡HARDEN, CONGEAL, DRY; 388] *Opposite:* thaw. **2** *v* **refrigerate**, chill, cool, preserve. [➡HARDEN, CONGEAL, DRY; 388] *Opposite:* thaw. **3** *v* **halt**, stop, stop in your tracks, stop dead, stiffen, immobilize. [➡STOP ACTING; 265] *Opposite:* relax. **4** *v* **suspend**, stop, halt, hold, break off, mothball, shelve. [➡CAUSE TO STOP; 267] *Opposite:* resume. **5** *v* **hold**, fix, restrict, stop, control, halt, immobilize, check, arrest. [➡CAUSE TO STOP; 267] *Opposite:* vary. **6** *n* **restriction**, halt, embargo, check, stoppage, suspension, interruption, stay. [➡END; 54] *Opposite:* resumption.

freeze out *v* **exclude**, ostracize, give the cold shoulder, be incapacitated, ignore, send to Coventry, neglect, reject, drive away. [➡REFUSING OR REJECTING RELATIONS; 975] *Opposite:* welcome.

freezer *type of* **cooling appliance**. [➡HEATING, REFRIGERATION, AND VENTILATION; 1141]

freeze up *v* **ice over**, ice up, harden, solidify, freeze. [➡HARDEN, CONGEAL, DRY; 388] *Opposite:* thaw.

freezing *adj* **cold**, subzero, icy, chilly, bitter, glacial. [➡COLD WEATHER; 1051] *Opposite:* hot.

freight **1** *n* **cargo**, goods, merchandise, consignment, load, goods in transit. [➡TRANSPORTATION, TRANSPORTERS, AND CARGOS; 323] **2** *n* **carriage**, shipping, conveyance, transport, transportatio-n, shipment. [➡TRANSPORTATION, TRANSPORTERS, AND CARGOS; 323]

freight car *part of* **train**. [➡RAILWAYS; 1106]

freighter *type of* **motor vessel**. [➡SHIPS AND BOATS; 1149]

French bean *type of* **pulse**. [➡BEANS AND PULSES; 1188]

French dressing *type of* **seasonings, sauces, and dips**. [➡SEASONINGS AND SAUCES; 1173]

French fries *type of* **processed potato**. [➡FRUIT AND VEGETABLES; 1175]

French horn *type of* **brass instrument**. [➡MUSICAL INSTRUMENTS; 910]

French kiss *v* [➡PHYSICAL CONTACT AS COMMUNICATION; 656]

French pleat *type of* **hairstyle**. [➡HAIR STYLES AND HAIR PIECES; 489]

French window *type of* **window**. [➡WINDOWS; 1099]

frenetic *adj* **frantic**, frenzied, hectic, distracted, feverish, chaotic, wild, uncontrolled, furious, intense. [➡DISORDER AND CHAOS; 246] *Opposite:* calm.

frenzied *adj* **frantic**, hyperactive, hysterical, feverish, hectic, overexcited, wild, furious, chaotic, violent. [➡IRRITATION AND ANGER; 542] *Opposite:* calm.

frenziedly *adv* **uncontrollably**, wildly, excitedly, hysterically, frantically, feverishly, chaotically, violently, hectically. [➡INCAUTIOUS AND CARELESS; 284] *Opposite:* calmly.

frenzy **1** *n* **fury**, turmoil, fever, rage, passion, state (*informal*), anger, agitation. [➡INSECURITY AND LOSS OF COMPOSURE; 545] *Opposite:* calmness. **2** *n* **whirl**, fit, tumult, rush, flurry, turmoil. [➡DISORDER AND CHAOS; 246]

frequency *n* **incidence**, occurrence, regularity, rate of recurrence, rate. [➡FREQUENT AND OFTEN; 107]

frequent **1** *adj* **recurrent**, common, everyday, normal, numerous, many, repeated, regular. [➡FREQUENT AND OFTEN; 107] *Opposite:* infrequent. **2** *v* **visit**, haunt, patronize, hang around, spend time at, go to regularly. [➡EXIST IN A PLACE; 19] *Opposite:* avoid.

fresco *n* **wall painting**, mural, frieze, wall, painting. [➡ARTWORKS; 898]

fresh **1** *adj* **at its best**, garden-fresh, crisp, moist, juicy. [➡TASTE; 704] *Opposite:* rotting. **2** *adj* **new**, renewed, additional, replacement, other, different. [➡NEW, MODERN; 167] *Opposite:* old. **3** *adj* **clean**, bright, unmarked, unsullied, immaculate, spanking new, brand-new. [➡CLEAN; 1232] *Opposite:* soiled. **4** *adj* **wholesome**, crisp, pleasant, airy, refreshing, clean, breezy, unpolluted. [➡IN GOOD REPAIR; 1231] *Opposite:* musty. **5** *adj* **novel**, original, new, inventive, innovative, creative. [➡EXTRAORDINARY: UNCOMMON; 206] *Opposite:* hackneyed. **6** *adj* **alert**, energetic, lively, vigorous, active, full of beans (*informal*). [➡WIDE AWAKE AND CONSCIOUS; 736] *Opposite:* tired.

See Compare and Contrast at **new**.

freshen *v* **tidy**, neaten, dust, clean, air, air out, ventilate, refresh, revive, clean up. [➡CLEAN AND POLISH; 404]

freshen up *v* **wash**, shower, change, powder your nose (*informal*), clean up, wash up (*US*). [➡CLEAN AND POLISH; 404]

fresher (*informal*) *n* **first-year student**, first year, undergraduate, student, novice. [➡STUDENTS AND PUPILS; 841] *Opposite:* finalist.

fresh-faced *adj* **innocent**, wide-eyed, naive, unsophisticated, young, impressionable, jejune. [➡FACIAL CHARACTERISTICS; 482]

freshly *adv* **newly**, recently, just now, a moment ago, just this minute, not long. [➡NEW, MODERN; 167]

freshness **1** *n* **crispness**, juiciness, flavour, moistness. [➡TASTE; 704] *Opposite:* staleness. **2** *n* **cleanness**, cleanliness, brightness, sparkle, brilliance. [➡CLEAN; 1232] *Opposite:* grubbiness. **3** *n* **novelty**, originality, newness, inventiveness, innovation, creativity. [➡EXTRAORDINARY: UNCOMMON; 206] *Opposite:* tiredness.

freshwater birds and fish

◆ *types of freshwater bird*
barnacle goose, bittern, Canada goose, canvasback, coot, crane, diver, duck, egret, flamingo, grebe, heron, ibis, kingfisher, loon (*US*), mallard, merganser, moorhen, snipe, spoonbill, stork, swan, teal

◆ *types of freshwater fish*
bass, bream, carp, catfish, crappie, goldfish, grayling, guppy, loach, minnow, mullet, Nile perch, perch, pike, piranha, roach, stickleback, tench, tilapia, trout

fret *v* **worry**, fuss, agonize, vex, trouble, bother, upset, hassle (*informal*). [➡BE CONCERNED AND CARE; 582] *Opposite:* calm down.

fretful *adj* **worried**, restless, agitated, unsettled, distressed, irritable, upset, touchy, nervous, anxious. [➡CONFUSION, ANXIETY, AND WORRY; 541] *Opposite:* calm.

fretfulness *n* **anxiety**, restlessness, agitation, distress, unease, worry, disquiet, irritation, nervousness, apprehension. [➡CONFUSION, ANXIETY, AND WORRY; 541] *Opposite:* calmness.

friability *n* [➡FRAGILE; 1208]

friable *adj* **crumbly**, powdery, workable, light. [➡FRAGILE; 1208] *Opposite:* heavy.

See Compare and Contrast at **fragile**.

friar *n* [➡RELIGIOUS PEOPLE; 779]

friary *n* **community**, monastery, building, house, convent, fraternity, brotherhood. [➡RELIGIOUS BUILDINGS; 1084]

fricassee *type of* **cooked dish**. [➡PREPARED DISHES; 1169]

friction 1 *n* **rubbing**, abrasion, contact, chafing, rasping, brushing. [➡ENERGY GENERAL; 1160] 2 *n* **hostility**, conflict, tension, antagonism, disagreement, discord, strife. [➡DISHARMONY; 157] *Opposite:* accord.

fridge *type of* **cooling appliance**. [➡HEATING, REFRIGERATION, AND VENTILATION; 1141]

fridge-freezer *type of* **cooling appliance**. [➡HEATING, REFRIGERATION, AND VENTILATION; 1141]

fried 1 *adj* [➡STATE OF PREPARED FOOD; 1170] 2 *adj* (*US slang*) **tired**, exhausted, run-down, weary, bushed (*informal*), beat (*informal*), done for (*informal*), spent, wiped out (*slang*). [➡TIRED, ASLEEP, AND UNCONSCIOUS; 739] *Opposite:* fresh.

friend 1 *n* **pal** (*informal*), chum (*informal*), mate, comrade, companion, buddy (*US informal*). [➡FRIENDS; 963]. *Opposite:* foe (*literary*) 2 *n* **acquaintance**, contact, colleague, associate, comrade, workmate. [➡FRIENDS; 963] *Opposite:* stranger. 3 *n* **ally**, helper, supporter, well-wisher, collaborator. [➡FRIENDS; 963] *Opposite:* rival.

friendless *adj* [➡SOLITARINESS; 941]

friendliness *n* **openness**, sociability, pleasantness, approachability, outgoingness, responsiveness, affability, kindliness. [➡FRIENDLINESS AND SOCIABILITY; 495] *Opposite:* reserve.

friendly *adj* **welcoming**, approachable, outgoing, open, pleasant, affable, kindly, responsive, sociable. [➡FRIENDLINESS AND SOCIABILITY; 495] *Opposite:* unfriendly.

friendship 1 *n* **bond**, relationship, alliance, attachment, acquaintance, rapport. [➡RELATIONSHIP TO ANOTHER; 973] 2 *n* **companionship**, amity (*formal*), comradeship, camaraderie, closeness, familiarity. [➡RELATIONSHIP TO ANOTHER; 973] *Opposite:* animosity.

fries *type of* **processed potato**. [➡FRUIT AND VEGETABLES; 1175]

frieze *n* **decoration**, band, strip, panel, mural, fresco, wall painting. [➡ARTWORKS; 898]

frigate *type of* **military vessel**. [➡SHIPS AND BOATS; 1149]

fright 1 *n* **fear**, terror, anxiety, foreboding, dread, panic. [➡FEELINGS ABOUT THE FUTURE; 534] *Opposite:* composure. 2 *n* **scare**, shock, start, turn, heart attack (*informal*), seizure. [➡SUDDEN EVENT; 52]

frighten *v* **scare**, terrify, alarm, startle, upset, worry, panic. [➡FRIGHTEN AND SHOCK; 569] *Opposite:* soothe.

frightened *adj* **scared**, afraid, terrified, alarmed, startled, anxious, upset, worried, panicky. [➡FEAR AND PANIC; 544] *Opposite:* calm.

frightening *adj* **scary** (*informal*), terrifying, alarming, startling, fearsome, fearful, redoubtable, upsetting. [➡FRIGHTENING; 232] *Opposite:* soothing.

frightful *adj* **appalling**, horrible, unpleasant, dreadful, awful, terrible. [➡BAD AND BADLY; 224] *Opposite:* pleasant.

frightfully *adv* **terribly**, extremely, awfully, dreadfully, excessively, very, fearfully, horribly, tremendously, monstrously. [➡CRITICALLY AND SERIOUSLY; 132] *Opposite:* rather.

frightfulness *n* **awfulness**, atrociousness, horrendousness, severity, badness, hideousness, horror, horridness, hatefulness, dreadfulness. [➡DISGUSTING AND REPULSIVE; 231] *Opposite:* pleasantness.

frigid 1 *adj* **unfriendly**, standoffish, cold, distant, frosty, forbidding, icy, aloof. [➡UNFRIENDLINESS AND UNSOCIABILITY; 505] *Opposite:* warm. 2 *adj* **cold**, frosty, chilly, icy, freezing, glacial. [➡TEMPERATURE: COLD; 1230] *Opposite:* torrid.

frigidity *n* **coldness**, frostiness, iciness, coldheartedness, aloofness, formality, reserve, standoffishness. [➡UNFRIENDLINESS AND UNSOCIABILITY; 505] *Opposite:* warmth.

frigidly *adv* **coldly**, icily, frostily, unemotionally, unfeelingly, distantly, coolly, cold-heartedly, uncaringly, impersonally. [➡RUDE AND HOSTILE; 626] *Opposite:* warmly.

frill 1 *n* **decoration**, flounce, trimming, ruffle, ruche, edging, lace. [➡ORNAMENTS AND DECORATIONS; 1247] 2 *n* **extra**, add-on, luxury, decoration, accompaniment, embellishment, gimmick, addition, superfluity. [➡ORNAMENTS AND DECORATIONS; 1247]

frills *n* **accompaniments**, trappings, added extras, embellishments, add-ons, additions, superfluities, trimmings, flourishes. [➡MORE AND EXCESS; 122]

frilly *adj* **lacy**, ruched, gathered, pleated, fancy, delicate, decorated. [➡ BEAUTY AND ATTRACTIVENESS; 190] *Opposite:* plain.

fringe 1 *n* **tassel**, edging, edge, border, trimming, trim. [➡ ORNAMENTS AND DECORATIONS; 1247] 2 *n* **periphery**, edge, extreme, perimeter, border, limit, margin. [➡ EXTREMITIES OF PHYSICAL OBJECTS; 1249] *Opposite:* centre. 3 *type of* **hairstyle**. [➡ HAIR STYLES AND HAIR PIECES; 489] 4 *adj* **peripheral**, outlying, marginal, far-flung, frontier, border. [➡ EXTREMITIES OF PHYSICAL OBJECTS; 1249] *Opposite:* central. 5 *adj* **unconventional**, extreme, radical, marginal, extremist, alternative. [➡ EXTRAORDINARY: UNCOMMON; 206] *Opposite:* mainstream.

fringe benefit *n* **extra**, compensation, perk, privilege, reward, perquisite (*formal*). [➡ GIFTS; 439]

frippery *n* [➡ RUBBISH AND USELESS OBJECTS; 1248]

frisk 1 *v* **play**, frolic, gambol, cavort, kick up your heels, leap, romp, dance. [➡ FIDGET AND FROLIC; 312] *Opposite:* plod. 2 *v* **search**, pat down, body search, examine, inspect, check. [➡ SEEK POSSESSION AND SEARCH; 457]

friskily *adv* **playfully**, energetically, excitably, excitedly, enthusiastically, bouncily. [➡ WITH ENTHUSIASM; 287] *Opposite:* lethargically.

friskiness *n* **playfulness**, excitability, excitement, liveliness, enthusiasm, bounciness. [➡ POSITIVE IMPATIENCE, ENTHUSIASM, AND ALERTNESS; 538] *Opposite:* lethargy.

frisky *adj* **playful**, frolicsome, excitable, excited, lighthearted, energetic, lively, bouncy, spirited. [➡ ENERGY AND ENTHUSIASM; 497] *Opposite:* lethargic.

fritter away *v* **dissipate**, waste, squander, misspend, gamble away, idle away, use up. [➡ USE UP AND WASTE; 475] *Opposite:* conserve.

frivolity 1 *n* **playfulness**, perkiness, lightheartedness, merriment, gaiety, giddiness (*dated*), dizziness, silliness. [➡ CHEERFULNESS OF OUTLOOK; 504] *Opposite:* seriousness. 2 *n* **triviality**, frivolousness, unimportance, inconsequentiality, superficiality, silliness, foolishness. [➡ UNIMPORTANT AND UNNECESSARY; 239] *Opposite:* seriousness.

frivolous 1 *adj* **trivial**, silly, inconsequential, idle, shallow, vain. [➡ UNIMPORTANT AND UNNECESSARY; 239] *Opposite:* serious. 2 *adj* **playful**, frolicsome, perky, lighthearted, giddy (*dated*), silly, flippant, dizzy (*informal*). [➡ NEGATIVE INTELLECTUAL CHARACTERISTICS; 526] *Opposite:* serious.

frivolously 1 *adv* **playfully**, lightheartedly, perkily, dizzily, giddily (*dated*), flippantly, lightly. [➡ MOCKING AND DISMISSIVE; 637] *Opposite:* seriously. 2 *adv* **thoughtlessly**, idly, inconsequentially, trivially, foolishly, vainly. [➡ GOOD-TEMPERED AND HUMOROUS; 628] *Opposite:* responsibly.

frizz *v* **curl**, crimp, frizzle, perm, kink. [➡ CHANGE OF SHAPE; 386] *Opposite:* straighten.

frizzed *adj* [➡ DESCRIBING HAIR; 487]

frizzle 1 *v* **burn**, shrivel, scorch, sear, dry up, wrinkle, char. [➡ FIRE, FLAMMABILITY, AND BURNING; 1164] 2 *v* **frizz**, curl, perm, crimp, kink. [➡ CHANGE OF SHAPE; 386] *Opposite:* straighten. 3 *v* **sizzle**, fry, pan-fry, sauté, grill, barbecue, heat. [➡ COOKING AND FOOD PREPARATION; 354]

frizzy *adj* **curled**, wiry, curly, kinky, frizzed. [➡ DESCRIBING HAIR; 487] *Opposite:* straight.

frock (*dated*) *type of* **dress**. [➡ GARMENTS AND OUTFITS; 865]

frock coat *type of* **overcoat**. [➡ GARMENTS AND OUTFITS; 865]

frog *type of* **amphibian**. [➡ AMPHIBIANS; 1008]

frogmarch *v* **propel**, march, bundle (*informal*), accompany, take, carry. [➡ ACCOMPANY AND FOLLOW; 338]

frogspawn *n* **eggs**, spawn, tadpoles, progeny, offspring. [➡ EGGS AND SPAWN; 728]

frolic *v* **play**, skip, cavort, frisk, gambol, leap, romp, dance, kick up your heels. [➡ FIDGET AND FROLIC; 312] *Opposite:* plod.

frolicsome *adj* **playful**, frisky, frivolous, lighthearted, spirited, lively. [➡ ENERGY AND ENTHUSIASM; 497] *Opposite:* solemn.

from hand to mouth *adv* **from payday to payday**, close to the line, with no slack, on a strict budget, from day to day, at the edge, on the breadline, from paycheque to paycheque, near the poverty line. [➡ POVERTY AND POOR; 892]

from the bottom of your heart *adv* **sincerely**, wholeheartedly, truly, honestly, unequivocally. [➡ HONEST AND OPEN; 631] *Opposite:* insincerely.

from the horse's mouth *adv* **from a reliable source**, on good authority, reliably, authoritatively, directly, at first hand. [➡ WORDS AND PHRASES EMPHASIZING THE TRUTH OF A MATTER; 173] *Opposite:* indirectly.

from time to time *adv* **occasionally**, now and then, now and again, once in a while, infrequently, periodically. [➡ NEVER AND INFREQUENCY; 97] *Opposite:* frequently.

frond *n* **leaf**, branch, palm leaf, fern leaf. [➡ PARTS OF TREES AND PLANTS; 1026]

front 1 *n* **façade**, face, frontage, obverse, head, fore (*literary*). [➡ EXTREMITIES OF PHYSICAL OBJECTS; 1249] *Opposite:* back. 2 *n* **cheek** (*informal*), bottle (*informal*), impertinence, cockiness, nerve, gall, chutzpah (*informal*), audacity, impudence. [➡ BAD MANNERS AND SOCIAL SKILLS; 522]

frontage *n* **front**, façade, face, outlook, front part. [➡ PARTS OF A BUILDING; 1094] *Opposite:* rear.

frontal *adj* **forward**, anterior, front, fore (*literary*) [➡ RELATIVE LOCATION; 162] *Opposite:* posterior (*formal*).

frontbencher *n* [➡ POLITICAL OFFICES AND POLITICIANS; 808]

front door *n* **main entrance**, main door, door, entrance, entry. [➡ DOORS AND ACCESS POINTS; 1100] *Opposite:* exit.

frontier *n* **border**, boundary, limit, edge, border line, front line. [➡ GEOGRAPHICAL BORDERS AND BOUNDARIES; 1068]

frontispiece *n* **illustration**, print, picture, photograph, drawing, image, sketch, reproduction, plate. [➡ PARTS OF BOOKS AND DOCUMENTS; 594]

front line 1 *n* **front**, war zone, battle zone, combat zone, ground zero. [➡ GEOGRAPHICAL BORDERS AND BOUNDARIES; 1068] 2 *n* **forefront**, cutting edge, leading edge, sharp end, vanguard, uncharted territory, firing line, fore (*literary*). [➡DIFFICULT SITUATIONS; 72]

front of house *n* [➡IN THE THEATRE; 906]

front-page *adj* **headline**, important, significant, momentous, attention-grabbing, eye-catching, far-reaching. [➡NEWSPAPERS; 606]

frontrunner (*informal*) *n* **leader**, number one (*informal*), head, favourite, prime candidate, top dog (*informal*). [➡IMPORTANT OR FAMOUS PEOPLE; 893] *Opposite:* straggler.

frontwards *adv* **ahead**, to the fore, forwards. [➡DIRECTION OF MOTION; 346] *Opposite:* backwards.

frost 1 *n* **ice**, rime, hoar frost. [➡COLD WEATHER; 1051] 2 *n* **cold**, frostiness, iciness, coolness, frigidity, chill. [➡COLD WEATHER; 1051] *Opposite:* warmth.

frosted *adj* **ice-covered**, frosty, iced, icy, snowy, white, frozen. [➡COLD WEATHER; 1051] *Opposite:* thawed.

frostily *adv* **coldly**, icily, coolly, frigidly, angrily, bitterly. [➡RUDE AND HOSTILE; 626] *Opposite:* warmly.

frostiness 1 *n* **iciness**, coldness, cold, chill, rawness, wintriness. [➡COLD WEATHER; 1051] *Opposite:* warmth. 2 *n* **coldness**, aloofness, frigidity, coolness, iciness, standoffishness, reserve. [➡UNFRIENDLINESS AND UNSOCIABILITY; 505] *Opposite:* warmth.

frosting 1 *n* **icing**, cake coating, decoration, royal icing, topping. [➡SUGAR AND PRESERVES; 1183] 2 *n* **dullness**, opaqueness, opacity, matt surface, matt finish, texturing. [➡VISUAL TEXTURE; 1220]

frosty 1 *adj* **icy**, cold, chilly, freezing, frigid, cool, glacial. [➡COLD WEATHER; 1051] *Opposite:* warm. 2 *adj* **cold**, unfriendly, cool, icy, frigid, standoffish, aloof, reserved, chilling, cold-hearted. [➡UNFRIENDLINESS AND UNSOCIABILITY; 505] *Opposite:* warm.

froth 1 *n* **foam**, bubbles, lather, spume (*literary*), head, fizz. [➡FROTH; 1272] 2 *n* **triviality**, trivia, frivolity, superficiality, shallowness, lightheartedness, inconsequentiality, nonsense. [➡MEANINGLESS SPEECH OR WRITING; 677] *Opposite:* substance. 3 *v* **lather**, lather up, foam, soap, cream. [➡EMIT AND EMANATE; 362] 4 *v* **to become foamy**, foam, bubble, lather, lather up, produce a head, fizz, ferment. [➡FROTH AND EFFERVESCE; 390]

frothiness 1 *n* **foaminess**, bubbliness, fizziness, fizz, soapiness, sudsiness. [➡VISUAL TEXTURE; 1220] 2 *n* **triviality**, insubstantiality, lightness, frivolity, pettiness, superficiality, shallowness, lightheartedness, inconsequentiality. [➡UNIMPORTANT AND UNNECESSARY; 239] *Opposite:* seriousness.

frothy 1 *adj* **foamy**, foam-covered, lathered, lathered up, bubbly, soapy, fizzing, sudsy. [➡VISUAL TEXTURE; 1220] 2 *adj* **light**, inconsequential, superficial, trivial, shallow, frivolous, lighthearted. [➡UNIMPORTANT AND UNNECESSARY; 239] *Opposite:* serious.

frown 1 *v* **knit your brow**, scowl, glare, glower, lower, pull a face. [➡FACIAL EXPRESSION; 652] *Opposite:* smile. 2 *n* **scowl**, glare, glower, grimace, puckered brow. [➡FACIAL EXPRESSION; 652] *Opposite:* smile.

frown on *v* **disapprove**, take a dim view of, frown upon, condemn, dislike, object to, oppose, disfavour, be against, deplore. [➡DISLIKE AND HATE; 578] *Opposite:* favour.

See Compare and Contrast at **disapprove**.

frown upon *v* **disapprove of**, take a dim view of, frown on, condemn, dislike, object to, oppose, disfavour, be against. [➡DISLIKE AND HATE; 578] *Opposite:* favour.

frowzy *adj* **unkempt**, dishevelled, frayed, messy, shabby, untidy, slovenly, frazzled (*informal*), rumpled, disorganized. [➡BADLY GROOMED; 484] *Opposite:* neat.

frozen 1 *adj* **ice-covered**, cold, solid, freezing, iced up, icy. [➡COLD WEATHER; 1051] 2 *adj* **immobile**, stationary, unmoving, still, motionless, petrified. [➡LACK OF ACTIVITY; 343] *Opposite:* mobile.

fructose *type of* **nutrient**. [➡FOOD COMPONENTS; 1187]

frugal *adj* **thrifty**, prudent, economical, sparing, penny-wise, careful, meagre, parsimonious, stingy (*informal*), penny-pinching (*informal*), tight. [➡FINANCIALLY MEAN AND GRASPING; 520] *Opposite:* profligate.

frugality *n* **thrift**, stinginess, penny-pinching (*informal*), parsimony, prudence, economy, thriftiness. [➡FINANCIALLY MEAN AND GRASPING; 520] *Opposite:* profligacy.

fruit 1 *n* **ovary**, berry, pod, capsule, achene, drupe, fruitlet. [➡PARTS OF TREES AND PLANTS; 1026] 2 *n* **produce**, bounty, harvest, crop, yield. [➡RESULTS AND OUTCOMES; 83] 3 *n* **product**, result, consequence, reward, fruition, maturing, outcome, end result. [➡RESULTS AND OUTCOMES; 83] 4 *v* **produce fruit**, bear fruit, ripen, mature. [➡GROW AND CULTIVATE; 352]

fruit

◆ *types of fruit*
apple, apricot, avocado, banana, cherry, damson, date, fig, grape, guava, kiwi fruit, mango, melon, nectarine, olive, papaya, passion fruit, peach, pear, pineapple, plum, pomegranate, quince, strawberry, watermelon

◆ *parts of a fruit*
flesh, juice, kernel, peel, pip, pit (*US*), pith, pulp, rind, seed, skin, stone

fruit bat *type of* **flying mammal**. [➡FLYING MAMMAL; 984]

fruitcake *type of* **cake**. [➡CAKES, BISCUITS, AND DESSERTS; 1180]

fruit fly *type of* **flying insect**. [➡FLYING INSECTS; 1013]

fruitful *adj* **productive**, fertile, rich, prolific, abundant, successful, profitable, rewarding, effective, prosperous. [➡SUCCESSFUL AND PROMISING; 81] *Opposite:* fruitless.

fruitfulness *n* **productivity**, abundance, profitability, prosperity, fertility, effectiveness, success, richness, prosperousness. [➡SUCCESS; 82] *Opposite:* fruitlessness.

fruition *n* **completion**, maturity, readiness, realization, fruitfulness, culmination, fulfilment. [➡END; 54]

fruit juice *n* [➡DRINKS; 1186]

fruitless *adj* **unsuccessful**, futile, useless, unproductive, wasted, unrewarding, ineffective. [➡UNSUCCESSFUL AND UNPROMISING; 76] *Opposite:* fruitful.

fruitlessness *n* **uselessness**, futility, unproductiveness, failure, inadequacy, ineffectiveness. [➡REDUNDANT AND USELESS; 241] *Opposite:* fruitfulness.

fruit salad *type of* **dessert**. [➡CAKES, BISCUITS, AND DESSERTS; 1180]

fruity 1 *adj* **rich**, sweet, tangy, zesty, lemony, plummy, grapey. [➡TASTE; 704] 2 *adj* **resonant**, rich, plummy, mellow, harmonious, mellifluous. [➡SOFT OR PLEASANT SOUNDS; 1264] *Opposite:* shrill.

frumpiness *n* [➡BADLY GROOMED; 484]

frumpy *adj* [➡BADLY GROOMED; 484]

frustrate 1 *v* **thwart**, prevent, foil, stop, block, hinder, obstruct, stymie. [➡MAKE IMPOSSIBLE; 277] *Opposite:* promote. 2 *v* **discourage**, exasperate, irritate, upset, disturb, annoy, bother, aggravate (*informal*), vex, try, infuriate. [➡ANGER AND ANNOY; 570] *Opposite:* encourage.

frustrated 1 *adj* **unfulfilled**, unsatisfied, irritated, upset, angry, exasperated, discouraged. [➡IRRITATION AND ANGER; 542] *Opposite:* satisfied. 2 *adj* **foiled**, blocked, stymied, obstructed, hindered, thwarted. [➡UNSUCCESSFUL AND UNPROMISING; 76] *Opposite:* successful.

frustrating *adj* **annoying**, unsatisfying, exasperating, infuriating, maddening, provoking, vexing, challenging, wearisome, trying, galling, aggravating (*informal*), irritating, upsetting, disturbing, discouraging, disappointing. [➡IRRITATING; 229] *Opposite:* satisfying.

frustration 1 *n* **prevention**, hindrance, blocking, foiling, defeat, obstruction, thwarting. [➡PROBLEM; 257] *Opposite:* success. 2 *n* **dissatisfaction**, irritation, disturbance, annoyance, nuisance, vexation, disappointment, exasperation, weariness, aggravation (*informal*), infuriation. [➡IRRITATION AND ANGER; 542] *Opposite:* satisfaction.

fry *v* **cook**, sauté, stir-fry, fry up, deep-fry, brown. [➡COOKING AND FOOD PREPARATION; 354]

frying pan *n* **pan**, skillet, omelette pan, spider (*US dated*). [➡TABLEWARE, CUTLERY, AND KITCHENWARE; 861]

fry-up (*informal*) *type of* **cooked dish**. [➡PREPARED DISHES; 1169]

fuchsia 1 *type of* **perennial flower**. [➡FLOWERS; 1032] 2 *type of* **pink**. [➡COLOURS; 1223]

fucus *type of* **alga**. [➡MICROORGANISMS, FUNGI, AND ALGAE; 1023]

fuddle 1 *v* **confuse**, bewilder, stupefy, muddle, dull, cloud, befuddle, bemuse, puzzle, befog (*literary*). [➡CONFUSE AND BEWILDER; 572] *Opposite:* clarify. 2 *n* **muddle**, state (*informal*), dither, mess. [➡CONFUSION, ANXIETY, AND WORRY; 541]

fuddled *adj* [➡CONFUSION, ANXIETY, AND WORRY; 541]

fuddy-duddy (*informal*) *n* **fogy**, stick-in-the-mud (*informal*), stuffed shirt (*informal*), reactionary, diehard. [➡UNCOOPERATIVE OR REBELLIOUS PERSON; 567]

fudge 1 *type of* **confectionery**. [➡CONFECTIONERY; 1181] 2 *n* (*informal*) **nonsense**, rubbish, waffle (*informal*), garbage, verbiage. [➡MEANINGLESS SPEECH OR WRITING; 677] 3 *v* (*informal*) **falsify**, fiddle (*informal*), doctor, fix (*informal*), alter, massage, fabricate, exaggerate, misrepresent, distort. [➡FALSIFY AND CHEAT; 177] 4 *v* (*informal*) **prevaricate**, waffle (*informal*), stall, beat about the bush, evade the issue. [➡SHIRK AND DELAY; 274]

fuel 1 *n* **petroleum**, firewood, oil, coal, petrol, fossil fuel, energy, gasoline (*US*), gas (*US*). [➡ENERGY SOURCES; 1161] 2 *v* **power**, fire, run, drive, operate, work. [➡USE TOOLS AND MACHINERY; 469] 3 *v* **stimulate**, increase, promote, fire, energize, encourage, invigorate, add to, feed. [➡CHANGE OF INTENSITY: MORE; 395] *Opposite:* quell.

fug *n* **fog**, smog, haze, smoke, miasma. [➡HOT WEATHER; 1050]

fuggy *adj* **stuffy**, smoky, stale, airless, suffocating, foggy, hazy, smoke-filled. [➡HOT WEATHER; 1050] *Opposite:* bracing.

fugitive 1 *n* **escapee**, deserter, absconder, outlaw, runaway. [➡RUNAWAYS AND ABSENTEES; 9] 2 *adj* **brief**, fleeting, elusive, short, quick. [➡HAPPENING QUICKLY; 104]

fugue 1 *n* **fugue state**, blackout, amnesia, memory loss. [➡TIRED, ASLEEP, AND UNCONSCIOUS; 739] 2 *type of* **instrumental music**. [➡MUSIC, SONGS, AND SINGING; 907]

fulcrum *n* **pivot**, hinge, swivel, support, point. [➡PARTS OF MACHINES AND TOOLS; 1117]

fulfil 1 *v* **achieve**, bear out, live up to, satisfy, justify, accomplish, realize, bring about, make happen, bring to fruition, follow through. [➡COMPLETE AN ACTION; 264] 2 *v* **carry out**, execute, follow, obey, complete, comply with, accomplish, perform, implement, discharge (*formal*). [➡OBEY AND ABIDE BY; 302] *Opposite:* neglect. 3 *v* **satisfy**, meet, conform to, be in conformity with, accord with, be in accordance with, agree with, be in agreement with, match. [➡HARMONY; 156] *Opposite:* fall short. 4 *v* **complete**, finish, go through with, get through, make it through, survive, see through. [➡COMPLETE AN ACTION; 264] *Opposite:* abandon. 5 *v* **supply**, fill, deliver, furnish (*formal*), provide. [➡GIVE AND PROVIDE; 431] *Opposite:* renege. 6 *v* **succeed**, do proud, gain fulfilment, make it (*informal*), make good, fulfil your potential. [➡SUCCEED AND WIN; 79] *Opposite:* fail.

See Compare and Contrast at **perform**.

fulfilled *adj* **satisfied**, content, happy, pleased, rewarded, contented. [➡APPRECIATION AND GRATITUDE; 536] *Opposite:* frustrated.

fulfilling *adj* **satisfying**, rewarding, pleasing, gratifying, enjoyable. [➡EMOTIONALLY PLEASANT; 188] *Opposite:* frustrating.

fulfilment 1 *n* **achievement**, realization, execution, completion, accomplishment, implementation, discharge (*formal*). [➡SUCCESS; 82] *Opposite:* neglect. 2 *n* **contentment**, serenity, inner peace, self-actualization, nirvana, satisfaction, gratification, self-realization, joy, success. [➡CALMNESS, CONFIDENCE, AND COMPOSURE; 537] *Opposite:* dissatisfaction.

fulguration (*formal*) *n* [➡WINDY AND STORMY WEATHER; 1053]

full 1 *adj* **occupied**, complete, jam-packed (*informal*), bursting, chock-full (*informal*), packed, chock-a-block (*informal*), full up, filled, crowded, crammed. [➡FULL; 1238] *Opposite:* empty. 2 *adj* **complete**, broad, extensive, comprehensive, detailed, inclusive, thorough. [➡WHOLENESS AND COMPLETENESS; 199] *Opposite:* sketchy. 3 *adj* **sonorous**, resonant, rich, deep, plummy, mellow, mellifluous, harmonious. [➡LOUD OR UNPLEASANT SOUNDS; 1265] *Opposite:* shrill. **4** *adj* **satiated**, satisfied, stuffed (*informal*), bursting, full up, sated, replete, gorged. [➡EAT AND NOT EAT; 711] *Opposite:* hungry. **5** *adj* **plump**, round, chubby, ample, broad, rounded, rotund, pudgy (*informal*). [➡BUILD; 478] *Opposite:* thin.

full-blooded *adj* **vigorous**, hearty, thoroughgoing, forceful, robust, out-and-out. [➡FIT AND STRONG; 737] *Opposite:* feeble.

full-blown *adj* **complete**, full, full-scale, full-size, developed, advanced, mature, total, out-and-out, all-out. [➡WHOLENESS AND COMPLETENESS; 199] *Opposite:* incomplete.

full-bodied *adj* **flavourful**, rich, intense, powerful, strong, tasty, aromatic. [➡TASTE; 704] *Opposite:* insipid.

full dress *n* **formal attire**, dress uniform, jacket and tie, evening dress, black tie, formal wear. [➡CLOTHES AND ACCESSORIES; 864]

full-fashioned (*US*) *adj* **shaped**, close-fitting, tailored, well-fitting, figure-hugging, tight. [➡DESCRIBING CLOTHES; 869] *Opposite:* loose-fitting.

full-frontal (*informal*) *adj* **all-out**, unrestrained, wholehearted, uninhibited, concerted, committed, unambiguous, direct, full-on, total, full, complete, full-scale. [➡HONEST AND OPEN; 631] *Opposite:* half-hearted.

full-length **1** *adj* **ankle-length**, floor-length, long. [➡WHOLENESS AND COMPLETENESS; 199] *Opposite:* short. **2** *adj* **head-to-toe**, whole-body, full, long, tall. [➡LENGTH: LONG; 1196] **3** *adj* **unabridged**, complete, uncut, unedited, unexpurgated, uncensored, standard-length, whole. [➡WHOLENESS AND COMPLETENESS; 199] *Opposite:* abridged.

fullness **1** *n* **completeness**, richness, abundance. [➡TASTE; 704] *Opposite:* emptiness. **2** *n* **roundness**, plumpness, chubbiness, ampleness, pudginess (*informal*). [➡BUILD; 478] *Opposite:* thinness.

full of *adj* **alive with**, awash with, beset with (*formal*), thick with, resplendent with, crammed with, replete with. [➡FULL; 1238]

full of beans (*informal*) *adj* **lively**, animated, bouncy, perky, energetic, active, happy, vigorous, spirited, bubbly, full of life. [➡ENERGY AND ENTHUSIASM; 497] *Opposite:* morose.

full of life *adj* **vivacious**, lively, perky, spirited, energetic, dynamic, animated, active, bubbly, vigorous, full of beans (*informal*). [➡ENERGY AND ENTHUSIASM; 497] *Opposite:* lethargic.

full of yourself *adj* **conceited**, vain, self-satisfied, self-centred, self-absorbed, egocentric, pompous, self-important, arrogant. [➡POMPOUS, LOUD, AND OVER-CONFIDENT; 636] *Opposite:* modest.

full-scale **1** *adj* **life-size**, full-size, complete, full. [➡WHOLENESS AND COMPLETENESS; 199] **2** *adj* **total**, full-blown, unrestrained, all-out, unlimited, complete, full, out-and-out. [➡WHOLENESS AND COMPLETENESS; 199] *Opposite:* partial.

full-size *adj* **normal**, standard, regular, ordinary. [➡LARGE; 1192]

full speed ahead *adv* [➡MOVING QUICKLY; 103]

full steam ahead *adv* [➡MOVING QUICKLY; 103]

full stop *type of* **punctuation mark**. [➡ASPECTS OF LANGUAGE; 683]

full-time *adj* **around the clock**, permanent, round-the-clock, twenty-four-hour, day and night, twenty-four-hour-a-day. [➡PERMANENCE: WITHOUT END; 94] *Opposite:* part-time.

full-timer *n* **full-time employee**, full-time worker, full-time member of staff. [➡WORKER; 836] *Opposite:* part-timer.

full to bursting *adj* [➡FULL; 1238]

full to capacity *adj* [➡FULL; 1238]

full to overflowing *adj* [➡FULL; 1238]

full up **1** *adj* **full**, stuffed (*informal*), bursting, satisfied, satiated, replete. [➡EAT AND NOT EAT; 711] *Opposite:* hungry. **2** *adj* **complete**, jam-packed (*informal*), bursting, chock-full (*informal*), filled, chock-a-block (*informal*), packed. [➡FULL; 1238] *Opposite:* empty.

fully *adv* **completely**, entirely, wholly, totally, altogether, quite, absolutely. [➡WHOLENESS AND COMPLETENESS; 199] *Opposite:* partially.

fully-fledged **1** *adj* **complete**, mature, well-developed, independent, self-sufficient. [➡WHOLENESS AND COMPLETENESS; 199] **2** *adj* **qualified**, out-and-out, full, genuine, actual, bona fide, experienced. [➡TRUE AND REAL; 172]

fully-grown *adj* **mature**, adult, full-sized, full, well-developed, grown up. [➡WHOLENESS AND COMPLETENESS; 199] *Opposite:* immature.

fulmar *type of* **seabird**. [➡SEABIRD; 1002]

fulminate *v* **rail**, rant and rave, rage, rant, thunder, criticize. [➡PROTEST AND EXPRESS DISAPPROVAL; 643] *Opposite:* praise.

fulsome *adj* **flattering**, excessive, immoderate (*formal*), effusive, overgenerous, lavish, fawning. [➡ENTHUSIASTIC AND INQUISITIVE; 629]

fulsomely *adv* [➡PHYSICALLY PLEASANT; 187]

fumble **1** *v* **grope**, scrabble, rummage, root, search, feel, dig. [➡SEEK POSSESSION AND SEARCH; 457] **2** *v* **bungle** (*informal*), mess up (*informal*), mishandle, botch, botch up, blunder, muddle, muddle up. [➡MESS UP AND MAKE MISTAKES; 473] **3** *n* **mistake**, error, blunder, mess-up (*informal*), botched job, botch-up (*informal*), mess, misstep, slip-up (*informal*). [➡MISTAKES; 251]

fume **1** *v* **seethe**, rage, bristle, be angry, be furious, simmer, smoulder. [➡GIVING VENT TO EMOTIONS; 680] **2** *n* **emission**, vapour, miasma, smog, smoke, haze, gas. [➡GASES; 1274] **3** *n* **stench**, smell, stink, reek, odour. [➡SMELL AND SMELLING; 706]

fumes *n* [➡GASES; 1274]

fumigate *v* **sterilize**, disinfect, decontaminate, delouse, smoke, cleanse, clean. [➡CLEAN AND POLISH; 404]

fumigation *n* **disinfection**, decontamination, smoking, delousing, cleansing, sterilization, cleaning. [➡CLEAN AND POLISH; 404]

fuming *adj* **furious**, irate, incensed, enraged, seething, livid, angry, cross, beside yourself, mad, teed off (*US informal*). [➡ IRRITATION AND ANGER; 542]

fun 1 *n* **amusement**, excitement, enjoyment, entertainment, merriment, pleasure, diversion. [➡ ENTERTAINMENT; 872] *Opposite:* boredom. 2 *adj* (*informal*) **amusing**, entertaining, enjoyable, exciting, pleasurable, cool (*slang*), great (*informal*). [➡ EMOTIONALLY PLEASANT; 188] *Opposite:* boring.

funambulist *n* [➡ PEOPLE IN SPORTS AND LEISURE; 876]

fun and games *n* [➡ JOKES AND TEASING; 675]

function 1 *n* **purpose**, meaning, role, job, occupation, task, utility. [➡ INTENTION AND PURPOSE; 773] 2 *n* **event**, gathering, meeting, affair, party, occasion, do (*informal*), soiree (*formal*). [➡ PARTIES, DANCES, AND CELEBRATIONS; 37] 3 *v* **work**, perform, operate, run, go, behave, act, serve. [➡ FUNCTION SUCCESSFULLY; 470] *Opposite:* malfunction.

functional 1 *adj* **practical**, useful, handy, purposeful, efficient, serviceable. [➡ USEFULNESS; 200] *Opposite:* worthless. 2 *adj* **operational**, operative, running, going, working. [➡ HAPPENING AND IN PROGRESS; 32] *Opposite:* inoperative.

functionary *n* **official**, representative, bureaucrat, lackey, minion (*archaic or literary*), dogsbody (*informal*), employee. [➡ SUBORDINATES AND ASSISTANTS; 966]

functionless *adj* [➡ REDUNDANT AND USELESS; 241]

fund 1 *n* **supply**, stock, store, source, collection, bank. [➡ AMOUNT AND QUANTITY; 112] 2 *n* **reserve**, account, supply, endowment, stock, trust, nest egg, deposit. [➡ ACCOUNTING, BANKING, AND BUDGETING; 799] 3 *v* **finance**, support, back, sponsor, subsidize, underwrite, pay for. [➡ ACCOUNTING, BANKING, AND BUDGETING; 799]

fundamental 1 *adj* **basic**, primary, original, essential, elementary, elemental, deep, deep-seated, underlying, structural. [➡ FUNDAMENTAL; 196] *Opposite:* secondary. 2 *adj* **central**, essential, vital, ultimate, major, necessary, important. [➡ IMPORTANT; 195] *Opposite:* superfluous.

fundamentalism *n* [➡ RELIGIOUS CONCEPTS; 777]

fundamentalist *n* [➡ RELIGIOUS PEOPLE; 779]

fundamentally *adv* **basically**, essentially, primarily, deeply, necessarily, profoundly. [➡ FUNDAMENTAL; 196] *Opposite:* superficially.

fundamentals *n* **basics**, rudiments, essentials, ground rules, brass tacks, first principles, nitty-gritty (*informal*), details. [➡ BASIC DETAILS; 689]

funding *n* **backing**, support, finance, subsidy, money, cash, capital, currency, aid, resources, income. [➡ ACCOUNTING, BANKING, AND BUDGETING; 799]

fundraiser 1 *n* **campaigner**, crusader, supporter, representative, moneymaker. [➡ CHARITY AND CHARITABLE INSTITUTIONS; 822] 2 *n* **appeal**, campaign, crusade, push, drive, telethon, fun run, flag day, tag day (*US*). [➡ MEETINGS AND ASSEMBLIES; 43]

funeral *n* **service**, memorial, interment (*formal*), burial, cremation, rites, wake, procession. [➡ BURIAL AND PREPARATION FOR BURIAL; 929]

funeral director *n* [➡ BURIAL AND PREPARATION FOR BURIAL; 929]

funeral home (*US*) *n* [➡ BURIAL AND PREPARATION FOR BURIAL; 929]

funeral Mass *n* [➡ BURIAL AND PREPARATION FOR BURIAL; 929]

funeral rites *n* [➡ BURIAL AND PREPARATION FOR BURIAL; 929]

funerary *adj* [➡ BURIAL AND PREPARATION FOR BURIAL; 929]

funereal *adj* **gloomy**, melancholy, sorrowful, elegiac (*formal*), mournful, sad, depressing, solemn, dismal, lugubrious. [➡ EMOTIONALLY UNPLEASANT AND UPSETTING; 228] *Opposite:* cheerful.

funfair *n* **fair**, fairground, theme park, amusement park, carnival (*US*). [➡ URBAN OUTDOOR SPACES; 1071]

fungal *adj* **fungiform**, mycological, fungoid, fungous. [➡ MICROORGANISMS, FUNGI, AND ALGAE; 1023]

fungus

◆ *types of fungus*
beefsteak fungus, boletus, bracket fungus, cep, chanterelle, death cap, destroying angel, fairy ring champignon, field mushroom, fly agaric, horn of plenty, ink-cap, lichen, mildew, morel, mould, mushroom, orange-peel fungus, oyster mushroom, puffball, stinkhorn, toadstool, truffle, yeast

funicular *type of* **rail vehicle**. [➡ RAILWAYS; 1106]

funicular railway *type of* **railway**. [➡ RAILWAYS; 1106]

funk 1 *n* (*US slang*) **stench**, smell, odour, stink, pong (*informal*). [➡ SMELL AND SMELLING; 706] 2 *type of* **popular music**. [➡ MUSIC, SONGS, AND SINGING; 907]

funky 1 *adj* (*slang*) **rhythmic**, driving, jazzy (*slang*). [➡ MUSICAL TERMS; 912] 2 *adj* (*informal*) **hip** (*slang*), groovy (*dated slang*), trendy (*informal*), cool (*slang*), fab (*dated informal*), far-out, happening (*informal*), up-to-date, fashionable, unconventional. [➡ NEW, MODERN; 167] 3 *adj* (*US slang*) **smelly**, fetid, stinky (*informal*), malodorous, putrid, rank (*literary*). [➡ SMELL AND SMELLING; 706]

fun-loving *adj* **playful**, joyful, high-spirited, frivolous, exuberant, outgoing, extrovert, gregarious, boisterous. [➡ CHEERFULNESS OF OUTLOOK; 504] *Opposite:* staid.

funnel 1 *n* **chimney**, pipe, flue, smokestack, conduit. [➡ ROOFS, ROOF PARTS, AND CEILINGS; 1102] 2 *v* **channel**, direct, focus, guide, concentrate, siphon. [➡ MOVE SOMETHING TO ANOTHER LOCATION; 325]

funnel cloud *type of* **cloud**. [➡ CLOUDY AND RAINY WEATHER; 1052]

funnel-web spider *type of* **arachnid**. [➡ ARACHNIDS; 1018]

funnily 1 *adv* **strangely**, curiously, surprisingly, oddly, unusually, remarkably, bizarrely. [➡ BIZARRE AND PECULIAR; 258] 2 *adv* **comically**, humorously, amusingly, hilariously, wittily, sidesplittingly, uproariously, drolly. [➡ FUNNY AND AMUSING; 217]

funniness *n* **humour**, comedy, comicalness, wit, wittiness, absurdity, laughableness. [➡ FUNNY AND AMUSING; 217] *Opposite:* solemnity.

funny 1 *adj* **comical**, hilarious, amusing, comic, droll, witty, humorous, facetious, waggish (*dated*), sidesplitting, uproarious. [➡ FUNNY AND AMUSING; 217] *Opposite:*

serious. 2 *adj* **strange**, odd, weird, curious, peculiar, unusual, perplexing. [➡BIZARRE AND PECULIAR; 258] *Opposite:* normal. 3 *adj* **quaint**, unconventional, eccentric, quirky, odd, offbeat, peculiar, off-the-wall (*informal*). [➡BIZARRE AND PECULIAR; 258] 4 *adj* **unwell**, sick, poorly (*informal*), off-colour, nauseous, faint, giddy (*dated*), peculiar. [➡UNFIT AND WEAK; 740] 5 *n* (*informal*) **joke**, pun, witticism, gag (*informal*), jest (*literary*), bon mot. [➡JOKES AND TEASING; 675]

Compare and Contrast: ***funny, comic, comical, droll, facetious, humorous, witty, hilarious, sidesplitting***

CORE MEANING: CAUSING OR INTENDED TO CAUSE AMUSEMENT

funny causing amusement or laughter, whether intentionally or not; ***comic*** used in the same way as *funny*, especially to describe books, poems, or plays; ***comical*** funny to the extent of being absurd, especially if this is unintentional; ***droll*** funny because it is whimsical or odd, or drily humorous; ***facetious*** supposed to be funny but ill-timed, inappropriate, or silly; ***humorous*** giving rise to amusement, smiles, or laughter, but more genial, sympathetic, or light-hearted than is necessarily the case with *funny*; ***witty*** using words in a clever, inventive, humorous way; ***hilarious*** extremely funny; ***sidesplitting*** very funny indeed, especially causing a great deal of uncontrollable laughter.

fur 1 *n* **hair**, pelt, fleece, coat, fuzz, down. [➡THE SKIN; 721] 2 *type of* **fabric from animals**. [➡FABRICS; 1131]

furious 1 *adj* **angry**, livid, fuming, irate, infuriated, upset, beside yourself, mad, hopping mad (*informal*). [➡IRRITATION AND ANGER; 542] *Opposite:* calm. 2 *adj* **energetic**, manic (*informal*), concerted, all-out, full-on, breakneck, violent, uncompromising, frantic, feverish, desperate, ferocious, vehement. [➡DISORDER AND CHAOS; 246]

furiously 1 *adv* **angrily**, irately, wrathfully, heatedly, crossly. [➡IRRITATION AND ANGER; 542] 2 *adv* **energetically**, feverishly, frantically, desperately, violently, ferociously, vehemently. [➡HAPPENING QUICKLY; 104] *Opposite:* sluggishly.

furiousness 1 *n* **anger**, rage, fury, wrath, ire (*literary*), crossness. [➡IRRITATION AND ANGER; 542] 2 *n* **violence**, energy, vigour, ferocity, passion, vehemence, desperation. [➡DISORDER AND CHAOS; 246]

furl *v* **roll up**, wrap up, curl, curl up, tie up, wind up, fold up. [➡POSITION SOMETHING: AROUND SOMETHING; 328] *Opposite:* unfurl.

furlough 1 *n* **leave of absence**, leave, absence, holiday, R and R, vacation (*US*). [➡PERIOD OF REST; 91] 2 *n* (*US*) **layoff**, shutdown, unemployment. [➡WORK-RELATED ACTIVITIES; 834]

furnace *n* **heater**, oven, kiln, boiler, blast furnace, incinerator. [➡FIRE, FLAMMABILITY, AND BURNING; 1164]

furnish (*formal*) *v* **supply**, provide, equip, give, deliver, hand over, endow, yield. [➡EQUIP AND SUPPLY; 436]

furnished *adj* **equipped**, fitted out, well-appointed, well-found. [➡FULL; 1238] *Opposite:* unfurnished.

furnishings *n* **furniture**, fittings, fixtures, tables, chairs, cabinets, beds. [➡SOFT FURNISHINGS, LINEN, AND DRAPERY; 860]

furniture *n* **fittings**, fixtures, tables, chairs, cabinets, beds, furnishings. [➡FURNITURE; 858]

furore 1 *n* **uproar**, outcry, commotion, controversy, protest, tumult, rumpus, disturbance, indignation, ruckus. [➡CHAOS AND UPROAR; 51] 2 *n* **excitement**, hysteria, hype, frenzy, ballyhoo, hoo-hah (*slang*), to-do (*informal*), hubbub, fuss, kerfuffle (*informal*), carry-on (*informal*). [➡CHAOS AND UPROAR; 51]

furred *adj* **hairy**, furry, fuzzy, downy, fleecy, woolly. [➡PHYSICAL TEXTURE; 1221]

furriness *n* **hairiness**, fuzziness, woolliness, fleeciness, fluffiness, downiness. [➡PHYSICAL TEXTURE; 1221] *Opposite:* baldness.

furrow 1 *n* **channel**, groove, rut, undulation, crease, gully, line, trough. [➡WATERCOURSES; 1110] 2 *v* **wrinkle**, crease, gather, draw, contract. [➡CHANGE OF SHAPE; 386]

furrowed *adj* **wrinkled**, crumply, creasy, wrinkly, crinkly. [➡IN BAD REPAIR; 1233] *Opposite:* smooth.

furry *adj* **hairy**, fuzzy, woolly, furred, downy, fleecy. [➡PHYSICAL TEXTURE; 1221]

further 1 *adj* **additional**, more, extra, added, supplementary, auxiliary. [➡MORE AND EXCESS; 122] 2 *v* **advance**, promote, foster, broaden, expand, spread, extend, help, boost. [➡CAUSE TO CONTINUE; 268] *Opposite:* prevent.

furthermore *adv* **also**, in addition, besides, additionally, moreover, what's more. [➡EXPRESSIONS INTRODUCING EXTRA INFORMATION; 137]

furthermost *adj* **farthest**, furthest, greatest, remotest, nethermost (*formal*). [➡DISTANCE; 161]

furthest *adj* **farthest**, utmost, uttermost, outermost, furthermost, extreme. [➡DISTANCE; 161]

furtive *adj* **secretive**, stealthy, secret, sly, sneaky, surreptitious, clandestine, shifty. [➡SECRET AND UNKNOWN; 180] *Opposite:* open.

See Compare and Contrast at **secret**.

furtiveness 1 *n* **secrecy**, stealth, covertness, surreptitiousness, discreetness, discretion, shiftiness, sneakiness. [➡SECRET AND UNKNOWN; 180] 2 *n* **sneakiness**, suspiciousness, guiltiness, slyness, craftiness. [➡DECEITFUL; 514]

furuncle (*technical*) *n* [➡CONDITIONS AFFECTING THE SKIN; 722]

fury *n* **anger**, rage, ire (*literary*), wrath, ferocity. [➡IRRITATION AND ANGER; 542]

See Compare and Contrast at **anger**.

fuse 1 *n* **anger**, rage, ferocity, vehemence, wrath, passion, temper. [➡IRRITATION AND ANGER; 542] *Opposite:* serenity. 2 *v* **combine**, blend, mingle, meld, coalesce, unite, merge. [➡COMBINE AND MIX; 401]

fuselage *part of* **aircraft**. [➡AIRCRAFT; 1147]

fusilier *n* [➡MILITARY PERSONNEL; 828]

fusilli *type of* **pasta**. [➡PASTA; 1179]

fusion *n* **synthesis**, union, combination, mixture, blend, merging, meld. [➡COMBINE AND MIX; 401]

fuss 1 *n* **commotion**, excitement, bother, to-do (*informal*), carry-on (*informal*), kerfuffle (*informal*), bustle, activity. [➡CHAOS AND UPROAR; 51] 2 *n* **worry**, concern, bother, trouble, hassle (*informal*), aggravation (*informal*). [➡PROBLEM; 257] 3 *n* **protest**, controversy, argument, complaint, reaction, noise, row, storm. [➡CHAOS AND UPROAR; 51] 4 *v* **worry**, fret, stew, bother, niggle. [➡BE CONCERNED AND CARE; 582]

fussbudget (*US informal*) *n* **fusspot** (*informal*), worrier, worryguts (*informal*), worrywart (*US informal*). [➡GRUMPY AND NEGATIVE PEOPLE; 953]

fussily 1 *adv* **trivially**, pedantically, obsessively, painstakingly, meticulously, scrupulously. [➡DIFFICULT TO PLEASE; 516] 2 *adv* **choosily**, dogmatically, inflexibly, fastidiously, scrupulously, exactingly, particularly. [➡DIFFICULT TO PLEASE; 516] 3 *adv* **elaborately**, extravagantly, excessively, overelaborately, ornately. [➡IN POOR TASTE; 230]

fussiness 1 *n* **trivialness**, pedantry, obsessiveness, prissiness, hairsplitting, preciseness, assiduousness, scrupulousness, niceness. [➡DIFFICULT TO PLEASE; 516] 2 *n* **choosiness**, meticulousness, dogmatism, inflexibility, fastidiousness, exactness. [➡DIFFICULT TO PLEASE; 516] 3 *n* **elaborateness**, frilliness, ornateness, overstatement. [➡IN POOR TASTE; 230]

fuss over *v* [➡TAKE CARE OF AND SPOIL; 301]

fusspot (*informal*) *n* **worryguts** (*informal*), worrier, worrywart (*US informal*), fussbudget (*US informal*). [➡INTERFERING PEOPLE AND TELLTALES; 950]

fussy 1 *adj* **trivial**, pedantic, obsessive, prissy, assiduous, scrupulous, painstaking. [➡DIFFICULT TO PLEASE; 516] 2 *adj* **picky**, particular, finicky, fastidious, selective, choosy (*informal*), inflexible, pernickety (*informal*), exacting. [➡DIFFICULT TO PLEASE; 516] *Opposite:* laid-back (*informal*). 3 *adj* **elaborate**, busy, frilly, ornate, overelaborate, precious, chintzy (*informal disapproving*). [➡IN POOR TASTE; 230]

See Compare and Contrast at **careful**.

fusty 1 *adj* **stale**, mouldy, damp, fetid, musty, mildewy, rotten. [➡DIRTY; 1234] 2 *adj* **stuffy**, antiquated, dull, boring, old-fashioned, outdated, conservative. [➡BORING AND UNINTERESTING; 235]. *Opposite:* trendy (*informal*).

futile *adj* **useless**, pointless, fruitless, unsuccessful, vain, ineffectual, wasted, ineffective. [➡REDUNDANT AND USELESS; 241] *Opposite:* useful.

futility *n* **uselessness**, pointlessness, ineffectiveness, ineffectuality, vainness, senselessness. [➡REDUNDANT AND USELESS; 241] *Opposite:* usefulness.

futon *type of* **bed**. [➡FURNITURE; 858]

future 1 *n* **prospect**, outlook, potential, time ahead, time to come, what's in store. [➡FUTURE; 86] *Opposite:* past. 2 *adj* **forthcoming**, coming, imminent, yet to come, impending, upcoming (*US*). [➡FUTURE; 86] *Opposite:* past.

futures *n* **stocks**, commodities, contracts, investments. [➡ACCOUNTING, BANKING, AND BUDGETING; 799]

futurism *type of* **20th-century art movement**. [➡ARTISTIC MOVEMENTS AND STYLES; 899]

futuristic *adj* **innovative**, revolutionary, ahead of its time, advanced, ultramodern, space-age, high-tech, science fiction. [➡NEW, MODERN; 167] *Opposite:* antiquated.

fuzz *n* **down**, hair, fur, lint, fluff, nap. [➡HAIR; 485]

fuzzily 1 *adv* **blurrily**, blearily, hazily, mistily, vaguely, indistinctly, unclearly. [➡VAGUENESS; 244] *Opposite:* clearly. 2 *adv* **incoherently**, ambiguously, vaguely, unclearly, indistinctly, uncertainly. [➡VAGUENESS; 244]

fuzziness 1 *n* **hairiness**, fluffiness, woolliness, down, wool, hair, fur, fuzz. [➡PHYSICAL TEXTURE; 1221] 2 *n* **blurriness**, unclearness, nebulousness, haziness, vagueness, mistiness, shadowiness, bleariness, indistinctness. [➡VISUAL TEXTURE; 1220] 3 *n* **uncertainty**, vagueness, unsureness, incoherence, ambiguity, indistinctness, unclearness. [➡VAGUENESS; 244] *Opposite:* clarity.

fuzzy 1 *adj* **hairy**, furry, fluffy, downy, woolly. [➡DESCRIBING HAIR; 487] 2 *adj* **blurry**, unclear, nebulous, hazy, vague, misty, shadowy, bleary, indistinct. [➡VAGUENESS; 244] *Opposite:* clear. 3 *adj* **unsure**, ambiguous, vague, unclear, indistinct, incoherent, uncertain, ill-defined, woolly. [➡UNCERTAIN; 176] *Opposite:* clear.

G

gab (*informal*) **1** *v* **chatter**, chat, natter (*informal*), prattle, rattle on, jabber, gas (*informal*), gossip, gush, go on, talk the hind legs off a donkey, spout, talk nineteen to the dozen, talk a mile a minute (*US*), talk ten to the dozen (*US*). [➡TWO-WAY COMMUNICATION; 608] **2** *n* **chat**, chitchat (*informal*), chatter, talk, conversation, natter (*informal*), gossip. [➡INFORMAL COMMUNICATION; 45]

gabardine 1 *n* **raincoat**, garment, mac (*informal*), mackintosh (*dated*). [➡GARMENTS AND OUTFITS; 865] **2** *type of* **fabric from animals.** [➡FABRICS; 1131]

gabbing (*informal*) *n* [➡INFORMAL COMMUNICATION; 45]

gabble 1 *v* **chat**, chatter, gab (*informal*), swap gossip, natter (*informal*), prattle, blather (*informal*), blab (*informal*), blether (*informal*), blabber, footle (*informal*). [➡WITTER AND BABBLE; 618] **2** *n* **gibberish**, chatter, twaddle (*informal*), gab (*informal*), rubbish, prattle, blather (*informal*), nonsense, blabber. [➡MEANINGLESS SPEECH OR WRITING; 677]

gabby (*informal*) *adj* **talkative**, chatty, garrulous, voluble, gushing, loquacious (*formal*). [➡ELOQUENT, TALKATIVE, AND LONG-WINDED; 633] *Opposite:* taciturn.

gable *part of* **building.** [➡PARTS OF A BUILDING; 1094]

gad (*humorous*) *v* **gallivant** (*informal*), socialize, party (*informal*), go partying, go clubbing, paint the town red (*informal*), have a night on the town, live it up (*slang*), rave (*dated slang*), rave it up (*dated slang*). [➡LEISURE AND RECREATION; 874]

gadabout (*humorous*) *n* **pleasure-seeker**, fun lover, social butterfly, gadder (*dated*), partygoer, raver (*informal*). [➡NOMADIC AND ROOTLESS LIFESTYLES; 884]

gadfly 1 *n* (*dated*) **nuisance**, pest, irritator, stirrer (*informal*), tormentor, meddler, pesterer, busybody (*informal*). [➡GRUMPY AND NEGATIVE PEOPLE; 953] **2** *type of* **parasitic insect.** [➡PARASITES; 1017]

gadget 1 *n* **device**, tool, appliance, implement, contraption, utensil, apparatus. [➡DEVICES; 1114] **2** *n* **thingamajig** (*informal*), thingamabob (*informal*), widget (*humorous*), doodah (*informal*), gizmo (*informal*), doohickey (*US informal*), jigger (*US informal*), doodad (*US informal*). [➡PHYSICAL OBJECTS; 1242]

gaff *part of* **sailing vessel.** [➡PARTS OF A SHIP OR BOAT; 1150]

gaffe *n* **blunder**, solecism, faux pas (*literary*), clanger (*informal*), howler (*informal*), bloomer (*informal humorous*), mistake, error, boo-boo (*informal*), blooper (*US informal humorous*). [➡MISTAKES; 251]

gaffer (*informal*) *n* **boss**, supervisor, owner, proprietor, manager, chief. [➡BOSSES AND MANAGEMENT; 965] *Opposite:* underling.

gaffsail *part of* **sailing vessel.** [➡PARTS OF A SHIP OR BOAT; 1150]

gag 1 *n* **restraint**, curb, muzzle, tape, binding. [➡FASTENERS, LINKS, AND NETWORKS; 1246] **2** *n* **ban**, gagging order, injunction, restriction, interdiction, prohibition, court order, gag order (*US*). [➡REFUSE PERMISSION AND NOT ALLOW; 671] **3** *n* (*informal*) **joke**, one-liner, funny, shaggy dog story, quip, crack (*informal*), witticism, practical joke. [➡JOKES AND TEASING; 675] **4** *v* **muzzle**, stifle, muffle, restrain, curb, bind up, seal somebody's lips. [➡CAPTIVITY AND LOSS OF FREEDOM; 249] **5** *v* **suppress**, silence, interdict, prohibit, ban, muzzle, restrict, bind over. [➡MAKE IMPOSSIBLE; 277] **6** *v* **choke**, retch, heave (*informal*), suffocate, stifle, hyperventilate. [➡VOMIT AND BELCH; 713]

gagging order *n* **restriction**, gag, injunction, prohibition, court order, interdiction, curb, ban, restraining order (*US*). [➡TRIAL, PUNISHMENT, AND LEGAL OUTCOMES; 819]

gaggle 1 *n* **crowd**, group, horde, throng, multitude, pack, mob, drove. [➡GROUPS OF PEOPLE; 935] **2** *type of* **flock.** [➡GROUP OF BIRDS; 1007]

gaiety *n* **joyfulness**, lightheartedness, happiness, liveliness, merriment, cheerfulness, vivacity, high spirits, vivaciousness. [➡PLEASURE, EXCITEMENT, AND ELATION; 535] *Opposite:* misery.

gaily *adv* **happily**, joyfully, cheerily, merrily, brightly, lightheartedly, vivaciously. [➡PLEASURE, EXCITEMENT, AND ELATION; 535] *Opposite:* sadly.

gain 1 *v* **get**, achieve, acquire, obtain, secure, collect, earn, reap. [➡GET; 421] *Opposite:* lose. **2** *v* **increase**, add, put on, grow, expand, enlarge, extend, multiply. [➡CHANGE OF SIZE: BIGGER; 393] *Opposite:* decrease. **3** *n* **achievement**, improvement, advantage, advance, increase, expansion, addition. [➡CHANGE OF INTENSITY: MORE; 395] *Opposite:* setback. **4** *n* **advantage**, profit, reward, benefit, return, acquisition, payback. [➡INCOME; 461] *Opposite:* loss.

See Compare and Contrast at **get**.

gain access *v* **get into**, enter, infiltrate, access, get permission, get hold of, get a hold of (*US*). [➡ARRIVE; 12]

gainful *adj* **profitable**, advantageous, lucrative, rewarding, useful, paid, productive, beneficial, remunerative. [➡USEFULNESS; 200] *Opposite:* unprofitable.

gain ground *v* **progress**, advance, improve, expand, spread, develop. [➡SUCCEED AND WIN; 79] *Opposite:* fall back.

gain on *v* **near**, close in on, approach, catch up on, close the gap, get closer to, get nearer to. [➡ACCOMPANY AND FOLLOW; 338]

gainsay (*formal*) *v* **oppose**, contradict, argue, refute, deny, contravene, disaffirm (*formal*), negate (*formal*), dispute, naysay (*US*). [➡DENY AND REJECT; 645] *Opposite:* agree.

gait *n* **walk**, step, pace, bearing, manner, style, posture. [➡TEMPERAMENT AND BEHAVIOUR; 493]

gala *n* **festival**, celebration, party, ball, festivity, social event, concert, entertainment, special occasion. [➡PARTIES, DANCES, AND CELEBRATIONS; 37]

galactic 1 *adj* (*informal*) **huge**, enormous, immense, vast, extensive, colossal, gargantuan, gigantic. [➡LARGE; 1192] *Opposite:* infinitesimal. 2 *adj* **celestial**, cosmic, planetary, astronomic, space. [➡THE SOLAR SYSTEM AND ASTRONOMY; 1059] *Opposite:* terrestrial.

galaxy 1 *n* **gathering**, assembly, meeting, cluster, collection, congregation. [➡COLLECTIONS AND MIXTURES OF THINGS; 1243] 2 *type of* **star or star system**. [➡CELESTIAL BODIES; 1060]

gale *n* **wind**, windstorm, storm, tempest, hurricane, howling wind, gust, blow (*informal*). [➡WINDY AND STORMY WEATHER; 1053] *Opposite:* breeze.

gale-force *adj* [➡WINDY AND STORMY WEATHER; 1053]

gall 1 *n* **audacity**, impudence, boldness, nerve, cheek (*informal*), face (*informal*), effrontery, insolence, moxie (*US slang*). [➡BAD MANNERS AND SOCIAL SKILLS; 522] 2 *n* **sore**, rub, irritation, lesion, wound, blister. [➡ILLNESSES AND DISORDERS; 733] 3 *v* **irritate**, annoy, infuriate, anger, vex, madden, provoke, incense, aggravate (*informal*), outrage. [➡ANGER AND ANNOY; 570] *Opposite:* please.

gallant 1 *adj* (*literary*) **brave**, courageous, heroic, valiant, dauntless (*literary*), fearless, intrepid (*literary or humorous*), noble, spirited, bold. [➡COURAGE; 499] *Opposite:* cowardly. 2 *adj* **courteous**, chivalrous, polite, gentlemanly, thoughtful, magnanimous, gracious. [➡GOOD MANNERS AND SOCIAL SKILLS; 521] *Opposite:* rude.

gallantry 1 *n* (*literary*) **courage**, bravery, heroism, valour, daring, nerve, fearlessness, boldness. [➡COURAGE; 499] *Opposite:* cowardice. 2 *n* **courtesy**, thoughtfulness, chivalry, politeness, attentiveness, gentility, graciousness. [➡GOOD MANNERS AND SOCIAL SKILLS; 521] *Opposite:* boorishness.

gallbladder *part of* **digestive tract**. [➡THE DIGESTIVE TRACT; 710]

galleon *type of* **historical vessel**. [➡SHIPS AND BOATS; 1149]

gallery 1 *n* **colonnade**, portico, arcade, galleria, corridor, walkway, passageway. [➡ANCILLARY BUILDINGS; 1079] 2 *n* **balcony**, veranda, porch. [➡STAIRS AND STOREYS; 1101] 3 *type of* **room in public buildings**. [➡TYPES OF ROOM; 1096]

galley 1 *part of* **ship or boat**. [➡PARTS OF A SHIP OR BOAT; 1150] 2 *type of* **historical vessel**. [➡SHIPS AND BOATS; 1149]

galling *adj* **frustrating**, annoying, irritating, infuriating, exasperating, maddening, vexing. [➡IRRITATING; 229] *Opposite:* soothing.

gallivant (*informal*) *v* **globetrot**, tour, travel around, gad (*humorous*), wander, rove, meander, ramble. [➡TRAVEL: WAYS OF TRAVELLING; 321] *Opposite:* stay put.

gallons *n* **lots**, loads (*informal*), tons (*informal*), masses (*informal*), heaps (*informal*), oodles (*informal*). [➡MANY, MUCH, LARGE AMOUNT; 117] *Opposite:* few.

gallop 1 *n* **sprint**, dash, charge, bolt, mad dash, run. [➡SUDDEN EVENT; 52] 2 *v* **dash**, career, hurtle, run, fly, bolt, sprint, charge, race. [➡MOVE FAST; 314]

gallows *n* **scaffold**, gibbet, gallows tree, crossbeam, arm, beam. [➡ANCIENT MANMADE STRUCTURES; 1088]

galore *adj* **abundant**, plentiful, copious, plenteous (*literary*), aplenty. [➡MANY, MUCH, LARGE AMOUNT; 117] *Opposite:* scant.

galoshes *type of* **boot**. [➡FOOTWEAR; 871]

galumph (*informal*) *v* [➡MOVE SLOWLY; 315]

galvanize *v* **stimulate**, spur, rouse, electrify, fire up, stir up, animate, incite. [➡CAUSE TO START; 266] *Opposite:* dampen.

gam *type of* **herd**. [➡GROUP OF ANIMALS; 993]

gambit *n* **stratagem**, manoeuvre, ploy, scheme, strategy, ruse. [➡WAYS OF DOING THINGS; 295]

gamble 1 *v* **bet**, wager, back, game, risk, stake, have a flutter (*informal*), put money on, lay bets. [➡GAMBLE AND TAKE RISKS; 467] 2 *v* **risk**, stake, venture, hazard, chance, speculate, bet. [➡GAMBLE AND TAKE RISKS; 467] *Opposite:* play safe. 3 *n* **wager**, bet, stake, flutter (*informal*). [➡GAMBLE AND TAKE RISKS; 467] 4 *n* **chance**, risk, hazard, venture, speculation. [➡GAMBLE AND TAKE RISKS; 467]

gamble away *v* **squander**, lose, fritter away, waste, throw away, pour down the drain. [➡GAMBLE AND TAKE RISKS; 467]

gambler 1 *n* **punter** (*informal*), bettor, risker, wagerer, speculator, high roller (*slang*), plunger (*informal*), gamester (*archaic*). [➡PEOPLE IN SPORTS AND LEISURE; 876] 2 *n* **risk-taker**, chancer (*informal*), adventurer, speculator, risker. [➡PEOPLE IN SPORTS AND LEISURE; 876]

gambling *n* **betting**, gaming, bookmaking. [➡GAMBLE AND TAKE RISKS; 467]

gambol *v* **frolic**, skip, hop, spring, leap, bound, caper, frisk, romp. [➡FIDGET AND FROLIC; 312]

game 1 *n* **pastime**, sport, diversion, amusement, entertainment, recreation. [➡LEISURE AND RECREATION; 874] 2 *n* **wild animals**, big game, game birds, game fish. [➡TYPES AND CUTS OF MEAT; 1176] 3 *n* **match**, fixture, competition, contest, derby, event. [➡NON-AGGRESSIVE/SPORTING EVENT; 40] 4 *adj* **willing**, ready, up for, disposed, inclined, on for. [➡THE WILL AND WILLINGNESS; 564] *Opposite:* unwilling. 5 *adj* **brave**, spirited, plucky, gutsy (*informal*), spunky (*informal*), feisty (*informal*), resolute, determined, tough. [➡COURAGE; 499] *Opposite:* spiritless.

game piece

◆ *types of game piece*
checker (*US*), chessman (*US*), chesspiece, chip, counter, domino, draught, jack, tiddlywink

gamekeeper *n* **game warden**, breeder, keeper, handler, steward, warden (*US*). [➡FARMERS, GARDENERS, AND MANUAL WORKERS; 849]

gamelan *type of* **percussion instrument**. [➡MUSICAL INSTRUMENTS; 910]

gamely *adv* **bravely**, sportingly, spiritedly, gutsily (*informal*), spunkily (*informal*), feistily (*informal*), stoically, determinedly, resolutely. [➡COURAGE; 499] *Opposite:* weakly.

game plan *n* **plan**, strategy, scheme, stratagem, ploy, manoeuvre. [➡WAYS OF DOING THINGS; 295]

games *n* **sports**, competition, tournament, cup, sports event, meet, knockout. [➡NON-AGGRESSIVE/SPORTING EVENT; 40]

game show *type of* **broadcast**. [➡TELEVISION AND RADIO; 607]

games room *type of* **room in public buildings**. [➡TYPES OF ROOM; 1096]

gammon *type of* **meat**. [➡TYPES AND CUTS OF MEAT; 1176]

gammy (*informal*) *adj* **sore**, stiff, painful, uncomfortable, aching, arthritic, injured, broken. [➡ILL AND SICK; 741]

gamut *n* **range**, scale, length, scope, extent, breadth, array. [➡DEGREE AND EXTENT; 110]

gander 1 *n* (*informal*) **look**, shufti (*informal*), peek, glimpse, glance, dekko (*informal*). [➡LOOKING AND LOOKS; 701] 2 *type of* **male or female bird**. [➡MALE OR FEMALE BIRD; 1005]

gang 1 *n* **mob**, band, ring, clique, posse (*slang*). [➡FRIENDS AND ACQUAINTANCES; 936] 2 *n* **team**, squad, crew (*informal*), group, posse (*slang*), lineup. [➡GROUPS OF PEOPLE; 935]

gangland *n* **underworld**, criminal world, organized crime, vice, racketeering. [➡CRIMES; 817]

gangling *adj* **lanky**, gangly, gawky (*informal*), tall, rangy, awkward. [➡BUILD; 478] *Opposite:* elegant.

ganglion *n* **swelling**, lump, knot, concentration, cyst, tumour. [➡ILLNESSES AND DISORDERS; 733]

gangly *adj* **lanky**, gangling, gawky (*informal*), tall, rangy, awkward. [➡BUILD; 478] *Opposite:* elegant.

gangplank *n* **bridge**, walkway, footway, footbridge, gangway, passage. [➡BRIDGES, TUNNELS, CROSSINGS, AND JUNCTIONS; 1111]

gangrene 1 *n* **infection**, decay, rot, decomposition, putrefaction, disease. [➡ILLNESSES AND DISORDERS; 733] *Opposite:* health. 2 *v* **fester**, putrefy, decompose, decay, rot, moulder. [➡GO BAD AND CORRODE; 391] *Opposite:* recover.

gangrenous *adj* **infected**, festering, diseased, decaying, rotting, decomposing, putrescent, putrid. [➡SICKNESS; 730] *Opposite:* healthy.

gangster *n* **criminal**, thug, hooligan (*informal*), hoodlum, racketeer, gorilla (*informal*), Mafioso, mobster (*US informal*), goon (*US*). [➡CRIMINALS; 821]

gang up on *v* **unite against**, join forces against, combine against, pick on, mob, surround, target, put pressure on. [➡ACCUSE, BLAME, AND CRITICIZE; 642]

gangway *n* **walkway**, footway, aisle, passage, passageway, corridor. [➡PATHWAYS; 1109]

gannet 1 *n* (*informal*) **glutton**, pig (*informal*), gourmand. [➡PLEASURE-SEEKERS AND HEDONISTS; 886] 2 *type of* **seabird**. [➡SEABIRD; 1002]

gantry *n* **scaffold**, framework, support. [➡MACHINES AND MACHINE PARTS; 1115]

gaol 1 *n* [➡BUILDINGS FOR CONFINING PEOPLE; 1093] 2 *see* **jail**.

gap 1 *n* **break**, opening, breach, slit, fissure, crack, aperture, cavity, hole. [➡HOLES, GAPS, AND FORKS; 1251] 2 *n* **interval**, hiatus, pause, break, interruption, lull, interlude, space. [➡PAUSES AND PHASES; 56] *Opposite:* continuity. 3 *n* **disparity**, difference, divergence, mismatch, inequality, disproportion, imparity, variance. [➡DIFFERENCE; 150] *Opposite:* parity. 4 *n* **chasm**, gorge, ravine, canyon, rift, gully, gulch (*US*). [➡GEOLOGICAL FEATURES; 1056]

gape 1 *v* **stare**, gawk (*informal*), gawp (*informal*), gaze, ogle, look hard, rubberneck (*informal*). [➡LOOKING AND LOOKS; 701] 2 *v* **part**, separate, divide, yawn, break open, fall open. [➡SEPARATE AND DIVIDE; 402]

See Compare and Contrast at **gaze**.

gaping *adj* **wide**, wide open, huge, yawning, cavernous, deep, abysmal. [➡WIDTH: WIDE; 1198]

garage 1 *n* **carport**, lockup, cover, shed, car stall, outbuilding, parking garage. [➡STORES AND STORAGE BUILDINGS; 1087] 2 *n* **service station**, petrol station, gas station (*US*). [➡ANCILLARY BUILDINGS; 1079] 3 *type of* **popular music**. [➡MUSIC, SONGS, AND SINGING; 907] 4 *type of* **industrial site**. [➡INDUSTRIAL BUILDINGS; 1086]

garage sale *n* [➡SALES AND SHOWS; 444]

garb 1 *n* **clothing**, dress, attire (*formal*), costume, apparel, outfit, duds (*informal*), weeds (*archaic or literary*), kit, gear (*informal*), threads (*US slang*). [➡CLOTHES AND ACCESSORIES; 864] 2 *v* **clothe**, dress, array (*literary*), attire (*formal*), do up, dress up. [➡DRESS, WEAR, AND UNDRESS; 868]

garbage 1 *n* **nonsense**, trivia, rubbish, drivel, hogwash (*informal*), baloney (*informal*). [➡MEANINGLESS SPEECH OR WRITING; 677] *Opposite:* sense. 2 *n* (*US*) **rubbish**, refuse, compost, debris, litter, junk (*informal*), waste, trash (*US*). [➡RUBBISH AND USELESS OBJECTS; 1248]

garbage can (*US*) *n* **rubbish bin**, waste bin, litter bin, trash can (*US*), ash can (*US*), wastebasket (*US*). [➡CONTAINERS, RECEPTACLES, AND PACKAGING; 1244]

garbage truck (*US*) *type of* **public service vehicle**. [➡VEHICLES; 1144]

garbagy *adj* [➡REDUNDANT AND USELESS; 241]

garbanzo *type of* **pulse**. [➡BEANS AND PULSES; 1188]

garbanzo bean *see* **garbanzo**.

garbed *adj* [➡DRESS, WEAR, AND UNDRESS; 868]

garble *v* **jumble**, confuse, muddle, mangle, distort, corrupt, pervert, twist. [➡CREATE DISORDER AND CAUSE CHAOS; 359]

garbled *adj* **jumbled**, confused, muddled, distorted, mangled, corrupted, twisted, misconstrued. [➡INARTICULATE, RAMBLING, AND AWKWARD; 634] *Opposite:* clear.

garden 1 *n* **plot**, allotment, kitchen garden, vegetable garden, vegetable plot, patch, flower garden, rose garden, rock garden, orchard, rockery, shrubbery, lawn. [➡GARDENS; 1073] 2 *n* **park**, gardens, public park, green, common, botanical garden, parkland. [➡GARDENS; 1073] 3 *v* **plant**, cultivate, tend, work, grow, weed, sow, raise. [➡HOBBIES, GAMES, AND SPORTS; 875]

garden apartment (*US*) *type of* **apartment.** [➡RESIDENTIAL BUILDINGS; 1077]

garden centre *type of* **retail outlet.** [➡RETAIL OUTLETS; 1082]

gardener *n* **horticulturist**, landscape gardener, grower, planter, weeder, landscape architect, landscaper (*US*). [➡FARMERS, GARDENERS, AND MANUAL WORKERS; 849]

garden flat *type of* **apartment.** [➡RESIDENTIAL BUILDINGS; 1077]

gardenia *type of* **shrub or bush.** [➡BUSHES AND SHRUBS; 1027]

garden party *n* [➡PARTIES, DANCES, AND CELEBRATIONS; 37]

garden shed *type of* **outbuilding.** [➡ANCILLARY BUILDINGS; 1079]

garden-variety (*US*) *adj* [➡ORDINARINESS; 245]

gargantuan *adj* **huge**, large, gigantic, enormous, vast, massive, colossal, immense. [➡LARGE; 1192] *Opposite:* tiny.

gargle 1 *v* **rinse your mouth**, rinse, wash out, disinfect, freshen, cleanse, swill. [➡CLEAN AND POLISH; 404] 2 *v* **gurgle**, bubble, burble, glug (*informal*). [➡EMIT CONTINUOUS SOUNDS; 367]

gargoyle *n* **ornament**, decoration, carving, figurehead, effigy. [➡SCULPTURE; 902]

garish *adj* **gaudy**, showy, lurid, vulgar, brash, loud, tasteless, tawdry, bright. [➡IN POOR TASTE; 230] *Opposite:* tasteful.

garishness *n* **gaudiness**, tawdriness, vulgarity, brashness, loudness, tastelessness, showiness, luridness, brightness. [➡IN POOR TASTE; 230] *Opposite:* subtlety.

garland 1 *n* **wreath**, chaplet, coronet, circlet, crown, lei. [➡ORNAMENTS AND DECORATIONS; 1247] 2 *n* **festoon**, swag, drape, chain. [➡ORNAMENTS AND DECORATIONS; 1247]

garlic *type of* **vegetable.** [➡FRUIT AND VEGETABLES; 1175]

garment *n* **clothing**, vestment, costume, frock (*dated*), dress, coat, skirt, attire (*formal*), apparel, raiment (*formal*). [➡CLOTHES AND ACCESSORIES; 864]

garment

◆ *parts of a garment*
brim, buckle, button, buttonhole, coat-tail, collar, cuff, décolletage, drawstring, gusset, hem, lace, lapel, leg, lining, neck, neckband, neckline, pocket, sash, sleeve, strap, turn-up, waistband, zip

garner 1 *v* **gather**, bring in, save, lay down, store, put away, harvest, reap. [➡GET; 421] *Opposite:* scatter. 2 *v* **acquire**, get, gain, collect, bring together, search out, earn, accumulate. [➡GET; 421] *Opposite:* squander.

garnet 1 *type of* **red.** [➡COLOURS; 1223] 2 *type of* **gemstone.** [➡PRECIOUS STONES; 1277]

garnish 1 *v* **enhance**, improve, set off, embellish, decorate, glaze, dress up, pretty up, prettify, deck (*literary*). [➡COOKING AND FOOD PREPARATION; 354] 2 *n* **enhancer**, sauce, accompaniment, relish, savoury, side dish, gravy, trimmings, fixings (*US informal*). [➡SEASONINGS AND SAUCES; 1173] 3 *n* **embellishment**, decoration, adornment, ornament, trimming, enhancement. [➡ORNAMENTS AND DECORATIONS; 1247]

garret *n* **attic**, loft, gable, penthouse, top storey, upper floor, roof space. [➡TYPES OF ROOM; 1096]

garrison *n* **barracks**, quarters, military base, casern. [➡UNDESIRABLE ACCOMMODATION; 856]

garrotte *v* [➡KILL; 923]

garrulous *adj* **talkative**, voluble, chatty, effusive, loquacious (*formal*), verbose, long-winded, gushing, gassy (*informal*), chattering, gaseous (*informal*). [➡ELOQUENT, TALKATIVE, AND LONG-WINDED; 633] *Opposite:* taciturn.

See Compare and Contrast at **talkative**.

garrulousness *n* **loquacity** (*formal*), verbosity, volubility, chattiness, gift of the gab (*informal*), prattling, long-windedness, talkativeness, effusiveness. [➡ELOQUENT, TALKATIVE, AND LONG-WINDED; 633] *Opposite:* taciturnity.

garter *type of* **lower body underwear.** [➡HABERDASHERY, MILLINERY, AND LINGERIE; 867]

garter snake *type of* **non-poisonous snake.** [➡SNAKE; 995]

gas 1 *n* **air**, vapour, fume, smoke. [➡GASES; 1274] 2 *n* (*informal*) **blast**, thrill, trip (*informal*), experience. [➡TREAT; 211] *Opposite:* drag. 3 *n* (*informal*) **chitchat** (*informal*), chatter, gab (*informal*), prattle, blather (*informal*), footle (*informal*), bunkum (*informal*), rubbish, nonsense, bombast, claptrap (*informal*), bunk (*slang*), poppycock (*dated informal*), balderdash. [➡MEANINGLESS SPEECH OR WRITING; 677] 4 *v* (*informal*) **chat**, gossip, chitchat (*informal*), natter (*informal*), yak (*informal*), jaw (*slang*), chew the fat (*slang*), chinwag (*US*). [➡GOSSIP; 679]

gas

◆ *types of gas*
acetylene, argon, butane, chlorine, coal gas, greenhouse gas, helium, hydrogen, inert gas, marsh gas, methane, mustard gas, natural gas, neon, nerve gas, nitrogen, nitrous oxide, noble gas, oxygen, poison gas, propellant, tear gas

gaseous 1 *adj* **vaporous**, gassy, steamy, smoky, fumy, gasiform. [➡FLUID AND NON-SOLID; 1212] 2 *adj* (*informal*) **talkative**, verbose, long-winded, chatty, gassy (*informal*), chattering, loquacious (*formal*), voluble, effusive, garrulous, gushing, prattling. [➡ELOQUENT, TALKATIVE, AND LONG-WINDED; 633] *Opposite:* tight-lipped. 3 *adj* **carbonated**, fizzy, bubbly, sparkling, effervescent, gassy. [➡FLUID AND NON-SOLID; 1212] *Opposite:* still.

gash 1 *n* **wound**, slash, cut, tear, laceration, incision. [➡HOLES, GAPS, AND FORKS; 1251] 2 *v* **cut**, slash, wound, tear, lacerate, gouge. [➡TEAR, BREAK, AND CUT; 361]

gasket 1 *n* **seal**, washer, ring, liner, lining. [➡PARTS OF MACHINES AND TOOLS; 1117] 2 *part of* **engine.** [➡PARTS OF AN ENGINE; 1143]

gasoline (*US*) *n* [➡ENERGY SOURCES; 1161]

gasometer *type of* **storage space.** [➡STORES AND STORAGE BUILDINGS; 1087]

gasp 1 *n* **wheeze**, pant, huff, puff, breath. [➡BREATHE AND NOT BREATHE; 717] 2 *type of* **human sound.** [➡SOUNDS MADE BY PEOPLE; 1261]

gasping 1 *adj* **out of breath**, puffed, winded, breathless, panting, wheezing, puffing. [➡ILL AND SICK; 741] 2 *adj* **thirsty**, parched, dry, dehydrated, thirsting. [➡DRINK; 712] 3 *adj* **desperate**, dying, longing, craving, yearning, burning. [➡DESIRE AND WANT; 580]

gas station (*US*) *n* **service station**, service area, garage, filling station, petrol station, petrol pumps, gas pumps (*US*). [➡RETAIL OUTLETS; 1082]

gassy 1 *adj* **carbonated**, fizzy, bubbly, sparkling, effervescent, gaseous. [➡FLUID AND NON-SOLID; 1212] *Opposite:* still. 2 *adj* **vaporous**, gaseous, steamy, smoky, fumy, gasiform. [➡FLUID AND NON-SOLID; 1212] 3 *adj* (*informal*) **talkative**, verbose, long-winded, chatty, gossipy, garrulous, chattering, gaseous, loquacious (*formal*), voluble, gushing, prattling. [➡ELOQUENT, TALKATIVE, AND LONG-WINDED; 633] *Opposite:* tight-lipped.

gastric *adj* **stomach**, abdominal, intestinal, digestive, gastrointestinal, tummy (*informal*). [➡THE DIGESTIVE TRACT; 710]

gastrointestinal *adj* **stomach**, abdominal, intestinal, digestive, gastric, tummy (*informal*). [➡THE DIGESTIVE TRACT; 710]

gastronome *n* **gourmet**, epicure, foodie (*informal*), food lover, connoisseur, bon vivant (*literary*), gourmand, bon viveur (*literary*). [➡EATERS, GOURMETS, AND DIETARY CHOICES; 715] *Opposite:* glutton.

gastronomic *adj* **culinary**, cooking, food, gourmet, epicurean. [➡FOOD; 1166]

gastronomy *n* **cookery**, cooking, cuisine, food, gourmet food, gourmandise, epicureanism. [➡FOOD; 1166]

gasworks *n* **gas plant**, power station, installation, power plant. [➡INDUSTRIAL BUILDINGS; 1086]

gate 1 *n* **entrance**, entry, door, gateway, opening, postern, doorway, access. [➡DOORS AND ACCESS POINTS; 1100] 2 *n* **attendance**, crowd, turnout, audience. [➡AUDIENCES AND ATTENDEES; 937] 3 *n* **receipts**, takings, proceeds, revenue, take. [➡INCOME; 461]

gateau *n* [➡CAKES, BISCUITS, AND DESSERTS; 1180]

gatecrash *v* **crash** (*informal*), sneak in, barge in, invade, intrude, trespass. [➡ARRIVE; 12]

gatecrasher *n* **intruder**, interloper, trespasser, invader, persona non grata. [➡STRANGERS; 972] *Opposite:* guest.

gatehouse *type of* **outbuilding.** [➡ANCILLARY BUILDINGS; 1079]

gateleg table *type of* **table.** [➡FURNITURE; 858]

gatepost *n* **support**, upright, post, frame, doorpost, door jamb. [➡STICKS, POLES, AND WEDGES; 1253]

gateway 1 *n* **entry**, doorway, entrance, opening, access, postern, door, entryway (*US*). [➡DOORS AND ACCESS POINTS; 1100] 2 *n* **opening**, first step, opportunity, access, way in, chance. [➡ADVANTAGE; 213]

gather 1 *v* **meet**, get together, collect, congregate, assemble, join together, gather round, gather together. [➡GET CLOSER TOGETHER; 311] *Opposite:* disperse. 2 *v* **collect**, bring together, draw together, amass, pull together, pile up, gather together, muster, marshal, round up, mobilize. [➡COMBINE AND MIX; 401] *Opposite:* distribute. 3 *v* **harvest**, pick, collect, garner, pluck, reap. [➡GET; 421] *Opposite:* scatter. 4 *v* **understand**, infer, conclude, hear, assume, deduce, surmise. [➡UNDERSTAND AND GRASP; 760] *Opposite:* misunderstand. 5 *v* **pleat**, fold, pucker, ruche, shirr, crimp, ruck, bunch. [➡CHANGE OF SHAPE; 386] *Opposite:* smooth. 6 *n* **fold**, pleat, pucker, wrinkle, ruck, crease. [➡ORNAMENTS AND DECORATIONS; 1247]

See Compare and Contrast at **collect.**

gathering *n* **meeting**, assembly, congregation, crowd, get-together (*informal*), jamboree, rally. [➡MEETINGS AND ASSEMBLIES; 43]

gathering place *n* **meeting place**, centre, assembly point, forum. [➡PUBLIC BUILDINGS AND MEETING PLACES; 1080]

gather together *v* [➡GET CLOSER TOGETHER; 311]

gather up *v* **pick up**, take up, draw up, scoop up, dredge up, haul up. [➡CONTACT: HOLD; 412] *Opposite:* put down.

gauche *adj* **awkward**, uncouth, tactless, callow, graceless, clumsy. [➡BAD MANNERS AND SOCIAL SKILLS; 522] *Opposite:* poised.

gaucheness *n* **uncouthness**, awkwardness, tactlessness, gracelessness, clumsiness, callowness. [➡BAD MANNERS AND SOCIAL SKILLS; 522] *Opposite:* poise.

gaucherie *n* [➡AGILITY OF THE BODY; 477]

gaudiness *n* **showiness**, luridness, flamboyance, garishness, tawdriness, loudness, tackiness (*informal*), cheapness, vividness, extravagance, colourfulness. [➡IN POOR TASTE; 230] *Opposite:* tastefulness.

gaudy *adj* **garish**, flashy, kitschy, loud, showy, colourful, lurid, extravagant, cheap, flamboyant, tawdry, tacky (*informal*). [➡IN POOR TASTE; 230] *Opposite:* tasteful.

gauge 1 *v* **evaluate**, judge, assess, determine, measure, appraise, estimate, test, calculate, guess, weigh. [➡EXAMINE AND ASSESS; 754] 2 *n* **measurement**, estimate, assessment, measure, test, yardstick, indication, criterion, standard, benchmark, indicator. [➡MEASURING DEVICES; 1122]

gaunt *adj* **thin**, skinny, lean, bony, emaciated, scrawny, skeletal, haggard. [➡BUILD; 478] *Opposite:* plump.

gauntness *n* **thinness**, skinniness, leanness, boniness, scrawniness, scragginess. [➡BUILD; 478] *Opposite:* plumpness.

gauze *type of* **fabric from plants.** [➡FABRICS; 1131]

gauzy *adj* **thin**, delicate, filmy, see-through, gossamer, light, diaphanous, transparent. [➡WIDTH: NARROW AND THIN; 1199] *Opposite:* heavy.

gawk (*informal*) *v* **gape**, stare, gawp (*informal*), gaze, goggle, watch, rubberneck (*informal*), ogle. [➡LOOKING AND LOOKS; 701] *Opposite:* ignore.

See Compare and Contrast at **gaze.**

gawkiness *(informal)* *n* **awkwardness**, clumsiness, inelegance, gracelessness, ungainliness. [➡AGILITY OF THE BODY; 477] *Opposite:* gracefulness.

gawky *(informal)* *adj* **awkward**, clumsy, gangling, gangly, ungainly, inelegant, graceless. [➡AGILITY OF THE BODY; 477] *Opposite:* graceful.

gawp *(informal)* *v* **stare**, gape, gawk *(informal)*, gaze, goggle, watch, ogle, rubberneck *(informal)*. [➡LOOKING AND LOOKS; 701] *Opposite:* ignore.

gaze 1 *v* **look**, stare, watch, contemplate, gape, eye, scrutinize, observe, gawk *(informal)*, gawp *(informal)*, goggle, rubberneck *(informal)*, ogle. [➡LOOKING AND LOOKS; 701] *Opposite:* ignore. 2 *n* **stare**, look, regard *(formal)*, contemplation, observation, scrutiny. [➡LOOKING AND LOOKS; 701]

Compare and Contrast: ***gaze, stare, gape, gawk, gawp, ogle, rubberneck***

CORE MEANING: TO LOOK AT SOMEBODY OR SOMETHING STEADILY OR AT LENGTH

gaze to look for a long time with unwavering attention; ***stare*** to look at somebody or something directly and intently without moving the eyes away, as a result of curiosity or surprise, or to express rudeness or defiance; ***gape*** to look at somebody or something in surprise or wonder, usually with an open mouth; ***gawk*** or ***gawp*** (*informal*) to stare stupidly or rudely; ***ogle*** to look steadily at somebody for sexual enjoyment or to show sexual interest; ***rubberneck*** (*informal*) to stare at somebody or something in an over-inquisitive or insensitive way.

gazebo *type of* **outbuilding.** [➡ANCILLARY BUILDINGS; 1079]

gazelle *type of* **deer or antelope.** [➡DEER AND ANTELOPE; 981]

gazette *n* **newspaper**, paper, journal, periodical, newsletter, newssheet, publication. [➡NEWSPAPERS; 606]

gazillion *(slang)* *n* [➡MANY, MUCH, LARGE AMOUNT; 117]

gazpacho *type of* **soup.** [➡SOUP; 1185]

gear 1 *n* *(informal)* **kit**, stuff, things, paraphernalia, tackle, trappings, equipment, apparatus. [➡POSSESSIONS; 462] 2 *n* *(informal)* **clothes**, clothing, kit, togs *(informal)*, outfit. [➡CLOTHES AND ACCESSORIES; 864] 3 *part of* **engine.** [➡PARTS OF AN ENGINE; 1143]

gearbox *part of* **engine.** [➡PARTS OF AN ENGINE; 1143]

geared up *adj* **ready**, prepared, set, equipped, operational, fitted out, outfitted. [➡ORDER AND ORGANIZATION; 207] *Opposite:* unprepared.

gearing *part of* **engine.** [➡PARTS OF AN ENGINE; 1143]

gear lever *type of* **controls.** [➡VEHICLES; 1144]

gearshift *(US)* *type of* **controls.** [➡VEHICLES; 1144]

gear to *v* **adjust to**, align with, adapt to, tailor, modify, customize. [➡CHANGE; 373]

gear up *v* **get ready**, prepare yourself, ready yourself, psych yourself up *(informal)*, prepare, mobilize. [➡PREPARE FOR ACTION; 290] *Opposite:* wind down.

gearwheel *n* [➡PARTS OF MACHINES AND TOOLS; 1117]

gecko *type of* **reptile.** [➡REPTILES; 994]

gee *(US informal)* *interj* [➡EXPRESSIONS OF SURPRISE; 547]

gee whiz *(US informal)* *interj* [➡EXPRESSIONS OF SURPRISE; 547]

geezer *(informal)* *n* [➡MALE PERSON; 934]

Geiger counter *type of* **measuring device.** [➡MEASURING DEVICES; 1122]

gel 1 *n* **cream**, lotion, balm, ointment, salve, emollient, unguent, liniment. [➡LOTIONS, PASTES, AND GELS; 1271] 2 *v* *(informal)* **come together**, take shape, crystallize, develop, form, hang together, materialize. [➡GRADUALLY COME INTO EXISTENCE; 1] *Opposite:* disperse. 3 *v* *(informal)* **hit it off** *(informal)*, click *(informal)*, see eye to eye, relate, get on, get on like a house on fire, get along, get along like a house on fire. [➡ESTABLISHING RELATIONSHIPS WITH OTHERS; 974] 4 *v* **congeal**, thicken, coagulate, clot, harden, set, solidify. [➡HARDEN, CONGEAL, DRY; 388] *Opposite:* liquefy.

gelatinous *adj* **jellylike**, gummy, gooey, sticky, gungy *(informal)*, viscous, glutinous. [➡PHYSICAL TEXTURE; 1221]

geld *v* **castrate**, neuter, spay, sterilize, emasculate *(formal or literary)*, vasectomize. [➡STERILIZE; 727]

gelignite *type of* **explosive material.** [➡EXPLOSIVES; 1154]

gem 1 *n* **jewel**, stone, precious stone, cut stone, rock *(informal)*, gemstone. [➡PRECIOUS STONES; 1277] 2 *n* *(informal)* **treasure**, pearl, peach *(informal)*, star, godsend, paragon, nugget, prize. [➡AMAZING THING; 212]

Gemini *type of* **star sign.** [➡FATE, DESTINY, AND ASTROLOGY; 783]

gemstone *n* **jewel**, stone, gem, precious stone, cut stone, rock *(informal)*. [➡PRECIOUS STONES; 1277]

gemstone

◆ *types of gemstone*
agate, amethyst, aquamarine, beryl, bloodstone, carnelian, chalcedony, chrysoprase, diamond, emerald, garnet, jade, lapis lazuli, moonstone, mother-of-pearl, onyx, opal, pearl, ruby, sapphire, sard, topaz, tourmaline, turquoise

gen *(informal)* *n* [➡KNOWLEDGE AND WISDOM; 559]

gender *n* **sex**, sexual category, sexual characteristics, masculinity, femininity, sexual role. [➡GENDER IDENTITY AND SEXUALITY; 932]

gender

◆ *types of male animal*
billy goat, boar, buck, bull, bullock, colt, hart, jackass, ram, stag, stallion, steer, tom, tomcat, wether

◆ *types of female animal*
bitch, cow, dam, doe, ewe, filly, heifer, hind, jenny, lioness, mare, nanny goat, sow, tigress, vixen

◆ *types of male or female bird*
capon, cob, cock, cockerel, drake, duck, gander, goose, hen, pen, rooster

genderless *adj* [➡GENDER IDENTITY AND SEXUALITY; 932]

gene *n* **genetic factor**, inheritable factor, protein sequence, DNA segment, RNA component, genetic material. [➡REPRODUCTION AND HEREDITY; 726]

genealogical *adj* **hereditary**, ancestral, family, pedigree. [➡THE FAMILY; 956]

genealogy *n* **family tree**, descent, lineage, pedigree, family, ancestors, forebears, descendants. [➡THE FAMILY; 956]

general 1 *adj* **overall**, universal, all-purpose, wide-ranging, broad, common, broad-spectrum. [➡WHOLENESS AND COMPLETENESS; 199] *Opposite:* specific. 2 *adj* **usual**, typical, conventional, customary, accustomed. [➡ORDINARINESS; 245] *Opposite:* unusual. 3 *adj* **widespread**, common, universal, wide-ranging, broad. [➡GENERAL LOCATIONS; 159] *Opposite:* unique. 4 *adj* **unspecific**, undefined, unclear, vague. [➡VAGUENESS; 244] *Opposite:* specific.

general election *n* [➡ELECTIONS AND SUFFRAGE; 807]

generalities *n* [➡BASIC DETAILS; 689]

generality 1 *n* **generalization**, sweeping statement, simplification, oversimplification, overview, broad view. [➡SUMMARIES, OUTLINES, AND EXCERPTS; 589] *Opposite:* detail. 2 *n* **platitude**, cliché, banality, bromide (*dated*), truism, chestnut (*informal*), axiom. [➡FIGURES OF SPEECH; 674]

generalization *n* **sweeping statement**, simplification, oversimplification, overview, generality, broad view. [➡SUMMARIES, OUTLINES, AND EXCERPTS; 589] *Opposite:* detail.

generalize *v* **simplify**, oversimplify, take a broad view, make a sweeping statement. [➡EXPLAIN AND CLARIFY; 611] *Opposite:* specify.

generalized *adj* **widespread**, sweeping, comprehensive, general, global, universal, indiscriminate. [➡WHOLENESS AND COMPLETENESS; 199] *Opposite:* isolated.

generally *adv* **usually**, normally, in general, in the main, by and large, commonly, mostly, largely, as a rule, all in all. [➡USUALLY; 108] *Opposite:* rarely.

generally speaking *adv* **in the main**, on the whole, in general, by and large, mostly, largely, as a rule, all in all, usually, normally. [➡SUMMARIZING EXPRESSIONS; 623] *Opposite:* exceptionally.

general public *n* **population**, populace, ordinary people, hoi polloi, rank and file. [➡GROUPS IN SOCIETY; 940] *Opposite:* elite.

general store (*US*) *type of* **retail outlet**. [➡RETAIL OUTLETS; 1082]

generate *v* **make**, produce, create, cause, engender, spawn, breed. [➡INSTITUTE AND INAUGURATE; 349] *Opposite:* prevent.

generation 1 *n* **age group**, peer group, peers, cohort, compeers (*formal*), group. [➡GROUPS OF PEOPLE; 935] 2 *n* **age**, era, epoch, period, aeon, phase. [➡EPOCHS AND ERAS; 89] 3 *n* **production**, making, creation, invention, initiation, origination. [➡CREATION; 347] *Opposite:* prevention.

generator 1 *n* **producer**, maker, creator, originator, initiator, author. [➡DESIGNERS, CREATORS, AND INSTIGATORS; 348] 2 *n* [➡ENERGY STORAGE AND GENERATION; 1162]

generic *adj* **general**, broad, common, basic, nonspecific, standard, universal, all-purpose. [➡ORDINARINESS; 245] *Opposite:* specific.

generically *adv* **generally**, broadly, commonly, basically, widely, loosely, universally. [➡USUALLY; 108] *Opposite:* specifically.

generosity *n* **kindness**, big-heartedness, openhandedness, liberality, bounty (*literary*), bounteousness (*literary*), munificence, charity. [➡GENEROSITY AND KINDNESS; 496] *Opposite:* stinginess.

generous 1 *adj* **kind**, liberal, big-hearted, openhanded, munificent, giving, charitable, magnanimous, bountiful (*literary*) [➡GENEROSITY AND KINDNESS; 496]. *Opposite:* stingy (*informal*). 2 *adj* **substantial**, large, lavish, liberal, plentiful, princely, unstinting. [➡MANY, MUCH, LARGE AMOUNT; 117] *Opposite:* meagre.

Compare and Contrast: *generous, magnanimous, munificent, bountiful, liberal*

CORE MEANING: GIVING READILY TO OTHERS

generous willing to give money, help, or time freely; ***magnanimous*** very generous, kind, or forgiving; ***munificent*** very generous, especially on a grand scale; ***bountiful*** (*literary*) generous, particularly to less fortunate people; ***liberal*** free with money, time, or other assets.

generously *adv* **kindly**, big-heartedly, openhandedly, liberally, munificently, charitably. [➡GENEROSITY AND KINDNESS; 496] *Opposite:* stingily.

genesis *n* **origin**, origins, beginning, start, birth, dawn, creation. [➡BEGINNING; 53]

genetic *adj* **hereditary**, inherited, heritable, inherent, genomic, chromosomal, innate, inborn, native, natural. [➡REPRODUCTION AND HEREDITY; 726] *Opposite:* learned.

genetics *type of* **bioscience**. [➡BIOLOGICAL SCIENCES; 1037]

genial *adj* **friendly**, amiable, warm, welcoming, hospitable, gracious, pleasant, kindly, cordial, convivial, sociable. [➡FRIENDLINESS AND SOCIABILITY; 495] *Opposite:* unfriendly.

geniality *n* **friendliness**, warmth, cordiality, amiability, conviviality, sociability, hospitableness, kindness, graciousness, pleasantness. [➡FRIENDLINESS AND SOCIABILITY; 495] *Opposite:* hostility.

genie *n* **sprite**, spirit, apparition, jinni, imp. [➡MYTHICAL BEINGS; 790]

genius 1 *n* **mastermind**, prodigy, whiz kid (*informal*), brain (*informal*), intellect, virtuoso. [➡TALENTED OR INTELLIGENT PERSON; 529] 2 *n* **brilliance**, intellect, brains, virtuosity, intelligence, gift, talent, knack, aptitude, capacity, ability, flair, smarts (*US informal*). [➡POSITIVE INTELLECTUAL CHARACTERISTICS; 525] *Opposite:* stupidity.

See Compare and Contrast at **talent**.

genocide *n* **killing**, slaughter, massacre, ethnic cleansing, liquidation, extermination, annihilation. [➡CAUSES OF DEATH; 921]

genre *n* **type**, sort, kind, category, field, variety, genus. [➡VARIETY, TYPE, KIND; 146]

See Compare and Contrast at **type**.

gent (*dated informal*) *n* **gentleman**, man, bloke (*informal*), guy (*informal*), fellow (*dated*). [➡MALE PERSON; 934]

genteel 1 *adj* **refined**, proper, polite, courteous, discreet, well-mannered, mannerly, civil, decorous. [➡GOOD MANNERS AND SOCIAL SKILLS; 521] *Opposite:* vulgar. 2 *adj* **pretentious**, snobbish, condescending, patronizing, snooty (*informal*), affected. [➡AFFECTATION, SELF-SATISFACTION, AND SNOBBISHNESS; 508] *Opposite:* modest.

genteelness *n* [➡GOOD MANNERS AND SOCIAL SKILLS; 521]

gentility *n* **refinement**, propriety, manners, breeding, decorum, courtesy, discretion, politeness, courteousness, urbanity, elegance, civility. [➡GOOD MANNERS AND SOCIAL SKILLS; 521] *Opposite:* vulgarity.

gentle 1 *adj* **mild**, calm, kind, tender, moderate, placid, temperate. [➡GENEROSITY AND KINDNESS; 496] 2 *adj* **soft**, light, soothing, mellow, restful, peaceful, quiet. [➡PEACEFULNESS AND GENTLENESS; 215] *Opposite:* rough.

gentleman 1 *n* **man**, fellow, chap (*informal*), guy (*informal*), bloke (*informal*), lad (*informal*), male, person. [➡MALE PERSON; 934] 2 *n* **nobleman**, aristocrat, squire, grandee. [➡CLASS STATUS; 889]

gentlemanly *adj* **chivalrous**, gallant, courteous, polite, civil, gracious, correct. [➡GOOD MANNERS AND SOCIAL SKILLS; 521] *Opposite:* rude.

gentleness 1 *n* **mildness**, calmness, kindness, tenderness, placidity. [➡GENEROSITY AND KINDNESS; 496] *Opposite:* harshness. 2 *n* **quietness**, softness, lightness, smoothness, mellowness, restfulness, peacefulness. [➡PEACEFULNESS AND GENTLENESS; 215] *Opposite:* harshness.

gently 1 *adv* **softly**, lightly, quietly, smoothly, soothingly, tenderly, kindly. [➡PEACEFULNESS AND GENTLENESS; 215] *Opposite:* harshly. 2 *adv* **mildly**, moderately, lightly, softly, slightly, gradually. [➡FEW, LITTLE, SMALL AMOUNT; 119] *Opposite:* rapidly.

gentrification *n* **redevelopment**, refurbishment, urban renewal, renovation, restoration, improvement, transformation. [➡SOCIAL, POLITICAL, AND ECONOMIC CHANGE; 374] *Opposite:* neglect.

gentrify *v* **redevelop**, refurbish, renovate, restore, improve, smarten up, spruce up, transform, do up, raise standards, move up the scale, move upmarket. [➡SOCIAL, POLITICAL, AND ECONOMIC CHANGE; 374]

gentry *n* **upper class**, nobility, aristocracy, elite, ruling class, landed gentry. [➡CLASS STATUS; 889] *Opposite:* working class.

genuflect 1 *v* **kneel**, bow, curtsy, bend the knee, bob. [➡GESTURES AND GESTICULATION; 654] 2 *v* **bow to**, defer to, kowtow, show respect for, grovel, crawl (*informal*), prostrate, respect. [➡GESTURES AND GESTICULATION; 654] *Opposite:* disrespect.

genuflection *n* **kneeling**, curtsy, bow, bob, dip. [➡GESTURES AND GESTICULATION; 654]

genuine 1 *adj* **real**, authentic, indisputable, true, unadulterated, actual, legitimate, valid. [➡TRUE AND REAL; 172] *Opposite:* fake. 2 *adj* **sincere**, honest, frank, open, unaffected, candid, unpretentious. [➡HONEST AND RELIABLE; 503] *Opposite:* false.

genuineness *n* **authenticity**, realness, substance, legitimacy, validity, truth, candidness, indisputability. [➡TRUE AND REAL; 172]

gen up (*informal*) *v* **research**, read up, swot up (*informal*), swot (*informal*), mug up (*informal*), study, revise. [➡STUDYING; 844]

genus *n* **type**, kind, sort, species, class, group, category, genre. [➡VARIETY, TYPE, KIND; 146]

geographic *adj* **physical**, topographical, terrestrial, earthly, environmental, geographical. [➡THE EARTH; 1039]

geographical *see* **geographic**.

geography *n* **topography**, natural features, characteristics, layout. [➡THE COUNTRYSIDE AND OUTDOOR SPACES; 1070]

geometric *adj* **regular**, symmetrical, ordered, orderly, linear, formal. [➡ORDER AND ORGANISATION; 207] *Opposite:* random.

geometry *n* [➡MATHS; 598]

Georgian *type of* **pre-20th-century architecture**. [➡BUILDING AND ARCHITECTURE; 1075]

geranium *type of* **perennial flower**. [➡FLOWERS; 1032]

gerbil *type of* **rodent**. [➡RODENT; 989]

geriatric *adj* **elderly**, aged, old, senior. [➡OLD AGE; 919] *Opposite:* young.

germ 1 *n* **bug** (*informal*), microbe, microorganism, bacteria, virus. [➡MICROORGANISMS, FUNGI, AND ALGAE; 1023] 2 *n* **origin**, seed, embryo, rudiment, kernel, spark, beginning, bud, nucleus. [➡BEGINNING; 53]

germane (*formal*) *adj* **relevant**, useful, connected, to the point, of interest, apropos (*formal*), suitable, appropriate. [➡FUNDAMENTAL; 196] *Opposite:* irrelevant.

German shepherd (*US*) *type of* **large dog**. [➡DOG; 980]

germ-free *adj* **sterile**, antiseptic, hygienic, sanitary, uninfected, sterilized, sanitized. [➡CLEAN; 1232] *Opposite:* contaminated.

germinate *v* **sprout**, grow, develop, take root, evolve, propagate, incubate. [➡GROW AND CULTIVATE; 352]

germination *n* **sprouting**, propagation, incubation, growth, development. [➡BEGINNING; 53]

gestation *n* **development**, growth, incubation, maturation, pregnancy. [➡REPRODUCTION AND HEREDITY; 726]

gesticulate *v* **gesture**, wave, signal, wigwag, motion, sign, indicate, point. [➡GESTURES AND GESTICULATION; 654]

gesticulation *n* **sign**, signal, gesture, wave, motion, movement. [➡GESTURES AND GESTICULATION; 654]

gesture 1 *n* **sign**, signal, gesticulation, motion, wave, shrug, nod, movement. [➡GESTURES AND GESTICULATION; 654] 2 *n* **act**, action, deed, token, intimation, indication, sign. [➡KIND ACTION OR BEHAVIOUR; 296] 3 *v* **gesticulate**, signal, shrug, nod, wave, motion, indicate, point. [➡GESTURES AND GESTICULATION; 654]

get 1 *v* **obtain**, acquire, find, dig up (*informal*), search out, get hold of, procure, annex, secure, gain, get a hold of (*US*). [➡GET; 421] 2 *v* **become**, grow, begin, have, attain. [➡GET; 421] 3 *v* **catch**, contract, acquire, develop, be infected with, pick up, come down with. [➡FALL ILL, TREAT, AND RECOVER; 729] 4 *v* **cause**, make, induce, persuade, urge, prevail on. [➡CAUSE OR COMPEL TO ACT; 272] 5 *v* **move**, step, progress, walk, climb. [➡PROCEED AND GO; 306] 6 *v* (*informal*) **understand**, comprehend, grasp, follow, perceive, learn. [➡UNDERSTAND AND GRASP; 760]

Compare and Contrast: ***get, acquire, obtain, gain, procure, secure***

CORE MEANING: TO COME INTO POSSESSION OF SOMETHING

get to become the owner of something or to succeed in finding and possessing it; ***acquire*** to come into possession of something, sometimes suggesting time or effort was involved; ***obtain*** to come into possession of something, especially by making an effort or having the necessary qualifications; ***gain*** to come into possession of something through effort, skill, or merit; ***procure*** to come into possession of something, especially with effort or special care; ***secure*** to come into possession of something, especially after using considerable effort to persuade somebody to grant or allow it.

get acquainted *v* [➡ESTABLISHING RELATIONSHIPS WITH OTHERS; 974]

get across *v* **put across**, put over, convey, impart, communicate, get over, pass on. [➡EXPLAIN AND CLARIFY; 611]

get a grip (*informal*) *v* **calm down**, get hold of yourself, compose yourself, control yourself, chill out (*slang*). [➡CHANGE OF MOOD AND COMPOSURE; 581]

get ahead *v* **advance**, climb the ladder, progress, make progress, prosper, be successful. [➡SUCCEED AND WIN; 79] *Opposite:* fail.

get ahead of *v* **pass**, pass by, be in front of, overtake. [➡MOVE PAST, INTO, OR THROUGH SOMETHING; 332] *Opposite:* hold back.

get a hold of (*US*) *v* **grasp**, catch, secure, grip, clutch, snare, trap, lay hands on, collar (*slang*). [➡CONTACT: HOLD; 412]

get along 1 *v* **survive**, get by, manage, cope, live, progress, fare, make out, muddle through. [➡CONTINUE TO EXIST; 17] 2 *v* (*US*) **like**, be compatible with, work well with, relate to, gel with (*informal*), get on. [➡ESTABLISHING RELATIONSHIPS WITH OTHERS; 974] *Opposite:* dislike.

get a move on (*informal*) *v* **speed up**, hurry up, get going, get moving, make tracks (*informal*), get cracking (*informal*), accelerate, step on it (*slang*), hurry, shift (*informal*), step on the gas (*US*), get the lead out (*US*). [➡CHANGE OF SPEED: MORE; 397] *Opposite:* slow down.

get angry *v* **bristle**, bridle, blow up (*informal*), explode, lose your rag (*slang*), lose your cool, hit the roof, lose your temper. [➡GIVING VENT TO EMOTIONS; 680]

get a raw deal *v* **suffer**, draw the short straw, be hard done by, be put upon, come off badly, be badly done by. [➡TOLERATE AND ENDURE; 767]

get at 1 *v* **reach**, find, contact, speak to, write to, call. [➡INITIATE AND ESTABLISH COMMUNICATION; 681] 2 *v* **annoy**, tease, get under your skin (*informal*), rub up the wrong way, irritate, get up somebody's nose (*informal*), get to. [➡ANGER AND ANNOY; 570]

get away *v* **leave**, go away, escape, flee, depart, absent yourself. [➡RUN AWAY AND AVOID; 10]

getaway *n* **escape**, exit, retreat, breakout, flight, departure. [➡END; 54]

get away from *v* **elude**, shake off, lose, escape from, outrun, evade. [➡AVOID OR ESCAPE CONTACT; 419]

get away with *v* **get off**, get off scot-free, pull off (*informal*), escape, evade, elude. [➡SUCCEED AND WIN; 79] *Opposite:* answer for.

get a word in edgeways *v* **get a word in**, get a chance to speak, have your say, voice your opinion, say anything, speak. [➡INTERRUPT AND BUTT IN; 620]

get back *v* **retrieve**, recoup, repossess, regain, recuperate, reclaim, recover. [➡REGAIN POSSESSION; 430] *Opposite:* lose.

get back at *v* **get even**, turn the tables on, take revenge, get your own back, even the score, fight back, pay back. [➡VENGEANCE AND REVENGE; 686]

get behind *v* **support**, endorse, back, join forces, put in a good word for. [➡APPROVE AND CONFIRM; 647] *Opposite:* oppose.

get better *v* **recover**, recuperate, improve, turn the corner, bounce back, convalesce, mend, pull through, buck up (*informal*), get well, ameliorate (*formal*). [➡GET BETTER; 376] *Opposite:* deteriorate.

get bigger *v* **swell**, grow, inflate, mount, expand, increase, wax, balloon, mushroom, swell up, distend. [➡CHANGE OF SIZE: BIGGER; 393] *Opposite:* shrink.

get by *v* **survive**, manage, cope, scrape by, get on, fare, make out, muddle through, get along. [➡CONTINUE TO EXIST; 17]

get carried away *v* [➡OVERDO SOMETHING; 291]

get cracking (*informal*) *v* **get going**, get a move on (*informal*), get on, make a start, get moving, get your skates on (*informal*). [➡START AN ACTION; 261]

get done *v* **accomplish**, effect (*formal*), achieve, complete, finish, do. [➡COMPLETE AN ACTION; 264]

get down *v* **descend**, get off, dismount, come down, climb down. [➡GO DOWNWARDS; 308]

get down to *v* **knuckle down** (*informal*), get to work, begin, get on, start, concentrate, focus. [➡START AN ACTION; 261] *Opposite:* put off.

get down to business *v* **get on with it**, get down to it, get down to brass tacks, get down to the nitty-gritty, stop beating about the bush, make a start, get to work. [➡START AN ACTION; 261]

get down to it *v* [➡START AN ACTION; 261]

get even *v* **get your own back**, get back at, take revenge, turn the tables, even the score, pay back, fight back, get you back (*US*). [➡VENGEANCE AND REVENGE; 686]

get free of *v* **get rid of**, exorcize, escape, jettison, eliminate, purge. [➡GET RID OF SOMETHING; 452]

get-go (*US informal*) *n* **beginning**, start, outset, commencement (*formal*), inception (*formal*), genesis. [➡BEGINNING; 53] *Opposite:* finish.

get going 1 *v* **get a move on** (*informal*), start, make a start, get cracking (*informal*), get on, hurry up, stir, push off, get your skates on (*informal*), buck up (*informal dated*). [➡START AN ACTION; 261] 2 *v* **start up**, turn on, activate, operate, actuate (*formal*), power. [➡CAUSE TO START; 266] *Opposite:* turn off.

get hitched (*informal*) *v* **get married**, marry, tie the knot (*informal*), wed (*formal or literary*), walk down the aisle. [➡ESTABLISHING RELATIONSHIPS WITH OTHERS; 974]

get hold of 1 *v* **obtain**, find, acquire, search out, lay hands on, locate, scare up (*US informal*). [➡GET; 421] 2 *v* **contact**, reach, find, get in touch with, talk to, run to ground, get through to, locate. [➡TELEPHONE AND PAGE; 682]

get hold of the wrong end of the stick *v* [➡MISUNDERSTAND AND FAIL TO GRASP; 762]

get in 1 *v* **arrive**, show up (*informal*), enter, appear. [➡ARRIVE; 12] *Opposite:* depart. 2 *v* **join**, be accepted, be included, make the grade, make the cut (*US*), make the team (*US*). [➡SUCCEED AND WIN; 79]

get in a lather (*informal*) *v* [➡GIVING VENT TO EMOTIONS; 680]

get in a state *v* [➡GIVING VENT TO EMOTIONS; 680]

get in good with (*US*) *v* [➡ESTABLISHING RELATIONSHIPS WITH OTHERS; 974]

get in on the act (*informal*) *v* **take part**, join in, be included, be involved, jump on the bandwagon, interfere, participate. [➡PARTICIPATE; 293]

get in the way *v* **obstruct**, hinder, impede, interfere, encumber, hamper. [➡AVOID, PREVENT, LIMIT, AND CONTROL; 278]

get into 1 *v* **gain entry**, enter, open, access, hack into, penetrate. [➡ARRIVE; 12] *Opposite:* get out of. 2 *v* **put on**, slip into, don (*formal*), change into, dress in. [➡DRESS, WEAR, AND UNDRESS; 868] *Opposite:* take off.

get in touch with *v* **call**, get hold of, contact, reach, ring up, speak to, write to, write, get a hold of (*US*). [➡TELEPHONE AND PAGE; 682]

get into your stride *v* **get going**, get up to speed, get the hang of something, get off the ground. [➡CARRY OUT AN ACTION; 270]

get involved *v* **interfere**, intervene, join in, be drawn in, muscle in (*informal*), put your oar in, step in. [➡PARTICIPATE; 293] *Opposite:* hold back.

get in with *v* **ingratiate yourself**, make friends with, curry favour, gain the favour of, associate with. [➡ESTABLISHING RELATIONSHIPS WITH OTHERS; 974]

get it *v* **understand**, see, cotton on (*informal*), get the drift, get the message (*informal*), get the picture (*informal*), follow, latch on (*informal*), comprehend. [➡UNDERSTAND AND GRASP; 760] *Opposite:* misunderstand.

get it in the neck (*informal*) *v* **take the blame**, carry the can (*informal*), take the rap (*slang*). [➡TOLERATE AND ENDURE; 767]

get it off your chest *v* **bare your soul**, tell somebody, let it out, unburden yourself, share. [➡ADMIT AND CONFESS; 616] *Opposite:* bottle up.

get it wrong *v* **misunderstand**, blunder, boob (*informal*), err, get the wrong idea, get the wrong end of the stick, make a mistake, misinterpret, misconstrue. [➡MISUNDERSTAND AND FAIL TO GRASP; 762]

get less *v* **subside**, die down, lessen, reduce, fall, decrease. [➡CHANGE OF SIZE: SMALLER; 394] *Opposite:* grow.

get longer *v* **lengthen**, elongate, grow, extend, spread out, draw out. [➡CHANGE OF SIZE: BIGGER; 393] *Opposite:* shorten.

get lost *v* **lose your way**, lose your bearings, go astray, go wrong, take a wrong turning, take a wrong turn (*US*). [➡AIMLESS AND ERRANT MOTION; 344]

get married *v* **marry**, walk down the aisle, get hitched (*informal*), tie the knot (*informal*), wed (*formal or literary*). [➡ESTABLISHING RELATIONSHIPS WITH OTHERS; 974]

get moving *v* **hurry up**, speed up, get a move on (*informal*), get going, make a move, shift (*informal*), get your skates on (*informal*), get the lead out (*US*), step on the gas (*US*). [➡CHANGE OF SPEED: MORE; 397]

get off 1 *v* **leave**, depart, exit, go, embark, quit, go away. [➡ABSENT ONESELF; 8] *Opposite:* arrive. 2 *v* **dismount**, get down, descend, come down, climb off, disembark. [➡TRAVEL: WAYS OF TRAVELLING; 321] *Opposite:* get on.

get on 1 *v* **deal with**, handle, manage, accept, progress. [➡CONTINUE AN ACTION; 263] *Opposite:* mismanage. 2 *v* **like**, be compatible, work well with, relate, gel (*informal*), get along (*US*). [➡ESTABLISHING RELATIONSHIPS WITH OTHERS; 974] *Opposite:* dislike. 3 *v* **board**, climb on, mount, get on board, embark. [➡TRAVEL: WAYS OF TRAVELLING; 321] *Opposite:* get off. 4 *v* **make a start**, get a move on (*informal*), get going, begin, start, get down to. [➡START AN ACTION; 261] *Opposite:* defer.

get on your high horse *v* **give yourself airs**, put on airs, act haughtily, lord it (*disapproving*). [➡GIVING VENT TO EMOTIONS; 680]

get on your nerves *v* **annoy**, aggravate (*informal*), irritate, bug (*informal*), bother, drive you up the wall (*informal*), put your back up. [➡ANGER AND ANNOY; 570]

get out *v* **leave**, depart, quit, evacuate, retreat, go away, clear out, exit, buzz off (*informal*). [➡RUN AWAY AND AVOID; 10] *Opposite:* enter.

get-out *n* [➡CLOTHES AND ACCESSORIES; 864]

get out of *v* **evade**, avoid, dodge, duck, get round, wriggle out of, sidestep, circumvent, escape, renege. [➡NOT DO AND REFUSE TO DO; 275] *Opposite:* participate.

get over 1 *v* **recover**, live through, endure, survive, get beyond, pass though, recuperate. [➡CONTINUE TO EXIST; 17] *Opposite:* succumb. **2** *v* **come to terms with**, accept, surmount, overcome, conquer, rise above, face up to. [➡FORGET, FORGIVE, AND ACCEPT; 749] **3** *v* **convey**, communicate, impart, pass on, get across, put over, put across. [➡INFORM AND ANNOUNCE; 612]

get ready *v* **prepare**, steel, prime, brace, organize, make ready, gear up. [➡PREPARE FOR ACTION; 290]

get rid of *v* **dispose of**, discard, throw away, throw out, chuck out (*informal*), get shot of (*informal*), jettison, dispense with, offload, dump. [➡GET RID OF SOMETHING; 452] *Opposite:* keep.

get round 1 *v* **become known**, break out, circulate, get out, be revealed, spread, leak. [➡APPEAR AND EMERGE; 3] **2** *v* **avoid**, go around, bypass, sidestep, evade, circumvent. [➡NOT DO AND REFUSE TO DO; 275] *Opposite:* comply.

get shot of (*informal*) *v* [➡GET RID OF SOMETHING; 452]

get smaller *v* **shrink**, shrivel up, narrow, deflate, recede, wane, decrease. [➡CHANGE OF SIZE: SMALLER; 394] *Opposite:* swell.

get somewhere *v* **make headway**, make progress, make inroads, achieve, make a breakthrough, progress. [➡SUCCEED AND WIN; 79] *Opposite:* fall behind.

get stirred up *v* [➡GIVING VENT TO EMOTIONS; 680]

get stuck in *v* [➡START AN ACTION; 261]

get the better of *v* **defeat**, beat, trounce, triumph over, get the upper hand. [➡BEAT AND DEFEAT; 80]

get the drift *v* **understand**, get the message (*informal*), see, follow, get it, cotton on (*informal*), get the picture (*informal*), latch on (*informal*). [➡UNDERSTAND AND GRASP; 760]

get the hang of *v* **learn**, pick up, understand, master. [➡UNDERSTAND AND GRASP; 760]

get the message (*informal*) *v* **understand**, get the drift, take the hint, grasp, follow, get it, see. [➡UNDERSTAND AND GRASP; 760]

get the most out of *v* **maximize**, make the most of, get the full benefit, exploit, milk (*informal*). [➡MAKE GOOD USE OF SOMETHING; 474]

get the picture (*informal*) *v* **understand**, catch on (*informal*), follow, cotton on (*informal*), get the message (*informal*), see, grasp, get it. [➡UNDERSTAND AND GRASP; 760]

get the wrong end of the stick *v* **misconstrue**, misinterpret, make a mistake, misunderstand, misread, get it wrong, err, take amiss. [➡MISUNDERSTAND AND FAIL TO GRASP; 762]

get the wrong idea *v* **misunderstand**, misread, misinterpret, misconstrue, misjudge, err, take amiss, get it wrong. [➡MISUNDERSTAND AND FAIL TO GRASP; 762]

get the wrong impression *v* [➡MISUNDERSTAND AND FAIL TO GRASP; 762]

get thinner *v* **narrow**, taper, slim down, lose weight, slenderize (*US dated*). [➡CHANGE OF SIZE: SMALLER; 394]

get through 1 *v* **survive**, come through, endure, weather, ride out, overcome. [➡CONTINUE TO EXIST; 17] **2** *v* **use**, consume, wear out, go through, expend, devour, eat, use up, finish. [➡USE UP AND WASTE; 475] **3** *v* **breach**, break through, penetrate, cross, pass, traverse, negotiate. [➡MOVE PAST, INTO, OR THROUGH SOMETHING; 332]

get to 1 *v* **annoy**, bother, bug (*informal*), affect, distract, irk, disturb. [➡ANGER AND ANNOY; 570] **2** *v* **reach**, make, arrive at, attain, deal with, address. [➡ARRIVE; 12]

get-together (*informal*) *n* **meeting**, gathering, social, assembly, rendezvous, powwow (*informal*). [➡MEETINGS AND ASSEMBLIES; 43]

get to grips with *v* [➡UNDERSTAND AND GRASP; 760]

get to know *v* **become acquainted with**, be introduced to, meet, become familiar with. [➡ESTABLISHING RELATIONSHIPS WITH OTHERS; 974]

get to work *v* [➡START AN ACTION; 261]

get to your feet *v* **stand up**, rise, stand, arise (*archaic or literary*), get up. [➡GO UPWARDS; 307]

get underway *v* **begin**, start, proceed, launch, kick off (*informal*), commence (*formal*). [➡START AN ACTION; 261] *Opposite:* come to a halt.

getup (*informal*) *n* **outfit**, gear (*informal*), clothes, costume, suit, dress, rig (*informal*), attire (*formal*), garb. [➡CLOTHES AND ACCESSORIES; 864]

get-up-and-go (*informal*) *n* **energy**, vitality, verve, life, drive, ambition, push, enthusiasm, vigour. [➡ENERGY AND ENTHUSIASM; 497]

get up to speed *v* [➡UNDERSTAND AND GRASP; 760]

get used to *v* **become accustomed to**, get into the habit, adjust, adapt, acclimatize, grow used to. [➡CHANGE; 373]

get wind of *v* [➡LEARN AND DISCOVER; 763]

get worse *v* [➡GET WORSE; 382]

get your bearings *v* **orient yourself**, find your way, find your feet, adjust, adapt, acquaint yourself with, get orientated, familiarize yourself with. [➡CHANGE; 373]

get your own back *v* **take revenge**, get even, retaliate, get back at, avenge yourself, even the score, turn the tables, fight back. [➡VENGEANCE AND REVENGE; 686]

gewgaw *n* [➡ORNAMENTS AND DECORATIONS; 1247]

geyser *n* **hot spring**, spring, natural spring, fountain, jet, spout. [➡RIVERS, LAKES, AND STREAMS; 1042]

ghastly **1** *adj* **horrifying**, shocking, upsetting, distressing, grisly, grim, horrific, gruesome, frightening, hair-raising. [➡FRIGHTENING; 232] *Opposite:* pleasant. **2** *adj* **terrible**, horrible, appalling, dreadful, nasty, rotten, foul, vile, horrid, disgusting, unbearable, unpleasant. [➡DISGUSTING AND REPULSIVE; 231] *Opposite:* pleasant. **3** *adj* (*informal*) **ill**, sick, unwell, poorly (*informal*), dreadful, bad, off-colour, under the weather. [➡ILL AND SICK; 741] *Opposite:* well. **4** *adj* (*literary*) **pale**, pallid, ashen, wan, deathly, cadaverous (*literary*). [➡COMPLEXION; 481] *Opposite:* rosy.

ghee *type of* **cooking fat and oil.** [➡FATS AND OILS; 1172]

gherkin *n* **pickled cucumber**, dill pickle, pickle, cornichon. [➡SEASONINGS AND SAUCES; 1173]

ghetto *n* [➡UNDESIRABLE ACCOMMODATION; 856]

ghost *n* [➡THE SUPERNATURAL; 788]

ghostlike *adj* **eerie**, wraithlike, spectral, ghostly, supernatural, ethereal, otherworldly, indistinct, creepy (*informal*), insubstantial, spooky (*informal*). [➡VAGUENESS; 244]

ghostly *adj* **ethereal**, wraithlike, spectral, indistinct, supernatural, eerie, ghostlike, insubstantial, otherworldly, creepy (*informal*), spooky (*informal*). [➡VAGUENESS; 244]

ghostwrite *v* **cowrite**, write, compose, author, coauthor, draft. [➡RECORD SOMETHING; 372]

ghostwriter *n* **cowriter**, writer, composer, author, co-author, drafter. [➡WRITERS AND STYLES; 914]

ghoul *n* [➡THE SUPERNATURAL; 788]

ghoulish **1** *adj* **morbid**, macabre, dark, chilling, ghastly, twisted, gloomy, unhealthy. [➡FRIGHTENING; 232] *Opposite:* innocent. **2** *adj* **cruel**, savage, brutal, fiendish, bloodthirsty, grim, grisly, gruesome, hideous. [➡SELFISH AND UNKIND; 506] *Opposite:* gentle.

ghoulishly **1** *adv* **morbidly**, darkly, chillingly, twistedly, gloomily, unhealthily. [➡BAD-TEMPERED AND HUMOURLESS; 627] *Opposite:* innocently. **2** *adv* **cruelly**, savagely, brutally, fiendishly, bloodthirstily, grimly, gruesomely, hideously. [➡RUDE AND HOSTILE; 626] *Opposite:* gently.

ghoulishness *n* [➡THE SUPERNATURAL; 788]

GI *n* **soldier**, private, enlisted person, volunteer, conscript, recruit, veteran, draftee (*US*). [➡MILITARY PERSONNEL; 828]

giant **1** *n* [➡BIG THINGS; 1193] **2** *n* [➡MYTHICAL BEINGS; 790] **3** *adj* **huge**, enormous, vast, large, massive, great. [➡LARGE; 1192] *Opposite:* tiny.

giant-sized *adj* [➡LARGE; 1192]

giant star *type of* **star or star system.** [➡CELESTIAL BODIES; 1060]

gibber *v* **babble**, rant, prattle, jabber, talk gibberish, gabble, prate. [➡WITTER AND BABBLE; 618]

gibbering *v* [➡WITTER AND BABBLE; 618]

gibberingly *adv* [➡INARTICULATE, RAMBLING, AND AWKWARD; 634]

gibberish *n* **nonsense**, prattle, babble, gabble, rubbish, drivel, rot (*informal*), twaddle (*informal*). [➡MEANINGLESS SPEECH OR WRITING; 677] *Opposite:* sense.

gibbon *type of* **primate.** [➡PRIMATE; 988]

gibe **1** *n* **jeer**, taunt, sneer, remark, joke, scoff, quip, jest (*literary*). [➡JOKES AND TEASING; 675] **2** *v* **taunt**, mock, tease, jeer, ridicule, rag (*dated*), twit (*dated*), scoff, sneer, razz (*US informal*), ride (*US informal*). [➡PROTEST AND EXPRESS DISAPPROVAL; 643]

giblets *n* **innards** (*informal*), guts, offal. [➡TYPES AND CUTS OF MEAT; 1176]

giddily **1** *adv* **dizzily**, unsteadily, lightheadedly, woozily, shakily, unstably. [➡GOOD-TEMPERED AND HUMOROUS; 628] *Opposite:* steadily. **2** *adv* (*dated*) **frivolously**, capriciously, volatilely, excitedly, flightily, foolishly, impulsively, scattily (*informal*). [➡LACK OF COMMITMENT AND UNRELIABILITY; 510] *Opposite:* sensibly.

giddiness **1** *n* **dizziness**, unsteadiness, lightheadedness, wooziness, shakiness, instability. [➡ILL AND SICK; 741] *Opposite:* steadiness. **2** *n* (*dated*) **frivolity**, capriciousness, volatility, overexcitement, flightiness, silliness, foolishness, impulsiveness, scattiness (*informal*). [➡INSECURITY AND LOSS OF COMPOSURE; 545] *Opposite:* seriousness.

giddy **1** *adj* **dizzy**, unsteady, off-balance, lightheaded, woozy, shaky, unstable. [➡ILL AND SICK; 741] *Opposite:* steady. **2** *adj* (*dated*) **frivolous**, scatterbrained, capricious, volatile, excited, flighty, silly, foolish, impulsive, scatty (*informal*). [➡LACK OF COMMITMENT AND UNRELIABILITY; 510] *Opposite:* serious.

gift **1** *n* **present**, donation, contribution, reward, bequest, award, endowment, grant, offering. [➡GIFTS; 439] **2** *n* **talent**, skill, ability, flair, knack, genius, aptitude, bent. [➡SKILLS, TALENTS, AND ABILITIES; 527]

See Compare and Contrast at **talent.**

gifted *adj* **talented**, skilled, able, exceptional, skilful, out of the ordinary, extraordinary, remarkable. [➡TALENTED AND SKILFUL; 528] *Opposite:* ordinary.

See Compare and Contrast at **intelligent.**

gift of the gab (*informal*) *n* [➡ELOQUENT, TALKATIVE, AND LONG-WINDED; 633]

giftwrap *v* **wrap**, wrap up, package, envelop, enclose, encase, decorate, adorn. [➡DECORATE, ADORN, AND APPLY COATINGS; 406]

gig (*informal*) *n* [➡PERFORMANCES AND SHOWS; 42]

gigantic *adj* **huge**, enormous, massive, vast, gargantuan, colossal, titanic, oversize, large, great. [➡LARGE; 1192] *Opposite:* tiny.

gigantically *adv* **hugely**, massively (*informal*), colossally, vastly, enormously, greatly. [➡TO A GREAT EXTENT; 130]

giggle **1** *v* **titter**, snigger, chuckle, laugh, chortle, twitter, snicker, cackle, snicker (*US*). [➡LAUGHTER; 650] **2** *n* **snigger**, titter, chuckle, laugh, chortle, twitter, cackle, snicker (*US*). [➡LAUGHTER; 650] **3** *type of* **human sound.** [➡SOUNDS MADE BY PEOPLE; 1261] **4** *n* (*informal*) [➡TREAT; 211]

giggly *adj* **silly**, hysterical, immature, tittering, sniggering, chuckling, laughing, chortling, twittering, snickering. [➡CHEERFULNESS OF OUTLOOK; 504] *Opposite:* serious.

gigolo *n* [➡PLEASURE-SEEKERS AND HEDONISTS; 886]

gila monster *type of* **reptile**. [➡REPTILES; 994]

gild *v* [➡DECORATE, ADORN, AND APPLY COATINGS; 406]

gilded *adj* **golden**, gold-plated, gilt, gold. [➡METALS; 1275]

gild the lily *v* **overdo it**, go over the top, get carried away, go too far, lay it on thick, over-egg the pudding. [➡OVERDO SOMETHING; 291]

gilet *type of* **top**. [➡GARMENTS AND OUTFITS; 865]

gill *part of* **fish**. [➡PARTS OF A FISH; 1011]

gilt 1 *n* **gold**, gold leaf, gold plate. [➡COVERS AND COATINGS; 1245] 2 *adj* **golden**, gold-plated, gilded, gold. [➡METALS; 1275]

gimmick *n* **trick**, ploy, stunt, device, promotion, tactic. [➡WAYS OF DOING THINGS; 295]

ginger 1 *type of* **orange**. [➡COLOURS; 1223] 2 *type of* **spice**. [➡HERBS AND SPICES; 1174]

gingerbread *type of* **cake**. [➡CAKES, BISCUITS, AND DESSERTS; 1180]

ginger group *n* [➡GROUPS WITH A COMMON INTEREST; 938]

gingerly *adv* **cautiously**, tentatively, warily, delicately, carefully, gently. [➡CAUTIOUS AND CAREFUL; 283] *Opposite:* boldly.

gingham *type of* **fabric from plants**. [➡FABRICS; 1131]

ginkgo *type of* **deciduous tree**. [➡DECIDUOUS TREES; 1028]

ginormous (*informal*) *adj* **huge**, enormous, vast, massive, immense, mammoth, gargantuan, monster. [➡LARGE; 1192] *Opposite:* tiny.

ginseng *type of* **spice**. [➡HERBS AND SPICES; 1174]

giraffe *type of* **large mammal**. [➡LARGE MAMMAL; 986]

girandole *type of* **firework**. [➡EXPLOSIVES; 1154]

gird (*literary*) *v* [➡DECORATE, ADORN, AND APPLY COATINGS; 406]

girder *n* **beam**, joist, bar, rafter, crossbeam, support. [➡BUILDING MATERIALS; 1076]

girdle *n* **belt**, sash, cummerbund, tie, drawstring, cord, band. [➡HABERDASHERY, MILLINERY, AND LINGERIE; 867]

gird your loins *v* **brace yourself**, get ready, grit your teeth, prepare yourself, steel yourself. [➡PREPARE FOR ACTION; 290]

girl *n* [➡FEMALE PERSON; 933]

girlfriend *n* **partner**, lover, sweetheart, fiancée, lady-friend (*informal humorous*), inamorata (*literary*). [➡SEXUAL AND ROMANTIC RELATIONSHIPS; 964] *Opposite:* boyfriend.

girlhood *n* **childhood**, youth, infancy, early years, adolescence, teens, salad days (*literary*), formative years. [➡BABYHOOD, CHILDHOOD, AND ADOLESCENCE; 917] *Opposite:* boyhood.

girlish *adj* [➡GENDER IDENTITY AND SEXUALITY; 932]

girlishness *n* [➡GENDER IDENTITY AND SEXUALITY; 932]

girth *n* **circumference**, breadth, width, span, thickness, wideness, size, bulk. [➡WIDTH: WIDE; 1198] *Opposite:* height.

gist *n* **idea**, essence, substance, general picture, point, meaning, sense, nucleus, kernel, nub. [➡MEANING; 691]

give 1 *v* **provide**, offer, contribute, present, furnish (*formal*), donate, bequeath, pass, hand, hand over, lend, deliver, give away. [➡GIVE AND PROVIDE; 431] *Opposite:* take. 2 *v* **grant**, bestow (*formal*), award, confer (*formal*), assign, allot, accord. [➡GIVE AND PROVIDE; 431] *Opposite:* withhold. 3 *v* **impart**, convey, communicate, pass on, afford (*formal*), share, lend. [➡DISPENSE, RATION, AND DISTRIBUTE; 435] *Opposite:* withhold. 4 *v* **perform**, put on, stage, produce, organize, deliver, carry out. [➡CARRY OUT AN ACTION; 270] 5 *v* **devote**, dedicate, give up, sacrifice, spend, surrender, allocate. [➡DISPENSE, RATION, AND DISTRIBUTE; 435] *Opposite:* withhold. 6 *v* **yield**, collapse, break, go, split, crack, fracture, shatter, crumble, give way. [➡TEAR, BREAK, AND CUT; 361] *Opposite:* hold up.

Compare and Contrast: ***give, present, confer, bestow, donate, grant***

CORE MEANING: TO HAND OVER SOMETHING TO SOMEBODY

give to hand over a possession to somebody else to keep or use; ***present*** to give something in a formal or ceremonial way; ***confer*** (*formal*) to give somebody an honour, privilege, or award, often at a formal ceremony; ***bestow*** (*formal*) to present somebody with something, especially something unexpected or undeserved; ***donate*** to give a contribution to a charitable organization or other good cause, or, in a medical context, to give blood for blood transfusions or organs for transplant; ***grant*** to agree to allow a request, favour, or privilege, especially at the discretion of a person in authority, or formally or officially to give money.

give a beating *v* **beat up** (*informal*), attack, assault, batter, hit, smack. [➡PHYSICAL ATTACK AND PUNISHMENT; 416]

give a bell (*informal*) *v* [➡TELEPHONE AND PAGE; 682]

give a boost *v* **strengthen**, boost, lift, encourage, boost up, give a lift, uplift, fortify, support, improve. [➡IMPROVE STRENGTH AND DURABILITY; 379] *Opposite:* deflate.

give a buzz (*informal*) *v* [➡TELEPHONE AND PAGE; 682]

give a call *v* [➡TELEPHONE AND PAGE; 682]

give a hand *v* [➡HELP; 294]

give a lift *v* **encourage**, boost, boost up, strengthen, fortify, give a boost, lift, uplift, support, improve. [➡ENCOURAGE; 577] *Opposite:* deflate.

give a miss (*informal*) *v* **stay away from**, abstain from, hold back from, give a wide berth, avoid, take a rain check (*US informal*). [➡NOT PAY ATTENTION; 765]

give-and-take (*informal*) *n* **cooperation**, compromise, reciprocity, collaboration, teamwork, helpfulness, understanding. [➡RECIPROCITY AND INTERDEPENDENCE; 148] *Opposite:* selfishness.

give a new lease of life *v* [➡ IMPROVE STRENGTH AND DURABILITY; 379]

give a ring *v* [➡ TELEPHONE AND PAGE; 682]

give a rough idea *v* [➡ EXPLAIN AND CLARIFY; 611]

give a shot (*informal*) *v* [➡ ATTEMPT AN ACTION; 262]

give a tinkle *v* [➡ TELEPHONE AND PAGE; 682]

give away 1 *v* **get rid of**, donate, offer, give, bestow (*formal*), pass on, give out, hand out, distribute, provide. [➡ DISPENSE, RATION, AND DISTRIBUTE; 435] *Opposite:* keep. 2 *v* **disclose**, reveal, let slip, betray, divulge, tell. [➡ BETRAY CONFIDENCES AND GOSSIP; 619] *Opposite:* keep secret.

giveaway 1 *n* **telltale sign**, clue, hint, indication, symptom, betrayal. [➡ EVIDENCE AND PROOF; 69] 2 *n* (*informal*) **gift**, freebie (*informal*), special offer, free sample, trial offer, promotion, gimmick. [➡ GIFTS; 439] 3 *adj* (*informal*) **bargain**, rock-bottom, low, introductory, special, exceptional, bargain-basement. [➡ CHEAP AND INEXPENSIVE; 222] *Opposite:* exorbitant.

give a wide berth *v* **steer clear**, keep well away, avoid, avoid like the plague, shun, keep at arm's length, keep your distance, give a miss (*informal*). [➡ AVOID OR ESCAPE CONTACT; 419] *Opposite:* seek out.

give back *v* **return**, restore, hand back, repay, refund, reimburse. [➡ GIVE AND PROVIDE; 431] *Opposite:* keep.

give chase (*formal*) *v* **pursue**, follow in hot pursuit, follow, go after, chase, run down. [➡ ACCOMPANY AND FOLLOW; 338]

give heed *v* [➡ PAY ATTENTION; 766]

give in 1 *v* **lose**, admit defeat, surrender, concede, submit, give up, quit, throw in the towel (*informal*), capitulate, defer. [➡ FORGET, FORGIVE, AND ACCEPT; 749] *Opposite:* stand your ground. 2 *v* **hand over**, hand in, deliver, submit, present, tender, proffer. [➡ PROFFER AND HAND OVER; 432] *Opposite:* withhold.

give instructions *v* **direct**, inform, brief, instruct, tell, guide, give orders. [➡ EXPLAIN AND CLARIFY; 611]

give it a try *v* [➡ ATTEMPT AN ACTION; 262]

give leave (*formal*) *v* [➡ PERMIT AND ALLOW; 670]

given 1 *adj* **known**, assumed, agreed, specified, prearranged, set, certain, particular, fixed. [➡ KNOWN AND FAMOUS; 182] 2 *prep* **because of**, in view of, as a result of, taking into consideration, taking into account. [➡ CAUSATION; 169]

given name *n* **first name**, Christian name, forename, name, moniker (*slang*). [➡ NAME AND DESCRIBE; 666]

give notice *v* [➡ REVOKE STATUS; 460]

given that *conj* **providing**, provided that, as long as, only if, assuming that, allowing that. [➡ CAUSATION; 169]

give off *v* **emit**, radiate, send out, discharge, exude, spew, give out. [➡ EMIT AND EMANATE; 362]

give or take *adv* [➡ APPROXIMATELY; 133]

give out 1 *v* **hand out**, distribute, provide, offer, allot, assign, hand over, give away, award. [➡ DISPENSE, RATION, AND DISTRIBUTE; 435] *Opposite:* keep. 2 *v* **declare**, announce, proclaim, pronounce, reveal, publish, make known, name. [➡ INFORM AND ANNOUNCE; 612] *Opposite:* withhold. 3 *v* **emit**, send out, transmit, give off, radiate, discharge, exude. [➡ EMIT AND EMANATE; 362] 4 *v* **run out**, dry up, fail, come to an end, end, finish, disappear. [➡ DISAPPEAR; 4] *Opposite:* hold out. 5 *v* **fail**, collapse, break, yield, go, give, snap, pack in (*informal*). [➡ FAIL OR CEASE TO FUNCTION; 471] *Opposite:* hold.

give over (*informal*) *v* **stop**, pack in (*informal*), lay off (*informal*), give a rest, desist, cease. [➡ STOP ACTING; 265] *Opposite:* continue.

give over to 1 *v* **dedicate**, devote, allocate, reserve, allot, use. [➡ PROFFER AND HAND OVER; 432] 2 *v* (*literary*) **give up**, relinquish, hand over, surrender, abandon, turn over to. [➡ PROFFER AND HAND OVER; 432]

give permission *v* **consent**, agree, allow, let, authorize, sanction, permit, give leave (*formal*). [➡ PERMIT AND ALLOW; 670] *Opposite:* forbid.

give refuge *v* [➡ TAKE CARE OF AND SPOIL; 301]

give rise to *v* [➡ CAUSE TO HAPPEN; 31]

give shelter to *v* [➡ TAKE CARE OF AND SPOIL; 301]

give somebody their cards *v* [➡ REVOKE STATUS; 460]

give somebody the slip *v* **lose**, shake off, get away from, escape from, avoid, slip through somebody's fingers. [➡ AVOID OR ESCAPE CONTACT; 419]

give the boot (*informal*) *v* [➡ REVOKE STATUS; 460]

give the brushoff *v* [➡ REFUSING OR REJECTING RELATIONS; 975]

give the bum's rush (*slang*) *v* [➡ REFUSING OR REJECTING RELATIONS; 975]

give the cold shoulder to *v* **ignore**, rebuff, exclude, look straight through, send to Coventry, freeze out, ostracize, snub, coldshoulder. [➡ REFUSING OR REJECTING RELATIONS; 975]

give the elbow (*informal*) *v* [➡ REVOKE STATUS; 460]

give the go-ahead *v* [➡ PERMIT AND ALLOW; 670]

give the heave-ho (*informal*) *v* [➡ REVOKE STATUS; 460]

give the lie to *v* **contradict**, belie, rebut, negate (*formal*), refute, conflict with, run counter to. [➡ DENY AND REJECT; 645]

give the once-over (*informal*) *v* **examine**, inspect, check out, scrutinize, look at, check over, vet. [➡ EXAMINE AND ASSESS; 754]

give the push (*informal*) *v* [➡ REVOKE STATUS; 460]

give the sack (*informal*) *v* [➡ REVOKE STATUS; 460]

give the third degree (*informal*) *v* [➡ ASK PEOPLE QUESTIONS; 667]

give up 1 *v* **admit defeat**, give in, surrender, concede, submit, quit, throw in the towel (*informal*), capitulate, defer. [➡ STOP ACTING; 265] *Opposite:* stand your ground. 2 *v* **hand over**, part with, surrender, relinquish, give away, deliver, convey, transfer, give in. [➡ PROFFER AND HAND OVER; 432] *Opposite:* keep. 3 *v* **stop**, quit, pack in (*informal*), leave off, renounce, abstain from, abandon. [➡ FOREGO AND DENY ONESELF; 450] *Opposite:* stick with. **4** *v* **despair**, abandon, lose hope, give up on. [➡ CHANGE OF MOOD AND COMPOSURE; 581] **5** *v* **devote**, dedicate, give, surrender, sacrifice, allocate, spend. [➡ GIVE AND PROVIDE; 431] *Opposite:* withhold. **6** *v* **reveal**, disclose, divulge, tell, let slip, betray. [➡ BETRAY CONFIDENCES AND GOSSIP; 619] *Opposite:* keep secret.

give up on 1 *v* **stop**, give up, quit, chuck (*informal*), abandon, leave off. [➡ STOP ACTING; 265] **2** *v* **despair**, abandon, lose hope, give up. [➡ CHANGE OF MOOD AND COMPOSURE; 581]

give up the ghost (*literary*) *v* [➡ DIE; 922]

give your word *v* **promise**, vow, swear, assure, give your assurance. [➡ PROMISE AND ASSURE; 685]

gizmo (*informal*) *n* **gadget**, device, contraption, appliance, thing, thingamabob (*informal*), thingamajig (*informal*), widget (*humorous*), doodah (*informal*), doodad (*US informal*), doohickey (*US informal*), jigger (*US informal*). [➡ DEVICES; 1114]

gizzard *part of* **bird**. [➡ PARTS OF A BIRD; 1006]

glacé *adj* [➡ STATE OF PREPARED FOOD; 1170]

glacial 1 *adj* **icy**, ice-cold, freezing, biting, bitter, cold, polar. [➡ COLD WEATHER; 1051] *Opposite:* tropical. **2** *adj* **hostile**, unfriendly, icy, cold, cool, withering, contemptuous. [➡ RUDE AND HOSTILE; 626] *Opposite:* warm.

glacial deposit *n* [➡ EROSION PRODUCTS AND SOIL; 1058]

glaciated valley *n* [➡ GEOLOGICAL FEATURES; 1056]

glacier *n* **ice field**, icecap, ice floe, iceberg, floe. [➡ MOUNTAINS AND HILLS; 1044]

glad 1 *adj* **delighted**, happy, pleased, content, grateful, thankful, appreciative. [➡ PLEASURE, EXCITEMENT, AND ELATION; 535] *Opposite:* sad. **2** *adj* **willing**, ready, prepared, happy, eager, set. [➡ THE WILL AND WILLINGNESS; 564] *Opposite:* unwilling.

gladden *v* **delight**, please, cheer, bring joy to, hearten, cheer up, elate. [➡ PLEASE AND AMUSE; 573] *Opposite:* sadden.

gladdened *adj* [➡ PLEASURE, EXCITEMENT, AND ELATION; 535]

glade *n* **clearing**, opening, dell (*literary*), gap, open space. [➡ THE COUNTRYSIDE AND OUTDOOR SPACES; 1070]

gladiator 1 *n* **fighter**, fencer, sword fighter, warrior, battler. [➡ COMPETITORS; 41] **2** *n* **campaigner**, lobbyist, supporter, advocate, champion, fighter, battler. [➡ DEVOTEES AND ADDICTED PEOPLE; 557]

gladiolus *type of* **flower grown from bulb**. [➡ FLOWERS FROM BULBS; 1030]

gladness *n* **happiness**, cheerfulness, delight, joy, pleasure, contentment. [➡ PLEASURE, EXCITEMENT, AND ELATION; 535] *Opposite:* sadness.

glad rags (*informal*) *n* **best clothes**, Sunday best, finery, best bib and tucker (*informal*), best togs (*informal*), black tie. [➡ CLOTHES AND ACCESSORIES; 864]

glamorize 1 *v* **romanticize**, idealize, exaggerate, embellish, dress up, giftwrap, varnish. [➡ IMPROVE APPEARANCE; 380] *Opposite:* understate. **2** *v* **beautify**, decorate, adorn, do up, dress up, doll up (*informal*). [➡ DECORATE, ADORN, AND APPLY COATINGS; 406]

glamorous *adj* **stylish**, fashionable, trendy (*informal*), glitzy, dazzling, splendid, beautiful, desirable, exciting, opulent. [➡ WELL GROOMED; 483] *Opposite:* drab.

glamour 1 *n* **allure**, charm, appeal, fascination, attraction, pull (*informal*), excitement, desirability, opulence. [➡ BEAUTY AND ATTRACTIVENESS; 190] *Opposite:* dullness. **2** *n* **good looks**, beauty, glitz, glitziness, style, stylishness, trendiness (*informal*). [➡ WELL GROOMED; 483] *Opposite:* drabness.

glam up (*slang*) *v* [➡ IMPROVE APPEARANCE; 380]

glance 1 *v* **look**, peep, peek, glimpse, squint, scan, skim, look over, look through. [➡ LOOKING AND LOOKS; 701] *Opposite:* gaze. **2** *v* **glint**, shine, glimmer, gleam, sheen (*regional*), glitter, flash, reflect. [➡ LIGHT EMISSION; 369] **3** *n* **peep**, look, peek, glimpse, squint, scan. [➡ LOOKING AND LOOKS; 701] *Opposite:* gaze.

glance off *v* **bounce off**, ricochet, reflect, deflect, rebound. [➡ CHANGE DIRECTION OF MOTION; 345]

glancing *adj* **sideways**, sidelong, lateral, slanting, tangential, partial, oblique. [➡ ORIENTATION AND ALIGNMENT; 1222]

glare 1 *v* **scowl**, stare, glower, frown, look daggers. [➡ FACIAL EXPRESSION; 652] **2** *v* **dazzle**, flash, glimmer, glitter, shine, gleam, reflect, shimmer, sheen. [➡ LIGHT EMISSION; 369] **3** *v* **stand out**, leap out, jump out, catch the eye, show. [➡ APPEAR AND EMERGE; 3] **4** *n* **dirty look**, stare, glower, scowl, frown. [➡ FACIAL EXPRESSION; 652] **5** *n* **shine**, brightness, dazzle, flash, shimmer, brilliance, glimmer, glitter, gleam, sheen (*regional*). [➡ LIGHT; 1163] *Opposite:* dullness.

glare at *v* [➡ FACIAL EXPRESSION; 652]

glaring 1 *adj* **conspicuous**, obvious, obtrusive, evident, blatant, clear, patent, manifest, stark, flagrant. [➡ PERCEPTIBLE; 25] *Opposite:* inconspicuous. **2** *adj* **dazzling**, brilliant, shimmering, bright, intense, glimmering, glittering, gleaming. [➡ DESCRIBING LIGHT; 1227] *Opposite:* dim. **3** *adj* **garish**, brash, gaudy, loud, clashing, jarring, bright. [➡ DESCRIBING LIGHT; 1227] *Opposite:* soft.

glaringly *adv* **conspicuously**, manifestly, painfully, blatantly, flagrantly, patently, starkly, utterly, obviously, obtrusively, clearly. [➡ PERCEPTIBLE; 25]

glass *n* **beaker**, tumbler, wineglass, goblet, flute, schooner. [➡ TABLEWARE, CUTLERY, AND KITCHENWARE; 861]

glass

◆ *types of glass*
bulletproof glass, crystal, cut glass, ground glass, lead glass, optical glass, plate glass, quartz glass, safety glass, stained glass, Venetian glass

glasses

◆ *types of glasses*
bifocals, dark glasses, eyeglasses (*US formal*), goggles, monocle, pince-nez, shades (*informal*), specs (*informal*), spectacles, sunglasses, sunspecs (*informal*)

glassful *n* [➡DRINK; 712]

glasshouse *type of* **outbuilding.** [➡ANCILLARY BUILDINGS; 1079]

glass snake *type of* **reptile.** [➡REPTILES; 994]

glassware *n* [➡TABLEWARE, CUTLERY, AND KITCHENWARE; 861]

glassy 1 *adj* **smooth**, slippery, shiny, glossy, slick, polished, gleaming, reflective, transparent, lustrous, glazed, varnished. [➡VISUAL TEXTURE; 1220] *Opposite:* dull. 2 *adj* **expressionless**, glazed, dazed, blank, vacant, distant, faraway, empty. [➡FACIAL EXPRESSION; 652] *Opposite:* alert.

glaze 1 *v* **varnish**, finish, seal, coat, cover, veneer, paint. [➡DECORATE, ADORN, AND APPLY COATINGS; 406] 2 *n* **coating**, varnish, finish, seal, cover, coat, veneer, paint. [➡COVERS AND COATINGS; 1245]

glazed 1 *adj* **glassy**, blank, fixed, expressionless, dull, faraway, vacant, distant, unfocused. [➡FACIAL EXPRESSION; 652] *Opposite:* alert. 2 *adj* **glossy**, shiny, smooth, lustrous, varnished, gleaming, polished, glassy. [➡VISUAL TEXTURE; 1220] *Opposite:* dull.

gleam 1 *v* **shine**, glow, beam, burn, blaze, glare. [➡LIGHT EMISSION; 369] 2 *v* **flash**, flicker, twinkle, shimmer, sparkle, glitter, glimmer, glisten, glint, flare. [➡LIGHT EMISSION; 369] 3 *n* **glow**, shine, beam, ray, blaze, glare. [➡DESCRIBING LIGHT; 1227] 4 *n* **flicker**, flash, twinkle, shimmer, sparkle, glitter, glimmer, glisten, glint, flare. [➡DESCRIBING LIGHT; 1227]

gleaming *adj* **shiny**, polished, luminous, lustrous, glossy, shining, glowing, glistening, glimmering. [➡VISUAL TEXTURE; 1220] *Opposite:* dull.

glean *v* [➡GET; 421]

glee 1 *n* **delight**, happiness, pleasure, joy, elation, excitement, cheerfulness, hilarity, merriment, laughter, amusement, gaiety, jollity. [➡PLEASURE, EXCITEMENT, AND ELATION; 535] *Opposite:* sadness. 2 *n* **triumph**, jubilation, smugness, exultance. [➡PLEASURE, EXCITEMENT, AND ELATION; 535] *Opposite:* despondency.

gleeful 1 *adj* **delighted**, happy, pleased, joyful, elated, thrilled, over the moon, excited, cheerful, merry, gay (*dated*), jolly. [➡PLEASURE, EXCITEMENT, AND ELATION; 535] *Opposite:* sad. 2 *adj* **triumphant**, jubilant, smug, gloating, exultant. [➡PLEASURE, EXCITEMENT, AND ELATION; 535] *Opposite:* despondent.

gleefulness *n* [➡PLEASURE, EXCITEMENT, AND ELATION; 535]

glen *n* **valley**, gorge, ravine, dale, vale (*literary*), dell (*literary*), cleft, hollow, dene, defile, chine. [➡GEOLOGICAL FEATURES; 1056]

glengarry *type of* **headgear.** [➡HABERDASHERY, MILLINERY, AND LINGERIE; 867]

glib 1 *adj* **persuasive**, fluent, smooth, convincing, slick, pat. [➡ELOQUENT, TALKATIVE, AND LONG-WINDED; 633] *Opposite:* hesitant. 2 *adj* **superficial**, shallow, facile, casual, simplistic. [➡UNINTERESTED AND DETACHED; 630] *Opposite:* profound.

glibness 1 *n* **persuasiveness**, fluency, slickness, smoothness. [➡ELOQUENT, TALKATIVE, AND LONG-WINDED; 633] *Opposite:* hesitation. 2 *n* **superficiality**, shallowness, facileness, casualness. [➡NEUTRALITY AND INDIFFERENCE; 554] *Opposite:* profoundness.

glide 1 *v* **slither**, slide, slide along, sashay (*humorous*), slip, skate, float. [➡PROCEED AND GO; 306] 2 *v* **fly**, soar, wheel, drift, coast, hover, float. [➡PROCEED AND GO; 306]

glider *type of* **civil aircraft.** [➡AIRCRAFT; 1147]

glimmer 1 *v* **twinkle**, shine, gleam, flicker, glow, reflect, sparkle, spark, glisten, shimmer. [➡LIGHT EMISSION; 369] 2 *n* **shine**, twinkle, gleam, flicker, glow, spark. [➡DESCRIBING LIGHT; 1227]

glimmering *adj* [➡DESCRIBING LIGHT; 1227]

glimpse 1 *n* **look**, glance, peek, peep, sight. [➡LOOKING AND LOOKS; 701] 2 *n* **hint**, sight, foretaste, indication, pointer, sign, preview. [➡FEW, LITTLE, SMALL AMOUNT; 119] 3 *v* **see**, catch sight of, glance at, peek at, peep at, look at. [➡SEE; 700]

glint 1 *v* **sparkle**, flash, wink, shine, twinkle, spark, gleam, shimmer, glimmer. [➡LIGHT EMISSION; 369] 2 *n* **flash**, sparkle, shine, twinkle, spark, gleam, shimmer, glimmer. [➡DESCRIBING LIGHT; 1227]

glinting *adj* [➡DESCRIBING LIGHT; 1227]

glisten 1 *v* **gleam**, sparkle, glint, flash, reflect, shine, shimmer, sheen (*regional*), glow. [➡LIGHT EMISSION; 369] 2 *n* **sparkle**, gleam, glint, flash, shine, shimmer, sheen, glow. [➡DESCRIBING LIGHT; 1227]

glistening *adj* **gleaming**, shining, sparkly, shiny, glittering, sparkling, glimmering, flashing, shimmering, glowing. [➡DESCRIBING LIGHT; 1227]

glitch *n* **hitch**, problem, malfunction, fault, bug (*informal*), anomaly, hiccup (*informal*). [➡PROBLEM; 257]

glitter 1 *v* **gleam**, sparkle, shine, dazzle, shimmer, glisten, flash, twinkle, glint. [➡LIGHT EMISSION; 369] 2 *n* **sparkle**, gleam, shimmer, flash, twinkle, glisten, glimmer. [➡LIGHT; 1163] 3 *n* **tinsel**, sequins, spangles. [➡ORNAMENTS AND DECORATIONS; 1247] 4 *n* **dazzle**, splendour, flashiness, glamour, showiness, glitziness, attraction, allure, charisma. [➡BEAUTY AND ATTRACTIVENESS; 190]

glitterati *n* [➡IMPORTANT OR FAMOUS PEOPLE; 893]

glittering *adj* **impressive**, sparkling, dazzling, splendid, scintillating, glitzy, gleaming, magnificent, showy, flashing, shimmering, star-studded, starry. [➡EXTRAORDINARY: AMAZING; 205]

glittery *adj* **shiny**, sparkly, shimmering, brilliant, dazzling, reflecting. [➡DESCRIBING LIGHT; 1227]

glitz *n* **glamour**, style, stylishness, glitziness, pizzazz (*informal*), showiness, ostentation. [➡WELL GROOMED; 483]

glitziness 1 *n* **glamour**, glitter, style, glitz, stylishness, pizzazz (*informal*). [➡WELL GROOMED; 483] 2 *n* **showiness**, tawdriness, snazziness (*informal*), flashiness, extravagance, flashness (*informal*), tastelessness, ostentatiousness, swankiness (*informal*). [➡IN POOR TASTE; 230]

glitzy *adj* **showy**, ostentatious, swanky (*informal*), flashy, extravagant, plush (*informal*), ritzy (*informal*). [➡IN POOR TASTE; 230]

gloat *v* **revel**, wallow, exult, rejoice (*literary*), smirk, delight. [➡BOAST; 617]

gloating *adj* [➡PLEASURE, EXCITEMENT, AND ELATION; 535]

glob (*informal*) *n* **blob**, gobbet, drop, globule, dollop (*informal*), lump, splodge, gob (*slang*), splotch (*US*). [➡AMOUNT OF SOLID OR SEMI-SOLID; 115]

global 1 *adj* **worldwide**, international. [➡WHOLENESS AND COMPLETENESS; 199] *Opposite:* local. 2 *adj* **universal**, comprehensive, total, inclusive, overall, large-scale. [➡LARGE; 1192]

globally 1 *adv* **internationally**, worldwide, universally. [➡ALL; 126] *Opposite:* locally. 2 *adv* **altogether**, as a whole, generally, universally, totally, comprehensively. [➡USUALLY; 108]

globe 1 *n* **sphere**, ball, orb, world, earth, rondure (*literary*). [➡ROUNDED SHAPE; 1217] 2 *n* **earth**, world, planet. [➡THE EARTH; 1039]

globetrot *v* **travel**, journey, tour, shuttle, backpack. [➡TRAVEL: WAYS OF TRAVELLING; 321]

globetrotter *n* **traveller**, tourist, backpacker, holidaymaker, journeyer, jet-setter (*informal*), adventurer, explorer, voyager, excursionist (*dated*), vacationer (*US*). [➡TRAVEL: TRAVELLERS AND WALKERS; 320]

globular *adj* **spherical**, round, circular, bulbous, rotund, orbicular (*formal*), rounded. [➡ROUNDED SHAPE; 1217]

globule *n* **drop**, blob, bead, bubble, glob (*informal*), gobbet, ball. [➡SMALL PIECE; 127]

glockenspiel *type of* **percussion instrument**. [➡MUSICAL INSTRUMENTS; 910]

gloom 1 *n* **darkness**, shade, murkiness, shadow, dimness, murk, gloominess, dreariness, obscurity. [➡DESCRIBING LIGHT; 1227] *Opposite:* brightness. 2 *n* **pessimism**, despair, sadness, dejection, unhappiness, misery, despondency, gloominess, depression, melancholy. [➡FEELINGS ABOUT THE FUTURE; 534] *Opposite:* happiness.

gloomily *adv* **miserably**, disconsolately, despondently, pessimistically, sullenly, glumly, unhopefully, unhappily, dolefully. [➡SADNESS, DISTRESS, AND DESPAIR; 540] *Opposite:* cheerfully.

gloominess 1 *n* **dimness**, darkness, murkiness, shade, shadow, murk, gloom, dreariness. [➡DESCRIBING LIGHT; 1227] *Opposite:* brightness. 2 *n* **despondency**, pessimism, gloom, depression, despair, dejection, misery, unhappiness. [➡FEELINGS ABOUT THE FUTURE; 534] *Opposite:* happiness.

gloomy 1 *adj* **dark**, depressing, dim, overcast, dull, dismal, murky. [➡DESCRIBING LIGHT; 1227] *Opposite:* bright. 2 *adj* **depressed**, low, low-spirited, melancholy, blue (*informal*), down in the dumps (*informal*), miserable, disconsolate, unhappy, sad, glum, woeful, pessimistic. [➡SADNESS, DISTRESS, AND DESPAIR; 540] *Opposite:* cheerful.

gloomy Gus (*US*) *n* [➡GRUMPY AND NEGATIVE PEOPLE; 953]

gloop (*informal*) *n* [➡UNPLEASANT AND DIRTY SUBSTANCES; 1267]

gloopy (*informal*) *adj* [➡FLUID AND NON-SOLID; 1212]

glop (*US informal*) *n* [➡UNPLEASANT AND DIRTY SUBSTANCES; 1267]

glorification *n* **adoration**, veneration, exaltation (*formal*), elevation, deification (*formal*), praise, worship, extolment. [➡PRAISE AND ENCOURAGE; 648]

glorify *v* **worship**, adore, lionize, exalt (*formal*), deify, elevate, venerate, praise, extol. [➡PRAISE AND ENCOURAGE; 648]

glorious *adj* **magnificent**, wonderful, splendid, celebrated, superb, outstanding. [➡EXTRAORDINARY: AMAZING; 205] *Opposite:* shameful.

glory 1 *n* **magnificence**, splendour, beauty, wonder, grandeur, brilliance, exaltation (*formal*). [➡TREAT; 211] 2 *n* **credit**, fame, praise, laurels, triumph, success, admiration, stardom. [➡SUCCESS; 82] *Opposite:* criticism.

glory days *n* [➡PLEASANT SITUATIONS; 74]

glory in *v* **enjoy**, lap up, wallow in, make the most of, revel in, exult in, take pride in, delight, jubilate (*archaic*). [➡LIKE, LOVE, VALUE, AND ENJOY; 579] *Opposite:* despise.

gloss 1 *n* **lustre**, polish, shine, brightness, sheen. [➡COVERS AND COATINGS; 1245] 2 *n* **interpretation**, explanation, spin (*slang*). [➡POINT OF VIEW; 768] *Opposite:* misinformation. 3 *n* **annotation**, commentary, footnote, explanation, comment, definition. [➡PARTS OF BOOKS AND DOCUMENTS; 594]

glossary *n* **lexicon**, dictionary, word list, vocabulary, thesaurus, appendix, supplement. [➡LISTS AND SCHEDULES; 588]

glossiness 1 *n* **shininess**, smoothness, sheen, patina, lustre, sleekness, finish, silkiness. [➡VISUAL TEXTURE; 1220] 2 *n* (*informal*) **veneer**, surface, façade. [➡COVERS AND COATINGS; 1245]

gloss over *v* **skim over**, pass over, dismiss, evade, dodge. [➡NOT PAY ATTENTION; 765] *Opposite:* dwell on.

glossy *adj* **sleek**, silky, silken, lustrous, shiny, polished, smooth, burnished, slick. [➡VISUAL TEXTURE; 1220] *Opposite:* dull.

glossy magazine *n* [➡NEWSPAPERS; 606]

glove 1 *type of* **sports equipment**. [➡SPORTS EQUIPMENT; 879] 2 *type of* **accessory**. [➡HABERDASHERY, MILLINERY, AND LINGERIE; 867]

glove compartment *type of* **internal feature**. [➡INTERNAL PARTS OF A VEHICLE; 1145]

glove puppet *type of* **toy**. [➡TOYS; 880]

glow 1 *n* **radiance**, ruddiness, light, luminosity, glimmering, afterglow. [➡LIGHT; 1163] 2 *v* **burn**, blaze, flame, shine, smoulder, flush, blush. [➡FACIAL EXPRESSION; 652]

glower *v* **glare**, frown, scowl, look daggers, look hard, stare. [➡FACIAL EXPRESSION; 652]

glowering *adj* **angry**, dark, scowling, sullen, surly. [➡IRRITATION AND ANGER; 542]

glowing 1 *adj* **bright**, shimmering, radiant, lustrous, shining, gleaming. [➡DESCRIBING LIGHT; 1227] *Opposite:* dull. 2 *adj* **fulsome**, complimentary, flattering, appreciative, congratulatory. [➡EXPRESSING RESPECT AND APPROVAL; 638] *Opposite:* derogatory. 3 *adj* **healthy-looking**, tanned, rosy, shining, radiant, blooming, blushing. [➡COMPLEXION; 481] *Opposite:* pale.

glowworm *type of* **insect stages of development**. [➡INSECT STAGES; 1020]

glucose *type of* **nutrient**. [➡FOOD COMPONENTS; 1187]

glue 1 *n* **adhesive**, paste, superglue, cement, gum. [➡ADHESIVES; 1270] 2 *v* **paste**, stick, fasten, attach, join, cement, bond. [➡FASTEN, LINK, AND JOIN; 409]

glue-like *adj* [➡FLUID AND NON-SOLID; 1212]

gluey *adj* **sticky**, gummy, tacky, glutinous, thick, viscous, gooey. [➡PHYSICAL TEXTURE; 1221]

glug (*informal*) *v* [➡DRINK; 712]

gluiness *n* [➡FLUID AND NON-SOLID; 1212]

glum *adj* **gloomy**, down, blue (*informal*), morose, sad, low, negative, depressed, sullen, sulky, miserable, dreary, saturnine. [➡SADNESS, DISTRESS, AND DESPAIR; 540] *Opposite:* cheerful.

glumness *n* **pessimism**, unhappiness, misery, depression, dejection, moodiness, sullenness, dreariness, gloominess. [➡SADNESS, DISTRESS, AND DESPAIR; 540] *Opposite:* cheerfulness.

glut *n* **excess**, surplus, superfluity, flood, overabundance, accumulation, surfeit, oversupply. [➡TOO MUCH; 118] *Opposite:* shortage.

glutinous *adj* **sticky**, gluey, gooey, tacky, gummy, viscous, gelatinous. [➡PHYSICAL TEXTURE; 1221]

glutton *n* **overeater**, gourmand, epicure, foodie (*informal*), epicurean, gorger (*US*). [➡PLEASURE-SEEKERS AND HEDONISTS; 886]

gluttonous *adj* **greedy**, voracious, insatiable, desirous (*formal*), excessive. [➡FINANCIALLY MEAN AND GRASPING; 520]

gluttony *n* **greed**, greediness, excess, piggishness, rapaciousness, gourmandizing, voraciousness. [➡MORALLY BAD; 776]

glyph *n* [➡SYMBOLS, SIGNS, AND NUMBERS; 597]

gnarled *adj* **knotted**, twisted, bent, knotty, crooked, knobbly, contorted, distorted. [➡IN BAD REPAIR; 1233] *Opposite:* straight.

gnash *v* **grind**, clench, grit, grate, rasp, gnaw. [➡FACIAL EXPRESSION; 652]

gnash your teeth *v* **be fuming**, be upset, grind your teeth, be frustrated. [➡GIVING VENT TO EMOTIONS; 680]

gnat 1 *n* **midge**, mosquito, fly, firefly, insect, bug, mozzie (*informal*), no-see-um (*US*), punkie (*US*). [➡INSECTS; 1012] 2 *type of* **flying insect.** [➡FLYING INSECTS; 1013]

gnaw *v* **worry**, trouble, bother, cause anxiety, concern, distress, aggravate (*informal*), bedevil, fret. [➡UPSET, DISTRESS, AND HUMILIATE; 568] *Opposite:* comfort.

gneiss *type of* **stone.** [➡STONES, ROCKS, AND BOULDERS; 1057]

gnome *n* **elf**, sprite, goblin, troll, leprechaun, fairy, brownie, pixie, fay (*literary*). [➡MYTHICAL BEINGS; 790]

gnu *type of* **deer or antelope.** [➡DEER AND ANTELOPE; 981]

go 1 *v* **leave**, go away, go off, depart, set off, set out, exit, walk off, move out, move, quit (*archaic*), be off, take off (*informal*). [➡ABSENT ONESELF; 8] *Opposite:* come. 2 *v* **move**, move on, proceed, progress, make for, travel. [➡TRAVEL: WAYS OF TRAVELLING; 321] 3 *v* **work**, run, function, operate, move, perform. [➡FUNCTION SUCCESSFULLY; 470] *Opposite:* stop. 4 *v* **reach**, extend, stretch, spread. [➡PROCEED AND GO; 306] 5 *v* **become**, get, grow, come to be. [➡CHANGE; 373] 6 *v* **die**, pass away, expire, depart (*formal*), pass on. [➡DIE; 922] *Opposite:* live. 7 *n* **energy**, liveliness, enthusiasm, spirit, verve, vigour, drive. [➡ENERGY AND ENTHUSIASM; 497] *Opposite:* lethargy. 8 *n* **try**, attempt, stab (*informal*), turn, chance, shot. [➡ATTEMPT AN ACTION; 262] 9 *n* (*informal*) **energy**, life, zip (*informal*), oomph, pizzazz (*informal*), zest. [➡POSITIVE IMPATIENCE, ENTHUSIASM, AND ALERTNESS; 538]

go about *v* **get on with**, perform, carry out, effect (*formal*), accomplish, transact, set about, approach, tackle, attempt, undertake, do. [➡CARRY OUT AN ACTION; 270]

goad 1 *v* **provoke**, prod, push, stir, stimulate, spur, incite, annoy, hound, badger, aggravate (*informal*), hassle (*informal*), drive. [➡CAUSE OR COMPEL TO ACT; 272] *Opposite:* calm. 2 *n* **stick**, prod, poker, rod, whip, crop, spur. [➡STICKS, POLES, AND WEDGES; 1253] 3 *n* **stimulus**, impetus, driving force, spur, stimulation, incitement, provocation. [➡BEGINNING; 53]

See Compare and Contrast at **motive.**

go adrift *v* **wander**, drift, stray, go astray, deviate, err. [➡AIMLESS AND ERRANT MOTION; 344]

go after *v* **try for**, go for (*informal*), aim for, target, go all-out for, bend over backwards, pull out all the stops, do your utmost. [➡ATTEMPT AN ACTION; 262]

go against *v* **violate**, disobey, infringe, buck (*informal*), fly in the face of. [➡DISOBEY; 303]

go-ahead (*informal*) *n* **permission**, consent, approval, green light, support, acceptance. [➡PERMIT AND ALLOW; 670]

goal 1 *n* **objective**, aim, end, ambition, purpose, target, object, aspiration. [➡INTENTION AND PURPOSE; 773] 2 *n* **goalmouth**, penalty area, box, area, goal line. [➡SPORTS TERMS; 877]

goalmouth *n* **penalty area**, box, area, goal line, line, goal. [➡SPORTS TERMS; 877]

go along with *v* **acquiesce**, concur, agree, grant, accept, accede, consent. [➡FORGET, FORGIVE, AND ACCEPT; 749] *Opposite:* refuse.

goanna *type of* **reptile.** [➡REPTILES; 994]

go around 1 *v* (*informal*) **accompany**, escort, tag along, spend time with, be together. [➡ACCOMPANY AND FOLLOW; 338] 2 *v* **travel**, go from place to place, ride, walk, move. [➡TRAVEL: WAYS OF TRAVELLING; 321] 3 *v* **revolve**, rotate, orbit, circumnavigate (*formal*), circulate, twirl, spin, twist, circle, gyrate, turn. [➡FIDGET AND FROLIC; 312]

go-around (*US informal*) *n* **argument**, disagreement, fight, tiff, quarrel, row, dispute, go-round (*US informal*). [➡ARGUMENT; 47] *Opposite:* agreement.

go around with (*informal*) *v* [➡ESTABLISHING RELATIONSHIPS WITH OTHERS; 974]

go astray *v* **stray**, get lost, transgress, go off the rails, deviate, err, wander. [➡AIMLESS AND ERRANT MOTION; 344]

goat 1 *type of* **farm animal.** [➡FARM ANIMAL; 982] 2 *type of* **meat.** [➡TYPES AND CUTS OF MEAT; 1176]

goatee *n* [➡FACIAL HAIR; 490]

goat moth *type of* **moth.** [➡MOTHS AND BUTTERFLIES; 1015]

go away 1 *v* **leave**, get away, move, quit (*archaic*), depart, be off, head off. [➡ABSENT ONESELF; 8] *Opposite:* stay. 2 *v* **disappear**, vanish, fade, fade away, recede, depart, leave. [➡DISAPPEAR; 4] *Opposite:* stay.

go AWOL *v* [➡RUN AWAY AND AVOID; 10]

go awry *v* [➡FAIL OR CEASE TO FUNCTION; 471]

gob (*slang*) 1 *n* **lump**, clot, glob (*informal*), blob, drop, spot. [➡AMOUNT OF SOLID OR SEMI-SOLID; 115] 2 *n* [➡THE MOUTH; 703] 3 *v* **spit**, expectorate, splutter, hawk, expel. [➡EXCRETION AND EXCRETA; 723]

go back *v* **return**, turn back, revert, revisit, retrace your steps, backtrack, double back, retreat. [➡GO BACKWARDS; 310] *Opposite:* advance.

go back on *v* **change your mind**, backtrack, break your promise, have second thoughts, retract, renege, reconsider, betray. [➡APOLOGIZE AND RETRACT; 684] *Opposite:* keep your word.

go back over *v* **reconsider**, re-examine, repeat, revise, return to, go back to, revisit, rethink. [➡THINK AND REFLECT; 744]

go backwards *v* **reverse**, retreat, regress, lose ground, fall back. [➡GO BACKWARDS; 310] *Opposite:* advance.

go bad *v* **decay**, go off, rot, decompose, putrefy, go mouldy, go sour, go rancid, sour, spoil, moulder. [➡GO BAD AND CORRODE; 391]

go ballistic (*slang*) *v* [➡GIVING VENT TO EMOTIONS; 680]

go bananas (*informal*) *v* [➡GIVING VENT TO EMOTIONS; 680]

go bankrupt *v* **fail**, collapse, fold, go out of business, go to the wall, go bust (*informal*). [➡FAIL OR BE UNSUCCESSFUL; 75]

gobbet *n* [➡AMOUNT OF SOLID OR SEMI-SOLID; 115]

gobble 1 *v* **guzzle** (*informal*), gobble up, gobble down, bolt, wolf, gorge, gulp, eat up, scarf down (*US slang*). [➡EAT AND NOT EAT; 711] *Opposite:* nibble. 2 *v* (*informal humorous*) **use up**, go through, run through, consume, eat into, use, spend. [➡USE UP AND WASTE; 475] *Opposite:* conserve.

gobbledegook (*informal disapproving*) *n* **nonsense**, waffle (*informal*), jargon, gibberish, mumbo jumbo (*informal*), drivel, bunkum (*informal*), rubbish, bunk (*slang*), claptrap (*informal*), footle (*informal*), poppycock (*dated informal*), balderdash. [➡MEANINGLESS SPEECH OR WRITING; 677]

gobble down *v* **gobble**, guzzle (*informal*), gobble up, bolt, wolf, gorge, gulp, eat up, scarf down (*US slang*). [➡EAT AND NOT EAT; 711] *Opposite:* nibble.

gobble up *v* **guzzle** (*informal*), eat up, gobble, bolt, wolf, gorge, gulp, scarf down (*US slang*). [➡USE UP AND WASTE; 475] *Opposite:* nibble.

go belly up *v* [➡FAIL OR BE UNSUCCESSFUL; 75]

go berserk *v* **lose control**, lose your temper, lose your cool, throw a fit (*informal*), throw a wobbly (*informal*), go mad, be beside yourself, go bananas (*informal*), hit the roof, be furious, lose it (*informal*), be angry. [➡GIVING VENT TO EMOTIONS; 680]

go beserk *v* [➡GIVING VENT TO EMOTIONS; 680]

go-between *n* **mediator**, intermediary, broker, arbitrator, messenger, agent, negotiator. [➡ADVISERS, JUDGES, AND ARBITERS; 971]

go beyond *v* **surpass**, outdo, rise above, overtake, pass, outrun, overdo, transcend, overshoot, overhaul. [➡OVERDO SOMETHING; 291]

goblet *n* **glass**, cup, chalice, wine glass. [➡TABLEWARE, CUTLERY, AND KITCHENWARE; 861]

goblin *n* **elf**, sprite, imp, gnome, troll, hobgoblin, brownie. [➡MYTHICAL BEINGS; 790]

gobsmacked (*slang*) *adj* [➡SURPRISE, SHOCK, AND AMAZEMENT; 546]

gobstopper *type of* **confectionery.** [➡CONFECTIONERY; 1181]

go bust (*informal*) *v* **go bankrupt**, bust (*informal*), go under, shut down, fail, go out of business, go to the wall, close down, cease trading, stop trading. [➡BUSINESS ACTIVITIES AND PHENOMENA; 795]

go by *v* **pass**, pass by, elapse, lapse. [➡HAPPEN; 27]

go-cart *type of* **leisure vehicle.** [➡VEHICLES; 1144]

god *n* **deity**, divinity, idol, spirit, supernatural being. [➡RELIGIOUS CONCEPTS; 777]

goddess *n* **deity**, divinity, idol, spirit, supernatural being. [➡RELIGIOUS CONCEPTS; 777]

go dead *v* [➡FAIL OR CEASE TO FUNCTION; 471]

godless *adj* [➡RELIGIOUS CONCEPTS; 777]

godlessness *n* [➡RELIGIOUS CONCEPTS; 777]

godlike *adj* **divine**, superhuman, transcendent, heavenly, holy, godly. [➡EXTRAORDINARY: AMAZING; 205]

godliness 1 *n* **religiousness**, holiness, devoutness, goodness, saintliness, righteousness, piousness. [➡RELIGIOUS CONCEPTS; 777] *Opposite:* wickedness. 2 *n* **divinity**, holiness, heavenliness, transcendence, sacredness. [➡RELIGIOUS CONCEPTS; 777]

godly (*formal*) 1 *adj* **religious**, devout, holy, pious, saintly, good, righteous. [➡RELIGIOUS CONCEPTS; 777] *Opposite:* wicked. 2 *adj* **divine**, holy, heavenly, transcendent, godlike, superhuman. [➡RELIGIOUS CONCEPTS; 777]

go down 1 *v* **descend**, drop, sink, dive, plunge, plummet, lower, fall, crash. [➡GO DOWNWARDS; 308] *Opposite:* go up. 2 *v* **deteriorate**, decline, slip, go downhill, get worse, worsen, weaken. [➡GET WORSE; 382] *Opposite:* improve. 3 *v* (*slang*) **happen**, occur, take place, go on, come about, transpire. [➡HAPPEN; 27] 4 *v* (*informal*) **lose**, be defeated, be beaten, go under, fail, suffer defeat, take a licking (*US informal*). [➡FAIL OR BE UNSUCCESSFUL; 75] *Opposite:* win.

go downhill *v* **deteriorate**, worsen, fail, get worse, go down, degenerate, flounder, decline, weaken, go to the dogs (*informal*), go from bad to worse. [➡GET WORSE; 382] *Opposite:* improve.

go down like a lead balloon (*slang*) *v* **fail**, crash, fizzle, bomb (*informal*), sink without trace. [➡FAIL OR BE UNSUCCESSFUL; 75]

go down the drain *v* [➡FAIL OR BE UNSUCCESSFUL; 75]

go down the tube (*informal*) *v* [➡FAIL OR BE UNSUCCESSFUL; 75]

go down with (*informal*) *v* **catch**, become ill with, contract, pick up, come down with. [➡ILL AND SICK; 741]

godparent *n* [➡ADOPTION, FOSTERING, AND EXTENDED FAMILY; 962]

gods (*informal*) *n* [➡IN THE THEATRE; 906]

God's Acre (*literary*) *n* [➡BURIAL PLACES AND ACCESSORIES; 930]

godsend *n* **blessing**, boon, stroke of luck, bonus, benefit. [➡SOURCE OF HAPPINESS, PLEASURE, OR IMPROVEMENT; 210] *Opposite:* disaster.

go easy on (*informal*) **1** *v* **treat gently**, indulge, sympathize, oblige, please, humour, cosset, coddle, pamper. [➡TAKE CARE OF AND SPOIL; 301] *Opposite:* punish. **2** *v* **take it easy**, slow down, take it steady, avoid, stint, temper. [➡UNDERDO SOMETHING; 292] *Opposite:* overdo.

gofer (*informal*) *n* **runner**, messenger, minion, assistant, lackey (*archaic*). [➡WORKER; 836]

go for **1** *v* (*informal*) **try for**, go after, target, aim for, set your sights on. [➡ATTEMPT AN ACTION; 262] **2** *v* (*informal*) **like**, enjoy, prefer, follow, love, go in for. [➡LIKE, LOVE, VALUE, AND ENJOY; 579] *Opposite:* dislike. **3** *v* (*informal*) **choose**, pick, select, prefer, opt for, settle on. [➡MAKE DECISIONS AND CHOICES; 753] *Opposite:* refuse. **4** *v* **attack**, lay into, set upon, assault, tear into, turn on. [➡PHYSICAL ATTACK AND PUNISHMENT; 416]

go for it (*slang*) *v* [➡ATTEMPT AN ACTION; 262]

go forward *v* **advance**, progress, go on, move along, proceed, move on, move ahead, move forward. [➡PROCEED AND GO; 306] *Opposite:* go back.

go from bad to worse *v* **worsen**, take a turn for the worse, go to pot (*informal*), go to the dogs (*informal*), deteriorate, degenerate, go downhill, fall apart, go to rack and ruin (*informal*), decline, disintegrate. [➡GET WORSE; 382] *Opposite:* improve.

go full tilt *v* [➡MOVE FAST; 314]

go-getter (*informal*) *n* **achiever**, doer, self-starter, high-flier, live wire (*informal*), live one (*informal*). [➡PEOPLE WHO ARE APPROVED OF; 955] *Opposite:* layabout.

go-getting (*informal*) *adj* **ambitious**, high-powered, determined, positive, can-do (*informal*), single-minded, proactive. [➡ENERGY AND ENTHUSIASM; 497]

goggle *v* **stare**, gaze, gape, ogle, gawk (*informal*), look, scrutinize, watch, gawp (*informal*). [➡LOOKING AND LOOKS; 701]

goggle-box (*dated informal*) *n* [➡TELEVISION AND RADIO; 607]

goggle-eyed *adj* [➡FACIAL EXPRESSION; 652]

goggles *type of* **glasses**. [➡GLASSES AND SPECTACLES; 1124]

go hard *v* **solidify**, set, set hard, harden, stiffen, go rigid, coagulate, congeal. [➡HARDEN, CONGEAL, DRY; 388] *Opposite:* soften.

go haywire (*informal*) *v* [➡FAIL OR CEASE TO FUNCTION; 471]

go in *v* **enter**, set foot in, gain admittance, step in, access. [➡ARRIVE; 12] *Opposite:* leave.

go in for **1** *v* **enter**, compete in, take part in, take up. [➡PARTICIPATE; 293] **2** *v* **like**, prefer, participate in, take part in, follow, love, practise, enjoy. [➡LIKE, LOVE, VALUE, AND ENJOY; 579] *Opposite:* dislike.

going **1** *n* **departure**, exit, disappearance. [➡END; 54] *Opposite:* arrival. **2** *n* **conditions**, circumstances, situation, case, setup, state of things. [➡WAYS OF DOING THINGS; 295] **3** *adj* **successful**, profitable, moneymaking, working. [➡SUCCESSFUL AND PROMISING; 81] *Opposite:* bankrupt. **4** *adj* **accepted**, standard, valid, current, present. [➡PRESENT AND AVAILABLE; 11] **5** *adj* **available**, obtainable, ready, free, open, on offer, untaken, existing, up for grabs (*informal*). [➡PRESENT AND AVAILABLE; 11] *Opposite:* taken.

going begging *adj* [➡PRESENT AND AVAILABLE; 11]

going on *adj* [➡HAPPENING AND IN PROGRESS; 32]

going on for *adv* **approximately**, around, about, close to, in the region of, nearly, not far off. [➡APPROXIMATELY; 133]

going-over (*informal*) **1** *n* **examination**, inspection, check, investigation, analysis, review, consideration, perusal. [➡EXAMINE AND ASSESS; 754] **2** *n* **overhaul**, service, restoration, checkup, improvement, wash, renovation, scrub, dust, makeover. [➡CLEAN AND POLISH; 404] **3** *n* **rebuke**, reprimand, scolding, talking-to (*informal*), telling-off (*informal*), roasting (*informal*). [➡CRITICISMS AND ANGRY OUTBURSTS; 50]

going rate *n* **market price**, standard, usual, average, price, rate, cost, salary, wage, pay. [➡MONEY, PAYMENTS, AND CHARGES; 800]

goings-on (*informal*) *n* **activity**, comings and goings, affairs, carry-on (*informal*), carryings-on (*informal*), toing and froing, hustle and bustle, huggermugger, high jinks (*informal*), palaver (*humorous*). [➡EVENTS AND OCCURRENCES; 35]

going strong *adj* [➡SUCCESSFUL AND PROMISING; 81]

go in search of *v* [➡SEEK POSSESSION AND SEARCH; 457]

go into **1** *v* **discuss**, go over, talk about, look into, examine, consider, assess. [➡EXAMINE AND ASSESS; 754] *Opposite:* ignore. **2** *v* **enter**, go in, set foot in, gain admittance, step in, access. [➡ARRIVE; 12] *Opposite:* leave.

go into detail *v* **elaborate**, enlarge on, amplify, expand, explain, specify. [➡EXPLAIN AND CLARIFY; 611]

go into liquidation *v* [➡FAIL OR BE UNSUCCESSFUL; 75]

go in with *v* **partner**, join, cooperate, merge, combine, associate. [➡ESTABLISHING RELATIONSHIPS WITH OTHERS; 974]

gold **1** *n* **treasure**, bullion, ingots, gold plate, sovereigns, doubloons, pieces of eight, jewellery, nuggets, bars. [➡FINANCIAL ASSETS; 463] **2** *n* **wealth**, money, assets, resources, riches, affluence, prosperity. [➡FINANCIAL ASSETS; 463] **3** *n* (*in-*

formal) **first place**, first prize, title, medal, trophy. [➡ADVANTAGE; 213] 4 *type of* **metal**. [➡METALS; 1275] 5 *type of* **orange**. [➡COLOURS; 1223] 6 *adj* **gilded**, gilt, gold-leaf, gold-plated, golden. [➡DESCRIBING LIGHT; 1227]

gold brick 1 *n* **fake**, fraud, fool's gold, counterfeit, swindle, forgery. [➡DECEPTION AND LIES; 661] 2 *n* (*informal*) **shirker**, slacker, evader, loafer, idler, layabout. [➡SUPERFICIAL OR INSINCERE PEOPLE; 951]

goldbrick (*informal*) *v* **shirk**, loaf, idle, slack, laze around, malinger (*disapproving*). [➡LACK OF ACTIVITY; 343]

goldbricker (*US informal*) *n* **shirker**, loafer, idler, slacker, malingerer (*disapproving*), layabout. [➡LAZY OR UNSUCCESSFUL PEOPLE; 948]

gold digger *n* [➡SUPERFICIAL OR INSINCERE PEOPLE; 951]

golden 1 *adj* **excellent**, unique, first-rate, wonderful, superb, one-off, first-class, terrific (*informal*), ideal. [➡EXTRAORDINARY: AMAZING; 205] 2 *adj* **idyllic**, best, peak, utopian, paradisiac, ideal. [➡GOOD, WELL, BETTER; 184] 3 *adj* **gold**, gold-plated, gold-leaf, gilt, gilded. [➡METALS; 1275] 4 *adj* **favoured**, superior, special, elite, select, esteemed, privileged, favourite, promising. [➡ADMIRABLE AND COMMENDABLE; 186] 5 *type of* **orange**. [➡COLOURS; 1223]

golden age *n* **peak**, pinnacle, apex, summit, zenith, best of times. [➡INTERMEDIATE STAGES; 55]

golden ager (*US*) *n* [➡OLD PERSON; 920]

golden eagle *type of* **bird of prey**. [➡BIRD OF PREY; 998]

golden-haired *adj* [➡HAIR COLOUR; 486]

golden handshake (*informal*) *n* [➡MONEY, PAYMENTS, AND CHARGES; 800]

golden mean *n* **middle**, midway, mean. [➡MEASUREABLE PORTION; 125] *Opposite:* extreme.

golden opportunity *n* **opportunity**, advantage, break (*informal*), chance, chance of a lifetime, good fortune. [➡SOURCE OF HAPPINESS, PLEASURE, OR IMPROVEMENT; 210]

golden parachute (*informal*) *n* [➡MONEY, PAYMENTS, AND CHARGES; 800]

goldenrod *type of* **weed**. [➡WEEDS AND THISTLES; 1034]

golden rule *n* **standard**, belief, tenet (*formal*), code, guide, guideline, principle. [➡WAYS OF DOING THINGS; 295]

golden syrup *n* [➡SUGAR AND PRESERVES; 1183]

goldfish *type of* **freshwater fish**. [➡FRESHWATER FISH; 1010]

gold mine *n* **moneymaker**, treasure-trove, treasure house, money-spinner (*informal*). [➡TREAT; 211]

gold-plated *adj* **gilded**, gilt, gold-leaf, golden, gold. [➡METALS; 1275]

gold standard *n* **benchmark**, system, yardstick, touchstone, criterion, paradigm. [➡WAYS OF DOING THINGS; 295]

golf *type of* **target ball game**. [➡HOBBIES, GAMES, AND SPORTS; 875]

golly (*dated informal*) *interj* **goodness**, blimey (*informal*), gosh (*informal*), heavens (*informal*), my word (*dated*), my, wow (*informal*), gee (*US informal*), oh my (*US informal*), gee whiz (*US informal*), heavens to Betsy (*US informal*). [➡EXPRESSIONS OF SURPRISE; 547]

go mad *v* **lose your temper**, blow up (*informal*), go off the deep end, go haywire (*informal*), blow your top (*informal*), hit the roof, lose your cool, lose your rag (*slang*). [➡GIVING VENT TO EMOTIONS; 680]

go missing *v* **disappear**, vanish, abscond, escape, go AWOL, do a bunk (*informal*). [➡RUN AWAY AND AVOID; 10]

go mouldy *v* [➡GO BAD AND CORRODE; 391]

gondola *type of* **small vessel**. [➡SHIPS AND BOATS; 1149]

gone 1 *adj* (*informal*) **dead**, deceased (*formal*), passed away, passed on, no more. [➡DEAD AND DYING; 925] *Opposite:* alive. 2 *adj* **absent**, away, left, disappeared, moved out, departed (*formal or literary*), vanished. [➡ABSENT AND UNAVAILABLE; 7] *Opposite:* present. 3 *adj* **used up**, spent, finished, consumed, depleted, drained, exhausted. [➡ABSENT AND UNAVAILABLE; 7] *Opposite:* remaining.

goner (*slang*) *n* **corpse**, dead body, cadaver, stiff (*slang*). [➡FAILURE; 77]

gonfalon *n* **pennant**, banner, flag, standard, ensign. [➡SYMBOLS, SIGNS, AND NUMBERS; 597]

gong 1 *n* (*slang*) **medal**, decoration, award, honour, distinction, title. [➡REWARDS AND AWARDS; 440] 2 *type of* **percussion instrument**. [➡MUSICAL INSTRUMENTS; 910]

gonzo (*US slang*) *adj* **exaggerated**, idiosyncratic, subjective, personalized, biased, partial. [➡BIZARRE AND PECULIAR; 258] *Opposite:* objective.

goo (*informal*) 1 *n* **gunge** (*informal*), sludge, slush, slop, gloop (*informal*), sticky stuff, gunk (*informal*), gook (*US informal*), goop (*US informal*). [➡UNPLEASANT AND DIRTY SUBSTANCES; 1267] 2 *n* **corn** (*informal*), slush, schmaltz (*informal*), sentimentality, emotionalism, slop (*informal*), mush. [➡IN POOR TASTE; 230]

good 1 *adj* **high-quality**, first-class, superior, fine (*informal*), excellent, first-rate. [➡GOOD, WELL, BETTER; 184] *Opposite:* poor. 2 *adj* **suitable**, helpful, beneficial, sound, safe, advantageous, reliable, trustworthy, useful. [➡USEFULNESS; 200] *Opposite:* useless. 3 *adj* **skilled**, skilful, able, proficient, accomplished, talented, capable, clever, competent, expert. [➡TALENTED AND SKILFUL; 528] *Opposite:* bad. 4 *adj* **virtuous**, decent, respectable, moral, upright, noble, worthy, blameless, wholesome. [➡MORALLY GOOD; 775] *Opposite:* bad. 5 *adj* **enjoyable**, pleasant, nice, lovely, satisfactory, agreeable, delightful. [➡EMOTIONALLY PLEASANT; 188] *Opposite:* bad. 6 *adj* **obedient**, well-behaved, well-mannered, polite, well-brought-up, courteous. [➡GOOD MANNERS AND SOCIAL SKILLS; 521] *Opposite:* naughty. 7 *adj* **nice**, fine (*informal*), lovely, clear, mild, pleasant, fair, sunny. [➡HOT WEATHER; 1050] *Opposite:* unpleasant. 8 *adj* **effective**, useful, valuable, right, appropriate, beneficial. [➡USEFULNESS; 200] *Opposite:* unsuitable. 9 *n* **benefit**, help, advantage, usefulness, profit, gain. [➡SOURCE OF HAPPINESS, PLEASURE, OR IMPROVEMENT; 210]

good afternoon *interj* [➡GREETINGS, FAREWELLS, AND SALUTATIONS; 660]

goodbye 1 *interj* **see you** (*informal*), bye (*informal*), see you later (*informal*), ta-ta (*informal*), bon voyage, ciao (*informal*), farewell (*literary*), hasta la vista (*informal*), so long (*informal*), later (*informal*), cheerio (*informal*). [➡GREETINGS, FAREWELLS, AND SALUTATIONS; 660] *Opposite:* hello. **2** *n* **departure**, farewell, valediction (*formal*), leave-taking (*literary*), sendoff, going, parting. [➡END; 54] *Opposite:* greeting.

good cause *n* **charitable organization**, voluntary organization, deserving cause, charity, benefit. [➡CHARITY AND CHARITABLE INSTITUTIONS; 822]

good day *interj* [➡GREETINGS, FAREWELLS, AND SALUTATIONS; 660]

good deed *n* **good turn**, favour, kindness, service. [➡KIND ACTION OR BEHAVIOUR; 296]

good enough *adj* **all right**, presentable, passable, satisfactory, sufficient, adequate. [➡ACCEPTABLE AND PASSABLE; 220] *Opposite:* inadequate.

good faith *n* **honesty**, lawfulness, sincerity, probity (*formal*), integrity, virtue. [➡MORALLY GOOD; 775]

good-for-nothing *adj* [➡REDUNDANT AND USELESS; 241]

good fortune *n* **luck**, fortuity, good luck, chance, a stroke of luck, lucky break. [➡LUCK; 784] *Opposite:* misfortune.

good guy (*US informal*) *n* **goody**, hero, winner. [➡PEOPLE WHO ARE APPROVED OF; 955] *Opposite:* baddie (*informal*).

good health *n* **fitness**, strength, healthiness, vigour, robustness. [➡FIT AND STRONG; 737] *Opposite:* illness.

goodhearted *adj* **kind-hearted**, kind, caring, generous, giving, decent, well-meaning. [➡GENEROSITY AND KINDNESS; 496]

good humour *n* [➡PLEASURE, EXCITEMENT, AND ELATION; 535]

good-humoured *adj* **friendly**, good-natured, good-tempered, easygoing, genial, affable, humorous, pleasant, happy, amiable, cheerful. [➡CHEERFULNESS OF OUTLOOK; 504] *Opposite:* ill-tempered.

good-humouredly *adv* **humorously**, good-naturedly, pleasantly, affably, amiably, genially, cheerfully. [➡GOOD-TEMPERED AND HUMOROUS; 628] *Opposite:* grumpily.

good job (*US*) *interj* [➡COMPLIMENTS; 658]

good judgment *n* **judiciousness**, acumen, astuteness, wisdom, perspicacity, good sense. [➡KNOWLEDGE AND WISDOM; 559]

good life *n* **luxury**, comfort, ease, life of ease, life of Riley, lap of luxury, a place in the sun. [➡PLEASANT SITUATIONS; 74]

good-looking *adj* **attractive**, handsome, beautiful, nice-looking, lovely, pretty, gorgeous, stunning. [➡PEOPLE'S PHYSICAL APPEARANCE; 476] *Opposite:* unattractive.

Compare and Contrast: ***good-looking, attractive, beautiful, handsome, lovely, pretty***

CORE MEANING: HAVING A PLEASING FACIAL APPEARANCE

good-looking having a pleasant personal, especially facial, appearance; ***attractive*** pleasing in appearance or manner, or sexually desirable; ***beautiful*** pleasing to the senses, especially pleasing to look at, and often used to describe women whose appearance is generally considered ideal or perfect; ***handsome*** with good facial features or a pleasing general appearance, generally used of men, but also of women who have strong but attractive features; ***lovely*** pleasing to look at, most often used of women; ***pretty*** with an attractive, pleasant face that is appealing, rather than outstandingly beautiful, most often used of women.

good looks *n* **beauty**, attractiveness, prettiness, handsomeness, loveliness, comeliness (*archaic or literary*). [➡PEOPLE'S PHYSICAL APPEARANCE; 476]

good luck *interj* [➡GREETINGS, FAREWELLS, AND SALUTATIONS; 660]

good luck charm *n* [➡LUCKY CHARMS; 786]

goodly *adj* **large**, substantial, fair, considerable, reasonable, sizable. [➡MANY, MUCH, LARGE AMOUNT; 117]

good-mannered *adj* [➡GOOD MANNERS AND SOCIAL SKILLS; 521]

good manners *n* **propriety**, manners, courtesy, decorum, etiquette, civility, courteousness. [➡GOOD MANNERS AND SOCIAL SKILLS; 521] *Opposite:* bad manners.

good morning *interj* [➡GREETINGS, FAREWELLS, AND SALUTATIONS; 660]

good name *n* **reputation**, repute (*formal*), credit, standing, status, prestige, popularity, renown. [➡SUCCESS; 82]

good-natured *adj* **pleasant**, cheerful, friendly, kind, happy, helpful, agreeable, genial, affable, amiable. [➡FRIENDLINESS AND SOCIABILITY; 495] *Opposite:* disagreeable.

good-naturedness *n* [➡FRIENDLINESS AND SOCIABILITY; 495]

goodness *n* **virtuousness**, decency, kindness, honesty, integrity, good, righteousness. [➡MORALLY GOOD; 775] *Opposite:* badness.

goodness gracious *interj* [➡EXPRESSIONS OF SURPRISE; 547]

goodnight *interj* **sleep well**, sleep tight, night (*informal*). [➡GREETINGS, FAREWELLS, AND SALUTATIONS; 660]

good offices *n* **intervention**, intercession, support, mediation, help, aid. [➡KIND ACTION OR BEHAVIOUR; 296]

good on you *interj* [➡COMPLIMENTS; 658]

goods **1** *n* **wares**, stock, articles, produce, supplies, commodities, merchandise. [➡BUSINESS PRODUCTS; 796] **2** *n* **property**, personal property, belongings, goods and chattels, things, possessions. [➡POSSESSIONS; 462] **3** *n* **merchandise**, imports, exports, cargo, freight, commodities, wares, produce. [➡BUSINESS PRODUCTS; 796]

goods and chattels *n* [➡POSSESSIONS; 462]

good sense *n* **prudence**, reason, nous (*informal*), practicality, gumption (*informal*), intelligence. [➡ KNOWLEDGE AND WISDOM; 559]

good-sized *adj* **sizable**, generous, big, substantial, large, considerable. [➡ LARGE; 1192] *Opposite:* small.

goods yard *n* [➡ URBAN OUTDOOR SPACES; 1071]

good taste *n* **discernment**, style, elegance, judgment, refinement, tastefulness, discrimination. [➡ BEAUTY AND ATTRACTIVENESS; 190] *Opposite:* bad taste.

good-tempered *adj* **placid**, good-natured, easygoing, good-humoured, amicable, genial, affable, friendly, sociable. [➡ CHEERFULNESS OF OUTLOOK; 504] *Opposite:* bad-tempered.

good-temperedly *adv* **good-humouredly**, placidly, amicably, genially, affably, sociably, good-naturedly. [➡ GOOD-TEMPERED AND HUMOROUS; 628]

good thing *n* **advantage**, blessing, plus (*informal*), boon, benefit. [➡ SOURCE OF HAPPINESS, PLEASURE, OR IMPROVEMENT; 210]

good turn *n* **favour**, kindness, good deed, service. [➡ KIND ACTION OR BEHAVIOUR; 296]

goodwill *n* **kindness**, friendliness, helpfulness, benevolence, generosity, concern, willingness, care, favour. [➡ LOVE, RESPECT, AND GOODWILL; 550] *Opposite:* malice.

good word *n* **recommendation**, testimonial, reference, character, defence. [➡ SOURCE OF HAPPINESS, PLEASURE, OR IMPROVEMENT; 210]

goody 1 *n* **treat**, perk, bonus, reward, extravagance, luxury. [➡ AMAZING THING; 212] 2 *n* **titbit**, sweet, snack, candy (*US*). [➡ CONFECTIONERY; 1181] 3 *n* **hero**, winner, good guy (*US*). [➡ PEOPLE WHO ARE APPROVED OF; 955]. *Opposite:* baddie (*informal*). 4 *interj* (*informal*) **good**, great (*informal*), super (*informal*), terrific (*informal*), splendid, wonderful, smashing. [➡ EXPRESSIONS OF SURPRISE; 547]

goody-goody (*informal*) 1 *n* **teacher's pet**, goody two-shoes (*informal*), bluenose (*US dated informal*) [➡ SUPERFICIAL OR INSINCERE PEOPLE; 951] 2 *adj* **sanctimonious**, smug, self-righteous (*disapproving*), self-satisfied, holier-than-thou (*informal*), prudish. [➡ AFFECTATION, SELF-SATISFACTION, AND SNOBBISHNESS; 508]

goody two-shoes (*informal*) *n* [➡ SUPERFICIAL OR INSINCERE PEOPLE; 951]

gooey 1 *adj* **sticky**, viscous, thick, glutinous, gummy, mushy, liquid, gelatinous, runny, gluey. [➡ PHYSICAL TEXTURE; 1221] 2 *adj* (*informal*) **slushy**, soppy (*informal*), corny, schmaltzy (*informal*), cloying, sentimental, mushy. [➡ IN POOR TASTE; 230]

gooeyness *n* [➡ FLUID AND NON-SOLID; 1212]

goof (*informal*) 1 *n* **error**, blunder, slip-up (*informal*), slip, gaffe, mistake, misstep, faux pas (*literary*). [➡ MISTAKES; 251] 2 *v* **slip up** (*informal*), mistake, get it wrong, make a blunder, blunder, miscue (*informal*), go wrong, boob (*informal*), err. [➡ MESS UP AND MAKE MISTAKES; 473] 3 *v* **botch**, mess up (*informal*), foul up (*informal*), bungle (*informal*), mix up, muddle. [➡ MESS UP AND MAKE MISTAKES; 473]

goof around (*US informal*) *v* [➡ JOKES AND TEASING; 675]

go off 1 *v* **go bad**, decay, rot, decompose, putrefy, moulder. [➡ GO BAD AND CORRODE; 391] 2 *v* **explode**, blow up, go up, detonate. [➡ DESTRUCTION AND DEMOLITION; 360] 3 *v* **leave**, go away, go, depart, set off, take off (*informal*). [➡ ABSENT ONESELF; 8] *Opposite:* stay.

go off in a huff *v* [➡ ABSENT ONESELF; 8]

go off the deep end *v* **lose your temper**, go mad, go bananas (*informal*), lose your cool, hit the roof, go berserk, lose control, throw a fit (*informal*), throw a wobbly (*informal*), be beside yourself. [➡ GIVING VENT TO EMOTIONS; 680] *Opposite:* calm down.

go off the rails *v* [➡ FAIL OR BE UNSUCCESSFUL; 75]

goof off (*US informal*) *v* [➡ JOKES AND TEASING; 675]

goofproof (*US informal*) *adj* [➡ SAFE AND SAFETY; 192]

gook (*US informal*) *n* [➡ UNPLEASANT AND DIRTY SUBSTANCES; 1267]

go on 1 *v* **continue**, last, keep on, keep up, persist, carry on, keep going. [➡ CONTINUE AN ACTION; 263] *Opposite:* stop. 2 *v* **occur**, happen, take place, come about. [➡ HAPPEN; 27] 3 *v* **blather** (*informal*), blab (*informal*), blabber, chatter, prattle, natter (*informal*), gab (*informal*), gas (*informal*), footle (*informal*). [➡ WITTER AND BABBLE; 618]

goon (*US*) *n* **thug**, gangster, attacker, assailant, hoodlum, criminal, gorilla (*informal*), hood (*US slang*). [➡ VILLAINS AND THUGS; 947]

go on at (*informal*) *v* **whine**, whinge (*informal*), moan (*informal*), complain, nag, criticize, grumble. [➡ COMPLAIN AND NAG; 687]

go one better *v* **surpass**, outdo, top, crown, better, beat. [➡ BEAT AND DEFEAT; 80]

go on the blink (*informal*) *v* [➡ FAIL OR CEASE TO FUNCTION; 471]

go on the rampage *v* [➡ GIVING VENT TO EMOTIONS; 680]

goop (*US informal*) *n* **goo** (*informal*), gunge (*informal*), gunk (*informal*), slime, mess, crud (*slang*), gook (*US informal*). [➡ UNPLEASANT AND DIRTY SUBSTANCES; 1267]

goopy (*US informal*) *adj* [➡ FLUID AND NON-SOLID; 1212]

goose 1 *type of* **fowl**. [➡ FOOD BIRD; 999] 2 *type of* **male or female bird**. [➡ MALE OR FEMALE BIRD; 1005] 3 *type of* **meat**. [➡ TYPES AND CUTS OF MEAT; 1176]

gooseberry *type of* **berry**. [➡ FRUIT AND VEGETABLES; 1175]

goose egg (*slang*) *n* [➡ NONE; 121]

goose pimples *n* [➡ CONDITIONS AFFECTING THE SKIN; 722]

goose step *v* **strut**, stride, tramp, pace, walk, march. [➡ PROCEED AND GO; 306]

go out 1 *v* **socialize**, party (*informal*), meet friends, go out on the town (*informal*), paint the town red (*informal*). [➡ LEISURE AND RECREATION; 874] 2 *v* **ebb**, recede, flow out. [➡ EMIT AND EMANATE; 362] *Opposite:* flow.

go out of business *v* **go bankrupt**, fold, close down, shut down, go bust (*informal*), go belly up, go under, fail, go to the wall, bust (*informal*). [➡ BUSINESS ACTIVITIES AND PHENOMENA; 795]

go over *v* **discuss**, go into, examine, look at, study, read, peruse, revise, look into, consider, review, revisit. [➡ EXAMINE AND ASSESS; 754] *Opposite:* ignore.

go over the top *v* **overdo it**, get carried away, go mad, gild the lily, over-egg the pudding, go to town (*informal*). [➡ OVERDO SOMETHING; 291]

go pale *v* [➡ FACIAL EXPRESSION; 652]

go pear-shaped (*informal*) *v* [➡ FAIL OR BE UNSUCCESSFUL; 75]

gopher *type of* **rodent.** [➡ RODENT; 989]

go postal (*US informal*) *v* [➡ GIVING VENT TO EMOTIONS; 680]

go rancid *v* [➡ GO BAD AND CORRODE; 391]

gore 1 *v* **wound**, pierce, stab, spear, stick, gouge, run through (*literary*). [➡ STAB; 417] 2 *n* **blood**, violence, blood-letting, slaughter, killing, carnage, bloodshed. [➡ CAUSES OF DEATH; 921]

go red *v* [➡ FACIAL EXPRESSION; 652]

gorge 1 *n* **valley**, ravine, canyon, defile, gap, chasm, gulch (*US*), arroyo (*US*). [➡ GEOLOGICAL FEATURES; 1056] 2 *part of* **bird.** [➡ PARTS OF A BIRD; 1006] 3 *v* **overeat**, stuff, binge, glut, sate, satiate. [➡ EAT AND NOT EAT; 711] 4 *v* **guzzle** (*informal*), devour, wolf, bolt, gobble, consume, eat, scarf down (*US slang*). [➡ EAT AND NOT EAT; 711] *Opposite:* nibble.

gorgeous *adj* **beautiful**, magnificent, stunning, elegant, attractive, striking, good-looking, dazzling, lovely, exquisite, adorable. [➡ BEAUTY AND ATTRACTIVENESS; 190] *Opposite:* unattractive.

gorgeousness *n* **elegance**, magnificence, beauty, splendour, exquisiteness, good looks, prettiness, attractiveness, loveliness. [➡ BEAUTY AND ATTRACTIVENESS; 190]

Gorgonzola *type of* **soft cheese.** [➡ DAIRY PRODUCTS AND CHEESES; 1182]

gorilla 1 *n* (*informal*) **thug**, brute, bully, heavy (*slang*), hoodlum, hood (*US slang*), goon (*US*). [➡ VILLAINS AND THUGS; 947] 2 *type of* **primate.** [➡ PRIMATE; 988]

gormless (*informal*) *adj* **stupid**, unintelligent, dull, obtuse, brainless, foolish. [➡ NEGATIVE INTELLECTUAL CHARACTERISTICS; 526] *Opposite:* bright.

go rotten *v* [➡ GO BAD AND CORRODE; 391]

go round *v* **visit**, call on, look in, drop in, pop by. [➡ ACCOMPANY AND FOLLOW; 338]

go-round (*US informal*) 1 *n* **round**, pass, turn, session, instance, occurrence. [➡ EVENTS AND OCCURRENCES; 35] 2 *n* **argument**, disagreement, fight, tiff, quarrel, row, dispute. [➡ ARGUMENT; 47] *Opposite:* agreement.

gorse *type of* **shrub or bush.** [➡ BUSHES AND SHRUBS; 1027]

gory 1 *adj* **bloody**, bloodstained, blood-soaked. [➡ IN BAD REPAIR; 1233] 2 *adj* **violent**, gruesome, brutal, bloodthirsty, fierce, horrific. [➡ PHYSICALLY UNPLEASANT; 227] *Opposite:* pleasant. 3 *adj* **disgusting**, gruesome, grisly, unpleasant, ghastly, horrible. [➡ DISGUSTING AND REPULSIVE; 231] *Opposite:* delightful.

go separate ways *v* [➡ SEPARATE AND DIVIDE; 402]

gosh (*informal*) *interj* **goodness**, my goodness, heavens (*informal*), goodness gracious, gracious, wow (*informal*), golly (*dated informal*), my, jeepers (*dated informal*), gee (*US informal*), oh my (*US informal*). [➡ EXPRESSIONS OF SURPRISE; 547]

go sky-high *v* [➡ CHANGE OF INTENSITY: MORE; 395]

gosling *type of* **young bird.** [➡ YOUNG BIRD; 1004]

go-slow *n* **stoppage**, strike, slowdown (*US*). [➡ WORK-RELATED ACTIVITIES; 834]

go sour *v* [➡ GO BAD AND CORRODE; 391]

gospel *type of* **popular music.** [➡ MUSIC, SONGS, AND SINGING; 907]

gossamer 1 *n* **filaments**, spider's web, cobwebs, threads (*US slang*). [➡ FASTENERS, LINKS, AND NETWORKS; 1246] 2 *adj* **delicate**, flimsy, sheer, filmy, ethereal, transparent, diaphanous, gauzy. [➡ VISUAL TEXTURE; 1220] *Opposite:* robust.

gossip 1 *n* **rumour**, hearsay, tittle-tattle, scandal, chit-chat (*informal*). [➡ GOSSIP; 679] 2 *n* **chatter**, chinwag (*informal*), chat, talk, conversation, natter (*informal*), blather (*informal*). [➡ INFORMAL COMMUNICATION; 45] 3 *n* **blabbermouth** (*informal*), tattler, telltale, bigmouth (*informal*), gossipmonger, scandalmonger, nosy parker (*informal*), rumourmonger, tattletale (*US informal*). [➡ INTERFERING PEOPLE AND TELLTALES; 950] 4 *v* **natter** (*informal*), chatter, chinwag (*informal*), talk, converse, chat. [➡ BETRAY CONFIDENCES AND GOSSIP; 619]

gossipmonger *n* **telltale**, gossip, bigmouth (*informal*), nosy parker (*informal*), scandalmonger, rumourmonger, blabbermouth (*informal*), tattler, tattletale (*US informal*). [➡ INTERFERING PEOPLE AND TELLTALES; 950]

go stale *v* [➡ GO BAD AND CORRODE; 391]

go the distance *v* **complete**, finish, achieve, accomplish, carry out, fulfil, realize. [➡ COMPLETE AN ACTION; 264] *Opposite:* give up.

Gothic 1 *adj* **supernatural**, creepy (*informal*), melodramatic, eerie, grotesque, gloomy, spooky (*informal*). [➡ FRIGHTENING; 232] 2 *type of* **pre-20th-century architecture.** [➡ BUILDING AND ARCHITECTURE; 1075]

Gothic revival *type of* **pre-20th-century architecture.** [➡ BUILDING AND ARCHITECTURE; 1075]

go through 1 *v* **experience**, endure, undergo, bear, suffer. [➡ EXPERIENCE AND ENCOUNTER; 583] 2 *v* **use**, get through, run through, consume, utilize, make use of, use up, spend. [➡ USE UP AND WASTE; 475] *Opposite:* keep. 3 *v* **examine**, look through, look over, go over, study, inspect, check. [➡ EXAMINE AND ASSESS; 754]

go through the roof *v* **soar**, rocket, rise, shoot up, spiral upwards, surge, spiral. [➡ CHANGE OF SIZE: BIGGER; 393] *Opposite:* plummet.

go to bed *v* **turn in** (*informal*), hit the hay (*informal*), hit the sack (*informal*), retire. [➡ SLEEP AND DREAM; 724]

go to meet your maker *v* [➡ DIE; 922]

go too far *v* [➡ OVERDO SOMETHING; 291]

go to pieces *v* **break down**, crack up (*informal*), crack, lose control, collapse, crumple, fall apart. [➡GIVING VENT TO EMOTIONS; 680]

go to pot (*informal*) *v* **deteriorate**, disintegrate, fall apart, go to the dogs (*informal*), go downhill, go to rack and ruin (*informal*), go from bad to worse, worsen, take a turn for the worse, degenerate, decline. [➡GET WORSE; 382] *Opposite:* improve.

go to rack and ruin (*informal*) *v* **deteriorate**, disintegrate, fall apart, go to the dogs (*informal*), go downhill, go to pot (*informal*), go from bad to worse, worsen, take a turn for the worse, degenerate, decline. [➡GET WORSE; 382] *Opposite:* improve.

go to seed *v* [➡FAIL OR BE UNSUCCESSFUL; 75]

go to sleep *v* **fall asleep**, nod off, doze off, drop off (*informal*), drift off. [➡SLEEP AND DREAM; 724] *Opposite:* wake up.

go to the dogs (*informal*) *v* **go downhill**, deteriorate, go to pot (*informal*), degenerate, decline, go from bad to worse, worsen, take a turn for the worse, go to rack and ruin (*informal*), fall apart. [➡GET WORSE; 382] *Opposite:* improve.

go to the wall *v* **go bankrupt**, fold, go under, fail, go bust (*informal*), close down, shut down. [➡BUSINESS ACTIVITIES AND PHENOMENA; 795]

go to waste *v* **be wasted**, go down the drain, squander, dissipate, throw away. [➡FAIL OR CEASE TO FUNCTION; 471]

got up (*informal*) *adj* [➡DRESS, WEAR, AND UNDRESS; 868]

gouache *n* [➡WRITING AND DRAWING IMPLEMENTS, AND MEDIA; 602]

Gouda *type of* **hard cheese**. [➡DAIRY PRODUCTS AND CHEESES; 1182]

gouge 1 *v* **scratch**, score, scrape, mark, cut into, gash, chisel. [➡EXTRACT AND SEVER; 342] 2 *v* (*US*) **extort**, extract, wring, wrest, squeeze, overcharge. [➡TAKE SOMETHING AWAY; 426] 3 *n* **score**, scratch, gash, groove, hollow, scrape, cavity. [➡HOLES, GAPS, AND FORKS; 1251]

gouge out *v* **dig out**, hollow out, press out, squeeze out, force out, chisel out, scoop, hollow. [➡EXTRACT AND SEVER; 342]

goulash *type of* **cooked dish**. [➡PREPARED DISHES; 1169]

go under 1 *v* **collapse**, go to the wall, go bust (*informal*), bite the dust (*informal*), fold, fail. [➡FAIL OR BE UNSUCCESSFUL; 75] 2 *v* **lose consciousness**, pass out, black out, faint. [➡FALL ILL, TREAT, AND RECOVER; 729]

go underground *v* [➡RUN AWAY AND AVOID; 10]

go up *v* **explode**, go off, detonate, blow up, ignite, go up in smoke. [➡FIRE, FLAMMABILITY, AND BURNING; 1164]

go up in smoke 1 *v* **burn**, catch fire, burst into flames, burn to a crisp, burn to the ground, catch light. [➡FIRE, FLAMMABILITY, AND BURNING; 1164] 2 *v* **fail**, fold, collapse, bomb (*informal*), go wrong, go awry. [➡FAIL OR BE UNSUCCESSFUL; 75]

gourmand *n* **food lover**, glutton, greedy guts (*informal*), gastronome, foodie (*informal*), gourmet, epicure. [➡EATERS, GOURMETS, AND DIETARY CHOICES; 715]

gourmandise *n* [➡EAT AND NOT EAT; 711]

gourmandizing *n* [➡EAT AND NOT EAT; 711]

gourmet *n* **gastronome**, foodie (*informal*), food lover, epicure, epicurean, connoisseur, gourmand. [➡EATERS, GOURMETS, AND DIETARY CHOICES; 715]

govern *v* **rule**, preside over, oversee, administer, administrate, direct, run, manage, head, reign, control, dominate, regulate, preside. [➡BE IN CHARGE; 271]

governess *n* **tutor**, teacher, instructor, schoolteacher, educator, coach. [➡EDUCATORS; 840]

government *n* **administration**, rule, management, direction, regime, control, supervision, command, authority, leadership. [➡GOVERNMENT AND POLITICS; 805]

governmental *adj* **administrative**, parliamentary, legislative, executive, constitutional, organizational, managerial, lawmaking. [➡GOVERNMENT AND POLITICS; 805]

governor *n* **director**, ruler, manager, administrator, chief, head, superintendent, regulator, controller. [➡BOSSES AND MANAGEMENT; 965]

governorship *n* **administration**, leadership, stewardship, directorship, captaincy, office, tenure. [➡POLITICAL OFFICES AND POLITICIANS; 808]

go well *v* [➡SUCCEED AND WIN; 79]

go white *v* [➡FACIAL EXPRESSION; 652]

go wild *v* **run riot**, rampage, run amok, go on the rampage, go mad, run wild. [➡GIVING VENT TO EMOTIONS; 680]

go with 1 *v* (*informal*) **date**, go out with, see, socialize, go steady. [➡ESTABLISHING RELATIONSHIPS WITH OTHERS; 974] 2 *v* **adopt**, accept, follow, run with, support, go along with, concur. [➡APPROVE AND CONFIRM; 647]

go without *v* **not have**, do without, be without, lack, want, be deprived, forgo. [➡FOREGO AND DENY ONESELF; 450] *Opposite:* have.

gown *n* **dress**, frock (*dated*), robe, evening dress, wedding dress, ballgown. [➡GARMENTS AND OUTFITS; 865]

go wrong 1 *v* **fail**, break down, not work, not succeed, go awry, be unsuccessful, be a failure. [➡FAIL OR BE UNSUCCESSFUL; 75] *Opposite:* succeed. 2 *v* **make a mistake**, slip up (*informal*), misjudge, blunder, err, goof (*informal*), boob (*informal*). [➡MESS UP AND MAKE MISTAKES; 473]

GP *n* **family doctor**, doctor, medic (*informal*), clinician, practitioner. [➡PEOPLE WHO WORK IN MEDICINE; 848]

grab 1 *v* **grasp**, clutch, grip, take hold of, seize, snatch, take. [➡CONTACT: HOLD; 412] *Opposite:* let go. 2 *v* **snatch**, seize, remove, steal, nick (*slang*), take, lift (*informal*), heist (*US slang*). [➡TAKE SOMETHING AWAY; 426] 3 *v* (*informal*) **affect**, appeal, impress, attract, please, influence. [➡APPEAL TO AND AROUSE INTEREST; 576]

grab bag (*US*) *n* [➡COLLECTIONS AND MIXTURES OF THINGS; 1243]

grab hold of *v* **grab**, grasp, grip, snatch, clutch, clench, take. [➡CONTACT: HOLD; 412]

grace 1 *n* **elegance**, refinement, loveliness, beauty, polish, style, poise, charm. [➡WELL GROOMED; 483] *Opposite:*

awkwardness. **2** *n* **kindness**, kindliness, decency, mercy, mercifulness, charity, benevolence, clemency, leniency, favour, reprieve. [➡MORALLY GOOD; 775] *Opposite:* unkindness. **3** *n* **blessing**, prayer, thanks, thanksgiving. [➡RELIGIOUS CONCEPTS; 777] **4** *v* **dignify**, honour, favour, distinguish. [➡IMPROVE SOMETHING; 375] *Opposite:* demean. **5** *v* **adorn**, embellish, enhance, decorate, ornament, beautify. [➡DECORATE, ADORN, AND APPLY COATINGS; 406] *Opposite:* deface.

graceful 1 *adj* **elegant**, beautiful, supple, agile, nimble, lithe, flowing, smooth, attractive, fluid. [➡AGILITY OF THE BODY; 477] *Opposite:* graceless. **2** *adj* **poised**, dignified, polished, refined, stylish, polite, charming, gracious. [➡GOOD MANNERS AND SOCIAL SKILLS; 521] *Opposite:* awkward. **3** *adj* **flowing**, fluid, smooth, easy on the eye, attractive, elegant. [➡BEAUTY AND ATTRACTIVENESS; 190] *Opposite:* ugly.

gracefully *adv* **stylishly**, with poise, charmingly, elegantly, graciously. [➡WELL GROOMED; 483] *Opposite:* awkwardly.

gracefulness 1 *n* **elegance**, grace, smoothness, fluidity, subtlety, delicacy, cleanness. [➡BEAUTY AND ATTRACTIVENESS; 190] *Opposite:* inelegance. **2** *n* **poise**, dignity, refinement, grace, restraint, politeness, delicacy, tact, diplomacy, graciousness. [➡GOOD MANNERS AND SOCIAL SKILLS; 521] *Opposite:* awkwardness.

graceless 1 *adj* **clumsy**, ungainly, inelegant, awkward, gawky (*informal*), bumbling (*informal*), maladroit (*formal*), ham-fisted (*informal*), ham-handed (*informal*). [➡AGILITY OF THE BODY; 477] *Opposite:* graceful. **2** *adj* **rude**, impolite, ill-mannered, boorish, offensive, crude, uncouth. [➡BAD MANNERS AND SOCIAL SKILLS; 522] *Opposite:* polite.

gracelessly 1 *adv* **inelegantly**, awkwardly, clumsily, maladroitly (*formal*), unskilfully, ham-fistedly (*informal*), ham-handedly (*informal*). [➡INCAUTIOUS AND CARELESS; 284] *Opposite:* gracefully. **2** *adv* **rudely**, impolitely, ill-manneredly, boorishly, offensively, crudely, uncouthly. [➡BAD MANNERS AND SOCIAL SKILLS; 522] *Opposite:* politely.

gracelessness 1 *n* **inelegance**, awkwardness, clumsiness, maladroitness (*formal*), ungainliness, unskilfulness. [➡UNSKILLED; 530] *Opposite:* gracefulness. **2** *n* **rudeness**, impoliteness, mannerlessness, bad manners, boorishness, offensiveness, crudeness, uncouthness. [➡BAD MANNERS AND SOCIAL SKILLS; 522] *Opposite:* politeness.

grace period *n* **extra time**, extension, overrun, overtime (*US*). [➡PAUSES AND PHASES; 56]

gracious 1 *adj* **kind**, polite, tactful, courteous, civil, diplomatic, amiable, cordial, affable. [➡GOOD MANNERS AND SOCIAL SKILLS; 521] *Opposite:* rude. **2** *adj* **condescending**, haughty, superior, snooty (*informal*), patronizing, high and mighty. [➡AFFECTATION, SELF-SATISFACTION, AND SNOBBISHNESS; 508] *Opposite:* genuine. **3** *adj* **luxurious**, elegant, comfortable, well-off, plush (*informal*), classy (*informal*). [➡WEALTH AND WEALTHY; 891] *Opposite:* harsh. **4** *adj* **merciful**, compassionate, lenient, humane, charitable, understanding. [➡MORALLY GOOD; 775] *Opposite:* harsh.

graciously 1 *adv* **kindly**, politely, tactfully, courteously, civilly, diplomatically, amiably, cordially, affably. [➡GOOD MANNERS AND SOCIAL SKILLS; 521] *Opposite:* rudely. **2** *adv* **luxuriously**, elegantly, comfortably. [➡PHYSICALLY PLEASANT; 187]

graciousness *n* **kindness**, courteousness, politeness, civility, affability, diplomacy, cordiality. [➡GOOD MANNERS AND SOCIAL SKILLS; 521] *Opposite:* rudeness.

gradation *n* **nuance**, degree, stage, progression, shift, shade. [➡DEGREE AND EXTENT; 110]

grade 1 *n* **score**, mark, rating, ranking, evaluation. [➡SCORES AND EVALUATIONS; 599] **2** *n* **rank**, position, status, standing, class, category, condition, quality, calibre, degree. [➡VARIETY, TYPE, KIND; 146] **3** *n* (*US*) **hill**, gradient, rise, slope, ascent, descent, incline, pitch. [➡MOUNTAINS AND HILLS; 1044] **4** *v* **classify**, categorize, sort, arrange, order, rate, rank, mark, score, group. [➡ARRANGE AND CREATE ORDER; 358]

Grade A *adj* [➡GOOD, WELL, BETTER; 184]

grade school (*US*) *type of* **school**. [➡EDUCATIONAL INSTITUTIONS; 813]

gradient *n* **slope**, incline, ramp, hill, rise, pitch, ascent, descent, grade (*US*). [➡MOUNTAINS AND HILLS; 1044]

gradual *adj* **slow**, measured, slow but sure, plodding, continuing, steady, regular, ongoing. [➡HAPPENING SLOWLY; 106] *Opposite:* rapid.

graduate 1 *v* **progress**, move up, advance, go forward, move on, proceed, go on, step up. [➡PROCEED AND GO; 306] *Opposite:* fall back. **2** *v* **mark off**, measure off, divide up, regulate. [➡SEPARATE AND DIVIDE; 402] **3** *v* **arrange**, order, categorize, classify, rank, rate, group. [➡ARRANGE AND CREATE ORDER; 358]

graduate school *n* [➡EDUCATIONAL INSTITUTIONS; 813]

graduate student *n* [➡STUDENTS AND PUPILS; 841]

graduation 1 *n* **matriculation**, qualification, completion, validation, attainment, valediction (*formal*), promotion, advancement. [➡LESSONS, COURSE WORK, AND EXAMINATIONS; 842] **2** *n* **award ceremony**, graduation day, ceremony, passing out, commencement (*US*). [➡CEREMONIES AND ANNIVERSARIES; 38] **3** *n* **mark**, division, line, unit, step, scale, point, scale point, calibration. [➡CHANGE; 373] **4** *n* **calibration**, division, measurement, marking up, marking out, verification, ranking, classification. [➡SEPARATE AND DIVIDE; 402]

graffiti *n* **drawing**, doodle, scrawl, scribble, writing, lettering. [➡WRITING; 584]

graft 1 *v* **splice**, attach, join, embed, implant, insert, transplant. [➡FASTEN, LINK, AND JOIN; 409] **2** *n* **implant**, insert, transplant, scion, slip, implantation. [➡COMBINE AND MIX; 401] **3** *n* (*informal*) **work**, labour, toil, slog, grind, struggle. [➡HARD WORK OR EFFORT; 299] **4** *v* (*informal*) **labour**, strive, work, slog, slave, toil, sweat (*informal*). [➡HARD WORK OR EFFORT; 299]

grain *part of* **spacecraft**. [➡SPACE VEHICLES; 1062]

grain elevator (*US*) *type of* **storage space**. [➡STORES AND STORAGE BUILDINGS; 1087]

graininess *n* [➡VISUAL TEXTURE; 1220]

grainy *adj* [➡VISUAL TEXTURE; 1220]

grammar *n* **syntax**, sentence structure, language rules, parsing. [➡ASPECTS OF LANGUAGE; 683]

grammar

◆ *types of grammatical term*
adjunct, affix, attributive, clause, conditional, conjugation, diphthong, indicative, infinitive, inflection, intransitive, modal, nominative, object, participle, plural, predicate, prefix, prenominal, preterite, sentence, subject, subjunctive, suffix, transitive

◆ *types of word class*
adjective, adverb, article, conjunction, definite article, determiner, indefinite article, interjection, modifier, noun, particle, phrasal verb, preposition, pronoun, proper noun, qualifier, quantifier, substantive, verb

grammar school *type of* **school**. [➡EDUCATIONAL INSTITUTIONS; 813]

grammatical 1 *adj* **linguistic**, syntactic, structural. [➡ASPECTS OF LANGUAGE; 683] 2 *adj* **correct**, well-formed, right, proper, standard, acceptable. [➡ASPECTS OF LANGUAGE; 683]

gramophone (*dated*) *type of* **audio equipment**. [➡AUDIO EQUIPMENT; 1138]

gramps (*informal*) *n* [➡OLDER GENERATION RELATIVES; 959]

grampus *type of* **marine mammal**. [➡MARINE MAMMAL; 987]

gran (*informal*) *n* **grandma** (*informal*), nana (*informal*), grandmother, granny (*informal*). [➡OLDER GENERATION RELATIVES; 959]

granary *n* **warehouse**, barn, silo, grain elevator (*US*), storeroom, hayloft. [➡STORES AND STORAGE BUILDINGS; 1087]

grand 1 *adj* **outstanding**, impressive, imposing, majestic, magnificent, splendid, striking, ostentatious, luxurious. [➡EXTRAORDINARY: AMAZING; 205] *Opposite:* humble. 2 *adj* **ambitious**, impressive, far-reaching, major, substantial, extensive, comprehensive, all-encompassing, all-inclusive. [➡LARGE; 1192] *Opposite:* limited. 3 *adj* **distinguished**, illustrious, celebrated, well-known, famous, revered, respected. [➡KNOWN AND FAMOUS; 182] *Opposite:* ordinary. 4 *adj* **wonderful**, fantastic, excellent, memorable, great, fine, good. [➡GOOD, WELL, BETTER; 184] *Opposite:* poor.

grandchild *type of* **younger relative**. [➡YOUNGER GENERATION RELATIVES; 958]

granddad (*informal*) *n* **grandfather**, grandpa (*informal*), gramps (*informal*). [➡OLDER GENERATION RELATIVES; 959]

granddaughter *type of* **younger relative**. [➡YOUNGER GENERATION RELATIVES; 958]

grandee *n* **dignitary**, notable, public figure, VIP, personage (*formal*), nob (*informal*), toff (*informal*). [➡IMPORTANT OR FAMOUS PEOPLE; 893]

grandeur *n* **splendour**, magnificence, sumptuousness, opulence, majesty, dignity, stateliness, greatness, grandness. [➡EXTRAORDINARY: AMAZING; 205] *Opposite:* austerity.

grandfather *n* **granddad** (*informal*), grandpa (*informal*), gramps (*informal*). [➡OLDER GENERATION RELATIVES; 959]

grandfather clock *type of* **clock**. [➡CLOCKS AND TIMERS; 1125]

grandiloquence *n* **pomposity**, bombast, orotundity, magniloquence, loftiness, fustian, rhetoric. [➡BOAST; 617]

grandiloquent *adj* **pompous**, lofty, haughty, bombastic, high-flown, high-sounding, magniloquent, orotund (*formal*). [➡POMPOUS, LOUD, AND OVER-CONFIDENT; 636] *Opposite:* plain.

grandiose 1 *adj* **pretentious**, pompous, flamboyant, ostentatious, extravagant, high-flying. [➡ELOQUENT, TALKATIVE AND LONG-WINDED; 633] *Opposite:* modest. 2 *adj* **magnificent**, lavish, splendid, impressive, stately, imposing, grand. [➡EXTRAORDINARY: AMAZING; 205] *Opposite:* modest. 3 *adj* **elaborate**, ambitious, complex, impenetrable, unfathomable. [➡DIFFICULTY AND COMPLEXITY; 243] *Opposite:* simple.

grandiosity 1 *n* **pretentiousness**, pompousness, self-importance, affectedness, pomposity, bombast. [➡BOAST; 617] *Opposite:* unpretentiousness. 2 *n* **magnificence**, lavishness, splendour, impressiveness, stateliness, imposingness, grandness. [➡EXTRAORDINARY: AMAZING; 205] *Opposite:* modesty. 3 *n* **elaborateness**, ambitiousness, complexity, impenetrability, unfathomability. [➡DIFFICULTY AND COMPLEXITY; 243] *Opposite:* simplicity.

grandly 1 *adv* **majestically**, magnificently, splendidly, luxuriously, impressively, imposingly. [➡EXTRAORDINARY: AMAZING; 205] *Opposite:* simply. 2 *adv* **ostentatiously** (*disapproving*), flamboyantly, pompously, extravagantly, pretentiously, loftily, haughtily. [➡POMPOUS, LOUD, AND OVER-CONFIDENT; 636] *Opposite:* humbly.

grandma (*informal*) *n* **grandmother**, granny (*informal*), gran (*informal*), nana (*informal*). [➡OLDER GENERATION RELATIVES; 959]

grandmother *n* **grandma** (*informal*), nana (*informal*), gran (*informal*), granny (*informal*). [➡OLDER GENERATION RELATIVES; 959]

grandness *n* **magnificence**, splendour, majesty, dignity, stateliness, greatness, grandeur, grandiosity. [➡EXTRAORDINARY: AMAZING; 205] *Opposite:* simplicity.

grandpa (*informal*) *n* **grandfather**, granddad (*informal*), gramps (*informal*). [➡OLDER GENERATION RELATIVES; 959]

grandparent *type of* **older relative**. [➡OLDER GENERATION RELATIVES; 959]

grand piano *type of* **keyboard**. [➡MUSICAL INSTRUMENTS; 910]

grandson *type of* **younger relative**. [➡YOUNGER GENERATION RELATIVES; 958]

grandstand (*US*) *v* **impress**, ham up, play to the gallery, show off, attract attention, showboat (*informal*). [➡BOAST; 617]

grand total *n* [➡ALL; 126]

grange *n* **farmhouse**, country house, manor house, homestead, ranch. [➡RESIDENTIAL BUILDINGS; 1077]

granite *type of* **stone**. [➡STONES, ROCKS, AND BOULDERS; 1057]

granny (*informal*) *n* **grandmother**, nana (*informal*), grandma (*informal*), gran (*informal*). [➡OLDER GENERATION RELATIVES; 959]

grant 1 *v* **allow**, permit, agree to, consent to, approve of, go along with, concede, admit. [➡AGREE; 646] *Opposite:* prohibit. 2 *v* **give**, accord, confer (*formal*), award, sign over, cede (*formal*), present, bestow (*formal*). [➡GIVE AND PROVIDE; 431] 3 *n* **funding**, scholarship, endowment, contribution, donation, award, gift, bequest, allowance. [➡GIFTS; 439]

See Compare and Contrast at **give**.

granular *adj* **gritty**, grainy, rough, coarse, granulated, granulose. [➡PHYSICAL TEXTURE; 1221] *Opposite:* smooth.

granulated *adj* **ground**, coarse, grainy, gritty, rough. [➡PHYSICAL TEXTURE; 1221]

granule *n* **grain**, pellet, particle, morsel, crumb, piece. [➡SMALL PIECE; 127]

grape *type of* **fruit**. [➡FRUIT AND VEGETABLES; 1175]

grapefruit *type of* **citrus**. [➡FRUIT AND VEGETABLES; 1175]

grapevine 1 *n* **rumour mill**, bush telegraph (*informal*), gossip, scuttlebutt (*US slang*). [➡GOSSIP; 679] 2 *type of* **climber**. [➡CLIMBERS; 1033]

graph *n* **chart**, diagram, grid, display. [➡DRAWINGS, CHARTS AND TABLES; 595]

graphic 1 *adj* **explicit**, realistic, vivid, striking, detailed, leaving nothing to the imagination, full, clear, lifelike. [➡CONCISE AND CLEAR; 203] *Opposite:* sketchy. 2 *adj* **illustrative**, pictorial, drawn, diagrammatic, decorative, visual. [➡ARTISTIC MOVEMENTS AND STYLES; 899]

graphic arts *n* [➡THE PICTORIAL ARTS; 897]

graphic designer *n* [➡DESIGNERS, CREATORS AND INSTIGATORS; 348]

graphic novel *n* [➡FICTION AND DRAMA; 913]

graphite *type of* **mineral**. [➡MINERALS; 1276]

grapple 1 *v* **struggle**, wrestle, seize, grab, grasp, tackle, fight. [➡CONTACT: HOLD; 412] 2 *v* **contend**, deal, cope, face, handle, tackle, struggle, wrestle, do battle. [➡COMPETE, CONTEND, AND COMBAT; 304]

grapple with *v* [➡ATTEMPT AN ACTION; 262]

grasp 1 *v* **take hold of**, clutch, grab, seize, grip, clasp, snatch, grapple, clench. [➡CONTACT: HOLD; 412] *Opposite:* let go. 2 *v* **understand**, comprehend, see the point of, follow, get, get the picture (*informal*), get the message (*informal*). [➡UNDERSTAND AND GRASP; 760] 3 *n* **grip**, hold, clutch, clasp, clench. [➡CONTACT: HOLD; 412] 4 *n* **understanding**, comprehension, knowledge, awareness, perception, sense. [➡KNOWLEDGE AND WISDOM; 559] 5 *n* **reach**, scope, extent, range, capacity, control. [➡DEGREE AND EXTENT; 110]

grasping *adj* **greedy**, avaricious, covetous, selfish, acquisitive, miserly. [➡FINANCIALLY MEAN AND GRASPING; 520] *Opposite:* generous.

graspingness *n* [➡FINANCIALLY MEAN AND GRASPING; 520]

grasp the nettle *v* [➡ATTEMPT AN ACTION; 262]

grass 1 *n* **lawn**, sward, grassland, meadow, pasture, prairie, greensward (*archaic or literary*). [➡THE COUNTRYSIDE AND OUTDOOR SPACES; 1070] 2 *n* (*slang*) **informant**, informer, traitor, snitch (*slang*), squealer (*slang disapproving*), nark (*slang*), supergrass (*informal*). [➡INTERFERING PEOPLE AND TELLTALES; 950] 3 *v* (*slang*) **inform**, betray, give away, snitch (*slang*), squeal (*slang disapproving*), grass up (*slang*), blow the whistle, sneak. [➡BETRAY CONFIDENCES AND GOSSIP; 619]

grass

◆ *types of grass*
bamboo, beach grass, bluegrass, bulrush, couch grass, crab grass, esparto, fescue, Kentucky bluegrass, lyme grass, marram, meadow fescue, pampas grass, reed, rye-grass, spinifex, sugar cane, sword grass, timothy

grass green *type of* **green**. [➡COLOURS; 1223]

grasshopper *type of* **flying insect**. [➡FLYING INSECTS; 1013]

grassland *n* **plains**, prairie, savanna, steppe, heath, downs, pampas, downland, moor, heathland, parkland, lea (*literary*). [➡DESERTS AND PLAINS; 1045]

grass on (*slang*) *v* [➡BETRAY CONFIDENCES AND GOSSIP; 619]

grassroots 1 *n* **masses**, hoi polloi, rank and file, ranks, also-rans, little men. [➡CLASS STATUS; 889] 2 *n* **basis**, origin, foundation, base, root, bedrock. [➡SUPPORTS AND BASES; 1254] 3 *adj* **popular**, proletarian, public, common, ordinary, mass. [➡BELONGING OR RELATING TO PEOPLE; 943]

grass snake *type of* **non-poisonous snake**. [➡SNAKE; 995]

grass up (*slang*) *v* **betray**, inform, blow the whistle on, turn in, sneak, give away, snitch (*slang*), squeal (*slang disapproving*). [➡BETRAY CONFIDENCES AND GOSSIP; 619]

grassy *adj* **green**, verdant, lush. [➡VEGETATION; 1025]

grate 1 *n* **grill**, lattice, grille, trellis, grid, pierced screen, screen, vent. [➡COVERS AND COATINGS; 1245] 2 *v* **shred**, scrape, rasp, file, grind, rub. [➡COOKING AND FOOD PREPARATION; 354] 3 *v* **irritate**, annoy, aggravate (*informal*), exasperate, peeve (*informal*), vex, nettle (*informal*), chafe, gravel. [➡ANGER AND ANNOY; 570] *Opposite:* please.

grateful 1 *adj* **thankful**, appreciative, obliged, indebted, glad. [➡APPRECIATION AND GRATITUDE; 536] *Opposite:* ungrateful. 2 *adj* (*archaic or literary*) **comforting**, gratifying, satisfying, pleasing, pleasant, refreshing. [➡EMOTIONALLY PLEASANT; 188] *Opposite:* unwelcome.

gratefully *adv* **appreciatively**, thankfully. [➡APPRECIATION AND GRATITUDE; 536] *Opposite:* ungratefully.

gratefulness *n* **thankfulness**, appreciativeness, appreciation, gratitude, thanks. [➡APPRECIATION AND GRATITUDE; 536] *Opposite:* ingratitude.

grater *type of* **utensil**. [➡TABLEWARE, CUTLERY, AND KITCHENWARE; 861]

gratification *n* **satisfaction**, fulfilment, indulgence, enjoyment, delight, pleasure. [➡APPRECIATION AND GRATITUDE; 536] *Opposite:* displeasure.

gratified *adj* [➡PLEASURE, EXCITEMENT, AND ELATION; 535]

gratify *v* **please**, satisfy, indulge, fulfil, oblige, humour, delight, enchant. [➡PLEASE AND AMUSE; 573] *Opposite:* displease.

gratifying *adj* **rewarding**, satisfying, agreeable, heart-warming, acceptable, pleasing, enjoyable. [➡EMOTIONALLY PLEASANT; 188]

grating 1 *n* **grille**, grate, lattice, grid, screen, vent. [➡COVERS AND COATINGS; 1245] 2 *adj* **rough**, harsh, raucous, strident, discordant, gruff, hoarse. [➡LOUD OR UNPLEASANT SOUNDS; 1265] *Opposite:* mellifluous. 3 *adj* **irritating**, annoying, infuriating, aggravating (*informal*), insensitive, vexing. [➡IRRITATING; 229] *Opposite:* pleasant.

gratis *adj* **free**, free of charge, on the house, complimentary, for nothing, gratuitous, costless, cost-free, toll-free (*US*). [➡GIFTS; 439]

gratitude *n* **thanks**, thankfulness, appreciation, gratefulness, appreciativeness. [➡APPRECIATION AND GRATITUDE; 536] *Opposite:* ingratitude.

gratuitous 1 *adj* **unwarranted**, uncalled-for, wanton, unjustified, unnecessary, unreasonable, needless, superfluous. [➡REDUNDANT AND USELESS; 241] *Opposite:* necessary. 2 *adj* **free**, gratis, complimentary, at no charge, costless, cost-free, for nothing, free of charge, on the house, toll-free (*US*). [➡GIFTS; 439]

gratuitously *adv* **unnecessarily**, irrelevantly, pointlessly, without cause, unreasonably, needlessly, wantonly, superfluously. [➡REDUNDANT AND USELESS; 241] *Opposite:* necessarily.

gratuitousness *n* **pointlessness**, needlessness, futility, unhelpfulness, unwarrantedness, wantonness, superfluousness. [➡REDUNDANT AND USELESS; 241]

gratuity *n* **tip**, perquisite, perk, token, donation. [➡GIFTS; 439]

grave 1 *n* **tomb**, crypt, vault, burial chamber, mausoleum, sepulchre. [➡BURIAL PLACES AND ACCESSORIES; 930] 2 *adj* **serious**, severe, weighty, momentous, crucial, critical, vital, important. [➡IMPORTANT; 195] *Opposite:* minor. 3 *adj* **solemn**, serious, sombre, grim, earnest, thoughtful, unsmiling, sober. [➡PENSIVENESS AND INTEREST; 539] *Opposite:* cheerful. 4 *adj* **ominous**, foreboding, forbidding, fateful, dire, dangerous. [➡DANGEROUS; 237] *Opposite:* favourable. 5 *type of* **diacritic.** [➡ASPECTS OF LANGUAGE; 683] 6 *type of* **musical term.** [➡MUSICAL TERMS; 912]

gravedigger *n* [➡BURIAL AND PREPARATION FOR BURIAL; 929]

gravel 1 *n* **stones**, pebbles, shingle, chippings. [➡STONES, ROCKS, AND BOULDERS; 1057] 2 *v* (*US*) **bewilder**, puzzle, confuse, perplex, baffle, buffalo (*US informal*). [➡CONFUSE AND BEWILDER; 572] 3 *v* (*US informal*) **annoy**, irritate, grate, vex, chafe, peeve (*informal*), nettle (*informal*), exasperate. [➡ANGER AND ANNOY; 570]

gravelly 1 *adj* **croaky**, gruff, hoarse, rough, harsh, rasping, raspy. [➡LOUD OR UNPLEASANT SOUNDS; 1265] *Opposite:* velvety. 2 *adj* **pebbly**, shingly, stony, rocky, gritty. [➡PHYSICAL TEXTURE; 1221]

gravely 1 *adv* **grimly**, sternly, austerely, seriously, solemnly, thoughtfully, sombrely. [➡BAD-TEMPERED AND HUMOURLESS; 627] *Opposite:* cheerfully. 2 *adv* **fatally**, dangerously, critically, incurably, mortally, grievously, badly. [➡CRITICALLY AND SERIOUSLY; 132]

grave mound *n* [➡BURIAL AND PREPARATION FOR BURIAL; 929]

graven image *n* [➡REPRESENTATIONS AND GENERAL EXAMPLES; 65]

gravestone *n* **headstone**, marker, cenotaph, tombstone, memorial, monument. [➡BURIAL PLACES AND ACCESSORIES; 930]

graveyard *n* **cemetery**, churchyard, necropolis, burial ground, boneyard (*informal*). [➡BURIAL PLACES AND ACCESSORIES; 930]

gravid (*technical*) *adj* [➡REPRODUCTION AND HEREDITY; 726]

gravidity (*technical*) *n* [➡REPRODUCTION AND HEREDITY; 726]

gravidness (*technical*) *n* [➡REPRODUCTION AND HEREDITY; 726]

gravitas (*formal*) *n* **seriousness**, gravity, sobriety, solemnness, sombreness. [➡IMPORTANCE AND SIGNIFICANCE; 193]

gravitate 1 *v* **incline**, lean, move, drift, be attracted, be drawn, be pulled. [➡PROCEED AND GO; 306] *Opposite:* repel. 2 *v* **sink**, settle, drop, fall, descend, drift down. [➡GO DOWNWARDS; 308] *Opposite:* rise.

gravitation *n* **movement**, attraction, gravity. [➡ENERGY GENERAL; 1160]

gravity 1 *n* **gravitation**, gravitational force, pull, draw. [➡ENERGY GENERAL; 1160] 2 *n* **seriousness**, importance, significance, severity, enormity, magnitude. [➡IMPORTANCE AND SIGNIFICANCE; 193] *Opposite:* insignificance. 3 *n* **solemnity**, grimness, sedateness, dignity, earnestness, thoughtfulness, sombreness. [➡SADNESS, DISTRESS, AND DESPAIR; 540] *Opposite:* cheerfulness.

gravy *type of* **seasonings, sauces, and dips.** [➡SEASONINGS AND SAUCES; 1173]

grayling *type of* **freshwater fish.** [➡FRESHWATER FISH; 1010]

graze 1 *v* **browse**, crop, nibble, forage, eat, feed. [➡EAT AND NOT EAT; 711] 2 *v* **scrape**, scratch, scuff, rub, skin, abrade, break. [➡WOUND A PERSON OR ANIMAL; 384] 3 *v* **glance**, brush, skim, sweep, touch. [➡CONTACT: TOUCH; 413] 4 *n* **scratch**, scrape, abrasion, lesion, scuff mark, scuff. [➡HOLES, GAPS, AND FORKS; 1251]

grease 1 *n* **fat**, lard, oil. [➡FATS AND OILS; 1172] 2 *v* **lubricate**, oil, smear. [➡DECORATE, ADORN, AND APPLY COATINGS; 406]

grease gun *type of* **general tool.** [➡HAND TOOLS; 1118]

greasepaint *n* [➡MAKEUP AND BEAUTY PRODUCTS; 491]

greasiness *n* **fattiness**, griminess, sliminess, oiliness, oleaginousness, unctuousness. [➡PHYSICAL TEXTURE; 1221]

greasy *adj* **oily**, fatty, slippery, slimy, oleaginous, unctuous, lubricious (*literary*). [➡PHYSICAL TEXTURE; 1221]

greasy spoon *type of* **eating place.** [➡HOTELS, RESTAURANTS, AND CLUBS; 1081]

great 1 *adj* **huge**, immense, enormous, vast, large, big, grand. [➡LARGE; 1192] *Opposite:* tiny. 2 *adj* **famous**, illustrious, eminent, distinguished, celebrated, impressive, remarkable, talented, skilful, notable. [➡KNOWN AND FAMOUS; 182] *Opposite:* ordinary. 3 *adj* **noble**, elevated, lofty, exalted (*formal*), imposing, stately, grand, impressive, heroic, splendid, majestic. [➡EXTRAORDINARY: AMAZING; 205] *Opposite:* lowly. 4 *adj* (*informal*) **wonderful**, fantastic, magnificent, excellent, terrific, cool (*slang*), groovy (*dated slang*), good. [➡EXTRAORDINARY:

AMAZING; 205] *Opposite:* awful. 5 *adj* **absolute**, utter, complete, downright, intense, profound, extreme. [➡ABSOLUTE AND ABSOLUTELY; 131] *Opposite:* slight. 6 *adj* **countless**, inordinate, prodigious, excessive, boundless, pronounced, abundant, numerous, unlimited. [➡MANY, MUCH, LARGE AMOUNT; 117] *Opposite:* limited. 7 *adj* **important**, significant, momentous, critical, major, weighty, serious. [➡IMPORTANT; 195] *Opposite:* unimportant.

great-aunt *type of* **older relative.** [➡OLDER GENERATION RELATIVES; 959]

greatcoat *type of* **overcoat.** [➡GARMENTS AND OUTFITS; 865]

greater *adj* **better**, superior, larger, bigger, more, grander. [➡SUPERIORITY; 153]

greatest *n* **most**, maximum, record, furthermost, utmost, supreme, best, peak. [➡MAJORITY; 139]

great-grandchild *type of* **younger relative.** [➡YOUNGER GENERATION RELATIVES; 958]

great-granddaughter *type of* **younger relative.** [➡YOUNGER GENERATION RELATIVES; 958]

great-grandfather *type of* **older relative.** [➡OLDER GENERATION RELATIVES; 959]

great-grandmother *type of* **older relative.** [➡OLDER GENERATION RELATIVES; 959]

great-grandparent *type of* **older relative.** [➡OLDER GENERATION RELATIVES; 959]

great-grandson *type of* **younger relative.** [➡YOUNGER GENERATION RELATIVES; 958]

greatly 1 *adv* **very much**, really, to a great extent, to the highest degree, deeply, seriously, considerably, wholly, completely, exceedingly, terribly, awfully. [➡TO A GREAT EXTENT; 130] *Opposite:* hardly. 2 *adv* **importantly**, significantly, momentously, critically, seriously, prominently, impressively. [➡EXTRAORDINARY: AMAZING; 205]

great-nephew *type of* **younger relative.** [➡YOUNGER GENERATION RELATIVES; 958]

greatness 1 *n* **magnitude**, enormity, immensity, vastness, size, largeness. [➡SIZE AND DIMENSIONS; 1191] 2 *n* **importance**, prominence, seriousness, significance, weightiness, magnitude. [➡IMPORTANCE AND SIGNIFICANCE; 193] *Opposite:* insignificance. 3 *n* **fame**, eminence, distinction, impressiveness, prominence, pre-eminence, renown, merit, excellence. [➡EXTRAORDINARY: AMAZING; 205] *Opposite:* commonness.

great-niece *type of* **younger relative.** [➡YOUNGER GENERATION RELATIVES; 958]

great-uncle *type of* **older relative.** [➡OLDER GENERATION RELATIVES; 959]

grebe *type of* **freshwater bird.** [➡FRESHWATER BIRD; 1000]

greed 1 *n* **gluttony**, voracity, ravenousness, greediness, insatiability, hunger, self-indulgence, appetite, craving. [➡MORALLY BAD; 776] *Opposite:* moderation. 2 *n* **avarice**, covetousness, greediness, materialism, acquisitiveness, passion, longing, desire. [➡FINANCIALLY MEAN AND GRASPING; 520] *Opposite:* generosity.

greedily 1 *adv* **voraciously**, ravenously, insatiably, hungrily, avidly, gluttonously. [➡WITH ENTHUSIASM; 287] *Opposite:* sparingly. 2 *adv* **covetously**, avariciously, acquisitively, materialistically, desirously (*formal*), passionately. [➡FINANCIALLY MEAN AND GRASPING; 520] *Opposite:* generously.

greediness 1 *n* **gluttony**, voracity, ravenousness, insatiability, greed, hunger, self-indulgence, appetite, craving. [➡MORALLY BAD; 776] *Opposite:* moderation. 2 *n* **greed**, avarice, covetousness, acquisitiveness, materialism, passion, longing, desire. [➡FINANCIALLY MEAN AND GRASPING; 520] *Opposite:* generosity.

greedy 1 *adj* **gluttonous**, voracious, ravenous, insatiable, hungry. [➡MORALLY BAD; 776] *Opposite:* moderate. 2 *adj* **avaricious**, covetous, grasping, materialistic, acquisitive, desirous (*formal*). [➡FINANCIALLY MEAN AND GRASPING; 520] *Opposite:* generous.

Greek *type of* **alphabet.** [➡SYMBOLS, SIGNS, AND NUMBERS; 597]

Greek coffee *n type of* **coffee.** [➡DRINKS; 1186]

green *type of* **colour.** [➡COLOURS; 1223]

green

◆ *types of green*
apple green, aquamarine, avocado, bottle green, chartreuse, emerald green, forest green, grass green, jade, jade green, lime green, Lincoln green, lovat, Nile green, olive green, pea green, sage green, sea green, viridian

green alga *type of* **alga.** [➡MICROORGANISMS, FUNGI, AND ALGAE; 1023]

green around the gills (*informal*) *adj* [➡ILL AND SICK; 741]

green belt *n* [➡THE COUNTRYSIDE AND OUTDOOR SPACES; 1070]

greenery *n* **foliage**, vegetation, plants, leaves, greens (*US*). [➡VEGETATION; 1025]

green-eyed *adj* [➡ENVY AND JEALOUSY; 549]

greenfield *adj* **undeveloped**, green belt, out-of-town, rural, country. [➡THE COUNTRYSIDE AND OUTDOOR SPACES; 1070] *Opposite:* urban.

greenfield site *n* [➡THE COUNTRYSIDE AND OUTDOOR SPACES; 1070]

greenfly *type of* **flying insect.** [➡FLYING INSECTS; 1013]

greengrocer's *type of* **food outlet.** [➡RETAIL OUTLETS; 1082]

greenhorn *n* **novice**, recruit, initiate, beginner, neophyte, newcomer, apprentice, tenderfoot (*informal*). [➡UNSKILLED PERSON; 531]

See Compare and Contrast at **beginner.**

greenhouse *n* **orangery**, glasshouse, hothouse, conservatory. [➡ANCILLARY BUILDINGS; 1079]

greenhouse gas *type of* **gas.** [➡GASES; 1274]

green light *n* **go-ahead** (*informal*), OK (*informal*), thumbs-up (*informal*), permission, clearance, consent, approval, stamp of approval. [➡AGREE; 646] *Opposite:* red light.

green onion (*US*) *type of* **salad vegetable**. [➡FRUIT AND VEGETABLES; 1175]

greens 1 *n* (*US*) **greenery**, foliage, vegetation, plants, leaves. [➡VEGETATION; 1025] 2 *type of* **vegetable**. [➡FRUIT AND VEGETABLES; 1175]

green with envy *adj* [➡ENVY AND JEALOUSY; 549]

greet 1 *v* **welcome**, meet, make the acquaintance of, receive. [➡ESTABLISHING RELATIONSHIPS WITH OTHERS; 974] 2 *v* **address**, speak to, acknowledge, hail, salute, accost. [➡GESTURES AND GESTICULATION; 654] *Opposite:* ignore. 3 *v* **respond to**, react to, receive, meet, hail, reply. [➡REPLY AND ANSWER; 669]

greeting *n* **salutation**, welcome, welcoming, reception, acknowledgement, address. [➡GREETINGS, FAREWELLS, AND SALUTATIONS; 660]

gregarious *adj* **outgoing**, sociable, social, extrovert, extroverted, expressive, expansive, unreserved, companionable, convivial. [➡FRIENDLINESS AND SOCIABILITY; 495] *Opposite:* shy.

gregariousness *n* **sociability**, friendliness, openness, unreservedness, conviviality, companionability. [➡FRIENDLINESS AND SOCIABILITY; 495] *Opposite:* shyness.

gremlin (*informal*) *n* **jinx**, bug (*informal*), malfunction, blip, glitch. [➡PROBLEM; 257]

grenade *type of* **projectile**. [➡PROJECTILES; 1158]

grey *type of* **colour**. [➡COLOURS; 1223]

grey

◆ *types of grey*
ash, battleship grey, charcoal grey, dove grey, grizzled, gunmetal, pearl grey, pewter, putty, silver grey, slate, steel grey, taupe

greyhound *type of* **large dog**. [➡DOG; 980]

grey whale *type of* **whale**. [➡WHALE; 991]

grid *n* **network**, lattice, net, web, gridiron, grating, trellis, framework, crisscross. [➡FASTENERS, LINKS, AND NETWORKS; 1246]

griddle *v* **grill**, sear, barbecue, cook, broil (*US*). [➡COOKING AND FOOD PREPARATION; 354]

griddlecake *type of* **pancake**. [➡CAKES, BISCUITS, AND DESSERTS; 1180]

gridiron *n* **grid**, lattice, grating, framework, network. [➡COVERS AND COATINGS; 1245]

gridlock 1 *n* **traffic jam**, jam, congestion, snarl-up, tailback, holdup, sig alert (*US*), backup (*US*), snarl (*US*). [➡TRAVEL: TRAFFIC PROBLEMS AND HOLDUPS; 324] 2 *n* **deadlock**, stalemate, standstill, logjam, impasse, standoff. [➡LACK OF ACTIVITY; 343]

grief *n* **sorrow**, heartache, anguish, misery, unhappiness, angst, woe, pain. [➡SADNESS, DISTRESS, AND DESPAIR; 540] *Opposite:* joy.

grief-stricken *adj* **grieving**, distraught, traumatized, inconsolable, heartbroken, devastated, anguished, desolate, despairing, brokenhearted, agonized, distressed, wretched, weeping, tearful. [➡SADNESS, DISTRESS, AND DESPAIR; 540] *Opposite:* happy.

grievance 1 *n* **complaint**, protest, criticism, objection, gripe (*informal*), grumble, moan (*informal*), whinge (*informal*). [➡COMPLAIN AND NAG; 687] 2 *n* **injustice**, wrong, cause of distress, ill-treatment, unfairness, infringement, injury, trial, tribulation. [➡NUISANCES; 254]

grieve 1 *v* **mourn**, feel sad, be sad, lament, be distressed, be upset, be unhappy, sorrow (*literary*), sadden, suffer. [➡GIVING VENT TO EMOTIONS; 680]. *Opposite:* rejoice (*literary*). 2 *v* **hurt**, afflict, pain, distress, aggrieve (*formal*), upset, sadden, depress. [➡UPSET, DISTRESS, AND HUMILIATE; 568] *Opposite:* cheer.

grieving *n* [➡DEATH AND BEREAVEMENT; 927]

grievous 1 *adj* **serious**, significant, critical, dangerous, grave, mortal. [➡BAD AND BADLY; 224] *Opposite:* slight. 2 *adj* **dreadful**, awful, terrible, shameful, painful, severe, grave. [➡EMOTIONALLY UNPLEASANT AND UPSETTING; 228]

grievously 1 *adv* **seriously**, significantly, critically, dangerously, gravely, mortally. [➡CRITICALLY AND SERIOUSLY; 132] *Opposite:* slightly. 2 *adv* **dreadfully**, awfully, terribly, shamefully, painfully, severely, gravely. [➡EMOTIONALLY UNPLEASANT AND UPSETTING; 228]

griffin *type of* **mythological creature**. [➡MYTHICAL CREATURES; 1036]

grill 1 *v* (*informal*) **question**, interrogate, examine, press, probe, quiz, put somebody through the mill (*informal*), give somebody the third degree (*informal*), cross-examine. [➡ASK PEOPLE QUESTIONS; 667] 2 *v* **cook**, barbecue, toast, brown, frizzle. [➡COOKING AND FOOD PREPARATION; 354] 3 *n* **griddle**, grate, barbecue, rotisserie. [➡HOUSEHOLD APPLIANCES; 1116]

See Compare and Contrast at **question**.

grille 1 *n* **grating**, lattice, framework, grid, trellis, grate, network. [➡COVERS AND COATINGS; 1245] 2 *part of* **external structure**. [➡EXTERNAL PARTS OF A VEHICLE; 1146]

grim 1 *adj* **depressing**, bleak, dismal, gloomy, cheerless, ominous, hopeless. [➡EMOTIONALLY UNPLEASANT AND UPSETTING; 228] *Opposite:* hopeful. 2 *adj* **forbidding**, ugly, unattractive, uninviting, grey, dingy. [➡UGLINESS AND UNATTRACTIVENESS; 234] *Opposite:* attractive. 3 *adj* **stern**, serious, dour, severe, morose, surly, unkind. [➡RUDE AND HOSTILE; 626] *Opposite:* kind. 4 *adj* **shocking**, ghastly, horrible, horrific, gruesome, grisly, macabre, repugnant, distasteful, hideous, unpleasant. [➡FRIGHTENING; 232] *Opposite:* pleasant. 5 *adj* (*informal*) **ill**, unwell, indisposed (*formal*), off-colour, poorly (*informal*). [➡ILL AND SICK; 741] *Opposite:* well. 6 *adj* (*informal*) **shoddy**, bad, awful, dire, appalling, terrible, execrable, inept. [➡BAD AND BADLY; 224] *Opposite:* excellent.

grimace 1 *n* **scowl**, frown, smirk, sneer, pout, long face. [➡FACIAL EXPRESSION; 652] *Opposite:* smile. 2 *v* **frown**, scowl, smirk, sneer, pout, pull a face, make a face. [➡FACIAL EXPRESSION; 652] *Opposite:* smile.

grime *n* **filth**, dirt, stain, soot, grunge (*informal*), dust, muck (*informal*). [➡UNPLEASANT AND DIRTY SUBSTANCES; 1267]

grim-faced *adj* [➡ FACIAL EXPRESSION; 652]

griminess *n* **dirtiness**, dinginess, filthiness, grubbiness, dustiness, muckiness (*informal*), squalidness. [➡ DIRTY; 1234] *Opposite:* cleanliness.

grimly 1 *adv* (*informal*) **shoddily**, badly, appallingly, execrably, poorly, ineptly. [➡ BAD AND BADLY; 224] *Opposite:* skilfully. 2 *adv* **depressingly**, bleakly, gloomily, dismally, cheerlessly, ominously. [➡ BAD-TEMPERED AND HUMOURLESS; 627] *Opposite:* cheerily. 3 *adv* **forbiddingly**, uninvitingly, unattractively, dingily, dismally, gloomily. [➡ EMOTIONALLY UNPLEASANT AND UPSETTING; 228] *Opposite:* warmly. 4 *adv* **sternly**, seriously, dourly, severely, morosely, unkindly. [➡ RUDE AND HOSTILE; 626] *Opposite:* kindly. 5 *adv* **shockingly**, horribly, horrifically, hideously, gruesomely, repugnantly, distastefully. [➡ FRIGHTENING; 232] *Opposite:* pleasantly.

grimness 1 *n* **bleakness**, cheerlessness, dismalness, ominousness, gloominess, hopelessness. [➡ EMOTIONALLY UNPLEASANT AND UPSETTING; 228] *Opposite:* brightness. 2 *n* **forbiddingness**, ugliness, unattractiveness, greyness, dinginess, gloominess. [➡ UGLINESS AND UNATTRACTIVENESS; 234] *Opposite:* attractiveness. 3 *n* **sternness**, seriousness, dourness, severity, moroseness, unkindness. [➡ BAD MANNERS AND SOCIAL SKILLS; 522] *Opposite:* kindness. 4 *n* **gruesomeness**, horror, hideousness, grisliness, dreadfulness, unpleasantness. [➡ FRIGHTENING; 232] *Opposite:* pleasantness.

grimy *adj* **dirty**, grubby, smudged, soiled, filthy, mucky (*informal*), dusty, grungy (*informal*). [➡ DIRTY; 1234] *Opposite:* clean.

See Compare and Contrast at **dirty**.

grin 1 *v* **smile**, beam, smirk, laugh, chortle, chuckle. [➡ LAUGHTER; 650] *Opposite:* frown. 2 *n* **beam**, smile, smirk, laugh, chortle, chuckle. [➡ FACIAL EXPRESSION; 652] *Opposite:* frown.

grin and bear it (*informal*) *v* **put up with**, lump (*informal*), take the rough with the smooth, take the bad with the good, weather, ride out. [➡ TOLERATE AND ENDURE; 767] *Opposite:* welcome.

grind 1 *v* **crush**, break up, mill, pound, mince, pulverize. [➡ TEAR, BREAK, AND CUT; 361] 2 *v* **grate**, rasp, gnash, scrape. [➡ EMIT SOUNDS THROUGH IMPACT AND ABRASION; 366] *Opposite:* glide. 3 *v* **sharpen**, file, whet, abrade, polish, smooth. [➡ CLEAN AND POLISH; 404] *Opposite:* blunt. 4 *n* (*informal*) **toil**, chore, slog, tedium, routine, drudgery. [➡ HARD WORK OR EFFORT; 299]

grind down 1 *v* **wear**, erode, eat away, abrade, rub, pound. [➡ TEAR, BREAK, AND CUT; 361] 2 *v* **oppress**, tyrannize, persecute, harass, weaken, destroy. [➡ UPSET, DISTRESS, AND HUMILIATE; 568] *Opposite:* nurture.

grinder *n* **mill**, mincer, crusher, pounder, pulverizer, mortar. [➡ TABLEWARE, CUTLERY, AND KITCHENWARE; 861]

grinding 1 *adj* **crushing**, oppressive, relentless, unending, never-ending, eternal. [➡ PHYSICALLY UNPLEASANT; 227] 2 *adj* **grating**, crunching, earsplitting, screeching, squealing, noisy, cacophonous. [➡ LOUD OR UNPLEASANT SOUNDS; 1265] *Opposite:* pleasant.

grindingly 1 *adv* **crushingly**, oppressively, relentlessly, unendingly, eternally, never-endingly. [➡ IRRITATING; 229] 2 *adv* **gratingly**, shrilly, noisily, stridently, cacophonously. [➡ LOUD OR UNPLEASANT SOUNDS; 1265] *Opposite:* pleasantly.

grind to a halt *v* [➡ FAIL OR CEASE TO FUNCTION; 471]

grinning *adj* [➡ FACIAL EXPRESSION; 652]

grip 1 *n* **grasp**, hold, clasp, clutch. [➡ CONTACT: HOLD; 412] *Opposite:* release. 2 *n* **control**, rule, command, authority, clutches, charge, power, sway. [➡ STRENGTH; 202] 3 *n* **understanding**, comprehension, grasp, command, appreciation, awareness, mastery. [➡ UNDERSTAND AND GRASP; 760] *Opposite:* ignorance. 4 *v* **grasp**, clasp, clutch, catch, seize, hold. [➡ CONTACT: HOLD; 412] *Opposite:* release. 5 *v* **stick**, adhere, cling, hang on, cleave to (*literary*). [➡ CONTACT: HOLD; 412] 6 *v* **overwhelm**, fill, pervade, suffuse, swamp, drown. [➡ HAPPEN TO SOMEBODY; 30] 7 *v* **fascinate**, enthral, rivet (*informal*), spellbind, transfix, mesmerize. [➡ APPEAL TO AND AROUSE INTEREST; 576] *Opposite:* bore.

gripe (*informal*) 1 *v* **complain**, moan (*informal*), whinge (*informal*), grumble, protest, object. [➡ COMPLAIN AND NAG; 687] 2 *n* **complaint**, grumble, moan (*informal*), grievance, whinge (*informal*), protest, objection. [➡ COMPLAIN AND NAG; 687] *Opposite:* compliment.

See Compare and Contrast at **complain**.

gripped *adj* **absorbed**, engrossed, rapt, obsessed, enthralled, spellbound, riveted (*informal*). [➡ PENSIVENESS AND INTEREST; 539] *Opposite:* bored.

gripping *adj* **fascinating**, spellbinding, enthralling, mesmerizing, riveting (*informal*), transfixing, absorbing, engrossing. [➡ INTERESTING AND MEANINGFUL; 191] *Opposite:* boring.

grisliness *n* **gruesomeness**, ghastliness, grimness, hideousness, dreadfulness, horror. [➡ FRIGHTENING; 232] *Opposite:* pleasantness.

grisly *adj* **gruesome**, ghastly, horrible, horrific, horrid, grim, dreadful, shocking, macabre, hideous, repugnant. [➡ FRIGHTENING; 232] *Opposite:* pleasant.

gristle *n* **cartilage**, tendon, sinew. [➡ THE BONES AND JOINTS; 720]

gristly *adj* **tough**, chewy, sinewy, stringy, leathery, rubbery, fibrous. [➡ STATE OF PREPARED FOOD; 1170] *Opposite:* tender.

grit 1 *n* **gravel**, stones, pebbles, sand, shingle. [➡ EROSION PRODUCTS AND SOIL; 1058] 2 *n* **determination**, perseverance, tenacity, bravery, fortitude, courage. [➡ COURAGE; 499] *Opposite:* cowardice. 3 *v* **clench**, grind, gnash, grate. [➡ CONTACT: EXERT PRESSURE; 415]

grits (*US*) *n* [➡ CEREAL FOODS; 1177]

gritty 1 *adj* **determined**, persistent, resolute, courageous, persevering, tenacious, brave. [➡ COURAGE; 499] *Opposite:* cowardly. 2 *adj* **realistic**, graphic, harsh, stark, uncompromising, unflinching. [➡ EMOTIONALLY UNPLEASANT AND UPSETTING; 228] *Opposite:* romantic. 3 *adj* **grainy**, coarse, rough, granular, sandy, gravelly. [➡ PHYSICAL TEXTURE; 1221] *Opposite:* smooth.

grit your teeth *v* **steel yourself**, nerve yourself, psych yourself up (*informal*), brace yourself, persevere, hold on tight. [➡ PREPARE FOR ACTION; 290] *Opposite:* knuckle under.

grizzle (*informal*) 1 *v* **cry**, whine, moan, whinge (*informal*), whimper, snivel. [➡ CRYING; 651] 2 *v* **grumble**, complain, moan, mutter, go on, whinge (*informal*), whine, murmur. [➡COMPLAIN AND NAG; 687]

grizzled *type of* **grey**. [➡COLOURS; 1223]

grizzly *adj* **fractious**, irritable, crying, whiny, whining, whingey (*informal*), whingeing (*informal*). [➡IRRITATION AND ANGER; 542]

groan 1 *v* **moan**, cry out, whimper, grunt, growl, sigh. [➡SOUND EMISSION BY PEOPLE; 364] *Opposite:* laugh. 2 *v* (*informal*) **grumble**, complain, whinge (*informal*), carp, moan, gripe (*informal*). [➡COMPLAIN AND NAG; 687] 3 *v* **creak**, squeak, squeal, screech, grind, grate. [➡EMIT SOUNDS THROUGH IMPACT AND ABRASION; 366] 4 *type of* **human sound**. [➡SOUNDS MADE BY PEOPLE; 1261]

groceries *n* **food**, shopping, provisions, rations, victuals, provender (*literary or humorous*), fare. [➡FOOD; 1166]

grocer's *type of* **food outlet**. [➡RETAIL OUTLETS; 1082]

grocery store (*US*) *type of* **food outlet**. [➡RETAIL OUTLETS; 1082]

groggily *adv* **weakly**, sleepily, unsteadily, dazedly, blearily, woozily, slowly, muzzily, shakily. [➡TIRED, ASLEEP, AND UNCONSCIOUS; 739] *Opposite:* alertly.

grogginess *n* **tiredness**, fatigue, sleepiness, unsteadiness, bleariness, wooziness, dizziness, faintness. [➡TIRED, ASLEEP, AND UNCONSCIOUS; 739] *Opposite:* alertness.

groggy *adj* **tired**, sleepy, slow, unsteady, bleary, muzzy, shaky, wobbly (*informal*), dazed, weak, woozy, faint, dizzy. [➡TIRED, ASLEEP, AND UNCONSCIOUS; 739] *Opposite:* alert.

groin *part of* **torso**. [➡TORSO; 694]

groom 1 *v* **prime**, train, coach, prepare, tutor, mentor. [➡IMPROVE SOMETHING; 375] *Opposite:* hinder. 2 *v* **clean**, clean up, brush, comb, tidy, spruce. [➡CLEAN AND POLISH; 404]

groomsman *n* [➡RELATIVES BY MARRIAGE; 960]

groove 1 *n* **channel**, furrow, rut, trench, indentation, hollow. [➡HOLES, GAPS, AND FORKS; 1251] *Opposite:* ridge. 2 *v* (*slang*) **listen**, harmonize, enjoy, dance, chill (*slang*), chill out (*slang*). [➡FIDGET AND FROLIC; 312]

groovy (*dated slang*) *adj* **fashionable**, wonderful, hip (*slang*), cool (*slang*), marvellous, great (*informal*), excellent, fantastic. [➡EMOTIONALLY PLEASANT; 188]

grope 1 *v* **fumble**, feel, cast about, scrabble, flounder, finger. [➡SEEK POSSESSION AND SEARCH; 457] 2 *v* (*informal*) **fondle**, touch, molest, caress, feel up (*informal*), touch up (*slang*). [➡CONTACT: TOUCH; 413]

gross 1 *adj* **aggregate**, combined, whole, overall, total. [➡ALL; 126] *Opposite:* net. 2 *adj* **flagrant**, blatant, glaring, arrant, serious, obvious, major, significant. [➡INTENTIONAL AND DELIBERATE; 280] *Opposite:* minor. 3 *adj* **coarse**, vulgar, crass, rude, crude, uncouth. [➡MORALLY BAD; 776] *Opposite:* polite. 4 *adj* **uncultured**, uncivilized, uncultivated, unsophisticated, unpolished, unrefined. [➡LEVEL OF EDUCATION AND SOPHISTICATION; 894] *Opposite:* cultured. 5 *adj* **overweight**, obese, fat, flabby (*informal*), heavy, stout. [➡BUILD; 478] *Opposite:* slim. 6 *adj* (*informal*) **disgusting**, unpleasant, sickening, foul, nasty, awful, dreadful, repugnant, repellent, revolting, nauseating, vile, abhorrent (*formal*), hideous. [➡DISGUSTING AND REPULSIVE; 231] *Opposite:* pleasant. 7 *v* **earn**, make, get, receive, bring in, clear (*informal*). [➡GET MONEY OR REWARD; 422] *Opposite:* lose.

grossly 1 *adv* **wholly**, totally, completely, utterly, unacceptably, obviously, clearly, exceptionally. [➡TO A GREAT EXTENT; 130] *Opposite:* slightly. 2 *adv* **rudely**, coarsely, uncouthly, crassly, crudely, vulgarly. [➡MORALLY BAD; 776] *Opposite:* politely. 3 *adv* (*informal*) **disgustingly**, revoltingly, nauseatingly, vilely, abhorrently (*formal*), hideously, repellently, sickeningly, unpleasantly. [➡DISGUSTING AND REPULSIVE; 231] *Opposite:* pleasantly.

grossness *n* [➡DISGUSTING AND REPULSIVE; 231]

gross out (*slang*) *v* **disgust**, sicken, nauseate, offend, repel, revolt. [➡UPSET, DISTRESS, AND HUMILIATE; 568] *Opposite:* delight.

gross revenue *n* [➡INCOME; 461]

grotesque 1 *adj* **distorted**, gross (*informal*), bizarre, misshapen, fantastic, monstrous. [➡UGLINESS AND UNATTRACTIVENESS; 234] *Opposite:* attractive. 2 *adj* **incongruous**, ridiculous, ludicrous, laughable, outrageous, outlandish, surreal, weird. [➡BIZARRE AND PECULIAR; 258] *Opposite:* fitting.

grotesquely 1 *adv* **disturbingly**, strangely, bizarrely, distortedly, monstrously, horrifically, terrifyingly. [➡UGLINESS AND UNATTRACTIVENESS; 234] 2 *adv* **incongruously**, ridiculously, ludicrously, laughably, outrageously, outlandishly, surreally, weirdly. [➡BIZARRE AND PECULIAR; 258] *Opposite:* fittingly.

grotto *n* **cavern**, pothole, hollow, cave. [➡GEOLOGICAL FEATURES; 1056]

grotty (*informal*) *adj* **shabby**, rundown, dingy, tatty, grubby, grim, unpleasant. [➡IN BAD REPAIR; 1233] *Opposite:* spotless.

grouch (*informal*) 1 *n* **complaint**, grumble, grouse (*informal*), moan (*informal*), gripe (*informal*), whinge (*informal*), whine. [➡COMPLAIN AND NAG; 687] *Opposite:* praise. 2 *n* **grumbler**, complainer, moaner (*informal*), whinger (*informal*), grouser (*informal*), malcontent, grump (*informal*), crank (*US informal*). [➡GRUMPY AND NEGATIVE PEOPLE; 953] 3 *v* **complain**, grumble, gripe (*informal*), moan (*informal*), whinge (*informal*), sulk, bellyache (*informal*). [➡COMPLAIN AND NAG; 687]

grouchily (*informal*) *adv* [➡BAD-TEMPERED AND HUMOURLESS; 627]

grouchiness (*informal*) *n* **peevishness**, irritability, cantankerousness, crabbiness, bad temper, grumpiness, tetchiness (*informal*), testiness (*informal*), petulance, crankiness (*US informal*). [➡DIFFICULT TO PLEASE; 516] *Opposite:* equanimity.

grouchy (*informal*) *adj* **bad-tempered**, complaining, testy (*informal*), grumpy, crabby, peevish, cantankerous, irritable, petulant, snappy, ill-tempered, snappish, cranky (*US informal*). [➡IRRITATION AND ANGER; 542] *Opposite:* even-tempered.

ground 1 *n* **earth**, soil, land, field, dry land, terra firma, terrain. [➡THE COUNTRYSIDE AND OUTDOOR SPACES; 1070] 2 *n* **playing field**, pitch, field, arena, stadium, ballpark (*US*). [➡URBAN OUTDOOR SPACES; 1071] 3 *adj* **crushed**, pulverized, broken up, milled, minced, pounded, powdered. [➡NOT IN A NATURAL STATE; 1214] 4 *v*

initiate, prepare, coach, instruct, tutor, train. [➡INSTRUCT AND TEACH; 610] 5 *v* **base**, substantiate, support, build, justify, found. [➡INSTITUTE AND INAUGURATE; 349] 6 *v* **punish**, deal with, chastise (*formal*). [➡REFUSE PERMISSION AND NOT ALLOW; 671]

ground beef *type of* **processed meat.** [➡TYPES AND CUTS OF MEAT; 1176]

groundbreaking *adj* **innovative**, pioneering, revolutionary, radical, trailblazing, brand-new, cutting-edge, leading-edge. [➡EXTRAORDINARY: AMAZING; 205] *Opposite:* old hat (*informal*).

ground cloth (*US*) *n* **tarpaulin**, tarp (*informal*), sheeting, cover, throw, rug. [➡COVERS AND COATINGS; 1245]

ground forces *n* [➡THE ARMED FORCES; 827]

ground glass *type of* **glass.** [➡GLASS; 1135]

groundhog *type of* **rodent.** [➡RODENT; 989]

grounding *n* **foundation**, basis, preparation, training, instruction, education. [➡KNOWLEDGE AND WISDOM; 559]

groundless *adj* **baseless**, unsupported, unjustified, unwarranted, unfounded, unsubstantiated. [➡REDUNDANT AND USELESS; 241] *Opposite:* sound.

ground meat *type of* **processed meat.** [➡TYPES AND CUTS OF MEAT; 1176]

groundnut *type of* **nut.** [➡NUTS; 1184]

ground plan 1 *n* **floor plan**, plan, scale drawing, blueprint, diagram, drawing. [➡DRAWINGS, CHARTS AND TABLES; 595] 2 *n* **outline**, sketch, blueprint, draft, preliminary design, plan. [➡DRAWINGS, CHARTS, AND TABLES; 595]

ground rule *n* **fundamental**, axiom, tenet (*formal*), stipulation, point of departure, modus operandi. [➡WAYS OF DOING THINGS; 295]

grounds 1 *n* **basis**, foundation, reason, justification, argument, proof. [➡CAUSATION; 169] 2 *n* **estate**, land, park, parkland, gardens, surroundings. [➡THE COUNTRYSIDE AND OUTDOOR SPACES; 1070] 3 *n* **dregs**, lees, sediment, residue, deposit, sludge. [➡UNPLEASANT AND DIRTY SUBSTANCES; 1267]

groundsheet *n* **tarpaulin**, sheeting, cover, throw, rug. [➡COVERS AND COATINGS; 1245]

groundswell 1 *n* **swell**, wave, storm, squall, heavy sea, tempest. [➡THE SEAS, OCEANS, AND SHORES; 1041] 2 *n* **upsurge**, wave, outpouring, rise, swell, feeling. [➡CHANGE OF SIZE: BIGGER; 393]

groundwork *n* **foundation**, basis, base, footing, underpinning, preliminaries. [➡WORK IN GENERAL; 298]

group 1 *n* **collection**, cluster, set, assemblage, assembly, clutch. [➡COLLECTIONS AND MIXTURES OF THINGS; 1243] *Opposite:* individual. 2 *n* **grouping**, set, faction, crowd, company, troop, troupe, party, band, knot, unit, clique. [➡GROUPS OF PEOPLE; 935] *Opposite:* individual. 3 *n* **musical group**, band, trio, duo, quartet, quintet, sextet, septet, octet, orchestra, ensemble. [➡MUSICIANS AND SINGERS; 908] *Opposite:* soloist. 4 *n* **alliance**, federation, consortium, amalgamation, confederation, confederacy. [➡GROUPS WITH A COMMON INTEREST; 938] 5 *v* **classify**, categorize, arrange, sort, bracket, class. [➡ARRANGE AND CREATE ORDER; 358] 6 *v* **gather**, assemble, congregate, convene, cluster, collect. [➡GET CLOSER TOGETHER; 311] *Opposite:* disperse.

groupie (*informal*) *n* **follower**, fan, enthusiast, aficionado, junkie (*informal*), supporter, aficionada, booster (*US*). [➡DEVOTEES AND ADDICTED PEOPLE; 557] *Opposite:* detractor.

grouping 1 *n* **alliance**, federation, consortium, assemblage, alignment, combination, group, confederacy. [➡GROUPS OF PEOPLE; 935] 2 *n* **category**, class, set, type, group, grade. [➡VARIETY, TYPE, KIND; 146]

group together *v* [➡GET CLOSER TOGETHER; 311]

grouse 1 *type of* **fowl.** [➡FOOD BIRD; 999] 2 *type of* **meat.** [➡TYPES AND CUTS OF MEAT; 1176] 3 *v* (*informal*) **complain**, grumble, moan, gripe (*informal*), bellyache (*informal*), whinge (*informal*). [➡COMPLAIN AND NAG; 687] 4 *n* (*informal*) **complaint**, grumble, moan (*informal*), gripe (*informal*), whinge (*informal*), objection, protest. [➡COMPLAIN AND NAG; 687]

See Compare and Contrast at **complain.**

grout 1 *n* **mortar**, filling, plaster, cement, putty, sealant. [➡BUILDING MATERIALS; 1076] 2 *v* **fill**, mortar, plaster, cement, render, face. [➡DECORATE, ADORN, AND APPLY COATINGS; 406]

grouts *n* **dregs**, lees, residue, sediment, deposit, sludge. [➡UNPLEASANT AND DIRTY SUBSTANCES; 1267]

grove *n* **copse**, coppice, orchard, wood, stand, plantation. [➡WOODS, FORESTS, AND JUNGLES; 1047]

grovel 1 *v* **plead**, beg, cringe (*disapproving*), fawn, bow and scrape, humble yourself, demean yourself, kowtow, crawl (*informal*), creep (*informal*). [➡FLATTER AND FAWN; 622] *Opposite:* alienate. 2 *v* **crawl**, creep (*informal*), crouch, stoop, kneel. [➡ASSUME A POSITION; 318] *Opposite:* stand up.

grow 1 *v* **develop**, grow up, mature, shoot up, sprout, flourish. [➡CHANGE OF SIZE: BIGGER; 393] 2 *v* **expand**, enlarge, swell, extend, spread, increase. [➡CHANGE OF SIZE: BIGGER; 393] *Opposite:* shrink. 3 *v* **increase**, multiply, intensify, escalate, strengthen, develop. [➡CHANGE OF SIZE: BIGGER; 393] *Opposite:* decrease. 4 *v* **produce**, cultivate, nurture, breed, raise, propagate. [➡GROW AND CULTIVATE; 352]

growing *adj* **rising**, mounting, upward, budding, emergent, increasing. [➡CHANGE OF SIZE: BIGGER; 393] *Opposite:* decreasing.

growl 1 *v* **roar**, snarl, bark, howl, rumble, yap. [➡SOUND EMISSION BY ANIMALS OR BIRDS; 365] 2 *n* **snarl**, bark, howl, rumble, roar, yap. [➡SOUNDS MADE BY ANIMALS; 1260]

grow less *v* **weaken**, wear off, fade, subside, decrease, abate (*formal or literary*). [➡CHANGE OF INTENSITY: LESS; 396] *Opposite:* increase.

grown *adj* **grown-up**, fully-fledged, adult, developed, mature, fully-grown. [➡ADULTHOOD; 918] *Opposite:* immature.

grown-up *adj* **adult**, mature, developed, grown, responsible, sensible, full-size, fully-fledged, fully-grown. [➡ADULTHOOD; 918] *Opposite:* immature.

growth 1 *n* **growing**, development, evolution, progress, advance, progression. [➡PROGRESS AND ADVANCEMENT; 214] *Opposite:* decay. 2 *n* **increase**, enlargement, expansion, augmentation, development, intensification, escalation. [➡CHANGE OF SIZE: BIGGER; 393] *Opposite:* reduction. **3** *n* **tumour**, cyst, lump, swelling, outgrowth, carcinoma. [➡ILLNESSES AND DISORDERS; 733]

grow up **1** *v* **grow**, develop, mature, evolve, flourish, come of age. [➡CHANGE; 373] **2** *v* **take shape**, arise, be born, develop, come about, evolve. [➡GRADUALLY COME INTO EXISTENCE; 1]

groyne *n* **breakwater**, mole, barrier, bulwark, jetty, projection. [➡BARRIERS; 1112]

grub **1** *v* **dig**, burrow, root out, excavate, pull up, uproot, dredge up, unearth, dig up. [➡MOVE SOMETHING: UPWARDS; 329] **2** *v* **search**, hunt, rummage, ferret, forage, scour. [➡SEEK POSSESSION AND SEARCH; 457] **3** *n* **larva**, maggot, caterpillar, creepy-crawly (*informal*), bug. [➡INSECT STAGES; 1020] **4** *n* (*informal*) **food**, nosh (*informal*), victuals, sustenance, feed, nourishment. [➡FOOD; 1166]

grubbiness **1** *n* **dirtiness**, griminess, filthiness, muckiness (*informal*), muddiness, sloppiness, dinginess, squalidness. [➡DIRTY; 1234] *Opposite:* cleanness. **2** *n* **sordidness**, squalidness, seediness, contemptibleness, despicableness, dishonourableness. [➡MORALLY BAD; 776] *Opposite:* purity.

grubby **1** *adj* **dirty**, grimy, soiled, filthy, mucky (*informal*), muddy, sloppy, dingy, squalid. [➡DIRTY; 1234] *Opposite:* clean. **2** *adj* **sordid**, squalid, seedy, contemptible, despicable, dishonourable, despised. [➡MORALLY BAD; 776] *Opposite:* honourable.

See Compare and Contrast at **dirty**.

grudge **1** *n* **complaint**, chip on your shoulder (*informal*), bitterness, resentment, dislike, hatred, antipathy, rancour. [➡ANTAGONISM; 553] **2** *v* **resent**, hold against, begrudge, loathe, mind, envy. [➡BE CONCERNED AND CARE; 582]

grudging *adj* **reluctant**, unwilling, complaining, resentful, rancorous, disinclined, loath. [➡UNWILLINGNESS AND STUBBORNNESS; 565] *Opposite:* willing.

gruel *type of* **cooked dish**. [➡PREPARED DISHES; 1169]

gruelling *adj* **arduous**, exhausting, demanding, taxing, tough, harsh, harrowing, hard, punishing, nerve-racking. [➡EMOTIONALLY UNPLEASANT AND UPSETTING; 228] *Opposite:* easy.

gruesome *adj* **grisly**, ghastly, horrible, horrific, horrid, dreadful, shocking, frightening, macabre, hideous, repugnant, ferocious. [➡FRIGHTENING; 232] *Opposite:* pleasant.

gruesomeness *n* **grisliness**, ghastliness, horror, dreadfulness, hideousness, repugnance, horridness. [➡FRIGHTENING; 232] *Opposite:* pleasantness.

gruff **1** *adj* **bad-tempered**, grumpy, angry, impatient, crotchety (*informal*), brusque, curt, stern, crusty, abrupt, surly, snippy (*informal*). [➡BAD-TEMPERED AND HUMOURLESS; 627] *Opposite:* friendly. **2** *adj* **hoarse**, husky, gravelly, rasping, harsh, throaty, deep, thick, croaky. [➡LOUD OR UNPLEASANT SOUNDS; 1265] *Opposite:* soft.

gruffness **1** *n* **grumpiness**, crotchetiness (*informal*), crustiness, abruptness, curtness, sternness, snippiness (*informal*). [➡BAD-TEMPERED AND HUMOURLESS; 627] *Opposite:* pleasantness. **2** *n* **hoarseness**, huskiness, thickness, throatiness, harshness, deepness. [➡LOUD OR UNPLEASANT SOUNDS; 1265] *Opposite:* softness.

grumble **1** *v* **complain**, moan (*informal*), grouse (*informal*), gripe (*informal*), protest, mutter, object, bellyache (*informal*), whinge (*informal*). [➡COMPLAIN AND NAG; 687] **2** *n* **complaint**, moan (*informal*), grouse (*informal*), gripe (*informal*), protest, objection, whinge (*informal*). [➡COMPLAIN AND NAG; 687]

See Compare and Contrast at **complain**.

grumbler *n* **grouch** (*informal*), complainer, moaner (*informal*), whinger (*informal*), malcontent, whiner, groaner. [➡GRUMPY AND NEGATIVE PEOPLE; 953]

grumpiness *n* **bad-temperedness**, irritability, cantankerousness, grouchiness (*informal*), petulance, crabbiness, testiness (*informal*), snappiness, crankiness (*US informal*). [➡IRRITATION AND ANGER; 542] *Opposite:* cheerfulness.

grumpy *adj* **bad-tempered**, irritable, sullen, cantankerous, ill-tempered, grouchy (*informal*), complaining, cross, petulant, crabby, sulky, testy (*informal*), snappy, cranky (*US informal*). [➡IRRITATION AND ANGER; 542] *Opposite:* cheerful.

grunge (*informal*) *n* **filth**, grime, dirt, muck (*informal*), rubbish, mess. [➡UNPLEASANT AND DIRTY SUBSTANCES; 1267] *Opposite:* cleanliness.

grunginess (*informal*) *n* [➡IN BAD REPAIR; 1233]

grungy (*informal*) *adj* **shabby**, mucky (*informal*), dirty, scruffy, unkempt, dilapidated, threadbare, tattered, ragged, untidy, worn-out. [➡IN BAD REPAIR; 1233] *Opposite:* clean.

grunt **1** *v* **mumble**, murmur, rumble, grumble, groan, snort. [➡SOUND EMISSION BY ANIMALS OR BIRDS; 365] **2** *n* **sound**, mumble, murmur, rumble, grumble, groan. [➡SOUNDS MADE BY PEOPLE; 1261] **3** *type of* **animal sound**. [➡SOUNDS MADE BY ANIMALS; 1260]

Gruyère *type of* **hard cheese**. [➡DAIRY PRODUCTS AND CHEESES; 1182]

G-string *type of* **lower body underwear**. [➡HABERDASHERY, MILLINERY, AND LINGERIE; 867]

guacamole *type of* **seasonings, sauces, and dips**. [➡SEASONINGS AND SAUCES; 1173]

guano *n* [➡UNPLEASANT AND DIRTY SUBSTANCES; 1267]

guarantee **1** *n* **assurance**, promise, pledge, agreement, security, surety, word. [➡CERTAIN; 175] **2** *n* **warranty**, certification, undertaking, contract, agreement, pledge. [➡OFFICIAL DOCUMENTS; 587] **3** *v* **assure**, ensure, promise, pledge, warrant, certify, secure. [➡PROMISE AND ASSURE; 685]

guaranteed *adj* **certain**, definite, sure, sure-fire (*informal*), cast-iron, fail-safe, assured, in the bag (*informal*). [➡CERTAIN; 175] *Opposite:* uncertain.

guarantor *n* **backer**, sponsor, underwriter, supporter, patron, angel. [➡PEOPLE INVOLVED IN FINANCE; 804]

See Compare and Contrast at **backer**.

guard 1 *v* **protect**, defend, safeguard, shield, watch over, secure, watch. [➡PREVENT CONTACT OR ATTACK; 420] 2 *n* **protector**, sentinel, sentry, picket, lookout, watch, bouncer. [➡PEOPLE WHO GUARD AND PROTECT; 846] 3 *n* **safeguard**, security, protection, shield, fortification, defence. [➡COVERS AND COATINGS; 1245]

See Compare and Contrast at **safeguard**.

guarded 1 *adj* **wary**, cautious, careful, circumspect, hesitant, restrained, cagey (*informal*), noncommittal. [➡INSECURITY AND LOSS OF COMPOSURE; 545] *Opposite:* open. 2 *adj* **protected**, secured, watched over, defended, safeguarded, shielded, fortified. [➡SAFE AND SAFETY; 192] *Opposite:* unprotected.

See Compare and Contrast at **cautious**.

guardedly *adv* **carefully**, cautiously, warily, suspiciously, cagily (*informal*), circumspectly. [➡RETICENT AND UNFORTHCOMING; 632] *Opposite:* openly.

guardhouse 1 *n* **prison**, jail, lockup, cells, detention centre, penitentiary (*US*). [➡BUILDINGS FOR CONFINING PEOPLE; 1093] 2 *type of* **outbuilding**. [➡ANCILLARY BUILDINGS; 1079]

guardian 1 *n* **protector**, guard, sentinel, keeper, custodian, warden. [➡SUPPORTERS, PROTECTORS, AND COMPATRIOTS; 970] 2 *n* **carer**, protector, godparent, custodian, caretaker, keeper, warden. [➡ADOPTION, FOSTERING, AND EXTENDED FAMILY; 962]

guardian angel (*informal*) *n* [➡PEOPLE WHO ARE APPROVED OF; 955]

guardianship *n* **protection**, custody, care, responsibility, supervision, charge, guard, keeping. [➡ADOPTION, FOSTERING, AND EXTENDED FAMILY; 962]

guardrail *n* **handrail**, rail, banister, railing, paling, balustrade. [➡STICKS, POLES, AND WEDGES; 1253]

guava *type of* **fruit**. [➡FRUIT AND VEGETABLES; 1175]

guerrilla *n* **freedom fighter**, rebel, insurgent, irregular, paramilitary, revolutionary. [➡UNCOOPERATIVE OR REBELLIOUS PERSON; 567]

guess 1 *v* **predict**, solve, fathom, work out, conjecture, estimate, guesstimate (*informal*). [➡EXAMINE AND ASSESS; 754] 2 *v* **deduce**, presume, speculate, suppose, estimate, conjecture. [➡GUESS; 755] 3 *n* **deduction**, conjecture, supposition, presumption, speculation, estimate, guesstimate (*informal*). [➡GUESS; 755]

guesstimate (*informal*) 1 *n* **guess**, estimate, conjecture, projection, reckoning, theory. [➡GUESS; 755] 2 *v* **estimate**, guess, reckon, conjecture, project, speculate. [➡GUESS; 755]

guesswork *n* **conjecture**, deduction, presumption, speculation, estimation, reasoning. [➡GUESS; 755]

guest *n* **visitor**, caller, invitee, boarder, visitant (*archaic*), lodger. [➡FRIENDS; 963] *Opposite:* host.

guesthouse *n* **hotel**, hostel, B & B (*informal*), bed and breakfast, boarding house, inn, lodging house (*dated*). [➡HOTELS, RESTAURANTS, AND CLUBS; 1081]

guestroom *n* **room**, bedroom, spare room. [➡TYPES OF ROOM; 1096]

guff (*informal*) *n* **nonsense**, rubbish, rigmarole, stuff, stuff and nonsense, verbiage, flimflam (*slang*), drivel, gobbledegook (*informal disapproving*), talk, waffle (*informal*), blether (*informal*), blather (*informal*), jive (*US slang*). [➡MEANINGLESS SPEECH OR WRITING; 677] *Opposite:* sense.

guffaw 1 *v* **laugh**, chuckle, chortle, roar, fall about (*informal*), howl (*slang*), crack up (*informal*), crease up (*informal*). [➡LAUGHTER; 650] 2 *n* **chuckle**, laugh, chortle, roar, belly laugh, horselaugh. [➡LAUGHTER; 650]

guidance 1 *n* **leadership**, direction, supervision, management, control, regulation. [➡RELATIONSHIP TO ANOTHER; 973] 2 *n* **help**, assistance, advice, support, counselling, direction. [➡ADVICE; 690]

guidance counsellor *n* **adviser**, counsellor, therapist, mediator. [➡ADVISERS, JUDGES, AND ARBITERS; 971]

guide 1 *v* **direct**, show, steer, lead, conduct, channel, funnel, point, pilot, escort, shepherd, usher. [➡ACCOMPANY AND FOLLOW; 338] 2 *v* **steer**, drive, pilot, direct, handle, manage. [➡TRAVEL: WAYS OF TRAVELLING; 321] 3 *n* **leader**, director, attendant, chaperon, controller, monitor. [➡ADVISERS, JUDGES, AND ARBITERS; 971] 4 *n* **tour guide**, courier, leader, escort, conductor, director, pilot. [➡TRAVEL: SIGHT-SEEING AND TOURISM; 322] 5 *n* **influence**, standard, model, ideal, guiding light, example, benchmark. [➡PERFECT EXAMPLES AND EMBODIMENTS; 67] 6 *n* **guidebook**, handbook, manual, instructions, vade mecum, compendium. [➡MANUALS AND INSTRUCTIONS; 590]

Compare and Contrast: ***guide, conduct, direct, lead, steer, usher***

CORE MEANING: TO SHOW SOMEBODY THE WAY TO SOMEWHERE

guide to take somebody in the right direction or to give a tour of a particular place; ***conduct*** to take somebody to or around a particular place, especially when the person showing the way has some kind of authority or specialized knowledge; ***direct*** to show or indicate the way; ***lead*** to show the way to others, usually by going ahead of them; ***steer*** to encourage somebody to take a particular course; ***usher*** to escort somebody to or from a place, especially a seat.

guidebook *n* **handbook**, instructions, travel guide, vade mecum, manual, compendium. [➡MANUALS AND INSTRUCTIONS; 590]

guided missile *type of* **explosive weapon**. [➡EXPLOSIVES; 1154]

guide dog *type of* **large dog**. [➡DOG; 980]

guideline *n* **advice**, recommendation, standard, guide, parameter, instruction, policy, rule, regulation, directions. [➡ADVICE; 690]

guidelines *n* [➡WAYS OF DOING THINGS; 295]

guiding principle *n* [➡WAYS OF DOING THINGS; 295]

guild *n* **club**, union, society, association, league, federation, company, organization. [➡INSTITUTIONS; 791]

guile *n* **cunning**, treachery, astuteness, slyness, wiliness, craftiness, cleverness, deviousness, deceit, duplicity, trickiness, deceitfulness. [➡DECEITFUL; 514] *Opposite:* frankness.

guileful *adj* **cunning**, treacherous, sly, astute, wily, crafty, clever, devious, shifty, sneaky, deceitful, underhand. [➡DECEITFUL; 514] *Opposite:* naive.

guileless *adj* **naive**, frank, candid, ingenuous, straightforward, open, honest, truthful, transparent. [➡NATURALNESS; 498] *Opposite:* guileful.

guilelessness *n* [➡NATURALNESS; 498]

guillemot *type of* **seabird.** [➡SEABIRD; 1002]

guillotine *v* **behead**, decapitate, execute, kill. [➡KILL; 923]

guilt 1 *n* **remorse**, shame, self-reproach, conscience, contriteness, compunction, contrition. [➡FEELINGS ABOUT THE PAST; 533] 2 *n* **fault**, responsibility, blame, culpability, guiltiness, onus. [➡MORALLY BAD; 776] *Opposite:* innocence.

guilt complex *n* [➡PSYCHOLOGY AND THE MIND; 770]

guiltiness 1 *n* **culpability**, guilt, responsibility, fault, sin, wrongdoing. [➡MORALLY BAD; 776] *Opposite:* innocence. 2 *n* **shame**, remorse, guilt, guilty conscience, self-reproach, regret, contrition. [➡FEELINGS ABOUT THE PAST; 533] *Opposite:* shamelessness.

guiltless *adj* **innocent**, blameless, faultless, unimpeachable, irreproachable, impeccable. [➡MORALLY GOOD; 775] *Opposite:* guilty.

guiltlessness *n* [➡MORALLY GOOD; 775]

guilt-ridden *adj* **guilty**, fearful, anguished, tormented, haunted, remorseful, mortified, awkward, uncomfortable. [➡EMBARRASSMENT AND HUMILIATION; 543] *Opposite:* unashamed.

guilty 1 *adj* **culpable**, responsible, at fault, blameworthy, in the wrong, to blame. [➡MORALLY BAD; 776] *Opposite:* innocent. 2 *adj* **shamefaced**, remorseful, embarrassed, mortified, guilt-ridden, uncomfortable, awkward. [➡EMBARRASSMENT AND HUMILIATION; 543] *Opposite:* unashamed.

guilty conscience *n* **guilt complex**, conscience, guilt trip (*slang*), twinge, pang. [➡FEELINGS ABOUT THE PAST; 533]

guilty party *n* [➡CRIMINALS; 821]

guinea fowl *type of* **fowl.** [➡FOOD BIRD; 999]

guinea pig *type of* **rodent.** [➡RODENT; 989]

guise 1 *n* **appearance**, semblance, show, pretext, excuse, façade, pretence. [➡REPRESENTATIONS AND GENERAL EXAMPLES; 65] 2 *n* **form**, appearance, shape, light, phase, manifestation. [➡APPEARANCE AND ATMOSPHERE; 1236] 3 *n* **costume**, disguise, dress, rig (*informal*), getup (*informal*), outfit, mask. [➡CLOTHES AND ACCESSORIES; 864]

guitar *type of* **stringed instrument.** [➡MUSICAL INSTRUMENTS; 910]

guitarist *n* [➡MUSICIANS AND SINGERS; 908]

gulch (*US*) *n* **ravine**, gorge, gully, valley, gap, chasm, arroyo (*US*). [➡GEOLOGICAL FEATURES; 1056]

gulf 1 *n* **bight**, bay, inlet, sound, cove, harbour. [➡THE SEAS, OCEANS, AND SHORES; 1041] 2 *n* **hole**, abyss, chasm, gap, hollow, vacuum. [➡HOLES, GAPS, AND FORKS; 1251]

gulfweed *type of* **alga.** [➡MICROORGANISMS, FUNGI, AND ALGAE; 1023]

gull *type of* **seabird.** [➡SEABIRD; 1002]

gullet *n* **crop**, maw, throat, craw, gorge, oesophagus. [➡THE DIGESTIVE TRACT; 710]

gullibility *n* **trustfulness**, innocence, credulity, unwariness, acceptance, naivety. [➡NEGATIVE INTELLECTUAL CHARACTERISTICS; 526] *Opposite:* shrewdness.

gullible *adj* **naive**, susceptible, innocent, trusting, accepting, credulous. [➡NEGATIVE INTELLECTUAL CHARACTERISTICS; 526] *Opposite:* discerning.

gully 1 *n* **ravine**, gorge, valley, gap, chasm, crevasse, channel, gulch (*US*), arroyo (*US*). [➡GEOLOGICAL FEATURES; 1056] 2 *n* **channel**, ditch, furrow, rut, culvert, drain. [➡HOLES, GAPS, AND FORKS; 1251]

gulp 1 *v* **guzzle** (*informal*), swig (*informal*), swallow, drink, knock back (*informal*), toss down, quaff (*literary or humorous*), slug (*informal*). [➡EAT AND NOT EAT; 711] *Opposite:* sip. 2 *n* **swallow**, guzzle (*informal*), swig (*informal*), drink, quaff (*literary or humorous*), slug (*informal*). [➡DRINK; 712] *Opposite:* sip. 3 *n* **mouthful**, swig (*informal*), slug (*informal*), drink, swallow, draught. [➡DRINK; 712] *Opposite:* sip.

gulp back *v* **stifle**, suppress, restrain, hold back, fight back, choke back. [➡WITHHOLD INFORMATION; 688]

gulp down *v* **wolf**, swill, swallow, down, gobble, stuff, chugalug (*US informal*), chug (*US informal*). [➡EAT AND NOT EAT; 711] *Opposite:* sip.

gum 1 *n* **secretion**, exudate, resin, latex, juice, sap. [➡PARTS OF TREES AND PLANTS; 1026] 2 *n* **glue**, adhesive, paste, cement, epoxy resin, superglue. [➡ADHESIVES; 1270] 3 *v* **stick**, glue, paste, bond, cement, affix. [➡FASTEN, LINK, AND JOIN; 409] *Opposite:* unstick. 4 *type of* **confectionery.** [➡CONFECTIONERY; 1181] 5 *part of* **mouth.** [➡THE MOUTH; 703]

gumbo *type of* **soup.** [➡SOUP; 1185]

gum boot *type of* **boot.** [➡FOOTWEAR; 871]

gumdrop *type of* **confectionery.** [➡CONFECTIONERY; 1181]

gumminess *n* [➡FLUID AND NON-SOLID; 1212]

gummy *adj* **sticky**, gooey, gluey, tacky, adhesive, viscid. [➡PHYSICAL TEXTURE; 1221]

gumption (*informal*) 1 *n* **common sense**, sense, horse sense (*informal*), shrewdness, practicality, presence of mind, initiative, resourcefulness, nous (*informal*). [➡POSITIVE INTELLECTUAL CHARACTERISTICS; 525] *Opposite:* stupidity. 2 *n* **courage**, nerve, bravery, mettle, guts (*slang*), pluck, moxie (*US slang*). [➡COURAGE; 499]

gum tree *type of* **evergreen tree.** [➡EVERGREEN AND CONIFEROUS TREES; 1029]

gun *n* **firearm**, shooter (*informal*), piece (*slang*), handgun. [➡WEAPONS FOR SHOOTING; 1155]

gun

◆ *types of gun*
air pistol, air rifle, antiaircraft gun, automatic, bazooka, blunderbuss, cannon, carbine, flamethrower, handgun, howitzer, machine gun, magnum, mortar, musket, pistol, revolver, rifle, sawed-off shotgun (*US*), sawn-off shotguns, semiautomatic, shotgun, submachine gun, Tommy gun (*informal*)

gunboat *type of* **military vessel**. [➡SHIPS AND BOATS; 1149]

gun down (*informal*) *v* **kill**, assassinate, shoot, shoot down, mow down, murder, blow away (*slang*). [➡KILL; 923]

gunfight *n* **gun battle**, shoot-out, firefight, fight, duel, shooting. [➡AGGRESSIVE EVENT; 39]

gunfire *n* **firing**, shooting, barrage of bullets, volley, salvo, barrage. [➡IMPACT SOUNDS; 1259]

gunge (*informal*) *n* **slime**, goo (*informal*), mess, gunk (*informal*), gloop (*informal*), dirt, filth, muck (*informal*), crud (*slang*), goop (*US informal*). [➡UNPLEASANT AND DIRTY SUBSTANCES; 1267]

gung ho (*informal*) **1** *adj* **combative**, belligerent, militaristic, bellicose, aggressive, trigger-happy (*informal*). [➡MILITARY; 829] *Opposite:* peaceable. **2** *adj* **enthusiastic**, eager, keen, zealous, bullish (*informal*), ardent. [➡ENERGY AND ENTHUSIASM; 497] *Opposite:* reluctant.

gungy (*informal*) *adj* **slimy**, messy, gunky (*informal*), gloopy (*informal*), dirty, filthy, mucky (*informal*), goopy (*US informal*). [➡DIRTY; 1234] *Opposite:* clean.

gunk (*informal*) *n* **grease**, mess, filth, muck (*informal*), dirt, slime. [➡UNPLEASANT AND DIRTY SUBSTANCES; 1267]

gunky (*informal*) *adj* **greasy**, slimy, messy, filthy, mucky (*informal*), dirty. [➡DIRTY; 1234] *Opposite:* clean.

gunman **1** *n* **sniper**, murderer, assassin, killer, gunslinger (*informal*), gangster, hit man (*slang*). [➡PEOPLE WHO KILL; 924] **2** *n* **marksman**, markswoman, shot, crack shot, good shot, deadeye (*US informal*). [➡PEOPLE WHO KILL; 924]

gunmetal *type of* **grey**. [➡COLOURS; 1223]

gunner *n* **soldier**, shooter, artilleryman, fusilier, rifleman, bombardier. [➡MILITARY PERSONNEL; 828]

gunpowder *type of* **explosive material**. [➡EXPLOSIVES; 1154]

guns *n* **weapons**, ordnance, firepower, artillery, arms, armaments, weaponry. [➡WEAPONS; 1153]

gunshot *n* **firing**, shooting, gunfire, volley, barrage, salvo. [➡IMPACT SOUNDS; 1259]

gunwale *part of* **ship or boat**. [➡PARTS OF A SHIP OR BOAT; 1150]

guppy *type of* **freshwater fish**. [➡FRESHWATER FISH; 1010]

gurdwara *type of* **place of worship**. [➡RELIGIOUS BUILDINGS; 1084]

gurgle **1** *v* **bubble**, slosh, splash, ripple, murmur, gush, babble, burble. [➡EMIT CONTINUOUS SOUNDS; 367] **2** *v* **babble**, burble, coo, warble, crow, croon. [➡SOUND EMISSION BY PEOPLE; 364] **3** *n* **slosh**, bubble, splash, ripple, murmur, gush, babble, burble. [➡CONTINUOUS SOUNDS; 1257] **4** *n* **burble**, babble, coo, murmur, warble. [➡CONTINUOUS SOUNDS; 1257]

guru **1** *n* **spiritual leader**, religious teacher, maharishi, sage (*literary*), spiritual guide, counsellor, spiritual advisor. [➡RELIGIOUS PEOPLE; 779] **2** *n* **leader**, authority, leading light, expert, pundit, specialist. [➡TALENTED OR INTELLIGENT PERSON; 529]

gush **1** *v* **pour**, flood, stream, surge, spurt, jet, flow. [➡LIQUID EMISSION; 371] *Opposite:* trickle. **2** *v* **be effusive**, prattle, flatter, ooze, admire, enthuse, babble. [➡WITTER AND BABBLE; 618] *Opposite:* criticize. **3** *n* **flood**, flow, spurt, jet, stream, surge, rush. [➡AMOUNT OF LIQUID; 114] *Opposite:* trickle.

gushing **1** *adj* **pouring**, flowing, overflowing, spouting, torrential, spurting. [➡MOVING QUICKLY; 103] *Opposite:* trickling. **2** *adj* **effusive**, voluble, enthusiastic, emotional, hammy (*informal*), sentimental, glib. [➡POMPOUS, LOUD, AND OVER-CONFIDENT; 636] *Opposite:* reserved.

gushingly *adv* **effusively**, volubly, enthusiastically, emotionally, hammily (*informal*), sentimentally, glibly. [➡ENTHUSIASTIC AND INQUISITIVE; 629] *Opposite:* reservedly.

gusset *n* **patch**, insert, inset, reinforcement, support, enlargement, extension. [➡PARTS OF A GARMENT; 870]

gussy up (*US informal*) *v* [➡IMPROVE APPEARANCE; 380]

gust **1** *n* **squall**, draught, flurry, breeze, blast, puff. [➡WINDY AND STORMY WEATHER; 1053] *Opposite:* calm. **2** *n* **burst**, explosion, expulsion, eruption, outburst, rush. [➡SUDDEN EVENT; 52] **3** *v* **blow**, bluster, squall. [➡WINDY AND STORMY WEATHER; 1053]

gusto *n* **enjoyment**, delight, enthusiasm, passion, zest, pleasure. [➡PLEASURE, EXCITEMENT, AND ELATION; 535] *Opposite:* apathy.

gusty *adj* **windy**, breezy, squally, blowy (*informal*), stormy, blustery. [➡WINDY AND STORMY WEATHER; 1053] *Opposite:* calm.

gut **1** *n* (*slang disapproving*) **belly**, stomach, paunch, spare tyre (*informal humorous*), beer gut (*slang*), beer belly (*slang*), bay window (*US slang*). [➡THE DIGESTIVE TRACT; 710] **2** *v* **disembowel**, eviscerate, clean, prepare, dress. [➡COOKING AND FOOD PREPARATION; 354] **3** *v* **ruin**, damage, destroy, burn, burn out (*informal*), raze. [➡FIRE, FLAMMABILITY, AND BURNING; 1164] *Opposite:* build up. **4** *v* **strip**, clear out, empty, empty out, plunder, ransack. [➡EMPTY AND UNLOAD; 408] **5** *adj* **instinctive**, intuitive, emotional, automatic, unconscious, instant, knee-jerk (*informal*). [➡THE NATURE OF IDEAS; 772] *Opposite:* considered.

gut feeling *n* **guess**, hunch, instinct, impression, intuition, gut reaction. [➡FEELINGS; 532] *Opposite:* fact.

gutless *adj* **cowardly**, spineless, spiritless, weak, timid, craven (*literary*). [➡COWARDICE AND WEAKNESS OF WILL; 509] *Opposite:* plucky.

See Compare and Contrast at **cowardly**.

gutlessness *n* [➡COWARDICE AND WEAKNESS OF WILL; 509]

gut reaction *n* **guess**, hunch, instinct, impression, intuition, gut feeling. [➡FEELINGS; 532] *Opposite:* fact.

guts **1** *n* **insides** (*informal*), intestines, innards (*informal*), bowels, stomach, viscera, entrails. [➡THE DIGESTIVE TRACT; 710]

2 *n* (*informal*) **glutton**, gannet (*informal*), pig (*informal*), greedy guts (*informal*), gourmand, guzzler (*informal*). [➡PLEASURE-SEEKERS AND HEDONISTS; 886] *Opposite:* ascetic. 3 *n* (*slang*) **courage**, bravery, strength of character, pluck, resolve, willpower, daring, mettle, nerve. [➡COURAGE; 499] *Opposite:* cowardice. 4 *n* **interior**, recesses, bowels, inner workings, heart, core, centre. [➡CENTRAL PARTS OF PHYSICAL OBJECTS; 1250]

See Compare and Contrast at **courage**.

gutsy (*informal*) 1 *adj* **brave**, plucky, courageous, fearless, intrepid (*literary or humorous*), determined, indomitable, daring. [➡COURAGE; 499] *Opposite:* cowardly. 2 *adj* **passionate**, impassioned, emotional, intense, fiery, heartfelt. [➡ENTHUSIASTIC AND INQUISITIVE; 629] *Opposite:* insipid. 3 *adj* **greedy**, gluttonous, insatiable, voracious, piggish, ravenous. [➡PLEASURE-SEEKING AND EXCESS; 885] *Opposite:* ascetic.

gutted 1 *adj* **cleaned**, disembowelled, eviscerated, prepared, dressed. [➡STATE OF PREPARED FOOD; 1170] 2 *adj* (*informal*) **devastated**, shattered, reeling, heartbroken, brokenhearted, distraught, traumatized, in a state of shock, disappointed. [➡SADNESS, DISTRESS, AND DESPAIR; 540] *Opposite:* pleased.

gutter 1 *n* **drain**, sewer, channel, trench, groove, trough, ditch. [➡WATERCOURSES; 1110] 2 *v* **flicker**, sputter, waver, drip, fade, fade out. [➡CEASE TO EXIST; 22] *Opposite:* flare.

guttering 1 *n* **gutters**, channels, trenches, grooves, sewers, troughs, ditching, drainage. [➡ROOFS, ROOF PARTS, AND CEILINGS; 1102] 2 *part of* **building**. [➡PARTS OF A BUILDING; 1094]

guttural *adj* **harsh**, rough, rasping, throaty, deep, low, gruff, grating, raucous. [➡LOUD OR UNPLEASANT SOUNDS; 1265] *Opposite:* melodious.

guv (*informal*) 1 *n* **pal** (*informal*), mate, chum (*informal*), guvnor (*dated informal*), man (*slang*), squire (*informal*). [➡MALE PERSON; 934] 2 *n* **boss**, superior, manager, chief, gaffer (*informal*), guvnor (*dated informal*). [➡BOSSES AND MANAGEMENT; 965]

guvnor (*dated informal*) 1 *n* **boss**, superior, manager, chief, gaffer (*informal*). [➡BOSSES AND MANAGEMENT; 965] 2 *n* **pal** (*informal*), mate, chum (*informal*), guv (*informal*), man (*slang*), squire (*informal*). [➡MALE PERSON; 934] 3 *n* **father**, pater (*dated slang or humorous*), pa (*informal*), papa (*informal dated*), dad (*informal*), pop (*informal*). [➡OLDER GENERATION RELATIVES; 959]

guy 1 *n* **effigy**, figure, model, manikin, scarecrow, image. [➡REPRESENTATIONS AND GENERAL EXAMPLES; 65] 2 *n* (*informal*) **man**, bloke (*informal*), chap (*informal*), fellow, fella (*informal*), type (*informal*), bod (*slang*), gent (*dated informal*), gentleman, lad (*informal*), boy, dude (*US slang*) [➡MALE PERSON; 934] 3 *v* (*regional informal*) **poke fun at**, send up (*informal*), imitate, tease, take off (*informal*), satirize. [➡JOKES AND TEASING; 675] *Opposite:* respect.

guyrope *n* **rope**, lashing, string, halyard, guy (*informal*), hawser. [➡FASTENERS, LINKS, AND NETWORKS; 1246]

guys (*informal*) *n* **people**, folks, gang, everybody. [➡FRIENDS AND ACQUAINTANCES; 936]

guzzle (*informal*) 1 *v* **gulp**, gobble, wolf, stuff, swig (*informal*), consume, eat, scoff (*informal*), drink, devour, swallow, knock back (*informal*), toss down. [➡EAT AND NOT EAT; 711] *Opposite:* nibble. 2 *v* **consume**, use, devour, burn up, use up, get through. [➡USE UP AND WASTE; 475] *Opposite:* conserve.

gym (*informal*) *n* **fitness centre**, exercise room, sports centre, leisure centre, sports club, health club, sports hall, aerobics studio, gymnasium. [➡BUILDINGS FOR PUBLIC ENTERTAINMENT; 1083]

gymkhana *n* **horse show**, riding show, equestrian show, showjumping competition, riding competition, horse-riding show. [➡NON-AGGRESSIVE/SPORTING EVENT; 40]

gymnasium *n* **fitness centre**, exercise room, sports centre, leisure centre, sports club, health club, sports hall, aerobics studio, gym (*informal*). [➡BUILDINGS FOR PUBLIC ENTERTAINMENT; 1083]

gymnast *n* [➡PEOPLE IN SPORTS AND LEISURE; 876]

gymnastic 1 *adj* **athletic**, acrobatic, sporty, sporting. [➡AGILITY OF THE BODY; 477] 2 *adj* **energetic**, athletic, acrobatic, lithe, supple, agile, active. [➡AGILITY OF THE BODY; 477] *Opposite:* stiff.

gymnastics *n* **physical exercises**, aerobics, calisthenics, keep fit, exercises, physical training. [➡HOBBIES, GAMES, AND SPORTS; 875]

gymslip *n* **dress**, uniform, pinafore. [➡GARMENTS AND OUTFITS; 865]

gypsum *type of* **mineral**. [➡MINERALS; 1276]

gypsy *n* **nomad**, traveller, drifter, wanderer. [➡NOMADIC AND ROOTLESS LIFESTYLES; 884]

gypsy moth *type of* **moth**. [➡MOTHS AND BUTTERFLIES; 1015]

gyrate *v* **rotate**, whirl, spin, revolve, twirl, spiral, turn, twist, twizzle (*informal*). [➡MOVE SOMETHING ON THE SPOT; 337]

gyration *n* **whirling**, twirling, spinning, turning, revolving, rotation, revolution, twisting. [➡MOVE SOMETHING ON THE SPOT; 337]

gyratory *adj* **spiral rotating**, revolving, spinning, whirling, turning, spiralling. [➡DIRECTION OF MOTION; 346] *Opposite:* still.

haberdashery (*US*) *n* [➡GARMENTS AND OUTFITS; 865]

habit 1 *n* **custom**, routine, tradition, convention, pattern, wont (*formal*), practice. [➡WAYS OF DOING THINGS; 295] *Opposite:* deviation. 2 *n* **tendency**, inclination, leaning, preference, fondness, bent. [➡TEMPERAMENT AND BEHAVIOUR; 493] 3 *n* **addiction**, problem, dependency, weakness, fixation, obsession. [➡UNDER THE INFLUENCE OF DRUGS OR ALCOHOL; 742] 4 *n* **uniform**, garb, apparel, attire (*formal*), outfit, garment. [➡CLOTHES AND ACCESSORIES; 864]

Compare and Contrast: ***habit, custom, tradition, practice, routine, wont***

CORE MEANING: ESTABLISHED PATTERN OF BEHAVIOUR

habit an action or behaviour pattern that is regular, repetitive, often unconscious, and sometimes compulsive; ***custom*** the way somebody normally or routinely behaves in a situation, or a traditional practice in a particular community or group of people; ***tradition*** a long-established action or pattern of behaviour in a particular community or group of people, especially one that has been handed down from generation to generation; ***practice*** an established way of doing something, especially one that has developed through experience and knowledge; ***routine*** a typical pattern of behaviour that is regularly followed on a day-to-day basis, sometimes with the suggestion that this is monotonous and tedious; ***wont*** (*formal*) something that somebody does regularly or habitually.

habitable *adj* **inhabitable**, livable, fit for human habitation, comfortable, fit to live in. [➡IN GOOD REPAIR; 1231] *Opposite:* uninhabitable.

habitat *n* **home**, locale, environment, surroundings, territory, haunt, habitation. [➡PLACE; 1064]

habitation 1 *n* **occupancy**, occupation, tenancy, inhabitation (*archaic*), inhabitance, residence. [➡ACCOMMODATION; 855] 2 *n* **house**, home, lodging, residence, abode (*literary*), dwelling (*formal*). [➡ACCOMMODATION; 855] 3 *n* **building**, structure, housing, construction, architecture, houses. [➡BUILDING AND ARCHITECTURE; 1075]

habitual 1 *adj* **regular**, usual, routine, customary, normal, consistent, ordinary. [➡ORDINARINESS; 245] *Opposite:* unusual. 2 *adj* **persistent**, addicted, chronic, long-term, ongoing, regular. [➡PERMANENCE: WITHOUT END; 94] *Opposite:* occasional. 3 *adj* **characteristic**, usual, customary, wonted (*formal*), typical, expected. [➡ORDINARINESS; 245] *Opposite:* uncharacteristic.

See Compare and Contrast at **usual**.

habitually *adv* **usually**, routinely, customarily, consistently, normally, regularly. [➡USUALLY; 108] *Opposite:* unusually.

habituate *v* **familiarize**, adjust, accustom, inure, acclimatize, orientate. [➡CHANGE OF MOOD AND COMPOSURE; 581] *Opposite:* disorientate.

habituation (*formal*) *n* **familiarization**, adjustment, acclimatization, orientation, adaptation, conditioning. [➡CHANGE; 373] *Opposite:* disorientation.

háček *type of* **diacritic**. [➡ASPECTS OF LANGUAGE; 683]

hacienda *type of* **house**. [➡RESIDENTIAL BUILDINGS; 1077]

hack 1 *v* **cut**, chop, slash, lacerate, scythe, hew, slice. [➡TEAR, BREAK, AND CUT; 361] *Opposite:* splice. 2 *v* (*informal*) **cope**, manage, succeed, make do, survive, get by. [➡TOLERATE AND ENDURE; 767] 3 *n* (*informal*) **drudge**, slave, flunky (*informal*), menial (*formal*), factotum, dogsbody (*informal*). [➡WORKER; 836] *Opposite:* specialist. 4 *n* (*informal*) **journalist**, scribbler, writer, stringer, journo (*informal*), reporter. [➡WORKERS IN ENTERTAINMENT AND MEDIA; 873] 5 *type of* **horse**. [➡HORSE; 985]

hacked off (*informal*) *adj* [➡IRRITATION AND ANGER; 542]

hackney cab *type of* **commercial or industrial vehicle**. [➡VEHICLES; 1144]

hackney carriage *type of* **commercial or industrial vehicle**. [➡VEHICLES; 1144]

hackneyed *adj* **trite**, clichéd, tired, stale, everyday, commonplace, unimaginative, worn-out. [➡BORING AND UNINTERESTING; 235] *Opposite:* original.

hack off (*informal*) *v* [➡ANGER AND ANNOY; 570]

haddock *type of* **sea fish**. [➡SEA FISH; 1009]

had it (*informal*) 1 *adj* **out of order**, broken, finished, no good, past its best, useless, kaput (*informal*). [➡IN BAD REPAIR; 1233] *Opposite:* brand-new. 2 *adj* **exhausted**, worn out, shattered, tired, weary, spent, beat (*informal*). [➡TIRED, ASLEEP, AND UNCONSCIOUS; 739] *Opposite:* fresh.

hadron *type of* **elementary particle**. [➡ELEMENTARY PARTICLES; 1278]

hadrosaur *type of* **dinosaur**. [➡DINOSAUR; 996]

haemorrhage 1 *n* **loss**, outflow, outpouring, seeping away, depletion, drop, seepage, flow. [➡LESS; 124] 2 *v* **lose**, flow away, seep away, pour out, drain away, gush, bleed. [➡THE BLOOD AND CIRCULATION; 718]

haggard *adj* **worn**, fatigued, tired, faded, exhausted, worn-down, gaunt, drawn, worn-out. [➡FACIAL CHARACTERISTICS; 482] *Opposite:* fresh.

haggle *v* **bargain**, barter, quibble, negotiate, wrangle, beat down (*informal*). [➡ARGUE AND FIGHT – TWO-WAY; 644]

hail 1 *n* **storm**, volley, burst, flood, barrage, shower, rain. [➡SUDDEN EVENT; 52] 2 *v* **greet**, welcome, address, speak to, call to, wave to. [➡GESTURES AND GESTICULATION; 654] *Opposite:* ignore.

3 *v* **acclaim**, acknowledge, salute, uphold, confirm, affirm. [➡APPROVE AND CONFIRM; 647] *Opposite:* reject. 4 *v* **summon**, call, call over, flag down, wave, signal, beckon. [➡GESTURES AND GESTICULATION; 654] *Opposite:* dismiss.

hair 1 *n* **locks** (*literary*), tresses, curls, mane (*literary or informal*), mop, shock. [➡HAIR; 485] 2 *n* **coat**, fur, wool, pelt, fleece, mane (*literary or informal*), beard, whiskers, fuzz, moustache. [➡THE SKIN; 721] 3 *part of* **head**. [➡HEAD; 693]

hairband *type of* **headgear**. [➡HABERDASHERY, MILLINERY, AND LINGERIE; 867]

hairbrush *type of* **cosmetic tool**. [➡HAND TOOLS; 1118]

haircut 1 *n* **trim**, cut, restyling, clip, restyle. [➡HAIR STYLES AND HAIR PIECES; 489] 2 *n* **hairdo** (*informal*), hairstyle, style, coiffure (*formal*). [➡HAIR STYLES AND HAIR PIECES; 489]

hairdo (*informal*) *n* **haircut**, hairstyle, style, coiffure (*formal*). [➡HAIR STYLES AND HAIR PIECES; 489]

hairdresser *n* **coiffeur** (*formal*), coiffeuse (*formal*), stylist, barber, hairstylist, cutter. [➡HAIR STYLISTS; 851]

hairdresser's *type of* **retail outlet**. [➡RETAIL OUTLETS; 1082]

hairdressing *n* **hair gel**, styling gel, mousse, hair cream, styling spray, hair spray. [➡HAIR STYLES AND HAIR PIECES; 489]

hairiness *n* **furriness**, shagginess, fuzziness, hirsuteness, fluffiness, downiness. [➡HAIR; 485] *Opposite:* baldness.

hairless *adj* **bald**, receding, thin on top, bald as a coot, shaved, shaven, baldheaded, beardless, clean-shaven, tonsured. [➡BALDNESS AND BALDING; 488] *Opposite:* hairy.

hairpiece *n* [➡HAIR STYLES AND HAIR PIECES; 489]

hair-raising *adj* **terrifying**, horrifying, extraordinary, scary (*informal*), spine-tingling, frightening, alarming, thrilling. [➡DANGEROUS; 237] *Opposite:* calming.

hair salon *type of* **retail outlet**. [➡RETAIL OUTLETS; 1082]

hairsplitting *n* **quibbling**, nitpicking, cavilling, pettifoggery, equivocation, pedantry. [➡COMPLAIN AND NAG; 687]

hairstyle *n* **hairdo** (*informal*), haircut, style, cut, coiffure (*formal*). [➡HAIR STYLES AND HAIR PIECES; 489]

hairstyle

◆ *types of hairstyle*
Afro, bangs (*US*), beehive, big hair (*informal*), bob, bouffant, braids, bun, bunches, buzz cut (*US*), chignon, cornrow, cowlick, crew cut, crop, dreadlocks, flat top, French pleat, fringe, mohawk (*US*), mohican, mullet, pageboy, pigtail, plait, pompadour, ponytail, quiff, ringlet, topknot

hair stylist *n* [➡HAIR STYLISTS; 851]

hairy 1 *adj* **hirsute**, bearded, bushy, furry, shaggy, long-haired, stubbly. [➡DESCRIBING HAIR; 487] *Opposite:* bald. 2 *adj* (*informal*) **dangerous**, hazardous, treacherous, scary (*informal*), risky, perilous. [➡DANGEROUS; 237] *Opposite:* safe.

hajj *n* [➡TRAVEL: JOURNEYS AND TRIPS; 319]

hajji *n* [➡TRAVEL: TRAVELLERS AND WALKERS; 320]

hake *type of* **sea fish**. [➡SEA FISH; 1009]

halcyon (*literary*) *adj* **untroubled**, calm, peaceful, still, tranquil, heavenly, quiet. [➡CALMING; 189] *Opposite:* turbulent.

halcyon days (*literary*) *n* [➡PLEASANT SITUATIONS; 74]

hale *adj* **healthy**, well, fit, robust, in good shape, in peak condition, lusty, vigorous, hearty. [➡FIT AND STRONG; 737] *Opposite:* unhealthy.

hale and hearty *adj* [➡FIT AND STRONG; 737]

half *n* [➡MEASUREABLE PORTION; 125]

half-baked (*informal*) 1 *adj* **unplanned**, ill-considered, impulsive, ill-conceived. [➡THE NATURE OF IDEAS; 772] *Opposite:* considered. 2 *adj* **impractical**, silly, unrealistic, idealistic, starry-eyed, romantic. [➡THE NATURE OF IDEAS; 772] *Opposite:* sensible.

half-hearted *adj* **unenthusiastic**, perfunctory, lukewarm, indifferent, lackadaisical, reluctant, unwilling, feeble, weak, spiritless, uninterested. [➡NEUTRALITY AND INDIFFERENCE; 554] *Opposite:* wholehearted.

half-heartedly *adv* **unenthusiastically**, perfunctorily, lukewarmly, indifferently, lackadaisically, reluctantly, unwillingly, feebly, weakly, spiritlessly, uninterestedly. [➡WITHOUT ENTHUSIASM; 288] *Opposite:* wholeheartedly.

half-truth *n* [➡DECEPTION AND LIES; 661]

halfway 1 *adv* **midway**, centrally, in the middle, between, in-between, medially, partway. [➡RELATIVE LOCATION; 162] 2 *adj* **middle**, central, intermediate, mid, midway, median, medial. [➡RELATIVE LOCATION; 162]

halibut *type of* **flatfish**. [➡SEA FISH; 1009]

hall 1 *n* **gallery**, great hall, room, public room, ballroom. [➡TYPES OF ROOM; 1096] 2 *n* **mansion**, manor, tower, castle, grange, lodge, country seat. [➡RESIDENTIAL BUILDINGS; 1077]

hallmark 1 *n* **seal**, stamp, trademark, symbol, mark, guarantee, assurance, promise, brand. [➡SYMBOLS, SIGNS, AND NUMBERS; 597] 2 *n* **characteristic**, feature, trait, property, quality, token. [➡QUALITIES AND CHARACTERISTICS; 1190]

hall of residence *n* **residence**, hall, student house, dorm (*informal*), lodgings (*dated*), dormitory, frat house (*US*). [➡RESIDENTIAL BUILDINGS; 1077]

hallow *v* **consecrate**, sanctify, bless, deify, revere, respect. [➡RELIGIONS AND RELIGIOUS PRACTICES; 778] *Opposite:* desecrate.

hallowed *adj* **sacred**, holy, sanctified, blessed, consecrated, deified, revered, respected. [➡RELIGIOUS CONCEPTS; 777] *Opposite:* profane.

hallucinate *v* **see things**, have delusions, have visions, fantasize, be delirious, imagine, have nightmares. [➡DREAM, IMAGINE, AND FANTASIZE; 750]

hallucination *n* **vision**, illusion, figment of the imagination, phantasm, mirage, delusion, delirium, fantasy, nightmare. [➡ NONEXISTENT THINGS; 23]

hallway *n* **hall**, entry, lobby, antechamber, vestibule, entrance, foyer, passage, corridor, passageway. [➡ DOORS AND ACCESS POINTS; 1100]

halo *n* **corona**, aureole, nimbus, aura, radiance, crown. [➡ ROUNDED SHAPE; 1217]

haloumi *type of* **hard cheese**. [➡ DAIRY PRODUCTS AND CHEESES; 1182]

halt 1 *n* **standstill**, stop, close, break, pause, cessation, termination, end. [➡ END; 54] *Opposite:* start. 2 *v* **stop**, pause, cease, freeze, come to an end, come to a close, come to a standstill, finish, bring to an end, bring to a close, arrest, cut short, close down, bring to a standstill, terminate (*formal*), immobilize. [➡ CAUSE TO STOP; 267] *Opposite:* begin.

halter 1 *n* **bridle**, rein, strap, lead, noose, collar, tether. [➡ FASTENERS, LINKS, AND NETWORKS; 1246] 2 *type of* **top**. [➡ GARMENTS AND OUTFITS; 865]

halting *adj* **hesitant**, uncertain, tentative, stumbling, faltering, awkward, ham-fisted (*informal*), ham-handed (*informal*). [➡ INSECURITY AND LOSS OF COMPOSURE; 545] *Opposite:* firm.

halve 1 *v* **bisect**, divide, cut in two, cut in half. [➡ SEPARATE AND DIVIDE; 402] *Opposite:* double. 2 *v* **split**, split fifty-fifty, go halves on, share, share out, divvy up (*informal*), carve up (*informal*), cut up. [➡ TEAR, BREAK, AND CUT; 361] 3 *v* **decrease**, reduce, cut, slash, cut down, cut back, pare down. [➡ CHANGE OF SIZE: SMALLER; 394] *Opposite:* double.

ham 1 *v* **overact**, lay it on thick, overplay, overdo it, mug, exaggerate. [➡ OVERDO SOMETHING; 291] 2 *type of* **processed meat**. [➡ TYPES AND CUTS OF MEAT; 1176]

hamburger *type of* **processed meat**. [➡ TYPES AND CUTS OF MEAT; 1176]

ham-fisted (*informal*) *adj* **clumsy**, inelegant, inept, blundering, awkward, all fingers and thumbs, ham-handed (*informal*). [➡ UNSKILLED; 530] *Opposite:* dexterous.

ham-fistedness (*informal*) *n* [➡ UNSKILLED; 530]

ham-handed (*informal*) *adj* **clumsy**, inelegant, inept, blundering, awkward, all fingers and thumbs, ham-fisted (*informal*). [➡ UNSKILLED; 530] *Opposite:* dexterous.

ham-handedness (*informal*) *n* [➡ UNSKILLED; 530]

ham it up *v* [➡ OVERDO SOMETHING; 291]

hamlet *n* **village**, settlement, homestead, community, colony. [➡ HUMAN SETTLEMENTS; 1069] *Opposite:* city.

hammer 1 *v* (*informal*) **batter**, beat, assault, attack, brutalize. [➡ PHYSICAL ATTACK AND PUNISHMENT; 416] 2 *v* **strike**, pound, hit, knock, beat, nail, batter, drum, drive. [➡ USE TOOLS AND MACHINERY; 469] 3 *v* (*informal*) **defeat**, beat, thrash, trounce, slaughter, walk over (*informal*), whip, paste, cream (*US informal*). [➡ BEAT AND DEFEAT; 80] 4 *v* (*informal*) **criticize**, put down (*informal*), slam (*informal*), disparage, condemn, censure. [➡ ACCUSE, BLAME, AND CRITICIZE; 642] 5 *type of* **carpentry tool**. [➡ HAND TOOLS; 1118]

hammering 1 *n* (*informal*) **defeat**, beating, thrashing, trouncing, hiding (*informal*), slaughter (*slang*). [➡ BEAT AND DEFEAT; 80] *Opposite:* victory. 2 *n* **pounding**, buffeting, battering, beating, lashing, pummelling. [➡ PHYSICAL ATTACK AND PUNISHMENT; 416]

hammer out 1 *v* **beat**, pound, forge, shape, craft, reshape. [➡ CHANGE OF SHAPE; 386] 2 *v* **accomplish**, establish, arrive at, reach, produce, settle, thrash out, agree, agree on, decide on, hash out (*US*). [➡ TWO-WAY COMMUNICATION; 608]

hammer throw *type of* **track and field**. [➡ HOBBIES, GAMES, AND SPORTS; 875]

hammock *type of* **bed**. [➡ FURNITURE; 858]

hammy (*informal*) *adj* [➡ AFFECTATION, SELF-SATISFACTION, AND SNOBBISHNESS; 508]

hamper 1 *n* **basket**, picnic basket, pannier. [➡ CONTAINERS, RECEPTACLES, AND PACKAGING; 1244] 2 *v* **hinder**, obstruct, get in the way of, impede, slow down, weigh down, hold back, fetter, shackle, encumber, debilitate. [➡ AVOID, PREVENT, LIMIT, AND CONTROL; 278] *Opposite:* facilitate.

See Compare and Contrast at **hinder**.

hamster *type of* **rodent**. [➡ RODENT; 989]

hamstring *type of* **muscle or tendon**. [➡ THE MUSCLES; 719]

hamstrung *adj* **constrained**, restricted, thwarted, confined, cramped, stymied. [➡ IN TROUBLE AND DISADVANTAGED; 73] *Opposite:* liberated.

hand 1 *n* **pointer**, needle, indicator, arrow, finger, big hand, small hand. [➡ PARTS OF MACHINES AND TOOLS; 1117] 2 *n* **influence**, part, share, role, involvement, participation. [➡ KIND ACTION OR BEHAVIOUR; 296] 3 *n* **clap**, ovation, standing ovation, round of applause, burst of applause, handclap, slow handclap. [➡ APPLAUSE; 653] *Opposite:* boo. 4 *n* **handwriting**, writing, script, scrawl, scribble, calligraphy. [➡ WRITING; 584] 5 *part of* **arm or hand**. [➡ ARM AND HAND; 696] 6 *v* **give**, hand over, offer, pass, tender, furnish (*formal*), dispense, administer, distribute. [➡ PROFFER AND HAND OVER; 432] *Opposite:* take.

handbag *n* **bag**, shoulder bag, clutch bag, backpack, purse (*US*), pocketbook (*US*). [➡ CONTAINERS, RECEPTACLES, AND PACKAGING; 1244]

hand basin *type of* **plumbing fittings**. [➡ FITTINGS; 859]

handbill *n* **leaflet**, flier, pamphlet, advertisement, circular, handout, tract, brochure. [➡ ADVERTISING AND PUBLICITY; 605]

handbook *n* **manual**, instruction manual, guide, guidebook, instruction book, reference book, reference, source book, almanac, booklet, brochure, encyclopedia. [➡ MANUALS AND INSTRUCTIONS; 590]

handcuff 1 *n* **manacles**, chains, cuffs (*slang*), shackles, fetters, irons, restraints. [➡ FASTENERS, LINKS, AND NETWORKS; 1246] 2 *v* **chain**, manacle, shackle, fasten, tie up, secure, restrain, cuff (*slang*). [➡ CAPTIVITY AND LOSS OF FREEDOM; 249] *Opposite:* release.

hand down *v* **leave**, bequeath, pass down, transmit, will, hand on, pass on. [➡ BEQUEATH AND BEQUESTS; 433]

handful 1 *n* **some**, a few, one or two, not many, hardly any, trickle, minority, a bit (*informal*), not much. [➡ FEW, LITTLE, SMALL AMOUNT; 119] *Opposite:* many. 2 *n* (*informal*) **test**, trial, problem, nuisance, tall order (*informal*), hard work. [➡PROBLEM; 257]

hand grenade *type of* **explosive weapon.** [➡EXPLOSIVES; 1154]

handgun *type of* **gun.** [➡WEAPONS FOR SHOOTING; 1155]

hand-held computer *type of* **computer.** [➡COMPUTERS AND COMPUTING; 1126]

hand-hot *adj* [➡TEMPERATURE: MEDIUM; 1229]

handicap *n* [➡FAULTS, FLAWS, AND WEAKNESSES; 252]

handicraft *n* **craft**, handcraft, handiwork, skill, art, ability. [➡CRAFTS AND CARVING; 356]

handicraft

◆ *types of handicraft*
appliqué, crochet, dressmaking, embroidery, knitting, lacemaking, macramé, needlepoint, needlework, sewing, smocking, stitching, tapestry, tatting, weaving

handily 1 *adv* **conveniently**, closely, accessibly, nearby, in easy reach, within reach, at hand. [➡CLOSENESS; 160] *Opposite:* inconveniently. 2 *adv* **skilfully**, dexterously, cleverly, neatly, ably, proficiently, competently, usefully, practically. [➡USEFULNESS; 200] *Opposite:* awkwardly.

hand in 1 *v* **submit**, give, give in, tender, offer, proffer, present. [➡PROFFER AND HAND OVER; 432] *Opposite:* withhold. 2 *v* **surrender**, return, give up, give back, hand over, relinquish. [➡PROFFER AND HAND OVER; 432] *Opposite:* withhold.

handiness 1 *n* **convenience**, proximity, closeness, accessibility. [➡CLOSENESS; 160] *Opposite:* inconvenience. 2 *n* **usefulness**, utility, efficacy, helpfulness, practicality, cleverness, usability, versatility, dexterity, neatness. [➡SKILLS, TALENTS, AND ABILITIES; 527] *Opposite:* uselessness. 3 *n* **skilfulness**, skill, dexterity, practicality, cleverness, ability, competence, proficiency. [➡SKILLS, TALENTS, AND ABILITIES; 527] *Opposite:* awkwardness.

handiwork 1 *n* **deed**, action, achievement, work, creation, accomplishment. [➡ACTIONS OR UNDERTAKINGS; 260] 2 *n* **handicraft**, craft, skill, art, dexterity, ability, proficiency. [➡SKILLS, TALENTS, AND ABILITIES; 527]

handkerchief *n* **hankie** (*informal*), tissue, paper handkerchief. [➡HABERDASHERY, MILLINERY, AND LINGERIE; 867]

handle 1 *n* **grip**, holder, handgrip. [➡PARTS OF MACHINES AND TOOLS; 1117] 2 *n* (*slang*) **name**, title, nickname, sobriquet, pet name, moniker (*slang*). [➡NAME AND DESCRIBE; 666] 3 *v* **touch**, finger, feel, move, hold, pick up. [➡CONTACT: TOUCH; 413] 4 *v* **control**, deal with, run, cope with, conduct, carry out, see to, get to grips with, treat. [➡CARRY OUT AN ACTION; 270] 5 *v* **manage**, operate, conduct, supervise, run, carry out. [➡USE; 468] 6 *v* **trade in**, sell, deal in, import, export, market. [➡SELL; 442]

handlebar moustache *n* [➡FACIAL HAIR; 490]

handlebars *part of* **bike** (*informal*). [➡BIKES, CARS, AND CARRIAGES; 1148]

handler *n* **trainer**, coach, manager, supervisor. [➡PEOPLE WHO GUARD AND PROTECT; 846]

handling *n* **treatment**, management, conduct, behaviour, supervision, control, hold, usage, use. [➡USE; 468]

hand-me-down *adj* **second-hand**, castoff, recycled, used, worn. [➡OLD, OLD-FASHIONED; 168] *Opposite:* brand-new.

hand on *v* [➡BEQUEATH AND BEQUESTS; 433]

hand out *v* **dispense**, distribute, administer, give away, give out, donate, award. [➡DISPENSE, RATION, AND DISTRIBUTE; 435] *Opposite:* take in.

handout 1 *n* **windfall**, bonus, gift, donation, contribution, gratuity, free sample, giveaway (*informal*), freebie (*informal*). [➡GIFTS; 439] 2 *n* **document**, fact sheet, leaflet, brochure, pamphlet, booklet, flier, handbill, press release, advertisement. [➡ADVERTISING AND PUBLICITY; 605]

hand over *v* **give up**, tender, surrender, entrust, relinquish, give away, renounce, devolve, extradite, deliver, abdicate, assign, confer (*formal*), bestow (*formal*), transfer, convey. [➡PROFFER AND HAND OVER; 432] *Opposite:* withhold.

handover *n* **delivery**, abdication, assignment, conferral, bestowal, transfer, transference, conveyance, surrender, devolution, extradition. [➡EXCHANGE AND INTERCHANGE; 449]

hand over fist *adv* **in large amounts**, copiously, prolifically, profusely, generously, freely, rapidly, quickly, easily. [➡MANY, MUCH, LARGE AMOUNT; 117] *Opposite:* gradually.

handpicked *adj* **select**, elite, exclusive, finest, top-quality, crack, chosen. [➡POPULAR AND WANTED; 221] *Opposite:* run-of-the-mill.

hand puppet (*US*) *type of* **toy.** [➡TOYS; 880]

handrail *n* **banister**, rail, railing, guardrail, balustrade, guiderail. [➡STICKS, POLES, AND WEDGES; 1253]

hand round *v* [➡DISPENSE, RATION, AND DISTRIBUTE; 435]

hands down *adv* **easily**, decisively, unquestionably, safely, unmistakably, indubitably (*formal*), incontrovertibly. [➡CERTAIN; 175] *Opposite:* questionably.

handset *n* **receiver**, earpiece, mouthpiece, phone, telephone. [➡AUDIO EQUIPMENT; 1138]

handshake *n* **handclasp**, grasp, greeting, grip, shake. [➡PHYSICAL CONTACT AS COMMUNICATION; 656]

hands-off *adj* **detached**, remote, distant, laid-back (*informal*), noninterventionist, laissez-faire. [➡NEUTRALITY AND INDIFFERENCE; 554] *Opposite:* hands-on.

handsome 1 *adj* **good-looking**, fine, attractive, striking, beautiful, gorgeous, fetching. [➡PEOPLE'S PHYSICAL APPEARANCE; 476] *Opposite:* ugly. 2 *adj* **generous**, substantial, sizable, attractive, liberal, considerable, abundant, ample, princely. [➡MANY, MUCH, LARGE AMOUNT; 117] *Opposite:* ungenerous.

See Compare and Contrast at **good-looking**.

handsomely *adv* **generously**, substantially, sizably, attractively, liberally, considerably, abundantly, amply. [➡MANY, MUCH, LARGE AMOUNT; 117] *Opposite:* ungenerously.

hands-on *adj* **practical**, active, applied, proactive, energetic, direct. [➡USEFULNESS; 200] *Opposite:* hands-off.

handspring *n* **somersault**, cartwheel, flip, flip-flop, vault. [➡ FIDGET AND FROLIC; 312]

hand-to-hand *adj* **unarmed**, close-range, face-to-face, direct, bareknuckle, head-on. [➡ CLOSENESS; 160]

handwork *n* **handiwork**, handicraft, skill, art, craft. [➡ CRAFTS AND CARVING; 356]

handwriting *n* **script**, writing, calligraphy, scrawl, scribble, hand. [➡ WRITING; 584]

handy 1 *adj* **convenient**, near, nearby, within reach, in easy reach, close, accessible, manageable, at hand. [➡ CLOSENESS; 160] *Opposite:* inconvenient. 2 *adj* **useful**, helpful, practical, clever, usable, versatile, multipurpose, nifty (*informal*), natty, neat. [➡ USEFULNESS; 200] *Opposite:* useless. 3 *adj* **skilful**, dexterous, practical, clever, skilled, able, competent, proficient. [➡ TALENTED AND SKILFUL; 528] *Opposite:* awkward.

hang 1 *v* **suspend**, dangle, droop, drape, hang down, swing, hang up, hang out (*informal*), sling, hook up (*informal*). [➡ POSITION SOMETHING; 326] *Opposite:* take down. 2 *v* **lynch**, suspend by the neck, execute, put to death, swing (*informal*). [➡ KILL; 923] 3 *v* **droop**, flop, drape, sag, trail, nod, fold. [➡ TAKE UP A NEW POSITION; 313] *Opposite:* stick up.

hang about 1 *v* **wait**, linger, loiter, lie around (*informal*), dawdle, remain, dally, stay, hover, kick your heels (*informal*), pass time, haunt, frequent, hang around. [➡ MOVE SLOWLY; 315] 2 *v* **associate**, mix, consort (*formal*), mess around (*informal*), hang around, keep company, go out. [➡ ESTABLISHING RELATIONSHIPS WITH OTHERS; 974]

hangar *type of* **storage space**. [➡ STORES AND STORAGE BUILDINGS; 1087]

hang around 1 *v* **wait**, linger, loiter, lie around (*informal*), dawdle, remain, dally, stay, hover, kick your heels (*informal*), pass time, haunt, frequent, hang about. [➡ MOVE SLOWLY; 315] 2 *v* **associate**, mix, consort (*formal*), mess around (*informal*), keep company, go out. [➡ ESTABLISHING RELATIONSHIPS WITH OTHERS; 974]

hang back *v* **hesitate**, drag your feet, drag your heels, linger, drop behind, drop back, lag behind, fall back, lag. [➡ MOVE SLOWLY; 315] *Opposite:* forge ahead.

hangdog *adj* **guilty**, dejected, furtive, intimidated, sheepish, humiliated, shamefaced, wretched, downcast, miserable. [➡ EMBARRASSMENT AND HUMILIATION; 543]. *Opposite:* chirpy (*informal*).

hang down *v* **sag**, dangle, droop, swing, hang, flop, nod, trail, drape. [➡ CHANGE OF SHAPE; 386] *Opposite:* stick up.

hanger *n* **coat hanger**, hook, peg, support, nail, knob. [➡ SUPPORTS AND BASES; 1254]

hanger-on *n* **follower**, groupie (*informal*), sycophant, disciple, proselyte, associate. [➡ DEVOTEES AND ADDICTED PEOPLE; 557]

hang fire *v* [➡ SHIRK AND DELAY; 274]

hang glider *type of* **civil aircraft**. [➡ AIRCRAFT; 1147]

hanging 1 *n* **execution**, lynching, killing. [➡ CAUSES OF DEATH; 921] 2 *n* **wall hanging**, tapestry, carpet, drape, drapery, swag. [➡ SOFT FURNISHINGS, LINEN, AND DRAPERY; 860]

hang loose (*informal*) *v* [➡ LACK OF ACTIVITY; 343]

hangnail *part of* **arm or hand**. [➡ ARM AND HAND; 696]

hang on 1 *v* **grip**, grasp, clutch, cling, hold on, keep a hold on, latch on. [➡ CONTACT: HOLD; 412] *Opposite:* let go. 2 *v* **persevere**, keep it up, stick it out, hold on, cling on, persist, see it through. [➡ CONTINUE AN ACTION; 263] *Opposite:* give up. 3 *v* **depend on**, hinge on, follow from, turn on, rely on. [➡ RECIPROCITY AND INTERDEPENDENCE; 148] 4 *v* **wait**, linger, hold on, remain, persevere, stick around (*informal*), hang around, hang about, kick your heels (*informal*), loiter. [➡ SHIRK AND DELAY; 274] *Opposite:* leave.

hang out 1 *v* **suspend**, dangle, drape, swing, hang up, hang, sling, hook up (*informal*). [➡ POSITION SOMETHING; 326] *Opposite:* take down. 2 *v* (*informal*) **spend time**, loiter, hang around, frequent, haunt, stay. [➡ LACK OF ACTIVITY; 343] 3 *v* (*informal*) **associate**, mix, consort (*formal*), be friendly, mess around (*informal*), hang around, interact, keep company, go around. [➡ ESTABLISHING RELATIONSHIPS WITH OTHERS; 974] 4 *v* (*informal*) **relax**, chill out (*slang*), hang about, hang around, laze about, lounge about, mess around (*informal*), loll around. [➡ LACK OF ACTIVITY; 343]

hangout (*informal*) *n* **haunt**, den, retreat, lair (*informal*), hidey-hole (*informal*), stamping ground (*informal*), meeting place. [➡ PUBLIC BUILDINGS AND MEETING PLACES; 1080]

hangover *n* **relic**, leftover, aftermath, aftereffect, inheritance, legacy. [➡ RESULTS AND OUTCOMES; 83]

hang together *v* **make sense**, add up, hold up, wash (*informal*), tell the complete story, give the full picture, cohere (*formal*). [➡ MEAN SOMETHING; 61] *Opposite:* fall apart.

hang up 1 *v* **suspend**, dangle, droop, drape, swing, hang out (*informal*), sling, hook up (*informal*). [➡ POSITION SOMETHING; 326] *Opposite:* take down. 2 *v* **ring off**, put the phone down, disconnect, get off the phone, replace the receiver. [➡ TELEPHONE AND PAGE; 682] *Opposite:* pick up.

hang-up (*informal*) *n* **anxiety**, worry, complex, neurosis (*dated*), inhibition, fixation, obsession, phobia, fear, problem. [➡ PSYCHOLOGY AND THE MIND; 770]

hank *n* **coil**, length, reel, skein, ball, bundle. [➡ AMOUNT OF SOLID OR SEMI-SOLID; 115]

hanker *v* **yearn**, crave, long, ache, hunger, thirst, have a yen, obsess. [➡ DESIRE AND WANT; 580]

hanker after *v* [➡ DESIRE AND WANT; 580]

hankering *n* **yearning**, craving, longing, desire, ache, hunger, thirst, yen, urge. [➡ DESIRE AND WANT; 580] *Opposite:* dislike.

haphazard *adj* **random**, chaotic, slapdash, disorganized, messy, jumbled, hit-and-miss, all over the place (*informal*), arbitrary, indiscriminate, unsystematic, irregular, unselective, unplanned, careless. [➡ DISORDER AND CHAOS; 246] *Opposite:* systematic.

haphazardness *n* [➡ DISORDER AND CHAOS; 246]

hapless *adj* **unfortunate**, unlucky, luckless, ill-fated, wretched, miserable, ill-starred (*formal*), star-crossed, doomed. [➡ BAD LUCK AND UNLUCKY; 785] *Opposite:* fortunate.

haplessness *n* **misfortune**, bad luck, ill fortune, wretchedness, misery, doom. [➡BAD LUCK AND UNLUCKY; 785] *Opposite:* luck.

happen *v* **occur**, take place, go on, come about, ensue, turn out, crop up (*informal*), transpire, materialize, chance, come to pass (*archaic or literary*), go down (*slang*). [➡HAPPEN; 27]

happenchance *n* [➡LUCK; 784]

happening 1 *n* **occurrence**, event, incident, episode, phenomenon, experience. [➡EVENTS AND OCCURRENCES; 35] 2 *adj* (*informal*) **trendy** (*informal*), fashionable, stylish, in, up-to-the-minute, bang up-to-date. [➡NEW, MODERN; 167] *Opposite:* old-fashioned.

happen on *v* [➡FIND; 464]

happenstance *n* **accident**, fluke (*informal*), coincidence, chance, happenchance. [➡CHANCE EVENT; 36]

happen upon *v* [➡FIND; 464]

happily 1 *adv* **luckily**, fortunately, thankfully, as good luck would have it, opportunely, well, favourably. [➡LUCK; 784] *Opposite:* sadly. 2 *adv* **gladly**, willingly, cheerfully, freely, voluntarily, unreservedly, enthusiastically, eagerly. [➡THE WILL AND WILLINGNESS; 564] *Opposite:* unwillingly. 3 *adv* **cheerfully**, contentedly, joyfully, gleefully, blissfully, merrily, gladly. [➡PLEASURE, EXCITEMENT, AND ELATION; 535] *Opposite:* sadly.

happiness *n* **contentment**, pleasure, gladness, cheerfulness, joy, glee, bliss, delight, exhilaration, ecstasy. [➡PLEASURE, EXCITEMENT, AND ELATION; 535] *Opposite:* sadness.

happy 1 *adj* **content**, contented, pleased, glad, joyful, cheerful, blissful, exultant, ecstatic, delighted, cheery, jovial, in high spirits, on cloud nine (*informal*). [➡PLEASURE, EXCITEMENT, AND ELATION; 535] *Opposite:* sad. 2 *adj* **lucky**, fortunate, favourable, opportune. [➡LUCK; 784] *Opposite:* unlucky. 3 *adj* (*informal*) [➡UNDER THE INFLUENCE OF DRUGS OR ALCOHOL; 742]

See Compare and Contrast at **lucky**.

happy-go-lucky *adj* **carefree**, optimistic, easygoing, lighthearted, nonchalant, blithe (*literary*). [➡CHEERFULNESS OF OUTLOOK; 504] *Opposite:* anxious.

hara-kiri *n* [➡CAUSES OF DEATH; 921]

harangue 1 *v* **berate**, lecture, criticize, rant, address, sermonize, scold, perorate (*formal*). [➡ACCUSE, BLAME, AND CRITICIZE; 642] 2 *n* **tirade**, diatribe, criticism, lecture, rant, address, scolding, jeremiad (*literary*). [➡CRITICISMS AND ANGRY OUTBURSTS; 50]

harass *v* **annoy**, pester, bother, pursue, hassle (*informal*), worry, badger, hound, bully, trouble, stress, harry. [➡ANGER AND ANNOY; 570]

harassed *adj* **stressed**, hassled (*informal*), under pressure, distraught, beleaguered, worried, strained, harried, agitated, put upon, pressured. [➡SADNESS, DISTRESS, AND DESPAIR; 540] *Opposite:* relaxed.

harassment *n* **pestering**, nuisance, annoyance, irritation, aggravation (*informal*), persecution, provocation, bother, agitation. [➡UNKIND ACTION OR BEHAVIOUR; 297]

harbinger *n* **forerunner**, herald, portent, omen, indication. [➡INDICATIONS, SIGNS, AND WARNINGS; 68]

harbour 1 *n* **port**, dock, anchorage, waterfront, wharf, quay, marina, haven (*literary*). [➡THE SEAS, OCEANS, AND SHORES; 1041] 2 *v* **believe**, entertain, hold, bear in mind, cherish, embrace. [➡THINK AND REFLECT; 744] 3 *v* **protect**, shelter, give refuge to, hide, conceal. [➡PREVENT CONTACT OR ATTACK; 420]

hard 1 *adj* **firm**, stiff, rigid, solid, tough, unbreakable, durable. [➡RIGID AND HARD; 1210] *Opposite:* soft. 2 *adj* **awkward**, difficult, problematical, tricky, tough, demanding, testing, challenging, gruelling, arduous, troublesome, laborious, strenuous. [➡DIFFICULTY AND COMPLEXITY; 243] *Opposite:* easy. 3 *adj* **intense**, fast, violent, brutal, fierce, powerful, relentless, remorseless. [➡DIFFICULTY AND COMPLEXITY; 243] *Opposite:* gentle. 4 *adj* **cruel**, callous, harsh, severe, unkind, tough, brutal, thick-skinned, strict, remorseless, pitiless. [➡SELFISH AND UNKIND; 506] *Opposite:* kind. 5 *adv* **intensely**, fast, violently, fiercely, powerfully, rigorously, relentlessly, remorselessly. [➡DIFFICULTY AND COMPLEXITY; 243] *Opposite:* gently.

Compare and Contrast: ***hard, difficult, strenuous, tough, arduous, laborious***

CORE MEANING: REQUIRING EFFORT OR EXERTION

hard requiring mental or physical effort or exertion to do or achieve; ***difficult*** requiring a lot of planning or effort to accomplish; ***strenuous*** requiring physical effort, energy, stamina, or strength; ***tough*** needing great effort to deal with; ***arduous*** requiring hard work or continuous physical effort; ***laborious*** requiring unwelcome, often tedious, effort and exertion.

hard as nails *adj* [➡SELFISH AND UNKIND; 506]

hard-bitten *adj* **tough**, hardened, cynical, hard-nosed (*informal*), stubborn, uncompromising, case-hardened, hard-edged. [➡SELFISH AND UNKIND; 506]

hard-boiled (*informal*) *adj* **unsentimental**, hardened, tough, cynical, case-hardened, unfeeling, hard-edged. [➡SELFISH AND UNKIND; 506] *Opposite:* soft-boiled.

hard-core *adj* **uncompromising**, committed, dedicated, staunch, faithful, unshakable, intransigent, diehard, obstinate. [➡UNWILLINGNESS AND STUBBORNNESS; 565]

hard disk *type of* **hardware**. [➡COMPUTERS AND COMPUTING; 1126]

harden 1 *v* **solidify**, set, freeze, consolidate, settle, coagulate, congeal. [➡HARDEN, CONGEAL, DRY; 388] *Opposite:* soften. 2 *v* **toughen**, strengthen, reinforce, stabilize, roughen, coarsen. [➡IMPROVE STRENGTH AND DURABILITY; 379] *Opposite:* weaken.

hardened *adj* **hard-bitten**, hard-boiled (*informal*), toughened, tough, cynical, case-hardened, unsentimental, hard-edged. [➡SELFISH AND UNKIND; 506]

hardened criminal *n* [➡CRIMINALS; 821]

hard feelings *n* [➡ANTAGONISM; 553]

hard graft *n* [➡HARD WORK OR EFFORT; 299]

hard hat *type of* **headgear.** [➡ HABERDASHERY, MILLINERY, AND LINGERIE; 867]

hardheaded *adj* **shrewd**, sharp, practical, no-nonsense, tough, businesslike, logical, pragmatic, hard-bitten. [➡ POSITIVE INTELLECTUAL CHARACTERISTICS; 525] *Opposite:* soft.

hardhearted *adj* **callous**, cold, hard, insensitive, unfeeling, unsympathetic, unemotional, uncaring, pitiless, stony. [➡ SELFISH AND UNKIND; 506] *Opposite:* kind.

hardheartedness *n* **callousness**, coldness, insensitivity, pitilessness, stoniness, hardness, heartlessness. [➡ SELFISH AND UNKIND; 506] *Opposite:* kindness.

hard-hitting *adj* [➡ STRENGTH; 202]

hardiness *n* **toughness**, hardihood, stamina, durability, robustness, resilience, endurance. [➡ STRENGTH OF WILL; 502] *Opposite:* frailty.

hard labour *n* [➡ HARD WORK OR EFFORT; 299]

hardline *adj* **uncompromising**, inflexible, rigid, extreme, radical, fanatical, strong, hard-nosed (*informal*). [➡ UNWILLINGNESS AND STUBBORNNESS; 565]

hardliner *n* [➡ GRUMPY AND NEGATIVE PEOPLE; 953]

hardly *adv* **barely**, only just, scarcely, by a hair's breadth, by the skin of your teeth, by a whisker. [➡ TO A CERTAIN EXTENT; 134]

hardly any *pron* [➡ TOO FEW, TOO LITTLE; 120]

hardly ever *adv* [➡ NEVER AND INFREQUENCY; 97]

hardness *n* **rigidity**, stiffness, firmness, inflexibility, solidity, resistance, toughness. [➡ RIGID AND HARD; 1210] *Opposite:* softness.

hard-nosed (*informal*) *adj* [➡ SELFISH AND UNKIND; 506]

hard-pressed *adj* [➡ IN TROUBLE AND DISADVANTAGED; 73]

hardship *n* **adversity**, privation, lack, poverty, destitution, need, want, suffering, difficulty. [➡ POVERTY AND POOR; 892] *Opposite:* comfort.

hard taskmaster *n* [➡ GRUMPY AND NEGATIVE PEOPLE; 953]

hard times *n* [➡ DIFFICULT SITUATIONS; 72]

hard to follow *adj* [➡ DIFFICULTY AND COMPLEXITY; 243]

hard to please *adj* [➡ DIFFICULT TO PLEASE; 516]

hard up (*informal*) *adj* **short of money**, poor, badly off, broke (*informal*), strapped (*informal*), impoverished, impecunious (*formal*), skint (*informal*), strapped for cash (*informal*), in a bad way (*US*). [➡ POVERTY AND POOR; 892] *Opposite:* well-off.

hardware *n* **equipment**, apparatus, tackle, gear, kit. [➡ DEVICES; 1114]

hard-wearing *adj* **durable**, long-lasting, strong, tough, resilient, indestructible, heavy-duty, weatherproof. [➡ STRENGTH; 202]

hard work *n* [➡ HARD WORK OR EFFORT; 299]

hard-working *adj* [➡ HARD-WORKING AND COMMITTED; 501]

hardy *adj* **robust**, resilient, enduring, tough, strong, resistant. [➡ COMPLEXION; 481] *Opposite:* frail.

hare 1 *type of* **small mammal.** [➡ SMALL MAMMAL; 990] 2 *type of* **meat.** [➡ TYPES AND CUTS OF MEAT; 1176]

haricot *type of* **pulse.** [➡ BEANS AND PULSES; 1188]

hark (*literary or humorous*) *v* **listen to**, hear, pay attention to, heed. [➡ PAY ATTENTION; 766]

hark back *v* **go back to**, revisit, recall, relive, revive, return to. [➡ REMIND; 748]

harm 1 *n* **damage**, hurt, injury, destruction, maltreatment, detriment, impairment. [➡ DESTRUCTION AND DEMOLITION; 360] *Opposite:* help. 2 *v* **hurt**, damage, spoil, injure, impair, cause detriment, wound. [➡ WOUND A PERSON OR ANIMAL; 384] *Opposite:* help.

Compare and Contrast: ***harm, damage, hurt, injure, wound***

CORE MEANING: TO WEAKEN OR IMPAIR SOMETHING OR SOMEBODY

harm to cause physical or mental impairment or deterioration; ***damage*** to cause physical deterioration that makes an object less useful, valuable, or able to function, or to impair something abstract such as a chance or somebody's reputation; ***hurt*** to cause physical or mental pain or harm to people and animals; ***injure*** to cause physical harm to a person or animal, usually causing at least a temporary loss of function or use, or to impair something abstract such as somebody's reputation or pride; ***wound*** to inflict physical harm on somebody, especially as a result of the use of a weapon, a violent incident, or a serious accident, or to upset or offend somebody.

harmattan *type of* **wind.** [➡ WINDY AND STORMY WEATHER; 1053]

harmed *adj* **injured**, damaged, hurt, wounded, impaired, abused, affected, maltreated. [➡ INJURED; 743] *Opposite:* untouched.

harmful *adj* **damaging**, injurious, destructive, detrimental, dangerous, unsafe, risky, toxic, poisonous. [➡ DANGEROUS; 237] *Opposite:* harmless.

harmless 1 *adj* **inoffensive**, innocuous, innocent, meaningless, anodyne (*literary*), bland, mild. [➡ MORALLY GOOD; 775] *Opposite:* offensive. 2 *adj* **safe**, risk-free, undamaging, nontoxic, unhazardous, undisruptive, sound. [➡ SAFE AND SAFETY; 192] *Opposite:* harmful.

harmlessness 1 *n* **inoffensiveness**, naivety, innocence, wholesomeness, blandness. [➡ MORALLY GOOD; 775] *Opposite:* offensiveness. 2 *n* **innocuousness**, safety, mildness, nontoxicity, unhazardousness. [➡ SAFE AND SAFETY; 192]

harmonic *adj* [➡ SOFT OR PLEASANT SOUNDS; 1264]

harmonica *type of* **wind instrument.** [➡ MUSICAL INSTRUMENTS; 910]

harmonious 1 *adj* **musical**, melodious, tuneful, pleasant-sounding, sweet, pleasant, symphonic. [➡ SOFT OR PLEASANT SOUNDS; 1264] *Opposite:* discordant. 2 *adj* **congruent** (*formal*), agreeable, congruous, balanced, matching, corresponding, concordant, consonant (*formal*). [➡ HARMONY; 156]

Opposite: discordant. 3 *adj* **friendly**, cordial, affable, agreeable, amicable, congenial. [➡RELATIONSHIP TO ANOTHER; 973] *Opposite:* hostile.

harmoniously 1 *adv* **musically**, tunefully, melodiously, sweetly, pleasantly, symphonically. [➡SOFT OR PLEASANT SOUNDS; 1264] *Opposite:* discordantly. 2 *adv* **amicably**, cordially, agreeably, pleasantly, affably, congenially. [➡RELATIONSHIP TO ANOTHER; 973] *Opposite:* acrimoniously.

harmoniousness *n* [➡SOFT OR PLEASANT SOUNDS; 1264]

harmonize 1 *v* **go with**, match, blend, complement, tone, correspond. [➡HARMONY; 156] *Opposite:* jar. 2 *v* **bring into line**, synchronize, standardize, make uniform, make conform, regularize, make proportionate, balance. [➡ARRANGE AND CREATE ORDER; 358]

harmonized *adj* **in line**, consistent, coordinated, matched, in step, coherent, in time, in agreement. [➡HARMONY; 156] *Opposite:* uncoordinated.

harmonizing *adj* **consistent**, congruent (*formal*), toning, matching, agreeing, coordinating, harmonious, complementary. [➡HARMONY; 156] *Opposite:* inconsistent.

harmony *n* **agreement**, accord, concord, synchronization, congruence, coordination, coherence. [➡HARMONY; 156] *Opposite:* discord.

harness 1 *v* **tie together**, strap up, yoke, bind, attach, connect, join, hitch, couple. [➡FASTEN, LINK, AND JOIN; 409] *Opposite:* separate. 2 *v* **control**, exploit, employ, channel, utilize, use. [➡USE; 468]

harp *type of* **stringed instrument**. [➡RECORDINGS AND PLAYERS; 911]

harp on *v* **complain**, moan (*informal*), go on, keep on, whine, grumble, dwell on, repeat, nag, whinge (*informal*), chunter (*informal*), rag (*dated*). [➡COMPLAIN AND NAG; 687]

harpoon *type of* **projectile**. [➡PROJECTILES; 1158]

harpsichord *type of* **keyboard**. [➡MUSICAL INSTRUMENTS; 910]

harried *adj* **harassed**, put upon, bothered, agitated, hassled (*informal*), stressed, distraught, under pressure, beleaguered, pressured. [➡SADNESS, DISTRESS, AND DESPAIR; 540] *Opposite:* calm.

harrowing *adj* **disturbing**, upsetting, traumatic, distressing, tormenting, vexing, dreadful, worrying, stressful. [➡EMOTIONALLY UNPLEASANT AND UPSETTING; 228] *Opposite:* relaxing.

harry *v* **harass**, hassle (*informal*), bother, pester, aggravate (*informal*), badger, annoy, irritate, worry, distress, stress, agitate, hound, bully, pursue. [➡COMPLAIN AND NAG; 687]

harsh 1 *adj* **severe**, bleak, austere, inhospitable, stark, bitter. [➡PHYSICALLY UNPLEASANT; 227] *Opposite:* mild. 2 *adj* **cruel**, unkind, unsympathetic, insensitive, callous, bitter, critical. [➡SELFISH AND UNKIND; 506] *Opposite:* kind. 3 *adj* **punitive**, exacting, strict, severe, unforgiving, tough. [➡PHYSICALLY UNPLEASANT; 227] *Opposite:* lenient. 4 *adj* **discordant**, loud, blaring, raucous, jangly, strident. [➡LOUD OR UNPLEASANT SOUNDS; 1265] *Opposite:* pleasant.

harsh conditions *n* [➡DIFFICULT SITUATIONS; 72]

harshness 1 *n* **severity**, austerity, ruggedness, bleakness, starkness, roughness. [➡PHYSICALLY UNPLEASANT; 227] *Opposite:* gentleness. 2 *n* **callousness**, cruelty, ruthlessness, strictness, severity, unkindness, insensitivity. [➡SELFISH AND UNKIND; 506] *Opposite:* gentleness.

hart *type of* **male animal**. [➡MALE OR FEMALE ANIMAL; 978]

harvest 1 *n* **crop**, yield, produce, return, fruitage, ingathering. [➡INCOME; 461] 2 *v* **reap**, gather, collect, bring in, pick, garner, mow, ingather. [➡GET; 421]

harvest mite *type of* **parasitic insect**. [➡PARASITES; 1017]

hash *v* **chop**, cut up, mince, grind, shred, dice. [➡COOKING AND FOOD PREPARATION; 354]

hash browns (*US*) *type of* **processed potato**. [➡FRUIT AND VEGETABLES; 1175]

hash up (*informal*) *v* [➡MESS UP AND MAKE MISTAKES; 473]

hasp *n* [➡FASTENERS, LINKS, AND NETWORKS; 1246]

hassle (*informal*) 1 *n* **bother**, annoyance, irritation, aggravation (*informal*), disturbance, stress, trouble, difficulty, agitation. [➡NUISANCES; 254] 2 *v* **harass**, irritate, annoy, bother, get on your nerves, aggravate (*informal*), pester, disturb, stress, agitate, badger, worry, trouble. [➡COMPLAIN AND NAG; 687] *Opposite:* leave alone.

hassled (*informal*) *adj* [➡CONFUSION, ANXIETY, AND WORRY; 541]

hassle-free (*informal*) *adj* [➡EASE AND SIMPLICITY; 201]

hassock *n* [➡FURNITURE; 858]

hasta la vista (*informal*) *interj* [➡GREETINGS, FAREWELLS, AND SALUTATIONS; 660]

haste *n* **speed**, swiftness, rapidity, alacrity, rush, hurriedness, quickness. [➡SPEED; 102] *Opposite:* slowness.

hasten *v* **hurry**, make haste, rush, speed up, speed, accelerate, move along, race. [➡MOVE FAST; 314]

hastily *adv* **hurriedly**, quickly, fast, at speed, speedily, in a hurry, at a fast pace, rapidly. [➡HAPPENING QUICKLY; 104] *Opposite:* slowly.

hastiness *n* **impulsiveness**, impetuosity, rashness, thoughtlessness. [➡LACK OF COMMITMENT AND UNRELIABILITY; 510] *Opposite:* carefulness.

hasty *adj* **quick**, speedy, hurried, swift, rapid, rushed, fast. [➡MOVING QUICKLY; 103] *Opposite:* slow.

hat 1 *type of* **headgear**. [➡HABERDASHERY, MILLINERY, AND LINGERIE; 867] 2 *type of* **accessory**. [➡HABERDASHERY, MILLINERY, AND LINGERIE; 867]

hatch 1 *v* **devise**, come up with, originate, formulate, plan, scheme. [➡DEVELOP THEORIES AND REASON; 745] 2 *v* **give forth**, emerge, produce, break open, come out. [➡ENGENDER; 351] 3 *v* **shade**, mark, crisscross, crosshatch, highlight. [➡CREATE IMAGES; 357]

hatchback *type of* **car**. [➡BIKES, CARS, AND CARRIAGES; 1148]

hatchet *type of* **cutting tool**. [➡CUTTING TOOLS; 1119]

hatchet man (*slang*) *n* [➡VILLAINS AND THUGS; 947]

hate 1 *v* **abhor** (*formal*), detest, loathe, dislike, despise.

[➡ DISLIKE AND HATE; 578] *Opposite:* love. **2** *n* **hatred**, abhorrence, detestation, odium, revulsion, disgust, dislike, animosity, aversion, distaste, loathing. [➡ IRRITATION AND ANGER; 542] *Opposite:* love.

See Compare and Contrast at **dislike**.

hated *adj* **loathed**, detested, abhorrent (*formal*), despicable, despised, unloved, unpopular. [➡ UNPOPULAR AND UNWANTED; 259] *Opposite:* loved.

hateful *adj* **horrible**, detestable, vile, odious, unbearable, intolerable, insufferable, revolting, repulsive, disgusting, terrible. [➡ DISGUSTING AND REPULSIVE; 231] *Opposite:* lovable.

hatred *n* **hate**, abhorrence, detestation, loathing, odium, revulsion, disgust, animosity, dislike, aversion. [➡ IRRITATION AND ANGER; 542] *Opposite:* love.

See Compare and Contrast at **dislike**.

hat stand *n* [➡ FURNITURE; 858]

haughtily *adv* **proudly**, arrogantly, snootily (*informal*), conceitedly, self-importantly, condescendingly. [➡ RUDE AND HOSTILE; 626] *Opposite:* modestly.

haughtiness *n* **arrogance**, conceit, pride, snootiness (*informal*), self-importance, overconfidence, superiority, hauteur (*formal*). [➡ AFFECTATION, SELF-SATISFACTION, AND SNOBBISHNESS; 508] *Opposite:* modesty.

haughty *adj* **supercilious**, proud, snooty (*informal*), self-important, superior, stuck-up (*informal*), high and mighty, self-aggrandizing, arrogant, conceited, condescending. [➡ UNFRIENDLINESS AND UNSOCIABILITY; 505] *Opposite:* humble.

haul *v* **tow**, drag, pull, lug, tug, heave. [➡ PUSH, PULL, SLIDE; 336] *Opposite:* shove.

See Compare and Contrast at **pull**.

haul over the coals *v* **rebuke**, tell off (*informal*), castigate (*formal*), take to task, scold, bawl out (*informal*), excoriate (*formal*), reprimand, chew out (*US informal*). [➡ ACCUSE, BLAME, AND CRITICIZE; 642]

haunch **1** *n* **upper leg**, hip, buttock, thigh, loin, hunkers (*dated informal*). [➡ LEG AND FOOT; 695] **2** *n* **loin**, side, flank, hindquarter, thigh, rump. [➡ TORSO; 694]

haunt **1** *v* **walk**, roam, frequent, prowl, inhabit, skulk in, lurk in, visit. [➡ EXIST IN A PLACE; 19] *Opposite:* leave. **2** *v* **trouble**, disturb, worry, bother, preoccupy, plague, discomfit (*formal*). [➡ ANGER AND ANNOY; 570] *Opposite:* soothe. **3** *n* **meeting place**, stamping ground (*informal*), rendezvous, hangout (*informal*). [➡ PUBLIC BUILDINGS AND MEETING PLACES; 1080]

haunted **1** *adj* **spooky** (*informal*), creepy (*informal*), ghostly, weird, sinister, eerie. [➡ FRIGHTENING; 232] **2** *adj* **troubled**, preoccupied, worried, disturbed, anxious, obsessed, terrified, frightened, unnerved. [➡ CONFUSION, ANXIETY, AND WORRY; 541] *Opposite:* relaxed.

haunting *adj* **lingering**, melancholy, poignant, evocative, moving, unforgettable, memorable, lasting, recurring. [➡ PERMANENCE: WITHOUT END; 94] *Opposite:* forgettable.

hauteur (*formal*) *n* **haughtiness**, arrogance, superiority, loftiness, snobbishness, self-importance, pride, superciliousness. [➡ POMPOUS, LOUD, AND OVER-CONFIDENT; 636] *Opposite:* humility.

haut monde *n* **elite**, jet set (*informal*), crème de la crème, high society, in-crowd (*informal*), rich and famous, aristocracy, upper class, upper crust (*informal*), top brass (*informal*). [➡ IMPORTANT OR FAMOUS PEOPLE; 893] *Opposite:* masses.

have **1** *v* **possess**, own, boast, exhibit, enjoy. [➡ POSSESS; 445] *Opposite:* lack. **2** *v* **must**, need, ought to, obligate, require, be necessary. [➡ NEED AND REQUIRE; 465] **3** *v* **receive**, obtain, grasp, get, gain, come up with, take. [➡ GET; 421] *Opposite:* lose. **4** *v* **consume**, take, partake, eat, drink, devour. [➡ EAT AND NOT EAT; 711] *Opposite:* abstain. **5** *v* **think of**, come up with, devise, develop, entertain, nurse. [➡ DEVELOP THEORIES AND REASON; 745] **6** *v* **experience**, undergo, partake, engage in, take part in, enjoy. [➡ EXPERIENCE AND ENCOUNTER; 583] *Opposite:* seek. **7** *v* **be affected by**, suffer from, suffer with, be inflicted with, be ill with, be sick with, be laid up with. [➡ ILL AND SICK; 741] **8** *v* **organize**, carry out, arrange, hold, give, put together. [➡ CAUSE TO HAPPEN; 31] **9** *v* **tolerate**, put up with, allow, permit, endure, suffer. [➡ TOLERATE AND ENDURE; 767] *Opposite:* encourage. **10** *v* **produce**, bear, give birth to, bring forth. [➡ ENGENDER; 351] **11** *v* **make sure**, make certain, ensure, be sure to do. [➡ CARRY OUT AN ACTION; 270]

have a bash (*informal*) *v* [➡ ATTEMPT AN ACTION; 262]

have a brush with *v* [➡ EXPERIENCE AND ENCOUNTER; 583]

have a crack (*informal*) *v* [➡ ATTEMPT AN ACTION; 262]

have a crush on (*informal*) *v* [➡ LIKE, LOVE, VALUE, AND ENJOY; 579]

have a fit (*informal*) *v* [➡ GIVING VENT TO EMOTIONS; 680]

have a flutter (*informal*) *v* [➡ GAMBLE AND TAKE RISKS; 467]

have a go (*informal*) *v* [➡ ATTEMPT AN ACTION; 262]

have a go at (*informal*) *v* **find fault with**, blast (*informal*), flay, criticize, get angry with, reprimand, attack. [➡ ACCUSE, BLAME, AND CRITICIZE; 642] *Opposite:* praise.

have a hand in *v* **partake in**, play a part in, play a role in, participate, be part of, contribute to, be involved in, make a contribution to, have a share in. [➡ PARTICIPATE; 293]

have a high opinion of *v* [➡ LIKE, LOVE, VALUE, AND ENJOY; 579]

have a high regard for *v* [➡ LIKE, LOVE, VALUE, AND ENJOY; 579]

have a horror of *v* **fear**, dread, be frightened of, be afraid of, be scared of, be terrified of. [➡ FEARS AND PHOBIAS; 555]

have a joke with *v* [➡ JOKES AND TEASING; 675]

have a lark *v* [➡ JOKES AND TEASING; 675]

have a laugh *v* [➡ JOKES AND TEASING; 675]

have a look at *v* [➡ LOOKING AND LOOKS; 701]

have a look-see (*US*) *v* [➡ LOOKING AND LOOKS; 701]

have a shot *v* [➡ATTEMPT AN ACTION; 262]

have a soft spot for *v* [➡LIKE, LOVE, VALUE, AND ENJOY; 579]

have a stab (*informal*) *v* [➡ATTEMPT AN ACTION; 262]

have a weakness for *v* [➡LIKE, LOVE, VALUE, AND ENJOY; 579]

have a yen for *v* [➡DESIRE AND WANT; 580]

have down pat (*US*) *v* [➡KNOWLEDGE AND WISDOM; 559]

have forty winks (*informal*) *v* [➡SLEEP AND DREAM; 724]

have hysterics (*informal*) *v* [➡LAUGHTER; 650]

have in mind *v* **propose**, suggest, be thinking of, come up with, intend, mean. [➡DREAM, IMAGINE, AND FANTASIZE; 750]

have it in for *v* **persecute**, harass, bully, victimize, target, pick on. [➡DISLIKE AND HATE; 578] *Opposite:* favour.

have kittens (*informal*) *v* [➡GIVING VENT TO EMOTIONS; 680]

have knowledge of *v* [➡KNOWLEDGE AND WISDOM; 559]

haven 1 *n* **refuge**, safe place, place of safety, sanctuary, shelter, asylum, retreat. [➡SAFE BUILDINGS OR PLACES; 1092] 2 *n* (*literary*) **harbour**, port, anchorage, dock, port of call. [➡THE SEAS, OCEANS, AND SHORES; 1041]

have need of *v* [➡NEED AND REQUIRE; 465]

have-nots *n* **disadvantaged**, poor, deprived, underprivileged, underclass, unfortunates. [➡POOR PEOPLE; 896] *Opposite:* privileged.

have off pat *v* [➡KNOWLEDGE AND WISDOM; 559]

have on 1 *v* **wear**, be dressed in, be clothed in, sport (*formal*), show off, flaunt, display, adorn, put on, cover. [➡DRESS, WEAR, AND UNDRESS; 868] 2 *v* (*informal*) **tease**, pull somebody's leg (*informal*), kid, fool, joke, deceive. [➡JOKES AND TEASING; 675]

have possession of *v* [➡POSSESS; 445]

haversack *n* **rucksack**, backpack, pack, knapsack, shoulder bag, bag, duffel bag, holdall, carryall (*US*). [➡CONTAINERS, RECEPTACLES, AND PACKAGING; 1244]

have second thoughts *v* **change your mind**, go back on, reconsider, think better of it, get cold feet, renege. [➡MAKE DECISIONS AND CHOICES; 753]

have to do with *v* **relate to**, concern, involve, be regarding, be in connection with, affect, deal with, touch on. [➡BE ABOUT SOMETHING; 62]

have up (*informal*) *v* **prosecute**, try, take to court, arrest, charge, arraign. [➡ACCUSE, BLAME, AND CRITICIZE; 642]

have your eye on *v* **want**, desire, aim for, be after, hanker, covet. [➡DESIRE AND WANT; 580]

havoc *n* **chaos**, mayhem (*informal*), destruction, disorder, turmoil, disaster, confusion, devastation. [➡DISORDER AND CHAOS; 246] *Opposite:* order.

Hawaiian guitar *type of* **stringed instrument**. [➡MUSICAL INSTRUMENTS; 910]

hawk 1 *type of* **bird of prey**. [➡BIRD OF PREY; 998] 2 *v* **sell**, peddle, flog (*informal*), push (*slang*), vend, deal. [➡SELL; 442] *Opposite:* buy.

hawker *n* **dealer**, vendor, seller, pusher (*slang*), marketer, salesperson. [➡SELLER; 443] *Opposite:* client.

hawk-eyed *adj* **eagle-eyed**, sharp-eyed, sharp-sighted, observant, perceptive, quick, alert. [➡SEE; 700] *Opposite:* unobservant.

hawkish *adj* **aggressive**, belligerent, warmongering, warlike, militant, combative, pugnacious. [➡REBELLIOUSNESS AND DISOBEDIENCE; 566] *Opposite:* peaceable.

hawk moth *type of* **moth**. [➡MOTHS AND BUTTERFLIES; 1015]

hawser *n* **cable**, rope, chain, towline, tow. [➡FASTENERS, LINKS, AND NETWORKS; 1246]

hawthorn *type of* **shrub or bush**. [➡BUSHES AND SHRUBS; 1027]

hay *n* **straw**, feed, fodder, dry feed, winter feed, silage, grass. [➡ANIMAL FEED; 1167]

hayloft *type of* **storage space**. [➡STORES AND STORAGE BUILDINGS; 1087]

hayrack *n* **rack**, trough, manger, feeder. [➡CONTAINERS, RECEPTACLES, AND PACKAGING; 1244]

haywire (*informal*) *adj* **wild**, out of order, erratic, nonfunctional, on the blink (*informal*), confused, fuddled, irrational. [➡DISORDER AND CHAOS; 246] *Opposite:* functional.

hazard 1 *n* **danger**, threat, risk, peril, deathtrap (*informal*), menace. [➡DANGER; 236] *Opposite:* safeguard. 2 *v* **suggest**, proffer, put forward, propose. [➡SUGGEST, HINT, AND COMMENT; 613] 3 *v* **risk**, take a chance, chance, gamble, venture, endanger, jeopardize, imperil (*formal*), put at risk. [➡GAMBLE AND TAKE RISKS; 467] *Opposite:* protect.

hazardous *adj* **dangerous**, unsafe, harmful, risky, lethal, perilous, menacing, precarious, threatening. [➡DANGEROUS; 237] *Opposite:* safe.

hazardousness *n* [➡DANGER; 236]

haze 1 *n* **mist**, fog, miasma, cloud, vapour, smog, smoke. [➡CLOUDY AND RAINY WEATHER; 1052] 2 *v* **become cloudy**, mist over, cloud over, darken. [➡CLOUDY AND RAINY WEATHER; 1052] *Opposite:* clear.

hazel *type of* **brown**. [➡COLOURS; 1223]

hazelnut *type of* **nut**. [➡NUTS; 1184]

hazily *adv* **indistinctly**, vaguely, dimly, fuzzily, imprecisely, unclearly, obscurely. [➡VAGUENESS; 244] *Opposite:* clearly.

haziness 1 *n* **mistiness**, fogginess, cloudiness, obscurity, smokiness, dimness, fuzziness. [➡CLOUDY AND RAINY WEATHER; 1052] *Opposite:* clarity. 2 *n* **confusion**, muddle, uncertainty, indistinctness, vagueness, obscurity. [➡VAGUENESS; 244] *Opposite:* clarity.

hazy 1 *adj* **misty**, foggy, cloudy, obscure, blurred, out-of-focus, dim, smoky, fuzzy. [➡CLOUDY AND RAINY WEATHER; 1052] *Opposite:* clear. 2 *adj* **unclear**, indistinct, muddled, confused, obscure, imprecise, vague. [➡VAGUENESS; 244] *Opposite:* distinct.

head 1 *n* [➡ EDUCATORS; 840] 2 *n* **skull**, cranium, pate (*archaic or humorous*), bonce (*informal*), dome, nut (*informal*), noodle (*slang*), crown, bean (*US slang*). [➡ HEAD; 693] 3 *n* **mind**, intelligence, intellect, sense, brain, brains, grey matter (*informal*), wit. [➡ POSITIVE INTELLECTUAL CHARACTERISTICS; 525] 4 *n* **boss**, leader, chief, president, controller, supervisor, master. [➡ BOSSES AND MANAGEMENT; 965] 5 *n* **top**, peak, crown, promontory, apex, height, summit. [➡ EXTREMITIES OF PHYSICAL OBJECTS; 1249] *Opposite:* base. 6 *n* **introduction**, beginning, start, opening, heading, header. [➡ BEGINNING; 53] *Opposite:* end. 7 *v* **go**, move, journey, advance, proceed, commence (*formal*), set out, travel. [➡ PROCEED AND GO; 306] 8 *v* **control**, rule, regulate, have control over, lead, supervise, command, be in charge, direct. [➡ BE IN CHARGE; 271] *Opposite:* support. 9 *v* **come first**, lead, be first, precede, be foremost. [➡ ACCOMPANY AND FOLLOW; 338] *Opposite:* follow.

head

◆ *parts of a head*
crown, ear, earlobe, face, forehead, hair, nape, scalp, temple

headache (*informal*) *n* **annoyance**, pain, bother, bore, nuisance, problem, worry, difficulty. [➡ NUISANCES; 254] *Opposite:* relief.

headband *n* **hairband**, Alice band, sweatband, bandeau, circlet, headdress. [➡ HABERDASHERY, MILLINERY, AND LINGERIE; 867]

headboard *n* [➡ FURNITURE; 858]

head-butt 1 *v* **hit**, strike, butt, jab, whack, thump. [➡ PHYSICAL ATTACK AND PUNISHMENT; 416] 2 *n* **blow**, hit, butt, jab, whack, thump. [➡ PHYSICAL ATTACK AND PUNISHMENT; 416]

headdress *type of* **headgear**. [➡ HABERDASHERY, MILLINERY, AND LINGERIE; 867]

header 1 *n* **shot**, pass, goal. [➡ SPORTS TERMS; 877] 2 *n* **heading**, title, caption, slogan, legend, banner, running head, running title, headpiece. [➡ PARTS OF BOOKS AND DOCUMENTS; 594] *Opposite:* footer.

headfirst *adv* **headlong**, head over heels, diving, pitching, plunging, somersaulting. [➡ DIRECTION OF MOTION; 346]

headgear

◆ *types of headgear*
Alice band, balaclava, bandeau, baseball cap, bearskin, beret, biretta, bobble hat, busby, cap, chaplet, cloth cap, cowl, crash helmet, fez, glengarry, hairband, hard hat, hat, headband, headdress, headscarf, headsquare, helmet, hood, mantilla, mobcap, nightcap, skullcap, tam-o'-shanter, tippet, topee, turban, yarmulke, yashmak

◆ *types of hat*
boater, bonnet, bowler hat, cloche, cowboy hat, deerstalker, derby (*US*), fedora, homburg, Panama hat, picture hat, pillbox, porkpie hat, rain hat, sailor hat, sombrero, sou'wester, stovepipe hat, sunhat, ten-gallon hat, top hat, topper, toque, trilby

head honcho (*US slang*) *n* [➡ IMPORTANT OR FAMOUS PEOPLE; 893]

headily 1 *adv* **exhilaratingly**, thrillingly, invigoratingly, excitingly, stimulatingly, giddily. [➡ EMOTIONALLY PLEASANT; 188] *Opposite:* dully. 2 *adv* **intoxicatingly** (*formal*), pungently, aromatically, strongly, richly, spicily, piquantly, potently. [➡ STRENGTH; 202] *Opposite:* mildly. 3 *adv* **impetuously**, imprudently (*formal*), impulsively, recklessly, rashly, hastily. [➡ INCAUTIOUS AND CARELESS; 284] *Opposite:* cautiously.

heading 1 *n* **title**, caption, headline, banner, header, slogan, legend. [➡ PARTS OF BOOKS AND DOCUMENTS; 594] 2 *n* **direction**, bearing, course, route, trajectory. [➡ NAVIGATION; 1140]

headland *n* **promontory**, cape, peninsula, point, bluff, cliff. [➡ THE SEAS, OCEANS, AND SHORES; 1041]

headlight *type of* **external feature**. [➡ VEHICLES; 1144]

headline 1 *n* **caption**, banner, title, heading, header, legend. [➡ NEWSPAPERS; 606] 2 *v* (*US*) **feature**, present, top, introduce, advertise, publicize, promote. [➡ ENTERTAINMENT; 872] 3 *v* (*US*) **top the bill**, feature, star, head, top, lead. [➡ THE PERFORMING ARTS; 904]

headlong 1 *adv* **headfirst**, head over heels, diving, pitching, plunging, tumbling, somersaulting. [➡ DIRECTION OF MOTION; 346] 2 *adv* **impetuously**, rashly, recklessly, hastily, hurriedly, impulsively, abruptly, precipitously. [➡ HAPPENING QUICKLY; 104] *Opposite:* carefully. 3 *adj* **impetuous**, rash, reckless, hasty, hurried, impulsive, abrupt, precipitous. [➡ HAPPENING QUICKLY; 104] *Opposite:* considered.

head louse *type of* **parasitic insect**. [➡ PARASITES; 1017]

headmaster *n* [➡ EDUCATORS; 840]

headmistress *n* [➡ EDUCATORS; 840]

head off 1 *v* **divert**, reroute, redirect, turn back, intercept, turn aside. [➡ CHANGE DIRECTION OF MOTION; 345] 2 *v* **forestall**, block, prevent, stop, avert, fend off. [➡ AVOID OR ESCAPE CONTACT; 419] *Opposite:* encourage. 3 *v* **leave**, go away, depart, take off, commence (*formal*), set off, go forward. [➡ ABSENT ONESELF; 8] *Opposite:* remain.

head office *n* **headquarters**, HQ, control centre, command centre, centre of operations, nerve centre, main centre. [➡ PLACE OF EMPLOYMENT; 832]

head of government *n* **leader**, ruler, prime minister, president, premier, head of state. [➡ POLITICAL OFFICES AND POLITICIANS; 808]

head of state *n* **premier**, president, leader, ruler, sovereign, monarch, chancellor, head of government. [➡ POLITICAL OFFICES AND POLITICIANS; 808]

head-on 1 *adv* **straight on**, straight ahead, frontally, directly, full steam ahead, full speed ahead. [➡ DIRECTION OF MOTION; 346] 2 *adv* **unflinchingly**, uncompromisingly, with guns blazing, confrontationally, bluntly, aggressively. [➡ RUDE AND HOSTILE; 626] *Opposite:* indirectly. 3 *adj* **face-to-face**, frontal, uncompromising, direct, confrontational, blunt, aggressive. [➡ CLOSENESS; 160] *Opposite:* indirect.

head over heels 1 *adv* **headfirst**, headlong, diving, plunging, pitching, somersaulting. [➡ DIRECTION OF MOTION; 346] 2 *adv* **deeply**, passionately, rapturously, madly, desperately, wildly, completely. [➡ APPRECIATION AND GRATITUDE; 536]

head over heels in love *adj* [➡APPRECIATION AND GRATITUDE; 536]

headphones *n* **phones** (*informal*), earphones, earpiece, headset, receiver. [➡AUDIO EQUIPMENT; 1138]

headpiece 1 *n* **header**, heading, design, ornament, decoration, pattern. [➡ORNAMENTS AND DECORATIONS; 1247] 2 *part of* **audio equipment.** [➡AUDIO EQUIPMENT; 1138]

headquarters *n* **head office**, HQ, control centre, command centre, centre of operations, nerve centre. [➡PLACE OF EMPLOYMENT; 832]

headrest *type of* **internal feature.** [➡INTERNAL PARTS OF A VEHICLE; 1145]

headscarf *type of* **headgear.** [➡HABERDASHERY, MILLINERY, AND LINGERIE; 867]

headset *n* **headphones**, receiver, earpiece, earphones, telephone, phone. [➡AUDIO EQUIPMENT; 1138]

headship *n* **leadership**, direction, management, control, regime, guidance, authority. [➡QUALIFICATIONS; 843]

headsquare *type of* **headgear.** [➡HABERDASHERY, MILLINERY, AND LINGERIE; 867]

head start *n* **advantage**, edge, lead, helping hand, help, boost, flying start. [➡ADVANTAGE; 213] *Opposite:* disadvantage.

headstone *n* **tombstone**, gravestone, stone, slab, memorial, memorial stone. [➡BURIAL PLACES AND ACCESSORIES; 930]

headstrong *adj* **impetuous**, impulsive, reckless, rash, wilful, determined, stubborn, obstinate, intractable (*formal*), pigheaded. [➡UNWILLINGNESS AND STUBBORNNESS; 565] *Opposite:* docile.

head teacher *n* **principal**, head, headmaster, headmistress, rector. [➡EDUCATORS; 840]

head-to-head 1 *adv* **adjacent**, next to, end-to-end, in line, together. [➡CLOSENESS; 160] 2 *adj* **one-to-one**, face-to-face, direct, intimate, personal, individual. [➡CLOSENESS; 160] 3 *n* **encounter**, meeting, discussion, dialogue, confrontation, showdown. [➡NEGOTIATION AND DEBATE; 46]

headway *n* **progress**, movement, advance, progression, improvement, inroads, advancement. [➡SUCCESS; 82]

headwind *n* **breeze**, wind, gale, gust. [➡WINDY AND STORMY WEATHER; 1053]

heady 1 *adj* **exhilarating**, thrilling, invigorating, exciting, stimulating, giddy. [➡EMOTIONALLY PLEASANT; 188] *Opposite:* dull. 2 *adj* **intoxicating** (*formal*), pungent, aromatic, strong, rich, spicy, piquant, potent. [➡SMELL AND SMELLING; 706] *Opposite:* mild. 3 *adj* **impetuous**, imprudent (*formal*), impulsive, reckless, rash, hasty. [➡LACK OF COMMITMENT AND UNRELIABILITY; 510] *Opposite:* cautious.

heal 1 *v* **cure**, restore to health, make well, nurse, mend, repair. [➡TAKE CARE OF AND SPOIL; 301] *Opposite:* worsen. 2 *v* **make good**, settle, patch up, reconcile, set right, restore, rebuild, rectify. [➡IMPROVE SOMETHING; 375] *Opposite:* damage.

healer *n* **doctor**, faith healer, naturopath, homeopath, therapist, shaman, witch doctor. [➡PEOPLE WHO WORK IN MEDICINE; 848]

healing 1 *n* **recovery**, restoration, recuperation, therapy, treatment, reinvigoration. [➡HEALING; 731] 2 *adj* **curative**, remedial, therapeutic, medicinal, curing, restorative, soothing, health-giving. [➡HEALING; 731]

health *n* **wellbeing**, fitness, condition, healthiness, strength, vigour, shape, physical condition. [➡PHYSICAL STATES; 735]

healthful *adj* **healthy**, good for your health, good for you, beneficial, wholesome, nourishing, nutritious, salubrious (*formal*), health-giving, advantageous. [➡CLEAN; 1232] *Opposite:* unhealthy.

healthiness *n* **health**, good condition, robustness, wellbeing, fitness, vigour. [➡PHYSICAL STATES; 735]

healthy 1 *adj* **fit**, well, strong, vigorous, in good physical shape, hale and hearty, in the pink (*dated*), in fine fettle. [➡FIT AND STRONG; 737] *Opposite:* sick. 2 *adj* **healthful**, good for your health, good for you, beneficial, nourishing, wholesome, nutritious, salubrious (*formal*), health-giving, advantageous. [➡CLEAN; 1232] *Opposite:* unhealthy.

heap 1 *n* **mound**, pile, stack, mountain, bundle, mass, load. [➡MANY, MUCH, LARGE AMOUNT; 117] 2 *v* **pile up**, pile, layer, mound, mass, build up, stack, collect, accumulate, arrange, gather. [➡COMBINE AND MIX; 401]

heaps (*informal*) 1 *n* **loads** (*informal*), masses (*informal*), lots, tons (*informal*), piles (*informal*), oodles (*informal*). [➡MANY, MUCH, LARGE AMOUNT; 117] 2 *adv* **a lot**, very much, a great deal, loads, lots, tons (*informal*), masses (*informal*). [➡MANY, MUCH, LARGE AMOUNT; 117]

heap up 1 *v* **pile up**, pile, mound, mass, stack, build up. [➡COMBINE AND MIX; 401] 2 *v* **collect**, amass, gather, accumulate, stockpile, hoard. [➡STORE AND KEEP; 454]

hear 1 *v* **make out**, catch, get, overhear, pick up, perceive. [➡HEAR; 708] 2 *v* **gather**, learn, find out, understand, pick up, get to know, get wind of. [➡LEARN AND DISCOVER; 763] 3 *v* **listen to**, catch, get, pick up, receive. [➡LISTEN AND LISTENERS; 709] 4 *v* **understand**, pay attention to, attend to, heed, take notice of, hearken (*archaic*), listen to, get. [➡LISTEN AND LISTENERS; 709] *Opposite:* miss. 5 *v* **sit in judgment**, try, judge, preside over, examine, consider. [➡TRIAL, PUNISHMENT, AND LEGAL OUTCOMES; 819]

hear from *v* **have news of**, have contact with, be in touch with, be contacted by, have a call from, have a letter from. [➡INITIATE AND ESTABLISH COMMUNICATION; 681]

hearing 1 *n* **earshot**, range, hearing distance, reach. [➡CLOSENESS; 160] 2 *n* **trial**, inquiry, investigation, examination, consideration. [➡TRIAL, PUNISHMENT, AND LEGAL OUTCOMES; 819]

hearing-impaired *adj* [➡HEAR; 708]

hearken (*archaic*) *v* [➡LISTEN AND LISTENERS; 709]

hear of *v* **countenance** (*formal*), consider, conceive, tolerate, allow (*formal*), permit, admit. [➡TOLERATE AND ENDURE; 767]

hearsay *n* **rumour**, gossip, tittle-tattle, idle talk, word of mouth, scuttlebutt (*US slang*). [➡GOSSIP; 679] *Opposite:* fact.

hearse *type of* **commercial or industrial vehicle.** [➡VEHICLES; 1144]

heart 1 *n* **core**, heart of hearts, mind, sentiment, soul, nature, temperament, mood, emotion, spirit. [➡TEMPERAMENT AND BEHAVIOUR; 493] 2 *n* **compassion**, sympathy, empathy, feeling, sensitivity, kindness, tenderness, affection, concern. [➡COMPASSION AND FORGIVENESS; 552] *Opposite:* cruelty. 3 *n* **spirit**, courage, bravery, fortitude, pluck, resolution. [➡COURAGE; 499] 4 *type of* **rounded shape.** [➡ROUNDED SHAPE; 1217]

heartache *n* **sorrow**, sadness, distress, anguish, despair, despondency, misery. [➡SADNESS, DISTRESS, AND DESPAIR; 540] *Opposite:* joy.

heart attack (*informal*) *n* **fit**, stroke, nervous breakdown, seizure, breakdown, coronary (*informal*), shock. [➡ILLNESSES AND DISORDERS; 733]

heartbreak *n* **grief**, despair, anguish, sorrow, pain, misery, suffering. [➡SADNESS, DISTRESS, AND DESPAIR; 540] *Opposite:* joy.

heartbreaking *adj* **tragic**, distressing, upsetting, sad, heartrending, moving, poignant, pitiful, pathetic, painful. [➡EMOTIONALLY UNPLEASANT AND UPSETTING; 228] *Opposite:* uplifting.

heartbroken *adj* **inconsolable**, forlorn, despairing, dejected, disconsolate, distraught, brokenhearted. [➡SADNESS, DISTRESS, AND DESPAIR; 540] *Opposite:* thrilled.

heartburn *n* **stomach pain**, acid stomach, indigestion, dyspepsia (*technical*), colic. [➡DISORDERS OF THE DIGESTIVE SYSTEM; 714]

hearten *v* **encourage**, inspire, raise your spirits, uplift, buoy, cheer up, cheer, gladden. [➡ENCOURAGE; 577] *Opposite:* dishearten.

heartened *adj* [➡CALMNESS, CONFIDENCE, AND COMPOSURE; 537]

heartening *adj* **encouraging**, promising, cheering, optimistic, reassuring, hopeful, positive, comforting. [➡CALMING; 189] *Opposite:* disheartening.

heartfelt *adj* **sincere**, genuine, earnest, warm, cordial, deepest, honest, profound, wholehearted. [➡TRUE AND REAL; 172] *Opposite:* superficial.

hearth 1 *n* **fireside**, fireplace, inglenook, grate. [➡ALCOVES, CUBICLES, AND COMPARTMENTS; 1095] 2 *n* **family life**, home sweet home, home, household. [➡THE FAMILY; 956]

hearth rug *n* [➡SOFT FURNISHINGS, LINEN, AND DRAPERY; 860]

heartily 1 *adv* **enthusiastically**, with gusto, energetically, vigorously, emphatically, wholeheartedly. [➡WITH ENTHUSIASM; 287] *Opposite:* feebly. 2 *adv* **jovially**, enthusiastically, cheerfully, warmly, genially, wholeheartedly. [➡GOOD-TEMPERED AND HUMOROUS; 628] 3 *adv* **thoroughly**, extremely, excessively, completely, utterly, wholly, totally, absolutely, very much. [➡TO A GREAT EXTENT; 130]

heartiness *n* **vigour**, enthusiasm, gusto, energy, cheerfulness, fervour, robustness. [➡ENERGY AND ENTHUSIASM; 497]

heartland *n* **centre**, core, hub, nucleus, focus, middle. [➡COUNTRIES AND REGIONS; 1066]

heartless *adj* **callous**, cruel, unfeeling, cold-blooded, merciless, pitiless, unkind. [➡SELFISH AND UNKIND; 506] *Opposite:* caring.

heartlessness *n* **cruelty**, callousness, cold-bloodedness, mercilessness, unkindness, pitilessness. [➡SELFISH AND UNKIND; 506] *Opposite:* kindness.

heartrending *adj* **heartbreaking**, tragic, distressing, pitiful, pathetic, upsetting, sad, poignant, moving, painful. [➡EMOTIONALLY UNPLEASANT AND UPSETTING; 228] *Opposite:* uplifting.

heart-searching *n* **soul-searching**, self-examination, self-analysis, introspection, deep thought, thought. [➡THINK AND REFLECT; 744]

heart-to-heart 1 *adj* **frank**, honest, open, candid, forthright, intimate, personal. [➡HONEST AND OPEN; 631] 2 *n* **talk**, tête-à-tête, one-to-one, chat, discussion, natter (*informal*), chinwag (*informal*). [➡INFORMAL COMMUNICATION; 45]

heartwarming *adj* **cheering**, positive, encouraging, heartening, pleasing, cheery, gratifying, uplifting, touching. [➡EMOTIONALLY PLEASANT; 188] *Opposite:* depressing.

hearty 1 *adj* **enthusiastic**, sincere, wholehearted, emphatic, vigorous, energetic, robust. [➡ENERGY AND ENTHUSIASM; 497] *Opposite:* half-hearted. 2 *adj* **jovial**, cheerful, warm, genial, welcoming, wholehearted. [➡GOOD-TEMPERED AND HUMOROUS; 628] 3 *adj* **strong**, sincere, abiding, deep, profound, deep-rooted, passionate. [➡HONEST AND OPEN; 631] 4 *adj* **substantial**, nourishing, filling, plentiful, abundant, ample. [➡FOOD; 1166] *Opposite:* meagre.

heat 1 *n* **warmth**, high temperature, temperature, hotness, warmness. [➡TEMPERATURE: HOT; 1228] *Opposite:* coldness. 2 *n* **passion**, emotion, fervour, ardour, intensity, excitement, stress, zeal, torridness. [➡INSECURITY AND LOSS OF COMPOSURE; 545] *Opposite:* indifference. 3 *v* **warm**, heat up, warm through, warm up, reheat, roast, boil, cook, microwave. [➡COOKING AND FOOD PREPARATION; 354] *Opposite:* cool.

heated *adj* **animated**, frenzied, impassioned, fiery, intense, excited, passionate, worked up (*informal*), angry. [➡ENTHUSIASTIC AND INQUISITIVE; 629] *Opposite:* calm.

heater *n* **fire**, stove, radiator, electric fire, electric heater, space heater, boiler. [➡HEATING, REFRIGERATION, AND VENTILATION; 1141]

heath *n* [➡DESERTS AND PLAINS; 1045]

heather *type of* **shrub or bush.** [➡BUSHES AND SHRUBS; 1027]

heathland *n* [➡DESERTS AND PLAINS; 1045]

heating 1 *n* **warming**, warming up, cooking, heating up, reheating, roasting (*informal*), boiling, microwaving. [➡COOKING AND FOOD PREPARATION; 354] 2 *n* **central heating**, heating system, solar heating, space heating, boiler. [➡HEATING, REFRIGERATION, AND VENTILATION; 1141]

heating

◆ *types of heating appliance*
boiler, electric fire, heater, immersion heater, quartz heater, radiator, space heater, storage heater

heat rash *n* [➡CONDITIONS AFFECTING THE SKIN; 722]

heat wave *n* **hot spell**, scorcher (*informal*), Indian summer, drought. [➡HOT WEATHER; 1050]

heave 1 *v* **haul**, drag, pull, yank, lug, tug. [➡PUSH, PULL, SLIDE; 336] *Opposite:* push. 2 *v* (*informal*) **toss**, chuck (*informal*), dump, throw, hurl (*slang*), pitch, fling. [➡THROW SOMETHING; 335] 3 *v* **rise and fall**, throb, palpitate, swell, surge. [➡BOUNCE, UNDULATE, AND VIBRATE; 309]

See Compare and Contrast at **throw**.

heave into view (*literary*) *v* [➡ARRIVE; 12]

heaven 1 *n* **bliss**, paradise, ecstasy, rapture, cloud nine, dreamland, heaven on earth. [➡RELIGIOUS CONCEPTS; 777] *Opposite:* hell. 2 *n* **air**, sky, cosmos, ether (*literary*), firmament (*literary*). [➡THE EARTH'S ATMOSPHERE; 1040]

heavenly 1 *adj* **divine**, holy, angelic, cherubic, saintly, blessed, spiritual. [➡RELIGIOUS CONCEPTS; 777] 2 *adj* **wonderful**, blissful, delightful, divine (*informal or humorous*), lovely, fantastic. [➡EMOTIONALLY PLEASANT; 188] *Opposite:* dreadful.

heavenly body [➡CELESTIAL BODIES; 1060]

heavenly body

◆ *types of heavenly body*
asteroid, bolide, comet, falling star, fireball, meteor, meteorite, moon, planet, shooting star

heaven on earth *n* [➡PLEASANT SITUATIONS; 74]

heavens (*informal*) *interj* [➡EXPRESSIONS OF SURPRISE; 547]

heavens to Betsy (*US informal*) *interj* [➡EXPRESSIONS OF SURPRISE; 547]

heavenwards *adv* **upward**, skyward, up, into the air, into the sky, to the heavens. [➡DIRECTION OF MOTION; 346] *Opposite:* earthwards.

heavily 1 *adv* **weightily**, forcefully, roughly, violently, brutally, powerfully, strongly, noisily. [➡STRENGTH; 202] *Opposite:* gently. 2 *adv* **slowly**, clumsily, laboriously, tiresomely, tediously, tiringly. [➡BORING AND UNINTERESTING; 235] *Opposite:* swiftly. 3 *adv* **greatly**, deeply, seriously, profoundly, comprehensively, severely, worryingly, cripplingly. [➡TO A GREAT EXTENT; 130] *Opposite:* slightly. 4 *adv* **sadly**, resignedly, sorrowfully, tearfully, exhaustedly, wearily, miserably, dispiritedly, dejectedly. [➡BAD-TEMPERED AND HUMOURLESS; 627] *Opposite:* cheerfully.

heaviness *n* **weight**, bulk, mass, substance, solidity, weightiness, immensity. [➡WEIGHT: HEAVY; 1204] *Opposite:* lightness.

heaving *adj* **crowded**, jam-packed (*informal*), bursting at the seams, full to overflowing, busy, packed, chock-a-block (*informal*), chock-full (*informal*). [➡FULL; 1238]

heavy 1 *adj* **weighty**, hefty, substantial, heavyweight. [➡WEIGHT: HEAVY; 1204] *Opposite:* light. 2 *adj* **thick**, dense, full, viscous, compact, opaque. [➡VISUAL TEXTURE; 1220] *Opposite:* thin. 3 *adj* **demanding**, onerous, burdensome, tiring, tedious, difficult, arduous, oppressive. [➡DIFFICULTY AND COMPLEXITY; 243] *Opposite:* easy. 4 *adj* **busy**, packed, tight, hectic, frenetic, difficult, intense. [➡DIFFICULTY AND COMPLEXITY; 243] *Opposite:* light. 5 *adj* **powerful**, forceful, violent, hard, jarring, crippling. [➡IMPORTANT; 195] *Opposite:* weak. 6 *adj* **serious**, profound, grave, deep, intense, weighty, important. [➡IMPORTANT; 195] *Opposite:* trivial. 7 *n* (*slang*) **thug**, hooligan (*informal*), minder (*informal*), bodyguard, bad guy, baddie (*informal*). [➡VILLAINS AND THUGS; 947]

heavy-duty 1 *adj* **hard-wearing**, forceful, tough, durable, long-lasting, strong. [➡STRENGTH; 202] *Opposite:* lightweight. 2 *adj* (*informal*) **serious**, important, intensive, intense, heavy (*slang*), high-level. [➡IMPORTANT; 195]

heavy-going *adj* [➡DIFFICULTY AND COMPLEXITY; 243]

heavy-handed 1 *adj* **clumsy**, rough, careless, ham-fisted (*informal*), awkward, butterfingered (*informal*), uncoordinated, gauche. [➡UNSKILLED; 530] *Opposite:* dexterous. 2 *adj* **oppressive**, harsh, forceful, hard, severe, despotic, brutal. [➡BOSSY AND OVERBEARING; 517]

heavy-handedness 1 *n* **clumsiness**, roughness, carelessness, ham-fistedness (*informal*), awkwardness, gaucheness. [➡AGILITY OF THE BODY; 477] 2 *n* **oppressiveness**, harshness, forcefulness, severity, brutality. [➡BOSSY AND OVERBEARING; 517]

heavy-hearted (*literary*) *adj* **unhappy**, sad, miserable, downcast, dispirited, low, blue (*informal*), depressed. [➡SADNESS, DISTRESS, AND DESPAIR; 540] *Opposite:* cheerful.

heavy labour *n* [➡HARD WORK OR EFFORT; 299]

heavy-laden (*literary*) *adj* **burdened**, encumbered, weighed down, troubled, distraught. [➡SADNESS, DISTRESS, AND DESPAIR; 540] *Opposite:* carefree.

heavyset *adj* **stocky**, well-built, sturdy, solid, thickset, bulky, chunky (*informal*), burly, hefty, brawny, beefy. [➡BUILD; 478] *Opposite:* slight.

heavy shower *n* [➡CLOUDY AND RAINY WEATHER; 1052]

heavyweight 1 *n* **muscleman**, bodyguard, bouncer, tough, toughie (*informal*), heavy (*slang*). [➡VILLAINS AND THUGS; 947] 2 *n* (*informal*) **big name**, leader, leading light, big cheese (*slang*), big shot (*informal*), big gun (*informal*), key player, colossus, titan. [➡IMPORTANT OR FAMOUS PEOPLE; 893]

heavy with child (*archaic or literary*) *adj* [➡REPRODUCTION AND HEREDITY; 726]

Hebrew *type of* **alphabet**. [➡SYMBOLS, SIGNS, AND NUMBERS; 597]

heckle *v* **jeer**, barrack (*informal*), interrupt, butt in, boo, shout down. [➡ACCUSE, BLAME, AND CRITICIZE; 642] *Opposite:* cheer.

heckler *n* **critic**, jeerer, interrupter, protester, barracker (*informal*), troublemaker. [➡UNCOOPERATIVE OR REBELLIOUS PERSON; 567] *Opposite:* supporter.

heckling *n* **criticism**, barracking (*informal*), jeering, interruption, protest, repartee, banter. [➡UNFAVOURABLE NONVERBAL RESPONSES; 655]

hectic *adj* **frantic**, frenzied, excited, confused, chaotic, frenetic, feverish, wild. [➡DISORDER AND CHAOS; 246] *Opposite:* calm.

hector *v* **bully**, intimidate, harass, badger, hassle (*informal*), push around (*informal*). [➡ACCUSE, BLAME, AND CRITICIZE; 642]

hedge 1 *n* **hedgerow**, privet, border, verge, windbreak, shrubbery. [➡BUSHES AND SHRUBS; 1027] 2 *v* **ring**, fence, enclose, protect, encircle, surround. [➡EXIST IN CLOSE PROXIMITY; 21] *Opposite:* expose. 3 *v* **evade**, prevaricate, fudge (*informal*), beat about the bush. [➡NOT PAY ATTENTION; 765]

hedgehog *type of* **small mammal**. [➡SMALL MAMMAL; 990]

hedgerow *n* **hedge**, border, verge, windbreak, shrubbery. [➡BUSHES AND SHRUBS; 1027]

hedge sparrow *type of* **songbird**. [➡SONGBIRD; 1003]

hedonism *n* **pleasure-seeking**, high-living, intemperance, self-indulgence, profligacy, self-satisfaction, debauchery, decadence. [➡PLEASURE-SEEKING AND EXCESS; 885] *Opposite:* asceticism.

hedonist *n* **pleasure-seeker**, debauchee (*formal*), rake, degenerate, roué (*literary*), sybarite, epicure. [➡PLEASURE-SEEKERS AND HEDONISTS; 886] *Opposite:* ascetic.

hedonistic *adj* **self-indulgent**, pleasure-seeking, profligate, debauched, sybaritic, epicurean, decadent. [➡PLEASURE-SEEKING AND EXCESS; 885] *Opposite:* ascetic.

heebie-jeebies (*slang*) *n* **shakes**, willies (*informal*), butterflies (*informal*), nerves (*informal*), bad vibe, anxiety. [➡FEAR AND PANIC; 544]

heed 1 *v* **pay attention to**, listen to, take note of, observe, notice, regard, note, follow. [➡PAY ATTENTION; 766] *Opposite:* ignore. 2 *n* **attention**, notice, note, regard, mindfulness, care, attentiveness. [➡ATTENTION AND ATTENTIVENESS; 764] *Opposite:* disregard.

heedful *adj* **mindful**, vigilant, watchful, thoughtful, careful, attentive. [➡POSITIVE IMPATIENCE, ENTHUSIASM, AND ALERTNESS; 538] *Opposite:* heedless.

heedless *adj* **neglectful**, oblivious, without regard, rash, reckless, careless, unmindful, thoughtless. [➡NEUTRALITY AND INDIFFERENCE; 554] *Opposite:* careful.

heedlessness *n* **thoughtlessness**, recklessness, carelessness, neglectfulness, rashness, obliviousness. [➡NEUTRALITY AND INDIFFERENCE; 554] *Opposite:* carefulness.

heel 1 *v* **repair**, resole, mend, fix, reinforce, patch up. [➡REPAIR AND MEND; 377] 2 *part of* **leg or foot**. [➡LEG AND FOOT; 695] 3 *part of* **arm or hand**. [➡ARM AND HAND; 696]

heel in *v* **dig in**, put in, bury, cover. [➡CAUSE TO DISAPPEAR; 6]

heft (*US*) 1 *v* **lift**, hoist, heave, raise, raise up, swing. [➡MOVE SOMETHING: UPWARDS; 329] 2 *n* **weight**, bulk, size, mass, immensity, heaviness. [➡WEIGHT: HEAVY; 1204] *Opposite:* lightness.

heftiness *n* **robustness**, burliness, stoutness, heaviness, stockiness, bulkiness, sturdiness, beefiness. [➡WEIGHT: HEAVY; 1204]

hefty 1 *adj* **bulky**, large, robust, sturdy, stocky, stout, beefy, brawny, thickset. [➡BUILD; 478] *Opposite:* slight. 2 *adj* **heavy**, weighty, substantial, cumbersome, awkward. [➡WEIGHT: HEAVY; 1204]

hegemony (*formal*) *n* **domination**, control, supremacy, dominion, power, authority. [➡STRENGTH; 202]

heifer 1 *type of* **female animal**. [➡MALE OR FEMALE ANIMAL; 978] 2 *type of* **young animal**. [➡YOUNG ANIMAL; 977]

height 1 *n* **tallness**, stature, altitude, loftiness, elevation. [➡HEIGHT: HIGH; 1202] *Opposite:* depth. 2 *n* **pinnacle**, summit, peak, top, apex, acme, zenith. [➡EXTREMITIES OF PHYSICAL OBJECTS; 1249] *Opposite:* nadir.

heighten *v* **intensify**, amplify, increase, enhance, add to, reinforce. [➡CHANGE OF INTENSITY: MORE; 395]

heinous *adj* **monstrous**, atrocious, odious, dreadful, shocking, scandalous, wicked, evil, terrible. [➡MORALLY BAD; 776]

heir *n* **successor**, inheritor, beneficiary, legatee, recipient, heritor (*archaic or technical*). [➡YOUNGER GENERATION RELATIVES; 958]

heirloom *n* **family treasure**, inheritance, valuable, gift, bequest, treasure. [➡BEQUEATH AND BEQUESTS; 433]

heist (*US slang*) *n* **robbery**, theft, raid, swoop, attack, lift (*informal*). [➡CRIMES; 817]

helical *adj* [➡ROUNDED SHAPE; 1217]

helicopter *type of* **civil aircraft**. [➡AIRCRAFT; 1147]

helicopter gunship *type of* **military aircraft**. [➡AIRCRAFT; 1147]

helideck *n* **landing pad**, helipad, heliport, helistop, landing strip, platform, runway. [➡AIRWAYS; 1108]

heliotrope *type of* **purple**. [➡COLOURS; 1223]

helipad *n* **landing pad**, helideck, heliport, helistop, landing strip, platform, runway. [➡AIRWAYS; 1108]

heliport *n* **landing pad**, helideck, helipad, helistop, landing strip, platform, runway. [➡AIRWAYS; 1108]

helistop *n* **landing pad**, helideck, heliport, helipad, landing strip, platform, runway. [➡AIRWAYS; 1108]

helium *type of* **gas**. [➡GASES; 1274]

helix *n* **spiral**, coil, corkscrew, spring, ringlet. [➡ROUNDED SHAPE; 1217]

hell 1 *n* (*formal*) **hades** (*informal*), underworld, nether world, perdition, inferno, abyss. [➡RELIGIOUS CONCEPTS; 777] *Opposite:* heaven. 2 *n* **torture**, misery, torment, agony, anguish, nightmare, suffering, pain. [➡DIFFICULT SITUATIONS; 72] *Opposite:* ecstasy.

hello *interj* **greetings**, hi (*informal*), good morning, good day, morning, good afternoon, ciao (*informal*), howdy (*US informal*). [➡GREETINGS, FAREWELLS, AND SALUTATIONS; 660] *Opposite:* goodbye.

helm *part of* **ship or boat**. [➡PARTS OF A SHIP OR BOAT; 1150]

helmet 1 *type of* **sports equipment**. [➡SPORTS EQUIPMENT; 879] 2 *type of* **headgear**. [➡HABERDASHERY, MILLINERY, AND LINGERIE; 867]

help 1 *v* **aid**, assist, help out, lend a hand, be of assistance, facilitate, rally round, abet. [➡HELP; 294] *Opposite:* hinder. 2 *v* **relieve**, improve, ameliorate (*formal*), ease, alleviate, amend, better. [➡IMPROVE SOMETHING; 375] *Opposite:* worsen. 3 *v* **avoid**, evade, dodge, stop, refrain from, prevent. [➡AVOID, PREVENT, LIMIT, AND CONTROL; 278] **4** *n* **assistance**, aid, benefit, support, service, relief, comfort, advantage, succour (*literary*). [➡KIND ACTION OR BEHAVIOUR; 296] *Opposite:* hindrance.

helper *n* **assistant**, aid, aide, collaborator, coworker, colleague, partner. [➡SUBORDINATES AND ASSISTANTS; 966]

helpful **1** *adj* **useful**, beneficial, advantageous, of use, effective, valuable. [➡USEFULNESS; 200] *Opposite:* useless. **2** *adj* **obliging**, accommodating, supportive, caring, cooperative. [➡THE WILL AND WILLINGNESS; 564] *Opposite:* unhelpful.

helpfully *adv* **carefully**, attentively, beneficially, favourably, obligingly, cooperatively, accommodatingly, supportively. [➡THE WILL AND WILLINGNESS; 564] *Opposite:* unhelpfully.

helpfulness **1** *n* **usefulness**, effectiveness, utility, benefit, advantageousness, value. [➡USEFULNESS; 200] *Opposite:* uselessness. **2** *n* **kindness**, neighbourliness, goodwill, concern, care, attentiveness, cooperation, support. [➡GENEROSITY AND KINDNESS; 496] *Opposite:* unhelpfulness.

helping *n* **serving**, plateful, portion, ration, selection. [➡AMOUNT AND QUANTITY; 112]

helping hand *n* **help**, assistance, support, aid, boost, push. [➡KIND ACTION OR BEHAVIOUR; 296]

helpless *adj* **powerless**, weak, feeble, dependent, vulnerable, unaided, defenceless. [➡COWARDICE AND WEAKNESS OF WILL; 509] *Opposite:* self-reliant.

helplessness *n* **powerlessness**, weakness, feebleness, vulnerability, dependence, defencelessness. [➡COWARDICE AND WEAKNESS OF WILL; 509] *Opposite:* confidence.

helpmate *n* **assistant**, associate, spouse, partner, coworker, helper, team-mate, companion. [➡SUBORDINATES AND ASSISTANTS; 966]

helpmeet (*archaic*) *n* [➡SUBORDINATES AND ASSISTANTS; 966]

help out *v* **help**, lend a hand, abet, aid, assist. [➡HELP; 294]

help yourself *v* **use**, make use of, appropriate, take, have. [➡GET; 421]

helter-skelter **1** *adv* **hurriedly**, in confusion, carelessly, haphazardly, pell-mell. [➡DISORDER AND CHAOS; 246] *Opposite:* calmly. **2** *adj* **chaotic**, disorganized, confused, haphazard. [➡DISORDER AND CHAOS; 246] *Opposite:* ordered.

hem **1** *v* **edge**, turn up, shorten, lengthen, sew up, stitch, tailor. [➡CRAFTS AND CARVING; 356] *Opposite:* let down. **2** *part of* **garment.** [➡PARTS OF A GARMENT; 870]

hem and haw *v* [➡HESITATE; 273]

hem in *v* **enclose**, close in, encircle, surround, circumscribe (*formal*), confine, restrict. [➡CAPTIVITY AND LOSS OF FREEDOM; 249] *Opposite:* release.

hemisphere *type of* **rounded shape.** [➡ROUNDED SHAPE; 1217]

hemispherical *adj* [➡ROUNDED SHAPE; 1217]

hemmed in *adj* [➡CAPTIVITY AND LOSS OF FREEDOM; 249]

hen *type of* **male or female bird.** [➡MALE OR FEMALE BIRD; 1005]

hence (*formal*) **1** *adv* **therefore**, for this reason, thus (*formal*), consequently (*formal*), that's why, and so, so. [➡CAUSATION; 169] **2** *adv* **from now**, from this time, henceforth (*formal*), later, hereafter (*formal*), in future, henceforward (*formal*). [➡FUTURE; 86]

henceforth (*formal*) *adv* **from now**, from this time, hereafter (*formal*), in future, henceforward (*formal*). [➡FUTURE; 86]

henceforward (*formal*) *adv* [➡FUTURE; 86]

henhouse *n* **coop**, pen, barn, shelter, shed, hutch. [➡ANIMAL OR BIRD ACCOMMODATION; 1078]

henna *type of* **brown.** [➡COLOURS; 1223]

heptathlon *type of* **track and field.** [➡HOBBIES, GAMES, AND SPORTS; 875]

herald **1** *n* **messenger**, crier, announcer, proclaimer, courier, representative. [➡MESSENGERS AND COURIERS; 852] **2** *n* (*literary*) **sign**, harbinger, indication, omen, portent, precursor, forerunner. [➡INDICATIONS, SIGNS, AND WARNINGS; 68] **3** *v* **proclaim**, announce, give out, publish, tout, publicize, make public. [➡INFORM AND ANNOUNCE; 612] **4** *v* **signal**, prefigure, foreshadow, presage, foreshow (*archaic*), indicate. [➡REPRESENT SOMETHING OR SOMEBODY; 59]

herb

◆ *types of herb*
angelica, basil, bay leaf, camomile, caraway, chervil, chive, cilantro (*US*), coriander, dill, fennel, hyssop, lemon grass, lovage, marjoram, mint, oregano, parsley, rosemary, sage, savory, spearmint, tarragon, thyme

herculean *adj* **superhuman**, colossal, enormous, phenomenal, staggering, extraordinary, huge, titanic. [➡LARGE; 1192] *Opposite:* small.

herd **1** *n* **people**, masses, mob, hoi polloi, crowd, sheep. [➡GROUPS OF PEOPLE; 935] **2** *v* **round up**, steer, gather together, collect, drove, drive. [➡ACCOMPANY AND FOLLOW; 338] **3** *v* **shepherd**, usher, direct, guide, funnel, channel, steer. [➡ACCOMPANY AND FOLLOW; 338]

herd

◆ *types of herd*
bevy, colony, drove, flock, gam, kennel, litter, pack, pod, pride, school, shoal, skulk, troop

here *adv* **at this time**, at this point, now, at this juncture. [➡PRESENT; 85]

hereabouts *adv* **nearby**, near, around here, close. [➡CLOSENESS; 160]

hereafter (*formal*) *adv* **after this**, in future, henceforth (*formal*), henceforward (*formal*), from now, from this time. [➡FUTURE; 86]

hereditarily *adv* **genetically**, by inheritance, heritably, transmissibly. [➡REPRODUCTION AND HEREDITY; 726]

hereditary **1** *adj* **genetic**, transmissible, inborn, inbred, inherited, innate. [➡REPRODUCTION AND HEREDITY; 726] 2 *adj* **inherited**, heritable, traditional, family. [➡THE FAMILY; 956]

heresy *n* **dissent**, deviation, unorthodoxy, profanation (*formal*), sacrilege, heterodoxy (*formal*). [➡MORALLY BAD; 776]

heretic *n* [➡RELIGIOUS CONCEPTS; 777]

heretical *adj* **unorthodox**, heterodox (*formal*), profane, sacrilegious, dissenting, unconventional, deviating. [➡MORALLY BAD; 776]

here today and gone tomorrow *adj* **short-lasting**, short-lived, temporary, brief, short, fleeting, transitory, transient, ephemeral. [➡FINITENESS, VARIABILITY, AND TRANSIENCE; 96] *Opposite:* lasting.

heretofore (*formal*) *adv* [➡PAST; 84]

herewith *adv* **with this**, together with this, enclosed, with, attached. [➡GENERAL LOCATIONS; 159]

heritable *adj* **inheritable**, transferable, transmissible, hereditary. [➡REPRODUCTION AND HEREDITY; 726]

heritage *n* **inheritance**, legacy, tradition, birthright, custom, culture. [➡BEQUEATH AND BEQUESTS; 433]

hermaphrodite *adj* **androgynous**, epicene, intersexual. [➡GENDER IDENTITY AND SEXUALITY; 932]

hermaphroditism *n* [➡GENDER IDENTITY AND SEXUALITY; 932]

hermetic *adj* **airtight**, enclosed, closed. [➡IN GOOD REPAIR; 1231]

hermit *n* **recluse**, loner, solitary, eremite (*literary*). [➡SOLITARY PEOPLE; 942]

hermitage *n* [➡RELIGIOUS BUILDINGS; 1084]

hermit crab *type of* **crustacean.** [➡AQUATIC INVERTEBRATE; 1022]

hero 1 *n* **superman**, champion, conqueror, idol. [➡PEOPLE WHO ARE APPROVED OF; 955] 2 *n* **male lead**, leading actor, leading man, star, protagonist, lead. [➡PEOPLE WHO ARE APPROVED OF; 955]

heroic *adj* **daring**, stout, valiant, brave, epic, superhuman, courageous, intrepid (*literary or humorous*), fearless, gallant (*literary*). [➡COURAGE; 499]

heroics *n* **recklessness**, rashness, derring-do (*literary*), irresponsibility, going over the top, overdoing it. [➡COURAGE; 499] *Opposite:* timidity.

heroine 1 *n* **superwoman**, champion, conqueror, idol. [➡PEOPLE WHO ARE APPROVED OF; 955] 2 *n* **female lead**, leading actress, leading lady, star, protagonist, lead. [➡PEOPLE WHO ARE APPROVED OF; 955]

heroism *n* **valour**, bravery, courageousness, fearlessness, boldness, pluckiness, pluck, gallantry, daring, intrepidness. [➡COURAGE; 499]

heron *type of* **freshwater bird.** [➡FRESHWATER BIRD; 1000]

hero worship *n* **adulation**, idolization, idealization, admiration, glorification, veneration, worship. [➡FADS, FETISHES, AND IDOLATRY; 556]

hero-worship *v* [➡LIKE, LOVE, VALUE, AND ENJOY; 579]

hero-worshipper *n* [➡DEVOTEES AND ADDICTED PEOPLE; 557]

herring *type of* **sea fish.** [➡SEA FISH; 1009]

hesitancy *n* **indecision**, caution, uncertainty, tentativeness, timidity, doubtfulness, reluctance, hesitation, disinclination, diffidence. [➡INSECURITY AND LOSS OF COMPOSURE; 545] *Opposite:* decisiveness.

hesitant *adj* **cautious**, tentative, timid, shy, undecided, doubtful, uncertain, diffident. [➡INSECURITY AND LOSS OF COMPOSURE; 545] *Opposite:* decisive.

See Compare and Contrast at **unwilling**.

hesitate 1 *v* **be uncertain**, be indecisive, vacillate, waver, falter, dither, shilly-shally, pause, dilly-dally, dawdle, delay, stumble. [➡HESITATE; 273] 2 *v* **be unwilling**, think twice, scruple, have qualms, be reluctant, hang back. [➡HESITATE; 273]

Compare and Contrast: ***hesitate, pause, falter, stumble, waver, vacillate***

CORE MEANING: TO SHOW UNCERTAINTY OR INDECISION

hesitate to be slow in doing something, or take a short break in an activity, as a result of uncertainty or reluctance; ***pause*** to stop doing something briefly before carrying on, or to wait intentionally for a short period before doing something; ***falter*** to show a loss of confidence, especially to speak or say something with a series of short stoppages, for example because of nervousness, fear, awkwardness, or incompetence; ***stumble*** to speak or act hesitatingly, confusedly, or incompetently; ***waver*** to become unsure or begin to change from a previous opinion; ***vacillate*** to be indecisive or irresolute, changing from one opinion to another.

hesitation 1 *n* **uncertainty**, indecision, vacillation, wavering, faltering, dithering, shilly-shallying, pause, delay, dilly-dallying, dawdling. [➡UNCERTAINTY; 560] *Opposite:* decisiveness. 2 *n* **unwillingness**, qualms, reluctance, disinclination, hesitancy, indecision. [➡UNWILLINGNESS AND STUBBORNNESS; 565] *Opposite:* willingness.

hessian *type of* **fibre.** [➡FABRICS; 1131]

heterogeneity *n* [➡DIFFERENCE; 150]

heterogeneous *adj* **varied**, mixed, assorted, diverse, various, dissimilar, unrelated. [➡UNRELATEDNESS AND SEPARATENESS; 147] *Opposite:* homogeneous.

het up (*informal*) *adj* **in a state** (*informal*), on edge, keyed up (*informal*), agitated, jittery, all of a flutter, jumpy, wound up (*informal*), excited, anxious, nervy (*informal*). [➡CONFUSION, ANXIETY, AND WORRY; 541]

heuristic *adj* **experiential**, empirical, experimental, investigative, exploratory. [➡THE NATURE OF IDEAS; 772]

hew 1 *v* **cut**, chop, fell, cleave, axe, slash, hack. [➡TEAR, BREAK, AND CUT; 361] 2 *v* **carve**, fashion, sculpt, shape, model. [➡CRAFTS AND CARVING; 356]

hex *n* **curse**, spell, jinx, voodoo. [➡BAD LUCK AND UNLUCKY; 785]

hexagonal *adj* [➡ANGULAR SHAPE; 1216]

heyday *n* **prime**, zenith, halcyon days (*literary*), glory days, peak. [➡PLEASANT SITUATIONS; 74]

hey presto (*informal*) *interj* [➡EXPRESSIONS OF SURPRISE; 547]

hi (*informal*) *interj* [➡GREETINGS, FAREWELLS, AND SALUTATIONS; 660]

hiatus *n* **pause**, break, interruption, space, lull, interval, time away, gap. [➡PAUSES AND PHASES; 56]

hibernate *v* **lie dormant**, take cover, overwinter, hide, hide away, sleep, keep cover, hole up (*slang*). [➡SLEEP AND DREAM; 724]

hiccup (*informal*) **1** *v* [➡VOMIT AND BELCH; 713] **2** *n* **hitch**, glitch, interruption, delay, setback. [➡PROBLEM; 257]

hickory *type of* **deciduous tree**. [➡DECIDUOUS TREES; 1028]

hickory nut *type of* **nut**. [➡NUTS; 1184]

hidden 1 *adj* **concealed**, out of sight, unseen, secreted, veiled, buried. [➡IMPERCEPTIBLE; 26] **2** *adj* **unknown**, secret, mysterious, clandestine, covert, obscure, cryptic, mystifying. [➡SECRET AND UNKNOWN; 180]

hidden agenda *n* **ulterior motive**, secret plan, motivation, driving force, impetus, incentive. [➡CAUSATION; 169]

hide 1 *v* **conceal**, put out of sight, hide from view, secrete, veil, bury, cover, screen, shroud, inter (*formal*). [➡CAUSE TO DISAPPEAR; 6] *Opposite:* flaunt. **2** *v* **go underground**, take cover, disappear, keep cover, hole up (*slang*). [➡RUN AWAY AND AVOID; 10] **3** *v* **keep secret**, withhold, hold back, keep back, suppress, hush up (*informal*), keep mum (*informal*), obscure, keep quiet. [➡WITHHOLD INFORMATION; 688] *Opposite:* disclose. **4** *type of* **leather**. [➡FABRICS; 1131]

hideaway *n* **hiding place**, refuge, sanctuary, hidey-hole (*informal*), asylum, retreat, safe place, hideout, lair (*informal*), den, safe house, place of escape. [➡SAFE BUILDINGS OR PLACES; 1092]

hidebound *adj* **narrow-minded**, prejudiced, conservative, conventional, parochial, reactionary. [➡CONSERVATIVE AND UNADVENTUROUS; 518] *Opposite:* broad-minded.

hideous *adj* **ugly**, revolting, repugnant, repulsive, unsightly, gruesome, shocking, dreadful. [➡UGLINESS AND UNATTRACTIVENESS; 234]

hideousness *n* **ugliness**, repulsiveness, unsightliness, gruesomeness, dreadfulness, repugnance, horribleness. [➡UGLINESS AND UNATTRACTIVENESS; 234]

hideout *n* **hideaway**, safe house, refuge, sanctuary, retreat, den, lair (*informal*), hiding place, hidey-hole (*informal*), place of escape, safe place, asylum. [➡SAFE BUILDINGS OR PLACES; 1092]

hidey-hole (*informal*) *n* **hiding place**, hideaway, safe house, safe place, hideout, nook, refuge, sanctuary, stash (*informal*), retreat, den, lair (*informal*). [➡SAFE BUILDINGS OR PLACES; 1092]

hiding (*informal*) *n* **beating**, walloping (*informal*), whacking, thumping, smacking, spanking, wallop (*informal*), whack, thump, smack, spank. [➡PHYSICAL ATTACK AND PUNISHMENT; 416]

hiding place *n* **hideaway**, hidey-hole (*informal*), lair (*informal*), hole, place of escape, den, safe house, safe place, hideout, sanctuary, retreat, refuge, asylum, recess, nook, stash (*informal*). [➡SAFE BUILDINGS OR PLACES; 1092]

hierarchical *adj* **ranked**, graded, tiered, ordered, classified, categorized. [➡ORDER AND ORGANISATION; 207]

hierarchy *n* **chain of command**, ladder, pecking order, grading, order, pyramid. [➡CONNECTION; 144]

hieroglyph *n* **symbol**, pictograph, picture, ideogram, cipher, glyph, pictogram, hieroglyphic. [➡SYMBOLS, SIGNS, AND NUMBERS; 597]

hieroglyphics *type of* **alphabet**. [➡SYMBOLS, SIGNS, AND NUMBERS; 597]

hifalutin (*informal*) *adj* **highfalutin** (*informal*), pretentious, affected, grandiose, la-di-da (*informal*), grandiloquent, high-flown, pompous, snobbish. [➡AFFECTATION, SELF-SATISFACTION, AND SNOBBISHNESS; 508] *Opposite:* down-to-earth.

hi-fi 1 *n* **sound system**, stereo system, stereo, CD player, cassette recorder, personal stereo. [➡RECORDINGS AND PLAYERS; 911] **2** *type of* **audio equipment**. [➡AUDIO EQUIPMENT; 1138]

higgledy-piggledy *adj* **untidy**, topsy-turvy, mixed-up (*informal*), in a mess, jumbled, confused, random, disordered, disorderly. [➡DISORDER AND CHAOS; 246] *Opposite:* ordered.

high 1 *adj* **tall**, lofty, elevated, towering, soaring, skyscraping. [➡HEIGHT: HIGH; 1202] *Opposite:* low. **2** *adj* **in height**, from top to bottom, from head to foot, from top to toe, tall, in elevation. [➡HEIGHT: HIGH; 1202] **3** *adj* **above average**, great, extraordinary, elevated, extreme, astronomical, prohibitive, abnormal. [➡EXPENSIVE AND OVERPRICED; 248] *Opposite:* normal. **4** *adj* **high-pitched**, shrill, piercing, penetrating, sharp, soprano, falsetto. [➡LOUD OR UNPLEASANT SOUNDS; 1265] *Opposite:* low-pitched. **5** *adj* **important**, exalted (*formal*), eminent, prominent, high-ranking, superior, distinguished, lofty, high-level. [➡IMPORTANT; 195] *Opposite:* low. **6** *n* **high point**, peak, climax, summit, high spot. [➡INTERMEDIATE STAGES; 55] *Opposite:* low point. **7** *n* (*informal*) **lift**, kick, boost, thrill, buzz (*informal*), tonic, pleasure, excitement. [➡TREAT; 211]

high achiever *n* **high flier**, go-getter (*informal*), success, star, winner, success story. [➡IMPORTANT OR FAMOUS PEOPLE; 893]

high and dry *adj* **helpless**, up the creek (*informal*), in the lurch, washed up, stranded, abandoned, destitute, deserted. [➡IN TROUBLE AND DISADVANTAGED; 73]

high and low *adv* **everywhere**, all over, here, there, and everywhere, in every nook and cranny, all over the place (*informal*), everyplace (*US informal*). [➡GENERAL LOCATIONS; 159]

high and mighty *adj* **arrogant**, disdainful, overbearing, conceited, stuck-up (*informal*), proud, haughty, self-important, full of yourself, condescending. [➡AFFECTATION, SELF-SATISFACTION, AND SNOBBISHNESS; 508]

highborn (*literary*) *adj* [➡CLASS STATUS; 889]

highboy (*US*) *type of* **cabinet**. [➡FURNITURE; 858]

highbrow 1 *adj* **intellectual**, cultured, academic, scholarly, exclusive, elitist, serious. [➡THE NATURE OF IDEAS; 772] *Oppo-*

site: lowbrow (*disapproving*). **2** *n* **intellectual**, academic, scholar, sage (*literary*), philosopher. [➡LEVEL OF EDUCATION AND SOPHISTICATION; 894]

highchair *type of* **seating**. [➡FURNITURE; 858]

high-class *adj* **swanky** (*informal*), high-quality, fancy, formal, swish (*informal*), elegant, superior, posh (*informal*), ritzy (*informal*), glitzy. [➡EXPENSIVE AND LUXURIOUS; 219] *Opposite:* cheap.

high court *n* **court**, principal court, supreme court (*US*). [➡TRIAL, PUNISHMENT, AND LEGAL OUTCOMES; 819]

highest *adj* **top**, topmost, utmost, ultimate, premier, record, supreme. [➡SUPERIORITY; 153]

highfalutin (*informal*) *adj* **pretentious**, pompous, affected, grandiose, snobbish, high-flown, la-di-da (*informal*), grandiloquent. [➡AFFECTATION, SELF-SATISFACTION, AND SNOBBISHNESS; 508] *Opposite:* down-to-earth.

high-fidelity *adj* [➡ACOUSTICS; 1137]

high-flier *n* **high achiever**, go-getter (*informal*), success, winner, success story, star. [➡IMPORTANT OR FAMOUS PEOPLE; 893]

high-flown *adj* **affected**, pretentious, exalted (*formal*), grandiose, high-sounding, highfalutin (*informal*), la-di-da (*informal*), grandiloquent, pompous, snobbish. [➡ELOQUENT, TALKATIVE AND LONG-WINDED; 633] *Opposite:* down-to-earth.

high-grade *adj* **high-quality**, quality, finest, superior, prime, select, best, first-class, choice, luxury, premium, super (*informal*), first-rate. [➡SUPERIORITY; 153] *Opposite:* low-grade.

high ground *n* **upland**, highland, plateau, hillside, hilltop, fell. [➡MOUNTAINS AND HILLS; 1044] *Opposite:* lowland.

high-handed *adj* **bossy**, autocratic, dominant, undemocratic, domineering, overbearing, imperious, cavalier, arrogant, inconsiderate. [➡BOSSY AND OVERBEARING; 517]

high-handedness *n* **bossiness**, arrogance, imperiousness, inconsiderateness, overbearingness, inconsideration. [➡BOSSY AND OVERBEARING; 517]

high jinks (*informal*) *n* **monkey business** (*informal*), mischief, mischievousness, carryings-on (*informal*), shenanigans (*informal*), trouble, no good. [➡CHAOS AND UPROAR; 51]

high jump *type of* **track and field**. [➡HOBBIES, GAMES, AND SPORTS; 875]

highland *n* **upland**, plateau, high ground, hilltop, moorland, fell. [➡MOUNTAINS AND HILLS; 1044] *Opposite:* lowland.

high-level *adj* **sophisticated**, elevated, advanced, complex, top, elite. [➡POSITIVELY COMPLEX OR COMPLICATED; 218] *Opposite:* unsophisticated.

high life *n* **good life**, life of Riley, life of ease, lap of luxury, easy street, clover, bed of roses, primrose path (*literary*). [➡PLEASANT SITUATIONS; 74]

highlight **1** *n* **high spot**, high point, climax, best bit, best part, icing on the cake, acme. [➡DECISIVE MOMENTS; 44] **2** *v* **emphasize**, draw attention to, underline, stress, show up, underscore, bring to light. [➡CLAIM, INSIST, AND EMPHASIZE; 615]

highlighter *type of* **pen**. [➡WRITING AND DRAWING IMPLEMENTS, AND MEDIA; 602]

highly **1** *adv* **extremely**, very, exceedingly, very much, greatly, decidedly, vastly. [➡TO A GREAT EXTENT; 130] *Opposite:* poorly. **2** *adv* **favourably**, approvingly, kindly, warmly, graciously, well, very well. [➡ENTHUSIASTIC AND INQUISITIVE; 629] *Opposite:* unfavourably.

highly-strung *adj* **excitable**, edgy, tense, jittery, easily upset, skittish, volatile, anxious, on edge, nervous, nervy (*informal*). [➡EXCESSIVE SENSITIVITY; 512]. *Opposite:* laid-back (*informal*).

highly unlikely *adj* [➡IMPOSSIBLE AND IMPROBABLE; 179]

high-minded *adj* **principled**, worthy, moral, noble, upright, fair, ethical, righteous. [➡HONEST AND RELIABLE; 503] *Opposite:* base.

high-pitched *adj* **shrill**, high, piercing, penetrating, sharp, falsetto, soprano. [➡LOUD OR UNPLEASANT SOUNDS; 1265]

high point *n* **best moment**, high spot, best bit, climax, icing on the cake, acme, highlight, best part. [➡DECISIVE MOMENTS; 44]

high-powered *adj* **successful**, dynamic, driven, go-getting (*informal*), ambitious, energetic, efficient, influential. [➡TALENTED AND SKILFUL; 528]

high-pressure *adj* **stressful**, difficult, relentless, pressured, intense, strenuous, demanding. [➡PHYSICALLY UNPLEASANT; 227] *Opposite:* easy.

high-profile *adj* **prominent**, prestigious, conspicuous, eminent, notorious (*archaic*). [➡IMPORTANT; 195] *Opposite:* discreet.

high profile *n* **prominence**, conspicuousness, eminence, celebrity, notoriety, prestige. [➡KNOWN AND FAMOUS; 182] *Opposite:* anonymity.

high-quality *adj* [➡GOOD, WELL, BETTER; 184]

high-ranking *adj* [➡CLASS STATUS; 889]

high-rise **1** *adj* **multistorey**, high, tall, big, lofty, soaring, towering. [➡HEIGHT: HIGH; 1202] **2** *n* **skyscraper**, block of flats, apartment block, tower block, office block, apartment house (*US*), office tower (*US*), apartment building (*US*). [➡RESIDENTIAL BUILDINGS; 1077]

high roller (*slang*) *n* [➡PEOPLE IN SPORTS AND LEISURE; 876]

high school *type of* **school**. [➡EDUCATIONAL INSTITUTIONS; 813]

high society *n* **upper classes**, upper crust (*informal*), elite, jet set (*informal*), polite society, beautiful people, Four Hundred (*US*). [➡CLASS STATUS; 889]

high-sounding *adj* **imposing**, high-flown, grandiloquent, grandiose, lofty, pompous, pretentious, extravagant. [➡POMPOUS, LOUD, AND OVER-CONFIDENT; 636]

high-spirited *adj* **lively**, exuberant, merry, cheerful, vivacious, excited, boisterous. [➡ENERGY AND ENTHUSIASM; 497] *Opposite:* lethargic.

high spirits *n* **liveliness**, exuberance, merriness, cheerfulness, vivacity, excitement, joie de vivre, brio (*literary*), happiness. [➡PLEASURE, EXCITEMENT, AND ELATION; 535] *Opposite:* depression.

high spot *n* **best moment**, high point, best bit, best part, climax, icing on the cake, acme, highlight. [➡DECISIVE MOMENTS; 44]

hightail it (*slang*) *v* [➡RUN AWAY AND AVOID; 10]

high tea *type of* **meal**. [➡MEALS AND PARTS OF MEALS; 1168]

high-tech *adj* **advanced**, technological, computerized, digital, modern, futuristic, sophisticated, multimedia, state-of-the-art. [➡DESCRIBING TECHNOLOGY; 1159]

high-up (*informal*) *n* **boss**, manager, director, bigwig (*informal*), top dog (*informal*), big boss. [➡CLASS STATUS; 889]

highway (*US*) *type of* **major road**. [➡ROADS; 1105]

highway robbery (*US informal*) *n* [➡CRIMES; 817]

hijack 1 *v* **take over**, seize, commandeer, capture, skyjack. [➡TAKE SOMETHING AWAY; 426] 2 *v* (*informal*) **steal**, appropriate, take over, commandeer, borrow, nick (*slang*). [➡STEAL AND ROB; 427] 3 *n* **takeover**, skyjacking, capture, seizure. [➡CRIMES; 817]

hijinks (*informal*) *n* **high jinks** (*informal*), mischievousness, mischief, shenanigans (*informal*), monkey business (*informal*), carryings-on (*informal*), trouble. [➡CHAOS AND UPROAR; 51]

hike 1 *v* **ramble**, trek, walk, climb, scramble, trudge, tramp, slog. [➡PROCEED AND GO; 306] 2 *n* **trek**, ramble, walk, climb, scramble, trudge, tramp, slog. [➡TRAVEL: JOURNEYS AND TRIPS; 319]

hiker *n* **walker**, rambler, backpacker, trekker, climber. [➡PEOPLE IN SPORTS AND LEISURE; 876]

hiking boot *type of* **boot**. [➡FOOTWEAR; 871]

hilarious *adj* **funny**, sidesplitting, hysterical (*informal*), comical, comic, humorous, entertaining, uproarious, riotous, mirthful, rib-tickling. [➡FUNNY AND AMUSING; 217]

See Compare and Contrast at **funny**.

hilariousness *n* **humour**, humorousness, uproariousness, comicalness, mirthfulness, funniness, amusingness. [➡FUNNY AND AMUSING; 217]

hilarity *n* **amusement**, laughter, hysterics (*informal*), merriment, mirth, glee, joviality, cheerfulness. [➡ENTERTAINMENT; 872] *Opposite:* sadness.

hill 1 *n* **mountain**, peak, knoll, mount, mound, hummock, tor. [➡MOUNTAINS AND HILLS; 1044] *Opposite:* valley. 2 *n* **gradient**, slope, incline, rise, drop. [➡MOUNTAINS AND HILLS; 1044]

hillock *n* **mound**, hummock, knoll, hill. [➡MOUNTAINS AND HILLS; 1044]

hilltop *n* **top**, summit, peak, pinnacle, brow, crown, crest. [➡MOUNTAINS AND HILLS; 1044] *Opposite:* base.

hilly *adj* **mountainous**, undulating, bumpy, alpine, craggy. [➡MOUNTAINS AND HILLS; 1044] *Opposite:* flat.

hind 1 *adj* **back**, rear, hindmost (*literary*), posterior (*formal*), rearmost. [➡RELATIVE LOCATION; 162] *Opposite:* fore (*literary*). 2 *type of* **female animal**. [➡MALE OR FEMALE ANIMAL; 978]

hinder *v* **hold back**, delay, deter, hamper, encumber, obstruct, get in the way, thwart, impede, block. [➡AVOID, PREVENT, LIMIT, AND CONTROL; 278] *Opposite:* facilitate.

Compare and Contrast: ***hinder, block, hamper, hold back, impede, obstruct***

CORE MEANING: TO PUT DIFFICULTIES IN THE WAY OF PROGRESS

hinder to delay or restrict the development or progress of something, either accidentally or by deliberate interference; ***block*** to prevent movement through, into, or out of something, or prevent something from taking place; ***hamper*** to restrict the free movement or action of somebody or something; ***hold back*** to keep something from happening or to restrain somebody from doing something; ***impede*** to interfere with the movement, progress, or development of somebody or something; ***obstruct*** to cause a serious delay in action or progress, or to cause a major physical blockage in a road or passageway.

hindleg *n* [➡LEG AND FOOT; 695]

hindmost (*literary*) *adj* **last**, rear, final, back, rearmost. [➡RELATIVE LOCATION; 162] *Opposite:* foremost.

hindquarters *n* **back**, rear, rear legs, hind legs. [➡HORSE; 985] *Opposite:* front.

hindrance 1 *n* **obstruction**, impediment, barrier, obstacle, encumbrance, difficulty, burden, deterrent. [➡PROBLEM; 257] 2 *n* **interference**, interruption, limitation, prevention, sabotage, obstruction, hampering. [➡PROBLEM; 257] *Opposite:* assistance.

hindsight *n* **reflection**, retrospection, perception, observation, remembrance, recall. [➡MEMORY; 746] *Opposite:* foresight.

hinge *n* **pivot**, axis, fulcrum, joint, centre, crux. [➡CENTRAL PARTS OF PHYSICAL OBJECTS; 1250]

hinge on *v* **depend on**, hang on, turn on, be dependent on, rest on, rely on, pivot on. [➡RECIPROCITY AND INTERDEPENDENCE; 148]

hint 1 *v* **suggest**, intimate, insinuate, imply, mention, indicate, signal. [➡SUGGEST, HINT, AND COMMENT; 613] 2 *n* **suggestion**, clue, intimation, mention, indication, tip-off (*informal*), insinuation, warning, telltale sign. [➡SUGGEST, HINT, AND COMMENT; 613] 3 *n* **tip**, advice, pointer, suggestion, clue, help. [➡ADVICE; 690] 4 *n* **trace**, tinge, suggestion, dash, taste, breath, whisper, whiff, touch, element. [➡FEW, LITTLE, SMALL AMOUNT; 119]

hinterland *n* **vicinity**, environs, surroundings, neighbourhood. [➡THE SEAS, OCEANS, AND SHORES; 1041] *Opposite:* heartland.

hip 1 *adj* (*slang*) **fashionable**, current, trendy (*informal*), all the rage, in vogue, à la mode (*dated*), modish, with-it (*dated informal*), stylish. [➡NEW, MODERN; 167] 2 *part of* **torso**. [➡TORSO; 694]

hip flask *n* [➡CONTAINERS, RECEPTACLES, AND PACKAGING; 1244]

hip-huggers (*US*) *type of* **trousers.** [➡GARMENTS AND OUTFITS; 865]

hipness (*slang*) *n* [➡NEW, MODERN; 167]

hippopotamus *type of* **large mammal.** [➡LARGE MAMMAL; 986]

hipster (*dated informal*) *n* [➡MALE PERSON; 934]

hipsters *type of* **trousers.** [➡GARMENTS AND OUTFITS; 865]

hire 1 *v* **employ,** appoint, take on, sign up, take into service, engage. [➡CONFER STATUS; 459] 2 *v* **rent,** lease, let, charter, engage, book. [➡LEND, LEASE, AND BORROW; 429]

Compare and Contrast: ***hire, rent, let, lease, charter***

CORE MEANING: TO GET OR GRANT THE TEMPORARY USE OF SOMETHING IN RETURN FOR PAYMENT

hire to get or grant the temporary use of something in return for payment, usually for a fairly short period of time; ***rent*** to get or grant the temporary use of property for residential or commercial purposes, cars or household equipment such as television sets in return for payment, usually for a longer period of time; ***let*** to grant the temporary use of property for residential or commercial purposes, in exchange for payment; ***lease*** to get or grant the temporary use of something for a specified period in return for periodic payments under the terms of a contract, known as a *lease*; ***charter*** to hire a large vehicle, boat, ship, or plane usually for exclusive use.

hired gun (*slang*) *n* [➡PEOPLE WHO KILL; 924]

hire out *v* **rent out,** rent, lend, lend out, lease, let. [➡LEND, LEASE, AND BORROW; 429]

hirsute *adj* **hairy,** long-haired, unshorn, unshaven, shaggy. [➡DESCRIBING HAIR; 487] *Opposite:* bald.

hirsuteness *n* [➡HAIR; 485]

hiss 1 *v* **jeer,** boo, hoot, mock, ridicule. [➡UNFAVOURABLE NON-VERBAL RESPONSES; 655] *Opposite:* cheer. 2 *v* **whisper,** murmur, rustle, whistle, susurrate. [➡EMIT CONTINUOUS SOUNDS; 367] 3 *n* [➡UNFAVOURABLE NON-VERBAL RESPONSES; 655] 4 *type of* **continuous sound.** [➡CONTINUOUS SOUNDS; 1257]

historic 1 *adj* **significant,** momentous, notable, famous, remarkable, extraordinary, celebrated, important. [➡IMPORTANT; 195] *Opposite:* insignificant. 2 *adj* **historical,** old, ancient, antique, past, bygone. [➡OLD, OLD-FASHIONED; 168] *Opposite:* modern.

historical *adj* **past,** old, ancient, antique, historic, bygone. [➡OLD, OLD-FASHIONED; 168] *Opposite:* modern.

historically 1 *adv* **for history,** in history, over all, factually, archaeologically. [➡PAST; 84] 2 *adv* **traditionally,** generally, usually, as a rule, in the main, by and large, in general. [➡USUALLY; 108]

history 1 *n* **past,** times gone by, times past, olden times, antiquity. [➡PAST; 84] *Opposite:* present. 2 *n* **account,** record, chronicle, narration, memoir, saga, description, story, annal (*dated*). [➡FICTION AND DRAMA; 913]

histrionic *adj* **theatrical,** dramatic, exaggerated, over-the-top (*informal*), melodramatic, unrestrained. [➡AFFECTATION, SELF-SATISFACTION, AND SNOBBISHNESS; 508] *Opposite:* restrained.

histrionics *n* **dramatics,** tantrums, hysterics, song and dance (*informal*), melodrama, drama. [➡CHAOS AND UPROAR; 51]

hit 1 *v* **strike,** punch, thump, slap, beat, smack, batter, knock, whack, bang, cuff, rap, sock (*informal*). [➡PHYSICAL ATTACK AND PUNISHMENT; 416] 2 *v* **crash into,** strike, bang into, bump into, collide with, run into, smash into, bash into (*informal*), ram. [➡CONTACT: IMPACT; 414] 3 *v* (*slang*) **reach,** attain, gain, win, achieve, arrive at, come to, rise to (*informal*), sink to, fall to. [➡ARRIVE; 12] 4 *v* **affect,** afflict, damage, hurt, disadvantage. [➡HAPPEN TO SOMEBODY; 30] 5 *n* **blow,** knock, smack, slap, bump, cuff, rap, thump, stroke, shot, punch, lick (*informal*). [➡CONTACT: IMPACT; 414] 6 *n* **success,** winner, triumph, sensation, market leader, knockout, smash. [➡AMAZING THING; 212] *Opposite:* flop (*informal*).

hit-and-miss *adj* **haphazard,** random, unpredictable, unplanned, careless, slapdash, casual, cursory, aimless, indiscriminate, chaotic. [➡DISORDER AND CHAOS; 246] *Opposite:* planned.

hit back *v* **retaliate,** get even, strike back, react, even the score, get your own back, get back, respond. [➡COMPETE, CONTEND, AND COMBAT; 304]

hitch 1 *v* **hitchhike,** get a lift, be given a lift, thumb a lift, put your thumb out, get a ride (*US*), be given a ride (*US*). [➡TRAVEL: WAYS OF TRAVELLING; 321] 2 *v* **fasten,** hook, harness, join, tether, attach, connect, tie, couple, lash, make fast, yoke. [➡FASTEN, LINK, AND JOIN; 409] *Opposite:* undo. 3 *n* **snag,** catch, drawback, glitch, delay, hindrance, problem, trouble, difficulty, holdup. [➡PROBLEM; 257]

hitchhike *v* **hitch,** get a lift, be given a lift, thumb a lift, put your thumb out, get a ride (*US*), be given a ride (*US*). [➡TRAVEL: WAYS OF TRAVELLING; 321]

hitchhiker *n* [➡TRAVEL: TRAVELLERS AND WALKERS; 320]

hi-tech *adj* [➡DESCRIBING TECHNOLOGY; 1159]

hither and thither *adv* **here and there,** backwards and forwards, all over the place (*informal*), back and forth, everywhere. [➡DIRECTION OF MOTION; 346]

hither and yon *adv* [➡DIRECTION OF MOTION; 346]

hitherto (*formal*) *adv* **up till now,** up till then, until now, until then, till now, till then, previously, thus far, so far, yet, before, until this time, until that time. [➡PAST; 84]

hit it off (*informal*) *v* **get on well,** connect, get on, make friends, click (*informal*), take to each other, get along like a house on fire, bond. [➡ESTABLISHING RELATIONSHIPS WITH OTHERS; 974] *Opposite:* clash.

hit man (*slang*) *n* **assassin,** murderer, killer, hired gun (*slang*), contract killer. [➡PEOPLE WHO KILL; 924]

hit on 1 *v* **think of,** chance upon, discover, realize, arrive at, find, stumble on, come up with, find out, uncover, detect, turn up. [➡LEARN AND DISCOVER; 763] 2 *v* (*US slang*) **chat up,** flirt, lead on, pick up (*informal*), make eyes at. [➡ESTABLISHING RELATIONSHIPS WITH OTHERS; 974]

hit out 1 *v* **criticize,** attack, assail, condemn, castigate (*formal*), lay into (*informal*). [➡PROTEST AND EXPRESS DISAPPROVAL;

643] 2 *v* **strike out**, lash out, lunge, go for, attack. [➡PHYSICAL ATTACK AND PUNISHMENT; 416]

hit squad (*slang*) *n* **task force**, working party, team, squad, unit, commando. [➡CRIMINALS; 821]

hit the big time (*slang*) *v* [➡SUCCEED AND WIN; 79]

hit the gas (*US*) *v* [➡MOVE FAST; 314]

hit the hay (*informal*) *v* **go to bed**, turn in (*informal*), hit the sack (*informal*), retire, say goodnight, get to sleep, get some shuteye (*informal*), get some rest. [➡SLEEP AND DREAM; 724]

hit the jackpot *v* [➡SUCCEED AND WIN; 79]

hit the road *v* [➡ABSENT ONESELF; 8]

hit the roof *v* **lose your temper**, see red (*informal*), be angry, blow your top (*informal*), go mad, fly off the handle (*informal*), lose it (*informal*), fly into a rage, go berserk. [➡GIVING VENT TO EMOTIONS; 680] *Opposite:* calm down.

hit the sack (*informal*) *v* **go to bed**, retire, turn in (*informal*), hit the hay (*informal*), say goodnight, get to sleep, get some shuteye (*informal*), get some rest. [➡SLEEP AND DREAM; 724]

hit upon *v* **stumble on**, chance upon, discover, realize, arrive at, uncover, come up with, think of, detect. [➡LEARN AND DISCOVER; 763]

hive *v* **store**, put away, save, put aside, hoard, squirrel, accumulate, amass, garner, stockpile, keep. [➡STORE AND KEEP; 454] *Opposite:* discard.

hive off *v* **cream off**, skim off, transfer, separate, split off, divide off, farm out, subdivide. [➡SEPARATE AND DIVIDE; 402] *Opposite:* merge.

hives *n* [➡CONDITIONS AFFECTING THE SKIN; 722]

hoagie (*US*) *n* [➡PREPARED DISHES; 1169]

hoard 1 *v* **save**, store, amass, stockpile, accumulate, collect, gather, put aside, hide away, squirrel, stash (*informal*). [➡STORE AND KEEP; 454] *Opposite:* throw away. 2 *n* **store**, pile, mass, reserve, supply, stockpile, heap, cache, collection, stash (*informal*). [➡COLLECTIONS AND MIXTURES OF THINGS; 1243]

See Compare and Contrast at **collect**.

hoarder *n* **collector**, saver, accumulator, squirrel (*informal*), magpie (*informal*), miser. [➡PEOPLE WHO COLLECT THINGS; 455]

hoarding *n* **billboard**, notice board, advertisement, placard, poster, bulletin board (*US*). [➡SIGNPOSTS, SIGNALS, AND BILLBOARDS; 596]

hoar frost *n* **frost**, ice, rime. [➡COLD WEATHER; 1051]

hoarse *adj* **croaky**, gruff, gravelly, husky, rough, throaty, raucous, guttural, rasping, grating. [➡LOUD OR UNPLEASANT SOUNDS; 1265] *Opposite:* smooth.

hoarseness *n* **croakiness**, gruffness, huskiness, roughness, harshness, throatiness, raucousness, gutturalness. [➡LOUD OR UNPLEASANT SOUNDS; 1265] *Opposite:* smoothness.

hoary 1 *adj* **overused**, old, ancient, age-old, stale, worn, worn-out, antediluvian (*informal*). [➡OLD, OLD-FASHIONED; 168] *Opposite:* fresh. 2 *adj* **white**, snow-white, whitened, snowy, grey, silvery, silver, silvered. [➡HAIR COLOUR; 486]

hoax 1 *n* **deception**, trick, practical joke, joke, swindle, ruse, prank, fraud, confidence trick, con trick (*informal*), put-up job (*informal*), con, con game (*US informal*), confidence game (*US*). [➡DECEPTION AND LIES; 661] 2 *v* **deceive**, trick, con, swindle, mislead, dupe, pull the wool over somebody's eyes, defraud. [➡DECEPTION AND LIES; 661]

hoaxer *n* **trickster**, practical joker, fraudster, joker, swindler, deceiver, con artist (*slang*). [➡PEOPLE WHO DECEIVE; 662]

hob *type of* **appliance**. [➡HOUSEHOLD APPLIANCES; 1116]

hobble 1 *v* **limp**, hop, shuffle, shamble, totter, stagger, stumble. [➡WALK UNSTEADILY; 316] 2 *n* **limp**, shuffle, stagger, shamble, stumble, totter. [➡PROCEED AND GO; 306]

hobble skirt *type of* **skirt**. [➡GARMENTS AND OUTFITS; 865]

hobby *n* **pastime**, leisure pursuit, diversion, relaxation, sideline, interest. [➡LEISURE AND RECREATION; 874] *Opposite:* job.

hobbyhorse *n* **favourite subject**, pet topic, idée fixe, bee in your bonnet, thing (*informal*), obsession, preoccupation. [➡FADS, FETISHES, AND IDOLATRY; 556]

hobgoblin *n* **goblin**, imp, elf, gremlin (*informal*), pixie, sprite, bugbear, fairy, fay (*literary*), brownie. [➡MYTHICAL BEINGS; 790]

hobnob (*disapproving*) *v* **socialize**, mix, fraternize, associate, go around, be in, mingle, hang out (*informal*). [➡ESTABLISHING RELATIONSHIPS WITH OTHERS; 974] *Opposite:* shun.

hobo *n* **traveller**, itinerant, vagrant, tramp, drifter. [➡NOMADIC AND ROOTLESS LIFESTYLES; 884]

hock 1 *type of* **cut**. [➡TYPES AND CUTS OF MEAT; 1176] 2 *part of* **horse**. [➡HORSE; 985] 3 *v* (*slang*) **pawn**, deposit, exchange, pledge. [➡EXCHANGE AND INTERCHANGE; 449] *Opposite:* redeem.

hockey *n* [➡HOBBIES, GAMES, AND SPORTS; 875]

hockey stick *type of* **sports equipment**. [➡SPORTS EQUIPMENT; 879]

hoe 1 *v* **turn over**, weed, dig, dig out, loosen. [➡USE TOOLS AND MACHINERY; 469] 2 *type of* **cutting tool**. [➡CUTTING TOOLS; 1119]

hoedown (*US*) *n* [➡PARTIES, DANCES, AND CELEBRATIONS; 37]

hog 1 *v* (*informal*) **monopolize**, take over, help yourself, take the lion's share of, hang onto, keep, corner. [➡TAKE SOMETHING AWAY; 426] 2 *type of* **farm animal**. [➡FARM ANIMAL; 982]

hoggish *adj* [➡BEASTLY AND BRUTISH; 511]

hoglike *adj* [➡BEASTLY AND BRUTISH; 511]

hogwash (*informal*) *n* **nonsense**, rubbish, gibberish, codswallop (*informal*), claptrap (*informal*), hooey (*informal*), bunkum (*informal*), humbug, twaddle (*informal*), garbage. [➡MEANINGLESS SPEECH OR WRITING; 677]

ho hum (*informal*) *interj* **oh no**, oh well, here we go again, what the hell (*informal*), what the heck (*informal*), well, OK (*informal*), right (*informal*). [➡EXPRESSIONS OF SURPRISE; 547]

hoi polloi *n* **common herd**, general public, masses, ordinary people, proletariat, populace, plebs, lower classes, public, commoners. [➡CLASS STATUS; 889] *Opposite:* aristocracy.

hoist 1 *v* **lift**, raise, pull, heave, erect, elevate, upraise, uplift, winch. [➡MOVE SOMETHING: UPWARDS; 329] 2 *n* **winch**, crane, lift, elevator, pulley. [➡MACHINES AND MACHINE PARTS; 1115]

See Compare and Contrast at **raise**.

hoity-toity (*informal*) *adj* **snooty** (*informal*), haughty, arrogant, snobbish, proud, disdainful, self-important, posh (*informal*). [➡AFFECTATION, SELF-SATISFACTION, AND SNOBBISHNESS; 508] *Opposite:* down-to-earth.

hokum (*US informal disapproving*) *n* **claptrap** (*informal*), hooey (*informal*), bunkum (*informal*), nonsense, hogwash (*informal*), rubbish, codswallop (*informal*), humbug, twaddle (*informal*), garbage. [➡MEANINGLESS SPEECH OR WRITING; 677]

hold 1 *v* **grasp**, clutch, grip, clasp, seize, cling to, embrace, cleave to (*literary*). [➡CONTACT: HOLD; 412] *Opposite:* release. 2 *v* **fix**, secure, fasten, bind, attach, keep, wedge. [➡FASTEN, LINK, AND JOIN; 409] 3 *v* **embrace**, hug, cuddle, enfold, squeeze, grasp, hold tight, hold close, clasp. [➡CONTACT: HOLD; 412] 4 *v* **contain**, accommodate, stow, carry, take in, have space for, comprise, seat, store, take. [➡HOLD AND CONTAIN; 456] 5 *v* **detain**, restrain, confine, shut in, imprison, keep, remand, lock up, incarcerate (*formal*). [➡REFUSE PERMISSION AND NOT ALLOW; 671] *Opposite:* let go. 6 *v* **arrange**, convene, call, conduct, have, run, call together, assemble, organize. [➡CAUSE TO HAPPEN; 31] 7 *v* **possess**, have, keep, retain, own, maintain, enjoy, occupy. [➡POSSESS; 445] 8 *v* **believe**, think, maintain, presume, consider, regard, view, deem (*formal*), reckon, feel, opine (*formal*). [➡DEVELOP THEORIES AND REASON; 745] 9 *v* **sustain**, maintain, continue, keep up, carry on, extend, draw out, stretch out. [➡CONTINUE TO EXIST; 17] 10 *v* **wait**, hold on, hang on, stay on the line. [➡CONTACT: HOLD; 412] *Opposite:* hang up. 11 *n* **grip**, grasp, clasp, clutch, embrace, clamp, clench. [➡CONTACT: HOLD; 412] 12 *n* **control**, power, influence, claim, sway, grasp, command, spell. [➡IMPORTANCE AND SIGNIFICANCE; 193] 13 *n* **storage space**, storeroom, cargo bay, compartment, storage. [➡STORES AND STORAGE BUILDINGS; 1087] 14 *part of* **ship or boat**. [➡PARTS OF A SHIP OR BOAT; 1150]

hold accountable *v* [➡ACCUSE, BLAME, AND CRITICIZE; 642]

holdall *n* **bag**, case, grip, suitcase, portmanteau, carryall (*US*). [➡CONTAINERS, RECEPTACLES, AND PACKAGING; 1244]

hold back 1 *v* **restrain**, inhibit, suppress, repress, contain, control, check, limit, hamper, obstruct, hinder, impede. [➡AVOID, PREVENT, LIMIT, AND CONTROL; 278] *Opposite:* let go. 2 *v* **keep back**, retain, keep, reserve, keep hold of, save, withhold, hide, conceal, delay, stifle. [➡STORE AND KEEP; 454] *Opposite:* release.

See Compare and Contrast at **hinder**.

hold captive *v* [➡CAPTIVITY AND LOSS OF FREEDOM; 249]

hold close *v* **hug**, embrace, hold tight, cuddle, enfold, squeeze, grasp, clasp. [➡CONTACT: HOLD; 412] *Opposite:* release.

hold dear *v* [➡LIKE, LOVE, VALUE, AND ENJOY; 579]

hold down (*informal*) *v* **keep**, retain, maintain, manage, hang onto, look after, keep hold of. [➡STORE AND KEEP; 454] *Opposite:* lose.

holder 1 *n* **container**, pouch, receptacle, vessel, box, frame, pocket. [➡CONTAINERS, RECEPTACLES, AND PACKAGING; 1244] 2 *n* **owner**, possessor, proprietor, controller, bearer, defender. [➡OWNERS; 447]

hold forth *v* **speak out**, harangue, preach, orate (*formal*), opine (*formal*), lecture, discourse, go on, rant. [➡WITTER AND BABBLE; 618] *Opposite:* bottle up.

hold in 1 *v* **keep in check**, restrain, keep back, hold back, control, bridle, constrain, inhibit. [➡NOT PAY ATTENTION; 765] *Opposite:* release. 2 *v* **restrain**, keep the lid on, control, bridle, suppress, repress, inhibit. [➡CAPTIVITY AND LOSS OF FREEDOM; 249] *Opposite:* let out.

hold in contempt *v* [➡DISLIKE AND HATE; 578]

holding 1 *n* **land**, field, property, farm, croft, plot, allotment. [➡THE COUNTRYSIDE AND OUTDOOR SPACES; 1070] 2 *n* **stock**, investment, share, property, interest, bond, asset. [➡POSSESSIONS; 462]

hold in high regard *v* **revere**, venerate, idolize, esteem, admire, think highly of, have a high opinion of. [➡LIKE, LOVE, VALUE, AND ENJOY; 579] *Opposite:* despise.

hold in the highest regard *v* [➡LIKE, LOVE, VALUE, AND ENJOY; 579]

hold off 1 *v* **refrain**, postpone, delay, put off, avoid, keep from, defer, adjourn, remit. [➡SHIRK AND DELAY; 274] *Opposite:* speed up. 2 *v* **resist**, fend off, keep away, keep off, repel, repulse, keep at bay, rebuff, rebut. [➡AVOID OR ESCAPE CONTACT; 419] *Opposite:* yield.

hold on 1 *v* **wait**, hang on, hold your horses (*informal*), be patient, wait a minute, wait up (*US informal*). [➡SHIRK AND DELAY; 274] 2 *v* **grasp**, grip, keep hold of, hold fast, stick, clasp, clutch, hang on. [➡CONTACT: HOLD; 412] *Opposite:* let go. 3 *v* **persist**, persevere, keep on, stand your ground, stand firm, stick at it, last out, stick it out, hold out, hang in there (*US informal*). [➡TOLERATE AND ENDURE; 767] *Opposite:* give up.

hold onto 1 *v* **retain**, keep, hang onto, save, hoard, store, set aside. [➡STORE AND KEEP; 454] *Opposite:* give up. 2 *v* **grasp**, clasp, clutch, grip, stick, keep hold of, hold fast, hang onto, cling to. [➡CONTACT: HOLD; 412] *Opposite:* release.

hold out 1 *v* **extend**, give, present, offer, proffer, stretch out. [➡PROFFER AND HAND OVER; 432] *Opposite:* withdraw. 2 *v* **endure**, stand your ground, persist, stand firm, withstand, persevere, stand fast, last, resist. [➡TOLERATE AND ENDURE; 767] *Opposite:* give in.

hold out on *v* **not tell**, keep something from, hide something from, withhold something from. [➡WITHHOLD INFORMATION; 688] *Opposite:* tell.

hold over *v* **defer**, delay, postpone, put off, suspend, adjourn, keep, hold up, shelve. [➡DELAY ACTION OR OCCURRENCE; 279] *Opposite:* bring forward.

hold prisoner *v* [➡CAPTIVITY AND LOSS OF FREEDOM; 249]

hold responsible *v* [➡ACCUSE, BLAME, AND CRITICIZE; 642]

hold sway *v* **have authority**, have influence, have power, be in power, be in control, reign, govern, rule, rule the roost. [➡BE IN CHARGE; 271]

hold the fort *v* **look after things**, take care of things, take over, take charge, mind things, attend to things. [➡PARTICIPATE; 293]

hold up 1 *v* **delay**, slow down, slow up, impede, hinder, set back, detain, hold back, remit, suspend, postpone, defer. [➡DELAY ACTION OR OCCURRENCE; 279] *Opposite:* speed up. 2 *v* **rob**, raid, mug, do (*slang*), stick up (*US informal*). [➡STEAL AND ROB; 427] 3 *v* **survive**, bear up, keep up, endure, keep going, hold out, last. [➡CONTINUE TO EXIST; 17] *Opposite:* give in. 4 *v* **support**, shore up, keep up, prop, sustain, buttress. [➡APPROVE AND CONFIRM; 647] *Opposite:* bring down.

holdup 1 *n* **theft**, raid, robbery, assault, mugging, stickup (*US informal*), heist (*US slang*). [➡CRIMES; 817] 2 *n* **delay**, snafu (*informal*), hitch, glitch, snag, stoppage, obstruction, difficulty, bottleneck, hindrance. [➡PROBLEM; 257]

See Compare and Contrast at **theft**.

hold with *v* **approve of**, endorse, support, subscribe to, agree with, like, countenance (*formal*), accept. [➡APPROVE AND CONFIRM; 647] *Opposite:* disapprove.

hold your own 1 *v* **match up**, stand your ground, stand firm, look after yourself, take care of yourself, give a good account of yourself, acquit yourself well (*formal*). [➡CONTINUE AN ACTION; 263] 2 *v* **bear up**, persevere, be stable, be comfortable, persist, endure, hang on. [➡TOLERATE AND ENDURE; 767] *Opposite:* succumb.

hole 1 *n* **cavity**, hollow, void, chasm, gulf, abyss, pit, dip. [➡HOLES, GAPS, AND FORKS; 1251] 2 *n* **aperture**, gap, opening, crack, break, outlet, puncture, fissure, tear, perforation. [➡HOLES, GAPS, AND FORKS; 1251] 3 *n* **burrow**, lair, retreat, run, sett, earth, warren, den. [➡ANIMAL OR BIRD ACCOMMODATION; 1078] 4 *n* (*informal*) **pigsty**, dump (*informal*), fleapit, hovel, slum, shack, fleabag (*US informal*), pigpen (*US*). [➡UNDESIRABLE ACCOMMODATION; 856] 5 *n* **flaw**, weakness, fault, error, defect, inconsistency. [➡FAULTS, FLAWS, AND WEAKNESSES; 252] *Opposite:* strength.

hole-and-corner *adj* **secret**, secretive, hidden, clandestine, private, undercover. [➡SECRET AND UNKNOWN; 180] *Opposite:* public.

hole-in-the-wall (*informal*) *n* **restaurant**, bar, dive (*informal*), bistro, café, joint (*slang*). [➡HOTELS, RESTAURANTS, AND CLUBS; 1081]

hole up (*slang*) *v* **hide**, shut up, hibernate, seclude, closet, retreat. [➡RUN AWAY AND AVOID; 10] *Opposite:* emerge.

holey *adj* **leaky**, porous, perforated, worn, torn, punctured. [➡IN BAD REPAIR; 1233]

holiday 1 *n* **day off**, break, long weekend, trip, outing, leave, R and R, personal day (*US*). [➡PERIOD OF REST; 91] 2 *n* **leave**, time off, hols (*informal*), break, vacation, sabbatical, leave of absence. [➡PERIOD OF REST; 91] *Opposite:* work. 3 *n* **festival**, bank holiday, anniversary, public holiday, feast, saint's day, carnival, legal holiday (*US*). [➡PARTIES, DANCES, AND CELEBRATIONS; 37] 4 *v* **be on holiday**, stay, relax, slob around (*informal*), sojourn (*literary*), vacation (*US*). [➡HOBBIES, GAMES, AND SPORTS; 875] *Opposite:* work.

holidaymaker *n* **traveller**, sightseer, visitor, tourist, day tripper, tripper (*informal*), vacationer (*US*). [➡TRAVEL: TRAVELLERS AND WALKERS; 320] *Opposite:* resident.

holier-than-thou (*informal*) *adj* **self-righteous** (*disapproving*), pious, smug, superior, sanctimonious, pompous. [➡AFFECTATION, SELF-SATISFACTION, AND SNOBBISHNESS; 508] *Opposite:* self-effacing.

holiness *n* **sanctity**, sacredness, piety, godliness, religiousness, saintliness, consecration, devoutness, devotion, purity. [➡RELIGIOUS CONCEPTS; 777]

holistic *adj* **all-inclusive**, rounded, full, complete, general, universal, whole. [➡HEALING; 731]

holler (*informal*) 1 *v* **shout**, yell, scream, shriek, howl, bawl, bellow, call. [➡SOUND EMISSION BY PEOPLE; 364] *Opposite:* whisper. 2 *n* **yell**, shout, scream, shriek, howl, bellow, call. [➡SOUNDS MADE BY PEOPLE; 1261] *Opposite:* whisper.

hollow 1 *adj* **empty**, void, unfilled, vacant, unoccupied. [➡EMPTY; 1237] *Opposite:* solid. 2 *adj* **concave**, depressed, sunken, indented, cavernous. [➡ROUNDED SHAPE; 1217] *Opposite:* convex. 3 *adj* **resonating**, echoing, deep, low, dull, muffled, muted, dead, heavy, reverberating, reverberant, resounding. [➡SOFT OR PLEASANT SOUNDS; 1264] *Opposite:* high-pitched. 4 *adj* **insincere**, empty, worthless, futile, vain, false, insignificant, unconvincing, cynical, meaningless. [➡REDUNDANT AND USELESS; 241] *Opposite:* sincere. 5 *n* **cavity**, recess, indentation, cup, nook, curve, hole, cave, cavern. [➡HOLES, GAPS, AND FORKS; 1251] *Opposite:* bulge. 6 *n* **valley**, crater, dip, depression, basin, dell (*literary*), trough, bowl. [➡HOLES, GAPS, AND FORKS; 1251] *Opposite:* hump. 7 *v* **excavate**, scoop, dig out, gouge, tunnel, burrow, scrape, carve out. [➡EMPTY AND UNLOAD; 408] *Opposite:* fill.

See Compare and Contrast at **vain**.

hollowly 1 *adv* **dully**, deeply, flatly, heavily, resoundingly, reverberantly. [➡SOFT OR PLEASANT SOUNDS; 1264] *Opposite:* shrilly. 2 *adv* **insincerely**, emptily, worthlessly, futilely, vainly, falsely, unconvincingly, cynically, meaninglessly. [➡INARTICULATE, RAMBLING, AND AWKWARD; 634] *Opposite:* sincerely.

hollowness 1 *n* **void**, empty space, cavity, emptiness, concavity, openness. [➡HOLES, GAPS, AND FORKS; 1251] *Opposite:* solidity. 2 *n* **insincerity**, emptiness, worthlessness, futility, vainness, falseness, unconvincingness, meaninglessness. [➡REDUNDANT AND USELESS; 241] *Opposite:* sincerity.

holly *type of* **evergreen tree**. [➡EVERGREEN AND CONIFEROUS TREES; 1029]

holocaust *n* [➡AGGRESSIVE EVENT; 39]

hols (*informal*) *n* [➡PERIOD OF REST; 91]

holy 1 *adj* **sacred**, consecrated, hallowed, sanctified, blessed, divine. [➡RELIGIOUS CONCEPTS; 777] *Opposite:* irreligious. 2 *adj* **saintly**, righteous, devout, religious, godly, pious, pure, virtuous, faithful. [➡RELIGIOUS CONCEPTS; 777]

holy day *n* [➡RELIGIOUS CONCEPTS; 777]

Holy Father *n* [➡RELIGIOUS PEOPLE; 779]

holy man *n* [➡RELIGIOUS PEOPLE; 779]

holy of holies *n* [➡RELIGIOUS CONCEPTS; 777]

holy rites *n* [➡RELIGIOUS CONCEPTS; 777]

holy sister *n* [➡RELIGIOUS PEOPLE; 779]

homage *n* **deference**, reverence, respect, service, duty, worship, praise, tribute, honour. [➡LOVE, RESPECT, AND GOODWILL; 550] *Opposite:* disrespect.

homburg *type of* **hat.** [➡HABERDASHERY, MILLINERY, AND LINGERIE; 867]

home 1 *n* **residence**, dwelling (*formal*), abode (*literary*), house, habitat, quarters, domicile (*formal*), address. [➡ACCOMMODATION; 855] 2 *n* **family**, household, family circle, family unit, background, home environment. [➡THE FAMILY; 956] 3 *n* **birthplace**, place of birth, homeland, home town, native land, fatherland, motherland, native soil. [➡COUNTRIES AND REGIONS; 1066] 4 *n* **institution**, residence, residential home, children's home, rest home, nursing home, establishment, hospice, assisted living (*US*), eldercare (*US*), Elderhostel (*US*). [➡PUBLIC BUILDINGS AND MEETING PLACES; 1080] 5 *adj* **internal**, domestic, inland, interior, local, national. [➡GOVERNMENT AND POLITICS; 805] *Opposite:* foreign. 6 *adj* **home-based**, household, homegrown, family, domestic, homespun, homemade, home-produced. [➡ACCOMMODATION; 855] *Opposite:* industrial. 7 *adv* **homewards**, back home, in, home sweet home, back at the ranch (*US informal*). [➡DIRECTION OF MOTION; 346]

home-brew *n* [➡DRINKS; 1186]

homecoming *n* **return**, arrival, repatriation, visit, revisiting. [➡ARRIVAL; 13] *Opposite:* emigration.

home fries (*US*) *type of* **processed potato.** [➡FRUIT AND VEGETABLES; 1175]

home help *n* **domestic**, cleaner, maid, au pair, carer, housekeeper. [➡DOMESTIC AND KITCHEN WORKERS; 850]

home in *v* **focus**, zoom in, move in, aim, take aim, point, zero in, bear down on, pinpoint. [➡ACCOMPANY AND FOLLOW; 338] *Opposite:* draw back.

homeland *n* **native country**, mother country, native land, fatherland, motherland, home, birthplace, land of birth, land of origin. [➡COUNTRIES AND REGIONS; 1066]

homeless *adj* **on the streets**, living rough, dispossessed, destitute, vagrant, displaced, itinerant, poor, adrift. [➡POVERTY AND POOR; 892] *Opposite:* housed.

homelessness *n* [➡POVERTY AND POOR; 892]

homely 1 *adj* **cosy**, simple, plain, ordinary, unpretentious, informal, comfortable. [➡ACCEPTABLE AND PASSABLE; 220] *Opposite:* fancy. 2 *adj* **unattractive**, plain, unappealing, ugly, mousy, unlovely. [➡PLAIN; 233] *Opposite:* attractive.

home page *n* **Web site**, site, location, Internet domain, Web page, URL, address, file. [➡THE INTERNET; 1127]

home rule *n* **self-government**, autonomy, self-rule, independence, separatism, nationalism, self-reliance. [➡STYLES AND SYSTEMS OF GOVERNMENT; 806]

homesick *adj* **nostalgic**, sad, melancholy, pining, unsettled, upset, wistful, unhappy. [➡SADNESS, DISTRESS, AND DESPAIR; 540] *Opposite:* content.

homesickness *n* [➡SADNESS, DISTRESS, AND DESPAIR; 540]

homespun *adj* **plain**, simple, ordinary, unsophisticated, down-to-earth, uncomplicated, straightforward, unpretentious. [➡PLAIN; 233] *Opposite:* sophisticated.

homestead 1 *n* **farm**, farmstead, ranch, smallholding, croft, estate. [➡HUMAN SETTLEMENTS; 1069] 2 *type of* **house.** [➡RESIDENTIAL BUILDINGS; 1077]

home town *n* **birthplace**, home, home base, back yard, home ground, turf (*informal*). [➡HUMAN SETTLEMENTS; 1069]

home truth *n* **fact**, truth, bitter pill, criticism. [➡ADVICE; 690] *Opposite:* lie.

homework 1 *n* **schoolwork**, exercise, lesson, study, assignment, coursework, project, prep (*informal*), task. [➡LESSONS, COURSE WORK, AND EXAMINATIONS; 842] 2 *n* (*informal*) **preparation**, legwork (*informal*), reading, research, groundwork, reading up, fact-finding. [➡LESSONS, COURSE WORK, AND EXAMINATIONS; 842]

homeworker *n* [➡WORKER; 836]

homeworking *n* [➡TYPES OF WORK; 835]

homicidal *adj* **murderous**, destructive, killer, killing, bloodthirsty, dangerous, violent, vindictive. [➡AGGRESSIVE AND BELLIGERENT; 519] *Opposite:* harmless.

homicide *n* **killing**, murder, slaughter, shooting, stabbing, manslaughter, assassination. [➡CAUSES OF DEATH; 921]

homily *n* **lecture**, sermon, talk, speech, discourse, oration. [➡NEUTRAL ONE-WAY COMMUNICATION; 49]

homing pigeon *type of* **pet bird.** [➡BIRD; 997]

hominid *n* **primate**, hominoid, anthropoid. [➡PERSON; 931]

hominoid *n* **primate**, hominid, anthropoid. [➡PERSON; 931]

homochromatic *adj* [➡DESCRIBING COLOURS; 1225]

homochromous *adj* [➡DESCRIBING COLOURS; 1225]

homogeneity 1 *n* **sameness**, similarity, equality, homogeneousness, consistency, regularity. [➡SAMENESS; 151] 2 *n* **uniformity**, consistency, evenness, regularity, smoothness, harmony. [➡SAMENESS; 151] *Opposite:* unevenness.

homogeneous 1 *adj* **same**, similar, standardized, consistent, equal, regular, identical. [➡SAMENESS; 151] *Opposite:* heterogeneous. 2 *adj* **uniform**, consistent, even, regular, smooth, harmonized. [➡SAMENESS; 151] *Opposite:* uneven.

homogeneously *adv* [➡SAMENESS; 151]

homogeneousness 1 *n* **sameness**, similarity, equality, homogeneity, consistency, regularity. [➡SAMENESS; 151]

2 *n* **uniformity**, regularity, consistency, evenness, smoothness, harmony. [➡ SAMENESS; 151] *Opposite:* unevenness.

homogenize 1 *v* **smooth**, emulsify, mix, beat, whip, combine, treat. [➡ COOKING AND FOOD PREPARATION; 354] *Opposite:* separate out. 2 *v* **standardize**, normalize, even out, regulate, make the same, make uniform. [➡ ARRANGE AND CREATE ORDER; 358] *Opposite:* distinguish.

homophobe *n* [➡ GRUMPY AND NEGATIVE PEOPLE; 953]

homophobic *adj* [➡ NEGATIVE INTELLECTUAL CHARACTERISTICS; 526]

homo sapiens *n* [➡ PERSON; 931]

honcho (*US slang*) *n* [➡ IMPORTANT OR FAMOUS PEOPLE; 893]

hone 1 *v* **improve**, refine, enhance, polish, sharpen, perfect, work on, practise, groom, prepare. [➡ IMPROVE SOMETHING; 375] *Opposite:* impair. 2 *v* **sharpen**, whet, file, grind, polish, point. [➡ CLEAN AND POLISH; 404] *Opposite:* blunt.

honest 1 *adj* **upright**, trustworthy, moral, good, decent, law-abiding, reliable, scrupulous, honourable. [➡ MORALLY BAD; 776] *Opposite:* immoral. 2 *adj* **truthful**, authentic, true, sincere, frank, candid, straightforward, direct, open. [➡ HONEST AND RELIABLE; 503] *Opposite:* untruthful.

honestly 1 *adv* **fairly**, justly, in all conscience, decently, reliably, scrupulously, honourably, in good conscience. [➡ HONEST AND OPEN; 631] *Opposite:* immorally. 2 *adv* **really**, truly, truthfully, candidly, openly, in all honesty, genuinely, sincerely. [➡ TRUE AND REAL; 172] *Opposite:* untruthfully.

honesty 1 *n* **uprightness**, morality, trustworthiness, goodness, scrupulousness, honour, decency, rectitude, righteousness, fairness, reliability. [➡ MORAL CONCEPTS; 774] *Opposite:* immorality. 2 *n* **sincerity**, truthfulness, integrity, frankness, candour, openness, authenticity, straightforwardness, directness. [➡ HONEST AND RELIABLE; 503] *Opposite:* untruthfulness.

honey 1 *type of* **preserve**. [➡ SUGAR AND PRESERVES; 1183] 2 *type of* **beige**. [➡ COLOURS; 1223] 3 *n* (*US informal*) **darling**, dear, dearest, sweetheart, sugar (*informal*), sweetie (*informal*), sweetie pie (*informal*), honeybunch (*US informal*), honeybun (*US informal*). [➡ ENDEARMENTS; 657]

honeybun (*US informal*) *n* [➡ ENDEARMENTS; 657]

honeybunch (*US informal*) *n* [➡ ENDEARMENTS; 657]

honeyed 1 *adj* **ingratiating**, sugarcoated, cloying, pleasing, soothing, flattering, fawning, persuasive. [➡ CALMING; 189] *Opposite:* sharp. 2 *adj* **melodious**, soft, dulcet, sweet, melodic, mellifluous. [➡ SOFT OR PLEASANT SOUNDS; 1264] *Opposite:* harsh.

honeymoon period *n* [➡ PLEASANT SITUATIONS; 74]

honey-pie (*US informal*) *n* [➡ ENDEARMENTS; 657]

honeysuckle *type of* **climber**. [➡ CLIMBERS; 1033]

honk 1 *n* **hoot**, toot, tootle (*informal*), beep, blare, blast, blow. [➡ RINGING AND TOOTING SOUNDS; 1258] 2 *type of* **continuous sound**. [➡ CONTINUOUS SOUNDS; 1257] 3 *v* **beep**, hoot, toot, tootle (*informal*), blare, blast, blow. [➡ EMIT RINGING AND TOOTING SOUNDS; 368]

honky-tonk (*US slang*) *n* [➡ BUILDINGS FOR PUBLIC ENTERTAINMENT; 1083]

honorarium *n* **payment**, fee, grant, scholarship, exhibition, stipend, allowance. [➡ GIFTS; 439]

See Compare and Contrast at **wage**.

honorary 1 *adj* **nominal**, token, symbolic, titular. [➡ EXTRAORDINARY: AMAZING; 205] 2 *adj* **unpaid**, voluntary, unwaged, unsalaried, amateur, volunteer, complimentary, pro bono. [➡ EMPLOYMENT STATUS; 831] *Opposite:* salaried.

honour 1 *n* **integrity**, decency, morality, righteousness, rectitude, principle, uprightness, scrupulousness, character. [➡ MORALLY GOOD; 775] *Opposite:* baseness. 2 *n* **respect**, admiration, esteem, regard, reverence, devotion. [➡ LOVE, RESPECT, AND GOODWILL; 550] *Opposite:* scorn. 3 *n* **dignity**, distinction, nobility, pride, decorum, graciousness. [➡ GOOD MANNERS AND SOCIAL SKILLS; 521] 4 *n* **reputation**, image, good name, name, renown, repute (*formal*). [➡ NAME AND DESCRIBE; 666] *Opposite:* disgrace. 5 *n* **distinction**, award, tribute, credit, accolade, compliment, commendation, commemoration, remembrance, medal, badge, certificate, medallion, degree, blue ribbon, gold medal. [➡ REWARDS AND AWARDS; 440] *Opposite:* blot. 6 *v* **keep**, stick to, fulfil, carry out. [➡ OBEY AND ABIDE BY; 302] *Opposite:* break. 7 *v* **esteem**, respect, admire, take your hat off to, revere, reverence, venerate, pay tribute to, pay homage to, exalt (*formal*), toast. [➡ LIKE, LOVE, VALUE, AND ENJOY; 579] *Opposite:* disparage.

honourable 1 *adj* **moral**, upright, noble, worthy, right, proper, ethical, decent, principled, good, fair, righteous. [➡ MORALLY GOOD; 775] *Opposite:* immoral. 2 *adj* **respectable**, decent, admirable, praiseworthy, worthy, laudable. [➡ MORALLY GOOD; 775] *Opposite:* shameful.

honoured *adj* **privileged**, pleased, flattered, grateful, thrilled. [➡ PLEASURE, EXCITEMENT, AND ELATION; 535] *Opposite:* insulted.

hooch (*US slang*) *n* [➡ DRINKS; 1186]

hood 1 *type of* **headgear**. [➡ HABERDASHERY, MILLINERY, AND LINGERIE; 867] 2 *n* (*US slang*) **hoodlum**, gangster, criminal, lawbreaker, thug, ruffian (*dated*), hooligan (*informal*), mobster (*US informal*). [➡ VILLAINS AND THUGS; 947] 3 *n* (*US slang*) **neighbourhood**, area, district, region, quarter. [➡ PLACE; 1064] 4 (*US*) *part of* **external structure**. [➡ EXTERNAL PARTS OF A VEHICLE; 1146]

hoodlum *n* **gangster**, criminal, lawbreaker, thug, ruffian (*dated*), hooligan (*informal*), yob (*informal*), yobbo (*informal*), mobster (*US informal*), hood (*US slang*). [➡ VILLAINS AND THUGS; 947]

hoodwink *v* **trick**, deceive, dupe, delude, take in, con, fool, pull the wool over somebody's eyes. [➡ DECEPTION AND LIES; 661]

hooey (*informal*) *n* **nonsense**, humbug, rubbish, hogwash (*informal*), bunkum (*informal*), twaddle (*informal*), gibberish, codswallop (*informal*), claptrap (*informal*), garbage, bunk (*slang*). [➡ MEANINGLESS SPEECH OR WRITING; 677] *Opposite:* fact.

hoof *part of* **horse**. [➡ HORSE; 985]

hoo-hah (*slang*) *n* **flap** (*informal*), scene, row, fuss, to-do (*informal*), commotion, hubbub, disturbance, hullabaloo, stir. [➡CHAOS AND UPROAR; 51]

hoojamaflip (*informal*) *n* [➡PHYSICAL OBJECTS; 1242]

hook 1 *n* **peg**, hanger, nail, knob, catch, fishhook, meat hook, boat hook. [➡FASTENERS, LINKS, AND NETWORKS; 1246] 2 *v* **fasten**, attach, secure, join, tie, couple, button, fix. [➡FASTEN, LINK, AND JOIN; 409]

hook and eye *n* **fastener**, fastening, clasp, catch, clip, closure. [➡FASTENERS, LINKS, AND NETWORKS; 1246]

hooked 1 *adj* **bent**, curved, bowed, curving, angular, aquiline. [➡ROUNDED SHAPE; 1217] *Opposite:* straight. 2 *adj* (*slang*) **obsessed**, infatuated, smitten (*humorous or literary*), enthusiastic, keen, captivated, passionate. [➡PENSIVENESS AND INTEREST; 539] *Opposite:* unenthusiastic.

hook up 1 *v* **connect**, link up, plug in, wire up, electrify. [➡FASTEN, LINK, AND JOIN; 409] *Opposite:* disconnect. 2 *v* (*informal*) **get together**, take up with, meet up, meet, pair off, make friends. [➡INITIATE AND ESTABLISH COMMUNICATION; 681] *Opposite:* part.

hooligan (*informal*) *n* **criminal**, gangster, lawbreaker, thug, ruffian (*dated*), hoodlum, yob (*informal*), yobbo (*informal*), mobster (*US informal*). [➡VILLAINS AND THUGS; 947]

hoop *n* **ring**, loop, band, circle, round, girdle. [➡ROUNDED SHAPE; 1217]

hoopla (*US informal*) *n* [➡MEANINGLESS SPEECH OR WRITING; 677]

hooray *interj* [➡EXPRESSIONS OF SURPRISE; 547]

hoot 1 *n* **beep**, honk, toot, tootle (*informal*), blare, blast. [➡RINGING AND TOOTING SOUNDS; 1258] 2 *n* (*slang*) **laugh** (*informal*), laughing stock, riot (*informal*), gas (*informal*), scream (*informal*). [➡FUNNY AND AMUSING; 217] 3 *n* **whoop**, howl, shout, roar, cry, guffaw, yell. [➡SOUNDS MADE BY BIRDS; 1262] 4 *type of* **continuous sound**. [➡CONTINUOUS SOUNDS; 1257] 5 *v* **shout**, howl, whoop, roar, cry out, guffaw, yell. [➡SOUND EMISSION BY PEOPLE; 364] 6 *v* **toot**, tootle (*informal*), beep, honk, blare, blow. [➡EMIT RINGING AND TOOTING SOUNDS; 368]

hoot owl *type of* **owl**. [➡OWL; 1001]

hop 1 *v* **jump**, skip, leap, bounce, pogo, dance. [➡BOUNCE, UNDULATE, AND VIBRATE; 309] 2 *v* **spring**, bound, leap, bounce, jump, vault. [➡BOUNCE, UNDULATE, AND VIBRATE; 309] 3 *n* **leap**, jump, skip, bound, step, spring. [➡PROCEED AND GO; 306] 4 *n* (*informal*) **flight**, journey, trip, stage, leg, step. [➡TRAVEL: JOURNEYS AND TRIPS; 319] 5 *n* (*dated informal*) **dance**, shindig (*informal*), do (*informal*), bop (*informal*), party, disco, barn dance, hoedown (*US*). [➡PARTIES, DANCES, AND CELEBRATIONS; 37]

hope 1 *v* **want**, expect, trust, anticipate, wish, yearn, long, look forward to. [➡PREDICT AND ANTICIPATE; 751] *Opposite:* despair. 2 *n* **confidence**, expectation, optimism, anticipation, faith, courage, hopefulness. [➡FEELINGS ABOUT THE FUTURE; 534] *Opposite:* despair. 3 *n* **likelihood**, prospect, possibility, promise, potential, chance. [➡POSSIBLE AND PROBABLE; 178] *Opposite:* impossibility. 4 *n* **desire**, aspiration, dream, expectation, plan, wish, goal. [➡DESIRE AND WANT; 580]

hopeful 1 *adj* **confident**, expectant, optimistic, positive, encouraged, buoyant, anticipative. [➡CALMNESS, CONFIDENCE, AND COMPOSURE; 537] *Opposite:* pessimistic. 2 *adj* **promising**, encouraging, positive, rosy, propitious, likely. [➡EMOTIONALLY PLEASANT; 188] *Opposite:* discouraging. 3 *adj* **aspiring**, prospective, would-be, potential, budding, embryonic, possible. [➡POSSIBLE AND PROBABLE; 178] 4 *n* **aspirant**, candidate, applicant, contender, seeker. [➡COMPETITORS; 41]

hopefully 1 *adv* **confidently**, expectantly, optimistically, positively, buoyantly. [➡CALMNESS, CONFIDENCE, AND COMPOSURE; 537] *Opposite:* despairingly. 2 *adv* **with any luck**, with a bit of luck, all being well. [➡POSSIBLE AND PROBABLE; 178]

hopefulness 1 *n* **confidence**, hope, optimism, expectation, anticipation, positiveness, positivity. [➡FEELINGS ABOUT THE FUTURE; 534] *Opposite:* despair. 2 *n* **promise**, encouragement, positiveness, positivity, rosiness, propitiousness. [➡FEELINGS ABOUT THE FUTURE; 534]

hopeless 1 *adj* **impossible**, desperate, unpromising, fruitless, bleak, doomed, bad. [➡EMOTIONALLY UNPLEASANT AND UPSETTING; 228] *Opposite:* promising. 2 *adj* **despairing**, desperate, in despair, despondent, disheartened, downhearted, forlorn, depressed, miserable, morose. [➡SADNESS, DISTRESS, AND DESPAIR; 540] *Opposite:* positive. 3 *adj* **useless**, bad, pathetic, inept, clueless (*informal*), incompetent, terrible. [➡UNSKILLED; 530] *Opposite:* excellent.

hopelessly 1 *adv* **despairingly**, in despair, desperately, despondently, downheartedly, forlornly, miserably, bleakly. [➡SADNESS, DISTRESS, AND DESPAIR; 540] *Opposite:* positively. 2 *adv* **terribly**, desperately, badly, completely, totally, utterly, awfully, very. [➡TO A GREAT EXTENT; 130] *Opposite:* slightly.

hopelessness 1 *n* **impossibility**, desperateness, fruitlessness, bleakness, futility. [➡IMPOSSIBLE AND IMPROBABLE; 179] *Opposite:* promise. 2 *n* **despair**, desperation, despondency, bleakness, depression, misery. [➡FEELINGS ABOUT THE FUTURE; 534] *Opposite:* hope. 3 *n* **uselessness**, ineptness, ineptitude, incompetence, cluelessness (*informal*), inability. [➡UNSKILLED; 530] *Opposite:* excellence.

hopping mad (*informal*) *adj* **enraged**, furious, irate, apoplectic, beside yourself, seething, angry, annoyed. [➡IRRITATION AND ANGER; 542] *Opposite:* calm.

horde *n* **throng**, crowd, mass, gang, group, multitude, host, flock, pack. [➡GROUPS OF PEOPLE; 935]

hordes *n* [➡MANY, MUCH, LARGE AMOUNT; 117]

horizon *n* **skyline**, distance, vanishing point, vista, prospect, limit. [➡POSSIBLE AND PROBABLE; 178]

horizontal *adj* **level**, flat, straight, plane. [➡ORIENTATION AND ALIGNMENT; 1222] *Opposite:* vertical.

horn 1 *n* **siren**, klaxon, hooter, alarm, buzzer, bleeper, alert. [➡AUDIO EQUIPMENT; 1138] 2 *n* **antler**, spine, barb, projection, tusk, point, spike. [➡EXTREMITIES OF PHYSICAL OBJECTS; 1249] 3 *type of* **controls**. [➡VEHICLES; 1144] 4 *type of* **brass instrument**. [➡MUSICAL INSTRUMENTS; 910]

hornblende *type of* **stone**. [➡STONES, ROCKS, AND BOULDERS; 1057]

horned lizard *type of* **reptile**. [➡REPTILES; 994]

horned toad *type of* **amphibian**. [➡AMPHIBIANS; 1008]

horned viper *type of* **poisonous snake**. [➡SNAKE; 995]

hornet *type of* **flying insect**. [➡FLYING INSECTS; 1013]

hornet's nest *n* [➡DIFFICULT SITUATIONS; 72]

horn in (*informal*) *v* [➡INTERRUPT AND BUTT IN; 620]

horn of plenty 1 *n* **cornucopia**, abundance, treasure chest, ready supply, never-ending supply, treasure house, treasury, Aladdin's cave. [➡MANY, MUCH, LARGE AMOUNT; 117] *Opposite:* famine. 2 *type of* **fungus**. [➡MICROORGANISMS, FUNGI, AND ALGAE; 1023]

horny *adj* [➡DIFFICULTY AND COMPLEXITY; 243]

horrendous 1 *adj* **dreadful**, awful, terrible, dire, unbearable, atrocious, unspeakable, horrific, ghastly, hideous, horrible, appalling, upsetting, shocking, staggering. [➡EMOTIONALLY UNPLEASANT AND UPSETTING; 228] *Opposite:* wonderful. 2 *adj* (*informal*) **outrageous**, exorbitant, sky-high, shocking, dreadful, terrible. [➡DISGUSTING AND REPULSIVE; 231]

horrible 1 *adj* **unpleasant**, bad, awful, vile, dreadful, disgusting, horrid, horrendous, terrible, unbearable, atrocious, unspeakable, ghastly, appalling. [➡EMOTIONALLY UNPLEASANT AND UPSETTING; 228] *Opposite:* pleasant. 2 *adj* **horrifying**, awful, terrible, nasty, atrocious, ghastly, hideous, horrific, repulsive, dreadful, upsetting, shocking, unspeakable, horrendous, appalling. [➡FRIGHTENING; 232] *Opposite:* lovely.

horribly 1 *adv* **unpleasantly**, dreadfully, badly, terribly, unbearably, disgustingly, hideously, awfully, atrociously, unspeakably, horrifically, horrendously, appallingly. [➡EMOTIONALLY UNPLEASANT AND UPSETTING; 228] *Opposite:* pleasantly. 2 *adv* **extremely**, greatly, very, totally, utterly, absolutely, unbearably, outrageously. [➡TO A GREAT EXTENT; 130]

horrid 1 *adj* **nasty** (*informal*), unkind, callous, mean, beastly (*dated informal*), rotten, despicable, vile, awful, unpleasant, hateful, horrible, dreadful, unspeakable, appalling, terrible. [➡EMOTIONALLY UNPLEASANT AND UPSETTING; 228] *Opposite:* pleasant. 2 *adj* **disgusting**, awful, dreadful, nasty, vile, horrible, unspeakable, loathsome, repellent. [➡DISGUSTING AND REPULSIVE; 231] *Opposite:* pleasing. 3 *adj* **dreadful**, shocking, appalling, horrific, frightful, hideous. [➡FRIGHTENING; 232]

horridness 1 *n* **nastiness**, beastliness, unpleasantness, hatefulness, meanness, unkindness. [➡UNKIND ACTION OR BEHAVIOUR; 297] *Opposite:* pleasantness. 2 *n* **disgustingness**, loathsomeness, vileness, dreadfulness, unpleasantness. [➡DISGUSTING AND REPULSIVE; 231] *Opposite:* attractiveness. 3 *n* **dreadfulness**, frightfulness, terribleness, awfulness, horror, shockingness. [➡FRIGHTENING; 232]

horrific *adj* **appalling**, dreadful, awful, horrendous, horrifying, shocking, ghastly, sickening, gruesome, horrible, terrible. [➡DISGUSTING AND REPULSIVE; 231] *Opposite:* wonderful.

horrified 1 *adj* **appalled**, shocked, aghast, sickened, disgusted, revolted, dismayed, horror-struck. [➡SURPRISE, SHOCK, AND AMAZEMENT; 546] *Opposite:* delighted. 2 *adj* **dismayed**, depressed, shocked, perplexed, disturbed, perturbed, confounded, upset, alarmed. [➡SADNESS, DISTRESS, AND DESPAIR; 540]

horrify 1 *v* **appal**, disgust, revolt, shock, sicken, repel. [➡FRIGHTEN AND SHOCK; 569] *Opposite:* delight. 2 *v* **dismay**, depress, shock, perplex, disturb, perturb, confound, upset, alarm. [➡UPSET, DISTRESS, AND HUMILIATE; 568]

horrifying 1 *adj* **horrific**, horrible, horrendous, terrible, sickening, appalling, shocking, gruesome, dreadful, awful, ghastly. [➡FRIGHTENING; 232] *Opposite:* delightful. 2 *adj* **dismaying**, depressing, shocking, perplexing, disturbing, upsetting, perturbing, alarming. [➡EMOTIONALLY UNPLEASANT AND UPSETTING; 228]

horror *n* **fear**, shock, revulsion, dismay, disgust, repulsion, dreadfulness, awfulness, terror, dread, distress, alarm, panic. [➡SADNESS, DISTRESS, AND DESPAIR; 540] *Opposite:* delight.

horror-stricken *adj* **horror-struck**, petrified, scared stiff, terrified, horrified, stunned, shocked, aghast, frightened, appalled, dismayed. [➡FEAR AND PANIC; 544]

horror-struck *adj* **horror-stricken**, petrified, scared stiff, terrified, horrified, stunned, shocked, aghast, frightened, appalled, dismayed. [➡SURPRISE, SHOCK, AND AMAZEMENT; 546]

hors de combat *adj* **wounded**, out of action, incapacitated, injured, in hospital, disabled, in the hospital (*US*). [➡INJURED; 743] *Opposite:* able.

hors d'oeuvre *n* **appetizer**, starter, entrée, first course, nibbles. [➡MEALS AND PARTS OF MEALS; 1168]

horse 1 *n* **mount**, pony, steed (*literary*), charger. [➡HORSE; 985] 2 *type of* **farm animal**. [➡FARM ANIMAL; 982]

> **horse**
>
> ◆ *parts of a horse*
> croup, fetlock, flank, foreleg, hindquarters, hock, hoof, mane, pastern, shank, withers
>
> ◆ *types of horse*
> Arabian horse, bronco, brood mare, carthorse, charger, cob, hack, hunter, mustang, packhorse, pony, racehorse, saddle horse, Shetland pony, shire horse, thoroughbred, trotter, warhorse, workhorse

horse about *v* [➡JOKES AND TEASING; 675]

horse around *v* **fool around**, play around, clown, act the fool, cavort, romp. [➡FIDGET AND FROLIC; 312]

horseback riding (*US*) *n* [➡HOBBIES, GAMES, AND SPORTS; 875]

horse chestnut 1 *type of* **deciduous tree**. [➡DECIDUOUS TREES; 1028] 2 *type of* **nut**. [➡NUTS; 1184]

horse-drawn carriage *type of* **wagon or carriage**. [➡BIKES, CARS, AND CARRIAGES; 1148]

horsefly 1 *type of* **flying insect**. [➡FLYING INSECTS; 1013] 2 *type of* **parasitic insect**. [➡PARASITES; 1017]

horsehair *type of* **fabric from animals**. [➡FABRICS; 1131]

horseman *n* **rider**, jockey, equestrian, huntsman, knight, cavalier. [➡PEOPLE IN SPORTS AND LEISURE; 876]

horseplay *n* **rough-and-tumble**, boisterousness, play, fun, horsing around, exuberance, roughhouse (*informal*). [➡LEISURE AND RECREATION; 874]

horse sense (*informal*) *n* **common sense**, nous (*informal*), sense, wit, judgment, wisdom. [➡POSITIVE INTELLECTUAL CHARACTERISTICS; 525]

horseshoe 1 *n* **lucky charm**, talisman, mascot, amulet, token. [➡LUCKY CHARMS; 786] 2 *n* **crescent**, curve, arc, loop, bend. [➡ROUNDED SHAPE; 1217]

horseshoe crab *type of* **crustacean**. [➡AQUATIC INVERTEBRATE; 1022]

horse show *n* [➡PERFORMANCES AND SHOWS; 42]

horse thief *n* [➡CRIMINALS; 821]

horsewoman *n* **rider**, jockey, equestrian, huntswoman. [➡PEOPLE IN SPORTS AND LEISURE; 876]

horsey *adj* **equine**, equestrian. [➡HORSE; 985]

horticultural *adj* **gardening**, garden, market garden, agricultural, viticultural, vinicultural, nursery. [➡AGRICULTURE AND FARMING; 1074]

horticulture *n* **gardening**, cultivation, propagation, agriculture, viticulture, viniculture, market gardening, truck farming. [➡AGRICULTURE AND FARMING; 1074]

hose 1 *n* **tube**, pipe, line, hosepipe, garden hose. [➡WATERCOURSES; 1110] 2 *v* **rinse**, water, spray, sluice, wash, soak, wash down, hose down. [➡CLEAN AND POLISH; 404]

hose down *v* **wash**, clean, sluice, rinse, hose, wash down. [➡CLEAN AND POLISH; 404] *Opposite:* dry.

hosepipe *n* **hose**, tube, pipe, garden hose. [➡WATERCOURSES; 1110]

hosiery *n* [➡HABERDASHERY, MILLINERY, AND LINGERIE; 867]

hospice *n* **nursing home**, hospital, rest home, sanatorium, clinic. [➡HOSPITALS AND CLINICS; 826]

hospitable *adj* **welcoming**, friendly, warm, open, generous, kind, cordial, sociable. [➡FRIENDLINESS AND SOCIABILITY; 495] *Opposite:* unfriendly.

hospital *n* **infirmary**, sanatorium, rest home, hospice, sickbay, clinic. [➡HOSPITALS AND CLINICS; 826]

hospitality *n* **welcome**, friendliness, warmth, kindness, generosity, cordiality, sociableness, openness. [➡FRIENDLINESS AND SOCIABILITY; 495] *Opposite:* unfriendliness.

host 1 *n* **entertainer**, master of ceremonies, emcee (*informal*), MC, presenter, compere. [➡WORKERS IN ENTERTAINMENT AND MEDIA; 873] 2 *v* **accommodate**, lay on, hold, present, introduce, put on, compere. [➡ENTERTAINMENT; 872] 3 *n* **crowd**, swarm, cloud, congregation, rout, mass, multitude, horde, army. [➡MANY, MUCH, LARGE AMOUNT; 117]

hostage *n* **captive**, prisoner, detainee, victim. [➡CAPTIVES AND PRISONERS; 250]

hostel 1 *n* **inn**, hotel, bed and breakfast, guesthouse, motel, pension, lodgings (*dated*). [➡HOTELS, RESTAURANTS, AND CLUBS; 1081] 2 *n* **shelter**, refuge, boarding house, dosshouse (*slang*), flophouse (*US informal*). [➡SAFE BUILDINGS OR PLACES; 1092]

hostelry (*archaic or humorous*) *type of* **eating place**. [➡HOTELS, RESTAURANTS, AND CLUBS; 1081]

hostess *n* **entertainer**, master of ceremonies, emcee (*informal*), MC, presenter, compere. [➡WORKERS IN ENTERTAINMENT AND MEDIA; 873]

hostile 1 *adj* **unfriendly**, aggressive, intimidating, antagonistic, unreceptive, unsympathetic, argumentative, inimical. [➡AGGRESSIVE AND BELLIGERENT; 519] *Opposite:* friendly. 2 *adj* **adverse**, harsh, unwelcoming, unfavourable, unpleasant, tough, inimical. [➡PHYSICALLY UNPLEASANT; 227] *Opposite:* pleasant.

hostilities *n* **fighting**, warfare, conflict, aggression. [➡AGGRESSIVE EVENT; 39]

hostility *n* **aggression**, anger, unfriendliness, resentment, antagonism, opposition, enmity, argumentativeness, intimidation, inimicalness. [➡ANTAGONISM; 553] *Opposite:* friendliness.

hot 1 *adj* **warm**, burning, scorching (*informal*), boiling, blistering, sizzling (*informal*), searing, broiling, fiery, heated, scalding. [➡TEMPERATURE: HOT; 1228] *Opposite:* cold. 2 *adj* **sweltering**, stifling, muggy, sultry, boiling, scorching (*informal*), oppressive, broiling. [➡HOT WEATHER; 1050] *Opposite:* fresh. 3 *adj* **spicy**, peppery, piquant, pungent, fiery, strong, red-hot. [➡TASTE; 704] *Opposite:* mild. 4 *adj* **passionate**, fierce, angry, emotional, strong, intense, excitable, vehement, ardent, fervent, stormy, torrid. [➡PLEASURE, EXCITEMENT, AND ELATION; 535] *Opposite:* dispassionate.

hot air (*informal*) *n* **nonsense**, rubbish, drivel, baloney (*informal*), stuff and nonsense, lies, twaddle (*informal*), bravado, bragging, boasting, malarkey (*informal*), blather (*informal*). [➡MEANINGLESS SPEECH OR WRITING; 677]

hot and bothered *adj* **worried**, worked up (*informal*), anxious, edgy, uptight (*informal*), flustered, in a flap (*informal*), in a panic, in a tizzy (*informal*). [➡CONFUSION, ANXIETY, AND WORRY; 541] *Opposite:* composed.

hotbed *n* **breeding ground**, source, focus, hothouse, centre. [➡BEGINNING; 53]

hot-blooded *adj* **passionate**, volatile, hot-tempered, ardent, fierce, temperamental, excitable, mercurial, fiery, impassioned, fervent. [➡AGGRESSIVE AND BELLIGERENT; 519] *Opposite:* cold-blooded.

hotcake (*US*) *type of* **pancake**. [➡CAKES, BISCUITS, AND DESSERTS; 1180]

hotchpotch *n* **jumble**, mixture, mishmash, mixed bag, miscellany, melange (*literary or formal*), potpourri, assortment, mass. [➡COLLECTIONS AND MIXTURES OF THINGS; 1243]

hotel

◆ *types of hotel*
B & B (*informal*), bed and breakfast, boarding house, guesthouse, hostel, inn, lodge, lodging house (*dated*), motel, pension, rooming house (*US*), youth hostel

hotelier *n* **innkeeper**, landlord, landlady, proprietor, manager, licensee. [➡BUSINESS PEOPLE; 794]

hotfoot *adv* **immediately**, at once, without delay, instantly, urgently, quickly, rapidly, fast, hastily, directly, straight, straightaway. [➡MOVING QUICKLY; 103] *Opposite:* slowly.

hothead *n* **firebrand**, tearaway, madcap. [➡UNCOOPERATIVE OR REBELLIOUS PERSON; 567]

hotheaded *adj* **impetuous**, volatile, rash, irascible, on a short fuse, reckless, impulsive, hasty, madcap, impatient, incautious, excitable, fiery. [➡LACK OF COMMITMENT AND UNRELIABILITY; 510] *Opposite:* prudent.

hotheadedness *n* [➡EXCESSIVE SENSITIVITY; 512]

hothouse *n* **greenhouse**, glasshouse, orangery, conservatory, winter garden. [➡ANCILLARY BUILDINGS; 1079]

hotly *adv* **passionately**, fiercely, ardently, fervently, vehemently, stormily, angrily, emotionally, strongly, intensely, excitably. [➡ENTHUSIASTIC AND INQUISITIVE; 629] *Opposite:* dispassionately.

hotness 1 *n* **heat**, high temperature, temperature, warmness, warmth. [➡TEMPERATURE: HOT; 1228] *Opposite:* coldness. 2 *n* **overheating**, sweatiness, stickiness, warmness, warmth, heat, feverishness, high temperature. [➡ILL AND SICK; 741] *Opposite:* freshness. 3 *n* **spiciness**, heat, fieriness, piquancy, pepperiness, strength. [➡TASTE; 704] *Opposite:* mildness.

hot pants *type of* **trousers**. [➡GARMENTS AND OUTFITS; 865]

hot potato *n* **difficulty**, controversy, tricky problem, knotty problem, sensitive issue, live issue, bone of contention, problem, issue. [➡PROBLEM; 257]

hot rod (*slang*) *type of* **car**. [➡BIKES, CARS, AND CARRIAGES; 1148]

hotshot (*informal*) *n* **high-flier**, achiever, go-getter (*informal*), star, bigwig (*informal*), expert, whiz (*informal*), big shot (*informal*), top gun (*US informal*). [➡IMPORTANT OR FAMOUS PEOPLE; 893]

hot-tempered *adj* **excitable**, fiery, hot-blooded, volatile, quick-tempered, impatient, irascible, irritable, bad-tempered, prickly (*informal*), ill-tempered, dyspeptic. [➡EXCESSIVE SENSITIVITY; 512] *Opposite:* relaxed.

hot toddy *n* [➡DRINKS; 1186]

hot tub *type of* **plumbing fittings**. [➡FITTINGS; 859]

hot under the collar (*informal*) *adj* **indignant**, worked up (*informal*), excited, angry, flustered, anxious. [➡IRRITATION AND ANGER; 542] *Opposite:* cool.

hot up (*informal*) *v* **intensify**, liven up, quicken, increase, speed up, grow. [➡CHANGE OF INTENSITY: MORE; 395] *Opposite:* cool down.

hot water (*informal*) *n* **trouble**, bother, difficulty, controversy, conflict. [➡DIFFICULT SITUATIONS; 72]

hound 1 *n* **dog**, wolfhound, deerhound, basset hound, foxhound, greyhound. [➡DOG; 980] 2 *v* **pursue**, chase, harass, pester, persecute, hunt, badger, dog. [➡ACCOMPANY AND FOLLOW; 338]

hour 1 *n* **60 minutes**, time, period, o'clock. [➡TIMES OF DAY; 87] 2 *n* **time**, period, era, age, day, epoch. [➡PERIOD OF TIME; 90]

hourglass *type of* **clock**. [➡CLOCKS AND TIMERS; 1125]

house 1 *n* **dwelling** (*formal*), residence, home, abode (*literary*), domicile (*formal*), address, building. [➡RESIDENTIAL BUILDINGS; 1077] 2 *n* **household**, family, dynasty, community, line, stock. [➡THE FAMILY; 956] 3 *n* **company**, firm, organization, business, outfit (*informal*), establishment, corporation, partnership. [➡BUSINESS ENTERPRISES AND RELATED BODIES; 793] 4 *v* **accommodate**, lodge, shelter, give shelter to, take in, put up. [➡EQUIP AND SUPPLY; 436] 5 *v* **contain**, keep, store, hold, retain, accommodate. [➡HOLD AND CONTAIN; 456]

house

◆ *types of house*
bothy, brownstone (*US*), bungalow, cabana (*US*), cabin, Cape Cod (*US*), chalet, chateau, cottage, country house, detached house, farmhouse, grange, hacienda, homestead, igloo, manor, manor house, mansion, pied-à-terre, ranch, ranch house (*US*), row house (*US*), semidetached, shack, stately home, terraced house, town house, villa

◆ *types of apartment*
apartment (*US*), bedsit, bedsitter, bedsitting room, condominium (*US*), duplex (*US*), efficiency apartment (*US*), flat, garden apartment (*US*), garden flat, loft, maisonette, penthouse, studio (*US*), studio flat

houseboat *type of* **motor vessel**. [➡SHIPS AND BOATS; 1149]

housebreaker (*US*) *n* [➡CRIMINALS; 821]

housecoat *n* **robe**, wrap, dressing gown, kimono, gown, bathrobe (*US*). [➡GARMENTS AND OUTFITS; 865]

house guest *n* **visitor**, guest, lodger, boarder. [➡FRIENDS; 963]

household 1 *n* **family**, home, family circle, family unit, ménage (*formal*), house. [➡THE FAMILY; 956] 2 *adj* **domestic**, home, family, everyday, domiciliary. [➡ACCOMMODATION; 855] *Opposite:* industrial.

household name *n* **celebrity**, star, superstar, megastar, luminary, public figure, celeb (*informal*). [➡IMPORTANT OR FAMOUS PEOPLE; 893] *Opposite:* unknown.

housekeeper *n* [➡DOMESTIC AND KITCHEN WORKERS; 850]

housekeeping 1 *n* **housework**, chores, cleaning, tidying, tidying up, tidiness. [➡WORK IN GENERAL; 298] 2 *n* (*US*) **maintenance**, upkeep, management, running, organization. [➡WORK IN GENERAL; 298]

house martin *type of* **common bird**. [➡BIRD; 997]

house of correction *n* [➡BUILDINGS FOR CONFINING PEOPLE; 1093]

house of God *n* [➡RELIGIOUS BUILDINGS; 1084]

house of worship *n* **house of God**, church, cathedral, synagogue, mosque, temple, chapel, minster. [➡RELIGIOUS BUILDINGS; 1084]

houseplant *n* **pot plant**, plant, bonsai, indoor plant, potted plant (*US*). [➡FOLIAGE PLANTS; 1035]

housing 1 *n* **accommodation**, lodging, shelter, board, home, accommodations (*US*). [➡ACCOMMODATION; 855] 2 *n* **cover**, covering, case, casing, frame, guard. [➡COVERS AND COATINGS; 1245]

housing development (*US*) *n* [➡HUMAN SETTLEMENTS; 1069]

housing estate *n* **estate**, development, urban development, residential area, council estate, housing development (*US*), housing project (*US*). [➡HUMAN SETTLEMENTS; 1069]

housing project (*US*) *n* [➡HUMAN SETTLEMENTS; 1069]

hove into view (*literary*) *v* [➡ARRIVE; 12]

hovel *n* **slum**, dump (*informal*), shack, fleapit, hole (*informal*), squat. [➡UNDESIRABLE ACCOMMODATION; 856]

hover 1 *v* **float**, hang, drift, soar, fly. [➡PROCEED AND GO; 306] *Opposite:* descend. 2 *v* **linger**, stay close, hang around, wait, remain, loiter. [➡EXIST IN A PLACE; 19] *Opposite:* leave.

hovercraft *type of* **motor vessel**. [➡SHIPS AND BOATS; 1149]

how *adv* **in what way**, by what means, by what method, in what manner, just how, exactly how. [➡WAYS OF DOING THINGS; 295]

howdy (*US informal*) *interj* [➡GREETINGS, FAREWELLS, AND SALUTATIONS; 660]

however *adv* **though**, but, on the other hand, yet, still, nevertheless, nonetheless, conversely, then again, in spite of this. [➡ALTHOUGH, NEVERTHELESS, AND DESPITE; 170] *Opposite:* also.

howitzer *type of* **gun**. [➡WEAPONS FOR SHOOTING; 1155]

howl 1 *v* **yowl**, bay, cry, wail, scream, shriek, whine, moan, holler (*informal*). [➡SOUND EMISSION BY ANIMALS OR BIRDS; 365] *Opposite:* murmur. 2 *n* **wail**, yowl, cry, scream, shriek, whine, moan, holler (*informal*). [➡SOUNDS MADE BY PEOPLE; 1261] *Opposite:* murmur. 3 *type of* **animal sound**. [➡SOUNDS MADE BY ANIMALS; 1260]

howl down *v* **drown out**, shout down, boo, jeer, mock, taunt, heckle. [➡DENY AND REJECT; 645] *Opposite:* cheer.

howler (*informal*) *n* **blunder**, gaffe, error, malapropism, mistake, bloomer (*informal humorous*), boner (*informal*), clanger (*informal*). [➡MISTAKES; 251]

howling *adj* **violent**, whistling, gale-force, hurricane-force, breathtaking, wailing, loud. [➡WINDY AND STORMY WEATHER; 1053] *Opposite:* gentle.

how the land lies *n* [➡SITUATIONS; 71]

how things stand *n* [➡SITUATIONS; 71]

hub 1 *n* **centre**, middle, boss, pivot. [➡CENTRAL PARTS OF PHYSICAL OBJECTS; 1250] *Opposite:* spoke. 2 *n* **core**, heart, focus, focal point, centre, nucleus. [➡CENTRAL PARTS OF PHYSICAL OBJECTS; 1250] *Opposite:* periphery.

hubbub *n* **noise**, racket (*informal*), hullabaloo, din, uproar, clamour, tumult. [➡CHAOS AND UPROAR; 51] *Opposite:* silence.

hubby (*informal*) *n* [➡RELATIVES BY MARRIAGE; 960]

hubcap *type of* **external feature**. [➡VEHICLES; 1144]

huckleberry *type of* **berry**. [➡FRUIT AND VEGETABLES; 1175]

huckster *n* [➡PEOPLE WHO DECEIVE; 662]

huddle 1 *n* **group**, cluster, knot, crowd, clump, mass, jumble. [➡GROUPS OF PEOPLE; 935] *Opposite:* scattering. 2 *v* **gather together**, crowd together, throng together, come together, bunch (*informal*), cluster. [➡GET CLOSER TOGETHER; 311] *Opposite:* scatter. 3 *v* **crouch**, bend, cower, nestle, hunch, curl up, snuggle up, huddle up. [➡ASSUME A POSITION; 318]

huddle together *v* [➡GET CLOSER TOGETHER; 311]

huddle up *v* [➡GET CLOSER TOGETHER; 311]

hue 1 *n* **colour**, tint, tinge, tone, shade. [➡DESCRIBING COLOURS; 1225] 2 *n* **type**, kind, sort, description, manner, variety. [➡VARIETY, TYPE, KIND; 146]

hue and cry *n* **uproar**, furore, commotion, protest, public outcry, public outrage. [➡CHAOS AND UPROAR; 51] *Opposite:* acceptance.

huff 1 *n* **sulk**, mood, bad mood, fit of pique, grumps (*informal*), temper. [➡IRRITATION AND ANGER; 542] 2 *v* **bluster**, grumble, complain, rant, anger, annoy, irritate. [➡COMPLAIN AND NAG; 687] *Opposite:* calm down. 3 *v* **puff**, pant, wheeze, gasp, blow, breathe, snort, huff and puff. [➡BREATHE AND NOT BREATHE; 717]

huffily *adv* **sulkily**, grumpily, indignantly, moodily, touchily, resentfully. [➡BAD-TEMPERED AND HUMOURLESS; 627] *Opposite:* good-naturedly.

huffiness *n* [➡DIFFICULT TO PLEASE; 516]

huffy *adj* **touchy**, sensitive, moody, grumpy, sulky, bad-tempered, piqued, offended. [➡SADNESS, DISTRESS, AND DESPAIR; 540] *Opposite:* good-natured.

hug 1 *v* **embrace**, hold close, enfold, cuddle, clasp, squeeze. [➡PHYSICAL CONTACT AS COMMUNICATION; 656] 2 *n* **cuddle**, clinch, clasp, bear hug, embrace, squeeze. [➡PHYSICAL CONTACT AS COMMUNICATION; 656]

huge 1 *adj* (*informal*) [➡EXTRAORDINARY: AMAZING; 205] 2 *adj* **enormous**, vast, gigantic, massive, giant, mammoth, colossal, titanic. [➡LARGE; 1192] *Opposite:* tiny.

hugely *adv* **enormously**, immensely, massively (*informal*), vastly, tremendously, incredibly, extremely. [➡TO A GREAT EXTENT; 130] *Opposite:* slightly.

huggermugger *n* [➡DISORDER AND CHAOS; 246]

hulk 1 *n* **giant**, goliath, colossus, titan, ogre, monster. [➡SHAPE; 1215] 2 *n* **shell**, skeleton, frame, carcass, wreck, remains, ruins. [➡EXTREMITIES OF PHYSICAL OBJECTS; 1249]

hulking *adj* **bulky**, vast, massive, colossal, enormous, large, husky (*US*). [➡LARGE; 1192] *Opposite:* dainty.

hull 1 *n* **body**, exterior, underside, keel, casing, structure. [➡EXTERNAL PARTS OF A VEHICLE; 1146] *Opposite:* interior. 2 *part of* **ship or boat**. [➡PARTS OF A SHIP OR BOAT; 1150]

hullaballoo *see* **hullabaloo**.

hullabaloo *n* **noise**, racket (*informal*), hubbub, din, uproar, clamour, tumult. [➡CHAOS AND UPROAR; 51] *Opposite:* silence.

hum 1 *v* **drone**, whine, purr, buzz, whirr, vibrate. [➡EMIT CONTINUOUS SOUNDS; 367] 2 *v* (*informal*) **smell**, whiff (*informal*), stink, reek, pong (*informal*), niff (*slang*). [➡SMELL EMISSION; 370] 3 *type of* **human sound**. [➡SOUNDS MADE BY PEOPLE; 1261] 4 *n* **whine**, drone, purr, buzz, whirr, vibration. [➡CONTINUOUS SOUNDS; 1257] 5 *n* (*informal*) **whiff** (*informal*), smell, stink, odour, pong (*informal*), niff (*slang*), reek, stench. [➡SMELL AND SMELLING; 706]

human 1 *adj* **humanoid**, hominid, hominoid, anthropological, anthropoid, social, mortal. [➡LIVING THINGS AND LIVING;

976] *Opposite:* animal. **2** *n* **person**, being, human being, individual, creature, homo sapiens, hominid. [➡PERSON; 931] **3** *type of* **primate.** [➡PRIMATE; 988]

human being *n* **person**, human, being, individual, creature, homo sapiens, hominid. [➡PERSON; 931]

hum and haw *v* [➡HESITATE; 273]

humane *adj* **compassionate**, caring, kind, gentle, humanitarian, kindly, benevolent, charitable. [➡GENEROSITY AND KINDNESS; 496] *Opposite:* cruel.

humanitarian *adj* **caring**, charitable, benevolent, philanthropic, public-spirited, altruistic. [➡MORALLY GOOD; 775] *Opposite:* uncaring.

humanities *n* [➡LESSONS, COURSE WORK, AND EXAMINATIONS; 842]

humanity **1** *n* **humankind**, people, human race, mortality, homo sapiens. [➡PERSON; 931] **2** *n* **kindness**, charity, compassion, sympathy, mercy, benevolence. [➡GENEROSITY AND KINDNESS; 496] *Opposite:* cruelty.

humanize **1** *v* **anthropomorphize**, personify, personalize. [➡NAME AND DESCRIBE; 666] **2** *v* **civilize**, cultivate, improve, soften, refine, tame. [➡IMPROVE SOMETHING; 375] *Opposite:* brutalize.

humanizing *adj* **civilizing**, improving, progressive, refining, softening, taming. [➡MORALLY GOOD; 775] *Opposite:* brutalizing.

humankind *n* **human race**, humanity, people, mortality, homo sapiens. [➡PERSON; 931]

humanly *adv* **at all**, feasibly, physically, realistically, in any way, by any means. [➡POSSIBLE AND PROBABLE; 178]

humanoid *n* [➡PERSON; 931]

human race *n* **humankind**, humanity, people, mortality, homo sapiens. [➡PERSON; 931]

human rights *n* **basic rights**, civil liberties, civil rights, citizens' rights, inalienable rights, rights. [➡THE LAW AND LEGAL AUTHORITY; 814]

humble **1** *adj* **modest**, unassuming, retiring, meek, self-effacing, unpretentious, shy. [➡RETICENT AND UNFORTHCOMING; 632] *Opposite:* arrogant. **2** *adj* **respectful**, subservient, servile, deferential, obliging, obsequious, meek. [➡LEVELS OF FORMALITY; 523] *Opposite:* brazen. **3** *adj* **lowly**, poor, simple, underprivileged, mean (*archaic*). [➡CLASS STATUS; 889] *Opposite:* privileged. **4** *v* **humiliate**, chasten, shame, bring down a peg, force to eat humble pie, bring down, put someone in their place. [➡UPSET, DISTRESS, AND HUMILIATE; 568] *Opposite:* glorify. **5** *v* **degrade**, debase, abase (*literary*), demean, lower, reduce. [➡INSULTS, ABUSE, AND SWEARING; 659] *Opposite:* exalt (*formal*).

humbled *adj* **shamed**, chastened, crestfallen, mortified, sheepish, humiliated. [➡EMBARRASSMENT AND HUMILIATION; 543] *Opposite:* proud.

humbleness *n* **humility**, modesty, meekness, self-effacement, shyness, unpretentiousness. [➡RETICENT AND UNFORTHCOMING; 632] *Opposite:* arrogance.

humbling *adj* **chastening**, mortifying, embarrassing, discomfiting (*formal*), shaming, awe-inspiring, awesome, overwhelming, sobering. [➡EXTRAORDINARY: AMAZING; 205] *Opposite:* exalting (*formal*).

humbly **1** *adv* **modestly**, unassumingly, meekly, simply, unpretentiously. [➡RETICENT AND UNFORTHCOMING; 632] *Opposite:* arrogantly. **2** *adv* **respectfully**, deferentially, obsequiously, subserviently, meekly, obligingly. [➡LEVELS OF FORMALITY; 523] *Opposite:* brazenly.

humbug **1** *n* **nonsense**, claptrap (*informal*), gibberish, twaddle (*informal*), bunkum (*informal*), codswallop (*informal*), hogwash (*informal*), hooey (*informal*), rubbish, baloney (*informal*), garbage. [➡MEANINGLESS SPEECH OR WRITING; 677] *Opposite:* fact. **2** *n* **deception**, hypocrisy, lies, deceit, pretence, propaganda, sham, insincerity, bunk (*slang*), hokum (*US informal disapproving*). [➡DECEPTION AND LIES; 661] *Opposite:* sincerity.

humdinger (*slang*) *n* [➡AMAZING THING; 212]

humdrum *adj* **dull**, boring, routine, unexciting, everyday, monotonous. [➡BORING AND UNINTERESTING; 235] *Opposite:* exciting.

humerus *type of* **bone.** [➡THE BONES AND JOINTS; 720]

humid *adj* **moist**, damp, steamy, tropical, sticky, clammy, muggy, sultry. [➡MOIST; 1240] *Opposite:* arid.

See Compare and Contrast at **wet.**

humidify *v* **moisten**, dampen, saturate, impregnate. [➡SOFTEN, LIQUEFY, DAMPEN; 389] *Opposite:* dry out.

humidity *n* **moisture**, moistness, dampness, clamminess, stickiness, damp, mugginess, wetness. [➡MOIST; 1240] *Opposite:* aridity.

humiliate *v* **chasten**, embarrass, demean, degrade, disgrace, shame, put down (*informal*), show up, humble, debase, dishonour. [➡UPSET, DISTRESS, AND HUMILIATE; 568] *Opposite:* dignify.

humiliated *adj* **chastened**, humbled, shamed, mortified, disgraced, demeaned, degraded, shown up, embarrassed, dishonoured. [➡EMBARRASSMENT AND HUMILIATION; 543] *Opposite:* proud.

humiliating *adj* **chastening**, humbling, embarrassing, mortifying, shameful, demeaning, degrading, crushing, dishonouring. [➡EMOTIONALLY UNPLEASANT AND UPSETTING; 228] *Opposite:* gratifying.

humiliation *n* **disgrace**, shame, mortification, embarrassment, dishonour, degradation. [➡EMBARRASSMENT AND HUMILIATION; 543] *Opposite:* dignity.

humility *n* **self-effacement**, unpretentiousness, humbleness, modesty, meekness, shyness. [➡RETICENT AND UNFORTHCOMING; 632] *Opposite:* arrogance.

humming **1** *adj* **droning**, whining, purring, buzzing, whirring, vibrating. [➡SOFT OR PLEASANT SOUNDS; 1264] *Opposite:* silent. **2** *adj* (*informal*) **smelly**, reeking, stinking, stinky (*informal*), malodorous, foul-smelling, pongy (*informal*), whiffy (*informal*). [➡SMELL AND SMELLING; 706]

hummock *n* **hillock**, mound, knoll, hill, rise. [➡MOUNTAINS AND HILLS; 1044] *Opposite:* dip.

humongous (*informal*) *adj* **enormous**, ginormous (*informal*), gigantic, colossal, massive, vast, huge. [➡ LARGE; 1192] *Opposite:* tiny.

humorist 1 *n* **comedian**, comic, standup comedian, impressionist, entertainer, satirist. [➡ WORKERS IN ENTERTAINMENT AND MEDIA; 873] 2 *n* **joker**, wit, wag (*dated*), satirist, punster, clown. [➡ JOKERS AND TEASES; 676]

humorous 1 *adj* **funny**, amusing, entertaining, hilarious, comical, comic, tongue in cheek, jokey, droll, witty. [➡ FUNNY AND AMUSING; 217] *Opposite:* serious. 2 *adj* **witty**, droll, funny, entertaining, amusing, waggish (*dated*). [➡ FUNNY AND AMUSING; 217] *Opposite:* dull.

See Compare and Contrast at **funny.**

humorously 1 *adv* **funnily**, amusingly, entertainingly, hilariously, jokily, wittily, comically, drolly. [➡ GOOD-TEMPERED AND HUMOROUS; 628] *Opposite:* seriously. 2 *adv* **wittily**, drolly, funnily, entertainingly, amusingly, waggishly (*dated*). [➡ GOOD-TEMPERED AND HUMOROUS; 628] *Opposite:* dully.

humour 1 *n* **funniness**, wit, comedy, comicality, comicalness, the funny side, absurdity, hilarity. [➡ FUNNY AND AMUSING; 217] *Opposite:* seriousness. 2 *n* **wit**, wittiness, sparkle, drollness, sense of humour, sense of fun. [➡ CHEERFULNESS OF OUTLOOK; 504] *Opposite:* dourness. 3 *n* **comedy**, satire, black humour, spoof, slapstick, joking, jesting (*literary*). [➡ JOKES AND TEASING; 675] 4 *v* **go along with**, pacify, indulge, accommodate, please, string along (*informal*). [➡ TAKE CARE OF AND SPOIL; 301] *Opposite:* oppose.

humourless 1 *adj* **sullen**, serious, po-faced, sour, dour, dull. [➡ NEGATIVE OF OUTLOOK; 515] *Opposite:* merry. 2 *adj* **unfunny**, unamusing, dull, straight, unwitty, serious. [➡ BORING AND UNINTERESTING; 235] *Opposite:* funny.

hump *n* **bulge**, bump, lump, swelling, protuberance, mound. [➡ ROUNDED SHAPE; 1217] *Opposite:* dip.

humpback bridge *type of* **bridge.** [➡ BRIDGES, TUNNELS, CROSSINGS, AND JUNCTIONS; 1111]

humpback whale *type of* **whale.** [➡ WHALE; 991]

humungous *see* **humongous.**

hunch 1 *n* **feeling**, gut feeling, sixth sense, premonition, intuition, instinct, idea. [➡ FEELINGS; 532] 2 *v* **bend**, huddle, stoop, lean forwards, bend forwards. [➡ ASSUME A POSITION; 318] *Opposite:* straighten.

hundred per cent *adj* [➡ ALL; 126]

hunger 1 *n* **appetite**, emptiness, craving, hungriness, ravenousness, famishment. [➡ EAT AND NOT EAT; 711] 2 *n* **starvation**, food shortage, lack of food, malnutrition, famine, deprivation. [➡ EAT AND NOT EAT; 711] *Opposite:* surfeit. 3 *n* **craving**, desire, need, wish, passion, yearning, longing, thirst, hankering. [➡ DESIRE AND WANT; 580] 4 *v* **crave**, yearn, long for, desire, hanker, thirst for. [➡ DESIRE AND WANT; 580] *Opposite:* spurn.

hunger after *v* [➡ DESIRE AND WANT; 580]

hungrily 1 *adv* **ravenously**, greedily, appreciatively, eagerly, enthusiastically, raveningly, voraciously. [➡ WITH ENTHUSIASM; 287] *Opposite:* unenthusiastically. 2 *adv* **eagerly**, impatiently, keenly, enthusiastically, excitedly, avidly. [➡ WITH ENTHUSIASM; 287] *Opposite:* nonchalantly.

hungry 1 *adj* **starving** (*informal*), famished, ravenous, starved (*informal*), peckish (*informal*), ravening, voracious. [➡ EAT AND NOT EAT; 711] *Opposite:* full. 2 *adj* (*informal*) **ambitious**, driven, thrusting, power-hungry, aggressive, keen. [➡ DESIRE AND WANT; 580] *Opposite:* content. 3 *adj* **avid**, eager, keen, desirous (*formal*), greedy, thirsty. [➡ POSITIVE IMPATIENCE, ENTHUSIASM, AND ALERTNESS; 538] *Opposite:* nonchalant.

hung up (*informal*) 1 *adj* **obsessed**, fixated, preoccupied, infatuated, possessed, captivated. [➡ APPRECIATION AND GRATITUDE; 536] *Opposite:* repelled. 2 *adj* **anxious**, worried, caught up, bothered, nervy (*informal*), concerned, nervous. [➡ CONFUSION, ANXIETY, AND WORRY; 541] *Opposite:* relaxed.

hunk *n* **chunk**, piece, lump, slab, wedge, doorstep (*informal*). [➡ LARGE PIECE; 128]

hunker *v* **squat**, crouch, cower, get on all fours, crawl, stoop, kneel. [➡ ASSUME A POSITION; 318] *Opposite:* stand.

hunker down *v* **squat down**, squat, crouch, crouch down, kneel, kneel down. [➡ ASSUME A POSITION; 318] *Opposite:* stand up.

hunky (*informal*) *adj* **muscular**, well-built, masculine, stocky, solid, brawny, handsome. [➡ PEOPLE'S PHYSICAL APPEARANCE; 476] *Opposite:* puny.

hunky-dory (*informal*) *adj* [➡ APPROPRIATE, SUITABLE, ADVISABLE; 185]

hunt 1 *v* **chase**, pursue, stalk, follow, track, prey on, trail. [➡ ACCOMPANY AND FOLLOW; 338] *Opposite:* flee. 2 *v* **seek out**, hunt down, track down, chase, pursue, hound. [➡ SEEK POSSESSION AND SEARCH; 457] *Opposite:* evade. 3 *v* **search**, seek, rummage, look, ferret about, rootle, ferret around. [➡ SEEK POSSESSION AND SEARCH; 457] *Opposite:* find. 4 *n* **search**, quest, chase, pursuit, expedition, rummage. [➡ SEEK POSSESSION AND SEARCH; 457]

hunt down *v* **find**, catch, track down, capture, get hold of, seek out. [➡ SEEK POSSESSION AND SEARCH; 457] *Opposite:* flee.

hunted *adj* **panic-stricken**, alarmed, startled, frightened, unsettled, disturbed. [➡ FEAR AND PANIC; 544] *Opposite:* relaxed.

hunter 1 *n* **stalker**, predator, tracker, killer, pursuer, chaser. [➡ PEOPLE WHO KILL; 924] *Opposite:* prey. 2 *n* **seeker**, pursuer, searcher, chaser. [➡ PEOPLE IN SPORTS AND LEISURE; 876] *Opposite:* prey. 3 *type of* **horse.** [➡ HORSE; 985]

hunting *n* **blood sport**, fox hunting, deer stalking, hare coursing, shooting, stalking. [➡ HOBBIES, GAMES, AND SPORTS; 875]

hurdle 1 *n* **obstacle**, difficulty, problem, stumbling block, snag, barrier, impediment. [➡ PROBLEM; 257] *Opposite:* aid. 2 *v* **jump**, leap, jump over, leap over, fly over, clear, vault, vault over. [➡ BOUNCE, UNDULATE, AND VIBRATE; 309]

hurl 1 *v* **fling**, throw, toss, chuck (*informal*), launch, heave. [➡ THROW SOMETHING; 335] 2 *v* (*slang*) **vomit**, be sick, throw up (*informal*), heave (*informal*), gag, retch, spew, puke (*slang*), barf (*US informal*). [➡ VOMIT AND BELCH; 713]

See Compare and Contrast at **throw.**

hurl abuse *v* [➡ACCUSE, BLAME, AND CRITICIZE; 642]

hurling *type of* **ball game.** [➡HOBBIES, GAMES, AND SPORTS; 875]

hurl insults *v* [➡ACCUSE, BLAME, AND CRITICIZE; 642]

hurly-burly *n* **commotion**, chaos, turmoil, confusion, bustle, hustle and bustle, turbulence. [➡CHAOS AND UPROAR; 51] *Opposite:* peace.

hurrah *interj* [➡EXPRESSIONS OF SURPRISE; 547]

hurricane *n* **storm**, gale, tempest, tornado, cyclone, typhoon, whirlwind, twister (*US informal*). [➡WINDY AND STORMY WEATHER; 1053]

hurricane lamp *type of* **light.** [➡LIGHT; 1163]

hurried 1 *adj* **quick**, rushed, speedy, swift, sudden, hasty, spur-of-the-moment, snatched. [➡HAPPENING QUICKLY; 104] *Opposite:* leisurely. 2 *adj* **hassled** (*informal*), rushed, pressurized, under pressure, harried. [➡SADNESS, DISTRESS, AND DESPAIR; 540] *Opposite:* relaxed.

hurriedly *adv* **quickly**, speedily, swiftly, suddenly, hastily, on the spur of the moment. [➡HAPPENING QUICKLY; 104] *Opposite:* slowly.

hurry 1 *v* **rush**, speed, hasten, run, dash, scurry, make haste. [➡MOVE FAST; 314] *Opposite:* delay. 2 *v* **speed up**, accelerate, quicken, hasten, hustle. [➡CHANGE OF SPEED: MORE; 397] *Opposite:* slow down. 3 *n* **haste**, rush, dash, flurry, frenzy, panic. [➡DISORDER AND CHAOS; 246] 4 *n* **urgency**, time pressure, panic, rush, haste, imperativeness, emergency. [➡DIFFICULT SITUATIONS; 72]

hurry up *v* **speed up**, accelerate, quicken, hasten, hustle. [➡CHANGE OF SPEED: MORE; 397] *Opposite:* slow down.

hurt 1 *v* **injure**, harm, wound, damage, mar, maim, bruise, impair, burn, cut, spoil, break. [➡WOUND A PERSON OR ANIMAL; 384] *Opposite:* benefit. 2 *v* **ache**, be sore, be painful, throb, trouble, sting, smart, kill (*informal*). [➡PAIN AND OTHER PHYSICAL SENSATIONS; 734] *Opposite:* soothe. 3 *v* **offend**, upset, insult, injure, cause offence, wound. [➡UPSET, DISTRESS, AND HUMILIATE; 568] *Opposite:* comfort. 4 *v* **impair**, damage, mar, spoil, ruin. [➡PUT AT RISK; 385] *Opposite:* improve. 5 *n* **upset**, pain, distress, sadness, damage, offence, injury, suffering. [➡SADNESS, DISTRESS, AND DESPAIR; 540] *Opposite:* gratification. 6 *n* **injury**, damage, harm, pain, soreness, ache, suffering, tenderness, discomfort. [➡PAIN AND OTHER PHYSICAL SENSATIONS; 734] *Opposite:* benefit. 7 *adj* **upset**, offended, miffed (*informal*), wounded, unhappy, indignant, injured. [➡SADNESS, DISTRESS, AND DESPAIR; 540] *Opposite:* gratified.

See Compare and Contrast at **harm.**

hurtful *adj* **upsetting**, unkind, cruel, spiteful, cutting, wounding, insensitive, tactless, inappropriate. [➡EMOTIONALLY UNPLEASANT AND UPSETTING; 228] *Opposite:* kind.

hurting *adj* **sad**, aching, heartbroken, brokenhearted, blue (*informal*), down, low. [➡SADNESS, DISTRESS, AND DESPAIR; 540] *Opposite:* happy.

hurtle *v* **dash**, career, tear, race, plunge, crash. [➡MOVE FAST; 314] *Opposite:* plod.

hurtling *adj* [➡MOVING QUICKLY; 103]

husband *n* **spouse**, partner, other half, significant other, man (*slang*), hubby (*informal*), mate. [➡RELATIVES BY MARRIAGE; 960] *Opposite:* wife.

husband-to-be *n* [➡RELATIVES BY MARRIAGE; 960]

hush 1 *v* **silence**, quieten, quieten down, shut up (*informal*), mute, shush (*informal*). [➡CAUSE TO STOP; 267] 2 *interj* **be quiet**, quiet, shut up (*informal*), shush, shut it (*informal*), silence, not a word. [➡UNFAVOURABLE NON-VERBAL RESPONSES; 655] 3 *n* **stillness**, silence, quiet, quietness, tranquillity, peace, peacefulness. [➡ABSENCE OF SOUND; 1256] *Opposite:* noise.

hushed *adj* **quiet**, silent, muted, soft, whispered, low. [➡SOFT OR PLEASANT SOUNDS; 1264] *Opposite:* loud.

hush-hush (*informal*) *adj* **secret**, confidential, top-secret, under wraps (*informal*), cloak-and-dagger, clandestine, undercover, classified. [➡SECRET AND UNKNOWN; 180] *Opposite:* public.

hush money (*informal*) *n* **bribe**, pacifier, sweetener (*informal*), backhander (*informal*), incentive, bung (*slang*), payoff (*informal*). [➡PROCEEDS OF CRIME; 428]

hush up (*informal*) *v* **cover up**, suppress, conceal, keep quiet, keep secret, sit on. [➡WITHHOLD INFORMATION; 688] *Opposite:* reveal.

husk *n* **shell**, casing, pod, covering, skin, outside, case. [➡PARTS OF TREES AND PLANTS; 1026] *Opposite:* kernel.

huskily *adv* **throatily**, hoarsely, roughly, gruffly, drily, croakily, gutturally, raspingly, gratingly. [➡LOUD OR UNPLEASANT SOUNDS; 1265] *Opposite:* clearly.

huskiness *n* **throatiness**, hoarseness, dryness, roughness, gruffness, croakiness, gutturalness, rasp. [➡LOUD OR UNPLEASANT SOUNDS; 1265] *Opposite:* clearness.

husky 1 *adj* **throaty**, hoarse, dry, rough, gruff, croaky, grating, rasping, raspy, gravelly, guttural. [➡LOUD OR UNPLEASANT SOUNDS; 1265] *Opposite:* clear. 2 *adj* (*US*) **burly**, strong, solid, broad, hulking, big, bulky. [➡BUILD; 478] 3 *type of* **large dog.** [➡DOG; 980]

hustle 1 *v* **propel**, bundle (*informal*), jostle, manhandle, push, shove. [➡MOVE SOMETHING TO ANOTHER LOCATION; 325] 2 *v* (*informal*) **hurry**, hurry up, get a move on (*informal*), get your skates on (*informal*), look sharp (*informal*), shift (*informal*), buck up (*informal dated*). [➡MOVE FAST; 314] *Opposite:* slow down. 3 *v* (*US slang*) **solicit**, tout, push, peddle. [➡SELL; 442]

hustle and bustle *n* **commotion**, chaos, turmoil, confusion, hurly-burly, fuss, hubbub, bustle. [➡CHAOS AND UPROAR; 51] *Opposite:* calm.

hustler *n* [➡PEOPLE WHO DECEIVE; 662]

hut *n* **shed**, lean-to, cabin, shelter, shack, shanty, outbuilding. [➡ANCILLARY BUILDINGS; 1079]

hutch *type of* **pen or cage.** [➡ANIMAL OR BIRD ACCOMMODATION; 1078]

hutzpah (*informal*) *n* **chutzpah** (*informal*), boldness, self-confidence, impudence, rudeness, pushiness (*informal*), self-assurance. [➡BAD MANNERS AND SOCIAL SKILLS; 522] *Opposite:* shyness.

hyacinth *type of* **flower grown from bulb.** [➡FLOWERS FROM BULBS; 1030]

hyaena *see* **hyena.**

hybrid *n* **cross**, crossbreed, mix, amalgam, mixture, fusion. [➡COMBINE AND MIX; 401]

hybridize *v* [➡COMBINE AND MIX; 401]

hydrangea *type of* **shrub or bush.** [➡BUSHES AND SHRUBS; 1027]

hydrofoil *type of* **motor vessel.** [➡SHIPS AND BOATS; 1149]

hydrogen *type of* **gas.** [➡GASES; 1274]

hydrogen bomb *type of* **explosive weapon.** [➡EXPLOSIVES; 1154]

hydrophobia *type of* **phobia.** [➡FEARS AND PHOBIAS; 555]

hydroplane *v* **skid**, slide, swerve, aquaplane, slew, veer. [➡PUSH, PULL, SLIDE; 336]

hyena *type of* **canine.** [➡CANINE; 979]

hygiene *n* **cleanliness**, sanitation, sanitariness, cleanness, sterility, sanitization, asepsis, asepticism, disinfection. [➡CLEAN; 1232]

hygienic *adj* **clean**, sterile, disinfected, sanitary, germ-free, sanitized, aseptic. [➡CLEAN; 1232] *Opposite:* unhygienic.

hymn **1** *n* **song**, chant, carol, chorus, anthem, canticle, psalm. [➡MUSIC, SONGS, AND SINGING; 907] **2** *v* **praise**, celebrate, eulogize (*formal*), extol, laud, acclaim, panegyrize (*formal*). [➡PRAISE AND ENCOURAGE; 648] *Opposite:* criticize.

hype **1** *n* **publicity**, propaganda, buildup, excitement, puff, hard sell, flimflam (*slang*), hot air (*informal*), hysteria. [➡ADVERTISING AND PUBLICITY; 605] **2** *v* **publicize**, advertise, build up, plug (*informal*), tout, push. [➡ADVERTISING AND PUBLICITY; 605]

hyper (*informal*) **1** *adj* **overexcited**, hyperactive, manic (*informal*), frenzied, restless, keyed up (*informal*), wired (*slang*), agitated, overactive. [➡INSECURITY AND LOSS OF COMPOSURE; 545] *Opposite:* calm. **2** *adj* **excitable**, hotheaded, on the edge, highly-strung, volatile, unbalanced, rash. [➡EXCESSIVE SENSITIVITY; 512] *Opposite:* placid.

hyperactive *adj* **agitated**, hyper (*informal*), wired (*slang*), restless, energetic, manic (*informal*), overactive. [➡EXCESSIVE SENSITIVITY; 512] *Opposite:* lethargic.

hyperbole *n* **exaggeration**, overstatement, overemphasis, magnification, inflation, embellishment. [➡FIGURES OF SPEECH; 674] *Opposite:* understatement.

hypercritical *adj* **overcritical**, censorious, nitpicking, finicky, negative, pedantic, fussy. [➡DIFFICULT TO PLEASE; 516] *Opposite:* lenient.

hypermarket *type of* **retail outlet.** [➡RETAIL OUTLETS; 1082]

hypersensitive *adj* **touchy**, oversensitive, thin-skinned, easily offended, easily hurt, quick to take offence. [➡IRRITATION AND ANGER; 542] *Opposite:* thick-skinned.

hypersensitivity *n* [➡EXCESSIVE SENSITIVITY; 512]

hyperventilate *v* [➡BREATHE AND NOT BREATHE; 717]

hyphen *type of* **punctuation mark.** [➡ASPECTS OF LANGUAGE; 683]

hypnotic (*informal*) *adj* **fascinating**, mesmerizing, entrancing, spellbinding, compelling, enthralling, magnetic, absorbing. [➡INTERESTING AND MEANINGFUL; 191] *Opposite:* uninteresting.

hypnotize *v* **fascinate**, mesmerize, spellbind, entrance, enthrall, compel, absorb. [➡APPEAL TO AND AROUSE INTEREST; 576] *Opposite:* bore.

hypnotizing *adj* [➡INTERESTING AND MEANINGFUL; 191]

hypochondriac *n* [➡GRUMPY AND NEGATIVE PEOPLE; 953]

hypocrisy *n* **insincerity**, double standard, pretence, duplicity, two-facedness, falseness. [➡DECEITFUL; 514] *Opposite:* sincerity.

hypocrite *n* **charlatan**, fraud, phoney, dissembler (*formal*), double-dealer, pretender. [➡PEOPLE WHO DECEIVE; 662]

hypocritical *adj* **insincere**, two-faced, duplicitous, deceitful, phoney, false. [➡DECEITFUL; 514] *Opposite:* genuine.

hypothesis *n* **theory**, premise, suggestion, supposition, proposition, guess, assumption, postulate, postulation. [➡IDEA AND THOUGHT; 771]

hypothesize *v* **imagine**, conjecture, put forward, assume, offer, theorize, posit (*formal*), postulate. [➡DEVELOP THEORIES AND REASON; 745]

hypothetical *adj* **theoretical**, imaginary, supposed, conjectural, proposed, assumed, putative, suppositious (*formal*), suppositional. [➡FALSE AND UNREAL; 174] *Opposite:* real.

hyrax *type of* **small mammal.** [➡SMALL MAMMAL; 990]

hyssop *type of* **herb.** [➡HERBS AND SPICES; 1174]

hysterectomy *n* [➡STERILIZE; 727]

hysteria *n* **panic**, hysterics, frenzy, madness, emotion, excitement, mania. [➡INSECURITY AND LOSS OF COMPOSURE; 545] *Opposite:* calm.

hysteric *adj* [➡FEAR AND PANIC; 544]

hysterical **1** *adj* **panic-stricken**, out of control, agitated, overexcited, feverish, frenetic, frenzied, frantic, hyper (*informal*), manic (*informal*), beside yourself, distraught, distracted, hysteric. [➡FEAR AND PANIC; 544] *Opposite:* composed. **2** *adj* **uncontrollable**, frenzied, intense, violent, unrestrained, wild, furious. [➡NEGATIVE INTELLECTUAL CHARACTERISTICS; 526] *Opposite:* controlled. **3** *adj* (*informal*) **hilarious**, uproarious, highly amusing, sidesplitting, comical, funny. [➡FUNNY AND AMUSING; 217] *Opposite:* sad.

hysterics **1** *n* (*informal*) **fits**, fits of laughter, stitches, laughter. [➡LAUGHTER; 650] **2** *n* **hysteria**, panic, frenzy, agitation, distraction, mania, overexcitement. [➡FEAR AND PANIC; 544] *Opposite:* calmness.

I

ibis *type of* **freshwater bird.** [➡ FRESHWATER BIRD; 1000]

ice 1 *n* **frost**, snow, hoar frost, rime, slush. [➡ COLD WEATHER; 1051] 2 *v* **freeze up**, freeze, freeze solid, freeze over, ice over, ice up. [➡ HARDEN, CONGEAL, DRY; 388] *Opposite:* thaw. 3 *v* **decorate**, finish off, frost, embellish, adorn. [➡ DECORATE, ADORN, AND APPLY COATINGS; 406] 4 *v* **chill**, cool, cool down. [➡ CHANGE OF TEMPERATURE; 387] *Opposite:* heat.

iceberg *n* [➡ GEOLOGICAL FEATURES; 1056]

ice blue *type of* **blue.** [➡ COLOURS; 1223]

icebox (*US*) *n* **refrigerator**, fridge, freezer, fridge-freezer. [➡ HEATING, REFRIGERATION, AND VENTILATION; 1141]

icebreaker *n* **opener**, starter, opening, introduction. [➡ NEUTRAL ONE-WAY COMMUNICATION; 49]

icecap *n* [➡ GEOLOGICAL FEATURES; 1056]

ice-cold *adj* **freezing**, frozen, icy, subzero, chilled, chilly, chill, bitter. [➡ COLD WEATHER; 1051] *Opposite:* red-hot.

ice cream *n* **cone**, cornet, ice-cream cone, ninety-nine, sherbet, sorbet, ice, gelato. [➡ CAKES, BISCUITS, AND DESSERTS; 1180]

iced *adj* **chilled**, cool, refrigerated, on the rocks (*informal*), frozen, cold. [➡ TEMPERATURE: COLD; 1230] *Opposite:* hot.

ice dancing *type of* **winter sport.** [➡ HOBBIES, GAMES, AND SPORTS; 875]

ice hockey *type of* **winter sport.** [➡ HOBBIES, GAMES, AND SPORTS; 875]

ice over *v* **freeze**, freeze over, freeze up, harden, solidify, ice up, ice. [➡ HARDEN, CONGEAL, DRY; 388] *Opposite:* thaw.

ice pack *n* **compress**, cold compress, wrapping, poultice. [➡ REMEDIES, TREATMENTS, AND OPERATIONS; 732]

ice up *v* **freeze**, freeze over, freeze up, ice over, frost up, ice. [➡ HARDEN, CONGEAL, DRY; 388]

ichthyosaur *type of* **dinosaur.** [➡ DINOSAUR; 996]

icily *adv* **coldly**, frostily, aloofly, unemotionally, distantly, remotely, coolly, disdainfully. [➡ RUDE AND HOSTILE; 626]

iciness *n* **coldness**, coolness, frostiness, unfriendliness, hostility, disdain, remoteness, aloofness. [➡ UNFRIENDLINESS AND UNSOCIABILITY; 505] *Opposite:* warmth.

icing 1 *n* **frosting**, decoration, glaze, glazing. [➡ COVERS AND COATINGS; 1245] 2 *n* **freezing**, freezing over, freezing up. [➡ HARDEN, CONGEAL, DRY; 388]

icing on the cake *n* [➡ AMAZING THING; 212]

icky (*informal*) 1 *adj* **nasty**, unpleasant, horrid, funny, uncomfortable, yucky (*informal*), horrible. [➡ DISGUSTING AND REPULSIVE; 231] 2 *adj* **sticky**, gooey, tacky, messy, disgusting, horrid, nasty. [➡ PHYSICAL TEXTURE; 1221] 3 *adj* **sentimental**, over-the-top (*informal*), sloppy (*informal*), schmaltzy (*informal*), too much, saccharine, tacky (*informal*). [➡ IN POOR TASTE; 230]

icon 1 *n* **idol**, star, model, symbol, embodiment, personification, incarnation, ideal, exemplar (*literary*). [➡ FADS, FETISHES, AND IDOLATRY; 556] 2 *n* **image**, likeness, representation, sign, picture, photograph, drawing, portrait. [➡ ARTWORKS; 898]

iconoclast *n* **revolutionary**, radical, free thinker, subversive, individualist, reformer, rebel. [➡ UNCOOPERATIVE OR REBELLIOUS PERSON; 567] *Opposite:* conservative.

iconoclastic *adj* **radical**, revolutionary, subversive, individualistic, free thinking. [➡ EXTRAORDINARY: UNCOMMON; 206] *Opposite:* conservative.

icy 1 *adj* **freezing**, frozen, frosty, ice-cold, subzero, cold, chilly, arctic (*informal*), polar, glacial, wintry, bitter. [➡ COLD WEATHER; 1051] 2 *adj* **unfriendly**, frosty, hostile, distant, aloof, cold, cool, disdainful. [➡ UNFRIENDLINESS AND UNSOCIABILITY; 505] *Opposite:* warm.

ID *n* **identification**, identity card, ID card (*informal*), passport, papers, documents. [➡ OFFICIAL DOCUMENTS; 587]

idea 1 *n* **opinion**, belief, view, viewpoint, outlook, judgment. [➡ IDEA AND THOUGHT; 771] 2 *n* **suggestion**, design, plan, scheme, proposal, initiative, recommendation. [➡ IDEA AND THOUGHT; 771] 3 *n* **concept**, impression, notion, understanding, perception, thought, sense, knowledge. [➡ IDEA AND THOUGHT; 771] 4 *n* **plan**, brain wave (*informal*), inspiration, solution, brainchild, notion, brainstorm (*US informal*). [➡ IDEA AND THOUGHT; 771] 5 *n* **aim**, objective, plan, object, goal, intention, intent (*formal*), purpose, point. [➡ INTENTION AND PURPOSE; 773] 6 *n* **gist**, précis, outline, sketch, snapshot, overview, summary. [➡ INDICATIONS, SIGNS, AND WARNINGS; 68]

ideal 1 *n* **epitome**, height, model, archetype, essence, stereotype, paradigm, icon, exemplar (*literary*). [➡ PERFECT EXAMPLES AND EMBODIMENTS; 67] 2 *n* **principle**, standard, belief, value. [➡ MORAL CONCEPTS; 774] 3 *adj* **best**, model, ultimate, idyllic, superlative, supreme, perfect. [➡ GOOD, WELL, BETTER; 184]

idealism 1 *n* **naivety**, romanticism, impracticality, optimism. [➡ NEGATIVE INTELLECTUAL CHARACTERISTICS; 526] *Opposite:* realism. 2 *n* **perfectionism**, fundamentalism, commitment, principle, morality, fanaticism, zeal, fervour. [➡ HARD-WORKING AND COMMITTED; 501]

idealist 1 *n* **perfectionist**, fundamentalist, crusader, zealot, fanatic. [➡ DEVOTEES AND ADDICTED PEOPLE; 557] 2 *n* **romantic**, optimist, dreamer. [➡ LAZY OR UNSUCCESSFUL PEOPLE; 948] *Opposite:* realist.

idealistic 1 *adj* **naive**, unrealistic, romantic, impractical, optimistic. [➡ NEGATIVE INTELLECTUAL CHARACTERISTICS; 526] *Opposite:* realistic. 2 *adj* **uncompromising**, principled, committed, unswerving, unwavering, perfectionist, fervent, ardent. [➡ HARD-WORKING AND COMMITTED; 501]

idealize *v* **romanticize**, put on a pedestal, view through rose-tinted spectacles, venerate, overemphasize, fetishize. [➡LIKE, LOVE, VALUE, AND ENJOY; 579]

idealized *adj* **perfect**, flawless, faultless, ideal, unrealistic, fanciful. [➡EXTRAORDINARY: UNCOMMON; 206]

ideally 1 *adv* **in an ideal world**, preferably, if possible, if at all possible. [➡POSSIBLE AND PROBABLE; 178] 2 *adv* **perfectly**, supremely, superlatively, well. [➡USEFULNESS; 200]

idée fixe *n* **obsession**, pet topic, thing (*informal*), hobbyhorse, fixation, bee in your bonnet. [➡IDEA AND THOUGHT; 771]

idem *adv* **the same**, the same thing, the same as before. [➡WRITTEN CONVENTIONS; 600]

identical *adj* **same**, indistinguishable, equal, matching, alike, like, duplicate, impossible to tell apart, one and the same, like peas in a pod. [➡SAMENESS; 151] *Opposite:* different.

identicalness *n* [➡SAMENESS; 151]

identifiable *adj* **recognizable**, distinguishable, perceptible, discernible, detectable, classifiable. [➡PERCEPTIBLE; 25]

identification 1 *n* **recognition**, classification, naming, detection, discovery. [➡NAME AND DESCRIBE; 666] 2 *n* **ID**, documentation, proof of identity, papers, credentials, documents. [➡OFFICIAL DOCUMENTS; 587] 3 *n* **empathy**, sympathy, affinity, rapport, bonding, association, connection, relationship, link. [➡COMPASSION AND FORGIVENESS; 552]

identify 1 *v* **recognize**, classify, name, find, categorize, detect, ascertain (*formal*), isolate, pinpoint, label, distinguish, characterize. [➡NAME AND DESCRIBE; 666] 2 *v* **equate**, connect, relate, link, associate. [➡CREATING CONNECTIONS; 145]

identify with *v* **empathize with**, sympathize with, relate to, feel for, have sympathy for, feel empathy with. [➡BE CONCERNED AND CARE; 582]

identity *n* **individuality**, uniqueness, distinctiveness, self, character, personality. [➡TEMPERAMENT AND BEHAVIOUR; 493]

identity card *n* **ID card** (*informal*), pass, card, passport. [➡OFFICIAL DOCUMENTS; 587]

ideogram *n* [➡SYMBOLS, SIGNS, AND NUMBERS; 597]

ideological *adj* **conceptual**, philosophical, moral, political, ethical, sociopolitical, religious. [➡PHILOSOPHIES AND BELIEFS; 781]

ideology *n* **philosophy**, belief, creed, dogma, line, system. [➡PHILOSOPHIES AND BELIEFS; 781]

idiocy *n* [➡NEGATIVE INTELLECTUAL CHARACTERISTICS; 526]

idiolect *n* **speech pattern**, turn of phrase, style, dialect, idiom, vocabulary, lexis, syntax, language. [➡ASPECTS OF LANGUAGE; 683]

idiom 1 *n* **expression**, phrase, set phrase, turn of phrase, saying, figure of speech. [➡FIGURES OF SPEECH; 674] 2 *n* **language**, dialect, speech, style, vernacular, syntax, lexicon, lexis. [➡ASPECTS OF LANGUAGE; 683]

idiomatic *adj* **natural**, fluent, colloquial, vernacular, native. [➡COMMUNICATIVE STYLE; 625] *Opposite:* stilted.

idiosyncrasy *n* **quirk**, peculiarity, eccentricity, foible, habit, characteristic, feature. [➡PERSONAL ECCENTRICITIES; 494]

idiosyncratic *adj* **characteristic**, personal, individual, distinctive, eccentric, peculiar, quirky, particular, unique, all your own. [➡EXTRAORDINARY: UNCOMMON; 206]

idiotic *adj* [➡BIZARRE AND PECULIAR; 258]

idle 1 *adj* **lazy**, indolent, shiftless, workshy, slothful (*formal*), sluggish. [➡LIFELESS, LAZY, AND UNENTHUSIASTIC; 507] *Opposite:* diligent. 2 *adj* **inactive**, inoperative, unoccupied, at rest, still, immobile, off, down. [➡LACK OF ACTIVITY; 343] *Opposite:* working. 3 *adj* **frivolous**, futile, pointless, worthless, useless, vain. [➡REDUNDANT AND USELESS; 241] 4 *adj* **unfounded**, baseless, groundless, frivolous, meaningless, speculative, casual. [➡THE NATURE OF IDEAS; 772] 5 *adj* **empty**, hollow, ineffectual, impotent, meaningless. [➡UNIMPORTANT AND UNNECESSARY; 239] 6 *v* **laze**, laze around, laze about, hang around, hang about, sit around, sit about, loaf around, loaf about, waste, while away, fritter away, goof off (*US informal*). [➡LACK OF ACTIVITY; 343] 7 *v* **tick over** (*informal*), turn over, run. [➡FUNCTION SUCCESSFULLY; 470] 8 *v* **lay off** (*informal*), dismiss, make redundant, can (*US slang*). [➡REVOKE STATUS; 460]

See Compare and Contrast at **vain**.

idle away *v* **while away**, fritter away, waste, pass, spend, occupy. [➡USE UP AND WASTE; 475]

idleness *n* **laziness**, sloth, slothfulness (*formal*), inertia, indolence, apathy, lethargy, sluggishness. [➡LACK OF ACTIVITY; 343] *Opposite:* willingness.

idler *n* **lazybones** (*informal*), slacker, skiver (*informal*), loafer, slouch (*informal*), sloth, malingerer (*disapproving*), timewaster, shirker. [➡LAZY OR UNSUCCESSFUL PEOPLE; 948] *Opposite:* workaholic.

idle rich *n* [➡RICH PEOPLE; 895]

idly 1 *adv* **lazily**, indolently, shiftlessly, slothfully (*formal*). [➡LIFELESS, LAZY, AND UNENTHUSIASTIC; 507] 2 *adv* **frivolously**, futilely, pointlessly, worthlessly, uselessly, vainly. [➡REDUNDANT AND USELESS; 241]

idol 1 *n* **hero**, star, pin-up, obsession, ideal, favourite. [➡PEOPLE WHO ARE APPROVED OF; 955] 2 *n* **icon**, graven image, statue, carving, sculpture, symbol, god, deity. [➡RELIGIOUS OBJECTS; 780]

idolater *n* **fan**, admirer, fanatic, devotee, hero-worshipper, aficionado, follower, worshipper, aficionada. [➡DEVOTEES AND ADDICTED PEOPLE; 557]

idolatry *n* **worship**, hero worship, adoration, admiration, veneration, idolization, adulation, reverence, fanaticism, devotion, obsession. [➡FADS, FETISHES, AND IDOLATRY; 556]

idolization *n* **worship**, hero worship, adoration, admiration, veneration, idolatry, adulation, reverence, fanaticism, devotion, obsession. [➡FADS, FETISHES, AND IDOLATRY; 556] *Opposite:* denigration.

idolize *v* **worship**, hero-worship, adore, look up to, admire, venerate, revere, put on a pedestal, exalt (*formal*). [➡LIKE, LOVE, VALUE, AND ENJOY; 579] *Opposite:* denigrate.

idyll *n* **nirvana**, honeymoon, honeymoon period, heaven, paradise, utopia, arcadia. [➡PLEASANT SITUATIONS; 74] *Opposite:* nightmare.

idyllic 1 *adj* **peaceful**, calm, tranquil, restful, relaxing, serene, heavenly, sublime, perfect, blissful, ideal, pleasant. [➡CALMING; 189] *Opposite:* nightmarish. 2 *adj* **picturesque**, scenic, unspoiled, serene, tranquil, calm, peaceful, beautiful, glorious, charming, delightful. [➡BEAUTY AND ATTRACTIVENESS; 190]

i.e. *adv* **that is to say**, that is, namely, viz, to be precise, to be exact, specifically, in so many words, in other words. [➡WRITTEN CONVENTIONS; 600]

if 1 *n* **doubt**, uncertainty, question mark, unknown, unknown quantity, gamble. [➡UNCERTAIN; 176] 2 *n* **stipulation**, condition, rider, proviso, qualification, but (*informal*), provision, reservation. [➡NECESSARY AND ESSENTIAL; 197]

iffy (*informal*) 1 *adj* **dodgy** (*informal*), dicey (*informal*), risky, chancy, shaky, suspicious, dubious, unreliable. [➡DANGEROUS; 237] *Opposite:* reliable. 2 *adj* **unsure**, undecided, doubtful, hesitant, up in the air, tentative, in doubt, touch and go, uncertain. [➡UNCERTAIN; 176] *Opposite:* certain.

if need be *adv* **if necessary**, if required, if essential, if needs must, if it comes to it, if it comes to the crunch, if push comes to shove, should it be necessary. [➡NECESSARY AND ESSENTIAL; 197]

if truth be told *adv* **to be honest**, to tell the truth, to be frank, frankly, in fact, as a matter of fact, in actual fact, actually. [➡WORDS AND PHRASES EMPHASIZING THE TRUTH OF A MATTER; 173]

if you ask me *adv* [➡EXPRESSIONS OF OPINION; 624]

igloo *type of* **house**. [➡RESIDENTIAL BUILDINGS; 1077]

ignite 1 *v* **catch fire**, catch light, go up in flames, burst into flames, flare up, kindle, burn, explode, go off. [➡FIRE, FLAMMABILITY, AND BURNING; 1164] *Opposite:* go out. 2 *v* **set fire to**, light, put a match to, set light to, set alight, kindle, burn, detonate, blow up. [➡FIRE, FLAMMABILITY, AND BURNING; 1164] *Opposite:* put out. 3 *v* **stir up**, stir, inflame, fan the flames of, kindle, awaken, provoke, incite, fire, fire up. [➡CAUSE TO HAPPEN; 31] *Opposite:* dampen.

ignition *n* **explosion**, detonation, eruption, burst, blast-off, start. [➡BEGINNING; 53]

ignoble *adj* **dishonourable**, shameful, despicable, immoral, dastardly, base, low, reprehensible, contemptible, shabby, disgraceful. [➡MORALLY BAD; 776] *Opposite:* honourable.

See Compare and Contrast at **mean**.

ignominious *adj* **humiliating**, embarrassing, discomfiting (*formal*), shameful, disgraceful, reprehensible, dishonourable, disreputable, despicable, discreditable. [➡EMOTIONALLY UNPLEASANT AND UPSETTING; 228] *Opposite:* honourable.

ignominy *n* **humiliation**, embarrassment, discomfiture (*formal*), shame, disgrace, dishonour, infamy, disrepute, discredit. [➡EMBARRASSMENT AND HUMILIATION; 543] *Opposite:* honour.

ignorance *n* **unawareness**, unfamiliarity, obliviousness, inexperience, illiteracy, witlessness. [➡IGNORANCE; 558] *Opposite:* knowledge.

ignorant *adj* **unaware**, uninformed, ill-informed, unfamiliar, oblivious, unconscious, unknowing, unwitting, unenlightened, in the dark, inexperienced, illiterate. [➡IGNORANCE; 558] *Opposite:* aware.

ignore *v* **pay no attention to**, take no notice of, close your eyes to, pay no heed to, disregard, not take into account, overlook, discount, dispense with, turn your back on, flout, snub, pass over, look through. [➡NOT PAY ATTENTION; 765] *Opposite:* notice.

ignored *adj* **overlooked**, unnoticed, disregarded, discounted, unheeded, passed over, flouted, snubbed. [➡IMPERCEPTIBLE; 26] *Opposite:* noted.

iguana *type of* **reptile**. [➡REPTILES; 994]

iguanodon *type of* **dinosaur**. [➡DINOSAUR; 996]

ilk *n* **type**, like, sort, kind, class, breed, manner, character, stripe, variety. [➡VARIETY, TYPE, KIND; 146]

ill 1 *adj* **unwell**, poorly (*informal*), sick, under the weather, ailing (*dated*), laid up, in poor health, off-colour, nauseous. [➡ILL AND SICK; 741] *Opposite:* well. 2 *adj* **unkind**, unfriendly, hostile, harsh, mean, cruel, hard, unpleasant, bad. [➡BAD AND BADLY; 224] *Opposite:* good. 3 *adj* **harmful**, adverse, detrimental, unfavourable, unpropitious, inauspicious, ominous, bad. [➡DANGEROUS; 237] *Opposite:* good. 4 *adj* **wicked**, evil, immoral, bad, iniquitous, sinful, reprobate. [➡MORALLY BAD; 776] *Opposite:* good. 5 *adv* **unkindly**, hostilely, harshly, cruelly, unpleasantly, poorly, shoddily, amiss, inadequately, inappropriately, badly. [➡BAD AND BADLY; 224] *Opposite:* well. 6 *adv* **unfavourably**, adversely, unpropitiously, inauspiciously, ominously, badly, harmfully, detrimentally. [➡DANGEROUS; 237] *Opposite:* well. 7 *adv* **hardly**, barely, scarcely. [➡TO A CERTAIN EXTENT; 134] *Opposite:* well. 8 *n* **harm**, evil, misfortune, trouble, mischief, bad luck, ill luck, injury. [➡NUISANCES; 254] *Opposite:* good.

ill-advised *adj* **foolish**, foolhardy, misguided, rash, reckless, hasty, unwise, imprudent (*formal*), incautious, ill-considered, ill-judged, injudicious, risky, irresponsible. [➡THE NATURE OF IDEAS; 772] *Opposite:* well-advised.

ill-advisedly *adv* **foolishly**, foolhardily, misguidedly, rashly, recklessly, hastily, unwisely, imprudently (*formal*), incautiously, injudiciously, riskily, irresponsibly. [➡NEGATIVE INTELLECTUAL CHARACTERISTICS; 526] *Opposite:* sensibly.

ill-assorted *adj* **incompatible**, mismatched, unsuited, incongruous, antagonistic, clashing. [➡DISHARMONY; 157] *Opposite:* compatible.

ill at ease *adj* **uncomfortable**, anxious, awkward, uneasy, edgy, on edge, jumpy, jittery, tense, self-conscious, nervous, nervy (*informal*). [➡INSECURITY AND LOSS OF COMPOSURE; 545] *Opposite:* relaxed.

ill-bred *adj* **rude**, impolite, boorish, bad-mannered, ill-mannered, ignorant, insensitive, inconsiderate, coarse, vulgar, common. [➡BAD MANNERS AND SOCIAL SKILLS; 522] *Opposite:* well-bred.

ill-conceived *adj* **half-baked** (*informal*), doomed, impractical, crackpot (*informal*), vague, ill-judged. [➡THE NATURE OF IDEAS; 772]

ill-considered *adj* **careless**, reckless, irresponsible, rash, hasty, imprudent (*formal*), unwise, ill-advised, ill-judged, foolhardy, foolish. [➡THE NATURE OF IDEAS; 772] *Opposite:* prudent.

ill-defined *adj* **imprecise**, vague, hazy, unclear, nebulous, blurred, inexact, inaccurate. [➡VAGUENESS; 244] *Opposite:* clear.

ill-disguised *adj* **obvious**, blatant, clear, apparent, plain, undisguised, unconcealed, glaring, visible, undoubted. [➡KNOWN AND FAMOUS; 182] *Opposite:* concealed.

ill-disposed *adj* **hostile**, unfriendly, cold, cool, antagonistic, negative, aggressive. [➡IRRITATION AND ANGER; 542] *Opposite:* well-disposed.

illegal *adj* **against the law**, unlawful, illicit, illegitimate, prohibited, banned, proscribed, forbidden, criminal, dishonest. [➡ILLEGAL; 816] *Opposite:* legal.

illegality 1 *n* **unlawfulness**, illicitness, illegitimacy, impropriety, wrongfulness, criminality, dishonesty. [➡ILLEGAL; 816] *Opposite:* legality. 2 *n* **crime**, misdemeanour, offence, felony, infraction, transgression, contravention, violation, infringement. [➡CRIMES; 817]

illegible *adj* **unreadable**, indecipherable, scrawled, scribbled, spidery, obscured. [➡DIFFICULTY AND COMPLEXITY; 243] *Opposite:* legible.

illegitimate *adj* **unlawful**, illegal, illicit, prohibited, banned, proscribed, forbidden, criminal, dishonest. [➡ILLEGAL; 816] *Opposite:* legitimate.

ill-fated *adj* **doomed**, ill-starred (*formal*), unlucky, unfortunate, hapless, star-crossed, fateful, ill-omened, disastrous. [➡BAD LUCK AND UNLUCKY; 785] *Opposite:* lucky.

ill-favoured *adj* **unattractive**, ugly, repulsive, repellent, hideous, unpleasant, horrible. [➡PEOPLE'S PHYSICAL APPEARANCE; 476] *Opposite:* good-looking.

ill feeling *n* **animosity**, hostility, ill will, antagonism, enmity, malice, resentment, antipathy, bitterness, hard feelings. [➡ANTAGONISM; 553] *Opposite:* friendliness.

ill-founded *adj* **illogical**, false, inaccurate, trumped-up, unreliable, dubious, unsubstantiated, unsound. [➡THE NATURE OF IDEAS; 772] *Opposite:* reliable.

ill-gotten *adj* **illegal**, illicit, fraudulent, contraband, unlawful, false, dishonest. [➡ILLEGAL; 816]

ill-gotten gains *n* [➡PROCEEDS OF CRIME; 428]

ill health *n* **infirmity**, illness, sickness, disease, frailty, weakness, debility, disability. [➡ILL AND SICK; 741] *Opposite:* good health.

ill humour *n* **bad mood**, mood, bad temper, foul mood, sulk, downer (*informal*), grumps (*informal*), pet. [➡IRRITATION AND ANGER; 542]

ill-humoured *adj* [➡NEGATIVE OF OUTLOOK; 515]

illiberal 1 *adj* **intolerant**, bigoted, narrow-minded, reactionary, parochial, proscriptive (*formal*), conservative. [➡NEGATIVE INTELLECTUAL CHARACTERISTICS; 526] *Opposite:* liberal. 2 *adj* (*formal*) **mean**, parsimonious, miserly, niggardly, tight, penny-pinching (*informal*), grudging, tightfisted, stingy (*informal*). [➡FINANCIALLY MEAN AND GRASPING; 520] *Opposite:* generous.

illicit *adj* **illegal**, unlawful, illegitimate, dishonest, criminal, against the law, prohibited, banned, forbidden, proscribed. [➡ILLEGAL; 816] *Opposite:* legal.

illicitness *n* [➡ILLEGAL; 816]

illiterate *adj* **uneducated**, untaught, unschooled, untrained, uninformed, ignorant. [➡UNSKILLED; 530] *Opposite:* literate.

ill-judged *adj* **misguided**, injudicious, inappropriate, unwise, imprudent (*formal*), rash, hasty, careless, thoughtless, ill-advised, ill-considered, ill-conceived. [➡THE NATURE OF IDEAS; 772] *Opposite:* prudent.

ill-mannered *adj* **rude**, bad-mannered, impolite, discourteous, disrespectful, common, ill-bred, vulgar, coarse, boorish, ignorant. [➡BAD MANNERS AND SOCIAL SKILLS; 522] *Opposite:* well-mannered.

ill-natured *adj* **unpleasant**, disagreeable, ill-tempered, bad-tempered, ill-humoured, irascible, irritable, surly, sulky, gruff, grumpy, cross, moody, prickly (*informal*), snippy (*informal*), crabby, grouchy (*informal*), curt, brusque, short, cantankerous, crotchety (*informal*). [➡AGGRESSIVE AND BELLIGERENT; 519] *Opposite:* good-natured.

illness 1 *n* **disease**, sickness, complaint, ailment, infection, virus, bug (*informal*), disorder, syndrome, malady, affliction. [➡ILL AND SICK; 741] 2 *n* **ill health**, sickness, disease, infirmity, disability, weakness, debility. [➡ILL AND SICK; 741] *Opposite:* good health.

illogical 1 *adj* **irrational**, unreasoned, unscientific, specious, unsound, unfounded, inconsistent, contradictory, invalid, irreconcilable, incongruous. [➡THE NATURE OF IDEAS; 772] *Opposite:* logical. 2 *adj* **unreasonable**, senseless, absurd, ludicrous, nonsensical, perverse. [➡THE NATURE OF IDEAS; 772] *Opposite:* logical.

illogicality 1 *n* **irrationality**, speciousness, unsoundness, inconsistency, contradiction, invalidity, irreconcilability, incongruity. [➡THE NATURE OF IDEAS; 772] 2 *n* **unreasonableness**, senselessness, absurdity, ludicrousness, nonsensicality, perverseness. [➡THE NATURE OF IDEAS; 772]

ill-omened *adj* **inauspicious**, unlucky, unfortunate, ominous, fateful, unpropitious, ill-starred (*formal*), ill-fated, doomed, hapless. [➡UNSUCCESSFUL AND UNPROMISING; 76] *Opposite:* blessed.

ill-starred (*formal*) *adj* **unlucky**, doomed, ill-fated, unfortunate, hapless, star-crossed, fateful, ill-omened, inauspicious, disastrous. [➡BAD LUCK AND UNLUCKY; 785] *Opposite:* lucky.

ill-tempered *adj* **bad-tempered**, short-tempered, ill-humoured, irascible, irritable, grumpy, cross, moody, prickly (*informal*), sulky, gruff, snippy (*informal*), grouchy (*informal*), cantankerous, crotchety (*informal*). [➡AGGRESSIVE AND BELLIGERENT; 519] *Opposite:* good-tempered.

ill-timed *adj* **inopportune**, mistimed, untimely, inconvenient, intrusive, unfortunate, inappropriate, misjudged, ill-judged. [➡PROMPTNESS: BADLY TIMED; 101] *Opposite:* opportune.

ill-treat *v* **abuse**, harm, mistreat, maltreat, ill-use, misuse, hurt, harass, torment, oppress, neglect, batter, knock about (*informal*). [➡WOUND A PERSON OR ANIMAL; 384] *Opposite:* look after.

See Compare and Contrast at **misuse**.

ill-treated *adj* **abused**, harmed, mistreated, maltreated, ill-used, misused, hurt, harassed, tormented, oppressed, neglected, battered, knocked about (*informal*). [➡INJURED; 743] *Opposite:* cherished.

ill-treatment *n* **abuse**, harm, maltreatment, mistreatment, cruelty, ill-use, misuse, hurt, harassment, torment, oppression, neglect. [➡UNKIND ACTION OR BEHAVIOUR; 297] *Opposite:* care.

illuminate 1 *v* **light up**, light, brighten, illumine (*literary*), lighten, irradiate, illume (*archaic or literary*). [➡LIGHT EMISSION; 369] *Opposite:* darken. 2 *v* **clarify**, elucidate (*formal*), explain, enlighten, put in the picture, inform, clear up, illustrate. [➡EXPLAIN AND CLARIFY; 611] *Opposite:* confuse.

illuminating *adj* **enlightening**, revealing, informative, instructive, educational, helpful. [➡INTERESTING AND MEANINGFUL; 191] *Opposite:* confusing.

illumination 1 *n* **light**, lighting, lights, brightness, brilliance, radiance. [➡LIGHT; 1163] 2 *n* **enlightenment**, clarification, elucidation (*formal*), explanation, insight, knowledge. [➡EXPLAIN AND CLARIFY; 611] *Opposite:* confusion.

illuminations *n* **lights**, Christmas lights, coloured lights, decorations, fairy lights. [➡LIGHT; 1163]

illumine (*literary*) *v* [➡LIGHT EMISSION; 369]

ill-use *v* **abuse**, harm, mistreat, maltreat, treat badly, be cruel to, ill-treat, misuse, hurt, harass, torment, oppress, neglect, batter, knock about (*informal*). [➡WOUND A PERSON OR ANIMAL; 384] *Opposite:* look after.

ill-used *adj* **mistreated**, maltreated, badly treated, abused, hurt, harmed, ill-treated, misused, harassed, tormented, oppressed, neglected, battered, knocked about (*informal*). [➡IN TROUBLE AND DISADVANTAGED; 73] *Opposite:* cherished.

illusion 1 *n* **fantasy**, daydream, figment of your imagination, chimera, mirage, dream, trick, deception, hallucination, figment. [➡NONEXISTENT THINGS; 23] *Opposite:* reality. 2 *n* **impression**, semblance, appearance, feeling, sensation, sense, idea, effect. [➡IDEA AND THOUGHT; 771] 3 *n* **delusion**, impression, misapprehension, deception, misconception, magic, trickery, artifice (*formal*), sleight of hand. [➡DECEPTION AND LIES; 661]

illusive *adj* **illusory**, deceptive, false, misleading, imagined, unreal, erroneous, sham. [➡FALSE AND UNREAL; 174] *Opposite:* real.

illusoriness *n* [➡FALSE AND UNREAL; 174]

illusory *adj* **deceptive**, false, illusive, imagined, misleading, unreal, sham, erroneous. [➡FALSE AND UNREAL; 174] *Opposite:* real.

illustrate *v* **exemplify**, demonstrate, show, point up, prove, explain, clarify, elucidate (*formal*), illuminate, point out. [➡REPRESENT SOMETHING OR SOMEBODY; 59]

illustration 1 *n* **picture**, drawing, design, figure, diagram, sketch, photograph, photo, image, graphic, artwork, visual, visual aid. [➡DRAWINGS, CHARTS AND TABLES; 595] 2 *n* **example**, demonstration, instance, case in point, exemplification, model, specimen, sample, representative. [➡REPRESENTATIONS AND GENERAL EXAMPLES; 65]

illustrations *n* [➡DRAWINGS, CHARTS, AND TABLES; 595]

illustrative *adj* **descriptive**, explanatory, graphic, expressive, demonstrative. [➡REPRESENTATIVE; 66]

illustrious *adj* **distinguished**, celebrated, renowned, famous, eminent, great, grand, glorious, admired, well-known. [➡KNOWN AND FAMOUS; 182] *Opposite:* obscure.

ill will *n* **animosity**, hostility, ill feeling, antagonism, enmity, malice, resentment, antipathy, bitterness, hard feelings. [➡ANTAGONISM; 553] *Opposite:* goodwill.

image 1 *n* **picture**, representation, drawing, icon, figure, likeness, illustration, reflection. [➡ARTWORKS; 898] 2 *n* **impression**, picture, idea, concept, notion, vision, view. [➡IDEA AND THOUGHT; 771] 3 *n* **copy**, twin, double, duplicate, spitting image (*informal*), carbon copy, doppelgänger. [➡REPRESENTATIONS AND GENERAL EXAMPLES; 65] 4 *n* **appearance**, look, persona, aura, air, aspect, semblance. [➡APPEARANCE AND ATMOSPHERE; 1236]

imagery *n* **images**, pictures, imaginings, descriptions, metaphors, similes. [➡REPRESENTATIONS AND GENERAL EXAMPLES; 65]

imaginable *adj* **conceivable**, possible, thinkable, supposable, presumable. [➡POSSIBLE AND PROBABLE; 178] *Opposite:* unimaginable.

imaginariness *n* [➡FALSE AND UNREAL; 174]

imaginary *adj* **fantasy**, make-believe, made-up, unreal, invented, pretend, imagined, fictional, illusory. [➡FALSE AND UNREAL; 174] *Opposite:* real.

imagination 1 *n* **mind's eye**, mind, head, thoughts, imaginings, dreams, fancy. [➡DREAM, IMAGINE, AND FANTASIZE; 750] 2 *n* **resourcefulness**, ingenuity, creativity, powers of invention, vision, inspiration, inventiveness. [➡POSITIVE INTELLECTUAL CHARACTERISTICS; 525]

imaginative *adj* **creative**, inventive, original, ingenious, inspired, artistic, resourceful, visionary, inspirational. [➡POSITIVE INTELLECTUAL CHARACTERISTICS; 525] *Opposite:* unimaginative.

imaginativeness *n* **creativeness**, inventiveness, originality, ingeniousness, resourcefulness. [➡POSITIVE INTELLECTUAL CHARACTERISTICS; 525]

imagine 1 *v* **picture**, envisage, visualize, see, conjure up, envision, conceive, fancy. [➡DREAM, IMAGINE, AND FANTASIZE; 750] 2 *v* **make up**, dream, dream up, invent, make believe, think up, think of, conceive of, concoct. [➡DREAM, IMAGINE, AND FANTASIZE; 750] 3 *v* **suppose**, think, expect, assume, presume, guess, dare say, understand, reckon. [➡DEVELOP THEORIES AND REASON; 745]

imagined *adj* **fictional**, imaginary, abstract, unreal, illusory, fantasy, make-believe, made-up, invented, pretend. [➡ FALSE AND UNREAL; 174] *Opposite:* real.

imago *type of* **insect stages of development**. [➡ INSECT STAGES; 1020]

imbalance *n* **inequity**, disparity, unevenness, disproportion, inequality, difference, discrepancy, one-sidedness. [➡ DIFFERENCE; 150] *Opposite:* balance.

imbibe (*formal or humorous*) *v* **drink**, down, swallow, take in, guzzle (*informal*), absorb, gulp. [➡ DRINK; 712]

imbroglio (*formal or literary*) *n* **mess**, embarrassment, entanglement, complication, enmeshment, confusion. [➡ DIFFICULT SITUATIONS; 72]

imbue *v* **instil**, fill, permeate, infuse, saturate, impregnate. [➡ FILL; 407]

imitate 1 *v* **copy**, reproduce, emulate, duplicate, replicate, try to be like. [➡ PRETEND AND MIMIC; 60] 2 *v* **mimic**, copy, impersonate, ape, pretend to be, take off (*informal*), do an impression. [➡ PRETEND AND MIMIC; 60]

Compare and Contrast: ***imitate, copy, emulate, mimic, take off, ape***

CORE MEANING: TO ADOPT THE BEHAVIOUR OF ANOTHER PERSON

imitate to copy somebody's behaviour, voice, or manner, sometimes in order to make fun of him or her; ***copy*** to do exactly what somebody else does; ***emulate*** to try to equal or surpass somebody or something successful or admired; ***mimic*** to imitate somebody in a deliberate and exaggerated way, especially to amuse; ***take off*** (*informal*) to imitate somebody to amuse; ***ape*** to imitate somebody or something in an absurd or grotesque way.

imitation 1 *n* **simulation**, reproduction, replication, copy, facsimile, mock-up. [➡ REPRESENTATIONS AND GENERAL EXAMPLES; 65] 2 *n* **impersonation**, impression, takeoff (*informal*), skit, parody, sendup (*informal*). [➡ REPRESENTATIONS AND GENERAL EXAMPLES; 65] 3 *adj* **mock**, fake, simulated, artificial, ersatz (*disapproving*), pretend, synthetic. [➡ FALSE AND UNREAL; 174] *Opposite:* real.

imitative *adj* **unoriginal**, derivative, plagiarized, copied, second-hand, clichéd, commonplace, trite. [➡ RELATED; 143] *Opposite:* original.

imitator 1 *n* **follower**, sheep, copycat (*informal*), copier, clone, imitation, pale imitation. [➡ REPRESENTATIONS AND GENERAL EXAMPLES; 65] *Opposite:* original. 2 *n* **impersonator**, impressionist, mimic, lookalike (*informal*), double, actor. [➡ WORKERS IN ENTERTAINMENT AND MEDIA; 873]

immaculate 1 *adj* **spotless**, perfect, neat and tidy, clean, tidy, spick-and-span. [➡ CLEAN; 1232] *Opposite:* messy. 2 *adj* **perfect**, flawless, faultless, pristine, pure, impeccable. [➡ CLEAN; 1232] *Opposite:* flawed.

immaculately *adv* **perfectly**, flawlessly, faultlessly, impeccably, spotlessly. [➡ TO A GREAT EXTENT; 130]

immanent (*formal*) *adj* **inherent**, intrinsic, innate, ingrained, internal, essential. [➡ PRESENT AND AVAILABLE; 11]

immaterial *adj* **irrelevant**, unimportant, of no importance, of no consequence, inconsequential, beside the point, neither here nor there, makes no difference. [➡ UNIMPORTANT AND UNNECESSARY; 239] *Opposite:* relevant.

immateriality *n* [➡ FALSE AND UNREAL; 174]

immaterialness *n* [➡ FALSE AND UNREAL; 174]

immature 1 *adj* **young**, undeveloped, small, unformed, juvenile, adolescent, unripe. [➡ BABYHOOD, CHILDHOOD, AND ADOLESCENCE; 917] *Opposite:* mature. 2 *adj* **childish**, babyish, infantile, juvenile, adolescent, puerile. [➡ BAD MANNERS AND SOCIAL SKILLS; 522] *Opposite:* mature.

immaturely *adv* **childishly**, babyishly, puerilely. [➡ BAD MANNERS AND SOCIAL SKILLS; 522] *Opposite:* maturely.

immaturity 1 *n* **adolescence**, infancy, reproductive immaturity, youth, babyhood, childhood. [➡ BABYHOOD, CHILDHOOD, AND ADOLESCENCE; 917] *Opposite:* maturity. 2 *n* **childishness**, irresponsibility, naivety, ingenuousness, silliness, stupidity, puerility, fatuity (*formal*). [➡ BAD MANNERS AND SOCIAL SKILLS; 522] *Opposite:* maturity. 3 *n* **naivety**, inexperience, greenness, rawness, awkwardness, crudeness, heavy-handedness. [➡ NEGATIVE INTELLECTUAL CHARACTERISTICS; 526] *Opposite:* maturity.

immeasurable *adj* **vast**, beyond measure, endless, infinite, incalculable, inestimable, immense, untold, massive, great, colossal, huge, enormous, considerable. [➡ LARGE; 1192] *Opposite:* slight.

immeasurably *adv* **infinitely**, vastly, incalculably, inestimably, immensely, massively (*informal*), greatly, colossally, hugely, enormously, considerably. [➡ TO A GREAT EXTENT; 130] *Opposite:* slightly.

immediate 1 *adj* **instant**, direct, instantaneous, abrupt, fast, speedy. [➡ HAPPENING QUICKLY; 104] 2 *adj* **direct**, close, near, proximate. [➡ CLOSENESS; 160] *Opposite:* distant. 3 *adj* **urgent**, current, pressing, high priority, burning, important. [➡ IMPORTANT; 195]

immediately 1 *adv* **right away**, straightaway, at once, without delay, instantly, directly, instantaneously, without further ado, right now, just now. [➡ HAPPENING QUICKLY; 104] 2 *adv* **directly**, closely, nearly, proximately. [➡ CLOSENESS; 160] 3 *conj* **as soon as**, the moment, the instant, the minute, the second. [➡ CONCURRENT AND CONTEMPORANEOUS; 165]

immemorial *adj* **ancient**, age-old, old, centuries old, timeworn, long-established. [➡ PERMANENCE: WITHOUT END; 94]

immense *adj* **huge**, vast, enormous, massive, gigantic, mammoth, giant, colossal, immeasurable, great, incalculable. [➡ LARGE; 1192] *Opposite:* tiny.

immensely *adv* **hugely**, vastly, enormously, massively (*informal*), immeasurably, greatly, incalculably, very, extremely, gigantically, colossally, infinitely. [➡ TO A GREAT EXTENT; 130]

immenseness *n* [➡ LARGE; 1192]

immensity *n* **hugeness**, vastness, enormity, sheer size, extent. [➡ LARGE; 1192]

immerse 1 *v* **submerge**, dip, plunge, duck, dunk, submerse. [➡ MOVE SOMETHING: DOWNWARDS; 330] 2 *v* **engross**, throw yourself into, absorb yourself in, engage, occupy. [➡ CHANGE OF MOOD AND COMPOSURE; 581]

immersed *adj* **engrossed**, wrapped up, absorbed, deep, occupied. [➡ PENSIVENESS AND INTEREST; 539] *Opposite:* distracted.

immersion 1 *n* **involvement**, engagement, absorption, entanglement, preoccupation, obsession. [➡ POSITIVE IMPATIENCE, ENTHUSIASM, AND ALERTNESS; 538] 2 *n* **dipping**, soaking, wetting, dunking, steeping, bathing, rinsing, submersion, covering. [➡ WET; 1239]

immersion heater *type of* **heating appliance**. [➡ HEATING, REFRIGERATION, AND VENTILATION; 1141]

immigrant *n* **settler**, émigré, migrant, refugee, colonist, colonizer. [➡ PEOPLE LIVING AWAY FROM HOME; 887] *Opposite:* emigrant.

immigrate *v* **settle**, arrive, colonize, discover, found, establish. [➡ TRAVEL: WAYS OF TRAVELLING; 321] *Opposite:* emigrate.

immigration *n* **migration**, settlement, arrival, entry, colonization. [➡ ARRIVAL; 13]

imminence *n* [➡ FUTURE; 86]

imminent *adj* **impending**, forthcoming, pending, looming, about to happen, coming up, in the offing, on the cards (*informal*), on the agenda, on the horizon, just round the corner, in the stars, in the pipeline, at hand. [➡ ABOUT TO HAPPEN; 33] *Opposite:* distant.

immobile 1 *adj* **motionless**, stationary, still, stock-still, inert, static, at a halt, at a standstill, at rest. [➡ LACK OF ACTIVITY; 343] *Opposite:* mobile. 2 *adj* **fixed**, immovable, secure, steady, permanent. [➡ RIGID AND HARD; 1210] *Opposite:* mobile.

immobility *n* **stillness**, motionlessness, immovability, fixity, stasis, rigidity. [➡ LACK OF ACTIVITY; 343] *Opposite:* mobility.

immobilize *v* **stop**, halt, restrain, arrest, bring to a halt, put out of action. [➡ CAUSE TO STOP; 267] *Opposite:* mobilize.

immoderate (*formal*) *adj* **excessive**, extreme, intemperate, over-the-top (*informal*), extravagant, unrestrained, debauched, wild, violent, riotous, uncontrolled, out of control, decadent. [➡ PLEASURE-SEEKING AND EXCESS; 885] *Opposite:* moderate.

immoderateness (*formal*) *n* [➡ TOO MUCH; 118]

immoderation (*formal*) *n* **excess**, intemperance, extravagance, prodigality, abandon, decadence, debauchery, riotousness, lack of control. [➡ PLEASURE-SEEKING AND EXCESS; 885] *Opposite:* moderation.

immodest *adj* **boastful**, bigheaded (*informal*), arrogant, conceited, ostentatious, bombastic, pretentious. [➡ AFFECTATION, SELF-SATISFACTION, AND SNOBBISHNESS; 508] *Opposite:* modest.

immodestly *adv* **boastfully**, arrogantly, conceitedly, ostentatiously, pretentiously, bombastically, bigheadedly (*informal*). [➡ POMPOUS, LOUD, AND OVER-CONFIDENT; 636] *Opposite:* modestly.

immodesty *n* **bigheadedness** (*informal*), arrogance, conceit, boastfulness, pretentiousness, ostentatiousness, showing off. [➡ BAD MANNERS AND SOCIAL SKILLS; 522] *Opposite:* modesty.

immolate 1 *v* (*formal*) **sacrifice**, offer up, slaughter, make an offering of, kill, burn, commit suicide, protest. [➡ KILL; 923] 2 *v* (*literary*) **give up**, sacrifice, renounce, do without, forgo, relinquish. [➡ FORGO AND DENY ONESELF; 450]

immolation (*formal*) *n* [➡ CAUSES OF DEATH; 921]

immoral *adj* **wicked**, depraved, corrupt, dissolute, dishonest, dissipated, decadent, debauched, sinful, iniquitous. [➡ MORALLY BAD; 776] *Opposite:* moral.

immorality *n* **wickedness**, sin, depravity, corruption, dissoluteness, dishonesty, dissipation, decadence, iniquity, debauchery. [➡ MORALLY BAD; 776] *Opposite:* morality.

immortal 1 *adj* **eternal**, everlasting, undying, perpetual, enduring, never-ending, endless, unending, abiding, that will live forever, that will never die. [➡ PERMANENCE: WITHOUT END; 94] *Opposite:* mortal. 2 *adj* **memorable**, well-known, famous, illustrious, unforgettable, remarkable. [➡ KNOWN AND FAMOUS; 182] *Opposite:* forgotten.

immortality *n* [➡ PERMANENCE: WITHOUT END; 94]

immortalize *v* **commemorate**, celebrate, exalt (*formal*), preserve, make immortal, memorialize, eternalize. [➡ REPRESENT SOMETHING OR SOMEBODY; 59]

immortally *adv* [➡ PERMANENCE: WITHOUT END; 94]

immovable 1 *adj* **fixed**, immobile, secure, steady, permanent. [➡ RIGID AND HARD; 1210] *Opposite:* movable. 2 *adj* **resolute**, unbending, rigid, stubborn, obstinate, inflexible, adamant, firm, steadfast, obdurate, set. [➡ UNWILLINGNESS AND STUBBORNNESS; 565] *Opposite:* irresolute.

immune 1 *adj* **resistant**, protected, invulnerable, safe, insusceptible (*formal*). [➡ HEALING; 731] *Opposite:* susceptible. 2 *adj* **exempt**, excepted, absolved, excused, not liable. [➡ FREEDOM AND LIBERTY; 209] *Opposite:* liable. 3 *adj* **impervious**, invulnerable, untouchable, untouched, unaffected, safe, proof. [➡ NEUTRALITY AND INDIFFERENCE; 554] *Opposite:* vulnerable.

immune system *n* **body's defences**, natural defences, immune response, white blood cells, natural resistance, antibodies, white corpuscles. [➡ HEALING; 731]

immunity 1 *n* **resistance**, protection, invulnerability, insusceptibility (*formal*). [➡ HEALING; 731] *Opposite:* susceptibility. 2 *n* **exemption**, exception, liberty, freedom, liberation. [➡ FREEDOM AND LIBERTY; 209] *Opposite:* liability. 3 *n* **invulnerability**, imperviousness, freedom, exception, protection. [➡ NEUTRALITY AND INDIFFERENCE; 554] *Opposite:* vulnerability.

immunization *n* **vaccination**, inoculation, injection, shot (*informal*), jab (*informal*). [➡ HEALING; 731]

immunize *v* **vaccinate**, inoculate, inject, protect, jab (*informal*). [➡ FALL ILL, TREAT, AND RECOVER; 729]

immure (*literary*) *v* **imprison**, confine, shut away, incarcerate (*formal*), shut up, hold captive, seclude. [➡ CAPTIVITY AND LOSS OF FREEDOM; 249] *Opposite:* free.

immutability *n* [➡ PERMANENCE: WITHOUT CHANGE; 95]

immutable *adj* **unchanging**, irreversible, fixed, absolute, unchangeable, unalterable, permanent. [➡ PERMANENCE: WITHOUT CHANGE; 95] *Opposite:* mercurial.

imp 1 *n* **elf**, goblin, gremlin (*informal*), pixie, sprite, fairy, demon. [➡MYTHICAL BEINGS; 790] 2 *n* **rascal** (*humorous*), scamp (*informal*), mischief, urchin, scallywag (*dated informal*), rapscallion (*archaic or humorous*). [➡MISCHIEVOUS OR BADLY-BEHAVED CHILD; 946]

impact 1 *n* **crash**, collision, shock, bang, blow, force, contact, brunt. [➡CONTACT: IMPACT; 414] 2 *n* **influence**, impression, effect, bearing, power, control, sway. [➡RESULTS AND OUTCOMES; 83]

impacted *adj* **wedged**, stuck, jammed, squeezed, obstructed, crushed, compressed. [➡LACK OF ACTIVITY; 343]

impair *v* **damage**, harm, spoil, weaken, worsen, prejudice, blight, mess up (*informal*), ruin, mar. [➡WORSEN SOMETHING; 381] *Opposite:* enhance.

impaired *adj* **reduced**, lessened, decreased, weakened, diminished, compromised. [➡IN BAD REPAIR; 1233] *Opposite:* unimpaired.

impairment *n* **damage**, injury, hurt, loss, weakening, deficiency, diminishing. [➡FAULTS, FLAWS, AND WEAKNESSES; 252] *Opposite:* enhancement.

impala *type of* **deer or antelope**. [➡DEER AND ANTELOPE; 981]

impale *v* **spear**, pierce, stab, bayonet, spike, skewer, run through (*literary*). [➡STAB; 417]

impalpability (*formal*) *n* [➡IMPERCEPTIBLE; 26]

impalpable (*formal*) *adj* **intangible**, shadowy, vague, unclear, indefinable, imperceptible, obscure, indescribable, mysterious. [➡IMPERCEPTIBLE; 26] *Opposite:* palpable.

impart *v* **communicate**, inform, tell, convey, report, teach, instruct, divulge, disclose, reveal, expose, pass on. [➡INFORM AND ANNOUNCE; 612]

impartial *adj* **neutral**, fair, unbiased, independent, objective, detached, unprejudiced, disinterested, open-minded, evenhanded, balanced, nonaligned. [➡NEUTRALITY AND INDIFFERENCE; 554] *Opposite:* biased.

impartiality *n* **neutrality**, fairness, independence, objectivity, detachment, lack of prejudice, disinterest, open-mindedness, nonalignment, balance, evenhandedness. [➡NEUTRALITY AND INDIFFERENCE; 554] *Opposite:* bias.

impassable *adj* **blocked**, impenetrable, treacherous, closed, obstructed, inaccessible. [➡IN BAD REPAIR; 1233] *Opposite:* open.

impasse *n* **stalemate**, standoff, deadlock, gridlock, bottleneck, dead end. [➡DIFFICULT SITUATIONS; 72]

impassioned *adj* **emotional**, ardent, fervent, passionate, heated, excited, heartfelt, from the heart, moving, touching. [➡ENTHUSIASTIC AND INQUISITIVE; 629] *Opposite:* impassive.

impassive 1 *adj* **expressionless**, blank, inexpressive, poker-faced, unrevealing, deadpan. [➡FACIAL EXPRESSION; 652] *Opposite:* expressive. 2 *adj* **emotionless**, unemotional, unmoved, stolid, stoical, phlegmatic, apathetic. [➡NEUTRALITY AND INDIFFERENCE; 554]

Compare and Contrast: ***impassive, apathetic, phlegmatic, stolid, stoical, unmoved***

CORE MEANING: SHOWING NO EMOTIONAL REPONSE OR INTEREST

impassive showing no outward sign of emotion, especially on the face; ***apathetic*** not taking any interest in anything, or not bothering to do anything; ***phlegmatic*** generally unemotional and difficult to arouse; ***stolid*** solemn, unemotional, and not easily excited or upset; ***stoical*** showing admirable patience and endurance in the face of adversity without complaining or getting upset; ***unmoved*** showing no emotion, surprise, or excitement when this would normally have been expected.

impassively *adv* **unemotionally**, blankly, without emotion, coolly, emotionlessly, aloofly. [➡UNINTERESTED AND DETACHED; 630] *Opposite:* expressively.

impassiveness *n* [➡NEUTRALITY AND INDIFFERENCE; 554]

impassivity *n* [➡NEUTRALITY AND INDIFFERENCE; 554]

impatience 1 *n* **annoyance**, irritation, edginess, intolerance, pique, displeasure, exasperation, touchiness, tetchiness (*informal*). [➡IRRITATION AND ANGER; 542] *Opposite:* patience. 2 *n* **eagerness**, keenness, anxiety, hurry, haste, impulsiveness, impetuosity, rashness, zeal, enthusiasm, excitement. [➡FEELINGS ABOUT THE FUTURE; 534] *Opposite:* patience.

impatient 1 *adj* **annoyed**, irritated, edgy, intolerant, exasperated, aggravated, irked, piqued, irascible, touchy, tetchy (*informal*), querulous. [➡IRRITATION AND ANGER; 542] *Opposite:* patient. 2 *adj* **eager**, keen, raring, anxious, in a hurry, hurried, hasty, impulsive, impetuous, rash, enthusiastic, excited, hotheaded, zealous. [➡POSITIVE IMPATIENCE, ENTHUSIASM, AND ALERTNESS; 538] *Opposite:* patient.

impeach *v* **indict**, accuse, arraign, charge, inculpate (*formal*), denunciate (*formal*). [➡TRIAL, PUNISHMENT, AND LEGAL OUTCOMES; 819]

impeccability *n* [➡GOOD, WELL, BETTER; 184]

impeccable *adj* **perfect**, flawless, faultless, unimpeachable, above reproach, immaculate, spotless, unsullied. [➡CORRECT; 183] *Opposite:* flawed.

impecunious (*formal*) *adj* **poor**, impoverished, penniless, struggling, underprivileged, deprived, disadvantaged, indigent (*formal*), broke (*informal*), on the breadline, strapped (*informal*), hard up (*informal*), skint (*informal*), poverty-stricken, needy, cleaned out (*informal*), ruined, destitute, insolvent, bankrupt, badly off. [➡POVERTY AND POOR; 892] *Opposite:* wealthy.

impecuniousness (*formal*) *n* [➡POVERTY AND POOR; 892]

impede *v* **obstruct**, hinder, hamper, slow down, delay, hold back, hold up, encumber, inhibit, block, get in the way of, get in the way. [➡AVOID, PREVENT, LIMIT, AND CONTROL; 278] *Opposite:* facilitate.

See Compare and Contrast at **hinder**.

impediment 1 *n* **obstacle**, obstruction, barrier, hurdle, hindrance, block, drawback, holdup, let (*archaic*).

[➡PROBLEM; 257] 2 *n* **impairment**, disablement, weakness, disorder, inhibition. [➡PROBLEM; 257]

impel 1 *v* **compel**, urge, force, drive, coerce, make, oblige, require, induce. [➡CAUSE OR COMPEL TO ACT; 272] *Opposite:* hold back. 2 *v* (*formal*) **propel**, force, drive, throw, push, fling, hurl, thrust. [➡PUSH, PULL, SLIDE; 336]

impend 1 *v* (*formal*) **loom**, approach, be on the horizon, be imminent, be in the offing, appear, be close, be on the cards (*informal*), be in the cards (*US informal*). [➡ABOUT TO HAPPEN; 33] *Opposite:* recede. 2 *v* (*literary*) **menace**, loom, threaten, hover, hang, overshadow. [➡ABOUT TO HAPPEN; 33]

impending *adj* **imminent**, looming, in the near future, awaiting, approaching, future, coming, just round the corner, on the horizon, at hand, forthcoming. [➡ABOUT TO HAPPEN; 33] *Opposite:* far-off.

impenetrability 1 *n* **impassability**, impermeability, density, denseness, thickness, darkness, murkiness. [➡DENSITY AND CONSISTENCY; 1206] 2 *n* **incomprehensibility**, complexity, opacity, intricacy, obscurity, denseness, inaccessibility, inscrutability. [➡DIFFICULTY AND COMPLEXITY; 243] *Opposite:* lucidity.

impenetrable 1 *adj* **impassable**, dense, tightly packed, thick, solid, impermeable, dark, murky. [➡DENSITY AND CONSISTENCY; 1206] 2 *adj* **incomprehensible**, unfathomable, indecipherable, inscrutable, unsolvable, obscure, mysterious, sphinxlike, enigmatic. [➡DIFFICULTY AND COMPLEXITY; 243] *Opposite:* understandable.

impenitent *adj* **unrepentant**, unremorseful, unapologetic, defiant, shameless, brazen. [➡IRRITATION AND ANGER; 542] *Opposite:* remorseful.

imperative 1 *adj* **necessary**, vital, crucial, essential, urgent, of the essence, important. [➡NECESSARY AND ESSENTIAL; 197] *Opposite:* unimportant. 2 *adj* (*formal*) **commanding**, domineering, bossy, imperious, overbearing, authoritative. [➡BOSSY AND OVERBEARING; 517] *Opposite:* subservient. 3 *n* **priority**, essential, requirement, necessity, rule, constraint, obligation, must, need. [➡MOST IMPORTANT THING; 198] *Opposite:* option.

imperativeness *n* [➡IMPORTANCE AND SIGNIFICANCE; 193]

imperceptibility *n* [➡IMPERCEPTIBLE; 26]

imperceptible *adj* **slight**, gradual, subtle, invisible, barely visible, faint, indiscernible, undetectable, light, small, tiny, unnoticeable. [➡IMPERCEPTIBLE; 26] *Opposite:* obvious.

imperceptibly *adv* **slightly**, gradually, invisibly, subtly, bit by bit, slowly, faintly, indiscernibly, undetectably, lightly, a little. [➡TO A CERTAIN EXTENT; 134] *Opposite:* obviously.

imperceptive *adj* [➡NEGATIVE INTELLECTUAL CHARACTERISTICS; 526]

imperfect *adj* **faulty**, defective, deficient, damaged, flawed, unsatisfactory, inadequate, incomplete, limited. [➡IN BAD REPAIR; 1233] *Opposite:* perfect.

imperfection 1 *n* **fault**, defect, deficiency, blemish, flaw, limitation, blot, failing, shortcoming, weakness. [➡FAULTS, FLAWS, AND WEAKNESSES; 252] 2 *n* **faultiness**, inadequacy, limitation, deficiency, failure, defectiveness. [➡FAULTS, FLAWS, AND WEAKNESSES; 252] *Opposite:* perfection.

See Compare and Contrast at **flaw**.

imperial *adj* **grand**, majestic, imposing, regal, stately, lordly, magnificent, royal. [➡ROYALNESS; 825]

imperialism *n* **expansionism**, colonialism, empire-building, colonization, interventionism, domination. [➡STYLES AND SYSTEMS OF GOVERNMENT; 806]

imperil (*formal*) *v* **endanger**, put in danger, risk, put at risk, jeopardize, expose, hazard, chance. [➡PUT AT RISK; 385] *Opposite:* protect.

imperilled (*formal*) *adj* [➡IN DANGER; 238]

imperious *adj* **domineering**, authoritative, commanding, arrogant, superior, haughty, high-handed, overbearing, bossy. [➡BOSSY AND OVERBEARING; 517] *Opposite:* humble.

imperiously *adv* **domineeringly**, authoritatively, commandingly, arrogantly, superiorly, haughtily, high-handedly, overbearingly, bossily. [➡BOSSY AND OVERBEARING; 517] *Opposite:* humbly.

imperiousness *n* **haughtiness**, overbearingness, arrogance, superiority, bossiness, high-handedness. [➡BOSSY AND OVERBEARING; 517] *Opposite:* humility.

imperishability 1 *n* **durability**, resilience, stability, endurance, hardiness, indestructibility. [➡DURABLE; 1209] 2 *n* (*literary*) **permanence**, immortality, everlastingness, enduringness. [➡PERMANENCE: WITHOUT END; 94] *Opposite:* transience.

imperishable 1 *adj* **permanent**, durable, indestructible, resilient, stable, enduring, hardy. [➡DURABLE; 1209] 2 *adj* (*literary*) **enduring**, eternal, everlasting, permanent, immortal, perpetual, inextinguishable. [➡PERMANENCE: WITHOUT END; 94] *Opposite:* transient.

imperishably (*literary*) *adv* **enduringly**, eternally, everlastingly, immortally, perpetually, permanently, indestructibly. [➡PERMANENCE: WITHOUT END; 94]

impermanence *n* **transience**, transitoriness, evanescence, ephemerality, temporariness, insubstantiality, incorporeity. [➡FINITENESS, VARIABILITY, AND TRANSIENCE; 96] *Opposite:* permanence.

impermanent *adj* **temporary**, transitory, passing, transient, evanescent, ephemeral. [➡FINITENESS, VARIABILITY, AND TRANSIENCE; 96] *Opposite:* permanent.

impermeability *n* **watertightness**, airtightness, waterproofness, protection, impenetrability, security. [➡DENSITY AND CONSISTENCY; 1206] *Opposite:* permeability.

impermeable *adj* **resistant**, impervious, waterproof, water-resistant, rainproof, watertight, solid. [➡DURABLE; 1209] *Opposite:* permeable.

impersonal 1 *adj* **objective**, cool, detached, measured, careful, neutral. [➡UNINTERESTED AND DETACHED; 630] *Opposite:* personal. 2 *adj* **anonymous**, faceless, soulless, featureless, grey, depersonalized, impassive, bureaucratic, monolithic, inhuman. [➡BORING AND UNINTERESTING; 235] **3** *adj* **unfriendly**, cool, cold, aloof, frosty, distant, remote, uncongenial, unwelcoming, inhospitable, formal. [➡RETICENT AND UNFORTHCOMING; 632] *Opposite:* friendly.

impersonate **1** *v* **mimic**, imitate, ape, copy, satirize, make fun of, take off (*informal*). [➡PRETEND AND MIMIC; 60] **2** *v* **pretend to be**, pose as, masquerade as, personate, pass off. [➡PRETEND AND MIMIC; 60]

impersonation **1** *n* **impression**, parody, caricature, takeoff (*informal*), sendup (*informal*). [➡REPRESENTATIONS AND GENERAL EXAMPLES; 65] **2** *n* **imitation**, pretence, masquerade, imposture (*formal*), personation. [➡REPRESENTATIONS AND GENERAL EXAMPLES; 65]

impertinence *n* **impudence**, cheek (*informal*), cheekiness (*informal*), insolence, disrespect, impoliteness, brazenness, sauce (*informal*), lip (*slang*). [➡BAD MANNERS AND SOCIAL SKILLS; 522] *Opposite:* respect.

impertinent (*formal*) *adj* **impudent**, cheeky, insolent, disrespectful, impolite, brazen, brash, rude. [➡RUDE AND HOSTILE; 626] *Opposite:* respectful.

impertinently (*formal*) *adv* **impudently**, cheekily (*informal*), insolently, disrespectfully, impolitely, brazenly. [➡BAD MANNERS AND SOCIAL SKILLS; 522] *Opposite:* respectfully.

imperturbability *n* [➡CONFIDENCE AND COMPOSURE; 500]

imperturbable *adj* **calm**, cool, unflappable, collected, composed, steady, serene, unflustered, level-headed, unruffled. [➡CONFIDENCE AND COMPOSURE; 500] *Opposite:* excitable.

impervious **1** *adj* **unreceptive**, unbending, unyielding, unwavering, rigid, obdurate, unmovable, unmoved, unaffected, unfeeling. [➡NEUTRALITY AND INDIFFERENCE; 554] *Opposite:* responsive. **2** *adj* **impermeable**, solid, resistant, waterproof, water-resistant, rainproof, invulnerable, watertight, proof. [➡DENSITY AND CONSISTENCY; 1206] *Opposite:* permeable.

imperviousness **1** *n* **unreceptiveness**, unyieldingness, rigidity, obduracy, inflexibility. [➡NEUTRALITY AND INDIFFERENCE; 554] *Opposite:* responsiveness. **2** *n* **impermeability**, resistance, invulnerability, watertightness, solidity. [➡DENSITY AND CONSISTENCY; 1206] *Opposite:* permeability.

impetuosity *n* **impulsiveness**, rashness, hastiness, suddenness, recklessness, spontaneity, impetuousness, hotheadedness. [➡LACK OF COMMITMENT AND UNRELIABILITY; 510] *Opposite:* consideration.

impetuous *adj* **impulsive**, rash, hasty, hotheaded, unthinking, sudden, reckless, spontaneous. [➡LACK OF COMMITMENT AND UNRELIABILITY; 510] *Opposite:* considered.

impetuousness *n* **impulsiveness**, rashness, hastiness, hotheadedness, suddenness, recklessness, spontaneity, impetuosity. [➡LACK OF COMMITMENT AND UNRELIABILITY; 510] *Opposite:* consideration.

impetus **1** *n* **push**, motivation, incentive, energy, stimulus, drive, impulse, spur, will. [➡CAUSATION; 169] **2** *n* **force**, momentum, impulsion, thrust, forward motion, motion, movement. [➡ENERGY GENERAL; 1160] *Opposite:* inertia.

impiety *n* **irreverence**, sinfulness, sin, wickedness, transgression, immorality, ungodliness, badness. [➡MORALLY BAD; 776] *Opposite:* piety.

impinge (*formal*) *v* **impose**, intrude, interrupt, encroach, invade, impact, have a bearing on, affect, have an effect on. [➡CHANGE; 373]

impious *adj* **sinful**, irreverent, wicked, bad, immoral, irreligious, ungodly. [➡MORALLY BAD; 776] *Opposite:* pious.

impiousness *n* **sinfulness**, irreverence, sin, wickedness, transgression, immorality, ungodliness, badness. [➡MORALLY BAD; 776] *Opposite:* piety.

impish *adj* **mischievous**, rascally (*humorous*), naughty, wicked, playful, puckish, roguish, waggish (*dated*). [➡LACK OF COMMITMENT AND UNRELIABILITY; 510]

impishness *n* **mischievousness**, naughtiness, wickedness, playfulness, puckishness, roguishness, waggishness (*dated*), mischief. [➡BAD BEHAVIOUR OR ACTION; 255]

implacability (*formal*) *n* **pitilessness**, mercilessness, relentlessness, ruthlessness, cruelty, hardheartedness, cold-heartedness, callousness, rigidity, unyieldingness, obduracy. [➡SELFISH AND UNKIND; 506] *Opposite:* kindness.

implacable (*formal*) *adj* **pitiless**, merciless, relentless, ruthless, cruel, hardhearted, cold-hearted, callous, rigid, unbending, unyielding, obdurate. [➡UNWILLINGNESS AND STUBBORNNESS; 565] *Opposite:* kind.

implant *v* **establish**, embed, plant, place, insert, instil, lodge, fix. [➡POSITION SOMETHING: BETWEEN, BESIDE, OR INSIDE SOMETHING; 327]

implantation *n* **embedding**, establishment, grafting, attaching, joining, splicing, inserting, attachment, insertion, fixing. [➡FASTEN, LINK, AND JOIN; 409]

implausibility *n* **improbability**, unlikelihood, inconceivability, inconceivableness, doubtfulness, questionability, unlikeliness. [➡IMPOSSIBLE AND IMPROBABLE; 179] *Opposite:* plausibility.

implausible *adj* **unlikely**, improbable, unbelievable, incredible, fantastic, far-fetched, doubtful, questionable. [➡IMPOSSIBLE AND IMPROBABLE; 179] *Opposite:* plausible.

implement **1** *n* **tool**, device, gadget, instrument, contrivance, gizmo (*informal*), appliance. [➡DEVICES; 1114] **2** *v* **carry out**, fulfil, put into practice, apply, realize, execute, employ, put into operation, put into service, put into action, instigate, put into effect, effect (*formal*). [➡CAUSE TO START; 266]

implementation *n* **carrying out**, application, putting into practice, operation, employment, execution, enactment. [➡CARRY OUT AN ACTION; 270] *Opposite:* proposal.

implicate *v* **connect**, involve, associate, link, incriminate, bring in, point to, point the finger at, finger (*slang*). [➡CREATING CONNECTIONS; 145] *Opposite:* clear.

implication *n* **insinuation**, inference, suggestion, allegation, consequence, repercussion, effect, knock-on effect, association. [➡MEANING; 691]

implicit **1** *adj* **understood**, implied, unspoken, tacit, hidden, embedded, indirect, inherent. [➡REPRESENTATIVE; 66] *Opposite:* explicit. **2** *adj* **unreserved**, absolute, total, complete, utter, perfect, unconditional, unqualified. [➡WHOLENESS AND COMPLETENESS; 199] *Opposite:* qualified.

implicitly 1 *adv* **indirectly**, covertly, tacitly, obliquely, subtly, subliminally, discreetly. [➡SECRET AND UNKNOWN; 180] 2 *adv* **unreservedly**, absolutely, totally, completely, wholly, utterly, perfectly, unconditionally, without reservation. [➡TO A GREAT EXTENT; 130]

implied *adj* **indirect**, understood, implicit, unspoken, tacit, veiled, oblique. [➡RETICENT AND UNFORTHCOMING; 632]

implode *v* **collapse**, fail, cave in, fall in, shrink, crash, founder, break down. [➡CEASE TO EXIST; 22] *Opposite:* explode.

implore (*formal*) *v* **beg**, plead, pray, appeal, entreat (*formal*), beseech (*literary*). [➡REQUEST AND DEMAND; 664]

imploring (*formal*) *adj* **pleading**, desperate, longing, beseeching (*literary*), suppliant (*formal*), heartfelt, supplicatory (*formal*). [➡REQUEST AND DEMAND; 664]

implosion *n* **collapse**, falling-in, subsidence, cave-in, disintegration, crumbling. [➡SUDDEN EVENT; 52] *Opposite:* explosion.

imply 1 *v* **suggest**, infer, hint at, point towards. [➡SUGGEST, HINT, AND COMMENT; 613] 2 *v* **involve**, entail, mean, indicate, denote. [➡MEAN SOMETHING; 61]

impolite *adj* **rude**, ill-mannered, bad-mannered, loutish, boorish, ignorant, disrespectful, indecorous, discourteous. [➡BAD MANNERS AND SOCIAL SKILLS; 522] *Opposite:* polite.

impoliteness *n* **rudeness**, bad manners, loutishness, boorishness, coarseness, discourteousness. [➡BAD MANNERS AND SOCIAL SKILLS; 522] *Opposite:* politeness.

impolitic (*formal*) *adj* **unwise**, inappropriate, misguided, ill-advised, ill-judged, injudicious, imprudent (*formal*). [➡THE NATURE OF IDEAS; 772] *Opposite:* wise.

imponderable 1 *adj* **unknown**, unquantifiable, incalculable, indeterminable, inestimable, immeasurable. [➡SECRET AND UNKNOWN; 180] 2 *n* **unknown**, mystery, enigma, paradox, uncertainty. [➡SECRETS AND MYSTERIES; 181]

import 1 *v* **bring in**, introduce, trade in, smuggle. [➡PURCHASE; 423] *Opposite:* export. 2 *n* **introduction**, importation, ingress (*formal*). [➡BUSINESS ACTIVITIES AND PHENOMENA; 795] *Opposite:* export. 3 *n* **significance**, importance, consequence (*formal*), meaning. [➡IMPORTANCE AND SIGNIFICANCE; 193]

importance 1 *n* **significance**, meaning, weight, consequence (*formal*), magnitude, import, substance, value, worth. [➡IMPORTANCE AND SIGNIFICANCE; 193] *Opposite:* triviality. 2 *n* **rank**, position, standing, status, reputation, prominence. [➡STATUS; 888]

important 1 *adj* **significant**, vital, imperative, central, chief, key, main, essential, principal, critical, crucial, weighty. [➡IMPORTANT; 195] *Opposite:* trivial. 2 *adj* **high-ranking**, eminent, worthy, notable, prominent, influential. [➡KNOWN AND FAMOUS; 182] *Opposite:* insignificant.

importantly *adv* **significantly**, notably, crucially, critically, vitally, relevantly, seriously. [➡IMPORTANT; 195]

important person *n* [➡IMPORTANT OR FAMOUS PEOPLE; 893]

importation *n* **import**, introduction, ingress (*formal*). [➡BUSINESS ACTIVITIES AND PHENOMENA; 795] *Opposite:* export.

importer *n* **trader**, shipper, carrier, haulier, distributor, wholesaler, retailer, broker, dealer. [➡BUSINESS PEOPLE; 794]

importunate (*formal*) *adj* **persistent**, demanding, unrelenting, annoying, overeager, forceful, avid. [➡BOSSY AND OVERBEARING; 517]

importune (*formal*) *v* **bother**, pester, badger, harass, plague, annoy, beleaguer, pursue. [➡COMPLAIN AND NAG; 687]

importunity (*formal*) 1 *n* **persistence**, demanding, pestering, insistence, clamouring, begging, supplication (*formal*). [➡DIFFICULT TO PLEASE; 516] 2 *n* **demand**, request, entreaty, appeal, petition, plea. [➡REQUEST AND DEMAND; 664]

impose 1 *v* **enforce**, levy, execute, carry out, enact. [➡MONEY, PAYMENTS, AND CHARGES; 800] 2 *v* **inflict**, force, foist, dump, insist, insist on. [➡GIVE TOO MUCH; 438] 3 *v* **intrude**, be in the way, be a nuisance, be a burden, disturb, trespass, inconvenience. [➡PARTICIPATE; 293]

imposing *adj* **impressive**, striking, grand, magnificent, stately, arresting, commanding. [➡EXTRAORDINARY: UNCOMMON; 206] *Opposite:* unimpressive.

imposition *n* **burden**, nuisance, annoyance, hassle (*informal*), bother, obligation. [➡NUISANCES; 254]

impossibility *n* **unfeasibility**, impracticality, hopelessness, ridiculousness, unlikelihood. [➡IMPOSSIBLE AND IMPROBABLE; 179] *Opposite:* possibility.

impossible 1 *adj* **irresolvable**, irresoluble, unfeasible, impracticable, unattainable, unachievable, unworkable, out of the question, unviable, impractical, hopeless, ridiculous, not on. [➡IMPOSSIBLE AND IMPROBABLE; 179] *Opposite:* possible. 2 *adj* **unbearable**, incredible, terrible, dreadful, intolerable, difficult, awkward, unmanageable, insufferable, unreasonable. [➡EMOTIONALLY UNPLEASANT AND UPSETTING; 228] *Opposite:* manageable.

impossibly *adv* **dreadfully**, terribly, hopelessly, unbearably, ridiculously, intolerably, insufferably, unbelievably, incredibly, extremely, unreasonably, unfeasibly. [➡TO A GREAT EXTENT; 130] *Opposite:* reasonably.

impostor *n* **deceiver**, imitator, impersonator, pretender, masquerader, fake, fraud, sham, plant (*informal*), charlatan. [➡PEOPLE WHO DECEIVE; 662] *Opposite:* the real McCoy (*informal*).

imposture (*formal*) *n* **deception**, impersonation, pretence, masquerade, imitation, faking, sham. [➡DECEPTION AND LIES; 661]

impotence *n* **ineffectiveness**, incapability, ineffectualness, feebleness, powerlessness, weakness, helplessness, inability, incapacity. [➡UNSKILLED; 530] *Opposite:* strength.

impotent *adj* **powerless**, weak, helpless, unable, incapable, ineffective, ineffectual, feeble. [➡UNSKILLED; 530] *Opposite:* powerful.

impound *v* **confiscate**, seize, lock up, take away, hold, store, possess. [➡TAKE SOMETHING AWAY; 426] *Opposite:* release.

impoverish *v* **deprive**, ruin, bankrupt, diminish, weaken, deplete, drain. [➡TAKE SOMETHING AWAY; 426] *Opposite:* enrich.

impoverished *adj* **needy**, poor, penniless, disadvantaged, broke (*informal*), underprivileged, insolvent, bankrupt, impecunious (*formal*), penurious (*literary*), indigent (*formal*), destitute, deprived, hard up (*informal*). [➡POVERTY AND POOR; 892] *Opposite:* rich.

impoverishment 1 *n* **destitution**, failure, disadvantage, poverty, insolvency, penury, privation, hardship, deprivation, bankruptcy, ruin. [➡POVERTY AND POOR; 892] *Opposite:* prosperity. 2 *n* **diminishment**, ruination, decline, depletion, degeneration, deterioration. [➡WORSEN SOMETHING; 381] *Opposite:* enrichment.

impracticability *n* **unworkability**, impossibility, impracticality, impracticableness, unworkableness, uselessness. [➡IMPOSSIBLE AND IMPROBABLE; 179] *Opposite:* feasibility.

impracticable *adj* **unviable**, useless, unrealistic, unfeasible, unpractical, unrealizable, unworkable, impossible, impractical. [➡IMPOSSIBLE AND IMPROBABLE; 179] *Opposite:* viable.

impractical 1 *adj* **unpractical**, unreasonable, unviable, unfeasible, unworkable, unrealizable, unusable, impossible, impracticable. [➡REDUNDANT AND USELESS; 241] *Opposite:* practical. 2 *adj* **unrealistic**, idealistic, useless, hopeless, clueless (*informal*), inept, incompetent. [➡NEGATIVE INTELLECTUAL CHARACTERISTICS; 526] *Opposite:* realistic.

impracticality *n* **unviability**, unfeasibility, impracticability, inconvenience, hopelessness, impossibility. [➡IMPOSSIBLE AND IMPROBABLE; 179] *Opposite:* practicality.

imprecate (*formal*) *v* **curse**, revile, call down, execrate (*literary or formal*), maledict (*literary*). [➡INSULTS, ABUSE, AND SWEARING; 659]

imprecation (*formal*) 1 *n* **oath**, insult, swearword, expletive, curse, malediction (*formal*), execration (*literary or formal*). [➡INSULTS, ABUSE, AND SWEARING; 659] 2 *n* **swearing**, execration (*literary or formal*), cursing, blasphemy, profanity, cussing (*informal*). [➡INSULTS, ABUSE, AND SWEARING; 659]

imprecise *adj* **sketchy**, vague, inexact, blurred, rough, inaccurate, hazy, fuzzy, indefinite, unfocused, unclear, ill-defined, indistinct, loose, woolly. [➡VAGUENESS; 244] *Opposite:* precise.

impreciseness *n* [➡VAGUENESS; 244]

imprecision *n* **fuzziness**, roughness, sketchiness, inaccuracy, inexactitude, sloppiness (*informal*), haziness, woolliness, vagueness, indistinctness. [➡VAGUENESS; 244] *Opposite:* accuracy.

impregnable *adj* **unassailable**, invincible, secure, unconquerable, impenetrable, invulnerable, indestructible. [➡STRENGTH; 202] *Opposite:* vulnerable.

impregnate *v* **saturate**, soak, steep, infuse, permeate, fill, imbue. [➡FILL; 407] *Opposite:* dry out.

impresario *n* **manager**, producer, promoter, agent, entrepreneur, organizer, business manager, entertainer. [➡IMPORTANT OR FAMOUS PEOPLE; 893]

impress 1 *v* **excite**, move, amaze, influence, affect, sway, astound, astonish, electrify, strike, stir. [➡SURPRISE AND IMPRESS; 575] *Opposite:* disappoint. 2 *v* **emphasize**, stress, drive home, drum in, din in, underline, highlight, imprint. [➡CLAIM, INSIST, AND EMPHASIZE; 615] *Opposite:* gloss over.

impressed *adj* [➡SURPRISE, SHOCK, AND AMAZEMENT; 546]

impression 1 *n* **feeling**, idea, notion, thought, sense, intuition, inkling, consciousness, fancy. [➡APPEARANCE AND ATMOSPHERE; 1236] *Opposite:* certainty. 2 *n* **imprint**, dent, mark, dint, hollow, dip, dimple, depression, impress, brand, stamp, ding (*US informal*). [➡HOLES, GAPS, AND FORKS; 1251] 3 *n* **mark**, impact, effect, influence, reaction, sway, vestige. [➡RESULTS AND OUTCOMES; 83] 4 *n* **impersonation**, imitation, sendup (*informal*), takeoff (*informal*), parody. [➡REPRESENTATIONS AND GENERAL EXAMPLES; 65]

impressionability *n* [➡NEGATIVE INTELLECTUAL CHARACTERISTICS; 526]

impressionable *adj* **susceptible**, suggestible, vulnerable, receptive, sensitive, gullible, pliable. [➡NEGATIVE INTELLECTUAL CHARACTERISTICS; 526] *Opposite:* unreceptive.

impressionableness *n* [➡NEGATIVE INTELLECTUAL CHARACTERISTICS; 526]

impressionism *type of* **pre-20th-century art movement**. [➡ARTISTIC MOVEMENTS AND STYLES; 899]

impressionist *n* **impersonator**, mimic, imitator, comic, entertainer, performer. [➡WORKERS IN ENTERTAINMENT AND MEDIA; 873]

impressionistic *adj* **ill-defined**, rough, loose, unfocused, imprecise, blurred, generalized, hazy, sketchy, vague, indistinct, inexplicit, undetailed. [➡VAGUENESS; 244] *Opposite:* detailed.

impressive *adj* **imposing**, inspiring, striking, remarkable, notable, extraordinary, exciting, moving, stirring. [➡EXTRAORDINARY: AMAZING; 205] *Opposite:* unimpressive.

impressiveness *n* **grandeur**, splendour, magnificence, brilliance, eminence, powerfulness, effectiveness. [➡EXTRAORDINARY: AMAZING; 205] *Opposite:* dowdiness.

imprint 1 *n* **impression**, print, mark, impress (*literary*), indentation, hollow, dent, dint, depression. [➡HOLES, GAPS, AND FORKS; 1251] 2 *n* **stamp**, inscription, name, print, printer's mark, watermark, colophon. [➡SYMBOLS, SIGNS, AND NUMBERS; 597] 3 *n* **hallmark**, emblem, stamp, seal, sign, symbol, identification mark, mark. [➡REPRESENTATIONS AND GENERAL EXAMPLES; 65] 4 *n* **indication**, mark, impression, effect, impress (*literary*), sign. [➡APPEARANCE AND ATMOSPHERE; 1236] 5 *v* **impress**, fix, establish, drive home, drum in, din in. [➡INSTRUCT AND TEACH; 610]

imprison *v* **put away** (*informal*), confine, detain, intern, incarcerate (*formal*), lock up, lock away, put inside (*informal*), send down (*slang*), jail. [➡THE POLICE, ARREST, AND PRETRIAL PROCEEDINGS; 818]

imprisoned *adj* **confined**, captive, restrained, trapped, caged, bound, held, shut in, constricted, inside (*informal*). [➡CAPTIVITY AND LOSS OF FREEDOM; 249] *Opposite:* free.

imprisonment *n* **custody**, incarceration (*formal*), captivity, detention, sentence, term, time (*informal*), internment, confinement. [➡CAPTIVITY AND LOSS OF FREEDOM; 249]

improbability *n* **unlikelihood**, implausibility, dubiousness, doubtfulness, questionability, improbableness, dubiety (*formal*), incredibility. [➡IMPOSSIBLE AND IMPROBABLE; 179] *Opposite:* probability.

improbable *adj* **unlikely**, doubtful, implausible, questionable, dubious, impracticable, unconvincing, unbelievable, incredible. [➡IMPOSSIBLE AND IMPROBABLE; 179] *Opposite:* likely.

improbably *adv* **strangely**, implausibly, unconvincingly, unbelievably, weirdly, doubtfully, oddly, unusually, surprisingly, incredibly, questionably. [➡BIZARRE AND PECULIAR; 258] *Opposite:* usually.

improbity (*formal*) *n* [➡MORALLY BAD; 776]

impromptu *adj* **unprepared**, unrehearsed, unplanned, spontaneous, spur-of-the-moment, unarranged, off-the-cuff, ad lib, improvised, unpremeditated, extempore, ad hoc. [➡UNINTENTIONAL AND ACCIDENTAL; 282] *Opposite:* prepared.

improper 1 *adj* (*formal*) **indecorous**, inappropriate, unsuitable, out of place, unfitting, inopportune, inadequate, wrong, incorrect. [➡MORALLY BAD; 776] *Opposite:* fitting. 2 *adj* **rude**, shocking, indecent, inappropriate, unacceptable, unseemly, offensive, reprehensible. [➡UNACCEPTABLE AND UNFORGIVEABLE; 226] *Opposite:* proper. 3 *adj* **dishonest**, irregular, illegal, crooked (*informal*), criminal, unlawful, shady, illicit. [➡MORALLY BAD; 776] *Opposite:* honest.

improperly 1 *adv* **rudely**, shockingly, inappropriately, unacceptably, offensively, reprehensively, indecently. [➡UNACCEPTABLE AND UNFORGIVEABLE; 226] *Opposite:* properly. 2 *adv* **dishonestly**, irregularly, illegally, crookedly (*informal*), unlawfully, shadily, illicitly, criminally. [➡MORALLY BAD; 776] *Opposite:* honestly. 3 *adv* (*formal*) **indecorously**, unsuitably, inappropriately, inadequately, wrongly, incorrectly, unfittingly, inopportunely. [➡INAPPROPRIATE AND UNSUITABLE; 225] *Opposite:* fittingly.

impropriety *n* **rudeness**, indecency, unseemliness, immodesty, indecorum, offensiveness, bad behaviour. [➡BAD MANNERS AND SOCIAL SKILLS; 522] *Opposite:* propriety.

improve 1 *v* **look up**, perk up, get better, rally, pick up (*informal*), mend, recover, advance, progress, develop, expand, increase. [➡GET BETTER; 376] *Opposite:* worsen. 2 *v* **better**, build up, enhance, perfect, develop, expand, further, enrich, upgrade, increase. [➡IMPROVE SOMETHING; 375] *Opposite:* deteriorate. 3 *v* **correct**, adjust, touch up, tweak (*informal*), titivate, amend. [➡IMPROVE SOMETHING; 375]

improved *adj* **better**, enhanced, amended, better-quality, upgraded, developed, value-added, enriched, perfected. [➡GOOD, WELL, BETTER; 184] *Opposite:* deteriorated.

improvement 1 *n* **amendment**, correction, development, step-up, upgrade, enhancement, advancement, progress, expansion, enlargement, increase. [➡PROGRESS AND ADVANCEMENT; 214] *Opposite:* deterioration. 2 *n* **recovery**, recuperation, progress, advance, upturn, convalescence. [➡PROGRESS AND ADVANCEMENT; 214] *Opposite:* decline.

improve on *v* **better**, go one better, top, beat, exceed, surpass, transcend, cap, outdo, outshine, outperform. [➡BEAT AND DEFEAT; 80]

improvident (*formal*) *adj* **imprudent** (*formal*), careless, reckless, negligent, irresponsible, wasteful, spendthrift, profligate, rash, extravagant. [➡INCAUTIOUS AND CARELESS; 284] *Opposite:* prudent.

improvisation 1 *n* **inventiveness**, invention, creativeness, lateral thinking. [➡WAYS OF DOING THINGS; 295] 2 *n* **extemporization**, ad-libbing, standup. [➡NEUTRAL ONE-WAY COMMUNICATION; 49]

improvise 1 *v* **ad-lib**, extemporize, wing it (*informal*), create, make up, invent, rely on your wits. [➡UTTER AND PRONOUNCE; 609] 2 *v* **contrive**, concoct, invent, create, devise, make up, cobble together, knock together (*informal*), rig up (*informal*), rig. [➡INSTITUTE AND INAUGURATE; 349]

improvised *adj* **unpremeditated**, ad hoc, unplanned, makeshift, spontaneous, offhand, spur-of-the-moment, unprepared, unarranged, unrehearsed, ad lib, impromptu, off-the-cuff, extempore. [➡UNINTENTIONAL AND ACCIDENTAL; 282] *Opposite:* prepared.

imprudence *n* **profligacy**, carelessness, indiscretion, rashness, injudiciousness, unwariness, haste, bad judgment, impulsiveness, recklessness, incaution, extravagance, foolishness, irresponsibility. [➡NEGATIVE INTELLECTUAL CHARACTERISTICS; 526] *Opposite:* prudence.

imprudent (*formal*) *adj* **foolish**, impulsive, indiscreet, irresponsible, rash, hasty, unwise, unconsidered, thoughtless, careless, improvident (*formal*), ill-considered, unwary, incautious, reckless. [➡INCAUTIOUS AND CARELESS; 284] *Opposite:* prudent.

impudence *n* **impertinence**, boldness, insolence, nerve, effrontery, audacity, rudeness, disrespect, impoliteness, mouthiness (*informal*), cheek (*informal*), presumption, sassiness (*US*). [➡BAD MANNERS AND SOCIAL SKILLS; 522] *Opposite:* respect.

impudent *adj* **bold**, brazen, impertinent (*formal*), insolent, rude, disrespectful, impolite, presumptuous, ill-mannered, mouthy (*informal*), cheeky, sassy (*US*). [➡BAD MANNERS AND SOCIAL SKILLS; 522] *Opposite:* respectful.

impugn (*formal*) *v* **question**, dispute, call into question, doubt, query, challenge, assail. [➡QUESTION THINGS; 752]

impulse 1 *n* **instinct**, desire, urge, whim, compulsion, wish, itch, yen, yearning, bent, fancy, inclination. [➡DESIRE AND WANT; 580] *Opposite:* aversion. 2 *n* **propulsion**, motive power, drive, stimulus, pressure, impetus, goad, spur, force, catalyst, incentive, motivation. [➡POSITIVE IMPATIENCE, ENTHUSIASM, AND ALERTNESS; 538] 3 *n* **tick**, pulse, nerve, pulsation, beat, signal, thrust. [➡ENERGY GENERAL; 1160]

impulsion 1 *n* **push**, propulsion, thrust, momentum, impetus, spur, drive. [➡BEGINNING; 53] 2 *n* **desire**, yen, compulsion, instinct, whim, urge, inclination, impulse, wish, stimulus, motivation. [➡DESIRE AND WANT; 580] *Opposite:* aversion.

impulsive *adj* **unwary**, thoughtless, impetuous, imprudent (*formal*), precipitate, spontaneous, rash, brash, reckless, hasty, irresponsible, offhand, madcap. [➡LACK OF COMMITMENT AND UNRELIABILITY; 510] *Opposite:* cautious.

impulsively *adv* **unwarily**, thoughtlessly, on impulse, imprudently (*formal*), impetuously, spontaneously, on a whim, precipitately, rashly, hastily, unwisely, irresponsibly. [➡AUTOMATIC AND INSTINCTIVE; 281] *Opposite:* deliberately.

impulsiveness *n* **precipitateness**, suddenness, thoughtlessness, impetuosity, spontaneity, recklessness, rashness, hastiness, irresponsibility. [➡LACK OF COMMITMENT AND UNRELIABILITY; 510] *Opposite:* deliberation (*formal*).

impunity *n* **exemption**, freedom, licence, liberty, latitude, immunity. [➡SAFE AND SAFETY; 192]

impure *adj* **contaminated**, adulterated, mixed, tainted, polluted, dirty, infected, poisoned, unclean. [➡DIRTY; 1234] *Opposite:* pure.

impurity *n* **contamination**, pollution, adulteration, uncleanness, infection, dirtiness, dirt. [➡UNPLEASANT AND DIRTY SUBSTANCES; 1267] *Opposite:* purity.

imputation *n* **accusation**, assertion, attribution, citation, reproach, complaint, allegation, insinuation, suggestion, charge. [➡CRITICISMS AND ANGRY OUTBURSTS; 50]

impute 1 *v* **credit**, chalk up, attribute, ascribe (*formal*), assign, accredit. [➡CREATING CONNECTIONS; 145] 2 *v* **complain**, accuse, implicate, allege, assert, challenge, cite, charge. [➡ACCUSE, BLAME, AND CRITICIZE; 642]

in 1 *prep* **inside**, within, around. [➡RELATIVE LOCATION; 162] *Opposite:* outside. 2 *adv* **around**, inside, accessible, available, at home, here, arrived, indoors, inwards. [➡GENERAL LOCATIONS; 159] *Opposite:* out. 3 *adj* **cutting-edge**, fashionable, trendy (*informal*), popular, hip (*slang*), happening (*informal*), now, in vogue, voguish, modish, all the rage, stylish. [➡NEW, MODERN; 167] *Opposite:* out.

in a bad mood *adj* [➡IRRITATION AND ANGER; 542]

in abeyance *adj* **suspended**, withdrawn, withheld, inoperative, out of action, pending, in remission, on ice, in limbo. [➡NOT HAPPENING; 34] *Opposite:* ongoing.

in a big way *adv* [➡MANY, MUCH, LARGE AMOUNT; 117]

inability *n* **incapability**, incapacity, powerlessness, helplessness, failure, incompetence, hopelessness. [➡UNSKILLED; 530] *Opposite:* ability.

in a bind *adj* [➡IN TROUBLE AND DISADVANTAGED; 73]

in a bit *adv* [➡FUTURE; 86]

in abundance *adv* **abundantly**, in great quantities, in large quantities, in profusion, aplenty, galore. [➡MANY, MUCH, LARGE AMOUNT; 117] *Opposite:* in short supply.

inaccessibility 1 *n* **unreachability**, remoteness, distance, isolation, unapproachability, solitariness, aloneness. [➡SOLITARINESS; 941] *Opposite:* approachability. 2 *n* **unattainability**, unavailability, unaffordability, unobtainability, confidentiality, impossibility. [➡IMPOSSIBLE AND IMPROBABLE; 179] *Opposite:* accessibility. 3 *n* **difficulty**, obscurity, obscureness, obliqueness, impenetrability, elitism, opaqueness. [➡DIFFICULTY AND COMPLEXITY; 243] *Opposite:* lucidity.

inaccessible 1 *adj* **unreachable**, out-of-the-way, unapproachable, difficult to get to, hard to find, remote, distant, faraway, isolated. [➡DISTANCE; 161] *Opposite:* approachable. 2 *adj* **difficult**, obscure, esoteric, abstruse, challenging, elitist, difficult to understand, hard to follow, oblique, impenetrable, opaque. [➡DIFFICULTY AND COMPLEXITY; 243] *Opposite:* simple.

in accordance *adj* **in conformity**, in line, in compliance, in keeping, in step. [➡APPROPRIATE, SUITABLE, ADVISABLE; 185] *Opposite:* at odds.

inaccuracy 1 *n* **imprecision**, inexactness, mistakenness, wrongness, erroneousness, incorrectness, impreciseness, inexactitude. [➡INCORRECT AND ERRONEOUS; 223] *Opposite:* precision. 2 *n* **error**, mistake, slip, flaw, blunder, typo (*informal*), typographical error. [➡MISTAKES; 251]

See Compare and Contrast at **mistake**.

inaccurate *adj* **imprecise**, inexact, mistaken, erroneous, wrong, incorrect, out, way-out (*informal*). [➡INCORRECT AND ERRONEOUS; 223] *Opposite:* precise.

in a cleft stick *adj* [➡UNCERTAINTY; 560]

inaction 1 *n* **failure to act**, indecision, procrastination, fumbling, delay, dithering, indecisiveness. [➡LACK OF ACTIVITY; 343] *Opposite:* decisiveness. 2 *n* **inactivity**, laziness, idleness, inertia, apathy, immobility, lethargy, sluggishness, sloth. [➡LACK OF ACTIVITY; 343] *Opposite:* energy.

inactivate *v* **deactivate**, put out of action, incapacitate, disable, render inoperative, render inactive, render inoperable, turn off, unplug, disarm, idle. [➡CAUSE TO STOP; 267] *Opposite:* set in motion.

inactive 1 *adj* **motionless**, stationary, unmoving, immobile, stopped, still. [➡LACK OF ACTIVITY; 343] *Opposite:* moving. 2 *adj* **idle**, dormant, out of action, reserve, unused, inoperative, out of order, static. [➡LACK OF ACTIVITY; 343] *Opposite:* working. 3 *adj* **sedentary**, lazy, slothful (*formal*), indolent, sluggish, deskbound, lethargic, quiet, sleepy, torpid. [➡LIFELESS, LAZY, AND UNENTHUSIASTIC; 507] *Opposite:* energetic.

inactivity 1 *n* **motionlessness**, immobility, stillness. [➡LACK OF ACTIVITY; 343] *Opposite:* motion. 2 *n* **idleness**, dormancy, inoperativeness. [➡LACK OF ACTIVITY; 343] *Opposite:* activity. 3 *n* **sedentariness**, laziness, sloth, slothfulness (*formal*), indolence, sluggishness, lethargy, quietness, sleepiness, torpidity, torpor. [➡LIFELESS, LAZY, AND UNENTHUSIASTIC; 507] *Opposite:* energy.

in actual fact *adv* **actually**, in fact, in reality, in truth, really, as it happens, in point of fact. [➡WORDS AND PHRASES EMPHASIZING THE TRUTH OF A MATTER; 173]

in a daze *adj* [➡SURPRISE, SHOCK, AND AMAZEMENT; 546]

in addition *adv* **furthermore**, moreover, as well, also, too, additionally, on top, besides, into the bargain, to boot. [➡EXPRESSIONS INTRODUCING EXTRA INFORMATION; 137]

in addition to *adv* **as well as**, along with, on top of, besides, over and above, not counting, other than. [➡EXPRESSIONS INTRODUCING EXTRA INFORMATION; 137]

inadequacy 1 *n* **insufficiency**, meagreness, scantiness, lack, shortage, shortfall. [➡TOO FEW, TOO LITTLE; 120] *Opposite:* sufficiency. 2 *n* **fault**, failure, failing, incompetence, defectiveness, hopelessness, shortcoming, defect, problem. [➡FAULTS, FLAWS, AND WEAKNESSES; 252] *Opposite:* asset.

inadequate 1 *adj* **insufficient**, scarce, too little, derisory, laughable, poor, short, scant, scanty. [➡TOO FEW, TOO LITTLE; 120] *Opposite:* sufficient. 2 *adj* **incompetent**, lacking, deficient, ineffective, inefficient, ineffectual, defective, imperfect, hopeless, unsatisfactory, incapable. [➡UNSKILLED; 530] *Opposite:* capable.

in a dilemma *adj* [➡UNCERTAINTY; 560]

inadmissible *adj* **unacceptable**, prohibited, precluded (*formal*), excluded, barred, disallowed, irrelevant, banned, censored. [➡REDUNDANT AND USELESS; 241] *Opposite:* acceptable.

in advance *adv* **beforehand**, before, prior to, ahead, earlier. [➡BEFORE, FIRST, AND PRECEDING; 164] *Opposite:* afterwards.

inadvertence 1 *n* **carelessness**, inattention, negligence, thoughtlessness, laxity, forgetfulness, inadvertency. [➡NEGATIVE INTELLECTUAL CHARACTERISTICS; 526] 2 *n* **oversight**, omission, error, mistake, slip-up (*informal*), blunder, inadvertency, faux pas (*literary*), fallacy, miscue (*informal*). [➡MISTAKES; 251]

inadvertency *see* **inadvertence**.

inadvertent *adj* **unintentional**, careless, unintended, involuntary, unplanned, accidental. [➡UNINTENTIONAL AND ACCIDENTAL; 282] *Opposite:* intentional.

inadvisable *adj* **ill-advised**, imprudent (*formal*), unwise, foolish, injudicious, impolitic (*formal*), inexpedient (*formal*). [➡DANGEROUS; 237] *Opposite:* wise.

in a fix (*informal*) *adj* **in trouble**, in difficulties, in hot water (*informal*), in a tight spot, in a spot of bother (*informal*), in a jam (*informal*), in extremis, in dire straits, up the creek (*informal*), in the soup (*informal*). [➡IN TROUBLE AND DISADVANTAGED; 73]

in a flap (*informal*) *adj* [➡CONFUSION, ANXIETY, AND WORRY; 541]

in a flash 1 *adv* **rapidly**, quickly, in (less than) no time, like a bat out of hell (*informal*), in the twinkling of an eye, hastily. [➡MOVING QUICKLY; 103] *Opposite:* slowly. 2 *adv* **suddenly**, immediately, right away, straight away, without hesitation, all of a sudden, like a bolt from the blue. [➡HAPPENING QUICKLY; 104] *Opposite:* gradually.

in a frenzy *adj* [➡CONFUSION, ANXIETY, AND WORRY; 541]

in a funk (*US informal*) *adj* [➡SADNESS, DISTRESS, AND DESPAIR; 540]

in agreement *adv* [➡HARMONY; 156]

in a huff (*informal*) *adj* **annoyed**, piqued, offended, affronted, nettled (*informal*), vexed, in high dudgeon, peeved (*informal*). [➡SADNESS, DISTRESS, AND DESPAIR; 540] *Opposite:* unconcerned.

in a hurry 1 *adj* **rushed**, pressed for time, short of time, in a rush, late. [➡HAPPENING QUICKLY; 104] *Opposite:* unrushed. 2 *adv* **in a rush**, hurriedly, quickly, rapidly, hastily, fast, at speed, with no time to spare, in a flash. [➡MOVING QUICKLY; 103] *Opposite:* slowly.

in a jam (*informal*) *adj* **in trouble**, in difficulties, in hot water (*informal*), in a tight spot, in a spot of bother (*informal*), in a fix (*informal*), in extremis, in dire straits, up the creek (*informal*), in the soup (*informal*). [➡IN TROUBLE AND DISADVANTAGED; 73]

in a jiffy (*informal*) *adv* **in a moment**, in a minute, in a second, in a tick (*informal*), shortly, right away, directly, in (less than) no time, immediately, straightaway, forthwith (*formal*). [➡FUTURE; 86]

in a jumble *adj* [➡DISORDER AND CHAOS; 246]

in a lather (*informal*) *adj* [➡CONFUSION, ANXIETY, AND WORRY; 541]

inalienable (*formal*) *adj* **unchallengeable**, absolute, immutable, unassailable, incontrovertible, indisputable, undeniable. [➡CERTAIN; 175] *Opposite:* disputable.

in a little while *adv* [➡FUTURE; 86]

in all *adv* **ultimately**, altogether, all in all, as a whole, all told, overall. [➡ALL; 126]

in all fairness *adv* [➡EXPRESSIONS OF OPINION; 624]

in all honesty *adv* [➡EXPRESSIONS OF OPINION; 624]

in all likelihood *adv* [➡EXPRESSIONS OF OPINION; 624]

in all probability *adv* [➡EXPRESSIONS OF OPINION; 624]

in a mess *adj* **untidy**, chaotic, in a muddle, in a state (*informal*), messy, cluttered, in disarray, upside down, disorganized, all over the place (*informal*), disordered. [➡DISORDER AND CHAOS; 246] *Opposite:* tidy.

in a minute *adv* [➡FUTURE; 86]

in a mood *adj* [➡SADNESS, DISTRESS, AND DESPAIR; 540]

inamorata (*literary*) *n* [➡SEXUAL AND ROMANTIC RELATIONSHIPS; 964]

in a muddle *adj* [➡DISORDER AND CHAOS; 246]

inane *adj* **silly**, unintelligent, absurd, ridiculous, stupid, frivolous, childish, immature, mindless, crass. [➡BIZARRE AND PECULIAR; 258] *Opposite:* sensible.

inaneness *n* [➡BIZARRE AND PECULIAR; 258]

inanimate 1 *adj* **lifeless**, dead, nonliving, inorganic, inert, extinct, deceased (*formal*). [➡DEAD AND DYING; 925] *Opposite:* alive. 2 *adj* **inactive**, dull, unresponsive, apathetic, impassive, listless, lethargic, spiritless, insensate, vacant. [➡LIFELESS, LAZY, AND UNENTHUSIASTIC; 507] *Opposite:* spirited.

inanity 1 *n* **meaninglessness**, senselessness, stupidity, ridiculousness, absurdity. [➡BIZARRE AND PECULIAR; 258] *Opposite:* logic. 2 *n* **silliness**, foolishness, frivolousness, stupidity, ridiculousness, childishness, immaturity, mindlessness, crassness. [➡NEGATIVE INTELLECTUAL CHARACTERISTICS; 526] *Opposite:* sensibleness.

in a nutshell *adv* **in short**, briefly, in a word, in brief, concisely, succinctly, to sum up, in a few words, all things considered, when all's said and done, in summary, to cut a long story short. [➡SUMMARIZING EXPRESSIONS; 623] *Opposite:* at length.

in any case 1 *adv* **anyway**, all in all, moreover, furthermore, besides, anyhow, at any rate, in any event. [➡EXPRESSIONS INTRODUCING EXTRA INFORMATION; 137] 2 *adv* **regardless**, anyway, nevertheless, nonetheless, whatever, in any event, come rain or shine, no matter what. [➡ALTHOUGH, NEVERTHELESS, AND DESPITE; 170]

in any event *adv* **anyhow**, anyway, in any case, at any rate, besides, moreover, furthermore, whatever happens, regardless, no matter what, even so. [➡ EXPRESSIONS INTRODUCING EXTRA INFORMATION; 137]

in a panic *adj* [➡ FEAR AND PANIC; 544]

inapplicability *n* **unsuitability**, inappropriateness, irrelevance, inappositeness (*formal*), inaptness, wrongness. [➡ INAPPROPRIATE AND UNSUITABLE; 225] *Opposite:* suitability.

inapplicable *adj* **unsuitable**, irrelevant, inappropriate, inapposite (*formal*), inapt, wrong, misplaced. [➡ INAPPROPRIATE AND UNSUITABLE; 225] *Opposite:* suitable.

inapposite (*formal*) *adj* **unsuitable**, out of place, inappropriate, inapt, unfitting, wrong, misplaced, misguided, irrelevant, inapplicable. [➡ INAPPROPRIATE AND UNSUITABLE; 225] *Opposite:* suitable.

inappositeness (*formal*) *n* **unsuitability**, inappropriateness, inaptness, wrongness, misguidedness, irrelevance, inapplicability. [➡ INAPPROPRIATE AND UNSUITABLE; 225] *Opposite:* suitability.

inappreciable *adj* **insignificant**, imperceptible, unperceivable, negligible, unimportant, immaterial, microscopic, minute. [➡ IMPERCEPTIBLE; 26] *Opposite:* significant.

inappreciably *adv* **insignificantly**, imperceptibly, unperceivably, negligibly, unimportantly, immaterially, microscopically, minutely. [➡ UNIMPORTANT AND UNNECESSARY; 239] *Opposite:* significantly.

inappropriate *adj* **unsuitable**, unfitting, untimely, unfortunate, inapt, wrong, incorrect, incongruous, inapplicable, inapposite (*formal*), ill-chosen, ill-timed, insensitive, misplaced, improper, tasteless, unseemly, tactless, unbecoming, unacceptable. [➡ INAPPROPRIATE AND UNSUITABLE; 225] *Opposite:* fitting.

inappropriateness *n* **unsuitability**, impropriety, wrongness, incorrectness, unseemliness, untimeliness, unfortunateness, inaptness, incongruity, indelicacy, indecorousness, tastelessness, unacceptability, insensitivity, inappositeness (*formal*), inapplicability. [➡ INAPPROPRIATE AND UNSUITABLE; 225] *Opposite:* appropriateness.

in a predicament *adj* [➡ IN TROUBLE AND DISADVANTAGED; 73]

inapt *adj* [➡ INAPPROPRIATE AND UNSUITABLE; 225]

inaptness *n* [➡ INAPPROPRIATE AND UNSUITABLE; 225]

in a quandary *adj* [➡ UNCERTAINTY; 560]

in a roundabout way *adv* **indirectly**, expansively, laboriously, circuitously, discursively, tangentially, long-windedly, obliquely, evasively. [➡ INARTICULATE, RAMBLING, AND AWKWARD; 634] *Opposite:* directly.

in a row *adv* **one after the other**, one behind the other, in single file, end to end, in succession, back-to-back, consecutively, in line, on the trot. [➡ AFTER, LAST, AND FOLLOWING; 166]

in arrears *adj* **behind**, overdue, late, in the red, behindhand. [➡ POVERTY AND POOR; 892] *Opposite:* ahead.

inarticulacy 1 *n* **incoherence**, hesitation, lack of fluency, stumbling, stuttering, stammering, speechlessness, awkwardness, clumsiness. [➡ INARTICULATE, RAMBLING, AND AWKWARD; 634] *Opposite:* eloquence. 2 *n* **unintelligibility**, incomprehensibility, inaudibility, indistinctness, unclearness. [➡ IMPERCEPTIBLE; 26] *Opposite:* clarity.

inarticulate 1 *adj* **tongue-tied**, incoherent, mumbling, hesitant, faltering, speechless, stuttering, stammering, stumbling, clumsy, awkward. [➡ INARTICULATE, RAMBLING, AND AWKWARD; 634] *Opposite:* eloquent. 2 *adj* **garbled**, muttered, incoherent, unintelligible, incomprehensible, mumbled, inaudible, indistinct, unclear. [➡ IMPERCEPTIBLE; 26] *Opposite:* clear.

inarticulateness *n* [➡ INARTICULATE, RAMBLING, AND AWKWARD; 634]

in a rush 1 *adj* **in a hurry**, rushed, short of time, pressed for time, late. [➡ IN TROUBLE AND DISADVANTAGED; 73] *Opposite:* unrushed. 2 *adv* **hurriedly**, hastily, quickly, at speed, rapidly, fast, swiftly, at the last minute. [➡ HAPPENING QUICKLY; 104] *Opposite:* slowly.

in a rut *adj* **bored**, stagnant, in the doldrums, unchanging, fixed, inflexible. [➡ NEUTRALITY AND INDIFFERENCE; 554] *Opposite:* dynamic.

in a second *adv* [➡ FUTURE; 86]

in a short time *adv* [➡ FUTURE; 86]

inasmuch as *conj* **because**, insofar as (*formal*), considering that, since, as, seeing that, as long as, whereas (*formal*). [➡ CAUSATION; 169]

in a spot of bother (*informal*) *adj* [➡ IN TROUBLE AND DISADVANTAGED; 73]

in a state (*informal*) 1 *adj* **upset**, worked up (*informal*), in a panic, anxious, overexcited, flustered, rattled, distressed, distraught, tense, in pieces, nervous, nervy (*informal*). [➡ SADNESS, DISTRESS, AND DESPAIR; 540] *Opposite:* calm. 2 *adj* **in a mess**, untidy, messy, in disarray, cluttered, chaotic, jumbled, upside down, in a muddle, all over the place (*informal*), disorganized, disordered. [➡ IN BAD REPAIR; 1233] *Opposite:* tidy.

in a state of shock *adj* [➡ SURPRISE, SHOCK, AND AMAZEMENT; 546]

in a strop (*informal*) *adj* [➡ SADNESS, DISTRESS, AND DESPAIR; 540]

in a tick (*informal*) *adv* [➡ FUTURE; 86]

in a tight corner *adj* [➡ IN TROUBLE AND DISADVANTAGED; 73]

in a tight spot *adj* [➡ IN TROUBLE AND DISADVANTAGED; 73]

in a tizzy (*informal*) *adj* [➡ POSITIVE IMPATIENCE, ENTHUSIASM, AND ALERTNESS; 538]

in a trice *adv* [➡ FUTURE; 86]

in attendance *adj* [➡ PRESENT AND AVAILABLE; 11]

inattention *n* **inattentiveness**, daydreaming, woolgathering, distraction, abstraction, carelessness, negligence, absent-mindedness, doziness. [➡ NOT PAY ATTENTION; 765] *Opposite:* concentration.

inattentive *adj* **careless**, daydreaming, distracted, abstracted, woolgathering, negligent, unmindful, absent-minded, dreamy, dozy. [➡ INCAUTIOUS AND CARELESS; 284] *Opposite:* careful.

inattentiveness *n* **carelessness**, inattention, daydreaming, distraction, abstraction, negligence, doziness, absent-mindedness, woolgathering. [➡NOT PAY ATTENTION; 765] *Opposite:* attention.

inaudibility *n* **quietness**, faintness, imperceptibility, noiselessness, silence, quiet, softness, stillness, soundlessness. [➡IMPERCEPTIBLE; 26] *Opposite:* audibility.

inaudible *adj* **quiet**, out of earshot, low, faint, soft, silent, noiseless, imperceptible, soundless, still. [➡IMPERCEPTIBLE; 26] *Opposite:* perceptible.

inaugural *adj* **opening**, initial, first, introductory, foundational, maiden, original, primary, germinal (*formal*). [➡BEFORE, FIRST, AND PRECEDING; 164]

inaugurate 1 *v* **swear in**, install, invest (*formal*), induct, instate, initiate. [➡CONFER STATUS; 459] *Opposite:* dismiss. 2 *v* **open**, launch, dedicate, initiate, unveil, start up, introduce, institute. [➡CAUSE TO START; 266] *Opposite:* close. 3 *v* **initiate**, establish, put in place, get underway, set up, start up, create, introduce, bring into being. [➡INSTITUTE AND INAUGURATE; 349] *Opposite:* terminate (*formal*).

inauguration 1 *n* **induction**, investiture, installation, swearing in, inaugural ceremony, appointment. [➡CEREMONIES AND ANNIVERSARIES; 38] *Opposite:* dismissal. 2 *n* **opening**, launch, opening ceremony, initiation ceremony, start, unveiling. [➡BEGINNING; 53] *Opposite:* closure. 3 *n* **initiation**, creation, introduction, setting up, conception, invention. [➡BEGINNING; 53] *Opposite:* closedown.

inauspicious *adj* **unpromising**, discouraging, ill-starred (*formal*), ill-fated, ominous, unfavourable, gloomy, fateful, adverse. [➡UNSUCCESSFUL AND UNPROMISING; 76] *Opposite:* promising.

inauthentic *adj* **false**, imitation, fake, forged, ersatz (*disapproving*), counterfeit, mock, synthetic. [➡FALSE AND UNREAL; 174] *Opposite:* genuine.

in awe *adv* [➡SURPRISE, SHOCK, AND AMAZEMENT; 546]

in awe of *adj* **frightened**, overcome, overwhelmed, impressed, daunted, intimidated, fearful, awed. [➡FEAR AND PANIC; 544] *Opposite:* unimpressed.

in a while *adv* **soon**, shortly, presently, afterwards, later, later on, before long, in good time, in your own good time. [➡FUTURE; 86] *Opposite:* immediately.

in a world of your own *adj* **in a dream**, in a daze, daydreaming, lost in thought, preoccupied, engrossed, absent-minded, far away. [➡NEUTRALITY AND INDIFFERENCE; 554]

in back (*US*) *adv* [➡GENERAL LOCATIONS; 159]

in bad odour *adj* [➡IN TROUBLE AND DISADVANTAGED; 73]

in bad repair *adj* [➡IN BAD REPAIR; 1233]

in bad shape *adj* **in bad condition**, unhealthy, unfit, out of condition, out of shape, flabby (*informal*), in poor health. [➡UNFIT AND WEAK; 740] *Opposite:* in good shape.

in bad taste *adj* **offensive**, tasteless, in poor taste, distasteful, ill-chosen, tactless, indelicate, insensitive, vulgar, crude, nasty, unpleasant. [➡IN POOR TASTE; 230] *Opposite:* tasteful.

in between *prep* **between**, amidst, next to, sandwiched by, in the middle of, amid, among, amongst. [➡RELATIVE LOCATION; 162]

in-between 1 *adj* **intermediate**, separating, isolating, halfway, indeterminate, vague, inconclusive, fuzzy. [➡RELATIVE LOCATION; 162] 2 *adv* **meanwhile**, in the interval, in the intervening time, between times, at the same time, intermediately, vaguely, inconclusively, fuzzily. [➡GENERAL LOCATIONS; 159]

in bits *adj* [➡IN BAD REPAIR; 1233]

inborn *adj* **innate**, natural, instinctive, intuitive, inherited, congenital, inherent. [➡REPRODUCTION AND HEREDITY; 726] *Opposite:* acquired.

inbound *adj* **incoming**, arriving, inward bound, coming in, heading toward. [➡DIRECTION OF MOTION; 346]

inbred *adj* **congenital**, inherited, hereditary, ingrained, deep-seated, inborn. [➡REPRODUCTION AND HEREDITY; 726] *Opposite:* acquired.

in brief *adv* **briefly**, in a few words, in short, to sum up, everything considered, when all's said and done, in a word, in summary, in a nutshell, to cut a long story short, to be brief, to come to the point, concisely. [➡SUMMARIZING EXPRESSIONS; 623] *Opposite:* at length.

in broad daylight *adv* **visibly**, noticeably, conspicuously, perceptibly, plainly, boldly, in full view, before your very eyes, right under your nose, openly. [➡INTENTIONAL AND DELIBERATE; 280] *Opposite:* surreptitiously.

in-built 1 *adj* **innate**, natural, inborn, inherent, instinctive, unlearned, intrinsic, intuitive, ingrained. [➡THE NATURE OF IDEAS; 772] *Opposite:* learned. 2 *adj* **incorporated**, integral, intrinsic, included, integrated, built-in, inboard, onboard, fitted. [➡RELATED; 143] *Opposite:* add-on.

in bulk *adv* **in large quantities**, wholesale. [➡MANY, MUCH, LARGE AMOUNT; 117] *Opposite:* piecemeal.

incalculable 1 *adj* **countless**, without number, innumerable, infinite, multitudinous, vast, huge, immense, untold, inestimable, immeasurable, limitless. [➡MANY, MUCH, LARGE AMOUNT; 117] *Opposite:* finite. 2 *adj* **unpredictable**, unforeseeable, indeterminable, uncertain, haphazard, hit-and-miss. [➡UNCERTAIN; 176] *Opposite:* predictable.

incalculably 1 *adv* **countlessly**, innumerably, immeasurably, infinitely, inestimably, immensely, multitudinously, hugely, vastly. [➡TO A GREAT EXTENT; 130] 2 *adv* **unpredictably**, unforeseeably, indeterminably, uncertainly, haphazardly. [➡UNCERTAIN; 176] *Opposite:* predictably.

in camera *adv* **in private**, in secret, clandestinely, covertly, confidentially, privately, secretly, behind closed doors. [➡SECRET AND UNKNOWN; 180] *Opposite:* openly.

incandesce *v* **glow**, radiate, shine, luminesce, fluoresce, burn, flame, beam, flare. [➡LIGHT EMISSION; 369]

incandescence *n* **glow**, luminosity, light, luminescence, fluorescence, burning, radiance, lustre. [➡LIGHT; 1163]

incandescent *adj* **glowing**, radiant, luminous, shining, bright, luminescent, aglow, burning, fluorescent, flaming, beaming, flaring. [➡DESCRIBING LIGHT; 1227]

incantation *n* **chant**, invocation, prayer, spell, charm, summons. [➡RELIGIONS AND RELIGIOUS PRACTICES; 778]

incapable 1 *adj* **unable**, powerless, inept, inexpert, unqualified, incompetent. [➡UNSKILLED; 530] *Opposite:* able. 2 *adj* **helpless**, weak, vulnerable, feeble, frail, dependent, incapacitated. [➡UNFIT AND WEAK; 740] *Opposite:* strong.

incapacitate *v* **debilitate**, injure, harm, disable, lay up, weaken, undermine. [➡WOUND A PERSON OR ANIMAL; 384] *Opposite:* enable.

incapacitated *adj* **debilitated**, injured, harmed, disabled, laid up, weakened, undermined. [➡UNFIT AND WEAK; 740] *Opposite:* fit.

incapacitating *adj* [➡PHYSICALLY UNPLEASANT; 227]

incapacity *n* **inability**, ineffectiveness, injury, incapability, powerlessness, failure, disability, weakness. [➡ILL AND SICK; 741] *Opposite:* ability.

incarcerate (*formal*) *v* **imprison**, jail, gaol, lock up, hold prisoner, intern, detain, put in prison, send to prison, keep under lock and key. [➡THE POLICE, ARREST, AND PRE-TRIAL PROCEEDINGS; 818] *Opposite:* free.

incarcerated (*formal*) *adj* [➡CAPTIVITY AND LOSS OF FREEDOM; 249]

incarceration *n* **imprisonment**, confinement, custody, captivity, internment, detention. [➡CAPTIVITY AND LOSS OF FREEDOM; 249] *Opposite:* freedom.

incarnate *adj* **personified**, in person, in the flesh, alive, embodied, in material form, come to life, made flesh. [➡REPRESENTATIVE; 66]

incarnation *n* **personification**, embodiment, manifestation, avatar, living form, life, materialization. [➡REPRESENTATIONS AND GENERAL EXAMPLES; 65]

in case *conj* **just in case**, in the event, lest, if, whether or no, whether or not. [➡UNCERTAIN; 176]

incautious *adj* **careless**, rash, reckless, impetuous, impulsive, unwary, unthinking, imprudent (*formal*), indiscreet, hasty. [➡INCAUTIOUS AND CARELESS; 284] *Opposite:* careful.

incendiary 1 *adj* **inflammable**, combustible, flammable. [➡FIRE, FLAMMABILITY, AND BURNING; 1164] 2 *adj* **inflammatory**, provocative, rabble-rousing, aggressive, stirring, rousing. [➡RUDE AND HOSTILE; 626] *Opposite:* conciliatory. 3 *n* (*formal*) **arsonist**, fire raiser, pyromaniac, burner, firebomber, torcher (*slang*), firebug (*slang*). [➡CRIMINALS; 821] 4 *n* (*formal*) **troublemaker**, agitator, demagogue, stirrer (*informal*), activist, firebrand, agent provocateur, rabble-rouser (*disapproving*). [➡UNCOOPERATIVE OR REBELLIOUS PERSON; 567]

incense *v* **enrage**, anger, rile (*informal*), exasperate, infuriate, annoy, make your blood boil. [➡ANGER AND ANNOY; 570] *Opposite:* calm.

incensed *adj* **enraged**, angry, riled (*informal*), exasperated, infuriated, annoyed, irate, furious. [➡IRRITATION AND ANGER; 542] *Opposite:* calm.

incentive *n* **inducement**, enticement, motivation, encouragement, spur, reason. [➡CAUSATION; 169] *Opposite:* disincentive.

See Compare and Contrast at **motive**.

inception (*formal*) *n* **beginning**, start, inauguration, initiation, foundation, origin, launch, establishment, commencement (*formal*). [➡BEGINNING; 53] *Opposite:* culmination.

incertitude *n* [➡UNCERTAINTY; 560]

incessant *adj* **nonstop**, never-ending, ceaseless, continuous, continual, unremitting, relentless, persistent, constant. [➡PERMANENCE: WITHOUT END; 94] *Opposite:* sporadic.

inch *v* **creep**, crawl, shuffle, edge. [➡MOVE SLOWLY; 315]

in charge *adj* **in command**, in control, at the helm, responsible, giving the orders, answerable, accountable, liable. [➡SUPERIORITY; 153]

inchoate (*formal*) *adj* **undeveloped**, incipient, immature, beginning, starting, budding, developing, emergent, early, embryonic. [➡VAGUENESS; 244] *Opposite:* mature.

in chorus *adv* **together**, in unison, all together, in harmony, harmoniously, as one, in concert, jointly. [➡ACTING WITH OTHERS; 286] *Opposite:* individually.

incidence *n* **occurrence**, frequency, rate, commonness, prevalence. [➡FREQUENT AND OFTEN; 107]

incident 1 *n* **event**, occurrence, occasion, happening, episode, instance, case. [➡EVENTS AND OCCURRENCES; 35] 2 *n* **confrontation**, clash, skirmish, fight, episode, scene. [➡ARGUMENT; 47]

incidental *adj* **related**, accompanying, secondary, subsidiary, supplementary, attendant, minor. [➡RELATED; 143] *Opposite:* essential.

incidentally *adv* **by the way**, by the by, while we're on the subject, before I forget, parenthetically. [➡EXPRESSIONS INTRODUCING EXTRA INFORMATION; 137]

incinerate *v* **burn**, burn up, set fire to, cremate, reduce to ashes, destroy. [➡FIRE, FLAMMABILITY, AND BURNING; 1164]

incineration *n* [➡FIRE, FLAMMABILITY, AND BURNING; 1164]

incinerator *n* **furnace**, brazier, kiln, oven, burner, firebox. [➡FIRE, FLAMMABILITY, AND BURNING; 1164]

incipient *adj* **emerging**, initial, embryonic, budding, early, developing, emergent, inchoate (*formal*). [➡FUTURE; 86] *Opposite:* final.

incise *v* **cut**, slit, notch, score, carve, chisel, engrave. [➡TEAR, BREAK, AND CUT; 361]

incision *n* **cut**, slit, opening, notch, scratch, score. [➡HOLES, GAPS, AND FORKS; 1251]

incisive *adj* **keen**, perceptive, insightful, sharp, penetrating, razor-sharp. [➡POSITIVE INTELLECTUAL CHARACTERISTICS; 525] *Opposite:* dull.

incisiveness *n* [➡POSITIVE INTELLECTUAL CHARACTERISTICS; 525]

incisor *type of* **tooth**. [➡THE MOUTH; 703]

incite *v* **provoke**, inflame, rouse, goad, spur, egg on, stimulate, motivate, push, stir up, instigate, whip up, breed, cause. [➡CAUSE OR COMPEL TO ACT; 272] *Opposite:* quell.

incitement *n* **provocation**, stimulation, agitation, encouragement, goad, spur, stimulus, motivation. [➡BEGINNING; 53] *Opposite:* deterrent.

incivility *n* **rudeness**, impoliteness, discourteousness, discourtesy, lack of respect, bad manners, coarseness, vulgarity. [➡BAD MANNERS AND SOCIAL SKILLS; 522] *Opposite:* politeness.

inclement *adj* **intemperate**, extreme, severe, bad, foul, rough, harsh, stormy, rainy, windy, squally. [➡COLD WEATHER; 1051] *Opposite:* pleasant.

inclination 1 *n* **feeling**, predisposition, disposition, leaning, proclivity, penchant, preference, liking, partiality, fondness, tendency. [➡LIKE, LOVE, VALUE, AND ENJOY; 579] *Opposite:* antipathy. 2 *n* **slope**, slant, incline, gradient, pitch, steepness. [➡ORIENTATION AND ALIGNMENT; 1222]

incline 1 *v* **predispose** (*formal*), dispose, persuade, prejudice, bias, bring round, lean, verge, favour, show a preference for. [➡LIKE, LOVE, VALUE, AND ENJOY; 579] *Opposite:* deter. 2 *v* **slant**, slope, tilt, rise, fall, lean. [➡ENCOURAGE; 577] 3 *n* **slope**, slant, gradient, rise, ascent, hill. [➡MOUNTAINS AND HILLS; 1044]

inclined 1 *adj* **motivated**, persuaded, tending, disposed, apt, liable, prone, of a mind. [➡APPRECIATION AND GRATITUDE; 536] *Opposite:* averse (*formal*). 2 *adj* **leaning**, sloping, slanting, tilting, orientated, oriented. [➡ORIENTATION AND ALIGNMENT; 1222]

in close proximity *adv* [➡CLOSENESS; 160]

in clover *adj* **well-off**, wealthy, affluent, rich, comfortable, in the lap of luxury, living high off the hog (*US slang*). [➡WEALTH AND WEALTHY; 891]

include 1 *v* **contain**, comprise, take in, consist of, take account of, embrace. [➡POSSESS; 445] *Opposite:* omit. 2 *v* **bring in**, incorporate, add in, enter, involve, rope in. [➡COMBINE AND MIX; 401] *Opposite:* reject.

included *adj* **contained within**, counted in, comprised, encompassed, involved. [➡PRESENT AND AVAILABLE; 11] *Opposite:* omitted.

including *prep* **counting**, as well as, with, together with, plus. [➡ALSO; 136] *Opposite:* excluding.

inclusion *n* **presence**, addition, enclosure, insertion, annexation, attachment. [➡MORE AND EXCESS; 122] *Opposite:* absence.

inclusive *adj* **comprehensive**, wide-ranging, all-encompassing, complete, broad, general. [➡WHOLENESS AND COMPLETENESS; 199] *Opposite:* narrow.

incognito *adv* **in disguise**, disguised, undercover, anonymously, secretly, in secret. [➡SECRET AND UNKNOWN; 180] *Opposite:* openly.

incoherence *n* **unintelligibility**, inarticulateness, disjointedness, illogicality, confusedness, confusion, disorganization. [➡VAGUENESS; 244] *Opposite:* coherence.

incoherent 1 *adj* **disjointed**, confused, jumbled, rambling, illogical, all over the place (*informal*). [➡INARTICULATE, RAMBLING, AND AWKWARD; 634] *Opposite:* clear. 2 *adj* **inarticulate**, unintelligible, incomprehensible, garbled, mumbled, slurred. [➡INARTICULATE, RAMBLING, AND AWKWARD; 634] *Opposite:* articulate.

in cold blood *adv* **mercilessly**, deliberately, premeditatedly, unemotionally, coolly, cruelly, cold-heartedly, pitilessly. [➡INTENTIONAL AND DELIBERATE; 280]

incombustible *adj* **fireproof**, flameproof, fire-resistant, flame-resistant, fire-retardant, flame-retardant. [➡FIRE, FLAMMABILITY, AND BURNING; 1164] *Opposite:* flammable.

income *n* **profits**, takings, proceeds, returns, revenue, earnings, wages, pay, salary, take-home pay. [➡INCOME; 461] *Opposite:* expenditure.

incomer *n* **settler**, immigrant, colonist, migrant, newcomer. [➡STRANGERS; 972]

income tax *n* **tax**, VAT, toll, duty, excise, tariff, levy, charge. [➡TAX AND TAXATION; 802]

incoming 1 *adj* **inbound**, inward bound, homeward bound, arriving, entering, inward. [➡DIRECTION OF MOTION; 346] *Opposite:* outgoing. 2 *adj* **new**, next, succeeding, newly appointed, newly elected, returning. [➡NEW, MODERN; 167] *Opposite:* outgoing.

incommensurate *adj* **disproportionate**, unequal, inadequate, insufficient, lacking parity, out of line (*informal*). [➡TOO FEW, TOO LITTLE; 120] *Opposite:* proportionate.

in commission *adj* **in service**, in use, operating, working, functioning. [➡HAPPENING AND IN PROGRESS; 32]

incommode (*formal*) *v* **inconvenience**, trouble, disturb, bother, put out, put to some trouble. [➡UPSET, DISTRESS, AND HUMILIATE; 568]

incommodious (*formal*) 1 *adj* **cramped**, restricted, confined, poky (*informal*), tiny, small. [➡SMALL; 1194] *Opposite:* roomy. 2 *adj* **inconvenient**, troublesome, awkward, annoying, bothersome, difficult. [➡PHYSICALLY UNPLEASANT; 227]

incommunicado *adj* **not in contact**, out of touch, not in communication, not able to communicate, unwilling to communicate, in solitary confinement. [➡SOLITARINESS; 941]

incomparable *adj* **unequalled**, unrivalled, unparalleled, unsurpassed, unmatched, outstanding, unique. [➡EXTRAORDINARY: AMAZING; 205] *Opposite:* ordinary.

incompatibility 1 *n* **mismatch**, unsuitability, discordancy, inharmoniousness, irreconcilability. [➡DISHARMONY; 157] 2 *n* **inconsistency**, illogicality, irreconcilability, incongruity, mismatch, conflict. [➡DISHARMONY; 157] *Opposite:* consistency.

incompatible *adj* **mismatched**, unsuited, discordant, unharmonious, dissenting, irreconcilable, ill-assorted. [➡DISHARMONY; 157] *Opposite:* like-minded.

incompetence *n* **ineptitude**, unskilfulness, inability, ineffectiveness, stupidity, uselessness. [➡UNSKILLED; 530] *Opposite:* ability.

incompetent *adj* **inept**, useless, bungling (*informal*), unskilled, ineffectual, hopeless, unapt, unable, incapable. [➡UNSKILLED; 530] *Opposite:* able.

incomplete 1 *adj* **imperfect**, partial, unfinished, inadequate, half-finished, piecemeal, lacking. [➡UNFINISHEDNESS; 240] *Opposite:* entire. 2 *adj* **unfinished**, undeveloped, curtailed, shortened, deficient, inchoate (*formal*). [➡UNFINISHEDNESS; 240] *Opposite:* finished.

incomprehensibility *n* [➡DIFFICULTY AND COMPLEXITY; 243]

incomprehensible *adj* **unintelligible**, unfathomable, impenetrable, inexplicable, inconceivable, perplexing. [➡DIFFICULTY AND COMPLEXITY; 243] *Opposite:* understandable.

incomprehension *n* **disbelief**, incredulity, incredulousness, perplexity, blankness. [➡SURPRISE, SHOCK, AND AMAZEMENT; 546] *Opposite:* understanding.

inconceivable *adj* **unimaginable**, unthinkable, beyond belief, unbelievable, incredible, implausible, mind-blowing (*informal*), mind-boggling (*informal*). [➡IMPOSSIBLE AND IMPROBABLE; 179] *Opposite:* imaginable.

in concert 1 *adv* **performing**, presenting, in recital, live, playing, singing, in performance, onstage, before a live audience. [➡MUSICAL TERMS; 912] 2 *adv* **in chorus**, harmoniously, together, as one, in unison, all together, jointly. [➡ACTING WITH OTHERS; 286] *Opposite:* individually.

inconclusive *adj* **indecisive**, questionable, unconvincing, unsatisfying, unsettled, inadequate, lacking, unfounded, groundless, unsound, uncertain. [➡UNCERTAIN; 176] *Opposite:* decisive.

in confidence *adv* **in secret**, confidentially, between ourselves, in private, privately, secretly, off the record. [➡SECRET AND UNKNOWN; 180] *Opposite:* openly.

incongruence *n* [➡DISHARMONY; 157]

incongruent *adj* [➡DISHARMONY; 157]

incongruity *n* **oddness**, strangeness, absurdity, inappropriateness, inaptness, unsuitableness, incompatibility, inconsistency, bizarreness, unsuitability, inharmoniousness. [➡BIZARRE AND PECULIAR; 258] *Opposite:* consistency.

incongruous *adj* **odd**, strange, out of place, incompatible, inappropriate, inconsistent, absurd, bizarre, unsuitable, inharmonious. [➡BIZARRE AND PECULIAR; 258] *Opposite:* consistent.

incongruousness *n* [➡DISHARMONY; 157]

in conjunction with *prep* **together with**, combined with, along with, with, in addition to, in tandem with, alongside, next to. [➡ALSO; 136] *Opposite:* apart from.

in consequence (*formal*) *adv* **accordingly**, as a result, consequently (*formal*), therefore, hence (*formal*), thus (*formal*), so. [➡RESULTS AND OUTCOMES; 83]

inconsequence *n* **unimportance**, irrelevance, insignificance, triviality, inconsequentiality, frivolity, inappropriateness, worthlessness. [➡UNIMPORTANT AND UNNECESSARY; 239] *Opposite:* importance.

inconsequential *adj* **unimportant**, trivial, petty, negligible, minor, insignificant, irrelevant, frivolous, inappropriate, worthless. [➡UNIMPORTANT AND UNNECESSARY; 239] *Opposite:* important.

inconsequentiality *n* **unimportance**, insignificance, triviality, frivolity, inconsequence, irrelevance, inappropriateness, worthlessness. [➡UNIMPORTANT AND UNNECESSARY; 239] *Opposite:* importance.

inconsiderable *adj* **small**, minor, tiny, paltry, negligible, trivial, petty, trifling. [➡UNIMPORTANT AND UNNECESSARY; 239] *Opposite:* sizable.

inconsiderate *adj* **selfish**, thoughtless, insensitive, uncharitable, unkind, uncaring, careless, discourteous. [➡SELFISH AND UNKIND; 506] *Opposite:* caring.

inconsiderateness *n* [➡SELFISH AND UNKIND; 506]

inconsistency *n* **discrepancy**, contradiction, variation, irregularity, changeability, unpredictability, conflict. [➡DIFFERENCE; 150]

inconsistent 1 *adj* **conflicting**, contradictory, incompatible, incoherent, incongruous, paradoxical, irreconcilable. [➡DISHARMONY; 157] *Opposite:* consistent. 2 *adj* **unpredictable**, varying, unreliable, erratic, uneven, shifting, fickle, changeable, variable, inconstant, mercurial, capricious. [➡FINITENESS, VARIABILITY, AND TRANSIENCE; 96] *Opposite:* constant.

inconsolable *adj* **grief-stricken**, brokenhearted, devastated, desolate, despairing, heartbroken, wretched. [➡SADNESS, DISTRESS, AND DESPAIR; 540] *Opposite:* ecstatic.

inconspicuous *adj* **unobtrusive**, discreet, unremarkable, ordinary, modest, quiet, low-key, unassuming. [➡IMPERCEPTIBLE; 26] *Opposite:* obvious.

inconspicuousness *n* [➡IMPERCEPTIBLE; 26]

inconstancy *n* [➡UNCERTAIN; 176]

inconstant 1 *adj* (*literary*) **unfaithful**, disloyal, fickle, deceitful, false, two-timing (*informal*). [➡DECEITFUL; 514] *Opposite:* faithful. 2 *adj* **changeable**, variable, irregular, unpredictable, fluctuating, varying. [➡FINITENESS, VARIABILITY, AND TRANSIENCE; 96] *Opposite:* unchanging.

incontestable *adj* **indisputable**, incontrovertible, irrefutable, unquestionable, indubitable (*formal*), undeniable, unarguable, obvious, undoubted. [➡CERTAIN; 175] *Opposite:* arguable.

incontrovertible *adj* **undeniable**, unquestionable, irrefutable, incontestable, indisputable, indubitable (*formal*), unarguable, unassailable. [➡CERTAIN; 175] *Opposite:* questionable.

inconvenience 1 *n* **troublesomeness**, tiresomeness, inopportuneness, untimeliness, awkwardness, embarrassment. [➡NUISANCES; 254] *Opposite:* benefit. 2 *n* **problem**, trouble, bother, hassle (*informal*), difficulty, nuisance, aggravation (*informal*), annoyance. [➡NUISANCES; 254] 3 *v* **disrupt**, put out, trouble, bother, incommode (*formal*), discommode (*formal*), disturb. [➡ANGER AND ANNOY; 570] *Opposite:* help.

inconvenient *adj* **troublesome**, tiresome, inopportune, problematic, untimely, awkward, ill-timed, bothersome, difficult, embarrassing. [➡PROMPTNESS: BADLY TIMED; 101] *Opposite:* beneficial.

inconveniently *adv* **awkwardly**, troublesomely, inopportunely, tiresomely, problematically, embarrassingly. [➡IRRITATING; 229] *Opposite:* beneficially.

in cooperation with *prep* **together with**, in association with, in collaboration with, alongside, in conjunction with. [➡ALSO; 136]

incorporate 1 *v* **join**, slot in, fit in, add in, slip in, include, integrate, unite, combine. [➡POSITION SOMETHING: BETWEEN, BESIDE, OR INSIDE SOMETHING; 327] *Opposite:* exclude. 2 *v* **merge**, combine, feature, contain, include, encompass, absorb, assimilate. [➡POSSESS; 445] *Opposite:* divide.

incorporated *adj* **combined**, united, unified, merged, fused, assimilated, amalgamated, integrated. [➡RELATED; 143] *Opposite:* separate.

incorporation *n* **combination**, amalgamation, integration, assimilation, merger, fusion, unification, absorption, union. [➡COMBINE AND MIX; 401] *Opposite:* separation.

incorporeal (*formal*) *adj* **intangible**, ethereal, spiritual, unreal, disembodied, ghostly. [➡FALSE AND UNREAL; 174] *Opposite:* tangible.

incorrect 1 *adj* **erroneous**, wrong, mistaken, untrue, inaccurate, false. [➡INCORRECT AND ERRONEOUS; 223] *Opposite:* right. 2 *adj* **improper**, unfitting, inappropriate, unseemly, unbecoming, indecorous, indelicate, indecent, impolite, offensive, unsuitable. [➡INAPPROPRIATE AND UNSUITABLE; 225] *Opposite:* proper.

incorrectness 1 *n* **erroneousness**, error, fallacy, wrongness, mistakenness, falseness, inaccuracy. [➡INCORRECT AND ERRONEOUS; 223] *Opposite:* correctness. 2 *n* **impropriety**, inappropriateness, unsuitability, unseemliness, indecorousness, indelicacy, indecency, impoliteness. [➡MORALLY BAD; 776] *Opposite:* propriety.

incorrigible *adj* **irredeemable**, habitual, inveterate, dyed-in-the-wool, persistent, incurable, hopeless. [➡UNWILLINGNESS AND STUBBORNNESS; 565] *Opposite:* tractable.

incorruptibility *n* [➡MORALLY GOOD; 775]

incorruptible 1 *adj* **moral**, principled, just, straight, honourable, honest, upright. [➡HONEST AND RELIABLE; 503] *Opposite:* venal. 2 *adj* **imperishable**, everlasting, immortal, indestructible, unchanging, constant. [➡PERMANENCE: WITHOUT CHANGE; 95] *Opposite:* perishable.

increase 1 *v* **enlarge**, extend, augment (*formal*), boost, amplify, swell, expand, multiply, improve, intensify, raise. [➡CHANGE OF SIZE: BIGGER; 393] *Opposite:* decrease. 2 *n* **upsurge**, surge, rise, growth, intensification, escalation, proliferation, upturn, spread, expansion, multiplication, buildup. [➡CHANGE OF INTENSITY: MORE; 395] *Opposite:* decrease.

> **Compare and Contrast:** ***increase, expand, enlarge, extend, augment, intensify, amplify***
>
> CORE MEANING: MAKE LARGER OR GREATER
>
> ***increase*** to become or cause to become larger in number, quantity, degree, or scope; ***expand*** to become or cause to become larger or more extensive; ***enlarge*** to become or cause to become larger generally, or to broaden in scope and detail; ***extend*** to make larger in terms of length, area, period of time, or other existing limits; ***augment*** (*formal*) to add to something in order to make it larger or more substantial; ***intensify*** to become or cause to become greater in strength or degree; ***amplify*** to become or cause to become louder, or greater in intensity or scope.

incredible 1 *adj* **unbelievable**, implausible, improbable, far-fetched, absurd, inconceivable. [➡FALSE AND UNREAL; 174] *Opposite:* believable. 2 *adj* **amazing**, astonishing, extraordinary, staggering, mind-blowing (*informal*), unbelievable, fantastic, remarkable, mind-boggling (*informal*). [➡EXTRAORDINARY: AMAZING; 205] *Opposite:* unremarkable. 3 *adj* (*informal*) **excellent**, superb, tremendous, prodigious, phenomenal. [➡MANY, MUCH, LARGE AMOUNT; 117] *Opposite:* mediocre.

incredibly 1 *adv* **unbelievably**, implausibly, inconceivably, absurdly, improbably. [➡FALSE AND UNREAL; 174] *Opposite:* believably. 2 *adv* (*informal*) **very**, extremely, unbelievably, amazingly, really, exceedingly, extraordinarily, exceptionally, awfully. [➡TO A GREAT EXTENT; 130]

in credit *adj* **in the black**, all straight, solvent. [➡WEALTH AND WEALTHY; 891] *Opposite:* overdrawn.

incredulity *n* **disbelief**, amazement, astonishment, doubt, scepticism, wonder, suspicion. [➡SURPRISE, SHOCK, AND AMAZEMENT; 546] *Opposite:* belief.

incredulous *adj* **disbelieving**, sceptical, unbelieving, doubtful, doubting, unconvinced, suspicious. [➡SURPRISE, SHOCK, AND AMAZEMENT; 546] *Opposite:* believing.

increment *n* **increase**, addition, augmentation, raise, rise, growth, boost. [➡CHANGE OF INTENSITY: MORE; 395] *Opposite:* cut.

incriminate *v* **implicate**, impeach, drop somebody in it, give away, lay the blame on, convict, point the finger. [➡ACCUSE, BLAME, AND CRITICIZE; 642] *Opposite:* exonerate.

in-crowd (*informal*) *n* **inner circle**, beau monde, high society, clique, elite, jet set (*informal*), in-group, beautiful people. [➡FRIENDS AND ACQUAINTANCES; 936]

incrustation *n* **coating**, crust, layer, covering, accumulation, shell, veneer. [➡COVERS AND COATINGS; 1245]

incubate *v* **hatch**, gestate, raise, rear, nurture, protect, nurse. [➡REPRODUCTION AND HEREDITY; 726]

incubation *n* **development**, gestation, cultivation, nurture, growth, increase, maturation, evolution. [➡SICKNESS; 730] *Opposite:* destruction.

incubus *n* [➡NUISANCES; 254]

inculcate *v* **impress upon**, teach, drum into, instruct, drill into, din, hammer into, instil, coach, train, indoctrinate. [➡ INSTRUCT AND TEACH; 610]

incumbency (*formal*) 1 *n* **tenure**, period of office, term of office, term, time, period. [➡ WORK-RELATED ACTIVITIES; 834] 2 *n* **post**, position, office, appointment. [➡ JOB; 833] 3 *n* **duty**, obligation, responsibility, office, task, role, commitment, charge. [➡ RESPONSIBILITY; 171]

incumbent 1 *adj* (*formal*) **obligatory**, mandatory, compulsory, binding, unavoidable, inescapable. [➡ EMPLOYMENT STATUS; 831] *Opposite:* optional. 2 *n* **official**, office holder, occupant, appointee, officer, executive. [➡ POLITICAL OFFICES AND POLITICIANS; 808]

incur 1 *v* **experience**, suffer, sustain, bring upon yourself, lay yourself open to, invite, acquire, earn, gain, deserve, meet with, encounter, come in for. [➡ CAUSE TO HAPPEN; 31] *Opposite:* avoid. 2 *v* **sustain**, meet with, encounter, experience, suffer, come in for. [➡ EXPERIENCE AND ENCOUNTER; 583]

incurable 1 *adj* **terminal**, fatal, deadly, inoperable, untreatable, grave, permanent. [➡ SICKNESS; 730] *Opposite:* curable. 2 *adj* **irredeemable**, inveterate, incorrigible, hopeless, undying, dyed-in-the wool, irrepressible, eternal. [➡ UNWILLINGNESS AND STUBBORNNESS; 565] *Opposite:* redeemable.

incurious *adj* **uninterested**, indifferent, unmoved, unconcerned, detached, apathetic. [➡ NEUTRALITY AND INDIFFERENCE; 554] *Opposite:* inquisitive.

incursion 1 *n* **raid**, night raid, attack, sortie, invasion, foray. [➡ AGGRESSIVE EVENT; 39] *Opposite:* retreat. 2 *n* (*formal*) **intrusion**, invasion, spread, infiltration, movement, arrival, inroad. [➡ ARRIVAL; 13]

in custody *n* **under arrest**, in prison, in detention, detained, remanded, arrested. [➡ CAPTIVITY AND LOSS OF FREEDOM; 249]

in danger *adj* [➡ IN DANGER; 238]

in debit *adj* **in the red**, in debt, overdrawn, in arrears, insolvent. [➡ FINANCE AND ECONOMICS; 797] *Opposite:* in credit.

in debt *adj* **in the red**, overdrawn, insolvent, in arrears, owing money, in debit, bankrupt, broke (*informal*). [➡ POVERTY AND POOR; 892] *Opposite:* in credit.

indebted *adj* **obligated**, obliged, grateful, thankful, in somebody's debt, beholden, owing a favour, appreciative. [➡ APPRECIATION AND GRATITUDE; 536] *Opposite:* ungrateful.

indebtedness *n* **obligation**, gratitude, appreciation, thankfulness, gratefulness, acknowledgement. [➡ RELATIONSHIP TO ANOTHER; 973] *Opposite:* ingratitude.

indecency 1 *n* **offensiveness**, coarseness, crudeness, lewdness, licentiousness (*formal*), obscenity, rudeness, filth. [➡ MORALLY BAD; 776] *Opposite:* decency. 2 *n* **impropriety**, unsuitability, unseemliness, indecorousness, indelicacy, inappropriateness. [➡ BAD BEHAVIOUR OR ACTION; 255] *Opposite:* propriety.

indecent 1 *adj* **offensive**, coarse, rude, crude, filthy, lewd, licentious (*formal*). [➡ MORALLY BAD; 776] *Opposite:* decorous. 2 *adj* **improper**, unsuitable, unseemly, indecorous, unbecoming, indelicate, shocking, inappropriate. [➡ MORALLY BAD; 776] *Opposite:* proper.

indecipherable 1 *adj* **illegible**, incomprehensible, unintelligible, unreadable, indistinct, unclear. [➡ DIFFICULTY AND COMPLEXITY; 243] *Opposite:* legible. 2 *adj* **impenetrable**, inscrutable, obscure, unfathomable, enigmatic, cryptic, incomprehensible, unintelligible. [➡ DIFFICULTY AND COMPLEXITY; 243] *Opposite:* clear.

indecision *n* **irresolution**, hesitancy, indecisiveness, uncertainty, vacillation, wavering. [➡ UNCERTAINTY; 560] *Opposite:* decisiveness.

indecisive 1 *adj* **irresolute**, in two minds, vacillating, wavering, hesitant, unsure, faltering, dithering, uncertain. [➡ NEGATIVE INTELLECTUAL CHARACTERISTICS; 526] *Opposite:* decisive. 2 *adj* **inconclusive**, indefinite, indeterminate, tentative, unclear. [➡ UNCERTAIN; 176] *Opposite:* conclusive.

indecisively *adv* **irresolutely**, vacillatingly, waveringly, hesitantly, uncertainly, ditheringly. [➡ NEGATIVE INTELLECTUAL CHARACTERISTICS; 526] *Opposite:* decisively.

indecisiveness 1 *n* **irresolution**, hesitancy, hesitation, vacillation, uncertainty. [➡ UNCERTAINTY; 560] *Opposite:* decisiveness. 2 *n* **indefiniteness**, inconclusiveness, woolliness, vagueness, indeterminacy, tentativeness, unclearness, uncertainty. [➡ UNCERTAIN; 176] *Opposite:* certainty.

indecorous *adj* **impolite**, rude, shocking, inappropriate, unseemly, improper, undignified, ill-mannered. [➡ BAD MANNERS AND SOCIAL SKILLS; 522] *Opposite:* polite.

indecorousness *n* [➡ BAD MANNERS AND SOCIAL SKILLS; 522]

indecorum *n* **impoliteness**, bad behaviour, rudeness, shockingness, offensiveness, impropriety, unseemliness, untowardness, solecism. [➡ BAD MANNERS AND SOCIAL SKILLS; 522] *Opposite:* politeness.

indeed 1 *adv* **in reality**, in fact, actually, in truth, as a matter of fact, in actual fact, if truth be told. [➡ TRUE AND REAL; 172] 2 *adv* **certainly**, really, to be sure, undeniably, definitely, without a doubt, truly. [➡ CERTAIN; 175]

in deep trouble *adj* [➡ IN TROUBLE AND DISADVANTAGED; 73]

in deep water *adj* [➡ IN TROUBLE AND DISADVANTAGED; 73]

indefatigable *adj* **untiring**, unflagging, unrelenting, remorseless, unfaltering, inexorable (*formal*), dogged, determined. [➡ STRENGTH OF WILL; 502] *Opposite:* half-hearted.

indefensible 1 *adj* **inexcusable**, unpardonable, unforgivable, unjustifiable, unwarrantable, reprehensible, uncalled-for. [➡ UNACCEPTABLE AND UNFORGIVEABLE; 226] *Opposite:* excusable. 2 *adj* **invalid**, untenable, unsustainable, shaky, weak, wrong. [➡ MORALLY BAD; 776] *Opposite:* valid. 3 *adj* **unprotected**, exposed, vulnerable, undefended, unfortified, defenceless, weak. [➡ WEAKNESS; 242] *Opposite:* impregnable.

indefensibly 1 *adv* **inexcusably**, unforgivably, unpardonably, unjustifiably, reprehensibly, shamefully. [➡ INAPPROPRIATE AND UNSUITABLE; 225] *Opposite:* excusably. 2 *adv* **invalidly**, untenably, unsustainably, shakily, weakly, wrongly. [➡ IMPOSSIBLE AND IMPROBABLE; 179]

indefinable *adj* **indescribable**, impalpable (*formal*), inexpressible, vague, indefinite, obscure. [➡ VAGUENESS; 244]

indefinite 1 *adj* **unlimited**, unfixed, unspecified, unknown, indeterminate, open-ended, undefined, undetermined. [➡UNCERTAIN; 176] *Opposite:* specified. 2 *adj* **unclear**, imprecise, vague, hazy, woolly, indistinct, blurred. [➡VAGUENESS; 244] *Opposite:* precise. 3 *adj* **vague**, uncertain, undecided, unclear, noncommittal, unsure. [➡UNCERTAIN; 176] *Opposite:* certain.

indefinite article *type of* **word class**. [➡ASPECTS OF LANGUAGE; 683]

indefinitely *adv* **until further notice**, for the foreseeable future, for life, forever, ad infinitum, indeterminately, open-endedly. [➡PERMANENCE: WITHOUT END; 94]

indelible 1 *adj* **permanent**, fixed, ineradicable, fast, stubborn. [➡PERMANENCE: WITHOUT END; 94] *Opposite:* temporary. 2 *adj* **unforgettable**, deep-seated, deep-rooted, lasting, enduring, ingrained. [➡PERMANENCE: WITHOUT END; 94] *Opposite:* temporary.

indelibly *adv* **permanently**, ineradicably, lastingly, forever, for good, for always. [➡PERMANENCE: WITHOUT END; 94] *Opposite:* temporarily.

indelicacy *n* **tactlessness**, offensiveness, tastelessness, crudeness, unseemliness, coarseness, impropriety, indecency, bad manners. [➡BAD MANNERS AND SOCIAL SKILLS; 522] *Opposite:* politeness.

indelicate *adj* **tactless**, offensive, improper, unseemly, impolite, indecent, coarse, bad-mannered, crude. [➡BAD MANNERS AND SOCIAL SKILLS; 522] *Opposite:* polite.

indelicateness *n* [➡BAD MANNERS AND SOCIAL SKILLS; 522]

in demand *adj* [➡POPULAR AND WANTED; 221]

indemnify 1 *v* **insure**, underwrite, cover, assure, protect, guarantee. [➡INSURANCE; 801] 2 *v* **reimburse**, compensate, repay, pay, refund, remunerate, settle. [➡GIVE MONEY; 434]

indemnity 1 *n* **insurance**, protection, cover, life assurance, security, guarantee, coverage, life insurance (*US*). [➡SAFE AND SAFETY; 192] 2 *n* **compensation**, reimbursement, remuneration, reparation, payment, repayment, settlement. [➡REWARDS AND AWARDS; 440]

indent 1 *v* **hollow out**, dent, depress, stave in, scoop, gouge, pockmark, pit. [➡CHANGE OF SHAPE; 386] 2 *v* **notch**, serrate, nick, pink, incise, score. [➡TEAR, BREAK, AND CUT; 361]

indentation 1 *n* **hollow**, dent, depression, scoop, gouge, dimple, pockmark. [➡HOLES, GAPS, AND FORKS; 1251] 2 *n* **notch**, groove, serration, nick, incision. [➡HOLES, GAPS, AND FORKS; 1251]

indenture *n* **contract**, arrangement, pact, deal, agreement, accord. [➡HARMONY; 156]

independence 1 *n* **self-government**, sovereignty, autonomy, self-rule, self-determination, freedom, liberty. [➡FREEDOM AND LIBERTY; 209] *Opposite:* subjection. 2 *n* **self-sufficiency**, self-reliance, self-determination, freedom, autonomy, individualism. [➡RELATIONSHIP TO ANOTHER; 973] *Opposite:* helplessness. 3 *n* **individuality**, freedom, liberation, unconventionality. [➡FREEDOM AND LIBERTY; 209] *Opposite:* conventionality. 4 *n* **impartiality**, objectivity, disinterest, neutrality, disinterestedness, nonalignment. [➡UNRELATEDNESS AND SEPARATENESS; 147] *Opposite:* partiality.

independent 1 *adj* **self-governing**, sovereign, autonomous, self-determining, self-regulating, free, liberated. [➡FREEDOM AND LIBERTY; 209] *Opposite:* dependent. 2 *adj* **self-sufficient**, self-reliant, autonomous, self-supporting, self-contained. [➡RELATIONSHIP TO ANOTHER; 973] *Opposite:* dependent. 3 *adj* **free**, liberated, individual, individualistic, unconventional, unconstrained, unfettered. [➡FREEDOM AND LIBERTY; 209] *Opposite:* conventional. 4 *adj* **impartial**, detached, objective, dispassionate, neutral, nonpartisan, unbiased, unprejudiced, nonaligned. [➡POSITIVE INTELLECTUAL CHARACTERISTICS; 525] *Opposite:* partial.

independently 1 *adv* **sovereignly**, autonomously, freely. [➡FREEDOM AND LIBERTY; 209] 2 *adv* **self-sufficiently**, self-reliantly, autonomously. [➡ACTING INDEPENDENTLY; 285] *Opposite:* helplessly. 3 *adv* **individualistically**, freely, individually, unconventionally. [➡UNRELATEDNESS AND SEPARATENESS; 147] *Opposite:* conventionally. 4 *adv* **impartially**, detachedly, dispassionately, objectively, disinterestedly, neutrally. [➡POSITIVE INTELLECTUAL CHARACTERISTICS; 525] *Opposite:* partially.

in depth *adv* **at length**, painstakingly, in detail, thoroughly, exhaustively, fully, comprehensively, profoundly, deeply, carefully. [➡WHOLENESS AND COMPLETENESS; 199] *Opposite:* superficially.

in-depth *adj* **painstaking**, detailed, exhaustive, thorough, comprehensive, considered, full, profound, careful, deep, extensive, far-reaching. [➡WHOLENESS AND COMPLETENESS; 199] *Opposite:* superficial.

indescribable 1 *adj* **indefinable**, inexpressible, unutterable, ineffable (*formal*), incommunicable, unspeakable. [➡EXTRAORDINARY: AMAZING; 205] 2 *adj* **extreme**, great, tremendous, intense, dramatic, powerful. [➡DIFFICULTY AND COMPLEXITY; 243]

indescribably 1 *adv* **indefinably**, unspeakably, inexpressibly, unutterably, ineffably (*formal*), incommunicably. [➡EXTRAORDINARY: AMAZING; 205] 2 *adv* **extremely**, greatly, tremendously, intensely, dramatically, powerfully. [➡TO A GREAT EXTENT; 130]

in despair *adj* [➡SADNESS, DISTRESS, AND DESPAIR; 540]

indestructibility *n* [➡PERMANENCE: WITHOUT END; 94]

indestructible 1 *adj* **abiding**, durable, everlasting, imperishable, eternal, immortal, enduring, unyielding. [➡PERMANENCE: WITHOUT END; 94] *Opposite:* perishable. 2 *adj* **unbreakable**, nonbreaking, resistant, shatterproof, rock-solid, reinforced, armoured, durable. [➡STRENGTH; 202] *Opposite:* fragile.

indestructibly *adv* **abidingly**, permanently, unyieldingly, durably, everlastingly, eternally, enduringly, imperishably (*literary*), immortally. [➡PERMANENCE: WITHOUT END; 94]

in detail *adv* **fully**, in depth, thoroughly, exhaustively, comprehensively, carefully, painstakingly, meticulously, scrupulously. [➡WHOLENESS AND COMPLETENESS; 199] *Opposite:* cursorily.

indeterminable 1 *adj* **unknowable**, indefinable, indescribable, impalpable (*formal*). [➡UNCERTAIN; 176] *Opposite:* knowable. 2 *adj* **unresolvable**, unanswerable, uncountable. [➡VAGUENESS; 244] *Opposite:* answerable.

indeterminacy *n* [➡UNCERTAIN; 176]

indeterminate 1 *adj* **unknown**, unspecified, unstipulated, unstated, unclassified, uncategorized. [➡UNCERTAIN; 176]

Opposite: known. 2 *adj* **undefined**, vague, undetermined, indefinite, unfixed, imprecise, unclear, uncertain. [➡VAGUENESS; 244] *Opposite:* definite.

indeterminately *adv* [➡UNCERTAIN; 176]

index 1 *n* **catalogue**, directory, guide, file, key, table. [➡LISTS AND SCHEDULES; 588] 2 *n* **indication**, indicator, symbol, pointer, sign, mark. [➡PERFECT EXAMPLES AND EMBODIMENTS; 67]

index finger *part of* **arm or hand**. [➡ARM AND HAND; 696]

Indiaman *type of* **historical vessel**. [➡SHIPS AND BOATS; 1149]

Indian summer *n* [➡HOT WEATHER; 1050]

indicate 1 *v* **point to**, point towards, point at, signpost, show, direct (*formal*), point out. [➡GESTURES AND GESTICULATION; 654] 2 *v* **denote**, signify, be a sign of, imply, suggest, hint at, show, reveal, be a symptom of. [➡MEAN SOMETHING; 61] 3 *v* **signal**, wink, flash. [➡LIGHT EMISSION; 369]

indication *n* **sign**, suggestion, signal, hint, warning, clue, symptom. [➡INDICATIONS, SIGNS, AND WARNINGS; 68]

See Compare and Contrast at **sign**.

indicative 1 *adj* **revealing**, symptomatic, telling, telltale, suggestive, symbolic. [➡REPRESENTATIVE; 66] 2 *type of* **grammatical term**. [➡ASPECTS OF LANGUAGE; 683]

indicator 1 *n* **pointer**, needle, gauge, dial, display, meter. [➡PARTS OF MACHINES AND TOOLS; 1117] 2 *type of* **external feature**. [➡VEHICLES; 1144]

indict *v* **accuse**, impeach, summons, prosecute, arraign, charge. [➡TRIAL, PUNISHMENT, AND LEGAL OUTCOMES; 819] *Opposite:* exonerate.

indictable *adj* **criminal**, unlawful, illegal, chargeable, felonious, prosecutable. [➡ILLEGAL; 816]

indictment 1 *n* **accusation**, impeachment, summons, prosecution, arraignment, charge. [➡TRIAL, PUNISHMENT, AND LEGAL OUTCOMES; 819] *Opposite:* exoneration. 2 *n* **condemnation**, denunciation, criticism, comment, censure, blame. [➡EVIDENCE AND PROOF; 69] *Opposite:* praise.

indifference 1 *n* **apathy**, coldness, coolness, unconcern, disinterest, uninterest. [➡NEUTRALITY AND INDIFFERENCE; 554] *Opposite:* concern. 2 *n* **unimportance**, insignificance, inconsequence, meaninglessness, irrelevance, triviality. [➡UNIMPORTANT AND UNNECESSARY; 239] *Opposite:* importance.

indifferent 1 *adj* **uncaring**, uninterested, unresponsive, apathetic, unsympathetic, unconcerned, unmoved, cold, cool. [➡NEUTRALITY AND INDIFFERENCE; 554] *Opposite:* concerned. 2 *adj* **average**, mediocre, moderate, undistinguished, so-so (*informal*), middling, tolerable, fair, unexceptional, poor. [➡ORDINARINESS; 245] *Opposite:* exceptional.

in difficulty *adj* [➡IN TROUBLE AND DISADVANTAGED; 73]

indigence (*formal*) *n* **poverty**, need, penury, deprivation, destitution, impecuniousness (*formal*), impoverishment, pennilessness. [➡POVERTY AND POOR; 892] *Opposite:* wealth.

See Compare and Contrast at **poverty**.

indigenous *adj* **native**, original, aboriginal, home-grown, local, ethnic. [➡COUNTRIES AND REGIONS; 1066] *Opposite:* immigrant.

See Compare and Contrast at **native**.

indigent (*formal*) *adj* **poor**, needy, impoverished, poverty-stricken, penniless, destitute, impecunious (*formal*), deprived, penurious (*literary*). [➡POVERTY AND POOR; 892] *Opposite:* wealthy.

indigestible 1 *adj* **stodgy** (*informal*), heavy, rich, tough, inedible. [➡FOOD; 1166] *Opposite:* edible. 2 *adj* **incomprehensible**, impenetrable, unreadable, complex, obscure, dense, dry. [➡DIFFICULTY AND COMPLEXITY; 243] *Opposite:* readable.

indigestion *n* **dyspepsia** (*technical*), heartburn, stomachache, upset stomach, colic, gastritis. [➡DISORDERS OF THE DIGESTIVE SYSTEM; 714]

indignant *adj* **angry**, furious, vexed, irate, in a huff (*informal*), outraged, incensed, put out, annoyed, piqued, cross. [➡IRRITATION AND ANGER; 542] *Opposite:* mollified.

indignantly *adv* **angrily**, furiously, irately, heatedly, crossly, huffily. [➡BAD-TEMPERED AND HUMOURLESS; 627] *Opposite:* delightedly.

indignation *n* **anger**, resentment, outrage, annoyance, crossness, exasperation, pique, irritation. [➡IRRITATION AND ANGER; 542] *Opposite:* delight.

See Compare and Contrast at **anger**.

indignity *n* **humiliation**, shame, disgrace, mortification, embarrassment, ignominy, dishonour. [➡DIFFICULT SITUATIONS; 72] *Opposite:* glory.

indigo *type of* **blue**. [➡COLOURS; 1223]

indirect 1 *adj* **circuitous**, roundabout, rambling, circumlocutory, tortuous, meandering. [➡DIRECTION OF MOTION; 346] *Opposite:* straight. 2 *adj* **unintended**, unplanned, secondary, ancillary, subsidiary, incidental, unforeseen. [➡UNINTENTIONAL AND ACCIDENTAL; 282] *Opposite:* intended. 3 *adj* **devious**, oblique, implicit, tacit, implied, understood, inferred, hinted at. [➡RETICENT AND UNFORTHCOMING; 632] *Opposite:* overt.

indirectly 1 *adv* **circuitously**, ramblingly, tortuously, meanderingly. [➡INARTICULATE, RAMBLING, AND AWKWARD; 634] *Opposite:* straight. 2 *adv* **incidentally**, secondarily, subsidiarily. [➡UNIMPORTANT AND UNNECESSARY; 239] 3 *adv* **deviously**, obliquely, implicitly, tacitly, subtly, tactfully, subliminally. [➡INARTICULATE, RAMBLING, AND AWKWARD; 634] *Opposite:* overtly.

in dire straits *adj* **in difficulties**, in extremis, in a jam (*informal*), in a fix (*informal*), in a tight spot, up the creek (*informal*), in trouble, in the soup (*informal*), in a spot of bother (*informal*), in hot water. [➡IN TROUBLE AND DISADVANTAGED; 73]

in disarray *adj* **confused**, in a mess, shambolic (*informal*), chaotic, in pieces, in a jumble, in a muddle, untidy, disorganized, all over the place (*informal*), disordered. [➡DISORDER AND CHAOS; 246] *Opposite:* orderly.

in disbelief *adj* **incredulous**, disbelieving, unbelieving, shocked, dumbfounded, gobsmacked (*slang*). [➡SURPRISE, SHOCK, AND AMAZEMENT; 546]

indiscernibility *n* [➡IMPERCEPTIBLE; 26]

indiscernible *adj* **imperceptible**, invisible, inaudible, unnoticeable, unfathomable, undetectable, impalpable (*formal*). [➡IMPERCEPTIBLE; 26] *Opposite:* perceptible.

indiscipline *n* **disorderliness**, rowdiness, unruliness, insubordination, disruptiveness. [➡REBELLIOUSNESS AND DISOBEDIENCE; 566] *Opposite:* control.

indiscreet 1 *adj* **careless**, injudicious, imprudent (*formal*), incautious, unthinking, reckless, rash. [➡NEGATIVE INTELLECTUAL CHARACTERISTICS; 526] *Opposite:* careful. 2 *adj* **tactless**, undiplomatic, unsubtle, garrulous, indelicate. [➡BAD MANNERS AND SOCIAL SKILLS; 522] *Opposite:* tactful.

indiscretion 1 *n* **carelessness**, injudiciousness, imprudence, lack of caution, recklessness, rashness, incaution, thoughtlessness, unthinkingness. [➡NEGATIVE INTELLECTUAL CHARACTERISTICS; 526] *Opposite:* carefulness. 2 *n* **tactlessness**, garrulousness, indelicateness, nosiness (*informal*). [➡NOSY AND INTERFERING; 513] 3 *n* **transgression**, impropriety, peccadillo, misdemeanour, misdeed (*formal*), lapse, folly, blunder, faux pas (*literary*), gaffe, slip, clanger (*informal*), boob (*informal*). [➡BAD BEHAVIOUR OR ACTION; 255]

indiscriminate 1 *adj* **unselective**, undiscriminating, undiscerning, undifferentiating, uncritical, catholic. [➡NEGATIVE INTELLECTUAL CHARACTERISTICS; 526] *Opposite:* selective. 2 *adj* **haphazard**, random, arbitrary, wholesale, blanket, unsystematic. [➡DISORDER AND CHAOS; 246] *Opposite:* planned.

in disgrace *adj* [➡IN TROUBLE AND DISADVANTAGED; 73]

indispensable *adj* **necessary**, essential, crucial, vital, required, obligatory, imperative, key. [➡NECESSARY AND ESSENTIAL; 197] *Opposite:* unnecessary.

See Compare and Contrast at **necessary.**

indispensably *adv* **necessarily**, essentially, crucially, vitally, imperatively, obligatorily. [➡IMPORTANT; 195] *Opposite:* unnecessarily.

indisposed (*formal*) 1 *adj* **sick**, unwell, ill, poorly (*informal*), laid up, under the weather. [➡ILL AND SICK; 741] *Opposite:* well. 2 *adj* **unwilling**, disinclined, reluctant, loath, loth. [➡UNWILLINGNESS AND STUBBORNNESS; 565] *Opposite:* willing.

indisposition 1 *n* **illness**, complaint, condition, problem, debility, sickness. [➡ILL AND SICK; 741] *Opposite:* health. 2 *n* **reluctance**, unwillingness, disinclination, refusal, resistance. [➡UNWILLINGNESS AND STUBBORNNESS; 565] *Opposite:* willingness.

indisputability *n* [➡CERTAIN; 175]

indisputable *adj* **indubitable** (*formal*), unquestionable, undeniable, beyond doubt, incontrovertible, irrefutable, certain, unarguable, incontestable. [➡CERTAIN; 175] *Opposite:* debatable.

indissoluble *adj* **binding**, unbreakable, enduring, everlasting, eternal, permanent. [➡PERMANENCE: WITHOUT END; 94] *Opposite:* temporary.

indistinct 1 *adj* **unclear**, blurry, hazy, dim, misty, inaudible, inarticulate, slurred, faint, muffled, low, mumbled, soft. [➡VAGUENESS; 244] *Opposite:* clear. 2 *adj* **vague**, imprecise, indistinguishable, indefinite, unintelligible. [➡IMPERCEPTIBLE; 26] *Opposite:* definite.

indistinctive *adj* **ordinary**, dull, everyday, unexceptional, unmemorable, undistinguished, unidentified, unspecified. [➡BORING AND UNINTERESTING; 235] *Opposite:* unique.

indistinctness 1 *n* **unclearness**, inarticulacy, faintness, softness. [➡VAGUENESS; 244] *Opposite:* clarity. 2 *n* **blurriness**, haziness, fuzziness, mistiness, dimness, faintness, imprecision, indefiniteness, inaudibility, unintelligibility. [➡IMPERCEPTIBLE; 26] *Opposite:* clarity.

indistinguishable 1 *adj* **undifferentiated**, homogeneous, identical, the same, interchangeable, like two peas in a pod. [➡SAMENESS; 151] *Opposite:* separable. 2 *adj* **vague**, blurry, hazy, fuzzy, misty, dim, faint. [➡VAGUENESS; 244] *Opposite:* clear. 3 *adj* **inaudible**, inarticulate, unintelligible, faint, soft, low. [➡IMPERCEPTIBLE; 26] *Opposite:* clear.

indistinguishably *adv* [➡IMPERCEPTIBLE; 26]

in distress *adj* [➡SADNESS, DISTRESS, AND DESPAIR; 540]

individual 1 *n* **person**, human being, entity, character, personality, personage (*formal*), being, creature, party. [➡PERSON; 931] 2 *adj* **separable**, singular, separate, discrete, distinct, single, specific, different. [➡UNRELATEDNESS AND SEPARATENESS; 147] 3 *adj* **particularized**, special, private, exclusive, particular, specific, personal. [➡BELONGING OR RELATING TO INDIVIDUALS; 944] *Opposite:* collective. 4 *adj* **unusual**, distinctive, original, idiosyncratic, individualistic, characteristic, peculiar, unique, singular, personal. [➡EXTRAORDINARY: UNCOMMON; 206] *Opposite:* ordinary.

individualism *n* **uniqueness**, egoism, individuality, independence, selfishness, distinctiveness, eccentricity. [➡POSITIVE INTELLECTUAL CHARACTERISTICS; 525] *Opposite:* conformity.

individualist *n* **free spirit**, nonconformist, eccentric, rebel, maverick, loner. [➡SOLITARY PEOPLE; 942] *Opposite:* conformist.

individuality *n* **independence**, uniqueness, eccentricity, personality, distinctiveness, originality, individualism. [➡UNRELATEDNESS AND SEPARATENESS; 147] *Opposite:* conformity.

individualize *v* **adapt**, modify, customize, personalize, convert, change, tailor, adjust. [➡CHANGE; 373]

individually *adv* **separately**, independently, alone, on your own, by yourself, in isolation, exclusively, discretely. [➡ACTING INDEPENDENTLY; 285] *Opposite:* together.

indivisible *adj* **inseparable**, undividable, united, amalgamated, blended, conjoined (*formal*). [➡RELATED; 143] *Opposite:* separable.

indoctrinate *v* **instruct**, programme, train, teach, coach, brainwash, proselytize, propagandize, inculcate. [➡INSTRUCT AND TEACH; 610]

indoctrination *n* **instruction**, programming, propaganda, brainwashing, training, teaching, coaching, proselytization. [➡EDUCATORS; 840]

indolence *n* **laziness**, idleness, lethargy, sloth,

inactivity, torpor, lassitude, apathy, sluggishness. [➡LIFELESS, LAZY, AND UNENTHUSIASTIC; 507] *Opposite:* energy.

indolent *adj* **lazy**, laid-back (*informal*), lethargic, idle, sluggish, slothful (*formal*), apathetic, torpid, lax, languid. [➡LIFELESS, LAZY, AND UNENTHUSIASTIC; 507] *Opposite:* energetic.

indomitability *n* [➡STRENGTH OF WILL; 502]

indomitable *adj* **unconquerable**, strong, resolute, determined, stubborn, tough, spirited, doughty (*literary*), invincible, steadfast, staunch. [➡STRENGTH OF WILL; 502] *Opposite:* submissive.

indoor *adj* **inside**, interior, covered, enclosed, internal. [➡GENERAL LOCATIONS; 159] *Opposite:* outdoor.

indoors *adv* **inside**, in, within, at home, in the house. [➡GENERAL LOCATIONS; 159] *Opposite:* outside.

in doubt *adj* **open to question**, in question, undecided, doubtful, dubious, unresolved, insecure, at risk, uncertain. [➡UNCERTAIN; 176] *Opposite:* assured.

indubitable (*formal*) *adj* **unquestionable**, definite, certain, positive, sure-fire (*informal*), concrete, undoubted, undeniable, conclusive, irrefutable. [➡CERTAIN; 175] *Opposite:* questionable.

induce 1 *v* **persuade**, encourage, tempt, make, bring, talk into, prevail upon, convince, prompt. [➡CAUSE OR COMPEL TO ACT; 272] *Opposite:* dissuade. 2 *v* **bring on**, bring about, provoke, stimulate, produce, cause, generate, engender. [➡CAUSE TO HAPPEN; 31] *Opposite:* deter.

inducement *n* **stimulus**, incentive, encouragement, carrot, enticement, bribe, lure, bait. [➡BRIBES; 441] *Opposite:* disincentive.

See Compare and Contrast at **motive**.

induct 1 *v* **inaugurate**, invest (*formal*), swear in, initiate, welcome, receive, instate, install. [➡CONFER STATUS; 459] 2 *v* **introduce**, initiate, train, instruct, educate, acquaint. [➡INSTRUCT AND TEACH; 610]

induction 1 *n* **bringing on**, stimulation, generation, production, provocation, initiation, bringing about, setting off. [➡BEGINNING; 53] 2 *n* **inauguration**, instalment, investiture, reception, swearing in. [➡CEREMONIES AND ANNIVERSARIES; 38] 3 *n* **introduction**, initiation, training, instruction, orientation, education. [➡TEACHING; 839]

in due course *adv* **afterwards**, eventually, in good time, ultimately, in the end, sooner or later, finally, in a while, later. [➡FUTURE; 86]

indulge *v* **treat**, spoil, pamper, pander, cosset, make a fuss of, coddle, humour. [➡TAKE CARE OF AND SPOIL; 301] *Opposite:* deny.

indulgence 1 *n* **treat**, luxury, extravagance, pleasure. [➡AMAZING THING; 212] *Opposite:* necessity. 2 *n* **tolerance**, lenience, understanding, clemency, sympathy, pardon, absolution, forbearance (*formal*), leniency. [➡KIND ACTION OR BEHAVIOUR; 296] *Opposite:* strictness.

indulgent *adj* **permissive**, kind, lenient, tolerant, generous, nonjudgmental, easygoing, understanding, forbearing (*formal*). [➡GENEROSITY AND KINDNESS; 496] *Opposite:* strict.

industrial 1 *adj* **manufacturing**, engineering, trade, business, work. [➡BUSINESS; 792] 2 *adj* **developed**, built-up, industrialized, mechanized, manufacturing, modern. [➡DESCRIBING TECHNOLOGY; 1159]

industrial action *n* **strike**, stoppage, work-to-rule, go-slow, general strike, wildcat strike, lightning strike, job action (*US*), slowdown (*US*). [➡WORK-RELATED ACTIVITIES; 834]

industrial espionage *n* **espionage**, spying, intelligence gathering, surveillance, bugging, phone tapping. [➡BUSINESS ACTIVITIES AND PHENOMENA; 795]

industrial estate 1 *n* **trading estate**, science park, enterprise zone, industrial zone, industrial development, business park, development, industrial park (*US*). [➡URBAN OUTDOOR SPACES; 1071] 2 *type of* **industrial site**. [➡INDUSTRIAL BUILDINGS; 1086]

industrialist *n* **manufacturer**, entrepreneur, businessperson, factory owner, capitalist, owner, mogul. [➡BUSINESS PEOPLE; 794]

industrialization *n* **industrial development**, economic development, development, economic growth, progress, social change, mechanization, mass production, automation. [➡SOCIAL, POLITICAL, AND ECONOMIC CHANGE; 374]

industrialize *v* **change**, mechanize, develop, mass-produce, automate. [➡SOCIAL, POLITICAL, AND ECONOMIC CHANGE; 374]

industrialized *adj* **industrial**, developed, technologically advanced, manufacturing, commercial. [➡STYLES AND SYSTEMS OF GOVERNMENT; 806] *Opposite:* agrarian.

industrial park (*US*) *n* **trading estate**, science park, enterprise zone, industrial zone, industrial development, business park, development, industrial estate. [➡INDUSTRIAL BUILDINGS; 1086]

industrial site

◆ *types of industrial site*
abattoir, business park, coalfield, colliery, depot, dock, dockyard, enterprise zone, garage, gasworks, industrial estate, industrial park, industrial zone, lab (*informal*), laboratory, mine, nuclear power plant (*US*), nuclear power station, nuclear reprocessing plant, office block, oil rig, pit, pithead, power plant, power station, quarry, refinery, rig, shipyard, slaughterhouse, tannery, winery (*US*)

industrial tribunal *n* **tribunal**, hearing, court, law court, magistrates' court, high court. [➡TRIAL, PUNISHMENT, AND LEGAL OUTCOMES; 819]

industrial zone *type of* **industrial site**. [➡INDUSTRIAL BUILDINGS; 1086]

industrious *adj* **diligent**, hard-working, busy, productive, conscientious, active, assiduous, energetic, bustling. [➡HARD-WORKING AND COMMITTED; 501] *Opposite:* indolent.

industriousness *n* **diligence**, hard work, industry (*formal or literary*), application, conscientiousness, productiveness, energy. [➡HARD-WORKING AND COMMITTED; 501] *Opposite:* indolence.

industry 1 *n* **manufacturing**, business, commerce, trade, engineering, production. [➡BUSINESS; 792] 2 *n* (*formal or literary*) **hard work**, diligence, productiveness, conscientiousness, activity, industriousness. [➡HARD WORK OR EFFORT; 299] *Opposite:* indolence.

in earnest *adv* **genuinely**, seriously, sincerely, earnestly, for real, passionately, intensely, wholeheartedly. [➡APPRECIATION AND GRATITUDE; 536] *Opposite:* jokingly.

in easy reach *adv* [➡CLOSENESS; 160]

inebriated (*formal*) *adj* **drunk**, intoxicated (*formal*), plastered (*informal*), smashed (*informal*), under the influence (*informal*), bombed (*slang*), stewed (*slang*), tanked (*slang*), tanked-up (*slang*), sloshed (*slang*), soused (*slang*), liquored up (*US informal*), loaded (*US slang*), crocked (*US slang*). [➡UNDER THE INFLUENCE OF DRUGS OR ALCOHOL; 742] *Opposite:* sober.

inebriation *n* [➡UNDER THE INFLUENCE OF DRUGS OR ALCOHOL; 742]

inedible *adj* **uneatable**, indigestible, unpalatable, revolting, bad, tough as old boots, disgusting, poisonous, unfit for human consumption, noxious. [➡FOOD; 1166] *Opposite:* edible.

ineffable (*formal*) *adj* **indescribable**, inexpressible, unutterable, beyond words, overwhelming, deep, unspeakable, indefinable. [➡EXTRAORDINARY: AMAZING; 205]

in effect *adv* **basically**, essentially, in fact, effectively, to all intents and purposes, really, actually. [➡TRUE AND REAL; 172]

ineffective *adj* **unsuccessful**, unproductive, useless, vain, futile, hopeless, fruitless, ineffectual, abortive, feeble. [➡REDUNDANT AND USELESS; 241] *Opposite:* successful.

ineffectiveness *n* **unsuccessfulness**, unproductiveness, uselessness, futility, hopelessness, vanity, feebleness. [➡REDUNDANT AND USELESS; 241] *Opposite:* success.

ineffectual *adj* **incompetent**, indecisive, weak, feeble, unimpressive, unsuccessful, useless, hopeless, inadequate, inefficient, inept, fruitless. [➡NEGATIVE INTELLECTUAL CHARACTERISTICS; 526] *Opposite:* competent.

ineffectuality *n* **incompetence**, indecisiveness, futility, fruitlessness, inadequacy, uselessness, feebleness, hopelessness, inefficiency, ineptness. [➡NEGATIVE INTELLECTUAL CHARACTERISTICS; 526] *Opposite:* competence.

ineffectualness *n* [➡NEGATIVE INTELLECTUAL CHARACTERISTICS; 526]

inefficiency *n* **disorganization**, incompetence, inadequacy, wastefulness, ineptitude, ineffectiveness, uselessness. [➡WASTEFUL AND UNECONOMICAL; 247] *Opposite:* competence.

inefficient *adj* **disorganized**, unproductive, wasteful, inept, bungling (*informal*), useless, uneconomical, incompetent, ineffective. [➡WASTEFUL AND UNECONOMICAL; 247] *Opposite:* competent.

inelastic *adj* **inflexible**, rigid, unbendable, stiff, unyielding, hard, brittle. [➡RIGID AND HARD; 1210] *Opposite:* stretchy.

inelegance 1 *n* **unstylishness**, unsophistication, tastelessness, bad taste, vulgarity. [➡IN POOR TASTE; 230] *Opposite:* stylishness. 2 *n* **clumsiness**, awkwardness, gracelessness, coarseness, roughness, gawkiness (*informal*), uncouthness. [➡BADLY GROOMED; 484] *Opposite:* grace.

inelegant 1 *adj* **unstylish**, unsophisticated, tasteless, vulgar, unpolished. [➡IN POOR TASTE; 230] *Opposite:* stylish. 2 *adj* **clumsy**, awkward, gawky (*informal*), ungainly, maladroit (*formal*), graceless, splay, uncouth. [➡AGILITY OF THE BODY; 477] *Opposite:* graceful.

inelegantly 1 *adv* **unstylishly**, unsophisticatedly, tastelessly, in bad taste, vulgarly. [➡IN POOR TASTE; 230] *Opposite:* stylishly. 2 *adv* **clumsily**, awkwardly, gracelessly, gawkily (*informal*), maladroitly (*formal*), uncouthly. [➡BADLY GROOMED; 484] *Opposite:* gracefully.

ineligible *adj* **unentitled**, unqualified, disqualified, barred, disallowed, unable, not qualified, banned. [➡UNPOPULAR AND UNWANTED; 259] *Opposite:* entitled.

ineluctable (*literary*) *adj* **unavoidable**, inescapable, inexorable (*formal*), inevitable, unpreventable, certain, sure. [➡CERTAIN; 175] *Opposite:* avoidable.

in employment *adj* [➡EMPLOYMENT STATUS; 831]

inept *adj* **incompetent**, inexpert, clumsy, ham-fisted (*informal*), maladroit (*formal*), useless, hopeless, unskilled, bungling (*informal*), heavy-handed, ham-handed (*informal*). [➡UNSKILLED; 530] *Opposite:* competent.

ineptitude *n* **incompetence**, ineptness, clumsiness, uselessness, ineffectiveness, lack of ability, lack of skill, maladroitness (*formal*). [➡UNSKILLED; 530] *Opposite:* competence.

ineptness *n* **incompetence**, clumsiness, uselessness, ineffectiveness, lack of ability, lack of skill, maladroitness (*formal*), ineptitude. [➡UNSKILLED; 530] *Opposite:* competence.

inequality *n* **disparity**, dissimilarity, variation, difference, discrimination, inequity, disproportion, imbalance, unfairness. [➡DIFFERENCE; 150] *Opposite:* parity.

inequitable *adj* **unfair**, unjust, unbalanced, undemocratic, unequal, discriminatory, prejudiced, biased. [➡MORALLY BAD; 776] *Opposite:* fair.

inequity (*formal*) *n* **unfairness**, injustice, discrimination, inequality, bias, disproportion, imbalance. [➡MORALLY BAD; 776] *Opposite:* fairness.

ineradicable *adj* **indelible**, enduring, ineffaceable (*formal*), lasting, ingrained, stubborn, deep-seated, unforgettable, deep-rooted, permanent. [➡PERMANENCE: WITHOUT END; 94] *Opposite:* fleeting.

inert 1 *adj* **motionless**, still, lifeless, immobile, unmoving, static. [➡LACK OF ACTIVITY; 343] *Opposite:* moving. 2 *adj* **sluggish**, unmotivated, slow, inactive, passive, torpid, indolent, lethargic, phlegmatic, stolid, unwilling. [➡MOVING SLOWLY; 105] *Opposite:* active.

inert gas *type of* **gas**. [➡GASES; 1274]

inertia *n* **apathy**, inactivity, torpor, lethargy, disinterest, inaction, indolence, sluggishness, unwillingness. [➡LACK OF ACTIVITY; 343] *Opposite:* activity.

inescapable *adj* **inevitable**, unavoidable, bound to happen, certain, unpreventable, inexorable (*formal*), patent, manifest, obvious. [➡CERTAIN; 175] *Opposite:* avoidable.

in essence *adv* **fundamentally**, intrinsically, basically, essentially, at heart, inherently, quintessentially, in reality, in effect, really, to all intents and purposes. [➡MAINLY AND PRIMARILY; 138]

inessential *adj* **unnecessary**, unneeded, superfluous, redundant, dispensable, extra, surplus. [➡UNIMPORTANT AND UNNECESSARY; 239] *Opposite:* necessary.

inestimable *adj* **incalculable**, immeasurable, great, fathomless, enormous, invaluable, infinite, tremendous. [➡LARGE; 1192] *Opposite:* measurable.

inestimably *adv* **incalculably**, immeasurably, enormously, immensely, tremendously, infinitely. [➡TO A GREAT EXTENT; 130] *Opposite:* measurably.

in evidence *adj* [➡PRESENT AND AVAILABLE; 11]

inevitability *n* **unavoidability**, predictability, certainty, inexorableness (*formal*), inescapability, irrevocability. [➡CERTAIN; 175]

inevitable *adj* **unavoidable**, predictable, expected, foreseeable, to be expected, to be anticipated, certain, inescapable, inexorable (*formal*), preordained. [➡CERTAIN; 175] *Opposite:* avoidable.

inevitably *adv* **unavoidably**, inexorably (*formal*), inescapably, without doubt, certainly, predictably, unsurprisingly. [➡AUTOMATIC AND INSTINCTIVE; 281]

inexact *adj* **imprecise**, inaccurate, vague, rough, approximate, indefinite, indistinct. [➡APPROXIMATELY; 133] *Opposite:* precise.

inexactness *n* **imprecision**, vagueness, uncertainty, roughness, approximation, inaccuracy, indefiniteness. [➡VAGUENESS; 244] *Opposite:* precision.

in excess of *prep* **more than**, beyond, above, over and above, exceeding, greater than. [➡MORE AND EXCESS; 122] *Opposite:* below.

inexcusable *adj* **unpardonable**, unforgivable, uncalled-for, intolerable, indefensible, unjustifiable, unwarrantable, rude, impolite. [➡UNACCEPTABLE AND UNFORGIVEABLE; 226] *Opposite:* excusable.

inexhaustible *adj* **everlasting**, infinite, unlimited, never-ending, bottomless, endless, limitless, vast, boundless. [➡MANY, MUCH, LARGE AMOUNT; 117] *Opposite:* limited.

in existence *adj* [➡PRESENT AND AVAILABLE; 11]

inexorability (*formal*) *n* **inevitability**, unavoidability, inescapability, relentlessness, certainty, inexorableness (*formal*), obdurateness, inflexibility. [➡CERTAIN; 175]

inexorable 1 *adj* (*formal*) **unstoppable**, inevitable, unavoidable, inescapable, unchangeable, relentless, inflexible. [➡PERMANENCE: WITHOUT CHANGE; 95] 2 *adj* **adamant**, obstinate, obdurate, unyielding, unbending, unwavering, immovable, stubborn. [➡UNWILLINGNESS AND STUBBORNNESS; 565]

inexorableness (*formal*) *n* **unavoidability**, inescapability, relentlessness, inevitability, certainty, inexorability (*formal*), obdurateness, inflexibility. [➡CERTAIN; 175]

inexorably (*formal*) *adv* **inevitably**, inescapably, relentlessly, unavoidably, unalterably, adamantly, unstoppably, obdurately. [➡PERMANENCE: WITHOUT CHANGE; 95]

inexpedient 1 *adj* **inconvenient**, impractical, inopportune, untimely, ill-timed. [➡PROMPTNESS: BADLY TIMED; 101] *Opposite:* convenient. 2 *adj* (*formal*) **inadvisable**, inappropriate, unwise, unsuitable, injudicious, ill-judged, imprudent (*formal*). [➡INAPPROPRIATE AND UNSUITABLE; 225] *Opposite:* advisable.

inexpensive *adj* **cheap**, low-cost, low-priced, economical, budget, reasonable, cheapo (*informal*). [➡CHEAP AND INEXPENSIVE; 222] *Opposite:* costly.

inexperience *n* **greenness**, rawness, innocence, immaturity, naivety, ingenuousness, unsophistication, amateurishness. [➡UNSKILLED; 530] *Opposite:* experience.

inexperienced *adj* **green**, inexpert, raw, new, innocent, untried, untested, unproven, unsophisticated, amateurish, naive. [➡UNSKILLED; 530] *Opposite:* seasoned.

inexpert *adj* **unskilled**, clumsy, inept, inexperienced, untrained, unprofessional, ham-fisted (*informal*), awkward, bungling (*informal*), amateurish, ham-handed (*informal*). [➡UNSKILLED; 530] *Opposite:* skilled.

inexplicable *adj* **unaccountable**, mysterious, incomprehensible, unfathomable, bizarre, curious, strange, perplexing, mystifying, puzzling, baffling, enigmatic. [➡BIZARRE AND PECULIAR; 258] *Opposite:* explicable.

inexplicit *adj* **imprecise**, vague, ambiguous, hazy, sketchy, indistinct, impressionistic, fuzzy, indefinite. [➡VAGUENESS; 244] *Opposite:* precise.

inexpressible *adj* **indescribable**, ineffable (*formal*), beyond words, overwhelming, deep, indefinable, unutterable, unspeakable. [➡EXTRAORDINARY: AMAZING; 205]

inexpressive *adj* **emotionless**, impassive, soulless, deadpan, unemotional, expressionless, blank, wooden, flat, bland. [➡UNINTERESTED AND DETACHED; 630] *Opposite:* animated.

inextinguishable *adj* [➡PERMANENCE: WITHOUT END; 94]

in extremis *adj* **critical**, dire, near-death, dying, at death's door, moribund. [➡DEAD AND DYING; 925] *Opposite:* alive and kicking (*informal*).

inextricable *adj* **complicated**, complex, tricky, involved, knotty, tangled, indissoluble, inseparable, indivisible. [➡DIFFICULTY AND COMPLEXITY; 243] *Opposite:* simple.

inextricably *adv* **indissolubly**, inseparably, indistinguishably, intimately, indivisibly, intricately. [➡RECIPROCITY AND INTERDEPENDENCE; 148]

in fact 1 *adv* **actually**, in actual fact, in effect, in reality, really, in truth, indeed. [➡WORDS AND PHRASES EMPHASIZING THE TRUTH OF A MATTER; 173] 2 *adv* **truthfully**, actually, in effect, in reality, really, as a matter of fact, in point of fact. [➡TRUE AND REAL; 172]

infallibility 1 *n* **perfection**, rightness, flawlessness, correctness, exactitude, accuracy. [➡CORRECT; 183] *Opposite:* inaccuracy. 2 *n* **dependability**, soundness, reliability, trustworthiness, steadiness, solidity, sureness. [➡CERTAIN; 175] *Opposite:* fallibility.

infallible 1 *adj* **perfect**, right, flawless, correct, exact, accurate, faultless, unerring, unfailing. [➡CORRECT; 183] *Opposite:* imperfect. 2 *adj* **dependable**, unfailing, foolproof, watertight, reliable, sound, fail-safe, sure-fire (*informal*), trustworthy, steady, solid, sure, certain. [➡CERTAIN; 175] *Opposite:* unreliable.

infallibly *adv* **dependably**, unfailingly, without fail, reliably, always, perfectly, unerringly, faultlessly. [➡CERTAIN; 175] *Opposite:* unreliably.

infamous 1 *adj* **notorious**, disreputable, ill-famed, ill-reputed, dishonourable, scandalous, shameful. [➡KNOWN AND FAMOUS; 182] *Opposite:* reputable. 2 *adj* **abominable**, villainous, wicked, iniquitous, loathsome, outrageous, evil, shameful, nefarious, ignoble, heinous. [➡MORALLY BAD; 776] *Opposite:* illustrious.

infamy 1 *n* **notoriety**, ill repute, ill fame, shame, disrepute, ignominy, dishonour. [➡KNOWN AND FAMOUS; 182] *Opposite:* repute (*formal*). 2 *n* **disgrace**, scandal, outrage, abomination, atrocity, villainy. [➡BAD BEHAVIOUR OR ACTION; 255] *Opposite:* good deed.

infancy 1 *n* **babyhood**, childhood, early years, youth, immaturity, early life, formative years. [➡BABYHOOD, CHILDHOOD, AND ADOLESCENCE; 917] *Opposite:* adulthood. 2 *n* **beginning**, early stages, embryonic stage, initial stages, first phase, start. [➡BEGINNING; 53] *Opposite:* conclusion.

infant *n* **baby**, child, newborn, babe in arms, toddler, tot (*informal*), kid (*informal*), nursling, suckling, preschooler (*US*). [➡CHILD OR YOUTH; 945] *Opposite:* adult.

infantile 1 *adj* **childish**, babyish, immature, puerile, juvenile, silly. [➡BAD MANNERS AND SOCIAL SKILLS; 522] *Opposite:* mature. 2 *adj* **childhood**, juvenile, infant, baby, youthful. [➡BABYHOOD, CHILDHOOD, AND ADOLESCENCE; 917] *Opposite:* adult.

infantry *n* [➡THE ARMED FORCES; 827]

infant school *type of* **school**. [➡EDUCATIONAL INSTITUTIONS; 813]

infatuated *adj* **in love**, lovesick, obsessed, besotted, crazy (*informal*), smitten (*humorous or literary*), captivated, enamoured, enchanted, enraptured (*formal*). [➡APPRECIATION AND GRATITUDE; 536] *Opposite:* disenchanted.

infatuation *n* **passion**, obsession, craze, love, fascination, crush (*informal*), fixation, rapture, enchantment. [➡LOVE, RESPECT, AND GOODWILL; 550] *Opposite:* disenchantment.

See Compare and Contrast at **love**.

in favour *adj* [➡APPRECIATION AND GRATITUDE; 536]

in favour of *prep* **for**, all for, supporting, on the side of, supportive of, in support of, pro, with, rooting for. [➡LIKE, LOVE, VALUE, AND ENJOY; 579] *Opposite:* against.

infect 1 *v* **contaminate**, pollute, taint, poison, blight, dirty. [➡DIRTY AND CONTAMINATE; 405] *Opposite:* cleanse. 2 *v* **pervert**, corrupt, defile (*formal*), deprave, debase, debauch (*formal*). [➡WOUND A PERSON OR ANIMAL; 384] *Opposite:* redeem. 3 *v* **influence**, affect, afflict, touch, inspire, move, overwhelm, enthuse. [➡APPEAL TO AND AROUSE INTEREST; 576]

infected 1 *adj* **contaminated**, polluted, tainted, poisoned, impure, diseased, dirty, blighted. [➡DECAYING OR INFESTED; 1235] *Opposite:* pure. 2 *adj* **ill**, diseased, sick, infested, disease-ridden, plague-ridden. [➡ILL AND SICK; 741] *Opposite:* healthy. 3 *adj* **septic**, festering, weeping, pussy, pus-filled, purulent, suppurating. [➡DECAYING OR INFESTED; 1235] *Opposite:* healthy. 4 *adj* **affected**, influenced, touched, inspired, moved, overwhelmed, enthused. [➡PLEASURE, EXCITEMENT, AND ELATION; 535] *Opposite:* untouched.

infection 1 *n* **contagion**, contamination, pollution, taint, poison, impurity, dirt, septicity, toxicity. [➡DIRTY AND CONTAMINATE; 405] 2 *n* **disease**, illness, virus, pestilence (*archaic*), blight, bug (*informal*). [➡ILLNESSES AND DISORDERS; 733] 3 *n* **corruption**, perversion (*disapproving*), defilement (*formal*), depravity, debasement, debauchery. [➡MORALLY BAD; 776]

infectious 1 *adj* **communicable**, catching, transferable, transmittable, transmissible, contagious, infective, virulent, catchable. [➡SICKNESS; 730] 2 *adj* **irresistible**, compelling, catching, contagious. [➡STRENGTH; 202]

infective *adj* **infectious**, communicable, catching, transferable, transmittable, transmissible, virulent, catchable, contagious. [➡SICKNESS; 730]

infer 1 *v* **conclude**, deduce, suppose, gather, understand, conjecture, surmise, assume, extrapolate, reckon, reason, judge, work out, figure out. [➡SOLVE AND INTERPRET; 761] *Opposite:* guess. 2 *v* **imply**, suggest, insinuate, hint. [➡SUGGEST, HINT, AND COMMENT; 613]

See Compare and Contrast at **deduce**.

inference 1 *n* **conclusion**, deduction, supposition, conjecture, presumption, assumption, reasoning, reckoning, judgement. [➡UNDERSTAND AND GRASP; 760] *Opposite:* guess. 2 *n* **implication**, extrapolation, corollary, interpretation, reading, insinuation. [➡SUGGEST, HINT, AND COMMENT; 613]

inferior 1 *adj* **lower**, junior, secondary, subordinate, subsidiary, minor, subservient. [➡RELATIONSHIP TO ANOTHER; 973] *Opposite:* superior. 2 *adj* **mediocre**, lesser, lower, substandard, poorer, low-grade, second-rate, not up to snuff (*informal*). [➡INFERIORITY; 154] *Opposite:* superior. 3 *n* **junior**, subordinate, underling, menial (*formal*), vassal, minion (*archaic or literary*). [➡SUBORDINATES AND ASSISTANTS; 966] *Opposite:* superior.

inferiority 1 *n* **lowliness**, humbleness, subordination, subservience, subsidiarity, dependency. [➡INFERIORITY; 154] *Opposite:* superiority. 2 *n* **mediocrity**, weakness, inadequacy, shoddiness, meanness, poor quality. [➡FAULTS, FLAWS, AND WEAKNESSES; 252] *Opposite:* superiority.

inferiority complex *n* **inadequacy**, anxiety, phobia, depression, obsession, fixation, neurosis (*dated*). [➡PSYCHOLOGY AND THE MIND; 770]

inferno 1 *n* **conflagration**, blaze, fire, firestorm, flames, oven, furnace. [➡FIRE, FLAMMABILITY, AND BURNING; 1164] **2** *n* **hellhole**, hell, Hades (*informal*), underworld, perdition, fire and brimstone. [➡RELIGIOUS CONCEPTS; 777] *Opposite:* heaven.

See Compare and Contrast at **fire**.

infertile *adj* **sterile**, unproductive, barren, unfruitful, childless, arid, bare. [➡REPRODUCTION AND HEREDITY; 726] *Opposite:* fertile.

infertility *n* **sterility**, barrenness, poverty, childlessness, aridity, unproductiveness, unfruitfulness. [➡REPRODUCTION AND HEREDITY; 726] *Opposite:* fertility.

infest *v* **overrun**, fill, invade, crowd, infiltrate, pervade, permeate, infect, plague, overwhelm, riddle. [➡PROSPER AND ABOUND; 16]

infestation *n* **plague**, invasion, swarm, influx, infiltration, incursion. [➡ARRIVAL; 13]

infested *adj* [➡DECAYING OR INFESTED; 1235]

infidelity *n* **unfaithfulness**, faithlessness, disloyalty, betrayal, adultery, cheating, perfidy (*literary*). [➡MORALLY BAD; 776] *Opposite:* faithfulness.

infighting *n* **internal strife**, backbiting, squabbling, bickering, wrangling, power struggle. [➡ARGUMENT; 47]

infiltrate *v* **penetrate**, permeate, gain access to, break into, creep into, subvert, intrude, insinuate. [➡MOVE PAST, INTO, OR THROUGH SOMETHING; 332]

infiltration *n* **penetration**, permeation, access, intrusion, insinuation, subversion. [➡GOVERNMENT POLICIES; 810]

infiltrator *n* **mole**, plant (*informal*), spy, secret agent, double agent, subversive, undercover agent. [➡INTERFERING PEOPLE AND TELLTALES; 950]

in fine fettle *adj* [➡FIT AND STRONG; 737]

infinite **1** *adj* **immeasurable**, never-ending, endless, countless, unbounded, boundless, vast, inestimable, unlimited, interminable, limitless. [➡PERMANENCE: WITHOUT END; 94] *Opposite:* limited. **2** *adj* **extreme**, stupendous, great, immense, large, huge, tremendous, vast. [➡LARGE; 1192] *Opposite:* slight.

infinitely *adv* **extremely**, enormously, markedly, a great deal, substantially, noticeably, by a long way, by a long chalk, interminably. [➡TO A GREAT EXTENT; 130] *Opposite:* slightly.

infinitesimal *adj* **tiny**, minute, minuscule, microscopic, insignificant, teeny (*informal*), inconsiderable, diminutive, indiscernible. [➡SMALL; 1194] *Opposite:* huge.

infinitive *type of* **grammatical term**. [➡ASPECTS OF LANGUAGE; 683]

infinitude *n* [➡PERMANENCE: WITHOUT END; 94]

infinity *n* **eternity**, immensity, endlessness, infinitude, boundlessness, limitlessness, perpetuity. [➡PERMANENCE: WITHOUT END; 94]

infirm *adj* **unwell**, sick, ill, frail, in poor health, ailing (*dated*), weak, feeble, sickly. [➡ILL AND SICK; 741] *Opposite:* healthy.

See Compare and Contrast at **weak**.

infirmary *n* **hospital**, sanatorium, sickbay, hospice, medical centre, medical wing, nursing home. [➡HOSPITALS AND CLINICS; 826]

infirmity *n* **ill health**, illness, frailty, disability, weakness, susceptibility, ailment, malady, indisposition, frailness, sickness. [➡ILL AND SICK; 741] *Opposite:* health.

in flagrante delicto *adv* **red-handed**, committing a crime, lawbreaking, offending, violating, committing an offence. [➡HAPPENING AND IN PROGRESS; 32]

inflame **1** *v* **arouse**, anger, fan, provoke, stir up, agitate, ignite, kindle. [➡ANGER AND ANNOY; 570] *Opposite:* calm. **2** *v* **exacerbate**, aggravate, fuel, intensify, increase, worsen. [➡WORSEN SOMETHING; 381] *Opposite:* diminish.

inflamed *adj* **reddened**, swollen, irritated, tender, sore, angry. [➡ILL AND SICK; 741]

in flames *adj* **burning**, alight, aflame, raging, ablaze, on fire. [➡FIRE, FLAMMABILITY, AND BURNING; 1164]

inflammable *adj* **flammable**, combustible, ignitable, burnable, incendiary. [➡FIRE, FLAMMABILITY, AND BURNING; 1164] *Opposite:* nonflammable.

inflammation *n* **irritation**, swelling, soreness, tenderness, redness, infection. [➡ILL AND SICK; 741]

inflammatory *adj* **provocative**, seditious, rabble-rousing, fiery, stirring, inspiring, incendiary, inciting, demagogic. [➡ELOQUENT, TALKATIVE, AND LONG-WINDED; 633] *Opposite:* placatory.

inflatable *adj* **blow-up**, pump-up, expandable. [➡CHANGE OF SHAPE; 386]

inflate **1** *v* **blow up**, pump up, fill with air, expand, fill, puff up, swell, bloat. [➡CHANGE OF SIZE: BIGGER; 393] *Opposite:* deflate. **2** *v* **exaggerate**, amplify, embellish, magnify, overestimate, overstate. [➡DECEPTION AND LIES; 661] *Opposite:* understate. **3** *v* **increase**, go up, drive up, escalate, boost, raise. [➡CHANGE OF INTENSITY: MORE; 395] *Opposite:* deflate.

inflated *adj* **exaggerated**, overstated, overblown, puffed up, magnified, extravagant, overestimated, bloated, swollen. [➡BIZARRE AND PECULIAR; 258] *Opposite:* understated.

inflation *n* **price rises**, rise, increase, price increases. [➡MARKET FORCES; 803] *Opposite:* deflation.

inflationary *adj* **price-raising**, price-increasing, spiralling. [➡FINANCE AND ECONOMICS; 797]

inflect *v* **change**, modulate, vary, adjust, modify, transform. [➡CHANGE; 373]

inflection *n* **modulation**, nuance, variation, variety, shade, accent, articulation, enunciation, intonation, tone, timbre, tonality. [➡ASPECTS OF LANGUAGE; 683]

inflexibility **1** *n* **stubbornness**, obstinacy, intransigence, rigidity, rigour, dogmatism, pigheadedness. [➡UNWILLINGNESS AND STUBBORNNESS; 565] *Opposite:* tractability. **2** *n* **rigidity**, stiffness, hardness, firmness, tautness, tension, solidness. [➡RIGID AND HARD; 1210] *Opposite:* flexibility.

inflexible 1 *adj* **unbending**, stubborn, obstinate, uncompromising, strict, fixed, set in your ways, unyielding, intransigent, rigid, hidebound, obdurate, pigheaded, recalcitrant. [➡UNWILLINGNESS AND STUBBORNNESS; 565] *Opposite:* tractable. 2 *adj* **rigid**, stiff, hard, unbendable, firm, unyielding, solid, taut. [➡RIGID AND HARD; 1210] *Opposite:* bendable.

inflexibly *adv* **unbendingly**, unyieldingly, stubbornly, obstinately, intransigently, dogmatically, uncompromisingly, rigidly. [➡UNWILLINGNESS AND STUBBORNNESS; 565]

inflict *v* **impose**, exact, mete out, wreak, perpetrate, visit, lay on, bring to bear, dump on. [➡CAUSE TO HAPPEN; 31] *Opposite:* remove.

in-flight *adj* **onboard**, mid-flight, airborne, midair. [➡AIRCRAFT; 1147]

in floods *adj* [➡CRYING; 651]

in floods of tears *adj* [➡CRYING; 651]

inflow *n* **influx**, arrival, invasion, incursion, introduction, entry. [➡ARRIVAL; 13] *Opposite:* outflow.

influence 1 *n* **effect**, inspiration, impact, stimulus, encouragement, guidance. [➡PSYCHOLOGY AND THE MIND; 770] 2 *n* **power**, sway, authority, weight, control, pressure, pull (*informal*), hold. [➡MOST IMPORTANT THING; 198] 3 *v* **sway**, manipulate, persuade, induce, win over, prompt, impel. [➡CAUSE OR COMPEL TO ACT; 272] 4 *v* **affect**, motivate, inspire, shape, have an effect on, guide, change. [➡CHANGE; 373]

influential *adj* **powerful**, important, significant, persuasive, dominant, leading, prominent, effective, instrumental, forceful. [➡STRENGTH; 202] *Opposite:* ineffectual.

influenza *n* **flu**, cold, virus, infection, bug (*informal*), respiratory tract infection. [➡ILLNESSES AND DISORDERS; 733]

influx *n* **arrival**, invasion, incursion, flood, entry, inflow. [➡ARRIVAL; 13] *Opposite:* outflow.

info (*informal*) 1 *n* **information**, data, statistics, facts, figures, gen (*informal*). [➡BASIC DETAILS; 689] 2 *n* **news**, report, tidings, word, communication, intelligence, knowledge. [➡BASIC DETAILS; 689]

in focus *adj* **sharp**, focused, clear, well-defined, crystal clear, distinct. [➡CONCISE AND CLEAR; 203] *Opposite:* blurred.

infomediary *n* [➡E-COMMERCE; 1128]

infomercial 1 *n* **commercial**, ad, advertisement, promotional film, promo (*informal*). [➡ADVERTISING AND PUBLICITY; 605] 2 *type of* **broadcast**. [➡TELEVISION AND RADIO; 607]

in for *adj* **due**, heading for, in line for. [➡ABOUT TO HAPPEN; 33]

in force 1 *adj* **effective**, valid, serviceable, working, applicable, in operation, in use, operational, in effect. [➡HAPPENING AND IN PROGRESS; 32] *Opposite:* invalid. 2 *adv* **strongly**, powerfully, monumentally, forcefully, solidly, in large numbers, in strength. [➡MANY, MUCH, LARGE AMOUNT; 117] *Opposite:* feebly.

inform 1 *v* **tell**, notify, let know, update, bring up-to-date, put in the picture, enlighten, apprise (*formal*), report to, advise, tip off. [➡INFORM AND ANNOUNCE; 612] *Opposite:* keep in the dark. 2 *v* **blow the whistle on**, betray, sneak on, denounce, tell on, tattle, snitch (*slang*), squeal (*slang disapproving*), grass up (*slang*), grass (*slang*). [➡BETRAY CONFIDENCES AND GOSSIP; 619] *Opposite:* keep mum (*informal*).

informal 1 *adj* **relaxed**, casual, familiar, easy, comfortable, unceremonious, easygoing, natural. [➡LEVELS OF FORMALITY; 523] *Opposite:* ceremonious. 2 *adj* **unofficial**, off-the-record, unauthorized, unsanctioned, confidential, unconfirmed. [➡SECRET AND UNKNOWN; 180] *Opposite:* official. 3 *adj* **colloquial**, idiomatic, vernacular, everyday, familiar. [➡ASPECTS OF LANGUAGE; 683] *Opposite:* formal.

informality *n* **casualness**, familiarity, ease, unpretentiousness, lack of formality, lack of ceremony. [➡LEVELS OF FORMALITY; 523] *Opposite:* formality.

informally 1 *adv* **casually**, nonchalantly, easily, unceremoniously, offhandedly, familiarly. [➡LEVELS OF FORMALITY; 523] *Opposite:* ceremoniously. 2 *adv* **unofficially**, off the record, confidentially. [➡SECRET AND UNKNOWN; 180] *Opposite:* officially.

informant *n* **informer**, sneak, spy, mole, grass (*slang*), stool pigeon (*slang*), snitch (*slang*), squealer (*slang disapproving*), rat (*slang*). [➡INTERFERING PEOPLE AND TELLTALES; 950]

information 1 *n* **info** (*informal*), data, statistics, facts, figures, gen (*informal*), material, evidence. [➡BASIC DETAILS; 689] 2 *n* **news**, report, tidings, word, communication, intelligence, knowledge. [➡BASIC DETAILS; 689]

information processing *n* **data processing**, data handling, data manipulation, data analysis, data transmission, computer processing, computing. [➡COMPUTERS AND COMPUTING; 1126]

information retrieval *n* **data storage and retrieval**, data storage, data retrieval, data processing, computer processing. [➡COMPUTERS AND COMPUTING; 1126]

information sheet *n* **newsletter**, brochure, leaflet, bulletin, communiqué, press release, handout. [➡MANUALS AND INSTRUCTIONS; 590]

information superhighway *n* **superhighway**, worldwide computer network, electronic telecommunication, the Net (*informal*), the Internet, electronic networks, computer networks, the Web (*informal*), electronic communications, electronic communications network, the World Wide Web. [➡THE INTERNET; 1127]

information technology *n* **IT**, computing, telecommunications, computer technology, electronic technology. [➡COMPUTERS AND COMPUTING; 1126]

informative *adj* **educational**, revealing, edifying, enlightening, useful, helpful, instructive, explanatory, illuminating. [➡INTERESTING AND MEANINGFUL; 191] *Opposite:* uncommunicative.

informed *adj* **knowledgeable**, well-versed, conversant, up-to-date, educated, clued-up (*informal*), cognizant (*formal*), abreast, primed, learned. [➡KNOWLEDGE AND WISDOM; 559] *Opposite:* ignorant.

informer *n* **informant**, sneak, spy, mole, grass (*slang*), stool pigeon (*slang*), snitch (*slang*), rat (*slang*), squealer (*slang disapproving*). [➡INTERFERING PEOPLE AND TELLTALES; 950]

infotainment *type of* **broadcast.** [➡TELEVISION AND RADIO; 607]

infraction *n* **breach**, violation, infringement, contravention, transgression, flouting, lawbreaking, trespass. [➡CRIMES; 817]

infra dig (*informal*) *adj* **beneath one's dignity**, undignified, unacceptable, improper, inappropriate, unsuitable. [➡INAPPROPRIATE AND UNSUITABLE; 225] *Opposite:* appropriate.

infrastructure 1 *n* **substructure**, organization, structure, setup, arrangement, frame, groundwork, foundation, base. [➡COMMUNICATION NETWORKS; 1104] 2 *n* **public services**, communications, public transport, power supplies, water supplies, broadcasting, radio, telecommunications, road and rail networks, transportation. [➡INSTITUTIONS; 791]

infrequency *n* **rarity**, irregularity, uncommonness, paucity, scarcity, scarceness. [➡NEVER AND INFREQUENCY; 97] *Opposite:* frequency.

infrequent *adj* **rare**, uncommon, occasional, few and far between (*informal*), intermittent, sporadic, irregular, scarce, few, fitful. [➡NEVER AND INFREQUENCY; 97] *Opposite:* frequent.

infringe 1 *v* **disobey**, disregard, breach, break, violate, contravene, flout, transgress. [➡DISOBEY; 303] *Opposite:* obey. 2 *v* **encroach on**, intrude on, interfere with, impinge on (*formal*), trespass, invade, overstep. [➡PARTICIPATE; 293] *Opposite:* respect.

infringement 1 *n* **breach**, violation, contravention, transgression, flouting, infraction. [➡CRIMES; 817] *Opposite:* compliance. 2 *n* **encroachment**, intrusion, invasion, interference, trespass, incursion. [➡ARRIVAL; 13]

in front 1 *adv* **ahead**, leading, in the lead, before, further on, at the front. [➡GENERAL LOCATIONS; 159] *Opposite:* behind. 2 *adv* **in the lead**, ahead, winning, beating, leading, up on, defeating, outplaying, outrunning, outpacing. [➡SUCCESSFUL AND PROMISING; 81] *Opposite:* losing.

in front of 1 *prep* **before**, ahead of, facing, opposite. [➡RELATIVE LOCATION; 162] *Opposite:* behind. 2 *prep* **in the presence of**, with, in the company of, before, watched by. [➡RELATIVE LOCATION; 162]

in full *adv* **completely**, fully, totally, in total, wholly, entirely, in its entirety, absolutely, one hundred per cent. [➡WHOLENESS AND COMPLETENESS; 199] *Opposite:* in part.

in full swing *adj* **well under way**, in progress, up and running, at full blast, well-advanced. [➡HAPPENING AND IN PROGRESS; 32]

in full view *adv* [➡PERCEPTIBLE; 25]

in funds *adj* [➡WEALTH AND WEALTHY; 891]

infuriate *v* **enrage**, madden, incense, make your blood boil, wind up (*informal*), annoy, irritate, anger, make see red, exasperate, inflame, rile (*informal*). [➡ANGER AND ANNOY; 570] *Opposite:* calm.

infuriated *adj* **enraged**, exasperated, furious, angry, incensed, irate, up in arms, wound up (*informal*), riled (*informal*), inflamed, mad. [➡IRRITATION AND ANGER; 542] *Opposite:* calm.

infuriating *adj* **maddening**, annoying, irritating, exasperating, galling, vexatious. [➡IRRITATING; 229] *Opposite:* calming.

infuse 1 *v* **pervade**, fill, permeate, suffuse, imbue, bathe. [➡FILL; 407] 2 *v* **instil**, impart, introduce, inculcate, imbue, implant, inspire, fortify. [➡INSTRUCT AND TEACH; 610] 3 *v* **steep**, soak, brew, immerse, saturate, souse. [➡SOFTEN, LIQUEFY, DAMPEN; 389] *Opposite:* drain.

infusion *n* **brew**, tea, distillation, fermentation, drink, mixture, potion. [➡COLLECTIONS AND MIXTURES OF THINGS; 1243]

in future *adv* [➡FUTURE; 86]

in general 1 *adv* **as a whole**, generally, altogether, overall. [➡USUALLY; 108] *Opposite:* in particular. 2 *adv* **in most cases**, generally, mainly, normally, usually, ordinarily, on the whole. [➡USUALLY; 108] *Opposite:* occasionally.

ingenious 1 *adj* **inventive**, clever, imaginative, resourceful, original, creative. [➡TALENTED AND SKILFUL; 528] *Opposite:* unimaginative. 2 *adj* **nifty** (*informal*), clever, effective, cunning, inspired. [➡INTERESTING AND MEANINGFUL; 191]

ingeniously *adv* **inventively**, imaginatively, cleverly, resourcefully, niftily (*informal*), skilfully, creatively, cunningly. [➡TALENTED AND SKILFUL; 528] *Opposite:* unimaginatively.

ingenuity *n* **inventiveness**, cleverness, resourcefulness, imagination, originality, skill, creativity, cunning, initiative. [➡POSITIVE INTELLECTUAL CHARACTERISTICS; 525] *Opposite:* unimaginativeness.

ingenuous 1 *adj* **innocent**, unworldly, artless, unsophisticated, gullible, inexperienced, naive, trusting, simple. [➡NEGATIVE INTELLECTUAL CHARACTERISTICS; 526] *Opposite:* artful. 2 *adj* **honest**, direct, frank, open, straightforward, sincere, candid. [➡NATURALNESS; 498] *Opposite:* dishonest.

ingenuously 1 *adv* **innocently**, artlessly, unpretentiously, gullibly, unsophisticatedly, simply, naively. [➡NEGATIVE INTELLECTUAL CHARACTERISTICS; 526] *Opposite:* artfully. 2 *adv* **honestly**, frankly, candidly, openly, directly, straightforwardly, sincerely. [➡HONEST AND OPEN; 631] *Opposite:* dishonestly.

ingenuousness 1 *n* **innocence**, unpretentiousness, unworldliness, gullibility, simplicity, naivety. [➡LEVEL OF EDUCATION AND SOPHISTICATION; 894] *Opposite:* artfulness. 2 *n* **openness**, straightforwardness, directness, honesty, artlessness, frankness, candour, sincerity. [➡NATURALNESS; 498] *Opposite:* dishonesty.

ingest *v* **absorb**, swallow, take in, consume, eat, drink, devour, gulp down, swig (*informal*), sip, gulp. [➡EAT AND NOT EAT; 711] *Opposite:* vomit.

inglenook *n* **hearthside**, fireside, nook, corner, recess, fireplace. [➡ALCOVES, CUBICLES, AND COMPARTMENTS; 1095]

inglorious *adj* **shameful**, dishonourable, disgraceful, humiliating, unsuccessful, ignominious, ignoble. [➡INAPPROPRIATE AND UNSUITABLE; 225] *Opposite:* glorious.

ingoing *adj* **incoming**, new, inward, moving. [➡DIRECTION OF MOTION; 346] *Opposite:* outgoing.

in good condition *adj* [➡FIT AND STRONG; 737]

in good form (*US*) *adj* [➡FIT AND STRONG; 737]

in good health *adj* [➡FIT AND STRONG; 737]

in good shape *adj* **in good condition**, healthy, fit, in good health, hale and hearty, well. [➡FIT AND STRONG; 737] *Opposite:* in bad shape.

in good spirits *adj* [➡PLEASURE, EXCITEMENT, AND ELATION; 535]

in good taste *adv* [➡APPROPRIATE, SUITABLE, ADVISABLE; 185]

in good time *adv* [➡PROMPTNESS: ON TIME; 99]

ingot *n* **slab**, nugget, lump, brick, block, bar. [➡AMOUNT OF SOLID OR SEMI-SOLID; 115]

ingrain *v* **impress**, etch, drill in, fix, root, hammer in, drum into, set, indoctrinate, instil. [➡INSTRUCT AND TEACH; 610]

ingrained *adj* **deep-seated**, in-built, entrenched, fixed, deep-rooted, rooted. [➡PERMANENCE: WITHOUT END; 94] *Opposite:* superficial.

ingratiate *v* **curry favour**, insinuate yourself, suck up (*informal*), toady, crawl (*informal*), get in with, grovel, cosy up. [➡ESTABLISHING RELATIONSHIPS WITH OTHERS; 974] *Opposite:* alienate.

ingratiating *adj* **sycophantic**, insinuative, obsequious, smarmy, deferential. [➡INGRATIATING; 639] *Opposite:* proud.

ingratitude *n* **rudeness**, unmannerliness, unappreciativeness, ungratefulness, thanklessness, boorishness. [➡BAD MANNERS AND SOCIAL SKILLS; 522] *Opposite:* gratitude.

ingredient *n* **element**, component, part, constituent, factor, feature, item. [➡PHYSICAL OBJECTS; 1242]

ingress (*formal*) *n* **entry**, entrance, opening, door, admission, doorway, right of way. [➡DOORS AND ACCESS POINTS; 1100]

in-group *n* **clique**, clan (*informal*), gang, faction, circle, elite, coterie, camp, cabal. [➡FRIENDS AND ACQUAINTANCES; 936]

ingrowing *adj* **ingrown**, impacted, malformed, deformed. [➡ILLNESSES AND DISORDERS; 733]

inhabit *v* **live**, reside, populate, occupy, squat, dwell (*literary*). [➡INHABIT; 20]

inhabitable *adj* **habitable**, up to scratch (*informal*), civilized, usable, hospitable, livable, residential. [➡IN GOOD REPAIR; 1231] *Opposite:* uninhabitable.

inhabitant *n* **occupant**, resident, citizen, dweller (*literary*), native, denizen, tenant, occupier. [➡INHABITANT; 857]

inhabited *adj* **populated**, populous, tenanted. [➡FULL; 1238] *Opposite:* uninhabited.

inhalation *n* **breath**, gulp, gasp, pant, mouthful. [➡BREATHE AND NOT BREATHE; 717]

inhale *v* **gasp**, gulp, huff, pant. [➡BREATHE AND NOT BREATHE; 717] *Opposite:* exhale.

inhaler *n* **bronchodilator**, nebulizer, spray. [➡REMEDIES, TREATMENTS, AND OPERATIONS; 732]

in half a shake *adv* [➡FUTURE; 86]

in hand 1 *adj* **under control**, receiving attention, under consideration, under deliberation, being dealt with. [➡HAPPENING AND IN PROGRESS; 32] *Opposite:* pending. 2 *adj* **unused**, remaining, spare, superfluous, available, to play with, over, extra, free, surplus, left over. [➡PRESENT AND AVAILABLE; 11]

inharmonious 1 *adj* **discordant**, clashing, unpleasant, harsh, jarring, unmusical, unmelodious, tuneless, dissonant, cacophonous. [➡LOUD OR UNPLEASANT SOUNDS; 1265] *Opposite:* harmonious. 2 *adj* **argumentative**, clashing, incompatible, disagreeable, antagonistic, conflicting, contradictory, discordant, at odds, at variance. [➡DISHARMONY; 157] *Opposite:* cordial.

in harmony *adv* [➡HARMONY; 156]

in haste *adv* [➡HAPPENING QUICKLY; 104]

inherent *adj* **characteristic**, essential, innate, natural, intrinsic, inborn, in-built, integral, fundamental. [➡RELATED; 143] *Opposite:* acquired.

inherit *v* **receive**, accede to, come into, succeed to, take over, get. [➡GET MONEY OR REWARD; 422] *Opposite:* bequeath.

inheritance *n* **heirloom**, tradition, legacy, bequest, birthright, heritage. [➡BEQUEATH AND BEQUESTS; 433]

inhibit 1 *v* **slow**, stop, hold back, restrain, hinder, hamper, stall, reduce. [➡AVOID, PREVENT, LIMIT, AND CONTROL; 278] 2 *v* **constrain**, hinder, prevent, impede, obstruct, deter, bar. [➡MAKE IMPOSSIBLE; 277]

inhibited *adj* **self-conscious**, reserved, introverted, repressed, subdued, withdrawn, shy, reticent. [➡COWARDICE AND WEAKNESS OF WILL; 509] *Opposite:* uninhibited.

inhibition *n* **reserve**, hang-up (*informal*), shyness, embarrassment, self-consciousness, reticence. [➡EMBARRASSMENT AND HUMILIATION; 543] *Opposite:* spontaneity.

in high dudgeon *adj* [➡CONFUSION, ANXIETY, AND WORRY; 541]

in high spirits *adj* [➡PLEASURE, EXCITEMENT, AND ELATION; 535]

inhospitable 1 *adj* **unwelcoming**, unfriendly, unreceptive, uncongenial, uninviting, hostile, cold. [➡UNFRIENDLINESS AND UNSOCIABILITY; 505] *Opposite:* hospitable. 2 *adj* **harsh**, forbidding, bleak, desolate, barren, hostile. [➡PHYSICALLY UNPLEASANT; 227] *Opposite:* inviting.

in hot water *adj* **in trouble**, in the soup (*informal*), in a spot of bother (*informal*), in difficulties, in extremis, up the creek (*informal*), in a jam (*informal*), in a fix (*informal*), in dire straits. [➡IN TROUBLE AND DISADVANTAGED; 73]

inhuman 1 *adj* **cruel**, vicious, cold-blooded, inhumane, brutal, ruthless. [➡BEASTLY AND BRUTISH; 511] *Opposite:* kind. 2 *adj* **cold-hearted**, unfeeling, insensitive, merciless, callous, heartless. [➡SELFISH AND UNKIND; 506] *Opposite:* sensitive. 3 *adj* **otherworldly**, weird, strange, unearthly, eerie, uncanny. [➡BIZARRE AND PECULIAR; 258] *Opposite:* earthly.

inhumane *adj* **cold-hearted**, cold-blooded, cruel, callous, brutal, merciless, sadistic, vicious, heartless, atrocious, appalling. [➡BEASTLY AND BRUTISH; 511] *Opposite:* humane.

inhumanity *n* **cruelty**, cold-heartedness, mercilessness, viciousness, ruthlessness, cold-bloodedness, brutality, sadism, heartlessness, atrociousness, callousness. [➡SELFISH AND UNKIND; 506] *Opposite:* humanity.

inhumanly 1 *adv* **cruelly**, cold-bloodedly, inhumanely, viciously, ruthlessly, brutally. [➡BEASTLY AND BRUTISH; 511] *Opposite:* kindly. 2 *adv* **cold-heartedly**, unfeelingly, insensitively, mercilessly, callously, heartlessly. [➡SELFISH AND UNKIND; 506] *Opposite:* sensitively.

inimical 1 *adj* **unfavourable**, contrary, opposed, adverse, detrimental, disadvantageous. [➡DANGEROUS; 237] *Opposite:* favourable. 2 *adj* **hostile**, unfriendly, unwelcoming, cold, ill-disposed. [➡IRRITATION AND ANGER; 542] *Opposite:* friendly.

inimitable *adj* **unique**, matchless, unmatched, incomparable, peerless, one-off, one and only. [➡EXTRAORDINARY: AMAZING; 205] *Opposite:* common.

iniquitous *adj* **wicked**, heinous, sinful, bad, evil, unjust, immoral, naughty. [➡MORALLY BAD; 776] *Opposite:* good.

iniquity *n* **wickedness**, evil, sin, vice, immorality, injustice, crime, heinousness. [➡MORALLY BAD; 776] *Opposite:* goodness.

in isolation *adv* **separately**, out of context, alone, individually, independently. [➡UNRELATEDNESS AND SEPARATENESS; 147] *Opposite:* together.

initial *adj* **first**, early, original, preliminary, opening, primary. [➡BEFORE, FIRST, AND PRECEDING; 164] *Opposite:* final.

initialize *v* **reset**, prime, prepare, set, make ready, adjust, modify. [➡COMPUTERS AND COMPUTING; 1126] *Opposite:* disable.

initiate 1 *v* **start**, introduce, originate, begin, kick off (*informal*), open, commence (*formal*), set off, instigate. [➡START AN ACTION; 261] *Opposite:* finish. 2 *v* **instruct**, induct, admit, introduce, teach, tutor, coach, train, catechize. [➡INSTRUCT AND TEACH; 610] *Opposite:* expel.

initiation 1 *n* **beginning**, start, opening, instigation, launch, origination, introduction, commencement (*formal*). [➡BEGINNING; 53] *Opposite:* end. 2 *n* **introduction**, admission, induction, admittance, instruction, training, catechesis. [➡TEACHING; 839] *Opposite:* expulsion.

initiative 1 *n* **inventiveness**, creativity, wits, enterprise, resourcefulness, ingenuity. [➡POSITIVE INTELLECTUAL CHARACTERISTICS; 525] 2 *n* **plan**, proposal, scheme, idea, programme, project. [➡IDEA AND THOUGHT; 771] 3 *n* **pole position**, upper hand, advantage, edge, lead, ascendancy. [➡SOURCE OF HAPPINESS, PLEASURE, OR IMPROVEMENT; 210]

initiator *n* **motivator**, inventor, originator, author, creator, architect, prime mover, spur. [➡DESIGNERS, CREATORS, AND INSTIGATORS; 348]

in its entirety *adv* [➡ALL; 126]

inject 1 *v* **vaccinate**, inoculate, give a jab (*informal*), insert, give a shot (*informal*). [➡FALL ILL, TREAT, AND RECOVER; 729] 2 *v* **bring**, add, introduce, instil, infuse. [➡POSITION SOMETHING: BETWEEN, BESIDE, OR INSIDE SOMETHING; 327] *Opposite:* remove.

injection 1 *n* **inoculation**, dose, jab (*informal*), vaccination, booster, shot (*informal*). [➡REMEDIES, TREATMENTS, AND OPERATIONS; 732] 2 *n* **addition**, instillation, instilment, insertion, introduction, infusion. [➡COMBINE AND MIX; 401] *Opposite:* removal.

in jeopardy *adj* [➡IN DANGER; 238]

in jest *adv* [➡JOKES AND TEASING; 675]

in-joke *n* **private joke**, joke, running joke, prank, witticism, jest (*literary*). [➡JOKES AND TEASING; 675]

injudicious *adj* **ill-advised**, unwise, foolish, imprudent (*formal*), careless, indiscreet, inadvisable. [➡THE NATURE OF IDEAS; 772] *Opposite:* judicious.

injudiciousness *n* **indiscretion**, imprudence, foolishness, rashness, impulsiveness, hastiness, carelessness, misjudgment. [➡THE NATURE OF IDEAS; 772] *Opposite:* prudence.

injunction *n* **ban**, sanction, embargo, restriction, order, command, ruling. [➡LEGISLATIVE BODIES AND LEGISLATION; 809]

injure *v* **damage**, harm, hurt, wound, cut, scar, burn. [➡WOUND A PERSON OR ANIMAL; 384] *Opposite:* heal.

See Compare and Contrast at **harm**.

injured *adj* **hurt**, incapacitated, wounded, battered, bruised, damaged, gammy. [➡INJURED; 743] *Opposite:* unscathed.

injurious *adj* **harmful**, distressing, damaging, adverse, detrimental, deleterious (*formal*), ruinous. [➡DANGEROUS; 237] *Opposite:* beneficial.

injury *n* **wound**, damage, grievance, wrong, hurt, harm. [➡PAIN AND OTHER PHYSICAL SENSATIONS; 734]

injury time *n* **extra time**, extension, overtime (*US*). [➡SPORTS TERMS; 877]

injustice *n* **discrimination**, unfairness, inequality, bias, prejudice, wrong. [➡MORALLY BAD; 776] *Opposite:* justice.

ink-cap *type of* **fungus**. [➡MICROORGANISMS, FUNGI, AND ALGAE; 1023]

in keeping *adj* **consistent with**, suitable for, in accordance with, in line with, according to, compliant with, in agreement with. [➡APPROPRIATE, SUITABLE, ADVISABLE; 185]

inkling *n* **suspicion**, hint, clue, hunch, feeling, idea, notion. [➡IDEA AND THOUGHT; 771] *Opposite:* certainty.

inkwell *n* **jar**, inkstand, pot, container, well, receptacle. [➡CONTAINERS, RECEPTACLES, AND PACKAGING; 1244]

inky *type of* **black**. [➡COLOURS; 1223]

inlaid *adj* **decorated**, veneered, enamelled, ornamented, mosaic, tessellated, tiled, inset. [➡DESCRIBING PATTERNS; 1226]

inland 1 *adj* **interior**, internal, upcountry, inward, central. [➡GENERAL LOCATIONS; 159] 2 *adv* **within**, inwards, towards, inshore, upcountry, inside, centrally. [➡DIRECTION OF MOTION; 346]

in-law (*informal*) *type of* **by marriage**. [➡RELATIVES BY MARRIAGE; 960]

inlay 1 *n* **stone**, glass, ivory, wood, enamel, tile, piece, ornament, inset. [➡ORNAMENTS AND DECORATIONS; 1247] 2 *n* **pattern**, decoration, ornament, mosaic, enamelling, marquetry, veneer. [➡ORNAMENTS AND DECORATIONS; 1247]

in less than no time *adv* **immediately**, at once, quickly, rapidly, instantly, in an instant, in a jiffy (*informal*), in a flash. [➡HAPPENING QUICKLY; 104] *Opposite:* slowly.

inlet *n* **bay**, cove, creek, fjord. [➡THE SEAS, OCEANS, AND SHORES; 1041]

in lieu *adv* **instead**, in place, in the place of, to compensate for, to make up for, as a replacement for, for. [➡DIFFERENCE; 150]

in limbo *adj* **in abeyance**, suspended, on hold, on the back burner, up in the air, on ice. [➡NOT HAPPENING; 34] *Opposite:* on the move.

in line 1 *adv* **in a row**, in order, in sequence, in turn, in rank, in formation, in single file. [➡ORIENTATION AND ALIGNMENT; 1222] 2 *adv* **in keeping**, in accordance, in agreement, in step, in harmony, in concordance. [➡HARMONY; 156] *Opposite:* against.

in line for *adj* **due**, due for, owed, worthy of, entitled to, in for, up for. [➡OWE AND DESERVE; 466]

in line with *prep* **in agreement with**, according to, in keeping with, corresponding to, consistent with, along the lines of, in proportion to. [➡HARMONY; 156]

in love *adj* [➡APPRECIATION AND GRATITUDE; 536]

in low spirits *adj* [➡SADNESS, DISTRESS, AND DESPAIR; 540]

in luck *adj* [➡LUCK; 784]

inmate *n* **prisoner**, internee, patient, convict, jailbird (*slang*). [➡CAPTIVES AND PRISONERS; 250]

in memoriam *prep* **in memory of**, in remembrance of, as a memorial to, in commemoration of, for. [➡FOREIGN WORDS AND PHRASES; 673]

in moderation *adv* **a bit** (*informal*), within reason, a little, within limits, within bounds, moderately, reasonably, sensibly. [➡TO A CERTAIN EXTENT; 134] *Opposite:* excessively.

inmost *adj* **innermost**, deepest, private, secret, intimate, personal. [➡SECRET AND UNKNOWN; 180] *Opposite:* outermost.

in most cases *adv* [➡USUALLY; 108]

in mourning *adj* [➡DEATH AND BEREAVEMENT; 927]

in my book *adv* **to my mind**, in my opinion, if you ask me, as far as I'm concerned, personally, in my view. [➡EXPRESSIONS OF OPINION; 624]

in my opinion *adv* [➡EXPRESSIONS OF OPINION; 624]

in my view *adv* [➡EXPRESSIONS OF OPINION; 624]

inn *type of* **hotel**. [➡HOTELS, RESTAURANTS, AND CLUBS; 1081]

in name only *adv* **theoretically**, supposedly, officially, in theory, on paper, in principle, nominally, notionally, technically. [➡FALSE AND UNREAL; 174] *Opposite:* really.

innards (*informal*) *n* **entrails**, guts, intestines, bowels, viscera, insides (*informal*). [➡THE DIGESTIVE TRACT; 710]

innate *adj* **essential**, inborn, native, distinctive, natural, characteristic, instinctive, inherent, intrinsic. [➡REPRODUCTION AND HEREDITY; 726]

in need *adj* [➡POVERTY AND POOR; 892]

inner 1 *adj* **innermost**, inward, internal, inside, central, middle, interior. [➡CENTRAL PARTS OF PHYSICAL OBJECTS; 1250] *Opposite:* outer. 2 *adj* **private**, secret, intimate, deep, hidden, personal, innermost. [➡SECRET AND UNKNOWN; 180] *Opposite:* public.

inner city *n* **city centre**, centre, town centre, downtown (*US*). [➡HUMAN SETTLEMENTS; 1069]

inner-city *adj* **city**, metropolitan, town, central, inner, urban, built-up, downtown (*US*). [➡HUMAN SETTLEMENTS; 1069] *Opposite:* suburban.

innermost *adj* **inmost**, deepest, private, secret, intimate, personal. [➡SECRET AND UNKNOWN; 180] *Opposite:* outermost.

in next to no time *adv* [➡HAPPENING QUICKLY; 104]

innings *n* **runs**, turn, batting, score, round, go, shot. [➡SPORTS TERMS; 877]

innocence 1 *n* **blamelessness**, goodness, guiltlessness, incorruptibility, virtue, virtuousness, purity. [➡MORALLY GOOD; 775] *Opposite:* guilt. 2 *n* **naivety**, inexperience, unworldliness, unsophistication, gullibility, ingenuousness, artlessness, simplicity. [➡NEGATIVE INTELLECTUAL CHARACTERISTICS; 526] *Opposite:* experience.

innocent 1 *adj* **blameless**, acquitted, guiltless, cleared, not guilty, above suspicion, in the clear. [➡MORALLY GOOD; 775] *Opposite:* guilty. 2 *adj* **harmless**, unknowing, unintended, unintentional, inoffensive, innocuous, safe. [➡SAFE AND SAFETY; 192] *Opposite:* malicious. 3 *adj* **virtuous**, untouched, pure (*literary*), unsullied, chaste, immaculate, spotless. [➡MORALLY GOOD; 775] *Opposite:* tainted. 4 *adj* **unsophisticated**, unworldly, artless, harmless, naive, childlike, gullible, ingenuous, simple, pure (*literary*). [➡LEVEL OF EDUCATION AND SOPHISTICATION; 894] *Opposite:* worldly.

innocently 1 *adv* **openly**, harmlessly, inoffensively, safely, innocuously, unknowingly, unintentionally. [➡SAFE AND SAFETY; 192] *Opposite:* maliciously. 2 *adv* **naively**, gullibly, unsophisticatedly, unpretentiously, ingenuously, simply, artlessly, openly. [➡NEGATIVE INTELLECTUAL CHARACTERISTICS; 526] *Opposite:* knowingly.

innocuous *adj* **inoffensive**, harmless, innocent, safe, mild, bland. [➡SAFE AND SAFETY; 192] *Opposite:* offensive.

in no doubt *adj* [➡CERTAINTY; 562]

in no time *adv* [➡HAPPENING QUICKLY; 104]

innovate *v* **invent**, modernize, originate, revolutionize, transform, update, renovate, renew, remodel. [➡IMPROVE SOMETHING; 375] *Opposite:* stagnate.

innovation *n* **novelty**, invention, revolution, modernization, origination, improvement, advance. [➡NEW, MODERN; 167] *Opposite:* stagnation.

innovative *adj* **groundbreaking**, advanced, state-of-the-art, pioneering, inventive, original, new, novel, modern. [➡NEW, MODERN; 167] *Opposite:* outdated.

innuendo *n* **insinuation**, ambiguity, double entendre, inference, intimation, suggestion, allusion, hint, overtone. [➡SUGGEST, HINT, AND COMMENT; 613]

innumerable *adj* **countless**, uncountable, numerous, incalculable, immeasurable, untold, inestimable, infinite. [➡MANY, MUCH, LARGE AMOUNT; 117]

inoculate *v* **immunize**, vaccinate, inject, protect, give a shot (*informal*). [➡FALL ILL, TREAT, AND RECOVER; 729] *Opposite:* infect.

inoculation *n* **vaccination**, jab (*informal*), injection, booster, immunization, shot (*informal*). [➡REMEDIES, TREATMENTS, AND OPERATIONS; 732]

inoffensive *adj* **innocuous**, harmless, bland, dull, safe, mild, unoffending. [➡SAFE AND SAFETY; 192] *Opposite:* offensive.

inoffensively *adv* **innocuously**, harmlessly, innocently, mildly, blandly, safely. [➡ACCEPTABLE AND PASSABLE; 220] *Opposite:* offensively.

in one fell swoop *adv* [➡HAPPENING QUICKLY; 104]

inoperable 1 *adj* **incurable**, untreatable, terminal, grave, fatal, deadly. [➡SICKNESS; 730] *Opposite:* operable. 2 *adj* **impracticable**, unworkable, unfeasible, impossible, unachievable, impractical. [➡IMPOSSIBLE AND IMPROBABLE; 179] *Opposite:* doable.

inoperative *adj* **out of action**, out of order, out of use, broken, broken down, defective. [➡IN BAD REPAIR; 1233] *Opposite:* operative.

inopportune *adj* **ill-timed**, unfortunate, inconvenient, mistimed, untimely, inappropriate, unpropitious. [➡PROMPTNESS: BADLY TIMED; 101] *Opposite:* opportune.

inopportunely *adv* **inconveniently**, unsuitably, inappropriately, unfortunately, awkwardly, regrettably. [➡IRRITATING; 229] *Opposite:* conveniently.

in opposition *adj* [➡DISHARMONY; 157]

in order 1 *adj* **correct**, appropriate, acceptable, all right, OK (*informal*), okay (*informal*), permissible, permitted, satisfactory, adequate. [➡ACCEPTABLE AND PASSABLE; 220] *Opposite:* incorrect. 2 *adv* **in turn**, in sequence, in line, in rank, consecutively, one at a time, one by one, sequentially, one after the other. [➡AFTER, LAST, AND FOLLOWING; 166] *Opposite:* out of order.

in order to *conj* **so as to**, to, with the intention of, with the purpose of, with the aim of, that, so that. [➡CAUSATION; 169]

inordinate *adj* **excessive**, undue, unwarranted, immoderate (*formal*), unreasonable, extravagant, disproportionate, unconscionable, exorbitant. [➡TOO MUCH; 118] *Opposite:* moderate.

inordinately *adv* [➡TO A GREAT EXTENT; 130]

inorganic *adj* **mineral**, inanimate, inert, lifeless. [➡NATURE AND THE ENVIRONMENT; 1038] *Opposite:* organic.

in other words *adv* [➡SUMMARIZING EXPRESSIONS; 623]

in pain *adj* [➡PAIN AND OTHER PHYSICAL SENSATIONS; 734]

in part *adv* **to some extent**, partly, partially, in some measure, in some way, to a certain extent, comparatively, relatively, to some degree, somewhat. [➡TO A CERTAIN EXTENT; 134] *Opposite:* completely.

in particular *adv* **specifically**, especially, specially, particularly, above all, singularly, expressly. [➡TO A GREAT EXTENT; 130] *Opposite:* in general.

in peak condition *adj* [➡FIT AND STRONG; 737]

in peril *adj* [➡IN DANGER; 238]

in perpetuity *adv* [➡PERMANENCE: WITHOUT END; 94]

in person *adv* **personally**, yourself, in the flesh, physically, individually. [➡ACTING INDEPENDENTLY; 285]

in pieces *adj* [➡IN BAD REPAIR; 1233]

in plain sight *adj* [➡PERCEPTIBLE; 25]

in plenty of time *adv* [➡PROMPTNESS: EARLY; 98]

in point of fact *adv* **genuinely**, irrefutably, in truth, in reality, in fact, as it happens, as a matter of fact, actually, really. [➡WORDS AND PHRASES EMPHASIZING THE TRUTH OF A MATTER; 173]

in poor condition *adj* [➡UNFIT AND WEAK; 740]

in poor health *adj* [➡ILL AND SICK; 741]

in poor taste *adj* [➡IN POOR TASTE; 230]

in principle *adv* **in theory**, theoretically, hypothetically, on paper, technically, in name only, notionally, supposedly, officially. [➡POSSIBLE AND PROBABLE; 178]

in print *adv* **published**, printed, available, in book form. [➡WRITING; 584]

in prison *adj* [➡CAPTIVITY AND LOSS OF FREEDOM; 249]

in progress *adj* [➡HAPPENING AND IN PROGRESS; 32]

input 1 *n* **contribution**, effort, say, participation, involvement, idea, feedback, response. [➡BASIC DETAILS; 689] 2 *v* **enter**, key, key in, record, store, keyboard. [➡RECORD SOMETHING; 372]

inquest *n* **investigation**, inquiry, examination, postmortem, autopsy, probe, review. [➡BURIAL AND PREPARATION FOR BURIAL; 929]

in question *adj* [➡UNCERTAIN; 176]

inquire *v* **ask**, query, request, question, find out, make inquiries. [➡ASK PEOPLE QUESTIONS; 667]

inquire into *v* **investigate**, go into, delve into, look into, probe into, research. [➡QUESTION THINGS; 752]

inquiring 1 *adj* **inquisitive**, interested, curious, questioning, analytical, probing, examining, investigative, speculative. [➡POSITIVE INTELLECTUAL CHARACTERISTICS; 525] *Opposite:* incurious. 2 *adj* **searching**, questioning, penetrating, probing, prying, intrusive, quizzical. [➡POSITIVE INTELLECTUAL CHARACTERISTICS; 525]

inquiry 1 *n* **review**, postmortem, autopsy, investigation, examination, analysis, survey, probe, inquest, study. [➡EXAMINE AND ASSESS; 754] 2 *n* **request**, question, query, interrogation, quiz. [➡ASK PEOPLE QUESTIONS; 667]

inquisition *n* **inquiry**, inquest, investigation, examination, interrogation, cross-questioning. [➡ASK PEOPLE QUESTIONS; 667]

inquisitive 1 *adj* **curious**, inquiring, interested, questioning, probing, keen. [➡POSITIVE INTELLECTUAL CHARACTERISTICS; 525] *Opposite:* indifferent. 2 *adj* **nosy** (*informal*), prying, intrusive, snooping (*informal*), prurient, meddlesome, officious, inquisitorial, interfering. [➡NOSY AND INTERFERING; 513] *Opposite:* incurious.

inquisitiveness 1 *n* **curiosity**, interest, keenness, desire for knowledge, thirst for knowledge, imagination. [➡POSITIVE INTELLECTUAL CHARACTERISTICS; 525] *Opposite:* indifference. 2 *n* **nosiness** (*informal*), prurience, meddlesomeness, prying, questioning, officiousness, intrusiveness. [➡NOSY AND INTERFERING; 513] *Opposite:* indifference.

inquisitor *n* **cross-examiner**, examiner, investigator, interrogator, questioner, interviewer. [➡QUESTIONERS; 668]

inquisitorial *adj* **interrogational**, cross-examining, investigative, interviewing, questioning, interrogative. [➡ENTHUSIASTIC AND INQUISITIVE; 629]

inquorate *adj* **insufficient**, inadequate, not enough, too few, under strength, undermanned. [➡TOO FEW, TOO LITTLE; 120]

in rags *adj* [➡IN BAD REPAIR; 1233]

in raptures *adj* [➡PLEASURE, EXCITEMENT, AND ELATION; 535]

in reality *adv* **in actual fact**, really, actually, in fact, in effect, as a matter of fact, in point of fact, in truth. [➡TRUE AND REAL; 172]

in retrospect 1 *adj* **on reflection**, with the benefit of hindsight, on second thoughts, all together, looking back, with hindsight. [➡PAST; 84] 2 *adv* **with hindsight**, looking back, retrospectively, on second thoughts, with the benefit of hindsight, on review. [➡PAST; 84]

in ruins *adj* [➡IN BAD REPAIR; 1233]

in safe hands *adj* [➡SAFE AND SAFETY; 192]

insalubrious (*formal*) *adj* **unhealthy**, unsavoury, unwholesome, harmful, unhygienic, seedy. [➡DIRTY; 1234] *Opposite:* healthy.

ins and outs *n* **details**, fine points, particulars, facts, minutiae, circumstances, nitty-gritty (*informal*), nuts and bolts (*informal*). [➡BASIC DETAILS; 689] *Opposite:* generalities.

insane *adj* **foolish**, silly, stupid, impractical, crazy (*informal*), ridiculous, senseless, unreasonable. [➡BIZARRE AND PECULIAR; 258] *Opposite:* sensible.

insanitary *adj* **unhygienic**, dirty, unclean, contaminated, unhealthy, unwholesome, septic, toxic, unsanitary. [➡DIRTY; 1234] *Opposite:* hygienic.

insanity *n* **foolishness**, stupidity, craziness (*informal*), irrationality, folly, senselessness, recklessness, absurdity. [➡ECCENTRICITY AND IRRATIONALITY; 563] *Opposite:* common sense.

insatiability *n* **voraciousness**, greed, greediness, gluttony, ravenousness, avidity. [➡FINANCIALLY MEAN AND GRASPING; 520]

insatiable *adj* **voracious**, greedy, avid, ravenous, unquenchable, unappeasable, unsatisfiable, limitless. [➡FINANCIALLY MEAN AND GRASPING; 520]

inscribe 1 *v* **engrave**, carve, etch, cut, scratch, incise, mark, print, pen, write, imprint, chisel, impress. [➡CREATE IMAGES; 357] *Opposite:* erase. 2 *v* **list**, enter, record, register, enrol, add. [➡RECORD SOMETHING; 372] *Opposite:* delete. 3 *v* **dedicate**, autograph, address, sign, assign, consecrate. [➡NAME AND DESCRIBE; 666]

inscription 1 *n* **writing**, caption, label, engraving, legend, words, lettering, imprinting, impression. [➡LETTERS AND WRITTEN MESSAGES; 585] 2 *n* **dedication**, autograph, signature, personal note, initials. [➡NAME AND DESCRIBE; 666]

inscrutability *n* **mystique**, mystery, mysteriousness, enigma, incomprehensibility, impenetrability. [➡RETICENT AND UNFORTHCOMING; 632] *Opposite:* clarity.

inscrutable *adj* **enigmatic**, sphinx-like, unfathomable, mysterious, impenetrable, unreadable, incomprehensible, indecipherable, unknowable, inexplicable. [➡RETICENT AND UNFORTHCOMING; 632] *Opposite:* transparent.

in secrecy *adv* [➡SECRET AND UNKNOWN; 180]

in secret *adv* **secretly**, privately, in private, confidentially, clandestinely, surreptitiously, furtively, in confidence, between ourselves, unbeknownst to others. [➡SECRET AND UNKNOWN; 180] *Opposite:* openly.

insect *n* **bug**, creepy-crawly (*informal*), pest, creature, fly, beetle, butterfly, moth, ant. [➡INSECTS; 1012]

insect

◆ *types of insect stages of development*
caterpillar, chrysalis, glowworm, grub, imago, larva, maggot, nit, pupa, silkworm, woodworm

◆ *parts of an insect*
abdomen, antenna, feeler, proboscis, thorax, wing

insecure 1 *adj* **unconfident**, anxious, self-doubting, uncertain, lacking confidence, timid, doubtful, apprehensive, diffident. [➡UNCERTAINTY; 560] *Opposite:* confident. 2 *adj* **vulnerable**, unprotected, unguarded, undefended, at risk, unsafe, endangered, exposed, precarious. [➡DANGEROUS; 237] *Opposite:* secure. 3 *adj* **shaky**, rickety, unstable, unsteady, loose, wobbly, unsound, frail, unreliable, tottering. [➡IN BAD REPAIR; 1233] *Opposite:* steady.

insecurely *adv* **anxiously**, uncertainly, tentatively, apprehensively, timidly, diffidently, doubtfully. [➡INSECURITY AND LOSS OF COMPOSURE; 545] *Opposite:* confidently.

insecurity *n* **lack of confidence**, anxiety, uncertainty, timidity, self-doubt, diffidence. [➡INSECURITY AND LOSS OF COMPOSURE; 545] *Opposite:* confidence.

inseminate *v* [➡REPRODUCTION AND HEREDITY; 726]

insemination *n* [➡REPRODUCTION AND HEREDITY; 726]

insensate 1 *adj* **unconscious**, comatose, inert, anaesthetized, numbed, numb, knocked out, insentient, insensible. [➡TIRED, ASLEEP, AND UNCONSCIOUS; 739] *Opposite:* animate. 2 *adj* (*literary*) **heartless**, callous, cold, insensitive, unsympathetic, hardhearted, unfeeling, uncaring. [➡SELFISH AND UNKIND; 506] *Opposite:* sympathetic. 3 *adj* (*literary*) **thoughtless**, inconsiderate, inattentive, heedless, unthinking, selfish. [➡SELFISH AND UNKIND; 506] *Opposite:* considerate.

insensible 1 *adj* **unconscious**, comatose, inert, insentient, numb, numbed, knocked out, anaesthetized, insensate. [➡TIRED, ASLEEP, AND UNCONSCIOUS; 739] *Opposite:* conscious. 2 *adj* **unaware**, unresponsive, insensitive, oblivious, numb, unfeeling. [➡IGNORANCE; 558] *Opposite:* sensitive. 3 *adj* **imperceptible**, indiscernible, unnoticeable, indistinguishable, inappreciable, invisible. [➡IMPERCEPTIBLE; 26] *Opposite:* obvious.

insensitive 1 *adj* **tactless**, thoughtless, inconsiderate, uncaring, unsympathetic, thick-skinned, inattentive, hardened, cold, callous. [➡SELFISH AND UNKIND; 506] *Opposite:* sensitive. 2 *adj* **numb**, unfeeling, insensate, insensible, dead, impervious, impassive. [➡IGNORANCE; 558] *Opposite:* sensitive. 3 *adj* **unresponsive**, impervious, oblivious, unmoved, inured to, indifferent, obtuse, unaffected, blasé. [➡NEUTRALITY AND INDIFFERENCE; 554] *Opposite:* responsive.

insensitively *adv* **tactlessly**, thoughtlessly, inconsiderately, inattentively, undiplomatically, coldly, callously. [➡SELFISH AND UNKIND; 506] *Opposite:* considerately.

insensitivity *n* **selfishness**, thoughtlessness, inconsiderateness, tactlessness, inattentiveness, coldness, callousness. [➡SELFISH AND UNKIND; 506] *Opposite:* sensitivity.

insentient *adj* **lifeless**, inert, inanimate, insensate, unconscious, numbed, comatose, knocked out, insensible, numb. [➡TIRED, ASLEEP, AND UNCONSCIOUS; 739] *Opposite:* sentient.

inseparable 1 *adj* **close**, devoted, intimate, joined at the hip, in each other's pocket, thick as thieves, attached. [➡RELATIONSHIP TO ANOTHER; 973] *Opposite:* distant. 2 *adj* **indivisible**, indissoluble, undividable, inextricable, conjoined (*formal*), united. [➡RECIPROCITY AND INTERDEPENDENCE; 148] *Opposite:* independent.

in sequence *adv* [➡AFTER, LAST, AND FOLLOWING; 166]

in serious trouble *adj* [➡IN TROUBLE AND DISADVANTAGED; 73]

insert 1 *v* **introduce**, implant, inject, put in, place in, pop in (*informal*), slot in, interleave, set in. [➡POSITION SOMETHING: BETWEEN, BESIDE, OR INSIDE SOMETHING; 327] *Opposite:* take out. 2 *v* **add**, include, enclose, append, incorporate, introduce. [➡POSITION SOMETHING: BETWEEN, BESIDE, OR INSIDE SOMETHING; 327] *Opposite:* extract. 3 *n* **supplement**, pullout, addition, enclosure, inset, insertion, attachment. [➡PARTS OF BOOKS AND DOCUMENTS; 594]

insertion 1 *n* **addition**, inclusion, incorporation, enclosure, attachment, introduction. [➡COMBINE AND MIX; 401] 2 *n* **supplement**, pullout, addition, inset, insert, enclosure, attachment. [➡PARTS OF BOOKS AND DOCUMENTS; 594]

in-service *adj* **work-related**, occupational, professional, vocational, job-related, on-the-job. [➡TYPES OF WORK; 835]

inset 1 *v* **insert**, put in, add, include, incorporate, place, position. [➡MOVE PAST, INTO, OR THROUGH SOMETHING; 332] *Opposite:* extract. 2 *n* **supplement**, insert, pullout, insertion, inclusion, addition, enclosure. [➡PARTS OF BOOKS AND DOCUMENTS; 594]

in seventh heaven *adj* [➡PLEASURE, EXCITEMENT, AND ELATION; 535]

in shape *adj* [➡FIT AND STRONG; 737]

in sharp contrast *adv* [➡DIFFERENCE; 150]

in shock *adj* [➡SURPRISE, SHOCK, AND AMAZEMENT; 546]

inshore *adv* **landwards**, coastwards, ashore, shorewards. [➡DIRECTION OF MOTION; 346]

in short *adv* **in brief**, briefly, in a word, in summary, in a nutshell, to sum up, to cut a long story short, to be brief, to come to the point, concisely. [➡SUMMARIZING EXPRESSIONS; 623] *Opposite:* at length.

in short supply *adj* **rare**, running low, few and far between (*informal*), at a premium, insufficient, lacking, scarce, scant. [➡TOO FEW, TOO LITTLE; 120] *Opposite:* plentiful.

in shreds *adj* [➡IN BAD REPAIR; 1233]

inside 1 *adv* **indoors**, in, within, in the interior, at home. [➡GENERAL LOCATIONS; 159] *Opposite:* outside. 2 *adj* (*informal*) **locked up**, imprisoned, put away (*informal*), doing time (*slang*), banged up (*informal*). [➡CAPTIVITY AND LOSS OF FREEDOM; 249] 3 *adj* **inner**, innermost, inmost, inward. [➡RELATIVE LOCATION; 162] *Opposite:* outer. 4 *adj* **indoor**, interior, internal. [➡GENERAL LOCATIONS; 159] *Opposite:* outside. 5 *adj* **confidential**, privileged, secret, private, exclusive, classified, esoteric, intimate, internal. [➡SECRET AND UNKNOWN; 180] 6 *n* **interior**, inner recesses, inner parts, contents. [➡CENTRAL PARTS OF PHYSICAL OBJECTS; 1250] *Opposite:* outside. 7 *prep* **in**, within, surrounded by, contained by. [➡RELATIVE LOCATION; 162] *Opposite:* outside.

inside out 1 *adj* **the wrong way round**, back to front, inverted, reversed, topsy-turvy, transposed. [➡ORIENTATION AND ALIGNMENT; 1222] 2 *adv* **really well**, like the back of your hand, back to front, thoroughly, backwards, exhaustively. [➡WHOLENESS AND COMPLETENESS; 199] *Opposite:* superficially.

insides (*informal*) *n* **innards** (*informal*), internal organs, guts, entrails, bowels, viscera, intestines. [➡THE DIGESTIVE TRACT; 710]

insidious *adj* **sinister**, treacherous, crafty, sneaky, deceptive, devious, stealthy, underhand. [➡DANGEROUS; 237] *Opposite:* harmless.

insidiousness *n* [➡DANGER; 236]

in sight *adv* [➡PERCEPTIBLE; 25]

insight *n* **vision**, understanding, awareness, intuition, perception, acumen, comprehension, discernment, perceptiveness. [➡POSITIVE INTELLECTUAL CHARACTERISTICS; 525]

insightful *adj* **perceptive**, astute, shrewd, understanding, discerning, aware, intuitive. [➡POSITIVE INTELLECTUAL CHARACTERISTICS; 525] *Opposite:* unperceptive.

insightfulness *n* **perspicacity**, perceptiveness, astuteness, discernment, sensitivity, understanding, insight, comprehension. [➡POSITIVE INTELLECTUAL CHARACTERISTICS; 525]

insignia *n* **emblem**, crest, badge, sign, symbol, motif, logo, decoration. [➡SYMBOLS, SIGNS, AND NUMBERS; 597]

insignificance *n* **unimportance**, irrelevance, inconsequentiality, triviality, paltriness, pettiness. [➡UNIMPORTANT AND UNNECESSARY; 239] *Opposite:* significance.

insignificant *adj* **unimportant**, irrelevant, immaterial, inconsequential, trivial, minor, paltry, petty, trifling, slight. [➡UNIMPORTANT AND UNNECESSARY; 239] *Opposite:* significant.

insincere *adj* **dishonest**, two-faced, hypocritical, disingenuous, deceitful, dissembling (*formal*), devious, double-dealing. [➡DECEITFUL; 514] *Opposite:* sincere.

insincerity *n* **dishonesty**, disingenuousness, hypocrisy, deceit, mendacity, deviousness. [➡DECEITFUL; 514] *Opposite:* sincerity.

insinuate 1 *v* **imply**, suggest, hint, intimate, indicate, allude, whisper. [➡SUGGEST, HINT, AND COMMENT; 613] *Opposite:* declare. **2** *v* **ingratiate yourself**, worm your way in, wheedle, cosy up, curry favour, get in with. [➡ESTABLISHING RELATIONSHIPS WITH OTHERS; 974] *Opposite:* insult.

insinuation *n* **suggestion**, implication, hint, intimation, allusion, indication, whisper. [➡SUGGEST, HINT, AND COMMENT; 613] *Opposite:* statement.

insipid 1 *adj* **dull**, bland, wishy-washy (*informal*), characterless, colourless, trite, tame, unexciting, uninteresting, boring, lifeless, inane, banal. [➡BORING AND UNINTERESTING; 235] *Opposite:* exciting. **2** *adj* **bland**, tasteless, unappetizing, flavourless, watery, weak, wishy-washy (*informal*), savourless. [➡TASTE; 704] *Opposite:* tasty.

insipidly *adv* **boringly**, uninterestingly, dully, blandly, feebly, unexcitingly, weakly, lifelessly, inanely, banally. [➡BORING AND UNINTERESTING; 235] *Opposite:* interestingly.

insipidness 1 *n* **dullness**, blandness, feebleness, characterlessness, colourlessness, lifelessness, banality, inanity. [➡BORING AND UNINTERESTING; 235] **2** *n* **tastelessness**, flavourlessness, blandness, wateriness, weakness, savourlessness, staleness. [➡TASTE; 704] *Opposite:* tastiness.

insist 1 *v* **maintain**, claim, assert, contend, swear, aver (*formal*), vow, hold. [➡CLAIM, INSIST, AND EMPHASIZE; 615] *Opposite:* deny. **2** *v* **require**, demand, press for, stipulate, enforce, claim. [➡REQUEST AND DEMAND; 664]

insistence *n* **persistence**, resolve, firmness, perseverance, doggedness, determination. [➡HARD-WORKING AND COMMITTED; 501]

insistent 1 *adj* **adamant**, firm, persistent, unrelenting, resolute, persevering, demanding, clamorous, imperative. [➡ELOQUENT, TALKATIVE, AND LONG-WINDED; 633] *Opposite:* half-hearted. **2** *adj* **incessant**, repeated, persistent, relentless, unrelenting, monotonous. [➡PERMANENCE: WITHOUT END; 94] *Opposite:* occasional.

in situ *adj* [➡PRESENT AND AVAILABLE; 11]

insofar as (*formal*) *conj* **inasmuch as**, insomuch as, to the extent that, to the degree that, because, since, in that. [➡CAUSATION; 169]

insolence *n* **cheekiness** (*informal*), impudence, impertinence, rudeness, cheek (*informal*), audacity, disrespect. [➡BAD MANNERS AND SOCIAL SKILLS; 522] *Opposite:* respect.

insolent *adj* **impudent**, impertinent (*formal*), rude, audacious, disrespectful, cheeky, brazen. [➡RUDE AND HOSTILE; 626] *Opposite:* respectful.

insolently *adv* **impudently**, impertinently (*formal*), rudely, audaciously, disrespectfully, cheekily (*informal*), brazenly. [➡BAD MANNERS AND SOCIAL SKILLS; 522] *Opposite:* respectfully.

insolubility *n* **mysteriousness**, insolvability, indecipherability, intricacy, difficulty, impenetrability, enigma, mystery, unfathomableness. [➡DIFFICULTY AND COMPLEXITY; 243] *Opposite:* solubility.

insoluble *adj* **inexplicable**, mysterious, unsolvable, unfathomable, indecipherable, impenetrable, difficult, intricate, enigmatic. [➡DIFFICULTY AND COMPLEXITY; 243] *Opposite:* solvable.

insolvency *n* **bankruptcy**, liquidation, indebtedness, ruin, collapse, failure. [➡ACCOUNTING, BANKING, AND BUDGETING; 799] *Opposite:* solvency.

insolvent *adj* **bankrupt**, broke (*informal*), bust (*informal*), ruined, in debt, in receivership. [➡POVERTY AND POOR; 892] *Opposite:* solvent.

insomnia *n* **sleeplessness**, wakefulness, restlessness. [➡SLEEP AND DREAM; 724]

insomuch as *conj* **insofar as** (*formal*), inasmuch as, to the extent that, to the degree that, because, since, in that. [➡CAUSATION; 169]

insouciance *n* **carefreeness**, nonchalance, indifference, happiness, unconcern. [➡NEUTRALITY AND INDIFFERENCE; 554] *Opposite:* worry.

insouciant *adj* [➡NEUTRALITY AND INDIFFERENCE; 554]

inspect *v* **look at**, review, examine, scrutinize, look over, study, give the once-over (*informal*), check. [➡EXAMINE AND ASSESS; 754] *Opposite:* ignore.

inspection *n* **review**, examination, scrutiny, checkup, going-over (*informal*), assessment, check. [➡EXAMINE AND ASSESS; 754]

inspector *n* **examiner**, superintendent, overseer, assessor, supervisor, checker. [➡SURVEYORS, EXAMINERS, AND JUDGES; 853]

inspiration 1 *n* **stimulus**, spur, motivation, stimulation, encouragement. [➡CAUSATION; 169] *Opposite:* disincentive. **2** *n* **creativeness**, inventiveness, brilliance, vision, creativity, muse. [➡POSITIVE INTELLECTUAL CHARACTERISTICS; 525] **3** *n* **brain wave** (*informal*), insight, flash, idea, revelation, brainstorm (*US informal*). [➡IDEA AND THOUGHT; 771]

inspirational *adj* **stimulating**, inspiring, stirring, rousing, moving, encouraging, motivating. [➡INTERESTING AND MEANINGFUL; 191] *Opposite:* boring.

inspire *v* **stimulate**, motivate, stir, instigate, encourage, enthuse, move, arouse, rouse. [➡APPEAL TO AND AROUSE INTEREST; 576] *Opposite:* bore.

inspired 1 *adj* **brilliant**, outstanding, superb, exceptional, virtuosic, dazzling. [➡EXTRAORDINARY: AMAZING; 205] *Opposite:* uninspired. **2** *adj* **stimulated**, stirred, moved, encouraged, motivated. [➡POSITIVE IMPATIENCE, ENTHUSIASM, AND ALERTNESS; 538] *Opposite:* uninspired.

inspiring *adj* **inspirational**, stirring, rousing, moving, exciting, stimulating. [➡INTERESTING AND MEANINGFUL; 191] *Opposite:* uninspiring.

in spite of *prep* **notwithstanding** (*formal*), despite, regardless of, in the face of. [➡ALTHOUGH, NEVERTHELESS, AND DESPITE; 170]

instability *n* **unpredictability**, variability, uncertainty, unsteadiness, volatility, shakiness, insecurity, flux. [➡DANGER; 236] *Opposite:* stability.

install 1 *v* **connect**, fit, put in, set up, fix, mount, bed in. [➡EQUIP AND SUPPLY; 436] *Opposite:* remove. 2 *v* **ordain**, establish, inaugurate, invest (*formal*), instate, induct, appoint. [➡INSTITUTE AND INAUGURATE; 349] *Opposite:* oust. 3 *v* **settle in**, settle, settle down, ensconce, position. [➡POSITION SOMETHING; 326]

installation 1 *n* **connection**, fitting, setting up, fixing, putting in, putting in place. [➡FASTEN, LINK, AND JOIN; 409] *Opposite:* removal. 2 *n* **system**, mechanism, machinery, equipment, apparatus. [➡DEVICES; 1114] 3 *n* **appointment**, ordination, inauguration, investiture, instatement, induction. [➡BEGINNING; 53] *Opposite:* removal.

instalment 1 *n* **payment**, segment, portion, part, section. [➡EVENTS AND OCCURRENCES; 35] 2 *n* **part**, episode, chapter. [➡FICTION AND DRAMA; 913]

instance *n* **example**, case, case in point, occurrence, illustration, occasion. [➡REPRESENTATIONS AND GENERAL EXAMPLES; 65]

instant 1 *adj* **prompt**, immediate, sudden, rapid, swift, instantaneous, on the spot, direct. [➡HAPPENING QUICKLY; 104] *Opposite:* gradual. 2 *adj* **prepared**, precooked, premixed, powdered, microwavable, fast. [➡STATE OF PREPARED FOOD; 1170] 3 *adj* **sudden**, immediate, instantaneous, rapid, swift. [➡HAPPENING QUICKLY; 104] 4 *adj* **urgent**, pressing, immediate. [➡FUNDAMENTAL; 196] 5 *n* **moment**, second, split second, the twinkling of an eye, minute, time. [➡SHORT PERIOD OF TIME; 93] *Opposite:* age.

instantaneous *adj* **prompt**, rapid, sudden, immediate, instant, direct, on the spot. [➡HAPPENING QUICKLY; 104] *Opposite:* gradual.

instantly *adv* **promptly**, rapidly, suddenly, right away, instantaneously, immediately, directly, at once, straightaway. [➡HAPPENING QUICKLY; 104] *Opposite:* gradually.

instate *v* **appoint**, ordain, invest (*formal*), inaugurate, establish, install. [➡INSTITUTE AND INAUGURATE; 349] *Opposite:* oust.

instead *adv* **in its place**, as an alternative, as a substitute, as a replacement for. [➡DIFFERENCE; 150]

instead of *prep* **in place of**, rather than, as opposed to, in preference to. [➡DIFFERENCE; 150]

in step 1 *adv* **in line**, in accordance, in harmony, in concordance, in agreement, in keeping, correspondingly. [➡HARMONY; 156] 2 *adv* **keeping pace**, in time, in synchronization, in sync (*informal*), keeping up, in harmony, simultaneously. [➡ACTING WITH OTHERS; 286]

instep *part of* **leg or foot**. [➡LEG AND FOOT; 695]

instigate *v* **bring about**, prompt, initiate, start, activate, set off, originate. [➡CAUSE TO HAPPEN; 31] *Opposite:* stifle.

instigation 1 *n* **start**, beginning, initiation, establishment, commencement (*formal*). [➡BEGINNING; 53] *Opposite:* end. 2 *n* **initiation**, prompting, urging, encouragement, provocation. [➡BEGINNING; 53] *Opposite:* discouragement.

instigator *n* **initiator**, prime mover, mastermind, troublemaker, ringleader, leader. [➡DESIGNERS, CREATORS, AND INSTIGATORS; 348]

instil 1 *v* **impart**, inculcate, drum in, drive into, impress upon, teach, drill, school. [➡INSTRUCT AND TEACH; 610] 2 *v* **drip**, pour, infuse, inject, introduce. [➡MOVE PAST, INTO, OR THROUGH SOMETHING; 332]

instinct 1 *n* **nature**, character, makeup, predisposition, disposition, constitution. [➡TEMPERAMENT AND BEHAVIOUR; 493] 2 *n* **drive**, reflex, feeling, impulse, urge, compulsion, need. [➡FEELINGS; 532] *Opposite:* reason. 3 *n* **feeling**, urge, intuition, impulse, gut feeling, sixth sense, sense. [➡FEELINGS; 532] 4 *n* **talent**, knack, gift, flair, ability, aptitude, feeling. [➡SKILLS, TALENTS, AND ABILITIES; 527]

instinctive 1 *adj* **involuntary**, automatic, reflex, natural, unconscious, intuitive. [➡AUTOMATIC AND INSTINCTIVE; 281] *Opposite:* conscious. 2 *adj* **natural**, intuitive, innate, inherent, inborn. [➡REPRODUCTION AND HEREDITY; 726] *Opposite:* learned.

instinctively *adv* **impulsively**, mechanically, on impulse, automatically, unconsciously, intuitively. [➡AUTOMATIC AND INSTINCTIVE; 281]

institute 1 *v* **introduce**, establish, set up, bring about, found, start, inaugurate. [➡INSTITUTE AND INAUGURATE; 349] 2 *n* **organization**, institution, establishment, foundation, association, society. [➡INSTITUTIONS; 791]

institution 1 *n* **establishment**, organization, body, association, society, foundation, institute. [➡INSTITUTIONS; 791] 2 *n* **tradition**, custom, convention, ritual. [➡WAYS OF DOING THINGS; 295] 3 *n* **introduction**, establishment, setting up, foundation, creation. [➡BEGINNING; 53] 4 *type of* **school**. [➡EDUCATIONAL INSTITUTIONS; 813]

institutional 1 *adj* **official**, recognized, formal, established, organized, influential. [➡KNOWN AND FAMOUS; 182] *Opposite:* unofficial. 2 *adj* **utilitarian**, uniform, dull, functional, ugly, ordinary, standard issue. [➡BORING AND UNINTERESTING; 235] *Opposite:* unique.

institutionalized *adj* **established**, existing, long-standing, traditional, entrenched, customary. [➡OLD, OLD-FASHIONED; 168] *Opposite:* innovative.

in store 1 *adj* [➡ABOUT TO HAPPEN; 33] 2 *adv* **to come**, coming up, in the making, for the future, waiting, in the offing, before you, ahead of you. [➡FUTURE; 86]

in strength *adv* **in force**, in large numbers, in their thousands, in crowds, in throngs, in floods. [➡MANY, MUCH, LARGE AMOUNT; 117]

instruct 1 *v* **teach**, train, coach, tutor, educate, drill, inculcate, initiate. [➡INSTRUCT AND TEACH; 610] 2 *v* **command**, order, tell, direct (*formal*), give orders to, charge. [➡CAUSE OR COMPEL TO ACT; 272]

See Compare and Contrast at **teach**.

instruction 1 *n* **teaching**, training, lessons, tuition, education, coaching, tutoring. [➡TEACHING; 839] 2 *n* **order**, command, direction, directive. [➡REQUEST AND DEMAND; 664]

instructive *adj* **informative**, educational, useful, helpful, enlightening, edifying. [➡INTERESTING AND MEANINGFUL; 191]

instructor *n* **teacher**, coach, tutor, trainer, mentor, lecturer. [➡EDUCATORS; 840]

instrument 1 *n* **tool**, gadget, device, utensil, apparatus, appliance, implement, mechanism, contraption. [➡DEVICES; 1114] 2 *n* **means**, channel, vehicle, method, medium, mechanism, catalyst. [➡WAYS OF DOING THINGS; 295] 3 *n* **musical instrument**. [➡MUSICAL INSTRUMENTS; 910]

instrument

◆ *types of keyboard*
accordion, baby grand, celesta, clavichord, concertina, grand piano, harpsichord, organ, piano, pianoforte, spinet, synthesizer, upright piano

◆ *types of percussion instrument*
bass drum, bongo drums, castanet, chimes, conga drum, cymbal, drum, gamelan, glockenspiel, gong, kettledrum, maraca, marimba, metallophone, snare drum, steel drum, tabla, tabor, tambourine, timpani, tom-tom, triangle, tubular bells, vibraphone, xylophone

◆ *types of stringed instrument*
balalaika, banjo, bass guitar, bouzouki, cello, double bass, electric guitar, fiddle, guitar, harp, Hawaiian guitar, lute, lyre, mandolin, sitar, Spanish guitar, steel guitar, ukulele, viol, viola, viola da gamba, violin, violoncello, zither

◆ *types of wind instrument*
bagpipes, bassoon, clarinet, cor anglais, crumhorn, didgeridoo, English horn (*US*), fife, flute, harmonica, nose flute, oboe, ocarina, panpipes, penny whistle, piccolo, recorder

◆ *types of brass instrument*
bugle, cornet, euphonium, flugelhorn, French horn, horn, post horn, saxhorn, saxophone, sousaphone, trombone, trumpet, tuba

instrumental *adj* **contributory**, active, involved, helpful, influential. [➡RELATED; 143] *Opposite:* tangential.

instrumentalist *n* **musician**, player, performer. [➡MUSICIANS AND SINGERS; 908]

instrumentation 1 *n* **arrangement**, composition, musical arrangement, music, score. [➡NOTES AND CHORDS; 909] 2 *n* **instrument panel**, equipment, instruments, controls, console, dials, control panel, dashboard. [➡MACHINERY; 1113]

instrument panel *n* [➡PARTS OF MACHINES AND TOOLS; 1117]

insubordinate *adj* **disobedient**, defiant, rebellious, mutinous, unruly, noncompliant. [➡REBELLIOUSNESS AND DISOBEDIENCE; 566] *Opposite:* obedient.

insubordination *n* **disobedience**, defiance, rebelliousness, mutiny, unruliness, noncompliance. [➡REBELLIOUSNESS AND DISOBEDIENCE; 566] *Opposite:* obedience.

insubstantial *adj* **flimsy**, light, slight, weak, frail, thin. [➡WEAKNESS; 242] *Opposite:* weighty.

insubstantiality *n* **weakness**, fragility, thinness, flimsiness, lightness, delicacy. [➡WEAKNESS; 242] *Opposite:* robustness.

in succession *adv* [➡AFTER, LAST, AND FOLLOWING; 166]

insufferable *adj* **excruciating**, unbearable, intolerable, insupportable, unendurable, beyond the pale, unspeakable. [➡IRRITATING; 229]

insufficiency 1 *n* **lack**, deficiency, dearth, absence, shortage, scarcity, paucity. [➡TOO FEW, TOO LITTLE; 120] 2 *n* **inadequacy**, deficiency, unfitness, failure, inefficiency, ineffectuality. [➡INAPPROPRIATE AND UNSUITABLE; 225] *Opposite:* adequacy.

insufficient *adj* **inadequate**, deficient, lacking, in short supply, unsatisfactory, scarce. [➡TOO FEW, TOO LITTLE; 120]

insular *adj* **inward-looking**, blinkered, narrow-minded, narrow, limited. [➡NEGATIVE INTELLECTUAL CHARACTERISTICS; 526] *Opposite:* open-minded.

insularity *n* **narrow-mindedness**, narrowness, blinkeredness. [➡NEGATIVE INTELLECTUAL CHARACTERISTICS; 526]

insulate 1 *v* **lag**, wad, line, fill, pad. [➡DECORATE, ADORN, AND APPLY COATINGS; 406] 2 *v* **cloister**, sequester (*formal*), protect, shield, cut off, isolate, separate, segregate. [➡SEPARATE AND DIVIDE; 402] *Opposite:* expose.

insulation 1 *n* **lining**, lagging, wadding, padding, filling. [➡COVERS AND COATINGS; 1245] 2 *n* **protection**, isolation, separation, segregation, sequestration. [➡SEPARATE AND DIVIDE; 402] *Opposite:* exposure.

insulator *n* **soundproofing**, heat-proofing, padding, lagging. [➡BUILDING MATERIALS; 1076]

insult 1 *v* **offend**, affront, abuse, slur, slight, upset. [➡INSULTS, ABUSE, AND SWEARING; 659] *Opposite:* praise. 2 *n* **affront**, offence, slight, slur, rudeness. [➡INSULTS, ABUSE, AND SWEARING; 659]

insulted *adj* [➡SADNESS, DISTRESS, AND DESPAIR; 540]

insulting *adj* **abusive**, offensive, rude, insolent, impertinent (*formal*), wounding, discourteous, slighting. [➡INSULTS, ABUSE, AND SWEARING; 659] *Opposite:* polite.

in sum *adv* [➡SUMMARIZING EXPRESSIONS; 623]

in summary *adv* [➡SUMMARIZING EXPRESSIONS; 623]

insuperability *n* [➡DIFFICULTY AND COMPLEXITY; 243]

insuperable *adj* **insurmountable**, impossible, unbeatable, challenging, undefeatable, overwhelming. [➡DIFFICULTY AND COMPLEXITY; 243] *Opposite:* easy.

insupportable *adj* **unbearable**, intolerable, unendurable, insufferable, unspeakable, unacceptable. [➡IRRITATING; 229] *Opposite:* bearable.

insurance *n* **cover**, indemnity, assurance, protection, coverage, indemnification. [➡INSURANCE; 801]

insurance policy 1 *n* **document**, contract, cover, agreement, guarantee, warranty. [➡OFFICIAL DOCUMENTS; 587] 2 *n* **safety net**, safeguard, precaution, protection, provision. [➡INSURANCE; 801]

insure *v* **protect**, cover, assure, indemnify, underwrite. [➡INSURANCE; 801]

insurer *n* **underwriter**, broker, guarantor. [➡INSURANCE; 801]

insurgence *n* **uprising**, rebellion, revolt, revolution, mutiny, riot. [➡AGGRESSIVE EVENT; 39]

insurgency *n* **insurrection**, insurgence, rebellion, revolution, revolt, uprising, mutiny, riot. [➡AGGRESSIVE EVENT; 39]

insurgent 1 *n* **rebel**, insurrectionary, revolutionary, guerrilla, mutineer, rioter, protester. [➡UNCOOPERATIVE OR REBELLIOUS PERSON; 567] 2 *adj* **mutinous**, rebellious, rebel, insurrectionary. [➡REBELLIOUSNESS AND DISOBEDIENCE; 566]

insurmountable *adj* **unbeatable**, insuperable, impossible, undefeatable, overwhelming. [➡DIFFICULTY AND COMPLEXITY; 243] *Opposite:* easy.

insurrection *n* **insurgence**, insurgency, rebellion, revolution, revolt, mutiny, uprising, rising, civil disobedience. [➡AGGRESSIVE EVENT; 39]

in suspense *adj* [➡POSITIVE IMPATIENCE, ENTHUSIASM, AND ALERTNESS; 538]

in sync (*informal*) *adv* [➡HARMONY; 156]

intact *adj* **complete**, whole, unbroken, in one piece, integral, undamaged, unharmed, together. [➡WHOLENESS AND COMPLETENESS; 199] *Opposite:* broken.

intake 1 *n* **consumption**, eating, drinking, ingestion. [➡AMOUNT AND QUANTITY; 112] 2 *n* **entry**, entrants, students. [➡STUDENTS AND PUPILS; 841] 3 *n* **opening**, pipe, tube, aperture, entry, inlet, duct. [➡WATERCOURSES; 1110] *Opposite:* outlet.

in tandem *adv* **in partnership**, together, concurrently, jointly, as a pair, as a team, with each other, collectively. [➡ACTING WITH OTHERS; 286] *Opposite:* independently.

intangibility 1 *n* **imperceptibility**, impalpability (*formal*), immateriality, immaterialness, untouchability, insubstantiality. [➡IMPERCEPTIBLE; 26] *Opposite:* tangibility. 2 *n* **indescribability**, elusiveness, vagueness, subtlety, unquantifiability, abstractness, ethereality. [➡VAGUENESS; 244]

intangible 1 *adj* **imperceptible**, incorporeal (*formal*), immaterial, insubstantial, impalpable (*formal*). [➡IMPERCEPTIBLE; 26] *Opposite:* concrete. 2 *adj* **unquantifiable**, elusive, vague, ethereal, subtle, indefinable, indescribable. [➡VAGUENESS; 244]

intangibly *adv* **elusively**, imperceptibly, unsubstantially, impalpably. [➡IMPERCEPTIBLE; 26]

in tatters *adj* [➡IN BAD REPAIR; 1233]

in tears *adj* [➡CRYING; 651]

integer *n* **whole number**, number, numeral, digit, figure. [➡MATHS; 598] *Opposite:* fraction.

integral 1 *adj* **essential**, vital, important, basic, fundamental, primary, central. [➡FUNDAMENTAL; 196] *Opposite:* unimportant. 2 *adj* **connected**, internal, central, at the heart of. [➡RELATED; 143] *Opposite:* unimportant. 3 *adj* **complete**, whole, intact, undivided, unbroken, full. [➡WHOLENESS AND COMPLETENESS; 199]

integrate 1 *v* **mix**, fit in, join in, assimilate, take part, participate. [➡PARTICIPATE; 293] 2 *v* **put together**, mix, incorporate, add, join together, amalgamate, combine, assimilate. [➡COMBINE AND MIX; 401] *Opposite:* separate. 3 *v* **open up**, desegregate, combine, mix, assimilate. [➡ESTABLISHING RELATIONSHIPS WITH OTHERS; 974]

integrated 1 *adj* **combined**, united, joined, unified, cohesive, assimilated, incorporated, included, amalgamated. [➡RELATED; 143] *Opposite:* separated. 2 *adj* **open**, desegregated, multiethnic, multicultural, multilingual, interracial. [➡HARMONY; 156] *Opposite:* segregated.

integrated circuit *type of* **hardware**. [➡COMPUTERS AND COMPUTING; 1126]

integration *n* **addition**, mixing, incorporation, combination, amalgamation, assimilation. [➡COMBINE AND MIX; 401]

integrity *n* **honesty**, truth, truthfulness, honour, veracity, reliability, uprightness. [➡MORALLY GOOD; 775] *Opposite:* dishonesty.

integument *n* [➡THE SKIN; 721]

intellect *n* **intelligence**, brainpower, brain, brains, mind, understanding. [➡DESCRIBING SOMEBODY'S INTELLECT; 524] *Opposite:* emotion.

intellectual 1 *adj* **knowledgeable**, intelligent, highbrow, academic, rational, logical, cerebral, scholarly. [➡POSITIVE INTELLECTUAL CHARACTERISTICS; 525] 2 *n* **philosopher**, thinker, academic, brain (*informal*), scholar, highbrow. [➡LEVEL OF EDUCATION AND SOPHISTICATION; 894]

intellectualize *v* [➡THINK AND REFLECT; 744]

intellectually *adv* **intelligently**, rationally, knowledgeably, mentally, logically, academically, cerebrally, in your head. [➡PSYCHOLOGY AND THE MIND; 770] *Opposite:* emotionally.

intelligence 1 *n* **brain**, cleverness, aptitude, intellect, brains, astuteness, brainpower, acumen. [➡POSITIVE INTELLECTUAL CHARACTERISTICS; 525] *Opposite:* stupidity. 2 *n* **information**, news, reports, communication, word, details. [➡BASIC DETAILS; 689]

intelligence quotient *n* **IQ**, mental ability, measure, measurement, degree, aptitude. [➡PSYCHOLOGY AND THE MIND; 770]

intelligent 1 *adj* **brainy** (*informal*), clever, bright, gifted, intellectual, sharp, quick, able, smart, scholarly, knowledgeable. [➡POSITIVE INTELLECTUAL CHARACTERISTICS; 525] *Opposite:* stupid. 2 *adj* **sensible**, rational, wise, logical, perceptive, shrewd, judicious, cerebral. [➡POSITIVE INTELLECTUAL CHARACTERISTICS; 525] *Opposite:* irrational.

Compare and Contrast: ***intelligent, bright, quick, smart, clever, able, gifted***

CORE MEANING: HAVING THE ABILITY TO LEARN AND UNDERSTAND EASILY

intelligent quick to learn and understand; ***bright*** showing an ability to think, learn, or respond quickly, especially used of younger people; ***quick*** alert, perceptive, and able to respond quickly; ***smart*** showing intelligence and mental alertness but sometimes suggesting insolent intelligence; ***clever*** having sharp mental abilities, but sometimes suggesting showy or superficial cleverness; ***able*** capable or talented, also used in educational circles of children who are intelligent; ***gifted*** talented, especially artistic or creative, also used in educational circles of children who are exceptionally intelligent.

intelligentsia *n* **intellectuals**, academics, literati (*formal*), highbrows, cognoscenti. [➡LEVEL OF EDUCATION AND SOPHISTICATION; 894]

intelligible *adj* **comprehensible**, understandable, clear, plain, lucid, logical. [➡CONCISE AND CLEAR; 203] *Opposite:* unintelligible.

intemperance *n* **self-indulgence**, overindulgence, excess, hedonism, gluttony, greed. [➡MORALLY BAD; 776] *Opposite:* moderation.

intemperate *adj* **self-indulgent**, uncontrolled, unrestrained, inordinate, immoderate (*formal*), unbalanced, extreme, severe, excessive, greedy, extravagant, unreasonable. [➡PLEASURE-SEEKING AND EXCESS; 885] *Opposite:* moderate.

intemperately *adv* **greedily**, immoderately (*formal*), excessively, self-indulgently, inordinately, extravagantly, unreasonably, extremely, severely. [➡PLEASURE-SEEKING AND EXCESS; 885] *Opposite:* temperately.

intend *v* **mean**, aim, propose, plan, have it in mind, anticipate, expect. [➡PREPARE FOR ACTION; 290]

intended 1 *adj* **envisioned**, future, planned, proposed, projected, wished-for, anticipated. [➡FUTURE; 86] 2 *adj* **planned**, intentional, deliberate, on purpose, premeditated, calculated. [➡INTENTIONAL AND DELIBERATE; 280] *Opposite:* accidental. 3 *n* (*dated or humorous*) **betrothed** (*formal*), fiancé, fiancée, husband-to-be, wife-to-be, girlfriend, boyfriend. [➡RELATIVES BY MARRIAGE; 960]

intense *adj* **penetrating**, strong, powerful, forceful, concentrated, deep, passionate, extreme, severe. [➡STRENGTH; 202] *Opposite:* moderate.

intensely *adv* **forcefully**, penetratingly, powerfully, strongly, deeply, very much, extremely, hugely, passionately, severely. [➡TO A GREAT EXTENT; 130] *Opposite:* mildly.

intensification *n* **strengthening**, increase, rise, escalation, spiralling, growth, amplification. [➡CHANGE OF INTENSITY: MORE; 395] *Opposite:* reduction.

intensify *v* **strengthen**, deepen, step up, exaggerate, increase, heap on, pile on, build up. [➡CHANGE OF INTENSITY: MORE; 395] *Opposite:* weaken.

See Compare and Contrast at **increase**.

intensity *n* **strength**, concentration, power, force, passion, amount, greatness. [➡STRENGTH; 202] *Opposite:* moderation.

intensive *adj* **concentrated**, rigorous, exhaustive, severe, thorough, demanding, serious. [➡STRENGTH; 202] *Opposite:* easy.

intensive care 1 *n* **monitoring**, nursing, specialist care, 24-hour care, one-to-one care. [➡HOSPITALS AND CLINICS; 826] 2 *n* **ward**, ICU, intensive care unit. [➡HOSPITALS AND CLINICS; 826]

intensive care unit *n* **intensive care**, ICU, ward. [➡HOSPITALS AND CLINICS; 826]

intent 1 *n* (*formal*) **intention**, aim, goal, target, objective, plan, meaning, purpose. [➡INTENTION AND PURPOSE; 773] 2 *adj* **concentrated**, absorbed, focused, directed, fixed, rapt, engaged. [➡PENSIVENESS AND INTEREST; 539] 3 *adj* **intending to**, bent on, determined, resolved, set on, committed. [➡DESIRE AND WANT; 580]

intention *n* **aim**, purpose, intent (*formal*), goal, target, objective, plan. [➡INTENTION AND PURPOSE; 773]

intentional *adj* **deliberate**, planned, intended, premeditated, calculated, purposeful. [➡INTENTIONAL AND DELIBERATE; 280] *Opposite:* accidental.

intently *adv* **closely**, fixedly, carefully, keenly, attentively, absorbedly, raptly. [➡WITH ENTHUSIASM; 287] *Opposite:* abstractedly.

intentness *n* **attentiveness**, concentration, focus, attention, close attention, raptness, fixedness, absorption. [➡ATTENTION AND ATTENTIVENESS; 764] *Opposite:* abstraction.

inter (*formal*) *v* **bury**, entomb, lay to rest. [➡BURIAL AND PREPARATION FOR BURIAL; 929]

interact *v* **interrelate**, act together, cooperate, relate, intermingle, network. [➡CREATING CONNECTIONS; 145]

interaction *n* **communication**, contact, interface, dealings, relations, collaboration. [➡COMMUNICATION; 603]

interactive *adj* **communicating**, collaborating, cooperating, collaborative, cooperative, shared. [➡RELATED; 143]

inter alia (*formal*) *adv* **among others**, among other things, and others, et cetera, and so on. [➡EXPRESSIONS INTRODUCING EXTRA INFORMATION; 137]

interbreed *v* **breed**, reproduce, multiply, mate, produce, propagate, spawn. [➡REPRODUCTION AND HEREDITY; 726]

intercalate *v* **insert**, introduce, interpolate, add, interpose, place. [➡POSITION SOMETHING: BETWEEN, BESIDE, OR INSIDE SOMETHING; 327] *Opposite:* extrapolate.

intercede *v* **intervene**, mediate, plead, negotiate, arbitrate. [➡PARTICIPATE; 293]

intercept *v* **cut off**, catch, interrupt, stop, seize, capture, divert. [➡CAUSE TO STOP; 267]

interception *n* **capture**, seizure, interruption, interference, intervention. [➡PAUSES AND PHASES; 56]

intercession *n* **intervention**, mediation, arbitration, negotiation. [➡NEGOTIATION AND DEBATE; 46]

interchange 1 *v* **switch**, swap (*informal*), trade, exchange, substitute, trade off. [➡EXCHANGE AND INTERCHANGE; 449] 2 *n* **trading**, exchange, transaction, swap (*informal*), swapping, substitution, trade-off. [➡EXCHANGE AND INTERCHANGE; 449] 3 *n* **crossroads**, junction, intersection. [➡BRIDGES, TUNNELS, CROSSINGS, AND JUNCTIONS; 1111]

interchangeable *adj* **substitutable**, identical, the same, similar, compatible, transposable, exchangeable, switchable, swappable. [➡SAMENESS; 151] *Opposite:* incompatible.

intercity *adj* **interurban**, long-distance. [➡COMMUNICATION NETWORKS; 1104] *Opposite:* local.

intercollegiate *adj* **intercollege**, interuniversity, interschool, intermural. [➡LESSONS, COURSE WORK, AND EXAMINATIONS; 842] *Opposite:* intramural.

intercom *type of* **telecommunications equipment**. [➡TELECOMMUNICATIONS; 1129]

intercommunicate *v* **talk**, communicate, converse, discuss, contact. [➡TWO-WAY COMMUNICATION; 608]

interconnect *v* **join**, intersect, connect, interrelate, interlock, communicate. [➡CREATING CONNECTIONS; 145]

intercontinental *adj* **international**, transnational, global, worldwide, large-scale. [➡WHOLENESS AND COMPLETENESS; 199] *Opposite:* national.

intercourse *n* **dealings**, contact, communication, interaction, association. [➡COMMUNICATION; 603]

intercut *v* **interpose**, insert, alternate, interweave, interject, interpolate. [➡POSITION SOMETHING: BETWEEN, BESIDE, OR INSIDE SOMETHING; 327]

interdenominational *adj* **interfaith**, interreligion, ecumenical, inclusive, mixed. [➡RELIGIONS AND RELIGIOUS PRACTICES; 778]

interdependent *adj* **symbiotic**, dependent, reliant, codependent. [➡RECIPROCITY AND INTERDEPENDENCE; 148]

interdict 1 *n* **order**, court order, ban, prohibition, veto, injunction, restraining order, exclusion order, embargo, sanction, proscription (*formal*), restriction. [➡REFUSE PERMISSION AND NOT ALLOW; 671] 2 *v* **ban**, prohibit, forbid, veto, embargo, exclude, proscribe, preclude (*formal*), bar. [➡REFUSE PERMISSION AND NOT ALLOW; 671] *Opposite:* permit.

interest 1 *n* **attention**, notice, curiosity, concentration, awareness, attentiveness, concern. [➡ATTENTION AND ATTENTIVENESS; 764] 2 *n* **hobby**, activity, pursuit, pastime, leisure activity, leisure pursuit. [➡LEISURE AND RECREATION; 874] 3 *n* **concern**, importance, significance, relevance, consequence (*formal*), note. [➡IMPORTANCE AND SIGNIFICANCE; 193] 4 *n* **good**, advantage, benefit, gain, profit. [➡SOURCE OF HAPPINESS, PLEASURE, OR IMPROVEMENT; 210] 5 *v* **attract**, draw, appeal, fascinate, be of interest, catch your eye. [➡APPEAL TO AND AROUSE INTEREST; 576]

interested *adj* **absorbed**, attentive, involved, concerned, attracted, fascinated, engrossed, intent, entranced, captivated, riveted (*informal*). [➡PENSIVENESS AND INTEREST; 539] *Opposite:* indifferent.

interest group 1 *n* **alliance**, association, society, cartel, trade union, league, pressure group, lobby group, lobby, faction, group. [➡GROUPS WITH A COMMON INTEREST; 938] 2 *n* **club**, association, group, society. [➡CLUBS AND SOCIETIES; 939]

interesting *adj* **stimulating**, attractive, thought-provoking, motivating, exciting, fascinating, attention-grabbing, out of the ordinary, remarkable, worthy of note, curious, noteworthy. [➡INTERESTING AND MEANINGFUL; 191] *Opposite:* boring.

interface 1 *n* **border**, boundary, line, crossing point, edge. [➡EXTREMITIES OF PHYSICAL OBJECTS; 1249] 2 *type of* **software**. [➡COMPUTERS AND COMPUTING; 1126]

interfere 1 *v* **pry**, intrude, stick your oar in, meddle, disturb, intervene, stick your nose in, snoop (*informal*), interlope. [➡INTERRUPT AND BUTT IN; 620] 2 *v* **delay**, inhibit, restrict, affect, get in the way, hinder, obstruct, impede, hold up, hamper. [➡AVOID, PREVENT, LIMIT, AND CONTROL; 278]

interference 1 *n* **meddling**, intrusion, prying, interfering, nosiness (*informal*), intervention, snooping (*informal*), interloping. [➡BAD BEHAVIOUR OR ACTION; 255] 2 *n* **restriction**, obstruction, hindrance, obstacle, delay, impediment, holdup. [➡PROBLEM; 257]

interfere with *v* [➡WOUND A PERSON OR ANIMAL; 384]

interfering *adj* **nosy** (*informal*), intrusive, meddlesome, prying, inquisitive, snooping (*informal*), meddling, interloping. [➡NOSY AND INTERFERING; 513]

intergalactic *adj* **interstellar**, interplanetary, space. [➡THE SOLAR SYSTEM AND ASTRONOMY; 1059]

intergovernmental *adj* **interstate**, international, diplomatic, foreign, high-level, transnational, geopolitical. [➡COUNTRIES AND REGIONS; 1066]

interim 1 *adj* **temporary**, provisional, short-term, intervening, acting, pro tem, ad hoc. [➡FINITENESS, VARIABILITY, AND TRANSIENCE; 96] *Opposite:* permanent. 2 *n* **interlude**, pause, break, interval, pause in the action, intermezzo. [➡PAUSES AND PHASES; 56]

interior 1 *n* **inside**, centre, core, heart. [➡CENTRAL PARTS OF PHYSICAL OBJECTS; 1250] *Opposite:* outside. 2 *adj* **internal**, inner, central, inland, inside. [➡GENERAL LOCATIONS; 159] *Opposite:* peripheral.

interior decoration *n* **decoration**, furnishings, decorating scheme, colour scheme, interior design, decor. [➡FITTINGS; 859]

interject *v* **butt in**, exclaim, interrupt, throw in, interpose, cut in, interpolate, speak. [➡INTERRUPT AND BUTT IN; 620]

interjection 1 *n* **exclamation**, outburst, cry, utterance, shout. [➡NEUTRAL ONE-WAY COMMUNICATION; 49] 2 *n* **interruption**, interpolation, introduction, addition, insertion. [➡NEUTRAL ONE-WAY COMMUNICATION; 49] 3 *type of* **word class**. [➡ASPECTS OF LANGUAGE; 683]

interlace *v* **interweave**, intertwine, interlock, entwine, knit, connect, intermingle, link, interconnect, interlink, join, intermesh, mesh. [➡POSITION SOMETHING: BETWEEN, BESIDE, OR INSIDE SOMETHING; 327]

interlard *v* **interpose**, insert, introduce, intersperse, interweave, intertwine, alternate, interpolate, vary. [➡POSITION SOMETHING: BETWEEN, BESIDE, OR INSIDE SOMETHING; 327]

interleave *v* **slot in**, put in, enclose, interweave, add, incorporate, include, insert. [➡POSITION SOMETHING: BETWEEN, BESIDE, OR INSIDE SOMETHING; 327]

interlink *v* **interweave**, intertwine, interlace, insert, intersperse, add, link, entwine, interconnect, knit, connect, intermingle, intermesh, mesh, join. [➡FASTEN, LINK, AND JOIN; 409]

interlock *v* **mesh**, dovetail, link, join, interconnect, connect, intertwine, knit, intermingle, interlink, interweave, intermesh. [➡POSITION SOMETHING: BETWEEN, BESIDE, OR INSIDE SOMETHING; 327]

interlocutor *n* **speaker**, talker, discusser, panelist, converser, debater. [➡SPEAKERS AND ORATORS; 604]

interloper 1 *n* **intruder**, trespasser, gatecrasher, persona non grata, impostor. [➡STRANGERS; 972] 2 *n* **meddler**, busybody (*informal*), snoop (*informal*), nosy parker (*informal*). [➡ INTERFERING PEOPLE AND TELLTALES; 950]

interlude *n* **interval**, break, rest, pause, interim, intermission, intermezzo. [➡ PAUSES AND PHASES; 56]

intermediary 1 *n* **intercessor**, arbitrator, negotiator, go-between, mediator, liaison, agent, conciliator, intermediate. [➡ REPRESENTATIVES AND PATRONS; 968] 2 *adj* **intermediate**, middle, midway, in-between, transitional, halfway. [➡ RELATIVE LOCATION; 162]

intermediate *adj* **middle**, midway, in-between, transitional, halfway, intermediary. [➡ RELATIVE LOCATION; 162] *Opposite:* extreme.

interment (*formal*) *n* **burial**, entombment, committal, funeral, funeral rites. [➡ BURIAL AND PREPARATION FOR BURIAL; 929]

intermesh *v* **join**, interlink, knit, mesh, interconnect, interlock, interlace, intertwine, intersperse, link, entwine. [➡ FASTEN, LINK, AND JOIN; 409]

intermezzo *type of* **instrumental music**. [➡ MUSIC, SONGS, AND SINGING; 907]

interminable *adj* **endless**, ceaseless, everlasting, perpetual, never-ending, incessant. [➡ PERMANENCE: WITHOUT END; 94] *Opposite:* finite.

intermingle *v* **intermix**, mingle, interact, combine, fuse, meld, amalgamate, coalesce. [➡ COMBINE AND MIX; 401]

intermission *n* **intermezzo**, interval, break, interlude, pause, rest. [➡ PAUSES AND PHASES; 56]

intermittent *adj* **spasmodic**, recurrent, erratic, irregular, sporadic, discontinuous, broken, alternating, occasional. [➡ FINITENESS, VARIABILITY, AND TRANSIENCE; 96] *Opposite:* constant.

See Compare and Contrast at **periodic**.

intermix *v* **meld**, intermingle, mix, mingle, blend, amalgamate, fuse, merge, combine, coalesce. [➡ COMBINE AND MIX; 401] *Opposite:* separate.

intern 1 *v* **imprison**, detain, confine, hold, jail. [➡ THE POLICE, ARREST, AND PRE-TRIAL PROCEEDINGS; 818] *Opposite:* release. 2 *n* **medical student**, med student, doctor, student doctor. [➡ STUDENTS AND PUPILS; 841]

internal 1 *adj* **interior**, inner, inside, core, heart, centre. [➡ CENTRAL PARTS OF PHYSICAL OBJECTS; 1250] *Opposite:* external. 2 *adj* **domestic**, in-house, home, intramural. [➡ BELONGING OR RELATING TO INDIVIDUALS; 944] *Opposite:* external.

internalize 1 *v* **adopt**, affect, take on, assume, co-opt. [➡ LEARN AND DISCOVER; 763] 2 *v* **stew**, mull over, bottle up, suppress. [➡ WITHHOLD INFORMATION; 688] *Opposite:* externalize.

international *adj* **global**, worldwide, intercontinental, universal, transnational. [➡ COUNTRIES AND REGIONS; 1066] *Opposite:* domestic.

internationalist *adj* **open-minded**, unprejudiced, unbigoted, unnationalistic. [➡ STYLES AND SYSTEMS OF GOVERNMENT; 806] *Opposite:* nationalist.

internecine 1 *adj* **internal**, inner, civil, domestic. [➡ BELONGING OR RELATING TO INDIVIDUALS; 944] 2 *adj* **destructive**, devastating, decimating, deadly, injurious, costly, havoc-wreaking. [➡ DANGEROUS; 237]

internee *n* **prisoner**, captive, detainee, hostage, inmate, political prisoner. [➡ CAPTIVES AND PRISONERS; 250]

Internet *n* [➡ THE INTERNET; 1127]

internment *n* **imprisonment**, captivity, confinement, custody, incarceration (*formal*), detention. [➡ CAPTIVITY AND LOSS OF FREEDOM; 249] *Opposite:* release.

internship (*US*) *n* **residency**, position, medical training, placement, job, medical school, training period, practicum (*US*). [➡ JOB; 833]

interpersonal *adj* **relational**, social, personal, interactive. [➡ RELATIONSHIP TO ANOTHER; 973] *Opposite:* solitary.

interplanetary *adj* **space**, planetary, interstellar, intergalactic, astronomical. [➡ THE SOLAR SYSTEM AND ASTRONOMY; 1059]

interplay *n* **chemistry**, interaction, relationship, interchange, back-and-forth. [➡ CONNECTION; 144]

interpolate 1 *v* **insert**, interpose, intercalate, incorporate, include, add, introduce. [➡ MOVE PAST, INTO, OR THROUGH SOMETHING; 332] 2 *v* **interrupt**, interject, interpose, throw in, cut in, butt in. [➡ INTERRUPT AND BUTT IN; 620]

interpose 1 *v* **interrupt**, cut in, throw in, interpolate, interject, butt in. [➡ POSITION SOMETHING: BETWEEN, BESIDE, OR INSIDE SOMETHING; 327] 2 *v* **intervene**, interfere, intercede, meddle, butt in, mediate, negotiate, arbitrate. [➡ INTERRUPT AND BUTT IN; 620]

interpret 1 *v* **explain**, clarify, account for, elucidate (*formal*), make clear, shed light on, illuminate. [➡ EXPLAIN AND CLARIFY; 611] 2 *v* **take to mean**, understand, read, construe, infer, read between the lines, deduce, take. [➡ SOLVE AND INTERPRET; 761] 3 *v* **translate**, decode, decipher, unravel, figure out. [➡ SOLVE AND INTERPRET; 761]

interpretation *n* **clarification**, understanding, reading, explanation, analysis, version, construal, elucidation (*formal*). [➡ EXPLAIN AND CLARIFY; 611]

interpretative *adj* **explanatory**, revelatory, informational, informative, revealing, interpretive. [➡ EXPLAIN AND CLARIFY; 611]

interpreter 1 *n* **translator**, linguist, transcriber, explainer, paraphraser, polyglot, commentator, exegetist, explicator. [➡ PEOPLE WHO WORK WITH LANGUAGE AND CODE; 854] 2 *n* **performer**, portrayer, exponent, promoter, medium, player, actor, musician, reader. [➡ WORKERS IN ENTERTAINMENT AND MEDIA; 873]

interpretive *adj* **explanatory**, revelatory, informational, informative, revealing, interpretative. [➡ EXPLAIN AND CLARIFY; 611]

interracial *adj* **mixed**, of mixed race, multicultural, multiethnic, integrated, mixed-race, multiracial. [➡ RECIPROCITY AND INTERDEPENDENCE; 148] *Opposite:* segregated.

interregnum *n* **interval**, pause, lag, lapse, wait, period, interruption, hiatus. [➡ PAUSES AND PHASES; 56]

interrelate *v* **interconnect**, relate, connect, link up, correlate, join up, interdepend. [➡CREATING CONNECTIONS; 145]

interrogate *v* **question**, cross-examine, quiz, grill (*informal*), interview, debrief, give the third degree (*informal*), catechize, probe. [➡ASK PEOPLE QUESTIONS; 667]

interrogation *n* **questioning**, examination, cross-examination, grilling, interview, debriefing. [➡ASK PEOPLE QUESTIONS; 667]

interrogative *adj* **questioning**, curious, inquisitive, inquiring, probing. [➡ENTHUSIASTIC AND INQUISITIVE; 629]

interrupt 1 *v* **butt in**, barge in, interject, disturb, intrude, interpose, intersect, interfere, cut in on. [➡INTERRUPT AND BUTT IN; 620] 2 *v* **break off**, cut short, disrupt, break up, stop, suspend, discontinue, disconnect. [➡CAUSE TO STOP; 267]

interruption *n* **break**, pause, disruption, stoppage, disturbance, intrusion, intermission, interlude, interval, disconnection. [➡PAUSES AND PHASES; 56]

intersect *v* **cross**, interconnect, meet, traverse, overlap, crisscross, pass across, transect. [➡CREATING CONNECTIONS; 145]

intersection 1 *n* **connection**, meeting, juncture (*formal*), node, joint, joining, crossing, coming together. [➡CONNECTION; 144] 2 *n* **junction**, crossroads, roundabout, T-junction, fork, traffic circle (*US*). [➡BRIDGES, TUNNELS, CROSSINGS, AND JUNCTIONS; 1111]

intersperse *v* **mix together**, combine, scatter, spread, intermingle, sprinkle, interpose, pepper, intermix, commingle (*literary*), punctuate, break up, dot, disperse, broadcast. [➡COMBINE AND MIX; 401]

interstate 1 *adj* **regional**, national, federal, political, administrative, judicial. [➡GOVERNMENT AND POLITICS; 805] 2 (*US*) *type of* **major road**. [➡ROADS; 1105]

interstellar *adj* **interplanetary**, space, star, intergalactic, stellar, astronomical. [➡THE SOLAR SYSTEM AND ASTRONOMY; 1059]

interstice *n* **space**, gap, crack, opening, aperture, chink, cranny, crevice, cleft, fissure. [➡HOLES, GAPS, AND FORKS; 1251]

intertwine *v* **interweave**, entwine, interlace, link, interleave, interlink, interlock, knit, interconnect, intermingle, connect, braid, crisscross, mesh. [➡POSITION SOMETHING: BETWEEN, BESIDE, OR INSIDE SOMETHING; 327] *Opposite:* divide.

intertwined *adj* [➡RELATIVE LOCATION; 162]

interval 1 *n* **intermission**, break, pause, interlude, recess, rest, wait, interim. [➡PAUSES AND PHASES; 56] 2 *n* **gap**, time, period, space, distance, hiatus, separation, rift, breach. [➡HOLES, GAPS, AND FORKS; 1251]

intervene 1 *v* **intercede**, arbitrate, mediate, interfere, get involved, intrude, interpose. [➡PARTICIPATE; 293] *Opposite:* hold back. 2 *v* **happen**, occur, take place, come to pass (*archaic or literary*), ensue, succeed, arise, befall (*archaic or literary*). [➡HAPPEN; 27]

intervention *n* **interference**, involvement, intrusion, intercession, interposition, interpolation, mediation, intermediation. [➡KIND ACTION OR BEHAVIOUR; 296]

interview 1 *n* **meeting**, talk, consultation, conference, discussion, question and answer session, conversation, round table, dialogue. [➡MEETINGS AND ASSEMBLIES; 43] 2 *v* **question**, interrogate, talk to, converse with, put questions to, cross-examine, quiz. [➡ASK PEOPLE QUESTIONS; 667]

interviewee *n* **applicant**, candidate, hopeful, aspirant, contender, entrant, examinee. [➡SUBORDINATES AND ASSISTANTS; 966] *Opposite:* interviewer.

interviewer 1 *n* **examiner**, assessor, questioner, interrogator, evaluator, investigator, cross-examiner. [➡BOSSES AND MANAGEMENT; 965] 2 *n* **presenter**, questioner, correspondent, personality, journalist. [➡WORKERS IN ENTERTAINMENT AND MEDIA; 873] *Opposite:* interviewee.

interweave *v* **intertwine**, interlace, mingle, intermingle, entwine, link, interleave, interlink, interlock, knit, interconnect, connect, crisscross, braid, mesh. [➡POSITION SOMETHING: BETWEEN, BESIDE, OR INSIDE SOMETHING; 327]

interwoven *adj* [➡RELATIVE LOCATION; 162]

intestate *adj* **without a will**, unrepresented, unaccounted for, voiceless, unheard. [➡LACK OF POSSESSION; 446]

intestinal *adj* **duodenal**, colonic, abdominal, stomach, bowel, celiac, gastric, gut, ventral, visceral. [➡THE DIGESTIVE TRACT; 710]

intestine *part of* **digestive tract**. [➡THE DIGESTIVE TRACT; 710]

in that *conj* **because**, as, since, given that. [➡CAUSATION; 169]

in the air *adj* **imminent**, about to happen, in the pipeline, forthcoming, coming, near, happening, threatening, in preparation. [➡ABOUT TO HAPPEN; 33]

in the altogether (*informal*) *adj* [➡DRESS, WEAR, AND UNDRESS; 868]

in the area *adv* [➡PRESENT AND AVAILABLE; 11]

in the ascendant *adj* [➡PLEASANT SITUATIONS; 74]

in the background *adv* [➡GENERAL LOCATIONS; 159]

in the bag (*informal*) *adj* **certain**, a sure thing (*informal*), guaranteed, a dead cert (*informal*), assured, definite. [➡CERTAIN; 175] *Opposite:* uncertain.

in the black *adj* **in credit**, solvent, in the money, in clover, flush (*informal*). [➡WEALTH AND WEALTHY; 891] *Opposite:* in the red.

in the blink of an eye *adv* [➡HAPPENING QUICKLY; 104]

in the buff (*informal*) *adj* [➡DRESS, WEAR, AND UNDRESS; 868]

in the chips (*US*) *adj* [➡WEALTH AND WEALTHY; 891]

in the clear *adj* **innocent**, let off, off the hook (*informal*), free of blame, cleared, guiltless, blameless, free to go, scot free, exonerated. [➡FREEDOM AND LIBERTY; 209] *Opposite:* guilty.

in the club (*slang*) *adj* [➡REPRODUCTION AND HEREDITY; 726]

in the course of *prep* [➡CONCURRENT AND CONTEMPORANEOUS; 165]

in the distance *adv* [➡DISTANCE; 161]

in the doghouse (*informal*) *adj* **in disgrace**, in trouble, out of favour, disgraced, in bad odour, under a cloud. [➡ IN TROUBLE AND DISADVANTAGED; 73] *Opposite:* popular.

in the doldrums *adj* [➡ SADNESS, DISTRESS, AND DESPAIR; 540]

in the dumps *adj* [➡ SADNESS, DISTRESS, AND DESPAIR; 540]

in the end *adv* **finally**, eventually, after some time, at long last, after a while, ultimately, at last, at the end of the day. [➡ AFTER, LAST, AND FOLLOWING; 166] *Opposite:* initially.

in the event *adv* **as it turned out**, as it was, unexpectedly, surprisingly, when it came to it, as it happened, anyway, anyhow, the thing was. [➡ RESULTS AND OUTCOMES; 83]

in the face of *prep* **despite**, in spite of, notwithstanding (*formal*), regardless of. [➡ ALTHOUGH, NEVERTHELESS, AND DESPITE; 170]

in the family way (*dated informal*) *adj* [➡ REPRODUCTION AND HEREDITY; 726]

in the flesh *adv* **in person**, personally, in real life, physically, individually, yourself. [➡ ACTING INDEPENDENTLY; 285]

in the fullness of time *adv* [➡ FUTURE; 86]

in the future *adv* [➡ FUTURE; 86]

in the know *adj* **informed**, in the picture, well-informed, aware, clued-up (*informal*), primed, enlightened, with it (*informal*), on the ball (*informal*). [➡ KNOWLEDGE AND WISDOM; 559] *Opposite:* ignorant.

in the lap of luxury *adj* [➡ PLEASANT SITUATIONS; 74]

in the lead *adj* [➡ PLEASANT SITUATIONS; 74]

in the light of *prep* **taking into consideration**, in view of, considering, taking into account, with regard to, given that, all in all. [➡ CAUSATION; 169]

in the limelight *adj* [➡ KNOWN AND FAMOUS; 182]

in the long run *adv* [➡ FUTURE; 86]

in the lurch *adj* [➡ IN TROUBLE AND DISADVANTAGED; 73]

in the main *adv* **largely**, in general, on the whole, generally, generally speaking, for the most part, by and large, when all's said and done, as a rule, ordinarily, commonly, usually. [➡ SUMMARIZING EXPRESSIONS; 623] *Opposite:* in part.

in the making *adj* **future**, potential, budding, prospective, to be, to come, up and coming, promising, upcoming (*US*). [➡ FUTURE; 86] *Opposite:* established.

in the midst of *adv* **in the middle of**, at the heart of, amid, among, between, in, amongst, within, inside. [➡ GENERAL LOCATIONS; 159]

in the money *adj* **rich**, in clover, well-off, affluent, prosperous, not short, in the black, rolling in it (*informal*), flush (*informal*), loaded (*slang*). [➡ WEALTH AND WEALTHY; 891] *Opposite:* poor.

in the name of *prep* **on behalf of**, for, for the benefit of, for the sake of, on the authority of. [➡ CAUSATION; 169]

in the near future *adj* [➡ FUTURE; 86]

in the nick of time *adv* [➡ PROMPTNESS: ON TIME; 99]

in the nude *adj* [➡ DRESS, WEAR, AND UNDRESS; 868]

in the offing *adj* **imminent**, coming up, on the cards (*informal*), on the agenda, on the horizon, forthcoming, in the pipeline, pending, looming, expected, likely, upcoming (*US*). [➡ ABOUT TO HAPPEN; 33]

in the open 1 *adj* **unhidden**, unconcealed, revealed, on show, public, public knowledge, known, in the public domain. [➡ KNOWN AND FAMOUS; 182] *Opposite:* concealed. 2 *adv* **openly**, publicly, in full view, for everyone to see, in public, without fear, unashamedly. [➡ PERCEPTIBLE; 25] *Opposite:* furtively.

in theory *adv* **theoretically**, technically, in principle, hypothetically, on paper, ideally. [➡ POSSIBLE AND PROBABLE; 178] *Opposite:* in fact.

in the past *adv* [➡ PAST; 84]

in the picture *adj* [➡ KNOWLEDGE AND WISDOM; 559]

in the pink (*dated*) *adj* [➡ FINE; 738]

in the pipeline *adj* **in preparation**, on the way, underway, on the go, planned, just round the corner, under discussion, coming up, forthcoming, on the cards (*informal*), imminent, on the agenda, up and coming, in the offing, on the horizon. [➡ ABOUT TO HAPPEN; 33]

in the public domain *adj* [➡ KNOWN AND FAMOUS; 182]

in the raw (*informal*) *adj* **naked**, stark-naked, nude, in the nude, with nothing on, in a state of undress, in the buff (*informal*), in your birthday suit (*slang humorous*), starkers (*informal*), au naturel (*humorous*), stripped, unclothed. [➡ DRESS, WEAR, AND UNDRESS; 868] *Opposite:* dressed.

in the rear (*US*) *adv* [➡ GENERAL LOCATIONS; 159]

in the red *adj* **overdrawn**, in debt, insolvent, broke (*informal*), in arrears, bankrupt, indebted. [➡ POVERTY AND POOR; 892] *Opposite:* in the black.

in the region of *adv* [➡ APPROXIMATELY; 133]

in the right *adj* **correct**, right, justified, blameless, not to blame, vindicated. [➡ MORALLY GOOD; 775] *Opposite:* wrong.

in the running *adj* **in contention**, in competition, up there, in with a shout (*informal*). [➡ POSSIBLE AND PROBABLE; 178]

in the short term *adv* [➡ FUTURE; 86]

in the soup (*informal*) *adj* **in trouble**, in hot water, in a tight spot, in a tight corner, in a spot of bother (*informal*), in a jam (*informal*), in a predicament, in dire straits, up the creek (*informal*), in difficulties, in a fix (*informal*). [➡ IN TROUBLE AND DISADVANTAGED; 73]

in the stars *adj* [➡ ABOUT TO HAPPEN; 33]

in the throes of *adv* **in the process of**, in the middle of, in the midst of, in the thick of, involved in. [➡ HAPPENING AND IN PROGRESS; 32]

in the twinkling of an eye *adv* [➡ HAPPENING QUICKLY; 104]

in the vicinity *adv* [➡ CLOSENESS; 160]

in the wind *adj* [➡ HAPPENING AND IN PROGRESS; 32]

in the works *adj* [➡HAPPENING AND IN PROGRESS; 32]

in the wrong 1 *adj* **to blame**, at fault, out of line (*informal*), culpable, responsible, blameworthy, guilty, blamable. [➡IN TROUBLE AND DISADVANTAGED; 73] *Opposite:* in the right. 2 *adj* **mistaken**, incorrect, wide of the mark, off beam, wrong, not thinking straight. [➡INCORRECT AND ERRONEOUS; 223] *Opposite:* in the right.

in this day and age *adv* [➡PRESENT; 85]

in throngs *adv* [➡MANY, MUCH, LARGE AMOUNT; 117]

intimacy 1 *n* **familiarity**, closeness, understanding, confidence, caring, tenderness, affection. [➡RELATIONSHIP TO ANOTHER; 973] *Opposite:* distance. 2 *n* **quietness**, seclusion, privacy, informality, friendliness, warmth. [➡LEVELS OF FORMALITY; 523] *Opposite:* formality.

intimate 1 *adj* **close**, dear, near, warm, friendly, bosom, cherished, familiar. [➡RELATIONSHIP TO ANOTHER; 973] *Opposite:* distant. 2 *adj* **cosy**, quiet, informal, friendly, warm, snug, comfortable, relaxed. [➡LEVELS OF FORMALITY; 523] *Opposite:* formal. 3 *adj* **personal**, confidential, private, secret, innermost, guarded. [➡SECRET AND UNKNOWN; 180] *Opposite:* public. 4 *adj* **thorough**, detailed, in-depth, profound, firsthand, exhaustive, deep, special, close. [➡WHOLENESS AND COMPLETENESS; 199] *Opposite:* superficial. 5 *v* **suggest**, hint, insinuate, imply, indicate, infer, allude, rumour. [➡SUGGEST, HINT, AND COMMENT; 613]

intimately 1 *adv* **closely**, warmly, familiarly, confidentially, personally, well. [➡CLOSENESS; 160] *Opposite:* distantly. 2 *adv* **quietly**, informally, cosily, warmly, comfortably, snugly. [➡LEVELS OF FORMALITY; 523] *Opposite:* coldly. 3 *adv* **thoroughly**, very well, fully, in detail, closely, through and through, deeply. [➡WHOLENESS AND COMPLETENESS; 199] *Opposite:* superficially.

intimation *n* **hint**, allusion, insinuation, suggestion, warning, inkling, indication, rumour. [➡SUGGEST, HINT, AND COMMENT; 613]

in time 1 *adv* **early enough**, soon enough, before you know it, early. [➡PROMPTNESS: EARLY; 98] *Opposite:* late. 2 *adv* **eventually**, after a while, over time, in the end, in due course, in the fullness of time, sooner or later, ultimately, at the end of the day. [➡FUTURE; 86] *Opposite:* instantly. 3 *adv* **in step**, keeping pace, in synchronization, in sync (*informal*), keeping up, together, synchronously, all together. [➡HARMONY; 156]

intimidate *v* **threaten**, frighten, scare, bully, coerce, terrorize, overawe, daunt, put off, terrify, alarm, browbeat. [➡FRIGHTEN AND SHOCK; 569]

intimidated *adj* **daunted**, scared, frightened, overwhelmed, unsettled, afraid, overawed, apprehensive, nervous, alarmed, terrified, browbeaten. [➡FEAR AND PANIC; 544] *Opposite:* relaxed.

intimidating *adj* **threatening**, unapproachable, frightening, scary (*informal*), daunting, menacing, nerve-racking, overwhelming, alarming, terrifying, browbeating. [➡FRIGHTENING; 232] *Opposite:* approachable.

intimidation *n* **coercion**, pressure, bullying, fear, threats, terrorization, extortion. [➡CRITICISMS AND ANGRY OUTBURSTS; 50]

in tiptop condition *adj* [➡IN GOOD REPAIR; 1231]

into *adj* **keen on**, addicted to, interested in, obsessed by, mad about, crazy about (*informal*), hooked on (*slang*). [➡APPRECIATION AND GRATITUDE; 536]

intolerable *adj* **unbearable**, insufferable, impossible, unendurable, painful, insupportable, excruciating, inexcusable. [➡EMOTIONALLY UNPLEASANT AND UPSETTING; 228] *Opposite:* bearable.

intolerance *n* **bigotry**, prejudice, narrow-mindedness, fanaticism, narrowness, bias, xenophobia, chauvinism, racism. [➡PREJUDICE; 551] *Opposite:* tolerance.

intolerant *adj* **bigoted**, prejudiced, narrow-minded, fanatical, blinkered, biased, chauvinistic, xenophobic, racist. [➡SELFISH AND UNKIND; 506] *Opposite:* tolerant.

intolerantly *adv* **narrow-mindedly**, bigotedly, prejudicially, biasedly, illiberally, unfairly, chauvinistically. [➡NEGATIVE INTELLECTUAL CHARACTERISTICS; 526] *Opposite:* tolerantly.

intonation 1 *n* **pitch**, inflection, lilt, cadence, timbre, modulation, tone, stress, accentuation. [➡THE SPOKEN WORD; 672] 2 *n* **chanting**, chant, incantation, invocation, intoning, singing, humming. [➡MUSIC, SONGS, AND SINGING; 907]

intone 1 *v* **say**, utter, speak, articulate, pronounce, declare. [➡UTTER AND PRONOUNCE; 609] 2 *v* (*formal*) **chant**, sing, croon, drone, hum. [➡MUSIC, SONGS, AND SINGING; 907]

in total *adv* [➡ALL; 126]

into the bargain *adv* [➡EXPRESSIONS INTRODUCING EXTRA INFORMATION; 137]

intoxicated (*formal*) *adj* [➡UNDER THE INFLUENCE OF DRUGS OR ALCOHOL; 742]

intoxicating 1 *adj* (*formal*) **alcoholic**, strong, powerful, heady, mind-altering, inebriating, hallucinogenic, hard. [➡STRENGTH; 202] *Opposite:* soft. 2 *adj* **exciting**, invigorating, stimulating, exhilarating, fascinating, enthralling, compulsive, enchanting, elating. [➡EMOTIONALLY PLEASANT; 188] *Opposite:* dull.

intoxication *n* **alcoholism**, drunkenness, inebriation, intemperance, boozing (*slang*), heavy drinking. [➡UNDER THE INFLUENCE OF DRUGS OR ALCOHOL; 742]

intractability 1 *n* (*formal*) **unmanageability**, uncontrollability, obstinacy, stubbornness, pigheadedness, rebelliousness, recalcitrance, recidivism. [➡UNWILLINGNESS AND STUBBORNNESS; 565] *Opposite:* tractability. 2 *n* **difficulty**, knottiness, insolvability, complexity, awkwardness, unwieldiness. [➡DIFFICULTY AND COMPLEXITY; 243] *Opposite:* simplicity.

intractable 1 *adj* (*formal*) **stubborn**, obstinate, obdurate, wilful, inflexible, pigheaded, headstrong, perverse, mulish. [➡UNWILLINGNESS AND STUBBORNNESS; 565] *Opposite:* easy-going. 2 *adj* **difficult**, problematic, troublesome, awkward, knotty, thorny. [➡DIFFICULTY AND COMPLEXITY; 243] *Opposite:* easy.

See Compare and Contrast at **unruly**.

intramural *adj* **internal**, inner, in-house, college, school. [➡EDUCATION; 838] *Opposite:* extramural.

intransigence *n* **inflexibility**, stubbornness, narrow-mindedness, obstinacy, unyieldingness, obduracy. [➡ UNWILLINGNESS AND STUBBORNNESS; 565] *Opposite:* flexibility.

intransigent 1 *adj* **inflexible**, stubborn, obdurate, narrow-minded, obstinate, uncompromising, intractable (*formal*), unyielding, unbending. [➡ UNWILLINGNESS AND STUBBORNNESS; 565] *Opposite:* flexible. 2 *n* (*formal*) **conservative**, dinosaur, diehard, reactionary, extremist, bigot. [➡ UNCOOPERATIVE OR REBELLIOUS PERSON; 567] *Opposite:* progressive.

intransitive *type of* **grammatical term**. [➡ ASPECTS OF LANGUAGE; 683]

intravenous *adj* **venous**, vein, arterial, blood, circulatory. [➡ THE BLOOD AND CIRCULATION; 718]

in-tray *n* **tray**, desk, pigeonhole, mailbag, postbag, mailbox (*US*). [➡ CONTAINERS, RECEPTACLES, AND PACKAGING; 1244]

intrepid (*literary or humorous*) *adj* **fearless**, brave, bold, courageous, valiant, heroic, daring, gallant (*literary*), resolute, audacious, plucky, dauntless (*literary*). [➡ COURAGE; 499] *Opposite:* cowardly.

intrepidity *n* [➡ COURAGE; 499]

intricacies *n* **details**, ins and outs, workings, particulars, minutiae, niceties, complexities, twists and turns, convolutions. [➡ BASIC DETAILS; 689]

intricacy *n* **complexity**, difficulty, obscurity, sophistication, convolutedness, multifariousness. [➡ POSITIVELY COMPLEX OR COMPLICATED; 218]

intricate *adj* **complicated**, complex, involved, difficult, elaborate, convoluted, sophisticated, tricky, knotty. [➡ DIFFICULTY AND COMPLEXITY; 243] *Opposite:* simple.

intrigue 1 *n* **plotting**, conspiracy, huggermugger, manoeuvring, trickery, scheming, secrecy. [➡ DECEPTION AND LIES; 661] 2 *n* **conspiracy**, plot, deception, scheme, stratagem, manoeuvre, ruse. [➡ WAYS OF DOING THINGS; 295] 3 *v* **interest**, fascinate, charm, attract, captivate, absorb, enthral, tickle your fancy (*informal*), titillate. [➡ APPEAL TO AND AROUSE INTEREST; 576]

intriguer *n* [➡ PEOPLE WHO DECEIVE; 662]

intriguing *adj* **interesting**, fascinating, exciting, stimulating, absorbing, captivating, enthralling, titillating. [➡ INTERESTING AND MEANINGFUL; 191] *Opposite:* uninteresting.

intrinsic *adj* **basic**, essential, inherent, fundamental, central, core, key, deep-down, deep-seated, deep-rooted, innate, underlying. [➡ FUNDAMENTAL; 196] *Opposite:* acquired.

intro (*informal*) *n* [➡ BEGINNING; 53]

introduce 1 *v* **present**, make known to, acquaint with, familiarize, announce, bring together. [➡ INFORM AND ANNOUNCE; 612] 2 *v* **host**, present, preside over, lead, head. [➡ ENTERTAINMENT; 872] 3 *v* **bring in**, set up, initiate, usher in, begin, commence (*formal*), pioneer, launch, establish, institute, start, propose, advance, create. [➡ INSTITUTE AND INAUGURATE; 349] *Opposite:* conclude. 4 *v* **make somebody aware of**, bring to somebody's attention, acquaint somebody with, turn somebody on to, get somebody into, give somebody a taste for, familiarize, initiate, inform. [➡ INSTRUCT AND TEACH; 610]

introduction 1 *n* **foreword**, opening, preface, prologue, preamble, beginning, overture. [➡ PARTS OF BOOKS AND DOCUMENTS; 594] *Opposite:* conclusion. 2 *n* **outline**, overview, primer, summary, starter, rough guide, taster. [➡ PARTS OF BOOKS AND DOCUMENTS; 594] 3 *n* **institution**, presentation, insertion, ushering in. [➡ BEGINNING; 53]

introductory 1 *adj* **preliminary**, initial, opening, starting, early, first, preparatory, exploratory, prefatory. [➡ BEFORE, FIRST, AND PRECEDING; 164] *Opposite:* final. 2 *adj* **basic**, entry-level, preliminary, first, simple. [➡ EASE AND SIMPLICITY; 201]

introspection *n* **self-examination**, contemplation, brooding, meditation, self-analysis, reflection, navel-gazing, solipsism, soul-searching. [➡ THINK AND REFLECT; 744]

introspective *adj* **self-examining**, self-absorbed, inward-looking, contemplative, brooding, solipsistic, lost in thought, deep in thought, meditative, thoughtful, soul-searching. [➡ PENSIVENESS AND INTEREST; 539]

in trouble *adj* **in difficulty**, having problems, struggling, failing, in distress, up the creek (*informal*), in the soup (*informal*), liable. [➡ IN TROUBLE AND DISADVANTAGED; 73]

introversion *n* **introspection**, self-absorption, inwardness, contemplation, navel-gazing, shyness, timidity, reserve, musing, soul-searching. [➡ PSYCHOLOGY AND THE MIND; 770] *Opposite:* extroversion.

introvert 1 *n* **recluse**, hermit, loner, homebody (*informal*), shrinking violet (*informal*). [➡ SOLITARY PEOPLE; 942] *Opposite:* extrovert. 2 *adj* **introverted**, shy, withdrawn, reclusive, reserved, reticent, timid, quiet. [➡ RETICENT AND UNFORTHCOMING; 632] *Opposite:* extrovert.

introverted *adj* **shy**, withdrawn, reclusive, reserved, reticent, timid, quiet, introvert. [➡ RETICENT AND UNFORTHCOMING; 632]

intrude *v* **encroach**, break in, interrupt, interfere, impose, butt in, intervene, interlope, meddle. [➡ INTERRUPT AND BUTT IN; 620]

intruder *n* **interloper**, burglar, trespasser, prowler, stalker, invader, gatecrasher, impostor. [➡ STRANGERS; 972]

intrusion *n* **disturbance**, interruption, imposition, interference, invasion, incursion, meddling, interloping, intervention. [➡ BAD BEHAVIOUR OR ACTION; 255]

intrusive *adj* **invasive**, indiscreet, pushy (*informal*), interfering, unpleasant, insensitive, upsetting, disturbing, meddling. [➡ NOSY AND INTERFERING; 513] *Opposite:* discreet.

intrusiveness *n* **invasiveness**, insensitivity, pushiness (*informal*), indiscreetness, inappropriateness, tactlessness. [➡ NOSY AND INTERFERING; 513] *Opposite:* discretion.

in truth *adv* [➡ WORDS AND PHRASES EMPHASIZING THE TRUTH OF A MATTER; 173]

intuit *v* **sense**, perceive, discern, feel, understand, be aware of. [➡ UNDERSTAND AND GRASP; 760]

intuition 1 *n* **instinct**, perception, insight, sixth sense, awareness, sensitivity, clairvoyance. [➡ THE SUPERNATURAL; 788] 2 *n* **hunch**, feeling, inkling, suspicion, sense, presentiment, instinct, surmise, flash. [➡ FEELINGS; 532]

intuitive 1 *adj* **instinctive**, spontaneous, innate, in-built, instinctual, untaught, natural, native, inborn. [➡THE NATURE OF IDEAS; 772] 2 *adj* **perceptive**, sensitive, shrewd, discerning, insightful, perspicacious. [➡POSITIVE INTELLECTUAL CHARACTERISTICS; 525]

intuitively *adv* **instinctively**, automatically, by instinct, spontaneously, naturally, unthinkingly, subconsciously, subliminally, innately. [➡THE NATURE OF IDEAS; 772]

intuitiveness *n* **instinctiveness**, instinct, perceptiveness, perception, insightfulness, insight, awareness, sensitivity, intuition. [➡POSITIVE INTELLECTUAL CHARACTERISTICS; 525]

in tune *adj* [➡HARMONY; 156]

in turmoil *adj* [➡SADNESS, DISTRESS, AND DESPAIR; 540]

in two minds *adj* [➡UNCERTAINTY; 560]

in two shakes of a lamb's tail *adv* [➡HAPPENING QUICKLY; 104]

inundate *v* **flood**, overwhelm, snow under, swamp, deluge, engulf, submerge, drown. [➡GIVE TOO MUCH; 438] *Opposite:* starve.

inundated 1 *adj* **snowed under**, flooded, swamped, overwhelmed, besieged, overcome, drowned. [➡TOO MUCH; 118] *Opposite:* starved. 2 *adj* **flooded**, immersed, waterlogged, submerged, submersed, covered, engulfed. [➡WET; 1239] *Opposite:* drained.

inundation (*formal*) 1 *n* **deluge**, flood, sea, stream, shower, tidal wave. [➡TOO MUCH; 118] *Opposite:* trickle. 2 *n* **flood**, blizzard, sea, wave, barrage, mound, heap, backlog, accumulation. [➡MANY, MUCH, LARGE AMOUNT; 117]

in unison *adv* [➡ACTING WITH OTHERS; 286]

inure *v* **harden**, toughen, accustom, season, habituate, acclimatize, desensitize, familiarize, naturalize. [➡SOOTHE AND CALM; 574]

inured to *adj* **accustomed to**, used to, conditioned to, insensible of, insensitive to, familiarized. [➡NEUTRALITY AND INDIFFERENCE; 554] *Opposite:* unaccustomed.

inurement *n* **hardening**, toughening, habituation (*formal*), acclimatization, seasoning, desensitization. [➡CHANGE; 373]

invade 1 *v* **attack**, occupy, enter, conquer, annex, march into, assault, overrun. [➡ARRIVE; 12] 2 *v* **overrun**, infect, infest, plague, colonize, parasitize. [➡ARRIVE; 12]

invader *n* **attacker**, aggressor, raider, intruder, assailant, trespasser, interloper. [➡ENEMIES AND TORMENTORS; 969]

in vain *adv* **without success**, unsuccessfully, uselessly, hopelessly, with little hope, fruitlessly, for nothing, to no avail, to no purpose, ineffectively, vainly, for no good reason, pointlessly, futilely. [➡UNSUCCESSFUL AND UNPROMISING; 76] *Opposite:* successfully.

invalid 1 *adj* **null and void**, unacceptable, unenforceable, illegal, worthless, unsound, void. [➡REDUNDANT AND USELESS; 241] *Opposite:* valid. 2 *adj* **unsound**, untrue, unfounded, illogical, untenable, worthless, unsustainable, null, void, unconvincing, fallacious. [➡FALSE AND UNREAL; 174] *Opposite:* valid. 3 *n* **convalescent**, patient, sick person. [➡UNFIT AND WEAK; 740] 4 *adj* **infirm**, enfeebled, debilitated, disabled, sick, ailing (*dated*), incapacitated. [➡UNFIT AND WEAK; 740] *Opposite:* well.

invalidate *v* **overturn**, cancel, annul, nullify, undo, quash, overthrow, undermine, refute, abrogate (*formal*), countermand, discredit. [➡ABOLISH AND ANNUL; 453] *Opposite:* validate.

See Compare and Contrast at **nullify**.

invalidation *n* **annulment**, undoing, overthrow, nullification, cancellation, refutation, abrogation (*formal*), countermanding, discrediting. [➡END; 54] *Opposite:* validation.

invalidity 1 *n* **unsoundness**, inaccuracy, baselessness, unjustifiability, irrationality, falsehood, inadequacy, fallaciousness, faultiness, unconvincingness. [➡INCORRECT AND ERRONEOUS; 223] *Opposite:* validity. 2 *n* **illegality**, inoperativeness, ineffectiveness, unenforceability, voidness, unsoundness, unsustainability, abrogation (*formal*). [➡REDUNDANT AND USELESS; 241] *Opposite:* legality.

invaluable *adj* **priceless**, irreplaceable, vital, instrumental, helpful, important, valuable, precious, unique, treasured, inestimable, rare, choice. [➡ADMIRABLE AND COMMENDABLE; 186] *Opposite:* worthless.

invaluableness *n* **pricelessness**, irreplaceability, helpfulness, importance, value, preciousness, uniqueness, rareness, choiceness. [➡IMPORTANCE AND SIGNIFICANCE; 193] *Opposite:* worthlessness.

invariability *n* [➡PERMANENCE: WITHOUT CHANGE; 95]

invariable *adj* **constant**, set, unchanging, inflexible, rigid, consistent, unwavering, habitual, uniform, unvarying, undeviating, unchangeable. [➡PERMANENCE: WITHOUT CHANGE; 95] *Opposite:* erratic.

invasion *n* **attack**, assault, incursion, raid, foray, offensive, annexation, conquest, subjugation, penetration, infiltration, aggression. [➡AGGRESSIVE EVENT; 39] *Opposite:* withdrawal.

invasive 1 *adj* **aggressive**, offensive, hostile, warlike, bellicose, martial. [➡PHYSICALLY UNPLEASANT; 227] 2 *adj* **intrusive**, disturbing, interfering, insensitive, imposing, annoying. [➡NOSY AND INTERFERING; 513] *Opposite:* discreet.

invective (*formal*) *n* **diatribe**, tirade, attack, broadside, counterblast, polemic, abuse, criticism, vituperation, denunciation, vilification, execration (*literary or formal*). [➡CRITICISMS AND ANGRY OUTBURSTS; 50] *Opposite:* eulogy.

inveigh (*formal*) *v* **protest**, complain, fulminate, criticize, rail, rant, denounce, castigate (*formal*), abuse. [➡PROTEST AND EXPRESS DISAPPROVAL; 643]

inveigle *v* **persuade**, entice, charm, cajole, trick, deceive, con (*informal*), wheedle, influence, convince, beguile, allure, seduce. [➡CAUSE OR COMPEL TO ACT; 272]

invent 1 *v* **create**, devise, formulate, originate, conceive, design, discover, develop, contrive, fashion. [➡CREATION; 347] 2 *v* **make up**, think up, concoct, fabricate, cook up (*informal*), contrive, dream up, conjure up. [➡DREAM, IMAGINE, AND FANTASIZE; 750]

invented *adj* **false**, made-up, fictitious, imaginary, pretend, concocted, hypothetical, make-believe, fabricated, fictional, contrived. [➡FALSE AND UNREAL; 174] *Opposite:* real.

invention 1 *n* **device**, innovation, contraption, gadget, design, contrivance, implement, apparatus. [➡DEVICES; 1114] 2 *n* **creation**, discovery, development, brainchild, baby (*slang*), origination. [➡CREATION; 347] 3 *n* **fabrication**, forgery, falsehood, deceit, lies, sham, fake, fiction, fantasy. [➡DECEPTION AND LIES; 661] *Opposite:* truth. 4 *n* **creativity**, imagination, ingenuity, inventiveness, resourcefulness, originality, innovativeness, fertility. [➡DESCRIBING SOMEBODY'S INTELLECT; 524]

inventive *adj* **creative**, imaginative, ingenious, resourceful, original, innovative, fertile. [➡POSITIVE INTELLECTUAL CHARACTERISTICS; 525] *Opposite:* unimaginative.

inventiveness *n* **ingenuity**, resourcefulness, originality, creativity, imagination, invention, initiative, cleverness, fertility. [➡POSITIVE INTELLECTUAL CHARACTERISTICS; 525]

inventor *n* **discoverer**, originator, creator, architect, author, designer, maker. [➡DESIGNERS, CREATORS, AND INSTIGATORS; 348]

inventory 1 *n* **list**, record, account, register, catalogue, portfolio, stock list, roster, roll. [➡LISTS AND SCHEDULES; 588] 2 *n* **supply**, range, array, stock, accounting, stock-taking. [➡COLLECTIONS AND MIXTURES OF THINGS; 1243]

inverse 1 *adj* **opposite**, converse, reverse, contrary, other, counter, antithetical (*formal*), transposed, inverted, backward. [➡OPPOSITE; 158] *Opposite:* same. 2 *n* **reverse**, opposite, other, contrary, converse, antithesis, flip side, counterpoint. [➡OPPOSITE; 158]

inversion 1 *n* **reversal**, overturn, downturn, upturn, capsizal, transposal, transposition. [➡CHANGE; 373] 2 *n* **reverse**, transposition, antithesis, contrary, converse. [➡CHANGE ONE THING FOR ANOTHER; 399]

invert *v* **turn over**, upset, capsize, overturn, reverse, upturn, turn upside down, double back, flip-flop (*informal*), upend. [➡MOVE SOMETHING: INTO A NEW POSITION OR OVERTURN; 331] *Opposite:* right.

invertebrate

◆ *types of aquatic invertebrate*
abalone, barnacle, clam, cockle, conch, coral, crustacean, cuttlefish, jellyfish, limpet, mollusc, mussel, octopus, oyster, Portuguese man-of-war, quahog, scallop, sea anemone, sea urchin, sponge, squid, starfish, whelk, winkle

◆ *types of crustacean*
bivalve, crab, crayfish, hermit crab, horseshoe crab, langoustine, lobster, prawn, sand flea (*US*), sand hopper, shellfish, shrimp, water flea

◆ *types of land invertebrate*
centipede, earthworm, millipede, slug, snail, woodlouse, worm

inverted comma *type of* **punctuation mark**. [➡ASPECTS OF LANGUAGE; 683]

invest 1 *v* **capitalize**, participate, put in, devote, advance, finance. [➡GIVE MONEY; 434] 2 *v* (*formal*) **appoint**, ordain, instate, inaugurate, establish, install. [➡CONFER STATUS; 459] 3 *v* **endow**, provide, supply, empower, authorize, arm, license, enable. [➡PERMIT AND ALLOW; 670]

investigate *v* **examine**, look into, explore, inspect, study, consider, probe, scrutinize, poke around, reconnoitre, recce (*slang*), research, delve into. [➡EXAMINE AND ASSESS; 754]

investigation *n* **study**, examination, search, exploration, analysis, research, survey, scrutiny, inspection, inquiry, reconnaissance, recce (*slang*), enquiry, probe, review. [➡EXAMINE AND ASSESS; 754]

investigative *adj* **analytical**, exploratory, undercover, fact-finding, research, probing, inspective. [➡EXAMINE AND ASSESS; 754]

investigator *n* **detective**, private detective, private eye (*informal*), sleuth (*informal*), private investigator, agent, gumshoe (*US informal*), dick (*US dated slang*), plain-clothesman (*US*). [➡PEOPLE IN LAW COURTS; 820]

investiture *n* **installation**, inauguration, swearing-in, instatement, admission, investment (*formal*), enthronement. [➡BEGINNING; 53]

investment 1 *n* (*formal*) [➡CONFER STATUS; 459] 2 *n* **savings**, speculation, venture, deal, asset, stock, share, venture capital, security, outlay, investing, capital spending, financing. [➡EXPENDITURE; 424]

investor 1 *n* **saver**, shareholder, depositor, stakeholder, stockholder, nominee, financier, venture capitalist. [➡PEOPLE INVOLVED IN FINANCE; 804] 2 *n* **backer**, sponsor, patron, guarantor, security. [➡PEOPLE INVOLVED IN FINANCE; 804]

inveterate *adj* **chronic**, confirmed, hardened, ingrained, incurable, incorrigible, seasoned, entrenched, habitual, deep-rooted, diehard, adamant. [➡UNWILLINGNESS AND STUBBORNNESS; 565] *Opposite:* occasional.

invidious *adj* **unpleasant**, discriminatory, unenviable, unfair, undesirable, tricky, odious, difficult, offensive, awkward, horrible, impossible, insulting, spiteful, malevolent. [➡EMOTIONALLY UNPLEASANT AND UPSETTING; 228] *Opposite:* pleasant.

in view of *prep* **considering**, bearing in mind, taking into consideration, in consideration of (*formal*), taking into account. [➡CAUSATION; 169] *Opposite:* notwithstanding (*formal*).

invigilate *v* **supervise**, monitor, inspect, observe, check, police, keep an eye on. [➡LOOKING AND LOOKS; 701]

invigilator *n* **supervisor**, inspector, monitor, overseer, scrutineer, examiner, official, verifier, observer. [➡LOOKERS AND SPECTATORS; 702]

invigorate *v* **energize**, revitalize, refresh, stimulate, enliven, animate, rejuvenate, strengthen, liven up, galvanize, exhilarate, fortify, quicken. [➡IMPROVE STRENGTH AND DURABILITY; 379] *Opposite:* exhaust.

invigorated *adj* **strengthened**, fortified, energized, refreshed, restored, revitalized, rejuvenated, exhilarated, perked up, pepped up (*informal*), galvanized, motivated, quickened. [➡ WIDE AWAKE AND CONSCIOUS; 736] *Opposite:* weakened.

invigorating *adj* **bracing**, brisk, stimulating, refreshing, revitalizing, energizing, reviving, vitalizing, enlivening, exhilarating, restorative, animating, rejuvenating. [➡ PHYSICALLY PLEASANT; 187] *Opposite:* enervating.

invincibility *n* **strength**, insuperability, invulnerability, impregnability, indomitability, dauntlessness (*literary*), unassailability, indestructability. [➡ STRENGTH; 202] *Opposite:* vulnerability.

invincible *adj* **unbeatable**, invulnerable, unconquerable, indomitable, impregnable, unassailable, insuperable, indestructible, supreme, unshakable, insurmountable, irrepressible. [➡ STRENGTH; 202] *Opposite:* vulnerable.

inviolable *adj* **unbreakable**, sacred, sacrosanct, firm, uninfringeable, unchallengeable, inviolate. [➡ STRENGTH; 202] *Opposite:* breakable.

inviolate 1 *adj* **unaltered**, unchanged, unbroken, intact, entire, perfect, immune, infrangible (*formal*), inviolable. [➡ SAFE AND SAFETY; 192] *Opposite:* altered. 2 *adj* **pure**, unsullied, untouched, whole, intact, virgin, perfect, unspoiled, unadulterated, uncontaminated. [➡ IN GOOD REPAIR; 1231] *Opposite:* contaminated.

invisibility *n* **hiddenness**, inconspicuousness, indiscernibility, faintness, indistinctness, lateness. [➡ IMPERCEPTIBLE; 26] *Opposite:* visibility.

invisible 1 *adj* **imperceptible**, unseen, indistinguishable, indiscernible, undetectable, obscure, unseeable. [➡ IMPERCEPTIBLE; 26] *Opposite:* visible. 2 *adj* **hidden**, concealed, disguised, unnoticed, obscured, out of sight, covered, masked, covert, veiled. [➡ SECRET AND UNKNOWN; 180] *Opposite:* obvious. 3 *adj* **imaginary**, nonexistent, impalpable (*formal*), intangible, shadowy, insubstantial, ghostly. [➡ FALSE AND UNREAL; 174] *Opposite:* palpable.

invisibly *adv* **imperceptibly**, indiscernibly, unnoticeably, undetectably, impalpably (*formal*), intangibly. [➡ IMPERCEPTIBLE; 26] *Opposite:* visibly.

invitation 1 *n* **offer**, invite (*informal*), request, call, summons, bidding, solicitation. [➡ REQUEST AND DEMAND; 664] 2 *n* **encouragement**, inducement, provocation, incitement, enticement, challenge, temptation, lure. [➡ ADVICE; 690] *Opposite:* discouragement.

invite 1 *n* (*informal*) **invitation**, request, call, summons, offer, bidding. [➡ REQUEST AND DEMAND; 664] 2 *v* **ask**, request, call, bid (*archaic*), summon. [➡ REQUEST AND DEMAND; 664] *Opposite:* blackball. 3 *v* **provoke**, incite, induce, attract, encourage, tempt, lure, welcome. [➡ APPEAL TO AND AROUSE INTEREST; 576] *Opposite:* forbid.

inviting *adj* **attractive**, appealing, alluring, tempting, pleasing, fascinating, engaging, welcoming, enticing. [➡ INTERESTING AND MEANINGFUL; 191] *Opposite:* unappealing.

invocation *n* **supplication** (*formal*), prayer, call, request, entreaty, petition, appeal, solicitation, plea. [➡ RELIGIONS AND RELIGIOUS PRACTICES; 778]

in vogue *adj* [➡ DESCRIBING CLOTHES; 869]

invoice 1 *n* **bill**, account, statement, demand, proof of purchase. [➡ RECEIPTS AND INVOICES; 592] 2 *v* **bill**, debit, charge. [➡ SELL; 442]

invoke 1 *v* **cite**, quote, use, refer, mention, bring up, resort to. [➡ NAME AND DESCRIBE; 666] 2 *v* **appeal**, call upon, call up, pray, beg, beseech (*literary*), summon, entreat (*formal*), petition, raise, implore (*formal*). [➡ REQUEST AND DEMAND; 664] 3 *v* **evoke**, call to mind, conjure up, incite, arouse, call forth, remind. [➡ CAUSE TO APPEAR; 5]

involuntarily *adv* **unwillingly**, reluctantly, unhappily, against your will, compulsorily, obligatorily. [➡ AUTOMATIC AND INSTINCTIVE; 281] *Opposite:* willingly.

involuntary 1 *adj* **compulsory**, obligatory, forced, unwilling, reluctant, unchosen. [➡ CAPTIVITY AND LOSS OF FREEDOM; 249] *Opposite:* willing. 2 *adj* **instinctive**, spontaneous, reflex, unintentional, automatic, unconscious, unthinking, uncontrolled. [➡ AUTOMATIC AND INSTINCTIVE; 281] *Opposite:* intentional.

involve 1 *v* **contain**, include, take in, comprise, consist of, encompass. [➡ CREATING CONNECTIONS; 145] 2 *v* **concern**, have to do with, affect, interest, encompass, embrace. [➡ BE ABOUT SOMETHING; 62] 3 *v* **implicate**, draw in, mix up, get into, embroil, entangle, enmesh. [➡ CAUSE OR COMPEL TO ACT; 272] 4 *v* **engage**, engross, absorb, grip, rivet (*informal*), occupy, preoccupy. [➡ APPEAL TO AND AROUSE INTEREST; 576] *Opposite:* bore. 5 *v* **imply**, mean, entail, necessitate, require. [➡ NEED AND REQUIRE; 465]

involved 1 *adj* **complicated**, complex, intricate, elaborate, knotty, tangled, convoluted, tortuous, difficult, labyrinthine. [➡ DIFFICULTY AND COMPLEXITY; 243] *Opposite:* simple. 2 *adj* **concerned**, caught up, mixed up, occupied, implicated, drawn in, immersed, enmeshed, entangled. [➡ RELATED; 143] *Opposite:* uninvolved.

involvement 1 *n* **attachment**, interest, concern, enthusiasm, connection, commitment, preoccupation, engagement. [➡ ATTENTION AND ATTENTIVENESS; 764] *Opposite:* detachment. 2 *n* **participation**, association, connection, contribution, engrossment, immersion, envelopment. [➡ CONNECTION; 144]

invulnerability *n* [➡ SAFE AND SAFETY; 192]

invulnerable *adj* **untouchable**, invincible, unassailable, safe, impenetrable, secure, indestructible, unconquerable, unbeatable, indomitable. [➡ STRENGTH OF WILL; 502] *Opposite:* vulnerable.

inward 1 *adj* **inner**, innermost, inmost, interior, internal, private, deep, deepest, secret, hidden, confidential. [➡ SECRET AND UNKNOWN; 180] *Opposite:* external. 2 *adj* **internal**, interior, inner, inner-directed, innermost, within, inmost. [➡ GENERAL LOCATIONS; 159] *Opposite:* outer. 3 *adj* **incoming**, ingoing, entering, inward bound, inflowing, return. [➡ DIRECTION OF MOTION; 346] *Opposite:* outward.

inwardly *adv* **secretly**, privately, to yourself, silently, deeply, interiorly. [➡ SECRET AND UNKNOWN; 180] *Opposite:* openly.

inwards *adv* **within**, inwardly, inside, in. [➡ DIRECTION OF MOTION; 346] *Opposite:* outwards.

in work *adj* [➡ EMPLOYMENT STATUS; 831]

in working order *adj* [➡ IN GOOD REPAIR; 1231]

in-your-face (*slang*) *adj* **direct**, forthright, provocative, outspoken, shocking, aggressive, full-on. [➡POMPOUS, LOUD, AND OVER-CONFIDENT; 636] *Opposite:* indirect.

in your own right *adv* **independently**, voluntarily, for yourself, by yourself, solo. [➡ACTING INDEPENDENTLY; 285]

in your prime *adj* [➡PLEASANT SITUATIONS; 74]

Ionic *type of* **pre-20th-century architecture.** [➡BUILDING AND ARCHITECTURE; 1075]

ionosphere *n* [➡THE EARTH'S ATMOSPHERE; 1040]

iota *n* **jot**, bit, scrap, speck, grain, particle, smidgen (*informal*), scintilla. [➡FEW, LITTLE, SMALL AMOUNT; 119] *Opposite:* lot.

ipso facto *adv* **as a result**, therefore, hence (*formal*), thus (*formal*), so, in consequence (*formal*), consequently (*formal*), in view of. [➡CAUSATION; 169]

IQ *n* **intelligence quotient**, level of intelligence, degree of intelligence, intelligence. [➡PSYCHOLOGY AND THE MIND; 770]

irascibility *n* [➡AGGRESSIVE AND BELLIGERENT; 519]

irascible *adj* **quick-tempered**, irritable, testy (*informal*), petulant, hot-tempered, short-tempered, grumpy, snappy, touchy, snappish, cantankerous, cross, ornery (*US informal*). [➡AGGRESSIVE AND BELLIGERENT; 519] *Opposite:* easy-going.

irate *adj* **angry**, incensed, furious, mad, irritated, enraged, fuming, infuriated, annoyed. [➡IRRITATION AND ANGER; 542] *Opposite:* calm.

ire (*literary*) *n* **fury**, rage, anger, wrath, annoyance, indignation, bile (*literary*). [➡IRRITATION AND ANGER; 542] *Opposite:* calmness.

See Compare and Contrast at **anger.**

ireful (*literary*) *adj* [➡IRRITATION AND ANGER; 542]

iridescent *adj* **lustrous**, rainbow-like, shimmering, rainbow, shimmery, colourful, shot, dazzling, kaleidoscopic, glittering, sparkling, shining, gleaming, glistening, flickering, shiny, opalescent, prismatic. [➡VISUAL TEXTURE; 1220] *Opposite:* monochrome.

iris 1 *n* [➡THE EYE; 699] 2 *type of* **flower grown from bulb.** [➡FLOWERS FROM BULBS; 1030]

Irish coffee *type of* **coffee.** [➡DRINKS; 1186]

Irish moss *type of* **alga.** [➡MICROORGANISMS, FUNGI, AND ALGAE; 1023]

Irish stew *type of* **cooked dish.** [➡PREPARED DISHES; 1169]

irk *v* **annoy**, vex, displease, trouble, bother, nag, rile (*informal*), rankle, peeve (*informal*), gall, irritate, exasperate, bug (*informal*). [➡ANGER AND ANNOY; 570] *Opposite:* please.

See Compare and Contrast at **annoy, bother.**

irked *adj* [➡IRRITATION AND ANGER; 542]

irksome *adj* **annoying**, irritating, exasperating, tiresome, wearing, tedious, bothersome, trying, galling, vexing. [➡IRRITATING; 229] *Opposite:* pleasant.

iron 1 *adj* **firm**, hard, strong, determined, tough, steely, rock-hard. [➡STRENGTH OF WILL; 502] *Opposite:* soft. 2 *v* **press**, smooth out, iron out, smooth, flatten, steam, even out. [➡CLEAN AND POLISH; 404] *Opposite:* crumple. 3 *type of* **appliance.** [➡HOUSEHOLD APPLIANCES; 1116] 4 *type of* **metal.** [➡METALS; 1275]

iron curtain *n* **obstacle**, impediment, hurdle, line, curtain, border. [➡GEOGRAPHICAL BORDERS AND BOUNDARIES; 1068]

ironic 1 *adj* **caustic**, dry, biting, sarcastic, satirical, sardonic, mocking, ironical, tongue-in-cheek. [➡RETICENT AND UNFORTHCOMING; 632] 2 *adj* **incongruous**, paradoxical, poignant, peculiar, odd, strange, weird, atypical, contradictory, curious. [➡FUNNY AND AMUSING; 217]

ironical *see* **ironic**

iron out *v* **sort out**, resolve, smooth over, clear up, settle, end. [➡CORRECT AND PUT RIGHT; 378]

iron-willed *adj* [➡UNWILLINGNESS AND STUBBORNNESS; 565]

ironwork *n* **wrought iron**, metalwork, ironmongery, ironware, iron object, hardware. [➡ORNAMENTS AND DECORATIONS; 1247]

irony 1 *n* **satire**, dryness, causticness, sardonicism, sarcasm, mockery, insincerity, wit, humour, double meaning. [➡JOKES AND TEASING; 675] *Opposite:* sincerity. 2 *n* **paradox**, incongruity, fatefulness, dramatic irony, contrariety, contrariness, absurdity. [➡DISHARMONY; 157]

irradiate 1 *v* **light up**, light, illuminate, brighten, illumine (*literary*), cast light on. [➡LIGHT EMISSION; 369] *Opposite:* darken. 2 *v* **enlighten**, clarify, inform, instruct, inspire, explain. [➡EXPLAIN AND CLARIFY; 611] *Opposite:* obfuscate.

irradiation 1 *n* **radioactivity**, radiation, contamination, X-ray, treatment. [➡LIGHT; 1163] 2 *n* **preservation**, treatment, sterilization, purification. [➡CLEAN AND POLISH; 404]

irrational *adj* **illogical**, unreasonable, foolish, crazy (*informal*), ridiculous, absurd, silly, senseless, unfounded, groundless, unsound, baseless, nonsensical. [➡BIZARRE AND PECULIAR; 258] *Opposite:* rational.

irrationality *n* **illogicality**, unreasonableness, foolishness, craziness (*informal*), ludicrousness, absurdity, ridiculousness, senselessness, pointlessness. [➡BIZARRE AND PECULIAR; 258] *Opposite:* sense.

irreconcilable *adj* **incompatible**, irresoluble, conflicting, opposing, opposed, clashing, contradictory. [➡DISHARMONY; 157] *Opposite:* compatible.

irrecoverable 1 *adj* **irretrievable**, gone, lost, given up, written off (*informal*). [➡ABSENT AND UNAVAILABLE; 7] 2 *adj* **irreparable**, beyond repair, irreversible, irredeemable, irremediable, irrevocable. [➡BAD AND BADLY; 224]

irredeemable *adj* **hopeless**, unalterable, absolute, complete, incorrigible, inveterate, incurable, lost. [➡UNWILLINGNESS AND STUBBORNNESS; 565] *Opposite:* redeemable.

irreducible *adj* **complex**, complicated, involved, intricate, difficult. [➡POSITIVELY COMPLEX OR COMPLICATED; 218]

irrefutable *adj* **indisputable**, certain, unquestionable, overwhelming, unassailable, convincing, undeniable, incontrovertible, watertight, proven. [➡CERTAIN; 175] *Opposite:* disputable.

irregular 1 *adj* **uneven**, unequal, asymmetrical, unbalanced, rough, crooked, jagged, bumpy, lopsided, broken. [➡ANGULAR SHAPE; 1216] *Opposite:* even. 2 *adj* **erratic**, variable, random, haphazard, intermittent, sporadic, patchy, fluctuating, fitful. [➡FINITENESS, VARIABILITY, AND TRANSIENCE; 96] *Opposite:* regular. 3 *adj* **improper**, unacceptable, abnormal, wrong, unsuitable, inappropriate, unconventional, unorthodox, unusual, nonconforming. [➡INAPPROPRIATE AND UNSUITABLE; 225] *Opposite:* proper.

irregularity 1 *n* **unevenness**, inequality, variability, randomness, haphazardness, patchiness, disproportion, asymmetry, roughness. [➡DIFFERENCE; 150] *Opposite:* regularity. 2 *n* **indiscretion**, abnormality, wrongdoing, misdeed (*formal*), anomaly, loophole, peccadillo. [➡BAD BEHAVIOUR OR ACTION; 255]

irregularly *adv* **erratically**, unevenly, sporadically, intermittently, haphazardly, occasionally, now and then, brokenly. [➡FINITENESS, VARIABILITY, AND TRANSIENCE; 96] *Opposite:* regularly.

irrelevance 1 *n* **insignificance**, unimportance, inappropriateness, worthlessness, inconsequence, inappositeness (*formal*), triviality. [➡UNIMPORTANT AND UNNECESSARY; 239] *Opposite:* relevance. 2 *n* **inconsequence**, side issue, detail, technicality, red herring, diversion. [➡UNIMPORTANT AND UNNECESSARY; 239]

irrelevant *adj* **immaterial**, neither here nor there, unrelated, inappropriate, extraneous, beside the point, unconnected, inapt, off base. [➡UNIMPORTANT AND UNNECESSARY; 239] *Opposite:* relevant.

irreligious *adj* **profane**, ungodly, unspiritual, nonreligious, blasphemous, sacrilegious, unbelieving, godless, impious. [➡RELIGIOUS CONCEPTS; 777] *Opposite:* devout.

irremediable *adj* **irreparable**, irreversible, irredeemable, beyond repair, irrevocable, irretrievable, unsalvageable. [➡BAD AND BADLY; 224]

irreparable *adj* **beyond repair**, irreversible, irretrievable, severe, lasting, irrevocable, irremediable, irredeemable, uncorrectable, unsalvageable. [➡PERMANENCE: WITHOUT CHANGE; 95]

irreplaceable *adj* **unique**, one-off, inimitable, matchless, exceptional, rare, nonpareil. [➡EXTRAORDINARY: UNCOMMON; 206] *Opposite:* common.

irrepressible *adj* **uncontrollable**, out of control, uncontainable, wild, unruly, disorderly, incorrigible, unmanageable, intractable (*formal*), wilful, unrestrainable, unquenchable. [➡ENERGY AND ENTHUSIASM; 497] *Opposite:* contained.

irreproachability *n* [➡MORALLY GOOD; 775]

irreproachable *adj* **blameless**, faultless, flawless, perfect, impeccable, spotless, immaculate, irreprehensible, stainless, unimpeachable. [➡HONEST AND RELIABLE; 503] *Opposite:* blameworthy.

irreproachably *adv* [➡MORALLY GOOD; 775]

irresistible 1 *adj* **overwhelming**, overpowering, uncontrollable, compelling, strong, overriding, uncontainable, powerful. [➡STRENGTH; 202] *Opposite:* weak. 2 *adj* **desirable**, tempting, appealing, enticing, alluring, mouthwatering, seductive, tantalizing. [➡INTERESTING AND MEANINGFUL; 191] *Opposite:* unappealing.

irresistibly *adv* **overwhelmingly**, overpoweringly, uncontrollably, compellingly, powerfully, strongly, seductively, tantalizingly. [➡STRENGTH; 202] *Opposite:* weakly.

irresolute *adj* **indecisive**, vacillating, unsure, weak, undetermined, wishy-washy (*informal*), wavering, procrastinating, unsteady. [➡UNCERTAINTY; 560] *Opposite:* determined.

irresoluteness *n* [➡UNCERTAINTY; 560]

irresolution *n* **indecision**, indecisiveness, vacillation, weakness, hesitancy, changeableness. [➡UNCERTAINTY; 560] *Opposite:* determination.

irrespective *adj* **regardless**, notwithstanding (*formal*), nevertheless, nonetheless, heedlessly, unrelatedly. [➡UNINTENTIONAL AND ACCIDENTAL; 282]

irrespective of *prep* **regardless of**, despite, notwithstanding (*formal*), no matter, in spite of, heedless of. [➡NOT; 135] *Opposite:* considering.

irresponsibility *n* **recklessness**, carelessness, inattention, negligence, rashness, imprudence, frivolity, flippancy, unreliability. [➡BAD BEHAVIOUR OR ACTION; 255] *Opposite:* responsibility.

irresponsible *adj* **reckless**, careless, negligent, rash, foolish, immature, undependable, unreliable, imprudent (*formal*). [➡LACK OF COMMITMENT AND UNRELIABILITY; 510] *Opposite:* responsible.

irretrievable *adj* **irreparable**, irreversible, irrevocable, lasting, severe, irrecoverable, lost. [➡ABSENT AND UNAVAILABLE; 7]

irreverence *n* **disrespect**, mockery, derision, impertinence, impudence, cheek (*informal*), discourtesy, ridicule, sauciness. [➡BAD MANNERS AND SOCIAL SKILLS; 522] *Opposite:* respect.

irreverent *adj* **disrespectful**, mocking, impertinent (*formal*), derisive, rude, impudent, flippant, bold, cheeky, saucy, discourteous. [➡RUDE AND HOSTILE; 626] *Opposite:* respectful.

irreversible *adj* **irreparable**, irretrievable, irrevocable, unalterable, irremediable, permanent. [➡PERMANENCE: WITHOUT CHANGE; 95] *Opposite:* temporary.

irrevocable *adj* **binding**, irreversible, final, unalterable, unchangeable, immutable, irretrievable, fixed, permanent, conclusive. [➡PERMANENCE: WITHOUT CHANGE; 95] *Opposite:* flexible.

irrevocably *adv* **irreversibly**, forever, permanently, once and for all, for all time, irretrievably, conclusively. [➡PERMANENCE: WITHOUT END; 94]

irrigate *v* **water**, flood, wet, moisten, hose down, hose. [➡GROW AND CULTIVATE; 352] *Opposite:* dry out.

irritability *n* **tetchiness** (*informal*), touchiness, bad temper, petulance, cantankerousness, prickliness (*informal*). [➡IRRITATION AND ANGER; 542] *Opposite:* equanimity.

irritable *adj* **bad-tempered**, short-tempered, ill-tempered, cross, prickly (*informal*), tetchy (*informal*), petulant, cantankerous, irascible, touchy, testy (*informal*), grouchy (*informal*). [➡IRRITATION AND ANGER; 542] *Opposite:* easygoing.

irritant *n* **nuisance**, annoyance, aggravation, irritation, pain (*informal*), bane, vexation. [➡NUISANCES; 254] *Opposite:* balm.

irritate 1 *v* **annoy**, get on somebody's nerves, aggravate (*informal*), infuriate, bother, exasperate, wind somebody up, rub up the wrong way, vex, peeve (*informal*), irk. [➡ANGER AND ANNOY; 570] *Opposite:* soothe. 2 *v* **inflame**, rub, chafe, sting, aggravate (*informal*), hurt, worsen. [➡PAIN AND OTHER PHYSICAL SENSATIONS; 734] *Opposite:* soothe.

See Compare and Contrast at **annoy**.

irritated *adj* **annoyed**, cross, angry, exasperated, wound up (*informal*), maddened, vexed, peeved (*informal*). [➡IRRITATION AND ANGER; 542] *Opposite:* unperturbed.

irritating *adj* **annoying**, exasperating, irksome, infuriating, frustrating, grating, nauseating, galling, vexing, peeving (*informal*). [➡IRRITATING; 229] *Opposite:* soothing.

irritation 1 *n* **annoyance**, crossness, frustration, impatience, exasperation, anger, irascibility, touchiness, testiness (*informal*), indignation. [➡IRRITATION AND ANGER; 542] *Opposite:* calmness. 2 *n* **nuisance**, pest (*informal*), bother, irritant, bane, pain. [➡NUISANCES; 254] 3 *n* **inflammation**, soreness, tenderness, itchiness, prickliness (*informal*), rash. [➡PAIN AND OTHER PHYSICAL SENSATIONS; 734]

island *n* **isle**, islet, atoll, desert island, key, landmass. [➡THE CONTINENTS AND ISLANDS; 1048]

islander *n* **inhabitant**, local, resident, occupant, native, dweller (*literary*). [➡INHABITANT; 857]

island-hop *v* **travel around**, tour, sail around, sail, cruise, visit, sail round. [➡TRAVEL: WAYS OF TRAVELLING; 321]

isle *n* **island**, islet, atoll, desert island, key. [➡THE CONTINENTS AND ISLANDS; 1048]

islet *n* **island**, isle, atoll, desert island, key. [➡THE CONTINENTS AND ISLANDS; 1048]

ism (*informal*) *n* **doctrine**, ideology, belief, belief system, principles, creed, philosophy, movement, practice. [➡IDEA AND THOUGHT; 771]

isobar *n* **line**, weather symbol, front, low, low front, high, high front. [➡WEATHER AND CLIMATE; 1049]

isolate *v* **cut off**, separate, segregate, detach, divorce, set apart, insulate, quarantine, sequester (*formal*). [➡SEPARATE AND DIVIDE; 402] *Opposite:* include.

isolated 1 *adj* **remote**, cut off, inaccessible, lonely, secluded, out-of-the-way, insulated, quarantined, sequestered (*formal*). [➡DISTANCE; 161] *Opposite:* nearby. 2 *adj* **lonely**, alone, solitary, insular, friendless, single. [➡SOLITARINESS; 941] 3 *adj* **one-off**, exceptional, unique, solitary, unrepeated, special, rare. [➡UNRELATEDNESS AND SEPARATENESS; 147] *Opposite:* common.

isolation *n* **separation**, segregation, remoteness, loneliness, seclusion, inaccessibility, sequestration, quarantine. [➡DISTANCE; 161] *Opposite:* inclusion.

isolationism *n* **separateness**, remoteness, seclusion, independence, standoffishness, pride. [➡STYLES AND SYSTEMS OF GOVERNMENT; 806]

isometrics *n* **exercise**, body building, workout, keep fit. [➡HOBBIES, GAMES, AND SPORTS; 875]

isotherm *n* **line**, weather symbol, front, warm front, cold front. [➡WEATHER AND CLIMATE; 1049]

isotope *n* **element**, form, variant, version. [➡VARIETY, TYPE, KIND; 146]

issue 1 *n* **subject**, matter, question, topic, problem, concern, dispute. [➡SUBJECT AREA; 769] 2 *n* **copy**, number, edition, back number, back copy, instalment, back issue (*US*). [➡NEWSPAPERS; 606] 3 *n* **production**, release, distribution, circulation, publication, delivery, issuance. [➡DISPENSE, RATION, AND DISTRIBUTE; 435] 4 *n* **progeny**, offspring, children, young, descendants, heirs, posterity (*formal*). [➡YOUNGER GENERATION RELATIVES; 958] 5 *v* **supply**, give out, hand out, deliver, distribute, deal out, dispense, allot. [➡DISPENSE, RATION, AND DISTRIBUTE; 435] 6 *v* **announce**, broadcast, send out, make, declare, put out. [➡INFORM AND ANNOUNCE; 612] 7 *v* **publish**, release, broadcast, disseminate, distribute, deliver, circulate. [➡NAME AND DESCRIBE; 666] *Opposite:* withdraw. 8 *v* **emanate**, emerge, issue forth, gush, flow, come out, erupt. [➡EMIT AND EMANATE; 362] 9 *v* **originate**, stem, come forth, spring, arise, rise, proceed, result, follow. [➡GRADUALLY COME INTO EXISTENCE; 1]

isthmus *n* **strip**, neck, bridge, peninsula, spit, bar, promontory, headland. [➡THE SEAS, OCEANS, AND SHORES; 1041]

IT *n* **information technology**, computer science, data processing, information processing, data retrieval. [➡COMPUTERS AND COMPUTING; 1126]

italic *adj* **sloping**, slanted, oblique. [➡PRINTING; 601] *Opposite:* roman.

itch 1 *v* **irritate**, prickle, scratch, tickle, crawl, tingle, creep. [➡PAIN AND OTHER PHYSICAL SENSATIONS; 734] *Opposite:* soothe. 2 *v* **long**, desire, wish, hanker, yearn, ache, burn, have a yen for, pine for, crave. [➡DESIRE AND WANT; 580] 3 *n* **itchiness**, tickle, irritation, prickling, tingling, prickliness. [➡PAIN AND OTHER PHYSICAL SENSATIONS; 734] 4 *n* **desire**, longing, wish, eagerness, hankering, yearning, craving, pining, yen, appetite. [➡DESIRE AND WANT; 580]

itchiness *n* **irritation**, tickle, inflammation, tingling, prickliness, prickling, prickly heat, heat rash, discomfort. [➡CONDITIONS AFFECTING THE SKIN; 722]

itching *adj* **eager**, longing, dying, keen, burning, impatient. [➡POSITIVE IMPATIENCE, ENTHUSIASM, AND ALERTNESS; 538] *Opposite:* reluctant.

itchy *adj* **prickly**, tickly, scratchy, uncomfortable, irritated, inflamed. [➡PAIN AND OTHER PHYSICAL SENSATIONS; 734]

itchy feet *n* [➡POSITIVE IMPATIENCE, ENTHUSIASM, AND ALERTNESS; 538]

item 1 *n* **thing**, article, piece, entry, point, element, note, detail, particular. [➡PHYSICAL OBJECTS; 1242] **2** *n* (*informal*) **couple**, pair, twosome, match, duo, lovers. [➡SEXUAL AND ROMANTIC RELATIONSHIPS; 964]

itemize *v* **list**, detail, enumerate, record, document, catalogue, note, enter, specify. [➡RECORD SOMETHING; 372]

iterate *v* **repeat**, restate, reiterate, recapitulate (*formal*), go over, retell, do again, rehearse, redo. [➡RECITE, REPEAT, AND NARRATE; 621]

iteration *n* **repetition**, restatement, reiteration, recapitulation (*formal*), rehearsal, duplication. [➡CLAIM, INSIST, AND EMPHASIZE; 615]

itinerant *adj* **peripatetic**, roving, wandering, nomadic, roaming, travelling, wayfaring (*literary*), migrant. [➡NOMADIC AND ROOTLESS LIFESTYLES; 884] *Opposite:* settled.

itinerary *n* **route**, schedule, journey, circuit, tour, programme, travel plan. [➡SUMMARIES, OUTLINES, AND EXCERPTS; 589]

itsy-bitsy (*informal*) *adj* **tiny**, teeny (*informal*), weeny (*informal*), teeny-weeny (*informal*), little, small, minute, minuscule, itty-bitty (*informal*), wee. [➡SMALL; 1194] *Opposite:* huge.

itty-bitty (*informal*) *adj* [➡SMALL; 1194]

ivory *type of* **white**. [➡COLOURS; 1223]

ivory tower *n* **seclusion**, isolation, retreat, remoteness, academe (*formal*), academic world. [➡EDUCATIONAL INSTITUTIONS; 813] *Opposite:* real world.

ivy *type of* **climber**. [➡CLIMBERS; 1033]

J

jab 1 *v* **punch**, prod, stab, thrust, dig, poke, nudge, tap, bump. [➡CONTACT: TOUCH; 413] 2 *n* **prod**, stab, thrust, dig, poke, punch, blow, hit. [➡CONTACT: TOUCH; 413] 3 *n* (*informal*) **injection**, immunization, inoculation, vaccination, jag (*informal*), booster, shot (*informal*). [➡REMEDIES, TREATMENTS, AND OPERATIONS; 732]

jabber *v* **chatter**, babble, prattle, gabble, ramble, natter (*informal*), prate, blather (*informal*), gab (*informal*). [➡WITTER AND BABBLE; 618]

jack 1 *type of* **game piece**. [➡GAMES PIECES; 878] 2 *type of* **general tool**. [➡HAND TOOLS; 1118]

jackal *type of* **canine**. [➡CANINE; 979]

jackass *type of* **male animal**. [➡MALE OR FEMALE ANIMAL; 978]

jackboot *type of* **boot**. [➡FOOTWEAR; 871]

jackdaw *type of* **scavenger**. [➡BIRD; 997]

jacket 1 *n* **cover**, covering, casing, sheathing, sheath, sleeve, skin, coat, insulation, lagging, wrapper, wrapping, envelope. [➡COVERS AND COATINGS; 1245] 2 *type of* **jacket**. [➡GARMENTS AND OUTFITS; 865]

jacket potato *type of* **processed potato**. [➡FRUIT AND VEGETABLES; 1175]

jack in (*informal*) *v* **stop**, give up, resign, abandon, leave, quit. [➡STOP ACTING; 265] *Opposite:* take up.

jack-in-the-box *type of* **toy**. [➡TOYS; 880]

jackknife 1 *v* **turn**, skid, swerve, veer, swivel, twist. [➡CHANGE DIRECTION OF MOTION; 345] 2 *type of* **knife**. [➡CUTTING TOOLS; 1119]

jackpot *n* **prize**, bonanza, rollover, winnings, windfall, pool. [➡ADVANTAGE; 213]

jack up 1 *v* **lift**, lift up, raise, raise up, put up, lever up. [➡MOVE SOMETHING: UPWARDS; 329] *Opposite:* lower. 2 *v* **increase**, raise, put up, hike up, boost, push up. [➡CHANGE OF INTENSITY: MORE; 395] *Opposite:* slash.

jade 1 *type of* **gemstone**. [➡PRECIOUS STONES; 1277] 2 *type of* **green**. [➡COLOURS; 1223]

jaded 1 *adj* **bored**, world-weary, jaundiced, fed up (*informal*), cynical, tired, weary, overstimulated. [➡NEGATIVE OF OUTLOOK; 515] *Opposite:* enthusiastic. 2 *adj* **tired**, weary, exhausted, worn-out, lacklustre, burned-out. [➡TIRED, ASLEEP, AND UNCONSCIOUS; 739] *Opposite:* fresh.

jade green *type of* **green**. [➡COLOURS; 1223]

jagged 1 *adj* **uneven**, rough, ragged, crude, irregular, bumpy, coarse, angular. [➡PHYSICAL TEXTURE; 1221] *Opposite:* even. 2 *adj* **sharp**, pointed, pointy, rough, serrated, spiky, toothed. [➡PHYSICAL TEXTURE; 1221] *Opposite:* smooth.

jaggedness 1 *n* **unevenness**, raggedness, roughness, sharpness, irregularity, bumpiness, coarseness, fluidity. [➡PHYSICAL TEXTURE; 1221] *Opposite:* evenness. 2 *n* **sharpness**, pointedness, pointiness, roughness, serration, serratedness, spikiness, toothiness, raggedness. [➡PHYSICAL TEXTURE; 1221] *Opposite:* smoothness.

jaguar *type of* **cat**. [➡FELINE; 983]

jai alai *type of* **court game**. [➡HOBBIES, GAMES, AND SPORTS; 875]

jail 1 *n* **prison**, detention centre, lockup, secure unit, open prison, borstal, dungeon, oubliette, remand home, penitentiary (*US*), detention home (*US*). [➡BUILDINGS FOR CONFINING PEOPLE; 1093] 2 *v* **imprison**, lock up, lock away, put away (*informal*), put behind bars, incarcerate (*formal*), confine, detain. [➡THE POLICE, ARREST, AND PRE-TRIAL PROCEEDINGS; 818] *Opposite:* free.

jailbird (*slang*) *n* **convict**, con (*slang*), prisoner, old lag (*slang*), inmate, detainee, offender. [➡CAPTIVES AND PRISONERS; 250]

jailbreak *n* **breakout**, escape, getaway, exodus, flight. [➡SUDDEN EVENT; 52]

jailed *adj* [➡CAPTIVITY AND LOSS OF FREEDOM; 249]

jailer *n* **prison officer**, guard, governor, warder, keeper, screw (*slang*), prison guard, warden (*US*). [➡PEOPLE WHO GUARD AND PROTECT; 846] *Opposite:* liberator.

jalopy (*dated informal*) *n* **banger** (*informal*), wreck, crate (*dated informal*), heap (*slang*), tin lizzie (*informal*), rattletrap (*informal*), beater (*US informal*). [➡BIKES, CARS, AND CARRIAGES; 1148]

jam 1 *v* **push**, squash, cram, stuff, pack, ram, shove, force, wedge, crush, squeeze, press. [➡CONTACT: EXERT PRESSURE; 415] 2 *v* **fill**, fill up, throng, pack, block, congest. [➡FILL; 407] 3 *v* **stop**, seize, seize up, grind to a halt, stick, bung up (*informal*), block, clog. [➡FAIL OR CEASE TO FUNCTION; 471] 4 *n* **traffic jam**, queue, gridlock, tailback, bottleneck, logjam, roadblock. [➡TRAVEL: TRAFFIC PROBLEMS AND HOLDUPS; 324] 5 *n* (*informal*) **predicament**, mess, scrape (*informal*), pickle (*informal*), fix (*informal*), quandary. [➡DIFFICULT SITUATIONS; 72] 6 *type of* **preserve**. [➡SUGAR AND PRESERVES; 1183]

jamb *n* **upright**, post, support, column, doorpost, vertical, side. [➡SUPPORTS AND BASES; 1254]

jamboree *n* **celebration**, party, fête, knees-up (*informal*), shindig (*informal*), do (*informal*), carnival, garden party, block party (*US*). [➡PARTIES, DANCES, AND CELEBRATIONS; 37]

jam jar *type of* **container**. [➡CONTAINERS, RECEPTACLES, AND PACKAGING; 1244]

jammed 1 *adj* **stuck**, wedged, stuck fast, lodged, caught, trapped. [➡LACK OF ACTIVITY; 343] *Opposite:* free. 2 *adj* **blocked**, congested, mobbed (*informal*), thronged, packed, crammed, full. [➡FULL; 1238] *Opposite:* deserted.

jammy (*informal*) *adj* **lucky**, fortunate, comfortable, easy. [➡LUCK; 784] *Opposite:* unlucky.

jam-pack (*informal*) *v* [➡FILL; 407]

jam-packed (*informal*) *adj* **crowded**, full up, chock-a-block (*informal*), heaving, chock-full (*informal*), packed out (*informal*), full, packed. [➡FULL; 1238] *Opposite:* empty.

jangle 1 *v* **rattle**, jingle, clank, clink, clatter, clang. [➡EMIT SOUNDS THROUGH IMPACT AND ABRASION; 366] 2 *n* **jingle**, rattle, clank, clink, clatter, clang. [➡RINGING AND TOOTING SOUNDS; 1258]

janitor *n* [➡PEOPLE WHO GUARD AND PROTECT; 846]

Japanese beetle *type of* **beetle**. [➡BEETLES AND WEEVILS; 1016]

jape (*archaic*) 1 *n* **prank**, jest (*literary*), trick, practical joke, joke, setup (*informal*), lark, wind-up (*informal*), caper, escapade. [➡JOKES AND TEASING; 675] 2 *v* **joke**, lark, lark about, lark around, mess about (*informal*), mess around (*informal*), fool around, make mischief, fool about, set up (*informal*), trick, wind up (*informal*), josh (*informal*). [➡JOKES AND TEASING; 675]

jar 1 *n* **pot**, jam jar, container, vessel, crock, urn, cruse (*archaic*). [➡CONTAINERS, RECEPTACLES, AND PACKAGING; 1244] 2 *v* **irritate**, grate, annoy, irk, get on somebody's nerves, nettle (*informal*), vex. [➡ANGER AND ANNOY; 570] 3 *v* **shake**, jolt, jerk, bash (*informal*), bump, hit, shudder, vibrate, judder. [➡MOVE SOMETHING ON THE SPOT; 337]

jargon 1 *n* **terminology**, slang, lingo (*informal*), argot, language. [➡ASPECTS OF LANGUAGE; 683] 2 *n* **gobbledegook** (*informal disapproving*), mumbo jumbo (*informal*), waffle (*informal*), nonsense, verbiage, cant, guff (*informal*). [➡MEANINGLESS SPEECH OR WRITING; 677]

jarring 1 *adj* **irritating**, upsetting, grating, annoying, unpleasant, unbearable. [➡EMOTIONALLY UNPLEASANT AND UPSETTING; 228] *Opposite:* calming. 2 *adj* **disturbing**, unsettling, shocking, destabilizing, uncomfortable, worrying, upsetting. [➡EMOTIONALLY UNPLEASANT AND UPSETTING; 228] *Opposite:* reassuring. 3 *adj* **clashing**, incongruous, uncharacteristic, discordant, inharmonious, uncomfortable, inappropriate, disturbing. [➡LOUD OR UNPLEASANT SOUNDS; 1265] *Opposite:* harmonious.

jasmine *type of* **climber**. [➡CLIMBERS; 1033]

jaundiced *adj* **cynical**, pessimistic, sceptical, unenthusiastic, jaded, negative. [➡NEGATIVE OF OUTLOOK; 515]

jaunt *n* **outing**, trip, excursion, break, day out, away day, spree, day away. [➡TRAVEL: JOURNEYS AND TRIPS; 319]

jauntily *adv* **cheerfully**, gaily, spryly, briskly, chirpily (*informal*), cheerily. [➡PLEASURE, EXCITEMENT, AND ELATION; 535]

jauntiness *n* **cheerfulness**, jolliness, gaiety, dash, spryness, cheeriness, self-confidence, chirpiness (*informal*), briskness. [➡PLEASURE, EXCITEMENT, AND ELATION; 535]

jaunty *adj* **carefree**, cheerful, cheery, jolly, spry, lively, brisk, merry, sprightly, chirpy (*informal*). [➡ENERGY AND ENTHUSIASM; 497]

javelin 1 *n* **spear**, projectile, missile, lance, harpoon. [➡PROJECTILES; 1158] 2 *type of* **sports equipment**. [➡SPORTS EQUIPMENT; 879] 3 *type of* **track and field**. [➡HOBBIES, GAMES, AND SPORTS; 875]

jaw 1 *v* (*slang*) [➡TWO-WAY COMMUNICATION; 608] 2 *n* **chin**, jawbone, jawline, jowl, mouth, chops (*informal*), mandible (*technical*), maxilla. [➡HEAD; 693]

jawbone *n* **jaw**, bone, chin, mandible (*technical*), maxilla. [➡THE BONES AND JOINTS; 720]

jawbreaker (*US*) *type of* **confectionery**. [➡CONFECTIONERY; 1181]

jawline *part of* **face**. [➡HEAD; 693]

jay *type of* **common bird**. [➡BIRD; 997]

jaywalk *v* **cross**, cross over, walk across, stroll across, go across, traverse. [➡PROCEED AND GO; 306]

jaywalker *n* **pedestrian**, walker, crosser, traverser, stroller. [➡TRAVEL: TRAVELLERS AND WALKERS; 320]

jazz 1 *n* (*slang*) **stuff**, gear (*informal*), things, paraphernalia, belongings, tackle, equipment. [➡PHYSICAL OBJECTS; 1242] 2 *n* (*slang*) **liveliness**, vivacity, enthusiasm, pizazz (*informal*), zip (*informal*), zing (*informal*), pep (*informal*), energy, joie de vivre, oomph. [➡ENERGY AND ENTHUSIASM; 497] 3 *n* (*US slang*) **nonsense**, rubbish, rigmarole, stuff, stuff and nonsense, verbiage, guff (*informal*), waffle (*informal*), flimflam (*slang*), blether (*informal*), drivel, gobbledegook (*informal disapproving*), talk, blather (*informal*), jive (*US slang*). [➡MEANINGLESS SPEECH OR WRITING; 677] 4 *type of* **popular music**. [➡MUSIC, SONGS, AND SINGING; 907]

jazz band *type of* **band**. [➡MUSICIANS AND SINGERS; 908]

jazz up (*informal*) *v* **enhance**, pep up (*informal*), spice, spice up, liven up, enliven, add zing to, add zest to, zest, brighten up. [➡IMPROVE APPEARANCE; 380]

jazzy (*slang*) *adj* **showy**, bright, flashy, gaudy, glitzy, smart, fancy, psychedelic, colourful. [➡DESCRIBING COLOURS; 1225] *Opposite:* sombre.

jealous 1 *adj* **envious**, covetous, resentful, desirous (*formal*), green with envy, green, green-eyed, bitter. [➡ENVY AND JEALOUSY; 549] 2 *adj* **protective**, suspicious, wary, watchful, mistrustful, possessive. [➡INSECURITY AND LOSS OF COMPOSURE; 545] *Opposite:* trusting.

jealousy 1 *n* **envy**, covetousness, resentment, resentfulness, desirousness (*formal*). [➡ENVY AND JEALOUSY; 549] 2 *n* **protectiveness**, suspicion, suspiciousness, wariness, watchfulness, mistrustfulness, distrust, possessiveness. [➡INSECURITY AND LOSS OF COMPOSURE; 545]

jeans *type of* **trousers**. [➡GARMENTS AND OUTFITS; 865]

jeep *type of* **military vehicle**. [➡VEHICLES; 1144]

jeepers (*dated informal*) *interj* [➡EXPRESSIONS OF SURPRISE; 547]

jeer 1 *v* **boo**, hiss, heckle, catcall, taunt, laugh at, mock, abuse, call names. [➡UNFAVOURABLE NON-VERBAL RESPONSES; 655] *Opposite:* applaud. 2 *n* **hiss**, boo, taunt, catcall, hoot, raspberry (*slang*), Bronx cheer (*US informal*). [➡INSULTS, ABUSE, AND SWEARING; 659]

jeer at *v* **insult**, taunt, sneer, mock, deride, ridicule, scoff. [➡INSULTS, ABUSE, AND SWEARING; 659] *Opposite:* cheer.

jeering 1 *n* **derision**, mockery, name-calling, mocking, taunting, scoffing, heckling, booing, hissing. [➡INSULTS,

ABUSE, AND SWEARING; 659] *Opposite:* applause. 2 *adj* **derisive**, scornful, mocking, sardonic, contemptuous, sneering, taunting. [➡ MOCKING AND DISMISSIVE; 637]

jejune 1 *adj* **boring**, undemanding, uninteresting, lightweight, insubstantial, superficial. [➡ BORING AND UNINTERESTING; 235] *Opposite:* interesting. 2 *adj* **childish**, immature, adolescent, unsophisticated, crude, simplistic. [➡ NEGATIVE INTELLECTUAL CHARACTERISTICS; 526] *Opposite:* mature.

jell 1 *v* **solidify**, set, congeal, firm, harden, thicken, gel. [➡ HARDEN, CONGEAL, DRY; 388] *Opposite:* liquefy. 2 *v* **take shape**, shape up, crystallize, come together, firm up, become clear, gel (*informal*). [➡ GRADUALLY COME INTO EXISTENCE; 1] *Opposite:* disintegrate. 3 *v* **bond**, get on, click (*informal*), be compatible, be on the same wavelength, hit it off (*informal*), gel (*informal*), get along (*US*). [➡ ESTABLISHING RELATIONSHIPS WITH OTHERS; 974] *Opposite:* clash.

jellied *adj* **gelatinous**, set, solid, congealed. [➡ STATE OF PREPARED FOOD; 1170]

jellify *v* **set**, jelly, gelatinize, congeal, jell, gel. [➡ HARDEN, CONGEAL, DRY; 388] *Opposite:* liquefy.

jelly 1 *n* **gelatin**, aspic, gel. [➡ CAKES, BISCUITS, AND DESSERTS; 1180] 2 *n* **petroleum jelly**, lubricant, ointment. [➡ LOTIONS, PASTES, AND GELS; 1271] 3 *type of* **shoe**. [➡ FOOTWEAR; 871] 4 *type of* **preserve**. [➡ SUGAR AND PRESERVES; 1183] 5 *v* **set**, thicken, jellify, gelatinize, congeal, jell, gel, firm. [➡ HARDEN, CONGEAL, DRY; 388] *Opposite:* liquefy.

jellybean *type of* **confectionery**. [➡ CONFECTIONERY; 1181]

jellyfish *type of* **aquatic invertebrate**. [➡ AQUATIC INVERTEBRATE; 1022]

jellylike *adj* [➡ MALLEABLE AND ELASTIC; 1211]

jelly roll (*US*) *type of* **cake**. [➡ CAKES, BISCUITS, AND DESSERTS; 1180]

jemmy 1 *v* **lever**, open, force, prise, crowbar, pry (*US*). [➡ UNFASTEN AND UNDO; 410] 2 *type of* **general tool**. [➡ HAND TOOLS; 1118]

je ne sais quoi *n* [➡ FOREIGN WORDS AND PHRASES; 673]

jenny *type of* **female animal**. [➡ MALE OR FEMALE ANIMAL; 978]

jeopardize *v* **put at risk**, risk, put in danger, endanger, lay on the line (*informal*), expose, threaten. [➡ PUT AT RISK; 385]

jeopardy *n* **danger**, risk, threat, peril, hazard, difficulty, trouble. [➡ DANGER; 236]

jerboa *type of* **rodent**. [➡ RODENT; 989]

jeremiad (*literary*) *n* [➡ CRITICISMS AND ANGRY OUTBURSTS; 50]

jerk 1 *v* **yank**, tug, pull, wrench, haul. [➡ PUSH, PULL, SLIDE; 336] 2 *v* **lurch**, jolt, shudder, judder, bump, shake, kangaroo (*informal*). [➡ PHYSICAL REACTIONS; 317] 3 *v* **twitch**, shudder, tremble, shake. [➡ MOVE SOMETHING ON THE SPOT; 337] 4 *n* **pull**, tug, yank, wrench, haul. [➡ CONTACT: TOUCH; 413] 5 *n* **jolt**, bump, shudder, judder, lurch, shake. [➡ MOVE SOMETHING ON THE SPOT; 337] 6 *n* **spasm**, twitch, shudder, tremble, shake. [➡ PHYSICAL REACTIONS; 317]

jerkin *n* **jacket**, body warmer, tunic, waistcoat, gilet, vest (*US*). [➡ GARMENTS AND OUTFITS; 865]

jerkiness *n* **bumpiness**, jumpiness, bounciness, lurching, shuddering, juddering, jolting, irregularity. [➡ DESCRIBING BODY MOVEMENTS; 289] *Opposite:* smoothness.

jerky *adj* **irregular**, spasmodic, erratic, fitful, bumpy, jumpy, bouncy, rough, shuddering, juddering, lurching, jolting. [➡ DESCRIBING BODY MOVEMENTS; 289] *Opposite:* smooth.

jerry-build *v* **throw together** (*informal*), throw up, fling up, knock together (*informal*). [➡ BUILD; 353]

jerry-built *adj* **thrown together** (*informal*), knocked together (*informal*), poor, shoddy, flimsy, ramshackle, cheap and nasty, slapdash, cheap. [➡ IN BAD REPAIR; 1233]

jerry can *n* **can**, container, canister. [➡ CONTAINERS, RECEPTACLES, AND PACKAGING; 1244]

jerry-rigged *adj* [➡ IN BAD REPAIR; 1233]

jersey 1 *type of* **fabric from animals**. [➡ FABRICS; 1131] 2 *type of* **sweater or cardigan**. [➡ GARMENTS AND OUTFITS; 865]

jest (*literary*) 1 *n* **joke**, prank, hoax, quip, gag (*informal*), canard (*literary*), spoof, jape (*archaic*). [➡ JOKES AND TEASING; 675] 2 *v* **banter**, joke, kid, tease, quip, clown. [➡ JOKES AND TEASING; 675]

jester *n* **fool**, clown, comedian, entertainer, comic, joker. [➡ JOKERS AND TEASES; 676]

jesting (*literary*) 1 *adj* **jokey**, lighthearted, flippant, funny, humorous, playful. [➡ GOOD-TEMPERED AND HUMOROUS; 628] *Opposite:* serious. 2 *n* **joking**, clowning, kidding, slapstick, fun, humour, banter. [➡ JOKES AND TEASING; 675]

jet 1 *n* **spurt**, spout, fountain, squirt, stream, gush. [➡ AMOUNT OF LIQUID; 114] 2 *type of* **civil aircraft**. [➡ AIRCRAFT; 1147] 3 *type of* **mineral**. [➡ MINERALS; 1276]

jet black *type of* **black**. [➡ COLOURS; 1223]

jet engine *part of* **aircraft**. [➡ AIRCRAFT; 1147]

jetsam *n* **odds and ends**, bits and pieces (*informal*), flotsam, debris, detritus, junk (*informal*), rubbish, miscellanea, trash (*US*). [➡ RUBBISH AND USELESS OBJECTS; 1248]

jet set (*informal*) *n* **glitterati**, high society, rich and famous, beautiful people, idle rich, café society. [➡ RICH PEOPLE; 895] *Opposite:* hoi polloi.

jet-setter (*informal*) *n* [➡ TRAVEL: TRAVELLERS AND WALKERS; 320]

jettison *v* **throw away**, throw out, get rid of, chuck (*informal*), chuck out (*informal*), abandon, discard, ditch (*informal*), dump. [➡ GET RID OF SOMETHING; 452] *Opposite:* keep.

jetty *n* **dock**, breakwater, quay, landing stage, pier, quayside, wharf. [➡ WATERWAYS AND SEAWAYS; 1107]

jewel 1 *n* **ornament**, trinket, charm, accessory, ring, brooch, necklace, bracelet, tiara, choker, earring. [➡ ORNAMENTS AND DECORATIONS; 1247] 2 *n* **gemstone**, gem, precious stone, semiprecious stone, rock (*informal*), crystal, sparkler (*informal*). [➡ PRECIOUS STONES; 1277]

jewel in the crown *n* [➡ AMAZING THING; 212]

jewellery *type of* **accessory**. [➡ HABERDASHERY, MILLINERY, AND LINGERIE; 867]

jewellery

◆ *types of jewellery*
anklet, armlet, badge, bangle, bracelet, brooch, cameo, charm, cuff link, eardrop, earring, necklace, nose ring, nose stud, pin, ring, stud, tiara, tie clasp (*US*), tie clip, tiepin, tie tack (*US*), wristlet

◆ *types of necklace*
beads, chain, choker, collar, locket, medallion, necklet, pendant, torque

jib 1 *part of* **sailing vessel.** [➡PARTS OF A SHIP OR BOAT; 1150] 2 *v* **baulk**, stop short, pull up, recoil, retreat, shy. [➡NOT DO AND REFUSE TO DO; 275]

jibe 1 *n* **taunt**, dig, crack (*informal*), sneer, insult, gibe. [➡INSULTS, ABUSE, AND SWEARING; 659] 2 *v* **sneer**, taunt, mock, ridicule, insult, belittle, gibe. [➡JOKES AND TEASING; 675]

jiff *n* [➡SHORT PERIOD OF TIME; 93]

jiffy (*informal*) *n* **moment**, second, minute, flash, instant, sec (*informal*), tick (*informal*), mo (*informal*). [➡SHORT PERIOD OF TIME; 93]

jig 1 *v* **jerk**, skip, hop, caper, leap, spring, dance. [➡FIDGET AND FROLIC; 312] 2 *type of* **dance.** [➡DANCE; 903]

jiggery-pokery (*informal*) *n* [➡DECEPTION AND LIES; 661]

jiggle *v* **wiggle**, waggle, shake, joggle, rattle, agitate, jostle. [➡MOVE SOMETHING ON THE SPOT; 337]

jigsaw 1 *n* **puzzle**, jigsaw puzzle, picture puzzle, Chinese puzzle, tangram, game. [➡TOYS; 880] 2 *type of* **carpentry tool.** [➡HAND TOOLS; 1118]

jigsaw puzzle *type of* **toy.** [➡TOYS; 880]

jilt *v* **reject**, turn down, break up, drop (*informal*), ditch (*informal*), split up, walk out, finish with (*informal*), leave, leave in the lurch, desert, abandon. [➡REFUSING OR REJECTING RELATIONS; 975] *Opposite:* stick by.

jim-dandy (*US informal*) *n* [➡AMAZING THING; 212]

jimsonweed (*US*) *type of* **weed.** [➡WEEDS AND THISTLES; 1034]

jingle 1 *n* **ringing**, ring, tinkle, tinkling, clink, clinking, clank, clanking, clatter, clattering, rattle, rattling. [➡RINGING AND TOOTING SOUNDS; 1258] 2 *n* **tune**, song, refrain, chorus, ditty. [➡MUSIC, SONGS, AND SINGING; 907] 3 *v* **tinkle**, rattle, ring, clink, clank, clatter. [➡EMIT SOUNDS THROUGH IMPACT AND ABRASION; 366]

jingoism *n* **chauvinism**, patriotism, nationalism, xenophobia, hostility, antipathy, antagonism, flag-waving, wrapping yourself in the flag. [➡PREJUDICE; 551]

jingoist *n* [➡SELF-IMPORTANT AND SELF-SEEKING PEOPLE; 949]

jingoistic *adj* **chauvinistic**, patriotic, nationalistic, xenophobic, hostile, antagonistic. [➡NEGATIVE INTELLECTUAL CHARACTERISTICS; 526]

jinx *n* **curse**, plague, gremlin (*informal*), evil eye, spell, bad luck, misfortune, whammy (*informal*), bugaboo. [➡PROBLEM; 257]

jitterbug *type of* **dance.** [➡DANCE; 903]

jitteriness *n* [➡CONFUSION, ANXIETY, AND WORRY; 541]

jitters (*informal*) *n* **nervousness**, nerves (*informal*), agitation, uneasiness, anxiety, apprehension, fright, fear, butterflies (*informal*), habdabs (*informal*), heebie-jeebies (*slang*), shakes, shivers (*informal*). [➡CONFUSION, ANXIETY, AND WORRY; 541] *Opposite:* calmness.

jittery *adj* **nervous**, nervy (*informal*), jumpy, on edge, edgy, strung up (*informal*), stressed out (*informal*), frazzled (*informal*), fidgety, skittish. [➡CONFUSION, ANXIETY, AND WORRY; 541] *Opposite:* calm.

jive 1 *type of* **dance.** [➡DANCE; 903] 2 *n* (*US slang*) **smooth talk**, sweet talk (*informal*), soft soap (*informal*), blarney (*informal*), weasel words (*informal*), flattery, blandishment (*formal*). [➡INGRATIATING; 639]

job 1 *n* **occupation**, work, trade, profession, career, employment, contract, business. [➡PROFESSIONS; 845] 2 *n* **task**, duty, responsibility, chore, assignment, activity, mission, affair, charge. [➡WORK IN GENERAL; 298] 3 *n* **position**, post, situation (*formal*), appointment, vacancy, role, function, engagement, spot, opening. [➡JOB; 833]

Compare and Contrast: *job, assignment, task, chore, duty*

CORE MEANING: A PIECE OF WORK TO BE DONE

job a paid occupation, or a piece of work to be done whether on one occasion or regularly; ***assignment*** a specific piece of work given to somebody as part of the workload of an occupation or course of study, often with a time limit for completion. It can also be a position, duty, or post allocated to somebody; ***task*** a piece of work to be done whether on one occasion or regularly; ***chore*** a short, routine, regularly performed activity, especially one that is unwelcome, unpleasant, or tedious; ***duty*** something that somebody is obliged to do for moral, legal, or religious reasons, or because it is part of a paid occupation.

jobbing *adj* **casual**, occasional, freelance, part-time, temporary, self-employed. [➡EMPLOYMENT STATUS; 831] *Opposite:* regular.

jobless *adj* **unemployed**, out of work, on the dole (*informal*), unwaged, on benefit, redundant, on welfare (*US*). [➡EMPLOYMENT STATUS; 831] *Opposite:* employed.

joblessness *n* [➡WORK-RELATED ACTIVITIES; 834]

job-sharer *n* [➡WORKER; 836]

job-sharing *n* **part-time work**, work-sharing, sharing. [➡WORK-RELATED ACTIVITIES; 834]

jockey 1 *n* **rider**, equestrian, steeplechaser, showjumper, eventer, competitor, point-to-pointer. [➡PEOPLE IN SPORTS AND LEISURE; 876] 2 *v* **ride**, race, steeplechase, showjump, compete, show, event. [➡HOBBIES, GAMES, AND SPORTS; 875] 3 *v* **manoeuvre**, compete, contend, fight, struggle, juggle, jostle. [➡COMPETE, CONTEND, AND COMBAT; 304] 4 *v* **manipulate**, cajole, trick, deceive, talk into, con, pressure, press, coax, persuade. [➡CAUSE OR COMPEL TO ACT; 272]

jockstrap *type of* **lower body underwear.** [➡HABERDASHERY, MILLINERY, AND LINGERIE; 867]

jocose (*literary*) *adj* [➡GOOD-TEMPERED AND HUMOROUS; 628]

jocular *adj* **jokey**, funny, joking, jovial, playful, witty, flippant, lighthearted, flip (*informal*), frivolous, waggish (*dated*), good-humoured, sportive, jocose (*literary*), facetious, roguish, humorous. [➡GOOD-TEMPERED AND HUMOROUS; 628] *Opposite:* solemn.

jocularity *n* **playfulness**, wittiness, comicality, humour, jokiness, humorousness, waggishness (*dated*), facetiousness, cheerfulness, joviality, sportiveness, roguishness. [➡JOKES AND TEASING; 675] *Opposite:* solemnity.

jocund (*literary*) *adj* [➡GOOD-TEMPERED AND HUMOROUS; 628]

jocundity (*literary*) *n* [➡GOOD-TEMPERED AND HUMOROUS; 628]

jodhpurs *type of* **trousers**. [➡GARMENTS AND OUTFITS; 865]

joey *type of* **young animal**. [➡YOUNG ANIMAL; 977]

jog 1 *v* **trot**, run, train, exercise, keep fit, sprint. [➡MOVE FAST; 314] 2 *v* **nudge**, prod, bump, push, bang, hit, shake, jerk, pull, twitch. [➡CONTACT: IMPACT; 414]

jogger *n* **runner**, sprinter, cross-country runner, harrier, athlete. [➡PEOPLE IN SPORTS AND LEISURE; 876]

joggle *v* **shake**, wiggle, waggle, jiggle, jerk, bump, knock. [➡MOVE SOMETHING ON THE SPOT; 337]

John Dory *type of* **sea fish**. [➡SEA FISH; 1009]

John Hancock (*US informal*) *n* [➡NAME AND DESCRIBE; 666]

johnnycake (*US*) *type of* **pancake**. [➡CAKES, BISCUITS, AND DESSERTS; 1180]

joie de vivre *n* **vitality**, enthusiasm, liveliness, exuberance, high-spiritedness, spiritedness, energy, élan (*literary*). [➡PLEASURE, EXCITEMENT, AND ELATION; 535] *Opposite:* lethargy.

join 1 *v* **link**, unite, connect, stick, fasten, fix, adhere, bond, unify, bind, paste. [➡FASTEN, LINK, AND JOIN; 409] *Opposite:* separate. 2 *v* **connect**, link up, merge, bring together, unite, link, put in touch, bridge, consolidate. [➡CREATING CONNECTIONS; 145] *Opposite:* disengage. 3 *v* **sign up**, enrol, enlist, join up, go in with, enter, subscribe to. [➡PARTICIPATE; 293] *Opposite:* leave. 4 *n* **joint**, seam, connection, intersection, link, junction, junctive. [➡FASTENERS, LINKS, AND NETWORKS; 1246]

joined 1 *adj* **linked**, united, combined, amalgamated, merged, fused. [➡RELATED; 143] *Opposite:* separated. 2 *adj* **fixed together**, hinged, hitched, linked, tied, bound, attached, coupled, yoked. [➡FASTEN, LINK, AND JOIN; 409] *Opposite:* detached. 3 *adj* **connected**, linked, coupled, attached, associated, allied, affiliated, twinned, bound. [➡RELATED; 143] *Opposite:* independent.

joinery *n* **woodwork**, cabinetmaking, furniture making, carving, carpentry, woodcraft (*US*). [➡CRAFTS AND CARVING; 356]

join forces *v* **team up**, collaborate, get together, come together, rally, merge, amalgamate, combine, consolidate. [➡ESTABLISHING RELATIONSHIPS WITH OTHERS; 974] *Opposite:* split.

join in *v* **participate**, become involved, take part, enter into, play, have a go (*informal*), contribute. [➡PARTICIPATE; 293] *Opposite:* leave.

joint 1 *adj* **combined**, dual, shared, multiparty, united, mutual, common, cooperative, communal, collaborative, allied. [➡ACTING WITH OTHERS; 286] *Opposite:* individual. 2 *n* **join**, linkage, link, junction, intersection, seam, connection, juncture (*formal*), coupling, hinge. [➡FASTENERS, LINKS, AND NETWORKS; 1246] 3 *n* (*slang*) **venue**, hangout (*informal*), dive (*informal*), place, establishment, locale, location. [➡HOTELS, RESTAURANTS, AND CLUBS; 1081] 4 *type of* **cut**. [➡TYPES AND CUTS OF MEAT; 1176]

join together *v* **merge**, amalgamate, integrate, dovetail, associate, federate, unite, consolidate, cooperate. [➡CREATING CONNECTIONS; 145] *Opposite:* split.

joint-stock company *n* [➡BUSINESS ENTERPRISES AND RELATED BODIES; 793]

joint venture *n* [➡BUSINESS ENTERPRISES AND RELATED BODIES; 793]

join up 1 *v* **enlist**, enrol, sign up, join, subscribe. [➡WARFARE AND WAR; 830] *Opposite:* quit. 2 *v* **meet up**, link, team up, come together, get together, combine, pair, unite, consolidate, amalgamate. [➡ESTABLISHING RELATIONSHIPS WITH OTHERS; 974]

joist *n* **beam**, spar, truss, support. [➡BUILDING MATERIALS; 1076]

joke 1 *n* **gag** (*informal*), witticism, shaggy dog story, tall story, pun, anecdote, yarn (*informal*), tale, jest (*literary*), put-on (*informal*), tall tale. [➡JOKES AND TEASING; 675] 2 *n* **laughing stock**, butt, object of ridicule, fool, buffoon, scapegoat. [➡LAZY OR UNSUCCESSFUL PEOPLE; 948] 3 *n* **prank**, trick, practical joke, stunt, hoax, act, gag (*informal*), caper, lark. [➡JOKES AND TEASING; 675] 4 *v* **kid**, pull somebody's leg (*informal*), mess about (*informal*), mess around (*informal*), jest (*literary*), pretend, clown, play the fool, josh (*informal*). [➡JOKES AND TEASING; 675]

joker *n* **clown**, fool, buffoon, comedian, comic, prankster, entertainer, wit, wag (*dated*), jester. [➡JOKERS AND TEASES; 676]

jokey *adj* **amusing**, good-humoured, lighthearted, flippant, flip (*informal*), funny, witty, comical, humorous, facetious, jesting (*literary*), joshing (*informal*). [➡GOOD-TEMPERED AND HUMOROUS; 628] *Opposite:* serious.

jokily *adv* **amusingly**, good-humouredly, jokingly, humorously, drolly, facetiously, wittily, comically, entertainingly, flippantly. [➡GOOD-TEMPERED AND HUMOROUS; 628] *Opposite:* seriously.

jokiness *n* [➡GOOD-TEMPERED AND HUMOROUS; 628]

joking 1 *adj* **jokey**, playful, flippant, lighthearted, facetious, funny, teasing, jesting (*literary*). [➡GOOD-TEMPERED AND HUMOROUS; 628] *Opposite:* serious. 2 *n* **clowning**, teasing, raillery, fooling around, fooling about, larking about, larking around, high jinks (*informal*), horseplay, playing the fool. [➡JOKES AND TEASING; 675]

jollification *n* **festivity**, revelry, celebration, merrymaking, party, revel, carousal (*literary*), feast, do (*informal*). [➡PARTIES, DANCES, AND CELEBRATIONS; 37]

jolliness *n* **cheerfulness**, jollity, joviality, fun, hilarity, gaiety, high-spiritedness, jauntiness, merriness, gleefulness, playfulness, ebullience. [➡PLEASURE, EXCITEMENT, AND ELATION; 535] *Opposite:* seriousness.

jollity *n* **cheerfulness**, fun, hilarity, joviality, jolliness, gaiety, high-spiritedness, jauntiness, gleefulness, merriness, high spirits, playfulness. [➡PLEASURE, EXCITEMENT, AND ELATION; 535] *Opposite:* seriousness.

jolly 1 *adj* **cheerful**, friendly, happy, fun, jovial, bright, ebullient, cheery, good-humoured, merry, gleeful, playful. [➡CHEERFULNESS OF OUTLOOK; 504] *Opposite:* sad. 2 *adv* (*dated informal*) **very**, really, tremendously, hugely, terrifically, extremely, terribly. [➡TO A GREAT EXTENT; 130]

jolt 1 *v* **shake**, jerk, bump, joggle, nudge, push, shove, lurch, quake. [➡MOVE SOMETHING ON THE SPOT; 337] 2 *n* **bump**, shake, jerk, joggle, bounce, judder, shudder, lurch, quake (*informal*). [➡MOVE SOMETHING ON THE SPOT; 337] 3 *n* **shock**, surprise, bolt from the blue, bombshell (*informal*), blow, reminder, jar, thunderbolt, trauma. [➡SUDDEN EVENT; 52]

jonquil *type of* **flower grown from bulb.** [➡FLOWERS FROM BULBS; 1030]

josh (*informal*) *v* **tease**, rib (*informal*), make fun of, pull somebody's leg (*informal*), chaff, ridicule, set up (*informal*), mock, twit (*dated*). [➡JOKES AND TEASING; 675]

josher (*US informal*) *n* [➡JOKERS AND TEASES; 676]

joshing (*informal*) *n* [➡JOKES AND TEASING; 675]

jostle *v* **push**, knock, bump, shove, elbow, push around (*informal*), manhandle, crowd, butt, shoulder. [➡CONTACT: IMPACT; 414]

jot *n* **iota**, atom, whit (*informal*), bit, speck, tittle, dot, mite, smidgen (*informal*). [➡FEW, LITTLE, SMALL AMOUNT; 119]

jot down *v* **write down**, make a note of, scribble down, put on paper, put down, note, list, record, enter. [➡RECORD SOMETHING; 372]

jotter *n* **notepad**, notebook, pad, personal organizer, writing pad. [➡WRITING AND DRAWING IMPLEMENTS, AND MEDIA; 602]

journal 1 *n* **periodical**, magazine, paper, weekly, monthly, quarterly, bulletin, newsletter. [➡NEWSPAPERS; 606] 2 *n* **diary**, log, chronicle, record, register, daybook. [➡RECORDS; 586]

journalism *n* **reporting**, reportage, broadcasting, commentary, recording, writing, fourth estate, press. [➡NEWSPAPERS; 606]

journalist *n* **correspondent**, reporter, broadcaster, newsreader, columnist, commentator, press officer, newswriter. [➡WORKERS IN ENTERTAINMENT AND MEDIA; 873]

journalistic *adj* **reporting**, editorial, writing, newspaper, broadsheet, tabloid, weekly, monthly, quarterly, magazine. [➡NEWSPAPERS; 606]

journey 1 *n* **trip**, voyage, expedition, ride, flight, passage, crossing, excursion, drive, tour, trek, outing. [➡TRAVEL: JOURNEYS AND TRIPS; 319] 2 *v* **travel**, tour, go, trek, voyage, fly, sail, sightsee, cruise, roam. [➡TRAVEL: WAYS OF TRAVELLING; 321]

journo (*informal*) *n* [➡WORKERS IN ENTERTAINMENT AND MEDIA; 873]

joust *v* **fight**, tilt, compete, battle, engage, contest, contend, spar, bicker, squabble, dispute, argue, wrangle. [➡ARGUE AND FIGHT – TWO-WAY; 644] *Opposite:* agree.

jovial *adj* **cheerful**, jolly, good-humoured, fun-loving, full of beans (*informal*), bright and breezy, breezy, happy, cheery, buoyant, merry, jocund (*literary*), blithe (*literary*). [➡CHEERFULNESS OF OUTLOOK; 504] *Opposite:* miserable.

joviality *n* **cheerfulness**, fun, jollity, jolliness, cheeriness, hilarity, bonhomie, good humour, jocundity (*literary*), merriness, blitheness (*literary*). [➡PLEASURE, EXCITEMENT, AND ELATION; 535] *Opposite:* glumness.

jovially *adv* **cheerfully**, happily, heartily, joyously, convivially, merrily, cheerily, enthusiastically. [➡GOOD-TEMPERED AND HUMOROUS; 628] *Opposite:* miserably.

jovialness *n* [➡GOOD-TEMPERED AND HUMOROUS; 628]

jowl *n* **jaw**, chin, jawbone, jawline, mandible (*technical*), muzzle, chops (*informal*). [➡HEAD; 693]

joy 1 *n* **happiness**, delight, enjoyment, bliss, ecstasy, elation, joyfulness, thrill, pleasure, gladness, exultation, rapture. [➡PLEASURE, EXCITEMENT, AND ELATION; 535] *Opposite:* sadness. 2 *n* **delight**, jewel, treasure, pearl, angel, wonder, prize, pride, gem (*informal*). [➡TREAT; 211]

joyful 1 *adj* **happy**, elated, ecstatic, thrilled, pleased, jubilant, glad, delighted, exultant. [➡PLEASURE, EXCITEMENT, AND ELATION; 535] *Opposite:* sad. 2 *adj* **welcome**, wonderful, blissful, pleasurable, fantastic, enjoyable, carefree, pleasant, happy, pleasing, heartwarming, delightful. [➡EMOTIONALLY PLEASANT; 188] *Opposite:* unpleasant.

joyfully *adv* **happily**, ecstatically, blissfully, merrily, gladly, cheerily, elatedly, jubilantly, exuberantly. [➡PLEASURE, EXCITEMENT, AND ELATION; 535] *Opposite:* sadly.

joyfulness *n* **happiness**, enjoyment, bliss, ecstasy, merriment, cheerfulness, jubilation, pleasure, gladness, exultation, rapture. [➡PLEASURE, EXCITEMENT, AND ELATION; 535] *Opposite:* sadness.

joyless *adj* **miserable**, cheerless, depressing, bleak, desolate, unhappy, dreary, gloomy, dour. [➡EMOTIONALLY UNPLEASANT AND UPSETTING; 228] *Opposite:* happy.

joylessness *n* **miserableness**, gloom, cheerlessness, misery, unhappiness, bleakness, desolation, despondency, dreariness, gloominess, dourness. [➡SADNESS, DISTRESS, AND DESPAIR; 540] *Opposite:* happiness.

joyous *adj* **happy**, merry, blissful, festive, jolly, cheerful, jubilant, exuberant, delighted, elated, exultant. [➡PLEASURE, EXCITEMENT, AND ELATION; 535] *Opposite:* sad.

joyousness *n* **happiness**, pleasure, bliss, joyfulness, jubilation, cheerfulness, elation, exuberance, joy, gladness, exultation, rapture. [➡PLEASURE, EXCITEMENT, AND ELATION; 535] *Opposite:* sadness.

joyride 1 *n* **carjacking**, speeding, twoc (*slang*), hot-rodding (*slang*). [➡CRIMES; 817] 2 *v* **carjack**, speed, twoc (*slang*), hot-rod (*slang*). [➡STEAL AND ROB; 427]

joyrider *n* **carjacker**, car thief, speeder, twoccer (*slang*), hot-rodder (*slang*). [➡CRIMINALS; 821]

joyriding *n* **carjacking**, car theft, speeding, hot-rodding (*slang*). [➡CRIMES; 817]

joystick 1 *type of* **hardware**. [➡COMPUTERS AND COMPUTING; 1126] 2 *part of* **aircraft**. [➡AIRCRAFT; 1147]

JP *n* **Justice of the Peace**, magistrate, justice, official, judge, arbitrator, administrator. [➡PEOPLE IN LAW COURTS; 820]

jubilant *adj* **triumphant**, proud, thrilled, ecstatic, over the moon, delighted, euphoric, glad, overjoyed, joyful, joyous. [➡PLEASURE, EXCITEMENT, AND ELATION; 535] *Opposite:* disappointed.

jubilation *n* **elation**, triumph, joyousness, euphoria, delight, joy. [➡PLEASURE, EXCITEMENT, AND ELATION; 535] *Opposite:* disappointment.

jubilee *n* **anniversary**, celebration, commemoration, festival, festivity, silver jubilee, diamond jubilee, golden jubilee. [➡CEREMONIES AND ANNIVERSARIES; 38]

judder 1 *v* **shake**, vibrate, shudder, quiver, tremble, quaver, roll, rock, jerk. [➡MOVE SOMETHING ON THE SPOT; 337] 2 *n* **shudder**, vibration, quiver, tremor, jerk, quaver. [➡MOVE SOMETHING ON THE SPOT; 337]

judge 1 *n* **magistrate**, justice, justice of the peace, judge advocate. [➡PEOPLE IN LAW COURTS; 820] 2 *n* **arbitrator**, adjudicator, moderator, umpire, referee. [➡SURVEYORS, EXAMINERS, AND JUDGES; 853] 3 *n* **evaluator**, critic, reviewer, arbiter, expert, authority, connoisseur, assessor, appraiser. [➡SURVEYORS, EXAMINERS, AND JUDGES; 853] 4 *v* **arbitrate**, adjudicate, mediate, referee, umpire, rule on, try, adjudge. [➡ASSESS QUALITY; 756] 5 *v* **assess**, evaluate, weigh, weigh up, look at, appraise, rate, rank, estimate. [➡EXAMINE AND ASSESS; 754] 6 *v* **consider**, reckon, think, believe, deem (*formal*), maintain, conclude. [➡HAVE AN OPINION OF SOMETHING; 757] 7 *v* **estimate**, guess, consider, say, assess, think, decide, ascertain (*formal*), find, resolve. [➡ASSESS QUANTITY; 758] 8 *v* **condemn**, criticize, sneer at, belittle, pass judgment on. [➡ACCUSE, BLAME, AND CRITICIZE; 642]

judgment 1 *n* **verdict**, ruling, decision, finding, sentence, conclusion, result, decree, adjudication, arbitration. [➡RESULTS AND OUTCOMES; 83] 2 *n* **discernment**, good sense, shrewdness, wisdom, common sense, discrimination, prudence, intelligence, judiciousness, perceptiveness, acumen. [➡DESCRIBING SOMEBODY'S INTELLECT; 524] 3 *n* **opinion**, view, considered opinion, feeling, thoughts, way of thinking, reasoning, belief, assessment, appraisal, conviction. [➡POINT OF VIEW; 768]

judgmental *adj* **critical**, hypercritical, condemnatory, negative, disapproving, disparaging, pejorative (*formal*). [➡SELFISH AND UNKIND; 506] *Opposite:* complimentary.

Judgment Day *n* [➡RELIGIOUS CONCEPTS; 777]

judicial *adj* **legal**, court, justice, jurisdictional, jurisdictive, official. [➡LEGAL; 815]

judicial proceedings *n* [➡THE POLICE, ARREST, AND PRE-TRIAL PROCEEDINGS; 818]

judiciary *n* **judges**, bench, courts, magistrates. [➡THE LAW AND LEGAL AUTHORITY; 814]

judicious *adj* **sensible**, wise, careful, shrewd, astute, prudent, cautious, thoughtful, sagacious (*formal*), just, discriminating. [➡POSITIVE INTELLECTUAL CHARACTERISTICS; 525] *Opposite:* foolish.

judiciousness *n* **wisdom**, prudence, shrewdness, sense, care, caution, judgment, discrimination, sagacity. [➡POSITIVE INTELLECTUAL CHARACTERISTICS; 525] *Opposite:* foolishness.

judo *type of* **combat sport**. [➡HOBBIES, GAMES, AND SPORTS; 875]

jug *n* **container**, flagon, carafe, milk jug, cream jug, pitcher, vessel, ewer, crock. [➡TABLEWARE, CUTLERY, AND KITCHENWARE; 861]

juggernaut *type of* **commercial or industrial vehicle**. [➡VEHICLES; 1144]

juggle 1 *v* **fit in**, manage, cope with, run, deal with, organize. [➡CARRY OUT AN ACTION; 270] 2 *v* **manipulate**, falsify, alter, misrepresent, tamper with, disguise, rearrange. [➡FALSIFY AND CHEAT; 177]

juggler *type of* **entertainer**. [➡WORKERS IN ENTERTAINMENT AND MEDIA; 873]

jugular vein *type of* **blood vessel**. [➡THE BLOOD AND CIRCULATION; 718]

juice 1 *n* **extract**, sap, liquid, fluid, liquor, nectar, essence. [➡LIQUIDS; 1268] 2 *part of* **fruit**. [➡FRUIT AND VEGETABLES; 1175]

juice extractor *type of* **utensil**. [➡TABLEWARE, CUTLERY, AND KITCHENWARE; 861]

juicer *type of* **utensil**. [➡TABLEWARE, CUTLERY, AND KITCHENWARE; 861]

juiciness *n* **succulence**, ripeness, lusciousness, moistness. [➡TASTE; 704] *Opposite:* dryness.

juicy 1 *adj* **succulent**, luscious, thirst-quenching, moist, ripe. [➡WET; 1239] *Opposite:* dry. 2 *adj* (*informal*) **titillating**, scandalous, spicy (*informal*), salacious, exciting, sensational, interesting, vivid, racy, lurid. [➡INTERESTING AND MEANINGFUL; 191] *Opposite:* dull.

juju *n* [➡LUCKY CHARMS; 786]

jukebox *type of* **audio equipment**. [➡AUDIO EQUIPMENT; 1138]

julienne *type of* **soup**. [➡SOUP; 1185]

jumble 1 *v* **mix up**, muddle, clutter, disarrange, mess up (*informal*), shuffle, strew. [➡CREATE DISORDER AND CAUSE CHAOS; 359] *Opposite:* tidy. 2 *n* **muddle**, heap, clutter, hotchpotch, mishmash, mixture, mess, confusion, disarray, tangle. [➡DISORDER AND CHAOS; 246] 3 *n* **junk** (*informal*), unwanted items, second-hand goods, castoffs, odds and ends. [➡RUBBISH AND USELESS OBJECTS; 1248]

jumbled *adj* **untidy**, topsy-turvy, muddled, chaotic, mixed-up (*informal*), disorderly, random, messy, tangled, cluttered, confused, higgledy-piggledy, disarrayed. [➡DISORDER AND CHAOS; 246] *Opposite:* orderly.

jumble sale *n* [➡SALES AND SHOWS; 444]

jumbo *adj* **oversize**, oversized, outsize, outsized, huge, gigantic, giant, whopping (*informal*), super (*informal*), massive, immense, mammoth, colossal, stupendous. [➡LARGE; 1192] *Opposite:* tiny.

jump 1 *v* **bound**, leap, hop, skip, soar, shoot, fly, hurdle, vault, spring, bounce. [➡BOUNCE, UNDULATE, AND VIBRATE; 309] **2** *v* **be startled**, be surprised, start, get a fright, be frightened, jerk, flinch, recoil. [➡PHYSICAL REACTIONS; 317] **3** *v* (*informal*) **obey**, do as you are told, conform, toe the line, play the game, kowtow. [➡OBEY AND ABIDE BY; 302] **4** *n* **leap**, bound, hop, skip, spring, caper, vault. [➡BOUNCE, UNDULATE, AND VIBRATE; 309] **5** *n* **obstacle**, hurdle, fence, wall, hedge, obstruction, barrier, barricade. [➡BARRIERS; 1112] **6** *n* **start**, jolt, jerk, lurch, jar, flinch. [➡PHYSICAL REACTIONS; 317]

jump back *v* **rebound**, recoil, bounce back, ricochet. [➡GO BACKWARDS; 310]

jumper **1** *n* **athlete**, high jumper, long jumper, hurdler, steeplechaser, showjumper. [➡PEOPLE IN SPORTS AND LEISURE; 876] **2** *type of* **sweater or cardigan.** [➡GARMENTS AND OUTFITS; 865] **3** (*US*) *type of* **dress.** [➡GARMENTS AND OUTFITS; 865]

jumpily **1** *adv* **anxiously**, nervously, edgily, restlessly, on edge, apprehensively, tensely. [➡POSITIVE IMPATIENCE, ENTHUSIASM, AND ALERTNESS; 538] *Opposite:* calmly. **2** *adv* **jerkily**, erratically, fitfully, suddenly, abruptly, unsteadily, joltingly. [➡DESCRIBING BODY MOVEMENTS; 289] *Opposite:* smoothly.

jump in *v* **make a start**, take the plunge, get going, leap in, take the bull by the horns, take action, be decisive. [➡START AN ACTION; 261]

jumpiness **1** *n* **jitteriness**, anxiety, nervousness, nerves (*informal*), agitation, edginess, restlessness, apprehensiveness, uneasiness. [➡CONFUSION, ANXIETY, AND WORRY; 541] *Opposite:* calm. **2** *n* **jerkiness**, erraticism, unsteadiness, suddenness, abruptness, shakiness, fitfulness. [➡DESCRIBING BODY MOVEMENTS; 289] *Opposite:* smoothness.

jump ship *v* [➡RUN AWAY AND AVOID; 10]

jump-start **1** *v* **kick-start**, start up, bump-start, start, push-start, get going, set in motion, rev up (*informal*). [➡CAUSE TO START; 266] **2** *v* **stimulate**, trigger, set off, start up, kick-start, spark, spark off, rouse, spur, spur on, bring about. [➡CAUSE TO HAPPEN; 31] **3** *n* **kick-start**, bump-start, push-start, startup, start. [➡BEGINNING; 53] **4** *n* **stimulus**, momentum, spur, start, impetus, thrust, push, drive. [➡SOURCE OF HAPPINESS, PLEASURE, OR IMPROVEMENT; 210]

jump suit *type of* **suit.** [➡GARMENTS AND OUTFITS; 865]

jumpy **1** *adj* **jittery**, anxious, nervous, nervy (*informal*), worried, tense, scared, frightened, agitated, on edge, edgy, restless, fidgety, skittish. [➡CONFUSION, ANXIETY, AND WORRY; 541] *Opposite:* calm. **2** *adj* **jerky**, erratic, unsteady, sudden, abrupt, shaky, fitful, jolting, lurching. [➡DESCRIBING BODY MOVEMENTS; 289] *Opposite:* smooth.

junction *n* **connection**, intersection, seam, link, joint, join, confluence, interchange, convergence, linkup. [➡CONNECTION; 144]

juncture **1** *n* **point in time**, stage, moment, occasion, interval, pass. [➡PAUSES AND PHASES; 56] **2** *n* (*formal*) **join**, connection, joint, link, seam, junction, confluence, intersection. [➡FASTENERS, LINKS, AND NETWORKS; 1246]

jungle **1** *n* **tropical forest**, rain forest, forest, wilderness, bush, wilds. [➡WOODS, FORESTS, AND JUNGLES; 1047] **2** *n* **tangle**, muddle, maze, jumble, mess, confusion, mass. [➡DISORDER AND CHAOS; 246]

junior **1** *adj* **low-ranking**, subordinate, inferior, lower, low-grade, lesser, secondary, minor. [➡INFERIORITY; 154] *Opposite:* senior. **2** *n* **subordinate**, underling, beginner, trainee, novice, apprentice. [➡UNSKILLED PERSON; 531]

junior high (*US*) *type of* **school.** [➡EDUCATIONAL INSTITUTIONS; 813]

junior school *type of* **school.** [➡EDUCATIONAL INSTITUTIONS; 813]

juniper **1** *type of* **berry.** [➡FRUIT AND VEGETABLES; 1175] **2** *type of* **evergreen tree.** [➡EVERGREEN AND CONIFEROUS TREES; 1029]

junk **1** *n* (*informal*) **rubbish**, scrap, debris, litter, refuse, waste, garbage (*US*), trash (*US*). [➡RUBBISH AND USELESS OBJECTS; 1248] **2** *n* (*informal*) **second-hand goods**, jumble, unwanted items, castoffs, odds and ends. [➡RUBBISH AND USELESS OBJECTS; 1248] **3** *v* (*informal*) **discard**, throw away, throw out, get rid of, scrap, chuck (*informal*), ditch (*informal*), jettison, dump. [➡GET RID OF SOMETHING; 452] *Opposite:* keep. **4** *type of* **sailing vessel.** [➡SHIPS AND BOATS; 1149]

junket **1** *n* **trip**, excursion, visit, outing, spree, freebie (*informal*). [➡TRAVEL: JOURNEYS AND TRIPS; 319] **2** *type of* **dessert.** [➡CAKES, BISCUITS, AND DESSERTS; 1180]

junk food *n* **snack food**, convenience food, fast food, junk (*informal*), TV dinner. [➡FOOD; 1166]

junk mail *n* **fliers**, mailshot, leaflets, brochures, direct mail. [➡ADVERTISING AND PUBLICITY; 605]

junky *adj* [➡IN BAD REPAIR; 1233]

junta **1** *n* **military government**, military rule, regime, martial law, government, leadership, dictatorship. [➡STYLES AND SYSTEMS OF GOVERNMENT; 806] **2** *n* **cabal**, faction, clique, gang, band. [➡GROUPS OF PEOPLE; 935] **3** *n* **council**, committee, legislative body, assembly, forum, cabinet. [➡LEGISLATIVE BODIES AND LEGISLATION; 809]

Jupiter *type of* **planet.** [➡CELESTIAL BODIES; 1060]

jurisdiction **1** *n* **authority**, dominion, influence, power, control, prerogative, rule, say. [➡THE LAW AND LEGAL AUTHORITY; 814] **2** *n* **area**, state, extent of power, territory, province, dominion, bailiwick, precinct, district, circuit. [➡SUBJECT AREA; 769]

juror *n* **jury member**, assessor, estimator, judge, adjudicator, panel member. [➡PEOPLE IN LAW COURTS; 820]

jury *n* **adjudicators**, judges, bench, panel, board. [➡TRIAL, PUNISHMENT, AND LEGAL OUTCOMES; 819]

just **1** *adv* **a minute ago**, a moment ago, a second ago, only this minute, in the past few minutes, a short time ago, recently, lately, not long ago. [➡AFTER, LAST, AND FOLLOWING; 166] **2** *adv* **at this moment**, now, immediately, presently, in a minute, very soon, right now, straightaway. [➡PRESENT; 85] *Opposite:* later. **3** *adv* **only**, merely, simply, solely, purely. [➡TO A CERTAIN EXTENT; 134] **4** *adv* **barely**, hardly, scarcely, slightly. [➡TO A CERTAIN EXTENT; 134] **5** *adv* **simply**, really, truly, definitely, emphatically, clearly, entirely, absolutely, completely, perfectly. [➡ABSOLUTE AND ABSOLUTELY; 131] **6** *adv* **exactly**, precisely, absolutely, emphatically, completely, totally. [➡EXACT; 204] **7** *adj* **fair**, impartial, objective, unbiased, unprejudiced, disinterested, evenhanded. [➡HONEST AND RELIABLE; 503] *Opposite:* unjust. **8** *adj* **correct**, moral, ethical, good, appropriate, proper, right, fitting. [➡MORALLY GOOD; 775] *Opposite:* wrong. **9** *adj* **reasonable**, valid, sensible, sound, balanced, well-grounded, justified, merited. [➡THE NATURE OF IDEAS; 772]

just about *adv* **almost**, very nearly, pretty nearly (*informal*), pretty well (*informal*), pretty much (*informal*), nearly, about, around, not quite, practically, approximately. [➡APPROXIMATELY; 133]

just deserts *n* [➡RESULTS AND OUTCOMES; 83]

just-folks (*US informal*) *adj* **simple**, unaffected, unsophisticated, folksy, friendly, informal, relaxed, unpretentious. [➡NATURALNESS; 498] *Opposite:* pretentious.

justice **1** *n* **fairness**, reasonableness, impartiality, even-handedness, righteousness, fair dealing, honesty, integrity, uprightness, rightness, justness. [➡MORALLY GOOD; 775] *Opposite:* unfairness. **2** *n* **validity**, legitimacy, rightfulness, acceptability, reasonableness, legitimateness, lawfulness. [➡TRUE AND REAL; 172] **3** *n* **judge**, magistrate, justice of the peace, judge advocate. [➡PEOPLE IN LAW COURTS; 820]

Justice of the Peace *n* [➡PEOPLE IN LAW COURTS; 820]

justifiable *adj* **defensible**, admissible, justified, reasonable, correct, right, acceptable, permissible, understandable, valid, fit, sound, proper, fair, arguable, maintainable. [➡MORALLY GOOD; 775] *Opposite:* indefensible.

justification *n* **defence**, reason, reasoning, explanation, validation, rationalization, excuse, account, confirmation, support. [➡EXPLAIN AND CLARIFY; 611]

justified *adj* **warranted**, defensible, vindicated, correct, right, acceptable, reasonable, necessary, befitting, supportable (*literary*), validated, confirmed. [➡POPULAR AND WANTED; 221] *Opposite:* unwarranted.

justify **1** *v* **defend**, validate, explain, rationalize, excuse, vindicate, substantiate, warrant, support. [➡EXPLAIN AND CLARIFY; 611] **2** *v* **align**, adjust, straighten up, line up. [➡ARRANGE AND CREATE ORDER; 358]

justly **1** *adv* **fairly**, impartially, rightly, reasonably, honestly, honourably, truthfully, righteously, morally, equitably (*formal*), evenhandedly. [➡MORALLY GOOD; 775] *Opposite:* unfairly. **2** *adv* **correctly**, morally, deservedly, reasonably, justifiably, with reason, with good reason, rightly, excusably, understandably, legitimately, befittingly. [➡MORALLY GOOD; 775] *Opposite:* unjustly.

just now **1** *adv* **a minute ago**, a moment ago, a second ago, only this minute, in the past few minutes, a short time ago, not long ago, recently, lately. [➡AFTER, LAST, AND FOLLOWING; 166] **2** *adv* **at this moment**, now, immediately, right now, straightaway, presently, in a minute, very soon. [➡PRESENT; 85] *Opposite:* later.

just reward *n* [➡RESULTS AND OUTCOMES; 83]

just right *adj* [➡GOOD, WELL, BETTER; 184]

just the same *adv* **nevertheless**, nonetheless, all the same, be that as it may, in any case. [➡ALTHOUGH, NEVERTHELESS, AND DESPITE; 170]

jut *v* **stick out**, protrude, overhang, poke out, project, extend, go beyond. [➡EXIST IN A PLACE; 19]

jute *type of* **fibre**. [➡PLANT MATERIALS; 1132]

juvenile **1** *adj* **youthful**, young, immature, adolescent, fresh-faced, baby-faced. [➡BAD MANNERS AND SOCIAL SKILLS; 522] *Opposite:* mature. **2** *adj* **childish**, infantile, babyish, puerile, immature, adolescent. [➡NEGATIVE INTELLECTUAL CHARACTERISTICS; 526] *Opposite:* grown-up. **3** *n* **youngster**, adolescent, young person, teenager, teen (*informal*), youth, child, minor. [➡CHILD OR YOUTH; 945] *Opposite:* adult.

juxtapose *v* **put side by side**, put together, put next to, put beside, put adjacent to, place alongside, contrast, compare, set against. [➡POSITION SOMETHING: BETWEEN, BESIDE, OR INSIDE SOMETHING; 327]

juxtaposition *n* **collocation**, association, apposition, comparison, contrast, connection. [➡CONNECTION; 144]

K

kaftan *type of* **dress.** [➡GARMENTS AND OUTFITS; 865]

kahikatea *type of* **evergreen tree.** [➡EVERGREEN AND CONIFEROUS TREES; 1029]

kahuna (*US informal*) *n* [➡IMPORTANT OR FAMOUS PEOPLE; 893]

kale *type of* **vegetable.** [➡FRUIT AND VEGETABLES; 1175]

kaleidoscope 1 *n* **complex pattern**, phantasmagoria, display, mixture, medley, changing scene. [➡COLLECTIONS AND MIXTURES OF THINGS; 1243] 2 *n* **series**, web, set, chain reaction, domino effect, chain of events. [➡CHAIN OF EVENTS; 163] 3 *type of* **toy.** [➡TOYS; 880]

kaleidoscopic *adj* **colourful**, variegated, multicoloured, many-coloured, motley, psychedelic, phantasmagoric, parti-coloured. [➡DESCRIBING COLOURS; 1225] *Opposite:* monochromatic.

kangaroo 1 *v* (*informal*) **jerk**, jump, leap, bump, jolt, bounce. [➡BOUNCE, UNDULATE, AND VIBRATE; 309] *Opposite:* glide. 2 *type of* **marsupial.** [➡MARSUPIAL; 992]

kaolin *n* **clay**, kaolinite, argil, potter's clay, potter's earth. [➡MINERALS; 1276]

kaon *type of* **elementary particle.** [➡ELEMENTARY PARTICLES; 1278]

kapok *type of* **fibre.** [➡PLANT MATERIALS; 1132]

kaput (*informal*) *adj* **broken**, ruined, wrecked, finished, ended, useless, defunct. [➡IN BAD REPAIR; 1233] *Opposite:* working.

karaoke *n* **singing**, singsong, karaoke night, music, entertainment, knees-up (*informal*), sing-along (*US*). [➡ENTERTAINMENT; 872]

karate *type of* **combat sport.** [➡HOBBIES, GAMES, AND SPORTS; 875]

karma 1 *n* **destiny**, fate, kismet, fortune, providence, predestination. [➡RELIGIOUS CONCEPTS; 777] 2 *n* (*informal*) **atmosphere**, aura, feeling, vibes (*slang*), vibrations (*informal*), ambience. [➡APPEARANCE AND ATMOSPHERE; 1236]

kauri *type of* **evergreen tree.** [➡EVERGREEN AND CONIFEROUS TREES; 1029]

kayak *type of* **small vessel.** [➡SHIPS AND BOATS; 1149]

kebab *n* **skewer**, brochette, satay, shish kebab, souvlakia, grill stick. [➡TYPES AND CUTS OF MEAT; 1176]

kedgeree *type of* **cooked dish.** [➡PREPARED DISHES; 1169]

keel 1 *v* **capsize**, keel over (*informal*), turn upside down, upset, overturn, turn over, tip over, roll over, tip, upturn. [➡MOVE SOMETHING: INTO A NEW POSITION OR OVERTURN; 331] *Opposite:* stabilize. 2 *part of* **ship or boat.** [➡PARTS OF A SHIP OR BOAT; 1150]

keel over (*informal*) 1 *v* **collapse**, fall over, faint, pass out, conk out (*informal*), lose consciousness, swoon. [➡TAKE UP A NEW POSITION; 313] *Opposite:* come to. 2 *v* **capsize**, keel, turn upside down, upset, overturn, turn over, tip over, roll over, tip, upturn. [➡MOVE SOMETHING: INTO A NEW POSITION OR OVERTURN; 331] *Opposite:* right.

keen 1 *adj* **eager**, enthusiastic, willing, desirous (*formal*), fanatical, dedicated, devoted, ardent, zealous, earnest. [➡ENERGY AND ENTHUSIASM; 497] *Opposite:* indifferent. 2 *adj* **acute**, quick, clever, perceptive, alert, intelligent, astute, sharp. [➡POSITIVE INTELLECTUAL CHARACTERISTICS; 525] *Opposite:* dull. 3 *adj* **sensitive**, sharp, precise, accurate, acute, perceptive, responsive, finely honed, finely tuned, well-developed. [➡STRENGTH; 202] *Opposite:* insensitive. 4 *adj* **intense**, strong, acute, deep, powerful, profound, extreme, ardent, lively. [➡STRENGTH; 202] *Opposite:* mild. 5 *adj* (*literary*) **sharp**, sharpened, whetted, bright, steely, well-honed, razor sharp, sharp-edged. [➡PHYSICAL TEXTURE; 1221] *Opposite:* blunt. 6 *adj* **icy**, bitter, cold, chilly, wintry, freezing, glacial, biting, penetrating. [➡COLD WEATHER; 1051] *Opposite:* mild. 7 *adj* **competitive**, low, cheap, attractive, affordable, effective. [➡CHEAP AND INEXPENSIVE; 222] *Opposite:* prohibitive. 8 *v* **cry out**, wail, howl, weep, sob, lament, grieve. [➡SOUND EMISSION BY PEOPLE; 364]

keenly 1 *adv* **eagerly**, enthusiastically, willingly, fanatically, devotedly, ardently, zealously, earnestly. [➡ENERGY AND ENTHUSIASM; 497] *Opposite:* indifferently. 2 *adv* **intensely**, strongly, acutely, deeply, powerfully, profoundly, extremely, clearly, painfully. [➡STRENGTH; 202] *Opposite:* faintly.

keenness 1 *n* **enthusiasm**, eagerness, zeal, passion, willingness, zest, fervour, ardour, gusto, interest. [➡ENERGY AND ENTHUSIASM; 497] *Opposite:* reluctance. 2 *n* **fondness**, attraction, enthusiasm, devotion, partiality, liking, love, affection, attachment, soft spot. [➡LIKE, LOVE, VALUE, AND ENJOY; 579] *Opposite:* aversion. 3 *n* **acuteness**, perception, quickness, cleverness, perceptiveness, sensitivity, alertness, acuity, intelligence, astuteness. [➡POSITIVE INTELLECTUAL CHARACTERISTICS; 525] *Opposite:* dullness. 4 *n* **sensitivity**, sharpness, precision, accuracy, acuity, responsiveness, perceptiveness. [➡POSITIVE INTELLECTUAL CHARACTERISTICS; 525] *Opposite:* insensitivity. 5 *n* **intensity**, intenseness, strength, acuteness, depth, powerfulness, profundity. [➡STRENGTH; 202] *Opposite:* mildness. 6 *n* (*literary*) **sharpness**, razor-sharpness, brightness, steeliness. [➡PHYSICAL TEXTURE; 1221] *Opposite:* bluntness. 7 *n* **iciness**, bitterness, coldness, chill, wintriness, bitter cold. [➡COLD WEATHER; 1051] *Opposite:* mildness. 8 *n* **competitiveness**, lowness, cheapness, attractiveness, affordability. [➡ECONOMICAL AND RESOURCEFUL; 208] *Opposite:* ineffectiveness.

keen on *adj* **fond of**, partial to, smitten with (*humorous or literary*), taken with, dotty about (*informal*), wild about, gone on (*informal*), potty about (*informal*), stuck on (*informal*). [➡APPRECIATION AND GRATITUDE; 536]

keen-sighted *adj* [➡SEE; 700]

keep 1 *v* **hang onto**, hold onto, save, retain, have, possess, cling to, preserve. [➡STORE AND KEEP; 454] *Opposite:* throw away. **2** *v* **hide**, conceal, repress, withhold, hold back, hold in, keep to yourself, stifle. [➡WITHHOLD INFORMATION; 688] *Opposite:* let out. **3** *v* **maintain**, hold, sustain, preserve, conserve, fix. [➡STORE AND KEEP; 454] *Opposite:* abandon. **4** *v* **store**, hold, stash, stack, shelve, file, deposit, stock. [➡STORE AND KEEP; 454] *Opposite:* get rid of. **5** *v* **continue**, go on, carry on, keep on, persist in, persevere with. [➡CONTINUE AN ACTION; 263] *Opposite:* stop. **6** *v* **honour**, fulfil, carry out, comply with, obey, adhere to, observe, respect. [➡OBEY AND ABIDE BY; 302] *Opposite:* break. **7** *v* **detain**, delay, hold up, hold back, keep back, retard. [➡AVOID, PREVENT, LIMIT, AND CONTROL; 278] *Opposite:* release. **8** *v* **take care of**, care for, tend, look after, watch over, mind, sit, watch, guard, house. [➡TAKE CARE OF AND SPOIL; 301] *Opposite:* turn away. **9** *v* **stay**, remain, be, keep yourself. [➡CONTINUE TO EXIST; 17] *Opposite:* become. **10** *v* **own**, look after, care for, farm, rear, breed. [➡POSSESS; 445] *Opposite:* get rid of.

keep abreast of *v* **stay current**, keep up on, be in the know, keep up to date, be well-informed, follow. [➡STUDYING; 844]

keep an eye on **1** *v* **watch closely**, keep a close watch on, keep tabs on (*informal*), observe, spy on, watch, monitor, keep track of, check. [➡LOOKING AND LOOKS; 701] **2** *v* **look after**, watch over, keep in check, mind, take care of, watch. [➡LOOKING AND LOOKS; 701]

keep a secret *v* **keep mum** (*informal*), not tell a soul, be discreet, keep quiet, be the soul of discretion, button your lip (*slang*). [➡WITHHOLD INFORMATION; 688] *Opposite:* spill the beans (*informal*).

keep a straight face *v* **have a poker face**, keep a stiff upper lip (*informal*), look blank, dissemble, show no emotion. [➡FACIAL EXPRESSION; 652]

keep at *v* **persevere**, beaver (*informal*), persist, soldier on, plough on, plough through, keep your nose to the grindstone, plug away (*informal*), stick to. [➡CONTINUE AN ACTION; 263] *Opposite:* give up.

keep at bay *v* **hold off**, keep away, ward off, stave off, fend off, repel, discourage. [➡AVOID OR ESCAPE CONTACT; 419] *Opposite:* encourage.

keep at it *v* [➡CONTINUE AN ACTION; 263]

keep away *v* **hold off**, ward off, keep at bay, stave off, fend off, repel, discourage. [➡AVOID OR ESCAPE CONTACT; 419] *Opposite:* encourage.

keep back **1** *v* **withhold**, keep secret, suppress, omit, hide, conceal, hush up (*informal*), retain, keep to yourself, sit on. [➡WITHHOLD INFORMATION; 688] *Opposite:* reveal. **2** *v* **reserve**, conserve, hold on to, save, withhold, set aside, put by. [➡STORE AND KEEP; 454] *Opposite:* use up. **3** *v* **restrain**, curb, control, restrict, limit, check. [➡AVOID, PREVENT, LIMIT, AND CONTROL; 278]

keep count *v* **record**, note, keep a record of, note down, keep a note of, keep track of, remember. [➡REMEMBER; 747] *Opposite:* lose track of.

keep down **1** *v* **oppress**, suppress, repress, subjugate, subdue, keep under. [➡CAPTIVITY AND LOSS OF FREEDOM; 249] *Opposite:* liberate. **2** *v* **limit**, curb, restrain, control, check, keep in check, keep a tight rein on. [➡AVOID, PREVENT, LIMIT, AND CONTROL; 278]

keeper *n* **custodian**, warder, guard, guardian, caretaker, attendant, groundsman, curator, ranger, groundskeeper (*US*), warden (*US*). [➡PEOPLE WHO GUARD AND PROTECT; 846]

keep fit **1** *n* **physical exercise**, exercise, working out, aerobics, gymnastics, physical education. [➡HOBBIES, GAMES, AND SPORTS; 875] **2** *v* **keep in shape**, exercise, work out, keep in trim, keep healthy (*informal*), train, keep trim (*US*). [➡HOBBIES, GAMES, AND SPORTS; 875]

keep from **1** *v* **withhold**, omit, hide, conceal, keep back, hush up (*informal*), retain, keep to yourself, save. [➡WITHHOLD INFORMATION; 688] *Opposite:* reveal. **2** *v* **prevent**, restrain, stop, deter, prohibit, put off, discourage. [➡MAKE IMPOSSIBLE; 277] *Opposite:* allow. **3** *v* **protect**, shield, shelter, save, cushion, safeguard, guard. [➡PREVENT CONTACT OR ATTACK; 420] *Opposite:* expose.

keep going *v* **persevere**, carry on, persist, hold up, last, sustain, survive, chug away (*informal*), plug away (*informal*), spin out. [➡CONTINUE AN ACTION; 263] *Opposite:* stop.

keep in *v* **hold in**, repress, withhold, hold back, retain, suppress, rein in, stifle. [➡STORE AND KEEP; 454] *Opposite:* let out.

keep in check *v* **control**, restrict, restrain, curb, limit, keep an eye on, monitor. [➡AVOID, PREVENT, LIMIT, AND CONTROL; 278]

keeping *n* **charge**, custody, possession, care, trust, protection, guardianship. [➡STORE AND KEEP; 454]

keep in mind *v* **bear in mind**, remember, recall, retain. [➡REMEMBER; 747] *Opposite:* forget.

keep in the dark *v* **keep in ignorance**, withhold information from, keep something back from, hold something back from, conceal something from. [➡WITHHOLD INFORMATION; 688] *Opposite:* inform.

keep mum (*informal*) *v* **keep quiet**, not tell a soul, be discreet, keep secret, keep under wraps, keep under your hat, button your lip (*slang*), be the soul of discretion. [➡WITHHOLD INFORMATION; 688] *Opposite:* spill the beans (*informal*).

keep off **1** *v* **hold off**, hold back, separate, shut out, ward off, prevent. [➡EJECT AND EXCLUDE; 341] *Opposite:* encourage. **2** *v* **abstain**, do without, go without, avoid, not touch, lay off (*informal*). [➡NOT DO AND REFUSE TO DO; 275] *Opposite:* indulge.

keep on *v* **continue**, persist, persevere, carry on, go on, soldier on. [➡CONTINUE AN ACTION; 263] *Opposite:* give up.

keep on at (*informal*) *v* **nag**, badger, hassle (*informal*), pester, harp on, harass, prompt, remind. [➡COMPLAIN AND NAG; 687] *Opposite:* give up on.

keep out *v* **exclude**, shut out, bar, ban, deny entry, proscribe, ostracize. [➡MAKE IMPOSSIBLE; 277] *Opposite:* admit.

keep quiet *v* [➡WITHHOLD INFORMATION; 688]

keepsake *n* **memento**, reminder, souvenir, gift, token, relic, remembrance. [➡ORNAMENTS AND DECORATIONS; 1247]

keep secret *v* **withhold**, suppress, sit on, keep from, keep under wraps, keep to yourself, keep under your hat, keep back, keep quiet. [➡WITHHOLD INFORMATION; 688] *Opposite:* let slip.

keep the ball rolling *v* **continue**, keep things moving, keep things going, keep up the momentum, maintain momentum, carry on, go on. [➡CAUSE TO CONTINUE; 268] *Opposite:* stop.

keep the lid on *v* **keep under control**, contain, control, suppress, restrain, check, curb, keep in check. [➡AVOID, PREVENT, LIMIT, AND CONTROL; 278]

keep to *v* **obey**, comply with, abide by, stick to, adhere to, go along with. [➡OBEY AND ABIDE BY; 302]

keep to yourself *v* [➡WITHHOLD INFORMATION; 688]

keep track of *v* **follow**, keep an eye on, keep up with, contain, keep up to date with, monitor. [➡EXAMINE AND ASSESS; 754] *Opposite:* lose track of.

keep under control *v* **keep in check**, restrain, contain, keep the lid on, suppress, curb, check. [➡AVOID, PREVENT, LIMIT, AND CONTROL; 278]

keep under wraps *v* **keep secret**, keep to yourself, keep back, keep quiet, hide, conceal, cover up, suppress, draw a veil over. [➡WITHHOLD INFORMATION; 688] *Opposite:* reveal.

keep under your hat *v* [➡WITHHOLD INFORMATION; 688]

keep up 1 *v* **continue**, sustain, maintain, carry on, persevere, preserve. [➡CONTINUE AN ACTION; 263] *Opposite:* stop. 2 *v* **stay beside**, keep abreast of, keep pace with, stay even with, match, stay shoulder to shoulder. [➡ACCOMPANY AND FOLLOW; 338] *Opposite:* fall behind.

keep up with *v* **stay in touch with**, keep in touch, keep in contact, hear from, correspond, write, communicate. [➡INITIATE AND ESTABLISH COMMUNICATION; 681]

keep your chin up *v* **make the best of things**, make the best of a bad job, take the rough with the smooth, take the bad with the good, look on the bright side, not let things get the better of you. [➡TOLERATE AND ENDURE; 767] *Opposite:* go under.

keep your cool *v* **stay calm**, keep your head, calm down, chill out (*slang*), cool it (*informal*), simmer down, cool off. [➡CHANGE OF MOOD AND COMPOSURE; 581]

keep your word *v* **be as good as your word**, stand by your promise, deliver on a promise, be true to your word, keep your side of the bargain. [➡PROMISE AND ASSURE; 685]

keg *n* **barrel**, cask, tub, firkin, drum, vat, puncheon. [➡CONTAINERS, RECEPTACLES, AND PACKAGING; 1244]

kelp *type of* **alga**. [➡MICROORGANISMS, FUNGI, AND ALGAE; 1023]

ken *n* **knowledge**, acquaintance, cognizance (*formal*), understanding, awareness, comprehension, wit. [➡KNOWLEDGE AND WISDOM; 559]

kendo *type of* **combat sport**. [➡HOBBIES, GAMES, AND SPORTS; 875]

kennel 1 *n* **house**, hut, shelter, lair, den. [➡ANIMAL OR BIRD ACCOMMODATION; 1078] 2 *type of* **herd**. [➡GROUP OF ANIMALS; 993] 3 *v* **lodge**, keep, shelter, house. [➡HOLD AND CONTAIN; 456]

Kentucky bluegrass *type of* **grass**. [➡GRASS; 1031]

kerfuffle (*informal*) *n* **commotion**, disturbance, disorder, agitation, hubbub, tumult, to-do (*informal*), melee, rumpus, ruckus, foofaraw, donnybrook. [➡CHAOS AND UPROAR; 51]

kernel 1 *n* **pip**, pit, stone. [➡FRUIT AND VEGETABLES; 1175] 2 *n* **core**, nub, root, heart, essence, crux, gist, marrow, pith. [➡CENTRAL PARTS OF PHYSICAL OBJECTS; 1250]

kerosene (*US*) *n* **fuel**, paraffin, paraffin oil, oil, fuel oil, lamp oil (*regional*). [➡ENERGY SOURCES; 1161]

kerosine *see* **kerosene**.

kestrel *type of* **bird of prey**. [➡BIRD OF PREY; 998]

ketch *type of* **sailing vessel**. [➡SHIPS AND BOATS; 1149]

ketchup *type of* **seasonings, sauces, and dips**. [➡SEASONINGS AND SAUCES; 1173]

kettle *n* **pot**, pan, cauldron, steamer, fish kettle, container, teakettle, teapot. [➡TABLEWARE, CUTLERY, AND KITCHENWARE; 861]

kettledrum *type of* **percussion instrument**. [➡MUSICAL INSTRUMENTS; 910]

kettle of fish *n* **mess**, predicament, difficulty, problem, quagmire, crisis, situation. [➡DIFFICULT SITUATIONS; 72]

key 1 *n* **solution**, answer, explanation, means, secret, meaning, interpretation, source, resolution, basis, recipe. [➡SOLUTION; 216] 2 *n* **pitch**, register, tone, scale, note. [➡NOTES AND CHORDS; 909] 3 *n* **skeleton key**, master key, passe-partout, passkey, latchkey, opener. [➡FASTENERS, LINKS, AND NETWORKS; 1246] 4 *n* **button**, knob, control. [➡PARTS OF MACHINES AND TOOLS; 1117] 5 *adj* **important**, main, crucial, significant, vital, major, strategic, basic, fundamental, central, keynote, essential, quintessential. [➡IMPORTANT; 195] *Opposite:* unimportant. 6 *v* **input**, keyboard, enter, key in, type, set, typeset. [➡RECORD SOMETHING; 372]

keyboard 1 *n* **control panel**, console, controls. [➡PARTS OF MACHINES AND TOOLS; 1117] 2 *type of* **hardware**. [➡COMPUTERS AND COMPUTING; 1126] 3 *v* **type**, key, key in, input, enter, typeset, set, input data. [➡RECORD SOMETHING; 372]

keyboarder *n* **keyboard operator.**, typist, data entry clerk, typesetter, inputter, secretary. [➡MUSICIANS AND SINGERS; 908]

keyed up (*informal*) *adj* **nervous**, tense, excited, jumpy, anxious, twitchy (*informal*), hyper (*informal*), edgy, jittery. [➡PLEASURE, EXCITEMENT, AND ELATION; 535] *Opposite:* relaxed.

keyhole *n* **hole**, aperture, orifice (*literary*), spyhole, peephole, opening. [➡HOLES, GAPS, AND FORKS; 1251]

key in *v* **key**, type, input, enter, typeset, input data, keyboard. [➡RECORD SOMETHING; 372]

keynote 1 *n* **theme**, essence, idea, gist, core, heart. [➡MOST IMPORTANT THING; 198] 2 *adj* **important**, crucial, major, essential, defining, significant, central. [➡IMPORTANT; 195] *Opposite:* insignificant.

key player *n* [➡IMPORTANT OR FAMOUS PEOPLE; 893]

keystone *n* **foundation**, basis, bedrock, underpinning, grounding, root, source, base, principle, cornerstone. [➡MOST IMPORTANT THING; 198]

khaki *type of* **brown.** [➡ COLOURS; 1223]

khakis *type of* **trousers.** [➡ GARMENTS AND OUTFITS; 865]

khamsin *type of* **wind.** [➡ WINDY AND STORMY WEATHER; 1053]

kibbutz *n* **collective**, commune, cooperative, kolkhoz, community, settlement, village, ashram. [➡ PLACE OF EMPLOYMENT; 832]

kick 1 *v* **boot**, strike, put the boot in, hack. [➡ PHYSICAL ATTACK AND PUNISHMENT; 416] 2 *v* **dribble**, punt, place-kick, kick off. [➡ CONTACT: IMPACT; 414] 3 *v* **jolt**, jerk, recoil, flex, reflex, thrust, hit out, strike out. [➡ PHYSICAL REACTIONS; 317] 4 *v* **give up**, quit, end, cease, stop, abandon, forsake. [➡ STOP ACTING; 265] *Opposite:* take up. 5 *n* **recoil**, rebound, return, reaction, reflex, backlash, jolt, jerk. [➡ PHYSICAL REACTIONS; 317] 6 *n* (*informal*) **thrill**, buzz (*informal*), high (*informal*), boost, pleasure, excitement, frisson, shudder. [➡ TREAT; 211]

kick back (*informal*) *v* [➡ LACK OF ACTIVITY; 343]

kickback *n* **bribe**, sweetener (*informal*), softener, cut (*informal*), payment, reward, inducement, boodle (*slang*), share, commission. [➡ BRIBES; 441]

kickboxing *type of* **combat sport.** [➡ HOBBIES, GAMES, AND SPORTS; 875]

kick in 1 *v* (*informal*) **take effect**, come on-stream, get going, get underway, start, begin, commence (*formal*). [➡ SUDDENLY COME INTO EXISTENCE; 2] *Opposite:* run out. 2 *v* **break down**, smash, demolish, flatten, destroy, knock down, batter. [➡ PHYSICAL ATTACK AND PUNISHMENT; 416]

kick in the teeth *n* **setback**, blow, shock, betrayal, letdown, knock (*informal*), body blow, knock-back (*informal*). [➡ PROBLEM; 257] *Opposite:* boost.

kick off (*informal*) *v* **start**, begin, start the ball rolling, get underway, commence (*formal*), open. [➡ START AN ACTION; 261] *Opposite:* end.

kickoff (*informal*) *n* **start**, beginning, opening, commencement (*formal*), inception (*formal*), initiation. [➡ BEGINNING; 53] *Opposite:* end.

kick out (*informal*) *v* **throw out**, chuck out (*informal*), sling out, eject, force out, sack (*informal*), fire (*informal*), make redundant, axe (*informal*), give the chop (*informal*), cast out (*formal*), show the door, give the bum's rush (*slang*). [➡ EJECT AND EXCLUDE; 341] *Opposite:* appoint.

kick-start 1 *v* **start up**, start, get going, turn over, rev up (*informal*), crank up. [➡ CAUSE TO START; 266] *Opposite:* stop. 2 *v* **restart**, start, revive, resuscitate, jump-start, revitalize, resurrect, rejuvenate, inject new life into. [➡ CAUSE TO START; 266] *Opposite:* kill off. 3 *n* (*informal*) **fillip**, shot in the arm, spur, stimulus, boost, reactivation, kickoff (*informal*), jump-start. [➡ BEGINNING; 53] 4 *n* **kick-starter**, pedal, starter, foot pedal, lever, treadle. [➡ EXTERNAL PARTS OF A VEHICLE; 1146]

kick the bucket (*slang*) *v* **die**, pass away, expire, pop off (*informal*), pop your clogs (*informal*), croak (*slang*). [➡ DIE; 922]

kick up a fuss *v* **protest**, rampage, make a scene, make a fuss, complain, make a song and dance (*informal*), go on about, grumble, grouse (*informal*). [➡ COMPLAIN AND NAG; 687] *Opposite:* smooth over.

kick up a rumpus *v* [➡ PROTEST AND EXPRESS DISAPPROVAL; 643]

kick up a storm *v* [➡ PROTEST AND EXPRESS DISAPPROVAL; 643]

kick up your heels *v* [➡ FIDGET AND FROLIC; 312]

kid 1 *n* (*informal*) **child**, teenager, adolescent, youngster, toddler, tot (*informal*), tyke, young'un (*informal*), teen (*informal*), sprog (*slang*). [➡ CHILD OR YOUTH; 945] *Opposite:* adult. 2 *type of* **leather.** [➡ FABRICS; 1131] 3 *type of* **young animal.** [➡ YOUNG ANIMAL; 977] 4 *v* **tease**, joke, rib (*informal*), poke fun at, make fun of, mock, ridicule, pull somebody's leg (*informal*), josh (*informal*), rag (*dated*), yank somebody's chain (*US informal*). [➡ JOKES AND TEASING; 675] 5 *v* (*informal*) **fool**, trick, delude, have on (*informal*), hoodwink, con, mislead, deceive, bamboozle (*informal*). [➡ DECEPTION AND LIES; 661]

See Compare and Contrast at **youth.**

kidder *n* **joker**, tease, trickster, clown, prankster. [➡ JOKERS AND TEASES; 676]

kiddo (*informal*) *n* [➡ ENDEARMENTS; 657]

kiddy (*informal*) *n* **youngster**, child, tot (*informal*), kid (*informal*), baby, sprog (*slang*), rug rat (*informal humorous*). [➡ CHILD OR YOUTH; 945]

kidnap *v* **abduct**, take hostage, capture, take prisoner, hijack, shanghai, snatch (*US informal*). [➡ CAPTIVITY AND LOSS OF FREEDOM; 249] *Opposite:* release.

kidnapper *n* [➡ CRIMINALS; 821]

kidney 1 *part of* **digestive tract.** [➡ THE DIGESTIVE TRACT; 710] 2 *type of* **rounded shape.** [➡ ROUNDED SHAPE; 1217]

kidney bean *type of* **pulse.** [➡ BEANS AND PULSES; 1188]

kid's stuff *n* [➡ EASY WORK; 300]

kill *v* **murder**, assassinate, execute, put to death, slaughter, slay (*formal or literary*), dispatch, massacre, put to sleep, destroy, exterminate, eradicate, bump off (*slang*). [➡ KILL; 923] *Opposite:* revive.

Compare and Contrast: ***kill, murder, assassinate, execute, put to death, slaughter, slay, put down, put to sleep***

CORE MEANING: TO DEPRIVE OF LIFE

kill to cause the death of a person or animal; ***murder*** to take the life of another person deliberately and not in self-defence in a serious criminal act; ***assassinate*** to murder a public figure by a sudden violent attack; ***execute*** to take somebody's life as part of a judicial or extrajudicial process; ***put to death*** to deliberately take somebody's life, especially in accordance with a legal death sentence; ***slaughter*** to kill farm animals for food, or to kill a person or large numbers of people brutally; ***slay*** (*formal or literary*) to kill a person or animal; ***put down*** or ***put to sleep*** to kill a sick or injured animal, especially when done by a vet.

killer 1 *n* **murderer**, assassin, slaughterer, executioner, destroyer, exterminator, eradicator, slayer (*formal or literary*), hit man (*slang*), hatchet man (*slang*). [➡ PEOPLE WHO KILL; 924] 2 *n* **disease**, destroyer, natural disaster, predator. [➡ DISASTERS; 253]

killer whale *type of* **whale**. [➡WHALE; 991]

killing *n* **murder**, assassination, butchery, slaughter, carnage, homicide, massacre, slaying, extermination, liquidation. [➡CAUSES OF DEATH; 921]

killjoy *n* **spoilsport**, party pooper (*informal*), sourpuss (*informal*), wet blanket (*informal*), misery (*informal*). [➡GRUMPY AND NEGATIVE PEOPLE; 953]

kill off *v* **put an end to**, stop, halt, finish (*informal*), destroy, end, ruin, scotch (*archaic*), eradicate. [➡CAUSE TO STOP; 267] *Opposite:* set up.

kill time *v* **pass the time**, waste time, wait, loiter, twiddle your thumbs, idle away the hours, fill in time, hang around. [➡LACK OF ACTIVITY; 343]

kill yourself *v* **commit suicide**, end it all, take your own life, top yourself (*slang*). [➡DIE; 922]

kill yourself laughing *v* **laugh your head off**, have hysterics (*informal*), split your sides (*informal*), crease up (*informal*), fall about (*informal*), double over. [➡LAUGHTER; 650]

kiln *n* **oven**, furnace, forge. [➡FIRE, FLAMMABILITY, AND BURNING; 1164]

kilt 1 *v* **pleat**, gather, fold, crease, smock, corrugate. [➡CHANGE OF SHAPE; 386] 2 *type of* **skirt**. [➡GARMENTS AND OUTFITS; 865]

kimono *n* **dressing gown**, negligée, peignoir, bathrobe, robe. [➡GARMENTS AND OUTFITS; 865]

kin *n* **family**, relatives, relations, nearest and dearest, people (*informal*), kith and kin, kinsfolk, flesh and blood, clan (*informal*), folks (*US*), kinfolk (*US*). [➡THE FAMILY; 956]

kind 1 *adj* **caring**, nice, generous, gentle, compassionate, thoughtful, benevolent, sympathetic, humane, kind-hearted, humanitarian, considerate, benign, kindly, charitable. [➡GENEROSITY AND KINDNESS; 496] *Opposite:* inhumane. 2 *n* **type**, sort, class, variety, category, breed, manner, style, nature, form, hue, caste, brand, genre, make. [➡VARIETY, TYPE, KIND; 146]

See Compare and Contrast at **type**.

kindergarten (*US*) *n* **nursery school**, playschool, pre-school playgroup, playgroup, nursery, crèche, day nursery. [➡EDUCATIONAL INSTITUTIONS; 813]

kind-hearted *adj* **kind**, caring, sympathetic, nice, gentle, compassionate, benevolent, thoughtful, humane, considerate, benign, kindly, charitable, friendly, generous, tenderhearted. [➡GENEROSITY AND KINDNESS; 496]

kind-heartedness *n* **kindness**, sympathy, compassion, benevolence, thoughtfulness, humanity, consideration, kindliness, helpfulness, charity. [➡GENEROSITY AND KINDNESS; 496] *Opposite:* cruelty.

kindle 1 *v* **encourage**, stimulate, stir up, fire up, promote, inspire, rouse, awaken, ignite, instil, provoke, incite. [➡CAUSE TO HAPPEN; 31] *Opposite:* quench. 2 *v* **spark**, light, set alight, burn, ignite, set on fire, torch (*slang*). [➡FIRE, FLAMMABILITY, AND BURNING; 1164] *Opposite:* douse.

kindliness *n* **kindness**, compassion, sympathy, amiability, gentleness, thoughtfulness, kind-heartedness, sensitivity, warmth, humanity, consideration, graciousness, charity. [➡GENEROSITY AND KINDNESS; 496] *Opposite:* cruelty.

kindly 1 *adj* **friendly**, sympathetic, generous, caring, kind, compassionate, kind-hearted, benevolent, nice, thoughtful, gentle, humane, considerate, benign, helpful, charitable. [➡GENEROSITY AND KINDNESS; 496] 2 *adv* **gently**, compassionately, sympathetically, benevolently, kind-heartedly, nicely, thoughtfully, humanely, considerately, benignly, helpfully. [➡GENEROSITY AND KINDNESS; 496] *Opposite:* cruelly.

kindness *n* **compassion**, gentleness, sympathy, kind-heartedness, benevolence, thoughtfulness, humanity, consideration, helpfulness, charity. [➡GENEROSITY AND KINDNESS; 496] *Opposite:* cruelty.

kind of (*informal*) *adv* **sort of** (*informal*), rather, a bit (*informal*), somewhat, fairly, in a way, quite. [➡TO A CERTAIN EXTENT; 134]

kindred 1 *adj* **associated**, close, like, alike, allied, attractive, corresponding, akin, similar, matching, analogous. [➡RELATED; 143] *Opposite:* dissimilar. 2 *n* **kinship**, family, kin, blood, ties, parentage, relatedness. [➡THE FAMILY; 956] 3 *n* **family**, relations, relatives, people (*informal*), kinsfolk, nearest and dearest, kin, kith and kin, folks (*US*), kinfolk (*US*). [➡THE FAMILY; 956]

kinfolk (*US*) *n* **family**, relatives, relations, kindred, kith and kin, nearest and dearest, kin, kinfolk, people (*informal*), folks (*US*). [➡THE FAMILY; 956]

king 1 *n* **monarch**, sovereign, ruler, royal (*informal*), rajah, tsar, liege, suzerain. [➡RULERS AND ARISTOCRACY; 823] *Opposite:* subject. 2 *n* **ruler**, chief, head, leader, dictator, despot. [➡RULERS AND ARISTOCRACY; 823] 3 *n* **leader**, star, superstar, luminary, leading light, kingpin (*informal*), principal, ace (*informal*), maven, honcho (*US slang*). [➡IMPORTANT OR FAMOUS PEOPLE; 893] 4 *v* **crown**, enthrone, install, invest (*formal*), honour, dignify. [➡CONFER STATUS; 459] *Opposite:* dethrone.

kingdom *n* **realm**, empire, monarchy, territory, domain, demesne (*formal*), dominion, nation, estate. [➡REALMS AND RULES; 824]

kingfish *type of* **tropical sea fish**. [➡SEA FISH; 1009]

kingfisher *type of* **freshwater bird**. [➡FRESHWATER BIRD; 1000]

kingly *adj* **magnificent**, stately, grand, majestic, regal, splendid, royal, imperial, monarchal. [➡ROYALNESS; 825]

kingpin (*informal*) *n* **key player**, top dog (*informal*), number one (*informal*), linchpin, leading light, superstar, ace (*informal*), principal, honcho (*US slang*). [➡IMPORTANT OR FAMOUS PEOPLE; 893]

kingship *n* **monarchy**, sovereignty, power, authority, supremacy, reign, rule, crown. [➡ROYALNESS; 825]

king-size *adj* **extra-large**, outsize, enormous, huge, giant, massive, vast, immense, mammoth. [➡LARGE; 1192] *Opposite:* miniature.

king-size bed *type of* **bed**. [➡FURNITURE; 858]

king snake *type of* **non-poisonous snake**. [➡SNAKE; 995]

kink *n* **bend**, twist, crook, hook, bow, knot, snarl, crimp, crinkle, curve. [➡ROUNDED SHAPE; 1217]

kinky 1 *adj* (*informal*) **unusual**, strange, idiosyncratic, quirky, unnatural, unconventional, odd, peculiar, eccentric, unorthodox. [➡BIZARRE AND PECULIAR; 258] *Opposite:* conventional. 2 *adj* **crinkled**, crinkly, twisty, knotted, twisted, warped. [➡IN BAD REPAIR; 1233] *Opposite:* straight.

kinsfolk *n* **family**, relatives, relations, kindred, kith and kin, nearest and dearest, kin, people (*informal*), kinfolk (*US*), folks (*US*). [➡THE FAMILY; 956]

kinship 1 *n* **relationship**, connection, tie, link, bond. [➡RELATIONSHIP TO ANOTHER; 973] 2 *n* **relatedness**, understanding, empathy, affiliation, affinity, connection, similarity, likeness. [➡CONNECTION; 144]

kinship

◆ *types of older relative*
aunt, biological parent, dad (*informal*), daddy (*informal*), father, gran, granddad (*informal*), grandfather, grandma (*informal*), grandmother, grandpa (*informal*), grandparent, granny (*informal*), great-aunt, great-grandfather, great-grandmother, great-grandparent, great-uncle, lone parent, mom (*US*), mother, mum (*informal*), parent, single parent, stepfather, stepmother, stepparent, uncle

◆ *types of same generation relative*
brother, cousin, second cousin, senior, sibling, sister, stepbrother, stepsister

◆ *types of younger relative*
child, daughter, dependant, grandchild, granddaughter, grandson, great-grandchild, great-granddaughter, great-grandson, great-nephew, great-niece, nephew, niece, son, stepchild, stepdaughter, stepson

◆ *types of in-law*
brother-in-law, daughter-in-law, father-in-law, mother-in-law, sister-in-law, son-in-law

kinsman (*formal*) *n* [➡THE FAMILY; 956]

kinswoman (*formal*) *n* [➡THE FAMILY; 956]

kiosk 1 *n* **booth**, stall, cabin, stand, hut. [➡RETAIL OUTLETS; 1082] 2 *type of* **outbuilding**. [➡ANCILLARY BUILDINGS; 1079]

kip (*informal*) *n* **nap**, snooze (*informal*), sleep, doze, forty winks (*informal*). [➡SLEEP AND DREAM; 724]

kipper *v* **smoke**, cure, preserve, dry, smoke-dry. [➡COOKING AND FOOD PREPARATION; 354]

kismet *n* **fate**, fortune, luck, destiny, doom, lot, portion (*literary*), providence, end, karma. [➡FATE, DESTINY, AND ASTROLOGY; 783]

kiss 1 *v* **osculate** (*formal or humorous*), caress, neck (*dated*), smooch (*informal*), peck, buss (*dated*), canoodle (*informal*). [➡PHYSICAL CONTACT AS COMMUNICATION; 656] 2 *v* **touch**, brush, glance, graze, caress, skim, rub. [➡CONTACT: TOUCH; 413] 3 *n* **osculation** (*formal or humorous*), peck, smacker (*informal*), smooch (*informal*), canoodle (*informal*), caress, embrace. [➡PHYSICAL CONTACT AS COMMUNICATION; 656] 4 *n* **caress**, light touch, contact, graze, pat, stroke. [➡PHYSICAL CONTACT AS COMMUNICATION; 656]

kiss-and-tell (*informal*) *adj* **revealing**, exposing, divulging, sensational, juicy (*informal*), scandalous, lurid. [➡IN POOR TASTE; 230]

kit 1 *n* **tackle**, gear (*informal*), tools, equipment, implements, supplies, necessaries (*informal*). [➡DEVICES; 1114] 2 *n* **set of clothes**, dress, gear (*informal*), strip, apparel, costume, clothing, outfit. [➡CLOTHES AND ACCESSORIES; 864] 3 *n* **belongings**, gear (*informal*), things, stuff, baggage, luggage, personal belongings, personal effects, possessions, trappings, paraphernalia, accoutrements. [➡POSSESSIONS; 462]

kitbag *n* **canvas bag**, knapsack, backpack, rucksack, duffel bag, holdall, tote bag, carryall (*US*). [➡CONTAINERS, RECEPTACLES, AND PACKAGING; 1244]

kitchen *n* **kitchenette**, galley, scullery. [➡TYPES OF ROOM; 1096]

kitchenette *type of* **room in the home**. [➡TYPES OF ROOM; 1096]

kitchen garden *n* [➡GARDENS; 1073]

kite 1 *type of* **toy**. [➡TOYS; 880] 2 *type of* **bird of prey**. [➡BIRD OF PREY; 998]

kith and kin *n* **relatives**, family, relations, kinsfolk, flesh and blood, nearest and dearest, people (*informal*), folks (*US*), kinfolk (*US*). [➡THE FAMILY; 956]

kit out *v* **equip**, prepare, provide, fit out, rig out (*informal*), supply, give, furnish (*formal*), fix up. [➡EQUIP AND SUPPLY; 436]

kitsch 1 *n* **vulgarity**, tastelessness, sentimentality, ostentation, showiness, brashness, tackiness (*informal*). [➡IN POOR TASTE; 230] *Opposite:* tastefulness. 2 *n* **junk** (*informal*), tack (*informal*), trash, frippery. [➡RUBBISH AND USELESS OBJECTS; 1248] 3 *adj* **tasteless**, vulgar, tacky (*informal*), brash, common, loud, cheap, crummy (*informal*), cheesy (*informal*). [➡IN POOR TASTE; 230] *Opposite:* tasteful.

kitschy *adj* **tasteless**, vulgar, loud, tacky (*informal*), cheesy (*informal*), cheap, naff (*informal*), common. [➡IN POOR TASTE; 230] *Opposite:* tasteful.

kitten *type of* **young animal**. [➡YOUNG ANIMAL; 977]

kittenish 1 *adj* **playful**, frisky, lively, coltish, frolicsome, fun-loving, mischievous, impish, sportive. [➡ENERGY AND ENTHUSIASM; 497] *Opposite:* staid. 2 *adj* **flirtatious**, coy, coquettish (*literary*), frisky, cute. [➡FLIRTATIOUS; 640]

kittiwake *type of* **seabird**. [➡SEABIRD; 1002]

kitty 1 *n* (*informal*) **puss** (*informal*), pussy (*informal*), pussycat (*informal*), cat, kitten. [➡FELINE; 983] 2 *n* **fund**, pool, stake, ante, pot (*US informal*). [➡MONEY; 140]

kitty-cornered (*US*) *adv* [➡ORIENTATION AND ALIGNMENT; 1222]

kiwi *type of* **flightless bird**. [➡BIRD; 997]

kiwi fruit *type of* **fruit**. [➡FRUIT AND VEGETABLES; 1175]

klaxon *n* **horn**, siren, alarm, signal, buzzer, bell. [➡SIGNALLING; 1139]

knack *n* **ability**, skill, talent, flair, aptitude, gift, capability, capacity, propensity (*formal*), facility, dexterity, expertise. [➡SKILLS, TALENTS, AND ABILITIES; 527]

See Compare and Contrast at **talent**.

knacker (*slang*) *v* **exhaust**, tire out, tire, wear out, fatigue, do in (*informal*). [➡USE UP AND WASTE; 475] *Opposite:* invigorate.

knackered (*slang*) *adj* **exhausted**, tired, tired out, fatigued, worn-out, done in (*informal*), bushed (*informal*). [➡TIRED, ASLEEP, AND UNCONSCIOUS; 739] *Opposite:* invigorated.

knapsack *n* **bag**, shoulder bag, rucksack, backpack, daypack, duffel bag. [➡CONTAINERS, RECEPTACLES, AND PACKAGING; 1244]

knead *v* **massage**, rub, work, mould, manipulate, press, squeeze. [➡CONTACT: EXERT PRESSURE; 415]

knee *part of* **leg or foot.** [➡LEG AND FOOT; 695]

kneecap *type of* **bone.** [➡THE BONES AND JOINTS; 720]

knee-deep *adj* **involved**, occupied, engrossed, absorbed, immersed, submerged, up to your ears, up to your elbows, up to your eyes, sunk, entangled. [➡PENSIVENESS AND INTEREST; 539] *Opposite:* uninvolved.

knee-highs *type of* **lower body underwear.** [➡HABERDASHERY, MILLINERY, AND LINGERIE; 867]

knee-jerk (*informal*) 1 *adj* **unthinking**, automatic, reflex, habitual, immediate, thoughtless, mindless. [➡AUTOMATIC AND INSTINCTIVE; 281] *Opposite:* considered. 2 *adj* **predictable**, prejudging, prejudiced, biased, dyed-in-the-wool, unchanging. [➡THE NATURE OF IDEAS; 772] *Opposite:* unpredictable.

kneel *v* **go down on your knees**, genuflect, kneel down, kowtow. [➡ASSUME A POSITION; 318] *Opposite:* rise.

knees-up (*informal*) *n* **party**, celebration, bash, get-together (*informal*), shindig (*informal*), festivity, do (*informal*), fiesta, blast (*US slang*). [➡PARTIES, DANCES, AND CELEBRATIONS; 37]

knell 1 *n* **toll**, ring, peal, sound, ringing, tolling. [➡RINGING AND TOOTING SOUNDS; 1258] 2 *v* **ring**, toll, sound, peal, chime, strike, resound, reverberate. [➡EMIT RINGING AND TOOTING SOUNDS; 368]

knickerbockers *type of* **trousers.** [➡GARMENTS AND OUTFITS; 865]

knickers *type of* **lower body underwear.** [➡HABERDASHERY, MILLINERY, AND LINGERIE; 867]

knick-knack *n* **trinket**, ornament, curio, souvenir, object, decoration, trifle, bauble, gewgaw, tchotchke (*US*). [➡ORNAMENTS AND DECORATIONS; 1247]

knife 1 *v* **stab**, spear, stick, wound, lacerate, cut, slash. [➡WOUND A PERSON OR ANIMAL; 384] 2 *type of* **cutlery.** [➡TABLEWARE, CUTLERY, AND KITCHENWARE; 861]

knife

◆ *types of knife*
bread knife, butcher's knife, carving knife, cleaver, flick knife, jackknife, paperknife, penknife, pocketknife (*US*), switchblade (*US*), table knife

knife-edge *n* **critical point**, decisive point, turning point, watershed, crisis, crux, crunch. [➡DECISIVE MOMENTS; 44]

knight 1 *n* **cavalier**, caballero, knight-errant, adventurer. [➡NOMADIC AND ROOTLESS LIFESTYLES; 884] 2 *type of* **aristocrat.** [➡RULERS AND ARISTOCRACY; 823]

knight in shining armour *n* [➡PEOPLE WHO ARE APPROVED OF; 955]

knish *type of* **processed potato.** [➡FRUIT AND VEGETABLES; 1175]

knit 1 *v* **heal**, mend, set, join, meld, get better, bond, attach. [➡REPAIR AND MEND; 377] 2 *v* **unite**, join, interweave, weave, interlace, bind, tie, braid, plait, interlock. [➡FASTEN, LINK, AND JOIN; 409]

knitting *type of* **handicraft.** [➡CRAFTS AND CARVING; 356]

knit your brow *v* [➡FACIAL EXPRESSION; 652]

knob 1 *n* **handle**, doorknob, dial, button, handhold, hold, grip. [➡PARTS OF MACHINES AND TOOLS; 1117] 2 *n* **lump**, bump, bulge, protuberance, protrusion, hump, knot, knurl, nub. [➡ROUNDED SHAPE; 1217]

knobbly *adj* **lumpy**, bumpy, ridged, bony, protuberant, uneven, rough, textured, knotty. [➡PHYSICAL TEXTURE; 1221] *Opposite:* smooth.

knock 1 *v* **bash** (*informal*), hit, bump, collide, bang, thump, crack, clout, whack, strike, smite (*archaic or literary*), slam, hammer, pound, tap, rap, beat. [➡PHYSICAL ATTACK AND PUNISHMENT; 416] 2 *v* (*informal*) **criticize**, put down (*informal*), slam (*informal*), disparage, condemn, censure, belittle, deprecate, abuse, do down (*informal*). [➡ACCUSE, BLAME, AND CRITICIZE; 642] *Opposite:* praise. 3 *n* **blow**, collision, hit, bash (*informal*), bump, bang, thump, crack (*informal*), clout, whack, stroke, thwack, rap, tap. [➡PHYSICAL ATTACK AND PUNISHMENT; 416] 4 *n* (*informal*) **blow**, setback, upset, knock-back (*informal*), kick in the teeth, misfortune. [➡CRITICISMS AND ANGRY OUTBURSTS; 50]

knock about (*informal*) 1 *v* **beat**, beat up (*informal*), hit, mistreat, abuse, batter. [➡PHYSICAL ATTACK AND PUNISHMENT; 416] 2 *v* **kick about** (*informal*), hang about, hang out (*informal*), spend time, relax, chill (*slang*), hang around. [➡LACK OF ACTIVITY; 343]

knockabout 1 *n* **slapstick**, physical comedy, visual comedy, clowning, buffoonery, farce. [➡JOKES AND TEASING; 675] 2 *n* (*informal*) **game**, informal game, friendly, friendly game, knock-up, practice, practice session. [➡NON-AGGRESSIVE/SPORTING EVENT; 40] 3 *adj* **sturdy**, stout, strong, solid, substantial, tough, casual, informal, everyday. [➡DESCRIBING CLOTHES; 869] *Opposite:* flimsy. 4 *adj* **physical**, slapstick, boisterous, rowdy, rough, visual, lively, spontaneous. [➡DISORDER AND CHAOS; 246] *Opposite:* decorous.

knock back (*informal*) *v* **down**, gulp, swallow, quaff (*literary or humorous*), drink, put back, toss back. [➡DRINK; 712]

knock down 1 *v* **floor**, fell, knock over, hit, deck (*informal*), strike, smite (*archaic or literary*), pound, smash. [➡MOVE SOMETHING: INTO A NEW POSITION OR OVERTURN; 331] 2 *v* **destroy**, demolish, dismantle, bulldoze, pull down, tear down, take down, flatten, raze, level. [➡DESTRUCTION AND DEMO-

LITION; 360] *Opposite:* build. **3** *v* **reduce the price of**, discount, mark down, lower, reduce. [➡SELL; 442] *Opposite:* put up.

knockdown *adj* **cheap**, reduced, low, rock-bottom, giveaway (*informal*), bargain, budget. [➡CHEAP AND INEXPENSIVE; 222] *Opposite:* inflated.

knocked for six (*informal*) *adj* **stunned**, flabbergasted (*informal*), taken aback, amazed, astounded, surprised, astonished, shocked, speechless, gobsmacked (*slang*). [➡SURPRISE, SHOCK, AND AMAZEMENT; 546]

knocked out 1 *adj* (*informal*) **bowled over**, awestruck, dazzled, amazed, knocked for six (*informal*), blown away (*US slang*). [➡SURPRISE, SHOCK, AND AMAZEMENT; 546] *Opposite:* unimpressed. **2** *adj* **unconscious**, stunned, anaesthetized, comatose, under (*informal*), out cold. [➡TIRED, ASLEEP, AND UNCONSCIOUS; 739]

knocker 1 *n* **door fixture**, knob, handle, bell, doorbell. [➡ORNAMENTS AND DECORATIONS; 1247] **2** *n* (*informal*) **critic**, faultfinder, detractor, carper, caviller, moaner (*informal*). [➡GRUMPY AND NEGATIVE PEOPLE; 953] *Opposite:* admirer.

knock for six (*informal*) *v* [➡SURPRISE AND IMPRESS; 575]

knock off 1 *v* (*informal*) **stop work**, finish, call it a day, down tools, pack in (*informal*), leave, head off. [➡STOP ACTING; 265] *Opposite:* start. **2** *v* (*informal*) **deduct**, take off, discount, subtract, reduce. [➡BUSINESS ACTIVITIES AND PHENOMENA; 795] **3** *v* (*informal*) **mass-produce**, churn out, knock out, turn out, rattle off, produce. [➡MANUFACTURE; 350] **4** *v* (*slang*) **kill**, murder, top (*slang*), do in (*informal*), do away with (*informal*), assassinate, eliminate, liquidate. [➡KILL; 923] **5** *v* (*slang*) **steal**, rob, pinch (*informal*), filch (*informal*), pilfer, thieve, nick (*slang*), make off with, embezzle, appropriate, lift (*informal*). [➡STEAL AND ROB; 427]

knockoff (*informal*) *n* **copy**, fake, forgery, reproduction, counterfeit, rip-off (*informal*). [➡COPIES AND REPLICAS; 152] *Opposite:* original.

knock-on effect *n* **consequence**, outcome, result, upshot, conclusion, chain reaction, chain of events, domino effect. [➡RESULTS AND OUTCOMES; 83]

knock out 1 *v* **make unconscious**, hit, floor, fell, deck (*informal*), knock down. [➡WOUND A PERSON OR ANIMAL; 384] **2** *v* **eliminate**, put out, defeat, overcome, beat, finish. [➡BEAT AND DEFEAT; 80]

knockout (*informal*) *n* **big success**, wow (*informal*), hit, sensation, triumph, winner, smash, stunner (*informal*). [➡AMAZING THING; 212] *Opposite:* dud (*informal*).

knock over 1 *v* **upset**, topple, overturn, tip over, spill, knock down, floor, fell, deck (*informal*). [➡MOVE SOMETHING: INTO A NEW POSITION OR OVERTURN; 331] **2** *v* (*informal*) **overwhelm**, impress, floor, bowl over, astound, amaze. [➡SURPRISE AND IMPRESS; 575]

knock together (*informal*) *v* **assemble**, improvise, knock up (*informal*), make up, rustle up (*informal*), concoct, scare up (*US informal*). [➡CREATION; 347]

knock up (*informal*) *v* **improvise**, assemble, knock together (*informal*), make up, rustle up (*informal*), concoct. [➡CREATION; 347]

knock-up *n* **practice**, practice session, knockabout (*informal*), rehearsal, training session. [➡PREPARATORY EVENT; 57]

knock your socks off *v* **surprise**, astonish, take aback, amaze, shock, astound, flabbergast (*informal*), bowl over, knock down with a feather. [➡SURPRISE AND IMPRESS; 575]

knoll *n* **hill**, hillock, hummock, mound, mount. [➡MOUNTAINS AND HILLS; 1044]

knot 1 *n* **tie**, loop, reef knot, granny knot, square knot (*US*). [➡FASTENERS, LINKS, AND NETWORKS; 1246] **2** *n* **lump**, bump, bulge, protuberance, nub. [➡ROUNDED SHAPE; 1217] **3** *n* **cluster**, huddle, clutch, band, collection, gathering, crowd, group, bunch, circle. [➡GROUPS OF PEOPLE; 935] **4** *v* **join**, tie, bind, tether, secure. [➡FASTEN, LINK, AND JOIN; 409] *Opposite:* untie.

knotted *adj* **tied**, tense, secured, taut, tangled, tight, snarled, hard, entwined, clenched, drawn, furrowed, knitted. [➡RIGID AND HARD; 1210] *Opposite:* relaxed.

knotty *adj* **tricky**, awkward, complicated, complex, thorny, tough, problematic, hard, difficult. [➡DIFFICULTY AND COMPLEXITY; 243] *Opposite:* simple.

know 1 *v* **understand**, be aware of, be knowledgeable about, comprehend, appreciate, realize, grasp, get (*informal*), recognize, see. [➡KNOWLEDGE AND WISDOM; 559] **2** *v* **experience**, go through, undergo. [➡EXPERIENCE AND ENCOUNTER; 583] **3** *v* **be acquainted with**, be familiar with, distinguish, see, tell, have knowledge of, be friendly with. [➡KNOWLEDGE AND WISDOM; 559]

knowable *adj* **intelligible**, comprehensible, understandable, coherent, identifiable, recognizable, fathomable. [➡PERCEPTIBLE; 25] *Opposite:* unknowable.

know-all (*informal*) *n* **smart aleck** (*informal*), clever Dick (*informal*), clever clogs (*informal*), smarty-pants (*informal*), wiseacre (*informal*), wise guy (*US informal*). [➡SELF-IMPORTANT AND SELF-SEEKING PEOPLE; 949]

know back to front *v* **know backwards**, know inside out, know like the back of your hand, know backward and forward (*US*). [➡KNOWLEDGE AND WISDOM; 559]

know backward and forward (*US*) *v* [➡KNOWLEDGE AND WISDOM; 559]

know backwards *v* **know back to front**, know inside out, know like the back of your hand, know backward and forward (*US*). [➡KNOWLEDGE AND WISDOM; 559]

know-how (*informal*) *n* **knowledge**, experience, expertise, savoir-faire, savvy (*informal*), proficiency, competence. [➡SKILLS, TALENTS, AND ABILITIES; 527]

knowing 1 *adj* **meaningful**, significant, expressive, eloquent, perceptive, shrewd. [➡KNOWLEDGE AND WISDOM; 559] *Opposite:* innocent. **2** *adj* **deliberate**, intentional, intended, conscious, calculating, aware. [➡INTENTIONAL AND DELIBERATE; 280] *Opposite:* unconscious.

knowledge 1 *n* **acquaintance**, familiarity, awareness, understanding, comprehension, realization, experience, expertise, skill, know-how (*informal*). [➡KNOWLEDGE AND WISDOM; 559] *Opposite:* ignorance. **2** *n* **information**, facts, data, gen (*informal*). [➡BASIC DETAILS; 689] **3** *n* **wisdom**, learning, education, scholarship, erudition, intelligence. [➡KNOWLEDGE AND WISDOM; 559]

Compare and Contrast: ***knowledge, erudition, information, learning, scholarship, wisdom***

CORE MEANING: WHAT CAN BE KNOWN

knowledge all the information, facts, truths, and principles acquired by experience; ***erudition*** knowledge acquired through study and learning; ***information*** facts or data; ***learning*** knowledge or skill gained through education; ***scholarship*** advanced academic learning or achievement; ***wisdom*** accumulated knowledge of life or of a particular sphere of activity that has been gained through experience.

knowledgeable *adj* **well-informed**, clued-up (*informal*), au fait, on the ball (*informal*), conversant, familiar, informed, educated, erudite, experienced, expert. [➡KNOWLEDGE AND WISDOM; 559] *Opposite:* ignorant.

known **1** *adj* **recognized**, identified, acknowledged, branded, notorious (*archaic*), well-known, famous, celebrated, renowned. [➡KNOWN AND FAMOUS; 182] **2** *adj* **accepted**, acknowledged, established, recognized, proven. [➡KNOWN AND FAMOUS; 182]

knuckle **1** *n* **protuberance**, projection, lump, prominence, bulge, knob, nub, knot. [➡ROUNDED SHAPE; 1217] **2** *part of* **arm or hand.** [➡ARM AND HAND; 696]

knuckle down (*informal*) *v* **work hard**, apply yourself, get down to it, buckle down (*informal*), get your head down. [➡HARD WORK OR EFFORT; 299]

knuckle under *v* **give in**, give up, admit defeat, concede defeat, concede, surrender, give way, throw in the towel (*informal*), yield, throw in the sponge (*informal*), throw in your hand (*informal*). [➡FAIL OR BE UNSUCCESSFUL; 75] *Opposite:* continue.

KO (*informal*) *v* [➡PHYSICAL ATTACK AND PUNISHMENT; 416]

koala *type of* **marsupial.** [➡MARSUPIAL; 992]

kohl *n* **eyeliner**, eye pencil, mascara. [➡MAKEUP AND BEAUTY PRODUCTS; 491]

Komodo dragon *type of* **reptile.** [➡REPTILES; 994]

kosher (*informal*) **1** *adj* **genuine**, authentic, true, real, bona fide. [➡TRUE AND REAL; 172] *Opposite:* fake. **2** *adj* **lawful**, acceptable, legitimate, aboveboard, proper. [➡APPROPRIATE, SUITABLE, ADVISABLE; 185] *Opposite:* unlawful.

kowtow **1** *v* **kneel**, bow, genuflect, prostrate oneself, salaam, stoop, bend. [➡GESTURES AND GESTICULATION; 654] **2** *v* **grovel**, be servile, be obsequious, show deference, bow and scrape, fawn, humble oneself. [➡GESTURES AND GESTICULATION; 654] **3** *n* **bow**, genuflection, prostration, salaam, homage, obeisance (*formal*). [➡GESTURES AND GESTICULATION; 654]

kudos *n* **glory**, praise, credit, fame, admiration, acclaim, honour, prestige, cachet, esteem. [➡SOURCE OF HAPPINESS, PLEASURE, OR IMPROVEMENT; 210] *Opposite:* discredit.

kudzu *type of* **climber.** [➡CLIMBERS; 1033]

kung fu *type of* **combat sport.** [➡HOBBIES, GAMES, AND SPORTS; 875]

kvetch (*informal*) *v* [➡COMPLAIN AND NAG; 687]

L

laager *n* **camp**, encampment, settlement, defensive position, shelter, stronghold. [➡ HUMAN SETTLEMENTS; 1069]

lab (*informal*) *n* **workroom**, workshop, test bed, test centre, laboratory. [➡ INDUSTRIAL BUILDINGS; 1086]

label 1 *n* **tag**, ticket, sticker, marker, sticky label. [➡ NAME AND DESCRIBE; 666] 2 *n* **make**, brand name, trade name, trademark, mark, marque, brand. [➡ NAME AND DESCRIBE; 666] 3 *n* **description**, categorization, classification, characterization. [➡ NAME AND DESCRIBE; 666] 4 *v* **put a label on**, mark, identify, stamp. [➡ NAME AND DESCRIBE; 666] 5 *v* **consider**, regard, describe, categorize, class, characterize, write off as (*informal*), pigeonhole, brand. [➡ NAME AND DESCRIBE; 666]

laboratory *n* **workroom**, workshop, test bed, test centre, research laboratory, test site. [➡ INDUSTRIAL BUILDINGS; 1086]

laborious *adj* **arduous**, backbreaking, painstaking, protracted, lengthy, strenuous, hard, tough, painful, difficult. [➡ DIFFICULTY AND COMPLEXITY; 243] *Opposite:* easy.

See Compare and Contrast at **hard**.

laboriousness *n* **difficulty**, arduousness, hardness, toughness, tedium. [➡ DIFFICULTY AND COMPLEXITY; 243] *Opposite:* ease.

labor union (*US*) *n* **syndicate**, trade union, organized labour, union, workers' association, staff association. [➡ BUSINESS ENTERPRISES AND RELATED BODIES; 793]

labour 1 *n* **work**, toil, hard work, manual labour, efforts, employment, exertions, industry (*formal or literary*), hard labour, blood, sweat, and tears. [➡ HARD WORK OR EFFORT; 299] 2 *n* **workers**, workforce, employees, labour force, hands, staff, personnel, manual workers, blue-collar workers, working class. [➡ THE WORK FORCE; 837] *Opposite:* management. 3 *n* **task**, job, chore, effort, exertion, mission, duty, activity, occupation. [➡ JOB; 833] 4 *n* **childbirth**, delivery, giving birth, confinement (*dated*), contractions. [➡ REPRODUCTION AND HEREDITY; 726] 5 *v* **strive**, strain, grind away, endeavour, keep at it, burn the candle at both ends, toil, slog, sweat blood, work like a dog, break your back, sweat (*informal*), struggle, plug away (*informal*). [➡ HARD WORK OR EFFORT; 299] *Opposite:* laze around. 6 *v* **struggle**, exert, grapple, wrestle, agonize. [➡ COMPETE, CONTEND, AND COMBAT; 304] 7 *v* **malfunction**, strain, complain, play up, seize up, stall, falter, crash, struggle. [➡ FAIL OR CEASE TO FUNCTION; 471] 8 *v* **drag yourself**, stagger, plod, lumber (*informal*), trudge, trail, slog, struggle. [➡ WALK UNSTEADILY; 316] *Opposite:* skip. 9 *v* **overemphasize**, go on, dwell on, exaggerate, drive home, overdo, stress, underline, accentuate, belabour. [➡ CLAIM, INSIST, AND EMPHASIZE; 615] *Opposite:* skim.

laboured *adj* **tortured**, tortuous, forced, strenuous, arduous, awkward, contrived, artificial, leaden, difficult. [➡ DIFFICULTY AND COMPLEXITY; 243] *Opposite:* effortless.

labourer *n* **manual worker**, blue-collar worker, hand, workhand, navvy (*dated*), worker, employee, drudge. [➡ WORKER; 836]

labour force *n* **workforce**, workers, labour, hands, staff, personnel. [➡ WORKER; 836]

labour-intensive *adj* [➡ DIFFICULTY AND COMPLEXITY; 243]

labour-saving *adj* [➡ EASE AND SIMPLICITY; 201]

labour the point *v* [➡ CLAIM, INSIST, AND EMPHASIZE; 615]

labour under *v* **suffer from**, struggle with, be disadvantaged by, be burdened with, be swayed by, be influenced by, persist, continue, suffer. [➡ EXPERIENCE AND ENCOUNTER; 583]

Labrador *type of* **large dog**. [➡ DOG; 980]

laburnum *type of* **deciduous tree**. [➡ DECIDUOUS TREES; 1028]

labyrinth *n* **maze**, warren, web, tangle, jumble, muddle. [➡ DISORDER AND CHAOS; 246]

labyrinthine *adj* **complex**, convoluted, intricate, complicated, tortuous, obscure, tangled, involved. [➡ DIFFICULTY AND COMPLEXITY; 243] *Opposite:* straightforward.

lace 1 *n* **tie**, shoelace, bootlace, cord. [➡ FASTENERS, LINKS, AND NETWORKS; 1246] 2 *v* **do up**, tie up, lace up, fasten. [➡ FASTEN, LINK, AND JOIN; 409] *Opposite:* undo. 3 *v* **spike**, mix, fortify, line. [➡ COMBINE AND MIX; 401] 4 *part of* **garment**. [➡ PARTS OF A GARMENT; 870]

lacemaking *type of* **handicraft**. [➡ CRAFTS AND CARVING; 356]

lacerate *v* **slash**, tear, cut, score, scratch, shred, gash, rip, slit, slice, hack. [➡ TEAR, BREAK, AND CUT; 361]

laceration *n* **cut**, slash, graze, scratch, tear, gash, rip, slit. [➡ HOLES, GAPS, AND FORKS; 1251]

lachrymose (*literary*) 1 *adj* **tearful**, weepy (*informal*), crying, easily moved, in tears, in floods of tears, with tears in your eyes, close to tears. [➡ SADNESS, DISTRESS, AND DESPAIR; 540] 2 *adj* **sad**, tragic, unhappy, moving, dismal, mournful, sorrowful. [➡ EMOTIONALLY UNPLEASANT AND UPSETTING; 228] *Opposite:* cheerful.

lack 1 *n* **shortage**, absence, want, dearth, deficiency, deficit. [➡ NONEXISTENCE; 24] 2 *v* **be short of**, not have, be deficient in, want for, need, require. [➡ NEED AND REQUIRE; 465] *Opposite:* have.

Compare and Contrast: ***lack, shortage, deficiency, deficit, want, dearth***

CORE MEANING: AN INSUFFICIENCY OR ABSENCE OF SOMETHING

lack a complete absence of a particular thing; ***shortage*** a lack of something that is needed or required; ***deficiency*** a shortfall in the amount of something necessary, e.g. a particular nutrient in the human body, or an inadequacy in the supply or performance of something; ***deficit*** the amount by which something falls short of a target amount or level; ***want*** *or* ***dearth*** a scarcity or absence of something.

lackadaisical *adj* **apathetic**, careless, lazy, relaxed, half-hearted, laid-back (*informal*), easygoing, laissez-faire, lax, casual, slapdash. [➡NEUTRALITY AND INDIFFERENCE; 554] *Opposite:* energetic.

lackey (*archaic*) *type of* **servant**. [➡DOMESTIC AND KITCHEN WORKERS; 850]

lacking *adj* **missing**, not there, wanting, absent. [➡ABSENT AND UNAVAILABLE; 7] *Opposite:* present.

lacking in *adj* **short of**, without, not having, bereft of, devoid of, deficient in. [➡TOO FEW, TOO LITTLE; 120] *Opposite:* full of.

lacklustre *adj* **dull**, lifeless, dreary, unexciting, uninspiring, flat, leaden, tame, bland, undistinguished. [➡BORING AND UNINTERESTING; 235] *Opposite:* brilliant.

laconic *adj* **terse**, brief, short, concise, economical, curt, to the point. [➡ELOQUENT, TALKATIVE, AND LONG-WINDED; 633] *Opposite:* long-winded.

laconicism *n* [➡ELOQUENT, TALKATIVE, AND LONG-WINDED; 633]

lacquer *n* **polish**, varnish, gloss. [➡COVERS AND COATINGS; 1245]

lacrosse *type of* **ball game**. [➡HOBBIES, GAMES, AND SPORTS; 875]

lacrosse stick *type of* **sports equipment**. [➡SPORTS EQUIPMENT; 879]

lactose *type of* **nutrient**. [➡FOOD COMPONENTS; 1187]

lacuna (*literary*) *n* **space**, empty space, void, hole, omission, gap. [➡HOLES, GAPS, AND FORKS; 1251]

lacy *adj* **delicate**, lacelike, net, filigree, fine. [➡VISUAL TEXTURE; 1220]

lad 1 *n* **boy**, young man, youngster, youth, kid (*informal*), teenager, adolescent, laddie (*informal*), son. [➡CHILD OR YOUTH; 945] *Opposite:* lass. **2** *n* (*informal*) **man**, chap (*informal*), bloke (*informal*), guy (*informal*), fella (*informal*), gentleman, fellow. [➡MALE PERSON; 934] *Opposite:* lass.

ladder 1 *n* **stepladder**, folding ladder, loft ladder, roof ladder, steps, rope ladder. [➡STAIRS AND STOREYS; 1101] **2** *n* **ranking**, tree, standings, pecking order. [➡CONNECTION; 144] **3** *v* **run**, rip, tear, snag. [➡TEAR, BREAK, AND CUT; 361]

ladder-back *type of* **seating**. [➡FURNITURE; 858]

laddie (*informal*) *n* **boy**, young man, youth, kid (*informal*), teenager, adolescent, lad. [➡MALE PERSON; 934] *Opposite:* lassie (*informal*).

laddish (*informal*) *adj* **male**, masculine, macho, sexist, chauvinist, stereotypical, archetypal. [➡GENDER IDENTITY AND SEXUALITY; 932]

la-de-da *see* **la-di-da**.

laden *adj* **weighed down**, burdened, overloaded, loaded. [➡FULL; 1238] *Opposite:* empty.

la-di-da (*informal*) *adj* **affected**, posh (*informal*), pretentious, snobbish, put-on, full of airs and graces, upper-class, genteel, refined, highfalutin (*informal*), precious. [➡AFFECTATION, SELF-SATISFACTION, AND SNOBBISHNESS; 508] *Opposite:* common.

ladle *n* [➡SPOONS, SCOOPS, AND SHOVELS; 1120]

lady *n* **woman**, female, matron. [➡FEMALE PERSON; 933]

ladybird *type of* **beetle**. [➡BEETLES AND WEEVILS; 1016]

ladybug (*US*) *type of* **beetle**. [➡BEETLES AND WEEVILS; 1016]

ladyfriend (*informal humorous*) *n* [➡SEXUAL AND ROMANTIC RELATIONSHIPS; 964]

lag 1 *v* **drop back**, drop behind, fall back, fall behind, trail, hang back, dawdle, loiter, linger, crawl, straggle, drag your feet, bring up the rear, dally. [➡MOVE SLOWLY; 315] *Opposite:* lead. **2** *v* **insulate**, wrap, wad, protect, pad. [➡DECORATE, ADORN, AND APPLY COATINGS; 406] **3** *n* **interval**, wait, delay, intermission, pause, halt. [➡PAUSES AND PHASES; 56]

laggard *n* **straggler**, dawdler, slowcoach (*informal*), foot-dragger (*informal*), lazybones (*informal*), shirker, slacker, idler, slowpoke (*US informal*). [➡LAZY OR UNSUCCESSFUL PEOPLE; 948] *Opposite:* leader.

lagging *n* **insulation**, wadding, padding, sleeve, skin, sheathing, covering, coat, casing, protection. [➡COVERS AND COATINGS; 1245]

lagoon 1 *n* **inlet**, creek, cove, bay. [➡THE SEAS, OCEANS, AND SHORES; 1041] **2** *n* **lake**, pond, pool, loch, lough, mere (*archaic or literary*). [➡RIVERS, LAKES, AND STREAMS; 1042]

lah-di-dah *see* **la-di-da**.

laid-back (*informal*) *adj* **relaxed**, easygoing, easy, phlegmatic, cool, casual, calm, chilled (*slang*), chilled out (*slang*). [➡CALMNESS, CONFIDENCE, AND COMPOSURE; 537] *Opposite:* tense.

laid off *adj* [➡EMPLOYMENT STATUS; 831]

laid up *adj* **unwell**, ill, sick, bedridden, under the weather, poorly (*informal*), below par (*informal*), ailing (*dated*), injured. [➡ILL AND SICK; 741] *Opposite:* well.

lair 1 *n* (*informal*) **hideout**, den, haunt, hangout (*informal*), retreat, hideaway. [➡UNDESIRABLE ACCOMMODATION; 856] **2** *type of* **den or nest**. [➡ANIMAL OR BIRD ACCOMMODATION; 1078]

laird *n* **landowner**, lord, landlord, owner, proprietor. [➡RICH PEOPLE; 895]

laissez-faire 1 *n* **noninterventionism**, nonintervention, noninvolvement, laxity. [➡NEUTRALITY AND INDIFFERENCE; 554] *Opposite:* intervention. **2** *adj* **noninterventionist**, unrestrictive, permissive, freewheeling, lax, hands-off, relaxed. [➡PERMIT AND ALLOW; 670] *Opposite:* proactive.

laity 1 *n* **laypeople**, congregation, worshippers. [➡RELIGIOUS PEOPLE; 779] *Opposite:* clergy. 2 *n* **nonprofessionals**, outsiders, amateurs, uninitiated. [➡UNSKILLED PERSON; 531]

lake *n* **pond**, lagoon, mere (*archaic or literary*), loch, lough, tarn, water, sea. [➡RIVERS, LAKES, AND STREAMS; 1042]

lakeside *n* **shore**, waterside, water's edge, bank, land, beach. [➡THE SEAS, OCEANS, AND SHORES; 1041]

lama *n* **monk**, priest, brother, Father, clergyman. [➡RELIGIOUS PEOPLE; 779]

lamb 1 *type of* **meat**. [➡TYPES AND CUTS OF MEAT; 1176] 2 *type of* **young animal**. [➡YOUNG ANIMAL; 977]

lambada *n* [➡DANCE; 903]

lambaste *v* **attack**, lay into (*informal*), castigate (*formal*), tell off (*informal*), upbraid, reprimand, criticize, reprove, scold, excoriate (*formal*), deride, slate, lash, condemn, have your knife in. [➡ACCUSE, BLAME, AND CRITICIZE; 642]

lambent 1 *adj* (*literary*) **gleaming**, glowing, radiant, luminous, shining, shimmering, glimmering, soft. [➡DESCRIBING LIGHT; 1227] *Opposite:* dull. 2 *adj* **brilliant**, scintillating, witty, sharp, rapier-like, quick. [➡POSITIVE INTELLECTUAL CHARACTERISTICS; 525] *Opposite:* leaden.

lambswool *type of* **fabric from animals**. [➡FABRICS; 1131]

lamé *type of* **synthetic fabric**. [➡FABRICS; 1131]

lame duck *n* [➡LAZY OR UNSUCCESSFUL PEOPLE; 948]

lament 1 *v* **mourn**, grieve, grieve over, grieve for, cry for, weep, bewail (*formal*), bemoan, howl, moan (*informal*). [➡GIVING VENT TO EMOTIONS; 680] *Opposite:* celebrate. 2 *n* **crying**, lamentation, cry, weeping, dirge, howling, wailing. [➡SOUNDS MADE BY PEOPLE; 1261] *Opposite:* celebration.

lamentable 1 *adj* **regrettable**, deplorable, inexcusable, execrable, appalling, dreadful, hopeless, terrible, bad, unsatisfactory, pitiful, disappointing. [➡BAD AND BADLY; 224] *Opposite:* laudable. 2 *adj* (*literary*) **woeful**, sad, mournful, pitiful. [➡EMOTIONALLY UNPLEASANT AND UPSETTING; 228]

lamentation *n* **lament**, weeping, crying, dirge, howling, mourning, cry. [➡SOUNDS MADE BY PEOPLE; 1261] *Opposite:* celebration.

laminaria *type of* **alga**. [➡MICROORGANISMS, FUNGI, AND ALGAE; 1023]

laminate *v* **cover**, seal, coat, protect, enclose. [➡DECORATE, ADORN, AND APPLY COATINGS; 406]

laminated *adj* **plastic-coated**, coated, covered, bonded, composite, layered, veneered. [➡PHYSICAL TEXTURE; 1221]

lammergeier *type of* **scavenger**. [➡BIRD; 997]

lammergeyer *see* **lammergeier**.

lamp *type of* **light**. [➡LIGHT; 1163]

lampoon 1 *v* **ridicule**, satirize, make fun of, parody, send up (*informal*), caricature. [➡JOKES AND TEASING; 675] 2 *n* **satire**, parody, skit, sketch, sendup (*informal*), caricature. [➡JOKES AND TEASING; 675]

lamppost *n* **streetlight**, streetlamp, light. [➡LIGHT; 1163]

lampshade *n* **shade**, lightshade, cover. [➡SOFT FURNISHINGS, LINEN, AND DRAPERY; 860]

lanai *n* [➡STAGES, PLATFORMS, AND RAISED AREAS; 1097]

lance 1 *n* **spear**, weapon, bayonet, javelin. [➡SWORDS AND KNIVES; 1156] 2 *v* **cut**, pierce, prick, slice into, slice open, puncture, incise, hack. [➡TEAR, BREAK, AND CUT; 361]

lancet *type of* **medical instrument**. [➡HAND TOOLS; 1118]

lancet window *type of* **window**. [➡WINDOWS; 1099]

land 1 *n* **earth**, ground, terrain, countryside. [➡THE COUNTRYSIDE AND OUTDOOR SPACES; 1070] 2 *n* **property**, plot, parcel, acreage, lot, estate, spread (*US regional*). [➡HUMAN SETTLEMENTS; 1069] 3 *n* **homeland**, nation, country, territory. [➡COUNTRIES AND REGIONS; 1066] 4 *v* **arrive**, set down, alight, come down, touch down. [➡ARRIVE BY TRANSPORT; 14] *Opposite:* take off. 5 *v* **acquire**, get, annex, gain, obtain, procure, secure, win. [➡GET; 421] *Opposite:* lose.

land army *n* [➡THE ARMED FORCES; 827]

landau *type of* **wagon or carriage**. [➡VEHICLES; 1144]

landaulet *type of* **wagon or carriage**. [➡VEHICLES; 1144]

landed *adj* **property-owning**, landowning, wealthy, propertied, rich, moneyed, powerful. [➡CLASS STATUS; 889] *Opposite:* landless.

landed gentry *n* [➡CLASS STATUS; 889]

lander *type of* **spacecraft**. [➡SPACE VEHICLES; 1062]

landfall 1 *n* **arrival**, landing, touchdown, docking, mooring. [➡ARRIVAL; 13] 2 *n* **land**, dry land, mainland, terra firma, shore, coast. [➡THE SEAS, OCEANS, AND SHORES; 1041]

landfill *type of* **storage space**. [➡STORES AND STORAGE BUILDINGS; 1087]

land forces *n* **army**, ground forces, troops, infantry, soldiers, foot soldiers, land army. [➡THE ARMED FORCES; 827]

landholder *n* **landowner**, landlord, property-owner, proprietor, owner. [➡OWNERS; 447]

landing 1 *n* **arrival**, alighting, touchdown, docking, mooring. [➡ARRIVAL; 13] 2 *n* **mooring**, pier, jetty, quay, landing stage. [➡WATERWAYS AND SEAWAYS; 1107] 3 *n* [➡STAIRS AND STOREYS; 1101]

landing field *n* **airstrip**, landing strip, runway, airfield, aerodrome, airdrome (*US*). [➡AIRWAYS; 1108]

landing gear *part of* **aircraft**. [➡AIRCRAFT; 1147]

landing stage *n* **jetty**, quay, mooring, landing. [➡WATERWAYS AND SEAWAYS; 1107]

landing strip *n* **runway**, airstrip, landing field, airfield, aerodrome, airdrome (*US*). [➡AIRWAYS; 1108]

landlady 1 *n* **property-owner**, landowner, landholder, proprietor, owner, lessor. [➡OWNERS; 447] *Opposite:* tenant. 2 *n* **licensee**, proprietor, manager, hotelier, innkeeper, lessee. [➡BUSINESS PEOPLE; 794]

landless *adj* **dispossessed**, evicted, ousted, powerless. [➡POVERTY AND POOR; 892] *Opposite:* landed.

landline *n* **cable**, line, phone line, wire, link. [➡TELECOMMUNICATIONS; 1129]

landlocked *adj* **closed in**, blocked-in, noncoastal, interior. [➡THE SEAS, OCEANS, AND SHORES; 1041] *Opposite:* coastal.

landlord 1 *n* **property-owner**, landowner, landholder, proprietor, owner, lessor. [➡OWNERS; 447] *Opposite:* tenant. 2 *n* **licensee**, proprietor, manager, hotelier, innkeeper, lessee. [➡BUSINESS PEOPLE; 794]

landmark 1 *n* **marker**, sight, attraction, sign, signpost, pointer, cairn. [➡PLACE; 1064] 2 *n* **breakthrough**, milestone, revolution, innovation, benchmark, standard, development. [➡DECISIVE MOMENTS; 44] 3 *adj* **milestone**, breakthrough, momentous, revolutionary, innovative, innovatory, groundbreaking, radical, pioneering, historic, significant. [➡MOST IMPORTANT AND MAIN; 194] *Opposite:* run-of-the-mill.

landmass *n* **continent**, land, landform, island, mainland. [➡THE CONTINENTS AND ISLANDS; 1048]

land of make-believe *n* [➡NON-EXISTENT PLACE; 1065]

land on your feet *v* **come out on top**, succeed, get lucky, come through unscathed, find yourself, survive, finish up, wind up (*informal*). [➡SUCCEED AND WIN; 79] *Opposite:* start out.

landowner *n* **property-owner**, landlord, owner, proprietor, landlady. [➡OWNERS; 447] *Opposite:* tenant.

landscape 1 *n* **scenery**, countryside, land, site, scene, setting, background, backdrop, backcloth, panorama, view, topography, geography, terrain, environment, surroundings. [➡THE COUNTRYSIDE AND OUTDOOR SPACES; 1070] 2 *n* **background**, backdrop, circumstances, situation, setting, scene. [➡SITUATIONS; 71] 3 *v* **design**, model, form, shape, plan out, improve, camouflage, disguise. [➡IMPROVE APPEARANCE; 380]

landslide 1 *n* **mudslide**, avalanche, landslip, rock fall. [➡EROSION AND WEATHERING; 1055] 2 *n* **victory**, rout, win, success, triumph, sweep. [➡SUCCESS; 82]

landslip *n* [➡EROSION AND WEATHERING; 1055]

landward *adj* **inland**, inward, inward-looking, inner, innermost. [➡DIRECTION OF MOTION; 346]

landwards *adv* **inland**, ashore, inwards, in. [➡DIRECTION OF MOTION; 346]

land with (*informal*) *v* **saddle with**, burden, dump with, encumber, load, lumber (*informal*). [➡GIVE TOO MUCH; 438]

land yacht *type of* **leisure vehicle**. [➡VEHICLES; 1144]

lane *n* **traffic lane**, right-hand lane, right lane, fast lane, slow lane, overtaking lane, inside lane, outside lane, passing lane, left lane (*US*). [➡ROADS; 1105]

langoustine *type of* **crustacean**. [➡AQUATIC INVERTEBRATE; 1022]

language 1 *n* **tongue**, idiom, lingo (*informal*), dialect, patois, argot, vernacular, jargon, lingua franca, idiolect, parlance. [➡ASPECTS OF LANGUAGE; 683] 2 *n* **communication**, speech, talking. [➡THE SPOKEN WORD; 672] 3 *n* **words**, vocabulary, writing, prose, poetry, style, expression. [➡ASPECTS OF LANGUAGE; 683]

Compare and Contrast: ***language, vocabulary, tongue, idiolect, dialect, slang, jargon, parlance, lingo, -speak, -ese***

CORE MEANING: COMMUNICATION BY WORDS

language the human use of spoken or written words as a communication system, or the particular system of communication prevailing in a specific country, nation, or community; ***vocabulary*** the body of words that make up a particular language; ***tongue*** a particular language used by a specific country, nation, or community; ***idiolect*** an individual person's speech habits or vocabulary; ***dialect*** a regional variety of a language, or a form of a language spoken by members of a particular social class or profession; ***slang*** words, expressions, and turns of phrase used instead of standard terms in casual speech or writing, or by a particular group of people; ***jargon*** terms associated with a particular specialized activity, profession, or culture, especially terms that are not generally understood by outsiders; ***parlance*** the style of speech or writing used by people in a particular context or profession; ***lingo*** (*informal*) the way of speaking associated with a particular, usually specialized, group of people; ***-speak*** a suffix added to nouns to describe the language used by a particular group of people or in a particular context, suggesting that this way of speaking or writing is obscure or difficult to follow; ***-ese*** a suffix added to nouns to describe the language associated with a group of people, especially when it is like a *jargon*.

languid *adj* **unhurried**, relaxed, languorous, lazy, indolent, lethargic, slow, dreamy, droopy, sleepy, somnolent, drowsy, leisurely. [➡MOVING SLOWLY; 105] *Opposite:* vigorous.

languish 1 *v* **suffer**, weaken, fail, flag, deteriorate, waste away, ail (*archaic or literary*). [➡GET WORSE; 382] *Opposite:* thrive. 2 *v* **decline**, fail, sink, teeter, diminish. [➡CEASE TO EXIST; 22] *Opposite:* thrive. 3 *v* **pine**, pine away, fade away, long for, grieve. [➡DESIRE AND WANT; 580]

languishing *adj* [➡TIRED, ASLEEP, AND UNCONSCIOUS; 739]

languor *n* **tiredness**, listlessness, lethargy, sluggishness, dreaminess, slowness, stillness, torpor, sleepiness. [➡LACK OF ACTIVITY; 343] *Opposite:* vigour.

languorous *adj* **tired**, listless, lethargic, languid, sluggish, dreamy, slow, still, torpid, sleepy, unhurried, relaxed. [➡MOVING SLOWLY; 105] *Opposite:* vigorous.

laniard *see* **lanyard**.

lank *adj* **limp**, lifeless, dull, thin, floppy. [➡DESCRIBING HAIR; 487]

lankiness *n* [➡BUILD; 478]

lanky *adj* **gangling**, gangly, long-legged, leggy, angular. [➡BUILD; 478] *Opposite:* rotund.

lantern *type of* **light**. [➡LIGHT; 1163]

lanyard *n* **rope**, cord, line, cable, halyard, vang, ratline. [➡FASTENERS, LINKS, AND NETWORKS; 1246]

lap 1 *part of* **leg or foot**. [➡LEG AND FOOT; 695] 2 *n* **circuit**, tour, round, circle. [➡ SPORTS TERMS; 877] **3** *n* **stage**, leg, part, segment, section, heat, phase. [➡ AREA AND RANGE; 111] **4** *v* **lick up**, slurp, lap up, drink. [➡ DRINK; 712]

lapdog *n* **minion**, toady, sycophant, yes man, lackey, creature. [➡ SUPERFICIAL OR INSINCERE PEOPLE; 951]

lapel *part of* **garment**. [➡ PARTS OF A GARMENT; 870]

lapis lazuli **1** *type of* **blue**. [➡ COLOURS; 1223] **2** *type of* **gemstone**. [➡ PRECIOUS STONES; 1277]

lap of luxury *n* [➡ PLEASANT SITUATIONS; 74]

lapse **1** *n* **error**, slip, failure, mistake, blunder, slip-up (*informal*), hiccup (*informal*). [➡ MISTAKES; 251] **2** *n* **interval**, space, break, delay, pause, wait, hiatus, gap, time lag. [➡ PERIOD OF TIME; 90] **3** *v* **decline**, tumble, descend, drop, fall, slide. [➡ GO DOWNWARDS; 308] *Opposite:* rise. **4** *v* **slip**, tail off, trail off, drift, falter, fade, fail. [➡ GET WORSE; 382] *Opposite:* start up. **5** *v* **come to an end**, end, fail, give up, lose, stop, expire, turn your back on. [➡ CEASE TO EXIST; 22] *Opposite:* renew.

lapsed *adj* **failed**, onetime, former, has-been (*informal*), erstwhile, recent. [➡ PAST; 84] *Opposite:* current.

lapse into **1** *v* **slide into**, slip into, fall into, drift into, resort to. [➡ START AN ACTION; 261] *Opposite:* choose. **2** *v* **revert**, regress, backslide, relapse, fall back, go back to, slide back, return to. [➡ GET WORSE; 382] *Opposite:* progress.

laptop *type of* **computer**. [➡ COMPUTERS AND COMPUTING; 1126]

lap up **1** *v* **lick up**, slurp up, lap. [➡ DRINK; 712] **2** *v* **enjoy**, soak up, bask in, love, glory in, get a kick out of. [➡ LIKE, LOVE, VALUE, AND ENJOY; 579] *Opposite:* hate. **3** *v* **swallow**, fall for, believe, be fooled by, take in, accept, eat up (*informal*). [➡ FORGET, FORGIVE, AND ACCEPT; 749] *Opposite:* disbelieve.

larcenist *n* [➡ CRIMINALS; 821]

larcenous *adj* [➡ ILLEGAL; 816]

larceny (*dated*) *n* **theft**, stealing, robbery, thieving, embezzlement, appropriation, pilfering, burglary, breaking and entering, shoplifting. [➡ CRIMES; 817]

See Compare and Contrast at **theft.**

larch *type of* **evergreen tree**. [➡ EVERGREEN AND CONIFEROUS TREES; 1029]

lard *type of* **cooking fat and oil**. [➡ FATS AND OILS; 1172]

larder *n* **pantry**, cold-room, storeroom, room, cupboard, store, cold store. [➡ STORES AND STORAGE BUILDINGS; 1087]

large **1** *adj* **big**, great, huge, fat, bulky, hefty, outsized, enormous. [➡ LARGE; 1192] *Opposite:* tiny. **2** *adj* **well-built**, big, larger, outsized, overweight, fat, chubby, obese, corpulent (*formal or literary*), heavy, portly, generously proportioned. [➡ BUILD; 478] *Opposite:* small. **3** *adj* **sizable**, considerable, not inconsiderable, great, greater, significant, substantial, generous, copious. [➡ MANY, MUCH, LARGE AMOUNT; 117] *Opposite:* insignificant.

large amount *n* [➡ MANY, MUCH, LARGE AMOUNT; 117]

large-hearted *adj* **generous**, giving, kind, kindly, kind-hearted, warm-hearted, soft-hearted, big-hearted, understanding, sympathetic. [➡ GENEROSITY AND KINDNESS; 496] *Opposite:* mean-spirited.

large intestine *part of* **digestive tract**. [➡ THE DIGESTIVE TRACT; 710]

large it (*informal*) *v* [➡ LEISURE AND RECREATION; 874]

largely *adv* **mainly**, in the main, mostly, for the most part, principally, basically, chiefly, on the whole, by and large, generally. [➡ MAINLY AND PRIMARILY; 138] *Opposite:* particularly.

largeness *n* **size**, bulk, expansiveness, mass, extent, scale. [➡ LARGE; 1192] *Opposite:* smallness.

larger-than-life *adj* **flamboyant**, confident, impressive, exaggerated, overstated, over-the-top (*informal*), blown up, attention-grabbing, arresting. [➡ AFFECTATION, SELF-SATISFACTION, AND SNOBBISHNESS; 508] *Opposite:* understated.

large-scale *adj* **major**, important, significant, extensive, sweeping, comprehensive, across-the-board, all-encompassing, far-reaching, wide-ranging, broad, wholesale, global, international, intercontinental, worldwide, leading, detailed. [➡ IMPORTANT; 195] *Opposite:* small-scale.

largesse **1** *n* **generosity**, charity, liberality, munificence, bounty (*literary*), benevolence. [➡ GENEROSITY AND KINDNESS; 496] *Opposite:* miserliness. **2** *n* **gifts**, handouts, aid, assistance, donations, favours, money. [➡ GIFTS; 439]

larghetto *type of* **musical term**. [➡ MUSICAL TERMS; 912]

largo *type of* **musical term**. [➡ MUSICAL TERMS; 912]

lariat (*US*) *n* **lasso**, noose, loop, rope, tether, riata. [➡ FASTENERS, LINKS, AND NETWORKS; 1246]

lark **1** *n* **game**, joke, prank, caper, high jinks (*informal*), laugh (*informal*), shines (*US*). [➡ JOKES AND TEASING; 675] **2** *type of* **songbird**. [➡ SONGBIRD; 1003]

lark about *v* **fool about**, mess about (*informal*), mess around (*informal*), lark around, play the fool, muck about (*informal*), fool around, goof around (*US informal*). [➡ JOKES AND TEASING; 675] *Opposite:* behave.

lark around *v* **fool around**, mess around (*informal*), have a lark, lark about, play the fool, muck about (*informal*), goof around (*US informal*), goof off (*US informal*). [➡ JOKES AND TEASING; 675] *Opposite:* behave.

larva *type of* **insect stages of development**. [➡ INSECT STAGES; 1020]

larynx *part of* **respiratory system**. [➡ RESPIRATORY ORGANS; 716]

lasagne *type of* **pasta**. [➡ PASTA; 1179]

lascivious *adj* [➡ MORALLY BAD; 776]

laser *type of* **optical instrument**. [➡ OPTICAL INSTRUMENTS; 1123]

lash **1** *n* **cat-o'-nine-tails**, cat, whip, belt, switch, strap, horsewhip. [➡ BLUNT INSTRUMENTS AND WHIPS; 1157] **2** *n* **hit**, whip, blow, stroke, belt (*informal*), whiplash. [➡ PHYSICAL ATTACK AND PUNISHMENT; 416] **3** *v* **smash**, pound, beat, impact, bump, slam. [➡ CONTACT: IMPACT; 414] **4** *v* **criticize**, lambaste, lay into (*informal*), upbraid, castigate (*formal*), slate, condemn. [➡ ACCUSE, BLAME, AND CRITICIZE; 642] **5** *v* **whip**, flog, flay, thrash, belt (*informal*), strike, hit, beat, punish. [➡PHYSICAL ATTACK AND PUNISHMENT; 416] **6** *v* **shake**, jerk, thrash, twitch, thump, whisk, beat. [➡MOVE SOMETHING ON THE SPOT; 337] **7** *v* **tie**, bind, fasten, knot, secure, rope, tie up, fix, attach. [➡FASTEN, LINK, AND JOIN; 409] *Opposite:* loosen.

lashings *n* **loads** (*informal*), lots, heaps (*informal*), masses (*informal*), piles (*informal*), plenty. [➡MANY, MUCH, LARGE AMOUNT; 117] *Opposite:* little.

lash out **1** *v* (*informal*) **spend**, fritter, squander, run through, shell out, splash out, lay out, blow (*slang*) [➡GIVE MONEY; 434] **2** *v* **yell at**, shout at, scream at, hit out, savage, go for, let have it, lay into (*informal*), have a go at (*informal*). [➡ACCUSE, BLAME, AND CRITICIZE; 642] **3** *v* **strike out**, hit out, tear into, let fly, flail around, savage, go for, set on, lay into. [➡PHYSICAL ATTACK AND PUNISHMENT; 416]

lass *n* **girl**, miss, mademoiselle, young woman, daughter, lassie (*informal*), teenager, adolescent. [➡FEMALE PERSON; 933] *Opposite:* lad.

lassie (*informal*) *n* **girl**, young woman, teenager, adolescent, lass, miss, mademoiselle, daughter. [➡FEMALE PERSON; 933] *Opposite:* laddie (*informal*).

lassitude *n* **weariness**, listlessness, apathy, lethargy, fatigue, tiredness, exhaustion, inertia, ennui, jadedness, inactivity, torpor. [➡LACK OF ACTIVITY; 343] *Opposite:* energy.

lasso *n* **noose**, rope, loop, tether, riata, lariat (*US*). [➡FASTENERS, LINKS, AND NETWORKS; 1246]

last **1** *adj* **previous**, latter, past, preceding, latest, former. [➡BEFORE, FIRST, AND PRECEDING; 164] *Opposite:* next. **2** *adj* **final**, end, ultimate, closing, concluding, finishing. [➡AFTER, LAST, AND FOLLOWING; 166] *Opposite:* first. **3** *adj* **remaining**, surviving, extant, final, sole remaining. [➡MORE AND EXCESS; 122] *Opposite:* original. **4** *v* **keep**, stay fresh, keep going, carry on, go on, last out. [➡CONTINUE TO EXIST; 17] *Opposite:* perish (*literary*).

last-ditch *adj* **final**, last-minute, one last, eleventh-hour, desperate, last. [➡AFTER, LAST, AND FOLLOWING; 166]

lasting *adj* **permanent**, long-lasting, long-term, lifelong, eternal, durable, enduring, fixed, undying, unchanging, ongoing, continuing. [➡PERMANENCE: WITHOUT END; 94] *Opposite:* temporary.

last leg *n* [➡END; 54]

lastly *adv* **finally**, last of all, to finish, to conclude, to end, in conclusion, to sum up. [➡SUMMARIZING EXPRESSIONS; 623] *Opposite:* firstly.

last minute *n* **eleventh hour**, final moment, last ditch, last gasp. [➡PROMPTNESS: LATE; 100]

last-minute *adj* **eleventh-hour**, final, last, last-ditch, emergency, rushed. [➡PROMPTNESS: LATE; 100] *Opposite:* early.

last nail in the coffin *n* [➡END; 54]

last name *n* **surname**, family name, name, patronymic, matronymic. [➡NAME AND DESCRIBE; 666] *Opposite:* given name.

last out *v* **survive**, live, go on, continue, persist, keep on, keep up, carry on, persevere. [➡CONTINUE TO EXIST; 17] *Opposite:* fail.

last resort *n* **last chance**, only hope, last-ditch effort, fallback. [➡END; 54]

last straw *n* **final straw**, limit, end, breaking point, bridge too far, finishing touch, deciding factor, end of the line, end of the road, coup de grâce. [➡END; 54]

latch *n* **fastener**, handle, bolt, key, bar, clasp. [➡FASTENERS, LINKS, AND NETWORKS; 1246]

latch on (*informal*) *v* **catch on** (*informal*), understand, get (*informal*), cotton on (*informal*), grasp, comprehend, get the hang of. [➡UNDERSTAND AND GRASP; 760]

latch onto **1** *v* **stay with**, stick to, fasten onto, befriend, take to. [➡ESTABLISHING RELATIONSHIPS WITH OTHERS; 974] *Opposite:* abandon. **2** *v* **take to**, discover, take up with, get into, go in for, pursue, hit on (*US slang*). [➡LIKE, LOVE, VALUE, AND ENJOY; 579]

late **1** *adj* **delayed**, tardy, overdue, belated, unpunctual, last-minute. [➡PROMPTNESS: LATE; 100] *Opposite:* early. **2** *adj* **later**, delayed, deferred, postponed. [➡PROMPTNESS: LATE; 100] *Opposite:* early. **3** *adj* **late-night**, nighttime, evening, twilight, dawn. [➡TIMES OF DAY; 87] *Opposite:* early. **4** *adj* **dead**, deceased (*formal*), dear departed (*formal or literary*), much lamented, late lamented, former, previous. [➡DEAD AND DYING; 925] *Opposite:* living. **5** *adj* **last-minute**, recent, eleventh-hour, last-ditch. [➡PROMPTNESS: LATE; 100] *Opposite:* early. **6** *adv* **belatedly**, unpunctually, tardily, behind schedule, behind time. [➡PROMPTNESS: LATE; 100] *Opposite:* early. **7** *adv* **at the last minute**, too late, late on, finally, at the end, in the nick of time. [➡PROMPTNESS: LATE; 100] *Opposite:* early. **8** *adv* **at night**, in the small hours, in the dead of night, in the evening, at dark, after dark, in the wee hours (*US*). [➡TIMES OF DAY; 87] *Opposite:* early. **9** *adv* **recently**, until recently, lately, of late, latterly. [➡AFTER, LAST, AND FOLLOWING; 166]

See Compare and Contrast at **dead.**

latecomer *n* **straggler**, dawdler, laggard. [➡LAZY OR UNSUCCESSFUL PEOPLE; 948]

lately *adv* **recently**, of late, these days, latterly, currently, just, just now, today, up till now, until now. [➡PAST; 84]

latency *n* **dormancy**, inexpression, inactivity, potential, expectancy, underdevelopment, unconsciousness, invisibility. [➡IMPERCEPTIBLE; 26] *Opposite:* expression.

lateness *n* **tardiness**, unpunctuality, delay, belatedness, deferment, postponement. [➡PROMPTNESS: LATE; 100] *Opposite:* promptness.

latent **1** *adj* **hidden**, covert, buried, concealed, invisible, imperceptible, unseen, undiscovered. [➡IMPERCEPTIBLE; 26] *Opposite:* manifest. **2** *adj* **dormant**, inactive, lurking, embryonic, underlying, suppressed, undeveloped. [➡SECRET AND UNKNOWN; 180]

later *adv* **afterwards**, later on, in a while, anon (*archaic or literary*), shortly, soon, presently. [➡AFTER, LAST, AND FOLLOWING; 166]

lateral *adj* **side**, on the side, adjacent, crossways, horizontal, cross, sideways. [➡ORIENTATION AND ALIGNMENT; 1222]

lateral thinking *n* [➡PSYCHOLOGY AND THE MIND; 770]

latest *adj* **newest**, up-to-the-minute, hottest, state-of-the-art, modern, up-to-date, cutting-edge. [➡NEW, MODERN; 167] *Opposite:* outdated.

latex 1 *n* **sap**, fluid, liquid, gutta-percha, rubber. [➡PARTS OF TREES AND PLANTS; 1026] 2 *type of* **plastic**. [➡PLASTICS; 1133]

lathe *type of* **general tool**. [➡HAND TOOLS; 1118]

lather 1 *n* **foam**, suds, froth, bubbles, soapsuds. [➡FROTH; 1272] 2 *n* (*informal*) **flap** (*informal*), agitation, tizzy (*informal*), anxiety, state (*informal*), panic, dither, pother. [➡FEAR AND PANIC; 544] *Opposite:* calmness. 3 *v* **soap**, lather up, soap up. [➡FROTH AND EFFERVESCE; 390]

latitude 1 *n* **position**, coordinate, location, place. [➡NAVIGATION; 1140] 2 *n* **leeway**, freedom, autonomy, liberty, room, room for manoeuvre, scope, opportunity, space (*informal*), rope, breathing space. [➡FREEDOM AND LIBERTY; 209]

latke *type of* **processed potato**. [➡FRUIT AND VEGETABLES; 1175]

latte *type of* **coffee**. [➡DRINKS; 1186]

latter *adj* **last**, final, concluding, second, end, later. [➡AFTER, LAST, AND FOLLOWING; 166] *Opposite:* former.

latter-day *adj* **modern**, modern-day, contemporary, current. [➡PRESENT; 85]

latterly 1 *adv* **recently**, lately, up till now, currently, of late, in recent times, these days, until now (*US*). [➡PAST; 84] *Opposite:* formerly. 2 *adv* **at the end**, towards the end, in the last part, finally. [➡AFTER, LAST, AND FOLLOWING; 166] *Opposite:* initially.

lattice *n* **frame**, mesh, framework, web, matrix, trellis, wood frame, open-mesh frame. [➡FASTENERS, LINKS, AND NETWORKS; 1246]

laud *v* **praise**, applaud, extol, acclaim, glorify, sing the praises of, praise to the skies, speak well of, pay tribute to, wax lyrical (*literary*), rave about. [➡PRAISE AND ENCOURAGE; 648] *Opposite:* criticize.

laudable *adj* **admirable**, praiseworthy, creditable, worthy, commendable, impressive, meritorious (*formal*). [➡ADMIRABLE AND COMMENDABLE; 186] *Opposite:* despicable.

laudatory *adj* **admiring**, congratulatory, praising, sycophantic, complimentary, approving, approbatory, acclamatory. [➡EXPRESSING RESPECT AND APPROVAL; 638] *Opposite:* damning.

laugh 1 *v* **chuckle**, chortle, guffaw, giggle, snigger, hoot, snort, cackle, titter, have hysterics (*informal*), fall about (*informal*), crease up (*informal*), double up, roll in the aisles, snicker (*US*), fall down laughing (*US*). [➡LAUGHTER; 650] *Opposite:* cry. 2 *n* (*informal*) **fun**, joke, teasing, giggle, hoot (*slang*), lark, prank, game. [➡JOKES AND TEASING; 675]

laughable *adj* **pathetic**, pitiful, derisory, inadequate, ridiculous, absurd, preposterous, ludicrous, embarrassing, unsatisfactory, unimpressive. [➡INAPPROPRIATE AND UNSUITABLE; 225] *Opposite:* impressive.

laugh at *v* **sneer**, jeer, mock, make fun of, tease, deride, disparage, put down (*informal*), ridicule, poke fun at, scoff at. [➡JOKES AND TEASING; 675] *Opposite:* respect.

See Compare and Contrast at **ridicule**.

laughing stock *n* **figure of fun**, joke, fool, clown (*informal*), buffoon, hoot (*slang*), butt. [➡JOKES AND TEASING; 675]

laugh off *v* **downplay**, trivialize, shrug off, joke about, dismiss, discount, take no notice of, ignore, pass over. [➡FORGET, FORGIVE, AND ACCEPT; 749] *Opposite:* face up to.

laugh out of court *v* **ridicule**, mock, make fun of, scoff at, pour scorn on, poke fun at, laugh at, deride, scorn. [➡JOKES AND TEASING; 675]

laughter *n* **happiness**, amusement, hilarity, mirth, merriment, glee, enjoyment. [➡LAUGHTER; 650] *Opposite:* sadness.

laugh your head off *v* [➡LAUGHTER; 650]

launch 1 *v* **dispatch**, send off, discharge (*formal*), send, shoot, fire, release, loose, let fly. [➡DESPATCH AND SEND; 334] 2 *v* **open**, start on (*informal*), start, begin, commence (*formal*), initiate, instigate, get underway, embark on, depart. [➡START AN ACTION; 261] 3 *v* **introduce**, present, inaugurate, unveil, unleash, reveal, market. [➡INSTITUTE AND INAUGURATE; 349] 4 *v* **hurl**, throw, toss, fling, propel, spring, jump, leap. [➡THROW SOMETHING; 335] 5 *n* **presentation**, introduction, promotion, unveiling, inauguration. [➡BEGINNING; 53] 6 *type of* **motor vessel**. [➡SHIPS AND BOATS; 1149]

launching pad *n* **take off point**, springboard, start, base, foundation. [➡BEGINNING; 53]

launch into *v* **start on** (*informal*), embark on, get going on, break into, begin, commence (*formal*). [➡START AN ACTION; 261]

launch out 1 *v* **start**, start afresh, start anew, start out, begin, give it a try. [➡START AN ACTION; 261] *Opposite:* finish. 2 *v* (*informal*) **splash out**, lash out (*informal*), go mad, treat yourself, indulge yourself, spend money like water, splurge. [➡GIVE MONEY; 434] *Opposite:* stint.

launch vehicle *type of* **spacecraft**. [➡SPACE VEHICLES; 1062]

launder 1 *v* **wash**, clean, dry-clean, valet. [➡CLEAN AND POLISH; 404] 2 *v* **legalize**, filter, clean, decontaminate. [➡STEAL AND ROB; 427]

laundry *n* **washing**, wash, clean washing, dirty washing. [➡CLOTHES AND ACCESSORIES; 864]

laurel *type of* **shrub or bush**. [➡BUSHES AND SHRUBS; 1027]

laurels *n* **success**, glory, honour, achievements. [➡SUCCESS; 82]

lava *type of* **stone**. [➡STONES, ROCKS, AND BOULDERS; 1057]

lavatory *type of* **room in public buildings**. [➡TYPES OF ROOM; 1096]

lavender 1 *type of* **shrub or bush**. [➡BUSHES AND SHRUBS; 1027] 2 *type of* **purple**. [➡COLOURS; 1223]

lavish 1 *adj* **abundant**, plentiful, bountiful (*literary*), sumptuous, generous, copious, prolific, fulsome. [➡MANY, MUCH, LARGE AMOUNT; 117] *Opposite:* scanty. 2 *adj* **lush**, luxuriant, luxurious, copious, abundant, rich. [➡MANY, MUCH, LARGE AMOUNT; 117] *Opposite:* sparse. 3 *adj* **extravagant**, profligate, wasteful, over-the-top (*informal*), immoderate (*formal*), unrestrained, excessive. [➡TOO MUCH; 118] *Opposite:* frugal. 4 *v* **heap**, pour, bestow (*formal*), smother, cover, load, shower. [➡GIVE TOO MUCH; 438] *Opposite:* deprive.

lavishly 1 *adv* **plentifully**, generously, abundantly, sumptuously, copiously, bountifully (*literary*), prolifically. [➡MANY, MUCH, LARGE AMOUNT; 117] *Opposite:* scantily. 2 *adv* **extravagantly**, profligately, wastefully, unrestrainedly, immoderately (*formal*), excessively. [➡TOO MUCH; 118] *Opposite:* frugally.

lavishness *n* **lushness**, luxuriousness, luxury, extravagance, richness, abundance, generosity, fulsomeness. [➡MANY, MUCH, LARGE AMOUNT; 117] *Opposite:* frugality.

law 1 *n* **rule**, regulation, decree, act, edict, ruling, commandment, directive, bylaw. [➡THE LAW AND LEGAL AUTHORITY; 814] 2 *n* **principle**, theory, formula, rule. [➡WAYS OF DOING THINGS; 295]

law-abiding *adj* **honest**, straight, upright, upstanding, peaceable, decent, just, respectable [➡MORALLY GOOD; 775] *Opposite:* crooked (*informal*).

law and order 1 *n* **law enforcement**, keeping the peace, order, orderliness, policing. [➡THE LAW AND LEGAL AUTHORITY; 814] *Opposite:* crime. 2 *n* **stability**, harmony, peace, peace and quiet, peacefulness, cooperation. [➡PEACEFULNESS AND GENTLENESS; 215] *Opposite:* unrest.

lawbreaker *n* **criminal**, felon, wrongdoer, convict, offender, delinquent. [➡CRIMINALS; 821]

law enforcement agency (*US*) *n* [➡THE POLICE, ARREST, AND PRE-TRIAL PROCEEDINGS; 818]

law enforcement officer *n* [➡THE POLICE, ARREST, AND PRE-TRIAL PROCEEDINGS; 818]

lawful *adj* **legal**, legalized, legitimate, official, endorsed, allowed, permitted, permissible, decriminalized, legit (*slang*), licit. [➡LEGAL; 815] *Opposite:* unlawful.

lawgiver *n* **lawmaker**, legislator, policymaker. [➡PEOPLE IN LAW COURTS; 820]

lawless *adj* **unruly**, anarchic, uncontrolled, unregulated, ungovernable, anarchistic, uncontrollable. [➡DISORDER AND CHAOS; 246] *Opposite:* law-abiding.

lawlessness *n* **anarchy**, chaos, disorder, mayhem (*informal*), unruliness. [➡CHAOS AND UPROAR; 51] *Opposite:* order.

lawmaker *n* **lawgiver**, legislator, policymaker. [➡POLITICAL OFFICES AND POLITICIANS; 808]

lawn *n* [➡GARDENS; 1073]

lawn bowling (*US*) *type of* **target ball game**. [➡HOBBIES, GAMES, AND SPORTS; 875]

lawsuit *n* **court case**, proceedings, litigation (*technical*), process. [➡TRIAL, PUNISHMENT, AND LEGAL OUTCOMES; 819]

lawyer *n* **legal representative**, brief (*informal*), notary, solicitor, barrister, trial lawyer, public prosecutor, attorney (*US*). [➡PEOPLE IN LAW COURTS; 820]

lax 1 *adj* **lenient**, soft, tolerant, permissive, accepting, nonjudgmental. [➡PERMIT AND ALLOW; 670] 2 *adj* **negligent**, slack, careless, slipshod, sloppy, laid-back (*informal*). [➡NEUTRALITY AND INDIFFERENCE; 554] *Opposite:* strict. 3 *adj* **limp**, loose, flaccid, relaxed, floppy, slack. [➡MALLEABLE AND ELASTIC; 1211] *Opposite:* tense.

laxity 1 *n* **leniency**, tolerance, permissiveness, softness, forbearance (*formal*). [➡LACK OF COMMITMENT AND UNRELIABILITY; 510] *Opposite:* severity. 2 *n* **carelessness**, negligence, sloppiness, slackness. [➡NEUTRALITY AND INDIFFERENCE; 554] *Opposite:* vigilance.

laxness 1 *n* **carelessness**, negligence, sloppiness, slackness. [➡NEUTRALITY AND INDIFFERENCE; 554] *Opposite:* vigilance. 2 *n* **leniency**, tolerance, permissiveness, softness, forbearance (*formal*). [➡LACK OF COMMITMENT AND UNRELIABILITY; 510] *Opposite:* severity.

lay 1 *v* **put down**, place, rest, put, arrange, leave, set, position. [➡MOVE SOMETHING: DOWNWARDS; 330] *Opposite:* pick up. 2 *adj* **untrained**, amateur, nonprofessional, uninitiated, unqualified. [➡UNSKILLED; 530] *Opposite:* professional.

layabout *n* **lazybones** (*informal*), slacker, slouch (*informal*), shirker, timewaster, idler, skiver (*informal*), lounger. [➡LAZY OR UNSUCCESSFUL PEOPLE; 948] *Opposite:* go-getter (*informal*).

lay about *v* **strike out**, hit out, thrash about, flail around, hit, strike, beat, set on, attack, lay into. [➡PHYSICAL ATTACK AND PUNISHMENT; 416]

lay a wager *v* [➡GAMBLE AND TAKE RISKS; 467]

lay bare *v* **reveal**, explain, show, expose, display, bare, uncover. [➡CAUSE TO APPEAR; 5] *Opposite:* cover up.

lay before *v* **set before**, present, put before, submit, set out, show, propose, suggest. [➡PROFFER AND HAND OVER; 432]

lay bets *v* [➡GAMBLE AND TAKE RISKS; 467]

lay claim to *v* **appropriate**, claim, stake a claim to, demand, insist on, request, annex, assume, take possession of, take over. [➡REQUEST AND DEMAND; 664] *Opposite:* renounce.

lay down 1 *v* **put down**, lay aside, put aside, finish with (*informal*), give up, surrender, let fall, set down. [➡MOVE SOMETHING: DOWNWARDS; 330] *Opposite:* take up. 2 *v* **ordain** (*formal*), decree, set down, put down, formulate, rule, dictate. [➡REQUEST AND DEMAND; 664]

lay down the law *v* **order**, boss, order around, boss around, dictate to, throw your weight around, call the tune. [➡REQUEST AND DEMAND; 664]

layer 1 *n* **stratum** (*formal*), level, tier, seam, gradation. [➡DEGREE AND EXTENT; 110] 2 *n* **coating**, coat, sheet, film, deposit, cover. [➡COVERS AND COATINGS; 1245]

layette *n* **baby clothes**, babywear, baby linen, outfit, nursery equipment. [➡SOFT FURNISHINGS, LINEN, AND DRAPERY; 860]

lay in *v* **store**, acquire, hoard, save, stock up, stockpile, squirrel, put by, salt away, gather. [➡GET; 421]

lay into 1 *v* (*informal*) **criticize**, attack, lambaste, get at, round on, tell off (*informal*). [➡ACCUSE, BLAME, AND CRITICIZE; 642] 2 *v* **hit**, attack, beat, thump, thrash, strike, set on. [➡PHYSICAL ATTACK AND PUNISHMENT; 416]

lay it on *v* **exaggerate**, embroider, embellish, overdo, pile on, lay it on thick, lay on with a trowel (*informal*), overstate, boast, ham it up. [➡BOAST; 617] *Opposite:* understate.

lay it on the line (*informal*) *v* **be honest**, be direct, be blunt, be straight, be clear, give somebody an ultimatum, be frank, not beat about the bush, tell it how it is (*informal*), come clean (*informal*). [➡EXPLAIN AND CLARIFY; 611] *Opposite:* lie.

lay it on thick *v* [➡CLAIM, INSIST, AND EMPHASIZE; 615]

lay it on with a trowel (*informal*) *v* [➡CLAIM, INSIST, AND EMPHASIZE; 615]

lay off 1 *v* **dismiss**, suspend, discharge (*formal*), make redundant, sack, let go. [➡EJECT AND EXCLUDE; 341] *Opposite:* take on. 2 *v* (*informal*) **stop**, cease, desist, discontinue, cut out. [➡STOP ACTING; 265] *Opposite:* continue.

layoff 1 *n* **dismissal**, redundancy, sacking (*informal*), discharge (*formal*), letting go, downsizing, rationalization, streamlining. [➡WORK-RELATED ACTIVITIES; 834] 2 *n* **unemployment**, career break, inactivity, rest, joblessness. [➡WORK-RELATED ACTIVITIES; 834] *Opposite:* employment.

lay on *v* **provide**, supply, make available, organize, cater. [➡EQUIP AND SUPPLY; 436]

lay out 1 *v* **explain**, present, describe, outline, set out, detail. [➡EXPLAIN AND CLARIFY; 611] 2 *v* **design**, plan, arrange, organize, prepare, draft. [➡POSITION SOMETHING; 326]

layout *n* **plan**, design, arrangement, outline, draft, blueprint. [➡DRAWINGS, CHARTS, AND TABLES; 595]

layover (*US*) *n* **stopover**, stop, halt, break, stay. [➡PAUSES AND PHASES; 56]

lay to rest *v* [➡BURIAL AND PREPARATION FOR BURIAL; 929]

lay waste *v* [➡DESTRUCTION AND DEMOLITION; 360]

laze *v* **idle**, lounge, loaf, bask, relax, lie, hang about, hang around, kill time. [➡LACK OF ACTIVITY; 343]

laze about *v* **relax**, waste time, dawdle, be idle, bask, loaf about, lie around (*informal*), lounge around, loll around, laze about. [➡LACK OF ACTIVITY; 343]

laze around *v* **relax**, waste time, dawdle, be idle, bask, loaf around, lie around (*informal*), lounge around, loll around, laze around. [➡LACK OF ACTIVITY; 343]

lazily *adv* **idly**, indolently, slowly, languidly, sluggishly, slothfully (*formal*), lethargically. [➡WITHOUT ENTHUSIASM; 288] *Opposite:* energetically.

laziness *n* **idleness**, lethargy, indolence, languor, sluggishness, slothfulness (*formal*). [➡LIFELESS, LAZY, AND UNENTHUSIASTIC; 507] *Opposite:* energy.

lazy *adj* **indolent**, idle, lethargic, languid, sluggish, slothful (*formal*). [➡LIFELESS, LAZY, AND UNENTHUSIASTIC; 507] *Opposite:* energetic.

lazybones (*informal*) *n* **layabout**, slacker, skiver (*informal*), shirker, loafer, idler, slouch (*informal*), sloth, parasite, bum (*informal*), lollygagger (*US dated*), goldbricker (*US informal*). [➡LAZY OR UNSUCCESSFUL PEOPLE; 948] *Opposite:* worker.

lea (*literary*) *n* **meadow**, field, pasture, grassland. [➡THE COUNTRYSIDE AND OUTDOOR SPACES; 1070]

leach *v* **leak**, filter, percolate, trickle, seep. [➡LIQUID EMISSION; 371]

lead 1 *v* **guide**, indicate, direct, escort, pilot, precede, steer, front, head, conduct, usher. [➡ACCOMPANY AND FOLLOW; 338] *Opposite:* follow. 2 *v* **be in charge of**, run, control, command, direct, manage, head, steer. [➡CAUSE TO HAPPEN; 31] 3 *v* **be in the lead**, take the lead, be the forerunner, be in front, have an advantage. [➡SUCCEED AND WIN; 79] *Opposite:* trail. 4 *n* **frontrunner** (*informal*), leader, spearhead, leading light, trailblazer, groundbreaker. [➡IMPORTANT OR FAMOUS PEOPLE; 893] 5 *n* **advantage**, advance, start, head start, flying start. [➡SOURCE OF HAPPINESS, PLEASURE, OR IMPROVEMENT; 210] 6 *n* **precedent**, example, style, pattern, model, practice. [➡INDICATIONS, SIGNS, AND WARNINGS; 68] 7 *n* **clue**, tip, indication, information, hint, pointer. [➡EVIDENCE AND PROOF; 69] 8 *n* **leash**, chain, tether, restraint, rope, halter, string. [➡FASTENERS, LINKS, AND NETWORKS; 1246] 9 *adj* **principal**, chief, main, central, prime, top. [➡MOST IMPORTANT AND MAIN; 194] 10 *type of* **metal**. [➡METALS; 1275]

See Compare and Contrast at **guide**.

lead astray *v* **mislead**, misinform, lead on, hoodwink, delude, deceive, trick, seduce, corrupt, lead up the garden path. [➡DECEPTION AND LIES; 661]

leaden 1 *adj* **grey**, steely, ashen, dull, grim, dark, gloomy, sombre, cloudy, overcast. [➡CLOUDY AND RAINY WEATHER; 1052] *Opposite:* bright. 2 *adj* **heavy**, ponderous, weighty, sluggish, stodgy (*informal*). [➡WEIGHT: HEAVY; 1204] *Opposite:* light. 3 *adj* **sluggish**, laboured, slow, dragging, crawling, plodding, unhurried, leisurely. [➡MOVING SLOWLY; 105] *Opposite:* quick. 4 *adj* **lifeless**, dull, dreary, flat, stodgy (*informal*), monotonous, boring, uninteresting, unexciting, forced. [➡DIFFICULTY AND COMPLEXITY; 243] *Opposite:* lively.

leader 1 *n* **guide**, director, organizer, mentor, guru, adviser. [➡IMPORTANT OR FAMOUS PEOPLE; 893] 2 *n* **frontrunner** (*informal*), spearhead, leading light, trailblazer, groundbreaker, lead, forerunner. [➡IMPORTANT OR FAMOUS PEOPLE; 893] 3 *n* **head**, chief, manager, superior, principal, boss, supervisor, kingpin (*informal*), top dog (*informal*). [➡BOSSES AND MANAGEMENT; 965]

leadership *n* **management**, control, guidance, headship, direction, governance (*formal*). [➡RELATIONSHIP TO ANOTHER; 973]

lead glass *type of* **glass**. [➡GLASS; 1135]

lead-in *n* **introduction**, preamble, preface, prelude, preliminary, way in, opener. [➡BEGINNING; 53] *Opposite:* conclusion.

leading *adj* **prominent**, foremost, important, principal, chief, top, primary. [➡MOST IMPORTANT AND MAIN; 194] *Opposite:* secondary.

leading article *n* **editorial**, leader, opinion, view, comment, piece. [➡NEWSPAPERS; 606]

leading edge *n* **forefront**, cutting edge, sharp end, vanguard, avant-garde, van, fore (*literary*), front, lead, spearhead. [➡BEGINNING; 53]

leading light *n* **big name**, top name, star, superstar, celebrity, luminary, kingpin (*informal*), expert, authority, leader, top dog (*informal*). [➡IMPORTANT OR FAMOUS PEOPLE; 893] *Opposite:* nobody.

lead off *v* **begin**, start, start off, commence (*formal*), open, kick off (*informal*), set in motion, set the ball rolling, get going. [➡START AN ACTION; 261] *Opposite:* end.

lead on *v* **entice**, lure, tempt, seduce, attract, cajole, persuade. [➡APPEAL TO AND AROUSE INTEREST; 576]

lead the way *v* **blaze a trail**, set a trend, originate, break new ground, break through, spearhead. [➡START AN ACTION; 261]

lead time *n* **notice**, run-up, advance notice, warning, notification, foreknowledge (*formal*). [➡FUTURE; 86]

lead to *v* **cause**, bring about, make possible, initiate, set in motion, produce, result in. [➡CAUSE TO HAPPEN; 31]

lead up the garden path *v* [➡DECEPTION AND LIES; 661]

lead up to 1 *v* **prepare for**, prepare the way, prepare the ground, sow the seeds, gear up, make ready, precede. [➡PREPARE FOR ACTION; 290] 2 *v* **approach**, come to, get to, get round to. [➡START AN ACTION; 261]

leaf 1 *n* **foliage**, greenery, sprig, spray, frond, shoot. [➡PARTS OF TREES AND PLANTS; 1026] 2 *n* **page**, sheet, folio, side. [➡PARTS OF BOOKS AND DOCUMENTS; 594] 3 *n* **sheet**, foil, plate, lamina, film, coating, patina. [➡COVERS AND COATINGS; 1245] 4 *n* **flap**, foldout, projection, section, piece. [➡EXTREMITIES OF PHYSICAL OBJECTS; 1249]

leafcutter ant *type of* **ant**. [➡ANTS; 1014]

leaflet *n* **booklet**, brochure, pamphlet, flier, handbill, handout, circular. [➡ADVERTISING AND PUBLICITY; 605]

leaf through *v* **look through**, flick through, skim, browse, flip, scan, riffle. [➡LOOKING AND LOOKS; 701]

leafy *adj* **green**, verdant, lush, luxuriant, rank. [➡VEGETATION; 1025] *Opposite:* bare.

league *n* **association**, group, union, confederation, club, alliance, coalition, federation, confederacy. [➡GROUPS WITH A COMMON INTEREST; 938]

leak 1 *n* **escape**, seepage, leakage, outflow, drip, trickle. [➡EMIT AND EMANATE; 362] 2 *n* **disclosure**, betrayal, giveaway, revelation, release. [➡INFORM AND ANNOUNCE; 612] 3 *v* **seep**, escape, pour out, trickle, drip, ooze. [➡LIQUID EMISSION; 371] 4 *v* **disclose**, reveal, give away, betray, uncover, let slip. [➡BETRAY CONFIDENCES AND GOSSIP; 619]

leakage *n* **leak**, escape, seepage, outflow, drip, trickle. [➡EMIT AND EMANATE; 362]

leak out *v* **emerge**, get out, slip out, come out, come to light, get round. [➡APPEAR AND EMERGE; 3]

leakproof *adj* **watertight**, waterproof, sealed, hermetic, rainproof, showerproof, damp-proof. [➡IN GOOD REPAIR; 1231] *Opposite:* leaky.

leaky 1 *adj* **leaking**, holey, sieve-like, dripping, drippy, permeable. [➡IN BAD REPAIR; 1233] *Opposite:* watertight. 2 *adj* (*informal*) **unsecured**, unsafe, indiscreet, loose, lax. [➡DANGEROUS; 237] *Opposite:* secure.

lean 1 *v* **bend**, bend over, bend forwards, incline, tilt, tip, slant, bow, slope. [➡ASSUME A POSITION; 318] 2 *v* **rest**, prop, support, place, put. [➡MOVE SOMETHING: INTO A NEW POSITION OR OVERTURN; 331] 3 *v* **tend**, incline, be disposed, favour, prefer, like better. [➡LIKE, LOVE, VALUE, AND ENJOY; 579] 4 *adj* **thin**, slender, slim, wiry, sinewy, spare, trim, bony, angular. [➡BUILD; 478] *Opposite:* stout.

See Compare and Contrast at **thin**.

leaning *n* **inclination**, tendency, bent, affinity, preference, proclivity, propensity (*formal*), liking, penchant, predilection (*formal*). [➡LIKE, LOVE, VALUE, AND ENJOY; 579] *Opposite:* aversion.

lean on 1 *v* **depend on**, rely on, trust, count on. [➡CERTAINTY; 562] 2 *v* (*informal*) **intimidate**, pressurize, put pressure on, oblige, coerce, induce, require. [➡CAUSE OR COMPEL TO ACT; 272]

lean-to *type of* **outbuilding**. [➡ANCILLARY BUILDINGS; 1079]

leap 1 *v* **jump**, bound, dive, soar, fly, hurdle, bounce, hop, spring, vault. [➡BOUNCE, UNDULATE, AND VIBRATE; 309] 2 *v* **increase**, rise, shoot up, go up, jump, mount, ascend, surge. [➡CHANGE OF SIZE: BIGGER; 393] *Opposite:* drop. 3 *n* **bound**, jump, dive, spring, hop. [➡BOUNCE, UNDULATE, AND VIBRATE; 309] 4 *n* **rise**, increase, jump, hike, climb, spike, surge. [➡CHANGE OF INTENSITY: MORE; 395] *Opposite:* drop.

leap at *v* **jump at**, seize, grab, go for (*informal*), clutch, accept. [➡TAKE SOMETHING AWAY; 426] *Opposite:* baulk.

leapfrog 1 *v* **jump**, vault, leap, bound, spring. [➡BOUNCE, UNDULATE, AND VIBRATE; 309] 2 *v* **advance**, shoot ahead, get ahead, get on, pull ahead, catapult, jump ahead, make strides. [➡MOVE PAST, INTO, OR THROUGH SOMETHING; 332] 3 *v* **overtake**, pass, leave behind, outstrip, leave standing, step over. [➡MOVE PAST, INTO, OR THROUGH SOMETHING; 332] 4 *v* **circumvent**, evade, avoid, sidestep, bypass, dodge. [➡NOT PAY ATTENTION; 765]

leap out at *v* **stand out**, stick out, jump out, hit somebody in the face, impact, strike. [➡APPEAR AND EMERGE; 3] *Opposite:* hide.

leap year *type of* **time period**. [➡TIMES OF YEAR; 88]

learn 1 *v* **study**, absorb, pick up, acquire, cram (*informal*), swot (*informal*), mug up (*informal*), hit the books (*US informal*). [➡STUDYING; 844] 2 *v* **find out**, hear, discover, realize, ascertain (*formal*), gather, understand, come to know. [➡LEARN AND DISCOVER; 763]

learned *adj* **erudite**, educated, scholarly, academic, cultured, well-read, well-educated, knowledgeable. [➡KNOWLEDGE AND WISDOM; 559] *Opposite:* uneducated.

learner *n* **beginner**, apprentice, student, pupil, novice, greenhorn, initiate. [➡UNSKILLED PERSON; 531] *Opposite:* expert.

learning *n* **knowledge**, education, erudition, scholarship, culture, wisdom, book learning. [➡KNOWLEDGE AND WISDOM; 559] *Opposite:* ignorance.

lease 1 *v* **rent out**, hire out, let, charter, let out. [➡LEND, LEASE, AND BORROW; 429] 2 *v* **rent**, hire, charter. [➡LEND, LEASE, AND BORROW; 429]

See Compare and Contrast at **hire**.

lease out *v* [➡LEND, LEASE, AND BORROW; 429]

leash *n* **lead**, chain, tether, string, rope, restraint, halter. [➡FASTENERS, LINKS, AND NETWORKS; 1246]

least *adj* **smallest**, slightest, tiniest, minimum. [➡FEW, LITTLE, SMALL AMOUNT; 119] *Opposite:* most.

leastways (*informal*) *adv* **in any case**, anyway, at least, at any rate, in spite of. [➡ALTHOUGH, NEVERTHELESS, AND DESPITE; 170]

leastwise (*US regional informal*) *adv* **in any case**, anyway, at least, at any rate, in spite of. [➡ALTHOUGH, NEVERTHELESS, AND DESPITE; 170]

leather

◆ *types of leather*
buckskin, calf, calfskin, chamois, hide, kid, morocco, patent leather, pigskin, rawhide, sheepskin, snakeskin, suede

leave 1 *v* **go away**, depart, go, run off, abscond, disappear, exit, vamoose (*US slang*). [➡ABSENT ONESELF; 8] *Opposite:* stay. 2 *v* **put down**, set down, put, put away, place, leave behind. [➡POSITION SOMETHING; 326] *Opposite:* remove. 3 *v* **bequeath**, pass on, hand down, donate, legate, consign, entrust, will. [➡BEQUEATH AND BEQUESTS; 433] 4 *v* **result in**, cause, effect (*formal*), bring about. [➡CAUSE TO HAPPEN; 31] 5 *v* **delay**, defer, put off, avoid, hold off, put aside. [➡SHIRK AND DELAY; 274] 6 *v* **abandon**, desert, renounce, ditch (*informal*), dump (*informal*), forsake, quit (*archaic*), drop. [➡REFUSING OR REJECTING RELATIONS; 975] 7 *v* **set aside**, allow, give, permit, assign, allot, hand over. [➡PERMIT AND ALLOW; 670] 8 *n* **holiday**, sabbatical, time off, time out (*US*), vacation. [➡PERIOD OF REST; 91] 9 *n* (*formal*) **permission**, consent, leave of absence, authority, authorization, dispensation. [➡PERMIT AND ALLOW; 670]

leave alone *v* **let alone**, let be, leave in peace, leave well enough alone, pay no attention, ignore, disregard, leave somebody to himself/herself, get off somebody's back (*slang*). [➡REFUSING OR REJECTING RELATIONS; 975] *Opposite:* harass.

leave be *v* **let alone**, let be, leave in peace, leave well enough alone, pay no attention, ignore, disregard, leave somebody to himself/herself, get off somebody's back (*slang*). [➡REFUSING OR REJECTING RELATIONS; 975] *Opposite:* harass.

leave behind 1 *v* **overtake**, outstrip, outpace, surpass, leave standing, shake off, outdo, move ahead of, get ahead of, outrun, leave in the dust (*US*). [➡BEAT AND DEFEAT; 80] *Opposite:* fall behind. 2 *v* **put behind you**, escape, evade, get away from, put to one side, put away, dismiss, forget, free yourself of, shed. [➡FORGET, FORGIVE, AND ACCEPT; 749] 3 *v* **abandon**, get rid of, cast off, leave, forget, walk out on (*informal*), forsake, desert, shed. [➡GET RID OF SOMETHING; 452] *Opposite:* retain.

leave in peace *v* **leave alone**, let be, let alone, leave somebody to himself/herself, go away, leave well enough alone, pay no attention, ignore, disregard, leave somebody to his/her own devices, get off somebody's back (*slang*), get off somebody's case (*slang*). [➡REFUSING OR REJECTING RELATIONS; 975] *Opposite:* harass.

leave much to be desired *v* **be unsatisfactory**, disappoint, let down, not make the grade, fall short, not be up to scratch (*informal*). [➡FAIL OR BE UNSUCCESSFUL; 75] *Opposite:* pass muster.

leave no stone unturned *v* **do all you can**, do your utmost, pull out all the stops, spare no effort, try everything, move heaven and earth, try your best, stop at nothing. [➡HARD WORK OR EFFORT; 299]

leave of absence *n* [➡PERIOD OF REST; 91]

leave off *v* **stop**, desist, cease, give over (*informal*), refrain, discontinue. [➡STOP ACTING; 265] *Opposite:* carry on.

leave out *v* **omit**, exclude, count out, ignore, except (*formal*), overlook. [➡NOT PAY ATTENTION; 765] *Opposite:* include.

leave-taking (*literary*) *n* **farewell**, goodbye, sendoff, departure, separation, parting, adieu, exit, going, valediction (*formal*). [➡END; 54] *Opposite:* greeting.

leavings *n* **leftovers**, scraps, dregs (*literary*), remnants, remains, castoffs, orts (*US*). [➡REMAINDER AND REMAINDERS; 123]

lecherous *adj* **lewd**, lustful, lascivious, libidinous (*formal*), randy (*informal*), lusty. [➡MORALLY BAD; 776]

lectern *n* **bookstand**, reading stand, reading desk, stand, bookrest. [➡FURNITURE; 858]

lecture 1 *n* **talk**, address, sermon, speech, homily, oration, discourse, allocution (*formal*). [➡NEUTRAL ONE-WAY COMMUNICATION; 49] 2 *n* **reprimand**, ticking-off (*informal*), talking-to (*informal*), dressing-down, scolding, telling-off (*informal*), tongue-lashing. [➡CRITICISMS AND ANGRY OUTBURSTS; 50] 3 *v* **teach**, address, instruct, talk, hold forth, pontificate. [➡INSTRUCT AND TEACH; 610] 4 *v* **harangue**, criticize, tell off (*informal*), tick off (*informal*), scold, reprove, censure, castigate (*formal*), reprimand, upbraid. [➡ACCUSE, BLAME, AND CRITICIZE; 642]

lecture hall *n* [➡BUILDINGS FOR PUBLIC ENTERTAINMENT; 1083]

lecturer *n* **speaker**, public speaker, speechmaker, orator, presenter, spokesperson, debater. [➡EDUCATORS; 840]

lecture room *n* [➡BUILDINGS FOR PUBLIC ENTERTAINMENT; 1083]

lecture theatre *n* [➡BUILDINGS FOR PUBLIC ENTERTAINMENT; 1083]

LED *type of* **light**. [➡LIGHT; 1163]

lederhosen *type of* **trousers**. [➡GARMENTS AND OUTFITS; 865]

ledge 1 *n* **shelf**, sill, niche, ridge, rack, bookshelf, mantelpiece, window ledge, windowsill, bracket. [➡WINDOWS; 1099] 2 *n* **outcrop**, ridge, sill, shelf, foothold, projection, protrusion, protuberance, bulge, extension. [➡EXTREMITIES OF PHYSICAL OBJECTS; 1249] 3 *n part of* **window**. [➡WINDOWS; 1099]

ledger *n* **book**, account book, record book, record, register, archive, journal. [➡RECORDS; 586]

lee *n* **shelter**, cover, protection, shadow, shade. [➡SAFE BUILDINGS OR PLACES; 1092]

leech *n* [➡SUPERFICIAL OR INSINCERE PEOPLE; 951]

leek *type of* **vegetable**. [➡FRUIT AND VEGETABLES; 1175]

leer 1 *v* **smirk**, ogle, eye, sneer, stare, make eyes. [➡FACIAL

EXPRESSION; 652] **2** *n* **sneer**, grimace, smirk, evil eye, stare. [➡ FACIAL EXPRESSION; 652]

leery (*informal*) *adj* **suspicious**, wary, doubting, doubtful, circumspect, cautious, skittish, untrusting, watchful, questioning, mistrustful, hesitant, sceptical. [➡ UNCERTAINTY; 560] *Opposite:* confident.

lees *n* [➡ REMAINDER AND REMAINDERS; 123]

leeward *adj* **protected**, sheltered, shielded. [➡ GENERAL LOCATIONS; 159]

leeway *n* **scope**, flexibility, margin, freedom, latitude, breathing space, breathing room. [➡ FREEDOM AND LIBERTY; 209]

left-hand *adj* **left**, leftward, port. [➡ GENERAL LOCATIONS; 159] *Opposite:* right-hand.

left-handed *adj* **anticlockwise**, right to left, circular, round, helical, spiral, counterclockwise (*US*). [➡ DIRECTION OF MOTION; 346] *Opposite:* right-handed.

leftie (*informal*) *n* [➡ PHILOSOPHICAL AND POLITICAL THINKERS; 782]

leftism *n* [➡ PHILOSOPHIES AND BELIEFS; 781]

leftist *n* [➡ PHILOSOPHICAL AND POLITICAL THINKERS; 782]

leftover *n* **relic**, hangover, vestige, remnant, remainder, residue, remains, legacy, inheritance. [➡ REMAINDER AND REMAINDERS; 123]

leftovers *n* **scraps**, remains, dregs (*literary*), what's left, table scraps, leavings, remnants, orts (*US*). [➡ REMAINDER AND REMAINDERS; 123]

left-wing *adj* **progressive**, reformist, leftist. [➡ STYLES AND SYSTEMS OF GOVERNMENT; 806] *Opposite:* right-wing.

left-winger *n* **progressive**, reformist, leftist. [➡ PHILOSOPHICAL AND POLITICAL THINKERS; 782] *Opposite:* right-winger.

leg **1** *n* **limb**, foreleg, hindleg, peg (*informal*), pins (*informal*). [➡ LEG AND FOOT; 695] **2** *n* **pole**, foot, support, stand, base, prop, rod, shaft, brace, bracket. [➡ SUPPORTS AND BASES; 1254] **3** *n* **stage**, phase, lap, step, part, section, segment. [➡ PAUSES AND PHASES; 56] **4** *type of* **cut**. [➡ TYPES AND CUTS OF MEAT; 1176] **5** *part of* **garment**. [➡ PARTS OF A GARMENT; 870]

leg

◆ *parts of a leg or foot*
ankle, big toe, calf, foot, haunch, heel, instep, knee, lap, little toe, shin, sole, thigh, toe, toenail

legacy **1** *n* **bequest**, inheritance, heirloom, heritage, birthright, gift, money. [➡ BEQUEATH AND BEQUESTS; 433] **2** *n* **relic**, hangover, vestige, remnant, remainder, residue, remains, consequence, leftover. [➡ REMAINDER AND REMAINDERS; 123]

legal *adj* **lawful**, permissible, permitted, allowed, authorized, aboveboard, legitimate, official, licit, rightful, legalized, decriminalized. [➡ LEGAL; 815] *Opposite:* illegal.

Compare and Contrast: *legal, lawful, decriminalized, legalized, legitimate, licit*

CORE MEANING: DESCRIBES SOMETHING THAT IS PERMITTED, RECOGNIZED, OR REQUIRED BY LAW

legal permitted, recognized, or required by law; ***lawful*** a less common word meaning the same as legal; ***decriminalized*** no longer categorized as a criminal offence; ***legalized*** previously categorized as illegal and now declared legal; ***legitimate*** complying with the law, or under the law; ***licit*** (*formal*) a rarely used word meaning the same as legal.

legal eagle (*slang*) *n* **lawyer**, barrister, solicitor, advocate, counsel. [➡ TRIAL, PUNISHMENT, AND LEGAL OUTCOMES; 819]

legalese *n* **jargon**, cant, gobbledegook (*informal disapproving*), terminology, mumbo jumbo (*informal*). [➡ MEANINGLESS SPEECH OR WRITING; 677]

legality *n* **validity**, lawfulness, rightfulness, legitimacy. [➡ LEGAL; 815]

legalization *n* **ratification**, authorization, certification, validation, endorsement. [➡ TRIAL, PUNISHMENT, AND LEGAL OUTCOMES; 819] *Opposite:* criminalization.

legalize *v* **decriminalize**, authorize, sanction, allow, permit, validate, enact, decree. [➡ TRIAL, PUNISHMENT, AND LEGAL OUTCOMES; 819] *Opposite:* prohibit.

legate *n* **representative**, envoy, ambassador, emissary, diplomat, messenger. [➡ REPRESENTATIVES AND PATRONS; 968]

legato *type of* **musical term**. [➡ MUSICAL TERMS; 912]

legend **1** *n* **fable**, myth, tale, lore, folklore, fairy tale, folk tale. [➡ THE ORAL TRADITION; 678] **2** *n* **star**, celebrity, big name, icon, personality, prodigy, superstar. [➡ IMPORTANT OR FAMOUS PEOPLE; 893]

legendary **1** *adj* **fabled**, mythical, mythological, imaginary, fabulous. [➡ FALSE AND UNREAL; 174] **2** *adj* **famous**, renowned, well-known, celebrated, great, illustrious, eminent. [➡ KNOWN AND FAMOUS; 182]

legerdemain *n* [➡ SKILLS, TALENTS, AND ABILITIES; 527]

leggings *type of* **trousers**. [➡ GARMENTS AND OUTFITS; 865]

leggy *adj* [➡ BUILD; 478]

legible *adj* **clear**, readable, intelligible, decipherable, understandable, comprehensible. [➡ CONCISE AND CLEAR; 203] *Opposite:* illegible.

legion *n* **multitude**, host, team, crowd, throng, mass, gang, band, group. [➡ GROUPS OF PEOPLE; 935]

legionnaire *n* [➡ MILITARY PERSONNEL; 828]

legislate *v* **enact**, pass, establish, lay down the law, decree, constitute (*formal*), authorize, promulgate (*formal*). [➡ TRIAL, PUNISHMENT, AND LEGAL OUTCOMES; 819]

legislation **1** *n* **lawmaking**, lawgiving, legislature, regulation. [➡ THE LAW AND LEGAL AUTHORITY; 814] **2** *n* **laws**, legal code, body of law, bill, rule, guidelines, statute, decree, code, law. [➡ THE LAW AND LEGAL AUTHORITY; 814]

legislative *adj* **lawmaking**, parliamentary, governmental, judicial, jurisdictive, statutory. [➡GOVERNMENT AND POLITICS; 805]

legislator *n* [➡THE POLICE, ARREST, AND PRE-TRIAL PROCEEDINGS; 818]

legislature *n* **government**, parliament, administration, senate, assembly, council. [➡LEGISLATIVE BODIES AND LEGISLATION; 809]

leg it (*informal*) *v* [➡RUN AWAY AND AVOID; 10]

legit (*slang*) *adj* [➡LEGAL; 815]

legitimacy 1 *n* **legality**, lawfulness, validity, rightfulness. [➡LEGAL; 815] 2 *n* **acceptability**, rightfulness, correctness, justice. [➡ACCEPTABLE AND PASSABLE; 220] 3 *n* **sincerity**, genuineness, realness, authenticity, validity, fairness. [➡TRUE AND REAL; 172]

legitimate 1 *adj* **lawful**, rightful, valid, legal. [➡LEGAL; 815] *Opposite:* unlawful. 2 *adj* **reasonable**, acceptable, justifiable, logical, valid, sensible, recognized. [➡ACCEPTABLE AND PASSABLE; 220] *Opposite:* unreasonable. 3 *adj* **genuine**, sincere, real, valid, authentic, appropriate, reasonable. [➡TRUE AND REAL; 172] *Opposite:* spurious.

legitimately 1 *adv* **legally**, lawfully, rightfully, validly. [➡LEGAL; 815] *Opposite:* unlawfully. 2 *adv* **reasonably**, acceptably, justifiably, logically, validly, sensibly. [➡TRUE AND REAL; 172] *Opposite:* unreasonably.

leg-pull (*informal*) *n* **joke**, practical joke, deception, trick, tease, wind-up (*informal*), laugh (*informal*). [➡JOKES AND TEASING; 675]

leg-pulling (*informal*) *n* [➡JOKES AND TEASING; 675]

legroom *n* **room**, elbowroom (*informal*), space, freedom. [➡FREEDOM AND LIBERTY; 209]

legume *n* **leguminous plant**, pea, pulse, bean. [➡FRUIT AND VEGETABLES; 1175]

legwarmer *n* **sock**, stocking, legging, gaiter, puttee, anklewarmer. [➡HABERDASHERY, MILLINERY, AND LINGERIE; 867]

legwork (*informal*) *n* **research**, preparation, homework, groundwork, spadework, dirty work. [➡HARD WORK OR EFFORT; 299]

lei *n* [➡ORNAMENTS AND DECORATIONS; 1247]

leisure *n* **free time**, spare time, time off, holiday, leisure time, freedom, relaxation, rest, ease, R and R, vacation, time out (*US*). [➡LEISURE AND RECREATION; 874] *Opposite:* work.

leisure centre *n* **sports centre**, gym (*informal*), gymnasium, club, swimming pool, swimming baths. [➡BUILDINGS FOR PUBLIC ENTERTAINMENT; 1083]

leisured *adj* **rich**, wealthy, affluent, moneyed, propertied, well-off, well-to-do, prosperous, well-heeled (*informal*), comfortable. [➡WEALTH AND WEALTHY; 891] *Opposite:* poor.

leisurely *adj* **unhurried**, easy, relaxed, restful, relaxing, laid-back (*informal*), slow, gentle. [➡MOVING SLOWLY; 105] *Opposite:* frantic.

leisure pursuit *n* [➡LEISURE AND RECREATION; 874]

leisure time *n* [➡PERIOD OF REST; 91]

leisurewear *n* **sportswear**, casualwear, casual clothes, casuals, mufti. [➡GARMENTS AND OUTFITS; 865]

leitmotif *n* **motif**, theme, strand, element, topic, subject, subject matter. [➡NOTES AND CHORDS; 909]

lekvar *type of* **preserve**. [➡SUGAR AND PRESERVES; 1183]

lemming 1 *n* **conformist**, sheep, copycat (*informal*), imitator, follower. [➡LAZY OR UNSUCCESSFUL PEOPLE; 948] *Opposite:* nonconformist. 2 *type of* **rodent**. [➡RODENT; 989]

lemon 1 *n* **lemonade**, bitter lemon, fruit juice, squash, cordial. [➡DRINKS; 1186] 2 *n* (*informal*) **dud** (*informal*), nonstarter (*informal*), no-hoper (*informal*), failure, washout (*informal*), flop (*informal*), old banger (*informal*), jalopy (*dated informal*). [➡FAILURE; 77] *Opposite:* winner. 3 *type of* **citrus**. [➡FRUIT AND VEGETABLES; 1175] 4 *type of* **yellow**. [➡COLOURS; 1223]

lemonade *n* [➡DRINKS; 1186]

lemon curd *type of* **preserve**. [➡SUGAR AND PRESERVES; 1183]

lemon grass *type of* **herb**. [➡HERBS AND SPICES; 1174]

lemon sole *type of* **flatfish**. [➡SEA FISH; 1009]

lemon squeezer *type of* **utensil**. [➡TABLEWARE, CUTLERY, AND KITCHENWARE; 861]

lemony *adj* **lemon-flavoured**, lemon, lemon-yellow, light-yellow, pale-yellow, yellow, citrus. [➡TASTE; 704] *Opposite:* sweet.

lemon yellow *type of* **yellow**. [➡COLOURS; 1223]

lemur *type of* **primate**. [➡PRIMATE; 988]

lend 1 *v* **loan**, advance, give, offer. [➡LEND, LEASE, AND BORROW; 429] *Opposite:* borrow. 2 *v* **provide**, offer, give, impart, afford (*formal*), add, inject, bestow (*formal*), contribute. [➡GIVE AND PROVIDE; 431] *Opposite:* take away.

lend a hand *v* **help**, help out, give somebody a hand, do your bit, chip in (*informal*), assist, pull your weight, do your part. [➡HELP; 294] *Opposite:* hinder.

lend an ear *v* [➡LISTEN AND LISTENERS; 709]

lender *n* **giver**, moneylender, financier, creditor, investor, mortgagee, owner, bank, building society. [➡PEOPLE INVOLVED IN FINANCE; 804]

length 1 *n* **distance**, span, measurement, extent, dimension, size, interval, stretch. [➡LENGTH: LONG; 1196] 2 *n* **duration**, time, time span, extent. [➡PERIOD OF TIME; 90] 3 *n* **piece**, strip, segment, section, bit, quantity, amount, part, chunk. [➡AMOUNT OF SOLID OR SEMI-SOLID; 115]

lengthen *v* **grow**, increase, extend, elongate, stretch, pull out, draw out, prolong, drag out. [➡CHANGE OF SIZE: BIGGER; 393] *Opposite:* shorten.

lengthiness *n* [➡LENGTH: LONG; 1196]

lengthways *adv* **lengthwise**, along, end to end, sideways, laterally. [➡ORIENTATION AND ALIGNMENT; 1222] *Opposite:* endways.

lengthwise *adv* **lengthways**, along, end to end, sideways, laterally. [➡ORIENTATION AND ALIGNMENT; 1222] *Opposite:* endwise.

lengthy *adj* **long**, long-lasting, extensive, prolonged, protracted, extended, drawn-out, overlong, interminable, long-winded. [➡ HAPPENING SLOWLY; 106] *Opposite:* brief.

lenience *n* **clemency**, leniency, mercy, compassion, humanity, tolerance, indulgence, kindness, forbearance (*formal*), forgiveness, mildness, moderation. [➡ GENEROSITY AND KINDNESS; 496] *Opposite:* severity.

leniency *n* **clemency**, lenience, mercy, compassion, humanity, tolerance, indulgence, kindness, forbearance (*formal*), forgiveness, mildness, moderation. [➡ GENEROSITY AND KINDNESS; 496] *Opposite:* severity.

lenient *adj* **compassionate**, merciful, humane, tolerant, indulgent, kind, forbearing (*formal*), forgiving, mild, temperate, moderate, soft, light. [➡ GENEROSITY AND KINDNESS; 496] *Opposite:* severe.

Leninism *n* [➡ PHILOSOPHIES AND BELIEFS; 781]

Leninist *adj* [➡ PHILOSOPHIES AND BELIEFS; 781]

lens 1 *n* [➡ THE EYE; 699] 2 *part of* **photographic equipment**. [➡ PHOTOGRAPHY AND PHOTOGRAPHIC EQUIPMENT; 1121]

lens cap *part of* **photographic equipment**. [➡ PHOTOGRAPHY AND PHOTOGRAPHIC EQUIPMENT; 1121]

lentil *type of* **pulse**. [➡ BEANS AND PULSES; 1188]

lentissimo *type of* **musical term**. [➡ MUSICAL TERMS; 912]

lento *type of* **musical term**. [➡ MUSICAL TERMS; 912]

Leo *type of* **star sign**. [➡ FATE, DESTINY, AND ASTROLOGY; 783]

leonine *adj* **impressive**, imposing, majestic, proud, dignified, magnificent. [➡ EXTRAORDINARY: AMAZING; 205]

leopard *type of* **cat**. [➡ FELINE; 983]

leotard *n* **one-piece**, body, body stocking, all-in-one, bodysuit, body suit (*US*). [➡ GARMENTS AND OUTFITS; 865]

leper *n* [➡ SOLITARY PEOPLE; 942]

leprechaun *n* **sprite**, elf, imp, pixie, dwarf, gnome, goblin. [➡ MYTHICAL BEINGS; 790]

lepton *type of* **elementary particle**. [➡ ELEMENTARY PARTICLES; 1278]

lèse majesté *see* **lese majesty**.

lese majesty 1 *n* **disrespect**, disregard, dishonour, contempt, disdain, irreverence, disparagement, belittlement. [➡ ANTAGONISM; 553] *Opposite:* respect. 2 *n* **treason**, high treason, sedition, betrayal, perfidy (*literary*), perfidiousness (*literary*), treachery, traitorousness, disloyalty. [➡ DECEPTION AND LIES; 661] *Opposite:* loyalty.

lesion *n* **wound**, injury, cut, graze, scratch, laceration, abrasion, gash. [➡ ILLNESSES AND DISORDERS; 733]

less 1 *adj* **a smaller amount of**, not as much of, a lesser amount of, a reduced amount of. [➡ LESS; 124] *Opposite:* more. 2 *prep* **minus**, take away, with a reduction of, excluding. [➡ LESS; 124] *Opposite:* plus.

lessen *v* **diminish**, decrease, decline, tail off, ease off, let up, die down, slacken, lower, cut, reduce, minimize. [➡ CHANGE OF INTENSITY: LESS; 396] *Opposite:* increase.

lesser *adj* **smaller**, slighter, minor, reduced. [➡ INFERIORITY; 154] *Opposite:* greater.

lesson 1 *n* **class**, lecture, session, tutorial, seminar, period. [➡ LESSONS, COURSE WORK, AND EXAMINATIONS; 842] 2 *n* **example**, message, moral, warning, object lesson, experience, punishment. [➡ MEANING; 691]

lest *conj* **in case**, for fear that, so as not to. [➡ UNCERTAIN; 176]

let 1 *v* **allow**, give permission, permit, agree to, consent to, give leave (*formal*), authorize, assent to, accede to. [➡ PERMIT AND ALLOW; 670] *Opposite:* forbid. 2 *v* **rent**, rent out, lease, lease out, hire, hire out, sublet, sublease. [➡ LEND, LEASE, AND BORROW; 429] 3 *n* **lease**, tenancy, occupancy, rent, agreement, contract. [➡ ACCOMMODATION; 855] 4 *n* (*archaic*) **problem**, difficulty, hindrance, impediment, complication, hurdle, hitch, stumbling block. [➡ NUISANCES; 254]

See Compare and Contrast at **hire**.

let alone *v* **leave be**, leave alone, let be, leave to yourself, get off somebody's back (*slang*), leave in peace, leave off. [➡ REFUSING OR REJECTING RELATIONS; 975] *Opposite:* pester.

let be *v* **leave alone**, leave in peace, leave be, let alone, leave to yourself, leave off, leave well enough alone, pay no attention, ignore, disregard, leave somebody to himself/herself, leave somebody to his/her own devices, get off somebody's back (*slang*). [➡ REFUSING OR REJECTING RELATIONS; 975] *Opposite:* bother.

let bygones be bygones *v* [➡ FORGET, FORGIVE, AND ACCEPT; 749]

let down 1 *v* **lower**, drop, sink, let fall, move down, take down. [➡ MOVE SOMETHING: DOWNWARDS; 330] *Opposite:* raise. 2 *v* **deflate**, empty, drain. [➡ CHANGE OF SIZE: SMALLER; 394] *Opposite:* inflate. 3 *v* **disappoint**, fail, abandon, betray, disillusion, desert, forsake. [➡ UPSET, DISTRESS, AND HUMILIATE; 568] 4 *v* **lengthen**, extend, let out, expand, enlarge, unfasten, undo, unpin. [➡ CHANGE OF SIZE: BIGGER; 393] *Opposite:* take up.

letdown *n* **disappointment**, anticlimax, damp squib (*informal*), failure, washout (*informal*), flop (*informal*), disillusionment, discouragement. [➡ FAILURE; 77] *Opposite:* success.

let drop *v* [➡ BETRAY CONFIDENCES AND GOSSIP; 619]

let fly 1 *v* **lose your temper**, hit the roof, go mad, let rip (*informal*), see red (*informal*), lose your rag (*slang*), explode, rage. [➡ GIVING VENT TO EMOTIONS; 680] *Opposite:* keep your cool. 2 *v* **throw**, fling, toss, hurl, pitch, launch, propel. [➡ THROW SOMETHING; 335]

let go *v* **release**, liberate, set free, free, set loose, unchain, unleash, drop, relinquish, give up, surrender, discard, shed. [➡ FREEDOM AND LIBERTY; 209] *Opposite:* retain.

lethal *adj* **deadly**, fatal, mortal, poisonous, toxic, dangerous, harmful, disastrous, destructive, ruinous. [➡ DANGEROUS; 237]

See Compare and Contrast at **deadly**.

lethally *adv* **fatally**, mortally, terminally, gravely, severely, seriously, incurably, critically, acutely, dangerously, disastrously. [➡CRITICALLY AND SERIOUSLY; 132] *Opposite:* slightly.

lethargic *adj* **sluggish**, tired, weary, exhausted, lacklustre, lazy, languid, indolent, slow, dull, lifeless, listless. [➡TIRED, ASLEEP, AND UNCONSCIOUS; 739] *Opposite:* energetic.

lethargically *adv* **sluggishly**, tiredly, wearily, lazily, languidly, indolently, slowly, dully, lifelessly, listlessly. [➡WITHOUT ENTHUSIASM; 288] *Opposite:* energetically.

lethargy *n* **sluggishness**, tiredness, weariness, exhaustion, fatigue, lassitude, laziness, indolence, stupor, slowness, dullness, lifelessness, listlessness. [➡TIRED, ASLEEP, AND UNCONSCIOUS; 739] *Opposite:* energy.

let in *v* **admit**, allow in, open the door to, show in, receive, let past, invite in, usher in, welcome in, take in. [➡PERMIT AND ALLOW; 670] *Opposite:* keep out.

let in for (*informal*) *v* **involve in**, entangle in, ensnare in, mix up in, entrap in, catch up in, embroil in. [➡CAUSE OR COMPEL TO ACT; 272] *Opposite:* get out of.

let in on *v* **make aware of**, tell, acquaint with, reveal to, disclose to, put somebody in the picture, share, let into, fill in on, inform of. [➡INFORM AND ANNOUNCE; 612] *Opposite:* keep from.

let into 1 *v* **let in on**, fill in on, share, tell, inform of, notify of, acquaint with, disclose to, let know, reveal to. [➡INFORM AND ANNOUNCE; 612] *Opposite:* keep from. 2 *v* **allow into**, admit to, receive into, welcome into, take into, invite into, show into, usher into. [➡PERMIT AND ALLOW; 670] 3 *v* **admit to**, accept into, receive into, welcome into, take into, allow into, enlist into, enrol into, induct into. [➡PERMIT AND ALLOW; 670]

let know *v* **tell**, inform, advise, alert, warn, update, put in the picture, acquaint, apprise (*formal*), impart, pass on. [➡INFORM AND ANNOUNCE; 612] *Opposite:* keep in the dark.

let loose *v* **let out**, let go, set free, set loose, release, free, liberate, unchain, unleash, unfetter. [➡FREEDOM AND LIBERTY; 209] *Opposite:* confine.

let off 1 *v* **excuse**, pardon, release, free, acquit, discharge (*formal*). [➡FORGET, FORGIVE, AND ACCEPT; 749] *Opposite:* punish. 2 *v* **fire** (*informal*), explode, detonate, discharge (*formal*), set off, shoot, put a match to. [➡FIRE, FLAMMABILITY, AND BURNING; 1164] *Opposite:* put out.

let off steam *v* [➡GIVING VENT TO EMOTIONS; 680]

let on 1 *v* **admit**, disclose, divulge, reveal, declare, say, acknowledge, avow (*formal*), confess, tell, own up. [➡ADMIT AND CONFESS; 616] *Opposite:* conceal. 2 *v* **pretend**, make out, claim, profess, act, affect, fake. [➡PRETEND AND MIMIC; 60] *Opposite:* come clean (*informal*).

let-out *n* **loophole**, escape clause, way out, technicality, window, opening. [➡ADVANTAGE; 213]

let out 1 *v* **emit**, give, utter, release, produce, give out, give off, give forth. [➡EMIT AND EMANATE; 362] *Opposite:* suppress. 2 *v* **free**, let go, release, set free, let loose, liberate, set loose. [➡FREEDOM AND LIBERTY; 209] *Opposite:* keep in. 3 *v* **enlarge**, expand, extend, widen, broaden, unfasten, release. [➡CHANGE OF SIZE: BIGGER; 393] *Opposite:* take in. 4 *v* **let slip**, reveal, divulge, disclose, blurt out, give away, leak. [➡BETRAY CONFIDENCES AND GOSSIP; 619] *Opposite:* conceal.

let pass 1 *v* **ignore**, let go, overlook, let ride, pay no attention to, take no notice of, disregard, close your eyes to, turn a blind eye to, pass over, forgive, excuse. [➡NOT PAY ATTENTION; 765] *Opposite:* pick up on (*informal*). 2 *v* **let through**, let by, let past, stand aside for, make way for, clear the way for, admit, allow in, let in, usher in, welcome in. [➡PERMIT AND ALLOW; 670] *Opposite:* bar.

let ride *v* **ignore**, close your eyes to, turn a blind eye to, let go, let pass, take no notice of, pay no attention to, pass over, disregard, forgive, excuse. [➡NOT PAY ATTENTION; 765] *Opposite:* stop.

let rip (*informal*) *v* [➡GIVING VENT TO EMOTIONS; 680]

let slip 1 *v* **reveal**, disclose, divulge, give away, let out, blurt out, tell, leak, betray. [➡BETRAY CONFIDENCES AND GOSSIP; 619] *Opposite:* hold back. 2 *v* **let go**, lose, lose track of, lose sight of, take your eyes off, miss, waste. [➡LOSE AND FORFEIT; 448]

letter 1 *n* **communication**, note, message, memo, dispatch, notelet, document, missive, epistle (*formal*). [➡LETTERS AND WRITTEN MESSAGES; 585] 2 *n* **character**, symbol, sign, capital, capital letter, uppercase, lower case. [➡SYMBOLS, SIGNS, AND NUMBERS; 597]

letterbox *n* **accommodation address**, poste restante, postbox, post office box, mailbox (*US*), general delivery (*US*), maildrop (*US*). [➡CONTAINERS, RECEPTACLES, AND PACKAGING; 1244]

letter card *n* **card**, letter, note, notelet, note card. [➡LETTERS AND WRITTEN MESSAGES; 585]

lettered *adj* **educated**, knowledgeable, cultured, cultivated, literary, literate, scholarly, erudite, learned, well-read, intellectual. [➡LEVEL OF EDUCATION AND SOPHISTICATION; 894] *Opposite:* uneducated.

lettering *n* **writing**, print, calligraphy, letters, inscription, script, words, characters, graffiti. [➡WRITING; 584]

letter-perfect (*US*) *adj* **word-perfect**, faultless, perfect, flawless, impeccable, consummate, prepared, precise, exact. [➡EXACT; 204] *Opposite:* unprepared.

letters *n* **literature**, culture, cultivation, knowledge, education, literacy, erudition. [➡LEVEL OF EDUCATION AND SOPHISTICATION; 894]

let the cat out of the bag *v* **spill the beans** (*informal*), talk, blab (*informal*), squeal (*slang disapproving*), let on, blow the gaff (*slang*). [➡BETRAY CONFIDENCES AND GOSSIP; 619] *Opposite:* keep mum (*informal*).

let through *v* **make way for**, stand aside for, clear the way for, let pass, let past, let by, admit, allow in, let in, usher in, welcome in. [➡MAKE POSSIBLE; 276] *Opposite:* block.

lettuce *type of* **salad vegetable**. [➡FRUIT AND VEGETABLES; 1175]

let up *v* **ease off**, ease, ease up, lessen, slacken, relent, relax, slow down, die down, tail off, abate (*formal or literary*), stop. [➡DISAPPEAR; 4] *Opposite:* intensify.

let-up (*informal*) *n* **respite**, break, rest, relief, interval, lull, relaxation, remission. [➡PAUSES AND PHASES; 56] *Opposite:* intensification.

let up on *v* **ease up on**, ease off on, slack off on, go easy on (*informal*), soften up on, spare. [➡TAKE CARE OF AND SPOIL; 301]

let your hair down *v* **relax**, have a good time, enjoy yourself, let yourself go, party (*informal*), have fun, have a knees-up (*informal*). [➡LEISURE AND RECREATION; 874]

let yourself go *v* [➡CHANGE OF MOOD AND COMPOSURE; 581]

levanter *type of* **wind**. [➡WINDY AND STORMY WEATHER; 1053]

levee 1 *n* **embankment**, earthwork, bank, wall, rampart, protection. [➡BARRIERS; 1112] 2 *n* **reception**, royal reception, royal function, court reception, court function. [➡PARTIES, DANCES, AND CELEBRATIONS; 37]

level 1 *adj* **flat**, smooth, flat as a pancake, even, dead flat. [➡PHYSICAL TEXTURE; 1221] *Opposite:* bumpy. 2 *adj* **horizontal**, parallel with the ground, even, flat. [➡ORIENTATION AND ALIGNMENT; 1222] 3 *adj* **equal**, neck and neck, side by side, close, near. [➡EQUALITY; 155] 4 *n* **height**, altitude, stage, point, plane, echelon, rank. [➡DEGREE AND EXTENT; 110] 5 *n* **intensity**, quantity, concentration, amount, degree, reading. [➡DEGREE AND EXTENT; 110] 6 (*US*) *type of* **measuring device**. [➡MEASURING DEVICES; 1122] 7 *v* **flatten**, smooth, steamroll, press flat, even out. [➡CHANGE OF SHAPE; 386] 8 *v* **aim**, direct, point, turn. [➡MOVE SOMETHING: UPWARDS; 329] 9 *v* **demolish**, knock down, raze, blow up, raze to the ground. [➡DESTRUCTION AND DEMOLITION; 360] *Opposite:* rebuild.

level crossing *n* **railway crossing**, crossing, grade crossing (*US*). [➡BRIDGES, TUNNELS, CROSSINGS, AND JUNCTIONS; 1111]

level-headed *adj* **sensible**, calm, sound, even-tempered, reliable, equable, composed, rational, dispassionate, unperturbed. [➡CONFIDENCE AND COMPOSURE; 500] *Opposite:* rash.

level-headedness *n* **composure**, equanimity, calmness, good sense, reliability, balance. [➡CONFIDENCE AND COMPOSURE; 500] *Opposite:* rashness.

levelly 1 *adv* **calmly**, steadily, sensibly, evenly, equably, unemotionally. [➡GOOD-TEMPERED AND HUMOROUS; 628] *Opposite:* excitedly. 2 *adv* **smoothly**, flatly, evenly. [➡PHYSICAL TEXTURE; 1221] *Opposite:* unevenly.

level off *v* **stabilize**, even out, settle, settle down, smooth out, steady. [➡CHANGE; 373]

level out *v* **settle down**, stabilize, settle, even out, even up, balance out, steady. [➡CHANGE; 373]

level pegging *n* **equality**, parity, same score, tie, draw, dead heat. [➡EQUALITY; 155] *Opposite:* inequality.

lever 1 *n* **handle**, control, regulator, knob. [➡PARTS OF MACHINES AND TOOLS; 1117] 2 *part of* **engine**. [➡PARTS OF AN ENGINE; 1143]

leverage *n* **influence**, power, force, control, pull (*informal*), weight, clout (*informal*). [➡STRENGTH; 202]

leveret *type of* **young animal**. [➡YOUNG ANIMAL; 977]

leviathan *n* [➡BIG THINGS; 1193]

levitate *v* **float**, rise up, ascend, drift up, soar, take off, fly up. [➡GO UPWARDS; 307] *Opposite:* sink.

levitation *n* **defiance of gravity**, rising, raising, hovering, floating, flying. [➡GO UPWARDS; 307]

levity *n* **lightheartedness**, cheerfulness, humour, lightness, flippancy, jokiness. [➡GOOD-TEMPERED AND HUMOROUS; 628] *Opposite:* gravity.

levy 1 *v* **impose**, tax, collect, put, charge. [➡MONEY, PAYMENTS, AND CHARGES; 800] 2 *n* **tax**, rates, toll, duty, tariff, charge. [➡TAX AND TAXATION; 802]

lewd *adj* [➡MORALLY BAD; 776]

lewdness *n* [➡MORALLY BAD; 776]

lexical *adj* **verbal**, word, vocabulary, philological, etymological. [➡ASPECTS OF LANGUAGE; 683]

lexicon 1 *n* **dictionary**, monolingual dictionary, bilingual dictionary, foreign language dictionary, reference book. [➡LISTS AND SCHEDULES; 588] 2 *n* **vocabulary**, vocabulary list, word list, lexis, idiolect, glossary, concordance. [➡ASPECTS OF LANGUAGE; 683]

lexis *n* [➡LISTS AND SCHEDULES; 588]

ley 1 *n* **grassland**, pasture, pastureland, pasturage, grazing, arable land. [➡THE COUNTRYSIDE AND OUTDOOR SPACES; 1070] 2 *n* **path**, pathway, footpath, bridle path, track, trail, walk, route. [➡PATHWAYS; 1109]

liability 1 *n* **legal responsibility**, obligation, accountability, responsibility, charge. [➡THE LAW AND LEGAL AUTHORITY; 814] 2 *n* **disadvantage**, problem, burden, millstone, disaster area (*informal*), jinx. [➡PROBLEM; 257]

liable 1 *adj* **legally responsible**, accountable, answerable, responsible. [➡RESPONSIBILITY; 171] *Opposite:* unaccountable. 2 *adj* **likely**, apt, predisposed, prone. [➡THE WILL AND WILLINGNESS; 564] *Opposite:* unlikely.

liaise *v* **act as a go-between**, communicate, link, bridge, mediate, coordinate, interact, get together with, network. [➡INITIATE AND ESTABLISH COMMUNICATION; 681]

liaison *n* **link**, connection, contact, cooperation, relationship, association. [➡CONNECTION; 144]

liana *type of* **climber**. [➡CLIMBERS; 1033]

liar *n* [➡PEOPLE WHO DECEIVE; 662]

libation 1 *n* (*humorous*) **drink**, alcoholic drink, beverage (*formal*), brew (*informal*), potation (*literary*), potion, bevvy (*slang*). [➡DRINKS; 1186] 2 *n* **offering**, oblation, offertory, sacrifice, tribute. [➡RELIGIOUS CONCEPTS; 777]

libel 1 *n* **defamation**, vilification, slander, smear, denigration, character assassination. [➡CRIMES; 817] *Opposite:* praise. 2 *v* **defame**, vilify, sully, tarnish, malign, slander. [➡DECEPTION AND LIES; 661] *Opposite:* praise.

See Compare and Contrast at **malign**.

libellous *adj* **defamatory**, vilifying, slanderous, unfounded. [➡ILLEGAL; 816] *Opposite:* admiring.

liberal 1 *adj* **open-minded**, broad-minded, moderate, noninterventionist, freethinking, tolerant, laissez-faire. [➡THE NATURE OF IDEAS; 772] *Opposite:* narrow-minded. 2 *adj* **generous**, copious, abundant, profuse, substantial, large. [➡ MANY, MUCH, LARGE AMOUNT; 117] *Opposite:* measly (*informal*).

See Compare and Contrast at **generous.**

liberalism *n* **tolerance**, broad-mindedness, open-mindedness, moderation, freethinking, laissez-faire. [➡ THE NATURE OF IDEAS; 772] *Opposite:* narrow-mindedness.

liberalize *v* **relax**, slacken, loosen, ease up, open, free up. [➡ CHANGE OF INTENSITY: LESS; 396] *Opposite:* tighten.

liberally *adv* **copiously**, generously, freely, abundantly, profusely, substantially. [➡ MANY, MUCH, LARGE AMOUNT; 117] *Opposite:* stingily.

liberate *v* **release**, free, set free, unshackle, unfetter. [➡ FREEDOM AND LIBERTY; 209]

liberated *adj* **unconventional**, open-minded, freethinking, modern, enlightened, progressive. [➡ POSITIVE INTELLECTUAL CHARACTERISTICS; 525] *Opposite:* unenlightened.

liberation *n* **deliverance** (*formal*), freedom, liberty, release, discharge, emancipation. [➡ FREEDOM AND LIBERTY; 209] *Opposite:* captivity.

liberator *n* **deliverer**, saviour, emancipator, releaser. [➡ PEOPLE WHO ARE APPROVED OF; 955] *Opposite:* captor.

libertine *n* [➡ PLEASURE-SEEKERS AND HEDONISTS; 886]

liberty 1 *n* **freedom**, independence, autonomy, emancipation, liberation. [➡ FREEDOM AND LIBERTY; 209] *Opposite:* captivity. 2 *n* **right**, freedom, authorization, authority, permission. [➡ PHILOSOPHIES AND BELIEFS; 781] *Opposite:* suppression.

libidinous (*formal*) *adj* [➡ MORALLY BAD; 776]

Libra *type of* **star sign.** [➡ FATE, DESTINY, AND ASTROLOGY; 783]

library 1 *n* **collection**, archive, books, papers, records. [➡ RECORDS; 586] 2 *type of* **room in public buildings.** [➡ TYPES OF ROOM; 1096]

librettist *n* **libretto writer**, lyricist, songwriter, writer, author. [➡ WRITERS AND STYLES; 914]

libretto *n* [➡ MUSICAL TERMS; 912]

licence 1 *n* **certificate**, authorization, warrant, pass, card, permit, ticket. [➡ OFFICIAL DOCUMENTS; 587] 2 *n* **excess**, immoderation (*formal*), abandon, lawlessness, unrestraint, intemperance. [➡ MORALLY BAD; 776] 3 *n* **freedom**, liberty, carte blanche, authority, permission, right, dispensation, privilege. [➡ FREEDOM AND LIBERTY; 209]

license *v* **certify**, permit, allow, authorize, accredit. [➡ PERMIT AND ALLOW; 670]

licensed *adj* **approved**, qualified, certified, accredited, registered. [➡ PERMIT AND ALLOW; 670]

license plate (*US*) *type of* **external feature.** [➡ VEHICLES; 1144]

licentiate *n* **licence holder**, licensee, certified professional, qualified practitioner. [➡ OWNERS; 447]

licentious (*formal*) *adj* [➡ MORALLY BAD; 776]

licentiousness (*formal*) *n* [➡ MORALLY BAD; 776]

lichen *type of* **fungus.** [➡ MICROORGANISMS, FUNGI, AND ALGAE; 1023]

licit *adj* **lawful**, legitimate, legal, valid, right, proper, acceptable, permissible, admissible, accepted, permitted, admitted, authorized, sanctioned by law. [➡ LEGAL; 815] *Opposite:* illegal.

See Compare and Contrast at **legal.**

lick (*informal*) *v* **defeat**, conquer, get the better of, overcome, thrash, clobber (*informal*), beat, cream (*US informal*). [➡ BEAT AND DEFEAT; 80]

lickety-split (*informal*) *adv* **quickly**, fast, at high speed, at a lick (*informal*), at a rate of knots, swiftly, rapidly, speedily, fast as a rabbit (*US*). [➡ HAPPENING QUICKLY; 104] *Opposite:* sluggishly.

licking (*informal*) *n* [➡ BEAT AND DEFEAT; 80]

lick your lips *v* **relish**, salivate, drool, anticipate, await, look forward to, hope for, long for. [➡ PREDICT AND ANTICIPATE; 751]

lid *n* **top**, cover, cap, closure. [➡ COVERS AND COATINGS; 1245]

lido 1 *n* **outdoor pool**, outdoor swimming pool, open-air pool, public swimming pool. [➡ URBAN OUTDOOR SPACES; 1071] 2 *n* **public beach**, bathing beach, beach. [➡ THE SEAS, OCEANS, AND SHORES; 1041]

lie 1 *v* **recline**, stretch out, lounge, lie down, slouch, laze, loll. [➡ ASSUME A POSITION; 318] 2 *v* **be positioned**, be arranged, be placed, be situated, sit, rest. [➡ EXIST IN A PLACE; 19] 3 *v* **remain**, rest, stay, be, stop, keep. [➡ CONTINUE TO EXIST; 17] 4 *v* **tell untruths**, perjure yourself, have on (*informal*), fib (*informal*), tell stories, be economical with the truth. [➡ DECEPTION AND LIES; 661] *Opposite:* tell the truth. 5 *n* **untruth**, falsehood, fib (*informal*), tall tale, story (*informal*), fabrication, white lie, invention. [➡ DECEPTION AND LIES; 661] *Opposite:* truth.

Compare and Contrast: ***lie, untruth, falsehood, fabrication, fib, white lie***

CORE MEANING: SOMETHING THAT IS NOT TRUE

lie a false statement made deliberately; ***untruth*** something that is presented as being true but is actually false; ***falsehood*** a *lie* or an *untruth*; ***fabrication*** a statement, story, or account devised with intent to deceive; ***fib*** (*informal*) an insignificant, harmless, or small *lie*; ***white lie*** a minor harmless *lie*, usually told to avoid hurting somebody's feelings.

lie about 1 *v* **be scattered about**, lie around (*informal*), be all over the place, clutter up the place, mess up the place (*informal*), be distributed, litter, be dispersed, be spread. [➡ EXIST IN A PLACE; 19] 2 *v* (*informal*) **laze**, idle, lie around (*informal*), loll, lounge around, loaf, relax, sprawl, bask. [➡ LACK OF ACTIVITY; 343]

lie around (*informal*) *v* **laze**, bask, laze about, lounge around, flop about, sit around, laze around, flop around, loaf, relax, sprawl. [➡ LACK OF ACTIVITY; 343]

lie back *v* **recline**, stretch out, lounge, sprawl, relax, rest, lie, loll, slump, flop. [➡ ASSUME A POSITION; 318]

lie down *v* **recline**, rest, stretch out, relax, lounge, sprawl. [➡ASSUME A POSITION; 318] *Opposite:* stand up.

lie-down (*informal*) *n* **sleep**, nap, rest, snooze (*informal*), doze, forty winks (*informal*). [➡SLEEP AND DREAM; 724]

lie in (*informal*) *v* **sleep late**, stay in bed, get up late, rise late. [➡SLEEP AND DREAM; 724]

lie-in (*informal*) *n* **late sleep**, late rise, rest, doze, long sleep. [➡PERIOD OF REST; 91]

lie in wait *v* **lurk**, hide, conceal yourself, ambush, prowl, stalk, wait in the shadows. [➡ABOUT TO HAPPEN; 33]

lie off *v* **remain near**, remain close, stay near, stay close, lie near, lie close. [➡EXIST IN CLOSE PROXIMITY; 21]

lie of the land (*informal*) *n* **general state**, general situation, prospect, state of affairs, picture, look of things, state of things, circumstances, appearance, how the land lies, how things stand. [➡SITUATIONS; 71]

lieutenant *n* [➡SUBORDINATES AND ASSISTANTS; 966]

life 1 *n* **existence**, being, living. [➡PERIOD OF TIME; 90] *Opposite:* death. 2 *n* **lifetime**, life span, life cycle, life expectancy, natural life. [➡THE STAGES OF LIFE; 916] 3 *n* **verve**, vivacity, animation, energy, excitement, soul, kick (*informal*), go (*informal*), get-up-and-go (*informal*), sparkle. [➡ENERGY AND ENTHUSIASM; 497]

life-and-death *adj* **critical**, crucial, vital, pivotal, paramount, momentous, fateful, life-or-death. [➡IMPORTANT; 195] *Opposite:* unimportant.

life and soul of the party *n* [➡PEOPLE WHO ARE APPROVED OF; 955]

lifeblood 1 *n* (*literary*) **blood**, sap, essence, life force, élan vital, vital spark, spark of life, vital signs. [➡THE BLOOD AND CIRCULATION; 718] 2 *n* **essential**, essence, quintessence, sine qua non, necessity, basic. [➡MOST IMPORTANT THING; 198]

lifeboat *type of* **motor vessel**. [➡SHIPS AND BOATS; 1149]

life cycle *n* **life span**, development, maturation, growth. [➡THE STAGES OF LIFE; 916]

life expectancy *n* **life span**, lifetime, allotted span, natural life. [➡THE STAGES OF LIFE; 916]

life form *n* [➡LIVING THINGS AND LIVING; 976]

lifeguard *n* **lifesaver** (*informal*), rescuer, beach attendant, swimming pool attendant, pool attendant. [➡PEOPLE WHO GUARD AND PROTECT; 846]

lifeless 1 *adj* **dead**, unconscious, unresponsive, unmoving, inert, motionless, comatose, limp, insensible. [➡TIRED, ASLEEP, AND UNCONSCIOUS; 739] *Opposite:* alive. 2 *adj* **unexciting**, dull, uninteresting, tedious, listless, flat. [➡BORING AND UNINTERESTING; 235] *Opposite:* animated.

See Compare and Contrast at **dead**.

lifelessly *adv* **inertly**, motionlessly, insensibly, limply, unresponsively, unconsciously. [➡TIRED, ASLEEP, AND UNCONSCIOUS; 739] *Opposite:* animatedly.

lifelessness *n* **motionlessness**, limpness, listlessness, unresponsiveness, inertness, unconsciousness, insensibility. [➡TIRED, ASLEEP, AND UNCONSCIOUS; 739] *Opposite:* animation.

lifelike *adj* **realistic**, natural, believable, convincing, credible, authentic, faithful. [➡TRUE AND REAL; 172] *Opposite:* unrealistic.

lifeline *n* **salvation**, link, help, support, helping hand, sustenance. [➡SAFE AND SAFETY; 192]

lifelong *adj* **enduring**, all-time, lifetime (*informal*), permanent, ultimate, lasting, constant. [➡PERMANENCE: WITHOUT END; 94] *Opposite:* temporary.

life of ease *n* [➡PLEASANT SITUATIONS; 74]

life of Riley *n* [➡PLEASANT SITUATIONS; 74]

life-or-death *see* **life-and-death**.

life raft *type of* **small vessel**. [➡SHIPS AND BOATS; 1149]

lifesaver (*informal*) *n* [➡TREAT; 211]

life-size *adj* **full-scale**, full-size, actual size. [➡LARGE; 1192] *Opposite:* miniature.

life span *n* **natural life**, lifetime, life cycle, life expectancy, life. [➡THE STAGES OF LIFE; 916]

lifestyle *n* **way of life**, standard of living, existence, routine, life, daily life, everyday life, regime. [➡LIFESTYLE; 881]

life-support system *part of* **spacecraft**. [➡SPACE VEHICLES; 1062]

life's work *n* **achievement**, accomplishment, success, attainment, lifework (*US*). [➡SUCCESS; 82]

life-threatening *adj* **dangerous**, serious, severe, grave, incurable, critical, acute, mortal, lethal, deadly, fatal. [➡DEADLY; 928]

lifetime 1 *n* **life**, time, life span, natural life, life cycle, life expectancy. [➡THE STAGES OF LIFE; 916] 2 *n* (*informal*) **forever** (*informal*), eternity, days, ages (*informal*), yonks (*slang*), donkey's years (*informal*). [➡LONG PERIOD OF TIME; 92] 3 *n* **era**, generation, time, period, days, epoch. [➡EPOCHS AND ERAS; 89]

lifework (*US*) *n* **product of working life**, result of working life, life's work, achievement, accomplishment, success, attainment. [➡SUCCESS; 82]

lift 1 *v* **winch up**, haul up, elevate, boost, raise, pick up. [➡MOVE SOMETHING: UPWARDS; 329] 2 *v* **revoke**, cancel, take back, relax, rescind, repeal. [➡APOLOGIZE AND RETRACT; 684] *Opposite:* impose. 3 *v* **lighten**, buoy up, brighten, elate, uplift, raise. [➡ENCOURAGE; 577] 4 *v* (*informal*) **steal**, pinch (*informal*), filch (*informal*), walk off with, help yourself, nick (*slang*), pocket, take, plagiarize. [➡STEAL AND ROB; 427] 5 *n* **boost**, kick (*informal*), high (*informal*), buzz (*informal*), revitalization, tonic, encouragement. [➡TREAT; 211] 6 *n* [➡STAIRS AND STOREYS; 1101]

See Compare and Contrast at **raise**.

liftoff *n* [➡BEGINNING; 53]

ligature 1 *n* **cord**, string, rope, tie, line, lace, thong, band. [➡FASTENERS, LINKS, AND NETWORKS; 1246] **2** *n* **tying**, binding, tying up, lashing, securing, tethering, trussing. [➡FASTEN, LINK, AND JOIN; 409] **3** *n* (*formal*) **bond**, connection, link, linkage, union, tie. [➡CONNECTION; 144]

ligger (*informal*) *n* [➡SUPERFICIAL OR INSINCERE PEOPLE; 951]

light **1** *n* **glow**, beam, brightness, luminosity, daylight, illumination, radiance. [➡DESCRIBING LIGHT; 1227] *Opposite:* darkness. **2** *adj* **bright**, sunny, sunlit, well-lit. [➡DESCRIBING LIGHT; 1227] *Opposite:* dark. **3** *adj* **pastel**, subtle, neutral, fair, pale, muted. [➡DESCRIBING COLOURS; 1225] *Opposite:* dark. **4** *v* **set alight**, set on fire, ignite, strike, set fire to. [➡FIRE, FLAMMABILITY, AND BURNING; 1164] *Opposite:* extinguish. **5** *adj* **weightless**, buoyant, fluffy, insubstantial, frothy, wispy, feathery, flimsy. [➡WEIGHT: LIGHT; 1205] *Opposite:* heavy. **6** *adj* **gentle**, delicate, soft, noiseless, featherlike, imperceptible. [➡IMPERCEPTIBLE; 26] *Opposite:* heavy. **7** *adj* **nimble**, graceful, dainty, elegant, agile, sprightly. [➡AGILITY OF THE BODY; 477] *Opposite:* heavy. **8** *adj* **carefree**, happy, cheerful, untroubled, blithe (*literary*), joyful. [➡PLEASURE, EXCITEMENT, AND ELATION; 535] *Opposite:* heavy. **9** *adj* **easy**, manageable, undemanding, simple, effortless, unexacting. [➡EASE AND SIMPLICITY; 201] *Opposite:* heavy. **10** *adj* **entertaining**, lightweight, fun, frivolous, amusing, playful, undemanding. [➡FUNNY AND AMUSING; 217] *Opposite:* heavy.

light

◆ *types of light*
arc lamp, chandelier, flashlight (*US*), floodlight, fluorescent lamp, footlights, hurricane lamp, lamp, lamppost, lantern, LED, light bulb, neon light, nightlight, penlight, searchlight, spotlight, standard lamp, streetlamp, streetlight, striplight, sunlamp, torch, torchlight, traffic light, uplighter

light aircraft *type of* **civil aircraft**. [➡AIRCRAFT; 1147]

light bulb *type of* **light**. [➡LIGHT; 1163]

light-coloured *adj* **pale**, light, pastel, subtle, fair, neutral, blonde, blond. [➡DESCRIBING COLOURS; 1225]

lighten **1** *v* **ease**, lessen, alleviate, reduce, lift, relieve, allay, assuage. [➡CHANGE OF INTENSITY: LESS; 396] **2** *v* **cheer up**, improve, lift, refresh, buoy up, lighten up (*informal*), relax, loosen up. [➡IMPROVE SOMETHING; 375]

lighten up (*informal*) *v* **relax**, take it easy, cool it (*informal*), loosen up, unwind, chill out (*slang*). [➡CHANGE OF MOOD AND COMPOSURE; 581]

lighter *type of* **motor vessel**. [➡SHIPS AND BOATS; 1149]

lightface *adj* **faint**, light. [➡PRINTING; 601] *Opposite:* bold.

light-fingered *adj* **thieving**, sticky-fingered (*informal*), kleptomaniacal, larcenous, dishonest. [➡MORALLY BAD; 776]

light-footed *adj* **nimble**, graceful, dainty, elegant, agile. [➡AGILITY OF THE BODY; 477] *Opposite:* clumsy.

lightheaded *adj* **dizzy**, faint, giddy, woozy, wobbly (*informal*), unsteady, groggy. [➡ILL AND SICK; 741]

lighthearted **1** *adj* **carefree**, happy-go-lucky, happy, cheerful, cheery, relaxed, upbeat (*informal*), merry, buoyant, blithe (*literary*). [➡PLEASURE, EXCITEMENT, AND ELATION; 535] *Opposite:* troubled. **2** *adj* **cheerful**, jokey, cheery, funny, optimistic, fun, blithe (*literary*), frivolous, bright, jocular, flippant, facetious, happy, humorous. [➡PLEASURE, EXCITEMENT, AND ELATION; 535] *Opposite:* gloomy. **3** *adj* **enjoyable**, entertaining, amusing, diverting, fun, delightful, pleasant, pleasing. [➡FUNNY AND AMUSING; 217] *Opposite:* serious.

lightheartedly *adv* **cheerfully**, cheerily, brightly, happily, blithely (*literary*), gaily. [➡PLEASURE, EXCITEMENT, AND ELATION; 535] *Opposite:* gloomily.

lighting *n* **illumination**, light, lights. [➡LIGHT; 1163]

light into (*informal*) *v* **attack**, tear into, set upon, pitch into (*informal*), lay into, let have it, let fly at, savage, maul. [➡PHYSICAL ATTACK AND PUNISHMENT; 416] *Opposite:* praise.

lightly **1** *adv* **gently**, softly, delicately, imperceptibly, quietly, noiselessly. [➡IMPERCEPTIBLE; 26] *Opposite:* heavily. **2** *adv* **flippantly**, frivolously, jokily, informally, casually, carelessly, nonchalantly, blithely (*literary*), without due consideration. [➡INCAUTIOUS AND CARELESS; 284] **3** *adv* **nimbly**, gracefully, trippingly, adeptly, dexterously, daintily. [➡AGILITY OF THE BODY; 477] *Opposite:* heavily.

light-minded *adj* **frivolous**, silly, foolish, vacuous, inane. [➡NEGATIVE INTELLECTUAL CHARACTERISTICS; 526] *Opposite:* serious-minded.

lightness **1** *n* **weightlessness**, buoyancy, fluffiness, frothiness, flimsiness. [➡WEIGHT: LIGHT; 1205] *Opposite:* heaviness. **2** *n* **nimbleness**, precision, grace, agility, dexterity, subtlety. [➡AGILITY OF THE BODY; 477] *Opposite:* heaviness.

lightning **1** *n* **flash of lightning**, forked lightning, sheet lightning, coruscation (*literary*), fulguration (*formal*). [➡WINDY AND STORMY WEATHER; 1053] **2** *adj* **fast**, quick, speedy, whirlwind, sudden, precipitous, headlong. [➡HAPPENING QUICKLY; 104] *Opposite:* slow.

light out (*informal*) *v* **run away**, run off, leave in a hurry, cut and run, run for it, bolt, skedaddle (*slang*), flee, take to flight, take to your heels, make yourself scarce (*informal*). [➡RUN AWAY AND AVOID; 10]

light plane (*US*) *type of* **civil aircraft**. [➡AIRCRAFT; 1147]

light railway *type of* **railway**. [➡RAILWAYS; 1106]

lightship *type of* **motor vessel**. [➡SHIPS AND BOATS; 1149]

lights out **1** *n* **bedtime**, time for bed, sleep time, byebyes (*babytalk*). [➡TIMES OF DAY; 87] **2** *n* **signal**, taps, bugle call, curfew, last post. [➡TIMES OF DAY; 87] *Opposite:* reveille.

light up **1** *v* **illuminate**, light, cast light on, shed light on, shine a light on, illumine (*literary*), brighten. [➡LIGHT EMISSION; 369] *Opposite:* darken. **2** *v* **shine**, glow, gleam, beam, burn, glimmer, flare, blaze, flame. [➡LIGHT EMISSION; 369] *Opposite:* darken. **3** *v* **cheer up**, brighten up, perk up, liven up, buck up (*informal*), brighten, animate, gladden. [➡CHANGE OF MOOD AND COMPOSURE; 581]

lightweight **1** *adj* **frivolous**, trivial, insubstantial, inconsequential, unimportant, frothy. [➡UNIMPORTANT AND UNNECESSARY; 239] *Opposite:* serious. **2** *n* **person of little consequence**, small fry, little man, little guy, pawn. *Opposite:* heavyweight. (*informal*). [➡LAZY OR UNSUCCESSFUL PEOPLE; 948]

ligneous *adj* [➡RIGID AND HARD; 1210]

likable *adj* **pleasant**, nice, affable, agreeable, amiable, genial, easygoing, congenial, friendly. [➡FRIENDLINESS AND SOCIABILITY; 495] *Opposite:* abominable.

like 1 *prep* **similar to**, akin to, approximating to, in the vein of, reminiscent of, resembling. [➡SIMILARITY; 149] *Opposite:* unlike. 2 *adj* **similar**, comparable, alike, corresponding, identical. [➡SIMILARITY; 149] 3 *v* **be fond of**, love, be keen on, enjoy, be partial to, adore. [➡LIKE, LOVE, VALUE, AND ENJOY; 579] *Opposite:* dislike.

like a bat out of hell (*informal*) *adv* [➡MOVING QUICKLY; 103]

like a bolt from the blue *adv* [➡HAPPENING QUICKLY; 104]

like a cat on a hot tin roof *adj* [➡POSITIVE IMPATIENCE, ENTHUSIASM, AND ALERTNESS; 538]

like a cat on hot bricks *adj* [➡POSITIVE IMPATIENCE, ENTHUSIASM, AND ALERTNESS; 538]

like a shot *adv* **quickly**, eagerly, enthusiastically, keenly, willingly, avidly. [➡HAPPENING QUICKLY; 104] *Opposite:* reluctantly.

like clockwork *adv* **smoothly**, without a hitch, regularly, efficiently, routinely, perfectly. [➡ORDER AND ORGANIZATION; 207]

like greased lightning *adv* **quick as a flash**, like a bat out of hell (*informal*), like the wind, in a jiffy (*informal*), in the twinkling of an eye, in a trice, with alacrity, in a flash, fast as a rabbit (*US*). [➡HAPPENING QUICKLY; 104]

likelihood *n* **probability**, possibility, prospect, chance, chances, odds. [➡POSSIBLE AND PROBABLE; 178]

likely 1 *adj* **probable**, possible, expected, prospective, to be expected, on the cards (*informal*), in the offing. [➡POSSIBLE AND PROBABLE; 178] *Opposite:* unlikely. 2 *adj* **liable**, apt, prone, tending, having a tendency to. [➡THE WILL AND WILLINGNESS; 564]

like mad *adv* **like crazy**, madly, intensely, like anything, like fury, energetically. [➡INCAUTIOUS AND CARELESS; 284]

like-minded *adj* **in agreement**, concurring, compatible, in accord, of one mind, on the same wavelength. [➡HARMONY; 156]

liken *v* **compare**, equate, relate, associate. [➡CREATING CONNECTIONS; 145] *Opposite:* contrast.

likeness 1 *n* **similarity**, resemblance, correspondence. [➡SIMILARITY; 149] 2 *n* **portrait**, image, reproduction, picture, rendering, representation. [➡REPRESENTATIONS AND GENERAL EXAMPLES; 65]

like so *adv* **like this**, this way, in this way, in this fashion, thus (*formal*). [➡WAYS OF DOING THINGS; 295]

like the back of your hand *adv* **thoroughly**, back to front, inside out, backwards. [➡KNOWLEDGE AND WISDOM; 559]

like the wind *adv* [➡MOVING QUICKLY; 103]

like two peas in a pod *adj* [➡SAMENESS; 151]

likewise *adv* **similarly**, the same, equally, also, as well, too. [➡EXPRESSIONS INTRODUCING EXTRA INFORMATION; 137]

liking *n* **taste**, fondness, partiality, love, penchant, predilection (*formal*), weakness, fancy, soft spot. [➡APPRECIATION AND GRATITUDE; 536] *Opposite:* dislike.

See Compare and Contrast at **love**.

lilac 1 *type of* **purple**. [➡COLOURS; 1223] 2 *type of* **shrub or bush**. [➡BUSHES AND SHRUBS; 1027]

lilt *n* [➡ASPECTS OF LANGUAGE; 683]

lily *type of* **flower grown from bulb**. [➡FLOWERS FROM BULBS; 1030]

lily-livered (*literary*) *adj* [➡COWARDICE AND WEAKNESS OF WILL; 509]

lily of the valley *type of* **perennial flower**. [➡FLOWERS; 1032]

lima bean *type of* **pulse**. [➡BEANS AND PULSES; 1188]

limb 1 *n* **member**, appendage, extremity, projection, branch, bough. [➡SUBDIVISIONS AND OFFSHOOTS; 1252] 2 *n* **extremity**, appendage, member. [➡TORSO; 694]

limber *adj* **lithe**, supple, agile, nimble, lissom, flexible. [➡AGILITY OF THE BODY; 477] *Opposite:* stiff.

limber up *v* **warm up**, loosen up, exercise, practise, prepare. [➡PREPARE FOR ACTION; 290]

limbo *n* [➡RELIGIOUS CONCEPTS; 777]

lime 1 *type of* **citrus**. [➡FRUIT AND VEGETABLES; 1175] 2 *type of* **mineral**. [➡MINERALS; 1276] 3 *type of* **deciduous tree**. [➡DECIDUOUS TREES; 1028]

lime green *type of* **green**. [➡COLOURS; 1223]

limelight *n* **attention**, public interest, public eye, fame, renown, publicity, glare of publicity. [➡KNOWN AND FAMOUS; 182]

limerick *n* [➡POETRY AND VERSE; 915]

limestone *type of* **stone**. [➡STONES, ROCKS, AND BOULDERS; 1057]

limit 1 *n* **boundary**, bounds, border, edge, perimeter, frontier. [➡EXTREMITIES OF PHYSICAL OBJECTS; 1249] 2 *n* **maximum value**, maximum, threshold, constraint, cutoff point, ceiling, cap, check. [➡MAJORITY; 139] 3 *v* **control**, regulate, restrain, curb, constrain, ration, keep a tight rein on, restrict, reduce, check. [➡AVOID, PREVENT, LIMIT, AND CONTROL; 278] *Opposite:* deregulate.

limitation *n* **drawback**, inadequacy, imperfection, weakness, weak point, shortcoming, snag. [➡FAULTS, FLAWS, AND WEAKNESSES; 252]

limited *adj* **incomplete**, imperfect, partial, inadequate, restricted, narrow. [➡UNFINISHEDNESS; 240] *Opposite:* boundless.

limited-access highway (*US*) *type of* **major road**. [➡ROADS; 1105]

limited company *n* **limited liability company**, public limited company, PLC, joint-stock company, company, corporation, firm, enterprise. [➡BUSINESS ENTERPRISES AND RELATED BODIES; 793]

limited edition *n* **special edition**, limited printing, limited issue, limited print run, deluxe edition. [➡BOOKS AND BOOKLETS; 591]

limited liability company *n* [➡BUSINESS ENTERPRISES AND RELATED BODIES; 793]

limiter *n* **regulator**, controller, control, restraint, check. [➡ELECTRONICS AND ELECTRICS; 1136]

limitless *adj* **boundless**, unbounded, immeasurable, infinite, vast, inexhaustible, never-ending, unlimited. [➡PERMANENCE: WITHOUT END; 94] *Opposite:* limited.

limitlessness *n* [➡PERMANENCE: WITHOUT END; 94]

limits *n* **bounds**, restrictions, confines, parameters, boundaries. [➡EXTREMITIES OF PHYSICAL OBJECTS; 1249]

limo (*informal*) *type of* **car**. [➡BIKES, CARS, AND CARRIAGES; 1148]

Limoges *type of* **pottery**. [➡POTTERY; 1134]

limousine *type of* **car**. [➡BIKES, CARS, AND CARRIAGES; 1148]

limp 1 *v* **hobble**, shuffle, shamble, stagger, wobble, hitch (*US*). [➡WALK UNSTEADILY; 316] 2 *adj* **floppy**, bendy, wilted, flaccid, lifeless, drooping, sagging, wilting, loose. [➡MALLEABLE AND ELASTIC; 1211] *Opposite:* stiff.

limpet *type of* **aquatic invertebrate**. [➡AQUATIC INVERTEBRATE; 1022]

limpid 1 *adj* **transparent**, clear, translucent, diaphanous, see-through, sheer, crystalline, crystal, pellucid (*literary*). [➡VISUAL TEXTURE; 1220] *Opposite:* opaque. 2 *adj* **lucid**, clear, crystal clear, clear as day, understandable, intelligible, comprehensible, unambiguous. [➡CONCISE AND CLEAR; 203] *Opposite:* obscure.

limpness *n* **floppiness**, flaccidity, droopiness, lifelessness, flabbiness (*informal*), sagginess, softness. [➡MALLEABLE AND ELASTIC; 1211] *Opposite:* stiffness.

limy *adj* **lime-flavoured**, lime, citrus. [➡TASTE; 704]

linchpin *n* **kingpin** (*informal*), fulcrum, cornerstone, hub, essential, prerequisite, sine qua non, requirement. [➡MOST IMPORTANT THING; 198] *Opposite:* accessory.

Lincoln green *type of* **green**. [➡COLOURS; 1223]

lindy hop *n* [➡DANCE; 903]

line 1 *n* **row**, column, procession, lineup, queue. [➡AREA AND RANGE; 111] 2 *n* **streak**, stripe, contour, mark, stroke. [➡PATTERNS; 1224] 3 *n* **boundary**, limit, border, edge, frontier. [➡EXTREMITIES OF PHYSICAL OBJECTS; 1249] 4 *n* **link**, route, track, connection, course, way, passage. [➡RAILWAYS; 1106] 5 *n* **string**, cable, rope, thread, twine, flex, wire, lead, cord. [➡FASTENERS, LINKS, AND NETWORKS; 1246] 6 *n* **ancestry**, family, lineage, descent, race, parentage, stock, heritage. [➡THE FAMILY; 956] 7 *n* **edge**, profile, contour, outline, silhouette, delineation. [➡EXTREMITIES OF PHYSICAL OBJECTS; 1249] 8 *n* **policy**, attitude, method, approach, ideology, position, stance, course, procedure. [➡TEMPERAMENT AND BEHAVIOUR; 493] 9 *n* **area**, occupation, field, interest, speciality, specialization, specialism, work, job, calling, pursuit. [➡SUBJECT AREA; 769] 10 *v* **coat**, cover, reinforce, pad. [➡DECORATE, ADORN, AND APPLY COATINGS; 406]

lineage *n* **ancestry**, family, line, heredity, extraction, pedigree, roots, family tree, stock, descent. [➡THE FAMILY; 956]

lineament (*literary*) *n* **facial feature**, feature, contour. [➡FACIAL CHARACTERISTICS; 482]

linear 1 *adj* **in lines**, lined, line. [➡ORIENTATION AND ALIGNMENT; 1222] 2 *adj* **straight**, rectilinear, direct, undeviating, right, true. [➡ORIENTATION AND ALIGNMENT; 1222]

lined 1 *adj* **wrinkled**, creased, wizened, furrowed, crinkled. [➡FACIAL CHARACTERISTICS; 482] *Opposite:* smooth. 2 *adj* **ruled**, feint. [➡DESCRIBING PATTERNS; 1226] *Opposite:* plain.

line dancing *type of* **dance**. [➡DANCE; 903]

line manager *n* **manager**, production manager, sales manager, boss, superior, supervisor. [➡BOSSES AND MANAGEMENT; 965]

linen *type of* **fabric from plants**. [➡FABRICS; 1131]

line of attack *n* [➡WAYS OF DOING THINGS; 295]

line officer *n* **combat officer**, frontline officer, fighting officer, field officer, officer, combatant. [➡MILITARY PERSONNEL; 828]

line of sight *n* **sightline**, line of vision, view. [➡SEE; 700]

line of work *n* [➡PROFESSIONS; 845]

liner *n* **lining**, bin liner, pool liner, facing, insert. [➡COVERS AND COATINGS; 1245]

line up 1 *v* **assemble**, queue, gather together, collect, align, organize. [➡ARRANGE AND CREATE ORDER; 358] 2 *v* **form ranks**, fall into line, marshal, order, align. [➡POSITION SOMETHING; 326] 3 *v* **plan**, organize, arrange, prepare, set up, get ready, sort, systematize, provide. [➡PREPARE FOR ACTION; 290] 4 *v* **arrange**, collect, order, organize, place, array (*formal*). [➡ARRANGE AND CREATE ORDER; 358] *Opposite:* disarrange.

lineup 1 *n* **team list**, roster, team, listing, side, cast. [➡GROUPS WITH A COMMON INTEREST; 938] 2 *n* **schedule**, listing, programme. [➡WORKERS IN ENTERTAINMENT AND MEDIA; 873] 3 *n* **group**, team, alliance, association, league, union, assembly, band, ensemble. [➡GROUPS OF PEOPLE; 935]

ling *type of* **sea fish**. [➡SEA FISH; 1009]

linger *v* **remain**, stay behind, hang on, loiter, stay, stick around (*informal*), delay, dawdle, hang back, hang around. [➡MOVE SLOWLY; 315] *Opposite:* leave.

lingerie *n* **underwear**, underclothes, underclothing, undergarments, undies (*informal*), smalls (*informal or humorous*). [➡HABERDASHERY, MILLINERY, AND LINGERIE; 867]

lingering 1 *adj* **drawn-out**, spun-out, slow, protracted, long-drawn-out, prolonged. [➡HAPPENING SLOWLY; 106] *Opposite:* quick. 2 *adj* **lasting**, remaining, persistent, enduring, haunting. [➡PERMANENCE: WITHOUT END; 94]

lingo (*informal*) *n* **language**, speech, idiom, vernacular, jargon, argot, dialect, patois, patter. [➡ASPECTS OF LANGUAGE; 683]

lingua franca *n* [➡ASPECTS OF LANGUAGE; 683]

linguine *type of* **pasta**. [➡PASTA; 1179]

linguist *n* [➡PEOPLE WHO WORK WITH LANGUAGE AND CODE; 854]

linguistic *adj* **language**, verbal, philological, dialectal, etymological, phonological, morphological, semantic, grammatical, syntactical. [➡ASPECTS OF LANGUAGE; 683]

linguistics *n* **dialectology**, etymology, phonology, morphology, semantics, grammar, syntax. [➡ASPECTS OF LANGUAGE; 683]

liniment *n* **ointment**, cream, unguent, rub, salve, lotion, balm, emollient, gel. [➡LOTIONS, PASTES, AND GELS; 1271]

lining 1 *n* **coating**, liner, insert, facing. [➡COVERS AND COATINGS; 1245] 2 *part of* **garment**. [➡PARTS OF A GARMENT; 870]

link 1 *n* **connection**, relation, association, relationship, linkage, tie, bond, yoke, nexus. [➡CONNECTION; 144] 2 *v* **connect**, relate, associate, bring together, link up, network, join, combine, couple, conjoin (*formal*). [➡CREATING CONNECTIONS; 145] *Opposite:* separate.

linkage *n* **connection**, relation, association, relationship, link, bond, tie, yoke, nexus. [➡CONNECTION; 144]

linked *adj* **related**, connected, accompanying, allied, associated, interconnected, interrelated, concomitant, concurrent, attendant. [➡RELATED; 143] *Opposite:* unrelated.

linkup *n* **connection**, association, link, linkage, bond, union, hookup (*informal*), tie-up. [➡CONNECTION; 144] *Opposite:* separation.

linnet *type of* **songbird**. [➡SONGBIRD; 1003]

lion *type of* **cat**. [➡FELINE; 983]

lioness *type of* **female animal**. [➡MALE OR FEMALE ANIMAL; 978]

lionhearted *adj* **brave**, courageous, intrepid (*literary or humorous*), stouthearted, bold, audacious, daring, fearless, dauntless (*literary*), unafraid, plucky, valorous, valiant, heroic, doughty (*literary*), gallant (*literary*). [➡COURAGE; 499] *Opposite:* cowardly.

lionheartedness *n* [➡COURAGE; 499]

lionize *v* **glorify**, idolize, praise, fete, celebrate, acclaim, applaud, hail, extol. [➡PRAISE AND ENCOURAGE; 648] *Opposite:* censure.

lion's share *n* **largest part**, bulk, most, majority, mass, vast majority. [➡MAJORITY; 139]

lip 1 *n* **edge**, rim, brim, brink. [➡EXTREMITIES OF PHYSICAL OBJECTS; 1249] 2 *n* (*slang*) **impertinence**, mouth (*informal*), impudence, rudeness, attitude, cheek, backchat (*informal*), back talk (*US*). [➡BAD MANNERS AND SOCIAL SKILLS; 522] *Opposite:* respect. 3 *part of* **mouth**. [➡THE MOUTH; 703]

lip-smacking *adj* [➡TASTE; 704]

lipstick *n* [➡MAKEUP AND BEAUTY PRODUCTS; 491]

liquefied *adj* [➡FLUID AND NON-SOLID; 1212]

liquefy *v* **dissolve**, soften, melt, run, thaw, deliquesce. [➡SOFTEN, LIQUEFY, DAMPEN; 389] *Opposite:* solidify.

liquescence *n* [➡FLUID AND NON-SOLID; 1212]

liquescent *adj* [➡FLUID AND NON-SOLID; 1212]

liquid 1 *n* **fluid**, water, juice, solution, liquor. [➡LIQUIDS; 1268] 2 *adj* **runny**, fluid, gooey, watery, melted, liquescent, molten, liquefied. [➡FLUID AND NON-SOLID; 1212] *Opposite:* solid.

liquid assets *n* [➡FINANCIAL ASSETS; 463]

liquidate 1 *v* **settle**, clear up, pay, honour, pay off, discharge (*formal*), satisfy, square, quit (*archaic*). [➡REWARD; 437] 2 *v* **shut down**, sell out, sell off, bankrupt, wind up. [➡BUSINESS ACTIVITIES AND PHENOMENA; 795] 3 *v* **kill**, murder, execute, eliminate, assassinate, exterminate, bump off (*slang*), knock off (*slang*), dispose of. [➡KILL; 923]

liquidation *n* **insolvency**, bankruptcy, closing, winding up, selling out, shutting down. [➡BUSINESS ACTIVITIES AND PHENOMENA; 795]

liquidator *n* **receiver**, official receiver, sequestrator, administrative receiver, overseer. [➡PEOPLE INVOLVED IN FINANCE; 804]

liquidity 1 *n* **liquidness**, fluidity, fluidness, wateriness, runniness, liquescence, liquescency. [➡FLUID AND NON-SOLID; 1212] *Opposite:* solidity. 2 *n* **assets**, liquid assets, convertible assets, resources, financial resources, cash, cash flow, funds, monies (*formal*), reserves. [➡FINANCIAL ASSETS; 463]

liquidize *v* **purée**, blend, pulverize, mash, pulp, mix, intermix, liquefy. [➡COOKING AND FOOD PREPARATION; 354]

liquidizer *type of* **utensil**. [➡TABLEWARE, CUTLERY, AND KITCHENWARE; 861]

liquor 1 *n* **alcohol**, spirits, whisky, malt. [➡DRINKS; 1186] 2 *n* **liquid**, fluid, solution, juice. [➡LIQUIDS; 1268]

liquored up (*US informal*) *adj* [➡UNDER THE INFLUENCE OF DRUGS OR ALCOHOL; 742]

liquorice *type of* **confectionery**. [➡CONFECTIONERY; 1181]

lissom 1 *adj* **lithe**, supple, flexible, willowy, svelte, limber. [➡AGILITY OF THE BODY; 477] *Opposite:* stiff. 2 *adj* **agile**, nimble, lively, quick, light, deft, graceful, adroit, spry, light on your feet, sprightly. [➡AGILITY OF THE BODY; 477] *Opposite:* awkward.

lissome *see* **lissom**.

list 1 *n* **catalogue**, register, record, roll, listing, directory, file, inventory. [➡LISTS AND SCHEDULES; 588] 2 *v* **record**, catalogue, register, itemize, enumerate, inventory. [➡RECORD SOMETHING; 372] 3 *n* **tilt**, slant, slope, gradient, lean, grade, incline, angle. [➡ORIENTATION AND ALIGNMENT; 1222] 4 *v* **slant**, tilt, incline, lean, bank, decline, recline, slope. [➡TAKE UP A NEW POSITION; 313]

listed *adj* **registered**, recorded, itemized, enumerated. [➡PRESENT AND AVAILABLE; 11] *Opposite:* unlisted.

listen *v* **pay attention**, take note, attend, pin your ears back (*informal*), heed, hang on. [➡LISTEN AND LISTENERS; 709] *Opposite:* ignore.

listener *n* **hearer**, auditor (*formal*), radio listener, audience member, audiophile, eavesdropper. [➡LISTEN AND LISTENERS; 709]

listen in *v* **eavesdrop**, snoop (*informal*), monitor, wiretap, bug. [➡LISTEN AND LISTENERS; 709]

listening post *n* **observation post**, lookout post, surveillance post, sentry post. [➡TOWERS; 1098]

listen up (*informal*) *v* **listen**, pay attention, attend, heed, pay heed, give heed, take notice, concentrate, lend an ear. [➡LISTEN AND LISTENERS; 709] *Opposite:* ignore.

listeria *type of* **microorganism**. [➡MICROORGANISMS, FUNGI, AND ALGAE; 1023]

listing 1 *n* **citation**, item, entry. [➡SUMMARIES, OUTLINES, AND EXCERPTS; 589] 2 *n* **list**, catalogue, register, record, roll, inventory, directory. [➡LISTS AND SCHEDULES; 588]

listings *n* **schedule**, programme, guide. [➡LISTS AND SCHEDULES; 588]

listless *adj* **languid**, lethargic, indolent, enervated, limp, apathetic, inactive, inert. [➡TIRED, ASLEEP, AND UNCONSCIOUS; 739] *Opposite:* energetic.

listlessness *n* [➡TIRED, ASLEEP, AND UNCONSCIOUS; 739]

litany 1 *n* **prayers**, liturgical prayers, petitions, invocations, responses, supplications (*formal*). [➡RELIGIONS AND RELIGIOUS PRACTICES; 778] 2 *n* **list**, listing, catalogue, series, recital, recitation, enumeration, inventory. [➡COLLECTIONS AND MIXTURES OF THINGS; 1243]

literacy 1 *n* **three Rs**, literateness, reading ability. [➡KNOWLEDGE AND WISDOM; 559] 2 *n* **knowledge**, learning, mastery, savvy (*informal*), nous. [➡KNOWLEDGE AND WISDOM; 559]

literal 1 *adj* **factual**, truthful, honest, exact, accurate, unembroidered, unembellished, plain, bare, unvarnished. [➡TRUE AND REAL; 172] *Opposite:* figurative. 2 *adj* **word for word**, verbatim, accurate, exact, correct, precise. [➡EXACT; 204] *Opposite:* inaccurate.

literally *adv* **factually**, accurately, exactly, plainly. [➡TRUE AND REAL; 172] *Opposite:* figuratively.

literary 1 *adj* **fictional**, mythical, legendary, storybook, fictitious. [➡FALSE AND UNREAL; 174] *Opposite:* historical. 2 *adj* **bookish**, erudite, scholarly, well-read, literate. [➡LEVEL OF EDUCATION AND SOPHISTICATION; 894]

literate *adj* **well-educated**, well-read, knowledgeable, cultured, erudite, literary, informed, scholarly, scholastic, learned. [➡LEVEL OF EDUCATION AND SOPHISTICATION; 894] *Opposite:* illiterate.

literati (*formal*) 1 *n* **intellectuals**, intellects, highbrows, intelligentsia, academics, scholars. [➡LEVEL OF EDUCATION AND SOPHISTICATION; 894] 2 *n* **authors**, writers, poets, playwrights, editors, publishers, littérateurs (*archaic*). [➡WRITERS AND STYLES; 914]

literature 1 *n* **writings**, works, collected works, texts, books, words, prose, poetry, fiction, nonfiction. [➡FICTION AND DRAMA; 913] 2 *n* **information**, sources, reading matter, brochures, pamphlets, leaflets, info (*informal*), bumf (*informal*), fliers. [➡BOOKS AND BOOKLETS; 591]

lithe *adj* **supple**, flexible, lissom, agile, nimble, limber. [➡AGILITY OF THE BODY; 477] *Opposite:* stiff.

litheness *n* [➡AGILITY OF THE BODY; 477]

lithesome (*archaic or literary*) *adj* **lithe**, supple, flexible, limber, lissom, loose-limbed, willowy. [➡AGILITY OF THE BODY; 477] *Opposite:* stiff.

lithograph *n* [➡DRAWINGS, CHARTS, AND TABLES; 595]

litigable *adj* **responsible**, liable, accountable, answerable, actionable, disputable, suable, arguable. [➡ILLEGAL; 816]

litigant *n* [➡THE POLICE, ARREST, AND PRE-TRIAL PROCEEDINGS; 818]

litigate *v* **take proceedings**, sue, contest, file, petition, prosecute, implead, arraign, impeach, accuse, charge, press charges. [➡TRIAL, PUNISHMENT, AND LEGAL OUTCOMES; 819]

litigation *n* **court case**, proceedings, lawsuit, legal action, legal process, trial, hearing, process. [➡TRIAL, PUNISHMENT, AND LEGAL OUTCOMES; 819]

litmus test *n* **acid test**, proof, confirmation, test, measure. [➡PERFECT EXAMPLES AND EMBODIMENTS; 67]

litter 1 *n* **waste**, rubbish, debris, refuse, trash (*US*), garbage (*US*). [➡RUBBISH AND USELESS OBJECTS; 1248] 2 *n* **disorder**, confusion, jumble, clutter, untidiness, mess. [➡DISORDER AND CHAOS; 246] 3 *n* **offspring**, young, progeny, brood, family. [➡GROUP OF ANIMALS; 993] 4 *v* **drop litter**, scatter, spoil, strew, clutter. [➡WORSEN APPEARANCE; 383] *Opposite:* clean up.

litterbug (*informal*) *n* **litter lout** (*informal disapproving*), litterer, dumper, fly-tipper. [➡DIRTY AND SLOVENLY PEOPLE; 954]

litter lout (*informal disapproving*) *n* **litterbug** (*informal*), litterer, fly-tipper, dumper. [➡DIRTY AND SLOVENLY PEOPLE; 954]

little 1 *adj* **small**, slight, petite, diminutive, tiny, minute, bantam, miniature, pint-sized (*informal*), pocket-sized. [➡SMALL; 1194] *Opposite:* large. 2 *adj* **unimportant**, trivial, slight, petty, trifling, inconsequential, negligible, piddling (*informal*), insignificant, minor. [➡UNIMPORTANT AND UNNECESSARY; 239] *Opposite:* major. 3 *pron* **bit**, touch, spot, some, tad (*informal*), pittance, minimum, trace. [➡FEW, LITTLE, SMALL AMOUNT; 119] *Opposite:* lot. 4 *adv* **not very**, not much, not sufficiently, insufficiently, inadequately, not enough, barely, hardly, slightly, scarcely. [➡TO A CERTAIN EXTENT; 134] *Opposite:* well.

little by little *adv* **gradually**, bit by bit, inch by inch, slowly, incrementally, imperceptibly, by degrees. [➡HAPPENING SLOWLY; 106] *Opposite:* all at once.

little finger *part of* **arm or hand**. [➡ARM AND HAND; 696]

little folk *see* **little people**

little green man (*humorous*) *n* **alien**, Martian, extraterrestrial. [➡SCIENCE FICTION; 1063]

little-known *adj* [➡SECRET AND UNKNOWN; 180]

little owl *type of* **owl**. [➡OWL; 1001]

little people *n* **little folk**, supernatural beings, imaginary beings, fairies, elves, pixies, leprechauns, gnomes. [➡MYTHICAL BEINGS; 790]

little toe *part of* **leg or foot**. [➡LEG AND FOOT; 695]

littoral 1 *adj* **coastal**, shoreline, seaside. [➡THE SEAS, OCEANS, AND SHORES; 1041] *Opposite:* inland. 2 *n* **shore**, coast, seaside, shoreline, beach, seafront, shorefront, oceanfront. [➡THE SEAS, OCEANS, AND SHORES; 1041]

liturgy *n* **church service**, mass, ritual, religious ceremony, rite, worship. [➡RELIGIONS AND RELIGIOUS PRACTICES; 778]

livable 1 *adj* **habitable**, functional, civilized, comfortable, agreeable, pleasant, convenient, cosy, enjoyable, accommodating, suitable. [➡PHYSICALLY PLEASANT; 187] *Opposite:* uninhabitable. 2 *adj* **bearable**, endurable, acceptable, tolerable, worthwhile, passable, supportable (*literary*). [➡ACCEPTABLE AND PASSABLE; 220] *Opposite:* intolerable.

live 1 *v* **exist**, be alive, be in this world, survive, subsist, breathe, be, be animate. [➡EXIST; 15] *Opposite:* die. 2 *v* **reside**, stay, have your home, dwell (*literary*), inhabit, settle, abide (*archaic*), occupy. [➡INHABIT; 20] 3 *adj* **living**, animate, conscious, breathing, aware, sentient, alive, quick (*archaic*), existent (*formal*), vital. [➡LIVING THINGS AND LIVING; 976] *Opposite:* dead.

liveable *see* **livable**.

lived-in 1 *adj* **homely**, comfortable, relaxed, laid-back (*informal*), dishevelled, untidy, homey. [➡IN GOOD REPAIR; 1231] 2 *adj* **careworn**, haggard, worn, lined, tired, weather-beaten, rundown. [➡FACIAL CHARACTERISTICS; 482]

live down *v* **get over**, recover, shake off, forget, survive, outlast. [➡FORGET, FORGIVE, AND ACCEPT; 749]

live it up (*slang*) *v* **enjoy life**, have a good time, paint the town red (*informal*), have fun, have a ball (*dated slang*). [➡LEISURE AND RECREATION; 874]

livelihood 1 *n* **living**, income, source of revenue, means of support, maintenance, funds. [➡INCOME; 461] 2 *n* **employment**, occupation, trade, business, work, job. [➡JOB; 833]

liveliness *n* **energy**, sparkle, vigour, joie de vivre, get-up-and-go (*informal*), vivacity, dynamism, spirit. [➡ENERGY AND ENTHUSIASM; 497] *Opposite:* lethargy.

lively *adj* **energetic**, vigorous, sparkling, active, vivacious, animated, sprightly, dynamic, bouncy, bubbly, buoyant, spirited. [➡ENERGY AND ENTHUSIASM; 497] *Opposite:* lethargic.

liven *v* **perk up**, cheer up, boost, quicken, energize, enliven. [➡ENCOURAGE; 577] *Opposite:* depress.

liven up *v* **enliven**, stimulate, revive, cheer up, perk up, brighten up, hot up (*informal*), raise, lift. [➡IMPROVE SOMETHING; 375]

live off *v* **rely on**, depend on, impose on, sponge, mooch (*informal*), skive (*informal*), leech (*informal*). [➡RECIPROCITY AND INTERDEPENDENCE; 148]

live on 1 *v* **remain**, continue, survive, persist, prevail, persevere. [➡CONTINUE TO EXIST; 17] *Opposite:* die away. 2 *v* **survive on**, get by on, exist on, subsist on, eke out a living, make ends meet. [➡CONTINUE TO EXIST; 17]

liver 1 *type of* **brown**. [➡COLOURS; 1223] 2 *part of* **digestive tract**. [➡THE DIGESTIVE TRACT; 710]

liveried *adj* **uniformed**, costumed, dressed up, caparisoned. [➡DRESS, WEAR, AND UNDRESS; 868]

liverish *adj* **irritable**, bad-tempered, moody, tetchy (*informal*), irascible, ill-humoured, volatile, hotheaded, touchy. [➡AGGRESSIVE AND BELLIGERENT; 519]

liver sausage *type of* **processed meat**. [➡TYPES AND CUTS OF MEAT; 1176]

liverwurst (*US*) *type of* **processed meat**. [➡TYPES AND CUTS OF MEAT; 1176]

livery 1 *n* (*literary*) **insignia**, colours, corporate colours, racing colours. [➡PATTERNS; 1224] 2 *n* **uniform**, dress, costume, attire (*formal*), vestments, regalia. [➡GARMENTS AND OUTFITS; 865]

livestock *n* [➡FARM ANIMAL; 982]

live through *v* **survive**, come through, get through, experience, undergo, go through, weather, withstand, brave, ride out. [➡EXPERIENCE AND ENCOUNTER; 583] *Opposite:* succumb.

live up to *v* **match**, achieve, reach, come up to, meet, compare. [➡SUCCEED AND WIN; 79]

live wire (*informal*) *n* **doer**, activist, high-flier, bright spark (*informal*), go-getter (*informal*), extrovert, live one (*informal*). [➡PEOPLE WHO ARE APPROVED OF; 955]

live with *v* **tolerate**, put up with, bear, endure, manage, cope, accept. [➡TOLERATE AND ENDURE; 767]

livid 1 *adj* **discoloured**, bruised, purple, contused (*technical*), black-and-blue. [➡INJURED; 743] 2 *adj* **furious**, enraged, up in arms, beside yourself, incensed, fuming, outraged, irate, mad, angry. [➡IRRITATION AND ANGER; 542] *Opposite:* pleased.

lividly *adv* **furiously**, angrily, irately, exasperatedly. [➡IRRITATION AND ANGER; 542]

living 1 *adj* **alive**, breathing, existing, live, active, animate, incarnate, corporeal, organic, extant, quick (*archaic*). [➡LIVING THINGS AND LIVING; 976] *Opposite:* dead. 2 *n* **livelihood**, income, living wage, source of revenue, subsistence, means of support, funds. [➡INCOME; 461]

> **Compare and Contrast:** ***living, alive, animate, extant***
>
> CORE MEANING: HAVING LIFE OR EXISTENCE
>
> ***living*** not dead, or, of inanimate things, still in existence; ***alive*** not dead; ***animate*** physically alive, epecially used to distinguish animals and plants from inanimate objects such as rocks, water, or buildings; ***extant*** still in existence.

living being *n* [➡LIVING THINGS AND LIVING; 976]

living quarters *n* [➡ACCOMMODATION; 855]

living room *type of* **room in the home**. [➡TYPES OF ROOM; 1096]

living thing *n* **creature**, being, living being, life form, organism, animal, beast, human, human being. [➡LIVING THINGS AND LIVING; 976]

lizard *type of* **reptile**. [➡REPTILES; 994]

llama *type of* **large mammal**. [➡LARGE MAMMAL; 986]

loach *type of* **freshwater fish**. [➡FRESHWATER FISH; 1010]

load 1 *n* **weight**, cargo, freight, consignment, shipment, burden, capacity, contents. [➡TRANSPORTATION, TRANSPORTERS, AND CARGOS; 323] 2 *v* **fill**, pack, stack, load up, pile, heap, stock, stuff, charge (*formal*). [➡FILL; 407] *Opposite:* unload. 3 *v* **put in**, insert, slot in, pop in (*informal*). [➡POSITION SOMETHING; 326] *Opposite:* eject. 4 *v* **burden**, encumber, weigh down, overload, oppress, worry, overwhelm, crush, hamper. [➡GIVE TOO MUCH; 438] *Opposite:* alleviate.

loaded 1 *adj* **laden**, weighed down, encumbered, burdened, overloaded, full, overburdened. [➡FULL; 1238] *Opposite:* empty. 2 *adj* (*slang*) **rich**, wealthy, well-off, well-heeled (*informal*), affluent, rolling in it (*informal*). [➡WEALTH AND WEALTHY; 891] *Opposite:* poor. 3 *adj* **biased**, leading, deceptive, trick, manipulative, unfair. [➡FALSE AND UNREAL; 174] *Opposite:* innocent.

loads (*informal*) *n* **many**, heaps (*informal*), masses (*informal*), oodles (*informal*), much, lots, tons (*informal*). [➡MANY, MUCH, LARGE AMOUNT; 117] *Opposite:* handful.

loadstone *see* **lodestone**.

load up *v* **fill up**, stack, pack, pile, fill, cram, stuff, heap up, charge (*formal*), load. [➡FILL; 407] *Opposite:* unload.

loaf *v* **be idle**, be unoccupied, hang out (*informal*), hang about, mooch (*slang*), laze, loiter, loll, lie around (*informal*), malinger (*disapproving*). [➡LACK OF ACTIVITY; 343]

loaf about *v* [➡LACK OF ACTIVITY; 343]

loaf around *v* [➡LACK OF ACTIVITY; 343]

loafer *n* **idler**, slacker, slouch (*informal*), shirker, sloth, lazybones (*informal*), loiterer (*disapproving*), malingerer (*disapproving*), goldbricker (*US informal*), lollygagger (*US dated*). [➡LAZY OR UNSUCCESSFUL PEOPLE; 948]

loam *n* [➡EROSION PRODUCTS AND SOIL; 1058]

loan 1 *n* **advance**, credit, finance, mortgage. [➡ACCOUNTING, BANKING, AND BUDGETING; 799] 2 *v* **lend**, advance, give a loan, give an advance, allow. [➡LEND, LEASE, AND BORROW; 429] *Opposite:* borrow.

loath *adj* **unwilling**, reluctant, wary, chary, against, opposed, averse (*formal*), disinclined. [➡UNWILLINGNESS AND STUBBORNNESS; 565] *Opposite:* eager.

See Compare and Contrast at **unwilling**.

loathe *v* **hate**, dislike, detest, can't stand, can't bear, despise, abhor (*formal*), abominate (*formal*), scorn, disdain. [➡DISLIKE AND HATE; 578] *Opposite:* adore.

loathed *adj* [➡UNPOPULAR AND UNWANTED; 259]

loathing *n* **hate**, hatred, dislike, antipathy, repugnance, detestation, abhorrence, disgust, aversion, revulsion, animus, animosity, hostility. [➡DISLIKE AND HATE; 578] *Opposite:* love.

See Compare and Contrast at **dislike**.

loathsome *adj* **hateful**, despicable, disgusting, repugnant, detestable, abhorrent (*formal*), nasty, vile, odious, obnoxious, repulsive, revolting, offensive. [➡DISGUSTING AND REPULSIVE; 231] *Opposite:* delightful.

lob 1 *v* **throw**, toss, fling, pitch, chuck (*informal*), hurl. [➡THROW SOMETHING; 335] 2 *v* **hit**, knock, strike, bat, whack. [➡CONTACT: IMPACT; 414] 3 *n* **toss**, throw, pitch, hit, ball. [➡THROW SOMETHING; 335]

lobby 1 *n* **entrance hall**, foyer, reception area, vestibule, atrium, entrance, hall, antechamber, anteroom, waiting room. [➡DOORS AND ACCESS POINTS; 1100] 2 *n* **pressure group**, interest group, ginger group, campaign group, special interest group, faction, alliance, lobby group. [➡GROUPS WITH A COMMON INTEREST; 938] 3 *type of* **room in public buildings**. [➡TYPES OF ROOM; 1096] 4 *v* **petition**, press your case, try to influence, apply pressure, sway opinion, push, promote, urge, pull strings. [➡REQUEST AND DEMAND; 664]

lobby group *n* **pressure group**, campaign group, interest group, lobby, alliance, faction, special interest group. [➡GROUPS WITH A COMMON INTEREST; 938]

lobe *n* **part**, section, portion, hemisphere. [➡EXTREMITIES OF PHYSICAL OBJECTS; 1249]

lobelia *type of* **annual flower**. [➡FLOWERS; 1032]

lobster *type of* **crustacean**. [➡AQUATIC INVERTEBRATE; 1022]

local 1 *adj* **restricted**, limited, confined, narrow, insular, parochial. [➡CLOSENESS; 160] *Opposite:* universal. 2 *adj* **home**, neighbouring, neighbourhood, community, district, regional, area, provincial. [➡CLOSENESS; 160] *Opposite:* national. 3 *adj* **native**, indigenous, resident, homegrown. [➡COUNTRIES AND REGIONS; 1066] *Opposite:* foreign. 4 *n* **resident**, inhabitant, citizen, native. [➡INHABITANT; 857] *Opposite:* stranger. 5 *type of* **bar or club**. [➡HOTELS, RESTAURANTS, AND CLUBS; 1081]

locale *n* **location**, setting, place, milieu (*formal*), area, locality, site, spot. [➡PLACE; 1064]

locality 1 *n* **area**, district, region, neighbourhood, zone, section, vicinity, quarter, ghetto. [➡PLACE; 1064] 2 *n* **position**, place, site, spot, setting, environment, locale. [➡PLACE; 1064]

localize 1 *v* **restrict**, confine, limit, focus, contain, concentrate. [➡CAPTIVITY AND LOSS OF FREEDOM; 249] 2 *v* **pinpoint**, locate, identify, find exactly, narrow down, specify. [➡FIND; 464]

localized *adj* **contained**, limited, restricted, confined, local. [➡CAPTIVITY AND LOSS OF FREEDOM; 249] *Opposite:* generalized.

locally *adv* **nearby**, close by, in the vicinity, in the neighbourhood. [➡CLOSENESS; 160]

locate 1 *v* **place**, put, position, situate (*formal*), set, fix (*informal*), establish, station, post. [➡POSITION SOMETHING; 326] 2 *v* **find**, trace, discover, track down, detect, pinpoint, localize, ferret out, uncover. [➡FIND; 464] *Opposite:* lose.

location *n* **site**, place, position, spot, setting, scene, locality, whereabouts, situation, locale. [➡PLACE; 1064]

loch 1 *n* **lake**, tarn, broad, water, lough, mere (*archaic or literary*). [➡RIVERS, LAKES, AND STREAMS; 1042] 2 *n* **inlet**, fjord, firth, creek, sea loch, sound, estuary. [➡RIVERS, LAKES, AND STREAMS; 1042]

lock 1 *n* **security device**, padlock, mortise lock, safety catch, combination lock, latch, bolt, catch, deadlock, dead bolt. [➡FASTENERS, LINKS, AND NETWORKS; 1246] 2 *v* **fasten**, bolt, secure, lock up, padlock, bar. [➡FASTEN, LINK, AND JOIN; 409] *Opposite:* unlock. 3 *v* **fix in place**, lodge, wedge, secure, confine. [➡BAR AND OBSTRUCT ACCESS; 411] *Opposite:* free. 4 *v* **brace**, clench, stiffen, tighten. [➡PHYSICAL REACTIONS; 317] *Opposite:* flex. 5 *v* **link**, clasp, intertwine, join, unite, interlink, clinch, interlock.

[➡ FASTEN, LINK, AND JOIN; 409] 6 *n* **curl**, strand, tuft, wisp, ringlet, tress, hank, skein. [➡ HAIR; 485]

lock away 1 *v* **imprison**, lock up, incarcerate (*formal*), jail, put away (*informal*), put inside (*informal*), send to prison, sentence to prison, intern, send down (*slang*), pen, cage, send up the river (*US*). [➡ CAPTIVITY AND LOSS OF FREEDOM; 249] 2 *v* **shut away**, keep safe, secure, stash (*informal*), seal up, hide away, conceal, put in store, squirrel, put away, store. [➡ STORE AND KEEP; 454] *Opposite:* bring out.

locked up *adj* [➡ CAPTIVITY AND LOSS OF FREEDOM; 249]

locket *type of* **necklace.** [➡ JEWELLERY; 866]

lock horns *v* **argue**, row, disagree, fight, contest, dispute, struggle. [➡ ARGUE AND FIGHT – TWO-WAY; 644]

lock on *v* **home in on**, track, follow, shadow. [➡ ACCOMPANY AND FOLLOW; 338]

lock, stock, and barrel *adv* **completely**, entirely, totally. [➡ ALL; 126]

lock up *v* **imprison**, put away (*informal*), put in jail, put in prison, put behind bars, confine, send down (*slang*), detain, incarcerate (*formal*), pen, coop up. [➡ THE POLICE, ARREST, AND PRE-TRIAL PROCEEDINGS; 818] *Opposite:* release.

lockup *n* **jail**, prison, detention centre, slammer (*slang*), reformatory, penitentiary (*US*). [➡ BUILDINGS FOR CONFINING PEOPLE; 1093]

locomotion *n* **movement**, motion, propulsion, kinetic energy, kinesis, drive. [➡ SELF-PROPULSION; 305] *Opposite:* immobility.

locomotive *n* **train**, engine, steam engine, tank engine. [➡ RAILWAYS; 1106]

locum *n* [➡ SUBORDINATES AND ASSISTANTS; 966]

locus *n* [➡ PLACE; 1064]

locust *type of* **flying insect.** [➡ FLYING INSECTS; 1013]

locution *n* [➡ ASPECTS OF LANGUAGE; 683]

loden *type of* **fabric from animals.** [➡ FABRICS; 1131]

lodge 1 *n* **small house**, cabin, cottage, chalet, hunting lodge, shooting lodge, gatehouse. [➡ RESIDENTIAL BUILDINGS; 1077] 2 *n* **hotel**, inn, resort, motel. [➡ HOTELS, RESTAURANTS, AND CLUBS; 1081] 3 *type of* **outbuilding.** [➡ ANCILLARY BUILDINGS; 1079] 4 *type of* **den or nest.** [➡ ANIMAL OR BIRD ACCOMMODATION; 1078] 5 *v* **stay**, live, board, be a lodger, take lodgings, stop, put up, sojourn (*literary*), room. [➡ INHABIT; 20] 6 *v* **accommodate**, board, billet, put up, quarter, entertain, harbour, shelter. [➡ TAKE CARE OF AND SPOIL; 301] 7 *v* **fix in place**, embed, implant, stick, catch, settle, become fixed. [➡ FASTEN, LINK, AND JOIN; 409]

lodger *n* **tenant**, boarder, paying guest, cotenant, lessee, occupier, resident, occupant, renter, roomer (*US*). [➡ INHABITANT; 857]

lodging *n* **accommodation**, room, space, place to stay, housing, billet, bed and board, accommodations (*US*). [➡ ACCOMMODATION; 855]

lodging house (*dated*) *type of* **hotel.** [➡ HOTELS, RESTAURANTS, AND CLUBS; 1081]

lodgings (*dated*) *n* **rooms**, quarters, bedsitter, digs (*dated informal*). [➡ ACCOMMODATION; 855]

loft 1 *type of* **apartment.** [➡ RESIDENTIAL BUILDINGS; 1077] 2 *type of* **room in the home.** [➡ TYPES OF ROOM; 1096] 3 *type of* **storage space.** [➡ STORES AND STORAGE BUILDINGS; 1087]

loftily *adv* **superciliously**, in a superior way, disdainfully, snootily (*informal*), arrogantly, proudly, haughtily. [➡ POMPOUS, LOUD, AND OVER-CONFIDENT; 636] *Opposite:* humbly.

loftiness *n* **haughtiness**, superior manner, disdain, arrogance, condescension, superciliousness. [➡ POMPOUS, LOUD, AND OVER-CONFIDENT; 636] *Opposite:* humility.

lofty 1 *adj* **supercilious**, superior, disdainful, snooty (*informal*), lordly, arrogant, aloof, proud, haughty, condescending, patronizing. [➡ POMPOUS, LOUD, AND OVER-CONFIDENT; 636] *Opposite:* humble. 2 *adj* **grand**, exalted (*formal*), elevated, noble, admirable, distinguished, dignified, imposing, stately, sublime (*informal*), majestic. [➡ SUPERIORITY; 153] *Opposite:* base. 3 *adj* **tall**, high, towering, soaring, high-ceilinged, elevated. [➡ HEIGHT: HIGH; 1202] *Opposite:* short.

log 1 *n* **record**, journal, notes, minutes, logbook, daybook, calendar, diary. [➡ RECORDS; 586] 2 *v* **make a note of**, chart, record, note down, note, register, list. [➡ RECORD SOMETHING; 372]

loganberry *type of* **berry.** [➡ FRUIT AND VEGETABLES; 1175]

logbook *n* **record**, record book, log, journal, report, register, diary. [➡ RECORDS; 586]

loge *n* **box**, enclosure, box seat (*US*), skybox (*US*). [➡ ALCOVES, CUBICLES, AND COMPARTMENTS; 1095]

loggia *n* [➡ STAGES, PLATFORMS, AND RAISED AREAS; 1097]

logic *n* **reason**, judgment, sense, common sense, lucidity, reasoning, rationality, sensibleness, soundness. [➡ IDEA AND THOUGHT; 771]

logical 1 *adj* **plausible**, reasonable, obvious, sensible, understandable, likely, compelling. [➡ POSSIBLE AND PROBABLE; 178] *Opposite:* implausible. 2 *adj* **rational**, reasonable, sound, commonsense, commonsensical, consistent, coherent, valid, analytical, cogent, lucid. [➡ POSITIVE INTELLECTUAL CHARACTERISTICS; 525] *Opposite:* illogical.

log in *v* **gain access**, open up, start, switch on, sign in, start up, commence (*formal*), begin, access, log on, initiate. [➡ USE TOOLS AND MACHINERY; 469]

logjam 1 *n* **deadlock**, standstill, standoff, stalemate, impasse, gridlock. [➡ LACK OF ACTIVITY; 343] 2 *n* **traffic jam**, holdup, tailback, buildup, snarl-up, snarl (*US*). [➡ TRAVEL: TRAFFIC PROBLEMS AND HOLDUPS; 324]

logo *n* **symbol**, sign, emblem, badge, insignia, design. [➡ SYMBOLS, SIGNS, AND NUMBERS; 597]

log off *v* **leave**, quit, exit, close down, shut down. [➡ STOP ACTING; 265] *Opposite:* log on.

logogram *type of* **wordplay.** [➡ JOKES AND TEASING; 675]

log on *v* **gain access**, open up, start, switch on, sign in, start up, commence (*formal*), begin, access, log in, initiate. [➡ USE TOOLS AND MACHINERY; 469]

log out *v* **log off**, close, exit, sign off, leave. [➡ USE TOOLS AND MACHINERY; 469]

logy (*US*) *adj* **tired**, run-down, enervated, sleepy, wiped out (*slang*), washed out, bushed (*informal*). [➡ TIRED, ASLEEP, AND UNCONSCIOUS; 739]

loin *type of* **cut**. [➡ TYPES AND CUTS OF MEAT; 1176]

loiter 1 *v* **amble**, stroll, wander, drift, dally, dawdle, idle. [➡ MOVE SLOWLY; 315] 2 *v* **wait**, linger, lurk, skulk, hang around, hang out (*informal*). [➡ LACK OF ACTIVITY; 343]

loll 1 *v* **lie**, lounge, lie back, sprawl, slouch, slump, recline, flop. [➡ TAKE UP A NEW POSITION; 313] 2 *v* **droop**, hang down, dangle, sag, flop. [➡ TAKE UP A NEW POSITION; 313]

loll around *v* [➡ LACK OF ACTIVITY; 343]

lollipop *type of* **confectionery on a stick**. [➡ CONFECTIONERY; 1181]

lollop 1 *v* **bound**, bounce, bumble, stride, lope, walk. [➡ PROCEED AND GO; 306] 2 *v* **relax**, take it easy, lounge, veg out (*informal*), chill out (*slang*), lie about (*informal*). [➡ LACK OF ACTIVITY; 343]

lolly (*informal*) 1 *n* **money**, cash, ready money, readies (*informal*), dough (*slang*), dosh (*slang*), bread (*dated slang*), ready cash. [➡ MONEY; 140] 2 *n* **ice lolly**, ice, lollipop. [➡ CONFECTIONERY; 1181]

lollygag (*dated*) *v* [➡ JOKES AND TEASING; 675]

lone 1 *adj* **solitary**, single, single-handed, solo. [➡ ACTING INDEPENDENTLY; 285] *Opposite:* accompanied. 2 *adj* **only**, sole, unique, singular. [➡ UNRELATEDNESS AND SEPARATENESS; 147] 3 *adj* **isolated**, lonely, separate, distinct, discrete, detached, solitary. [➡ SOLITARINESS; 941]

loneliness *n* **aloneness**, solitude, isolation, seclusion, lonesomeness (*US*). [➡ SOLITARINESS; 941] *Opposite:* companionship.

lonely 1 *adj* **forlorn**, lost, alone, friendless, without a friend in the world, abandoned, deserted, lonesome (*US*). [➡ SOLITARINESS; 941] 2 *adj* **isolated**, solitary, secluded, cut off, deserted, remote, desolate, lone, lonesome (*US*). [➡ DISTANCE; 161]

lone parent *type of* **older relative**. [➡ OLDER GENERATION RELATIVES; 959]

loner *n* **recluse**, hermit, lone wolf, outsider. [➡ SOLITARY PEOPLE; 942]

lonesome (*US*) 1 *adj* **lonely**, forlorn, lost, alone, friendless, without a friend in the world, abandoned, deserted. [➡ SOLITARINESS; 941] 2 *adj* **solitary**, isolated, secluded, lonely, cut off, deserted, remote, desolate. [➡ DISTANCE; 161]

lonesomeness (*US*) *n* [➡ SOLITARINESS; 941]

lone wolf *n* [➡ SOLITARY PEOPLE; 942]

long 1 *adj* **extended**, extensive, elongated, lengthy, stretched. [➡ LENGTH: LONG; 1196] *Opposite:* short. 2 *adj* **time-consuming**, protracted, lengthy, slow, prolonged, lingering, sustained. [➡ HAPPENING SLOWLY; 106] *Opposite:* brief.

long ago *n* [➡ PAST; 84]

long-ago *adj* **past**, old, historic, olden (*archaic or literary*), early, prehistoric, ancient, primitive. [➡ PAST; 84] *Opposite:* modern.

longboat *type of* **historical vessel**. [➡ SHIPS AND BOATS; 1149]

long bone *type of* **bone**. [➡ THE BONES AND JOINTS; 720]

longbow *type of* **bow**. [➡ WEAPONS FOR SHOOTING; 1155]

longcase clock *type of* **clock**. [➡ CLOCKS AND TIMERS; 1125]

long-drawn-out *adj* **protracted**, prolonged, lengthy, drawn-out, dragged-out, long-winded, rambling, tedious, boring. [➡ HAPPENING SLOWLY; 106] *Opposite:* concise.

long-eared owl *type of* **owl**. [➡ OWL; 1001]

longed-for *adj* [➡ POPULAR AND WANTED; 221]

long-established *adj* **age-old**, time-honoured, time-worn, ancient, old, traditional, established, deep-rooted, customary, usual. [➡ OLD, OLD-FASHIONED; 168] *Opposite:* new.

longevity *n* **long life**, permanence, durability, endurance. [➡ PERMANENCE: WITHOUT END; 94]

long face *n* [➡ FACIAL EXPRESSION; 652]

long for *v* **want**, yearn, crave, desire, hunger, ache, pine. [➡ DESIRE AND WANT; 580]

See Compare and Contrast at **want**.

long-gone *adj* [➡ ABSENT AND UNAVAILABLE; 7]

long haul (*informal*) 1 *n* **ordeal**, marathon, trial, struggle, endurance test, uphill battle. [➡ HARD WORK OR EFFORT; 299] 2 *n* **trek**, hike, distance, way, big picture (*US*), schlep (*US informal*). [➡ TRAVEL: JOURNEYS AND TRIPS; 319]

longing *n* **desire**, wish, yearning, hunger, craving, ache, pining, lust. [➡ DESIRE AND WANT; 580]

longitude *n* **position**, place, coordinate, location. [➡ NAVIGATION; 1140]

long johns *type of* **lower body underwear**. [➡ HABERDASHERY, MILLINERY, AND LINGERIE; 867]

long jump *type of* **track and field**. [➡ HOBBIES, GAMES, AND SPORTS; 875]

long-lasting *adj* **long-term**, continuing, enduring, lifelong, abiding, ongoing. [➡ PERMANENCE: WITHOUT END; 94] *Opposite:* short-lived.

long-life *adj* **UHT**, tinned, canned. [➡ STATE OF PREPARED FOOD; 1170] *Opposite:* fresh.

long-lived *adj* **long-lasting**, long-standing, prolonged, abiding, long-term, enduring. [➡ PERMANENCE: WITHOUT END; 94] *Opposite:* short-lived.

long-lost (*humorous*) *adj* **lost**, gone, forgotten, missing. [➡ ABSENT AND UNAVAILABLE; 7]

long-range *adj* **long-term**, future, distant, far-off. [➡ FUTURE; 86]

longship *type of* **historical vessel**. [➡ SHIPS AND BOATS; 1149]

long shot *n* **slim chance**, long odds, poor prospect, remote possibility, outside chance, fat chance (*informal*). [➡ATTEMPT AN ACTION; 262]

long-sighted *adj* [➡SEE; 700]

long-standing *adj* **established**, long-lasting, age-old, ancient, enduring, time-honoured. [➡PERMANENCE: WITHOUT END; 94] *Opposite:* recent.

long-suffering *adj* **forgiving**, resigned, tolerant, accommodating, patient, selfless. [➡GENEROSITY AND KINDNESS; 496] *Opposite:* intolerant.

long-term *adj* **lasting**, long-standing, enduring, continuing, durable, abiding. [➡PERMANENCE: WITHOUT END; 94] *Opposite:* short-term.

long-winded *adj* **long-drawn-out**, rambling, interminable, lengthy, prolix, loquacious (*formal*), wordy, verbose, discursive, circuitous, expansive. [➡INARTICULATE, RAMBLING, AND AWKWARD; 634] *Opposite:* concise.

See Compare and Contrast at **wordy.**

long-windedly *adv* **verbosely**, wordily, volubly, prolixly, loquaciously (*formal*), discursively, circuitously, at length, in detail, in depth, expansively. [➡ELOQUENT, TALKATIVE, AND LONG-WINDED; 633] *Opposite:* concisely.

long-windedness *n* **verbosity**, wordiness, volubility, prolixity, verbiage, discursiveness, circumlocution, circuitousness, lengthiness, loquaciousness (*formal*), expansiveness. [➡ELOQUENT, TALKATIVE, AND LONG-WINDED; 633] *Opposite:* conciseness.

loofah *n* **sponge**, scrubber, exfoliator. [➡PERSONAL HYGIENE; 492]

look 1 *v* **observe**, watch, see, behold (*archaic or literary*), view, consider (*formal*), regard, eye, gaze, contemplate. [➡LOOKING AND LOOKS; 701] 2 *v* **examine**, inspect, scrutinize, eyeball (*informal*), pore over, study, scan, survey. [➡EXAMINE AND ASSESS; 754] 3 *v* **seem**, appear, come across, seem to be. [➡SEEM TO BE SOMETHING; 58] 4 *v* **explore**, investigate, examine, consider, discuss, tackle. [➡EXAMINE AND ASSESS; 754] 5 *v* **focus on**, gaze, stare, glare, gawk (*informal*), gawp (*informal*), glance, peep, peek, peer. [➡LOOKING AND LOOKS; 701] 6 *n* **appearance**, expression, air, aspect, guise, mien (*literary*). [➡APPEARANCE AND ATMOSPHERE; 1236]

look after *v* **care for**, take care of, see to, watch over, guard, tend, oversee, mind. [➡TAKE CARE OF AND SPOIL; 301]

look ahead *v* **look forward**, project, plan, anticipate, think about. [➡PREDICT AND ANTICIPATE; 751]

lookalike (*informal*) *n* **double**, twin, doppelgänger, mirror image, duplicate, match, spitting image, clone. [➡COPIES AND REPLICAS; 152]

look back 1 *v* **remember**, reminisce, recall, recollect, relive. [➡REMEMBER; 747] *Opposite:* look ahead. 2 *v* **review**, check, return, revisit. [➡LOOKING AND LOOKS; 701]

look daggers *v* **glare**, glower, scowl, give somebody a dirty look. [➡FACIAL EXPRESSION; 652]

look down on *v* **scorn**, disdain, despise, frown on, abhor (*formal*). [➡DISLIKE AND HATE; 578] *Opposite:* look up to.

looked-for *adj* **anticipated**, expected, awaited, foreseen, hoped-for, desired, wanted, required, necessary. [➡POPULAR AND WANTED; 221] *Opposite:* unexpected.

looker *n* **observer**, watcher, spectator, viewer, onlooker, bystander. [➡LOOKERS AND SPECTATORS; 702]

look for *v* **search for**, seek, hunt for, rummage. [➡SEEK POSSESSION AND SEARCH; 457]

look forward to *v* **anticipate**, hope for, expect, await, wait for, long for. [➡PREDICT AND ANTICIPATE; 751] *Opposite:* dread.

looking glass (*archaic*) *n* **mirror**, glass, hand mirror, shaving mirror. [➡FITTINGS; 859]

look into *v* **investigate**, go into, check out, research, study, examine, explore, delve, dig, probe, inquire. [➡QUESTION THINGS; 752]

look like *v* **resemble**, be like, be similar to, mimic. [➡PRETEND AND MIMIC; 60]

look on the bright side *v* **be positive**, be optimistic, make the best of something, make the best of a bad job, make the best of things, hope for the best, keep your chin up, grin and bear it (*informal*). [➡CHANGE OF MOOD AND COMPOSURE; 581] *Opposite:* despair.

look out 1 *v* **watch out**, beware, take care, pay attention, be alert, be watchful, keep your eyes open, mind. [➡PAY ATTENTION; 766] 2 *v* **look over**, look on to, look out on, give on to, face front, overlook. [➡EXIST IN A PLACE; 19]

lookout 1 *n* **guard**, sentry, sentinel, watch. [➡PEOPLE WHO GUARD AND PROTECT; 846] 2 *n* **viewpoint**, vantage point, lookout tower, crow's nest, belvedere. [➡TOWERS; 1098]

lookout tower *n* [➡TOWERS; 1098]

look over *v* **inspect**, examine, check, give the once-over (*informal*), peruse, scan, flick through, skim, flip through. [➡EXAMINE AND ASSESS; 754]

lookover (*informal*) *n* **inspection**, once-over (*informal*), examination, dekko (*informal*), shufti (*informal*), scan, glance, skim. [➡SEE; 700]

look-see (*informal*) *n* **shufti** (*informal*), dekko (*informal*), look, glance, inspection, scan, examination, skim, once-over (*informal*). [➡SEE; 700]

look through *v* **ignore**, take no notice of, give the cold shoulder, snub, cut, walk by, pass by, sail by. [➡REFUSING OR REJECTING RELATIONS; 975] *Opposite:* acknowledge.

look up 1 *v* **search**, hunt, research, find, consult. [➡FIND; 464] 2 *v* **get better**, improve, take a turn for the better, be on the up (*informal*), mend, recuperate, convalesce, pick up (*informal*). [➡GET BETTER; 376] *Opposite:* worsen. 3 *v* **visit**, call on, contact, get in touch, locate. [➡INITIATE AND ESTABLISH COMMUNICATION; 681]

look up to *v* **admire**, respect, esteem, worship, adore, revere. [➡LIKE, LOVE, VALUE, AND ENJOY; 579] *Opposite:* look down on.

loom 1 *v* **appear**, emerge, come out, materialize, show, reveal. [➡APPEAR AND EMERGE; 3] *Opposite:* recede. 2 *v* **impend**

(*formal*), hang over, approach, come up, threaten, menace. [➡ABOUT TO HAPPEN; 33] *Opposite:* recede.

looming *adj* **impending**, pending, forthcoming, coming up, approaching, imminent, future, on the horizon, in the offing, at hand. [➡ABOUT TO HAPPEN; 33]

loon (*US*) *type of* **freshwater bird**. [➡FRESHWATER BIRD; 1000]

loop 1 *n* **ring**, coil, twist, circlet, hoop, eye, circle. [➡ROUNDED SHAPE; 1217] 2 *v* **wind**, twist, coil, entwine, encircle, encompass, ring, surround, circle. [➡POSITION SOMETHING: AROUND SOMETHING; 328]

loophole *n* **dodge**, get-out, gap, ambiguity, excuse, escape. [➡FAULTS, FLAWS, AND WEAKNESSES; 252]

loose 1 *adj* **movable**, slack, wobbly, unfastened, free, unattached. [➡MALLEABLE AND ELASTIC; 1211] *Opposite:* fixed. 2 *adj* **floppy**, relaxed, supple, slack, droopy, sagging, limp. [➡SHAPELESSNESS; 1218] *Opposite:* tight. 3 *adj* **loose-fitting**, baggy, unrestricting, flowing, roomy, voluminous, ample, shapeless, formless. [➡DESCRIBING CLOTHES; 869] *Opposite:* tight. 4 *adj* **free**, freed, at liberty, unchained, untied, flowing, unconfined, at large. [➡FREEDOM AND LIBERTY; 209] *Opposite:* secure. 5 *adj* **assorted**, diverse, free, miscellaneous, eclectic. [➡DIFFERENCE; 150] 6 *adj* (*dated*) **irresponsible**, lax, slack, relaxed, free, unprofessional, careless, weak, sloppy. [➡LACK OF COMMITMENT AND UNRELIABILITY; 510] *Opposite:* strict.

loose-fitting *adj* **loose**, baggy, voluminous, roomy, ample, floppy, shapeless, formless. [➡DESCRIBING CLOTHES; 869] *Opposite:* tight.

loose-limbed *adj* **supple**, lissom, agile, lithe, elastic. [➡AGILITY OF THE BODY; 477] *Opposite:* stiff.

loosely 1 *adv* **insecurely**, slackly, roughly, lightly. [➡MALLEABLE AND ELASTIC; 1211] *Opposite:* tightly. 2 *adv* **limply**, slackly, droopily, freely, heavily, floppily. [➡SHAPELESSNESS; 1218] 3 *adv* (*dated*) **inaccurately**, sloppily, freely, carelessly, laxly. [➡INCAUTIOUS AND CARELESS; 284] *Opposite:* accurately.

loosen *v* **come loose**, work loose, untie, undo, release, relax, slacken, slacken off. [➡UNFASTEN AND UNDO; 410] *Opposite:* tighten.

looseness 1 *n* (*dated*) **irresponsibility**, laxity, slackness, freeness, carelessness, sloppiness, negligence. [➡LACK OF COMMITMENT AND UNRELIABILITY; 510] *Opposite:* strictness. 2 *n* **bagginess**, shapelessness, roominess, ampleness. [➡SHAPELESSNESS; 1218] *Opposite:* tightness.

loosen up 1 *v* **warm up**, limber up, stretch, exercise, prepare. [➡FIDGET AND FROLIC; 312] 2 *v* **relax**, kick back (*informal*), let your hair down, take it easy, chill out (*slang*). [➡CHANGE OF MOOD AND COMPOSURE; 581]

loot 1 *n* **booty**, spoils, swag (*slang*), plunder. [➡PROCEEDS OF CRIME; 428] 2 *n* (*informal*) **money**, cash, wealth, assets, dough (*slang*), dosh (*slang*). [➡MONEY; 140] 3 *v* **burgle**, plunder, ransack, pillage, rob, do over (*slang*), sack. [➡STEAL AND ROB; 427]

looter *n* **robber**, raider, plunderer, burglar, thief, pillager. [➡CRIMINALS; 821]

lop 1 *v* **cut**, chop, hack, sever, crop, trim, slice, prune, pare. [➡EXTRACT AND SEVER; 342] *Opposite:* graft. 2 *v* **cut off**, chop off, slice off, remove, amputate. [➡EXTRACT AND SEVER; 342] *Opposite:* attach. 3 *v* **deduct**, take off, subtract, discount, reduce, decrease, lower. [➡REMOVE SOMETHING; 339] *Opposite:* add.

lope *n* [➡PROCEED AND GO; 306]

lopsided *adj* **uneven**, askew, crooked, cockeyed, wonky (*informal*), disproportionate, skewed, skewwhiff (*informal*), unequal, irregular. [➡ORIENTATION AND ALIGNMENT; 1222] *Opposite:* even.

lopsidedness *n* **unevenness**, crookedness, skewedness, imbalance, disproportionateness, wonkiness (*informal*), irregularity. [➡ORIENTATION AND ALIGNMENT; 1222] *Opposite:* evenness.

loquacious (*formal*) *adj* **talkative**, garrulous, chatty, voluble, verbose, prolix, wordy, effusive, noisy, gabby (*informal*), windy (*informal*), talky (*US*). [➡ELOQUENT, TALKATIVE, AND LONG-WINDED; 633] *Opposite:* silent.

See Compare and Contrast at **talkative**.

loquaciousness (*formal*) *n* [➡ELOQUENT, TALKATIVE, AND LONG-WINDED; 633]

lore *n* **wisdom**, tradition, teachings, knowledge, experience, beliefs, legends, folklore. [➡THE ORAL TRADITION; 678]

lorry *type of* **commercial or industrial vehicle**. [➡VEHICLES; 1144]

lose 1 *v* **misplace**, be unable to find, mislay, drop, miss. [➡LOSE AND FORFEIT; 448] *Opposite:* find. 2 *v* **be defeated**, go down (*informal*), be beaten, go under, fail, suffer defeat, take a licking (*US informal*). [➡FAIL OR BE UNSUCCESSFUL; 75] *Opposite:* win. 3 *v* **shake off**, evade, give somebody the slip, leave behind, get away from, elude, escape, drop. [➡GET RID OF SOMETHING; 452] *Opposite:* find. 4 *v* **waste**, squander, exhaust, use up, consume, spend. [➡USE UP AND WASTE; 475] *Opposite:* save.

lose consciousness *v* **faint**, blackout, pass out, swoon, collapse. [➡FALL ILL, TREAT, AND RECOVER; 729] *Opposite:* come to.

lose control *v* **lose it** (*informal*), get carried away, go berserk, hit the roof, lose your rag (*slang*), blow up (*informal*), see red (*informal*). [➡GIVING VENT TO EMOTIONS; 680]

lose heart *v* **become despondent**, become demoralized, give up, give in, lose motivation, falter, flag. [➡CHANGE OF MOOD AND COMPOSURE; 581] *Opposite:* take heart.

lose it (*informal*) *v* **lose your temper**, blow up (*informal*), lose your rag (*slang*), blow your top (*informal*), hit the roof, see red (*informal*), lose control, lose your cool (*informal*). [➡GIVING VENT TO EMOTIONS; 680] *Opposite:* keep your cool.

lose out (*informal*) *v* **miss out**, get the worst of it, come off second best, fail to benefit, miss the boat, miss an opportunity, miss a chance. [➡FAIL OR BE UNSUCCESSFUL; 75] *Opposite:* gain.

loser *n* **failure**, also-ran, underdog, dud (*informal*), has-been (*informal*). [➡LAZY OR UNSUCCESSFUL PEOPLE; 948]

lose the thread *v* **get off the point**, lose the point, digress, go off at a tangent, deviate, stray, drift, lose concentration, falter, hesitate. [➡HESITATE; 273] *Opposite:* follow.

lose track of *v* **misplace**, lose sight of, lose, be unable to follow, mislay, forget. [➡LOSE AND FORFEIT; 448] *Opposite:* keep track of.

lose weight *v* **diet**, go on a diet, slim, watch your weight, count the calories, cut down, fast. [➡EAT AND NOT EAT; 711]

lose your bearings *v* **get lost**, lose your way, stray, become disorientated, take a wrong turn (*US*). [➡AIMLESS AND ERRANT MOTION; 344]

lose your cool (*informal*) *v* **go off the deep end**, go berserk, lose it (*informal*), hit the roof, see red (*informal*), blow up (*informal*), blow your top (*informal*), lose your head, flip your lid (*slang*). [➡GIVING VENT TO EMOTIONS; 680] *Opposite:* keep your cool.

lose your footing *v* **stumble**, trip, trip up, fall over, slip, tumble, take a tumble, falter, fall, lose your balance. [➡TAKE UP A NEW POSITION; 313]

lose your nerve *v* **go to pieces**, lose your cool, bottle out (*informal*), get flustered, give up, chicken out (*slang*), lose your head. [➡CHANGE OF MOOD AND COMPOSURE; 581] *Opposite:* keep your cool.

lose your patience *v* **lose your cool** (*informal*), flare up, snap, lose it (*informal*), hit the roof, see red (*informal*), blow up (*informal*), blow your top (*informal*). [➡GIVING VENT TO EMOTIONS; 680] *Opposite:* keep your cool.

lose your rag (*slang*) *v* **lose your temper**, blow up (*informal*), blow a fuse (*informal*), see red (*informal*), flip your lid (*slang*), lose it (*informal*), go off the deep end, hit the roof. [➡GIVING VENT TO EMOTIONS; 680] *Opposite:* keep your cool.

lose your temper *v* **fly into a rage**, fly off the handle (*informal*), throw a fit (*informal*), go mad, blow your top (*informal*), see red (*informal*), explode, lose your rag (*slang*), lose it (*informal*), hit the roof. [➡GIVING VENT TO EMOTIONS; 680] *Opposite:* keep your cool.

lose your way *v* **lose your bearings**, get lost, become disorientated, stray, go wrong, take a wrong turn (*US*). [➡AIMLESS AND ERRANT MOTION; 344]

losing *adj* **behind**, trailing, bringing up the rear, down. [➡IN TROUBLE AND DISADVANTAGED; 73] *Opposite:* winning.

loss 1 *n* **bereavement**, passing, passing away, demise (*formal*), death. [➡DEATH AND BEREAVEMENT; 927] 2 *n* **deficit**, debit, deficiency, shortfall. [➡TOO FEW, TOO LITTLE; 120] *Opposite:* profit. 3 *n* **defeat**, beating, thrashing, hammering (*informal*), pasting (*informal*), trouncing, slaughter (*slang*), failure. [➡FAILURE; 77] *Opposite:* victory. 4 *n* **damage**, harm, injury, cost, forfeiture, hurt. [➡NUISANCES; 254]

lossmaking *adj* **uneconomic**, running at a loss, unprofitable, not viable, inefficient, impracticable. [➡FINANCE AND ECONOMICS; 797] *Opposite:* profitable.

loss of consciousness *n* **blackout**, faint, fainting fit, swoon, collapse. [➡TIRED, ASLEEP, AND UNCONSCIOUS; 739]

lost 1 *adj* **misplaced**, mislaid, missing, gone, nowhere to be found, gone astray, vanished, absent. [➡ABSENT AND UNAVAILABLE; 7] *Opposite:* found. 2 *adj* **off-course**, disorientated, adrift, astray. [➡AIMLESS AND ERRANT MOTION; 344] 3 *adj* **confused**, bewildered, bemused, at sea, stumped, puzzled, perplexed, mystified, baffled, flummoxed (*informal*). [➡CONFUSION, ANXIETY, AND WORRY; 541] 4 *adj* **forlorn**, vulnerable, abandoned, alone, aimless, helpless. [➡IN TROUBLE AND DISADVANTAGED; 73] 5 *adj* **deep in thought**, spellbound, entranced, rapt, engrossed, absorbed, preoccupied. [➡PENSIVENESS AND INTEREST; 539]

lost in thought *adj* **faraway**, dreamy, engrossed, absorbed, deep in thought, pensive, distant, bemused. [➡PENSIVENESS AND INTEREST; 539]

lot 1 *n* **batch**, set, assortment, grouping, bundle, delivery, quantity, group, bunch (*informal*). [➡COLLECTIONS AND MIXTURES OF THINGS; 1243] 2 *n* **ration**, share, slice, proportion, percentage, allocation, allotment, allowance, measure, quota, portion (*literary*). [➡AMOUNT AND QUANTITY; 112] 3 *n* **fate**, destiny, luck, kismet, fortune, plight. [➡FATE, DESTINY, AND ASTROLOGY; 783]

loth *see* **loath**.

Lothario (*literary*) *n* [➡PLEASURE-SEEKERS AND HEDONISTS; 886]

lotion *n* **oil**, ointment, liniment, unguent, rub, salve, gel, balm, cream. [➡LOTIONS, PASTES, AND GELS; 1271]

lots *n* **plenty**, many, heaps (*informal*), bags of (*informal*), loads (*informal*), masses (*informal*), oodles (*informal*), tons (*informal*), stacks (*informal*). [➡MANY, MUCH, LARGE AMOUNT; 117] *Opposite:* few.

lottery 1 *n* **draw**, sweepstake, raffle, lotto, bingo, tombola, pools. [➡GAMBLE AND TAKE RISKS; 467] 2 *n* **risk**, gamble, chance, fortune, luck, the luck of the draw. [➡LUCK; 784] *Opposite:* certainty.

lotus *type of* **perennial flower**. [➡FLOWERS; 1032]

lotus-eater *n* **lazy person**, hedonist, dreamer, daydreamer, idler. [➡LAZY OR UNSUCCESSFUL PEOPLE; 948]

louche *adj* **disreputable**, shady, dubious, immoral, suspect, corrupt. [➡MORALLY BAD; 776] *Opposite:* respectable.

loud 1 *adj* **noisy**, deafening, piercing, strident, thunderous, booming, shrill, earsplitting. [➡LOUD OR UNPLEASANT SOUNDS; 1265] *Opposite:* quiet. 2 *adj* **vociferous**, rowdy, boisterous, raucous, noisy, loudmouthed (*informal*), forceful, voluble, riotous, blaring. [➡POMPOUS, LOUD, AND OVER-CONFIDENT; 636] *Opposite:* gentle. 3 *adj* **lurid**, flamboyant, brash, flashy, gaudy, vulgar, garish, showy, ostentatious. [➡IN POOR TASTE; 230] *Opposite:* muted.

loudly 1 *adv* **noisily**, deafeningly, piercingly, stridently, at the top of your voice, at full volume. [➡LOUD OR UNPLEASANT SOUNDS; 1265] *Opposite:* quietly. 2 *adv* **vociferously**, rowdily, boisterously, raucously, noisily, forcefully, brashly. [➡POMPOUS, LOUD, AND OVER-CONFIDENT; 636] *Opposite:* quietly.

loudmouth (*informal*) *n* [➡SELF-IMPORTANT AND SELF-SEEKING PEOPLE; 949]

loudmouthed (*informal*) *adj* **blustering**, loud, noisy, vociferous, voluble, brash. [➡POMPOUS, LOUD, AND OVER-CONFIDENT; 636] *Opposite:* quiet.

loudness *n* **volume**, noise, decibels, level, intensity. [➡LOUD OR UNPLEASANT SOUNDS; 1265] *Opposite:* quietness.

loudspeaker *part of* **audio equipment**. [➡AUDIO EQUIPMENT; 1138]

lough 1 *n* **lake**, tarn, broad, water, loch, mere (*archaic or literary*). [➡RIVERS, LAKES, AND STREAMS; 1042] 2 *n* **inlet**, fjord, firth, creek, sea loch, sound, estuary. [➡RIVERS, LAKES, AND STREAMS; 1042]

lounge 1 *n* **living room**, drawing room, sitting room, family room, salon. [➡TYPES OF ROOM; 1096] 2 *v* **lie around** (*informal*), sprawl, recline, laze, loaf, loll, relax, take it easy, idle, dawdle, hang (*slang*), chill (*slang*). [➡LACK OF ACTIVITY; 343]

lounge about *v* [➡LACK OF ACTIVITY; 343]

lounge around *v* [➡LACK OF ACTIVITY; 343]

lounger *n* **reclining seat**, recliner, sunbed, folding chair, deck chair, tanning bed (*US*). [➡FURNITURE; 858]

louse *type of* **parasitic insect**. [➡PARASITES; 1017]

louse-ridden *adj* [➡DECAYING OR INFESTED; 1235]

lousy (*informal*) 1 *adj* **awful**, rotten, miserable, fed up (*informal*), dreadful, abysmal, nasty, terrible. [➡SADNESS, DISTRESS, AND DESPAIR; 540] *Opposite:* great (*informal*). 2 *adj* **useless**, worthless, stupid, crummy (*informal*), second-rate, mean, inferior, horrible. [➡BAD AND BADLY; 224] *Opposite:* great (*informal*).

loutish *adj* **coarse**, impolite, rough, uncouth, rude, ill-mannered, boorish. [➡BAD MANNERS AND SOCIAL SKILLS; 522] *Opposite:* genteel.

loutishness *n* **uncouthness**, rudeness, incivility, vulgarity, boorishness, bad behaviour. [➡BAD MANNERS AND SOCIAL SKILLS; 522] *Opposite:* politeness.

lovable *adj* **endearing**, adorable, enchanting, attractive, delightful, affable, congenial, amiable, engaging, winning, captivating, cute. [➡BEAUTY AND ATTRACTIVENESS; 190] *Opposite:* despicable.

lovage *type of* **herb**. [➡HERBS AND SPICES; 1174]

lovat *type of* **green**. [➡COLOURS; 1223]

love 1 *v* **feel affection for**, adore, worship, be in love with, be devoted to, care for, find irresistible, be keen on, be fond of, hold dear, fancy (*informal*). [➡LIKE, LOVE, VALUE, AND ENJOY; 579] *Opposite:* hate. 2 *v* **like**, enjoy, appreciate, be keen on, be partial to, have a weakness for, go for (*informal*), have a thing about (*informal*), be attracted to. [➡LIKE, LOVE, VALUE, AND ENJOY; 579] *Opposite:* dislike. 3 *n* **affection**, friendship, feeling, adoration, tenderness, fondness, devotion, passion, ardour, amity (*formal*), liking. [➡LOVE, RESPECT, AND GOODWILL; 550] *Opposite:* hatred. 4 *n* **darling**, dear, dearest, sweetheart, honey (*US informal*). [➡ENDEARMENTS; 657]

Compare and Contrast: ***love, liking, affection, fondness, passion, infatuation, crush***

CORE MEANING: A STRONG POSITIVE FEELING TOWARDS SOMEBODY OR SOMETHING

love an intense feeling of tender affection and compassion, especially strong romantic or sexual feelings between people; ***liking*** a feeling of enjoying something or of finding it pleasant, or personal taste or choice; ***affection*** fond or tender feelings towards somebody or something; ***fondness*** a feeling of affection or preference; ***passion*** intense or overpowering emotion, either love for somebody, usually of a strong sexual nature, or strong liking or enthusiasm for something; ***infatuation*** an intense but short-lived and often unrealistic love for somebody, usually of a romantic or sexual nature; ***crush*** (*informal*) a temporary romantic infatuation, especially in teenagers and young people.

lovebird *type of* **pet bird**. [➡BIRD; 997]

loved *adj* **precious**, treasured, respected, important, adored, worshipped, valued, esteemed, prized. [➡POPULAR AND WANTED; 221] *Opposite:* detested.

loved ones *n* **family**, nearest and dearest, relations, relatives, kin, kith and kin. [➡THE FAMILY; 956]

love handles (*informal*) *n* [➡EXTRA WEIGHT; 479]

love-in-a-mist *type of* **annual flower**. [➡FLOWERS; 1032]

loveless *adj* **harsh**, hard, unhappy, unkind, cruel, insensitive, unsympathetic, callous. [➡SELFISH AND UNKIND; 506] *Opposite:* loving.

love-lies-bleeding *type of* **perennial flower**. [➡FLOWERS; 1032]

loveliness *n* **beauty**, attractiveness, good looks, exquisiteness, charm, allure, comeliness (*archaic or literary*). [➡PEOPLE'S PHYSICAL APPEARANCE; 476] *Opposite:* ugliness.

lovely 1 *adj* **beautiful**, attractive, pretty, good-looking, gorgeous, exquisite, charming, divine (*informal or humorous*), handsome, adorable, fetching, enchanting, comely (*archaic or literary*). [➡BEAUTY AND ATTRACTIVENESS; 190] *Opposite:* ugly. 2 *adj* **pleasant**, agreeable, delightful, perfect, wonderful, superb, nice, good, splendid, fine. [➡EMOTIONALLY PLEASANT; 188] *Opposite:* unpleasant.

See Compare and Contrast at **good-looking**.

love seat *type of* **seating**. [➡FURNITURE; 858]

lovesick *adj* **infatuated**, sentimental, overly affectionate, obsessed, pining, overemotional, yearning, icky (*informal*), longing, soppy (*informal*), sloppy (*informal*). [➡APPRECIATION AND GRATITUDE; 536]

love-struck *adj* [➡APPRECIATION AND GRATITUDE; 536]

lovey (*informal*) *n* [➡ENDEARMENTS; 657]

loving *adj* **affectionate**, tender, fond, devoted, caring, warm, adoring, amorous, doting, sympathetic, benevolent, solicitous. [➡FRIENDLINESS AND SOCIABILITY; 495] *Opposite:* cold.

low 1 *adj* **near to the ground**, low down, short, small, little, squat, low-slung, stumpy, truncated. [➡HEIGHT: LOW; 1203] *Opposite:* high. 2 *adj* **depleted**, at a low level, down, short, in short supply, dwindling, minimal, run-down. [➡TOO FEW, TOO LITTLE; 120] *Opposite:* high. 3 *adj* **soft**, muted, soothing, muffled, subdued, gentle, subtle, hushed, faint, quiet. [➡SOFT OR PLEASANT SOUNDS; 1264] *Opposite:* loud. 4 *adj* **sad**, miserable, unhappy, down, blue (*informal*), depressed, gloomy, down in the dumps (*informal*), sorry for yourself, glum, despondent, downcast, forlorn, dejected, disheartened, dispirited, fed up (*informal*). [➡SADNESS, DISTRESS, AND DESPAIR; 540] *Opposite:* cheerful. 5 *n* **low point**, slump, depression, depths, nadir, trough. [➡INTERMEDIATE STAGES; 55] *Opposite:* peak.

See Compare and Contrast at **mean**.

lowboy *type of* **cabinet**. [➡FURNITURE; 858]

lowbrow (*disapproving*) *adj* **popular**, mass-market, philistine, undemanding, middle-of-the-road. [➡THE NATURE OF IDEAS; 772] *Opposite:* highbrow.

low-cut *adj* [➡DESCRIBING CLOTHES; 869]

lowdown (*informal*) *n* [➡BASIC DETAILS; 689]

lower 1 *adj* **inferior**, subordinate, lesser, junior, poorer, worse, minor. [➡INFERIORITY; 154] *Opposite:* superior. 2 *v* **let down**, drop, let fall, hand down, sink, pull down, depress, take down. [➡MOVE SOMETHING: DOWNWARDS; 330] *Opposite:* raise. 3 *v* **lessen**, drop, cut, bring down, decrease, slash, reduce. [➡CHANGE OF INTENSITY: LESS; 396] *Opposite:* raise.

lower class *n* **working class**, masses, hoi polloi, lower classes, proletariat. [➡CLASS STATUS; 889] *Opposite:* upper class.

lower-class *adj* **working-class**, blue-collar, popular, plebeian. [➡CLASS STATUS; 889] *Opposite:* aristocratic.

lower ground floor *n* [➡STAIRS AND STOREYS; 1101]

lowermost *adj* **lowest**, bottommost, deepest, bottom, last. [➡RELATIVE LOCATION; 162]

lower yourself *v* **deign**, condescend, cheapen yourself, stoop, humiliate yourself, humble yourself. [➡CHANGE OF MOOD AND COMPOSURE; 581]

low-grade *adj* **low-quality**, inferior, cheap, substandard, second-rate. [➡ORDINARINESS; 245] *Opposite:* premium.

low-key *adj* **simple**, unglamorous, unspectacular, understated, subdued, discreet, unpretentious, muted, restrained, toned-down. [➡PLAIN; 233] *Opposite:* elaborate.

lowland *n* **plain**, fen, flat, valley, swamp, wetland. [➡DESERTS AND PLAINS; 1045]

lowlife (*informal*) *n* [➡LAZY OR UNSUCCESSFUL PEOPLE; 948]

lowliness *n* **humbleness**, meekness, submissiveness, inferiority, commonness, modesty. [➡CLASS STATUS; 889] *Opposite:* eminence.

lowly *adj* **humble**, poor, deprived, mean (*archaic*), ordinary, modest, simple, common, meek, submissive. [➡ORDINARINESS; 245] *Opposite:* exalted (*formal*).

low-lying *adj* **low**, lowland, sea-level, below sea level, coastal, sunken. [➡HEIGHT: LOW; 1203] *Opposite:* high.

low-minded *adj* **coarse**, common, vulgar, base, uncouth, rude. [➡BAD MANNERS AND SOCIAL SKILLS; 522] *Opposite:* refined.

low-necked *adj* [➡DESCRIBING CLOTHES; 869]

low-pitched *adj* **low**, deep, throaty, gruff. [➡SOFT OR PLEASANT SOUNDS; 1264] *Opposite:* high.

low point *n* **low**, all-time low, nadir, rock bottom. [➡INTERMEDIATE STAGES; 55] *Opposite:* high point.

low-rise *adj* **double-storey**, single-storey, small, low. [➡HEIGHT: LOW; 1203] *Opposite:* high-rise.

loyal *adj* **faithful**, trustworthy, devoted, reliable, dependable, dedicated, steadfast, trusty, constant. [➡HARD-WORKING AND COMMITTED; 501] *Opposite:* disloyal.

loyalist *n* **stalwart**, partisan, supporter, devotee, advocate, proponent. [➡DEVOTEES AND ADDICTED PEOPLE; 557] *Opposite:* rebel.

loyalty *n* **faithfulness**, allegiance, constancy, fidelity, devotion, trustworthiness, reliability, dependability, steadfastness. [➡HARD-WORKING AND COMMITTED; 501] *Opposite:* disloyalty.

lozenge 1 *n* **pastille**, tablet, pill. [➡REMEDIES, TREATMENTS, AND OPERATIONS; 732] 2 *type of* **angular shape**. [➡ANGULAR SHAPE; 1216]

LP *n* [➡RECORDINGS AND PLAYERS; 911]

lubricate *v* **oil**, grease, loosen. [➡DECORATE, ADORN, AND APPLY COATINGS; 406]

lucid 1 *adj* **articulate**, clear, well-spoken, silver-tongued, smooth-tongued, eloquent, thought through, coherent, plain, simple, sound. [➡ELOQUENT, TALKATIVE, AND LONG-WINDED; 633] *Opposite:* incoherent. 2 *adj* **rational**, sane, sober, clear-headed, compos mentis, in your right mind, logical, cogent, reasoned. [➡CALMNESS, CONFIDENCE, AND COMPOSURE; 537] *Opposite:* delirious. 3 *adj* **luminous**, shining, luminescent, limpid, translucent, bright. [➡DESCRIBING LIGHT; 1227] *Opposite:* dull.

lucidity 1 *n* **intelligibility**, lucidness, unambiguousness, perspicuity, fluency, eloquence, articulacy. [➡CONCISE AND CLEAR; 203] *Opposite:* ambiguousness. 2 *n* **rationality**, lucidness, clarity, reason, sanity, logic, saneness, soberness. [➡POSITIVE INTELLECTUAL CHARACTERISTICS; 525] *Opposite:* confusion. 3 *n* **luminousness**, luminescence, limpidness, lucidness, translucence, brightness. [➡DESCRIBING LIGHT; 1227] *Opposite:* dullness.

lucidness 1 *n* **clarity**, logic, intelligibleness, coherence, plainness, simplicity, clearness. [➡CONCISE AND CLEAR; 203] *Opposite:* incoherence. 2 *n* **saneness**, soberness, clear-headedness, rationality, judgment, cogency (*formal*). [➡CONFIDENCE AND COMPOSURE; 500] *Opposite:* irrationality.

luck 1 *n* **good fortune**, good luck, fluke (*informal*), stroke of luck, windfall, blessing, godsend, break (*informal*), providence. [➡LUCK; 784] *Opposite:* misfortune. 2 *n* **chance**, fate, fortune, destiny, providence, accident, coincidence, kismet. [➡FATE, DESTINY, AND ASTROLOGY; 783]

luckless *adj* **hapless**, unlucky, unfortunate, jinxed, ill-fated, doomed, unsuccessful. [➡BAD LUCK AND UNLUCKY; 785] *Opposite:* lucky.

luck of the draw *n* [➡LUCK; 784]

lucky *adj* **fortunate**, blessed, jammy (*informal*), fluky (*informal*), auspicious, propitious, providential, timely, happy. [➡LUCK; 784] *Opposite:* unlucky.

Compare and Contrast: ***lucky, fortunate, happy, providential***

CORE MEANING: RELATING TO ADVANTAGE OR GOOD FORTUNE

lucky bringing or gaining success or advantage, especially when this seems to happen by chance; ***fortunate*** bringing or enjoying success or advantage, especially when this is greater than was expected or deserved; ***happy*** giving rise to something pleasant or welcome; ***providential*** happening at a favourable time.

lucky break *n* [➡LUCK; 784]

lucky charm *n* **amulet**, mascot, good luck charm, juju, talisman. [➡LUCKY CHARMS; 786]

lucky dip *n* **raffle**, draw, lottery, tombola, drawing, lotto, grab bag (*US*). [➡LUCK; 784]

lucrative *adj* **profitable**, well-paid, rewarding, worthwhile, money-spinning (*informal*), beneficial, productive. [➡USEFULNESS; 200] *Opposite:* unprofitable.

ludicrous *adj* **absurd**, ridiculous, preposterous, nonsensical, comical, farcical, foolish, stupid, daft (*informal*), outrageous. [➡BIZARRE AND PECULIAR; 258] *Opposite:* sensible.

ludicrousness *n* **absurdity**, ridiculousness, unreasonableness, foolishness, nonsensicalness, irrationality, illogicality, preposterousness, farce, silliness, stupidity. [➡BIZARRE AND PECULIAR; 258] *Opposite:* sensibleness.

lug *v* **drag**, heave, cart, carry, haul, pull, tow, tug, draw. [➡PUSH, PULL, SLIDE; 336]

luge *type of* **leisure vehicle**. [➡VEHICLES; 1144]

luggage *n* **baggage**, bags, cases, gear (*informal*), suitcases, stuff, kit, belongings. [➡CONTAINERS, RECEPTACLES, AND PACKAGING; 1244]

luggage compartment 1 *n* **hold**, boot, locker, trunk (*US*). [➡STORES AND STORAGE BUILDINGS; 1087] 2 *part of* **train**. [➡RAILWAYS; 1106]

luggage rack (*US*) *type of* **external feature**. [➡EXTERNAL PARTS OF A VEHICLE; 1146]

lugubrious *adj* **sad**, mournful, gloomy, depressing, doleful, melancholic, sombre, cheerless, miserable, dismal, morose. [➡EMOTIONALLY UNPLEASANT AND UPSETTING; 228] *Opposite:* cheerful.

lugubriousness *n* **moroseness**, gloominess, melancholy, depression, sadness, misery, mournfulness, dolefulness, sombreness, seriousness, cheerlessness. [➡SADNESS, DISTRESS, AND DESPAIR; 540] *Opposite:* cheerfulness.

lukewarm 1 *adj* **tepid**, warm, hand-hot, cool. [➡TEMPERATURE: MEDIUM; 1229] 2 *adj* **unenthusiastic**, half-hearted, cool, unexcited, indifferent, subdued, apathetic, uninterested. [➡NEUTRALITY AND INDIFFERENCE; 554] *Opposite:* enthusiastic.

lukewarmly *adv* [➡NEUTRALITY AND INDIFFERENCE; 554]

lull 1 *v* **soothe**, calm, reassure, quieten, settle down, comfort, pacify, hush. [➡SOOTHE AND CALM; 574] *Opposite:* rouse. 2 *n* **quiet**, calm, stillness, silence, pause, break, let-up (*informal*), respite, hiatus. [➡PAUSES AND PHASES; 56] *Opposite:* flare-up (*informal*).

lullaby *n* **cradlesong**, song, ditty, child's bedtime song, lilt, serenade, chorus. [➡MUSIC, SONGS, AND SINGING; 907]

lumbago *n* **backache**, back pain, bad back. [➡PAIN AND OTHER PHYSICAL SENSATIONS; 734]

lumber 1 *v* (*informal*) **burden**, encumber, weigh down, land, impose, trouble, inflict, load. [➡GIVE TOO MUCH; 438] *Opposite:* unload. 2 *v* **trudge**, shamble, hobble, plod, clump, stagger. [➡WALK UNSTEADILY; 316] 3 *n* (*US*) **wood**, timber, boards, planks, logs. [➡BUILDING MATERIALS; 1076]

lumbering *adj* **awkward**, bumbling (*informal*), clumsy, unwieldy, hulking, graceless. [➡AGILITY OF THE BODY; 477] *Opposite:* dainty.

luminary *n* **celebrity**, star, achiever, personality, top name, face (*informal*), VIP, leading light. [➡IMPORTANT OR FAMOUS PEOPLE; 893] *Opposite:* nobody.

luminesce *v* [➡LIGHT EMISSION; 369]

luminescence *n* [➡DESCRIBING LIGHT; 1227]

luminescent *adj* [➡DESCRIBING LIGHT; 1227]

luminosity *n* **glow**, light, brilliance, radiance, shine, sheen, brightness, glare, incandescence, gleam. [➡DESCRIBING LIGHT; 1227]

luminous *adj* **glowing**, shining, brilliant, bright, radiant, gleaming, shimmering, incandescent, resplendent. [➡DESCRIBING LIGHT; 1227] *Opposite:* dull.

lump 1 *n* **bump**, swelling, protuberance, knob, inflammation, bulge, tumour. [➡ROUNDED SHAPE; 1217] 2 *n* **piece**, chunk, morsel, block, section, hunk, mass, slab, slice. [➡AMOUNT OF SOLID OR SEMI-SOLID; 115] 3 *v* **group**, collect, combine, join, amalgamate, mass, consolidate, conjoin (*formal*). [➡COMBINE AND MIX; 401] *Opposite:* split. 4 *v* (*informal*) **put up with**, grin and bear it (*informal*), deal with, take, endure, bear, suffer. [➡TOLERATE AND ENDURE; 767]

lump together *v* [➡COMBINE AND MIX; 401]

lumpy 1 *adj* **lump-filled**, clumpy, uneven, bumpy, unsmooth. [➡ROUNDED SHAPE; 1217] 2 *adj* **cumbersome**, awkward, lumbering, unwieldy, graceless, bumbling (*informal*). [➡AGILITY OF THE BODY; 477] *Opposite:* graceful.

luna moth *type of* **moth**. [➡MOTHS AND BUTTERFLIES; 1015]

lunar *adj* **lunate**, lunular (*technical*), semilunar. [➡THE SOLAR SYSTEM AND ASTRONOMY; 1059]

lunar module *type of* **spacecraft**. [➡SPACE VEHICLES; 1062]

lunar month *type of* **time period**. [➡TIMES OF YEAR; 88]

lunch *type of* **meal**. [➡MEALS AND PARTS OF MEALS; 1168]

lunch break *n* [➡PERIOD OF REST; 91]

luncheonette (*US*) *type of* **eating place.** [➡HOTELS, RESTAURANTS, AND CLUBS; 1081]

lunchroom (*US*) *type of* **eating place.** [➡HOTELS, RESTAURANTS, AND CLUBS; 1081]

lunchtime *n* [➡TIMES OF DAY; 87]

lung *part of* **respiratory system.** [➡RESPIRATORY ORGANS; 716]

lunge 1 *n* **swipe**, grab, swing, thrust, stab, plunge. [➡CONTACT: HOLD; 412] 2 *v* **attack**, dive, spring, leap, charge, pounce, plunge, pitch. [➡MOVE FAST; 314] 3 *v* **grab**, swipe, swing, thrust, stab, make for. [➡CONTACT: HOLD; 412]

lupin *type of* **perennial flower.** [➡FLOWERS; 1032]

lurch 1 *v* **pitch**, stagger, rock, tilt, list, reel, roll, sway, wobble, heave, yaw, lean. [➡TAKE UP A NEW POSITION; 313] 2 *v* **totter**, stagger, stumble, sway, reel, falter, stammer. [➡AIMLESS AND ERRANT MOTION; 344]

lure 1 *v* **entice**, tempt, attract, decoy, draw in, ensnare, allure, trap, persuade. [➡APPEAL TO AND AROUSE INTEREST; 576] 2 *n* **bait**, trap, decoy, enticement, temptation, pull (*informal*), appeal, attraction, allure. [➡BEAUTY AND ATTRACTIVENESS; 190]

lurid 1 *adj* **shocking**, explicit, sensational, vivid, juicy (*informal*). [➡IN POOR TASTE; 230] *Opposite:* bland. 2 *adj* **loud**, garish, gaudy, bright, colourful, vivid, striking, shocking. [➡DESCRIBING COLOURS; 1225] *Opposite:* dull.

luridness *n* **garishness**, brightness, vividness, gaudiness, colourfulness. [➡DESCRIBING COLOURS; 1225]

lurk *v* **lie in wait for**, loiter, prowl, hang about, skulk, wait, creep around. [➡LACK OF ACTIVITY; 343]

luscious *adj* **juicy**, moist, delicious, succulent, sweet, tasty, scrumptious (*informal*). [➡TASTE; 704] *Opposite:* dry.

lusciousness *n* **juiciness**, succulence, moistness, palatability, sweetness, tastiness, scrumptiousness (*informal*). [➡TASTE; 704] *Opposite:* dryness.

lush 1 *adj* **verdant**, abundant, green, flourishing, thriving, luxuriant, fertile, blossoming, grassy, leafy, blooming. [➡MANY, MUCH, LARGE AMOUNT; 117] *Opposite:* arid. 2 *adj* **luxurious**, plush (*informal*), lavish, opulent, swanky (*informal*), sumptuous, deluxe, upmarket, rich. [➡EXPENSIVE AND LUXURIOUS; 219] *Opposite:* downmarket.

lushness 1 *n* **greenness**, abundance, fertility, leafiness, luxuriance, verdure, grassiness. [➡MANY, MUCH, LARGE AMOUNT; 117] *Opposite:* aridity. 2 *n* **luxury**, lavishness, plushness (*informal*), sumptuousness, opulence, richness, magnificence, extravagance, swankiness (*informal*), luxuriance. [➡EXPENSIVE AND LUXURIOUS; 219]

lust 1 *n* **desire**, envy, covetousness, longing, yearning, hankering, hunger, thirst, itch. [➡LOVE, RESPECT, AND GOODWILL; 550] 2 *v* **yearn**, desire, long, hanker, hunger, ache, covet, thirst, itch. [➡DESIRE AND WANT; 580]

lustful *adj* [➡MORALLY BAD; 776]

lustre *n* **sheen**, shine, patina, gleam, glint, gloss, polish. [➡VISUAL TEXTURE; 1220] *Opposite:* lustrelessness.

lustreless *adj* **dull**, mat, drab, faded, unpolished, lacklustre, lifeless. [➡DESCRIBING LIGHT; 1227] *Opposite:* shiny.

lustrous *adj* **shiny**, glossy, radiant, gleaming, shimmering, glistening. [➡DESCRIBING LIGHT; 1227] *Opposite:* dull.

lusty *adj* **hearty**, healthy, vigorous, forceful, robust, strong. [➡FIT AND STRONG; 737] *Opposite:* feeble.

lute *type of* **stringed instrument.** [➡MUSICAL INSTRUMENTS; 910]

luxuriance *n* **lavishness**, luxury, extravagance, abundance, richness, lushness, opulence. [➡MANY, MUCH, LARGE AMOUNT; 117]

luxuriant 1 *adj* **lush**, flourishing, thriving, fertile, rich, dense, verdant. [➡MANY, MUCH, LARGE AMOUNT; 117] *Opposite:* sparse. 2 *adj* **abundant**, lavish, plentiful, copious, ample. [➡MANY, MUCH, LARGE AMOUNT; 117] *Opposite:* meagre.

luxuriate *v* **enjoy**, wallow, indulge, bask, relish, revel, delight. [➡LIKE, LOVE, VALUE, AND ENJOY; 579]

luxurious 1 *adj* **deluxe**, sumptuous, opulent, expensive, lavish, well-appointed, swish (*informal*), plush (*informal*). [➡EXPENSIVE AND LUXURIOUS; 219] *Opposite:* meagre. 2 *adj* **extravagant**, indulgent, sensual, decadent, epicurean, bohemian, pleasure-loving, frugal. [➡PLEASURE-SEEKING AND EXCESS; 885]

luxuriousness *n* **expensiveness**, luxury, sumptuousness, magnificence, fulsomeness, richness, extravagance, opulence, lavishness, grandness, splendour. [➡EXPENSIVE AND LUXURIOUS; 219]

luxury 1 *n* **treat**, extra, extravagance, indulgence, bonus, amenity, frill, superfluity. [➡AMAZING THING; 212] 2 *n* **lavishness**, comfort, sumptuousness, opulence, magnificence, extravagance. [➡EXPENSIVE AND LUXURIOUS; 219]

lying 1 *adj* **deceitful**, dishonest, two-faced, insincere, untruthful, mendacious, double-dealing, false. [➡DECEITFUL; 514] *Opposite:* truthful. 2 *n* **dishonesty**, deceit, duplicity, falseness, untruthfulness, insincerity, mendaciousness. [➡DECEPTION AND LIES; 661] *Opposite:* truthfulness.

lyme grass *type of* **grass.** [➡GRASS; 1031]

lymph *n* [➡EXCRETION AND EXCRETA; 723]

lynch *v* **hang**, string up, murder, mob, assassinate, kill. [➡KILL; 923]

lynchpin *see* **linchpin.**

lynx *type of* **cat.** [➡FELINE; 983]

lyre *type of* **stringed instrument.** [➡MUSICAL INSTRUMENTS; 910]

lyric 1 *adj* **poetic**, romantic, emotional, expressive, inspired, sentimental. [➡EMOTIONALLY PLEASANT; 188] 2 *adj* **musical**, melodic, harmonious, tuneful, lilting. [➡SOFT OR PLEASANT SOUNDS; 1264]

lyrical *adj* **poetic**, romantic, emotional, expressive, inspired, sentimental. [➡ELOQUENT, TALKATIVE, AND LONG-WINDED; 633]

lyricist *n* [➡MUSICIANS AND SINGERS; 908]

lyrics *n* **words**, lines, libretto, stanza. [➡MUSIC, SONGS, AND SINGING; 907]

M

ma (*informal*) *n* **mother**, mum (*informal*), mummy (*informal*), mam (*regional informal*), mama (*informal*), mammy (*informal*), mamma (*informal*), mater (*dated informal or humorous*), mom (*US informal*), mommy (*US informal*), momma (*US informal*). [➡ OLDER GENERATION RELATIVES; 959]

mac (*informal*) *type of* **overcoat**. [➡ GARMENTS AND OUTFITS; 865]

macabre *adj* **ghoulish**, ghastly, grisly, chilling, gruesome, horrid, morbid, cadaverous (*formal or literary*), deathly, horrific. [➡ FRIGHTENING; 232]

macadam *n* **asphalt**, tar, blacktop (*US*), pavement (*US*), paving (*US*). [➡ COVERS AND COATINGS; 1245]

macadamia nut *type of* **nut**. [➡ NUTS; 1184]

macaque *type of* **primate**. [➡ PRIMATE; 988]

macaroni *type of* **pasta**. [➡ PASTA; 1179]

macaroon *type of* **cake**. [➡ CAKES, BISCUITS, AND DESSERTS; 1180]

macaw *type of* **pet bird**. [➡ BIRD; 997]

mace 1 *type of* **club**. [➡ BLUNT INSTRUMENTS AND WHIPS; 1157] 2 *type of* **spice**. [➡ HERBS AND SPICES; 1174]

macerate 1 *v* **soften**, soak, steep, marinate, marinade, drench, saturate, infuse. [➡ SOFTEN, LIQUEFY, DAMPEN; 389] 2 *v* **break up**, separate, soak, mash, pulp, puree, deliquesce. [➡ CHANGE OF SHAPE; 386] 3 *v* **waste away**, starve, fast, slim, lose weight, shed pounds, reduce. [➡ CHANGE OF SIZE: SMALLER; 394]

machete 1 *type of* **cutting tool**. [➡ CUTTING TOOLS; 1119] 2 *type of* **sword or knife**. [➡ SWORDS AND KNIVES; 1156]

Machiavellian *adj* **cunning**, unscrupulous, tricky, amoral, devious, treacherous, deceitful, opportunist, scheming, conniving. [➡ DECEITFUL; 514] *Opposite:* honest.

machinate *v* **plot**, scheme, conspire, intrigue, hatch, cook up (*informal*), manoeuvre. [➡ DEVELOP THEORIES AND REASON; 745]

machination *n* **intrigue**, plotting, manoeuvring, scheming, planning. [➡ DECEPTION AND LIES; 661]

machine 1 *n* **mechanism**, engine, appliance, apparatus, contraption, device, instrument, contrivance. [➡ DEVICES; 1114] 2 *n* **system**, machinery, structure, procedure, mechanism, organization. [➡ WAYS OF DOING THINGS; 295] 3 *n* **automaton**, robot, cyborg, android. [➡ PERSON; 931]

machine gun *type of* **gun**. [➡ WEAPONS FOR SHOOTING; 1155]

machine-gun 1 *v* **shoot**, kill, fire at, blaze, strafe, attack, mow down. [➡ DESTRUCTION AND DEMOLITION; 360] 2 *adj* **staccato**, rapid, abrupt, fast, quick, rapid-fire, speedy. [➡ HAPPENING QUICKLY; 104] *Opposite:* slow.

machinery 1 *n* **mechanism**, moving parts, workings, works, cogs. [➡ PARTS OF MACHINES AND TOOLS; 1117] 2 *n* **machines**, apparatus, tackle, gear, technology, equipment. [➡ MACHINERY; 1113] 3 *n* **organization**, system, procedure, machine, structure, mechanism, arrangement. [➡ WAYS OF DOING THINGS; 295]

machine shop *type of* **factory**. [➡ INDUSTRIAL BUILDINGS; 1086]

machine tool *type of* **general tool**. [➡ HAND TOOLS; 1118]

machinist *n* **machine operator**, operator, factory worker, operative, technician, mechanic. [➡ FARMERS, GARDENERS, AND MANUAL WORKERS; 849]

machismo *n* **manliness**, masculinity, masculineness, maleness, virility. [➡ GENDER IDENTITY AND SEXUALITY; 932]

macho *adj* **manly**, masculine, virile, laddish. [➡ GENDER IDENTITY AND SEXUALITY; 932]

mackerel *type of* **sea fish**. [➡ SEA FISH; 1009]

mackintosh (*dated*) *type of* **overcoat**. [➡ GARMENTS AND OUTFITS; 865]

macramé *type of* **handicraft**. [➡ CRAFTS AND CARVING; 356]

macro *n* **instruction**, command, key code, function, short cut. [➡ COMPUTERS AND COMPUTING; 1126]

macrobiotic *adj* **wholefood**, vegan, vegetarian, organic, wholegrain, natural, unrefined, unprocessed. [➡ RAW AND NATURAL; 1213]

macrocosm *n* **system**, structure, formation, composition, whole. [➡ REPRESENTATIONS AND GENERAL EXAMPLES; 65] *Opposite:* microcosm.

mad 1 *adj* **angry**, furious, livid, irate, infuriated, fuming, annoyed, beside yourself, up in arms, wrathful, outraged, ireful (*literary*), choleric (*literary*). [➡ IRRITATION AND ANGER; 542] *Opposite:* calm. 2 *adj* **uncontrolled**, crazy (*informal*), frenzied, frenetic, panic-stricken, frantic, wild. [➡ REBELLIOUSNESS AND DISOBEDIENCE; 566] *Opposite:* calm. 3 *adj* **passionate**, mad on, wild, keen on, crazy (*informal*), nuts (*slang*), infatuated with, enthusiastic. [➡ APPRECIATION AND GRATITUDE; 536] *Opposite:* indifferent.

madcap *adj* **crazy** (*informal*), wacky (*informal*), silly, zany, daft (*informal*), chaotic, wild. [➡ FUNNY AND AMUSING; 217] *Opposite:* sensible.

madden *v* **infuriate**, enrage, annoy, anger, drive mad (*informal*), irritate, exasperate, make somebody's blood boil, drive somebody up the wall (*informal*), wind up (*informal*), frustrate, gall, rile (*informal*). [➡ ANGER AND ANNOY; 570] *Opposite:* pacify.

maddened *adj* **infuriated**, incensed, annoyed, angered, enraged, exasperated, irritated, frustrated. [➡ IRRITATION AND ANGER; 542] *Opposite:* calm.

maddening *adj* **infuriating**, annoying, irritating,

exasperating, frustrating, enraging, vexing, galling. [➡ IRRITATING; 229] *Opposite:* pleasing.

Madeira cake *type of* **cake**. [➡ CAKES, BISCUITS, AND DESSERTS; 1180]

madeleine *type of* **cake**. [➡ CAKES, BISCUITS, AND DESSERTS; 1180]

mademoiselle *n* [➡ FEMALE PERSON; 933]

made-to-measure *adj* **tailor-made**, custom-made, customized, custom-built, bespoke, made-to-order (*US*). [➡ EXTRAORDINARY: UNCOMMON; 206] *Opposite:* off-the-peg.

made-to-order (*US*) *adj* **custom-made**, custom-built, made-to-measure, tailor-made, bespoke. [➡ EXTRAORDINARY: UNCOMMON; 206] *Opposite:* mass-produced.

made-up *adj* **pretend**, invented, concocted, fictional, fictitious, imaginary, make-believe. [➡ FALSE AND UNREAL; 174] *Opposite:* real.

madly 1 *adv* **intensely**, extremely, strongly, deeply, very, utterly, totally. [➡ TO A GREAT EXTENT; 130] 2 *adv* **wildly**, frantically, frenetically, rashly, riotously, uncontrollably. [➡ WITH ENTHUSIASM; 287] *Opposite:* calmly.

madness *n* **folly**, foolishness, stupidity, foolhardiness. [➡ NEGATIVE INTELLECTUAL CHARACTERISTICS; 526]

madrigal *type of* **vocal music**. [➡ MUSIC, SONGS, AND SINGING; 907]

maelstrom *n* **tumult**, turbulence, flurry, whirl, turmoil, scramble, frenzy, vortex. [➡ DISORDER AND CHAOS; 246]

maestro *n* **genius**, ace (*informal*), talent, whiz (*informal*), virtuoso, marvel, whiz kid (*informal*), expert. [➡ TALENTED OR INTELLIGENT PERSON; 529] *Opposite:* amateur.

mafia *n* **clique**, gang, coterie, faction, set, circle. [➡ CRIMINALS; 821]

Mafioso *n* [➡ CRIMINALS; 821]

mag (*informal*) *n* [➡ NEWSPAPERS; 606]

magazine 1 *n* **periodical**, publication, glossy magazine, journal, mag (*informal*), weekly, monthly, quarterly, fortnightly, slick (*US*). [➡ NEWSPAPERS; 606] 2 *n* **arsenal**, depot, repository, ordnance, stockpile, storeroom, storehouse. [➡ STORES AND STORAGE BUILDINGS; 1087]

magenta *type of* **red**. [➡ COLOURS; 1223]

maggot *type of* **insect stages of development**. [➡ INSECT STAGES; 1020]

maggoty *adj* [➡ DECAYING OR INFESTED; 1235]

magic 1 *n* **enchantment**, sorcery, witchcraft, voodoo, augury, alchemy. [➡ THE SUPERNATURAL; 788] 2 *n* **conjuring**, tricks, trickery, illusion, sleight of hand, artifice (*formal*). [➡ FALSE AND UNREAL; 174] 3 *n* **mystery**, charm, appeal, allure, attraction, fascination, charisma, magnetism, sparkle, je ne sais quoi. [➡ BEAUTY AND ATTRACTIVENESS; 190] 4 *adj* **enchanted**, magical, fairylike, charmed, dreamlike, mystic, fairy-tale. [➡ FALSE AND UNREAL; 174] 5 *adj* **supernatural**, magical, paranormal, mysterious, miraculous. [➡ THE SUPERNATURAL; 788] *Opposite:* normal. 6 *adj* **thrilling**, magical, enchanting, delightful, wonderful, lovely, captivating, charming, astonishing, breathtaking. [➡ EXTRAORDINARY: AMAZING; 205] *Opposite:* mundane. 7 *adj* **powerful**, special, key, all-important, famous. [➡ MOST IMPORTANT AND MAIN; 194]

magical 1 *adj* **enchanted**, magic, fairylike, charmed, dreamlike, mystic, fairy-tale. [➡ FALSE AND UNREAL; 174] 2 *adj* **supernatural**, magic, paranormal, mysterious, miraculous. [➡ THE SUPERNATURAL; 788] *Opposite:* normal. 3 *adj* **thrilling**, magic, enchanting, delightful, wonderful, lovely, captivating, charming, astonishing, breathtaking. [➡ EXTRAORDINARY: AMAZING; 205] *Opposite:* mundane.

magician 1 *n* **conjurer**, illusionist, prestidigitator (*formal*), entertainer, escape artist, performer. [➡ WORKERS IN ENTERTAINMENT AND MEDIA; 873] 2 *n* **sorcerer**, wizard, warlock, enchanter, necromancer (*literary*). [➡ PEOPLE WITH SUPERNATURAL POWERS; 789] 3 *n* **genius**, virtuoso, expert, wizard, whiz (*informal*), whiz kid (*informal*), marvel, ace (*informal*). [➡ TALENTED OR INTELLIGENT PERSON; 529]

magisterial 1 *adj* **august** (*formal*), commanding, authoritative, majestic, stately, dignified, imposing, regal. [➡ EXTRAORDINARY: AMAZING; 205] *Opposite:* lightweight. 2 *adj* **overbearing**, arrogant, superior, domineering, imperious, dictatorial. [➡ BOSSY AND OVERBEARING; 517] *Opposite:* diffident. 3 *adj* **masterly**, authoritative, expert, able, knowledgeable, scholarly. [➡ TALENTED AND SKILFUL; 528]

magisterially 1 *adv* **augustly** (*formal*), commandingly, authoritatively, majestically, imposingly, regally. [➡ BOSSY AND OVERBEARING; 517] 2 *adv* **domineeringly**, dictatorially, overbearingly, imperiously, arrogantly. [➡ POMPOUS, LOUD, AND OVERCONFIDENT; 636] *Opposite:* diffidently. 3 *adv* **authoritatively**, expertly, ably, commandingly, knowledgeably. [➡ TALENTED AND SKILFUL; 528] *Opposite:* inexpertly.

magistrate *n* **law officer**, justice of the peace, judge, JP, justice, public officer, judicial officer, official. [➡ PEOPLE IN LAW COURTS; 820]

magma *n* **molten rock**, lava, tuff, igneous rock, pumice. [➡ STONES, ROCKS, AND BOULDERS; 1057]

magnanimity *n* **nobility**, high-mindedness, fairness, generousness, generosity, benevolence, altruism. [➡ GENEROSITY AND KINDNESS; 496] *Opposite:* pettiness.

magnanimous *adj* **generous**, high-minded, noble, big, worthy, upright, benevolent, altruistic, considerate, kindly, forgiving. [➡ GENEROSITY AND KINDNESS; 496] *Opposite:* petty.

See Compare and Contrast at **generous**.

magnate *n* **tycoon**, mogul, entrepreneur, industrialist, baron, plutocrat, big cheese (*slang*), honcho (*US slang*), kahuna (*US informal*). [➡ RICH PEOPLE; 895]

magnesium *type of* **metal**. [➡ METALS; 1275]

magnet 1 *n* **magnetic body**, lodestone, horseshoe magnet, electromagnet, bar magnet, fridge magnet, refrigerator magnet (*US*). [➡ ENERGY GENERAL; 1160] 2 *n* **lure**, draw, attraction, pull, enticement, crowd puller, inducement, centre of attention. [➡ TREAT; 211]

magnetic *adj* **attractive**, charming, compelling, alluring, captivating, charismatic, hypnotic (*informal*), irresistible, mesmeric, fascinating. [➡ INTERESTING AND MEANINGFUL; 191] *Opposite:* repellent.

magnetism 1 *n* **magnetic field**, attraction, pull. [➡ENERGY GENERAL; 1160] 2 *n* **charisma**, appeal, allure, charm, magic, fascination, pull (*informal*), draw, enticement, attraction, mesmerism. [➡INTERESTING AND MEANINGFUL; 191]

magnetize *v* **attract**, charm, influence, draw, pull (*informal*), fascinate, entice. [➡APPEAL TO AND AROUSE INTEREST; 576] *Opposite:* repel.

magnification *n* **exaggeration**, intensification, enlargement, increase, amplification. [➡CHANGE OF SIZE: BIGGER; 393] *Opposite:* reduction.

magnificence *n* **splendour**, glory, brilliance, radiance, majesty, grandeur, grandness, impressiveness, marvellousness, beauty. [➡BEAUTY AND ATTRACTIVENESS; 190]

magnificent *adj* **superb**, wonderful, splendid, glorious, brilliant, outstanding, superlative, bravura, stunning, marvellous, resplendent, grand, beautiful, impressive. [➡EXTRAORDINARY: AMAZING; 205] *Opposite:* unimpressive.

magnify 1 *v* **enlarge**, blow up, expand, amplify, increase, augment (*formal*), extend, heighten, boost. [➡CHANGE OF SIZE: BIGGER; 393] *Opposite:* shrink. 2 *v* (*formal*) **worship**, praise, extol, exalt (*formal*), laud, glorify, venerate, bless, adore. [➡PRAISE AND ENCOURAGE; 648]

magnifying glass *type of* **optical instrument**. [➡OPTICAL INSTRUMENTS; 1123]

magniloquence *n* [➡POMPOUS, LOUD, AND OVER-CONFIDENT; 636]

magniloquent *adj* [➡POMPOUS, LOUD, AND OVER-CONFIDENT; 636]

magnitude 1 *n* **greatness**, size, extent, degree, amount, enormousness, level, scale. [➡LARGE; 1192] 2 *n* **importance**, significance, enormity, weight, consequence (*formal*), moment (*formal*). [➡IMPORTANCE AND SIGNIFICANCE; 193] *Opposite:* triviality.

magnolia 1 *type of* **white**. [➡COLOURS; 1223] 2 *type of* **shrub or bush**. [➡BUSHES AND SHRUBS; 1027]

magnum 1 *n* **bottle**, jeroboam, demijohn. [➡CONTAINERS, RECEPTACLES, AND PACKAGING; 1244] 2 *type of* **gun**. [➡WEAPONS FOR SHOOTING; 1155]

magnum opus *n* [➡ARTWORKS; 898]

magpie 1 *n* (*informal*) **chatterer**, babbler, prattler, talker, chatterbox (*informal*), yammerer (*informal*), gossip, yapper (*informal*). [➡INTERFERING PEOPLE AND TELLTALES; 950] 2 *n* (*informal*) **collector**, squirrel (*informal*), hoarder, saver, accumulator, pack rat (*US informal*). [➡PEOPLE WHO COLLECT THINGS; 455] 3 *type of* **scavenger**. [➡BIRD; 997]

magus *n* [➡PEOPLE WITH SUPERNATURAL POWERS; 789]

maharajah *type of* **aristocrat**. [➡RULERS AND ARISTOCRACY; 823]

maharani *type of* **aristocrat**. [➡RULERS AND ARISTOCRACY; 823]

maharishi *n* **religious teacher**, guru, sage (*literary*), mahatma, prophet, evangelist, swami. [➡RELIGIOUS PEOPLE; 779] *Opposite:* follower.

mahi-mahi *type of* **tropical sea fish**. [➡SEA FISH; 1009]

mahogany 1 *type of* **brown**. [➡COLOURS; 1223] 2 *type of* **evergreen tree**. [➡EVERGREEN AND CONIFEROUS TREES; 1029]

maid *type of* **servant**. [➡DOMESTIC AND KITCHEN WORKERS; 850]

maiden 1 *n* **girl**, lass, maid, young woman, young lady, damsel (*archaic or literary*). [➡FEMALE PERSON; 933] 2 *adj* **first**, earliest, initial, original. [➡BEFORE, FIRST, AND PRECEDING; 164]

maidservant *type of* **servant**. [➡DOMESTIC AND KITCHEN WORKERS; 850]

mail 1 *n* **letters**, post, correspondence, packages, parcels, junk mail, circulars, bulk mail (*US*). [➡LETTERS AND WRITTEN MESSAGES; 585] 2 *v* (*US*) **post**, send, dispatch, transmit, email. [➡DESPATCH AND SEND; 334]

mailbag 1 *n* **postbag**, sack, bag, satchel, shoulder bag, mail sack (*US*), mail pouch (*US*). [➡CONTAINERS, RECEPTACLES, AND PACKAGING; 1244] 2 *n* **correspondence**, postbag, feedback, mail, post, letters, communications, messages. [➡LETTERS AND WRITTEN MESSAGES; 585]

mailbox (*US*) *n* **letterbox**, pillar box, box, post box, inbox, post office box, maildrop (*US*), mail slot (*US*). [➡CONTAINERS, RECEPTACLES, AND PACKAGING; 1244]

maildrop (*US*) *n* [➡CONTAINERS, RECEPTACLES, AND PACKAGING; 1244]

mailer 1 *n* **envelope**, padded envelope, carton, mailing tube, container. [➡CONTAINERS, RECEPTACLES, AND PACKAGING; 1244] 2 *n* (*US*) **advertisement**, circular, flier, leaflet, brochure, handbill. [➡ADVERTISING AND PUBLICITY; 605]

mailing list *n* **distribution list**, register, circulation list, newsgroup, address book, clientele. [➡LISTS AND SCHEDULES; 588]

mail order *n* **home shopping**, teleshopping, teleordering, electronic shopping, virtual shopping, online shopping, cybershopping. [➡PURCHASE; 423]

mailshot *n* **advertisement**, circular, leaflet, letter, brochure, pamphlet, junk mail. [➡ADVERTISING AND PUBLICITY; 605]

mail slot (*US*) *n* [➡HOLES, GAPS, AND FORKS; 1251]

maim *v* **wound**, injure, hurt, mutilate, damage, lacerate. [➡WOUND A PERSON OR ANIMAL; 384]

main *adj* **major**, chief, key, foremost, core, focal, central, highest, leading, principal, head. [➡MOST IMPORTANT AND MAIN; 194] *Opposite:* minor.

main course *part of* **meal**. [➡MEALS AND PARTS OF MEALS; 1168]

mainframe *type of* **computer**. [➡COMPUTERS AND COMPUTING; 1126]

mainland *n* **landmass**, continent, land. [➡THE CONTINENTS AND ISLANDS; 1048] *Opposite:* island.

main line *n* **rail route**, principal route, major route, line, trunk route (*US*). [➡RAILWAYS; 1106]

mainline *adj* **main**, chief, central, inter-city, principal. [➡COMMUNICATION NETWORKS; 1104] *Opposite:* local.

mainly *adv* **mostly**, largely, chiefly, for the most part, primarily, principally, generally, essentially, above all, predominantly, first and foremost. [➡USUALLY; 108]

main road *type of* **major road**. [➡ROADS; 1105]

mainsail *part of* **sailing vessel**. [➡PARTS OF A SHIP OR BOAT; 1150]

mainspring *n* **driving force**, motive force, motivating force, chief reason, chief motive, impelling cause, impetus, dynamo. [➡MOST IMPORTANT THING; 198]

mainstay 1 *n* **cornerstone**, linchpin, keystone, foundation, basis, backbone. [➡MOST IMPORTANT THING; 198] 2 *part of* **sailing vessel.** [➡PARTS OF A SHIP OR BOAT; 1150]

mainstream *adj* **normal**, typical, conventional, ordinary, middle-of-the-road, majority, vanilla (*slang*). [➡ORDINARINESS; 245] *Opposite:* unconventional.

maintain 1 *v* **uphold**, keep, keep up, continue, sustain, retain, conserve, keep alive, preserve. [➡CAUSE TO CONTINUE; 268] *Opposite:* destroy. 2 *v* **argue**, claim, insist, assert, hold, swear, be adamant, avow (*formal*), declare, affirm, state. [➡CLAIM, INSIST, AND EMPHASIZE; 615] *Opposite:* deny. 3 *v* **look after**, care for, take care of, keep up, keep in good condition, continue, support. [➡REPAIR AND MEND; 377] *Opposite:* neglect.

maintenance 1 *n* **preservation**, upholding, protection, continuation, continuance, safeguarding. [➡PERMANENCE: WITHOUT END; 94] *Opposite:* destruction. 2 *n* **repairs**, upkeep, looking after, care, keep, conservation, preservation. [➡WORK IN GENERAL; 298] *Opposite:* neglect. 3 *n* **alimony**, allowance, child support, child maintenance, grant. [➡MONEY, PAYMENTS, AND CHARGES; 800]

maisonette *type of* **apartment.** [➡RESIDENTIAL BUILDINGS; 1077]

maize *type of* **cereal.** [➡CEREAL FOODS; 1177]

majestic 1 *adj* **impressive**, superb, grand, wonderful, splendid, awesome, sublime, magnificent. [➡EXTRAORDINARY: AMAZING; 205] *Opposite:* modest. 2 *adj* **regal**, royal, grand, stately, imposing, grandiose, resplendent, august (*formal*), impressive. [➡LEVELS OF FORMALITY; 523] *Opposite:* humble.

majesty *n* **magnificence**, splendour, dignity, grandeur, illustriousness, stateliness, gravitas (*formal*). [➡EXTRAORDINARY: AMAZING; 205]

major 1 *adj* **main**, chief, key, foremost, leading, greatest, principal. [➡MOST IMPORTANT AND MAIN; 194] *Opposite:* minor. 2 *adj* **significant**, important, weighty, substantial, crucial, big. [➡IMPORTANT; 195] *Opposite:* trivial. 3 *adj* **serious**, grave, life-threatening. [➡DANGEROUS; 237] *Opposite:* minor.

major-domo *type of* **servant.** [➡DOMESTIC AND KITCHEN WORKERS; 850]

majority 1 *n* **bulk**, preponderance, mass, greater part, lion's share, best part. [➡MAJORITY; 139] 2 *n* **margin**, difference, gap, advantage, lead, edge. [➡MAJORITY; 139] 3 *n* **adulthood**, maturity, manhood, womanhood, adult years, independence, seniority, legal age. [➡ADULTHOOD; 918] *Opposite:* childhood. 4 *adj* **mainstream**, popular, common, widely held, middle-of-the-road. [➡BELONGING OR RELATING TO PEOPLE; 943] *Opposite:* minority.

make 1 *v* **create**, fashion, compose, craft, build, construct, formulate. [➡CREATION; 347] *Opposite:* destroy. 2 *v* **put together**, assemble, make up, put up, knock together (*informal*), cobble together. [➡BUILD; 353] 3 *v* **manufacture**, produce, fabricate, churn out, yield, turn out. [➡MANUFACTURE; 350] *Opposite:* consume. 4 *v* **cause**, bring about, create, give rise to, effect (*formal*), generate, occasion, render (*formal*). [➡CAUSE TO HAPPEN; 31] 5 *v* **cook**, prepare, concoct, produce, create, brew, bake, rustle up (*informal*), throw together (*informal*). [➡COOKING AND FOOD PREPARATION; 354] 6 *v* **earn**, bring in, get, take home, get paid, receive. [➡GET MONEY OR REWARD; 422] *Opposite:* spend. 7 *v* **force**, compel, pressurize, pressure, command, cause, oblige, constrain, require. [➡CAUSE OR COMPEL TO ACT; 272] *Opposite:* ask. 8 *v* **become**, turn into, change into, be. [➡GRADUALLY COME INTO EXISTENCE; 1] 9 *v* **appoint**, elect, designate, nominate, name. [➡CONFER STATUS; 459] 10 *v* **achieve**, get into, get on to, succeed, progress to, be selected for. [➡SUCCEED AND WIN; 79] *Opposite:* miss. 11 *v* **form**, make up, constitute, comprise, be, add up to. [➡POSSESS; 445] 12 *v* **manage**, accomplish, find time for, fit in, finish, do. [➡COMPLETE AN ACTION; 264] 13 *v* **reach**, get to, make it to, get as far as, arrive at, attain. [➡ARRIVE; 12] 14 *n* **sort**, type, kind, style, variety, mark, brand. [➡VARIETY, TYPE, KIND; 146]

Compare and Contrast: ***make, produce, create, fashion, manufacture***

CORE MEANING: TO BRING SOMETHING INTO EXISTENCE

make to bring something into existence; ***produce*** to make something in large quantities or in a commercial setting; ***create*** to make something using imagination and artistic skill or to cause something such as a job or opportunity to exist; ***fashion*** to make something by shaping and working raw materials, especially when using only the hands or hand-held tools; ***manufacture*** to make something in large numbers, usually in a factory using machinery, or to make something quickly and cynically, especially something that normally requires time and artistic skill.

make a beeline for *v* **make straight for**, go directly to, head for, target. [➡MOVE FAST; 314]

make a big thing of *v* **make a show of**, make a big deal out of (*informal*), make a mountain out of a molehill, make a point of. [➡CLAIM, INSIST, AND EMPHASIZE; 615] *Opposite:* play down.

make a break for it *v* [➡RUN AWAY AND AVOID; 10]

make a clean breast of things *v* **confess**, own up, tell the truth, come clean (*informal*), tell all, admit, fess up (*US informal*). [➡ADMIT AND CONFESS; 616]

make a dash for it *v* [➡RUN AWAY AND AVOID; 10]

make a difference *v* **have an effect**, matter, be important, change things. [➡CHANGE; 373]

make a dog's breakfast/dinner of *v* **mess up** (*informal*), bungle (*informal*), foul up (*informal*), make a pig's ear, make a mess, hash up (*informal*), botch. [➡MESS UP AND MAKE MISTAKES; 473]

make a fool of *v* **trick**, mislead, dupe, con, make a monkey of (*informal*), take for a ride, make somebody look an idiot, deceive, fool. [➡DECEPTION AND LIES; 661]

make a fool of yourself *v* **embarrass yourself**, humiliate yourself, appear foolish, put your foot in it (*informal*), make an exhibition of yourself, expose yourself to ridicule. [➡CHANGE OF MOOD AND COMPOSURE; 581]

make a fuss *v* **complain**, fuss, make a scene, kick up a fuss, make a mountain out of a molehill, make a song and dance (*informal*). [➡COMPLAIN AND NAG; 687]

make a fuss of *v* **make much of**, indulge, spoil, cosset, coddle, pamper, fuss over, baby. [➡TAKE CARE OF AND SPOIL; 301] *Opposite:* ignore.

make a hash of (*informal*) *v* **muddle**, confuse, jumble, mess up (*informal*), spoil, mix up. [➡MESS UP AND MAKE MISTAKES; 473]

make allowances *v* **take into account**, bear in mind, consider, take into consideration, cut somebody some slack (*US*). [➡TOLERATE AND ENDURE; 767]

make amends *v* **make up for**, compensate for, recompense, pay back, make reparations, atone (*formal*), redress the balance, repent. [➡APOLOGIZE AND RETRACT; 684]

make a mess of *v* **botch**, mess up (*informal*), mishandle, mismanage, manage badly, spoil, bodge (*informal*), ruin, put a spanner in the works, do badly, bungle (*informal*), botch up, make a hash of (*informal*), make a dog's dinner of, foul up (*informal*). [➡MESS UP AND MAKE MISTAKES; 473]

make a mistake *v* [➡MESS UP AND MAKE MISTAKES; 473]

make a monkey of (*informal*) *v* [➡UPSET, DISTRESS, AND HUMILIATE; 568]

make a mountain out of a molehill *v* **make a fuss**, exaggerate, make a big deal out of something (*informal*), overstate, make too much of something, make a big thing of something, make a song and dance about (*informal*). [➡CLAIM, INSIST, AND EMPHASIZE; 615]

make a name for yourself *v* **succeed**, rise to fame, make it to the top, become known, gain respect. [➡SUCCEED AND WIN; 79]

make an effort *v* **put yourself out**, try, attempt, endeavour, work hard. [➡HARD WORK OR EFFORT; 299]

make an exhibition of yourself *v* **make a fool of yourself**, expose yourself to ridicule, embarrass yourself, behave foolishly, show off. [➡CHANGE OF MOOD AND COMPOSURE; 581]

make a note of 1 *v* **notice**, mark, memorize, remark upon, observe, pick up on (*informal*). [➡REMEMBER; 747] 2 *v* **write down**, jot down, take down, keep a record. [➡RECORD SOMETHING; 372]

make a pig's ear of *v* [➡MESS UP AND MAKE MISTAKES; 473]

make a point of 1 *v* **make a show of**, make a big thing of, make a song and dance about (*informal*), let people know about, make a fuss. [➡OVERDO SOMETHING; 291] 2 *v* **make sure to**, don't forget to, take care to, remember to, make an effort to, try to. [➡REMEMBER; 747]

make a racket *v* [➡SOUND EMISSION; 363]

make a run for it *v* [➡RUN AWAY AND AVOID; 10]

make a scene *v* **be angry**, carry on, make an exhibition of yourself, make a fuss, throw a tantrum, have hysterics (*informal*), have kittens (*informal*). [➡GIVING VENT TO EMOTIONS; 680]

make a sharp exit *v* [➡RUN AWAY AND AVOID; 10]

make a splash *v* **make an impression**, impress, get noticed, make an impact, turn heads, make your presence felt. [➡SUCCEED AND WIN; 79]

make a stab at (*informal*) *v* **attempt**, try, endeavour, strive at, essay (*formal*), assay (*literary*). [➡ATTEMPT AN ACTION; 262]

make a start *v* **get going**, get cracking (*informal*), jump in, begin, start. [➡START AN ACTION; 261] *Opposite:* procrastinate.

make a statement *v* **say something**, send a message, catch the eye, turn heads, make an impact. [➡MEAN SOMETHING; 61]

make available *v* **free up**, find, set aside, release, provide, grant access to, supply. [➡DISPENSE, RATION, AND DISTRIBUTE; 435] *Opposite:* refuse.

make believe *v* **pretend**, imagine, fantasize, daydream, muse. [➡DREAM, IMAGINE, AND FANTASIZE; 750]

make-believe 1 *n* **fantasy**, pretence, role-playing, play-acting, story, game. [➡DREAM, IMAGINE, AND FANTASIZE; 750] *Opposite:* reality. 2 *adj* **pretend**, imaginary, fantasy, made-up, invented, fake, mock. [➡FALSE AND UNREAL; 174] *Opposite:* real.

make better *v* **cure**, heal, treat, alleviate, relieve, improve, remedy, palliate, ameliorate (*formal*). [➡IMPROVE SOMETHING; 375]

make certain *v* **ensure**, make sure, double-check, be in no doubt, ascertain (*formal*), check. [➡CAUSE TO HAPPEN; 31]

make clear *v* **clarify**, elucidate (*formal*), spell out, explain, give details, illuminate, shed light on, make obvious, ram home. [➡EXPLAIN AND CLARIFY; 611] *Opposite:* obscure.

make contact *v* **speak to**, approach, communicate, touch base, get in touch, contact. [➡INITIATE AND ESTABLISH COMMUNICATION; 681] *Opposite:* drop.

make contacts *v* **meet people**, exchange cards, introduce yourself, make friends, network, schmooze (*slang*). [➡ESTABLISHING RELATIONSHIPS WITH OTHERS; 974]

make do *v* **manage**, put up with, cope, accept, tolerate, live with, cut your coat according to your cloth. [➡CONTINUE TO EXIST; 17]

make ends meet *v* **cope**, manage, pay your bills, break even, get by, eke out a living. [➡CONTINUE TO EXIST; 17]

make enquiries *see* **make inquiries**.

make for 1 *v* **head for**, head towards, go towards, proceed towards, aim for, approach. [➡PROCEED AND GO; 306] 2 *v* **produce**, create, bring about, give rise to, effect (*formal*), generate, occasion. [➡CAUSE TO HAPPEN; 31]

make friends *v* **befriend**, take up with, get in with, get to know, become acquainted, strike up a friendship, win peoples' hearts, make contacts. [➡ESTABLISHING RELATIONSHIPS WITH OTHERS; 974] *Opposite:* repel.

make fun of *v* **mock**, poke fun at, laugh at, tease, send up (*informal*), ridicule, scoff at, satirize, burlesque, lampoon. [➡JOKES AND TEASING; 675] *Opposite:* respect.

make good *v* **succeed**, make it (*informal*), arrive, be somebody, do well, become successful, come out on top. [➡SUCCEED AND WIN; 79] *Opposite:* fail.

make happen *v* **cause**, effect (*formal*), bring about, realize, make real, produce. [➡CAUSE TO HAPPEN; 31]

make headway *v* **make progress**, progress, get somewhere, get on, make ground, make inroads. [➡SUCCEED AND WIN; 79]

make inquiries *v* **research**, investigate, explore, look into, inspect, analyse. [➡ASK PEOPLE QUESTIONS; 667]

make inroads 1 *v* **produce a result**, have an effect on, get somewhere, make something happen, make headway, make progress. [➡SUCCEED AND WIN; 79] 2 *v* **encroach**, creep up on, dent, overstep, infringe, intrude, trespass. [➡APPEAR AND EMERGE; 3]

make it (*informal*) *v* **succeed**, achieve, accomplish, attain, manage, pull off (*informal*), make good, hit the big time (*slang*), come out on top, do well. [➡SUCCEED AND WIN; 79] *Opposite:* give up.

make known *v* **publicize**, announce, communicate, proclaim, broadcast. [➡INFORM AND ANNOUNCE; 612]

make light of *v* **play down**, make little of, minimize, underestimate, understate, slough off, dismiss, belittle, underplay, underrate, talk down. [➡UNDERDO SOMETHING; 292] *Opposite:* overstate.

make merry *v* [➡LEISURE AND RECREATION; 874]

make mincemeat of *v* **defeat heavily**, thrash, hammer (*informal*), rout, overwhelm, overpower, crush, slaughter (*slang*), cream (*US informal*). [➡BEAT AND DEFEAT; 80]

make much of *v* **make a fuss of**, mollycoddle, baby, pet, pat, fuss over, indulge, spoil, cosset, pamper. [➡OVERDO SOMETHING; 291]

make off *v* **run away**, run off, decamp, make a break for it, make a run for it, take off (*informal*), scarper (*slang*), head off, flee, bolt, beat a hasty retreat, escape, vamoose (*US slang*). [➡ABSENT ONESELF; 8] *Opposite:* come back.

make off with *v* **appropriate**, run away with, steal, remove, pilfer, thieve, lift (*informal*), take. [➡STEAL AND ROB; 427] *Opposite:* return.

make out 1 *v* **distinguish**, see, hear, perceive, pick out, recognize, discern. [➡LOOKING AND LOOKS; 701] 2 *v* **understand**, work out, decipher, decode, figure out, comprehend. [➡SOLVE AND INTERPRET; 761] 3 *v* **fill in**, write out, make, compose, draw up, complete, write. [➡RECORD SOMETHING; 372] 4 *v* **imply**, suggest, give the impression, make somebody believe, insinuate, hint. [➡MEAN SOMETHING; 61] 5 *v* **get by**, get on, manage, fare, do, get along. [➡SUCCEED AND WIN; 79]

makeover 1 *n* **transformation**, change, restyling, cosmetic treatment, beautification, alteration. [➡IMPROVE APPEARANCE; 380] 2 *n* **remodelling**, renovation, rehab (*informal*), restoration, transformation, alteration, conversion. [➡IMPROVE APPEARANCE; 380]

make overtures *v* [➡ESTABLISHING RELATIONSHIPS WITH OTHERS; 974]

make points with (*US*) *v* **butter up** (*informal*), get on the good side of, pander to, ingratiate yourself, flatter, suck up to (*informal*), get in good with (*US*). [➡ESTABLISHING RELATIONSHIPS WITH OTHERS; 974]

make preparations *v* [➡PREPARE FOR ACTION; 290]

make progress 1 *v* **make headway**, progress, advance, get somewhere, forge ahead, make inroads, come on, proceed. [➡SUCCEED AND WIN; 79] *Opposite:* stall. 2 *v* **recover**, get well, get better, improve, be on the mend. [➡GET BETTER; 376] *Opposite:* deteriorate.

make public *v* **publicize**, publish, release, put out, reveal, make known, expose, air, announce. [➡INFORM AND ANNOUNCE; 612]

maker *n* **creator**, manufacturer, fabricator, producer, architect, cause. [➡DESIGNERS, CREATORS, AND INSTIGATORS; 348] *Opposite:* destroyer.

make redundant *v* [➡REVOKE STATUS; 460]

make reparations *v* [➡APOLOGIZE AND RETRACT; 684]

make sense *v* **add up**, fit, seem sensible, seem right. [➡MEAN SOMETHING; 61]

make sense of *v* **understand**, decode, decipher, follow, grasp, get (*informal*), work out, comprehend, figure out. [➡SOLVE AND INTERPRET; 761] *Opposite:* misunderstand.

makeshift *adj* **rough-and-ready**, crude, temporary, improvised, provisional, ersatz (*disapproving*), do-it-yourself. [➡IN BAD REPAIR; 1233] *Opposite:* permanent.

make short work of *v* **make short shrift of**, do quickly, dash off (*informal*), rush through, dash through, make mincemeat of. [➡CARRY OUT AN ACTION; 270]

make small talk *v* [➡TWO-WAY COMMUNICATION; 608]

make somebody's acquaintance *v* **meet for the first time**, meet, get to know, become acquainted, bump into, come across. [➡ESTABLISHING RELATIONSHIPS WITH OTHERS; 974]

make somebody's blood boil *v* **anger**, annoy, wind up (*informal*), drive mad (*informal*), exasperate, irritate, enrage, infuriate, incense, madden. [➡ANGER AND ANNOY; 570] *Opposite:* delight.

make somebody's hackles rise *v* **anger**, antagonize, get up somebody's nose, annoy, get somebody's back up, infuriate, incense, enrage. [➡ANGER AND ANNOY; 570] *Opposite:* placate.

make sure *v* **validate**, confirm, certify, take care, ensure, verify, make certain, check. [➡APPROVE AND CONFIRM; 647] *Opposite:* assume.

make the best of a bad job *v* **make the best of things**, take the rough with the smooth, take the bad with the good, keep smiling, keep your chin up, look on the bright side, grin and bear it (*informal*). [➡TOLERATE AND ENDURE; 767] *Opposite:* complain.

make the best of things *v* **take the rough with the smooth**, take the bad with the good, make the best of a bad job, look on the bright side, keep your chin up, keep smiling, grin and bear it (*informal*). [➡TOLERATE AND ENDURE; 767] *Opposite:* complain.

make the grade *v* **meet the standards**, come up to

scratch (*informal*), be good enough, measure up, hit the mark, come up with the goods, satisfy, deliver. [➡SUCCEED AND WIN; 79] *Opposite:* fail.

make the most of *v* **capitalize on**, take advantage of, make hay while the sun shines (*informal*), maximize, profit from. [➡MAKE GOOD USE OF SOMETHING; 474] *Opposite:* squander.

make tracks (*informal*) *v* **leave**, depart, go away, make a move, hit the road, take off (*informal*), vamoose (*US slang*). [➡ABSENT ONESELF; 8] *Opposite:* stay.

makeup 1 *n* **cosmetics**, face paint, greasepaint, powder and paint, face (*informal*), maquillage. [➡MAKEUP AND BEAUTY PRODUCTS; 491] 2 *n* **composition**, constitution, structure, formation, construction. [➡QUALITIES AND CHARACTERISTICS; 1190] 3 *n* **temperament**, character, personality, nature, disposition, complexion, individuality, humour. [➡TEMPERAMENT AND BEHAVIOUR; 493]

make up 1 *v* **prepare**, make ready, get ready, set up, put together. [➡CREATION; 347] 2 *v* **contribute**, add, supply, chip in (*informal*), come up with, provide. [➡GIVE AND PROVIDE; 431] *Opposite:* deduct. 3 *v* **form**, comprise, constitute, add up to, make, be, join up, compose. [➡AMOUNT TO AND EQUAL; 70] 4 *v* **invent**, concoct, forge, fabricate, think up, dream up. [➡DREAM, IMAGINE, AND FANTASIZE; 750] 5 *v* **top up**, subsidize, augment (*formal*), supplement, round up, bring up, complete. [➡CHANGE OF SIZE: BIGGER; 393] 6 *v* **be reconciled**, make peace, forgive and forget, kiss and make up, bury the hatchet, settle your differences. [➡ESTABLISHING RELATIONSHIPS WITH OTHERS; 974] *Opposite:* fall out. 7 *v* **compensate**, make amends, make good, recompense, atone for (*formal*), balance, offset, redeem. [➡CORRECT AND PUT RIGHT; 378]

makeup remover *n* [➡MAKEUP AND BEAUTY PRODUCTS; 491]

make up your mind *v* **decide**, come to a decision, resolve, determine. [➡MAKE DECISIONS AND CHOICES; 753]

make use of *v* **utilize**, use, draw on, take advantage of, avail yourself, exploit. [➡USE; 468]

make waves *v* **kick up a fuss**, create a stir, rock the boat, dissent, revolt, rebel, disturb, criticize. [➡PROTEST AND EXPRESS DISAPPROVAL; 643]

makeweight 1 *n* **counterpoise**, weight, counterbalance, ballast, counterweight. [➡WEIGHT: HEAVY; 1204] 2 *n* **extra**, complement, supplement, compensation, reinforcement, offset. [➡MORE AND EXCESS; 122]

make your mark *v* **succeed**, arrive, make it (*informal*), make an impact, make an impression, make your presence felt, impact, impress. [➡SUCCEED AND WIN; 79]

make yourself known *v* **introduce yourself**, say who you are, identify yourself, give your name, come forward, show yourself. [➡INITIATE AND ESTABLISH COMMUNICATION; 681]

make yourself scarce (*informal*) *v* [➡ABSENT ONESELF; 8]

make yourself useful *v* **help out**, be of service, lend a hand, assist, rally round. [➡HELP; 294] *Opposite:* hinder.

make your way *v* **go**, move, head, wend your way, pick your way, progress, proceed. [➡PROCEED AND GO; 306]

making *n* **creation**, manufacture, production, construction, assembly, building. [➡CREATION; 347]

makings 1 *n* **ingredients**, requirements, components, elements, materials, pieces, parts. [➡PHYSICAL OBJECTS; 1242] 2 *n* **qualities**, potential, wherewithal, what it takes, assets, ability, talent. [➡SKILLS, TALENTS, AND ABILITIES; 527]

malachite *type of* **stone**. [➡STONES, ROCKS, AND BOULDERS; 1057]

maladjusted *adj* **disturbed**, neurotic (*informal*), unstable, confused, alienated, estranged. [➡PSYCHOLOGY AND THE MIND; 770] *Opposite:* well-adjusted.

maladjustment *n* **instability**, disturbance, neurosis (*dated*), confusion, alienation, estrangement. [➡PSYCHOLOGY AND THE MIND; 770] *Opposite:* balance.

maladroit (*formal*) *adj* **awkward**, clumsy, inept, gauche, ungainly, inelegant, graceless, gawky (*informal*), unskilful, insensitive, ham-fisted (*informal*), ham-handed (*informal*). [➡UNSKILLED; 530] *Opposite:* dexterous.

maladroitness (*formal*) *n* **clumsiness**, insensitivity, awkwardness, ham-fistedness (*informal*), ham-handedness (*informal*), ineptitude, gaucheness, inelegance, gracelessness, gawkiness (*informal*). [➡UNSKILLED; 530]

malady *n* **sickness**, illness, disease, disorder, condition, malaise. [➡SICKNESS; 730]

malaise 1 *n* **sickness**, illness, disease, disorder, condition, malady. [➡SICKNESS; 730] 2 *n* **dissatisfaction**, discontent, unease, disquiet, anxiety, depression, discomfort. [➡SADNESS, DISTRESS, AND DESPAIR; 540]

malapropism *type of* **wordplay**. [➡JOKES AND TEASING; 675]

malarkey (*informal*) *n* [➡MEANINGLESS SPEECH OR WRITING; 677]

malcontent 1 *n* **complainer**, mischief-maker, protester, rebel, whiner, agitator, grouch (*informal*), troublemaker, dissident, whinger (*informal*). [➡UNCOOPERATIVE OR REBELLIOUS PERSON; 567] 2 *adj* **discontented**, disgruntled, dissatisfied, unhappy, complaining, rebellious, grumbling. [➡SADNESS, DISTRESS, AND DESPAIR; 540] *Opposite:* happy.

male 1 *adj* **masculine**, mannish, manlike, manly, virile, macho. [➡GENDER IDENTITY AND SEXUALITY; 932] *Opposite:* feminine. 2 *n* **man**, guy (*informal*), fellow, bloke (*informal*), chap (*informal*), boy, fella (*informal*), dude (*US slang*). [➡MALE PERSON; 934] *Opposite:* female.

malediction (*formal*) *n* **curse**, spell, blight, charm, hex. [➡BAD LUCK AND UNLUCKY; 785] *Opposite:* blessing.

malefactor (*formal*) *n* **lawbreaker**, wrongdoer, criminal, outlaw, offender, miscreant (*literary*), villain. [➡CRIMINALS; 821]

maleficence *n* [➡MORALLY BAD; 776]

maleficent *adj* [➡MORALLY BAD; 776]

malevolence *n* **wickedness**, malice, ill will, evil, spite, nastiness, unkindness, meanness. [➡MORALLY BAD; 776] *Opposite:* benevolence.

malevolent *adj* **malicious**, spiteful, wicked, nasty, mean, unkind, vindictive, malign, malignant, evil. [➡MORALLY BAD; 776] *Opposite:* benevolent.

malfeasance *n* [➡MORALLY BAD; 776]

malformation *n* **deformity**, defect, fault, abnormality, distortion, disfigurement, aberration, crookedness, twistedness. [➡ORIENTATION AND ALIGNMENT; 1222]

malformed *adj* **misshapen**, deformed, abnormal, crooked, distorted, twisted. [➡ORIENTATION AND ALIGNMENT; 1222] *Opposite:* perfect.

malfunction 1 *v* **break down**, go wrong, fail, act up, play up, flop (*informal*), bomb (*informal*), crash. [➡FAIL OR CEASE TO FUNCTION; 471] 2 *n* **fault**, breakdown, failure, error, blip, glitch. [➡FAILURE; 77]

malice *n* **hatred**, spite, malevolence, meanness, nastiness, cruelty, wickedness, mischievousness, evil. [➡ANTAGONISM; 553] *Opposite:* kindness.

malicious *adj* **hateful**, spiteful, malevolent, mean, nasty, cruel, wicked, mischievous, evil. [➡SELFISH AND UNKIND; 506] *Opposite:* kind.

maliciousness *n* [➡SELFISH AND UNKIND; 506]

malign 1 *v* **slander**, defame, criticize, smear, libel, vilify, denigrate, disparage, slur, badmouth (*slang*), asperse (*formal*). [➡INSULTS, ABUSE, AND SWEARING; 659] *Opposite:* praise. 2 *adj* **harmful**, hurtful, damaging, destructive, negative, evil, injurious, aspersive (*formal*). [➡DANGEROUS; 237] *Opposite:* benign.

Compare and Contrast: ***malign, defame, slander, libel, vilify***

CORE MEANING: TO SAY OR WRITE SOMETHING DAMAGING ABOUT SOMEBODY

malign to criticize somebody in a spiteful and false or misleading way; ***defame*** to make an attack on somebody's good name or reputation with a view to damaging or destroying it; ***slander*** in legal terms, to make spoken false damaging accusations about somebody injurious to the person's reputation; ***libel*** in legal terms, to make false damaging accusations about somebody in writing, signs, or pictures; ***vilify*** to make viciously defamatory statements about somebody.

malignancy 1 *n* **distortion**, spite, warp, malevolence, menace, evil, malice, enmity, hostility, unkindness, vindictiveness. [➡SELFISH AND UNKIND; 506] *Opposite:* kindness. 2 *n* **melanoma**, tumour, disease, growth, cancer, sarcoma. [➡SICKNESS; 730]

malignant 1 *adj* **evil**, malevolent, hateful, spiteful, malicious, menacing, wicked, nasty, unkind, vindictive, cruel, mean. [➡SELFISH AND UNKIND; 506] *Opposite:* kind. 2 *adj* **cancerous**, spreading, harmful, fatal. [➡DEADLY; 928]

malignantly *adv* **malevolently**, menacingly, malignly, maliciously, unkindly, spitefully, vindictively, meanly, nastily, wickedly. [➡SELFISH AND UNKIND; 506] *Opposite:* kindly.

malignly *adv* **malevolently**, maliciously, spitefully, unkindly, harmfully, nastily, vindictively, malignantly. [➡SELFISH AND UNKIND; 506] *Opposite:* benignly.

malinger (*disapproving*) *v* **shirk**, skive (*informal*), bunk off (*informal*), take a sickie (*informal*), play hooky (*informal*), go AWOL, duck, sidestep, shun. [➡NOT DO AND REFUSE TO DO; 275]

malingerer (*disapproving*) *n* [➡LAZY OR UNSUCCESSFUL PEOPLE; 948]

mall (*US*) *n* **shopping centre**, shopping mall, shopping precinct, plaza (*US*). [➡RETAIL OUTLETS; 1082]

mallard *type of* **freshwater bird**. [➡FRESHWATER BIRD; 1000]

malleability 1 *n* **flexibility**, pliability, softness, plasticity, ductility, bendiness, suppleness. [➡MALLEABLE AND ELASTIC; 1211] *Opposite:* rigidity. 2 *n* **impressionability**, pliability, manipulability, compliance, acquiescence. [➡THE WILL AND WILLINGNESS; 564] *Opposite:* inflexibility.

malleable 1 *adj* **soft**, supple, flexible, bendy, pliable, ductile, plastic. [➡MALLEABLE AND ELASTIC; 1211] *Opposite:* rigid. 2 *adj* **impressionable**, compliant, acquiescent, manipulable, biddable, persuadable, pliable. [➡NEGATIVE INTELLECTUAL CHARACTERISTICS; 526]

See Compare and Contrast at **pliable**.

mallet *type of* **carpentry tool**. [➡HAND TOOLS; 1118]

malnourished *adj* **underfed**, undernourished, underweight, starving, famished, half-starved, hungry, emaciated, wasted, thin. [➡EAT AND NOT EAT; 711] *Opposite:* well-fed.

malnourishment *n* [➡DISORDERS OF THE DIGESTIVE SYSTEM; 714]

malnutrition *n* **undernourishment**, malnourishment, underfeeding, starvation, famine, hunger. [➡DISORDERS OF THE DIGESTIVE SYSTEM; 714]

malodorous *adj* **stinking**, foul-smelling, smelly, foul, fetid, putrid, rank (*literary*), reeking, humming (*informal*), pongy (*informal*), whiffy (*informal*), ripe (*informal*), offensive. [➡SMELL AND SMELLING; 706] *Opposite:* sweet-smelling.

malpractice *n* **misconduct**, negligence, abuse, dereliction, mismanagement, misuse. [➡MISUSE AND ABUSE; 472]

maltreat *v* **mistreat**, hurt, injure, harm, damage, abuse, neglect, misuse. [➡WOUND A PERSON OR ANIMAL; 384]

See Compare and Contrast at **misuse**.

maltreatment *n* **mistreatment**, abuse, ill-treatment, harm, damage, cruelty, injury, hurt, neglect. [➡UNKIND ACTION OR BEHAVIOUR; 297]

mam (*regional informal*) *n* [➡OLDER GENERATION RELATIVES; 959]

mama (*informal*) *n* **mother**, mummy (*informal*), mum (*informal*), mam (*regional informal*), mammy (*informal*), mamma (*informal*), mommy (*US informal*), mom (*US informal*), momma (*US informal*). [➡OLDER GENERATION RELATIVES; 959]

mamba *type of* **poisonous snake**. [➡SNAKE; 995]

mambo 1 *type of* **popular music**. [➡MUSIC, SONGS, AND SINGING; 907] 2 *type of* **dance**. [➡DANCE; 903]

mamma (*informal*) *see* **mama**.

mammal *n* **animal**, marsupial, placental mammal, marine mammal. [➡LIVING THINGS AND LIVING; 976]

mammal

◆ *types of large mammal*
alpaca, bactrian camel, bear, bison, boar, buffalo, camel, dromedary, elephant, giraffe, hippopotamus, llama, panda, polar bear, rhinoceros, wart hog

◆ *types of small mammal*
anteater, armadillo, badger, ferret, hare, hedgehog, hyrax, marten, mink, mongoose, otter, pine marten, polecat, porcupine, rabbit, raccoon, skunk, sloth, stoat, weasel, wolverine

◆ *types of marine mammal*
dolphin, dugong, grampus, manatee, porpoise, seal, sea lion, walrus, whale

mammon (*disapproving*) *n* **riches**, wealth, money, lucre (*dated or humorous*), greed, ambition, loot. [➡FINANCIAL ASSETS; 463]

mammoth *adj* **enormous**, huge, massive, immense, epic, gargantuan, colossal, vast, titanic. [➡LARGE; 1192] *Opposite:* tiny.

mammy (*informal*) *n* [➡OLDER GENERATION RELATIVES; 959]

man 1 *n* **gentleman**, bloke (*informal*), guy (*informal*), chap (*informal*), male, gent (*dated informal*), fellow, fella (*informal*), dude (*US slang*). [➡MALE PERSON; 934] *Opposite:* woman. 2 *v* **operate**, staff, crew, work, manage, handle. [➡USE TOOLS AND MACHINERY; 469]

manacle 1 *n* **handcuff**, chain, shackle, bond, fetter, irons. [➡FASTENERS, LINKS, AND NETWORKS; 1246] 2 *v* **bind**, handcuff, chain up, shackle, fetter, chain, enchain (*formal or literary*), pinion. [➡CAPTIVITY AND LOSS OF FREEDOM; 249] *Opposite:* release.

manage 1 *v* **achieve**, accomplish, succeed, be able to, bring about. [➡SUCCEED AND WIN; 79] *Opposite:* fail. 2 *v* **cope**, fare, get on, do, get by, get along, make do, survive, muddle through. [➡CONTINUE TO EXIST; 17] *Opposite:* give up. 3 *v* **run**, direct, administer, supervise, be in charge, oversee, operate, govern. [➡BE IN CHARGE; 271] 4 *v* **handle**, deal with, control, cope with. [➡CARRY OUT AN ACTION; 270] 5 *v* **control**, discipline, master, dominate, boss. [➡AVOID, PREVENT, LIMIT, AND CONTROL; 278]

manageable *adj* **controllable**, handy, untroublesome, practicable, adaptable, wieldy. [➡USEFULNESS; 200] *Opposite:* unwieldy.

management 1 *n* **organization**, running, administration, supervision, managing, controlling. [➡BUSINESS ACTIVITIES AND PHENOMENA; 795] 2 *n* **directors**, managers, executives, employers, board, bosses. [➡BOSSES AND MANAGEMENT; 965]

manager *n* **boss**, director, executive, administrator, supervisor, leader, chief, superior. [➡BUSINESS PEOPLE; 794]

managerial *adj* **executive**, management, supervisory, directorial, decision-making, organizational, administrative, professional, white-collar. [➡TYPES OF WORK; 835]

manatee *type of* **marine mammal**. [➡MARINE MAMMAL; 987]

mandarin 1 *n* **bureaucrat**, official, public servant, civil servant, manager. [➡POLITICAL OFFICES AND POLITICIANS; 808] 2 *type of* **citrus**. [➡FRUIT AND VEGETABLES; 1175]

mandate 1 *n* **order**, command, directive, decree, dictate, instruction, fiat, obligation. [➡REQUEST AND DEMAND; 664] 2 *n* **permission**, authorization, consent, go-ahead (*informal*), authority, support. [➡PERMIT AND ALLOW; 670] 3 *n* **term of office**, reign, tenure, stay. [➡POLITICAL OFFICES AND POLITICIANS; 808] 4 *v* **instruct**, authorize, direct (*formal*), delegate, assign, require, command. [➡PERMIT AND ALLOW; 670]

mandatory *adj* **obligatory**, compulsory, required, fixed, binding, needed. [➡NECESSARY AND ESSENTIAL; 197] *Opposite:* optional.

mandible 1 *n* **jaw**, jawbone, maxilla, mouth, mouthpiece, bill, beak. [➡HEAD; 693] 2 *type of* **parts of insects**. [➡PARTS OF AN INSECT; 1019]

mandolin *type of* **stringed instrument**. [➡MUSICAL INSTRUMENTS; 910]

mandrill *type of* **primate**. [➡PRIMATE; 988]

mane 1 *n* (*literary or informal*) **locks** (*literary*), tresses, curls, shock, head of hair. [➡HAIR; 485] 2 *part of* **horse**. [➡HORSE; 985]

man-eating *adj* **carnivorous**, ferocious, fierce, wild, aggressive. [➡DANGEROUS; 237]

manful *adj* **brave**, strong, resolute, bold, determined, intrepid (*literary or humorous*), courageous. [➡COURAGE; 499] *Opposite:* cowardly.

mangel-wurzel *type of* **root vegetable**. [➡FRUIT AND VEGETABLES; 1175]

manger *n* **trough**, feeding-box, container, crib. [➡CONTAINERS, RECEPTACLES, AND PACKAGING; 1244]

mangetout *type of* **pulse**. [➡BEANS AND PULSES; 1188]

mangle *v* **crush**, mash, smash, contort, twist, batter, maul, injure, mar, disfigure. [➡WOUND A PERSON OR ANIMAL; 384]

mangled *adj* [➡IN BAD REPAIR; 1233]

mango *type of* **fruit**. [➡FRUIT AND VEGETABLES; 1175]

mangrove *type of* **evergreen tree**. [➡EVERGREEN AND CONIFEROUS TREES; 1029]

mangy (*informal*) *adj* **dirty**, disgusting, filthy, foul, messy, mucky (*informal*), grungy (*informal*), gunky (*informal*), rank (*literary*), unpleasant, sticky, gungy (*informal*), shabby, scuzzy (*US slang*). [➡IN BAD REPAIR; 1233] *Opposite:* pristine.

manhandle *v* **push**, shove, bundle (*informal*), jostle, hustle, move. [➡PHYSICAL ATTACK AND PUNISHMENT; 416]

manhood 1 *n* **maturity**, independence, adulthood. [➡ADULTHOOD; 918] 2 *n* **strength**, courage, determination, virility, boldness, manliness. [➡COURAGE; 499] 3 *n* **men**, menfolk, males. [➡MALE PERSON; 934]

mania *n* **obsession**, desire, love, craze, thing (*informal*), passion, fad, fashion, enthusiasm, hysteria, fever. [➡FADS, FETISHES, AND IDOLATRY; 556]

maniac *n* **enthusiast**, fanatic, nut (*informal*), zealot, fiend, freak (*informal*). [➡DEVOTEES AND ADDICTED PEOPLE; 557]

manic (*informal*) *adj* **overexcited**, hyper (*informal*), agitated, hectic, frenzied, busy, hysterical, feverish, frantic, excited. [➡PLEASURE, EXCITEMENT, AND ELATION; 535] *Opposite:* calm.

manicure *v* **trim**, file, shape, cut, clip, pare, crop. [➡IMPROVE APPEARANCE; 380]

manifest 1 *adj* **apparent**, unmistakable, clear, obvious, distinct, noticeable. [➡PERCEPTIBLE; 25] *Opposite:* unclear. 2 *v* **make plain**, establish, demonstrate, display, reveal, show, exhibit, express. [➡CAUSE TO APPEAR; 5]

manifestation *n* **sign**, indication, index, indicator, appearance, display, exhibition, expression, demonstration. [➡REPRESENTATIONS AND GENERAL EXAMPLES; 65]

manifestly *adv* **apparently**, unmistakably, clearly, obviously, distinctly, noticeably. [➡CERTAIN; 175]

manifesto *n* **declaration**, statement, policy, guidelines, proposal, philosophy, plan, platform, programme, beliefs, strategy. [➡OFFICIAL DOCUMENTS; 587]

manifold *adj* **various**, diverse, many, multiple, assorted, multifarious. [➡MANY, MUCH, LARGE AMOUNT; 117] *Opposite:* uniform.

manipulate 1 *v* **operate**, work, use, deploy, employ, handle. [➡USE; 468] 2 *v* **influence**, control, bias, direct, sway, affect, impress. [➡CAUSE OR COMPEL TO ACT; 272] 3 *v* **manoeuvre**, direct, control, stage-manage, engineer. [➡CARRY OUT AN ACTION; 270]

manipulation 1 *n* **operation**, handling, management, use, guidance, influence, employment. [➡USE; 468] 2 *n* **running**, control, manoeuvring, exploitation, persuasion, wheeler-dealing (*informal*), scheming, capitalizing on. [➡CARRY OUT AN ACTION; 270] 3 *n* **falsification**, forgery, alteration, tweaking (*informal*), misuse, tampering with, misapplication. [➡MISUSE AND ABUSE; 472] 4 *n* **osteopathy**, massage, movement, flexing, rub, kneading, therapy, physiotherapy, treatment. [➡REMEDIES, TREATMENTS, AND OPERATIONS; 732]

manipulative *adj* **scheming**, calculating, controlling, devious, unscrupulous, cunning, Machiavellian, serpentine (*literary*). [➡DECEITFUL; 514]

manipulator *n* **Machiavelli**, wheeler-dealer (*informal*), spin doctor (*slang*), exploiter, schemer, Svengali. [➡VILLAINS AND THUGS; 947]

mankind 1 *n* **human race**, humankind, humanity, human beings, people. [➡PERSON; 931] 2 *n* (*dated*) **men**, menfolk, manhood, males. [➡MALE PERSON; 934]

manliness *n* **masculinity**, machismo, manhood. [➡GENDER IDENTITY AND SEXUALITY; 932]

manly *adj* **virile**, mannish, male, masculine, macho. [➡GENDER IDENTITY AND SEXUALITY; 932] *Opposite:* womanly.

man-made *adj* **artificial**, synthetic, manufactured, substitute, imitation, faux. [➡FALSE AND UNREAL; 174] *Opposite:* natural.

manna 1 *n* **food**, sustenance, victuals, provender (*literary or humorous*), fodder, provisions, vittles (*archaic*). [➡FOOD; 1166] 2 *n* **godsend**, blessing, boon, gift, help, benefit, lifesaver (*informal*). [➡SOURCE OF HAPPINESS, PLEASURE, OR IMPROVEMENT; 210]

mannequin *n* **dummy**, model, figure, tailor's dummy, dressmaker's dummy, figurine, manikin. [➡REPRESENTATIONS AND GENERAL EXAMPLES; 65]

manner 1 *n* **way**, means, method, style, custom, routine, mode, fashion, modus. [➡WAYS OF DOING THINGS; 295] 2 *n* **type**, kind, sort. [➡TEMPERAMENT AND BEHAVIOUR; 493]

mannered *adj* **affected**, artificial, put-on, false, simpering, genteel. [➡AFFECTATION, SELF-SATISFACTION, AND SNOBBISHNESS; 508] *Opposite:* natural.

mannerism 1 *n* **gesture**, trait, characteristic, gesticulation, habit, idiosyncrasy, quirk, trick. [➡GESTURES AND GESTICULATION; 654] 2 *n* **affectation**, show, act, display, pretence, parade. [➡DECEPTION AND LIES; 661]

Mannerism *type of* **pre-20th-century art movement**. [➡ARTISTIC MOVEMENTS AND STYLES; 899]

mannerly *adj* **well-behaved**, polite, refined, well-mannered, respectful, decent, gallant, polished, gracious, well-bred, decorous, courteous, respectable, civilized, well brought-up, courtly. [➡GOOD MANNERS AND SOCIAL SKILLS; 521] *Opposite:* rude.

manners 1 *n* **etiquette**, protocol, good manners. [➡GOOD MANNERS AND SOCIAL SKILLS; 521] 2 *n* **behaviour**, conduct, comportment (*formal*), demeanour, deportment (*formal*), manner. [➡TEMPERAMENT AND BEHAVIOUR; 493]

manoeuvre 1 *n* **move**, movement, operation, exercise. [➡ACTIONS OR UNDERTAKINGS; 260] 2 *n* **ploy**, trick, plot, tactic, plan, move, scheme, stratagem, gambit, ruse, artifice (*formal*), feint. [➡WAYS OF DOING THINGS; 295] 3 *v* **manipulate**, plot, contrive, plan, scheme, finesse, play, machinate. [➡FALSIFY AND CHEAT; 177]

man-of-war *type of* **historical vessel**. [➡SHIPS AND BOATS; 1149]

manor *type of* **house**. [➡RESIDENTIAL BUILDINGS; 1077]

manor house *type of* **house**. [➡RESIDENTIAL BUILDINGS; 1077]

manqué *adj* **failed**, wannabe (*informal disapproving*), near, would-be, ersatz (*disapproving*), unfulfilled, unsuccessful. [➡UNSUCCESSFUL AND UNPROMISING; 76] *Opposite:* successful.

mansard *n* **attic**, loft, roof, eaves, rafters. [➡ROOFS, ROOF PARTS, AND CEILINGS; 1102]

manse *n* **vicarage**, rectory, parsonage, residence, church house. [➡RELIGIOUS BUILDINGS; 1084]

manservant *type of* **servant**. [➡DOMESTIC AND KITCHEN WORKERS; 850]

mansion *type of* **house**. [➡RESIDENTIAL BUILDINGS; 1077]

manslaughter *n* **murder**, homicide, killing, assassination, slaying, slaughter, unlawful death, massacre. [➡CAUSES OF DEATH; 921]

manta (*US*) *type of* **flatfish**. [➡SEA FISH; 1009]

manta ray *type of* **flatfish**. [➡SEA FISH; 1009]

mantel *type of* **general fittings**. [➡FITTINGS; 859]

mantelpiece *type of* **general fittings**. [➡FITTINGS; 859]

mantilla *type of* **headgear.** [➡HABERDASHERY, MILLINERY, AND LINGERIE; 867]

mantle 1 *n* (*literary*) **layer**, blanket, covering, shroud, veil, cloak. [➡COVERS AND COATINGS; 1245] 2 *n* (*formal*) **responsibility**, function, role, position, duty, onus. [➡RESPONSIBILITY; 171]

mantra *n* **chant**, intonation, repetition, refrain, sacred word, hymn, song, word. [➡RELIGIONS AND RELIGIOUS PRACTICES; 778]

manual 1 *adj* **physical**, labour-intensive, blue-collar. [➡TYPES OF WORK; 835] *Opposite:* mental. 2 *n* **instruction booklet**, guide, handbook, guidebook, instruction manual, booklet, instructions. [➡MANUALS AND INSTRUCTIONS; 590]

manual labour *n* [➡TYPES OF WORK; 835]

manual labourer *n* [➡WORKER; 836]

manual worker *n* [➡WORKER; 836]

manufacture 1 *v* **build**, assemble, construct, produce, create, turn out, make, form, fashion, fabricate. [➡MANUFACTURE; 350] 2 *n* **production**, making, creation, building, assembly, manufacturing, construction, fabrication. [➡CREATION; 347]

See Compare and Contrast at **make.**

manufactured *adj* **factory-made**, mass-produced, industrial, man-made, synthetic, artificial. [➡NOT IN A NATURAL STATE; 1214]

manufacturer *n* **builder**, producer, constructor, creator, industrialist, maker. [➡DESIGNERS, CREATORS, AND INSTIGATORS; 348]

manufacturing *n* **production**, manufacture, making, assembly, construction, building, fabrication, creation. [➡CREATION; 347]

manumission (*formal*) *n* [➡FREEDOM AND LIBERTY; 209]

manure *n* **dung**, compost, guano, muck, fertilizer, droppings. [➡EXCRETION AND EXCRETA; 723]

manuscript *n* **document**, copy, text, script. [➡BOOKS AND BOOKLETS; 591]

Manx cat *type of* **cat.** [➡FELINE; 983]

many *adj* **a lot of**, lots of, numerous, loads of (*informal*), countless, several, various, scores of, sundry, voluminous. [➡MANY, MUCH, LARGE AMOUNT; 117] *Opposite:* few.

many-coloured *adj* [➡DESCRIBING COLOURS; 1225]

many-hued *adj* [➡DESCRIBING COLOURS; 1225]

many-sided *adj* **multifaceted**, complex, complicated, deep, multidimensional. [➡POSITIVELY COMPLEX OR COMPLICATED; 218] *Opposite:* one-dimensional.

Maoism *n* [➡PHILOSOPHIES AND BELIEFS; 781]

Maoist *adj* [➡PHILOSOPHIES AND BELIEFS; 781]

map 1 *n* **plan**, plot, chart, atlas, record, drawing, diagram. [➡DRAWINGS, CHARTS, AND TABLES; 595] 2 *v* **chart**, plot, plan, record, draw, represent. [➡CREATE IMAGES; 357]

maple *type of* **deciduous tree.** [➡DECIDUOUS TREES; 1028]

maple syrup *n* [➡SUGAR AND PRESERVES; 1183]

map out *v* **work out**, plan, devise, outline, arrange, design. [➡CREATION; 347]

map reading *n* **route-planning**, routing, direction-finding, orienteering, triangulation. [➡NAVIGATION; 1140]

maquiladora (*US*) *type of* **factory.** [➡INDUSTRIAL BUILDINGS; 1086]

maquillage *n* [➡MAKEUP AND BEAUTY PRODUCTS; 491]

mar *v* **deface**, ruin, mutilate, damage, disfigure, stain, injure, blemish, harm, impair. [➡WORSEN SOMETHING; 381] *Opposite:* repair.

marabou *type of* **scavenger.** [➡BIRD; 997]

maraca *type of* **percussion instrument.** [➡MUSICAL INSTRUMENTS; 910]

marathon 1 *adj* **lengthy**, epic, long-drawn-out, gruelling, difficult, long-winded. [➡HAPPENING SLOWLY; 106] 2 *type of* **track and field.** [➡HOBBIES, GAMES, AND SPORTS; 875]

maraud *v* **raid**, plunder, ransack, loot, pillage. [➡STEAL AND ROB; 427]

marauder *n* **raider**, robber, bandit, pillager, plunderer, brigand (*literary*). [➡VILLAINS AND THUGS; 947]

marble 1 *n* **toy**, glass ball, agate, cat's eye. [➡TOYS; 880] 2 *type of* **stone.** [➡STONES, ROCKS, AND BOULDERS; 1057]

marbled *adj* **veined**, streaked, mottled, lined, shot through, patterned, moiré. [➡DESCRIBING PATTERNS; 1226]

marbles (*slang*) *n* **wits**, mind, reason, sense, commonsense. [➡PSYCHOLOGY AND THE MIND; 770]

march 1 *v* **parade**, file, step, troop, process, walk. [➡PROCEED AND GO; 306] 2 *v* **stride**, stomp, storm, sweep, flounce, stalk. [➡PROCEED AND GO; 306] 3 *n* **hike**, trek, walk, tramp, trudge. [➡TRAVEL: JOURNEYS AND TRIPS; 319] 4 *n* **protest**, picket, mass lobby, rally, demonstration, campaign, demo (*informal*). [➡AGGRESSIVE EVENT; 39]

marcher *n* **demonstrator**, protester, walker, campaigner, supporter, activist, picketer. [➡UNCOOPERATIVE OR REBELLIOUS PERSON; 567]

marchioness *type of* **aristocrat.** [➡RULERS AND ARISTOCRACY; 823]

marchpast *n* **parade**, review, muster, procession. [➡PERFORMANCES AND SHOWS; 42]

mare *type of* **female animal.** [➡MALE OR FEMALE ANIMAL; 978]

mare's-tail *type of* **cloud.** [➡CLOUDY AND RAINY WEATHER; 1052]

margarine *type of* **cooking fat and oil.** [➡FATS AND OILS; 1172]

margin 1 *n* **boundary**, border, brim, sideline, edge, verge, fringe, side, perimeter. [➡EXTREMITIES OF PHYSICAL OBJECTS; 1249] 2 *n* **surplus**, room, leeway, allowance, scope, space, play, latitude, slack. [➡DEGREE AND EXTENT; 110]

marginal 1 *adj* **negligible**, minimal, low, minor, slight, small, tiny. [➡FEW, LITTLE, SMALL AMOUNT; 119] *Opposite:* major. 2 *adj*

irrelevant, insignificant, unimportant, borderline, fringe. [➡ UNIMPORTANT AND UNNECESSARY; 239] *Opposite:* central.

marginalization *n* **relegation**, sidelining, demotion, downgrading, disregarding, freezing out, ostracism, banishment. [➡ SEPARATE AND DIVIDE; 402]

marginalize *v* **relegate**, sideline, demote, downgrade, disregard, freeze out, banish, ostracize. [➡ SEPARATE AND DIVIDE; 402] *Opposite:* include.

marginally *adv* **slightly**, a bit (*informal*), a little, a tad (*informal*), a touch. [➡ TO A CERTAIN EXTENT; 134]

marigold *type of* **annual flower.** [➡ FLOWERS; 1032]

marimba *type of* **percussion instrument.** [➡ MUSICAL INSTRUMENTS; 910]

marina *n* **harbour**, port, dock, quay. [➡ WATERWAYS AND SEAWAYS; 1107]

marinade 1 *n* **dressing**, sauce, flavouring, juices, infusion. [➡ SEASONINGS AND SAUCES; 1173] 2 *see* **marinate.**

marinate *v* **steep**, soak, infuse, immerse, douse. [➡ COOKING AND FOOD PREPARATION; 354]

marinated *adj* [➡ STATE OF PREPARED FOOD; 1170]

marine 1 *adj* **saltwater**, seawater, sea, aquatic. [➡ THE SEAS, OCEANS, AND SHORES; 1041] 2 *adj* **nautical**, oceangoing, naval, seafaring, seagoing, oceanic, maritime. [➡ THE SEAS, OCEANS, AND SHORES; 1041]

mariner *n* **sailor**, seafarer, seadog, tar (*archaic informal*), old salt. [➡ TRAVEL: TRAVELLERS AND WALKERS; 320]

marital *adj* **conjugal**, nuptial, wedded, spousal, matrimonial, connubial (*formal*). [➡ MARRIED STATE; 961]

maritime 1 *adj* **nautical**, naval, oceanic, seafaring, seagoing, marine. [➡ THE SEAS, OCEANS, AND SHORES; 1041] 2 *adj* **seaside**, coastal, shoreline, littoral. [➡ THE SEAS, OCEANS, AND SHORES; 1041]

marjoram *type of* **herb.** [➡ HERBS AND SPICES; 1174]

mark 1 *n* **spot**, scratch, dent, stain, smear, blot, smudge, streak. [➡ FAULTS, FLAWS, AND WEAKNESSES; 252] 2 *n* **sign**, indication, feature, characteristic, symbol, indicator, index, symptom, evidence. [➡ INDICATIONS, SIGNS, AND WARNINGS; 68] 3 *n* **score**, point, assessment, evaluation, grade. [➡ SCORES AND EVALUATIONS; 599] 4 *v* **stain**, scratch, smudge, smear, blot, taint, besmear, soil, sully (*literary*), streak, tarnish, mar. [➡ DIRTY AND CONTAMINATE; 405] 5 *v* **indicate**, denote, show, demonstrate, evidence, exhibit. [➡ MEAN SOMETHING; 61] 6 *v* **celebrate**, commemorate, keep, observe, solemnize. [➡ PRAISE AND ENCOURAGE; 648] 7 *v* **correct**, assess, evaluate, score, grade (*US*). [➡ ASSESS QUALITY; 756]

markdown *n* **discount**, price cutting, reduction, concession. [➡ MONEY, PAYMENTS, AND CHARGES; 800] *Opposite:* mark-up.

marked *adj* **clear**, apparent, evident, noticeable, conspicuous, pronounced, blatant, obvious, arresting, prominent, striking, significant, decided, distinct. [➡ PERCEPTIBLE; 25]

marker 1 *n* **indicator**, sign, indication, symbol, pointer. [➡ INDICATIONS, SIGNS, AND WARNINGS; 68] 2 *type of* **pen.** [➡ WRITING AND DRAWING IMPLEMENTS, AND MEDIA; 602]

market 1 *n* **marketplace**, souk, bazaar, shop, arcade, fair, flea market. [➡ URBAN OUTDOOR SPACES; 1071] 2 *v* **sell**, promote, advertise, peddle, trade, merchandise, package. [➡ SELL; 442]

marketable *adj* **in demand**, sought-after, wanted, vendible, merchantable, saleable, merchandisable. [➡ POPULAR AND WANTED; 221]

market analyst *n* [➡ PEOPLE INVOLVED IN FINANCE; 804]

market garden *n* [➡ AGRICULTURE AND FARMING; 1074]

marketing *n* **advertising**, selling, presentation, publicizing, promotion. [➡ BUSINESS ACTIVITIES AND PHENOMENA; 795]

marketplace 1 *n* **bazaar**, market, souk, flea market, open market, covered market, square, fair. [➡ URBAN OUTDOOR SPACES; 1071] 2 *n* **trading floor**, sphere, arena, market. [➡ BUSINESS; 792]

market square *n* [➡ URBAN OUTDOOR SPACES; 1071]

marking *n* **pattern**, coloration, design. [➡ PATTERNS; 1224]

mark out 1 *v* **outline**, demarcate, sketch, delimit (*formal*), delineate, map out, establish, define, draw, set down, bound, determine. [➡ NAME AND DESCRIBE; 666] 2 *v* **distinguish**, differentiate, single out, identify, characterize, highlight. [➡ NAME AND DESCRIBE; 666]

mark-up *n* **price increase**, rise, hike, profit, profit margin. [➡ MONEY, PAYMENTS, AND CHARGES; 800] *Opposite:* markdown.

marlin *type of* **tropical sea fish.** [➡ SEA FISH; 1009]

marmalade *type of* **preserve.** [➡ SUGAR AND PRESERVES; 1183]

marmoset *type of* **primate.** [➡ PRIMATE; 988]

marmot *type of* **rodent.** [➡ RODENT; 989]

maroon 1 *v* **abandon**, leave high and dry, leave, cast aside, cast ashore, isolate, forsake, strand, desert. [➡ REFUSING OR REJECTING RELATIONS; 975] 2 *type of* **red.** [➡ COLOURS; 1223]

marooned *adj* **stranded**, deserted, abandoned, isolated, stuck, forsaken, left. [➡ SOLITARINESS; 941]

marque *n* **make**, label, trademark, brand. [➡ NAME AND DESCRIBE; 666]

marquee *n* **tent**, pavilion, canvas, shelter, erection (*formal*). [➡ BUILDINGS FOR PUBLIC ENTERTAINMENT; 1083]

marquess *type of* **aristocrat.** [➡ RULERS AND ARISTOCRACY; 823]

marquetry 1 *n* **inlay**, pattern, design, veneer. [➡ ORNAMENTS AND DECORATIONS; 1247] 2 *type of* **woodwork.** [➡ CRAFTS AND CARVING; 356]

marram *type of* **grass.** [➡ GRASS; 1031]

marred *adj* **blemished**, flawed, stained, disfigured, tarnished, tainted, soiled, smudged, scratched, spoiled. [➡ IN BAD REPAIR; 1233] *Opposite:* unblemished.

marriage 1 *n* **wedding**, matrimony, nuptials (*literary*), wedding ceremony, marriage ceremony. [➡ CEREMONIES AND ANNIVERSARIES; 38] *Opposite:* divorce. 2 *n* **union**, fusion, combination, coming together, alliance, coalition, merger. [➡ COLLECTIONS AND MIXTURES OF THINGS; 1243] *Opposite:* separation.

marriageability *n* **eligibility**, suitability, availability, fitness. [➡ MARITAL STATUS; 890]

marriageable *adj* **eligible**, suitable, available, adult, grown-up. [➡ MARITAL STATUS; 890]

married *adj* **wedded**, matrimonial, nuptial, conjugal, connubial (*formal*), marital. [➡ MARRIED STATE; 961]

marrow 1 *n* (*literary*) **core**, heart, soul, spirit, essence, substance, centre, nucleus. [➡ MOST IMPORTANT THING; 198] 2 *type of* **vegetable**. [➡ FRUIT AND VEGETABLES; 1175]

marrow squash (*US*) *type of* **vegetable**. [➡ FRUIT AND VEGETABLES; 1175]

marry *v* **get married**, tie the knot (*informal*), walk down the aisle, wed (*formal or literary*), join in matrimony, espouse (*archaic*). [➡ ESTABLISHING RELATIONSHIPS WITH OTHERS; 974]

Mars *type of* **planet**. [➡ CELESTIAL BODIES; 1060]

marsh *n* **bog**, swamp, quagmire, swampland, marshland, fen, fenland, peat bog, wetland, morass, everglade (*US*). [➡ WETLANDS; 1043]

marshal 1 *n* **officer**, deputy, law officer, sheriff (*US*). [➡ THE POLICE, ARREST, AND PRE-TRIAL PROCEEDINGS; 818] 2 *v* **assemble**, position, gather together, collect, shepherd, line up, group, organize. [➡ COMBINE AND MIX; 401] *Opposite:* disperse. 3 *v* **arrange**, order, sort out, put in order, organize, rationalize, clarify. [➡ ARRANGE AND CREATE ORDER; 358] *Opposite:* muddle.

marsh gas *type of* **gas**. [➡ GASES; 1274]

marshland *n* **bog**, swamp, swampland, marsh, wetland, fen, fenland, peat bog, quagmire, everglade (*US*). [➡ WETLANDS; 1043]

marshmallow *type of* **confectionery**. [➡ CONFECTIONERY; 1181]

marshy *adj* **boggy**, swampy, soggy, muddy, peaty, squelchy. [➡ WET; 1239] *Opposite:* dry.

marsupial

◆ *types of marsupial*
bandicoot, bettong, bilby, kangaroo, koala, opossum, phalanger, potoroo, Tasmanian devil, thylacine, wallaby, wombat

mart *n* **auction**, sale, market, saleroom, hypermarket, store, trading place. [➡ RETAIL OUTLETS; 1082]

marten *type of* **small mammal**. [➡ SMALL MAMMAL; 990]

martial 1 *adj* **military**, soldierly, warlike, battle-hardened, fighting, paramilitary. [➡ MILITARY; 829] *Opposite:* civilian. 2 *adj* **warlike**, fierce, aggressive, belligerent, hostile, antagonistic, bellicose. [➡ AGGRESSIVE AND BELLIGERENT; 519] *Opposite:* peaceful.

martial law *n* **stratocracy** (*formal*), state of emergency, militarism, junta, dictatorship, emergency powers, military rule. [➡ STYLES AND SYSTEMS OF GOVERNMENT; 806]

Martian *n* **alien**, extraterrestrial, ET, spaceman, invader, space invader, little green man (*humorous*). [➡ SCIENCE FICTION; 1063] *Opposite:* terrestrial.

martin *type of* **common bird**. [➡ BIRD; 997]

martinet *n* **disciplinarian**, stickler, despot, hardliner, perfectionist, tyrant. [➡ GRUMPY AND NEGATIVE PEOPLE; 953] *Opposite:* softy (*informal*).

martyr 1 *n* **sacrifice**, sacrificial victim, victim, scapegoat, ransom (*literary*). [➡ DEAD PERSON; 926] 2 *n* **idealist**, witness, believer, supporter. [➡ RELIGIOUS PEOPLE; 779] 3 *n* **sufferer**, invalid, patient. [➡ UNFIT AND WEAK; 740]

martyrdom 1 *n* **death**, killing, slaughter, torture, ritual murder, execution. [➡ CAUSES OF DEATH; 921] 2 *n* **suffering**, misery, pain, sacrifice, torment, agony, passion, persecution, endurance. [➡ SADNESS, DISTRESS, AND DESPAIR; 540]

marvel 1 *n* **wonder**, miracle, spectacle, sight, curiosity, phenomenon, sensation. [➡ AMAZING THING; 212] 2 *n* **genius**, prodigy, whiz (*informal*), ace (*informal*), phenomenon, wunderkind. [➡ TALENTED OR INTELLIGENT PERSON; 529] 3 *v* **be amazed**, be surprised, be impressed, admire, wonder, be awed, gaze in awe. [➡ PRAISE AND ENCOURAGE; 648] *Opposite:* deride.

marvellous 1 *adj* **amazing**, impressive, remarkable, magnificent, superb, stunning, outstanding, excellent, spectacular, awe-inspiring, splendid. [➡ EXTRAORDINARY: AMAZING; 205] *Opposite:* ordinary. 2 *adj* **great**, brilliant, wonderful, fantastic, fabulous, cool (*slang*). [➡ EXTRAORDINARY: AMAZING; 205]

marvellously *adv* **amazingly**, impressively, extraordinarily, remarkably, spectacularly, stunningly, brilliantly, wonderfully, fantastically, fabulously, splendidly, magnificently, superbly, outstandingly, awe-inspiringly. [➡ EXTRAORDINARY: AMAZING; 205] *Opposite:* ordinarily.

Marxism *n* [➡ PHILOSOPHIES AND BELIEFS; 781]

Marxist *adj* [➡ PHILOSOPHIES AND BELIEFS; 781]

marzipan *type of* **confectionery**. [➡ CONFECTIONERY; 1181]

mascara *n* [➡ MAKEUP AND BEAUTY PRODUCTS; 491]

mascarpone *type of* **soft cheese**. [➡ DAIRY PRODUCTS AND CHEESES; 1182]

mascot *n* **symbol**, charm, talisman, amulet, periapt. [➡ LUCKY CHARMS; 786] *Opposite:* hex.

masculine *adj* **male**, manly, mannish, macho, virile, boyish. [➡ GENDER IDENTITY AND SEXUALITY; 932] *Opposite:* feminine.

masculinity *n* **maleness**, manliness, mannishness, manhood, boyhood, boyishness, virility, machismo. [➡ GENDER IDENTITY AND SEXUALITY; 932] *Opposite:* femininity.

mash 1 *n* **purée**, pulp, mush. [➡ PREPARED DISHES; 1169] 2 *type of* **processed potato**. [➡ FRUIT AND VEGETABLES; 1175] 3 *v* **pulp**, squash, pound, crush, smash, purée, mush, pulverize. [➡ CHANGE OF SHAPE; 386]

mask 1 *n* **cover**, disguise, guise, façade, front, veneer, concealment. [➡ REPRESENTATIONS AND GENERAL EXAMPLES; 65] 2 *v* **hide**, conceal, disguise, cover, camouflage, screen, veil, cloak. [➡ CAUSE TO DISAPPEAR; 6] *Opposite:* expose.

masked 1 *adj* **disguised**, incognito, camouflaged, concealed, screened, veiled, covered. [➡ IMPERCEPTIBLE; 26] *Opposite:* exposed. 2 *adj* **undetectable**, imperceptible, latent, hidden, invisible, concealed, disguised, covered up. [➡IMPERCEPTIBLE; 26] *Opposite:* detectable.

masonry *n* **stonework**, brickwork, building materials, granite, sandstone, stone, brick, bricks and mortar. [➡BUILDING MATERIALS; 1076]

masque 1 *n* **performance**, allegory, theatricals, play, opera, entertainment, show. [➡PERFORMANCES AND SHOWS; 42] 2 *n* **dance**, ball, masked ball. [➡PARTIES, DANCES, AND CELEBRATIONS; 37]

masquerade 1 *n* **pretence**, deception, cover-up, subterfuge, ruse, charade, trick, concealment. [➡DECEPTION AND LIES; 661] 2 *v* **pretend to be**, impersonate, pose, disguise yourself, make-believe, make as if, imitate. [➡PRETEND AND MIMIC; 60]

mass 1 *n* **form**, figure, frame, physique, build, bulk. [➡SHAPE; 1215] 2 *n* **quantity**, corpus, amount, area, reservoir, supply. [➡SIZE AND DIMENSIONS; 1191] 3 *n* **bulk**, main part, essence, majority, better part, lion's share. [➡CENTRAL PARTS OF PHYSICAL OBJECTS; 1250] 4 *v* **gather**, assemble, group, congregate, collect, huddle. [➡GET CLOSER TOGETHER; 311] *Opposite:* disperse. 5 *adj* **general**, widespread, common, universal, wholesale, large. [➡WHOLENESS AND COMPLETENESS; 199] 6 *type of* **vocal music**. [➡MUSIC, SONGS, AND SINGING; 907]

massacre 1 *n* **extermination**, annihilation, carnage, butchery, mass slaughter, holocaust, destruction, bloodbath, genocide. [➡CAUSES OF DEATH; 921] 2 *v* **slaughter**, murder, wipe out (*informal*), exterminate, butcher, mow down, annihilate, decimate, blow away (*slang*). [➡KILL; 923]

massage 1 *n* **manipulation**, pressure, kneading, rubbing, reflexology, acupressure, shiatsu, bodywork. [➡CONTACT: EXERT PRESSURE; 415] 2 *v* **knead**, manipulate, rub, rub down. [➡CONTACT: EXERT PRESSURE; 415] 3 *v* **falsify**, manipulate, alter, amend, misrepresent, fiddle (*informal*). [➡FALSIFY AND CHEAT; 177]

masses 1 *n* **common people**, crowd, multitude, commonality, hoi polloi, the many, the multitude, the people, grassroots. [➡CLASS STATUS; 889] *Opposite:* elite. 2 *n* (*informal*) **lots**, loads (*informal*), tons (*informal*), heaps (*informal*), oodles (*informal*). [➡MANY, MUCH, LARGE AMOUNT; 117]

massif *n* **mountain range**, chain, sierra, ridge, line. [➡MOUNTAINS AND HILLS; 1044]

massive 1 *adj* **bulky**, heavy, solid, weighty, vast, colossal, great. [➡WEIGHT: HEAVY; 1204] *Opposite:* slight. 2 *adj* **huge**, enormous, gigantic, immense, colossal, substantial, considerable, great, vast, mammoth, giant. [➡LARGE; 1192] *Opposite:* tiny.

massively (*informal*) *adv* **enormously**, immensely, hugely, tremendously, vastly, greatly, colossally, extremely, very. [➡TO A GREAT EXTENT; 130] *Opposite:* slightly.

mass-produce *v* **churn out**, turn out, manufacture, process, knock out, spit out (*US*). [➡MANUFACTURE; 350]

mass-produced *adj* **high-street**, off-the-peg, ready-to-wear, off-the-shelf, ready-made, machine-made. [➡ORDINARINESS; 245] *Opposite:* custom-made.

mast 1 *part of* **sailing vessel**. [➡PARTS OF A SHIP OR BOAT; 1150] 2 *type of* **telecommunications equipment**. [➡TELECOMMUNICATIONS; 1129]

master 1 *n* **controller**, ruler, leader, chief, boss. [➡BOSSES AND MANAGEMENT; 965] *Opposite:* underling. 2 *n* **expert**, virtuoso, maestro, genius, prodigy, wizard (*informal*), ace (*informal*). [➡TALENTED OR INTELLIGENT PERSON; 529] 3 *n* **teacher**, guru, tutor, instructor, guide, leader, trainer. [➡ADVISERS, JUDGES, AND ARBITERS; 971] *Opposite:* pupil. 4 *adj* **chief**, principal, main, major, leading, dominant, controlling, directing. [➡MOST IMPORTANT AND MAIN; 194] *Opposite:* secondary. 5 *v* **conquer**, gain control of, overcome, subdue, get the better of, control, surmount. [➡BEAT AND DEFEAT; 80] 6 *v* **become skilled at**, become proficient at, grasp, learn, understand, get to grips with. [➡STUDYING; 844] *Opposite:* fail.

masterful 1 *adj* **expert**, skilled, proficient, skilful, accomplished, adept, consummate. [➡TALENTED AND SKILFUL; 528] *Opposite:* incompetent. 2 *adj* **authoritative**, commanding, imposing, assured, forceful, firm. [➡STRENGTH; 202] *Opposite:* weak.

masterly *adj* **skilled**, skilful, proficient, talented, gifted, accomplished, expert. [➡TALENTED AND SKILFUL; 528] *Opposite:* incompetent.

mastermind 1 *n* **brains**, brain (*informal*), architect, organizer, instigator, intelligence. [➡TALENTED OR INTELLIGENT PERSON; 529] 2 *v* **plan**, engineer, oversee, organize, devise, instigate, think up, conceive, come up with, hatch. [➡INSTITUTE AND INAUGURATE; 349] *Opposite:* carry out.

masterpiece *n* **work of art**, masterwork, magnum opus, tour de force, chef-d'oeuvre (*formal*), stroke of genius. [➡ARTWORKS; 898]

masterwork *n* **masterpiece**, magnum opus, tour de force, chef-d'oeuvre (*formal*), stroke of genius, work of art. [➡ARTWORKS; 898]

mastery 1 *n* **expertise**, skill, knowledge, proficiency, command, ability. [➡SKILLS, TALENTS, AND ABILITIES; 527] 2 *n* **control**, power, supremacy, authority, command, sway. [➡STRENGTH; 202]

masthead *n* **title**, banner, strip, spread (*informal*), logo, header. [➡NEWSPAPERS; 606]

masticate *v* **chew**, munch, crunch, chomp (*informal*), champ, grind, pulverize, eat. [➡EAT AND NOT EAT; 711]

mastication *n* **chewing**, munching, eating, chomping (*informal*), grinding, champing. [➡EAT AND NOT EAT; 711]

mastiff *type of* **large dog**. [➡DOG; 980]

mat 1 *n* **rug**, carpet, doormat, bathmat, floorcovering, runner. [➡SOFT FURNISHINGS, LINEN, AND DRAPERY; 860] 2 *n* **table mat**, place mat, doily, coaster, pad. [➡SOFT FURNISHINGS, LINEN, AND DRAPERY; 860] 3 *v* **tangle**, entwine, entangle, intertwine, knot, snarl, tangle up. [➡COMBINE AND MIX; 401] *Opposite:* disentangle.

match 1 *n* **competition**, bout, contest, game, tie, cup tie. [➡NON-AGGRESSIVE/SPORTING EVENT; 40] 2 *n* **equal**, counterpart, equivalent, pair, partner. [➡EQUALITY; 155] 3 *v* **be alike**, correspond, be identical, tally, fit, equal, pair, match up, marry up, partner. [➡EQUALITY; 155] *Opposite:* differ. 4 *v* **go with**, complement, harmonize, accord, coordinate, agree with, be compatible. [➡HARMONY; 156] *Opposite:* clash.

matching 1 *adj* **corresponding**, identical, similar, alike, same, equivalent. [➡SAMENESS; 151] *Opposite:* different. 2 *adj*

toning, harmonizing, complementary, coordinative, coordinating, accordant (*formal*). [➡HARMONY; 156] *Opposite:* clashing.

matchless *adj* **peerless**, outstanding, unrivalled, unparalleled, incomparable, perfect, unique, inimitable, without equal, beyond compare. [➡EXTRAORDINARY: AMAZING; 205] *Opposite:* ordinary.

matchmaker *n* **marriage broker**, go-between, fixer, intermediary, cupid. [➡SEXUAL AND ROMANTIC RELATIONSHIPS; 964]

mate 1 *n* **friend**, pal (*informal*), chum (*informal*), comrade, companion, buddy (*US informal*). [➡FRIENDS; 963] *Opposite:* rival. 2 *n* **helper**, assistant, colleague, partner, coworker. [➡COLLEAGUES AND EQUALS; 967] 3 *v* **breed**, reproduce, couple (*formal*), copulate (*formal*). [➡REPRODUCTION AND HEREDITY; 726]

mater (*dated informal or humorous*) *n* [➡OLDER GENERATION RELATIVES; 959]

materfamilias (*literary*) *n* [➡OLDER GENERATION RELATIVES; 959]

material 1 *n* **substance**, matter, raw material, stuff. [➡SUBSTANCES; 1266] 2 *n* **data**, information, ideas, facts, notes, background. [➡BASIC DETAILS; 689] 3 *n* **fabric**, textile, stuff, cloth, yard goods, piece goods. [➡TEXTILES AND THREADS; 1130] 4 *adj* **physical**, substantial, solid, factual, quantifiable, sensible, measurable, visible. [➡TRUE AND REAL; 172] *Opposite:* insubstantial. 5 *adj* **significant**, relevant, pertinent, important, central, associated, substantive. [➡IMPORTANT; 195] *Opposite:* immaterial.

materialism *n* **acquisitiveness**, avariciousness, avarice, covetousness, cupidity (*formal*), avidity, greediness, greed. [➡PHILOSOPHIES AND BELIEFS; 781] *Opposite:* detachment.

materialistic *adj* **money-orientated**, grasping, acquisitive, avaricious, covetous, greedy, worldly. [➡FINANCIALLY MEAN AND GRASPING; 520] *Opposite:* spiritual.

materialization *n* **appearance**, arrival, advent, embodiment, manifestation, incarnation, realization, emergence. [➡BEGINNING; 53] *Opposite:* disappearance.

materialize 1 *v* **come into existence**, happen, occur, exist, take shape, come about, become manifest, shape up, emerge. [➡GRADUALLY COME INTO EXISTENCE; 1] *Opposite:* evaporate. 2 *v* **appear**, turn up, show up, arrive, reveal yourself, pop up (*informal*), emerge. [➡APPEAR AND EMERGE; 3] *Opposite:* disappear.

materially *adv* **significantly**, considerably, substantially, importantly, essentially, greatly, immensely, pertinently, centrally, substantively. [➡IMPORTANT; 195] *Opposite:* slightly.

materials *n* **resources**, supplies, ingredients, constituents, equipment, tackle, tools, provisions, things, stuff. [➡PHYSICAL OBJECTS; 1242]

maternal 1 *adj* **motherly**, parental, nurturing, protective, guiding. [➡RELATIONSHIP TO ANOTHER; 973] 2 *adj* **caring**, devoted, kind, tender, gentle, affectionate, warm, loving. [➡GENEROSITY AND KINDNESS; 496] *Opposite:* uncaring.

maternally *adv* **caringly**, tenderly, devotedly, protectively, gently, warmly, lovingly, affectionately. [➡GENEROSITY AND KINDNESS; 496] *Opposite:* neglectfully.

maternity *n* **motherhood**, childbearing, parenthood. [➡RELATIONSHIP TO ANOTHER; 973]

matey *adj* **friendly**, comradely, companionable, warm, amiable, genial, pally (*informal*), chummy (*informal*), buddy-buddy (*informal*). [➡RELATIONSHIP TO ANOTHER; 973] *Opposite:* unfriendly.

mathematical 1 *adj* **arithmetical**, numerical, arithmetic, geometric, algebraic, statistical. [➡MATHS; 598] 2 *adj* **exact**, precise, scientific, accurate, measured, calculated. [➡EXACT; 204] *Opposite:* random.

mathematics *n* **calculation**, reckoning, sums (*informal*), maths, algebra, arithmetic, calculus, geometry, statistics, trigonometry. [➡MATHS; 598]

matinée *n* **afternoon showing**, show, performance, presentation. [➡PERFORMANCES AND SHOWS; 42]

matiness *n* [➡FRIENDLINESS AND SOCIABILITY; 495]

matriarch *n* **mother**, matron, materfamilias (*literary*), grandmother, older woman. [➡OLDER GENERATION RELATIVES; 959] *Opposite:* patriarch.

matriculate 1 *v* **admit**, register, enrol, enlist, inscribe, enter. [➡STUDYING; 844] *Opposite:* strike off. 2 *v* **be admitted**, sign up, join, be enrolled, register, enter, enrol. [➡PARTICIPATE; 293] *Opposite:* drop out.

matriculation *n* **admission**, registration, admittance, enrolment, enlistment, inscription, entry, signing up. [➡LESSONS, COURSE WORK, AND EXAMINATIONS; 842] *Opposite:* expulsion.

matrimonial *adj* **marital**, wedded, married, nuptial, conjugal, connubial (*formal*), spousal. [➡MARRIED STATE; 961] *Opposite:* single.

matrimony *n* **marriage**, wedlock, wedding, nuptials (*literary*), ceremony, service, ritual, vows, marriage vows. [➡MARRIED STATE; 961] *Opposite:* divorce.

matrix 1 *n* **substance**, medium, carrier, solution, base, bed, ground. [➡SUBSTANCES; 1266] 2 *n* **situation**, environment, milieu (*formal*), conditions, background, interaction. [➡PLACE; 1064] 3 *n* **template**, mould, format, pattern, mint, plate. [➡EXTREMITIES OF PHYSICAL OBJECTS; 1249]

matron *n* **older woman**, mature woman, middle-aged woman, matriarch, doyenne, woman of a certain age. [➡FEMALE PERSON; 933]

matronly *adj* **full-figured**, plump, portly, stout, well-rounded, mature. [➡BUILD; 478]

matronymic *n* [➡NAME AND DESCRIBE; 666]

matte *adj* **dull**, lustreless, nonglossy, muted. [➡VISUAL TEXTURE; 1220] *Opposite:* glossy.

matted *adj* **tangled**, entwined, entangled, dishevelled, intertwined, knotted, knotty. [➡IN BAD REPAIR; 1233]

matter 1 *n* **subject**, topic, theme, issue, affair, question. [➡SUBJECT AREA; 769] 2 *n* **trouble**, problem, difficulty, worry, concern, complication. [➡PROBLEM; 257] 3 *n* **substance**, stuff, stock, staple, material. [➡SUBSTANCES; 1266] 4 *v* **be of importance**, be important, count, signify, be significant, carry some weight, make a difference, have a bearing, be relevant. [➡MEAN SOMETHING; 61]

See Compare and Contrast at **subject.**

matter-of-fact 1 *adj* **down-to-earth**, straightforward, rational, unemotional, realistic, practical, sensible, no-nonsense, pragmatic, straight-thinking, hardheaded, with both feet on the ground, literal. [➡HONEST AND OPEN; 631] 2 *adj* **factual**, unvarnished, down-to-earth, literal, unembroidered, unembellished, plain, exact, accurate, faithful, undistorted, truthful. [➡TRUE AND REAL; 172] *Opposite:* fictional.

matter-of-factness *n* [➡HONEST AND OPEN; 631]

matting *n* **floorcovering**, tatami, mats, coconut matting, rush matting, sisal, coir, jute. [➡PLANT MATERIALS; 1132]

mattress *n* **palliasse**, futon, air mattress, air bed, cushion, pad, bed. [➡SOFT FURNISHINGS, LINEN, AND DRAPERY; 860]

maturation *n* **maturing**, ripening, mellowing, development, growth, evolution, progress, fruition. [➡CHANGE; 373]

mature 1 *adj* **grown-up**, adult, fully-grown, middle-aged, older, in your prime. [➡ADULTHOOD; 918] *Opposite:* immature. 2 *adj* **experienced**, responsible, prudent, wise, sensible, stable, settled. [➡POSITIVE INTELLECTUAL CHARACTERISTICS; 525] *Opposite:* naive. 3 *adj* **established**, developed, advanced, settled, matured, complete. [➡IN GOOD REPAIR; 1231] *Opposite:* undeveloped. 4 *adj* **ripe**, mellow, ready, strong, sweet, aged, flavoursome, flavourful. [➡TASTE; 704] *Opposite:* young. 5 *v* **grow up**, develop, ripen, mellow, age, season. [➡CHANGE; 373]

matured *adj* **mature**, ripe, ripened, mellowed, aged, seasoned, developed. [➡IN GOOD REPAIR; 1231] *Opposite:* young.

maturely *adv* **wisely**, sensibly, responsibly, prudently. [➡POSITIVE INTELLECTUAL CHARACTERISTICS; 525] *Opposite:* immaturely.

maturity 1 *n* **adulthood**, prime of life, middle age, old age. [➡ADULTHOOD; 918] *Opposite:* youth. 2 *n* **ripeness**, mellowness, development, age. [➡OLD, OLD-FASHIONED; 168] *Opposite:* youth. 3 *n* **wisdom**, experience, responsibility, reliability, sensibleness. [➡KNOWLEDGE AND WISDOM; 559] *Opposite:* inexperience.

matzo *type of* **bread.** [➡BREAD, FLOUR, AND BREAD PRODUCTS; 1178]

maudlin *adj* **oversentimental**, mawkish, soppy (*informal*), slushy, mushy, syrupy, overemotional, weepy (*informal*), self-pitying, tearful, saccharine. [➡IN POOR TASTE; 230] *Opposite:* unemotional.

maul 1 *v* **claw**, attack, ill-treat, paw, mangle, batter, injure, knock about (*informal*), assault, beat, rough up (*informal*), savage. [➡PHYSICAL ATTACK AND PUNISHMENT; 416] 2 *v* **criticize**, attack, slate, slam (*informal*), pan (*informal*), put down (*informal*), badmouth (*slang*), savage. [➡ACCUSE, BLAME, AND CRITICIZE; 642]

mauling *n* **criticism**, disparagement, censure, barrage, blast, panning (*slang*). [➡CRITICISMS AND ANGRY OUTBURSTS; 50]

maunder *v* [➡MOVE SLOWLY; 315]

mausoleum *n* **tomb**, vault, sepulchre, crypt, resting place, grave, burial chamber, burial place, catacomb, last resting place. [➡MONUMENTS; 1091]

mauve *type of* **purple.** [➡COLOURS; 1223]

maven *n* **expert**, doyen, doyenne, enthusiast, pundit, connoisseur, aficionado, devotee, ace (*informal*). [➡TALENTED OR INTELLIGENT PERSON; 529]

maverick *n* **nonconformist**, eccentric, individualist, rebel, odd one out, dissident, one of a kind. [➡SOLITARY PEOPLE; 942] *Opposite:* conformist.

maw *n* [➡THE MOUTH; 703]

mawkish *adj* **oversentimental**, slushy, mushy, syrupy, overemotional, weepy (*informal*), soppy (*informal*). [➡IN POOR TASTE; 230] *Opposite:* unemotional.

mawkishness *n* **sentimentality**, oversentimentality, weepiness (*informal*), tearfulness, soppiness (*informal*), mushiness, slushiness. [➡IN POOR TASTE; 230]

max (*US slang*) *v* [➡SUCCEED AND WIN; 79]

maxi *adj* **large**, mega, big, jumbo, king-size, giant. [➡LARGE; 1192] *Opposite:* mini.

maxilla *n* [➡HEAD; 693]

maxim 1 *n* **saying**, adage, proverb, saw, aphorism, truism, axiom, dictum (*formal*), motto. [➡FIGURES OF SPEECH; 674] 2 *n* **rule**, tenet (*formal*), guideline, truth, precept (*formal*), principle. [➡IDEA AND THOUGHT; 771]

maximal *adj* **best**, greatest, most, utmost, highest, top, leading, biggest, first-rate, first-class, maximum. [➡CORRECT; 183] *Opposite:* minimal.

maximization *n* **expansion**, growth, enlargement, extension, intensification, boosting. [➡CHANGE OF SIZE: BIGGER; 393]

maximize 1 *v* **make the most of**, make best use of, exploit, take full advantage of, capitalize on, get the most out of, take advantage of, get the best out of, exhaust the possibilities, use to the full. [➡MAKE GOOD USE OF SOMETHING; 474] *Opposite:* minimize. 2 *v* **increase**, expand, amplify, make bigger, boost, augment (*formal*), extend, enlarge, raise. [➡CHANGE OF SIZE: BIGGER; 393] *Opposite:* minimize.

maximum 1 *n* **most**, greatest, highest, utmost. [➡MANY, MUCH, LARGE AMOUNT; 117] *Opposite:* minimum. 2 *n* **limit**, ceiling, greatest extent, top figure, upper limit. [➡MAJORITY; 139] *Opposite:* minimum.

maybe *adv* **perhaps**, possibly, it could be, perchance (*archaic or literary*), mayhap (*archaic*). [➡POSSIBLE AND PROBABLE; 178] *Opposite:* definitely.

mayday *n* **SOS**, distress signal, emergency call, distress call, 999 call, alert, call for help, 911 call (*US*). [➡SIGNPOSTS, SIGNALS, AND BILLBOARDS; 596]

mayfly *type of* **flying insect.** [➡FLYING INSECTS; 1013]

mayhem (*informal*) *n* **chaos**, disorder, confusion, turmoil, havoc, pandemonium, bedlam, anarchy. [➡DISORDER AND CHAOS; 246] *Opposite:* order.

mayonnaise *type of* **seasonings, sauces, and dips.** [➡SEASONINGS AND SAUCES; 1173]

maypole *n* **column**, post, pole, support. [➡STICKS, POLES, AND WEDGES; 1253]

maze 1 *n* **labyrinth**, warren, web, network. [➡FASTENERS, LINKS, AND NETWORKS; 1246] 2 *n* **confusion**, muddle, jumble, mess, intricacy, tangle. [➡DISORDER AND CHAOS; 246] *Opposite:* order.

MC *n* **presenter**, host, toastmaster, emcee (*informal*), moderator. [➡WORKERS IN ENTERTAINMENT AND MEDIA; 873]

m-commerce *n* [➡E-COMMERCE; 1128]

MD *n* [➡BUSINESS PEOPLE; 794]

meadow *n* **field**, pasture, paddock, grazing land, lea (*literary*). [➡THE COUNTRYSIDE AND OUTDOOR SPACES; 1070]

meadow fescue *type of* **grass.** [➡GRASS; 1031]

meadowland *n* [➡THE COUNTRYSIDE AND OUTDOOR SPACES; 1070]

meadowlark *type of* **songbird.** [➡SONGBIRD; 1003]

meagre *adj* **small**, slight, insufficient, inadequate, sparse, poor, scant, stingy (*informal*), paltry, measly (*informal*), miserable, mean, skimpy. [➡TOO FEW, TOO LITTLE; 120] *Opposite:* plentiful.

meagreness *n* **insufficiency**, inadequacy, scantness, stinginess, sparseness. [➡TOO FEW, TOO LITTLE; 120] *Opposite:* abundance.

meal 1 *n* **food**, bite, snack, something to eat. [➡FOOD; 1166] 2 *type of* **flour.** [➡BREAD, FLOUR, AND BREAD PRODUCTS; 1178]

meal

◆ *parts of a meal*
afters (*informal*), antipasto, aperitif, appetizer, canapé, delicacy, dessert, entrée, hors d'oeuvre, main course, meze, nibbles, pud (*informal*), pudding, side dish, starter, sweet, sweet course, tapas

◆ *types of meal*
banquet, barbecue, breakfast, brunch, buffet, clambake, cookout (*US*), dinner, elevenses, English breakfast, high tea, lunch, picnic, ready-made meal, snack, supper, takeaway, takeout (*US*), tea, titbit, TV dinner

mealtime *n* **breakfast time**, lunchtime, dinnertime, suppertime, tea-time. [➡TIMES OF DAY; 87]

mealy-mouthed (*disapproving*) *adj* **diffident**, restrained, hypocritical, insincere, euphemistic, indirect, devious. [➡DECEITFUL; 514] *Opposite:* frank.

mean 1 *v* **denote**, signify, indicate, stand for, represent, connote, imply, suggest, insinuate, purport (*formal*), portend, presage. [➡MEAN SOMETHING; 61] 2 *v* **intend**, propose, aim, plan, want, wish, have in mind, be thinking about. [➡PREPARE FOR ACTION; 290] 3 *v* **entail**, involve, require, lead to, necessitate, cause, result in. [➡CAUSE TO HAPPEN; 31] 4 *adj* (*archaic*) **humble**, lowly, poor, simple, underprivileged. [➡POVERTY AND POOR; 892] 5 *adj* **miserly**, niggardly, close-fisted (*informal*), tightfisted, parsimonious, penny-pinching (*informal*), ungenerous, stingy (*informal*). [➡FINANCIALLY MEAN AND GRASPING; 520] *Opposite:* generous. 6 *adj* **nasty**, unkind, cruel, callous, uncaring, malicious, despicable, vile, shameful, unpleasant. [➡SELFISH AND UNKIND; 506] *Opposite:* kind. 7 *adj* **paltry**, measly (*informal*), derisory, meagre, miserable, scanty, insufficient, inadequate, skimpy, scant, small, stingy (*informal*). [➡TOO FEW, TOO LITTLE; 120] *Opposite:* plentiful. 8 *adj* **poor**, shabby, squalid, humble, lowly, miserable, wretched. [➡IN BAD REPAIR; 1233] *Opposite:* comfortable. 9 *adj* **middle**, mid, average, normal, standard, median. [➡MATHS; 598] *Opposite:* extreme. 10 *n* **average**, norm, median, middle, midpoint. [➡MEASUREABLE PORTION; 125] *Opposite:* extremity.

Compare and Contrast: *mean, nasty, vile, low, base, ignoble*

CORE MEANING: REFERRING TO SOMEBODY OR SOMETHING BELOW NORMAL STANDARDS OF DECENCY

mean unkind or malicious; ***nasty*** showing spitefulness, malice, or ill-nature; ***vile*** despicable or shameful; ***low*** without principles or morals; ***base*** lacking proper social values or moral principles; ***ignoble*** dishonourable and contrary to the high standards of conduct expected.

mean business *v* **be serious**, mean what you say, mean it, be determined, be deadly serious, be in earnest, not be joking, be resolute. [➡MAKE DECISIONS AND CHOICES; 753]

meander 1 *v* **wind**, zigzag, twist and turn, twist, snake, bend, curve. [➡CHANGE DIRECTION OF MOTION; 345] 2 *v* **wander**, roam, amble, ramble, stroll, rove. [➡AIMLESS AND ERRANT MOTION; 344] *Opposite:* rush.

meandering *adj* **twisting**, winding, twisty, bendy, tortuous, snaking, windy, snaky, zigzagging, curving, sinuous, circuitous, indirect, zigzag, roundabout, meandrous. [➡ROUNDED SHAPE; 1217] *Opposite:* straight.

meanie (*informal*) *n* **miser**, penny pincher (*informal*), niggard, skinflint, scrooge (*informal*), cheapskate (*informal*), pinchpenny. [➡FINANCIALLY MEAN PEOPLE; 952]

meaning 1 *n* **sense**, connotation, denotation, import, gist. [➡MEANING; 691] 2 *n* **significance**, importance, implication, consequence (*formal*), worth, value. [➡IMPORTANCE AND SIGNIFICANCE; 193] *Opposite:* insignificance.

meaningful 1 *adj* **expressive**, evocative, telling, eloquent, speaking, feeling. [➡INTERESTING AND MEANINGFUL; 191] 2 *adj* **significant**, important, consequential, momentous, deep, profound. [➡IMPORTANT; 195] *Opposite:* meaningless.

meaningfulness *n* **meaning**, importance, significance, seriousness, relevance, consequence (*formal*). [➡IMPORTANCE AND SIGNIFICANCE; 193] *Opposite:* meaninglessness.

meaningless 1 *adj* **empty**, worthless, throwaway, hollow, pointless, futile, insincere, vain. [➡REDUNDANT AND USELESS; 241] *Opposite:* meaningful. 2 *adj* **unimportant**, trivial, inconsequential, irrelevant, insignificant. [➡UNIMPORTANT AND UNNECESSARY; 239] *Opposite:* significant.

meaninglessness *n* **emptiness**, insignificance, futility, purposelessness, worthlessness, vanity. [➡UNIMPORTANT AND UNNECESSARY; 239] *Opposite:* importance.

mean it *v* **be in earnest**, not be joking, be deadly serious, mean business, mean what you say, be determined. [➡MAKE DECISIONS AND CHOICES; 753]

meanly 1 *adv* **cruelly**, unkindly, spitefully, callously, despicably, shamefully, contemptibly. [➡SELFISH AND UNKIND; 506] *Opposite:* kindly. 2 *adv* **niggardly**, parsimoniously, ungenerously, tightfistedly, grudgingly, stingily. [➡FINANCIALLY MEAN AND GRASPING; 520] *Opposite:* generously. 3 *adv* **squalidly**, humbly, miserably, poorly. [➡POVERTY AND POOR; 892] *Opposite:* affluently.

mean-minded *adj* [➡SELFISH AND UNKIND; 506]

mean-mindedness *n* [➡SELFISH AND UNKIND; 506]

meanness 1 *n* **nastiness**, unkindness, cruelty, callousness, spitefulness, malice, heartlessness. [➡SELFISH AND UNKIND; 506] *Opposite:* kindness. 2 *n* **miserliness**, stinginess, niggardliness, parsimoniousness, tightfistedness, closefistedness (*informal*). [➡FINANCIALLY MEAN AND GRASPING; 520] *Opposite:* generosity.

means 1 *n* **way**, method, process, measures, channel, course, instrument, agency. [➡WAYS OF DOING THINGS; 295] 2 *n* **income**, earnings, resources, revenue, funds, capital, wealth, worth. [➡INCOME; 461]

mean-spirited *adj* **ungenerous**, uncharitable, harsh, mean, unkind, cruel, uncaring, spiteful, nasty, heartless, malicious. [➡SELFISH AND UNKIND; 506] *Opposite:* generous.

mean-spiritedness *n* [➡SELFISH AND UNKIND; 506]

meant 1 *adj* **inevitable**, preordained, fated, predestined, ordained (*formal*), destined. [➡FATE, DESTINY, AND ASTROLOGY; 783] *Opposite:* accidental. 2 *adj* **intended**, designed, planned, aimed, purposed, targeted. [➡INTENTIONAL AND DELIBERATE; 280] *Opposite:* unexpected.

meantime *n* **interim**, intervening time, period in-between, the time being. [➡PAUSES AND PHASES; 56]

mean well *v* **have good intentions**, have your heart in the right place, try to do the right thing, try hard, have the best intentions, have the right intentions. [➡TAKE CARE OF AND SPOIL; 301]

meanwhile *adv* **in the meantime**, for the meantime, in the interim, in the intervening time, for now, for the time being, temporarily, for the moment. [➡PRESENT; 85]

measly (*informal*) *adj* **meagre**, ungenerous, mean, derisory, paltry, miserable, small, inadequate, insufficient, stingy (*informal*). [➡TOO FEW, TOO LITTLE; 120] *Opposite:* ample.

measurable 1 *adj* **quantifiable**, assessable, gaugeable, computable, calculable, determinate, reckonable. [➡LARGE; 1192] *Opposite:* indeterminate. 2 *adj* **considerable**, appreciable, noticeable, detectable, perceptible, discernible, significant. [➡PERCEPTIBLE; 25] *Opposite:* imperceptible.

measurably *adv* **noticeably**, evidently, significantly, demonstrably, obviously, visibly, detectably. [➡TO A GREAT EXTENT; 130] *Opposite:* insignificantly.

measure 1 *n* **amount**, degree, quantity, portion, ration, quota, size, extent. [➡DEGREE AND EXTENT; 110] 2 *n* **measuring device**, gauge, meter, counter. [➡MEASURING DEVICES; 1122] 3 *v* **gauge**, calculate, compute, determine, assess, quantify, evaluate, appraise, rate. [➡ASSESS QUANTITY; 758]

measured 1 *adj* **deliberate**, calculated, precise, exact, careful, considered, reasonable. [➡CAUTIOUS AND CAREFUL; 283] *Opposite:* unthinking. 2 *adj* **slow**, unhurried, unrushed, restrained, stately, dignified, sedate, leisurely. [➡MOVING SLOWLY; 105] *Opposite:* hurried.

measureless (*literary*) *adj* **incalculable**, immeasurable, immense, vast, without limit, boundless, unbounded, great, limitless. [➡LARGE; 1192] *Opposite:* negligible.

measurement *n* **dimension**, size, extent, quantity, amount, capacity, height, depth, width, breadth, length, weight, volume, area, magnitude. [➡SIZE AND DIMENSIONS; 1191]

measure up *v* **come up to scratch** (*informal*), hit the mark, satisfy, deliver, fulfil requirements, do, meet the required standards, be good enough, be okay (*informal*), be alright, be satisfactory. [➡ACCEPTABLE AND PASSABLE; 220] *Opposite:* fall short.

measuring device *n* **gauge**, measure, meter, counter. [➡MEASURING DEVICES; 1122]

measuring device

◆ *types of measuring device*
altimeter, anemometer, aneroid barometer, balance, barograph, barometer, callipers, clock, compass, dipstick, dividers, dropper, Geiger counter, level (*US*), measuring tape, micrometer, mileometer, odometer (*US*), pipette, protractor, quadrant, rule, scale, speedo, speedometer, spirit level, statoscope, tachometer, tape, tape measure, theodolite, thermometer, weather vane, weighbridge, weighing machine, weighing scale (*US*), weighing scales, wind gauge, windsock

measuring tape *type of* **measuring device.** [➡MEASURING DEVICES; 1122]

meat 1 *n* **flesh**, food, carrion. [➡TYPES AND CUTS OF MEAT; 1176] 2 *n* **substance**, heart, gist, pith, kernel, essence, core, nub. [➡MOST IMPORTANT THING; 198]

meat

◆ *types of meat*
beef, chicken, duck, gammon, goat, goose, grouse, hare, lamb, mutton, partridge, pheasant, pork, rabbit, turkey, veal, venison, wild boar

◆ *types of processed meat*
bacon, bologna (*US*), burger, frankfurter, ground beef, ground meat, ham, hamburger, liver sausage, liverwurst (*US*), meatball, meat loaf, mince, minced beef, minced meat, mincemeat, mortadella, pâté, patty, pepperoni, rissole, salami, sausage, saveloy, wiener (*US*), wienerwurst (*US*)

◆ *types of steak*
Chateaubriand, fillet, porterhouse steak, rump, sirloin, T-bone steak, tenderloin

◆ *types of cut*
best end, breast, brisket, chop, chuck, chump, cutlet, drumstick, flank, foreshank, hock, joint, leg, loin, neck, rasher, rib, round, scrag end, shoulder, side, silverside, sparerib, steak, top round (*US*), topside, wing

meatball *type of* **processed meat.** [➡TYPES AND CUTS OF MEAT; 1176]

meat loaf *type of* **processed meat.** [➡TYPES AND CUTS OF MEAT; 1176]

meat pie *n* [➡PREPARED DISHES; 1169]

meaty 1 *adj* **brawny**, burly, muscular, hunky (*informal*), chunky (*informal*), fleshy, husky (*US*). [➡MUSCLES AND MUSCULATURE; 480] *Opposite:* weedy. 2 *adj* **substantial**, profound, deep, weighty, solid, interesting, significant, full of meaning. [➡INTERESTING AND MEANINGFUL; 191] *Opposite:* lightweight.

mecca *n* **focus**, focal point, magnet, hub, centre, seat, heart. [➡CENTRAL PARTS OF PHYSICAL OBJECTS; 1250]

mechanic *n* [➡FARMERS, GARDENERS, AND MANUAL WORKERS; 849]

mechanical 1 *adj* **motorized**, powered, power-driven, machine-driven, automated, automatic. [➡ENGINES AND HYDRAULICS; 1142] *Opposite:* manual. 2 *adj* **automatic**, perfunctory, unconscious, unthinking, reflex, involuntary, routine, knee-jerk (*informal*), machine-like, mechanistic, robotic, systematic. [➡AUTOMATIC AND INSTINCTIVE; 281] *Opposite:* spontaneous.

mechanics *n* **workings**, technicalities, procedure, mechanism, process, method, ins and outs, system. [➡WAYS OF DOING THINGS; 295]

mechanism 1 *n* **device**, instrument, apparatus, machine, machinery, appliance, tool, contrivance, gadget. [➡DEVICES; 1114] 2 *n* **means**, method, system, procedure, process, way, structure. [➡WAYS OF DOING THINGS; 295]

mechanistic *adj* **automatic**, mechanical, machine-like, automatous, robotic, systematic, cold, unfeeling, perfunctory, unthinking, routine. [➡AUTOMATIC AND INSTINCTIVE; 281] *Opposite:* spontaneous.

mechanization *n* **automation**, computerization, streamlining, modernization, systematization, industrialization. [➡MACHINERY; 1113]

mechanize *v* **automate**, power, systematize, industrialize, program, preset, computerize. [➡MANUFACTURE; 350]

mechanized *adj* **automated**, mechanical, industrialized, automatic, computerized, modern, programmed, preset, streamlined. [➡MACHINERY; 1113]

medal *n* **award**, decoration, honour, distinction, laurel, accolade. [➡ORNAMENTS AND DECORATIONS; 1247]

medallion 1 *n* **medal**, decoration, pendant, rondure (*literary*), ornament. [➡ORNAMENTS AND DECORATIONS; 1247] 2 *type of* **necklace.** [➡JEWELLERY; 866]

medallist *n* **champion**, winner, runner-up, gold medallist, silver medallist, bronze medallist, prizewinner, victor. [➡COMPETITORS; 41]

meddle *v* **interfere**, butt in, stick your nose in, intrude, put your oar in, pry, stir, gossip, snoop (*informal*), horn in (*informal*), invade. [➡INTERRUPT AND BUTT IN; 620]

meddler *n* **busybody** (*informal*), stirrer (*informal*), troublemaker, nuisance, pest (*informal*), gossip, nosy parker (*informal*), snoop (*informal*), interferer. [➡INTERFERING PEOPLE AND TELLTALES; 950]

meddlesome *adj* **interfering**, intrusive, meddling, nosy (*informal*), officious, prying, snoopy, gossipy. [➡NOSY AND INTERFERING; 513] *Opposite:* detached.

meddle with *v* [➡MISUSE AND ABUSE; 472]

meddling 1 *n* **interference**, nosiness (*informal*), inquisitiveness, intrusion, prying, intrusiveness, officiousness, intervention. [➡NOSY AND INTERFERING; 513] 2 *adj* **interfering**, meddlesome, nosy (*informal*), inquisitive, snooping (*informal*), intrusive, prying, officious. [➡NOSY AND INTERFERING; 513] *Opposite:* uninterested.

media *n* **mass media**, television, radio, newspapers, magazines, broadcasting. [➡ADVERTISING AND PUBLICITY; 605]

median *n* **mean**, midpoint, middle, norm, standard, par, golden mean, average, centre. [➡MATHS; 598]

mediate *v* **arbitrate**, intercede, facilitate, intermediate, referee, umpire, intervene, reconcile, negotiate, resolve. [➡TWO-WAY COMMUNICATION; 608] *Opposite:* provoke.

mediation *n* **arbitration**, intercession, conciliation, intervention, negotiation, facilitation, intermediation. [➡NEGOTIATION AND DEBATE; 46] *Opposite:* provocation.

mediator *n* **go-between**, intermediary, third party, arbitrator, negotiator, moderator, facilitator, referee, umpire, intercessor, conciliator. [➡ADVISERS, JUDGES, AND ARBITERS; 971]

medic (*informal*) *n* **doctor**, medical student, houseman, physician, registrar, consultant, surgeon, general practitioner, medical practitioner, GP, intern, resident (*US*), family practitioner (*US*). [➡PEOPLE WHO WORK IN MEDICINE; 848]

medical 1 *adj* **medicinal**, remedial, health, homeopathic, curative, therapeutic, healing, restorative. [➡REMEDIES, TREATMENTS, AND OPERATIONS; 732] 2 *n* **checkup**, health check, examination. [➡REMEDIES, TREATMENTS, AND OPERATIONS; 732]

medical practitioner *n* [➡PEOPLE WHO WORK IN MEDICINE; 848]

medical school *n* [➡EDUCATIONAL INSTITUTIONS; 813]

medical student *n* [➡STUDENTS AND PUPILS; 841]

medical training *n* [➡LESSONS, COURSE WORK, AND EXAMINATIONS; 842]

medicament *n* **medicine**, remedy, treatment, pharmaceutical, curative, drug, ointment, unguent, lotion, salve, balm. [➡REMEDIES, TREATMENTS, AND OPERATIONS; 732]

medicated *adj* **medicinal**, antiseptic, antibacterial, antiviral, analgesic, therapeutic, curative, tonic. [➡REMEDIES, TREATMENTS, AND OPERATIONS; 732]

medication *n* **drug**, pharmaceutical, pill, tablet, capsule, suppository, medicine. [➡REMEDIES, TREATMENTS, AND OPERATIONS; 732]

medicinal *adj* **medicated**, remedial, healing, therapeutic, curative, homeopathic, pharmaceutical, restorative, tonic. [➡REMEDIES, TREATMENTS, AND OPERATIONS; 732]

medicine *n* **drug**, remedy, medication, treatment, prescription, dose. [➡REMEDIES, TREATMENTS, AND OPERATIONS; 732]

medieval *adj* **old-fashioned**, out-of-date, primitive, feudal, unenlightened, barbaric, passé, benighted. [➡OLD, OLD-FASHIONED; 168] *Opposite:* modern.

mediocre *adj* **middling**, average, unexceptional, ordinary, middle-of-the-road, run-of-the-mill, second-rate, pedestrian, commonplace. [➡ORDINARINESS; 245] *Opposite:* excellent.

mediocrity *n* **patchiness**, unevenness, poorness, weakness, averageness, ordinariness. [➡ORDINARINESS; 245] *Opposite:* excellence.

meditate *v* **contemplate**, ponder, think, consider, deliberate, turn over, mull over, reflect, ruminate, muse. [➡THINK AND REFLECT; 744]

meditation *n* **thought**, consideration, deliberation (*formal*), contemplation, reflection, rumination, musing, introspection, concentration. [➡THINK AND REFLECT; 744]

meditative *adj* **thoughtful**, reflective, contemplative, pensive, introspective, preoccupied, serious, absorbed, lost in thought, brooding, wistful. [➡PENSIVENESS AND INTEREST; 539] *Opposite:* active.

medium 1 *adj* **average**, intermediate, middle, middling, standard, mediocre, moderate. [➡ACCEPTABLE AND PASSABLE; 220] *Opposite:* extraordinary. 2 *n* **means**, vehicle, channel, mode, method, way, avenue, form, agent, instrument, organ. [➡WAYS OF DOING THINGS; 295]

medium-large *adj* [➡MEDIUM; 1195]

medium-sized *adj* [➡MEDIUM; 1195]

medley *n* **mixture**, combination, assortment, mix, jumble, variety, miscellany, pastiche, patchwork. [➡COLLECTIONS AND MIXTURES OF THINGS; 1243]

meek 1 *adj* **mild**, quiet, humble, gentle, docile, modest, lowly. [➡MORALLY GOOD; 775] *Opposite:* overbearing. 2 *adj* **timid**, compliant, weak, cowed, fearful, tame, submissive. [➡THE WILL AND WILLINGNESS; 564] *Opposite:* assertive.

meekness 1 *n* **humbleness**, quietness, docility, humility, gentleness, modesty, mildness. [➡MORALLY GOOD; 775] 2 *n* **timidity**, submissiveness, fearfulness, compliance, weakness, tameness. [➡THE WILL AND WILLINGNESS; 564] *Opposite:* assertiveness.

meet 1 *v* **come across**, encounter, bump into, run into, chance on, see, happen, chance, light. [➡EXPERIENCE AND ENCOUNTER; 583] *Opposite:* avoid. 2 *v* **be introduced to**, make somebody's acquaintance, get to know, greet, become acquainted with, know. [➡ESTABLISHING RELATIONSHIPS WITH OTHERS; 974] 3 *v* **gather**, get together, come together, convene, assemble, congregate, rally, meet up, reunite. [➡GET CLOSER TOGETHER; 311] *Opposite:* disperse. 4 *v* **experience**, encounter, come across, endure, go through, suffer, undergo, sustain. [➡EXPERIENCE AND ENCOUNTER; 583] 5 *v* **touch**, contact, connect, join, converge, come together, unite, link, cross, intersect. [➡CREATING CONNECTIONS; 145] *Opposite:* separate. 6 *adj* (*archaic*) [➡APPROPRIATE, SUITABLE, ADVISABLE; 185]

meeting 1 *n* **business meeting**, conference, assembly, summit, seminar, board meeting, consultation, get-together (*informal*), gathering, convention. [➡MEETINGS AND ASSEMBLIES; 43] 2 *n* **encounter**, introduction, reunion, appointment, engagement, date, assignation. [➡MEETINGS AND ASSEMBLIES; 43]

meeting house *type of* **church**. [➡RELIGIOUS BUILDINGS; 1084]

meeting room *type of* **room in a public building**. [➡TYPES OF ROOM; 1096]

mega *adj* [➡LARGE; 1192]

megalith *n* **prehistoric monument**, standing stone, menhir, dolmen, sarsen, stele, plinth, monolith. [➡ANCIENT MANMADE STRUCTURES; 1088]

megalomania *n* **power lust**, overbearingness, tyranny, totalitarianism, autocracy, despotism. [➡BOSSY AND OVERBEARING; 517]

megalomaniac 1 *n* **tyrant**, dictator, autocrat, despot. [➡SELF-IMPORTANT AND SELF-SEEKING PEOPLE; 949] 2 *adj* **power-hungry**, power-crazy, self-important, tyrannical, dictatorial, despotic, totalitarian, autocratic. [➡BOSSY AND OVERBEARING; 517]

megalosaur *type of* **dinosaur**. [➡DINOSAUR; 996]

megaphone *n* **loudhailer**, loudspeaker, amplifier, PA, mike (*informal*), public-address system, bullhorn (*US*). [➡AUDIO EQUIPMENT; 1138]

megastar *n* [➡IMPORTANT OR FAMOUS PEOPLE; 893]

Meissen (*US*) *type of* **pottery**. [➡POTTERY; 1134]

melamine *type of* **plastic**. [➡PLASTICS; 1133]

melancholic *adj* **dejected**, sad, unhappy, miserable, forlorn, gloomy, mournful, despondent, sorrowful, lamenting, morose, nostalgic, dark, moody, down, plaintive, elegiac (*formal*). [➡SADNESS, DISTRESS, AND DESPAIR; 540] *Opposite:* cheerful.

melancholy 1 *adj* **sad**, downhearted, miserable, down in the dumps (*informal*), down, low, glum, gloomy, unhappy, despondent, dejected, dismal. [➡SADNESS, DISTRESS, AND DESPAIR; 540] *Opposite:* cheerful. 2 *n* **sadness**, unhappiness, dejection, sorrow, the blues, downheartedness, depression, gloominess, despondency. [➡SADNESS, DISTRESS, AND DESPAIR; 540] *Opposite:* cheerfulness.

melange (*literary or formal*) *n* **mixture**, mix, jumble, potpourri, mishmash, medley, blend, muddle, assortment, mixed bag, crazy quilt, hotchpotch. [➡COLLECTIONS AND MIXTURES OF THINGS; 1243]

mélange *see* **melange**.

melanoma *n* [➡CONDITIONS AFFECTING THE SKIN; 722]

meld 1 *v* **mix**, merge, blend, fuse, combine, amalgamate, mingle, commingle (*literary*). [➡COMBINE AND MIX; 401] *Opposite:* separate. 2 *n* **combination**, mix, mixture, blend, amalgamation, fusion, mingling. [➡COLLECTIONS AND MIXTURES OF THINGS; 1243]

melding *n* [➡COLLECTIONS AND MIXTURES OF THINGS; 1243]

melee 1 *n* **fight**, commotion, brawl, fracas, riot, uproar, tussle, skirmish, to-do (*informal*), scrap (*informal*), scuffle, clash, confusion, struggle, rumpus, free-for-all (*informal*), ruckus, hullabaloo, fray, donnybrook. [➡AGGRESSIVE EVENT; 39] **2** *n* **muddle**, jumble, mix, confusion, mixture, mishmash, medley, blend, miscellany, potpourri, hotchpotch, hash. [➡COLLECTIONS AND MIXTURES OF THINGS; 1243]

mêlée *see* **melee**.

mellifluous *adj* **pleasant**, soothing, sweet, melodious, honeyed, mellow, dulcet, musical. [➡SOFT OR PLEASANT SOUNDS; 1264] *Opposite:* jarring.

mellifluousness *n* [➡SOFT OR PLEASANT SOUNDS; 1264]

mellow **1** *adj* **smooth**, rich, full, warm, soft, deep, mellifluous. [➡SOFT OR PLEASANT SOUNDS; 1264] *Opposite:* harsh. **2** *adj* **mature**, full-flavoured, ripe, aged, strong, full-bodied. [➡TASTE; 704] *Opposite:* young. **3** *adj* **laid-back** (*informal*), easygoing, good-humoured, tolerant, approachable, genial, equable, affable, relaxed, placid, calm, sedate. [➡CONFIDENCE AND COMPOSURE; 500] *Opposite:* uptight (*informal*). **4** *v* **mature**, soften, develop, ripen, improve, fill out, age, grow. [➡IMPROVE SOMETHING; 375] *Opposite:* deteriorate. **5** *v* **calm down**, ease up, settle down, relax, mature, soften, expand. [➡CHANGE OF MOOD AND COMPOSURE; 581]

mellowness **1** *n* **smoothness**, richness, warmth, fullness, mellifluousness, pleasantness, softness. [➡SOFT OR PLEASANT SOUNDS; 1264] *Opposite:* harshness. **2** *n* **ripeness**, sweetness, fullness, matureness, maturity, softness. [➡TASTE; 704] *Opposite:* rawness. **3** *n* **geniality**, equanimity, amiability, warmth, affability, good humour, kind-heartedness, expansiveness. [➡GENEROSITY AND KINDNESS; 496]

melodic *adj* **tuneful**, harmonious, musical, melodious, easy on the ear, mellow, euphonious, pleasant, lyrical, dulcet. [➡SOFT OR PLEASANT SOUNDS; 1264] *Opposite:* discordant.

melodious *adj* **tuneful**, harmonious, musical, melodic, easy on the ear, mellow, euphonious, pleasant, lyrical, dulcet. [➡SOFT OR PLEASANT SOUNDS; 1264] *Opposite:* discordant.

melodiousness *n* **tunefulness**, musicalness, pleasantness, euphoniousness, euphony, melody, harmoniousness, lyricism. [➡SOFT OR PLEASANT SOUNDS; 1264]

melodrama **1** *n* **fuss**, drama, scene, to-do (*informal*), storm in a teacup, exaggeration, commotion, stir, ruckus, quarrel, tempest in a teapot (*US*). [➡CHAOS AND UPROAR; 51] **2** *n* **play**, drama, tragedy, comedy, farce, stage show, act. [➡FICTION AND DRAMA; 913]

melodramatic *adj* **histrionic**, overdramatic, overemotional, over-the-top (*informal*), exaggerated, sensational, theatrical, acting up. [➡AFFECTATION, SELF-SATISFACTION, AND SNOBBISHNESS; 508] *Opposite:* low-key.

melody *n* **tune**, song, air, phrase, strain, descant. [➡MUSIC, SONGS, AND SINGING; 907]

melon *type of* **fruit**. [➡FRUIT AND VEGETABLES; 1175]

melt **1** *v* **thaw**, thaw out, dissolve, soften, liquefy, melt down, liquesce, flux. [➡SOFTEN, LIQUEFY, DAMPEN; 389] *Opposite:* freeze. **2** *v* **disappear**, dissolve, fade, vanish, evaporate, vaporize, dissipate. [➡DISAPPEAR; 4] *Opposite:* materialize.

melt away *v* [➡DISAPPEAR; 4]

meltdown (*informal*) *n* **collapse**, breakdown, failure, disaster, disintegration, ruin, destruction, decay, extinction. [➡FAILURE; 77] *Opposite:* success.

melting *adj* **tender**, sweet, loving, soppy (*informal*), sentimental, soft, gentle. [➡EMOTIONALLY PLEASANT; 188] *Opposite:* harsh.

melting pot *n* **mixture**, mix, mishmash, blend, hotchpotch, fusion, jumble, medley. [➡COLLECTIONS AND MIXTURES OF THINGS; 1243]

member **1** *n* **associate**, affiliate, fellow, adherent, participant, follower, supporter, colleague, partner, representative, delegate. [➡BUSINESS PEOPLE; 794] **2** *n* **limb**, appendage, organ, extremity, leg, arm. [➡TORSO; 694] **3** *n* **part**, constituent, component, element, portion, item, unit. [➡PHYSICAL OBJECTS; 1242]

member of parliament *n* [➡POLITICAL OFFICES AND POLITICIANS; 808]

membership **1** *n* **association**, affiliation, involvement, connection, relationship, attachment, participation, belonging, inclusion, admission. [➡CONNECTION; 144] *Opposite:* exclusion. **2** *n* **members**, associates, affiliates, fellows, adherents, participants, followers, supporters, colleagues, partners, representatives, delegates. [➡GROUPS WITH A COMMON INTEREST; 938]

membrane *n* **skin**, film, sheath, casing, tissue, crust, covering, coating, layer, rind, peel. [➡THE SKIN; 721]

memento *n* **souvenir**, reminder, vestige, keepsake, token, relic. [➡ORNAMENTS AND DECORATIONS; 1247]

memo *n* **memorandum**, note, minute, letter, message, communication, document, dispatch, missive. [➡LETTERS AND WRITTEN MESSAGES; 585]

memoir **1** *n* **account**, biography, history, chronicle, description, record, diary, journal, dossier. [➡RECORDS; 586] **2** *n* **essay**, article, report, paper, thesis, dissertation, treatise, study. [➡ANALYTICAL NONFICTION WRITING; 593]

memoirist *n* [➡WRITERS AND STYLES; 914]

memoirs *n* **autobiography**, journal, life story, life history, diary, account, chronicle, record, reminiscences, recollections, confessions. [➡BOOKS AND BOOKLETS; 591]

memorabilia *n* **collectables**, collector's items, souvenirs, mementos, ephemera, keepsakes, personal effects, possessions, tokens, relics. [➡COLLECTIONS AND MIXTURES OF THINGS; 1243]

memorability *n* **importance**, consequence (*formal*), moment (*formal*), note, momentousness, uncommonness, impressiveness, fame. [➡EXTRAORDINARY: UNCOMMON; 206] *Opposite:* inconsequence.

memorable *adj* **unforgettable**, notable, remarkable, outstanding, impressive, striking, extraordinary, haunting, stamped on your memory, noteworthy. [➡EXTRAORDINARY: AMAZING; 205] *Opposite:* forgettable.

memorandum *n* **memo**, note, minute, letter, message, communication, document, dispatch, missive. [➡LETTERS AND WRITTEN MESSAGES; 585]

memorial *n* **monument**, cenotaph, statue, bust, plaque, stone, memorial stone. [➡MONUMENTS; 1091]

memorial stone *n* [➡MONUMENTS; 1091]

memorize *v* **learn by heart**, learn by rote, learn, commit to memory, remember. [➡REMEMBER; 747] *Opposite:* forget.

memory 1 *n* **reminiscence**, recollection, recall, remembrance, retention. [➡MEMORY; 746] 2 *n* **commemoration**, remembrance, celebration, memorial. [➡CEREMONIES AND ANNIVERSARIES; 38] 3 *type of* **software.** [➡COMPUTERS AND COMPUTING; 1126]

menace 1 *n* **threat**, danger, hazard, peril, jeopardy, risk. [➡DANGER; 236] *Opposite:* reassurance. 2 *n* (*informal*) **thorn in the flesh**, nuisance, pain in the neck (*informal*), troublemaker, pest (*informal*), annoyance, bother, thorn in one's side. [➡NUISANCES; 254] 3 *v* **endanger**, threaten, jeopardize, imperil (*formal*), hang over, loom over. [➡PUT AT RISK; 385] 4 *v* **threaten**, intimidate, terrorize, frighten, alarm, scare, bully, pick on. [➡FRIGHTEN AND SHOCK; 569] *Opposite:* reassure.

menacing *adj* **threatening**, ominous, frightening, alarming, intimidating, looming, foreboding, dark, ugly, scary (*informal*). [➡DANGEROUS; 237] *Opposite:* reassuring.

menagerie *n* **zoo**, zoological gardens, city farm, farm park, petting zoo (*US*). [➡URBAN OUTDOOR SPACES; 1071]

mend 1 *v* **repair**, fix, put right, put back together, restore, patch up, stick, glue. [➡REPAIR AND MEND; 377] *Opposite:* break. 2 *v* **stitch**, sew, sew up, patch, patch up, darn, repair. [➡REPAIR AND MEND; 377] *Opposite:* rip. 3 *v* **improve**, amend, rectify, reform, transform, work on, make better. [➡CORRECT AND PUT RIGHT; 378] 4 *v* **recover**, get better, get well, recuperate, heal. [➡GET BETTER; 376] *Opposite:* deteriorate. 5 *n* **patch**, darn, repair. [➡REPAIR AND MEND; 377]

mendacious 1 *adj* **untruthful**, dishonest, deceitful, unreliable, lying, inaccurate. [➡DECEITFUL; 514] *Opposite:* truthful. 2 *adj* **untrue**, misleading, false, spurious, untruthful, dishonest, deceitful, unreliable. [➡FALSE AND UNREAL; 174] *Opposite:* true.

mendaciously *adv* **untruthfully**, dishonestly, deceitfully, falsely, unreliably, misleadingly, spuriously, inaccurately. [➡DECEITFUL; 514] *Opposite:* truthfully.

mendaciousness *n* [➡DECEPTION AND LIES; 661]

mendacity *n* **lies**, deception, deceit, falsehood, fabrication, dishonesty, deceitfulness, untruthfulness, unreliability, spuriousness, inaccuracy. [➡DECEITFUL; 514] *Opposite:* truthfulness.

mendicant 1 *adj* **begging**, homeless, vagrant, vagabond, indigent (*formal*), penniless. [➡POVERTY AND POOR; 892] 2 *n* (*formal*) **beggar**, vagrant, tramp, down-and-out, homeless person, hobo, street person, vagabond, panhandler (*US*). [➡POOR PEOPLE; 896]

mending *n* **sewing**, darning, stitching, fixing, patching, repairing, needlecraft, needlework, hemming. [➡REPAIR AND MEND; 377]

menfolk *n* **kinsmen**, men, boys, husbands, sons, brothers. [➡THE FAMILY; 956]

menial *adj* **unskilled**, boring, tedious, basic, lowly, humble, low. [➡BORING AND UNINTERESTING; 235] *Opposite:* skilled.

mensch (*informal*) *n* [➡PERSON; 931]

men's clothing *n* [➡GARMENTS AND OUTFITS; 865]

men's room (*US*) *type of* **room in a public building.** [➡TYPES OF ROOM; 1096]

menswear *n* **men's clothing**, sportswear, outerwear, haberdashery (*US*). [➡GARMENTS AND OUTFITS; 865]

mental *adj* **psychological**, cerebral, rational, intellectual, spiritual, emotional, conceptual, perceptual, abstract. [➡PSYCHOLOGY AND THE MIND; 770] *Opposite:* physical.

mental image *n* [➡IDEA AND THOUGHT; 771]

mentality *n* **attitude**, approach, outlook, mindset, state of mind, frame of mind, point of view, temperament, character, personality. [➡POINT OF VIEW; 768]

mental picture *n* [➡IDEA AND THOUGHT; 771]

mention 1 *v* **talk about**, state, say, cite, bring up, comment on, remark on, touch on, refer to, allude to, declare, reveal, point out. [➡SUGGEST, HINT, AND COMMENT; 613] *Opposite:* conceal. 2 *n* **reference**, indication, discussion, remark, comment, allusion, declaration, statement, citation. [➡SUGGEST, HINT, AND COMMENT; 613]

mentor *n* **adviser**, counsellor, guide, tutor, teacher, guru, supporter. [➡ADVISERS, JUDGES, AND ARBITERS; 971] *Opposite:* pupil.

menu *n* **bill of fare**, carte du jour, tariff, blackboard, set menu. [➡LISTS AND SCHEDULES; 588]

mephitic (*literary*) *adj* [➡DANGEROUS; 237]

mercantile *adj* **merchant**, commercial, trade, trading, business. [➡BUSINESS; 792]

mercenary 1 *n* **soldier of fortune**, dog of war, soldier, legionnaire, freedom fighter, guerrilla. [➡MILITARY PERSONNEL; 828] 2 *adj* **acquisitive**, grasping, greedy, avaricious, covetous, gold-digging, moneygrubbing, venal. [➡SELFISH AND UNKIND; 506] *Opposite:* altruistic.

merchandise 1 *n* **goods**, products, produce, commodities, stock, range. [➡BUSINESS PRODUCTS; 796] 2 *v* **sell**, retail, trade in, deal in, handle, buy, import, export, market, promote. [➡SELL; 442]

merchant 1 *n* **retailer**, seller, vendor, shopkeeper, tradesperson, storekeeper (*US*). [➡SELLER; 443] 2 *n* **wholesaler**, dealer, trader, supplier, broker, importer, exporter. [➡BUSINESS PEOPLE; 794]

merchant navy *n* [➡THE ARMED FORCES; 827]

merciful 1 *adj* **compassionate**, kind, kind-hearted, lenient, humane, generous, sympathetic, understanding, forgiving, forbearing (*formal*), gracious, benevolent. [➡GENEROSITY AND KINDNESS; 496] *Opposite:* hardhearted. 2 *adj* **thankful**, fortunate, welcome, lucky, happy, timely, opportune. [➡LUCK; 784] *Opposite:* unfortunate.

mercifulness *n* [➡GENEROSITY AND KINDNESS; 496]

merciless *adj* **cruel**, hardhearted, pitiless, harsh, heartless, unpitying, ruthless, unforgiving, severe, unsympathetic, uncompromising, hard, unfeeling, callous, cold-blooded. [➡SELFISH AND UNKIND; 506] *Opposite:* kind.

mercilessness *n* **cruelty**, hardheartedness, pitilessness, harshness, heartlessness, ruthlessness, severity, callousness, cold-bloodedness, unkindness, nastiness. [➡SELFISH AND UNKIND; 506] *Opposite:* kindness.

mercurial *adj* **changeable**, unpredictable, lively, active, impulsive, inconstant, volatile, witty, fast-talking, brilliant. [➡LACK OF COMMITMENT AND UNRELIABILITY; 510] *Opposite:* consistent.

mercury *type of* **metal**. [➡METALS; 1275]

Mercury *type of* **planet**. [➡CELESTIAL BODIES; 1060]

mercy 1 *n* **compassion**, pity, clemency, kindness, leniency, humanity, generosity, sympathy, understanding, forgiveness, forbearance (*formal*), grace, benevolence. [➡COMPASSION AND FORGIVENESS; 552] *Opposite:* cruelty. 2 *n* **blessing**, relief, kindness, stroke of luck, piece of luck, godsend. [➡TREAT; 211] *Opposite:* blow.

mere 1 *adj* **ordinary**, simple, sheer, plain, unadorned. [➡PLAIN; 233] 2 *adj* **scant**, meagre, paltry, mean, miserable. [➡TOO FEW, TOO LITTLE; 120] 3 *n* (*archaic or literary*) **lake**, loch, lough, lagoon, broad, tarn. [➡RIVERS, LAKES, AND STREAMS; 1042]

merely *adv* **just**, only, simply, purely. [➡TO A CERTAIN EXTENT; 134]

merengue *n* [➡DANCE; 903]

meretricious 1 *adj* (*formal*) **superficial**, flashy, flash (*informal*), vulgar, tawdry, showy, glitzy, kitschy. [➡IN POOR TASTE; 230] 2 *adj* **plausible**, specious, glib, persuasive, insincere, deceiving, deceptive, false. [➡FALSE AND UNREAL; 174] *Opposite:* genuine.

merganser *type of* **freshwater bird**. [➡FRESHWATER BIRD; 1000]

merge 1 *v* **combine**, unite, come together, join, amalgamate, become one, join together, team up, fuse, unify. [➡ESTABLISHING RELATIONSHIPS WITH OTHERS; 974] *Opposite:* separate. 2 *v* **blend**, meld, blur, fuse, unify, mix, mingle, conflate. [➡COMBINE AND MIX; 401] *Opposite:* separate.

merger 1 *n* **amalgamation**, union, combination, joining, fusion, unification. [➡BUSINESS ACTIVITIES AND PHENOMENA; 795] *Opposite:* separation. 2 *n* **blend**, meld, blur, fusion, union, unification, mix, mixture, conflation, amalgamation, combination. [➡COLLECTIONS AND MIXTURES OF THINGS; 1243] *Opposite:* separation.

meridian (*literary*) *n* **zenith**, height, high point, peak, apogee, apex. [➡EXTREMITIES OF PHYSICAL OBJECTS; 1249] *Opposite:* nadir.

meringue *type of* **dessert**. [➡CAKES, BISCUITS, AND DESSERTS; 1180]

merit 1 *n* **value**, worth, quality, excellence, distinction, virtue, importance, weight. [➡IMPORTANCE AND SIGNIFICANCE; 193] *Opposite:* worthlessness. 2 *n* **advantage**, good point, pro, plus (*informal*), plus point, asset, virtue, quality, redeeming feature. [➡SOURCE OF HAPPINESS, PLEASURE, OR IMPROVEMENT; 210] *Opposite:* disadvantage. 3 *n* **ability**, accomplishment, capability, aptitude, skill, worth, excellence. [➡SKILLS, TALENTS, AND ABILITIES; 527] *Opposite:* worthlessness. 4 *v* **deserve**, warrant, earn, call for, be worthy of, be deserving of, be entitled to. [➡OWE AND DESERVE; 466]

meritorious (*formal*) *adj* **commendable**, praiseworthy, estimable, admirable, laudable, worthy. [➡ADMIRABLE AND COMMENDABLE; 186] *Opposite:* despicable.

mermaid *type of* **mythological creature**. [➡MYTHICAL CREATURES; 1036]

merriment *n* **cheerfulness**, happiness, fun, high spirits, jollity, gaiety, laughter, glee, joy, joyfulness, cheer, amusement. [➡PLEASURE, EXCITEMENT, AND ELATION; 535] *Opposite:* misery.

merry *adj* **cheerful**, happy, cheery, jolly, joyful, joyous, laughing, lively. [➡PLEASURE, EXCITEMENT, AND ELATION; 535] *Opposite:* miserable.

merry-go-round *n* **whirl**, round, series, succession, string, sequence, flurry. [➡EVENTS AND OCCURRENCES; 35]

merrymaker *n* **reveller**, partygoer, carouser (*literary*), raver (*informal*), party guest, life and soul of the party, social butterfly. [➡PLEASURE-SEEKERS AND HEDONISTS; 886] *Opposite:* killjoy.

merrymaking *n* **celebration**, revels, partying, carousing (*literary*), jollification, jollity, fun, fun and games, high jinks (*informal*), enjoyment. [➡PARTIES, DANCES, AND CELEBRATIONS; 37] *Opposite:* misery.

mesa *n* **butte**, hill, mound, tor, peak, cliff, rock formation. [➡MOUNTAINS AND HILLS; 1044]

mesh 1 *n* **net**, web, network, netting, webbing, wire, weave, lattice, trellis. [➡FASTENERS, LINKS, AND NETWORKS; 1246] 2 *v* **interlock**, interconnect, engage, fit together, enmesh, tangle, entangle, interlace, knit, go together, suit, complement. [➡FASTEN, LINK, AND JOIN; 409] *Opposite:* separate.

mesmeric *adj* **hypnotic** (*informal*), mesmerizing, fascinating, absorbing, attractive, compelling, compulsive, enthralling, riveting (*informal*), entrancing, spellbinding, captivating, alluring, appealing, enticing, magnetic, gripping, charming. [➡INTERESTING AND MEANINGFUL; 191] *Opposite:* boring.

mesmerize *v* **hypnotize**, fascinate, absorb, enthral, rivet (*informal*), entrance, spellbind, captivate, excite, charm, thrill. [➡APPEAL TO AND AROUSE INTEREST; 576] *Opposite:* bore.

mesmerized *adj* [➡PENSIVENESS AND INTEREST; 539]

mesmerizing *adj* **hypnotic** (*informal*), mesmeric, fascinating, absorbing, attractive, compelling, compulsive, enthralling, riveting (*informal*), entrancing, spellbinding, captivating, alluring, appealing, enticing, magnetic, gripping, charming. [➡INTERESTING AND MEANINGFUL; 191] *Opposite:* boring.

meson *type of* **elementary particle**. [➡ELEMENTARY PARTICLES; 1278]

mesosphere *n* [➡THE EARTH'S ATMOSPHERE; 1040]

mesquite *type of* **deciduous tree**. [➡DECIDUOUS TREES; 1028]

mess 1 *n* **untidiness**, muddle, chaos, confusion, clutter, jumble, disorder, disarray, state (*informal*), tip, heap, tangle. [➡DISORDER AND CHAOS; 246] *Opposite:* order. 2 *n* **fix**

(*informal*), tight spot, jam (*informal*), disaster, predicament, plight, bind, hole (*informal*), tight corner, trouble, scrape (*informal*), pickle (*informal*), stew (*informal*). [➡DIFFICULT SITUATIONS; 72] **3** *n* **canteen**, refectory, dining room, dining hall, restaurant, mess hall. [➡HOTELS, RESTAURANTS, AND CLUBS; 1081]

mess about (*informal*) **1** *v* **waste time**, mess around (*informal*), muck about (*informal*), lounge around, fool around, faff about (*informal*), mooch (*slang*), play. [➡LACK OF ACTIVITY; 343] *Opposite:* behave. **2** *v* **relax**, laze around, lounge around, chill out (*slang*), loll around, rest up. [➡LACK OF ACTIVITY; 343] **3** *v* **tamper**, fiddle, meddle, interfere, mess, muck about (*informal*), tinker, play. [➡CONTACT: TOUCH; 413] **4** *v* **hang around**, associate, go around, go out, spend time. [➡ESTABLISHING RELATIONSHIPS WITH OTHERS; 974] **5** *v* **joke**, have a laugh, mess around (*informal*), fool around, muck about (*informal*), play the fool, act the fool, lark around, tease, kid, clown around, clown, pull somebody's leg (*informal*), have a lark, josh (*informal*). [➡JOKES AND TEASING; 675] **6** *v* **mistreat**, treat badly, treat unfairly, muck about (*informal*), fool with, toy with. [➡WOUND A PERSON OR ANIMAL; 384] *Opposite:* look after. **7** *v* **potter**, tinker, dabble, fiddle, mess around (*informal*), play around, toy. [➡CONTACT: TOUCH; 413]

message **1** *n* **communication**, memo, memorandum, note, letter, missive, dispatch. [➡LETTERS AND WRITTEN MESSAGES; 585] **2** *n* **meaning**, significance, point, lesson, moral, idea, implication. [➡MEANING; 691]

mess around (*informal*) **1** *v* **waste time**, mess about (*informal*), muck about (*informal*), lounge around, fool around, faff about (*informal*), mooch (*slang*), play. [➡LACK OF ACTIVITY; 343] *Opposite:* behave. **2** *v* **relax**, laze around, lounge around, chill out (*slang*), loll around, rest up. [➡LACK OF ACTIVITY; 343] **3** *v* **tamper**, fiddle, meddle, interfere, mess, muck about (*informal*), tinker, play. [➡CONTACT: TOUCH; 413] **4** *v* **hang around**, associate, go around, go out, spend time. [➡ESTABLISHING RELATIONSHIPS WITH OTHERS; 974] **5** *v* **joke**, have a laugh, mess about (*informal*), fool around, muck about (*informal*), play the fool, act the fool, lark around, tease, kid, clown around, clown, pull somebody's leg (*informal*), have a lark, josh (*informal*). [➡JOKES AND TEASING; 675] **6** *v* **mistreat**, treat badly, treat unfairly, muck about (*informal*), fool with, toy with. [➡WOUND A PERSON OR ANIMAL; 384] **7** *v* **potter**, tinker, dabble, fiddle, mess about (*informal*), play around, toy, play around, toy with. [➡CONTACT: TOUCH; 413]

messed up (*informal*) *adj* [➡IN BAD REPAIR; 1233]

messenger *n* **courier**, envoy, go-between, emissary, herald, runner, dispatch rider. [➡MESSENGERS AND COURIERS; 852]

mess hall *type of* **eating place**. [➡HOTELS, RESTAURANTS, AND CLUBS; 1081]

messiah *n* **saviour**, champion, liberator, leader, defender, guardian angel (*informal*). [➡PEOPLE WHO ARE APPROVED OF; 955]

messiness **1** *n* **untidiness**, disorderliness, scruffiness, dirtiness, scrappiness, disarray, muddle, chaos, confusion, clutter, state (*informal*), disorganization, disorder. [➡DISORDER AND CHAOS; 246] *Opposite:* neatness. **2** *n* **unpleasantness**, acrimony, bitterness, awkwardness, complexity, nastiness, trickiness, difficulty, distress, painfulness. [➡EMOTIONALLY UNPLEASANT AND UPSETTING; 228]

mess-up (*informal*) *n* **muddle**, mix-up, mess, confusion, muddle-up, blunder, mistake, botch (*informal*), bungle (*informal*). [➡MISTAKES; 251]

mess up (*informal*) **1** *v* **spoil**, ruin, wreck, muck up (*informal*), botch, bungle (*informal*), scupper, blunder, make a mistake, flub (*US slang*). [➡MESS UP AND MAKE MISTAKES; 473] **2** *v* **make untidy**, muddle up, mix up, make a mess, clutter, dirty. [➡CREATE DISORDER AND CAUSE CHAOS; 359] *Opposite:* tidy up. **3** *v* **upset**, confuse, throw (*informal*), put out, put you off your stride, knock for six (*informal*). [➡CONFUSE AND BEWILDER; 572] *Opposite:* sort out.

messy **1** *adj* **untidy**, muddled, chaotic, confused, cluttered, in a state (*informal*), shambolic (*informal*), in disarray, disorganized, disordered, scruffy, dirty, scrappy. [➡DISORDER AND CHAOS; 246] *Opposite:* neat. **2** *adj* **unpleasant**, acrimonious, bitter, awkward, complicated, complex, nasty (*informal*), tricky, difficult, problematic, distressing, painful. [➡EMOTIONALLY UNPLEASANT AND UPSETTING; 228] *Opposite:* amicable.

metabolism *n* **breakdown**, absorption, digestion, uptake, use, metabolic rate. [➡EAT AND NOT EAT; 711]

metabolize *v* **break down**, absorb, digest, take up, make use of, process. [➡EAT AND NOT EAT; 711]

metal

◆ *types of metal*
aluminium, aluminum (*US*), brass, chromium, copper, gold, iron, lead, magnesium, mercury, molybdenum, nickel, pewter, platinum, radium, silver, stainless steel, steel, tin, titanium, tungsten, uranium, zinc

metallic **1** *adj* **metal**, iron, steel, copper, brass, stainless steel, gold, silver, pewter, platinum, titanium. [➡METALS; 1275] **2** *adj* **shiny**, reflective, glossy, glittering, polished. [➡VISUAL TEXTURE; 1220] *Opposite:* dull. **3** *adj* **tinny**, brassy, ringing, clanging, sharp, hard, harsh, unpleasant, jarring. [➡LOUD OR UNPLEASANT SOUNDS; 1265] *Opposite:* soft.

metallophone *type of* **percussion instrument**. [➡MUSICAL INSTRUMENTS; 910]

metamorphose *v* **change**, transform, transmute, mutate, alter, convert, become, turn, morph, transfigure. [➡CHANGE; 373]

metamorphosis *n* **transformation**, change, mutation, conversion, alteration, transmutation, transfiguration. [➡CHANGE; 373]

metaphor *n* **symbol**, image, figure of speech, allegory, comparison, representation. [➡FIGURES OF SPEECH; 674]

metaphoric *adj* [➡FALSE AND UNREAL; 174]

metaphorical *adj* **figurative**, symbolic, allegorical, emblematic, representational. [➡FALSE AND UNREAL; 174] *Opposite:* literal.

metaphysical *adj* **abstract**, theoretical, philosophical, hypothetical, conjectural, philosophic, supernatural, incorporeal (*formal*), speculative, ontological. [➡PHILOSOPHIES AND BELIEFS; 781]

meteor *type of* **heavenly body.** [➡CELESTIAL BODIES; 1060]

meteoric *adj* **dramatic**, sudden, swift, spectacular, impressive, rapid, brilliant, dazzling, speedy, quick, fast. [➡HAPPENING QUICKLY; 104] *Opposite:* gradual.

meteorite *type of* **heavenly body.** [➡CELESTIAL BODIES; 1060]

meteorological *adj* **climatological**, climatic, atmospheric, weather, weather-related, barometric. [➡WEATHER AND CLIMATE; 1049]

meteorology *n* **weather forecasting**, climatology, weather prediction, weathercasting. [➡WEATHER AND CLIMATE; 1049]

mete out *v* **give out**, deal out, allocate, impose, bestow (*formal*), exact, wreak, dispense, dole out (*informal*), dish out (*informal*). [➡DISPENSE, RATION, AND DISTRIBUTE; 435]

meter 1 *n* **measuring device**, gauge, counter. [➡MEASURING DEVICES; 1122] 2 *n* **rhythm**, beat, tempo, pulse, pattern, stress, cadence, measure, rhyme. [➡NOTES AND CHORDS; 909]

methane *type of* **gas.** [➡GASES; 1274]

method 1 *n* **means**, way, process, system, procedure, approach, practice, technique, modus. [➡WAYS OF DOING THINGS; 295] 2 *n* **orderliness**, organization, order, form, structure, pattern, design. [➡WAYS OF DOING THINGS; 295]

methodical *adj* **systematic**, logical, disciplined, precise, orderly, regular, meticulous, careful, painstaking. [➡CAUTIOUS AND CAREFUL; 283] *Opposite:* haphazard.

methodological *adj* **procedural**, organizational, working, running, operational, practical. [➡ORDER AND ORGANIZATION; 207]

methodology *n* **organizing system**, practice, procedure, organization, policy, method, approach, style, system. [➡WAYS OF DOING THINGS; 295]

meticulous *adj* **careful**, scrupulous, thorough, particular, painstaking, duteous, punctilious, assiduous, conscientious. [➡HARD-WORKING AND COMMITTED; 501] *Opposite:* careless.

See Compare and Contrast at **careful**.

meticulously *adv* **exactly**, accurately, precisely, squarely, methodically, punctiliously, fastidiously. [➡CAUTIOUS AND CAREFUL; 283] *Opposite:* carelessly.

meticulousness *n* **care**, thoroughness, strictness, diligence, perfectionism, precision, exactness, fastidiousness, punctiliousness, scrupulousness. [➡HARD-WORKING AND COMMITTED; 501] *Opposite:* carelessness.

métier *n* **vocation**, occupation, profession, calling, sphere, pursuit, lifework (*US*). [➡PROFESSIONS; 845]

metro *type of* **railway.** [➡RAILWAYS; 1106]

metronome *n* [➡CLOCKS AND TIMERS; 1125]

metropolis *n* **city**, conurbation, capital, metropolitan area, megalopolis, municipality. [➡HUMAN SETTLEMENTS; 1069]

See Compare and Contrast at **city**.

metropolitan *adj* **city**, urban, municipal, civic. [➡HUMAN SETTLEMENTS; 1069]

mettle *n* **courage**, bravery, determination, spirit, grit, nerve, pluck, resolve, valour, vigour, guts (*slang*), cojones (*US slang*). [➡COURAGE; 499]

See Compare and Contrast at **courage**.

mettlesome *adj* **lively**, spirited, high-spirited, courageous, plucky, frisky, energetic, fiery, spunky (*informal*). [➡ENERGY AND ENTHUSIASM; 497] *Opposite:* lethargic.

mew 1 *v* **cry**, miaow, sob, whimper, yowl, whine, howl, screech, wail. [➡SOUND EMISSION BY ANIMALS OR BIRDS; 365] 2 *n* **miaow**, cry, sob, whimper, yowl, whine, howl, screech, wail. [➡SOUNDS MADE BY ANIMALS; 1260]

mews *type of* **minor road.** [➡ROADS; 1105]

meze *part of* **meal.** [➡MEALS AND PARTS OF MEALS; 1168]

mezzanine *n* **mezzanine floor**, entresol, storey, level. [➡STAIRS AND STOREYS; 1101]

mezzanine floor *n* [➡STAIRS AND STOREYS; 1101]

mezzo-soprano *type of* **musical register.** [➡MUSICAL TERMS; 912]

miaow 1 *n* **mew**, purr, cry, caterwaul, whimper, yowl, whine, howl, screech, wail. [➡SOUNDS MADE BY ANIMALS; 1260] 2 *v* **cry**, purr, mew, caterwaul, whimper, yowl, whine, howl, screech, wail. [➡SOUND EMISSION BY ANIMALS OR BIRDS; 365] 3 *see* **meow**.

miasma *n* **mist**, fog, haze, cloud, murk, steam, pall, film, brume (*literary*), mistiness. [➡GASES; 1274]

mica *type of* **mineral.** [➡MINERALS; 1276]

microbe *n* **microorganism**, bug (*informal*), germ. [➡MICRO-ORGANISMS, FUNGI, AND ALGAE; 1023]

microbial *adj* [➡MICROORGANISMS, FUNGI, AND ALGAE; 1023]

microbiological *adj* **biological**, bacteriological, fungal, viral, microparasitic. [➡BIOLOGICAL SCIENCES; 1037]

microbiology *type of* **bioscience.** [➡BIOLOGICAL SCIENCES; 1037]

microchip *type of* **hardware.** [➡COMPUTERS AND COMPUTING; 1126]

microcomputer *type of* **computer.** [➡COMPUTERS AND COMPUTING; 1126]

microcosm *n* **small-scale version**, version in miniature, miniature copy, miniature. [➡REPRESENTATIONS AND GENERAL EXAMPLES; 65] *Opposite:* macrocosm.

microfiche *type of* **photographic equipment.** [➡PHOTOGRAPHY AND PHOTOGRAPHIC EQUIPMENT; 1121]

microfilm *type of* **photographic equipment.** [➡PHOTOGRAPHY AND PHOTOGRAPHIC EQUIPMENT; 1121]

microlight *type of* **civil aircraft.** [➡AIRCRAFT; 1147]

micromanage *v* **interfere**, intervene, nitpick, breathe down somebody's neck, control, meddle. [➡AVOID, PREVENT, LIMIT, AND CONTROL; 278]

micrometer *type of* **measuring device.** [➡MEASURING DEVICES; 1122]

microorganism *n* **microbe**, bug (*informal*), germ. [➡MICROORGANISMS, FUNGI, AND ALGAE; 1023]

microorganism

◆ *types of microorganism*
amoeba, bacteriophage, bacterium, botulinum, candida, ciliate, coccus, E. coli, flagellate, listeria, mycoplasma, protozoan, rhizopod, salmonella, spirillum, spirochaete, staphylococcus, stentor, streptococcus, virus

microphone *part of* **audio equipment.** [➡AUDIO EQUIPMENT; 1138]

microprocessor *type of* **hardware.** [➡COMPUTERS AND COMPUTING; 1126]

microscope *type of* **optical instrument.** [➡OPTICAL INSTRUMENTS; 1123]

microscopic *adj* **tiny**, minute, infinitesimal, minuscule, atomic, mini (*informal*), minuscular. [➡SMALL; 1194] *Opposite:* gigantic.

microscopically *adv* **meticulously**, minutely, closely, carefully, painstakingly, scrupulously, diligently, thoroughly. [➡CAUTIOUS AND CAREFUL; 283]

microwave 1 *v* **heat**, heat up, warm, warm up, warm through, cook, zap (*informal*), nuke (*informal*). [➡COOKING AND FOOD PREPARATION; 354] 2 *type of* **appliance.** [➡HOUSEHOLD APPLIANCES; 1116]

microwaved *adj* [➡STATE OF PREPARED FOOD; 1170]

microwave oven *type of* **appliance.** [➡HOUSEHOLD APPLIANCES; 1116]

mid *adj* **middle**, median, medium, midway, central, halfway, equidistant, medial, midmost. [➡RELATIVE LOCATION; 162] *Opposite:* extreme.

midair 1 *adj* **air**, airborne, in-flight, mid-flight, midcourse. [➡GENERAL LOCATIONS; 159] 2 *adj* **in the air**, up in the air, in the sky, overhead, above the ground, aloft, high up. [➡GENERAL LOCATIONS; 159]

midday *n* **noon**, noontime, twelve noon, lunchtime, the middle of the day. [➡TIMES OF DAY; 87]

middle 1 *n* **centre**, heart, focus, core, hub, central point, focal point. [➡CENTRAL PARTS OF PHYSICAL OBJECTS; 1250] 2 *n* **midpoint**, halfway point, median, mean, norm. [➡CENTRAL PARTS OF PHYSICAL OBJECTS; 1250] 3 *adj* **central**, mid, internal, intermediate, inside, medium, interior, inner, equidistant, midmost. [➡RELATIVE LOCATION; 162] 4 *adj* **median**, average, intermediate, medium, middling, moderate. [➡ACCEPTABLE AND PASSABLE; 220]

middlebrow (*informal*) *adj* **unintellectual**, conventional, unchallenging, middle-of-the-road, mediocre, unexceptional, bourgeois. [➡NEGATIVE INTELLECTUAL CHARACTERISTICS; 526]

middle-class *adj* [➡CLASS STATUS; 889]

middle finger *part of* **arm or hand.** [➡ARM AND HAND; 696]

middleman 1 *n* **trader**, distributor, wholesaler, retailer, broker, shopkeeper. [➡BUSINESS PEOPLE; 794] 2 *n* **intermediary**, agent, go-between, mediator, negotiator, envoy. [➡REPRESENTATIVES AND PATRONS; 968]

middle name *n* [➡NAME AND DESCRIBE; 666]

middle-of-the-road *adj* **normal**, mainstream, majority, standard, typical, run-of-the-mill, ordinary. [➡ORDINARINESS; 245]

middle school *type of* **school.** [➡EDUCATIONAL INSTITUTIONS; 813]

middling 1 *adj* **usual**, typical, ordinary, average, run-of-the-mill, moderate, medium. [➡ORDINARINESS; 245] 2 *adj* **adequate**, all right, so-so (*informal*), okay (*informal*), tolerable, fair, passable, average, mediocre, modest, satisfactory, unexceptional. [➡ACCEPTABLE AND PASSABLE; 220] *Opposite:* exceptional.

midge *type of* **flying insect.** [➡FLYING INSECTS; 1013]

midnight *n* **twelve o'clock**, twelve midnight, middle of the night, night, nighttime, the wee small hours, the wee hours. [➡TIMES OF DAY; 87]

midnight blue *type of* **blue.** [➡COLOURS; 1223]

midpoint *n* **centre**, middle, nucleus, median, mean. [➡CENTRAL PARTS OF PHYSICAL OBJECTS; 1250]

midriff *n* **waist**, stomach, tummy (*informal*), tum (*informal*), belly, middle, abdomen, diaphragm, love handles (*informal*). [➡TORSO; 694]

midst *n* **middle**, centre, heart, focus, core, hub. [➡CENTRAL PARTS OF PHYSICAL OBJECTS; 1250]

midstream *adv* **halfway through**, midway, in the middle, in full flow. [➡HAPPENING AND IN PROGRESS; 32]

midsummer *n* **middle of the summer**, summertime, summer solstice, dog days, the height of summer. [➡TIMES OF YEAR; 88] *Opposite:* midwinter.

midway 1 *adv* **central**, middle, mid, halfway. [➡GENERAL LOCATIONS; 159] 2 *adv* **halfway**, in the middle, midstream, in full flow, halfway through. [➡HAPPENING AND IN PROGRESS; 32]

midweek *n* **the middle of the week**, the midweek period, weekdays. [➡TIMES OF YEAR; 88]

midwife toad *type of* **amphibian.** [➡AMPHIBIANS; 1008]

midwinter *n* **middle of winter**, wintertime, winter solstice, the winter months, the depths of winter. [➡TIMES OF YEAR; 88] *Opposite:* midsummer.

mien (*literary*) *n* **appearance**, bearing, expression, manner, look, aspect, demeanour, air, deportment (*formal*), presence. [➡TEMPERAMENT AND BEHAVIOUR; 493]

miff (*informal*) *v* **irritate**, upset, annoy, vex, peeve, irk. [➡ANGER AND ANNOY; 570]

miffed (*informal*) *adj* **annoyed**, peeved (*informal*), displeased, put out, chagrined, bothered, irked, narked (*informal*), hurt, cheesed off (*informal*), perturbed, agitated. [➡SADNESS, DISTRESS, AND DESPAIR; 540]

might *n* **strength**, power, force, capacity, valour, potency, powerfulness, influence. [➡ STRENGTH; 202]

mightily *adv* **tremendously**, greatly, extremely, awfully, decidedly, exceedingly, terribly, hugely, strongly, powerfully. [➡ TO A GREAT EXTENT; 130] *Opposite:* slightly.

mighty 1 *adj* **powerful**, strong, forceful, potent, great, almighty, impressive, grand, influential. [➡ STRENGTH; 202] *Opposite:* weak. 2 *adj* **huge**, enormous, vast, expansive, massive, monumental, colossal, immense, gigantic, large, titanic, gargantuan. [➡ LARGE; 1192] *Opposite:* insignificant.

migrant 1 *n* **wanderer**, traveller, nomad, itinerant, wayfarer (*literary*). [➡ NOMADIC AND ROOTLESS LIFESTYLES; 884] *Opposite:* resident. 2 *n* **refugee**, immigrant, emigrant, asylum seeker. [➡ PEOPLE LIVING AWAY FROM HOME; 887] 3 *adj* **migratory**, travelling, wandering, drifting, itinerant, nomadic, seasonal, mobile. [➡ NOMADIC AND ROOTLESS LIFESTYLES; 884] *Opposite:* resident.

migrate *v* **travel**, journey, wander, drift, roam, move about, transfer, voyage, rove, trek, move around. [➡ TRAVEL: WAYS OF TRAVELLING; 321]

migration *n* **relocation**, immigration, passage, exodus, movement, journey, voyage, trek, resettlement. [➡ TRAVEL: JOURNEYS AND TRIPS; 319]

migratory *adj* **travelling**, wandering, drifting, migrant, itinerant, nomadic, seasonal. [➡ NOMADIC AND ROOTLESS LIFESTYLES; 884]

mild 1 *adj* **gentle**, kind, soft, easygoing, meek, placid, calm, serene, docile, lenient, peaceable. [➡ GENEROSITY AND KINDNESS; 496] *Opposite:* harsh. 2 *adj* **weak**, bland, tasteless, insipid, flat, distasteful. [➡ TASTE; 704] *Opposite:* strong. 3 *adj* **slight**, unimportant, insignificant, trifling, trivial, minor. [➡ UNIMPORTANT AND UNNECESSARY; 239] *Opposite:* serious. 4 *adj* **warm**, balmy, pleasant, clement, temperate, moderate, benign. [➡ HOT WEATHER; 1050]

mildew *type of* **fungus**. [➡ MICROORGANISMS, FUNGI, AND ALGAE; 1023]

mildewed *adj* [➡ DECAYING OR INFESTED; 1235]

mildewy *adj* [➡ DECAYING OR INFESTED; 1235]

mildly 1 *adv* **gently**, kindly, meekly, placidly, calmly, serenely, leniently. [➡ GENEROSITY AND KINDNESS; 496] *Opposite:* harshly. 2 *adv* **slightly**, a little, somewhat, a touch, unimportantly, insignificantly, a bit (*informal*). [➡ TO A CERTAIN EXTENT; 134] *Opposite:* considerably.

mild-mannered *adj* **gentle**, kind, polite, good-natured, placid, calm, easygoing, affable, amiable, genial. [➡ GOOD MANNERS AND SOCIAL SKILLS; 521] *Opposite:* fierce.

mildness *n* **gentleness**, kindness, leniency, tenderness, warmth, mercy, compassion, consideration, clemency. [➡ PEACEFULNESS AND GENTLENESS; 215] *Opposite:* harshness.

mileage 1 *n* **distance**, travelling distance, range, extent, way, stretch. [➡ AREA AND RANGE; 111] 2 *n* (*informal*) **benefit**, profit, advantage, usefulness, assistance, gain, good. [➡ SOURCE OF HAPPINESS, PLEASURE, OR IMPROVEMENT; 210]

mileometer *type of* **measuring device**. [➡ MEASURING DEVICES; 1122]

milepost *n* **marker**, sign, mark, indicator, signpost, landmark, milestone. [➡ ANCIENT MANMADE STRUCTURES; 1088]

miles (*informal*) 1 *n* **a long way**, a great distance, miles and miles, miles away, a long way away, a long way off. [➡ DISTANCE; 161] 2 *adv* **much**, very much, lots, loads (*informal*), heaps (*informal*), a lot, far, considerably. [➡ MANY, MUCH, LARGE AMOUNT; 117]

miles away *adj* [➡ NEUTRALITY AND INDIFFERENCE; 554]

milestone 1 *n* **sign**, signpost, indicator, mark, marker, milepost. [➡ DRAWINGS, CHARTS AND TABLES; 595] 2 *n* **landmark**, highlight, high point, achievement, record, goal, target, objective, aim, purpose, ambition. [➡ DECISIVE MOMENTS; 44]

milieu (*formal*) *n* **setting**, environment, scene, background, surroundings, situation, location, locale, ambience, atmosphere, climate. [➡ PLACE; 1064]

militancy *n* **aggressiveness**, combativeness, belligerency, forcefulness, violence, pugnaciousness. [➡ REBELLIOUSNESS AND DISOBEDIENCE; 566]

militant 1 *adj* **confrontational**, aggressive, radical, revolutionary, combative, rebellious, belligerent, bellicose, pugnacious. [➡ REBELLIOUSNESS AND DISOBEDIENCE; 566] *Opposite:* peaceable. 2 *n* **activist**, revolutionary, radical, fighter, supporter, rebel. [➡ UNCOOPERATIVE OR REBELLIOUS PERSON; 567]

militarism *n* **belligerence**, aggression, aggressiveness, pugnaciousness, bellicosity, hostility, hawkishness. [➡ PHILOSOPHIES AND BELIEFS; 781]

militarist *adj* **bellicose**, militaristic, aggressive, warmongering, martial, military, belligerent, pugnacious, hawkish, warlike. [➡ PHILOSOPHIES AND BELIEFS; 781] *Opposite:* pacific.

militaristic *adj* **militarist**, martial, bellicose, aggressive, warmongering, military, belligerent, pugnacious, warlike, hawkish. [➡ PHILOSOPHIES AND BELIEFS; 781] *Opposite:* pacific.

militarized *adj* **mobilized**, armed, battle-ready, prepared, organized, trained, equipped, on a war footing. [➡ MILITARY; 829]

military 1 *adj* **armed**, martial, soldierly, fighting. [➡ MILITARY; 829] *Opposite:* civilian. 2 *n* **services**, forces, armed forces, military establishment, army, navy, air force. [➡ THE ARMED FORCES; 827]

military attaché *n* [➡ MILITARY PERSONNEL; 828]

military establishment *n* [➡ THE ARMED FORCES; 827]

military government *n* [➡ STYLES AND SYSTEMS OF GOVERNMENT; 806]

military rule *n* [➡ STYLES AND SYSTEMS OF GOVERNMENT; 806]

military unit *n* [➡ THE ARMED FORCES; 827]

militate *v* **influence**, inspire, affect, work, act on, count, have an effect on, weigh. [➡ CHANGE; 373]

militia *n* **territorial army**, reservists, local militia, paramilitaries, mercenaries, soldiers, guerrillas, soldiers of fortune, legionnaires. [➡ THE ARMED FORCES; 827]

milk (*informal*) *v* **exploit**, drain, bleed (*informal*), tap, take advantage of, cash in on, profit from, benefit from, extract, make the most of. [➡ MAKE GOOD USE OF SOMETHING; 474]

milk tooth *type of* **tooth**. [➡THE MOUTH; 703]

milky *adj* **cloudy**, chalky, creamy, pale, translucent, whitish, opaque. [➡VISUAL TEXTURE; 1220] *Opposite:* clear.

Milky Way *n* [➡THE SOLAR SYSTEM AND ASTRONOMY; 1059]

mill 1 *type of* **factory**. [➡INDUSTRIAL BUILDINGS; 1086] 2 *type of* **utensil**. [➡TABLEWARE, CUTLERY, AND KITCHENWARE; 861]

millennial *adj* **utopian**, idealistic, visionary, romantic, optimistic, futuristic, millenarian, millenary, revolutionary. [➡EXTRAORDINARY: UNCOMMON; 206]

millennium *n* **epoch**, era, age, period, time. [➡EPOCHS AND ERAS; 89]

millet *type of* **cereal**. [➡CEREAL FOODS; 1177]

millionaire *n* **tycoon**, mogul, magnate, billionaire, baron. [➡RICH PEOPLE; 895] *Opposite:* pauper.

millions *n* **lots**, masses, loads (*informal*), heaps (*informal*), oodles (*informal*), many. [➡MANY, MUCH, LARGE AMOUNT; 117]

millipede *type of* **land invertebrate**. [➡LAND INVERTEBRATE; 1021]

millpond *n* [➡THE COUNTRYSIDE AND OUTDOOR SPACES; 1070]

millstone *n* **burden**, weight, dead weight, albatross, shackle, chain, load, responsibility. [➡PROBLEM; 257]

mime 1 *v* **act out**, represent, simulate, express, symbolize. [➡REPRESENT SOMETHING OR SOMEBODY; 59] 2 *v* **mimic**, satirize, caricature, parody, take off (*informal*), ape, mock, ridicule. [➡PRETEND AND MIMIC; 60] 3 *type of* **entertainer**. [➡WORKERS IN ENTERTAINMENT AND MEDIA; 873]

mimeograph *n* [➡SYMBOLS, SIGNS, AND NUMBERS; 597]

mimetic *adj* **imitative**, derivative, copied, representational, simulated, faked. [➡SIMILARITY; 149] *Opposite:* original.

mimic 1 *v* **caricature**, ape, satirize, parody, mock, ridicule, make fun of. [➡JOKES AND TEASING; 675] 2 *v* **imitate**, impersonate, take off (*informal*), represent, mirror, simulate, copy, copycat (*informal*). [➡PRETEND AND MIMIC; 60] 3 *n* **impersonator**, impressionist, imitator, copycat (*informal*), caricaturist, parodist, satirist, simulator. [➡JOKERS AND TEASES; 676]

See Compare and Contrast at **imitate**.

mimicry *n* **imitation**, impersonation, impression, parody, caricature, simulation, act. [➡REPRESENTATIONS AND GENERAL EXAMPLES; 65]

mimosa *type of* **deciduous tree**. [➡DECIDUOUS TREES; 1028]

minaret *n* **turret**, tower, spire. [➡TOWERS; 1098]

mince 1 *v* **shred**, cut up, chop up, crumble, hash, grind, chop. [➡TEAR, BREAK, AND CUT; 361] 2 *n* **mincemeat**, minced meat, minced beef, ground beef, hamburger (*US*). [➡TYPES AND CUTS OF MEAT; 1176]

minced beef *type of* **processed meat**. [➡TYPES AND CUTS OF MEAT; 1176]

minced meat *type of* **processed meat**. [➡TYPES AND CUTS OF MEAT; 1176]

mincemeat 1 *n* **mince**, minced meat, minced beef, ground beef, ground meat, hamburger. [➡TYPES AND CUTS OF MEAT; 1176] 2 *type of* **preserve**. [➡SUGAR AND PRESERVES; 1183]

mince pie *type of* **cake**. [➡CAKES, BISCUITS, AND DESSERTS; 1180]

mincer *type of* **utensil**. [➡TABLEWARE, CUTLERY, AND KITCHENWARE; 861]

mincing *adj* **affected**, foppish, dainty, prim, fussy, precious [➡AGILITY OF THE BODY; 477]

mind 1 *n* **brain**, intellect, wits, brains, brainpower, psyche, mentality, intelligence. [➡DESCRIBING SOMEBODY'S INTELLECT; 524] 2 *n* **attention**, concentration, thoughts, awareness, cognizance (*formal*), observance, notice. [➡ATTENTION AND ATTENTIVENESS; 764] 3 *n* **point of view**, mentality, opinion, thinking, view, viewpoint, approach, attitude, belief, conviction, sentiment. [➡POINT OF VIEW; 768] 4 *n* **thinker**, brain (*informal*), intellect, intellectual, boffin (*informal*), egghead (*informal*). [➡TALENTED OR INTELLIGENT PERSON; 529] 5 *v* **pay attention**, take care, beware, heed, be careful, watch out, look out. [➡PAY ATTENTION; 766] 6 *v* **object**, care, take offence, demur, resent, disagree, disapprove, be bothered, be offended. [➡BE CONCERNED AND CARE; 582] *Opposite:* approve. 7 *v* **look after**, tend, care for, attend to, take care of, watch, look out for, guard, keep an eye on. [➡TAKE CARE OF AND SPOIL; 301]

mind-bending (*informal*) *adj* **overwhelming**, mind-boggling (*informal*), complex, difficult, complicated, puzzling, baffling, confusing, challenging. [➡DIFFICULTY AND COMPLEXITY; 243] *Opposite:* simple.

mind-blowing (*informal*) *adj* **astonishing**, amazing, incredible, inconceivable, astounding, stupefying, staggering. [➡EXTRAORDINARY: AMAZING; 205] *Opposite:* unexceptional.

mind-boggling (*informal*) *adj* **overwhelming**, mind-bending (*informal*), complex, difficult, complicated, puzzling, baffling, confusing, challenging. [➡DIFFICULTY AND COMPLEXITY; 243] *Opposite:* simple.

minded (*formal*) *adj* **inclined**, of a mind to, intent, set, prepared, ready, willing. [➡THE WILL AND WILLINGNESS; 564] *Opposite:* disinclined.

minder 1 *n* **child minder**, carer, sitter, babysitter. [➡PEOPLE WHO GUARD AND PROTECT; 846] 2 *n* (*informal*) **guard**, guardian, escort, lookout, attendant, bodyguard, heavy, watcher, protector, handler. [➡PEOPLE WHO GUARD AND PROTECT; 846]

mindful *adj* **watchful**, aware, wary, heedful, alert, careful, attentive, chary, sensible (*formal*), thoughtful, conscious. [➡POSITIVE IMPATIENCE, ENTHUSIASM, AND ALERTNESS; 538] *Opposite:* unwary.

See Compare and Contrast at **aware**.

mindfulness *n* [➡POSITIVE IMPATIENCE, ENTHUSIASM, AND ALERTNESS; 538]

mindless 1 *adj* **tedious**, dull, boring, monotonous, mechanical, undemanding, humdrum, mind-numbing. [➡BORING AND UNINTERESTING; 235] *Opposite:* enthralling. 2 *adj* **senseless**, gratuitous, unnecessary, pointless, needless, meaningless, uncalled-for, purposeless, motiveless. [➡BAD AND BADLY; 224]

mindlessly 1 *adv* **automatically**, mechanically, unconsciously, unthinkingly, robotically, instinctively, routinely. [➡ INCAUTIOUS AND CARELESS; 284] 2 *adv* **senselessly**, stupidly, thoughtlessly, carelessly, foolishly, idiotically, crassly, asininely. [➡ BAD AND BADLY; 224] *Opposite:* thoughtfully.

mindlessness *n* [➡ INCORRECT AND ERRONEOUS; 223]

mind-numbing *adj* **boring**, dull, tedious, tiresome, wearisome, monotonous, tiring, humdrum, uninteresting, mindless. [➡ BORING AND UNINTERESTING; 235] *Opposite:* interesting.

mindset *n* **attitude**, outlook, mind, mentality, way of thinking, approach, frame of mind, belief, conviction. [➡ POINT OF VIEW; 768]

mind your own business *v* **keep your nose out of it**, keep yourself to yourself, keep off, keep out of it, keep it to yourself (*US*), butt out (*US slang*), mind your own beeswax (*US*). [➡ NOT PAY ATTENTION; 765]

mine 1 *n* **pit**, excavation, colliery, coalfield, coalmine, coalface, pithead. [➡ INDUSTRIAL BUILDINGS; 1086] 2 *n* **source**, repository, fund, gold mine, store, abundance, reserve, hoard, wealth. [➡ MANY, MUCH, LARGE AMOUNT; 117] *Opposite:* dearth. 3 *v* **extract**, excavate, quarry, dig, dig out, hew, unearth, burrow, drill, scoop. [➡ CAUSE TO APPEAR; 5] 4 *type of* **explosive weapon.** [➡ EXPLOSIVES; 1154]

minefield *n* **problem**, trial, test, ordeal, hazard, obstacle, block. [➡ DIFFICULT SITUATIONS; 72]

miner *n* **tunneller**, sapper, coalminer, collier, driller, mineworker, pit worker. [➡ FARMERS, GARDENERS, AND MANUAL WORKERS; 849]

mineral *type of* **nutrient.** [➡ FOOD COMPONENTS; 1187]

mineral

◆ *types of mineral*
arsenic, asbestos, asphalt, bauxite, carbon, clay, coal, coke, feldspar, fluorite, graphite, gypsum, jet, kaolin, lime, mica, pyrite, quartz, silicate, sulphur

minestrone *type of* **soup.** [➡ SOUP; 1185]

minesweeper *type of* **military vessel.** [➡ SHIPS AND BOATS; 1149]

mingle 1 *v* **mix**, blend, fuse, join, unite, fold in, stir in, dilute. [➡ COMBINE AND MIX; 401] *Opposite:* separate. 2 *v* **circulate**, associate, intermingle, socialize, mix, blend, intersperse, move around. [➡ ESTABLISHING RELATIONSHIPS WITH OTHERS; 974]

mingy (*informal*) *adj* **mean**, stingy (*informal*), ungenerous, inadequate, sparse, scant, slight, insufficient, meagre. [➡ TOO FEW, TOO LITTLE; 120] *Opposite:* generous.

mini *adj* **small**, miniature, baby, diminutive, tiny, minute, little, minuscule. [➡ SMALL; 1194] *Opposite:* maxi.

miniature *adj* **small-scale**, small, tiny, minute, little, mini (*informal*), baby, minuscule, diminutive. [➡ SMALL; 1194]

miniaturist *n* [➡ ARTISTS; 900]

miniaturization *n* **reduction**, shrinking, contraction, diminishment. [➡ CHANGE OF SIZE: SMALLER; 394] *Opposite:* enlargement.

miniaturize *v* **reduce**, scale down, shrink, contract, diminish. [➡ CHANGE OF SIZE: SMALLER; 394] *Opposite:* enlarge.

minibar *n* **bar**, fridge, cupboard, cooler, cocktail cabinet. [➡ HOUSEHOLD APPLIANCES; 1116]

minibreak (*informal*) *n* **long weekend**, weekend, holiday, break, vacation, getaway. [➡ PERIOD OF REST; 91]

minibus *type of* **public service vehicle.** [➡ VEHICLES; 1144]

minicab *type of* **commercial or industrial vehicle.** [➡ VEHICLES; 1144]

minicomputer *type of* **computer.** [➡ COMPUTERS AND COMPUTING; 1126]

minimal 1 *adj* **negligible**, trifling, slight, nominal, token, insignificant, marginal. [➡ FEW, LITTLE, SMALL AMOUNT; 119] *Opposite:* large. 2 *adj* **least**, smallest, minimum, tiniest, minutest, infinitesimal. [➡ SMALL; 1194] *Opposite:* maximum.

minimalism 1 *n* **simplicity**, plainness, unfussiness, cleanness, austereness, starkness, restraint. [➡ EASE AND SIMPLICITY; 201] *Opposite:* elaboration. 2 *type of* **20th-century art movement.** [➡ ARTISTIC MOVEMENTS AND STYLES; 899]

minimalist *adj* **simple**, uncluttered, understated, discreet, plain, unfussy, austere, restrained, stark, clean. [➡ EASE AND SIMPLICITY; 201] *Opposite:* baroque.

minimally *adv* **slightly**, negligibly, triflingly, marginally, nominally, insignificantly. [➡ TO A CERTAIN EXTENT; 134] *Opposite:* significantly.

minimize 1 *v* **minimalize**, diminish, curtail, lessen, abate (*formal or literary*), reduce. [➡ CHANGE OF INTENSITY: LESS; 396] *Opposite:* maximize. 2 *v* **play down**, make light of, reduce, dismiss, shrug off, brush off, belittle, disparage, write off (*informal*). [➡ UNDERDO SOMETHING; 292] *Opposite:* exaggerate.

minimum 1 *n* **least**, bare minimum, smallest amount, iota, jot, modicum, smidgen (*informal*), speck. [➡ FEW, LITTLE, SMALL AMOUNT; 119] *Opposite:* maximum. 2 *adj* **smallest**, least, lowest, tiniest, minutest, slightest, bottom. [➡ SMALL; 1194] *Opposite:* maximum.

minion *n* **follower**, assistant, hanger-on, crony (*disapproving*), underling, subordinate, gofer (*informal*), slave, dogsbody (*informal*), sycophant, toady. [➡ SUBORDINATES AND ASSISTANTS; 966] *Opposite:* superior.

miniseries *n* **series**, serial, soap, drama, serialization. [➡ TELEVISION AND RADIO; 607]

miniskirt *type of* **skirt.** [➡ GARMENTS AND OUTFITS; 865]

minister 1 *n* **priest**, vicar, rector, parson, reverend, clergyman, clergywoman, cleric. [➡ RELIGIOUS PEOPLE; 779] 2 *v* (*formal*) **attend**, look after, care, tend, nurse, wait on, comfort, aid, support. [➡ TAKE CARE OF AND SPOIL; 301] *Opposite:* neglect.

ministerial *adj* **governmental**, parliamentary, cabinet, official, legislative, departmental, executive. [➡ GOVERNMENT AND POLITICS; 805]

ministration (*formal*) *n* **care**, support, attention, nurture, aid, assistance, comfort, help, treatment, service. [➡KIND ACTION OR BEHAVIOUR; 296] *Opposite:* neglect.

ministry *n* **office**, bureau, department, agency, organization, government. [➡PLACE OF EMPLOYMENT; 832]

minivan *type of* **car.** [➡BIKES, CARS, AND CARRIAGES; 1148]

mink *type of* **small mammal.** [➡SMALL MAMMAL; 990]

minke whale *type of* **whale.** [➡WHALE; 991]

minnow 1 *n* **small fry**, little man, little guy, spear carrier (*informal*), nobody, sprat. [➡LAZY OR UNSUCCESSFUL PEOPLE; 948] **2** *type of* **freshwater fish.** [➡FRESHWATER FISH; 1010]

minor 1 *adj* **slight**, small, negligible, inconsequential, trivial, unimportant, trifling, petty, inconsiderable, minimal, marginal, insignificant. [➡FEW, LITTLE, SMALL AMOUNT; 119] *Opposite:* major. **2** *adj* **lesser**, inferior, junior, secondary, lower, insignificant, minor-league (*US*). [➡INFERIORITY; 154] *Opposite:* major. **3** *n* **juvenile**, youth, adolescent, child, teenager, youngster. [➡CHILD OR YOUTH; 945] *Opposite:* adult.

minority 1 *n* **section**, faction, interest group, subgroup, sector, component, element. [➡GROUPS WITH A COMMON INTEREST; 938] **2** *adj* **alternative**, underground, marginal, sectional, pressure, smaller, lesser. [➡BELONGING OR RELATING TO INDIVIDUALS; 944] *Opposite:* majority.

minster *type of* **church.** [➡RELIGIOUS BUILDINGS; 1084]

minstrel *n* **musician**, troubadour, wandering minstrel, player, entertainer, singer, songster, versifier, poet. [➡MUSICIANS AND SINGERS; 908]

mint 1 *type of* **herb.** [➡HERBS AND SPICES; 1174] **2** *n* (*informal*) **fortune**, packet (*informal*), bundle (*slang*), pile (*informal*), millions, billions. [➡LARGE AMOUNT OF MONEY; 141] *Opposite:* pittance. **3** *v* **cast**, issue, imprint, make, strike, coin, produce, stamp. [➡MANUFACTURE; 350] **4** *type of* **factory.** [➡INDUSTRIAL BUILDINGS; 1086]

mint sauce *type of* **seasonings, sauces, and dips.** [➡SEASONINGS AND SAUCES; 1173]

minuet *type of* **dance.** [➡DANCE; 903]

minus 1 *prep* **less**, take away, excluding, reduced by, with the subtraction of. [➡NOT; 135] *Opposite:* plus. **2** *prep* **without**, lacking, excluding, exclusive of, excepting (*formal*), with the exception of, sans (*literary or humorous*), wanting. [➡LACK OF POSSESSION; 446] *Opposite:* including. **3** *n* **deficiency**, loss, drop, fall, decrease, difference, deduction. [➡LESS; 124] *Opposite:* addition. **4** *n* **disadvantage**, detriment, handicap, hindrance, drawback, demerit. [➡NUISANCES; 254] *Opposite:* plus.

minuscule *adj* **tiny**, minute, microscopic, infinitesimal, little, miniature, diminutive. [➡SMALL; 1194] *Opposite:* gigantic.

minute 1 *n* **moment**, instant, second, flash, sec (*informal*), jiffy (*informal*), tick (*informal*), mo (*informal*). *Opposite:* ages. (*informal*). [➡SHORT PERIOD OF TIME; 93] **2** *v* **record**, summarize, write down, précis, transcribe, log, report, take notes. [➡RECORD SOMETHING; 372] **3** *adj* **miniature**, tiny, minuscule, microscopic, infinitesimal, little, small, diminutive, insignificant. [➡SMALL; 1194] *Opposite:* enormous. **4** *adj* **close**, detailed, thorough, exhaustive, painstaking, meticulous, exact, precise. [➡EXACT; 204] *Opposite:* cursory.

minutely *adv* **closely**, thoroughly, carefully, meticulously, painstakingly, microscopically, exhaustively, exactly, in great detail, precisely, with a fine-tooth comb. [➡CAUTIOUS AND CAREFUL; 283] *Opposite:* cursorily.

minuteness *n* **smallness**, tininess, shortness, compactness. [➡SMALL; 1194]

minutes *n* **notes**, record, proceedings, transcript, transcription, summary, résumé, follow-up, log, report. [➡RECORDS; 586]

minutiae *n* **details**, niceties, intricacies, particulars, ins and outs, workings. [➡BASIC DETAILS; 689] *Opposite:* gist.

miracle *n* **wonder**, phenomenon, marvel, sensation, vision, dream. [➡AMAZING THING; 212]

miraculous *adj* **amazing**, astounding, astonishing, incredible, unbelievable, phenomenal, marvellous, extraordinary, mind-blowing (*informal*), inexplicable, wonderful, wondrous. [➡EXTRAORDINARY: AMAZING; 205] *Opposite:* mundane.

mirage *n* **hallucination**, optical illusion, illusion, vision, delusion, fantasy, figment, imagining, phantasm. [➡NON-EXISTENT THINGS; 23] *Opposite:* reality.

mire *n* **swamp**, marsh, mud, sludge, slush, morass, bog, quagmire. [➡WETLANDS; 1043]

mired *adj* [➡CONFUSION, ANXIETY, AND WORRY; 541]

mirror 1 *n* **looking glass** (*archaic*), glass, hand mirror, shaving mirror. [➡FITTINGS; 859] **2** *v* **reflect**, echo, copy, parallel, emulate, imitate, image. [➡PRETEND AND MIMIC; 60] **3** *v* **represent**, symbolize, illustrate, typify, signify, correspond, embody, epitomize. [➡REPRESENT SOMETHING OR SOMEBODY; 59]

mirror image *n* **spitting image** (*informal*), chip off the old block (*informal*), double, twin, copy, replica, dead ringer (*informal*), likeness. [➡COPIES AND REPLICAS; 152]

mirth *n* **laughter**, hilarity, humour, jollity, fun, merriment, entertainment, delight, glee, joy, joyfulness, cheer, merrymaking. [➡LAUGHTER; 650] *Opposite:* sadness.

mirthful *adj* **joyful**, merry, gleeful, jovial, cheery, jolly, happy. [➡PLEASURE, EXCITEMENT, AND ELATION; 535] *Opposite:* mirthless.

mirthfully *adv* **merrily**, cheerily, laughingly, gleefully, happily, brightly, joyfully, jovially. [➡GOOD-TEMPERED AND HUMOROUS; 628] *Opposite:* mirthlessly.

mirthfulness *n* [➡LAUGHTER; 650]

mirthless *adj* **cheerless**, dour, gloomy, grim, dismal, dreary, humourless. [➡NEGATIVE OF OUTLOOK; 515] *Opposite:* cheerful.

misadventure *n* **accident**, mishap, misfortune, disaster, calamity, catastrophe. [➡DISASTERS; 253]

misaligned *adj* **askew**, skewed, awry, cockeyed, crooked, uneven, out of true, asymmetrical, twisted, disorderly, wonky (*informal*), lopsided. [➡ORIENTATION AND ALIGNMENT; 1222] *Opposite:* straight.

misalliance *n* **mismatch**, inequality, bad match, disparity, mésalliance, incongruity, incompatibility. [➡ DISHARMONY; 157]

misanthrope *n* **pessimist**, recluse, loner, cynic, malcontent, misanthropist. [➡ GRUMPY AND NEGATIVE PEOPLE; 953] *Opposite:* philanthropist.

misanthropic *adj* **cynical**, pessimistic, distrustful, disdainful, sardonic, reclusive. [➡ BAD MANNERS AND SOCIAL SKILLS; 522] *Opposite:* philanthropic.

misanthropist *n* **misanthrope**, recluse, loner, pessimist, cynic, malcontent. [➡ GRUMPY AND NEGATIVE PEOPLE; 953] *Opposite:* philanthropist.

misanthropy *n* **cynicism**, pessimism, distrust, disdain, sardonicism, reclusiveness. [➡ PREJUDICE; 551] *Opposite:* philanthropy.

misapplication *n* **misuse**, abuse, misemployment, mishandling, exploitation, mismanagement, misappropriation. [➡ MISUSE AND ABUSE; 472]

misapply *v* **misuse**, abuse, misemploy, mishandle, mismanage, misappropriate, exploit. [➡ MISUSE AND ABUSE; 472]

misapprehend (*formal*) *v* **mistake**, misunderstand, misinterpret, misconstrue, misjudge, misread, get the wrong end of the stick, get the wrong idea, confuse, get the wrong impression, miscomprehend, get wrong. [➡ MISUNDERSTAND AND FAIL TO GRASP; 762]

misapprehension *n* **misunderstanding**, misinterpretation, wrong idea, false impression, misconception, delusion, misreading. [➡ MISUNDERSTAND AND FAIL TO GRASP; 762] *Opposite:* comprehension.

misappropriate *v* **steal**, embezzle, pocket, take, help yourself, siphon off, fiddle (*informal*), defraud, misuse. [➡ STEAL AND ROB; 427] *Opposite:* reimburse.

See Compare and Contrast at **steal**.

misappropriation *n* **embezzlement**, misuse, stealing, dishonesty, fraud, deceit, appropriation, fiddling (*informal*), cheating, double-dealing. [➡ CRIMES; 817]

misbegotten *adj* **ill-conceived**, bad, inappropriate, foolish, deplorable, malapropos (*formal*), improper. [➡ THE NATURE OF IDEAS; 772]

misbehave *v* **be naughty**, be bad, play up, act up, behave badly, disobey, cut up (*US slang*). [➡ DISOBEY; 303] *Opposite:* behave.

misbehaviour *n* **naughtiness**, misconduct, mischief, disobedience, waywardness, troublesomeness, mischievousness. [➡ MORALLY BAD; 776]

miscalculate *v* **misjudge**, underestimate, overestimate, get it wrong, misconstrue, overvalue, overrate, undervalue, underrate, misunderstand. [➡ MISUNDERSTAND AND FAIL TO GRASP; 762]

miscalculation *n* **error**, mistake, inaccuracy, slip-up (*informal*), blunder, slip, fault, faux pas (*literary*), oversight, misstep. [➡ MISTAKES; 251]

miscarriage 1 *n* [➡ REPRODUCTION AND HEREDITY; 726] 2 *n* (*formal*) **failure**, lapse, breakdown, insufficiency, mistake, blunder, debacle. [➡ MISTAKES; 251]

miscarriage of justice *n* **wrongful conviction**, unfair ruling, injustice, judicial error, mistake, error, travesty. [➡ TRIAL, PUNISHMENT, AND LEGAL OUTCOMES; 819]

miscarry (*formal*) *v* **fail**, founder, backfire, go wrong, go amiss, come to nothing, fall through, fall short. [➡ FAIL OR BE UNSUCCESSFUL; 75]

miscellanea *n* [➡ COLLECTIONS AND MIXTURES OF THINGS; 1243]

miscellaneous *adj* **various**, varied, assorted, mixed, diverse, sundry, jumbled, disparate. [➡ DIFFERENCE; 150] *Opposite:* homogeneous.

miscellany *n* **assortment**, collection, selection, grouping, medley, pastiche, variety, diversity, hotchpotch, jumble, mixed bag, mishmash, mixture. [➡ COLLECTIONS AND MIXTURES OF THINGS; 1243]

mischance *n* **misfortune**, ill fortune, bad luck, ill luck, misadventure. [➡ BAD LUCK AND UNLUCKY; 785]

mischief 1 *n* **misbehaviour**, naughtiness, trouble, monkey business (*informal*), tomfoolery (*informal*), disobedience, waywardness, troublesomeness. [➡ BAD BEHAVIOUR OR ACTION; 255] 2 *n* **harm**, damage, trouble, disruption, injury, hurt, malice. [➡ NUISANCES; 254] 3 *n* **troublemaker**, rascal (*humorous*), scamp (*informal*), monkey (*informal*), pest (*informal*), nuisance. [➡ MISCHIEVOUS OR BADLY-BEHAVED CHILD; 946]

mischief-maker *n* **meddler**, troublemaker, stirrer (*informal*), mixer (*informal*), gossip, rabble-rouser (*disapproving*), ringleader, instigator. [➡ UNCOOPERATIVE OR REBELLIOUS PERSON; 567]

mischievous 1 *adj* **naughty**, playful, impish, roguish, ill-behaved, bad, tricksy, rascally (*humorous*), disobedient. [➡ BAD MANNERS AND SOCIAL SKILLS; 522] *Opposite:* well-behaved. 2 *adj* (*formal*) **harmful**, damaging, malicious, wicked, negative, hurtful, bad, malign, spiteful, nasty (*informal*). [➡ SELFISH AND UNKIND; 506] *Opposite:* harmless.

See Compare and Contrast at **bad**.

mischievously *adv* **playfully**, naughtily, impishly, roguishly. [➡ BAD MANNERS AND SOCIAL SKILLS; 522]

mischievousness 1 *n* **naughtiness**, bad behaviour, impishness, playfulness, disobedience. [➡ BAD BEHAVIOUR OR ACTION; 255] 2 *n* (*formal*) **malice**, hatred, harm, animosity, spite, ill will, damage. [➡ UNFRIENDLINESS AND UNSOCIABILITY; 505]

miscomprehend *v* [➡ MISUNDERSTAND AND FAIL TO GRASP; 762]

misconceive *v* **misunderstand**, misapprehend (*formal*), misinterpret, get the wrong impression, get the wrong idea, get the wrong end of the stick, miscomprehend, mistake, misconstrue. [➡ MISUNDERSTAND AND FAIL TO GRASP; 762] *Opposite:* understand.

misconceived *adj* **ill-conceived**, ill-thought-out, flawed, misguided, inappropriate, doomed, misjudged, misunderstood, misconstrued, mistaken. [➡ THE NATURE OF IDEAS; 772]

misconception *n* **fallacy**, delusion, misapprehension, misconstruction, mistaken belief, false impression, misunderstanding, misreading, error. [➡MISTAKES; 251] *Opposite:* fact.

misconduct *n* **bad behaviour**, misbehaviour, delinquency, transgression, wrongdoing. [➡MORALLY BAD; 776]

misconstruction *n* **misinterpretation**, misunderstanding, misreading, false impression, misjudgment, wrong idea, error, fallacy. [➡MISUNDERSTAND AND FAIL TO GRASP; 762] *Opposite:* understanding.

misconstrue *v* **misinterpret**, misunderstand, misread, get the wrong idea about, get the wrong impression about, get the wrong end of the stick, misapprehend (*formal*), miscomprehend. [➡MISUNDERSTAND AND FAIL TO GRASP; 762] *Opposite:* understand.

miscount *v* **lose count**, miscalculate, make a mistake, err, underestimate, overestimate. [➡ASSESS QUANTITY; 758]

miscreant (*literary*) *n* **troublemaker**, scoundrel, mischief-maker, malefactor (*formal*), wrongdoer, criminal, reprobate, offender, villain, lowlife (*informal*). [➡VILLAINS AND THUGS; 947]

misdeed (*formal*) *n* **misdemeanour**, crime, offence, wrong, transgression, fault, error. [➡MORALLY BAD; 776]

misdemeanour 1 *n* **petty larceny**, crime, offence, malfeasance, transgression, infringement, violation. [➡CRIMES; 817] 2 *n* **misdeed** (*formal*), wrongdoing, lapse, transgression, foul, indiscretion, wrong, breach, slip, faux pas (*literary*), misconduct, misbehaviour. [➡BAD BEHAVIOUR OR ACTION; 255]

misdirect 1 *v* **point in the wrong direction**, lead astray, send off course, send on a wild goose chase. [➡DESPATCH AND SEND; 334] *Opposite:* direct. 2 *v* **misallocate**, misuse, misapply, waste, misemploy, mismanage. [➡MISUSE AND ABUSE; 472]

misemploy *v* [➡MISUSE AND ABUSE; 472]

miser 1 *n* **hoarder**, accumulator, saver, squirrel (*informal*), magpie (*informal*), collector. [➡PEOPLE WHO COLLECT THINGS; 455] 2 *n* **penny pincher** (*informal*), cheapskate (*informal*), scrooge (*informal*), skinflint, pinchpenny, meanie (*informal*), niggard. [➡FINANCIALLY MEAN PEOPLE; 952]

miserable 1 *adj* **unhappy**, sad, fed up (*informal*), depressed, down, despondent, dejected, wretched, glum, dismal, low, woeful. [➡SADNESS, DISTRESS, AND DESPAIR; 540] *Opposite:* happy. 2 *adj* **depressing**, cheerless, wretched, desolate, gloomy, dismal, glum, melancholy. [➡EMOTIONALLY UNPLEASANT AND UPSETTING; 228] *Opposite:* cheery. 3 *adj* **inadequate**, measly (*informal*), paltry, derisory, miserly, mean, meagre, contemptible, pitiable, piddling (*informal*). [➡SMALL; 1194] *Opposite:* generous. 4 *adj* **gloomy**, dull, grey, overcast, dreary. [➡COLD WEATHER; 1051] *Opposite:* bright.

miserably *adv* **unhappily**, sadly, despondently, dejectedly, wretchedly, glumly, gloomily, desolately, sorrowfully. [➡SADNESS, DISTRESS, AND DESPAIR; 540] *Opposite:* happily.

miserliness *n* **stinginess**, greed, greediness, parsimoniousness, tightfistedness, avariciousness, meanness, close-fistedness (*informal*), tightness. [➡FINANCIALLY MEAN AND GRASPING; 520] *Opposite:* generosity.

miserly 1 *adj* **mean**, tightfisted, penny-pinching (*informal*), parsimonious, close-fisted (*informal*), tight, niggardly, scrounging (*informal*), mingy (*informal*), stingy (*informal*). [➡FINANCIALLY MEAN AND GRASPING; 520] *Opposite:* generous. 2 *adj* **measly** (*informal*), paltry, derisory, meagre, stingy (*informal*), mean, miserable, piddling (*informal*), mingy (*informal*). [➡SMALL; 1194] *Opposite:* generous.

misery 1 *n* (*informal*) **wet blanket** (*informal*), grouch (*informal*), grumbler, moaner (*informal*), whiner, whinger (*informal*). [➡GRUMPY AND NEGATIVE PEOPLE; 953] 2 *n* **unhappiness**, sadness, depression, desolation, gloom, wretchedness, melancholy, despair, grief, sorrow, indigence (*formal*), agony, misfortune. [➡SADNESS, DISTRESS, AND DESPAIR; 540] *Opposite:* happiness. 3 *n* **suffering**, deprivation, privation, destitution, poverty, distress. [➡POVERTY AND POOR; 892]

misfire *v* **go wrong**, backfire, fail, fall through, miscarry, not come off, fall flat. [➡FAIL OR BE UNSUCCESSFUL; 75] *Opposite:* succeed.

misfit *n* **oddity**, eccentric, loner, odd one out, nonconformist, crank (*informal*). [➡SOLITARY PEOPLE; 942] *Opposite:* conformist.

misfortune *n* **disaster**, calamity, trial, tribulation, misadventure, catastrophe, accident. [➡DISASTERS; 253] *Opposite:* opportunity.

misgiving *n* **scruple**, qualm, doubt, niggle, suspicion, hesitation, worry, unease, mistrust, reservation, uncertainty, fear. [➡FEELINGS ABOUT THE FUTURE; 534]

misguided *adj* **mistaken**, foolish, ill-advised, unwise, erroneous, injudicious, wrong, imprudent (*formal*). [➡THE NATURE OF IDEAS; 772] *Opposite:* wise.

mishandle 1 *v* **mismanage**, mess up (*informal*), make a mess of, botch, make a hash of (*informal*), bungle (*informal*), misapply, misuse, abuse. [➡MESS UP AND MAKE MISTAKES; 473] 2 *v* **abuse**, rough up (*informal*), knock about (*informal*), mistreat, exploit, ill-treat. [➡PHYSICAL ATTACK AND PUNISHMENT; 416]

mishap *n* **accident**, calamity, misfortune, disaster, catastrophe, misadventure, casualty. [➡DISASTERS; 253]

mishear *v* **hear wrong**, get wrong, pick up wrong, not get, be mistaken, get the wrong end of the stick, misunderstand. [➡MISUNDERSTAND AND FAIL TO GRASP; 762]

mishit 1 *v* **botch**, miss, nick, clip, hit a foul, slice, hook, fluff (*informal*), foul (*US*). [➡MISUSE AND ABUSE; 472] 2 *n* **error**, slice, hook, miss, nick, clip, foul ball, foul (*US*). [➡MISTAKES; 251]

mishmash *n* **hotchpotch**, jumble, muddle, miscellany, mixture, mixed bag, pastiche, assortment, collection. [➡COLLECTIONS AND MIXTURES OF THINGS; 1243]

misinform *v* **mislead**, deceive, lie to, lead on, lead astray, delude, misrepresent, distort, fabricate, propagandize, hoodwink, bamboozle (*informal*). [➡DECEPTION AND LIES; 661]

misinformation *n* **propaganda**, dishonesty, distortion, fabrication, bending of the truth, half-truth, misrepresentation, spin (*slang*), deception. [➡DECEPTION AND LIES; 661] *Opposite:* fact.

misinterpret *v* **misconstrue**, misunderstand, misread, get the wrong idea about, get the wrong impression about, get the wrong end of the stick, miss the point, mistake, misjudge, misapprehend (*formal*). [➡ MISUNDERSTAND AND FAIL TO GRASP; 762] *Opposite:* understand.

misinterpretation *n* **misunderstanding**, misconception, misapprehension, misreading, confusion, mix-up, misconstruction. [➡ MISUNDERSTAND AND FAIL TO GRASP; 762] *Opposite:* understanding.

misjudge *v* **miscalculate**, underestimate, overestimate, be wrong about, get the wrong idea, get the wrong impression, misapprehend (*formal*), mistake, misinterpret. [➡ MISUNDERSTAND AND FAIL TO GRASP; 762]

misjudgment 1 *n* **poor judgment**, error of judgment, error, miscalculation, slip-up (*informal*), slip, faux pas (*literary*), mistake, oversight. [➡ MISUNDERSTAND AND FAIL TO GRASP; 762] 2 *n* **wrong impression**, misinterpretation, misconstruction, false reading, prejudice, prejudgment, irrationality. [➡ MISTAKES; 251] *Opposite:* understanding.

mislaid *adj* **lost**, missing, nowhere to be found, gone astray, misplaced. [➡ ABSENT AND UNAVAILABLE; 7]

mislay *v* **lose**, misplace, be unable to find, miss, put in the wrong place, drop, leave behind, forget. [➡ LOSE AND FORFEIT; 448] *Opposite:* find.

mislead *v* **give the wrong impression**, misinform, deceive, lie, delude, take in, lead on, misrepresent, distort, fabricate, hoodwink, bamboozle (*informal*). [➡ DECEPTION AND LIES; 661]

misleading *adj* **deceptive**, ambiguous, confusing, false, disingenuous, misrepresentative, distorted. [➡ FALSE AND UNREAL; 174] *Opposite:* truthful.

mismanage *v* **mishandle**, mess up (*informal*), make a mess of, botch, make a hash of (*informal*), bungle (*informal*), misuse, manage badly. [➡ MISUSE AND ABUSE; 472]

mismanagement *n* **mishandling**, bungling (*informal*), misconduct, negligence, malpractice, maladministration. [➡ MISUSE AND ABUSE; 472] *Opposite:* efficiency.

mismatch *n* **incongruity**, discrepancy, gap, disparity, misalliance, bad fit, divergence, incompatibility. [➡ DISHARMONY; 157] *Opposite:* harmony.

mismatched *adj* **incompatible**, unequal, uneven, unjust, one-sided, inequitable, lopsided, asymmetric, off-balance. [➡ DISHARMONY; 157]

misnomer *n* **misleading term**, inaccurate term, poor description, loose term, contradiction, inaccuracy, incongruity. [➡ NAME AND DESCRIBE; 666]

misperceive *v* [➡ MISUNDERSTAND AND FAIL TO GRASP; 762]

misplace *v* **lose**, mislay, be unable to put your hands on, drop, leave behind, forget. [➡ LOSE AND FORFEIT; 448] *Opposite:* find.

misplaced 1 *adj* **inappropriate**, erroneous, misdirected, out-of-place, inapt, improper, illogical. [➡ INAPPROPRIATE AND UNSUITABLE; 225] *Opposite:* appropriate. 2 *adj* **mislaid**, nowhere to be found, missing, lost, gone astray, absent. [➡ ABSENT AND UNAVAILABLE; 7]

misprint *n* **typo** (*informal*), typographical error, error, mistake, literal, blunder, oversight. [➡ MISTAKES; 251]

mispronounce *v* **say wrong**, distort, mangle, make a mess of, stumble through, mess up (*informal*), misstate. [➡ WITTER AND BABBLE; 618] *Opposite:* articulate.

mispronunciation *n* **distortion**, error, misstatement, slip, blunder, mistake. [➡ THE SPOKEN WORD; 672]

misquote *v* **put words in somebody's mouth**, misreport, misrepresent, misattribute, quote out of context, overstate. [➡ RECITE, REPEAT, AND NARRATE; 621]

misread *v* **misjudge**, misinterpret, misunderstand, misconstrue, get the wrong idea, get the wrong impression, miss the point, get the wrong end of the stick, mistake, garble, misapprehend (*formal*). [➡ MISUNDERSTAND AND FAIL TO GRASP; 762] *Opposite:* interpret.

misrepresent *v* **parody**, pervert, twist, distort, pass off, bias, falsify, slant. [➡ FALSIFY AND CHEAT; 177]

misrepresentation *n* **parody**, caricature, distortion, falsification, twisting, slanting, perversion (*disapproving*). [➡ REPRESENTATIONS AND GENERAL EXAMPLES; 65]

misrule 1 *n* **misgovernment**, mishandling, corruption, maladministration, mismanagement, tyranny, abuse of power. [➡ STYLES AND SYSTEMS OF GOVERNMENT; 806] 2 *n* **lawlessness**, anarchy, unruliness, chaos, turmoil, disorder. [➡ DISORDER AND CHAOS; 246] *Opposite:* order.

miss 1 *v* **overlook**, fail to spot, let pass, fail to notice, fail to see, neglect, ignore, fail to catch. [➡ MISUNDERSTAND AND FAIL TO GRASP; 762] *Opposite:* see. 2 *v* **skip**, fail to attend, escape, avoid, forget, pass on. [➡ FORGET, FORGIVE, AND ACCEPT; 749] *Opposite:* attend. 3 *v* **forego**, lose, pass up, let pass, let go, let slip, disregard. [➡ FOREGO AND DENY ONESELF; 450] *Opposite:* take up. 4 *v* **pine for**, long for, yearn for, wish for, grieve for, want, lack. [➡ DESIRE AND WANT; 580] 5 *n* **omission**, oversight, delinquency, neglect, mistake, loss. [➡ MISTAKES; 251] 6 *n* **failure**, false step, error, slip, miscue, blunder. [➡ MISTAKES; 251]

missal *n* **service book**, prayer book, liturgical book, breviary, psalter, hymn book, hymnal. [➡ RELIGIOUS OBJECTS; 780]

misshapen *adj* **distorted**, twisted, deformed, malformed, warped, contorted, disproportionate, crooked, irregular. [➡ ORIENTATION AND ALIGNMENT; 1222] *Opposite:* shapely.

misshapenness *n* [➡ SHAPELESSNESS; 1218]

missile *type of* **explosive weapon**. [➡ EXPLOSIVES; 1154]

missing *adj* **lost**, absent, gone astray, misplaced, mislaid, gone, omitted, disappeared, unaccounted for, AWOL. [➡ ABSENT AND UNAVAILABLE; 7] *Opposite:* present.

mission 1 *n* **assignment**, task, job, work, undertaking, duty, operation, exercise, errand, enterprise, quest, charge. [➡ WORK IN GENERAL; 298] 2 *n* **calling**, vocation, purpose, goal, aim, objective, duty, pursuit, raison d'être. [➡ PROFESSIONS; 845] 3 *n* **delegation**, deputation, task force, legation, embassy, group. [➡ ADMINISTRATIVE OFFICERS; 811]

missionary 1 *n* **evangelist**, proselytizer, preacher, minister, priest, apostle, teacher. [➡ RELIGIOUS PEOPLE; 779] 2 *n*

campaigner, champion, crusader, proselytizer, propagandist, activist. [➡ PHILOSOPHICAL AND POLITICAL THINKERS; 782]

missive *n* **letter**, communiqué, note, communication, memo, memorandum, notification, dispatch, message, epistle (*formal*). [➡ LETTERS AND WRITTEN MESSAGES; 585]

miss out 1 *v* **omit**, leave out, disregard, miss, exclude, overlook. [➡ NOT PAY ATTENTION; 765] *Opposite:* include. 2 *v* **lose out** (*informal*), fail to benefit from, forego, miss the boat, miss an opportunity, miss a chance. [➡ LOSE AND FORFEIT; 448] *Opposite:* benefit.

misspelling *n* **spelling mistake**, wrong spelling, misspelt word, slip, error, orthographical error, mistake. [➡ MISTAKES; 251]

misspend *v* **squander**, fritter away, waste, throw away, misuse, dissipate. [➡ MISUSE AND ABUSE; 472] *Opposite:* save.

misspent *adj* **wasted**, squandered, frittered away, misused, thrown away, dissipated, misapplied. [➡ WASTEFUL AND UNECONOMICAL; 247] *Opposite:* profitable.

misstep *n* **mistake**, slip, gaffe, blunder, error, lapse, faux pas (*literary*), solecism, shortcoming, indiscretion, miscalculation, slip-up (*informal*), boo-boo (*informal*), bloomer (*informal humorous*), blooper (*US informal humorous*). [➡ MISTAKES; 251]

miss the boat *v* **miss an opportunity**, lose out (*informal*), miss a chance, miss out, fail to benefit from, forego. [➡ LOSE AND FORFEIT; 448]

miss the point *v* **misunderstand**, misinterpret, misconstrue, fail to understand, misread, not get the point, get hold of the wrong end of the stick, misapprehend (*formal*). [➡ MISUNDERSTAND AND FAIL TO GRASP; 762] *Opposite:* understand.

mist *n* **haze**, fog, vapour, smog, spray, steam, film. [➡ CLOUDY AND RAINY WEATHER; 1052]

mistake 1 *n* **blunder**, gaffe, slip, lapse, miscalculation, misstep, faux pas (*literary*), slip-up (*informal*), clanger (*informal*), bloomer (*informal humorous*), blooper (*US informal humorous*). [➡ MISTAKES; 251] 2 *n* **error**, fault, inaccuracy, oversight, misspelling, misprint. [➡ MISTAKES; 251] 3 *v* **misunderstand**, misjudge, misinterpret, misconstrue, confuse, miscalculate, misapprehend (*formal*). [➡ MISUNDERSTAND AND FAIL TO GRASP; 762] *Opposite:* understand. 4 *v* **confuse with**, take for, mix up with, confound, mix, muddle up, misidentify. [➡ MISUNDERSTAND AND FAIL TO GRASP; 762] *Opposite:* recognize.

Compare and Contrast: ***mistake, error, inaccuracy, slip, blunder, faux pas***

CORE MEANING: SOMETHING INCORRECT OR IMPROPER

mistake an incorrect, unwise, or unfortunate act or decision caused by bad judgment or a lack of information or care; ***error*** something that unintentionally deviates from a recognized standard or guide; ***inaccuracy*** something that is incorrect because it has been measured, calculated, copied, or conveyed incorrectly; ***slip*** a minor mistake or oversight, especially one caused by carelessness; ***blunder*** a serious or embarassing mistake, usually the result of carelessness or ignorance; ***faux pas*** (*literary*) an embarassing mistake that breaks a social convention.

mistaken *adj* **wrong**, incorrect, false, erroneous, faulty, flawed, fallacious, inaccurate, unfounded. [➡ INCORRECT AND ERRONEOUS; 223] *Opposite:* correct.

mistime *v* **misjudge**, miss the boat, anticipate, jump the gun, pre-empt, lag behind. [➡ CREATE DISORDER AND CAUSE CHAOS; 359] *Opposite:* coordinate.

mistimed *adj* [➡ PROMPTNESS: BADLY TIMED; 101]

mistiness 1 *n* **haziness**, murkiness, duskiness, cloudiness, fogginess, darkness, smogginess. [➡ CLOUDY AND RAINY WEATHER; 1052] *Opposite:* clarity. 2 *n* **vagueness**, indistinctness, obscurity, opacity, lack of clarity, fuzziness. [➡ VAGUENESS; 244] *Opposite:* clarity.

mistletoe *type of* **shrub or bush**. [➡ BUSHES AND SHRUBS; 1027]

mist over *v* **mist**, mist up, fog over, become hazy, become clouded, cloud up, cloud over, glaze over, film over, become indistinct, become obscure. [➡ CAUSE TO DISAPPEAR; 6] *Opposite:* clear.

mistral *type of* **wind**. [➡ WINDY AND STORMY WEATHER; 1053]

mistreat *v* **abuse**, maltreat, ill-treat, harm, mishandle, rough up (*informal*), knock about (*informal*), misuse, ill-use, oppress. [➡ MISUSE AND ABUSE; 472] *Opposite:* pamper.

See Compare and Contrast at **misuse**.

mistreated *adj* **abused**, neglected, wronged, injured, victimized, ill-treated, maltreated, ill-used, oppressed. [➡ IN TROUBLE AND DISADVANTAGED; 73] *Opposite:* pampered.

mistreatment *n* **maltreatment**, exploitation, abuse, ill-treatment, neglect, harm, oppression, ill-use. [➡ UNKIND ACTION OR BEHAVIOUR; 297] *Opposite:* pampering.

mistress 1 *n* **lover**, concubine, courtesan, kept woman, ladyfriend (*informal humorous*), paramour (*literary*). [➡ SEXUAL AND ROMANTIC RELATIONSHIPS; 964] *Opposite:* wife. 2 *n* **owner**, trainer, keeper, rider. [➡ OWNERS; 447] 3 *n* **expert**, specialist, queen, doyenne, leading exponent, authority, dab hand (*informal*). [➡ TALENTED OR INTELLIGENT PERSON; 529] *Opposite:* novice. 4 *n* **teacher**, schoolmistress, governess, instructress, schoolteacher, tutor. [➡ EDUCATORS; 840] *Opposite:* pupil. 5 *n* **manager**, employer, controller, proprietor, owner, boss, ruler. [➡ BOSSES AND MANAGEMENT; 965] *Opposite:* servant.

mistrial *n* **invalid trial**, unfair trial, miscarriage of justice, travesty, injustice, unfairness. [➡ TRIAL, PUNISHMENT, AND LEGAL OUTCOMES; 819]

mistrust 1 *n* **suspicion**, distrust, doubt, wariness, uncertainty, caution, misgiving, scepticism, caginess (*informal*). [➡ UNCERTAINTY; 560] *Opposite:* trust. 2 *v* **distrust**, doubt, suspect, be wary of, be suspicious of, have doubts about, disbelieve. [➡ DISLIKE AND HATE; 578] *Opposite:* trust.

mistrustful *adj* **distrustful**, wary, suspicious, doubtful, sceptical, cautious, chary, cagey (*informal*). [➡ INSECURITY AND LOSS OF COMPOSURE; 545] *Opposite:* trusting.

misty 1 *adj* **hazy**, foggy, murky, cloudy, steamy, vaporous, dewy. [➡ CLOUDY AND RAINY WEATHER; 1052] *Opposite:* clear. 2 *adj*

indistinct, vague, obscure, dim, opaque, unclear, fuzzy, murky, nebulous, cloudy. [➡VAGUENESS; 244] *Opposite:* clear.

misty-eyed 1 *adj* **tearful**, emotional, weepy (*informal*), teary, teary-eyed, close to tears, lachrymose (*literary*), sad. [➡CRYING; 651] *Opposite:* dry-eyed. 2 *adj* **sentimental**, nostalgic, romantic, weepy (*informal*), sloppy (*informal*), soppy (*informal*). [➡APPRECIATION AND GRATITUDE; 536] *Opposite:* unsentimental.

misunderstand *v* **get the wrong idea**, misinterpret, misread, misconstrue, get the wrong impression, get the wrong end of the stick, miss the point, misjudge, mistake, miscalculate, misapprehend (*formal*). [➡MISUNDERSTAND AND FAIL TO GRASP; 762] *Opposite:* understand.

misunderstanding 1 *n* **mistake**, mix-up, confusion, misinterpretation, misconstruction, misapprehension, miscalculation, false impression. [➡MISUNDERSTAND AND FAIL TO GRASP; 762] 2 *n* **quarrel**, row, argument, difference of opinion, disagreement, falling-out, squabble, dispute, rift, fight. [➡ARGUMENT; 47] *Opposite:* agreement.

misunderstood *adj* **unacknowledged**, unrecognized, unappreciated, undervalued, misjudged, unvalued. [➡IN TROUBLE AND DISADVANTAGED; 73] *Opposite:* valued.

misuse 1 *n* **misappropriation**, misapplication, waste, ill use, mismanagement. [➡MISUSE AND ABUSE; 472] 2 *v* **waste**, misappropriate, squander, misapply, mishandle, mismanage. [➡MISUSE AND ABUSE; 472] 3 *v* **abuse**, exploit, mistreat, rough up (*informal*), maltreat, ill-treat, ill-use, wrong, knock about (*informal*). [➡WOUND A PERSON OR ANIMAL; 384] *Opposite:* cherish.

Compare and Contrast: ***misuse, abuse, ill-treat, maltreat, mistreat***

CORE MEANING: TO TREAT SOMEBODY OR SOMETHING WRONGLY OR BADLY

misuse to put something to an inappropriate use or purpose, or (*archaic*) to treat a person or animal badly or harshly; ***abuse*** to use in a wrong or inappropriate way something that should be used responsibly, such as power, privilege, or a substance, such as alcohol or a drug. It is also used to refer to cruel or violent treatment of a person or animal, especially on a regular or habitual basis; ***ill-treat or maltreat*** to behave cruelly toward s a person or animal, or to treat something roughly and carelessly; ***mistreat*** to treat a person badly, inconsiderately, or unfairly, not necessarily involving physical cruelty, or to treat something roughly and carelessly.

mite 1 *n* (*dated*) **jot**, bit, scrap, speck, grain, iota, smidgen (*informal*), scintilla. [➡FEW, LITTLE, SMALL AMOUNT; 119] 2 *type of* **arachnid.** [➡ARACHNIDS; 1018] 3 *type of* **parasitic insect.** [➡PARASITES; 1017]

mitigate *v* **alleviate**, lessen, ease, allay, moderate, take the edge off, diminish, tone down, dull, soften, assuage, relieve, mollify, palliate, abate (*formal or literary*). [➡CHANGE OF INTENSITY: LESS; 396] *Opposite:* aggravate.

mitigating *adj* **justifying**, extenuating, modifying, qualifying, vindicating, moderating, alleviating. [➡CALMING; 189] *Opposite:* aggravating.

mitigation 1 *n* **extenuation**, vindication, justification, qualification, moderation, modification. [➡CAUSATION; 169] 2 *n* **alleviation**, easing, improvement, lessening, relief, palliation. [➡CHANGE OF INTENSITY: LESS; 396] *Opposite:* intensification.

mitt 1 *n* (*slang*) **hand**, paw (*informal*), appendage. [➡ARM AND HAND; 696] 2 *type of* **sports equipment.** [➡SPORTS EQUIPMENT; 879] 3 *type of* **accessory.** [➡HABERDASHERY, MILLINERY, AND LINGERIE; 867]

mitten *type of* **accessory.** [➡HABERDASHERY, MILLINERY, AND LINGERIE; 867]

mix 1 *v* **mix up**, mingle, intermingle, blend, intersperse, combine, jumble, stir together, admix. [➡COMBINE AND MIX; 401] *Opposite:* separate. 2 *v* **combine**, blend, unite, merge, join, amalgamate, mingle, fuse. [➡COMBINE AND MIX; 401] *Opposite:* separate out. 3 *v* **fraternize**, mingle, associate, get together, socialize, hang out (*informal*), consort (*formal*), hobnob (*disapproving*). [➡ESTABLISHING RELATIONSHIPS WITH OTHERS; 974] 4 *v* **go together**, accord, agree, fit, harmonize, match. [➡HARMONY; 156] *Opposite:* clash. 5 *n* **combination**, mixture, blend, assortment, fusion, amalgam, synthesis, mingling, assembly. [➡COLLECTIONS AND MIXTURES OF THINGS; 1243]

mixed 1 *adj* **varied**, diverse, assorted, sundry, miscellaneous, motley, diversified, variegated, hybrid. [➡DIFFERENCE; 150] *Opposite:* uniform. 2 *adj* **cosmopolitan**, integrated, international, interracial, unsegregated, multiracial, blended, multicultural, multinational, mingled. [➡DIFFERENCE; 150] *Opposite:* segregated.

mixed bag *n* **ragbag**, assortment, combination, jumble, variety, hotchpotch. [➡COLLECTIONS AND MIXTURES OF THINGS; 1243]

mixed grill *type of* **cooked dish.** [➡PREPARED DISHES; 1169]

mixed-up (*informal*) 1 *adj* **confused**, muddled, bewildered, puzzled, perplexed, upset. [➡CONFUSION, ANXIETY, AND WORRY; 541] *Opposite:* clear. 2 *adj* **disturbed**, maladjusted, confused, troubled, rebellious, alienated. [➡PSYCHOLOGY AND THE MIND; 770] *Opposite:* well-adjusted.

mixer *type of* **utensil.** [➡TABLEWARE, CUTLERY, AND KITCHENWARE; 861]

mixture *n* **combination**, mix, blend, assortment, concoction, jumble, muddle, fusion, admixture, amalgam. [➡COLLECTIONS AND MIXTURES OF THINGS; 1243]

Compare and Contrast: ***mixture, blend, combination, compound, alloy, amalgam***

CORE MEANING: SOMETHING FORMED BY MIXING MATERIALS

mixture a number of elements or ingredients brought together; ***blend*** something formed by putting together two or more different kinds of things, especially in a skilled way, to form a new whole; ***combination*** something formed by the association of two or more things that retain their distinctness; ***compound*** a technical word for a chemical formed from two or more elements, also used generally to describe anything composed of two or more separate parts; ***alloy*** a technical word for a metal such as steel that is formed by combining two or more different metallic elements; ***amalgam*** a technical word for an alloy formed by combining mercury with another metal, also used generally to describe something that is a mixture of two or more elements or characteristics.

mix up 1 *v* **confuse**, puzzle, perplex, bewilder, mistake, muddle up, straighten out. [➡MISUNDERSTAND AND FAIL TO GRASP; 762] 2 *v* **mix**, combine, merge, blend, fuse, unite, incorporate, mingle, amalgamate. [➡COMBINE AND MIX; 401] *Opposite:* separate.

mix-up *n* **mistake**, muddle, misunderstanding, confusion, error, tangle. [➡MISTAKES; 251]

mizzen *part of* **sailing vessel**. [➡PARTS OF A SHIP OR BOAT; 1150]

mizzle (*regional*) *n* [➡CLOUDY AND RAINY WEATHER; 1052]

mnemonic *n* **aide-mémoire** (*formal*), memory aid, reminder, prompt, cue. [➡NAME AND DESCRIBE; 666]

mo (*informal*) *n* **tick** (*informal*), sec (*informal*), half a tick (*informal*), half a sec (*informal*), moment, minute, bit, twinkling, trice. [➡SHORT PERIOD OF TIME; 93]

moan 1 *v* **groan**, sigh, whine, whimper, mutter, wail, lament, bemoan, keen. [➡SOUND EMISSION BY PEOPLE; 364] 2 *v* (*informal*) **complain**, grumble, whinge (*informal*), whine, lament, gripe (*informal*), grouse (*informal*). [➡COMPLAIN AND NAG; 687] 3 *n* **sigh**, groan, whine, whimper, sob, wail, lament, keening. [➡SOUNDS MADE BY PEOPLE; 1261] 4 *n* (*informal*) **complaint**, grumble, gripe (*informal*), whinge (*informal*), grouse (*informal*), lament, sob, wail. [➡COMPLAIN AND NAG; 687] *Opposite:* compliment.

moaner (*informal*) *n* **grumbler**, grouch (*informal*), complainer, whiner, wailer, whinger (*informal*), objector, protester. [➡GRUMPY AND NEGATIVE PEOPLE; 953]

moat *n* **ditch**, trench, fosse, channel, dyke, defence, earthwork. [➡WATERCOURSES; 1110] *Opposite:* bank.

mob 1 *n* **crowd**, horde, mass, multitude, throng, gang, pack, flock, crush, herd, rabble. [➡GROUPS OF PEOPLE; 935] 2 *v* **besiege**, descend on, crowd round, crowd around, surround, swarm around, encircle, converge. [➡ACCOMPANY AND FOLLOW; 338] *Opposite:* avoid. 3 *v* **attack**, jostle, pester, set upon, set about, assail. [➡PHYSICAL ATTACK AND PUNISHMENT; 416] *Opposite:* defend. 4 *n* (*informal*) **masses**, populace, plebs, hoi polloi, rabble, the masses, rank and file, proletariat, the great unwashed. [➡CLASS STATUS; 889] *Opposite:* elite.

mobcap *type of* **headgear**. [➡HABERDASHERY, MILLINERY, AND LINGERIE; 867]

mobile 1 *adj* **active**, flexible, limber, supple, agile, energetic. [➡FIT AND STRONG; 737] *Opposite:* immobile. 2 *adj* **expressive**, changing, changeable, lively, communicative, eloquent. [➡FACIAL EXPRESSION; 652] *Opposite:* inexpressive. 3 *adj* **movable**, portable, transportable, itinerant, peripatetic, travelling, ambulatory, rootless, nomadic. [➡TRANSPORTATION, TRANSPORTERS, AND CARGOS; 323] *Opposite:* fixed. 4 *adj* **upwardly mobile**, successful, ambitious, aspiring, rising. [➡SUCCESSFUL AND PROMISING; 81] *Opposite:* unambitious.

mobile home *type of* **leisure vehicle**. [➡VEHICLES; 1144]

mobile phone *type of* **telecommunications equipment**. [➡TELECOMMUNICATIONS; 1129]

mobility 1 *n* **flexibility**, freedom of movement, agility, suppleness, movement, motion, kinesis. [➡SELF-PROPULSION; 305] *Opposite:* stasis. 2 *n* **progress**, social mobility, upward mobility, success, promotion, social climbing (*disapproving*). [➡SUCCESS; 82]

mobilization *n* **enlistment**, deployment, armament, organization, utilization, conscription, recruitment, enrolment, draft (*US*). [➡BEGINNING; 53] *Opposite:* demobilization.

mobilize *v* **rally**, assemble, muster, drum up, gather together, marshal, activate, call up, organize, summon, call to arms. [➡GET CLOSER TOGETHER; 311] *Opposite:* demobilize.

mobster (*US informal*) *n* **gangster**, hoodlum, thug, heavy (*slang*), crook (*informal*), tough, racketeer. [➡VILLAINS AND THUGS; 947]

moccasin *type of* **shoe**. [➡FOOTWEAR; 871]

mocha 1 *type of* **brown**. [➡COLOURS; 1223] 2 *type of* **coffee**. [➡DRINKS; 1186]

mock 1 *v* **ridicule**, tease, make fun of, laugh at, poke fun at, scorn, scoff at, deride, send up (*informal*), taunt, jeer at, burlesque, lampoon. [➡JOKES AND TEASING; 675] *Opposite:* praise. 2 *v* **mimic**, imitate, parody, ape, simulate, caricature, satirize. [➡PRETEND AND MIMIC; 60] 3 *adj* **fake**, pretend, simulated, imitation, artificial, faux, ersatz (*disapproving*), pseudo. [➡FALSE AND UNREAL; 174] *Opposite:* genuine.

See Compare and Contrast at **ridicule**.

mocker *n* **ridiculer**, derider, scorner, scoffer, caricaturist, satirist, lampooner. [➡JOKERS AND TEASES; 676]

mockery 1 *n* **ridicule**, scorn, derision, contempt, disdain, sarcasm, jeering. [➡JOKES AND TEASING; 675] *Opposite:* respect. 2 *n* **travesty**, charade, farce, sham, caricature, parody, lampoon, burlesque. [➡DECEPTION AND LIES; 661] *Opposite:* exemplar (*literary*).

mocking *adj* **scornful**, derisive, contemptuous, disdainful, sardonic, sarcastic, disrespectful, insulting, jeering. [➡MOCKING AND DISMISSIVE; 637] *Opposite:* respectful.

mock-up *n* **replica**, copy, model, sample, dummy, facsimile, likeness, prototype, simulation, test case, beta version. [➡REPRESENTATIONS AND GENERAL EXAMPLES; 65]

modal *type of* **grammatical term**. [➡ASPECTS OF LANGUAGE; 683]

mode *n* **form**, style, manner, method, means, approach, type, sort, way, kind, genre, fashion, course, rule. [➡VARIETY, TYPE, KIND; 146]

model 1 *n* **replica**, mock-up, representation, copy, reproduction, facsimile, prototype, simulation, dummy. [➡REPRESENTATIONS AND GENERAL EXAMPLES; 65] 2 *n* **type**, sort, style, kind, version, mode, genre, brand. [➡VARIETY, TYPE, KIND; 146] 3 *n* **example**, paradigm, pattern, standard, archetypal, classic, exemplar (*literary*), prototype, template. [➡PERFECT EXAMPLES AND EMBODIMENTS; 67] 4 *v* **demonstrate**, show, exhibit, display, show off. [➡CAUSE TO APPEAR; 5] 5 *v* **sculpt**, mould, form, shape, fashion, develop, pattern, cast. [➡CRAFTS AND CARVING; 356] 6 *adj* **perfect**, classical, prototypical, typical, archetypal, classic, exemplary, ideal, consummate, standard, representative. [➡APPROPRIATE, SUITABLE, ADVISABLE; 185] *Opposite:* atypical.

modem 1 *type of* **hardware.** [➡COMPUTERS AND COMPUTING; 1126] 2 *type of* **telecommunications equipment.** [➡TELECOMMUNICATIONS; 1129]

moderate 1 *adj* **reasonable**, modest, sensible, restrained, judicious, fair, temperate, enough, adequate, sufficient, relative, mild, rational, measured. [➡ENOUGH AND SUFFICIENT; 129] *Opposite:* excessive. 2 *adj* **average**, medium, normal, balanced, middling, ordinary, adequate, modest. [➡ACCEPTABLE AND PASSABLE; 220] *Opposite:* extraordinary. 3 *v* **curb**, control, tone down, play down, diminish, restrain, regulate, temper, lessen, subdue, tame. [➡CHANGE OF INTENSITY: LESS; 396] *Opposite:* intensify. 4 *v* **arbitrate**, mediate, referee, facilitate, umpire, orchestrate, regulate, direct, manage, conduct. [➡AVOID, PREVENT, LIMIT, AND CONTROL; 278]

moderately *adv* **reasonably**, rather, somewhat, fairly, comparatively, quite. [➡TO A CERTAIN EXTENT; 134] *Opposite:* excessively.

moderation *n* **restraint**, control, self-control, temperance, fairness, balance, reasonableness, equability. [➡GOOD MANNERS AND SOCIAL SKILLS; 521] *Opposite:* excess.

moderato *type of* **musical term.** [➡MUSICAL TERMS; 912]

moderator *n* **mediator**, go-between, arbiter, arbitrator, diplomat, referee, broker, representative, intermediary, agent, facilitator, MC. [➡ADVISERS, JUDGES, AND ARBITERS; 971]

modern 1 *adj* **contemporary**, current, up-to-date, up-to-the-minute, recent, new, present, fresh, prevailing, modern-day. [➡NEW, MODERN; 167] *Opposite:* old-fashioned. 2 *adj* **state-of-the-art**, latest, cutting-edge, leading-edge, novel, innovative. [➡NEW, MODERN; 167] *Opposite:* outdated. 3 *adj* **progressive**, enlightened, forward-looking, avant-garde, advanced, novel. [➡THE NATURE OF IDEAS; 772] *Opposite:* traditional.

See Compare and Contrast at **new.**

modern-day *adj* **contemporary**, modern, current, recent, present-day, today's, new, latter-day. [➡PRESENT; 85] *Opposite:* past.

moderne *type of* **20th-century architecture.** [➡BUILDING AND ARCHITECTURE; 1075]

modernism *n* **innovation**, innovativeness, novelty, originality, modernization, radicalism, progress, avant-gardism. [➡ARTISTIC MOVEMENTS AND STYLES; 899] *Opposite:* traditionalism.

modernist *type of* **20th-century architecture.** [➡BUILDING AND ARCHITECTURE; 1075]

modernistic *adj* **ultramodern**, modern, radical, futuristic, avant-garde, high-tech, state-of-the-art. [➡ARTISTIC MOVEMENTS AND STYLES; 899] *Opposite:* traditional.

modernity *n* **modernism**, innovation, innovativeness, freshness, newness, stylishness, avant-gardism, contemporaneousness, trendiness (*informal*). [➡NEW, MODERN; 167] *Opposite:* traditionalism.

modernization *n* **transformation**, upgrading, innovation, reconstruction, renewal, rejuvenation, renovation, rebuilding, development. [➡SOCIAL, POLITICAL, AND ECONOMIC CHANGE; 374]

modernize *v* **update**, renovate, streamline, revolutionize, reform, improve, remodel, redevelop, upgrade, transform. [➡SOCIAL, POLITICAL, AND ECONOMIC CHANGE; 374]

modernizer *n* **innovator**, pacesetter, trendsetter, new broom, visionary, avant-gardist, reformer. [➡PHILOSOPHICAL AND POLITICAL THINKERS; 782]

modern pentathlon *type of* **track and field.** [➡HOBBIES, GAMES, AND SPORTS; 875]

modest 1 *adj* **self-effacing**, unassuming, unpretentious, humble, reserved, discreet. [➡NATURALNESS; 498] *Opposite:* arrogant. 2 *adj* **shy**, meek, diffident, unsure, uncertain, retiring, unassertive. [➡RETICENT AND UNFORTHCOMING; 632] *Opposite:* overbearing. 3 *adj* **unexceptional**, ordinary, humble, unpretentious, plain, simple, restrained, reserved, discreet, diffident, limited, quiet. [➡ORDINARINESS; 245] *Opposite:* showy. 4 *adj* **moderate**, reasonable, acceptable, small, low, token, fair. [➡SMALL; 1194] *Opposite:* excessive.

modestly 1 *adv* **humbly**, diffidently, discreetly, unassumingly, self-effacingly, unpretentiously, unassertively. [➡RETICENT AND UNFORTHCOMING; 632] *Opposite:* arrogantly. 2 *adv* **moderately**, reasonably, acceptably, fairly. [➡TO A CERTAIN EXTENT; 134] *Opposite:* excessively.

modesty *n* **humility**, reserve, reticence, diffidence, shyness, unpretentiousness, decorum, restraint, simplicity, discretion. [➡GOOD MANNERS AND SOCIAL SKILLS; 521] *Opposite:* arrogance.

modicum *n* **little**, bit, degree, scrap, ounce, measure, smidgen (*informal*), mite, drop. [➡FEW, LITTLE, SMALL AMOUNT; 119]

modification *n* **change**, alteration, adjustment, amendment, reform, revision, reformation, adaptation, adaption, conversion, variation. [➡CHANGE; 373]

modified *adj* **adapted**, altered, changed, improved, revised, reformed, adjusted, amended. [➡CHANGE; 373] *Opposite:* unmodified.

modifier *type of* **word class.** [➡ASPECTS OF LANGUAGE; 683]

modify 1 *v* **alter**, change, adapt, adjust, amend, vary, transform, revise, refashion, rework. [➡CHANGE; 373] *Opposite:* maintain. 2 *v* **lessen**, reduce, restraint, moderate, curb, control, tone down, play down, temper, modulate, lower, restrict, limit. [➡CHANGE OF INTENSITY: LESS; 396] *Opposite:* intensify.

See Compare and Contrast at **change.**

modish *adj* **fashionable**, stylish, in, chic, up-to-the-minute, trendy (*informal*), in vogue, classy (*informal*), voguish, current, à la mode (*dated*), smart, faddish (*US*). [➡WELL GROOMED; 483] *Opposite:* unfashionable.

modular *adj* **linked**, flexible, integrated, prefabricated, segmental, sectional. [➡RECIPROCITY AND INTERDEPENDENCE; 148]

modulate 1 *v* **adjust**, alter, amend, vary, modify, change, adapt, revise, temper, shift. [➡CHANGE; 373] 2 *v* **moderate**, curb, control, tone down, play down, temper, lessen, restrain, modify, reduce, regulate, lower. [➡CHANGE OF INTENSITY: LESS; 396] *Opposite:* intensify.

modulation 1 *n* **adjustment**, change, alteration, swing, variation, tempering. [➡CHANGE; 373] 2 *n* **inflection**, variation, variety, intonation, accent, lilt, cadence. [➡THE SPOKEN WORD; 672] *Opposite:* flatness.

module *n* **unit**, component, part, element, section, segment, building block. [➡AREA AND RANGE; 111]

modus *n* [➡WAYS OF DOING THINGS; 295]

modus operandi *n* **method**, formula, technique, way, protocol, procedure, approach, plan, practice, means. [➡WAYS OF DOING THINGS; 295]

modus vivendi 1 *n* **compromise**, arrangement, settlement, deal, bargain, truce, agreement. [➡WAYS OF DOING THINGS; 295] 2 *n* **practice**, way of life, lifestyle, standard of living, habit, routine, pattern, wont (*formal*). [➡LIFESTYLE; 881]

moggy (*slang*) *n* **cat**, puss (*informal*), pussy (*informal*). [➡FELINE; 983]

mogul *n* **tycoon**, entrepreneur, magnate, industrialist, kingpin (*informal*), dynast, power, czar, big shot (*informal*). [➡RICH PEOPLE; 895]

mohair *type of* **fabric from animals**. [➡FABRICS; 1131]

mohawk (*US*) *type of* **hairstyle**. [➡HAIR STYLES AND HAIR PIECES; 489]

mohican *type of* **hairstyle**. [➡HAIR STYLES AND HAIR PIECES; 489]

moist *adj* **damp**, wet, humid, soggy, clammy. [➡MOIST; 1240] *Opposite:* dry.

See Compare and Contrast at **wet**.

moisten *v* **dampen**, wet, moisturize, humidify, sprinkle, spray, irrigate. [➡SOFTEN, LIQUEFY, DAMPEN; 389] *Opposite:* dry.

moistness *n* **dampness**, humidity, wetness, clamminess, sogginess, mugginess, dankness. [➡MOIST; 1240] *Opposite:* aridity.

moisture *n* **damp**, dampness, wetness, humidity, moistness, vapour. [➡MOIST; 1240] *Opposite:* dryness.

moisturize 1 *v* **nourish**, soothe, oil, condition, treat, massage, cleanse, cream [➡CLEAN AND POLISH; 404] *Opposite:* dry. 2 *v* **moisten**, dampen, wet, humidify, spray, sprinkle, irrigate. [➡SOFTEN, LIQUEFY, DAMPEN; 389]

moisturizer *n* **cold cream**, cream, lotion, conditioner, night cream. [➡MAKEUP AND BEAUTY PRODUCTS; 491]

molar *type of* **tooth**. [➡THE MOUTH; 703]

molasses *n* **black treacle**, blackstrap molasses, treacle, golden syrup, syrup. [➡SUGAR AND PRESERVES; 1183]

mole 1 *n* **spy**, infiltrator, secret agent, undercover agent, plant. [➡INTERFERING PEOPLE AND TELLTALES; 950] 2 *type of* **rodent**. [➡RODENT; 989]

molecular biology *type of* **bioscience**. [➡BIOLOGICAL SCIENCES; 1037]

molecule *n* **particle**, bit, smidgen (*informal*), iota, speck, shred. [➡SMALL PIECE; 127]

moleskin *type of* **fabric from plants**. [➡FABRICS; 1131]

molest 1 *v* **assault**, mistreat, abuse, attack, touch up (*slang*), feel up (*informal*), interfere with. [➡PHYSICAL ATTACK AND PUNISHMENT; 416] 2 *v* **bother**, pester, annoy, bug (*informal*), torment, harass, tease, disturb, harry, trouble. [➡ANGER AND ANNOY; 570]

mollify *v* **pacify**, calm, placate, appease, calm down, soothe, moderate, quell, still. [➡SOOTHE AND CALM; 574] *Opposite:* enrage.

mollusc 1 *type of* **land invertebrate**. [➡LAND INVERTEBRATE; 1021] 2 *type of* **aquatic invertebrate**. [➡AQUATIC INVERTEBRATE; 1022]

mollycoddle *v* **pamper**, fuss over, spoil, overprotect, cosset, indulge, humour, pander, overindulge, baby, pet. [➡TAKE CARE OF AND SPOIL; 301]

moloch *type of* **reptile**. [➡REPTILES; 994]

Molotov cocktail *type of* **explosive weapon**. [➡EXPLOSIVES; 1154]

molten *adj* **melted**, liquefied, liquid, fluid, heated, flowing, smelted, igneous, red-hot. [➡FLUID AND NON-SOLID; 1212] *Opposite:* solid.

molybdenum *type of* **metal**. [➡METALS; 1275]

mom (*US informal*) *type of* **older relative**. [➡OLDER GENERATION RELATIVES; 959]

mom-and-pop store (*US*) *type of* **retail outlet**. [➡RETAIL OUTLETS; 1082]

moment 1 *n* **instant**, second, minute, tick (*informal*), jiffy (*informal*), split second, flash, mo (*informal*), twinkling, trice. [➡SHORT PERIOD OF TIME; 93] *Opposite:* age. 2 *n* (*formal*) **importance**, significance, weight, consequence (*formal*), import, substance. [➡IMPORTANCE AND SIGNIFICANCE; 193]

momentarily 1 *adv* **for a moment**, briefly, temporarily, fleetingly, transitorily, quickly. [➡HAPPENING QUICKLY; 104] 2 *adv* (*US*) **soon**, right away, in a moment, before long, any time now, in next to no time, presently. [➡FUTURE; 86]

momentariness *n* [➡SPEED; 102]

momentary *adj* **brief**, fleeting, passing, temporary, transitory, short-lived, quick, short, transient, ephemeral. [➡HAPPENING QUICKLY; 104] *Opposite:* interminable.

momentous *adj* **important**, significant, historic, earth-shattering, crucial, vital, meaningful, big, considerable, critical, decisive, fateful. [➡IMPORTANT; 195] *Opposite:* insignificant.

momentousness *n* [➡IMPORTANCE AND SIGNIFICANCE; 193]

momentum *n* **impetus**, thrust, energy, force, drive, motion, push. [➡ENERGY GENERAL; 1160] *Opposite:* brake.

momma (*US informal*) *n* [➡OLDER GENERATION RELATIVES; 959]

mommy (*US informal*) *n* [➡OLDER GENERATION RELATIVES; 959]

monarch *n* **ruler**, sovereign, crowned head, emperor, king, queen, tsar, imperator. [➡RULERS AND ARISTOCRACY; 823] *Opposite:* subject.

monarch butterfly *type of* **butterfly.** [➡MOTHS AND BUTTERFLIES; 1015]

monarchism *n* **royalism**, imperialism, elitism, anti-republicanism, tsarism, traditionalism, absolutism, divine right. [➡STYLES AND SYSTEMS OF GOVERNMENT; 806] *Opposite:* republicanism.

monarchist *n* **royalist**, loyalist, counter-revolutionary, traditionalist, imperialist, old guard. [➡DEVOTEES AND ADDICTED PEOPLE; 557] *Opposite:* revolutionary.

monarchy *n* **realm**, kingdom, dominion, domain, empire, demesne (*formal*). [➡REALMS AND RULES; 824] *Opposite:* republic.

monastery *n* **religious foundation**, religious community, cloister, friary, abbey, priory, hermitage, convent, nunnery. [➡RELIGIOUS BUILDINGS; 1084]

monastic *adj* **austere**, reclusive, simple, Spartan, frugal, ascetic, hermetic, monkish, cloistral. [➡ABSTEMIOUSNESS AND SELF-DENIAL; 882]

monetary *adj* **financial**, fiscal, economic, monetarist, pecuniary, budgetary, regulatory. [➡FINANCE AND ECONOMICS; 797]

money 1 *n* **cash**, currency, ready money, ready cash, coins, coinage, change, ready (*informal*), dosh (*slang*), dough (*slang*), bread (*dated slang*), bucks (*US informal*), greenbacks (*US slang*). [➡MONEY; 140] 2 *n* **capital**, funds, riches, means, wherewithal, wealth, income, earnings, wages, stock, equities, assets, affluence, big bucks (*US slang*). [➡MONEY, PAYMENTS, AND CHARGES; 800]

moneybags (*informal*) *n* **millionaire**, multimillionaire, billionaire, fat cat (*slang*), bankroller (*informal*), tycoon, mogul. [➡RICH PEOPLE; 895]

money box *n* **piggy bank**, cash box, collecting box, safe. [➡CONTAINERS, RECEPTACLES, AND PACKAGING; 1244]

moneyed *adj* **wealthy**, rich, well-heeled (*informal*), affluent, prosperous, comfortable, well-off, successful, well-fixed (*US informal*). [➡WEALTH AND WEALTHY; 891]

moneygrubbing *adj* [➡FINANCIALLY MEAN AND GRASPING; 520]

moneylender *n* **lender**, usurer, financier, bankroller (*informal*), banker, loan shark, pawnbroker. [➡PEOPLE INVOLVED IN FINANCE; 804]

moneymaker 1 *n* **tycoon**, speculator, magnate, investor, mogul, millionaire, multimillionaire, billionaire. [➡RICH PEOPLE; 895] 2 *n* **hit**, cash cow (*slang*), success, gold mine, profit centre, money-spinner (*informal*). [➡ADVANTAGE; 213]

moneymaking *adj* **profitable**, commercial, economic, fruitful, lucrative, worthwhile, helpful, gainful, beneficial, productive, well-paying, renumerative. [➡SUCCESSFUL AND PROMISING; 81]

money spider *type of* **arachnid.** [➡ARACHNIDS; 1018]

money-spinner (*informal*) *n* **hit**, moneymaker, cash cow (*slang*), going concern, success, gold mine, profit centre. [➡ADVANTAGE; 213]

money-spinning (*informal*) *adj* **economic**, profitable, lucrative, fruitful, worthwhile, moneymaking, beneficial, productive. [➡SUCCESSFUL AND PROMISING; 81]

mongoose *type of* **small mammal.** [➡SMALL MAMMAL; 990]

mongrel *n* **dog**, cur, hound, crossbreed, mutt (*slang*), pye-dog, pooch (*informal*). [➡DOG; 980] *Opposite:* pedigree.

moniker (*slang*) *n* **name**, first name, signature, nickname, given name, Christian name, surname, initials, sobriquet, appellation (*formal*), cognomen (*formal*), handle (*slang*). [➡NAME AND DESCRIBE; 666]

monitor 1 *n* **screen**, display, VDU, video display unit, television set, closed-circuit television, CCTV. [➡COMPUTERS AND COMPUTING; 1126] 2 *n* **observer**, supervisor, overseer, inspector, invigilator, duty officer, proctor, disciplinarian. [➡ADVISERS, JUDGES, AND ARBITERS; 971] 3 *v* **observe**, keep an eye on, supervise, scrutinize, examine, check, watch, censor. [➡EXAMINE AND ASSESS; 754]

monitor lizard *type of* **reptile.** [➡REPTILES; 994]

monk *n* **holy man**, religious, monastic, friar, abbot, prior, brother, hermit. [➡RELIGIOUS PEOPLE; 779]

monkey 1 *n* (*informal*) **fool**, laughing stock, dupe, ass, butt, buffoon, figure of fun. [➡VICTIMS OF DECEIT; 663] 2 *n* (*informal*) **rascal** (*humorous*), scamp (*informal*), mischief, rogue, scallywag (*dated informal*). [➡MISCHIEVOUS OR BADLY-BEHAVED CHILD; 946] 3 *type of* **primate.** [➡PRIMATE; 988]

monkey around *v* **fool around**, mess around (*informal*), joke, play the fool, clown around, lark, horse around, muck about (*informal*). [➡JOKES AND TEASING; 675]

monkey business (*informal*) *n* **tricks**, mischief, trouble, pranks, high jinks (*informal*), tomfoolery (*informal*), shenanigans (*informal*), monkeyshines (*US*). [➡BAD BEHAVIOUR OR ACTION; 255]

monkey nut *type of* **nut.** [➡NUTS; 1184]

monkey puzzle *type of* **evergreen tree.** [➡EVERGREEN AND CONIFEROUS TREES; 1029]

monkey with *v* **tamper**, meddle, interfere, fiddle, tinker, mess, mess around (*informal*). [➡CONTACT: TOUCH; 413]

monkfish *type of* **sea fish.** [➡SEA FISH; 1009]

monkish *adj* **reclusive**, austere, withdrawn, cloistered, simple, ascetic, self-denying. [➡SOLITARINESS; 941] *Opposite:* worldly.

mono 1 *n* **monophonic sound reproduction**, monophonic sound, monaural sound, audio. [➡ACOUSTICS; 1137] *Opposite:* stereo. 2 *adj* **monophonic**, monaural, audio, one-track, simple. [➡ACOUSTICS; 1137] *Opposite:* stereo.

monochromatic 1 *adj* **unicolour**, homochromous, self-coloured, homochromatic, shaded, monochrome, black-and-white, monotone, tinted. [➡DESCRIBING COLOURS; 1225] 2 *adj* **dull**, indistinct, undistinctive, samey (*informal*), neutral, uniform, boring, insipid, monotonous, unvarying. [➡BORING AND UNINTERESTING; 235] *Opposite:* colourful.

monochrome 1 *adj* **neutral**, colourless, dull, undistinctive, indeterminate, toneless, uniform, monotonous, unvarying. [➡BORING AND UNINTERESTING; 235] *Opposite:* colourful. 2 *adj* **unicolour**, homochromous, homochromatic, self-coloured, monochromatic, shaded. [➡DESCRIBING COLOURS; 1225]

monocle *n* **eyeglass**, glass, lens. [➡GLASSES AND SPECTACLES; 1124]

monogamous *adj* **faithful**, exclusive, committed, married, steady, one-to-one. [➡RELATIONSHIP TO ANOTHER; 973]

monogamy *n* **exclusivity**, fidelity, commitment, marriage, coupledom, stability. [➡RELATIONSHIP TO ANOTHER; 973]

monogram 1 *n* **initials**, signet, logo, seal, stamp, symbol, design, emblem. [➡ORNAMENTS AND DECORATIONS; 1247] 2 *v* **mark**, initial, sign, seal, identify, brand, stamp, decorate. [➡CREATE IMAGES; 357]

monograph *n* **book**, article, paper, essay, thesis, profile, critique. [➡BOOKS AND BOOKLETS; 591]

monolith *n* **standing stone**, menhir, megalith, sarsen, stone, monument, pillar, column, stele. [➡ANCIENT MANMADE STRUCTURES; 1088]

monolithic *adj* **colossal**, monumental, massive, uniform, immovable, solid, huge, gigantic. [➡LARGE; 1192]

monologue 1 *n* **soliloquy**, speech, prologue, epilogue, aside, solo, oration, address, lecture. [➡THE SPOKEN WORD; 672] *Opposite:* dialogue. 2 *n* **drone**, harangue, rant, speech, running commentary, lecture. [➡NEUTRAL ONE-WAY COMMUNICATION; 49] *Opposite:* conversation.

monophonic *adj* [➡LOUD OR UNPLEASANT SOUNDS; 1265]

monoplane *type of* **civil aircraft**. [➡AIRCRAFT; 1147]

monopolistic *adj* **anticompetitive**, unchallenged, controlling, autocratic, exploitative, dominant. [➡STYLES AND SYSTEMS OF GOVERNMENT; 806] *Opposite:* competitive.

monopolization *n* **control**, domination, appropriation, takeover, expropriation, exploitation, seizure. [➡TAKE SOMETHING AWAY; 426] *Opposite:* cooperation.

monopolize *v* **control**, dominate, hog (*informal*), take over, corner, exploit, cartelize. [➡TAKE SOMETHING AWAY; 426] *Opposite:* share.

monopoly *n* **control**, domination, cartel, corner, trust (*US*). [➡BUSINESS ACTIVITIES AND PHENOMENA; 795]

monorail *type of* **railway**. [➡RAILWAYS; 1106]

monosyllabic *adj* **uncommunicative**, curt, gruff, brief, short, terse, abrupt, laconic. [➡RETICENT AND UNFORTHCOMING; 632] *Opposite:* verbose.

monosyllable *n* **word**, syllable, grunt, squeak. [➡ASPECTS OF LANGUAGE; 683]

monotheism *n* **theism**, deism. [➡RELIGIOUS CONCEPTS; 777] *Opposite:* polytheism.

monotone *n* **drone**, whine, chant, intonation, mutter. [➡LOUD OR UNPLEASANT SOUNDS; 1265]

monotonous *adj* **dull**, repetitious, uninteresting, droning, repetitive, samey (*informal*), boring, tedious, wearisome, unvaried, colourless, dreary, pedestrian. [➡BORING AND UNINTERESTING; 235] *Opposite:* varied.

See Compare and Contrast at **boring**.

monotony 1 *n* **tedium**, dullness, wearisomeness, boredom, flatness, dreariness, deadliness (*informal*). [➡BORING AND UNINTERESTING; 235] *Opposite:* excitement. 2 *n* **uniformity**, repetitiousness, sameness, flatness, repetitiveness, predictability, dreariness. [➡SAMENESS; 151] *Opposite:* variety.

monsoon 1 *n* **rainy season**, wet season, rains. [➡CLOUDY AND RAINY WEATHER; 1052] 2 *type of* **wind**. [➡WINDY AND STORMY WEATHER; 1053]

monster 1 *n* **fiend**, ogre, beast, brute. [➡VILLAINS AND THUGS; 947] 2 *n* **whopper** (*informal*), giant, biggie (*informal*), behemoth, leviathan. [➡BIG THINGS; 1193] 3 *adj* **huge**, enormous, giant, monstrous, gigantic, massive, mammoth, colossal, prodigious. [➡LARGE; 1192] *Opposite:* small.

monstrosity *n* **eyesore**, blot on the landscape, atrocity, sight, horror, miscreation. [➡NUISANCES; 254]

monstrous 1 *adj* **atrocious**, outrageous, horrific, immoral, evil, shocking, scandalous, lurid, grisly, unfair. [➡UNACCEPTABLE AND UNFORGIVEABLE; 226] 2 *adj* **huge**, enormous, giant, monster, gigantic, massive, colossal, mammoth, prodigious. [➡LARGE; 1192] *Opposite:* small. 3 *adj* **hideous**, grotesque, gruesome, ugly, horrible, horrid, ghastly. [➡UGLINESS AND UNATTRACTIVENESS; 234] *Opposite:* lovely.

monstrously *adv* **preposterously**, shockingly, offensively, unbelievably, prodigiously, horribly, enormously, dreadfully, hugely. [➡TO A GREAT EXTENT; 130] *Opposite:* unexceptionally.

montage *n* **mosaic**, tableau, medley, mixture, pastiche, hotchpotch, assortment, mishmash, collage. [➡COLLECTIONS AND MIXTURES OF THINGS; 1243]

Monterey Jack *type of* **hard cheese**. [➡DAIRY PRODUCTS AND CHEESES; 1182]

month *type of* **time period**. [➡TIMES OF YEAR; 88]

monthly 1 *adj* **regular**, periodic, frequent, once-a-month, scheduled, continuing, prearranged, recurrent, cyclic. [➡FREQUENT AND OFTEN; 107] *Opposite:* occasional. 2 *adj* **month-long**, 30-day, period, season, medium-term. [➡TIMES OF YEAR; 88] 3 *adv* **regularly**, once a month, periodically, frequently, at monthly intervals, every month, by the month, cyclically. [➡TIMES OF YEAR; 88] *Opposite:* irregularly. 4 *n* **magazine**, publication, periodical, journal, bulletin, review. [➡NEWSPAPERS; 606]

monument 1 *n* **headstone**, marker, tombstone, gravestone. [➡MONUMENTS; 1091] 2 *n* **memorial**, testimonial, testament, tribute. [➡BURIAL AND PREPARATION FOR BURIAL; 929]

monumental 1 *adj* **colossal**, epic, immense, massive, enormous, huge, mammoth, vast, titanic, prodigious. [➡LARGE; 1192] *Opposite:* small. 2 *adj* **historic**, classic, significant, important, epic, towering, overwhelming. [➡IMPORTANT; 195] *Opposite:* minor.

monumentally *adv* **hugely**, overwhelmingly, intensely, prodigiously, massively (*informal*), enormously, extremely. [➡TO A GREAT EXTENT; 130] *Opposite:* moderately.

moo *type of* **animal sound.** [➡SOUNDS MADE BY ANIMALS; 1260]

mooch 1 *v* (*slang*) **wander**, amble, meander, roam, ramble, knock about (*informal*), saunter, walk, drift, range, mosey (*informal*). [➡MOVE SLOWLY; 315] **2** *v* (*informal*) **cadge** (*informal*), scrounge (*informal*), wheedle, sponge, freeload (*informal*), beg. [➡OBTAIN POSSESSION BY PERSUASION; 458] **3** *v* (*US slang*) **sneak**, steal, prowl, lurk, stalk, loiter. [➡LACK OF ACTIVITY; 343] **4** *v* (*US slang*) **steal**, take, rob, pilfer, swipe (*informal*), make away with. [➡STEAL AND ROB; 427]

moocher (*informal*) *n* **cadger** (*informal*), scrounger, freeloader (*informal*), sponger (*informal*), taker. [➡VILLAINS AND THUGS; 947]

mood 1 *n* **frame of mind**, disposition, temper, attitude, temperament, humour, vein. [➡FEELINGS; 532] **2** *n* **temper**, bad temper, sulk, the doldrums, anger, state (*informal*). [➡IRRITATION AND ANGER; 542] **3** *n* **atmosphere**, feel, vibes (*slang*), ambience, air, feeling, aura, tone. [➡APPEARANCE AND ATMOSPHERE; 1236]

moodily *adv* **sulkily**, sullenly, glumly, irritably, grumpily, morosely. [➡DIFFICULT TO PLEASE; 516] *Opposite:* cheerily.

moodiness *n* **sulkiness**, changeableness, sullenness, grumpiness, glumness, irritability. [➡LACK OF COMMITMENT AND UNRELIABILITY; 510] *Opposite:* cheeriness.

moody *adj* **temperamental**, morose, sulky, sullen, glum, irritable, short-tempered, grumpy, unstable. [➡DIFFICULT TO PLEASE; 516] *Opposite:* predictable.

moon 1 *v* **wander**, drift, meander, amble, dawdle, mooch (*slang*), mosey (*informal*). [➡MOVE SLOWLY; 315] **2** *v* (*literary or humorous*) **fantasize**, dream, daydream, languish, pine, long, yearn. [➡DREAM, IMAGINE, AND FANTASIZE; 750] **3** *type of* **heavenly body.** [➡CELESTIAL BODIES; 1060]

moonbeam *n* **ray**, moonlight, shaft of light, moonshine, glint, glimmer, shimmer, beam, gleam. [➡LIGHT; 1163] *Opposite:* sunbeam.

moonlight (*informal*) *v* **do work on the side**, do two jobs, supplement your income, have a second job, have a night job, make some pocket money, work double, work illegally, burn the midnight oil. [➡WORK-RELATED ACTIVITIES; 834]

moonscape *n* **wasteland**, desert, wilderness, barren land, waste, dust bowl. [➡DESERTS AND PLAINS; 1045]

moonshine 1 *n* (*informal*) **poteen**, bootleg alcohol, firewater (*dated slang*), home-brew, white lightning (*US regional*), mountain dew (*US informal*), hooch (*US slang*). [➡DRINKS; 1186] **2** *n* **nonsense**, fantasy, silliness, fiction, gibberish, corn (*informal*), drivel, balderdash. [➡MEANINGLESS SPEECH OR WRITING; 677]

moonshot *n* **rocket launch**, launch, lunar expedition, lunar exploration, mission, space mission, liftoff. [➡SPACE TRAVEL AND EXPLORATION; 1061]

moonstone *type of* **gemstone.** [➡PRECIOUS STONES; 1277]

moonstruck (*informal humorous*) *adj* **dazed**, confused, irrational, distracted, in a daze, in another world, dreamy. [➡CONFUSION, ANXIETY, AND WORRY; 541] *Opposite:* alert.

moor 1 *n* **heath**, moorland, common, upland, fell, hill. [➡DESERTS AND PLAINS; 1045] **2** *v* **tie**, fix, secure, chain, attach, fasten, cable, anchor. [➡FASTEN, LINK, AND JOIN; 409] *Opposite:* untie.

moorhen *type of* **freshwater bird.** [➡FRESHWATER BIRD; 1000]

mooring *n* **anchorage**, berth, tie-up, bay, reserved space, parking bay, parking space. [➡WATERWAYS AND SEAWAYS; 1107]

Moorish *type of* **pre-20th-century architecture.** [➡BUILDING AND ARCHITECTURE; 1075]

moorland *n* **heath**, moor, common, upland, fell, hill. [➡DESERTS AND PLAINS; 1045]

moose (*US*) *type of* **deer or antelope.** [➡DEER AND ANTELOPE; 981]

moot 1 *adj* **debatable**, arguable, doubtful, controversial, unresolved, disputable, unlikely, unsettled. [➡UNCERTAIN; 176] *Opposite:* established. **2** *v* **propose**, put forward, suggest, bring up, introduce, present. [➡SUGGEST, HINT, AND COMMENT; 613]

mop 1 *n* [➡HAND TOOLS; 1118] **2** *v* **wipe**, clean, swab, dust, mop up, wipe up, clear up, wash, clean up. [➡CLEAN AND POLISH; 404]

mope *v* **brood**, languish, pine, sulk, pout, despond (*archaic or literary*). [➡CHANGE OF MOOD AND COMPOSURE; 581]

moped *type of* **bike** (*informal*). [➡BIKES, CARS, AND CARRIAGES; 1148]

moppet (*informal*) *n* **child**, toddler, tot (*informal*), little one, kid (*informal*), kiddy (*informal*). [➡CHILD OR YOUTH; 945]

mop up 1 *v* **wipe up**, clear up, mop, wipe, swab, clean up, wash. [➡CLEAN AND POLISH; 404] **2** *v* (*informal*) **finish off**, dispose of, see to, deal with, polish off, complete, wrap up (*informal*). [➡COMPLETE AN ACTION; 264]

moquette *type of* **synthetic fabric.** [➡FABRICS; 1131]

moraine *n* **glacial deposit**, debris, rubble, residue, lateral moraine, terminal moraine. [➡EROSION PRODUCTS AND SOIL; 1058]

moral 1 *adj* **ethical**, good, right, honest, decent, proper, honourable, just, principled. [➡MORALLY GOOD; 775] *Opposite:* immoral. **2** *n* **message**, meaning, significance, rule, maxim, point, lesson, truism, aphorism, axiom, dictum (*formal*). [➡MEANING; 691]

morale *n* **confidence**, self-esteem, spirits, self-confidence, assurance, optimism, drive, determination. [➡FEELINGS; 532] *Opposite:* aimlessness.

moralist 1 *n* **moralizer**, censor, preacher, critic, philosopher. [➡PHILOSOPHICAL AND POLITICAL THINKERS; 782] **2** *n* **virtuous person**, upright person, puritan, saint, prude. [➡ASCETIC PEOPLE; 883]

moralistic *adj* **moralizing**, didactic, strait-laced, serious, upright, high-minded. [➡AFFECTATION, SELF-SATISFACTION, AND SNOBBISHNESS; 508]

morality 1 *n* **ethics**, morals, principles, standards, scruples, mores. [➡MORAL CONCEPTS; 774] **2** *n* **goodness**, decency, probity (*formal*), honesty, integrity, honour, virtue, godliness, saintliness. [➡MORALLY GOOD; 775] *Opposite:* wickedness.

moralize *v* **preach**, lecture, sermonize, criticize, nag, advise. [➡ACCUSE, BLAME, AND CRITICIZE; 642]

moralizing 1 *n* **lecturing**, sermonizing, instruction, remonstration, admonishment, censure, criticism. [➡CRITICISMS AND ANGRY OUTBURSTS; 50] 2 *adj* **lecturing**, critical, preaching, exhorting, hectoring, improving, holier-than-thou (*informal*), sanctimonious. [➡ACCUSATORY AND DISAPPROVING; 635] *Opposite:* unprincipled.

morals *n* **ethics**, morality, standards, scruples, principles, mores. [➡MORAL CONCEPTS; 774]

morass 1 *n* **bog**, marsh, mire, swamp, wetland. [➡WETLANDS; 1043] 2 *n* **mess**, chaos, muddle, quagmire, mire, tangle, knot, jungle. [➡DISORDER AND CHAOS; 246]

moratorium *n* **suspension**, freeze, halt, pause, cessation, standstill, delay. [➡PAUSES AND PHASES; 56]

morbid 1 *adj* **morose**, gloomy, dark, moody, melancholic, sullen, saturnine. [➡SADNESS, DISTRESS, AND DESPAIR; 540] *Opposite:* cheerful. 2 *adj* **gruesome**, dark, sinister, macabre, perverse, gloomy, grisly, ominous, baleful, maleficent. [➡FRIGHTENING; 232]

morbidity *n* **illness**, injury, disease, ill health, indisposition, sickness. [➡TIRED, ASLEEP AND UNCONSCIOUS; 739] *Opposite:* health.

mordant *adj* **caustic**, astringent, acerbic, penetrating, sarcastic, biting, scathing, corrosive, harsh, sardonic, acid, acrid. [➡RUDE AND HOSTILE; 626] *Opposite:* gentle.

more *adj* **additional**, extra, supplementary, added, further, new, other. [➡MORE AND EXCESS; 122] *Opposite:* less.

moreish (*informal*) *adj* **yummy**, scrumptious (*informal*), tasty, delectable, tempting, delicious, scrummy (*informal*). [➡TASTE; 704] *Opposite:* unappealing.

morel *type of* **fungus**. [➡MICROORGANISMS, FUNGI, AND ALGAE; 1023]

more often than not *adv* **usually**, typically, routinely, normally, frequently, as a rule, customarily. [➡USUALLY; 108]

more or less *adv* **relatively**, comparatively, essentially, roughly, thereabouts, approximately, almost. [➡APPROXIMATELY; 133]

moreover *adv* **furthermore**, what is more, in addition, besides, also, additionally, likewise. [➡EXPRESSIONS INTRODUCING EXTRA INFORMATION; 137]

mores *n* **customs**, values, habits, traditions, patterns, behaviour, ethics, morals, standards, principles, scruples. [➡WAYS OF DOING THINGS; 295]

morgue *n* **mortuary**, undertaker's, funeral home (*US*). [➡STORES AND STORAGE BUILDINGS; 1087]

moribund 1 *adj* **dying**, failing, expiring, on your last legs, at death's door, on your deathbed. [➡DEAD AND DYING; 925] *Opposite:* well. 2 *adj* **declining**, on the way out, waning, past its best, on its last legs, dilapidated, seen better days. [➡IN BAD REPAIR; 1233] *Opposite:* thriving.

morning *n* **dawn**, daybreak, sunrise, break of day, first light, crack of dawn, daylight, cockcrow (*archaic or literary*), sunup (*US*). [➡TIMES OF DAY; 87]

morning glory *type of* **climber**. [➡CLIMBERS; 1033]

morocco *type of* **leather**. [➡FABRICS; 1131]

morose *adj* **miserable**, glum, depressed, down, low, gloomy, pessimistic, down in the dumps (*informal*), blue (*informal*), sad, sullen. [➡SADNESS, DISTRESS, AND DESPAIR; 540] *Opposite:* cheery.

moroseness *n* [➡SADNESS, DISTRESS, AND DESPAIR; 540]

morph *v* **transform**, alter, switch, convert, adapt, change, mutate, transmute, metamorphose. [➡CHANGE; 373]

morphology *n* **shape**, form, contours, formation. [➡SHAPE; 1215]

morsel *n* **scrap**, crumb, bit, piece, fragment, speck, ort (*US*), titbit. [➡SMALL PIECE; 127] *Opposite:* chunk.

mortadella *type of* **processed meat**. [➡TYPES AND CUTS OF MEAT; 1176]

mortal 1 *adj* **earthly**, worldly, human, corporeal, finite, temporal. [➡RELIGIOUS CONCEPTS; 777] *Opposite:* immortal. 2 *adj* **deadly**, fatal, lethal, life-threatening, terminal, pestilent. [➡DEADLY; 928] 3 *adj* **extreme**, great, grave, severe, serious, excessive, inordinate, intense. [➡ABSOLUTE AND ABSOLUTELY; 131] *Opposite:* mild. 4 *n* **human being**, human, person, individual, body (*informal*), soul, man, woman. [➡PERSON; 931]

See Compare and Contrast at **deadly**.

mortality *n* **humanity**, death, transience, impermanence. [➡THE STAGES OF LIFE; 916]

mortally 1 *adv* **fatally**, lethally, incurably, terminally. [➡CRITICALLY AND SERIOUSLY; 132] 2 *adv* **extremely**, severely, seriously, greatly, very, highly, gravely. [➡TO A GREAT EXTENT; 130] *Opposite:* mildly.

mortar 1 *n* [➡BUILDING MATERIALS; 1076] 2 *type of* **gun**. [➡WEAPONS FOR SHOOTING; 1155] 3 *type of* **utensil**. [➡TABLEWARE, CUTLERY, AND KITCHENWARE; 861]

mortgage 1 *n* **loan**, bank loan, advance, secured loan, debt, second mortgage, bridging loan, remortgage, hypothecation, home equity loan (*US*). [➡ACCOUNTING, BANKING, AND BUDGETING; 799] 2 *v* **pledge**, forfeit, offer as security, use as a guarantee, pawn, hypothecate, promise, guarantee. [➡ACCOUNTING, BANKING, AND BUDGETING; 799]

mortician (*US*) *n* [➡BURIAL AND PREPARATION FOR BURIAL; 929]

mortification *n* **shame**, degradation, indignity, embarrassment, chagrin, humiliation, loss of face. [➡EMBARRASSMENT AND HUMILIATION; 543]

mortified *adj* **ashamed**, embarrassed, humiliated, horrified, offended, affronted, chagrined. [➡EMBARRASSMENT AND HUMILIATION; 543] *Opposite:* proud.

mortify *v* **degrade**, humiliate, take down, embarrass, crush, confound, shame, put down (*informal*), humble, abase (*literary*). [➡UPSET, DISTRESS, AND HUMILIATE; 568]

mortifying *adj* **humiliating**, shameful, embarrassing, degrading, chastening, appalling, ignominious. [➡EMOTIONALLY UNPLEASANT AND UPSETTING; 228] *Opposite:* uplifting.

mortuary *n* **morgue**, undertaker's, funeral home (*US*). [➡STORES AND STORAGE BUILDINGS; 1087]

mosaic *n* **medley**, assortment, mixture, variety, montage, miscellany. [➡COLLECTIONS AND MIXTURES OF THINGS; 1243]

mosasaur *type of* **dinosaur**. [➡DINOSAUR; 996]

Moses basket *type of* **bed**. [➡FURNITURE; 858]

mosey (*informal*) *v* **saunter**, wander, amble, stroll, dawdle, drift, mooch (*slang*). [➡MOVE SLOWLY; 315] *Opposite:* rush.

mosque *type of* **place of worship**. [➡RELIGIOUS BUILDINGS; 1084]

mosquito *type of* **flying insect**. [➡FLYING INSECTS; 1013]

moss *type of* **foliage plant**. [➡FOLIAGE PLANTS; 1035]

mossy *adj* **moss-covered**, moss-grown, moss-topped, overgrown, green. [➡VEGETATION; 1025]

most 1 *pron* **the majority**, nearly everyone, nearly all, a good number, a large amount, the largest part, maximum, majority. [➡MAJORITY; 139] *Opposite:* few. 2 *adv* **very**, highly, extremely, really, truly, terribly, best. [➡TO A GREAT EXTENT; 130] *Opposite:* fairly.

most likely *adv* [➡POSSIBLE AND PROBABLE; 178]

mostly 1 *adv* **for the most part**, above all, mainly, generally, on the whole, principally, largely, in general, particularly, chiefly, predominantly, primarily, greatly. [➡MAINLY AND PRIMARILY; 138] 2 *adv* **usually**, more often than not, normally, typically, commonly, generally, as a rule, more or less. [➡USUALLY; 108] *Opposite:* rarely.

most of all *adv* [➡MAINLY AND PRIMARILY; 138]

most probably *adv* [➡POSSIBLE AND PROBABLE; 178]

mote *n* **speck**, particle, jot, iota, bit, grain, spot, piece. [➡SMALL PIECE; 127] *Opposite:* mass.

motel *type of* **hotel**. [➡HOTELS, RESTAURANTS, AND CLUBS; 1081]

moth *type of* **insect**. [➡INSECTS; 1012]

moth

◆ *types of moth*
cinnabar moth, clearwing, clothes moth, death's head moth, emperor moth, goat moth, gypsy moth, hawk moth, luna moth, peppered moth, pyralid, tiger moth, tussock moth, underwing

mothball 1 *v* **postpone**, delay, put on the back burner, put aside, put on ice, defer, put off, suspend, table (*US*). [➡DELAY ACTION OR OCCURRENCE; 279] 2 *v* **shut up**, pack away, decommission, put into storage, put out of commission. [➡CAUSE TO STOP; 267] *Opposite:* open up.

moth-eaten *adj* **tattered**, threadbare, tatty, dog-eared, worn, holey, decrepit, ragged, shabby. [➡IN BAD REPAIR; 1233] *Opposite:* brand-new.

mother 1 *v* **look after**, care for, protect, nurse, tend, cherish, pamper, cosset, nurture, raise, rear, mind. [➡TAKE CARE OF AND SPOIL; 301] *Opposite:* neglect. 2 *type of* **older relative**. [➡OLDER GENERATION RELATIVES; 959]

motherboard *type of* **hardware**. [➡COMPUTERS AND COMPUTING; 1126]

motherhood *n* **maternity**, parenthood, kinship. [➡REPRODUCTION AND HEREDITY; 726] *Opposite:* fatherhood.

mother-in-law *type of* **in-law**. [➡RELATIVES BY MARRIAGE; 960]

motherland *n* **mother country**, native country, birthplace, homeland, fatherland, native land, native soil, land of your birth, place of origin, home. [➡COUNTRIES AND REGIONS; 1066]

motherly *adj* **maternal**, protective, caring, loving, kind, kindly, tender, devoted. [➡GENEROSITY AND KINDNESS; 496] *Opposite:* uncaring.

mother-of-pearl *type of* **gemstone**. [➡PRECIOUS STONES; 1277]

motif 1 *n* **design**, pattern, image, decoration, shape, ornamentation, logo. [➡ARTWORKS; 898] 2 *n* **theme**, idea, subject, topic, keynote, style, treatment. [➡SUBJECT AREA; 769]

motion 1 *n* **movement**, action, activity, change, mobility, flow, kinesis. [➡SELF-PROPULSION; 305] *Opposite:* stillness. 2 *n* **gesture**, wave, signal, sign, gesticulation, nod, indication, cue. [➡GESTURES AND GESTICULATION; 654] 3 *n* **proposal**, suggestion, proposition, submission, recommendation, presentation, request. [➡SUGGEST, HINT, AND COMMENT; 613] 4 *v* **signal**, indicate, wave, gesture, beckon, gesticulate, nod. [➡GESTURES AND GESTICULATION; 654]

motionless *adj* **stationary**, immobile, still, stock-still, static, frozen, unmoving, quiet, inert, immovable, fixed. [➡LACK OF ACTIVITY; 343] *Opposite:* moving.

motionlessness *n* **stillness**, calm, immobility, paralysis, rigidity, lifelessness, inertness. [➡LACK OF ACTIVITY; 343] *Opposite:* mobility.

motion picture (*formal or technical*) *n* **film**, movie, talkie, picture, feature film, video, flick (*informal*). [➡FILM; 901]

motivate 1 *v* **cause**, prompt, provoke, induce, spur, trigger off, impel, activate, move. [➡CAUSE TO HAPPEN; 31] *Opposite:* deter. 2 *v* **inspire**, stimulate, encourage, egg on, persuade, arouse, provoke, influence, prompt. [➡CAUSE OR COMPEL TO ACT; 272] *Opposite:* discourage.

motivated *adj* **interested**, driven, inspired, moved, stirred, encouraged, enthused, striving, determined, ambitious. [➡ENERGY AND ENTHUSIASM; 497] *Opposite:* unmotivated.

motivating *adj* **stimulating**, interesting, inspiring, galvanizing, encouraging, fascinating, exciting, moving, stirring, rousing, provoking, influencing, prompting. [➡INTERESTING AND MEANINGFUL; 191] *Opposite:* uninspiring.

motivation 1 *n* **incentive**, inspiration, enthusiasm, impetus, stimulus, provocation, spur, impulse, drive, driving force. [➡FEELINGS ABOUT THE FUTURE; 534] *Opposite:* disincentive. 2 *n* **reason**, cause, motive, purpose, rationale, aim, goal. [➡CAUSATION; 169]

motivator *n* **instigator**, persuader, stimulus, cheerleader, driving force, promoter, reason, carrot, influence, inspiration. [➡CAUSATION; 169]

motive *n* **reason**, motivation, motivating force, incentive, inducement, spur, goad, stimulus, cause. [➡CAUSATION; 169] *Opposite:* deterrent.

Compare and Contrast: ***motive, incentive, inducement, spur, goad***

CORE MEANING: SOMETHING THAT PROMPTS ACTION

motive the reason for doing something or behaving in a particular way; ***incentive*** something external that inspires extra enthusiasm or effort, often some kind of reward; ***inducement*** something external that persuades or attracts somebody to a course of action, especially something that is offered as a reward; ***spur*** something such as the hope of a reward or the fear of punishment that encourages action or effort or energy; ***goad*** a stimulus that motivates somebody or stirs somebody into often unwilling action.

motiveless *adj* **unprovoked**, gratuitous, wanton, senseless, unwarranted, needless, groundless, mindless. [➡UNINTENTIONAL AND ACCIDENTAL; 282] *Opposite:* justified.

motley *adj* **assorted**, miscellaneous, diverse, varied, mixed, contrasting, dissimilar, heterogeneous, disparate, variegated. [➡DIFFERENCE; 150] *Opposite:* uniform.

motocross *n* **scrambling**, MX, cross-country, trail biking, motorcycle racing, motorcycle race. [➡HOBBIES, GAMES, AND SPORTS; 875]

motor 1 *n* **engine**, petrol engine, diesel engine, internal combustion engine, electric motor, gasoline engine (*US*). [➡ENGINES AND HYDRAULICS; 1142] 2 *n* (*dated or informal*) **car**, vehicle, automobile, wheels (*slang*). [➡BIKES, CARS, AND CARRIAGES; 1148] 3 *adj* **motorized**, motor-powered, petrol-powered, diesel-powered, electrically powered, mechanical, gas-powered (*US*). [➡ENGINES AND HYDRAULICS; 1142] 4 *v* **drive**, travel, proceed, journey, ride, cruise. [➡TRAVEL: WAYS OF TRAVELLING; 321] 5 *v* (*informal*) **zoom**, speed, tear along, race, zip (*informal*), hurtle. [➡MOVE FAST; 314] *Opposite:* dawdle. 6 *v* (*slang*) **progress**, get on, make progress, forge ahead, make strides. [➡SUCCEED AND WIN; 79] *Opposite:* get behind.

motorbike *type of* **bike** (*informal*). [➡BIKES, CARS, AND CARRIAGES; 1148]

motorboat *type of* **motor vessel**. [➡SHIPS AND BOATS; 1149]

motorcade *n* **convoy**, procession, parade, file, escort, cavalcade, cortege. [➡GROUPS OF VEHICLES; 1151]

motorcycle *type of* **bike** (*informal*). [➡BIKES, CARS, AND CARRIAGES; 1148]

motor home (*US*) *type of* **leisure vehicle**. [➡VEHICLES; 1144]

motorist *n* **driver**, car driver, car user, car owner, chauffeur. [➡DRIVERS; 1152] *Opposite:* passenger.

motorized *adj* **motor**, motor-powered, petrol-powered, diesel-powered, electrically powered, mechanical, gas-powered (*US*). [➡ENGINES AND HYDRAULICS; 1142]

motor scooter *type of* **bike** (*informal*). [➡BIKES, CARS, AND CARRIAGES; 1148]

motorway *type of* **major road**. [➡ROADS; 1105]

mottle *v* [➡DECORATE, ADORN, AND APPLY COATINGS; 406]

mottled *adj* **dappled**, spotted, spotty, blotchy, speckled, stippled, motley, parti-coloured, varicoloured. [➡DESCRIBING PATTERNS; 1226] *Opposite:* plain.

motto *n* **slogan**, saying, maxim, dictum (*formal*), axiom, aphorism, adage, watchword, proverb, byword. [➡FIGURES OF SPEECH; 674]

mould 1 *n* **cast**, container, form, die, tin, dish, shape, bowl. [➡CONTAINERS, RECEPTACLES, AND PACKAGING; 1244] 2 *n* **frame**, pattern, template, stencil, outline, guide, matrix. [➡EXTREMITIES OF PHYSICAL OBJECTS; 1249] 3 *n* **conformation**, character, type, variety, vein, style, kind, sort, shape, contour, line. [➡VARIETY, TYPE, KIND; 146] 4 *n* **moulding**, cornice, coving, dado rail, ceiling rose, beading, picture rail. [➡ORNAMENTS AND DECORATIONS; 1247] 5 *n* **mildew**, fungus, fungal growth, decay, rust, rot. [➡UNPLEASANT AND DIRTY SUBSTANCES; 1267] 6 *type of* **fungus**. [➡MICROORGANISMS, FUNGI, AND ALGAE; 1023] 7 *v* **shape**, fashion, style, sculpt, form, create, cast, construct, make. [➡MANUFACTURE; 350] 8 *v* **influence**, change, guide, form, shape, make, remodel, render (*formal*), modify, connect. [➡CHANGE; 373] 9 *v* **cling**, hug, follow, fit around, wrap around, press. [➡EXIST IN CLOSE PROXIMITY; 21]

moulder *v* **rot**, gather dust, disintegrate, crumble, decay, fester, perish, decompose, break down, go stale. [➡GO BAD AND CORRODE; 391]

mouldering *adj* [➡DECAYING OR INFESTED; 1235]

mouldiness *n* **decay**, disintegration, mustiness, mildew, rottenness, decomposition. [➡DECAYING OR INFESTED; 1235]

moulding *n* **decoration**, detail, cornice, beading, dado, coving, ceiling rose. [➡BUILDING MATERIALS; 1076]

mouldy 1 *adj* **mildewed**, festering, fungal, decaying, decayed, rotting, rotten, old. [➡DECAYING OR INFESTED; 1235] *Opposite:* fresh. 2 *adj* **stale**, neglected, dirty, musty, fusty, old, seedy, crumbling, shabby. [➡DIRTY; 1234] *Opposite:* fresh. 3 *adj* **boring**, dull, dreary, drab, insipid, banal. [➡BORING AND UNINTERESTING; 235] *Opposite:* exciting.

moult *v* **shed**, cast, peel, slough, scale, flake. [➡LOSE AND FORFEIT; 448]

mound 1 *n* **knoll**, hillock, embankment, bank, hill, rise, dune, mount. [➡MOUNTAINS AND HILLS; 1044] *Opposite:* valley. 2 *n* **pile**, stack, mass, bundle, mountain, heap, load. [➡MANY, MUCH, LARGE AMOUNT; 117]

mount 1 *v* **prepare**, set up, produce, launch, arrange, organize. [➡INSTITUTE AND INAUGURATE; 349] 2 *v* **rise**, mount up, increase, accumulate, grow, get bigger, swell, escalate, multiply, intensify, build up, soar, surge. [➡CHANGE OF INTENSITY: MORE; 395] *Opposite:* decrease. 3 *v* **get on**, climb on, jump on, board, go on, clamber on, straddle. [➡ASSUME A POSITION; 318] *Opposite:* dismount. 4 *v* **climb**, ascend, go up, climb up, clamber up, scale. [➡GO UPWARDS; 307] *Opposite:* descend. 5 *v* **frame**, box, encase, inset, affix, exhibit, display, install, fit, equip. [➡FASTEN, LINK, AND JOIN; 409] 6 *n* **base**, stand, support, pedestal, plinth, post. [➡SUPPORTS AND BASES; 1254] 7 *n* **horse**, mule, ass, donkey, pony, mare, steed (*literary*). [➡HORSE; 985]

mountain 1 *n* **peak**, mount, crag, fell, massif, foothill, elevation, highland, alp. [➡MOUNTAINS AND HILLS; 1044] *Opposite:* valley. 2 *n* **pile**, mass, stack, bundle, mound, heap, load. [➡MANY, MUCH, LARGE AMOUNT; 117]

mountain bike *type of* **bike** (*informal*). [➡BIKES, CARS, AND CARRIAGES; 1148]

mountain climbing *n* [➡HOBBIES, GAMES, AND SPORTS; 875]

mountaineer *n* **climber**, alpinist, rock climber. [➡PEOPLE IN SPORTS AND LEISURE; 876]

mountaineering *n* [➡HOBBIES, GAMES, AND SPORTS; 875]

mountain lion (*US*) *type of* **cat**. [➡FELINE; 983]

mountainous 1 *adj* **hilly**, high, steep, precipitous, rocky, rugged. [➡MOUNTAINS AND HILLS; 1044] *Opposite:* flat. 2 *adj* **huge**, enormous, immense, monumental, gigantic, colossal, massive, vast. [➡LARGE; 1192] *Opposite:* tiny.

mountainside *n* **slope**, shoulder, gradient, incline, ramp. [➡MOUNTAINS AND HILLS; 1044] *Opposite:* foothill.

mountaintop *n* **peak**, summit, pike, crest, hilltop, pinnacle. [➡MOUNTAINS AND HILLS; 1044] *Opposite:* bottom.

mountebank (*literary*) *n* **fraud**, deceiver, trickster, con artist (*slang*), cheat, fraudster, charlatan, quack, huckster. [➡PEOPLE WHO DECEIVE; 662]

mounted 1 *adj* **on horseback**, equestrian, astride, straddling, riding, on. [➡TRAVEL: WAYS OF TRAVELLING; 321] *Opposite:* on foot. 2 *adj* **attached**, fixed, affixed, screwed on, displayed, framed, set, fitted, installed. [➡FASTEN, LINK, AND JOIN; 409] *Opposite:* loose.

mounting *adj* **rising**, increasing, growing, swelling, escalating, intensifying. [➡CHANGE OF INTENSITY: MORE; 395] *Opposite:* decreasing.

mourn *v* **grieve**, lament, grieve for, grieve over, weep for, bewail (*formal*), bemoan, sorrow (*literary*), pine, keen. *Opposite:* rejoice. (*literary*). [➡GIVING VENT TO EMOTIONS; 680]

mourner *n* **bereaved person**, funeral-goer, griever, widow, widower, pallbearer. [➡DEATH AND BEREAVEMENT; 927]

mournful *adj* **sad**, sorrowful, sombre, woeful, doleful, despondent, desolate. [➡SADNESS, DISTRESS, AND DESPAIR; 540] *Opposite:* cheerful.

mournfulness *n* **sadness**, sombreness, melancholy, gloominess, despondency, dolefulness. [➡SADNESS, DISTRESS, AND DESPAIR; 540] *Opposite:* cheerfulness.

mourning *n* **grief**, bereavement, sorrow, sadness, lamentation, woe, grieving. [➡DEATH AND BEREAVEMENT; 927] *Opposite:* rejoicing.

mourning cloak (*US*) *type of* **butterfly**. [➡MOTHS AND BUTTERFLIES; 1015]

mouse 1 *type of* **rodent**. [➡RODENT; 989] 2 *type of* **hardware**. [➡COMPUTERS AND COMPUTING; 1126]

mousse *type of* **dessert**. [➡CAKES, BISCUITS, AND DESSERTS; 1180]

moustache *n* [➡FACIAL HAIR; 490]

mousy *type of* **brown**. [➡COLOURS; 1223]

mouth 1 *n* **trap** (*informal*), gob (*slang*), cakehole (*slang*), maw. [➡THE MOUTH; 703] 2 *n* **entrance**, opening, door, doorway, aperture, gate, gateway, means of access, entry, way in, way out, exit. [➡EXTREMITIES OF PHYSICAL OBJECTS; 1249] 3 *n* (*informal*) **insolence**, impertinence, cheek (*informal*), backchat (*informal*), lip (*slang*), rudeness, back talk (*US*). [➡BAD MANNERS AND SOCIAL SKILLS; 522] 4 *n* **estuary**, outlet, bay, inlet. [➡THE SEAS, OCEANS, AND SHORES; 1041] 5 *v* **say**, mime, state, utter, reply, pronounce, speak. [➡UTTER AND PRONOUNCE; 609] 6 *part of* **face**. [➡HEAD; 693]

mouth

◆ *parts of a mouth*
adenoids, denture, gum, lip, palate, roof, soft palate, taste bud, tongue, tonsils, tooth, uvula

mouthful 1 *n* **bite**, taste, piece, spoonful, forkful, sip, gulp, draught, swallow, swig (*informal*), slurp (*informal*). [➡DRINK; 712] 2 *n* **harangue**, invective (*formal*), earful (*informal*), sermon, lecture, tirade. [➡CRITICISMS AND ANGRY OUTBURSTS; 50]

mouthiness (*informal*) *n* [➡POMPOUS, LOUD, AND OVER-CONFIDENT; 636]

mouth off (*informal*) *v* [➡BOAST; 617]

mouthpiece *n* **spokesperson**, representative, agent, ambassador, delegate, messenger. [➡REPRESENTATIONS AND GENERAL EXAMPLES; 65]

mouth-to-mouth *n* **artificial respiration**, kiss of life, resuscitation, cardiopulmonary resuscitation, CPR, rescue, emergency procedure, mouth-to-mouth resuscitation. [➡BREATHE AND NOT BREATHE; 717]

mouthwash *n* **gargle**, rinse, breath freshener, mouth spray. [➡MAKEUP AND BEAUTY PRODUCTS; 491]

mouthwatering *adj* **delicious**, delectable, lip-smacking, luscious, tasty, appetizing, yummy, succulent, scrumptious (*informal*), scrummy (*informal*). [➡TASTE; 704] *Opposite:* revolting.

mouthy (*informal*) *adj* [➡POMPOUS, LOUD, AND OVER-CONFIDENT; 636]

movable 1 *adj* **portable**, transportable, transferable, mobile, detachable, flexible, removable. [➡TRANSPORTATION, TRANSPORTERS, AND CARGOS; 323] *Opposite:* fixed. 2 *adj* **changeable**, variable, mutable, impermanent, adjustable, alterable, separable. [➡FINITENESS, VARIABILITY, AND TRANSIENCE; 96] *Opposite:* fixed.

move 1 *v* **reposition**, shift, budge, shove, stir, push, pull, rearrange, move about, transfer, redistribute. [➡POSITION SOMETHING; 326] 2 *v* **go**, progress, transport, walk, shuffle, step, jump, run, travel, turn, dance, proceed, advance. [➡PROCEED AND GO; 306] 3 *v* **transfer**, progress, relocate, refocus, redeploy, change, shift, transplant. [➡MOVE SOMETHING TO ANOTHER LOCATION; 325] *Opposite:* stay put. 4 *v* **cause**, provoke, persuade, encourage, prod, nudge, propose, suggest, influence, induce, lead. [➡CAUSE OR COMPEL TO ACT; 272] 5 *n* **change**, transfer, traffic, interchange, passage, travel, transport, exchange. [➡CHANGE; 373] 6 *n* **attempt**, effort, step, start, action, movement. [➡ACTIONS OR UNDERTAKINGS; 260] 7 *n* **shift**, step, realignment, rearrangement, repositioning, relocation, change, movement. [➡MOVE SOMETHING TO ANOTHER LOCATION; 325]

move ahead *v* **progress**, move on, press forward, go on, move forward, get going, go forward, press on, proceed, advance, make headway, forge ahead. [➡PROCEED AND GO; 306] *Opposite:* retreat.

move along 1 *v* **proceed**, hasten, go on, advance, press on, hurry, go forward, run. [➡PROCEED AND GO; 306] 2 *v* **move aside**, move over, make way, make room, shift, change position, change places. [➡TAKE UP A NEW POSITION; 313] *Opposite:* stay put.

move away *v* **retreat**, back off, diverge, distance, deviate, regress, remove. [➡GO BACKWARDS; 310] *Opposite:* move into.

move back *v* **recoil**, recede, shrink back, retreat, regress, draw back, shy away, fall back, return. [➡GO BACKWARDS; 310] *Opposite:* advance.

move fast *v* **streak**, zoom, speed, tear, whiz, fly, zip (*informal*). [➡MOVE FAST; 314]

move forward *v* **advance**, progress, push on, go ahead, proceed, move ahead, go forward, forge ahead, make headway. [➡PROCEED AND GO; 306] *Opposite:* fall back.

move heaven and earth *v* **do your utmost**, pull out all the stops, make every effort, move mountains, leave no stone unturned. [➡HARD WORK OR EFFORT; 299]

move in on *v* **approach**, surround, converge, come closer, draw near, sneak up on, creep up on, move towards. [➡PROCEED AND GO; 306] *Opposite:* retreat.

move into *v* **enter**, start, enter on, begin, set the ball rolling, initiate, take the first step. [➡START AN ACTION; 261] *Opposite:* back out.

movement 1 *n* **motion**, mobility, locomotion, circulation. [➡SELF-PROPULSION; 305] 2 *n* **drive**, programme, crusade, undertaking, measure, effort. [➡WAYS OF DOING THINGS; 295] 3 *n* **pressure group**, association, society, lobby, faction, group, sect, action group, interest group, organization. [➡GROUPS WITH A COMMON INTEREST; 938] 4 *n* **progress**, advance, development, improvement, headway, increase, rise, change, deterioration, drop, fall, decrease. [➡PROGRESS AND ADVANCEMENT; 214]

movements *n* **actions**, activities, travels, schedule, arrangements, appointments, engagements, whereabouts, programme. [➡ACTIONS OR UNDERTAKINGS; 260]

move mountains *v* [➡HARD WORK OR EFFORT; 299]

move on 1 *v* **leave**, depart, take off (*informal*), go, make off, set off, move out. [➡ABSENT ONESELF; 8] *Opposite:* stay put. 2 *v* **progress**, get going, go on, take the next step, uproot, advance, move ahead. [➡GET BETTER; 376] *Opposite:* backtrack.

move out *v* **leave**, depart, go, relocate, move on, move away. [➡ABSENT ONESELF; 8] *Opposite:* stay put.

move over *v* **move aside**, make way, make room, shift, move along, change position. [➡PROCEED AND GO; 306] *Opposite:* stay put.

mover 1 *n* **motivator**, driving force, powerhouse (*informal*), agent, doer, goer, force, mover and shaker, animator. [➡IMPORTANT OR FAMOUS PEOPLE; 893] 2 *n* **initiator**, proposer, presenter, introducer, advocate, sponsor. [➡SUGGEST, HINT, AND COMMENT; 613] *Opposite:* seconder.

mover and shaker *n* [➡IMPORTANT OR FAMOUS PEOPLE; 893]

move towards *v* **come closer**, draw near, move in on, approach, converge, creep up on. [➡GET CLOSER TOGETHER; 311] *Opposite:* move away.

move up *v* **go up**, rise, increase, progress, advance, shift up, ascend. [➡GO UPWARDS; 307] *Opposite:* drop.

movie (*US*) *n* **film**, picture, show, flick (*informal*), moving picture, motion picture (*US formal or technical*), picture show (*US*). [➡FILM; 901]

movie camera (*US*) *type of* **photographic equipment**. [➡PHOTOGRAPHY AND PHOTOGRAPHIC EQUIPMENT; 1121]

movies (*US*) *n* **cinema**, big screen, pictures (*dated informal*), flicks (*dated informal*), silver screen, movie industry. [➡FILM; 901]

movie star (*US*) *type of* **entertainer**. [➡WORKERS IN ENTERTAINMENT AND MEDIA; 873]

moving *adj* **touching**, poignant, affecting, stirring, heartrending, heartwarming, emotional, inspiring, pathetic, tender, emotive. [➡EMOTIONALLY UNPLEASANT AND UPSETTING; 228]

Compare and Contrast: ***moving, pathetic, pitiful, poignant, touching, heartwarming, heartrending***

CORE MEANING: AROUSING EMOTION

moving causing deep feelings, especially of sadness or compassion; ***pathetic*** arousing feelings of compassion and pity, often centred on somebody who is vulnerable, helpless, or unfortunate; ***pitiful*** arousing compassion and pity, or arousing contempt or derision; ***poignant*** causing strong, often bitter-sweet feelings of sadness, pity, or regret; ***touching*** causing feelings of warmth, sympathy, and tenderness; ***heartwarming*** inspiring warm or kindly feelings, usually by showing life and human nature in a positive and reassuring light; ***heartrending*** causing intense sadness or distress, especially in sympathy with somebody else's unhappiness or hardship because it involves suffering or tragic events.

moving parts *n* **mechanism**, machinery, workings, components, gears, apparatus, works. [➡PARTS OF MACHINES AND TOOLS; 1117]

moving picture *n* [➡FILM; 901]

mow *v* **cut**, scythe, cut down, shear, trim, clip. [➡EXTRACT AND SEVER; 342]

mow down 1 *v* **shoot**, gun down (*informal*), kill, slaughter, massacre, butcher, wipe out (*slang*), blow away (*slang*), shoot down. [➡KILL; 923] 2 *v* **knock down**, run over, knock over, deck (*informal*), floor, topple. [➡MOVE SOMETHING: INTO A NEW POSITION OR OVERTURN; 331]

moxie (*US slang*) *n* [➡POSITIVE INTELLECTUAL CHARACTERISTICS; 525]

mozzarella *type of* **soft cheese**. [➡DAIRY PRODUCTS AND CHEESES; 1182]

MP *n* [➡POLITICAL OFFICES AND POLITICIANS; 808]

much 1 *adv* **significantly**, noticeably, considerably, greatly, substantially, extensively, sizably, largely. [➡ MANY, MUCH, LARGE AMOUNT; 117] 2 *adv* **often**, frequently, over and over again, time and again, repeatedly, habitually, a lot, regularly. [➡ FREQUENT AND OFTEN; 107] 3 *adj* **good deal**, great deal, lots, loads (*informal*), heaps (*informal*), abundant, ample, considerable, copious, plentiful. [➡ MANY, MUCH, LARGE AMOUNT; 117]

much-admired *adj* [➡ POPULAR AND WANTED; 221]

much-loved *adj* **adored**, favourite, preferred, chosen, desired, sought after, singled out. [➡ POPULAR AND WANTED; 221]

muck 1 *n* **manure**, sewage, waste, sludge, dung. [➡ UNPLEASANT AND DIRTY SUBSTANCES; 1267] 2 *n* (*informal*) **dirt**, mess, grime, grunge (*informal*), mud, filth. [➡ UNPLEASANT AND DIRTY SUBSTANCES; 1267]

muck about (*informal*) *v* **fool about**, lark about, mess about (*informal*), mess around (*informal*), waste time, be silly, fool around, lark. [➡ LEISURE AND RECREATION; 874]

muckiness (*informal*) *n* **filthiness**, muddiness, dirtiness, grubbiness, griminess. [➡ DIRTY; 1234]

muckraker *n* **scandalmonger**, gossipmonger, troublemaker, mudslinger, slanderer, stirrer (*informal*). [➡ INTERFERING PEOPLE AND TELLTALES; 950]

muckraking *n* **scandalmongering**, dishing the dirt, mudslinging, slander, libel, exposure, exposé. [➡ GOSSIP; 679]

muck up (*informal*) *v* **mess up** (*informal*), spoil, ruin, make a mess of, botch, damage, muddy up (*US*). [➡ MESS UP AND MAKE MISTAKES; 473]

mucky (*informal*) *adj* **dirty**, muddy, messy, grubby, grotty, smeared, tarnished, filthy, grimy, soiled, unclean. [➡ DIRTY; 1234] *Opposite:* clean.

mucous *adj* **self-lubricating**, slimy, slippery, lubricated. [➡ PHYSICAL TEXTURE; 1221]

mucus *n* **slime**, secretion, saliva, lubricant, phlegm, coating, liquid. [➡ EXCRETION AND EXCRETA; 723]

mud *n* **mire**, sludge, muck (*informal*), dirt. [➡ EROSION PRODUCTS AND SOIL; 1058]

muddiness 1 *n* **dirtiness**, muckiness (*informal*), grubbiness, filthiness, griminess. [➡ DIRTY; 1234] *Opposite:* cleanness. 2 *n* **cloudiness**, murkiness, dullness, opacity, thickness, darkness. [➡ VISUAL TEXTURE; 1220] *Opposite:* clarity.

muddle 1 *v* **mix up**, mess up (*informal*), jumble, disorder, disorganize, tangle, spoil, muff, botch, fumble, mistake. [➡ CREATE DISORDER AND CAUSE CHAOS; 359] *Opposite:* disentangle. 2 *v* **confuse**, bewilder, baffle, puzzle, bamboozle (*informal*), perplex, stupefy, nonplus, confound. [➡ CONFUSE AND BEWILDER; 572] *Opposite:* clarify. 3 *n* **disorder**, jumble, confusion, mix-up, chaos, bewilderment, tangle, upheaval, commotion, shambles, mess, disorganization, disarray, clutter. [➡ DISORDER AND CHAOS; 246] *Opposite:* order.

muddled 1 *adj* **jumbled**, scrambled, mixed up, topsy-turvy, upside down, higgledy-piggledy, disarrayed, cluttered. [➡ DISORDER AND CHAOS; 246] *Opposite:* ordered. 2 *adj* **confused**, befuddled, bewildered, bemused, perplexed, mixed up, puzzled, baffled, bamboozled (*informal*), stupefied, nonplussed, confounded. [➡ CONFUSION, ANXIETY, AND WORRY; 541] *Opposite:* clear.

muddleheaded 1 *adj* **baffled**, mixed up, confused, befuddled, bewildered, bemused, perplexed, puzzled, stupefied, nonplussed, confounded. [➡ NEGATIVE INTELLECTUAL CHARACTERISTICS; 526] *Opposite:* clear-headed. 2 *adj* **inept**, illogical, impractical, random, ineffective, disordered, confusing, unclear. [➡ THE NATURE OF IDEAS; 772] *Opposite:* logical.

muddle up *v* **confuse**, disturb, mix up, mess up (*informal*), hash up (*informal*), mistake, disorder, spoil, muff, tangle. [➡ CREATE DISORDER AND CAUSE CHAOS; 359]

muddy 1 *adj* **mucky** (*informal*), mud-spattered, dirty, grubby, grimy, filthy, slimy. [➡ DIRTY; 1234] *Opposite:* clean. 2 *adj* **cloudy**, murky, unclear, opaque, thick, dark. [➡ VISUAL TEXTURE; 1220] *Opposite:* clear.

mud flap 1 *n* **mudguard**, flap, shield, guard, cover, splashguard (*US*). [➡ EXTERNAL PARTS OF A VEHICLE; 1146] 2 *type of* **external feature**. [➡ VEHICLES; 1144]

mudflat *n* [➡ WETLANDS; 1043]

mudguard 1 *part of* **external structure**. [➡ EXTERNAL PARTS OF A VEHICLE; 1146] 2 *part of* **bike** (*informal*). [➡ BIKES, CARS, AND CARRIAGES; 1148]

mudpack *n* **face mask**, facial, face pack, treatment, beauty treatment. [➡ MAKEUP AND BEAUTY PRODUCTS; 491]

mudslide *n* [➡ EROSION AND WEATHERING; 1055]

mudslinger *n* **slanderer**, defamer, denigrator, character assassin, attacker, backbiter, exposer. [➡ INTERFERING PEOPLE AND TELLTALES; 950]

mudslinging *n* **defamation**, backbiting, slander, denigration, character assassination, libel. [➡ GOSSIP; 679] *Opposite:* praise.

mud-spattered *adj* [➡ DIRTY; 1234]

muff 1 *v* **miss**, drop, fumble, mishit, mishandle. [➡ MESS UP AND MAKE MISTAKES; 473] 2 *v* **bungle** (*informal*), mess up (*informal*), get wrong, make a hash of (*informal*), botch, blow (*slang*), fluff (*informal*), foul up (*informal*), mishandle. [➡ MESS UP AND MAKE MISTAKES; 473] 3 *type of* **accessory**. [➡ HABERDASHERY, MILLINERY, AND LINGERIE; 867]

muffin 1 *type of* **roll or bun**. [➡ BREAD, FLOUR, AND BREAD PRODUCTS; 1178] 2 *type of* **cake**. [➡ CAKES, BISCUITS, AND DESSERTS; 1180]

muffle *v* **deaden**, dampen, quieten, silence, mute, stifle. [➡ CHANGE OF INTENSITY: LESS; 396] *Opposite:* amplify.

muffled *adj* **stifled**, muted, inaudible, soft, lowered, silenced, subdued, hushed, quiet. [➡ SOFT OR PLEASANT SOUNDS; 1264] *Opposite:* loud.

muffler 1 *type of* **accessory**. [➡ HABERDASHERY, MILLINERY, AND LINGERIE; 867] 2 (*US*) *type of* **external feature**. [➡ VEHICLES; 1144]

mufti *n* **casuals**, civvies, civilian clothes, ordinary clothes, street clothes, casual wear. [➡ GARMENTS AND OUTFITS; 865] *Opposite:* uniform.

mug 1 *n* (*informal*) **face**, countenance, features, visage (*literary*), phizog (*slang*), phiz (*slang*). [➡ HEAD; 693] 2 *n* (*slang*) **fool**, dupe, sucker (*informal*), fall guy (*informal*), pushover (*informal*), gull. [➡ VICTIMS OF DECEIT; 663] 3 *v* **attack**, assault, rob, ambush, hold up, jump (*informal*). [➡PHYSICAL ATTACK AND PUNISHMENT; 416]

mugger 1 *n* **robber**, assailant, thug, attacker, assaulter, aggressor, thief, bag-snatcher, pickpocket. [➡CRIMINALS; 821] 2 *type of* **reptile**. [➡REPTILES; 994]

mugginess *n* **humidity**, closeness, clamminess, oppressiveness, warmth, moistness, dampness, heat, stickiness, sweatiness, stifling heat. [➡HOT WEATHER; 1050] *Opposite:* freshness.

mugging *n* **attack**, assault, bag-snatch, robbery, ambush, theft, holdup, purse-snatch (*US*). [➡CRIMES; 817]

See Compare and Contrast at **theft**.

muggy *adj* **humid**, close, sultry, clammy, oppressive, stifling, warm, sticky, sweaty, moist, damp, steamy. [➡HOT WEATHER; 1050] *Opposite:* fresh.

mug shot *n* **photo**, portrait, close-up, passport photo, photograph, snap, snapshot. [➡PHOTOGRAPHY AND PHOTOGRAPHIC EQUIPMENT; 1121]

mug up (*informal*) *v* **learn**, study, absorb, cram (*informal*), swot (*informal*), hit the books (*US informal*). [➡STUDYING; 844]

mukluk *type of* **boot**. [➡FOOTWEAR; 871]

mulberry *type of* **berry**. [➡FRUIT AND VEGETABLES; 1175]

mulch 1 *n* **covering**, protection, insulation, organic matter, leaves, straw, bark, peat, plastic sheeting. [➡COVERS AND COATINGS; 1245] 2 *v* **cover**, protect, insulate, dress, top dress. [➡GROW AND CULTIVATE; 352]

mule 1 *type of* **shoe**. [➡FOOTWEAR; 871] 2 *type of* **farm animal**. [➡FARM ANIMAL; 982]

mulish *adj* **stubborn**, obstinate, defiant, headstrong, obdurate, determined, wilful, pigheaded, recalcitrant. [➡UNWILLINGNESS AND STUBBORNNESS; 565] *Opposite:* amenable.

mulishness *n* **stubbornness**, obstinacy, defiance, obduracy, determination, pigheadedness, wilfulness. [➡UNWILLINGNESS AND STUBBORNNESS; 565] *Opposite:* amenability.

mull *v* **reflect**, think, cogitate (*formal*), consider, dwell on, ponder, muse, deliberate. [➡THINK AND REFLECT; 744]

mulled *adj* **spiced**, flavoured, warmed, sweetened, warm, heated, hot. [➡STATE OF PREPARED FOOD; 1170]

mullet *type of* **freshwater fish**, *type of* **hairstyle**. [➡HAIR STYLES AND HAIR PIECES; 489]

mulligatawny *type of* **soup**. [➡SOUP; 1185]

mull over *v* **think over**, consider, dwell on, think about, reflect, ponder, muse, think through, contemplate, ruminate, meditate, chew over, weigh up, deliberate, cogitate (*formal*), weigh, pore over, reflect on. [➡THINK AND REFLECT; 744]

multicolour *adj* **colourful**, rainbow, variegated, many-hued, polychrome, polychromatic, multicoloured, mottled, dappled, iridescent, flecked, coloured. [➡DESCRIBING COLOURS; 1225]

multicultural *adj* **diverse**, multiethnic, multiracial, inclusive, all-inclusive, open, culturally diverse, multinational. [➡DIFFERENCE; 150]

multifaceted *adj* **multilayered**, complex, complicated, many-sided, polygonal, manifold, multidimensional. [➡POSITIVELY COMPLEX OR COMPLICATED; 218] *Opposite:* simple.

multifarious *adj* **diverse**, varied, assorted, mixed, miscellaneous, different, manifold, diversified, various, heterogeneous. [➡DIFFERENCE; 150] *Opposite:* homogeneous.

multifariousness *n* [➡MANY, MUCH, LARGE AMOUNT; 117]

multilateral 1 *adj* **many-sided**, polygonal, multifaceted, multidimensional. [➡ORIENTATION AND ALIGNMENT; 1222] 2 *adj* **mutual**, all-party, multiparty, joint, bilateral, simultaneous. [➡RECIPROCITY AND INTERDEPENDENCE; 148] *Opposite:* unilateral.

multilingual *adj* **polyglot**, trilingual, bilingual. [➡ASPECTS OF LANGUAGE; 683]

multimedia 1 *n* **hypermedia**, software, interactive program, program. [➡COMPUTERS AND COMPUTING; 1126] 2 *n* **collage**, combination, montage, assemblage, construction. [➡COLLECTIONS AND MIXTURES OF THINGS; 1243]

multimillionaire *n* **millionaire**, magnate, billionaire, tycoon, moneybags (*informal*), mogul. [➡RICH PEOPLE; 895]

multinational 1 *adj* **international**, cosmopolitan, transnational, global, worldwide, offshore. [➡COUNTRIES AND REGIONS; 1066] *Opposite:* national. 2 *n* **conglomerate**, transnational, corporation, international business, international company, group, holding company. [➡BUSINESS ENTERPRISES AND RELATED BODIES; 793]

multipartite *adj* **multiple**, multifarious, multifaceted, composite, compound, manifold. [➡DIFFERENCE; 150]

multiple *adj* **manifold**, numerous, many, several, various, compound. [➡MANY, MUCH, LARGE AMOUNT; 117] *Opposite:* few.

multiplex *n* **multiscreen cinema**, cinema complex, picture house (*dated*), movie theater complex (*US*). [➡BUILDINGS FOR PUBLIC ENTERTAINMENT; 1083]

multiplication *n* **increase**, growth, development, reproduction, duplication, proliferation, exponentiation. [➡CHANGE OF INTENSITY: MORE; 395] *Opposite:* decrease.

multiplicity *n* **array**, diversity, variety, large quantity, range, assortment, collection, wealth. [➡MANY, MUCH, LARGE AMOUNT; 117] *Opposite:* dearth.

multiply *v* **increase**, grow, reproduce, burgeon (*literary*), swell, proliferate, enlarge, magnify, augment (*formal*). [➡CHANGE OF SIZE: BIGGER; 393] *Opposite:* decrease.

multipurpose *adj* **versatile**, flexible, adaptable, multiuse. [➡USEFULNESS; 200] *Opposite:* dedicated.

multiracial *adj* **interracial**, multicultural, multiethnic, inclusive, all-inclusive, all-embracing. [➡DIFFERENCE; 150] *Opposite:* exclusive.

multistage rocket *type of* **spacecraft**. [➡SPACE VEHICLES; 1062]

multistorey *adj* **high-rise**, multilevel, tall, high, towering, multitiered. [➡HEIGHT: HIGH; 1202] *Opposite:* low-rise.

multitalented *adj* [➡TALENTED AND SKILFUL; 528]

multitude 1 *n* **crowd**, horde, host, mass, throng, swarm, assembly, gathering, congregation, mob, legion. [➡GROUPS OF PEOPLE; 935] *Opposite:* handful. 2 *n* **variety**, assortment, array, collection, wealth, large quantity, multiplicity. [➡MANY, MUCH, LARGE AMOUNT; 117] *Opposite:* few.

multitudinous *adj* [➡MANY, MUCH, LARGE AMOUNT; 117]

mum (*informal*) 1 *n* **mother**, mummy (*informal*), mama (*informal*), ma (*informal*), mammy (*informal*), mamma (*informal*), mammie (*informal*), mom (*US informal*), mommy (*US informal*), momma (*US informal*). [➡OLDER GENERATION RELATIVES; 959] 2 *adj* **silent**, tight-lipped, mute, quiet, dumb, wordless, still, closemouthed, taciturn. [➡RETICENT AND UNFORTHCOMING; 632] *Opposite:* communicative.

mumble *v* **mutter**, murmur, drone, intone, gabble, stammer, stutter, slur, babble, garble. [➡WITTER AND BABBLE; 618] *Opposite:* enunciate.

mumbled *adj* **muttered**, murmured, muffled, inaudible, slurred, low, incomprehensible, unintelligible, incoherent, faint, inarticulate, garbled, stammered, stuttered. [➡INARTICULATE, RAMBLING, AND AWKWARD; 634] *Opposite:* enunciated.

mumbo jumbo (*informal*) *n* **jargon**, gobbledegook (*informal disapproving*), gibberish, doublespeak, cant, technobabble, legalese. [➡MEANINGLESS SPEECH OR WRITING; 677] *Opposite:* sense.

mummify 1 *v* **embalm**, preserve, wrap up, pickle, prepare, dress. [➡BURIAL AND PREPARATION FOR BURIAL; 929] 2 *v* **shrivel**, dry out, dry up, wrinkle, wither, desiccate. [➡HARDEN, CONGEAL, DRY; 388] *Opposite:* flourish.

mummy (*informal*) 1 *n* **mother**, mum (*informal*), mammy (*informal*), mama (*informal*), mommy (*US informal*), mom (*US informal*). [➡OLDER GENERATION RELATIVES; 959] 2 *n* **mummified body**, body, cadaver, corpse. [➡BURIAL AND PREPARATION FOR BURIAL; 929]

munch *v* **chew**, masticate, crunch, chomp (*informal*), grind, eat, champ. [➡EAT AND NOT EAT; 711]

mundane *adj* **ordinary**, dull, routine, everyday, commonplace, boring, unexciting, humdrum, dreary, monotonous, tedious, prosaic, banal, uninteresting. [➡BORING AND UNINTERESTING; 235] *Opposite:* exotic.

mundaneness *n* **routineness**, tedium, flatness, ordinariness, unimaginativeness, dullness. [➡BORING AND UNINTERESTING; 235] *Opposite:* excitement.

mung bean *type of* **pulse**. [➡BEANS AND PULSES; 1188]

municipal *adj* **civic**, public, community, urban, metropolitan. [➡HUMAN SETTLEMENTS; 1069] *Opposite:* private.

municipality *n* **city**, metropolis, town, borough, burg (*US*). [➡HUMAN SETTLEMENTS; 1069]

See Compare and Contrast at **city**.

munificence *n* **generosity**, largesse, benevolence, kindness, philanthropy, bounty (*literary*), charity, magnanimousness. [➡GENEROSITY AND KINDNESS; 496] *Opposite:* miserliness.

munificent *adj* **generous**, liberal, magnanimous, unstinting, unsparing, openhanded, charitable, bountiful (*literary*), freehanded (*US*). [➡GENEROSITY AND KINDNESS; 496] *Opposite:* miserly.

See Compare and Contrast at **generous**.

munitions *n* **weaponry**, ammunition, arms, guns, armaments, firepower, military capability. [➡WEAPONS; 1153]

muon *type of* **elementary particle**. [➡ELEMENTARY PARTICLES; 1278]

mural *n* **wall painting**, fresco, frieze, painting. [➡ARTWORKS; 898]

murder 1 *n* **homicide**, manslaughter, assassination, killing, slaying, unlawful death, contract killing, slaughter, massacre, wasting. [➡CAUSES OF DEATH; 921] 2 *v* **kill**, assassinate, execute, put to death, slaughter, massacre, slay (*formal or literary*), bump off (*slang*), waste (*slang*), snuff (*informal*), do (*slang*). [➡KILL; 923]

See Compare and Contrast at **kill**.

murderer *n* **killer**, assassin, slayer (*formal or literary*), butcher, slaughterer, executioner, contract killer. [➡PEOPLE WHO KILL; 924]

murderous 1 *adj* **fatal**, lethal, mortal, deadly, homicidal, brutal, vicious, cruel. [➡DEADLY; 928] 2 *adj* (*informal*) **difficult**, testing, arduous, rigorous, exhausting, strenuous. [➡PHYSICALLY UNPLEASANT; 227] *Opposite:* easy.

murk *n* **gloom**, darkness, shadows, dark, dimness, shade, obscurity. [➡DESCRIBING LIGHT; 1227] *Opposite:* light.

murkiness *n* **darkness**, fogginess, mistiness, cloudiness, gloom, shadows, dark, dimness, shade. [➡CLOUDY AND RAINY WEATHER; 1052] *Opposite:* brightness.

murky *adj* **dark**, gloomy, foggy, misty, cloudy, muddy, shadowy, dim, overcast. [➡CLOUDY AND RAINY WEATHER; 1052] *Opposite:* clear.

murmur 1 *v* **whisper**, mutter, mumble, purr, croon, susurrate, babble. [➡WITTER AND BABBLE; 618] 2 *v* **complain**, grumble, grouse (*informal*), grouch, mutter, bellyache (*informal*). [➡COMPLAIN AND NAG; 687] 3 *type of* **human sound**. [➡SOUNDS MADE BY PEOPLE; 1261]

murmured *adj* [➡SOFT OR PLEASANT SOUNDS; 1264]

Murphy bed (*US*) *type of* **bed**. [➡FURNITURE; 858]

muscle 1 *n* **sinew**, brawn, musculature, thew (*literary*). [➡THE MUSCLES; 719] 2 *n* **influence**, power, authority, force, control, weight, sway, pressure, pull. [➡STRENGTH; 202] 3 *n* (*informal*) **strength**, vigour, power, force, elbow grease (*informal*). [➡STRENGTH; 202]

muscle

◆ *types of muscle or tendon*
abdominals, Achilles tendon, biceps, diaphragm, hamstring, pectoral, quadriceps, sinew, smooth muscle, sphincter, striated muscle, tendon, triceps

muscle in (*informal*) *v* **intrude**, intervene, barge in, butt in, interfere, push in, get involved. [➡ INTERRUPT AND BUTT IN; 620]

muscly *adj* [➡ MUSCLES AND MUSCULATURE; 480]

muscular *adj* **brawny**, beefy, well-built, burly, well-developed, powerfully built, strapping (*informal*), strong, powerful. [➡ MUSCLES AND MUSCULATURE; 480] *Opposite:* puny.

muscularity *n* [➡ MUSCLES AND MUSCULATURE; 480]

muse *v* **think**, ponder, consider, mull over, cogitate (*formal*), deliberate, reflect on, chew over, ruminate, contemplate, recollect, meditate. [➡ THINK AND REFLECT; 744]

museum *n* **gallery**, exhibition hall, arts centre, academy, institution. [➡ BUILDINGS FOR PUBLIC ENTERTAINMENT; 1083]

mush 1 *n* **pap**, purée, mash, paste, slop, slush, pulp. [➡ LOTIONS, PASTES, AND GELS; 1271] 2 *n* **sentimentality**, sentimentalism, slush, slop (*informal*), schmaltz (*informal*), goo (*informal*), soppiness (*informal*), sugariness. [➡ IN POOR TASTE; 230]

mushiness *n* [➡ FLUID AND NON-SOLID; 1212]

mushroom 1 *v* **grow**, increase, expand, flourish, swell, thrive, spread out, proliferate, burgeon (*literary*). [➡ CHANGE OF SIZE: BIGGER; 393] *Opposite:* decline. 2 *type of* **fungus**. [➡ MICRO-ORGANISMS, FUNGI, AND ALGAE; 1023]

mushy 1 *adj* **soggy**, soft, squashy, squishy, squidgy, spongy. [➡ MALLEABLE AND ELASTIC; 1211] *Opposite:* firm. 2 *adj* **soppy**, oversentimental, mawkish, maudlin, syrupy, gooey (*informal*), bathetic, romantic, slushy, schmaltzy (*informal*), sloppy (*informal*). [➡ IN POOR TASTE; 230]

music *n* **melody**, tune, harmony, composition, song. [➡ MUSIC, SONGS, AND SINGING; 907]

music

◆ *types of musical register*
alto, baritone, bass, countertenor, falsetto, mezzo-soprano, soprano, tenor

◆ *types of musical term*
a cappella, adagio, allegro, andante, appassionato, arpeggio, capriccioso, con brio, crescendo, decrescendo (*US*), diminuendo, forte, fortissimo, grave, larghetto, largo, legato, lentissimo, lento, moderato, pianissimo, piano, pizzicato, sotto voce, staccato

◆ *types of instrumental music*
capriccio, concerto, fantasia, fugue, intermezzo, nocturne, overture, prelude, rondo, scherzo, sinfonia, sonata, suite, symphony

◆ *types of vocal music*
yodel, requiem, spiritual, anthem, aria, ballad, cantata, canticle, chorale, coloratura, folk song, hymn, madrigal, mass, oratorio, pop song, song

◆ *types of popular music*
bebop, bhangra, blues, calypso, country, drum and bass, dub, folk, funk, garage, gospel, jazz, mambo, pop, punk, rap, reggae, rhythm and blues, rock, rock and roll, salsa, samba, ska, soul, swing

◆ *types of classical music*
operetta, early music, Baroque, chamber music, comic opera, opera, Romantic, twelve-tone

musical *adj* **melodic**, harmonious, melodious, tuneful, easy on the ear, pleasant-sounding, pleasing, sweet. [➡ SOFT OR PLEASANT SOUNDS; 1264] *Opposite:* discordant.

music hall *n* [➡ BUILDINGS FOR PUBLIC ENTERTAINMENT; 1083]

musician 1 *n* **performer**, instrumentalist, player, artiste, composer, singer, conductor, picker (*informal*). [➡ MUSICIANS AND SINGERS; 908] 2 *type of* **entertainer**. [➡ WORKERS IN ENTERTAINMENT AND MEDIA; 873]

musing 1 *n* **thinking**, reflection, cogitation (*formal*), reverie, daydream, consideration, contemplation, ponderings, recollection, deliberation (*formal*), meditation. [➡ IDEA AND THOUGHT; 771] 2 *adj* **thoughtful**, reflective, pensive, contemplative, absorbed, speculative. [➡ PENSIVENESS AND INTEREST; 539]

musk *n* **perfume**, scent, smell, fragrance, aroma, bouquet. [➡ SMELL AND SMELLING; 706]

musket *type of* **gun**. [➡ WEAPONS FOR SHOOTING; 1155]

muskrat *type of* **rodent**. [➡ RODENT; 989]

musky *adj* **pungent**, perfumed, scented, odorous, aromatic, spicy. [➡ SMELL AND SMELLING; 706]

muslin *type of* **fabric from plants**. [➡ FABRICS; 1131]

mussel *type of* **aquatic invertebrate**. [➡ AQUATIC INVERTEBRATE; 1022]

must 1 *v* **have to**, have got to, be obliged to, ought to, should, be required to, need, want. [➡ NEED AND REQUIRE; 465] 2 *n* **necessity**, obligation, duty, essential, requirement, requisite (*formal*), need, commitment, precondition. [➡ MOST IMPORTANT THING; 198] *Opposite:* option.

mustang *type of* **horse**. [➡ HORSE; 985]

mustard 1 *type of* **spice**. [➡ HERBS AND SPICES; 1174] 2 *type of* **yellow**. [➡ COLOURS; 1223]

mustard gas *type of* **gas**. [➡ GASES; 1274]

muster 1 *v* **gather**, gather together, congregate, collect, get together, assemble, meet, rally, marshal, rendezvous, aggregate. [➡ GET CLOSER TOGETHER; 311] *Opposite:* disperse. 2 *n* **gathering**, assembly, meeting, congregation, congress, assemblage, collection, aggregation. [➡ MEETINGS AND ASSEMBLIES; 43]

mustiness *n* **dankness**, staleness, mouldiness, stuffiness, fustiness, fetidness, rankness (*literary*). [➡ DIRTY; 1234] *Opposite:* freshness.

musty *adj* **mildewed**, mouldy, stale, fusty, rank (*literary*), stuffy, fetid, malodorous, smelly. [➡ DIRTY; 1234] *Opposite:* fresh.

mutability *n* [➡ FINITENESS, VARIABILITY, AND TRANSIENCE; 96]

mutable *adj* **changeable**, alterable, changing, variable, fluctuating, inconsistent, unsettled, capricious. [➡FINITENESS, VARIABILITY, AND TRANSIENCE; 96] *Opposite:* fixed.

mutant *adj* **distorted**, misshapen, malformed, transformed, altered, changed, transmuted, modified. [➡ORIENTATION AND ALIGNMENT; 1222]

mutate *v* **change**, alter, transform, transmute, metamorphose, transfigure, modify. [➡CHANGE; 373]

mutation *n* **change**, alteration, transformation, transmutation, metamorphosis, transfiguration, modification. [➡CHANGE; 373]

mute *adj* **silent**, speechless, voiceless, unspeaking, quiet, taciturn, dumb, mum (*informal*), wordless. [➡ABSENCE OF SOUND; 1256] *Opposite:* vocal.

muted *adj* **subdued**, hushed, soft, quiet, gentle, low-key, muffled. [➡SOFT OR PLEASANT SOUNDS; 1264] *Opposite:* loud.

mutilate *v* **maim**, injure, hurt, disfigure, harm, damage, spoil, deface, mar, dismember. [➡DESTRUCTION AND DEMOLITION; 360]

mutilated *adj* [➡IN BAD REPAIR; 1233]

mutilation *n* **disfigurement**, defacement, damage, injury, maiming, dismemberment, hurt. [➡DESTRUCTION AND DEMOLITION; 360]

mutineer *n* **rebel**, insurgent, rioter, radical, insurrectionist, revolutionary. [➡UNCOOPERATIVE OR REBELLIOUS PERSON; 567]

mutinous *adj* **rebellious**, revolutionary, seditious, subversive, riotous (*formal*), disobedient, insubordinate, defiant, recalcitrant, unruly, wayward. [➡REBELLIOUSNESS AND DISOBEDIENCE; 566] *Opposite:* obedient.

mutiny *n* **rebellion**, revolt, sedition, uprising, insubordination, defiance, recalcitrance, revolution, riot, insurgence, insurrection. [➡AGGRESSIVE EVENT; 39]

mutt (*slang*) *n* [➡DOG; 980]

mutter 1 *v* **mumble**, murmur, drone, burble, witter (*informal*), slur, gabble. [➡WITTER AND BABBLE; 618] 2 *v* **complain**, grouch, grouse (*informal*), grumble, murmur, bellyache (*informal*). [➡COMPLAIN AND NAG; 687] 3 *type of* **human sound**. [➡SOUNDS MADE BY PEOPLE; 1261]

mutton *type of* **meat**. [➡TYPES AND CUTS OF MEAT; 1176]

muttonchops *n* [➡FACIAL HAIR; 490]

mutual *adj* **joint**, shared, common, communal, reciprocated, reciprocal, conjoint, related. [➡RECIPROCITY AND INTERDEPENDENCE; 148]

muumuu *type of* **dress**. [➡GARMENTS AND OUTFITS; 865]

muzzily *adv* **woozily**, confusedly, vaguely, dazedly, groggily, dizzily, blearily. [➡ILL AND SICK; 741]

muzzle *v* **silence**, gag, shut up (*informal*), hush, quieten, stifle, suppress. [➡MAKE IMPOSSIBLE; 277]

muzzy 1 *adj* **vague**, fuzzy, out of focus, bleary, indistinct, faint, shadowy. [➡VAGUENESS; 244] *Opposite:* clear. 2 *adj* **fuzzy**, woozy, groggy, wobbly (*informal*), bleary, shaky, dizzy. [➡ILL AND SICK; 741] *Opposite:* clear-headed.

my *interj* [➡EXPRESSIONS OF SURPRISE; 547]

mycoplasma *type of* **microorganism**. [➡MICROORGANISMS, FUNGI, AND ALGAE; 1023]

my goodness *interj* [➡EXPRESSIONS OF SURPRISE; 547]

myopia 1 *n* **short-sightedness**, poor sight, nearsightedness (*US*). [➡SEE; 700] 2 *n* **bigotry**, prejudice, bias, intolerance, narrow-mindedness. [➡NEGATIVE INTELLECTUAL CHARACTERISTICS; 526]

myopic 1 *adj* **short-sighted**, owlish, nearsighted (*US*). [➡SEE; 700] 2 *adj* **narrow-minded**, bigoted, parochial, prejudiced, intolerant, biased. [➡NEGATIVE INTELLECTUAL CHARACTERISTICS; 526] *Opposite:* broad-minded.

myriad 1 *adj* **countless**, innumerable, numberless, numerous, many, uncountable, unnumbered, untold. [➡MANY, MUCH, LARGE AMOUNT; 117] *Opposite:* few. 2 *n* **multitude**, mass, host, army, crowd, wealth, variety, heap (*informal*). [➡MANY, MUCH, LARGE AMOUNT; 117] *Opposite:* few.

mysterious 1 *adj* **strange**, unexplained, inexplicable, unsolved, odd, puzzling, mystifying, baffling, peculiar, weird. [➡BIZARRE AND PECULIAR; 258] 2 *adj* **secretive**, enigmatic, shadowy, furtive, cagey (*informal*), cryptic, covert, stealthy, surreptitious. [➡RETICENT AND UNFORTHCOMING; 632] *Opposite:* open.

mysteriousness *n* **strangeness**, oddness, weirdness, curiousness, inexplicableness, peculiarity. [➡BIZARRE AND PECULIAR; 258] *Opposite:* normality.

mystery 1 *n* **problem**, puzzle, conundrum, enigma, riddle. [➡SECRETS AND MYSTERIES; 181] 2 *n* **secrecy**, obscurity, ambiguity, inscrutability, vagueness, anonymity. [➡SECRET AND UNKNOWN; 180] 3 *adj* **unknown**, anonymous, unidentified, secret, clandestine, furtive, enigmatic, covert, cryptic. [➡SECRET AND UNKNOWN; 180] 4 *n* **whodunit**, detective novel, thriller, crime novel. [➡FICTION AND DRAMA; 913]

See Compare and Contrast at **problem**.

mystic 1 *n* **spiritualist**, medium, shaman, sage (*literary*), sorcerer, wizard. [➡PEOPLE WITH SUPERNATURAL POWERS; 789] 2 *adj* **mystical**, spiritual, supernatural, numinous, magical, cabalistic, sorcerous. [➡THE SUPERNATURAL; 788]

mystical *adj* **spiritual**, mystic, numinous, magical, supernatural, magic, transcendent, preternatural. [➡THE SUPERNATURAL; 788]

mystification *n* **bewilderment**, confusion, perplexity, bafflement, puzzlement, stupefaction, incomprehension, disorientation. [➡CONFUSION, ANXIETY, AND WORRY; 541]

mystified *adj* **puzzled**, confused, bewildered, bamboozled (*informal*), baffled, perplexed. [➡CONFUSION, ANXIETY, AND WORRY; 541] *Opposite:* enlightened.

mystify *v* **puzzle**, confuse, bewilder, confound, bamboozle (*informal*), baffle, stump, perplex, stymie, stupefy, floor, muddle. [➡CONFUSE AND BEWILDER; 572]

mystifying *adj* **mysterious**, baffling, inexplicable, puzzling, confusing, strange, perplexing, enigmatic, stupefying. [➡ BIZARRE AND PECULIAR; 258]

mystique *n* **air of mystery**, air of secrecy, aura, charisma, magic, charm, inscrutability, mysteriousness, secretiveness. [➡ SECRET AND UNKNOWN; 180]

myth 1 *n* **legend**, fable, saga, fairy story, fairy tale, allegory, parable, lore, mythos, apologue. [➡ THE ORAL TRADITION; 678] 2 *n* **falsehood**, fiction, illusion, invention, fabrication, untruth, figment, creation. [➡ NONEXISTENT THINGS; 23] *Opposite:* fact.

mythic *see* **mythical**.

mythical 1 *adj* **legendary**, mythological, fabled, fabulous, storybook, fairy-tale. [➡ FALSE AND UNREAL; 174] *Opposite:* factual. 2 *adj* **imaginary**, untrue, fictitious, fictional, made-up, make-believe, invented, unreal, false. [➡ FALSE AND UNREAL; 174] *Opposite:* real.

mythological *adj* **mythical**, mythic, fabulous, fairy-tale, fabled, storybook, allegorical, epic. [➡ FALSE AND UNREAL; 174] *Opposite:* factual.

mythological

◆ *types of mythological creature*
centaur, Chimera, dragon, griffin, mermaid, sphinx, unicorn, vampire, werewolf

mythology *n* **myths**, legends, folklore, tradition, mythos, lore. [➡ THE ORAL TRADITION; 678]

my word (*dated*) *interj* [➡ EXPRESSIONS OF SURPRISE; 547]

N

nab 1 *v* (*informal*) **arrest**, seize, capture, detain, catch, hold, apprehend. [➡THE POLICE, ARREST, AND PRE-TRIAL PROCEEDINGS; 818] 2 *v* **steal**, pinch (*informal*), rip off (*informal*), swipe (*informal*), walk off with, snitch (*slang*), lift (*informal*). [➡STEAL AND ROB; 427]

nadir *n* **lowest point**, all-time low, depths of despair, pits (*informal*), depths, base, foot, rock bottom. [➡DIFFICULT SITUATIONS; 72] *Opposite:* zenith.

naevus *n* [➡CONDITIONS AFFECTING THE SKIN; 722]

naff (*informal*) *adj* **tasteless**, unfashionable, unstylish, ridiculous, crass, vulgar. [➡IN POOR TASTE; 230] *Opposite:* fashionable.

nag 1 *v* **badger**, pester, plague, harass, hassle (*informal*), harry, keep on at (*informal*), carp at, needle. [➡COMPLAIN AND NAG; 687] 2 *v* **criticize**, find fault, carp, grouse (*informal*), grumble, complain. [➡ACCUSE, BLAME, AND CRITICIZE; 642] 3 *v* **irritate**, annoy, worry, trouble, torment, irk, disturb, vex, bother, distress. [➡ANGER AND ANNOY; 570]

See Compare and Contrast at **complain.**

nagging *adj* **irritating**, niggling, troublesome, distressing, irksome, harassing, pesky (*US informal*). [➡IRRITATING; 229]

naiad *n* [➡MYTHICAL BEINGS; 790]

nail 1 *n* **pin**, spike, tack, peg. [➡FASTENERS, LINKS, AND NETWORKS; 1246] 2 *v* **tack**, pin, fix, fasten, attach, secure. [➡FASTEN, LINK, AND JOIN; 409]

nail-biting *adj* **nerve-racking**, tense, exciting, stressful, anxious, worrying, scary (*informal*), edgy, uneasy. [➡FRIGHTENING; 232] *Opposite:* relaxing.

nail bomb *type of* **explosive weapon.** [➡EXPLOSIVES; 1154]

nailbrush *type of* **cosmetic tool.** [➡HAND TOOLS; 1118]

nail clippers *type of* **cosmetic tool.** [➡HAND TOOLS; 1118]

nail down *v* **pin down**, get an agreement on, get a decision on, settle, confirm, agree, decide. [➡EXPLAIN AND CLARIFY; 611]

nail file *type of* **cosmetic tool.** [➡HAND TOOLS; 1118]

nail polish *n* [➡MAKEUP AND BEAUTY PRODUCTS; 491]

nail scissors *type of* **cosmetic tool.** [➡HAND TOOLS; 1118]

naissance *n* [➡BEGINNING; 53]

naive 1 *adj* **simple**, trusting, innocent, childlike, inexperienced, ingenuous, guileless. [➡NATURALNESS; 498] *Opposite:* suspicious. 2 *adj* **unsophisticated**, gullible, wet behind the ears, green, foolish, credulous, unwise. [➡NEGATIVE INTELLECTUAL CHARACTERISTICS; 526] *Opposite:* shrewd.

naivety *n* **innocence**, ingenuousness, candour, artlessness, naturalness, inexperience, gullibility, simplicity. [➡NATURALNESS; 498] *Opposite:* sophistication.

naked 1 *adj* **bare**, nude, unclothed, stark-naked, stripped, starkers (*informal*), in the altogether (*informal*), undressed, in your birthday suit (*slang humorous*), in the buff (*informal*), with nothing on, buck naked (*US*). [➡DRESS, WEAR, AND UNDRESS; 868] *Opposite:* clothed. 2 *adj* **uncovered**, unprotected, exposed, unsheathed, unwrapped, unguarded. [➡PERCEPTIBLE; 25] *Opposite:* covered. 3 *adj* **open**, undisguised, unadorned, unadulterated, unvarnished, blatant, stark, obvious, plain, simple, overt. [➡PERCEPTIBLE; 25] *Opposite:* hidden.

Compare and Contrast: ***naked, bare, nude, undressed, unclothed***

CORE MEANING: DEVOID OF CLOTHES OR COVERING

naked not covered or concealed, especially not covered by clothing on any part of the body; ***bare*** without the usual furnishings or decorations, or not covered by clothing; ***nude*** not wearing any clothes at all, especially in artistic contexts; ***undressed*** not wearing any or many clothes, used specially when clothes have just been removed or are about to be put on; ***unclothed*** not wearing any clothes.

nakedly *adv* **openly**, blatantly, starkly, obviously, overtly, plainly, simply. [➡INTENTIONAL AND DELIBERATE; 280] *Opposite:* covertly.

nakedness 1 *n* **nudity**, bareness, state of undress. [➡DRESS, WEAR, AND UNDRESS; 868] 2 *n* **defencelessness**, helplessness, exposure, vulnerability. [➡DANGER; 236] 3 *n* **blatancy**, obviousness, openness, overtness, starkness, plainness, evidence. [➡PERCEPTIBLE; 25] *Opposite:* covertness.

namby-pamby (*informal*) *adj* **feeble**, soft, pathetic (*informal*), wishy-washy (*informal*), spineless, ineffectual. [➡COWARDICE AND WEAKNESS OF WILL; 509] *Opposite:* tough.

name 1 *n* **first name**, Christian name, forename, given name, surname, family name, middle name, maiden name, pet name, nickname, last name, handle (*slang*), moniker (*slang*). [➡NAME AND DESCRIBE; 666] 2 *n* **designation**, term, appellation (*formal*), tag, title, label, style (*formal*). [➡NAME AND DESCRIBE; 666] 3 *n* **reputation**, repute (*formal*), renown, character, respectability, honour, fame, celebrity. [➡KNOWN AND FAMOUS; 182] *Opposite:* notoriety. 4 *n* **celebrity**, star, big name, public figure, VIP, luminary, famous person, bigwig (*informal*). [➡IMPORTANT OR FAMOUS PEOPLE; 893] *Opposite:* nobody. 5 *v* **call**, christen, baptize, nickname, label, term, dub, entitle. [➡NAME AND DESCRIBE; 666] 6 *v* **identify**, specify, refer to, mention, cite, brand. [➡NAME AND DESCRIBE; 666] *Opposite:* conceal. 7 *v* **nominate**, appoint, assign, choose, suggest, propose, select. [➡CONFER STATUS; 459] *Opposite:* reject.

name-calling *n* **abuse**, insults, foul language, invective (*formal*), swearing. [➡INSULTS, ABUSE, AND SWEARING; 659]

named *adj* **called**, baptized, christened, entitled, titled, known as, so-called, termed. [➡NAME AND DESCRIBE; 666] *Opposite:* nameless.

name-drop *v* **boast**, brag, show off, swank (*informal*), vaunt. [➡NAME AND DESCRIBE; 666]

name-dropper *n* **boaster**, bragger, braggart, show-off (*informal*), bigmouth (*informal*), blower (*US informal*). [➡SELF-IMPORTANT AND SELF-SEEKING PEOPLE; 949]

nameless 1 *adj* **anonymous**, unknown, unidentified, unnamed, unspecified, mysterious, shadowy. [➡SECRET AND UNKNOWN; 180] *Opposite:* named. 2 *adj* **indescribable**, awful, dreadful, horrible, ghastly, fearsome, terrible. [➡EMOTIONALLY UNPLEASANT AND UPSETTING; 228]

namely *adv* **that is**, that is to say, viz, specifically, explicitly, to be exact, to be precise, i.e., to wit, for example, such as. [➡EXPRESSIONS INTRODUCING EXAMPLES; 64]

nameplate *n* **plate**, sign, plaque, notice, panel. [➡SIGNPOSTS, SIGNALS AND BILLBOARDS; 596]

naming *n* **identification**, designation, nomenclature, christening, baptism. [➡NAME AND DESCRIBE; 666]

nan 1 *n* (*informal*) [➡OLDER GENERATION RELATIVES; 959] 2 *type of* **bread**. [➡BREAD, FLOUR, AND BREAD PRODUCTS; 1178]

nana (*informal*) *n* [➡OLDER GENERATION RELATIVES; 959]

nanny 1 *n* **child minder**, au pair, carer, minder, caretaker (*US*), caregiver (*US*). [➡PEOPLE WHO GUARD AND PROTECT; 846] 2 *n* (*informal*) **nana** (*informal*), nan (*informal*), granny (*informal*), gran (*informal*), grandma (*informal*), grandmother. [➡OLDER GENERATION RELATIVES; 959]

nanny goat *type of* **female animal**. [➡MALE OR FEMALE ANIMAL; 978]

nanosecond *n* **moment**, split second, second, instant, trice, jiffy (*informal*), tick (*informal*). [➡SHORT PERIOD OF TIME; 93]

nap 1 *n* **doze**, snooze (*informal*), catnap, siesta, shuteye (*informal*), sleep, lie-down (*informal*), rest, kip (*informal*), zizz (*informal*), forty winks (*informal*). [➡SLEEP AND DREAM; 724] 2 *v* **snooze** (*informal*), sleep, catnap, have a siesta, doze, drowse, have a lie-down (*informal*), have forty winks (*informal*), get some shuteye (*informal*), kip (*informal*), zizz (*informal*), catch some z's (*US informal*). [➡SLEEP AND DREAM; 724] 3 *n* **pile**, surface, finish, weave, texture, down, fibre, shag. [➡TEXTURE; 1219]

napalm *type of* **explosive material**. [➡EXPLOSIVES; 1154]

nape *part of* **head**. [➡HEAD; 693]

napkin *n* **serviette**, bib, paper towel, napery (*archaic*), table linen. [➡SOFT FURNISHINGS, LINEN, AND DRAPERY; 860]

narcissism *n* **self-love**, self-admiration, self-absorption, egotism, conceit, self-importance, selfishness, self-centredness, vanity. [➡AFFECTATION, SELF-SATISFACTION, AND SNOBBISHNESS; 508] *Opposite:* selflessness.

narcissist *n* [➡SELF-IMPORTANT AND SELF-SEEKING PEOPLE; 949]

narcissistic *adj* **vain**, self-absorbed, egotistic, egotistical, selfish, conceited, self-important, self-loving, self-admiring. [➡AFFECTATION, SELF-SATISFACTION, AND SNOBBISHNESS; 508] *Opposite:* selfless.

narcissus *type of* **flower grown from bulb**. [➡FLOWERS FROM BULBS; 1030]

nark 1 *v* (*informal*) **provoke**, incense, drive mad (*informal*), aggravate (*informal*), madden, wind up (*informal*), annoy, bother, infuriate, frustrate, put out, get on your nerves, upset, exasperate, irritate, anger, displease. [➡ANGER AND ANNOY; 570] *Opposite:* please. 2 *v* (*informal*) **complain**, grumble, whine, whinge (*informal*), carp, find fault, nitpick, moan (*informal*), grouse. [➡COMPLAIN AND NAG; 687] 3 *n* (*slang*) **informer**, decoy, grass (*slang*), supergrass (*informal*), stool pigeon (*slang*). [➡INTERFERING PEOPLE AND TELLTALES; 950]

narked (*informal*) *adj* [➡IRRITATION AND ANGER; 542]

narrate *v* **relate**, recount, tell, describe, recite, report. [➡RECITE, REPEAT, AND NARRATE; 621]

narration 1 *n* **telling**, recitation, relating, unfolding, recounting, describing. [➡NEUTRAL ONE-WAY COMMUNICATION; 49] 2 *n* **tale**, account, description, chronicle, history, story. [➡THE ORAL TRADITION; 678]

narrative 1 *n* **tale**, account, description, chronicle, history, story. [➡THE ORAL TRADITION; 678] 2 *n* **plot**, story line, sequence of events. [➡THE ORAL TRADITION; 678]

narrator *n* **storyteller**, speaker, raconteur, teller of tales, relator, chronicler, reporter. [➡THE ORAL TRADITION; 678] *Opposite:* listener.

narrow 1 *adj* **thin**, fine, slim, slender, slight, tapered, contracted, constricted, tight, limited, restricted. [➡WIDTH: NARROW AND THIN; 1199] *Opposite:* wide. 2 *v* **get thinner**, get smaller, taper, contract, tighten, constrict. [➡CHANGE OF SIZE: SMALLER; 394] *Opposite:* widen. 3 *v* **restrict**, limit, narrow down, confine, focus, reduce. [➡CHANGE OF SIZE: SMALLER; 394] *Opposite:* broaden.

narrow boat *type of* **small vessel**. [➡SHIPS AND BOATS; 1149]

narrow down *v* **focus**, restrict, limit, confine, concentrate, fix on, centre on, zero in. [➡CHANGE OF SIZE: SMALLER; 394] *Opposite:* broaden.

narrow escape *n* **close call**, near thing (*informal*), near miss, narrow squeak, close shave, lucky escape. [➡RESULTS AND OUTCOMES; 83]

narrowing *n* **tapering**, contraction, thinning, reduction, tightening, lessening. [➡CHANGE OF SIZE: SMALLER; 394]

narrowly 1 *adv* **only just**, barely, hardly, scarcely, by a hair's breadth, by a whisker. [➡TO A CERTAIN EXTENT; 134] 2 *adv* **closely**, intently, carefully, attentively, assiduously, with care. [➡CAUTIOUS AND CAREFUL; 283]

narrow-minded *adj* **bigoted**, blinkered, insular, intolerant, prejudiced, biased, reactionary, parochial, provincial (*disapproving*), pigheaded. [➡NEGATIVE INTELLECTUAL CHARACTERISTICS; 526] *Opposite:* broad-minded.

narrow-mindedness *n* **bigotry**, insularity, prejudice, bias, intolerance, parochialism, provinciality (*dis-*

approving). [➡NEGATIVE INTELLECTUAL CHARACTERISTICS; 526] *Opposite:* broad-mindedness.

narrowness *n* **thinness**, fineness, slimness, slightness, constriction, tightness, slenderness, restriction. [➡WIDTH: NARROW AND THIN; 1199] *Opposite:* width.

narrow squeak *n* **narrow escape**, close shave, close call, lucky escape, near miss, near thing (*informal*). [➡RESULTS AND OUTCOMES; 83]

narwhal *type of* **whale**. [➡WHALE; 991]

nasal *adj* [➡THE NOSE; 705]

nascent *adj* **budding**, promising, embryonic, emerging, blossoming, burgeoning, growing. [➡FUTURE; 86] *Opposite:* moribund.

nasi goreng *type of* **cooked dish**. [➡PREPARED DISHES; 1169]

nastily *adv* **spitefully**, meanly, maliciously, viciously, cruelly, horribly, unkindly, unpleasantly, obnoxiously, objectionably, offensively. [➡SELFISH AND UNKIND; 506] *Opposite:* kindly.

nastiness *n* **spite**, meanness, malice, viciousness, cruelty, unkindness, unpleasantness, offensiveness, maliciousness, spitefulness, malevolence, wickedness, obnoxiousness. [➡UNKIND ACTION OR BEHAVIOUR; 297] *Opposite:* kindness.

nasturtium *type of* **annual flower**. [➡FLOWERS; 1032]

nasty 1 *adj* **spiteful**, mean, malicious, vicious, cruel, horrible, malevolent, wicked. [➡SELFISH AND UNKIND; 506] *Opposite:* kind. 2 *adj* **foul**, horrid, horrible, revolting, offensive, bad, disgusting, nauseating, sickening, vile, ghastly, unpleasant, repugnant. [➡DISGUSTING AND REPULSIVE; 231] *Opposite:* pleasant. 3 *adj* **severe**, painful, horrible, serious, grave, worrying, dangerous. [➡DANGEROUS; 237] *Opposite:* slight. 4 *adj* (*informal*) **obscene**, offensive, indecent, vulgar, crude, vile. [➡MORALLY BAD; 776] 5 *adj* (*informal*) **difficult**, tricky, hard, complicated, knotty, thorny, complex. [➡DIFFICULTY AND COMPLEXITY; 243]

See Compare and Contrast at **mean**.

nation 1 *n* **state**, country, land, realm, homeland, nation-state. [➡COUNTRIES AND REGIONS; 1066] 2 *n* **people**, population, inhabitants, residents, populace. [➡GROUPS IN SOCIETY; 940]

national 1 *adj* **nationwide**, countrywide, state, general, coast-to-coast, domestic, home. [➡GENERAL LOCATIONS; 159] *Opposite:* local. 2 *adj* **state**, public, nationalized, state-run, state-owned, federal. [➡BELONGING OR RELATING TO PEOPLE; 943] *Opposite:* private. 3 *n* **resident**, citizen, inhabitant, subject, native. [➡INHABITANT; 857] *Opposite:* visitor.

national guard *n* [➡THE ARMED FORCES; 827]

nationalism 1 *n* **independence**, autonomy, home rule, self-rule, self-government, separatism. [➡STYLES AND SYSTEMS OF GOVERNMENT; 806] 2 *n* **patriotism**, chauvinism, jingoism, xenophobia. [➡PHILOSOPHIES AND BELIEFS; 781]

nationalist *n* **separatist**, autonomist, separationist. [➡POLITICAL OFFICES AND POLITICIANS; 808]

nationalistic *adj* **patriotic**, jingoistic, chauvinistic, xenophobic. [➡PHILOSOPHIES AND BELIEFS; 781] *Opposite:* internationalist.

nationality *n* **people**, population, race, ethnic group. [➡COUNTRIES AND REGIONS; 1066]

nationalize *v* **make public**, take over, municipalize. [➡SOCIAL, POLITICAL, AND ECONOMIC CHANGE; 374] *Opposite:* privatize.

nationalized *adj* **state-owned**, publicly owned, public sector, state, national. [➡BELONGING OR RELATING TO PEOPLE; 943] *Opposite:* private.

nationally *adv* **countrywide**, all over the country, on a national scale, nationwide, generally. [➡COUNTRIES AND REGIONS; 1066] *Opposite:* locally.

national park *n* [➡THE COUNTRYSIDE AND OUTDOOR SPACES; 1070]

nation-state *n* **state**, country, land, nation, sovereign state, realm. [➡COUNTRIES AND REGIONS; 1066]

nationwide 1 *adj* **countrywide**, general, national, state, coast-to-coast, from Land's End to John O'Groats. [➡GENERAL LOCATIONS; 159] *Opposite:* local. 2 *adv* **nationally**, countrywide, all over the country, on a national scale, generally. [➡COUNTRIES AND REGIONS; 1066] *Opposite:* locally.

native 1 *adj* **innate**, natural, inborn, instinctive, inherent, built-in, intrinsic, intuitive. [➡TRUE AND REAL; 172] *Opposite:* acquired. 2 *adj* **indigenous**, local, aboriginal, resident, autochthonous. [➡COUNTRIES AND REGIONS; 1066] *Opposite:* foreign. 3 *n* **inhabitant**, resident, local, citizen, subject, national, aboriginal. [➡INHABITANT; 857] *Opposite:* foreigner.

Compare and Contrast: ***native, aboriginal, indigenous, autochthonous***

CORE MEANING: ORIGINATING IN A PARTICULAR PLACE

native born or originating in a particular place; ***aboriginal*** existing in a region from the earliest known times; ***indigenous*** originating in and typical of a region or country; ***autochthonous*** originating where currently found, especially used of rocks and minerals that were formed in their present position, or flora, fauna or inhabitants decended from those present in a region from earliest times.

native land *n* **land of origin**, land of birth, birthplace, native country, motherland, fatherland, mother country, home, homeland. [➡COUNTRIES AND REGIONS; 1066]

nativity *n* **origin**, birth, genesis, conception, dawn, beginning. [➡BEGINNING; 53] *Opposite:* demise (*informal*).

natter (*informal*) 1 *v* **have a chat**, chat, chatter, chinwag, gossip, blether (*informal*), jaw (*slang*), talk, rabbit on (*informal*), prattle, blather (*informal*). [➡TWO-WAY COMMUNICATION; 608] 2 *n* **chat**, chinwag (*informal*), conversation, gossip, talk, chitchat (*informal*). [➡INFORMAL COMMUNICATION; 45]

nattering (*informal*) *n* [➡MEANINGLESS SPEECH OR WRITING; 677]

natterjack toad *type of* **amphibian**. [➡AMPHIBIANS; 1008]

natty *adj* **smart**, fashionable, trim, dapper, chic, spruce, nifty (*informal*), snazzy (*informal*), trendy (*informal*), neat. [➡WELL GROOMED; 483] *Opposite:* unfashionable.

natural 1 *adj* **usual**, normal, ordinary, accepted, expected, regular, likely. [➡ORDINARINESS; 245] *Opposite:* unusual. 2 *adj* **physical**, biological, environmental, ecological, geographical, geological. [➡BIOLOGICAL SCIENCES; 1037] *Opposite:* technological. 3 *adj* **innate**, native, inborn, instinctive, effortless, inherent. [➡TRUE AND REAL; 172] *Opposite:* learned. 4 *adj* **unaffected**, unpretentious, spontaneous, genuine, artless, sincere, relaxed, open. [➡NATURALNESS; 498] *Opposite:* affected. 5 *adj* **untreated**, unprocessed, pure, raw, crude, organic. [➡RAW AND NATURAL; 1213] *Opposite:* artificial. 6 *adj* **biological**, physical, birth, true, actual, real. [➡TRUE AND REAL; 172] *Opposite:* adoptive.

natural ability *n* [➡SKILLS, TALENTS, AND ABILITIES; 527]

natural disaster *n* [➡VOLCANOES AND EARTHQUAKES; 1054]

natural fibre *n* [➡TEXTILES AND THREADS; 1130]

natural gas *type of* **gas.** [➡GASES; 1274]

natural gift *n* [➡SKILLS, TALENTS, AND ABILITIES; 527]

naturalistic *adj* **realistic**, real, true-to-life, natural, lifelike, representational, real-life. [➡TRUE AND REAL; 172]

naturalize 1 *v* **accept**, adopt, enfranchise. [➡ELECTIONS AND SUFFRAGE; 807] 2 *v* **adapt**, become established, grow wild, grow naturally, acclimatize. [➡CHANGE; 373]

naturally 1 *adv* **of course**, obviously, logically, as expected, unsurprisingly, certainly, indeed. [➡EXPRESSIONS OF AGREEMENT; 649] *Opposite:* surprisingly. 2 *adv* **innately**, inherently, instinctively, intuitively, effortlessly. [➡TRUE AND REAL; 172] 3 *adv* **unaffectedly**, unpretentiously, spontaneously, genuinely, artlessly, sincerely, in a relaxed manner, openly, easily, effortlessly. [➡NATURALNESS; 498] *Opposite:* pretentiously. 4 *adv* **in nature**, physically, biologically, geographically, geologically, organically, purely. [➡RAW AND NATURAL; 1213] *Opposite:* artificially.

naturalness *n* **unaffectedness**, spontaneity, genuineness, artlessness, sincerity, openness. [➡NATURALNESS; 498] *Opposite:* affectedness.

natural resource *n* **raw material**, mineral, mineral deposit, reserve, resource. [➡SUBSTANCES; 1266]

natural world *n* **environment**, nature, biosphere, ecosphere. [➡NATURE AND THE ENVIRONMENT; 1038]

nature 1 *n* **Mother Nature**, countryside, natural surroundings, wildlife, flora, fauna, landscape, natural world, environment. [➡NATURE AND THE ENVIRONMENT; 1038] 2 *n* **class**, kind, sort, type, description, character, quality, characteristics, features, ilk, stripe. [➡VARIETY, TYPE, KIND; 146] 3 *n* **character**, personality, temperament, disposition, spirit, makeup, complexion, humour. [➡TEMPERAMENT AND BEHAVIOUR; 493]

nature preserve (*US*) *n* [➡THE COUNTRYSIDE AND OUTDOOR SPACES; 1070]

nature reserve *n* [➡THE COUNTRYSIDE AND OUTDOOR SPACES; 1070]

naturopath *n* [➡PEOPLE WHO WORK IN MEDICINE; 848]

naughtiness *n* **disobedience**, bad behaviour, wickedness, ill-discipline, waywardness, mischief, impishness. [➡REBELLIOUSNESS AND DISOBEDIENCE; 566] *Opposite:* obedience.

naughty *adj* **disobedient**, bad, badly behaved, wicked, ill-disciplined, wayward, mischievous, impish. [➡REBELLIOUSNESS AND DISOBEDIENCE; 566] *Opposite:* good.

See Compare and Contrast at **bad.**

nausea 1 *n* **biliousness**, queasiness, sickness, vomiting, unsettled stomach, seasickness, motion sickness. [➡ILL AND SICK; 741] 2 *n* (*literary*) **revulsion**, repugnance, repulsion, abhorrence, disgust, aversion, detestation, hatred. [➡DISLIKE AND HATE; 578]

nauseate *v* **sicken**, disgust, repel, revolt, turn your stomach, make you feel sick, upset, put off. [➡UPSET, DISTRESS, AND HUMILIATE; 568] *Opposite:* please.

nauseated *adj* [➡ILL AND SICK; 741]

nauseating *adj* **disgusting**, sickening, repellent, revolting, repulsive, hideous, upsetting, off-putting, gross. [➡DISGUSTING AND REPULSIVE; 231] *Opposite:* pleasant.

nauseous 1 *adj* **sick**, bilious, queasy, unwell, nauseated, woozy, seasick. [➡ILL AND SICK; 741] *Opposite:* well. 2 *adj* **disgusting**, sickening, repellent, revolting, repulsive, upsetting, gross, detestable, hideous. [➡DISGUSTING AND REPULSIVE; 231] *Opposite:* pleasant.

nautical *adj* **maritime**, naval, seafaring, sailing, marine, navigational. [➡THE SEAS, OCEANS, AND SHORES; 1041]

naval *adj* **nautical**, maritime, seafaring, sailing, marine, navigational. [➡THE SEAS, OCEANS, AND SHORES; 1041]

nave *n* [➡PARTS OF RELIGIOUS BUILDINGS; 1085]

navel *n* **umbilicus** (*technical*), tummy button (*informal*), bellybutton (*informal*). [➡TORSO; 694]

navel-gazing *n* **self-analysis**, reflection, rumination, brooding, self-absorption, meditation, contemplation, daydreaming, woolgathering. [➡THE NATURE OF IDEAS; 772]

navigable 1 *adj* **passable**, negotiable, crossable, traversable. [➡IN GOOD REPAIR; 1231] *Opposite:* impassable. 2 *adj* **manoeuvrable**, controllable, pilotable, seaworthy, sturdy, steerable. [➡IN GOOD REPAIR; 1231]

navigate 1 *v* **find the way**, plot a course, plot a route, map read, follow the map. [➡TRAVEL: WAYS OF TRAVELLING; 321] 2 *v* **sail across**, circumnavigate (*formal*), steer, pilot, take the helm, direct, pass through, travel through, cross, traverse. [➡TRAVEL: WAYS OF TRAVELLING; 321]

navigation *n* **direction finding**, steering, course plotting, map reading, celestial navigation, triangulation. [➡NAVIGATION; 1140]

navigational *adj* **directional**, direction-finding, course-plotting, route-finding. [➡NAVIGATION; 1140]

navigator *n* **guide**, autopilot, skipper, pilot, direction finder, route finder. [➡NAVIGATION; 1140]

navvy (*dated*) *n* **manual worker**, labourer, manual labourer, worker, hand. [➡FARMERS, GARDENERS, AND MANUAL WORKERS; 849]

navy *n* **fleet**, armada, flotilla, merchant navy, merchant marine (*US*). [➡THE ARMED FORCES; 827]

navy bean (*US*) *type of* **pulse.** [➡BEANS AND PULSES; 1188]

navy blue *type of* **blue.** [➡COLOURS; 1223]

nay (*archaic or literary*) *adv* **or rather**, and also, more correctly, indeed, even, truly, verily (*archaic*). [➡EXPRESSIONS INTRODUCING EXTRA INFORMATION; 137]

naysay (*US*) *v* [➡DENY AND REJECT; 645]

NB *adv* [➡WRITTEN CONVENTIONS; 600]

near 1 *prep* **close to**, by, next to, in close proximity to, in the vicinity of, in the neighbourhood, in front of. [➡CLOSENESS; 160] *Opposite:* far from. 2 *prep* **like**, close to, similar to, resembling, approaching. [➡SIMILARITY; 149] 3 *prep* **on the verge of**, approaching, nearing, close to, bordering on, touching on. [➡CLOSENESS; 160] 4 *adv* **nearby**, close, close by, close to, close at hand, in close proximity, hard by, to hand, in the vicinity, in the neighbourhood, nigh. [➡CLOSENESS; 160] 5 *adv* **almost**, nearly, virtually, practically, just about, all but, not quite, about. [➡TO A CERTAIN EXTENT; 134] 6 *adj* **close**, nearby, neighbouring, adjacent, adjoining, immediate, nigh, proximate. [➡CLOSENESS; 160] *Opposite:* far. 7 *v* **approach**, reach, draw up to, draw near to, go up to, come up to, border on, verge on, touch on, come close to. [➡MOVE PAST, INTO OR THROUGH SOMETHING; 332] *Opposite:* leave.

nearby 1 *adj* **close**, near, neighbouring, adjacent, adjoining, proximate, immediate, nigh. [➡CLOSENESS; 160] *Opposite:* distant. 2 *adv* **near**, close, close by, close to, close at hand, in close proximity, hard by, to hand, in the vicinity, in the neighbourhood, nigh. [➡CLOSENESS; 160]

near enough *adv* [➡APPROXIMATELY; 133]

nearest and dearest *n* [➡THE FAMILY; 956]

nearly *adv* **closely**, approximately, almost, near, virtually, practically, all but, just about, not quite, more or less. [➡TO A CERTAIN EXTENT; 134]

near miss *n* **lucky escape**, close thing, close call, near thing (*informal*), close shave, narrow escape, narrow squeak. [➡RESULTS AND OUTCOMES; 83]

nearness *n* **immediacy**, imminence, proximity, closeness, propinquity (*formal*), juxtaposition, contiguity (*formal*). [➡CLOSENESS; 160] *Opposite:* distance.

nearside (*US*) *adj* **passenger side**, kerbside, inside. [➡RELATIVE LOCATION; 162]

nearsighted (*US*) *adj* **short-sighted**, myopic, owlish. [➡SEE; 700] *Opposite:* farsighted.

nearsightedness (*US*) *n* [➡SEE; 700]

near thing (*informal*) *n* **narrow squeak**, lucky escape, close shave, close thing, close call, near miss, narrow escape. [➡RESULTS AND OUTCOMES; 83]

neat 1 *adj* **well-ordered**, in order, straight, arranged, immaculate, spotless, shipshape, spick-and-span, tidy, orderly, trim. [➡ORDER AND ORGANISATION; 207] *Opposite:* untidy. 2 *adj* **well-organized**, organized, methodical, systematic, careful, painstaking, orderly, tidy, efficient, precise, regular. [➡ORDER AND ORGANISATION; 207] *Opposite:* disorganized. 3 *adj* **straight**, undiluted, unmixed, full-strength, pure, plain, unadulterated. [➡RAW AND NATURAL; 1213] *Opposite:* diluted. 4 *adj* **simple**, ingenious, elegant, clever, convenient, effective, well-thought-out, handy, useful, nifty (*informal*). [➡THE NATURE OF IDEAS; 772] 5 *adj* **graceful**, effortless, practised, precise, deft, skilful. [➡DESCRIBING BODY MOVEMENTS; 289] *Opposite:* clumsy. 6 *adj* **natty**, trim, compact, well-designed, elegant, simple, handy. [➡SMALL; 1194] *Opposite:* cumbersome.

neat and tidy *adj* [➡IN GOOD REPAIR; 1231]

neaten *v* **order**, tidy, tidy up, arrange, sort out, put in order. *Opposite:* mess up. (*informal*). [➡ARRANGE AND CREATE ORDER; 358]

neatly 1 *adv* **carefully**, tidily, in order, efficiently, precisely, painstakingly, trimly, nattily, immaculately. [➡ORDER AND ORGANISATION; 207] *Opposite:* messily. 2 *adv* **ingeniously**, elegantly, cleverly, effectively, handily, usefully, conveniently. [➡THE NATURE OF IDEAS; 772] *Opposite:* ineffectively. 3 *adv* **gracefully**, effortlessly, deftly, precisely, skilfully. [➡DESCRIBING BODY MOVEMENTS; 289] *Opposite:* clumsily.

neatness 1 *n* **tidiness**, orderliness, carefulness, efficiency, precision, trimness, immaculateness. [➡ORDER AND ORGANISATION; 207] *Opposite:* messiness. 2 *n* **ingeniousness**, elegance, cleverness, effectiveness, handiness, usefulness, convenience. [➡THE NATURE OF IDEAS; 772] *Opposite:* ineffectiveness. 3 *n* **gracefulness**, effortlessness, preciseness, deftness, skilfulness. [➡DESCRIBING BODY MOVEMENTS; 289] *Opposite:* clumsiness. 4 *n* **simplicity**, elegance, nattiness, trimness, compactness, handiness. [➡EASE AND SIMPLICITY; 201]

nebula *type of* **star or star system.** [➡CELESTIAL BODIES; 1060]

nebulous *adj* **unclear**, vague, imprecise, hazy, unformulated, tenuous, ill-defined, indefinable. [➡VAGUENESS; 244] *Opposite:* precise.

nebulousness *n* [➡VAGUENESS; 244]

necessary *adj* **essential**, needed, required, compulsory, obligatory, indispensable, basic, crucial, vital, de rigueur (*formal*), requisite (*formal*), mandatory. [➡NECESSARY AND ESSENTIAL; 197] *Opposite:* optional.

> **Compare and Contrast:** ***necessary, essential, vital, indispensable, requisite, needed***
>
> CORE MEANING: DESCRIBES SOMETHING THAT IS REQUIRED
>
> ***necessary*** important in order to achieve a desired result, or required by authority or convention; ***essential*** of the highest importance for achieving something; ***vital*** extremely important to the survival or continuing effectiveness of something; ***indispensable*** not to be done without, or extremely desirable or useful; ***requisite*** (*formal*) necessary for a particular purpose; ***needed*** required or desired.

necessitate *v* **require**, demand, need, call for, dictate, force, impose, oblige, compel, take. [➡NEED AND REQUIRE; 465]

necessitous (*formal*) *adj* [➡NECESSARY AND ESSENTIAL; 197]

necessitude *n* **need**, necessity, demand, requirement, requisite (*formal*), want, obligation. [➡IMPORTANCE AND SIGNIFICANCE; 193]

necessity 1 *n* **essential**, requirement, requisite (*formal*), prerequisite, basic, necessary, must. [➡MOST IMPORTANT THING; 198] *Opposite:* luxury. 2 *n* **need**, requirement, inevitability, obligation, stipulation, compulsion. [➡NECESSARY AND ESSENTIAL; 197]

neck 1 *n* **narrow part**, stem, shank, shaft. [➡EXTREMITIES OF PHYSICAL OBJECTS; 1249] 2 *v* (*dated*) **kiss**, cuddle, hug, smooch (*informal*), embrace, canoodle (*informal*), snog (*slang*). [➡PHYSICAL CONTACT AS COMMUNICATION; 656] 3 *part of* **torso**. [➡TORSO; 694] 4 *part of* **garment**. [➡PARTS OF A GARMENT; 870] 5 *type of* **cut**. [➡TYPES AND CUTS OF MEAT; 1176]

neck and neck (*informal*) *adv* **equal**, level, close, too close to call, even-steven (*informal*), level pegging, with nothing to choose between them. [➡EQUALITY; 155]

neckband *part of* **garment**. [➡PARTS OF A GARMENT; 870]

neckerchief (*dated*) *n* **bandanna**, cravat, scarf, tie, band. [➡HABERDASHERY, MILLINERY, AND LINGERIE; 867]

necklace *n* **chain**, necklet, string, choker, band, rope. [➡JEWELLERY; 866]

necklet *n* **necklace**, chain, choker, string, band, rope. [➡JEWELLERY; 866]

neckline *part of* **garment**. [➡PARTS OF A GARMENT; 870]

neck of the woods *n* [➡PLACE; 1064]

necktie (*US*) *n* **cravat**, scarf, bandanna, tie. [➡HABERDASHERY, MILLINERY, AND LINGERIE; 867]

necrophobia *type of* **phobia**. [➡FEARS AND PHOBIAS; 555]

necropolis *n* **cemetery**, burial ground, graveyard, resting place, churchyard, catacomb, boneyard (*informal*). [➡BURIAL PLACES AND ACCESSORIES; 930]

nectar *n* **liquid**, juice, sap, fluid, syrup. [➡PARTS OF TREES AND PLANTS; 1026]

nectarine *type of* **fruit**. [➡FRUIT AND VEGETABLES; 1175]

née *adj* **formerly**, previously, originally. [➡NAME AND DESCRIBE; 666]

need 1 *v* **demand**, require, call for, want, necessitate, crave, take. [➡NEED AND REQUIRE; 465] 2 *v* **have to**, must, should, ought. [➡NEED AND REQUIRE; 465] 3 *n* **essential**, necessity, requirement, want, requisite (*formal*), prerequisite, basic, necessary, must, demand. [➡MOST IMPORTANT THING; 198] *Opposite:* option. 4 *n* **privation**, poverty, want, hardship, neediness, indigence (*formal*), penury, destitution. [➡POVERTY AND POOR; 892] *Opposite:* luxury.

See Compare and Contrast at **necessary**.

needed *adj* [➡NECESSARY AND ESSENTIAL; 197]

needful 1 *adj* (*formal or archaic*) **necessary**, obligatory, compulsory, mandatory, essential, vital, prerequisite, requisite (*formal*). [➡NECESSARY AND ESSENTIAL; 197] 2 *adj* (*formal*) **requiring**, necessitating, demanding, calling for, needing, lacking, without. [➡LACK OF POSSESSION; 446]

neediness *n* **indigence** (*formal*), need, poverty, want, penury, destitution, privation, hardship, deprivation, poorness. [➡POVERTY AND POOR; 892]

needle 1 *n* **pointer**, indicator, hand. [➡PARTS OF MACHINES AND TOOLS; 1117] 2 *n* **spine**, spike, prickle, barb, sticker, pine needle. [➡PARTS OF TREES AND PLANTS; 1026] 3 *v* (*informal*) **nettle** (*informal*), irritate, provoke, rile (*informal*), annoy, aggravate (*informal*), pester, hassle (*informal*), niggle, enrage, bedevil, irk, gnaw, tease. [➡ANGER AND ANNOY; 570]

needlecraft *n* [➡CRAFTS AND CARVING; 356]

needlepoint *type of* **handicraft**. [➡CRAFTS AND CARVING; 356]

needless *adj* **unnecessary**, pointless, uncalled-for, useless, unneeded, unwanted, inessential, unrequired. [➡REDUNDANT AND USELESS; 241] *Opposite:* necessary.

needlessness *n* **uselessness**, unhelpfulness, fruitlessness, impracticality, pointlessness, senselessness. [➡REDUNDANT AND USELESS; 241] *Opposite:* usefulness.

needlework *type of* **handicraft**. [➡CRAFTS AND CARVING; 356]

needy *adj* **poor**, in need, deprived, disadvantaged, destitute, penurious (*literary*), indigent (*formal*). [➡POVERTY AND POOR; 892]

ne'er-do-well (*dated*) *n* **layabout**, waster, lazybones (*informal*), scallywag (*dated informal*), idler, slacker, shirker. [➡LAZY OR UNSUCCESSFUL PEOPLE; 948]

nefarious *adj* **wicked**, evil, despicable, immoral, reprehensible, disreputable, degenerate, infamous, perverse. [➡MORALLY BAD; 776] *Opposite:* reputable.

nefariousness *n* [➡MORALLY BAD; 776]

negate (*formal*) 1 *v* **refute**, contradict, disprove, disavow (*formal*), deny, repudiate, contravene, disaffirm (*formal*). [➡DENY AND REJECT; 645] *Opposite:* affirm. 2 *v* **invalidate**, cancel, reverse, render null and void, annul, remove, wipe out, cancel out, abolish, abrogate (*formal*), nullify. [➡DENY AND REJECT; 645] *Opposite:* validate.

See Compare and Contrast at **nullify**.

negation 1 *n* **denial**, annulment, nullification, repudiation, disavowal (*formal*), cancellation, reversal. [➡DENY AND REJECT; 645] *Opposite:* affirmation. 2 *n* **opposite**, contrary, absence, lack, antithesis. [➡OPPOSITE; 158] *Opposite:* confirmation.

negative 1 *adj* **unenthusiastic**, unconstructive, unhelpful, pessimistic, downbeat, disapproving, off-putting, discouraging, depressing. [➡SADNESS, DISTRESS, AND DESPAIR; 540] *Opposite:* encouraging. 2 *adj* **bad**, undesirable, adverse, harmful, damaging, destructive, deleterious (*formal*). [➡DANGEROUS; 237] *Opposite:* positive. 3 *n* **rejection**, rebuff, veto, nix (*US dated slang*), thumbs-down (*informal*), no, refusal, denial. [➡REFUSE PERMISSION AND NOT ALLOW; 671] *Opposite:* approval.

negatively 1 *adv* **in the negative**, with a no, with a refusal, with a denial. [➡NOT; 135] *Opposite:* affirmatively. 2 *adv* **damagingly**, harmfully, destructively, undesirably, depressingly, deleteriously (*formal*), adversely. [➡BAD AND BADLY; 224] *Opposite:* positively. 3 *adv* **offputtingly**, discouragingly, unenthusiastically, unconstructively, unhelpfully, pessimistically, disapprovingly. [➡SADNESS, DISTRESS, AND DESPAIR; 540] *Opposite:* encouragingly.

negativity *n* **unconstructiveness**, unhelpfulness, pessimism, disapproval. [➡ FEELINGS ABOUT THE FUTURE; 534] *Opposite:* enthusiasm.

neglect 1 *v* **abandon**, desert, forget, forsake, ignore, pass over. [➡ NOT PAY ATTENTION; 765] *Opposite:* look after. **2** *v* **omit**, forget, overlook, ignore, disregard, fail. [➡ NOT DO AND REFUSE TO DO; 275] **3** *n* **negligence**, abandonment, desertion, disregard, inattention, mistreatment, lack of care, carelessness. [➡ NOT PAY ATTENTION; 765] *Opposite:* care.

Compare and Contrast: ***neglect, forget, omit, overlook***

CORE MEANING: TO FAIL TO DO SOMETHING

neglect to fail to give the the proper or required care and attention to somebody or something, or to fail to do something, especially because of carelessness, forgetfulness, or indifference; ***forget*** to fail, or fail to remember, to give due attention to somebody or something; ***omit*** to fail to do something either deliberately or accidentally; ***overlook*** to fail to notice or check something as a result of inattention, preoccupation, or haste.

neglected *adj* **deserted**, abandoned, unkempt, uncared for, mistreated, ignored, unloved. [➡ IN TROUBLE AND DISADVANTAGED; 73] *Opposite:* looked after.

neglectful *adj* **negligent**, careless, slipshod, remiss, lax, slack, casual, forgetful, inattentive. [➡ LACK OF COMMITMENT AND UNRELIABILITY; 510] *Opposite:* attentive.

negligée *n* **nightdress**, nightgown, nightie (*informal*), dressing gown, peignoir. [➡ GARMENTS AND OUTFITS; 865]

negligence *n* **neglect**, inattention, abandonment, disregard, laxity, slackness, casualness, forgetfulness, carelessness. [➡ NOT PAY ATTENTION; 765] *Opposite:* attention.

negligent 1 *adj* **neglectful**, careless, inattentive, slipshod, remiss, lax, slack, casual, forgetful. [➡ LACK OF COMMITMENT AND UNRELIABILITY; 510] *Opposite:* careful. **2** *adj* (*literary*) **nonchalant**, relaxed, casual, informal, easy, indifferent. [➡ NEUTRALITY AND INDIFFERENCE; 554] *Opposite:* attentive.

negligible *adj* **insignificant**, tiny, small, slight, unimportant, minor, trifling, trivial. [➡ UNIMPORTANT AND UNNECESSARY; 239] *Opposite:* significant.

negligibly *adv* **not noticeably**, unimportantly, just, insignificantly, trivially, marginally, slightly. [➡ TO A CERTAIN EXTENT; 134] *Opposite:* significantly.

negotiable 1 *adj* **open to discussion**, up for grabs (*informal*), unfixed, flexible, open-ended. [➡ UNCERTAIN; 176] *Opposite:* nonnegotiable. **2** *adj* **transferable**, exchangeable, convertible, assignable, movable, flexible. [➡ FINANCE AND ECONOMICS; 797] **3** *adj* **passable**, navigable, crossable, traversable, accessible, reachable, open. [➡ IN GOOD REPAIR; 1231] *Opposite:* impassable.

negotiate 1 *v* **talk**, discuss, confer, consult, bargain, parley, agree, settle, cooperate, collaborate. [➡ TWO-WAY COMMUNICATION; 608] **2** *v* **sell**, transfer, exchange, convert, convey, assign. [➡ ACCOUNTING, BANKING, AND BUDGETING; 799] **3** *v* **get past**, pass, navigate, go around, cross, cope with, traverse, deal with. [➡ MOVE PAST, INTO OR THROUGH SOMETHING; 332]

negotiation *n* **arbitration**, mediation, discussion, cooperation, diplomacy, intercession, intervention. [➡ NEGOTIATION AND DEBATE; 46]

negotiations *n* **talks**, discussions, conference, consultation, dialogue, debate, parley. [➡ NEGOTIATION AND DEBATE; 46]

negotiator *n* **speaker**, representative, envoy, delegate, mediator, diplomat. [➡ REPRESENTATIVES AND PATRONS; 968]

Nehru jacket *type of* **jacket**. [➡ GARMENTS AND OUTFITS; 865]

neigh *type of* **animal sound**. [➡ SOUNDS MADE BY ANIMALS; 1260]

neighbour *v* [➡ EXIST IN CLOSE PROXIMITY; 21]

neighbourhood *n* **area**, district, region, locality, zone, quarter, community, environs, proximity. [➡ PLACE; 1064]

neighbouring *adj* **nearby**, local, adjoining, surrounding, bordering, close, immediate, adjacent, next door, near, next. [➡ CLOSENESS; 160] *Opposite:* distant.

neighbourliness *n* **friendliness**, kindness, helpfulness, consideration, sociability, hospitality, care, cooperation. [➡ FRIENDLINESS AND SOCIABILITY; 495] *Opposite:* unfriendliness.

neighbourly *adj* **helpful**, kind, pleasant, sociable, friendly, amiable. [➡ FRIENDLINESS AND SOCIABILITY; 495] *Opposite:* antisocial.

neither here nor there *adj* **beside the point**, irrelevant, inappropriate, unimportant, inconsequential, not worth worrying about, not the issue. [➡ UNIMPORTANT AND UNNECESSARY; 239] *Opposite:* to the point.

nemesis 1 *n* (*literary*) **avenger**, retaliator, revenger, vindicator. [➡ ENEMIES AND TORMENTORS; 969] **2** *n* (*literary*) **punishment**, vengeance, retribution, fate, doom, revenge. [➡ FATE, DESTINY, AND ASTROLOGY; 783] **3** *n* (*US literary*) **opponent**, archenemy, archrival, adversary, competitor, rival, antagonist, foe (*literary*). [➡ ENEMIES AND TORMENTORS; 969]

neoclassical *type of* **pre-20th-century architecture**. [➡ BUILDING AND ARCHITECTURE; 1075]

neologism *n* **new word**, coinage, buzzword (*informal*). [➡ ASPECTS OF LANGUAGE; 683]

neon *type of* **gas**. [➡ GASES; 1274]

neonatal *adj* **newborn**, new, brand-new. [➡ BABYHOOD, CHILDHOOD AND ADOLESCENCE; 917]

neonate *n* [➡ CHILD OR YOUTH; 945]

neon light *type of* **light**. [➡ LIGHT; 1163]

neophyte *n* **novice**, beginner, recruit, tenderfoot (*informal*), learner, trainee, raw recruit, newcomer, greenhorn, amateur, rookie (*US informal*), apprentice, tyro. [➡ UNSKILLED PERSON; 531]

neoprene *type of* **plastic**. [➡ PLASTICS; 1133]

nephew *type of* **younger relative**. [➡ YOUNGER GENERATION RELATIVES; 958]

ne plus ultra (*formal*) *n* [➡ GOOD, WELL, BETTER; 184]

nepotism *n* **favouritism**, preferential treatment, partiality, bias, preference, discrimination, prejudice, one-sidedness. [➡PREJUDICE; 551]

Neptune *type of* **planet.** [➡CELESTIAL BODIES; 1060]

nerve 1 *n* **courage**, bravery, spirit, audacity, bravado, guts (*slang*), daring, pluck, mettle, fearlessness. [➡COURAGE; 499] *Opposite:* cowardice. 2 *n* **boldness**, cheek (*informal*), face (*informal*), impudence, insolence, effrontery, bravado, audacity. [➡BAD MANNERS AND SOCIAL SKILLS; 522]

See Compare and Contrast at **courage.**

nerve centre *n* **hub**, centre of operations, control room, headquarters, HQ, nexus, command post, head office. [➡CENTRAL PARTS OF PHYSICAL OBJECTS; 1250]

nerve gas *type of* **gas.** [➡GASES; 1274]

nerve-racking *adj* **anxious**, nervous, worrying, tense, panicky, terrifying, scary (*informal*), nail-biting, menacing, intimidating. [➡EMOTIONALLY UNPLEASANT AND UPSETTING; 228]

nerves (*informal*) *n* **anxiety**, worry, tension, stress, mental strain, nervous tension, concern, uneasiness, nervousness. [➡FEELINGS ABOUT THE FUTURE; 534]

nerve-wracking *see* **nerve-racking.**

nerve yourself *v* [➡CHANGE OF MOOD AND COMPOSURE; 581]

nerviness *n* **edginess**, anxiety, jumpiness, tenseness, uneasiness, nervousness, tension. [➡FEELINGS ABOUT THE FUTURE; 534] *Opposite:* calmness.

nervous *adj* **anxious**, worried, edgy, jumpy, panicky, tense, uneasy, nervy (*informal*). [➡CONFUSION, ANXIETY, AND WORRY; 541] *Opposite:* calm.

nervous breakdown *n* [➡PSYCHOLOGY AND THE MIND; 770]

nervousness *n* **anxiety**, edginess, jumpiness, tenseness, uneasiness, nerviness (*informal*), nerves (*informal*), apprehension, tension. [➡FEELINGS ABOUT THE FUTURE; 534] *Opposite:* calmness.

nervous tension *n* [➡PSYCHOLOGY AND THE MIND; 770]

nervy 1 *adj* (*informal*) **nervous**, anxious, worried, edgy, jumpy, panicky, tense, uneasy. [➡CONFUSION, ANXIETY, AND WORRY; 541] *Opposite:* calm. 2 *adj* (*US informal*) **fearless**, brave, gutsy (*informal*), daring, bold. [➡COURAGE; 499]

nest *type of* **den or nest.** [➡ANIMAL OR BIRD ACCOMMODATION; 1078]

nest egg *n* **savings**, reserve, capital, fund, store, stash (*informal*), contingency, something for a rainy day. [➡MONEY; 140]

nestle 1 *v* **cosy up**, cuddle up, huddle, nuzzle, settle, burrow, snuggle. [➡GET CLOSER TOGETHER; 311] 2 *v* **cushion**, place, lie, soften, shelter, protect. [➡AVOID OR ESCAPE CONTACT; 419]

nestling *type of* **young bird.** [➡YOUNG BIRD; 1004]

net 1 *n* **mesh**, web, netting, lattice, grid, meshwork, network. [➡FASTENERS, LINKS, AND NETWORKS; 1246] 2 *v* (*informal*) **get**, catch, achieve, obtain, procure, acquire, win. [➡GET; 421] 3 *adj* **remaining**, disposable, clear, after deductions, left, take-home. [➡TAX AND TAXATION; 802] *Opposite:* gross. 4 *v* **earn**, make, gain, clear (*informal*), make a profit of, profit. [➡GET MONEY OR REWARD; 422]

netball *type of* **ball game.** [➡HOBBIES, GAMES, AND SPORTS; 875]

nether (*formal*) *adj* **posterior** (*formal*), rear, hindmost (*literary*), hind, hinder, back, after. [➡RELATIVE LOCATION; 162]

nether world 1 *n* (*literary*) [➡CRIMINALS; 821] 2 *n* (*formal*) **hell**, inferno, purgatory, underworld, perdition. [➡RELIGIOUS CONCEPTS; 777]

net income *n* [➡INCOME; 461]

netting *n* **mesh**, net, web, fabric, meshwork. [➡FASTENERS, LINKS, AND NETWORKS; 1246]

nettle 1 *v* (*informal*) **irritate**, annoy, aggravate (*informal*), infuriate, bother, exasperate, irk, get on somebody's nerves. [➡ANGER AND ANNOY; 570] 2 *type of* **weed.** [➡WEEDS AND THISTLES; 1034]

nettled (*informal*) *adj* [➡IRRITATION AND ANGER; 542]

network *n* **net**, system, grid, web, link, linkage. [➡FASTENERS, LINKS, AND NETWORKS; 1246]

neurological *adj* **nervous**, nerve, neural. [➡PSYCHOLOGY AND THE MIND; 770]

neurosis (*dated*) *n* **hang-up** (*informal*), quirk, complex, obsession, inhibition, idiosyncrasy, phobia, problem, fixation. [➡PSYCHOLOGY AND THE MIND; 770]

neurosurgeon *n* [➡PEOPLE WHO WORK IN MEDICINE; 848]

neurotic (*informal*) *adj* **anxious**, fearful, phobic, fixated, hung up (*informal*), disturbed, irrational, obsessed, over-anxious. [➡PSYCHOLOGY AND THE MIND; 770] *Opposite:* rational.

neuter *v* **spay**, sterilize, castrate, fix. [➡STERILIZE; 727]

neutral 1 *adj* **unbiased**, impartial, disinterested, dispassionate, middle-of-the-road, not taking sides, on the fence, impersonal, nonaligned. [➡NEUTRALITY AND INDIFFERENCE; 554] *Opposite:* biased. 2 *adj* **drab**, light-coloured, indistinct, indeterminate, wishy-washy (*informal*), colourless, pale. [➡DESCRIBING COLOURS; 1225] *Opposite:* colourful.

neutrality *n* **impartiality**, detachment, objectivity, non-involvement, disinterest, nonalignment. [➡NEUTRALITY AND INDIFFERENCE; 554] *Opposite:* bias.

neutralization *n* **cancelling out**, nullification, off-setting, frustration, counteraction, removal, counter-balancing, deactivation. [➡END; 54] *Opposite:* activation.

neutralize *v* **counteract**, counterbalance, defuse, deactivate, nullify, offset, cancel out, counterweight. [➡CORRECT AND PUT RIGHT; 378]

neutrally *adv* **impartially**, disinterestedly, dispassionately, objectively, without taking sides, impersonally. [➡NEUTRALITY AND INDIFFERENCE; 554]

neutrino *type of* **elementary particle.** [➡ELEMENTARY PARTICLES; 1278]

neutron *type of* **elementary particle.** [➡ELEMENTARY PARTICLES; 1278]

neutron bomb *type of* **explosive weapon.** [➡EXPLOSIVES; 1154]

never 1 *adv* **not ever**, not once, on no occasion, at no time. [➡NEVER AND INFREQUENCY; 97] *Opposite:* always. 2 *adv* **certainly not**, under no circumstances, by no means, in no way, not at all, on no account, for no reason, no way (*informal*). [➡NOT; 135] *Opposite:* certainly.

never-ending *adj* **endless**, everlasting, continual, continuous, nonstop, constant, incessant, interminable, unremitting, eternal, infinite, permanent. [➡PERMANENCE: WITHOUT END; 94]

never-never land *n* [➡NON-EXISTENT PLACE; 1065]

nevertheless *adv* **yet**, but, however, nonetheless, on the other hand, all the same, even so, still, though. [➡ALTHOUGH, NEVERTHELESS, AND DESPITE; 170]

never-to-be-repeated *adj* [➡EXTRAORDINARY: UNCOMMON; 206]

new 1 *adj* **novel**, newfangled, original, innovative, fresh, different, firsthand. [➡EXTRAORDINARY: UNCOMMON; 206] *Opposite:* old. 2 *adj* **recent**, latest, up-to-the-minute, contemporary, up-to-date, modern, modernistic, neoteric. [➡NEW, MODERN; 167] *Opposite:* outmoded. 3 *adj* **brand-new**, pristine, newborn, in mint condition, newfound, spanking. [➡IN GOOD REPAIR; 1231] *Opposite:* used. 4 *adj* **another**, additional, extra, further, different, fresh, more, other. [➡MORE AND EXCESS; 122] 5 *adj* **inexperienced**, new to the job, just starting out, wet behind the ears, green, recent, unfamiliar, unaccustomed. [➡UNSKILLED; 530] *Opposite:* experienced.

Compare and Contrast: ***new, fresh, modern, newfangled, novel, original***

CORE MEANING: NEVER EXPERIENCED BEFORE OR HAVING RECENTLY COME INTO BEING

new recently invented, discovered, made, bought or experienced, or not previously known or encountered; ***fresh*** excitingly or refreshingly different from what has been done or experienced previously; ***modern*** of the latest kind, or characterized by up-to-date ideas, techniques, design, and equipment; ***newfangled*** puzzlingly or worryingly new or different, especially because it seems gimmicky or overcomplicated; ***novel*** original and different, often interestingly, unusually, or inventively different; ***original*** unique and not copied or derived from anything else.

New Age traveller *n* [➡TRAVEL: TRAVELLERS AND WALKERS; 320]

newborn 1 *adj* **new**, brand-new, neonatal. [➡BABYHOOD, CHILDHOOD AND ADOLESCENCE; 917] 2 *adj* **newfound**, new, brand-new, fresh, recent. [➡NEW, MODERN; 167] *Opposite:* established. 3 *n* **baby**, infant, babe (*literary or archaic*), child, neonate. [➡CHILD OR YOUTH; 945]

newcomer 1 *n* **new arrival**, stranger, Johnny-come-lately (*informal*). [➡STRANGERS; 972] 2 *n* **novice**, recruit, beginner, neophyte, trainee, greenhorn, apprentice, tenderfoot (*informal*). [➡UNSKILLED PERSON; 531] *Opposite:* old hand.

newfangled *adj* **novel**, new, innovative, up-to-date, up-to-the-minute, modern. [➡NEW, MODERN; 167] *Opposite:* old-fashioned.

See Compare and Contrast at **new**.

newly 1 *adv* **recently**, lately, freshly, just now, just this minute, only just. [➡PRESENT; 85] 2 *adv* **afresh**, anew, again, once more. [➡AGAIN; 109]

newlywed *n* **just marrieds**, wedding couple, happy couple, bride and groom, bride, groom, couple. [➡RELATIVES BY MARRIAGE; 960]

newness *n* **novelty**, innovation, originality, freshness, inventiveness, individuality. [➡EXTRAORDINARY: UNCOMMON; 206]

new potato *type of* **root vegetable**. [➡FRUIT AND VEGETABLES; 1175]

news 1 *n* **information**, reports, intelligence, gossip, rumour, hearsay. [➡BASIC DETAILS; 689] 2 *n* **news bulletin**, news broadcast, newscast, news summary, news flash, news update, bulletin, broadcast, update, summary, news report, news hour (*US*). [➡TELEVISION AND RADIO; 607]

newscast *n* **news**, news bulletin, news broadcast, news summary, news flash, news update, broadcast, bulletin, update, summary, news report, news hour (*US*). [➡TELEVISION AND RADIO; 607]

news flash *n* **news update**, news bulletin, news broadcast, newscast. [➡TELEVISION AND RADIO; 607]

newshawk (*US informal*) *n* **reporter**, journalist, investigative reporter, correspondent, newsgatherer. [➡WORKERS IN ENTERTAINMENT AND MEDIA; 873]

newshound (*informal*) *n* **reporter**, journalist, investigative journalist, newsgatherer, correspondent, newshawk (*US informal*). [➡WORKERS IN ENTERTAINMENT AND MEDIA; 873]

newsletter *n* **information sheet**, newssheet, bulletin, circular. [➡ADVERTISING AND PUBLICITY; 605]

newsman *n* **reporter**, journalist, broadcaster, correspondent, newshound (*informal*), newspaperman, newshawk (*US informal*). [➡WORKERS IN ENTERTAINMENT AND MEDIA; 873]

newspaper 1 *n* **paper**, broadsheet, tabloid, daily, weekly, rag (*informal*), red-top (*informal*), broadside (*US*). [➡NEWSPAPERS; 606] 2 *n* **newsprint**, printing paper, coarse paper. [➡NEWSPAPERS; 606]

newspaperman *n* **reporter**, journalist, correspondent, newshound (*informal*), newsman, newshawk (*US informal*). [➡WORKERS IN ENTERTAINMENT AND MEDIA; 873]

newspaperwoman *n* **reporter**, journalist, correspondent, newshound (*informal*), newshawk (*US informal*), newswoman. [➡WORKERS IN ENTERTAINMENT AND MEDIA; 873]

newsprint *n* **newspaper**, printing paper, coarse paper. [➡NEWSPAPERS; 606]

newsreader *n* **presenter**, broadcaster, anchor, anchorperson. [➡WORKERS IN ENTERTAINMENT AND MEDIA; 873]

newsreel *n* **news film**, documentary, news report, news bulletin, news footage, news movie (*US*). [➡TELEVISION AND RADIO; 607]

newsroom *n* **news studio**, broadcasting studio, TV studio. [➡TELEVISION AND RADIO; 607]

newssheet *n* **newsletter**, bulletin, press release, information sheet, data sheet, fact file, newspaper. [➡NEWSPAPERS; 606]

newsstand *n* **kiosk**, stand, stall, booth. [➡RETAIL OUTLETS; 1082]

newswoman *n* **reporter**, broadcaster, correspondent, journalist, newshound (*informal*), newspaperwoman, newshawk (*US informal*). [➡WORKERS IN ENTERTAINMENT AND MEDIA; 873]

newsworthy *adj* **interesting**, exciting, remarkable, out of the ordinary, extraordinary, important. [➡INTERESTING AND MEANINGFUL; 191] *Opposite:* unremarkable.

newsy *adj* **chatty**, gossipy, friendly, interesting, informative, explanatory, informational. [➡INTERESTING AND MEANINGFUL; 191]

newt *type of* **amphibian**. [➡AMPHIBIANS; 1008]

next *adv* **after that**, then, afterwards, after, thereafter, consequently (*formal*), subsequently, behind, later. [➡AFTER, LAST, AND FOLLOWING; 166] *Opposite:* first.

next door *adv* **nearby**, close, round the corner, in the vicinity, around the corner. [➡CLOSENESS; 160]

next-door *adj* **adjacent**, adjoining, neighbouring, flanking, next, nearby. [➡CLOSENESS; 160]

next of kin *n* **close relative**, blood relation, blood relative, spouse, partner, parent, kinsman, kinswoman, kin, kinsfolk, kinfolk. [➡THE FAMILY; 956]

next to last *adj* [➡AFTER, LAST, AND FOLLOWING; 166]

next world *n* [➡RELIGIOUS CONCEPTS; 777]

nexus *n* **connection**, link, tie, relationship, node, join, interconnection, bond, yoke. [➡CONNECTION; 144]

nib *n* **tip**, point, end. [➡EXTREMITIES OF PHYSICAL OBJECTS; 1249]

nibble 1 *v* **chew**, nip, peck, gnaw, bite [➡EAT AND NOT EAT; 711]. *Opposite:* chomp (*informal*). 2 *n* **bite**, morsel, titbit, crumb, speck, particle, fragment. [➡SMALL PIECE; 127]

nibbles *n* **snacks**, finger food, canapés, appetizers, hors d'oeuvres, cocktail snacks. [➡MEALS AND PARTS OF MEALS; 1168]

nice 1 *adj* **enjoyable**, agreeable, pleasant, good, fine (*informal*), lovely, amusing, wonderful. [➡EMOTIONALLY PLEASANT; 188] *Opposite:* unpleasant. 2 *adj* **polite**, considerate, friendly, courteous, charming, kind, sympathetic, warm-hearted, cordial. [➡GENEROSITY AND KINDNESS; 496] *Opposite:* nasty. 3 *adj* **respectable**, proper, refined, virtuous, genteel, correct, seemly, acceptable. [➡GOOD MANNERS AND SOCIAL SKILLS; 521] *Opposite:* improper. 4 *adj* **attractive**, lovely, pleasant, delightful, appealing, fine (*informal*), good-looking. [➡BEAUTY AND ATTRACTIVENESS; 190] *Opposite:* unattractive. 5 *adj* **fine** (*informal*), precise, exact, fine-drawn, meticulous, narrow, subtle. [➡CONCISE AND CLEAR; 203] *Opposite:* broad. 6 *adj* **choosy** (*informal*), discriminating, painstaking, particular, scrupulous, precise, fastidious, meticulous, fussy, exact, finicky, careful. [➡DIFFICULTY AND COMPLEXITY; 243]

nice-looking *adj* **good-looking**, pretty, lovely, attractive, handsome, appealing, pleasing, striking, beautiful. [➡PEOPLE'S PHYSICAL APPEARANCE; 476] *Opposite:* unattractive.

nicely 1 *adv* **suitably**, effectively, satisfactorily, accurately, carefully, adequately, exactly, well, agreeably, properly. [➡CORRECT; 183] *Opposite:* unsatisfactorily. 2 *adv* **agreeably**, kindly, well, politely, courteously, attractively, pleasantly. [➡GOOD MANNERS AND SOCIAL SKILLS; 521] *Opposite:* unpleasantly. 3 *adv* **carefully**, meticulously, finely, subtly, narrowly, precisely, fastidiously, neatly. [➡CONCISE AND CLEAR; 203] *Opposite:* broadly.

nicety 1 *n* **distinction**, precision, detail, small point, refinement, subtlety. [➡BASIC DETAILS; 689] 2 *n* **delicacy**, tactfulness, particularity, finesse, polish, subtlety, meticulousness, exactness. [➡CONCISE AND CLEAR; 203]

niche 1 *n* **alcove**, bay, nook, hidey-hole (*informal*), cubbyhole, recess, cranny, corner, hollow. [➡ALCOVES, CUBICLES, AND COMPARTMENTS; 1095] 2 *n* **place**, position, slot, function, role, forte, calling, vocation, métier. [➡PROFESSIONS; 845]

nick 1 *n* **incision**, groove, mark, notch, cut, scratch, score, chip. [➡HOLES, GAPS, AND FORKS; 1251] 2 *v* **score**, incise, mark, cut, scratch, notch, dent, deface. [➡TEAR, BREAK, AND CUT; 361] 3 *n* (*slang*) **prison**, jail, custody. [➡BUILDINGS FOR CONFINING PEOPLE; 1093] 4 *v* (*slang*) **purloin** (*formal*), misappropriate, steal, pinch (*informal*), walk off with, make off with, make away with, pocket, filch (*informal*), pilfer, lift (*informal*). [➡STEAL AND ROB; 427]

See Compare and Contrast at **steal**.

nickel *type of* **metal**. [➡METALS; 1275]

nick-nack *see* **knick-knack**.

nickname 1 *n* **name**, pet name, moniker (*slang*), handle (*slang*), epithet, sobriquet, cognomen (*formal*), diminutive. [➡NAME AND DESCRIBE; 666] 2 *v* **label**, call, name, designate, dub, tag. [➡NAME AND DESCRIBE; 666]

niece *type of* **younger relative**. [➡YOUNGER GENERATION RELATIVES; 958]

niff (*slang*) 1 *n* **odour**, pong (*informal*), reek, whiff, hum (*informal*), stink, stench, smell. [➡SMELL AND SMELLING; 706] *Opposite:* fragrance. 2 *v* **stink**, whiff (*informal*), pong (*informal*), reek, hum (*informal*), smell. [➡SMELL EMISSION; 370]

niffy (*slang*) *adj* **smelly**, reeking, pongy (*informal*), whiffy (*informal*), stinking, humming (*informal*), stinky (*informal*). [➡SMELL AND SMELLING; 706] *Opposite:* sweet-smelling.

niftiness (*informal*) *n* [➡USEFULNESS; 200]

nifty 1 *adj* (*informal*) **useful**, handy, convenient, effective, ingenious, clever, neat. [➡USEFULNESS; 200] *Opposite:* useless. 2 *adj* **good**, quick, clever, skilful, neat, slick, agile, adroit, deft. [➡DESCRIBING BODY MOVEMENTS; 289] *Opposite:* clumsy. 3 *adj* **smart**, attractive, well-designed, neat, natty, stylish. [➡BEAUTY AND ATTRACTIVENESS; 190] *Opposite:* unattractive.

niggard *n* **miser**, skinflint, penny pincher (*informal*), scrooge (*informal*), cheapskate (*informal*), meanie (*informal*), pinchpenny. [➡FINANCIALLY MEAN PEOPLE; 952]

niggardliness *n* [➡FINANCIALLY MEAN AND GRASPING; 520]

niggardly 1 *adj* **ungenerous**, stingy (*informal*), mean, miserly, tight, measly (*informal*), parsimonious, cheap (*US*). [➡FINANCIALLY MEAN AND GRASPING; 520] *Opposite:* generous. 2 *adj* **miserable**, meagre, wretched, insufficient, paltry, poor, beggarly, sorry. [➡TOO FEW, TOO LITTLE; 120]

niggle 1 *v* **criticize**, cavil, carp, nag, nitpick, find fault, grouse (*informal*). [➡COMPLAIN AND NAG; 687] 2 *v* **trouble**, bother, nag, annoy, irritate, worry. [➡ANGER AND ANNOY; 570] 3 *n* **complaint**, grumble, objection, grievance, criticism. [➡COMPLAIN AND NAG; 687] 4 *n* **doubt**, anxiety, twinge, misgiving, concern, worry. [➡CONFUSION, ANXIETY, AND WORRY; 541]

niggling 1 *adj* **trivial**, petty, unimportant, inconsequential, insignificant, minor, small, trifling, piddling (*informal*). [➡UNIMPORTANT AND UNNECESSARY; 239] *Opposite:* important. 2 *adj* **irritating**, awkward, finicky, troublesome, difficult, nagging, tricky, bothersome, worrying, troubling. [➡IRRITATING; 229]

nigh *adj* **imminent**, close, near, at hand, approaching, coming, nearly here. [➡CLOSENESS; 160] *Opposite:* remote.

nigh on *adv* **almost**, close on, about, approaching, nearly, not far off, just about, practically, virtually. [➡APPROXIMATELY; 133]

night 1 *n* **nighttime**, hours of darkness, dark, darkness, nightfall, dusk. [➡TIMES OF DAY; 87] *Opposite:* day. 2 *n* **early hours**, small hours, middle of the night, evening. [➡TIMES OF DAY; 87] 3 *interj* (*informal*) **goodnight**, sleep well, sleep tight. [➡GREETINGS, FAREWELLS, AND SALUTATIONS; 660]

nightcap 1 *n* **drink**, bedtime drink, hot drink, hot toddy. [➡DRINKS; 1186] 2 *n* **bedcap**, sleeping cap, hat. [➡HABERDASHERY, MILLINERY, AND LINGERIE; 867] 3 *type of* **sleepwear**. [➡GARMENTS AND OUTFITS; 865]

nightclothes *n* **pyjamas**, nightwear, sleepwear (*US*). [➡GARMENTS AND OUTFITS; 865]

nightclub *type of* **bar or club**. [➡HOTELS, RESTAURANTS, AND CLUBS; 1081]

nightdress *n* **negligée**, nightgown, nightie (*informal*), nightshirt. [➡GARMENTS AND OUTFITS; 865]

nightfall *n* **dusk**, twilight, evening, sunset, end of the day, sundown, eventide (*literary*). [➡TIMES OF DAY; 87] *Opposite:* daybreak.

nightgown (*US*) *n* **negligée**, nightdress, nightie (*informal*), nightshirt. [➡GARMENTS AND OUTFITS; 865]

nightie (*informal*) *n* **nightwear**, negligée, nightdress, nightgown, nightshirt. [➡GARMENTS AND OUTFITS; 865]

nightingale *type of* **songbird**. [➡SONGBIRD; 1003]

nightjar *type of* **songbird**. [➡SONGBIRD; 1003]

nightlife *n* **nightspots**, social life, entertainment, club scene, discos, pubs and clubs, bars, nightclubs. [➡ENTERTAINMENT; 872]

nightlight *type of* **light**. [➡LIGHT; 1163]

nightly 1 *adj* **night**, evening, nocturnal. [➡TIMES OF DAY; 87] 2 *adv* **every night**, night by night, once a night, nocturnally, through the night. [➡TIMES OF DAY; 87]

nightmare 1 *n* **dream**, bad dream, hallucination, vision, incubus. [➡SLEEP AND DREAM; 724] 2 *adj* **traumatic**, frightening, dreadful, terrible, nightmarish, horrendous, terrifying. [➡FRIGHTENING; 232] *Opposite:* wonderful.

nightmarish *adj* **nightmare**, frightening, terrifying, horrendous, terrible, dreadful. [➡FRIGHTENING; 232] *Opposite:* lovely.

nightshirt *n* [➡GARMENTS AND OUTFITS; 865]

nightspot *n* **bar**, nightclub, disco, club. [➡HOTELS, RESTAURANTS, AND CLUBS; 1081]

nightstick (*US*) *type of* **club**. [➡BLUNT INSTRUMENTS AND WHIPS; 1157]

night table (*US*) *type of* **table**. [➡FURNITURE; 858]

nighttime *n* **night**, evening, dark, hours of darkness, middle of the night, early hours. [➡TIMES OF DAY; 87] *Opposite:* daytime.

night watchman *n* [➡PEOPLE WHO GUARD AND PROTECT; 846]

nightwear *n* **sleepwear**, nightclothes, pyjamas. [➡GARMENTS AND OUTFITS; 865]

nihilism *n* **negativism**, pessimism, nothingness, emptiness, anarchism, scepticism. [➡PHILOSOPHIES AND BELIEFS; 781]

nihilist *n* **pessimist**, existentialist, anarchist, revolutionary, radical, rebel, destroyer. [➡PHILOSOPHICAL AND POLITICAL THINKERS; 782]

nihilistic *adj* **negativistic**, pessimistic, existentialist, destructive, anarchic, revolutionary, rebellious, radical. [➡PHILOSOPHIES AND BELIEFS; 781]

nil *n* **nothing**, zilch (*informal*), zero, none, null, nullity, nought, nix (*US dated slang*). [➡NONE; 121]

Nile green *type of* **green**. [➡COLOURS; 1223]

Nile perch *type of* **freshwater fish**. [➡FRESHWATER FISH; 1010]

nimble *adj* **sprightly**, lithe, deft, agile, quick, dexterous, lively, lissom, light-footed, spry. [➡AGILITY OF THE BODY; 477] *Opposite:* awkward.

nimbleness *n* **sprightliness**, litheness, agility, quickness, dexterity, liveliness, spryness. [➡AGILITY OF THE BODY; 477] *Opposite:* awkwardness.

nimbus 1 *n* **circle of light**, halo, corona, aura, radiance. [➡LIGHT; 1163] 2 *type of* **cloud**. [➡CLOUDY AND RAINY WEATHER; 1052]

nip 1 *v* **squeeze**, compress, grasp, grab, grip, pinch, tweak. [➡CONTACT: TOUCH; 413] 2 *v* (*informal*) **race**, hurry, dash, rush, run, zip (*informal*). [➡MOVE FAST; 314] *Opposite:* dawdle. 3 *v* **peck**, nibble, snap, gnaw, bite, lop, snip, clip, dock. [➡TEAR, BREAK, AND CUT; 361] 4 *v* (*US*) **steal**, purloin (*formal*), snatch, lift (*informal*), pilfer, make off with, make away with, swipe (*informal*). [➡STEAL AND ROB; 427] 5 *n* **pinch**, tweak, grasp, grab, squeeze. [➡CONTACT: TOUCH; 413] 6 *n* **sip**, drink, swig (*informal*), swallow, tot, shot (*informal*). [➡DRINKS; 1186] 7 *n* **peck**, bite, nibble, snippet, clipping, cutting. [➡SMALL PIECE; 127]

nip in the bud (*informal*) *v* **stop**, prevent, hinder, block, thwart, stymie, abort, nix (*US slang*). [➡CAUSE TO STOP; 267] *Opposite:* encourage.

nipper 1 *n* **pincer**, claw, gripper, appendage. [➡ARM AND HAND; 696] 2 *n* (*informal*) **baby**, rug rat (*informal humorous*), child, kid (*informal*), toddler, tot (*informal*), little one, sprog (*slang*). [➡CHILD OR YOUTH; 945]

nipple *part of* **torso.** [➡TORSO; 694]

nippy 1 *adj* **cold**, chilly, freezing, biting, icy, cool. [➡COLD WEATHER; 1051] *Opposite:* warm. 2 *adj* **quick**, fast, speedy, rapid, swift. [➡MOVING QUICKLY; 103] *Opposite:* slow.

nirvana 1 *n* **enlightenment**, spiritual enlightenment, state of grace. [➡RELIGIOUS CONCEPTS; 777] 2 *n* **bliss**, heaven, joy, paradise, pleasure, glory, Eden, seventh heaven, promised land. [➡PLEASANT SITUATIONS; 74] *Opposite:* hell.

nit *type of* **insect stages of development.** [➡INSECT STAGES; 1020]

nitpick *v* **cavil**, complain, quibble, find fault, criticize, carp, pick holes, take apart (*informal*). [➡COMPLAIN AND NAG; 687]

See Compare and Contrast at **criticize.**

nitpicker *n* **faultfinder**, critic, carper, nagger, pedant, fusspot (*informal*). [➡INTERFERING PEOPLE AND TELLTALES; 950]

nitpicking 1 *n* **criticism**, faultfinding, carping, hair-splitting, quibbling, fussiness, pickiness. [➡DIFFICULTY AND COMPLEXITY; 243] 2 *adj* **critical**, faultfinding, carping, finicky, fussy, hypercritical, unfavourable, disapproving. [➡DIFFICULT TO PLEASE; 516]

nitrogen *type of* **gas.** [➡GASES; 1274]

nitroglycerine *type of* **explosive material.** [➡EXPLOSIVES; 1154]

nitrous oxide *type of* **gas.** [➡GASES; 1274]

nitty-gritty (*informal*) *n* **essentials**, brass tacks, fundamentals, basics, crux of the matter, details, nuts and bolts (*informal*). [➡BASIC DETAILS; 689]

nix 1 *n* (*US dated slang*) **zero**, nil, nothing, zilch (*informal*), nought, none, null, nullity. [➡NONE; 121] 2 *v* (*US slang*) **refuse**, forbid, veto, overturn, nullify, annul, reverse, invalidate, negate (*formal*). [➡CAUSE TO STOP; 267]

no 1 *n* **rejection**, negative, denial, rebuff, refusal, veto, thumbs-down (*informal*). [➡REFUSE PERMISSION AND NOT ALLOW; 671] 2 *adv* **on no account**, not at all, certainly not, definitely not, by no means, no way (*informal*), nope (*slang*). [➡NOT; 135] 3 *adj* **not any**, not one, not at all. [➡NONE; 121]

nob (*informal*) *n* **toff** (*informal*), grandee, aristo, big shot (*informal*), bigwig (*informal*), big cheese (*slang*), VIP. [➡CLASS STATUS; 889]

no ball *n* **foul throw**, misthrow, foul ball (*US*). [➡SPORTS TERMS; 877]

nobble (*informal*) 1 *v* **persuade**, win over, sway, convince, influence. [➡APPEAL TO AND AROUSE INTEREST; 576] 2 *v* **coerce**, affect, force, intimidate, bribe, rig, fix. [➡CAUSE OR COMPEL TO ACT; 272] 3 *v* **dope**, incapacitate, fix, tamper with, drug. [➡PHYSICAL ATTACK AND PUNISHMENT; 416] 4 *v* **accost**, waylay, buttonhole (*informal*), confront, approach, detain, stop. [➡INITIATE AND ESTABLISH COMMUNICATION; 681]

nobility 1 *n* **aristocracy**, upper class, landed gentry, upper crust (*informal*). [➡CLASS STATUS; 889] 2 *n* **dignity**, graciousness, decency, goodness, nobleness, superiority. [➡MORALLY GOOD; 775]

noble 1 *adj* **honourable**, principled, moral, decent, upright, gallant, polite, self-sacrificing, magnanimous, virtuous, just. [➡MORALLY GOOD; 775] *Opposite:* unprincipled. 2 *adj* **magnificent**, impressive, imposing, fine, splendid, gracious, great, superior. [➡SUPERIORITY; 153] *Opposite:* unimpressive. 3 *adj* **aristocratic**, patrician, blue-blooded, titled, upper-class, highborn (*literary*), princely. [➡CLASS STATUS; 889] 4 *n* **nobleman**, noblewoman, lord, lady, earl, duke, duchess, baron, baronet, baroness, aristocrat, peer, patrician. [➡RULERS AND ARISTOCRACY; 823] *Opposite:* commoner.

noble gas *type of* **gas.** [➡GASES; 1274]

nobleman *n* **noble**, aristocrat, lord, peer, patrician. [➡RULERS AND ARISTOCRACY; 823] *Opposite:* commoner.

nobleness *n* **honourableness**, honour, morality, magnanimity, dignity, decency, goodness, gallantry, nobility, righteousness, graciousness, greatness, superiority, sublime. [➡MORALLY GOOD; 775]

noblewoman *n* **noble**, peer, lady, aristocrat, patrician. [➡RULERS AND ARISTOCRACY; 823]

nobly *adv* **decently**, magnanimously, graciously, kindly, virtuously, gallantly, splendidly, uprightly, justly. [➡GOOD MANNERS AND SOCIAL SKILLS; 521] *Opposite:* poorly.

nobody 1 *pron* **not one person**, not a single person, no one, not a soul. [➡NONE; 121] *Opposite:* everybody. 2 *n* **nonentity**, mediocrity, unknown, upstart, nothing. [➡LAZY OR UNSUCCESSFUL PEOPLE; 948]

nocturnal *adj* **nighttime**, night, nightly. [➡TIMES OF DAY; 87] *Opposite:* diurnal.

nocturne *type of* **instrumental music.** [➡MUSIC, SONGS, AND SINGING; 907]

nod 1 *v* **move**, bow, bob, jiggle, dip, waggle, move up and down, shake. [➡MOVE SOMETHING ON THE SPOT; 337] 2 *n* **permission**, go-ahead (*informal*), thumbs-up (*informal*), affirmation, okay (*informal*), signal, sign, gesture. [➡GESTURES AND GESTICULATION; 654]

noddle (*dated informal*) *n* **head**, nut (*informal*), bonce (*informal*), napper (*dated informal*), noggin (*dated informal*). [➡HEAD; 693]

node 1 *n* **bulge**, protuberance, lump, swelling, bump, knob, knot, nodule, burl, bud. [➡ROUNDED SHAPE; 1217] 2 *n* **meeting point**, join, connection, intersection, point, joint. [➡FASTENERS, LINKS, AND NETWORKS; 1246]

no different *adj* **identical**, the same, equal, alike, equivalent. [➡SAMENESS; 151]

nod off *v* **doze off**, drop off (*informal*), fall asleep, drift off, doze, snooze (*informal*), catnap, nap, drowse. [➡SLEEP AND DREAM; 724] *Opposite:* wake up.

no doubt *adv* **undoubtedly**, surely, certainly, for sure (*informal*), without a doubt. [➡CERTAIN; 175]

nod to *v* **acknowledge**, greet, signal to, salute. [➡GESTURES AND GESTICULATION; 654]

nodule *n* **node**, knot, knob, lump, bump, protuberance, swelling. [➡ROUNDED SHAPE; 1217]

no end of (*informal*) *pron* **a lot of**, a great deal of, very much, lots of, plenty of. [➡MANY, MUCH, LARGE AMOUNT; 117]

no-frills *(informal) adj* **basic**, utilitarian, unadorned, economy, generic, plain, straightforward. [➡PLAIN; 233] *Opposite:* luxury.

noggin *(dated informal) n* **head**, noddle *(dated informal)*, bonce *(informal)*, napper *(dated informal)*, nut *(informal)*. [➡HEAD; 693]

no good *adj* [➡REDUNDANT AND USELESS; 241]

no great shakes *adj* [➡REDUNDANT AND USELESS; 241]

no holds barred *adv* **unrestrained**, unconstrained, uninhibited, free, without restraint, without fear or favour. [➡INCAUTIOUS AND CARELESS; 284]

noise *n* **sound**, din, racket *(informal)*, clamour, clatter, blast, blare, uproar, hullabaloo, commotion. [➡SOUNDS; 1255] *Opposite:* silence.

noiseless *adj* **soundless**, silent, muted, hushed, quiet, still, inaudible. [➡ABSENCE OF SOUND; 1256] *Opposite:* noisy.

noiselessness *n* [➡ABSENCE OF SOUND; 1256]

noisiness *n* [➡LOUD OR UNPLEASANT SOUNDS; 1265]

noisome *adj* **foul**, offensive, disgusting, repulsive, repellent, repugnant, horrible, awful, putrid. [➡DISGUSTING AND REPULSIVE; 231] *Opposite:* pleasant.

noisy *adj* **loud**, deafening, earsplitting, piercing, raucous, strident, boisterous, blaring. [➡LOUD OR UNPLEASANT SOUNDS; 1265] *Opposite:* quiet.

no joke *adj* **a serious matter**, no laughing matter, not a trivial issue, hard work. [➡DIFFICULTY AND COMPLEXITY; 243]

no longer with us *adj* [➡DEAD AND DYING; 925]

nomad *n* **wanderer**, traveller, itinerant, migrant, drifter, rover. [➡NOMADIC AND ROOTLESS LIFESTYLES; 884]

nomadic *adj* **itinerant**, travelling, roaming, wandering, roving, drifting. [➡NOMADIC AND ROOTLESS LIFESTYLES; 884]

no matter what *adv* **come what may**, anyhow, regardless, by hook or by crook, anyway, in any case. [➡EXPRESSIONS OF AGREEMENT; 649]

nom de guerre *n* [➡NAME AND DESCRIBE; 666]

nom de plume *n* **pen name**, pseudonym, alias, assumed name, nom de guerre. [➡NAME AND DESCRIBE; 666]

nomenclature 1 *n* **classification**, taxonomy, codification, categorization, organization, arrangement, catalogue. [➡NAME AND DESCRIBE; 666] **2** *n* **terminology**, vocabulary, language, terms, jargon. [➡ASPECTS OF LANGUAGE; 683]

nominal 1 *adj* **supposed**, ostensible, so-called, in name only, titular. [➡FALSE AND UNREAL; 174] *Opposite:* actual. **2** *adj* **small**, trifling, token, minimal, insignificant, minor, peppercorn. [➡SMALL; 1194] *Opposite:* great.

nominally *adv* **supposedly**, ostensibly, by name, technically, in name only. [➡FALSE AND UNREAL; 174]

nominate 1 *v* **propose**, put forward, suggest, name, submit, recommend. [➡CONFER STATUS; 459] *Opposite:* reject. **2** *v* **appoint**, elect, designate, choose, select, pick, commission. [➡CONFER STATUS; 459] *Opposite:* reject.

nomination 1 *n* **proposal**, suggestion, recommendation, submission. [➡APPROVE AND CONFIRM; 647] **2** *n* **choice**, selection, appointment, nominee, candidate. [➡CONFER STATUS; 459]

nominative *type of* **grammatical term**. [➡ASPECTS OF LANGUAGE; 683]

nominee *n* **candidate**, entrant, applicant, nomination, contender. [➡COMPETITORS; 41]

nonaggression *n* **pacifism**, peaceful coexistence, nonbelligerence, nonviolence, inaction. [➡PEACEFULNESS AND GENTLENESS; 215] *Opposite:* aggression.

nonalcoholic *adj* **soft**, lite, low-alcohol. [➡DRINKS; 1186] *Opposite:* alcoholic.

nonaligned *adj* **neutral**, independent, unallied, unconnected, unrelated, autonomous, impartial. [➡STYLES AND SYSTEMS OF GOVERNMENT; 806] *Opposite:* aligned.

nonalignment *n* **neutrality**, independence, autonomy, self-determination, impartiality. [➡STYLES AND SYSTEMS OF GOVERNMENT; 806] *Opposite:* alignment.

nonattendance 1 *n* **truancy**, default, skiving *(informal)*, wagging *(slang)*, playing truant, bunking off *(informal)*, playing hooky *(US)*, cutting class *(US)*. [➡ABSENT AND UNAVAILABLE; 7] *Opposite:* attendance. **2** *n* **absence**, default, absenteeism, nonappearance. [➡ABSENT AND UNAVAILABLE; 7] *Opposite:* presence.

nonbeliever *n* **disbeliever**, unbeliever, doubter, sceptic, agnostic, atheist. [➡RELIGIOUS PEOPLE; 779] *Opposite:* believer.

nonchalance *n* **indifference**, detachment, disinterest, calmness, dispassion, casualness, insouciance. [➡NEUTRALITY AND INDIFFERENCE; 554] *Opposite:* interest.

nonchalant *adj* **casual**, offhand, cool, calm, laid-back *(informal)*, relaxed, blasé, indifferent, detached, unconcerned, dispassionate, imperturbable, unflappable, insouciant. [➡NEUTRALITY AND INDIFFERENCE; 554] *Opposite:* concerned.

noncombatant *n* **civilian**, citizen, nonfighter. [➡MILITARY PERSONNEL; 828] *Opposite:* soldier.

noncommittal *adj* **guarded**, evasive, vague, wary, tactful, reserved, cautious, careful, discreet, unrevealing, ambiguous. [➡RETICENT AND UNFORTHCOMING; 632] *Opposite:* definite.

noncompliance *n* **nonconformity**, refusal, failure, denial, defiance, disobedience, rebellion, rebelliousness, nonfulfilment. [➡REBELLIOUSNESS AND DISOBEDIENCE; 566] *Opposite:* compliance.

noncompliant *adj* **disobedient**, recalcitrant, rebellious, uncooperative, dissenting, nonconforming, defiant. [➡REBELLIOUSNESS AND DISOBEDIENCE; 566] *Opposite:* cooperative.

nonconformist 1 *adj* **unconventional**, way-out *(informal)*, eccentric, alternative, rebellious, radical, individualistic. [➡REBELLIOUSNESS AND DISOBEDIENCE; 566] *Opposite:* conformist. **2** *n* **rebel**, dissenter, maverick, radical, eccentric, free spirit, individualist. [➡UNCOOPERATIVE OR REBELLIOUS PERSON; 567] *Opposite:* conformist.

nonconformity 1 *n* **unconventionality**, originality,

eccentricity, idiosyncrasy, individuality, free-spiritedness, individualism, rebelliousness. [➡DIFFERENCE; 150] *Opposite:* conformity. **2** *n* **noncooperation**, noncompliance, divergence, variation, difference, disobedience, rebellion, variance. [➡REBELLIOUSNESS AND DISOBEDIENCE; 566] *Opposite:* conformity.

noncooperation *n* **defiance**, disobedience, insubordination, rebellion, rebelliousness, nonconformity, insolence, boldness, noncompliance. [➡UNWILLINGNESS AND STUBBORNNESS; 565] *Opposite:* cooperation.

nondescript *adj* **unremarkable**, ordinary, unexceptional, dull, uninteresting, commonplace, characterless, plain. [➡PLAIN; 233] *Opposite:* special.

nondiscriminatory *adj* **fair**, equal, unbiased, even-handed, just, fair-minded. [➡EQUALITY; 155] *Opposite:* discriminatory.

none **1** *pron* **no one**, nobody, not a soul, not a single person. [➡NONE; 121] **2** *pron* **not any**, nothing, not a bit, not an iota, not a hint. [➡NONE; 121] *Opposite:* some.

nonentity *n* **nobody**, unknown, mediocrity, nothing. [➡LAZY OR UNSUCCESSFUL PEOPLE; 948] *Opposite:* somebody.

nonessential **1** *adj* **luxury**, extra, supplementary, additional, dispensable, unnecessary, unneeded. [➡UNIMPORTANT AND UNNECESSARY; 239] *Opposite:* essential. **2** *n* **extra**, luxury, perk. [➡AMAZING THING; 212] *Opposite:* essential.

nonetheless *adv* **however**, nevertheless, even so, on the other hand. [➡ALTHOUGH, NEVERTHELESS, AND DESPITE; 170]

nonevent *n* **failure**, anticlimax, disappointment, letdown, flop, dud (*informal*), bummer (*slang*), bomb (*informal*). [➡DISASTERS; 253] *Opposite:* success.

nonexistence **1** *n* **absence**, lack, want, dearth, deficiency. [➡TOO FEW, TOO LITTLE; 120] *Opposite:* existence. **2** *n* **nothingness**, unreality, fictionality. [➡NONEXISTENCE; 24] *Opposite:* existence.

nonexistent *adj* **missing**, unreal, fictional, imaginary, absent. *Opposite:* existent. (*formal*). [➡FALSE AND UNREAL; 174]

nonfatal *adj* [➡SAFE AND SAFETY; 192]

nonfiction *adj* **factual**, true-life, reference, fact-based. [➡TRUE AND REAL; 172] *Opposite:* fiction.

nonflammable *adj* **noninflammable**, fireproof, flameproof, fire-retardant, fire-resistant. [➡FIRE, FLAMMABILITY, AND BURNING; 1164] *Opposite:* inflammable.

nonhazardous *adj* [➡SAFE AND SAFETY; 192]

nonintervention *n* **inaction**, noninvolvement, noninterventionism, laissez-faire, abstention, neutrality. [➡STYLES AND SYSTEMS OF GOVERNMENT; 806] *Opposite:* intervention.

noninterventionist *adj* **laissez-faire**, noninterfering, neutral, nonaligned, nonpartisan. [➡STYLES AND SYSTEMS OF GOVERNMENT; 806]

noniron *adj* **crease-resistant**, easy-care, drip-dry, wash-and-wear, permanent-press. [➡DESCRIBING CLOTHES; 869]

nonjudgmental *adj* **indulgent**, lax, easygoing, relaxed, lenient, open-minded, broad-minded, liberal, unprejudiced, tolerant. [➡POSITIVE INTELLECTUAL CHARACTERISTICS; 525] *Opposite:* judgmental.

nonmember *n* **outsider**, visitor, guest. [➡STRANGERS; 972] *Opposite:* member.

nonnegotiable **1** *adj* **firm**, immutable, unchanging, inflexible, fixed. [➡PERMANENCE: WITHOUT CHANGE; 95] *Opposite:* negotiable. **2** *adj* **nontransferable**, unmarketable, nonsalable, nonexchangeable, nonconvertible. [➡FINANCE AND ECONOMICS; 797] *Opposite:* transferable.

no-no (*informal*) *n* **impossibility**, nonstarter (*informal*), no-go (*informal*), hopeless case. [➡PROBLEM; 257] *Opposite:* possibility.

no-nonsense *adj* **straightforward**, plain, practical, down-to-earth, plain-speaking, blunt. *Opposite:* airy-fairy. (*informal*). [➡HONEST AND OPEN; 631]

nonpareil *adj* **unparalleled**, peerless, best, unequalled, unique, matchless, choice, elite. [➡EXTRAORDINARY: UNCOMMON; 206] *Opposite:* common.

nonpartisan *adj* **unbiased**, impartial, unprejudiced, independent, neutral, nonaligned. [➡NEUTRALITY AND INDIFFERENCE; 554] *Opposite:* partisan.

nonpayment *n* **defaulting**, evasion, default, avoidance. [➡ACCOUNTING, BANKING, AND BUDGETING; 799] *Opposite:* payment.

nonperformance (*US*) *n* **delinquency**, default, arrears. [➡MONEY, PAYMENTS, AND CHARGES; 800]

nonplus *v* **unnerve**, throw (*informal*), flummox (*informal*), befuddle, stump, bewilder, mystify, baffle, puzzle, alarm, bemuse, confuse, perplex. [➡CONFUSE AND BEWILDER; 572]

nonplussed *adj* **confused**, thrown (*informal*), flummoxed (*informal*), baffled, bewildered, puzzled, stumped, at a loss, mystified, perplexed, bemused, befuddled. [➡CONFUSION, ANXIETY, AND WORRY; 541]

nonprofessional *adj* **amateur**, blue-collar, manual, lay. [➡TYPES OF WORK; 835] *Opposite:* professional.

nonprofitmaking *adj* **charitable**, public, state, not-for-profit. [➡CHARITY AND CHARITABLE INSTITUTIONS; 822] *Opposite:* profit-making.

nonproliferation *n* **limitation**, reduction, control, prevention. [➡AVOID, PREVENT, LIMIT, AND CONTROL; 278] *Opposite:* proliferation.

nonresident **1** *adj* **transient**, visiting, commuting, holidaying, vacationing (*US*). [➡NOMADIC AND ROOTLESS LIFESTYLES; 884] *Opposite:* resident. **2** *n* **visitor**, transient, guest, holidaymaker, tourist, vacationer (*US*). [➡STRANGERS; 972] *Opposite:* resident.

nonsense *n* **rubbish**, twaddle (*informal*), claptrap (*informal*), drivel, gobbledegook (*informal disapproving*), gibberish, hot air (*informal*), noise, poppycock (*dated informal*), babble, balderdash, jabber, garbage, baloney (*informal*). [➡MEANINGLESS SPEECH OR WRITING; 677] *Opposite:* sense.

nonsensical *adj* **ridiculous**, stupid, senseless, absurd, illogical, silly, ludicrous, preposterous, unreasonable, asinine, irrational. [➡BIZARRE AND PECULIAR; 258] *Opposite:* sensible.

nonspecific *adj* **generic**, general, broad, broad-based, broad-spectrum, common, basic. [➡VAGUENESS; 244] *Opposite:* specific.

nonstandard *adj* **unusual**, out of the ordinary, atypical, special, modified, altered, special-order, custom-made, custom-built, nonconforming. [➡EXTRAORDINARY: UNCOMMON; 206] *Opposite:* standard.

nonstarter (*informal*) *n* **hopeless case**, loser, failure, nonrunner, dud (*informal*). [➡FAILURE; 77] *Opposite:* winner.

nonstick *adj* **coated**, protected, surfaced, covered. [➡DECORATE, ADORN, AND APPLY COATINGS; 406]

nonstop *adj* **continuous**, never-ending, uninterrupted, around-the-clock, constant, round-the-clock, unending, endless, interminable, ceaseless, unbroken, relentless, unceasing, incessant, steady. [➡PERMANENCE: WITHOUT END; 94] *Opposite:* intermittent.

nontoxic *adj* **harmless**, safe, nonhazardous, innocuous, risk-free. [➡SAFE AND SAFETY; 192] *Opposite:* toxic.

nonverbal communication *n* [➡COMMUNICATION; 603]

nonviolence *n* **pacifism**, passivity, nonaggression, civil disobedience. [➡PEACEFULNESS AND GENTLENESS; 215] *Opposite:* violence.

nonviolent *adj* **peaceful**, nonaggressive, pacific, peaceable, passive. [➡PEACEFULNESS AND GENTLENESS; 215] *Opposite:* violent.

noodle (*slang*) *n* [➡HEAD; 693]

nook *n* **corner**, alcove, cranny, niche, recess. [➡ALCOVES, CUBICLES, AND COMPARTMENTS; 1095]

noon *n* **midday**, twelve noon, noontime, noonday (*literary*). [➡TIMES OF DAY; 87]

noonday (*literary*) *n* **noon**, midday, twelve o'clock, middle of the day. [➡TIMES OF DAY; 87] *Opposite:* midnight.

no one *pron* **not one person**, not a single person, nobody, not a soul. [➡NONE; 121] *Opposite:* everyone.

noose 1 *n* **loop**, lasso, halter, rope, riata, lariat (*US*). [➡FASTENERS, LINKS, AND NETWORKS; 1246] 2 *n* **snare**, trap, booby trap, trick, con, ruse. [➡DECEPTION AND LIES; 661]

no problem (*informal*) *interj* **you're welcome**, all right, don't mention it, yes, it's no trouble, sure, it was nothing, certainly, my pleasure, fair enough (*informal*), that's okay (*informal*), agreed, not at all, okay (*informal*), of course. [➡EXPRESSIONS OF AGREEMENT; 649]

norm *n* **standard**, average, custom, rule, model, type, pattern. [➡PERFECT EXAMPLES AND EMBODIMENTS; 67]

normal *adj* **usual**, standard, ordinary, typical, customary, common, average, natural, habitual, routine, conventional, regular. [➡ACCEPTABLE AND PASSABLE; 220] *Opposite:* abnormal.

normalcy (*US*) *see* **normality**.

normality *n* **routine**, regularity, status quo, normalcy (*US*). [➡ORDER AND ORGANIZATION; 207]

normalization *n* **regularization**, standardization, stabilization, regulation, control. [➡CHANGE; 373] *Opposite:* deviation.

normalize *v* **regularize**, standardize, regulate, put on a normal footing, control, stabilize. [➡IMPROVE SOMETHING; 375] *Opposite:* destabilize.

normally 1 *adv* **usually**, in general, as a rule, on the whole, by and large, more often than not, on average, generally, typically, customarily, ordinarily, habitually, routinely. [➡USUALLY; 108] *Opposite:* rarely. 2 *adv* **as normal**, as usual, naturally, unexceptionally, conventionally. [➡ACCEPTABLE AND PASSABLE; 220] *Opposite:* abnormally.

Norman *type of* **pre-20th-century architecture**. [➡BUILDING AND ARCHITECTURE; 1075]

northeaster *type of* **wind**. [➡WINDY AND STORMY WEATHER; 1053]

northwester *type of* **wind**. [➡WINDY AND STORMY WEATHER; 1053]

nose 1 *n* **snout**, muzzle, beak, proboscis, conk (*slang*), hooter (*slang humorous*), schnozzle (*US slang*). [➡THE NOSE; 705] 2 *v* (*informal*) **snoop** (*informal*), poke around, watch, nose around (*informal*), sneak, pry. [➡SEEK POSSESSION AND SEARCH; 457] 3 *part of* **face**. [➡HEAD; 693]

nose about (*informal*) *v* [➡SEEK POSSESSION AND SEARCH; 457]

nose around (*informal*) *v* [➡SEEK POSSESSION AND SEARCH; 457]

nosebag *n* **feedbag**, bag, container. [➡CONTAINERS, RECEPTACLES, AND PACKAGING; 1244]

nosebleed *n* **bloody nose**, blood, blood loss, haemorrhage. [➡THE BLOOD AND CIRCULATION; 718]

nose cone 1 *part of* **aircraft** [➡AIRCRAFT; 1147] 2 *part of* **spacecraft**. [➡SPACE VEHICLES; 1062]

nose dive 1 *n* **dive**, fall, drop, plunge, tumble, plummet. [➡GO DOWNWARDS; 308] *Opposite:* ascent. 2 *n* **decrease**, fall, deterioration, drop, crash, tumble, slump, plunge, dive, collapse. [➡DISASTERS; 253] *Opposite:* increase.

nose-dive 1 *v* **plummet**, drop, plunge, dive, tumble, fall. [➡GO DOWNWARDS; 308] *Opposite:* ascend. 2 *v* **decrease**, deteriorate, plummet, drop, slump, crash, tumble, plunge, dive, rocket. [➡FAIL OR BE UNSUCCESSFUL; 75]

no-see-um (*US*) *type of* **flying insect**. [➡FLYING INSECTS; 1013]

nose flute *type of* **wind instrument**. [➡MUSICAL INSTRUMENTS; 910]

nosegay *n* **posy**, spray, bouquet, bunch, sprig. [➡COLLECTIONS AND MIXTURES OF THINGS; 1243]

nose ring *type of* **jewellery**. [➡JEWELLERY; 866]

nose stud *type of* **jewellery**. [➡JEWELLERY; 866]

nose wheel *part of* **aircraft**. [➡AIRCRAFT; 1147]

nosh (*informal*) 1 *n* **snack**, food, grub (*informal*), chow (*slang*), eats (*slang*), rations, tuck, goodies. [➡FOOD; 1166] 2 *v* **eat**, munch, champ, chomp (*informal*), tuck in (*informal*), eat up, consume. [➡EAT AND NOT EAT; 711]

no-show *n* **absentee**, nonarriver, nonattender, dropout. [➡ABSENT AND UNAVAILABLE; 7]

nosh-up (*informal*) *n* **big meal**, feast, binge, blowout (*slang*). [➡MEALS AND PARTS OF MEALS; 1168]

nosiness (*informal*) *n* [➡NOSY AND INTERFERING; 513]

nostalgia *n* **homesickness**, reminiscence, wistfulness, longing, melancholy. [➡FEELINGS ABOUT THE PAST; 533]

nostalgic *adj* **sentimental**, wistful, misty, longing, yearning, regretful. [➡PENSIVENESS AND INTEREST; 539] *Opposite:* expectant.

nostril *n* [➡THE NOSE; 705]

nostrum *n* **remedy**, plan, scheme, big idea, solution, recipe. [➡REMEDIES, TREATMENTS AND OPERATIONS; 732]

nosy (*informal*) *adj* **inquisitive**, curious, interfering, prying, meddlesome, snooping (*informal*), intrusive. [➡NOSY AND INTERFERING; 513]

nosy parker (*informal*) *n* [➡INTERFERING PEOPLE AND TELLTALES; 950]

notability 1 *n* **famous person**, celebrity, dignitary, VIP, notable, personality, personage (*formal*), public figure, somebody. [➡IMPORTANT OR FAMOUS PEOPLE; 893] *Opposite:* nobody. 2 *n* **significance**, importance, relevance, import, weight. [➡IMPORTANCE AND SIGNIFICANCE; 193]

notable 1 *adj* **noteworthy**, distinguished, outstanding, prominent, extraordinary, famous, remarkable, important, significant, noted. [➡EXTRAORDINARY: AMAZING; 205] *Opposite:* insignificant. 2 *n* **personage** (*formal*), celebrity, dignity, VIP, personality, somebody, public figure, notability. [➡IMPORTANT OR FAMOUS PEOPLE; 893] *Opposite:* nobody.

not allowed *adj* **inadmissible**, forbidden, prohibited, banned, proscribed, unacceptable. [➡REFUSE PERMISSION AND NOT ALLOW; 671] *Opposite:* permitted.

notarize *v* **authenticate**, certify, endorse, validate, rubber stamp. [➡TRIAL, PUNISHMENT, AND LEGAL OUTCOMES; 819]

notary *n* **lawyer**, solicitor, legal official, legal clerk, attorney (*US*). [➡PEOPLE IN LAW COURTS; 820]

notation 1 *n* **representation**, symbolization, system, code, cipher, scheme. [➡SYMBOLS, SIGNS, AND NUMBERS; 597] 2 *n* **note**, footnote, jotting, memo, annotation. [➡PARTS OF BOOKS AND DOCUMENTS; 594]

not bad *adj* **reasonable**, average, fair, acceptable, passable, pretty good. [➡ACCEPTABLE AND PASSABLE; 220] *Opposite:* terrible.

notch 1 *n* **nick**, indentation, cut, mark, slash, score, gash, scratch. [➡HOLES, GAPS, AND FORKS; 1251] 2 *n* **level**, degree, step, stage, rung, grade. [➡DEGREE AND EXTENT; 110]

not counting *prep* **apart from**, excluding, aside from, besides, except, not including, other than, with the exception of, over and above, excepting (*formal*), leaving out. [➡NOT; 135]

note 1 *n* **letter**, memo, memorandum, message, communication, reminder. [➡LETTERS AND WRITTEN MESSAGES; 585] 2 *n* **footnote**, annotation, gloss, comment, addendum, commentary. [➡PARTS OF BOOKS AND DOCUMENTS; 594] 3 *n* **tone**, edge, tinge, shade, hint, suggestion. [➡FEW, LITTLE, SMALL AMOUNT; 119] 4 *v* **notice**, take note of, take notice of, take in, observe, be aware of, see, perceive. [➡LEARN AND DISCOVER; 763] *Opposite:* disregard. 5 *v* **mention**, observe, state, say, remark. [➡SUGGEST, HINT, AND COMMENT; 613] 6 *v* **make a note of**, note down, write down, record, jot down, log, write, document. [➡RECORD SOMETHING; 372]

notebook *type of* **computer**. [➡COMPUTERS AND COMPUTING; 1126]

noted *adj* **renowned**, well-known, famous, distinguished, celebrated, illustrious, eminent, prominent, notable. [➡KNOWN AND FAMOUS; 182]

note down *v* [➡RECORD SOMETHING; 372]

notelet *n* **card**, note card, letter card. [➡LETTERS AND WRITTEN MESSAGES; 585]

notepad *n* **writing pad**, pad of paper, jotter, memo pad, block, pad, scribbling pad, scratchpad (*US*). [➡WRITING AND DRAWING IMPLEMENTS, AND MEDIA; 602]

notepaper *n* **writing paper**, writing pad, stationery, headed paper, letterhead. [➡WRITING AND DRAWING IMPLEMENTS, AND MEDIA; 602]

noteworthy *adj* **of note**, notable, striking, remarkable, important, significant, worth mentioning. [➡EXTRAORDINARY: AMAZING; 205] *Opposite:* insignificant.

nothing 1 *pron* **nought**, nil, zilch (*informal*), zero. [➡NONE; 121] 2 *n* **nonentity**, nobody, unknown. [➡LAZY OR UNSUCCESSFUL PEOPLE; 948]

nothing like *adj* [➡DIFFERENCE; 150]

nothingness *n* **oblivion**, nothing, emptiness, void, vacuum, nonexistence, nihility. [➡NONEXISTENCE; 24]

nothing special *adj* [➡ORDINARINESS; 245]

nothing to write home about *adj* [➡ORDINARINESS; 245]

no through road *type of* **minor road**. [➡ROADS; 1105]

notice 1 *n* **sign**, poster, announcement, advertisement, bill. [➡SIGNPOSTS, SIGNALS AND BILLBOARDS; 596] 2 *n* **warning**, notification, announcement, communication. [➡ADVISE AND WARN; 614] 3 *v* **become aware of**, see, take in, observe, perceive, note, discern, detect, remark, spot, sight, make out. [➡LEARN AND DISCOVER; 763]

noticeable *adj* **obvious**, clear, visible, perceptible, conspicuous, evident, manifest, in plain sight, in full view, plain. [➡PERCEPTIBLE; 25] *Opposite:* inconspicuous.

noticeboard *n* **display board**, information board, bulletin board (*US*). [➡SIGNPOSTS, SIGNALS AND BILLBOARDS; 596]

notification *n* **announcement**, notice, warning, statement, report. [➡INFORM AND ANNOUNCE; 612]

notify *v* **inform**, alert, advise, warn, report, let know, give notice, tell, acquaint, tip off. [➡INFORM AND ANNOUNCE; 612]

notion 1 *n* **idea**, view, concept, belief, conception, impression, opinion, perception, thought. [➡IDEA AND THOUGHT; 771] 2 *n* **impulse**, urge, whim, fancy, instinct. [➡FEELINGS; 532]

notional 1 *adj* **theoretical**, estimated, speculative, academic, hypothetical, abstract. [➡UNCERTAIN; 176] 2 *adj* **imaginary**, unreal, fancied, fanciful, whimsical, nonexistent, all in the mind. [➡FALSE AND UNREAL; 174] *Opposite:* real.

notionally *adv* **theoretically**, on paper, hypothetically, speculatively. [➡UNCERTAIN; 176]

not many *adj* [➡FEW, LITTLE, SMALL AMOUNT; 119]

not much *n* [➡FEW, LITTLE, SMALL AMOUNT; 119]

not on *adj* [➡UNACCEPTABLE AND UNFORGIVEABLE; 226]

notoriety *n* **disrepute**, infamy, dishonour, bad reputation, bad name, ill repute. [➡KNOWN AND FAMOUS; 182]

notorious 1 *adj* **infamous**, disreputable, dishonourable, tarnished. [➡MORALLY BAD; 776] *Opposite:* reputable. 2 *adj* (*archaic*) **famous**, renowned, eminent, familiar, recognized, celebrated, distinguished, illustrious. [➡KNOWN AND FAMOUS; 182] *Opposite:* unknown.

notoriously *adv* **particularly**, especially, extremely, very. [➡TO A GREAT EXTENT; 130]

not quite *adv* **almost**, virtually, as good as, roughly, nearly, just about, approximately, nigh on. [➡TO A CERTAIN EXTENT; 134]

not unlike *adj* [➡SIMILARITY; 149]

notwithstanding (*formal*) 1 *prep* **despite**, in spite of, aside from, excluding, setting aside, apart from. [➡NOT; 135] 2 *adv* **nevertheless**, all the same, nonetheless, anyhow. [➡ALTHOUGH, NEVERTHELESS, AND DESPITE; 170]

nougat *type of* **confectionery.** [➡CONFECTIONERY; 1181]

nought *n* **zero**, nothing, nil, zilch (*informal*). [➡NONE; 121]

noun *type of* **word class.** [➡ASPECTS OF LANGUAGE; 683]

nourish 1 *v* **nurture**, give food to, sustain, suckle, feed. [➡EAT AND NOT EAT; 711] 2 *v* **encourage**, promote, cultivate, support, foster, develop. [➡IMPROVE STRENGTH AND DURABILITY; 379]

nourishing *adj* **nutritious**, wholesome, beneficial, healthful. [➡FOOD; 1166] *Opposite:* unhealthy.

nourishment *n* **food**, sustenance, diet, nutrition. [➡FOOD; 1166]

nous 1 *n* (*informal*) **common sense**, good sense, sense, wisdom, horse sense, judgment. [➡KNOWLEDGE AND WISDOM; 559] 2 *n* **intellect**, ability, intelligence, rationality, reason, mind. [➡POSITIVE INTELLECTUAL CHARACTERISTICS; 525]

no use *adj* [➡REDUNDANT AND USELESS; 241]

nouveau riche *adj* [➡WEALTH AND WEALTHY; 891]

nova *type of* **star or star system.** [➡CELESTIAL BODIES; 1060]

novel 1 *n* **book**, narrative, work of fiction, tale, story. [➡BOOKS AND BOOKLETS; 591] 2 *adj* **original**, new, fresh, different, innovative, unusual, unique. [➡EXTRAORDINARY: UNCOMMON; 206] *Opposite:* well-worn.

See Compare and Contrast at **new.**

novelette *n* **short novel**, short story, novella, tale, fable. [➡FICTION AND DRAMA; 913]

novelist *n* **writer**, author, story writer. [➡WRITERS AND STYLES; 914]

novella *n* **short story**, short novel, novelette, tale, fable. [➡FICTION AND DRAMA; 913]

novelty *n* **innovation**, originality, newness, freshness, uniqueness. [➡EXTRAORDINARY: UNCOMMON; 206]

novice *n* **beginner**, learner, trainee, apprentice, greenhorn, neophyte, rookie (*US informal*). [➡UNSKILLED PERSON; 531] *Opposite:* old hand.

See Compare and Contrast at **beginner.**

now 1 *adv* **at the present**, at the moment, at this time, currently, at present, nowadays, at this moment, at this instant, at this point. [➡PRESENT; 85] *Opposite:* then. 2 *adv* **immediately**, right away, straightaway, at once, instantly, promptly, without hesitation, right now, pronto (*informal*), in half a shake, in a jiffy (*informal*). [➡HAPPENING QUICKLY; 104] *Opposite:* later.

nowadays *adv* **these days**, today, now, at the present time, at the moment, currently, in our time, in this day and age. [➡PRESENT; 85] *Opposite:* formerly.

now and again *adv* **from time to time**, once in a while, sometimes, at times, occasionally, every so often, now and then, sporadically, at irregular intervals. [➡NEVER AND INFREQUENCY; 97] *Opposite:* regularly.

now and then *adv* **from time to time**, sometimes, at times, now and again, occasionally, every so often, once in a while. [➡NEVER AND INFREQUENCY; 97] *Opposite:* regularly.

no-win situation *n* [➡DIFFICULT SITUATIONS; 72]

noxious 1 *adj* **harmful**, toxic, poisonous, deadly, lethal, venomous, injurious, deleterious (*formal*), pernicious. [➡DANGEROUS; 237] *Opposite:* harmless. 2 *adj* **nasty**, unpleasant, offensive, foul, horrible, disgusting. [➡DISGUSTING AND REPULSIVE; 231] *Opposite:* pleasant.

noxiousness *n* [➡DANGER; 236]

nozzle *n* **spout**, jet, control valve, spigot, outlet, tap. [➡FITTINGS; 859]

nuance *n* **tone**, gradation, distinction, tinge, hint, degree, touch, trace, note, shade. [➡FEW, LITTLE, SMALL AMOUNT; 119]

nub *n* **crux**, crucial point, essence, core, heart, nitty-gritty (*informal*), root, gist. [➡MOST IMPORTANT THING; 198]

nubbin *n* [➡EXTREMITIES OF PHYSICAL OBJECTS; 1249]

nub end *n* [➡EXTREMITIES OF PHYSICAL OBJECTS; 1249]

nuclear *adj* **atomic**, nuclear-powered, fissile, fissionable. [➡ENERGY SOURCES; 1161]

nuclear family *n* [➡THE FAMILY; 956]

nuclear missile *type of* **explosive weapon.** [➡EXPLOSIVES; 1154]

nuclear power plant (*US*) *type of* **industrial site.** [➡INDUSTRIAL BUILDINGS; 1086]

nuclear power station *type of* **industrial site.** [➡INDUSTRIAL BUILDINGS; 1086]

nuclear reprocessing plant *type of* **industrial site.** [➡INDUSTRIAL BUILDINGS; 1086]

nuclear warhead *type of* **explosive weapon.** [➡EXPLOSIVES; 1154]

nuclear weapon *type of* **explosive weapon.** [➡EXPLOSIVES; 1154]

nucleus *n* **centre**, basis, core, heart, nub, focus. [➡CENTRAL PARTS OF PHYSICAL OBJECTS; 1250]

nude *adj* **unclothed**, in the nude, undressed, in the buff (*informal*), in a state of undress, in your birthday suit (*slang humorous*), stripped, stark-naked, bare, naked, starkers (*informal*), with nothing on, buck naked (*US*). [➡DRESS, WEAR, AND UNDRESS; 868] *Opposite:* clothed.

See Compare and Contrast at **naked.**

nudge 1 *v* **push**, bump, elbow, shove, jolt, prod. [➡CONTACT: TOUCH; 413] 2 *n* **prod**, push, shove, bump, jolt. [➡CONTACT: TOUCH; 413]

nudity *n* **bareness**, nakedness, undress, deshabille. [➡DRESS, WEAR, AND UNDRESS; 868]

nugatory *adj* **trifling**, petty, insignificant, trivial, unimportant, irrelevant. [➡TOO FEW, TOO LITTLE; 120] *Opposite:* significant.

nugget *n* **piece**, bit, chunk, lump, hunk, titbit. [➡AMOUNT OF SOLID OR SEMI-SOLID; 115]

nuisance *n* **irritation**, annoyance, pest (*informal*), bother, trouble, irritant, pain (*informal*). [➡NUISANCES; 254]

nuke (*slang*) *v* **bomb**, obliterate, blow up, destroy, annihilate, wipe out (*informal*). [➡DESTRUCTION AND DEMOLITION; 360]

null 1 *adj* **invalid**, null and void, void, unacceptable, unsound, untrue. [➡ILLEGAL; 816] *Opposite:* valid. 2 *adj* **worthless**, valueless, unimportant, insignificant, useless. [➡UNIMPORTANT AND UNNECESSARY; 239]

null and void *adj* **invalid**, void, null, unacceptable, flawed. [➡ILLEGAL; 816] *Opposite:* valid.

nullify *v* **invalidate**, annul, cancel out, abolish, negate (*formal*), reverse, repeal, quash, abrogate (*formal*). [➡ABOLISH AND ANNUL; 453] *Opposite:* validate.

Compare and Contrast: ***nullify, abrogate, annul, repeal, invalidate, negate***

CORE MEANING: TO PUT AN END TO THE EFFECTIVE EXISTENCE OF SOMETHING

nullify to make something legally invalid or ineffective, or to cancel something out; ***abrogate*** (*formal*) to end an agreement or contract formally and publicly; ***annul*** to declare something officially or legally invalid or ineffective; ***repeal*** to end a law officially; ***invalidate*** to deprive something of its legal force or value, e.g. by failing to comply with certain terms and conditions; ***negate*** (*formal*) to render something ineffective, e.g. by doing something that counterbalances its force or effectiveness.

numb 1 *adj* **frozen**, anaesthetized, dead, deadened, unfeeling, insensitive, sensationless. [➡PAIN AND OTHER PHYSICAL SENSATIONS; 734] 2 *adj* **emotionless**, shocked, dazed, disoriented, distressed. [➡NEUTRALITY AND INDIFFERENCE; 554] *Opposite:* animated. 3 *v* **deaden**, freeze, anaesthetize, stun, dull, blunt. [➡PAIN AND OTHER PHYSICAL SENSATIONS; 734]

number 1 *n* **figure**, numeral, digit, integer. [➡SYMBOLS, SIGNS, AND NUMBERS; 597] 2 *n* **amount**, quantity, sum. [➡AMOUNT AND QUANTITY; 112] 3 *v* **come to**, add up to, total, amount to, run to. [➡AMOUNT TO AND EQUAL; 70]

numberless *adj* **countless**, innumerable, numerous, endless, myriad. [➡MANY, MUCH, LARGE AMOUNT; 117] *Opposite:* few.

number one 1 *adj* (*informal*) **excellent**, high quality, first-rate, top, top quality, top-class, top-grade, best-selling, first-class, world-class. [➡ADMIRABLE AND COMMENDABLE; 186] 2 *n* (*informal*) **important person**, key player, top dog (*informal*), linchpin, leader, prime candidate, main contender. [➡IMPORTANT OR FAMOUS PEOPLE; 893] 3 *n* (*informal*) **chief executive officer**, managing director, chief executive, boss, chief, head, head honcho (*US*). [➡IMPORTANT OR FAMOUS PEOPLE; 893] 4 *adj* **first**, top, leading, best, most important, favourite, chosen, successful, winning. [➡MOST IMPORTANT AND MAIN; 194]

number plate *type of* **external feature.** [➡VEHICLES; 1144]

numbing 1 *adj* **deadening**, freezing, anaesthetizing. [➡PAIN AND OTHER PHYSICAL SENSATIONS; 734] 2 *adj* **shocking**, distressing, dazing, upsetting, traumatic. [➡EMOTIONALLY UNPLEASANT AND UPSETTING; 228]

numbly *adv* **dazedly**, dully, torpidly, emotionlessly, impassively, expressionlessly. [➡NEUTRALITY AND INDIFFERENCE; 554] *Opposite:* animatedly.

numbness 1 *n* **deadness**, unresponsiveness, lack of sensation. [➡PAIN AND OTHER PHYSICAL SENSATIONS; 734] *Opposite:* sensation. 2 *n* **emotionlessness**, impassiveness, coldness, detachment, shock. [➡NEUTRALITY AND INDIFFERENCE; 554]

numeracy *n* **mathematical ability**, numerical competence, skill, proficiency, expertise, accomplishment, facility. [➡KNOWLEDGE AND WISDOM; 559]

numeral *n* **number**, figure, digit, cipher. [➡MATHS; 598]

numerate *adj* **mathematically competent**, good with numbers, proficient, accomplished, competent. [➡KNOWLEDGE AND WISDOM; 559]

numerical *adj* **mathematical**, arithmetic, arithmetical, statistical. [➡MATHS; 598]

numeric keypad *type of* **hardware**. [➡COMPUTERS AND COMPUTING; 1126]

numerous *adj* **many**, frequent, plentiful, abundant, several, copious, various. [➡MANY, MUCH, LARGE AMOUNT; 117] *Opposite:* few.

numerousness *n* [➡MANY, MUCH, LARGE AMOUNT; 117]

nun *n* [➡RELIGIOUS PEOPLE; 779]

nunnery *n* **convent**, monastery, abbey, religious foundation, religious community. [➡RELIGIOUS BUILDINGS; 1084]

nuptial *adj* **marriage**, wedding, bridal, matrimonial, marital, conjugal, connubial (*formal*). [➡CEREMONIES AND ANNIVERSARIES; 38]

nuptials (*literary or humorous*) *n* **wedding**, marriage, happy day. [➡CEREMONIES AND ANNIVERSARIES; 38]

nurse 1 *n* [➡PEOPLE WHO WORK IN MEDICINE; 848] 2 *v* **care for**, look after, take care of, tend, foster, nurture. [➡TAKE CARE OF AND SPOIL; 301] *Opposite:* neglect. 3 *v* **harbour**, cherish, nurture, have, foster, indulge. [➡CAUSE TO CONTINUE; 268]

nursery 1 *n* **nursery school**, day nursery, playgroup, kindergarten. [➡EDUCATIONAL INSTITUTIONS; 813] 2 *n* **plant sales outlet**, garden centre, plant market. [➡RETAIL OUTLETS; 1082]

nursery school *type of* **school**. [➡EDUCATIONAL INSTITUTIONS; 813]

nursing home *n* [➡HOSPITALS AND CLINICS; 826]

nurture 1 *v* **care for**, look after, take care of, raise, rear, foster. [➡TAKE CARE OF AND SPOIL; 301] 2 *v* **cultivate**, cherish, develop, support, encourage, foster. [➡CAUSE TO CONTINUE; 268]

nut (*informal*) 1 *n* **skull**, cranium, pate (*archaic or humorous*), bonce (*informal*), dome, bean (*US slang*), noodle (*slang*), crown. [➡HEAD; 693] 2 *n* **enthusiast**, fan, aficionado, buff, devotee, follower, admirer, aficionada. [➡DEVOTEES AND ADDICTED PEOPLE; 557]

nut

◆ *types of nut*
acorn, almond, brazil nut, cashew, chestnut, cob, cobnut, coconut, cola nut, groundnut, hazelnut, hickory nut, horse chestnut, macadamia nut, monkey nut, peanut, pecan, pine nut, pistachio, walnut

nut-brown *type of* **brown**. [➡COLOURS; 1223]

nutcracker *type of* **utensil**. [➡TABLEWARE, CUTLERY, AND KITCHENWARE; 861]

nuthatch *type of* **common bird**. [➡BIRD; 997]

nutmeg *type of* **spice**. [➡HERBS AND SPICES; 1174]

nutrient

◆ *types of nutrient*
amino acid, carbohydrate, dextrose, fat, fibre, fructose, glucose, lactose, mineral, protein, salt, starch, sucrose, sugar, vitamin

nutrition *n* **nourishment**, diet, food, sustenance. [➡FOOD; 1166]

nutritional *adj* **nutritious**, nourishing, nutritive, dietary, alimentary, dietetic, food. [➡FOOD; 1166]

nutritious *adj* **nourishing**, healthy, wholesome, healthful, beneficial, nutritive. [➡FOOD; 1166] *Opposite:* unhealthy.

nutritive 1 *adj* **nutritional**, dietary, dietetic, alimentary, food. [➡FOOD; 1166] 2 *adj* **nutritious**, nourishing, healthy, wholesome, healthful, beneficial. [➡FOOD; 1166] *Opposite:* unhealthy.

nuts (*slang*) *adj* [➡ECCENTRICITY AND IRRATIONALITY; 563]

nuts and bolts (*informal*) *n* **basics**, brass tacks, nitty-gritty (*informal*), practicalities, fundamentals, details, foundations. [➡BASIC DETAILS; 689]

nutshell *n* **husk**, casing, shell, outer. [➡COVERS AND COATINGS; 1245]

nuzzle *v* **nestle**, cuddle, burrow, snuggle, push, rub. [➡CONTACT: TOUCH; 413]

nyctophobia *type of* **phobia**. [➡FEARS AND PHOBIAS; 555]

nylon *type of* **synthetic fabric**. [➡FABRICS; 1131]

nylons *type of* **lower body underwear**. [➡HABERDASHERY, MILLINERY, AND LINGERIE; 867]

nymph *n* **fairy**, sprite, spirit, dryad, elf, leprechaun. [➡MYTHICAL BEINGS; 790]

O

oak *type of* **deciduous tree.** [➡DECIDUOUS TREES; 1028]

OAP *n* [➡OLD PERSON; 920]

oar *n* **paddle**, scull, sweep, blade. [➡PARTS OF A SHIP OR BOAT; 1150]

oarlock (*US*) *part of* **ship or boat.** [➡PARTS OF A SHIP OR BOAT; 1150]

oasis *n* **retreat**, refuge, haven, sanctuary, escape. [➡SAFE BUILDINGS OR PLACES; 1092]

oat *type of* **cereal.** [➡CEREAL FOODS; 1177]

oath 1 *n* **promise**, pledge, vow, word, assurance, word of honour. [➡PROMISE AND ASSURE; 685] 2 *n* **curse**, swearword, expletive, four-letter word, imprecation (*formal*), cussword (*US informal*). [➡INSULTS, ABUSE, AND SWEARING; 659]

oatmeal *type of* **beige.** [➡COLOURS; 1223]

obduracy *n* **obstinacy**, stubbornness, inflexibility, mulishness, pigheadedness, determination, implacability (*formal*), immovability. [➡UNWILLINGNESS AND STUBBORNNESS; 565] *Opposite:* compliance.

obdurate 1 *adj* **obstinate**, stubborn, inflexible, unyielding, unbending, pigheaded, adamant, immovable, implacable (*formal*), mulish, stiff-necked. [➡UNWILLINGNESS AND STUBBORNNESS; 565] *Opposite:* compliant. 2 *adj* **hardhearted**, callous, unfeeling, heartless, pitiless, ruthless, unsympathetic, hard-boiled (*informal*). [➡SELFISH AND UNKIND; 506] *Opposite:* warm-hearted.

obdurately *adv* **obstinately**, stubbornly, implacably (*formal*), mulishly, inflexibly, unbendingly, unyieldingly, pigheadedly, adamantly, immovably. [➡UNWILLINGNESS AND STUBBORNNESS; 565] *Opposite:* compliantly.

obdurateness *n* [➡UNWILLINGNESS AND STUBBORNNESS; 565]

obedience *n* **compliance**, agreement, submission, respect, duty, deference, tractability, docility, conformity, subservience, meekness. [➡THE WILL AND WILLINGNESS; 564] *Opposite:* disobedience.

obedient *adj* **compliant**, dutiful, submissive, respectful, biddable, deferential, well-trained, docile, tractable, amenable, subservient, meek, tame, unquestioning. [➡EXPRESSING RESPECT AND APPROVAL; 638] *Opposite:* disobedient.

obeisance 1 *n* (*formal*) **bow**, curtsy, bob, nod, genuflection, kowtow. [➡GESTURES AND GESTICULATION; 654] 2 *n* **homage**, respect, deference, duty, loyalty, genuflection. [➡LOVE, RESPECT, AND GOODWILL; 550]

obelisk *n* **pillar**, column, pylon, needle, tower, monument. [➡MONUMENTS; 1091]

obese *adj* **fat**, overweight, heavy, stout, plump, large, corpulent (*formal or literary*), chunky (*informal*). [➡BUILD; 478] *Opposite:* underweight.

obesity *n* **overweightness**, heaviness, stoutness, plumpness, largeness, chunkiness (*informal*), fatness, corpulence (*formal or literary*). [➡BUILD; 478] *Opposite:* thinness.

obey *v* **do as you are told**, submit, follow, comply with, act upon, observe, abide by, conform, mind, defer to. [➡OBEY AND ABIDE BY; 302] *Opposite:* disobey.

obfuscate *v* **obscure**, complicate, confuse, muddy, cloud, mystify, muddle, befuddle, befog (*literary*). [➡CREATE DISORDER AND CAUSE CHAOS; 359] *Opposite:* clarify.

obfuscation *n* **complication**, mystification, confusion, muddying, clouding, smoke screen. [➡DECEPTION AND LIES; 661] *Opposite:* clarification.

obituary 1 *n* **tribute**, obit, article, announcement, feature, eulogy, epitaph. [➡BURIAL AND PREPARATION FOR BURIAL; 929] 2 *adj* **funerary**, funereal, memorial, epitaphic, death, valedictory (*formal*). [➡BURIAL AND PREPARATION FOR BURIAL; 929]

object 1 *n* **thing**, article, item, entity, body, piece. [➡PHYSICAL OBJECTS; 1242] 2 *n* **purpose**, objective, aim, point, idea, goal, intention, intent (*formal*), reason. [➡INTENTION AND PURPOSE; 773] 3 *v* **oppose**, protest, complain, challenge, demur, baulk, remonstrate, expostulate, take exception to, grumble, carp. [➡PROTEST AND EXPRESS DISAPPROVAL; 643] *Opposite:* approve. 4 *type of* **grammatical term.** [➡ASPECTS OF LANGUAGE; 683]

Compare and Contrast: ***object, protest, demur, remonstrate, expostulate***

CORE MEANING: TO INDICATE OPPOSITION TO SOMETHING

object to be opposed or averse to something, or express opposition to it; ***protest*** to express strong disapproval of or disagreement with something, or to refuse to obey or accept something, often by making a formal statement or taking action in public; ***demur*** to raise objections in a hesitant or tentative way; ***remonstrate*** to reason or argue forcefully with somebody about something; ***expostulate*** to express disagreement or disapproval vehemently, or to attempt to dissuade somebody from doing something.

objectify 1 *v* **actualize**, realize, represent, portray, reify, symbolize. [➡REPRESENT SOMETHING OR SOMEBODY; 59] 2 *v* **diminish**, reduce, simplify, trivialize. [➡CHANGE; 373]

objection 1 *n* **opposition**, protest, protestation, hostility, demurral, complaint. [➡CRITICISMS AND ANGRY OUTBURSTS; 50] *Opposite:* approval. 2 *n* **doubt**, concern, problem, worry, niggle, difficulty. [➡PROBLEM; 257] *Opposite:* confidence.

objectionable *adj* **offensive**, obnoxious, horrible, unpleasant, intolerable, abhorrent (*formal*), distasteful, disagreeable, loathsome, unacceptable. [➡DISGUSTING AND REPULSIVE; 231] *Opposite:* inoffensive.

objective 1 *adj* **impartial**, detached, neutral, unbiased, unprejudiced, independent, dispassionate, disinterested, fair. [➡THE NATURE OF IDEAS; 772] *Opposite:* subjective. **2** *adj* **factual**, actual, tangible, fact-based, demonstrable, quantitative, empirical, real. [➡TRUE AND REAL; 172] *Opposite:* subjective. **3** *n* **object**, purpose, aim, point, idea, goal, intention, intent (*formal*), reason. [➡INTENTION AND PURPOSE; 773]

objectivity *n* **impartiality**, detachment, independence, neutrality, fairness. [➡THE NATURE OF IDEAS; 772] *Opposite:* subjectivity.

objet d'art *n* **work of art**, masterpiece, creation, piece, ornament, curio. [➡ARTWORKS; 898]

obligate *v* **compel**, oblige, force, make, require, coerce, necessitate. [➡CAUSE OR COMPEL TO ACT; 272] *Opposite:* request.

obligated *adj* [➡APPRECIATION AND GRATITUDE; 536]

obligation **1** *n* **debt**, contract, commitment, promise, agreement, understanding. [➡PROMISE AND ASSURE; 685] **2** *n* **duty**, responsibility, requirement, compulsion, commitment, onus. [➡WORK IN GENERAL; 298] *Opposite:* option.

obligatory **1** *adj* **required**, statutory, mandatory, binding, the law. [➡NECESSARY AND ESSENTIAL; 197] *Opposite:* discretionary. **2** *adj* **compulsory**, required, requisite (*formal*), necessary, essential, de rigueur (*formal*). [➡NECESSARY AND ESSENTIAL; 197] *Opposite:* optional.

oblige **1** *v* **compel**, obligate, force, make, require, coerce, necessitate. [➡CAUSE OR COMPEL TO ACT; 272] *Opposite:* request. **2** *v* **gratify**, please, indulge, accommodate, help, assist. [➡PLEASE AND AMUSE; 573] *Opposite:* disappoint.

obliged *adj* **grateful**, thankful, appreciative, gratified, indebted. [➡APPRECIATION AND GRATITUDE; 536]

obliging *adj* **helpful**, kind, considerate, willing, agreeable, polite, courteous, accommodating, cooperative. [➡THE WILL AND WILLINGNESS; 564] *Opposite:* unhelpful.

oblique **1** *adj* **slanting**, slanted, tilted, sloping, leaning, askew, diagonal. [➡ORIENTATION AND ALIGNMENT; 1222] *Opposite:* upright. **2** *adj* **indirect**, implicit, implied, roundabout, circuitous, backhanded. [➡INARTICULATE, RAMBLING, AND AWKWARD; 634] *Opposite:* direct.

obliqueness **1** *n* **tilt**, inclination, slant, steepness, lean, slope, cant. [➡ORIENTATION AND ALIGNMENT; 1222] **2** *n* **indirectness**, circuitousness, circumlocution, obscureness, opaqueness, opacity. [➡VAGUENESS; 244] *Opposite:* directness.

obliterate *v* **destroy**, wipe out (*informal*), demolish, eliminate, eradicate, annihilate, abolish. [➡DESTRUCTION AND DEMOLITION; 360] *Opposite:* create.

obliteration *n* **destruction**, annihilation, eradication, elimination, abolition, demolition. [➡DESTRUCTION AND DEMOLITION; 360] *Opposite:* creation.

oblivion **1** *n* **forgetfulness**, unconsciousness, stupor, insensibility, obliviousness. [➡IGNORANCE; 558] *Opposite:* awareness. **2** *n* **obscurity**, extinction, the past, the annals of history, nothingness, silence. [➡NONEXISTENCE; 24] *Opposite:* existence.

oblivious *adj* **unaware**, unconscious, unmindful, ignorant, insensible. [➡IGNORANCE; 558] *Opposite:* conscious.

oblong *type of* **angular shape.** [➡ANGULAR SHAPE; 1216]

obloquy (*formal or literary*) **1** *n* **censure**, criticism, defamation, blame, opprobrium, bad press, attack, character assassination. [➡CRITICISMS AND ANGRY OUTBURSTS; 50] *Opposite:* praise. **2** *n* **disgrace**, shame, infamy, ignominy, disfavour, dishonour, humiliation, odium, disrepute. [➡DIFFICULT SITUATIONS; 72]

obnoxious *adj* **loathsome**, hateful, horrible, insufferable, intolerable, detestable, unbearable, abhorrent (*formal*), abominable, despicable, repugnant, repellent, offensive, unpleasant. [➡DISGUSTING AND REPULSIVE; 231] *Opposite:* delightful.

obnoxiousness *n* [➡DISGUSTING AND REPULSIVE; 231]

oboe *type of* **wind instrument.** [➡MUSICAL INSTRUMENTS; 910]

obscene **1** *adj* **indecent**, lewd, explicit, offensive, blue (*informal*), X-rated (*informal*), crude, rude. [➡MORALLY BAD; 776] *Opposite:* decent. **2** *adj* **disgusting**, nauseating, sickening, offensive, rude, crass, excessive, beyond the pale. [➡DISGUSTING AND REPULSIVE; 231] *Opposite:* decent.

obscenity **1** *n* **indecency**, lewdness, offensiveness, explicitness, crudeness, rudeness. [➡MORALLY BAD; 776] *Opposite:* decency. **2** *n* **offensiveness**, atrocity, tastelessness, vulgarity, rudeness, crassness. [➡DISGUSTING AND REPULSIVE; 231] *Opposite:* tastefulness. **3** *n* **curse**, swearword, four-letter word, expletive, cuss word (*informal*). [➡INSULTS, ABUSE, AND SWEARING; 659]

obscurantism *n* **conservatism**, traditionalism, dogmatism, reaction, illiberalism, opposition. [➡STYLES AND SYSTEMS OF GOVERNMENT; 806] *Opposite:* liberalism.

obscurantist **1** *adj* **reactionary**, conservative, backward-looking, traditionalist, old-fashioned, diehard, hidebound, doctrinaire, illiberal. [➡THE NATURE OF IDEAS; 772] *Opposite:* liberal. **2** *n* **conservative**, reactionary, traditionalist, diehard, dogmatist, obscurant. [➡UNCOOPERATIVE OR REBELLIOUS PERSON; 567] *Opposite:* liberal.

obscure **1** *adj* **incomprehensible**, unclear, vague, ambiguous, abstruse, enigmatic, cryptic, unintelligible, arcane, recondite. [➡DIFFICULTY AND COMPLEXITY; 243] *Opposite:* clear. **2** *adj* **indistinct**, faint, shadowy, murky, blurry, dim, foggy, muddy, opaque. [➡IMPERCEPTIBLE; 26] *Opposite:* clear. **3** *adj* **unknown**, little-known, minor, unseen, unheard of, humble. [➡SECRET AND UNKNOWN; 180] *Opposite:* famous. **4** *v* **confuse**, disguise, conceal, complicate, obfuscate, muddy, muddle. [➡CREATE DISORDER AND CAUSE CHAOS; 359] *Opposite:* clarify. **5** *v* **darken**, cloak, mask, hide, shroud, veil, eclipse, block out. [➡CAUSE TO DISAPPEAR; 6] *Opposite:* disclose.

Compare and Contrast: ***obscure, abstruse, recondite, arcane, cryptic, enigmatic***

CORE MEANING: DIFFICULT TO UNDERSTAND

obscure difficult to understand because it is expressed in a complicated way or because it involves areas of knowledge or study that are not known to most people; ***abstruse*** not easy to understand, often because it involves specialist knowledge or is expressed in specialist language; ***recondite*** requiring a high degree of scholarship or specialist knowledge to be understood;

arcane requiring information that is secret or known only to a few people in order to be understood; ***cryptic*** deliberately mysterious or ambiguous and seeming to have a hidden meaning; ***enigmatic*** having a quality of mystery and ambiguity that makes it difficult to understand or interpret.

obscurely 1 *adv* **indistinctly**, faintly, murkily, blurrily, dimly. [➡IMPERCEPTIBLE; 26] *Opposite:* clearly. 2 *adv* **incomprehensibly**, unclearly, vaguely, ambiguously, abstrusely, murkily, unintelligibly. [➡DIFFICULTY AND COMPLEXITY; 243] *Opposite:* clearly.

obscurity 1 *n* **anonymity**, insignificance, unimportance, inconspicuousness, oblivion. [➡SECRET AND UNKNOWN; 180] *Opposite:* fame. 2 *n* **incomprehensibility**, vagueness, ambiguousness, doubt, opacity, abstruseness, murkiness, unintelligibility. [➡VAGUENESS; 244] *Opposite:* clarity.

obsequious *adj* **servile**, sycophantic, flattering, toadying, submissive, fawning, compliant, deferential, reverential, grovelling, unctuous, smarmy. [➡INGRATIATING; 639] *Opposite:* assertive.

obsequiousness *n* **sycophancy**, servility, flattery, submissiveness, sweet talk (*informal*), compliance, deference, unctuousness, smarminess, reverence. [➡INGRATIATING; 639] *Opposite:* assertiveness.

observable *adj* **noticeable**, visible, apparent, evident, obvious, discernible, recognizable, perceptible, plain, clear, detectable. [➡PERCEPTIBLE; 25] *Opposite:* imperceptible.

observance 1 *n* **adherence**, compliance, execution, performance, observation, fulfilment, obedience. [➡THE WILL AND WILLINGNESS; 564] *Opposite:* violation. 2 *n* **ritual**, ceremony, ceremonial, rite, celebration, practice. [➡CEREMONIES AND ANNIVERSARIES; 38]

observant *adj* **sharp-eyed**, alert, attentive, watchful, vigilant, on the ball (*informal*), wide-awake, perceptive. [➡POSITIVE INTELLECTUAL CHARACTERISTICS; 525] *Opposite:* unobservant.

observation 1 *n* **surveillance**, scrutiny, watching, inspection, examination, study. [➡SEE; 700] *Opposite:* neglect. 2 *n* **remark**, comment, opinion, thought, reflection, statement. [➡SUGGEST, HINT, AND COMMENT; 613]

observation tower *n* [➡TOWERS; 1098]

observatory *n* **building**, station, laboratory, telescope, viewpoint. [➡TOWERS; 1098]

observe 1 *v* **detect**, perceive, witness, see, spot, note, discern, notice. [➡LEARN AND DISCOVER; 763] *Opposite:* miss. 2 *v* **watch**, view, scrutinize, monitor, study, examine, survey. [➡LOOKING AND LOOKS; 701] *Opposite:* ignore. 3 *v* **remark**, comment, say, declare, state, opine (*formal*), reflect. [➡UTTER AND PRONOUNCE; 609] 4 *v* **abide by**, respect, follow, comply with, heed, conform to, keep, adhere to, perform. [➡OBEY AND ABIDE BY; 302] *Opposite:* violate. 5 *v* **celebrate**, keep, remember, take part in, perform. [➡PARTICIPATE; 293] *Opposite:* break.

observer *n* **spectator**, witness, viewer, onlooker, bystander, eyewitness. [➡LOOKERS AND SPECTATORS; 702] *Opposite:* participant.

obsess *v* **preoccupy**, grip, consume, fixate, possess, fascinate. [➡APPEAL TO AND AROUSE INTEREST; 576] *Opposite:* bore.

obsessed *adj* **fanatical**, gripped, preoccupied, infatuated, fixated, passionate, possessed. [➡PENSIVENESS AND INTEREST; 539] *Opposite:* indifferent.

obsession *n* **mania**, fascination, fixation, passion, preoccupation, thing (*informal*). [➡FADS, FETISHES, AND IDOLATRY; 556] *Opposite:* indifference.

obsessional *adj* [➡NEGATIVE INTELLECTUAL CHARACTERISTICS; 526]

obsessive *adj* **compulsive**, fanatical, fixated, infatuated, neurotic (*informal*), preoccupied, possessed. [➡NEGATIVE INTELLECTUAL CHARACTERISTICS; 526] *Opposite:* easygoing.

obsessiveness *n* [➡FADS, FETISHES, AND IDOLATRY; 556]

obsolescence *n* **uselessness**, desuetude (*formal*), undesirability, outmodedness, oldness, unfashionableness. [➡OLD, OLD-FASHIONED; 168] *Opposite:* modernity.

obsolescent *adj* **dated**, old, antiquated, out-of-date, passé, unfashionable, old-fashioned, outmoded, archaic, antediluvian (*informal*), superseded, obsolete, undesirable. [➡OLD, OLD-FASHIONED; 168] *Opposite:* up-to-date.

obsolete *adj* **archaic**, superseded, outmoded, antiquated, antediluvian (*informal*), passé, unfashionable, outdated, out-of-date, obsolescent, dated, old, old-fashioned. [➡OLD, OLD-FASHIONED; 168] *Opposite:* up-to-date.

See Compare and Contrast at **old-fashioned.**

obstacle 1 *n* **problem**, difficulty, hindrance, impediment, complication, hurdle, hitch, stumbling block. [➡PROBLEM; 257] *Opposite:* help. 2 *n* **obstruction**, barrier, blockage, blockade, impediment. [➡PROBLEM; 257]

obstinacy *n* **stubbornness**, determination, pigheadedness, inflexibility, unreasonableness, persistence, tenacity, intransigence, mulishness, wrong-headedness. [➡UNWILLINGNESS AND STUBBORNNESS; 565] *Opposite:* compliance.

obstinate *adj* **stubborn**, determined, pigheaded, fixed, inflexible, adamant, unmoved, persistent, tenacious, mulish, headstrong, wrong-headed. [➡UNWILLINGNESS AND STUBBORNNESS; 565] *Opposite:* compliant.

obstreperous *adj* **disruptive**, rowdy, disorderly, loud, noisy, undisciplined, unruly, rough. [➡REBELLIOUSNESS AND DISOBEDIENCE; 566] *Opposite:* demure.

See Compare and Contrast at **unruly.**

obstreperousness *n* [➡REBELLIOUSNESS AND DISOBEDIENCE; 566]

obstruct 1 *v* **block**, barricade, impede, hold up, stop, bar. [➡AVOID, PREVENT, LIMIT, AND CONTROL; 278] *Opposite:* clear. 2 *v* **hinder**, thwart, frustrate, hamper, complicate, prohibit, check. [➡AVOID, PREVENT, LIMIT, AND CONTROL; 278] *Opposite:* assist.

See Compare and Contrast at **hinder.**

obstruction *n* **obstacle**, barrier, block, blockade, barricade, impediment, hindrance, stumbling block, hitch, difficulty. [➡PROBLEM; 257] *Opposite:* help.

obstructionism *n* **timewasting**, stalling, filibustering, sabotage, hindrance, blocking. [➡AVOID, PREVENT, LIMIT, AND CONTROL; 278] *Opposite:* helpfulness.

obstructionist 1 *adj* **stalling**, timewasting, filibustering, delaying, delay. [➡AVOID, PREVENT, LIMIT, AND CONTROL; 278] 2 *n* **staller**, timewaster, filibusterer, wrecker, saboteur, delayer. [➡INTERFERING PEOPLE AND TELLTALES; 950]

obstructive *adj* **disruptive**, uncooperative, unhelpful, obstreperous, awkward, hindering, frustrating. [➡REBELLIOUSNESS AND DISOBEDIENCE; 566] *Opposite:* helpful.

obstructiveness *n* [➡REBELLIOUSNESS AND DISOBEDIENCE; 566]

obtain *v* **get**, get hold of, acquire, procure, attain, secure, gain, achieve. [➡GET; 421] *Opposite:* lose.

See Compare and Contrast at **get**.

obtainable *adj* **available**, accessible, reachable, attainable. [➡PRESENT AND AVAILABLE; 11] *Opposite:* unavailable.

obtrude 1 *v* **interfere**, impose, meddle, pry, interrupt, interpose, horn in (*informal*), intercede. [➡INTERRUPT AND BUTT IN; 620] 2 *v* **extend**, thrust, stick out, push out. [➡APPEAR AND EMERGE; 3]

obtrusive 1 *adj* **conspicuous**, unmistakable, blatant, prominent, garish, flagrant, flashy, obvious, bald, sheer. [➡PERCEPTIBLE; 25] *Opposite:* inconspicuous. 2 *adj* **interfering**, intruding, meddlesome, pushy (*informal*), forward, presumptuous. [➡NOSY AND INTERFERING; 513]

obtuse *adj* **insensitive**, dull-witted, simple-minded, imperceptive, stupid, dull. [➡NEGATIVE INTELLECTUAL CHARACTERISTICS; 526] *Opposite:* astute.

obtuseness *n* [➡DIFFICULTY AND COMPLEXITY; 243]

obverse 1 *n* **front**, head, heads, side, face, top. [➡EXTREMITIES OF PHYSICAL OBJECTS; 1249] 2 *n* **counterpart**, complement, opposite, equivalent, opposite number, supplement. [➡OPPOSITE; 158] 3 *adj* **front**, forward-facing, opposite, visible, anterior. [➡OPPOSITE; 158] *Opposite:* reverse. 4 *adj* **equivalent**, complementary, opposite, other, opposing. [➡OPPOSITE; 158]

obviate *v* **do away with**, avoid, remove, preclude (*formal*), forestall, prevent, avert, ward off, stave off, fend off. [➡AVOID, PREVENT, LIMIT, AND CONTROL; 278]

obvious *adj* **clear**, understandable, palpable, noticeable, apparent, evident, observable, recognizable, discernible. [➡PERCEPTIBLE; 25] *Opposite:* obscure.

obviousness *n* **clearness**, undoubtedness, certainty, patentness, overtness, unmistakableness, conspicuousness, plainness, inevitability, unavoidability, blatancy. [➡PERCEPTIBLE; 25] *Opposite:* obscurity.

ocarina *type of* **wind instrument**. [➡MUSICAL INSTRUMENTS; 910]

occasion 1 *n* **time**, juncture, case, instance, event, incident, occurrence, circumstance, point, spot, position. [➡EVENTS AND OCCURRENCES; 35] 2 *n* **possibility**, opportunity, opening, season, contingency, stage, chance. [➡BEGINNING; 53] 3 *n* **reason**, cause, motive, justification, rationale, explanation, excuse, basis, ground. [➡CAUSATION; 169] 4 *v* **cause**, motivate, give rise to, bring about, induce, prompt, elicit, effect (*formal*). [➡CAUSE TO HAPPEN; 31]

occasional *adj* **infrequent**, irregular, chance, sporadic, rare, intermittent, random. [➡NEVER AND INFREQUENCY; 97] *Opposite:* regular.

See Compare and Contrast at **periodic**.

occasional table *type of* **table**. [➡FURNITURE; 858]

occlude 1 *v* **block**, stop up, close off, seal, shut off, obstruct, clog up, cork. [➡BAR AND OBSTRUCT ACCESS; 411] *Opposite:* free. 2 *v* **cut off**, cut out, close, block off, shut, block out, seal, stem, stop, obscure. [➡BAR AND OBSTRUCT ACCESS; 411] *Opposite:* open.

occlusion 1 *n* **blocking**, obstruction, stopping up, closing off, sealing, shutting off, clogging up, constriction. [➡FASTEN, LINK, AND JOIN; 409] 2 *n* **cutting off**, cutting out, closure, blocking, sealing, blocking off, blocking out, stemming, stopping, obscuring. [➡END; 54]

occult *adj* [➡THE SUPERNATURAL; 788]

occultist *n* [➡PEOPLE WITH SUPERNATURAL POWERS; 789]

occupancy *n* **tenancy**, tenure, habitation, possession, residence, use. [➡POSSESS; 445] *Opposite:* vacancy.

occupant *n* **inhabitant**, tenant, dweller (*literary*), lodger, resident, occupier, denizen. [➡INHABITANT; 857]

occupation 1 *n* **job**, profession, work, career, livelihood, living, employment, business, vocation, calling, position, post. [➡PROFESSIONS; 845] 2 *n* **activity**, pursuit, enterprise, task. [➡WORK IN GENERAL; 298]

occupational *adj* **work-related**, job-related, professional, industrial, working, business. [➡TYPES OF WORK; 835]

occupied 1 *adj* **busy**, engaged, employed, unavailable, working. [➡ABSENT AND UNAVAILABLE; 7] *Opposite:* free. 2 *adj* **in use**, full, engaged, tied down, taken, tied up. [➡ABSENT AND UNAVAILABLE; 7] *Opposite:* empty. 3 *adj* **conquered**, subjugated, subject, dominated, ruled, captured, seized, oppressed. [➡CAPTIVITY AND LOSS OF FREEDOM; 249] *Opposite:* liberated.

occupier *n* **inhabitant**, resident, tenant, occupant, dweller (*literary*), lodger. [➡INHABITANT; 857]

occupy 1 *v* **live in**, inhabit, reside in, dwell in (*literary*), lodge (*dated*). [➡INHABIT; 20] *Opposite:* vacate. 2 *v* **interest**, engage, divert, take up, entertain, absorb, amuse, concern. [➡APPEAL TO AND AROUSE INTEREST; 576] 3 *v* **conquer**, subjugate, dominate, rule, seize, oppress, capture. [➡CAPTIVITY AND LOSS OF FREEDOM; 249] *Opposite:* liberate.

occur 1 *v* **happen**, take place, crop up (*informal*), befall (*archaic or literary*), arise, come about, transpire, ensue, follow. [➡HAPPEN; 27] 2 *v* **hit**, strike, cross your mind, appear, come to mind. [➡APPEAR AND EMERGE; 3]

occurrence 1 *n* **incidence**, rate, amount, existence, manifestation. [➡FREQUENT AND OFTEN; 107] 2 *n* **happening**, event, incident, episode, occasion, circumstance, fact, experience. [➡EVENTS AND OCCURRENCES; 35]

ocean 1 *n* **sea**, deep, water, briny. [➡THE SEAS, OCEANS, AND SHORES; 1041] 2 *adj* **marine**, sea, deep-sea, oceanic. [➡THE SEAS, OCEANS, AND SHORES; 1041]

oceangoing *adj* **seagoing**, sea, seaworthy, maritime, seafaring. [➡TRANSPORTATION, TRANSPORTERS, AND CARGOS; 323]

oceanic *adj* **sea**, deep-sea, ocean, saltwater, marine. [➡THE SEAS, OCEANS, AND SHORES; 1041]

ocelot *type of* **cat**. [➡FELINE; 983]

ochlocracy *n* [➡STYLES AND SYSTEMS OF GOVERNMENT; 806]

ochre *type of* **orange**. [➡COLOURS; 1223]

octagonal *adj* [➡ANGULAR SHAPE; 1216]

octet *type of* **band**. [➡MUSICIANS AND SINGERS; 908]

octopus *type of* **aquatic invertebrate**. [➡AQUATIC INVERTEBRATE; 1022]

ocular *adj* **visual**, optical, ophthalmic. [➡SEE; 700]

odd *adj* **strange**, peculiar, unusual, abnormal, anomalous, weird, funny, offbeat, incongruous, eccentric, idiosyncratic, unconventional, uncommon, unorthodox, individual. [➡BIZARRE AND PECULIAR; 258] *Opposite:* ordinary.

oddball (*informal*) *adj* [➡BIZARRE AND PECULIAR; 258]

oddity 1 *n* **peculiarity**, quirk, foible, idiosyncrasy, twist, kink, tic, eccentricity. [➡PERSONAL ECCENTRICITIES; 494] 2 *n* **strangeness**, peculiarity, quirkiness, oddness, bizarreness, abnormality, incongruousness. [➡BIZARRE AND PECULIAR; 258] *Opposite:* normality. 3 *n* **eccentric**, character, original, exception, case (*informal*), misfit, crank (*informal*). [➡SOLITARY PEOPLE; 942] 4 *n* **curiosity**, rarity, phenomenon, freak. [➡BIZARRE AND PECULIAR; 258]

oddments 1 *n* **odds and ends**, bits and pieces (*informal*), leftovers, offcuts, bits, fragments, odds and sods. [➡REMAINDER AND REMAINDERS; 123] 2 *n* **knick-knacks**, notions, sundries, curios, gewgaws, novelties. [➡ORNAMENTS AND DECORATIONS; 1247]

oddness *n* **strangeness**, peculiarity, mysteriousness, incongruity, weirdness, abnormality, quaintness, deviation, aberration. [➡BIZARRE AND PECULIAR; 258] *Opposite:* normality.

odd one out *n* [➡DIFFERENCE; 150]

odds *n* **chances**, probability, likelihood, balance. [➡GAMBLE AND TAKE RISKS; 467]

odds and ends *n* **bits and pieces** (*informal*), bits and bobs (*informal*), remnants, leftovers, loose ends, offcuts, fragments. [➡RUBBISH AND USELESS OBJECTS; 1248]

odds and sods *n* [➡RUBBISH AND USELESS OBJECTS; 1248]

odds-on (*informal*) *adv* **probably**, most likely, like enough, likely, dependably, reliably. [➡POSSIBLE AND PROBABLE; 178] *Opposite:* unlikely.

ode *n* **poem**, elegy, verse, song (*literary*), sonnet. [➡POETRY AND VERSE; 915]

odious *adj* **hateful**, horrible, abhorrent (*formal*), loathsome, revolting, detestable, repellent, repulsive, obnoxious, abominable, execrable. [➡DISGUSTING AND REPULSIVE; 231] *Opposite:* delightful.

odium *n* **abhorrence**, hatred, disgust, revulsion, hate, loathing, abomination, execration (*literary or formal*), detestation. [➡DISLIKE AND HATE; 578] *Opposite:* approval.

odometer (*US*) *type of* **measuring device**. [➡MEASURING DEVICES; 1122]

odoriferous (*formal or technical*) *adj* [➡SMELL AND SMELLING; 706]

odorous (*literary*) *adj* **scented**, aromatic, redolent, fragrant, perfumed, odoriferous (*formal or technical*). [➡SMELL AND SMELLING; 706]

odour 1 *n* **scent**, perfume, stink, aroma, stench, redolence, fragrance, bouquet, pong (*informal*). [➡SMELL AND SMELLING; 706] 2 *n* **air**, aura, atmosphere, flavour, spirit, feeling, quality, essence, sense. [➡APPEARANCE AND ATMOSPHERE; 1236]

See Compare and Contrast at **smell**.

odourless *adj* **unscented**, fragrance-free, neutral. [➡SMELL AND SMELLING; 706] *Opposite:* scented.

odyssey *n* **journey**, trek, crusade, pilgrimage, wanderings, travels, peregrination (*literary*). [➡TRAVEL: JOURNEYS AND TRIPS; 319]

oedema *n* [➡CONDITIONS AFFECTING THE SKIN; 722]

oesophagus *part of* **digestive tract**. [➡THE DIGESTIVE TRACT; 710]

oeuvre (*formal*) *n* **work**, piece, composition, opus, works, legacy, productions, creations. [➡ARTWORKS; 898]

of a kind *adj* [➡SIMILARITY; 149]

of course 1 *adv* **obviously**, unquestionably, undeniably, indubitably (*formal*), certainly. [➡CERTAIN; 175] 2 *adv* **yes**, certainly, naturally, evidently, no problem (*informal*), sure (*informal*), for sure (*informal*). [➡EXPRESSIONS OF AGREEMENT; 649] 3 *adv* **naturally**, not surprisingly, sure enough, needless to say. [➡CERTAIN; 175] *Opposite:* surprisingly.

off *adj* **rotten**, rancid, bad, tainted, mouldy, sour, inedible. [➡DECAYING OR INFESTED; 1235] *Opposite:* fresh.

offal *n* [➡TYPES AND CUTS OF MEAT; 1176]

off and on *adv* **intermittently**, infrequently, by fits and starts, discontinuously. [➡FINITENESS, VARIABILITY, AND TRANSIENCE; 96] *Opposite:* regularly.

off balance *adv* [➡ORIENTATION AND ALIGNMENT; 1222]

off beam *adj* **mistaken**, inaccurate, wrong, wide of the mark, off course, off track, erroneous, incorrect. [➡INCORRECT AND ERRONEOUS; 223]

offbeat *adj* **unusual**, unconventional, eccentric, off-the-wall (*informal*), quirky, bizarre, different. [➡BIZARRE AND PECULIAR; 258] *Opposite:* typical.

off-centre 1 *adj* **asymmetrical**, skewed, uneven, unbalanced, eccentric. [➡ORIENTATION AND ALIGNMENT; 1222] 2 *adj* **off-the-wall** (*informal*), quirky, eccentric, unconventional, odd, out in left field (*US*). [➡BIZARRE AND PECULIAR; 258]

off chance *n* **likelihood**, probability, possibility, chance, prospect, outside chance. [➡POSSIBLE AND PROBABLE; 178]

off-colour 1 *adj* **unwell**, sick, ill, under the weather, poorly (*informal*), unfit. [➡ILL AND SICK; 741] *Opposite:* well. 2 *adj* (*informal*) **risqué**, indecorous, improper, indiscreet, racy, spicy (*informal*), suggestive, broad, raunchy (*informal*), smutty (*informal*), dirty, blue (*informal*), adult, bawdy. [➡MORALLY BAD; 776]

off course *adj* **disorientated**, lost, out, astray, adrift, at sea. [➡AIMLESS AND ERRANT MOTION; 344]

off duty *adj* **on holiday**, on leave, not working, having a break, on vacation (*US*). [➡EMPLOYMENT STATUS; 831]

offence 1 *n* **crime**, wrongdoing, felony, fault, violation, infraction, breach, infringement, sin, misdemeanour. [➡CRIMES; 817] 2 *n* **insult**, affront, outrage, slight, slur, dig, barb, aspersion. [➡INSULTS, ABUSE, AND SWEARING; 659] 3 *n* **umbrage**, resentment, pique, indignation. [➡IRRITATION AND ANGER; 542] 4 *n* **attack**, offensive, assault, onslaught, bombardment, aggression. [➡AGGRESSIVE EVENT; 39] *Opposite:* defence.

offend 1 *v* **hurt somebody's feelings**, upset, insult, affront, be rude to, cause offence, rub up the wrong way. [➡UPSET, DISTRESS, AND HUMILIATE; 568] 2 *v* **commit an offence**, commit a crime, commit a felony, transgress, break the law. [➡DISOBEY; 303]

offended *adj* **affronted**, insulted, hurt, upset, slighted, snubbed. [➡SADNESS, DISTRESS, AND DESPAIR; 540]

offender *n* **criminal**, wrongdoer, reprobate, delinquent, lawbreaker. [➡CRIMINALS; 821]

offensive 1 *adj* **unpleasant**, nasty (*informal*), distasteful, disgusting, odious, hateful. [➡DISGUSTING AND REPULSIVE; 231] *Opposite:* agreeable. 2 *adj* **insulting**, rude, impolite, provoking, provocative, abusive, impertinent (*formal*). [➡BAD MANNERS AND SOCIAL SKILLS; 522] *Opposite:* courteous. 3 *adj* **aggressive**, attacking, violent, invasive, belligerent, bellicose. [➡IRRITATION AND ANGER; 542] *Opposite:* peaceful.

offensively *adv* **rudely**, abusively, impertinently (*formal*), impolitely, indecently, unpleasantly, vulgarly, nastily, outrageously, disgracefully. [➡BAD MANNERS AND SOCIAL SKILLS; 522] *Opposite:* politely.

offensiveness *n* **rudeness**, impoliteness, indecency, vulgarity, abusiveness, nastiness (*informal*), tastelessness, unpleasantness. [➡BAD MANNERS AND SOCIAL SKILLS; 522] *Opposite:* politeness.

offer 1 *v* **proffer**, tender, present, bid. [➡DISPENSE, RATION, AND DISTRIBUTE; 435] 2 *v* **propose**, suggest, pose, recommend, put forward, submit, propound, extend, advance, move. [➡SUGGEST, HINT, AND COMMENT; 613] *Opposite:* withdraw. 3 *n* **proposal**, suggestion, bid, proposition, bargain, agreement, compromise, deal, submission, motion, advance, approach, overture. [➡SUGGEST, HINT, AND COMMENT; 613]

offering *n* **contribution**, gift, donation, present, submission, subscription. [➡GIFTS; 439]

off-guard *adj* **unready**, unawares, napping, unprepared. [➡NEUTRALITY AND INDIFFERENCE; 554] *Opposite:* ready.

offhand 1 *adj* **impromptu**, extemporaneous, improvised, unrehearsed, spontaneous. [➡UNINTENTIONAL AND ACCIDENTAL; 282] *Opposite:* premeditated. 2 *adj* **informal**, casual, nonchalant, easygoing, indifferent, blasé. [➡UNINTERESTED AND DETACHED; 630] *Opposite:* serious.

offhandedly 1 *adv* **extemporaneously**, spontaneously. [➡UNINTENTIONAL AND ACCIDENTAL; 282] *Opposite:* deliberately. 2 *adv* **informally**, casually, nonchalantly. [➡UNINTERESTED AND DETACHED; 630] *Opposite:* seriously.

offhandness *n* [➡UNINTERESTED AND DETACHED; 630]

office 1 *n* **bureau**, workplace, administrative centre, headquarters, agency. [➡PLACE OF EMPLOYMENT; 832] 2 *type of* **room in public buildings**. [➡TYPES OF ROOM; 1096]

office assistant *n* [➡OFFICE WORKERS; 847]

office block *type of* **industrial site**. [➡INDUSTRIAL BUILDINGS; 1086]

office holder *n* **official**, officer, politician, public servant, elected official, civil servant. [➡POLITICAL OFFICES AND POLITICIANS; 808]

officer 1 *n* **major**, captain, colonel, brigadier, field marshal, general, soldier of rank. [➡MILITARY PERSONNEL; 828] 2 *n* **constable**, sergeant, police officer, detective, policeman, policewoman, patrolman, cop (*slang*), peace officer (*US*). [➡THE POLICE, ARREST, AND PRE-TRIAL PROCEEDINGS; 818] 3 *n* **official**, bureaucrat, representative, administrator, office holder, executive, manager, exec (*informal*). [➡BUSINESS PEOPLE; 794]

office worker *n* [➡WORKER; 836]

official 1 *n* **bureaucrat**, administrator, representative, spokesperson, officer, executive, exec (*informal*). [➡BUSINESS PEOPLE; 794] 2 *adj* **authorized**, certified, endorsed, sanctioned, allowed, approved, formal, authoritative, legitimate. [➡TRUE AND REAL; 172] *Opposite:* informal.

officialdom (*informal*) *n* **the powers that be**, bureaucracy, administrative system, red tape (*informal*). [➡ADMINISTRATIVE OFFICERS; 811]

officiate *v* **preside**, manage, perform official duties, carry out official duties, solemnize, celebrate, oversee, be in charge. [➡BE IN CHARGE; 271]

officious *adj* **meddlesome**, bossy, bureaucratic, self-important, overbearing, interfering, intrusive, fussy. [➡BOSSY AND OVERBEARING; 517]

officiousness *n* [➡BOSSY AND OVERBEARING; 517]

off-key 1 *adj* **out of key**, tuneless, out of tune, discordant, screeching, caterwauling, unmusical. [➡LOUD OR UNPLEASANT SOUNDS; 1265] *Opposite:* melodious. 2 *adv* **tunelessly**, out of tune, discordantly, unmusically. [➡LOUD OR UNPLEASANT SOUNDS; 1265] *Opposite:* melodiously.

off-limits *adj* **forbidden**, prohibited, proscribed, outlawed, verboten, out of bounds. [➡REFUSE PERMISSION AND NOT ALLOW; 671] *Opposite:* permitted.

off-line *adj* **off**, disconnected, down. [➡COMPUTERS AND COMPUTING; 1126] *Opposite:* online.

offload 1 *v* (*informal*) **relieve of**, divest, rid, free from, unburden. [➡GET RID OF SOMETHING; 452] 2 *v* **discharge**, unload, deposit, dump, leave, unlade, debark, disburden (*archaic*). [➡MOVE SOMETHING TO ANOTHER LOCATION; 325] *Opposite:* load. **3** *v* **pass on**, get rid of, dump, deposit, devolve, unload, leave, abandon, delegate, distribute. [➡GET RID OF SOMETHING; 452] *Opposite:* keep.

off-peak *adj* [➡TIMES OF DAY; 87]

off-putting **1** *adj* **repellent**, repulsive, disgusting, distasteful, offensive. [➡DISGUSTING AND REPULSIVE; 231] *Opposite:* attractive. **2** *adj* **forbidding**, disconcerting, upsetting, disturbing, daunting. [➡EMOTIONALLY UNPLEASANT AND UPSETTING; 228] *Opposite:* comforting.

offset **1** *n* **counterbalance**, balance, counterpoise, equipoise (*formal*), counterweight, equalizer, compensation. [➡EQUALITY; 155] **2** *v* **counterweigh**, equipoise (*formal*), counterbalance, make up for, counteract, compensate, equalize, balance, counterpoise. [➡CORRECT AND PUT RIGHT; 378]

offshoot **1** *n* **sideshoot**, sprout, sucker, branch, twig, sprig, shoot, outgrowth. [➡PARTS OF TREES AND PLANTS; 1026] **2** *n* **derivative**, subsidiary, consequence, result, outcome, development, branch, byproduct, spin-off. [➡RESULTS AND OUTCOMES; 83]

offspring *n* **descendants**, progeny, children, issue, young, brood, litter, posterity (*formal*). [➡YOUNGER GENERATION RELATIVES; 958]

offspring

◆ *types of offspring*
only child, quadruplet, quintuplet, singleton, triplet, twin

off the beam (*US*) *adj* [➡ORIENTATION AND ALIGNMENT; 1222]

off the beaten path (*US*) *adj* [➡DISTANCE; 161]

off the beaten track (*informal*) *adj* **secluded**, remote, isolated, out-of-the-way, far-flung, distant. [➡DISTANCE; 161]

off-the-cuff *adj* **impromptu**, spontaneous, improvised, unprepared, unrehearsed, unscripted, ad lib, ad hoc. [➡UNINTENTIONAL AND ACCIDENTAL; 282]

off-the-peg *adj* **ready-made**, ready-to-wear, standard-size, mass-produced, prêt-à-porter. [➡DESCRIBING CLOTHES; 869] *Opposite:* made-to-measure.

off the record *adj* **private**, confidential, secret, privy (*archaic*), unofficial. [➡SECRET AND UNKNOWN; 180] *Opposite:* official.

off-the-shelf *adj* **standard**, regular, bog-standard (*informal*), mass-produced, ordinary, run-of-the-mill, common or garden, common, garden-variety (*US*). [➡ORDINARINESS; 245]

off-the-wall (*informal*) *adj* **bizarre**, strange, eccentric, unusual, wacky (*informal*), unconventional, funny, weird, offbeat, out in left field (*US*). [➡BIZARRE AND PECULIAR; 258]

off-white *type of* **white**. [➡COLOURS; 1223]

of interest *adj* [➡INTERESTING AND MEANINGFUL; 191]

of its own accord *adv* **by itself**, on its own, unaided, voluntarily. [➡AUTOMATIC AND INSTINCTIVE; 281]

of late *adv* **lately**, recently, latterly. [➡PAST; 84]

of necessity *adv* **necessarily**, unavoidably, automatically, inevitably. [➡NECESSARY AND ESSENTIAL; 197]

of no account *adj* **unimportant**, of no consequence, inconsequential, insignificant, minor. [➡UNIMPORTANT AND UNNECESSARY; 239] *Opposite:* important.

of no consequence *adj* **irrelevant**, insignificant, a minor point, inconsequential, immaterial, neither here nor there, beside the point, unimportant, trivial. [➡UNIMPORTANT AND UNNECESSARY; 239] *Opposite:* important.

of no importance *adj* [➡UNIMPORTANT AND UNNECESSARY; 239]

of note *adj* **important**, well-known, worth mentioning, notable, acclaimed, famous, noteworthy. [➡IMPORTANT; 195] *Opposite:* unknown.

of no use *adj* [➡REDUNDANT AND USELESS; 241]

of no value *adj* [➡REDUNDANT AND USELESS; 241]

of one mind *adj* [➡HARMONY; 156]

often *adv* **frequently**, over and over again, time and again, repeatedly, habitually, a lot, regularly. [➡FREQUENT AND OFTEN; 107] *Opposite:* seldom.

of the essence *adj* **vital**, very important, crucial, imperative. [➡NECESSARY AND ESSENTIAL; 197] *Opposite:* unimportant.

of the order of *adv* [➡APPROXIMATELY; 133]

of use *adj* [➡USEFULNESS; 200]

of your own accord *adv* **voluntarily**, willingly, spontaneously, independently, by choice, autonomously. [➡THE WILL AND WILLINGNESS; 564]

ogle *v* **scrutinize**, eye, look at, stare, gaze, keep an eye on, rubberneck (*informal*), gawk. [➡LOOKING AND LOOKS; 701] *Opposite:* ignore.

See Compare and Contrast at **gaze**.

ogre *n* **giant**, troll, tyrant, monster, fiend. [➡MYTHICAL BEINGS; 790]

oh my (*US informal*) *interj* [➡EXPRESSIONS OF SURPRISE; 547]

oil **1** *n* **lubricant**, emollient, grease. [➡LIQUIDS; 1268] **2** *n* **grease**, fat, lard. [➡FATS AND OILS; 1172] **3** *v* **apply oil**, lubricate, smear with oil, grease, loosen. [➡DECORATE, ADORN, AND APPLY COATINGS; 406]

oil

◆ *types of cooking fat and oil*
suet, corn oil, shortening (*US*), peanut oil, butter, canola oil, dripping, ghee, lard, margarine, olive oil, rape oil, sesame oil, sunflower oil, vegetable oil

oil painting *n* [➡ARTWORKS; 898]

oil pan (*US*) *part of* **engine**. [➡PARTS OF AN ENGINE; 1143]

oil rig *type of* **industrial site**. [➡INDUSTRIAL BUILDINGS; 1086]

oily *adj* **greasy**, fatty, slick, slippery, oleaginous, unctuous. [➡PHYSICAL TEXTURE; 1221]

oink *type of* **animal sound.** [➡SOUNDS MADE BY ANIMALS; 1260]

ointment *n* **gel**, liniment, lotion, balm, salve, cream, unguent. [➡LOTIONS, PASTES, AND GELS; 1271]

OK (*informal*) *adv* [➡EXPRESSIONS OF AGREEMENT; 649]

okapi *type of* **deer or antelope.** [➡DEER AND ANTELOPE; 981]

okay (*informal*) 1 *interj* **fine** (*informal*), all right, sure (*informal*), of course, certainly, no problem (*informal*), yes, agreed, yep (*informal*). [➡EXPRESSIONS OF AGREEMENT; 649] 2 *adj* **satisfactory**, acceptable, all right, tolerable, passable, up to scratch (*informal*). [➡ACCEPTABLE AND PASSABLE; 220] *Opposite:* unacceptable. 3 *v* **green light**, approve, agree to, sanction, give the nod to, give the go-ahead to (*informal*), endorse, authorize, certify. [➡APPROVE AND CONFIRM; 647] *Opposite:* veto. 4 *n* **approval**, consent, go-ahead (*informal*), permission, sanction, endorsement. [➡APPROVE AND CONFIRM; 647]

okeydokey (*informal humorous*) *adv* [➡EXPRESSIONS OF AGREEMENT; 649]

okra *type of* **vegetable.** [➡FRUIT AND VEGETABLES; 1175]

old 1 *adj* **aged**, elderly, older, mature, getting on, not getting any younger. [➡OLD AGE; 919] *Opposite:* young. 2 *adj* **from the past**, ancient, from way back, long-standing, childhood, long forgotten, deep-rooted, hoary, timeworn. [➡OLD, OLD-FASHIONED; 168] *Opposite:* recent. 3 *adj* **previous**, last, other, former, erstwhile, onetime, archaic, dated, outmoded, antiquated. [➡PAST; 84] *Opposite:* current.

old banger (*informal*) *n* [➡BIKES, CARS, AND CARRIAGES; 1148]

olden (*archaic or literary*) *adj* **past**, ancient, historic, bygone, aged, hoary, age-old. [➡OLD, OLD-FASHIONED; 168] *Opposite:* modern.

old-fashioned 1 *adj* **antiquated**, archaic, antediluvian (*informal*), unfashionable, behind the times, outmoded, passé, out-of-date, outdated, obsolete. [➡OLD, OLD-FASHIONED; 168] *Opposite:* up-to-date. 2 *adj* **fogyish**, traditional, conservative, conventional, old-school. [➡OLD, OLD-FASHIONED; 168] *Opposite:* modern.

Compare and Contrast: *old-fashioned, outdated, antiquated, archaic, obsolete, passé, antediluvian*

CORE MEANING: NO LONGER IN CURRENT USE OR NO LONGER CONSIDERED FASHIONABLE

old-fashioned no longer considered fashionable or suitable because of changes in taste or technology, or, nostalgically favouring or maintaining the style of a former time; ***outdated*** no longer relevant to modern life because it has been superseded by something better, more fashionable, or more technologically advanced; ***antiquated*** regarded as in need of updating or replacing, though still functioning or in use; ***archaic*** belonging to a much earlier period of time, often suggesting a lack of relevance to modern life; ***obsolete*** superseded by something new, and in some cases therefore no longer in use; ***passé*** dismissed as no longer current or fashionable; ***antediluvian*** (*informal*) extremely old-fashioned and outdated.

old flame (*informal*) *n* [➡SEXUAL AND ROMANTIC RELATIONSHIPS; 964]

old fogy *n* [➡OLD PERSON; 920]

old gold *type of* **orange.** [➡COLOURS; 1223]

old hand *n* **veteran**, expert, professional, connoisseur, authority. [➡TALENTED OR INTELLIGENT PERSON; 529] *Opposite:* novice.

old hat (*informal*) *adj* **outmoded**, obsolete, clichéd, out-of-date, dated, anachronistic, ancient, old-fashioned, corny. [➡OLD, OLD-FASHIONED; 168] *Opposite:* up-to-date.

old lag (*slang*) *n* [➡CRIMINALS; 821]

old master *n* [➡ARTWORKS; 898]

old person *n* [➡OLD PERSON; 920]

old-style *adj* **traditional**, outdated, outmoded, out-of-date, old, old-fashioned. [➡OLD, OLD-FASHIONED; 168] *Opposite:* modern.

old-time *adj* **old-fashioned**, outdated, outmoded, traditional, old-style, quaint, old-world. [➡OLD, OLD-FASHIONED; 168] *Opposite:* modern.

old-timer *n* [➡OLD PERSON; 920]

old-world *adj* **outdated**, outmoded, quaint, traditional, old-style, old-fashioned. [➡OLD, OLD-FASHIONED; 168] *Opposite:* modern.

oleaginous *adj* [➡PHYSICAL TEXTURE; 1221]

oleaginousness *n* [➡PHYSICAL TEXTURE; 1221]

olive *type of* **fruit.** [➡FRUIT AND VEGETABLES; 1175]

olive branch *n* **peace offering**, compromise, concession, gesture, apology, reconciliation. [➡APOLOGIZE AND RETRACT; 684]

olive green *type of* **green.** [➡COLOURS; 1223]

olive oil *type of* **cooking fat and oil.** [➡FATS AND OILS; 1172]

olive-skinned *adj* [➡COMPLEXION; 481]

ombudsman *n* [➡SURVEYORS, EXAMINERS, AND JUDGES; 853]

omen *n* **sign**, portent, warning, forecast, premonition, augury, foretoken (*literary*), presage. [➡INDICATIONS, SIGNS, AND WARNINGS; 68]

ominous *adj* **threatening**, warning, worrying, gloomy, portentous, menacing, ill-omened, unpromising. [➡DANGEROUS; 237] *Opposite:* promising.

omission 1 *n* **oversight**, lapse, slip, error, blunder, faux pas (*literary*), inadvertence. [➡MISTAKES; 251] 2 *n* **exclusion**, exception, absence, leaving out, noninclusion, hiatus, blank, gap, lacuna (*literary*). [➡ABSENT AND UNAVAILABLE; 7] *Opposite:* inclusion.

omit 1 *v* **leave out**, miss out, pass over, skip, skip over, exclude. [➡EJECT AND EXCLUDE; 341] *Opposite:* include. 2 *v* **neglect**, forget, not take the trouble, not bother, overlook, ignore, fail. [➡NOT DO AND REFUSE TO DO; 275] *Opposite:* remember.

See Compare and Contrast at **neglect.**

omitted *adj* [➡ABSENT AND UNAVAILABLE; 7]

omnibus *n* **compilation**, collection, anthology, edition, album, florilegium (*archaic*). [➡COLLECTIONS AND MIXTURES OF THINGS; 1243]

omnipotence *n* **authority**, power, all-powerfulness, supremacy, influence, control, might, invincibility. [➡STRENGTH; 202] *Opposite:* powerlessness.

omnipotent *adj* **almighty**, all-powerful, invincible, unstoppable, supreme, godlike. [➡STRENGTH; 202] *Opposite:* powerless.

omnipresent *adj* **ubiquitous**, all-pervading, universal, ever-present, pervasive, all over. [➡PRESENT AND AVAILABLE; 11] *Opposite:* absent.

omniscience *n* **knowledge**, awareness, insight, wisdom, sapience, sagacity. [➡KNOWLEDGE AND WISDOM; 559] *Opposite:* ignorance.

omniscient *adj* **all-knowing**, all-seeing, wise, well-informed, sagacious (*formal*). [➡KNOWLEDGE AND WISDOM; 559]

on 1 *prep* **sitting on**, on top of, resting on, lying on, atop (*literary*), upon. [➡RELATIVE LOCATION; 162] *Opposite:* under. **2** *prep* **at**, next to, by the side of, by. [➡RELATIVE LOCATION; 162] **3** *adv* **happening**, taking place, scheduled, arranged, proceeding, going on. [➡HAPPENING AND IN PROGRESS; 32] *Opposite:* off. **4** *adv* **without stopping**, continuously, without a break, never-endingly. [➡PERMANENCE: WITHOUT END; 94]

on account of *prep* **owing to**, because of, due to, through, in consequence of (*formal*), as a result of, in view of. [➡CAUSATION; 169]

on and off *adv* **occasionally**, intermittently, sporadically, with breaks, now and then, now and again. [➡FREQUENT AND OFTEN; 107] *Opposite:* continuously.

on an even keel *adj* **stable**, well-balanced, reliable, dependable, steady, poised, steadfast. [➡ORDER AND ORGANISATION; 207] *Opposite:* unstable.

on a par *adj* [➡SIMILARITY; 149]

on a par with *adj* **on an equal footing with**, level pegging with, equal to, similar to, parallel to, equivalent to. [➡EQUALITY; 155]

on a shoestring *adv* **cheaply**, on the cheap (*informal*), on a tight budget, inexpensively, economically, for next to nothing, frugally. [➡ECONOMICAL AND RESOURCEFUL; 208] *Opposite:* extravagantly.

on a slope *adj* [➡ORIENTATION AND ALIGNMENT; 1222]

on a tight rein *adj* **under control**, restricted, closely controlled, regimented, disciplined. [➡CAPTIVITY AND LOSS OF FREEDOM; 249]

on a whim *adv* [➡UNINTENTIONAL AND ACCIDENTAL; 282]

on balance *adv* **all things considered**, all in all, at the end of the day, taking everything into account. [➡MAINLY AND PRIMARILY; 138]

on benefit *adj* [➡EMPLOYMENT STATUS; 831]

on board *adj* **involved**, committed, on the team, on the project, on our side. [➡PRESENT AND AVAILABLE; 11]

onboard *adj* **aboard**, on the ship, on the train, on the bus. [➡TRAVEL: WAYS OF TRAVELLING; 321]

on call *adj* **on duty**, working, on call-out, available, on hand, on standby. [➡EMPLOYMENT STATUS; 831] *Opposite:* off duty.

once 1 *adv* **some time ago**, formerly, previously, a long time ago, once upon a time, in the past, then. [➡PAST; 84] *Opposite:* now. **2** *adv* **as soon as**, when, after, the minute. [➡AFTER, LAST, AND FOLLOWING; 166]

once again *adv* [➡AGAIN; 109]

once in a blue moon (*informal*) *adv* [➡NEVER AND INFREQUENCY; 97]

once-in-a-lifetime *adj* [➡NEVER AND INFREQUENCY; 97]

once in a while *adv* **every so often**, every now and then, now and again, from time to time, occasionally, sometimes, on occasion, infrequently. [➡NEVER AND INFREQUENCY; 97] *Opposite:* frequently.

once more *adv* [➡AGAIN; 109]

once-over (*informal*) *n* **examination**, inspection, check, review, survey, shufti (*informal*), going-over (*informal*). [➡EXAMINE AND ASSESS; 754]

once upon a time *adv* [➡PAST; 84]

on cloud nine (*informal*) *adj* **happy**, elated, excited, ecstatic, pleased, in seventh heaven, joyful, in raptures, delighted, enraptured (*formal*). [➡PLEASURE, EXCITEMENT, AND ELATION; 535] *Opposite:* down in the dumps.

oncoming *adj* **approaching**, looming, nearing, advancing, onrushing. [➡ABOUT TO HAPPEN; 33]

on display *adj* [➡PERCEPTIBLE; 25]

one *adj* **unique**, single, solitary, lone, individual, one and only. [➡EXTRAORDINARY: UNCOMMON; 206]

one after another *adv* **one by one**, consecutively, in sequence, in succession, back-to-back, end-to-end, sequentially, one after the other, singly, in turn. [➡AFTER, LAST, AND FOLLOWING; 166]

one after the other *adv* **in a row**, one by one, consecutively, in sequence, in succession, back-to-back, end-to-end, sequentially, one after another, singly, in turn. [➡AFTER, LAST, AND FOLLOWING; 166]

one and all *pron* **everyone**, everybody, all, all and sundry, ladies and gentlemen. [➡ALL; 126] *Opposite:* nobody.

one and only *adj* **unique**, inimitable, incomparable, amazing, incredible. [➡EXTRAORDINARY: UNCOMMON; 206] *Opposite:* common.

one and the same *adj* **identical**, the same, the very same. [➡SAMENESS; 151] *Opposite:* different.

one by one *adv* **one after another**, one after the other, one at a time, sequentially, separately, consecutively, in succession, singly, in sequence, in turn. [➡AFTER, LAST, AND FOLLOWING; 166] *Opposite:* all together.

on edge *adj* **edgy**, irritated, touchy, nervy (*informal*), jumpy, tense, uneasy, jittery, nervous, anxious. [➡CONFUSION, ANXIETY, AND WORRY; 541] *Opposite:* calm.

one-dimensional *adj* **superficial**, lacking in depth, simplistic, simple-minded, basic. [➡ORDINARINESS; 245]

one-liner *n* **joke**, gag (*informal*), witticism, wisecrack (*informal*), quip, jest (*literary*), bon mot, crack (*informal*), epigram. [➡JOKES AND TEASING; 675]

on end *adv* **successively**, consecutively, continuously, continually, without end, running, on the run, on the trot. [➡PERMANENCE: WITHOUT END; 94]

oneness 1 *n* **singleness**, cohesion, coherence. [➡SAMENESS; 151] *Opposite:* diversity. 2 *n* **agreement**, unanimity, unity, togetherness, solidarity. [➡HARMONY; 156] *Opposite:* divergence.

one of a kind *adj* **unique**, exceptional, irreplaceable, special, inimitable, incomparable. [➡EXTRAORDINARY: UNCOMMON; 206] *Opposite:* commonplace.

one-off 1 *adj* **unique**, once-in-a-lifetime, never-to-be-repeated, limited-edition, special, unrepeatable. [➡EXTRAORDINARY: UNCOMMON; 206] 2 *n* **rarity**, limited edition, one in a million. [➡EXTRAORDINARY: UNCOMMON; 206]

one of these days *adv* [➡FUTURE; 86]

one or two *adj* **a few**, a couple, a handful, some, not many. [➡FEW, LITTLE, SMALL AMOUNT; 119] *Opposite:* lots.

one over the eight (*informal*) *adj* [➡UNDER THE INFLUENCE OF DRUGS OR ALCOHOL; 742]

one-piece *n* [➡GARMENTS AND OUTFITS; 865]

onerous *adj* **difficult**, burdensome, arduous, heavy, tiring, time-consuming, tedious. [➡DIFFICULTY AND COMPLEXITY; 243] *Opposite:* easy.

onerousness *n* [➡DIFFICULTY AND COMPLEXITY; 243]

one-sided *adj* **biased**, unfair, prejudiced, weighted, unrepresentative, misleading, partisan, partial, inequitable. [➡THE NATURE OF IDEAS; 772] *Opposite:* balanced.

one-sidedness *n* **bias**, biasedness, partiality, unfairness, prejudice, inequity, unrepresentativeness. [➡THE NATURE OF IDEAS; 772]

onetime *adj* **former**, previous, ex, past, old, erstwhile. [➡PAST; 84] *Opposite:* current.

one-to-one 1 *adj* **individual**, private, personal, intimate, personalized, individualized. [➡BELONGING OR RELATING TO INDIVIDUALS; 944] 2 *adj* **corresponding**, identical, matching. [➡SAMENESS; 151] 3 *adv* **individually**, privately, personally, alone. [➡BELONGING OR RELATING TO INDIVIDUALS; 944] 4 *n* **conversation**, natter (*informal*), chinwag (*informal*), heart-to-heart, tête-à-tête, gossip, discussion, chitchat (*informal*), yak (*informal*). [➡INFORMAL COMMUNICATION; 45]

one-way *adj* **single**, outward. [➡DIRECTION OF MOTION; 346] *Opposite:* return.

on fire 1 *adj* **burning**, alight, ablaze, blazing, in flames, afire, fiery. [➡FIRE, FLAMMABILITY, AND BURNING; 1164] 2 *adj* **passionate**, enthusiastic, fervent, ardent, bubbling over, fired up, fiery, eager. [➡PLEASURE, EXCITEMENT, AND ELATION; 535] *Opposite:* apathetic.

on foot *adv* **walking**, by shank's pony, under your own steam. [➡TRAVEL: WAYS OF TRAVELLING; 321]

on form *adj* [➡FINE; 738]

ongoing *adj* **continuing**, rolling, in progress, current, open-ended, constant. [➡PERMANENCE: WITHOUT END; 94]

on hand *adv* **nearby**, available, to hand, at hand, close by, convenient, there, around, close at hand. [➡PRESENT AND AVAILABLE; 11] *Opposite:* unavailable.

on hold *adj* [➡NOT HAPPENING; 34]

on ice *adj* [➡NOT HAPPENING; 34]

on impulse *adv* [➡UNINTENTIONAL AND ACCIDENTAL; 282]

onion *type of* **vegetable**. [➡FRUIT AND VEGETABLES; 1175]

on its last legs *adj* **falling apart**, dilapidated, run-down, decrepit, ramshackle, crumbling. [➡IN BAD REPAIR; 1233]

online *adj* **connected**, on, operational, working, available, accessible, wired, virtual, cyber-, real-time, on-screen, electronic. [➡COMPUTERS AND COMPUTING; 1126]

online banking *n* [➡E-COMMERCE; 1128]

on loan *adj* **borrowed**, lent, rented, hired out, loaned out (*US*). [➡ABSENT AND UNAVAILABLE; 7]

onlooker *n* **bystander**, spectator, viewer, observer, witness, watcher. [➡LOOKERS AND SPECTATORS; 702]

only 1 *adv* **merely**, simply, just, barely, no more than. [➡TO A CERTAIN EXTENT; 134] 2 *adj* **single**, lone, solitary, individual, one. [➡SOLITARINESS; 941]

only child *type of* **offspring**. [➡YOUNGER GENERATION RELATIVES; 958]

on no account *adv* **in no way**, for no reason, by no means, certainly not, never, under no circumstances. [➡NOT; 135]

on paper *adv* **in theory**, theoretically, notionally, hypothetically, conjecturally, suppositionally, abstractly. [➡FALSE AND UNREAL; 174] *Opposite:* in reality.

on purpose *adv* **consciously**, knowingly, deliberately, purposely, intentionally, by design, with intent, explicitly. [➡INTENTIONAL AND DELIBERATE; 280] *Opposite:* accidentally.

onrush *n* **surge**, rush, wave, tide, deluge, flood. [➡SUDDEN EVENT; 52]

onrushing *adj* **oncoming**, surging, rushing, approaching, nearing, advancing. [➡ABOUT TO HAPPEN; 33]

on sale *adj* **being sold**, available, on offer, for sale, reduced, discounted, selling at knockdown prices, on special offer, for a song. [➡SELL; 442]

on-screen *adj* **televised**, television, TV (*informal*), live, on-air, televisual, public. [➡TELEVISION AND RADIO; 607]

onset *n* **start**, beginning, inception (*formal*), arrival, commencement (*formal*). [➡BEGINNING; 53] *Opposite:* conclusion.

on show *adj* [➡PERCEPTIBLE; 25]

onside 1 *adj* **legal**, safe, clear, in the clear. [➡SAFE AND SAFETY; 192] 2 *adv* **legally**, safely, legitimately. [➡SAFE AND SAFETY; 192]

onslaught *n* **attack**, assault, offensive, ambush, blitz, blitzkrieg. [➡AGGRESSIVE EVENT; 39]

on stand-by *adv* **on call**, standing by, ready to step in, as backup, in case of emergency, available. [➡PRESENT AND AVAILABLE; 11]

on tap *adj* **at hand**, on hand, ready, obtainable, available, accessible, attainable, procurable. [➡PRESENT AND AVAILABLE; 11]

on tenterhooks *adj* **in suspense**, excited, anxious, apprehensive, on edge, agitated, nervous. [➡CONFUSION, ANXIETY, AND WORRY; 541]

on the agenda *adj* [➡ABOUT TO HAPPEN; 33]

on the air *adj* **live**, being broadcast, on air, recording, on TV, on the radio. [➡TELEVISION AND RADIO; 607]

on the alert *adj* **on the lookout**, aware, wary, vigilant, observant, prepared, on your guard, attentive, alert, heedful, watchful, on the ball (*informal*). [➡POSITIVE IMPATIENCE, ENTHUSIASM, AND ALERTNESS; 538]

on the back burner *adj* [➡NOT HAPPENING; 34]

on the ball (*informal*) *adj* **aware**, clued up, with it (*informal*), alert, with your wits about you, on your toes, awake, apprehensive, sensible. [➡POSITIVE INTELLECTUAL CHARACTERISTICS; 525]

on the blink (*informal*) *adj* **broken**, out of order, not working, faulty, playing up, malfunctioning, broken-down, busted (*US informal*). [➡IN BAD REPAIR; 1233]

on the breadline *adj* [➡POVERTY AND POOR; 892]

on the button (*informal*) *adv* **exactly**, precisely, spot-on (*informal*), dead right, on the nail, dead on, plumb (*informal*), on the nose (*US*). [➡EXACT; 204]

on the cards (*informal*) *adj* **possible**, imminent, likely, in the offing, in the pipeline, potential. [➡POSSIBLE AND PROBABLE; 178] *Opposite:* unlikely.

on the cheap (*informal*) *adv* **discounted**, cheaply, economically, inexpensively, for next to nothing, on a shoestring, for a song, at a low price. [➡CHEAP AND INEXPENSIVE; 222]

on the contrary *adv* **quite the reverse**, in contrast, quite the opposite, not at all, absolutely not. [➡NOT; 135]

on the cross *adv* [➡ORIENTATION AND ALIGNMENT; 1222]

on the dole (*informal*) *adj* [➡EMPLOYMENT STATUS; 831]

on the dot *adv* **on time**, punctually, precisely, promptly, exactly, squarely. [➡PROMPTNESS: ON TIME; 99] *Opposite:* late.

on the face of it *adv* [➡EXPRESSIONS OF UNCERTAINTY; 561]

on the fence *adj* **undecided**, noncommittal, hedging your bets, equivocal, indecisive, unsettled. [➡UNCERTAINTY; 560] *Opposite:* decided.

on the go *adj* **occupied**, bustling, active, busy, on the move, lively. [➡HAPPENING AND IN PROGRESS; 32]

on the horizon *adj* [➡ABOUT TO HAPPEN; 33]

on the horns of a dilemma *adj* **in a quandary**, between a rock and a hard place, at a stalemate, in a cleft stick, in a predicament, in a bind. [➡IN TROUBLE AND DISADVANTAGED; 73]

on the house *adj* **free of charge**, for free, free, complimentary, gratis. [➡GIFTS; 439]

on the level (*informal*) *adj* **trustworthy**, honest, straight, telling the truth, reliable, truthful. [➡HONEST AND RELIABLE; 503] *Opposite:* underhand.

on the loose *adv* **at large**, free, roaming freely, running wild, loose, unrestrained, unconfined. [➡FREEDOM AND LIBERTY; 209]

on the market *adv* **on sale**, on offer, for sale, available, purchasable, obtainable. [➡SELL; 442]

on the mend *adj* **getting better**, on the road to recovery, improving, recovering, recuperating, getting your strength back, convalescing. [➡HEALING; 731]

on the move 1 *adv* **moving ahead**, succeeding, making headway, progressing, making progress, forging ahead. [➡SUCCESSFUL AND PROMISING; 81] 2 *adv* **travelling**, touring, travelling around, travelling about, on the road, moving about. [➡TRAVEL: WAYS OF TRAVELLING; 321] 3 *adj* **bustling**, on the go, active, busy, moving, lively, energetic. [➡HAPPENING AND IN PROGRESS; 32]

on the nail *adv* [➡EXACT; 204]

on the nose (*US informal*) *adv* **exactly**, precisely, on the button, spot-on (*informal*), on the nail, dead on, squarely. [➡EXACT; 204]

on the other hand *adv* **instead**, conversely, alternatively, then again, in contrast, oppositely, contrariwise. [➡OPPOSITE; 158]

on the point of *adv* **about to**, near to, bordering on, on the threshold of, considering, all set to, set to, getting ready to, on the verge of, close to, just going to, ready to, likely to. [➡ABOUT TO HAPPEN; 33]

on the road *adj* **on the move**, travelling, touring, on tour, doing a tour. [➡TRAVEL: WAYS OF TRAVELLING; 321]

on the rocks (*informal*) *adj* **in trouble**, in danger, failing, collapsing, breaking up. [➡IN DANGER; 238]

on the run *adj* **runaway**, escaping, absconding, fleeing, running scared, in retreat, in flight, routed. [➡FREEDOM AND LIBERTY; 209]

on the same wavelength *adj* **compatible**, in tune, similar, coming from the same direction, singing the same song, consistent, consonant (*formal*). [➡HARMONY; 156] *Opposite:* incompatible.

on the skids (*slang*) *adj* [➡POVERTY AND POOR; 892]

on the slant *adv* [➡ORIENTATION AND ALIGNMENT; 1222]

on the sly *adv* **secretly**, behind your back, slyly, surreptitiously, sneakily, covertly. [➡SECRET AND UNKNOWN; 180] *Opposite:* openly.

on the spot 1 *adv* **immediately**, instantly, then and there, there and then, without delay, at once, right away. [➡HAPPENING QUICKLY; 104] *Opposite:* later. **2** *adj* **in a difficult situation**, in a tight corner, under pressure, in a tricky situation. [➡IN TROUBLE AND DISADVANTAGED; 73] *Opposite:* in the clear.

on the spur of the moment *adv* **impulsively**, on impulse, suddenly, impetuously, on a whim, spontaneously, off the cuff, abruptly. [➡AUTOMATIC AND INSTINCTIVE; 281] *Opposite:* deliberately.

on the streets *adj* [➡POVERTY AND POOR; 892]

on the strength of *prep* **because of**, on the basis of, on account of, by reason of, by virtue of, due to. *Opposite:* notwithstanding. (*formal*). [➡CAUSATION; 169]

on the subject of *prep* **concerning**, with reference to, apropos (*formal*), regarding, as regards, re, about, as to. [➡EXPRESSIONS OF REFERENCE; 63]

on the surface *adv* **superficially**, on the face of it, at first glance, at first sight, to the outsider, from the outside, apparently, ostensibly. [➡PERCEPTIBLE; 25] *Opposite:* in reality.

on the threshold of *prep* **on the brink of**, on the point of, at the start of, verging on, bordering on, on the cusp of. [➡FUTURE; 86]

on the trot *adv* **consecutively**, in succession, without a break, nonstop, successively, running, one after the other, sequentially, in a row, without stopping. [➡AFTER, LAST, AND FOLLOWING; 166]

on the up and up *adv* (*informal*) **doing well**, successful, up and coming, doing nicely, prosperous, wealthy, improving, on the increase, shooting up, rocketing, on an upward curve, on a winning streak, on the way, rising, on the up. [➡SUCCESSFUL AND PROMISING; 81]

on the verge of *adv* **on the brink of**, on the edge of, bordering on, on the threshold of, on the point of, close to, near. [➡ABOUT TO HAPPEN; 33]

on the wagon *adj* [➡ABSTEMIOUSNESS AND SELF-DENIAL; 882]

on the warpath (*informal*) *adj* **furious**, looking for trouble, gunning for somebody, spoiling for a fight, in high dudgeon, up in arms, on the offensive. [➡IRRITATION AND ANGER; 542]

on the way *adv* **imminent**, just round the corner, near, close, about to happen, under discussion, on the horizon, on the cards (*informal*), in the offing, in the pipeline. [➡ABOUT TO HAPPEN; 33]

on the whole *adv* **in general**, overall, generally, generally speaking, usually, mostly, for the most part, largely, by and large. [➡USUALLY; 108]

on time **1** *adj* **punctual**, prompt, in time, in good time. [➡PROMPTNESS: ON TIME; 99] *Opposite:* late. **2** *adv* **punctually**, promptly, in good time, with time to spare, in plenty of time, on the dot, in time. [➡PROMPTNESS: ON TIME; 99] *Opposite:* late.

on top *adv* **ahead**, leading, with the upper hand, in the lead, in front, in pole position, in control, in the driver's seat. [➡SUCCESSFUL AND PROMISING; 81]

on top form *adj* [➡FINE; 738]

on top of **1** *prep* **over**, lying on, resting on, on, above, covering, across. *Opposite:* beneath. (*formal*). [➡RELATIVE LOCATION; 162] **2** *adj* **ahead of**, in control of, dealing with, abreast of, aware of. [➡KNOWLEDGE AND WISDOM; 559]

on tour *adv* **on the road**, touring, travelling. [➡TRAVEL: WAYS OF TRAVELLING; 321]

on track *adj* [➡HAPPENING AND IN PROGRESS; 32]

on unemployment (*US*) *adj* [➡EMPLOYMENT STATUS; 831]

onus *n* **responsibility**, burden, obligation, duty. [➡RESPONSIBILITY; 171]

on view *adj* [➡PERCEPTIBLE; 25]

onward **1** *adj* **forward**, headlong. [➡DIRECTION OF MOTION; 346] *Opposite:* backward. **2** *adv* **on**, forwards, ahead, headlong, straight on. [➡DIRECTION OF MOTION; 346] *Opposite:* backwards.

onwards *see* **onward**.

on welfare (*US*) *adj* [➡EMPLOYMENT STATUS; 831]

on your mettle *adv* **alert**, with all your wits about you, on your toes, on top form, ready for anything, on guard. [➡POSITIVE IMPATIENCE, ENTHUSIASM, AND ALERTNESS; 538]

on your own **1** *adv* **alone**, all alone, by yourself, on your tod (*informal*), unaccompanied, single-handedly, unaided, solo, single-handed. [➡ACTING INDEPENDENTLY; 285] **2** *adj* **by yourself**, alone, all alone, on your tod (*informal*), unmarried, unattached, single. [➡MARITAL STATUS; 890]

onyx *type of* **gemstone**. [➡PRECIOUS STONES; 1277]

oodles (*informal*) *n* **loads** (*informal*), heaps (*informal*), plenty, lots, piles (*informal*), masses (*informal*), tons (*informal*). [➡MANY, MUCH, LARGE AMOUNT; 117]

oomph *n* **energy**, enthusiasm, life, go (*informal*), brio (*literary*), dynamism, vigour, vivacity, liveliness, get-up-and-go (*informal*), gusto, vim (*informal*), verve. [➡ENERGY AND ENTHUSIASM; 497]

ooze **1** *v* **seep**, leach, leak, trickle, dribble, drip, exude, come out of, emerge. [➡LIQUID EMISSION; 371] **2** *v* **exude**, be full of, reek of, radiate, overflow with, be bursting with, be brimming with. [➡EMIT AND EMANATE; 362]

opacity **1** *n* **opaqueness**, imperviousness, impenetrability, denseness, cloudiness, muddiness, mistiness, smokiness, milkiness, dullness. [➡VISUAL TEXTURE; 1220] *Opposite:* transparency. **2** *n* **obscurity**, obtuseness, impenetrability, complexity, vagueness, difficulty. [➡DIFFICULTY AND COMPLEXITY; 243] *Opposite:* transparency.

opal *type of* **gemstone**. [➡PRECIOUS STONES; 1277]

opalescent *adj* [➡VISUAL TEXTURE; 1220]

opaque **1** *adj* **impervious**, cloudy, muddy, milky, misty, smoky, dense, solid, thick. [➡VISUAL TEXTURE; 1220] *Opposite:* transparent. **2** *adj* **obscure**, unclear, incomprehensible, impenetrable, difficult, hard, dense. [➡DIFFICULTY AND COMPLEXITY; 243] *Opposite:* clear.

opaqueness *n* [➡VISUAL TEXTURE; 1220]

op art *type of* **20th-century art movement.** [➡ARTISTIC MOVEMENTS AND STYLES; 899]

open 1 *adj* **unlocked**, ajar, wide open, gaping. [➡UNFASTEN AND UNDO; 410] *Opposite:* closed. 2 *adj* **exposed**, uncluttered, sweeping, undeveloped, unspoilt. [➡THE COUNTRYSIDE AND OUTDOOR SPACES; 1070] *Opposite:* built-up. 3 *adj* **accessible**, public, unrestricted, free. [➡PRESENT AND AVAILABLE; 11] *Opposite:* restricted. 4 *adj* **approachable**, friendly, amenable, receptive, amicable. [➡FRIENDLINESS AND SOCIABILITY; 495] *Opposite:* standoffish. 5 *adj* **honest**, unguarded, direct, straight, frank, sincere, candid. [➡HONEST AND OPEN; 631] *Opposite:* guarded. 6 *adj* **vulnerable**, exposed, undefended, unprotected, unguarded. [➡IN DANGER; 238] *Opposite:* safe. 7 *v* **begin**, start, commence (*formal*), initiate, launch, set off, kick off (*informal*). [➡START AN ACTION; 261] *Opposite:* conclude. 8 *v* **unlock**, unbolt, undo, unfasten, release, untie, unwrap, unseal. [➡UNFASTEN AND UNDO; 410] *Opposite:* close.

open-air *adj* **outside**, outdoor, alfresco, uncovered. [➡GENERAL LOCATIONS; 159] *Opposite:* indoor.

open-and-shut *adj* **simple**, clear, straightforward, clear-cut, obvious. [➡EASE AND SIMPLICITY; 201] *Opposite:* ambiguous.

open-ended *adj* **open**, flexible, undecided, unrestricted, fluid. [➡VAGUENESS; 244] *Opposite:* fixed.

opener 1 *n* **bottle opener**, tin opener, can opener, corkscrew. [➡TABLEWARE, CUTLERY, AND KITCHENWARE; 861] 2 *n* (*informal*) **starter**, introduction, icebreaker, preamble. [➡BEGINNING; 53]

openhanded *adj* **generous**, unstinting, lavish, bountiful (*literary*), unselfish, philanthropic. [➡GENEROSITY AND KINDNESS; 496] *Opposite:* ungenerous.

openhandedness *n* **generosity**, lavishness, bountifulness (*literary*), bounty (*literary*), unselfishness, philanthropy. [➡GENEROSITY AND KINDNESS; 496] *Opposite:* selfishness.

openhearted *adj* **sincere**, genuine, honest, open, kind, loving, warm, generous, magnanimous. [➡GENEROSITY AND KINDNESS; 496]

openheartedness *n* **sincerity**, genuineness, honesty, kindness, love, warmth, generosity, magnanimity. [➡GENEROSITY AND KINDNESS; 496]

opening 1 *n* **gap**, breach, aperture, hole, fissure, cavity. [➡HOLES, GAPS, AND FORKS; 1251] 2 *n* **start**, beginning, introduction, intro (*informal*), lead-in, prologue, preamble, overture. [➡BEGINNING; 53] *Opposite:* end. 3 *n* **opportunity**, chance, lucky break, break (*informal*). [➡PROGRESS AND ADVANCEMENT; 214]

openly *adv* **candidly**, explicitly, frankly, honestly, plainly, overtly. [➡HONEST AND OPEN; 631] *Opposite:* secretly.

open-minded *adj* **unbiased**, unprejudiced, tolerant, liberal, progressive, flexible, easygoing, broad-minded, impartial. [➡POSITIVE INTELLECTUAL CHARACTERISTICS; 525] *Opposite:* narrow-minded.

open-mindedness *n* **broad-mindedness**, impartiality, tolerance, liberalism, progressiveness. [➡POSITIVE INTELLECTUAL CHARACTERISTICS; 525] *Opposite:* narrow-mindedness.

open-mouthed *adj* **astonished**, amazed, astounded, horrified, aghast, enthralled. [➡SURPRISE, SHOCK, AND AMAZEMENT; 546]

openness *n* **honesty**, directness, frankness, sincerity, candidness, plainness. [➡HONEST AND OPEN; 631] *Opposite:* reticence.

open out 1 *v* **unfold**, spread out, open, open up, stretch out, fan out, unfurl. [➡CHANGE OF SHAPE; 386] *Opposite:* fold up. 2 *v* **open up**, divide, separate, spread out, radiate. [➡TAKE UP A NEW POSITION; 313] 3 *v* **expand**, flower, spread, spread wide, get bigger, swell, inflate, blossom, grow, enlarge, spread out, bloom, develop, flourish, widen out, widen, open. [➡CHANGE OF SIZE: BIGGER; 393]

open to attack *adj* [➡IN DANGER; 238]

open to question *adj* [➡UNCERTAIN; 176]

open up 1 *v* **unfold**, expand, spread out, open out, stretch, stretch out, unfurl. [➡TAKE UP A NEW POSITION; 313] 2 *v* (*informal*) **accelerate**, put your foot down, open the throttle, speed up, get going. [➡CHANGE OF SPEED: MORE; 397] *Opposite:* slow down. 3 *v* **excavate**, cut through, open, dig out, expose. [➡TEAR, BREAK, AND CUT; 361] 4 *v* **unwrap**, open, uncover, expose. [➡CAUSE TO APPEAR; 5] 5 *v* **speak freely**, bare your soul, unwind, speak your mind, speak openly, talk freely, talk openly. [➡GIVING VENT TO EMOTIONS; 680] *Opposite:* clam up (*informal*). 6 *v* **open fire**, start firing, start shooting. [➡USE TOOLS AND MACHINERY; 469] 7 *v* **begin trading**, open, unlock. [➡BUSINESS ACTIVITIES AND PHENOMENA; 795] *Opposite:* close.

opera *type of* **classical music.** [➡MUSIC, SONGS, AND SINGING; 907]

operable 1 *adj* **treatable**, curable, nonfatal, nonterminal. [➡HEALING; 731] *Opposite:* inoperable. 2 *adj* **practicable**, doable, possible, feasible, workable, realizable. [➡POSSIBLE AND PROBABLE; 178] *Opposite:* impracticable.

opera glasses *type of* **optical instrument.** [➡OPTICAL INSTRUMENTS; 1123]

opera house *n* [➡BUILDINGS FOR PUBLIC ENTERTAINMENT; 1083]

operate 1 *v* **function**, work, run, go, activate, control, manoeuvre, drive, use. [➡FUNCTION SUCCESSFULLY; 470] 2 *v* **trade**, work, manage, run, carry on, carry out, conduct, direct, organize. [➡CARRY OUT AN ACTION; 270]

operating 1 *n* **running**, functioning, managing, operation, performing, working. [➡USE; 468] 2 *adj* **functional**, functioning, in force, operational, in service, going, effective, working, in use, in action, operative. [➡HAPPENING AND IN PROGRESS; 32]

operating room (*US*) *type of* **room in public buildings.** [➡TYPES OF ROOM; 1096]

operation 1 *n* **control**, management, use, controlling, manoeuvring, working. [➡USE; 468] 2 *n* **business**, company, venture, undertaking, outfit (*informal*). [➡BUSINESS ENTERPRISES AND RELATED BODIES; 793] 3 *n* **process**, action, act, procedure, manoeuvre, job, task, setup. [➡WAYS OF DOING THINGS; 295] 4 *n* **surgical procedure**, surgical treatment, procedure, surgery. [➡REMEDIES, TREATMENTS AND OPERATIONS; 732] 5 *n* **campaign**, manoeuvre, procedure, raid, attack, strategy, tactic. [➡WARFARE AND WAR; 830]

operational *adj* **in use**, in operation, in order, working, active, in force, operative, in effect, effective, functioning, operating. [➡HAPPENING AND IN PROGRESS; 32]

operative 1 *adj* **in effect**, functioning, working, effective, operational, running, active, in force, in operation. [➡HAPPENING AND IN PROGRESS; 32] *Opposite:* inoperative. 2 *n* **worker**, operator, machinist, hand, technician. [➡WORKER; 836]

operator *n* **worker**, operative, machinist, hand. [➡WORKER; 836]

operetta *type of* **classical music**. [➡MUSIC, SONGS, AND SINGING; 907]

operose (*formal*) *adj* **arduous**, taxing, difficult, strenuous, hard, back-breaking, exacting. [➡PHYSICALLY UNPLEASANT; 227] *Opposite:* easy.

ophthalmic *adj* [➡SEE; 700]

opine (*formal*) *v* **pronounce**, hold forth, discourse, lecture, preach, rant, speak out. [➡CLAIM, INSIST, AND EMPHASIZE; 615]

opinion *n* **view**, estimation, belief, judgment, attitude, outlook. [➡POINT OF VIEW; 768]

opinionated *adj* **voluble**, bigoted, narrow-minded, partisan, prejudiced, biased, rigid. [➡NEGATIVE INTELLECTUAL CHARACTERISTICS; 526] *Opposite:* open-minded.

opinion poll *n* **survey**, poll, questionnaire, investigation. [➡ASK PEOPLE QUESTIONS; 667]

opossum *type of* **marsupial**. [➡MARSUPIAL; 992]

opponent *n* **adversary**, enemy, foe (*literary*), rival, challenger, antagonist. [➡ENEMIES AND TORMENTORS; 969] *Opposite:* ally.

opportune *adj* **favourable**, fitting, appropriate, apt, right, suitable, timely, well-timed, convenient, auspicious, propitious, lucky. [➡APPROPRIATE, SUITABLE, ADVISABLE; 185] *Opposite:* inopportune.

opportuneness *n* [➡APPROPRIATE, SUITABLE, ADVISABLE; 185]

opportunism *n* **resourcefulness**, unscrupulousness, cunning, deviousness, speculation, buccaneering, carpetbaggery. [➡MORALLY BAD; 776]

opportunist *n* **chancer** (*informal*), freebooter, speculator, fortune hunter, buccaneer, swashbuckler, carpetbagger. [➡SUPERFICIAL OR INSINCERE PEOPLE; 951]

opportunistic *n* **unscrupulous**, resourceful, unprincipled, devious, cunning, adaptable. [➡MORALLY BAD; 776] *Opposite:* principled.

opportunity *n* **occasion**, opening, break (*informal*), prospect, chance. [➡PROGRESS AND ADVANCEMENT; 214]

oppose 1 *v* **be against**, resist, fight, contest, combat, counter, disagree with, dissent, dispute. [➡COMPETE, CONTEND, AND COMBAT; 304] 2 *v* **compete with**, face, compete against, do battle with, clash with, be in conflict with, be in competition with, be pitted against. [➡COMPETE, CONTEND, AND COMBAT; 304]

opposed *adj* **opposite**, different, contrasting, divergent, conflicting, disparate. [➡OPPOSITE; 158] *Opposite:* similar.

opposed to *adj* **against**, anti (*informal*), hostile to, antagonistic to, resistant to. [➡UNWILLINGNESS AND STUBBORNNESS; 565] *Opposite:* in favour of.

opposing 1 *adj* **opposite**, contrasting, differing, disparate, conflicting, divergent, contradictory. [➡OPPOSITE; 158] *Opposite:* similar. 2 *adj* **rival**, opposite, hostile, competing, antagonistic, opposed. [➡UNWILLINGNESS AND STUBBORNNESS; 565] *Opposite:* allied.

opposite 1 *adj* **far**, other, furthest, facing, opposing, parallel. [➡DISTANCE; 161] *Opposite:* adjacent. 2 *adj* **conflicting**, contradictory, differing, reverse, contrary, opposed, contrasting. [➡OPPOSITE; 158] *Opposite:* matching. 3 *n* **contrary**, reverse, converse, inverse, opposite number, counterpart. [➡OPPOSITE; 158] *Opposite:* same. 4 *prep* **facing**, across from, in front of, overlooking. [➡RELATIVE LOCATION; 162] *Opposite:* beside.

opposite number *n* **counterpart**, equivalent, parallel, equal, match, partner. [➡COLLEAGUES AND EQUALS; 967]

opposition 1 *n* **resistance**, antagonism, hostility, disapproval, disagreement, obstruction, unfriendliness. [➡UNWILLINGNESS AND STUBBORNNESS; 565] *Opposite:* friendliness. 2 *n* **opponent**, challenger, competitor, enemy, rival, foe (*literary*), adversary. [➡ENEMIES AND TORMENTORS; 969]

oppress 1 *v* **keep down**, coerce, tyrannize, dominate, repress, subjugate, persecute, harry, harass, hound, beset. [➡CAPTIVITY AND LOSS OF FREEDOM; 249] *Opposite:* liberate. 2 *v* **afflict**, worry, torment, depress, distress, burden. [➡UPSET, DISTRESS, AND HUMILIATE; 568] *Opposite:* relieve.

oppressed *adj* [➡IN TROUBLE AND DISADVANTAGED; 73]

oppression *n* **domination**, coercion, cruelty, tyranny, repression, subjugation, persecution, harassment. [➡UNKIND ACTION OR BEHAVIOUR; 297]

oppressive 1 *adj* **cruel**, harsh, domineering, tyrannical, repressive, despotic, unfair, unjust, overbearing. [➡MORALLY BAD; 776] *Opposite:* fair. 2 *adj* **overwhelming**, crushing, depressing, distressing, stressful, burdensome, worrying, troubling, uncomfortable, dispiriting, disheartening. [➡EMOTIONALLY UNPLEASANT AND UPSETTING; 228] *Opposite:* relaxing. 3 *adj* **humid**, hot, close, muggy, stifling, sticky, airless. [➡HOT WEATHER; 1050] *Opposite:* fresh.

oppressively *adv* **cruelly**, harshly, with a rod of iron, tyrannically, despotically, repressively, unjustly, domineeringly, overbearingly. [➡MORALLY BAD; 776] *Opposite:* fairly.

oppressor *n* **autocrat**, despot, persecutor, bully, tyrant, dictator, tormentor, intimidator, teaser, authoritarian. [➡VILLAINS AND THUGS; 947] *Opposite:* liberator.

opprobrious 1 *adj* **scornful**, contemptuous, excoriating (*formal*), damning, dismissive, reproachful, critical, censorious, disapproving. [➡MOCKING AND DISMISSIVE; 637] *Opposite:* approving. 2 *adj* **shameful**, humiliating, ignominious, embarrassing, belittling, degrading, mortifying, disgraceful, dishonourable, inglorious. [➡EMOTIONALLY UNPLEASANT AND UPSETTING; 228] *Opposite:* glorious.

opprobriousness 1 *n* **scorn**, contempt, censoriousness, dismissiveness, reproachfulness, disapproval. [➡IRRITATION AND ANGER; 542] *Opposite:* approval. 2 *n* **shamefulness**, shame, humiliation, ignominy, embarrassment, ingloriousness, degradation, mortification, disgrace, dishonour. [➡EMBARRASSMENT AND HUMILIATION; 543] *Opposite:* glory.

opprobrium 1 *n* **scorn**, contempt, excoriation (*formal*), condemnation, criticism, reproach, censure, disapproval. [➡IRRITATION AND ANGER; 542] *Opposite:* approval. 2 *n* **shame**, disgrace, ignominy, humiliation, embarrassment, mortification, dishonour. [➡EMBARRASSMENT AND HUMILIATION; 543] *Opposite:* glory.

opt *v* **choose**, elect, decide, determine, plump for, go for (*informal*), decide on, select, pick. [➡MAKE DECISIONS AND CHOICES; 753]

optical *adj* **visual**, ocular, ophthalmic, photosensitive. [➡SEE; 700]

optical

◆ *types of optical instrument*
astronomical telescope, binoculars, electron microscope, laser, magnifying glass, microscope, optometer, periscope, spyglass, telescope

optical glass *type of* **glass**. [➡GLASS; 1135]

optical illusion 1 *n* **illusion**, impression, effect, visual effect, mirage, fata morgana (*literary*), will-o'-the-wisp. [➡NONEXISTENT THINGS; 23] 2 *n* **trick**, illusion, trick of the light, special effect, visual effect, conjuring trick, trompe l'oeil. [➡NONEXISTENT THINGS; 23]

optimal *adj* **best**, ideal, optimum, top, finest, peak, prime. [➡GOOD, WELL, BETTER; 184] *Opposite:* worst.

optimism 1 *n* **hopefulness**, sanguinity, confidence, positiveness, positivity, brightness. [➡FEELINGS ABOUT THE FUTURE; 534] *Opposite:* pessimism. 2 *n* **cheerfulness**, confidence, assurance, enthusiasm, buoyancy, sunniness. [➡FEELINGS ABOUT THE FUTURE; 534] *Opposite:* pessimism.

optimist *n* **idealist**, romantic, utopian, visionary, hoper. [➡PEOPLE WHO ARE APPROVED OF; 955] *Opposite:* pessimist.

optimistic *adj* **hopeful**, positive, bright, cheerful, expectant, sanguine, confident, buoyant, enthusiastic. [➡CHEERFULNESS OF OUTLOOK; 504] *Opposite:* pessimistic.

optimize *v* **enhance**, improve, augment (*formal*), adjust, heighten, elevate, raise, boost. [➡IMPROVE SOMETHING; 375]

optimum 1 *n* **ideal situation**, best-case scenario, goal, ideal, best, target. [➡GOOD, WELL, BETTER; 184] 2 *adj* **best**, ideal, optimal, top, finest, peak, prime. [➡SUPERIORITY; 153] *Opposite:* worst.

option *n* **choice**, alternative, possibility, route, opportunity, preference, selection, decision. [➡MAKE DECISIONS AND CHOICES; 753]

optional *adj* **elective**, noncompulsory, voluntary, discretionary, possible, uncompelled, free. [➡POSSIBLE AND PROBABLE; 178] *Opposite:* compulsory.

optometer *type of* **optical instrument**. [➡OPTICAL INSTRUMENTS; 1123]

opt out (*informal*) *v* **bow out**, bail out, withdraw, get out, leave, wriggle out, decline, refuse, abandon, give a miss (*informal*). [➡NOT DO AND REFUSE TO DO; 275]

opulence 1 *n* **wealth**, affluence, riches, prosperity, fortune. [➡WEALTH AND WEALTHY; 891] *Opposite:* poverty. 2 *n* **lavishness**, luxury, richness, magnificence, sumptuousness, abundance. [➡EXPENSIVE AND LUXURIOUS; 219] *Opposite:* simplicity.

opulent 1 *adj* **wealthy**, lavish, luxurious, rich, magnificent, affluent, sumptuous, prosperous. [➡EXPENSIVE AND LUXURIOUS; 219] *Opposite:* poor. 2 *adj* **abundant**, ample, lavish, profuse, rich, plentiful. [➡MANY, MUCH, LARGE AMOUNT; 117] *Opposite:* sparse.

opus *n* **composition**, oeuvre (*formal*), work, piece, production, brainchild, creation. [➡ARTWORKS; 898]

oracle 1 *n* **prophet**, augur, soothsayer, seer, visionary, psychic, sage (*literary*), sibyl. [➡PEOPLE WITH SUPERNATURAL POWERS; 789] 2 *n* **prophesy**, vision, revelation, foreshadowing, prediction, answer, truth, advice, forewarning. [➡FEELINGS ABOUT THE FUTURE; 534]

oracular *adj* [➡THE SUPERNATURAL; 788]

oral *adj* **spoken**, verbal, uttered, said, verbalized, voiced, viva voce, sounded. [➡THE SPOKEN WORD; 672] *Opposite:* written.

See Compare and Contrast at **verbal**.

oral tradition *n* [➡THE ORAL TRADITION; 678]

orange 1 *type of* **colour**. [➡COLOURS; 1223] 2 *type of* **citrus**. [➡FRUIT AND VEGETABLES; 1175]

orange

◆ *types of orange*
amber, apricot, flame, ginger, gold, golden, ochre, old gold, peach, tangerine, titian

orange-peel fungus *type of* **fungus**. [➡MICROORGANISMS, FUNGI, AND ALGAE; 1023]

orangery *n* **greenhouse**, glasshouse, hothouse, conservatory, winter garden. [➡ANCILLARY BUILDINGS; 1079]

orang-utan *type of* **primate**. [➡PRIMATE; 988]

orate 1 *v* **speak**, lecture, speechify (*informal*), make a speech, take the floor, discourse. [➡INSTRUCT AND TEACH; 610] 2 *v* (*formal*) **hold forth**, preach, lecture, speak, declaim, pronounce, moralize, sermonize, rant. [➡UTTER AND PRONOUNCE; 609]

oration *n* **speech**, discourse, address, lecture, sermon, proclamation. [➡NEUTRAL ONE-WAY COMMUNICATION; 49]

orator *n* **speaker**, debater, lecturer, raconteur, storyteller, speechmaker, declaimer. [➡SPEAKERS AND ORATORS; 604]

oratorical *adj* **rhetorical**, debating, declamatory, speechmaking, eloquent, silver-tongued, high-flown, fluent. [➡ELOQUENT, TALKATIVE AND LONG-WINDED; 633] *Opposite:* halting.

oratorio *type of* **vocal music**. [➡MUSIC, SONGS, AND SINGING; 907]

oratory 1 *n* **debating**, discussion, rhetoric, eloquence, declamation, speechifying (*informal*). [➡COMMUNICATION; 603] 2 *n* **eloquence**, persuasiveness, cogency (*formal*), skill, style, technique. [➡ELOQUENT, TALKATIVE AND LONG-WINDED; 633] 3 *n* **pomposity**, prolixity, grandiloquence, verbosity, speechifying (*informal*), hot air (*informal*). [➡ MEANINGLESS SPEECH OR WRITING; 677]

orb *n* **globe**, sphere, planet, ball, round, circle. [➡ ROUNDED SHAPE; 1217]

orbicular (*formal*) *adj* [➡ ROUNDED SHAPE; 1217]

orbit 1 *n* **path**, track, trajectory, flight path, course, revolution, range, circle, circuit. [➡ DIRECTION OF MOTION; 346] 2 *n* **scope**, range, compass, influence, ambit, circle. [➡ DEGREE AND EXTENT; 110] 3 *n* [➡ THE EYE; 699] 4 *v* **circle**, circumnavigate (*formal*), loop, encircle, revolve. [➡ TRAVEL: WAYS OF TRAVELLING; 321]

orbital space station *type of* **spacecraft**. [➡ SPACE VEHICLES; 1062]

orbiter *type of* **spacecraft**. [➡ SPACE VEHICLES; 1062]

orchard *n* **plantation**, wood, copse, grove, coppice, spinney. [➡ WOODS, FORESTS, AND JUNGLES; 1047]

orchestra *type of* **band**. [➡ MUSICIANS AND SINGERS; 908]

orchestral *adj* **instrumental**, classical, symphonic, musical. [➡ MUSICAL TERMS; 912]

orchestrate 1 *v* **score**, arrange, compose, write, rewrite. [➡ INSTITUTE AND INAUGURATE; 349] 2 *v* **plan out**, work out, arrange, coordinate, organize, stage-manage, plan, preplan, choreograph, devise. [➡ CAUSE TO HAPPEN; 31] *Opposite:* improvise.

orchestration 1 *n* **instrumentation**, transposition, arrangement, scoring, composition, adaptation. [➡ MUSIC, SONGS, AND SINGING; 907] 2 *n* **planning**, organization, stage-management, arrangement, preplanning, choreography. [➡ ARRANGE AND CREATE ORDER; 358] *Opposite:* improvisation.

orchid *type of* **perennial flower**. [➡ FLOWERS; 1032]

ordain 1 *v* [➡ CONFER STATUS; 459] 2 *v* (*formal*) **order**, decree, proclaim, enact, command, lay down, rule, adjudge, determine, establish. [➡ REQUEST AND DEMAND; 664] *Opposite:* suggest.

ordeal *n* **trial**, torment, suffering, tribulation, test, nightmare, trouble, affliction. [➡ DIFFICULT SITUATIONS; 72]

order 1 *n* **instruction**, command, directive, direction, demand, edict, mandate, imperative. [➡ REQUEST AND DEMAND; 664] *Opposite:* suggestion. 2 *n* **sequence**, succession, rank, classification, arrangement, categorization, series. [➡ CONNECTION; 144] *Opposite:* chaos. 3 *n* **orderliness**, neatness, tidiness, method, regulation, uniformity, regularity, symmetry, organization. [➡ ORDER AND ORGANISATION; 207] *Opposite:* disorder. 4 *n* **stability**, calm, harmony, peace, peacefulness, tranquillity, lawfulness, serenity. [➡ PEACEFULNESS AND GENTLENESS; 215] *Opposite:* upheaval. 5 *n* **contract**, purchase, sale, request, requisition, demand. [➡ REQUEST AND DEMAND; 664] 6 *n* **sect**, organization, group, class, lodge, society, fraternity, sisterhood, fellowship, company, association, union. [➡ CLUBS AND SOCIETIES; 939] 7 *v* **command**, direct (*formal*), instruct, tell, bid (*archaic*), enjoin (*formal*), require, charge. [➡ REQUEST AND DEMAND; 664] *Opposite:* request. 8 *v* **requisition**, request, ask for, send for, send off for, buy. [➡ PURCHASE; 423] *Opposite:* supply. 9 *v* **arrange**, organize, regulate, classify, categorize, sort, array (*formal*), tidy, systematize, sort out. [➡ ARRANGE AND CREATE ORDER; 358] *Opposite:* confuse.

order about *v* **boss around**, boss about, bully, push around (*informal*), lord it over (*disapproving*), order around. [➡ CAUSE OR COMPEL TO ACT; 272]

order around *v* **boss around**, boss about, bully, push around (*informal*), lord it over (*disapproving*), order about. [➡ CAUSE OR COMPEL TO ACT; 272]

ordered 1 *adj* **well-ordered**, neat, tidy, methodical, well-organized, well thought-out, well-arranged, orderly, systematic. [➡ ORDER AND ORGANISATION; 207] *Opposite:* disorganized. 2 *adj* **controlled**, regimented, consistent, steady, efficient, regular, strict, rigid, structured, disciplined, self-controlled. [➡ ORDER AND ORGANISATION; 207] *Opposite:* irregular.

orderliness *n* **neatness**, order, tidiness, method, organization, regulation, uniformity, regularity, symmetry. [➡ ORDER AND ORGANISATION; 207] *Opposite:* disorderliness.

orderly 1 *adj* **obedient**, disciplined, well-behaved, decorous, compliant, amenable. [➡ HONEST AND RELIABLE; 503] *Opposite:* disorderly. 2 *adj* **arranged**, tidy, methodical, neat, logical, systematic, organized, well-ordered. [➡ ORDER AND ORGANISATION; 207] *Opposite:* disorderly.

ordinance *n* **decree**, order, rule, regulation, law, edict, writ, dictate, dictum (*formal*), injunction, fiat, sanction. [➡ OFFICIAL DOCUMENTS; 587]

ordinarily *adv* **normally**, usually, generally, customarily, in general, as a rule, typically. [➡ USUALLY; 108] *Opposite:* unusually.

ordinariness 1 *n* **normality**, commonplaceness, usualness, commonness, familiarity, routineness, customariness, averageness. [➡ ORDINARINESS; 245] 2 *n* **dullness**, triteness, drabness, dreariness, predictability, staleness, monotony, commonplaceness. [➡ BORING AND UNINTERESTING; 235]

ordinary 1 *adj* **normal**, commonplace, usual, regular, common, everyday, conventional, average, familiar, routine. [➡ ORDINARINESS; 245] *Opposite:* out of the ordinary. 2 *adj* **dull**, trite, drab, dreary, predictable, stale, monotonous, boring, routine, commonplace. [➡ ORDINARINESS; 245] *Opposite:* extraordinary.

ordination *n* **investiture**, consecration, ceremony, conferment, installation, initiation. [➡ RELIGIONS AND RELIGIOUS PRACTICES; 778]

ordnance *n* **weapons**, artillery, arms, guns, weaponry, armaments. [➡ WEAPONS; 1153]

ordure (*formal*) *n* **excrement**, filth, dung, manure, faeces, dirt, muck. [➡ UNPLEASANT AND DIRTY SUBSTANCES; 1267]

ore *n* **mineral**, rock, metal, element, aggregate, raw material. [➡ STONES, ROCKS, AND BOULDERS; 1057]

oregano *type of* **herb**. [➡ HERBS AND SPICES; 1174]

organ 1 *n* **body part**, tissue, structure. [➡ BODY; 692] 2 *n* (*formal*) **agency**, organization, body, representative, voice, front, cover, means, medium, vehicle. [➡ WAYS OF DOING THINGS; 295] 3 *n* (*formal*) **publication**, mouthpiece, newspaper, magazine, periodical, newsletter, journal. [➡ NEWSPAPERS; 606] 4 *type of* **keyboard**. [➡ MUSICAL INSTRUMENTS; 910]

organdy *type of* **fabric from plants**. [➡ FABRICS; 1131]

organic 1 *adj* **carbon-based**, biological, living, animate, animal, plant. [➡ LIVING THINGS AND LIVING; 976] *Opposite:* inorganic. **2** *adj* **gradual**, natural, spontaneous, slow, unforced, free. [➡ HAPPENING SLOWLY; 106] *Opposite:* artificial. **3** *adj* **natural**, unprocessed, unrefined, untreated, raw, nonchemical, green, GM-free. [➡ FOOD; 1166] *Opposite:* synthetic.

organic matter *n*

organism *n* **living thing**, creature, animal, plant, virus, bacterium, being, beast, entity. [➡ LIVING THINGS AND LIVING; 976]

organization **1** *n* **group**, body, society, association, party, union, institute, business, company, corporation, establishment. [➡ GROUPS OF PEOPLE; 935] **2** *n* **arrangement**, configuration, design, format, composition, constitution, make-up, pattern, structure. [➡ QUALITIES AND CHARACTERISTICS; 1190] **3** *n* **orderliness**, order, method, regulation, neatness, tidiness. [➡ ORDER AND ORGANIZATION; 207] *Opposite:* chaos.

organizational *adj* **structural**, administrative, legislative, executive, logistic, managerial, directorial, governmental, clerical. [➡ TYPES OF WORK; 835]

organize **1** *v* **establish**, form, shape, unify, unite, consolidate, bring together, start up, get off the ground. [➡ CAUSE TO HAPPEN; 31] **2** *v* **coordinate**, manage, control, run, set up, fix (*informal*). [➡ AVOID, PREVENT, LIMIT, AND CONTROL; 278] **3** *v* **systematize**, arrange, sort out, classify, categorize, combine, structure. [➡ ARRANGE AND CREATE ORDER; 358] *Opposite:* disarrange.

organized **1** *adj* **prearranged**, structured, ordered, systematized, well thought-out, controlled, planned, prepared. [➡ ORDER AND ORGANISATION; 207] *Opposite:* spontaneous. **2** *adj* **methodical**, logical, orderly, reasonable, sensible, systematic, regular. [➡ HARD-WORKING AND COMMITTED; 501] *Opposite:* disorganized.

organized crime *n* [➡ CRIMES; 817]

organizer **1** *n* **manager**, director, coordinator, planner, controller, arranger. [➡ BOSSES AND MANAGEMENT; 965] **2** *n* **diary**, agenda, schedule, daybook, log book. [➡ LISTS AND SCHEDULES; 588]

orgy *n* [➡ PARTIES, DANCES, AND CELEBRATIONS; 37]

orient **1** *v* **position**, turn, angle, place, face, orientate. [➡ MOVE SOMETHING: INTO A NEW POSITION OR OVERTURN; 331] **2** *v* **familiarize**, adjust, learn about, orientate, adapt, accommodate. [➡ LEARN AND DISCOVER; 763]

orientate **1** *v* **position**, turn, angle, face, place, orient. [➡ MOVE SOMETHING: INTO A NEW POSITION OR OVERTURN; 331] **2** *v* **familiarize**, adjust, learn about, orient, adapt, accommodate. [➡ LEARN AND DISCOVER; 763]

orientation **1** *n* **location**, alignment, direction, positioning, angle, bearings, placement, coordination. [➡ NAVIGATION; 1140] **2** *n* **emphasis**, focus, character, slant, thrust, inclination. [➡ ORIENTATION AND ALIGNMENT; 1222] **3** *n* **leaning**, tendency, proclivity, preference, inclination, nature. [➡ LIKE, LOVE, VALUE, AND ENJOY; 579] **4** *n* **adjustment**, acclimatization, assimilation, acclimation, settling in, finding your feet. [➡ CHANGE; 373] **5** *n* **initiation**, briefing, reception, welcome, induction, training. [➡ BEGINNING; 53]

oriented *adj* **concerned with**, in favour of, focused on, preoccupied with, slanted towards, adapted to. [➡ EXPRESSING RESPECT AND APPROVAL; 638]

orienteering *n* [➡ HOBBIES, GAMES, AND SPORTS; 875]

orifice (*literary*) *n* **opening**, hole, vent, cavity, outlet, slit. [➡ HOLES, GAPS, AND FORKS; 1251]

origin *n* **source**, derivation, provenance, beginning, cause, root, basis, foundation. [➡ BEGINNING; 53]

Compare and Contrast: ***origin, source, derivation, provenance, root***

CORE MEANING: THE BEGINNING OF SOMETHING

origin the beginning of something in terms of the time, place, situation, or idea from which it arose, or somebody's ancestry, social background, or country; ***source*** the place, person, or thing through which something has come into being or from which it has been obtained; ***derivation*** the origin or source of something, especially a word, phrase, or name; ***provenance*** the place of origin of something, or the source and ownership history of a work of art or archaeological artefact; ***root*** the fundamental cause, basis, or origin of something, especially a feeling or a problem.

original **1** *adj* **first**, initial, previous, fundamental, primary, prime. [➡ BEFORE, FIRST, AND PRECEDING; 164] *Opposite:* last. **2** *adj* **unique**, innovative, novel, inventive, creative, new, unusual, imaginative, unprecedented, singular, special. [➡ EXTRAORDINARY: UNCOMMON; 206] *Opposite:* unoriginal. **3** *n* **real McCoy** (*informal*), prototype, genuine article, pattern, archetype, exemplar (*literary*), template, form, mould. [➡ PERFECT EXAMPLES AND EMBODIMENTS; 67] *Opposite:* copy.

See Compare and Contrast at **new.**

originality *n* **innovation**, novelty, uniqueness, inventiveness, creativity, freshness, imagination, ingenuity. [➡ EXTRAORDINARY: AMAZING; 205] *Opposite:* unoriginality.

originally *adv* **first**, initially, in the beginning, formerly, at first, firstly. [➡ PAST; 84] *Opposite:* eventually.

originate **1** *v* **begin**, derive, stem from, start, commence (*formal*), initiate, inaugurate. [➡ GRADUALLY COME INTO EXISTENCE; 1] *Opposite:* finish. **2** *v* **create**, invent, initiate, instigate, start off, make, devise, patent, coin. [➡ INSTITUTE AND INAUGURATE; 349]

origination *n* [➡ BEGINNING; 53]

originator *n* **inventor**, creator, instigator, designer, maker, discoverer, initiator, prime mover. [➡ DESIGNERS, CREATORS AND INSTIGATORS; 348]

oriole *type of* **songbird.** [➡ SONGBIRD; 1003]

ornament **1** *n* **knick-knack**, figurine, objet d'art, bauble, decoration, trinket. [➡ ORNAMENTS AND DECORATIONS; 1247] **2** *n* **decoration**, adornment, embellishment, pattern, enhancement, enrichment, trimming, garnish, beautification. [➡ ORNAMENTS AND DECORATIONS; 1247] **3** *v* **adorn**, decorate, beautify, embellish, paint, prettify, smarten up, trim, embroider, elaborate, festoon, deck out. [➡ DECORATE, ADORN, AND APPLY COATINGS; 406]

ornamental *adj* **decorative**, attractive, for show, ornate, patterned. [➡ BEAUTY AND ATTRACTIVENESS; 190] *Opposite:* functional.

ornamentation *n* **decoration**, adornment, embellishment, enhancement, garnishing, beautification, trimming. [➡ IMPROVE APPEARANCE; 380]

ornate 1 *adj* **decorative**, overelaborate, baroque, elaborate, ornamental, sumptuous, rich, opulent, lavish. [➡ EXPENSIVE AND LUXURIOUS; 219] *Opposite:* unadorned. 2 *adj* **high-flown**, flowery, wordy, verbose, elaborate, complex, overelaborate, metaphorical, highly wrought, complicated, flamboyant. [➡ DIFFICULTY AND COMPLEXITY; 243] *Opposite:* plain.

ornately *adv* **overelaborately**, baroquely, elaborately, lavishly, richly, sumptuously, opulently, ornamentally, flamboyantly. [➡ EXPENSIVE AND LUXURIOUS; 219]

ornateness *n* [➡ POSITIVELY COMPLEX OR COMPLICATED; 218]

ornery (*US informal*) *adj* **irritable**, crabby, grouchy (*informal*), cantankerous, bad-tempered, awkward, uncooperative, cranky (*US informal*). [➡ REBELLIOUSNESS AND DISOBEDIENCE; 566] *Opposite:* good-tempered.

ornithologist *n* [➡ PEOPLE IN SPORTS AND LEISURE; 876]

orotund (*formal*) 1 *adj* **loud**, clear, strong, ringing, stentorian, robust. [➡ SOFT OR PLEASANT SOUNDS; 1264] *Opposite:* soft. 2 *adj* **wordy**, verbose, grandiloquent, pompous, bombastic, long-winded, self-important. [➡ POMPOUS, LOUD, AND OVER-CONFIDENT; 636] *Opposite:* humble.

orotundity *n* [➡ POMPOUS, LOUD, AND OVER-CONFIDENT; 636]

orotundly (*formal*) *adv* [➡ POMPOUS, LOUD, AND OVER-CONFIDENT; 636]

orphan 1 *n* **child**, baby, boy, girl, waif, foundling (*dated*), urchin. [➡ CHILD OR YOUTH; 945] 2 *v* **bereave**, leave alone, leave all alone, leave, make an orphan, leave parentless. [➡ REFUSING OR REJECTING RELATIONS; 975]

orphanage *n* **home**, residential home, hostel, poorhouse, workhouse, institution, children's home, residential care. [➡ CHARITY AND CHARITABLE INSTITUTIONS; 822]

or so *adv* [➡ APPROXIMATELY; 133]

ort (*US*) *n* [➡ REMAINDER AND REMAINDERS; 123]

orthodox *adj* **conventional**, accepted, traditional, mainstream, conformist, standard, approved, established. [➡ ACCEPTABLE AND PASSABLE; 220] *Opposite:* unorthodox.

orthodoxy *n* **accepted view**, convention, accepted belief, prevailing attitude, tenet (*formal*), belief, canon, custom. [➡ POINT OF VIEW; 768]

oscillate 1 *v* **swing**, move back and forth, move to and fro, move backwards and forwards, fluctuate, vacillate, alternate, undulate. [➡ BOUNCE, UNDULATE, AND VIBRATE; 309] 2 *v* **waver**, hesitate, vacillate, blow hot and cold, dither, equivocate, be indecisive, run hot and cold, fluctuate. [➡ HESITATE; 273]

oscillation *n* **swaying**, fluctuation, vacillation, alternation, swinging, undulation, wavering. [➡ BOUNCE, UNDULATE, AND VIBRATE; 309]

osculate (*formal or humorous*) *v* **kiss**, give a kiss, French kiss, give a smacker, canoodle with (*informal*), snog (*slang*), smooch (*informal*). [➡ PHYSICAL CONTACT AS COMMUNICATION; 656]

osculation (*formal or humorous*) *n* [➡ PHYSICAL CONTACT AS COMMUNICATION; 656]

osprey *type of* **bird of prey**. [➡ BIRD OF PREY; 998]

ossification *n* [➡ HARDEN, CONGEAL, DRY; 388]

ossified *adj* [➡ RIGID AND HARD; 1210]

ossify *v* **petrify**, fossilize, harden, become inflexible, become fixed, solidify, fix, paralyze. [➡ HARDEN, CONGEAL, DRY; 388]

ossuary (*formal*) *n* **vault**, grave, tomb, crypt, charnel house, urn, catacomb. [➡ BURIAL PLACES AND ACCESSORIES; 930]

ostensible *adj* **ostensive** (*formal*), apparent, professed, supposed, perceived, seeming, alleged, superficial. [➡ UNCERTAIN; 176] *Opposite:* real.

ostensive (*formal*) *adj* [➡ UNCERTAIN; 176]

ostentation *n* **flashiness**, showiness, display, flamboyance, pretension, affectation, brazenness, vulgarity. [➡ IN POOR TASTE; 230] *Opposite:* modesty.

ostentatious *adj* **flashy**, showy, flamboyant, affected, pretentious, grandiose, brazen. [➡ IN POOR TASTE; 230] *Opposite:* modest.

ostentatiousness *n* [➡ IN POOR TASTE; 230]

ostinato *n* [➡ MUSICAL TERMS; 912]

ostracism *n* **shunning**, snubbing, exclusion, barring, keeping out, sending to Coventry, banishment, isolation, excommunication, expulsion. [➡ UNKIND ACTION OR BEHAVIOUR; 297] *Opposite:* inclusion.

ostracize *v* **coldshoulder**, exclude, banish, shun, ignore, snub, send to Coventry, excommunicate, expel, blackball, blacklist. [➡ REFUSING OR REJECTING RELATIONS; 975] *Opposite:* include.

ostracized *adj* [➡ IN TROUBLE AND DISADVANTAGED; 73]

ostrich *type of* **flightless bird**. [➡ BIRD; 997]

other *adj* **additional**, new, more, fresh, extra, another, further. [➡ MORE AND EXCESS; 122]

other half *n* [➡ SEXUAL AND ROMANTIC RELATIONSHIPS; 964]

otherness *n* **strangeness**, difference, uniqueness, distinctiveness, oddness, apartness, dissimilarity, unlikeness. [➡ UNRELATEDNESS AND SEPARATENESS; 147] *Opposite:* normality.

otherwise *adv* **or else**, if not, else, alternatively. [➡ ALTHOUGH, NEVERTHELESS, AND DESPITE; 170]

otherworldliness *n* [➡ BIZARRE AND PECULIAR; 258]

otherworldly *adj* [➡ BIZARRE AND PECULIAR; 258]

otiose *adj* **futile**, ineffectual, useless, impractical, ineffective, hopeless. [➡ REDUNDANT AND USELESS; 241] *Opposite:* effective.

OTT (*informal*) *adj* [➡ TOO MUCH; 118]

otter *type of* **small mammal**. [➡ SMALL MAMMAL; 990]

ottoman *n* **divan**, couch, day bed, chaise longue, settee, sofa, seat. [➡ FURNITURE; 858]

oubliette *n* **prison cell**, dungeon, prison, cell. [➡ BUILDINGS FOR CONFINING PEOPLE; 1093]

ounce *n* **grain**, jot, scrap, small amount, modicum, smidgeon (*informal*), iota, particle, speck. [➡FEW, LITTLE, SMALL AMOUNT; 119]

oust *v* **expel**, throw out, get rid of, drive out, exile, overthrow, cast out (*formal*), eject, force out, banish, deport. [➡EJECT AND EXCLUDE; 341] *Opposite:* appoint.

ousted *adj* [➡IN TROUBLE AND DISADVANTAGED; 73]

ouster *n* **removal**, ejection, dismissal, expulsion, coup, upheaval, overthrow. [➡AGGRESSIVE EVENT; 39]

out 1 *adv* **outdoors**, out-of-doors, in the open, in the open air, alfresco, outside, without (*regional or archaic*). [➡GENERAL LOCATIONS; 159] 2 *adv* **elsewhere**, not in, not at home, away, away from home, absent, gone. [➡ABSENT AND UNAVAILABLE; 7] *Opposite:* in. 3 *adj* **exposed**, revealed, given away, made known, shown, publicized, open, uncovered. [➡KNOWN AND FAMOUS; 182] *Opposite:* hidden. 4 *adj* **available**, on view, obtainable, ready, on show, on sale, purchasable. [➡PRESENT AND AVAILABLE; 11] *Opposite:* unavailable. 5 *adj* **unacceptable**, impossible, improbable, not worth it, not on, unthinkable. [➡IMPOSSIBLE AND IMPROBABLE; 179] *Opposite:* acceptable. 6 *adj* **old-fashioned**, unfashionable, outdated, dated, passé, old hat (*informal*), outmoded, antiquated. [➡OLD, OLD-FASHIONED; 168] *Opposite:* fashionable. 7 *adj* **banned**, prohibited, disallowed, barred, prevented, vetoed, not permitted, forbidden, contraband, censored. [➡REFUSE PERMISSION AND NOT ALLOW; 671] *Opposite:* legitimate. 8 *adj* **out for the count** (*informal*), unconscious, out cold, comatose, dazed, in a daze. [➡TIRED, ASLEEP AND UNCONSCIOUS; 739] *Opposite:* conscious.

out-and-out *adj* **complete**, blatant, obvious, outright, utter, absolute, total, shameless, brazen, glaring. [➡ABSOLUTE AND ABSOLUTELY; 131]

outback *n* **wilderness**, scrubland, wilds, desert, badlands. [➡REMOTE PLACES; 1046]

outbid *v* **offer more than**, outspend, outdo, leave standing, overpay, up the ante (*informal*). [➡GAMBLE AND TAKE RISKS; 467]

outboard *adj* **external**, on the outside, outside, outward, exterior. [➡GENERAL LOCATIONS; 159]

outboard motor *part of* **ship or boat.** [➡PARTS OF A SHIP OR BOAT; 1150]

outbound *adj* [➡DIRECTION OF MOTION; 346]

outbrave (*archaic*) *v* **defy**, confront, brave, stand up to, face up to, outface, face, resist. [➡COMPETE, CONTEND, AND COMBAT; 304]

outbreak *n* **eruption**, outburst, epidemic, occurrence, rash, spate, plague, burst. [➡SUDDEN EVENT; 52]

outbuilding *n* **shed**, outhouse, lean-to, barn, shack. [➡ANCILLARY BUILDINGS; 1079]

outbuilding

◆ *types of outbuilding*
barn, booth, byre (*regional*), carport, conservatory, cowshed, garage, garden shed, gatehouse, gazebo, glasshouse, greenhouse, guardhouse, hothouse, hut, kiosk, lean-to, lodge, orangery, outhouse, pavilion, pergola, potting shed, privy (*informal*), sentry box, shed, stall, stand, summerhouse

outburst *n* **outpouring**, upsurge, surge, eruption, explosion, outbreak, burst, flare-up (*informal*), gust, frenzy. [➡SUDDEN EVENT; 52]

outcast *n* **untouchable**, exile, pariah, recluse, outsider, castaway, leper. [➡SOLITARY PEOPLE; 942]

outclass *v* **surpass**, outshine, excel, do better than, better, outdo, exceed, outstep, outrun. [➡BEAT AND DEFEAT; 80]

out cold *adj* [➡TIRED, ASLEEP AND UNCONSCIOUS; 739]

outcome *n* **consequence**, result, ending, product, conclusion, upshot, effect, aftermath, sequel, aftereffect. [➡RESULTS AND OUTCOMES; 83]

outcrop *n* **rocky outcrop**, crag, ridge, bluff, boulder, outlier, protrusion, protuberance, projection. [➡GEOLOGICAL FEATURES; 1056]

outcry 1 *n* **protest**, disagreement, objection, chorus of disapproval, quarrel. [➡CRITICISMS AND ANGRY OUTBURSTS; 50] *Opposite:* acceptance. 2 *n* **uproar**, hullabaloo, hue and cry, turmoil, clamour, row, din, commotion, tumult. [➡CHAOS AND UPROAR; 51]

outdated *adj* **antiquated**, passé, outmoded, obsolete, dated, archaic, out-of-date, old-fashioned. [➡OLD, OLD-FASHIONED; 168] *Opposite:* up-to-date.

See Compare and Contrast at **old-fashioned**.

outdistance *v* **outdo**, beat, do better than, outrun, outstrip, leave behind, overtake. [➡BEAT AND DEFEAT; 80]

outdo *v* **exceed**, surpass, top, outdistance, outshine, outclass, do better than, outstrip, beat, excel. [➡BEAT AND DEFEAT; 80]

outdoor *adj* **outside**, open-air, out-of-doors, alfresco. [➡GENERAL LOCATIONS; 159] *Opposite:* indoor.

outdoors *adv* **out-of-doors**, outside, in the open, in the open air, alfresco. [➡GENERAL LOCATIONS; 159] *Opposite:* indoors.

outer *adj* **outside**, external, on the outside, surface, superficial, exterior, outward. [➡EXTREMITIES OF PHYSICAL OBJECTS; 1249] *Opposite:* inner.

outer ear *n* [➡THE EAR; 707]

outermost *adj* **furthest**, farthest, remotest, outmost. [➡DISTANCE; 161] *Opposite:* innermost.

outer space *n* **space**, the heavens, the universe, the solar system, the cosmos, interstellar space. [➡THE SOLAR SYSTEM AND ASTRONOMY; 1059]

outerwear *n* [➡GARMENTS AND OUTFITS; 865]

outface 1 *v* **stare out**, outstare, psych out (*informal*), stare down (*US*). [➡COMPETE, CONTEND, AND COMBAT; 304] *Opposite:* give in. 2 *v* **brave**, stand up to, face up to, defy, confront, beat, overcome, outbrave (*archaic*). [➡BEAT AND DEFEAT; 80] *Opposite:* capitulate.

outfall *n* **vent**, mouth, duct, channel, culvert, drain, waste pipe, outlet. [➡WATERCOURSES; 1110]

outfit 1 *n* **suit**, clothes, clothing, getup (*informal*), ensemble, dress, guise. [➡CLOTHES AND ACCESSORIES; 864] 2 *n* (*informal*) **company**, team, business, group, unit, setup, party, corps, troop. [➡GROUPS OF PEOPLE; 935] 3 *v* **supply**, furnish (*formal*), equip, kit out, fit out, arm. [➡EQUIP AND SUPPLY; 436]

outflank 1 *v* **go around**, attack from behind, attack from the rear, outmanoeuvre. [➡WARFARE AND WAR; 830] 2 *v* **outwit**, outmanoeuvre, outdo, bypass, outclass, outfox, beat, outthink, outsmart. [➡BEAT AND DEFEAT; 80]

outflow 1 *n* **discharge**, drainage, seepage, leakage, depletion, loss. [➡EMIT AND EMANATE; 362] *Opposite:* influx. 2 *n* **expenditure**, debit, expenses, spending, outlay, disbursement. [➡MONEY, PAYMENTS, AND CHARGES; 800] *Opposite:* income.

out for the count (*informal*) 1 *adj* **unconscious**, out, out cold, knocked out, comatose, dazed, insensible. [➡TIRED, ASLEEP AND UNCONSCIOUS; 739] *Opposite:* conscious. 2 *adj* **asleep**, dead to the world, sleeping, sound asleep, out, unconscious. [➡TIRED, ASLEEP AND UNCONSCIOUS; 739] *Opposite:* awake.

outfox *v* **defeat**, outwit, get the better of, outflank, take in, con, outsmart, outthink. [➡BEAT AND DEFEAT; 80]

outgoing 1 *adj* **outward-bound**, outbound, outward, departing, leaving. [➡DIRECTION OF MOTION; 346] *Opposite:* incoming. 2 *adj* **retiring**, leaving, departing, withdrawing, resigning. [➡PAST; 84] *Opposite:* incoming. 3 *adj* **sociable**, friendly, gregarious, extrovert, genial, affable, demonstrative, expansive. [➡FRIENDLINESS AND SOCIABILITY; 495] *Opposite:* introvert.

outgoings *n* **expenses**, expenditure, costs, overhead, outlay, spending, disbursement. [➡EXPENDITURE; 424] *Opposite:* income.

outgrow 1 *v* **get too large for**, grow too big for, get too big for, enlarge, grow up, expand, fill out. [➡CHANGE OF SIZE: BIGGER; 393] 2 *v* **move beyond**, be too grown-up for, be too old for, mature, develop, surpass. [➡GET BETTER; 376] 3 *v* **grow bigger than**, grow larger than, grow faster than, grow quicker than, outnumber, outstrip, overwhelm, exceed. [➡BEAT AND DEFEAT; 80]

outgrowth *n* **extension**, result, development, product, consequence, effect, outcome. [➡RESULTS AND OUTCOMES; 83]

outhouse *n* (*US*) **outdoor toilet**, latrine, privy (*informal*), toilet. [➡ANCILLARY BUILDINGS; 1079]

outing *n* **visit**, excursion, trip, day trip, jaunt, day out, junket, getaway. [➡TRAVEL: JOURNEYS AND TRIPS; 319]

out in left field (*US*) *adj* [➡BIZARRE AND PECULIAR; 258]

out in the open *adj* [➡KNOWN AND FAMOUS; 182]

outjockey *v* **outfox**, outdo, outwit, outmanoeuvre, outflank, beat. [➡BEAT AND DEFEAT; 80]

outlandish *adj* **unusual**, bizarre, peculiar, strange, eccentric, weird, odd. [➡BIZARRE AND PECULIAR; 258] *Opposite:* usual.

outlandishness *n* [➡BIZARRE AND PECULIAR; 258]

outlast *v* **outlive**, survive, live longer than, last longer than, endure, carry on. [➡CONTINUE TO EXIST; 17]

outlaw 1 *n* **runaway**, criminal, fugitive, bandit, brigand (*literary*), desperado (*literary*). [➡RUNAWAYS AND ABSENTEES; 9] 2 *v* **forbid**, ban, prohibit, proscribe, veto, bar, censure, suppress. [➡REFUSE PERMISSION AND NOT ALLOW; 671] *Opposite:* allow.

outlay 1 *n* **expenditure**, expense, cost, spending, sum, amount, disbursement. [➡EXPENDITURE; 424] 2 *v* **expend**, spend, lay out, pay out, disburse, shell out (*informal*), fork out (*informal*). [➡GIVE MONEY; 434]

outlet 1 *n* **opening**, passage, vent, exit, channel, hole, pipe, orifice (*literary*), aperture, egress (*formal*). [➡HOLES, GAPS, AND FORKS; 1251] 2 *n* **means**, channel, conduit, vent, instrument, vehicle. [➡WAYS OF DOING THINGS; 295] 3 *n* **department store**, shop, retailer, market, store, showroom. [➡BUSINESS ENTERPRISES AND RELATED BODIES; 793]

outline 1 *n* **shape**, form, figure, contour, silhouette, profile. [➡SHAPE; 1215] 2 *n* **plan**, rough draft, summary, sketch, rough idea, skeleton, framework. [➡SUMMARIES, OUTLINES, AND EXCERPTS; 589] 3 *v* **draw round**, sketch, draw, delineate, chart, border, bound, define, edge. [➡CREATE IMAGES; 357] *Opposite:* fill in. 4 *v* **summarize**, sketch out, delineate, run through, give a rough idea, make a rough draft. [➡EXPLAIN AND CLARIFY; 611] *Opposite:* expand.

outlive *v* **live longer than**, outlast, survive, last longer than, endure, carry on. [➡CONTINUE TO EXIST; 17]

outlook 1 *n* **viewpoint**, view, attitude, position, point of view, stance. [➡POINT OF VIEW; 768] 2 *n* **future**, prospect, time to come, time ahead. [➡FUTURE; 86] 3 *n* **view**, panorama, vista. [➡VIEWS AND OUTLOOKS; 1072]

out loud *adv* **loudly**, audibly, distinctly, aloud, vocally. [➡LOUD OR UNPLEASANT SOUNDS; 1265] *Opposite:* inaudibly.

outlying *adj* **remote**, out-of-the-way, distant, faraway, far-off, far-flung. [➡DISTANCE; 161] *Opposite:* neighbouring.

outmanoeuvre *v* **get the better of**, outsmart, outfox, outwit, outflank, beat, outdo. [➡BEAT AND DEFEAT; 80]

outmoded 1 *adj* **unfashionable**, dated, passé, old-fashioned, out-of-date, outdated. [➡OLD, OLD-FASHIONED; 168] *Opposite:* fashionable. 2 *adj* **obsolete**, out of use, out of commission, archaic, antiquated, worn-out. [➡REDUNDANT AND USELESS; 241]

outmodedness *n* [➡OLD, OLD-FASHIONED; 168]

outmost *adj* **outermost**, remotest, furthest, most remote, extreme, furthermost, utmost. [➡DISTANCE; 161]

outnumber *v* **be more than**, be more numerous than, outstrip. [➡BEAT AND DEFEAT; 80]

out of bounds *adj* **off-limits**, forbidden, prohibited, banned, barred, not accessible, inaccessible. [➡CAPTIVITY AND LOSS OF FREEDOM; 249] *Opposite:* open.

out of breath *adj* **breathless**, panting, gasping, puffing, winded, wheezy, puffed (*informal*). [➡ ILL AND SICK; 741]

out of cash *adj* [➡ POVERTY AND POOR; 892]

out of commission *adj* **out of order**, out of action, not working, not in use, broken-down, broken, inoperative, bust (*informal*), incapacitated, inactive, busted (*US informal*). [➡ IN BAD REPAIR; 1233] *Opposite:* functional.

out of condition *adj* [➡ UNFIT AND WEAK; 740]

out-of-date *adj* **outdated**, obsolete, outmoded, old-fashioned, dated, archaic, passé, antiquated. [➡ OLD, OLD-FASHIONED; 168] *Opposite:* up-to-date.

out-of-doors *adv* **outdoors**, outside, in the open, in the open air, alfresco. [➡ GENERAL LOCATIONS; 159] *Opposite:* indoors.

out of fashion *adj* [➡ OLD, OLD-FASHIONED; 168]

out of favour *adj* [➡ IN TROUBLE AND DISADVANTAGED; 73]

out of focus *adj* [➡ IMPERCEPTIBLE; 26]

out of harm's way *adj* [➡ SAFE AND SAFETY; 192]

out of it *adj* [➡ UNDER THE INFLUENCE OF DRUGS OR ALCOHOL; 742]

out of kilter *adj* [➡ ORIENTATION AND ALIGNMENT; 1222]

out of order 1 *adj* **not working**, unusable, broken, out of commission, out of use, inoperative, incapacitated, inactive, bust (*informal*), busted (*US informal*). [➡ IN BAD REPAIR; 1233] *Opposite:* functional. 2 *adj* (*regional informal*) **inappropriate**, wrong, beyond the pale, improper, incorrect, unacceptable, unsuitable. [➡ INAPPROPRIATE AND UNSUITABLE; 225] *Opposite:* appropriate.

out of shape *adj* [➡ UNFIT AND WEAK; 740]

out of sight *adj* **out of view**, hidden, hidden from view, hidden from sight, obscured, concealed, veiled. [➡ IMPERCEPTIBLE; 26]

out of sorts 1 *adj* **poorly** (*informal*), unwell, off-colour, below par (*informal*), down in the mouth (*informal*), not yourself, ill. [➡ ILL AND SICK; 741] *Opposite:* well. 2 *adj* **irritable**, grumpy, tetchy (*informal*), ill-tempered, cross, impatient, grouchy (*informal*). [➡ IRRITATION AND ANGER; 542] *Opposite:* good-tempered.

out of stock *adj* [➡ ABSENT AND UNAVAILABLE; 7]

out of sync *adj* [➡ PROMPTNESS: BADLY TIMED; 101]

out of the blue *adv* **unexpectedly**, without warning, all of a sudden, suddenly, surprisingly, from nowhere. [➡ HAPPENING QUICKLY; 104]

out of the ordinary *adj* **unusual**, exceptional, atypical, extraordinary, uncommon, rare, remarkable. [➡ EXTRAORDINARY: UNCOMMON; 206] *Opposite:* ordinary.

out of the question *adj* **impossible**, unthinkable, unacceptable, highly unlikely, improbable, not feasible. [➡ IMPOSSIBLE AND IMPROBABLE; 179] *Opposite:* possible.

out-of-the-way 1 *adj* **distant**, off the beaten track, remote, isolated, desolate, outlying, faraway, off the beaten path (*US*). [➡ DISTANCE; 161] *Opposite:* accessible. 2 *adj* **uncommon**, unconventional, different, out of the ordinary, special, unusual, singular, unique, extraordinary. [➡ EXTRAORDINARY: UNCOMMON; 206] *Opposite:* common.

out of this world (*informal*) *adj* **exceptional**, superb, wonderful, fabulous, terrific (*informal*), amazing, marvellous. [➡ EXTRAORDINARY: AMAZING; 205] *Opposite:* unexceptional.

out of true *adj* [➡ ORIENTATION AND ALIGNMENT; 1222]

out of view *adj* [➡ IMPERCEPTIBLE; 26]

outpace *v* **outstrip**, outperform, overtake, outdo, beat, leave standing, leave behind. [➡ BEAT AND DEFEAT; 80]

outperform *v* **outdo**, outstrip, outpace, outclass, beat, overtake, leave behind. [➡ BEAT AND DEFEAT; 80] *Opposite:* underperform.

outpost *n* **garrison**, base, station, settlement, colony, post. [➡ HUMAN SETTLEMENTS; 1069]

outpouring *n* **expression**, outburst, torrent, spate, flood, deluge, inundation (*formal*). [➡ CRITICISMS AND ANGRY OUTBURSTS; 50]

output *n* **production**, productivity, amount produced, yield, harvest, crop. [➡ CREATION; 347]

outrage 1 *n* **crime**, barbarity, disgrace, scandal, horror, atrocity, violence. [➡ BAD BEHAVIOUR OR ACTION; 255] 2 *n* **indignation**, anger, rage, fury, ire (*literary*), annoyance, wrath. [➡ IRRITATION AND ANGER; 542] 3 *v* **infuriate**, offend, insult, anger, enrage, affront, wrong, incense. [➡ ANGER AND ANNOY; 570] *Opposite:* placate.

outraged *adj* **angry**, incensed, livid, infuriated, furious, shocked, scandalized. [➡ IRRITATION AND ANGER; 542] *Opposite:* calm.

outrageous *adj* **disgraceful**, shameful, shocking, offensive, contemptible, despicable, extreme. [➡ UNACCEPTABLE AND UNFORGIVEABLE; 226] *Opposite:* commendable.

outré *adj* **shocking**, eccentric, unconventional, excessive, over-the-top (*informal*), too much, beyond the pale, de trop, outrageous. [➡ UNACCEPTABLE AND UNFORGIVEABLE; 226]

outride 1 *v* **outpace**, outstrip, outclass, beat, overtake, leave behind. [➡ BEAT AND DEFEAT; 80] 2 *v* **survive**, last out, endure, ride out, make it through, last. [➡ CONTINUE TO EXIST; 17]

outrider *n* **patrol**, guard, bodyguard, attendant, escort. [➡ SUPPORTERS, PROTECTORS, AND COMPATRIOTS; 970]

outrigger *part of* **ship or boat**. [➡ PARTS OF A SHIP OR BOAT; 1150]

outright 1 *adv* **completely**, entirely, totally, fully, absolutely, wholly. [➡ ABSOLUTE AND ABSOLUTELY; 131] *Opposite:* partially. 2 *adv* **immediately**, straightaway, right away, without hesitation, at once, instantly. [➡ HAPPENING QUICKLY; 104] *Opposite:* hesitantly. 3 *adv* **openly**, unreservedly, frankly, forthrightly, unequivocally, candidly. [➡ HONEST AND OPEN; 631] *Opposite:* equivocally. 4 *adj* **absolute**, complete, total, utter, out-and-out, entire, consummate, downright. [➡ ABSOLUTE AND ABSOLUTELY; 131] *Opposite:* partial. 5 *adj* **out-and-out**, clear, transparent, obvious, direct, overt. [➡ PERCEPTIBLE; 25]

outrun 1 *v* **outpace**, outstrip, outclass, beat, overtake, leave behind, run faster than. [➡ BEAT AND DEFEAT; 80] 2 *v* **leave behind**, flee, run faster than, elude, get away from, escape.

[➡AVOID OR ESCAPE CONTACT; 419] **3** *v* **go beyond**, overrun, exceed, excel, surpass, outshine, outdo. [➡BEAT AND DEFEAT; 80]

outsell *v* **beat**, overtake, outpace, outstrip, sell more than, outperform. [➡SELL; 442] *Opposite:* underperform.

outset *n* **beginning**, start, kickoff (*informal*), onset, inception (*formal*). [➡BEGINNING; 53]

outshine *v* **surpass**, outdo, outstrip, outperform, do better than, overtake, beat. [➡BEAT AND DEFEAT; 80]

outside **1** *adv* **outdoors**, in the open air, alfresco, out of doors, in the fresh air, in the street, in the garden, in the road. [➡GENERAL LOCATIONS; 159] **2** *adv* **beyond**, out there, yonder (*regional*), elsewhere. [➡GENERAL LOCATIONS; 159] **3** *adj* **outdoor**, external, separate, open-air, exterior, freestanding. [➡GENERAL LOCATIONS; 159] **4** *adj* **external**, unknown, unfamiliar, independent, freelance, foreign. [➡SECRET AND UNKNOWN; 180] **5** *adj* **slight**, faint, remote, scarce, slim. [➡IMPOSSIBLE AND IMPROBABLE; 179] *Opposite:* strong. **6** *prep* **beyond**, out of, further than, farther than, past, in front of, beside. [➡CLOSENESS; 160] *Opposite:* within. **7** *n* **exterior**, outer surface, surface, external surface. [➡EXTREMITIES OF PHYSICAL OBJECTS; 1249] *Opposite:* inside.

outsider *n* **stranger**, foreigner, unknown, interloper, outcast, recluse. [➡SOLITARY PEOPLE; 942] *Opposite:* native.

outsize *adj* **enormous**, massive, vast, huge, immense, gigantic, whopping (*informal*), capacious, extra-large, big, giant-sized, oversized, hefty, giant. [➡LARGE; 1192]

out-sized *see* **outsize**.

outskirts *n* **border**, fringes, periphery, bounds, outer reaches, environs, suburbs, limit. [➡HUMAN SETTLEMENTS; 1069] *Opposite:* centre.

outsmart *v* **outwit**, outfox, outmanoeuvre, get the better of, overcome, best, beat. [➡BEAT AND DEFEAT; 80]

outspoken *adj* **frank**, opinionated, honest, candid, open, blunt, forthright. [➡HONEST AND OPEN; 631] *Opposite:* tactful.

outspokenness *n* **frankness**, honesty, candour, openness, bluntness, forthrightness. [➡HONEST AND OPEN; 631] *Opposite:* tact.

outspread **1** *adj* **extended**, spread-out, stretched, widely spread, open, outstretched, unfolded. [➡ORIENTATION AND ALIGNMENT; 1222] *Opposite:* folded. **2** *v* **extend**, expand, stretch, spread, spread out, hold out. [➡CHANGE OF SIZE: BIGGER; 393] *Opposite:* close in.

outstanding **1** *adj* **exceptional**, terrific (*informal*), wonderful, stupendous, dazzling, marvellous, excellent, great, superior, remarkable. [➡EXTRAORDINARY: AMAZING; 205] *Opposite:* abysmal. **2** *adj* **unresolved**, unsettled, unpaid, remaining, owing, due. [➡OWE AND DESERVE; 466] *Opposite:* settled.

outstandingly *adv* **exceptionally**, terrifically, wonderfully, stupendously, marvellously, dazzlingly, excellently, staggeringly. [➡EXTRAORDINARY: AMAZING; 205] *Opposite:* abysmally.

outstay *v* **outlast**, outlive, survive, stay longer than. [➡CONTINUE TO EXIST; 17]

outstretched *adj* **outspread**, extended, stretched out, spread-out, stretched, widely spread, open, unfolded. [➡ORIENTATION AND ALIGNMENT; 1222] *Opposite:* folded.

outstrip *v* **outdo**, outshine, surpass, exceed, do better than, outperform, better, beat, overtake. [➡BEAT AND DEFEAT; 80] *Opposite:* fall behind.

out to lunch (*slang*) *adj* [➡BIZARRE AND PECULIAR; 258]

outward *adj* **visible**, external, apparent, obvious, noticeable. [➡PERCEPTIBLE; 25] *Opposite:* inward.

outward-bound *adj* [➡DIRECTION OF MOTION; 346]

outwards *adv* **out**, outward, away, centrifugally. [➡DIRECTION OF MOTION; 346] *Opposite:* inwards.

outweigh *v* **overshadow**, be more important than, prevail over, be greater than, dwarf. [➡MOST IMPORTANT AND MAIN; 194]

outwit *v* **outsmart**, outfox, outmanoeuvre, get the better of, take in, beat. [➡BEAT AND DEFEAT; 80]

outworker *n* [➡WORKER; 836]

outworking *n* [➡TYPES OF WORK; 835]

outworn *adj* **obsolete**, outmoded, out-of-date, antiquated, archaic, ancient, old. [➡OLD, OLD-FASHIONED; 168] *Opposite:* current.

ova *n* [➡EGGS AND SPAWN; 728]

oval *type of* **rounded shape**. [➡ROUNDED SHAPE; 1217]

ovary *n* [➡REPRODUCTION AND HEREDITY; 726]

ovate *adj* **oval**, egg-shaped, ellipsoid. [➡ROUNDED SHAPE; 1217]

ovation *n* **standing ovation**, cheer, thumbs-up (*informal*), vote of confidence, endorsement. [➡APPLAUSE; 653]

oven *n* **cooker**, kiln, range, rotisserie, tandoor. [➡TABLEWARE, CUTLERY, AND KITCHENWARE; 861]

oven dish *n* [➡TABLEWARE, CUTLERY, AND KITCHENWARE; 861]

oven tray *n* [➡TABLEWARE, CUTLERY, AND KITCHENWARE; 861]

ovenware *n* [➡TABLEWARE, CUTLERY, AND KITCHENWARE; 861]

over **1** *prep* **throughout**, around, the length and breadth of, round, across, all round, all around, all across. [➡RELATIVE LOCATION; 162] **2** *prep* **in excess of**, more than, greater than, larger than, above, older than, faster than, heavier than, taller than, longer than. [➡MORE AND EXCESS; 122] *Opposite:* under. **3** *prep* **on top of**, above, on, upon. [➡RELATIVE LOCATION; 162] *Opposite:* beneath (*formal*). **4** *adj* **ended, finished**, done, completed, concluded, terminated. [➡ABSENT AND UNAVAILABLE; 7]

overabundance *n* **excess**, surplus, glut, superfluity, flood, surfeit, plethora, oversupply. [➡TOO MUCH; 118] *Opposite:* shortage.

overabundant *adj* [➡TOO MUCH; 118]

overact *v* **ham it up**, ham, overdo it, exaggerate, overplay. [➡OVERDO SOMETHING; 291]

overactive *adj* **feverish**, overexcited, overcharged, intense, fervid, fanciful, febrile. [➡NEGATIVE INTELLECTUAL CHARACTERISTICS; 526]

over again *adv* [➡AGAIN; 109]

overall 1 *adj* **general**, complete, total, global, inclusive, whole. [➡WHOLENESS AND COMPLETENESS; 199] 2 *adv* **on the whole**, in general, generally, taken as a whole, largely, by and large. [➡USUALLY; 108] *Opposite:* in particular.

overalls *type of* **suit**. [➡GARMENTS AND OUTFITS; 865]

over and above *prep* **in addition to**, besides, as well as, added to, on top of. [➡ALSO; 136]

over and done with *adj* **over**, finished, done with, done, ended, complete, completed, concluded. [➡PAST; 84]

over and over *adv* [➡AGAIN; 109]

over and over again *adv* [➡AGAIN; 109]

overarching *adj* **all-embracing**, main, all-encompassing, predominant, principal, primary, central, supreme, key. [➡MOST IMPORTANT AND MAIN; 194]

overawe *v* **intimidate**, scare, impress, subdue. [➡FRIGHTEN AND SHOCK; 569]

overawed *adj* [➡SURPRISE, SHOCK, AND AMAZEMENT; 546]

overbearing *adj* **arrogant**, domineering, bossy, imperious, pompous, haughty. [➡BOSSY AND OVERBEARING; 517] *Opposite:* meek.

overbearingness *n* [➡BOSSY AND OVERBEARING; 517]

overblown 1 *adj* **overdone**, excessive, exaggerated, unrestrained, immoderate (*formal*), extravagant, overstated, inflated. [➡BIZARRE AND PECULIAR; 258] *Opposite:* understated. 2 *adj* **pretentious**, pompous, puffed-up, extravagant. [➡POMPOUS, LOUD, AND OVER-CONFIDENT; 636] *Opposite:* unassuming.

overburden *v* **overload**, overtax, overstrain, burden, load, tax, overstretch. [➡GIVE TOO MUCH; 438]

overburdened *adj* [➡IN TROUBLE AND DISADVANTAGED; 73]

overcast *adj* **cloudy**, grey, gloomy, dark, dull, dreary. [➡CLOUDY AND RAINY WEATHER; 1052] *Opposite:* bright.

overcharge *v* **charge too much**, fleece (*informal*), take advantage of, cheat, swindle, rip off (*informal*). [➡TAKE SOMETHING AWAY; 426]

overcoat *type of* **overcoat**. [➡GARMENTS AND OUTFITS; 865]

overcome 1 *v* **overwhelm**, overpower, incapacitate, disable, knock out, kill, asphyxiate, choke, poison. [➡WOUND A PERSON OR ANIMAL; 384] 2 *v* **carry away**, affect, move to tears, reduce to tears, grip, seize. [➡UPSET, DISTRESS, AND HUMILIATE; 568] 3 *v* **surmount**, prevail over, rise above, triumph over, conquer, defeat. [➡BEAT AND DEFEAT; 80] *Opposite:* yield. 4 *v* **conquer**, defeat, beat, trounce, triumph over, vanquish. [➡BEAT AND DEFEAT; 80] *Opposite:* lose.

See Compare and Contrast at **defeat**.

overcompensate *v* **overreact**, overcorrect, overplay, give too much weight to, try too hard. [➡OVERDO SOMETHING; 291]

overconfidence *n* **arrogance**, overoptimism, boldness, pride, nerve, self-confidence, bullishness (*informal*), brashness. [➡BOSSY AND OVERBEARING; 517] *Opposite:* caution.

overconfident *adj* **arrogant**, full of yourself, brash, overoptimistic, bullish (*informal*). [➡BOSSY AND OVERBEARING; 517] *Opposite:* modest.

overcook *v* **overdo**, stew, burn, char, spoil, ruin. [➡COOKING AND FOOD PREPARATION; 354] *Opposite:* undercook.

overcooked *adj* **overdone**, burnt, well done, chewy, hard, stewed, charred, tough. [➡STATE OF PREPARED FOOD; 1170] *Opposite:* underdone.

overcritical *adj* **harsh**, hypercritical, censorious, severe, critical, contemptuous, disapproving, stern, judgmental, disparaging. [➡DIFFICULT TO PLEASE; 516]

overcrowded *adj* **stuffed** (*informal*), filled to capacity, congested, overloaded, teeming, swarming, heaving, jammed, clogged. [➡FULL; 1238] *Opposite:* empty.

overcrowding *n* **congestion**, overloading, overpopulation, excess, excess numbers. [➡TOO MUCH; 118]

overdo 1 *v* **overcook**, burn, stew, char, spoil, ruin. [➡COOKING AND FOOD PREPARATION; 354] *Opposite:* undercook. 2 *v* **exaggerate**, overstate, overplay, overemphasize. [➡OVERDO SOMETHING; 291] *Opposite:* play down.

overdo it *v* [➡OVERDO SOMETHING; 291]

overdone *adj* **overcooked**, burnt, stewed, charred, spoilt, spoiled, ruined. [➡STATE OF PREPARED FOOD; 1170] *Opposite:* underdone.

overdo things *v* **strain yourself**, burn the candle at both ends, overtax yourself, overexert yourself, overdo it, overwork, work too hard, burn the midnight oil. [➡OVERDO SOMETHING; 291] *Opposite:* relax.

overdramatize *v* [➡OVERDO SOMETHING; 291]

overdrawn *adj* **in debt**, in the red, overspent, insolvent, over your limit. [➡POVERTY AND POOR; 892] *Opposite:* in credit.

overdue *adj* **late**, tardy, unpaid, unsettled, belated. [➡PROMPTNESS: LATE; 100] *Opposite:* early.

overeat *v* **overindulge**, eat too much, gorge, stuff yourself, binge, overdose. [➡OVERDO SOMETHING; 291]

over-egg the pudding *v* [➡OVERDO SOMETHING; 291]

overemotional *adj* **emotional**, sentimental, weepy (*informal*), melodramatic, maudlin, histrionic, mawkish, slushy, mushy, syrupy, tearful, gushing. [➡EXCESSIVE SENSITIVITY; 512] *Opposite:* unemotional.

overemphasize *v* **exaggerate**, overstate, overstress, stress, go over the top about, go on and on about, lay it on with a trowel (*informal*). [➡CLAIM, INSIST, AND EMPHASIZE; 615]

overenthusiasm *n* **fanaticism**, mania, obsessiveness, obsession, ardour, fervour, fever, feverishness, zeal. [➡FADS, FETISHES, AND IDOLATRY; 556]

overenthusiastic *adj* **overzealous**, over-the-top (*informal*), carried away, fanatical, manic (*informal*), obsessive, obsessional, ardent, fervent, feverish. [➡NEGATIVE INTELLECTUAL CHARACTERISTICS; 526]

overestimate 1 *v* **misjudge**, overrate, miscalculate, overvalue, allow too much for. [➡OVERDO SOMETHING; 291] *Opposite:* underestimate. 2 *v* **overrate**, expect too much of, misjudge, miscalculate, overemphasize. [➡ASSESS QUALITY; 756] *Opposite:* underestimate.

overexcite *v* **work up**, excite, wind up (*informal*), get in a state, get in a lather (*informal*), get carried away. [➡UPSET, DISTRESS, AND HUMILIATE; 568]

overexcited *adj* **worked up** (*informal*), carried away, in a lather (*informal*), in a state (*informal*), hyper (*informal*), keyed up (*informal*), manic (*informal*), high, frenzied, in a frenzy, feverish, nervous, anxious. [➡PLEASURE, EXCITEMENT, AND ELATION; 535] *Opposite:* calm.

overexcitement *n* **frenzy**, mania, feverishness, anxiety, emotion, excitement, hyperactivity. [➡FADS, FETISHES, AND IDOLATRY; 556]

overextend *v* **overstretch**, overreach, go too far, bite off more than you can chew, exceed your limit. [➡OVERDO SOMETHING; 291]

overflow 1 *v* **run over**, flood, spill over, brim over, pour out, burst. [➡FILL; 407] 2 *n* **excess**, runoff, extra, surfeit, surplus, overspill. [➡MORE AND EXCESS; 122] *Opposite:* lack.

overflowing *adj* **spilling over**, teeming, swarming, brimming, abundant, brimful. [➡FULL; 1238] *Opposite:* empty.

overflow with *v* **be full of**, brim with, abound with, bubble with, be bursting at the seams with, exude, be brimming with. [➡PROSPER AND ABOUND; 16] *Opposite:* lack.

overgrown *adj* **dense**, thick, overrun, lush, untidy, unkempt, wild. [➡IN BAD REPAIR; 1233] *Opposite:* tidy.

overhang 1 *v* **project**, extend, jut out, hang over, extend beyond, jut out over. [➡EXIST IN A PLACE; 19] 2 *n* **projection**, extension, outcrop, ledge, outcropping. [➡GEOLOGICAL FEATURES; 1056]

overhaul 1 *v* **repair**, renovate, fix, refit, refurbish, service, revamp, strip down. [➡REPAIR AND MEND; 377] 2 *v* **overtake**, surpass, leave behind, outdo, pass, go past. [➡BEAT AND DEFEAT; 80] *Opposite:* fall behind. 3 *n* **service**, refit, refurbishment. [➡IMPROVE SOMETHING; 375]

overhead *adv* **above**, in the air, upstairs, directly above, above your head. [➡GENERAL LOCATIONS; 159] *Opposite:* below.

overheads *n* **costs**, outgoings, expenses, payments, business costs, bills. [➡MONEY, PAYMENTS, AND CHARGES; 800]

overhear *v* **eavesdrop**, listen in, hear, eavesdrop on, listen to, earwig (*humorous*). [➡LISTEN AND LISTENERS; 709]

overheated *adj* **excited**, worked up (*informal*), hot under the collar (*informal*), impassioned, agitated, inflamed, hot and bothered, upset. [➡IRRITATION AND ANGER; 542] *Opposite:* cool.

overindulge *v* **overeat**, eat too much, stuff yourself, gorge, gorge yourself, binge. [➡OVERDO SOMETHING; 291]

overindulgence *n* **excess**, greed, immoderation (*formal*), intemperance, hedonism, gluttony, dissipation, debauchery, gourmandise, abandonment, overkill. [➡MORALLY BAD; 776]

overindulgent *adj* **excessive**, greedy, immoderate (*formal*), intemperate, hedonistic, debauched, dissipated. [➡MORALLY BAD; 776]

overjoyed *adj* **delighted**, joyful, elated, ecstatic, jubilant, thrilled, over the moon. [➡PLEASURE, EXCITEMENT, AND ELATION; 535] *Opposite:* disappointed.

overkill *n* **excess**, too much, overstatement, overegging the pudding, too much of a good thing, heavy-handedness, overindulgence, overload. [➡TOO MUCH; 118] *Opposite:* restraint.

overladen *adj* **overloaded**, overfilled, crammed, stuffed (*informal*), overburdened, weighed down. [➡FULL; 1238]

overlap 1 *v* **partly cover**, overlie, meet, touch, cover. [➡EXIST IN CLOSE PROXIMITY; 21] 2 *v* **coincide**, correspond, intersect, meet, come together, interrelate, correspond with, bring together. [➡CREATING CONNECTIONS; 145] 3 *n* **overlay**, intersection, edge, join, connection. [➡EXTREMITIES OF PHYSICAL OBJECTS; 1249] 4 *n* **correspondence**, intersection, connection, similarity, common ground, commonality. [➡CONNECTION; 144]

overlay *v* **cover**, coat, put over, overlap, drape, shroud, blanket. [➡DECORATE, ADORN, AND APPLY COATINGS; 406]

overlie *v* [➡EXIST IN CLOSE PROXIMITY; 21]

overload 1 *v* **overburden**, overwork, tax, strain, weigh down, overexert. [➡GIVE TOO MUCH; 438] 2 *n* **excess**, surplus, overwork, burden, overkill. [➡TOO MUCH; 118] *Opposite:* lack.

overloaded *adj* **weighed down**, weighted down, loaded, laden, full, burdened, encumbered, bogged down (*informal*). [➡FULL; 1238]

overlook 1 *v* **ignore**, miss, forget, skip, neglect, omit. [➡NOT PAY ATTENTION; 765] *Opposite:* notice. 2 *v* **excuse**, condone, spare, let pass, pardon, wink at (*informal*), forgive. [➡FORGET, FORGIVE, AND ACCEPT; 749] *Opposite:* punish. 3 *v* **give onto**, be opposite, face. [➡EXIST IN A PLACE; 19] 4 *v* **supervise**, oversee, superintend, boss, observe, manage, direct, administer, guide, watch, regulate. [➡BE IN CHARGE; 271] 5 *v* **inspect**, survey, examine, peruse, scan. [➡LOOKING AND LOOKS; 701]

See Compare and Contrast at **neglect**.

overlooked *adj* [➡IN TROUBLE AND DISADVANTAGED; 73]

overly *adv* **excessively**, too, desperately, exaggeratedly, exceedingly, very. [➡TO A GREAT EXTENT; 130] *Opposite:* slightly.

overmuch 1 *adv* **excessively**, too much, very much, unnecessarily, overly, immoderately (*formal*), extravagantly, unduly, inordinately. [➡TOO MUCH; 118] 2 *adj* **excessive**, extreme, too, very, a lot, immoderate (*formal*), extravagant, undue, inordinate. [➡TOO MUCH; 118] 3 *n* **excess**, superfluity, surplus, overage. [➡TOO MUCH; 118]

overnight 1 *adv* **suddenly**, at once, quickly, instantly, abruptly, immediately, instantaneously. [➡HAPPENING QUICKLY; 104] *Opposite:* gradually. 2 *adj* **instant**, immediate, abrupt, instantaneous, sudden, rapid, dramatic, meteoric. [➡HAPPENING QUICKLY; 104] *Opposite:* gradual.

overnight bag *type of* **baggage.** [➡CONTAINERS, RECEPTACLES, AND PACKAGING; 1244]

overpass *type of* **bridge.** [➡BRIDGES, TUNNELS, CROSSINGS, AND JUNCTIONS; 1111]

overpitch *v* **exaggerate**, overdo, overcompensate, overplay, overemphasize, overstress, make too much of, overstate, give too much weight to. [➡OVERDO SOMETHING; 291]

overplay *v* **overemphasize**, exaggerate, overdo, overstress, overstate. [➡CLAIM, INSIST, AND EMPHASIZE; 615] *Opposite:* underplay.

overpower 1 *v* **subdue**, override, suppress, subjugate, conquer, subsume, stretch, defeat, overcome, overdevelop, overdraw, master, prevail. [➡BEAT AND DEFEAT; 80] *Opposite:* yield. 2 *v* **overwhelm**, overshadow, floor, overcome, dumbfound, daze, stagger, stun, overawe, throw (*informal*). [➡UPSET, DISTRESS, AND HUMILIATE; 568]

overpowered *adj* [➡BEATEN AND DEFEATED; 78]

overpowering *adj* **overwhelming**, intense, overriding, uncontrollable, consuming, unbearable, overshadowing, strong. [➡STRENGTH; 202] *Opposite:* weak.

overpoweringly *adv* **irresistibly**, overwhelmingly, devastatingly, strongly, intensely, extremely, powerfully, distinctly, tremendously, greatly, deeply, keenly, very much, fearsomely, astonishingly, formidably, strikingly, amazingly, awesomely. [➡TO A GREAT EXTENT; 130]

overprice *v* **overrate**, overvalue, hike up, write up, mark up. [➡MONEY, PAYMENTS, AND CHARGES; 800] *Opposite:* underprice.

overpriced *adj* **high-priced**, costly, extortionate, steep (*informal*), expensive, exorbitant, dear, stiff. [➡EXPENSIVE AND OVERPRICED; 248] *Opposite:* cheap.

overprotect *v* **cosset**, fuss over, cocoon, indulge, protect, mollycoddle, baby, coddle, pamper, spoil. [➡OVERDO SOMETHING; 291] *Opposite:* neglect.

overrate *v* **overprize**, overestimate, exaggerate, overvalue. [➡CLAIM, INSIST, AND EMPHASIZE; 615] *Opposite:* underrate.

overrated *adj* **overvalued**, overestimated, hyped, puffed up, glorified. [➡ORDINARINESS; 245] *Opposite:* underrated.

overreach 1 *v* **overdo**, bite off more than you can chew, overstretch, overextend, outreach, strain. [➡OVERDO SOMETHING; 291] 2 *v* **outwit**, outsmart, outfox, outplay, deceive, trick. [➡DECEPTION AND LIES; 661]

overreact *v* **exaggerate**, react excessively, make a big deal, overdramatize, overplay, overstretch, go over the top. [➡OVERDO SOMETHING; 291]

override 1 *v* **disregard**, overrule, defy, flout, countermand, reverse, ignore. [➡NOT PAY ATTENTION; 765] *Opposite:* follow. 2 *v* **supersede**, dominate, prevail, predominate, overrule, outweigh. [➡CHANGE ONE THING FOR ANOTHER; 399]

overriding *adj* **overruling**, superseding, intervening, dominant, prevailing, prime, principal, preponderant, paramount, supreme. [➡MOST IMPORTANT AND MAIN; 194] *Opposite:* insignificant.

overrule 1 *v* **override**, cancel, rule against, refuse, make null and void, annul, reject, disallow, veto. [➡MAKE IMPOSSIBLE; 277] 2 *v* **master**, exercise authority, domineer, pull rank. [➡REFUSE PERMISSION AND NOT ALLOW; 671]

overrun 1 *v* **invade**, attack, assail, assault, besiege, ravage, plunder. [➡PHYSICAL ATTACK AND PUNISHMENT; 416] 2 *adj* **swarming**, infested, teeming, flooded, swamped, choked, clogged, filled. [➡FULL; 1238]

overseas 1 *adj* **foreign**, external, ultramarine (*literary*). [➡COUNTRIES AND REGIONS; 1066] 2 *adv* **abroad**, out of the country, in foreign parts. [➡COUNTRIES AND REGIONS; 1066]

oversee *v* **supervise**, manage, superintend, run, direct, watch over, administer, mastermind, keep an eye on. [➡BE IN CHARGE; 271]

overseer *n* **supervisor**, manager, administrator, chief, boss, superintendent. [➡BOSSES AND MANAGEMENT; 965]

oversell *v* **overpraise**, overvalue, overrate, exaggerate, hype. [➡CLAIM, INSIST, AND EMPHASIZE; 615] *Opposite:* undersell.

oversensitive *adj* **emotional**, thin-skinned, hypersensitive, vulnerable, touchy, prickly (*informal*). [➡EXCESSIVE SENSITIVITY; 512] *Opposite:* thick-skinned.

oversensitivity *n* [➡EXCESSIVE SENSITIVITY; 512]

oversentimental *adj* **slushy**, mawkish, syrupy, maudlin, sad, mushy, overemotional, gooey (*informal*), weepy (*informal*), tearful, emotional, schmaltzy (*informal*). [➡EXCESSIVE SENSITIVITY; 512] *Opposite:* callous.

overshadow *v* **outshine**, outdo, dominate, surpass, eclipse, dwarf, put in the shade, minimize, reduce, detract from. [➡BEAT AND DEFEAT; 80]

overshoot *v* **pass**, exceed, overreach, overpass, overrun, overextend, miss. [➡PROCEED AND GO; 306] *Opposite:* hit.

oversight 1 *n* **mistake**, failure to notice, slip, omission, misunderstanding, error, lapse, inaccuracy, bungle (*informal*), flub (*US slang*). [➡MISTAKES; 251] 2 *n* **supervision**, control, overseeing, management, administration, managing, surveillance. [➡ARRANGE AND CREATE ORDER; 358]

oversimplify *v* **generalize**, overgeneralize, simplify, distort. [➡OVERDO SOMETHING; 291] *Opposite:* complicate.

oversize *adj* **oversized**, king-size, extra large, large, huge, monster, gigantic, extremely large, enormous, gargantuan, colossal, massive, maxi. [➡LARGE; 1192]

oversized *see* **oversize.**

oversleep *v* **sleep in**, sleep late, lie in (*informal*). [➡SLEEP AND DREAM; 724]

overspill 1 *n* **flood**, overflow, runoff, excess, surplus, extra. [➡TOO MUCH; 118] 2 *v* **spill over**, overflow, brim over, pour out, flood, run over. [➡EMPTY AND UNLOAD; 408]

overstate *v* **exaggerate**, make too much of, overdo, overstress, overemphasize, overplay. [➡CLAIM, INSIST, AND EMPHASIZE; 615] *Opposite:* understate.

overstated *adj* **exaggerated**, extravagant, excessive, inflated, overelaborate, loud, blown up, flamboyant, larger-than-life, overdone, garish, puffed up, gaudy, overblown, showy, flashy, attention-grabbing, over-the-top (*informal*), overemphasized. [➡IN POOR TASTE; 230] *Opposite:* understated.

overstatement *n* **exaggeration**, hyperbole, overemphasis. [➡CLAIM, INSIST, AND EMPHASIZE; 615] *Opposite:* understatement.

overstay *v* **prolong**, protract, spin out, extend. [➡OVERDO SOMETHING; 291]

overstep 1 *v* **exceed**, go beyond, pass, surpass, step over. [➡OVERDO SOMETHING; 291] 2 *v* **transgress**, violate, disregard, disobey, contravene, break. [➡DISOBEY; 303] *Opposite:* obey.

overstrain *v* **overstretch**, overstress, overreach, overtax, overload, burden, overdo. [➡OVERDO SOMETHING; 291]

overstress 1 *v* **overemphasize**, overplay, overpitch, overstate, overdo, dwell on. [➡CLAIM, INSIST, AND EMPHASIZE; 615] 2 *v* **overstretch**, overstrain, overreach, overtax, overload, burden. [➡GIVE TOO MUCH; 438] 3 *n* **overstating**, overplaying, overdoing, dwelling on, going on about. [➡CLAIM, INSIST, AND EMPHASIZE; 615]

overstretch *v* **overstrain**, overstress, overreach, overtax, overload, overdo, go too far, bite off more than you can chew, strain, tax. [➡OVERDO SOMETHING; 291]

overstretched *adj* [➡IN TROUBLE AND DISADVANTAGED; 73]

overstrung *adj* **nervous**, tense, oversensitive, highly-strung, temperamental, excitable, touchy, emotional, volatile. [➡CONFUSION, ANXIETY, AND WORRY; 541] *Opposite:* placid.

overstuffed *adj* **brimming**, overfilled, brimful, overflowing, bursting at the seams, packed. [➡FULL; 1238] *Opposite:* empty.

oversupply 1 *n* **overflow**, excess, surplus, glut, superfluity, flood, surfeit. [➡TOO MUCH; 118] 2 *v* **glut**, overwhelm, flood, inundate, swamp, saturate. [➡GIVE TOO MUCH; 438]

overt *adj* **obvious**, unconcealed, explicit, evident, open, clear, plain, manifest, blatant, apparent. [➡PERCEPTIBLE; 25] *Opposite:* covert.

overtake 1 *v* **pass**, go beyond, go past, overhaul, leave behind, outdo, surpass, run by, reach. [➡ACCOMPANY AND FOLLOW; 338] *Opposite:* fall behind. 2 *v* **hit**, sweep over, engulf, assail, strike, catch off-guard. [➡UPSET, DISTRESS, AND HUMILIATE; 568]

overtax *v* **strain**, overload, overdo it, overstretch, overstrain, overburden, burn the candle at both ends, overwork, load, overextend, burden, exhaust. [➡GIVE TOO MUCH; 438]

over-the-hill *adj* **old**, past your prime, past your sell-by date, ancient, decrepit (*archaic or humorous*). [➡OLD AGE; 919]

over the moon *adj* **overjoyed**, delighted, thrilled, ecstatic, chuffed (*informal*), exultant, jubilant, glad, pleased, thrilled to bits (*informal*). [➡PLEASURE, EXCITEMENT, AND ELATION; 535]

over-the-top (*informal*) *adj* **exaggerated**, excessive, overdone, extravagant, overblown, OTT (*informal*), melodramatic, theatrical, overemotional, dramatic, overdramatic, histrionic, unrestrained, immoderate (*formal*). [➡TOO MUCH; 118] *Opposite:* understated.

overthrow *v* **conquer**, defeat, dethrone, bring down, depose, oust, topple. [➡BEAT AND DEFEAT; 80] *Opposite:* uphold.

overtime 1 *n* **extra pay**, extra hours, time and a half, additional hours, double time, extra work, bonus, late shift. [➡WORK-RELATED ACTIVITIES; 834] 2 *adv* **energetically**, tirelessly, actively, strenuously, intensely. [➡DIFFICULTY AND COMPLEXITY; 243]

overtness *n* [➡PERCEPTIBLE; 25]

overtone *n* **implication**, association, hint, undertone, connotation, nuance, insinuation, tinge, suggestion. [➡SUGGEST, HINT, AND COMMENT; 613]

overture *type of* **instrumental music**. [➡MUSIC, SONGS, AND SINGING; 907]

overturn 1 *v* **turn over**, knock over, tip over, upend, capsize, upset, keel over (*informal*), spill over, topple. [➡MOVE SOMETHING: INTO A NEW POSITION OR OVERTURN; 331] *Opposite:* right. 2 *v* **nullify**, abolish, invalidate, annul, reverse, throw out, cancel, negate (*formal*), veto, nix (*slang*). [➡MAKE IMPOSSIBLE; 277]

overturned *adj* [➡ORIENTATION AND ALIGNMENT; 1222]

overuse 1 *n* **overemployment**, overdoing, misuse, abuse, overplay. [➡USE UP AND WASTE; 475] 2 *v* **overemploy**, overdo, go to extremes, run riot, misuse, abuse. [➡OVERDO SOMETHING; 291]

overused *adj* **overworked**, clichéd, hackneyed, commonplace, trite, corny, stereotyped. [➡BORING AND UNINTERESTING; 235]

overvalue *v* **overrate**, overprize, overestimate. [➡OVERDO SOMETHING; 291] *Opposite:* undervalue.

overview *n* **indication**, summary, outline, gestalt, synopsis. [➡IDEA AND THOUGHT; 771]

overweening *adj* **arrogant**, conceited, pompous, presumptuous, haughty. [➡BOSSY AND OVERBEARING; 517] *Opposite:* unassuming.

overweight *adj* **overheavy**, heavy, big, large, weighty, cumbersome, bulky. [➡BUILD; 478] *Opposite:* underweight.

overwhelm *v* **overpower**, overcome, engulf, devastate, crush, rout, overthrow, annihilate, beat. [➡BEAT AND DEFEAT; 80]

overwhelmed 1 *adj* **overcome**, overawed, speechless, dazed, stunned, incredulous, flabbergasted (*informal*), astounded, gobsmacked (*slang*), amazed, dumbfounded, knocked for six (*informal*). [➡SURPRISE, SHOCK, AND AMAZEMENT; 546] *Opposite:* unimpressed. 2 *adj* **overpowered physically**, overcome, beaten, conquered, crushed, subjugated, routed, vanquished, trounced. [➡BEATEN AND DEFEATED; 78] 3 *adj* **inundated**, snowed under, swamped, flooded, exhausted. [➡SADNESS, DISTRESS, AND DESPAIR; 540]

overwhelming *adj* **irresistible**, overpowering, devastating, crushing, awe-inspiring, awesome, prodigious, vast, great, tremendous. [➡STRENGTH; 202] *Opposite:* insignificant.

overwhelmingly *adv* **overpoweringly**, devastatingly,

crushingly, prodigiously, tremendously, awesomely. [➡TO A GREAT EXTENT; 130] *Opposite:* insignificantly.

overwinter *v* **hibernate**, lie dormant, stagnate, vegetate, lie fallow, hole up (*slang*), hide away. [➡CONTINUE TO EXIST; 17]

overwork *v* **burn the midnight oil**, overdo it, overburden, overtax, overtask, overextend, overstrain, overload, burn the candle at both ends. [➡HARD WORK OR EFFORT; 299]

overworked *adj* [➡IN TROUBLE AND DISADVANTAGED; 73]

overwrought *adj* **tense**, stressed, distraught, emotional, strained, overexcited, excitable, jumpy, fidgety, touchy, nervous, highly-strung. [➡CONFUSION, ANXIETY, AND WORRY; 541] *Opposite:* calm.

ovoid *adj* [➡ROUNDED SHAPE; 1217]

ovule *n* [➡EGGS AND SPAWN; 728]

ovum *n* [➡EGGS AND SPAWN; 728]

owe *v* **be beholden**, be obligated. [➡OWE AND DESERVE; 466] *Opposite:* repay.

owed *adj* **owing**, unpaid, outstanding, due, payable, remaining, unsettled, in arrears, in the red. [➡OWE AND DESERVE; 466] *Opposite:* paid.

owing *adj* **in arrears**, owed, due, in the red. [➡OWE AND DESERVE; 466] *Opposite:* paid.

owing to *prep* **because of**, due to, on account of, thanks to, as a result of, in consequence of (*formal*). [➡CAUSATION; 169]

owl

◆ *types of owl*
barn owl, fish owl, hoot owl, little owl, long-eared owl, screech owl, short-eared owl, snowy owl, tawny owl

owlet *type of* **young bird.** [➡YOUNG BIRD; 1004]

owlish *adj* **owl-like**, serious, wise, solemn, bespectacled, myopic. [➡FACIAL CHARACTERISTICS; 482]

owl-like *adj* [➡FACIAL CHARACTERISTICS; 482]

own 1 *adj* **individual**, private, particular, peculiar, specific, identifiable, personal. [➡BELONGING OR RELATING TO INDIVIDUALS; 944] 2 *v* **possess**, have, have possession of, keep, retain, preserve, maintain, hold, be in possession of. [➡POSSESS; 445] 3 *v* (*formal*) **confess**, admit, own up, acknowledge, profess, express, utter, declare, accept, concede. [➡ADMIT AND CONFESS; 616] *Opposite:* deny.

owner *n* **proprietor**, landlord, possessor, holder, title-holder, vendor. [➡OWNERS; 447]

ownership *n* **possession**, rights, tenure, title, proprietorship. [➡POSSESS; 445]

own goal *n* **self-defeating action**, blunder, mistake, misjudgment, miscalculation, slip up (*informal*), faux pas (*literary*). [➡MISTAKES; 251]

own up *v* **confess**, admit, profess, carry the can (*informal*), express, utter, declare. [➡ADMIT AND CONFESS; 616]

ox *n* **bull**, bullock, steer. [➡FARM ANIMAL; 982]

oxblood *type of* **red.** [➡COLOURS; 1223]

oxford *type of* **shoe.** [➡FOOTWEAR; 871]

oxidation *n* [➡GO BAD AND CORRODE; 391]

oxidization *n* **reaction**, rust, tarnishing, corrosion, verdigris, decomposition. [➡GO BAD AND CORRODE; 391]

oxidize *v* **react**, rust, tarnish, corrode, dissolve, flake, crumble. [➡GO BAD AND CORRODE; 391]

oxygen *type of* **gas.** [➡GASES; 1274]

oxymoron *n* [➡ASPECTS OF LANGUAGE; 683]

oyster 1 *type of* **white.** [➡COLOURS; 1223] 2 *type of* **aquatic invertebrate.** [➡AQUATIC INVERTEBRATE; 1022]

oystercatcher *type of* **seabird.** [➡SEABIRD; 1002]

oyster mushroom *type of* **fungus.** [➡MICROORGANISMS, FUNGI, AND ALGAE; 1023]

ozonosphere *n* [➡THE EARTH'S ATMOSPHERE; 1040]

P

P2P *adv* [➡E-COMMERCE; 1128]

PA *n* **public-address system**, loudspeaker, speaker, amplifier, amp. [➡AUDIO EQUIPMENT; 1138]

pace 1 *n* **speed**, rapidity, swiftness, velocity, rate of knots. [➡SPEED; 102] 2 *n* **rate**, speed, tempo, time, regularity, frequency. [➡SPEED; 102] 3 *n* **step**, stride, leap, bound, hop, skip, jump. [➡PROCEED AND GO; 306] 4 *v* **walk**, stride, march, walk back and forth, walk up and down, walk to and fro, patrol, wander. [➡PROCEED AND GO; 306] 5 *v* **govern**, regulate, restrict, manage, limit, control, monitor. [➡BE IN CHARGE; 271]

pacemaker *n* **leader**, pacesetter, pacer, innovator, trendsetter, leading light, modernizer, pioneer. [➡IMPORTANT OR FAMOUS PEOPLE; 893]

pacific 1 *adj* **soothing**, appeasing, conciliatory, comforting, placatory. [➡EMOTIONALLY PLEASANT; 188] *Opposite:* antagonistic. 2 *adj* **tranquil**, peaceful, calm, untroubled, gentle, relaxing. [➡PEACEFULNESS AND GENTLENESS; 215] *Opposite:* violent.

pacifist 1 *n* **peace lover**, conscientious objector, dove, peacemaker, peacekeeper. [➡PHILOSOPHICAL AND POLITICAL THINKERS; 782] 2 *adj* **pacific**, appeasing, conciliatory, placatory, comforting, soothing. [➡EMOTIONALLY PLEASANT; 188] *Opposite:* antagonistic.

pacify *v* **calm**, soothe, mollify, placate, calm down, appease. [➡SOOTHE AND CALM; 574] *Opposite:* antagonize.

pack 1 *v* **store**, arrange, put, place, sort, put away. [➡ARRANGE AND CREATE ORDER; 358] 2 *v* **package**, wrap, wrap up, box, bundle, parcel. [➡DECORATE, ADORN, AND APPLY COATINGS; 406] *Opposite:* unpack. 3 *v* **fill**, cram, stuff, jam, load, cover. [➡FILL; 407] 4 *v* **compact**, press, compress, squash, flatten, tamp. [➡CONTACT: EXERT PRESSURE; 415] 5 *n* **carton**, packet, box, parcel, container, drum, package. [➡CONTAINERS, RECEPTACLES, AND PACKAGING; 1244] 6 *n* **folder**, packet, wallet, dossier, file, portfolio. [➡CONTAINERS, RECEPTACLES, AND PACKAGING; 1244] 7 *n* **set**, bunch, group, quantity, collection, bundle, wad. [➡COLLECTIONS AND MIXTURES OF THINGS; 1243] 8 *n* **bag**, rucksack, backpack, haversack, daypack, bundle. [➡CONTAINERS, RECEPTACLES, AND PACKAGING; 1244] 9 *n* **crowd**, horde, mob, gang, bunch, group, herd, flock, army. [➡GROUPS OF PEOPLE; 935] 10 *type of* **herd**. [➡GROUP OF ANIMALS; 993]

package 1 *n* **parcel**, packet, box, envelope, file, wallet. [➡CONTAINERS, RECEPTACLES, AND PACKAGING; 1244] 2 *n* **set**, bundle, suite, raft, compendium, platform, file, array. [➡COLLECTIONS AND MIXTURES OF THINGS; 1243] 3 *v* **pack**, wrap, wrap up, parcel, box, bundle. [➡DECORATE, ADORN, AND APPLY COATINGS; 406] *Opposite:* unwrap. 4 *v* **promote**, present, market, advertise, put across, portray. [➡BUSINESS ACTIVITIES AND PHENOMENA; 795]

packaging *n* **wrapping**, packing, wrapper, packet, box, bag, pack, container. [➡CONTAINERS, RECEPTACLES, AND PACKAGING; 1244]

packed *adj* **crowded**, crammed, full, full to capacity, heaving, filled, bursting, overflowing, jam-packed (*informal*), chock-full (*informal*), chock-a-block (*informal*). [➡FULL; 1238] *Opposite:* empty.

packet *n* **pack**, package, sachet, container, carton, envelope, wallet, box. [➡CONTAINERS, RECEPTACLES, AND PACKAGING; 1244]

packhorse *type of* **horse**. [➡HORSE; 985]

pack in 1 *v* **attract**, interest, excite, fill the seats, be a box office success. [➡APPEAL TO AND AROUSE INTEREST; 576]. *Opposite:* flop (*informal*). 2 *v* (*informal*) **stop**, give up, quit, abandon, drop, ditch (*informal*), dump (*informal*). [➡STOP ACTING; 265] *Opposite:* take up.

packing *n* **stuffing**, filling, filler, wadding, padding. [➡CENTRAL PARTS OF PHYSICAL OBJECTS; 1250]

pack up 1 *v* **stop**, give up, quit, abandon, drop, cease. [➡STOP ACTING; 265] *Opposite:* start. 2 *v* (*informal*) **stop working**, break down, conk out (*informal*), go on the blink (*informal*), fail, give up the ghost (*literary*), seize, jam, die. [➡FAIL OR CEASE TO FUNCTION; 471]

pact *n* **deal**, agreement, treaty, contract, accord, concord, concordat, settlement, compact. [➡PROMISE AND ASSURE; 685]

pad 1 *n* **cushion**, cloth, wad, swab, plug (*informal*), pack. [➡CENTRAL PARTS OF PHYSICAL OBJECTS; 1250] 2 *n* **notepad**, sketchpad, notebook, jotter, sketchbook. [➡WRITING AND DRAWING IMPLEMENTS, AND MEDIA; 602] 3 *n* (*slang dated*) **place**, house, flat, bedsit, lodgings (*dated*), apartment (*US*). [➡ACCOMMODATION; 855] 4 *n* (*US*) **mat**, place mat, coaster, doily, table mat. [➡SOFT FURNISHINGS, LINEN, AND DRAPERY; 860] 5 *v* **creep**, tiptoe, steal, walk, sneak. [➡MOVE SLOWLY; 315] 6 *v* **line**, cover, fill, stuff, wad, cushion, lag, protect. [➡IMPROVE STRENGTH AND DURABILITY; 379] 7 *v* **fill out**, flesh out, amplify, lengthen, expand, stretch out, embellish. [➡CHANGE OF SIZE: BIGGER; 393] 8 *type of* **sports equipment**. [➡SPORTS EQUIPMENT; 879]

padding 1 *n* **stuffing**, filling, wadding, lining, packing, packaging, insulation. [➡CENTRAL PARTS OF PHYSICAL OBJECTS; 1250] 2 *n* **waffle** (*informal*), verbiage, gobbledegook (*informal disapproving*), circumlocution, periphrasis, garbage, rubbish. [➡MEANINGLESS SPEECH OR WRITING; 677]

paddle 1 *n* **oar**, scull, sweep, blade. [➡PARTS OF A SHIP OR BOAT; 1150] 2 *v* **row**, scull, propel. [➡TRAVEL: WAYS OF TRAVELLING; 321]

paddock *n* [➡THE COUNTRYSIDE AND OUTDOOR SPACES; 1070]

paddy (*informal*) *n* [➡CRITICISMS AND ANGRY OUTBURSTS; 50]

padlock *n* [➡FASTENERS, LINKS, AND NETWORKS; 1246]

pad out *v* [➡FILL; 407]

padre *n* [➡RELIGIOUS PEOPLE; 779]

paella *type of* **cooked dish**. [➡PREPARED DISHES; 1169]

page 1 *n* **sheet**, piece of paper, sheet of paper, side, leaf, folio. [➡WRITING AND DRAWING IMPLEMENTS, AND MEDIA; 602] **2** *v* **call**, contact, bleep, summon. [➡TELEPHONE AND PAGE; 682]

pageant *n* **procession**, parade, cavalcade, display, carnival, spectacle, show, play. [➡PARTIES, DANCES, AND CELEBRATIONS; 37]

pageantry *n* **spectacle**, display, pomp, ceremony, ritual, tradition. [➡PARTIES, DANCES, AND CELEBRATIONS; 37]

pageboy *type of* **hairstyle**. [➡HAIR STYLES AND HAIR PIECES; 489]

pager *type of* **telecommunications equipment**. [➡TELECOMMUNICATIONS; 1129]

paid *adj* **waged**, salaried, professional, funded. [➡TYPES OF WORK; 835] *Opposite:* unpaid.

pail *n* [➡CONTAINERS, RECEPTACLES, AND PACKAGING; 1244]

pain **1** *n* **discomfort**, agony, aching, hurt, ache, sting, soreness, throbbing, smarting, stinging, twinge. [➡PAIN AND OTHER PHYSICAL SENSATIONS; 734] *Opposite:* pleasure. **2** *n* **grief**, sorrow, anguish, ache, torture, agony, heartache. [➡SADNESS, DISTRESS, AND DESPAIR; 540] *Opposite:* joy. **3** *n* (*informal*) **nuisance**, bother, drag (*informal*), bind, pest (*informal*), menace. [➡NUISANCES; 254] *Opposite:* pleasure. **4** *v* **sadden**, distress, upset, disturb, grieve, displease, worry. [➡UPSET, DISTRESS, AND HUMILIATE; 568] *Opposite:* hearten.

pained *adj* **hurt**, aggrieved, indignant, wounded, injured, disappointed. [➡SADNESS, DISTRESS, AND DESPAIR; 540]

painful **1** *adj* **tender**, aching, raw, throbbing, excruciating, hurting, agonizing, burning, sore, uncomfortable. [➡PAIN AND OTHER PHYSICAL SENSATIONS; 734] *Opposite:* painless. **2** *adj* **sorrowful**, distressing, anguished, heartbreaking, upsetting, harrowing, heartrending. [➡EMOTIONALLY UNPLEASANT AND UPSETTING; 228] *Opposite:* pleasant. **3** *adj* **laborious**, troublesome, awkward, laboured, tedious, slow. [➡DIFFICULTY AND COMPLEXITY; 243] *Opposite:* easy. **4** *adj* **awful**, excruciating, dire, dreadful, agonizing, embarrassing, terrible. [➡BAD AND BADLY; 224] *Opposite:* wonderful.

painfully **1** *adv* **agonizingly**, uncomfortably, excruciatingly, terribly, awfully, horribly. [➡PHYSICALLY UNPLEASANT; 227] **2** *adv* **distressingly**, uncomfortably, upsettingly, harrowingly, agonizingly, disturbingly. [➡EMOTIONALLY UNPLEASANT AND UPSETTING; 228] *Opposite:* pleasantly. **3** *adv* **laboriously**, with difficulty, awkwardly, stiffly. [➡MOVING SLOWLY; 105] *Opposite:* easily. **4** *adv* **excruciatingly**, agonizingly, embarrassingly, hideously, grotesquely. [➡BAD AND BADLY; 224] *Opposite:* wonderfully.

pain in the neck (*informal*) *n* [➡NUISANCES; 254]

painkiller *n* **analgesic**, sedative, anaesthetic, drug. [➡REMEDIES, TREATMENTS AND OPERATIONS; 732]

painkilling *adj* **analgesic**, calming, sedative, deadening, numbing, palliative, soothing. [➡PHYSICALLY PLEASANT; 187]

painless *adj* **effortless**, easy, trouble-free, simple, unproblematic, straightforward. [➡EASE AND SIMPLICITY; 201] *Opposite:* problematic.

pains *n* **care**, effort, trouble, lengths. [➡HARD WORK OR EFFORT; 299]

painstaking *adj* **thorough**, careful, meticulous, conscientious, scrupulous, particular, assiduous. [➡HARD-WORKING AND COMMITTED; 501] *Opposite:* careless.

See Compare and Contrast at **careful**.

paint **1** *v* **coat**, decorate, smear, daub, splatter, undercoat, brush. [➡DECORATE, ADORN, AND APPLY COATINGS; 406] **2** *v* **portray**, render (*formal*), capture, catch, show. [➡NAME AND DESCRIBE; 666]

painted lady *type of* **butterfly**. [➡MOTHS AND BUTTERFLIES; 1015]

painter *n* **artist**, watercolourist, portraitist, miniaturist. [➡ARTISTS; 900]

painting **1** *n* **picture**, work of art, image, canvas, watercolour, oil painting, landscape, portrait, still life. [➡ARTWORKS; 898] **2** *n* **art**, fine art, portraiture, landscape, watercolour, oils, acrylics. [➡THE PICTORIAL ARTS; 897]

paint the town red (*informal*) *v* **celebrate**, have a good time, have fun, whoop it up (*informal*), party (*informal*), revel, large it (*informal*), go out, socialize, live it up (*slang*), let your hair down, go out on the town (*informal*), have a night on the town, have a ball (*dated slang*). [➡LEISURE AND RECREATION; 874]

pair **1** *n* **couple**, duo, twosome, brace, set. [➡AMOUNT AND QUANTITY; 112] **2** *v* **pair off**, team up, join up, match up, put together, combine. [➡CREATING CONNECTIONS; 145] *Opposite:* separate.

paisley *n* [➡PATTERNS; 1224]

pal (*informal*) *n* **friend**, mate, chum (*informal*), comrade, crony (*disapproving*), buddy (*US informal*). [➡FRIENDS; 963]

palace *n* [➡RESIDENTIAL BUILDINGS; 1077]

palatable **1** *adj* **edible**, pleasant, tasty, appetizing, toothsome, delicious. [➡TASTE; 704] *Opposite:* inedible. **2** *adj* **acceptable**, agreeable, satisfactory, pleasant, passable. [➡ACCEPTABLE AND PASSABLE; 220] *Opposite:* disagreeable.

palate *part of* **mouth**. [➡THE MOUTH; 703]

palatial *adj* **luxurious**, lavish, grand, impressive, splendid, regal, extravagant, opulent. [➡EXPENSIVE AND LUXURIOUS; 219] *Opposite:* miserable.

palaver **1** *n* **fuss**, bother, trouble, nuisance, hassle (*informal*), commotion, uproar, to-do (*informal*). [➡CHAOS AND UPROAR; 51] **2** *n* **chatter**, chat, chitchat (*informal*), nattering (*informal*), gossip, talk. [➡INFORMAL COMMUNICATION; 45]

pale **1** *adj* **light**, pastel, soft, whitish, insipid, watery, wishy-washy (*informal*). [➡DESCRIBING COLOURS; 1225] *Opposite:* dark. **2** *adj* **pallid**, fair, colourless, ashen, white, pasty, sallow, anaemic, wan. [➡COMPLEXION; 481] **3** *v* **diminish**, reduce, recede, lessen, fade. [➡CHANGE OF INTENSITY: LESS; 396] *Opposite:* intensify. **4** *adj* **faint**, dim, feeble, weak, watery. [➡DESCRIBING LIGHT; 1227] *Opposite:* strong. **5** *v* **go white**, whiten, go pale, blanch, bleach. [➡CHANGE OF COLOUR; 392] *Opposite:* colour. **6** *v* **fade**, lose colour, become washed out, soften, lighten. [➡CHANGE OF COLOUR; 392] *Opposite:* deepen.

palimpsest *n* [➡BOOKS AND BOOKLETS; 591]

palindrome *type of* **wordplay**. [➡JOKES AND TEASING; 675]

paling *n* [➡BARRIERS; 1112]

palisade *n* [➡BARRIERS; 1112]

pall 1 *v* **lose its attraction**, fade, diminish, wither, go sour, outstay its welcome. [➡GET WORSE; 382] 2 *n* **cloud**, blanket, shroud, sheet, wall, column. [➡AMOUNT OF GAS; 116] 3 *n* **gloom**, despair, sadness, depression, melancholy, despondency. [➡NUISANCES; 254]

Palladian *type of* **pre-20th-century architecture**. [➡BUILDING AND ARCHITECTURE; 1075]

pallbearer *n* [➡BURIAL AND PREPARATION FOR BURIAL; 929]

pallet *n* [➡SOFT FURNISHINGS, LINEN, AND DRAPERY; 860]

palliasse *n* [➡SOFT FURNISHINGS, LINEN, AND DRAPERY; 860]

palliate *v* [➡IMPROVE SOMETHING; 375]

palliation *n* [➡IMPROVE SOMETHING; 375]

palliative 1 *adj* **analgesic**, painkilling, anaesthetic, sedative. [➡PHYSICALLY PLEASANT; 187] 2 *adj* **soothing**, calming, relaxing, comforting, mollifying, reassuring. [➡CALMING; 189]

pallid *adj* **pale**, white, ashen, pasty, colourless, sallow, anaemic, wan. [➡COMPLEXION; 481] *Opposite:* dark.

pallor *n* **paleness**, whiteness, pastiness, wanness, sallowness. [➡COMPLEXION; 481]

pally (*informal*) *adj* [➡RELATIONSHIP TO ANOTHER; 973]

palm *part of* **arm or hand**. [➡ARM AND HAND; 696]

palmcorder *type of* **video equipment**. [➡PHOTOGRAPHY AND PHOTOGRAPHIC EQUIPMENT; 1121]

palm off *v* [➡GIVE TOO MUCH; 438]

palmtop *type of* **computer**. [➡COMPUTERS AND COMPUTING; 1126]

palpability *n* [➡PERCEPTIBLE; 25]

palpable 1 *adj* **intense**, tangible, physical, real, deep, profound, substantial. [➡PERCEPTIBLE; 25] *Opposite:* intangible. 2 *adj* **obvious**, clear, demonstrable, unmistakable, evident, self-evident, unambiguous, definite. [➡PERCEPTIBLE; 25] *Opposite:* hidden.

palpitate *v* **flutter**, pound, race, tremble, quiver, twitch. [➡PHYSICAL REACTIONS; 317]

paltriness *n* [➡TOO FEW, TOO LITTLE; 120]

paltry 1 *adj* **worthless**, measly (*informal*), trivial, trifling, miserable, insignificant. [➡TOO FEW, TOO LITTLE; 120] *Opposite:* substantial. 2 *adj* **despicable**, wretched, mean, miserable, contemptible, low, poor, base. [➡UNACCEPTABLE AND UNFORGIVEABLE; 226]

pampas *n* [➡DESERTS AND PLAINS; 1045]

pampas grass *type of* **grass**. [➡GRASS; 1031]

pamper *v* **spoil**, indulge, coddle, mollycoddle, cosset, baby, treat. [➡TAKE CARE OF AND SPOIL; 301]

pamphlet *n* **leaflet**, brochure, booklet, guide, tract, fact sheet. [➡BOOKS AND BOOKLETS; 591]

pan 1 *n* **pot**, saucepan, casserole, wok, frying pan, skillet, pressure cooker. [➡TABLEWARE, CUTLERY, AND KITCHENWARE; 861] 2 *v* (*informal*) **criticize**, slate, slam (*informal*), roast (*informal*), berate, disparage, deride. [➡ACCUSE, BLAME, AND CRITICIZE; 642] *Opposite:* praise.

panacea *n* **cure-all**, cure, solution, answer, remedy, magic potion, magic bullet. [➡SOLUTION; 216]

panache *n* **flair**, flamboyance, style, élan (*literary*), spirit, confidence, elegance. [➡ENERGY AND ENTHUSIASM; 497] *Opposite:* awkwardness.

Panama hat *type of* **hat**. [➡HABERDASHERY, MILLINERY, AND LINGERIE; 867]

pancake

◆ *types of pancake*
blini, blintz, crêpe, drop scone, flapjack (*US*), griddlecake, hotcake (*US*), johnnycake (*US*), battercake (*US*), waffle

pancreas *part of* **digestive tract**. [➡THE DIGESTIVE TRACT; 710]

panda *type of* **large mammal**. [➡LARGE MAMMAL; 986]

panda car (*informal*) *type of* **public service vehicle**. [➡VEHICLES; 1144]

pandemic *n* **epidemic**, plague, contagion, sickness, disease, illness. [➡SICKNESS; 730]

pandemonium *n* **chaos**, mayhem (*informal*), bedlam, racket (*informal*), uproar, hubbub. [➡CHAOS AND UPROAR; 51]

pander to *v* **indulge**, satisfy, gratify, bow to, go along with, be a slave to. [➡ESTABLISHING RELATIONSHIPS WITH OTHERS; 974] *Opposite:* resist.

pane *n* **windowpane**, glass, window, sheet, panel, piece. [➡WINDOWS; 1099]

panegyric (*formal*) *n* [➡NEUTRAL ONE-WAY COMMUNICATION; 49]

panegyrize (*formal*) *v* [➡AGREE; 646]

panel 1 *n* **piece**, board, pane, sheet, plate, section, square, rectangle. [➡AREA AND RANGE; 111] 2 *n* **board**, team, jury, group, council, committee. [➡GROUPS OF PEOPLE; 935]

pan-fry *v* [➡COOKING AND FOOD PREPARATION; 354]

pang *n* **twinge**, spasm, paroxysm, shooting pain, cramp, stitch, pain, wrench. [➡PAIN AND OTHER PHYSICAL SENSATIONS; 734]

panhandler (*US*) *n* [➡POOR PEOPLE; 896]

panic 1 *n* **fear**, anxiety, fright, terror, dread, alarm, horror. [➡FEAR AND PANIC; 544] *Opposite:* calm. 2 *v* **be frightened**, be terrified, lose your nerve, lose it (*informal*), go to pieces, get flustered, freak out (*informal*), freak (*slang*). [➡GIVING VENT TO EMOTIONS; 680] *Opposite:* calm down. 3 *v* **terrify**, unnerve, scare, frighten, fluster, throw into disarray, spook, rattle. [➡FRIGHTEN AND SHOCK; 569]

panicked *adj* [➡FEAR AND PANIC; 544]

panicky *adj* **frightened**, scared, alarmed, fearful, anxious, unnerved, jumpy, edgy. [➡FEAR AND PANIC; 544] *Opposite:* calm.

panic-stricken *adj* **terrified**, unnerved, frightened, fearful, scared out of your wits, shocked. [➡FEAR AND PANIC; 544] *Opposite:* calm.

pannier *type of* **baggage**. [➡CONTAINERS, RECEPTACLES, AND PACKAGING; 1244]

panoply *n* **display**, array, show, parade, exhibition. [➡COLLECTIONS AND MIXTURES OF THINGS; 1243]

panorama *n* **view**, scene, vista, outlook, landscape, prospect. [➡VIEWS AND OUTLOOKS; 1072]

pan out (*informal*) *v* **turn out**, work out, develop, end up, resolve itself, conclude, end. [➡HAPPEN; 27]

panpipes *type of* **wind instrument**. [➡MUSICAL INSTRUMENTS; 910]

pansy *type of* **annual flower**. [➡FLOWERS; 1032]

pant *v* **gasp**, puff, wheeze, blow, gasp for air, huff. [➡BREATHE AND NOT BREATHE; 717]

pantheism *n* [➡PHILOSOPHIES AND BELIEFS; 781]

panther *type of* **cat**. [➡FELINE; 983]

panties (*informal*) *type of* **lower body underwear**. [➡HABERDASHERY, MILLINERY, AND LINGERIE; 867]

pantomime (*informal*) *n* **farce**, joke, rigmarole, drama. [➡JOKES AND TEASING; 675]

pantry *type of* **storage space**. [➡STORES AND STORAGE BUILDINGS; 1087]

pants *type of* **lower body underwear**. [➡HABERDASHERY, MILLINERY, AND LINGERIE; 867]

pantsuit (*US*) *type of* **suit**. [➡GARMENTS AND OUTFITS; 865]

pantyhose (*US*) *type of* **lower body underwear**. [➡HABERDASHERY, MILLINERY, AND LINGERIE; 867]

pap *n* **drivel**, nonsense, rubbish, trash, garbage, dreck (*US*). [➡MEANINGLESS SPEECH OR WRITING; 677]

papa (*informal dated*) *n* [➡OLDER GENERATION RELATIVES; 959]

paparazzo *n* [➡WORKERS IN ENTERTAINMENT AND MEDIA; 873]

papaya *type of* **fruit**. [➡FRUIT AND VEGETABLES; 1175]

paper 1 *n* **newspaper**, daily, weekly, broadsheet, tabloid, rag (*informal*), red-top (*informal*), broadside (*US*). [➡NEWSPAPERS; 606] 2 *n* **document**, manuscript, thesis, dissertation, essay, article, piece, lecture, term paper (*US*). [➡ANALYTICAL NONFICTION WRITING; 593]

paperback *n* **book**, softback, softcover, novel. [➡BOOKS AND BOOKLETS; 591]

paperclip *n* [➡FASTENERS, LINKS, AND NETWORKS; 1246]

paperknife *type of* **knife**. [➡CUTTING TOOLS; 1119]

paper over 1 *v* **wallpaper**, cover, cover up, obscure, disguise, hide. [➡DECORATE, ADORN, AND APPLY COATINGS; 406] *Opposite:* strip. 2 *v* **conceal**, sweep under the carpet, hide, cover up, make light of, minimize. [➡CAUSE TO DISAPPEAR; 6] *Opposite:* highlight.

paper-pusher (*informal*) *n* [➡WORKER; 836]

paper-thin *adj* [➡WIDTH: NARROW AND THIN; 1199]

paperwork *n* **form-filling**, accounts, bookkeeping, correspondence, administration, filing. [➡WORK-RELATED ACTIVITIES; 834]

papery *adj* **flimsy**, frail, thin, paper-thin, delicate, dry, diaphanous. [➡FRAGILE; 1208]

paprika *type of* **spice**. [➡HERBS AND SPICES; 1174]

papyrus *n* [➡WRITING AND DRAWING IMPLEMENTS, AND MEDIA; 602]

par *n* **average**, standard, norm, the usual. [➡MATHS; 598]

parable *n* **allegory**, fable, moral tale, folk tale, tale, legend, story. [➡THE ORAL TRADITION; 678]

parade 1 *n* **procession**, pageant, cavalcade, display, carnival, spectacle, line. [➡PARTIES, DANCES, AND CELEBRATIONS; 37] 2 *v* **process**, march, file, strut, turn out. [➡PROCEED AND GO; 306] 3 *v* **show off**, exhibit, display, trumpet, flaunt, flourish. [➡CAUSE TO APPEAR; 5] *Opposite:* hide. 4 *v* **walk**, stalk, march, strut, stroll, posture. [➡PROCEED AND GO; 306] *Opposite:* skulk. 5 *type of* **minor road**. [➡ROADS; 1105]

paradiddle *n* [➡IMPACT SOUNDS; 1259]

paradigm 1 *n* **model**, template, prototype, standard, pattern, example. [➡PERFECT EXAMPLES AND EMBODIMENTS; 67] 2 *n* **epitome**, archetype, model, exemplar (*literary*), example. [➡PERFECT EXAMPLES AND EMBODIMENTS; 67] *Opposite:* antithesis.

paradise 1 *n* **heaven**, bliss, cloud nine, ecstasy, seventh heaven, nirvana, utopia, El Dorado. [➡RELIGIOUS CONCEPTS; 777] *Opposite:* hell. 2 *n* (*informal*) **dreamworld**, wonderland, heaven, happy hunting ground, ideal. [➡NON-EXISTENT PLACE; 1065] *Opposite:* nightmare.

paradisiac *adj* [➡PHYSICALLY PLEASANT; 187]

paradox *n* **inconsistency**, absurdity, irony, contradiction, contradiction in terms, oxymoron, enigma, puzzle. [➡SECRETS AND MYSTERIES; 181]

paradoxical *adj* **inconsistent**, absurd, ironic, contradictory, illogical, impossible, enigmatic, puzzling. [➡BIZARRE AND PECULIAR; 258] *Opposite:* logical.

paradoxically 1 *adv* **illogically**, absurdly, inconsistently, puzzlingly, unexpectedly, in contradiction. [➡BIZARRE AND PECULIAR; 258] *Opposite:* logically. 2 *adv* **strangely enough**, oddly enough, funnily enough, surprisingly, ironically, bizarrely, in actual fact. [➡EXPRESSIONS OF SURPRISE; 547]

paraffin *n* [➡ENERGY SOURCES; 1161]

paraffin oil *n* [➡ENERGY SOURCES; 1161]

paraglider *type of* **civil aircraft**. [➡AIRCRAFT; 1147]

paragon *n* **model**, shining example, epitome, archetype, quintessence, paradigm, exemplar (*literary*), ideal. [➡PERFECT EXAMPLES AND EMBODIMENTS; 67]

paragraph 1 *n* **section**, subsection, passage, part, clause. [➡ASPECTS OF LANGUAGE; 683] 2 *n* **article**, piece, item, story, editorial, column. [➡PARTS OF BOOKS AND DOCUMENTS; 594]

parakeet *type of* **pet bird**. [➡BIRD; 997]

parallel 1 *adj* **similar**, equivalent, corresponding, analogous, matching, comparable. [➡EQUALITY; 155] *Opposite:* dissimilar. **2** *n* **counterpart**, match, equal, equivalent, peer, twin, like. [➡ EQUALITY; 155] *Opposite:* opposite. **3** *n* **similarity**, correspondence, equivalence, resemblance, analogy, comparison, congruence. [➡ EQUALITY; 155] *Opposite:* dissimilarity.

parallelogram *type of* **angular shape.** [➡ ANGULAR SHAPE; 1216]

paralyse *v* [➡ MAKE IMPOSSIBLE; 277]

paralytic (*informal*) *adj* [➡ UNDER THE INFLUENCE OF DRUGS OR ALCOHOL; 742]

parameter *n* **limit**, stricture (*formal*), boundary, limitation, restriction, constraint, bound, factor, consideration. [➡ DEGREE AND EXTENT; 110]

paramilitary **1** *adj* **guerrilla**, rebel, revolutionary, terrorist. [➡ MILITARY; 829] **2** *n* **rebel**, revolutionary, terrorist, guerrilla, fighter, partisan, soldier. [➡ MILITARY PERSONNEL; 828]

paramount *adj* **supreme**, utmost, dominant, chief, principal, top, overriding, vital. [➡ MOST IMPORTANT AND MAIN; 194] *Opposite:* minimal.

paramour (*literary*) *n* [➡ SEXUAL AND ROMANTIC RELATIONSHIPS; 964]

paranoia *n* **fear**, suspicion, mistrust, distrust, obsession, terror. [➡ FEARS AND PHOBIAS; 555] *Opposite:* confidence.

paranoid *adj* **suspicious**, fearful, mistrustful, distrustful, obsessed, unreasonable. [➡ INSECURITY AND LOSS OF COMPOSURE; 545] *Opposite:* trusting.

paranormal *adj* [➡ THE SUPERNATURAL; 788]

parapet *n* [➡ PARTS OF FORTRESSES; 1090]

paraphernalia *n* **things**, stuff, equipment, kit, bits and pieces (*informal*), gear (*informal*), trappings, accoutrements, odds and ends. [➡ POSSESSIONS; 462]

paraphrase **1** *v* **rephrase**, summarize, reword, interpret, translate, restate. [➡ RECITE, REPEAT, AND NARRATE; 621] **2** *n* **summary**, rewording, précis, translation, interpretation, restatement. [➡ SUMMARIES, OUTLINES, AND EXCERPTS; 589]

parapsychological *adj* [➡ THE SUPERNATURAL; 788]

parapsychologist *n* [➡ PEOPLE WITH SUPERNATURAL POWERS; 789]

parasite **1** *n* **pest**, bug, bloodsucker, insect, flea, louse. [➡ PARASITES; 1017] *Opposite:* host. **2** *n* **scrounger** (*informal*), sponger (*informal*), sponge (*informal*), freeloader (*informal*), leech. [➡ LAZY OR UNSUCCESSFUL PEOPLE; 948]

parasite

◆ *types of parasitic insect*
bedbug, botfly, chigoe, crab louse, deer tick, flea, gadfly, harvest mite, head louse, horsefly, louse, mite, sand flea (*US*), sandfly, tapeworm, tick

parasitic **1** *adj* **biting**, bloodsucking, dependent, opportunistic. [➡ PARASITES; 1017] *Opposite:* host. **2** *adj* **scrounging** (*informal*), sponging (*informal*), freeloading (*informal*), dependent, lazy. [➡ SELFISH AND UNKIND; 506]

parasol *n* **sunshade**, umbrella, shade, brolly (*informal*). [➡ COVERS AND COATINGS; 1245]

parboil *v* [➡ COOKING AND FOOD PREPARATION; 354]

parcel **1** *n* **package**, packet, bundle, carton, box, pack. [➡ CONTAINERS, RECEPTACLES, AND PACKAGING; 1244] **2** *n* **tract**, plot, piece, section, portion, allotment, lot. [➡ AREA AND RANGE; 111] **3** *v* **pack**, package, wrap, wrap up, box, bundle. [➡ DECORATE, ADORN, AND APPLY COATINGS; 406] *Opposite:* unwrap.

parcel out *v* **distribute**, divide, share out, give out, hand out, apportion, dispense, allocate, allot. [➡ DISPENSE, RATION, AND DISTRIBUTE; 435]

parcel up *v* **wrap up**, wrap, parcel, bundle, pack, box, package. [➡ DECORATE, ADORN, AND APPLY COATINGS; 406] *Opposite:* unwrap.

parch *v* **dry**, dry out, scorch, dehydrate, desiccate. [➡ HARDEN, CONGEAL, DRY; 388]

parched **1** *adj* (*informal*) **thirsty**, gasping, dehydrated, dry, panting, thirsting. [➡ DRINK; 712] *Opposite:* refreshed. **2** *adj* **dry**, arid, dried up, dried out, scorched, dehydrated, desiccated, waterless. [➡ DRY; 1241] *Opposite:* waterlogged.

See Compare and Contrast at **dry.**

parchment *n* [➡ WRITING AND DRAWING IMPLEMENTS, AND MEDIA; 602]

pardon **1** *v* **forgive**, absolve, exonerate, let off, acquit, release, let go. [➡ FORGET, FORGIVE, AND ACCEPT; 749] *Opposite:* condemn. **2** *v* **excuse**, forgive, overlook, let pass, take no notice of, ignore. [➡ NOT PAY ATTENTION; 765] *Opposite:* resent. **3** *n* **forgiveness**, absolution, exoneration, amnesty, mercy, acquittal, release, remission. [➡ RELIGIOUS CONCEPTS; 777]

pare **1** *v* **cut**, trim, clip, cut back, tidy up. [➡ EXTRACT AND SEVER; 342] *Opposite:* grow. **2** *v* **peel**, skin, strip, trim, shave, prepare. [➡ COOKING AND FOOD PREPARATION; 354]

pare down *v* **cut back**, cut down, reduce, scale down, pare, shave, trim. [➡ CHANGE OF SIZE: SMALLER; 394] *Opposite:* increase.

parent *type of* **older relative.** [➡ OLDER GENERATION RELATIVES; 959]

parentage **1** *n* **ancestry**, background, pedigree, origin, derivation, descent, family, line. [➡ THE FAMILY; 956] **2** *n* **parents**, paternity, maternity. [➡ RELATIONSHIP TO ANOTHER; 973]

parental *adj* **parent**, maternal, paternal. [➡ THE FAMILY; 956]

parenthesis **1** *n* **digression**, afterthought, addition, aside, comment, interpolation. [➡ FIGURES OF SPEECH; 674] **2** *type of* **punctuation mark.** [➡ ASPECTS OF LANGUAGE; 683]

parenthood *n* **parentage**, fatherhood, motherhood, parenting, paternity, maternity, guardianship. [➡ RELATIONSHIP TO ANOTHER; 973]

parenting *n* **childcare**, child-rearing, babycare, nurturing, child raising, education. [➡ TEACHING; 839]

parget *n* [➡ BUILDING MATERIALS; 1076]

pargeting *n* [➡ BUILDING MATERIALS; 1076]

pariah *n* [➡ LAZY OR UNSUCCESSFUL PEOPLE; 948]

parings *n* [➡ REMAINDER AND REMAINDERS; 123]

parish *n* **community**, neighbourhood, district, village, locality, area. [➡HUMAN SETTLEMENTS; 1069]

parish priest *n* [➡RELIGIOUS PEOPLE; 779]

parity *n* **equivalence**, equality, uniformity, similarity, correspondence. [➡EQUALITY; 155] *Opposite:* disparity.

park 1 *n* **gardens**, botanical gardens, common, green, grounds, country park, estate. [➡URBAN OUTDOOR SPACES; 1071] 2 *v* (*informal*) **sit**, settle, plonk, plunk, put, be seated, settle down. [➡POSITION SOMETHING; 326]

parka *type of* **overcoat**. [➡GARMENTS AND OUTFITS; 865]

parking *n* **space**, bays, car parks, places, room. [➡URBAN OUTDOOR SPACES; 1071]

parking light (*US*) *type of* **external feature**. [➡VEHICLES; 1144]

parkland *n* **grassland**, land, fields, meadows, estate, reserve. [➡THE COUNTRYSIDE AND OUTDOOR SPACES; 1070]

parkway (*US*) *type of* **major road**. [➡ROADS; 1105]

parky (*informal*) *adj* [➡COLD WEATHER; 1051]

parlance *n* **idiom**, turn of phrase, phraseology, phrasing, jargon, vernacular, dialect. [➡THE SPOKEN WORD; 672]

parley 1 *v* **confer**, negotiate, talk, discuss, deliberate, consult. [➡TWO-WAY COMMUNICATION; 608] 2 *n* **conference**, meeting, discussion, confab (*informal*), negotiations, deliberations (*formal*), consultation, talks, huddle (*informal*). [➡NEGOTIATION AND DEBATE; 46]

parliament *n* **government**, legislative body, legislature, assembly, MPs. [➡LEGISLATIVE BODIES AND LEGISLATION; 809]

parliamentarian *n* **member of parliament**, MP, politician, backbencher, legislator, minister, frontbencher. [➡POLITICAL OFFICES AND POLITICIANS; 808]

parliamentary *adj* **governmental**, legislative, lawmaking, congressional, senatorial, deliberative (*formal*), legislatorial. [➡STYLES AND SYSTEMS OF GOVERNMENT; 806]

parliamentary government *n* [➡STYLES AND SYSTEMS OF GOVERNMENT; 806]

parlour 1 *n* **business premises**, salon, business establishment, shop, studio, store. [➡RETAIL OUTLETS; 1082] 2 *type of* **room in the home**. [➡TYPES OF ROOM; 1096]

parlous (*archaic or humorous*) *adj* **dangerous**, perilous, risky, unsafe, uncertain, difficult. [➡DANGEROUS; 237] *Opposite:* comfortable.

Parmesan *type of* **hard cheese**. [➡DAIRY PRODUCTS AND CHEESES; 1182]

parochial *adj* **narrow**, narrow-minded, closed-minded, provincial, insular, hidebound, unsophisticated. [➡NEGATIVE INTELLECTUAL CHARACTERISTICS; 526] *Opposite:* broad-minded.

parochialism *n* **narrow-mindedness**, provincialism, insularity, closed-mindedness, narrowness. [➡NEGATIVE INTELLECTUAL CHARACTERISTICS; 526] *Opposite:* broad-mindedness.

parodist *n* **satirist**, humorist, imitator, lampooner, burlesquer, impersonator, caricaturist. [➡WRITERS AND STYLES; 914]

parody 1 *n* **caricature**, imitation, lampoon, satire, burlesque, takeoff (*informal*), spoof, mockery. [➡JOKES AND TEASING; 675] 2 *n* **distortion**, travesty, misrepresentation, perversion (*disapproving*), pale imitation, insult. [➡REPRESENTATIONS AND GENERAL EXAMPLES; 65] *Opposite:* model. 3 *v* **distort**, pervert, misrepresent, twist. [➡PRETEND AND MIMIC; 60] 4 *v* **lampoon**, imitate, caricature, satirize, burlesque, make fun of, take the mickey, mock, ape. [➡JOKES AND TEASING; 675]

parole 1 *n* **conditional release**, early release, bail, liberation. [➡TRIAL, PUNISHMENT, AND LEGAL OUTCOMES; 819] 2 *v* **release on parole**, release conditionally, liberate, bail, give terms. [➡TRIAL, PUNISHMENT, AND LEGAL OUTCOMES; 819]

paroxysm 1 *n* **outburst**, fit, frenzy, outpouring, explosion, eruption. [➡CRITICISMS AND ANGRY OUTBURSTS; 50] 2 *n* **convulsion**, spasm, fit, seizure, attack, outbreak. [➡PAIN AND OTHER PHYSICAL SENSATIONS; 734]

paroxysmal *adj* **convulsive**, violent, spasmodic, uncontrollable, involuntary. [➡PAIN AND OTHER PHYSICAL SENSATIONS; 734]

parp *v* [➡EMIT RINGING AND TOOTING SOUNDS; 368]

parquet *n* **flooring**, parquetry, floor, floorboards, inlay. [➡BUILDING MATERIALS; 1076]

parquetry *n* [➡BUILDING MATERIALS; 1076]

parricide *n* [➡CAUSES OF DEATH; 921]

parrot 1 *n* **imitator**, mimic, impressionist, copycat (*informal*), impersonator, copier. [➡REPRESENTATIONS AND GENERAL EXAMPLES; 65] 2 *v* **mimic**, imitate, copy, impersonate, echo, ape, repeat back. [➡PRETEND AND MIMIC; 60] 3 *type of* **pet bird**. [➡BIRD; 997]

parrot-fashion (*informal*) *adv* **mindlessly**, by rote, mechanically, automatically, unthinkingly, uncomprehendingly. [➡UNINTERESTED AND DETACHED; 630]

parry 1 *v* **deflect**, block, fend off, shield yourself from, dodge, duck. [➡AVOID OR ESCAPE CONTACT; 419] *Opposite:* take. 2 *v* **evade**, avoid, dodge, elude, sidestep, deflect, circumvent. [➡WITHHOLD INFORMATION; 688] *Opposite:* answer.

parse *v* **analyse**, describe, break down, explain, construe, deconstruct. [➡EXAMINE AND ASSESS; 754]

parsimonious *adj* **stingy** (*informal*), thrifty, mean, frugal, ungenerous, miserly, penny-pinching (*informal*), tightfisted, tight, sparing. [➡FINANCIALLY MEAN AND GRASPING; 520] *Opposite:* extravagant.

parsimoniousness *n* **stinginess**, thrift, thriftiness, meanness, frugality, ungenerousness, miserliness, penny-pinching (*informal*), tightfistedness, parsimony. [➡FINANCIALLY MEAN AND GRASPING; 520] *Opposite:* extravagance.

parsimony *n* **stinginess**, thrift, thriftiness, meanness, frugality, ungenerousness, miserliness, penny-pinching (*informal*), tightfistedness, parsimoniousness. [➡FINANCIALLY MEAN AND GRASPING; 520] *Opposite:* extravagance.

parsley *type of* **herb**. [➡HERBS AND SPICES; 1174]

parsnip *type of* **root vegetable**. [➡FRUIT AND VEGETABLES; 1175]

parson *n* **cleric**, priest, minister, pastor, parish priest, rector, vicar, preacher, beneficiary. [➡RELIGIOUS PEOPLE; 779]

parsonage *n* **church house**, rectory, vicarage, manse, residence. [➡ RELIGIOUS BUILDINGS; 1084]

part 1 *n* **portion**, division, section, fraction, piece, bit, segment. [➡ AREA AND RANGE; 111] *Opposite:* whole. 2 *n* **feature**, ingredient, element, component, bit, piece. [➡ AMOUNT OF SOLID OR SEMI-SOLID; 115] 3 *n* **share**, portion, fragment, cut (*informal*), slice, chunk, amount, quantity, measure. [➡ AMOUNT AND QUANTITY; 112] *Opposite:* whole. 4 *n* **function**, role, duty, job, position, capacity, involvement. [➡ JOB; 833] 5 *v* **divide**, separate, open, split, segregate, put asunder (*formal*), draw apart. [➡ SEPARATE AND DIVIDE; 402] *Opposite:* join.

partake 1 *v* (*formal*) **consume**, dine, eat, drink, taste, touch. [➡ EAT AND NOT EAT; 711] *Opposite:* abstain. 2 *v* **participate**, share, contribute, take part, play a part, join. [➡ PARTICIPATE; 293] *Opposite:* refrain.

Parthian shot *n* [➡ CRITICISMS AND ANGRY OUTBURSTS; 50]

partial 1 *adj* **incomplete**, fractional, limited, restricted, unfinished, half-. [➡ UNFINISHEDNESS; 240] *Opposite:* complete. 2 *adj* **biased**, prejudiced, subjective, one-sided, inequitable, preferential. [➡ THE NATURE OF IDEAS; 772] *Opposite:* impartial.

partiality 1 *n* **fondness**, predilection (*formal*), liking, penchant, inclination, affection, soft spot. [➡ LIKE, LOVE, VALUE AND ENJOY; 579] *Opposite:* dislike. 2 *n* **bias**, prejudice, preference, leaning, favouritism, subjectivity, one-sidedness. [➡ THE NATURE OF IDEAS; 772] *Opposite:* impartiality.

partially *adv* **partly**, in part, incompletely, to some extent, somewhat, moderately, to a degree, in some measure. [➡ TO A CERTAIN EXTENT; 134] *Opposite:* completely.

partially sighted *adj* [➡ SEE; 700]

partial to *adj* **keen on**, fond of, into. [➡ APPRECIATION AND GRATITUDE; 536]

participant *n* **member**, contributor, contestant, applicant, partaker, accomplice. [➡ COMPETITORS; 41] *Opposite:* observer.

participate *v* **contribute**, partake, chip in (*informal*), take part, join, join in, share, play a part. [➡ PARTICIPATE; 293] *Opposite:* observe.

participation *n* **contribution**, input, sharing, partaking, involvement, membership. [➡ KIND ACTION OR BEHAVIOUR; 296] *Opposite:* observation.

participatory *adj* **taking part**, participating, sharing, partaking, hands-on, involved. [➡ PRESENT AND AVAILABLE; 11]

participle *type of* **grammatical term**. [➡ ASPECTS OF LANGUAGE; 683]

particle 1 *n* **bit**, speck, spot, crumb, grain, fragment, fleck, flake, shard. [➡ SMALL PIECE; 127] 2 *n* **smidgen** (*informal*), iota, bit, jot, whit (*informal*), crumb, grain, fragment, scrap, shred. [➡ SMALL PIECE; 127] 3 *type of* **word class**. [➡ ASPECTS OF LANGUAGE; 683]

parti-coloured *adj* **variegated**, multicoloured, pied, piebald, rainbow, motley. [➡ DESCRIBING COLOURS; 1225] *Opposite:* monochrome.

particular 1 *adj* **specific**, precise, certain, exact, actual, individual. [➡ EXACT; 204] *Opposite:* vague. 2 *adj* **individual**, distinct, noteworthy, special, unique, specific. [➡ EXTRAORDINARY: UNCOMMON; 206] *Opposite:* general. 3 *adj* **exacting**, meticulous, scrupulous, fastidious, fussy, finicky, picky. [➡ DIFFICULT TO PLEASE; 516] *Opposite:* relaxed.

particularity 1 *n* **fastidiousness**, meticulousness, fussiness, carefulness, discrimination, exactitude, accuracy. [➡ DIFFICULT TO PLEASE; 516] *Opposite:* recklessness. 2 *n* **peculiarity**, characteristic, trait, idiosyncrasy, quirk, eccentricity. [➡ PERSONAL ECCENTRICITIES; 494] 3 *n* **individuality**, distinctiveness, idiosyncrasy, singularity, originality, specialness, difference. [➡ DIFFERENCE; 150] *Opposite:* similarity.

particularize *v* **detail**, itemize, specify, enumerate, stipulate, spell out, describe, list, delineate (*formal*), relate. [➡ NAME AND DESCRIBE; 666]

particularly 1 *adv* **chiefly**, mainly, above all, predominantly, mostly, on the whole, principally. [➡ MAINLY AND PRIMARILY; 138] 2 *adv* **exceptionally**, intensely, acutely, especially, specifically, remarkably, outstandingly, markedly. [➡ TO A GREAT EXTENT; 130] *Opposite:* unexceptionally.

particulars *n* **details**, facts, information, essentials, basics, statistics, data, the whole story, nitty-gritty (*informal*). [➡ BASIC DETAILS; 689]

parting *n* **leaving**, departure, separation, going, leave-taking (*literary*), goodbye, sendoff, farewell, valediction (*formal*). [➡ END; 54] *Opposite:* reunion.

parting shot *n* **final remark**, Parthian shot, last word, retort, hostile remark, valediction (*formal*). [➡ CRITICISMS AND ANGRY OUTBURSTS; 50]

partisan 1 *n* **supporter**, follower, adherent, fan, member, enthusiast, devotee, sponsor, backer, champion. [➡ DEVOTEES AND ADDICTED PEOPLE; 557] *Opposite:* opponent. 2 *adj* **biased**, prejudiced, opinionated, one-sided, bigoted, limited, parochial, narrow-minded. [➡ NEGATIVE INTELLECTUAL CHARACTERISTICS; 526] *Opposite:* impartial.

partisanship 1 *n* **support**, devotion, membership, sponsorship, adherence, allegiance. [➡ FADS, FETISHES, AND IDOLATRY; 556] 2 *n* **bias**, prejudice, bigotry, narrow-mindedness, one-sidedness. [➡ PREJUDICE; 551] *Opposite:* impartiality.

partition 1 *n* **divider**, panel, dividing wall, screen, sliding doors, room divider, wall, barrier. [➡ WALLS AND PARTITIONS; 1103] 2 *n* **separation**, division, rift, split, dividing up, detachment, breaking up, severance. [➡ SEPARATE AND DIVIDE; 402] 3 *v* **divide**, separate, wall off, fence off, split, segregate, break up, divvy up (*informal*), divide up, subdivide, apportion. [➡ SEPARATE AND DIVIDE; 402]

partly *adv* **partially**, in part, somewhat, partway, moderately, comparatively, fairly, relatively, incompletely. [➡ TO A CERTAIN EXTENT; 134] *Opposite:* wholly.

partner 1 *n* **spouse**, wife, husband, mate, other half, lover, companion, significant other. [➡ RELATIVES BY MARRIAGE; 960] 2 *n* **associate**, colleague, collaborator, equal, mate, coworker, affiliate. [➡ COLLEAGUES AND EQUALS; 967] *Opposite:* superior. 3 *v* **team up**, unite, join, link up, consort (*formal*), accompany, escort. [➡ ACCOMPANY AND FOLLOW; 338]

partner in crime *n* **accessory**, accomplice, associate, sidekick (*informal*), buddy (*US informal*), crony (*disapproving*). [➡CRIMINALS; 821]

partnership 1 *n* **affiliation**, association, collaboration, companionship, alliance, relationship, interest, connection, cooperation. [➡RELATIONSHIP TO ANOTHER; 973] *Opposite:* opposition. 2 *n* **company**, business, firm, corporation, enterprise, joint venture, conglomerate, trust, syndicate, cartel, combine, organization. [➡BUSINESS ENTERPRISES AND RELATED BODIES; 793]

partridge 1 *type of* **fowl**. [➡FOOD BIRD; 999] 2 *type of* **meat**. [➡TYPES AND CUTS OF MEAT; 1176]

part-time *adj* **job-sharing**, evening, weekend, freelance, casual. [➡EMPLOYMENT STATUS; 831] *Opposite:* full-time.

part-timer *n* **part-time worker**, job-sharer, freelance, freelancer, casual, employee. [➡WORKER; 836] *Opposite:* full-timer.

part-time work *n* [➡TYPES OF WORK; 835]

part-time worker *n* [➡WORKER; 836]

parturition (*formal*) *n* [➡REPRODUCTION AND HEREDITY; 726]

partway *adv* **partly**, partially, halfway, in part, somewhat, incompletely. [➡TO A CERTAIN EXTENT; 134] *Opposite:* completely.

party 1 *n* **social gathering**, gathering, get-together (*informal*), festivity, shindig (*informal*), revelry, bash, event, social, merrymaking, celebration, thrash (*dated informal*). [➡PARTIES, DANCES, AND CELEBRATIONS; 37] 2 *n* **faction**, political party, interest group, society, splinter group, cabal, caucus, coalition, bloc, group, organization. [➡GROUPS WITH A COMMON INTEREST; 938] 3 *n* **participant**, accomplice, accessory, partaker, contributor, assistant, associate, partner. [➡SUPPORTERS, PROTECTORS, AND COMPATRIOTS; 970] 4 *n* **company**, band, gang, crew, contingent, team, sector, faction, section, delegation, sect, troop, denomination, side, group, outfit (*informal*). [➡GROUPS OF PEOPLE; 935] 5 *n* **individual**, person, one, person concerned, someone. [➡PERSON; 931] 6 *v* (*informal*) **celebrate**, have fun, whoop it up (*informal*), paint the town red (*informal*), get down (*US informal*), let your hair down (*informal*), hang loose (*informal*), groove (*informal dated*), revel. [➡LEISURE AND RECREATION; 874]

party animal (*informal*) *n* [➡PLEASURE-SEEKERS AND HEDONISTS; 886]

partygoer *n* **celebrator**, party animal (*informal*), socializer, guest, sociable person, attendee, partyer, socialite. [➡PLEASURE-SEEKERS AND HEDONISTS; 886]

party line *n* **official policy**, official position, party policy, official line, dogma, doctrine, policy. [➡GOVERNMENT POLICIES; 810]

party piece *n* [➡ENTERTAINMENT; 872]

party pooper (*informal*) *n* **spoilsport**, killjoy, wet blanket (*informal*), nonparticipant, bore. [➡GRUMPY AND NEGATIVE PEOPLE; 953]

parvenu *n* **upstart**, nouveau riche, social climber (*disapproving*), arriviste (*disapproving*), pretender. [➡CLASS STATUS; 889]

pashmina *type of* **accessory**. [➡HABERDASHERY, MILLINERY, AND LINGERIE; 867]

pass 1 *v* **go by**, overtake, exceed, outdo, surpass, overstep, bypass. [➡MOVE PAST, INTO OR THROUGH SOMETHING; 332] *Opposite:* stop. 2 *v* **throw**, kick, hit, toss, lob, pitch, fling, flip, cast, hurl, chuck (*informal*). [➡THROW SOMETHING; 335] 3 *v* **hand over**, give, deliver, hand, forward, hand out, distribute, dispatch, spread, send on, circulate, disseminate. [➡DISPENSE, RATION, AND DISTRIBUTE; 435] *Opposite:* withhold. 4 *v* **elapse**, go by, pass by, lapse, go, slip away. [➡HAPPEN; 27] 5 *v* **succeed**, qualify, make the grade, excel, exceed, surpass. [➡SUCCEED AND WIN; 79] *Opposite:* fail. 6 *v* **approve**, ratify, adopt, permit, accept, authorize. [➡APPROVE AND CONFIRM; 647] 7 *v* **happen**, occur, arise, take place, come about, befall (*archaic or literary*), appear, come up, issue, ensue. [➡HAPPEN; 27] 8 *n* **permit**, licence, authorization, card, documentation, badge, clearance, permission. [➡OFFICIAL DOCUMENTS; 587] *Opposite:* ban. 9 *n* **toss**, kick, hit, throw, lob, fling, pitch, cast, hurl, flip. [➡THROW SOMETHING; 335] 10 *n* **passage**, gorge, route, corridor, valley, road, way, gap. [➡MOUNTAINS AND HILLS; 1044] 11 *n* **state of affairs**, state, plight, predicament, fix (*informal*), jam (*informal*), circumstances, condition, situation. [➡DIFFICULT SITUATIONS; 72]

passable 1 *adj* **acceptable**, adequate, good enough, all right, respectable, tolerable, satisfactory, fair, decent. [➡ACCEPTABLE AND PASSABLE; 220] *Opposite:* unacceptable. 2 *adj* **traversable**, crossable, drivable, safe, okay (*informal*), penetrable. [➡IN GOOD REPAIR; 1231] *Opposite:* impassable.

passably *adv* **acceptably**, adequately, tolerably, reasonably, respectably, satisfactorily. [➡ACCEPTABLE AND PASSABLE; 220] *Opposite:* inadequately.

passage 1 *n* **corridor**, pathway, walkway, hall, hallway, alleyway, path, trail. [➡PATHWAYS; 1109] 2 *n* **way through**, way, passageway, road, channel, course, means of access, route, opening, path, track. [➡PATHWAYS; 1109] 3 *n* **section**, part, episode, chapter, paragraph, segment, incident, bit, extract, article, clause, piece. [➡PARTS OF BOOKS AND DOCUMENTS; 594] 4 *n* **migration**, movement, exodus, flood, transit, progress, growth, motion. [➡TRAVEL: JOURNEYS AND TRIPS; 319] 5 *n* **journey**, voyage, transfer, run, crossing, expedition, transit, trip. [➡TRAVEL: JOURNEYS AND TRIPS; 319] 6 *n* **approval**, enactment, passing, ratification, acceptance, establishment, validation, legitimization. [➡SUCCESS; 82]

passageway *n* **passage**, corridor, pathway, hallway, hall, walkway, gangway. [➡PATHWAYS; 1109]

pass away 1 *v* **die**, expire, succumb, depart (*formal*), kick the bucket (*slang*), pass on. [➡DIE; 922] 2 *v* **come to an end**, finish, end, cease, terminate (*formal*). [➡CEASE TO EXIST; 22]

pass by 1 *v* **disregard**, overlook, pass over, ignore, look the other way, let pass, close the eyes to. [➡NOT PAY ATTENTION; 765] 2 *v* **overtake**, go by, pass, surpass, leave behind, overstep, elude, outstrip, outrun, exceed. [➡MOVE PAST, INTO OR THROUGH SOMETHING; 332] 3 *v* **reject**, turn down, decline, refuse, ignore, decide against. [➡DENY AND REJECT; 645]

pass down *v* [➡BEQUEATH AND BEQUESTS; 433]

passé *adj* **out-of-date**, old, faded, aged, worn-out, archaic, done to death, obsolescent, unfashionable, obsolete, old hat (*informal*), dated, old-fashioned, outdated, outmoded, behind the times, antiquated, outworn. [➡ OLD, OLD-FASHIONED; 168] *Opposite:* fashionable.

See Compare and Contrast at **old-fashioned**.

passed on *adj* [➡ DEAD AND DYING; 925]

passenger *n* **traveller**, customer, fare, commuter, rail user. [➡ TRAVEL: TRAVELLERS AND WALKERS; 320]

passenger seat *type of* **internal feature**. [➡ INTERNAL PARTS OF A VEHICLE; 1145]

passer-by *n* **onlooker**, bystander, spectator, witness, passer, pedestrian, watcher. [➡ STRANGERS; 972]

pass for *v* **impersonate**, pass as, look like, go as, do as, pose as, masquerade, carry off. [➡ PRETEND AND MIMIC; 60]

passim (*formal*) *adv* **here and there**, throughout, frequently, in various places, in several places, everywhere. [➡ WRITTEN CONVENTIONS; 600]

passing 1 *adj* **transitory**, short-lived, ephemeral, fleeting, fly-by-night, momentary, temporary, perishable, impermanent, fugitive, transient. [➡ HAPPENING QUICKLY; 104] *Opposite:* permanent. 2 *adj* **cursory**, quick, casual, superficial, surface, hasty, shallow, slight, slapdash. [➡ HAPPENING QUICKLY; 104] *Opposite:* in depth. 3 *n* **departure**, departing, leaving, leave-taking (*literary*), disappearance, desertion. [➡ END; 54] 4 *n* **death**, dying, passing away, demise (*formal*), end, departure, passing on. [➡ DEATH AND BEREAVEMENT; 927]

passing comment *n* [➡ NEUTRAL ONE-WAY COMMUNICATION; 49]

passion 1 *n* **fervour**, ardour, obsession, infatuation, excitement, enthusiasm, zeal, craze, delight, fervidness, emotion, fervency. [➡ POSITIVE IMPATIENCE, ENTHUSIASM, AND ALERTNESS; 538] 2 *n* **desire**, hunger, thirst, appetite, craving, lust, urge, ache. [➡ DESIRE AND WANT; 580] 3 *n* **rage**, fury, outburst, fever, furore, anger, fit, paroxysm, storm, dudgeon, wrath, ire (*literary*), temper, choler (*archaic or literary*). [➡ IRRITATION AND ANGER; 542]

See Compare and Contrast at **love**.

passionate 1 *adj* **fervent**, ardent, zealous, avid, obsessive, fanatical, adoring, loving, impassioned, vehement, fervid, enthusiastic. [➡ POSITIVE IMPATIENCE, ENTHUSIASM, AND ALERTNESS; 538] *Opposite:* indifferent. 2 *adj* **fiery**, quick-tempered, incensed, inflamed, enraged, fuming, infuriated, raving, hot-blooded. [➡ EXCESSIVE SENSITIVITY; 512] *Opposite:* easygoing.

passionately *adv* **fervently**, ardently, avidly, single-mindedly, overpoweringly, keenly, zealously, vehemently, fervidly, enthusiastically. [➡ POSITIVE IMPATIENCE, ENTHUSIASM, AND ALERTNESS; 538] *Opposite:* indifferently.

passionflower *type of* **climber**. [➡ CLIMBERS; 1033]

passion fruit *type of* **fruit**. [➡ FRUIT AND VEGETABLES; 1175]

passionless *adj* **loveless**, detached, unromantic, emotionless, frigid, dispassionate, unloving, calm, unemotional, cold, cold-blooded, insensitive, impervious, thick-skinned. [➡ NEUTRALITY AND INDIFFERENCE; 554] *Opposite:* passionate.

passive *adj* **inert**, inactive, unreceptive, reflexive, flaccid, lifeless, submissive, impassive, unresponsive, docile. [➡ LIFELESS, LAZY, AND UNENTHUSIASTIC; 507] *Opposite:* active.

passiveness *n* **inactiveness**, inaction, inactivity, non-participation, indifference, apathy, impassiveness, unresponsiveness, passivity, submissiveness, docility. [➡ LIFELESS, LAZY, AND UNENTHUSIASTIC; 507] *Opposite:* activeness.

passivity *n* **inactivity**, inactiveness, inaction, non-participation, indifference, apathy, unresponsiveness, impassiveness, passiveness, docility. [➡ LIFELESS, LAZY, AND UNENTHUSIASTIC; 507] *Opposite:* activeness.

pass judgment *v* **give opinion**, judge, criticize, condemn, deliver judgment, adjudicate. [➡ PROTEST AND EXPRESS DISAPPROVAL; 643]

pass muster *v* **measure up**, be alright, check out, be okay (*informal*), qualify, come up to scratch (*informal*), do. [➡ ACCEPTABLE AND PASSABLE; 220]

pass off *v* **masquerade**, pretend, misrepresent, palm off, falsify, fob off. [➡ DECEPTION AND LIES; 661]

pass on *v* **convey**, send, forward, impart, communicate, contaminate, infect, transmit. [➡ INFORM AND ANNOUNCE; 612]

pass out 1 *v* **faint**, black out, keel over (*informal*), lose consciousness, conk out (*informal*), have a fainting fit, swoon. [➡ FALL ILL, TREAT, AND RECOVER; 729] *Opposite:* come to. 2 *v* **distribute**, hand out, give out, dish out (*informal*), assign, share out, deal out, administer, circulate, dispense, spread. [➡ DISPENSE, RATION, AND DISTRIBUTE; 435]

pass over *v* **ignore**, neglect, discount, disregard, let go, omit. [➡ NOT PAY ATTENTION; 765] *Opposite:* consider.

passport 1 *n* **official document**, travel document, ID, papers, permit, visa, pass, travel permit, credentials. [➡ OFFICIAL DOCUMENTS; 587] 2 *n* **access**, gateway, entry, opening, door, key, entrance, channel, admission, portal (*literary*), avenue. [➡ BEGINNING; 53]

pass the buck (*informal*) *v* **shift the blame**, evade responsibility, lay something at somebody's door. [➡ ACCUSE, BLAME, AND CRITICIZE; 642]

pass through *v* **cross**, go through, lead through, traverse, move across, navigate. [➡ TRAVEL: WAYS OF TRAVELLING; 321]

pass up *v* [➡ FOREGO AND DENY ONESELF; 450]

pass with flying colours *v* [➡ SUCCEED AND WIN; 79]

password *n* **code word**, open sesame, secret word, PIN, key, secret code, watchword, key word. [➡ ASPECTS OF LANGUAGE; 683]

past 1 *adj* **elapsed**, completed, accomplished, over and done, done, ended, gone, forgotten, over, ancient history, spent. [➡ PAST; 84] *Opposite:* ongoing. 2 *adj* **previous**, historical, earlier, former, bygone, ancient, older, preceding, long-ago, early, late, prior. [➡ BEFORE, FIRST, AND PRECEDING; 164] *Opposite:* future. 3 *n* **history**, earlier period, ancient times, times of yore, antiquity, long ago, yesterday, yesteryear, bygone days. [➡ PAST; 84] *Opposite:* future.

pasta

◆ *types of pasta*
cannelloni, capellini, cappelletti, conchiglie, fettuccine, fusilli, lasagne, linguine, macaroni, penne, ravioli, rigatoni, spaghetti, tagliatelle, tortellini, vermicelli

paste 1 *n* **adhesive**, glue, gum, fixative, wallpaper paste, cement. [➡ADHESIVES; 1270] 2 *n* **gunge** (*informal*), gloop (*informal*), gunk (*informal*), goo (*informal*), goop (*US informal*), glop (*US informal*), slime. [➡LOTIONS, PASTES, AND GELS; 1271] 3 *v* **glue**, stick, gum, fix, bond, attach. [➡FASTEN, LINK, AND JOIN; 409]

pastel 1 *adj* **pale**, light, soft, muted, neutral, gentle, wishy-washy (*informal*). [➡DESCRIBING COLOURS; 1225] *Opposite:* vivid. 2 *n* **crayon**, chalk, coloured chalk, oil pastel. [➡WRITING AND DRAWING IMPLEMENTS, AND MEDIA; 602]

pastern *part of* **horse**. [➡HORSE; 985]

pasteurization *n* **sterilization**, heat treatment, purification, decontamination, disinfection, sanitization. [➡CLEAN AND POLISH; 404]

pasteurize *v* **sterilize**, heat, purify, decontaminate, disinfect, sanitize. [➡COOKING AND FOOD PREPARATION; 354]

pasteurized *adj* **sterilized**, treated, purified, decontaminated, disinfected, sanitized. [➡NOT IN A NATURAL STATE; 1214]

past history *n* [➡PAST; 84]

pastiche *n* **takeoff** (*informal*), imitation, spoof, satire, lampoon, parody. [➡JOKES AND TEASING; 675]

pastime *n* **hobby**, interest, activity, pursuit, amusement, distraction, diversion, entertainment. [➡LEISURE AND RECREATION; 874]

pastiness *n* [➡COMPLEXION; 481]

pasting (*informal*) *n* **beating**, defeat, thrashing, hammering (*informal*), licking (*informal*), hiding (*informal*), drubbing, whipping (*informal*), pounding, battering. [➡BEAT AND DEFEAT; 80]

past love *n* **ex** (*informal*), old flame (*informal*), first love, blast from the past (*informal*). [➡SEXUAL AND ROMANTIC RELATIONSHIPS; 964]

pastor *n* **minister**, priest, vicar, clergyman, cleric. [➡RELIGIOUS PEOPLE; 779]

pastoral *adj* **rural**, rustic, countryside, countrified, idyllic, bucolic. [➡THE COUNTRYSIDE AND OUTDOOR SPACES; 1070] *Opposite:* urban.

pastry 1 *n* **dough**, shortcrust pastry, puff pastry, flaky pastry, choux pastry, filo pastry, crust. [➡BREAD, FLOUR, AND BREAD PRODUCTS; 1178] 2 *n* **pie**, tart, tartlet, flan, Danish pastry. [➡CAKES, BISCUITS, AND DESSERTS; 1180]

pastry fork *type of* **cutlery**. [➡TABLEWARE, CUTLERY, AND KITCHENWARE; 861]

pastry slice *type of* **cutlery**. [➡TABLEWARE, CUTLERY, AND KITCHENWARE; 861]

pasturage *n* [➡THE COUNTRYSIDE AND OUTDOOR SPACES; 1070]

pasture *n* **meadow**, meadowland, fallow, grassland, prairie, grass. [➡THE COUNTRYSIDE AND OUTDOOR SPACES; 1070]

pastureland *n* [➡THE COUNTRYSIDE AND OUTDOOR SPACES; 1070]

pasty 1 *n* **pie**, Cornish pasty, meat pie, sausage roll, steak pie, turnover, pastry. [➡BREAD, FLOUR, AND BREAD PRODUCTS; 1178] 2 *adj* **pale**, unhealthy-looking, ashen, pallid, wan, anaemic, sickly, grey, white, pasty-faced. [➡COMPLEXION; 481]

pasty-faced *adj* **pasty**, pale, unhealthy-looking, ashen, pallid, wan, anaemic, sickly, white, grey. [➡COMPLEXION; 481]

pat 1 *v* **tap**, touch, stroke, caress, massage, slap, palm. [➡CONTACT: TOUCH; 413] 2 *v* **shape**, smooth, mould, work, knead, flatten. [➡CONTACT: EXERT PRESSURE; 415] 3 *n* **touch**, tap, stroke. [➡CONTACT: TOUCH; 413] 4 *adv* **perfectly**, faultlessly, fluently, impeccably, by heart, word for word, verbatim. [➡EXACT; 204]

patch 1 *n* **cover**, reinforcement, covering, square. [➡COVERS AND COATINGS; 1245] 2 *n* **area**, spot, blotch, bit, smear, piece, stain. [➡AREA AND RANGE; 111] 3 *n* **badge**, award, stripe, tag, square, decoration, insignia. [➡SYMBOLS, SIGNS, AND NUMBERS; 597] 4 *v* **repair**, cover, mend, strengthen, reinforce, fix, patch up. [➡REPAIR AND MEND; 377]

patchiness 1 *n* **unevenness**, intermittence, bittiness, sparseness. [➡UNFINISHEDNESS; 240] *Opposite:* evenness. 2 *n* **variability**, inconsistency, unreliability, irregularity, unevenness. [➡FINITENESS, VARIABILITY, AND TRANSIENCE; 96] *Opposite:* consistency.

patchouli *n* **aromatic oil**, oil, perfume, scent, essential oil, aromatherapy oil, fragrance. [➡PERSONAL HYGIENE; 492]

patch up *v* **mend**, repair, fix, strengthen, reinforce, cover, sew up, patch. [➡REPAIR AND MEND; 377]

patchwork 1 *n* **mixture**, hotchpotch, mix, collage, mélange (*literary or formal*), assortment, potpourri, mixed bag, mess, crazy quilt. [➡COLLECTIONS AND MIXTURES OF THINGS; 1243] 2 *adj* (*US*) **pieced together**, jerry-rigged, makeshift, jerry-built, piecemeal, collaged. [➡IN BAD REPAIR; 1233]

patchy 1 *adj* **occasional**, irregular, sporadic, intermittent, sparse. [➡UNFINISHEDNESS; 240] 2 *adj* **variable**, inconsistent, unreliable, erratic, unpredictable, irregular, intermittent. [➡FINITENESS, VARIABILITY, AND TRANSIENCE; 96]

pate (*archaic or humorous*) *n* **head**, crown, cranium, skull, noggin (*dated informal*), bonce (*informal*), poll (*archaic*). [➡HEAD; 693]

pâté *type of* **processed meat**. [➡TYPES AND CUTS OF MEAT; 1176]

patella (*technical*) *type of* **bone**. [➡THE BONES AND JOINTS; 720]

paten *n* [➡RELIGIOUS OBJECTS; 780]

patent 1 *n* **copyright**, charter, right. [➡OFFICIAL DOCUMENTS; 587] 2 *adj* **clear**, obvious, blatant, flagrant, barefaced, out-and-out, manifest, self-evident, arrant, bald-faced (*US*). [➡PERCEPTIBLE; 25] *Opposite:* unclear.

patent leather *type of* **leather**. [➡FABRICS; 1131]

pater (*dated slang or humorous*) *n* **father**, dad (*informal*), daddy (*informal*), pop (*informal*), papa (*informal dated*), poppa (*US*). [➡OLDER GENERATION RELATIVES; 959]

paterfamilias *n* **father**, head, headman, paternalist. [➡OLDER GENERATION RELATIVES; 959]

paternal *adj* **fatherly**, parental, nurturing, protective, guiding. [➡RELATIONSHIP TO ANOTHER; 973]

paternalism *n* **authoritarianism**, interventionism, protectiveness, overprotectiveness, control. [➡RELATIONSHIP TO ANOTHER; 973]

paternalistic *adj* **authoritarian**, patriarchal, protective, overprotective. [➡RELATIONSHIP TO ANOTHER; 973]

paternal name *n* [➡NAME AND DESCRIBE; 666]

paternity *n* **fatherhood**, parenthood, role, status, responsibility. [➡RELATIONSHIP TO ANOTHER; 973]

paternoster 1 *n* **lift**, platform, compartment, elevator (*US*). [➡STAIRS AND STOREYS; 1101] 2 *part of* **building**. [➡PARTS OF A BUILDING; 1094]

path 1 *n* **track**, trail, pathway, footpath, route. [➡PATHWAYS; 1109] 2 *n* **course**, route, way, orbit, direction, line. [➡DIRECTION OF MOTION; 346] 3 *type of* **minor road**. [➡ROADS; 1105]

pathetic 1 *adj* **pitiful**, sad, moving, tragic, doleful, pitiable, wretched, touching, distressing, heartbreaking, heartrending. [➡EMOTIONALLY UNPLEASANT AND UPSETTING; 228] 2 *adj* (*informal*) **contemptible**, useless, risible, derisory, laughable, feeble, woeful, pitiful, ridiculous, lamentable, absurd, ludicrous. [➡INAPPROPRIATE AND UNSUITABLE; 225]

See Compare and Contrast at **moving**.

pathfinder *n* **leader**, trailblazer, scout, pioneer, guide. [➡TRAVEL: TRAVELLERS AND WALKERS; 320]

pathological 1 *adj* **medical**, clinical, scientific, diagnostic, immunological, biochemical, cellular. [➡SICKNESS; 730] 2 *adj* **morbid**, systemic, allergic, viral, bacteriological. [➡SICKNESS; 730] 3 *adj* **extreme**, compulsive, uncontrolled, unreasonable, unreasoning, obsessive, irrational, neurotic (*informal*). [➡ECCENTRICITY AND IRRATIONALITY; 563]

pathos *n* **sadness**, tragedy, bleakness, despair, anguish. [➡SADNESS, DISTRESS, AND DESPAIR; 540]

pathway *n* **trail**, path, way, lane, alleyway, conduit, corridor, passageway, route. [➡PATHWAYS; 1109]

patience 1 *n* **endurance**, staying power, stamina, persistence, perseverance. [➡STRENGTH OF WILL; 502] *Opposite:* impatience. 2 *n* **tolerance**, fortitude, forbearance (*formal*), serenity, imperturbability, unflappability, placidity. [➡CONFIDENCE AND COMPOSURE; 500] *Opposite:* impatience.

patient 1 *adj* **enduring**, persistent, persevering, easygoing. [➡STRENGTH OF WILL; 502] 2 *adj* **tolerant**, long-suffering, serene, forbearing (*formal*), fortitudinous, imperturbable, unflappable, good-natured, understanding, uncomplaining. [➡CONFIDENCE AND COMPOSURE; 500]

patiently *adv* **uncomplainingly**, long-sufferingly, tolerantly, good-naturedly, unwearyingly. [➡CONFIDENCE AND COMPOSURE; 500] *Opposite:* impatiently.

patina 1 *n* **discoloration**, tarnishing, staining, coating, verdigris. [➡DESCRIBING COLOURS; 1225] 2 *n* **sheen**, shine, lustre, gloss. [➡VISUAL TEXTURE; 1220] 3 *n* **layer**, veneer, covering, coating, coat, skin. [➡COVERS AND COATINGS; 1245]

patio *n* [➡GARDENS; 1073]

patois 1 *n* **dialect**, vernacular, idiom, language, lingo (*informal*), speech. [➡THE SPOKEN WORD; 672] 2 *n* **jargon**, slang, cant, patter, lingo (*informal*), argot. [➡ASPECTS OF LANGUAGE; 683]

pat on the back (*informal*) *n* **handshake**, round of applause, endorsement, seal of approval. [➡GESTURES AND GESTICULATION; 654]

patriarch 1 *n* **head of family**, paterfamilias, father, head, headman. [➡OLDER GENERATION RELATIVES; 959] *Opposite:* matriarch. 2 *n* **bishop**, archbishop, prelate, leader. [➡RELIGIOUS PEOPLE; 779]

patriarchal *adj* **male-controlled**, male, masculine, macho. [➡STYLES AND SYSTEMS OF GOVERNMENT; 806]

patrician 1 *n* **aristocrat**, noble, peer, squire. [➡RULERS AND ARISTOCRACY; 823] 2 *adj* **aristocratic**, refined, upper-class, noble, blue-blooded, titled, highborn (*literary*), well-bred. [➡CLASS STATUS; 889]

patricide 1 *n* **murder**, killing, parricide, slaughter, manslaughter, homicide. [➡CAUSES OF DEATH; 921] 2 *n* **murderer**, killer, parricide, slaughterer, slayer (*formal or literary*), homicide. [➡PEOPLE WHO KILL; 924]

patriot *n* **nationalist**, loyalist, flag-waver. [➡DEVOTEES AND ADDICTED PEOPLE; 557]

patriotic *adj* **nationalistic**, loyal, jingoistic, xenophobic, chauvinistic. [➡PHILOSOPHIES AND BELIEFS; 781]

patriotism *n* **loyalty**, partisanship, nationalism, jingoism, xenophobia, chauvinism. [➡PHILOSOPHIES AND BELIEFS; 781]

patrol 1 *n* **tour**, round, beat, circuit, perambulation, guard, duty. [➡WORK-RELATED ACTIVITIES; 834] 2 *n* **unit**, detachment, squad, troop, group. [➡MILITARY PERSONNEL; 828] 3 *v* **guard**, watch, tour, make the rounds, walk the beat, traverse. [➡PROCEED AND GO; 306]

patron 1 *n* **sponsor**, benefactor, supporter, investor, backer, donor. [➡REPRESENTATIVES AND PATRONS; 968] 2 *n* **customer**, client, diner, user, punter (*informal*), shopper. [➡PURCHASER; 425]

See Compare and Contrast at **backer**.

patronage *n* **investment**, backing, aid, sponsorship, benefaction. [➡GIFTS; 439]

patronize 1 *v* **be condescending to**, demean, denigrate, belittle, talk down to. [➡INSULTS, ABUSE, AND SWEARING; 659] 2 *v* (*formal*) **frequent**, shop at, use, utilize, visit, go to. [➡EXIST IN A PLACE; 19]

patronizing *adj* **condescending**, superior, denigrating, belittling, full of yourself, supercilious. [➡MOCKING AND DISMISSIVE; 637]

patronymic *n* [➡NAME AND DESCRIBE; 666]

patter 1 *n* **spiel** (*informal*), speech, script, talk. [➡ NEUTRAL ONE-WAY COMMUNICATION; 49] 2 *v* **tap**, drum, beat, pitter-patter, knock, clatter. [➡ EMIT SOUNDS THROUGH IMPACT AND ABRASION; 366] 3 *n* **jargon**, lingo (*informal*), slang, cant, patois, argot. [➡ ASPECTS OF LANGUAGE; 683] 4 *v* **jabber**, prattle, rattle on, burble (*informal*), rant, go on and on. [➡ WITTER AND BABBLE; 618] 5 *n* **tapping**, drumming, beating, pitter-patter, rhythm, drumbeat. [➡ IMPACT SOUNDS; 1259]

pattern 1 *n* **design**, decoration, shape, outline, form, arrangement, configuration, array, display, repetition, tessellation. [➡ PATTERNS; 1224] 2 *n* **prototype**, outline, model, example, blueprint, guide, mould, sample, precedent, archetype. [➡ REPRESENTATIONS AND GENERAL EXAMPLES; 65]

patterned *adj* **decorated**, spotted, lined, squared, dotted, checked, chequered, striped, tartan, plaid, paisley, psychedelic, speckled, floral, flowery, decorative, mottled, marbled, stippled, dappled, veined. [➡ DESCRIBING PATTERNS; 1226]

patty 1 *n* **cake**, burger, rissole. [➡ TYPES AND CUTS OF MEAT; 1176] 2 *n* **pie**, pasty, pastry, meat pie. [➡ BREAD, FLOUR, AND BREAD PRODUCTS; 1178]

paucity *n* **dearth**, scarcity, rareness, scantiness, lack, rarity, scarceness. [➡ TOO FEW, TOO LITTLE; 120]

paunch *n* **stomach**, belly, gut, potbelly, beer belly (*slang*), beer gut (*slang*), spare tyre (*informal humorous*), pot (*informal*), bay window (*US slang*). [➡ EXTRA WEIGHT; 479]

paunchy *adj* **potbellied**, portly, corpulent (*formal or literary*), fleshy, plump, tubby (*informal*). [➡ BUILD; 478]

pauper *n* **poor person**, down-and-out, bankrupt, indigent (*formal*). [➡ POOR PEOPLE; 896]

pause 1 *v* **stop**, wait, break off, rest, stop what you're doing, adjourn, hesitate. [➡ STOP ACTING; 265] *Opposite:* continue. 2 *v* **linger**, stop, rest, tarry, halt, hang back. [➡ STOP ACTING; 265] *Opposite:* move on. 3 *v* **hesitate**, falter, waver, wait, hold back, stall. [➡ HESITATE; 273] 4 *n* **break**, recess, suspension, intermission, breather (*informal*), hiatus, stop. [➡ PERIOD OF REST; 91] *Opposite:* continuation. 5 *n* **silence**, awkward moment, hiatus, gap. [➡ PAUSES AND PHASES; 56]

See Compare and Contrast at **hesitate**.

pave *v* **cover**, surface, floor, tile, flag, concrete. [➡ DECORATE, ADORN, AND APPLY COATINGS; 406]

paved *adj* **cemented**, flagged, surfaced, covered, tiled, concreted, concrete. [➡ DECORATE, ADORN, AND APPLY COATINGS; 406]

pavement 1 *n* **path**, footpath, pathway, roadside, walkway, sidewalk (*US*). [➡ PATHWAYS; 1109] 2 *n* (*US*) **road surface**, asphalt, roadway, street, Tarmac. [➡ ROADS; 1105]

pave the way *v* [➡ PREPARE FOR ACTION; 290]

pavilion *type of* **outbuilding**. [➡ ANCILLARY BUILDINGS; 1079]

paving *n* **flagging**, tiling, flooring, concrete, stonework, pavement (*US*). [➡ BUILDING MATERIALS; 1076]

paving slab *n* [➡ BUILDING MATERIALS; 1076]

paving stone *n* [➡ BUILDING MATERIALS; 1076]

paw 1 *n* (*informal*) **hand**, mitt (*slang*), appendage. [➡ ARM AND HAND; 696] 2 *v* **maul**, molest, fondle, stroke, pet, touch, grope (*slang*). [➡ CONTACT: TOUCH; 413]

pawl *n* [➡ PARTS OF MACHINES AND TOOLS; 1117]

pawn *v* **trade in**, wager, put up, place as collateral, pledge, forfeit, stake, hock (*slang*). [➡ SELL; 442] *Opposite:* redeem.

pay 1 *v* **disburse**, reimburse, shell out (*informal*), compensate, forfeit, recompense, give, remunerate, repay. [➡ GIVE MONEY; 434] *Opposite:* receive. 2 *n* **wage**, salary, recompense, reimbursement, earnings, compensation, remuneration, fee, emolument (*formal or humorous*), hire, stipend. [➡ INCOME; 461]

See Compare and Contrast at **wage**.

payable *adj* **owed**, billed, due, to be paid, mature, outstanding, unsettled, allocated (*US*). [➡ OWE AND DESERVE; 466]

pay-as-you-earn *n* [➡ TAX AND TAXATION; 802]

pay attention *v* [➡ PAY ATTENTION; 766]

payback *n* **return**, reimbursement, profit, remuneration, repayment, settlement, benefits. [➡ INCOME; 461]

pay back 1 *v* **repay**, reimburse, pay off, settle up, restore, ante up (*US informal*). [➡ REWARD; 437] *Opposite:* keep. 2 *v* **retaliate**, get even, take revenge, give tit for tat, settle scores, get someone (*informal*), make somebody pay, square. [➡ VENGEANCE AND REVENGE; 686]

pay cheque *n* **wages**, salary, pay, payment, earnings, income. [➡ INCOME; 461]

pay court to (*dated*) *v* [➡ ESTABLISHING RELATIONSHIPS WITH OTHERS; 974]

PAYE *n* **pay-as-you-earn**, income tax, revenue, tax, tax at source, direct tax. [➡ TAX AND TAXATION; 802]

payee *n* **recipient**, beneficiary, receiver, collector, acceptor, heir. [➡ PEOPLE INVOLVED IN FINANCE; 804] *Opposite:* payer.

payer *n* **spender**, financier, customer, client, paymaster, bursar. [➡ BUSINESS PEOPLE; 794] *Opposite:* payee.

pay heed *v* [➡ PAY ATTENTION; 766]

pay homage to *v* [➡ PRAISE AND ENCOURAGE; 648]

pay in *v* **deposit**, bank, put away, put in, save, invest, lay aside, coffer. [➡ ACCOUNTING, BANKING, AND BUDGETING; 799] *Opposite:* withdraw.

paying guest *n* [➡ INHABITANT; 857]

payload *n* **cargo**, load, freight, shipment, consignment, goods, contents, lading, burden. [➡ AMOUNT AND QUANTITY; 112]

payment *n* **sum**, expense, compensation, recompense, disbursement, fee. [➡ INCOME; 461]

payment gateway *n* [➡ E-COMMERCE; 1128]

pay no attention *v* [➡ NOT PAY ATTENTION; 765]

pay no heed *v* [➡ NOT PAY ATTENTION; 765]

payoff (*informal*) 1 *n* **payment**, settlement, reckoning, payout, remuneration. [➡INCOME; 461] 2 *n* **bribe**, graft, take, inducement, bribery, fix (*informal*). [➡BRIBES; 441]

pay off 1 *v* **settle**, square, repay, pay back, reimburse, compensate, recompense, amortize, discharge (*formal*), liquidate. [➡REWARD; 437] 2 *v* **succeed**, bear fruit, work, be effective, prosper, flourish. [➡SUCCEED AND WIN; 79]

payola (*US informal*) *n* **payment**, bribe, bribery, inducement, graft, palm greasing (*informal*), payoff (*informal*), fix (*informal*). [➡BRIBES; 441]

payout 1 *n* **disbursement**, expenditure, expenses, outgoing, charge, overhead. [➡EXPENDITURE; 424] *Opposite:* income. 2 *n* **payment**, pay, payoff (*informal*), wages, money, cash, salary. [➡INCOME; 461]

pay packet *n* **wages**, salary, paycheque, payment, earnings, income, emolument (*formal or humorous*), hire, stipend. [➡INCOME; 461]

payphone *type of* **telecommunications equipment**. [➡TELECOMMUNICATIONS; 1129]

payroll *n* **employees**, personnel, staff, workforce, workers, labour force. [➡ACCOUNTING, BANKING, AND BUDGETING; 799]

payslip *n* **statement**, slip, record, note, pay, paycheque, pay packet, payment, pay envelope (*US*), paystub (*US*). [➡RECEIPTS AND INVOICES; 592]

paystub (*US*) *n* **statement**, stub, record, note, pay, paycheque, payment, pay packet, pay envelope (*US*). [➡INCOME; 461]

pay tribute *v* [➡PRAISE AND ENCOURAGE; 648]

PC 1 *n* [➡THE POLICE, ARREST, AND PRE-TRIAL PROCEEDINGS; 818] 2 *type of* **computer**. [➡COMPUTERS AND COMPUTING; 1126]

pdq (*informal*) *adv* **immediately**, pretty damn quick (*informal*), at once, quickly, fast, right away, a.s.a.p., stat, forthwith (*formal*), instantly. [➡HAPPENING QUICKLY; 104] *Opposite:* at your leisure.

PE *n* [➡LESSONS, COURSE WORK, AND EXAMINATIONS; 842]

pea *type of* **pulse**. [➡BEANS AND PULSES; 1188]

peace 1 *n* **concord**, peacetime, harmony, amity (*formal*), armistice, reconciliation, ceasefire, accord, goodwill. [➡HARMONY; 156] *Opposite:* war. 2 *n* **harmony**, calm, quiet, stillness, tranquillity, silence, serenity. [➡PEACEFULNESS AND GENTLENESS; 215] *Opposite:* uproar.

peaceable 1 *adj* **peace-loving**, amiable, agreeable, easygoing, willing to please, compliant, unwarlike, nonbelligerent, nonviolent, diplomatic. [➡FRIENDLINESS AND SOCIABILITY; 495] *Opposite:* aggressive. 2 *adj* **tranquil**, peaceful, serene, harmonious, calm, quiet, ordered, restful. [➡PEACEFULNESS AND GENTLENESS; 215] *Opposite:* chaotic.

peaceably 1 *adv* **peacefully**, quietly, amiably, placidly, nonviolently, nonbelligerently, agreeably, compliantly, diplomatically. [➡FRIENDLINESS AND SOCIABILITY; 495] *Opposite:* belligerently. 2 *adv* **tranquilly**, peacefully, calmly, quietly, serenely, restfully, harmoniously. [➡PEACEFULNESS AND GENTLENESS; 215] *Opposite:* noisily.

peace agreement *n* **treaty**, truce, ceasefire, armistice, agreement. [➡HARMONY; 156]

peace and quiet *n* [➡PEACEFULNESS AND GENTLENESS; 215]

peaceful 1 *adj* **quiet**, serene, calm, still, peaceable, undisturbed. [➡PEACEFULNESS AND GENTLENESS; 215] *Opposite:* disordered. 2 *adj* **nonviolent**, passive, diplomatic, peaceable, pacific. [➡PEACEFULNESS AND GENTLENESS; 215] *Opposite:* violent.

peaceful coexistence *n* [➡RELATIONSHIP TO ANOTHER; 973]

peacefully *adv* **quietly**, serenely, calmly, peaceably, tranquilly. *Opposite:* manically. (*informal*). [➡PEACEFULNESS AND GENTLENESS; 215]

peacefulness *n* **serenity**, tranquillity, repose, placidity, quietness, quiet, hush. [➡PEACEFULNESS AND GENTLENESS; 215]

peacekeeper *n* **intermediary**, mediator, go-between, diplomat, pacifist, negotiator, broker, interceder, conciliator. [➡ADVISERS, JUDGES, AND ARBITERS; 971]

peacekeeping *n* **mediation**, intermediation, diplomacy, pacification, negotiation, international relations. [➡PEACEFULNESS AND GENTLENESS; 215]

peace-loving *adj* [➡GENEROSITY AND KINDNESS; 496]

peacemaker *n* **negotiator**, arbitrator, diplomat, mediator, intermediary, go-between, appeaser, pacifier. [➡ADVISERS, JUDGES, AND ARBITERS; 971] *Opposite:* fighter.

peacemaking *n* **reconciliation**, conciliation, mediation, arbitration, appeasement, pacification. [➡HARMONY; 156]

peace offering *n* **olive branch**, apology, overture, approach, gesture, flag of truce. [➡PEACEFULNESS AND GENTLENESS; 215]

peace of mind *n* [➡PEACEFULNESS AND GENTLENESS; 215]

peacetime *n* **peace**, harmony, amity (*formal*), armistice, truce, ceasefire, reconciliation. [➡PEACEFULNESS AND GENTLENESS; 215]

peach 1 *n* (*informal*) **beauty**, cracker (*informal*), humdinger (*slang*), wow (*informal*), pearl, dilly (*US slang*), jim-dandy (*US informal*), honey (*US informal*). [➡AMAZING THING; 212]. *Opposite:* turkey (*US slang*). 2 *type of* **orange**. [➡COLOURS; 1223] 3 *type of* **fruit**. [➡FRUIT AND VEGETABLES; 1175]

peachy 1 *adj* **peachlike**, downy, fuzzy, velvety, soft, smooth. [➡PHYSICAL TEXTURE; 1221] 2 *adj* (*informal*) **excellent**, wonderful, great (*informal*), nice, fine (*informal*), splendid, cool (*slang*). [➡GOOD, WELL, BETTER; 184] *Opposite:* terrible.

peacock 1 *n* **show-off** (*informal*), egoist, exhibitionist, dandy (*dated*), fop, coxcomb (*archaic*). [➡SELF-IMPORTANT AND SELF-SEEKING PEOPLE; 949] 2 *type of* **flightless bird**. [➡BIRD; 997]

peacock blue *type of* **blue**. [➡COLOURS; 1223]

peacock butterfly *type of* **butterfly**. [➡MOTHS AND BUTTERFLIES; 1015]

pea green *type of* **green**. [➡COLOURS; 1223]

peak 1 *n* **mountain**, mountaintop, summit, crest, point, height, mount, alp. [➡MOUNTAINS AND HILLS; 1044] *Opposite:* valley.

2 *n* **tip**, pinnacle, zenith, top, summit, height, apex, apogee. [➡EXTREMITIES OF PHYSICAL OBJECTS; 1249] *Opposite:* base. 3 *v* **climax**, crest, summit, top, max out (*US*). [➡SUCCEED AND WIN; 79] *Opposite:* dip. 4 *adj* **top**, highest, crowning, topmost, ultimate, greatest, uttermost. [➡SUPERIORITY; 153] *Opposite:* bottom.

peaked 1 *adj* **pointed**, sharp, pointy, spiky, tipped. [➡ANGULAR SHAPE; 1216] *Opposite:* rounded. 2 *adj* (*US*) **sickly-looking**, pale, thin, wan, emaciated, drawn, off-colour, peaky, sickly. [➡UNFIT AND WEAK; 740]

peaky *adj* **sickly-looking**, pale, thin, wan, emaciated, drawn, off-colour, peaked (*US*), sickly. [➡UNFIT AND WEAK; 740]

peal 1 *n* **clangour**, ringing, tolling, din, clang, ding-dong, knell, chime. [➡RINGING AND TOOTING SOUNDS; 1258] 2 *v* **ring**, toll, clang, sound, resonate, boom, bong, knell. [➡EMIT RINGING AND TOOTING SOUNDS; 368]

peanut *type of* **nut**. [➡NUTS; 1184]

peanut butter *type of* **preserve**. [➡SUGAR AND PRESERVES; 1183]

peanut oil *type of* **cooking fat and oil**. [➡FATS AND OILS; 1172]

peanuts (*informal*) *n* **a small sum**, a trifling amount, trifle, a trifling sum, chicken feed (*informal*), a paltry sum. [➡SMALL AMOUNT OF MONEY; 142] *Opposite:* fortune.

pear *type of* **fruit**. [➡FRUIT AND VEGETABLES; 1175]

pearl 1 *n* **gem** (*informal*), treasure, precious thing, nugget, prize. *Opposite:* dud. (*informal*). [➡AMAZING THING; 212] 2 *type of* **white**. [➡COLOURS; 1223] 3 *type of* **gemstone**. [➡PRECIOUS STONES; 1277]

pearl grey *type of* **grey**. [➡COLOURS; 1223]

pearly *adj* **iridescent**, lustrous, gleaming, shining, translucent, glowing, burnished, glistening, sheeny, nacreous. [➡VISUAL TEXTURE; 1220] *Opposite:* dull.

pear-shaped *adj* **bottom-heavy**, broadening, widening, bulging, billowing, rotund, plump, thickset. [➡BUILD; 478] *Opposite:* top-heavy.

peasant 1 *n* **farmer**, labourer, farm hand, farmworker, crofter. [➡FARMERS, GARDENERS, AND MANUAL WORKERS; 849] 2 *n* **country-dweller**, rustic, provincial (*disapproving*), bumpkin (*informal*), hillbilly (*US informal*). [➡CLASS STATUS; 889]

pea soup *type of* **soup**. [➡SOUP; 1185]

peasouper *n* [➡CLOUDY AND RAINY WEATHER; 1052]

peat *n* **mulch**, moss, compost, fertilizer, turf. [➡EROSION PRODUCTS AND SOIL; 1058]

pebble *n* **stone**, nugget, grit, shingle. [➡STONES, ROCKS, AND BOULDERS; 1057]

pebbledash *n* **facing**, finish, plaster, roughcast, encrustation, pebbles, cladding. [➡BUILDING MATERIALS; 1076]

pecan *type of* **nut**. [➡NUTS; 1184]

peccadillo *n* **sin**, offence, failing, indulgence, crime, transgression, wrong, wrongdoing, fault, infringement, breach. [➡MORALLY BAD; 776] *Opposite:* virtue.

peck 1 *v* **strike**, bite, jab, poke, dig, tap, hit. [➡CONTACT: TOUCH; 413] 2 *v* **nibble**, pick at, eat, play with, toy with, sniff at. [➡EAT AND NOT EAT; 711] *Opposite:* gobble. 3 *v* **kiss**, brush, caress, osculate (*formal or humorous*), buss (*dated*). [➡PHYSICAL CONTACT AS COMMUNICATION; 656] 4 *n* (*informal*) **kiss**, brush, caress, osculation (*formal or humorous*), buss (*dated*), smack. [➡PHYSICAL CONTACT AS COMMUNICATION; 656] 5 *n* **bite**, blow, stroke, jab, dig, poke. [➡CONTACT: TOUCH; 413]

pecking order *n* **hierarchy**, class structure, social order, social structure, ladder, society. [➡CONNECTION; 144]

peckish (*informal*) *adj* **hungry**, famished, starving (*informal*), ravenous, starved (*informal*). [➡EAT AND NOT EAT; 711] *Opposite:* full.

pecorino *type of* **hard cheese**. [➡DAIRY PRODUCTS AND CHEESES; 1182]

pectoral *type of* **muscle or tendon**. [➡THE MUSCLES; 719]

pectoral fin *part of* **fish**. [➡PARTS OF A FISH; 1011]

peculate (*formal*) *v* [➡STEAL AND ROB; 427]

peculiar 1 *adj* **unusual**, odd, strange, weird, irregular, abnormal, uncharacteristic, atypical, curious, eccentric, unconventional. [➡BIZARRE AND PECULIAR; 258] *Opposite:* normal. 2 *adj* **unique**, idiosyncratic, local, individual, special, distinctive, particular, inimitable. [➡EXTRAORDINARY: UNCOMMON; 206] *Opposite:* universal.

peculiarity 1 *n* **individuality**, idiosyncrasy, distinctiveness, particularity, uniqueness, inimitableness. [➡EXTRAORDINARY: UNCOMMON; 206] 2 *n* **oddness**, strangeness, weirdness, eccentricity, abnormality, irregularity, curiousness. [➡BIZARRE AND PECULIAR; 258] *Opposite:* normality.

peculiarly 1 *adv* **uniquely**, abnormally, unusually, curiously, strangely, markedly, noticeably. [➡BIZARRE AND PECULIAR; 258] *Opposite:* typically. 2 *adv* **particularly**, especially, extremely, very, massively (*informal*), extraordinarily. [➡TO A GREAT EXTENT; 130] *Opposite:* slightly.

pecuniary *adj* **monetary**, financial, fiscal, economic, commercial, budgetary. [➡FINANCE AND ECONOMICS; 797]

pedagogic *see* **pedagogical**.

pedagogical *adj* **educational**, academic, instructive, tutorial, didactic, informative, instructional, pedagogic, teaching, scholastic. [➡EDUCATION; 838]

pedagogics (*formal*) *n* [➡TEACHING; 839]

pedagogue *n* **teacher**, educator, schoolteacher, instructor, tutor, lecturer. [➡EDUCATORS; 840]

pedagogy *n* **teaching**, education, pedagogics (*formal*), instruction, training, tutoring, schooling. [➡TEACHING; 839]

pedal 1 *n* **lever**, device, control, treadle. [➡VEHICLES; 1144] 2 *v* **cycle**, bike (*informal*), ride, drive, steer, travel. [➡TRAVEL: WAYS OF TRAVELLING; 321] 3 *v* **ride**, operate, propel, control, guide, steer, impel. [➡TRAVEL: WAYS OF TRAVELLING; 321] 4 *part of* **bike** (*informal*). [➡BIKES, CARS, AND CARRIAGES; 1148]

pedalo *type of* **small vessel**. [➡SHIPS AND BOATS; 1149]

pedal pushers *type of* **trousers**. [➡GARMENTS AND OUTFITS; 865]

pedant *n* **doctrinaire**, obfuscator, nitpicker, sophist, hairsplitter, scholar, theoretician. [➡GRUMPY AND NEGATIVE PEOPLE; 953] *Opposite:* dilettante.

pedantic *adj* **finicky**, plodding, obscure, arcane, dull, doctrinaire, sophistic, hairsplitting, nitpicking, fussy. [➡NEGATIVE INTELLECTUAL CHARACTERISTICS; 526] *Opposite:* dilettante.

pedantry *n* **literalism**, laboriousness, sophistry, meticulousness, thoroughness, unimaginativeness. [➡NEGATIVE INTELLECTUAL CHARACTERISTICS; 526] *Opposite:* creativity.

peddle 1 *v* **sell**, tout, hawk, vend, retail, market, push (*slang*), flog (*informal*), get rid of. [➡SELL; 442] 2 *v* **promote**, market, hype, espouse, push (*slang*), advocate, publicize. [➡SELL; 442]

pedestal *n* **base**, plinth, stand, dais, platform, podium, support, foundation, understructure, foot. [➡SUPPORTS AND BASES; 1254]

pedestrian 1 *n* **rambler**, walker, ambler, hiker, strider. [➡TRAVEL: TRAVELLERS AND WALKERS; 320] 2 *adj* **dull**, ordinary, unimaginative, uninspired, prosaic, everyday, humdrum, unexciting, boring, tedious. [➡ORDINARINESS; 245] *Opposite:* exciting.

pedestrian crossing *n* **crossing**, pelican crossing, zebra crossing, crosswalk (*US*). [➡BRIDGES, TUNNELS, CROSSINGS, AND JUNCTIONS; 1111]

pedestrianized *adj* **pedestrian**, converted, nonvehicle, nonvehicular, closed off. [➡PATHWAYS; 1109]

pedestrian precinct *n* [➡PATHWAYS; 1109]

pedicure *n* **beauty treatment**, foot massage, cosmetic treatment, cosmetic session, chiropody treatment, chiropody session. [➡PERSONAL HYGIENE; 492]

pedigree 1 *n* **lineage**, family background, ancestry, derivation, history, bloodline, birth, extraction, parentage. [➡THE FAMILY; 956] 2 *adj* **purebred**, full-blooded, thoroughbred, noble, aristocratic, blue-blooded. [➡CLASS STATUS; 889]

pedlar *n* **seller**, dealer, street trader, trader, pusher (*slang*), vendor, hawker, supplier, retailer, wholesaler. [➡SELLER; 443]

peek 1 *v* **peep**, glance, peer, steal a look, sneak a quick look, have a look-see (*US*). [➡LOOKING AND LOOKS; 701] *Opposite:* stare. 2 *n* **look**, glance, peep, glimpse, once-over (*informal*), gander (*informal*), look-see (*informal*). [➡LOOKING AND LOOKS; 701] *Opposite:* gaze.

peel 1 *v* **unpeel**, skin, strip, unwrap, pare, hull, bark, flay, shed. [➡COOKING AND FOOD PREPARATION; 354] 2 *n* **skin**, rind, peelings, covering, shell, crust, wrapping, bark, husk. [➡FRUIT AND VEGETABLES; 1175]

peeler *n* **potato peeler**, paring knife, scraper. [➡TABLEWARE, CUTLERY, AND KITCHENWARE; 861]

peeling *adj* **flaking**, shedding, cracking, coming off, coming loose, detaching. [➡IN BAD REPAIR; 1233] *Opposite:* smooth.

peelings *n* **parings**, skin, peel, rind, shavings, bark, husk, wrapping, covering, shell. [➡REMAINDER AND REMAINDERS; 123]

peep 1 *v* **peek**, peer, steal a look, glance, sneak a look, glimpse. [➡LOOKING AND LOOKS; 701] *Opposite:* gaze. 2 *n* **peek**, glance, glimpse, gander (*informal*), gawp (*informal*), look. [➡LOOKING AND LOOKS; 701] 3 *v* **chirp**, twitter, tweet, chirrup, squeak, beep, cheep. [➡SOUND EMISSION BY ANIMALS OR BIRDS; 365] 4 *n* **chirp**, cheep, twitter, squeak, tweet, beep, chirrup. [➡SOUNDS MADE BY BIRDS; 1262] 5 *n* **sound**, utterance, noise, word. [➡SOUNDS MADE BY PEOPLE; 1261]

peephole 1 *n* **opening**, crack, hole, aperture, knothole. [➡HOLES, GAPS, AND FORKS; 1251] 2 *n* **spyhole**, eyehole, keyhole. [➡HOLES, GAPS, AND FORKS; 1251]

Peeping Tom *n* [➡CRIMINALS; 821]

peer 1 *v* **look**, scrutinize, gaze, stare, examine, look closely, go over, take in, squint. [➡LOOKING AND LOOKS; 701] *Opposite:* glance. 2 *n* **noble**, aristocrat, lord, earl, duke, viscount, patrician, peer of the realm. [➡RULERS AND ARISTOCRACY; 823] 3 *n* **equal**, colleague, contemporary, friend, match, like, partner, associate, mate, fellow (*dated*). [➡COLLEAGUES AND EQUALS; 967]

peerage 1 *n* **peers**, aristocracy, nobility, nobles, aristocrats, upper classes, peers of the realm. [➡RULERS AND ARISTOCRACY; 823] 2 *n* **hereditary peerage**, life peerage, dukedom, title, honour. [➡CLASS STATUS; 889]

peer group *n* **cohort**, coequals, generation, age group, classmates, colleagues, contemporaries, equals. [➡COLLEAGUES AND EQUALS; 967]

peerless *adj* **incomparable**, matchless, unequalled, unrivalled, without equal, nonpareil, unsurpassed, unmatched. [➡SUPERIORITY; 153] *Opposite:* commonplace.

peer of the realm *n* **earl**, duke, viscount, peer, noble, aristocrat, lord, patrician. [➡RULERS AND ARISTOCRACY; 823]

peeve (*informal*) 1 *v* **miff** (*informal*), vex, annoy, irritate, irk, upset, pique, provoke, nettle (*informal*), chafe, rile (*informal*). [➡ANGER AND ANNOY; 570] *Opposite:* please. 2 *n* **gripe** (*informal*), bugbear, irritation, vexation, nuisance, bother, annoyance, irritant, headache (*informal*), hassle (*informal*). [➡NUISANCES; 254] *Opposite:* pleasure.

peeved (*informal*) *adj* **riled** (*informal*), annoyed, irritated, irked, piqued, upset, put out, vexed, provoked, nettled (*informal*), miffed (*informal*). [➡IRRITATION AND ANGER; 542] *Opposite:* pleased.

peevish *adj* **irritable**, crabby, bad-tempered, cross, grumpy, spiteful, petulant, touchy, testy (*informal*), grouchy (*informal*), cranky (*US informal*). [➡IRRITATION AND ANGER; 542] *Opposite:* good-tempered.

peevishness *n* **irritability**, crabbiness, spitefulness, crossness, grumpiness, pettiness, grouchiness (*informal*), crankiness (*US informal*). [➡IRRITATION AND ANGER; 542]

peewee *adj* **mini** (*informal*), toy, pint-size (*informal*), miniature, undersized, tiny, small. [➡SMALL; 1194] *Opposite:* jumbo.

peg 1 *n* **pin**, fastener, dowel, hook, bolt, hanger, nail, spike, tack. [➡FASTENERS, LINKS, AND NETWORKS; 1246] 2 *n* (*informal*) [➡LEG AND FOOT; 695] 3 *v* **fasten**, secure, attach, fix, hang, nail, make fast. [➡FASTEN, LINK, AND JOIN; 409] *Opposite:* detach. 4 *v* **mark**, keep score, track, gauge, measure, note down.

[➡ASSESS QUALITY; 756] **5** *v* **freeze**, fix, set, control, limit. [➡AVOID, PREVENT, LIMIT, AND CONTROL; 278] *Opposite:* free.

peignoir *type of* **sleepwear.** [➡GARMENTS AND OUTFITS; 865]

pejorative (*formal*) *adj* **disapproving**, judgmental, harsh, scornful, derogatory, uncomplimentary, negative, depreciative, depreciatory, critical, sneering, sniping, disparaging, belittling, downgrading. [➡ACCUSATORY AND DISAPPROVING; 635] *Opposite:* positive.

Pekingese *type of* **small dog.** [➡DOG; 980]

pelargonium *type of* **perennial flower.** [➡FLOWERS; 1032]

pelican *type of* **seabird.** [➡SEABIRD; 1002]

pelican crossing *n* **crossing**, zebra crossing, pedestrian crossing, crosswalk (*US*). [➡BRIDGES, TUNNELS, CROSSINGS, AND JUNCTIONS; 1111]

pellet *type of* **projectile.** [➡PROJECTILES; 1158]

pell-mell **1** *adv* **helter-skelter**, hurriedly, headlong, recklessly, tumultuously, precipitously, impulsively, rashly, impetuously. [➡HAPPENING QUICKLY; 104] *Opposite:* carefully. **2** *adv* **untidily**, higgledy-piggledy, haphazardly, chaotically, topsy-turvily, randomly. [➡DISORDER AND CHAOS; 246] *Opposite:* neatly.

pellucid (*literary*) *adj* [➡VISUAL TEXTURE; 1220]

pellucidity (*literary*) *n* [➡VISUAL TEXTURE; 1220]

pelmet *n* **valance**, decoration, drapery, board, frill. [➡SOFT FURNISHINGS, LINEN, AND DRAPERY; 860]

pelt **1** *n* **hide**, fur, skin, hair, coat, covering, fleece. [➡THE SKIN; 721] **2** *v* **bombard**, assail, assault, strafe, attack, shell, mortar, shower. [➡THROW SOMETHING; 335] **3** *v* **pour**, chuck it down (*informal*), cascade, come down in sheets (*informal*), bucket down (*informal*), rain cats and dogs (*informal*). [➡CLOUDY AND RAINY WEATHER; 1052] *Opposite:* drizzle.

pelt down *v* [➡CLOUDY AND RAINY WEATHER; 1052]

pelvic *adj* **pubic**, lumbar, sacral, genital, iliac. [➡THE BONES AND JOINTS; 720]

pelvic fin *part of* **fish.** [➡PARTS OF A FISH; 1011]

pelvis *type of* **bone.** [➡THE BONES AND JOINTS; 720]

pelycosaur *type of* **dinosaur.** [➡DINOSAUR; 996]

Pembroke table *type of* **table.** [➡FURNITURE; 858]

pen **1** *n* **enclosure**, run, cage, coop. [➡ANIMAL OR BIRD ACCOMMODATION; 1078] **2** *n* (*US slang*) [➡BUILDINGS FOR CONFINING PEOPLE; 1093] **3** *v* **dash off** (*informal*), scribble, jot, compose, scrawl, write, author. [➡RECORD SOMETHING; 372] **4** *v* **confine**, shut in, hold in, trap, capture, hem in, keep, imprison, cage in, corral (*US*). [➡CAPTIVITY AND LOSS OF FREEDOM; 249] *Opposite:* release. **5** *type of* **male or female bird.** [➡MALE OR FEMALE BIRD; 1005]

pen

◆ *types of pen*
ballpoint, crayon, felt-tipped pen, fountain pen, highlighter, marker, quill, rollerball

penal *adj* **punitive**, punishing, disciplinary, corrective. [➡TRIAL, PUNISHMENT, AND LEGAL OUTCOMES; 819]

penal colony *n* [➡BUILDINGS FOR CONFINING PEOPLE; 1093]

penal complex (*US*) *n* [➡BUILDINGS FOR CONFINING PEOPLE; 1093]

penal institution *n* [➡BUILDINGS FOR CONFINING PEOPLE; 1093]

penalization *n* **castigation** (*formal*), imprisonment, punishment, disciplining, fining, discipline, correction. [➡THE LAW AND LEGAL AUTHORITY; 814] *Opposite:* rewarding.

penalize *v* **punish**, discipline, fine, reprimand, correct, castigate (*formal*), chasten, imprison. [➡ACCUSE, BLAME, AND CRITICIZE; 642] *Opposite:* let off.

penalty **1** *n* **punishment**, fine, sentence, penalization. [➡TRIAL, PUNISHMENT, AND LEGAL OUTCOMES; 819] **2** *n* **consequence**, disadvantage, drawback, forfeit, price. [➡RESULTS AND OUTCOMES; 83] *Opposite:* advantage.

penance *n* **self-punishment**, reparation, forfeit, atonement, amends, propitiation, repentance, contrition, self-flagellation. [➡APOLOGIZE AND RETRACT; 684]

penchant *n* **liking**, fondness, partiality, taste, predilection (*formal*), proclivity, desire, weakness, inclination. [➡APPRECIATION AND GRATITUDE; 536] *Opposite:* antipathy.

pencil *v* **write**, draw, mark, colour, sketch, trace, outline, delineate. [➡RECORD SOMETHING; 372]

pencil case *type of* **container.** [➡CONTAINERS, RECEPTACLES, AND PACKAGING; 1244]

pencil moustache *n* [➡FACIAL HAIR; 490]

pencil pusher (*US*) *n* [➡WORKER; 836]

pendant **1** *adj* **undecided**, incomplete, unresolved, awaiting, pending. [➡ABOUT TO HAPPEN; 33] **2** *type of* **necklace.** [➡JEWELLERY; 866]

pendent **1** *adj* **hanging**, suspended, dangling, sagging, pendulous, trailing, overhanging, drooping. [➡ORIENTATION AND ALIGNMENT; 1222] **2** *adj* (*formal or literary*) **pending**, incomplete, unresolved, awaiting, undecided. [➡ABOUT TO HAPPEN; 33]

pending **1** *adj* **undecided**, incomplete, pendent (*formal or literary*), awaiting, unresolved. [➡ABOUT TO HAPPEN; 33] **2** *adj* **imminent**, impending, expected, approaching, forthcoming, round the corner. [➡ABOUT TO HAPPEN; 33] **3** *prep* **awaiting**, until, till. [➡FUTURE; 86] **4** *prep* **during**, throughout, in the course of. [➡CONCURRENT AND CONTEMPORANEOUS; 165]

pendulous **1** *adj* **hanging**, swinging, overhanging, drooping, loose, sagging, oscillating, pendent, dangling. [➡ORIENTATION AND ALIGNMENT; 1222] **2** *adj* **undecided**, wavering, vacillating, uncommitted, uncertain, unsure. [➡UNCERTAINTY; 560] *Opposite:* decided.

pendulum *n* **weight**, bob, plumb, swing. [➡PARTS OF MACHINES AND TOOLS; 1117]

penetrability *n* [➡DENSITY AND CONSISTENCY; 1206]

penetrable *adj* [➡DENSITY AND CONSISTENCY; 1206]

penetrate **1** *v* **enter**, pass through, go through, go in, break in, break through, pierce, infiltrate, access, breach, stab, gore, spear, lance, spike. [➡MOVE PAST, INTO OR THROUGH SOMETHING; 332] **2** *v* **diffuse**, seep in, soak in, infiltrate, imbue, invade, infuse, seep into, permeate, creep into, saturate, filter through, transfuse. [➡SOFTEN, LIQUEFY, DAMPEN; 389] **3** *v* **work out**, solve, crack (*informal*), decipher, figure out, understand, fathom, apprehend. [➡SOLVE AND INTERPRET; 761] **4** *v* **grasp**, see into, perceive, figure out, comprehend, understand, apprehend, discern. [➡UNDERSTAND AND GRASP; 760]

penetrating **1** *adj* **all-pervading**, powerful, pungent, sharp, piercing, strong. [➡STRENGTH; 202] **2** *adj* **probing**, piercing, searching, questioning, inquiring, sharp, penetrative. [➡FACIAL EXPRESSION; 652] **3** *adj* **sharp**, intelligent, astute, perceptive, insightful, clever, acute, keen, discriminating. [➡POSITIVE INTELLECTUAL CHARACTERISTICS; 525] *Opposite:* obtuse. **4** *adj* **piercing**, shrill, high-pitched, earsplitting, sharp, strident, loud. [➡LOUD OR UNPLEASANT SOUNDS; 1265]

penetration **1** *n* **diffusion**, infiltration, saturation, dispersion, dissemination, permeation. [➡DISPENSE, RATION, AND DISTRIBUTE; 435] **2** *n* **perception**, astuteness, understanding, discernment, comprehension, insight, acumen, shrewdness, intelligence. [➡POSITIVE INTELLECTUAL CHARACTERISTICS; 525] **3** *n* **incursion**, access, breach, entrance, infringement, invasion. [➡ARRIVAL; 13]

penetrative **1** *adj* **infiltratory**, penetrating, piercing, penetrant, permeating, pervasive. [➡STRENGTH; 202] **2** *adj* **keen**, perceptive, insightful, acute, sharp, discerning. [➡POSITIVE INTELLECTUAL CHARACTERISTICS; 525] *Opposite:* unperceptive.

pen friend *n* **pen pal** (*informal*), correspondent, letter writer, friend, pal (*informal*), acquaintance. [➡FRIENDS; 963]

penguin *type of* **flightless bird.** [➡BIRD; 997]

peninsula *n* **neck of land**, finger of land, cape, point, headland. [➡THE CONTINENTS AND ISLANDS; 1048]

penitence *n* **shame**, repentance, contrition, atonement, remorse, regret, sorrow, compunction. [➡APOLOGIZE AND RETRACT; 684] *Opposite:* shamelessness.

penitent *adj* **repentant**, repenting, contrite, remorseful, regretful, apologetic, rueful, conscience-stricken, sorry. [➡EMBARRASSMENT AND HUMILIATION; 543] *Opposite:* unrepentant.

penitential *adj* **penitent**, sorrowful, repentant, penitentiary, atoning, regretful, contrite, remorseful. [➡EMBARRASSMENT AND HUMILIATION; 543] *Opposite:* unrepentant.

penitentiary (*US*) *n* **prison**, jail, penal institution, labour camp, penal colony, nick (*slang*), reformatory, house of correction, pen (*US slang*). [➡BUILDINGS FOR CONFINING PEOPLE; 1093]

penknife *type of* **knife.** [➡CUTTING TOOLS; 1119]

penlight *type of* **light.** [➡LIGHT; 1163]

pen name *n* **pseudonym**, nom de plume, alias, nom de guerre. [➡NAME AND DESCRIBE; 666]

pennant **1** *n* **banner**, flag, ensign, emblem, streamer, pennon, bunting. [➡SYMBOLS, SIGNS, AND NUMBERS; 597] **2** *part of* **sailing vessel.** [➡PARTS OF A SHIP OR BOAT; 1150]

penne *type of* **pasta.** [➡PASTA; 1179]

penniless *adj* **poor**, impoverished, broke (*informal*), flat broke (*informal*), impecunious (*formal*), destitute, bankrupt, ruined, cleaned out (*informal*), insolvent. [➡POVERTY AND POOR; 892] *Opposite:* rich.

pennilessness *n* [➡POVERTY AND POOR; 892]

pennon *n* **flag**, pennant, banner, standard, emblem, streamer, bunting. [➡SYMBOLS, SIGNS, AND NUMBERS; 597]

penny-farthing [➡BIKES, CARS, AND CARRIAGES; 1148]

penny pincher (*informal*) *n* **cheapskate** (*informal*), skinflint, scrooge (*informal*), miser, niggard, pinchpenny, meanie (*informal*). [➡FINANCIALLY MEAN PEOPLE; 952] *Opposite:* spendthrift.

penny-pinching (*informal*) *adj* **frugal**, thrifty, tight-fisted, parsimonious, stingy (*informal*), economizing. [➡FINANCIALLY MEAN AND GRASPING; 520] *Opposite:* generous.

penny whistle *type of* **wind instrument.** [➡MUSICAL INSTRUMENTS; 910]

penny-wise *adj* [➡FINANCIALLY MEAN AND GRASPING; 520]

pen pal (*informal*) *n* **pen friend**, correspondent, letter writer, friend, pal (*informal*), acquaintance. [➡FRIENDS; 963]

penpusher (*informal*) *n* **bureaucrat**, clerk, writer, scribe, office worker, paper-pusher (*informal*), pencil pusher (*US*). [➡WORKER; 836]

pension **1** *n* **retirement pension**, retirement fund, annuity, income, retirement income, fixed income, allowance, social security (*US*). [➡MONEY, PAYMENTS, AND CHARGES; 800] **2** *type of* **hotel.** [➡HOTELS, RESTAURANTS, AND CLUBS; 1081]

pensioner *n* **retiree**, retired person, senior citizen, senior, OAP. [➡OLD PERSON; 920]

pensive *adj* **thoughtful**, meditative, contemplative, thinking, brooding, pondering, preoccupied, lost in thought, absorbed, engrossed, reflective. [➡PENSIVENESS AND INTEREST; 539]

pensiveness *n* **thoughtfulness**, dreaminess, wistfulness, meditativeness, reflectiveness, preoccupation, contemplativeness, musing. [➡ATTENTION AND ATTENTIVENESS; 764]

pentagon *type of* **angular shape.** [➡ANGULAR SHAPE; 1216]

pentagonal *adj* [➡ANGULAR SHAPE; 1216]

penthouse *type of* **apartment.** [➡RESIDENTIAL BUILDINGS; 1077]

pent-up *adj* **repressed**, stifled, unexpressed, contained, constrained, bottled up, curbed, restrained. [➡SECRET AND UNKNOWN; 180] *Opposite:* voiced.

penultimate *adj* **last but one**, one before the last, next to last, second to last (*US*). [➡AFTER, LAST, AND FOLLOWING; 166]

penumbra **1** *n* **shadow**, shade, darkness. [➡DESCRIBING LIGHT; 1227] **2** *n* **obscurity**, uncertainty, cloudiness, indistinctness. [➡VAGUENESS; 244]

pen up *v* **cage**, round up, shut within, enclose, hold, trap, capture, hem in, keep, imprison, corral (*US*). [➡CAPTIVITY AND LOSS OF FREEDOM; 249] *Opposite:* free.

penurious (*literary*) **1** *adj* **poor**, impoverished, destitute, indigent (*formal*), needy, penniless, impecunious (*formal*), broke (*informal*), strapped (*informal*). [➡POVERTY

AND POOR; 892] *Opposite:* well-off. **2** *adj* **stingy** (*informal*), grudging, scanty, cheap, miserly, niggardly, frugal, mean. [➡FINANCIALLY MEAN AND GRASPING; 520] *Opposite:* generous.

penury *n* **poverty**, pennilessness, destitution, indigence (*formal*), neediness, impecuniousness (*formal*), impoverishment. [➡POVERTY AND POOR; 892] *Opposite:* luxury.

See Compare and Contrast at **poverty**.

peony *type of* **perennial flower**. [➡FLOWERS; 1032]

people **1** *n* **nation**, community, nationality, populace, population, inhabitants. [➡INHABITANT; 857] **2** *n* **persons**, folks, individuals, public, general public, society. [➡GROUPS IN SOCIETY; 940] **3** *n* (*informal*) **relatives**, relations, family, folks, ancestors. [➡THE FAMILY; 956] **4** *v* **populate**, fill, inhabit, immigrate, colonize, pioneer, occupy. [➡INHABIT; 20]

people carrier *type of* **car**. [➡BIKES, CARS, AND CARRIAGES; 1148]

pep (*informal*) *n* **energy**, liveliness, vim (*informal*), vigour, perkiness, zest, verve, activeness, potency, moxie (*US slang*). [➡ENERGY AND ENTHUSIASM; 497]

pepper **1** *v* **sprinkle**, shower, spray, scatter, speckle, dot, stipple. [➡SPREAD AND SCATTER; 333] **2** *v* **scatter**, intersperse, sprinkle, interleave, infuse, interrupt, interfuse, interlace. [➡SPREAD AND SCATTER; 333] **3** *type of* **spice**. [➡HERBS AND SPICES; 1174] **4** *type of* **salad vegetable**. [➡FRUIT AND VEGETABLES; 1175]

pepper-and-salt *adj* **flecked**, streaked, greying, grizzled, patchy, mottled. [➡DESCRIBING PATTERNS; 1226]

peppercorn *type of* **spice**. [➡HERBS AND SPICES; 1174]

peppered moth *type of* **moth**. [➡MOTHS AND BUTTERFLIES; 1015]

pepperiness *n* [➡TASTE; 704]

peppermint *type of* **confectionery**. [➡CONFECTIONERY; 1181]

pepperoni *type of* **processed meat**. [➡TYPES AND CUTS OF MEAT; 1176]

peppery *adj* **spicy**, piquant, hot, fiery, pungent, strong, zesty, gingery. [➡TASTE; 704] *Opposite:* mild.

peppy (*informal*) *adj* **lively**, vigorous, sprightly, perky, frisky, playful, spry, animated, vivacious, energetic. [➡ENERGY AND ENTHUSIASM; 497] *Opposite:* lethargic.

pep talk (*informal*) *n* **team talk**, talking-to (*informal*), speech, support, encouragement, inspiration, boost. [➡NEUTRAL ONE-WAY COMMUNICATION; 49]

peptic *adj* [➡THE DIGESTIVE TRACT; 710]

pep up (*informal*) *v* **spice up**, give a bit of zing (*informal*), add zest, liven up, jazz up (*informal*), make something go with a bang (*informal*), make something swing. [➡IMPROVE SOMETHING; 375]

per *prep* **for each**, apiece, for every, each, per capita. [➡APPORTIONMENT; 113]

perambulate (*formal*) *v* [➡PROCEED AND GO; 306]

perambulator (*formal*) *n* **pram**, pushchair, buggy, baby buggy (*US regional*), stroller (*US*), baby carriage (*US*). [➡BIKES, CARS, AND CARRIAGES; 1148]

per annum *adv* **each year**, by year, yearly, annually, every year, once a year. [➡TIMES OF YEAR; 88]

percale *type of* **synthetic fabric**. [➡FABRICS; 1131]

per capita *adj* **each one**, each person, per person, per head, apiece, per. [➡APPORTIONMENT; 113]

perceivable *adj* [➡PERCEPTIBLE; 25]

perceive **1** *v* **notice**, observe, see, take in, remark, distinguish, recognize, pick out, identify, make out. [➡SEE; 700] *Opposite:* ignore. **2** *v* **understand**, comprehend, sense, feel, become aware of, realize. [➡UNDERSTAND AND GRASP; 760]

per cent **1** *adv* **out of a hundred**, out of each hundred, in each hundred, in a hundred, per hundred. [➡MATHS; 598] **2** *n* **percentage**, part, proportion, ratio, percentile, fraction. [➡MEASUREABLE PORTION; 125]

percentage **1** *n* **fraction**, proportion, ratio, part, section, measurement, calculation. [➡DEGREE AND EXTENT; 110] **2** *n* (*informal*) **commission**, cut (*informal*), proportion, fraction, take, profit, entitlement, gain. [➡MEASUREABLE PORTION; 125]

percentile *n* [➡MEASUREABLE PORTION; 125]

perceptibility *n* [➡PERCEPTIBLE; 25]

perceptible *adj* **noticeable**, traceable, observable, appreciable, visible, definite, distinguishable, distinctive, perceivable, detectable. [➡PERCEPTIBLE; 25] *Opposite:* invisible.

perception **1** *n* **reading**, view, opinion, picture, take, slant, assessment, experience. [➡POINT OF VIEW; 768] **2** *n* **insight**, acuity, awareness, discernment, observation, sensitivity. [➡THE SENSES; 697]

perceptive *adj* **discerning**, sensitive, insightful, keen, observant, understanding, aware, sharp. [➡POSITIVE INTELLECTUAL CHARACTERISTICS; 525] *Opposite:* insensitive.

perceptiveness *n* **insight**, insightfulness, understanding, intuition, discernment, astuteness, acuity, sensitivity, discrimination, sharpness. [➡POSITIVE INTELLECTUAL CHARACTERISTICS; 525]

perch **1** *v* **rest**, sit, settle, balance, alight, land, light. [➡EXIST IN A PLACE; 19] **2** *type of* **freshwater fish**. [➡FRESHWATER FISH; 1010]

perchance (*archaic or literary*) *adv* **perhaps**, maybe, possibly, by chance, conceivably, feasibly. [➡POSSIBLE AND PROBABLE; 178] *Opposite:* definitely.

percipience *n* **insight**, insightfulness, perceptiveness, discernment, understanding, intuition. [➡POSITIVE INTELLECTUAL CHARACTERISTICS; 525] *Opposite:* insensitivity.

percipient *adj* **insightful**, perceptive, observant, discerning, understanding, intuitive. [➡POSITIVE INTELLECTUAL CHARACTERISTICS; 525] *Opposite:* insensitive.

percolate **1** *v* **drip**, filter, trickle, ooze, leach. [➡MOVE SLOWLY; 315] **2** *v* **seep into**, infiltrate, permeate, penetrate, get into, infect, saturate. [➡MOVE PAST, INTO OR THROUGH SOMETHING; 332]

percolator *n* **coffeepot**, coffee maker, coffee machine. [➡HOUSEHOLD APPLIANCES; 1116]

percussion (*formal*) *n* **drumming**, beating, striking, hitting, bass beat, thumping, tapping. [➡IMPACT SOUNDS; 1259]

percussionist *n* [➡MUSICIANS AND SINGERS; 908]

per diem *adj* **by the day**, daily, quotidian (*formal*), day-by-day, part-time, day-to-day, every day. [➡TIMES OF DAY; 87]

perdition *n* **hell**, purgatory, punishment, damnation, abyss, inferno, hades (*informal*), nether world, underworld. [➡RELIGIOUS CONCEPTS; 777]

peregrination (*literary*) *n* **journey**, voyage, passage, traversing, crossing, trip, expedition, excursion, pilgrimage, safari. [➡TRAVEL: JOURNEYS AND TRIPS; 319]

peregrine falcon *type of* **bird of prey**. [➡BIRD OF PREY; 998]

peremptorily *adv* **dictatorially**, imperatively, imperiously, urgently, dogmatically, commandingly, authoritatively, definitively, emphatically, positively. [➡POMPOUS, LOUD, AND OVER-CONFIDENT; 636] *Opposite:* meekly.

peremptory 1 *adj* **dictatorial**, authoritative, unconditional, absolute, dogmatic, imperious, commanding, definite. [➡POMPOUS, LOUD, AND OVER-CONFIDENT; 636] *Opposite:* polite. 2 *adj* **decisive**, no-nonsense, quick, hasty, direct, unthinking, snap, determined, resolute. [➡CERTAINTY; 562] *Opposite:* roundabout.

perennial *adj* **recurrent**, returning, perpetual, constant, persistent, lasting, continuing, permanent, enduring, regular, unfailing. [➡PERMANENCE: WITHOUT END; 94] *Opposite:* occasional.

perestroika *n* **restructuring**, reform, reconstruction, reorganization, modernization, transformation. [➡SOCIAL, POLITICAL, AND ECONOMIC CHANGE; 374]

perfect 1 *adj* **faultless**, flawless, textbook, picture-perfect, seamless, unspoiled, unadulterated, impeccable, unflawed. [➡IN GOOD REPAIR; 1231] *Opposite:* flawed. 2 *adj* **complete**, absolute, unqualified, whole, finished, total, entire, intact. [➡WHOLENESS AND COMPLETENESS; 199] *Opposite:* incomplete. 3 *adj* **ideal**, just right, just the thing, great (*informal*), wonderful, just what the doctor ordered. [➡GOOD, WELL, BETTER; 184] *Opposite:* wrong. 4 *adj* **precise**, exact, accurate, spot-on (*informal*), on target, just right. [➡EXACT; 204] 5 *v* **improve**, refine, hone, tighten up, work on, sharpen, round off, put the finishing touches to. [➡IMPROVE SOMETHING; 375] *Opposite:* spoil. 6 *v* **achieve**, finish, complete, finalize, reach the summit of, top off. [➡COMPLETE AN ACTION; 264] *Opposite:* work on.

perfection 1 *n* **excellence**, rightness, faultlessness, exactness, precision, flawlessness, aptness. [➡CORRECT; 183] 2 *n* **accomplishment**, fulfilment, completion, realization, achievement, working out. [➡END; 54] *Opposite:* abandonment.

perfectionism *n* **fastidiousness**, fussiness, nitpicking, hairsplitting, pedantry, meticulousness, conscientiousness, rigorousness. [➡HARD-WORKING AND COMMITTED; 501] *Opposite:* carelessness.

perfectionist *n* **stickler**, purist, pedant, obsessive, quibbler, hairsplitter, fusspot (*informal*), fussbudget (*US informal*). [➡GRUMPY AND NEGATIVE PEOPLE; 953]

perfectly 1 *adv* **flawlessly**, faultlessly, impeccably, effortlessly, seamlessly, like a dream, without a glitch, dreamily. [➡GOOD, WELL, BETTER; 184] *Opposite:* badly. 2 *adv* **completely**, entirely, wholly, absolutely, utterly, thoroughly, extremely. [➡WHOLENESS AND COMPLETENESS; 199] *Opposite:* partially.

perfidious (*literary*) *adj* **disloyal**, treacherous, deceitful, dishonest, lying, untrue, base, low. [➡DECEITFUL; 514] *Opposite:* honest.

perfidiousness (*literary*) *n* [➡DECEITFUL; 514]

perfidy (*literary*) *n* **treachery**, disloyalty, deceit, duplicity, betrayal, lying, dishonesty. [➡DECEPTION AND LIES; 661] *Opposite:* honesty.

perforate *v* **puncture**, prick, pierce, hole, go through, burst, punch. [➡TEAR, BREAK, AND CUT; 361]

perforation *n* **hole**, puncture, tear, rip, slash, gap. [➡HOLES, GAPS, AND FORKS; 1251]

perforce (*literary*) *adv* **unavoidably**, inevitably, of necessity, necessarily, inescapably, helplessly. [➡NECESSARY AND ESSENTIAL; 197]

perform 1 *v* **do**, carry out, fulfil, achieve, discharge (*formal*), execute, complete, accomplish, implement, act upon, make. [➡CARRY OUT AN ACTION; 270] 2 *v* **present**, act, play, put on, stage, do, enact, impersonate. [➡THE PERFORMING ARTS; 904] 3 *v* **function**, work, behave, act, go, run, operate, react. [➡CARRY OUT AN ACTION; 270]

Compare and Contrast: ***perform, do, carry out, fulfil, discharge, execute***

CORE MEANING: TO COMPLETE A TASK

perform to complete an action or accomplish a task, especially when this requires skill or care or when it forms part of a set procedure; ***do*** to complete an action or accomplish a task of any kind; ***carry out*** to complete any action or task; ***fulfil*** to do what is necessary to achieve the successful accomplishment or realization of something planned, promised, or anticipated; ***discharge*** (*formal*) to complete duties or responsibilities successfully; ***execute*** to put an instruction or plan into effect, or to complete an action or procedure that requires skill and expertise.

performance 1 *n* **presentation**, recital, act, routine, concert, show, piece, enactment. [➡PERFORMANCES AND SHOWS; 42] 2 *n* **functioning**, implementation, execution, performing, carrying out, operation, running, working. [➡CARRY OUT AN ACTION; 270] 3 *n* **feat**, deed, act, accomplishment, occurrence. [➡ACTIONS OR UNDERTAKINGS; 260]

performance art *n* [➡THE PERFORMING ARTS; 904]

performer 1 *n* **player**, actor, musician, recitalist, actress, artist, entertainer. [➡PERFORMERS; 905] *Opposite:* spectator. 2 *n* **doer**, perpetrator, executor, architect, operator. [➡WORKER; 836]

performing arts *n* [➡THE PERFORMING ARTS; 904]

perfume 1 *n* **fragrance**, scent, cologne, body spray, toilet water, body mist, balm, incense. [➡PERSONAL HYGIENE; 492] 2 *n* **smell**, aroma, scent, odour, fragrance, essence, whiff, bouquet, redolence. [➡SMELL AND SMELLING; 706] **3** *v* **scent**, fragrance, imbue, freshen, lace, anoint, aromatize. [➡DECORATE, ADORN, AND APPLY COATINGS; 406]

See Compare and Contrast at **smell.**

perfumed *adj* **scented**, sweet-smelling, sweet-scented, aromatic, fragrant, fragranced, odorous (*literary*), pleasant-smelling, sweetly perfumed. [➡SMELL AND SMELLING; 706]

perfunctory **1** *adj* **unthinking**, automatic, mechanical, dutiful, obligatory, token, routine, careless, cursory. [➡AUTOMATIC AND INSTINCTIVE; 281] *Opposite:* thoughtful. **2** *adj* **hasty**, superficial, quick, fleeting, hurried, passing, rapid, brief. [➡INCAUTIOUS AND CARELESS; 284] *Opposite:* thorough.

pergola *n* **arch**, trellis, framework, arbour, structure, passageway, pavilion, arcade, walkway, bower. [➡ANCILLARY BUILDINGS; 1079]

perhaps *adv* **maybe**, possibly, conceivably, perchance (*archaic or literary*), feasibly, imaginably. [➡POSSIBLE AND PROBABLE; 178] *Opposite:* definitely.

per head *adj* [➡APPORTIONMENT; 113]

peril *n* **danger**, threat, risk, hazard, jeopardy, liability, exposure. [➡DANGER; 236] *Opposite:* safety.

perilous *adj* **dangerous**, unsafe, hazardous, risky, death-defying, terrifying, exposed, extreme. [➡DANGEROUS; 237] *Opposite:* safe.

perilousness *n* [➡DANGER; 236]

perimeter *n* **boundary**, border, edge, limit, outskirts, outside. [➡EXTREMITIES OF PHYSICAL OBJECTS; 1249]

perinatal *adj* [➡REPRODUCTION AND HEREDITY; 726]

period **1** *n* **interval**, episode, interlude, phase, cycle, time, extent. [➡PERIOD OF TIME; 90] **2** *n* **era**, age, epoch, stage, phase, time, day. [➡EPOCHS AND ERAS; 89] **3** (*US*) *type of* **punctuation mark.** [➡ASPECTS OF LANGUAGE; 683]

periodic **1** *adj* **episodic**, intermittent, interrupted, sporadic, occasional, broken, intervallic. [➡FINITENESS, VARIABILITY, AND TRANSIENCE; 96] *Opposite:* constant. **2** *adj* **cyclic**, recurring, recurrent, serial, regular, continuing, seasonal. [➡FREQUENT AND OFTEN; 107] *Opposite:* irregular.

Compare and Contrast: ***periodic, intermittent, occasional, sporadic***

CORE MEANING: RECURRING OVER A PERIOD OF TIME

periodic recurring or reappearing from time to time with a degree of regularity; ***intermittent*** occurring at irregular intervals; ***occasional*** occurring infrequently at irregular intervals; ***sporadic*** occuring irregularly and unpredictably.

periodical *n* **journal**, bulletin, magazine, review, publication, monthly, weekly, quarterly. [➡NEWSPAPERS; 606]

peripatetic *adj* **itinerant**, travelling, nomadic, wandering, roving, roaming. [➡EMPLOYMENT STATUS; 831] *Opposite:* settled.

peripheral **1** *adj* **outlying**, marginal, fringe, bordering, exterior, outer. [➡RELATIVE LOCATION; 162] *Opposite:* central. **2** *adj* **minor**, incidental, tangential, marginal, unimportant, nonessential, sideline, secondary, superficial. [➡UNIMPORTANT AND UNNECESSARY; 239] *Opposite:* central.

peripherally *adv* **incidentally**, superficially, unimportantly, marginally, tangentially, irrelevantly, nonessentially, secondarily. [➡UNIMPORTANT AND UNNECESSARY; 239] *Opposite:* significantly.

periphery *n* **boundary**, margin, edge, sideline, border, fringe, outside. [➡EXTREMITIES OF PHYSICAL OBJECTS; 1249] *Opposite:* centre.

periscope *type of* **optical instrument.** [➡OPTICAL INSTRUMENTS; 1123]

perish (*literary*) *v* **die**, expire, pass away, breathe your last (*literary*), depart this life (*formal*), give up the ghost (*literary*), take your last breath, succumb, decease (*formal*). [➡DIE; 922] *Opposite:* live.

perishable *adj* **unpreserved**, fresh, untreated. [➡RAW AND NATURAL; 1213] *Opposite:* preserved.

perished (*informal*) *adj* **cold**, freezing, frozen, shivering, perishing, chilled, raw. [➡TEMPERATURE: COLD; 1230] *Opposite:* boiling.

perishing *adj* **cold**, freezing, bitter, raw, chilly, nippy, arctic (*informal*), frozen, shivering. [➡COLD WEATHER; 1051] *Opposite:* boiling.

periwig *n* **wig**, hairpiece, toupee, rug (*informal*), peruke (*archaic*). [➡HAIR STYLES AND HAIR PIECES; 489]

perjure *v* **lie**, bear false witness, commit perjury, forswear (*archaic or literary*), fabricate, stretch the truth, be economical with the truth, equivocate, prevaricate. [➡DECEPTION AND LIES; 661] *Opposite:* tell the truth.

perjurer *n* [➡PEOPLE WHO DECEIVE; 662]

perjury *n* **lying**, untruthfulness, lie, falsehood, untruth, fabrication, falsification, mendacity, equivocation, prevarication. [➡DECEPTION AND LIES; 661] *Opposite:* honesty.

perk *n* **bonus**, benefit, incentive, perquisite, extra, plus (*informal*), plus point, privilege, gratuity, freebie (*informal*), advantage, pro, sweetener (*informal*). [➡REWARDS AND AWARDS; 440] *Opposite:* disadvantage.

perkily **1** *adv* **cheerfully**, energetically, jauntily, pertly, happily, animatedly, buoyantly, spryly, bouncily, briskly, spiritedly, vibrantly. [➡WITH ENTHUSIASM; 287] *Opposite:* despondently. **2** *adv* **overconfidently**, confidently, self-confidently, self-importantly, self-assuredly, cockily, bumptiously. [➡POMPOUS, LOUD, AND OVER-CONFIDENT; 636] *Opposite:* timidly.

perkiness **1** *n* **liveliness**, cheerfulness, energy, jauntiness, pertness, sprightliness, pep (*informal*), zest, verve, vigour, happiness, animation, buoyancy, bounciness, spryness, briskness, spiritedness, spirit, vibrancy. [➡ENERGY AND ENTHUSIASM; 497] **2** *n* **overconfidence**, confidence, self-confidence, self-importance, self-assurance, cockiness, cocksureness, bumptiousness. [➡POMPOUS, LOUD, AND OVER-CONFIDENT; 636] *Opposite:* timidity.

perk up **1** *v* **liven up**, cheer up, brighten up, pep up (*informal*), wake up, awaken, animate, get into the mood, spice up, enliven, brighten, cheer. [➡ENCOURAGE; 577] 2 *v* **stick up**, stand up, prick up, cock up, pop up, straighten up. [➡GO UPWARDS; 307] *Opposite:* droop.

perky 1 *adj* **lively**, cheerful, energetic, jaunty, pert, sprightly, happy, animated, buoyant, bouncy, spry, brisk, spirited, vibrant. [➡CHEERFULNESS OF OUTLOOK; 504] *Opposite:* despondent. 2 *adj* **overconfident**, confident, self-confident, self-important, self-assured, cocky (*informal*), cocksure, bumptious. [➡POMPOUS, LOUD, AND OVER-CONFIDENT; 636] *Opposite:* timid.

perm *v* **curl**, wave, kink, crimp, frizz. [➡CHANGE OF SHAPE; 386] *Opposite:* straighten.

permafrost *n* [➡EROSION PRODUCTS AND SOIL; 1058]

permanence *n* **perpetuity**, durability, durableness, longevity, solidity, stability, immovability, lastingness. [➡PERMANENCE: WITHOUT END; 94] *Opposite:* transience.

permanency *see* **permanence**.

permanent *adj* **perpetual**, enduring, lasting, eternal, everlasting, long-lasting, undying, stable, undeviating, unending, constant. [➡PERMANENCE: WITHOUT END; 94] *Opposite:* temporary.

permanent-press *adj* [➡DESCRIBING CLOTHES; 869]

permeability *n* **porousness**, penetrability, perviousness, absorbency, absorptivity, sponginess. [➡DENSITY AND CONSISTENCY; 1206] *Opposite:* impermeability.

permeable *adj* **porous**, penetrable, pervious, absorbent, absorptive, spongy, holey, leaky. [➡DENSITY AND CONSISTENCY; 1206] *Opposite:* impermeable.

permeate 1 *v* **infuse**, pervade, flood, fill, saturate, soak, infiltrate, invade, spread through. [➡FILL; 407] 2 *v* **filter**, seep, leak, pervade, penetrate, soak, percolate, impregnate, pass, infiltrate, enter. [➡MOVE PAST, INTO OR THROUGH SOMETHING; 332]

permeation 1 *n* **infusion**, pervasion, flood, saturation, infiltration, invasion, spread. [➡MORE AND EXCESS; 122] 2 *n* **filtration**, seepage, leakage, pervasion, entrance, penetration, percolation, impregnation, diffusion. [➡DENSITY AND CONSISTENCY; 1206]

permissible *adj* **allowable**, allowed, permitted, acceptable, accepted, tolerable, tolerated, approved, admissible, legitimate, legal, lawful. [➡PERMIT AND ALLOW; 670] *Opposite:* unacceptable.

permission *n* **consent**, authorization, approval, agreement, leave (*formal*), acquiescence, go-ahead (*informal*), green light, clearance, sanction, blessing, carte blanche, OK (*informal*), say-so (*informal*). [➡REFUSE PERMISSION AND NOT ALLOW; 671]

permissive *adj* **tolerant**, lenient, liberal, accommodating, lax, laissez-faire, hands-off, broad-minded, nonjudgmental, free, loose, indulgent, progressive, open-minded. [➡CONFIDENCE AND COMPOSURE; 500] *Opposite:* strict.

permissively *adv* **tolerantly**, leniently, liberally, accommodatingly, laxly, broad-mindedly, nonjudgmentally, freely, loosely, indulgently, progressively, open-mindedly. [➡POSITIVE INTELLECTUAL CHARACTERISTICS; 525] *Opposite:* strictly.

permissiveness *n* **tolerance**, leniency, liberalism, laxness, laxity, broad-mindedness, licence, indulgence, progressiveness, open-mindedness, flexibility, openness. [➡POSITIVE INTELLECTUAL CHARACTERISTICS; 525] *Opposite:* strictness.

permit 1 *v* **authorize**, allow, let, approve, consent to, agree to, sanction, acquiesce to, pass, clear, give the go-ahead, give your blessing, give the green light, give carte blanche, OK (*informal*), give leave (*formal*), tolerate, enable, facilitate. [➡PERMIT AND ALLOW; 670] *Opposite:* forbid. 2 *n* **licence**, document, certification, certificate, authorization, authority, warrant, card, badge. [➡OFFICIAL DOCUMENTS; 587]

permitted *adj* **allowed**, allowable, permissible, acceptable, accepted, approved, tolerable, tolerated, admissible, legitimate, legal, lawful. [➡PERMIT AND ALLOW; 670] *Opposite:* forbidden.

permutation *n* **variation**, transformation, version, arrangement, rearrangement, combination, alternative, change, vicissitude, mutation. [➡CHANGE; 373]

pernicious 1 *adj* **malicious**, wicked, evil, malevolent, malign, malignant, maleficent, spiteful, bad. [➡MORALLY BAD; 776] *Opposite:* benign. 2 *adj* **destructive**, harmful, deadly, fatal, insidious, ruinous, malignant, damaging, deleterious (*formal*), noxious. [➡DANGEROUS; 237] *Opposite:* harmless.

perniciousness 1 *n* **maliciousness**, malice, wickedness, evil, malevolence, malignity, maleficence, spite, badness. [➡MORALLY BAD; 776] *Opposite:* benignity. 2 *n* **destructiveness**, harmfulness, deadliness, insidiousness, ruinousness, malignancy, deleteriousness (*formal*), noxiousness. [➡DANGER; 236] *Opposite:* harmlessness.

pernicketiness (*informal*) *n* [➡DIFFICULT TO PLEASE; 516]

pernickety (*informal*) 1 *adj* **meticulous**, exacting, demanding, finicky, fussy, picky, painstaking, nit-picking, pedantic, particular, choosy (*informal*), fastidious, punctilious, nice. [➡DIFFICULT TO PLEASE; 516] *Opposite:* slapdash. 2 *adj* **detailed**, exacting, fiddly (*informal*), painstaking, precise, finicky, fine, complex, complicated. [➡DIFFICULTY AND COMPLEXITY; 243] *Opposite:* straightforward.

perorate (*formal*) *v* [➡INSTRUCT AND TEACH; 610]

peroration (*formal*) *n* **speech**, oration, discourse, address, talk, lecture, declamation. [➡NEUTRAL ONE-WAY COMMUNICATION; 49]

peroxide 1 *n* **hydrogen peroxide**, bleaching agent, bleach, tint. [➡DYES AND COLOURANTS; 1269] 2 *v* **bleach**, tint, lighten, dye, colour, rinse, fade, discolour. [➡CHANGE OF COLOUR; 392]

perp (*US slang*) *n* [➡CRIMINALS; 821]

perpend (*archaic*) *v* [➡THINK AND REFLECT; 744]

perpendicular 1 *adj* **vertical**, at right angles, upright, bolt upright, erect, sheer, abrupt, steep. [➡ORIENTATION AND ALIGNMENT; 1222] *Opposite:* parallel. 2 *type of* **pre-20th-century architecture**. [➡BUILDING AND ARCHITECTURE; 1075]

per person *adj* [➡APPORTIONMENT; 113]

perpetrate *v* **commit**, carry out, pull off (*informal*), do, be responsible for, be behind, enact, execute, perform, effect (*formal*). [➡CARRY OUT AN ACTION; 270]

perpetration *n* **commission**, enactment, transaction, action, responsibility, performance, execution. [➡CARRY OUT AN ACTION; 270]

perpetrator *n* **culprit**, criminal, wrongdoer, guilty party, offender, committer, agent, perp (*US slang*). [➡CRIMINALS; 821]

perpetual *adj* **continuous**, everlasting, uninterrupted, lasting, unending, long-lasting, eternal, continual, permanent, constant, enduring, undying. [➡PERMANENCE: WITHOUT END; 94] *Opposite:* temporary.

perpetuate *v* **continue**, preserve, prolong, carry on, spread, disseminate, keep up, maintain, keep alive, propagate, extend, immortalize. [➡CAUSE TO CONTINUE; 268] *Opposite:* stop.

perpetuation *n* **continuation**, continuance, preservation, prolongation, spread, dissemination, maintenance, propagation, endurance, extension, immortalization. [➡PERMANENCE: WITHOUT END; 94] *Opposite:* ending.

perpetuity *n* **eternity**, time without end, all time, infinity, permanence, endlessness, timelessness, imperishability. [➡PERMANENCE: WITHOUT END; 94]

perplex *v* **puzzle**, baffle, confuse, stun, throw (*informal*), mystify, confound, stump, flummox (*informal*), fox, bewilder, befuddle, bamboozle (*informal*), disconcert. [➡CONFUSE AND BEWILDER; 572] *Opposite:* enlighten.

perplexed *adj* **puzzled**, baffled, confused, at a loss, stunned, thrown (*informal*), mystified, confounded, stumped, flummoxed (*informal*), foxed, bewildered, befuddled, bamboozled (*informal*), disconcerted, blank, uncomprehending. [➡CONFUSION, ANXIETY, AND WORRY; 541] *Opposite:* comprehending.

perplexing *adj* **puzzling**, baffling, confusing, mystifying, confounding, bewildering, disconcerting, impenetrable, difficult, befuddling. [➡DIFFICULTY AND COMPLEXITY; 243] *Opposite:* simple.

perplexity *n* **puzzlement**, bafflement, confusion, bewilderment, mystification, blankness, incomprehension. [➡CONFUSION, ANXIETY, AND WORRY; 541] *Opposite:* comprehension.

perquisite (*formal*) *n* **privilege**, gratuity, freebie (*informal*), perk, bonus, benefit, extra, advantage, incentive, plus, plus point, sweetener (*informal*). [➡REWARDS AND AWARDS; 440] *Opposite:* disadvantage.

per se (*formal*) *adv* **as such**, by itself, for itself, in isolation, intrinsically. [➡FOREIGN WORDS AND PHRASES; 673]

persecute 1 *v* **oppress**, hound, harass, maltreat, pursue, hunt, single out, discriminate against, bully, torture, torment, tyrannize, intimidate. [➡UPSET, DISTRESS, AND HUMILIATE; 568] *Opposite:* protect. 2 *v* **pester**, harass, torment, hassle (*informal*), bother, bait, badger, annoy, irritate. [➡COMPLAIN AND NAG; 687] *Opposite:* leave alone.

persecuted *adj* [➡IN TROUBLE AND DISADVANTAGED; 73]

persecution 1 *n* **oppression**, harassment, maltreatment, pursuit, discrimination, torture, torment, tyranny, intimidation, subjection. [➡UNKIND ACTION OR BEHAVIOUR; 297] *Opposite:* protection. 2 *n* **harassment**, torment, hassle (*informal*), annoyance, irritation, suffering, vexation. [➡COMPLAIN AND NAG; 687]

persecutor 1 *n* **oppressor**, harasser, pursuer, bully, torturer, tormentor, tyrant, intimidator. [➡ENEMIES AND TORMENTORS; 969] *Opposite:* protector. 2 *n* **pesterer**, harasser, tormentor, nuisance, baiter, heckler, aggravator, gadfly, a thorn in somebody's flesh. [➡ENEMIES AND TORMENTORS; 969]

perseverance *n* **persistence**, determination, resolve, resolution, doggedness, diligence, grit, insistence, tenacity, obstinacy, stubbornness, tirelessness, endurance, steadfastness, purpose, dedication, devotion, drive. [➡STRENGTH OF WILL; 502]

persevere *v* **persist**, continue, keep at, keep it up, keep on, carry on, stick it out, stick, insist, endure, proceed, press on. [➡CONTINUE AN ACTION; 263] *Opposite:* give up.

persevering *adj* **persistent**, determined, resolute, resolved, dogged, diligent, insistent, tenacious, obstinate, stubborn, tireless, enduring, steadfast, purposeful, dedicated, devoted, driven, staunch, unrelenting, unwavering, indomitable, single-minded. [➡STRENGTH OF WILL; 502] *Opposite:* irresolute.

Persian cat *type of* **cat**. [➡FELINE; 983]

persist 1 *v* **persevere**, continue, keep at, keep it up, keep on, carry on, stick it out, stick at. [➡CONTINUE AN ACTION; 263] *Opposite:* give up. 2 *v* **continue**, endure, live on, stay, stick around (*informal*), go on, hang on, refuse to go away. [➡CONTINUE TO EXIST; 17] *Opposite:* fade away.

persistence 1 *n* **perseverance**, determination, tenacity, resolve, resolution, doggedness, diligence, importunity (*formal*), insistence, obstinacy, stubbornness, tirelessness, endurance, steadfastness, purpose, dedication, devotion, drive, grit, pushiness (*informal*). [➡STRENGTH OF WILL; 502] 2 *n* **continuance**, continuation, endurance, permanence, preservation, maintenance, continuity, durability. [➡PERMANENCE: WITHOUT END; 94] *Opposite:* transience.

persistent 1 *adj* **tenacious**, determined, obstinate, insistent, dogged, stubborn, tireless, untiring, pushy (*informal*), assiduous, importunate (*formal*), steadfast. [➡STRENGTH OF WILL; 502] *Opposite:* irresolute. 2 *adj* **continuing**, continual, continued, unrelenting, incessant, constant, relentless, permanent, lasting, remaining, enduring. [➡PERMANENCE: WITHOUT END; 94] *Opposite:* fleeting.

person 1 *n* **being**, human being, individual, creature, soul, type, party, one, somebody, anybody, human. [➡PERSON; 931] 2 *n* **body**, form, frame, figure. [➡BODY; 692] 3 *n* (*formal*) **appearance**, persona, personality, character, ego, mien (*literary*). [➡PSYCHOLOGY AND THE MIND; 770]

persona 1 *n* **character**, figure, person, role, part, personage (*formal*). [➡PERSON; 931] 2 *n* **identity**, role, guise, personality, character, qualities, façade, front, face, image. [➡REPRESENTATIONS AND GENERAL EXAMPLES; 65]

personable *adj* **amiable**, friendly, pleasant, affable, agreeable, likable, charming, attractive. [➡FRIENDLINESS AND SOCIABILITY; 495] *Opposite:* disagreeable.

personage (*formal*) *n* **VIP**, celebrity, star, public figure, dignitary, somebody, notable, grandee. [➡ IMPORTANT OR FAMOUS PEOPLE; 893] *Opposite:* nobody.

personal 1 *adj* **individual**, private, own, special, particular, peculiar, subjective, respective, delicate, intimate. [➡ BELONGING OR RELATING TO INDIVIDUALS; 944] *Opposite:* public. 2 *adj* **offensive**, rude, derogatory, familiar, intrusive, impertinent (*formal*), cheeky. [➡ EMOTIONALLY UNPLEASANT AND UPSETTING; 228] *Opposite:* complimentary. 3 *n* (*US*) **classified ad**, ad, advertisement, announcement, public notice, classified advertisement, advert (*informal*), classifieds (*informal*), personal ad, want ad (*US informal*). [➡ ADVERTISING AND PUBLICITY; 605]

personal ad *n* **classified ad**, ad, advert (*informal*), advertisement, announcement, public notice, classified advertisement, classifieds (*informal*), want ad (*US informal*), personal (*US*). [➡ ADVERTISING AND PUBLICITY; 605]

personal assistant *n* **PA**, secretary, assistant, administrative assistant, administrator, right arm, aide. [➡ SUBORDINATES AND ASSISTANTS; 966]

personal belongings *n* [➡ POSSESSIONS; 462]

personal computer *n* **PC**, computer, terminal, laptop, notebook, palmtop, workstation, word processor. [➡ COMPUTERS AND COMPUTING; 1126]

personal effects *n* **belongings**, possessions, personal property, effects (*formal*), things, stuff, gear (*informal*). [➡ POSSESSIONS; 462]

personal hygiene *n* [➡ PERSONAL HYGIENE; 492]

personality 1 *n* **character**, nature, disposition, temperament, makeup, traits, qualities, persona, behaviour. [➡ TEMPERAMENT AND BEHAVIOUR; 493] 2 *n* **celebrity**, star, public figure, somebody, VIP, dignitary. [➡ IMPORTANT OR FAMOUS PEOPLE; 893] *Opposite:* nobody.

personalize 1 *v* **initial**, monogram, mark, engrave, identify, brand, distinguish, tattoo. [➡ DECORATE, ADORN, AND APPLY COATINGS; 406] 2 *v* **customize**, individualize, differentiate, specify, change, modify. [➡ CHANGE; 373] *Opposite:* generalize.

personally 1 *adv* **for myself**, in my opinion, in my view, for my part, myself. [➡ EXPRESSIONS OF OPINION; 624] *Opposite:* generally. 2 *adv* **in person**, face to face, individually, myself, directly. [➡ BELONGING OR RELATING TO INDIVIDUALS; 944] *Opposite:* indirectly.

personal organizer 1 *n* **diary**, planner, appointment book, address book, engagement book, aide-mémoire (*formal*), calendar, datebook (*US*). [➡ LISTS AND SCHEDULES; 588] 2 *n* **hand-held computer**, electronic planner, palmtop, electronic organizer. [➡ COMPUTERS AND COMPUTING; 1126]

personal possessions *n* [➡ POSSESSIONS; 462]

personal property *n* [➡ POSSESSIONS; 462]

personal stereo *type of* **audio equipment**. [➡ AUDIO EQUIPMENT; 1138]

persona non grata *n* [➡ LAZY OR UNSUCCESSFUL PEOPLE; 948]

personate *v* [➡ REPRESENT SOMETHING OR SOMEBODY; 59]

personation *n* [➡ REPRESENTATIONS AND GENERAL EXAMPLES; 65]

personification *n* **epitome**, image, embodiment, incarnation, representation, characterization, distillation, exemplification. [➡ REPRESENTATIONS AND GENERAL EXAMPLES; 65]

personify 1 *v* **epitomize**, embody, incarnate, exemplify, characterize, typify, represent, show. [➡ REPRESENT SOMETHING OR SOMEBODY; 59] 2 *v* **anthropomorphize**, humanize, personalize, give a human face, bring alive. [➡ PRETEND AND MIMIC; 60]

personnel *n* **workers**, staff, employees, workforce, human resources, people, recruits, labourers. [➡ THE WORK FORCE; 837]

perspective 1 *n* **viewpoint**, standpoint, outlook, view, perception, point of view, side, angle, take, evaluation, assessment. [➡ POINT OF VIEW; 768] 2 *n* **proportion**, scale, ratio, size, depth, range, distance. [➡ DEGREE AND EXTENT; 110] 3 *n* **vista**, view, prospect, scene, lookout, outlook, overlook. [➡ VIEWS AND OUTLOOKS; 1072]

perspicacious *adj* **discerning**, perceptive, astute, insightful, wise, sagacious (*formal*), sharp, smart, clear-sighted. [➡ POSITIVE INTELLECTUAL CHARACTERISTICS; 525] *Opposite:* obtuse.

perspicacity *n* **discernment**, perceptiveness, astuteness, shrewdness, clear-sightedness, cleverness, intelligence, insightfulness, wisdom, acuity, sharpness. [➡ POSITIVE INTELLECTUAL CHARACTERISTICS; 525]

perspicuity *n* [➡ POSITIVE INTELLECTUAL CHARACTERISTICS; 525]

perspicuous *adj* [➡ POSITIVE INTELLECTUAL CHARACTERISTICS; 525]

perspiration *n* **sweat**, fluid, exudate, secretion, moisture, dampness, wetness. [➡ EXCRETION AND EXCRETA; 723]

perspire *v* **sweat**, exude, ooze, swelter, drip, secrete. [➡ EXCRETION AND EXCRETA; 723]

persuade 1 *v* **encourage**, coax, influence, induce, motivate, convince, prevail upon, sway, plead with. [➡ CAUSE OR COMPEL TO ACT; 272] *Opposite:* dissuade. 2 *v* **convince**, win over, sway, convert, bring round. [➡ ENCOURAGE; 577]

persuaded *adj* [➡ CERTAINTY; 562]

persuasion 1 *n* **persuading**, encouragement, coaxing, influence, urging, arguments, wiles, inducement, conversion. [➡ ELOQUENT, TALKATIVE AND LONG-WINDED; 633] 2 *n* **affiliation**, belief, order, denomination, faith, conviction, opinion, view, creed, credo. [➡ POINT OF VIEW; 768]

persuasive *adj* **convincing**, influential, winning, swaying, believable, credible, cogent. [➡ ELOQUENT, TALKATIVE AND LONG-WINDED; 633] *Opposite:* unconvincing.

persuasiveness *n* **persuasion**, influence, cogency (*formal*), smoothness, eloquence, articulateness, slickness. [➡ ELOQUENT, TALKATIVE AND LONG-WINDED; 633]

pert *adj* **cheeky**, chirpy (*informal*), lively, flippant, flip (*informal*), impertinent (*formal*), impudent, perky, breezy, animated, jaunty, vivacious, sassy (*US*). [➡ CHEERFULNESS OF OUTLOOK; 504]

pertain to *v* **relate**, refer to, apply to, belong to, affect, connect to. [➡ BE ABOUT SOMETHING; 62]

pertinacious *adj* **resolute**, stubborn, obstinate, persistent, headstrong, perverse, tenacious, wilful, obdurate, mulish, unshakable. [➡ UNWILLINGNESS AND STUBBORNNESS; 565] *Opposite:* malleable.

pertinence *n* **relevance**, relatedness, appositeness, appropriateness, germaneness (*formal*), suitability, aptness, applicability. [➡ CONNECTION; 144] *Opposite:* irrelevance.

pertinent *adj* **relevant**, related, apposite, appropriate, germane (*formal*), applicable, relatable, apt, valid. [➡ IMPORTANT; 195] *Opposite:* irrelevant.

pertly *adv* **cheekily** (*informal*), chirpily (*informal*), flippantly, perkily, breezily, animatedly, impertinently (*formal*), impudently, jauntily, vivaciously, sassily (*US*). [➡ GOOD-TEMPERED AND HUMOROUS; 628] *Opposite:* bashfully.

pertness *n* **cheekiness** (*informal*), chirpiness (*informal*), liveliness, flippancy, perkiness, breeziness, impertinence (*formal*), jauntiness, vivacity, impudence, sassiness (*US*). [➡ CHEERFULNESS OF OUTLOOK; 504]

perturb *v* **trouble**, bother, disturb, worry, agitate, upset, discompose (*formal*), shake up, ruffle, fluster, flurry. [➡ UPSET, DISTRESS, AND HUMILIATE; 568]

perturbation *n* **alarm**, worry, agitation, disquiet, trepidation, discomposure, disconcertion, uneasiness, unrest, distress. [➡ SADNESS, DISTRESS, AND DESPAIR; 540] *Opposite:* composure.

perturbed *adj* **troubled**, disturbed, worried, anxious, disconcerted, agitated, uneasy, distressed, nervous. [➡ CONFUSION, ANXIETY, AND WORRY; 541] *Opposite:* composed.

perturbing *adj* [➡ EMOTIONALLY UNPLEASANT AND UPSETTING; 228]

perusal *n* **examination**, scrutiny, inspection, checking, readthrough, survey, review. [➡ EXAMINE AND ASSESS; 754]

peruse *v* **read**, examine, scan, pore over, scrutinize, inspect, check. [➡ READ; 759] *Opposite:* skim.

pervade *v* **permeate**, pass through, saturate, spread through, infuse, suffuse, diffuse, transfuse, infiltrate. [➡ MOVE PAST, INTO OR THROUGH SOMETHING; 332]

pervasive *adj* **extensive**, universal, general, inescapable, prevalent, widespread, ubiquitous, omnipresent, persistent, rife. [➡ PRESENT AND AVAILABLE; 11] *Opposite:* localized.

pervasiveness *n* **extensiveness**, universality, generality, ubiquity, ubiquitousness, inescapability, prevalence, omnipresence, rifeness, commonness. [➡ PRESENT AND AVAILABLE; 11]

perverse 1 *adj* **aberrant**, irrational, deviant, abnormal, unreasonable, contrary, rebellious, disobedient, contradictory, difficult. [➡ DIFFICULT TO PLEASE; 516] *Opposite:* obliging. 2 *adj* **obstinate**, wilful, stubborn, awkward, headstrong, pertinacious, tenacious, obdurate, dogged. [➡ UNWILLINGNESS AND STUBBORNNESS; 565] *Opposite:* malleable.

perverseness 1 *n* **aberrance**, irrationality, deviance, disobedience, unreasonableness, contrariness, rebelliousness. [➡ BAD BEHAVIOUR OR ACTION; 255] 2 *n* **wilfulness**, stubbornness, contrariness, recalcitrance. [➡ UNWILLINGNESS AND STUBBORNNESS; 565] *Opposite:* malleability.

perversion (*disapproving*) *n* **distortion**, misinterpretation, twisting, corruption, misapplication, falsification. [➡ MISUSE AND ABUSE; 472]

perversity *n* **obstinacy**, wilfulness, stubbornness, unreasonableness, contrariness, intransigence. [➡ UNWILLINGNESS AND STUBBORNNESS; 565] *Opposite:* malleability.

pervert 1 *v* **deprave**, corrupt, debauch (*formal*), lead astray, spoil, warp. [➡ WORSEN SOMETHING; 381] 2 *v* **distort**, misinterpret, twist, misrepresent, alter, spoil, change, garble. [➡ FALSIFY AND CHEAT; 177]

perverted 1 *adj* **depraved**, corrupt, debauched, warped, degenerate, wayward, deviant, deviate, aberrant, spoiled, abnormal. [➡ MORALLY BAD; 776] 2 *adj* **distorted**, misinterpreted, twisted, garbled, changed, misrepresented, altered. [➡ FALSE AND UNREAL; 174] *Opposite:* undistorted.

pervious 1 *adj* **porous**, penetrable, absorbent, permeable. [➡ DENSITY AND CONSISTENCY; 1206] *Opposite:* impervious. 2 *adj* **receptive**, amenable, responsive, flexible, open. [➡ POSITIVE INTELLECTUAL CHARACTERISTICS; 525] *Opposite:* impervious.

perviousness *n* [➡ DENSITY AND CONSISTENCY; 1206]

pesky (*US informal*) *adj* **irritating**, troublesome, annoying, harassing, bothersome, irksome, vexatious, galling, chafing. [➡ IRRITATING; 229]

pessimism *n* **negativity**, cynicism, doubt, distrust, gloom, glumness, nihilism, suspicion, hopelessness. [➡ FEELINGS ABOUT THE FUTURE; 534] *Opposite:* optimism.

pessimist *n* **cynic**, doubter, worrier, nihilist, defeatist, wet blanket (*informal*), doomsayer, doom merchant, doomster (*informal*), worryguts (*informal*), naysayer (*US literary*), worrywart (*US informal*), gloomy Gus (*US*). [➡ GRUMPY AND NEGATIVE PEOPLE; 953] *Opposite:* optimist.

pessimistic *adj* **negative**, cynical, doubtful, distrustful, gloomy, glum, unenthusiastic, suspicious. [➡ NEGATIVE OF OUTLOOK; 515] *Opposite:* optimistic.

pest 1 *n* **vermin**, bug, insect, fly, mosquito. [➡ INSECTS; 1012] 2 *n* (*informal*) **bother**, nuisance, annoyance, vexation, hassle (*informal*), irritant, pain in the neck (*informal*). [➡ NUISANCES; 254]

pester *v* **annoy**, harass, worry, beleaguer, disturb, bedevil, tease, hector, hound, dog, nag, pick on, ride (*US informal*). [➡ ANGER AND ANNOY; 570] *Opposite:* delight.

pesticide *n* **insecticide**, insect repellent, fly spray, bug juice (*US slang*). [➡ UNPLEASANT AND DIRTY SUBSTANCES; 1267]

pestilence (*archaic*) *n* **plague**, epidemic, virus, disease, bubonic plague, endemic, pandemic. [➡ SICKNESS; 730]

pestilent 1 *adj* **infected**, plague-ridden, contaminated, polluted, bug-ridden, infested, toxic, diseased. [➡ DIRTY; 1234] *Opposite:* healthy. 2 *adj* **deadly**, lethal, fatal, virulent, killer, pestilential, infectious, contagious. [➡ DANGEROUS; 237] *Opposite:* mild. 3 *adj* (*literary or humorous*) **annoying**, irksome, irritating, bothersome, troublesome, pesky (*US informal*). [➡ IRRITATING; 229] *Opposite:* pleasing.

pestilential *adj* [➡ DECAYING OR INFESTED; 1235]

pestle *type of* **utensil**. [➡ TABLEWARE, CUTLERY, AND KITCHENWARE; 861]

pest-ridden *adj* [➡DECAYING OR INFESTED; 1235]

pet 1 *n* **animal**, domestic animal, domesticated animal, tame animal, companion, four-legged friend. [➡LIVING THINGS AND LIVING; 976] 2 *n* **favourite**, darling, treasure, jewel, idol, beloved, apple of somebody's eye. [➡PEOPLE WHO ARE APPROVED OF; 955] 3 *n* **dear**, love, darling, precious, dearest, sweetheart, babe (*slang*), baby (*slang*), sweetie (*informal*), honey (*US informal*). [➡ENDEARMENTS; 657] 4 *n* **sulk**, huff, pique, temper, tantrum, tiff, miff (*informal*). [➡IRRITATION AND ANGER; 542] 5 *adj* **favourite**, special, cherished, indulged, preferred, beloved, dearest, precious, prized, dear. [➡POPULAR AND WANTED; 221] 6 *v* **stroke**, pat, fondle, caress, nuzzle, rub. [➡CONTACT: TOUCH; 413] 7 *v* **indulge**, pamper, cosset, mollycoddle, spoil, fuss over, make a fuss of, coddle. [➡TAKE CARE OF AND SPOIL; 301]

peter out *v* **disappear**, dwindle, fade, recede, decrease, go away, diminish, die out, melt away, dissolve. [➡DISAPPEAR; 4] *Opposite:* grow.

petite *adj* **small**, diminutive, short, little, tiny, elfin. [➡BUILD; 478]

petition 1 *n* **request**, appeal, entreaty, requisition, supplication (*formal*), application, plea. [➡LISTS AND SCHEDULES; 588] 2 *v* **appeal**, lobby, request, beg, implore (*formal*), plead, ask, solicit. [➡REQUEST AND DEMAND; 664]

petitioner *n* **supplicant** (*formal*), lobbyist, activist, campaigner, requester, asker, suitor, solicitor. [➡PEOPLE WHO MAKE REQUESTS; 665]

petits pois *type of* **pulse**. [➡BEANS AND PULSES; 1188]

pet name *n* **name**, nickname, sobriquet, diminutive, moniker (*slang*), epithet, handle (*slang*). [➡NAME AND DESCRIBE; 666]

petrification *n* [➡HARDEN, CONGEAL, DRY; 388]

petrified 1 *adj* **frightened**, terrified, scared, alarmed, scared stiff, horrified. [➡FEAR AND PANIC; 544] *Opposite:* reassured. 2 *adj* **fossilized**, hardened, solidified, fixed, calcified, rigidified, ossified. [➡RIGID AND HARD; 1210]

petrify 1 *v* **frighten**, terrify, scare, alarm, fill with fear, horrify. [➡FRIGHTEN AND SHOCK; 569] *Opposite:* reassure. 2 *v* **fossilize**, harden, solidify, ossify, fix, rigidify, turn into stone, calcify, set. [➡HARDEN, CONGEAL, DRY; 388]

petrifying *adj* **frightening**, terrifying, scary (*informal*), horrifying, shocking, spine-chilling, bloodcurdling, chilling, startling, terrorizing. [➡FRIGHTENING; 232] *Opposite:* reassuring.

petrol *n* [➡ENERGY SOURCES; 1161]

petrol bomb *type of* **explosive weapon**. [➡EXPLOSIVES; 1154]

petroleum *n* [➡ENERGY SOURCES; 1161]

petrol station *n* **filling station**, garage, service station, gas station (*US*). [➡RETAIL OUTLETS; 1082]

petticoat *type of* **lower body underwear**. [➡HABERDASHERY, MILLINERY, AND LINGERIE; 867]

pettifoggery *n* [➡NEGATIVE INTELLECTUAL CHARACTERISTICS; 526]

pettifogging *adj* **trivial**, petty, unimportant, minor, insignificant, trifling, niggling, picayune (*US informal*). [➡UNIMPORTANT AND UNNECESSARY; 239] *Opposite:* important.

pettiness 1 *n* **triviality**, unimportance, inconsequence, paltriness, irrelevance, insignificance. [➡UNIMPORTANT AND UNNECESSARY; 239] *Opposite:* importance. 2 *n* **petty-mindedness**, mean-mindedness, triviality, pettifoggery, narrow-mindedness. [➡NEGATIVE INTELLECTUAL CHARACTERISTICS; 526] 3 *n* **spitefulness**, grudgingness, resentfulness, maliciousness, vindictiveness, mean-spiritedness, meanness. [➡SELFISH AND UNKIND; 506]

pettish *adj* **grouchy** (*informal*), peevish, irritable, sulky, bad-tempered, petulant, irascible, sore (*informal*), touchy, testy (*informal*), cranky (*US informal*). [➡IRRITATION AND ANGER; 542] *Opposite:* even-tempered.

petty 1 *adj* **trivial**, unimportant, inconsequential, insignificant, paltry, irrelevant, trifling, small, niggling, minor, little. [➡UNIMPORTANT AND UNNECESSARY; 239] *Opposite:* important. 2 *adj* **petty-minded**, mean-minded, niggling, narrow-minded, trivial. [➡NEGATIVE INTELLECTUAL CHARACTERISTICS; 526] 3 *adj* **spiteful**, grudging, resentful, malicious, vindictive, mean-spirited, mean. [➡SELFISH AND UNKIND; 506] *Opposite:* generous.

petty cash *n* **cash fund**, office fund, float, coffee fund (*US*). [➡MONEY, PAYMENTS, AND CHARGES; 800]

petty larceny *n* [➡CRIMES; 817]

petty-minded *adj* [➡NEGATIVE INTELLECTUAL CHARACTERISTICS; 526]

petty-mindedness *n* [➡NEGATIVE INTELLECTUAL CHARACTERISTICS; 526]

petty thief *n* [➡CRIMINALS; 821]

petulance *n* **sulkiness**, crabbiness, peevishness, sullenness, moodiness, cantankerousness, grouchiness (*informal*), bad temper, irritability, grumpiness, tantrums, touchiness, testiness (*informal*), querulousness. [➡IRRITATION AND ANGER; 542] *Opposite:* affability.

petulant *adj* **sulky**, crabby, peevish, grumpy, sullen, moody, cantankerous, bad-tempered, irritable, touchy, testy (*informal*), querulous, snappy, grouchy (*informal*), ill-tempered, huffy, snappish. [➡IRRITATION AND ANGER; 542] *Opposite:* affable.

petunia *type of* **annual flower**. [➡FLOWERS; 1032]

pew *n* **bench**, form, seat, bleacher (*US*). [➡FURNITURE; 858]

pewter 1 *type of* **metal**. [➡METALS; 1275] 2 *type of* **grey**. [➡COLOURS; 1223]

phaeton *type of* **wagon or carriage**. [➡VEHICLES; 1144]

phalanger *type of* **marsupial**. [➡MARSUPIAL; 992]

phalanx *n* **group**, body, mass, unit, formation, assemblage. [➡GROUPS OF PEOPLE; 935]

phantasm *n* **ghost**, spirit, apparition, spectre, phantom, shade (*literary*), spook (*informal*). [➡THE SUPERNATURAL; 788]

phantasmagoria *n* **images**, dream, hallucination, optical illusion, mirage, fantasy. [➡NONEXISTENT THINGS; 23]

phantasmagoric *adj* **dreamlike**, bizarre, surreal,

psychedelic, fantastical, hallucinatory. [➡ BIZARRE AND PECULIAR; 258]

phantasmagory *see* **phantasmagoria**.

phantom *n* **ghost**, apparition, spirit, spectre, phantasm, spook (*informal*), shade (*literary*). [➡ THE SUPERNATURAL; 788]

Pharaoh *n* **ruler**, king, sovereign, monarch, emperor, sultan. [➡ RULERS AND ARISTOCRACY; 823]

Pharaoh ant *type of* **ant**. [➡ ANTS; 1014]

pharmaceutical 1 *adj* **medicinal**, medical, pharmacological, therapeutic, curative. [➡ REMEDIES, TREATMENTS AND OPERATIONS; 732] 2 *n* **drug**, medicine, medication, treatment, narcotic, analgesic, antibiotic. [➡ REMEDIES, TREATMENTS, AND OPERATIONS; 732]

pharmacist *n* **chemist**, dispensing chemist, apothecary (*archaic*), pharmacologist, posologist, druggist (*US*). [➡ PEOPLE WHO WORK IN MEDICINE; 848]

pharmacologist *n* [➡ PEOPLE WHO WORK IN MEDICINE; 848]

pharmacy *n* **chemist's**, dispensary, dispensing chemist's, apothecary (*archaic*), druggist's (*US*), drugstore (*US*). [➡ RETAIL OUTLETS; 1082]

pharynx *part of* **respiratory system**. [➡ RESPIRATORY ORGANS; 716]

phase *n* **stage**, point, chapter, time, segment, part, period, level, rung. [➡ PAUSES AND PHASES; 56]

phase in *v* [➡ CAUSE TO START; 266]

phase out *v* [➡ CAUSE TO STOP; 267]

pheasant 1 *type of* **meat**. [➡ TYPES AND CUTS OF MEAT; 1176] 2 *type of* **fowl**. [➡ FOOD BIRD; 999]

phenomenal 1 *adj* **remarkable**, extraordinary, impressive, prodigious, outstanding, astonishing, unbelievable, incredible, astounding, exceptional, unique, unusual, rare, extra special, out of the ordinary, unparalleled. [➡ EXTRAORDINARY: AMAZING; 205] *Opposite:* unremarkable. 2 *adj* (*informal*) **fantastic**, marvellous, huge (*informal*), wonderful, amazing, brilliant, great (*informal*), sensational. [➡ EXTRAORDINARY: AMAZING; 205] *Opposite:* moderate.

phenomenon 1 *n* **occurrence**, fact, experience, happening, incident, event, trend. [➡ EVENTS AND OCCURRENCES; 35] 2 *n* **marvel**, wonder, singularity, miracle, spectacle, portent (*formal*), sensation. [➡ AMAZING THING; 212] 3 *n* **prodigy**, genius, bright star, whiz kid (*informal*), enfant terrible. [➡ TALENTED OR INTELLIGENT PERSON; 529]

phial *n* **vial**, bottle, vessel, flask, flagon, ampoule. [➡ CONTAINERS, RECEPTACLES, AND PACKAGING; 1244]

philanderer (*disapproving*) *n* **womanizer** (*disapproving*), flirt, Casanova, adulterer, lady-killer, stud (*informal*), wolf (*informal*), Lothario (*literary*), Romeo, ladies' man. [➡ PLEASURE-SEEKERS AND HEDONISTS; 886]

philandering (*disapproving*) *adj* [➡ PLEASURE-SEEKING AND EXCESS; 885]

philanthropic *adj* **charitable**, benevolent, humanitarian, generous, big-hearted, giving, goodhearted, altruistic. [➡ GENEROSITY AND KINDNESS; 496] *Opposite:* misanthropic.

philanthropist *n* **patron**, humanitarian, donor, sponsor, promoter, contributor, backer, guarantor. [➡ PEOPLE WHO ARE APPROVED OF; 955] *Opposite:* misanthropist.

philanthropy *n* **charity**, compassion, humanity, patronage, generosity, benevolence, altruism, clemency, goodwill, amity (*formal*). [➡ KIND ACTION OR BEHAVIOUR; 296] *Opposite:* misanthropy.

philharmonic *adj* [➡ MUSICAL TERMS; 912]

philippic *n* **diatribe**, tirade, discourse, denunciation, invective (*formal*), insult, harangue, rant, jeremiad (*literary*). [➡ CRITICISMS AND ANGRY OUTBURSTS; 50]

philistine (*disapproving*) 1 *n* **barbarian**, vulgarian, boor. [➡ GRUMPY AND NEGATIVE PEOPLE; 953] *Opposite:* aesthete. 2 *adj* **uncultured**, barbarous, unsophisticated, uninformed, untutored, boorish. [➡ LEVEL OF EDUCATION AND SOPHISTICATION; 894] *Opposite:* cultured.

philistinism (*disapproving*) *n* **barbarism**, unsophistication, boorishness, ignorance. [➡ LEVEL OF EDUCATION AND SOPHISTICATION; 894]

philosopher *n* **theorist**, thinker, logician, truth-seeker, academic, dreamer. [➡ PHILOSOPHICAL AND POLITICAL THINKERS; 782] *Opposite:* realist.

philosophic 1 *adj* **logical**, ethical, metaphysical, moral, theoretical, rational. [➡ PHILOSOPHIES AND BELIEFS; 781] *Opposite:* scientific. 2 *adj* **deep-thinking**, learned, thoughtful, studious, enlightened, wise, erudite, scholarly, rational. [➡ POSITIVE INTELLECTUAL CHARACTERISTICS; 525] *Opposite:* shallow. 3 *adj* **calm**, resigned, restrained, stoical, patient, uncomplaining, wise, accepting, unruffled. [➡ CALMNESS, CONFIDENCE, AND COMPOSURE; 537] *Opposite:* emotional.

philosophical 1 *adj* **logical**, ethical, metaphysical, moral, theoretical, rational. [➡ THE NATURE OF IDEAS; 772] *Opposite:* scientific. 2 *adj* **deep-thinking**, learned, thoughtful, studious, enlightened, wise, erudite, scholarly, rational. [➡ POSITIVE INTELLECTUAL CHARACTERISTICS; 525] *Opposite:* shallow. 3 *adj* **calm**, resigned, restrained, stoical, patient, uncomplaining, wise, accepting, unruffled. [➡ CALMNESS, CONFIDENCE, AND COMPOSURE; 537] *Opposite:* emotional.

philosophize *v* **moralize**, speculate, theorize, pronounce, meditate, reason. [➡ DEVELOP THEORIES AND REASON; 745]

philosophy *n* **beliefs**, viewpoint, thinking, values, attitude, idea, way of life. [➡ PHILOSOPHIES AND BELIEFS; 781]

philtre (*literary*) *n* **potion**, charm, drug, aphrodisiac, magic potion, draught (*dated*). [➡ LUCKY CHARMS; 786]

phiz (*slang*) *n* **face**, phizog (*slang*), mug (*informal*), puss (*slang*). [➡ HEAD; 693]

phizog (*slang*) *n* [➡ HEAD; 693]

phlegm 1 *n* **mucus**, catarrh, rheum. [➡ EXCRETION AND EXCRETA; 723] 2 *n* **calmness**, composure, unflappability, self-possession, imperturbability, coolness, equanimity. [➡ CONFIDENCE AND COMPOSURE; 500] *Opposite:* nervousness.

phlegmatic *adj* **calm**, unemotional, composed, unflappable, apathetic, indifferent, unconcerned, undemonstrative, matter-of-fact, placid, impassive, dry, stoic, stolid. [➡ LIFELESS, LAZY, AND UNENTHUSIASTIC; 507] *Opposite:* nervous.

See Compare and Contrast at **impassive.**

phlegmatically *adv* **calmly**, unemotionally, unflappably, stoically, impassively, apathetically, stolidly, placidly, undemonstratively. [➡ LIFELESS, LAZY, AND UNENTHUSIASTIC; 507] *Opposite:* nervously.

phobia *n* **fear**, terror, dread, horror, thing (*informal*), fright, obsession, paranoia, anxiety. [➡ FEARS AND PHOBIAS; 555]

phobia

◆ *types of phobia*
acrophobia, agoraphobia, ailurophobia, arachnophobia, claustrophobia, hydrophobia, necrophobia, nyctophobia, photophobia, pyrophobia, technophobia, theophobia, zoophobia

phobic 1 *adj* **fearful**, scared, terrified, nervous, anxious, neurotic (*informal*), overanxious, paranoid. [➡ FEAR AND PANIC; 544] 2 *adj* **irrational**, neurotic (*informal*), obsessed, disturbed, fixated, hung up (*informal*), paranoid. [➡ FEARS AND PHOBIAS; 555]

phone 1 *n* **telephone**, touchtone phone, mobile phone, mobile, cellphone, cellular phone. [➡ TELECOMMUNICATIONS; 1129] 2 *v* **call**, ring, ring up, buzz (*informal*), telephone, make a call, give a ring, call up, drop a dime on (*US*). [➡ TELEPHONE AND PAGE; 682]

phone call *n* [➡ TELEPHONE COMMUNICATION; 48]

phonecard *type of* **telecommunications equipment.** [➡ TELECOMMUNICATIONS; 1129]

phone-in *type of* **broadcast.** [➡ TELEVISION AND RADIO; 607]

phonetic alphabet *type of* **alphabet.** [➡ SYMBOLS, SIGNS, AND NUMBERS; 597]

phone up *v* [➡ TELEPHONE AND PAGE; 682]

phoney 1 *adj* **false**, fake, counterfeit, bogus, artificial, feigned, forged, spurious, sham, ersatz (*disapproving*). [➡ FALSE AND UNREAL; 174] *Opposite:* genuine. 2 *adj* **affected**, pretentious, deceiving, insincere, deceptive, sham, put-on, mannered. [➡ DECEITFUL; 514] *Opposite:* sincere. 3 *n* **fake**, counterfeit, impostor, hypocrite, forgery, fraud, sham, charlatan, dissembler (*formal*), hoax, pretender. [➡ PEOPLE WHO DECEIVE; 662]

phoniness *n* [➡ FALSE AND UNREAL; 174]

phonograph (*US*) *type of* **audio equipment.** [➡ AUDIO EQUIPMENT; 1138]

phony *see* **phoney.**

photo *n* **photograph**, picture, snapshot, print, snap, shot. [➡ PHOTOGRAPHY AND PHOTOGRAPHIC EQUIPMENT; 1121]

photocopy 1 *n* **copy**, duplicate, reproduction, print. [➡ PHOTOGRAPHY AND PHOTOGRAPHIC EQUIPMENT; 1121] 2 *v* **copy**, reproduce, make a copy of, run off, duplicate, replicate, reduplicate. [➡ COPY AND DUPLICATE; 403]

photo finish *n* **close contest**, neck-and-neck finish (*informal*), close thing, tie. [➡ NON-AGGRESSIVE/SPORTING EVENT; 40]

photogenic *adj* **camera-friendly**, attractive, picturesque, appealing, good-looking, striking, beautiful, pretty. [➡ PEOPLE'S PHYSICAL APPEARANCE; 476]

photograph 1 *n* **photo**, picture, snap, shot, snapshot, print. [➡ PHOTOGRAPHY AND PHOTOGRAPHIC EQUIPMENT; 1121] 2 *v* **photo**, snap, shoot, get on film. [➡ CREATE IMAGES; 357]

photographer *n* **professional photographer**, press photographer, paparazzo, amateur photographer, photojournalist, snapper (*informal*), shutterbug (*US informal*). [➡ PEOPLE IN SPORTS AND LEISURE; 876]

photographic 1 *adj* **pictorial**, graphic, picturesque, photogenic, camera-friendly. [➡ ARTISTIC MOVEMENTS AND STYLES; 899] 2 *adj* **vivid**, clear, accurate, exact, detailed, precise, graphic, acute, rich, intense. [➡ EXACT; 204]

photography *n* **cinematography**, filmmaking, picture making, shooting, camerawork. [➡ THE PICTORIAL ARTS; 897]

photography

◆ *parts of photographic equipment*
autofocus, diaphragm, exposure meter, film, filter, fisheye lens, flash, lens, lens cap, rangefinder, shutter, telephoto lens, viewfinder, zoom lens

◆ *types of photographic equipment*
box camera, camera, cine camera, darkroom, developer, disc camera, enlarger, microfiche, microfilm, movie camera (*US*), pinhole camera, printer, projector, reflex camera, single-lens reflex, speed camera, tripod, twin-lens reflex

photojournalism *n* **photography**, news photography, reportage, camerawork, filmmaking, journalism. [➡ NEWSPAPERS; 606]

photon *type of* **elementary particle.** [➡ ELEMENTARY PARTICLES; 1278]

photo opportunity *n* **publicity stunt**, photo shoot, photo op, media event, public-relations exercise, press interview, TV interview, interview, publicity event. [➡ TELEVISION AND RADIO; 607]

photophobia *type of* **phobia.** [➡ FEARS AND PHOBIAS; 555]

photorealism *type of* **20th-century art movement.** [➡ ARTISTIC MOVEMENTS AND STYLES; 899]

photosensitive *adj* **light sensitive**, sensitive, reactive, light reactive, hypersensitive, photophobic. [➡ SEE; 700]

phrasal *adj* **linguistic**, verbal, expressive, semantic, phraseological, terminological. [➡ ASPECTS OF LANGUAGE; 683]

phrasal verb *type of* **word class.** [➡ ASPECTS OF LANGUAGE; 683]

phrase 1 *n* **expression**, saying, idiom, axiom, slogan, turn of phrase, locution, catch phrase, watchword. [➡ ASPECTS OF LANGUAGE; 683] 2 *v* **express**, couch, put, say, put into words, verbalize, formulate, word. [➡ UTTER AND PRONOUNCE; 609]

phrase book *n* **glossary**, bilingual dictionary, foreign-language dictionary, dictionary, lexicon, vocabulary list, thesaurus. [➡ BOOKS AND BOOKLETS; 591]

phraseology *n* **phrasing**, wording, choice of words,

word choice, terminology, turn of phrase, expression, style. [➡ASPECTS OF LANGUAGE; 683]

phrasing *n* **wording**, turn of phrase, style, word choice, diction, language, idiom, expression, phraseology, choice of words, manner of speaking. [➡ASPECTS OF LANGUAGE; 683]

physical 1 *adj* **bodily**, corporeal, animal, corporal, carnal (*formal*), fleshly, somatic. [➡LIVING THINGS AND LIVING; 976] *Opposite:* mental. 2 *adj* **substantial**, material, objective, natural, real, tangible, sensible, touchable. [➡PERCEPTIBLE; 25] *Opposite:* ethereal. 3 *adj* **brute**, instinctive, visceral, instinctual, basic, base. [➡STRENGTH; 202] *Opposite:* refined.

physical education *n* **sports**, gymnastics, games, exercise, aerobics, athletics. [➡LESSONS, COURSE WORK, AND EXAMINATIONS; 842]

physically *adv* **bodily**, actually, in the flesh, really, materially, substantially, tangibly. [➡TRUE AND REAL; 172] *Opposite:* mentally.

physical therapy (*US*) *n* **treatment**, physical exercises, remedial exercise, rehabilitation, physiotherapy, physio (*informal*), exercise. [➡REMEDIES, TREATMENTS AND OPERATIONS; 732]

physician *n* **doctor**, medical doctor, doctor of medicine, general practitioner, GP, surgeon. [➡PEOPLE WHO WORK IN MEDICINE; 848]

physics *n* **dynamics**, forces, physical processes, interactions, properties. [➡QUALITIES AND CHARACTERISTICS; 1190]

physiognomy *n* **appearance**, face, features, characteristics, physical appearance, physical characteristics. [➡HEAD; 693]

physiological *adj* **physical**, bodily, biological, functional. [➡BIOLOGICAL SCIENCES; 1037]

physiology *type of* **bioscience**. [➡BIOLOGICAL SCIENCES; 1037]

physiotherapy *n* **remedial exercise**, exercise, rehabilitation, physio (*informal*), physical therapy (*US*). [➡REMEDIES, TREATMENTS, AND OPERATIONS; 732]

physique *n* **build**, body type, physical type, figure, form, body, shape, size, structure, frame. [➡BUILD; 478]

phytoplankton *type of* **alga**. [➡MICROORGANISMS, FUNGI, AND ALGAE; 1023]

pianissimo *type of* **musical term**. [➡MUSICAL TERMS; 912]

pianist *n* [➡MUSICIANS AND SINGERS; 908]

piano 1 *type of* **musical term**. [➡MUSICAL TERMS; 912] 2 *type of* **keyboard**. [➡MUSICAL INSTRUMENTS; 910]

pianoforte (*formal*) *type of* **keyboard**. [➡MUSICAL INSTRUMENTS; 910]

piazza *n* **square**, forum, gathering place, village square, town square, quadrangle, market square. [➡URBAN OUTDOOR SPACES; 1071]

picaresque *adj* **roguish**, mischievous, rascally, impish, villainous, cheating. [➡SELFISH AND UNKIND; 506]

picayune (*US informal*) *adj* [➡NEGATIVE INTELLECTUAL CHARACTERISTICS; 526]

piccalilli *type of* **pickle**. [➡SEASONINGS AND SAUCES; 1173]

piccolo *type of* **wind instrument**. [➡MUSICAL INSTRUMENTS; 910]

pick 1 *v* **harvest**, gather, cut, collect, pluck, reap. [➡GROW AND CULTIVATE; 352] 2 *v* **select**, single out, choose, pick and choose, accept, make a choice, elect to choose, decide on, settle on, elect, opt. [➡MAKE DECISIONS AND CHOICES; 753] 3 *n* **best choice**, top choice, choice, cream of the crop, pick of the litter, preference, prize, best, elite. [➡SOURCE OF HAPPINESS, PLEASURE, OR IMPROVEMENT; 210]

pick and choose *v* [➡MAKE DECISIONS AND CHOICES; 753]

pickaxe *type of* **cutting tool**. [➡CUTTING TOOLS; 1119]

picked *adj* **chosen**, selected, select, elect, handpicked, elite, exclusive. [➡SUPERIORITY; 153]

picket 1 *n* **stake**, post, fence post, peg, rod, pole, stick, paling. [➡STICKS, POLES, AND WEDGES; 1253] 2 *n* **striker**, protester, boycotter, blockader. [➡UNCOOPERATIVE OR REBELLIOUS PERSON; 567] 3 *n* **lookout**, sentinel, watch, sentry, guard, patrol. [➡WORK-RELATED ACTIVITIES; 834] 4 *v* **protest**, strike, demonstrate, strike against, demonstrate at, blockade, besiege. [➡PROTEST AND EXPRESS DISAPPROVAL; 643] 5 *v* **enclose**, fence, restrain, hedge in, pen in, corral (*US*). [➡BAR AND OBSTRUCT ACCESS; 411]

pick holes in *v* **find fault with**, fault, criticize, attack, tear to shreds, slate (*informal*), slam (*informal*), rubbish (*informal*), disparage. [➡ACCUSE, BLAME, AND CRITICIZE; 642] *Opposite:* praise.

pickiness *n* [➡DIFFICULT TO PLEASE; 516]

pickings *n* **earnings**, profits, takings, proceeds, spoils, loot, plunder, swag (*slang*), ill-gotten gains, booty. [➡PROCEEDS OF CRIME; 428]

pickle 1 *n* (*informal*) **difficulty**, bind, fix (*informal*), jam (*informal*), scrape (*informal*), spot (*informal*), predicament, tight spot (*informal*), plight, quandary, mess. [➡DIFFICULT SITUATIONS; 72] 2 *v* **preserve**, marinate, cure, keep, conserve, soak, store. [➡COOKING AND FOOD PREPARATION; 354]

> **pickle**
>
> ◆ *types of pickle*
> chutney, cornichon, gherkin, piccalilli, pickled cucumber

pickled *adj* **preserved**, soused, marinated. [➡STATE OF PREPARED FOOD; 1170]

pickled cucumber *type of* **pickle**. [➡SEASONINGS AND SAUCES; 1173]

pick-me-up (*informal*) *n* **refreshment**, stimulant, shot in the arm, drink, hair of the dog, tonic, catalyst, impetus, incentive, motivation. [➡TREAT; 211]

pick of the bunch *n* [➡SOURCE OF HAPPINESS, PLEASURE, OR IMPROVEMENT; 210]

pick of the litter *n* [➡SOURCE OF HAPPINESS, PLEASURE, OR IMPROVEMENT; 210]

pick on *v* **tease**, make fun of, bully, harass, criticize, be critical of, single out, persecute, annoy, harry, pester, bedevil. [➡JOKES AND TEASING; 675]

pick out 1 *v* **choose**, make a choice, select, pick, pull out, single out, elect, opt. [➡MAKE DECISIONS AND CHOICES; 753] 2 *v* **identify**, distinguish, isolate, recognize, single out, discern, differentiate, discriminate. [➡NAME AND DESCRIBE; 666] 3 *v* **highlight**, outline, emphasize. [➡MAKE DECISIONS AND CHOICES; 753]

pickpocket *n* **thief**, sneak thief, robber, bag-snatcher, crook (*informal*), purse snatcher (*US*). [➡CRIMINALS; 821]

pick-up *type of* **commercial or industrial vehicle.** [➡VEHICLES; 1144]

pick up 1 *v* **lift**, raise, hoist, raise up, elevate, uplift. [➡MOVE SOMETHING: UPWARDS; 329] *Opposite:* put down. 2 *v* (*informal*) **improve**, recover, bounce back, buck up, change for the better, look up, get better, rally. [➡GET BETTER; 376] *Opposite:* deteriorate. 3 *v* **give a ride to**, give a lift to, collect, come and get somebody, call for somebody, stop for somebody, come by, take on, load up, transport, convey, carry. *Opposite:* drop off. (*informal*). [➡ACCOMPANY AND FOLLOW; 338] 4 *v* **learn**, understand, grasp, get the hang of, remember, become familiar with, master, memorize, realize. [➡UNDERSTAND AND GRASP; 760] 5 *v* **speed up**, accelerate, go faster, get better, improve, be more exciting, liven up, quicken, stimulate. [➡CHANGE OF SPEED: MORE; 397] *Opposite:* slow down. 6 *v* **restart**, take up again, continue, carry on, jump back in. [➡CONTINUE AN ACTION; 263] *Opposite:* drop.

pick up on (*informal*) *v* **notice**, point out, focus on, single out, call attention to, mention, raise, remark on, comment on. [➡UNDERSTAND AND GRASP; 760] *Opposite:* miss.

pick up speed *v* [➡CHANGE OF SPEED: MORE; 397]

pick up the pace *v* [➡CHANGE OF SPEED: MORE; 397]

picky *adj* **fastidious**, fussy, pernickety (*informal*), choosy (*informal*), hard to please, finicky, particular, exacting. [➡DIFFICULT TO PLEASE; 516] *Opposite:* easygoing.

picnic 1 *n* (*informal*) **doddle** (*informal*), walkover (*informal*), cinch (*informal*), piece of cake (*informal*), breeze (*informal*), nothing. [➡EASY WORK; 300] 2 *v* **have a picnic**, eat al fresco, eat outside. [➡HOBBIES, GAMES, AND SPORTS; 875] 3 *type of* **meal.** [➡MEALS AND PARTS OF MEALS; 1168]

picnic basket *type of* **container.** [➡CONTAINERS, RECEPTACLES, AND PACKAGING; 1244]

pictogram *n* [➡DRAWINGS, CHARTS AND TABLES; 595]

pictograph *n* **symbol**, hieroglyph, primitive writing, character, drawing, picture. [➡SYMBOLS, SIGNS, AND NUMBERS; 597]

pictographic *adj* **graphic**, symbolic, pictorial, illustrative, visual. [➡ARTISTIC MOVEMENTS AND STYLES; 899]

pictorial *adj* **graphic**, symbolic, illustrative, pictographic, clear, vivid. [➡ARTISTIC MOVEMENTS AND STYLES; 899]

picture 1 *n* **image**, depiction, portrait, representation, photograph, photo, print, painting, drawing, sketch, delineation, portrayal, illustration, likeness. [➡ARTWORKS; 898] 2 *n* **film**, movie (*US*), motion picture (*US formal or technical*), flick (*informal*), feature. [➡FILM; 901] 3 *n* **embodiment**, epitome, perfect example, essence, personification, archetype, image, living example, model, mould, paragon, mirror. [➡REPRESENTATIONS AND GENERAL EXAMPLES; 65] 4 *v* **imagine**, create in your mind, visualize, see, conceive of, see in your mind's eye, conjure up, dream of, evoke, fancy. [➡DREAM, IMAGINE, AND FANTASIZE; 750] 5 *v* **describe**, depict, illustrate, draw, show, give, portray, represent, delineate. [➡NAME AND DESCRIBE; 666]

picture book *n* **illustrated book**, children's book, story book, annual, coffee-table book, comic book. [➡BOOKS AND BOOKLETS; 591]

picture hat *type of* **hat.** [➡HABERDASHERY, MILLINERY, AND LINGERIE; 867]

picture house (*dated*) *n* [➡BUILDINGS FOR PUBLIC ENTERTAINMENT; 1083]

picture molding (*US*) *type of* **general fittings.** [➡FITTINGS; 859]

picture-perfect *adj* [➡BEAUTY AND ATTRACTIVENESS; 190]

picture-postcard *adj* **picturesque**, attractive, pretty, chocolate-box, scenic, charming, appealing, pleasant, quaint, twee. [➡BEAUTY AND ATTRACTIVENESS; 190] *Opposite:* unattractive.

picture rail *type of* **general fittings.** [➡FITTINGS; 859]

picturesque 1 *adj* **attractive**, pretty, scenic, charming, chocolate-box, striking, quaint, pleasing. [➡BEAUTY AND ATTRACTIVENESS; 190] *Opposite:* unattractive. 2 *adj* **pictorial**, graphic, symbolic, pictographic, vivid, colourful. [➡CONCISE AND CLEAR; 203]

picturesquely *adv* **attractively**, prettily, scenically, charmingly, appealingly, pleasantly. [➡BEAUTY AND ATTRACTIVENESS; 190] *Opposite:* unattractively.

picturesqueness *n* [➡BEAUTY AND ATTRACTIVENESS; 190]

picture window *type of* **window.** [➡WINDOWS; 1099]

piddling (*informal*) *adj* **measly** (*informal*), petty, small, puny, paltry, trifling, trivial, unimportant, insignificant, minor, skimpy, piffling (*informal*), slight, picayune (*US informal*). [➡FEW, LITTLE, SMALL AMOUNT; 119] *Opposite:* enormous.

pidgin *n* **lingua franca**, creole, patois, dialect, lingo (*informal*). [➡THE SPOKEN WORD; 672]

pie *type of* **dessert.** [➡CAKES, BISCUITS, AND DESSERTS; 1180]

piebald *adj* **parti-coloured**, pied, skewbald, spotted, mottled, speckled, dappled, flecked, two-coloured. [➡DESCRIBING PATTERNS; 1226] *Opposite:* plain.

piece 1 *n* **part**, fragment, bit, member, part of a set, part of the pack, section. [➡AREA AND RANGE; 111] *Opposite:* whole. 2 *n* **bit**, portion, hunk, wedge, slice, cut (*informal*), chunk, fragment, amount, quantity. [➡AMOUNT OF SOLID OR SEMI-SOLID; 115] *Opposite:* whole. 3 *n* **example**, case, sample, instance, occurrence, specimen. [➡REPRESENTATIONS AND GENERAL EXAMPLES; 65] 4 *v* **patch**, mend, repair, restore, fix. [➡REPAIR AND MEND; 377]

pièce de résistance *n* [➡SOURCE OF HAPPINESS, PLEASURE, OR IMPROVEMENT; 210]

piecemeal 1 *adv* **gradually**, by degrees, little by little, a little at a time, a bit at a time, slowly, inchmeal, progressively. [➡UNFINISHEDNESS; 240] *Opposite:* all at once. **2** *adv* **piece by piece**, bit by bit, one by one, separately, one at a time, individually, fractionally. [➡APPORTIONMENT; 113] **3** *adj* **fragmentary**, disjointed, disconnected, disorganized, haphazard, bitty, fractional, spasmodic. [➡UNFINISHEDNESS; 240] *Opposite:* cohesive.

piece of cake (*informal*) *n* **doddle** (*informal*), child's play, nothing, breeze (*informal*), cinch (*informal*), gift (*informal*), snap (*US*). [➡EASY WORK; 300]

piece of music *n* **composition**, creation, tune, melody, work, piece. [➡MUSIC, SONGS, AND SINGING; 907]

piece of writing *n* **article**, essay, composition, report, discourse, treatise, thesis, book. [➡ANALYTICAL NONFICTION WRITING; 593]

piece out **1** *v* **apportion**, mete out, share out, dispense, hand out, distribute. [➡DISPENSE, RATION, AND DISTRIBUTE; 435] **2** *v* (*US*) **piece together**, work out, reconstruct, restore, make sense of, rationalize. [➡DEVELOP THEORIES AND REASON; 745]

piece together **1** *v* **work out**, reconstruct, make sense of, rationalize, piece out (*US*). [➡DEVELOP THEORIES AND REASON; 745] **2** *v* **assemble**, join, fix, repair, mend, put together, reconstruct, patch, restore. [➡BUILD; 353] *Opposite:* take apart.

piecework *n* **freelance work**, part-time work, casual work, commission. [➡TYPES OF WORK; 835]

piechart *n* **graph**, chart, diagram, illustration, figure. [➡DRAWINGS, CHARTS AND TABLES; 595]

pied *adj* **multicoloured**, variegated, mottled, piebald, flecked, brindled, dappled, parti-coloured. [➡DESCRIBING PATTERNS; 1226] *Opposite:* plain.

pied-à-terre *n* **second home**, holiday home, city apartment, town flat, flat, studio, apartment (*US*), vacation home (*US*). [➡RESIDENTIAL BUILDINGS; 1077]

pied wagtail *type of* **songbird**. [➡SONGBIRD; 1003]

pier *n* **dock**, wharf, berth, jetty, landing-stage, quay, landing place, landing, levee, piling, slip. [➡WATERWAYS AND SEAWAYS; 1107]

pierce **1** *v* **bore into**, stab, impale, cut, slice, slice open, penetrate, prick, perforate, puncture, drill, stick, spear, lance. [➡TEAR, BREAK, AND CUT; 361] **2** *v* **hurt**, sting, pain, wound, affront, grieve, distress. [➡UPSET, DISTRESS, AND HUMILIATE; 568] *Opposite:* heal.

piercing **1** *adj* **penetrating**, intense, sharp, loud, ear-splitting, high-pitched, shrill, deafening, discordant, strident, acute, stabbing, painful, keen, cutting, knife-like. [➡LOUD OR UNPLEASANT SOUNDS; 1265] *Opposite:* soothing. **2** *adj* **perceptive**, searching, shrewd, acute, keen, penetrating, intense, sharp. [➡POSITIVE INTELLECTUAL CHARACTERISTICS; 525] *Opposite:* gentle. **3** *adj* **cold**, bitter, freezing, wintry, raw, biting, chilling, penetrating. [➡COLD WEATHER; 1051] *Opposite:* mild.

piercingly **1** *adv* **penetratingly**, intensely, sharply, loudly, earsplittingly, shrilly, deafeningly, discordantly, stridently, acutely, painfully, keenly. [➡LOUD OR UNPLEASANT SOUNDS; 1265] *Opposite:* soothingly. **2** *adv* **perceptively**, searchingly, shrewdly, acutely, keenly, penetratingly, intensely, sharply. [➡POSITIVE INTELLECTUAL CHARACTERISTICS; 525] *Opposite:* gently.

piety **1** *n* **piousness**, devoutness, devotion, religiousness, virtue, goodness, faithfulness, godliness (*formal*), holiness, reverence, respect. [➡MORALLY GOOD; 775] *Opposite:* impiety. **2** *n* **self-righteousness** (*disapproving*), sanctimoniousness, moralizing, hypocrisy, smugness. [➡AFFECTATION, SELF-SATISFACTION, AND SNOBBISHNESS; 508]

piffle (*informal*) *n* **nonsense**, rubbish, twaddle (*informal*), bunkum (*informal*), tosh (*dated informal*), tripe (*informal*), claptrap (*informal*), garbage, rot (*informal*). [➡MEANINGLESS SPEECH OR WRITING; 677] *Opposite:* sense.

piffling (*informal*) *adj* **trifling**, unimportant, trivial, insignificant, petty, minor, small, paltry. [➡UNIMPORTANT AND UNNECESSARY; 239] *Opposite:* important.

pig **1** *n* (*informal*) **glutton**, greedy pig (*informal*), guzzler (*informal*), greedy guts (*informal*), gourmand. [➡PLEASURE-SEEKERS AND HEDONISTS; 886] **2** *n* (*informal*) **brute**, beast, monster, rat (*slang*), skunk (*slang*). [➡VILLAINS AND THUGS; 947] **3** *type of* **farm animal**. [➡FARM ANIMAL; 982]

pigeon **1** *n* (*informal*) **sitting duck** (*informal*), easy target, dupe, sucker (*informal*), mark (*slang*), chump (*dated informal*). [➡VICTIMS OF DECEIT; 663] **2** *type of* **fowl**. [➡FOOD BIRD; 999] **3** *type of* **common bird**. [➡BIRD; 997]

pigeon-breasted *adj* **barrel-chested**, top-heavy, stout. [➡BUILD; 478]

pigeonhole **1** *n* **cubbyhole**, compartment, box, shelf, slot, niche, cubicle. [➡CONTAINERS, RECEPTACLES, AND PACKAGING; 1244] **2** *n* **category**, class, slot, classification, compartment, label. [➡VARIETY, TYPE, KIND; 146] **3** *v* **categorize**, class, classify, label, compartmentalize, sort, slot, partition, rank, break down, sort out, group. [➡NAME AND DESCRIBE; 666]

piggery *type of* **pen or cage**. [➡ANIMAL OR BIRD ACCOMMODATION; 1078]

piggish **1** *adj* **greedy**, gluttonous, hoggish, self-indulgent. [➡BEASTLY AND BRUTISH; 511] *Opposite:* abstemious. **2** *adj* **stubborn**, uncooperative, obstructive, selfish, self-centred. [➡SELFISH AND UNKIND; 506] *Opposite:* considerate.

piggy *adj* **greedy**, piggish, gluttonous, hoggish, self-indulgent. [➡BEASTLY AND BRUTISH; 511] *Opposite:* abstemious.

piggyback *adj* **allied**, attached, associated, linked, added. [➡RELATED; 143]

piggy bank *n* **money box**, cash box, collecting box, savings box. [➡CONTAINERS, RECEPTACLES, AND PACKAGING; 1244]

piggy in the middle *n* **go-between**, pig in the middle, mediator, intermediary, negotiator, peacemaker. [➡ADVISERS, JUDGES, AND ARBITERS; 971]

pigheaded *adj* **stubborn**, obstinate, mulish, intractable (*formal*), dogged, single-minded, intransigent, obdurate, inflexible, unyielding, tenacious, headstrong, wilful. [➡UNWILLINGNESS AND STUBBORNNESS; 565] *Opposite:* flexible.

pigheadedness *n* **stubbornness**, obstinacy, mulishness, intractability (*formal*), single-mindedness, intransigence, obduracy, inflexibility, unyieldingness, tenacity, perseverance, doggedness, persistence. [➡UNWILLINGNESS AND STUBBORNNESS; 565] *Opposite:* flexibility.

piglet *type of* **young animal.** [➡YOUNG ANIMAL; 977]

pigment *n* **colour**, dye, stain, tint, colouring, tincture, colourant, dyestuff. [➡DYES AND COLOURANTS; 1269]

pigmentation *n* **colouring**, coloration, skin-colour, pigment, colour, natural colouring, skin-colouring. [➡PATTERNS; 1224]

pig out (*informal*) *v* **guzzle** (*informal*), gobble, gorge, devour, scoff (*informal*), eat. [➡EAT AND NOT EAT; 711]

pigpen (*US*) *n* **filthy surroundings**, mess, pigsty, pit, tip (*informal*), dump (*informal*), hole (*informal*). [➡UNDESIRABLE ACCOMMODATION; 856]

pigskin 1 *n* (*US*) **football**, ball, oval. [➡SPORTS EQUIPMENT; 879] 2 *type of* **leather.** [➡FABRICS; 1131]

pigsty 1 *n* **untidy place**, mess, pit, tip (*informal*), hole (*informal*), dump (*informal*). [➡UNDESIRABLE ACCOMMODATION; 856] 2 *type of* **pen or cage.** [➡ANIMAL OR BIRD ACCOMMODATION; 1078]

pigswill *n* **slops**, pig food, scraps, mash, leftovers. [➡ANIMAL FEED; 1167]

pigtail *type of* **hairstyle.** [➡HAIR STYLES AND HAIR PIECES; 489]

pike *type of* **freshwater fish.** [➡FRESHWATER FISH; 1010]

pilaf (*US*) *type of* **cooked dish.** [➡PREPARED DISHES; 1169]

pilaster *n* [➡SUPPORTS AND BASES; 1254]

pilau *type of* **cooked dish.** [➡PREPARED DISHES; 1169]

pilchard *type of* **sea fish.** [➡SEA FISH; 1009]

pile 1 *n* **mound**, mountain, quantity, mass, heap, stack, load, batch, accumulation, hoard. [➡MANY, MUCH, LARGE AMOUNT; 117] 2 *n* (*informal*) **big money**, fortune, mint (*informal*), packet (*informal*), bomb (*informal*), wad (*US informal*), megabucks (*US slang*). [➡LARGE AMOUNT OF MONEY; 141] 3 *n* **stake**, post, support, pillar, column, piling, upright. [➡STICKS, POLES, AND WEDGES; 1253] 4 *n* **soft surface**, down, nap, fibre, fur. [➡TEXTURE; 1219] 5 *v* **heap**, load, stack, pile up, amass, superimpose, swell, assemble, accumulate. [➡POSITION SOMETHING; 326] *Opposite:* scatter.

pile up *v* **stack**, heap up, amass, mound, collect, pile, heap, accumulate, assemble, load. [➡COMBINE AND MIX; 401] *Opposite:* scatter.

pile-up (*informal*) *n* **crash**, car crash, collision, road accident, accident, smash, bump, smash-up. [➡TRAFFIC ACCIDENTS; 256]

pilfer *v* **steal**, rob, thieve, pinch (*informal*), swipe (*informal*), nick (*slang*), knock off (*slang*), poach, purloin (*formal*), filch (*informal*), take. [➡STEAL AND ROB; 427]

See Compare and Contrast at **steal.**

pilferer *n* **crook** (*informal*), thief, petty thief, sneak thief, robber, shoplifter, burglar. [➡CRIMINALS; 821]

pilfering *n* [➡CRIMES; 817]

pilgrim *n* **hajji**, traveller, tourist, visitor, wayfarer (*literary*). [➡TRAVEL: TRAVELLERS AND WALKERS; 320]

pilgrimage *n* **journey**, trip, visit, hajj, tour, excursion. [➡RELIGIONS AND RELIGIOUS PRACTICES; 778]

pill *n* **tablet**, capsule, medication. [➡REMEDIES, TREATMENTS AND OPERATIONS; 732]

pillage 1 *v* **plunder**, sack, rob, loot, steal, embezzle, despoil. [➡STEAL AND ROB; 427] 2 *n* **loot**, spoils, plunder, booty, prize, taking. [➡PROCEEDS OF CRIME; 428]

pillager *n* **plunderer**, robber, looter, raider, thief, burglar, rustler. [➡CRIMINALS; 821]

pillar 1 *n* **support**, column, post, prop, mast, stake. [➡STICKS, POLES, AND WEDGES; 1253] 2 *n* **rock**, mainstay, tower of strength, stalwart. [➡PEOPLE WHO ARE APPROVED OF; 955]

pillar box *n* **postbox**, letterbox, mailbox (*US*), maildrop (*US*). [➡CONTAINERS, RECEPTACLES, AND PACKAGING; 1244]

pillar-box red *type of* **red.** [➡COLOURS; 1223]

pillbox 1 *n* **box**, tin, container, étui. [➡CONTAINERS, RECEPTACLES, AND PACKAGING; 1244] 2 *n* **lookout post**, shelter, gun emplacement, gun shelter. [➡FORTRESSES AND FORTIFICATIONS; 1089] 3 *type of* **hat.** [➡HABERDASHERY, MILLINERY, AND LINGERIE; 867]

pillory *v* **ridicule**, denounce, scorn, deride, humiliate, brand, pour scorn on, tear to pieces. [➡ACCUSE, BLAME, AND CRITICIZE; 642] *Opposite:* praise.

pillow 1 *n* **cushion**, support, throw cushion, pad, throw pillow, bolster, head rest, padding. [➡SOFT FURNISHINGS, LINEN, AND DRAPERY; 860] 2 *v* **protect**, support, prop up, hold up. [➡PREVENT CONTACT OR ATTACK; 420]

pillowcase *n* **pillowslip**, slipcover, slipcase, bedding, slip, linen, sham (*US*), pillow sham (*US*). [➡SOFT FURNISHINGS, LINEN, AND DRAPERY; 860]

pillow sham (*US*) *n* [➡SOFT FURNISHINGS, LINEN, AND DRAPERY; 860]

pillowslip *n* [➡SOFT FURNISHINGS, LINEN, AND DRAPERY; 860]

pilot 1 *n* [➡DRIVERS; 1152] 2 *v* **guide**, conduct, control, navigate, lead, direct, steer, handle. [➡TRAVEL: WAYS OF TRAVELLING; 321] 3 *adj* **experimental**, trial, model, test, preliminary, initial. [➡DESCRIBING TECHNOLOGY; 1159]

pilot whale *type of* **whale.** [➡WHALE; 991]

pimple *n* **spot**, blemish, zit (*slang*), blackhead, boil, pustule. [➡CONDITIONS AFFECTING THE SKIN; 722]

pimpled *adj* [➡COMPLEXION; 481]

pimply *adj* **spotty**, blemished, acned. [➡COMPLEXION; 481] *Opposite:* clear.

pin 1 *n* (*dated informal*) **iota**, tittle, smidgen (*informal*), pinch, bit, dash, soupçon, touch, jot. [➡FEW, LITTLE, SMALL AMOUNT; 119] 2 *n* **brooch**, badge, stick pin. [➡JEWELLERY; 866] 3 *v* **fasten**, attach, fix, secure. [➡FASTEN, LINK, AND JOIN; 409] 4 *v* **hold**, pin down, hold down, restrain, stick, pinion, trap, immobilize. [➡CAPTIVITY AND LOSS OF FREEDOM; 249]

pinafore *n* **apron**, overall, pinny (*informal*). [➡GARMENTS AND OUTFITS; 865]

pince-nez *type of* **glasses.** [➡GLASSES AND SPECTACLES; 1124]

pincers *type of* **general tool.** [➡HAND TOOLS; 1118]

pinch 1 *v* **squeeze**, nip, tweak, grasp, press, grip. [➡CONTACT: EXERT PRESSURE; 415] 2 *v* (*informal*) **steal**, take, make off with, pilfer, thieve, nick (*slang*). [➡STEAL AND ROB; 427] 3 *n* **touch**, dash, smidgen (*informal*), soupçon, bit, taste, jot, iota, tittle. [➡FEW, LITTLE, SMALL AMOUNT; 119]

See Compare and Contrast at **steal**.

pinched *adj* **haggard**, gaunt, drawn, pale, thin, tired, shrunken, withered, wan, tense, careworn, strained, drained. [➡FACIAL CHARACTERISTICS; 482]

pinchpenny 1 *adj* **stingy** (*informal*), ungenerous, miserly, tightfisted, niggardly, mean. [➡FINANCIALLY MEAN AND GRASPING; 520] *Opposite:* generous. 2 *n* **miser**, skinflint, penny pincher (*informal*), niggard, meanie (*informal*), scrooge (*informal*), cheapskate (*informal*). [➡FINANCIALLY MEAN PEOPLE; 952]

pin down 1 *v* **identify**, determine, locate, pinpoint, isolate, find. [➡FIND; 464] 2 *v* **hold down**, restrain, trap, pinion, pin, hold, immobilize. [➡CAPTIVITY AND LOSS OF FREEDOM; 249]

pine 1 *v* **long**, yearn, ache, want, wish for, crave, hunger. [➡DESIRE AND WANT; 580] 2 *v* **waste away**, fade, fade away, suffer, go downhill, languish, mope, fail. [➡DESIRE AND WANT; 580] *Opposite:* thrive. 3 *type of* **evergreen tree.** [➡EVERGREEN AND CONIFEROUS TREES; 1029]

pineapple *type of* **fruit.** [➡FRUIT AND VEGETABLES; 1175]

pine cone *n* **cone**, fir cone, seed case. [➡PARTS OF TREES AND PLANTS; 1026]

pine marten *type of* **small mammal.** [➡SMALL MAMMAL; 990]

pine nut *type of* **nut.** [➡NUTS; 1184]

ping 1 *v* **sound**, ring, ding, beep, tinkle, chime, clang, bleep, peep. [➡EMIT RINGING AND TOOTING SOUNDS; 368] 2 *type of* **ringing sound.** [➡RINGING AND TOOTING SOUNDS; 1258]

pinhole camera *type of* **photographic equipment.** [➡PHOTOGRAPHY AND PHOTOGRAPHIC EQUIPMENT; 1121]

pinion *v* **hold down**, trap, restrain, pin down, immobilize, hold, pin. [➡CONTACT: EXERT PRESSURE; 415]

pink 1 *adj* **flushed**, red, rosy, glowing, blushing, ruddy, healthy-looking. [➡COMPLEXION; 481] 2 *adj* **undercooked**, rare, underdone, raw. [➡STATE OF PREPARED FOOD; 1170] 3 *type of* **perennial flower.** [➡FLOWERS; 1032] 4 *type of* **colour.** [➡COLOURS; 1223]

pink

◆ *types of pink*
cerise, coral, fuchsia, raspberry, rose, salmon pink, shell pink, shocking pink

pinkie (*informal*) *part of* **arm or hand.** [➡ARM AND HAND; 696]

pin money *n* **pocket money**, spending money, allowance, change, small change, chump change (*US slang*). [➡SMALL AMOUNT OF MONEY; 142]

pinnacle 1 *n* **summit**, peak, height, top, apex. [➡EXTREMITIES OF PHYSICAL OBJECTS; 1249] *Opposite:* base. 2 *n* **high point**, peak, acme, zenith, apex. [➡PLEASANT SITUATIONS; 74] *Opposite:* nadir.

pinpoint *v* **locate**, identify, pin down, isolate, find, determine. [➡FIND; 464]

pinprick *n* **hole**, puncture, pinhole, perforation, prick, cut, incision. [➡HOLES, GAPS, AND FORKS; 1251]

pins (*informal*) *n* [➡LEG AND FOOT; 695]

pins and needles *n* **tingling**, prickling, numbness. [➡PAIN AND OTHER PHYSICAL SENSATIONS; 734]

pinto bean *type of* **pulse.** [➡BEANS AND PULSES; 1188]

pint-size (*informal*) *adj* **miniature**, pocket-sized, pocket-size, little, minuscule, minute, mini (*informal*), undersized, undersize, tiny, small, diminutive, pint-sized (*informal*). [➡SMALL; 1194]

pint-sized (*informal*) *adj* [➡SMALL; 1194]

pinwheel (*US*) *type of* **firework.** [➡EXPLOSIVES; 1154]

pin your ears back (*informal*) *v* [➡LISTEN AND LISTENERS; 709]

pion *type of* **elementary particle.** [➡ELEMENTARY PARTICLES; 1278]

pioneer 1 *n* **innovator**, inventor, forerunner, developer, creator, discoverer. [➡DESIGNERS, CREATORS AND INSTIGATORS; 348] 2 *v* **lead the way**, open up, forge, found, initiate, break new ground, establish, prepare. [➡START AN ACTION; 261]

pioneering *adj* **groundbreaking**, revolutionary, original, new, inventive, innovative. [➡DESCRIBING TECHNOLOGY; 1159]

pious 1 *adj* **devout**, religious, virtuous, moral, sincere, spiritual, reverent, holy, saintly, godly (*formal*). [➡RELIGIOUS CONCEPTS; 777] *Opposite:* impious. 2 *adj* **self-righteous** (*disapproving*), sanctimonious, holier-than-thou (*informal*), goody-goody (*informal*), moralizing, hypocritical, smug. [➡AFFECTATION, SELF-SATISFACTION, AND SNOBBISHNESS; 508]

piousness 1 *n* **piety**, devoutness, devotion, religiousness, virtue, holiness, spirituality, saintliness, godliness (*formal*). [➡MORALLY GOOD; 775] *Opposite:* impiety. 2 *n* **self-righteousness** (*disapproving*), sanctimoniousness, moralizing, hypocrisy, smugness. [➡AFFECTATION, SELF-SATISFACTION, AND SNOBBISHNESS; 508]

pip 1 *n* **seed**, fruit seed, stone, nut, kernel, pit (*US*). [➡FRUIT AND VEGETABLES; 1175] 2 *n* **peep**, beep, bleep, ping, ding, chime, ding-dong, cheep, chirp, squawk. [➡RINGING AND TOOTING SOUNDS; 1258] 3 *n* **spot**, speck, blemish, dot, mark. [➡SMALL PIECE; 127] 4 *v* (*informal*) **beat**, defeat, pip to the post (*informal*). [➡BEAT AND DEFEAT; 80]

pipe 1 *n* **tube**, cylinder, channel, conduit, pipeline, duct. [➡WATERCOURSES; 1110] 2 *v* **supply**, channel, convey, transmit, bring in. [➡EQUIP AND SUPPLY; 436] 3 *v* **whistle**, twitter, tweet, cheep, peep, shrill. [➡MUSIC, SONGS, AND SINGING; 907]

pipe band *type of* **band.** [➡MUSICIANS AND SINGERS; 908]

pipe down (*informal*) *v* **quiet down**, shut up (*informal*), keep it down, be quiet, belt up (*slang*), hush, hush up (*informal*). [➡SOUND EMISSION; 363]

pipe dream *n* **fantasy**, aspiration, ambition, castle in the air, castle in Spain, daydream, wish, dream, hope, plan, idea, aim. [➡NONEXISTENT THINGS; 23]

pipeline *n* **conduit**, pipe, duct, channel, tube. [➡WATERCOURSES; 1110]

pipette *type of* **measuring device.** [➡MEASURING DEVICES; 1122]

pipe up *v* **speak up**, speak, make yourself heard, have your say, chip in (*informal*). [➡INTERRUPT AND BUTT IN; 620]

piping 1 *n* **pipes**, tubing, plumbing. [➡BUILDING MATERIALS; 1076] 2 *n* **edging**, trimming, fringing. [➡ORNAMENTS AND DECORATIONS; 1247] 3 *adj* **high-pitched**, shrill, piercing, penetrating, high, fluting, strident. [➡LOUD OR UNPLEASANT SOUNDS; 1265]

piping hot *adj* [➡TEMPERATURE: HOT; 1228]

pipistrelle *type of* **flying mammal.** [➡FLYING MAMMAL; 984]

pipit *type of* **songbird.** [➡SONGBIRD; 1003]

pip to the post (*informal*) *v* [➡BEAT AND DEFEAT; 80]

piquancy *n* **spiciness**, tastiness, sharpness, heat, tang, kick, tartness, spice, zest, bite. [➡TASTE; 704] *Opposite:* blandness.

piquant 1 *adj* **spicy**, tasty, sharp, hot, tangy, strong, tart, zesty. [➡TASTE; 704] *Opposite:* bland. 2 *adj* **stimulating**, provocative, interesting, exciting. [➡INTERESTING AND MEANINGFUL; 191] 3 *adj* **critical**, biting, severe, sharp, harsh, brusque. [➡RUDE AND HOSTILE; 626]

pique 1 *n* **temper**, resentment, annoyance, anger, ill will, bad feeling, displeasure, irritation. [➡IRRITATION AND ANGER; 542] 2 *v* **irritate**, annoy, upset, rile (*informal*), offend, bother, displease, anger, vex. [➡ANGER AND ANNOY; 570] 3 *v* **interest**, intrigue, attract, stimulate, arouse, grab, awake. [➡APPEAL TO AND AROUSE INTEREST; 576] *Opposite:* bore.

piqued *adj* **resentful**, irritated, annoyed, upset, in high dudgeon, in a huff (*informal*), indignant, nettled (*informal*), riled (*informal*), vexed, peeved (*informal*), cross, put out, affronted, offended, in a bad mood, hurt, sulky. [➡IRRITATION AND ANGER; 542]

piranha *type of* **freshwater fish.** [➡FRESHWATER FISH; 1010]

piratic *adj* **freebooting**, marauding, attacking, robbing, lawless, illegal. [➡ILLEGAL; 816]

pirogue *type of* **small vessel.** [➡SHIPS AND BOATS; 1149]

pirouette 1 *n* **spin**, twirl, whirl, turn, revolution. [➡DANCE; 903] 2 *v* **twirl**, rotate, spin, turn, whirl, turn round, revolve, go round, spin around, go around. [➡MOVE SOMETHING ON THE SPOT; 337]

Pisces *type of* **star sign.** [➡FATE, DESTINY, AND ASTROLOGY; 783]

pistachio *type of* **nut.** [➡NUTS; 1184]

pistol *type of* **gun.** [➡WEAPONS FOR SHOOTING; 1155]

piston *part of* **engine.** [➡PARTS OF AN ENGINE; 1143]

pit 1 *n* **hole**, ditch, well, crater, trench, abyss. [➡HOLES, GAPS, AND FORKS; 1251] 2 *n* **coal mine**, mine, quarry, colliery. [➡INDUSTRIAL BUILDINGS; 1086] 3 *n* **dent**, pock, indentation, hollow, depression, cavity. [➡HOLES, GAPS, AND FORKS; 1251] 4 *n* **nadir**, bottom, depths. [➡EXTREMITIES OF PHYSICAL OBJECTS; 1249] 5 *v* **set as rivals**, set against, fight, oppose. [➡COMPETE, CONTEND, AND COMBAT; 304] 6 (*US*) *part of* **fruit.** [➡FRUIT AND VEGETABLES; 1175]

pitch 1 *v* **throw**, hurl, lob, toss, fling, chuck (*informal*). [➡THROW SOMETHING; 335] *Opposite:* catch. 2 *v* **erect**, set up, fix, plant, put up, place. [➡BUILD; 353] 3 *v* **sway**, move, teeter, fall, stumble, lurch, plunge. [➡TAKE UP A NEW POSITION; 313] 4 *v* **slope**, slant, fall away, descend, dip. [➡GO DOWNWARDS; 308] 5 *v* **roll**, lurch, plunge, rock, buck, list, toss, wobble. [➡BOUNCE, UNDULATE, AND VIBRATE; 309] 6 *v* **propose**, sell, throw, offer, deliver. [➡SUGGEST, HINT, AND COMMENT; 613] 7 *n* **playing field**, area, terrain, field, arena, ground. [➡URBAN OUTDOOR SPACES; 1071] 8 *n* **tone**, highness, lowness, note. [➡LOUD OR UNPLEASANT SOUNDS; 1265]

pitch and toss *v* [➡BOUNCE, UNDULATE, AND VIBRATE; 309]

pitch-black 1 *adj* **dark**, black, inky, jet-black, pitch-dark, black as night, unlit. [➡COLOURS; 1223] *Opposite:* bright. 2 *type of* **black.** [➡COLOURS; 1223]

pitch-dark *adj* **dark**, pitch-black, black, inky, jet-black, black as night, unlit. [➡DESCRIBING LIGHT; 1227] *Opposite:* bright.

pitched battle *n* **argument**, disagreement, fight, head-to-head, battle, set-to (*informal*). [➡AGGRESSIVE EVENT; 39]

pitcher *n* **jug**, decanter, carafe. [➡TABLEWARE, CUTLERY, AND KITCHENWARE; 861]

pitchfork 1 *v* **turn**, lift, fork, toss. [➡USE TOOLS AND MACHINERY; 469] 2 *v* **thrust**, push, force, propel, drive, throw. [➡THROW SOMETHING; 335]

pitch in *v* [➡HELP; 294]

pitching *adj* **rolling**, lurching, plunging, rocking, bucking, listing, tossing, wobbling, motion, movement. [➡DIRECTION OF MOTION; 346]

piteous *adj* **pathetic**, pitiful, wretched, sad, pitiable, doleful, distressing, mournful, heartbreaking. [➡EMOTIONALLY UNPLEASANT AND UPSETTING; 228] *Opposite:* enviable.

pitfall *n* **drawback**, snare, snag, danger, downside, difficulty, trap, hazard, consequence. [➡PROBLEM; 257] *Opposite:* advantage.

pith 1 *n* **essence**, crux, heart, nub, core, kernel, quintessence, spirit, soul, gist, substance, zest, nucleus, nitty-gritty (*informal*). [➡MOST IMPORTANT THING; 198] 2 *part of* **fruit.** [➡FRUIT AND VEGETABLES; 1175]

pithead *n* **colliery**, pit, coalmine, mineshaft, mine, mine workings, excavation. [➡INDUSTRIAL BUILDINGS; 1086]

pithiness *n* **concision**, terseness, brevity, wit, succinctness, briefness, sharpness, acuteness, forcefulness, laconicism, curtness. [➡SUCCINCT AND TO-THE-POINT; 641] *Opposite:* long-windedness.

pithy *adj* **concise**, terse, to the point, brief, witty, succinct, cutting, sharp, acute, forceful, epigrammatic, aphoristic, laconic, curt. [➡SUCCINCT AND TO-THE-POINT; 641] *Opposite:* long-winded.

pitiable 1 *adj* **contemptible**, wretched, deplorable, disgraceful, miserable, abject, dismal, sorry, despicable, pathetic. [➡WEAKNESS; 242] *Opposite:* admirable. 2 *adj* **pitiful**, pathetic, unfortunate, sad, piteous, doleful, poor, wretched, miserable, sorry. [➡WEAKNESS; 242] *Opposite:* heartening.

pitiful 1 *adj* **disgraceful**, deplorable, contemptible, derisible (*formal*), abject, despicable, pathetic, sorry, woeful. [➡BAD AND BADLY; 224] *Opposite:* admirable. 2 *adj* **piteous**, pathetic, pitiable, unfortunate, sad, doleful, poor, miserable, wretched, distressing, heartbreaking, sorry. [➡WEAKNESS; 242] *Opposite:* heartening. 3 *adj* **meagre**, inadequate, derisory, small, paltry, miserable, cheap, shabby, worthless, beggarly, insignificant. [➡SMALL; 1194] *Opposite:* magnanimous.

pitifully 1 *adv* **piteously**, pathetically, pitiably, unfortunately, sadly, dolefully, poorly, miserably, wretchedly, distressingly, heartbreakingly, sorrily. [➡BAD AND BADLY; 224] 2 *adv* **disgracefully**, deplorably, contemptibly, derisibly (*formal*), abjectly, despicably, pathetically, sorrily, woefully. [➡WEAKNESS; 242] *Opposite:* admirably.

pitiless *adj* **merciless**, heartless, callous, hard, unfeeling, ruthless, unforgiving, harsh, cruel, unkind, hardhearted, cold-hearted, unsympathetic, cold-blooded, cold. [➡SELFISH AND UNKIND; 506] *Opposite:* compassionate.

pitilessness *n* **mercilessness**, heartlessness, callousness, ruthlessness, harshness, cruelty, unkindness, hardheartedness, cold-heartedness, cold-bloodedness, coldness. [➡SELFISH AND UNKIND; 506] *Opposite:* compassion.

pit stop *n* **refuelling stop**, stop, break, servicing stop, rest, rest stop (*US*). [➡PAUSES AND PHASES; 56]

pitta *type of* **bread**. [➡BREAD, FLOUR, AND BREAD PRODUCTS; 1178]

pittance *n* **subsistence wage**, chicken feed (*informal*), peanuts (*informal*), small change, trifle, small potatoes (*informal*), nothing, mite, nickels and dimes (*US*). [➡SMALL AMOUNT OF MONEY; 142] *Opposite:* fortune.

pitted *adj* **potholed**, rutted, eroded, rough, bumpy, uneven, pockmarked, pocked, holey, indented. [➡PHYSICAL TEXTURE; 1221] *Opposite:* smooth.

pitter-patter *type of* **impact sound**. [➡IMPACT SOUNDS; 1259]

pit viper *type of* **poisonous snake**. [➡SNAKE; 995]

pity 1 *n* **sympathy**, compassion, mercy, mercifulness, kindliness, empathy, understanding, solicitousness, benevolence. [➡COMPASSION AND FORGIVENESS; 552] *Opposite:* pitilessness. 2 *n* **shame**, disappointment, bad luck, tough luck, letdown, misfortune. [➡DISASTERS; 253] *Opposite:* luck. 3 *v* **sympathize**, commiserate, empathize, be there for somebody, show concern, comfort, console. [➡BE CONCERNED AND CARE; 582] *Opposite:* blame.

pitying *adj* **sympathetic**, understanding, compassionate, concerned, solicitous, comforting, commiserative, condolatory (*formal*), consolatory, benevolent. [➡GENEROSITY AND KINDNESS; 496] *Opposite:* unsympathetic.

pivot 1 *n* **hinge**, axle, axis, swivel, spindle, reel, spool, fulcrum. [➡PARTS OF MACHINES AND TOOLS; 1117] 2 *v* **spin**, revolve, twist, rotate, whirl, swivel, hinge, swing, turn. [➡MOVE SOMETHING ON THE SPOT; 337]

pivotal *adj* **essential**, key, crucial, fundamental, critical, central, focal, vital, decisive, momentous, important, paramount. [➡FUNDAMENTAL; 196] *Opposite:* unimportant.

pixel *type of* **software**. [➡COMPUTERS AND COMPUTING; 1126]

pixie *n* **fairy**, elf, sprite, gnome, gremlin (*informal*), hobgoblin, Puck. [➡MYTHICAL BEINGS; 790]

pizza *type of* **cooked dish**. [➡PREPARED DISHES; 1169]

pizzazz (*informal*) *n* **vitality**, spark, zest, style, glamour, go (*informal*), zing (*informal*), dash, energy, flair. [➡INTERESTING AND MEANINGFUL; 191] *Opposite:* dullness.

pizzeria *type of* **eating place**. [➡HOTELS, RESTAURANTS, AND CLUBS; 1081]

pizzicato *type of* **musical term**. [➡MUSICAL TERMS; 912]

placard *n* **poster**, sign, board, advertisement, notice, hoarding, broadside, billboard, bill. [➡SIGNPOSTS, SIGNALS AND BILLBOARDS; 596]

placate *v* **appease**, pacify, mollify, propitiate (*formal*), conciliate, calm down, soothe, calm, satisfy, please. [➡SOOTHE AND CALM; 574] *Opposite:* enrage.

placation *n* **appeasement**, pacification, mollification, propitiation (*formal*), conciliation, satisfaction, comfort. [➡APOLOGIZE AND RETRACT; 684]

placatory *adj* **appeasing**, mollifying, propitiatory (*formal*), conciliatory, calming, soothing, satisfying, pleasing, comforting. [➡CALMING; 189] *Opposite:* inflammatory.

place 1 *n* **space**, spot, position, point, area, corner. [➡PLACE; 1064] 2 *n* **location**, spot, area, position, locality, site, locale, situation, whereabouts. [➡PLACE; 1064] 3 *n* **home**, house, residence, dwelling (*formal*), room, flat, domicile (*formal*), abode (*literary*), habitation, accommodation, housing, apartment (*US*), accommodations (*US*). [➡ACCOMMODATION; 855] 4 *n* **status**, rank, position, station, circumstance, condition, state, standing, grade, class, estate. [➡STATUS; 888] 5 *v* **assign**, hire, employ, engage, retain, enlist, sign on, take on. [➡CONFER STATUS; 459] *Opposite:* fire. 6 *v* **position**, put, set, set down, lay, leave, station, locate, site, situate (*formal*), rest, deposit, posit (*formal*), target. [➡POSITION SOMETHING; 326] *Opposite:* jettison. 7 *v* **consign**, identify, file, locate, arrange, categorize, rank, order, dispose (*formal*). [➡POSITION SOMETHING; 326]

placebo *n* **dummy**, palliative, control, try-on (*informal*), sample. [➡REMEDIES, TREATMENTS AND OPERATIONS; 732] *Opposite:* treatment.

place mat *n* **table mat**, mat, cover, cloth, coaster, doily. [➡TABLEWARE, CUTLERY, AND KITCHENWARE; 861]

placement 1 *n* **siting**, positioning, location, arrangement, situation, fixing, hanging, setting, laying. [➡MOVE SOMETHING TO ANOTHER LOCATION; 325] 2 *n* **location**, settlement, assignment, situation, employment, engagement, appointment. [➡JOB; 833]

place of safety *n* [➡SAFE BUILDINGS OR PLACES; 1092]

place of worship

◆ *types of place of worship*
church, gurdwara, mosque, shrine, synagogue, temple

place setting *n* **setting**, cover, place, tableware, cutlery, utensils, glassware. [➡TABLEWARE, CUTLERY, AND KITCHENWARE; 861]

placid *adj* **calm**, equable, even-tempered, imperturbable, easygoing, docile, good-natured, mild, peaceful, serene, tranquil, still, quiet, gentle, sedate. [➡CONFIDENCE AND COMPOSURE; 500] *Opposite:* excitable.

placidity *n* **calmness**, equability, serenity, imperturbability, even-temperedness, mildness, good-naturedness, tranquillity, docility, peacefulness, stillness, quietness, gentleness, sedateness. [➡CALMNESS, CONFIDENCE, AND COMPOSURE; 537] *Opposite:* excitability.

plagiarism *n* **copy**, piracy, theft, bootlegging, fraud, thieving, lifting (*informal*), stealing, imitation, deception. [➡CRIMES; 817]

plagiarist *n* **copyist**, pirate, bootlegger, imitator, cheat, fraud, purloiner (*formal*), deceiver, thief. [➡CRIMINALS; 821] *Opposite:* originator.

plagiarize *v* **copy**, pirate, bootleg, steal, lift (*informal*), pass off as your own, imitate, purloin. [➡COPY AND DUPLICATE; 403] *Opposite:* originate.

plague 1 *n* **epidemic**, disease, infection, pandemic, wave, outbreak, pestilence (*archaic*). [➡SICKNESS; 730] 2 *n* **curse**, affliction, scourge, blight, visitation, calamity, adversity. [➡NUISANCES; 254] *Opposite:* blessing. 3 *v* **afflict**, trouble, pursue, hound, harass, torture, torment, persecute, dog. [➡UPSET, DISTRESS, AND HUMILIATE; 568] *Opposite:* bless. 4 *v* **pester**, badger, bother, harass, trouble, agitate, upset, perturb, annoy, beleaguer, vex, dog. [➡ANGER AND ANNOY; 570] *Opposite:* leave off.

plague-ridden *adj* [➡DECAYING OR INFESTED; 1235]

plaice *type of* **flatfish**. [➡SEA FISH; 1009]

plaid *adj* **checked**, chequered, tartan. [➡DESCRIBING PATTERNS; 1226] *Opposite:* plain.

plain 1 *adj* **simple**, basic, unadorned, natural, pure, bare, ordinary, normal, stark, everyday, austere, dull, commonplace. [➡PLAIN; 233] *Opposite:* elaborate. 2 *adj* **clear**, evident, obvious, apparent, pronounced, manifest, palpable, tangible, patent, unmistakable, transparent, unambiguous, comprehensible, lucid. [➡PERCEPTIBLE; 25] *Opposite:* obscure. 3 *adj* **blunt**, straightforward, direct, frank, open, blatant, forthright, candid, bald. [➡HONEST AND OPEN; 631] *Opposite:* evasive. 4 *adj* **plain-featured**, ordinary, homely, unattractive, unappealing. [➡PEOPLE'S PHYSICAL APPEARANCE; 476] *Opposite:* pretty. 5 *n* **prairie**, savanna, steppe, pampas. [➡DESERTS AND PLAINS; 1045]

plain as a pikestaff *adj* [➡CONCISE AND CLEAR; 203]

plain-clothes *adj* **undercover**, ununiformed, secret, disguised, out of uniform. [➡DESCRIBING CLOTHES; 869]

plain flour *type of* **flour**. [➡BREAD, FLOUR, AND BREAD PRODUCTS; 1178]

plainly 1 *adv* **simply**, normally, basically, naturally, purely, barely. [➡PLAIN; 233] *Opposite:* elaborately. 2 *adv* **clearly**, evidently, obviously, apparently, pronouncedly, palpably, tangibly, patently, unmistakably, manifestly. [➡PERCEPTIBLE; 25] *Opposite:* obscurely. 3 *adv* **bluntly**, straightforwardly, directly, frankly, openly, blatantly, forthrightly, candidly, baldly, straight from the shoulder. [➡HONEST AND OPEN; 631] *Opposite:* evasively.

plainness 1 *n* **simplicity**, ordinariness, naturalness, purity, bareness, starkness, everydayness, austerity, dullness, commonplaceness. [➡EASE AND SIMPLICITY; 201] 2 *n* **clarity**, clearness, palpability, tangibility, transparency, unambiguousness, comprehensibility, lucidity. [➡PERCEPTIBLE; 25] *Opposite:* obscurity. 3 *n* **bluntness**, straightforwardness, directness, frankness, openness, forthrightness, candidness, baldness. [➡HONEST AND OPEN; 631] *Opposite:* evasiveness.

plain sailing *adj* [➡EASE AND SIMPLICITY; 201]

plain-speaking *adj* [➡HONEST AND OPEN; 631]

plain-spoken *adj* **direct**, frank, blunt, forthright, bald, candid, open, honest, straight-talking, straightforward. *Opposite:* mealy-mouthed. (*disapproving*). [➡HONEST AND OPEN; 631]

plain-spokenness *n* [➡HONEST AND OPEN; 631]

plaint *n* **plea**, charge, accusation, complaint, action, suit, indictment, grievance. [➡TRIAL, PUNISHMENT, AND LEGAL OUTCOMES; 819] *Opposite:* defence.

plaintiff *n* **accuser**, applicant, complainant, petitioner, litigant, claimant, appellant. [➡TRIAL, PUNISHMENT, AND LEGAL OUTCOMES; 819] *Opposite:* defendant.

plaintive *adj* **mournful**, lamenting, elegiac (*formal*), nostalgic, sorrowful, wistful, sad, melancholy. [➡SADNESS, DISTRESS, AND DESPAIR; 540] *Opposite:* cheerful.

plait 1 *v* **braid**, interweave, weave, intertwine, crisscross, interlace, splice, twill. [➡FASTEN, LINK, AND JOIN; 409] *Opposite:* unravel. 2 *type of* **hairstyle**. [➡HAIR STYLES AND HAIR PIECES; 489]

plan 1 *n* **strategy**, scheme, idea, proposal, plot, design, disposition, organization, blueprint, ground plan. [➡WAYS OF DOING THINGS; 295] 2 *v* **work out**, arrange, scheme, plot, organize, design, devise, develop, form, formulate, shape, fashion, conceive, mould. [➡CAUSE TO HAPPEN; 31] *Opposite:* improvise. 3 *v* **intend**, propose, mean, line up, schedule, project, set up, arrange, organize, prearrange, prepare. [➡ARRANGE AND CREATE ORDER; 358]

plane 1 *n* **aircraft**, aeroplane, airplane (*US*). [➡AIRCRAFT; 1147] 2 *type of* **carpentry tool**. [➡HAND TOOLS; 1118]

planet 1 *n* **earth**, world, globe. [➡THE EARTH; 1039] 2 *type of* **heavenly body**. [➡CELESTIAL BODIES; 1060]

planet

◆ *types of planet*
Earth, Jupiter, Mars, Mercury, Neptune, Pluto, Saturn, Uranus, Venus

planetarium *n* [➡BUILDINGS FOR PUBLIC ENTERTAINMENT; 1083]

planetary *adj* **terrestrial**, earthly, environmental, global, universal, world. [➡THE SOLAR SYSTEM AND ASTRONOMY; 1059]

plane tree *type of* **deciduous tree**. [➡DECIDUOUS TREES; 1028]

plangent *adj* [➡SOFT OR PLEASANT SOUNDS; 1264]

plank *n* [➡BUILDING MATERIALS; 1076]

planking *n* [➡BUILDING MATERIALS; 1076]

planned *adj* **deliberate**, intentional, prearranged, strategic, premeditated, on purpose, scheduled, intended, calculated, designed, organized, prepared. [➡INTENTIONAL AND DELIBERATE; 280] *Opposite:* unplanned.

planner 1 *n* **town planner**, organizer, developer, city planner, designer, arranger, proposer, architect, engineer, manager, schemer, director, urban planner. [➡DESIGNERS, CREATORS AND INSTIGATORS; 348] 2 *n* **diary**, calendar, appointment book, wall chart, planning aid, chart, notebook. [➡LISTS AND SCHEDULES; 588]

planning *n* **preparation**, setting up, development, arrangement, scheduling, design, forecasting, organization, formation, projection, provision. [➡BEGINNING; 53]

plant 1 *n* **shrub**, bush, flower, herb, vegetable, pot plant, houseplant, cutting, seedling, potted plant (*US*). [➡PLANTS AND TREES; 1024] 2 *n* (*informal*) **spy**, informant, infiltrator, secret agent, agent. [➡PEOPLE WHO DECEIVE; 662] 3 *v* **sow**, seed, scatter, root, transplant, pot, replant, put in, bed. [➡GROW AND CULTIVATE; 352] 4 *v* **place**, fix, stand, transplant, deposit, set, lodge. [➡POSITION SOMETHING; 326] 5 *v* **introduce**, lodge, establish, implant, fix, embed, ingrain, root. [➡POSITION SOMETHING; 326] *Opposite:* erase. 6 *v* **conceal**, hide, bury, frame somebody, incriminate somebody, shop somebody (*slang*). [➡POSITION SOMETHING; 326] 7 *type of* **factory**. [➡INDUSTRIAL BUILDINGS; 1086]

plantation *n* **estate**, farm, homestead, farmstead, manor. [➡THE COUNTRYSIDE AND OUTDOOR SPACES; 1070]

planter *n* **pot**, flower pot, container, window box, urn, plant-holder. [➡CONTAINERS, RECEPTACLES, AND PACKAGING; 1244]

plaque *n* **sign**, panel, commemoration, inscription, plate, tablet, tile. [➡SIGNPOSTS, SIGNALS AND BILLBOARDS; 596]

plasma *n* [➡THE BLOOD AND CIRCULATION; 718]

plasma engine *part of* **spacecraft**. [➡SPACE VEHICLES; 1062]

plaster 1 *n* [➡BUILDING MATERIALS; 1076] 2 *n* **sticking plaster** (*formal*), bandage, dressing, covering, adhesive bandage (*US*). [➡COVERS AND COATINGS; 1245] 3 *v* **surface**, coat, cover, face, plaster over, mortar, daub. [➡DECORATE, ADORN, AND APPLY COATINGS; 406]

plasterboard *n* [➡BUILDING MATERIALS; 1076]

plastered (*informal*) *adj* [➡UNDER THE INFLUENCE OF DRUGS OR ALCOHOL; 742]

plasterwork *n* **plaster**, stuccowork, stucco, pargeting, moulding, frieze, decoration, parget, scagliola. [➡BUILDING MATERIALS; 1076]

plastic 1 *adj* **malleable**, soft, pliable, elastic, flexible, manipulable. [➡MALLEABLE AND ELASTIC; 1211] *Opposite:* hard. 2 *adj* **artificial**, fake, synthetic, false, forced, unnatural. [➡FALSE AND UNREAL; 174] *Opposite:* genuine.

plastic

◆ *types of plastic*
acetate, celluloid, epoxide, latex, melamine, neoprene, polyethylene (*US*), polystyrene, polythene, polyurethane, vinyl

plastic bullet *type of* **projectile**. [➡PROJECTILES; 1158]

plastic explosive *type of* **explosive material**. [➡EXPLOSIVES; 1154]

plasticity *n* **malleability**, softness, pliability, elasticity, flexibility, manipulability. [➡MALLEABLE AND ELASTIC; 1211] *Opposite:* hardness.

plastic surgeon *n* [➡PEOPLE WHO WORK IN MEDICINE; 848]

plastic surgery *n* **skin grafting**, cosmetic surgery, surgical repair (*US*). [➡REMEDIES, TREATMENTS AND OPERATIONS; 732]

plate 1 *n* **dish**, platter, salver, serving dish, bowl. [➡TABLEWARE, CUTLERY, AND KITCHENWARE; 861] 2 *n* **number plate**, registration, license plate (*US*). [➡EXTERNAL PARTS OF A VEHICLE; 1146] 3 *v* **cover**, coat, overlay, protect, shield, laminate, sheet, finish, electroplate. [➡DECORATE, ADORN, AND APPLY COATINGS; 406]

plateau 1 *n* **upland**, highland, hill, mesa, tableland, table. [➡DESERTS AND PLAINS; 1045] 2 *n* **level**, stage, period, phase. [➡PAUSES AND PHASES; 56]

plated *adj* **coated**, overlaid, gold-plated, covered, finished, electroplated, silver-plated, gilded. [➡PHYSICAL TEXTURE; 1221] *Opposite:* solid.

plateful *n* [➡AMOUNT OF SOLID OR SEMI-SOLID; 115]

plate glass *type of* **glass**. [➡GLASS; 1135]

platform 1 *n* **stage**, display place, raised area, podium, stand, dais, boards. [➡STAGES, PLATFORMS, AND RAISED AREAS; 1097] 2 *n* **policy**, proposal, manifesto, programme. [➡GOVERNMENT POLICIES; 810] 3 *type of* **shoe**. [➡FOOTWEAR; 871]

plating 1 *n* **electroplating**, silver-plating, gilding, coating, lustre. [➡COVERS AND COATINGS; 1245] 2 *n* **armour**, armour plate, cladding, metal casing, outer casing, reinforcement, strengthening, protection. [➡EXTREMITIES OF PHYSICAL OBJECTS; 1249] *Opposite:* core.

platinum 1 *type of* **metal**. [➡METALS; 1275] 2 *type of* **white**. [➡COLOURS; 1223]

platitude 1 *n* **cliché**, inanity, tired expression, commonplace, banality, bromide (*dated*), prosaicism. [➡FIGURES OF SPEECH; 674] 2 *n* **dullness**, boredom, insipidity, triteness, plainness, vapidity, inaneness. [➡BORING AND UNINTERESTING; 235]

platitudinous *adj* **clichéd**, trite, banal, corny, hackneyed, old hat (*informal*), unoriginal, prosaic. [➡BORING AND UNINTERESTING; 235] *Opposite:* original.

platonic *adj* **spiritual**, companionable, friendly, nonsexual, nonphysical, sexless, amicable, neighbourly. [➡RELATIONSHIP TO ANOTHER; 973]

platoon *n* **squad**, legion, team, detachment, subdivision, section, unit, group. [➡MILITARY PERSONNEL; 828]

platter *n* **plate**, serving dish, salver, dish, tray. [➡TABLEWARE, CUTLERY, AND KITCHENWARE; 861]

plaudit *n* **applause**, approval, praise, positive feedback, appreciation, recognition, acclaim. [➡PRAISE AND ENCOURAGE; 648] *Opposite:* criticism.

plausibility *n* **believability**, credibility, reasonableness, probability, conceivability, likelihood, possibility, acceptability, plausibleness. [➡POSSIBLE AND PROBABLE; 178] *Opposite:* implausibility.

plausible *adj* **believable**, credible, reasonable, probable, conceivable, likely, possible, acceptable. [➡POSSIBLE AND PROBABLE; 178] *Opposite:* implausible.

play 1 *v* **enjoy yourself**, occupy yourself, amuse yourself, have fun, frolic, fool around. [➡LEISURE AND RECREATION; 874] 2 *v* **joke**, tease, mess about (*informal*), mess around (*informal*), fool about, fool around, kid (*informal*), jest (*literary*). [➡JOKES AND TEASING; 675] 3 *v* **participate**, take part, join in, compete, engage in, cooperate. [➡PARTICIPATE; 293] 4 *v* **perform**, act, play-act, portray, star as, be, enact, personate. [➡PRETEND AND MIMIC; 60] 5 *n* **recreation**, amusement, fun, diversion, games, sport, sports. [➡LEISURE AND RECREATION; 874] *Opposite:* work. 6 *n* **production**, drama, show, piece, performance, comedy, tragedy, composition, work. [➡PERFORMANCES AND SHOWS; 42] 7 *type of* **broadcast**. [➡TELEVISION AND RADIO; 607]

play-act (*informal*) *v* **pretend**, ham it up, put it on, put on an act, play to the gallery, fake, sham, posture, make believe. [➡PRETEND AND MIMIC; 60]

play a part *v* [➡PARTICIPATE; 293]

playback *n* **replay**, rerun, reshowing, repetition, reproduction. [➡RECORDINGS AND PLAYERS; 911] *Opposite:* recording.

play down *v* **minimize**, make light of, underplay, underestimate, make little of. [➡UNDERDO SOMETHING; 292] *Opposite:* accentuate.

player 1 *n* **participant**, team member, competitor, contestant. [➡PEOPLE IN SPORTS AND LEISURE; 876] 2 *n* **actor**, thespian, performer, entertainer, play-actor, trouper. [➡PERFORMERS; 905]

playfellow (*dated*) *n* **friend**, playmate, chum (*informal*), pal (*informal*), mate, buddy (*US informal*). [➡FRIENDS; 963] *Opposite:* enemy.

playful 1 *adj* **lively**, bouncy, full of fun, full of life, frisky, full of beans (*informal*), spirited. [➡ENERGY AND ENTHUSIASM; 497] *Opposite:* subdued. 2 *adj* **good-humoured**, lighthearted, good-natured, teasing, jokey, mischievous, humorous, impish, naughty, roguish. [➡CHEERFULNESS OF OUTLOOK; 504] *Opposite:* serious.

playfully 1 *adv* **bouncily**, friskily, spiritedly. [➡ENERGY AND ENTHUSIASM; 497] 2 *adv* **good-humouredly**, lightheartedly, good-naturedly, teasingly, impishly, humorously, jokingly, mischievously, naughtily, roguishly. [➡GOOD-TEMPERED AND HUMOROUS; 628] *Opposite:* seriously.

playfulness 1 *n* **liveliness**, bounce, bounciness, friskiness, spirit. [➡ENERGY AND ENTHUSIASM; 497] 2 *n* **good humour**, lightheartedness, teasing, mischief, impishness, mischievousness, naughtiness, roguishness. [➡CHEERFULNESS OF OUTLOOK; 504] *Opposite:* seriousness.

play games with *v* **deceive**, trick, mess about (*informal*), confuse, mess around (*informal*), string along (*informal*), mistreat, abuse. [➡DECEPTION AND LIES; 661]

playgoer *n* **theatre buff**, theatregoer, spectator, punter (*informal*). [➡IN THE THEATRE; 906]

playground 1 *n* **park**, play area, community playground, adventure playground, outdoor play area (*US*). [➡URBAN OUTDOOR SPACES; 1071] 2 *n* **school yard**, school grounds, play area, recreation area, concourse, forecourt. [➡URBAN OUTDOOR SPACES; 1071] *Opposite:* classroom.

play hooky (*informal*) *v* **play truant**, truant, skip classes, miss school, absent yourself. [➡RUN AWAY AND AVOID; 10] *Opposite:* attend.

playhouse 1 *n* **theatre**, auditorium, studio, venue. [➡BUILDINGS FOR PUBLIC ENTERTAINMENT; 1083] 2 *n* **Wendy house**, tree house, den. [➡TOYS; 880]

playing field *n* **sports ground**, sports field, pitch, park, ground, field, court. [➡URBAN OUTDOOR SPACES; 1071]

playmate *n* **friend**, pal (*informal*), chum (*informal*), playfellow (*dated*), mate, buddy (*US informal*). [➡FRIENDS; 963] *Opposite:* enemy.

play-off *n* **final**, final round, semifinal, quarterfinal, tiebreaker, competition, contest, game, match. [➡NON-AGGRESSIVE/SPORTING EVENT; 40]

play off *v* **oppose**, set against, pit against, go against, challenge. [➡COMPETE, CONTEND, AND COMBAT; 304]

playroom *type of* **room in the home**. [➡TYPES OF ROOM; 1096]

play safe *v* **take no risks**, hedge your bets, take care, be cautious, be careful, go easy (*informal*). [➡PAY ATTENTION; 766] *Opposite:* gamble.

playschool *n* **playgroup**, nursery, preschool, kindergarten (*US*). [➡EDUCATIONAL INSTITUTIONS; 813]

play the game *v* **toe the line**, follow the rules, conform, comply, obey, act honestly. [➡OBEY AND ABIDE BY; 302] *Opposite:* act up.

plaything *n* **toy**, doll, bauble, curio, knick-knack, game. [➡TOYS; 880]

playtime *n* **break**, interval, free time, leisure time, lunchtime, recess (*US*). [➡PERIOD OF REST; 91]

play to the gallery *v* **show off**, play up, posture, perform, play to the crowd, ham it up, put on an act. [➡OVERDO SOMETHING; 291]

play truant *v* [➡RUN AWAY AND AVOID; 10]

play up 1 *v* **exaggerate**, emphasize, embellish, highlight, draw attention to, stress. [➡CLAIM, INSIST, AND EMPHASIZE; 615] *Opposite:* play down. 2 *v* **misbehave**, act up, malfunction, go wrong. [➡OVERDO SOMETHING; 291] *Opposite:* behave.

play up to *v* **flatter**, win the favour of, butter up (*informal*), toady, ingratiate yourself with, creep (*informal*), crawl (*informal*), suck up to (*informal*). [➡PRAISE AND ENCOURAGE; 648]

playwright *n* **dramatist**, writer, author, tragedian, dramaturge, scriptwriter. [➡WRITERS AND STYLES; 914]

play your cards close to your chest *v* **be secretive**, be a dark horse, keep quiet, keep mum (*informal*). [➡WITHHOLD INFORMATION; 688]

plaza 1 *n* **square**, piazza, marketplace, court, mall (*US*). [➡URBAN OUTDOOR SPACES; 1071] 2 *n* (*US*) **shopping centre**, precinct, arcade, mall (*US*). [➡RETAIL OUTLETS; 1082]

PLC *n* [➡BUSINESS ENTERPRISES AND RELATED BODIES; 793]

plea 1 *n* **appeal**, entreaty, prayer, supplication (*formal*), imploration (*formal*), request, petition. [➡REQUEST AND DEMAND; 664] *Opposite:* demand. 2 *n* **statement**, claim, defence, declaration, assertion. [➡TRIAL, PUNISHMENT, AND LEGAL OUTCOMES; 819] *Opposite:* denial. 3 *n* **excuse**, pretext, reason, explanation, alibi. [➡EXPLAIN AND CLARIFY; 611]

plea-bargain *v* **plead guilty**, do a deal, negotiate, come to an agreement, contract, compromise, cop a plea (*US slang*). [➡TRIAL, PUNISHMENT, AND LEGAL OUTCOMES; 819]

plead 1 *v* **beg**, appeal, pray, beseech (*literary*), implore (*formal*), entreat (*formal*), importune (*formal*), supplicate (*formal*), request, petition. [➡REQUEST AND DEMAND; 664] *Opposite:* demand. 2 *v* **declare**, assert, claim, state, put forward, allege. [➡CLAIM, INSIST, AND EMPHASIZE; 615] 3 *v* **support**, defend, argue, contend, vindicate, assert. [➡APPROVE AND CONFIRM; 647]

pleading *adj* **begging**, suppliant (*formal*), beseeching (*literary*), imploring (*formal*), entreating (*formal*), piteous, persuasive. [➡REQUEST AND DEMAND; 664]

pleasant 1 *adj* **enjoyable**, agreeable, pleasing, lovely, nice, pleasurable, satisfying, amusing. [➡EMOTIONALLY PLEASANT; 188] *Opposite:* unpleasant. 2 *adj* **amiable**, friendly, congenial, likable, genial, affable, nice, cheery, good-humoured, good-natured. [➡FRIENDLINESS AND SOCIABILITY; 495] *Opposite:* nasty.

pleasantness 1 *n* **appeal**, loveliness, niceness, pleasurableness, satisfaction, enjoyableness, agreeableness. [➡TREAT; 211] *Opposite:* unpleasantness. 2 *n* **amiability**, friendliness, congeniality, likability, likableness, niceness, geniality, affableness, cheeriness, good humour, good-naturedness. [➡FRIENDLINESS AND SOCIABILITY; 495] *Opposite:* nastiness.

pleasantries *n* **small talk**, chat, gossip, banter, chitchat (*informal*), conversation. [➡INFORMAL COMMUNICATION; 45]

pleasantry *n* **remark**, civility, banality, politeness, observation, comment, passing comment. [➡NEUTRAL ONE-WAY COMMUNICATION; 49] *Opposite:* insult.

please 1 *v* **satisfy**, gratify, make happy, delight, make somebody's day, thrill, entertain, content. [➡PLEASE AND AMUSE; 573] *Opposite:* displease. 2 *v* **like**, prefer, choose, desire, wish, want. [➡MAKE DECISIONS AND CHOICES; 753] *Opposite:* dislike.

pleased *adj* **satisfied**, happy, content, delighted, contented, thrilled. [➡PLEASURE, EXCITEMENT, AND ELATION; 535] *Opposite:* displeased.

pleasing *adj* **agreeable**, pleasant, enjoyable, lovely, nice, pleasurable, satisfying, gratifying, delightful, welcome. [➡EMOTIONALLY PLEASANT; 188] *Opposite:* disagreeable.

pleasing to the eye *adj* [➡BEAUTY AND ATTRACTIVENESS; 190]

pleasurable *adj* **agreeable**, enjoyable, pleasing, pleasant, gratifying, satisfying, congenial, delightful. [➡EMOTIONALLY PLEASANT; 188] *Opposite:* disagreeable.

pleasure 1 *n* **enjoyment**, happiness, delight, bliss, contentment, satisfaction, gratification, joy. [➡PLEASURE, EXCITEMENT, AND ELATION; 535] *Opposite:* displeasure. 2 *n* **gratification**, indulgence, hedonism, decadence, sensuality, carnality. [➡PLEASURE, EXCITEMENT, AND ELATION; 535] 3 *n* **amusement**, recreation, fun, leisure, diversion, relaxation, delectation (*formal*). [➡ENTERTAINMENT; 872] *Opposite:* work. 4 *n* (*formal or literary*) **desire**, preference, wish, choice, liking, inclination, will. [➡MAKE DECISIONS AND CHOICES; 753] *Opposite:* displeasure.

pleasure-lover *n* [➡PLEASURE-SEEKERS AND HEDONISTS; 886]

pleasure-loving *adj* [➡PLEASURE-SEEKING AND EXCESS; 885]

pleasure-seeker *n* [➡PLEASURE-SEEKERS AND HEDONISTS; 886]

pleasure-seeking *n* [➡PLEASURE-SEEKING AND EXCESS; 885]

pleat 1 *n* **crease**, fold, tuck, gather, crimp, corrugation, furrow, wrinkle. [➡CHANGE OF SHAPE; 386] 2 *v* **fold**, crease, tuck, gather, crimp, wrinkle. [➡CHANGE OF SHAPE; 386]

plebe (*US*) *n* [➡STUDENTS AND PUPILS; 841]

plebiscite *n* **referendum**, poll, vote, ballot, opinion poll, survey, direct vote. [➡ELECTIONS AND SUFFRAGE; 807]

pledge 1 *n* **vow**, oath, promise, assurance, guarantee, undertaking, word of honour, word. [➡PROMISE AND ASSURE; 685] 2 *n* **security**, deposit, guarantee, warranty, collateral, down payment, advance, guaranty, token. [➡GIFTS; 439] 3 *n* (*US*) **initiate**, new member, recruit, inductee, newcomer, freshman (*US*), pledgee. [➡UNSKILLED PERSON; 531] 4 *v* **promise**, vow, swear, guarantee, give your word, swear an oath, assure, vouchsafe, covenant, plight, undertake. [➡PROMISE AND ASSURE; 685]

plenary 1 *adj* (*formal*) **full**, complete, entire, whole, quorate, unlimited. [➡WHOLENESS AND COMPLETENESS; 199] 2 *n* **meeting**, session, general assembly, plenary meeting, plenary session, plenum, lecture. [➡MEETINGS AND ASSEMBLIES; 43]

plenary meeting *n* [➡MEETINGS AND ASSEMBLIES; 43]

plenary session *n* [➡MEETINGS AND ASSEMBLIES; 43]

plenipotentiary 1 *adj* **presiding**, all-powerful, in charge, officiating, supreme, absolute, authoritative. [➡STRENGTH; 202] *Opposite:* powerless. 2 *n* **minister**, minister plenipotentiary, ambassador, special envoy, envoy, delegate, representative. [➡REPRESENTATIVES AND PATRONS; 968] *Opposite:* pawn.

plenteous (*literary*) *adj* **plentiful**, abundant, copious, overflowing, bounteous (*literary*), bountiful (*literary*), ample, profuse, lavish. [➡MANY, MUCH, LARGE AMOUNT; 117] *Opposite:* sparse.

plentiful *adj* **abundant**, copious, plenteous (*literary*), overflowing, bountiful (*literary*), ample, bounteous (*literary*), lavish, profuse. [➡MANY, MUCH, LARGE AMOUNT; 117] *Opposite:* scarce.

plenty 1 *n* **prosperity**, abundance, copiousness, bounty (*literary*), profusion, plethora. [➡ MANY, MUCH, LARGE AMOUNT; 117] *Opposite:* insufficiency. 2 *adj* (*informal*) **ample**, a lot, lots, loads (*informal*), a load, heaps (*informal*), masses (*informal*), sufficient, enough, adequate, stacks (*informal*). [➡ ENOUGH AND SUFFICIENT; 129] *Opposite:* inadequate. 3 *adv* (*US informal*) **sufficiently**, quite, adequately, amply, abundantly, profusely, plenteously (*literary*), copiously, loads (*informal*), very. [➡ ENOUGH AND SUFFICIENT; 129] *Opposite:* insufficiently.

plenum *n* **general assembly**, meeting, session, plenary meeting, plenary session, plenary. [➡ MEETINGS AND ASSEMBLIES; 43]

pleonasm *n* [➡ MEANINGLESS SPEECH OR WRITING; 677]

plesiosaur *type of* **dinosaur**. [➡ DINOSAUR; 996]

plethora *n* **overabundance**, excess, surfeit, glut, surplus, superfluity. [➡ TOO MUCH; 118] *Opposite:* shortage.

pliability 1 *n* **flexibility**, bendability, suppleness, pliancy, bendiness, elasticity, malleability, plasticity, softness. [➡ MALLEABLE AND ELASTIC; 1211] *Opposite:* rigidity. 2 *n* **compliance**, pliancy, adaptability, flexibility, meekness, obedience, docility, manipulability, suggestibility, tractability, impressionability. [➡ COWARDICE AND WEAKNESS OF WILL; 509] *Opposite:* inflexibility.

pliable 1 *adj* **flexible**, bendable, supple, workable, pliant, bendy, elastic, malleable, plastic, ductile, soft. [➡ MALLEABLE AND ELASTIC; 1211] *Opposite:* rigid. 2 *adj* **compliant**, pliant, adaptable, adjustable, flexible, agreeable, accommodating, meek, obedient, docile, manipulable, yielding, easily swayed, biddable, suggestible, tractable, impressionable. [➡ THE WILL AND WILLINGNESS; 564] *Opposite:* inflexible.

Compare and Contrast: ***pliable, ductile, malleable, elastic, pliant***

CORE MEANING: READY TO BE BENT OR MOULDED

pliable flexible and easily bent or moulded; ***ductile*** describes metals that are able to be easily drawn out into a long continuous wire or hammered into thin sheets; ***malleable*** describes metals that can be hammered or pressed into various shapes without breaking or cracking; ***elastic*** describes substances or materials that can be stretched without breaking and then return to their original shape; ***pliant*** supple and springy and therefore easily bent.

pliancy 1 *n* **pliability**, flexibility, bendability, suppleness, bendiness, elasticity, malleability, plasticity, softness. [➡ MALLEABLE AND ELASTIC; 1211] *Opposite:* stiffness. 2 *n* **compliance**, pliability, adaptability, adjustability, flexibility, meekness, obedience, docility, manipulability, suggestibility, tractability, impressionability. [➡ THE WILL AND WILLINGNESS; 564] *Opposite:* obstinacy.

pliant 1 *adj* **pliable**, flexible, bendable, supple, workable, elastic, bendy, plastic, malleable, soft. [➡ MALLEABLE AND ELASTIC; 1211] *Opposite:* inflexible. 2 *adj* **compliant**, pliable, adaptable, adjustable, flexible, agreeable, accommodating, meek, obedient, docile, manipulable, yielding, easily swayed, biddable, tractable, impressionable. [➡ THE WILL AND WILLINGNESS; 564]. *Opposite:* rebellious, suggestible.

See Compare and Contrast at **pliable**.

pliers *type of* **general tool**. [➡ HAND TOOLS; 1118]

plight *n* **dilemma**, trouble, predicament, difficulty, quandary, scrape (*informal*). [➡ DIFFICULT SITUATIONS; 72]

plimsoll *type of* **shoe**. [➡ FOOTWEAR; 871]

plinth *n* **pedestal**, platform, base, stand, support, podium, dais. [➡ SUPPORTS AND BASES; 1254]

plod *v* **trudge**, slog, tread, traipse (*informal*), lumber, tramp, clump, clomp, walk. [➡ MOVE SLOWLY; 315] *Opposite:* race.

plodder *n* **slowcoach** (*informal*), snail, toiler, slogger, idler, slowpoke (*US informal*). [➡ LAZY OR UNSUCCESSFUL PEOPLE; 948] *Opposite:* high-flier.

plodding *adj* **slow**, dull, slow but sure, ponderous, tedious, steady, slow-moving, laboured. [➡ MOVING SLOWLY; 105] *Opposite:* rapid.

plonk 1 *v* **place**, put, put down, set down, stick (*informal*), pop (*informal*), plop (*informal*), dump, lay, bung (*informal*). [➡ POSITION SOMETHING; 326] 2 *n* (*informal*) **vino** (*informal*), house red, house white, vin de table, booze (*slang*). [➡ DRINKS; 1186]

plop 1 *v* (*informal*) **place**, put, put down, set down, stick (*informal*), pop (*informal*), plonk, dump, lay, bung (*informal*). [➡ POSITION SOMETHING; 326] 2 *type of* **impact sound**. [➡ IMPACT SOUNDS; 1259]

plop down *v* **sit**, sit down, plonk down (*informal*), settle, flop down, plunk down (*US*). [➡ ASSUME A POSITION; 318]

plot 1 *n* **conspiracy**, plan, scheme, subversion, strategy, design, intrigue, stratagem. [➡ WAYS OF DOING THINGS; 295] 2 *n* **story line**, action, scenario, outline, narrative, story. [➡ THE ORAL TRADITION; 678] 3 *n* **area**, section, parcel, piece, lot. [➡ AREA AND RANGE; 111] 4 *v* **plan**, scheme, strategize, conspire, design, contrive, intrigue, connive. [➡ CAUSE TO HAPPEN; 31] 5 *v* **chart**, map, draw, mark, map out, outline, calculate. [➡ RECORD SOMETHING; 372]

plotter *n* **schemer**, conspirator, conniver, contriver, strategist, planner. [➡ PEOPLE WHO DECEIVE; 662]

plough 1 *v* **cultivate**, till, turn over, work. [➡ USE TOOLS AND MACHINERY; 469] 2 *type of* **cutting tool**. [➡ CUTTING TOOLS; 1119]

plough into *v* **crash into**, bang into, drive into, run into, career into, collide with. [➡ CONTACT: IMPACT; 414]

plough on *v* **keep at it**, struggle on, persevere, persist, plug away (*informal*), keep your nose to the grindstone. [➡ CONTINUE AN ACTION; 263]

plough through *v* **keep at**, struggle on, plough on, persevere, persist, plug away (*informal*). [➡ CONTINUE AN ACTION; 263]

plough under *v* **bury**, cover, cover over, turn over. [➡ CAUSE TO DISAPPEAR; 6] *Opposite:* dig up.

plover *type of* **seabird**. [➡ SEABIRD; 1002]

ploy *n* **trick**, manoeuvre, strategy, plan, ruse, tactic, scheme, gambit, stratagem. [➡ WAYS OF DOING THINGS; 295]

pluck 1 *v* **pull**, tug, pick at, grasp, take, grab. [➡REMOVE SOMETHING; 339] 2 *v* **pull out**, remove, yank, tweak, uproot. [➡EXTRACT AND SEVER; 342] 3 *v* **strum**, play, twang, plunk, pick. [➡MUSIC, SONGS, AND SINGING; 907] 4 *v* **pick**, collect, gather, harvest. [➡GET; 421] 5 *n* **courage**, determination, bravery, fortitude, resolve, nerve, guts (*slang*), backbone, bottle (*informal*), fearlessness. [➡COURAGE; 499] *Opposite:* cowardice.

See Compare and Contrast at **courage**.

pluckiness *n* **bravery**, courage, pluck, guts (*informal*), fearlessness, boldness, audacity, audaciousness, spirit, intrepidity, daring, determination. [➡COURAGE; 499] *Opposite:* cowardice.

pluck up courage *v* **dare**, screw up, take the plunge, brace yourself, take a deep breath, steel yourself, get up, muster. [➡PREPARE FOR ACTION; 290]. *Opposite:* chicken out (*slang*).

plucky *adj* **brave**, courageous, gutsy (*informal*), fearless, bold, audacious, spirited, intrepid (*dated or humorous*), daring, determined. [➡COURAGE; 499] *Opposite:* cowardly.

plug 1 *n* **stopper**, cork, cap, bung, top. [➡COVERS AND COATINGS; 1245] 2 *n* (*informal*) **socket**, point, outlet, power point, wall outlet. [➡ELECTRONICS AND ELECTRICS; 1136] 3 *n* (*informal*) **advertisement**, advert (*informal*), ad, mention, promotion, publicity. [➡ADVERTISING AND PUBLICITY; 605] 4 *n* **sample**, core, piece, wedge, extract, section, cross section. [➡REPRESENTATIONS AND GENERAL EXAMPLES; 65] 5 *n* **wad**, mass, lump, wodge (*informal*), wadding, padding, pad. [➡AMOUNT OF SOLID OR SEMI-SOLID; 115] 6 *v* (*informal*) **work**, carry on, keep at it, keep going, persevere, press on, beaver (*informal*), soldier on, keep your nose to the grindstone, keep your head down, struggle, persist, labour, plough. [➡CONTINUE AN ACTION; 263] 7 *v* (*informal*) **puff**, hype, sell, push, spin, endorse, advertise, promote, publicize. [➡ADVERTISING AND PUBLICITY; 605] *Opposite:* run down. 8 *v* **stop**, cap, bung, cork, seal, block, close, bung up (*informal*), clog, congest, plug up. [➡FILL; 407] *Opposite:* unplug.

plug away (*informal*) *v* [➡CONTINUE AN ACTION; 263]

plugged-in (*informal*) *adj* **informed**, involved, connected, in tune, in touch, aware, alert, clued-up (*informal*), switched on (*informal*). [➡KNOWLEDGE AND WISDOM; 559]

plughole *n* **outlet**, drainhole, bunghole, drain, hole. [➡HOLES, GAPS, AND FORKS; 1251]

plug in *v* **connect**, hook up (*informal*), link up. [➡FASTEN, LINK, AND JOIN; 409] *Opposite:* unplug.

plum 1 *n* (*informal*) **reward**, award, bonus, windfall, trophy, catch, prize. [➡AMAZING THING; 212] 2 *adj* (*informal*) **desirable**, choice, covetable, prestigious, profitable, preferable. [➡ADMIRABLE AND COMMENDABLE; 186] 3 *type of* **fruit**. [➡FRUIT AND VEGETABLES; 1175] 4 *type of* **purple**. [➡COLOURS; 1223]

plumage *n* **feathers**, down, fluff, fuzz. [➡PARTS OF A BIRD; 1006]

plumb 1 *adv* (*informal*) **exactly**, precisely, slap (*informal*), right, bang, slap-bang (*informal*), smack-dab (*US informal*). [➡EXACT; 204] 2 *adv* (*US informal*) **completely**, truly, totally, absolutely, utterly, entirely, very, extremely. [➡TO A GREAT EXTENT; 130] 3 *v* **comprehend**, understand, fathom, grasp, know, follow. [➡UNDERSTAND AND GRASP; 760] 4 *v* **experience**, undergo, face, suffer, go through, live through. [➡EXPERIENCE AND ENCOUNTER; 583] 5 *adj* **perpendicular**, upright, vertical, true, aligned, straight. [➡ORIENTATION AND ALIGNMENT; 1222] *Opposite:* horizontal.

plumbing *n* **drains**, sanitation, drainage system, water system, heating system, pipes, fixtures. [➡FITTINGS; 859]

plumb line *type of* **general tool**. [➡HAND TOOLS; 1118]

plume 1 *n* **trail**, cloud, spiral, column, curl. [➡AMOUNT OF GAS; 116] 2 *part of* **bird**. [➡PARTS OF A BIRD; 1006]

plummet *v* **plunge**, drop, dive, tumble, crash, nose-dive, fall. [➡GO DOWNWARDS; 308] *Opposite:* climb.

plummy 1 *adj* **resonant**, mellow, rich, sonorous. [➡SOFT OR PLEASANT SOUNDS; 1264] *Opposite:* reedy. 2 *adj* **upper-class**, posh (*informal*), public-school, patrician, affected. [➡AFFECTATION, SELF-SATISFACTION, AND SNOBBISHNESS; 508] *Opposite:* common.

plump 1 *adj* **fat**, overweight, chubby, stout, fleshy, curvy, obese, round. [➡BUILD; 478] *Opposite:* slender. 2 *v* **flop down**, drop, plonk down (*informal*), plop down, flop, fall, collapse, plunk down (*US*). [➡ASSUME A POSITION; 318] *Opposite:* stand up.

plump down *v* [➡POSITION SOMETHING; 326]

plump for *v* **choose**, decide on, opt for, take, go for (*informal*), settle on. [➡MAKE DECISIONS AND CHOICES; 753]

plumpness *n* **fatness**, chubbiness, fleshiness, curviness, obesity, roundness. [➡BUILD; 478] *Opposite:* slenderness.

plump up *v* **fatten**, shake up, plump, fluff up. [➡CHANGE OF SIZE: BIGGER; 393]

plunder 1 *v* **steal**, rob, loot, pillage, raid, ransack. [➡STEAL AND ROB; 427] 2 *n* **stolen goods**, loot, booty, spoils, ill-gotten gains, swag. [➡PROCEEDS OF CRIME; 428]

plunge 1 *v* **thrust**, force, throw, push, pitch, sink, stab. [➡MOVE SOMETHING: DOWNWARDS; 330] 2 *v* **rush**, jump, leap, lurch, throw yourself, immerse yourself, rush headlong, charge, embark. [➡MOVE FAST; 314] *Opposite:* hesitate. 3 *v* **drop**, dive, plummet, sink, nose-dive, fall, dip, tumble. [➡GO DOWNWARDS; 308] *Opposite:* soar. 4 *n* **dive**, drop, plummet, nose dive, fall. [➡GO DOWNWARDS; 308] *Opposite:* climb.

plunger *type of* **general tool**. [➡HAND TOOLS; 1118]

plunging 1 *adj* **plummeting**, dipping, dropping, tumbling, reducing, falling, sinking, downward. [➡MOVING QUICKLY; 103] *Opposite:* rising. 2 *adj* **low**, low-cut, revealing, décolleté. [➡DESCRIBING CLOTHES; 869] *Opposite:* high.

plunk 1 *v* **twang**, strum, plonk, play, pick, pluck. [➡EMIT SOUNDS THROUGH IMPACT AND ABRASION; 366] 2 *v* **throw**, push, drop, toss, fall, dump. [➡GET RID OF SOMETHING; 452] 3 *n* **twang**, strum, plonk. [➡IMPACT SOUNDS; 1259]

plunk down *v* **plump down**, flop down, plop down, drop down, collapse, fall, plonk down (*informal*). [➡ASSUME A POSITION; 318] *Opposite:* stand up.

plural *type of* **grammatical term**. [➡ASPECTS OF LANGUAGE; 683]

pluralism *n* **variety**, diversity, multiplicity, heterogeneity. [➡DIFFERENCE; 150] *Opposite:* homogeneity.

pluralistic *adj* **varied**, mixed, diverse, multicultural, multiethnic, pluralist. [➡DIFFERENCE; 150] *Opposite:* homogeneous.

plurality 1 *n* **number**, range, variety, multiplicity, multitude, group. [➡MANY, MUCH, LARGE AMOUNT; 117] *Opposite:* single. 2 *n* (*US*) **majority**, landslide, margin. [➡MAJORITY; 139]

plus 1 *prep* **in addition to**, added to, as well as, along with, together with, and also, and. [➡ALSO; 136] *Opposite:* minus. 2 *adj* **desirable**, positive, advantageous, favourable, good. [➡ADMIRABLE AND COMMENDABLE; 186] *Opposite:* minus. 3 *adj* **and above**, and over, and more. [➡ALSO; 136] 4 *n* (*informal*) **advantage**, bonus, benefit, good thing, boon, pro, good point, plus point (*informal*). [➡SOURCE OF HAPPINESS, PLEASURE, OR IMPROVEMENT; 210] *Opposite:* minus.

plus fours *type of* **trousers**. [➡GARMENTS AND OUTFITS; 865]

plush (*informal*) *adj* **lush**, luxurious, expensive, rich, lavish, luxury, posh (*informal*), swish (*informal*), swanky (*informal*), deluxe. [➡EXPENSIVE AND LUXURIOUS; 219]

plus point *n* **plus** (*informal*), good point, advantage, bonus, good thing, pro, benefit, boon. [➡SOURCE OF HAPPINESS, PLEASURE, OR IMPROVEMENT; 210]

Pluto *type of* **planet**. [➡CELESTIAL BODIES; 1060]

plutocrat *n* **tycoon**, magnate, mogul, big shot (*informal*). [➡RICH PEOPLE; 895]

ply 1 *v* **work**, practise, pursue, carry out, wage, carry on, exercise. [➡CARRY OUT AN ACTION; 270] 2 *v* **use**, work with, apply, utilize, employ. [➡USE; 468] 3 *v* **supply**, pile, furnish (*formal*), load, provide. [➡EQUIP AND SUPPLY; 436] 4 *v* **badger**, hound, harass, overwhelm, bombard, barrage. [➡COMPLAIN AND NAG; 687] 5 *n* **layer**, thickness, strand, tier. [➡COVERS AND COATINGS; 1245]

plywood *n* [➡BUILDING MATERIALS; 1076]

p.m. *adj* **afternoon**, after lunch, evening, night. [➡TIMES OF DAY; 87] *Opposite:* a.m..

PM *n* [➡POLITICAL OFFICES AND POLITICIANS; 808]

pneumatic *adj* **air-filled**, inflated, inflatable, air. [➡DESCRIBING TECHNOLOGY; 1159] *Opposite:* solid.

poach 1 *v* **steal**, thieve, rustle, pilfer, plunder, rob. [➡STEAL AND ROB; 427] 2 *v* **simmer**, boil, steam, braise. [➡COOKING AND FOOD PREPARATION; 354]

poached *adj* [➡STATE OF PREPARED FOOD; 1170]

poacher *n* **thief**, rustler, robber, pilferer. [➡CRIMINALS; 821]

pocked *adj* **pitted**, pockmarked, dented, cratered, scarred, marked, blemished. [➡CONDITIONS AFFECTING THE SKIN; 722] *Opposite:* unblemished.

pocket 1 *n* **pouch**, compartment, receptacle, sack, bag. [➡CONTAINERS, RECEPTACLES, AND PACKAGING; 1244] 2 *v* **help yourself**, pinch (*informal*), snaffle, purloin (*formal*), steal, appropriate, take. [➡STEAL AND ROB; 427] 3 *adj* **concise**, abridged, reduced, short, small, compact, portable, mini (*informal*), pocket-sized, little, handy. [➡SMALL; 1194] 4 *part of* **garment**. [➡PARTS OF A GARMENT; 870]

pocketbook (*US*) 1 *n* **purse**, shoulder bag, handbag. [➡CONTAINERS, RECEPTACLES, AND PACKAGING; 1244] 2 *n* **wallet**, purse, notecase (*dated*), case, organizer. [➡CONTAINERS, RECEPTACLES, AND PACKAGING; 1244]

pocketknife *type of* **knife**. [➡CUTTING TOOLS; 1119]

pocket money *n* **spending money**, pin money, expenses, extra cash, personal money. [➡SMALL AMOUNT OF MONEY; 142]

pocket-size *see* **pocket-sized**.

pocket-sized *adj* **little**, small, handy, compact, portable, mini (*informal*), pocket. [➡SMALL; 1194] *Opposite:* bulky.

pocket watch *type of* **clock**. [➡CLOCKS AND TIMERS; 1125]

pockmark *n* **blemish**, scar, indentation, hollow, blotch, pit. [➡CONDITIONS AFFECTING THE SKIN; 722]

pockmarked *adj* **pitted**, pocked, dented, cratered, scarred, marked, blemished. [➡CONDITIONS AFFECTING THE SKIN; 722] *Opposite:* unblemished.

pod 1 *n* **shell**, husk, peapod, case, hull, shuck (*US*). [➡PARTS OF TREES AND PLANTS; 1026] 2 *type of* **herd**. [➡GROUP OF ANIMALS; 993] 3 *part of* **spacecraft**. [➡SPACE VEHICLES; 1062]

podginess *n* [➡BUILD; 478]

podgy *adj* **fat**, overweight, chubby, stout, fleshy, curvy, obese, round, pudgy (*US informal*). [➡BUILD; 478] *Opposite:* slim.

podium 1 *n* **dais**, platform, stage, plinth. [➡STAGES, PLATFORMS, AND RAISED AREAS; 1097] 2 *n* (*US*) **lectern**, pedestal, stand, support. [➡SUPPORTS AND BASES; 1254]

poem *n* **verse**, rhyme, ode, sonnet, elegy, limerick, couplet, epic. [➡POETRY AND VERSE; 915] *Opposite:* prose.

poesy (*archaic or literary*) *n* [➡POETRY AND VERSE; 915]

poet *n* **bard** (*literary or humorous*), writer, lyricist, rhymester, versifier, composer. [➡WRITERS AND STYLES; 914]

poetaster *n* [➡WRITERS AND STYLES; 914]

poetic 1 *adj* **lyrical**, elegiac, graceful, rhythmical, flowing, expressive, whimsical, romantic, elevated, uplifting. [➡ELOQUENT, TALKATIVE AND LONG-WINDED; 633] *Opposite:* prosaic. 2 *adj* **sensitive**, full of feeling, profound, deep, moving, perceptive, insightful, imaginative. [➡EMOTIONALLY PLEASANT; 188] *Opposite:* insensitive.

poetry *n* **verse**, rhyme, poems, rhymes, poesy (*archaic or literary*), lyrics. [➡POETRY AND VERSE; 915] *Opposite:* prose.

po-faced *adj* **disapproving**, solemn, serious, strait-laced, humourless, dour. [➡BAD-TEMPERED AND HUMOURLESS; 627] *Opposite:* jovial.

pogo *v* [➡BOUNCE, UNDULATE, AND VIBRATE; 309]

pogrom *n* **persecution**, extermination, massacre, devastation, slaughter, holocaust, ethnic cleansing. [➡CAUSES OF DEATH; 921]

poignance *n* **pathos**, sadness, tragedy, nostalgia, expressiveness, tenderness. [➡SADNESS, DISTRESS, AND DESPAIR; 540]

poignancy *n* **pathos**, sadness, tragedy, nostalgia, tenderness, expressiveness. [➡SADNESS, DISTRESS, AND DESPAIR; 540]

poignant *adj* **moving**, emotional, touching, distressing, sad, affecting, heartrending, heartbreaking, upsetting, tender, agonizing, expressive, nostalgic. [➡EMOTIONALLY UNPLEASANT AND UPSETTING; 228] *Opposite:* unemotional.

poinsettia *type of* **foliage plant.** [➡FOLIAGE PLANTS; 1035]

point 1 *n* **opinion**, fact, idea, argument, theme, topic. [➡SUBJECT AREA; 769] 2 *n* **instant**, time, stage, crux, juncture (*formal*), moment. [➡SHORT PERIOD OF TIME; 93] 3 *n* **aim**, meaning, central theme, intention, heart, crux, thrust. [➡MEANING; 691] 4 *n* **purpose**, advantage, use, sense, object, objective, aim, goal, usefulness. [➡INTENTION AND PURPOSE; 773] 5 *n* **argument**, statement, line of reasoning, thrust, viewpoint, view. [➡POINT OF VIEW; 768] 6 *n* **detail**, item, feature, aspect, thing, article, element, step. [➡SUBJECT AREA; 769] 7 *n* **position**, spot, place, situation, site, location, locus, station. [➡PLACE; 1064] 8 *n* **tip**, end, top, summit, peak, apex, cusp, prong. [➡EXTREMITIES OF PHYSICAL OBJECTS; 1249] 9 *n* **headland**, cape, promontory, spit, peninsula, foreland, head. [➡THE SEAS, OCEANS, AND SHORES; 1041] 10 *n* **socket**, power point, plug, contact, outlet. [➡ELECTRONICS AND ELECTRICS; 1136] 11 *v* **direct**, aim, face, indicate, draw attention to, steer, train. [➡POSITION SOMETHING; 326] 12 *type of* **punctuation mark.** [➡ASPECTS OF LANGUAGE; 683]

point and click agreement *n* [➡E-COMMERCE; 1128]

point-blank 1 *adv* **at close range**, straight on, dead on, close up, close to, closely, immediately. [➡CLOSENESS; 160] 2 *adv* **frankly**, bluntly, outright, straightforwardly, directly, abruptly, straight out. [➡HONEST AND OPEN; 631] *Opposite:* indirectly.

pointed 1 *adj* **sharp**, piercing, keen, pointy, jagged. [➡ANGULAR SHAPE; 1216] *Opposite:* blunt. 2 *adj* **barbed**, critical, meaningful, incisive, sharp, cutting, trenchant, acerbic, emphatic, insightful. [➡RUDE AND HOSTILE; 626] *Opposite:* mild.

pointedly *adv* **deliberately**, purposely, intentionally, meaningfully, openly, emphatically. [➡RUDE AND HOSTILE; 626] *Opposite:* subtly.

pointer 1 *n* **cane**, baton, stick, pole. [➡STICKS, POLES, AND WEDGES; 1253] 2 *n* **needle**, indicator, hand, cursor. [➡PARTS OF MACHINES AND TOOLS; 1117] 3 *n* **tip**, advice, hint, suggestion, warning, indication. [➡ADVICE; 690]

pointillism *type of* **pre-20th-century art movement.** [➡ARTISTIC MOVEMENTS AND STYLES; 899]

pointiness *n* [➡ANGULAR SHAPE; 1216]

pointing *n* **mortar**, cement, grout, filling. [➡BUILDING MATERIALS; 1076]

pointless *adj* **useless**, futile, senseless, meaningless, worthless, stupid, inane, purposeless, hopeless, needless, aimless, vain. [➡REDUNDANT AND USELESS; 241] *Opposite:* useful.

pointlessness *n* **uselessness**, futility, senselessness, meaninglessness, worthlessness, stupidity, inanity, purposelessness, hopelessness, needlessness, aimlessness, vanity. [➡REDUNDANT AND USELESS; 241] *Opposite:* usefulness.

point of departure *n* [➡BEGINNING; 53]

point of no return *n* [➡DECISIVE MOMENTS; 44]

point of view *n* **opinion**, attitude, standpoint, viewpoint, position, approach, judgment, perspective. [➡POINT OF VIEW; 768]

point out 1 *v* **indicate**, show, reveal, point at, identify. [➡INFORM AND ANNOUNCE; 612] 2 *v* **call attention to**, draw attention to, highlight, indicate, mention, spotlight, emphasize. [➡CLAIM, INSIST, AND EMPHASIZE; 615] *Opposite:* hide.

point the finger *v* [➡ACCUSE, BLAME, AND CRITICIZE; 642]

point-to-point *n* **steeplechase**, horse race, equestrian event, cross-country racing (*US*). [➡NON-AGGRESSIVE/SPORTING EVENT; 40]

point up *v* **emphasize**, draw attention to, underline, make clear, show, reveal, underscore, put the accent on, highlight, demonstrate, accentuate, focus. [➡CLAIM, INSIST, AND EMPHASIZE; 615]

pointy *adj* [➡ANGULAR SHAPE; 1216]

poise 1 *n* **composure**, dignity, self-assurance, self-confidence, self-control, sang-froid (*formal*), aplomb, self-possession, gracefulness, calm, cool. [➡CONFIDENCE AND COMPOSURE; 500] 2 *n* **grace**, bearing, deportment (*formal*), carriage (*formal*), good posture, composure, mien (*literary*). [➡TEMPERAMENT AND BEHAVIOUR; 493] 3 *v* **hover**, balance, float, perch, hang, suspend. [➡ASSUME A POSITION; 318]

poised 1 *adj* **ready**, prepared, primed, in position, in place. [➡ABOUT TO HAPPEN; 33] *Opposite:* unprepared. 2 *adj* **balanced**, suspended, hovering, on the edge, on the brink, perched, hanging, floating. [➡LACK OF ACTIVITY; 343] 3 *adj* **composed**, dignified, self-assured, self-confident, controlled, self-possessed, graceful, calm, cool, easygoing, placid. [➡CONFIDENCE AND COMPOSURE; 500] *Opposite:* insecure.

poison 1 *n* **venom**, toxin, contagion, toxic substance. [➡UNPLEASANT AND DIRTY SUBSTANCES; 1267] 2 *v* **kill**, murder, exterminate, destroy, harm, injure, assassinate, slaughter, attack. [➡KILL; 923] 3 *v* **pollute**, taint, corrupt, contaminate, adulterate, spoil, dirty, sully, debase, turn. [➡DIRTY AND CONTAMINATE; 405]

poisoner *n* **murderer**, killer, exterminator, assassin, slaughterer, attacker. [➡PEOPLE WHO KILL; 924]

poison gas *type of* **gas.** [➡GASES; 1274]

poison ivy *type of* **weed.** [➡WEEDS AND THISTLES; 1034]

poison oak *type of* **weed.** [➡WEEDS AND THISTLES; 1034]

poisonous 1 *adj* **toxic**, venomous, noxious, fatal, lethal, deadly, mephitic (*literary*), pestilential. [➡DEADLY; 928] *Opposite:* harmless. 2 *adj* **malicious**, evil, wicked, ill-intentioned, nasty, spiteful, vicious, hostile, venomous, malevolent, vituperative. [➡AGGRESSIVE AND BELLIGERENT; 519] *Opposite:* kindly.

poisonously *adv* **maliciously**, evilly, wickedly, nastily, spitefully, viciously, hostilely, venomously, malevolently, vituperatively. [➡AGGRESSIVE AND BELLIGERENT; 519]

poke 1 *v* **jab**, stab, push, prod, thrust, dig, nudge, punch, stick. [➡CONTACT: TOUCH; 413] 2 *v* **protrude**, stick out, project, jut, extend. [➡ARRIVE; 12] 3 *v* **search through**, nose around (*informal*), look through, root, browse, rummage, search, ferret about. [➡SEEK POSSESSION AND SEARCH; 457] 4 *n* **stab**, jab, push, prod, thrust, dig, nudge. [➡CONTACT: TOUCH; 413]

poke around *v* [➡SEEK POSSESSION AND SEARCH; 457]

poke fun at *v* **make fun of**, ridicule, tease, mock, laugh at, rag (*dated*), razz (*US informal*). [➡JOKES AND TEASING; 675]

poker *type of* **general tool**. [➡HAND TOOLS; 1118]

poker-faced *adj* **expressionless**, reactionless, blank, impassive, emotionless, deadpan, straight-faced. [➡FACIAL EXPRESSION; 652] *Opposite:* expressive.

pokey (*US dated slang*) *n* [➡BUILDINGS FOR CONFINING PEOPLE; 1093]

poky 1 *adj* (*informal*) **small**, tiny, cramped, restricted, tight, boxy. [➡SMALL; 1194] *Opposite:* spacious. 2 *adj* (*US*) **slow**, plodding, sluggish, leaden, dilatory. [➡MOVING SLOWLY; 105] *Opposite:* quick. 3 *adj* (*US*) **frumpy**, dowdy, shabby, drab, plain, unfashionable, old-fashioned. [➡OLD, OLD-FASHIONED; 168]

polar *adj* **glacial**, Arctic, Antarctic. [➡COLD WEATHER; 1051] *Opposite:* tropical.

polar bear *type of* **large mammal**. [➡LARGE MAMMAL; 986]

polarity *n* **division**, split, schism, divergence, polarization, separation, opposition. [➡OPPOSITE; 158] *Opposite:* convergence.

polarization *n* **divergence**, separation, division, opposition, schism, split, polarity. [➡SEPARATE AND DIVIDE; 402] *Opposite:* union.

polarize *v* **diverge**, split, drive apart, separate, create a rift in, differentiate, divide, oppose. [➡SEPARATE AND DIVIDE; 402] *Opposite:* unite.

pole 1 *n* **opposite**, extreme, extremity, limit, end. [➡OPPOSITE; 158] 2 *n* **rod**, shaft, stick, post, dowel, staff, baton, stake. [➡STICKS, POLES, AND WEDGES; 1253] 3 *v* **push**, propel, raft, punt, shove, thrust, drive. [➡PUSH, PULL, SLIDE; 336]

poleaxe 1 *v* **astonish**, amaze, stupefy, stun, shock, dumbfound. [➡CONFUSE AND BEWILDER; 572] 2 *type of* **sword or knife**. [➡SWORDS AND KNIVES; 1156]

polecat *type of* **small mammal**. [➡SMALL MAMMAL; 990]

polemic 1 *n* **argument**, plea, diatribe, speech, discourse, attack, defence. [➡CRITICISMS AND ANGRY OUTBURSTS; 50] 2 *adj* **controversial**, outspoken, impassioned, uncompromising, bold, polemical, passionate, persuasive. [➡HONEST AND OPEN; 631] *Opposite:* dispassionate.

polemicist *n* **debater**, orator, speaker, essayist, lecturer, thinker, campaigner, activist. [➡SPEAKERS AND ORATORS; 604]

pole position *n* **prime position**, lead, front, advantage. [➡SOURCE OF HAPPINESS, PLEASURE, OR IMPROVEMENT; 210] *Opposite:* rear.

poles apart *adj* **complete opposites**, diametrically opposed, nothing like each other, like chalk and cheese (*informal*), completely different. [➡DIFFERENCE; 150]

pole-vault *v* **jump**, vault, leap, bound. [➡GO UPWARDS; 307]

pole vault *type of* **track and field event**. [➡HOBBIES, GAMES, AND SPORTS; 875]

police 1 *n* **police force**, force, constabulary, law, crime squad, drug squad, vice squad, fraud squad, riot police, police department (*US*), law enforcement agency (*US*). [➡THE POLICE, ARREST, AND PRE-TRIAL PROCEEDINGS; 818] 2 *v* **regulate**, control, keep watch over, monitor, patrol, supervise, watch. [➡AVOID, PREVENT, LIMIT, AND CONTROL; 278]

police cadet *n* [➡THE POLICE, ARREST, AND PRE-TRIAL PROCEEDINGS; 818]

police car *type of* **public service vehicle**. [➡VEHICLES; 1144]

police constable *n* [➡THE POLICE, ARREST, AND PRE-TRIAL PROCEEDINGS; 818]

police department (*US*) *n* [➡THE POLICE, ARREST, AND PRE-TRIAL PROCEEDINGS; 818]

police force *n* crime squad, drug squad, vice squad, fraud squad, riot police, police, force, constabulary, law, law enforcement agency (*US*), police department (*US*). [➡THE POLICE, ARREST, AND PRE-TRIAL PROCEEDINGS; 818]

policeman *n* **law enforcement officer**, bobby (*dated informal*), copper, cop (*slang*), police constable, PC, police officer, detective, sergeant, peace officer (*US*), sheriff (*US*). [➡THE POLICE, ARREST, AND PRE-TRIAL PROCEEDINGS; 818]

police officer *n* **bobby** (*dated informal*), copper, cop (*slang*), police constable, PC, WPC, policeman, policewoman, detective, law enforcement officer, sergeant, sheriff (*US*), peace officer (*US*). [➡THE POLICE, ARREST, AND PRE-TRIAL PROCEEDINGS; 818]

policewoman *n* **law enforcement officer**, bobby (*dated informal*), copper, cop (*slang*), police constable, WPC, police officer, detective, sergeant, peace officer (*US*), sheriff (*US*). [➡THE POLICE, ARREST, AND PRE-TRIAL PROCEEDINGS; 818]

policy 1 *n* **course of action**, rule, strategy, plan, guiding principle, guidelines, procedure, dogma, programme. [➡WAYS OF DOING THINGS; 295] 2 *n* **contract**, document, certificate, statement, papers, testament, record, schedule. [➡OFFICIAL DOCUMENTS; 587]

polish 1 *v* **shine**, buff, buff up, rub, clean, dust, furbish. [➡CLEAN AND POLISH; 404] *Opposite:* tarnish. 2 *v* **improve**, enhance, refine, perfect, hone, brush up, work on, practise, mend. [➡IMPROVE SOMETHING; 375] 3 *n* **shine**, lustre, gleam, sheen, brilliance, smoothness, gloss. [➡VISUAL TEXTURE; 1220] *Opposite:* dullness. 4 *n* **refinement**, skill, control, sophistication, grace, style, sparkle, culture, elegance. [➡GOOD MANNERS AND SOCIAL SKILLS; 521]

polished 1 *adj* **refined**, elegant, cultured, sophisticated, graceful, genteel. [➡GOOD MANNERS AND SOCIAL SKILLS; 521] *Opposite:* coarse. 2 *adj* **practised**, skilful, accomplished, professional, impeccable, expert. [➡TALENTED AND SKILFUL; 528] *Opposite:* amateur. 3 *adj* **smooth**, shiny, gleaming, glossy, slippery, bright. [➡VISUAL TEXTURE; 1220] *Opposite:* dull.

polish off *v* **finish**, finish off, dispose of, complete, eliminate, eat, eat up, gobble, wolf, bolt, demolish (*informal*), scarf down (*US slang*). [➡EAT AND NOT EAT; 711] *Opposite:* leave.

polish up 1 *v* **shine**, buff, rub, clean, dust, furbish. [➡CLEAN AND POLISH; 404] *Opposite:* tarnish. 2 *v* **refine**, improve, practise, brush up, work on, perfect, hone, enhance. [➡IMPROVE SOMETHING; 375] *Opposite:* let go.

polish up on *v* **refine**, improve, practise, brush up, work on, perfect, hone, enhance. [➡PREPARE FOR ACTION; 290] *Opposite:* let go.

polite 1 *adj* **well-mannered**, good-mannered, civil, well-bred, gracious, courteous, respectful, mannerly. [➡GOOD MANNERS AND SOCIAL SKILLS; 521] *Opposite:* rude. 2 *adj* **refined**, cultured, sophisticated, polished, elegant, genteel, urbane, poised. [➡LEVEL OF EDUCATION AND SOPHISTICATION; 894] *Opposite:* coarse.

politely *adv* **civilly**, graciously, courteously, respectfully. [➡GOOD MANNERS AND SOCIAL SKILLS; 521] *Opposite:* rudely.

politeness *n* **good manners**, graciousness, manners, civility, breeding, courtesy, respect. [➡GOOD MANNERS AND SOCIAL SKILLS; 521] *Opposite:* rudeness.

politesse *n* [➡GOOD MANNERS AND SOCIAL SKILLS; 521]

politic *adj* **tactful**, diplomatic, prudent, wise, expedient, sensible, discreet, shrewd, astute, crafty, canny, cunning, sly. [➡POSITIVE INTELLECTUAL CHARACTERISTICS; 525] *Opposite:* foolish.

political 1 *adj* **party-political**, politically aware, radical, partisan, dogmatic. [➡THE NATURE OF IDEAS; 772] 2 *adj* **governmental**, administrative, electoral, civil, diplomatic, constitutional, doctrinal, ethical, civic. [➡GOVERNMENT AND POLITICS; 805]

political correctness *n* **appropriateness**, sensitivity, awareness, tactfulness, inclusiveness, inoffensiveness. [➡GOOD MANNERS AND SOCIAL SKILLS; 521] *Opposite:* insensitivity.

politically correct *adj* **inclusive**, appropriate, sensitive, aware, tactful, inoffensive, right-on (*dated informal*). [➡GOOD MANNERS AND SOCIAL SKILLS; 521] *Opposite:* politically incorrect.

politically incorrect *adj* **exclusive**, insensitive, inappropriate, unaware, tactless, prejudiced, offensive, insulting, inconsiderate. [➡BAD MANNERS AND SOCIAL SKILLS; 522] *Opposite:* politically correct.

politician *n* **political figure**, representative, candidate, official, legislator, office-bearer, statesman, stateswoman. [➡POLITICAL OFFICES AND POLITICIANS; 808]

politicization *n* **awareness raising**, consciousness raising, lobbying. [➡SOCIAL, POLITICAL, AND ECONOMIC CHANGE; 374]

politicize *v* **raise awareness of**, put on the agenda, debate, discuss, air, lobby, campaign. [➡SOCIAL, POLITICAL, AND ECONOMIC CHANGE; 374] *Opposite:* depoliticize.

politicking *n* **campaigning**, speechmaking, lobbying, politics, scheming, intriguing. [➡GOVERNMENT POLICIES; 810]

politics 1 *n* **government**, political affairs, affairs of state, policy, policymaking, legislation. [➡GOVERNMENT AND POLITICS; 805] 2 *n* **beliefs**, principles, opinions, views, theory, philosophy, dogma. [➡POINT OF VIEW; 768]

polity *n* **political entity**, organization, institution, state, society, community. [➡INSTITUTIONS; 791]

polka *type of* **dance**. [➡DANCE; 903]

poll 1 *n* **election**, census, survey, opinion poll, sample, ballot, referendum, market research. [➡ELECTIONS AND SUFFRAGE; 807] 2 *v* **sample**, survey, question, ask, interview, ballot. [➡ASK PEOPLE QUESTIONS; 667]

pollinate *v* **fertilize**, cross-fertilize, self-fertilize, cross-pollinate, self-pollinate. [➡GROW AND CULTIVATE; 352]

pollination *n* **fertilization**, cross-fertilization, self-fertilization, cross-pollination, self-pollination, allogamy, autogamy. [➡GROW AND CULTIVATE; 352]

polling *n* **voting**, casting your vote, balloting, going to the polls. [➡ELECTIONS AND SUFFRAGE; 807]

polling booth *n* **cubicle**, voting booth, booth, stall, box, compartment. [➡ELECTIONS AND SUFFRAGE; 807]

pollutant *n* **contaminant**, impurity, toxin, poison, waste product, chemical. [➡UNPLEASANT AND DIRTY SUBSTANCES; 1267]

pollute 1 *v* **contaminate**, poison, adulterate, infest, infect, foul, spoil, litter, dirty, taint. [➡DIRTY AND CONTAMINATE; 405] *Opposite:* clean. 2 *v* **corrupt**, defile (*formal*), pervert, demoralize, violate, damage, impair, blight. [➡MISUSE AND ABUSE; 472] *Opposite:* purify.

polluted *adj* **contaminated**, dirty, poisoned, adulterated, unclean, insanitary, unhygienic, diseased, infested, infected, fouled, foul, rank (*literary*), fetid, impure, tainted. [➡DIRTY; 1234] *Opposite:* clean.

polluter *n* **contaminator**, fly-tipper, dumper, poisoner, emitter, discharger. [➡DIRTY AND SLOVENLY PEOPLE; 954] *Opposite:* environmentalist.

pollution 1 *n* [➡DIRTY AND CONTAMINATE; 405] 2 *n* **contamination**, toxic waste, effluence, greenhouse gasses, smog, fumes, litter, trash (*US*). [➡UNPLEASANT AND DIRTY SUBSTANCES; 1267]

polo neck *type of* **sweater or cardigan**. [➡GARMENTS AND OUTFITS; 865]

polo shirt *type of* **top**. [➡GARMENTS AND OUTFITS; 865]

poltergeist *n* **ghost**, spirit, manifestation, apparition, spectre, phantom, presence. [➡THE SUPERNATURAL; 788]

poly (*informal*) *n* [➡EDUCATIONAL INSTITUTIONS; 813]

polychromatic *adj* [➡DESCRIBING COLOURS; 1225]

polychrome *adj* [➡DESCRIBING COLOURS; 1225]

polyester *type of* **synthetic fabric**. [➡FABRICS; 1131]

polyethylene (*US*) *type of* **plastic**. [➡PLASTICS; 1133]

polyglot *n* **linguist**, multilingual person, bilingual person. [➡PEOPLE WHO WORK WITH LANGUAGE AND CODE; 854]

polygon *type of* **angular shape**. [➡ANGULAR SHAPE; 1216]

polygonal *adj* **many-sided**, multilateral, triangular, quadrilateral, pentagonal, hexagonal, octagonal, geometric. [➡ANGULAR SHAPE; 1216]

polygraph *n* **detector**, lie detector, recorder, tester. [➡THE POLICE, ARREST, AND PRE-TRIAL PROCEEDINGS; 818]

polymath *n* **fount of knowledge**, Renaissance man, Renaissance woman, walking encyclopedia, sage (*literary*), mine of information. [➡TALENTED OR INTELLIGENT PERSON; 529] *Opposite:* specialist.

polyp *n* **growth**, tumour, cyst, nodule, swelling, lump. [➡ ILLNESSES AND DISORDERS; 733]

polystyrene *type of* **plastic**. [➡ PLASTICS; 1133]

polysyllabic *adj* **long**, compound, complex, multisyllabic. [➡ ASPECTS OF LANGUAGE; 683] *Opposite:* monosyllabic.

polysyllable *n* **long word**, compound, complex word. [➡ ASPECTS OF LANGUAGE; 683] *Opposite:* monosyllable.

polytechnic *n* **college**, poly (*informal*), tech (*informal*), technical college, college of further education, training college, university. [➡ EDUCATIONAL INSTITUTIONS; 813]

polytheism *n* **dualism**, animism, pantheism. [➡ RELIGIOUS CONCEPTS; 777] *Opposite:* monotheism.

polythene *type of* **plastic**. [➡ PLASTICS; 1133]

polyurethane *type of* **plastic**. [➡ PLASTICS; 1133]

pomegranate *type of* **fruit**. [➡ FRUIT AND VEGETABLES; 1175]

pomelo *type of* **citrus**. [➡ FRUIT AND VEGETABLES; 1175]

pomfret *type of* **tropical sea fish**. [➡ SEA FISH; 1009]

pomp *n* **splendour**, spectacle, display, ceremony, show, showiness, pageantry, solemnity, magnificence, grandeur. [➡ CEREMONIES AND ANNIVERSARIES; 38] *Opposite:* understatement.

pompadour *type of* **hairstyle**. [➡ HAIR STYLES AND HAIR PIECES; 489]

pompano *type of* **flatfish**. [➡ SEA FISH; 1009]

pompom *n* **bobble**, tassel, powder puff, decoration, detail, ball. [➡ ORNAMENTS AND DECORATIONS; 1247]

pomposity *n* **self-importance**, arrogance, pretentiousness, pretension, snobbishness, affectation, affectedness, ostentation, portentousness, haughtiness, exaggeration, pompousness, grandiosity, vanity. [➡ AFFECTATION, SELF-SATISFACTION, AND SNOBBISHNESS; 508] *Opposite:* modesty.

pompous 1 *adj* **self-important**, arrogant, pretentious, snobbish, affected, ostentatious, portentous, haughty, exaggerated, grandiose, vain. [➡ AFFECTATION, SELF-SATISFACTION, AND SNOBBISHNESS; 508] *Opposite:* modest. 2 *adj* **showy**, flaunting, spectacular, magnificent, grand, splendid, overstated. [➡ IN POOR TASTE; 230] *Opposite:* modest.

pompousness 1 *n* **self-importance**, arrogance, pretentiousness, pretension, snobbishness, affectedness, ostentation, portentousness, haughtiness, pomposity, grandiosity, vanity. [➡ AFFECTATION, SELF-SATISFACTION, AND SNOBBISHNESS; 508] *Opposite:* modesty. 2 *n* **spectacle**, magnificence, pomp, grandeur, ceremony, pageantry, splendour, display, show, showiness, overstatement. [➡ IN POOR TASTE; 230] *Opposite:* modesty.

poncho *n* **cloak**, cape, wrap. [➡ GARMENTS AND OUTFITS; 865]

pond *n* **pool**, tarn, mere (*archaic or literary*), fishpond, millpond. [➡ RIVERS, LAKES, AND STREAMS; 1042]

ponder *v* **consider**, think about, think over, contemplate, deliberate, wonder about, muse, brood over, mull over, weigh up, medidate upon. [➡ THINK AND REFLECT; 744]

ponderable *adj* **appreciable**, significant, considerable, substantial, weighty, palpable. [➡ IMPORTANT; 195] *Opposite:* insignificant.

ponderous 1 *adj* **heavy**, laborious, lumbering, weighty, unwieldy, cumbersome, bulky, hefty. [➡ WEIGHT: HEAVY; 1204] *Opposite:* light. 2 *adj* **tedious**, boring, laborious, tiresome, dull, slow, verbose, long-winded. [➡ BORING AND UNINTERESTING; 235] *Opposite:* lively.

ponderously *adv* **heavily**, laboriously, slowly, tediously, boringly, tiresomely. [➡ BORING AND UNINTERESTING; 235] *Opposite:* briskly.

ponderousness *n* [➡ LARGE; 1192]

pond scum *type of* **alga**. [➡ MICROORGANISMS, FUNGI, AND ALGAE; 1023]

pong (*informal*) 1 *n* **stink**, smell, whiff (*informal*), niff (*slang*), reek, stench, hum (*informal*). [➡ SMELL AND SMELLING; 706] 2 *v* **smell**, stink, whiff (*informal*), niff (*slang*), reek, stench, hum (*informal*). [➡ SMELL EMISSION; 370]

pongy (*informal*) *adj* **stinky** (*informal*), whiffy (*informal*), niffy (*slang*), cheesy, high, rank (*literary*). [➡ SMELL AND SMELLING; 706] *Opposite:* fragrant.

pontiff *n* **pope**, bishop of Rome, Holy Father. [➡ RELIGIOUS PEOPLE; 779]

pontifical 1 *adj* **episcopal**, papal, prelatic. [➡ RELIGIONS AND RELIGIOUS PRACTICES; 778] 2 *adj* **pompous**, self-important, pontificating, grandiose, portentous, pretentious, swaggering. [➡ AFFECTATION, SELF-SATISFACTION, AND SNOBBISHNESS; 508] *Opposite:* humble.

pontificate *v* **hold forth**, preach, go on, sound off. [➡ UTTER AND PRONOUNCE; 609]

pontoon *n* **platform**, float, buoy, support, base, raft. [➡ SUPPORTS AND BASES; 1254]

pontoon bridge *type of* **bridge**. [➡ BRIDGES, TUNNELS, CROSSINGS, AND JUNCTIONS; 1111]

pony *type of* **horse**. [➡ HORSE; 985]

ponytail *type of* **hairstyle**. [➡ HAIR STYLES AND HAIR PIECES; 489]

pony-trekking *n* **hacking**, horse-riding, riding, riding out, equitation (*formal*), horseback riding (*US*). [➡ HOBBIES, GAMES, AND SPORTS; 875]

pooch (*informal*) *n* **doggy** (*babytalk*), dog, lapdog, canine companion, canine, hound, pet. [➡ DOG; 980]

poodle *type of* **small dog**. [➡ DOG; 980]

pooh-pooh *v* **reject**, dismiss, spurn, scorn, scoff at, express contempt, undermine, put down (*informal*), turn up your nose at. [➡ DENY AND REJECT; 645] *Opposite:* praise.

pool 1 *n* **pond**, puddle, lake, swimming pool, tarn, mere (*archaic or literary*), loch. [➡ RIVERS, LAKES, AND STREAMS; 1042] 2 *n* **team**, band, collection, consortium, collective, group. [➡ GROUPS OF PEOPLE; 935] 3 *n* **kitty**, fund, pot (*US informal*). [➡ MONEY; 140] 4 *v* **share**, combine, bring together, put together, assemble, merge, amalgamate. [➡ COMBINE AND MIX; 401] 5 *type of* **target ball game**. [➡ HOBBIES, GAMES, AND SPORTS; 875]

poop *part of* **ship or boat**. [➡ PARTS OF A SHIP OR BOAT; 1150]

pooped (*informal*) *adj* **exhausted**, shattered, tired out, worn out, dead beat (*informal*), wiped out (*slang*), bushed (*informal*), whacked (*informal*), dog-tired (*informal*), done in (*informal*), drained, ready to drop. [➡TIRED, ASLEEP AND UNCONSCIOUS; 739] *Opposite:* invigorated.

poor 1 *adj* **broke** (*informal*), needy, destitute, skint (*informal*), hard up (*informal*), badly off, poverty-stricken, indigent (*formal*), impoverished, penniless. [➡POVERTY AND POOR; 892] *Opposite:* rich. 2 *adj* **deprived**, unfortunate, underprivileged, meagre, reduced, pitiable, humble, lowly, modest. [➡POVERTY AND POOR; 892] *Opposite:* privileged. 3 *adj* **weak**, inadequate, feeble, meagre, bad, inferior, scanty, deficient, mediocre. [➡WEAKNESS; 242] *Opposite:* superior. 4 *adj* **humble**, lowly, modest, insignificant. [➡CLASS STATUS; 889] *Opposite:* noble.

poorly 1 *adv* **badly**, inadequately, weakly, feebly, scantily, defectively, unsuccessfully, disappointingly. [➡WEAKNESS; 242] *Opposite:* well. 2 *adj* (*informal*) **ill**, unwell, under the weather, sick, out of sorts, below par (*informal*), off-colour, ailing (*dated*). [➡ILL AND SICK; 741] *Opposite:* healthy.

poorly maintained *adj* [➡IN BAD REPAIR; 1233]

poorness 1 *n* **poverty**, impoverishment, destitution, indigence (*formal*), pennilessness, neediness, deprivation. [➡POVERTY AND POOR; 892] *Opposite:* wealth. 2 *n* **weakness**, inadequacy, feebleness, inferiority, poor quality, poor standard, deficiency, mediocrity. [➡ORDINARINESS; 245] *Opposite:* superiority.

poor person *n* [➡POOR PEOPLE; 896]

poor-quality *adj* **cheap**, shoddy, trashy, thrown together (*informal*), jerry-built, second-class, second-rate, mediocre, rubbishy, substandard. [➡IN BAD REPAIR; 1233] *Opposite:* first-rate.

poor quality *n* **cheapness**, tawdriness, mediocrity, inferiority, weakness, worthlessness, atrociousness. [➡IN BAD REPAIR; 1233] *Opposite:* quality.

pop 1 *n* **explosion**, bang, crack, report, snap. [➡IMPACT SOUNDS; 1259] 2 *v* **explode**, burst, go off, crack. [➡EMIT SOUNDS THROUGH IMPACT AND ABRASION; 366] 3 *v* (*informal*) **dash**, dart, nip (*informal*), go, call. [➡MOVE FAST; 314] 4 *v* (*informal*) **put**, place, insert, drop, shove, stick (*informal*), push. [➡POSITION SOMETHING; 326] 5 *adj* (*informal*) **popular**, modern, current, accessible, easy, simple, contemporary, superficial. [➡NEW, MODERN; 167] 6 *type of* **popular music**. [➡MUSIC, SONGS, AND SINGING; 907]

pop art *type of* **20th-century art movement**. [➡ARTISTIC MOVEMENTS AND STYLES; 899]

pop by *v* [➡ARRIVE; 12]

pope *n* **pontiff**, bishop of Rome, Holy Father. [➡RELIGIOUS PEOPLE; 779]

popeyed *adj* **bug-eyed** (*informal*), goggle-eyed, swollen-eyed, wide-eyed. [➡FACIAL CHARACTERISTICS; 482]

pop group *type of* **band**. [➡MUSICIANS AND SINGERS; 908]

popgun *type of* **toy**. [➡TOYS; 880]

pop in (*informal*) *v* **call in**, visit, go, stop at, look in on, drop in on, call round. [➡ARRIVE; 12]

poplar *type of* **deciduous tree**. [➡DECIDUOUS TREES; 1028]

poplin *type of* **fabric from plants**. [➡FABRICS; 1131]

poppa (*US*) *n* [➡OLDER GENERATION RELATIVES; 959]

poppadom *type of* **bread**. [➡BREAD, FLOUR, AND BREAD PRODUCTS; 1178]

popper *n* [➡FASTENERS, LINKS, AND NETWORKS; 1246]

poppet (*informal*) *n* **dear**, love, lovey (*informal*), darling, sweetie (*informal*), sweetie pie (*informal*), honey (*US informal*), honey-pie (*US informal*). [➡ENDEARMENTS; 657]

poppy *type of* **annual flower**. [➡FLOWERS; 1032]

poppycock (*dated informal*) *n* **nonsense**, absurdity, untruth, rubbish, twaddle (*informal*), codswallop (*informal*). [➡MEANINGLESS SPEECH OR WRITING; 677]

pop round (*informal*) *v* [➡ARRIVE; 12]

pop song *type of* **vocal music**. [➡MUSIC, SONGS, AND SINGING; 907]

populace *n* **public**, population, general public, common people, lay people, masses, inhabitants. [➡GROUPS IN SOCIETY; 940]

popular 1 *adj* **well-liked**, accepted, admired, trendy (*informal*), in style, all the rage, fashionable. [➡POPULAR AND WANTED; 221] *Opposite:* unpopular. 2 *adj* **common**, general, prevalent, widely held, current, widespread, standard. [➡KNOWN AND FAMOUS; 182] *Opposite:* rare.

popularity *n* **admiration**, approval, acceptance, fame, status, reputation, attractiveness, regard, esteem, recognition. [➡KNOWN AND FAMOUS; 182] *Opposite:* infamy.

popularization 1 *n* **promotion**, spread, commercialization, propagation, universalization, dissemination. [➡INFORM AND ANNOUNCE; 612] 2 *n* **simplification**, vulgarization, interpretation, explanation, universalization. [➡EXPLAIN AND CLARIFY; 611]

popularize 1 *v* **make popular**, promote, spread, propagate, commercialize, disseminate. [➡INFORM AND ANNOUNCE; 612] 2 *v* **simplify**, interpret, vulgarize, put in layperson's terms, explain, gloss, universalize. [➡EXPLAIN AND CLARIFY; 611]

popularly *adv* **generally**, commonly, prevalently, readily, widely, usually, universally, traditionally. [➡USUALLY; 108] *Opposite:* rarely.

populate *v* **inhabit**, people, settle, colonize, fill, crowd, occupy. [➡INHABIT; 20] *Opposite:* desert.

population *n* **inhabitants**, populace, people, residents. [➡GROUPS IN SOCIETY; 940]

populist *adj* **antielitist**, majority, mainstream, democratic, general, accessible. [➡STYLES AND SYSTEMS OF GOVERNMENT; 806] *Opposite:* elitist.

populous *adj* **crowded**, overcrowded, populated, full of people, packed. [➡FULL; 1238]

pop-up *adj* **spring-operated**, automatic, self-opening, folding, foldaway. [➡CHANGE OF SHAPE; 386]

pop your clogs (*informal*) *v* [➡DIE; 922]

porcelain *type of* **pottery.** [➡POTTERY; 1134]

porch *part of* **building.** [➡PARTS OF A BUILDING; 1094]

porcine *adj* **piggy**, piggish, swinish, hoglike. [➡BEASTLY AND BRUTISH; 511]

porcupine *type of* **small mammal.** [➡SMALL MAMMAL; 990]

pore *n* **hole**, opening, aperture, stoma. [➡HOLES, GAPS, AND FORKS; 1251]

pore over *v* **examine**, scour, read, study, go over, go through, scrutinize, peruse. [➡EXAMINE AND ASSESS; 754]

pork *type of* **meat.** [➡TYPES AND CUTS OF MEAT; 1176]

porkpie hat *type of* **hat.** [➡HABERDASHERY, MILLINERY, AND LINGERIE; 867]

porky (*slang*) *n* [➡DECEPTION AND LIES; 661]

porosity *n* [➡DENSITY AND CONSISTENCY; 1206]

porous *adj* **absorbent**, permeable, leaky, spongy. [➡DENSITY AND CONSISTENCY; 1206] *Opposite:* impermeable.

porousness *n* [➡DENSITY AND CONSISTENCY; 1206]

porpoise *type of* **marine mammal.** [➡MARINE MAMMAL; 987]

porridge *n* **breakfast cereal**, gruel, oatmeal, oats. [➡CEREAL FOODS; 1177]

port 1 *n* **harbour**, seaport, anchorage, haven (*literary*), dock. [➡THE SEAS, OCEANS, AND SHORES; 1041] 2 *type of* **hardware.** [➡COMPUTERS AND COMPUTING; 1126]

portability *n* **movability**, transportability, transferability, lightness, compactness, handiness, convenience, manageability. [➡WEIGHT: LIGHT; 1205] *Opposite:* bulkiness.

portable *adj* **movable**, transportable, transferable, handy, convenient, manageable, compact, light. [➡WEIGHT: LIGHT; 1205] *Opposite:* fixed.

portal (*literary*) *n* **gateway**, doorway, porch, entrance, entry, threshold, portico, entryway (*US*), entranceway. [➡DOORS AND ACCESS POINTS; 1100]

portcullis *n* **gate**, door, grating, drawbridge, entry, entryway (*US*). [➡PARTS OF FORTRESSES; 1090]

portend *v* **foreshadow**, foretell, signify, mean, warn of, herald, threaten, indicate, presage. [➡MEAN SOMETHING; 61]

portent 1 *n* **omen**, sign, presage, warning, indication, signal, augury, threat, foreshadowing, herald. [➡INDICATIONS, SIGNS, AND WARNINGS; 68] 2 *n* (*formal*) **marvel**, phenomenon, prodigy, wonder, miracle. [➡AMAZING THING; 212]

portentous 1 *adj* **significant**, important, crucial, ominous, fateful, threatening. [➡IMPORTANT; 195] *Opposite:* trivial. 2 *adj* **pompous**, pretentious, self-important, haughty, arrogant, solemn, grave, serious. [➡AFFECTATION, SELF-SATISFACTION, AND SNOBBISHNESS; 508] *Opposite:* modest.

portentously 1 *adv* **significantly**, importantly, crucially, ominously, fatefully, threateningly. [➡IMPORTANT; 195] 2 *adv* (*disapproving*) **pompously**, pretentiously, self-importantly, haughtily, solemnly, gravely, arrogantly, seriously. [➡AFFECTATION, SELF-SATISFACTION, AND SNOBBISHNESS; 508] *Opposite:* modestly.

portentousness *n* [➡AFFECTATION, SELF-SATISFACTION, AND SNOBBISHNESS; 508]

porter *n* **gatekeeper**, doorkeeper, concierge, caretaker, janitor, receptionist. [➡PEOPLE WHO GUARD AND PROTECT; 846]

porterhouse steak *type of* **steak.** [➡TYPES AND CUTS OF MEAT; 1176]

portfolio 1 *n* **case**, folder, file, wallet. [➡CONTAINERS, RECEPTACLES, AND PACKAGING; 1244] 2 *n* (*formal*) **range**, collection, selection, group, set, assortment. [➡COLLECTIONS AND MIXTURES OF THINGS; 1243]

portfolio worker *n* [➡WORKER; 836]

porthole *type of* **window.** [➡WINDOWS; 1099]

portico *n* **porch**, entrance, doorway, entry, entryway (*US*), entranceway. [➡DOORS AND ACCESS POINTS; 1100]

portion 1 *n* **helping**, share, slice, serving, percentage, quota, ration, lot, measure, quantity, allotment. [➡DEGREE AND EXTENT; 110] 2 *n* **fraction**, piece, bit, part, segment, section, fragment, scrap, division. [➡AMOUNT AND QUANTITY; 112] *Opposite:* whole. 3 *n* (*literary*) **fate**, destiny, lot, karma, kismet. [➡FATE, DESTINY, AND ASTROLOGY; 783] 4 *v* **divide**, distribute, allocate, assign, share out, apportion, mete out, dole out (*informal*), parcel out. [➡DISPENSE, RATION, AND DISTRIBUTE; 435]

portliness *n* **stoutness**, stockiness, roundness, heaviness, heftiness, chubbiness. [➡BUILD; 478] *Opposite:* slimness.

portly *adj* **overweight**, stout, stocky, round, heavy, hefty, chubby. [➡BUILD; 478] *Opposite:* slim.

portmanteau 1 *n* **suitcase**, case, bag, valise, holdall, carryall (*US*). [➡CONTAINERS, RECEPTACLES, AND PACKAGING; 1244] 2 *adj* **multiple**, combination, hybrid, blended, general-purpose, multipurpose. [➡SAMENESS; 151]

portrait *n* **picture**, representation, portrayal, likeness, photograph, sketch, depiction, study, painting, drawing. [➡REPRESENTATIONS AND GENERAL EXAMPLES; 65]

portraitist *n* [➡AN ARTIST/PHOTOGRAPHER; 914]

portraiture *n* **portrait making**, portrait painting, photography, painting, drawing, self-portraiture. [➡THE PICTORIAL ARTS; 897]

portray *v* **depict**, represent, describe, show, render (*formal*), interpret, picture. [➡REPRESENT SOMETHING OR SOMEBODY; 59]

portrayal *n* **representation**, interpretation, depiction, picture, description, rendering, reading. [➡REPRESENTATIONS AND GENERAL EXAMPLES; 65]

Portuguese man-of-war *type of* **aquatic invertebrate.** [➡AQUATIC INVERTEBRATE; 1022]

pose 1 *n* (*disapproving*) **pretence**, sham, fake, front, façade, masquerade, affectation. [➡DECEPTION AND LIES; 661] 2 *v* **model**, stand, sit, sit for, posture, position yourself. [➡ASSUME A POSITION; 318] 3 *v* **impersonate**, pretend, play the part of, masquerade, profess, disguise yourself, pass off, feign. [➡PRETEND AND MIMIC; 60] 4 *v* **ask**, put, put forward, present, propound, inquire, question, propose. [➡ASK PEOPLE QUESTIONS; 667] **5** *v* **present**, cause, create, set, establish, throw up, proffer, tender. [➡CREATION; 347] **6** *n* **posture**, stance, position, attitude, carriage (*formal*). [➡TEMPERAMENT AND BEHAVIOUR; 493]

poser 1 *n* (*informal disapproving*) [➡SUPERFICIAL OR INSINCERE PEOPLE; 951] **2** *n* **problem**, question, puzzle, conundrum, challenge, riddle, enigma. [➡SECRETS AND MYSTERIES; 181]

poseur *n* **poser** (*informal disapproving*), show-off (*informal*), exhibitionist, posturer, narcissist, swaggerer, peacock. [➡SUPERFICIAL OR INSINCERE PEOPLE; 951]

posh (*informal*) **1** *adj* **upmarket**, elegant, fashionable, expensive, luxurious, exclusive, smart. [➡EXPENSIVE AND LUXURIOUS; 219] *Opposite:* downmarket. **2** *adj* **upper-class**, well-to-do, genteel, aristocratic. [➡CLASS STATUS; 889] *Opposite:* common.

posit (*formal*) *v* **put forward**, postulate, suggest, theorize, speculate, hypothesize, advance. [➡DEVELOP THEORIES AND REASON; 745]

position **1** *n* **location**, place, site, spot, point, situation, locus, station. [➡PLACE; 1064] **2** *n* **posture**, stance, pose, arrangement, attitude. [➡TEMPERAMENT AND BEHAVIOUR; 493] **3** *n* **rank**, status, standing, station. [➡STATUS; 888] **4** *n* **view**, opinion, policy, stance, perception, side, attitude, thinking, outlook, standpoint, take. [➡POINT OF VIEW; 768] **5** *v* **put**, place, locate, stand, sit, set, arrange. [➡POSITION SOMETHING; 326]

positive **1** *adj* **sure**, certain, clear, convinced, assured, confident. [➡CERTAINTY; 562] *Opposite:* uncertain. **2** *adj* **irrefutable**, definite, explicit, clear-cut, conclusive, categorical, decisive, unquestionable, confirmed, certain. [➡CERTAIN; 175] *Opposite:* dubious. **3** *adj* **optimistic**, confident, constructive, helpful, encouraging, affirmative, progressive, up, upbeat (*informal*). [➡CHEERFULNESS OF OUTLOOK; 504] *Opposite:* negative.

positively **1** *adv* **definitely**, absolutely, completely, really, certainly, surely, confidently, clearly. [➡CERTAIN; 175] **2** *adv* **encouragingly**, confidently, optimistically, supportively, constructively, helpfully, progressively. [➡ENTHUSIASTIC AND INQUISITIVE; 629] *Opposite:* negatively.

positron *type of* **elementary particle**. [➡ELEMENTARY PARTICLES; 1278]

posse (*informal*) *n* **gang**, band, party, group, company, body of people, clique, crew (*informal*). [➡FRIENDS AND ACQUAINTANCES; 936]

possess **1** *v* **own**, have, hold, enjoy, keep, retain. [➡POSSESS; 445] *Opposite:* lack. **2** *v* **take control**, influence, take, occupy, seize, hold, have power over, take over, control, dominate. [➡POSSESS; 445]

possessed *adj* **controlled**, influenced, obsessed, crazed, overcome, infatuated, haunted. [➡ECCENTRICITY AND IRRATIONALITY; 563]

possession *n* **ownership**, control, tenure, custody, proprietorship. [➡POSSESS; 445]

possessions *n* **property**, belongings, wealth, goods, assets, personal effects, chattels, movables. [➡POSSESSIONS; 462]

possessive **1** *adj* **domineering**, jealous, controlling, overprotective, covetous, suspicious, envious. [➡BOSSY AND OVERBEARING; 517] *Opposite:* trusting. **2** *adj* **selfish**, greedy, grasping, tightfisted, mean, stingy (*informal*), ungenerous. [➡SELFISH AND UNKIND; 506] *Opposite:* generous.

possessiveness **1** *n* **selfishness**, greed, tightfistedness, meanness, stinginess, greediness. [➡SELFISH AND UNKIND; 506] *Opposite:* generosity. **2** *n* **jealousy**, jealousness, suspiciousness, overprotectiveness, insecurity, covetousness, suspicion, envy, enviousness. [➡ENVY AND JEALOUSY; 549]

possessor *n* **owner**, holder, bearer, keeper, proprietor, inheritor. [➡OWNERS; 447]

possibility *n* **likelihood**, prospect, risk, chance, probability. [➡POSSIBLE AND PROBABLE; 178]

possible **1** *adj* **likely**, conceivable, imaginable, thinkable, probable, potential, promising. [➡POSSIBLE AND PROBABLE; 178] *Opposite:* unlikely. **2** *adj* **achievable**, doable, feasible, on the cards (*informal*), viable, workable. [➡POSSIBLE AND PROBABLE; 178] *Opposite:* impossible.

possibly *adv* **perhaps**, maybe, perchance (*archaic or literary*), probably, conceivably, feasibly. [➡POSSIBLE AND PROBABLE; 178] *Opposite:* certainly.

post **1** *n* **pole**, column, stake, upright, marker, boundary marker, pillar, support. [➡STICKS, POLES, AND WEDGES; 1253] **2** *n* **position**, placement, job, station, situation (*formal*), place, workplace. [➡JOB; 833] **3** *v* **display**, announce, advertise, put up, publish, declare, publicize. [➡INFORM AND ANNOUNCE; 612] **4** *v* **send**, dispatch, forward, airmail, mail. [➡DESPATCH AND SEND; 334] *Opposite:* receive.

postage *n* **stamp price**, postage fee, postage charge, postage cost, first-class postage, second-class postage. [➡EXPENDITURE; 424]

postbag **1** *n* **sack**, mailbag, bag, satchel, delivery bag, mailer, mail sack (*US*). [➡CONTAINERS, RECEPTACLES, AND PACKAGING; 1244] **2** *n* **correspondence**, mail, letters, mailbag, postal communications. [➡LETTERS AND WRITTEN MESSAGES; 585]

postbox *n* **letterbox**, posting box, pillar box, collection box, collection point, mailbox (*US*), maildrop (*US*). [➡CONTAINERS, RECEPTACLES, AND PACKAGING; 1244]

postcard *n* **card**, picture postcard, message, note, letter, missive. [➡LETTERS AND WRITTEN MESSAGES; 585]

poster **1** *n* **picture**, print, reproduction, artwork, photograph. [➡SIGNPOSTS, SIGNALS AND BILLBOARDS; 596] **2** *n* **advertisement**, placard, notice, bill, announcement. [➡SIGNPOSTS, SIGNALS AND BILLBOARDS; 596]

posterior (*formal*) *adj* **latter**, subsequent, following, next, later, after. [➡AFTER, LAST, AND FOLLOWING; 166] *Opposite:* earlier.

posterity *n* **future generations**, later generations, generations to come, successors, future, years to come, descendants, children, heirs. [➡FUTURE; 86]

postgrad (*informal*) *n* [➡STUDENTS AND PUPILS; 841]

postgraduate *n* **student**, postgraduate student, graduate student, postgrad (*informal*), PhD student, graduate. [➡STUDENTS AND PUPILS; 841]

posthaste *adv* **fast**, immediately, right away, quickly, straight away, without delay. [➡HAPPENING QUICKLY; 104] *Opposite:* slowly.

post horn *type of* **brass instrument**. [➡MUSICAL INSTRUMENTS; 910]

posthumous *adj* **subsequent**, retrospective, delayed, following, post-obit (*formal*), postmortem. [➡BURIAL AND PREPARATION FOR BURIAL; 929]

postimpressionism *type of* **pre-20th-century art movement**. [➡ARTISTIC MOVEMENTS AND STYLES; 899]

posting *n* **placement**, situation (*formal*), relocation, position, post, military posting, stationing, appointment. [➡JOB; 833]

postmark 1 *n* **date stamp**, frank, stamp, mark, rubber stamp, proof of posting. [➡RECEIPTS AND INVOICES; 592] 2 *v* **frank**, stamp, date, mark, rubber-stamp, validate. [➡CREATE IMAGES; 357]

postmodern *type of* **20th-century art movement**. [➡ARTISTIC MOVEMENTS AND STYLES; 899]

postmodernism *type of* **20th-century art movement**. [➡ARTISTIC MOVEMENTS AND STYLES; 899]

postmortem 1 *n* **autopsy**, postmortem examination, medical examination, examination, inquest. [➡BURIAL AND PREPARATION FOR BURIAL; 929] 2 *n* **investigation**, analysis, examination, inquest, review, debriefing. [➡EXAMINE AND ASSESS; 754]

postmortem examination *n* [➡BURIAL AND PREPARATION FOR BURIAL; 929]

postnatal *adj* **postpartum**, post-delivery, perinatal. [➡REPRODUCTION AND HEREDITY; 726]

post-obit (*formal*) *adj* [➡BURIAL AND PREPARATION FOR BURIAL; 929]

post office 1 *n* **PO**, GPO, sorting office, mailroom, mail depot (*US*). [➡RETAIL OUTLETS; 1082] 2 *n* **mail system**, mail service, postal service, postal communications, mail. [➡RETAIL OUTLETS; 1082]

postpartum *adj* [➡REPRODUCTION AND HEREDITY; 726]

postpone *v* **delay**, put off, put back, shelve, put on the back burner, defer, suspend, stall, reschedule, adjourn, take a rain check on (*US informal*). [➡DELAY ACTION OR OCCURRENCE; 279] *Opposite:* bring forward.

postponed *adj* [➡NOT HAPPENING; 34]

postponement *n* **delay**, rescheduling, rearrangement, deferment, adjournment, deferral, suspension. [➡DELAY ACTION OR OCCURRENCE; 279]

postscript *n* **afterthought**, addition, supplement, afterword, epilogue, message. [➡PARTS OF BOOKS AND DOCUMENTS; 594] *Opposite:* preface.

postulate 1 *v* **assume**, guess, hypothesize, suggest, claim, put forward, propose, advance. [➡DEVELOP THEORIES AND REASON; 745] 2 *v* (*formal*) **nominate**, propose, select, choose, put forward, solicit, submit. [➡MAKE DECISIONS AND CHOICES; 753]

posture *n* **carriage** (*formal*), bearing, stance, attitude, position, pose, deportment (*formal*), mien (*literary*). [➡TEMPERAMENT AND BEHAVIOUR; 493]

posturing *n* **self-importance**, pomposity, swagger, bravado, bluster, airs, posing, affectation, pretence, pretentiousness, pretension. [➡AFFECTATION, SELF-SATISFACTION, AND SNOBBISHNESS; 508]

posy *n* **bouquet**, bunch of flowers, spray, nosegay, arrangement, buttonhole, boutonniere (*US formal*). [➡COLLECTIONS AND MIXTURES OF THINGS; 1243]

pot 1 *n* **container**, pan, vessel, jar, tub, crock. [➡CONTAINERS, RECEPTACLES, AND PACKAGING; 1244] 2 *n* (*informal*) [➡EXTRA WEIGHT; 479] 3 *v* **shoot**, bag, catch, get, hit. [➡GET; 421] 4 *v* **preserve**, seal, pickle, can, tin. [➡COOKING AND FOOD PREPARATION; 354]

potable *adj* **drinkable**, clean, filtered, fit to drink, drinking. [➡ACCEPTABLE AND PASSABLE; 220]

potage *type of* **soup**. [➡SOUP; 1185]

potation (*literary*) *n* [➡DRINKS; 1186]

potato *n* **tuber**, new potato, seed potato, spud (*informal*), tater (*regional*), murphy (*dated informal*). [➡FRUIT AND VEGETABLES; 1175]

potato

◆ *types of processed potato*
knish, latke, home fries (*US*), hash browns (*US*), chip, crisp, croquette, French fries, fries, jacket potato, mash, potato cake, potato chip, potato pancake, rösti

potato cake *type of* **processed potato**. [➡FRUIT AND VEGETABLES; 1175]

potato chip *type of* **processed potato**. [➡FRUIT AND VEGETABLES; 1175]

potato pancake *type of* **processed potato**. [➡FRUIT AND VEGETABLES; 1175]

potbellied *adj* [➡BUILD; 478]

potbelly *n* [➡EXTRA WEIGHT; 479]

potboiler *n* [➡WRITERS AND STYLES; 914]

poteen *n* **bootleg whisky**, bootleg alcohol, moonshine (*informal*), firewater (*dated slang*), spirit, whisky, white lightning (*US regional*), mountain dew (*US informal*), hooch (*US slang*). [➡DRINKS; 1186]

potency *n* **strength**, force, muscle (*informal*), power, might, vigour, energy. [➡STRENGTH; 202] *Opposite:* weakness.

potent 1 *adj* **strong**, effective, powerful, forceful, mighty, vigorous, puissant (*literary*). [➡STRENGTH; 202] *Opposite:* weak. 2 *adj* **persuasive**, convincing, influential, forceful. [➡STRENGTH; 202]

potentate *n* **monarch**, ruler, leader, emperor, sovereign, czar, king, queen, empress. [➡RULERS AND ARISTOCRACY; 823]

potential 1 *n* **ability**, capacity, possibility, makings, what it takes, aptitude, capability. [➡SKILLS, TALENTS, AND

ABILITIES; 527] **2** *adj* **possible**, hypothetical, conceivable, likely, probable, imaginable, thinkable. [➡POSSIBLE AND PROBABLE; 178] *Opposite:* unlikely.

pothole **1** *n* **rut**, hole, dip, depression, fault, fissure. [➡HOLES, GAPS, AND FORKS; 1251] **2** *n* **cave**, cavern, catacomb, pit, hole. [➡GEOLOGICAL FEATURES; 1056]

potholed *adj* **rutted**, pitted, holed, eroded, uneven, bumpy, rough, broken. [➡PHYSICAL TEXTURE; 1221] *Opposite:* smooth.

potholer *n* **speleologist**, caver, spelunker. [➡PEOPLE IN SPORTS AND LEISURE; 876]

potion *n* **liquid**, medicine, concoction, mixture, brew, tonic, remedy. [➡COLLECTIONS AND MIXTURES OF THINGS; 1243]

potluck *n* **luck of the draw**, whatever is going, whatever is on offer, chance, whatever is available. [➡LUCK; 784]

potoroo *type of* **marsupial**. [➡MARSUPIAL; 992]

pot plant *n* [➡FOLIAGE PLANTS; 1035]

potpourri *n* **miscellany**, mixture, ragbag (*informal*), assortment, hotchpotch, collection, jumble, variety, medley, assembly. [➡COLLECTIONS AND MIXTURES OF THINGS; 1243]

pots (*informal*) *n* **heaps** (*informal*), piles (*informal*), tons (*informal*), loads (*informal*), bags. [➡MANY, MUCH, LARGE AMOUNT; 117]

potshot *n* **shot**, pot, go, aim, try, attempt. [➡ATTEMPT AN ACTION; 262]

potted **1** *adj* **preserved**, sealed, conserved, pickled, canned, tinned. [➡STATE OF PREPARED FOOD; 1170] *Opposite:* fresh. **2** *adj* (*informal*) **abridged**, summarized, brief, concise, shortened, short, condensed. [➡CHANGE OF SIZE: SMALLER; 394] *Opposite:* full.

potted plant (*US*) *n* [➡FOLIAGE PLANTS; 1035]

potter **1** *v* **dabble**, mess about (*informal*), mess, mooch (*slang*), fiddle, tinker, toy, play, mess around (*informal*). [➡LACK OF ACTIVITY; 343] **2** *v* **go slowly**, dawdle, shuffle, toddle (*informal*), amble. [➡MOVE SLOWLY; 315] *Opposite:* hurry.

pottery **1** *n* **ceramic objects**, earthenware, stoneware, ceramics. [➡ORNAMENTS AND DECORATIONS; 1247] **2** *type of* **factory**. [➡INDUSTRIAL BUILDINGS; 1086]

pottery

◆ *types of pottery*
bone china, ceramic, china, delft, Dresden china, earthenware, enamel, faience, Limoges, Meissen (*US*), porcelain, Sèvres, stoneware, terracotta

potting shed *type of* **outbuilding**. [➡ANCILLARY BUILDINGS; 1079]

potty (*informal*) *adj* **foolish**, irrational, crazy (*informal*), batty (*informal*), eccentric, silly, ridiculous, absurd. [➡ECCENTRICITY AND IRRATIONALITY; 563] *Opposite:* sensible.

potty-train (*informal*) *v* **toilet train**, housetrain, socialize, train, bring up, raise, housebreak (*US*). [➡INSTRUCT AND TEACH; 610]

potty-training (*informal*) *n* **toilet training**, continence training, housetraining, personal hygiene, socialization, housebreaking (*US*). [➡TEACHING; 839]

pouch *n* **bag**, pocket, money bag, purse, sack. [➡CONTAINERS, RECEPTACLES, AND PACKAGING; 1244]

pouf *n* **stool**, beanbag, seat, cushion, floor cushion, footrest, hassock. [➡FURNITURE; 858]

poultice *n* **dressing**, compress, bandage, plaster. [➡COVERS AND COATINGS; 1245]

pounce **1** *v* **spring**, swoop, leap, jump, dive, bound. [➡GO UPWARDS; 307] *Opposite:* recoil. **2** *v* **attack**, seize upon, seize, tackle, ambush, snatch, grab. [➡PHYSICAL ATTACK AND PUNISHMENT; 416] **3** *n* **leap**, jump, spring, bound, swoop, dive. [➡BOUNCE, UNDULATE, AND VIBRATE; 309]

pound **1** *n* **quid** (*informal*), pound sterling, smacker (*informal*), nicker (*slang*). [➡CURRENCIES; 798] **2** *v* **hit**, strike, batter, beat, hammer, thump, clobber (*informal*), pummel, buffet, thrash. [➡CONTACT: IMPACT; 414] **3** *v* **grind**, crush, pulverize, bruise, mash, squash, smash, stamp. [➡TEAR, BREAK, AND CUT; 361] **4** *v* **throb**, thump, beat, pulsate, pulse, palpitate, hammer. [➡PHYSICAL REACTIONS; 317] **5** *type of* **pen or cage**. [➡ANIMAL OR BIRD ACCOMMODATION; 1078]

pounding **1** *n* **throbbing**, thumping, pulsation, pulse, hammering, beating, beat. [➡PHYSICAL REACTIONS; 317] **2** *n* **beating**, thrashing, pasting (*informal*), hammering (*informal*), drubbing, defeat, whitewash (*informal*). [➡BEAT AND DEFEAT; 80]

pour **1** *v* **decant**, drizzle, dispense, discharge, transfer, empty, tip. [➡EMPTY AND UNLOAD; 408] **2** *v* **spill out**, gush, stream, flow, rush, surge, cascade, course. [➡LIQUID EMISSION; 371] *Opposite:* trickle. **3** *v* **rain**, rain cats and dogs (*informal*), bucket (*informal*), chuck it down (*informal*), tip down (*informal*), sheet down, drench, lash. [➡CLOUDY AND RAINY WEATHER; 1052] *Opposite:* drizzle. **4** *v* **swarm**, crowd, teem, stream, rush, flow. [➡MOVE FAST; 314] *Opposite:* trickle.

pouring *adj* **torrential**, heavy, bucketing (*informal*), sheeting down, hammering, driving. [➡CLOUDY AND RAINY WEATHER; 1052] *Opposite:* light.

pour out *v* **reveal**, blurt out, disclose, give away, tell. [➡BETRAY CONFIDENCES AND GOSSIP; 619]

pour scorn on *v* [➡PROTEST AND EXPRESS DISAPPROVAL; 643]

pour with rain *v* [➡CLOUDY AND RAINY WEATHER; 1052]

pout **1** *v* **purse your lips**, pucker, frown, scowl, glower, grimace. [➡FACIAL EXPRESSION; 652] *Opposite:* smile. **2** *v* **sulk**, mope, glower, scowl, grouch (*informal*). [➡FACIAL EXPRESSION; 652] *Opposite:* smile.

poverty **1** *n* **neediness**, destitution, hardship, deprivation, privation, indigence (*formal*), penury, impecuniousness (*formal*), impecuniosity (*formal*), impoverishment, want. [➡POVERTY AND POOR; 892] *Opposite:* affluence. **2** *n* **lack**, deficiency, scarcity, shortage, dearth, paucity, scarceness, insufficiency. [➡TOO FEW, TOO LITTLE; 120] *Opposite:* surplus.

Compare and Contrast: ***poverty, destitution, indigence, deprivation, penury, want***

CORE MEANING: INSUFFICIENCY OF RESOURCES ON WHICH TO LIVE

poverty the state of being without enough money or resources to take care of basic needs such as food, clothing, and housing; ***destitution*** *or* indigence *(formal)* complete lack of the basic necessities of life; ***deprivation*** the state of being without or denied something, especially of lacking adequate food and shelter and the material benefits that others enjoy; ***penury*** a severe state of economic need; ***want*** the state of being poor.

poverty-stricken *adj* **destitute**, in need, poor, broke (*informal*), penniless, skint (*informal*), impoverished, indigent (*formal*), impecunious (*formal*), penurious (*literary*), needy. [➡POVERTY AND POOR; 892] *Opposite:* rich.

powder 1 *n* **fine particles**, dust, residue, precipitate, ash, shavings, concentrate, face powder, gunpowder, triturate. [➡SOLIDS; 1273] 2 *v* **crush**, grind, pound, pulverize, mill, process, triturate, comminute. [➡CHANGE OF SHAPE; 386]

powder blue *type of* **blue**. [➡COLOURS; 1223]

powdered *adj* **ground**, crushed, pulverized, milled, processed, pounded, triturated, comminuted. [➡PHYSICAL TEXTURE; 1221] *Opposite:* whole.

powder keg *n* **tinderbox**, minefield, time bomb, recipe for disaster, explosive combination. [➡DANGER; 236]

powder room *type of* **room in public building**. [➡TYPES OF ROOM; 1096]

powdery *adj* **fine**, crumbly, chalky, dusty, dry, powdered, granular. [➡PHYSICAL TEXTURE; 1221]

power 1 *n* **ability**, capacity, faculty, potential, capability, competence, function, aptitude, skill. [➡SKILLS, TALENTS, AND ABILITIES; 527] *Opposite:* inability. 2 *n* **strength**, force, might, energy, muscle (*informal*), capability, brawn, weight, potency, sinew (*literary*). [➡STRENGTH; 202] *Opposite:* weakness. 3 *n* **control**, influence, authority, supremacy, rule, command, clout (*informal*), muscle (*informal*), sway, dominance, dominion, sovereignty. [➡RELATIONSHIP TO ANOTHER; 973] *Opposite:* powerlessness. 4 *n* **authority**, right, prerogative, licence, privilege, ability. [➡PERMIT AND ALLOW; 670] *Opposite:* powerlessness. 5 *n* **nation**, country, state, player, superpower, world power, nation-state, sovereign state. [➡TERRITORIES AND GROUPS OF NATIONS; 1067]

power base *n* **stronghold**, seat of power, headquarters, home base, base. [➡PLACE; 1064]

powerboat *type of* **motor vessel**. [➡SHIPS AND BOATS; 1149]

powerful 1 *adj* **influential**, commanding, authoritative, controlling, prevailing, dominant, potent, great, mighty, formidable, weighty. [➡STRENGTH; 202] *Opposite:* powerless. 2 *adj* **strong**, mighty, brawny, muscular, sturdy, robust, hard, vigorous, sinewy. [➡MUSCLES AND MUSCULATURE; 480] *Opposite:* weak. 3 *adj* **effective**, potent, strong, pungent, overwhelming, overpowering, intense, distinct. [➡STRENGTH; 202] *Opposite:* impotent. 4 *adj* **persuasive**, compelling, forceful, effective, convincing, impressive, moving, evocative, eloquent, deep, haunting, emotive, effectual (*formal*). [➡EXTRAORDINARY: AMAZING; 205] *Opposite:* unimpressive.

powerfully 1 *adv* **strongly**, mightily, sturdily, muscularly, robustly, forcefully, hard, vigorously, violently. [➡STRENGTH; 202] *Opposite:* weakly. 2 *adv* **effectively**, potently, intensely, strongly, overpoweringly, overwhelmingly, distinctly, pungently, very, extremely. [➡TO A GREAT EXTENT; 130] *Opposite:* somewhat. 3 *adv* **persuasively**, compellingly, forcefully, effectively, convincingly, impressively, eloquently, movingly, evocatively, hauntingly, emotively. [➡EXTRAORDINARY: AMAZING; 205] *Opposite:* weakly.

powerhouse (*informal*) *n* **driving force**, capital, heart, centre, dynamo, live wire (*informal*). [➡TALENTED OR INTELLIGENT PERSON; 529]

powerless *adj* **helpless**, incapable, unable, weak, feeble, ineffective, defenceless. [➡WEAKNESS; 242] *Opposite:* powerful.

powerlessness *n* **helplessness**, hopelessness, weakness, feebleness, ineffectiveness, defencelessness, subjection, incapability, inability, incapacity. [➡WEAKNESS; 242]

power line *n* **electricity cable**, overhead cable, cable, wire, overhead wire, high-voltage line. [➡ELECTRONICS AND ELECTRICS; 1136]

power plant (*US*) *type of* **industrial site**. [➡INDUSTRIAL BUILDINGS; 1086]

power point *n* **socket**, point, electric socket, plug, hookup, outlet. [➡ELECTRONICS AND ELECTRICS; 1136]

power station *type of* **industrial site**. [➡INDUSTRIAL BUILDINGS; 1086]

power struggle *n* [➡ARGUMENT; 47]

powwow (*informal*) *n* [➡INFORMAL COMMUNICATION; 45]

practicability *n* **feasibility**, viability, workability, attainability, operability, possibility, practicality, achievability. [➡POSSIBLE AND PROBABLE; 178] *Opposite:* impossibility.

practicable *adj* **feasible**, realistic, possible, workable, attainable, operable, achievable, practical, viable, doable. [➡POSSIBLE AND PROBABLE; 178] *Opposite:* impossible.

practical 1 *adj* **applied**, real-world, hands-on, everyday, real, useful. [➡TRUE AND REAL; 172] *Opposite:* theoretical. 2 *adj* **useful**, sensible, feasible, sound, workable, practicable, handy, step-by-step, helpful, user-friendly, realistic, viable. [➡USEFULNESS; 200] *Opposite:* useless. 3 *adj* **realistic**, down-to-earth, level-headed, sensible, pragmatic, reasonable, hardheaded, rational, businesslike, matter-of-fact, sober. [➡POSITIVE INTELLECTUAL CHARACTERISTICS; 525] *Opposite:* unrealistic. 4 *adj* **everyday**, workaday, serviceable, functional, plain, useful, convenient, utilitarian. [➡USEFULNESS; 200] *Opposite:* decorative.

practicality 1 *n* **usefulness**, sensibleness, feasibility, soundness, workability, reasonableness, helpfulness, applicability, practicability, user-friendliness. [➡USEFULNESS; 200] *Opposite:* uselessness. 2 *n* **realism**, common sense, level-headedness, pragmatism, sensibleness, reasonableness, soberness. [➡POSITIVE INTELLECTUAL CHARACTERISTICS; 525] *Opposite:* impracticality.

practical joke *n* **trick**, prank, wind-up (*informal*), joke, lark, hoax, escapade, caper, shenanigan (*informal*). [➡JOKES AND TEASING; 675]

practically 1 *adv* **almost**, nearly, virtually, just about, nigh on, well-nigh, all but, as good as, essentially, in effect. [➡TO A CERTAIN EXTENT; 134] 2 *adv* **realistically**, sensibly, rationally, reasonably, level-headedly, pragmatically, expediently. [➡POSITIVE INTELLECTUAL CHARACTERISTICS; 525]

practice 1 *n* **repetition**, rehearsal, exercise, preparation, training, run-through, drill. [➡PREPARATORY EVENT; 57] 2 *n* **habit**, custom, tradition, way, system, routine, procedure, ritual, manner, praxis (*formal*), method. [➡WAYS OF DOING THINGS; 295]

See Compare and Contrast at **habit**.

practice session *n* [➡PREPARATORY EVENT; 57]

practise 1 *v* **rehearse**, prepare, exercise, go through, run through, repeat, try, attempt, drill. [➡PREPARE FOR ACTION; 290] *Opposite:* perform. 2 *v* **do**, put into practice, live out, carry out, perform, apply, follow, observe. [➡CARRY OUT AN ACTION; 270] *Opposite:* reject.

practised *adj* **skilful**, experienced, trained, expert, adept, proficient, accomplished, able. [➡TALENTED AND SKILFUL; 528] *Opposite:* untrained.

practitioner *n* **doctor**, medical practitioner, general practitioner, GP, physician, consultant, health worker. [➡PEOPLE WHO WORK IN MEDICINE; 848]

praenomen *n* [➡NAME AND DESCRIBE; 666]

pragmatic *adj* **practical**, realistic, logical, rational, reasonable, sensible, hardheaded, hard-nosed (*informal*), matter-of-fact, no-nonsense, down-to-earth. [➡POSITIVE INTELLECTUAL CHARACTERISTICS; 525] *Opposite:* idealistic.

pragmatism *n* **practicality**, realism, logicality, rationality, reasonableness, common sense, uncomplicatedness, matter-of-factness, hardheadedness. [➡POSITIVE INTELLECTUAL CHARACTERISTICS; 525] *Opposite:* idealism.

pragmatist *n* **practical person**, down-to-earth person, realist, doer, rationalist, logician. [➡PEOPLE WHO ARE APPROVED OF; 955] *Opposite:* idealist.

prairie *n* **plain**, savanna, steppe, pampas. [➡DESERTS AND PLAINS; 1045]

prairie dog *type of* **rodent**. [➡RODENT; 989]

prairie schooner *type of* **wagon or carriage**. [➡VEHICLES; 1144]

praise 1 *n* **admiration**, commendation, approval, acclaim, tribute, applause, compliment, recommendation. [➡PRAISE AND ENCOURAGE; 648] *Opposite:* criticism. 2 *n* **worship**, honour, adoration, devotion, thanks, glory, celebration, blessing. [➡RELIGIONS AND RELIGIOUS PRACTICES; 778] *Opposite:* vilification. 3 *v* **admire**, commend, extol, compliment, honour, eulogize (*formal*), congratulate, pay tribute to, go into raptures over, applaud, acclaim, hail. [➡PRAISE AND ENCOURAGE; 648] *Opposite:* criticize. 4 *v* **glorify**, honour, laud, worship, adore, exalt (*formal*), magnify (*formal*), bless, celebrate, extol. [➡RELIGIONS AND RELIGIOUS PRACTICES; 778] *Opposite:* vilify.

praise to the skies *v* [➡PRAISE AND ENCOURAGE; 648]

praiseworthy *adj* **admirable**, commendable, laudable, worthy, exemplary, creditable. [➡ADMIRABLE AND COMMENDABLE; 186] *Opposite:* blameworthy.

praline *type of* **confectionery**. [➡CONFECTIONERY; 1181]

pram *n* **perambulator** (*formal*), buggy, pushchair, stroller (*US*), baby carriage (*US*). [➡BIKES, CARS, AND CARRIAGES; 1148]

prance 1 *v* **cavort**, dance, frolic, gambol, caper, frisk, romp, revel. [➡FIDGET AND FROLIC; 312] 2 *v* **swagger**, strut, parade, flounce, sashay (*humorous*). [➡MOVE FAST; 314]

prang (*informal*) *v* **crash**, smash, write off, bump, bash (*informal*), dent, damage, wreck. [➡CONTACT: IMPACT; 414]

prank *n* **trick**, practical joke, hoax, joke, wind-up (*informal*), lark. [➡JOKES AND TEASING; 675]

prankster *n* **trickster**, joker, practical joker, mischief-maker, imp, Puck. [➡JOKERS AND TEASES; 676]

prate *v* **chatter**, gibber, prattle, babble, jabber, rant, blether (*informal*), jaw (*slang*), witter (*informal*), burble (*informal*), natter (*informal*), blather (*informal*). [➡WITTER AND BABBLE; 618]

prattle 1 *v* **witter** (*informal*), gibber, chatter, burble (*informal*), jabber, babble, natter (*informal*), blether (*informal*), prate, blather (*informal*). [➡WITTER AND BABBLE; 618] 2 *n* **chatter**, gibber, burble (*informal*), blether (*informal*), nattering (*informal*), wittering (*informal*), drivel, nonsense, jabber, babble, blather (*informal*). [➡MEANINGLESS SPEECH OR WRITING; 677]

prattling *adj* [➡INARTICULATE, RAMBLING, AND AWKWARD; 634]

prawn *type of* **crustacean**. [➡AQUATIC INVERTEBRATE; 1022]

praxis (*formal*) *n* [➡WAYS OF DOING THINGS; 295]

pray 1 *v* **meditate**, contemplate, say your prayers, call upon, invoke, call up, summon, deliberate. [➡RELIGIONS AND RELIGIOUS PRACTICES; 778] 2 *v* **hope**, wish, cross your fingers, hope against hope, yearn, long, ache, yen. [➡DESIRE AND WANT; 580] 3 *v* **request**, implore (*formal*), plead, beg, crave, ask, entreat (*formal*), urge, beseech (*literary*), appeal, importune (*formal*). [➡REQUEST AND DEMAND; 664]

prayer 1 *n* **invocation**, meditation, contemplation, devotions, chant, petition, supplication (*formal*), appeal, imploration (*formal*). [➡RELIGIONS AND RELIGIOUS PRACTICES; 778] 2 *n* **entreaty**, appeal, plea, request, desire, hope, wish, supplication, imploration (*formal*), petition. [➡REQUEST AND DEMAND; 664]

prayer book *n* [➡RELIGIOUS OBJECTS; 780]

preach 1 *v* **give a sermon**, speak, discourse, talk, deliver an address, address, orate (*formal*), expound. [➡INSTRUCT AND TEACH; 610] 2 *v* **advise**, lecture, sermonize, moralize, advocate, urge, persuade. [➡ADVISE AND WARN; 614]

preacher *n* **minister**, pastor, missionary, lay preacher, vicar, celebrant, parson, evangelist. [➡RELIGIOUS PEOPLE; 779]

preadolescent *adj* [➡BABYHOOD, CHILDHOOD AND ADOLESCENCE; 917]

preamble *n* **introduction**, preface, foreword, prelude, overture, opening, explanation. [➡PARTS OF BOOKS AND DOCUMENTS; 594] *Opposite:* postscript.

preamplifier *type of* **audio equipment**. [➡AUDIO EQUIPMENT; 1138]

prearrange *v* **organize**, set up, arrange, plan, settle upon, decide upon, preset, schedule, agree. [➡CAUSE TO HAPPEN; 31]

prearranged *adj* **planned**, arranged, agreed, preset, programmed, controlled, specified, established, selected, given, intended, scheduled, determined, allotted, chosen, fixed, set. [➡INTENTIONAL AND DELIBERATE; 280] *Opposite:* chance.

prebake *v* [➡COOKING AND FOOD PREPARATION; 354]

precarious *adj* **shaky**, unstable, insecure, wobbly, unsteady, uncertain, unsafe. [➡DANGEROUS; 237] *Opposite:* stable.

precariousness *n* [➡DANGER; 236]

precatory (*formal*) *adj* [➡RELIGIOUS CONCEPTS; 777]

precaution *n* **protection**, safety measure, preventive measure, insurance, safeguard, provision, security, deterrent. [➡ACTIONS OR UNDERTAKINGS; 260]

precautionary *adj* **protective**, defensive, safety, cautionary, preventive, preventative, counteractive, prophylactic, anticipatory. [➡SAFE AND SAFETY; 192] *Opposite:* remedial.

precede *v* **lead**, come first, go before, pave the way, herald, head. [➡BEFORE, FIRST, AND PRECEDING; 164] *Opposite:* follow.

precedence *n* **superiority**, priority, preference, primacy, antecedence, precedency. [➡SUPERIORITY; 153]

precedent *n* **example**, model, guide, pattern, standard, instance, practice. [➡REPRESENTATIONS AND GENERAL EXAMPLES; 65]

preceding *adj* **previous**, earlier, prior, former, past, above, foregoing, antecedent, anterior. [➡BEFORE, FIRST, AND PRECEDING; 164] *Opposite:* following.

precept (*formal*) *n* **principle**, teaching, rule, guideline, instruction, edict, dictum (*formal*), law. [➡IDEA AND THOUGHT; 771]

precinct *n* **district**, zone, area, sector, quarter, division, ward, borough. [➡PLACE; 1064]

precincts *n* **grounds**, confines, area, limits, boundaries, surroundings, environs. [➡URBAN OUTDOOR SPACES; 1071]

precious 1 *adj* **valuable**, costly, expensive, dear, treasurable, exquisite, priceless, prized. [➡EXPENSIVE AND LUXURIOUS; 219] *Opposite:* worthless. 2 *adj* **valued**, loved, beloved, important, dear, treasured, cherished, favourite. [➡POPULAR AND WANTED; 221] *Opposite:* despised. 3 *adj* **fastidious**, affected, overrefined, fussy, self-conscious, dainty, pretentious, artificial. [➡AFFECTATION, SELF-SATISFACTION, AND SNOBBISHNESS; 508] *Opposite:* natural.

preciously *adv* **fastidiously**, affectedly, fussily, self-consciously, daintily, pretentiously, artificially. [➡AFFECTATION, SELF-SATISFACTION, AND SNOBBISHNESS; 508] *Opposite:* naturally.

preciousness 1 *n* **valuableness**, value, costliness, expensiveness, dearness, exquisiteness, pricelessness. [➡EXPENSIVE AND LUXURIOUS; 219] *Opposite:* worthlessness. 2 *n* **fastidiousness**, affectation, fussiness, self-consciousness, daintiness, overrefinement, pretentiousness, artificiality. [➡AFFECTATION, SELF-SATISFACTION, AND SNOBBISHNESS; 508] *Opposite:* naturalness.

precious stone *n* **gemstone**, jewel, stone, gem, sparkler (*informal*), rock (*informal*). [➡PRECIOUS STONES; 1277]

precipice *n* **rock face**, cliff, crag, sheer drop, abyss, height, face. [➡GEOLOGICAL FEATURES; 1056]

precipitate 1 *adj* **rash**, impulsive, impetuous, careless, reckless. [➡INCAUTIOUS AND CARELESS; 284] *Opposite:* considered. 2 *adj* **hurried**, hasty, swift, quick, rapid, precipitous. [➡MOVING QUICKLY; 103] *Opposite:* slow. 3 *adj* **abrupt**, sudden, unexpected, surprising, unforeseen. [➡HAPPENING QUICKLY; 104] *Opposite:* expected. 4 *v* **hasten**, bring on, cause, lead to, occasion, give rise to, trigger, advance. [➡CAUSE TO HAPPEN; 31] *Opposite:* retard.

precipitateness *n* [➡SPEED; 102]

precipitation *n* **rain**, rainfall, snow, sleet, hail, drizzle. [➡CLOUDY AND RAINY WEATHER; 1052]

precipitous 1 *adj* **rash**, quick, hurried, swift, impulsive, hasty, precipitate. [➡INCAUTIOUS AND CARELESS; 284] *Opposite:* careful. 2 *adj* **steep**, sheer, abrupt, high, vertical, lofty. [➡ORIENTATION AND ALIGNMENT; 1222] *Opposite:* gentle.

precipitousness *n* [➡SPEED; 102]

précis 1 *n* **summary**, synopsis, résumé, abstract, sketch, thumbnail sketch, digest, compendium. [➡SUMMARIES, OUTLINES, AND EXCERPTS; 589] 2 *v* **summarize**, sum up, condense, outline, abridge, digest. [➡EXPLAIN AND CLARIFY; 611] *Opposite:* expand.

precise 1 *adj* **exact**, detailed, accurate, specific, particular, clear-cut, defined, fixed, correct, complete. [➡EXACT; 204] *Opposite:* vague. 2 *adj* **meticulous**, scrupulous, particular, careful, fastidious, strict. [➡HARD-WORKING AND COMMITTED; 501] *Opposite:* careless.

preciseness *n* [➡CONCISE AND CLEAR; 203]

precision *n* **exactness**, accuracy, exactitude, care, meticulousness, correctness, fastidiousness, strictness. [➡EXACT; 204] *Opposite:* vagueness.

preclude (*formal*) *v* **prevent**, impede, stop, rule out, exclude, disqualify, prohibit, bar. [➡MAKE IMPOSSIBLE; 277] *Opposite:* permit.

preclusion (*formal*) *n* **prevention**, exclusion, disqualification, prohibition, deterrence, impediment, bar, hindrance, obstacle. [➡AVOID, PREVENT, LIMIT, AND CONTROL; 278] *Opposite:* encouragement.

precocious *adj* **advanced**, developed, intelligent, bright, gifted, talented, mature, articulate, clever. [➡TALENTED AND SKILFUL; 528] *Opposite:* immature.

precociousness *n* **talent**, cleverness, brightness, intelligence, precocity, maturity, giftedness. [➡SKILLS, TALENTS, AND ABILITIES; 527] *Opposite:* immaturity.

precocity *n* **talent**, cleverness, brightness, intelligence, precociousness, maturity, giftedness. [➡SKILLS, TALENTS, AND ABILITIES; 527] *Opposite:* immaturity.

precognition *n* **clairvoyance**, foreknowledge (*formal*), premonition, foresight, second sight, sixth sense. [➡KNOWLEDGE AND WISDOM; 559]

preconceived *adj* **fixed**, set, defined, rigid, inflexible, predetermined, prejudiced, biased. [➡THE NATURE OF IDEAS; 772] *Opposite:* unprejudiced.

preconception *n* **prejudice**, bias, fixed idea, presumption, notion, predetermination. [➡POINT OF VIEW; 768]

precondition *n* **condition**, requirement, prerequisite, qualification, must, necessity. [➡NECESSARY AND ESSENTIAL; 197]

precook *v* **parboil**, boil, cook, prepare, soften, simmer. [➡COOKING AND FOOD PREPARATION; 354]

precooked *adj* [➡STATE OF PREPARED FOOD; 1170]

precursor *n* **forerunner**, ancestor, predecessor, antecedent, pioneer, herald, originator, sign, foundation, foretaste. [➡INDICATIONS, SIGNS, AND WARNINGS; 68] *Opposite:* successor.

predate *v* **precede**, go before, antedate, exist before, pre-exist, antecede, prelude, come before. [➡BEFORE, FIRST, AND PRECEDING; 164]

predator *n* **marauder**, killer, slayer (*formal or literary*), hunter, pillager, raider. [➡VILLAINS AND THUGS; 947]

predatory *adj* **greedy**, destructive, rapacious, grasping, voracious, predacious (*formal*), vulturine. [➡SELFISH AND UNKIND; 506]

predecessor *n* **precursor**, forerunner, ancestor, antecedent, prototype. [➡BEFORE, FIRST, AND PRECEDING; 164] *Opposite:* successor.

predestination *n* **destiny**, fate, doom, kismet, lot, predetermination, foreordination (*formal*), foreordainment (*formal*), preordination, preordainment. [➡FATE, DESTINY, AND ASTROLOGY; 783] *Opposite:* free will.

predestine *v* **destine**, fate, preordain, doom, predetermine, foreordain (*formal*), decide, prearrange. [➡CAUSE TO HAPPEN; 31]

predestined *adj* **fated**, destined, bound, preordained, foreordained (*formal*), appointed, predetermined, prearranged, inexorable (*formal*), inevitable. [➡FATE, DESTINY, AND ASTROLOGY; 783]

predetermination 1 *n* **prearrangement**, arrangement, intention, decision, resolution, resolve, intent (*formal*), agreement, plan. [➡WAYS OF DOING THINGS; 295] 2 *n* **predestination**, preordination, preordainment, foreordination (*formal*), foreordainment (*formal*), lot, destiny, fate, doom, kismet. [➡FATE, DESTINY, AND ASTROLOGY; 783] *Opposite:* free will.

predetermine 1 *v* **set**, programme, encode, determine, decide, fix, prearrange, schedule. [➡MAKE DECISIONS AND CHOICES; 753] 2 *v* **predestine**, destine, fate, preordain, foreordain (*formal*), doom. [➡CAUSE TO HAPPEN; 31]

predetermined 1 *adj* **prearranged**, programmed, encoded, fixed, determined, set, preset, scheduled. [➡BEFORE, FIRST, AND PRECEDING; 164] 2 *adj* **predestined**, destined, fated, bound, preordained, foreordained (*formal*), inexorable (*formal*), inevitable. [➡FATE, DESTINY, AND ASTROLOGY; 783]

predicament *n* **difficulty**, quandary, jam (*informal*), pickle (*informal*), fix (*informal*), dilemma, tight spot, tight corner, mess. [➡DIFFICULT SITUATIONS; 72]

predicate 1 *v* (*formal*) **base**, establish, found, ground, build, centre, rest. [➡INSTITUTE AND INAUGURATE; 349] 2 *type of* **grammatical term.** [➡ASPECTS OF LANGUAGE; 683]

predict *v* **forecast**, foresee, envisage, expect, guess, calculate, foretell, see coming, prophesy. [➡PREDICT AND ANTICIPATE; 751]

predictability 1 *n* **expectedness**, obviousness, certainty, likelihood, probability, liability, sureness, predictableness. [➡CERTAIN; 175] *Opposite:* unlikelihood. 2 *n* **unoriginality**, banality, triteness, obviousness, staleness, tiredness, predictableness. [➡BORING AND UNINTERESTING; 235] *Opposite:* originality.

predictable 1 *adj* **foreseeable**, expectable, expected, likely, probable, liable, anticipated, sure, certain. [➡POSSIBLE AND PROBABLE; 178] *Opposite:* unlikely. 2 *adj* **unsurprising**, unoriginal, banal, trite, obvious, stale, tired, hackneyed. [➡BORING AND UNINTERESTING; 235] *Opposite:* original.

predictableness 1 *n* **likelihood**, obviousness, expectedness, probability, predictability, liability, sureness, certainty. [➡CERTAIN; 175] *Opposite:* unlikelihood. 2 *n* **unoriginality**, banality, triteness, obviousness, staleness, tiredness, predictability. [➡BORING AND UNINTERESTING; 235] *Opposite:* originality.

predicted *adj* **foretold**, forecast, foreseen, prophesied, projected, expected, anticipated. [➡PREDICT AND ANTICIPATE; 751] *Opposite:* unforeseen.

prediction *n* **forecast**, guess, calculation, estimate, prophecy, expectation, likelihood, extrapolation, prognostication, projection. [➡PREDICT AND ANTICIPATE; 751]

predictive *adj* **prognostic**, extrapolative, prophetic, projecting, foretelling. [➡PREDICT AND ANTICIPATE; 751]

predilection (*formal*) *n* **liking**, preference, fondness, partiality, penchant, taste, weakness, tendency. [➡APPRECIATION AND GRATITUDE; 536] *Opposite:* dislike.

predispose (*formal*) *v* **incline**, dispose, prompt, influence, prejudice, bias, affect. [➡ENCOURAGE; 577]

predisposed (*formal*) *adj* **inclined**, disposed, subject, liable, susceptible, prone, given. [➡THE WILL AND WILLINGNESS; 564] *Opposite:* unwilling.

predisposition *n* **tendency**, disposition, inclination, predilection (*formal*), penchant, bias, susceptibility. [➡TEMPERAMENT AND BEHAVIOUR; 493]

predominance 1 *n* **superiority**, power, dominance, control, supremacy, leadership. [➡SUPERIORITY; 153] 2 *n* **majority**, prevalence, preponderance, numerousness. [➡MANY, MUCH, LARGE AMOUNT; 117] *Opposite:* minority.

predominant *adj* **main**, major, chief, principal, prime, biggest, largest, leading, prevalent. [➡MOST IMPORTANT AND MAIN; 194] *Opposite:* minor.

predominantly *adv* **mainly**, mostly, largely, chiefly, principally, primarily, in the main, for the most part. [➡MAINLY AND PRIMARILY; 138] *Opposite:* partially.

predominate *v* **prevail**, dominate, outweigh, preponderate, be in the majority, lead. [➡PROSPER AND ABOUND; 16]

pre-eminence *n* **superiority**, authority, excellence, eminence, renown, prestige, prominence. [➡SUPERIORITY; 153] *Opposite:* obscurity.

pre-eminent *adj* **distinguished**, outstanding, excellent, exalted (*formal*), eminent, renowned, prestigious, prominent, famous, well-known, foremost, leading, dominant. [➡KNOWN AND FAMOUS; 182] *Opposite:* obscure.

pre-eminently *adv* **to a great extent**, in large part, first and foremost, predominantly, principally, overwhelmingly, far and away, dominantly, primarily. [➡TO A GREAT EXTENT; 130] *Opposite:* partly.

pre-empt *v* **forestall**, anticipate, obstruct, block, prevent, head off, avert, deter, stave off. [➡AVOID, PREVENT, LIMIT, AND CONTROL; 278] *Opposite:* react.

pre-emption *n* **preemptive action**, preventive action, preventive measures, prevention, anticipation. [➡AVOID, PREVENT, LIMIT, AND CONTROL; 278] *Opposite:* reaction.

pre-emptive *adj* **preventive**, preventative, proactive, anticipatory, blocking, defensive, tactical. [➡AVOID, PREVENT, LIMIT, AND CONTROL; 278] *Opposite:* reactive.

preen *v* **groom**, smarten, clean, tidy, smooth, trim. [➡IMPROVE APPEARANCE; 380]

pre-exist *v* **predate**, precede, antecede, go before, prelude, antedate, forerun. [➡BEFORE, FIRST, AND PRECEDING; 164]

pre-existing *adj* **previous**, prior, earlier, former, established, pre-existent, foregoing, antecedent, preceding. [➡BEFORE, FIRST, AND PRECEDING; 164] *Opposite:* new.

prefabricate *v* **manufacture**, make up, assemble, produce, mass-produce. [➡MANUFACTURE; 350]

preface 1 *n* **foreword**, preamble, introduction, prologue, prelude. [➡PARTS OF BOOKS AND DOCUMENTS; 594] *Opposite:* postscript. **2** *v* **prefix**, precede, introduce, start, begin. [➡START AN ACTION; 261]

prefect *n* **senior pupil**, monitor, captain, head boy, head girl. [➡STUDENTS AND PUPILS; 841]

prefer *v* **favour**, have a preference, like better, rather, wish, fancy (*informal*), desire, choose, select, single out. [➡LIKE, LOVE, VALUE AND ENJOY; 579]

preferable *adj* **better**, desirable, nicer, superior, choice. [➡GOOD, WELL, BETTER; 184] *Opposite:* inferior.

preference *n* **favourite**, first choice, partiality, penchant, predilection (*formal*), fondness, liking, inclination. [➡APPRECIATION AND GRATITUDE; 536] *Opposite:* dislike.

preferential *adj* **special**, favoured, privileged, superior, better, partisan. [➡SUPERIORITY; 153] *Opposite:* disadvantageous.

preferment (*formal*) *n* **promotion**, upgrading, appointment, advancement, elevation. [➡CONFER STATUS; 459] *Opposite:* demotion.

preferred *adj* **favoured**, favourite, chosen, number one, in, ideal. [➡POPULAR AND WANTED; 221]

prefigure *v* **anticipate**, herald, foreshadow, portend, presage, predict, suggest. [➡BEFORE, FIRST, AND PRECEDING; 164]

prefix 1 *v* **preface**, precede, begin, start, start off, attach, put in front, introduce, add. [➡START AN ACTION; 261] **2** *type of* **grammatical term**. [➡ASPECTS OF LANGUAGE; 683]

pregnancy 1 *n* **gravidity** (*technical*), gravidness (*technical*), condition (*informal*), gestation, confinement (*dated*), lying-in (*archaic*), antenatal period, prenatal period, perinatal period. [➡REPRODUCTION AND HEREDITY; 726] **2** *n* **significance**, importance, import, meaning. [➡IMPORTANCE AND SIGNIFICANCE; 193]

pregnant 1 *adj* **expectant**, expecting (*informal*), with child (*archaic or literary*), in the family way (*dated informal*), heavy with child (*archaic or literary*), gravid (*technical*), antenatal, prenatal. [➡REPRODUCTION AND HEREDITY; 726] **2** *adj* **charged**, significant, weighty, meaningful, pointed, loaded. [➡INTERESTING AND MEANINGFUL; 191]

preheat *v* **heat**, heat up, warm, warm up, turn on. [➡COOKING AND FOOD PREPARATION; 354] *Opposite:* cool.

prehistoric 1 *adj* **primeval**, primitive, antediluvian, early, ancient, old, primordial, primal. [➡PAST; 84] **2** *adj* **old-fashioned**, out-of-date, ancient, old, antiquated, archaic, outmoded, antediluvian. [➡OLD, OLD-FASHIONED; 168] *Opposite:* modern.

prehistory *n* **early history**, olden days, times gone by, dawn of time, Stone Age, Bronze Age, Iron Age, ancient history. [➡PAST; 84]

prejudge *v* **jump to conclusions**, presume, presuppose, anticipate, assume, posit (*formal*). [➡PREDICT AND ANTICIPATE; 751]

prejudice 1 *n* **bias**, preconception, prejudgment, predisposition, partiality. [➡THE NATURE OF IDEAS; 772] *Opposite:* impartiality. **2** *n* **bigotry**, chauvinism, narrow-mindedness, discrimination, intolerance, injustice, unfairness, partisanship. [➡PREJUDICE; 551] *Opposite:* tolerance. **3** *v* **influence**, bias, sway, slant, distort, incline, predispose (*formal*), prepossess. [➡APPEAL TO AND AROUSE INTEREST; 576]

prejudiced *adj* **biased**, intolerant, bigoted, narrow-minded, discriminatory, unfair, opinionated, partisan, blinkered, unjust. [➡NEGATIVE INTELLECTUAL CHARACTERISTICS; 526] *Opposite:* tolerant.

prejudicial *adj* **harmful**, detrimental, hurtful, damaging, injurious, deleterious (*formal*). [➡DANGEROUS; 237] *Opposite:* helpful.

prelate *n* **bishop**, archbishop, cardinal, abbot, prior, cleric, minister. [➡RELIGIOUS PEOPLE; 779]

preliminary 1 *adj* **initial**, first, opening, pilot, introductory, maiden, primary, earliest. [➡BEFORE, FIRST, AND PRECEDING; 164] *Opposite:* closing. **2** *n* **beginning**, first round, introduction, opening, groundwork, preface, prelude, inception (*formal*), initiation. [➡BEGINNING; 53] *Opposite:* finale.

prelude 1 *n* **introduction**, run-up, overture, prologue, preface, foreword, preamble. [➡BEGINNING; 53] *Opposite:* finale. 2 *type of* **instrumental music.** [➡MUSIC, SONGS, AND SINGING; 907]

premature *adj* **early**, untimely, hasty, rash, precipitate, impulsive, previous (*informal*). [➡PROMPTNESS: EARLY; 98] *Opposite:* overdue.

premeditated *adj* **planned**, deliberate, intentional, calculated, thought-out, intended, conscious, studied. [➡INTENTIONAL AND DELIBERATE; 280] *Opposite:* spontaneous.

premeditation 1 *n* **planning**, calculation, cold-bloodedness, coldness, contemplation, scheming, design. [➡THINK AND REFLECT; 744] *Opposite:* impulsiveness. 2 *n* **reflection**, contemplation, thought, consideration, cogitation (*formal*), deliberation (*formal*). [➡IDEA AND THOUGHT; 771] *Opposite:* spontaneity.

premier 1 *adj* **best**, first, leading, foremost, highest, chief, primary, principal, arch. [➡SUPERIORITY; 153] *Opposite:* worst. 2 *n* **prime minister**, PM, leader, head of state, ruler, head of government, minister. [➡POLITICAL OFFICES AND POLITICIANS; 808]

premiere *n* **opening**, first night, first performance, first showing, debut. [➡PERFORMANCES AND SHOWS; 42]

premiership 1 *n* **leadership**, prime ministership, presidency, chancellorship, office, tenure. [➡POLITICAL OFFICES AND POLITICIANS; 808] 2 *n* **premier league championship**, league championship, championship competition, championship, premier championship, premier league. [➡NON-AGGRESSIVE/SPORTING EVENT; 40]

premise 1 *n* **evidence**, principle, idea, foundation, ground, statement. [➡IDEA AND THOUGHT; 771] 2 *n* **proposition**, supposition, hypothesis, assertion, thesis, presupposition, grounds, basis, assumption, postulate, presumption. [➡POINT OF VIEW; 768]

premises *n* **building**, grounds, location, site, property, place. [➡PLACE; 1064]

premium 1 *n* **payment**, percentage, bonus, reward, perk, extra, dividend, prize. [➡MONEY, PAYMENTS, AND CHARGES; 800] 2 *adj* **best**, top, finest, quality, first-class, first-rate, superior, exceptional. [➡SUPERIORITY; 153] *Opposite:* low-grade.

premolar *type of* **tooth.** [➡THE MOUTH; 703]

premonition 1 *n* **intuition**, presentiment, feeling, hunch, fear, sense, suspicion, foreboding. [➡FEELINGS ABOUT THE FUTURE; 534] 2 *n* **warning**, omen, sign, portent, indication, admonition, forewarning. [➡THE SUPERNATURAL; 788]

premonitory 1 *adj* **intuitive**, predictive, clairvoyant, prophetic, precognitive, psychic, mantic, vatic. [➡PREDICT AND ANTICIPATE; 751] 2 *adj* **warning**, prognostic, precautionary, cautionary, sobering, worrying, ominous, admonitory. [➡THE SUPERNATURAL; 788]

prenatal *adj* [➡REPRODUCTION AND HEREDITY; 726]

prenominal *type of* **grammatical term.** [➡ASPECTS OF LANGUAGE; 683]

preoccupation *n* **worry**, obsession, anxiety, concern, fixation, niggle, bee in your bonnet, care, uneasiness. [➡CONFUSION, ANXIETY, AND WORRY; 541]

preoccupied *adj* **worried**, anxious, lost in thought, elsewhere, inattentive, in a world of your own, distant, thoughtful, pensive, engrossed, absent-minded. [➡CONFUSION, ANXIETY, AND WORRY; 541] *Opposite:* carefree.

preoccupy *v* **worry**, concern, disturb, trouble, bug (*informal*), consume, possess, eat away at, get to, haunt, grip, obsess. [➡UPSET, DISTRESS, AND HUMILIATE; 568]

preordained *adj* **inevitable**, fated, predetermined, destined, doomed, predicted, inescapable, certain, unavoidable, foreordained (*formal*). [➡CERTAIN; 175]

prep (*informal*) *n* [➡LESSONS, COURSE WORK, AND EXAMINATIONS; 842]

preparation 1 *n* **groundwork**, training, grounding, homework, research, tuition. [➡TEACHING; 839] 2 *n* **planning**, provision, arrangement, formulation, organization. [➡BEGINNING; 53]

preparatory *adj* **introductory**, foundation, preliminary, elementary, opening, preparative (*formal*). [➡BEFORE, FIRST, AND PRECEDING; 164] *Opposite:* final.

prepare 1 *v* **get ready**, arrange, organize, plan, set up, practise, put in order. [➡PREPARE FOR ACTION; 290] 2 *v* **train**, groom, coach, prime, make ready, warm up. [➡INSTRUCT AND TEACH; 610] 3 *v* **make**, cook, get ready, fix (*informal*), concoct, formulate. [➡MEAL PREPARATION; 355]

prepared *adj* **ready**, set, equipped, geared up, organized, arranged, all set, primed, willing, able. [➡POSITIVE IMPATIENCE, ENTHUSIASM, AND ALERTNESS; 538]

preparedness *n* **readiness**, preparation, alertness, attentiveness, awareness, vigilance. [➡POSITIVE IMPATIENCE, ENTHUSIASM, AND ALERTNESS; 538]

prepare the ground *v* [➡PREPARE FOR ACTION; 290]

prepare the way *v* [➡PREPARE FOR ACTION; 290]

prepare yourself *v* **steel yourself**, brace yourself, nerve yourself, compose yourself, get ready. [➡PREPARE FOR ACTION; 290]

prepayment *n* **advance payment**, down payment, payment, advance, deposit, instalment. [➡EXPENDITURE; 424] *Opposite:* debt.

preplan *v* [➡PREPARE FOR ACTION; 290]

preponderance (*formal*) 1 *n* **majority**, mass, great number, multitude, many. [➡MANY, MUCH, LARGE AMOUNT; 117] *Opposite:* minority. 2 *n* **dominance**, superiority, prevalence, predominance, weight, majority, supremacy. [➡IMPORTANCE AND SIGNIFICANCE; 193]

preponderant *adj* **greater**, more numerous, more powerful, more important, more significant, preeminent. [➡MOST IMPORTANT AND MAIN; 194] *Opposite:* lesser.

preponderantly *adv* **generally**, largely, in the main, by and large, for the most part, on the whole. [➡MAINLY AND PRIMARILY; 138]

preposition *type of* **word class.** [➡ASPECTS OF LANGUAGE; 683]

prepossessing (*formal*) *adj* **attractive**, pleasant, alluring, good-looking, nice-looking, eye-catching, beautiful, handsome, striking, pleasing. [➡BEAUTY AND ATTRACTIVENESS; 190] *Opposite:* unattractive.

preposterous *adj* **outrageous**, absurd, ridiculous, ludicrous, unbelievable, laughable, silly, outlandish, unreasonable. [➡BIZARRE AND PECULIAR; 258] *Opposite:* sensible.

preposterousness *n* **outrageousness**, absurdity, ludicrousness, ridiculousness, silliness, outlandishness, unreasonableness. [➡BIZARRE AND PECULIAR; 258] *Opposite:* sensibleness.

preppy (*US informal*) *adj* **yuppie**, conservative, classic, neat, well-groomed, traditional, tailored, smart. [➡DESCRIBING CLOTHES; 869]

preproduction *n* **planning**, groundwork, organization, scheduling, planning stage, preparation. [➡BEGINNING; 53]

prep school *type of* **school**. [➡EDUCATIONAL INSTITUTIONS; 813]

prepubescent **1** *adj* **preadolescent**, preteen, preteenager, young, childish, childlike, juvenile. [➡BABYHOOD, CHILDHOOD AND ADOLESCENCE; 917] *Opposite:* adult. **2** *n* **youngster**, preadolescent, preteenager, preteen, subteen, child, kid (*informal*), youth, moppet (*informal*). [➡CHILD OR YOUTH; 945] *Opposite:* adult.

prequel *n* **prelude**, prologue, spin-off. [➡FICTION AND DRAMA; 913] *Opposite:* sequel.

Pre-Raphaelitism *type of* **pre-20th-century art movement**. [➡ARTISTIC MOVEMENTS AND STYLES; 899]

prerecord *v* **record**, tape, film, copy, video. [➡RECORD SOMETHING; 372]

prerequisite *n* **precondition**, requirement, condition, qualification, criterion, essential, must, necessity. [➡NECESSARY AND ESSENTIAL; 197]

prerogative *n* **right**, privilege, due, entitlement, birthright, perquisite. [➡SOURCE OF HAPPINESS, PLEASURE, OR IMPROVEMENT; 210]

presage **1** *n* **portent**, omen, sign, warning, signal, indication, augury, herald. [➡THE SUPERNATURAL; 788] **2** *v* **foretell**, foreshadow, portend, bode, sanction, augur, betoken (*literary*), signify. [➡MEAN SOMETHING; 61]

presbyter *n* [➡RELIGIOUS PEOPLE; 779]

preschool **1** *adj* **young**, toddler, infant, kindergarten, nursery, infantile. [➡BABYHOOD, CHILDHOOD AND ADOLESCENCE; 917] **2** *type of* **school**. [➡EDUCATIONAL INSTITUTIONS; 813]

preschooler (*US*) *n* **young child**, preschool child, under-five, toddler, infant, tot (*informal*), baby, youngster, child. [➡STUDENTS AND PUPILS; 841]

prescience *n* **foresight**, precognition, clairvoyance, prophecy, prediction, divination, insight, intuition, foreknowledge (*formal*). [➡PREDICT AND ANTICIPATE; 751] *Opposite:* hindsight.

prescient *adj* **prophetic**, psychic, clairvoyant, discerning, perceptive, mantic, vatic, revelatory. [➡PREDICT AND ANTICIPATE; 751]

prescribe **1** *v* **recommend**, suggest, advise, propose, counsel (*formal or literary*), advocate, commend. [➡ADVISE AND WARN; 614] **2** *v* **lay down**, stipulate, impose, order, set down, demand, fix, specify, particularize. [➡REQUEST AND DEMAND; 664]

prescribed *adj* **set**, agreed, arranged, prearranged, given, approved. [➡BEFORE, FIRST, AND PRECEDING; 164]

prescript (*formal*) *n* **rule**, regulation, law, convention, canon, decree, edict, ordinance, statute. [➡REQUEST AND DEMAND; 664]

prescription *n* **medicine**, treatment, drug, preparation, remedy, medicament. [➡REMEDIES, TREATMENTS AND OPERATIONS; 732]

prescriptive *adj* **narrow**, rigid, strict, unbending, inflexible, dogmatic, doctrinaire, authoritarian. [➡THE NATURE OF IDEAS; 772] *Opposite:* lax.

prescriptiveness *n* **narrowness**, rigidity, strictness, unbendingness, inflexibility, dogmatism, authoritarianism. [➡THE NATURE OF IDEAS; 772] *Opposite:* laxity.

presence **1** *n* **attendance**, company, occurrence, incidence, existence, manifestation. [➡PRESENT AND AVAILABLE; 11] *Opposite:* absence. **2** *n* **dignity**, charisma, aura, authority, poise, air, bearing, comportment (*formal*), mien (*literary*). [➡TEMPERAMENT AND BEHAVIOUR; 493] **3** *n* **ghost**, apparition, spirit, ghoul, manifestation, spectre, phantom, phantasm. [➡THE SUPERNATURAL; 788]

presence of mind *n* **nerve**, composure, level-headedness, common sense, sense, alertness, gumption (*informal*). [➡POSITIVE INTELLECTUAL CHARACTERISTICS; 525]

present **1** *v* **give**, hand over, award, bestow (*formal*), donate, offer, give away, hand out. [➡PROFFER AND HAND OVER; 432] *Opposite:* deny. **2** *v* **cause**, throw up, represent, raise, produce, bring about, pose. [➡CAUSE TO HAPPEN; 31] **3** *v* (*formal*) **submit**, impart, offer, put forward, expound, state, communicate. [➡SUGGEST, HINT, AND COMMENT; 613] **4** *v* **introduce**, acquaint with, put forward. [➡INFORM AND ANNOUNCE; 612] **5** *v* **stage**, show, put on, exhibit, organize, display, mount, perform. [➡CAUSE TO APPEAR; 5] **6** *v* **portray**, represent, depict, cast, describe, render (*formal*). [➡REPRESENT SOMETHING OR SOMEBODY; 59] **7** *v* **appear**, report, arrive, turn up, visit, attend. [➡ARRIVE; 12] **8** *n* **gift**, offering, grant, dowry, largesse, benevolence. [➡GIFTS; 439] **9** *n* **now**, here and now, present day, today, nowadays, this day and age, these days. [➡PRESENT; 85] *Opposite:* past. **10** *adj* **current**, contemporary, present-day, existing, extant, contemporaneous, existent (*formal*). [➡PRESENT; 85] *Opposite:* past. **11** *adj* **there**, here, in attendance, at hand, near, nearby. [➡PRESENT AND AVAILABLE; 11] *Opposite:* absent.

See Compare and Contrast at **give**.

presentable **1** *adj* **respectable**, personable, fit to be seen, smart, well-dressed, well turned-out, neat, tidy. [➡WELL GROOMED; 483] *Opposite:* scruffy. **2** *adj* **reasonable**, acceptable, satisfactory, good enough, OK (*informal*), okay (*informal*), passable, tolerable. [➡ACCEPTABLE AND PASSABLE; 220] *Opposite:* unsatisfactory.

presentation **1** *n* **performance**, exhibition, demonstration, appearance, arrangement, staging, production, management, exposition. [➡SALES AND SHOWS; 444] **2** *n* **award**, donation, giving, offer, bestowment (*formal*), bestowal, benefaction, contribution. [➡DISPENSE, RATION, AND DISTRIBUTE; 435] **3** *n* **talk**, lecture, seminar, speech, address, allocution (*formal*), report. [➡NEUTRAL ONE-WAY COMMUNICATION; 49]

present circumstances *n* [➡SITUATIONS; 71]

present day *n* **now**, here and now, present, today, nowadays, this day and age, these days. [➡PRESENT; 85] *Opposite:* past.

present-day *adj* **contemporary**, current, existing, present, modern, extant. [➡PRESENT; 85] *Opposite:* past.

presenter *n* **announcer**, broadcaster, anchor, TV presenter, radio presenter, host, newsreader. [➡WORKERS IN ENTERTAINMENT AND MEDIA; 873]

presentiment *n* **feeling**, intuition, foreboding, fear, sense, hunch, premonition, suspicion, awareness. [➡FEELINGS ABOUT THE FUTURE; 534]

presently **1** *adv* **soon**, shortly, in a short time, in a while, before long. [➡FUTURE; 86] **2** *adv* **currently**, at the moment, at present, right now, now. [➡PRESENT; 85]

preservation **1** *n* **protection**, conservation, safeguarding, defence, conservancy, salvation. [➡PREVENT CONTACT OR ATTACK; 420] *Opposite:* destruction. **2** *n* **maintenance**, continuation, perpetuation, keeping, upholding, support. [➡PERMANENCE: WITHOUT END; 94] *Opposite:* abolition.

preservative **1** *adj* **preserving**, conserving, protective, antibacterial, antifungal, stabilizing. [➡SAFE AND SAFETY; 192] *Opposite:* destructive. **2** *n* **additive**, preserver, E number, stabilizer. [➡ADDITIVES; 1171]

preserve **1** *v* **maintain**, uphold, keep, continue, carry on, sustain, save, conserve. [➡STORE AND KEEP; 454] *Opposite:* destroy. **2** *n* **realm**, domain, sphere, field, territory, ambit, compass, orbit, purview. [➡SUBJECT AREA; 769] **3** *n* (*US*) **game reserve**, reserve, reservation, sanctuary, game preserve (*US*). [➡THE COUNTRYSIDE AND OUTDOOR SPACES; 1070]

preserve

◆ *types of preserve*
compote, conserve, honey, jam, jelly, lekvar, lemon curd, marmalade, mincemeat, peanut butter

preserved **1** *adj* **conserved**, well-looked-after, well-maintained, well-preserved, well-kept-up, well-kept, unspoiled. [➡IN GOOD REPAIR; 1231] *Opposite:* dilapidated. **2** *adj* **treated**, pickled, frozen, dried, salted, canned, smoked, bottled, cured, tinned. [➡STATE OF PREPARED FOOD; 1170] *Opposite:* fresh.

preserver *n* **protector**, guard, guardian, saviour, conserver. [➡SUPPORTERS, PROTECTORS, AND COMPATRIOTS; 970] *Opposite:* destroyer.

preset *adj* **set**, predetermined, fixed, stipulated, specific, stated, firm, certain. [➡BEFORE, FIRST, AND PRECEDING; 164]

preshrunk *adj* [➡DESCRIBING CLOTHES; 869]

preside *v* **take the chair**, chair, control, supervise, head, lead, manage, direct, run, oversee, reign, govern. [➡BE IN CHARGE; 271]

presidency **1** *n* **premiership**, position, job, function, term, term of office, role, tenure. [➡POLITICAL OFFICES AND POLITICIANS; 808] **2** *n* **post**, status, function, office, authority, responsibility. [➡JOB; 833]

president *n* **leader**, premier, head, head of state, chair, chief, commander. [➡POLITICAL OFFICES AND POLITICIANS; 808]

presidential **1** *adj* **political**, constitutional, high-level, governmental, top-level, diplomatic, official, executive. [➡STYLES AND SYSTEMS OF GOVERNMENT; 806] **2** *adj* **dignified**, authoritative, monarchic, judicious, regal, diplomatic, imperial, powerful, authoritarian, awe-inspiring, self-assured, commanding. [➡CONFIDENCE AND COMPOSURE; 500]

presidentially *adv* **authoritatively**, monarchically, judiciously, regally, powerfully, imperially, confidently, commandingly, with dignity. [➡CONFIDENCE AND COMPOSURE; 500]

presidium *n* **executive committee**, committee, council, group, body, authority. [➡BUSINESS ENTERPRISES AND RELATED BODIES; 793]

press **1** *v* **push**, depress, force down, bear down on, compress, squash. [➡CONTACT: EXERT PRESSURE; 415] *Opposite:* pull. **2** *v* **iron**, smooth, steam, flatten, hot-press. [➡CHANGE OF SHAPE; 386] **3** *v* **force**, urge, push, compel, oblige, hound, pressure. [➡CAUSE OR COMPEL TO ACT; 272] **4** *v* **pursue**, lobby, beg, implore (*formal*), importune (*formal*), entreat (*formal*), enjoin, bug (*informal*). [➡REQUEST AND DEMAND; 664] **5** *v* (*literary*) **surge**, crowd, swarm, mill, cluster, herd, huddle, throng. [➡GET CLOSER TOGETHER; 311] **6** *n* **journalists**, media, reporters, newspapers, correspondents, fourth estate, print media. [➡WORKERS IN THE MEDIA; 873] **7** *n* **crowd**, horde, throng, mob, multitude, swarm, host, crush. [➡GROUPS OF PEOPLE; 935] **8** *type of* **cabinet.** [➡FURNITURE; 858]

press ahead *v* [➡CONTINUE AN ACTION; 263]

press conference *n* **news conference**, question and answer session, interview, conference, photo opportunity, meeting. [➡MEETINGS AND ASSEMBLIES; 43]

pressed *adj* **busy**, pushed, hard-pressed, constrained, compelled, forced. [➡IN TROUBLE AND DISADVANTAGED; 73]

pressed for time *adj* [➡IN TROUBLE AND DISADVANTAGED; 73]

press for *v* **demand**, seek, urge, push for, campaign for, lobby for, advocate. [➡REQUEST AND DEMAND; 664]

press-gang *v* **force**, coerce, bully, pressurize, pressure, bulldoze (*informal*), make, compel, shanghai. [➡CAUSE OR COMPEL TO ACT; 272]

pressing **1** *adj* **urgent**, important, serious, crucial, vital, burning, imperative, necessary, critical. [➡IMPORTANT; 195] *Opposite:* unimportant. **2** *adj* **persistent**, insistent, unrelenting, unyielding, demanding, irresistible, tenacious, persuasive, crying, clamouring, importunate (*formal*). [➡THE WILL AND WILLINGNESS; 564] *Opposite:* half-hearted.

press officer *n* **spokesperson**, media spokesperson, press liaison officer, press agent. [➡WORKERS IN ENTERTAINMENT AND MEDIA; 873]

press on *v* **continue**, push on, forge ahead, keep going, carry on, persist, press ahead, persevere. [➡CONTINUE AN ACTION; 263] *Opposite:* give up.

press release *n* **statement**, document, announcement, bulletin. [➡ADVERTISING AND PUBLICITY; 605]

press stud *n* **popper**, press fastener, fastening, fastener, stud, snap (*US*). [➡FASTENERS, LINKS, AND NETWORKS; 1246]

press together *v* **squeeze together**, force together, clamp, join together, close, purse, clump, crowd, cluster, huddle. [➡GET CLOSER TOGETHER; 311] *Opposite:* pull apart.

pressure **1** *n* **force**, weight, heaviness, burden, compression, gravity, density. [➡ENERGY GENERAL; 1160] **2** *n* **stress**, anxiety, weight, strain, tension, demands, care, difficulty, burden, hassle (*informal*), load. [➡DIFFICULT SITUATIONS; 72] **3** *v* **coerce**, pressurize, force, bulldoze (*informal*), bully, insist, compel, hassle (*informal*). [➡CAUSE OR COMPEL TO ACT; 272]

pressure cooker *n* [➡TABLEWARE, CUTLERY, AND KITCHENWARE; 861]

pressured *adj* **worried**, stressed, under pressure, strung out (*informal*), overstretched, edgy, distressed, tense, anxious, careworn. [➡SADNESS, DISTRESS, AND DESPAIR; 540] *Opposite:* relaxed.

pressure sore *n* [➡CONDITIONS AFFECTING THE SKIN; 722]

pressurize *v* **force**, coerce, compel, make, bully, bulldoze (*informal*), press-gang, press, pressure. [➡CAUSE OR COMPEL TO ACT; 272]

prestige *n* **status**, standing, stature, kudos, esteem, reputation, regard, cachet, fame, celebrity, repute (*formal*), notability, distinction, respect. [➡KNOWN AND FAMOUS; 182] *Opposite:* notoriety.

prestigious *adj* **admired**, respected, significant, important, impressive, high-status, prominent, esteemed, celebrated, exalted (*formal*), influential, major, famed, notable, respectable. [➡KNOWN AND FAMOUS; 182] *Opposite:* insignificant.

presumably *adv* **most probably**, I assume, I imagine, in all probability, most likely, it would seem, seemingly, apparently, doubtless, probably, likely, ostensibly. [➡POSSIBLE AND PROBABLE; 178]

presume **1** *v* **believe**, assume, guess, deduce, imagine, suppose, take as read, take for granted, postulate, posit (*formal*), gather, think. [➡PREDICT AND ANTICIPATE; 751] *Opposite:* know. **2** *v* **venture**, dare, be so bold, take the liberty, make free, have the audacity, have the nerve. [➡UTTER AND PRONOUNCE; 609]

presumption **1** *n* **belief**, assumption, conjecture, supposition, presupposition, guess, deduction, opinion, hypothesis, premise, speculation. [➡POINT OF VIEW; 768] **2** *n* **cheek** (*informal*), impertinence, audacity, nerve, gall, impudence, front, boldness, effrontery, brass (*informal*). [➡BAD MANNERS AND SOCIAL SKILLS; 522]

presumptive (*formal*) *adj* **probable**, likely, plausible, convincing, reasonable, possible, ostensible, apparent. [➡UNCERTAIN; 176] *Opposite:* implausible.

presumptuous *adj* **rude**, presuming, audacious, insolent, bold, rash, disrespectful, inconsiderate, overconfident, overfamiliar, arrogant, improper, pushy (*informal*), impolite, inappropriate, shameless. [➡BAD MANNERS AND SOCIAL SKILLS; 522] *Opposite:* modest.

presumptuousness *n* **rudeness**, arrogance, impropriety, disrespect, inappropriateness, presumption, audacity, insolence, boldness, rashness, inconsiderateness, overfamiliarity, overconfidence, shamelessness, pushiness (*informal*), chutzpah (*informal*). [➡BAD MANNERS AND SOCIAL SKILLS; 522] *Opposite:* modesty.

presuppose *v* **assume**, take for granted, take as read, take as fact, presume, suppose, accept. [➡PREDICT AND ANTICIPATE; 751]

presupposition *n* **assumption**, supposition, conjecture, belief, guess, deduction, presumption, premise, opinion, hypothesis. [➡POINT OF VIEW; 768]

prêt-à-porter *adj* **off-the-peg**, ready-made, ready-to-wear, mass-produced. [➡DESCRIBING CLOTHES; 869] *Opposite:* made-to-measure.

preteen *n* [➡CHILD OR YOUTH; 945]

preteenager *n* [➡CHILD OR YOUTH; 945]

pretence **1** *n* **trick**, con, sham, hoax, fabrication, invention, deception, subterfuge, cover, pretext, deceit, charade, façade. [➡DECEPTION AND LIES; 661] **2** *n* **claim**, suggestion, allegation, hint, supposition, presumption, pretension. [➡INTENTION AND PURPOSE; 773] **3** *n* **make-believe**, fantasy, fancy, imagination, castles in the air, nonsense. [➡NONEXISTENT THINGS; 23] *Opposite:* reality.

pretend **1** *v* **make believe**, imagine, fantasize, make up, play, play-act (*informal*). [➡DREAM, IMAGINE, AND FANTASIZE; 750] **2** *v* **feign**, put on, affect, profess, simulate, fake, imitate. [➡PRETEND AND MIMIC; 60] **3** *adj* **imaginary**, make-believe, made-up, invented, false, sham, fictitious. [➡FALSE AND UNREAL; 174] *Opposite:* real.

pretended *adj* [➡FALSE AND UNREAL; 174]

pretender *n* **aspirant**, aspiring leader, candidate, opponent, claimant. [➡COMPETITORS; 41]

pretend to be *v* **impersonate**, masquerade as, pose as, imitate, pass for, pass yourself off as, mimic, play-act. [➡PRETEND AND MIMIC; 60]

pretension *n* **affectation**, pretentiousness, airs, posing, posturing, pretence, self-importance. [➡AFFECTATION, SELF-SATISFACTION, AND SNOBBISHNESS; 508] *Opposite:* humility.

pretentious *adj* **affected**, ostentatious, showy, exaggerated, pompous, conceited, hollow, fake. [➡AFFECTATION, SELF-SATISFACTION, AND SNOBBISHNESS; 508] *Opposite:* down-to-earth.

pretentiousness *n* **affectation**, pretension, pretence, airs, posing, posturing, self-importance, showing off, pompousness, display. [➡AFFECTATION, SELF-SATISFACTION, AND SNOBBISHNESS; 508] *Opposite:* humility.

preterite *type of* **grammatical term**. [➡ASPECTS OF LANGUAGE; 683]

preternatural (*literary*) *adj* **supernatural**, paranormal, uncanny, unnatural, otherworldly, occult, unearthly, weird, bizarre. [➡THE SUPERNATURAL; 788] *Opposite:* natural.

pretext *n* **excuse**, cause, con, ploy, ruse, grounds. [➡CAUSATION; 169]

prettify *v* **smarten up**, do up, beautify, improve, adorn, decorate, gentrify, ornament. *Opposite:* mess up. (*informal*). [➡IMPROVE APPEARANCE; 380]

prettiness *n* **good looks**, handsomeness, attractiveness, beauty, loveliness, cuteness (*US*). [➡PEOPLE'S PHYSICAL APPEARANCE; 476] *Opposite:* ugliness.

pretty 1 *adj* **attractive**, beautiful, handsome, nice-looking, good-looking, appealing, comely (*archaic or literary*), lovely, cute (*US*), sweet. [➡PEOPLE'S PHYSICAL APPEARANCE; 476] *Opposite:* unattractive. 2 *adv* **rather**, fairly, reasonably, quite, moderately, somewhat, adequately, satisfactorily. [➡TO A CERTAIN EXTENT; 134]

See Compare and Contrast at **good-looking**.

pretty up *v* [➡IMPROVE APPEARANCE; 380]

prevail 1 *v* **triumph**, win through, succeed, be victorious, overcome, win out, conquer, carry the day. [➡SUCCEED AND WIN; 79] *Opposite:* fail. 2 *v* (*formal*) **exist**, reign, be happening, occur, predominate, abound, be present, be current. [➡PROSPER AND ABOUND; 16]

prevailing 1 *adj* **current**, existing, customary, established, popular, general, widespread. [➡PRESENT; 85] 2 *adj* **usual**, main, dominant, predominant, principal, fundamental, prevalent, normal, preponderant. [➡ORDINARINESS; 245] *Opposite:* underlying.

prevail on *v* **persuade**, convince, cajole, sway, coax into, influence, talk into, induce, nag into. [➡CAUSE OR COMPEL TO ACT; 272]

prevail upon *v* [➡CAUSE OR COMPEL TO ACT; 272]

prevalence *n* **occurrence**, commonness, pervasiveness, incidence, frequency, popularity. [➡PRESENT AND AVAILABLE; 11]

prevalent *adj* **common**, dominant, predominant, widespread, rampant, ubiquitous, established, customary, prevailing, numerous, frequent. [➡PRESENT AND AVAILABLE; 11] *Opposite:* rare.

See Compare and Contrast at **widespread**.

prevaricate *v* **hedge**, evade, beat about the bush, quibble, stall, put off, dither, fib (*informal*), dissemble, misstate, fudge (*informal*). [➡DECEPTION AND LIES; 661]

prevarication *n* **evasiveness**, evasion, equivocation, avoidance, hedging, stonewalling (*informal*), fudging (*informal*). [➡DECEPTION AND LIES; 661] *Opposite:* forthrightness.

prevaricator *n* [➡PEOPLE WHO DECEIVE; 662]

prevent *v* **stop**, avert, avoid, foil, thwart, put a stop to, preclude (*formal*), nip in the bud (*informal*), inhibit, counteract, block, ward off, check. [➡MAKE IMPOSSIBLE; 277] *Opposite:* encourage.

preventable *adj* **avoidable**, needless, unnecessary, avertible, escapable, inevitable. [➡UNIMPORTANT AND UNNECESSARY; 239]

prevention 1 *n* **avoidance**, deterrence, anticipation, preclusion (*formal*), stoppage, inhibition, hindrance. [➡AVOID, PREVENT, LIMIT, AND CONTROL; 278] *Opposite:* promotion. 2 *n* **obstacle**, hindrance, impediment, inhibition, restraint, bar. [➡PROBLEM; 257]

preventive 1 *adj* **anticipatory**, pre-emptive, defensive, prophylactic, deterrent, protective, proactive. [➡AVOID, PREVENT, LIMIT, AND CONTROL; 278] 2 *n* **protection**, defence, anticipatory measure, pre-emptive measure, deterrent, disincentive, preventative, preemptive measure. [➡SAFE AND SAFETY; 192]

preview 1 *n* **showing**, performance, broadcast, screening, opening, promo (*informal*). [➡PERFORMANCES AND SHOWS; 42] 2 *n* **trailer**, promo (*informal*), ad, clip, taster, advert (*informal*), foretaste, extract. [➡ADVERTISING AND PUBLICITY; 605] 3 *v* **show**, perform, broadcast, screen, promote, advertise. [➡CAUSE TO APPEAR; 5] 4 *v* **review**, describe, introduce, promote, advertise, trail. [➡NAME AND DESCRIBE; 666]

previous *adj* **preceding**, earlier, prior, former, aforementioned (*formal*), foregoing, erstwhile. [➡BEFORE, FIRST, AND PRECEDING; 164] *Opposite:* subsequent.

prey *n* **quarry**, victim, target, kill, game. [➡DEAD PERSON; 926]

prey on 1 *v* **live on**, live off, feed on, hunt, kill, exploit. [➡KILL; 923] 2 *v* **worry**, preoccupy, bug (*informal*), bother, haunt, oppress, depress. [➡UPSET, DISTRESS, AND HUMILIATE; 568] 3 *v* **take advantage of**, exploit, victimize, intimidate, bully, extort. [➡MISUSE AND ABUSE; 472]

price 1 *n* **cost**, worth, fee, face value, amount, bill, rate, expense, value, charge. [➡EXPENDITURE; 424] 2 *n* **penalty**, cost, punishment, consequences, fine. [➡RESULTS AND OUTCOMES; 83] 3 *v* **set a price**, assess, estimate, rate, evaluate, appraise, value. [➡ASSESS QUALITY; 756]

priceless 1 *adj* **invaluable**, inestimable, beyond price, incalculable, costly, expensive, irreplaceable, incomparable, peerless, precious. [➡EXPENSIVE AND LUXURIOUS; 219] *Opposite:* worthless. 2 *adj* (*informal*) **hilarious**, funny, comic, amusing, entertaining, sidesplitting. [➡FUNNY AND AMUSING; 217]

pricey (*informal*) *adj* **costly**, expensive, dear, steep (*informal*), high-priced, exorbitant, overpriced. [➡EXPENSIVE AND OVERPRICED; 248] *Opposite:* cheap.

prick 1 *v* **pierce**, stab, puncture, perforate, jab, make a hole in, cut, lance. [➡TEAR, BREAK, AND CUT; 361] 2 *n* **hole**, puncture, perforation, pinhole. [➡HOLES, GAPS, AND FORKS; 1251]

prickle 1 *n* **spike**, spine, barb, thorn, quill, needle. [➡EXTREMITIES OF PHYSICAL OBJECTS; 1249] 2 *n* **itch**, tickle, sting, irritation, tingling. [➡CONDITIONS AFFECTING THE SKIN; 722] 3 *v* **sting**, itch, tickle, prick, irritate, tingle. [➡PAIN AND OTHER PHYSICAL SENSATIONS; 734]

prickling *n* **scratchiness**, pricking, itchiness, itching, prickle, tingling, sting, tickle, irritation. [➡CONDITIONS AFFECTING THE SKIN; 722]

prickly 1 *adj* **spiny**, thorny, barbed, bristly, spiky. [➡PHYSICAL TEXTURE; 1221] *Opposite:* smooth. 2 *adj* **itchy**, tickly, scratchy, stinging, tingling. [➡CONDITIONS AFFECTING THE SKIN; 722] 3 *adj* (*informal*) **sensitive**, snappy, tetchy (*informal*), irritable, grumpy, snappish, cantankerous, touchy. [➡EXCESSIVE SENSITIVITY; 512] *Opposite:* impervious.

prickly heat *n* [➡CONDITIONS AFFECTING THE SKIN; 722]

pride 1 *n* **arrogance**, conceit, smugness, superiority, self-importance, egotism, vanity, immodesty. [➡MORALLY BAD; 776] *Opposite:* humility. 2 *n* **satisfaction**, delight, gratification, enjoyment, joy, happiness, pleasure, self-satisfaction. [➡APPRECIATION AND GRATITUDE; 536] 3 *n* **self-respect**, dignity, self-esteem, honour. [➡CONFIDENCE AND COMPOSURE; 500] 4 *type of* **herd**. [➡GROUP OF ANIMALS; 993]

pride and joy *n* **most prized possession**, the apple of your eye, poster child (*US*), treasure, pride, showpiece, obsession. [➡TREAT; 211]

pride yourself on *v* **be proud of**, take satisfaction in, revel in, take pride in, glory in, exult. [➡LIKE, LOVE, VALUE AND ENJOY; 579]

priest *n* **minister**, pastor, vicar, rector, presbyter, celebrant, chief priest, high priest, cleric, ecclesiastic. [➡RELIGIOUS PEOPLE; 779]

priesthood *n* **clergy**, ministry, cloth. [➡RELIGIOUS PEOPLE; 779] *Opposite:* laity.

priestly (*formal or literary*) *adj* **religious**, holy, pastoral, ecclesiastical, church, clerical. [➡RELIGIONS AND RELIGIOUS PRACTICES; 778]

prim 1 *adj* **prudish**, prissy, strait-laced, puritanical, moralistic. [➡EXCESSIVE SENSITIVITY; 512] *Opposite:* broad-minded. 2 *adj* **formal**, proper, dignified, starchy, stiff, correct, demure, snobbish. [➡LEVELS OF FORMALITY; 523] *Opposite:* informal. 3 *adj* **tidy**, orderly, precise, meticulous, fussy, fastidious, neat. [➡ORDER AND ORGANISATION; 207] *Opposite:* messy.

primacy 1 *n* **pre-eminence**, importance, predominance, dominance, prevalence, superiority, supremacy, priority. [➡IMPORTANCE AND SIGNIFICANCE; 193] 2 *n* **archbishopric**, primate, bishopric. [➡RELIGIOUS PEOPLE; 779]

prima facie 1 *adv* **at first glance**, on the face of it, apparently, ostensibly, seemingly, superficially. [➡FOREIGN WORDS AND PHRASES; 673] 2 *adj* **apparent**, clear, clear-cut, obvious, unambiguous. [➡CONCISE AND CLEAR; 203]

primal *adj* **primitive**, primeval, aboriginal, primordial, prehistoric, original, ancient. [➡PAST; 84] *Opposite:* new.

primarily *adv* **first and foremost**, above all, chiefly, mainly, principally, for the most part, mostly, largely, predominantly. [➡MAINLY AND PRIMARILY; 138]

primary 1 *adj* **first**, initial, top, leading, foremost. [➡BEFORE, FIRST, AND PRECEDING; 164] *Opposite:* last. 2 *adj* **main**, chief, most important, key, prime, principal, major, crucial. [➡MOST IMPORTANT AND MAIN; 194] *Opposite:* secondary. 3 *adj* **basic**, core, central, fundamental, essential, important. [➡FUNDAMENTAL; 196] *Opposite:* minor.

primary school *type of* **school**. [➡EDUCATIONAL INSTITUTIONS; 813]

primate *n* **archbishop**, bishop, prelate, cardinal. [➡RELIGIOUS PEOPLE; 779]

primate

◆ *types of primate*

ape, aye-aye, baboon, Barbary ape, bonnet monkey, capuchin, chimp, chimpanzee, colobus, gibbon, gorilla, human, lemur, macaque, mandrill, marmoset, monkey, orang-utan, proboscis monkey, rhesus monkey, spider monkey

prime 1 *adj* **top**, superior, superlative, best, premier, first-class, foremost, first-rate. [➡SUPERIORITY; 153] *Opposite:* inferior. 2 *adj* **major**, main, key, chief, leading, primary, principal, crucial. [➡MOST IMPORTANT AND MAIN; 194] 3 *n* **peak**, zenith, heyday, summit, high point, pinnacle, best part. [➡INTERMEDIATE STAGES; 55] *Opposite:* nadir. 4 *v* **prepare**, ready, get ready, make ready. [➡INSTRUCT AND TEACH; 610] 5 *v* **brief**, fill in, give somebody the lowdown (*informal*), instruct. [➡INSTRUCT AND TEACH; 610]

primed 1 *adj* **prepared**, ready, set, in position, in place, at the ready. [➡ABOUT TO HAPPEN; 33] 2 *adj* **aware**, well-informed, geared up, clued-up (*informal*), informed, in the picture, with it (*informal*), on the ball (*informal*), au courant, clued in (*US*). [➡KNOWLEDGE AND WISDOM; 559] *Opposite:* unprepared.

prime minister *n* **premier**, chief minister, head of cabinet, PM, head of government. [➡POLITICAL OFFICES AND POLITICIANS; 808]

prime of life *n* [➡ADULTHOOD; 918]

primer *n* **textbook**, reader, grammar, introduction. [➡MANUALS AND INSTRUCTIONS; 590]

primeval 1 *adj* **prehistoric**, original, ancient, archaic. [➡PAST; 84] *Opposite:* modern. 2 *adj* **primitive**, primordial, primal, basic, instinctive, intuitive. [➡PSYCHOLOGY AND THE MIND; 770] *Opposite:* considered.

primitive 1 *adj* **embryonic**, primeval, original, aboriginal, nascent. [➡PAST; 84] *Opposite:* developed. 2 *adj* **simple**, basic, uncomplicated, unsophisticated, crude, rough, coarse. [➡BAD MANNERS AND SOCIAL SKILLS; 522] *Opposite:* sophisticated. 3 *adj* **prehistoric**, ancient, primordial, primal, archaic, primeval, original. [➡OLD, OLD-FASHIONED; 168] *Opposite:* modern.

primitiveness 1 *n* **antiquity**, ancientness, primitive stage, early stage, primeval stage, early stage of development, earliness. [➡OLD, OLD-FASHIONED; 168] 2 *n* **crudeness**, basicness, simplicity, roughness, coarseness, unsophisticatedness, plainness. [➡ORDINARINESS; 245] *Opposite:* sophistication.

primness 1 *n* **prudishness**, narrowness, shockability, oversensitivity, strait-lacedness, politeness, prissiness. [➡EXCESSIVE SENSITIVITY; 512] *Opposite:* broad-mindedness. 2 *n* **formality**, properness, starchiness, propriety, stiffness, correctness, demureness. [➡LEVELS OF FORMALITY; 523] *Opposite:* informality. 3 *n* **neatness**, tidiness, orderliness, fastidiousness, meticulousness, fussiness. [➡DIFFICULT TO PLEASE; 516] *Opposite:* messiness.

primordial 1 *adj* **primeval**, prehistoric, primal, ancient, primitive, elemental, aboriginal. [➡PAST; 84] 2 *adj* **embryonic**, developing, early, nascent. [➡OLD, OLD-FASHIONED; 168]

primp *v* **fuss**, fuss over, groom, preen, adorn, admire, gussy up (*US informal*). [➡IMPROVE APPEARANCE; 380]

primrose *type of* **perennial flower**. [➡FLOWERS; 1032]

primrose path (*literary*) *n* [➡PLEASANT SITUATIONS; 74]

prince 1 *n* **leader**, leading figure, leading light, doyen, big shot (*informal*), big gun (*informal*). [➡IMPORTANT OR FAMOUS PEOPLE; 893] 2 *n* (*US informal*) **gentleman**, mensch (*informal*), trump (*informal*). [➡MALE PERSON; 934] *Opposite:* egotist. 3 *type of* **aristocrat**. [➡RULERS AND ARISTOCRACY; 823]

princely *adj* **generous**, handsome, large, significant, huge, sizable, substantial. *Opposite:* measly. (*informal*). [➡MANY, MUCH, LARGE AMOUNT; 117]

princess *type of* **aristocrat**. [➡RULERS AND ARISTOCRACY; 823]

principal 1 *adj* **main**, major, chief, most important, primary, prime, key, foremost, basic, fundamental. [➡MOST IMPORTANT AND MAIN; 194] 2 *n* **head of school**, head teacher, head, headmaster, headmistress, dean, provost, superintendent. [➡BOSSES AND MANAGEMENT; 965] 3 *n* **leader**, chief, doyenne, doyen, head, big shot (*informal*), big gun (*informal*), leading light. [➡IMPORTANT OR FAMOUS PEOPLE; 893] *Opposite:* follower.

principality *n* **princedom**, territory, country, domain. [➡COUNTRIES AND REGIONS; 1066]

principally *adv* **mainly**, chiefly, above all, first and foremost, primarily, predominantly, mostly, largely, essentially, for the most part. [➡MAINLY AND PRIMARILY; 138]

principle 1 *n* **rule**, theory, notion, tenet (*formal*), dogma, assumption, law. [➡WAYS OF DOING THINGS; 295] 2 *n* **code**, standard, belief, attitude, value, opinion, norm. [➡IDEA AND THOUGHT; 771] 3 *n* **source**, wellspring, origin, cause, basis, antecedent, determinant. [➡BEGINNING; 53]

principled *adj* **honourable**, righteous, upright, ethical, just, moral. [➡HONEST AND RELIABLE; 503] *Opposite:* unethical.

print 1 *n* **pattern**, design, motif. [➡ARTWORKS; 898] 2 *n* **reproduction**, copy, photograph, photocopy, facsimile, duplication, imitation, replica, version. [➡PHOTOGRAPHY AND PHOTOGRAPHIC EQUIPMENT; 1121] 3 *v* **turn out**, produce, make, issue, run off. [➡CREATE IMAGES; 357] 4 *v* **publish**, carry, make known, advertise, broadcast, disseminate, feature. [➡UTTER AND PRONOUNCE; 609] 5 *v* **stamp**, imprint, engrave, emboss. [➡CREATE IMAGES; 357]

printed *adj* **in print**, in black and white, on paper, published, reproduced. [➡WRITING; 584]

printed circuit *type of* **hardware**. [➡COMPUTERS AND COMPUTING; 1126]

printer 1 *type of* **hardware**. [➡COMPUTERS AND COMPUTING; 1126] 2 *type of* **photographic equipment**. [➡PHOTOGRAPHY AND PHOTOGRAPHIC EQUIPMENT; 1121]

printing 1 *n* **production**, reproduction, lithography, offset lithography, letterpress, photogravure, laser printing, silk-screening, block printing. [➡PRINTING; 601] 2 *n* **text**, lettering, words, writing, wording, information. [➡PRINTING; 601] 3 *n* **writing**, lettering, hand, capitals, upper case, lower case, block lettering, print. [➡WRITING; 584] *Opposite:* script. 4 *n* **edition**, print run, run, impression. [➡PRINTING; 601]

prior *adj* **previous**, preceding, past, erstwhile, former, earlier, aforementioned (*formal*). [➡BEFORE, FIRST, AND PRECEDING; 164] *Opposite:* subsequent.

prioritization *n* **ordering**, ranking, arranging, arrangement, listing, prioritizing. [➡ARRANGE AND CREATE ORDER; 358]

prioritize 1 *v* **order**, rank, arrange, list, line up, place in order. [➡ARRANGE AND CREATE ORDER; 358] 2 *v* **concentrate on**, give precedence to, select, highlight, rank first, spotlight, focus on. [➡MAKE DECISIONS AND CHOICES; 753]

priority *n* **importance**, precedence, urgency, import, significance, primacy. [➡MOST IMPORTANT THING; 198]

prior to *adv* **before**, previous to, earlier than, preceding, in advance of. [➡BEFORE, FIRST, AND PRECEDING; 164] *Opposite:* after.

priory *n* **monastery**, convent, religious community, abbey, ashram. [➡RELIGIOUS BUILDINGS; 1084]

prise 1 *v* **lever**, open, force, work loose, work free. [➡UNFASTEN AND UNDO; 410] 2 *v* **extract**, drag out, wheedle, coax, cajole, force, bully, squeeze. [➡OBTAIN POSSESSION BY PERSUASION; 458]

prise open *v* [➡UNFASTEN AND UNDO; 410]

prismatic *adj* [➡DESCRIBING COLOURS; 1225]

prison 1 *n* **jail**, top-security prison, secure unit, detention centre, young offenders' institution, slammer (*slang*), clink (*dated slang*), reformatory, penitentiary (*US*), pen (*US slang*), penal complex (*US*), pokey (*US slang*). [➡BUILDINGS FOR CONFINING PEOPLE; 1093] 2 *n* **incarceration** (*formal*), imprisonment, confinement, solitary confinement, detention, custody. [➡CAPTIVITY AND LOSS OF FREEDOM; 249]

prison cell *n* [➡BUILDINGS FOR CONFINING PEOPLE; 1093]

prison chaplain *n* [➡RELIGIOUS PEOPLE; 779]

prisoner 1 *n* **detainee**, inmate, convict, jailbird (*slang*), political prisoner, prisoner of war, prisoner of conscience, recidivist. [➡CAPTIVES AND PRISONERS; 250] 2 *n* **captive**, hostage, kidnap victim. [➡CAPTIVES AND PRISONERS; 250]

prissiness *n* **primness**, prudishness, properness, starchiness, stiffness, formality, strait-lacedness. [➡LEVELS OF FORMALITY; 523] *Opposite:* informality.

prissy *adj* **prim**, prudish, proper, starchy, stiff, formal, strait-laced. [➡LEVELS OF FORMALITY; 523] *Opposite:* informal.

pristine 1 *adj* **immaculate**, perfect, faultless, spotless, pure, unsullied. [➡CLEAN; 1232] *Opposite:* soiled. 2 *adj* **unspoiled**, untouched, primeval, original, virgin. [➡CLEAN; 1232] *Opposite:* developed.

privacy 1 *n* **solitude**, time alone, space, seclusion, isolation, retreat. [➡SOLITARINESS; 941] *Opposite:* company. 2 *n* **confidentiality**, discretion, secrecy, concealment. [➡SECRET AND UNKNOWN; 180] *Opposite:* disclosure.

private 1 *adj* **confidential**, secret, concealed, undisclosed, classified, clandestine, personal, hush-hush (*informal*). [➡SECRET AND UNKNOWN; 180] *Opposite:* public. 2 *adj* **secluded**, set apart, isolated, remote, sequestered (*formal*), cloistered. [➡DISTANCE; 161] 3 *adj* **privileged**, restricted, not in the public domain, exclusive, reserved. [➡BELONGING OR RELATING TO INDIVIDUALS; 944] *Opposite:* public. 4 *adj* **reserved**, secretive, tight-lipped, self-contained, unrevealing. [➡RETICENT AND UNFORTHCOMING; 632] *Opposite:* forthcoming.

private detective *n* **private investigator**, private eye (*informal*), PI (*US*), dick (*US dated slang*), gumshoe (*US informal*). [➡THE POLICE, ARREST, AND PRE-TRIAL PROCEEDINGS; 818]

private eye (*informal*) *n* **private detective**, private investigator, dick (*US dated slang*), gumshoe (*US informal*), PI (*US*). [➡THE POLICE, ARREST, AND PRE-TRIAL PROCEEDINGS; 818]

private investigator *n* **private detective**, private eye (*informal*), dick (*US dated slang*), gumshoe (*US informal*), PI (*US*). [➡THE POLICE, ARREST, AND PRE-TRIAL PROCEEDINGS; 818]

private joke *n* [➡JOKES AND TEASING; 675]

privately *adv* **confidentially**, in confidence, in private, secretly, in secret, behind closed doors, surreptitiously, on the sly. [➡SECRET AND UNKNOWN; 180] *Opposite:* publicly.

private residence *n* [➡ACCOMMODATION; 855]

private school *type of* **school**. [➡EDUCATIONAL INSTITUTIONS; 813]

privation *n* **hardship**, deprivation, adversity, poverty, need, misery. [➡POVERTY AND POOR; 892]

privatization *n* **sale**, transfer, denationalization. [➡BUSINESS ACTIVITIES AND PHENOMENA; 795]

privatize *v* **sell**, transfer, denationalize, go public. [➡BUSINESS ACTIVITIES AND PHENOMENA; 795] *Opposite:* nationalize.

privet *type of* **shrub or bush**. [➡BUSHES AND SHRUBS; 1027]

privilege 1 *n* **freedom**, licence, opportunity, dispensation, advantage, benefit, concession, right. [➡FREEDOM AND LIBERTY; 209] 2 *n* **honour**, source of pride, treat, pleasure, joy. [➡TREAT; 211] 3 *v* **favour**, show partiality towards, benefit. [➡LIKE, LOVE, VALUE AND ENJOY; 579]

privileged 1 *adj* **advantaged**, lucky, fortunate, honoured. [➡WEALTH AND WEALTHY; 891] *Opposite:* disadvantaged. 2 *adj* **confidential**, private, restricted, controlled, limited, top secret. [➡SECRET AND UNKNOWN; 180] *Opposite:* public.

privy 1 *adj* **in the know**, sharing in, aware of, party to, partaking of, in on. [➡KNOWLEDGE AND WISDOM; 559] 2 *n* (*informal*) **outside toilet**, outside lavatory, outside loo, latrine, garderobe, toilet, lavatory, outhouse (*US*). [➡ANCILLARY BUILDINGS; 1079]

prize 1 *n* **award**, reward, trophy, accolade, honour. [➡REWARDS AND AWARDS; 440] 2 *v* **treasure**, cherish, value, respect, esteem, appreciate, hold dear. [➡LIKE, LOVE, VALUE AND ENJOY; 579]

prized *adj* **award-winning**, high-quality, valued, respected, esteemed, appreciated, cherished. [➡POPULAR AND WANTED; 221]

prizewinning *adj* **award-winning**, victorious, successful, triumphant, winning, number-one, champion. [➡SUCCESSFUL AND PROMISING; 81] *Opposite:* unsuccessful.

pro 1 *prep* **for**, in favour of, all for, in support of. [➡EXPRESSING RESPECT AND APPROVAL; 638] *Opposite:* against. 2 *n* **professional**, authority, maven, expert, specialist, ace (*informal*). [➡TALENTED OR INTELLIGENT PERSON; 529] *Opposite:* amateur.

proactive *adj* **practical**, taking the initiative, hands-on, active, down to business, positive, upbeat (*informal*), preemptive. [➡ENERGY AND ENTHUSIASM; 497] *Opposite:* passive.

probability *n* **likelihood**, prospect, odds, possibility, chance. [➡POSSIBLE AND PROBABLE; 178]

probable *adj* **likely**, credible, possible, feasible, plausible, apparent. [➡POSSIBLE AND PROBABLE; 178] *Opposite:* unlikely.

probate *n* **certification**, validation, confirmation, validity. [➡THE LAW AND LEGAL AUTHORITY; 814]

probation *n* **trial**, test, audition, experimentation, tryout. [➡PREPARATORY EVENT; 57]

probationary *adj* **provisional**, trial, test, experimental, sample, introductory, exploratory. [➡EMPLOYMENT STATUS; 831] *Opposite:* permanent.

probe 1 *n* **investigation**, inquiry, review, examination, analysis, postmortem. [➡EXAMINE AND ASSESS; 754] 2 *v* **investigate**, research, delve, inquire, look into, explore. [➡EXAMINE AND ASSESS; 754] 3 *type of* **medical instrument**. [➡HAND TOOLS; 1118]

probing *adj* **searching**, penetrating, analytical, inquisitive, curious, investigative, exploratory, examining, interested, pointed, thorough, researching, incisive, inquiring. [➡EXAMINE AND ASSESS; 754] *Opposite:* cursory.

probity (*formal*) *n* **correctness**, scrupulousness, rectitude, righteousness, integrity, justice, morality, honour. [➡MORALLY GOOD; 775] *Opposite:* immorality.

problem 1 *n* **difficulty**, setback, hitch, drawback, glitch, hindrance, catch (*informal*), obstruction, snag, obstacle. [➡PROBLEM; 257] 2 *n* **puzzle**, question, conundrum, challenge, poser, mystery, enigma, riddle. [➡SECRETS AND MYSTERIES; 181] 3 *adj* **problematic**, tricky, unruly, badly-behaved, delinquent, difficult. [➡DIFFICULTY AND COMPLEXITY; 243] *Opposite:* easy.

Compare and Contrast: *problem, mystery, puzzle, riddle, conundrum, enigma*

CORE MEANING: SOMETHING DIFFICULT TO SOLVE OR UNDERSTAND

problem a difficult situation, matter, or person; ***mystery*** an event or situation that has never been fully explained or understood, or a person who is puzzling or mysterious; ***puzzle*** a problem whose solution requires ingenuity, or a situation that it is difficult to resolve, or somebody whose behaviour or motives are difficult to understand; ***riddle*** a perplexing or confusing issue; ***conundrum*** something puzzling, confusing, or mysterious; ***enigma*** somebody or something that is mysterious and hard to understand.

problematic *adj* **tricky**, challenging, sticky, awkward, knotty, problematical, difficult. [➡DIFFICULTY AND COMPLEXITY; 243] *Opposite:* easy.

problematical *adj* **uncertain**, debatable, questionable, doubtful, dubious, unpredictable. [➡UNCERTAIN; 176] *Opposite:* certain.

problematically 1 *adv* **not without difficulty**, awkwardly, trickily, challengingly, ticklishly, knottily. [➡DIFFICULTY AND COMPLEXITY; 243] *Opposite:* clearly. 2 *adv* (*US*) **uncertainly**, debatably, questionably, in question, unpredictably. [➡UNCERTAIN; 176] *Opposite:* definitely.

pro bono *adj* [➡FOREIGN WORDS AND PHRASES; 673]

proboscis *n* **nose**, snout, feeler, trunk, antenna. [➡PARTS OF AN INSECT; 1019]

proboscis monkey *type of* **primate**. [➡PRIMATE; 988]

procedural *adj* **technical**, practical, bureaucratic, routine, ritual, ceremonial. [➡ORDER AND ORGANISATION; 207]

procedure *n* **process**, modus operandi, way, technique, method, course of action, system, formula, route, practice. [➡WAYS OF DOING THINGS; 295]

proceed *v* **go on**, carry on, continue, ensue, advance, keep, keep on, progress. [➡CONTINUE AN ACTION; 263] *Opposite:* recede.

proceedings 1 *n* **events**, actions, measures, trial, procedures, dealings. [➡EVENTS AND OCCURRENCES; 35] 2 *n* **minutes**, records, account, report, chronicle. [➡RECORDS; 586]

proceeds *n* **profits**, income, earnings, takings, gate, box office. [➡INCOME; 461]

process 1 *n* **procedure**, course, activity, development, progression, method, route, course of action, manner, means. [➡WAYS OF DOING THINGS; 295] 2 *v* **deal with**, handle, treat, sort out, administer, see to, manage. [➡CARRY OUT AN ACTION; 270]

processed *adj* [➡NOT IN A NATURAL STATE; 1214]

procession 1 *n* **march**, parade, pageant, demonstration, demo (*informal*), march past, convoy, motorcade. [➡MEETINGS AND ASSEMBLIES; 43] 2 *n* **sequence**, succession, string, series, line, chain, row. [➡COLLECTIONS AND MIXTURES OF THINGS; 1243]

processional *adj* **ceremonial**, ritual, commemorative, celebratory, sacred, formal, regimented. [➡CEREMONIES AND ANNIVERSARIES; 38]

processor *type of* **hardware**. [➡COMPUTERS AND COMPUTING; 1126]

proclaim *v* **state publicly**, announce, declare, state, make known, decree, assert, pronounce, broadcast. [➡INFORM AND ANNOUNCE; 612]

proclamation *n* **public statement**, announcement, declaration, decree, assertion, edict. [➡INFORM AND ANNOUNCE; 612]

proclivity *n* **liking**, appetite, taste, penchant, inclination, tendency, bent. [➡APPRECIATION AND GRATITUDE; 536]

procrastinate *v* **put off**, delay, postpone, adjourn, dally, drag your feet, hang fire, defer, dawdle, take a raincheck (*US informal*). [➡SHIRK AND DELAY; 274]

procrastination *n* **deferment**, putting off, postponement, stalling, delay, adjournment. [➡DELAY ACTION OR OCCURRENCE; 279] *Opposite:* action.

procreate *v* [➡REPRODUCTION AND HEREDITY; 726]

procreation *n* [➡REPRODUCTION AND HEREDITY; 726]

procreative *adj* [➡REPRODUCTION AND HEREDITY; 726]

procurable *adj* [➡PRESENT AND AVAILABLE; 11]

procure *v* **obtain**, acquire, secure, get hold of, get, land, buy, gain, attain, pick up. [➡GET; 421]

See Compare and Contrast at **get**.

procurement 1 *n* **gaining**, obtaining, finding, locating, tracking down, winning, earning, attaining. [➡FIND; 464] *Opposite:* giving up. 2 *n* **buying**, purchasing, ordering, obtaining. [➡BUSINESS ACTIVITIES AND PHENOMENA; 795] *Opposite:* sale.

procurer *n* **buyer**, purchaser, customer, client, consumer, punter (*informal*). [➡PURCHASER; 425]

prod 1 *v* **elbow**, nudge, dig, jab, push, poke. [➡CONTACT: TOUCH; 413] 2 *v* **urge**, stimulate, stir, prompt, provoke, egg on. [➡CAUSE OR COMPEL TO ACT; 272] 3 *n* **nudge**, elbow, dig, jab, push, poke. [➡CONTACT: TOUCH; 413]

prodigal *adj* **wasteful**, reckless, dissolute, profligate, uncontrolled, extravagant. [➡PLEASURE-SEEKING AND EXCESS; 885] *Opposite:* cautious.

prodigality *n* [➡PLEASURE-SEEKING AND EXCESS; 885]

prodigious 1 *adj* **huge**, vast, copious, giant, gigantic, immense, enormous, profuse, massive. [➡LARGE; 1192] *Opposite:* small. 2 *adj* **abnormal**, extraordinary, phenomenal, unusual, exceptional, remarkable, wonderful, amazing, impressive. [➡EXTRAORDINARY: AMAZING; 205] *Opposite:* average.

prodigiously 1 *adv* **enormously**, hugely, massively (*informal*), immensely, tremendously, colossally, inordinately, vastly, stupendously. [➡TO A GREAT EXTENT; 130] *Opposite:* minutely. 2 *adv* **amazingly**, exceptionally, remarkably, marvellously, fabulously, fantastically, phenomenally, strikingly. [➡EXTRAORDINARY: AMAZING; 205] *Opposite:* ordinarily.

prodigiousness 1 *n* **hugeness**, enormousness, vastness, massiveness, immenseness, immensity, tremendousness. [➡LARGE; 1192] *Opposite:* smallness. 2 *n* **stupendousness**, remarkableness, amazingness, exceptional nature, fabulousness, marvellousness. [➡EXTRAORDINARY: AMAZING; 205] *Opposite:* ordinariness.

prodigy *n* **genius**, sensation, phenomenon, wonder, star, boy wonder, wunderkind. [➡TALENTED OR INTELLIGENT PERSON; 529]

produce 1 *v* **create**, make, manufacture, construct, fabricate, bring into being, turn out, generate. [➡CREATION; 347] 2 *v* **give**, give off, yield, churn out, be the source of, engender, emit, supply, deliver. [➡EMIT AND EMANATE; 362] 3 *n* **crop**, foodstuffs, harvest, products, goods, food, yield. [➡FOOD; 1166]

See Compare and Contrast at **make**.

producer *n* **creator**, manufacturer, maker, fabricator. [➡DESIGNERS, CREATORS AND INSTIGATORS; 348]

product 1 *n* **manufactured article**, creation, produce, item for consumption, invention, merchandise, artefact. [➡PHYSICAL OBJECTS; 1242] 2 *n* **result**, outcome, upshot, consequence, effect. [➡RESULTS AND OUTCOMES; 83]

production *n* **manufacture**, making, construction, creation, invention, fabrication, assembly. [➡CREATION; 347]

productive 1 *adj* **creative**, prolific, fecund, industrious, fruitful, dynamic. [➡ECONOMICAL AND RESOURCEFUL; 208] *Opposite:* destructive. 2 *adj* **useful**, helpful, constructive, beneficial, valuable, practical, positive. [➡USEFULNESS; 200] *Opposite:* negative.

productiveness *n* **usefulness**, constructiveness, use, utility, fruitfulness, productivity. [➡USEFULNESS; 200]

productivity *n* **output**, efficiency, yield, production, throughput. [➡BUSINESS PRODUCTS; 796]

profanation (*formal*) *n* [➡MORALLY BAD; 776]

profane *adj* **blasphemous**, irreverent, irreligious, disrespectful, wicked, sacrilegious. [➡MORALLY BAD; 776] *Opposite:* sacred.

profanely (*formal*) *adv* [➡MORALLY BAD; 776]

profanity *n* **blasphemy**, oath, vulgarity, curse, swear-word, expletive, sacrilege. [➡INSULTS, ABUSE, AND SWEARING; 659]

profess *v* **admit**, own (*formal*), own up, confess, acknowledge, agree, allow (*formal*), recognize. [➡ADMIT AND CONFESS; 616]

professed 1 *adj* **declared**, avowed (*formal*), acknowledged, open, stated, blatant. [➡KNOWN AND FAMOUS; 182] *Opposite:* unspoken. 2 *adj* **supposed**, alleged, so-called, ostensible, seeming, apparent, ersatz (*disapproving*), soi-disant (*literary*). [➡FALSE AND UNREAL; 174] *Opposite:* proven.

professedly *adv* **supposedly**, allegedly, ostensibly, seemingly, apparently. [➡FALSE AND UNREAL; 174] *Opposite:* in fact.

profession *n* **job**, work, occupation, line of work, career, vocation, business, living. [➡PROFESSIONS; 845]

professional 1 *adj* **specialized**, qualified, proficient, skilled, trained, practised, certified, licensed, expert, career. [➡EMPLOYMENT STATUS; 831] *Opposite:* amateur. 2 *n* **specialist**, expert, authority, pro, maven. [➡TALENTED OR INTELLIGENT PERSON; 529] *Opposite:* amateur.

professionalism *n* **skill**, competence, expertise, know-how (*informal*), proficiency, efficiency, experience, effectiveness, ability. [➡SKILLS, TALENTS, AND ABILITIES; 527] *Opposite:* incompetence.

professionally 1 *adv* **for work**, for money, for a living, as a job, jobwise, workwise. [➡EMPLOYMENT STATUS; 831] *Opposite:* casually. 2 *adv* **skilfully**, expertly, competently, proficiently, efficiently, discreetly, with the minimum of fuss, ably. [➡TALENTED AND SKILFUL; 528] *Opposite:* ineptly.

professor *n* **university teacher**, lecturer, fellow, don, tutor, dean, instructor (*US*). [➡EDUCATORS; 840]

professorial *adj* **academic**, pedagogical, intellectual, educational, senior. [➡EDUCATION; 838]

proffer *v* **offer**, hold out, extend, tender, volunteer, submit, give. [➡PROFFER AND HAND OVER; 432] *Opposite:* withdraw.

proficiency *n* **skill**, ability, talent, expertise, aptitude, knack, adeptness, competence, know-how (*informal*). [➡SKILLS, TALENTS, AND ABILITIES; 527] *Opposite:* incompetence.

proficient *adj* **capable**, talented, expert, gifted, adroit, skilled, dexterous, competent, adept, skilful, practised. [➡TALENTED AND SKILFUL; 528] *Opposite:* incompetent.

profile 1 *n* **outline**, side view, shape, silhouette, contour, mug shot. [➡SHAPE; 1215] 2 *n* **summary**, sketch, outline, report, précis, rundown, synopsis. [➡SUMMARIES, OUTLINES, AND EXCERPTS; 589] 3 *v* **summarize**, sketch, outline, report, sum up, describe. [➡NAME AND DESCRIBE; 666]

profit 1 *n* **income**, earnings, revenue, proceeds, turnover, return, yield, takings. [➡INCOME; 461] *Opposite:* loss. 2 *n* **advantage**, gain, benefit, use, reward, good. [➡REWARDS AND AWARDS; 440] *Opposite:* loss. 3 *v* **earn**, bring in, make, make money on, turn a profit. [➡GET MONEY OR REWARD; 422] *Opposite:* lose. 4 *v* **benefit**, gain, be of advantage to, help, aid, serve. [➡IMPROVE SOMETHING; 375]

profitability 1 *n* **success**, effectiveness, productivity, viability, cost-effectiveness, lucrativeness. [➡ECONOMICAL AND RESOURCEFUL; 208] *Opposite:* cost. 2 *n* **usefulness**, worth, fruitfulness, use, value, point. [➡USEFULNESS; 200] *Opposite:* uselessness.

profitable 1 *adj* **lucrative**, moneymaking, gainful, money-spinning (*informal*), commercial, cost-effective. [➡ECONOMICAL AND RESOURCEFUL; 208] *Opposite:* unprofitable. 2 *adj* **advantageous**, beneficial, rewarding, useful, valuable, worthwhile, helpful. [➡USEFULNESS; 200] *Opposite:* unhelpful.

profit and loss *n* [➡ACCOUNTING, BANKING, AND BUDGETING; 799]

profiteer 1 *v* **exploit**, take advantage of, make use of, racketeer, abuse. [➡MAKE GOOD USE OF SOMETHING; 474] 2 *n* **swindler**, racketeer, con man (*informal*), scammer (*slang*), crook (*informal*), embezzler. [➡PEOPLE WHO DECEIVE; 662]

profitmaking *adj* **profitable**, viable, moneymaking, economic, cost-effective, lucrative, commercial, going, prosperous. [➡ECONOMICAL AND RESOURCEFUL; 208] *Opposite:* draining.

profit margin *n* [➡ACCOUNTING, BANKING, AND BUDGETING; 799]

profligacy *n* **wastefulness**, recklessness, licentiousness (*formal*), dissolution, decadence, extravagance. [➡PLEASURE-SEEKING AND EXCESS; 885] *Opposite:* parsimony.

profligate 1 *adj* **wasteful**, reckless, spendthrift, squandering, decadent, extravagant. [➡WASTEFUL AND UNECONOMICAL; 247] *Opposite:* parsimonious. 2 *adj* **dissolute**, licentious (*formal*), immoral, wicked, shameless. [➡MORALLY BAD; 776]

profligately *adv* **wastefully**, recklessly, licentiously (*formal*), dissolutely, decadently, extravagantly. [➡WASTEFUL AND UNECONOMICAL; 247] *Opposite:* parsimoniously.

pro forma *n* [➡FOREIGN WORDS AND PHRASES; 673]

profound 1 *adj* **deep**, thoughtful, reflective, philosophical, weighty, insightful. [➡PENSIVENESS AND INTEREST; 539] *Opposite:* superficial. 2 *adj* **intense**, great, overpowering, overwhelming, extreme, acute, sincere. [➡STRENGTH; 202] *Opposite:* shallow.

profoundly *adv* **intensely**, greatly, overpoweringly, overwhelmingly, extremely, strongly, very much, severely. [➡TO A GREAT EXTENT; 130] *Opposite:* superficially.

profoundness 1 *n* **degree**, extent, intensity, strength, depth, completeness, acuteness, profundity. [➡STRENGTH; 202] 2 *n* **perceptiveness**, wisdom, acuity, insight, depth, weight, perspicacity, profundity. [➡THE NATURE OF IDEAS; 772] **3** *n* **depth**, immensity, cavernousness, fathomlessness, extent, reach, profundity. [➡DEPTH: DEEP; 1200]

profundity 1 *n* **understanding**, perceptiveness, wisdom, acuity, perspicacity, profoundness, insight, insightfulness, depth. [➡THE NATURE OF IDEAS; 772] *Opposite:* superficiality. **2** *n* **complexity**, abstruseness, difficulty, depth, intricacy. [➡DIFFICULTY AND COMPLEXITY; 243] *Opposite:* simplicity. **3** *n* **intensity**, greatness, strength, seriousness, enormity, extensiveness, extent. [➡STRENGTH; 202] *Opposite:* mildness. **4** *n* **depth**, immensity, cavernousness, fathomlessness, extent, reach. [➡DEPTH: DEEP; 1200]

profuse *adj* **plentiful**, copious, abundant, teeming, generous, bountiful (*literary*), prolific. [➡MANY, MUCH, LARGE AMOUNT; 117] *Opposite:* scanty.

profusion *n* **abundance**, large amount, excess, cornucopia, plethora, glut, surplus, wealth. [➡MANY, MUCH, LARGE AMOUNT; 117] *Opposite:* dearth.

progenitor 1 *n* **ancestor**, forerunner, forebear, antecedent, predecessor, precursor. [➡OLDER GENERATION RELATIVES; 959] *Opposite:* descendant. **2** *n* **antecedent**, originator, forerunner, prototype, predecessor, precursor. [➡BEGINNING; 53] *Opposite:* copy.

progeny *n* **offspring**, children, young, descendants, posterity (*formal*), issue, scions. [➡YOUNGER GENERATION RELATIVES; 958]

prognosis *n* **forecast**, prediction, projection, scenario, diagnosis, prospects. [➡PREDICT AND ANTICIPATE; 751]

prognosticate 1 *v* **predict**, divine, foresee, foretell, forecast, prophesy, soothsay, portend. [➡PREDICT AND ANTICIPATE; 751] *Opposite:* recall. **2** *v* **indicate**, suggest, point to, augur, betoken (*literary*), signify, herald, portend, presage. [➡MEAN SOMETHING; 61] *Opposite:* prove.

prognostication 1 *n* **prediction**, prognosis, projection, divination, foreseeing, foretelling, forecast, prophecy, soothsaying. [➡PREDICT AND ANTICIPATE; 751] *Opposite:* recollection. **2** *n* **indication**, suggestion, pointer, token, portent, foretoken (*literary*), augury. [➡INDICATIONS, SIGNS, AND WARNINGS; 68] *Opposite:* proof.

prognosticator *n* **predictor**, diviner, prophet, seer, clairvoyant, psychic, forecaster, haruspex, soothsayer. [➡PEOPLE WITH SUPERNATURAL POWERS; 789]

program 1 *n* **setting**, option, cycle, mode, instruction, set of instructions. [➡COMPUTERS AND COMPUTING; 1126] **2** *v* **write instructions**, load instructions, write software, load software, set, adjust, calibrate. [➡COMPUTERS AND COMPUTING; 1126]

programme 1 *n* **plan**, agenda, schedule, timetable, list, curriculum, syllabus, rubric, calendar, docket. [➡LISTS AND SCHEDULES; 588] **2** *n* **broadcast**, production, show, transmission, game show, talk show, quiz show, presentation. [➡TELEVISION AND RADIO; 607] **3** *n* **brochure**, booklet, synopsis, listing, timetable, itinerary, pamphlet. [➡LISTS AND SCHEDULES; 588] **4** *n* **system**, procedure, course, series, setup. [➡WAYS OF DOING THINGS; 295] **5** *v* **schedule**, arrange, lay on, book, plan, line up, design, map out. [➡ARRANGE AND CREATE ORDER; 358] **6** *v* **train**, condition, compel, brainwash, hypnotize, manipulate, order. [➡CAUSE TO HAPPEN; 31]

programmed *adj* **automatic**, involuntary, planned, automated, set, preset. [➡INTENTIONAL AND DELIBERATE; 280] *Opposite:* spontaneous.

programmer *n* **computer operator**, computer programmer, computer scientist, program writer, systems analyst, IT worker. [➡COMPUTERS AND COMPUTING; 1126]

programming *n* **software design**, program design, program writing, user interface design, software development. [➡COMPUTERS AND COMPUTING; 1126]

progress 1 *n* **development**, improvement, advancement, evolution, growth, headway, steps forward, movement, evolvement. [➡SUCCESS; 82] *Opposite:* regression. **2** *v* **improve**, develop, advance, evolve, increase, grow, move on, get better, make progress, make headway. [➡GET BETTER; 376] *Opposite:* regress. **3** *v* **move forward**, advance, proceed, continue, make progress, move on, march, forge ahead. [➡PROCEED AND GO; 306] *Opposite:* retreat.

progression 1 *n* **development**, evolution, movement, advance, advancement, progress, headway. [➡PROGRESS AND ADVANCEMENT; 214] *Opposite:* regression. **2** *n* **series**, sequence, succession, string, chain, cycle, sequel, train. [➡CHAIN OF EVENTS; 163]

progressive 1 *adj* **gradual**, ongoing, increasing, continuing, developing, advancing, step-by-step, piecemeal. [➡HAPPENING AND IN PROGRESS; 32] *Opposite:* acute. **2** *adj* **liberal**, reformist, open-minded, broad-minded, radical, enlightened, advanced, tolerant. [➡POSITIVE INTELLECTUAL CHARACTERISTICS; 525] *Opposite:* reactionary.

progressively *adv* **increasingly**, more and more, with time, gradually, little by little, ever more. [➡HAPPENING AND IN PROGRESS; 32] *Opposite:* suddenly.

progressiveness *n* **liberalism**, reformism, progressivism, modernism, tolerance, open-mindedness, permissiveness, broad-mindedness, enlightenment, radicalism. [➡POSITIVE INTELLECTUAL CHARACTERISTICS; 525]

progressivism *n* **liberalism**, reformism, modernism, radicalism, leftism. [➡PHILOSOPHIES AND BELIEFS; 781]

prohibit *v* **forbid**, ban, proscribe, disallow, veto, outlaw, bar, exclude, rule out, interdict. [➡REFUSE PERMISSION AND NOT ALLOW; 671] *Opposite:* permit.

prohibited *adj* **forbidden**, banned, verboten, illegal, proscribed, taboo, outlawed, illicit, barred. [➡ILLEGAL; 816] *Opposite:* permitted.

prohibition *n* **ban**, exclusion, proscription (*formal*), embargo, prevention, ruling out, veto, injunction, bar. [➡THE LAW AND LEGAL AUTHORITY; 814] *Opposite:* permission.

prohibitive *adj* **high-priced**, excessive, exorbitant, extortionate, unaffordable, unreasonable, expensive. [➡EXPENSIVE AND OVERPRICED; 248] *Opposite:* affordable.

project 1 *n* **scheme**, assignment, task, undertaking, job, plan, blueprint, design, strategy. [➡ACTIONS OR UNDERTAKINGS; 260] **2** *v* **forecast**, predict, estimate, foresee, foretell, envisage, envision. [➡PREDICT AND ANTICIPATE; 751] **3** *v* **stick out**, jut out, protrude, bulge, distend. [➡ARRIVE; 12] **4** *v* **throw**, launch, shoot, propel, cast, impel, send off, fling, hurl, pitch. [➡THROW SOMETHING; 335] **5** *v* **plan**, envisage, propose, intend, anticipate, expect, plan ahead. [➡PREDICT AND ANTICIPATE; 751]

projected *adj* **estimated**, planned, proposed, outlined, expected, anticipated, future. [➡ABOUT TO HAPPEN; 33] *Opposite:* actual.

projectile [➡PROJECTILES; 1158]

projectile

◆ *types of projectile*
arrow, arrowhead, assegai, bolt, boomerang, brickbat, buckshot, bullet, cannonball, dart, dumdum bullet, grenade, harpoon, javelin, lance, pellet, plastic bullet, rubber bullet, shell, shot, slug, spear

projection **1** *n* **forecast**, prediction, plan, prognosis, estimate, prognostication. [➡PREDICT AND ANTICIPATE; 751] *Opposite:* analysis. **2** *n* **outcrop**, protuberance, bulge, protrusion, ledge, shelf, ridge, jut, overhang. [➡EXTREMITIES OF PHYSICAL OBJECTS; 1249]

projector *type of* **photographic equipment**. [➡PHOTOGRAPHY AND PHOTOGRAPHIC EQUIPMENT; 1121]

proletarian *adj* **popular**, grassroots, people's, working-class, blue-collar, plebeian, democratic. [➡BELONGING OR RELATING TO PEOPLE; 943] *Opposite:* aristocratic.

proletariat *n* **hoi polloi**, grassroots, working class, workers, masses, blue-collars, public. [➡CLASS STATUS; 889] *Opposite:* gentry.

proliferate **1** *v* **multiply**, thrive, flourish, boom, increase, bloom, burgeon (*literary*), grow, mushroom. [➡PROSPER AND ABOUND; 16] *Opposite:* dwindle. **2** *v* **reproduce**, propagate, multiply, breed, procreate, beget, replicate. [➡REPRODUCTION AND HEREDITY; 726] *Opposite:* die out.

proliferation *n* **propagation**, explosion, spread, multiplying, production, creation, increase, rise. [➡MORE AND EXCESS; 122]

prolific **1** *adj* **productive**, creative, fertile, inexhaustible, high-volume, fruitful. [➡SUCCESSFUL AND PROMISING; 81] *Opposite:* unproductive. **2** *adj* (*formal*) **abundant**, abounding, plentiful, copious, profuse, teeming, fruitful, rich, bountiful (*literary*). [➡MANY, MUCH, LARGE AMOUNT; 117] *Opposite:* scarce.

prolix *adj* **wordy**, verbose, long-winded, flowery, protracted, rambling, diffuse. [➡INARTICULATE, RAMBLING, AND AWKWARD; 634] *Opposite:* concise.

See Compare and Contrast at **wordy**.

prolixity *n* [➡MEANINGLESS SPEECH OR WRITING; 677]

prologue *n* **introduction**, preface, foreword, preamble, opening, prelude. [➡BEGINNING; 53] *Opposite:* epilogue.

prolong *v* **extend**, lengthen, protract, draw out, spin out, delay, stretch, elongate, persist. [➡CAUSE TO CONTINUE; 268] *Opposite:* curtail.

prolongation *n* **continuation**, perpetuation, drawing out, protraction, extension, maintenance, elongation. [➡PERMANENCE: WITHOUT END; 94] *Opposite:* curtailment.

prolonged *adj* **lengthy**, protracted, long, continued, extended, sustained, elongated, persistent. [➡PERMANENCE: WITHOUT END; 94] *Opposite:* curtailed.

prom **1** *n* **promenade**, seafront, walkway, path, esplanade, boardwalk. [➡PATHWAYS; 1109] **2** *n* (*US*) **dance**, college dance, formal dance, high-school dance, ball. [➡PARTIES, DANCES, AND CELEBRATIONS; 37]

promenade **1** *n* **walkway**, sea front, path, boardwalk, esplanade, prom. [➡PATHWAYS; 1109] **2** *n* (*formal*) **stroll**, walk, saunter, amble, constitutional. [➡PROCEED AND GO; 306] **3** *v* (*formal*) **walk**, stroll, amble, saunter, swan (*informal*), wander, roam, drift, mosey (*informal*). [➡PROCEED AND GO; 306] **4** *type of* **minor road**. [➡ROADS; 1105]

prominence **1** *n* **fame**, importance, distinction, celebrity, eminence, reputation, standing, status, notoriety. [➡KNOWN AND FAMOUS; 182] *Opposite:* obscurity. **2** *n* **bump**, lump, bulge, swelling, protrusion, protuberance, projection. [➡ROUNDED SHAPE; 1217] *Opposite:* crater.

prominent **1** *adj* **protuberant**, protruding, projecting, bulbous, bulging. [➡ROUNDED SHAPE; 1217] *Opposite:* flat. **2** *adj* **noticeable**, conspicuous, obvious, blatant, flagrant, pronounced, glaring. [➡PERCEPTIBLE; 25] *Opposite:* subtle. **3** *adj* **famous**, well-known, important, high-up (*informal*), high-flying, top, major, outstanding, leading, foremost, notorious, renowned. [➡KNOWN AND FAMOUS; 182] *Opposite:* obscure.

prominently *adv* **conspicuously**, obviously, blatantly, flagrantly, glaringly. [➡PERCEPTIBLE; 25] *Opposite:* subtly.

promiscuous (*disapproving*) *adj* **immoral**, loose, licentious (*formal*), wanton, uninhibited, unrestrained, philandering (*disapproving*). [➡MORALLY BAD; 776]

promise **1** *v* **assure**, swear, vow, undertake, guarantee, give your word, pledge, confirm, engage, ensure. [➡PROMISE AND ASSURE; 685] **2** *v* **suggest**, augur, bode, look like, show all the signs, indicate, imply, insinuate, hint at, forebode, foreshadow. [➡MEAN SOMETHING; 61] **3** *n* **assurance**, undertaking, guarantee, agreement, contract, word, oath, pledge, vow. [➡PROMISE AND ASSURE; 685] **4** *n* **potential**, possibilities, aptitude, ability, capacity, talent. [➡SKILLS, TALENTS, AND ABILITIES; 527]

promised land *n* [➡RELIGIOUS CONCEPTS; 777]

promising **1** *adj* **talented**, gifted, capable, able. [➡TALENTED AND SKILFUL; 528] **2** *adj* **auspicious**, hopeful, likely, encouraging, favourable. [➡SUCCESSFUL AND PROMISING; 81] *Opposite:* disappointing.

promisingly *adv* **favourably**, auspiciously, hopefully, well, nicely, encouragingly. [➡SUCCESSFUL AND PROMISING; 81] *Opposite:* disappointingly.

promo (*informal*) *n* **promotion**, advertisement, publicity stunt, publicity, profile-raiser, photo-shoot, hook (*informal*). [➡ADVERTISING AND PUBLICITY; 605]

promontory *n* **cape**, headland, peninsula, outcrop, point, cliff. [➡THE SEAS, OCEANS, AND SHORES; 1041]

promote **1** *v* **advance**, upgrade, further, elevate, put forward, raise. [➡CONFER STATUS; 459] *Opposite:* demote. **2** *v* **endorse**, encourage, help, support, stimulate, sponsor, campaign for, uphold, prop up, foster. [➡APPROVE AND CONFIRM; 647] *Opposite:* suppress. **3** *v* **advertise**, publicize, make known, market, plug (*informal*), push, disseminate, advocate, boost, propagandize. [➡ADVERTISING AND PUBLICITY; 605] *Opposite:* defame. **4** *v* **further**, progress, move forward, stage, put on, organize, arrange. [➡CAUSE TO HAPPEN; 31] *Opposite:* prevent.

promoter *n* **organizer**, agent, sponsor, advocate, supporter, publicist, marketer, developer, backer, PR man, PR woman. [➡BUSINESS PEOPLE; 794]

promotion **1** *n* **upgrade**, preferment (*formal*), advancement, elevation, rise. [➡CONFER STATUS; 459] *Opposite:* demotion. **2** *n* **advertising**, marketing, publicity, campaign, offer, plug (*informal*). [➡ADVERTISING AND PUBLICITY; 605] *Opposite:* defamation. **3** *n* **endorsement**, encouragement, help, support, stimulation, sponsorship, backup, backing. [➡APPROVE AND CONFIRM; 647]

promotional *adj* **publicity**, advertising, public relations, PR, positive, profile-raising, persuasive, marketing. [➡ADVERTISING AND PUBLICITY; 605] *Opposite:* defamatory.

prompt **1** *adj* **quick**, rapid, swift, without delay, speedy, hasty, early, ready, apt. [➡HAPPENING QUICKLY; 104] *Opposite:* slow. **2** *adj* **punctual**, on time, at the appointed time, without delay, timely. [➡PROMPTNESS: ON TIME; 99] *Opposite:* late. **3** *v* **stimulate**, encourage, provoke, incite, urge, inspire, pressurize, pressure, motivate, exhort, prod. [➡CAUSE OR COMPEL TO ACT; 272] *Opposite:* prevent. **4** *v* **bring about**, induce, effect (*formal*), occasion, set off, trigger, start off, prevail, persuade. [➡CAUSE TO HAPPEN; 31] *Opposite:* prevent. **5** *n* **stimulus**, prod, goad, reminder, aide-mémoire (*formal*), heads-up (*US*). [➡BEGINNING; 53]

prompting *n* **encouragement**, warning, pressure, motivation, instigation. [➡BEGINNING; 53]

promptness **1** *n* **speed**, rapidity, swiftness, alacrity, velocity, pace, haste, celerity (*formal*). [➡SPEED; 102] *Opposite:* slowness. **2** *n* **punctuality**, timeliness, timekeeping. [➡PROMPTNESS: ON TIME; 99] *Opposite:* tardiness.

promulgate (*formal*) **1** *v* **declare**, proclaim, decree, announce, pronounce, endorse, state. [➡INFORM AND ANNOUNCE; 612] *Opposite:* withdraw. **2** *v* **publicize**, spread, disseminate, circulate, transmit, broadcast, propagate. [➡INFORM AND ANNOUNCE; 612] *Opposite:* suppress.

promulgation (*formal*) **1** *n* **declaration**, proclamation, decree, announcement, pronouncement, statement, endorsement. [➡INFORM AND ANNOUNCE; 612] *Opposite:* withdrawal. **2** *n* **publicizing**, spreading, dissemination, circulation, broadcasting, transmission, propagation. [➡INFORM AND ANNOUNCE; 612] *Opposite:* suppression.

prone **1** *adj* **disposed to**, predisposed to, susceptible to, inclined to, likely to, liable to. [➡THE WILL AND WILLINGNESS; 564] **2** *adj* **flat**, horizontal, lying, flat out, face down, motionless. [➡ORIENTATION AND ALIGNMENT; 1222] *Opposite:* upright.

prong *n* **point**, spike, spine, tine. [➡EXTREMITIES OF PHYSICAL OBJECTS; 1249]

pronoun *type of* **word class**. [➡ASPECTS OF LANGUAGE; 683]

pronounce **1** *v* **say**, speak, utter, articulate, voice, enunciate, phonate. [➡UTTER AND PRONOUNCE; 609] **2** *v* **state**, assert, declare, announce, decree, lay down the law, proclaim, maintain, pontificate. [➡INFORM AND ANNOUNCE; 612]

pronounced *adj* **marked**, noticeable, distinct, definite, obvious, prominent, evident, unmistakable, manifest. [➡PERCEPTIBLE; 25] *Opposite:* subtle.

pronouncement *n* **statement**, assertion, declaration, announcement, decree, verdict, proclamation. [➡INFORM AND ANNOUNCE; 612]

pronto (*informal*) *adv* **straightaway**, right away, quick, quickly, at once, promptly, immediately, right now, this instant, rapidly, a.s.a.p., at the double. [➡HAPPENING QUICKLY; 104] *Opposite:* sluggishly.

pronunciation *n* **articulation**, accent, elocution, intonation, enunciation, diction, phonation. [➡THE SPOKEN WORD; 672]

proof **1** *n* **evidence**, testimony, verification, confirmation, attestation, corroboration, substantiation, testimonial, witness. [➡EVIDENCE AND PROOF; 69] **2** *adj* **resistant**, resilient, impervious, immune. [➡STRENGTH; 202] *Opposite:* vulnerable.

proof of identity *n* [➡EVIDENCE AND PROOF; 69]

proof of ownership *n* [➡EVIDENCE AND PROOF; 69]

proof of posting *n* [➡RECEIPTS AND INVOICES; 592]

proof of purchase *n* [➡RECEIPTS AND INVOICES; 592]

proof positive *n* [➡EVIDENCE AND PROOF; 69]

proofread *v* **check**, correct, check through, check over, look through, look over, mark up, edit. [➡READ; 759]

proofreader *n* **checker**, reader, editor, copy editor, corrector. [➡WORKERS IN ENTERTAINMENT AND MEDIA; 873]

prop **1** *n* **support**, leg, crutch, buttress, pile, strut, brace, underpinning. [➡SUPPORTS AND BASES; 1254] **2** *v* **hold up**, support, prop up, sustain, buttress, bolster, uphold, buoy, brace. [➡CONTACT: HOLD; 412] *Opposite:* destabilize.

propaganda **1** *n* **publicity**, advertising, marketing, literature, information, bumf (*informal*), puffery (*informal*), hype, buildup, hoopla (*US informal*). [➡ADVERTISING AND PUBLICITY; 605] **2** *n* **misinformation**, disinformation, party line, half-truths, cant, indoctrination. [➡DECEPTION AND LIES; 661]

propagandist **1** *n* **publicist**, polemicist, essayist, writer, speaker, orator, satirist. [➡WRITERS AND STYLES; 914] **2** *n* **partisan**, apologist, mouthpiece, sophist, spin doctor (*slang*). [➡SPEAKERS AND ORATORS; 604] **3** *adj* **slanted**, distorted, one-sided, polemical, partisan, extremist, manipulative. [➡FALSE AND UNREAL; 174]

propagate **1** *v* **breed**, grow, raise, reproduce, proliferate, generate. [➡GROW AND CULTIVATE; 352] **2** *v* **spread**, broadcast, proliferate, circulate, disseminate, promulgate (*formal*), transmit, publicize. [➡INFORM AND ANNOUNCE; 612]

propagation **1** *n* **breeding**, reproduction, proliferation, procreation. [➡GROW AND CULTIVATE; 352] **2** *n* **spread**, proliferation, circulation, dissemination, transmission, promulgation (*formal*). [➡INFORM AND ANNOUNCE; 612]

propagator **1** *n* **spreader**, broadcaster, transmitter, communicator, diffuser. [➡DESIGNERS, CREATORS AND INSTIGATORS; 348] **2** *n* **tray**, box, seed tray, cloche, pan. [➡CONTAINERS, RECEPTACLES, AND PACKAGING; 1244]

propel *v* **push**, drive, force, boost, thrust, impel. [➡THROW SOMETHING; 335]

propellant 1 *type of* **explosive material.** [➡EXPLOSIVES; 1154] 2 *type of* **gas.** [➡GASES; 1274]

propeller *part of* **aircraft.** [➡AIRCRAFT; 1147]

propensity (*formal*) *n* **tendency**, inclination, partiality, bent, proclivity, predisposition, susceptibility, predilection (*formal*), penchant. [➡TEMPERAMENT AND BEHAVIOUR; 493]

proper 1 *adj* **good**, correct, appropriate, suitable, right, apt, apposite, accurate, fitting. [➡APPROPRIATE, SUITABLE, ADVISABLE; 185] *Opposite:* wrong. 2 *adj* **polite**, modest, decorous, prim, genteel, respectable, courteous. [➡GOOD MANNERS AND SOCIAL SKILLS; 521] *Opposite:* improper. 3 *adj* **own**, personal, characteristic, identifiable, individual. [➡EXTRAORDINARY: UNCOMMON; 206]

properly *adv* **correctly**, right, appropriately, as it should be, by the book, suitably, accurately, well. [➡APPROPRIATE, SUITABLE, ADVISABLE; 185] *Opposite:* incorrectly.

proper noun *type of* **word class.** [➡ASPECTS OF LANGUAGE; 683]

propertied *adj* **property-owning**, land-owning, landed, affluent, moneyed, titled. [➡WEALTH AND WEALTHY; 891] *Opposite:* dispossessed.

property 1 *n* **possessions**, belongings, goods, assets, material goods, chattels, things, stuff. [➡POSSESSIONS; 462] 2 *n* **land**, home, house, estate, acreage. [➡PLACE; 1064]

property owner *n* **proprietor**, owner, landowner, homeowner, property holder, landholder. [➡RICH PEOPLE; 895] *Opposite:* tenant.

prophecy *n* **prediction**, forecast, divination, foretelling, insight, foresight. [➡PREDICT AND ANTICIPATE; 751]

prophesy *v* **predict**, forecast, divine, foretell, see the future, prefigure, portend, presage, envisage. [➡PREDICT AND ANTICIPATE; 751]

prophet *n* **clairvoyant**, forecaster, fortune teller, seer, prescient, psychic, diviner, mystic, telepathist, spiritualist, parapsychologist, sibyl. [➡PEOPLE WITH SUPERNATURAL POWERS; 789]

prophetic *adj* **visionary**, farsighted, predictive, foretelling, forewarning, oracular, divinatory. [➡PREDICT AND ANTICIPATE; 751]

propinquity (*formal*) *n* **nearness**, closeness, proximity, convenience, relationship. [➡CLOSENESS; 160] *Opposite:* remoteness.

propitiate (*formal*) *v* **appease**, placate, mollify, pacify, soothe, calm down, conciliate. *Opposite:* aggravate. (*informal*). [➡SOOTHE AND CALM; 574]

propitiation (*formal*) *n* **placation**, appeasement, mollification, pacification, soothing, calming, conciliation. [➡APOLOGIZE AND RETRACT; 684] *Opposite:* provocation.

propitiatory (*formal*) *adj* **placatory**, conciliatory, soothing, mollifying, calming, pacifying. [➡CALMING; 189] *Opposite:* provocative.

propitious *adj* [➡SUCCESSFUL AND PROMISING; 81]

propitiousness *n* [➡SUCCESS; 82]

proponent *n* **advocate**, supporter, exponent, protagonist, follower, fan, champion. [➡DEVOTEES AND ADDICTED PEOPLE; 557] *Opposite:* opponent.

proportion 1 *n* **amount**, quantity, part, share, percentage, fraction. [➡DEGREE AND EXTENT; 110] 2 *n* **ratio**, comparison, relative amount, relationship. [➡MEASUREABLE PORTION; 125]

proportional *adj* **relative**, comparative, relational, related, proportionate. [➡EQUALITY; 155]

proportionate *adj* **balanced**, proportional, comparable, equal, equivalent. [➡EQUALITY; 155]

proportions *n* [➡SIZE AND DIMENSIONS; 1191]

proposal *n* **suggestion**, offer, application, tender, bid, plan, scheme, request, proposition. [➡SUGGEST, HINT, AND COMMENT; 613]

propose 1 *v* **suggest**, offer, recommend, proposition, advise, put forward. [➡SUGGEST, HINT, AND COMMENT; 613] 2 *v* **intend**, plan, have in mind, aim, mean, insinuate. [➡PREPARE FOR ACTION; 290]

proposer *n* **nominator**, supporter, sponsor, advocate, advocator, backer, exponent, champion. [➡DEVOTEES AND ADDICTED PEOPLE; 557]

proposition *n* **proposal**, plan, scheme, intention, suggestion, offer. [➡SUGGEST, HINT, AND COMMENT; 613]

propound *v* **put forward**, advocate, submit, set out, offer, bring forward, yield, propose, promote, promulgate (*formal*). [➡SUGGEST, HINT, AND COMMENT; 613]

proprietary 1 *adj* **branded**, exclusive, patented, registered, trademarked, copyrighted, named, brand-named. [➡FINANCE AND ECONOMICS; 797] *Opposite:* generic. 2 *adj* **private**, privately-owned, privately-run, privately-operated, commercial. [➡BELONGING OR RELATING TO INDIVIDUALS; 944] 3 *adj* **protective**, jealous, territorial, possessive, suspicious, watchful. [➡SELFISH AND UNKIND; 506]

proprietor *n* **owner**, manager, administrator, landowner, property owner, landlord. [➡OWNERS; 447]

proprietorial *adj* **possessive**, protective, jealous, suspicious, territorial, proprietary. [➡BOSSY AND OVERBEARING; 517]

propriety 1 *n* **politeness**, decorum, modesty, good manners, respectability, decency. [➡GOOD MANNERS AND SOCIAL SKILLS; 521] *Opposite:* impropriety. 2 *n* **correctness**, aptness, appropriateness, decency, suitability. [➡MORALLY GOOD; 775] *Opposite:* impropriety.

propulsion *n* **force**, forward motion, thrust, impulsion, momentum, impetus, driving force. [➡ENERGY GENERAL; 1160]

prop up *v* **hold up**, support, prop, sustain, buttress, bolster, uphold, stand, place, set. [➡MOVE SOMETHING: INTO A NEW POSITION OR OVERTURN; 331] *Opposite:* destabilize.

pro rata *adv* [➡FOREIGN WORDS AND PHRASES; 673]

prosaic 1 *adj* **straightforward**, matter-of-fact, simple, plain, ordinary, routine. [➡ORDINARINESS; 245] 2 *adj* **banal**, mundane, everyday, dull, humdrum, colourless, run-of-the-mill, pedestrian, plain, vanilla (*slang*), characterless, ordinary, commonplace. [➡BORING AND UNINTERESTING; 235] *Opposite:* extraordinary.

prosaicness *n* **plainness**, dullness, flatness, woodenness, pedestrianism. [➡BORING AND UNINTERESTING; 235] *Opposite:* poetry.

proscribe *v* **ban**, bar, forbid, exclude, make illegal, veto, disallow, rule out, prohibit. [➡REFUSE PERMISSION AND NOT ALLOW; 671] *Opposite:* permit.

proscribed *adj* **prohibited**, banned, forbidden, verboten, inadmissible, barred, illegal, illicit, unacceptable, taboo, outlawed. [➡REFUSE PERMISSION AND NOT ALLOW; 671] *Opposite:* permissible.

proscription (*formal*) *n* **prohibition**, banning, exclusion, forbidding, interdiction, outlawing, veto. [➡REFUSE PERMISSION AND NOT ALLOW; 671]

proscriptive (*formal*) *adj* [➡REFUSE PERMISSION AND NOT ALLOW; 671]

prose *n* **writing style**, style, text. [➡FICTION AND DRAMA; 913]

prosecute *v* **put on trial**, act against, impeach, arraign, indict, take legal action, accuse, bring to court, sue. [➡TRIAL, PUNISHMENT, AND LEGAL OUTCOMES; 819]

prosecuting attorney *n* [➡PEOPLE IN LAW COURTS; 820]

prosecution *n* **trial**, action, suit, examination, hearing, tribunal. [➡TRIAL, PUNISHMENT, AND LEGAL OUTCOMES; 819]

prosecutor (*US*) *n* **prosecuting attorney**, DA (*US*), district attorney (*US*), public prosecutor. [➡PEOPLE IN LAW COURTS; 820]

proselyte *n* [➡SUPPORTERS, PROTECTORS, AND COMPATRIOTS; 970]

proselytization *n* **preaching**, evangelization, agitation, propagandizing, campaigning, tireless support, boundless enthusiasm. [➡APPROVE AND CONFIRM; 647]

proselytize *v* **preach**, agitate, evangelize, persuade, cajole, spread the word, convert, make see the light, bend somebody's ear. [➡INSTRUCT AND TEACH; 610]

proselytizer *n* **preacher**, evangelist, missionary, zealot, agitator, lecturer, tireless campaigner, polemicist. [➡SPEAKERS AND ORATORS; 604]

prospect 1 *n* **view**, scene, vision, outlook, panorama, vista, viewpoint, overlook (*US*). [➡VIEWS AND OUTLOOKS; 1072] 2 *n* **hope**, possibility, expectation, outlook, vision, likelihood, probability, potential, option, chance. [➡POSSIBLE AND PROBABLE; 178] 3 *v* **search**, mine, dig, seek, pan, hunt. [➡SEEK POSSESSION AND SEARCH; 457]

prospective *adj* **potential**, future, forthcoming, likely, probable, soon-to-be, eventual, approaching, latent, upcoming (*US*). [➡FUTURE; 86]

prospectus *n* **brochure**, list, catalogue, booklet, leaflet, pamphlet. [➡MANUALS AND INSTRUCTIONS; 590]

prosper 1 *v* **flourish**, thrive, do well, get on, grow, burgeon (*literary*). [➡PROSPER AND ABOUND; 16] *Opposite:* decline. 2 *v* **succeed**, make money, show a profit, be in the black. [➡SUCCEED AND WIN; 79]

prospering *adj* [➡SUCCESSFUL AND PROMISING; 81]

prosperity *n* **wealth**, affluence, opulence, riches, success, richness, fortune. [➡WEALTH AND WEALTHY; 891] *Opposite:* poverty.

prosperous 1 *adj* **wealthy**, affluent, rich, well-off, well-to-do. [➡WEALTH AND WEALTHY; 891] *Opposite:* poor. 2 *adj* **flourishing**, thriving, successful, booming. [➡SUCCESSFUL AND PROMISING; 81] *Opposite:* failing.

prosperously *adv* **wealthily**, affluently, richly, comfortably, successfully, well. [➡WEALTH AND WEALTHY; 891]

prostrate 1 *adj* **flat**, face down, horizontal, level, prone. [➡ORIENTATION AND ALIGNMENT; 1222] *Opposite:* upright. 2 *adj* **drained**, exhausted, desperate, powerless, at a low ebb, miserable, depressed, low, dispirited. [➡SADNESS, DISTRESS, AND DESPAIR; 540]

prostrate yourself *v* **bow**, genuflect, bend low, abase yourself (*literary*), humble yourself, grovel. [➡GESTURES AND GESTICULATION; 654]

prostration 1 *n* **bowing**, kneeling, falling down, worship, adoration, abasement (*literary*), kowtowing. [➡GESTURES AND GESTICULATION; 654] 2 *n* **incapacitation**, breakdown, exhaustion, helplessness, weakness. [➡TIRED, ASLEEP AND UNCONSCIOUS; 739] *Opposite:* robustness.

protagonist *n* **character**, hero, central character, leading role, good guy (*US informal*). [➡PEOPLE WHO ARE APPROVED OF; 955]

protean *adj* **variable**, changeable, mutable, adjustable, fluctuating, erratic, inconsistent. [➡FINITENESS, VARIABILITY, AND TRANSIENCE; 96] *Opposite:* constant.

protect *v* **defend**, guard, keep, look after, care for, save from harm, shield, shelter, safeguard, watch over. [➡PREVENT CONTACT OR ATTACK; 420] *Opposite:* neglect.

See Compare and Contrast at **safeguard**.

protected 1 *adj* **endangered**, threatened, nearing extinction, dwindling. [➡IN DANGER; 238] *Opposite:* thriving. 2 *adj* **sheltered**, safe, secure, safeguarded, shielded, covered. [➡SAFE AND SAFETY; 192] *Opposite:* exposed. 3 *adj* **locked**, tamperproof, inaccessible, sealed, impenetrable. [➡IN GOOD REPAIR; 1231] *Opposite:* open.

protection *n* **defence**, guard, shield, fortification, safeguard, safety, security, shelter, armour. [➡SAFE AND SAFETY; 192]

protectionism *n* **isolationism**, protection, tariff barriers, trade barriers. [➡STYLES AND SYSTEMS OF GOVERNMENT; 806]

protectionist 1 *n* **isolationist**, nationalist, patriot, xenophobe. [➡STYLES AND SYSTEMS OF GOVERNMENT; 806] 2 *adj* **protective**, isolationist, nationalist, preferential, xenophobic, patriotic. [➡STYLES AND SYSTEMS OF GOVERNMENT; 806]

protective *adj* **defensive**, caring, shielding, protecting, defending. [➡SAFE AND SAFETY; 192]

protective clothing *n* [➡GARMENTS AND OUTFITS; 865]

protective covering *n* **shell**, armour, cladding, shield. [➡COVERS AND COATINGS; 1245]

protectiveness 1 *n* **safety**, security, secureness, strength, robustness, rigidity, thickness. [➡SAFE AND SAFETY; 192] 2 *n* **solicitousness**, jealousness, jealousy, possessiveness, suspicion. [➡ENVY AND JEALOUSY; 549] *Opposite:* hostility. 3 *n* **protectionism**, isolationism, protection, tariff barriers, trade barriers. [➡BUSINESS ACTIVITIES AND PHENOMENA; 795]

protector 1 *n* **shield**, armour, mask, apron. [➡COVERS AND COATINGS; 1245] 2 *n* **guard**, guardian, minder, defender, handler, bodyguard. [➡SUPPORTERS, PROTECTORS, AND COMPATRIOTS; 970]

protectorate *n* **dominion**, colony, dependency, region, territory, satellite. [➡TERRITORIES AND GROUPS OF NATIONS; 1067]

protégé *n* **charge** (*formal*), ward, pupil, dependant, apprentice, acolyte, disciple, understudy. [➡ADOPTION, FOSTERING, AND EXTENDED FAMILY; 962] *Opposite:* protector.

protein *type of* **nutrient**. [➡FOOD COMPONENTS; 1187]

pro tem 1 *adv* **for the time being**, in the short term, temporarily, in the interim, for the moment, for now, for the present, at present. [➡FOREIGN WORDS AND PHRASES; 673] 2 *adj* **short-term**, present, intervening, provisional, temporary, acting. [➡FOREIGN WORDS AND PHRASES; 673] *Opposite:* long-term.

protest 1 *v* **complain**, object, gripe (*informal*), remonstrate, dissent, dispute, voice disapproval, moan (*informal*), make an objection, oppose, carp, grumble, murmur. [➡PROTEST AND EXPRESS DISAPPROVAL; 643] 2 *v* **declare**, affirm, assert, insist, claim, announce, avow (*formal*). [➡CLAIM, INSIST, AND EMPHASIZE; 615] 3 *n* **complaint**, objection, gripe (*informal*), remonstration, dissent, dispute, disapproval. [➡COMPLAIN AND NAG; 687] 4 *n* **demonstration**, march, rally, campaign, dispute, picket, strike, walkout, work to rule. [➡MEETINGS AND ASSEMBLIES; 43]

See Compare and Contrast at **complain, object.**

protestation *n* **assertion**, declaration, affirmation, pronouncement, avowal (*formal*), disclosure. [➡CRITICISMS AND ANGRY OUTBURSTS; 50]

protester *n* **activist**, campaigner, demonstrator, marcher, picketer, striker, dissenter. [➡UNCOOPERATIVE OR REBELLIOUS PERSON; 567] *Opposite:* supporter.

protest march *n* **demonstration**, demo (*informal*), march, rally, protest rally, protest. [➡MEETINGS AND ASSEMBLIES; 43]

protest rally *n* **demonstration**, demo (*informal*), march, protest march, rally, protest. [➡MEETINGS AND ASSEMBLIES; 43]

protocol *n* **procedure**, etiquette, conventions, code of behaviour, rules, modus operandi, proprieties, good form, decorum. [➡WAYS OF DOING THINGS; 295]

proton *type of* **elementary particle**. [➡ELEMENTARY PARTICLES; 1278]

prototype *n* **example**, sample, model, original, archetype, exemplar (*literary*), pattern. [➡PERFECT EXAMPLES AND EMBODIMENTS; 67] *Opposite:* copy.

prototypical *adj* [➡REPRESENTATIVE; 66]

protozoan *type of* **microorganism**. [➡MICROORGANISMS, FUNGI, AND ALGAE; 1023]

protract *v* **draw out**, prolong, extend, spin out, drag out, expand, lengthen, delay, stretch out. [➡CAUSE TO CONTINUE; 268] *Opposite:* shorten.

protracted *adj* **long-drawn-out**, prolonged, extended, lingering, expanded, lengthy, lengthened, delayed, stretched out. [➡HAPPENING SLOWLY; 106] *Opposite:* brief.

protraction 1 *n* **extension**, lengthening, drawing out, continuation. [➡PERMANENCE: WITHOUT END; 94] *Opposite:* shortening. 2 *n* **scale drawing**, plan, elevation, blueprint, diagram, drawing. [➡DRAWINGS, CHARTS AND TABLES; 595]

protractor *type of* **measuring device**. [➡MEASURING DEVICES; 1122]

protrude *v* **stick out**, jut, project, overhang, obtrude, extend beyond, bulge, swell. [➡EXIST IN A PLACE; 19]

protruding *adj* [➡PERCEPTIBLE; 25]

protrusion *n* **lump**, lip, flange, overhang, outcrop, protuberance, projection, bulge, extension, overlap. [➡EXTREMITIES OF PHYSICAL OBJECTS; 1249]

protrusive 1 *adj* **prominent**, bulging, swelling, jutting, extending, proud. [➡PERCEPTIBLE; 25] *Opposite:* sunken. 2 *adj* **brash**, forward, presumptuous, impertinent (*formal*), fresh (*informal*), rude. [➡POMPOUS, LOUD, AND OVER-CONFIDENT; 636] *Opposite:* retiring.

protuberance *n* **swelling**, bulge, bump, lump, knob, distension, protrusion, prominence, projection, convexity. [➡ROUNDED SHAPE; 1217]

protuberant *adj* **sticking out**, prominent, bulging, swelling, popping, bulgy, swollen, convex. [➡ROUNDED SHAPE; 1217] *Opposite:* concave.

proud 1 *adj* **pleased**, satisfied, gratified, honoured, delighted, fulfilled. [➡PLEASURE, EXCITEMENT, AND ELATION; 535] *Opposite:* ashamed. 2 *adj* **impressive**, stately, majestic, noble, magnificent, great, grand, lordly. [➡EXTRAORDINARY: UNCOMMON; 206] 3 *adj* **arrogant**, conceited, smug, superior, self-important, pompous, self-righteous (*disapproving*), bigheaded (*informal*), vain, egotistical, self-satisfied, overbearing. [➡AFFECTATION, SELF-SATISFACTION, AND SNOBBISHNESS; 508] *Opposite:* humble. 4 *adj* **independent**, self-sufficient, dignified, scrupulous, honourable, self-respecting. [➡GOOD MANNERS AND SOCIAL SKILLS; 521] 5 *adj* **rewarding**, satisfying, pleasurable, pleasing, uplifting, fulfilling. [➡EMOTIONALLY PLEASANT; 188] 6 *adj* **projecting**, prominent, jutting, bulging, protrusive, sticking out. [➡PERCEPTIBLE; 25] *Opposite:* sunken.

Compare and Contrast: *proud, arrogant, conceit, egotistic, vain*

CORE MEANING: DESCRIBING SOMEBODY WHO IS PLEASED WITH HIMSELF OR HERSELF

proud justifiably pleased and satisfied about a situation, or self-satisfied and having an exaggerated opinion of self worth; ***arrogant*** feeling or showing self-importance and contempt for others; ***conceited*** showing excessive satisfaction with one's personal qualities or abilities; ***egotistic*** having an inflated sense of self- importance, especially when this is shown through constantly talking or thinking about oneself; ***vain*** excessively self-satisfied, especially overconcerned with and admiring one's personal appearance.

proudly *adv* **arrogantly**, conceitedly, smugly, self-importantly, pompously, bigheadedly (*informal*). [➡AFFECTATION, SELF-SATISFACTION, AND SNOBBISHNESS; 508] *Opposite:* humbly.

provable *adj* **demonstrable**, verifiable, watertight, incontestable, unarguable. [➡CERTAIN; 175]

prove 1 *v* **show**, establish, confirm, demonstrate, verify, evidence, attest, bear out, substantiate, ascertain (*formal*), corroborate, uphold, support, sustain. [➡APPROVE AND CONFIRM; 647] *Opposite:* disprove. 2 *v* **turn out**, develop, grow, grow up, be, show yourself, end up. [➡GRADUALLY COME INTO EXISTENCE; 1]

proven *adj* **established**, confirmed, demonstrated, verified, recognized, sure, upheld, supported, sustained. [➡CERTAIN; 175] *Opposite:* unproven.

provenance *n* **origin**, derivation, attribution, source, birthplace, background. [➡BEGINNING; 53]

See Compare and Contrast at **origin**.

provender 1 *n* (*archaic*) **fodder**, feed, hay, forage, silage. [➡ANIMAL FEED; 1167] 2 *n* (*literary or humorous*) **food**, fare, provisions, comestibles (*formal*), grub (*informal*), nosh (*informal*), eatables (*informal*), victuals, chow (*slang*), eats (*slang*). [➡FOOD; 1166]

proverb *n* **maxim**, axiom, adage, saying, aphorism, saw, truism, epigram. [➡FIGURES OF SPEECH; 674]

proverbial 1 *adj* **well-known**, axiomatic, familiar, legendary, famous, famed, reputed, notorious (*archaic*). [➡KNOWN AND FAMOUS; 182] 2 *adj* **archetypal**, clichéd, typical, regular, common, usual, traditional. [➡ORDINARINESS; 245] *Opposite:* novel.

provide 1 *v* **give**, supply, present, endow, grant, impart, bestow (*formal*), furnish (*formal*), offer. [➡EQUIP AND SUPPLY; 436] *Opposite:* withhold. 2 *v* **make available**, deliver, offer, arrange for, run, be responsible for, afford (*formal*). [➡GIVE AND PROVIDE; 431] *Opposite:* withdraw. 3 *v* **stipulate**, postulate, specify, require. [➡REQUEST AND DEMAND; 664] 4 *v* **take care of**, support, look after, care for, keep, feed, finance, prepare, arrange, plan, cater. [➡GIVE AND PROVIDE; 431] *Opposite:* neglect.

provided *conj* **on condition that**, if, only if, as long as, so long as, providing, in case, granted. [➡CAUSATION; 169]

provided that *conj* **on condition that**, if, only if, as long as, so long as, providing, in case, granted. [➡CAUSATION; 169]

provide for *v* [➡TAKE CARE OF AND SPOIL; 301]

providence 1 *n* **wisdom**, foresight, prudence, sense, frugality, thrift, farsightedness, forethought, provision. [➡POSITIVE INTELLECTUAL CHARACTERISTICS; 525] 2 *n* **fate**, luck, destiny, fortune, divine intervention, outside influence. [➡FATE, DESTINY, AND ASTROLOGY; 783]

provident 1 *adj* **prudent**, foresighted, well-prepared, wise, careful, sensible, farsighted. *Opposite:* improvident. (*formal*). [➡POSITIVE INTELLECTUAL CHARACTERISTICS; 525] 2 *adj* **frugal**, thrifty, cautious, careful, sparing, mean, parsimonious, economical. [➡ECONOMICAL AND RESOURCEFUL; 208] *Opposite:* spendthrift.

providential 1 *adj* **preordained**, destined, fated, God-given, divine, heaven-sent. [➡FATE, DESTINY, AND ASTROLOGY; 783] *Opposite:* arbitrary. 2 *adj* **fortunate**, lucky, beneficial, advantageous. [➡LUCK; 784] *Opposite:* unfortunate.

See Compare and Contrast at **lucky**.

providentially *adv* **fortunately**, luckily, conveniently, beneficially, advantageously, opportunely. [➡LUCK; 784] *Opposite:* unfortunately.

provider 1 *n* **supplier**, source, contributor, donor, bringer, giver. [➡REPRESENTATIVES AND PATRONS; 968] *Opposite:* beneficiary. 2 *n* **breadwinner**, wage-earner, earner, worker, billpayer, benefactor. [➡SUPPORTERS, PROTECTORS, AND COMPATRIOTS; 970] *Opposite:* dependant.

providing *conj* **on condition that**, if, only if, as long as, so long as, provided that, in case, granted. [➡CAUSATION; 169]

province 1 *n* **area**, sphere, field, jurisdiction, domain, authority. [➡SUBJECT AREA; 769] 2 *n* **region**, area, state, county, prefecture, territory, department (*informal*), district, realm. [➡COUNTRIES AND REGIONS; 1066]

provinces *n* **outlying areas**, shires, countryside, sticks (*informal*), backwaters, boonies (*US informal*), boondocks (*US informal*). [➡COUNTRIES AND REGIONS; 1066] *Opposite:* capital.

provincial 1 *adj* **local**, regional, county, district, small-town, rural, bucolic, rustic, country. [➡HUMAN SETTLEMENTS; 1069] *Opposite:* central. 2 *adj* (*disapproving*) **unsophisticated**, unfashionable, simple, outmoded, parochial, narrow-minded, insular. [➡LEVEL OF EDUCATION AND SOPHISTICATION; 894] *Opposite:* worldly.

provincialism (*disapproving*) *n* **lack of sophistication**, lack of refinement, parochialism, narrow-mindedness, insularity. [➡NEGATIVE INTELLECTUAL CHARACTERISTICS; 526] *Opposite:* worldliness.

provision 1 *n* **delivery**, facility, running, setting up, establishment, providing, endowment, donation. [➡DISPENSE, RATION, AND DISTRIBUTE; 435] 2 *n* **anticipation**, prearrangement, forethought, wherewithal, readiness, precaution. [➡POSITIVE INTELLECTUAL CHARACTERISTICS; 525] 3 *n* **stipulation**, rider, condition, proviso, but (*informal*), if, prerequisite, specification, requirement, obligation. [➡NECESSARY AND ESSENTIAL; 197]

provisional *adj* **temporary**, interim, conditional, makeshift, short-term, impermanent, draft, outline, rough. [➡FINITENESS, VARIABILITY, AND TRANSIENCE; 96] *Opposite:* permanent.

provisions *n* **supplies**, necessities, requirements, food, rations, eatables (*informal*), comestibles (*formal*), sustenance. [➡FOOD; 1166]

proviso *n* **stipulation**, rider, condition, provision, but (*informal*), if, disclaimer, prerequisite, specification, requirement, limitation. [➡NECESSARY AND ESSENTIAL; 197]

provisory *adj* **conditional**, subject to, dependent upon, provisional, contingent, limited. [➡FINITENESS, VARIABILITY, AND TRANSIENCE; 96] *Opposite:* unconditional.

provocation 1 *n* **incitement**, needling, goading, baiting, aggravation (*informal*), niggling, hassle (*informal*).

[➡NUISANCES; 254] **2** *n* **vexation**, frustration, irritation, annoyance, aggravation (*informal*), affront. [➡NUISANCES; 254]

provocative **1** *adj* **challenging**, provoking, stimulating, inflammatory, incendiary, confrontational, rabble-rousing, aggressive, offensive, insulting, annoying, aggravating (*informal*), vexing. [➡RUDE AND HOSTILE; 626] *Opposite:* conciliatory. **2** *adj* **suggestive**, enticing, seductive, alluring, cheeky, encouraging, tantalizing, beguiling, bewitching. [➡INTERESTING AND MEANINGFUL; 191] *Opposite:* forbidding.

provoke **1** *v* **incite**, aggravate (*informal*), hassle (*informal*), needle, goad, bait, irritate, niggle, inflame, rouse, whip up. [➡ANGER AND ANNOY; 570] *Opposite:* soothe. **2** *v* **cause**, elicit, produce, trigger, bring about, stir, activate, prompt. [➡CAUSE TO HAPPEN; 31] *Opposite:* prevent.

provoked *adj* **irritated**, annoyed, angered, goaded, frustrated, aggravated (*informal*). [➡IRRITATION AND ANGER; 542] *Opposite:* unaffected.

provoking *adj* **infuriating**, irritating, aggravating (*informal*), annoying, frustrating, maddening. [➡IRRITATING; 229] *Opposite:* soothing.

provost *n* **principal**, director, head, chancellor, leader, dean, chief. [➡EDUCATORS; 840]

prow *part of* **ship or boat.** [➡SHIPS AND BOATS; 1149]

prowess **1** *n* **ability**, skill, expertise, competence, dexterity, competency, aptitude, proficiency, know-how (*informal*), knack, talent. [➡SKILLS, TALENTS, AND ABILITIES; 527] *Opposite:* incompetence. **2** *n* **bravery**, heroism, gallantry, courage, daring, valour. [➡COURAGE; 499] *Opposite:* cowardice.

prowl *v* **stalk**, lurk, skulk, lie in wait, hang about, hang around, scavenge. [➡PROCEED AND GO; 306]

prowl car (*US dated*) *type of* **public service vehicle.** [➡VEHICLES; 1144]

prowler *n* **stalker**, pursuer, intruder, tormentor, Peeping Tom, lurker. [➡VILLAINS AND THUGS; 947]

proximate *adj* [➡CLOSENESS; 160]

proximity *n* **nearness**, closeness, juxtaposition, vicinity, immediacy, propinquity (*formal*), contiguity (*formal*). [➡CLOSENESS; 160] *Opposite:* remoteness.

proxy **1** *n* **indirect means**, substitution, deputation, commission, delegation, representation. [➡REPRESENTATIVES AND PATRONS; 968] **2** *n* **substitute**, stand-in, deputy, delegate, understudy, surrogate, replacement, alternate (*US*). [➡REPRESENTATIONS AND GENERAL EXAMPLES; 65]

prudence *n* **practicality**, carefulness, caution, cautiousness, discretion, forethought, farsightedness, judiciousness, good sense, common sense, shrewdness, judgment, pragmatism, wisdom, calculation, foresight, providence, care. [➡POSITIVE INTELLECTUAL CHARACTERISTICS; 525] *Opposite:* imprudence.

prudent *adj* **practical**, careful, cautious, sensible, discreet, wise, judicious, farsighted, shrewd, pragmatic. *Opposite:* imprudent. (*formal*). [➡POSITIVE INTELLECTUAL CHARACTERISTICS; 525]

See Compare and Contrast at **cautious.**

prudential *adj* **sensible**, wise, sagacious (*formal*), provident, practical, commonsensical. [➡POSITIVE INTELLECTUAL CHARACTERISTICS; 525] *Opposite:* foolish.

prudery *n* **prudishness**, primness, stuffiness, reserve, puritanism, prissiness, narrow-mindedness. [➡EXCESSIVE SENSITIVITY; 512] *Opposite:* permissiveness.

prudish *adj* **prim**, stuffy, strait-laced, starchy, formal, proper, prissy, squeamish, puritanical, narrow-minded. [➡EXCESSIVE SENSITIVITY; 512] *Opposite:* relaxed.

prudishness *n* **prudery**, primness, stuffiness, reserve, puritanism, prissiness, narrow-mindedness. [➡EXCESSIVE SENSITIVITY; 512] *Opposite:* permissiveness.

prune **1** *v* **clip**, trim, snip, cut back, cut, thin, lop, crop. [➡EXTRACT AND SEVER; 342] **2** *v* **shorten**, cut, abridge, condense, tighten up, curtail, reduce, trim, abbreviate. [➡CHANGE OF SIZE: SMALLER; 394] *Opposite:* expand.

prurience *n* [➡MORALLY BAD; 776]

prurient *adj* **unwholesome**, unhealthy, immodest, indecent, salacious, voyeuristic, lustful, libidinous (*formal*), lascivious. [➡MORALLY BAD; 776] *Opposite:* healthy.

Prussian blue *type of* **blue.** [➡COLOURS; 1223]

pry **1** *v* **interfere**, poke your nose in, meddle, snoop (*informal*), inquire, peer, be inquisitive, be nosy (*informal*). [➡ASK PEOPLE QUESTIONS; 667] *Opposite:* leave alone. **2** *v* (*US*) **lever open**, force, force open, wrench, wrest, prise. [➡UNFASTEN AND UNDO; 410]

prying *adj* **snooping** (*informal*), interfering, inquisitive, nosy (*informal*), curious, meddling, peeping, peering. [➡NOSY AND INTERFERING; 513] *Opposite:* incurious.

pry open (*US*) *v* [➡UNFASTEN AND UNDO; 410]

PS *adv* **postscript**, addendum, afterthought, addition, stop press, coda. [➡WRITTEN CONVENTIONS; 600]

psalm *n* **sacred song**, hymn, poem, canticle, prayer, song, song of praise. [➡RELIGIOUS OBJECTS; 780]

psalter *n* **book of psalms**, prayer book, breviary, hymnal, missal. [➡RELIGIOUS OBJECTS; 780]

pseud *n* **poser** (*informal disapproving*), know-all (*informal*), fraud, fake, pseudointellectual. [➡SELF-IMPORTANT AND SELF-SEEKING PEOPLE; 949]

pseudo *adj* [➡FALSE AND UNREAL; 174]

pseudonym *n* **alias**, false name, assumed name, fictitious name, stage name, pen name, nom de plume. [➡NAME AND DESCRIBE; 666]

psych (*US*) **1** *v* **panic**, frighten, scare, worry, trouble, bother. [➡UPSET, DISTRESS, AND HUMILIATE; 568] **2** *v* **nerve**, steel, brace, motivate, gear up, wind up, prepare, get ready. [➡PREPARE FOR ACTION; 290]

psyche **1** *n* **soul**, spirit, inner self, essence, being. [➡PSYCHOLOGY AND THE MIND; 770] **2** *n* **mind**, consciousness, awareness, ego, intellect, mentality, personality. [➡ PSYCHOLOGY AND THE MIND; 770]

psychedelic 1 *adj* **hallucinogenic**, mind-altering, mind-blowing (*informal*), mind-expanding, mood-altering, intoxicating (*formal*). [➡ PAIN AND OTHER PHYSICAL SENSATIONS; 734] 2 *adj* **coloured**, patterned, vibrant, vivid, loud, exuberant, kaleidoscopic. [➡ DESCRIBING COLOURS; 1225] *Opposite:* dull.

psyched up (*informal*) *adj* [➡ POSITIVE IMPATIENCE, ENTHUSIASM, AND ALERTNESS; 538]

psychiatrist *n* [➡ PEOPLE WHO WORK IN MEDICINE; 848]

psychiatry *n* [➡ PSYCHOLOGY AND THE MIND; 770]

psychic 1 *adj* **mental**, cerebral, intellectual, cognitive, psychosomatic, emotional. [➡ PSYCHOLOGY AND THE MIND; 770] 2 *adj* **supernatural**, extrasensory, mysterious, unexplained, paranormal, spiritual, out-of-body. [➡ THE SUPERNATURAL; 788] *Opposite:* physical. 3 *adj* **telepathic**, clairvoyant, intuitive, second-sighted, stargazing, spiritualistic. [➡ THE SUPERNATURAL; 788] 4 *n* **clairvoyant**, spiritualist, soothsayer, sensitive, diviner, medium. [➡ PEOPLE WITH SUPERNATURAL POWERS; 789]

psychical *adj* **supernatural**, paranormal, spiritual, extrasensory, subliminal, subconscious, clairvoyant. [➡ THE SUPERNATURAL; 788] *Opposite:* physical.

psychoanalysis *n* [➡ PSYCHOLOGY AND THE MIND; 770]

psychoanalyst *n* [➡ PEOPLE WHO WORK IN MEDICINE; 848]

psychological *adj* **mental**, emotional, inner, spiritual, psychosomatic. [➡ PSYCHOLOGY AND THE MIND; 770] *Opposite:* physical.

psychology *n* **mind**, thinking, mindset, makeup, sensibility, consciousness, attitude, feeling. [➡ PSYCHOLOGY AND THE MIND; 770]

psychosis *n* [➡ PSYCHOLOGY AND THE MIND; 770]

psychosomatic *adj* **self-induced**, mental, psychological, inner, all in the mind. [➡ PSYCHOLOGY AND THE MIND; 770]

psychotherapist *n* [➡ PEOPLE WHO WORK IN MEDICINE; 848]

psychotherapy *n* [➡ PSYCHOLOGY AND THE MIND; 770]

psych out (*informal*) *v* [➡ CONFUSE AND BEWILDER; 572]

psych up (*informal*) *v* **nerve**, steel, gear up, wind up, prepare, get ready, brace, motivate. [➡ PREPARE FOR ACTION; 290]

PT *n* **physical training**, games, physical education, PE, gymnastics, sports education. [➡ HOBBIES, GAMES, AND SPORTS; 875]

PT boat (*US*) *type of* **military vessel**. [➡ PARTS OF A SHIP OR BOAT; 1150]

pteranodon *type of* **dinosaur**. [➡ DINOSAUR; 996]

pterodactyl *type of* **dinosaur**. [➡ DINOSAUR; 996]

pterosaur *type of* **dinosaur**. [➡ DINOSAUR; 996]

PTO *adv* [➡ WRITTEN CONVENTIONS; 600]

pub *type of* **bar or club**. [➡ HOTELS, RESTAURANTS, AND CLUBS; 1081]

pubertal *adj* [➡ BABYHOOD, CHILDHOOD AND ADOLESCENCE; 917]

puberty *n* **sexual maturity**, adolescence, youth, teens. [➡ BABYHOOD, CHILDHOOD AND ADOLESCENCE; 917]

pubescent *adj* **pubertal**, teenage, teen (*informal*), adolescent. [➡ BABYHOOD, CHILDHOOD AND ADOLESCENCE; 917]

public 1 *adj* **community**, civic, communal, municipal, free, open, unrestricted. [➡ BELONGING OR RELATING TO PEOPLE; 943] *Opposite:* private. 2 *adj* **freely available**, shared, known, open, in the public domain, broadcast. [➡ PRESENT AND AVAILABLE; 11] *Opposite:* secret. 3 *n* **everyone**, people, populace, community, society, nation, the world at large. [➡ GROUPS IN SOCIETY; 940]

public amenities *n* [➡ SOCIAL WELFARE; 812]

publication *n* **book**, magazine, newspaper, journal, periodical, pamphlet. [➡ BOOKS AND BOOKLETS; 591]

public defender (*US*) *n* [➡ PEOPLE IN LAW COURTS; 820]

public disgrace *n* **dishonour**, disgrace, ignominy, humiliation, exposure, shaming, naming and shaming. [➡ CRITICISMS AND ANGRY OUTBURSTS; 50]

public disturbance *n* [➡ CRIMES; 817]

public figure *n* **celebrity**, name, personality, personage, household name, VIP, star. [➡ IMPORTANT OR FAMOUS PEOPLE; 893]

public holiday *n* [➡ PERIOD OF REST; 91]

public image *n* **façade**, front, public face, persona, identity. [➡ TEMPERAMENT AND BEHAVIOUR; 493]

publicity *n* **advertising**, promotion, exposure, hype, media hype, public relations. [➡ ADVERTISING AND PUBLICITY; 605]

publicize *v* **make public**, make known, broadcast, advertise, announce, expose, publish, air. [➡ INFORM AND ANNOUNCE; 612] *Opposite:* suppress.

public limited company *n* [➡ BUSINESS ENTERPRISES AND RELATED BODIES; 793]

publicly *adv* **openly**, in public, overtly, widely, freely, visibly. [➡ KNOWN AND FAMOUS; 182] *Opposite:* secretly.

public nuisance *n* [➡ CRIMES; 817]

public prosecutor *n* [➡ PEOPLE IN LAW COURTS; 820]

public relations *n* **image management**, publicity, media, relations, self-promotion, spin doctoring (*slang*). [➡ ADVERTISING AND PUBLICITY; 605]

public school *type of* **school**. [➡ EDUCATIONAL INSTITUTIONS; 813]

public services *n* [➡ SOCIAL WELFARE; 812]

public-spirited *adj* **philanthropic**, charitable, altruistic, humanitarian, benevolent, unselfish. [➡ GENEROSITY AND KINDNESS; 496] *Opposite:* selfish.

public transport *n* [➡ SOCIAL WELFARE; 812]

publish 1 *v* **issue**, put out, bring out, print, distribute, circulate. [➡ INFORM AND ANNOUNCE; 612] 2 *v* **make public**, make known, announce, broadcast, advertise, print. [➡ INFORM AND ANNOUNCE; 612] *Opposite:* keep secret.

publisher *n* **producer**, originator, commissioner, editor, issuer. [➡WORKERS IN ENTERTAINMENT AND MEDIA; 873]

publishing *n* **publication**, printing, issuing, reproducing, dissemination, broadcasting. [➡CREATION; 347]

puce *type of* **red**. [➡COLOURS; 1223]

puck *type of* **sports equipment**. [➡SPORTS EQUIPMENT; 879]

pucker 1 *v* **wrinkle**, crease, gather, pull together, ruck up, crumple. [➡CHANGE OF SHAPE; 386] *Opposite:* smooth. 2 *n* **gather**, wrinkle, crease, ruck, pull. [➡CHANGE OF SHAPE; 386]

puckish *adj* **mischievous**, cheeky, playful, naughty, rascally (*humorous*), impish, elfin. [➡CHEERFULNESS OF OUTLOOK; 504]

puckishly *adv* **mischievously**, cheekily (*informal*), playfully, naughtily, impishly, wickedly. [➡GOOD-TEMPERED AND HUMOROUS; 628]

pud (*informal*) *part of* **meal**. [➡MEALS AND PARTS OF MEALS; 1168]

pudding 1 *n* **dessert**, sweet, afters (*informal*). [➡MEALS AND PARTS OF MEALS; 1168] 2 *type of* **dessert**. [➡CAKES, BISCUITS, AND DESSERTS; 1180]

puddle 1 *n* **pool**, slick, wet patch. [➡AMOUNT OF LIQUID; 114] 2 *v* **potter**, mosey around, dawdle, idle, lounge about, mooch (*slang*), lounge around. [➡AIMLESS AND ERRANT MOTION; 344] 3 *v* **splash**, dabble, paddle, splosh, wade. [➡PROCEED AND GO; 306]

pudginess (*informal*) *n* [➡BUILD; 478]

pudgy (*informal*) *adj* **fat**, chubby, stubby, podgy, heavy, round, obese, overweight, portly, stocky, tubby. [➡BUILD; 478]

puerile *adj* **childish**, immature, infantile, foolish, silly, trivial, trifling, fatuous. [➡NEGATIVE INTELLECTUAL CHARACTERISTICS; 526] *Opposite:* mature.

puerility *n* **immaturity**, childishness, silliness, foolishness, inanity, fatuity (*formal*), fatuousness. [➡NEGATIVE INTELLECTUAL CHARACTERISTICS; 526]

puff 1 *n* **gust**, breath, draught, current, flurry. [➡WINDY AND STORMY WEATHER; 1053] 2 *n* **cloud**, wisp, waft, billow. [➡AMOUNT OF GAS; 116] 3 *n* **praise**, recommendation, advertisement, publicity, blurb (*slang*). [➡PRAISE AND ENCOURAGE; 648] 4 *v* **blow**, exhale, breathe out, breathe. [➡BREATHE AND NOT BREATHE; 717] *Opposite:* inhale. 5 *v* **pant**, breathe heavily, wheeze, gasp, gasp for breath, be short of breath. [➡BREATHE AND NOT BREATHE; 717]

puff adder *type of* **poisonous snake**. [➡SNAKE; 995]

puffball *type of* **fungus**. [➡MICROORGANISMS, FUNGI, AND ALGAE; 1023]

puffed *adj* **out of breath**, breathless, breathing heavily, panting, gasping, puffed out, winded. [➡TIRED, ASLEEP, AND UNCONSCIOUS; 739]

puffed out *adj* [➡TIRED, ASLEEP AND UNCONSCIOUS; 739]

puffed-up *adj* **pompous**, self-important, arrogant, conceited, boastful, self-satisfied, swaggering, superior, swollen with pride, haughty, proud, egotistic. [➡POMPOUS, LOUD, AND OVER-CONFIDENT; 636] *Opposite:* humble.

puffin *type of* **seabird**. [➡SEABIRD; 1002]

puffiness 1 *n* **swelling**, enlargement, inflammation, oedema, distension, engorgement. [➡SICKNESS; 730] 2 *n* **pomposity**, pompousness, arrogance, haughtiness, pride, egotism. [➡POMPOUS, LOUD, AND OVER-CONFIDENT; 636] *Opposite:* humility.

puffing 1 *n* **wheezing**, wheeziness, breathlessness, heavy breathing, breathing, panting, gasping. [➡BREATHE AND NOT BREATHE; 717] 2 *adj* **breathless**, out of breath, panting, gasping, winded, wheezy, fighting for breath. [➡BREATHE AND NOT BREATHE; 717]

puff out *v* **enlarge**, swell, expand, puff up, distend, bulge. [➡CHANGE OF SIZE: BIGGER; 393] *Opposite:* deflate.

puff pastry *n* [➡BREAD, FLOUR, AND BREAD PRODUCTS; 1178]

puff up *v* **enlarge**, swell, inflate, expand, puff out, bulge. [➡CHANGE OF SIZE: BIGGER; 393] *Opposite:* deflate.

puffy *adj* **swollen**, distended, inflated, bloated, bulbous, bulging. [➡ROUNDED SHAPE; 1217]

pug 1 *n* (*informal*) **pugilist**, boxer, fighter, prizefighter, wrestler. [➡PEOPLE IN SPORTS AND LEISURE; 876] 2 *type of* **small dog**. [➡DOG; 980]

pugilism *n* **boxing**, fighting, prizefighting. [➡HOBBIES, GAMES, AND SPORTS; 875]

pugilist *n* **boxer**, fighter, pug (*informal*), prizefighter. [➡PEOPLE IN SPORTS AND LEISURE; 876]

pugnacious *adj* **aggressive**, confrontational, belligerent, truculent, argumentative, contentious. [➡AGGRESSIVE AND BELLIGERENT; 519] *Opposite:* peaceable.

pugnaciousness *n* **aggression**, fierceness, forcefulness, confrontational attitude, intimidating manner, pugnacity. [➡AGGRESSIVE AND BELLIGERENT; 519]

pugnacity *n* **aggression**, fierceness, forcefulness, confrontational attitude, intimidating manner, pugnaciousness. [➡BAD MANNERS AND SOCIAL SKILLS; 522]

pug-nosed *adj* [➡FACIAL CHARACTERISTICS; 482]

puissant (*literary*) *adj* [➡STRENGTH; 202]

puke (*slang*) 1 *v* **vomit**, be sick, throw up (*informal*), spew, retch, bring up, upchuck (*informal*), gag. [➡VOMIT AND BELCH; 713] 2 *n* **vomit**, spew, sick. [➡VOMIT AND BELCH; 713]

pukka 1 *adj* **fine**, well-made, excellent, high-quality, first-class, topnotch (*informal*). [➡ADMIRABLE AND COMMENDABLE; 186] 2 *adj* (*informal*) **genuine**, authentic, real, correct, proper, kosher (*informal*). [➡TRUE AND REAL; 172] 3 *adj* (*informal*) **respectable**, high-class, upper-class, well-placed, superior, well-respected. [➡CLASS STATUS; 889]

pull 1 *v* **drag**, draw, heave, haul, tow, lug, cart. [➡PUSH, PULL, SLIDE; 336] *Opposite:* push. 2 *v* **tug**, jerk, yank, wrench, pluck, twitch. [➡CONTACT: EXERT PRESSURE; 415] 3 *v* **attract**, draw, bring in, pull in, lure, entice. [➡APPEAL TO AND AROUSE INTEREST; 576] *Opposite:* put off. 4 *v* **strain**, sprain, damage, injure, tear. [➡WOUND A PERSON OR ANIMAL; 384] 5 *v* **remove**, extract, withdraw, draw out, pluck out, pull out. [➡EXTRACT AND SEVER; 342] *Opposite:* put in. 6 *n* (*informal*) **attraction**, appeal, power, influence, draw, magnetism, allure. [➡INTERESTING AND MEANINGFUL; 191] 7 *n* jerk, tug, yank, twitch, tweak, wrench. [➡CONTACT: EXERT PRESSURE; 415]

Compare and Contrast: ***pull, drag, draw, haul, tow, tug, yank***

CORE MEANING: MOVE SOMETHING TOWARDS YOU OR IN THE SAME DIRECTION AS YOU

pull to move something towards you or in the same direction as you; ***drag*** to move something large or heavy with effort across a surface; ***draw*** to pull something with a smooth movement; ***haul*** to pull something with a steady strong movement, often involving strenuous effort; ***tow*** to pull something along behind by means of a rope or chain; ***tug*** to pull at something with a sharp, forceful movement, without necessarily moving object; ***yank*** to pull something suddenly and sharply with a single strong movement.

pull a face *v* [➡FACIAL EXPRESSION; 652]

pull a fast one (*slang*) *v* **deceive**, trick, con, put one over (*informal*), swindle, bamboozle (*informal*). [➡DECEPTION AND LIES; 661]

pull apart *v* **disintegrate**, tear apart, dismantle, pull to pieces, demolish, separate. [➡TEAR, BREAK, AND CUT; 361] *Opposite:* assemble.

pull away *v* [➡ABSENT ONESELF; 8]

pull back *v* **recoil**, shrink, shrink away, back off, retract, baulk. [➡GO BACKWARDS; 310]

pull down *v* **demolish**, tear down, destroy, fell, flatten, raze. [➡DESTRUCTION AND DEMOLITION; 360] *Opposite:* build up.

pullet *type of* **young bird.** [➡YOUNG BIRD; 1004]

pulley *n* **winch**, hoist, block and tackle. [➡PARTS OF MACHINES AND TOOLS; 1117]

pull in 1 *v* (*slang*) [➡CAPTIVITY AND LOSS OF FREEDOM; 249] **2** *v* **attract**, draw, bring in, pull, encourage, entice. [➡APPEAL TO AND AROUSE INTEREST; 576] *Opposite:* put off.

pull-in (*dated*) *n* **roadside café**, transport café, service area, service station. [➡ROADS; 1105]

Pullman *part of* **train.** [➡RAILWAYS; 1106]

pull off (*informal*) *v* **achieve**, succeed, be successful, accomplish, carry out, execute, realize. [➡SUCCEED AND WIN; 79] *Opposite:* fail.

See Compare and Contrast at **accomplish.**

pull out 1 *v* **remove**, extract, withdraw, draw out, pluck out, pull. [➡EXTRACT AND SEVER; 342] *Opposite:* insert. **2** *v* **leave**, depart, abandon, drop out, go away, draw out. [➡ABSENT ONESELF; 8] *Opposite:* remain.

pullout 1 *n* **insert**, supplement, enclosure, addendum. [➡PARTS OF BOOKS AND DOCUMENTS; 594] **2** *n* **retreat**, withdrawal, departure. [➡END; 54]

pull out all the stops *v* **do your utmost**, go all-out, move heaven and earth, go for it (*slang*), make a supreme effort, do all you can, give your all. [➡HARD WORK OR EFFORT; 299]

pullover *type of* **sweater or cardigan.** [➡GARMENTS AND OUTFITS; 865]

pull somebody's leg (*informal*) *v* [➡JOKES AND TEASING; 675]

pull somebody's leg (*informal*) *v* **tease somebody**, joke, kid somebody (*informal*), have a joke on somebody, have a laugh, tell stories. [➡JOKES AND TEASING; 675]

pull the plug *v* **end**, terminate (*formal*), discontinue, close down, finish off (*informal*), cut off, wind up. [➡CAUSE TO STOP; 267]

pull the wool over somebody's eyes *v* **deceive**, delude, hoodwink, swindle, con, cheat. [➡DECEPTION AND LIES; 661]

pull through *v* **recover**, get better, pick up, survive, get through, get over, rally, revive. [➡GET BETTER; 376]

pull together 1 *v* **unite**, join forces, rally, cooperate, team up, pool your resources. [➡HELP; 294] **2** *v* **organize**, arrange, assemble, draw together, bring together, form. [➡ARRANGE AND CREATE ORDER; 358]

pull to pieces 1 *v* **dismantle**, pull to bits, pull apart, take to pieces, rip to pieces, rip to shreds. [➡EXTRACT AND SEVER; 342] **2** *v* **criticize**, vilify, slate, make short work of, make mincemeat of, rip to shreds. [➡ACCUSE, BLAME, AND CRITICIZE; 642]

pull up 1 *v* **stop**, halt, draw to halt, brake, pull in. [➡ARRIVE BY TRANSPORT; 14] **2** *v* **criticize**, tell off (*informal*), reprimand, rebuke, take to task, have words with. [➡ACCUSE, BLAME, AND CRITICIZE; 642]

pull yourself together (*informal*) *v* **compose**, regain your composure, think straight, calm down, get a grip (*informal*), regain your self-control, control yourself, get a hold of yourself. [➡CHANGE OF MOOD AND COMPOSURE; 581]

pulmonary *adj* **pulmonic**, lung, respiratory. [➡RESPIRATORY ORGANS; 716]

pulp 1 *n* **soft tissue**, fleshy tissue, tissue, flesh. [➡CENTRAL PARTS OF PHYSICAL OBJECTS; 1250] **2** *n* **paste**, mush, mash, blend, soft mass, smooth mixture. [➡LOTIONS, PASTES, AND GELS; 1271] **3** *v* **mash**, crush, squash, pound, grind, pulverize. [➡CHANGE OF SHAPE; 386] **4** *part of* **fruit.** [➡FRUIT AND VEGETABLES; 1175]

pulpit 1 *n* **podium**, dais, stand, lectern, reading desk. [➡RELIGIOUS OBJECTS; 780] **2** *n* **clergy**, church, church authorities. [➡RELIGIOUS PEOPLE; 779]

pulsar *type of* **star or star system.** [➡CELESTIAL BODIES; 1060]

pulsate *v* **throb**, beat, pulse, thump, thud, pound. [➡PHYSICAL REACTIONS; 317]

pulsation *n* **throb**, beat, pulse, rhythm, pounding, thump. [➡PHYSICAL REACTIONS; 317]

pulse 1 *n* **throb**, pulsation, rhythm, pounding, thump, beat. [➡PHYSICAL REACTIONS; 317] **2** *v* **throb**, beat, pulsate, pound, palpitate, vibrate. [➡PHYSICAL REACTIONS; 317]

pulse

◆ *types of pulse*
bean, black bean, black-eyed bean, black-eyed pea (*US*), broad bean, butter bean, chickpea, fava bean (*US*), French bean, garbanzo, haricot, kidney bean, lentil, lima bean, mangetout, mung bean, navy bean (*US*), pea, petits pois, pinto bean, runner bean, snow pea (*US*), soya bean, string bean

pulverization 1 *n* **maceration**, liquidation, crushing, reduction, grinding. [➡DESTRUCTION AND DEMOLITION; 360] 2 *n* (*informal*) **defeat**, humiliation, thrashing, beating, whipping, drubbing. [➡BEAT AND DEFEAT; 80]

pulverize 1 *v* **grind**, crush, macerate, pulp, mash, chop up, chop into pieces, pound. [➡TEAR, BREAK, AND CUT; 361] 2 *v* (*informal*) **thrash**, crush, annihilate, hammer (*informal*), destroy, defeat, lick (*informal*), trounce. [➡BEAT AND DEFEAT; 80]

puma *type of* **cat**. [➡FELINE; 983]

pumice *type of* **stone**. [➡STONES, ROCKS, AND BOULDERS; 1057]

pummel *v* **beat**, thump, bash (*informal*), thrash, pound, punch, wallop (*informal*). [➡PHYSICAL ATTACK AND PUNISHMENT; 416]

pummelling *n* [➡PHYSICAL ATTACK AND PUNISHMENT; 416]

pump 1 *v* **force**, drive, impel, propel, inflate, thrust, deflate, push, send, inject, fill, expand. [➡EJECT AND EXCLUDE; 341] 2 *v* **question**, interrogate, cross examine (*informal*), grill (*informal*), quiz, probe, debrief. [➡ASK PEOPLE QUESTIONS; 667] 3 *part of* **engine**. [➡PARTS OF AN ENGINE; 1143] 4 *type of* **shoe**. [➡FOOTWEAR; 871] 5 *type of* **general tool**. [➡HAND TOOLS; 1118]

pumpernickel *type of* **bread**. [➡BREAD, FLOUR, AND BREAD PRODUCTS; 1178]

pumpkin *type of* **vegetable**. [➡FRUIT AND VEGETABLES; 1175]

pump out *v* **produce**, give off, generate, churn out, emit, expel, broadcast, disseminate, release. [➡EMIT AND EMANATE; 362]

pump up *v* **inflate**, blow up, puff up, puff out, expand, fill, dilate, distend. [➡CHANGE OF SIZE: BIGGER; 393] *Opposite:* deflate.

pun 1 *n* **witticism**, joke, gag (*informal*), jest (*literary*), double entendre, quip, bon mot. [➡JOKES AND TEASING; 675] 2 *v* **play with words**, joke, quip, make a joke, banter, jest (*literary*). [➡JOKES AND TEASING; 675]

punch 1 *v* **stamp**, press, perforate, cut, pierce. [➡TEAR, BREAK, AND CUT; 361] 2 *v* **hit**, beat, strike, pummel, thump, clout, cuff, smite, box, whack, clobber, sock (*informal*). [➡PHYSICAL ATTACK AND PUNISHMENT; 416] 3 *n* **blow**, hit, thump, clout, knock, cuff, stroke, sock (*informal*), box. [➡PHYSICAL ATTACK AND PUNISHMENT; 416] 4 *n* **vigour**, drive, energy, power, vim (*informal*), verve, oomph, pep (*informal*), punchiness, liveliness, pizzazz (*informal*). [➡ENERGY AND ENTHUSIASM; 497] 5 *type of* **general tool**. [➡HAND TOOLS; 1118]

punch-drunk (*informal*) *adj* **dazed**, confused, bewildered, stupefied, stunned, punchy (*informal*). [➡CONFUSION, ANXIETY, AND WORRY; 541] *Opposite:* alert.

punchiness *n* **vigour**, energy, verve, liveliness, pizzazz (*informal*), drive, power, vim (*informal*), oomph, pep (*informal*). [➡INTERESTING AND MEANINGFUL; 191] *Opposite:* lethargy.

punch-up (*informal*) *n* **fight**, scrap (*informal*), brawl, set-to (*informal*), fist fight, scuffle. [➡AGGRESSIVE EVENT; 39]

punchy 1 *adj* **pithy**, hard-hitting, forceful, terse, effective, succinct. [➡HONEST AND OPEN; 631] *Opposite:* bland. 2 *adj* **punch-drunk** (*informal*), dazed, confused, bewildered, stupefied, stunned. [➡CONFUSION, ANXIETY, AND WORRY; 541] *Opposite:* alert.

punctilious 1 *adj* **correct**, seemly, courteous, polite, civil, proper. [➡GOOD MANNERS AND SOCIAL SKILLS; 521] *Opposite:* boorish. 2 *adj* **fastidious**, scrupulous, painstaking, assiduous, meticulous, conscientious, thorough, exact, precise, correct. *Opposite:* sloppy. (*informal*). [➡HARD-WORKING AND COMMITTED; 501]

See Compare and Contrast at **careful**.

punctiliousness 1 *n* **propriety**, courteousness, correctness, politeness, decorum. [➡GOOD MANNERS AND SOCIAL SKILLS; 521] *Opposite:* boorishness. 2 *n* **fastidiousness**, precision, correctness, exactitude, efficiency, rectitude (*formal*), assiduity, thoroughness, sedulousness (*literary*), attention to detail, nitpicking. [➡HARD-WORKING AND COMMITTED; 501] *Opposite:* carelessness.

punctual *adj* **on time**, in good time, prompt, on the dot. [➡PROMPTNESS: ON TIME; 99] *Opposite:* late.

punctuality *n* **promptness**, timekeeping, reliability, regularity. [➡PROMPTNESS: ON TIME; 99] *Opposite:* lateness.

punctuate 1 *v* **mark**, edit, correct, mark up, proofread, proof, hyphenate, bracket. [➡RECORD SOMETHING; 372] 2 *v* **interrupt**, intersperse, scatter, interpose, pepper, dot, litter, speckle, disrupt, break, sprinkle, lace. [➡SPREAD AND SCATTER; 333]

punctuation mark

◆ *types of punctuation mark*
asterisk, backslash, bracket, colon, comma, dash, exclamation mark, full stop, hyphen, inverted comma, parenthesis, period (*US*), point, question mark, quotation mark, square bracket, swung dash

puncture 1 *n* **hole**, perforation, wound, lesion, pinhole, cut, break, rupture. [➡HOLES, GAPS, AND FORKS; 1251] 2 *v* **pierce**, stab, perforate, prick, stick in, penetrate, wound, nick. [➡TEAR, BREAK, AND CUT; 361] 3 *v* **undermine**, deflate, erode, ruin, destroy, demolish (*informal*), shoot down. [➡DESTRUCTION AND DEMOLITION; 360] *Opposite:* inflate.

punctured *adj* [➡IN BAD REPAIR; 1233]

pundit *n* **expert**, specialist, authority, commentator, guru, analyst. [➡TALENTED OR INTELLIGENT PERSON; 529]

pungency 1 *n* **spiciness**, strong flavour, bitterness, sharpness, tanginess, acidity, hotness. [➡TASTE; 704] *Opposite:* blandness. 2 *n* **pithiness**, pointedness, wit, force, bite, causticness. [➡ELOQUENT, TALKATIVE AND LONG-WINDED; 633] *Opposite:* mildness.

pungent 1 *adj* **strong**, powerful, spicy, hot, overpowering, sharp, bitter, sharp-tasting, piquant, stimulating. [➡TASTE; 704] *Opposite:* bland. 2 *adj* **caustic**, pithy, pointed, witty, forceful, biting, cutting, acerbic, trenchant, sharp, piercing. [➡ELOQUENT, TALKATIVE AND LONG-WINDED; 633] *Opposite:* mild.

punish *v* **chastise** (*formal*), discipline, penalize, castigate (*formal*), reprove, rebuke, reprimand, correct, admonish, chasten. [➡ACCUSE, BLAME, AND CRITICIZE; 642] *Opposite:* commend.

punishable *adj* **disciplinary**, indictable, bookable, hanging, capital, illegal, serious. [➡UNACCEPTABLE AND UNFORGIVEABLE; 226]

punishing *adj* **gruelling**, exhausting, demanding, tiring, arduous, laborious, strenuous, harsh, severe, unremitting. [➡PHYSICALLY UNPLEASANT; 227] *Opposite:* undemanding.

punishment 1 *n* **sentence**, penalty, chastisement (*formal*), castigation (*formal*), reprimand, retribution, penance, price, deserts. [➡RESULTS AND OUTCOMES; 83] *Opposite:* reward. 2 *n* **rough treatment**, abuse, mistreatment, heavy use, stick (*informal*), ill-use, maltreatment. [➡UNKIND ACTION OR BEHAVIOUR; 297]

punitive *adj* **disciplinary**, castigatory (*formal*), penal, corrective, retaliatory, retributive, retributory, punishing, revengeful, vindictive. [➡VENGEANCE AND REVENGE; 686]

punk 1 *adj* (*informal*) **inferior**, second rate, cheap, nasty, poor, rotten, weak, unimpressive. [➡IN POOR TASTE; 230] 2 *type of* **popular music**. [➡MUSIC, SONGS, AND SINGING; 907]

punkie (*US*) *type of* **flying insect**. [➡FLYING INSECTS; 1013]

punnet *n* **basket**, tray, carton, box, container. [➡CONTAINERS, RECEPTACLES, AND PACKAGING; 1244]

punning *adj* [➡JOKES AND TEASING; 675]

punster *n* [➡JOKERS AND TEASES; 676]

punt 1 *type of* **small vessel**. [➡SHIPS AND BOATS; 1149] 2 *v* **kick**, hit, strike, boot, shoot, send, lob. [➡THROW SOMETHING; 335] 3 *n* **bet**, gamble, stake, wager, flutter. [➡GAMBLE AND TAKE RISKS; 467]

punter (*informal*) *n* **customer**, client, consumer, shopper, viewer, listener. [➡PURCHASER; 425]

puny 1 *adj* **small**, weak, tiny, feeble, frail, stunted, scrawny, undersized, pint-sized (*informal*), underdeveloped. [➡BUILD; 478] *Opposite:* robust. 2 *adj* **inadequate**, trifling, paltry, minor, feeble, insignificant, useless, worthless, meagre. [➡REDUNDANT AND USELESS; 241] *Opposite:* considerable.

pup 1 *n* **upstart**, brat, whippersnapper (*dated*), puppy (*informal*), know-all (*informal*), smart aleck (*informal*). [➡MISCHIEVOUS OR BADLY-BEHAVED CHILD; 946] 2 *v* **whelp**, litter, bear, deliver, give birth, drop. [➡REPRODUCTION AND HEREDITY; 726] 3 *type of* **young animal**. [➡YOUNG ANIMAL; 977]

pupa *type of* **insect stages of development**. [➡INSECT STAGES; 1020]

pupil 1 *n* **student**, follower, apprentice, acolyte, understudy, scholar, learner, beginner, novice, trainee. [➡STUDENTS AND PUPILS; 841] *Opposite:* teacher. 2 *n* [➡THE EYE; 699]

pupillage (*formal*) *n* [➡LESSONS, COURSE WORK, AND EXAMINATIONS; 842]

puppet 1 *n* **marionette**, dummy, doll, glove puppet, hand puppet, finger-puppet, string-puppet, mannequin. [➡TOYS; 880] 2 *n* **pawn**, flunky (*informal*), lackey, instrument, tool, lapdog, creature, cat's paw, minion. [➡SUBORDINATES AND ASSISTANTS; 966]

puppy 1 *n* **brat**, upstart, whippersnapper (*dated*), pup, know-all (*informal*), smart aleck (*informal*). [➡MISCHIEVOUS OR BADLY-BEHAVED CHILD; 946] 2 *type of* **young animal**. [➡YOUNG ANIMAL; 977]

purchase 1 *v* **buy**, pay for, acquire, obtain, procure, get, pick up. [➡PURCHASE; 423] *Opposite:* sell. 2 *v* **obtain**, win, gain, secure, acquire. [➡GET; 421] 3 *n* **acquisition**, buying, obtaining, procurement, securing, consumption. [➡BUSINESS ACTIVITIES AND PHENOMENA; 795] 4 *n* **buy**, acquisition, goods, merchandise, item. [➡PURCHASE; 423] 5 *n* **grip**, grasp, hold, leverage, foothold, firm footing, toehold. [➡CONTACT: HOLD; 412]

purchaser *n* **buyer**, procurer, customer, client, consumer, payer. [➡PURCHASER; 425] *Opposite:* seller.

purdah 1 *n* **seclusion**, withdrawal, separation, retirement, isolation, exclusion, restriction. [➡RELIGIONS AND RELIGIOUS PRACTICES; 778] 2 *n* **screen**, curtain, barrier, divider, shield. [➡WALLS AND PARTITIONS; 1103]

pure 1 *adj* **unmixed**, one hundred per cent, genuine, real, authentic, natural. [➡TRUE AND REAL; 172] 2 *adj* **uncontaminated**, unadulterated, unpolluted, clean, untainted, wholesome, unalloyed. [➡CLEAN; 1232] *Opposite:* tainted. 3 *adj* **sheer**, complete, utter, absolute, downright, out-and-out, total. [➡ABSOLUTE AND ABSOLUTELY; 131] 4 *adj* **theoretical**, abstract, fundamental, basic, higher. [➡THE NATURE OF IDEAS; 772] *Opposite:* applied. 5 *adj* (*literary*) **chaste**, unsullied, uncorrupted, innocent, sinless, moral, virtuous. [➡MORALLY GOOD; 775] *Opposite:* corrupt. 6 *adj* **clear**, vivid, strong, vibrant, rich, deep. [➡SOFT OR PLEASANT SOUNDS; 1264] *Opposite:* weak.

purebred *adj* **thoroughbred**, pedigree, pure. [➡CLASS STATUS; 889]

puree *v* [➡COOKING AND FOOD PREPARATION; 354]

purée 1 *n* **pulp**, paste, mush, pap, sauce, coulis. [➡LOTIONS, PASTES, AND GELS; 1271] 2 *v* **mash**, blend, process, liquidize, pound. [➡COOKING AND FOOD PREPARATION; 354]

purely 1 *adv* **entirely**, wholly, totally, thoroughly, completely, absolutely. [➡ABSOLUTE AND ABSOLUTELY; 131] *Opposite:* partly. 2 *adv* **merely**, only, simply, just, solely, essentially. [➡MAINLY AND PRIMARILY; 138] 3 *adv* **chastely**, virtuously, decently, morally, innocently, virginally. [➡MORALLY GOOD; 775] *Opposite:* indecently.

pureness 1 *n* **cleanliness**, wholesomeness, spotlessness, clarity, transparency, limpidness, cleanness, stainlessness. [➡CLEAN; 1232] *Opposite:* dirtiness. 2 *n* **clearness**, vividness, strength, vibrancy, richness, depth. [➡SOFT OR PLEASANT SOUNDS; 1264]

purgative (*formal*) 1 *n* **enema**, emetic, suppository, laxative, purge, cathartic. [➡EXCRETION AND EXCRETA; 723] 2 *adj* **cleansing**, emetic, laxative, emptying, purging. [➡EXCRETION AND EXCRETA; 723]

purgatory *n* **agony**, limbo, hell, anguish, despair, suffering, torment, torture. [➡DIFFICULT SITUATIONS; 72]

purge 1 *v* **get rid of**, eliminate, remove, eradicate, do away with, expel, expunge, liquidate, oust, dismiss. [➡GET

RID OF SOMETHING; 452] 2 *v* (*formal*) **pardon**, exonerate, absolve, forgive, excuse, shrive, atone for (*formal*). *Opposite:* castigate. (*formal*). [➡FORGET, FORGIVE, AND ACCEPT; 749] 3 *v* **wash out**, cleanse, clean, flush out, sluice, clean up, purify. [➡CLEAN AND POLISH; 404] 4 *n* **laxative**, purgative (*formal*), cathartic, emetic. [➡REMEDIES, TREATMENTS AND OPERATIONS; 732] 5 *n* **elimination**, removal, eradication, expulsion, ridding, housecleaning (*US informal*), shakeup. [➡REMOVE SOMETHING; 339]

puri *type of* **bread.** [➡BREAD, FLOUR, AND BREAD PRODUCTS; 1178]

purification *n* **cleansing**, sanitization, decontamination, distillation, refinement, refining, ablution. [➡CLEAN AND POLISH; 404]

purified *adj* [➡NOT IN A NATURAL STATE; 1214]

purifier *n* **cleanser**, filter, sterilizer, disinfectant, antiseptic, decontaminant. [➡CLEANING AGENTS; 863]

purify *v* **cleanse**, disinfect, sanitize, decontaminate, clean, get rid of impurities, distil, filter, refine, sterilize. [➡CLEAN AND POLISH; 404] *Opposite:* contaminate.

purist *n* **traditionalist**, perfectionist, stickler, pedant, conformist, conservative. [➡GRUMPY AND NEGATIVE PEOPLE; 953]

puritan *n* [➡ASCETIC PEOPLE; 883]

puritanical *adj* [➡ABSTEMIOUSNESS AND SELF-DENIAL; 882]

puritanism *n* [➡ABSTEMIOUSNESS AND SELF-DENIAL; 882]

purity 1 *n* **cleanliness**, spotlessness, clarity, transparency, limpidness, concentration, pureness. [➡CLEAN; 1232] *Opposite:* dirtiness. 2 *n* **innocence**, wholesomeness, virtue, virtuousness, chasteness, chastity. [➡MORALLY GOOD; 775]

purl 1 *n* **thread**, gold thread, silver thread, wire, filigree. [➡TEXTILES AND THREADS; 1130] 2 *n* **border**, edge, frill, trim, fringe, decoration. [➡ORNAMENTS AND DECORATIONS; 1247] 3 *n* (*literary*) **ripple**, babble, murmur, gurgle, tinkle, plash (*literary*). [➡CONTINUOUS SOUNDS; 1257] 4 *v* (*literary*) **flow**, ripple, babble, murmur, gurgle, tinkle, plash (*literary*). [➡EMIT CONTINUOUS SOUNDS; 367]

purlieu 1 *n* **suburb**, commuter belt, outskirts, suburbia, vicinity, neighbourhood, district, exurb (*US*). [➡PLACE; 1064] 2 *n* (*formal*) **ghetto**, shanty town, slum. [➡UNDESIRABLE ACCOMMODATION; 856]

purloin (*formal*) *v* **steal**, pinch (*informal*), nick (*slang*), pilfer, appropriate, walk off with, pocket, filch (*informal*), lift (*informal*), help yourself to, thieve, shoplift. [➡STEAL AND ROB; 427]

See Compare and Contrast at **steal.**

purple 1 *adj* **elaborate**, exaggerated, florid, overwritten, ornate, over-the-top (*informal*), excessive, overheated. [➡IN POOR TASTE; 230] 2 *type of* **colour.** [➡COLOURS; 1223]

purple

◆ *types of purple*
amethyst, aubergine, heliotrope, lavender, lilac, mauve, plum, violet

purport 1 *v* **claim**, assert, allege, profess, contend, maintain, declare, seem. [➡CLAIM, INSIST, AND EMPHASIZE; 615] 2 *v* (*formal*) **intend**, aim, mean, plan. [➡PREPARE FOR ACTION; 290] 3 *n* **sense**, significance, importance, meaning, implication, relevance, import, reason, rationale. [➡IMPORTANCE AND SIGNIFICANCE; 193] 4 *n* **purpose**, intention, intent (*formal*), aim, design, plan, end, object, objective. [➡INTENTION AND PURPOSE; 773]

purported (*formal*) *adj* **supposed**, claimed, alleged, ostensible, unsupported, unsubstantiated, professed, maintained. [➡FALSE AND UNREAL; 174]

purpose 1 *n* **intention**, intent (*formal*), aim, object, objective, goal, target, end. [➡INTENTION AND PURPOSE; 773] 2 *n* **determination**, resolution, resolve, persistence, perseverance, tenacity, single-mindedness, commitment, purposefulness, devotion, dedication, drive. [➡POSITIVE IMPATIENCE, ENTHUSIASM, AND ALERTNESS; 538] *Opposite:* indifference.

purpose-built *adj* **tailor-made**, custom-made, custom-built, individual, exclusive, unique, one-off. [➡BUILDING AND ARCHITECTURE; 1075] *Opposite:* standard.

purposeful *adj* **focused**, determined, decisive, resolute, firm, fixed, decided, persistent. [➡POSITIVE INTELLECTUAL CHARACTERISTICS; 525] *Opposite:* indecisive.

purposefully *adv* **decisively**, firmly, resolutely, persistently, tenaciously. [➡WITH ENTHUSIASM; 287] *Opposite:* aimlessly.

purposefulness *n* **determination**, resolution, single-mindedness, commitment, tenacity, devotion, dedication, drive, resolve, persistence, perseverance, purpose. [➡HARD-WORKING AND COMMITTED; 501] *Opposite:* aimlessness.

purposeless 1 *adj* **pointless**, irrational, useless, illogical, unreasonable. [➡REDUNDANT AND USELESS; 241] 2 *adj* **empty**, aimless, meaningless, pointless, senseless, useless. [➡REDUNDANT AND USELESS; 241] *Opposite:* meaningful.

purposelessly *adv* [➡REDUNDANT AND USELESS; 241]

purposelessness *n* [➡REDUNDANT AND USELESS; 241]

purposely *adv* **deliberately**, intentionally, on purpose, knowingly, wittingly, with intent, expressly. [➡INTENTIONAL AND DELIBERATE; 280] *Opposite:* accidentally.

purr 1 *n* **purring**, hum, whirr, buzz, vibration, drone. [➡CONTINUOUS SOUNDS; 1257] 2 *v* **vibrate**, hum, whirr, rumble, buzz, drone. [➡SOUND EMISSION BY ANIMALS OR BIRDS; 365] 3 *type of* **animal sound.** [➡SOUNDS MADE BY ANIMALS; 1260]

purse 1 *n* **reward**, winnings, takings, prize. [➡INCOME; 461] 2 *n* **wallet**, pouch, money bag, change purse (*US*). [➡CONTAINERS, RECEPTACLES, AND PACKAGING; 1244] 3 *v* **pucker**, tighten, squeeze, press, compress. [➡CHANGE OF SHAPE; 386] *Opposite:* relax.

purse-snatch (*US*) *v* [➡STEAL AND ROB; 427]

purse snatcher (*US*) *n* [➡CRIMINALS; 821]

purse your lips *v* [➡FACIAL EXPRESSION; 652]

pursuance (*formal*) *n* **enactment**, undertaking, achievement, acquirement, fulfilment, carrying out. [➡CARRY OUT AN ACTION; 270]

pursue 1 *v* **follow**, chase, hunt, trail, track, tail, shadow, dog, hound, stalk. [➡ACCOMPANY AND FOLLOW; 338] 2 *v* **practise**, engage in, work at, go in for, take up, carry out. [➡CARRY OUT AN ACTION; 270]

See Compare and Contrast at **follow.**

pursuer *n* **follower**, chaser, hunter, trailer, tracker, tail (*informal*), shadow. [➡ENEMIES AND TORMENTORS; 969]

pursuit 1 *n* **chase**, hunt, search, quest, detection. [➡SEEK POSSESSION AND SEARCH; 457] 2 *n* **hobby**, recreation, activity, pastime, interest. [➡LEISURE AND RECREATION; 874]

purulent *adj* **infected**, pus-filled, pussy, weeping, oozing. [➡CONDITIONS AFFECTING THE SKIN; 722]

purvey 1 *v* (*formal*) **sell**, provide, supply, deal in, furnish (*formal*). [➡SELL; 442] *Opposite:* buy. 2 *v* **gossip**, tattle, whisper, spread, tell. [➡GOSSIP; 679]

purveyor (*formal*) 1 *n* **supplier**, stockist, seller, vendor, outlet, source. [➡SELLER; 443] 2 *n* **spreader**, gossipmonger, teller, tattler, source, scandalmonger, whisperer. [➡SPEAKERS AND ORATORS; 604]

pus *n* **discharge**, secretion, excretion, fluid, infection. [➡EXCRETION AND EXCRETA; 723]

pus-filled *adj* [➡DECAYING OR INFESTED; 1235]

push 1 *v* **shove**, thrust, ram, press on, set in motion, drive, move forward. [➡PUSH, PULL, SLIDE; 336] *Opposite:* pull. 2 *v* **impel**, urge, goad, force, make, induce, exhort, persuade, press. [➡CAUSE OR COMPEL TO ACT; 272] *Opposite:* restrain. 3 *v* **advocate**, promote, advance, endorse, plug (*informal*), boost, get behind, back. [➡APPROVE AND CONFIRM; 647] *Opposite:* oppose. 4 *v* (*slang*) **sell**, flog (*informal*), vend, hawk, peddle, tout. [➡SELL; 442] *Opposite:* buy. 5 *n* **ambition**, energy, get-up-and-go (*informal*), force, vigour, impetus, motivation, drive. [➡CAUSATION; 169] *Opposite:* apathy.

push-bike (*dated informal*) *type of* **bike** (*informal*). [➡BIKES, CARS, AND CARRIAGES; 1148]

push-button *adj* **automatic**, high-tech, remote-control, electronic. [➡MACHINERY; 1113] *Opposite:* manual.

pushcart *n* **barrow**, cart, handcart, trolley, wagon. [➡BIKES, CARS, AND CARRIAGES; 1148]

pushchair *n* **buggy**, stroller, carriage, baby carriage (*US*). [➡BIKES, CARS, AND CARRIAGES; 1148]

pushed (*informal*) 1 *adj* **lacking**, strapped (*informal*), hard up (*informal*), broke (*informal*). [➡POVERTY AND POOR; 892] 2 *adj* **hard-pressed**, pressed, busy, struggling, hard at it. [➡IN TROUBLE AND DISADVANTAGED; 73]

pusher (*slang*) *n* **dealer**, supplier, peddler, hawker. [➡SELLER; 443]

push for *v* [➡REQUEST AND DEMAND; 664]

push in *v* **jump the queue**, skip the queue, cut in, barge in, shove in, squeeze in, muscle in (*informal*), butt in. [➡MOVE PAST, INTO OR THROUGH SOMETHING; 332]

pushiness *n* **forcefulness**, front, nerve, cheek (*informal*), aggression, assertiveness, brashness, insistence. [➡BOSSY AND OVERBEARING; 517] *Opposite:* reluctance.

pushing 1 *adj* **approaching**, nearly, almost, just about, roughly, near enough, close to. [➡APPROXIMATELY; 133] 2 *adj* **assertive**, forceful, aggressive, strident, brash, insistent, nervy (*US informal*), loudmouthed (*informal*), go-ahead (*informal*). [➡POMPOUS, LOUD, AND OVER-CONFIDENT; 636] *Opposite:* retiring.

push into *v* [➡CAUSE OR COMPEL TO ACT; 272]

push off 1 *v* **cast off**, shove off, embark, depart, set sail. [➡ABSENT ONESELF; 8] 2 *v* (*informal*) **go away**, leave, depart, get going, set out, shove off (*informal*), clear off (*informal*), head off. [➡ABSENT ONESELF; 8] *Opposite:* remain.

pushover (*informal*) *n* **dupe**, soft touch, softy (*informal*), sucker (*informal*), gull, mark (*slang*), target. [➡VICTIMS OF DECEIT; 663]

push-start *n* [➡BEGINNING; 53]

push the boat out (*informal*) *v* [➡OVERDO SOMETHING; 291]

push through *v* **put into force**, enforce, enact, introduce, force through, drive through, rush through. [➡CAUSE TO HAPPEN; 31]

pushy (*informal*) *adj* **assertive**, forceful, aggressive, loudmouthed (*informal*), strident, brash, insistent, nervy (*US informal*). [➡BOSSY AND OVERBEARING; 517] *Opposite:* retiring.

pusillanimity (*formal*) *n* **timidity**, fear, cowardliness, nervousness, hesitation, trepidation, spinelessness, tremulousness, fearfulness, faint-heartedness. [➡COWARDICE AND WEAKNESS OF WILL; 509] *Opposite:* confidence.

pusillanimous (*formal*) *adj* **timid**, cowardly, faint-hearted, lily-livered (*literary*), spineless, fearful, tremulous, nervous, gutless, craven. [➡COWARDICE AND WEAKNESS OF WILL; 509] *Opposite:* brave.

See Compare and Contrast at **cowardly.**

puss 1 *n* (*slang*) [➡HEAD; 693] 2 *n* (*informal*) **cat**, pussy (*informal*), pussycat (*informal*), moggy (*slang*), kitty (*informal*), kitten. [➡FELINE; 983]

pussy 1 *n* (*informal*) **cat**, puss (*informal*), pussycat (*informal*), moggy (*slang*), kitty (*informal*), kitten. [➡FELINE; 983] 2 *adj* **infected**, purulent, pus-filled, weeping, oozing. [➡DECAYING OR INFESTED; 1235]

pussycat 1 *n* **cat**, pussy (*informal*), puss (*informal*), moggy (*slang*), kitty (*informal*), kitten. [➡FELINE; 983] 2 *n* (*informal*) **softy** (*informal*), dear, sweetie (*informal*), soft touch. [➡PEOPLE WHO ARE APPROVED OF; 955]

pussyfoot (*informal*) 1 *v* **hesitate**, waver, wander, prevaricate, procrastinate, sit on the fence, fudge (*informal*). [➡HESITATE; 273] 2 *v* **tiptoe**, creep, steal, pick your way, ghost, glide. [➡MOVE SLOWLY; 315]

pussy willow *type of* **shrub or bush**. [➡BUSHES AND SHRUBS; 1027]

pustule *n* **boil**, abscess, eruption, furuncle (*technical*), spot, pimple. [➡CONDITIONS AFFECTING THE SKIN; 722]

put *v* **place**, set, lay, position, situate (*formal*), locate, plant, deposit, leave, plonk, plunk. [➡POSITION SOMETHING; 326] *Opposite:* remove.

put about *v* **spread**, circulate, tell, inform, give out, make known, disseminate. [➡INFORM AND ANNOUNCE; 612] *Opposite:* keep secret.

put across *v* **get across**, express, transmit, articulate, explain, communicate. [➡EXPLAIN AND CLARIFY; 611]

put a damper on *v* **deflate**, spoil, mess up (*informal*), mar, subdue, depress. [➡WORSEN SOMETHING; 381] *Opposite:* enliven.

put a match to *v* **set light to**, set alight, set fire to, set on fire, light, burn, burn down. [➡FIRE, FLAMMABILITY, AND BURNING; 1164] *Opposite:* put out.

put an end to *v* **stop**, terminate (*formal*), discontinue, halt, suspend, call a halt, bring to an end, put a stop to, pull the plug on. [➡CAUSE TO STOP; 267] *Opposite:* continue.

put a premium on *v* **value**, appreciate, prize, favour, rate. [➡LIKE, LOVE, VALUE AND ENJOY; 579]

put aside 1 *v* **save**, earmark, allocate, put by, set aside, put to one side, put away, stash away. [➡STORE AND KEEP; 454] 2 *v* **disregard**, ignore, close your eyes to, forget, waive, set aside. [➡NOT PAY ATTENTION; 765] 3 *v* **set down**, set aside, deposit, lay down, put down, put to one side. [➡MOVE SOMETHING TO ANOTHER LOCATION; 325]

put a spanner in the works *v* [➡MAKE IMPOSSIBLE; 277]

put a spoke in somebody's wheel *v* **foil**, thwart, frustrate, put a spanner in the works, put a wrench in the works, wreak havoc, cause havoc. [➡MAKE IMPOSSIBLE; 277] *Opposite:* help.

put a stop to *v* **put an end to**, stop, bring to an end, terminate (*formal*), pull the plug on, call a halt, discontinue, halt, suspend. [➡CAUSE TO STOP; 267] *Opposite:* continue.

putative 1 *adj* **supposed**, reputed, alleged, assumed, presumed. [➡UNCERTAIN; 176] 2 *adj* **accepted**, acknowledged, recognized, known, believed. [➡KNOWN AND FAMOUS; 182]

put at risk *v* **imperil** (*formal*), endanger, jeopardize, gamble with, risk. [➡PUT AT RISK; 385]

put away 1 *v* **tidy up**, pack away, clear up, tidy away, pack up, show. [➡ARRANGE AND CREATE ORDER; 358] *Opposite:* scatter. 2 *v* (*informal*) **consume**, eat, drink, swallow, devour, wolf, scarf down (*US slang*), bolt, chow down (*US informal*). [➡EAT AND NOT EAT; 711] 3 *v* **save**, put aside, keep, stash away, put by, set aside, earmark, allocate, put to one side. [➡STORE AND KEEP; 454] 4 *v* (*informal*) **imprison**, jail, commit, confine. [➡THE POLICE, ARREST, AND PRE-TRIAL PROCEEDINGS; 818]

put a wrench in the works (*US*) *v* **foil**, thwart, cause havoc, put a spanner in the works, put a spoke in somebody's wheel, frustrate, wreak havoc. [➡MAKE IMPOSSIBLE; 277] *Opposite:* help.

put back 1 *v* **postpone**, defer, suspend, put on hold, put off, reschedule, delay, hold up, set back, retard. [➡DELAY ACTION OR OCCURRENCE; 279] 2 *v* **drink**, throw back, put away, gulp down, swallow down, quaff (*literary or humorous*). [➡DRINK; 712] 3 *v* **put away**, replace, pack away, return, clear away, tidy. [➡MOVE SOMETHING TO ANOTHER LOCATION; 325] 4 *v* **pay back**, reimburse, compensate, recompense, remunerate. [➡GIVE MONEY; 434]

put back together *v* **mend**, repair, reassemble, rebuild, reconstruct. [➡REPAIR AND MEND; 377] *Opposite:* take apart.

put behind bars *v* [➡THE POLICE, ARREST, AND PRE-TRIAL PROCEEDINGS; 818]

put behind you *v* **forget**, get over, recover from, put down to experience, get out of your system, turn your back on. [➡FORGET, FORGIVE, AND ACCEPT; 749] *Opposite:* brood.

put by *v* **save**, put aside, stash away, earmark, put away, allocate, set aside, put to one side. [➡STORE AND KEEP; 454]

put down 1 *v* **set down**, lay down, down, deposit, leave, plonk, plop (*informal*), put aside. [➡MOVE SOMETHING: DOWNWARDS; 330] *Opposite:* pick up. 2 *v* **enter**, write down, put in writing, record, log, note, file. [➡RECORD SOMETHING; 372] 3 *v* (*informal*) **ridicule**, mock, criticize, deride, disparage, deprecate. [➡ACCUSE, BLAME, AND CRITICIZE; 642] *Opposite:* praise. 4 *v* **quell**, crush, suppress, quash, repress. [➡CAUSE TO STOP; 267]

See Compare and Contrast at **kill**.

putdown (*informal*) *n* **insult**, attack, jibe, criticism, slap in the face (*informal*), dig. [➡CRITICISMS AND ANGRY OUTBURSTS; 50] *Opposite:* compliment.

put forth (*formal*) 1 *v* **state**, set forth (*formal*), make known, publish, present, give, propose, submit, offer. [➡SUGGEST, HINT, AND COMMENT; 613] 2 *v* **leave**, set out, depart, head off, start out, move off. [➡ABSENT ONESELF; 8]

put forward 1 *v* **state**, set forth (*formal*), make known, publish, present, give. [➡INFORM AND ANNOUNCE; 612] 2 *v* **suggest**, propose, present, submit, offer. [➡SUGGEST, HINT, AND COMMENT; 613]

put in 1 *v* **denote**, dedicate, allocate, give, spend. [➡GIVE MONEY; 434] 2 *v* **present**, submit, offer, make, claim, apply, request. [➡SUGGEST, HINT, AND COMMENT; 613] 3 *v* **interrupt**, break in, interpose, interject, butt in. [➡INTERRUPT AND BUTT IN; 620]

put in an appearance *v* **attend**, show up (*informal*), drop in, appear, show (*informal*), turn up, be present, roll up, arrive, show your face. [➡ARRIVE; 12]

put in danger *v* **imperil** (*formal*), jeopardize, endanger, hazard, risk, compromise, menace. [➡PUT AT RISK; 385]

put in jail *v* [➡THE POLICE, ARREST, AND PRE-TRIAL PROCEEDINGS; 818]

put in prison *v* [➡THE POLICE, ARREST, AND PRE-TRIAL PROCEEDINGS; 818]

put in the shade *v* **outshine**, be head and shoulders above, eclipse, be streets ahead of, surpass, overshadow, be way ahead of (*US*). [➡BEAT AND DEFEAT; 80]

put into *v* **invest in**, plough into, sink in, tie up in, devote to, give to, donate to. [➡GIVE MONEY; 434]

put into action *v* **implement**, put into practice, apply, realize, carry out, put into effect, enforce, exercise. [➡CARRY OUT AN ACTION; 270]

put into effect *v* **enforce**, put into practice, exercise, apply, carry out, put into action, implement, realize. [➡CARRY OUT AN ACTION; 270]

put into operation *v* **implement**, put into action, put into practice, apply, set up, put into effect, carry out. [➡CARRY OUT AN ACTION; 270]

put into practice *v* **carry out**, do, practise, realize, implement, put into effect, achieve, accomplish, put into action. [➡CARRY OUT AN ACTION; 270]

put into words *v* **phrase**, articulate, formulate, express, convey, say. [➡EXPLAIN AND CLARIFY; 611]

put in writing *v* **put down on paper**, put down in black and white, put down, confirm in writing, write down, record. [➡RECORD SOMETHING; 372]

put money on *v* [➡GAMBLE AND TAKE RISKS; 467]

put off 1 *v* **postpone**, delay, defer, shelve, suspend, adjourn, hold over, leave to another time, put on the back burner, put on ice, put on hold. [➡DELAY ACTION OR OCCURRENCE; 279] *Opposite:* bring forward. 2 *v* **disgust**, repel, offend, sicken, revolt, repulse. [➡UPSET, DISTRESS, AND HUMILIATE; 568] *Opposite:* attract. 3 *v* **hinder**, delay, obstruct, prevent, impede. [➡MAKE IMPOSSIBLE; 277] 4 *v* **confuse**, distract, divert, disconcert, fluster, put somebody off his or her stride. [➡CONFUSE AND BEWILDER; 572]

put-on 1 *adj* **pretend**, false, fake, sham, feigned, artificial, assumed, phony. [➡FALSE AND UNREAL; 174] *Opposite:* genuine. 2 *n* (*informal*) **deception**, simulation, trick, hoax, con, pose (*disapproving*), act. [➡DECEPTION AND LIES; 661]

put on 1 *v* **dress in**, wear, change into, get into, don (*formal*). [➡DRESS, WEAR, AND UNDRESS; 868] *Opposite:* take off. 2 *v* **pretend**, feign, simulate, fake, play-act, sham, assume, adopt. [➡PRETEND AND MIMIC; 60] 3 *v* **stage**, present, produce, direct, dramatize, show. [➡CAUSE TO HAPPEN; 31] 4 *v* **gain**, add, increase, accumulate, acquire. [➡CHANGE OF SIZE: BIGGER; 393] *Opposite:* lose.

put on a brave front *v* **keep a stiff upper lip** (*informal*), put a brave face on it, keep up appearances, be brave, keep your chin up. [➡TOLERATE AND ENDURE; 767]

put on an act *v* **pretend**, put it on, put on a pretence, sham, feign, play-act, ham, play to the gallery. [➡PRETEND AND MIMIC; 60]

put on a pedestal *v* **elevate**, idolize, worship, admire, regard highly, look up to, lionize, adulate. [➡PRAISE AND ENCOURAGE; 648]

put on hold *v* **put off**, delay, postpone, adjourn, defer, set aside, put to one side, shelve, put on the back burner, put on ice. [➡DELAY ACTION OR OCCURRENCE; 279]

put on ice *v* **put off**, delay, postpone, adjourn, defer, set aside, shelve, put on hold, put on the back burner. [➡DELAY ACTION OR OCCURRENCE; 279]

put on the back burner *v* **put off**, delay, postpone, adjourn, defer, set aside, put to one side, shelve, put on hold, put on ice. [➡DELAY ACTION OR OCCURRENCE; 279]

put on the market *v* **offer for sale**, put up for sale, market, advertise. [➡SELL; 442]

put out 1 *v* **extinguish**, douse, snuff out, stifle, snuff. [➡CAUSE TO STOP; 267] *Opposite:* light. 2 *v* **make public**, make known, publicize, circulate, spread, issue, publish, release, put about, disseminate. [➡INFORM AND ANNOUNCE; 612] *Opposite:* keep secret. 3 *v* **annoy**, irritate, aggravate (*informal*), exasperate, inconvenience, disturb, vex, provoke, niggle. [➡ANGER AND ANNOY; 570] *Opposite:* please.

put paid to (*informal*) *v* [➡CAUSE TO STOP; 267]

put pressure on *v* [➡CAUSE OR COMPEL TO ACT; 272]

putrefaction *n* **decay**, decomposition, rot, breakdown, corruption, degeneration. [➡DECAYING OR INFESTED; 1235]

putrefied *adj* [➡DECAYING OR INFESTED; 1235]

putrefy *v* **rot**, decay, decompose, go bad, go off, go mouldy, deteriorate, become rancid, spoil, turn. [➡GO BAD AND CORRODE; 391]

putrescent *adj* [➡DECAYING OR INFESTED; 1235]

putrid *adj* **rotten**, rotting, decayed, decaying, decomposed, decomposing, tainted, putrescent, bad, spoiled, foetid, rancid, rank (*literary*), mouldy, off. [➡DECAYING OR INFESTED; 1235] *Opposite:* fresh.

put right *v* **repair**, fix, mend, rectify, restore, redress, correct, straighten out. [➡CORRECT AND PUT RIGHT; 378]

putsch *n* **coup**, insurrection, uprising, revolution, revolt, overthrow. [➡ELECTIONS AND SUFFRAGE; 807]

put somebody's back up (*informal*) *v* **annoy**, irritate, wind up (*informal*), get on somebody's nerves, get up somebody's nose, aggravate (*informal*), get on the wrong side of, provoke, bother, vex, put out. [➡ANGER AND ANNOY; 570]

putt 1 *v* **hit**, tap, stroke, knock, push, drive. [➡PUSH, PULL, SLIDE; 336] 2 *n* **tap**, stroke, hit, knock, push, shove. [➡PUSH, PULL, SLIDE; 336]

put the arm on (*US informal*) *v* [➡CAUSE OR COMPEL TO ACT; 272]

put the boot in *v* [➡PHYSICAL ATTACK AND PUNISHMENT; 416]

put the lid on *v* [➡CAUSE TO STOP; 267]

put to death *v* **kill**, execute, murder, assassinate, liquidate, decapitate, guillotine, exterminate, bump off (*slang*), massacre, slaughter, slay (*formal or literary*), waste (*slang*). [➡KILL; 923]

put together 1 *v* **assemble**, piece together, construct, build, fabricate, make. [➡BUILD; 353] 2 *v* **draw up**, formulate, devise, develop, prepare, run up, rustle up (*informal*), concoct, make up, invent. [➡CREATION; 347]

put to good use *v* **use**, apply, exploit, exercise, make use of, utilize, find a use for. [➡MAKE GOOD USE OF SOMETHING; 474] *Opposite:* discard.

put to sleep *v* **knock out**, sedate, anaesthetize, put under, numb, dope. [➡REMEDIES, TREATMENTS AND OPERATIONS; 732]

put to use *v* [➡USE; 468]

putty 1 *n* [➡BUILDING MATERIALS; 1076] 2 *type of* **grey**. [➡COLOURS; 1223]

put under *v* **sedate**, put to sleep, anaesthetize, put out, knock out. [➡REMEDIES, TREATMENTS AND OPERATIONS; 732] *Opposite:* bring round.

put up 1 *v* **erect**, raise, build, construct, create. [➡BUILD; 353] *Opposite:* tear down. 2 *v* **accommodate**, house, lodge. [➡TAKE CARE OF AND SPOIL; 301] *Opposite:* evict. 3 *v* **offer**, provide, proffer, extend, advance, give. [➡GIVE MONEY; 434]

put-upon *adj* **overburdened**, exploited, used, overworked, abused. [➡IN TROUBLE AND DISADVANTAGED; 73]

put up to *v* **induce**, persuade, encourage, make, cause, incite, prompt, urge. [➡CAUSE OR COMPEL TO ACT; 272] *Opposite:* dissuade.

put up with *v* **tolerate**, endure, bear, stand, submit, swallow, stomach, suffer, shoulder. [➡TOLERATE AND ENDURE; 767]

put your back into *v* **try hard**, give your all, use elbow grease (*informal*), give it your best shot, give it all you've got, buckle down (*informal*), slog, go for it (*slang*), go all out. [➡HARD WORK OR EFFORT; 299]

put your faith in *v* **trust**, rely on, count on, have confidence in, bank on, believe. [➡CERTAINTY; 562]

put your feet up *v* **relax**, rest, nap, take five (*informal*), catch forty winks (*informal*), stop, put your head down, chill out (*slang*), take a breather (*informal*), take it easy, lounge around, lie down, catch some 'z' s (*US informal*). [➡STOP ACTING; 265]

put your foot down *v* **demand**, stand firm, stand fast, be resolute, be determined, insist. [➡CLAIM, INSIST, AND EMPHASIZE; 615]

put your foot in it (*informal*) *v* **blunder**, boob (*informal*), put your foot in your mouth (*informal*), err, goof, slip up (*informal*), speak out of turn, be indiscreet, be tactless. [➡BETRAY CONFIDENCES AND GOSSIP; 619]

put your foot in your mouth (*informal*) *v* **blunder**, put your foot in it (*informal*), be indiscreet, be tactless, speak out of turn, goof, boob (*informal*), slip up (*informal*), err. [➡BETRAY CONFIDENCES AND GOSSIP; 619]

put your oar in *v* **interfere**, meddle, stick your nose in, intrude, butt in, intervene. [➡INTERRUPT AND BUTT IN; 620]

puzzle 1 *v* **mystify**, bewilder, perplex, baffle, confuse, bamboozle (*informal*), wonder, mull, brood, ponder, stump. [➡CONFUSE AND BEWILDER; 572] 2 *n* **mystery**, enigma, conundrum, problem, dilemma, brainteaser, riddle, poser, puzzler. [➡SECRETS AND MYSTERIES; 181] *Opposite:* explanation.

See Compare and Contrast at **problem.**

puzzled *adj* **mystified**, bewildered, perplexed, baffled, confused, bamboozled (*informal*), all at sea, at a complete loss, nonplussed, confounded. [➡CONFUSION, ANXIETY, AND WORRY; 541] *Opposite:* enlightened.

puzzlement *n* **bafflement**, perplexity, uncertainty, disorientation, bemusement, confusion, bewilderment, mystification. [➡CONFUSION, ANXIETY, AND WORRY; 541] *Opposite:* understanding.

puzzle out *v* **work out**, solve, figure out, resolve, decipher, find the answer, decode. [➡SOLVE AND INTERPRET; 761]

puzzler *n* **conundrum**, puzzle, mystery, riddle, brainteaser, challenge. [➡SECRETS AND MYSTERIES; 181]

puzzling *adj* **mystifying**, bewildering, perplexing, baffling, confusing, bamboozling (*informal*). [➡DIFFICULTY AND COMPLEXITY; 243] *Opposite:* enlightening.

PVC *type of* **synthetic fabric.** [➡FABRICS; 1131]

pye-dog *n* [➡DOG; 980]

pygmy *adj* **miniature**, small, tiny, dwarf, little, undersized, diminutive, midget, toy. [➡SMALL; 1194]

pyjamas *type of* **sleepwear.** [➡GARMENTS AND OUTFITS; 865]

pylon *n* **tower**, mast, post, pillar. [➡TOWERS; 1098]

pyralid *type of* **moth.** [➡MOTHS AND BUTTERFLIES; 1015]

pyramid *type of* **angular shape.** [➡ANGULAR SHAPE; 1216]

pyre *n* **fire**, bonfire, furnace. [➡FIRE, FLAMMABILITY, AND BURNING; 1164]

pyrite *type of* **mineral.** [➡MINERALS; 1276]

pyromania *n* [➡FADS, FETISHES, AND IDOLATRY; 556]

pyromaniac *n* **fire raiser**, fire setter, arsonist, torcher. [➡DEVOTEES AND ADDICTED PEOPLE; 557]

pyrophobia *type of* **phobia.** [➡FEARS AND PHOBIAS; 555]

pyrotechnics *n* [➡FIRE, FLAMMABILITY, AND BURNING; 1164]

python *type of* **non-poisonous snake.** [➡SNAKE; 995]

QC *n* **Queen's Counsel**, counsel, barrister, brief (*informal*). [➡PEOPLE IN LAW COURTS; 820]

quack 1 *n* **charlatan**, fraud, con artist (*slang*), fake, sham, pretender. [➡PEOPLE WHO DECEIVE; 662] 2 *type of* **bird sound**. [➡SOUNDS MADE BY BIRDS; 1262]

quackery *n* **deception**, trickery, dishonesty, fraud, deceit, charlatanism, flimflam (*slang*). [➡DECEPTION AND LIES; 661] *Opposite:* honesty.

quad (*informal*) *n* **courtyard**, square, patio, piazza, plaza, yard, quadrangle. [➡URBAN OUTDOOR SPACES; 1071]

quadrangle 1 *n* **courtyard**, quad (*informal*), square, piazza, plaza, patio. [➡URBAN OUTDOOR SPACES; 1071] 2 *n* **four-sided figure**, rectangle, oblong, quadrilateral, parallelogram, rhombus, lozenge, diamond, square. [➡ANGULAR SHAPE; 1216]

quadrant *type of* **measuring device**. [➡MEASURING DEVICES; 1122]

quadriceps *type of* **muscle or tendon**. [➡THE MUSCLES; 719]

quadrilateral 1 *n* **rectangle**, oblong, square, parallelogram, rhombus, lozenge, diamond, four-sided figure, tetragon, trapezoid, trapezium. [➡ANGULAR SHAPE; 1216] 2 *adj* **four-sided**, quadrangular, quadrate, rectangular, square, rhomboid, diamond, trapezoidal. [➡ANGULAR SHAPE; 1216]

quadrille *type of* **dance**. [➡DANCE; 903]

quadruped *n* **animal**, four-footed animal, tetrapod. [➡LIVING THINGS AND LIVING; 976]

quadruple *v* **increase fourfold**, multiply, times, magnify, augment, expand. [➡CHANGE OF SIZE: BIGGER; 393] *Opposite:* decrease.

quadruplet *type of* **offspring**. [➡YOUNGER GENERATION RELATIVES; 958]

quaff (*literary or humorous*) *v* **drink**, swig (*informal*), gulp down, guzzle (*informal*), put away, knock back (*informal*), throw back, swallow down, swill, imbibe (*formal or humorous*). [➡DRINK; 712]

quagmire 1 *n* **swamp**, marsh, bog, mire, quicksand, morass. [➡WETLANDS; 1043] 2 *n* **predicament**, dilemma, quandary, sticky situation, muddle, imbroglio (*formal or literary*), crisis, perplexity, entanglement. [➡DIFFICULT SITUATIONS; 72]

quahog *type of* **aquatic invertebrate**. [➡AQUATIC INVERTEBRATE; 1022]

quail 1 *type of* **fowl**. [➡FOOD BIRD; 999] 2 *v* **flinch**, recoil, cringe, baulk. [➡PHYSICAL REACTIONS; 317]

See Compare and Contrast at **recoil**.

quaint 1 *adj* **old-world**, old-fashioned, picturesque, antiquated, charming, pretty, attractive, appealing. [➡BEAUTY AND ATTRACTIVENESS; 190] *Opposite:* modern. 2 *adj* **strange**, peculiar, odd, curious, bizarre, weird, extraordinary, unusual. [➡BIZARRE AND PECULIAR; 258] *Opposite:* ordinary.

quaintness 1 *n* **strangeness**, peculiarity, oddness, weirdness, curiousness, curiosity. [➡BIZARRE AND PECULIAR; 258] *Opposite:* ordinariness. 2 *n* **picturesqueness**, antiquatedness, antiqueness, charm, appeal, attraction, attractiveness, prettiness. [➡BEAUTY AND ATTRACTIVENESS; 190] *Opposite:* modernity.

quake 1 *v* **quail**, tremble, quaver, cower, flinch, cringe, show fear, take fright. [➡PHYSICAL REACTIONS; 317] 2 *v* **shake**, tremble, quiver, shudder, shiver, wobble, vibrate. [➡BOUNCE, UNDULATE, AND VIBRATE; 309] 3 *n* (*informal*) **earthquake**, tremor, seism (*technical*), seismic wave, seismic activity. [➡VOLCANOES AND EARTHQUAKES; 1054]

qualification 1 *n* [➡QUALIFICATIONS; 843] 2 *n* **skill**, quality, attribute, ability, aptitude, talent, characteristic, fitness, experience. [➡SKILLS, TALENTS, AND ABILITIES; 527] *Opposite:* failing. 3 *n* **requirement**, condition, prerequisite, criterion, sine qua non, stipulation, proviso, rider. [➡NECESSARY AND ESSENTIAL; 197] 4 *n* **restriction**, modification, limitation, tempering. [➡CHANGE OF INTENSITY: LESS; 396]

qualified 1 *adj* **eligible**, short-listed, accepted, nominated, seeded, authorized, certified, licensed, enrolled. [➡NAME AND DESCRIBE; 666] *Opposite:* unqualified. 2 *adj* **suitable**, fitted, eligible, capable, competent, skilled, trained, practised, experienced. [➡APPROPRIATE, SUITABLE, ADVISABLE; 185] *Opposite:* unsuitable.

qualifier *type of* **word class**. [➡ASPECTS OF LANGUAGE; 683]

qualify 1 *v* **be suitable**, be in the running, meet the requirements, be eligible, make the grade, be nominated, succeed, be licensed, be certified. [➡SUCCEED AND WIN; 79] *Opposite:* fail. 2 *v* **restrict**, limit, modify, temper, lessen, soften, reduce. [➡CHANGE OF INTENSITY: LESS; 396]

quality 1 *n* **characteristic**, feature, attribute, property, trait, condition. [➡QUALITIES AND CHARACTERISTICS; 1190] 2 *n* **excellence**, superiority, class, eminence, worth, value. [➡GOOD, WELL, BETTER; 184] *Opposite:* inferiority.

qualm 1 *n* **scruple**, pang of conscience, remorse, contrition, regret, repentance, shame. [➡FEELINGS ABOUT THE PAST; 533] 2 *n* **misgiving**, doubt, pang, fear, apprehensiveness, uneasiness, forebodingness, trepidation, disquiet. [➡FEELINGS ABOUT THE FUTURE; 534] *Opposite:* hunch.

quandary *n* **dilemma**, predicament, fix (*informal*), jam (*informal*), difficulty, cleft stick, catch-22. [➡DIFFICULT SITUATIONS; 72]

quantifiable *adj* **calculable**, computable, measurable, assessable, reckonable, finite, countable, specifiable, ratable. [➡MATHS; 598] *Opposite:* unquantifiable.

quantifier *type of* **word class.** [➡ASPECTS OF LANGUAGE; 683]

quantify *v* **calculate**, count, enumerate, measure, compute, tell, reckon, put a figure on. [➡ASSESS QUANTITY; 758]

quantitative 1 *adj* **numerical**, enumerative, finite, arithmetical, mathematical, variable. [➡MATHS; 598] 2 *adj* **measurable**, quantifiable, calculable, numerical, computable, assessable, reckonable, ratable. [➡MATHS; 598] *Opposite:* unquantifiable.

quantity *n* **amount**, number, measure, extent, size, magnitude, capacity, mass. [➡AMOUNT AND QUANTITY; 112]

quantum *adj* **major**, dramatic, significant, important, considerable, substantial, huge. [➡MOST IMPORTANT AND MAIN; 194] *Opposite:* minor.

quarantine 1 *n* **isolation**, seclusion, confinement, solitary confinement, cordon sanitaire, separation. [➡REMEDIES, TREATMENTS AND OPERATIONS; 732] *Opposite:* integration. 2 *v* **isolate**, seclude, set apart, confine, separate, cordon off. [➡FALL ILL, TREAT, AND RECOVER; 729] *Opposite:* integrate. 3 *v* **detain**, imprison, hold, lock up, intern, confine, keep under lock and key, put in solitary. [➡CAPTIVITY AND LOSS OF FREEDOM; 249] *Opposite:* release.

quark *type of* **elementary particle.** [➡ELEMENTARY PARTICLES; 1278]

quarrel 1 *n* **argument**, dispute, squabble, disagreement, row, tiff, difference of opinion, clash, fight, spat, wrangle. [➡ARGUMENT; 47] *Opposite:* reconciliation. 2 *v* **argue**, row, fall out, have a tiff, clash, fight, wrangle. [➡ARGUE AND FIGHT – TWO-WAY; 644] *Opposite:* make up.

quarrelsome *adj* **argumentative**, cantankerous, irritable, petulant, confrontational, querulous, grouchy (*informal*), hot-tempered, difficult. [➡DIFFICULT TO PLEASE; 516] *Opposite:* agreeable.

quarry 1 *n* **mine**, excavation, pit, diggings. [➡INDUSTRIAL BUILDINGS; 1086] 2 *v* **mine**, dig out, extract, excavate, dig up, gouge out, cut. [➡EXTRACT AND SEVER; 342] 3 *n* **prey**, victim, target, kill, game, objective. [➡DEAD PERSON; 926] *Opposite:* hunter.

quarter 1 *n* **district**, neighbourhood, sector, section, part, area, barrio, quartier. [➡HUMAN SETTLEMENTS; 1069] 2 *n* **fourth**, division, part, section, quadrant, quartile. [➡MEASUREABLE PORTION; 125] 3 *v* **divide**, subdivide, cut up, section, split up, slice. [➡SEPARATE AND DIVIDE; 402] 4 *v* **lodge**, house, billet, accommodate, put up, find a bed for. [➡TAKE CARE OF AND SPOIL; 301] *Opposite:* evict. 5 *type of* **time period.** [➡TIMES OF YEAR; 88]

quarterfinal *n* **round**, heat, leg, match, game. [➡NON-AGGRESSIVE/SPORTING EVENT; 40]

quarterly 1 *adj* **three-monthly**, trimestral, four times a year. [➡TIMES OF YEAR; 88] 2 *n* **magazine**, periodical, journal, publication, glossy magazine, slick (*US*). [➡NEWSPAPERS; 606]

quarters *n* **rooms**, lodgings (*dated*), accommodation, digs (*dated informal*), billet, housing, accommodations (*US*). [➡ACCOMMODATION; 855]

quartet *type of* **band.** [➡MUSICIANS AND SINGERS; 908]

quartile *n* [➡MEASUREABLE PORTION; 125]

quartz *type of* **mineral.** [➡MINERALS; 1276]

quartz glass *type of* **glass.** [➡GLASS; 1135]

quartz heater *type of* **heating appliance.** [➡HEATING, REFRIGERATION, AND VENTILATION; 1141]

quartzite *type of* **stone.** [➡STONES, ROCKS, AND BOULDERS; 1057]

quasar *type of* **star or star system.** [➡CELESTIAL BODIES; 1060]

quash 1 *v* **put down**, suppress, quell, crush, repress, overwhelm, defeat, conquer. [➡BEAT AND DEFEAT; 80] *Opposite:* allow. 2 *v* **nullify**, cancel, repeal, overturn, annul, invalidate, make void. [➡ABOLISH AND ANNUL; 453] *Opposite:* validate.

quasi *adj* **virtual**, as it were (*formal*), to all intents and purposes, pseudo, would-be, wannabe (*informal disapproving*), self-styled, mock. [➡FALSE AND UNREAL; 174] *Opposite:* through and through.

quatrain *n* **verse**, stanza, rhyme. [➡POETRY AND VERSE; 915]

quaver 1 *v* **tremble**, shake, quiver, quake, quail, flinch. [➡PHYSICAL REACTIONS; 317] 2 *v* **trill**, warble, wobble, vibrate, quiver, waver. [➡EMIT RINGING AND TOOTING SOUNDS; 368]

quavering *adj* [➡SOFT OR PLEASANT SOUNDS; 1264]

quay *n* **dockside**, wharf, quayside, dock, pier, harbour, seafront, jetty. [➡WATERWAYS AND SEAWAYS; 1107]

quayside *n* **dock**, quay, dockside, wharf, harbour, seafront. [➡WATERWAYS AND SEAWAYS; 1107]

queasily *adv* **nauseously**, biliously, dizzily, groggily, woozily. [➡ILL AND SICK; 741]

queasiness *n* **nausea**, sickness, biliousness, vomiting, upset stomach, dizziness, faintness. [➡ILL AND SICK; 741]

queasy 1 *adj* **nauseous**, sick, ill, green around the gills (*informal*), seasick, odd, groggy, woozy, unsettled, queer (*dated*). [➡ILL AND SICK; 741] *Opposite:* well. 2 *adj* **uneasy**, uncomfortable, doubtful, dubious, troubling, unsettling. [➡INSECURITY AND LOSS OF COMPOSURE; 545] *Opposite:* reassuring.

queen 1 *n* **monarch**, sovereign, ruler, crowned head, empress. [➡RULERS AND ARISTOCRACY; 823] 2 *n* **icon**, star, doyenne, epitome, model, crème de la crème, ideal. [➡IMPORTANT OR FAMOUS PEOPLE; 893]

queenly *adj* **majestic**, royal, regal, dignified, stately, noble. [➡ROYALNESS; 825]

Queen's Counsel *n* [➡PEOPLE IN LAW COURTS; 820]

queen-size *adj* **large**, largish, medium-large. [➡LARGE; 1192]

queen-size bed *type of* **bed.** [➡FURNITURE; 858]

queer (*dated*) 1 *adj* **unusual**, unexpected, strange, surprising, funny, odd, peculiar, out of the ordinary, atypical. [➡BIZARRE AND PECULIAR; 258] *Opposite:* commonplace. 2 *adj* **eccentric**, unconventional, cranky (*informal*), idiosyncratic, out of the ordinary, strange, peculiar, curious, bizarre, unusual. [➡BIZARRE AND PECULIAR; 258] *Opposite:* normal. 3 *adj* **unwell**, sick, nauseous, queasy, faint, dizzy, groggy, woozy. [➡ILL AND SICK; 741] *Opposite:* well.

queerly (*dated*) 1 *adv* **eccentrically**, unconventionally, strangely, idiosyncratically, crankily (*informal*), peculiarly, funnily, oddly, unusually, curiously, bizarrely. [➡ BIZARRE AND PECULIAR; 258] *Opposite:* normally. **2** *adv* **unusually**, oddly, funnily, unexpectedly, surprisingly, strangely, peculiarly, atypically. [➡ BIZARRE AND PECULIAR; 258] *Opposite:* typically.

queerness (*dated*) *n* **eccentricity**, oddness, strangeness, peculiarity, abnormality, crankiness (*informal*), bizarreness. [➡ BIZARRE AND PECULIAR; 258] *Opposite:* normality.

quell **1** *v* **suppress**, put down, subdue, crush, quash, repress, control, overwhelm, defeat, conquer. [➡ CAUSE TO STOP; 267] *Opposite:* incite. **2** *v* **allay**, assuage, alleviate, mollify, mitigate, soothe, calm, disperse. [➡ CHANGE OF INTENSITY: LESS; 396] *Opposite:* aggravate.

quench **1** *v* **slake**, satisfy, satiate, reduce, sate, appease. [➡ DRINK; 712] *Opposite:* stimulate. **2** *v* **extinguish**, put out, douse, smother, stifle, snuff out. [➡ CAUSE TO STOP; 267] *Opposite:* ignite.

querulous **1** *adj* **complaining**, carping, critical, difficult, hard to please, fussy, negative, censorious. [➡ ACCUSATORY AND DISAPPROVING; 635] *Opposite:* equable. **2** *adj* **whining**, whingeing (*informal*), cantankerous, moaning (*informal*), grumbling, complaining, grouchy (*informal*). [➡ BAD-TEMPERED AND HUMOURLESS; 627] *Opposite:* good-natured.

querulously *adv* **complainingly**, carpingly, cantankerously, critically, fussily, negatively, censoriously. [➡ ACCUSATORY AND DISAPPROVING; 635] *Opposite:* positively.

querulousness *n* **peevishness**, negativity, cantankerousness, criticalness, argumentativeness, quarrelsomeness, provocativeness, petulance. [➡ BAD-TEMPERED AND HUMOURLESS; 627]

query **1** *n* **inquiry**, question, request, interrogation, demand, probe. [➡ ASK PEOPLE QUESTIONS; 667] *Opposite:* answer. **2** *n* **doubt**, uncertainty, reservation, question, question mark, objection. [➡ UNCERTAINTY; 560] *Opposite:* certainty. **3** *v* **question**, cast doubt on, doubt, suspect, challenge, mistrust, distrust, have reservations about. [➡ QUESTION THINGS; 752] *Opposite:* trust. **4** *v* **inquire**, ask, interrogate, quiz, demand, question, probe, grill (*informal*), look into. [➡ ASK PEOPLE QUESTIONS; 667] *Opposite:* answer.

quest **1** *n* **mission**, expedition, pursuit, search, hunt, journey. [➡ SEEK POSSESSION AND SEARCH; 457] **2** *v* **search**, hunt, seek, chase, pursue, go in search of. [➡ SEEK POSSESSION AND SEARCH; 457] *Opposite:* find.

question **1** *n* **inquiry**, query, interrogation, request, demand. [➡ ASK PEOPLE QUESTIONS; 667] *Opposite:* answer. **2** *n* **uncertainty**, doubt, reservation, query, question mark, hesitation, anxiety. [➡ UNCERTAINTY; 560] *Opposite:* certainty. **3** *n* **issue**, subject, matter, point at issue, problem, difficulty. [➡ SUBJECT AREA; 769] *Opposite:* resolution. **4** *v* **interrogate**, quiz, ask, grill (*informal*), give the third degree (*informal*), probe, examine, look into. [➡ ASK PEOPLE QUESTIONS; 667] *Opposite:* reply. **5** *v* **doubt**, suspect, mistrust, distrust, query, have reservations about, cast doubt on. [➡ QUESTION THINGS; 752] *Opposite:* trust.

Compare and Contrast: ***question, quiz, interrogate, grill, give the third degree***

CORE MEANING: TO ASK FOR INFORMATION

question to ask for information on a particular subject, especially formally or officially; ***quiz*** to subject somebody to persistent questions; ***interrogate*** to question somebody systematically and intensively in a formal or official context, such as in a police investigation or court case; ***grill*** (*informal*) to question somebody intensively; ***give the third degree*** (*informal*) to question somebody intensively, especially in an aggressive way.

questionable *adj* **dubious**, doubtful, open to discussion, open to doubt, moot, disputed, problematic, debatable, uncertain. [➡ UNCERTAIN; 176] *Opposite:* indisputable.

questionably *adv* **doubtfully**, uncertainly, debatably, dubiously, problematically, disputably. [➡ UNCERTAIN; 176] *Opposite:* indisputably.

questioner *n* **interviewer**, interrogator, cross-examiner, asker, inquirer, examiner. [➡ QUESTIONERS; 668] *Opposite:* interviewee.

questioning *adj* **interrogative**, inquisitorial, searching, quizzical, inquiring, probing, prying, nosy (*informal*), inquisitive, curious. [➡ ENTHUSIASTIC AND INQUISITIVE; 629] *Opposite:* responsive.

question mark **1** *n* **doubt**, uncertainty, reservation, query, question, issue. [➡ UNCERTAINTY; 560] *Opposite:* certainty. **2** *type of* **punctuation mark**. [➡ ASPECTS OF LANGUAGE; 683]

question master *n* **host**, interviewer, questioner, chair, examiner. [➡ WORKERS IN ENTERTAINMENT AND MEDIA; 873] *Opposite:* contestant.

questionnaire *n* **survey**, opinion poll, inquiry form, form, feedback form. [➡ ASK PEOPLE QUESTIONS; 667]

queue **1** *n* **line**, file, row, crocodile, column, train. [➡ AREA AND RANGE; 111] **2** *n* **tailback**, backlog, log jam, train, string, succession. [➡ TRAVEL: TRAFFIC PROBLEMS AND HOLDUPS; 324] **3** *v* **line up**, queue up, form a queue, get in line, wait your turn, stand in line, wait in line. [➡ GET CLOSER TOGETHER; 311]

queue-jump *v* **push in**, move ahead, leapfrog, overtake, butt in, push ahead, gain an advantage. [➡ MOVE PAST, INTO OR THROUGH SOMETHING; 332]

quibble **1** *v* **equivocate**, hedge, split hairs, nitpick, cavil, be pedantic. [➡ PROTEST AND EXPRESS DISAPPROVAL; 643] *Opposite:* agree. **2** *n* **objection**, cavil, equivocation, quiddity (*formal*). [➡ DISHARMONY; 157]

quiche *n* **tart**, egg pie, flan, tartlet, pastry. [➡ BREAD, FLOUR, AND BREAD PRODUCTS; 1178]

quick **1** *adj* **rapid**, fast, speedy, swift, nippy, hasty, hurried. [➡ MOVING QUICKLY; 103] *Opposite:* slow. **2** *adj* **alert**, clever, bright, quick-thinking, quick-witted, sharp-witted, smart, adroit, quick on the uptake (*informal*), shrewd, astute, intelligent, quick off the mark, on the ball (*informal*). [➡ POSITIVE INTELLECTUAL CHARACTERISTICS; 525] **3** *adj* **nimble**, lively, sprightly, spry, agile, nifty (*informal*). [➡ DESCRIBING BODY MOVEMENTS; 289] *Opposite:* sluggish. **4** *adj*

sudden, immediate, instant, prompt, abrupt, swift, rapid. [➡HAPPENING QUICKLY; 104] *Opposite:* delayed. 5 *adj* **brief**, short, cursory, fleeting, momentary, passing, transient. [➡HAPPENING QUICKLY; 104] *Opposite:* lasting.

See Compare and Contrast at **intelligent**.

quick as a flash *adv* [➡HAPPENING QUICKLY; 104]

quicken *v* **speed up**, accelerate, hasten, pick up speed, go faster, get faster, open up (*informal*). [➡CHANGE OF SPEED: MORE; 397] *Opposite:* slow down.

quick-fire *adj* **rapid**, swift, successive, automatic, fast, brisk, speedy, quick. [➡HAPPENING QUICKLY; 104] *Opposite:* measured.

quickly 1 *adv* **rapidly**, fast, speedily, swiftly, hurriedly, hastily, nippily. [➡MOVING QUICKLY; 103] *Opposite:* slowly. 2 *adv* **suddenly**, immediately, promptly, without delay, at once, instantly, abruptly, hurriedly, hastily. [➡HAPPENING QUICKLY; 104] *Opposite:* slowly. 3 *adv* **briefly**, cursorily, fleetingly, momentarily, passingly, transiently. [➡FINITENESS, VARIABILITY, AND TRANSIENCE; 96] *Opposite:* lastingly.

quickness 1 *n* **rapidity**, speed, speediness, swiftness, nippiness, promptness. [➡SPEED; 102] *Opposite:* sluggishness. 2 *n* **alertness**, cleverness, quick-wittedness, adroitness, sharpness, responsiveness, intelligence. [➡POSITIVE INTELLECTUAL CHARACTERISTICS; 525]

quick off the mark *adj* [➡POSITIVE INTELLECTUAL CHARACTERISTICS; 525]

quick on the uptake (*informal*) *adj* **bright**, smart, quick-witted, alert, intelligent, sharp, with it (*informal*), on the ball (*informal*), quick. [➡POSITIVE INTELLECTUAL CHARACTERISTICS; 525]

quicksand *n* **swamp**, marsh, quagmire, bog, mire, morass. [➡WETLANDS; 1043]

quicksilver *adj* **volatile**, mercurial, changeable, inconstant, unpredictable, unstable. [➡EXCESSIVE SENSITIVITY; 512] *Opposite:* constant.

quickstep *type of* **dance**. [➡DANCE; 903]

quick-tempered *adj* **fiery**, temperamental, excitable, volatile, passionate, hotheaded, hot-blooded. [➡EXCESSIVE SENSITIVITY; 512] *Opposite:* calm.

quick-thinking *adj* [➡POSITIVE INTELLECTUAL CHARACTERISTICS; 525]

quick-witted *adj* **smart**, intelligent, clever, bright, sharp, quick, brilliant, alert, adroit, inventive, perceptive, astute. [➡POSITIVE INTELLECTUAL CHARACTERISTICS; 525]

quick-wittedness *n* **adroitness**, inventiveness, sharpness, intelligence, cleverness, perceptiveness, keenness, astuteness. [➡POSITIVE INTELLECTUAL CHARACTERISTICS; 525]

quid (*informal*) *n* [➡CURRENCIES; 798]

quid pro quo *n* **deal**, trade, agreement, exchange, trade-off, bribe, tit for tat, an eye for an eye. [➡HARMONY; 156]

quiescence (*formal*) *n* **inactivity**, rest, stillness, inertness, calm, dormancy, motionlessness, latency, inertia, lifelessness, stagnation, sluggishness. [➡LACK OF ACTIVITY; 343] *Opposite:* action.

quiescent (*formal*) *adj* **calm**, inactive, dormant, gentle, sluggish, inert, still, motionless, latent, lifeless. [➡LACK OF ACTIVITY; 343] *Opposite:* active.

quiescently (*formal*) *adv* **calmly**, gently, sluggishly, inertly. [➡LACK OF ACTIVITY; 343] *Opposite:* actively.

quiet 1 *adj* **silent**, noiseless, inaudible, low, soft, discreet, unobtrusive, soundless. [➡ABSENCE OF SOUND; 1256] *Opposite:* noisy. 2 *adj* **peaceful**, still, tranquil, uninterrupted, undisturbed, serene, calm, halcyon (*literary*). [➡PEACEFULNESS AND GENTLENESS; 215] *Opposite:* noisy. 3 *adj* **private**, discreet, unofficial, off-the-record, confidential, intimate. [➡SECRET AND UNKNOWN; 180] *Opposite:* public. 4 *adj* **trouble-free**, straightforward, uncomplicated, simple, easy, hassle-free (*informal*). [➡EASE AND SIMPLICITY; 201] 5 *adj* **relaxing**, restful, leisurely, peaceful, pleasant, untroubled, relaxed. [➡EMOTIONALLY PLEASANT; 188] *Opposite:* busy. 6 *adj* **discreet**, modest, subtle, subdued, muted, understated, restrained, unobtrusive. [➡IMPERCEPTIBLE; 26] *Opposite:* showy. 7 *n* **silence**, hush, peace, stillness, tranquillity, peace and quiet, quietude. [➡ABSENCE OF SOUND; 1256] *Opposite:* noise.

See Compare and Contrast at **silent**.

quieten 1 *v* **fall silent**, calm down, settle down, calm, hush, silence. [➡CHANGE OF INTENSITY: LESS; 396] *Opposite:* animate. 2 *v* **alleviate**, allay, soothe, assuage, quell, mollify, banish, dispel, still. [➡CHANGE OF INTENSITY: LESS; 396] *Opposite:* aggravate.

quieten down *v* **stop talking**, fall silent, keep it down, shut up (*informal*), belt up (*slang*), shut it (*informal*), quieten, cool it (*informal*). [➡SOUND EMISSION; 363]

quietly 1 *adv* **silently**, gently, inaudibly, softly, in silence, soundlessly, noiselessly, unobtrusively. [➡ABSENCE OF SOUND; 1256] *Opposite:* loudly. 2 *adv* **calmly**, peacefully, tranquilly, serenely, uninterrupted, undisturbed. [➡CALMNESS, CONFIDENCE, AND COMPOSURE; 537] *Opposite:* noisily. 3 *adv* **peacefully**, tranquilly, pleasantly, agreeably, restfully. [➡EMOTIONALLY PLEASANT; 188]

quietness 1 *n* **silence**, softness, quiet, noiselessness, inaudibility, lowness, discreetness, unobtrusiveness, soundlessness. [➡ABSENCE OF SOUND; 1256] *Opposite:* noise. 2 *n* **peace**, stillness, tranquillity, serenity, calm, quiet. [➡PEACEFULNESS AND GENTLENESS; 215]

quiff *type of* **hairstyle**. [➡HAIR STYLES AND HAIR PIECES; 489]

quill 1 *n* **feather**, plume, barb, spine, spike. [➡PARTS OF A BIRD; 1006] 2 *type of* **pen**. [➡WRITING AND DRAWING IMPLEMENTS, AND MEDIA; 602]

quilt *n* **bedcover**, bedspread, eiderdown, counterpane (*dated*), coverlet, duvet, comforter (*US*). [➡SOFT FURNISHINGS, LINEN, AND DRAPERY; 860]

quince *type of* **fruit**. [➡FRUIT AND VEGETABLES; 1175]

quintessence *n* **essence**, embodiment, epitome, personification, soul, heart, ideal. [➡PERFECT EXAMPLES AND EMBODIMENTS; 67]

quintessential *adj* **typical**, essential, archetypal, prototypical, model, exemplary, classic, ideal. [➡REPRESENTATIVE; 66] *Opposite:* atypical.

quintet *type of* **band.** [➡MUSICIANS AND SINGERS; 908]

quintuplet *type of* **offspring.** [➡YOUNGER GENERATION RELATIVES; 958]

quip 1 *n* **witticism**, joke, jibe, wisecrack (*informal*), one-liner, clever remark, pun, retort, bon mot. [➡JOKES AND TEASING; 675] 2 *v* **joke**, jibe, remark, wisecrack (*informal*), jest (*literary*), banter, retort, kid. [➡JOKES AND TEASING; 675]

quirk 1 *n* **twist of fate**, fluke (*informal*), coincidence, accident, chance, oddity, twist. [➡CHANCE EVENT; 36] 2 *n* **idiosyncrasy**, peculiarity, foible, oddity, habit, eccentricity, trait, whim. [➡PERSONAL ECCENTRICITIES; 494]

quirkiness *n* **strangeness**, oddness, nonconformity, eccentricity, weirdness, peculiarity, idiosyncrasy. [➡BIZARRE AND PECULIAR; 258] *Opposite:* normality.

quirky *adj* **idiosyncratic**, individual, unusual, peculiar, odd, strange, eccentric, unpredictable. [➡BIZARRE AND PECULIAR; 258] *Opposite:* normal.

quit 1 *v* **resign**, leave, walk out, abandon, vacate, give notice, desert, give up. [➡ABSENT ONESELF; 8] *Opposite:* stay. 2 *v* **give up**, stop, relinquish, refrain from, renounce, suspend. [➡STOP ACTING; 265] *Opposite:* take up.

quite 1 *adv* **fairly**, rather, pretty (*informal*), moderately, relatively, reasonably, somewhat. [➡TO A CERTAIN EXTENT; 134] *Opposite:* extremely. 2 *adv* **entirely**, completely, very, totally, utterly, absolutely, extremely, fully, wholly. [➡ABSOLUTE AND ABSOLUTELY; 131] *Opposite:* slightly.

quits (*informal*) *adj* **even**, square, settled, level, even-steven (*informal*). [➡EQUALITY; 155]

quitter (*informal*) *n* **defeatist**, deserter, loser, pessimist, coward, fatalist. *Opposite:* go-getter. (*informal*). [➡LAZY OR UNSUCCESSFUL PEOPLE; 948]

quiver 1 *v* **tremble**, shake, shudder, shiver, quake, vibrate, quaver. [➡PHYSICAL REACTIONS; 317] 2 *n* **shudder**, shiver, tremble, palpitation, tremor, spasm, vibration. [➡PHYSICAL REACTIONS; 317]

quivering 1 *adj* **trembling**, quaking, quavering, unsteady, shaky, shaking, wobbly, weak. [➡DESCRIBING BODY MOVEMENTS; 289] *Opposite:* steady. 2 *n* **pulsation**, vibration, spasm, palpitation, tremor. [➡DESCRIBING BODY MOVEMENTS; 289]

quixotic *adj* **romantic**, unrealistic, idealistic, impractical, impracticable, dreamy. [➡NEGATIVE INTELLECTUAL CHARACTERISTICS; 526] *Opposite:* down-to-earth.

quiz 1 *n* **test**, puzzle, game, contest, competition, exercise, examination. [➡NON-AGGRESSIVE/SPORTING EVENT; 40] 2 *v* **question**, interrogate, cross-examine, interview, examine, grill (*informal*), sound out, cross-question, debrief, query, catechize. [➡ASK PEOPLE QUESTIONS; 667]

See Compare and Contrast at **question**.

quizzical *adj* **questioning**, curious, puzzled, surprised, perplexed, inquiring, amused, sardonic, ironic. [➡ENTHUSIASTIC AND INQUISITIVE; 629]

quorum *n* **minimum**, minimum number, least, required number, lower limit. [➡ENOUGH AND SUFFICIENT; 129]

quota *n* **share**, allocation, allowance, part, ration, slice, proportion, measure, lot, portion. [➡MEASUREABLE PORTION; 125]

quotation 1 *n* **quote**, citation, line, passage, extract, reference, excerpt, reading. [➡SUMMARIES, OUTLINES, AND EXCERPTS; 589] 2 *n* **estimate**, price, figure, costing, quote, appraisal, estimation, assessment. [➡SCORES AND EVALUATIONS; 599]

quotation mark *type of* **punctuation mark.** [➡ASPECTS OF LANGUAGE; 683]

quote 1 *v* **cite**, recite, repeat, refer to, mention, allude to, parrot. [➡RECITE, REPEAT, AND NARRATE; 621] 2 *v* **give an estimate**, estimate, give a price of, give a figure of, price, offer. [➡ASSESS QUANTITY; 758] 3 *n* **quotation**, citation, line, passage, extract, reference, excerpt. [➡SUMMARIES, OUTLINES, AND EXCERPTS; 589] 4 *n* **estimate**, price, figure, costing, quotation, appraisal, estimation, assessment. [➡SCORES AND EVALUATIONS; 599]

quotidian (*formal*) *adj* [➡TIMES OF DAY; 87]

quotient *n* **proportion**, measure, amount, share, percentage. [➡MEASUREABLE PORTION; 125]

R

rabbi *n* **religious leader**, scholar, teacher, official, leader. [➡ RELIGIOUS PEOPLE; 779]

rabbit 1 *n* **bunny**, coney, cottontail. [➡ SMALL MAMMAL; 990] 2 *v* (*informal*) **chat**, chatter, gossip, witter (*informal*), natter (*informal*), go on, run on, blather (*informal*), blether (*informal*), ramble, prattle. [➡ WITTER AND BABBLE; 618] 3 *type of* **meat.** [➡ TYPES AND CUTS OF MEAT; 1176]

rabbit on (*informal*) *v* [➡ WITTER AND BABBLE; 618]

rabble *n* **mob**, crowd, swarm, throng, horde, multitude, army, herd. [➡ GROUPS OF PEOPLE; 935]

rabble-rouser (*disapproving*) *n* **troublemaker**, agitator, demagogue, stirrer (*informal*), activist, firebrand, agent provocateur. [➡ UNCOOPERATIVE OR REBELLIOUS PERSON; 567]

rabble-rousing 1 *n* **troublemaking**, sedition, provocation, agitation, activism. [➡ BAD BEHAVIOUR OR ACTION; 255] 2 *adj* **provocative**, inflammatory, seditious, incendiary, troublemaking. [➡ REBELLIOUSNESS AND DISOBEDIENCE; 566]

rabid 1 *adj* **diseased**, sick, ill, infected, unwell. [➡ ILL AND SICK; 741] *Opposite:* well. 2 *adj* **fanatical**, extreme, radical, uncompromising, militant, dedicated. [➡ APPRECIATION AND GRATITUDE; 536] *Opposite:* lukewarm. 3 *adj* **intense**, fervent, ardent, violent, zealous, naked. [➡ STRENGTH; 202] *Opposite:* moderate.

rabidly *adv* **fervently**, ardently, intensely, single-mindedly, zealously. [➡ APPRECIATION AND GRATITUDE; 536] *Opposite:* moderately.

raccoon *type of* **small mammal.** [➡ SMALL MAMMAL; 990]

race 1 *n* **contest**, competition, sprint, marathon, steeplechase, relay race. [➡ NON-AGGRESSIVE/SPORTING EVENT; 40] 2 *n* **ethnic group**, nation, people (*informal*), tribe, line. [➡ GROUPS IN SOCIETY; 940] 3 *n* **competition**, contest, battle, duel, fight, rivalry, meeting. [➡ NON-AGGRESSIVE/SPORTING EVENT; 40] 4 *v* **compete**, take part, run, sprint, contest, battle, vie. [➡ COMPETE, CONTEND, AND COMBAT; 304] *Opposite:* withdraw. 5 *v* **speed**, go fast, run, sprint, hurry, dash, rush, fly, zip (*informal*), gallop. [➡ MOVE FAST; 314] *Opposite:* crawl.

racecourse *n* **track**, turf, course, hippodrome. [➡ URBAN OUTDOOR SPACES; 1071]

racehorse *type of* **horse.** [➡ HORSE; 985]

racer *n* **competitor**, contender, entrant, sprinter, runner, athlete. [➡ PEOPLE IN SPORTS AND LEISURE; 876]

racetrack *n* **track**, stadium, running track, circuit, speedway. [➡ URBAN OUTDOOR SPACES; 1071]

raceway 1 *n* **channel**, race, conduit, canal, course, gutter, trough, aqueduct. [➡ WATERCOURSES; 1110] 2 *n* **track**, circuit, course, stadium, racetrack. [➡ URBAN OUTDOOR SPACES; 1071]

racial *adj* **ethnic**, cultural, tribal, national. [➡ BELONGING OR RELATING TO PEOPLE; 943]

racing bike *type of* **bike** (*informal*). [➡ BIKES, CARS, AND CARRIAGES; 1148]

racing car *type of* **car.** [➡ BIKES, CARS, AND CARRIAGES; 1148]

racism *n* **racial discrimination**, discrimination, prejudice, bigotry, intolerance, xenophobia, bias, racialism (*dated*). [➡ PREJUDICE; 551]

racist *adj* **chauvinistic**, bigoted, xenophobic, racialist (*dated*), prejudiced, discriminatory. [➡ NEGATIVE INTELLECTUAL CHARACTERISTICS; 526] *Opposite:* tolerant.

rack 1 *n* **stand**, frame, framework, holder, shelf, support. [➡ SUPPORTS AND BASES; 1254] 2 *v* **shake**, rock, devastate, play havoc with, wreck, damage. [➡ DESTRUCTION AND DEMOLITION; 360] *Opposite:* restore. 3 *v* **store**, shelve, stack, stow, put away, keep, pack. [➡ POSITION SOMETHING; 326] *Opposite:* unpack. 4 *v* **afflict**, torment, plague, torture, beset, disturb, pain, agonize, try. [➡ EXPERIENCE AND ENCOUNTER; 583] *Opposite:* comfort.

racket 1 *n* (*informal*) **row**, noise, din, rumpus, commotion, hullabaloo, clamour, uproar. [➡ CHAOS AND UPROAR; 51] 2 *n* (*informal*) **swindle**, fiddle (*informal*), con, scam (*slang*), fraud, scheme. [➡ CRIMES; 817] 3 *type of* **sports equipment.** [➡ SPORTS EQUIPMENT; 879]

racketeer *n* **criminal**, shark (*informal*), swindler, con artist (*slang*), fraudster, hoodlum, hood (*US slang*). [➡ CRIMINALS; 821]

racketeering *n* [➡ CRIMES; 817]

rackets *type of* **court game.** [➡ HOBBIES, GAMES, AND SPORTS; 875]

racking *adj* [➡ PHYSICALLY UNPLEASANT; 227]

rack up (*informal*) *v* **accumulate**, chalk up, notch up (*slang*), score, make, achieve, collect. [➡ GET MONEY OR REWARD; 422]

rack your brains *v* **try to remember**, think hard, concentrate, make an effort, focus. [➡ THINK AND REFLECT; 744]

raconteur *n* **narrator**, storyteller, conversationalist, after-dinner speaker, wit. [➡ SPEAKERS AND ORATORS; 604]

racquets *see* **rackets.**

racy *adj* **indecent**, spicy (*informal*), indelicate, improper, off-colour (*informal*), sexy, rude, shocking, lewd, lascivious. [➡ MORALLY BAD; 776] *Opposite:* chaste.

radar *n* **detector**, locater, sensor, locating system, position finder. [➡ NAVIGATION; 1140]

raddled *adj* **haggard**, debauched, worn-out, dishevelled, unkempt, worn. [➡ BADLY GROOMED; 484] *Opposite:* fresh.

radial *adj* **circular**, outward, centrifugal, radiated, outspread, radiating. [➡ORIENTATION AND ALIGNMENT; 1222]

radiance 1 *n* **happiness**, sparkle, joy, vivacity, joie de vivre, warmth, glow. [➡PLEASURE, EXCITEMENT, AND ELATION; 535] *Opposite:* dullness. 2 *n* **light**, brightness, glow, luminosity, brilliance, gleam, glare. [➡LIGHT; 1163]

radiant 1 *adj* **happy**, healthy, glowing, beaming, sunny, joyful, ecstatic. [➡PLEASURE, EXCITEMENT, AND ELATION; 535] *Opposite:* unhappy. 2 *adj* **shining**, luminous, brilliant, bright, dazzling, glowing, resplendent. [➡DESCRIBING LIGHT; 1227] *Opposite:* dull.

radiate 1 *v* **give out**, give off, emit, discharge, issue, release. [➡EMIT AND EMANATE; 362] 2 *v* **exude**, emanate, glow with, bristle with, brim with, overflow with, burst with. [➡EMIT AND EMANATE; 362] 3 *v* **spread out**, branch out, diverge, spread, circulate, diffuse, strew. [➡CHANGE DIRECTION OF MOTION; 345]

radiation *n* **particle emission**, energy, radioactivity, fallout, contamination, pollution. [➡ENERGY SOURCES; 1161]

radiator 1 *n* **heater**, room heater, storage heater, space heater. [➡HEATING, REFRIGERATION, AND VENTILATION; 1141] 2 *type of* **general fittings**. [➡FITTINGS; 859] 3 *part of* **engine**. [➡PARTS OF AN ENGINE; 1143]

radical 1 *adj* **basic**, fundamental, essential, profound, deep-seated, deep-rooted. [➡FUNDAMENTAL; 196] 2 *adj* **sweeping**, pervasive, thorough, far-reaching, profound, drastic, major. [➡WHOLENESS AND COMPLETENESS; 199] *Opposite:* minor. 3 *adj* **revolutionary**, extreme, extremist, uncompromising, militant, fanatical. [➡REBELLIOUSNESS AND DISOBEDIENCE; 566] *Opposite:* conservative. 4 *n* **extremist**, activist, militant, revolutionary, fanatic. [➡UNCOOPERATIVE OR REBELLIOUS PERSON; 567] *Opposite:* conservative.

radicalism *n* **extremism**, militancy, fanaticism, ardour, zealotry, radicalness. [➡PHILOSOPHIES AND BELIEFS; 781]

radically *adv* **very**, fundamentally, thoroughly, drastically, completely, totally, deeply, profoundly. [➡ABSOLUTE AND ABSOLUTELY; 131] *Opposite:* superficially.

radicchio *type of* **salad vegetable**. [➡FRUIT AND VEGETABLES; 1175]

radio *n* **radio set**, wireless (*dated*), transistor, hi-fi, receiver. [➡AUDIO EQUIPMENT; 1138]

radioactive *adj* **emitting radiation**, dangerous, harmful, hot, active. [➡ENERGY SOURCES; 1161]

radioactivity *n* **radiation**, particle emission, energy, fallout. [➡ENERGY SOURCES; 1161]

radio-controlled *adj* **remote-controlled**, automatic, remote. [➡DESCRIBING TECHNOLOGY; 1159]

radio presenter *n* [➡WORKERS IN ENTERTAINMENT AND MEDIA; 873]

radio set *type of* **audio equipment**. [➡AUDIO EQUIPMENT; 1138]

radish *type of* **salad vegetable**. [➡FRUIT AND VEGETABLES; 1175]

radium *type of* **metal**. [➡METALS; 1275]

radius 1 *n* **line**, distance, length. [➡WIDTH: WIDE; 1198] 2 *n* **area**, range, circle, ambit, extent, bounds, span, limit, compass, purview. [➡ROUNDED SHAPE; 1217] 3 *n* **scope**, range, area of influence, umbrella, reach, remit, sweep. [➡DEGREE AND EXTENT; 110] 4 *type of* **bone**. [➡THE BONES AND JOINTS; 720]

raffia *n* **straw**, fibre, grass, natural fibre. [➡PLANT MATERIALS; 1132]

raffish 1 *adj* **unconventional**, dashing, rakish, disreputable, louche, free-spirited, colourful, individual, unusual. [➡BAD MANNERS AND SOCIAL SKILLS; 522] *Opposite:* conventional. 2 *adj* **showy**, ostentatious, gaudy, loud, garish, brash. [➡IN POOR TASTE; 230] *Opposite:* discreet.

raffle 1 *n* **lottery**, draw, tombola, sweepstake, drawing. [➡SALES AND SHOWS; 444] 2 *v* **offer**, give away, award, present, donate, proffer, tender. [➡GIVE AND PROVIDE; 431]

raft 1 *n* (*informal*) **bundle**, number, tranche, portfolio, range, host, amount. [➡MANY, MUCH, LARGE AMOUNT; 117] 2 *type of* **small vessel**. [➡SHIPS AND BOATS; 1149]

rafter *n* **beam**, roof beam, support, joist, strut, girder, timber. [➡BUILDING MATERIALS; 1076]

rag 1 *n* (*informal*) [➡NEWSPAPERS; 606] 2 *n* **cloth**, duster, scrap, wisp, tatter, thread. [➡RUBBISH AND USELESS OBJECTS; 1248] 3 *v* (*dated*) **tease**, taunt, make fun of, rib (*informal*), call names, poke fun at, bait, mock, razz (*US informal*). [➡JOKES AND TEASING; 675]

ragamuffin (*dated*) *n* **urchin**, waif, child. [➡CHILD OR YOUTH; 945]

ragbag (*informal*) *n* **mixture**, mixed bag, miscellany, jumble, hotchpotch, assortment, potpourri, melange (*literary or formal*). [➡COLLECTIONS AND MIXTURES OF THINGS; 1243]

rag doll *type of* **toy**. [➡TOYS; 880]

rage 1 *n* **fury**, anger, wrath, temper, ire (*literary*), frenzy, indignation. [➡IRRITATION AND ANGER; 542] *Opposite:* calmness. 2 *v* **fume**, rant and rave, storm, seethe, thunder, fulminate, explode, erupt. [➡GIVING VENT TO EMOTIONS; 680]

> *See Compare and Contrast at* **anger**.

ragged 1 *adj* **tattered**, torn, worn-out, raggedy, in tatters, frayed, worn to shreds, shabby. [➡IN BAD REPAIR; 1233] *Opposite:* pristine. 2 *adj* **unkempt**, untidy, shabby, raggedy, in rags, scruffy, tatty, ragtag. [➡BADLY GROOMED; 484] *Opposite:* smart. 3 *adj* **jagged**, serrated, uneven, irregular, rough, notched. [➡ANGULAR SHAPE; 1216] *Opposite:* even.

raggedly 1 *adv* **untidily**, shabbily, scruffily, sloppily, messily, tattily. [➡BADLY GROOMED; 484] *Opposite:* neatly. 2 *adv* **unevenly**, jaggedly, roughly, irregularly, sharply, ruggedly, brokenly. [➡ANGULAR SHAPE; 1216] *Opposite:* smoothly.

raggedness 1 *n* **untidiness**, shabbiness, scruffiness, sloppiness, messiness, dishevelment. [➡BADLY GROOMED; 484] *Opposite:* neatness. 2 *n* **unevenness**, jaggedness, roughness, irregularity, sharpness, serration, ruggedness, brokenness. [➡ANGULAR SHAPE; 1216] *Opposite:* smoothness.

raggedy 1 *adj* **ragged**, torn, worn out, in tatters, frayed, worn to shreds, old, shabby, tattered. [➡IN BAD REPAIR; 1233] *Opposite:* pristine. 2 *adj* **unkempt**, untidy, shabby, ragged, in rags, scruffy, tatty, ragtag. [➡BADLY GROOMED; 484] *Opposite:* smart.

raging *adj* **powerful**, intense, furious, strong, rampant, violent, uncontrolled, wild. [➡STRENGTH; 202] *Opposite:* mild.

ragout *type of* **cooked dish**. [➡PREPARED DISHES; 1169]

ragtag 1 *adj* **motley**, disparate, assorted, dubious, miscellaneous, multifarious. [➡DIFFERENCE; 150] 2 *adj* **untidy**, shabby, unkempt, scruffy, ragged, raggedy, messy, sloppy. [➡BADLY GROOMED; 484] *Opposite:* neat.

ragweed *type of* **weed**. [➡WEEDS AND THISTLES; 1034]

raid 1 *n* **attack**, search, forced entry, break-in, incursion, invasion, foray, bust (*slang*), swoop. [➡SUDDEN EVENT; 52] 2 *v* **storm**, attack, invade, search, break into, ransack, maraud, swoop, assault. [➡ARRIVE; 12] 3 *v* **rob**, loot, plunder, hold up, knock off (*slang*), burgle, burglarize (*US*). [➡STEAL AND ROB; 427]

raider *n* **attacker**, thief, robber, marauder, invader, plunderer, ravager, looter. [➡CRIMINALS; 821]

rail 1 *n* **railing**, handrail, banister, bar, support, barrier, fence. [➡STICKS, POLES, AND WEDGES; 1253] 2 *v* **protest**, complain, kick (*informal*), kick up (*informal*), object, criticize, condemn, denounce, attack, inveigh (*formal*), vociferate, fulminate. [➡PROTEST AND EXPRESS DISAPPROVAL; 643] *Opposite:* accept.

railhead *n* **terminus**, starting point, end of the line. [➡RAILWAYS; 1106]

railing *n* **fence**, paling, barrier, balustrade, boundary line, rails, rail. [➡BARRIERS; 1112]

raillery *n* **teasing**, joking, banter, repartee, backchat (*informal*), jesting (*literary*), joshing (*informal*), sport (*formal*), kidding, badinage. [➡JOKES AND TEASING; 675] *Opposite:* bullying.

rail line *n* [➡RAILWAYS; 1106]

rail network *n* [➡RAILWAYS; 1106]

railroad (*informal*) *v* **push**, force, steamroller, bulldoze, shove, press. [➡CAUSE OR COMPEL TO ACT; 272]

railroad station *n* [➡RAILWAYS; 1106]

rail route *n* [➡RAILWAYS; 1106]

rail terminal *n* [➡RAILWAYS; 1106]

rail transportation system (*US*) *n* [➡RAILWAYS; 1106]

rail transport system *n* [➡RAILWAYS; 1106]

railway 1 *n* **track**, line, train track, route, railroad (*US*). [➡RAILWAYS; 1106] 2 *n* **rail network**, rail transport system, train system, train network, railroad (*US*), rail transportation system (*US*). [➡RAILWAYS; 1106]

railway

◆ *parts of a train*
cabin, caboose (*US*), car, carriage, coach, compartment, dining car (*US*), freight car, locomotive, luggage compartment, Pullman, restaurant car, sleeper, sleeping car, smoker, steam engine, smoking car, smoking carriage, smoking compartment, tank engine, wagon

◆ *types of rail vehicle*
cable car, funicular, locomotive, steam engine, streetcar (*US*), train, tram

◆ *types of railway*
cable railroad (*US*), cable railway, funicular railway, light railway, metro, monorail, streetcar line (*US*), subway (*US*), tramway, tube (*UK*), underground

railway crossing *n* [➡BRIDGES, TUNNELS, CROSSINGS, AND JUNCTIONS; 1111]

raiment (*formal*) *n* **clothing**, apparel, clothes, wear, dress, attire (*formal*), costume, garments, habiliment (*formal*). [➡CLOTHES AND ACCESSORIES; 864]

rain 1 *n* **rainfall**, drizzle, precipitation, rainwater, raindrops, driving rain, Scotch mist, mizzle (*regional*). [➡CLOUDY AND RAINY WEATHER; 1052] 2 *n* **volley**, hail, stream, torrent, flood, deluge, shower, barrage, fall, spate, plethora. [➡SUDDEN EVENT; 52] 3 *v* **pour**, bucket (*informal*), drizzle, spit, rain cats and dogs (*informal*), pelt down, shower, sprinkle (*US*). [➡CLOUDY AND RAINY WEATHER; 1052] 4 *v* **lavish**, shower, pour, stream, deluge, overwhelm, bombard, sprinkle (*US*). [➡GIVE TOO MUCH; 438]

rain barrel (*US*) *n* [➡CONTAINERS, RECEPTACLES, AND PACKAGING; 1244]

rainbow 1 *n* **arc**, arch, bow. [➡CLOUDY AND RAINY WEATHER; 1052] 2 *adj* **multicoloured**, colourful, variegated, spectral, polychromatic, polychromatous, kaleidoscopic. [➡DESCRIBING COLOURS; 1225] *Opposite:* monochrome.

rain cats and dogs (*informal*) *v* **pour with rain**, teem, pour down, bucket (*informal*), come down in torrents, come down in buckets, come down in sheets (*informal*). [➡CLOUDY AND RAINY WEATHER; 1052]

rain check (*US informal*) *n* [➡DELAY ACTION OR OCCURRENCE; 279]

rain cloud *type of* **cloud**. [➡CLOUDY AND RAINY WEATHER; 1052]

raincoat *type of* **overcoat**. [➡GARMENTS AND OUTFITS; 865]

raindrops *n* [➡CLOUDY AND RAINY WEATHER; 1052]

rainfall *n* **rain**, shower, drizzle, Scotch mist, precipitation, rainwater, raindrops, mizzle (*regional*). [➡CLOUDY AND RAINY WEATHER; 1052] *Opposite:* sunshine.

rain forest *n* [➡WOODS, FORESTS, AND JUNGLES; 1047]

rain hat *type of* **hat**. [➡HABERDASHERY, MILLINERY, AND LINGERIE; 867]

rainmaker (*US informal*) *n* **achiever**, triumph, success, star, celebrity, somebody, winner. [➡PEOPLE WHO ARE APPROVED OF; 955] *Opposite:* failure.

rain off *v* **postpone**, cancel, put back, call off, move on, move forward, rain out (*US*). [➡MAKE IMPOSSIBLE; 277] *Opposite:* bring forward.

rain out (*US*) *v* **postpone**, cancel, put back, call off, move on, move forward, rain off. [➡MAKE IMPOSSIBLE; 277] *Opposite:* bring forward.

rainproof *adj* **impermeable**, water-resistant, waterproof, showerproof, impervious, watertight, impregnable. [➡IN GOOD REPAIR; 1231] *Opposite:* permeable.

rainstorm *n* **cloudburst**, downpour, deluge, thunderstorm, shower, squall. [➡CLOUDY AND RAINY WEATHER; 1052]

rainwater *n* **rain**, precipitation, rainfall, raindrops, freshwater. [➡CLOUDY AND RAINY WEATHER; 1052]

rainy *adj* **wet**, raining, drizzling, showery, drizzly, damp, pouring, inclement. [➡CLOUDY AND RAINY WEATHER; 1052] *Opposite:* dry.

rainy season *n* [➡CLOUDY AND RAINY WEATHER; 1052]

raise 1 *v* **hoist**, lift up, uplift, elevate, move up, lift. [➡MOVE SOMETHING: UPWARDS; 329] *Opposite:* let down. 2 *v* **look after**, bring up, foster, grow, breed, produce, educate, cultivate, nurse, develop, nurture, rear. [➡TAKE CARE OF AND SPOIL; 301] *Opposite:* neglect. 3 *v* **increase**, put up, inflate, augment (*formal*), boost, jack up. [➡CHANGE OF SIZE: BIGGER; 393] *Opposite:* lower. 4 *v* **build**, erect, set up, construct, put up. [➡BUILD; 353] 5 *v* **improve**, better, enhance, augment (*formal*), uplift, advance, upgrade. [➡IMPROVE SOMETHING; 375] *Opposite:* deteriorate. 6 *v* **mention**, bring up, present, put forward, moot, broach, introduce. [➡SUGGEST, HINT, AND COMMENT; 613] *Opposite:* withdraw. 7 *v* **solicit**, canvass, obtain, bring in, procure, amass. [➡OBTAIN POSSESSION BY PERSUASION; 458] 8 *v* **lift**, end, terminate (*formal*), conclude. [➡CAUSE TO STOP; 267] 9 *v* **cause**, elicit, stimulate, induce, excite, rouse, precipitate, result in, provoke, produce, create. [➡CAUSE TO HAPPEN; 31] *Opposite:* quell.

> **Compare and Contrast:** ***raise, elevate, lift, hoist, uplift***
>
> CORE MEANING: TO PLACE SOMETHING IN A HIGHER POSITION
>
> ***raise*** to move something to a higher position; ***elevate*** to move something to a higher position, rarely involving major physical effort; ***lift*** to move something from a low level to a higher level, often involving physical effort; ***hoist*** to raise something by mechanical means, or sometimes by heavy manual effort; ***uplift*** to raise or lift something, also used in Scotland, South Africa, and New Zealand to mean 'to collect or pick up something such as a parcel'.

raise a fuss *v* [➡PROTEST AND EXPRESS DISAPPROVAL; 643]

raise a ruckus (*US*) *v* [➡PROTEST AND EXPRESS DISAPPROVAL; 643]

raise objections *v* **object**, protest about, demur, remonstrate, contest, disagree, oppose. [➡PROTEST AND EXPRESS DISAPPROVAL; 643] *Opposite:* agree.

raise the spirits *v* [➡LEISURE AND RECREATION; 874]

raise your spirits *v* **cheer up**, lift your spirits, gladden, hearten, buoy up, liven up, inspire, give confidence, cheer. [➡ENCOURAGE; 577] *Opposite:* depress.

raisin *type of* **berry**. [➡FRUIT AND VEGETABLES; 1175]

raison d'état *n* **national interest**, realpolitik, expediency, diplomacy, politics, consideration. [➡STYLES AND SYSTEMS OF GOVERNMENT; 806]

raison d'être *n* **meaning**, purpose, rationale, motivation, inspiration, ethos, philosophy, belief, hope. [➡INTENTION AND PURPOSE; 773]

rajah *n* **king**, prince, maharajah, chief, ruler, sovereign, leader. [➡RULERS AND ARISTOCRACY; 823] *Opposite:* subject.

rake 1 *v* **gather**, clear up, scrape, collect, scrape up, rake up (*informal*), rake over. [➡USE TOOLS AND MACHINERY; 469] *Opposite:* scatter. 2 *v* **enfilade**, pepper, spray, shoot. [➡SPREAD AND SCATTER; 333] 3 *v* **search through**, go through, sift, rummage, comb, hunt for, scour, ransack. [➡SEEK POSSESSION AND SEARCH; 457] *Opposite:* find. 4 *n* **reprobate**, degenerate, inebriate (*archaic or literary*), prodigal, profligate, squanderer, drunkard, gambler, voluptuary, libertine, roué (*literary*). [➡VILLAINS AND THUGS; 947] *Opposite:* paragon.

rake it in (*informal*) *v* [➡GET MONEY OR REWARD; 422]

rake-off (*informal*) *n* **bribe**, backhander (*informal*), sweetener (*informal*), kickback, cut (*informal*), payoff (*informal*), favour. [➡MONEY, PAYMENTS, AND CHARGES; 800] *Opposite:* cost.

rake over the coals (*US*) *v* [➡ACCUSE, BLAME, AND CRITICIZE; 642]

rake up (*informal*) *v* **mention**, drag up, dredge up, bring up, dig up, allude to. [➡SUGGEST, HINT, AND COMMENT; 613] *Opposite:* keep mum (*informal*).

rakish 1 *adj* **dashing**, stylish, sporty, jaunty, casual, confident, breezy, dapper, debonair. [➡WELL GROOMED; 483] *Opposite:* bland. 2 *adj* **dissolute**, profligate, degenerate, louche, dubious, disreputable, depraved, lecherous, dissipated, raffish. [➡MORALLY BAD; 776] *Opposite:* upright.

rakishly *adv* [➡MORALLY BAD; 776]

rally 1 *v* **come together**, gather, call together, bring together, unite, assemble, collect, support, join forces, reassemble, reconvene, reunite. [➡GET CLOSER TOGETHER; 311] *Opposite:* disperse. 2 *v* **revive**, improve, recover, pull through, get better, recuperate, perk up, make a comeback, pick up. [➡CHANGE OF MOOD AND COMPOSURE; 581] *Opposite:* decline. 3 *n* **gathering**, meeting, assembly, convention, demonstration, demo (*informal*), march, caucus. [➡MEETINGS AND ASSEMBLIES; 43]

rally round *v* [➡HELP; 294]

ram *type of* **male animal**. [➡MALE OR FEMALE ANIMAL; 978]

RAM *type of* **software**. [➡COMPUTERS AND COMPUTING; 1126]

ramble 1 *n* **hike**, walk, roam, stroll, wander, amble, saunter. [➡PROCEED AND GO; 306] 2 *v* **go on**, digress, blether (*informal*), blather (*informal*), go off at a tangent, ramble on, rabbit on (*informal*), witter on (*informal*), rattle on. [➡WITTER AND BABBLE; 618] *Opposite:* focus. 3 *v* **walk**, hike, wander, roam, go for a walk, stroll, saunter, amble, perambulate (*formal*), traipse, drift. [➡PROCEED AND GO; 306]

ramble on *v* **go on**, ramble, digress, go off at a tangent, blether (*informal*), blather (*informal*), rabbit on (*informal*), witter on (*informal*), rattle on. [➡WITTER AND BABBLE; 618] *Opposite:* focus.

rambler *n* **walker**, hiker, backpacker, roamer, wanderer, stroller. [➡TRAVEL: TRAVELLERS AND WALKERS; 320]

rambling 1 *adj* **pointless**, inconsequential, confused, incoherent, tedious, wordy, long-winded, prolix, digressive, discursive. [➡INARTICULATE, RAMBLING, AND AWKWARD; 634] *Opposite:* concise. 2 *adj* **spread out**, sprawling, trailing, straggling, irregular, shaggy, all over the place (*informal*). [➡LARGE; 1192] *Opposite:* compact.

See Compare and Contrast at **wordy**.

ramblingly *adv* [➡INARTICULATE, RAMBLING, AND AWKWARD; 634]

rambunctious *adj* **rowdy**, high-spirited, lively, disorderly, riotous, noisy, boisterous, rollicking, uproarious. [➡CHEERFULNESS OF OUTLOOK; 504] *Opposite:* mellow.

rambunctiousness *n* **rowdiness**, high spirits, liveliness, riotousness, unruliness, disorderliness, boisterousness, uproariousness. [➡CHEERFULNESS OF OUTLOOK; 504] *Opposite:* mellowness.

ramekin *n* **dish**, cocotte, pot, container, vessel, baking dish, bowl. [➡TABLEWARE, CUTLERY, AND KITCHENWARE; 861]

ramequin *see* **ramekin**.

ram home *v* **emphasize**, stress, accentuate, drive home, underline, highlight, make clear. [➡CLAIM, INSIST, AND EMPHASIZE; 615] *Opposite:* pass over.

ramie *type of* **fibre**. [➡PLANT MATERIALS; 1132]

ramification *n* **complication**, difficulty, consequence, result, implication, corollary, effect, upshot, sequel, development. [➡RESULTS AND OUTCOMES; 83]

ramify 1 *v* **branch**, divide, subdivide, fork, split, separate. [➡SEPARATE AND DIVIDE; 402] *Opposite:* unite. 2 *v* **complicate**, confuse, confound, compound, intensify, multiply, proliferate, increase. [➡CHANGE OF INTENSITY: MORE; 395] *Opposite:* simplify.

ramp 1 *n* **slope**, incline, rise, upgrade, gradient, bank. [➡PATHWAYS; 1109] 2 *n* **hump**, ridge, bump, speed bump, rumble strip, sleeping policeman (*dated*). [➡ROADS; 1105]

rampage *v* **run riot**, riot, rage, run amok, tear, storm, go wild, go berserk, charge. [➡GIVING VENT TO EMOTIONS; 680]

rampant 1 *adj* **unchecked**, unrestrained, threatening, out of control, uncontrolled, unbridled, raging, epidemic. [➡DISORDER AND CHAOS; 246] *Opposite:* contained. 2 *adj* **wild**, widespread, extensive, lush, fecund (*formal*), rambling, proliferating, flourishing, multiplying, rife, epidemic, pandemic. [➡SUCCESSFUL AND PROMISING; 81] *Opposite:* tamed.

rampantly *adv* **wildly**, violently, like wildfire, profusely, uncontrollably, unrestrainedly. [➡SUCCESSFUL AND PROMISING; 81] *Opposite:* gently.

rampart *n* **fortification**, embankment, bastion, wall, earthwork, battlement, parapet, barricade, barrier, bulwark. [➡PARTS OF FORTRESSES; 1090]

ram-raid *v* **loot**, break in, force an entry, plunder, rob, heist (*US slang*). [➡STEAL AND ROB; 427]

ram-raider *n* **burglar**, robber, looter, thief, plunderer, heister (*slang*). [➡CRIMINALS; 821]

ramshackle *adj* **rickety**, tumbledown, dilapidated, broken down, falling to pieces, decrepit, derelict, rundown, crumbling. [➡IN BAD REPAIR; 1233] *Opposite:* sturdy.

ranch 1 *n* **farm**, smallholding, farmstead, stud, estate, hacienda, rancho (*US*), spread (*US regional*). [➡AGRICULTURE AND FARMING; 1074] 2 *type of* **house**. [➡RESIDENTIAL BUILDINGS; 1077]

rancher *n* **farmer**, livestock farmer, smallholder, landowner, squire, planter, breeder. [➡FARMERS, GARDENERS, AND MANUAL WORKERS; 849]

ranch hand (*US*) *n* [➡FARMERS, GARDENERS, AND MANUAL WORKERS; 849]

ranch house (*US*) *type of* **house**. [➡RESIDENTIAL BUILDINGS; 1077]

rancid *adj* **reeking**, fetid, rank (*literary*), sour, off, bad, rotten, stinking, putrid, foul. [➡TASTE; 704] *Opposite:* fresh.

rancidness *n* **sourness**, rankness, fetidness, rottenness, smelliness, foulness, putrefaction. [➡TASTE; 704] *Opposite:* freshness.

rancorous *adj* **acrimonious**, bitter, malicious, resentful, vindictive, spiteful, mean, nasty, malevolent, virulent, hostile, splenetic. [➡IRRITATION AND ANGER; 542] *Opposite:* amicable.

rancorousness *n* **acrimoniousness**, maliciousness, spitefulness, bitterness, resentfulness, vindictiveness, malevolence, virulence, hostility, spleen. [➡ANTAGONISM; 553] *Opposite:* friendliness.

rancour *n* **acrimony**, bitterness, malice, resentment, vindictiveness, spite, meanness, nastiness, hatred, ill will, hostility, malevolence, spleen, venom. [➡ANTAGONISM; 553]

random *adj* **haphazard**, arbitrary, accidental, casual, hit and miss, indiscriminate, chance, unsystematic, unplanned, unintentional. [➡DISORDER AND CHAOS; 246] *Opposite:* deliberate.

randomness *n* **haphazardness**, arbitrariness, casualness, chanciness, unpredictability, uncertainty, chance. [➡UNRELATEDNESS AND SEPARATENESS; 147] *Opposite:* predictability.

range 1 *n* **variety**, choice, series, assortment, array, sort, kind, collection, scope, gamut, selection, run. [➡COLLECTIONS AND MIXTURES OF THINGS; 1243] 2 *n* **scope**, span, breadth, reach, extent, scale, limit, radius, bounds. [➡AREA AND RANGE; 111] 3 *v* **vary between**, fluctuate, vacillate, oscillate, alternate, reach, go, extend, stretch. [➡CHANGE; 373] 4 *type of* **appliance**. [➡HOUSEHOLD APPLIANCES; 1116]

rangefinder *part of* **photographic equipment**. [➡PHOTOGRAPHY AND PHOTOGRAPHIC EQUIPMENT; 1121]

ranger 1 *n* **wanderer**, roamer, rambler, walker, hiker, backpacker. [➡TRAVEL: TRAVELLERS AND WALKERS; 320] 2 *n* **park ranger**, steward, overseer, guardian, guard, warden (*US*). [➡BOSSES AND MANAGEMENT; 965]

ranginess *n* [➡BUILD; 478]

rangy *adj* **long-legged**, tall, lanky, gangling, gangly, stringy, leggy. [➡BUILD; 478] *Opposite:* thickset.

rani *n* **queen**, princess, maharani, consort. [➡RULERS AND ARISTOCRACY; 823]

rank 1 *n* **status**, title, category, position, level, order, class, echelon, grade, type, sort, ranking. [➡STATUS; 888] 2 *v* **rate**, position, place, categorize, class, grade, order, classify, organize, arrange. [➡ASSESS QUALITY; 756] 3 *adj* **vigorous**, rampant, exuberant, fecund (*formal*), abundant, flourishing, overgrown, luxuriant, overabundant. [➡SUCCESSFUL AND PROMISING; 81] *Opposite:* sparse. 4 *adj* **sheer**, utter, complete, blatant, absolute, total, bald, unmitigated, downright. [➡ABSOLUTE AND ABSOLUTELY; 131] *Opposite:* minimal. 5 *adj* (*literary*) **pungent**, fetid, smelly, bad, foul, reeking, rancid. [➡SMELL AND SMELLING; 706] *Opposite:* fresh.

rank and file *n* [➡GROUPS IN SOCIETY; 940]

ranking *n* **position**, status, place, standing, rank, level, grade, classification. [➡STATUS; 888]

rankle *v* **irritate**, fester, gnaw, eat up, irk, gall, needle, rile (*informal*), annoy, infuriate, chafe. [➡ANGER AND ANNOY; 570] *Opposite:* soothe.

rankness *n* [➡SMELL AND SMELLING; 706]

ransack 1 *v* **search**, go through, rummage, turn upside down, turn out, rake, comb, scour. [➡SEEK POSSESSION AND SEARCH; 457] *Opposite:* find. 2 *v* **rob**, despoil, vandalize, strip, loot, raid, pillage, plunder, ravage, sack, rifle. [➡STEAL AND ROB; 427] *Opposite:* guard.

ransom 1 *n* **payment**, payoff (*informal*), money, sum, deal, exchange, redemption. [➡PROCEEDS OF CRIME; 428] 2 *v* **redeem**, buy back, set free, strike a deal, pay up, exchange, pay off, rescue, secure the release of, release, deliver (*literary*), restore. [➡FREEDOM AND LIBERTY; 209]

rant 1 *v* **rage**, go on, bluster, fume, seethe, shout, harangue, rave, fulminate. *Opposite:* sweet-talk. (*informal*). [➡GIVING VENT TO EMOTIONS; 680] 2 *n* **outburst**, bombast, histrionics, bluster, tirade, rage. [➡CRITICISMS AND ANGRY OUTBURSTS; 50] *Opposite:* calm.

rant and rave *v* **rage**, go on, keep on, bluster, shout, yell, harangue, rave, fulminate. [➡GIVING VENT TO EMOTIONS; 680] *Opposite:* calm down.

rap 1 *n* **blow**, tap, knock, smack, crack, thwack, thump. [➡PHYSICAL ATTACK AND PUNISHMENT; 416] *Opposite:* caress. 2 *v* **hit**, thwack, strike, tap, crack, knock, smack, thump, drum. [➡PHYSICAL ATTACK AND PUNISHMENT; 416] 3 *v* (*US slang*) **chat**, talk, gas (*informal*), natter (*informal*), yap (*informal*), chew the fat, converse, schmooze (*US slang*), chinwag (*US*). [➡TWO-WAY COMMUNICATION; 608] 4 *type of* **popular music**. [➡MUSIC, SONGS, AND SINGING; 907]

rapacious 1 *adj* **grasping**, greedy, avid, voracious, avaricious, gluttonous, ravenous, insatiable, covetous, mercenary. [➡FINANCIALLY MEAN AND GRASPING; 520] *Opposite:* temperate. 2 *adj* **destructive**, vicious, harmful, aggressive, dangerous, damaging, violent. [➡DANGEROUS; 237] *Opposite:* harmless.

rapaciousness 1 *n* **graspingness**, voraciousness, greediness, avidness, unscrupulousness, mercenariness, greed, avarice, voracity, rapacity. [➡FINANCIALLY MEAN AND GRASPING; 520] 2 *n* **destructiveness**, violence, viciousness, harmfulness, aggressiveness, dangerousness. [➡DANGER; 236] *Opposite:* gentleness.

rape oil *type of* **cooking fat and oil**. [➡FATS AND OILS; 1172]

rapid *adj* **swift**, quick, fast, speedy, hasty, express, hurried, brisk, prompt, fleet, instant, precipitous. [➡MOVING QUICKLY; 103] *Opposite:* slow.

rapid-fire *adj* [➡HAPPENING QUICKLY; 104]

rapidity *n* **swiftness**, quickness, speed, speediness, haste, hurry, briskness, promptness, fleetness (*literary*). [➡SPEED; 102] *Opposite:* slowness.

rapidness *n* [➡SPEED; 102]

rapids *n* **fast-moving water**, white water, torrents, waterfall, fall, cascade. [➡RIVERS, LAKES, AND STREAMS; 1042]

rapier *type of* **sword or knife**. [➡SWORDS AND KNIVES; 1156]

rap on/over the knuckles (*informal*) *v* **tell off** (*informal*), haul over the coals, wig (*dated informal*), give a talking-to (*informal*), tick off (*informal*), reprimand, scold, rebuke, put in your place, censure, upbraid. [➡ACCUSE, BLAME, AND CRITICIZE; 642] *Opposite:* praise.

rap out *v* **bark**, shout, spit (*informal*), snap, bawl, holler, yell. [➡UTTER AND PRONOUNCE; 609] *Opposite:* whisper.

rapper *n* **singer**, vocalist, rhymer, performer. [➡MUSICIANS AND SINGERS; 908]

rapport *n* **relationship**, bond, understanding, link, affinity, fellow feeling, empathy, connection, camaraderie, affiliation, fellowship. [➡CONNECTION; 144] *Opposite:* friction.

rapprochement (*formal*) *n* **reconciliation**, reunion, understanding, settlement, compromise, coming together, agreement, accord, entente, conciliation. [➡HARMONY; 156] *Opposite:* hostility.

rapscallion (*archaic or humorous*) *n* [➡MISCHIEVOUS OR BADLY-BEHAVED CHILD; 946]

rapt 1 *adj* **engrossed**, fascinated, absorbed, captivated, gripped, enthralled, spellbound, wrapped up, immersed, interested, attentive. [➡PENSIVENESS AND INTEREST; 539] *Opposite:* bored. 2 *adj* **happy**, blissful, delighted, content, joyful, ecstatic. [➡PLEASURE, EXCITEMENT, AND ELATION; 535] *Opposite:* sullen.

rapture *n* **bliss**, ecstasy, euphoria, delight, joy, heaven, elation. [➡PLEASURE, EXCITEMENT, AND ELATION; 535] *Opposite:* depression.

rapturous *adj* **delighted**, enthusiastic, thrilled, overjoyed, elated, euphoric, ecstatic, blissful, joyful. [➡PLEASURE, EXCITEMENT, AND ELATION; 535] *Opposite:* unenthusiastic.

rare 1 *adj* **infrequent**, occasional, sporadic, intermittent, erratic, uncommon, unusual, exceptional, atypical. [➡NEVER AND INFREQUENCY; 97] *Opposite:* frequent. 2 *adj* **valuable**, unique, singular, scarce, exceptional, matchless. [➡EXTRAORDINARY: UNCOMMON; 206] *Opposite:* common. 3 *adj* **underdone**, bloody, juicy, red, pink, blue. [➡STATE OF PREPARED FOOD; 1170]

rarefied *adj* **esoteric**, abstruse, exclusive, obscure, complex, highbrow, refined, recondite. [➡EXTRAORDINARY: UNCOMMON; 206] *Opposite:* simple.

rarely *adv* **seldom**, infrequently, once in a blue moon (*informal*), on the odd occasion, hardly ever, not often, hardly. [➡NEVER AND INFREQUENCY; 97] *Opposite:* often.

rareness 1 *n* **scarcity**, paucity, dearth, lack, scarceness, scantiness, rarity. [➡TOO FEW, TOO LITTLE; 120] *Opposite:* abundance. 2 *n* **uniqueness**, matchlessness, exclusivity, exceptionality, individuality, inimitability, rarity. [➡EXTRAORDINARY: UNCOMMON; 206] *Opposite:* commonness.

rarified *see* **rarefied**.

raring *adj* **enthusiastic**, eager, keen, ready, impatient, revitalized, refreshed, restored, game, impetuous, in a hurry. [➡THE WILL AND WILLINGNESS; 564] *Opposite:* reluctant.

rarity 1 *n* **infrequency**, shortage, scarcity, uncommonness, fewness, intermittence, paucity. [➡TOO FEW, TOO LITTLE; 120] 2 *n* **one-off**, find, unusual object, curiosity, oddity, gem (*informal*), singularity. [➡EXTRAORDINARY: UNCOMMON; 206]

rascal 1 *n* (*humorous*) **tease**, joker, prankster, trickster, jester, puck, imp. [➡JOKERS AND TEASES; 676] 2 *n* **rogue**, scamp (*informal*), mischief, scoundrel, scallywag (*dated informal*), reprobate. [➡MISCHIEVOUS OR BADLY-BEHAVED CHILD; 946]

rascally 1 *adj* (*humorous*) **mischievous**, impish, naughty, puckish, playful, elfin. [➡BAD MANNERS AND SOCIAL SKILLS; 522] *Opposite:* well-behaved. 2 *adj* **dishonest**, wicked, bad, mean, untrustworthy, evil. [➡MORALLY BAD; 776] *Opposite:* good.

rash 1 *adj* **impetuous**, thoughtless, hasty, impulsive, reckless, foolish, sudden, careless, imprudent (*formal*), precipitous, brash. [➡INCAUTIOUS AND CARELESS; 284] *Opposite:* sensible. 2 *n* **eruption**, spots, reaction, itchiness, inflammation, irritation, pimples, hives. [➡CONDITIONS AFFECTING THE SKIN; 722] 3 *n* **outbreak**, flush, spate, string, eruption, wave, flood, epidemic. [➡SUDDEN EVENT; 52] *Opposite:* incident.

rasher 1 *n* **slice**, strip, piece, sliver. [➡AMOUNT OF SOLID OR SEMI-SOLID; 115] 2 *type of* **cut**. [➡TYPES AND CUTS OF MEAT; 1176]

rashness *n* **impetuousness**, thoughtlessness, haste, recklessness, foolishness, imprudence, impulsiveness, indiscretion, lack of caution, carelessness, precipitousness, hastiness, brashness. [➡LACK OF COMMITMENT AND UNRELIABILITY; 510] *Opposite:* prudence.

rasp 1 *n* **file**, scraper, tool. [➡HAND TOOLS; 1118] 2 *v* **grate**, bark, snarl, growl. [➡EMIT SOUNDS THROUGH IMPACT AND ABRASION; 366] *Opposite:* murmur. 3 *n* **scraping**, rasping, rubbing, grating, grinding, scratching. [➡CONTINUOUS SOUNDS; 1257] 4 *v* **scrape**, rub, grate, chafe, grind, scratch, file, abrade. [➡USE TOOLS AND MACHINERY; 469] *Opposite:* caress.

raspberry 1 *n* (*slang*) [➡UNFAVOURABLE NON-VERBAL RESPONSES; 655] 2 *type of* **berry**. [➡FRUIT AND VEGETABLES; 1175] 3 *type of* **pink**. [➡COLOURS; 1223]

rasping *adj* **harsh**, rough, grating, hoarse, jarring. [➡LOUD OR UNPLEASANT SOUNDS; 1265] *Opposite:* smooth.

rat 1 *n* (*slang*) **swine**, rascal, scoundrel, good-for-nothing, rogue, traitor, sneak. [➡VILLAINS AND THUGS; 947] 2 *type of* **rodent**. [➡RODENT; 989]

rat-arsed (*slang*) *adj* [➡UNDER THE INFLUENCE OF DRUGS OR ALCOHOL; 742]

ratatat-tat *type of* **impact sound**. [➡IMPACT SOUNDS; 1259]

ratatouille *type of* **cooked dish**. [➡PREPARED DISHES; 1169]

ratchet 1 *n* **notch**, tooth, cog, wheel, pawl. [➡PARTS OF MACHINES AND TOOLS; 1117] 2 *v* **intensify**, inflame, step up, stir up, increase, heighten, force up. [➡CHANGE OF INTENSITY: MORE; 395] *Opposite:* lessen.

rate 1 *n* **speed**, tempo, pace, velocity. [➡SPEED; 102] 2 *n* **amount**, frequency, speed, level, degree, proportion, percentage, ratio, quotient, scale. [➡DEGREE AND EXTENT; 110] 3 *n* **charge**, fee, price, tariff, toll, cost, figure. [➡EXPENDITURE; 424] 4 *v* **value**, regard, rank, esteem, appraise, evaluate, grade, assess, measure, assay, valuate. [➡ASSESS QUALITY; 756]

rather 1 *adv* **quite**, somewhat, to a certain extent, slightly, pretty, fairly, relatively, moderately. [➡TO A CERTAIN EXTENT; 134] 2 *adv* **very**, considerably, significantly, noticeably, extremely, quite. [➡TO A GREAT EXTENT; 130] *Opposite:* hardly. 3 *adv* **sooner**, preferably, instead, by preference. [➡DIFFERENCE; 150]

ratification *n* **approval**, sanction, endorsement, confirmation, authorization, agreement, consent, permission. [➡APPROVE AND CONFIRM; 647] *Opposite:* rejection.

ratify *v* **approve**, sanction, endorse, confirm, authorize, consent, back, be behind, disapprove. [➡APPROVE AND CONFIRM; 647] *Opposite:* reject.

rat-infested *adj* [➡DECAYING OR INFESTED; 1235]

rating 1 *n* **assessment**, score, evaluation, grade, ranking, mark. [➡SCORES AND EVALUATIONS; 599] 2 *n* **sailor**, seaman, hand. [➡MILITARY PERSONNEL; 828]

ratio *n* **proportion**, relative amount, relation, percentage, share, part, fraction, quotient, relationship. [➡MEASUREABLE PORTION; 125]

ratiocination (*formal*) *n* [➡IDEA AND THOUGHT; 771]

ration 1 *n* **share**, portion, allowance, quota, allotment, helping, measure, allocation. [➡AMOUNT AND QUANTITY; 112] 2 *v* **restrict**, control, limit, put a ceiling on, regulate, curb, prorate, allocate, allot. [➡DISPENSE, RATION, AND DISTRIBUTE; 435] *Opposite:* lavish.

rational 1 *adj* **reasonable**, sensible, logical, realistic, sound, wise, judicious. [➡THE NATURE OF IDEAS; 772] *Opposite:* illogical. 2 *adj* **lucid**, balanced, sane, normal, cogent, coherent. [➡POSITIVE INTELLECTUAL CHARACTERISTICS; 525] *Opposite:* irrational.

rationale *n* **reasoning**, basis, foundation, justification, motivation, grounds, raison d'être, validation, logic. [➡IDEA AND THOUGHT; 771]

rationalist *n* [➡PEOPLE WHO ARE APPROVED OF; 955]

rationality *n* **logic**, reason, shrewdness, judgment, lucidity, clear-headedness, equanimity, wisdom, sensibleness, saneness, level-headedness, reasonableness. [➡POSITIVE INTELLECTUAL CHARACTERISTICS; 525] *Opposite:* irrationality.

rationalization 1 *n* **streamlining**, restructuring,

reorganization, rearrangement, reshuffling. [➡ARRANGE AND CREATE ORDER; 358] 2 *n* **justification**, explanation, reasoning, validation, excuse, reason. [➡EXPLAIN AND CLARIFY; 611]

rationalize 1 *v* **adjust**, tune, level, straighten out, unravel, improve, enhance. [➡CORRECT AND PUT RIGHT; 378] 2 *v* **justify**, give good reason for, vindicate, excuse, explain, account for. [➡DEVELOP THEORIES AND REASON; 745] 3 *v* **streamline**, make more efficient, downsize, slim down, scale down, scale back (*US*), reduce. [➡ARRANGE AND CREATE ORDER; 358] *Opposite:* increase.

ration out *v* **distribute**, share out, apportion, divide up, allot, allocate, dispense, dole out (*informal*), hand out, give out, assign. [➡DISPENSE, RATION, AND DISTRIBUTE; 435] *Opposite:* pool.

rations *n* **provisions**, supplies, food, consignment, distribution. [➡FOOD; 1166]

rat on (*informal*) 1 *v* **abandon**, give up on, walk out on (*informal*), go back on, renege on, let down, fail, default on. [➡NOT DO AND REFUSE TO DO; 275] *Opposite:* stick to. 2 *v* **betray**, tell on, inform on, set up, spill the beans on (*informal*), grass on (*slang*), squeal on (*US slang disapproving*). [➡BETRAY CONFIDENCES AND GOSSIP; 619]

rat snake *type of* **non-poisonous snake.** [➡SNAKE; 995]

rattan 1 *type of* **climber.** [➡CLIMBERS; 1033] 2 *type of* **fibre.** [➡PLANT MATERIALS; 1132]

rattily (*informal*) 1 *adv* [➡IRRITATION AND ANGER; 542] 2 *adv* **messily**, shabbily, tattily, raggedly, scruffily, untidily. [➡BADLY GROOMED; 484] *Opposite:* tidily.

rattle 1 *v* **shake**, clatter, bang, crash, jangle, knock. [➡EMIT SOUNDS THROUGH IMPACT AND ABRASION; 366] 2 *v* **unnerve**, fluster, shock, throw (*informal*), disconcert, put off, perturb, disturb, unsettle. [➡UPSET, DISTRESS, AND HUMILIATE; 568] *Opposite:* calm. 3 *n* **clatter**, jangle, bang, crash, commotion. [➡CONTINUOUS SOUNDS; 1257]

rattle off *v* **say quickly**, reel off, run through, list, recite, repeat. [➡RECITE, REPEAT, AND NARRATE; 621] *Opposite:* stammer.

rattle on *v* **chatter**, blather (*informal*), go on and on, drone on, witter (*informal*), witter on (*informal*), rabbit on (*informal*), talk nineteen to the dozen, blether (*informal*), jabber, blabber. *Opposite:* clam up. (*informal*). [➡WITTER AND BABBLE; 618]

rattler *type of* **poisonous snake.** [➡SNAKE; 995]

rattlesnake *type of* **poisonous snake.** [➡SNAKE; 995]

rattle through *v* **rush through**, dash off (*informal*), dash through, make short work of. [➡MOVE FAST; 314] *Opposite:* labour.

rattletrap (*informal*) *n* **banger** (*informal*), jalopy (*dated informal*), boneshaker (*informal*), heap (*slang*), wreck, rust bucket (*informal humorous*). [➡BIKES, CARS, AND CARRIAGES; 1148]

rattling *adj* **quick-fire**, pacey, fast, brisk, lively, speedy, fast-moving, rapid-fire. [➡MOVING QUICKLY; 103] *Opposite:* plodding.

ratty 1 *adj* (*informal*) **irritable**, short-tempered, bad-tempered, crabby, tetchy (*informal*), irascible, cranky, crotchety (*informal*), grumpy, moody, testy (*informal*). [➡IRRITATION AND ANGER; 542] *Opposite:* easygoing. 2 *adj* (*informal*) **messy**, unkempt, shabby, seedy, tatty, ragged. [➡BADLY GROOMED; 484] *Opposite:* tidy. 3 *adj* (*US informal*) **dilapidated**, shabby, tatty, worn, seedy, decrepit, rundown, falling apart, ragged, tattered. [➡IN BAD REPAIR; 1233] *Opposite:* pristine.

raucous *adj* **loud**, harsh, rough, hoarse, disorderly, boisterous, unruly, riotous, rowdy, noisy, wild. [➡REBELLIOUSNESS AND DISOBEDIENCE; 566] *Opposite:* subdued.

raucousness *n* **boisterousness**, wildness, disorderliness, unruliness, riotousness, rowdiness, noisiness, loudness, roughness, harshness, hoarseness. [➡CHAOS AND UPROAR; 51] *Opposite:* quietness.

raunchy (*informal*) *adj* [➡MORALLY BAD; 776]

ravage 1 *v* **wreck**, devastate, destroy, ruin, damage, wreak havoc on, raze, desolate. [➡DESTRUCTION AND DEMOLITION; 360] *Opposite:* create. 2 *v* **despoil**, pillage, plunder, sack, lay waste, ransack. [➡DESTRUCTION AND DEMOLITION; 360] *Opposite:* restore.

ravages *n* **effects**, consequences, results, aftereffects. [➡RESULTS AND OUTCOMES; 83]

rave 1 *v* **rant**, rage, fume, fulminate, hold forth, thunder, babble. [➡WITTER AND BABBLE; 618] *Opposite:* reason. 2 *v* **enthuse**, praise, go on about, laud, extol. [➡PRAISE AND ENCOURAGE; 648] *Opposite:* criticize. 3 *n* **party**, bash, event, thrash (*dated informal*), shindig (*informal*), revelry, festivity, celebration. [➡PARTIES, DANCES, AND CELEBRATIONS; 37]

ravel *v* **tangle**, knot, twist, snag, catch, snarl. [➡COMBINE AND MIX; 401] *Opposite:* untangle.

raven 1 *type of* **black.** [➡COLOURS; 1223] 2 *v* (*literary*) **scoff** (*informal*), wolf, wolf down, gobble, gobble up, bolt, gulp, gulp down. [➡EAT AND NOT EAT; 711] 3 *type of* **scavenger.** [➡BIRD; 997]

ravening *adj* **voracious**, greedy, hungry, predatory, vicious, ravenous, insatiable. [➡FINANCIALLY MEAN AND GRASPING; 520] *Opposite:* sated.

ravenous 1 *adj* **hungry**, famished, starving (*informal*), starved (*informal*). [➡EAT AND NOT EAT; 711] *Opposite:* sated. 2 *adj* **greedy**, voracious, rapacious, ravening, predatory, gluttonous, insatiable. [➡FINANCIALLY MEAN AND GRASPING; 520] *Opposite:* generous.

ravenously *adv* **hungrily**, greedily, voraciously, rapaciously, gluttonously, insatiably. [➡WITH ENTHUSIASM; 287] *Opposite:* generously.

ravenousness *n* **greediness**, insatiability, hunger, greed, gluttony, voraciousness. [➡EAT AND NOT EAT; 711] *Opposite:* generosity.

raver (*informal*) *n* **partygoer**, party animal (*informal*), carouser (*literary*), bon viveur (*literary*), clubber, hedonist, sybarite. [➡PLEASURE-SEEKERS AND HEDONISTS; 886]

rave-up (*dated slang*) *n* **party**, rave (*slang*), shindig (*informal*), bash, do (*informal*), knees-up (*informal*). [➡PARTIES, DANCES, AND CELEBRATIONS; 37]

ravine *n* **valley**, gorge, gully, canyon, chasm, abyss, rift, gulch (*US*). [➡GEOLOGICAL FEATURES; 1056]

raving *adj* **frenzied**, gibbering, crazed, raging, delirious, rampant, frantic, furious, wild, uncontrollable, irrational, angry. [➡ECCENTRICITY AND IRRATIONALITY; 563] *Opposite:* controlled.

ravioli *type of* **pasta**. [➡PASTA; 1179]

ravish *v* **overwhelm**, overcome, transport, overpower, delight, entrance, enchant, stun, enrapture (*formal*), bewitch. [➡APPEAL TO AND AROUSE INTEREST; 576]

ravishing *adj* **beautiful**, stunning, gorgeous, striking, eye-catching, entrancing, delightful, enchanting. [➡PEOPLE'S PHYSICAL APPEARANCE; 476] *Opposite:* ordinary.

raw 1 *adj* **uncooked**, fresh, rare, red, underdone, pink, blue. [➡STATE OF PREPARED FOOD; 1170] *Opposite:* cooked. 2 *adj* **unprocessed**, unrefined, untreated, crude, basic, natural. [➡RAW AND NATURAL; 1213] *Opposite:* synthetic. 3 *adj* **painful**, sore, sensitive, tender, bleeding, bloody, inflamed, angry, red. [➡PAIN AND OTHER PHYSICAL SENSATIONS; 734] 4 *adj* **inexperienced**, green, untrained, wet behind the ears, untried, new. [➡UNSKILLED; 530] *Opposite:* experienced. 5 *adj* **bitter**, chilly, perishing, bleak, freezing, inclement, icy, cold, harsh. [➡COLD WEATHER; 1051] *Opposite:* mild. 6 *adj* **visceral**, brutal, crude, rude, primal, atavistic, primitive, simple, gut-wrenching, direct, authentic, no-holds-barred, vivid, intense. [➡STRENGTH; 202] *Opposite:* bland.

rawboned *adj* [➡BUILD; 478]

rawhide *type of* **leather**. [➡FABRICS; 1131]

raw material *n* [➡SUBSTANCES; 1266]

rawness 1 *n* **inflammation**, painfulness, soreness, pain, redness, abrasion. [➡CONDITIONS AFFECTING THE SKIN; 722] 2 *n* **inexperience**, naivety, ingenuousness, innocence, immaturity, greenness. [➡UNSKILLED; 530] *Opposite:* poise. 3 *n* **cold**, chill, bitterness, bitingness, iciness, chilliness, coldness. [➡COLD WEATHER; 1051] *Opposite:* mildness. 4 *n* **brutality**, crudeness, rudeness, primitiveness, atavism, simplicity, directness, authenticity, vividness, intensity. [➡STRENGTH; 202] *Opposite:* polish.

raw recruit *n* [➡UNSKILLED PERSON; 531]

ray 1 *n* **beam**, shaft, gleam, glimmer, flicker, spark. [➡LIGHT; 1163] 2 *type of* **flatfish**. [➡SEA FISH; 1009]

ray of sunshine *n* [➡PEOPLE WHO ARE APPROVED OF; 955]

rayon *type of* **synthetic fabric**. [➡FABRICS; 1131]

raze *v* **destroy**, demolish, annihilate, level, flatten, lay waste, wreck, ruin, devastate, knock down, tear down. [➡DESTRUCTION AND DEMOLITION; 360] *Opposite:* build.

raze to the ground *v* [➡DESTRUCTION AND DEMOLITION; 360]

razor 1 *v* **shave**, cut, trim, style, clip, shear. [➡TEAR, BREAK, AND CUT; 361] 2 *type of* **cosmetic tool**. [➡HAND TOOLS; 1118]

razor blade *type of* **cutting tool**. [➡CUTTING TOOLS; 1119]

razz (*US informal*) *v* **tease**, taunt, make fun of, poke fun at, ridicule, mock. [➡JOKES AND TEASING; 675]

razzle-dazzle *n* [➡INTERESTING AND MEANINGFUL; 191]

razzmatazz *n* **showiness**, flashiness, hype, razzle-dazzle, snazziness (*informal*), glitziness. [➡INTERESTING AND MEANINGFUL; 191] *Opposite:* dullness.

re *prep* **on the subject of**, with regard to, with reference to, concerning, regarding, about, apropos (*formal*), pertaining to, relating to. [➡EXPRESSIONS OF REFERENCE; 63]

reach 1 *v* **stretch**, touch, get hold of, get (*informal*), grasp, extend. [➡GET; 421] 2 *v* **go**, move, feel, fumble, lunge, dive, grasp, grab. [➡CONTACT: HOLD; 412] 3 *v* **arrive at**, get to, attain, make, achieve, accomplish, turn up, show up (*informal*). [➡ARRIVE; 12] 4 *v* **influence**, touch, affect, impact on, get to, speak to, sway, move. [➡APPEAL TO AND AROUSE INTEREST; 576] 5 *v* **contact**, get in touch with, access, get through to, get hold of, make contact with, get a message to, connect with, catch, communicate. [➡INITIATE AND ESTABLISH COMMUNICATION; 681] 6 *n* **scope**, spread, range, grasp, influence, extent. [➡DEGREE AND EXTENT; 110]

reachable *adj* **within reach**, on hand, nearby, easy to get to, accessible, local, at hand. [➡PRESENT AND AVAILABLE; 11] *Opposite:* remote.

react 1 *v* **respond**, counter, retort, answer, reply, rejoin. [➡REPLY AND ANSWER; 669] *Opposite:* ignore. 2 *v* **change**, alter, oxidize, reduce, bond, ionize. [➡CHANGE; 373]

reaction *n* **response**, reply, answer, feedback, rejoinder (*formal*), retort, return, antiphon (*literary*). [➡REPLY AND ANSWER; 669]

reactionary 1 *adj* **backward-looking**, conservative, illiberal, unreceptive, unreasonable, intolerant, bigoted, intransigent, diehard, medieval, prehistoric, outdated. [➡NEGATIVE INTELLECTUAL CHARACTERISTICS; 526] *Opposite:* progressive. 2 *n* **conservative**, dinosaur, diehard, intransigent (*formal*), extremist, bigot. [➡UNCOOPERATIVE OR REBELLIOUS PERSON; 567] *Opposite:* progressive.

reactivate *v* **restart**, reboot, galvanize, resuscitate, revitalize, revive, resurrect, reenergize. [➡RECOMMENCE AND RESUME; 269] *Opposite:* deactivate.

reactive *adj* **responsive**, sensitive, oversensitive, volatile, mercurial, touchy, irritable, combative. [➡EXCESSIVE SENSITIVITY; 512] *Opposite:* phlegmatic.

reactor *n* **device**, apparatus, vessel, container, receptacle, cauldron. [➡ENERGY STORAGE AND GENERATION; 1162]

read 1 *v* **interpret**, study, examine, translate, convert, understand, comprehend, make sense of. [➡READ; 759] 2 *v* **peruse**, scan, glance at, look at, study, look through, look over, skim, browse, leaf through, flick through, inspect, examine, go through. [➡LOOKING AND LOOKS; 701] 3 *v* **read out**, recite, deliver, speak, declaim, reel off, orate, state. [➡RECITE, REPEAT, AND NARRATE; 621] 4 *v* **interpret**, understand, comprehend, decipher, figure out, make sense of, follow. [➡SOLVE AND INTERPRET; 761] 5 *v* **study**, take, do, do a degree in, research. [➡STUDYING; 844]

readable *adj* **clear**, legible, decipherable, understandable, comprehensible. [➡CONCISE AND CLEAR; 203] *Opposite:* illegible.

read between the lines *v* [➡SOLVE AND INTERPRET; 761]

reader *n* **booklover**, bookworm (*informal*), bibliophile. [➡DEVOTEES AND ADDICTED PEOPLE; 557]

readership *n* **circulation**, audience, distribution, market share, niche. [➡GROUPS WITH A COMMON INTEREST; 938]

readies (*informal*) *n* [➡MONEY; 140]

readily 1 *adv* **willingly**, gamely, eagerly, voluntarily, gladly, with good grace, with pleasure, enthusiastically, cheerfully, freely, graciously, ungrudgingly. [➡THE WILL AND WILLINGNESS; 564] *Opposite:* grudgingly. 2 *adv* **promptly**, unhesitatingly, quickly, straightaway, at once, without delay, swiftly, speedily, immediately, instantly, pronto (*informal*), right away. [➡HAPPENING QUICKLY; 104] *Opposite:* belatedly. 3 *adv* **without difficulty**, easily, effortlessly, with no trouble, smoothly, facilely, dexterously. [➡EASE AND SIMPLICITY; 201] *Opposite:* painfully.

readiness 1 *n* **willingness**, gameness, eagerness, keenness, enthusiasm, inclination. [➡THE WILL AND WILLINGNESS; 564] *Opposite:* unwillingness. 2 *n* **promptness**, speediness, quickness, alacrity, skill, ease. [➡SPEED; 102] *Opposite:* delay.

reading 1 *n* **understanding**, comprehension, construing, interpretation, analysis, appraisal, evaluation, impression, sense, imagination, conception. [➡EXAMINE AND ASSESS; 754] *Opposite:* incomprehension. 2 *n* **recitation**, recital, rendition, performance, presentation, delivery. [➡PERFORMANCES AND SHOWS; 42]

reading desk *n* [➡FURNITURE; 858]

reading stand *n* [➡FURNITURE; 858]

readjust 1 *v* **get used to**, readapt, settle, settle in, accommodate, come to terms with. [➡CHANGE; 373] 2 *v* **rearrange**, realign, modify, calibrate, rectify, straighten, change, manipulate. [➡ARRANGE AND CREATE ORDER; 358] *Opposite:* leave alone.

readjustment *n* **rearrangement**, change, modification, alteration, reformation, revision. [➡CHANGE; 373]

read out *v* **announce**, recite, deliver, declaim, reel off, read, state, orate. [➡RECITE, REPEAT, AND NARRATE; 621]

readout 1 *n* **data**, information, figures, statistics, info (*informal*), details. [➡COMPUTERS AND COMPUTING; 1126] 2 *n* **display**, retrieval, record, screen, monitor. [➡RECORDS; 586]

read the riot act *v* [➡ACCUSE, BLAME, AND CRITICIZE; 642]

read up *v* **study**, find out about, gen up (*informal*), look into, investigate, research. [➡STUDYING; 844]

ready 1 *adj* **prepared**, set, all set, complete, standing by, geared up, equipped, organized, arranged. [➡CALMNESS, CONFIDENCE, AND COMPOSURE; 537] *Opposite:* unprepared. 2 *adj* **likely to**, about to, on the verge of, on the point of, liable to, close to, on the brink of, just about. [➡FUTURE; 86] *Opposite:* unlikely. 3 *adj* **willing**, eager, prepared, disposed, keen, glad, raring to go, inclined, game, prone. [➡THE WILL AND WILLINGNESS; 564] *Opposite:* unwilling. 4 *adj* **quick**, prompt, apt, timely, swift, flexible, immediate, alacritous, punctual, speedy, expeditious. [➡HAPPENING QUICKLY; 104] *Opposite:* slow. 5 *adj* **perceptive**, discerning, attentive, wide-awake, astute, acute. [➡POSITIVE INTELLECTUAL CHARACTERISTICS; 525] *Opposite:* dull. 6 *v* **prepare**, set, arrange, prime, make plans for, lay out, organize, equip, fit out. [➡PREPARE FOR ACTION; 290]

ready and waiting *adj* [➡CALMNESS, CONFIDENCE, AND COMPOSURE; 537]

ready cash *n* [➡MONEY; 140]

ready for action *adj* [➡CALMNESS, CONFIDENCE, AND COMPOSURE; 537]

ready for anything *adj* [➡CALMNESS, CONFIDENCE, AND COMPOSURE; 537]

ready-made *adj* **off-the-peg**, ready-to-wear, prêt-à-porter, retail, high-street, convenient, handy. [➡DESCRIBING CLOTHES; 869] *Opposite:* custom-made.

ready-made meal *type of* **meal**. [➡MEALS AND PARTS OF MEALS; 1168]

ready money *n* [➡MONEY; 140]

ready to drop *adj* [➡TIRED, ASLEEP AND UNCONSCIOUS; 739]

ready-to-wear *adj* **ready-made**, mass-produced, off-the-peg, retail, high-street, convenient, prêt-à-porter. [➡DESCRIBING CLOTHES; 869] *Opposite:* custom-made.

ready yourself *v* [➡PREPARE FOR ACTION; 290]

reaffirm *v* **repeat**, reassert, confirm, reiterate, endorse, restate. [➡CLAIM, INSIST, AND EMPHASIZE; 615] *Opposite:* contradict.

reaffirmation *n* **restatement**, repetition, reiteration, endorsement, confirmation, reassertion. [➡CLAIM, INSIST, AND EMPHASIZE; 615] *Opposite:* contradiction.

reagent *n* **substance**, component, element, chemical, mixture. [➡SUBSTANCES; 1266]

real 1 *adj* **existent** (*formal*), physical, actual, factual, material, tangible. [➡TRUE AND REAL; 172] *Opposite:* nonexistent. 2 *adj* **genuine**, original, authentic, bona fide, valid, true, unquestionable. [➡TRUE AND REAL; 172] *Opposite:* false. 3 *adj* **sincere**, unfeigned, genuine, frank, heartfelt, unaffected, authentic, truthful, honest. [➡HONEST AND RELIABLE; 503] *Opposite:* artificial. 4 *adv* (*US informal*) **very**, extremely, really, truly, honestly, absolutely. [➡TO A GREAT EXTENT; 130] *Opposite:* hardly.

real estate (*US*) *n* **land**, property, realty, estate, real property, assets. [➡POSSESSIONS; 462]

realign *v* **readjust**, straighten, manipulate, rearrange, restore, calibrate. [➡ARRANGE AND CREATE ORDER; 358] *Opposite:* disarrange.

realignment *n* **readjustment**, rearrangement, shift, repositioning, relocation, change, manipulation. [➡ARRANGE AND CREATE ORDER; 358]

realism 1 *n* **practicality**, pragmatism, level-headedness, common sense, sanity, saneness. [➡POSITIVE INTELLECTUAL CHARACTERISTICS; 525] *Opposite:* impracticality. 2 *type of* **pre-20th-century art movement**. [➡ARTISTIC MOVEMENTS AND STYLES; 899]

realist *n* **pragmatist**, doer, experimenter, radical, stoic, humanist. [➡PHILOSOPHICAL AND POLITICAL THINKERS; 782] *Opposite:* idealist.

realistic 1 *adj* **practical**, sensible, pragmatic, down-to-earth, level-headed, reasonable, rational, matter-of-fact. [➡POSITIVE INTELLECTUAL CHARACTERISTICS; 525] *Opposite:* impractical. 2 *adj* **convincing**, lifelike, representative, truthful, accurate, faithful, genuine, true, credible, true-to-life, natural, authentic. [➡TRUE AND REAL; 172] *Opposite:* unnatural.

reality 1 *n* **realism**, authenticity, truth, certainty, veracity, genuineness, representativeness. [➡TRUE AND REAL; 172] *Opposite:* idealism. 2 *n* **actuality**, the everyday, experience, existence, life, the here and now, corporeality, materiality. [➡TRUE AND REAL; 172] *Opposite:* make-believe.

realizable *adj* **achievable**, attainable, realistic, viable, possible, doable, reachable, practicable, feasible. [➡POSSIBLE AND PROBABLE; 178] *Opposite:* unattainable.

realization 1 *n* **understanding**, comprehension, consciousness, awareness, recognition, apprehension, insight, grasp. [➡UNDERSTAND AND GRASP; 760] 2 *n* **achievement**, fulfilment, accomplishment, carrying out, attainment, completion. [➡SUCCESS; 82] *Opposite:* failure.

realize 1 *v* **understand**, comprehend, become conscious, appreciate, grasp, apprehend, recognize, take in, gather, get (*informal*), fathom. [➡UNDERSTAND AND GRASP; 760] *Opposite:* misunderstand. 2 *v* **achieve**, fulfil, accomplish, carry out, bring to fruition, make happen, complete, reach, attain, consummate, execute, do, reorganize. [➡CARRY OUT AN ACTION; 270] *Opposite:* fail.

See Compare and Contrast at **accomplish**.

real life *n* [➡TRUE AND REAL; 172]

real-life *adj* **actual**, true, factual, real, realistic, genuine, everyday, tangible, palpable. [➡TRUE AND REAL; 172] *Opposite:* imaginary.

reallocate *v* **redistribute**, reshuffle, reorganize, transfer, rationalize, sort out, restructure, rearrange, change round, reorder. [➡ARRANGE AND CREATE ORDER; 358]

really 1 *adv* **actually**, in fact, in truth, in reality, truly, in actual fact, if truth be told, certainly, indeed, categorically, surely. [➡WORDS AND PHRASES EMPHASIZING THE TRUTH OF A MATTER; 173] *Opposite:* on the contrary. 2 *adv* **very**, thoroughly, truly, genuinely, sincerely, exceedingly, especially, truthfully. [➡TO A GREAT EXTENT; 130] *Opposite:* hardly.

realm 1 *n* **scope**, area, range, domain, sphere, field, ambit, province, orbit. [➡SUBJECT AREA; 769] 2 *n* **kingdom**, monarchy, dominion, empire, land, territory, jurisdiction, demesne (*formal*), country, state. [➡TERRITORIES AND GROUPS OF NATIONS; 1067]

realness *n* **reality**, actuality, authenticity, genuineness, sincerity, trueness, truth. [➡TRUE AND REAL; 172]

realpolitik *n* [➡STYLES AND SYSTEMS OF GOVERNMENT; 806]

real-time *adj* [➡COMPUTERS AND COMPUTING; 1126]

realty *n* **real property**, land, property, estate, real estate (*US*). [➡POSSESSIONS; 462]

real-world *adj* **practical**, actual, everyday, real, real-life, true. [➡TRUE AND REAL; 172] *Opposite:* imaginary.

real world *n* **reality**, life, everyday, the world, actuality, hurly-burly, real life, everyday life, the big bad world. [➡TRUE AND REAL; 172] *Opposite:* ivory tower.

ream *n* **quantity**, amount, pack, pile. [➡AMOUNT OF SOLID OR SEMI-SOLID; 115]

reamer (*US*) *type of* **utensil**. [➡TABLEWARE, CUTLERY, AND KITCHENWARE; 861]

reanimate *v* **revive**, restore, reawaken, awaken, resuscitate, resurrect, bring round. [➡IMPROVE STRENGTH AND DURABILITY; 379] *Opposite:* deaden.

reap 1 *v* **gather**, harvest, garner, collect, pick, bring in, get in, glean. [➡GET; 421] *Opposite:* sow. 2 *v* **obtain**, acquire, gain, earn, secure, win, get in, procure, realize, derive. [➡GET MONEY OR REWARD; 422] *Opposite:* lose.

reaper *n* **gatherer**, harvester, cutter, gleaner, mower, farmer. [➡FARMERS, GARDENERS, AND MANUAL WORKERS; 849]

reappear *v* **come back**, recur, resurface, return, come again, re-emerge, repeat. [➡HAPPEN AGAIN; 28] *Opposite:* disappear.

reappearance *n* **recurrence**, repetition, re-emergence, return, comeback, revival. [➡REPETITION; 29] *Opposite:* disappearance.

reappraisal *n* **reassessment**, re-evaluation, re-examination, review, reconsideration, check, second look, revision. [➡SCORES AND EVALUATIONS; 599]

reappraise *v* **reassess**, re-evaluate, check, reconsider, re-examine, review. [➡EXAMINE AND ASSESS; 754]

rear 1 *v* **raise**, bring up, care for, nurture, take care of, tend, look after, watch over, train, educate, cultivate. [➡GROW AND CULTIVATE; 352] *Opposite:* neglect. 2 *n* **back**, stern, tail, tail end, back end, end, posterior (*formal*). [➡EXTREMITIES OF PHYSICAL OBJECTS; 1249] *Opposite:* front.

rear-end (*US*) *v* **collide**, crash into, bang into, bump into, hit, smash into. [➡CONTACT: IMPACT; 414]

rear-ender (*US*) *n* [➡TRAFFIC ACCIDENTS; 256]

rearguard *n* **tail end**, rear, back end, tail, back, rear end. [➡EXTREMITIES OF PHYSICAL OBJECTS; 1249] *Opposite:* vanguard.

rear its head *v* **appear**, loom, turn up, crop up (*informal*), materialize, rise up. [➡APPEAR AND EMERGE; 3] *Opposite:* disappear.

rearm 1 *v* **arm**, equip, provide, supply, sell, trade. [➡EQUIP AND SUPPLY; 436] 2 *v* **re-equip**, build up, upgrade, reinforce, fortify, secure. [➡IMPROVE STRENGTH AND DURABILITY; 379] *Opposite:* disarm.

rearmament 1 *n* **equipment**, armament, provision, supply, sale, trade, arming. [➡WARFARE AND WAR; 830] 2 *n* **buildup**, re-equipment, upgrade, fortification, reinforcement, securement, re-equipping. [➡IMPROVE STRENGTH AND DURABILITY; 379] *Opposite:* disarmament.

rearmost *adj* **backmost**, last, hindmost (*literary*), hinder, final, ultimate, terminal, end, posterior (*formal*). [➡RELATIVE LOCATION; 162] *Opposite:* foremost.

rearrange 1 *v* **reorder**, reorganize, reposition, move, redispose, relocate, readjust, reshuffle. [➡ARRANGE AND CREATE ORDER; 358] **2** *v* **reschedule**, change the date, postpone, delay, adjourn, put off. [➡DELAY ACTION OR OCCURRENCE; 279] *Opposite:* bring forward.

rearrangement **1** *n* **reorganization**, reordering, movement, redisposition, change, relocation, readjustment, reshuffle. [➡ARRANGE AND CREATE ORDER; 358] **2** *n* **rescheduling**, postponement, change of date, delay, adjournment, transferral. [➡DELAY ACTION OR OCCURRENCE; 279]

rearview mirror *type of* **internal feature.** [➡INTERNAL PARTS OF A VEHICLE; 1145]

rearward **1** *adj* **backward**, to the rear, towards the back, back, behind, rear. [➡RELATIVE LOCATION; 162] *Opposite:* forward. **2** *adv* **backward**, towards the back, behind, back, to the rear, over your shoulder. [➡DIRECTION OF MOTION; 346] *Opposite:* forward.

rearwards **1** *adv* **backwards**, towards the back, behind, back, to the rear, over your shoulder. [➡DIRECTION OF MOTION; 346] *Opposite:* forward. **2** *adj* **backward**, behind, back, to the rear, over your shoulder, towards the back. [➡DIRECTION OF MOTION; 346] *Opposite:* forward.

reason **1** *n* **justification**, explanation, basis, grounds, cause, excuse, rationale, pretext, occasion. [➡CAUSATION; 169] **2** *n* **motive**, cause, aim, end, goal, purpose, object, intention, motivation. [➡INTENTION AND PURPOSE; 773] **3** *n* **thought**, judgment, logic, sense, mind, brains, intelligence, wit, comprehension. [➡DESCRIBING SOMEBODY'S INTELLECT; 524] **4** *n* **sanity**, right mind, mind, wits, senses, intelligence, brains, faculties. [➡PSYCHOLOGY AND THE MIND; 770] *Opposite:* insanity. **5** *v* **think**, rationalize, deduce, work out, infer, apply your mind, figure out, solve, analyse, conclude. [➡DEVELOP THEORIES AND REASON; 745] **6** *v* **argue**, debate, discuss, influence, persuade, talk through, talk over, dispute. [➡CLAIM, INSIST, AND EMPHASIZE; 615]

See Compare and Contrast at **deduce.**

reasonable **1** *adj* **sensible**, rational, judicious, practical, realistic, level-headed, sound, equitable (*formal*), intelligent, wise, logical, evenhanded. [➡POSITIVE INTELLECTUAL CHARACTERISTICS; 525] *Opposite:* unreasonable. **2** *adj* **inexpensive**, affordable, cheap, moderate, economical, equitable (*formal*). [➡CHEAP AND INEXPENSIVE; 222] *Opposite:* expensive. **3** *adj* **not bad**, quite good, passable, tolerable, all right, sufficient, acceptable, good enough, satisfactory, fair. [➡ACCEPTABLE AND PASSABLE; 220] *Opposite:* appalling.

See Compare and Contrast at **valid.**

reasonableness *n* **sensibleness**, rationality, equanimity, fairness, common sense, level-headedness, practicality, moderation, balance, intelligence, wisdom, logicality. [➡POSITIVE INTELLECTUAL CHARACTERISTICS; 525] *Opposite:* irrationality.

reasonably **1** *adv* **sensibly**, rationally, judiciously, level-headedly, soundly, equitably (*formal*), practically, realistically, commonsensically, intelligently, wisely, logically. [➡POSITIVE INTELLECTUAL CHARACTERISTICS; 525] *Opposite:* irrationally. **2** *adv* **quite**, fairly, moderately, rather, relatively, tolerably, acceptably, satisfactorily, well enough, somewhat. [➡TO A CERTAIN EXTENT; 134] *Opposite:* extremely.

reasoned *adj* **rational**, coherent, logical, lucid, analytic, well-structured, consistent, articulate, systematic, clear, thought through, plain, sound, cogent, methodical. [➡THE NATURE OF IDEAS; 772] *Opposite:* illogical.

reasoning *n* **analysis**, logic, calculation, reckoning, interpretation, deduction, ratiocination (*formal*), thought, thinking. [➡IDEA AND THOUGHT; 771]

reassemble **1** *v* **meet again**, reconvene, reunite, get back together, congregate, collect. [➡GET CLOSER TOGETHER; 311] *Opposite:* disperse. **2** *v* **put back together**, reconstruct, rebuild, repair, mend, restore. [➡BUILD; 353] *Opposite:* take apart.

reassert *v* **restate**, reaffirm, repeat, reiterate, confirm, insist. [➡CLAIM, INSIST, AND EMPHASIZE; 615] *Opposite:* abandon.

reassertion *n* **reaffirmation**, restatement, repetition, reiteration, confirmation, insistence, saying again. [➡CLAIM, INSIST, AND EMPHASIZE; 615] *Opposite:* abandonment.

reassess *v* **reconsider**, review, re-evaluate, re-examine, have another look at, think again, check, go back over, go over. [➡EXAMINE AND ASSESS; 754] *Opposite:* accept.

reassessment *n* **reconsideration**, review, re-evaluation, check, revision, second look, re-examination. [➡SCORES AND EVALUATIONS; 599]

reassurance *n* **comfort**, assurance, support, encouragement, hope, faith, guarantee. [➡CALMNESS, CONFIDENCE, AND COMPOSURE; 537] *Opposite:* discouragement.

reassure *v* **assure**, comfort, support, encourage, set your mind at rest, soothe, calm, bolster, uplift, cheer. [➡SOOTHE AND CALM; 574] *Opposite:* discourage.

reassured *adj* [➡CALMNESS, CONFIDENCE, AND COMPOSURE; 537]

reassuring *adj* **encouraging**, comforting, supportive, cheering, heartening, soothing, calming, uplifting. [➡CALMING; 189] *Opposite:* discouraging.

reawaken *v* **stir up**, revive, bring back, rekindle, resuscitate, recall, resurrect. [➡RECOMMENCE AND RESUME; 269] *Opposite:* obliterate.

rebarbative (*formal*) *adj* **unpleasant**, unattractive, objectionable, annoying, forbidding, antipathetic, repugnant. [➡DISGUSTING AND REPULSIVE; 231] *Opposite:* pleasant.

rebate *n* **refund**, repayment, return, discount, reimbursement, allowance, reduction. [➡MONEY, PAYMENTS, AND CHARGES; 800] *Opposite:* supplement.

rebel **1** *n* **protester**, objector, campaigner, agitator, radical, dissenter, revolutionary, mutineer, insurgent, maverick, renegade, iconoclast, nonconformist. [➡UNCOOPERATIVE OR REBELLIOUS PERSON; 567] *Opposite:* loyalist. **2** *v* **revolt**, rise up, mutiny, resist, mount the barricades, take up arms, fight. [➡NOT DO AND REFUSE TO DO; 275] *Opposite:* comply. **3** *v* **protest**, campaign, agitate, defy, dissent, take on, fight. [➡COMPETE, CONTEND, AND COMBAT; 304] *Opposite:* obey.

rebellion *n* **revolt**, uprising, insurgence, upheaval, mutiny, revolution, rising, agitation, insurrection. [➡AGGRESSIVE EVENT; 39] *Opposite:* compliance.

rebellious 1 *adj* **revolutionary**, militant, armed, treacherous, mutinous, disloyal, seditious. [➡UNWILLINGNESS AND STUBBORNNESS; 565] *Opposite:* law-abiding. 2 *adj* **disobedient**, unruly, insubordinate, recalcitrant, defiant, stubborn, unmanageable, uncontrollable, refractory, contrary, fractious, iconoclastic, nonconformist. [➡REBELLIOUSNESS AND DISOBEDIENCE; 566] *Opposite:* obedient.

rebelliousness 1 *n* **revolution**, insurrection, sedition, mutiny, treachery, seditiousness, disloyalty, dissent, iconoclasm, nonconformity. [➡UNWILLINGNESS AND STUBBORNNESS; 565] *Opposite:* compliance. 2 *n* **disobedience**, unruliness, recalcitrance, insubordination, defiance, noncompliance. [➡REBELLIOUSNESS AND DISOBEDIENCE; 566] *Opposite:* obedience.

rebirth 1 *n* **regeneration**, renewal, restoration, revitalization, rejuvenation, new beginning, revival. [➡BEGINNING; 53] *Opposite:* degeneration. 2 *n* **revival**, renaissance, reawakening, renascence, return, resurgence. [➡REPETITION; 29] *Opposite:* disappearance.

reboot *v* **restart**, start up again, open again, boot up. [➡COMPUTERS AND COMPUTING; 1126] *Opposite:* shut down.

reborn *adj* **born again**, recreated, regenerated, renewed, revitalized, brought back to life, resurrected, reincarnated. [➡NEW, MODERN; 167]

rebound 1 *v* **spring back**, recoil, ricochet, jump back, return. [➡CHANGE DIRECTION OF MOTION; 345] 2 *v* **recover**, bounce back, rally, pick up, return to normal, get back, make a comeback. [➡FALL ILL, TREAT, AND RECOVER; 729]

rebuff 1 *v* **reject**, snub, refuse, repulse, slight, spurn, give the cold shoulder, decline, turn down. [➡REFUSING OR REJECTING RELATIONS; 975] *Opposite:* accept. 2 *n* **rejection**, refusal, snub, slight, denial, putdown (*informal*). [➡DENY AND REJECT; 645] *Opposite:* acceptance.

rebuild 1 *v* **reconstruct**, build, restructure, re-erect, remake, reconstitute, re-establish. [➡IMPROVE STRENGTH AND DURABILITY; 379] *Opposite:* destroy. 2 *v* **restore**, renovate, recreate, reconstitute, do up, remodel, reform, overhaul. [➡REPAIR AND MEND; 377] *Opposite:* neglect.

rebuke 1 *v* **reprimand**, reprove, censure, reproach, take to task, haul over the coals, scold, admonish, chide (*literary*), criticize, give a talking-to. [➡ACCUSE, BLAME, AND CRITICIZE; 642] *Opposite:* praise. 2 *n* **reproach**, reproof, censure, reprimand, scolding, admonition, telling-off (*informal*), lecture, criticism, slap on the wrist (*informal*). [➡CRITICISMS AND ANGRY OUTBURSTS; 50] *Opposite:* compliment.

rebut *v* **refute**, disprove, deny, invalidate, confute (*formal*), contradict, controvert (*formal*). [➡DENY AND REJECT; 645] *Opposite:* accept.

rebuttal *n* **refutation**, disproof, confutation (*formal*), denial, negation, contradiction. [➡DENY AND REJECT; 645] *Opposite:* endorsement.

recalcitrance *n* **resistance**, noncooperation, stubbornness, obstinacy, obduracy, defiance, insubordination, mutiny, rebellion, disobedience, waywardness. [➡REBELLIOUSNESS AND DISOBEDIENCE; 566] *Opposite:* cooperation.

recalcitrant *adj* **unruly**, intractable (*formal*), refractory, disobedient, wayward, headstrong, obstinate, unmanageable, noncompliant, stubborn, uncooperative. [➡REBELLIOUSNESS AND DISOBEDIENCE; 566] *Opposite:* cooperative.

See Compare and Contrast at **unruly**.

recall 1 *v* **remember**, bring to mind, evoke, call to mind, recollect, summon up, bear in mind, educe (*formal*), elicit. [➡REMEMBER; 747] *Opposite:* forget. 2 *v* **call back**, call in, take back, withdraw, take out, retract, abjure, recant. [➡APOLOGIZE AND RETRACT; 684] 3 *n* **memory**, recollection, remembrance, reminiscence. [➡MEMORY; 746] *Opposite:* amnesia.

recant *v* **take back**, renounce, repudiate, disavow (*formal*), retract, withdraw, deny, revoke. *Opposite:* avow. (*formal*). [➡APOLOGIZE AND RETRACT; 684]

recantation *n* **denial**, withdrawal, repudiation, retraction, revocation, renege, negation. [➡APOLOGIZE AND RETRACT; 684] *Opposite:* affirmation.

recap 1 *v* **recapitulate** (*formal*), sum up, summarize, go over, run through, review, repeat, reiterate, restate. [➡EXPLAIN AND CLARIFY; 611] 2 *n* **summary**, outline, summing up, review, restatement, repetition, recapitulation (*formal*). [➡SUMMARIES, OUTLINES, AND EXCERPTS; 589]

recapitulate (*formal*) *v* **sum up**, recap, summarize, run through, review, go over, repeat, reiterate. [➡EXPLAIN AND CLARIFY; 611]

recapitulation (*formal*) *n* **recap**, summary, restatement, review, outline, repetition. [➡SUMMARIES, OUTLINES, AND EXCERPTS; 589]

recapture 1 *v* **regain**, retake, take back, reclaim, repossess, recover. [➡REGAIN POSSESSION; 430] 2 *v* **summon up**, recall, evoke, bring back, recollect, take back, educe (*formal*). [➡REMEMBER; 747]

recast 1 *v* **reorganize**, re-present, re-form, modify, alter, change, vary. [➡CHANGE; 373] 2 *v* **reassign**, reallocate, reselect, redistribute. [➡THE PERFORMING ARTS; 904]

recce (*slang*) 1 *n* **reconnaissance**, exploration, look, lookout, watch, patrol. [➡LOOKING AND LOOKS; 701] 2 *v* **reconnoitre**, explore, look out, look, watch, patrol. [➡LOOKING AND LOOKS; 701]

recede 1 *v* **move away**, retreat, go back, withdraw, draw back, draw away, ebb, retrocede, regress. [➡GO BACKWARDS; 310] *Opposite:* advance. 2 *v* **diminish**, lessen, decline, wane, fade, dwindle, decrease, abate (*formal or literary*). [➡CHANGE OF INTENSITY: LESS; 396] *Opposite:* increase.

receding *adj* **retreating**, withdrawing, disappearing, ebbing, declining, waning, fading. [➡DIRECTION OF MOTION; 346] *Opposite:* growing.

receipt 1 *n* **acknowledgment**, proof of purchase, note, chit (*dated*), slip, voucher, tab (*US informal*). [➡RECEIPTS AND INVOICES; 592] *Opposite:* invoice. 2 *n* **receiving**, reception, delivery, unloading, acceptance. [➡ACCEPT POSSESSION; 451] *Opposite:* dispatch.

receive 1 *v* **get**, obtain, accept, take, have, take delivery of, be given, collect. [➡ACCEPT POSSESSION; 451] *Opposite:* dispatch. **2** *v* **hear**, catch, sense, gather, grasp, pick up, convert. [➡HEAR; 708] **3** *v* **entertain**, have round, greet, welcome, meet. [➡ESTABLISHING RELATIONSHIPS WITH OTHERS; 974]

Received Pronunciation *n* [➡ASPECTS OF LANGUAGE; 683]

receiver *type of* **telecommunications equipment.** [➡TELECOMMUNICATIONS; 1129]

receivership *n* **bankruptcy**, insolvency, failure, ruin, destitution, dissolution. [➡BUSINESS ACTIVITIES AND PHENOMENA; 795]

receiving benefit *adj* [➡EMPLOYMENT STATUS; 831]

recent *adj* **new**, of late, fresh, current, topical, hot, modern, up to date, latest, contemporary. [➡NEW, MODERN; 167] *Opposite:* old.

recently *adv* **lately**, only just, in recent times, a moment ago, a short time ago, newly, freshly, not long ago, just now. [➡PAST; 84]

receptacle *n* **container**, vessel, holder, repository, magazine, depot, store. [➡CONTAINERS, RECEPTACLES, AND PACKAGING; 1244]

reception **1** *n* **receipt**, receiving, delivery, unloading, acceptance. [➡ACCEPT POSSESSION; 451] *Opposite:* dispatch. **2** *n* **welcome**, greeting, reaction, response, treatment. [➡GREETINGS, FAREWELLS, AND SALUTATIONS; 660] **3** *n* **party**, function, do (*informal*), drinks party, cocktail party, gathering, get-together (*informal*), soirée (*formal*). [➡PARTIES, DANCES, AND CELEBRATIONS; 37] **4** *n* **signal**, clarity, picture, sound. [➡TELEVISION AND RADIO; 607]

receptionist *n* **receiver**, welcomer, greeter, telephonist, switchboard operator, administrator. [➡OFFICE WORKERS; 847]

reception room *type of* **room in a public building.** [➡TYPES OF ROOM; 1096]

receptive **1** *adj* **open**, amenable, accessible, interested, approachable, friendly, sympathetic. [➡FRIENDLINESS AND SOCIABILITY; 495] *Opposite:* hostile. **2** *adj* **alert**, sensitive, responsive, sharp, bright, quick. [➡POSITIVE INTELLECTUAL CHARACTERISTICS; 525] *Opposite:* slow.

receptively *adv* **openly**, amenably, accessibly, approachably, sympathetically. [➡FRIENDLINESS AND SOCIABILITY; 495] *Opposite:* antagonistically.

receptiveness **1** *n* **receptivity**, openness, accessibility, interest, approachability, friendliness. [➡FRIENDLINESS AND SOCIABILITY; 495] *Opposite:* hostility. **2** *n* **alertness**, sensitivity, responsiveness, acuteness, brightness, sharpness. [➡POSITIVE INTELLECTUAL CHARACTERISTICS; 525] *Opposite:* slowness.

receptivity *n* **receptiveness**, openness, accessibility, interest, approachability, friendliness, sociableness. [➡FRIENDLINESS AND SOCIABILITY; 495] *Opposite:* hostility.

recess **1** *n* **alcove**, nook, indentation, niche, bay, depression. [➡ALCOVES, CUBICLES, AND COMPARTMENTS; 1095] **2** *n* **break**, vacation, time off, rest, retreat, holiday, leave, respite, adjournment. [➡PERIOD OF REST; 91]

recession *n* **depression**, slump, downturn, collapse, decline, stagnation. [➡MARKET FORCES; 803] *Opposite:* boom.

recessionary *adj* **falling**, declining, failing, in slump, in depression, in recession. [➡FINANCE AND ECONOMICS; 797] *Opposite:* booming.

recessive **1** *adj* **receding**, falling, retreating, ebbing, declining, lowering. [➡DIRECTION OF MOTION; 346] *Opposite:* growing. **2** *adj* **latent**, suppressed, dormant, hidden, masked, unrevealed. [➡IMPERCEPTIBLE; 26] *Opposite:* dominant.

recharge *v* **renew**, refresh, boost, revive, revitalize, restore, rejuvenate. [➡IMPROVE STRENGTH AND DURABILITY; 379] *Opposite:* drain.

recherché *adj* **rare**, exotic, obscure, exquisite, unusual, extraordinary. [➡EXTRAORDINARY: UNCOMMON; 206] *Opposite:* ordinary.

recidivism *n* **reoffending**, repetition, habit, tendency, backsliding. [➡TRIAL, PUNISHMENT, AND LEGAL OUTCOMES; 819]

recidivist *n* **reoffender**, hardened criminal, old lag (*slang*), repeat offender, backslider, lawbreaker, criminal, malefactor (*formal*). [➡CRIMINALS; 821]

recipe *n* **formula**, guidelines, instructions, method, steps, way, procedure, technique, process. [➡WAYS OF DOING THINGS; 295]

recipe for disaster *n* [➡DANGER; 236]

recipient *n* **receiver**, beneficiary, heir, addressee, inheritor, heritor (*archaic or technical*). [➡OWNERS; 447] *Opposite:* donor.

reciprocal *adj* **mutual**, give-and-take (*informal*), joint, shared, equal, common, communal. [➡RECIPROCITY AND INTERDEPENDENCE; 148] *Opposite:* one-sided.

reciprocate *v* **give in return**, respond, return, give back, counter, reply, share, interchange. [➡GIVE AND PROVIDE; 431]

reciprocation *n* **giving in return**, correspondence, exchange, trade, complementation, interchange, sharing. [➡RECIPROCITY AND INTERDEPENDENCE; 148]

reciprocity *n* **mutual benefit**, mutuality, exchange, trade, trade-off, interchange, switch. [➡RECIPROCITY AND INTERDEPENDENCE; 148] *Opposite:* isolation.

recital *n* **performance**, concert, presentation, reading, recitation, narration, solo. [➡PERFORMANCES AND SHOWS; 42]

recitation *n* **recital**, reading, performance, narration, presentation, oration. [➡PERFORMANCES AND SHOWS; 42]

recitative *n* **declamation**, narrative, oratorio, opera, singing. [➡PERFORMANCES AND SHOWS; 42]

recite **1** *v* **declaim**, narrate, perform, rehearse, speak publicly, deliver, recount, relate. [➡RECITE, REPEAT, AND NARRATE; 621] **2** *v* **list**, enumerate, reel off, regurgitate, itemize, detail, count, number. [➡RECITE, REPEAT, AND NARRATE; 621]

reckless *adj* **irresponsible**, wild, thoughtless, uncontrolled, out of control, inattentive, hasty, careless, rash, heedless. [➡LACK OF COMMITMENT AND UNRELIABILITY; 510] *Opposite:* cautious.

recklessness *n* **irresponsibility**, unruliness, wildness, thoughtlessness, carelessness, haste, rashness. [➡LACK OF COMMITMENT AND UNRELIABILITY; 510] *Opposite:* caution.

reckon 1 *v* **calculate**, add up, total, tot up, count, number, estimate, figure. [➡ASSESS QUANTITY; 758] 2 *v* **think**, consider, imagine, suppose, feel, deem (*formal*), guess, surmise, account, regard, view. [➡DEVELOP THEORIES AND REASON; 745] *Opposite:* know.

reckoning 1 *n* **calculation**, estimate, sums (*informal*), weighing up, computation, arithmetic. [➡MATHS; 598] 2 *n* **opinion**, judgment, view, estimation. [➡POINT OF VIEW; 768]

reckon on (*informal*) *v* **depend**, rely, count on, bank on, be prepared, bargain, anticipate, assume, expect. [➡PREDICT AND ANTICIPATE; 751]

reckon with *v* **allow for**, bargain for, be prepared for, expect, anticipate, take into account, take seriously. [➡PREDICT AND ANTICIPATE; 751]

reclaim *v* **get back**, regain, retrieve, recover, repossess, recoup, salvage, rescue. [➡REGAIN POSSESSION; 430]

reclamation *n* **recovery**, retrieval, repossession, recuperation, renovation, salvage. [➡REGAIN POSSESSION; 430]

recline *v* **lie down**, lie back, stretch out, loll, lounge, tilt back, rest, sprawl. [➡ASSUME A POSITION; 318] *Opposite:* stand.

recliner *type of* **seating**. [➡FURNITURE; 858]

recluse *n* **hermit**, loner, outsider, lone wolf, solitary, anchorite, eremite (*literary*). [➡SOLITARY PEOPLE; 942]

reclusive *adj* **isolated**, cloistered, solitary, withdrawn, secluded, lone, antisocial. [➡SOLITARINESS; 941] *Opposite:* sociable.

reclusiveness *n* [➡SOLITARINESS; 941]

recognition 1 *n* **identification**, detection, distinguishing, perception, differentiation, establishing, apperception. [➡KNOWLEDGE AND WISDOM; 559] 2 *n* **credit**, gratitude, acknowledgment, thanks, appreciation, respect. [➡APPRECIATION AND GRATITUDE; 536] *Opposite:* blame. 3 *n* **detection**, identification, recall, recollection, remembering. [➡MEMORY; 746]

recognizable *adj* **familiar**, identifiable, decipherable, detectable, distinguishable, perceptible, noticeable. [➡KNOWN AND FAMOUS; 182] *Opposite:* unfamiliar.

recognize 1 *v* **know**, identify, distinguish, make out, be familiar with, be aware of, be acquainted with, be on familiar terms with, diagnose, spot. [➡LEARN AND DISCOVER; 763] 2 *v* **acknowledge**, credit, cherish, value, have appreciation for, attach importance to, be grateful for, be thankful for. [➡PRAISE AND ENCOURAGE; 648] 3 *v* **accept**, acknowledge, appreciate, understand, admit, comprehend, concede, grant, realize, see, agree. [➡UNDERSTAND AND GRASP; 760] *Opposite:* deny.

recognized 1 *adj* **documented**, familiar, known, standard, predictable, renowned, accepted, acknowledged, well-known, recognizable. [➡KNOWN AND FAMOUS; 182] *Opposite:* unknown. 2 *adj* **established**, acclaimed, professional, accepted, important, highly praised, much-admired. [➡POPULAR AND WANTED; 221]

recoil 1 *v* **shrink back**, withdraw, quail, draw back, jump back, back away, wince, react, flinch, dodge. [➡GO BACKWARDS; 310] *Opposite:* confront. 2 *n* **shrinking**, wince, withdrawal, start, retreat, hesitation, shudder. [➡PHYSICAL REACTIONS; 317]

Compare and Contrast: ***recoil, flinch, quail, shrink, wince***

CORE MEANING: TO DRAW BACK IN FEAR OR DISTASTE

recoil to draw back suddenly, or react mentally, in fear, horror, disgust, or distaste; ***flinch*** to draw back physically because of fear or pain, or to avoid confronting something unpleasant; ***quail*** to tremble or cower with fear or apprehension; ***shrink*** to move away physically from something because of fear or disgust, or to feel reluctance to do something because of fear or apprehension; ***wince*** to make an involuntary movement away from something in response to a stimulus such as pain or embarrassment.

recollect *v* **remember**, recall, call to mind, summon up, think of, reminisce. [➡REMEMBER; 747] *Opposite:* forget.

recollection *n* **memory**, recall, remembrance, reminiscence, calling to mind. [➡MEMORY; 746]

recommence *v* **begin again**, restart, resume, take up again, continue, carry on, pick up where you left off, start again, pick up, carry on with. [➡RECOMMENCE AND RESUME; 269]

recommencement *n* [➡REPETITION; 29]

recommend 1 *v* **suggest**, advocate, propose, counsel (*formal or literary*), advise, urge. [➡ADVISE AND WARN; 614] *Opposite:* oppose. 2 *v* **endorse**, commend, vouch for, mention, put in a good word for, acclaim, applaud, praise. [➡APPROVE AND CONFIRM; 647] *Opposite:* criticize.

Compare and Contrast: ***recommend, advise, advocate, counsel, suggest***

CORE MEANING: TO PUT FOWARD IDEAS TO SOMEBODY DECIDING ON A COURSE OF ACTION

recommend to put forward a course of action as being worthy of acceptance in the circumstances; ***advise*** to give advice in a relatively open and objective way; ***advocate*** to support or speak in favour of something; ***counsel*** (*formal or literary*) to advise somebody on a particular course of action; ***suggest*** to propose something in a tentative way as a possible course of action, for somebody else to consider.

recommendation 1 *n* **reference**, endorsement, commendation, blessing, approval, sanction, good word. [➡APPROVE AND CONFIRM; 647] *Opposite:* disparagement. 2 *n* **advice**, proposal, suggestion, counsel (*formal or literary*). [➡ADVICE; 690]

recompense 1 *v* **reward**, compensate, repay, pay, remunerate, reimburse, make up for, requite. [➡REWARD; 437] *Opposite:* charge. 2 *n* **payment**, reward, remuneration, repayment, return, compensation, reparation, restitution, quittance. [➡REWARDS AND AWARDS; 440] *Opposite:* cost.

reconcile *v* **settle**, bring together, square, reunite, resolve, merge, patch up, put to rights, join. [➡CORRECT AND PUT RIGHT; 378] *Opposite:* fall out.

reconciliation *n* **settlement**, understanding, squaring off, resolution, compromise, reunion, ceasefire, bringing together, appeasement. [➡SOLUTION; 216] *Opposite:* conflict.

recondite *adj* **obscure**, abstruse, complex, out-of-the-way, little known, esoteric, hidden, concealed. [➡SECRET AND UNKNOWN; 180] *Opposite:* mainstream.

See Compare and Contrast at **obscure**.

recondition *v* **overhaul**, service, tune, clean, repair, mend, get into shape, renovate. [➡REPAIR AND MEND; 377]

See Compare and Contrast at **renew**.

reconnaissance *n* **investigation**, scouting, inspection, exploration, survey, recce (*slang*). [➡EXAMINE AND ASSESS; 754]

reconnect *v* **connect up**, rewire, rejoin, relink, recouple, recombine. [➡FASTEN, LINK, AND JOIN; 409] *Opposite:* sever.

reconnection *n* **connecting again**, connecting up, rejoining, relinking, rewiring, recoupling, recombination. [➡FASTEN, LINK, AND JOIN; 409] *Opposite:* severance.

reconnoitre 1 *v* **explore**, scout, investigate, survey, search, inspect, scrutinize, spy, patrol, probe, keep an eye out. [➡EXAMINE AND ASSESS; 754] 2 *n* **investigation**, reconnaissance, exploration, survey, scouting, search, inspection, spying, scrutinizing, patrol, look, watch. [➡LOOKING AND LOOKS; 701]

reconsider *v* **reassess**, re-evaluate, review, think again, go back over, re-examine. [➡EXAMINE AND ASSESS; 754]

reconsideration *n* **reassessment**, re-evaluation, review, re-examination. [➡EXAMINE AND ASSESS; 754]

reconstitute 1 *v* **reconstruct**, rebuild, re-form, put back together, build again, make again. [➡BUILD; 353] *Opposite:* take apart. 2 *v* **alter**, change, reorganize, modify, revise, vary, refashion. [➡CHANGE; 373]

reconstitution 1 *n* **reconstruction**, rebuilding, re-formation, putting back together, building again, making again. [➡CREATION; 347] *Opposite:* break up. 2 *n* **alteration**, modification, reorganization, revision, change, rearrangement. [➡CHANGE; 373]

reconstruct *v* **rebuild**, renovate, recreate, redo, restructure, modernize, re-form. [➡BUILD; 353] *Opposite:* take apart.

reconstructed *adj* **rebuilt**, recreated, reassembled, restored, renovated, remodelled. [➡CHANGE; 373] *Opposite:* original.

reconstruction *n* **rebuilding**, renovation, reform, modernization, renewal, restoration, refurbishment, re-establishment. [➡CREATION; 347]

reconvene *v* **resume**, come together again, call together again, gather again, call again, reunite, bring together again, convene again, begin again, continue, carry on, restart, pick up where you left off, start again, pick up, carry on with, take up again. [➡RECOMMENCE AND RESUME; 269]

recook *v* [➡COOKING AND FOOD PREPARATION; 354]

record 1 *n* **past performance**, track record, reputation, background, history, profile, highest achievement, top score. [➡SCORES AND EVALUATIONS; 599] 2 *n* **personal best**, top score, high, world record, best. [➡ADVANTAGE; 213] 3 *v* **note down**, make a note, keep a note, take notes, keep details, keep information, write down, log, chronicle, note, verify, document, detail. [➡RECORD SOMETHING; 372] 4 *v* **make a recording**, tape, video, film, pick up. [➡RECORD SOMETHING; 372] 5 *part of* **audio equipment**. [➡AUDIO EQUIPMENT; 1138]

recorder *type of* **wind instrument**. [➡MUSICAL INSTRUMENTS; 910]

recording *n* **footage**, video recording, copy, soundtrack, demo (*informal*), tape, cassette, CD, record. [➡RECORDINGS AND PLAYERS; 911]

record player *type of* **audio equipment**. [➡AUDIO EQUIPMENT; 1138]

recount *v* **tell**, narrate, relate, report, describe, give an account, communicate, detail. [➡RECITE, REPEAT, AND NARRATE; 621]

re-count 1 *n* **verification**, second opinion, check. [➡SCORES AND EVALUATIONS; 599] 2 *v* **count again**, verify, tally up, check. [➡ASSESS QUANTITY; 758]

recoup *v* **get back**, earn, make back, recover, regain, make good, recuperate, retrieve, recapture. [➡REGAIN POSSESSION; 430] *Opposite:* lose.

recouple *v* [➡FASTEN, LINK, AND JOIN; 409]

recourse *n* **option**, alternative, remedy, way out, choice, route, resort. [➡SOLUTION; 216]

recover 1 *v* **get well**, get better, pull through, recuperate, make progress, convalesce, improve, mend, restore your health, pick up. [➡FALL ILL, TREAT, AND RECOVER; 729] *Opposite:* deteriorate. 2 *v* **get back**, claim, regain, recuperate, recoup, retrieve, salvage, recapture, repossess. [➡REGAIN POSSESSION; 430] *Opposite:* lose.

recovery 1 *n* **revival**, upturn, recuperation, mending, healing, improvement, resurgence, revitalization, renewal. [➡PROGRESS AND ADVANCEMENT; 214] *Opposite:* deterioration. 2 *n* **retrieval**, salvage, recapture, repossession, regaining, rescue, reclamation. [➡REGAIN POSSESSION; 430] *Opposite:* loss.

recreate *v* [➡CREATION; 347]

re-create *v* **reproduce**, copy, redesign, redevise, reinvent, reconstruct, rebuild, remake, re-establish, restructure, restore, re-form, redo. [➡CREATION; 347]

See Compare and Contrast at **copy**.

recreation 1 *n* **leisure**, hobby, pastime, exercise, play, activity, amusement, sport. [➡LEISURE AND RECREATION; 874] *Opposite:* work. 2 *n* **regeneration**, rebirth, reformation, restoration, restitution, refreshment. [➡CREATION; 347] *Opposite:* exhaustion.

recreational *adj* **leisure**, spare time, fun, frivolous, entertaining, amusing. [➡EMOTIONALLY PLEASANT; 188]

recreation area *n* [➡URBAN OUTDOOR SPACES; 1071]

recreation ground *n* [➡URBAN OUTDOOR SPACES; 1071]

recreation room *n* **rec room**, den (*US*), study, family room, living room, playroom. [➡TYPES OF ROOM; 1096]

recrimination *n* **accusation**, blame, reproach, allegation, retort, retaliation. [➡CRITICISMS AND ANGRY OUTBURSTS; 50] *Opposite:* appeasement.

recriminatory *adj* **counter-accusatory**, accusing, retaliatory, counterattacking. [➡VENGEANCE AND REVENGE; 686] *Opposite:* placatory.

rec room (*US*) *type of* **room in the home.** [➡TYPES OF ROOM; 1096]

recrudescence *n* **reactivation**, recurrence, breaking out again, repetition, happening again, renaissance, rebirth, revival. [➡REPETITION; 29]

recruit 1 *v* **employ**, take on, enlist, engage, conscript, hire, sign up, enrol, draft (*US*). *Opposite:* fire. (*informal*). [➡WORK-RELATED ACTIVITIES; 834] 2 *n* **employee**, trainee, beginner, novice, newcomer, apprentice, convert, rookie (*US informal*). [➡SUBORDINATES AND ASSISTANTS; 966] *Opposite:* old hand.

recruitment *n* **staffing**, employment, enrolment, conscription, enlistment. [➡WORK-RELATED ACTIVITIES; 834] *Opposite:* dismissal.

rectangle *type of* **angular shape.** [➡ANGULAR SHAPE; 1216]

rectangular *adj* **four-sided**, quadrilateral, quadrangular, oblong. [➡ANGULAR SHAPE; 1216]

rectification *n* **correction**, improvement, adjustment, minor adjustment, modification, alteration, refinement, amendment, tweak. [➡IMPROVE SOMETHING; 375]

rectify *v* **put right**, set right, correct, remedy, cure, repair, fix, resolve, mend. [➡CORRECT AND PUT RIGHT; 378] *Opposite:* damage.

rectilinear *adj* **straight-lined**, with straight lines, direct, unbending, uncurving, straight. [➡ANGULAR SHAPE; 1216] *Opposite:* serpentine.

rectitude 1 *n* **righteousness**, morality, goodness, correctness, decency, integrity, uprightness. [➡MORALLY GOOD; 775] *Opposite:* immorality. 2 *n* (*formal*) **correctness**, rightness, precision, accuracy, exactness, exactitude, infallibility. [➡CORRECT; 183]

rector 1 *n* **minister**, cleric, parson, priest, vicar, reverend. [➡RELIGIOUS PEOPLE; 779] 2 *n* **principal**, head, director, chancellor, dean, president. [➡EDUCATORS; 840]

rectory *n* **vicarage**, lodge, manse, church house, residence, house. [➡RELIGIOUS BUILDINGS; 1084]

rectum *part of* **digestive tract.** [➡THE DIGESTIVE TRACT; 710]

recumbent (*literary*) *adj* **lying down**, leaning, lying back, reclining, resting, horizontal. [➡ORIENTATION AND ALIGNMENT; 1222] *Opposite:* upright.

recuperate 1 *v* **convalesce**, build up your strength, recover, get better, get well, restore your form, improve, pull through, mend. [➡FALL ILL, TREAT, AND RECOVER; 729] *Opposite:* deteriorate. 2 *v* **get back**, retrieve, reclaim, recover, recapture, salvage, regain, rescue, claim, recoup, repossess. [➡REGAIN POSSESSION; 430] *Opposite:* lose.

recuperation 1 *n* **convalescence**, healing, recovery, getting better, restoration, improvement. [➡HEALING; 731] *Opposite:* deterioration. 2 *n* **retrieval**, recovery, repossession, salvage, reclamation, recapture, regaining, rescue. [➡REGAIN POSSESSION; 430] *Opposite:* loss.

recuperative *adj* **curative**, restorative, invigorating, convalescent, healing, recovering, soothing, uplifting. [➡HEALING; 731]

recur *v* **happen again**, persist, return, come back, reappear, come again, relapse, repeat. [➡HAPPEN AGAIN; 28] *Opposite:* cease.

recurrence *n* **reappearance**, return, repetition, relapse. [➡REPETITION; 29] *Opposite:* cessation.

recurrent *adj* **recurring**, repeated, persistent, frequent, periodic, intermittent, continuing, continual, chronic, regular, spasmodic. [➡FREQUENT AND OFTEN; 107] *Opposite:* finished.

recurring *adj* **recurrent**, periodic, frequent, repeated, habitual, repetitive, regular, cyclical. [➡FREQUENT AND OFTEN; 107] *Opposite:* finished.

recurvate *adj* **curved**, bowed, arched, rounded, bent. [➡ROUNDED SHAPE; 1217] *Opposite:* straight.

recyclable *adj* [➡ECONOMICAL AND RESOURCEFUL; 208]

recycle *v* **reprocess**, salvage, reuse, recover, reutilize, recondition. [➡MAKE GOOD USE OF SOMETHING; 474] *Opposite:* throw away.

recycled *adj* [➡ECONOMICAL AND RESOURCEFUL; 208]

red *type of* **colour.** [➡COLOURS; 1223]

> **red**
>
> ◆ *types of red*
> wine, blood red, brick red, burgundy, carmine, carnation, cherry red, claret, crimson, damask, garnet, magenta, maroon, oxblood, pillar-box red, puce, ruby, scarlet, vermilion

red admiral *type of* **butterfly.** [➡MOTHS AND BUTTERFLIES; 1015]

red alga *type of* **alga.** [➡MICROORGANISMS, FUNGI, AND ALGAE; 1023]

red ant *type of* **ant.** [➡ANTS; 1014]

red-blooded *adj* **vigorous**, strong, robust, hearty, lusty, hale. [➡FIT AND STRONG; 737] *Opposite:* weak.

red-carpet *adj* **preferential**, VIP, no-expense-spared, special, favoured, privileged, superior. [➡SUPERIORITY; 153]

red corpuscle *n* [➡THE BLOOD AND CIRCULATION; 718]

redcurrant *type of* **berry.** [➡FRUIT AND VEGETABLES; 1175]

redden *v* **flush**, blush, embarrass, shame, shock, anger. [➡CHANGE OF COLOUR; 392]

redecorate *v* **revamp**, spruce up, refurbish, restore, repaint, repaper, renovate, transform. [➡DECORATE, ADORN, AND APPLY COATINGS; 406]

redeem 1 *v* **cash in**, cash, trade in, exchange, convert, use, buy back, transfer. [➡EXCHANGE AND INTERCHANGE; 449] *Opposite:* keep. 2 *v* **compensate for**, make up for, make amends for, restore, redress, save. [➡REWARD; 437] **3** *v* **release**, liberate, free, emancipate, deliver, rescue, save. [➡FREEDOM AND LIBERTY; 209] *Opposite:* arrest.

redeemable *adj* **saving**, exchangeable, valid, good, convertible, equivalent, tradable. [➡USEFULNESS; 200] *Opposite:* irredeemable.

redeeming *adj* **saving**, good, positive, abiding, compensatory, restorative. [➡GOOD, WELL, BETTER; 184]

redeeming feature *n* [➡SOURCE OF HAPPINESS, PLEASURE, OR IMPROVEMENT; 210]

redeeming quality *n* [➡SOURCE OF HAPPINESS, PLEASURE, OR IMPROVEMENT; 210]

redemption **1** *n* **salvation**, deliverance (*formal*), rescue, release, liberation, emancipation, recovery. [➡FREEDOM AND LIBERTY; 209] *Opposite:* downfall. **2** *n* **improvement**, recovery, renovation, reclamation, refurbishment, revitalization, restoration. [➡IMPROVE SOMETHING; 375] *Opposite:* deterioration. **3** *n* **exchange**, use, conversion, trade-in, swap (*informal*). [➡EXCHANGE AND INTERCHANGE; 449]

redemptive *adj* **liberating**, redeeming, saving, rescuing, delivering, emancipating, releasing. [➡FREEDOM AND LIBERTY; 209]

redeploy *v* **redistribute**, divert, post, send, dispatch, reassign, reorganize. [➡DESPATCH AND SEND; 334]

redeployment *n* **redistribution**, posting, reorganization, relocation, rearrangement, reassignment. [➡MOVE SOMETHING TO ANOTHER LOCATION; 325]

redesign *v* [➡CREATION; 347]

redevelop *v* **improve**, revitalize, renovate, revamp, restore, regenerate, renew, revive, rekindle. [➡BUILD; 353] *Opposite:* neglect.

redevelopment *n* **improvement**, renovation, revitalization, revamping, restoration, regeneration, renewal, revival, rekindling. [➡CREATION; 347] *Opposite:* neglect.

redevise *v* [➡INSTITUTE AND INAUGURATE; 349]

red-faced **1** *adj* **blushing**, flushed, embarrassed, hot and bothered, sweating, ashamed. [➡EMBARRASSMENT AND HUMILIATION; 543] **2** *adj* **ruddy**, weather-beaten, rosy, florid, rubicund (*literary*). [➡COMPLEXION; 481]

red giant *type of* **star or star system**. [➡CELESTIAL BODIES; 1060]

redheaded *adj* **auburn**, chestnut-haired, auburn-haired, ginger, sandy. [➡HAIR COLOUR; 486]

red herring *n* **decoy**, trick, ploy, lure, diversion, deviation, device. [➡DECEPTION AND LIES; 661]

red-hot *adj* **burning**, boiling, scalding, scorching (*informal*), sizzling (*informal*), fiery. [➡TEMPERATURE: HOT; 1228] *Opposite:* cold.

redirect *v* **forward**, send, readdress, send on, transmit, convey, relay, pass on. [➡DESPATCH AND SEND; 334]

redirection *n* **sending on**, resending, redispatch, rerouting, transferral, forwarding, redistribution. [➡MOVE SOMETHING TO ANOTHER LOCATION; 325]

rediscover *v* **find again**, revive, experience again, remember, relive, re-experience. [➡REMEMBER; 747]

rediscovery *n* **finding again**, discovering again, reawakening, seeing afresh, rekindling, renewal, renaissance. [➡REPETITION; 29]

redistribute *v* **reallocate**, reorder, sort out, restructure, rearrange, redeploy, reorganize. [➡ARRANGE AND CREATE ORDER; 358]

redistribution *n* **redeployment**, rearrangement, relocation, reorganization, restructuring, reallocation. [➡CHANGE; 373]

red-letter day *n* **special day**, day to remember, occasion, event, turning point. [➡DECISIVE MOMENTS; 44]

red light **1** *n* **traffic light**, warning signal, warning light, stop light, stop sign, signal. [➡SIGNALLING; 1139] *Opposite:* green light. **2** *n* (*informal*) **rejection**, disapproval, thumbs-down (*informal*), refusal, no, prohibition, declining. [➡REFUSE PERMISSION AND NOT ALLOW; 671] *Opposite:* approval.

redness **1** *n* **blush**, flush, rosiness, glow, pinkness, ruddiness, high colour, reddishness. [➡COMPLEXION; 481] *Opposite:* pallor. **2** *n* **soreness**, rawness, tenderness, inflammation, painfulness, irritation. [➡CONDITIONS AFFECTING THE SKIN; 722]

redo *v* **rebuild**, do from scratch, do again, recreate, start again, go back to the beginning, repeat, restart. [➡RECOMMENCE AND RESUME; 269]

redolence **1** *n* **suggestion**, hint, trace, evocation, reminiscence, idea, whisper. [➡REPRESENTATIONS AND GENERAL EXAMPLES; 65] **2** *n* (*literary*) **fragrance**, scent, aroma, smell, bouquet, odour. [➡SMELL AND SMELLING; 706]

redolent **1** *adj* **suggestive**, reminiscent, evocative, indicative, recalling. [➡REPRESENTATIVE; 66] **2** *adj* **scented**, aromatic, fragrant, sweet-smelling, perfumed, smelling, odorous (*literary*). [➡SMELL AND SMELLING; 706]

redolently *adv* [➡REPRESENTATIVE; 66]

redouble *v* **intensify**, renew, increase, augment (*formal*), multiply, amplify. [➡CHANGE OF INTENSITY: MORE; 395] *Opposite:* reduce.

redoubt (*literary*) *n* **stronghold**, castle, fortification, fort, fortress, citadel, keep. [➡FORTRESSES AND FORTIFICATIONS; 1089]

redoubtable *adj* **formidable**, impressive, terrible, mighty, fearsome, awesome. [➡EXTRAORDINARY: AMAZING; 205] *Opposite:* unimpressive.

redraft **1** *n* **rewrite**, reworking, alteration, modification, change, revision, amendment. [➡CHANGE; 373] **2** *v* **rewrite**, reword, rework, revise, rephrase, alter, modify, change, say differently, reshape, amend. [➡CORRECT AND PUT RIGHT; 378]

redress **1** *n* **compensation**, reparation, damages, recompense, reimbursement, amends. [➡REWARDS AND AWARDS; 440] **2** *v* **restore**, level out, equalize, right, rectify, remedy, put right, even out, set right, balance out. [➡CORRECT AND PUT RIGHT; 378]

red tape (*informal*) *n* **formalities**, bureaucracy, paperwork, official procedure, rules and regulations, procedures, regulations, rules. [➡WAYS OF DOING THINGS; 295]

reduce 1 *v* **decrease**, lessen, diminish, cut, trim down, condense, shrink, ease, moderate, lower. [➡CHANGE OF INTENSITY: LESS; 396] *Opposite:* increase. 2 *v* **downgrade**, cut down, demote, degrade, slash, bring down, drive down, relegate. [➡WORSEN SOMETHING; 381] *Opposite:* upgrade.

reduced *adj* **cheap**, bargain, cut-price, low-price, on sale, cut-rate (*US*). [➡CHEAP AND INEXPENSIVE; 222]

reduce speed *v* [➡CHANGE OF SPEED: LESS; 398]

reduce to ashes *v* [➡DESTRUCTION AND DEMOLITION; 360]

reduce to rubble *v* [➡DESTRUCTION AND DEMOLITION; 360]

reduce to tears *v* [➡UPSET, DISTRESS, AND HUMILIATE; 568]

reduce to the ranks *v* [➡REVOKE STATUS; 460]

reduction *n* **discount**, decrease, lessening, drop, saving, bargain, fall, decline, diminution, cutback, cut. [➡CHANGE OF SIZE: SMALLER; 394] *Opposite:* increase.

redundancy *n* **unemployment**, job loss, dismissal, severance, termination, firing, laying-off. [➡WORK-RELATED ACTIVITIES; 834] *Opposite:* employment.

redundant 1 *adj* **laid off**, let go, out of work, out of a job, jobless, fired, dismissed, terminated. [➡EMPLOYMENT STATUS; 831] *Opposite:* employed. 2 *adj* **superfluous**, outmoded, disused, surplus, unneeded, unnecessary, uncalled-for, unwanted. [➡REDUNDANT AND USELESS; 241] *Opposite:* needed.

redundantly *adv* **superfluously**, unnecessarily, unwantedly, excessively, in surplus. [➡REDUNDANT AND USELESS; 241] *Opposite:* necessarily.

reduplicate *v* **repeat**, double, copy, redo, recast, duplicate, reproduce, imitate. [➡COPY AND DUPLICATE; 403]

reduplication *n* **repetition**, copying, imitation, doubling, duplication, reproduction. [➡SAMENESS; 151]

redwood *type of* **evergreen tree**. [➡EVERGREEN AND CONIFEROUS TREES; 1029]

re-echo *v* [➡SOUND EMISSION; 363]

reed *n* **cane**, stalk, stem. [➡GRASS; 1031]

reediness *n* **squeakiness**, shrillness, stridency, screechiness, squawkiness, thinness. [➡SOFT OR PLEASANT SOUNDS; 1264] *Opposite:* sonority.

re-educate *v* **retrain**, reskill, re-equip, requalify, reinstruct, rehabilitate, reorient. [➡INSTRUCT AND TEACH; 610]

re-education *n* **retraining**, reskilling, re-equipping, requalification, reinstruction, rehabilitation, reorientation. [➡TEACHING; 839]

reedy 1 *adj* **high-pitched**, thin, shrill, high, feeble. [➡LOUD OR UNPLEASANT SOUNDS; 1265] *Opposite:* full-bodied. 2 *adj* **thin**, narrow, slim, skinny, long, elongated, flexible. [➡BUILD; 478] *Opposite:* squat.

reef *n* **ridge**, bar, bank, mound, range. [➡THE SEAS, OCEANS, AND SHORES; 1041]

reefer (*US*) *type of* **jacket**. [➡GARMENTS AND OUTFITS; 865]

reefer jacket *type of* **jacket**. [➡GARMENTS AND OUTFITS; 865]

reek 1 *v* **stink**, smell, pong (*informal*), stench. [➡SMELL EMISSION; 370] 2 *v* **show signs**, smack, smell, suggest, be redolent of, stink, evidence. [➡SEEM TO BE SOMETHING; 58] 3 *n* **stench**, stink, smell, odour, pong (*informal*), whiff. [➡SMELL AND SMELLING; 706]

See Compare and Contrast at **smell**.

reel 1 *n* **roll**, spool, cylinder, bobbin, roller, winder. [➡CONTAINERS, RECEPTACLES, AND PACKAGING; 1244] 2 *v* **lurch**, stagger, totter, stumble, wobble, sway. [➡WALK UNSTEADILY; 316] 3 *v* **wind**, whirl, spin, go round and round, revolve, twirl. [➡FIDGET AND FROLIC; 312]

re-elect *v* **vote in again**, reappoint, reconfirm, endorse, reinstall, reselect, appoint again, reinstate. [➡ELECTIONS AND SUFFRAGE; 807]

re-election *n* **reappointment**, endorsement, confirmation. [➡CONFER STATUS; 459] *Opposite:* defeat.

reel off *v* **recite**, rattle off, list, repeat, go through, enumerate. [➡RECITE, REPEAT, AND NARRATE; 621] *Opposite:* stammer.

re-emerge *v* [➡HAPPEN AGAIN; 28]

re-enter *v* **return**, retrace one's steps, go back into, withdraw into, retire into, turn back into. [➡ARRIVE; 12] *Opposite:* leave.

re-entry *n* **return**, going back into, going into again, going in again. [➡ARRIVAL; 13]

re-establish *v* **establish again**, create again, regenerate, reinvent, rebuild, recreate, restore, reconstruct, reinstate, reproduce, redevise, remake, redesign, put back. [➡CREATION; 347]

re-examination *n* **reappraisal**, reconsideration, reassessment, re-evaluation, rechecking, review, revision, check, second look. [➡EXAMINE AND ASSESS; 754]

re-examine *v* **reconsider**, go back over, review, reassess, check, go over, return to, re-evaluate, have another look at, revisit, go back to, revise. [➡EXAMINE AND ASSESS; 754]

ref (*informal*) *n* **referee**, umpire, arbitrator, adjudicator, mediator, arbiter, judge. [➡PEOPLE IN SPORTS AND LEISURE; 876]

refectory 1 *n* **cafeteria**, dining hall, mess hall, lunchroom (*US*), diner (*US*). [➡TYPES OF ROOM; 1096] 2 *type of* **eating place**. [➡HOTELS, RESTAURANTS, AND CLUBS; 1081]

refer 1 *v* **consult**, check, turn to, look up, examine, search. [➡EXAMINE AND ASSESS; 754] *Opposite:* ignore. 2 *v* **mention**, denote, talk about, bring up, speak of, state, comment on, discuss, raise. [➡SUGGEST, HINT, AND COMMENT; 613] 3 *v* **signify**, mean, indicate, suggest, insinuate, stand for, represent, imply, denote, describe. [➡MEAN SOMETHING; 61] 4 *v* **send to**, direct to, pass on to, consign to, turn over to, deliver to, hand over, transfer. [➡DESPATCH AND SEND; 334] 5 *v* **apply to**, relate to, concern, belong, be relevant to, connect with. [➡BE ABOUT SOMETHING; 62]

referee 1 *n* **umpire**, arbitrator, judge, arbiter, adjudicator, ref (*informal*). [➡ADVISERS, JUDGES, AND ARBITERS; 971] *Opposite:* partisan. 2 *v* **arbitrate**, adjudicate, umpire, mediate, judge, decide. [➡EXAMINE AND ASSESS; 754]

reference 1 *n* **orientation**, position, situation, location, locus, place. [➡NAVIGATION; 1140] 2 *n* **allusion**, mention, suggestion, indication, citation, quotation, note. [➡SUGGEST, HINT, AND COMMENT; 613] 3 *n* **recommendation**, testimonial, character reference, good word. [➡LETTERS AND WRITTEN MESSAGES; 585]

referendum *n* **vote**, poll, plebiscite, survey, ballot. [➡ELECTIONS AND SUFFRAGE; 807]

referral *n* **transfer**, recommendation, appointment, medical appointment. [➡EXCHANGE AND INTERCHANGE; 449]

refill *v* **replenish**, top up, fill up, restock, stock up. [➡FILL; 407] *Opposite:* empty.

refine 1 *v* **purify**, process, treat, filter, distil, get rid of impurities. [➡CLEAN AND POLISH; 404] *Opposite:* contaminate. 2 *v* **improve**, polish, perfect, hone, enhance, sharpen up, upgrade, make better, cultivate. [➡IMPROVE SOMETHING; 375] *Opposite:* coarsen.

refined *adj* **sophisticated**, advanced, superior, polished, distinguished, developed, experienced, cultured, gracious, cultivated. [➡GOOD MANNERS AND SOCIAL SKILLS; 521] *Opposite:* coarse.

refinement 1 *n* **modification**, alteration, minor change, improvement, enhancement, tweak, fine-tuning. [➡IMPROVE SOMETHING; 375] 2 *n* **sophistication**, finesse, class, maturity, delicacy, subtlety, culture, style, taste, civility, elegance. [➡GOOD MANNERS AND SOCIAL SKILLS; 521] *Opposite:* coarseness.

refinery *type of* **industrial site**. [➡INDUSTRIAL BUILDINGS; 1086]

refining 1 *n* **improving**, cultivating, educating, taming, enlightening, improvement, refinement, civilizing. [➡IMPROVE SOMETHING; 375] *Opposite:* coarsening. 2 *n* **purifying**, sanitizing, decontaminating, cleansing, filtering. [➡CLEAN AND POLISH; 404] *Opposite:* adulterating. 3 *adj* **improving**, educating, cultivating, civilizing, enlightening, taming. [➡MORALLY GOOD; 775] *Opposite:* coarsening.

refit 1 *v* **overhaul**, renovate, re-equip, service, repair, refurbish, fit out, revamp, set up, kit out. [➡REPAIR AND MEND; 377] 2 *n* **overhaul**, re-equipping, repair, refurbishment, service, fitting out, fitting up, kitting out, renovation. [➡REPAIR AND MEND; 377]

reflate *v* **expand**, increase, stimulate, spur on, build up, boost, inject. [➡ACCOUNTING, BANKING, AND BUDGETING; 799] *Opposite:* deflate.

reflation *n* **expansion**, increase, stimulation, boost, advance, broadening. [➡MARKET FORCES; 803] *Opposite:* deflation.

reflect 1 *v* **reproduce**, mirror, imitate, replicate, redirect, echo, return. [➡PRETEND AND MIMIC; 60] 2 *v* **be a sign of**, reveal, expose, suggest, signal, indicate, point towards, show, display, manifest, exhibit, signify. [➡REPRESENT SOMETHING OR SOMEBODY; 59] 3 *v* **think**, consider, ponder, mull over, contemplate, ruminate, wonder, think about, cogitate (*formal*), chew over. [➡THINK AND REFLECT; 744]

reflection 1 *n* **indication**, sign, manifestation, suggestion, expression, evidence, signal. [➡REPRESENTATIONS AND GENERAL EXAMPLES; 65] 2 *n* **consideration**, thinking, thought, contemplation, deliberation (*formal*), musing, rumination. [➡THINK AND REFLECT; 744] *Opposite:* impulse. 3 *n* **mirror image**, likeness, echo, image, replication, reproduction. [➡COPIES AND REPLICAS; 152]

reflective *adj* **thoughtful**, pensive, wistful, meditative, contemplative, deep, profound, studious, serious, quiet, sober. [➡PENSIVENESS AND INTEREST; 539] *Opposite:* impulsive.

reflector *part of* **bike** (*informal*). [➡BIKES, CARS, AND CARRIAGES; 1148]

reflex *n* **reaction**, impulse, spontaneous effect, response. [➡RESULTS AND OUTCOMES; 83]

reflex camera *type of* **photographic equipment**. [➡PHOTOGRAPHY AND PHOTOGRAPHIC EQUIPMENT; 1121]

reflexive *adj* **automatic**, impulsive, spontaneous, involuntary, instinctive, knee-jerk (*informal*). [➡AUTOMATIC AND INSTINCTIVE; 281] *Opposite:* premeditated.

reflexology *n* **massage**, alternative therapy, manipulation. [➡REMEDIES, TREATMENTS AND OPERATIONS; 732]

reform 1 *v* **improve**, restructure, revolutionize, ameliorate (*formal*), remodel, modernize, rearrange, upgrade, amend, restore, reorganize. [➡IMPROVE SOMETHING; 375] 2 *n* **improvement**, reorganization, restructuring, modification, transformation, alteration, development, amendment, change. [➡PROGRESS AND ADVANCEMENT; 214]

re-form *v* **recreate**, reconstruct, re-fashion, reinvent, refabricate. [➡CHANGE; 373]

reformat *v* [➡CHANGE; 373]

reformation *n* **improvement**, renovation, reorganization, restructuring, overhaul, restoration, rectification. [➡PROGRESS AND ADVANCEMENT; 214]

reformatory *n* **institution**, detention centre, secure unit, jail, prison, penal complex (*US*), pokey (*US slang*), penitentiary (*US*). [➡BUILDINGS FOR CONFINING PEOPLE; 1093]

reformed *adj* **rehabilitated**, transformed, changed, converted, renewed, new, improved. [➡MORALLY GOOD; 775]

reformer *n* **improver**, campaigner, activist, crusader, agitator, reorganizer. [➡PHILOSOPHICAL AND POLITICAL THINKERS; 782] *Opposite:* conservative.

reformist *n* **supporter of reform**, improver, corrector, campaigner, activist, crusader, agitator, reorganizer. [➡PHILOSOPHICAL AND POLITICAL THINKERS; 782] *Opposite:* conservative.

refract *v* **bend**, divert, change course, detour, deflect, alter. [➡CHANGE DIRECTION OF MOTION; 345]

refraction *n* **bending**, change of direction, change of course, diversion, detour, deflection, alteration. [➡CHANGE DIRECTION OF MOTION; 345]

refractory *adj* **headstrong**, stubborn, rebellious, obstinate, intractable (*formal*), wayward, recalcitrant, noncompliant, unruly, unmanageable, disobedient. [➡REBELLIOUSNESS AND DISOBEDIENCE; 566] *Opposite:* placid.

refrain 1 *v* **desist**, abstain, hold back, leave off, cease, renounce, avoid doing. [➡STOP ACTING; 265] *Opposite:* persist. 2 *n* **catch phrase**, exhortation (*formal*), chorus, buzzword (*informal*). [➡FIGURES OF SPEECH; 674]

refresh *v* **revive**, cool down, enliven, invigorate, rejuvenate, energize, restore, pep up (*informal*), recharge, revitalize. [➡IMPROVE STRENGTH AND DURABILITY; 379] *Opposite:* wear out.

refreshed *adj* [➡WIDE AWAKE AND CONSCIOUS; 736]

refresher *n* **reminder**, revision, update, review. [➡SUMMARIES, OUTLINES, AND EXCERPTS; 589]

refreshing *adj* **stimulating**, uplifting, inspirational, invigorating, energizing, bracing, revitalizing, cool, thirst-quenching. [➡PHYSICALLY PLEASANT; 187] *Opposite:* draining.

refreshingly *adv* **pleasingly**, excitingly, unusually, thrillingly, differently, interestingly, stirringly, bracingly. [➡INTERESTING AND MEANINGFUL; 191] *Opposite:* mundanely.

refreshment *n* **drink**, food, nourishment, sustenance, nutriment, nutrition. [➡FOOD; 1166]

refreshment break *n* [➡PERIOD OF REST; 91]

refreshments *n* **food and drink**, snacks, drinks, munchies (*slang*), nibbles, hors d'oeuvres, appetizers. [➡FOOD; 1166]

refreshment stand *type of* **retail outlet**. [➡RETAIL OUTLETS; 1082]

refrigerate *v* **keep cold**, store at a low temperature, cool, ice, chill. [➡CHANGE OF TEMPERATURE; 387] *Opposite:* heat.

refrigeration *n* **cooling**, chilling, preservation, freezing, conserving. [➡HEATING, REFRIGERATION, AND VENTILATION; 1141]

refrigerator *type of* **cooling appliance**. [➡HEATING, REFRIGERATION, AND VENTILATION; 1141]

refrigerator magnet (*US*) *n* [➡ORNAMENTS AND DECORATIONS; 1247]

refry *v* [➡COOKING AND FOOD PREPARATION; 354]

refuel *v* **refill**, replenish, top up, restock, resupply. [➡FILL; 407] *Opposite:* run down.

refuge *n* **haven**, sanctuary, shelter, harbour, protection, place of safety, bolthole, asylum, retreat. [➡SAFE BUILDINGS OR PLACES; 1092]

refugee *n* **person in exile**, immigrant, migrant, expatriate, exile, evacuee, expat (*informal*), emigrant. [➡PEOPLE LIVING AWAY FROM HOME; 887]

refulgence (*literary*) *n* **brilliance**, splendour, shine, brightness, glitter, lustre. [➡DESCRIBING LIGHT; 1227] *Opposite:* dullness.

refulgent (*literary*) *adj* **brilliant**, shining, bright, sparkling, glittering, lustrous. [➡DESCRIBING LIGHT; 1227] *Opposite:* dull.

refund 1 *v* **repay**, reimburse, give back, pay back, compensate, restore, return. [➡GIVE MONEY; 434] *Opposite:* keep. 2 *n* **repayment**, reimbursement, money back, compensation, recompense. [➡REGAIN POSSESSION; 430] *Opposite:* payment.

refurbish *v* **renovate**, restore, do up, smarten up, redecorate, renew, revamp, overhaul, repair. [➡DECORATE, ADORN, AND APPLY COATINGS; 406]

refurbishment *n* **restoration**, renovation, overhaul, renewal, repair, refit, redecoration, revamp. [➡REPAIR AND MEND; 377]

refusal *n* **negative response**, snub, denial, rejection, negation, rebuttal, repudiation, rebuff, knock-back (*informal*). [➡DENY AND REJECT; 645] *Opposite:* acceptance.

refuse 1 *v* **say no**, decline, reject, snub, rebuff, turn down, repudiate, deny, negate (*formal*). [➡FOREGO AND DENY ONESELF; 450] *Opposite:* accept. 2 *n* **waste**, garbage, rubbish, litter, junk (*informal*), trash (*US*). [➡RUBBISH AND USELESS OBJECTS; 1248]

refutation *n* **repudiation**, disproof, negation, rejection, contradiction, rebuff, retraction, confutation (*formal*), dismissal, denial, disclaimer, refusal, disavowal (*formal*). [➡DENY AND REJECT; 645] *Opposite:* confirmation.

refute *v* **disprove**, contest, rebut, counter, repudiate, negate (*formal*), contradict. [➡DENY AND REJECT; 645] *Opposite:* prove.

regain *v* **recover**, get back, recuperate, recoup, reclaim, salvage, take back, recapture, redeem. [➡REGAIN POSSESSION; 430] *Opposite:* lose.

regain consciousness *v* [➡WAKE AND REGAIN CONSCIOUSNESS; 725]

regal *adj* **royal**, majestic, noble, imperial, stately, magnificent, kingly. [➡ROYALNESS; 825]

regale *v* **entertain**, amuse, delight, divert. [➡PLEASE AND AMUSE; 573]

regalia *n* **symbols of office**, ceremonial objects, ceremonial dress, insignia. [➡ORNAMENTS AND DECORATIONS; 1247]

regard 1 *v* **look upon**, stare, observe, gaze at, view, watch. [➡LOOKING AND LOOKS; 701] 2 *v* **consider**, hold, think, deem (*formal*), see, view, interpret. [➡HAVE AN OPINION OF SOMETHING; 757] 3 *v* **relate to**, concern, touch on, connect with, have to do with, involve, pertain to. [➡BE ABOUT SOMETHING; 62] 4 *n* **respect**, esteem, favour, affection, repute (*formal*), honour, admiration. [➡LOVE, RESPECT, AND GOODWILL; 550] 5 *n* (*formal*) **look**, stare, gaze, glance. [➡SEE; 700]

Compare and Contrast: ***regard, admiration, esteem, favour, respect, reverence, veneration***

CORE MEANING: APPRECIATION OF THE WORTH OF SOMEBODY OR SOMETHING

regard a mixture of liking and appreciation of somebody or something; ***admiration*** warm approval and appreciation of somebody or something, often suggesting a desire to copy or resemble somebody; ***esteem*** a high opinion and appreciation of somebody or something; ***favour*** a liking and preference for somebody or something; ***respect*** a strong acknowledgment and appreciation of somebody's abilities and achievements; ***reverence*** a feeling of deep respect and devotion combined with a slight sense of awe; ***veneration*** a profound feeling of respect and awe.

regard highly *v* [➡LIKE, LOVE, VALUE AND ENJOY; 579]

regarding *prep* **concerning**, about, on the subject of, on the topic of, as regards, apropos (*formal*), re, vis-à-vis. [➡EXPRESSIONS OF REFERENCE; 63]

regardless *prep* **in spite of**, despite, apart from, not considering. [➡NOT; 135]

regatta *n* **boat race competition**, race, gala, competition, contest, competitive event, meet. [➡NON-AGGRESSIVE/SPORTING EVENT; 40]

regenerate *v* **renew**, restore, revive, redevelop, reinforce, stimulate, restart, rejuvenate, revitalize, rekindle. [➡CORRECT AND PUT RIGHT; 378] *Opposite:* degenerate.

regeneration *n* **renewal**, rebirth, revival, renaissance, rejuvenation, restoration, redevelopment, reinforcement. [➡PROGRESS AND ADVANCEMENT; 214]

regenerative *adj* **growing back**, reformative, recreating, re-forming, recovering, renewing. [➡GOOD, WELL, BETTER; 184] *Opposite:* degenerative.

regent *n* **substitute**, proxy, replacement, advisor. [➡RULERS AND ARISTOCRACY; 823]

reggae *type of* **popular music.** [➡MUSIC, SONGS, AND SINGING; 907]

regime 1 *n* **government**, command, rule, administration, management, system, establishment, organization. [➡GOVERNMENT AND POLITICS; 805] 2 *n* **routine**, system, regimen, treatment, course of therapy, schedule, scheme, procedure, method. [➡WAYS OF DOING THINGS; 295]

regimen *n* **routine**, schedule, treatment, regime, course of therapy, procedure, programme. [➡WAYS OF DOING THINGS; 295]

regiment 1 *n* **military unit**, troop, squadron, battalion, brigade, company, team, contingent, squad, division, corps. [➡MILITARY PERSONNEL; 828] 2 *v* **control strictly**, regulate, oppress, suppress, order, discipline, control. [➡AVOID, PREVENT, LIMIT, AND CONTROL; 278] *Opposite:* liberate. 3 *v* **organize systematically**, arrange, order, file, organize, group, categorize. [➡ARRANGE AND CREATE ORDER; 358]

regimental *adj* **strict**, rigid, disciplined, harsh, ordered, severe. [➡ORDER AND ORGANISATION; 207] *Opposite:* lax.

regimentation *n* **control**, regulation, oppression, suppression, organization, arrangement, order. [➡ARRANGE AND CREATE ORDER; 358]

regimented *adj* **strictly controlled**, well-ordered, disciplined, on a tight rein, restricted, closely controlled, strict, rigid, ordered, well-organized, regular. [➡ORDER AND ORGANISATION; 207] *Opposite:* undisciplined.

region *n* **area**, district, county, section, province, state, constituency, borough, territory, zone, locality. [➡COUNTRIES AND REGIONS; 1066]

regional *adj* **local**, area, district, provincial, county. [➡COUNTRIES AND REGIONS; 1066] *Opposite:* national.

regionalism 1 *n* **regional loyalty**, regional prejudice, decentralization, home loyalty, area loyalty. [➡STYLES AND SYSTEMS OF GOVERNMENT; 806] 2 *n* **linguistic feature**, local expression, dialect word. [➡ASPECTS OF LANGUAGE; 683]

regionalization *n* [➡SOCIAL, POLITICAL, AND ECONOMIC CHANGE; 374]

regionalize *v* [➡SOCIAL, POLITICAL, AND ECONOMIC CHANGE; 374]

register 1 *n* **list**, record, catalogue, roll, index, inventory, chronicle, schedule. [➡LISTS AND SCHEDULES; 588] 2 *v* **enter**, list, record, catalogue, keep details, put in, chronicle. [➡RECORD SOMETHING; 372] 3 *v* **enrol**, join, sign up, enlist, sign on, go into, put your name down. [➡PARTICIPATE; 293] 4 *v* **reach**, touch, record, measure, indicate. [➡CAUSE TO APPEAR; 5] 5 *v* **reveal**, disclose, show, convey, score, express, transmit, display. [➡CAUSE TO APPEAR; 5] *Opposite:* hide.

registrar 1 *n* **public official**, recorder, public administrator, record-keeper, clerk. [➡ADMINISTRATIVE OFFICERS; 811] 2 *n* **administrative officer**, school administrator, university official, administrator, bursar. [➡ADMINISTRATIVE OFFICERS; 811] 3 *n* **senior hospital doctor**, specialist, consultant. [➡PEOPLE WHO WORK IN MEDICINE; 848]

registration 1 *n* **registering**, recording, record-keeping, process, action, cataloguing, listing, chronicling. [➡ADMINISTRATIVE OFFICERS; 811] 2 *n* **roll call**, register, muster, check, entry, list, listing. [➡BEGINNING; 53] 3 *n* **enrolment**, enlisting, signing up, signing on, course enrolment, class enrolment, school enrolment. [➡BEGINNING; 53]

registry *n* **records office**, register office, archive, administrative office, office. [➡ADMINISTRATIVE OFFICERS; 811]

regress 1 *v* **relapse**, revert, lapse, backslide, retrogress, degenerate. [➡GET WORSE; 382] *Opposite:* progress. 2 *v* **go back**, lose headway, lose ground, retreat, move back, fall back. [➡FAIL OR BE UNSUCCESSFUL; 75] *Opposite:* advance.

regression 1 *n* **recession**, retreat, retrogression, return. [➡GO BACKWARDS; 310] *Opposite:* advance. 2 *n* **reversion**, deterioration, relapse, worsening, getting worse, lapse. [➡WORSEN SOMETHING; 381] *Opposite:* progression.

regressive *adj* **reverting**, returning, going back, degenerating, deteriorating, backsliding, relapsing. [➡WORSEN SOMETHING; 381] *Opposite:* progressive.

regret 1 *v* **be sorry**, be apologetic, apologize for, be repentant, feel sorry. [➡CHANGE OF MOOD AND COMPOSURE; 581] 2 *v* (*formal*) **be disappointed**, be unhappy, lament, be remorseful, express grief, mourn, grieve over, bemoan. [➡APOLOGIZE AND RETRACT; 684] 3 *n* **remorse**, guilt, repentance, compunction, pang of conscience, shame, pang of guilt. [➡FEELINGS ABOUT THE PAST; 533] *Opposite:* shamelessness. 4 *n* **disappointment**, sorrow, unhappiness, grief, distress. [➡SADNESS, DISTRESS, AND DESPAIR; 540] *Opposite:* contentment.

regretful *adj* **apologetic**, remorseful, repentant, sorry, penitent, ashamed, contrite. [➡EMBARRASSMENT AND HUMILIATION; 543] *Opposite:* unapologetic.

regretfully 1 *adv* **apologetically**, remorsefully, repentantly, with regret, contritely, penitently. [➡EMBARRASSMENT AND HUMILIATION; 543] 2 *adv* **disappointedly**, unhappily, sorrowfully, sadly, with sadness. [➡SADNESS, DISTRESS, AND DESPAIR; 540] *Opposite:* contentedly.

regrettable *adj* **unfortunate**, deplorable, lamentable, a pity, undesirable, unwelcome, inopportune, disappointing. [➡EMOTIONALLY UNPLEASANT AND UPSETTING; 228] *Opposite:* fortunate.

regroup *v* **reform**, recover, rearrange, recuperate, reorder, change round, reorganize. [➡ARRANGE AND CREATE ORDER; 358] *Opposite:* scatter.

regular 1 *adj* **even**, steady, unvarying, consistent, systematic, fixed. [➡ORDER AND ORGANISATION; 207] *Opposite:* irregular. 2 *adj* **recurring**, recurrent, frequent, repeated, fixed, uniform, set. [➡FREQUENT AND OFTEN; 107] *Opposite:* intermittent. 3 *adj* **ordered**, methodical, even, consistent, reliable, steady, routine. [➡ORDER AND ORGANISATION; 207] *Opposite:* inconsistent. 4 *adj* **usual**, normal, standard, ordinary, customary, habitual, expected, accepted, conventional, common. [➡ACCEPTABLE AND PASSABLE; 220] *Opposite:* unusual. 5 *n* **soldier**, combatant, legionnaire, squaddie (*slang*), GI. [➡MILITARY PERSONNEL; 828]

regularity *n* **orderliness**, symmetry, uniformity, consistency, constancy, sameness, monotony, predictability. [➡SAMENESS; 151] *Opposite:* inconsistency.

regularize *v* **standardize**, normalize, make conform, legalize. [➡IMPROVE SOMETHING; 375]

regularly 1 *adv* **consistently**, evenly, smoothly, methodically, systematically, steadily. [➡ORDER AND ORGANISATION; 207] *Opposite:* irregularly. 2 *adv* **frequently**, often, on a regular basis, habitually, repeatedly, recurrently, commonly. [➡FREQUENT AND OFTEN; 107] *Opposite:* rarely.

regulate 1 *v* **control**, order, adjust, set, synchronize. [➡ARRANGE AND CREATE ORDER; 358] 2 *v* (*formal*) **normalize**, legalize, standardize, make conform, police. [➡ARRANGE AND CREATE ORDER; 358]

regulation 1 *n* **rule**, directive, guideline, parameter, instruction, ruling, bylaw, law, decree, order. [➡WAYS OF DOING THINGS; 295] 2 *n* **control**, adjustment, adaptation, alteration, management, supervision, government, organizing. [➡CHANGE; 373]

regulator 1 *n* **device**, valve, mechanism, controller, rheostat, circuit breaker, governor, switch. [➡PARTS OF MACHINES AND TOOLS; 1117] 2 *n* **watchdog**, controller, supervisory body, manager, supervisor, official. [➡ADVISERS, JUDGES, AND ARBITERS; 971]

regulatory *adj* **controlling**, supervisory, governing, monitoring, directing, adjusting, guiding. [➡ORDER AND ORGANISATION; 207]

regurgitate 1 *v* **bring up**, vomit, throw up (*informal*), spew up, sick up (*informal*), spit up. [➡VOMIT AND BELCH; 713] 2 *v* **repeat**, rehearse, go over, do again, reiterate, say again, restate, recite, churn out. [➡RECITE, REPEAT, AND NARRATE; 621]

regurgitation 1 *n* **bringing up**, vomiting, sicking up, spitting out, spewing, spewing out, throwing up (*informal*), spitting up (*US*). [➡VOMIT AND BELCH; 713] 2 *n* **repetition**, rehearsal, restating, churning out, recitation, reiteration. [➡NEUTRAL ONE-WAY COMMUNICATION; 49]

rehabilitate 1 *v* **restore**, recover, mend, repair, re-establish, revitalize, regenerate. [➡IMPROVE SOMETHING; 375] 2 *v* **assimilate**, acclimatize, re-educate, naturalize, reorient, socialize. [➡INSTRUCT AND TEACH; 610]

rehabilitation *n* **reintegration**, restoration, therapy, recuperation, convalescence, analysis, recovery, psychotherapy, help, remedy, psychoanalysis, physiotherapy. [➡PROGRESS AND ADVANCEMENT; 214]

rehash *v* **rework**, reuse, do again, go over, repeat, revise, return to, go back to. [➡RECOMMENCE AND RESUME; 269]

rehearsal *n* **practice**, preparation, trial, run through, dummy run, dry run, tryout (*US*). [➡PREPARATORY EVENT; 57] *Opposite:* performance.

rehearse *v* **practise**, go over, run through, prepare, train, repeat, study, review. [➡PREPARE FOR ACTION; 290]

rehearsed *adj* **practised**, prepared, learned, studied, planned out, thought out. [➡KNOWN AND FAMOUS; 182] *Opposite:* ad-lib.

reheat *v* **heat up**, warm up, warm through, warm, heat, refry, recook, rewarm. [➡COOKING AND FOOD PREPARATION; 354]

rehoboam *n* [➡CONTAINERS, RECEPTACLES, AND PACKAGING; 1244]

rehouse *v* **move**, transfer, relocate, resettle. [➡MOVE SOMETHING TO ANOTHER LOCATION; 325]

reign 1 *n* **rule**, sovereignty, control, supremacy, sway, time in power, period in office, period of influence. [➡REALMS AND RULES; 824] 2 *v* **rule**, hold sway, govern, control, lead, administrate, be in power. [➡BE IN CHARGE; 271]

reimburse *v* **repay**, pay back, give money back, compensate, refund, recompense. [➡GIVE MONEY; 434]

reimbursement *n* **repayment**, compensation, recompense, settlement, damages, refund. [➡REGAIN POSSESSION; 430]

rein *n* **bridle**, restraint, harness, leash, lead, strap, restriction. [➡FASTENERS, LINKS, AND NETWORKS; 1246]

rein back *v* [➡AVOID, PREVENT, LIMIT, AND CONTROL; 278]

reincarnate *v* **revive**, bring back, revitalize, rejuvenate, reawaken, restore, re-embody. [➡IMPROVE STRENGTH AND DURABILITY; 379]

reincarnation *n* **re-embodiment**, rebirth, re-creation, reawakening, restoration. [➡RELIGIOUS CONCEPTS; 777]

reindeer *type of* **deer or antelope**. [➡DEER AND ANTELOPE; 981]

reinforce 1 *v* **strengthen**, support, underpin, buttress, bolster, fortify, shore up. [➡IMPROVE STRENGTH AND DURABILITY; 379] *Opposite:* weaken. 2 *v* **emphasize**, underline, highlight, add force to, boost. [➡CLAIM, INSIST, AND EMPHASIZE; 615] *Opposite:* weaken.

reinforcement 1 *n* **strengthening**, support, underpinning, fortification, buttressing, shoring up, bolstering. [➡IMPROVE STRENGTH AND DURABILITY; 379] *Opposite:* weakening. 2 *n* **emphasis**, underlining, underscoring, corroboration, backup, highlighting, boosting. [➡CLAIM, INSIST, AND EMPHASIZE; 615] *Opposite:* weakening.

reinforcements *n* [➡MORE AND EXCESS; 122]

rein in *v* **hold back**, cut back, restrain, reduce, decrease, temper, curb, contain, inhibit, control. [➡AVOID, PREVENT, LIMIT, AND CONTROL; 278]

reinstate *v* **restore**, return, give back, re-establish, put back, replace, recall. [➡CONFER STATUS; 459]

reinstatement *n* **restoration**, return, recall, replacement, re-establishment. [➡REPETITION; 29]

reinsurance *n* **provision**, extra cover, protection, additional coverage (*US*). [➡INSURANCE; 801]

reinsure *v* **take out extra cover**, transfer, make extra provision. [➡INSURANCE; 801]

reintroduce *v* **introduce again**, bring into effect again, reinstate, restore, re-establish, bring back. [➡INSTITUTE AND INAUGURATE; 349]

reintroduction *n* **reinstatement**, restoration, re-establishment. [➡BEGINNING; 53]

reinvent *v* [➡CHANGE; 373]

reinvigorated *adj* [➡WIDE AWAKE AND CONSCIOUS; 736]

reissue 1 *v* **rerelease**, redistribute, recirculate, republish, send out again, reprint, reproduce. [➡INSTITUTE AND INAUGURATE; 349] 2 *n* **new issue**, reprint, rerelease, new edition, new copy. [➡BEGINNING; 53]

reiterate *v* **repeat**, go over, restate, do again, recap, retell, echo. [➡RECITE, REPEAT, AND NARRATE; 621]

reiteration *n* **repetition**, replication, restatement, echo, recap. [➡CLAIM, INSIST, AND EMPHASIZE; 615]

reject *v* **refuse**, rebuff, decline, snub, throw out, discard, disallow, eliminate, deny. [➡FOREGO AND DENY ONESELF; 450] *Opposite:* accept.

rejection *n* **refusal**, denial, rebuff, denunciation, refutation, dismissal, elimination, negative. [➡DENY AND REJECT; 645] *Opposite:* acceptance.

rejig (*informal*) *v* **rearrange**, alter, readjust, reorganize, change, juggle. [➡ARRANGE AND CREATE ORDER; 358]

rejoice (*literary*) *v* **celebrate**, be pleased about, cheer, exult, be glad, delight. [➡GIVING VENT TO EMOTIONS; 680]

rejoin (*formal*) *v* **reply**, answer, respond, retort, return, come back with. [➡REPLY AND ANSWER; 669]

rejoinder (*formal*) *n* **response**, answer, reply, comeback, retort, riposte, return. [➡REPLY AND ANSWER; 669]

See Compare and Contrast at **answer**.

rejuvenate *v* **revitalize**, invigorate, revive, make younger, revivify, refresh, renew, restore, regenerate. [➡IMPROVE STRENGTH AND DURABILITY; 379]

rejuvenated *adj* [➡WIDE AWAKE AND CONSCIOUS; 736]

rejuvenating *adj* [➡PHYSICALLY PLEASANT; 187]

rejuvenation *n* **revitalization**, reinvigoration, regeneration, renewal, renovation, restoration, rebirth, restitution, revival. [➡IMPROVE SOMETHING; 375]

rekindle *v* **renew**, reawaken, revive, regenerate, relight, revitalize, refresh, restore. [➡CAUSE TO HAPPEN; 31] *Opposite:* kill.

rekindling *n* [➡REPETITION; 29]

relapse 1 *v* **go back to**, revert, deteriorate, degenerate, fall back, worsen, lapse. [➡GET WORSE; 382] *Opposite:* improve. 2 *n* **deterioration**, decline, degeneration, reversion, waning, setback. [➡PROBLEM; 257] *Opposite:* improvement.

relate 1 *v* **connect**, link, associate, correlate, link up, join, attach. [➡CREATING CONNECTIONS; 145] 2 *v* **interact**, get on, form a relationship, hit it off (*informal*), connect, cooperate, associate. [➡ESTABLISHING RELATIONSHIPS WITH OTHERS; 974] 3 *v* **tell**, narrate, speak about, recount, relay, transmit, communicate, share, convey, report. [➡RECITE, REPEAT, AND NARRATE; 621]

related *adj* **connected**, linked, associated, correlated, interrelated, allied, interconnected. [➡RELATED; 143] *Opposite:* unconnected.

relatedness *n* [➡CONNECTION; 144]

relating to *prep* **about**, regarding, re, apropos of, in relation to, pertaining to, with regard to, vis-à-vis, in connection with, as regards, respecting, with respect to, with reference to, in respect of, concerning, on the subject of, in connection to (*US*). [➡EXPRESSIONS OF REFERENCE; 63]

relations 1 *n* **family members**, relatives, family, kindred. [➡THE FAMILY; 956] 2 *n* **relationships**, dealings, associations, affairs, contact, interaction. [➡RELATIONSHIP TO ANOTHER; 973]

relationship *n* **association**, connection, affiliation, rapport, liaison, link, correlation, bond. [➡CONNECTION; 144]

relative 1 *adj* **comparative**, qualified, virtual. [➡TO A CERTAIN EXTENT; 134] *Opposite:* absolute. 2 *n* **family member**, relation, next of kin, kin, kith and kin. [➡THE FAMILY; 956]

relative to *prep* **in relation to**, compared with, proportionate to, corresponding to. [➡EXPRESSIONS OF REFERENCE; 63]

relativism *n* **contingency**, belief, doctrine. [➡PHILOSOPHIES AND BELIEFS; 781] *Opposite:* absolutism.

relativist 1 *n* **equivocator**, fence sitter, trimmer, agnostic, waverer, vacillator. [➡PHILOSOPHICAL AND POLITICAL THINKERS; 782] 2 *adj* **contingent**, dependent, relative. [➡PHILOSOPHIES AND BELIEFS; 781]

relativity *n* **relativeness**, dependence, contingency. [➡CONNECTION; 144]

relax 1 *v* **loosen**, slacken, ease. [➡CHANGE OF INTENSITY: LESS; 396] *Opposite:* tense. 2 *v* **rest**, put your feet up, take it easy, have a break, chill out (*slang*), lie down, be calm. [➡LACK OF ACTIVITY; 343] 3 *v* **unwind**, calm down, slow down, let go, loosen up, lighten up (*informal*), settle down. [➡CHANGE OF MOOD AND COMPOSURE; 581] 4 *v* **lessen**, decrease, diminish, lower, ease, reduce. [➡CHANGE OF INTENSITY: LESS; 396] *Opposite:* increase.

relaxation 1 *n* **recreation**, leisure, entertainment, rest, repose, respite. [➡LEISURE AND RECREATION; 874] 2 *n* **reduction**, lessening, let-up (*informal*), easing, slackening, moderation. [➡LESS; 124] *Opposite:* increase.

relaxed 1 *adj* **tranquil**, calm, comfortable, stress-free, hassle-free (*informal*), unperturbed, peaceful, undisturbed, cosy. [➡EMOTIONALLY PLEASANT; 188] *Opposite:* tense. 2 *adj* **lenient**, easygoing, laid-back (*informal*), untroubled, casual. [➡PEACEFULNESS AND GENTLENESS; 215] *Opposite:* strict.

relaxing *adj* **calming**, soothing, comforting, peaceful, tranquil. [➡CALMING; 189] *Opposite:* tense.

relay *v* **communicate**, pass on, transmit, spread, convey, impart, dispatch, send. [➡INFORM AND ANNOUNCE; 612]

relay race *type of* **track and field.** [➡HOBBIES, GAMES, AND SPORTS; 875]

release 1 *v* **let go**, free, discharge, liberate, let loose, leave go of, emancipate. [➡FREEDOM AND LIBERTY; 209] *Opposite:* hold. 2 *v* **make public**, make available, announce, publish, circulate, issue, emit, publicize, distribute. [➡INFORM AND ANNOUNCE; 612] *Opposite:* withhold. 3 *n* **relief**, discharge, freedom, liberation, emancipation, delivery. [➡FREEDOM AND LIBERTY; 209] 4 *n* **announcement**, issue, statement, publication, proclamation. [➡BASIC DETAILS; 689]

release on bail *n* [➡TRIAL, PUNISHMENT, AND LEGAL OUTCOMES; 819]

release on parole *v* [➡TRIAL, PUNISHMENT, AND LEGAL OUTCOMES; 819]

relegate *v* **demote**, downgrade, transfer, consign, refer, reduce in importance, lower. [➡REVOKE STATUS; 460] *Opposite:* promote.

relegation *n* **demotion**, sending down, transfer down, lowering of rank, downgrade, being demoted. [➡REVOKE STATUS; 460] *Opposite:* promotion.

relent *v* **give in**, cave in, change your mind, concede, yield, take a softer line, give up, surrender, sympathize. [➡FORGET, FORGIVE, AND ACCEPT; 749] *Opposite:* stand firm.

relentless *adj* **persistent**, unyielding, unremitting, inexorable (*formal*), insistent, harsh, unrelenting, ruthless, uncompromising, obstinate. [➡PERMANENCE: WITHOUT END; 94] *Opposite:* moderate.

relentlessness 1 *n* **ceaselessness**, unremittingness, persistence, remorselessness, intensity, steadiness, endlessness. [➡PERMANENCE: WITHOUT END; 94] *Opposite:* moderation. 2 *n* **remorselessness**, mercilessness, implacability (*formal*), pitilessness, ruthlessness, inexorability (*formal*), harshness, strictness, heartlessness, cold-bloodedness. [➡EMOTIONALLY UNPLEASANT AND UPSETTING; 228]

relevance *n* **significance**, bearing, application, importance, weight, consequence (*formal*), applicability, germaneness (*formal*). [➡IMPORTANCE AND SIGNIFICANCE; 193]

relevant *adj* **pertinent**, applicable, germane (*formal*), related, appropriate, significant, important. [➡IMPORTANT; 195] *Opposite:* unrelated.

relevantly *adv* **pertinently**, appositely, appropriately, fittingly, relatedly, aptly, suitably, connectedly. [➡APPROPRIATE, SUITABLE, ADVISABLE; 185] *Opposite:* irrelevantly.

reliability *n* **dependability**, consistency, steadfastness, trustworthiness. [➡HONEST AND RELIABLE; 503] *Opposite:* untrustworthiness.

reliable *adj* **dependable**, consistent, steadfast, unswerving, unfailing, trustworthy. [➡HONEST AND RELIABLE; 503] *Opposite:* undependable.

reliance *n* **dependence**, confidence, trust, belief, faith, support. [➡RECIPROCITY AND INTERDEPENDENCE; 148] *Opposite:* independence.

reliant *adj* **dependent**, needful, conditional, subject to, contingent, trusting. [➡RELATIONSHIP TO ANOTHER; 973] *Opposite:* independent.

relic *n* **historical object**, artefact, remnant, remains, vestige, leftover. [➡REMAINDER AND REMAINDERS; 123]

relief 1 *n* **assistance**, aid, help, reinforcement, support, alleviation. [➡KIND ACTION OR BEHAVIOUR; 296] 2 *n* **respite**, release, reprieve, break, liberation, help. [➡FREEDOM AND LIBERTY; 209]

relieve 1 *v* **ease**, release, alleviate, reduce, mitigate, lessen, lighten, allay. [➡CHANGE OF INTENSITY: LESS; 396] *Opposite:* exacerbate. 2 *v* **take somebody's place**, take over for, substitute for, stand in for, replace. [➡CHANGE ONE THING FOR ANOTHER; 399] 3 *v* **dismiss**, release, let go, sack (*informal*), discharge, fire (*informal*), get rid of, boot out (*informal*). [➡REVOKE STATUS; 460] *Opposite:* appoint.

relieved *adj* **reassured**, thankful, calmed, pleased, comforted. [➡CALMNESS, CONFIDENCE, AND COMPOSURE; 537] *Opposite:* worried.

religion *n* **faith**, belief, creed, conviction. [➡RELIGIONS AND RELIGIOUS PRACTICES; 778]

religious 1 *adj* **spiritual**, sacred, devout, pious, holy. [➡RELIGIOUS CONCEPTS; 777] *Opposite:* secular. 2 *adj* **thorough**, conscientious, dutiful, faithful, reliable, loyal. [➡HONEST AND RELIABLE; 503] *Opposite:* unreliable.

religious education *n* [➡LESSONS, COURSE WORK, AND EXAMINATIONS; 842]

religious fervour *n* [➡FADS, FETISHES, AND IDOLATRY; 556]

religious instruction *n* [➡LESSONS, COURSE WORK, AND EXAMINATIONS; 842]

religiously *adv* **dutifully**, faithfully, consistently, thoroughly, conscientiously, unfailingly, devotedly, loyally, reliably. [➡HONEST AND RELIABLE; 503] *Opposite:* carelessly.

religiousness *n* **devoutness**, piousness, spirituality, sense of God, faithfulness, conscientiousness. [➡RELIGIOUS CONCEPTS; 777]

religious studies *n* [➡LESSONS, COURSE WORK, AND EXAMINATIONS; 842]

religious zeal *n* [➡FADS, FETISHES, AND IDOLATRY; 556]

relinquish *v* **give up**, surrender, hand over, abandon, renounce, resign, turn down, let go by, let pass. [➡FOREGO AND DENY ONESELF; 450] *Opposite:* retain.

reliquary *n* **repository**, casket, container, shrine. [➡RELIGIOUS OBJECTS; 780]

relish 1 *v* **enjoy**, delight in, savour, take pleasure in, like, appreciate. [➡LIKE, LOVE, VALUE AND ENJOY; 579] *Opposite:* dislike. 2 *n* **enjoyment**, delight, pleasure, elation, appreciation, bliss. [➡PLEASURE, EXCITEMENT, AND ELATION; 535] *Opposite:* displeasure.

relive *v* **experience again**, go through again, live through again, remember, recall, re-experience, recreate. [➡REMEMBER; 747] *Opposite:* forget.

reload *v* **refill**, fill, load again, replenish, fill up. [➡FILL; 407] *Opposite:* unload.

relocate *v* **move**, change place, reposition, transfer, displace, shuffle, put somewhere else, rearrange. [➡MOVE SOMETHING TO ANOTHER LOCATION; 325] *Opposite:* remain.

relocation *n* **transfer**, moving, rearrangement, repositioning, replacement, removal, move. [➡MOVE SOMETHING TO ANOTHER LOCATION; 325]

reluctance *n* **unwillingness**, lack of enthusiasm, disinclination, foot-dragging (*informal*), hesitancy, averseness (*formal*). [➡FEELINGS ABOUT THE FUTURE; 534] *Opposite:* enthusiasm.

reluctant *adj* **unwilling**, unenthusiastic, disinclined, loath, hesitant, indisposed (*formal*), averse (*formal*). [➡UNWILLINGNESS AND STUBBORNNESS; 565] *Opposite:* enthusiastic.

See Compare and Contrast at **unwilling**.

reluctantly *adv* **unwillingly**, unenthusiastically, half-heartedly, grudgingly, hesitantly, aversely (*formal*). [➡WITHOUT ENTHUSIASM; 288] *Opposite:* willingly.

rely *v* **depend on**, bank on, count on, trust, be sure of, be dependent on, have faith in, put your faith in, be certain about, have confidence in. [➡RECIPROCITY AND INTERDEPENDENCE; 148] *Opposite:* distrust.

remain 1 *v* **stay**, stay put, stay behind, stay on, linger, wait, hang about, hang around. [➡EXIST IN A PLACE; 19] *Opposite:* leave. 2 *v* **continue**, keep on, endure, persist, go on. [➡CONTINUE TO EXIST; 17] *Opposite:* stop.

remainder *n* **rest**, residue, remnants, remains, leftovers, what's left, balance. [➡REMAINDER AND REMAINDERS; 123]

remainders *n* [➡REMAINDER AND REMAINDERS; 123]

remaining *adj* **residual**, outstanding, left over, lingering, enduring, lasting, left behind. [➡PERMANENCE: WITHOUT END; 94]

remains 1 *n* **leftovers**, remnants, relics, remainder, ruins, vestiges, residue, what's left, rest, orts, scraps. [➡REMAINDER AND REMAINDERS; 123] 2 *n* **dead body**, corpse, cadaver, ashes, carcass, skeleton, body. [➡DEAD PERSON; 926]

remake 1 *n* **new version**, cover version, cover, new edition, re-creation. [➡ARTWORKS; 898] 2 *v* **produce again**, re-create, re-form, change the format, reshape, reconstruct, redesign, remodel, restyle, reproduce, reformat. [➡CREATION; 347]

remand 1 *v* **return to custody**, return to prison, commit to custody, release on bail, incarcerate (*formal*), imprison, jail. [➡TRIAL, PUNISHMENT, AND LEGAL OUTCOMES; 819] 2 *n* **return to custody**, return to prison, committal to custody, release on bail, custody, prison, imprisonment. [➡TRIAL, PUNISHMENT, AND LEGAL OUTCOMES; 819]

remand home *n* [➡BUILDINGS FOR CONFINING PEOPLE; 1093]

remark 1 *n* **comment**, statement, observation, aside, mention, quip. [➡SUGGEST, HINT, AND COMMENT; 613] 2 *v* **say**, comment, state, observe, pronounce, mention. [➡SUGGEST, HINT, AND COMMENT; 613]

remarkability *n* [➡EXTRAORDINARY: AMAZING; 205]

remarkable *adj* **extraordinary**, amazing, notable, outstanding, noteworthy, significant, incredible, astonishing. [➡EXTRAORDINARY: AMAZING; 205] *Opposite:* ordinary.

remarkableness *n* [➡EXTRAORDINARY: AMAZING; 205]

remarry *v* **get married again**, marry again, wed again (*formal or literary*), get wed again, re-wed. [➡ESTABLISHING RELATIONSHIPS WITH OTHERS; 974]

rematch *n* **replay**, a second go, another game. [➡NON-AGGRESSIVE/SPORTING EVENT; 40]

rematerialize *v* [➡APPEAR AND EMERGE; 3]

remedial *adj* **corrective**, counteractive, helpful, educative, curative. [➡USEFULNESS; 200]

remedy 1 *n* **solution**, cure, answer, antidote, resolution, alleviation, treatment. [➡SOLUTION; 216] 2 *n* **medicine**, medication, preparation, mixture, therapy, cure, tonic, remedying. [➡REMEDIES, TREATMENTS AND OPERATIONS; 732] 3 *v* **cure**, relieve, improve, alleviate, ease, treat, fix. [➡CORRECT AND PUT RIGHT; 378] 4 *v* **resolve**, deal with, correct, improve, make better, solve, sort out, take care of, fix. [➡CORRECT AND PUT RIGHT; 378] *Opposite:* exacerbate.

remember 1 *v* **keep in mind**, bear in mind, retain, memorize, learn, have off pat, commit to memory, consider, take into account, have down pat (*US*). [➡REMEMBER; 747] *Opposite:* forget. 2 *v* **recall**, think of, recollect, dredge up, hark back to, reminisce, evoke, summon up, bring to mind. [➡REMEMBER; 747] *Opposite:* forget.

remembrance *n* **commemoration**, memory, tribute, recollection, reminiscence, celebration. [➡MEMORY; 746]

remind 1 *v* **be reminiscent**, ring a bell (*informal*), strike a chord, take you back, jog your memory. [➡REMIND; 748] 2 *v* **repeat**, retell, prompt, recap, run by again, hark back, tell again. [➡INFORM AND ANNOUNCE; 612]

reminder 1 *n* **cue**, aide-mémoire (*formal*), notice, prompt, recap. [➡INDICATIONS, SIGNS, AND WARNINGS; 68] 2 *n* **souvenir**, token, memento, knick-knack, keepsake, remembrance. [➡ORNAMENTS AND DECORATIONS; 1247]

reminisce *v* **recall**, talk about, hark back to, muse over, evoke, recollect, bring to mind, ponder, ruminate. [➡REMEMBER; 747]

reminiscence 1 *n* **nostalgia**, recollection, looking back, musing, rumination. [➡MEMORY; 746] 2 *n* **memory**, recollection, reminder. [➡MEMORY; 746]

reminiscent *adj* **suggestive**, evocative, resonant, redolent, similar, like. [➡SIMILARITY; 149]

remiss *adj* **careless**, negligent, lax, slipshod, slapdash, inattentive, thoughtless, inconsistent. [➡INCAUTIOUS AND CARELESS; 284] *Opposite:* diligent.

remission *n* **reduction**, decrease, lessening, diminution, cutback, retardation. [➡CHANGE OF SIZE: SMALLER; 394]

remissive *adj* **pardoning**, forgiving, absolving, exonerating. [➡GENEROSITY AND KINDNESS; 496]

remit 1 *v* **send**, forward, dispatch, pay, settle, square. [➡DESPATCH AND SEND; 334] 2 *v* **submit**, refer, pass on. [➡GIVE MONEY; 434] *Opposite:* handle. 3 *v* **slacken**, decrease, lessen, diminish, cancel, reduce, abate (*formal or literary*). [➡CHANGE OF INTENSITY: LESS; 396] *Opposite:* increase. 4 *n* **responsibility**, concern, sphere of activity, job, brief, sphere, scope. [➡SUBJECT AREA; 769]

remittance 1 *n* **payment**, transfer of funds, transmittal, fee, transfer, settlement. [➡MONEY, PAYMENTS, AND CHARGES; 800] 2 *n* **release**, discharge (*formal*), dispatch. [➡FREEDOM AND LIBERTY; 209]

remix 1 *v* **produce new version**, rehash, rejig (*informal*), reproduce, alter, change, revise. [➡CREATION; 347] 2 *n* **new recording**, different version, new version, latest version, revised version. [➡RECORDINGS AND PLAYERS; 911]

remnant *n* **remainder**, remains, relic, residue, trace, vestige, scrap, end, last part, leftover. [➡REMAINDER AND REMAINDERS; 123]

remnants *n* [➡REMAINDER AND REMAINDERS; 123]

remodel *v* **alter**, modify, modernize, adapt, adjust, amend, transform, renovate, change, refashion. [➡IMPROVE SOMETHING; 375]

remonstrance 1 *n* **argument**, evidence, backup, proof, case, point. [➡POINT OF VIEW; 768] 2 *n* **protest**, complaint, objection, petition, dispute, civil disobedience. [➡CRITICISMS AND ANGRY OUTBURSTS; 50]

remonstrate *v* **argue**, protest, object, oppose, complain, squabble, bicker, dispute, gripe (*informal*). [➡PROTEST AND EXPRESS DISAPPROVAL; 643] *Opposite:* agree.

See Compare and Contrast at **object**.

remorse *n* **regret**, sorrow, repentance, penitence, guilt, compunction, shame. [➡FEELINGS ABOUT THE PAST; 533]

remorseful *adj* **regretful**, repentant, penitent, contrite, apologetic, rueful, sorry. [➡EMBARRASSMENT AND HUMILIATION; 543] *Opposite:* unrepentant.

remorseless 1 *adj* **pitiless**, ruthless, merciless, callous, cruel, hard, brutal, compassionless, unforgiving, coldhearted. [➡IRRITATION AND ANGER; 542] *Opposite:* merciful. 2 *adj* **inexorable**, implacable (*formal*), indefatigable, unbending, unyielding, unstoppable, relentless. [➡PERMANENCE: WITHOUT END; 94]

remorselessness *n* [➡PERMANENCE: WITHOUT END; 94]

remote 1 *adj* **distant**, isolated, inaccessible, far-flung, far-off, in the sticks, secluded, out-of-the-way, faraway, apart. [➡DISTANCE; 161] *Opposite:* nearby. 2 *adj* **aloof**, detached, withdrawn, reserved, cool, cold, frosty, uninvolved, inaccessible, diffident. [➡UNFRIENDLINESS AND UNSOCIABILITY; 505] *Opposite:* approachable. 3 *adj* **slight**, outside, unlikely, improbable, faint, small. [➡IMPOSSIBLE AND IMPROBABLE; 179] *Opposite:* likely.

remotely 1 *adv* **distantly**, tenuously, slightly, a little, somewhat, vaguely. [➡TO A CERTAIN EXTENT; 134] *Opposite:* closely. 2 *adv* **at all**, in the least, the least bit, the slightest bit. [➡FEW, LITTLE, SMALL AMOUNT; 119] *Opposite:* greatly.

remoteness 1 *n* **isolation**, seclusion, distance, solitude, inaccessibility. [➡DISTANCE; 161] *Opposite:* closeness. 2 *n* **aloofness**, detachment, reserve, inaccessibility, coolness, frostiness, diffidence. [➡UNFRIENDLINESS AND UNSOCIABILITY; 505] *Opposite:* approachability.

remount *v* **get on again**, get back on, mount again, ride again, get back in the saddle, climb on again. [➡TRAVEL: WAYS OF TRAVELLING; 321]

removable *adj* **detachable**, not fixed, comes off, can be removed, changeable, transferable. [➡UNRELATEDNESS AND SEPARATENESS; 147] *Opposite:* attached.

removal *n* **taking away**, elimination, exclusion, subtraction, deletion, amputation, confiscation, deduction, abstraction, ejection. [➡REMOVE SOMETHING; 339] *Opposite:* addition.

removal van *type of* **commercial or industrial vehicle**. [➡VEHICLES; 1144]

remove 1 *v* **take away**, get rid of, eliminate, do away with, eradicate, take out, confiscate. [➡REMOVE SOMETHING; 339] *Opposite:* add. 2 *v* **take off**, detach, cut off, amputate, disconnect, strip off, subtract, delete. [➡DELETE AND ERASE; 340]

remunerate *v* **pay**, reward, compensate, recompense, repay, reimburse. [➡GIVE MONEY; 434]

remuneration *n* **payment**, fee, salary, wage, compensation, recompense, pay, reward, return, stipend, reimbursement. [➡INCOME; 461]

See Compare and Contrast at **wage**.

renaissance *n* **rebirth**, new start, new beginning, resurgence, revitalization, revival, regeneration, recovery, reawakening. [➡REPETITION; 29] *Opposite:* decline.

Renaissance 1 *type of* **pre-20th-century art movement**. [➡ARTISTIC MOVEMENTS AND STYLES; 899] 2 *type of* **pre-20th-century architecture**. [➡BUILDING AND ARCHITECTURE; 1075]

rename *v* **name again**, give new name, retitle, rechristen, give name again, change name, give another name. [➡NAME AND DESCRIBE; 666]

renascent *adj* **becoming active**, budding, burgeoning, appearing, becoming popular, reviving, re-emerging. [➡ABOUT TO HAPPEN; 33]

rend *v* **tear**, tear apart, rip, come apart, split, slash, shred, slit. [➡TEAR, BREAK, AND CUT; 361] *Opposite:* mend.

See Compare and Contrast at **tear**.

render 1 *v* (*formal*) **decide**, decree, judge, adjudicate, declare. [➡MAKE DECISIONS AND CHOICES; 753] 2 *v* (*formal*) **provide**, give, deliver, submit, afford (*formal*), make available, hand over, supply, bestow (*formal*). [➡EQUIP AND SUPPLY; 436] 3 *v* (*formal*) **portray**, depict, represent, execute, translate, perform. [➡CAUSE TO APPEAR; 5] 4 *v* **melt down**, reduce, condense, concentrate, boil down, purify, extract, solidify. [➡SOFTEN, LIQUEFY, DAMPEN; 389]

rendering 1 *n* **portrayal**, depiction, picture, image, portrait, shooting, reproduction, description, delivery. [➡REPRESENTATIONS AND GENERAL EXAMPLES; 65] 2 *n* **version**, translation, interpretation, interpreting, execution, representation, transcription, adaptation. [➡REPRESENTATIONS AND GENERAL EXAMPLES;

65] 3 *n* **plaster coating**, plaster, pebbledash, coating, cladding, siding, coat. [➡COVERS AND COATINGS; 1245]

render speechless *v* [➡CONFUSE AND BEWILDER; 572]

rendezvous 1 *n* **engagement**, meeting, appointment, tryst, assignation, date. [➡MEETINGS AND ASSEMBLIES; 43] 2 *n* **meeting place**, meeting point, assembly point, location, site, resort, hangout (*informal*), muster, station. [➡PUBLIC BUILDINGS AND MEETING PLACES; 1080] 3 *v* **meet**, come together, make contact, get together, assemble, gather, congregate. [➡INITIATE AND ESTABLISH COMMUNICATION; 681]

rendition *n* **version**, interpretation, performance, rendering, execution, delivery. [➡NEUTRAL ONE-WAY COMMUNICATION; 49]

renegade *n* **apostate**, traitor, rebel, turncoat, betrayer, defector, deserter. [➡VILLAINS AND THUGS; 947] *Opposite:* loyalist.

renege *v* **go back on**, break your word, break a promise, back out, default. [➡NOT DO AND REFUSE TO DO; 275]

renew 1 *v* **return to**, reintroduce, repeat, restart, recommence (*formal*), begin again. [➡RECOMMENCE AND RESUME; 269] 2 *v* **restore**, rekindle, revitalize, rejuvenate, refresh, recharge, revive, regenerate, reinstate, recall. [➡IMPROVE SOMETHING; 375] 3 *v* **recondition**, renovate, refurbish, repair, restore, mend, make good, revamp. [➡REPAIR AND MEND; 377]

Compare and Contrast: ***renew, recondition, renovate, restore, revamp***

CORE MEANING: TO IMPROVE THE CONDITION OF SOMETHING

renew to replace something worn or broken; ***recondition*** to bring something such as a machine or appliance back to a good condition or working state by means of repairs or replacement of parts; ***renovate*** to bring something such as a building back to a former better state by means of repairs, redecoration, or refurbishment; ***restore*** to bring something back to an original state after it has been damaged or fallen into a bad condition; ***revamp*** to improve the appearance or condition of something.

renewal *n* **regeneration**, restitution, rekindling, revitalization, rejuvenation, rebirth, replenishment, restoration, repair. [➡IMPROVE SOMETHING; 375]

renounce 1 *v* **relinquish**, surrender, hand over, turn down, disown, refuse, give up, abdicate, demit. [➡FOREGO AND DENY ONESELF; 450] *Opposite:* accept. 2 *v* **disavow** (*formal*), repudiate, give up, reject, abandon, forsake, desert, quit. [➡FOREGO AND DENY ONESELF; 450] *Opposite:* embrace.

renovate *v* **renew**, recondition, modernize, refurbish, repair, restore, mend, do up, revamp, remodel, redecorate, fix up. [➡REPAIR AND MEND; 377]

See Compare and Contrast at **renew.**

renovated *adj* [➡IN GOOD REPAIR; 1231]

renovation *n* **facelift**, revamp, makeover, restoration, redecoration, repair, overhaul, renewal, reformation, transformation, reconstruction. [➡IMPROVE SOMETHING; 375]

renown *n* **fame**, celebrity, repute (*formal*), notoriety, prominence, popularity, reputation, recognition, distinction. [➡KNOWN AND FAMOUS; 182] *Opposite:* obscurity.

renowned *adj* **famous**, well-known, celebrated, notorious (*archaic*), prominent, popular, distinguished, legendary, recognized, established. [➡KNOWN AND FAMOUS; 182] *Opposite:* unknown.

rent 1 *n* **rental**, rent payment, hire charge, fee, payment, charge. [➡INCOME; 461] 2 *n* **hole**, tear, rip, split, slash, fissure, gash, crack, cleft, slit, divide. [➡HOLES, GAPS, AND FORKS; 1251] 3 *v* **let**, hire out, lend out, rent out, charter, lease. [➡LEND, LEASE, AND BORROW; 429]

See Compare and Contrast at **hire.**

rental 1 *n* **rent payment**, fee, payment, hire charge, charge, rent. [➡MONEY, PAYMENTS, AND CHARGES; 800] 2 *n* **hire**, leasing, letting, charter. [➡INCOME; 461]

rent out *v* [➡LEND, LEASE, AND BORROW; 429]

renunciation 1 *n* **repudiation**, abandonment, denial, renouncement, disavowal (*formal*), rejection. [➡DENY AND REJECT; 645] *Opposite:* acceptance. 2 *n* **rejection**, repudiation, abandonment, denial, refusal, disallowance, refutation. [➡REFUSE PERMISSION AND NOT ALLOW; 671] *Opposite:* acceptance. 3 *n* **surrender**, disowning, refusal, resignation, abdication, relinquishment. [➡FOREGO AND DENY ONESELF; 450]

reoccurrence *n* [➡REPETITION; 29]

reoffender *n* [➡CRIMINALS; 821]

reorder *v* **rearrange**, reorganize, regroup, restructure, move around, change round, alter, mix up, sort out. [➡ARRANGE AND CREATE ORDER; 358]

reorganization *n* **reform**, restructuring, reshuffle, redeployment, reformation, sort-out, shake-up. [➡ARRANGE AND CREATE ORDER; 358]

reorganize *v* **regroup**, move around, reorder, rearrange, restructure, change round, alter, reschedule, sort out, tidy up, change. [➡ARRANGE AND CREATE ORDER; 358]

rep (*informal*) *n* **sales rep** (*informal*), representative, agent, courier, delegate, deputy. [➡REPRESENTATIVES AND PATRONS; 968]

repaint *v* **redecorate**, do over again (*informal*), renovate, touch up, patch up, freshen the paint, recoat. [➡DECORATE, ADORN, AND APPLY COATINGS; 406]

repair 1 *v* **overhaul**, mend, fix, patch up, restore, darn, put back together, get working again. [➡REPAIR AND MEND; 377] 2 *n* **overhaul**, reparation, restoration, patch-up, mending, healing, renovation, darning. [➡REPAIR AND MEND; 377]

repaper *v* [➡DECORATE, ADORN, AND APPLY COATINGS; 406]

reparation *n* **amends**, compensation, damages, recompense, reimbursement, restitution. [➡MONEY, PAYMENTS, AND CHARGES; 800]

repartee *n* **banter**, wit, wordplay, badinage, raillery. [➡JOKES AND TEASING; 675]

repast (*literary*) *n* **meal**, banquet, feast, spread (*informal*), buffet, collation, refection (*literary*). [➡MEALS AND PARTS OF MEALS; 1168]

repatriate *v* **send home**, deport, send back, banish, exile, expel, oust. [➡EJECT AND EXCLUDE; 341]

repatriation *n* **sending home**, going home, deportation, return, exile, banishment, expulsion, ouster. [➡MOVE SOMETHING TO ANOTHER LOCATION; 325]

repay *v* **pay**, pay back, reimburse, refund, pay off, settle up, recompense, square. [➡REWARD; 437]

repayment *n* **payment**, refund, reimbursement, settlement, compensation, recompense. [➡MONEY, PAYMENTS, AND CHARGES; 800]

repeal *v* **cancel**, revoke, rescind, annul, retract, abolish, dismantle, reverse. [➡ABOLISH AND ANNUL; 453] *Opposite:* enact.

repeat 1 *v* **reiterate**, recap, go over, echo, retell, say again, recite, resay, restate, iterate. [➡RECITE, REPEAT, AND NARRATE; 621] 2 *v* **do again**, replicate, duplicate, show again, copy, imitate. [➡RECOMMENCE AND RESUME; 269] 3 *n* **recurrence**, replication, reiteration, duplication, reappearance, echo, recap, reprise, repetition. [➡REPETITION; 29]

repeated *adj* **recurrent**, frequent, recurring, repetitive, constant, continual. [➡FREQUENT AND OFTEN; 107] *Opposite:* rare.

repeat offender *n* [➡CRIMINALS; 821]

repel 1 *v* **disgust**, revolt, nauseate, repulse, make you feel sick, sicken. [➡UPSET, DISTRESS, AND HUMILIATE; 568] 2 *v* **keep away**, fend off, drive back, keep at bay, deter, resist, prevent, hold off, ward off. [➡EJECT AND EXCLUDE; 341] *Opposite:* attract.

repellant *adj* [➡DISGUSTING AND REPULSIVE; 231]

repelled *adj* [➡IRRITATION AND ANGER; 542]

repellent 1 *adj* **disgusting**, revolting, nauseating, repulsive, repugnant, off-putting, sickening, hideous, vile, disconcerting. [➡DISGUSTING AND REPULSIVE; 231] *Opposite:* attractive. 2 *adj* **impervious**, impermeable, resistant, proof, tight. [➡SAFE AND SAFETY; 192]

repent *v* **regret**, be sorry, apologize, ask forgiveness, feel sorrow, be penitent, atone (*formal*), be remorseful. [➡APOLOGIZE AND RETRACT; 684]

repentance *n* **regret**, sorrow, remorse, penitence, atonement, shame, contrition, penance, contriteness. [➡FEELINGS ABOUT THE PAST; 533]

repentant *adj* **regretful**, remorseful, apologetic, penitent, rueful, contrite, sorry. [➡EMBARRASSMENT AND HUMILIATION; 543] *Opposite:* unrepentant.

repercussion *n* **consequence**, effect, upshot, impact, aftermath, outcome, ramification, corollary, influence, implication, result. [➡RESULTS AND OUTCOMES; 83]

repertoire *n* **repertory**, collection, selection, series, stock, range, group. [➡COLLECTIONS AND MIXTURES OF THINGS; 1243]

repertory 1 *n* **staging**, production, performance. [➡PERFORMANCES AND SHOWS; 42] 2 *n* **theatre company**, theatre group, company, repertory theatre, theatre, repertory company. [➡THE PERFORMING ARTS; 904] 3 *n* **repertoire**, selection, series, stock, range, collection, store. [➡COLLECTIONS AND MIXTURES OF THINGS; 1243]

repertory company *n* [➡PERFORMERS; 905]

repertory theatre *n* [➡THE PERFORMING ARTS; 904]

repetition *n* **recurrence**, replication, duplication, reiteration, reappearance, echo, reverberation, reprise, repeat. [➡REPETITION; 29]

repetitious *adj* **repetitive**, boring, monotonous, tedious, dull, tiresome, pedestrian, dreary. [➡BORING AND UNINTERESTING; 235] *Opposite:* innovative.

repetitiousness *n* [➡REPETITION; 29]

repetitive *adj* **boring**, dull, monotonous, tedious, tiresome, uninteresting, pedestrian, dreary. [➡BORING AND UNINTERESTING; 235] *Opposite:* varied.

repetitively *adv* **repeatedly**, continually, over and over again, cyclically, frequently. [➡FREQUENT AND OFTEN; 107] *Opposite:* infrequently.

repetitiveness *n* [➡REPETITION; 29]

repetitive strain injury *n* [➡THE BONES AND JOINTS; 720]

rephrase *v* **restate**, retell, say differently, put another way, reshape, rearticulate, resay. [➡RECITE, REPEAT, AND NARRATE; 621]

replace 1 *v* **substitute**, swap (*informal*), trade, use instead, exchange, switch, interchange, take the place of, supplant, change, supersede. [➡CHANGE ONE THING FOR ANOTHER; 399] 2 *v* **replenish**, put back, restore, return, reinstate, restitute. [➡POSITION SOMETHING; 326]

replacement *n* **substitute**, stand-in, substitution, proxy, surrogate, alternative, understudy, alternate (*US*). [➡SUBSTITUTES AND STAND-INS; 400] *Opposite:* original.

replay 1 *v* **play again**, rerun, repeat, retell, reiterate, restate. [➡RECOMMENCE AND RESUME; 269] 2 *n* **rerun**, repetition, reiteration, echo, repeat. [➡REPETITION; 29]

replenish *v* **replace**, refill, fill, stock up, top up, restock, reload. [➡FILL; 407] *Opposite:* deplete.

replenishment *n* **replacement**, refill, top up, renewal. [➡MORE AND EXCESS; 122]

replete 1 *adj* **full**, complete, supplied, abounding, chock-full (*informal*), brimming, awash, rife. [➡FULL; 1238] *Opposite:* lacking. 2 *adj* **sated**, full up, stuffed (*informal*), satisfied, satiated, full. [➡EAT AND NOT EAT; 711] *Opposite:* hungry.

replica *n* **copy**, reproduction, imitation, model, facsimile, duplication, mock-up, carbon copy. [➡COPIES AND REPLICAS; 152] *Opposite:* original.

replicate *v* **duplicate**, repeat, copy, imitate, reproduce, photocopy, redo. [➡COPY AND DUPLICATE; 403]

See Compare and Contrast at **copy**.

replication *n* **repetition**, duplication, imitation, copying, reproduction. [➡REPRESENTATIONS AND GENERAL EXAMPLES; 65]

reply 1 *v* **respond**, answer, retort, answer back, react, rejoin (*formal*), counter, come back with. [➡REPLY AND ANSWER; 669] 2 *n* **response**, account, answer, retort, rejoinder (*formal*), riposte, comeback, reaction. [➡REPLY AND ANSWER; 669]

See Compare and Contrast at **answer.**

report 1 *v* **give an account**, tell, state, describe, give details, testify, convey, inform, recount, relate, narrate. [➡RECITE, REPEAT, AND NARRATE; 621] 2 *v* **register**, check in, present yourself, turn up, show up, arrive. [➡ARRIVE; 12] 3 *n* **tale**, statement, description, testimony, story, account, chronicle, narrative, version. [➡NEUTRAL ONE-WAY COMMUNICATION; 49] 4 *n* **loud noise**, bang, boom, crash, explosion, shot, noise, echo. [➡IMPACT SOUNDS; 1259]

reportage *n* **news coverage**, reporting, coverage, mention, analysis, exposure. [➡NEWSPAPERS; 606]

reportedly *adv* **allegedly**, supposedly, apparently, seemingly, so they say, purportedly (*formal*). [➡UNCERTAIN; 176] *Opposite:* in fact.

reporter *n* **foreign correspondent**, special correspondent, journalist, correspondent, writer, newsperson. [➡WORKERS IN ENTERTAINMENT AND MEDIA; 873]

repose 1 *n* **inactivity**, sleep, rest, relaxation, restfulness, ease, leisure. [➡PERIOD OF REST; 91] *Opposite:* activity. 2 *n* **calmness**, peace, stillness, tranquillity, calm, peacefulness. [➡LACK OF ACTIVITY; 343] *Opposite:* agitation. 3 *v* (*formal*) **relax**, rest, take it easy, recline, put your feet up, lounge, stretch out, lie, lie down. [➡LACK OF ACTIVITY; 343]

reposition *v* **shift**, transpose, move, relocate. [➡POSITION SOMETHING; 326]

repositioning *n* **transposition**, relocation, moving, move. [➡MOVE SOMETHING TO ANOTHER LOCATION; 325]

repository 1 *n* **store**, container, storage area, storage place, receptacle, storeroom, vessel, storehouse, warehouse. [➡STORES AND STORAGE BUILDINGS; 1087] 2 *n* **source**, fountain, mine, fount (*literary*), storehouse, origin. [➡BEGINNING; 53]

repossess *v* **recoup**, take back, reclaim, recover, recuperate, retrieve, recall, get back, regain. [➡REGAIN POSSESSION; 430]

repossession *n* **recovery**, reclamation, retrieval, taking back, seizure, recouping. [➡REGAIN POSSESSION; 430]

repot *v* **transplant**, transfer, replant, pot on, pot up, pot. [➡GROW AND CULTIVATE; 352]

reprehend *v* [➡ACCUSE, BLAME, AND CRITICIZE; 642]

reprehensible *adj* **wrong**, bad, disgraceful, shameful, inexcusable, unacceptable. [➡UNACCEPTABLE AND UNFORGIVEABLE; 226] *Opposite:* praiseworthy.

reprehension *n* **criticism**, censure, condemnation, telling off, admonition, reproof, censoriousness. [➡IRRITATION AND ANGER; 542] *Opposite:* praise.

reprehensive *adj* **condemnatory**, reproachful, accusing, reproving, blameful, critical, censorious. [➡ACCUSATORY AND DISAPPROVING; 635] *Opposite:* praiseworthy.

reprehensively *adv* [➡UNACCEPTABLE AND UNFORGIVEABLE; 226]

represent 1 *v* **act for**, speak for, stand for, stand in for. [➡REPRESENT SOMETHING OR SOMEBODY; 59] 2 *v* **stand for**, symbolize, correspond to, signify, exemplify, characterize, embody, be a symbol of, denote, epitomize. [➡REPRESENT SOMETHING OR SOMEBODY; 59] *Opposite:* misrepresent.

representation 1 *n* **picture**, image, symbol, depiction, illustration, demonstration, sign, exemplification. [➡REPRESENTATIONS AND GENERAL EXAMPLES; 65] 2 *n* **statement**, complaint, submission, argument. [➡CLAIM, INSIST, AND EMPHASIZE; 615] 3 *n* **account**, version, portrayal, description, interpretation, depiction. [➡REPRESENTATIONS AND GENERAL EXAMPLES; 65]

representational *adj* **mimetic**, representative, figurative, depictive, realistic. [➡REPRESENTATIVE; 66] *Opposite:* abstract.

representative 1 *n* **envoy**, delegate, agent, spokesperson, diplomat, commissioner, ambassador. [➡REPRESENTATIVES AND PATRONS; 968] 2 *n* **agent**, courier, rep (*informal*), sales rep (*informal*), delegate, deputy. [➡SUBORDINATES AND ASSISTANTS; 966] 3 *adj* **symbolic**, descriptive, illustrative, evocative, expressive. [➡REPRESENTATIVE; 66] 4 *adj* **illustrative**, typical, characteristic, demonstrative, archetypal. [➡REPRESENTATIVE; 66]

repress 1 *v* **curb**, block, suppress, contain, keep inside, hold back, bottle up, limit, inhibit, stifle, internalize. [➡WITHHOLD INFORMATION; 688] *Opposite:* express. 2 *v* **dominate**, subdue, overpower, subjugate, quell, suppress, crush. [➡CAPTIVITY AND LOSS OF FREEDOM; 249]

repressed 1 *adj* **stifled**, bottled-up, suppressed, blocked, curbed, inhibited. [➡SECRET AND UNKNOWN; 180] *Opposite:* expressed. 2 *adj* **intimidated**, crushed, suppressed, subjugated, overpowered, oppressed. [➡CAPTIVITY AND LOSS OF FREEDOM; 249] *Opposite:* liberated.

repression *n* **suppression**, subjugation, domination, authoritarianism, tyranny, despotism, cruelty, control, oppression. [➡CAPTIVITY AND LOSS OF FREEDOM; 249]

repressive *adj* **oppressive**, suppressive, tyrannical, authoritarian, brutal, cruel, exploitive, despotic. [➡CAPTIVITY AND LOSS OF FREEDOM; 249] *Opposite:* liberal.

reprieve 1 *v* **let off**, pardon, grant a stay of execution, acquit, stay, remit, excuse, liberate. [➡FORGET, FORGIVE, AND ACCEPT; 749] *Opposite:* punish. 2 *n* **official pardon**, stay of execution, amnesty, pardon, acquittal, absolution, exculpation (*formal*), exoneration, stay. [➡TRIAL, PUNISHMENT, AND LEGAL OUTCOMES; 819]

reprimand 1 *v* **chastise** (*formal*), reproach, lecture, scold, chide (*literary*), tell off (*informal*), castigate (*formal*), admonish, reprove, criticize, tick off (*informal*), chew out (*US informal*). [➡ACCUSE, BLAME, AND CRITICIZE; 642] *Opposite:* praise. 2 *n* **rebuke**, admonishment, warning, dressing-down, talking-to (*informal*), slap on the wrist (*informal*), ticking-off (*informal*), reproof, lecture, telling off, scolding. [➡CRITICISMS AND ANGRY OUTBURSTS; 50]

reprint 1 *v* **reissue**, print again, publish again, produce again, republish, reproduce, recopy, redistribute. [➡COPY AND DUPLICATE; 403] 2 *n* **reissue**, copy, edition, new copy, new edition, new version. [➡COPIES AND REPLICAS; 152]

reprisal *n* **retaliation**, revenge, act of vengeance, punishment, payback. [➡VENGEANCE AND REVENGE; 686]

reprise 1 *n* **reappearance**, echo, recap, repeat, repetition, return, recurrence. [➡NOTES AND CHORDS; 909] 2 *v* **repeat**, reinterpret, re-enact, re-present. [➡RECOMMENCE AND RESUME; 269]

reproach 1 *v* **admonish**, accuse, reprove, criticize, scold, rebuke, reprimand, blame, point the finger at, chide (*literary*). [➡ACCUSE, BLAME, AND CRITICIZE; 642] *Opposite:* praise. 2 *n* **criticism**, censure, reprimand, blame, accusation, reproof, rebuke, scolding. [➡CRITICISMS AND ANGRY OUTBURSTS; 50] *Opposite:* praise.

reproachful *adj* **censorious**, accusing, disapproving, reproving, critical, judgmental, faultfinding. [➡ACCUSATORY AND DISAPPROVING; 635] *Opposite:* approving.

reproachfulness *n* [➡ANTAGONISM; 553]

reprobate *n* **degenerate**, rascal, troublemaker, ne'er-do-well (*dated*), sinner, wrongdoer. [➡VILLAINS AND THUGS; 947]

reprocess *v* **process again**, reuse, recycle, recover, reclaim, salvage. [➡MAKE GOOD USE OF SOMETHING; 474]

reproduce 1 *v* **copy**, replicate, duplicate, repeat, imitate, mimic, clone, re-create. [➡COPY AND DUPLICATE; 403] 2 *v* **have children**, produce offspring, produce young, breed, give birth, procreate, produce. [➡REPRODUCTION AND HEREDITY; 726]

See Compare and Contrast at **copy**.

reproduction 1 *n* **copy**, imitation, replica, duplicate, facsimile, model. [➡COPIES AND REPLICAS; 152] *Opposite:* original. 2 *n* **breeding**, procreation, propagation, generation, multiplication. [➡REPRODUCTION AND HEREDITY; 726] 3 *adj* **imitation**, replica, fake, faux. [➡FALSE AND UNREAL; 174] *Opposite:* genuine.

reproductive *adj* **generative**, multiplicative, procreative, procreant, propagative. [➡REPRODUCTION AND HEREDITY; 726]

reproductive cell *n* [➡EGGS AND SPAWN; 728]

reproof *n* **criticism**, blame, accusation, rebuke, scolding, reprimand, telling off, ticking-off (*informal*), dressing-down, admonition, chastisement (*formal*). [➡CRITICISMS AND ANGRY OUTBURSTS; 50] *Opposite:* compliment.

reprove *v* **criticize**, take to task, accuse, rebuke, scold, reprimand, tell off (*informal*), tick off (*informal*), admonish, haul over the coals, chide (*literary*), reproach, chastise (*formal*). [➡ACCUSE, BLAME, AND CRITICIZE; 642]

reproving *adj* **disapproving**, condemnatory, reproachful, admonitory, censorious, withering, contemptuous, critical. [➡ACCUSATORY AND DISAPPROVING; 635] *Opposite:* approving.

reptile

◆ *types of reptile*
alligator, basilisk, bearded dragon, cayman, chameleon, crocodile, gecko, gila monster, glass snake, goanna, horned lizard, iguana, Komodo dragon, lizard, moloch, monitor lizard, mugger, skink, slowworm, terrapin, tortoise, turtle

reptilian *adj* **cold-blooded**, unfriendly, emotionless, inhuman, stony, cold. [➡BEASTLY AND BRUTISH; 511] *Opposite:* warm.

republic *n* **state**, nation, democracy. [➡COUNTRIES AND REGIONS; 1066] *Opposite:* monarchy.

republican 1 *n* **democrat**, antiroyalist, antimonarchist. [➡POLITICAL OFFICES AND POLITICIANS; 808] *Opposite:* monarchist. 2 *adj* **pro-republic**, democrat, antiroyalist, antimonarchist. [➡STYLES AND SYSTEMS OF GOVERNMENT; 806] *Opposite:* monarchist.

republicanism *n* **antimonarchism**, antiroyalism, political belief. [➡STYLES AND SYSTEMS OF GOVERNMENT; 806] *Opposite:* monarchism.

repudiate *v* **reject**, disclaim, renounce, deny, not accept, rebut, retract, disavow (*formal*), turn your back on, wash your hands of. [➡DENY AND REJECT; 645] *Opposite:* acknowledge.

repudiation 1 *n* **refutation**, retraction, disavowal (*formal*), renunciation, rejection. [➡DENY AND REJECT; 645] *Opposite:* acknowledgment. 2 *n* **denial**, refutation, negation, disclaimer, rejection, abandonment, refusal, disallowance. [➡DENY AND REJECT; 645] *Opposite:* acceptance.

repugnance *n* **disgust**, revulsion, hatred, dislike, hate, abhorrence, repulsion, loathing, aversion. [➡DISLIKE AND HATE; 578] *Opposite:* attraction.

See Compare and Contrast at **dislike**.

repugnant 1 *adj* **offensive**, objectionable, distasteful, unacceptable, obnoxious, obscene, shocking. [➡DISGUSTING AND REPULSIVE; 231] *Opposite:* agreeable. 2 *adj* **disgusting**, revolting, nauseating, repulsive, hideous, gross (*slang*), vile, foul, abhorrent (*formal*), repellent, loathsome, abominable, sickening. [➡DISGUSTING AND REPULSIVE; 231] *Opposite:* attractive.

repulse 1 *v* **repel**, drive away, force away, hold back, hold off, ward off, resist, deter, force back, fight off, keep at bay, drive back. [➡AVOID OR ESCAPE CONTACT; 419] *Opposite:* yield. 2 *v* **reject**, rebuff, resist, spurn, snub, turn away. [➡REFUSING OR REJECTING RELATIONS; 975] *Opposite:* welcome.

repulsed *adj* **disgusted**, nauseated, revolted, repelled, sickened. [➡IRRITATION AND ANGER; 542] *Opposite:* attracted.

repulsion *n* **disgust**, revulsion, nausea, loathing, repugnance, dislike, abhorrence. [➡DISLIKE AND HATE; 578] *Opposite:* attraction.

repulsive *adj* **disgusting**, revolting, nauseating, hideous, gross (*slang*), vile, foul, abhorrent (*formal*), repellent, stomach-turning. [➡DISGUSTING AND REPULSIVE; 231] *Opposite:* attractive.

repulsiveness *n* **revoltingness**, hideousness, repugnance, foulness, abhorrence, vileness, grossness, offensiveness. [➡DISGUSTING AND REPULSIVE; 231] *Opposite:* attractiveness.

reputable *adj* **of good repute** (*formal*), highly regarded, trustworthy, well-thought-of, sound, upright, honest, decent, dependable, reliable, respectable, of good standing. [➡ADMIRABLE AND COMMENDABLE; 186] *Opposite:* disreputable.

reputation *n* **standing**, status, name, repute (*formal*), character. [➡STATUS; 888]

repute (*formal*) *n* **standing**, status, name, reputation, character. [➡STATUS; 888]

reputed *adj* **supposed**, alleged, presumed, apparent, believed, fabled. [➡UNCERTAIN; 176] *Opposite:* actual.

request 1 *v* **ask for**, demand, apply for, call for, entreat (*formal*), invite, wish, bid (*archaic*). [➡REQUEST AND DEMAND; 664] 2 *n* **appeal**, call, demand, application, entreaty, invitation, wish, bid. [➡REQUEST AND DEMAND; 664]

requiem 1 *n* **service**, Mass, funeral, funeral Mass, service for the dead. [➡RELIGIONS AND RELIGIOUS PRACTICES; 778] 2 *n* **funeral music**, lament, dirge, funeral hymn, funeral song. [➡MUSIC, SONGS, AND SINGING; 907]

require 1 *v* **need**, necessitate, want, have need of, entail, involve, call for. [➡NEED AND REQUIRE; 465] 2 *v* **oblige**, compel, demand, expect, force, make, command. [➡CAUSE OR COMPEL TO ACT; 272]

required *adj* **necessary**, obligatory, compulsory, mandatory, essential, vital, prerequisite, requisite (*formal*). [➡NECESSARY AND ESSENTIAL; 197] *Opposite:* optional.

requirement *n* **obligation**, condition, requisite (*formal*), prerequisite, must, necessity, constraint. [➡NECESSARY AND ESSENTIAL; 197] *Opposite:* option.

requisite (*formal*) *adj* **necessary**, mandatory, vital, essential, indispensable, basic, required, obligatory, prerequisite, called for. [➡NECESSARY AND ESSENTIAL; 197] *Opposite:* optional.

See Compare and Contrast at **necessary**.

requisition 1 *n* **demand**, request, application, summons. [➡REQUEST AND DEMAND; 664] 2 *v* **take over**, commandeer, seize, take possession of, appropriate, occupy. [➡TAKE SOMETHING AWAY; 426] *Opposite:* relinquish. 3 *v* **demand**, apply for, call for, request, put in for, summons. [➡REQUEST AND DEMAND; 664]

reread *v* **revise**, revisit, look back over, check through, go through, read again, come back to, review. [➡READ; 759]

rerun 1 *v* **replay**, repeat, play again, air again, show again. [➡TELEVISION AND RADIO; 607] 2 *n* **repeat**, repeat showing, replay. [➡TELEVISION AND RADIO; 607]

reschedule *v* **postpone**, rearrange, defer, reorganize, suspend, carry over. [➡DELAY ACTION OR OCCURRENCE; 279] *Opposite:* bring forward.

rescheduling *n* **postponement**, deferment, putting off, rearrangement, rearranging, reorganizing. [➡DELAY ACTION OR OCCURRENCE; 279]

rescind *v* **withdraw**, annul, cancel, repeal, overturn, quash, void, retract, revoke, make null and void. [➡ABOLISH AND ANNUL; 453] *Opposite:* authorize.

rescue 1 *v* **save**, free, set free, liberate, release, salvage, let go. [➡FREEDOM AND LIBERTY; 209] *Opposite:* abandon. 2 *n* **release**, liberation, saving, salvage. [➡FREEDOM AND LIBERTY; 209]

rescuer *n* **saviour**, champion, liberator, salvation, Redeemer. [➡SUPPORTERS, PROTECTORS, AND COMPATRIOTS; 970]

research 1 *n* **investigation**, study, exploration, examination, enquiries. [➡EXAMINE AND ASSESS; 754] 2 *v* **investigate**, study, explore, do research, delve into, examine, make enquiries, follow a line of investigation, seek, look into, make inquiries. [➡EXAMINE AND ASSESS; 754]

researcher *n* **investigator**, academic, scholar, scientist, student, assistant. [➡STUDENTS AND PUPILS; 841]

resemblance *n* **similarity**, likeness, semblance, similitude (*formal*), sameness, alikeness, closeness. [➡SIMILARITY; 149] *Opposite:* difference.

resemble *v* **look like**, bear a resemblance to, be similar to, be like, look a lot like, remind you of, take after, bring to mind, seem like, smack of. [➡SEEM TO BE SOMETHING; 58] *Opposite:* differ.

resembling *adj* **like**, similar to, not unlike, close to, reminiscent of, bordering on, approaching, in the vein of, approximating, akin to. [➡SIMILARITY; 149]

resent 1 *v* **begrudge**, bear a grudge, feel bitter about, have hard feelings about, feel aggrieved. [➡DISLIKE AND HATE; 578] *Opposite:* accept. 2 *v* **dislike**, not like, hate, be offended by, show antipathy towards, take exception to, rail against. [➡DISLIKE AND HATE; 578] *Opposite:* like.

resentful *adj* **angry**, bitter, indignant, offended, aggrieved, annoyed, insulted. [➡IRRITATION AND ANGER; 542]

resentfulness *n* [➡ENVY AND JEALOUSY; 549]

resentment *n* **anger**, bitterness, dislike, hatred, antipathy, offence, umbrage, bile (*literary*). [➡FEELINGS ABOUT THE PAST; 533]

reservation 1 *n* **advance booking**, booking, registration, reserved seat, arrangement, reserved table, reserved room, reserved ticket. [➡BUSINESS ACTIVITIES AND PHENOMENA; 795] 2 *n* **reserve**, protected area, game park, game reserve, preserve (*US*), sanctuary, wildlife santcuary, wildlife refuge, refuge, park. [➡THE COUNTRYSIDE AND OUTDOOR SPACES; 1070] 3 *n* **unwillingness**, reluctance, hesitation, distance, aloofness, formality, reserve, shyness, coolness, detachment, coldness, diffidence. [➡UNFRIENDLINESS AND UNSOCIABILITY; 505] *Opposite:* enthusiasm. 4 *n* **condition**, proviso, rider, corollary, stipulation. [➡NECESSARY AND ESSENTIAL; 197]

reservations *n* **misgivings**, doubts, hesitation, questions, uncertainties, difficulties, issues, objections. [➡UNCERTAINTY; 560]

reserve 1 *v* **set aside**, keep, keep back, hold back, put to one side, store, salt away, hoard, stockpile, save, stash, preserve. [➡STORE AND KEEP; 454] *Opposite:* use. 2 *v* **book**, retain, put your name down for, make a reservation. [➡LEND, LEASE, AND BORROW; 429] *Opposite:* cancel. 3 *n* **store**, cache, hoard, stock, emergency supply, supply, stockpile, stash (*informal*). [➡COLLECTIONS AND MIXTURES OF THINGS; 1243] 4 *n* **reservation**, park, game park, protected area, game reserve, sanctuary, wildlife sanctuary, wildlife refuge, preserve (*US*). [➡THE COUNTRYSIDE AND OUTDOOR SPACES; 1070] 5 *n* **substitute**, stand-in, locum, extra, fallback, replacement, alternate (*US*). [➡COLLEAGUES AND EQUALS; 967]

reserved 1 *adj* **booked**, retained, taken, engaged. [➡ABSENT AND UNAVAILABLE; 7] *Opposite:* free. 2 *adj* **earmarked**, kept, set aside, held in reserve, kept back. [➡ABSENT AND UNAVAILABLE; 7] *Opposite:* used. 3 *adj* **aloof**, reticent, standoffish, snobbish, distant, unfriendly, cold, detached, cool, shy, diffident. [➡UNFRIENDLINESS AND UNSOCIABILITY; 505] *Opposite:* outgoing.

reservedly *adv* **diffidently**, quietly, reticently, timidly, warily, bashfully, coyly. [➡RETICENT AND UNFORTHCOMING; 632] *Opposite:* demonstratively.

reserves 1 *n* **assets**, funds, contingency fund, financial resources, capital, investments, cash, monies (*formal*), nest egg, stash (*informal*), money. [➡MONEY, PAYMENTS, AND CHARGES; 800] 2 *n* **stocks**, supplies, hoard, resources, stores. [➡FINANCIAL ASSETS; 463]

reservist *n* **soldier**, reserve, reserve member, part-time soldier, Territorial. [➡MILITARY PERSONNEL; 828]

reservoir *n* **tank**, pool, basin, lake, artificial lake. [➡RIVERS, LAKES, AND STREAMS; 1042]

reset *v* **rearrange**, reorganize, retune, change, right, set something to rights. [➡CHANGE; 373]

resettle *v* **relocate**, transfer, transplant, emigrate, immigrate, migrate, move, shift. [➡MOVE SOMETHING TO ANOTHER LOCATION; 325]

resettlement *n* **relocation**, immigration, emigration, migration, transfer, transplantation, movement. [➡MOVE SOMETHING TO ANOTHER LOCATION; 325]

reshape *v* **redesign**, reform, rewrite, restructure, reformat, restyle, remodel, remake. [➡CHANGE; 373]

reshuffle 1 *n* **reorganization**, rearrangement, rationalization, reallocation, reordering, restructuring. [➡ARRANGE AND CREATE ORDER; 358] 2 *v* **reorganize**, rearrange, rationalize, reallocate, reorder, restructure, change. [➡ARRANGE AND CREATE ORDER; 358]

reside 1 *v* **live**, live in, inhabit, dwell (*literary*), have your home, be a resident of. [➡INHABIT; 20] 2 *v* **exist in**, be inherent in, be located in, be a feature of, be present in, be vested in, belong to. [➡EXIST IN A PLACE; 19]

residence *n* **house**, home, dwelling (*formal*), abode (*literary*), seat, habitation. [➡ACCOMMODATION; 855]

residency *n* **placement**, position, job, post, internship. [➡JOB; 833]

resident *n* **occupant**, inhabitant, denizen, tenant, occupier, dweller (*literary*). [➡INHABITANT; 857]

residential *adj* **domestic**, suburban, housing, domiciliary. [➡HUMAN SETTLEMENTS; 1069] *Opposite:* business.

residential area *n* [➡HUMAN SETTLEMENTS; 1069]

residential care *n* [➡HOSPITALS AND CLINICS; 826]

residential home *n* [➡HOSPITALS AND CLINICS; 826]

residual *adj* **left over**, remaining, lingering, left behind, outstanding, lasting, enduring. [➡MORE AND EXCESS; 122]

residue *n* **remains**, remainder, rest, deposit, scum, lees, dregs, filtrate, excess. [➡UNPLEASANT AND DIRTY SUBSTANCES; 1267]

resign *v* **leave**, leave your job, quit, walk out, give notice, hand in your notice, give up your job, step down. [➡WORK-RELATED ACTIVITIES; 834] *Opposite:* sign on.

resignation 1 *n* **notice**, notification, letter of resignation. [➡LETTERS AND WRITTEN MESSAGES; 585] 2 *n* **acceptance**, acquiescence, acknowledgment, submission, forbearance (*formal*). [➡FEELINGS ABOUT THE PAST; 533] *Opposite:* defiance.

resigned *adj* **reconciled**, accepting, acquiescent, submissive, stoic, fatalistic, long-suffering, forbearing (*formal*). [➡THE WILL AND WILLINGNESS; 564] *Opposite:* resistant.

resignedly *adv* **reluctantly**, long-sufferingly, stoically, with a sigh, wearily, despairingly, unenthusiastically, tiredly. [➡WITHOUT ENTHUSIASM; 288] *Opposite:* enthusiastically.

resign yourself *v* **accept**, acknowledge, give in to, yield to, reconcile yourself, come to terms. [➡FORGET, FORGIVE, AND ACCEPT; 749] *Opposite:* resist.

resilience 1 *n* **pliability**, flexibility, elasticity, suppleness, bounciness, springiness. [➡DURABLE; 1209] *Opposite:* rigidity. 2 *n* **buoyancy**, spirit, hardiness, toughness, resistance, strength. [➡STRENGTH OF WILL; 502] *Opposite:* defeatism.

resilient 1 *adj* **hardy**, strong, tough, robust, buoyant, irrepressible, spirited, resistant. [➡STRENGTH OF WILL; 502] *Opposite:* defeatist. 2 *adj* **elastic**, pliable, flexible, supple, resistant, tough, durable, sturdy. [➡DURABLE; 1209] *Opposite:* rigid.

resiliently *adv* **buoyantly**, robustly, irrepressibly, spiritedly, sturdily, stoutly. [➡STRENGTH OF WILL; 502] *Opposite:* feebly.

resin *n* **mastic**, gum, balm, kauri gum, gamboge, dammar, pitch, tolu. [➡PARTS OF TREES AND PLANTS; 1026]

resinous *adj* **sticky**, viscous, tacky, gummy. [➡PHYSICAL TEXTURE; 1221]

resist 1 *v* **fight**, battle, struggle, fight back, attack, counterattack, repel. [➡COMPETE, CONTEND, AND COMBAT; 304] *Opposite:* surrender. 2 *v* **oppose**, defy, stand firm, contest, challenge, forbear (*formal*). [➡ACCUSE, BLAME, AND CRITICIZE; 642] *Opposite:* accept. 3 *v* **withstand**, survive, endure, weather, be proof against. [➡TOLERATE AND ENDURE; 767] *Opposite:* succumb. 4 *v* **keep from**, avoid, refuse, refrain, withstand, abstain. [➡NOT DO AND REFUSE TO DO; 275] *Opposite:* give in.

resistance 1 *n* **confrontation**, fight, battle, fighting, struggle, conflict, opposition. [➡UNWILLINGNESS AND STUBBORNNESS; 565] *Opposite:* surrender. 2 *n* **opposition**, defiance, challenge, endurance, forbearance (*formal*). [➡REBELLIOUSNESS AND DISOBEDIENCE; 566] *Opposite:* acceptance.

resistant 1 *adj* **opposed**, dead set against, anti (*informal*), unwilling, defiant, challenging, opposing. [➡REBELLIOUSNESS AND DISOBEDIENCE; 566] *Opposite:* accepting. 2 *adj* **resilient**, hardy, unaffected, impervious, tough, strong, sturdy. [➡STRENGTH; 202] *Opposite:* weak.

resistor *n* **device**, controller, regulator, rheostat. [➡ELECTRONICS AND ELECTRICS; 1136]

resit 1 *n* **retake**, re-examination, re-test, repeat. [➡LESSONS, COURSE WORK, AND EXAMINATIONS; 842] 2 *v* **take again**, retake, repeat, sit again. [➡RECOMMENCE AND RESUME; 269]

resolute *adj* **firm**, staunch, unyielding, stubborn,

unbendable, definite, determined, unwavering, steadfast, tenacious, persevering, purposeful. [➡CERTAINTY; 562] *Opposite:* irresolute.

resoluteness *n* **firmness**, determination, steadfastness, staunchness, single-mindedness, sense of purpose, confidence, stubbornness, decisiveness. [➡STRENGTH OF WILL; 502] *Opposite:* indecisiveness.

resolution 1 *n* **decree**, declaration, decision, motion, ruling. [➡MAKE DECISIONS AND CHOICES; 753] 2 *n* **promise**, pledge, oath, vow. [➡PROMISE AND ASSURE; 685] 3 *n* **resolve**, determination, steadfastness, tenacity, firmness, perseverance, doggedness, purpose. [➡STRENGTH OF WILL; 502] *Opposite:* indecision. 4 *n* **solution**, answer, end, upshot, outcome. [➡SOLUTION; 216]

resolve 1 *v* **make up your mind**, decide, determine, make a decision, undertake, agree. [➡MAKE DECISIONS AND CHOICES; 753] 2 *v* **solve**, come to a decision, get to the bottom of, sort out, put an end to, settle, answer, work out. [➡SOLVE AND INTERPRET; 761] 3 *n* **resolution**, determination, steadfastness, tenacity, doggedness, firmness. [➡STRENGTH OF WILL; 502] *Opposite:* indecision.

resolved *adj* **determined**, set, resolute, fixed, committed. [➡CERTAINTY; 562] *Opposite:* undecided.

resonance 1 *n* **timbre**, character, quality, tone, reverberation, echo. [➡SOFT OR PLEASANT SOUNDS; 1264] 2 *n* **significance**, meaning, importance, suggestion, echo, hint, reverberation, reminiscence. [➡MEANING; 691]

resonant 1 *adj* **booming**, ringing, echoing, reverberating, resounding, deep, rich. [➡LOUD OR UNPLEASANT SOUNDS; 1265] *Opposite:* tinny. 2 *adj* **significant**, meaningful, important, evocative, indicative, reminiscent. [➡IMPORTANT; 195] *Opposite:* insignificant.

resonate *v* **reverberate**, vibrate, resound, ring, echo, boom. [➡EMIT RINGING AND TOOTING SOUNDS; 368]

resonating *adj* [➡LOUD OR UNPLEASANT SOUNDS; 1265]

resort *n* **option**, recourse, alternative, course of action, possibility, choice, help. [➡MAKE DECISIONS AND CHOICES; 753]

resort to *v* **turn to**, give in to, have recourse to, fall back on, avail yourself of, employ, make use of, use. [➡USE; 468]

resound *v* **echo**, resonate, boom, ring, reverberate. [➡SOUND EMISSION; 363]

resounding 1 *adj* **loud**, booming, echoing, ringing, resonant, reverberating, deep, rich. [➡LOUD OR UNPLEASANT SOUNDS; 1265] *Opposite:* weak. 2 *adj* **unqualified**, categorical, unambiguous, definite, unquestionable, decisive. [➡CERTAIN; 175] *Opposite:* qualified.

resource *n* **reserve**, supply, source, means, store. [➡COLLECTIONS AND MIXTURES OF THINGS; 1243]

resourceful *adj* **ingenious**, imaginative, inventive, practical, quick-witted, creative, capable. [➡POSITIVE INTELLECTUAL CHARACTERISTICS; 525] *Opposite:* unimaginative.

resourcefulness *n* **ingenuity**, imagination, inventiveness, wits, originality, creativity. [➡POSITIVE INTELLECTUAL CHARACTERISTICS; 525]

resources *n* **capital**, income, possessions, wealth, property, funds, assets, wherewithal, means. [➡FINANCIAL ASSETS; 463]

respect 1 *n* **admiration**, high opinion, deference, esteem, reverence, veneration. [➡LOVE, RESPECT, AND GOODWILL; 550] *Opposite:* disrespect. 2 *n* **detail**, regard, matter, particular, point, way, sense, manner, characteristic. [➡SUBJECT AREA; 769] 3 *v* **value**, revere, think a lot of, esteem, defer to, have a high opinion of, look up to, admire, venerate. [➡LIKE, LOVE, VALUE, AND ENJOY; 579] *Opposite:* disrespect. 4 *v* **show consideration for**, appreciate, regard, have a high regard for, recognize, pay attention to. [➡PAY ATTENTION; 766] *Opposite:* disregard. 5 *v* **follow**, abide by, comply with, obey, acknowledge, accept. [➡OBEY AND ABIDE BY; 302] *Opposite:* deny.

See Compare and Contrast at **regard**.

respectability *n* **decency**, propriety, uprightness, decorum, morality. [➡MORALLY GOOD; 775] *Opposite:* indecency.

respectable 1 *adj* **reputable**, highly regarded, well-thought-of, decent, good, upright, proper, suitable. [➡ADMIRABLE AND COMMENDABLE; 186] *Opposite:* disreputable. 2 *adj* **adequate**, decent, reasonable, acceptable, satisfactory, fair. [➡ACCEPTABLE AND PASSABLE; 220] *Opposite:* inadequate.

respected *adj* **reliable**, authoritative, distinguished, venerable, esteemed, valued, appreciated, prized (*US*). [➡POPULAR AND WANTED; 221]

respectful *adj* **deferential**, reverential, reverent, humble, dutiful. [➡GOOD MANNERS AND SOCIAL SKILLS; 521] *Opposite:* disrespectful.

respectfulness *n* **deference**, respect, consideration, regard, honour, veneration. [➡LOVE, RESPECT, AND GOODWILL; 550] *Opposite:* contemptuousness.

respecting *prep* **with regard to**, regarding, with respect to, in respect of, relating to, about, concerning. [➡EXPRESSIONS OF REFERENCE; 63]

respective *adj* **own**, individual, particular, separate, corresponding, one-to-one. [➡BELONGING OR RELATING TO INDIVIDUALS; 944]

respects *n* **compliments**, good wishes, greetings, salutations (*formal*). [➡PRAISE AND ENCOURAGE; 648]

respiration *n* **breathing**, inhalation, exhalation. [➡BREATHE AND NOT BREATHE; 717]

respirator *n* **breathing apparatus**, ventilator, gas mask, oxygen mask. [➡BREATHE AND NOT BREATHE; 717]

respiratory *adj* **breathing**, lung, respirational. [➡BREATHE AND NOT BREATHE; 717]

respiratory

◆ *parts of a respiratory system*
trachea, throat, air sac, airway, alveolus, bronchial tube, bronchiole, bronchus, larynx, lung, pharynx, vocal cords, voice box, windpipe

respire *v* **breathe**, take breaths, inhale, exhale. [➡BREATHE AND NOT BREATHE; 717]

respite 1 *n* **interval**, break, breather (*informal*), breathing space, lull, relief, let-up (*informal*), breathing room. [➡PERIOD OF REST; 91] 2 *n* **reprieve**, delay, adjournment, hiatus, break, postponement. [➡PAUSES AND PHASES; 56]

resplendent *adj* **splendid**, dazzling, magnificent, glorious, brilliant, stunning, glittering, impressive. [➡BEAUTY AND ATTRACTIVENESS; 190] *Opposite:* unimpressive.

respond 1 *v* **reply**, answer, retort, answer back, rejoin, return. [➡REPLY AND ANSWER; 669] 2 *v* **react**, act in response, take action, counter, act, act on. [➡CARRY OUT AN ACTION; 270] *Opposite:* ignore.

respondent *n* **defendant**, accused, plaintiff. [➡PEOPLE IN LAW COURTS; 820]

response *n* **reply**, answer, retort, onus, rejoinder (*formal*), comeback, reaction, riposte. [➡REPLY AND ANSWER; 669]

See Compare and Contrast at **answer**.

responsibility 1 *n* **accountability**, duty, charge, concern, obligation, bond, restraint. [➡RESPONSIBILITY; 171] 2 *n* **blame**, onus, liability, guilt, answerability, fault. [➡RESPONSIBILITY; 171] 3 *n* **task**, remit, brief, assignment, concern, job, commission. [➡WORK IN GENERAL; 298]

responsible 1 *adj* **accountable**, in charge, in control, in authority, answerable. [➡RESPONSIBILITY; 171] 2 *adj* **to blame**, liable, guilty, at fault, blamable. [➡MORALLY BAD; 776] 3 *adj* **dependable**, conscientious, trustworthy, reliable, sensible, mature. [➡HONEST AND RELIABLE; 503] *Opposite:* irresponsible.

responsibly *adv* **sensibly**, correctly, dutifully, dependably, reliably, maturely, conscientiously. [➡HONEST AND RELIABLE; 503] *Opposite:* irresponsibly.

responsive *adj* **receptive**, open, approachable, reactive, quick to respond, alert. [➡FRIENDLINESS AND SOCIABILITY; 495] *Opposite:* sluggish.

responsively *adv* **quickly**, quick-wittedly, instinctively, rapidly, swiftly, instantaneously. [➡HAPPENING QUICKLY; 104] *Opposite:* sluggishly.

responsiveness *n* **receptiveness**, openness, reaction, sensitivity, awareness, approachability, alertness. [➡FRIENDLINESS AND SOCIABILITY; 495] *Opposite:* sluggishness.

rest 1 *n* **break**, respite, breather (*informal*), time out, relaxation, recreation, cessation, repose. [➡PERIOD OF REST; 91] 2 *n* **remainder**, residue, leftovers, remnants, surplus, balance, excess. [➡REMAINDER AND REMAINDERS; 123] 3 *n* **stand**, support, holder, rack, frame. [➡SUPPORTS AND BASES; 1254] 4 *v* **relax**, take it easy, have a rest, take a break, have a break, put your feet up, repose, sleep. [➡LACK OF ACTIVITY; 343] 5 *v* **lie**, lean, lay, place, put, support, uphold. [➡MOVE SOMETHING: INTO A NEW POSITION OR OVERTURN; 331]

restart 1 *v* **resume**, take up, start again, pick up, start over (*US*). [➡RECOMMENCE AND RESUME; 269] 2 *v* **revive**, resurrect, save, renew, reopen, regenerate. [➡CAUSE TO HAPPEN; 31] *Opposite:* wind down.

restate *v* **repeat**, reaffirm, reiterate, say again, regurgitate, paraphrase, iterate. [➡RECITE, REPEAT, AND NARRATE; 621]

restaurant *n* [➡HOTELS, RESTAURANTS, AND CLUBS; 1081]

restaurant

◆ *types of eating place*
bistro, brasserie, café, cafeteria, canteen, coffee bar, coffee shop, commons, diner, dining hall, eatery, greasy spoon, hole-in-the-wall (*informal*), hostelry (*archaic or humorous*), luncheonette (*US*), lunchroom (*US*), mess, mess hall, pizzeria, roadside café, self-service restaurant, snack bar, steakhouse, tearoom, transport café, trattoria, truck stop (*US*)

restaurant car *part of* **train**. [➡RAILWAYS; 1106]

rested *adj* **refreshed**, relaxed, restored, reinvigorated, revitalized, raring to go. [➡FIT AND STRONG; 737] *Opposite:* exhausted.

restful *adj* **soothing**, relaxing, soporific, calming, peaceful, quiet. [➡CALMING; 189] *Opposite:* stimulating.

restfulness *n* [➡CALMING; 189]

rest home *n* [➡HOSPITALS AND CLINICS; 826]

resting place *n* [➡BURIAL PLACES AND ACCESSORIES; 930]

restitution 1 *n* **compensation**, recompense, reimbursement, amends, repayment, refund. [➡REWARDS AND AWARDS; 440] 2 *n* **restoration**, return, reinstatement, compensation. [➡REGAIN POSSESSION; 430]

restive *adj* **restless**, fidgety, twitchy (*informal*), agitated, edgy, impatient, on edge, uneasy. [➡POSITIVE IMPATIENCE, ENTHUSIASM, AND ALERTNESS; 538] *Opposite:* calm.

restiveness *n* **restlessness**, impatience, agitation, edginess, nervousness, uneasiness. [➡POSITIVE IMPATIENCE, ENTHUSIASM, AND ALERTNESS; 538] *Opposite:* calmness.

restless *adj* **fidgety**, restive, twitchy (*informal*), agitated, edgy, impatient, on edge. [➡POSITIVE IMPATIENCE, ENTHUSIASM, AND ALERTNESS; 538] *Opposite:* relaxed.

restlessness *n* **agitation**, impatience, restiveness, edginess, anxiety, disquiet. [➡POSITIVE IMPATIENCE, ENTHUSIASM, AND ALERTNESS; 538] *Opposite:* calmness.

restock *v* **refill**, replenish, top up, fill up, replace, top off (*US*). [➡FILL; 407]

rest on *v* **hinge on**, turn on, depend on, rely, hang on, pend. [➡BE ABOUT SOMETHING; 62]

restoration 1 *n* **reinstatement**, re-establishment, return, restitution, reinstallation. [➡CONFER STATUS; 459] *Opposite:* abolition. 2 *n* **refurbishment**, renovation, repair, renewal, rebuilding. [➡REPAIR AND MEND; 377]

restorative *adj* **healing**, uplifting, invigorating, soothing, recuperative, curative. [➡CALMING; 189] *Opposite:* draining.

restore 1 *v* **reinstate**, re-establish, bring back, return, give back. [➡INSTITUTE AND INAUGURATE; 349] 2 *v* **refurbish**, renovate, repair, do up, rebuild, recondition, touch up, fix, fix up. [➡REPAIR AND MEND; 377]

See Compare and Contrast at **renew**.

restrain 1 *v* **hold back**, prevent, stop, keep, deter, inhibit, forestall. [➡AVOID, PREVENT, LIMIT, AND CONTROL; 278] 2 *v* **control**, bring under control, keep under control, keep in check, check, curtail, limit, restrict, stem, contain. [➡AVOID, PREVENT, LIMIT, AND CONTROL; 278] 3 *v* **confine**, detain, jail, lock up, imprison, put away. [➡CAPTIVITY AND LOSS OF FREEDOM; 249] *Opposite:* free.

restrained *adj* **reserved**, controlled, in control of yourself, self-possessed, calm, unemotional, undemonstrative, nonaggressive. [➡RETICENT AND UNFORTHCOMING; 632] *Opposite:* demonstrative.

restraining order *n* **injunction**, court order, gagging order, stay, gag order (*US*). [➡TRIAL, PUNISHMENT, AND LEGAL OUTCOMES; 819]

restraint 1 *n* **self-control**, control, command, self-possession, self-discipline, moderation. [➡CONFIDENCE AND COMPOSURE; 500] *Opposite:* self-indulgence. 2 *n* **limit**, limitation, curb, ceiling, restriction, control, check. [➡CAPTIVITY AND LOSS OF FREEDOM; 249] 3 *n* **captivity**, arrest, imprisonment, confinement, detention. [➡CAPTIVITY AND LOSS OF FREEDOM; 249] *Opposite:* freedom. 4 *n* **belt**, chain, shackle, fetter, bond, attachment. [➡FASTENERS, LINKS, AND NETWORKS; 1246]

restrict *v* **limit**, confine, put a ceiling on, curb, control, contain, hamper, hold back, constrain, impede, inhibit, keep a tight rein on, check, constrict, cramp. [➡AVOID, PREVENT, LIMIT, AND CONTROL; 278] *Opposite:* loosen.

restricted 1 *adj* **limited**, controlled, constrained, delimited (*formal*), circumscribed (*formal*), regulated. [➡CAPTIVITY AND LOSS OF FREEDOM; 249] *Opposite:* open. 2 *adj* **classified**, top-secret, secret, confidential, privileged. [➡SECRET AND UNKNOWN; 180] *Opposite:* public.

restriction *n* **limit**, constraint, restraint, control, ceiling, curb, limitation, check. [➡CAPTIVITY AND LOSS OF FREEDOM; 249]

restrictive *adj* **preventive**, obstructive, limiting, deterring, restraining, constricting, cramping, holding back, restricting, hampering, off-putting. [➡CAPTIVITY AND LOSS OF FREEDOM; 249] *Opposite:* free.

rest room *type of* **room in a public building**. [➡TYPES OF ROOM; 1096]

restructure *v* **rearrange**, reorganize, reform, reshuffle, redistribute, streamline. [➡ARRANGE AND CREATE ORDER; 358]

restructuring *n* **rearrangement**, reorganization, shake-up, reform, reshuffle, streamlining, reformation. [➡ARRANGE AND CREATE ORDER; 358]

rest up *v* [➡LACK OF ACTIVITY; 343]

result 1 *n* **consequence**, outcome, upshot, effect, product, end result, end. [➡RESULTS AND OUTCOMES; 83] 2 *n* **mark**, grade, score, outcome. [➡SCORES AND EVALUATIONS; 599] 3 *n* **calculation**, solution, answer, findings, conclusion. [➡SOLUTION; 216] 4 *v* **cause**, bring about, give rise to, occasion, lead to. [➡CAUSE TO HAPPEN; 31] 5 *v* **ensue**, be caused by, stem, rise, be brought about by, develop, follow. [➡HAPPEN; 27]

resultant *adj* **subsequent**, ensuing, resulting, consequential, follow-on, secondary. [➡AFTER, LAST, AND FOLLOWING; 166]

resulting *adj* **subsequent**, resultant, ensuing, consequential, follow-on. [➡AFTER, LAST, AND FOLLOWING; 166]

resume 1 *v* **recommence**, start again, continue, begin again, pick up where you left off, restart, take up again, carry on. [➡RECOMMENCE AND RESUME; 269] *Opposite:* stop. 2 *v* **return**, go back, reoccupy, take up again. [➡RECOMMENCE AND RESUME; 269]

résumé *n* **précis**, review, potted version, outline, rundown, summary. [➡SUMMARIES, OUTLINES, AND EXCERPTS; 589]

resumption *n* **recommencement**, continuation, carrying on, renewal, reopening. [➡REPETITION; 29]

resurface 1 *v* **float up**, come up, break the surface, rise, reappear, re-emerge. [➡HAPPEN AGAIN; 28] *Opposite:* sink. 2 *v* **reappear**, come back, rematerialize, re-emerge, return. [➡ARRIVE; 12] 3 *v* **coat**, cover, skim, overlay, surface. [➡DECORATE, ADORN, AND APPLY COATINGS; 406]

resurgence *n* **revival**, renaissance, rebirth, resurrection, recovery, reappearance. [➡REPETITION; 29] *Opposite:* disappearance.

resurgent *adj* **burgeoning**, growing, rising, increasing, reviving, renascent, on the up. [➡ABOUT TO HAPPEN; 33]

resurrect 1 *v* **resuscitate**, bring back to life, raise from the dead, restore to life, revive. [➡FALL ILL, TREAT, AND RECOVER; 729] *Opposite:* kill. 2 *v* **save**, breathe new life into, revive, revivify, restart, resuscitate, revitalize. [➡IMPROVE STRENGTH AND DURABILITY; 379]

resurrection *n* **revival**, renaissance, rebirth, revivification, reappearance, restoration, resurgence, renewal, revitalization. [➡REPETITION; 29]

resuscitate 1 *v* **give the kiss of life to**, give artificial respiration to, bring round, save. [➡FALL ILL, TREAT, AND RECOVER; 729] *Opposite:* asphyxiate. 2 *v* **breathe new life into**, revive, revivify, resurrect, boost, save, revitalize, renew. [➡IMPROVE STRENGTH AND DURABILITY; 379]

resuscitation 1 *n* **artificial respiration**, cardiac massage, revival, recovery. [➡HEALING; 731] 2 *n* **restoration**, resurgence, renewal, revival, revitalization, resurrection. [➡REPETITION; 29]

retail 1 *n* **trade**, selling, marketing, merchandising, wholesale, sales. [➡BUSINESS ACTIVITIES AND PHENOMENA; 795] 2 *v* **sell**, trade, put on the market, put up for sale, vend. [➡SELL; 442] *Opposite:* wholesale.

retailer 1 *n* **shop**, store, retail outlet. [➡RETAIL OUTLETS; 1082] 2 *n* **seller**, vendor, merchant, trader, dealer. [➡SELLER; 443]

retail outlet *n* [➡RETAIL OUTLETS; 1082]

retail store *n* [➡RETAIL OUTLETS; 1082]

retain 1 *v* **keep**, keep hold of, hold on to, hold, hang on to, maintain, save, preserve. [➡STORE AND KEEP; 454] *Opposite:* let go. 2 *v* **recall**, recollect, keep in mind, remember, hold. [➡REMEMBER; 747]

retainer *n* **deposit**, down payment, fee, payment. [➡MONEY, PAYMENTS, AND CHARGES; 800]

retake 1 *v* **take back**, recapture, regain, reconquer, win back. [➡GET; 421] 2 *v* **repeat**, redo, resit. [➡RECOMMENCE AND RESUME; 269] 3 *n* **resit**, exam, examination, repeat. [➡LESSONS, COURSE WORK, AND EXAMINATIONS; 842]

retaliate *v* **hit back**, strike back, get even, even the score, react, get your own back, get revenge, give as good as you get, get back at, give tit for tat. [➡VENGEANCE AND REVENGE; 686] *Opposite:* forgive.

retaliation *n* **reprisal**, revenge, vengeance, retribution. [➡VENGEANCE AND REVENGE; 686] *Opposite:* forgiveness.

retaliatory *adj* **tit-for-tat**, reciprocal, reactive, punitive, revengeful, vengeful, avenging. [➡VENGEANCE AND REVENGE; 686] *Opposite:* forgiving.

retard *v* **delay**, slow down, hold up, hold back, hinder, impede, check. [➡DELAY ACTION OR OCCURRENCE; 279] *Opposite:* speed up.

retardation *n* **delay**, check, obstruction, hindrance, impedance (*formal*), obstacle. [➡PROBLEM; 257] *Opposite:* acceleration.

retarded *adj* **underdeveloped**, slow, stunted, arrested, lagging. [➡HAPPENING SLOWLY; 106] *Opposite:* accelerated.

retch *v* **vomit**, heave (*informal*), gag, throw up (*informal*), be sick, puke (*slang*). [➡VOMIT AND BELCH; 713]

retell *v* **repeat**, restate, go over, reiterate, recite. [➡RECITE, REPEAT, AND NARRATE; 621]

retention 1 *n* **holding**, retaining, preservation, withholding, maintenance, custody. [➡STORE AND KEEP; 454] *Opposite:* release. 2 *n* **remembering**, memorizing, recalling, memory, recollection. [➡MEMORY; 746] *Opposite:* forgetting.

retentive *adj* **retaining**, absorbent, spongy. [➡POSITIVE INTELLECTUAL CHARACTERISTICS; 525]

rethink 1 *v* **reconsider**, change your mind, change direction, change tack, change course, think again, start afresh, do a volte-face, have second thoughts, do an about-turn, do an about-face (*US*). [➡MAKE DECISIONS AND CHOICES; 753] 2 *n* **reconsideration**, change of mind, change of heart, second thoughts, volte-face, about-turn, about-face (*US*), changeround, consideration. [➡THINK AND REFLECT; 744]

reticence 1 *n* **reserve**, caginess (*informal*), silence, uncommunicativeness, discretion, restraint. [➡RETICENT AND UNFORTHCOMING; 632] *Opposite:* openness. 2 *n* **shyness**, bashfulness, reserve, quietness, modesty, introversion. [➡RETICENT AND UNFORTHCOMING; 632] *Opposite:* boldness.

reticent *adj* **cagey** (*informal*), discreet, reserved, restrained, unforthcoming, uncommunicative, taciturn, silent, quiet. [➡RETICENT AND UNFORTHCOMING; 632] *Opposite:* talkative.

See Compare and Contrast at **silent**.

reticule *n* **bag**, handbag, purse, container. [➡CONTAINERS, RECEPTACLES, AND PACKAGING; 1244]

retina *n* [➡THE EYE; 699]

retinue *n* **entourage**, followers, attendants, servants, aides, cortege. [➡FRIENDS AND ACQUAINTANCES; 936]

retire 1 *v* **give up work**, stop working, step down, be pensioned off, be superannuated, be put out to pasture. [➡WORK-RELATED ACTIVITIES; 834] 2 *v* **go to bed**, turn in (*informal*), hit the sack (*informal*), call it a day, hit the hay (*informal*). [➡ASSUME A POSITION; 318] 3 *v* **leave**, take your leave, withdraw, go away, go off, retreat. [➡ABSENT ONESELF; 8]

retired *adj* **superannuated**, pensioned off, discharged, emeritus, emerita, elderly, aged, old. [➡EMPLOYMENT STATUS; 831] *Opposite:* working.

retirement 1 *n* **superannuation**, departure, leaving, giving up work, stepping down. [➡PERIOD OF REST; 91] 2 *n* **withdrawal**, retreat, sequestration, seclusion. [➡END; 54]

retiring *adj* **reticent**, self-effacing, unassuming, shy, reserved, timid, diffident, introverted. [➡RETICENT AND UNFORTHCOMING; 632]

retort 1 *v* **respond**, snap, rejoin, come back, counter, bite back. [➡REPLY AND ANSWER; 669] 2 *n* **reply**, rejoinder (*formal*), response, riposte, answer, squelch (*slang*). [➡REPLY AND ANSWER; 669]

See Compare and Contrast at **answer**.

retouch *v* **touch up**, correct, restore, renovate, improve. [➡IMPROVE APPEARANCE; 380]

retrace *v* **review**, redo, go back over, repeat. [➡GO BACKWARDS; 310]

retract 1 *v* **draw in**, draw back, pull in, pull back, withdraw. [➡MOVE SOMETHING: INTO A NEW POSITION OR OVERTURN; 331] *Opposite:* extend. 2 *v* **deny**, take back, withdraw, apologize, recant, rescind. [➡APOLOGIZE AND RETRACT; 684] *Opposite:* stand by.

retractable *adj* **telescopic**, folding, able to be drawn in, sheathable, coverable. [➡CHANGE OF SHAPE; 386]

retraction *n* **withdrawal**, refutation, disavowal (*formal*), disclaimer, denial, negation, renunciation, repudiation. [➡APOLOGIZE AND RETRACT; 684] *Opposite:* confirmation.

retreat 1 *n* **departure**, withdrawal, flight, evacuation. [➡END; 54] *Opposite:* advance. 2 *n* **haven**, hideaway, sanctuary, refuge, shelter. [➡SAFE BUILDINGS OR PLACES; 1092] 3 *v* **move away**, move back, draw back, back away, run away, recoil, withdraw, leave, give ground, flee. [➡GO BACKWARDS; 310] *Opposite:* advance.

retrench *v* **cut back**, economize, save, save money, tighten your belt, draw in your horns, make savings, make economies, make cuts. [➡BUSINESS ACTIVITIES AND PHENOMENA; 795]

retrenchment *n* **cutback**, economizing, cuts, cost-cutting, belt-tightening. [➡BUSINESS ACTIVITIES AND PHENOMENA; 795]

retribution *n* **vengeance**, revenge, reprisal, reckoning, justice, payback. [➡VENGEANCE AND REVENGE; 686]

retributive *adj* **punitive**, retaliatory, vengeful, punishing, revengeful, avenging. [➡VENGEANCE AND REVENGE; 686]

retrieval *n* **recovery**, repossession, rescue, reclamation, salvage. [➡REGAIN POSSESSION; 430] *Opposite:* loss.

retrieve *v* **save**, get back, recover, regain, repossess, salvage, rescue, reclaim, take back. [➡REGAIN POSSESSION; 430] *Opposite:* lose.

retriever *type of* **large dog.** [➡DOG; 980]

retro *adj* **period**, old-fashioned, dated, historical, passé. [➡OLD, OLD-FASHIONED; 168]

retroactive *adj* **backdated**, retrospective, ex post facto. [➡PAST; 84]

retrograde 1 *adj* **backward**, reversing, rearward. [➡DIRECTION OF MOTION; 346] *Opposite:* forward. 2 *adj* **regressive**, declining, worsening, getting worse, deteriorating, reverting. [➡WORSEN SOMETHING; 381] *Opposite:* improving.

retrogress 1 *v* **regress**, decline, revert, degenerate, worsen, get worse, deteriorate. [➡GET WORSE; 382] *Opposite:* progress. 2 *v* **move backwards**, reverse, go back, retreat, draw back, withdraw, move back. [➡GO BACKWARDS; 310] *Opposite:* move forward.

retrogression *n* **decline**, regression, return, relapse, deterioration, worsening, lapse. [➡WORSEN SOMETHING; 381] *Opposite:* progression.

retrogressive 1 *adj* **regressive**, reverting, degenerating, worsening, getting worse, deteriorating, declining. [➡WORSEN SOMETHING; 381] *Opposite:* progressive. 2 *adj* **reversing**, retreating, withdrawing, moving back, drawing back. [➡DIRECTION OF MOTION; 346]

retropack *part of* **spacecraft.** [➡SPACE VEHICLES; 1062]

retrospect *n* **recollection**, remembrance, review, reconsideration, survey. [➡MEMORY; 746] *Opposite:* prospect.

retrospective 1 *adj* **reviewing**, reflective, surveying, reconsidering. [➡EXAMINE AND ASSESS; 754] 2 *adj* **retroactive**, backdated, ex post facto. [➡PAST; 84] 3 *adj* **backward-looking**, nostalgic, retrograde, traditional, conservative. [➡THE NATURE OF IDEAS; 772] *Opposite:* forward-thinking. 4 *n* **exhibition**, show, presentation, showcase, display, demonstration, exposition, showing. [➡PERFORMANCES AND SHOWS; 42]

retrospectively *adv* **on reflection**, in retrospect, with hindsight, with the benefit of hindsight, on second thoughts, looking back. [➡PAST; 84]

return 1 *v* **revisit**, come back, go again, come again, go back. [➡ARRIVE; 12] *Opposite:* depart. 2 *v* **send back**, take back, replace, restore. [➡DESPATCH AND SEND; 334] *Opposite:* remove. 3 *v* **resume**, go back, revert, revisit, begin again. [➡GO BACKWARDS; 310] *Opposite:* stop. 4 *v* **repay**, pay back, refund, reimburse, give back. [➡GIVE AND PROVIDE; 431] *Opposite:* keep. 5 *n* **coming back**, reappearance, reoccurrence, arrival, homecoming. [➡ARRIVAL; 13] *Opposite:* departure. 6 *n* **profit**, earnings, yield, revenue, proceeds, gain, benefit. [➡INCOME; 461]

returns *n* **revenue**, earnings, yield, proceeds, takings, income, profits. [➡INCOME; 461] *Opposite:* outlay.

reunification *n* **reunion**, reconsolidation, amalgamation, recombination, reintegration. [➡STYLES AND SYSTEMS OF GOVERNMENT; 806]

reunify *v* **reunite**, come together, rejoin, bring together, reintegrate, reassemble, reconcile, recombine. [➡SOCIAL, POLITICAL, AND ECONOMIC CHANGE; 374]

reunion 1 *n* **gathering**, meeting, get-together (*informal*), event. [➡MEETINGS AND ASSEMBLIES; 43] 2 *n* **reunification**, reintegration, recombination, reconsolidation. [➡HARMONY; 156]

reunite *v* **reunify**, unite, bring together, unify, come together, join up. [➡COMBINE AND MIX; 401] *Opposite:* split.

reusable *adj* **refillable**, returnable, recyclable, green, ecofriendly, environmentally friendly, ecological. [➡ECONOMICAL AND RESOURCEFUL; 208] *Opposite:* disposable.

reuse *v* **recycle**, reclaim, reprocess, salvage. [➡MAKE GOOD USE OF SOMETHING; 474] *Opposite:* discard.

rev 1 *n* **revolution**, cycle, rotation, turn, revolution per minute, rpm. [➡MOVE SOMETHING ON THE SPOT; 337] 2 *v* **race**, roar, scream, increase power, accelerate, open up (*informal*), gun (*informal*), throttle. [➡CHANGE OF SPEED: MORE; 397]

revaluation *n* **revision**, reappraisal, reassessment, readjustment, redefinition, adjustment. [➡EXAMINE AND ASSESS; 754]

revalue 1 *v* **raise**, increase, up, enhance, augment (*formal*). [➡BUSINESS ACTIVITIES AND PHENOMENA; 795] *Opposite:* devalue. 2 *v* **reappraise**, re-evaluate, adjust, reset, change, reassess. [➡EXAMINE AND ASSESS; 754]

revamp 1 *v* **makeover**, do up, refurbish, restore, overhaul, give a facelift, titivate. [➡IMPROVE APPEARANCE; 380] 2 *n* **facelift**, refurbishment, restoration, renovation, overhaul, makeover. [➡IMPROVE APPEARANCE; 380]

See Compare and Contrast at **renew.**

rev counter (*informal*) *type of* **controls.** [➡VEHICLES; 1144]

reveal 1 *v* **make known**, disclose, divulge, expose, make public, let slip, tell. [➡BETRAY CONFIDENCES AND GOSSIP; 619] *Opposite:* conceal. 2 *v* **expose**, uncover, show, bare, bring to light. [➡CAUSE TO APPEAR; 5] *Opposite:* cover up.

revealing 1 *adj* **skimpy**, see-through, figure-hugging, close-fitting, tight-fitting. [➡DESCRIBING CLOTHES; 869] 2 *adj* **enlightening**, illuminating, telling, telltale, informative, educational. [➡INTERESTING AND MEANINGFUL; 191] *Opposite:* obscure.

revealingly *adv* **tellingly**, significantly, interestingly, importantly, conspicuously, noticeably. [➡INTERESTING AND MEANINGFUL; 191]

reveille 1 *n* **wake-up call**, early-morning call, bugle call. [➡SIGNALLING; 1139] 2 *n* **early morning**, daybreak, dawn, sunrise, cockcrow (*archaic or literary*), the crack of dawn, sun up (*US*). [➡TIMES OF DAY; 87]

revel 1 *v* **delight**, enjoy, take pleasure in, luxuriate, bask, wallow, take pride, take satisfaction, lap up, glory, exult. [➡LIKE, LOVE, VALUE AND ENJOY; 579] 2 *v* **make merry**, party (*informal*), celebrate, have fun, let your hair down, go to town (*informal*), rejoice (*literary*), carouse (*literary*), socialize. [➡LEISURE AND RECREATION; 874] 3 *n* **celebration**, party, festivities, do (*informal*), carnival, merrymaking, carousal (*literary*). [➡PARTIES, DANCES, AND CELEBRATIONS; 37]

revelation 1 *n* **exposé**, exposure, disclosure, leak, admission. [➡ADMIT AND CONFESS; 616] 2 *n* **surprise**, shock, eye opener. [➡INFORM AND ANNOUNCE; 612]

reveller *n* **partygoer**, roisterer, merrymaker, pleasure-seeker, celebrator, carouser (*literary*), drinker, party animal (*informal*). [➡PLEASURE-SEEKERS AND HEDONISTS; 886]

revelry *n* **festivities**, revels, celebrations, carousing (*literary*), partying, merriment, gaiety. [➡PARTIES, DANCES, AND CELEBRATIONS; 37]

revels *n* [➡PARTIES, DANCES, AND CELEBRATIONS; 37]

revenge 1 *n* **retaliation**, vengeance, retribution, settling of scores, reprisal, payback. [➡VENGEANCE AND REVENGE; 686] 2 *v* **requite**, avenge, even the score, get your own back, retaliate. [➡VENGEANCE AND REVENGE; 686]

revengeful *adj* [➡IRRITATION AND ANGER; 542]

revenue *n* **income**, proceeds, profits, returns, takings. [➡INCOME; 461] *Opposite:* expenses.

revenue system *n* [➡TAX AND TAXATION; 802]

reverberant *adj* [➡LOUD OR UNPLEASANT SOUNDS; 1265]

reverberate *v* **echo**, resound, ring, vibrate, resonate. [➡SOUND EMISSION; 363]

reverberating *adj* **resounding**, echoing, resonant, rich, rumbling, ringing, booming, deep, loud. [➡LOUD OR UNPLEASANT SOUNDS; 1265]

reverberation *n* **echo**, sound, noise, boom. [➡SOUNDS; 1255]

reverberations *n* **aftershock**, aftereffects, impact, shock. [➡RESULTS AND OUTCOMES; 83]

revere *v* **admire**, respect, look up to, hold in the highest regard, be in awe of, worship, venerate. [➡LIKE, LOVE, VALUE AND ENJOY; 579] *Opposite:* despise.

revered 1 *adj* **respected**, valued, illustrious, distinguished, august (*formal*), esteemed, well-regarded, admired, honoured, celebrated. [➡POPULAR AND WANTED; 221] *Opposite:* vilified. 2 *adj* **holy**, sacred, blessed, venerated, hallowed, consecrated, sanctified. [➡RELIGIOUS CONCEPTS; 777] *Opposite:* vilified.

reverence *n* **respect**, admiration, worship, awe, veneration, astonishment, amazement, devotion. [➡LOVE, RESPECT, AND GOODWILL; 550] *Opposite:* contempt.

See Compare and Contrast at **regard**.

reverend 1 *adj* (*formal*) **respected**, revered, venerated, worthy, noble, hallowed. [➡POPULAR AND WANTED; 221] 2 *adj* **ecclesiastical**, clerical, priestly (*formal or literary*), ministerial. [➡RELIGIONS AND RELIGIOUS PRACTICES; 778] 3 *n* **vicar**, priest, cleric, minister, parson. [➡RELIGIOUS PEOPLE; 779]

reverent *adj* **deferential**, reverential, respectful, worshipful, awed, humble. [➡EXPRESSING RESPECT AND APPROVAL; 638] *Opposite:* irreverent.

reverential *adj* **respectful**, deferential, reverent, humble, awed. [➡EXPRESSING RESPECT AND APPROVAL; 638] *Opposite:* disrespectful.

reverie *n* **daydream**, dream, trance, musing, contemplation, brown study. [➡DREAM, IMAGINE, AND FANTASIZE; 750]

reversal 1 *n* **turnaround**, U-turn, volte-face, about-turn, about-face (*US*). [➡DECISIVE MOMENTS; 44] 2 *n* **setback**, hitch, problem, reverse, blow, snag, misfortune, difficulty. [➡PROBLEM; 257]

reverse 1 *v* **overturn**, turn round, undo, annul, invalidate, repeal, quash, render null and void. [➡ABOLISH AND ANNUL; 453] *Opposite:* carry out. 2 *v* **move backwards**, back up, drive backwards, go backwards, retreat, withdraw. [➡GO BACKWARDS; 310] *Opposite:* advance. 3 *v* **swap** (*informal*), transpose, switch, invert, reorder, rearrange, change. [➡CHANGE ONE THING FOR ANOTHER; 399] 4 *n* **contrary**, opposite, antithesis, converse. [➡OPPOSITE; 158] 5 *n* **back**, rear, underneath, other side, opposite side. [➡EXTREMITIES OF PHYSICAL OBJECTS; 1249] *Opposite:* front. 6 *adj* **opposite**, contrary, converse, inverse. [➡OPPOSITE; 158] *Opposite:* same. 7 *n* **setback**, reversal, hitch, problem, misfortune, difficulty, blow, snag. [➡PROBLEM; 257]

reversible 1 *adj* **rescindable**, revocable, alterable, adjustable, changeable, mutable, flexible. [➡FINITENESS, VARIABILITY, AND TRANSIENCE; 96] *Opposite:* irreversible. 2 *adj* **two-sided**, dual-purpose, multipurpose, double-sided, two-in-one. [➡DESCRIBING CLOTHES; 869]

reversion 1 *n* **return**, decline, deterioration, degeneration, retreat, relapse, lapse. [➡WORSEN SOMETHING; 381] 2 *n* **reversal**, turnaround, about-turn, U-turn, volte-face, change of direction, about-face (*US*). [➡DECISIVE MOMENTS; 44]

revert 1 *v* **return**, go back, take a step back, relapse, regress, lapse. [➡GO BACKWARDS; 310] 2 *v* **go back**, revisit, go over again, take another look at, return, reinvestigate, re-examine, retrace your steps, reopen. [➡EXAMINE AND ASSESS; 754] 3 *v* **regress**, change back, return, mutate, degenerate, deteriorate. [➡GET WORSE; 382] 4 *v* **lapse**, backslide, go back to your old ways, slip back, reoffend, slide back. [➡GET WORSE; 382] 5 *v* **be returned**, pass, pass back, return, go back, restore. [➡GO BACKWARDS; 310]

review 1 *v* **reconsider**, re-examine, reassess, go over, check, re-evaluate, make another study of, have another look at. [➡EXAMINE AND ASSESS; 754] 2 *v* **appraise**, evaluate, assess, look at, examine, study, go through. [➡EXAMINE AND ASSESS; 754] 3 *v* (*US*) **study**, go over, go through, look over, reread, brush up, revise, swot (*informal*). [➡STUDYING; 844] 4 *n* **publication**, magazine, journal, periodical. [➡NEWSPAPERS; 606] 5 *n* **appraisal**, evaluation, assessment, examination, analysis, criticism. [➡EXAMINE AND ASSESS; 754] 6 *n* **reconsideration**, re-examination, reassessment, check, re-evaluation, revision. [➡EXAMINE AND ASSESS; 754]

reviewer *n* **critic**, commentator, assessor, referee. [➡WORKERS IN ENTERTAINMENT AND MEDIA; 873]

revile *v* **insult**, abuse, scorn, condemn, censure, despise, berate, disparage. [➡INSULTS, ABUSE, AND SWEARING; 659] *Opposite:* praise.

reviled *adj* [➡UNPOPULAR AND UNWANTED; 259]

revise 1 *v* **amend**, modify, adjust, alter, change, correct, improve, rework. [➡CORRECT AND PUT RIGHT; 378] 2 *v* **study**, brush up, go over, look over, go through, reread, bone up (*informal*), swot (*informal*), mug up (*informal*), review (*US*). [➡STUDYING; 844]

revision 1 *n* [➡LESSONS, COURSE WORK, AND EXAMINATIONS; 842] 2 *n*

amendment, reconsideration, modification, adjustment, alteration, correction, improvement, review, change. [➡IMPROVE SOMETHING; 375]

revisionism *n* **reassessment**, reconsideration, reinterpretation, pragmatism, heterodoxy (*formal*), alteration, modification, readjustment, heresy. [➡STYLES AND SYSTEMS OF GOVERNMENT; 806]

revisionist 1 *adj* **pragmatic**, heterodox (*formal*), heretical, progressive, modernizing, ideological, political, controversial. [➡STYLES AND SYSTEMS OF GOVERNMENT; 806] 2 *n* **pragmatist**, modernizer, heretic, liberal. [➡PHILOSOPHICAL AND POLITICAL THINKERS; 782]

revisit 1 *v* **return to**, go back to, come back to, retreat to, re-enter. [➡TRAVEL: WAYS OF TRAVELLING; 321] *Opposite:* abandon. 2 *v* **reconsider**, re-examine, reassess, re-evaluate, rethink, reopen. [➡EXAMINE AND ASSESS; 754]

revitalization *n* **renewal**, renaissance, revival, new life, recovery, regeneration. [➡IMPROVE SOMETHING; 375] *Opposite:* decline.

revitalize *v* **refresh**, invigorate, revive, rejuvenate, regenerate, renew, give a new lease of life. [➡IMPROVE STRENGTH AND DURABILITY; 379] *Opposite:* wear out.

revitalized *adj* [➡WIDE AWAKE AND CONSCIOUS; 736]

revitalizing *adj* **energizing**, vitalizing, stimulating, uplifting, invigorating, refreshing, thirst-quenching, bracing, inspirational, fortifying, reviving, restorative, enlivening. [➡PHYSICALLY PLEASANT; 187]

revival 1 *n* **revitalization**, renewal, restoration, stimulation, reinforcement, recovery, resumption, resurgence, rebirth, rehabilitation. [➡CHANGE; 373] *Opposite:* disappearance. 2 *n* **resuscitation**, recovery, waking, bringing round, coming to, bringing around. [➡HEALING; 731] *Opposite:* relapse.

revive 1 *v* **resuscitate**, come round, recover, come to, bring round, regain consciousness, recuperate, wake up. [➡FALL ILL, TREAT, AND RECOVER; 729] *Opposite:* lose consciousness. 2 *v* **recover**, pick up, perk up, resume, develop, flourish. [➡GET BETTER; 376] *Opposite:* die down. 3 *v* **revitalize**, renew, breathe life into, restore, refresh, restart, stimulate, reinforce, reawaken. [➡IMPROVE STRENGTH AND DURABILITY; 379] *Opposite:* kill. 4 *v* **put on**, stage, restage, perform, redo, repeat, show again. [➡CAUSE TO APPEAR; 5]

revived *adj* [➡WIDE AWAKE AND CONSCIOUS; 736]

revivify *v* **rejuvenate**, breathe new life into, refresh, resurrect, resuscitate, give a boost to. [➡IMPROVE STRENGTH AND DURABILITY; 379] *Opposite:* exhaust.

revocation *n* **cancellation**, withdrawal, reversal, overturning, annulment. [➡CHANGE; 373] *Opposite:* enactment.

revoke *v* **cancel**, annul, rescind, withdraw, retract, repeal, invalidate. [➡ABOLISH AND ANNUL; 453]

revolt 1 *v* **rebel**, rise up, mutiny, riot. [➡PROTEST AND EXPRESS DISAPPROVAL; 643] 2 *v* **repel**, repulse, sicken, nauseate, turn your stomach, turn off (*informal*), put off. [➡UPSET, DISTRESS, AND HUMILIATE; 568] *Opposite:* attract. 3 *n* **rebellion**, revolution, uprising, upheaval, insurgency, insurrection, mutiny, riot. [➡AGGRESSIVE EVENT; 39]

revolted *adj* **nauseated**, appalled, horror-struck, horror-stricken, dismayed, sickened, aghast, disgusted, shocked, offended, repelled, repulsed. [➡IRRITATION AND ANGER; 542] *Opposite:* charmed.

revolting *adj* **disgusting**, repellent, repulsive, sickening, nauseating, horrible, horrendous, awful, dreadful, horrid. [➡DISGUSTING AND REPULSIVE; 231] *Opposite:* appealing.

revolution 1 *n* **rebellion**, revolt, uprising, upheaval, insurgency, insurrection, mutiny, riot. [➡AGGRESSIVE EVENT; 39] 2 *n* **transformation**, upheaval, conversion, alteration, development, change, reform, innovation, modernization. [➡CHANGE; 373] 3 *n* **rotation**, turn, spin, cycle, circle, orbit, gyration. [➡MOVE SOMETHING ON THE SPOT; 337]

revolutionary 1 *adj* **rebellious**, radical, insurgent, riotous (*formal*), mutinous, anarchist. [➡REBELLIOUSNESS AND DISOBEDIENCE; 566] 2 *adj* **radical**, groundbreaking, world-shattering, innovative, innovatory, new, avant-garde, progressive. [➡EXTRAORDINARY: UNCOMMON; 206] *Opposite:* conventional. 3 *n* **rebel**, radical, insurgent, rioter, mutineer, anarchist, insurrectionist. [➡UNCOOPERATIVE OR REBELLIOUS PERSON; 567]

revolutionize *v* **transform**, transfigure, reform, alter, change, modernize, update. [➡CHANGE; 373] *Opposite:* maintain.

revolve *v* **rotate**, turn, spin, circle, orbit, turn round, gyrate. [➡MOVE SOMETHING ON THE SPOT; 337]

revolver *type of* **gun**. [➡WEAPONS FOR SHOOTING; 1155]

revolving *adj* **rotating**, turning, spinning, circling, gyrating, gyratory. [➡DIRECTION OF MOTION; 346]

revue *n* **variety show**, show, skit, sketch show, satire, lampoon, vaudeville, burlesque, cabaret. [➡PERFORMANCES AND SHOWS; 42]

revulsion *n* **disgust**, repulsion, repugnance, nausea, distaste, horror, loathing, dislike, aversion. [➡DISLIKE AND HATE; 578] *Opposite:* attraction.

revulsive *adj* [➡DISGUSTING AND REPULSIVE; 231]

reward 1 *n* **recompense**, payment, repayment, return, remuneration, incentive, compensation, gift, bonus, prize. [➡REWARDS AND AWARDS; 440] *Opposite:* penalty. 2 *v* **recompense**, pay, repay, remunerate, compensate. [➡REWARD; 437] *Opposite:* penalize.

rewarding *adj* **satisfying**, worthwhile, gratifying, pleasing, fulfilling. [➡EMOTIONALLY PLEASANT; 188] *Opposite:* disappointing.

rewind *v* **wind back**, spool back, reverse. [➡MOVE SOMETHING ON THE SPOT; 337]

rewire *v* **redo**, renovate, renew, refurbish, revamp, modernize. [➡REPAIR AND MEND; 377]

reword *v* **rephrase**, redraft, rewrite, rework, revise, amend, alter, modify, change. [➡CORRECT AND PUT RIGHT; 378]

rework *v* **revise**, redraft, rephrase, rewrite, reword, amend, alter, modify, change. [➡CORRECT AND PUT RIGHT; 378]

rewrite 1 *v* **redraft**, rephrase, reword, rework, revise, amend, alter, modify, change, reshape, adjust. [➡CORRECT AND PUT RIGHT; 378] 2 *n* **revision**, amendment, alteration, modification. [➡CHANGE; 373]

rhapsodic *adj* **ecstatic**, enthusiastic, lyrical, rapturous, fervent, ardent, passionate, extravagant, over-the-top (*informal*), eulogistic. [➡ENTHUSIASTIC AND INQUISITIVE; 629] *Opposite:* unenthusiastic.

rhapsodize *v* **enthuse**, be ecstatic, go over the top, go on, wax lyrical (*literary*), eulogize (*formal*). [➡PRAISE AND ENCOURAGE; 648]

rhapsody *n* **ecstasy**, rapture, bliss, enthusiasm, eagerness, joy. [➡PLEASURE, EXCITEMENT, AND ELATION; 535] *Opposite:* gloom.

rheostat *n* **control**, regulator, resistor, controller. [➡ELECTRONICS AND ELECTRICS; 1136]

rhesus monkey *type of* **primate**. [➡PRIMATE; 988]

rhetoric 1 *n* **oratory**, public speaking, speechmaking, speechifying (*informal*). [➡THE SPOKEN WORD; 672] 2 *n* **bombast**, pomposity, grandiloquence, fustian, orotundity, magniloquence. [➡BOAST; 617] 3 *n* **language**, expression, style, idiom, words, vocabulary, speech, writing. [➡ASPECTS OF LANGUAGE; 683]

rhetorical 1 *adj* **bombastic**, pompous, pretentious, periphrastic, voluble, showy, flashy, declamatory, theatrical, contrived, effusive, high-flown, highfalutin (*informal*). [➡POMPOUS, LOUD, AND OVER-CONFIDENT; 636] 2 *adj* **oratorical**, verbal, linguistic, stylistic. [➡ASPECTS OF LANGUAGE; 683]

rhetorician *n* **orator**, speaker, public speaker, debater, advocate. [➡SPEAKERS AND ORATORS; 604]

rheum *n* [➡BREATHE AND NOT BREATHE; 717]

rheumatic *adj* **stiff**, aching, sore, inflexible, rigid, unbending. [➡THE BONES AND JOINTS; 720] *Opposite:* flexible.

rheumy *adj* [➡BREATHE AND NOT BREATHE; 717]

rhinestone *n* **paste**, strass, diamanté. [➡ORNAMENTS AND DECORATIONS; 1247]

rhinoceros *type of* **large mammal**. [➡LARGE MAMMAL; 986]

rhinoceros beetle *type of* **beetle**. [➡BEETLES AND WEEVILS; 1016]

rhizome *n* **stem**, shoot, root, tuber, corm, bulb. [➡PARTS OF TREES AND PLANTS; 1026]

rhizopod *type of* **microorganism**. [➡MICROORGANISMS, FUNGI, AND ALGAE; 1023]

rhododendron *type of* **shrub or bush**. [➡BUSHES AND SHRUBS; 1027]

rhomboid *n* **parallelogram**, diamond, lozenge. [➡ANGULAR SHAPE; 1216]

rhombus *n* **diamond**, lozenge, parallelogram. [➡ANGULAR SHAPE; 1216]

rhubarb (*US*) *n* **argument**, quarrel, fight, disagreement, dispute, row. [➡ARGUMENT; 47]

rhyme 1 *n* **assonance**, consonance, rhyming. [➡POETRY AND VERSE; 915] 2 *n* **poem**, verse, nursery rhyme, jingle, limerick, couplet, quatrain. [➡POETRY AND VERSE; 915]

rhyme or reason *n* **sense**, logic, meaning, pattern. [➡IDEA AND THOUGHT; 771]

rhythm 1 *n* **beat**, pace, tempo, time, measure, cadence, pulse. [➡NOTES AND CHORDS; 909] 2 *n* **regularity**, pattern, progression, sequence. [➡FREQUENT AND OFTEN; 107]

rhythm and blues *type of* **popular music**. [➡MUSIC, SONGS, AND SINGING; 907]

rhythmic 1 *adj* **recurring**, regular, periodic, pulsing, recurrent. [➡FREQUENT AND OFTEN; 107] 2 *adj* **musical**, cadenced, metrical. [➡MUSICAL TERMS; 912]

rib 1 *n* **beam**, strut, spoke, spine, spar. [➡BUILDING MATERIALS; 1076] 2 *v* (*informal*) **tease**, make fun of, laugh at, mock, rag (*dated*), kid, josh (*informal*), have on (*informal*), razz (*US informal*), ride (*US informal*). [➡JOKES AND TEASING; 675] 3 *type of* **bone**. [➡THE BONES AND JOINTS; 720] 4 *type of* **cut**. [➡TYPES AND CUTS OF MEAT; 1176]

ribald *adj* **coarse**, vulgar, bawdy, rude, lewd, funny, humorous. [➡MORALLY BAD; 776] *Opposite:* refined.

ribbed *adj* **grooved**, corrugated, ridged, bumpy, uneven, textured, striped. [➡PHYSICAL TEXTURE; 1221]

ribbing (*informal*) *n* [➡JOKES AND TEASING; 675]

ribbon 1 *n* **band**, tie, trimming, decoration, tape. [➡ORNAMENTS AND DECORATIONS; 1247] 2 *n* **strip**, stretch, band, length, taper. [➡AMOUNT OF SOLID OR SEMI-SOLID; 115] 3 *n* **decoration**, award, honour, badge of honour, medal, badge, emblem. [➡ORNAMENTS AND DECORATIONS; 1247]

rib cage *part of* **torso**. [➡TORSO; 694]

rib-tickling (*informal*) *adj* [➡FUNNY AND AMUSING; 217]

rice *type of* **cereal**. [➡CEREAL FOODS; 1177]

rich 1 *adj* **wealthy**, well-off, affluent, prosperous, well-heeled (*informal*), moneyed, well-to-do, loaded (*slang*). [➡WEALTH AND WEALTHY; 891] *Opposite:* poor. 2 *adj* **full**, abounding, plentiful, stuffed, heavy, dripping, loaded (*slang*). [➡MANY, MUCH, LARGE AMOUNT; 117] *Opposite:* lacking. 3 *adj* **opulent**, gorgeous, plush (*informal*), lush, luxuriant, splendid, valuable, expensive, ornate, costly, fine, precious. [➡EXPENSIVE AND LUXURIOUS; 219] *Opposite:* shabby. 4 *adj* **heavy**, indigestible, calorific, cloying, unhealthy, creamy, buttery, fatty, sweet. [➡TASTE; 704] *Opposite:* light. 5 *adj* **productive**, fertile, abundant, plentiful, fruitful, lush, full, prolific. [➡ECONOMICAL AND RESOURCEFUL; 208] *Opposite:* infertile. 6 *adj* **intense**, deep, strong, full, powerful, vivid, resonant, full-bodied. [➡STRENGTH; 202] *Opposite:* weak. 7 *adj* (*informal*) **ironic**, amusing, irritating, annoying, ridiculous, unlikely. [➡BIZARRE AND PECULIAR; 258]

rich and famous *n* [➡WEALTH AND WEALTHY; 891]

riches *n* **resources**, treasures, reserves, materials, raw materials, assets, possessions. [➡FINANCIAL ASSETS; 463]

richly 1 *adv* **opulently**, luxuriantly, luxuriously, splendidly, ornately, handsomely, abundantly, elaborately. [➡ EXPENSIVE AND LUXURIOUS; 219] *Opposite:* shabbily. 2 *adv* **thoroughly**, fully, completely, totally, deeply, well, absolutely, suitably. [➡ TO A GREAT EXTENT; 130] *Opposite:* barely.

richness 1 *n* **prosperity**, fortune, affluence, wealth. [➡ FINANCIAL ASSETS; 463] *Opposite:* poverty. 2 *n* **opulence**, luxury, sumptuousness, splendour, luxuriousness, lavishness, magnificence. [➡ EXPENSIVE AND LUXURIOUS; 219] *Opposite:* shabbiness. 3 *n* **fertility**, fruitfulness, productivity, lushness, fullness, abundance. [➡ USEFULNESS; 200] *Opposite:* infertility. 4 *n* **intensity**, depth, strength, fullness, power, vibrancy, vividness, resonance. [➡ STRENGTH; 202] *Opposite:* weakness.

rick *v* **twist**, pull, sprain, crick, put out, dislocate, injure, strain, wrench. [➡ WOUND A PERSON OR ANIMAL; 384]

ricketiness *n* [➡ IN BAD REPAIR; 1233]

rickety *adj* **wobbly** (*informal*), shaky, unsteady, unstable, rocky, unbalanced, unsound, insecure. [➡ IN BAD REPAIR; 1233] *Opposite:* firm.

rickshaw *type of* **bike** (*informal*). [➡ BIKES, CARS, AND CARRIAGES; 1148]

ricochet 1 *v* **recoil**, rebound, glance off, bounce off, reflect, reverberate, echo. [➡ CHANGE DIRECTION OF MOTION; 345] 2 *n* **rebound**, recoil, reverberation, reflection, echo, bounce. [➡ IMPACT SOUNDS; 1259]

ricotta *type of* **soft cheese**. [➡ DAIRY PRODUCTS AND CHEESES; 1182]

rictus *n* **grimace**, grin, fixed expression, contortion. [➡ FACIAL EXPRESSION; 652]

rid *v* **free**, clear, purge, liberate, divest, do away with, relieve, exonerate, get rid of. [➡ GET RID OF SOMETHING; 452]

riddle 1 *n* **puzzle**, conundrum, question, mystery, enigma, brainteaser, challenge. [➡ JOKES AND TEASING; 675] 2 *v* **pierce**, perforate, puncture, pepper, damage, poke. [➡ TEAR, BREAK, AND CUT; 361] 3 *v* **sift**, screen, sieve, separate. [➡ SEPARATE AND DIVIDE; 402]

See Compare and Contrast at **problem**.

ride 1 *v* **gallop**, canter, trot, jockey. [➡ TRAVEL: WAYS OF TRAVELLING; 321] 2 *v* **travel**, journey, go, be carried, be conveyed. [➡ PROCEED AND GO; 306] *Opposite:* walk. 3 *v* **depend on**, rest on, centre on, rely, be contingent on, be affected by, be decided by. [➡ RECIPROCITY AND INTERDEPENDENCE; 148] 4 *v* (*US informal*) **tease**, torment, criticise, mock, provoke, bother. [➡ JOKES AND TEASING; 675] 5 *n* **trip**, outing, jaunt, journey, cycle, drive. [➡ TRAVEL: JOURNEYS AND TRIPS; 319]

ride out *v* **endure**, brave, stick out, survive, live through, weather, come through, withstand, pass through. [➡ TOLERATE AND ENDURE; 767] *Opposite:* succumb.

rider *n* **proviso**, qualification, provision, condition, stipulation, requirement, criterion, clause, specification, prerequisite, disclaimer. [➡ PARTS OF BOOKS AND DOCUMENTS; 594]

ride up *v* **roll up**, slide up, wriggle up, move up, wrinkle, pucker. [➡ GO UPWARDS; 307] *Opposite:* fall down.

ridge 1 *n* **edge**, point, crest, rim, elevation, range. [➡ EXTREMITIES OF PHYSICAL OBJECTS; 1249] 2 *v* **fold**, crumple, crinkle, crease, wrinkle, pucker, pleat. [➡ CHANGE OF SHAPE; 386]

ridicule 1 *v* **mock**, deride, scorn, scoff at, laugh at, make fun of, poke fun at, send up (*informal*), jeer at, tease. [➡ PROTEST AND EXPRESS DISAPPROVAL; 643] 2 *n* **mockery**, scorn, derision, laughter, mimicry. [➡ JOKES AND TEASING; 675]

Compare and Contrast: ***ridicule, deride, laugh at, mock, send up***

CORE MEANING: TO BELITTLE OR MAKE FUN OF SOMEBODY OR SOMETHING

ridicule to belittle somebody or something in a cruel contemptuous way; ***deride*** to show utter contempt for somebody or something; ***laugh at*** to show amusement, contempt, or disrespect for somebody or something; ***mock*** to treat somebody or something with scorn or contempt, often involving cruel mimicking; ***send up*** (*informal*) to make fun of somebody or something by humorous imitation.

ridiculed *adj* [➡ UNPOPULAR AND UNWANTED; 259]

ridiculous *adj* **ludicrous**, preposterous, absurd, silly, outlandish, outrageous, bizarre, unreasonable, incredible, nonsensical. [➡ BIZARRE AND PECULIAR; 258] *Opposite:* sensible.

ridiculousness *n* **ludicrousness**, preposterousness, absurdity, nonsensicality, irrationality, outlandishness, silliness, outrageousness. [➡ BIZARRE AND PECULIAR; 258] *Opposite:* sense.

riding *n* **pony-trekking**, show jumping, racing, hunting, dressage, cross-country. [➡ HOBBIES, GAMES, AND SPORTS; 875]

rife 1 *adj* **widespread**, common, endemic, extensive, prevalent, ubiquitous, predominant, rampant, plentiful. [➡ PRESENT AND AVAILABLE; 11] *Opposite:* rare. 2 *adj* **full**, abounding, stuffed (*informal*), bursting, laden, loaded, packed. [➡ FULL; 1238] *Opposite:* lacking.

See Compare and Contrast at **widespread**.

riff 1 *n* **phrase**, refrain, melody, tune, groove, loop, sample, ostinato. [➡ NOTES AND CHORDS; 909] 2 *v* **play**, jam, improvise, strum, noodle (*slang*), perform. [➡ MUSIC, SONGS, AND SINGING; 907]

riffle 1 *v* **flick through**, turn pages, peruse, glance at, scan, skim through, cast your eyes over, browse, leaf through, thumb. [➡ LOOKING AND LOOKS; 701] 2 *v* **shuffle**, mix, mix up, randomize, jumble up, recombine. [➡ CREATE DISORDER AND CAUSE CHAOS; 359] 3 *v* **ripple**, roughen, undulate, get choppy, ruffle, dimple. [➡ CHANGE OF SHAPE; 386] 4 *n* **flick**, quick look, glance, perusal, skim, scan, browse. [➡ LOOKING AND LOOKS; 701]

rifle 1 *v* **ransack**, search, search through, rummage, go through, scour, shuffle through, turn over. [➡ SEEK POSSESSION AND SEARCH; 457] 2 *type of* **gun**. [➡ WEAPONS FOR SHOOTING; 1155]

rifleman *n* [➡ MILITARY PERSONNEL; 828]

rift 1 *n* **crack**, hole, fissure, split, crevice, cleft, aperture, fracture, opening, gap, fault, rupture. [➡ HOLES, GAPS, AND FORKS; 1251] 2 *n* **disagreement**, difference, conflict, falling-out, quarrel, dispute. [➡ ARGUMENT; 47]

rig 1 *v* **fix**, engineer, arrange, prepare, fit, put together, assemble, equip, furnish (*formal*). [➡BUILD; 353] 2 *v* **improvise**, fix up, invent, set up, assemble, provide, slap together, make up. [➡ARRANGE AND CREATE ORDER; 358] *Opposite:* plan. 3 *n* **oil rig**, platform, derrick. [➡INDUSTRIAL BUILDINGS; 1086] 4 *n* (*informal*) **dress**, clothes, clothing, getup (*informal*), rigout, gear (*informal*), togs (*informal*), attire (*formal*), outfit, threads (*US slang*). [➡CLOTHES AND ACCESSORIES; 864] 5 *v* **manipulate**, falsify, mock up, fix, set up, arrange, swindle, trick. [➡FALSIFY AND CHEAT; 177]

rigatoni *type of* **pasta**. [➡PASTA; 1179]

rigging *n* **ropes**, chains, wires, supports, pulleys, controls. [➡FASTENERS, LINKS, AND NETWORKS; 1246]

right 1 *adj* **correct**, accurate, true, exact, precise, spot-on (*informal*), dead-on (*informal*), factual, veracious. [➡CORRECT; 183] *Opposite:* wrong. 2 *adj* **appropriate**, respectable, fitting, proper, desirable, best, reasonable, suited, decent, suitable. [➡APPROPRIATE, SUITABLE, ADVISABLE; 185] *Opposite:* inappropriate. 3 *adj* **just**, proper, fair, moral, honourable, upright, righteous, acceptable, justified, nondiscriminatory. [➡MORALLY GOOD; 775] *Opposite:* immoral. 4 *adj* **well**, healthy, in shape, fit, fine (*informal*), very well, satisfactory, hale. [➡FINE; 738] *Opposite:* ill. 5 *adv* **correctly**, exactly, accurately, precisely, directly, perfectly, dead on, plumb (*informal*), on the nose (*US informal*). [➡CORRECT; 183] *Opposite:* inexactly. 6 *adv* **appropriately**, as it should be, acceptably, suitably, properly, aptly, reasonably, well. [➡APPROPRIATE, SUITABLE, ADVISABLE; 185] *Opposite:* unsuitably. 7 *adv* **utterly**, entirely, completely, absolutely, totally, straight, intensely, very. [➡TO A GREAT EXTENT; 130] 8 *n* **truth**, honesty, goodness, morality, fairness, justice. [➡MORALLY GOOD; 775] *Opposite:* wrong. 9 *n* **entitlement**, privilege, due, birthright, justification, claim, permission, merit. [➡THE LAW AND LEGAL AUTHORITY; 814] 10 *v* **redress**, rectify, amend, remedy, correct, restore. [➡CORRECT AND PUT RIGHT; 378]

right and proper *adj* [➡MORALLY GOOD; 775]

right-angled *adj* **angled**, square, rectilinear, ninety-degree, right-angle. [➡ANGULAR SHAPE; 1216]

right away *adv* **immediately**, straightaway, at once, instantaneously, right now, just now, without ado, at this instant, without delay, pronto (*informal*). [➡HAPPENING QUICKLY; 104]

righteous *adj* **virtuous**, moral, good, just, blameless, upright, honourable, honest, respectable, decent. [➡MORALLY GOOD; 775] *Opposite:* sinful.

righteousness *n* **virtue**, morality, justice, decency, uprightness, rectitude, honesty, blamelessness. [➡MORALLY GOOD; 775] *Opposite:* wickedness.

rightful *adj* **fair**, equitable (*formal*), correct, legal, due, just, apt, in principle. [➡LEGAL; 815] *Opposite:* unlawful.

rightfulness *n* **truth**, fairness, correctness, legality, lawfulness, justice, impartiality, legitimacy. [➡LEGAL; 815]

right hand *n* **assistant**, aide, deputy, lieutenant, helper, helping hand. [➡SUBORDINATES AND ASSISTANTS; 966]

See Compare and Contrast at **assistant**.

right-hand 1 *adj* **right**, rightward, starboard. [➡GENERAL LOCATIONS; 159] *Opposite:* left-hand. 2 *adj* **trusted**, important, reliable, principal, main, favourite. [➡RELATIONSHIP TO ANOTHER; 973]

right-handed *adj* **clockwise**, left to right, circular, round, helical, spiral. [➡DIRECTION OF MOTION; 346] *Opposite:* left-handed.

rightio (*dated informal*) *see* **righto**.

rightist *adj* **right-wing**, conservative, traditionalist. [➡STYLES AND SYSTEMS OF GOVERNMENT; 806]

rightly 1 *adv* **correctly**, truly, exactly, accurately, precisely, justly, properly, appropriately. [➡CORRECT; 183] *Opposite:* wrongly. 2 *adv* **justly**, fittingly, justifiably, equitably (*formal*), suitably, rightfully, legally, lawfully, correctly, duly, fairly. [➡LEGAL; 815] *Opposite:* unreasonably. 3 *adv* (*informal*) **for certain**, without a shadow of a doubt, justifiably, for sure, certainly, positively, absolutely. [➡CERTAIN; 175]

right-minded *adj* **reasonable**, sensible, fair-minded, decent, rational, right-thinking. [➡POSITIVE INTELLECTUAL CHARACTERISTICS; 525]

rightness 1 *n* **rectitude**, correctness, faultlessness, truth, precision, accuracy, exactness. [➡CORRECT; 183] 2 *n* **aptness**, suitability, appropriateness, timeliness, properness, equitableness (*formal*). [➡APPROPRIATE, SUITABLE, ADVISABLE; 185] *Opposite:* inappropriateness.

right now *adv* [➡PRESENT; 85]

righto (*dated informal*) *adv* **okay** (*informal*), okeydokey (*informal humorous*), right, sure (*informal*), all right. [➡EXPRESSIONS OF AGREEMENT; 649]

right oh (*dated informal*) *see* **righto**.

right-thinking *adj* [➡POSITIVE INTELLECTUAL CHARACTERISTICS; 525]

rightward *adj* [➡DIRECTION OF MOTION; 346]

right whale *type of* **whale**. [➡WHALE; 991]

right-wing *adj* **conservative**, rightist, traditionalist. [➡STYLES AND SYSTEMS OF GOVERNMENT; 806] *Opposite:* left-wing.

right-winger *n* **conservative**, rightist, traditionalist. [➡PHILOSOPHICAL AND POLITICAL THINKERS; 782] *Opposite:* liberal.

rigid 1 *adj* **unbending**, inflexible, stiff, firm, unyielding, inelastic. [➡RIGID AND HARD; 1210] *Opposite:* floppy. 2 *adj* **severe**, strict, harsh, set, stern, inflexible. [➡DIFFICULT TO PLEASE; 516] *Opposite:* lax.

rigidity 1 *n* **stiffness**, inflexibility, inelasticity, firmness, rigour. [➡RIGID AND HARD; 1210] *Opposite:* floppiness. 2 *n* **inflexibility**, firmness, severity, strictness, stringency. [➡DIFFICULT TO PLEASE; 516] *Opposite:* laxness.

rigidly *adv* **strictly**, severely, firmly, inflexibly, unbendingly, tightly, harshly. [➡DIFFICULT TO PLEASE; 516] *Opposite:* loosely.

rigmarole 1 *n* **explanation**, account, excuse, palaver, verbiage, waffle (*informal*), overelaboration. [➡MEANINGLESS SPEECH OR WRITING; 677] 2 *n* **hassle** (*informal*), carry-on (*informal*), fuss, bother, ritual, to-do (*informal*), business. [➡NUISANCES; 254]

rigor mortis *n* [➡DEATH AND BEREAVEMENT; 927]

rigorous 1 *adj* **hard**, severe, harsh, demanding, laborious, rough, arduous, difficult. [➡DIFFICULTY AND COMPLEXITY; 243] *Opposite:* mild. 2 *adj* **exact**, thorough, precise, meticulous, painstaking, accurate, careful, scrupulous. [➡EXACT; 204] *Opposite:* slapdash.

rigorousness 1 *n* **strictness**, discipline, severity, harshness, difficulty, arduousness. [➡DIFFICULTY AND COMPLEXITY; 243] *Opposite:* lenience. 2 *n* **exactness**, thoroughness, discipline, meticulousness, scrupulousness, carefulness. [➡EXACT; 204] *Opposite:* negligence.

rigour 1 *n* **severity**, strictness, harshness, intransigence, dogmatism, rigidity, intolerance, inflexibility, firmness. [➡DIFFICULT TO PLEASE; 516] *Opposite:* flexibility. 2 *n* **thoroughness**, consistency, exactitude, precision, meticulousness, accuracy, scrupulousness, attention to detail, care. [➡POSITIVE INTELLECTUAL CHARACTERISTICS; 525] *Opposite:* negligence. 3 *n* **hardship**, difficulty, adversity, hard time, difficult time, demand, stricture (*formal*), restriction, trial, trouble. [➡DIFFICULTY AND COMPLEXITY; 243] *Opposite:* mildness. 4 *n* **stiffness**, rigidity, unresponsiveness, stiffening, rigor mortis. [➡RIGID AND HARD; 1210] *Opposite:* flexibility.

rigout *n* [➡CLOTHES AND ACCESSORIES; 864]

rig out (*informal*) 1 *v* **equip**, provide, prepare, furnish (*formal*), arrange, fit out. [➡EQUIP AND SUPPLY; 436] 2 *v* **dress up**, kit out, clothe, get up (*informal*), attire (*formal*). [➡DRESS, WEAR, AND UNDRESS; 868]

rig up *v* **improvise**, cobble together, set up, assemble, fix up, provide. [➡CREATION; 347] *Opposite:* plan.

rile (*informal*) *v* **anger**, enrage, annoy, irritate, bug (*informal*), irk, peeve (*informal*), aggravate (*informal*), vex. [➡ANGER AND ANNOY; 570] *Opposite:* placate.

riled (*informal*) *adj* [➡IRRITATION AND ANGER; 542]

rim *n* **edge**, border, lip, perimeter, circumference, brim. [➡EXTREMITIES OF PHYSICAL OBJECTS; 1249] *Opposite:* centre.

rime *n* **frost**, hoar frost, ice. [➡COLD WEATHER; 1051]

rind *n* **peel**, skin, husk, crust, coat, coating, outer layer, integument. [➡FRUIT AND VEGETABLES; 1175] *Opposite:* flesh.

ring 1 *n* **circle**, loop, hoop, band, halo. [➡ROUNDED SHAPE; 1217] 2 *type of* **jewellery**. [➡JEWELLERY; 866] 3 *type of* **ringing sound**. [➡RINGING AND TOOTING SOUNDS; 1258] 4 *n* **phone call**, telephone call, buzz (*informal*), bell (*informal*). [➡TELEPHONE COMMUNICATION; 48] 5 *n* **group**, band, gang, organization, team, cartel, mob. [➡CRIMINALS; 821] 6 *n* **impression**, semblance, appearance, feel, air. [➡APPEARANCE AND ATMOSPHERE; 1236] 7 *v* **peal**, tinkle, chime, toll, ding-dong, jingle. [➡EMIT RINGING AND TOOTING SOUNDS; 368] 8 *v* **call**, phone, telephone, ring up, give a bell (*informal*), give a buzz (*informal*), give a tinkle. [➡TELEPHONE AND PAGE; 682] 9 *v* **resonate**, resound, ring out, reverberate, echo, re-echo. [➡SOUND EMISSION; 363] 10 *v* **encircle**, enclose, circle, surround. [➡EXIST IN CLOSE PROXIMITY; 21].

ring a bell (*informal*) *v* **strike a chord**, jog somebody's memory, sound familiar, be reminiscent, remind. [➡REMIND; 748]

ring-fence 1 *v* **set aside**, isolate, restrict, stipulate, protect, separate, specify, limit. [➡AVOID, PREVENT, LIMIT, AND CONTROL; 278] 2 *n* **restriction**, limitation, specification, separation, reservation, agreement. [➡CAPTIVITY AND LOSS OF FREEDOM; 249] 3 *n* **fence**, barrier, boundary, perimeter, border. [➡BARRIERS; 1112]

ring finger *part of* **arm or hand**. [➡ARM AND HAND; 696]

ringhals *type of* **poisonous snake**. [➡SNAKE; 995]

ringleader *n* **gang leader**, leader of the pack, agitator, instigator, inciter, leader, stirrer (*informal*). [➡INTERFERING PEOPLE AND TELLTALES; 950]

ringlet *n* **curl**, lock, twist, coil, spiral, wisp, whorl, wave. [➡HAIR; 485]

ringlets 1 *n* [➡HAIR; 485] 2 *type of* **hairstyle**. [➡HAIR STYLES AND HAIR PIECES; 489]

ringmaster *n* **master of ceremonies**, MC, emcee (*informal*), host, presenter, chair, chairperson. [➡WORKERS IN ENTERTAINMENT AND MEDIA; 873]

ring off *v* **hang up**, put the receiver down, finish, go. [➡TELEPHONE AND PAGE; 682] *Opposite:* hang on.

ring out *v* **be heard**, sound, rise, pierce the silence, blast out, blare out, peal out. [➡EMIT RINGING AND TOOTING SOUNDS; 368]

ring road *type of* **major road**. [➡ROADS; 1105]

ringside *adj* **front row**, grandstand, touch line, unimpeded, unobstructed, clear, good, perfect. [➡APPROPRIATE, SUITABLE, ADVISABLE; 185]

ring up *v* **call**, phone, telephone, ring, give a bell (*informal*), give a buzz (*informal*), give a tinkle. [➡TELEPHONE AND PAGE; 682]

rink *n* **arena**, floor, space, area. [➡BUILDINGS FOR PUBLIC ENTERTAINMENT; 1083]

rinse 1 *n* **wash**, clean, bathe, sluice, dip, wet, soak, douse, sponge down, bath. [➡CLEAN AND POLISH; 404] 2 *n* **solution**, colourant, dye, tint, bleach, stain. [➡DYES AND COLOURANTS; 1269]

riot 1 *n* **uprising**, insurrection, disturbance, unrest, demonstration, insurgence, mutiny, rebellion, revolt, revolution. [➡AGGRESSIVE EVENT; 39] 2 *n* (*informal*) **laugh** (*informal*), hoot (*slang*), scream (*informal*), gas (*informal*). [➡FUNNY AND AMUSING; 217] 3 *v* **mutiny**, demonstrate, run riot, rebel, revolt, rampage, rise up, run amok, take to the streets. [➡PROTEST AND EXPRESS DISAPPROVAL; 643]

rioter *n* **demonstrator**, rebel, revolutionary, insurgent, protester, mutineer, marcher, dissident. [➡UNCOOPERATIVE OR REBELLIOUS PERSON; 567]

riotous 1 *adj* **violent**, disorderly, unruly, uncontrolled, uncontained, lawless, mutinous, rebellious, revolutionary, anarchic. [➡REBELLIOUSNESS AND DISOBEDIENCE; 566] *Opposite:* peaceful. 2 *adj* **wild**, debauched, uncontrolled, out of control, hedonistic, intemperate, immoderate (*formal*), rowdy, rambunctious. [➡DISORDER AND CHAOS; 246] *Opposite:* subdued.

riotously 1 *adv* **hilariously**, madly, side-splittingly, screamingly, wildly, raucously. [➡FUNNY AND AMUSING; 217] 2 *adv* **raucously**, rowdily, wildly, rambunctiously, noisily, uproariously. [➡DISORDER AND CHAOS; 246] *Opposite:* quietly.

riotousness *n* [➡DISORDER AND CHAOS; 246]

riot police *n* [➡THE POLICE, ARREST, AND PRE-TRIAL PROCEEDINGS; 818]

rip 1 *v* **tear**, split, cleave, shred, scratch, slash, slit, break, gash. [➡TEAR, BREAK, AND CUT; 361] 2 *v* **snatch**, tear, seize, grab, pluck, pull. [➡TAKE SOMETHING AWAY; 426] 3 *v* **speed**, tear, dash, rush, fly, pelt, zip (*informal*), zoom, whiz, dart. [➡MOVE FAST; 314] 4 *n* **tear**, split, scratch, cleft, slash, slit, gash, opening, break, rupture. [➡HOLES, GAPS, AND FORKS; 1251]

See Compare and Contrast at **tear**.

rip apart *v* [➡TEAR, BREAK, AND CUT; 361]

ripcord *n* **cord**, line, string, cable, rope, release, handle. [➡FASTENERS, LINKS, AND NETWORKS; 1246]

ripe 1 *adj* (*informal*) **pungent**, strong, sour, strong-smelling, off, smelly. [➡SMELL AND SMELLING; 706] *Opposite:* sweet. 2 *adj* **mature**, ready, grown, fully grown, matured, seasoned, developed, ripened. [➡IN GOOD REPAIR; 1231] *Opposite:* unripe. 3 *adj* **ready**, suitable, prepared, crying out, disposed, apt, set, developed. [➡ORDER AND ORGANISATION; 207]

ripen *v* **mature**, season, grow, develop, evolve. [➡CHANGE; 373]

ripeness *n* **maturity**, readiness, mellowness, age. [➡OLD, OLD-FASHIONED; 168]

rip-off (*informal*) *n* **swindle**, swizz, con, cheat, diddle (*informal*). [➡DECEPTION AND LIES; 661]

rip off (*informal*) *v* **overcharge**, cheat, swindle, do (*informal*), fleece (*informal*), diddle (*informal*), dupe, deceive. [➡STEAL AND ROB; 427]

rip open *v* [➡TEAR, BREAK, AND CUT; 361]

riposte 1 *n* **reply**, retort, comeback, wisecrack (*informal*), rejoinder (*formal*), response, answer, return. [➡REPLY AND ANSWER; 669] 2 *v* **retort**, reply, come back, return, counter, answer, fight back, rejoin (*formal*), respond. [➡REPLY AND ANSWER; 669]

See Compare and Contrast at **answer**.

ripped *adj* [➡IN BAD REPAIR; 1233]

ripping (*dated informal*) *adj* [➡EXTRAORDINARY: UNCOMMON; 206]

ripple 1 *v* **undulate**, swell, flow, move, rise and fall, heave. [➡BOUNCE, UNDULATE, AND VIBRATE; 309] 2 *n* **wave**, undulation, swell, current, wrinkle. [➡BOUNCE, UNDULATE, AND VIBRATE; 309] *Opposite:* stillness.

rip-roaring (*informal*) *adj* **exciting**, uproarious, boisterous, rollicking, ripping (*dated informal*), energetic, riotous. [➡EXTRAORDINARY: UNCOMMON; 206] *Opposite:* boring.

rip to pieces *v* [➡TEAR, BREAK, AND CUT; 361]

rip to shreds *v* [➡TEAR, BREAK, AND CUT; 361]

rip up *v* **tear up**, shred, pull apart, chew up, pull to pieces, destroy. [➡TEAR, BREAK, AND CUT; 361] *Opposite:* piece together.

rise 1 *v* **stand up**, get up, get to your feet, arise (*archaic or literary*). [➡GO UPWARDS; 307] *Opposite:* sit down. 2 *v* **go up**, increase, climb, mount, get higher, ascend, augment (*formal*), grow, escalate, levitate, soar, rocket. [➡GO UPWARDS; 307] *Opposite:* drop. 3 *v* **rebel**, revolt, mutiny, rise up, riot. [➡PROTEST AND EXPRESS DISAPPROVAL; 643] 4 *v* **originate**, begin, start, come out of, set in motion. [➡GRADUALLY COME INTO EXISTENCE; 1] *Opposite:* end. 5 *v* **emerge**, come up, appear, arise, be apparent, tower, come into view, materialize, come out. [➡APPEAR AND EMERGE; 3] *Opposite:* disappear. 6 *v* **wake up**, get up, get out of bed, arise, awaken, come to life. [➡GO UPWARDS; 307] *Opposite:* retire. 7 *n* **increase**, promotion, advance, elevation. [➡CHANGE OF INTENSITY: MORE; 395] 8 *n* **increase**, growth, upsurge, intensification, escalation, upswing, augmentation, enlargement. [➡CHANGE OF INTENSITY: MORE; 395] *Opposite:* decrease. 9 *n* **growth**, spread, development, expansion, advance, progress, improvement, amelioration, upturn. [➡CHANGE OF INTENSITY: MORE; 395] *Opposite:* decline. 10 *n* **hill**, slope, incline, acclivity, elevation, gradient, bank, mount, hillock, mound, knoll. [➡MOUNTAINS AND HILLS; 1044] *Opposite:* hollow. 11 *n* **climb**, ascent, elevation. [➡GO UPWARDS; 307] *Opposite:* fall.

rise above *v* **surmount**, overcome, conquer, triumph over, surpass. [➡BEAT AND DEFEAT; 80]

rise and fall *n* **swell**, undulation, ripple, movement, rolling, fluctuation. [➡BOUNCE, UNDULATE, AND VIBRATE; 309] *Opposite:* stability.

rise to (*informal*) *v* **respond**, meet, shine, succeed, perform, behave. [➡BEAT AND DEFEAT; 80]

rise to the bait *v* **respond**, react, get angry, be provoked, answer, rejoin (*formal*), retort. [➡CHANGE OF MOOD AND COMPOSURE; 581] *Opposite:* ignore.

rise up 1 *v* **rebel**, revolt, riot, rise, mutiny, rampage, run amok, run riot, demonstrate. [➡PROTEST AND EXPRESS DISAPPROVAL; 643] 2 *v* **emerge**, stand up, arise (*archaic or literary*), float up, soar. [➡GRADUALLY COME INTO EXISTENCE; 1] *Opposite:* sink.

risibility 1 *n* (*formal*) **humorousness**, sense of humour, happiness, wit, humour. [➡CHEERFULNESS OF OUTLOOK; 504] *Opposite:* soberness. 2 *n* **ridiculousness**, ludicrousness, absurdity, laughableness, stupidity, foolishness. [➡BIZARRE AND PECULIAR; 258] *Opposite:* seriousness.

risible 1 *adj* **laughable**, ludicrous, absurd, ridiculous, stupid, foolish. [➡BIZARRE AND PECULIAR; 258] *Opposite:* serious. 2 *adj* (*formal*) **humorous**, good-humoured, happy, cheerful, cheery, hearty. [➡CHEERFULNESS OF OUTLOOK; 504] *Opposite:* sombre.

risibly *adv* [➡BIZARRE AND PECULIAR; 258]

rising 1 *adj* **increasing**, growing, going up, mounting, getting higher, getting bigger, intensifying, expanding, escalating, climbing. [➡CHANGE OF INTENSITY: MORE; 395] *Opposite:* falling. 2 *n* **uprising**, rebellion, revolt, mutiny, riot, insurrection, revolution, insurgence. [➡AGGRESSIVE EVENT; 39]

risk 1 *n* **danger**, jeopardy, peril, hazard, menace, threat. [➡DANGER; 236] *Opposite:* safety. 2 *n* **possibility**, chance, danger, hazard, gamble, probability, stake, consequence.

[➡POSSIBLE AND PROBABLE; 178] **3** *v* **endanger**, imperil (*formal*), jeopardize, lay bare, expose. [➡PUT AT RISK; 385] *Opposite:* protect. **4** *v* **chance**, hazard, attempt, gamble, venture, run the risk of, take the risk of, take a chance. [➡GAMBLE AND TAKE RISKS; 467] *Opposite:* play safe.

risk factor *n* [➡DANGER; 236]

risk-free *adj* [➡SAFE AND SAFETY; 192]

riskiness *n* **hazardousness**, perilousness, precariousness, dangerousness, audaciousness, insecurity. [➡DANGER; 236] *Opposite:* safety.

risky *adj* **dangerous**, hazardous, chancy, dicey (*informal*), dodgy (*informal*), precarious, perilous, unsafe, uncertain. [➡DANGEROUS; 237] *Opposite:* safe.

risotto *type of* **cooked dish.** [➡PREPARED DISHES; 1169]

risqué *adj* **racy**, rude, lewd, salacious, blue (*informal*), naughty, suggestive, smutty (*informal*), bawdy, ribald. [➡MORALLY BAD; 776] *Opposite:* decorous.

rissole *type of* **processed meat.** [➡TYPES AND CUTS OF MEAT; 1176]

rite **1** *n* **ritual**, ceremony, formal procedure, service, sacrament, formality. [➡RELIGIONS AND RELIGIOUS PRACTICES; 778] **2** *n* **custom**, habit, practice, routine, procedure, convention, tradition, usage. [➡WAYS OF DOING THINGS; 295]

ritual **1** *n* **rite**, ceremony, service, formal procedure, sacrament, formality, ceremonial. [➡RELIGIONS AND RELIGIOUS PRACTICES; 778] **2** *n* **custom**, habit, practice, routine, procedure, schedule, convention, tradition, usage. [➡WAYS OF DOING THINGS; 295] **3** *adj* **ceremonial**, procedural, ceremonious, sacramental, formal. [➡CEREMONIES AND ANNIVERSARIES; 38] **4** *adj* **customary**, habitual, usual, normal, expected, predictable, routine, traditional, conventional. [➡ORDINARINESS; 245]

ritualistic *adj* **ceremonial**, formalized, formulaic, ritualized, sacred. [➡CEREMONIES AND ANNIVERSARIES; 38]

ritually *adv* **formally**, officially, ceremonially, ritualistically, repetitively, prescriptively. [➡CEREMONIES AND ANNIVERSARIES; 38]

ritzy (*informal*) *adj* [➡IN POOR TASTE; 230]

rival **1** *n* **competitor**, opponent, adversary, contender, challenger, enemy, foe (*literary*). [➡ENEMIES AND TORMENTORS; 969] *Opposite:* ally. **2** *n* **equal**, match, counterpart, peer, equivalent. [➡EQUALITY; 155] **3** *v* **match**, equal, be the equal of, be similar to, compare with, resemble. [➡EQUALITY; 155] **4** *v* **oppose**, compete with, challenge, go up against, be against, contest, confront. [➡COMPETE, CONTEND, AND COMBAT; 304] **5** *v* **outdo**, surpass, exceed, beat, top, outshine. [➡BEAT AND DEFEAT; 80] **6** *adj* **competing**, opposing, challenging, contending, enemy, conflicting. [➡RELATIONSHIP TO ANOTHER; 973]

rivalry *n* **competition**, opposition, contention, competitiveness, enmity, conflict, challenge, jealousy. [➡RELATIONSHIP TO ANOTHER; 973] *Opposite:* cooperation.

rive (*literary*) *v* [➡TEAR, BREAK, AND CUT; 361]

riven (*literary*) *adj* **split**, torn apart, torn asunder (*formal*), divided, rent asunder (*formal*), fragmented. [➡IN BAD REPAIR; 1233] *Opposite:* united.

river *n* **stream**, waterway, tributary, brook, canal, watercourse. [➡RIVERS, LAKES, AND STREAMS; 1042]

riverbank *n* [➡RIVERS, LAKES, AND STREAMS; 1042]

riverside *n* **waterside**, water's edge, bank, shore. [➡RIVERS, LAKES, AND STREAMS; 1042]

rivet **1** *n* **pin**, nail, fastener, press stud, bolt, screw, snap (*US*). [➡FASTENERS, LINKS, AND NETWORKS; 1246] **2** *v* (*informal*) **fascinate**, enthral, entrance, interest, mesmerize. [➡APPEAL TO AND AROUSE INTEREST; 576] *Opposite:* bore. **3** *v* **fasten**, hold, pin, bolt, nail, fix, attach, join, weld, screw. [➡FASTEN, LINK, AND JOIN; 409]

riveted (*informal*) *adj* [➡PENSIVENESS AND INTEREST; 539]

riveting (*informal*) *adj* **fascinating**, enthralling, exciting, spellbinding, entrancing, interesting, mesmeric, exhilarating, thrilling, captivating. [➡INTERESTING AND MEANINGFUL; 191] *Opposite:* boring.

rivulet *n* **stream**, brook, burn, creek (*US*), gully. [➡RIVERS, LAKES, AND STREAMS; 1042]

RNA *n* **nucleic acid**, ribonucleic acid, genetic material. [➡REPRODUCTION AND HEREDITY; 726]

roach **1** *type of* **freshwater fish.** [➡FRESHWATER FISH; 1010] **2** (*informal*) *type of* **beetle.** [➡BEETLES AND WEEVILS; 1016]

road *n* **street**, thoroughfare, lane, way. [➡ROADS; 1105]

road

◆ *types of major road*
A-road, artery, avenue, beltway (*US*), boulevard, bypass, clearway, divided highway (*US*), dual carriageway, expressway (*US*), flyover, freeway (*US*), highway, interstate (*US*), limited-access highway (*US*), main road, motorway, parkway, ring road, speedway (*US*), superhighway (*US*), throughway (*US*), thruway (*US*), toll road, trunk road, trunk route (*US*), turnpike

◆ *types of minor road*
access road, access strip, alley, alleyway, B-road, backstreet, blind alley, byroad, byway, cart track, cul-de-sac, dead end, dirt track, esplanade, lane, mews, parade, path, promenade, ramp (*US*), side road, side street, slip road, street, track

roadblock *n* **barricade**, barrier, sentry post, obstruction, blockade. [➡BARRIERS; 1112]

roadhouse (*dated*) *n* **hotel**, pub, bar, transport café, tavern, greasy spoon, motel, inn. [➡HOTELS, RESTAURANTS, AND CLUBS; 1081]

roadroller *type of* **commercial or industrial vehicle.** [➡VEHICLES; 1144]

road show **1** *n* **radio show**, live broadcast, open-air broadcast, broadcast, tour. [➡PERFORMANCES AND SHOWS; 42] **2** *n* **campaign**, publicity campaign, advertising campaign, tour, circus. [➡ADVERTISING AND PUBLICITY; 605]

roadside café *type of* **eating place.** [➡HOTELS, RESTAURANTS, AND CLUBS; 1081]

road sign *n* **sign**, signpost, notice, stop sign, one-way sign, chevrons, signal, yield sign (*US*). [➡ SIGNPOSTS, SIGNALS AND BILLBOARDS; 596]

road-test *v* **try out**, test, test drive, trial, run, analyse. [➡ EXAMINE AND ASSESS; 754]

road test 1 *n* **test**, drive, test drive. [➡ PREPARATORY EVENT; 57] 2 *n* **controlled test**, test, trial, field test, experiment, assay, analysis. [➡ EXAMINE AND ASSESS; 754]

roadway *n* **road**, street, thoroughfare, highway. [➡ ROADS; 1105]

roadworks *n* **road repairs**, carriageway repairs, maintenance work, construction work, repair work, contraflow. [➡ TRAVEL: TRAFFIC PROBLEMS AND HOLDUPS; 324]

roadworthiness *n* **safety**, soundness, reliability, working order. [➡ SAFE AND SAFETY; 192]

roadworthy *adj* **safe**, fit, legal, driveable, suitable, sound. [➡ SAFE AND SAFETY; 192]

roam *v* **wander**, rove, travel, journey, stray, ramble, meander. [➡ AIMLESS AND ERRANT MOTION; 344] *Opposite:* settle.

roamer *n* **wanderer**, traveller, rover, itinerant, nomad, drifter. [➡ TRAVEL: TRAVELLERS AND WALKERS; 320]

roaming *adj* **wandering**, roving, itinerant, nomadic, peripatetic, drifting, travelling. [➡ NOMADIC AND ROOTLESS LIFESTYLES; 884] *Opposite:* stationary.

roan *type of* **brown**. [➡ COLOURS; 1223]

roar 1 *type of* **continuous sound**. [➡ CONTINUOUS SOUNDS; 1257] 2 *type of* **animal sound**. [➡ SOUNDS MADE BY ANIMALS; 1260]

roaring 1 *adj* **busy**, thriving, prosperous, active. [➡ SUCCESSFUL AND PROMISING; 81] *Opposite:* slack. 2 *adj* **noisy**, loud, deafening, boisterous, thunderous. [➡ LOUD OR UNPLEASANT SOUNDS; 1265] *Opposite:* quiet.

roast *v* **bake**, cook, heat. [➡ COOKING AND FOOD PREPARATION; 354]

roasting (*informal*) *adj* **boiling**, hot, red-hot, sweltering, burning up, burning, scorching (*informal*). [➡ HOT WEATHER; 1050] *Opposite:* cool.

rob 1 *v* **steal from**, take from, hold up, raid, pickpocket, mug, stick up (*US informal*). [➡ STEAL AND ROB; 427] 2 *v* **deprive**, cheat, strip, fleece (*informal*), drain. [➡ STEAL AND ROB; 427]

robber *n* **thief**, burglar, pickpocket, shoplifter, mugger, raider. [➡ CRIMINALS; 821]

robbery *n* **theft**, burglary, break-in, mugging, stealing, raid, shoplifting, pilfering, nicking (*slang*). [➡ CRIMES; 817]

See Compare and Contrast at **theft**.

robe *n* **dressing gown**, negligée, housecoat, bathrobe, gown, kimono. [➡ GARMENTS AND OUTFITS; 865]

robin *type of* **common bird**. [➡ BIRD; 997]

robot *n* **automaton**, android, machine, computer, mechanical device. [➡ DEVICES; 1114]

robotic 1 *adj* **mechanical**, mechanized, automated, automatic, cybernetic, computerized. [➡ MACHINERY; 1113] 2 *adj* **machine-like**, mechanical, unresponsive, unfeeling, humourless, unemotional, cold. [➡ NEUTRALITY AND INDIFFERENCE; 554] *Opposite:* warm.

robotics *n* **cybernetics**, automation, engineering, manufacturing, science, computing. [➡ MACHINERY; 1113]

robust *adj* **healthy**, vigorous, hearty, strong, tough, forceful, stout, hardy. [➡ FIT AND STRONG; 737] *Opposite:* weak.

robustness *n* **heftiness**, sturdiness, strength, toughness, forcefulness, stoutness, healthiness, vigour, hardiness. [➡ FIT AND STRONG; 737] *Opposite:* weakness.

rock 1 *n* **stone**, boulder, pebble. [➡ STONES, ROCKS, AND BOULDERS; 1057] 2 *n* **pillar**, mainstay, tower of strength, stalwart. [➡ PEOPLE WHO ARE APPROVED OF; 955] 3 *v* **sway**, swing, shake, move up and down, pitch. [➡ MOVE SOMETHING ON THE SPOT; 337] 4 *v* (*informal*) **astound**, shock, shake, stun, disturb, upset. [➡ SURPRISE AND IMPRESS; 575] 5 *type of* **popular music**. [➡ MUSIC, SONGS, AND SINGING; 907]

rock and roll *type of* **popular music**. [➡ MUSIC, SONGS, AND SINGING; 907]

rock bottom *n* **the lowest**, the bottom, the depths, all-time low, nadir, the pits (*informal*). [➡ DIFFICULT SITUATIONS; 72]

rock climber *n* [➡ PEOPLE IN SPORTS AND LEISURE; 876]

rock climbing *n* [➡ HOBBIES, GAMES, AND SPORTS; 875]

rocker 1 *n* **biker**, greaser, Hell's Angel, motorcyclist, youth, teenager. [➡ PEOPLE IN SPORTS AND LEISURE; 876] 2 *n* (*informal*) **rock star**, rock musician, rock singer, rock and roller, guitarist, bassist, singer, drummer, pop star. [➡ MUSICIANS AND SINGERS; 908] 3 *n* (*informal*) **rock fan**, fan, teddy boy, ted, devotee, aficionado, music lover. [➡ DEVOTEES AND ADDICTED PEOPLE; 557]

rockery *n* **garden**, rock garden, alpine garden, terrace. [➡ GARDENS; 1073]

rocket 1 *v* **speed**, whiz, hurtle, fly, zoom, career. [➡ MOVE FAST; 314] 2 *v* (*informal*) **shoot up**, soar, increase rapidly, go through the roof, go sky-high. [➡ CHANGE OF SIZE: BIGGER; 393] *Opposite:* plummet. 3 *type of* **firework**. [➡ EXPLOSIVES; 1154] 4 *type of* **spacecraft**. [➡ SPACE VEHICLES; 1062]

rocket engine *part of* **spacecraft**. [➡ SPACE VEHICLES; 1062]

rocket ship (*US*) *n* [➡ SPACE VEHICLES; 1062]

rock face *n* **cliff face**, face, precipice, crag, cliff, overhang, sheer drop, sea cliff. [➡ MOUNTAINS AND HILLS; 1044]

rock garden *n* **garden**, rockery, alpine garden, terrace. [➡ GARDENS; 1073]

rock-hard *adj* **solid**, firm, cast-iron, hard as nails, like granite, indestructible. [➡ RIGID AND HARD; 1210] *Opposite:* soft.

rockiness *n* **shakiness**, unsteadiness, uncertainty, insecurity, instability. [➡ DANGER; 236] *Opposite:* steadiness.

rocking chair *type of* **seating**. [➡ FURNITURE; 858]

rocking horse *type of* **toy**. [➡ TOYS; 880]

rock musician *n* [➡ MUSICIANS AND SINGERS; 908]

rock singer *n* [➡ MUSICIANS AND SINGERS; 908]

rock-solid 1 *adj* **firm**, unshakable, solid, rigid, unyielding, unwavering. [➡ SAFE AND SAFETY; 192] *Opposite:* shaky. 2 *adj* **durable**, unbreakable, strong, firm, enduring, permanent. [➡ DURABLE; 1209] *Opposite:* breakable.

rock star *n* [➡ MUSICIANS AND SINGERS; 908]

rock-strewn *adj* **stony**, rocky, gravelly, pebbly, rough. [➡ PHYSICAL TEXTURE; 1221] *Opposite:* smooth.

rock the boat (*informal*) *v* **cause an argument**, cause an upset, cause trouble. [➡ PROTEST AND EXPRESS DISAPPROVAL; 643]

rockweed *type of* **alga**. [➡ MICROORGANISMS, FUNGI, AND ALGAE; 1023]

rocky 1 *adj* **stony**, rock-strewn, pebbly, gravelly. [➡ PHYSICAL TEXTURE; 1221] 2 *adj* **difficult**, troubled, uncertain, not easy, hard, trying, strenuous, tough. [➡ DIFFICULTY AND COMPLEXITY; 243] *Opposite:* easy. 3 *adj* **shaky**, unsteady, wobbly, unsound, insecure, unstable, inconstant, wavering, quaking. [➡ DANGEROUS; 237] *Opposite:* stable.

rococo *type of* **pre-20th-century architecture**. [➡ BUILDING AND ARCHITECTURE; 1075]

rod *n* **bar**, pole, stick, shaft, dowel, fishing rod. [➡ STICKS, POLES, AND WEDGES; 1253]

rodent

◆ *types of rodent*
beaver, capybara, chinchilla, chipmunk, coypu, dormouse, gerbil, gopher, groundhog, guinea pig, hamster, jerboa, lemming, marmot, mole, mouse, muskrat, prairie dog, rat, shrew, squirrel, vole, woodchuck

rodeo *n* **competition**, display, festival, meet, fair, trial. [➡ NON-AGGRESSIVE/SPORTING EVENT; 40]

roe *part of* **fish**. [➡ EGGS AND SPAWN; 728]

roger (*informal*) *interj* **OK** (*informal*), right (*informal*), fine, yeah (*informal*), great (*informal*), yes. [➡ EXPRESSIONS OF AGREEMENT; 649]

rogue *n* **scoundrel**, rascal, reprobate, ne'er-do-well (*dated*), cad (*dated*), scallywag (*dated informal*). [➡ VILLAINS AND THUGS; 947]

roguery 1 *n* **dishonesty**, deceit, unscrupulousness, double-dealing, sharp practice, criminality, cheating, knavery (*archaic*). [➡ DECEITFUL; 514] *Opposite:* honesty. 2 *n* **mischief**, mischievousness, playfulness, naughtiness, tricks, pranks. [➡ BAD BEHAVIOUR OR ACTION; 255]

roguish 1 *adj* **dishonest**, deceitful, unscrupulous, double-dealing, criminal, cheating. [➡ DECEITFUL; 514] *Opposite:* honest. 2 *adj* **mischievous**, naughty, impish, wicked, malicious, wayward. [➡ BAD MANNERS AND SOCIAL SKILLS; 522]

roguishness 1 *n* **unscrupulousness**, dishonesty, deceit, double-dealing, sharp practice, criminality, cheating, knavery (*archaic*). [➡ DECEITFUL; 514] *Opposite:* honesty. 2 *n* **mischievousness**, mischief, playfulness, naughtiness, tricks, pranks. [➡ BAD BEHAVIOUR OR ACTION; 255]

roister 1 *v* **revel**, party (*informal*), make merry, celebrate, carouse (*literary*), drink. [➡ LEISURE AND RECREATION; 874] 2 *v* **brag**, boast, show off, swagger, gloat, exult. [➡ BOAST; 617]

roisterer 1 *n* **reveller**, partygoer, merrymaker, pleasure-seeker, celebrator, carouser (*literary*), drinker, party animal (*informal*). [➡ PLEASURE-SEEKERS AND HEDONISTS; 886] 2 *n* **show-off** (*informal*), loudmouth (*informal*), bigmouth (*informal*), braggart, boaster. [➡ SELF-IMPORTANT AND SELF-SEEKING PEOPLE; 949]

role 1 *n* **part**, character, person, title role, starring role, hero, heroine, protagonist. [➡ PERFORMERS; 905] 2 *n* **position**, function, responsibility, job, task, part. [➡ JOB; 833]

role model *n* **example**, model, exemplar (*literary*), paradigm. [➡ PERFECT EXAMPLES AND EMBODIMENTS; 67]

role-play *v* **act**, act out, enact, play, imagine, work through, work out. [➡ PRETEND AND MIMIC; 60]

role-playing *n* **acting**, acting out, game-playing, imagination, play-acting, role-play. [➡ THE PERFORMING ARTS; 904]

roll 1 *v* **bowl**, trundle, troll, set rolling, roll along, move. [➡ PUSH, PULL, SLIDE; 336] 2 *v* **revolve**, turn, turn over, turn round, spin, rotate. [➡ TAKE UP A NEW POSITION; 313] 3 *n* **reel**, cylinder, spool, tube. [➡ CONTAINERS, RECEPTACLES, AND PACKAGING; 1244] 4 *type of* **roll or bun**. [➡ BREAD, FLOUR, AND BREAD PRODUCTS; 1178]

roll call 1 *n* **attendance check**, register check, checkup, check, monitoring, supervision. [➡ LISTS AND SCHEDULES; 588] 2 *n* **time**, slot, period, session, allotted time, regular time. [➡ TIMES OF DAY; 87]

roller *n* **breaker**, wave, whitecap. [➡ THE SEAS, OCEANS, AND SHORES; 1041]

rollerball *type of* **pen**. [➡ WRITING AND DRAWING IMPLEMENTS, AND MEDIA; 602]

roller-skate *v* **skate**, blade, skateboard. [➡ HOBBIES, GAMES, AND SPORTS; 875]

rollicking 1 *adj* **boisterous**, rowdy, loud, ripping (*dated informal*), carefree, swashbuckling, noisy, thumping (*informal*). [➡ EXTRAORDINARY: UNCOMMON; 206] 2 *n* (*informal*) **telling-off** (*informal*), reprimand, dressing-down, talking-to (*informal*), scolding. [➡ CRITICISMS AND ANGRY OUTBURSTS; 50]

roll in *v* **arrive**, enter, land, roll up, appear, breeze in. [➡ ARRIVE; 12] *Opposite:* leave.

rolling 1 *adj* **undulating**, rising and falling, gently sloping. [➡ ROUNDED SHAPE; 1217] *Opposite:* steep. 2 *adj* **progressing**, continuing, systematic, regular, developing. [➡ HAPPENING AND IN PROGRESS; 32]

rolling in it (*informal*) *adj* **rich**, wealthy, in the money, loaded (*slang*). *Opposite:* broke. (*informal*). [➡ WEALTH AND WEALTHY; 891]

roll in the aisles *v* [➡ LAUGHTER; 650]

roll out the red carpet *v* **treat like royalty**, give a hero's welcome, lionize, make a fuss of, welcome. [➡ TAKE CARE OF AND SPOIL; 301]

roll-top desk *type of* **table**. [➡ FURNITURE; 858]

roll up 1 *v* **appear**, turn up, ride up, show up, roll in.

[➡ARRIVE; 12] *Opposite:* leave. **2** *v* **turn up**, push back, furl. [➡CHANGE OF SHAPE; 386] *Opposite:* unroll.

ROM *type of* **software**. [➡COMPUTERS AND COMPUTING; 1126]

roman **1** *adj* **upright**, straight, plain. [➡PRINTING; 601] *Opposite:* italic. **2** *adj* **in classical style**, classical, ancient. [➡OLD, OLD-FASHIONED; 168]

Roman alphabet *type of* **alphabet**. [➡SYMBOLS, SIGNS, AND NUMBERS; 597]

Roman candle *type of* **firework**. [➡EXPLOSIVES; 1154]

romance **1** *n* **relationship**, love affair, affair, involvement, fling (*informal*). [➡RELATIONSHIP TO ANOTHER; 973] **2** *n* **love**, passion, amorousness, ardour, sex, eroticism, desire, sexual love. [➡SEXUAL AND ROMANTIC RELATIONSHIPS; 964] **3** *n* **allure**, excitement, adventure, nostalgia, feeling, sensation, exoticism, sense of adventure, sense of excitement, sense of history. [➡FEELINGS ABOUT THE PAST; 533] **4** *n* **fascination**, enthusiasm, passion, love, love affair, involvement, association. [➡PLEASURE, EXCITEMENT, AND ELATION; 535] **5** *n* **love story**, romantic story, romantic novel, romantic short story, romantic film, weepie (*informal*), romantic comedy, romantic tale. [➡FICTION AND DRAMA; 913] *Opposite:* tragedy. **6** *n* **adventure story**, adventure, tale, yarn (*informal*), romp (*informal*), story, narrative. [➡FICTION AND DRAMA; 913] **7** *n* **fantasy**, story, tall tale, fiction, daydream, tissue of lies. [➡DECEPTION AND LIES; 661] **8** *n* **short piece of music**, song, piece. [➡MUSIC, SONGS, AND SINGING; 907] **9** *v* **tell stories**, fantasize, romanticize. [➡DREAM, IMAGINE, AND FANTASIZE; 750] **10** *v* **be romantic**, act romantically, moon (*literary or humorous*), swoon, daydream, be in love, gush. [➡LIKE, LOVE, VALUE AND ENJOY; 579] **11** *v* **court** (*dated*), woo (*literary*), pay court to (*dated*), put on a pedestal. [➡ESTABLISHING RELATIONSHIPS WITH OTHERS; 974] **12** *v* **have an affair with**, have a love affair with, have a relationship with, step out with (*informal*), date, have a fling with, be involved with, sleep with (*informal*). [➡ESTABLISHING RELATIONSHIPS WITH OTHERS; 974]

Romanesque *type of* **pre-20th-century architecture**. [➡BUILDING AND ARCHITECTURE; 1075]

romantic **1** *adj* **loving**, passionate, tender, amorous, adoring, sexual. [➡APPRECIATION AND GRATITUDE; 536] *Opposite:* platonic. **2** *adj* **idealistic**, dreamy, quixotic, impractical, starry-eyed. [➡NEGATIVE INTELLECTUAL CHARACTERISTICS; 526] *Opposite:* prosaic.

Romantic *type of* **classical music**. [➡MUSIC, SONGS, AND SINGING; 907]

romanticism *n* **idealization**, fantasy, nostalgia, soft focus, rose-tinted glasses, invention, idealism, naivety. [➡DREAM, IMAGINE, AND FANTASIZE; 750]

Romanticism *type of* **pre-20th-century art movement**. [➡ARTISTIC MOVEMENTS AND STYLES; 899]

romanticize **1** *v* **idealize**, glamorize, sentimentalize, put on a pedestal, view through rose-tinted spectacles, exaggerate, look at through rose-colored glasses (*US*). [➡LIKE, LOVE, VALUE AND ENJOY; 579] **2** *v* **daydream**, swoon, gush, dream, rhapsodize, moon (*literary or humorous*). [➡DREAM, IMAGINE, AND FANTASIZE; 750]

Romeo *n* **Don Juan**, Casanova, seducer, wolf, Lothario (*literary*), womanizer (*disapproving*). [➡PLEASURE-SEEKERS AND HEDONISTS; 886]

romp **1** *v* **cavort**, frolic, horse around, caper, prance, play, gambol, leap about, let off steam, bound about, kick up your heels. [➡FIDGET AND FROLIC; 312] **2** *v* (*informal*) **win**, coast, excel yourself, surpass yourself, walk it (*informal*). [➡SUCCEED AND WIN; 79] *Opposite:* lose. **3** *v* **sail**, steam, coast, cruise, zip (*informal*), whiz. [➡MOVE FAST; 314] *Opposite:* struggle. **4** *n* **frolic**, frisk, gambol, run, scramble, caper. [➡FIDGET AND FROLIC; 312] **5** *n* (*informal*) **frolic**, page-turner, thriller, chiller, potboiler. [➡FICTION AND DRAMA; 913] *Opposite:* bore. **6** *n* (*informal*) **piece of cake** (*informal*), foregone conclusion, one-horse race, cinch (*informal*), walkover (*informal*), doddle (*informal*). *Opposite:* whitewash. (*informal*). [➡EASY WORK; 300]

rondo *type of* **instrumental music**. [➡MUSIC, SONGS, AND SINGING; 907]

rondure (*literary*) *n* [➡ROUNDED SHAPE; 1217]

roof **1** *part of* **building**, *part of* **mouth**. [➡PARTS OF A BUILDING; 1094] **2** *part of* **mouth**. [➡THE MOUTH; 703]

roofed *adj* **covered**, enclosed, vaulted, ceiled, topped. [➡BUILDING AND ARCHITECTURE; 1075] *Opposite:* open.

roofing *n* **tiling**, slating, tiles, slates, shingles, thatch, guttering, gutters. [➡BUILDING MATERIALS; 1076]

roof rack *type of* **external feature**. [➡EXTERNAL PARTS OF A VEHICLE; 1146]

roof space *n* [➡ROOFS, ROOF PARTS, AND CEILINGS; 1102]

rooftop *n* **roof**, top, tiles, slates, gable, ridge. [➡ROOFS, ROOF PARTS, AND CEILINGS; 1102]

rook *type of* **scavenger**. [➡BIRD; 997]

rookie (*US informal*) *n* **beginner**, novice, trainee, learner, apprentice, recruit, neophyte, greenhorn, tyro. [➡UNSKILLED PERSON; 531] *Opposite:* old hand.

room **1** *n* **space**, scope, accommodation, extent, span, capacity. [➡DEGREE AND EXTENT; 110] **2** *n* **apartment** (*formal*), chamber (*archaic or literary*), area. [➡TYPES OF ROOM; 1096] **3** *n* **scope**, opportunity, possibility, occasion, chance, leeway. [➡POSSIBLE AND PROBABLE; 178]

room

◆ *types of room in public buildings*
antechamber, anteroom, ballroom, boardroom, cell, changing room, classroom, cloakroom, dormitory, dressing room, entrance hall, foyer, gallery, games room, hall, lavatory, library, lobby, lounge, meeting room, men's room (*US*), office, operating room (*US*), powder room, reception room, refectory, restroom (*US*), schoolroom, stateroom, surgery, vault, waiting room, ward, washroom (*US*)

◆ *types of room in the home*
atelier, attic, bathroom, bedchamber (*archaic or literary*), bedroom, boudoir, boxroom, closet (*US*), day room, den, dining room, drawing room, family room, garret, guestroom, kitchen, kitchenette, living room, loft, parlour, playroom, rec room (*US*), recreation room, salon, scullery, sitting room, sleeping quarters, spare room, study, sun lounge, sunroom (*US*), toilet, utility room

roomer (*US*) *n* **lodger**, tenant, occupant, dweller (*literary*), resident, renter. [➡INHABITANT; 857]

roomie (*US informal*) *n* **flatmate**, roommate, lodger, cotenant, pal (*informal*), colleague, buddy (*US informal*). [➡COLLEAGUES AND EQUALS; 967]

roominess *n* **spaciousness**, largeness, capaciousness, generousness, sizableness, voluminousness. [➡LARGE; 1192] *Opposite:* smallness.

rooming house (*US*) *type of* **hotel**. [➡HOTELS, RESTAURANTS, AND CLUBS; 1081]

roommate *n* **colleague**, pal (*informal*), cotenant, lodger, flatmate, roomie (*US informal*), buddy (*US informal*). [➡COLLEAGUES AND EQUALS; 967]

rooms *n* **lodgings** (*dated*), housing, quarters, place, accommodation, digs (*dated informal*), accommodations (*US*). [➡ACCOMMODATION; 855]

roomy *adj* **spacious**, large, generous, sizable, capacious, voluminous. [➡LARGE; 1192] *Opposite:* cramped.

roost *v* **settle**, rest, stay, perch, sleep, nestle. [➡EXIST IN A PLACE; 19]

rooster *type of* **male or female bird**. [➡MALE OR FEMALE BIRD; 1005]

root 1 *n* **stem**, rhizome, tuber, radicle, radix, corm. [➡PARTS OF TREES AND PLANTS; 1026] 2 *n* **origin**, cause, source, basis, starting place, derivation, core, essence, foundation. [➡BEGINNING; 53] 3 *v* **dig**, grub, rootle, forage, delve, burrow. [➡SEEK POSSESSION AND SEARCH; 457] 4 *v* **search**, nose (*informal*), rummage, delve, rifle, burrow. [➡SEEK POSSESSION AND SEARCH; 457] 5 *v* **cheer**, shout, applaud, yell, clap. [➡PRAISE AND ENCOURAGE; 648]

See Compare and Contrast at **origin**.

rooted *adj* **entrenched**, ingrained, fixed, deep-rooted, deep-seated, embedded, established. [➡PERMANENCE: WITHOUT END; 94]

root for *v* [➡PRAISE AND ENCOURAGE; 648]

rootle *v* [➡SEEK POSSESSION AND SEARCH; 457]

rootless *adj* **drifting**, freewheeling, roving, nomadic, itinerant, disenfranchised, peripatetic, homeless, travelling. [➡NOMADIC AND ROOTLESS LIFESTYLES; 884] *Opposite:* rooted.

root out 1 *v* **eradicate**, remove, get rid of, do away with, eliminate, obliterate, wipe out (*informal*). [➡GET RID OF SOMETHING; 452] 2 *v* **find**, discover, locate, turn up, unearth, produce. [➡SEEK POSSESSION AND SEARCH; 457] *Opposite:* hide.

roots *n* **origins**, ancestry, background, heritage, pedigree, stock. [➡BEGINNING; 53]

root to the spot *v* [➡FRIGHTEN AND SHOCK; 569]

rope 1 *n* **cord**, line, cable, lead, twine, string. [➡FASTENERS, LINKS, AND NETWORKS; 1246] 2 *v* **tie**, fasten, lash, secure, attach, moor, link, bind. [➡FASTEN, LINK, AND JOIN; 409] *Opposite:* untie.

rope in *v* [➡CAUSE OR COMPEL TO ACT; 272]

ropiness (*informal*) *n* [➡IN BAD REPAIR; 1233]

ropy (*informal*) 1 *adj* **poor**, shoddy, grotty (*informal*), cruddy (*slang*), trashy, cheap and nasty, rubbishy. [➡IN BAD REPAIR; 1233] *Opposite:* excellent. 2 *adj* **poorly** (*informal*), sick, grotty (*informal*), bad, unwell, off-colour. [➡UNFIT AND WEAK; 740] *Opposite:* fine.

Roquefort *type of* **soft cheese**. [➡DAIRY PRODUCTS AND CHEESES; 1182]

rose 1 *n* **design**, rosette, ornament, representation, emblem, badge. [➡ORNAMENTS AND DECORATIONS; 1247] 2 *n* **sprinkler**, jet, nozzle, spray, attachment, irrigator. [➡FITTINGS; 859] 3 *n* **ceiling rose**, fitting, boss, connector, socket. [➡ROOFS, ROOF PARTS, AND CEILINGS; 1102] 4 *type of* **perennial flower**. [➡FLOWERS; 1032] 5 *type of* **shrub or bush**. [➡BUSHES AND SHRUBS; 1027] 6 *type of* **pink**. [➡COLOURS; 1223]

roseate *adj* **reddish**, rose, fuchsia, magenta, rose-coloured, pink. [➡DESCRIBING COLOURS; 1225]

rosebud *n* **bud**, bloom, rose, flower, blossom, floret. [➡PARTS OF TREES AND PLANTS; 1026]

rose-coloured *adj* **optimistic**, idealistic, assured, sanguine, trusting, hopeful, rose-tinted. [➡EMOTIONALLY PLEASANT; 188] *Opposite:* pessimistic.

rose garden *n* [➡GARDENS; 1073]

rosemary *type of* **herb**. [➡HERBS AND SPICES; 1174]

rose-tinted *adj* **rose-coloured**, optimistic, idealistic, sanguine, trusting, hopeful. [➡EMOTIONALLY PLEASANT; 188] *Opposite:* pessimistic.

rosette 1 *n* **badge**, decoration, prize, emblem, insignia, ornament. [➡ORNAMENTS AND DECORATIONS; 1247] 2 *n* **ornament**, design, rose, shape, representation, decoration. [➡ORNAMENTS AND DECORATIONS; 1247]

rose window *type of* **window**. [➡WINDOWS; 1099]

rosiness *n* **blush**, flush, pinkness, redness, glow, ruddiness, colour. [➡COMPLEXION; 481]

roster *n* **rota**, list, schedule, roll, register. [➡LISTS AND SCHEDULES; 588]

rösti *type of* **processed potato**. [➡FRUIT AND VEGETABLES; 1175]

rostrum *n* **platform**, podium, stage, dais, stand, pulpit. [➡STAGES, PLATFORMS, AND RAISED AREAS; 1097]

rosy 1 *adj* **pink**, reddish, pinkish, rose, roseate, rose-coloured. [➡DESCRIBING COLOURS; 1225] 2 *adj* **blushing**, flushed, glowing, healthy, ruddy, rubicund (*literary*). [➡COMPLEXION; 481] *Opposite:* pale. 3 *adj* **promising**, auspicious, successful, happy, favourable, bright. [➡SUCCESSFUL AND PROMISING; 81] *Opposite:* unpromising. 4 *adj* **optimistic**, idealistic, unrealistic, hopeful, encouraging, sunny. [➡EMOTIONALLY PLEASANT; 188] *Opposite:* pessimistic.

rot 1 *v* **decompose**, decay, putrefy, disintegrate, go off, perish, break down. [➡GO BAD AND CORRODE; 391] 2 *n* **decay**, deterioration, putrefaction, decomposition, corrosion, corruption. [➡GO BAD AND CORRODE; 391] 3 *n* (*informal*) **nonsense**, twaddle (*informal*), balderdash, poppycock (*dated informal*), claptrap (*informal*), rubbish. [➡MEANINGLESS SPEECH OR WRITING; 677] *Opposite:* sense.

rota *n* **roster**, list, schedule, register, roll. [➡LISTS AND SCHEDULES; 588]

rotary *adj* **rotating**, turning, revolving, rotational, gyratory, rotatory. [➡DIRECTION OF MOTION; 346]

rotate 1 *v* **turn**, revolve, go, spin, swivel, pivot. [➡MOVE SOMETHING ON THE SPOT; 337] 2 *v* **replace**, switch, interchange, alternate, exchange, swap (*informal*). [➡CHANGE ONE THING FOR ANOTHER; 399] 3 *v* **alternate**, take tums, interchange, swap (*informal*), switch, revolve. [➡EXCHANGE AND INTERCHANGE; 449]

rotation 1 *n* **revolution**, turning, spin, gyration. [➡MOVE SOMETHING ON THE SPOT; 337] 2 *n* **alternation**, variation, interchange, replacement, cycle, sequence. [➡EXCHANGE AND INTERCHANGE; 449]

rote *n* **repetition**, memorization, routine, habit, rotation, conditioning. [➡MEMORY; 746]

roti *type of* **bread**. [➡BREAD, FLOUR, AND BREAD PRODUCTS; 1178]

rotisserie *n* **spit**, skewer, brochette, grill, barbecue, tandoor. [➡HOUSEHOLD APPLIANCES; 1116]

rotor *n* **blade**, propeller, aerofoil. [➡AIRCRAFT; 1147]

rotten 1 *adj* **decayed**, putrid, bad, decomposed, rotted, disintegrating, mouldy, off. [➡DECAYING OR INFESTED; 1235] *Opposite:* fresh. 2 *adj* (*informal*) **awful**, bad, nasty, terrible, foul (*informal*), unpleasant, unfortunate. [➡EMOTIONALLY UNPLEASANT AND UPSETTING; 228] *Opposite:* pleasant. 3 *adj* (*informal*) **inferior**, poor, bad, dreadful, incompetent, inadequate. [➡BAD AND BADLY; 224] *Opposite:* good. 4 *adj* (*informal*) **unwell**, ill, sick, poorly (*informal*), seedy (*informal*), off-colour. *Opposite:* fine. (*informal*). [➡ILL AND SICK; 741] 5 *adj* (*informal*) **unhappy**, uncomfortable, guilty, embarrassed, bad, wretched. [➡SADNESS, DISTRESS, AND DESPAIR; 540] *Opposite:* happy. 6 *adv* (*informal*) **terribly**, unduly, excessively, overly, outrageously, dreadfully. [➡BAD AND BADLY; 224] *Opposite:* slightly.

rottenly (*informal*) *adv* **shabbily**, badly, terribly, awfully, dreadfully, appallingly, poorly, unfairly, atrociously. [➡BAD AND BADLY; 224] *Opposite:* well.

rottenness 1 *n* **decay**, mouldiness, dry rot, wet rot, badness, decomposition, degradation, disintegration. [➡DECAYING OR INFESTED; 1235] *Opposite:* freshness. 2 *n* (*informal*) **unpleasantness**, awfulness, dreadfulness, hideousness, ghastliness, grottiness (*informal*), nastiness. [➡DISGUSTING AND REPULSIVE; 231] *Opposite:* pleasantness. 3 *n* (*informal*) **beastliness**, nastiness, cruelness, cruelty, horridness, awfulness, unpleasantness. [➡BAD BEHAVIOUR OR ACTION; 255] *Opposite:* goodness.

rotter (*informal dated*) *n* **scoundrel**, cad (*dated*), liar, swindler, cheat. [➡VILLAINS AND THUGS; 947] *Opposite:* angel.

rotting *adj* **decomposing**, decaying, putrid, bad, contaminated, tainted. [➡DECAYING OR INFESTED; 1235] *Opposite:* fresh.

Rottweiler *type of* **large dog**. [➡DOG; 980]

rotund *adj* **overweight**, stout, fat, plump, curved, corpulent (*formal or literary*), round. [➡BUILD; 478] *Opposite:* slender.

rotunda *n* **pavilion**, tower, dome, cupola. [➡TOWERS; 1098]

rotundity *n* **roundness**, sphericalness, rotundness, overweight, stoutness, fatness, plumpness. [➡BUILD; 478] *Opposite:* slenderness.

rotundness *n* [➡BUILD; 478]

roué (*literary*) *n* [➡PLEASURE-SEEKERS AND HEDONISTS; 886]

rouge (*dated*) 1 *n* **blusher**, lipstick, blush, makeup, face paint, colouring, red. [➡MAKEUP AND BEAUTY PRODUCTS; 491] 2 *v* **make up**, redden, highlight, paint, beautify, colour. [➡CHANGE OF COLOUR; 392]

rough 1 *adj* **uneven**, coarse, bumpy, irregular, jagged, lumpy. [➡PHYSICAL TEXTURE; 1221] *Opposite:* even. 2 *adj* **coarse**, shaggy, hairy, bristly, bushy, tangled. [➡PHYSICAL TEXTURE; 1221] *Opposite:* smooth. 3 *adj* **turbulent**, stormy, tempestuous, squally, wild. [➡WINDY AND STORMY WEATHER; 1053] *Opposite:* calm. 4 *adj* **rugged**, wild, uncultivated, rocky, hilly, craggy. [➡PHYSICAL TEXTURE; 1221] *Opposite:* level. 5 *adj* **violent**, forceful, tough, physical, forcible, brutal. [➡PHYSICALLY UNPLEASANT; 227] *Opposite:* gentle. 6 *adj* **unrefined**, impolite, rough-and-ready, coarse, crude, uncultured. [➡BAD MANNERS AND SOCIAL SKILLS; 522] *Opposite:* refined. 7 *adj* **harsh**, grating, jarring, discordant, rasping. [➡LOUD OR UNPLEASANT SOUNDS; 1265] *Opposite:* smooth. 8 *adj* **approximate**, sketchy, vague, estimated, imprecise, ballpark (*US informal*). [➡APPROXIMATELY; 133] *Opposite:* exact. 9 *adj* (*informal*) **unwell**, seedy (*informal*), sickly, poorly (*informal*), ill, out of sorts. [➡ILL AND SICK; 741] *Opposite:* well. 10 *adj* **rowdy**, boisterous, noisy, violent, tough, tempestuous. [➡DISORDER AND CHAOS; 246] *Opposite:* quiet. 11 *n* **outline**, sketch, summary, draft, mock-up, cartoon. [➡DRAWINGS, CHARTS AND TABLES; 595]

roughage *n* **bulk**, cellulose, bran, fibre. [➡FOOD COMPONENTS; 1187]

rough-and-ready 1 *adj* **crude**, simple, basic, primitive, serviceable, practical, usable, rustic. [➡IN BAD REPAIR; 1233] *Opposite:* sophisticated. 2 *adj* **down-to-earth**, unpretentious, honest, rough-hewn, kind-hearted, decent, warm, unsophisticated, unrefined, homely, downhome (*US informal*). [➡NATURALNESS; 498] *Opposite:* refined.

rough-and-tumble *n* **hurly-burly**, cut and thrust, infighting, sparring, free-for-all (*informal*), fracas. [➡CHAOS AND UPROAR; 51]

roughcast *n* **coating**, cladding, facing, plasterwork, rendering, pebbledash. [➡BUILDING MATERIALS; 1076]

rough copy *n* **outline**, sketch, summary, draft, rough, mock-up. [➡SUMMARIES, OUTLINES, AND EXCERPTS; 589]

roughen *v* **coarsen**, toughen, scratch, abrade, rough, crumple. [➡WORSEN APPEARANCE; 383] *Opposite:* soften.

rough-hewn 1 *adj* **rough**, unfinished, undressed, incomplete. [➡PHYSICAL TEXTURE; 1221] 2 *adj* **crude**, basic, primitive, simple, rough, unfinished. [➡RAW AND NATURAL; 1213] 3 *adj* **rugged**, rough, unrefined, coarse, crude, uncouth. [➡BAD MANNERS AND SOCIAL SKILLS; 522]

roughhouse (*informal*) *n* **rowdiness**, boisterousness, rough-and-tumble, horseplay, roughness, high spirits. [➡CHAOS AND UPROAR; 51]

roughly 1 *adv* **unevenly**, coarsely, jaggedly, bumpily, crudely, incompletely. [➡PHYSICAL TEXTURE; 1221] *Opposite:* evenly. 2 *adv* **violently**, physically, forcefully, forcibly, brutally, rudely. [➡PHYSICALLY UNPLEASANT; 227] *Opposite:* gently. 3 *adv* **approximately**, about, around, more or less, almost, nearly. [➡APPROXIMATELY; 133] *Opposite:* exactly.

roughly speaking *adv* [➡APPROXIMATELY; 133]

roughneck (*informal*) *n* **thug**, yobbo (*informal*), ruffian (*dated*), hooligan (*informal*), rowdy, hoodlum. [➡VILLAINS AND THUGS; 947]

roughness 1 *n* **unevenness**, coarseness, bumpiness, irregularity, jaggedness, lumpiness. [➡PHYSICAL TEXTURE; 1221] *Opposite:* smoothness. 2 *n* **coarseness**, shagginess, hairiness, bristliness, bushiness, fuzziness. [➡TEXTURE; 1219] *Opposite:* smoothness. 3 *n* **turbulence**, storminess, tempestuousness, wildness. [➡WINDY AND STORMY WEATHER; 1053] *Opposite:* calmness. 4 *n* **ruggedness**, wildness, rockiness, hilliness, cragginess, stoniness. [➡PHYSICAL TEXTURE; 1221] *Opposite:* evenness. 5 *n* **violence**, force, toughness, power, brutality, severity. [➡PHYSICALLY UNPLEASANT; 227] *Opposite:* gentleness. 6 *n* **brusqueness**, rudeness, gruffness, harshness, coarseness. [➡BAD MANNERS AND SOCIAL SKILLS; 522] *Opposite:* refinement. 7 *n* **harshness**, discordance, astringency, gruffness, raucousness. [➡LOUD OR UNPLEASANT SOUNDS; 1265] *Opposite:* smoothness. 8 *n* **vagueness**, sketchiness, ambiguity, inexactness, haziness, imprecision. [➡VAGUENESS; 244] *Opposite:* exactness. 9 *n* (*informal*) **seediness** (*informal*), sickliness, poorliness (*informal*), illness, sickness, ropiness (*informal*). [➡ILL AND SICK; 741] *Opposite:* healthiness. 10 *n* **rowdiness**, boisterousness, noisiness, violence, toughness, tempestuousness. [➡DISORDER AND CHAOS; 246]

rough out *v* **draft**, outline, prepare, sketch, block out, plan. [➡RECORD SOMETHING; 372] *Opposite:* finalize.

rough up (*informal*) *v* **maltreat**, mistreat, abuse, batter, manhandle, beat, beat up (*informal*), harm, ill-treat, knock about (*informal*). [➡WOUND A PERSON OR ANIMAL; 384] *Opposite:* take care of.

round 1 *prep* **surrounding**, around, about, encircling, encompassing, on all sides of. [➡RELATIVE LOCATION; 162] 2 *adv* **around**, about, near, on all sides. [➡DIRECTION OF MOTION; 346] 3 *v* **turn**, circumnavigate (*formal*), negotiate, skirt round, skirt, pass. [➡PROCEED AND GO; 306] 4 *n* **circle**, disc, slice, ring, band. [➡ROUNDED SHAPE; 1217] 5 *type of* **cut**. [➡TYPES AND CUTS OF MEAT; 1176]

round about *prep* **around**, circa, say, in the region of, nigh on. [➡APPROXIMATELY; 133]

roundabout 1 *n* **merry-go-round**, carousel, ride, attraction. [➡ENTERTAINMENT; 872] 2 *n* **traffic island**, traffic junction, junction, intersection, crossroads, traffic circle (*US*). [➡BRIDGES, TUNNELS, CROSSINGS, AND JUNCTIONS; 1111] 3 *adj* **indirect**, oblique, circuitous, winding, meandering, ambiguous. [➡INARTICULATE, RAMBLING, AND AWKWARD; 634] *Opposite:* direct.

rounded *adj* **curved**, smoothed, smooth-edged, round, curvy, plump. [➡ROUNDED SHAPE; 1217] *Opposite:* pointed.

rounders *type of* **ball game**. [➡HOBBIES, GAMES, AND SPORTS; 875]

round-eyed *adj* **open-mouthed**, amazed, gaping, gawping (*informal*), staring, fascinated, disbelieving. [➡FACIAL EXPRESSION; 652]

round here *adv* [➡CLOSENESS; 160]

roundly *adv* **severely**, forcefully, completely, utterly, bluntly, outright, plainly. [➡ABSOLUTE AND ABSOLUTELY; 131]

roundness *n* **roundedness**, plumpness, chubbiness. [➡BUILD; 478]

round of applause *n* [➡APPLAUSE; 653]

round-shouldered *adj* **stooping**, hunched, slouching, bent, bent over, huddled. [➡BUILD; 478] *Opposite:* erect.

round table *n* **discussion**, negotiation, debate, forum, meeting, consultation. [➡MEETINGS AND ASSEMBLIES; 43]

round the bend (*informal*) *adj* **crazy** (*informal*), batty (*informal*), barmy (*informal*), off your head, wild. [➡ECCENTRICITY AND IRRATIONALITY; 563]

round-the-clock *adj* **24-hour**, day-and-night, continuous, permanent, constant, unceasing, ceaseless. [➡PERMANENCE: WITHOUT END; 94]

round the twist (*slang*) *adj* **crazy**, batty (*informal*), round the bend (*informal*), off your head, insane, daft (*informal*), crazed. [➡ECCENTRICITY AND IRRATIONALITY; 563]

round trip *n* **both ways**, return journey, return trip, return, circuit, tour. [➡TRAVEL: JOURNEYS AND TRIPS; 319]

round-up 1 *n* **assembly**, capture, hunt, herding, rodeo, muster. [➡CAPTIVITY AND LOSS OF FREEDOM; 249] *Opposite:* release. 2 *n* **summary**, rundown, review, summing up, recap, overview. [➡SUMMARIES, OUTLINES, AND EXCERPTS; 589]

round up *v* **capture**, gather together, collect, arrest, amass, bring together. [➡CAPTIVITY AND LOSS OF FREEDOM; 249] *Opposite:* disperse.

rouse 1 *v* **stir**, wake up, revive, awaken, disturb, arouse. [➡APPEAL TO AND AROUSE INTEREST; 576] *Opposite:* lull. 2 *v* **stir up**, wind up (*informal*), provoke, incite, move, galvanize. [➡CAUSE OR COMPEL TO ACT; 272] *Opposite:* lull.

rousing *adj* **stirring**, inspiring, moving, exciting, stimulating, upbeat (*informal*). [➡EMOTIONALLY PLEASANT; 188] *Opposite:* soothing.

rout 1 *n* **retreat**, flight, stampede, surrender, collapse, disarray. [➡FAILURE; 77] *Opposite:* advance. 2 *n* **defeat**, massacre, landslide, pasting (*informal*), thrashing, beating. [➡BEAT AND DEFEAT; 80] *Opposite:* victory. 3 *n* **tumult**, disorder, riot, disturbance, hubbub. [➡CHAOS AND UPROAR; 51] 4 *v* **beat back**, overpower, overwhelm, beat, defeat, overthrow, crush, trounce. [➡BEAT AND DEFEAT; 80] *Opposite:* retreat.

route 1 *n* **road**, path, way, itinerary, track. [➡ROADS; 1105] 2 *n* **course**, means, method, way, direction, path. [➡WAYS OF DOING THINGS; 295] 3 *v* **direct**, send, transmit, move, channel, guide. [➡DESPATCH AND SEND; 334]

router *n* [➡THE INTERNET; 1127]

routine 1 *n* **procedure**, practice, habit, custom, sequence, schedule. [➡WAYS OF DOING THINGS; 295] 2 *adj* **usual**, standard, everyday, normal, customary, habitual, regular, scheduled. [➡ORDINARINESS; 245] *Opposite:* unusual. 3 *adj* **monotonous**, dull, tedious, repetitive, humdrum, mundane, predictable, unchanging. [➡BORING AND UNINTERESTING; 235] *Opposite:* exciting.

See Compare and Contrast at **habit**.

routinely *adv* **regularly**, as a matter of course, normally, habitually, usually, customarily, consistently, characteristically. [➡USUALLY; 108] *Opposite:* unusually.

routineness *n* [➡ORDINARINESS; 245]

rove *v* **wander**, roam, range, meander, travel, journey, ramble, stray. [➡AIMLESS AND ERRANT MOTION; 344]

rover 1 *n* **wanderer**, traveller, rolling stone, nomad, drifter, itinerant, rambler. [➡TRAVEL: TRAVELLERS AND WALKERS; 320] 2 *type of* **spacecraft**. [➡SPACE VEHICLES; 1062]

roving 1 *adj* **roaming**, travelling, wandering, rambling, nomadic, itinerant, drifting, peripatetic, meandering, moving, rootless. [➡NOMADIC AND ROOTLESS LIFESTYLES; 884] *Opposite:* stationary. 2 *adj* **erratic**, wandering, fickle, capricious, inconsistent, whimsical. [➡LACK OF COMMITMENT AND UNRELIABILITY; 510] *Opposite:* steady.

row 1 *n* **line**, chain, string, file, queue, rank, strip. [➡AREA AND RANGE; 111] 2 *v* **paddle**, scull, punt, take the oars, propel, manoeuvre. [➡TRAVEL: WAYS OF TRAVELLING; 321] 3 *n* **disagreement**, dispute, quarrel, controversy, argument, fight, wrangle. [➡ARGUMENT; 47] *Opposite:* agreement. 4 *n* **noise**, racket (*informal*), rumpus, din, commotion, disorder, disturbance, clamour, ruckus. [➡CHAOS AND UPROAR; 51] *Opposite:* lull. 5 *v* **fight**, quarrel, have a row, disagree, argue, dispute, wrangle. [➡ARGUE AND FIGHT – TWO-WAY; 644]

rowan 1 *type of* **berry**. [➡FRUIT AND VEGETABLES; 1175] 2 *type of* **deciduous tree**. [➡DECIDUOUS TREES; 1028]

rowdily *adv* **noisily**, wildly, loudly, raucously, disruptively, boisterously. [➡REBELLIOUSNESS AND DISOBEDIENCE; 566] *Opposite:* quietly.

rowdiness *n* **disorderliness**, unruliness, noisiness, loudness, raucousness, disruptiveness, boisterousness. [➡CHAOS AND UPROAR; 51] *Opposite:* restraint.

rowdy *adj* **disorderly**, unruly, noisy, loud, raucous, disruptive, boisterous, wild. [➡REBELLIOUSNESS AND DISOBEDIENCE; 566] *Opposite:* restrained.

rower *n* **oarsperson**, galley slave, sculler, coxswain, cox, sportsperson. [➡PEOPLE IN SPORTS AND LEISURE; 876]

row house (*US*) *n* **terraced house**, terrace, town house. [➡RESIDENTIAL BUILDINGS; 1077]

rowing boat *type of* **small vessel**. [➡SHIPS AND BOATS; 1149]

rowlock *part of* **ship or boat**. [➡PARTS OF A SHIP OR BOAT; 1150]

royal 1 *adj* **regal**, imperial, majestic, stately, noble, kingly, queenly. [➡ROYALNESS; 825] 2 *adj* **magnificent**, splendid, noble, excellent, grand, extravagant. [➡EXPENSIVE AND LUXURIOUS; 219] *Opposite:* ordinary.

royal blue *type of* **blue**. [➡COLOURS; 1223]

royal family *n* [➡RULERS AND ARISTOCRACY; 823]

royalist *n* **monarchist**, traditionalist, constitutionalist, conservative, loyal subject. [➡DEVOTEES AND ADDICTED PEOPLE; 557] *Opposite:* republican.

royally *adv* **regally**, magnificently, splendidly, nobly, majestically, imperially. [➡ROYALNESS; 825]

royals *n* **royalty**, crowned heads, monarchs, sovereigns, royal family, heads of state. [➡RULERS AND ARISTOCRACY; 823]

royalty 1 *n* **royals**, crowned heads, monarchs, sovereigns, royal family, heads of state. [➡RULERS AND ARISTOCRACY; 823] 2 *n* **fee**, payment, percentage, credit, cut (*informal*), token. [➡INCOME; 461]

RP *n* **Received Pronunciation**, BBC English, the Queen's English, Standard English, British English, Southern Educated Standard. [➡ASPECTS OF LANGUAGE; 683]

RSI *n* **repetitive strain injury**, industrial injury, work-related injury, tenosynovitis, injury, strain. [➡ILLNESSES AND DISORDERS; 733]

rub 1 *v* **massage**, stroke, caress, knead, pat. [➡CONTACT: EXERT PRESSURE; 415] 2 *v* **polish**, wipe, buff, shine, clean, dry. [➡CLEAN AND POLISH; 404] 3 *v* **chafe**, hurt, gall, irritate, scrape, squeeze. [➡WOUND A PERSON OR ANIMAL; 384] *Opposite:* soothe.

rubber 1 *n* **India rubber**, foam rubber, neoprene, gum, elastic, latex, sap, vulcanized rubber. [➡SOLIDS; 1273] 2 (*US*) *type of* **boot**. [➡FOOTWEAR; 871]

rubber bullet *type of* **projectile**. [➡PROJECTILES; 1158]

rubberneck (*informal*) *v* **stare**, gape, goggle, gaze, gawk (*informal*), gawp (*informal*). [➡LOOKING AND LOOKS; 701]

See Compare and Contrast at **gaze**.

rubbernecked (*informal*) *adj* **gawking** (*informal*), staring, gawping (*informal*), gazing, ogling, gaping. [➡NOSY AND INTERFERING; 513]

rubbernecking (*informal*) *n* [➡LOOKING AND LOOKS; 701]

rubber plant *type of* **foliage plant**. [➡FOLIAGE PLANTS; 1035]

rubber-stamp *v* **approve**, agree to, authorize, consent to, sanction, nod through (*informal*), okay (*informal*). [➡APPROVE AND CONFIRM; 647] *Opposite:* veto.

rubber stamp *n* **stamping device**, stamp, seal, stamper, signet, office stamp. [➡WRITING AND DRAWING IMPLEMENTS, AND MEDIA; 602]

rubbery *adj* **tough**, elastic, chewy, hard, overcooked, overdone. [➡STATE OF PREPARED FOOD; 1170] *Opposite:* tender.

rubbing 1 *n* **impression**, brass rubbing, copy, reproduction, relief. [➡ARTWORKS; 898] 2 *n* **friction**, scraping, abrasion, resistance, chafing, drag. [➡ENERGY GENERAL; 1160] 3 *n* **soreness**, chafing, irritation, blistering, saddle sores, pressure sores. [➡CONDITIONS AFFECTING THE SKIN; 722]

rubbish 1 *n* **refuse**, debris, litter, waste, junk (*informal*), garbage (*US*), trash (*US*). [➡RUBBISH AND USELESS OBJECTS; 1248] 2 *n* **nonsense**, drivel, twaddle (*informal*), claptrap (*informal*), hogwash (*informal*), dross. [➡MEANINGLESS SPEECH OR WRITING; 677] 3 *v* (*informal*) **pooh-pooh**, criticize, dismiss, ridicule, slate (*informal*), disparage, pick holes in, slam (*informal*), pan (*informal*). [➡ACCUSE, BLAME, AND CRITICIZE; 642] *Opposite:* praise.

rubbish bin *n* **dustbin**, bin, wheelie bin, waste bin, waste paper bin, bucket, trash can (*US*), garbage can (*US*), wastebasket (*US*). [➡CONTAINERS, RECEPTACLES, AND PACKAGING; 1244]

rubbish dump *type of* **storage space**. [➡STORES AND STORAGE BUILDINGS; 1087]

rubbishy *adj* **inferior**, poor quality, poor, dodgy (*informal*), ropy (*informal*), bad. [➡IN BAD REPAIR; 1233] *Opposite:* quality.

rubble *n* **debris**, ruins, wreckage, remains, bricks, stones. [➡RUBBISH AND USELESS OBJECTS; 1248]

rub down 1 *v* **finish**, wipe down, sand, scour, prepare, scrub. [➡CLEAN AND POLISH; 404] 2 *v* **massage**, rub, go over, oil, stroke, caress. [➡CONTACT: EXERT PRESSURE; 415] 3 *v* **dry**, rub, dry off, towel dry, towel. [➡CLEAN AND POLISH; 404]

rubicund (*literary*) *adj* **red**, rosy, ruddy, red-faced, flushed, healthy, hale, hearty, reddish. [➡COMPLEXION; 481] *Opposite:* pale.

rub out *v* **erase**, delete, wipe, expunge, efface, remove. [➡DELETE AND ERASE; 340]

rubric 1 *n* **title**, heading, header, head, introduction, preface. [➡SYMBOLS, SIGNS, AND NUMBERS; 597] 2 *n* **rules**, instructions, guidelines, directions, rulebook, procedures, comments, documentation. [➡MANUALS AND INSTRUCTIONS; 590] 3 *n* **custom**, tradition, practice, system, convention, rule. [➡WAYS OF DOING THINGS; 295] 4 *n* **class**, category, classification, division, type, family. [➡CONNECTION; 144]

rub up the wrong way *v* **irritate**, annoy, make somebody's hackles rise, infuriate, aggravate (*informal*), offend. [➡ANGER AND ANNOY; 570]

ruby 1 *type of* **gemstone**. [➡PRECIOUS STONES; 1277] 2 *type of* **red**. [➡COLOURS; 1223]

ruched *adj* **pleated**, gathered, frilled, frilly, edged, fancy. [➡PHYSICAL TEXTURE; 1221] *Opposite:* plain.

ruck 1 *n* **mass**, pile, heap, accumulation, conglomeration, number. [➡AMOUNT OF SOLID OR SEMI-SOLID; 115] 2 *v* **wrinkle**, crease, fold, crumple, gather, pucker, rumple, ruck up. [➡CHANGE OF SHAPE; 386] *Opposite:* smooth. 3 *n* **crease**, wrinkle, fold, crumple, rumple. [➡CHANGE OF SHAPE; 386]

rucksack *n* **backpack**, haversack, knapsack, frame rucksack, daypack. [➡CONTAINERS, RECEPTACLES, AND PACKAGING; 1244]

ruckus *n* **commotion**, disturbance, rumpus, riot, uproar, turmoil. [➡CHAOS AND UPROAR; 51]

ruction *n* **quarrel**, fight, dispute, disturbance, row, scene. [➡CHAOS AND UPROAR; 51]

ructions *n* **rumpus**, fuss, uproar, to-do (*informal*), dispute, controversy, disturbance. [➡CHAOS AND UPROAR; 51]

rudder 1 *part of* **aircraft**. [➡AIRCRAFT; 1147] 2 *part of* **ship or boat**. [➡PARTS OF A SHIP OR BOAT; 1150]

ruddiness *n* **redness**, rosiness, glow, blush, flush, reddishness. [➡COMPLEXION; 481] *Opposite:* pallor.

ruddy *adj* **reddish**, rosy, flushed, glowing, healthy-looking, red. [➡COMPLEXION; 481] *Opposite:* pale.

rude 1 *adj* **impolite**, discourteous, insolent, bad-mannered, ill-mannered, uncouth, boorish, disrespectful, offensive, vulgar. [➡RUDE AND HOSTILE; 626] *Opposite:* polite. 2 *adj* **foul**, crude, offensive, vulgar, foul-mouthed, obscene, indecent. [➡BAD MANNERS AND SOCIAL SKILLS; 522] *Opposite:* polite.

rudeness *n* **impoliteness**, insolence, discourtesy, offensiveness, vulgarity, boorishness, disrespect. [➡BAD MANNERS AND SOCIAL SKILLS; 522] *Opposite:* politeness.

rudimentary *adj* **basic**, elementary, simple, fundamental, primary, undeveloped. [➡EASE AND SIMPLICITY; 201] *Opposite:* advanced.

rudiments *n* **basics**, essentials, fundamentals, principles, beginnings, bare bones (*informal*). [➡BASIC DETAILS; 689]

rue *v* **regret**, lament, repent, deplore, feel sorry about, be sorry for. [➡CHANGE OF MOOD AND COMPOSURE; 581]

rueful *adj* **regretful**, remorseful, apologetic, repentant, contrite, sheepish, doleful. [➡EMBARRASSMENT AND HUMILIATION; 543] *Opposite:* cheerful.

ruff *part of* **bird**. [➡PARTS OF A BIRD; 1006]

ruffian (*dated*) *n* **hooligan** (*informal*), thug, tough guy, gangster, hood (*US slang*). [➡VILLAINS AND THUGS; 947]

ruffle 1 *v* **disturb**, mess up (*informal*), tousle, rumple, upset, dishevel, make a mess of. [➡WORSEN APPEARANCE; 383] *Opposite:* smooth. 2 *v* **perturb**, upset, annoy, disrupt, distress, unsettle. [➡ANGER AND ANNOY; 570] *Opposite:* calm.

rug 1 *n* **carpet**, mat, hearth rug, sheepskin, runner. [➡SOFT FURNISHINGS, LINEN, AND DRAPERY; 860] 2 *n* (*informal*) **wig**, toupee, hairpiece, periwig. [➡HAIR STYLES AND HAIR PIECES; 489] 3 *n* **blanket**, car rug, throw, cover, bedspread. [➡SOFT FURNISHINGS, LINEN, AND DRAPERY; 860]

rugby *type of* **ball game**. [➡HOBBIES, GAMES, AND SPORTS; 875]

rugged 1 *adj* **rocky**, rough, craggy, uneven, jagged, sharp, harsh, bleak. [➡PHYSICAL TEXTURE; 1221] *Opposite:* rolling. 2 *adj* **strong-featured**, craggy, chiselled, weathered, furrowed, rough, masculine, manly. [➡COMPLEXION; 481] 3 *adj* **strong**, hardy, tough, robust, resilient, muscular, sinewy. [➡STRENGTH; 202] *Opposite:* weak. 4 *adj* **testing**, demanding, difficult, harsh, tough, severe, punishing, unforgiving. [➡PHYSICALLY UNPLEASANT; 227] *Opposite:* easy. 5 *adj* **well-built**, sturdy, tough, robust, strong, resilient. [➡BUILD; 478] *Opposite:* flimsy.

ruggedness 1 *n* **roughness**, rockiness, harshness, jaggedness, cragginess, unevenness, sharpness, bleakness. [➡PHYSICAL TEXTURE; 1221] *Opposite:* smoothness. 2 *n* **strong features**, cragginess, handsomeness, manliness, masculinity. [➡BUILD; 478] *Opposite:* roundness. 3 *n* **toughness**, resilience, stamina, endurance, strength, survival skills, staying power. [➡STRENGTH OF WILL; 502] *Opposite:* weakness. 4 *n* **unforgiving nature**, difficulty, harshness, toughness, severity, punishing nature, demanding nature. [➡PHYSICALLY UNPLEASANT; 227] 5 *n* **resilience**, sturdiness, toughness, robustness, strength, rugged construction. [➡STRENGTH; 202] *Opposite:* flimsiness.

rugger (*informal*) *n* **game**, rugby, sport. [➡HOBBIES, GAMES, AND SPORTS; 875]

rug rat (*US informal humorous*) *n* [➡CHILD OR YOUTH; 945]

ruin 1 *n* **remains**, wreck, debris, wreckage, shell. [➡REMAINDER AND REMAINDERS; 123] 2 *n* **devastation**, shambles, decay, destruction, collapse, disintegration, deterioration, loss. [➡DIFFICULT SITUATIONS; 72] *Opposite:* regeneration. 3 *n* **decline**, downfall, defeat, fall, disaster, death. [➡FAILURE; 77] *Opposite:*

improvement. 4 *v* **trash** (*informal*), damage, wreck, spoil, mess up (*informal*), destroy, devastate, reduce to rubble, impair. [➡DESTRUCTION AND DEMOLITION; 360] *Opposite:* mend.

ruination 1 *n* **destruction**, loss, ruin, perdition (*archaic or literary*), calamity, devastation. [➡DIFFICULT SITUATIONS; 72] *Opposite:* salvation. 2 *n* **undoing**, downfall, ruin, curse, nemesis (*literary*), destruction. [➡END; 54] *Opposite:* making.

ruined 1 *adj* **tumbledown**, crumbling, derelict, abandoned, uninhabited, in ruins. [➡IN BAD REPAIR; 1233] *Opposite:* renovated. 2 *adj* **bankrupt**, insolvent, broke (*informal*), cleaned out (*informal*), skint (*informal*), out of business, bust (*informal*). [➡UNSUCCESSFUL AND UNPROMISING; 76] *Opposite:* solvent.

ruinous *adj* **disastrous**, damaging, harmful, devastating, catastrophic, dire. [➡DANGEROUS; 237] *Opposite:* advantageous.

rule 1 *n* **instruction**, law, regulation, decree, statute, imperative, canon, tenet (*formal*), ruling, directive. [➡THE LAW AND LEGAL AUTHORITY; 814] 2 *n* **regime**, power, control, leadership, reign, government, management, administration. [➡REALMS AND RULES; 824] 3 *v* **govern**, reign, run, administrate, have power over, lead, control, preside over, direct, manage. [➡BE IN CHARGE; 271] *Opposite:* follow. 4 *type of* **measuring device.** [➡MEASURING DEVICES; 1122]

rulebook *n* **manual**, rules, instructions, directory, rubric, guidelines, directions, procedures. [➡MANUALS AND INSTRUCTIONS; 590]

rule out 1 *v* **exclude**, dismiss, reject, discount, discard, forget about. [➡NOT PAY ATTENTION; 765] *Opposite:* consider. 2 *v* **prevent**, put paid to (*informal*), preclude (*formal*), exclude, ban, prohibit, forbid. [➡REFUSE PERMISSION AND NOT ALLOW; 671] *Opposite:* facilitate.

ruler *n* **monarch**, sovereign, leader, head of state, potentate. [➡RULERS AND ARISTOCRACY; 823] *Opposite:* subject.

rules and regulations *n* [➡WAYS OF DOING THINGS; 295]

rule the roost *v* **be in control**, be in charge, reign supreme, be top dog (*informal*), be in the saddle, be in the driving seat. [➡BE IN CHARGE; 271]

ruling 1 *adj* **presiding**, reigning, governing, dominant, sovereign, chief. [➡MOST IMPORTANT AND MAIN; 194] *Opposite:* subordinate. 2 *n* **decision**, verdict, edict, judgment, declaration, decree. [➡TRIAL, PUNISHMENT, AND LEGAL OUTCOMES; 819]

ruling body *n* **council**, administration, government, assembly, legislative body. [➡LEGISLATIVE BODIES AND LEGISLATION; 809]

rum (*dated informal*) *adj* **odd**, strange, extraordinary, weird, bizarre, unusual, curious, uncommon. [➡BIZARRE AND PECULIAR; 258] *Opposite:* usual.

rumba *type of* **dance.** [➡DANCE; 903]

rumble 1 *v* **grumble**, thunder, crash, growl, roll, roar, reverberate, resound, boom. [➡EMIT CONTINUOUS SOUNDS; 367] 2 *n* **roar**, thunder, crash, growl, grumble, roll, reverberation, boom. [➡CONTINUOUS SOUNDS; 1257]

rumbling (*informal*) *n* **indication**, early sign, beginning, warning sign, rumour, intimation, hint, suggestion, whispering. [➡SUGGEST, HINT, AND COMMENT; 613]

rumbustious *adj* **boisterous**, exuberant, unruly, swashbuckling, cavalier, swaggering. [➡POMPOUS, LOUD, AND OVER-CONFIDENT; 636] *Opposite:* reticent.

ruminant *adj* **reflective**, thoughtful, contemplative, speculative, deep, meditative, philosophical, deliberative (*formal*), calculating, retrospective, pensive, cogitative (*formal*), musing. [➡PENSIVENESS AND INTEREST; 539] *Opposite:* thoughtless.

ruminate 1 *v* **chew**, graze, browse, crop, pasture, chew the cud. [➡EAT AND NOT EAT; 711] 2 *v* **ponder**, think over, reflect, cogitate (*formal*), chew over, meditate, mull over, deliberate, contemplate, muse. [➡THINK AND REFLECT; 744]

rumination 1 *n* **chewing**, grazing, browsing, chewing the cud. [➡EAT AND NOT EAT; 711] 2 *n* **cogitation** (*formal*), reflection, ponderings, contemplation, musing, thoughts, meditation. [➡THINK AND REFLECT; 744]

ruminative *adj* **thoughtful**, pensive, reflective, cogitative (*formal*), contemplative, speculative, deep, meditative, philosophical, deliberative (*formal*), calculating, retrospective. [➡PENSIVENESS AND INTEREST; 539] *Opposite:* thoughtless.

rummage *v* **search**, look through, grope, fumble, poke around, delve, ferret about, ferret out. [➡SEEK POSSESSION AND SEARCH; 457]

rummage sale (*US*) *n* **sale**, jumble sale, car boot sale, garage sale, yard sale (*US*). [➡SALES AND SHOWS; 444]

rumour 1 *n* **unconfirmed report**, claim, report, story (*informal*), tale, allegation, anecdote, opinion. [➡THE ORAL TRADITION; 678] *Opposite:* fact. 2 *n* **speculation**, opinion, gossip, talk, tittle-tattle, chitchat (*informal*), word, buzz (*informal*), the word on the street. [➡THE ORAL TRADITION; 678] 3 *v* **say**, believe, allege, claim, speculate, opine (*formal*), spread the word. [➡GOSSIP; 679] *Opposite:* confirm.

rumoured *adj* **supposed**, thought, whispered, alleged, believed, said, understood, assumed, held. [➡UNCERTAIN; 176] *Opposite:* true.

rumour has it that *adv* [➡EXPRESSIONS OF UNCERTAINTY; 561]

rumour mill *n* **grapevine**, bush telegraph (*informal*), network, newsmongers, gossips, tattlers. [➡INTERFERING PEOPLE AND TELLTALES; 950]

rumourmonger *n* **gossip**, telltale, scandalmonger, gossipmonger, tattletale (*US*). [➡INTERFERING PEOPLE AND TELLTALES; 950]

rumourmongering *n* [➡GOSSIP; 679]

rump 1 *n* **hindquarters**, back end, rear, buttocks, rear end. [➡TORSO; 694] 2 *type of* **steak.** [➡TYPES AND CUTS OF MEAT; 1176]

rumple *v* **wrinkle**, crumple, crease, crinkle, pucker, scrunch up, mess up (*informal*). [➡CHANGE OF SHAPE; 386] *Opposite:* tidy.

rumpled *adj* **crumpled**, creased, untidy, messy, bedraggled, dishevelled, puckered, unkempt, scruffy, wrinkled. [➡IN BAD REPAIR; 1233] *Opposite:* tidy.

rumpus *n* **disturbance**, commotion, furore, to-do (*informal*), brouhaha (*formal*), fuss, stir, hullabaloo, tumult, outcry. [➡CHAOS AND UPROAR; 51]

run 1 *v* **sprint**, jog, lope, scuttle, scamper, dart, dash, scurry, rush, hurry. [➡MOVE FAST; 314] 2 *v* **compete**, enter, participate, take part, contend. [➡COMPETE, CONTEND, AND COMBAT; 304] 3 *v* **operate**, function, process. [➡USE; 468] 4 *v* **manage**, administer, govern, administrate, lead, control, be in charge, be in power, handle, manipulate, direct, rule, organize. [➡BE IN CHARGE; 271] 5 *v* **flow**, stream, trickle, course, pour out, seep, gush, flood, spill. [➡MOVE FAST; 314] 6 *v* **proceed**, happen, go, progress, move along, pass, go by, pass by, move forward. [➡HAPPEN; 27] 7 *v* **move**, pass, cast, throw. [➡MOVE SOMETHING TO ANOTHER LOCATION; 325] 8 *v* **continue**, extend, reach, stretch, go, last, carry on, persist, keep on, go on. [➡CONTINUE TO EXIST; 17] 9 *n* **outing**, trip, ride, excursion, visit. [➡TRAVEL: JOURNEYS AND TRIPS; 319] 10 *n* **sequence**, series, chain, string, list, spate, succession, cycle, train. [➡PERIOD OF TIME; 90] 11 *n* **course**, track, route, lane, path. [➡PATHWAYS; 1109] 12 *n* **enclosure**, pen, cage, coop, paddock. [➡ANIMAL OR BIRD ACCOMMODATION; 1078] 13 *n* **sprint**, race, lope, dart, dash, scuttle. [➡PROCEED AND GO; 306]

runabout 1 *n* **small vehicle**, small car, small boat, plane, small plane, small motorboat. [➡BIKES, CARS, AND CARRIAGES; 1148] 2 *n* **wanderer**, rover, rolling stone, nomad, traveller, drifter. [➡NOMADIC AND ROOTLESS LIFESTYLES; 884]

run after *v* **pursue**, chase, go after, follow, hound. [➡ACCOMPANY AND FOLLOW; 338]

run aground *adj* [➡LACK OF ACTIVITY; 343]

run along *v* **go away**, go, leave, depart, take leave, take off (*informal*), split (*slang*), scram (*informal*). [➡ABSENT ONESELF; 8] *Opposite:* stay.

run amok *v* **go berserk**, be in a frenzy, run riot, go on the rampage, go wild, rampage, riot. [➡GIVING VENT TO EMOTIONS; 680]

run a risk *v* **take a risk**, play a dangerous game, sail close to the wind, court disaster, play Russian roulette. [➡GAMBLE AND TAKE RISKS; 467]

run around *v* **associate**, spend time, hang out (*informal*), hang (*slang*), keep company. [➡ESTABLISHING RELATIONSHIPS WITH OTHERS; 974]

run around after *v* [➡TAKE CARE OF AND SPOIL; 301]

run away *v* **escape**, flee, run off, abscond, elope, abandon, turn your back on. [➡RUN AWAY AND AVOID; 10]

runaway 1 *n* **escapee**, absentee, absconder, fugitive. [➡RUNAWAYS AND ABSENTEES; 9] 2 *adj* (*informal*) **bestselling**, blockbusting, hit, roaring, huge. [➡SUCCESSFUL AND PROMISING; 81]

runaway success *n* **blockbuster** (*informal*), big hit, smash, smash hit, barnburner (*US informal*). [➡SUCCESS; 82]

runaway victory *n* [➡SUCCESS; 82]

run by *v* **explain**, describe, tell, apprise (*formal*), impart, acquaint, pass on. [➡EXPLAIN AND CLARIFY; 611]

run counter to *v* [➡DIFFERENCE; 150]

run down 1 *v* **bring to an end**, close down, wind up, shut down, peter out. [➡DISAPPEAR; 4] *Opposite:* start. 2 *v* **belittle**, criticize, knock, disparage, put down, rubbish. [➡ACCUSE, BLAME, AND CRITICIZE; 642] *Opposite:* praise.

rundown *n* **details**, list, listing, inventory, record, account, enumeration. [➡SUMMARIES, OUTLINES, AND EXCERPTS; 589]

run-down 1 *adj* **exhausted**, tired, weak, wearied, fried (*US slang*), wasted (*slang*), worn-out, shattered, knackered (*slang*). [➡TIRED, ASLEEP AND UNCONSCIOUS; 739] *Opposite:* energetic. 2 *adj* **tired**, worn out, weary, washed out, under the weather, below par (*informal*). [➡UNFIT AND WEAK; 740] *Opposite:* well. 3 *adj* **dilapidated**, ramshackle, shabby, neglected, derelict, in bad repair, in bad condition, badly maintained, in a state (*informal*), tumbledown, beat-up (*informal*), ragged, worn, seedy. [➡IN BAD REPAIR; 1233] *Opposite:* well-kept.

rune *n* **character**, letter, symbol, sign, hieroglyph, hieroglyphic. [➡SYMBOLS, SIGNS, AND NUMBERS; 597]

run for it *v* [➡RUN AWAY AND AVOID; 10]

rung *n* **step**, stair, tread, stage. [➡SUPPORTS AND BASES; 1254]

runic *type of* **alphabet**. [➡SYMBOLS, SIGNS, AND NUMBERS; 597]

run-in (*informal*) *n* **argument**, confrontation, quarrel, clash, disagreement, altercation, face-off, fight, row, barney (*informal*), tiff. [➡ARGUMENT; 47]

run into 1 *v* **come across**, bump into, meet by chance, encounter. [➡EXPERIENCE AND ENCOUNTER; 583] 2 *v* **hit**, bump into, crash into, collide with, run over, smash into, knock down. [➡CONTACT: IMPACT; 414] *Opposite:* miss.

runnel *n* [➡WATERCOURSES; 1110]

runner 1 *n* **sprinter**, jogger, racer, contender, competitor. [➡PEOPLE IN SPORTS AND LEISURE; 876] 2 *n* **candidate**, contender, entrant, participant, competitor, contestant. [➡COMPETITORS; 41] 3 *n* **messenger**, courier, gofer (*informal*). [➡MESSENGERS AND COURIERS; 852]

See Compare and Contrast at **candidate**.

runner bean *type of* **pulse**. [➡BEANS AND PULSES; 1188]

runner-up *n* **second place**, person in second place, silver medallist, second to finish, next best person, person with consolation prize. [➡PEOPLE IN SPORTS AND LEISURE; 876]

runniness *n* [➡FLUID AND NON-SOLID; 1212]

running 1 *n* **management**, administration, organization, operation, controlling, overseeing. [➡CARRY OUT AN ACTION; 270] 2 *adv* **in a row**, consecutively, on the trot, successively, in succession, seriatim. [➡AFTER, LAST, AND FOLLOWING; 166]

running joke *n* [➡JOKES AND TEASING; 675]

runny *adj* **liquid**, fluid, gooey, soft, thin. [➡FLUID AND NON-SOLID; 1212] *Opposite:* set.

run off *v* **flee**, escape, run away, decamp, scarper (*slang*). [➡RUN AWAY AND AVOID; 10]

run-of-the-mill *adj* **mediocre**, ordinary, middling, average, undistinguished, common or garden, basic, unremarkable, commonplace, no-frills (*informal*), everyday, plain, mundane, regular. [➡ORDINARINESS; 245] *Opposite:* extraordinary.

run on *v* **go on**, carry on, continue, keep going. [➡CONTINUE AN ACTION; 263] *Opposite:* stop.

run out *v* **end**, expire, come to an end, finish. [➡DISAPPEAR; 4]

run over 1 *v* **crush**, hit, squash, flatten, collide with, run into, knock down. [➡CONTACT: IMPACT; 414] **2** *v* **explain**, summarize, go over, run through, cover, recap, recapitulate (*formal*). [➡EXPLAIN AND CLARIFY; 611]

run rings around *v* **outshine**, beat, outdo, outstrip, outperform, surpass, trample over, walk over (*informal*), thrash, hammer (*informal*). [➡BEAT AND DEFEAT; 80]

run rings round *see* **run rings around**.

run riot *v* **run amok**, go on the rampage, riot, go berserk, go wild, rampage. [➡GIVING VENT TO EMOTIONS; 680]

runt *n* **smallest**, weakest, littlest. [➡LAZY OR UNSUCCESSFUL PEOPLE; 948]

run the gauntlet *v* **undergo**, experience, face, suffer, endure, bear. [➡EXPERIENCE AND ENCOUNTER; 583]

run through **1** *v* **use up**, exhaust, eat through, go through, deplete, get through, waste. [➡USE UP AND WASTE; 475] *Opposite:* conserve. **2** *v* **review**, go over, examine, consider, look over. [➡READ; 759] **3** *v* **pervade**, spread through, underlie, permeate. [➡EXIST IN A PLACE; 19] **4** *v* **rehearse**, practise, try out, go through. [➡CARRY OUT AN ACTION; 270] **5** *v* (*literary*) **spear**, impale, stab, jab. [➡STAB; 417] **6** *v* **infect**, contaminate, pollute. [➡MOVE PAST, INTO OR THROUGH SOMETHING; 332]

run-through **1** *n* **rehearsal**, practice, dry run, test run, test, trial, drill, tryout (*US*). [➡PREPARATORY EVENT; 57] **2** *n* **review**, survey, summary, overview, résumé. [➡SUMMARIES, OUTLINES, AND EXCERPTS; 589]

run to *v* [➡AMOUNT TO AND EQUAL; 70]

run to ground *v* [➡GET; 421]

run up **1** *v* **accumulate**, amass, collect, incur, build up. [➡GET; 421] *Opposite:* discharge. **2** *v* **sew**, create, make, put together. [➡CRAFTS AND CARVING; 356]

run-up **1** *n* **run**, approach, advance. [➡PAST; 84] **2** *n* **approach**, lead-in, introduction, buildup. [➡BEGINNING; 53]

runway *n* **landing strip**, airstrip, landing field, taxiway, flight strip, takeoff strip. [➡AIRWAYS; 1108]

rupture **1** *n* **break**, crack, tear, split, fissure, opening, gash, breach, gap. [➡HOLES, GAPS, AND FORKS; 1251] **2** *n* **disagreement**, falling-out, split, breakup, separation, estrangement, division, break, breach, rift. [➡ARGUMENT; 47] **3** *v* **break**, crack, burst, come apart, rip apart, rip open, shatter. [➡TEAR, BREAK, AND CUT; 361]

rural *adj* **country**, rustic, pastoral, bucolic, countryside. [➡THE COUNTRYSIDE AND OUTDOOR SPACES; 1070] *Opposite:* urban.

ruse *n* **trick**, dodge, subterfuge, wile, con, scam (*slang*), hoax, deception, ploy, stunt, plot. [➡DECEPTION AND LIES; 661]

rush **1** *v* **hurry**, precipitate, hustle (*informal*), hasten, dash, bolt. [➡OVERDO SOMETHING; 291] **2** *v* **run**, hurry, dash, sprint, flash, scurry, scuttle, tear, get a move on (*informal*), get your skates on (*informal*), charge. [➡MOVE FAST; 314] *Opposite:* dawdle. **3** *n* **blast**, current, gale, gust, blow, stream, draught. [➡SUDDEN EVENT; 52] **4** *n* **haste**, hurry, urgency, flash. [➡SPEED; 102]

rushed *adj* **hurried**, quick, swift, hasty. [➡HAPPENING QUICKLY; 104] *Opposite:* leisurely.

rushes *n* **unedited prints**, dailies, first prints, raw footage, footage. [➡FILM; 901]

russet *type of* **brown**. [➡COLOURS; 1223]

rust **1** *n* **corrosion**, oxidation, erosion, corruption, decomposition, tarnishing. [➡GO BAD AND CORRODE; 391] **2** *v* **corrode**, oxidize, tarnish, erode, decompose, corrupt. [➡GO BAD AND CORRODE; 391]

rust bucket (*informal humorous*) *n* [➡BIKES, CARS, AND CARRIAGES; 1148]

rust-free *adj* [➡IN GOOD REPAIR; 1231]

rustic *adj* **rural**, country, pastoral, bucolic, countryside. [➡THE COUNTRYSIDE AND OUTDOOR SPACES; 1070] *Opposite:* urban.

rustle *n* **crackle**, crunch, whisper, swish. [➡CONTINUOUS SOUNDS; 1257]

rustler *n* **thief**, poacher, robber, horse thief, cattle thief, livestock thief. [➡CRIMINALS; 821]

rustle up (*informal*) *v* **prepare**, concoct, put together, make, produce, find, knock together (*informal*), knock up (*informal*), whip up. [➡MEAL PREPARATION; 355]

rustproof **1** *adj* **nonrusting**, rust-free, rustproofed, stainless-steel, corrosion-proof, nonreactive, inert, coated, sealed, waterproofed. [➡DURABLE; 1209] **2** *v* **seal**, make rustproof, waterproof, coat, paint, prime, proof, treat. [➡DECORATE, ADORN, AND APPLY COATINGS; 406]

rusty **1** *adj* **corroded**, oxidized, tarnished, eroded. [➡IN BAD REPAIR; 1233] **2** *adj* **out of practice**, out of form, unpractised, unaccustomed, off form, unhabituated, out of shape. [➡UNSKILLED; 530]

rut *n* **furrow**, groove, channel, runnel, pothole. [➡HOLES, GAPS, AND FORKS; 1251]

rutabaga (*US*) *type of* **root vegetable**. [➡FRUIT AND VEGETABLES; 1175]

ruthless *adj* **cruel**, callous, brutal, pitiless, merciless, cold-blooded, hard-nosed (*informal*), unfeeling, hard-hearted, heartless. [➡SELFISH AND UNKIND; 506] *Opposite:* merciful.

ruthlessness *n* **callousness**, cruelty, mercilessness, brutality, heartlessness, cold-bloodedness, hard-heartedness. [➡SELFISH AND UNKIND; 506] *Opposite:* mercy.

rutted *adj* **uneven**, furrowed, potholed, bumpy. [➡PHYSICAL TEXTURE; 1221] *Opposite:* smooth.

RV **1** *n* **recreational vehicle**, camper, motor caravan, mobile home, trailer, motor home (*US*). [➡BIKES, CARS, AND CARRIAGES; 1148] **2** *type of* **leisure vehicle**. [➡VEHICLES; 1144]

rye *type of* **cereal**. [➡CEREAL FOODS; 1177]

rye bread *type of* **bread**. [➡BREAD, FLOUR, AND BREAD PRODUCTS; 1178]

rye-grass *type of* **grass**. [➡GRASS; 1031]

S

sabbatical *n* **study leave**, leave, time off, retreat, time out (*US*). [➡PERIOD OF REST; 91]

sable *type of* **black**. [➡COLOURS; 1223]

sabotage 1 *n* **disruption**, damage, interference, interruption. [➡AVOID, PREVENT, LIMIT, AND CONTROL; 278] 2 *v* **disrupt**, damage, interfere with, interrupt, harm, incapacitate, impair. [➡MAKE IMPOSSIBLE; 277]

saboteur *n* **hunt saboteur**, ecowarrior, computer hacker, vandal, sab (*slang*). [➡UNCOOPERATIVE OR REBELLIOUS PERSON; 567]

sabre *type of* **sword or knife**. [➡SWORDS AND KNIVES; 1156]

sabre-rattler *n* [➡UNCOOPERATIVE OR REBELLIOUS PERSON; 567]

sabre rattling *n* **display of force**, bravado, empty, threats, bluffing, aggression. [➡CRITICISMS AND ANGRY OUTBURSTS; 50]

sac *n* **bag**, pouch, case, pod, bladder. [➡CONTAINERS, RECEPTACLES, AND PACKAGING; 1244]

saccharine 1 *adj* **sugary**, sickly, sweet, syrupy, treacly. [➡TASTE; 704] *Opposite:* sour. 2 *adj* **sentimental**, slushy, mawkish, cloying, sickly, sickly-sweet, treacly. [➡IN POOR TASTE; 230] *Opposite:* unsentimental.

sacerdotal *adj* **clerical**, ecclesiastic, religious, spiritual, priestly (*formal or literary*). [➡RELIGIONS AND RELIGIOUS PRACTICES; 778]

sachet *n* **envelope**, packet, pouch. [➡CONTAINERS, RECEPTACLES, AND PACKAGING; 1244]

sack 1 *v* (*informal*) **dismiss**, fire (*informal*), discharge (*formal*), kick out (*informal*), give somebody notice, give somebody their cards, give the elbow (*informal*), throw out, give somebody the boot (*informal*), boot out (*informal*), can (*US slang*). [➡REVOKE STATUS; 460] *Opposite:* employ. 2 *v* **ransack**, plunder, destroy, pillage, tear apart, ruin, despoil. [➡DESTRUCTION AND DEMOLITION; 360]

sacking (*informal*) 1 *n* **dismissal**, firing (*informal*), discharge, job loss, notice, the boot (*informal*), the elbow (*informal*), walking papers (*US informal*), pink slip (*US informal*). [➡REVOKE STATUS; 460] 2 *type of* **fabric from plants**. [➡FABRICS; 1131]

sacrament *n* **rite**, ceremony, ritual, service, mass. [➡RELIGIONS AND RELIGIOUS PRACTICES; 778]

sacred *adj* **holy**, blessed, consecrated, hallowed, revered, sanctified, sacrosanct. [➡RELIGIOUS CONCEPTS; 777] *Opposite:* secular.

sacredness *n* [➡RELIGIOUS CONCEPTS; 777]

sacrifice *v* **give up**, forgo, forfeit, let go, surrender, lose. [➡FOREGO AND DENY ONESELF; 450]

sacrilege *n* **blasphemy**, desecration, profanity, irreverence, violation, disrespect. [➡RELIGIOUS CONCEPTS; 777] *Opposite:* sacred.

sacrilegious *adj* **blasphemous**, profane, irreverent, heretical, impious, disrespectful. [➡RELIGIOUS CONCEPTS; 777] *Opposite:* reverent.

sacrosanct *adj* **inviolable**, sacred, revered, holy, untouchable, sanctified. [➡RELIGIOUS CONCEPTS; 777]

sad 1 *adj* **unhappy**, miserable, depressed, gloomy, down, blue (*informal*), wretched, dejected, despondent, desolate, forlorn, sorrowful, melancholy, woeful. [➡SADNESS, DISTRESS, AND DESPAIR; 540] *Opposite:* happy. 2 *adj* **depressing**, gloomy, miserable, cheerless, distressing, heartbreaking, poignant, moving. [➡EMOTIONALLY UNPLEASANT AND UPSETTING; 228] *Opposite:* cheerful.

sadden *v* **depress**, distress, upset, dismay, pain, bring down. [➡UPSET, DISTRESS, AND HUMILIATE; 568] *Opposite:* cheer.

saddened *adj* [➡SADNESS, DISTRESS, AND DESPAIR; 540]

saddening *adj* [➡EMOTIONALLY UNPLEASANT AND UPSETTING; 228]

saddlebag *n* **basket**, bag, pannier, holdall. [➡CONTAINERS, RECEPTACLES, AND PACKAGING; 1244]

saddle horse *type of* **horse**. [➡HORSE; 985]

saddle with *v* **burden**, lumber, encumber, weigh down, dump, land, load, leave, impose. [➡GIVE TOO MUCH; 438]

sadism *n* [➡UNKIND ACTION OR BEHAVIOUR; 297]

sadistic *adj* **cruel**, nasty, callous, heartless, vicious, brutal, aggressive, inhuman, violent, merciless, gloating. [➡AGGRESSIVE AND BELLIGERENT; 519] *Opposite:* human.

sadly 1 *adv* **unhappily**, miserably, gloomily, wretchedly, dejectedly, despondently, desolately, forlornly, sorrowfully, woefully. [➡SADNESS, DISTRESS, AND DESPAIR; 540] *Opposite:* happily. 2 *adv* **unfortunately**, unluckily, regrettably, alas. [➡EXPRESSIONS OF REGRET; 548] *Opposite:* luckily.

sadness *n* **unhappiness**, misery, depression, gloom, blues (*informal*), wretchedness, dejection, despondency, desolation, sorrow, melancholy, grief, woe. [➡SADNESS, DISTRESS, AND DESPAIR; 540] *Opposite:* happiness.

safari *n* **trek**, expedition, trip, search, quest, field trip. [➡TRAVEL: JOURNEYS AND TRIPS; 319]

safari park *n* [➡THE COUNTRYSIDE AND OUTDOOR SPACES; 1070]

safe 1 *adj* **harmless**, benign, innocuous, innocent, nonviolent, nontoxic, anodyne (*literary*). [➡SAFE AND SAFETY; 192] *Opposite:* dangerous. 2 *adj* **secure**, protected, sheltered, in safe hands, out of harm's way, safe and sound. [➡SAFE AND SAFETY; 192] *Opposite:* unsafe. 3 *adj* **unharmed**, undamaged, uninjured, unhurt, unscathed, safe and sound, secure, alive and well, untouched, all right. [➡FINE; 738] 4 *adj* **reli-**

able, dependable, trustworthy, careful, cautious, prudent, sound. [➡HONEST AND RELIABLE; 503] *Opposite:* unsafe.

safe and sound *adj* **unharmed**, undamaged, uninjured, unhurt, unscathed, safe, secure, alive and well, untouched, all right. [➡FINE; 738]

safe as houses *adj* [➡SAFE AND SAFETY; 192]

safe bet *n* [➡CERTAIN; 175]

safeguard 1 *n* **protection**, precaution, defence, safety measure, safety device, safety net. [➡SAFE AND SAFETY; 192] 2 *v* **defend**, protect, preserve, maintain, uphold, guard, look after, shield. [➡PREVENT CONTACT OR ATTACK; 420] *Opposite:* endanger.

Compare and Contrast: ***safeguard, protect, defend, guard, shield***

CORE MEANING: TO KEEP SAFE FROM ACTUAL OR POTENTIAL DAMAGE OR ATTACK OF ANY KIND

safeguard to take steps to prevent somebody or something from being harmed or damaged; ***protect*** to keep somebody or something from any kind of harm or damage; ***defend*** to deter an actual or threatened attack; ***guard*** to work to prevent damage, loss, or attack by being vigilant and taking defensive measures; ***shield*** to prevent harm, damage, or attack by using a physical barrier or by intervening in a protective way.

safeguarding *n* **protection**, preservation, conservation, defence, maintenance, upkeep, continuation, continuance. [➡PREVENT CONTACT OR ATTACK; 420] *Opposite:* destruction.

safe haven *n* **refuge**, asylum, haven, sanctuary. [➡SAFE BUILDINGS OR PLACES; 1092]

safe house *n* **refuge**, hideaway, retreat, hideout, hidey-hole (*informal*). [➡SAFE BUILDINGS OR PLACES; 1092]

safekeeping *n* **protection**, care, security, custody, safety, trust, good hands, charge. [➡SAFE AND SAFETY; 192]

safely *adv* **securely**, without harm, in one piece, safe and sound, all right, out of harm's way. [➡SAFE AND SAFETY; 192]

safe place *n* **refuge**, safe haven, hideaway, haven, sanctuary, retreat, asylum. [➡SAFE BUILDINGS OR PLACES; 1092]

safety *n* **care**, security, protection, shelter, wellbeing, welfare. [➡SAFE AND SAFETY; 192] *Opposite:* danger.

safety belt 1 *n* **seat belt**, strap, restraint, harness, safety harness. [➡FASTENERS, LINKS, AND NETWORKS; 1246] 2 *type of* **internal feature.** [➡VEHICLES; 1144]

safety glass *type of* **glass.** [➡GLASS; 1135]

safety net *n* **safety device**, safeguard, fail-safe, guard, shield, screen, fallback. [➡SAFE AND SAFETY; 192]

safety valve 1 *n* **fail-safe**, valve, safety device, safety precaution, overflow. [➡PARTS OF MACHINES AND TOOLS; 1117] 2 *n* **release**, channel, outlet. [➡SAFE AND SAFETY; 192]

saffron 1 *type of* **yellow.** [➡COLOURS; 1223] 2 *type of* **spice.** [➡HERBS AND SPICES; 1174]

sag 1 *v* **droop**, wilt, slump, flag, drop, hang down, loll, bend. [➡CHANGE OF SHAPE; 386] 2 *n* **drop**, slump, dip, fall, depression, slackness. [➡CHANGE OF INTENSITY: LESS; 396]

saga *n* **epic**, account, chronicle, tale, legend, narrative, history, story, yarn (*informal*). [➡THE ORAL TRADITION; 678]

sagacious (*formal*) *adj* **wise**, knowledgeable, learned, erudite, perceptive, intelligent, astute, clever, shrewd, discerning, sage (*literary*). [➡POSITIVE INTELLECTUAL CHARACTERISTICS; 525] *Opposite:* foolish.

sagaciousness (*formal*) *n* [➡KNOWLEDGE AND WISDOM; 559]

sagacity *n* **wisdom**, sagaciousness (*formal*), knowledge, erudition, perceptiveness, intelligence, insight, shrewdness, understanding, discernment, prudence. [➡KNOWLEDGE AND WISDOM; 559] *Opposite:* stupidity.

sage 1 *n* (*literary*) **adviser**, mentor, elder, statesman, savant, solon (*literary*). [➡TALENTED OR INTELLIGENT PERSON; 529] 2 *type of* **herb.** [➡HERBS AND SPICES; 1174]

sagebrush *type of* **shrub or bush.** [➡BUSHES AND SHRUBS; 1027]

sage green *type of* **green.** [➡COLOURS; 1223]

sagely (*literary*) *adv* **wisely**, prudently, sensibly, astutely, judiciously, sagaciously (*formal*), shrewdly. [➡POSITIVE INTELLECTUAL CHARACTERISTICS; 525] *Opposite:* foolishly.

sagginess *n* [➡SHAPELESSNESS; 1218]

sagging *adj* **drooping**, wilting, flaccid, flabby (*informal*), floppy, slumped, bending, baggy, saggy. [➡SHAPELESSNESS; 1218]

saggy *adj* [➡SHAPELESSNESS; 1218]

Sagittarius *type of* **star sign.** [➡FATE, DESTINY, AND ASTROLOGY; 783]

said *adj* **aforesaid** (*formal*), aforementioned (*formal*), alleged, supposed, assumed. [➡EXPRESSIONS OF REFERENCE; 63]

sail 1 *v* **set sail**, navigate, cruise, put out to sea. [➡TRAVEL: WAYS OF TRAVELLING; 321] 2 *v* **glide**, float, flow, drift, fly. [➡MOVE FAST; 314]

sailboat (*US*) *type of* **sailing vessel.** [➡SHIPS AND BOATS; 1149]

sailfish *type of* **tropical sea fish.** [➡SEA FISH; 1009]

sailing *n* [➡HOBBIES, GAMES, AND SPORTS; 875]

sailing boat *type of* **sailing vessel.** [➡SHIPS AND BOATS; 1149]

sailor *n* [➡TRAVEL: TRAVELLERS AND WALKERS; 320]

sailor hat *type of* **hat.** [➡HABERDASHERY, MILLINERY, AND LINGERIE; 867]

sail through *v* **do well**, do with ease, pass with flying colours, breeze through, ace (*US slang*). [➡SUCCEED AND WIN; 79] *Opposite:* fail.

saint *n* [➡RELIGIOUS PEOPLE; 779]

Saint Bernard *type of* **large dog.** [➡DOG; 980]

saintliness *n* **virtue**, goodness, piety, holiness, devoutness, righteousness, godliness. [➡RELIGIOUS CONCEPTS; 777] *Opposite:* evil.

saintly *adj* **virtuous**, good, holy, pious, devout, righteous, godly, angelic. [➡RELIGIOUS CONCEPTS; 777] *Opposite:* evil.

saint's day *n* [➡RELIGIOUS CONCEPTS; 777]

salaam 1 *n* **greeting**, salutation, bow, nod, acknowledgment. [➡GREETINGS, FAREWELLS, AND SALUTATIONS; 660] 2 *v* **greet**, bow, salute, nod, acknowledge. [➡GESTURES AND GESTICULATION; 654]

salacious *adj* **prurient** (*disapproving*), risqué, indecent, crude, improper, obscene. [➡MORALLY BAD; 776]

salad

◆ *types of salad vegetable*
alfalfa, bean sprout, capsicum, celery, chicory, coleslaw, cress, cucumber, endive, green onion (*US*), lettuce, pepper, radicchio, radish, scallion, sorrel, spring onion, sweet pepper, tomato, watercress

salad cream *type of* **seasonings, sauces, and dips.** [➡SEASONINGS AND SAUCES; 1173]

salad days (*literary*) *n* [➡PLEASANT SITUATIONS; 74]

salamander *type of* **amphibian.** [➡AMPHIBIANS; 1008]

salami *type of* **processed meat.** [➡TYPES AND CUTS OF MEAT; 1176]

salaried *adj* **remunerated**, paid, compensated, waged. [➡EMPLOYMENT STATUS; 831]

salary *n* **income**, pay, earnings, remuneration, payment, wages, wage, money. [➡INCOME; 461]

See Compare and Contrast at **wage**.

sale 1 *n* **transaction**, deal, selling, retailing, vending, trade. [➡BUSINESS ACTIVITIES AND PHENOMENA; 795] *Opposite:* purchase. 2 *n* **auction**, jumble sale, car boot sale, garage sale, rummage sale (*US*). [➡SALES AND SHOWS; 444]

saleable *adj* **vendible**, marketable, commercial, commercially viable. [➡SELL; 442]

saleroom *type of* **retail outlet.** [➡RETAIL OUTLETS; 1082]

sales assistant *n* **salesperson**, shop assistant, floorwalker, salesclerk (*US*). [➡SELLER; 443]

salesclerk (*US*) *n* [➡SELLER; 443]

sales manager *n* [➡SELLER; 443]

salesperson 1 *n* **sales rep** (*informal*), rep, seller, trader, marketer, vendor, pedlar, hawker, purveyor (*formal*). [➡BUSINESS ACTIVITIES AND PHENOMENA; 795] 2 *n* **sales assistant**, shop assistant, floorwalker, salesclerk (*US*). [➡SELLER; 443]

sales rep (*informal*) *n* [➡SELLER; 443]

sales representative *n* **sales rep** (*informal*), salesperson, rep, seller, trader, marketer, vendor, pedlar, hawker, purveyor (*formal*). [➡SELLER; 443]

salient *adj* **noticeable**, striking, prominent, outstanding, relevant, significant, leading, main. [➡MOST IMPORTANT AND MAIN; 194] *Opposite:* minor.

saline *adj* **salty**, salt, brackish, briny, salted. [➡TASTE; 704]

saliva *n* **spittle**, spit, drool, dribble, slobber, slaver. [➡EXCRETION AND EXCRETA; 723]

salivate *v* **drool**, dribble, slobber, slaver. [➡EXCRETION AND EXCRETA; 723]

sallow *adj* **yellow**, sickly, wan, washed-out, ashen, pallid, pale. [➡COMPLEXION; 481]

sallowness *n* [➡COMPLEXION; 481]

sally 1 *n* **attack**, sortie, breakout, breakthrough, raid, incursion. [➡SUDDEN EVENT; 52] 2 *n* **rush**, charge, dash, push. [➡SUDDEN EVENT; 52] 3 *v* **attack**, charge, raid, strike. [➡PHYSICAL ATTACK AND PUNISHMENT; 416] 4 *v* **go forth**, go out, venture forth, venture out, set out. [➡ABSENT ONESELF; 8] *Opposite:* retreat.

salmon *type of* **sea fish.** [➡SEA FISH; 1009]

salmonella *type of* **microorganism.** [➡MICROORGANISMS, FUNGI, AND ALGAE; 1023]

salmon pink *type of* **pink.** [➡COLOURS; 1223]

salon 1 *n* **soiree** (*formal*), gathering, get-together (*informal*), rendezvous, meeting, group. [➡MEETINGS AND ASSEMBLIES; 43] 2 *n* **beauty salon**, hair salon, hairdresser's, barbershop, barber's. [➡RETAIL OUTLETS; 1082] 3 *type of* **room in the home.** [➡TYPES OF ROOM; 1096]

saloon 1 *type of* **car.** [➡BIKES, CARS, AND CARRIAGES; 1148] 2 *type of* **bar or club.** [➡HOTELS, RESTAURANTS, AND CLUBS; 1081]

salopettes *type of* **trousers.** [➡GARMENTS AND OUTFITS; 865]

salsa 1 *type of* **dance.** [➡DANCE; 903] 2 *type of* **popular music.** [➡MUSIC, SONGS, AND SINGING; 907]

salt *type of* **nutrient.** [➡FOOD COMPONENTS; 1187]

salt away *v* **hoard**, stash (*informal*), save, squirrel away, put by, set aside, amass, accumulate. [➡STORE AND KEEP; 454] *Opposite:* fritter away.

salt flat *n* [➡WETLANDS; 1043]

salt water *n* **brine**, sea water, saline. [➡LIQUIDS; 1268]

salty *adj* **salt**, saline, brackish, salted, briny. [➡TASTE; 704] *Opposite:* sweet.

salubrious (*formal*) *adj* **healthy**, wholesome, respectable, decent, hygienic, clean. *Opposite:* insalubrious. (*formal*). [➡CLEAN; 1232]

salutary *adj* **beneficial**, helpful, useful, valuable, constructive, productive. [➡USEFULNESS; 200]

salutation *n* **greeting**, acknowledgment, welcome, gesture, salute, nod, salaam. [➡GREETINGS, FAREWELLS, AND SALUTATIONS; 660]

salutations (*formal*) *n* [➡GREETINGS, FAREWELLS, AND SALUTATIONS; 660]

salute 1 *v* **acknowledge**, greet, welcome, gesture, wave, nod. [➡GESTURES AND GESTICULATION; 654] 2 *n* **sign of respect**, salutation, greeting, acknowledgment, signal, gesture. [➡GESTURES AND GESTICULATION; 654]

salvage *v* **save**, recover, rescue, retrieve, reclaim, recoup, pick up. [➡REGAIN POSSESSION; 430]

salvation *n* **redemption**, deliverance (*formal*), rescue, recovery, escape. [➡FREEDOM AND LIBERTY; 209]

salve 1 *n* **lotion**, ointment, balm, balsam, liniment, unguent, cream. [➡LOTIONS, PASTES, AND GELS; 1271] *Opposite:* irritant. 2 *v* **appease**, soothe, comfort, calm, ease, relieve, pacify. [➡SOOTHE AND CALM; 574] *Opposite:* irritate.

salver *n* **tray**, platter, plate, serving dish, dish, paten. [➡TABLEWARE, CUTLERY, AND KITCHENWARE; 861]

salvo *n* **barrage**, bombardment, round, torrent, hail, deluge, volley. [➡SUDDEN EVENT; 52]

samba 1 *type of* **dance**. [➡DANCE; 903] 2 *type of* **popular music**. [➡MUSIC, SONGS, AND SINGING; 907]

same 1 *adj* **identical**, alike, matching, similar, equal, equivalent. [➡SAMENESS; 151] *Opposite:* different. 2 *adj* **unchanged**, constant, consistent, uniform, even, invariable, unaffected. [➡PERMANENCE: WITHOUT CHANGE; 95] *Opposite:* changed.

sameness 1 *n* **similarity**, likeness, resemblance, similitude (*formal*), uniformity, equivalence, equality, identicalness. [➡SAMENESS; 151] *Opposite:* difference. 2 *n* **monotony**, repetitiveness, uniformity, consistency, evenness, regularity, similarity. [➡BORING AND UNINTERESTING; 235] *Opposite:* variety.

samey (*informal*) *adj* **repetitive**, unvaried, unchanging, monotonous, similar, boring. [➡BORING AND UNINTERESTING; 235] *Opposite:* varied.

samovar *n* **tea urn**, urn, teapot, jug, kettle. [➡TABLEWARE, CUTLERY, AND KITCHENWARE; 861]

sampan *type of* **small vessel**. [➡SHIPS AND BOATS; 1149]

sample 1 *n* **example**, taster, model, trial, illustration, mock-up, tester. [➡REPRESENTATIONS AND GENERAL EXAMPLES; 65] 2 *v* **test**, try, appraise, try out, check out, taste, experiment. [➡EXAMINE AND ASSESS; 754]

sampler 1 *n* **technician**, tester, analyst, quality control analyst, laboratory technician. [➡SURVEYORS, EXAMINERS, AND JUDGES; 853] 2 *n* **selection**, sample, cross section, sampling, representative selection, test group, control group. [➡REPRESENTATIONS AND GENERAL EXAMPLES; 65] 3 *n* **sample**, tryout, example, taste, illustration, taster. [➡REPRESENTATIONS AND GENERAL EXAMPLES; 65] 4 *n* **embroidery**, sewing, needlework, handwork. [➡CRAFTS AND CARVING; 356]

sampling *n* **sample**, specimen, cross section, selection, test group, sampler, control group, random sample, straw poll, straw vote. [➡REPRESENTATIONS AND GENERAL EXAMPLES; 65]

sanatorium *n* **clinic**, hospital, infirmary, hospice, spa, health resort. [➡HOSPITALS AND CLINICS; 826]

sanctification *n* [➡RELIGIOUS CONCEPTS; 777]

sanctified *adj* **sacred**, holy, blessed, consecrated, hallowed, dedicated, purified. [➡RELIGIOUS CONCEPTS; 777] *Opposite:* desecrated.

sanctify *v* **bless**, consecrate, hallow, dedicate, purify. [➡RELIGIONS AND RELIGIOUS PRACTICES; 778] *Opposite:* desecrate.

sanctimonious (*disapproving*) *adj* **self-righteous** (*disapproving*), holier-than-thou (*informal*), smug, pious, pompous, self-satisfied, superior, censorious. [➡AFFECTATION, SELF-SATISFACTION, AND SNOBBISHNESS; 508] *Opposite:* humble.

sanctimoniously *adv* [➡POMPOUS, LOUD, AND OVER-CONFIDENT; 636]

sanctimoniousness *n* [➡AFFECTATION, SELF-SATISFACTION, AND SNOBBISHNESS; 508]

sanction 1 *n* **authorization**, permission, approval, agreement, consent, endorsement. [➡PERMIT AND ALLOW; 670] *Opposite:* prohibition. 2 *n* **support**, approval, encouragement, agreement, affirmation, favour. [➡APPROVE AND CONFIRM; 647] 3 *n* **restriction**, penalty, ban, punishment, injunction, measure, action. [➡REFUSE PERMISSION AND NOT ALLOW; 671] 4 *v* **authorize**, permit, approve, allow, pass, endorse, OK (*informal*). [➡PERMIT AND ALLOW; 670] *Opposite:* veto.

sanctity *n* **holiness**, blessedness, sacredness, inviolability, purity, sacrosanctity. [➡RELIGIOUS CONCEPTS; 777] *Opposite:* profanity.

sanctuary 1 *n* **refuge**, asylum, shelter, safe haven, haven, safe house. [➡SAFE BUILDINGS OR PLACES; 1092] 2 *n* **safety**, protection, refuge, asylum, shelter, immunity. [➡SAFE AND SAFETY; 192] 3 *n* **reserve**, reservation, national park, nature reserve, preserve, nature preserve. [➡THE COUNTRYSIDE AND OUTDOOR SPACES; 1070]

sanctum 1 *n* **holy of holies**, sanctum sanctorum, temple, altar, shrine. [➡RELIGIOUS BUILDINGS; 1084] 2 *n* **retreat**, den, refuge, study, hideaway, office, lair (*informal*), sanctum sanctorum. [➡SAFE BUILDINGS OR PLACES; 1092]

sand 1 *n* [➡BUILDING MATERIALS; 1076] 2 *n* **shingle**, grit, gravel, powder, silt, soil. [➡EROSION PRODUCTS AND SOIL; 1058] 3 *n* **beach**, strand, shore. [➡THE SEAS, OCEANS, AND SHORES; 1041] 4 *v* **rub down**, smooth, sandpaper, polish, rub, scrape. [➡CLEAN AND POLISH; 404]

sandal *type of* **shoe**. [➡FOOTWEAR; 871]

sandalwood *type of* **evergreen tree**. [➡EVERGREEN AND CONIFEROUS TREES; 1029]

sandbank *n* **sandbar**, dune, mound, bank, hummock, hill, ridge. [➡THE SEAS, OCEANS, AND SHORES; 1041]

sandbar *n* **sandbank**, ridge, shallows. [➡THE SEAS, OCEANS, AND SHORES; 1041]

sander *type of* **carpentry tool**. [➡HAND TOOLS; 1118]

sand flea (*US*) 1 *type of* **parasitic insect**. [➡PARASITES; 1017] 2 *type of* **crustacean**. [➡LAND INVERTEBRATE; 1021]

sandfly *type of* **parasitic insect**. [➡PARASITES; 1017]

sand hopper *type of* **crustacean**. [➡LAND INVERTEBRATE; 1021]

sandpaper *v* **rub down**, smooth, sand, polish, rub, scrape. [➡CLEAN AND POLISH; 404]

sandshoe *type of* **shoe**. [➡FOOTWEAR; 871]

sandstone *type of* **stone**. [➡STONES, ROCKS, AND BOULDERS; 1057]

sandwich 1 *n* **snack**, club sandwich, double-decker, sarnie (*informal*), butty (*informal*), roll, toasty (*informal*), submarine, hoagie (*US*). [➡PREPARED DISHES; 1169] 2 *v* **squeeze in**, squash in, pack in, cram, slot in, insert, fit in. [➡POSITION SOMETHING: BETWEEN, BESIDE, OR INSIDE SOMETHING; 327]

sane 1 *adj* **well-balanced**, compos mentis, rational, stable, healthy, lucid. [➡POSITIVE INTELLECTUAL CHARACTERISTICS; 525] *Opposite:* insane. 2 *adj* **sensible**, reasonable, rational, sound, wise, commonsensical. [➡THE NATURE OF IDEAS; 772] *Opposite:* irrational.

saneness *n* [➡POSITIVE INTELLECTUAL CHARACTERISTICS; 525]

sang-froid (*formal*) *n* **self-possession**, calmness, poise, aplomb, self-assurance, self-control, composure, cool (*informal*). [➡CONFIDENCE AND COMPOSURE; 500] *Opposite:* anxiety.

sanguinary (*formal*) 1 *adj* **bloody**, gory, brutal, grim, gruesome, bloodied. [➡DISGUSTING AND REPULSIVE; 231] 2 *adj* **bloodthirsty**, murderous, ruthless, savage, cruel, merciless, homicidal. [➡UNFRIENDLINESS AND UNSOCIABILITY; 505]

sanguine *adj* **confident**, optimistic, cheerful, hopeful, positive, upbeat (*informal*). [➡CALMNESS, CONFIDENCE, AND COMPOSURE; 537] *Opposite:* pessimistic.

sanguinity *n* [➡CALMNESS, CONFIDENCE, AND COMPOSURE; 537]

sanitariness *n* [➡CLEAN; 1232]

sanitary *adj* **hygienic**, clean, healthy, salubrious (*formal*), wholesome, sterile. [➡CLEAN; 1232] *Opposite:* insanitary.

sanitation *n* **hygiene**, cleanliness, cleanness, public health, health. [➡SOCIAL WELFARE; 812]

sanitize *v* **disinfect**, clean, cleanse, wash, sterilize, decontaminate. [➡CLEAN AND POLISH; 404] *Opposite:* contaminate.

sanitized *adj* [➡CLEAN; 1232]

sanity 1 *n* **saneness**, rationality, stability, lucidity, reason. [➡POSITIVE INTELLECTUAL CHARACTERISTICS; 525] *Opposite:* insanity. 2 *n* **reasonableness**, sense, rationality, soundness, wisdom, understanding, common sense, reason, judgment. [➡THE NATURE OF IDEAS; 772] *Opposite:* unreasonableness.

sans (*literary or humorous*) *prep* [➡NOT; 135]

sansevieria *type of* **foliage plant**. [➡FOLIAGE PLANTS; 1035]

Santa Ana *type of* **wind**. [➡WINDY AND STORMY WEATHER; 1053]

sap 1 *n* **juice**, fluid, liquid, latex. [➡PARTS OF TREES AND PLANTS; 1026] 2 *n* **energy**, vitality, health, strength, life, vigour. [➡ENERGY AND ENTHUSIASM; 497] 3 *v* **dig down**, burrow, bore, tunnel, mine. [➡SEEK POSSESSION AND SEARCH; 457] 4 *v* **weaken**, drain, undermine, deplete, eat away, debilitate, reduce. [➡CHANGE OF INTENSITY: LESS; 396] *Opposite:* boost.

sapience *n* [➡KNOWLEDGE AND WISDOM; 559]

sapient *adj* **wise**, learned, educated, intelligent, sage (*literary*), knowing, discerning. [➡KNOWLEDGE AND WISDOM; 559] *Opposite:* unwise.

sapling 1 *n* **tree**, seedling, plantlet, sprout, scion, sprig. [➡PLANTS AND TREES; 1024] 2 *n* (*literary*) **youth**, adolescent, youngster, juvenile, teenager, teen (*informal*). [➡CHILD OR YOUTH; 945]

sapphire 1 *type of* **blue**. [➡COLOURS; 1223] 2 *type of* **gemstone**. [➡PRECIOUS STONES; 1277]

sarcasm *n* **irony**, mockery, cynicism, derision, acerbity, scorn, disdain. [➡MOCKING AND DISMISSIVE; 637]

sarcastic *adj* **ironic**, mocking, sardonic, cynical, acerbic, mordant, derisive, satirical, caustic. [➡MOCKING AND DISMISSIVE; 637]

Compare and Contrast: ***sarcastic, ironic, sardonic, satirical, caustic***

CORE MEANING: USED TO DESCRIBE REMARKS THAT ARE DESIGNED TO HURT OR MOCK

sarcastic contemptuous, scornful, or mocking and intended to hurt or belittle; ***ironic*** deliberately stating the opposite of the truth, usually with the intention of being amusing; ***sardonic*** mocking and cynical or disdainful, though not deliberately hurtful; ***satirical*** using ridicule to criticize somebody's or something's faults, especially in the arts; ***caustic*** harsh and bitter and intended to mock, offend, or belittle.

sarcoma *n* [➡ILLNESSES AND DISORDERS; 733]

sarcophagus *n* **coffin**, tomb, casket (*US*). [➡BURIAL PLACES AND ACCESSORIES; 930]

sard *type of* **gemstone**. [➡PRECIOUS STONES; 1277]

sardine *type of* **sea fish**. [➡SEA FISH; 1009]

sardonic *adj* **mocking**, scornful, ironic, sarcastic, derisive, satirical, cutting, mordant, scathing, disdainful. [➡MOCKING AND DISMISSIVE; 637]

See Compare and Contrast at **sarcastic**.

sardonicism *n* [➡MOCKING AND DISMISSIVE; 637]

sari *type of* **dress**. [➡GARMENTS AND OUTFITS; 865]

sarnie (*informal*) *n* [➡PREPARED DISHES; 1169]

sarong *type of* **skirt**. [➡GARMENTS AND OUTFITS; 865]

sarsaparilla *type of* **climber**. [➡CLIMBERS; 1033]

sarsen *n* **rock**, boulder, stone, cairn, block. [➡STONES, ROCKS, AND BOULDERS; 1057]

sartorial *adj* **clothing**, dress, tailored. [➡WELL GROOMED; 483]

sash 1 *n* **band**, ribbon, belt, cummerbund, tie, girdle. [➡PARTS OF A GARMENT; 870] 2 *type of* **accessory**. [➡HABERDASHERY, MILLINERY, AND LINGERIE; 867]

sashay (*humorous*) *v* **flounce**, sway, shimmy, strut, prance, swagger. [➡MOVE FAST; 314]

sash window *type of* **window**. [➡WINDOWS; 1099]

sasquatch *n* **humanoid**, Bigfoot. [➡MYTHICAL BEINGS; 790]

sassafras *type of* **deciduous tree**. [➡DECIDUOUS TREES; 1028]

sassiness (*US*) 1 *n* **impudence**, impertinence, brazenness, insolence, impishness, mischief, disrespect, nerve, cheek (*informal*), cheekiness. [➡BAD MANNERS AND SOCIAL SKILLS; 522] *Opposite:* respectfulness. 2 *n* **liveliness**, high spirits, feistiness (*informal*), jauntiness, vivacity, vivaciousness, bubbliness, playfulness. [➡ENERGY AND ENTHUSIASM; 497] *Opposite:* lifelessness.

sassy (*US*) 1 *adj* **impudent**, impertinent (*formal*), brazen, insolent, impish, mischievous, disrespectful, cheeky. [➡BAD MANNERS AND SOCIAL SKILLS; 522] *Opposite:* respectful. 2 *adj* **lively**, high-spirited, feisty (*informal*), spirited, jaunty, vivacious, bubbly, playful. [➡ENERGY AND ENTHUSIASM; 497] *Opposite:* lifeless.

satay *type of* **seasonings, sauces, and dips.** [➡SEASONINGS AND SAUCES; 1173]

satchel *n* **bag**, shoulder bag, haversack, school bag. [➡CONTAINERS, RECEPTACLES, AND PACKAGING; 1244]

sate *v* **fill up**, fill, satiate, stuff, gorge, satisfy, feed, glut. [➡FILL; 407]

sated *adj* **full**, full up, satiated, stuffed (*informal*), gorged, bursting, satisfied, replete. [➡EAT AND NOT EAT; 711] *Opposite:* hungry.

sateen *type of* **synthetic fabric.** [➡FABRICS; 1131]

satellite 1 *n* **dependency**, protectorate, colony, subject population. [➡TERRITORIES AND GROUPS OF NATIONS; 1067] 2 *n* **satellite television**, satellite TV, satellite broadcasting, digital television, digital TV, cable. [➡TELECOMMUNICATIONS; 1129] 3 *type of* **spacecraft.** [➡SPACE VEHICLES; 1062]

satellite dish *type of* **telecommunications equipment.** [➡TELECOMMUNICATIONS; 1129]

satellite television *n* [➡TELEVISION AND RADIO; 607]

satiate 1 *v* **glut**, fill, satisfy, sate, fill up, overindulge. [➡FILL; 407] 2 *v* **gratify**, satisfy, quench, sate, slake, assuage, appease. [➡CHANGE OF INTENSITY: LESS; 396]

satiated 1 *adj* **full**, satisfied, replete, sated, full up. [➡EAT AND NOT EAT; 711] *Opposite:* unsatisfied. 2 *adj* **gratified**, satisfied, quenched, sated, slaked, assuaged, appeased. [➡PLEASURE, EXCITEMENT, AND ELATION; 535]

satin *type of* **synthetic fabric.** [➡FABRICS; 1131]

satiny *adj* **lustrous**, luminous, shiny, radiant, glossy, smooth, glowing, sheeny. [➡VISUAL TEXTURE; 1220] *Opposite:* dull.

satire 1 *n* **mockery**, irony, sarcasm, ridicule, wit, parody, invective (*formal*). [➡JOKES AND TEASING; 675] 2 *n* **parody**, lampoon, burlesque, caricature, sendup (*informal*), travesty, spoof, mockery. [➡JOKES AND TEASING; 675]

satirical *adj* **mocking**, ironic, sardonic, humorous, sarcastic, tongue-in-cheek, spoof. [➡MOCKING AND DISMISSIVE; 637]

See Compare and Contrast at **sarcastic.**

satirist *n* **humorist**, wit, joker, satirizer, comic, wag (*dated*), lampooner. [➡WORKERS IN ENTERTAINMENT AND MEDIA; 873]

satirize *v* **mock**, ridicule, parody, lampoon, deride, send up (*informal*), caricature. [➡JOKES AND TEASING; 675]

satisfaction 1 *n* **contentment**, pleasure, happiness, joy, enjoyment, pride. [➡PLEASURE, EXCITEMENT, AND ELATION; 535] *Opposite:* dissatisfaction. 2 *n* **gratification**, consummation, fulfilment. [➡PLEASURE, EXCITEMENT, AND ELATION; 535] 3 *n* **approval**, liking, taste, contentment, agreement, pleasure. [➡APPRECIATION AND GRATITUDE; 536] *Opposite:* dissatisfaction. 4 *n* **redress**, reparation, compensation, settlement, repayment, recompense. [➡TREAT; 211]

satisfactory *adj* **acceptable**, reasonable, pleasing, fitting, agreeable, adequate, suitable, all right. [➡ACCEPTABLE AND PASSABLE; 220] *Opposite:* unsatisfactory.

satisfied *adj* **content**, pleased, happy, gratified, fulfilled, contented. [➡PLEASURE, EXCITEMENT, AND ELATION; 535] *Opposite:* dissatisfied.

satisfy 1 *v* **content**, please, gratify, mollify, placate, fulfil. [➡PLEASE AND AMUSE; 573] *Opposite:* dissatisfy. 2 *v* **gratify**, satiate, quench, sate, slake, assuage, appease. [➡CHANGE OF INTENSITY: LESS; 396] 3 *v* **convince**, assure, persuade, reassure, win over. [➡SOOTHE AND CALM; 574] 4 *v* **fulfil**, comply with, meet, suit, fill, fit, discharge (*formal*). [➡HARMONY; 156]

satisfying 1 *adj* **pleasing**, gratifying, fulfilling, rewarding, enjoyable, agreeable. [➡EMOTIONALLY PLEASANT; 188] *Opposite:* dissatisfying. 2 *adj* **filling**, sustaining, nourishing, substantial, satiating, sufficient, adequate. [➡ENOUGH AND SUFFICIENT; 129] *Opposite:* insufficient.

satsuma *type of* **citrus.** [➡FRUIT AND VEGETABLES; 1175]

saturate 1 *v* **soak**, drench, wet through, douse, steep, marinate, flood, inundate, waterlog. [➡SOFTEN, LIQUEFY, DAMPEN; 389] *Opposite:* dry out. 2 *v* **oversupply**, overwhelm, overload, flood, inundate, overfill, fill. [➡GIVE TOO MUCH; 438]

saturated 1 *adj* **soaked**, soaking, drenched, wet through, wet, wringing wet, dripping wet, flooded, inundated, waterlogged, steeped, marinated. [➡WET; 1239] *Opposite:* dry. 2 *adj* **packed**, full, brimming, brimful, overfull, flooded, inundated, overwhelmed, replete, overloaded. [➡FULL; 1238] *Opposite:* empty.

saturated fat *n* [➡FOOD COMPONENTS; 1187]

saturated fatty acid *n* [➡FOOD COMPONENTS; 1187]

saturation 1 *n* **wetness**, soaking, drenching, wetting, moistening. [➡WET; 1239] *Opposite:* dryness. 2 *n* **fullness**, capacity, overload, inundation (*formal*), satiety, permeation. [➡FULL; 1238]

saturation bombing *n* [➡WARFARE AND WAR; 830]

Saturn *type of* **planet.** [➡CELESTIAL BODIES; 1060]

saturnalia *n* **orgy**, celebration, bacchanalia, revel, party, debauch (*formal*), carousal (*literary*). [➡PARTIES, DANCES, AND CELEBRATIONS; 37]

saturnine *adj* **melancholy**, morose, gloomy, sad, sullen, dejected, depressed. [➡SADNESS, DISTRESS, AND DESPAIR; 540] *Opposite:* cheerful.

satyr *n* [➡PLEASURE-SEEKERS AND HEDONISTS; 886]

sauce (*informal*) *n* **impudence**, impertinence, rudeness, insolence, nerve, sauciness, insouciance, cheek (*informal*), sassiness (*US*). [➡BAD MANNERS AND SOCIAL SKILLS; 522]

sauce

◆ *types of seasonings, sauces, and dips*
apple sauce, barbecue sauce, béchamel sauce, brown sauce, chilli sauce, coulis, dressing, French dressing, gravy, guacamole, ketchup, marinade, mayonnaise, mint sauce, salad cream, satay, soy sauce, stock, tartare sauce, Thousand Island dressing, vinegar, Worcester sauce

saucepan *n* **pan**, pot, cooking pot. [➡TABLEWARE, CUTLERY, AND KITCHENWARE; 861]

saucer *n* **plate**, bowl, dish. [➡TABLEWARE, CUTLERY, AND KITCHENWARE; 861]

saucy *adj* **cheeky**, impertinent (*formal*), impudent, smart, rude, smart-alecky (*informal*), sassy (*US*). [➡BAD MANNERS AND SOCIAL SKILLS; 522]

sault (*US*) *n* **waterfall**, rapids, race, chute, white water. [➡RIVERS, LAKES, AND STREAMS; 1042]

sauna *n* **steam bath**, Turkish bath. [➡FITTINGS; 859]

saunter 1 *v* **stroll**, walk, amble, meander, ramble, wander, promenade (*formal*), mosey (*informal*). [➡MOVE SLOWLY; 315] *Opposite:* hurry. 2 *n* **walk**, stroll, amble, ramble, meander, wander, promenade (*formal*). [➡PROCEED AND GO; 306]

sausage *type of* **processed meat.** [➡TYPES AND CUTS OF MEAT; 1176]

sauté *v* **fry**, stir-fry, pan-fry, brown. [➡COOKING AND FOOD PREPARATION; 354]

sautéed *adj* [➡STATE OF PREPARED FOOD; 1170]

savage 1 *adj* **violent**, unrestrained, vicious, fierce, ferocious, brutal. [➡SELFISH AND UNKIND; 506] *Opposite:* gentle. 2 *adj* **severe**, harsh, drastic, stringent, ruthless, brutal, unsparing. [➡SELFISH AND UNKIND; 506] *Opposite:* mild. 3 *adj* **undomesticated**, wild, ferocious, fierce, feral, untamed. [➡DANGEROUS; 237] *Opposite:* tame. 4 *n* **barbarian**, brute, ruffian, boor, thug, beast. [➡VILLAINS AND THUGS; 947] 5 *v* **attack**, brutalize, mug, jump (*informal*), maul, mangle. [➡PHYSICAL ATTACK AND PUNISHMENT; 416] 6 *v* **criticize**, tear apart, maul, destroy, attack, weigh into (*informal*), blast (*informal*), castigate (*formal*). [➡ACCUSE, BLAME, AND CRITICIZE; 642] *Opposite:* praise.

savagely 1 *adv* **violently**, unrestrainedly, viciously, fiercely, ferociously, brutally. [➡SELFISH AND UNKIND; 506] *Opposite:* gently. 2 *adv* **severely**, harshly, ruthlessly, brutally, cruelly, callously. [➡TO A GREAT EXTENT; 130] *Opposite:* mildly.

savagery *n* **cruelty**, violence, barbarity, viciousness, barbarism, ferocity. [➡UNKIND ACTION OR BEHAVIOUR; 297] *Opposite:* gentleness.

savanna *n* **grassland**, pampas, plains, prairie. [➡DESERTS AND PLAINS; 1045]

savant *n* **guru**, philosopher, thinker, pundit, expert, scholar, sage (*literary*). [➡TALENTED OR INTELLIGENT PERSON; 529]

save 1 *v* **rescue**, recover, salvage, bail out, revive, resuscitate. [➡FREEDOM AND LIBERTY; 209] *Opposite:* abandon. 2 *v* **accumulate**, bank, salt away, collect. [➡STORE AND KEEP; 454] *Opposite:* spend. 3 *v* **keep back**, set aside, put aside, put away, hold back, hoard. [➡STORE AND KEEP; 454] *Opposite:* use up. 4 *v* **avoid**, prevent, stop, avert, preclude (*formal*), bar, spare. [➡AVOID, PREVENT, LIMIT, AND CONTROL; 278] 5 *prep* **but**, except, apart from, with the exception of, excluding, bar. [➡NOT; 135] *Opposite:* including.

save for *prep* [➡NOT; 135]

saveloy *type of* **processed meat.** [➡TYPES AND CUTS OF MEAT; 1176]

saver *n* **investor**, collector, hoarder, squirrel (*informal*), magpie (*informal*), gatherer. [➡PEOPLE WHO COLLECT THINGS; 455]

saving *n* **economy**, reduction, cutback, discount, cut. [➡MONEY, PAYMENTS, AND CHARGES; 800] *Opposite:* increase.

saving grace *n* **merit**, advantage, strong point, strong suit, virtue, compensation, redeeming feature, redeeming quality. [➡SOURCE OF HAPPINESS, PLEASURE, OR IMPROVEMENT; 210] *Opposite:* failing.

savings *n* **investments**, reserves, nest egg, funds, hoard, stash (*informal*), money, assets. [➡FINANCIAL ASSETS; 463] *Opposite:* expenditure.

saviour *n* **redeemer**, rescuer, knight in shining armour, liberator, deliverer, protector. [➡PEOPLE WHO ARE APPROVED OF; 955]

savoir-faire *n* **confidence**, style, flair, poise, savvy (*informal*), sense, know-how (*informal*), nous (*informal*). [➡KNOWLEDGE AND WISDOM; 559] *Opposite:* gaucheness.

savory *type of* **herb.** [➡HERBS AND SPICES; 1174]

savour 1 *v* **enjoy**, relish, appreciate, delight in, cherish, treasure, value. [➡LIKE, LOVE, VALUE AND ENJOY; 579] 2 *n* **taste**, smell, flavour, aroma, tang, bouquet. [➡TASTE; 704]

savourless *adj* [➡TASTE; 704]

savourlessness *n* [➡TASTE; 704]

savoury 1 *adj* **salty**, salt, spicy, piquant, pungent, aromatic, sharp. [➡TASTE; 704] *Opposite:* sweet. 2 *adj* **respectable**, pleasant, acceptable, nice, wholesome, congenial. [➡APPROPRIATE, SUITABLE, ADVISABLE; 185] *Opposite:* unsavoury. 3 *adj* **appetizing**, tasty, flavoursome, palatable, delicious, delectable, mouthwatering. [➡TASTE; 704] *Opposite:* insipid.

savvy (*informal*) *n* **shrewdness**, practicality, knowledge, perception, understanding, know-how (*informal*). [➡KNOWLEDGE AND WISDOM; 559] *Opposite:* ignorance.

saw 1 *v* **cut**, slice, sever, divide, chop. [➡USE TOOLS AND MACHINERY; 469] 2 *type of* **carpentry tool.** [➡HAND TOOLS; 1118] 3 *n* **saying**, proverb, adage, maxim, motto, aphorism, axiom. [➡FIGURES OF SPEECH; 674]

sawfish *type of* **tropical sea fish.** [➡SEA FISH; 1009]

sawmill *type of* **factory.** [➡INDUSTRIAL BUILDINGS; 1086]

sawn-off shotgun *type of* **gun.** [➡WEAPONS FOR SHOOTING; 1155]

saxe blue *type of* **blue.** [➡COLOURS; 1223]

saxhorn *type of* **brass instrument.** [➡MUSICAL INSTRUMENTS; 910]

saxophone *type of* **brass instrument.** [➡MUSICAL INSTRUMENTS; 910]

say 1 *v* **speak**, utter, articulate, declare, pronounce, state, cry, verbalize, exclaim. [➡UTTER AND PRONOUNCE; 609] 2 *v* **convey**, indicate, reveal, give away, tell, disclose, express, display, impart. [➡BETRAY CONFIDENCES AND GOSSIP; 619] **3** *n* **input**, voice, opinion, view, pennyworth, right of speech. [➡POINT OF VIEW; 768] **4** *adv* **approximately**, roughly, about, around, give or take, round about, at a guess. [➡APPROXIMATELY; 133] *Opposite:* exactly.

saying *n* **proverb**, adage, maxim, axiom, motto, saw, aphorism, dictum (*formal*). [➡FIGURES OF SPEECH; 674]

sayonara *interj* **goodbye**, ciao (*informal*), farewell (*literary*), bye (*informal*), cheerio (*informal*), bye-bye (*informal*), see you (*informal*), hasta la vista (*informal*), adios (*informal*), later (*informal*). [➡GREETINGS, FAREWELLS, AND SALUTATIONS; 660] *Opposite:* hello.

say-so (*informal*) *n* **authorization**, authority, permission, approval, agreement, sanction, accord, consent, endorsement, acquiescence. [➡PERMIT AND ALLOW; 670] *Opposite:* veto.

say sorry *v* **apologize**, excuse yourself, crawl, grovel, beg forgiveness, swallow your pride, say you're sorry. [➡APOLOGIZE AND RETRACT; 684]

say yes *v* **agree**, accept, consent, acquiesce, assent, jump at the chance. [➡AGREE; 646] *Opposite:* refuse.

say your piece *v* **speak out**, speak up, protest, take a stand, make a stand, stand your ground, fight your corner. [➡PROTEST AND EXPRESS DISAPPROVAL; 643] *Opposite:* hold back.

scab *n* **crust**, layer, skin, shell, covering, casing, coating. [➡CONDITIONS AFFECTING THE SKIN; 722]

scabbard *n* **sheath**, case, covering, cover, casing. [➡CONTAINERS, RECEPTACLES, AND PACKAGING; 1244]

scabby **1** *adj* **mangy**, scaly, diseased, shabby, dirty, moth-eaten, grotty. [➡IN BAD REPAIR; 1233] *Opposite:* unblemished. **2** *adj* (*slang*) **despicable**, dislikable, contemptible, detestable, low, shabby. [➡UNACCEPTABLE AND UNFORGIVEABLE; 226] *Opposite:* admirable.

scabrous *adj* **rough**, flaky, scaly, mangy, leprous. [➡CONDITIONS AFFECTING THE SKIN; 722] *Opposite:* smooth.

scads (*informal*) *n* **lots**, tons (*informal*), heaps (*informal*), buckets (*informal*), piles (*informal*), loads (*informal*). [➡MANY, MUCH, LARGE AMOUNT; 117] *Opposite:* none.

scaffold **1** *n* **support**, framework, frame, platform, shell, skeleton, scaffolding. [➡SUPPORTS AND BASES; 1254] **2** *n* **gallows**, gibbet, halter, noose. [➡ANCIENT MANMADE STRUCTURES; 1088]

scaffolding *n* **support**, framework, frame, platform, shell, skeleton, scaffold. [➡SUPPORTS AND BASES; 1254]

scalawag *see* **scallywag**.

scald **1** *v* **burn**, blister, singe, sear, injure, hurt, damage. [➡FIRE, FLAMMABILITY, AND BURNING; 1164] **2** *v* **sterilize**, boil, steam, autoclave, heat, disinfect, clean, sanitize. [➡CLEAN AND POLISH; 404] *Opposite:* contaminate. **3** *v* **bring to the boil**, boil, heat, warm, simmer. [➡COOKING AND FOOD PREPARATION; 354] *Opposite:* chill.

scalding **1** *adj* **boiling**, piping hot, scorching (*informal*), baking, burning, blistering, searing, broiling, sweltering, torrid, roasting (*informal*), red-hot, hot. [➡TEMPERATURE: HOT; 1228] *Opposite:* icy. **2** *adj* **scathing**, blistering, critical, fierce, scornful, withering, caustic, cutting, biting. [➡ACCUSATORY AND DISAPPROVING; 635] *Opposite:* complimentary.

scale **1** *n* **weighing machine**, balance, scales, weighbridge, measure. [➡MEASURING DEVICES; 1122] **2** *n* **plate**, flake, skin, scab, piece. [➡SMALL PIECE; 127] **3** *n* **gradation**, hierarchy, gamut, tier, band, ratio, progression, calibration, measurement. [➡DEGREE AND EXTENT; 110] **4** *n* **extent**, size, range, degree, level, amount, magnitude, dimension. [➡AREA AND RANGE; 111] **5** *n* **deposit**, crust, fur, covering, plaque, tartar. [➡COVERS AND COATINGS; 1245] **6** *part of* **fish**. [➡PARTS OF A FISH; 1011]

scale down *v* **reduce**, decrease, lower, cut back, cut down, trim, shave, pare, scale back, step down. [➡CHANGE OF INTENSITY: LESS; 396] *Opposite:* scale up.

scale up *v* **increase**, expand, extend, raise, step up, upgrade, improve, develop, widen, broaden. [➡CHANGE OF INTENSITY: MORE; 395] *Opposite:* scale down.

scallion *type of* **salad vegetable**. [➡FRUIT AND VEGETABLES; 1175]

scallop **1** *n* **pinking**, edging, scalloping, piping, border, decoration. [➡ORNAMENTS AND DECORATIONS; 1247] **2** *type of* **aquatic invertebrate**. [➡AQUATIC INVERTEBRATE; 1022]

scallywag (*dated informal*) *n* **mischief-maker**, rogue, scamp (*informal*), rascal (*humorous*), monkey (*informal*), scoundrel, rapscallion (*archaic or humorous*), imp. [➡MISCHIEVOUS OR BADLY-BEHAVED CHILD; 946]

scalp *part of* **head**. [➡HEAD; 693]

scalpel *type of* **medical instrument**. [➡HAND TOOLS; 1118]

scaly *adj* **flaking**, peeling, crusty, encrusted, scabby, rough. [➡PHYSICAL TEXTURE; 1221] *Opposite:* smooth.

scam (*slang*) **1** *n* **con**, rip-off (*informal*), swindle, trick, fiddle (*informal*), cheat, dodge, sting (*US slang*). [➡DECEPTION AND LIES; 661] **2** *v* **cheat**, trick, con, swindle, rip off (*informal*), fiddle (*informal*). [➡DECEPTION AND LIES; 661]

scammer (*slang*) *n* [➡PEOPLE WHO DECEIVE; 662]

scamp (*informal*) *n* **rascal** (*humorous*), rogue, imp, urchin, scallywag (*dated informal*), monkey (*informal*), mischief-maker, scoundrel, rapscallion (*archaic or humorous*). [➡MISCHIEVOUS OR BADLY-BEHAVED CHILD; 946] *Opposite:* angel.

scamper *v* **scurry**, scuttle, run, hurry, dash, dart, scoot (*informal*), tear, zip (*informal*). [➡MOVE FAST; 314] *Opposite:* dawdle.

scampi *n* [➡SEA FOOD; 1189]

scan **1** *v* **scrutinize**, examine, look into, inspect, search, look at, check. [➡EXAMINE AND ASSESS; 754] **2** *v* **skim**, skim through, glance at, glance over, peruse, look over, flick through, cast an eye over. [➡LOOKING AND LOOKS; 701] *Opposite:* study. **3** *v* **examine**, photograph, visualize, image, X-ray, shoot, probe, test. [➡EXAMINE AND ASSESS; 754] **4** *n* **perusal**, skim, examination, inspection, look, glance, once-over (*informal*). [➡EXAMINE AND ASSESS; 754] **5** *n* **image**, X-ray, CT scan, MRI, examination, photograph, shot, test, probe. [➡PHOTOGRAPHY AND PHOTOGRAPHIC EQUIPMENT; 1121]

scandal **1** *n* **disgrace**, shame, dishonour, humiliation, outrage, indignity. [➡NUISANCES; 254] 2 *n* **gossip**, tittle-tattle, rumour, talk, rumourmongering, chat. [➡GOSSIP; 679]

scandalize *v* **horrify**, outrage, shock, disgust, dismay, appal. [➡FRIGHTEN AND SHOCK; 569] *Opposite:* impress.

scandalized *adj* [➡SURPRISE, SHOCK, AND AMAZEMENT; 546]

scandalmonger *n* **gossip**, rumourmonger, gossipmonger, newsmonger, snoop (*informal*). [➡INTERFERING PEOPLE AND TELLTALES; 950]

scandalmongering *n* [➡GOSSIP; 679]

scandalous *adj* **shocking**, outrageous, disgraceful, immoral, shameful, indecent, disreputable, appalling, reprehensible, wicked. [➡MORALLY BAD; 776] *Opposite:* admirable.

scanner *type of* **hardware**. [➡COMPUTERS AND COMPUTING; 1126]

scant *adj* **slight**, limited, negligible, little, scarce, inadequate, insufficient, meagre, measly (*informal*). [➡TOO FEW, TOO LITTLE; 120] *Opposite:* extensive.

scantily *adv* **insufficiently**, inadequately, meagrely, poorly, skimpily, sparsely. [➡DESCRIBING CLOTHES; 869] *Opposite:* fully.

scantiness *n* [➡TOO FEW, TOO LITTLE; 120]

scantness *n* [➡TOO FEW, TOO LITTLE; 120]

scanty 1 *adj* **insufficient**, inadequate, meagre, little, scarce, sparse, negligible, limited, measly (*informal*). [➡TOO FEW, TOO LITTLE; 120] *Opposite:* abundant. 2 *adj* **revealing**, flimsy, light, low-cut, tight, short, small. [➡DESCRIBING CLOTHES; 869]

scapegoat 1 *n* **stooge**, victim, accused, culprit, fall guy (*slang*). [➡VICTIMS OF DECEIT; 663] 2 *v* **blame**, incriminate, condemn, accuse, reproach, censure, single out. [➡ACCUSE, BLAME, AND CRITICIZE; 642] *Opposite:* exonerate.

scar 1 *n* **mark**, blemish, mutilation, scratch, wound, scab, weal, welt, burn. [➡CONDITIONS AFFECTING THE SKIN; 722] 2 *n* **effect**, wound, trauma, hurt, aftereffect, hangover, legacy, trace, damage. [➡RESULTS AND OUTCOMES; 83] 3 *v* **damage**, mark, blemish, mutilate, disfigure, scratch, scrape, score, wound. [➡WORSEN APPEARANCE; 383] 4 *v* **traumatize**, hurt, affect, damage, mark, devastate. [➡UPSET, DISTRESS, AND HUMILIATE; 568]

scarab *type of* **beetle**. [➡BEETLES AND WEEVILS; 1016]

scarce 1 *adj* **in short supply**, limited, insufficient, inadequate, scant, sparse, meagre. [➡TOO FEW, TOO LITTLE; 120] *Opposite:* abundant. 2 *adj* **rare**, uncommon, unusual, infrequent, threatened, occasional. [➡EXTRAORDINARY: UNCOMMON; 206] *Opposite:* common.

scarcely *adv* **barely**, hardly, not quite, only just, just, narrowly, not at all. [➡TO A CERTAIN EXTENT; 134] *Opposite:* fully.

scarceness 1 *n* **shortage**, lack, dearth, insufficiency, scarcity, paucity, inadequacy. [➡TOO FEW, TOO LITTLE; 120] *Opposite:* abundance. 2 *n* **rarity**, uncommonness, infrequency, lack, want, absence. [➡EXTRAORDINARY: UNCOMMON; 206] *Opposite:* commonness.

scarcity 1 *n* **shortage**, lack, dearth, insufficiency, scarceness, paucity, inadequacy. [➡TOO FEW, TOO LITTLE; 120] *Opposite:* abundance. 2 *n* **rarity**, uncommonness, infrequency, lack, want, absence. [➡EXTRAORDINARY: UNCOMMON; 206] *Opposite:* commonness.

scare 1 *v* **frighten**, terrify, petrify, startle, alarm, panic, worry, shock, intimidate, jolt. [➡FRIGHTEN AND SHOCK; 569] *Opposite:* reassure. 2 *n* **fright**, shock, start, jolt, alarm, alert, panic, worry, anxiety. [➡FEAR AND PANIC; 544] *Opposite:* reassurance.

scarecrow *n* **figure**, effigy, guy, mannequin. [➡REPRESENTATIONS AND GENERAL EXAMPLES; 65]

scared *adj* **frightened**, afraid, fearful, terrified, petrified, nervous, startled, alarmed, worried, anxious, timid, timorous. [➡FEAR AND PANIC; 544] *Opposite:* fearless.

scared rigid *adj* [➡FEAR AND PANIC; 544]

scared stiff *adj* [➡FEAR AND PANIC; 544]

scared to death *adj* [➡FEAR AND PANIC; 544]

scaredy-cat (*informal*) *n* [➡LAZY OR UNSUCCESSFUL PEOPLE; 948]

scaremonger *n* **alarmist**, doomsayer, troublemaker, rumourmonger, newsmonger, gossip. [➡GRUMPY AND NEGATIVE PEOPLE; 953] *Opposite:* optimist.

scare off *v* **frighten away**, drive away, chase off, scare away, frighten, warn off, deter, discourage, put off. [➡FRIGHTEN AND SHOCK; 569] *Opposite:* welcome.

scare up (*US informal*) 1 *v* [➡MEAL PREPARATION; 355] 2 *v* **get**, get hold of, lay hands on, search out, locate, find. [➡GET; 421]

scarf 1 *n* **muffler**, headscarf, cravat, shawl, stole, wrap, pashmina, mantilla. [➡HABERDASHERY, MILLINERY, AND LINGERIE; 867] 2 *v* (*US slang*) **gobble**, wolf, bolt, devour, scoff (*informal*), scarf down (*US slang*). [➡EAT AND NOT EAT; 711] *Opposite:* refuse.

scarf down (*US slang*) *v* **gobble**, wolf, bolt, devour, scoff (*informal*), scarf (*US slang*). [➡EAT AND NOT EAT; 711] *Opposite:* refuse.

scarify 1 *v* **lacerate**, scratch, incise, cut, score, lance. [➡TEAR, BREAK, AND CUT; 361] 2 *v* (*informal*) **scare**, frighten, alarm, worry, startle, terrify, petrify, panic, shock. [➡FRIGHTEN AND SHOCK; 569] *Opposite:* reassure.

scariness *n* [➡FRIGHTENING; 232]

scarlet *type of* **red**. [➡COLOURS; 1223]

scarp *n* **escarpment**, ridge, cliff, bluff, crag, incline, slope. [➡MOUNTAINS AND HILLS; 1044]

scarper (*slang*) *v* **run away**, bolt, run for it, clear off (*informal*), beat it (*informal*), run off, hightail (*slang*), get away, flee. [➡RUN AWAY AND AVOID; 10] *Opposite:* stand your ground.

scarred *adj* [➡IN BAD REPAIR; 1233]

scary (*informal*) *adj* **frightening**, creepy (*informal*), chilling, terrifying, petrifying, daunting, forbidding, bloodcurdling, intimidating, menacing, startling, alarming, worrying. [➡FRIGHTENING; 232] *Opposite:* reassuring.

scat (*informal*) *v* [➡RUN AWAY AND AVOID; 10]

scathing *adj* **scornful**, mocking, derisive, sarcastic, contemptuous, cutting, biting, wounding, hurtful, caustic, scalding, critical, blistering, withering, fierce. [➡ACCUSATORY AND DISAPPROVING; 635] *Opposite:* complimentary.

scatter 1 *v* **throw**, strew, fling, toss, sprinkle, distribute, disseminate, broadcast, dot. [➡SPREAD AND SCATTER; 333] *Opposite:* collect. 2 *v* **disperse**, spread out, spread, flee, take flight, break up, fly away, fly apart. [➡SEPARATE AND DIVIDE; 402] *Opposite:* gather.

Compare and Contrast: ***scatter, broadcast, distribute, disseminate***

CORE MEANING: TO SPREAD AROUND

scatter to spread things around physically, especially in a random widespread manner; ***broadcast*** to spread or transmit information, especially by means of radio or television, or to scatter seeds over the ground; ***distribute*** to allocate, share, or give out something in a structured or organized way, or to spread something over a particular surface or area; ***disseminate*** to spread ideas or information, or abstract things such as good will.

scatterbrained *adj* **absent-minded**, vague, forgetful, dizzy (*informal*), woolly-headed, careless, unreliable, scatty (*informal*). [➡NEGATIVE INTELLECTUAL CHARACTERISTICS; 526] *Opposite:* focused.

scattered 1 *adj* **dispersed**, distributed, strewn, sprinkled, disseminated, spread, speckled, spread out, dotted. [➡GENERAL LOCATIONS; 159] *Opposite:* concentrated. 2 *adj* **infrequent**, isolated, discrete, separate, occasional, sporadic. [➡NEVER AND INFREQUENCY; 97] *Opposite:* frequent.

scattering *n* **handful**, sprinkling, trickle, bit, smattering, dusting, sprinkle, dash. [➡FEW, LITTLE, SMALL AMOUNT; 119]

scattershot *adj* **disorganized**, indiscriminate, random, chaotic, slapdash, careless, haphazard, unfocused. [➡DISORDER AND CHAOS; 246] *Opposite:* focused.

scattiness (*informal*) *n* [➡NEGATIVE INTELLECTUAL CHARACTERISTICS; 526]

scatty (*informal*) *adj* **empty-headed**, forgetful, absent-minded, scatterbrained, dizzy (*informal*), vague, woolly-headed, unreliable, eccentric, frivolous, thoughtless, careless, slapdash. [➡NEGATIVE INTELLECTUAL CHARACTERISTICS; 526] *Opposite:* organized.

scavenge *v* **hunt**, forage, search, rummage, sift, go through. [➡SEEK POSSESSION AND SEARCH; 457]

scenario *n* **situation**, state of affairs, state, setup, circumstances, setting, picture, development, consequence. [➡SITUATIONS; 71]

scene 1 *n* **act**, division, part, section, passage, extract. [➡THE ORAL TRADITION; 678] 2 *n* **setting**, site, place, background, location, area, field, arena. [➡PLACE; 1064] 3 *n* **sight**, prospect, picture, panorama, view, landscape, outlook, vista, tableau. [➡VIEWS AND OUTLOOKS; 1072] 4 *n* **fuss**, to-do (*informal*), commotion, carry-on (*informal*), exhibition, incident, spectacle, display, outburst. [➡CHAOS AND UPROAR; 51]

scenery 1 *n* **set**, backdrop, backcloth, background, decor, setting, staging. [➡IN THE THEATRE; 906] 2 *n* **landscape**, panorama, vista, outlook, view, countryside. [➡VIEWS AND OUTLOOKS; 1072]

scenic *adj* **picturesque**, beautiful, attractive, lovely, charming, pretty. [➡BEAUTY AND ATTRACTIVENESS; 190] *Opposite:* unsightly.

scent 1 *n* **smell**, odour, aroma, perfume, bouquet, whiff. [➡SMELL AND SMELLING; 706] 2 *n* **trail**, trace, track, aroma, odour, spoor. [➡EVIDENCE AND PROOF; 69] 3 *n* **perfume**, fragrance, cologne, toilet water, eau de cologne, eau de toilette, aftershave. [➡PERSONAL HYGIENE; 492] 4 *n* **hint**, trace, air, whiff, suggestion, indication. [➡FEW, LITTLE, SMALL AMOUNT; 119] 5 *v* **predict**, foresee, foretell, sense, feel, expect. [➡PREDICT AND ANTICIPATE; 751] 6 *v* **sniff**, smell, detect, sense, pick up, perceive. [➡SMELL AND SMELLING; 706] 7 *v* **imbue**, perfume, fill, infuse, suffuse, tinge. [➡DECORATE, ADORN, AND APPLY COATINGS; 406]

See Compare and Contrast at **smell**.

scented *adj* **perfumed**, fragrant, aromatic, sweet-smelling, smelly, spicy. [➡SMELL AND SMELLING; 706]

sceptic *n* **cynic**, disbeliever, doubter, doubting Thomas, questioner. [➡UNCERTAINTY; 560] *Opposite:* believer.

sceptical *adj* **cynical**, disbelieving, doubtful, doubting, unconvinced, incredulous, uncertain, distrustful, dubious, suspicious, questioning, unsure. [➡UNCERTAINTY; 560] *Opposite:* convinced.

See Compare and Contrast at **doubtful**.

scepticism *n* **cynicism**, disbelief, doubt, incredulity, uncertainty, suspicion, distrust. [➡UNCERTAINTY; 560] *Opposite:* conviction.

sceptre *n* **staff**, staff of office, mace, rod, insignia, wand. [➡STICKS, POLES, AND WEDGES; 1253]

schedule 1 *n* **agenda**, timetable, diary, calendar, list, plan, rota, roster, programme, to-do list. [➡LISTS AND SCHEDULES; 588] 2 *v* **arrange**, plan, timetable, programme, book, organize, list, reserve, slate (*US*). [➡PREPARE FOR ACTION; 290] *Opposite:* cancel.

scheduled *adj* **arranged**, planned, timetabled, programmed, listed, booked, organized, reserved, slated (*US*). [➡INTENTIONAL AND DELIBERATE; 280] *Opposite:* unplanned.

schema *n* **plan**, diagram, scheme, schematic, representation, graphic, chart, outline, draft. [➡SUMMARIES, OUTLINES, AND EXCERPTS; 589]

schematize *v* **systematize**, arrange, structure, organize, draft, set out, outline. [➡ARRANGE AND CREATE ORDER; 358] *Opposite:* disarrange.

scheme 1 *n* **plan**, plot, conspiracy, ploy, ruse, intrigue. [➡INTENTION AND PURPOSE; 773] 2 *n* **arrangement**, system, structure, outline, organization, pattern, order. [➡ORDER AND ORGANIZATION; 207] *Opposite:* chaos. 3 *n* **plan**, method, stratagem, format, idea, proposal, design, policy, programme, arrangement, system. [➡WAYS OF DOING THINGS; 295] 4 *n* **diagram**, plan, schematic, graphic, representation, chart, schema. [➡DRAWINGS, CHARTS AND TABLES; 595] 5 *v* **plot**, conspire, intrigue, connive, plan, machinate. [➡PREPARE FOR ACTION; 290]

schemer *n* **plotter**, conspirator, conniver, traitor, intriguer. [➡ PEOPLE WHO DECEIVE; 662]

scheming *adj* **devious**, calculating, conniving, conspiratorial, treacherous, cunning, underhand, wily, tricky. [➡ DECEITFUL; 514] *Opposite:* honest.

scherzo *type of* **instrumental music.** [➡ MUSIC, SONGS, AND SINGING; 907]

schism *n* **split**, break, division, rupture, rift, gulf, breakup, faction. [➡ DISHARMONY; 157] *Opposite:* union.

schismatic *adj* **factional**, divisive, clashing, conflicting, controversial, polemical, dissonant, dissenting. [➡ DISHARMONY; 157] *Opposite:* unifying.

schist *type of* **stone.** [➡ STONES, ROCKS, AND BOULDERS; 1057]

schlep (*informal*) **1** *v* **lug**, haul, heave, drag, cart. [➡ MOVE SLOWLY; 315] **2** *n* **trek**, trudge, hike, bore, bind, chore. [➡ HARD WORK OR EFFORT; 299]

schlock (*US slang*) *n* **junk** (*informal*), garbage, crud (*informal*), trash, rubbish, tripe (*informal*). [➡ RUBBISH AND USELESS OBJECTS; 1248]

schlocky (*US slang*) *adj* **junky**, cheap, worthless, garbagy, cruddy (*informal*), trashy, rubbishy. [➡ IN POOR TASTE; 230]

schmaltz (*informal*) *n* **sentimentality**, slush, mush, corniness, mawkishness, emotionalism. [➡ IN POOR TASTE; 230]

schmaltziness (*informal*) *n* [➡ IN POOR TASTE; 230]

schmaltzy (*informal*) *adj* **sentimental**, cloying, sugary, saccharine, slushy, mushy, soppy (*informal*), corny, mawkish, emotional, soft. [➡ IN POOR TASTE; 230] *Opposite:* hardheaded.

schmooze (*slang*) **1** *v* **chat**, chitchat (*informal*), chatter, yak (*informal*), socialize, converse, banter, talk, gossip. [➡ TWO-WAY COMMUNICATION; 608] **2** *n* **conversation**, chat, chitchat (*informal*), yak (*informal*), chinwag (*informal*), talk, gossip, dialogue. [➡ INFORMAL COMMUNICATION; 45]

schmoozer (*slang*) *n* **conversationalist**, chatterer, talker, gossip, banterer, raconteur, speaker. [➡ SPEAKERS AND ORATORS; 604]

schnozzle (*US slang*) *n* [➡ THE NOSE; 705]

scholar *n* **academic**, researcher, don, professor, doctor, intellectual, specialist, sage (*literary*). [➡ TALENTED OR INTELLIGENT PERSON; 529]

scholarly *adj* **learned**, academic, erudite, intellectual, educated, studious, bookish, cerebral, knowledgeable, well-read, highbrow, donnish. *Opposite:* lowbrow. (*disapproving*). [➡ LEVEL OF EDUCATION AND SOPHISTICATION; 894]

scholarship **1** *n* **grant**, bursary, studentship, subsidy, allowance. [➡ MONEY, PAYMENTS, AND CHARGES; 800] **2** *n* **learning**, erudition, study, knowledge, research, skill, science. [➡ KNOWLEDGE AND WISDOM; 559] *Opposite:* ignorance.

scholastic *adj* **educational**, academic, pedagogic, school, college, collegiate, university. [➡ EDUCATION; 838]

school **1** *n* **educational institution**, place of learning. [➡ EDUCATIONAL INSTITUTIONS; 813] **2** *n* **group**, set, coterie, brotherhood, sisterhood. [➡ GROUPS OF PEOPLE; 935] *Opposite:* individual. **3** *v* **train**, instruct, educate, discipline, teach, tutor, drill, coach, prepare. [➡ INSTRUCT AND TEACH; 610] **4** *type of* **herd.** [➡ GROUP OF ANIMALS; 993] **5** *n* (*US*) **university**, college, seminary, conservatory, graduate school, trade school, vocational school, institute. [➡ EDUCATIONAL INSTITUTIONS; 813]

school

◆ *types of school*
academy, boarding school, comprehensive, elementary school (*US*), grade school (*US*), grammar school, high school, infant school, junior high (*US*), junior school, kindergarten (*US*), middle school, nursery school, prep school, preschool, primary school, private school, public school, state school, vocational school (*US*)

See Compare and Contrast at **teach.**

schoolboy *n* [➡ STUDENTS AND PUPILS; 841]

schoolchild *n* **pupil**, student, scholar, schoolkid (*informal*), schoolboy, schoolgirl, schoolmate. [➡ STUDENTS AND PUPILS; 841]

schoolgirl *n* [➡ STUDENTS AND PUPILS; 841]

schooling *n* **education**, teaching, training, instruction, tuition, coaching. [➡ TEACHING; 839]

schoolkid (*informal*) *n* [➡ STUDENTS AND PUPILS; 841]

schoolmate *n* [➡ FRIENDS; 963]

school of dance *n* [➡ EDUCATIONAL INSTITUTIONS; 813]

school of the arts *n* [➡ EDUCATIONAL INSTITUTIONS; 813]

school of thought *n* **philosophy**, doctrine, ideology, outlook, attitude, viewpoint. [➡ POINT OF VIEW; 768]

schoolroom *type of* **room in a public building.** [➡ TYPES OF ROOM; 1096]

schoolteacher *n* [➡ EDUCATORS; 840]

schoolwork *n* [➡ LESSONS, COURSE WORK, AND EXAMINATIONS; 842]

school yard *n* [➡ URBAN OUTDOOR SPACES; 1071]

schooner *type of* **sailing vessel.** [➡ SHIPS AND BOATS; 1149]

sciatica *n* [➡ ILLNESSES AND DISORDERS; 733]

science *n* **discipline**, knowledge, skill, art, learning, scholarship. [➡ SUBJECT AREA; 769]

science fiction *n* [➡ FICTION AND DRAMA; 913]

science park *n* [➡ URBAN OUTDOOR SPACES; 1071]

scientific *adj* **technical**, methodical, systematic, logical, precise, exact, controlled. [➡ EXACT; 204] *Opposite:* unscientific.

scimitar *type of* **sword or knife.** [➡ SWORDS AND KNIVES; 1156]

scintilla *n* **jot**, iota, scrap, shred, speck, ounce, bit, spark, trace, particle. [➡FEW, LITTLE, SMALL AMOUNT; 119]

scintillate 1 *v* **sparkle**, glitter, gleam, flash, glint, glisten, twinkle, shine. [➡LIGHT EMISSION; 369] 2 *v* **fascinate**, dazzle, charm, shine, sparkle, stimulate, delight, bewitch. [➡APPEAL TO AND AROUSE INTEREST; 576] *Opposite:* bore.

scintillating *adj* **sparkling**, dazzling, brilliant, bright, shining, glittering, amusing, entertaining, fascinating, stimulating, witty, animated, lively. [➡INTERESTING AND MEANINGFUL; 191] *Opposite:* dull.

scintillation *n* **sparkling**, glittering, gleaming, flashing, glinting, glistening, twinkling. [➡LIGHT; 1163] *Opposite:* dullness.

scion 1 *n* **cutting**, graft, shoot, implant, implantation, insert, splice. [➡PARTS OF TREES AND PLANTS; 1026] 2 *n* **offspring**, child, heir, descendant, son, daughter. [➡YOUNGER GENERATION RELATIVES; 958] *Opposite:* parent.

scirocco *see* **sirocco**.

scissors *type of* **cutting tool**. [➡CUTTING TOOLS; 1119]

scoff 1 *v* **jeer**, sneer, mock, ridicule, make fun of, laugh at, poke fun at, pooh-pooh, deride. [➡PROTEST AND EXPRESS DISAPPROVAL; 643] *Opposite:* praise. 2 *v* (*informal*) **eat**, guzzle (*informal*), gobble, stuff your face, bolt, wolf, scarf down (*US*). [➡EAT AND NOT EAT; 711] *Opposite:* nibble.

scoffing *adj* [➡MOCKING AND DISMISSIVE; 637]

scold *v* **tell off** (*informal*), admonish, reprimand, reproach, rebuke, caution, discipline, haul over the coals, yell at, tick off (*informal*), chew out (*US informal*). [➡ACCUSE, BLAME, AND CRITICIZE; 642] *Opposite:* praise.

scolding *n* **telling-off** (*informal*), admonishment, reprimand, reproach, rebuke, caution, ticking-off (*informal*), dressing-down. [➡CRITICISMS AND ANGRY OUTBURSTS; 50] *Opposite:* praise.

sconce *n* **light fixture**, bracket, light fitting, lamp fitting, candleholder. [➡LIGHTING; 862]

scoop 1 *n* **ladle**, dipper, serving spoon, server, soup ladle, punch ladle. [➡SPOONS, SCOOPS, AND SHOVELS; 1120] 2 *n* (*informal*) **news story**, story, exclusive, revelation, exposé, sensation. [➡NEWSPAPERS; 606] 3 *v* **dig**, hollow, scrape, shovel, excavate, gouge. [➡USE TOOLS AND MACHINERY; 469] *Opposite:* fill. 4 *v* **lift**, gather up, pick up, raise, take, bundle (*informal*). [➡GET; 421] *Opposite:* drop.

scoot (*informal*) 1 *v* **go away**, leave, scat (*informal*), skedaddle (*slang*), make yourself scarce (*informal*), vamoose (*US slang*). [➡RUN AWAY AND AVOID; 10] *Opposite:* arrive. 2 *v* **move quickly**, rush, hurry, scurry, dash, run, race, career. [➡MOVE FAST; 314] *Opposite:* dawdle.

scooter *type of* **bike** (*informal*). [➡BIKES, CARS, AND CARRIAGES; 1148]

scope 1 *n* **possibility**, choice, room, opportunity, space, latitude. [➡POSSIBLE AND PROBABLE; 178] *Opposite:* constraint. 2 *n* **range**, extent, capacity, span, reach, compass, bounds. [➡DEGREE AND EXTENT; 110]

scorch *v* **burn**, singe, sear, char, blacken, mark, brand. [➡FIRE, FLAMMABILITY, AND BURNING; 1164]

scorched 1 *adj* **burnt**, singed, seared, charred, blackened, marked, branded. [➡IN BAD REPAIR; 1233] 2 *adj* **dried**, dry as a bone, dry, parched, baked, dried up, dried out, bone dry, desiccated, arid. [➡DRY; 1241] *Opposite:* drenched.

scorching (*informal*) *adj* **boiling**, baking, sweltering, sizzling (*informal*), blazing, burning, blistering, roasting (*informal*). [➡HOT WEATHER; 1050] *Opposite:* freezing.

score 1 *n* **total**, tally, mark, result, count, grade. [➡SCORES AND EVALUATIONS; 599] 2 *n* **notch**, cut, slash, groove, nick, mark. [➡HOLES, GAPS, AND FORKS; 1251] 3 *v* **achieve**, chalk up, attain, make, gain, get, notch up (*slang*). [➡GET MONEY OR REWARD; 422] 4 *v* **keep count**, keep a tally, keep score, count, tot up, record. [➡ASSESS QUANTITY; 758] 5 *v* **slash**, notch, nick, slice, cut, mark off, mark. [➡TEAR, BREAK, AND CUT; 361] 6 *v* **scratch**, etch, carve, mark, scrape, cut. [➡TEAR, BREAK, AND CUT; 361]

scoreboard *n* **display**, board, panel, notice board, bulletin board (*US*). [➡SIGNPOSTS, SIGNALS AND BILLBOARDS; 596]

scorecard *n* **tally**, scoresheet, record, card. [➡RECORDS; 586]

scores *n* [➡MANY, MUCH, LARGE AMOUNT; 117]

scoresheet *n* **sheet**, scorecard, tally, record. [➡RECORDS; 586]

scorn 1 *n* **contempt**, disdain, disrespect, derision, scornfulness, disparagement, ridicule, sneering, mockery. [➡ANTAGONISM; 553] *Opposite:* admiration. 2 *v* **show contempt for**, despise, disdain, belittle, deride, pour scorn on, disparage, ridicule, sneer at, mock, revile. [➡PROTEST AND EXPRESS DISAPPROVAL; 643] *Opposite:* admire. 3 *v* **reject**, spurn, rebuff, turn down, refuse, disdain, disregard, hate. [➡DENY AND REJECT; 645] *Opposite:* choose.

scorned 1 *adj* **despised**, disdained, belittled, derided, disparaged, reviled. [➡UNPOPULAR AND UNWANTED; 259] *Opposite:* admired. 2 *adj* **rejected**, spurned, rebuffed, turned down, refused, disdained, disregarded. [➡UNPOPULAR AND UNWANTED; 259] *Opposite:* chosen.

scornful *adj* **contemptuous**, disdainful, disrespectful, mocking, derisive, disparaging, sneering. [➡MOCKING AND DISMISSIVE; 637] *Opposite:* admiring.

scornfulness *n* [➡ANTAGONISM; 553]

Scorpio *type of* **star sign**. [➡FATE, DESTINY, AND ASTROLOGY; 783]

scorpion *type of* **arachnid**. [➡ARACHNIDS; 1018]

scotch *v* **stop**, spoil, foil, scuttle, scupper, mess up (*informal*), ruin. [➡MAKE IMPOSSIBLE; 277] *Opposite:* initiate.

Scotch broth *type of* **soup**. [➡SOUP; 1185]

scot-free *adv* **unpunished**, without punishment, with impunity, lightly, easily. [➡FREEDOM AND LIBERTY; 209]

scoundrel *n* **crook** (*informal*), rogue, rascal, villain, rat (*slang*), cheat. [➡VILLAINS AND THUGS; 947] *Opposite:* hero.

scour 1 *v* **scrub**, rub, clean, wash, polish, burnish. [➡CLEAN AND POLISH; 404] *Opposite:* dirty. 2 *v* **search**, comb, hunt, go over with a fine-tooth comb, rake through. [➡SEEK POSSESSION AND SEARCH; 457]

scourge 1 *n* **bane**, blight, plague, curse, menace, thorn in your flesh, thorn in your side, tormentor. [➡NUISANCES; 254] *Opposite:* blessing. 2 *v* **plague**, curse, afflict, terrorize, torment, devastate. [➡FRIGHTEN AND SHOCK; 569] *Opposite:* bless.

scout 1 *n* **lookout**, spy, watch, undercover agent, detective, emissary, pathfinder, guide, mole. [➡PEOPLE WHO GUARD AND PROTECT; 846] 2 *v* **search**, hunt, scout around, look around, cast around, nose around (*informal*), scout out, seek, look for, look out for, search for. [➡SEEK POSSESSION AND SEARCH; 457] *Opposite:* find. 3 *v* **check out**, reconnoitre, survey, investigate, spy out, explore, recce (*slang*). [➡LOOKING AND LOOKS; 701]

scout around *v* [➡SEEK POSSESSION AND SEARCH; 457]

scowl 1 *n* **dirty look**, black look, glare, frown, glower, grimace, stare, pout. [➡FACIAL EXPRESSION; 652] *Opposite:* smile. 2 *v* **look daggers**, glare, frown, glower, grimace, pout. [➡FACIAL EXPRESSION; 652] *Opposite:* smile.

scrabble 1 *v* **scratch**, dig, scrape, claw, pick, worry. [➡CONTACT: TOUCH; 413] 2 *v* **grope**, fumble, clutch, rummage, rootle, scrape around, feel. [➡SEEK POSSESSION AND SEARCH; 457]

scrag end *type of* **cut**. [➡TYPES AND CUTS OF MEAT; 1176]

scragginess *n* [➡IN BAD REPAIR; 1233]

scraggly *adj* **messy**, untidy, dishevelled, unkempt, tangled, tousled, bedraggled. [➡BADLY GROOMED; 484] *Opposite:* tidy.

scraggy *adj* **scrawny**, bony, thin, emaciated, gaunt, skinny. [➡BUILD; 478] *Opposite:* plump.

See Compare and Contrast at **thin**.

scram (*informal*) *v* **run off**, run away, get out, get away, bolt, skedaddle (*slang*), scat (*informal*), beat it (*informal*), scarper (*slang*), vamoose (*US slang*). [➡RUN AWAY AND AVOID; 10]

scramble 1 *v* **climb**, clamber, crawl, scrabble, struggle, swarm, scale. [➡GO UPWARDS; 307] *Opposite:* descend. 2 *v* **move quickly**, rush, run, scuttle, jostle, push, stampede, dash. [➡MOVE FAST; 314] *Opposite:* plod. 3 *v* **mix up**, jumble, mix, muddle, confuse, disorganize. [➡CREATE DISORDER AND CAUSE CHAOS; 359] *Opposite:* unscramble. 4 *n* **ascent**, climb, clamber, hike. [➡GO UPWARDS; 307] *Opposite:* descent. 5 *n* **rush**, run, stampede, commotion, free-for-all (*informal*), dash. [➡SUDDEN EVENT; 52] *Opposite:* calm.

scrap 1 *n* **piece**, bit, fragment, slip, wisp, particle, crumb, morsel. [➡SMALL PIECE; 127] 2 *v* **cancel**, abandon, get rid of, write off (*informal*), ditch (*informal*), do away with, give up, bin. [➡ABOLISH AND ANNUL; 453] *Opposite:* adopt. 3 *n* (*informal*) **fight**, scuffle, tussle, row, clash, fracas, brawl, punch-up (*informal*), disagreement. [➡AGGRESSIVE EVENT; 39] 4 *v* **scuffle**, fight, tussle, spar, brawl, wrestle, come to blows, clash, argue. [➡COMPETE, CONTEND, AND COMBAT; 304]

scrape 1 *v* **rub**, scratch, scuff, abrade, scour, rasp, scrub. [➡WORSEN APPEARANCE; 383] 2 *v* **graze**, scratch, scuff, mark, abrade, chafe, bark, skin, cut. [➡TEAR, BREAK, AND CUT; 361] 3 *n* (*informal*) **fight**, brawl, clash, fracas, scuffle, tussle. [➡AGGRESSIVE EVENT; 39] 4 *n* (*informal*) **fix** (*informal*), pickle (*informal*), jam (*informal*), predicament, plight, problem. [➡DIFFICULT SITUATIONS; 72] 5 *n* **scratch**, scuff, graze, mark, abrasion, cut. [➡HOLES, GAPS, AND FORKS; 1251]

scrape by *v* **make do**, survive, make ends meet, get by, scratch a living, eke out a living, scratch out a living. [➡CONTINUE TO EXIST; 17] *Opposite:* prosper.

scrape out *v* **hollow out**, scoop out, gouge out, carve out, gouge, scoop, dig out. [➡EMPTY AND UNLOAD; 408] *Opposite:* fill.

scrape together *v* **collect**, amass, put by, put aside, scrape up, save, gather, assemble, garner, glean, scrounge (*informal*), scratch together. [➡GET; 421] *Opposite:* disperse.

scrapheap *n* **rubbish dump**, junkyard, landfill, tip, garbage dump (*US*). [➡URBAN OUTDOOR SPACES; 1071]

scrappy 1 *adj* **fragmentary**, fragmented, bitty, patchy, piecemeal, incomplete, patchwork. [➡UNFINISHEDNESS; 240] *Opposite:* complete. 2 *adj* **disjointed**, inconsistent, disconnected, incoherent, patchy, untidy. [➡DISORDER AND CHAOS; 246] *Opposite:* uniform. 3 *adj* **plucky**, courageous, determined, spirited, spunky (*informal*), aggressive. [➡COURAGE; 499] *Opposite:* timid. 4 *adj* **argumentative**, contrary, confrontational, hotheaded, quarrelsome, belligerent. [➡AGGRESSIVE AND BELLIGERENT; 519] *Opposite:* docile.

scraps *n* **leftovers**, scrapings, slops, crumbs, leavings, odds and ends, remainders, outs (*US*). [➡REMAINDER AND REMAINDERS; 123]

scrapyard *n* [➡URBAN OUTDOOR SPACES; 1071]

scratch 1 *v* **scrape**, graze, grate, rub, cut, score, nick, scuff, abrade, mark. [➡WORSEN APPEARANCE; 383] 2 *v* **itch**, rub, scrabble, scrape, worry at. [➡CONTACT: TOUCH; 413] 3 *v* **cancel**, abandon, forget, scrap, leave out, delete. [➡ABOLISH AND ANNUL; 453] *Opposite:* keep. 4 *v* **pull out**, drop out, bow out, withdraw, abandon, leave. [➡CAUSE TO STOP; 267] *Opposite:* continue. 5 *n* **cut**, scrape, graze, score, nick, scuff, abrasion, mark. [➡HOLES, GAPS, AND FORKS; 1251]

scratched *adj* [➡IN BAD REPAIR; 1233]

scratchpad (*US*) *n* [➡WRITING AND DRAWING IMPLEMENTS, AND MEDIA; 602]

scratch together *v* **collect**, amass, put by, put aside, scratch up, scrape together, save, gather, assemble, garner, glean, scrounge (*informal*). [➡GET; 421] *Opposite:* disperse.

scratchy *adj* **itchy**, prickly, tickly, irritating, uncomfortable, rough. [➡PHYSICAL TEXTURE; 1221] *Opposite:* soft.

scrawl 1 *v* **scribble**, doodle, dash off (*informal*), pencil, write, draw. [➡RECORD SOMETHING; 372] 2 *n* **illegible writing**, scribble, doodle, graffiti, writing, squiggle. [➡WRITING; 584]

scrawled *adj* **indecipherable**, illegible, incomprehensible, scribbled, untidy, messy. [➡WRITING; 584] *Opposite:* neat.

scrawniness *n* [➡BUILD; 478]

scrawny *adj* **skinny**, scraggy, gaunt, bony, undernourished, emaciated, thin, lean, skeletal. [➡BUILD; 478] *Opposite:* plump.

See Compare and Contrast at **thin**.

screak (*US*) 1 *v* **screech**, howl, yowl, yell, scream, holler (*informal*), squeal. [➡SOUND EMISSION BY PEOPLE; 364] *Opposite:* murmur. 2 *v* **creak**, groan, grate, squeak, squeal, squawk. [➡SOUND EMISSION BY ANIMALS OR BIRDS; 365] 3 *type of* **human sound**. [➡SOUNDS MADE BY PEOPLE; 1261] 4 *type of* **bird sound**. [➡SOUNDS MADE BY BIRDS; 1262]

scream 1 *n* **shriek**, yell, cry, yelp, shout, screech, squeal, squawk. [➡SOUNDS MADE BY PEOPLE; 1261] *Opposite:* murmur. 2 *n* (*informal*) **laugh** (*informal*), riot (*informal*), gas (*informal*), card (*dated informal*), hoot (*slang*). [➡JOKERS AND TEASES; 676] 3 *v* **shout**, shriek, yell, cry, screech, bawl, squeal, squawk. [➡SOUND EMISSION BY PEOPLE; 364] *Opposite:* whisper.

scream with laughter *v* [➡LAUGHTER; 650]

scree *n* **rock debris**, talus, rubble, gravel, stones, rock. [➡EROSION PRODUCTS AND SOIL; 1058]

screech 1 *n* **scream**, shriek, squeal, cry, yelp, yell, squawk, shout. [➡SOUNDS MADE BY PEOPLE; 1261] *Opposite:* whisper. 2 *v* **shriek**, scream, squeal, cry, yelp, yell, squawk, shout. [➡SOUND EMISSION BY PEOPLE; 364] *Opposite:* whisper. 3 *v* **skid**, judder, shudder, squeal, scream, career. [➡MOVE FAST; 314] *Opposite:* glide. 4 *type of* **bird sound**. [➡SOUNDS MADE BY BIRDS; 1262]

screech owl *type of* **owl**. [➡OWL; 1001]

screen 1 *n* **partition**, divider, panel, shield, guard, barrier. [➡WALLS AND PARTITIONS; 1103] 2 *n* **shade**, awning, canopy, shelter, curtain. [➡COVERS AND COATINGS; 1245] 3 *n* **monitor**, display, VDU, computer screen, television, VDT (*US*). [➡COMPUTERS AND COMPUTING; 1126] 4 *v* **test**, inspect, examine, diagnose, check, check out. [➡EXAMINE AND ASSESS; 754] 5 *v* **hide**, conceal, cover, protect, shelter, shield, guard. [➡CAUSE TO DISAPPEAR; 6] *Opposite:* reveal. 6 *v* **partition**, separate, divide, mark off, curtain. [➡SEPARATE AND DIVIDE; 402] *Opposite:* open out. 7 *v* **broadcast**, put on, show, transmit, project, air, put on air. [➡TELEVISION AND RADIO; 607] 8 *v* **vet**, select, assess, investigate, inspect, test, examine, check out, sift, weed out. [➡EXAMINE AND ASSESS; 754] 9 *n type of* **hardware**. [➡COMPUTERS AND COMPUTING; 1126]

screening 1 *n* **show**, showing, viewing, programme, projection, matinée. [➡PERFORMANCES AND SHOWS; 42] 2 *n* **broadcast**, showing, transmission, run, airing, repeat, rerun. [➡FILM; 901] 3 *n* **inspection**, testing, examination, diagnosis, checking, check. [➡EXAMINE AND ASSESS; 754] 4 *n* **selection**, vetting, assessment, investigation, inspection, examination. [➡EXAMINE AND ASSESS; 754]

screenplay *n* **script**, dialogue, scenario, text, writing. [➡FILM; 901]

screen test *n* [➡FILM; 901]

screenwriter *n* **scriptwriter**, writer, dramatist, author, playwright. [➡WRITERS AND STYLES; 914]

screw 1 *v* **twist**, rotate, coil, turn, wind, spin. [➡MOVE SOMETHING ON THE SPOT; 337] *Opposite:* unscrew. 2 *v* **attach**, bolt, fasten, fix, secure. [➡FASTEN, LINK, AND JOIN; 409] *Opposite:* unscrew. 3 *v* **crumple**, twist, distort, contort, crinkle, fold, scrunch, crunch, wrinkle, furrow. [➡CHANGE OF SHAPE; 386] *Opposite:* smooth.

screwdriver *type of* **general tool**. [➡HAND TOOLS; 1118]

screw up *v* **muster**, gather, summon, call up, pluck up, concentrate, get up. [➡GET; 421] *Opposite:* lose.

scribble 1 *v* **scrawl**, jot, write, dash off (*informal*). [➡RECORD SOMETHING; 372] 2 *n* **doodle**, scrawl, jotting, squiggle, design, cartoon, drawing. [➡DRAWINGS, CHARTS AND TABLES; 595] 3 *v* **draw**, doodle, scrawl, jot, squiggle. [➡RECORD SOMETHING; 372] 4 *n* **writing**, handwriting, scrawl, lettering. [➡WRITING; 584]

scribbled *adj* **scrawled**, jotted, dashed off (*informal*), untidy, illegible, indecipherable, unreadable, incomprehensible, hurried. [➡WRITING; 584] *Opposite:* neat.

scribbler *n* [➡WRITING AND DRAWING IMPLEMENTS, AND MEDIA; 602]

scribbling pad *n* [➡WRITING AND DRAWING IMPLEMENTS, AND MEDIA; 602]

scribe *n* **transcriber**, copyist, clerk, illuminator. [➡WRITERS AND STYLES; 914]

scrimmage 1 *n* **fight**, battle, skirmish, clash, fray, brawl, scuffle, affray. [➡AGGRESSIVE EVENT; 39] 2 *n* **struggle**, tussle, fray, scrum, free-for-all (*informal*), conflict, ruckus. [➡CHAOS AND UPROAR; 51]

scrimp *v* **economize**, save, skimp, tighten your belt, draw in your horns, go easy (*informal*), pull in your horns (*US*). [➡FOREGO AND DENY ONESELF; 450] *Opposite:* squander.

script 1 *n* **screenplay**, text, words, libretto, play, speech. [➡FICTION AND DRAMA; 913] 2 *n* **writing**, calligraphy, handwriting, hand, cursive, lettering. [➡WRITING; 584]

scriptwriter *n* **writer**, author, playwright, screenwriter, dramatist. [➡WRITERS AND STYLES; 914]

scroll *n* **roll**, parchment, document, certificate, manuscript, spool. [➡OFFICIAL DOCUMENTS; 587]

scrooge (*informal*) *n* **miser**, skinflint, niggard, penny pincher (*informal*), pinchpenny, cheapskate (*informal*), meanie (*informal*). [➡FINANCIALLY MEAN PEOPLE; 952]

scrounge (*informal*) 1 *v* **beg**, borrow, cadge (*informal*), sponge, solicit, bum (*informal*). [➡OBTAIN POSSESSION BY PERSUASION; 458] *Opposite:* give. 2 *v* **scavenge**, rummage, forage, go through, search, hunt. [➡SEEK POSSESSION AND SEARCH; 457]

scrounger (*informal*) *n* **beggar**, borrower, cadger (*informal*), sponger (*informal*), bum (*informal*), freeloader (*informal*). [➡LAZY OR UNSUCCESSFUL PEOPLE; 948] *Opposite:* donor.

scrub 1 *v* **clean**, rub, scour, polish, brush, cleanse, burnish. [➡CLEAN AND POLISH; 404] *Opposite:* dirty. 2 *v* (*informal*) **cancel**, delete, erase, forget about, scratch, postpone. [➡ABOLISH AND ANNUL; 453] *Opposite:* schedule. 3 *n* **rub**, clean, scour, polish, brush, burnish. [➡CLEAN AND POLISH; 404] 4 *n* **undergrowth**, brush, bush, brushwood, vegetation, thicket, scrubland. [➡VEGETATION; 1025]

scrubby *adj* [➡IN BAD REPAIR; 1233]

scrubland *n* [➡DESERTS AND PLAINS; 1045]

scruffy *adj* **untidy**, shabby, tatty, unkempt, dishevelled, messy, ratty (*informal*), grubby, sloppy. [➡BADLY GROOMED; 484] *Opposite:* tidy.

scrum *n* **tussle**, fray, scuffle, free-for-all (*informal*), scrimmage, struggle, jostle. [➡CHAOS AND UPROAR; 51]

scrummy (*informal*) *adj* **delicious**, delectable, mouthwatering, tasty, delightful, yummy, gorgeous, delish (*slang*), scrumptious. [➡TASTE; 704] *Opposite:* revolting.

scrumptious (*informal*) *adj* **delicious**, delectable, mouthwatering, tasty, delightful, yummy, gorgeous, delish (*slang*), scrummy (*informal*). [➡TASTE; 704] *Opposite:* revolting.

scrumptiousness (*informal*) *n* [➡TASTE; 704]

scrunch *v* **crumple**, crush, crunch, crease, wrinkle, squeeze. [➡CHANGE OF SHAPE; 386] *Opposite:* smooth.

scruple *n* **misgiving**, doubt, qualm, compunction, hesitation, regret, second thought, pang of conscience. [➡UNCERTAINTY; 560]

scrupulous 1 *adj* **conscientious**, meticulous, thorough, careful, rigorous, painstaking, fussy, fastidious, punctilious, assiduous. [➡HARD-WORKING AND COMMITTED; 501] *Opposite:* sloppy. 2 *adj* **trustworthy**, reliable, dependable, trusty. [➡HONEST AND RELIABLE; 503]

See Compare and Contrast at **careful**.

scrupulousness *n* [➡HONEST AND RELIABLE; 503]

scrutinize *v* **examine**, inspect, study, pore over, analyse, dissect, search. [➡EXAMINE AND ASSESS; 754] *Opposite:* glance.

scrutiny *n* **examination**, inspection, study, analysis, search, inquiry. [➡EXAMINE AND ASSESS; 754]

scuba dive *v* [➡HOBBIES, GAMES, AND SPORTS; 875]

scuba diver *n* [➡PEOPLE IN SPORTS AND LEISURE; 876]

scud *v* **speed**, sweep, fly, sail, rush, hurry, tear, bowl along, zoom, zip (*informal*). [➡MOVE FAST; 314] *Opposite:* crawl.

scuff 1 *v* **scrape**, wear away, rub, graze, scratch, abrade. [➡WORSEN APPEARANCE; 383] 2 *n* **scratch**, scrape, graze, abrasion. [➡FAULTS, FLAWS, AND WEAKNESSES; 252]

scuffle 1 *n* **fight**, brawl, punch-up, scrap (*informal*), fracas, fray. [➡AGGRESSIVE EVENT; 39] 2 *v* **wrestle**, fight, come to blows, exchange blows, scrap. [➡COMPETE, CONTEND, AND COMBAT; 304]

scull 1 *n* **oar**, paddle, blade, sweep. [➡PARTS OF A SHIP OR BOAT; 1150] 2 *v* **row**, paddle, propel, canoe. [➡TRAVEL: WAYS OF TRAVELLING; 321] 3 *type of* **small vessel**. [➡SHIPS AND BOATS; 1149]

scullery *type of* **room in the home**. [➡TYPES OF ROOM; 1096]

sculpt *v* **carve**, shape, mould, form, fashion, chisel. [➡CRAFTS AND CARVING; 356]

sculptor *n* [➡ARTISTS; 900]

sculpture *n* **statue**, statuette, figure, figurine, carving, monument. [➡SCULPTURE; 902]

scum *n* **impurities**, filth, layer, froth, foam, crust, skin. [➡UNPLEASANT AND DIRTY SUBSTANCES; 1267]

scummy *adj* [➡DIRTY; 1234]

scupper *v* **wreck**, stymie, thwart, ruin, spoil, foil, scuttle, damage, scotch, undo, mess up (*informal*). [➡MAKE IMPOSSIBLE; 277]

scurf 1 *n* **dandruff**, dead skin, flakes. [➡CONDITIONS AFFECTING THE SKIN; 722] 2 *n* **encrustation**, scale, crust, deposit, coat, coating, layer. [➡COVERS AND COATINGS; 1245]

scurrilous *adj* **scandalous**, slanderous, libellous, defamatory, outrageous, abusive, insulting. [➡RUDE AND HOSTILE; 626] *Opposite:* complimentary.

scurry *v* **dash**, scuttle, scamper, dart, rush, hurry, bustle. [➡MOVE FAST; 314] *Opposite:* saunter.

scuttle 1 *v* **destroy**, stymie, thwart, spoil, ruin, foil, scupper, wreck, scotch, mess up (*informal*). [➡MAKE IMPOSSIBLE; 277] 2 *v* **scurry**, scamper, dart, dash, rush. [➡MOVE FAST; 314] *Opposite:* saunter.

scuttlebutt (*US slang*) *n* [➡GOSSIP; 679]

scuzzy (*US slang*) *adj* [➡DIRTY; 1234]

scythe 1 *v* **cut**, cut down, hack, slice, sweep, mow, reap. [➡EXTRACT AND SEVER; 342] 2 *type of* **cutting tool**. [➡CUTTING TOOLS; 1119]

sea 1 *n* **ocean**, deep, depths, briny. [➡THE SEAS, OCEANS, AND SHORES; 1041] 2 *adj* **maritime**, aquatic, oceanic, marine. [➡THE SEAS, OCEANS, AND SHORES; 1041] *Opposite:* land.

sea anemone *type of* **aquatic invertebrate**. [➡AQUATIC INVERTEBRATE; 1022]

seabird

◆ *types of seabird*
wader, albatross, auk, avocet, cormorant, fulmar, gannet, guillemot, gull, kittiwake, oystercatcher, pelican, plover, puffin, seagull, shag, skua, storm petrel, tern

seaboard *n* **coast**, coastline, shore, seashore, shoreline, seacoast, seaside. [➡THE SEAS, OCEANS, AND SHORES; 1041] *Opposite:* interior.

sea bream *type of* **sea fish**. [➡SEA FISH; 1009]

sea change *n* **transformation**, metamorphosis, shift, turnaround, U-turn, reversal, volte-face, about-turn, conversion, alteration, total change, change, about-face (*US*). [➡CHANGE; 373]

seacoast *n* **shore**, shoreline, coast, coastline, seaboard, seashore, beach. [➡THE SEAS, OCEANS, AND SHORES; 1041] *Opposite:* interior.

sea eagle *type of* **bird of prey**. [➡BIRD OF PREY; 998]

seafaring *adj* **maritime**, nautical, naval, seagoing, marine. [➡TRANSPORTATION, TRANSPORTERS, AND CARGOS; 323]

sea fish

◆ *types of tropical sea fish*
stingray, sailfish, barracuda, flying fish, kingfish, mahi-mahi, marlin, pomfret, sawfish, snapper, swordfish, tuna

◆ *types of sea fish*
anchovy, anglerfish, cod, coley, dogfish, eel, haddock, hake, herring, John Dory, ling, mackerel, monkfish, pilchard, salmon, sardine, sea bream, shark, sprat, sturgeon, whitebait, whiting

seafront *n* **waterfront**, promenade, prom, esplanade, boardwalk, beach, seashore, shore, shoreline, coast. [➡THE SEAS, OCEANS, AND SHORES; 1041]

seagoing *adj* **seafaring**, oceangoing, maritime, nautical, marine. [➡TRANSPORTATION, TRANSPORTERS, AND CARGOS; 323] *Opposite:* land.

sea green *type of* **green**. [➡COLOURS; 1223]

seagull *type of* **seabird**. [➡SEABIRD; 1002]

seal 1 *n* **stamp**, hallmark, impress (*literary*), impression, signet, sigil. [➡WRITING AND DRAWING IMPLEMENTS, AND MEDIA; 602] 2 *n* **closure**, cover, stopper, lid, cap. [➡COVERS AND COATINGS; 1245] 3 *v* **close**, fasten, stick, close up, shut, stop, stick down. [➡FASTEN, LINK, AND JOIN; 409] *Opposite:* open. 4 *v* **guarantee**, settle, finalize, wrap up, confirm, clinch. [➡COMPLETE AN ACTION; 264] 5 *part of* **engine**. [➡PARTS OF AN ENGINE; 1143] 6 *type of* **marine mammal**. [➡MARINE MAMMAL; 987]

sea lane *n* **seaway**, shipping lane, sea route, channel, corridor, passage. [➡WATERWAYS AND SEAWAYS; 1107]

sealant *n* [➡BUILDING MATERIALS; 1076]

sealed 1 *adj* **closed**, stuck down, wrapped, taped up. [➡FASTEN, LINK, AND JOIN; 409] *Opposite:* unsealed. 2 *adj* **impenetrable**, hermetically sealed, vacuum-packed, airtight, watertight, coated. [➡DECORATE, ADORN, AND APPLY COATINGS; 406] *Opposite:* unsealed.

sea lettuce *type of* **alga**. [➡MICROORGANISMS, FUNGI, AND ALGAE; 1023]

sea lion *type of* **marine mammal**. [➡MARINE MAMMAL; 987]

seal off *v* **close off**, cordon off, fence off, isolate, block, enclose, shut in. [➡BAR AND OBSTRUCT ACCESS; 411] *Opposite:* open.

seam 1 *n* **join**, closure, ridge. [➡EXTREMITIES OF PHYSICAL OBJECTS; 1249] 2 *n* **layer**, join, joint, stratum, vein, lode. [➡COVERS AND COATINGS; 1245]

seamless 1 *adj* **unified**, all-in-one, one-piece, whole, continuous, unbroken. [➡IN GOOD REPAIR; 1231] *Opposite:* joined. 2 *adj* **smooth**, perfect, faultless, uniform, unified, harmonious. [➡GOOD, WELL, BETTER; 184]

seamy *adj* **unpleasant**, degenerate, sordid, squalid, seedy, unsavoury, debauched, rough. [➡DISGUSTING AND REPULSIVE; 231] *Opposite:* wholesome.

seaplane *type of* **civil aircraft**. [➡AIRCRAFT; 1147]

seaport *n* **harbour**, port, coastal town, haven (*literary*), dock. [➡THE SEAS, OCEANS, AND SHORES; 1041]

sear *v* **burn**, scorch, solder, singe, char, flame, blister. [➡FIRE, FLAMMABILITY, AND BURNING; 1164]

search 1 *v* **examine**, rifle, comb, look for, seek, hunt, explore, seek out, investigate, rummage. [➡SEEK POSSESSION AND SEARCH; 457] 2 *n* **examination**, hunt, quest, pursuit, exploration. [➡SEEK POSSESSION AND SEARCH; 457]

searching *adj* **thorough**, penetrating, incisive, probing, pointed, sharp. [➡ENTHUSIASTIC AND INQUISITIVE; 629] *Opposite:* superficial.

searchlight *n* **light**, spotlight, beam, lamp, torch, flashlight (*US*). [➡LIGHT; 1163]

search out *v* **discover**, uncover, find out, find, reveal, get, get hold of, get a hold of (*US*). [➡FIND; 464]

search party *n* **searchers**, rescue party, rescuers, rescue patrol, emergency workers, volunteers. [➡GROUPS WITH A COMMON INTEREST; 938]

search through *v* **sift through**, sort through, rummage, hunt through, ransack, rifle, scour, comb. [➡SEEK POSSESSION AND SEARCH; 457]

searing 1 *adj* **scorching** (*informal*), blistering, sizzling (*informal*), sweltering, roasting (*informal*). [➡HOT WEATHER; 1050] *Opposite:* freezing. 2 *adj* **intense**, shooting, stabbing, agonizing, burning. [➡PHYSICALLY UNPLEASANT; 227] *Opposite:* mild.

sea serpent *n* [➡SNAKE; 995]

seashore *n* **coastline**, seaboard, shore, shoreline, coast, beach, sand, seaside. [➡THE SEAS, OCEANS, AND SHORES; 1041]

seasick *adj* **sick**, nauseous, queasy, travel-sick, ill, green around the gills (*informal*). [➡ILL AND SICK; 741]

seaside *n* **seashore**, coast, shore, beach. [➡THE SEAS, OCEANS, AND SHORES; 1041]

sea snake *type of* **poisonous snake**. [➡SNAKE; 995]

season 1 *n* **period**, term, spell, time, time of year. [➡TIMES OF YEAR; 88] 2 *v* **flavour**, spice, spike, pepper. [➡COOKING AND FOOD PREPARATION; 354]

seasonable *adj* **appropriate**, fitting, timely, opportune, suitable. [➡APPROPRIATE, SUITABLE, ADVISABLE; 185] *Opposite:* unseasonable.

seasonal 1 *adj* **cyclical**, periodic, cyclic, recurrent, regular, spring, summer, autumn, winter. [➡TIMES OF YEAR; 88] *Opposite:* year-round. 2 *adj* **limited**, sporadic, intermittent, temporary, casual. [➡FINITENESS, VARIABILITY, AND TRANSIENCE; 96] *Opposite:* permanent.

seasonal worker *n* [➡WORKER; 836]

seasoned *adj* **experienced**, veteran, hardened, tested, weathered, expert, versed in, well up in, au fait. [➡TALENTED AND SKILFUL; 528] *Opposite:* inexperienced.

seasoning *n* **flavouring**, flavour, zest, zing (*informal*). [➡SEASONINGS AND SAUCES; 1173]

seat 1 *n* **chair**, bench, pew, stool, armchair. [➡FURNITURE; 858] 2 *n* **base**, HQ, control centre, headquarters, centre, station, capital. [➡PLACE; 1064] 3 *v* **place**, sit, sit down, install, settle. [➡POSITION SOMETHING; 326] 4 *v* **accommodate**, hold, sit, contain, take. [➡HOLD AND CONTAIN; 456] **5** *part of* **bike** (*informal*). [➡BIKES, CARS, AND CARRIAGES; 1148]

seat belt *type of* **internal feature.** [➡INTERNAL PARTS OF A VEHICLE; 1145]

seating *n* **seats**, chairs, spaces, places, orchestra, stalls, front row, balcony. [➡FURNITURE; 858]

seating

◆ *types of seating*
Adirondack chair (*US*), armchair, bench, bleachers (*US*), Boston rocker, bucket seat, carver, chair, chaise longue, chesterfield, couch, davenport (*US*), deck chair, easy chair, highchair, ladder-back, lounger, love seat, pew, recliner, rocking chair, settee, sofa, stall, stool, sunlounger, swivel chair, Windsor chair, wing chair

sea urchin *type of* **aquatic invertebrate.** [➡AQUATIC INVERTEBRATE; 1022]

sea wall *n* **dike**, jetty, breakwater, embankment, barricade, barrier, dam. [➡BARRIERS; 1112]

seawards *adv* [➡DIRECTION OF MOTION; 346]

seaway *n* **channel**, sea lane, shipping lane, sea route, canal, corridor, passage. [➡WATERWAYS AND SEAWAYS; 1107]

seaweed *type of* **alga.** [➡MICROORGANISMS, FUNGI, AND ALGAE; 1023]

sea wrack *type of* **alga.** [➡MICROORGANISMS, FUNGI, AND ALGAE; 1023]

secateurs *type of* **cutting tool.** [➡CUTTING TOOLS; 1119]

secede *v* **withdraw**, break away, break from, disaffiliate, pull out, split, separate, become independent. [➡SEPARATE AND DIVIDE; 402] *Opposite:* affiliate.

secession *n* **withdrawal**, departure, separation, retreat, retirement, resignation, breakaway. [➡END; 54]

seclude *v* **isolate**, separate, keep away, keep apart, remove, pull out, withdraw, split off, segregate. [➡SEPARATE AND DIVIDE; 402]

secluded *adj* **private**, sheltered, quiet, isolated, out-of-the-way. [➡SECRET AND UNKNOWN; 180] *Opposite:* public.

seclusion *n* **privacy**, shelter, isolation, quiet, solitude. [➡SECRET AND UNKNOWN; 180]

second **1** *adj* **additional**, another, next, subsequent, following, succeeding. [➡AFTER, LAST, AND FOLLOWING; 166] **2** *v* **support**, agree with, uphold, back, go along with, be with, back up. [➡APPROVE AND CONFIRM; 647] *Opposite:* oppose. **3** *n* **moment**, minute, instant, jiffy (*informal*), trice, flash. [➡SHORT PERIOD OF TIME; 93] *Opposite:* age. **4** *v* **transfer**, assign, post, attach, send. [➡DESPATCH AND SEND; 334]

secondary **1** *adj* **subordinate**, minor, inferior, lesser, tributary, ancillary, unimportant. [➡UNIMPORTANT AND UNNECESSARY; 239] *Opposite:* primary. **2** *adj* **derived**, derivative, resulting, resultant, consequent, consequential. [➡RESULTS AND OUTCOMES; 83] *Opposite:* original.

second best *adj* **second-rate**, second-class, second choice, minor, inferior. [➡ORDINARINESS; 245] *Opposite:* best.

second-class *adj* **second-rate**, mediocre, indifferent, middling, second best, substandard. [➡UNACCEPTABLE AND UNFORGIVEABLE; 226] *Opposite:* first-class.

second cousin *type of* **same generation relative.** [➡SAME GENERATION RELATIVES; 957]

seconder *n* **supporter**, endorser, backer, advocate, assenter, follower, sponsor, subscriber. [➡SUPPORTERS, PROTECTORS, AND COMPATRIOTS; 970]

second-guess *v* **predict**, guess, foretell, anticipate, work out. [➡PREDICT AND ANTICIPATE; 751]

second-hand **1** *adj* **used**, hand-me-down, nearly new. [➡OLD, OLD-FASHIONED; 168] *Opposite:* new. **2** *adv* **indirectly**, circuitously, through the grapevine. [➡GOSSIP; 679] *Opposite:* first-hand.

secondly *adv* **then**, furthermore, in addition, what is more, also, next, moreover, again, in the second place. [➡EXPRESSIONS INTRODUCING EXTRA INFORMATION; 137] *Opposite:* firstly.

second name *n* [➡NAME AND DESCRIBE; 666]

second-rate *adj* **inadequate**, mediocre, unsatisfactory, poor, below standard, cheap, tawdry, tacky (*informal*), second-class. [➡INFERIORITY; 154] *Opposite:* first-rate.

second sight *n* **clairvoyance**, foresight, foreknowledge (*formal*), precognition, intuition, ESP, prediction. [➡THE SUPERNATURAL; 788]

second-sighted *adj* [➡THE SUPERNATURAL; 788]

second thoughts *n* **reconsideration**, pangs, doubts, qualms, misgivings, regrets, compunction, reservations. [➡FEELINGS ABOUT THE FUTURE; 534]

secrecy *n* **concealment**, clandestineness, confidentiality, privacy, mystery, silence. [➡SECRET AND UNKNOWN; 180] *Opposite:* openness.

secret **1** *adj* **clandestine**, covert, hush-hush (*informal*), undisclosed, surreptitious, furtive, stealthy, cloak-and-dagger, hole-and-corner, underhand, closet, underground. [➡SECRET AND UNKNOWN; 180] *Opposite:* open. **2** *adj* **confidential**, private, classified, top-secret, restricted, hush-hush (*informal*). [➡SECRET AND UNKNOWN; 180] *Opposite:* public. **3** *n* **confidence**, skeleton in the cupboard, mystery, riddle, enigma. [➡SECRETS AND MYSTERIES; 181]

Compare and Contrast: *secret, clandestine, covert, furtive, stealthy, surreptitious*

CORE MEANING: CONVEYING A DESIRE OR NEED FOR CONCEALMENT

secret intentionally withheld from general knowledge; ***clandestine*** describes an activity that needs to be concealed, usually because it is illegal or unauthorized; ***covert*** not intended to be known, seen, or found out, suggesting a lack of honesty or openness; ***furtive*** cautious and careful in order to escape notice; ***stealthy*** quiet, slow, and cautious in order to escape notice; ***surreptitious*** done in a concealed or underhand way to escape notice.

secret agent *n* **spy**, undercover agent, double agent, mole, infiltrator, private eye (*informal*), detective. [➡INTERFERING PEOPLE AND TELLTALES; 950]

secretary 1 *n* **clerical worker**, PA, personal assistant, office assistant, typist, clerk, administrator. [➡OFFICE WORKERS; 847] 2 *type of* **cabinet**. [➡FURNITURE; 858]

secretary-general *n* **chief executive officer**, CEO, head, chief, chair, chairperson, president. [➡BUSINESS PEOPLE; 794]

secret ballot *n* [➡ELECTIONS AND SUFFRAGE; 807]

secrete 1 *v* **hide**, hide away, conceal, stow, stash (*informal*), squirrel away. [➡CAUSE TO DISAPPEAR; 6] *Opposite:* display. 2 *v* **discharge** (*formal*), exude, ooze, emit, produce, squirt. [➡LIQUID EMISSION; 371] *Opposite:* absorb.

secreted *adj* [➡IMPERCEPTIBLE; 26]

secretion *n* **discharge**, excretion, exudation, emission, ooze. [➡EMIT AND EMANATE; 362]

secretive *adj* **private**, mysterious, enigmatic, guarded, reticent, reserved, cagey (*informal*), cautious. [➡RETICENT AND UNFORTHCOMING; 632] *Opposite:* open.

secretiveness *n* [➡SECRET AND UNKNOWN; 180]

secretly *adv* **clandestinely**, covertly, in secret, furtively, surreptitiously, behind somebody's back, behind closed doors, on the sly. [➡SECRET AND UNKNOWN; 180] *Opposite:* openly.

sect *n* **group**, clique, faction, camp, party, cult, division, offshoot, branch. [➡GROUPS WITH A COMMON INTEREST; 938]

sectarian 1 *adj* **religious**, denominational, sectional, factional. [➡RELIGIONS AND RELIGIOUS PRACTICES; 778] 2 *adj* **dogmatic**, intolerant, bigoted, biased, partisan, prejudiced, narrow-minded, rigid. [➡NEGATIVE INTELLECTUAL CHARACTERISTICS; 526] *Opposite:* tolerant.

section 1 *n* **part**, unit, piece, segment, slice, sector, division, subdivision, fragment, portion. [➡AREA AND RANGE; 111] *Opposite:* whole. 2 *v* **divide**, divide up, partition, split, segment. [➡SEPARATE AND DIVIDE; 402] *Opposite:* combine.

sector 1 *n* **part**, division, subdivision, segment, area. [➡AREA AND RANGE; 111] *Opposite:* whole. 2 *n* **area**, zone, region, quarter, district. [➡COUNTRIES AND REGIONS; 1066]

secular *adj* **earthly**, worldly, nonspiritual, profane, lay, material, irreligious, of this world, materialistic. [➡RELIGIOUS CONCEPTS; 777] *Opposite:* spiritual.

secure 1 *adj* **safe**, protected, locked, safe and sound, safe as houses, sheltered. [➡SAFE AND SAFETY; 192] *Opposite:* vulnerable. 2 *adj* **confident**, assured, self-confident, sure of yourself, self-assured. [➡CONFIDENCE AND COMPOSURE; 500] *Opposite:* insecure. 3 *adj* **fixed firmly**, closed, fastened, locked. [➡IN GOOD REPAIR; 1231] *Opposite:* unfastened. 4 *adj* **dependable**, reliable, safe, stable, steady. [➡SAFE AND SAFETY; 192] *Opposite:* unreliable. 5 *v* **make safe**, safeguard, fortify, lock, lock up. [➡BAR AND OBSTRUCT ACCESS; 411] 6 *v* **obtain**, acquire, get, get hold of, capture, procure, get your hands on. [➡GET; 421] *Opposite:* lose. 7 *v* **fix**, fasten, make fast, position, attach, tighten. [➡FASTEN, LINK, AND JOIN; 409] *Opposite:* loosen. 8 *v* **guarantee**, ensure, give security, indemnify, assure. [➡INSURANCE; 801]

See Compare and Contrast at **get**.

secure electronic transaction *n* [➡E-COMMERCE; 1128]

securely *adv* **firmly**, steadily, tightly, strongly, fast. [➡SAFE AND SAFETY; 192]

secure unit *n* [➡BUILDINGS FOR CONFINING PEOPLE; 1093]

securities broker *n* [➡PEOPLE INVOLVED IN FINANCE; 804]

security 1 *n* **safety**, refuge, sanctuary, haven, safe-keeping, retreat. [➡SAFE AND SAFETY; 192] *Opposite:* danger. 2 *n* **precautions**, safety measures, defence, protection. [➡SAFE AND SAFETY; 192] 3 *n* **confidence**, wellbeing, self-assurance, reassurance, self-confidence. [➡CONFIDENCE AND COMPOSURE; 500] *Opposite:* insecurity. 4 *n* **guarantee**, collateral, surety, insurance, indemnity, underwriting. [➡MONEY, PAYMENTS, AND CHARGES; 800]

security guard *n* [➡PEOPLE WHO GUARD AND PROTECT; 846]

security officer *n* [➡PEOPLE WHO GUARD AND PROTECT; 846]

sedan (*US*) *type of* **car**. [➡BIKES, CARS, AND CARRIAGES; 1148]

sedate 1 *adj* **dignified**, calm, cool, demure, serene, stately, placid, composed, unflappable. [➡CONFIDENCE AND COMPOSURE; 500] *Opposite:* boisterous. 2 *adj* **staid**, unexciting, dull, slow-moving, slow. [➡MOVING SLOWLY; 105] *Opposite:* exciting. 3 *v* **anaesthetize**, tranquillize, drug, put under sedation, knock out. [➡FALL ILL, TREAT, AND RECOVER; 729] *Opposite:* revive.

sedated *adj* [➡UNDER THE INFLUENCE OF DRUGS OR ALCOHOL; 742]

sedately *adv* **calmly**, coolly, demurely, serenely, placidly. [➡CONFIDENCE AND COMPOSURE; 500] *Opposite:* boisterously.

sedateness *n* [➡CONFIDENCE AND COMPOSURE; 500]

sedation *n* **calm**, restfulness, drowsiness, torpor, tranquillity, peacefulness. [➡REMEDIES, TREATMENTS AND OPERATIONS; 732] *Opposite:* excitement.

sedative 1 *n* **tranquillizer**, narcotic, downer (*slang*). [➡REMEDIES, TREATMENTS AND OPERATIONS; 732] 2 *adj* **tranquillizing**, calming, soothing, relaxing, soporific. [➡CALMING; 189] *Opposite:* stimulating.

sedentary *adj* **sitting**, inactive, deskbound, desk. [➡TYPES OF WORK; 835] *Opposite:* active.

sediment *n* **residue**, deposit, dregs, remains. [➡SUBSTANCES; 1266]

sedimentary *adj* [➡EROSION PRODUCTS AND SOIL; 1058]

sedition *n* **incitement to rebellion**, agitation, treason, subversion, rabble-rousing, troublemaking. [➡UNWILLINGNESS AND STUBBORNNESS; 565]

seditious *adj* **rebellious**, subversive, treasonable, disloyal, mutinous, up in arms. [➡UNWILLINGNESS AND STUBBORNNESS; 565] *Opposite:* loyal.

seditiousness *n* [➡UNWILLINGNESS AND STUBBORNNESS; 565]

seduce *v* [➡CAUSE OR COMPEL TO ACT; 272]

sedulity (*literary*) *n* [➡HARD-WORKING AND COMMITTED; 501]

sedulous (*literary*) *adj* **zealous**, assiduous, diligent, hard-working, keen, conscientious, determined, painstaking, careful. [➡HARD-WORKING AND COMMITTED; 501] *Opposite:* lazy.

sedulousness (*literary*) *n* [➡HARD-WORKING AND COMMITTED; 501]

see 1 *v* **perceive**, observe, distinguish, notice, witness, spot, glimpse, catch sight of, catch a glimpse of, set eyes on, make out. [➡SEE; 700] 2 *v* **understand**, get (*informal*), realize, perceive, grasp, appreciate, get the drift, get the message (*informal*), comprehend. [➡UNDERSTAND AND GRASP; 760] *Opposite:* misunderstand. 3 *v* **meet**, visit, pay a visit to, go to see, call on. [➡INITIATE AND ESTABLISH COMMUNICATION; 681] 4 *v* **find out**, establish, investigate, look into, ascertain (*formal*), check. [➡LEARN AND DISCOVER; 763] 5 *v* **imagine**, picture, envisage, predict, foresee, envision. [➡DREAM, IMAGINE, AND FANTASIZE; 750] 6 *v* **make sure**, see to it, ensure, make certain, guarantee. [➡CAUSE TO HAPPEN; 31] 7 *v* **consider it** (*formal*), think about it, refer to, give it some thought, think it over, reflect on it, mull it over. [➡THINK AND REFLECT; 744] 8 *v* **escort**, accompany, go with, go out with, date. [➡ACCOMPANY AND FOLLOW; 338] 9 *v* **look at**, refer to, consult, view, regard. [➡LOOKING AND LOOKS; 701]

see about *v* **take care of**, look into, investigate, find out about, attend to. [➡EXAMINE AND ASSESS; 754] *Opposite:* leave alone.

seed 1 *n* **kernel**, pip, spore, germ, stone, pit. [➡FRUIT AND VEGETABLES; 1175] 2 *n* **source**, beginning, start, starting point, nucleus, germ. [➡BEGINNING; 53] 3 *v* **sow**, plant, broadcast, scatter. [➡GROW AND CULTIVATE; 352] *Opposite:* harvest.

seedcake *type of* **cake**. [➡CAKES, BISCUITS, AND DESSERTS; 1180]

seed capital *n* **seed money**, startup funds, pump priming funds, venture capital, initial investment, working capital. [➡MONEY, PAYMENTS, AND CHARGES; 800]

seed case *n* [➡PARTS OF TREES AND PLANTS; 1026]

seed husk *n* [➡PARTS OF TREES AND PLANTS; 1026]

seediness (*informal*) *n* [➡ILL AND SICK; 741]

seedling *n* **sprout**, sapling, plantlet, slip, twig. [➡PLANTS AND TREES; 1024]

seed money *n* **seed capital**, startup funds, pump priming funds, venture capital, initial investment, working capital. [➡MONEY, PAYMENTS, AND CHARGES; 800]

seed pod *n* [➡PARTS OF TREES AND PLANTS; 1026]

seedy 1 *adj* (*informal*) **unwell**, ill, sick, poorly (*informal*), pale, wan, sickly, healthy. [➡ILL AND SICK; 741] 2 *adj* **dingy**, sordid, shabby, dodgy (*informal*), squalid, ropy (*informal*), sleazy, seamy. [➡BAD AND BADLY; 224] *Opposite:* respectable.

see eye to eye *v* **agree**, see things the same way, have the same opinion, be of the same mind. [➡AGREE; 646] *Opposite:* disagree.

seeing *conj* **considering**, bearing in mind, as, since, in view of. [➡EXPRESSIONS OF REFERENCE; 63]

seeing as *conj* [➡EXPRESSIONS OF REFERENCE; 63]

seeing that *conj* [➡EXPRESSIONS OF REFERENCE; 63]

see into *v* **discern**, understand, penetrate, comprehend, figure out, grasp, get a handle on. [➡UNDERSTAND AND GRASP; 760]

see in your mind's eye *v* **imagine**, picture, visualize, envision, see, conjure up. [➡DREAM, IMAGINE, AND FANTASIZE; 750]

seek 1 *v* **search for**, try to find, hunt for, pursue, seek out, look for. [➡SEEK POSSESSION AND SEARCH; 457] *Opposite:* find. 2 *v* **strive for**, try for, go for (*informal*), go after, work towards, pursue. [➡ATTEMPT AN ACTION; 262] *Opposite:* achieve. 3 *v* **ask for**, get, enquire about, request, inquire about. [➡REQUEST AND DEMAND; 664] *Opposite:* obtain.

seek out *v* **look for**, seek, search for, try to find, hunt for. [➡SEEK POSSESSION AND SEARCH; 457] *Opposite:* find.

seek to *v* **try to**, aspire to, endeavour to, aim to, attempt to, strive to. [➡ATTEMPT AN ACTION; 262] *Opposite:* succeed.

seem *v* **appear**, give the impression, seem like, look, look as if, look like. [➡SEEM TO BE SOMETHING; 58]

seeming *adj* **apparent**, outward, ostensible, surface, superficial, to all appearances. [➡FALSE AND UNREAL; 174] *Opposite:* real.

seemingly 1 *adv* **by all acounts**, on the face of it, rumour has it, or so it seems, at first glance, at first sight. [➡EXPRESSIONS OF UNCERTAINTY; 561] 2 *adv* **apparently**, outwardly, ostensibly, superficially. [➡UNCERTAIN; 176] *Opposite:* really.

seemliness *n* [➡MORALLY GOOD; 775]

seemly *adj* **appropriate**, decorous, fitting, fit, decent, proper, becoming, right. [➡APPROPRIATE, SUITABLE, ADVISABLE; 185] *Opposite:* unseemly.

seen better days *adj* [➡IN BAD REPAIR; 1233]

see off 1 *v* **say goodbye to**, bid farewell to, send off, take to the station, take to the airport, go with, accompany. [➡ACCOMPANY AND FOLLOW; 338] *Opposite:* welcome. 2 *v* (*informal*) **get rid of**, get shot of (*informal*), chase off, chase away, force to go, fend off, keep away. [➡GET RID OF SOMETHING; 452] *Opposite:* invite. 3 *v* **defeat**, beat, withstand, fend off, put paid to (*informal*). [➡BEAT AND DEFEAT; 80]

see out 1 *v* **stay**, last, last out, live out, survive, endure. [➡CONTINUE TO EXIST; 17] 2 *v* **show to the door**, show out, accompany, go with, say goodbye to, escort out, escort. [➡ACCOMPANY AND FOLLOW; 338]

seep *v* **leak**, ooze, trickle, dribble, soak, leach, bleed, percolate, escape. [➡LIQUID EMISSION; 371]

seepage *n* **leakage**, leak, outflow, waste, escape, ooze, discharge. [➡EMIT AND EMANATE; 362]

seer *n* **prophet**, soothsayer, clairvoyant, oracle, fortune-teller, psychic. [➡PEOPLE WITH SUPERNATURAL POWERS; 789]

see red (*informal*) *v* **lose your temper**, lose it (*informal*), go berserk, be enraged, fly into a rage, go wild, rage, lose your head, lose your rag (*slang*). [➡GIVING VENT TO EMOTIONS; 680] *Opposite:* calm down.

seesaw *v* **alternate**, go up and down, oscillate, fluctuate, swing. [➡BOUNCE, UNDULATE, AND VIBRATE; 309] *Opposite:* stabilize.

seethe 1 *v* **boil**, bubble, froth, foam, churn. [➡FROTH AND EFFERVESCE; 390] 2 *v* **fume**, rage, be furious, be livid, be hopping mad (*informal*), boil with rage. [➡GIVING VENT TO EMOTIONS; 680] *Opposite:* calm down. 3 *v* **teem**, swarm, be alive with, be crawling with. [➡PROSPER AND ABOUND; 16]

seething 1 *adj* **fuming**, furious, livid, beside yourself, enraged, incensed, apoplectic, irate, hopping mad (*informal*). [➡IRRITATION AND ANGER; 542] *Opposite:* calm. 2 *adj* **boiling**, bubbling, foaming, on the boil, simmering. [➡FLUID AND NON-SOLID; 1212] *Opposite:* still. 3 *adj* **bustling**, busy, frantic, heaving, teeming, packed, crowded, jam-packed (*informal*), full to bursting, bursting at the seams. [➡FULL; 1238] *Opposite:* quiet.

see-through *adj* **transparent**, translucent, sheer, diaphanous, gauzy, filmy. [➡VISUAL TEXTURE; 1220] *Opposite:* opaque.

see through 1 *v* **understand**, get to the bottom of, be wise to, know inside out, read like a book, penetrate, rumble (*informal*). [➡UNDERSTAND AND GRASP; 760] 2 *v* **persevere with**, persist at, stick at, stay with, carry out, finish, continue. [➡CONTINUE AN ACTION; 263] *Opposite:* quit.

see to *v* **deal with**, sort out, handle, take care of, manage, attend to, do. [➡CARRY OUT AN ACTION; 270]

see to it *v* **make sure**, see, ensure, make certain, guarantee. [➡CAUSE TO HAPPEN; 31]

see you (*informal*) *interj* [➡GREETINGS, FAREWELLS, AND SALUTATIONS; 660]

see you later (*informal*) *interj* [➡GREETINGS, FAREWELLS, AND SALUTATIONS; 660]

segment 1 *n* **section**, part, piece, slice, sector, division, subdivision, fragment, portion, bit, wedge. [➡AREA AND RANGE; 111] *Opposite:* whole. 2 *v* **divide**, split, subdivide, section, carve up (*informal*), portion. [➡SEPARATE AND DIVIDE; 402]

segmentation *n* **division**, subdivision, separation, splitting up, dissection, breakdown. [➡SEPARATE AND DIVIDE; 402] *Opposite:* integration.

segregate *v* **separate**, separate out, isolate, ghettoize, keep apart, set apart, set aside. [➡EJECT AND EXCLUDE; 341] *Opposite:* integrate.

segregation *n* **separation**, isolation, exclusion, setting apart, apartheid, seclusion, discrimination, ghettoization. [➡EJECT AND EXCLUDE; 341] *Opposite:* integration.

seismic *adj* [➡VOLCANOES AND EARTHQUAKES; 1054]

seismic activity *n* [➡VOLCANOES AND EARTHQUAKES; 1054]

seismic wave *n* [➡VOLCANOES AND EARTHQUAKES; 1054]

seize 1 *v* **take hold of**, grab, grab hold of, get hold of, snatch, grasp, clutch. [➡CONTACT: HOLD; 412] *Opposite:* relinquish. 2 *v* **appropriate**, confiscate, take away, sequester, remove, take possession of, commandeer. [➡TAKE SOMETHING AWAY; 426] *Opposite:* return. 3 *v* **take control of**, capture, take, take over, annex, overrun, conquer. [➡TAKE SOMETHING AWAY; 426] *Opposite:* lose. 4 *v* **arrest**, capture, take into custody, apprehend, take hostage, snatch, abduct. [➡CAPTIVITY AND LOSS OF FREEDOM; 249] *Opposite:* release. 5 *v* **take advantage of**, grab, jump at, take. [➡GET; 421]

seize up 1 *v* **grind to a halt**, jam, fail, stop working, stall, pack up, conk out (*informal*). [➡FAIL OR CEASE TO FUNCTION; 471] 2 *v* **stiffen**, stiffen up, stop working, freeze up, stick, cramp. [➡FAIL OR CEASE TO FUNCTION; 471]

seizure 1 *n* **attack**, fit, spasm, convulsion. [➡PHYSICAL REACTIONS; 317] 2 *n* **capture**, arrest, abduction, apprehension. [➡CAPTIVITY AND LOSS OF FREEDOM; 249] *Opposite:* release. 3 *n* **appropriation**, confiscation, commandeering, annexation, capture, removal. [➡TAKE SOMETHING AWAY; 426] *Opposite:* return.

seldom *adv* **not often**, hardly ever, rarely, infrequently, occasionally, once in a while. [➡NEVER AND INFREQUENCY; 97] *Opposite:* often.

select 1 *v* **choose**, pick, pick out, decide on, opt for, plump for, go for (*informal*). [➡MAKE DECISIONS AND CHOICES; 753] 2 *adj* **choice**, top quality, first-class, excellent, first-rate, handpicked. [➡SUPERIORITY; 153] *Opposite:* inferior. 3 *adj* **exclusive**, elite, privileged, cliquey, restricted, limited. [➡SUPERIORITY; 153]

selected *adj* **carefully chosen**, designated, nominated, particular, certain, a number of, a selection of. [➡AMOUNT AND QUANTITY; 112] *Opposite:* all.

selection *n* **range**, assortment, collection, choice, variety, miscellany, mixture, medley. [➡COLLECTIONS AND MIXTURES OF THINGS; 1243]

selective *adj* **discerning**, discriminating, discriminatory, choosy (*informal*), careful. [➡POSITIVE INTELLECTUAL CHARACTERISTICS; 525] *Opposite:* indiscriminate.

selectivity *n* **discrimination**, choosiness, fussiness, discernment. [➡POSITIVE INTELLECTUAL CHARACTERISTICS; 525]

selector *n* **chooser**, picker, committee member, jury member, panel member, member of selection panel. [➡SURVEYORS, EXAMINERS, AND JUDGES; 853]

self *n* **personality**, nature, character, identity, person, ego. [➡PSYCHOLOGY AND THE MIND; 770]

self-abasement *n* **humbling**, humiliation, mortification, prostration, crawling (*informal*), eating humble pie, self-effacement. [➡EMBARRASSMENT AND HUMILIATION; 543] *Opposite:* self-aggrandizement.

self-absorbed *adj* **full of yourself**, self-regarding, self-centred, narcissistic, egocentric, egoistic, egotistic, egotistical, selfish. [➡SELFISH AND UNKIND; 506] *Opposite:* considerate.

self-absorption *n* **self-preoccupation**, egotism, egoism, egocentricity, self-centredness, narcissism, self-importance, self-interest, self-regard, selfishness. [➡SELFISH AND UNKIND; 506] *Opposite:* generosity.

self-acting *adj* **self-operating**, automatic, automated, mechanized, mechanical, robotic. [➡DESCRIBING TECHNOLOGY; 1159]

self-admiring *adj* [➡POMPOUS, LOUD, AND OVER-CONFIDENT; 636]

self-aggrandizement *n* **ambition**, self-promotion, self-importance, self-glorification, self-glory, self-flattery, boasting, bragging. [➡BOAST; 617]

self-aggrandizing *adj* [➡POMPOUS, LOUD, AND OVER-CONFIDENT; 636]

self-assertive *adj* **confident**, self-confident, forceful, assured, aggressive, pushy (*informal*), bossy, strong. [➡CONFIDENCE AND COMPOSURE; 500] *Opposite:* timid.

self-assurance *n* **confidence**, self-confidence, self-possession, poise, assurance, composure. [➡CONFIDENCE AND COMPOSURE; 500] *Opposite:* timidity.

self-assured *adj* **confident**, self-confident, poised, assured, self-possessed, sure of yourself, well-balanced. [➡CONFIDENCE AND COMPOSURE; 500] *Opposite:* timid.

self-assuredness *n* [➡CONFIDENCE AND COMPOSURE; 500]

self-centred *adj* **selfish**, self-interested, egocentric, egotistic, egotistical, egoistic, self-absorbed, self-seeking, narcissistic. [➡SELFISH AND UNKIND; 506] *Opposite:* altruistic.

self-centredness *n* **selfishness**, self-interest, egocentricity, egotism, egoism, self-regard, self-absorption, narcissism. [➡SELFISH AND UNKIND; 506] *Opposite:* altruism.

self-coloured *adj* **uniform**, plain, single-colour, unpatterned. [➡DESCRIBING PATTERNS; 1226] *Opposite:* patterned.

self-conceit *n* **smugness**, arrogance, swollen head, boastfulness, conceit, superiority, superciliousness, pride, imperiousness. [➡AFFECTATION, SELF-SATISFACTION, AND SNOBBISHNESS; 508] *Opposite:* modesty.

self-confessed *adj* **admitted**, by your own admission, self-proclaimed, acknowledged, known. [➡TRUE AND REAL; 172] *Opposite:* closet.

self-confidence *n* **confidence**, self-assurance, self-possession, poise, assurance. [➡CONFIDENCE AND COMPOSURE; 500] *Opposite:* insecurity.

self-confident *adj* **confident**, self-assured, self-possessed, poised, assured. [➡CONFIDENCE AND COMPOSURE; 500] *Opposite:* insecure.

self-congratulation *n* **self-satisfaction**, smugness, self-praise, self-glorification, self-flattery, self-love, self-regard. [➡BOAST; 617] *Opposite:* self-hatred.

self-conscious *adj* **ill at ease**, awkward, uncomfortable, embarrassed, insecure, unsure of yourself. [➡INSECURITY AND LOSS OF COMPOSURE; 545] *Opposite:* self-confident.

self-consciousness *n* [➡INSECURITY AND LOSS OF COMPOSURE; 545]

self-contained *adj* **independent**, self-sufficient, self-reliant, autonomous. [➡RELATIONSHIP TO ANOTHER; 973] *Opposite:* dependent.

self-contempt *n* [➡INSECURITY AND LOSS OF COMPOSURE; 545]

self-contradictory *adj* **inconsistent**, self-contradicting, contradictory, illogical, unreasonable, incongruous. [➡DISORDER AND CHAOS; 246] *Opposite:* consistent.

self-control *n* **self-discipline**, discipline, willpower, restraint, strength of mind, strength of will, self-will. [➡STRENGTH OF WILL; 502] *Opposite:* self-indulgence.

self-controlled *adj* [➡STRENGTH OF WILL; 502]

self-critical *adj* **self-deprecatory**, self-deprecating, self-effacing, reticent, humble, modest. [➡NEGATIVE OF OUTLOOK; 515]

self-defence *n* **self-protection**, self-preservation, defence, resistance. [➡SAFE AND SAFETY; 192]

self-denial *n* **abstinence**, abstemiousness, frugality, asceticism, self-discipline, austerity. [➡ABSTEMIOUSNESS AND SELF-DENIAL; 882] *Opposite:* self-indulgence.

self-denying *adj* [➡ABSTEMIOUSNESS AND SELF-DENIAL; 882]

self-deprecating *adj* **self-critical**, self-deprecatory, self-effacing, modest, humble, overly modest, reticent. [➡RETICENT AND UNFORTHCOMING; 632] *Opposite:* boastful.

self-deprecation *n* **self-criticism**, self-depreciation, self-effacement, modesty, humility, reticence, hiding your light under a bushel. [➡RETICENT AND UNFORTHCOMING; 632] *Opposite:* boasting.

self-determination *n* **autonomy**, self-rule, self-government, freedom, independence, sovereignty, free will. [➡STYLES AND SYSTEMS OF GOVERNMENT; 806]

self-discipline *n* **self-control**, discipline, willpower, restraint, strength of mind, strength of will, self-will. [➡STRENGTH OF WILL; 502] *Opposite:* self-indulgence.

self-disciplined *adj* [➡STRENGTH OF WILL; 502]

self-disgust *n* [➡INSECURITY AND LOSS OF COMPOSURE; 545]

self-dislike *n* [➡INSECURITY AND LOSS OF COMPOSURE; 545]

self-doubt *n* **uncertainty**, lack of confidence, insecurity, self-loathing, self-hatred. [➡INSECURITY AND LOSS OF COMPOSURE; 545] *Opposite:* self-confidence.

self-effacing *adj* **modest**, quiet, meek, diffident, unassuming, shy, humble. [➡NATURALNESS; 498] *Opposite:* brash.

self-employed *adj* **freelance**, your own boss, independent, freelancing, entrepreneurial, self-starting. [➡EMPLOYMENT STATUS; 831] *Opposite:* employed.

self-esteem *n* **confidence**, self-confidence, self-worth, sense of worth, self-respect, self-image, self-regard, self-assurance, pride. [➡PSYCHOLOGY AND THE MIND; 770] *Opposite:* insecurity.

self-evident *adj* **obvious**, clear, plain, manifest, undeniable, indisputable, palpable, incontrovertible, explicit. [➡CERTAIN; 175] *Opposite:* unclear.

self-explanatory *adj* **clear**, easy to understand, easy to follow, transparent, understandable, palpable, plain. [➡CONCISE AND CLEAR; 203] *Opposite:* unclear.

self-expression *n* **creativity**, making a statement, assertiveness, individualism, expressing your identity, making yourself heard, expressiveness. [➡COMMUNICATION; 603]

self-fertilization *n* **self-fertilizing**, self-pollination, self-pollinating, autogamy, hermaphroditism, androgyny. [➡REPRODUCTION AND HEREDITY; 726] *Opposite:* cross-fertilization.

self-flattery *n* **self-congratulation**, self-satisfaction, self-praise, self-glorification, self-aggrandizement, self-glory, self-promotion, boasting, bragging, vanity, conceit. [➡BOAST; 617] *Opposite:* self-abasement.

self-glorification *n* **self-promotion**, self-congratulation, self-satisfaction, self-praise, self-flattery, self-aggrandizement, boasting, bragging, vanity, conceit. [➡BOAST; 617] *Opposite:* self-deprecation.

self-governing *adj* **autonomous**, independent, sovereign, self-determining, self-sufficient. [➡STYLES AND SYSTEMS OF GOVERNMENT; 806] *Opposite:* dependent.

self-government *n* **autonomy**, independence, self-governance, sovereignty, self-rule, self-determination, self-sufficiency. [➡STYLES AND SYSTEMS OF GOVERNMENT; 806] *Opposite:* dependence.

self-gratification *n* **self-indulgence**, hedonism, pleasure-seeking, high living, selfishness, pleasure, over-indulgence, intemperance. [➡PLEASURE-SEEKING AND EXCESS; 885] *Opposite:* self-sacrifice.

self-hatred *n* **self-contempt**, self-loathing, self-disgust, self-denigration, self-dislike, self-abasement. [➡INSECURITY AND LOSS OF COMPOSURE; 545] *Opposite:* self-love.

self-help *n* **support**, mutual support, group support, help, counselling, do-it-yourself. [➡PSYCHOLOGY AND THE MIND; 770]

self-help group *n* [➡GROUPS WITH A COMMON INTEREST; 938]

self-image *n* **opinion of yourself**, self-perception, self-esteem, self-regard, self-respect, sense of worth. [➡PSYCHOLOGY AND THE MIND; 770]

self-immolation (*formal*) *n* **suicide**, self-sacrifice, hara-kiri, martyrdom, self-destruction, ultimate sacrifice. [➡CAUSES OF DEATH; 921]

self-importance *n* **arrogance**, pride, haughtiness, pomposity, conceit, bumptiousness, officiousness, swagger, narcissism. [➡POMPOUS, LOUD, AND OVER-CONFIDENT; 636] *Opposite:* humility.

self-important *adj* **arrogant**, pompous, conceited, bumptious, officious, self-opinionated, full of yourself, puffed-up, swaggering. [➡POMPOUS, LOUD, AND OVER-CONFIDENT; 636] *Opposite:* humble.

self-imposed *adj* **chosen**, voluntary, self-inflicted, self-induced, of your own free will. [➡INTENTIONAL AND DELIBERATE; 280] *Opposite:* enforced.

self-incrimination *n* **self-accusation**, self-implication, confession, admission of guilt, self-blame. [➡ADMIT AND CONFESS; 616]

self-indulgence 1 *n* **decadence**, indulgence, hedonism, pleasure, luxury, pleasure-seeking, high living, intemperance. [➡PLEASURE-SEEKING AND EXCESS; 885] *Opposite:* restraint. **2** *n* **abandon**, self-pity, childishness, selfishness, self-centredness, self-absorption. [➡SELFISH AND UNKIND; 506] *Opposite:* restraint.

self-indulgent 1 *adj* **decadent**, indulgent, hedonistic, epicurean, luxurious, pleasure-seeking. [➡PLEASURE-SEEKING AND EXCESS; 885] *Opposite:* restrained. **2** *adj* **abandoned**, self-pitying, wallowing, childish, selfish, self-centred, self-absorbed. [➡SELFISH AND UNKIND; 506] *Opposite:* restrained.

self-interest *n* **selfishness**, self-centredness, egotism, self-regard, egocentricity, self-absorption. [➡SELFISH AND UNKIND; 506] *Opposite:* altruism.

self-interested *adj* **selfish**, self-centred, egocentric, egoistic, egotistic, egotistical, self-absorbed, self-regarding. [➡SELFISH AND UNKIND; 506] *Opposite:* altruistic.

selfish *adj* **self-centred**, self-seeking, self-interested, egotistical, egotistic, egoistic, egocentric, self-regarding, greedy, venal, mercenary. [➡SELFISH AND UNKIND; 506] *Opposite:* selfless.

selfishness *n* **self-centredness**, self-interest, egotism, egoism, egocentricity, egocentrism, self-regard, greediness. [➡SELFISH AND UNKIND; 506] *Opposite:* selflessness.

selfless *adj* **unselfish**, self-sacrificing, altruistic, generous, noble, gallant, self-effacing. [➡GENEROSITY AND KINDNESS; 496] *Opposite:* selfish.

selflessness *n* **unselfishness**, self-sacrifice, altruism, generosity, gallantry, self-abnegation. [➡GENEROSITY AND KINDNESS; 496] *Opposite:* selfishness.

self-loathing *n* [➡INSECURITY AND LOSS OF COMPOSURE; 545]

self-love *n* **egotism**, selfishness, egocentricity, narcissism, egoism, self-centredness, self-interest, self-esteem, self-respect, amour-propre (*formal*), vanity, conceit. [➡SELFISH AND UNKIND; 506] *Opposite:* modesty.

self-motivated *adj* **energetic**, dynamic, go-ahead (*informal*), keen, enthusiastic, driven, committed, forceful, vigorous, ambitious, self-directed, self-starting. [➡ENERGY AND ENTHUSIASM; 497] *Opposite:* unmotivated.

self-obsessed *adj* **self-centred**, egocentric, egocentric, egotistical, narcissistic, self-absorbed, self-seeking. [➡SELFISH AND UNKIND; 506]

self-opinionated 1 *adj* **overconfident**, sure of yourself, cocksure, self-confident, opinionated, pompous, bumptious, arrogant, overbearing, self-opinioned. [➡POMPOUS, LOUD, AND OVER-CONFIDENT; 636] *Opposite:* diffident. **2** *adj* **conceited**, vain, bigheaded (*informal*), full of yourself, self-satisfied, too big for your boots (*informal*), too big for your britches, self-opinioned. [➡BOSSY AND OVERBEARING; 517] *Opposite:* self-deprecating.

self-opinioned *see* **self-opinionated**.

self-pity *n* **self-indulgence**, misery, unhappiness, defeatism, self-absorption, depression. [➡SADNESS, DISTRESS, AND DESPAIR; 540] *Opposite:* cheerfulness.

self-pitying *adj* **self-absorbed**, wallowing, defeatist, sorry for yourself, miserable, melancholic, self-indulgent. [➡SADNESS, DISTRESS, AND DESPAIR; 540] *Opposite:* happy-go-lucky.

self-possessed *adj* **confident**, self-assured, self-confident, assured, poised, well-balanced, sure of yourself. [➡CONFIDENCE AND COMPOSURE; 500] *Opposite:* insecure.

self-possession *n* **confidence**, self-assurance, self-confidence, assurance, poise, composure, coolness. [➡CONFIDENCE AND COMPOSURE; 500] *Opposite:* insecurity.

self-preservation *n* **self-protection**, self-defence, survival, preservation instinct, survival instinct. [➡PSYCHOLOGY AND THE MIND; 770]

self-promotion *n* **self-aggrandizement**, self-importance, self-glorification, self-glory, self-praise, self-flattery, boasting, bragging. [➡BOAST; 617] *Opposite:* self-deprecation.

self-raising flour *type of* **flour**. [➡BREAD, FLOUR, AND BREAD PRODUCTS; 1178]

self-regard 1 *n* **self-interest**, self-centredness, selfishness, egotism, egocentricity, egoism, narcissism, self-absorption. [➡SELFISH AND UNKIND; 506] *Opposite:* altruism. **2** *n*

self-respect, self-esteem, self-worth, dignity, pride, sense of self. [➡CONFIDENCE AND COMPOSURE; 500] *Opposite:* self-hatred.

self-regarding *adj* **selfish**, self-centred, egocentric, egotistical, egotistic, self-absorbed, self-interested, vain, conceited. [➡SELFISH AND UNKIND; 506] *Opposite:* selfless.

self-reliance *n* **independence**, self-sufficiency, autonomy, self-confidence, self-assurance, self-containment, resourcefulness. [➡RELATIONSHIP TO ANOTHER; 973] *Opposite:* dependence.

self-reliant *adj* **independent**, self-sufficient, autonomous, self-confident, self-assured, self-contained, self-starting, resourceful, enterprising. [➡RELATIONSHIP TO ANOTHER; 973] *Opposite:* dependent.

self-reproach *n* **self-criticism**, remorse, contrition, shame, guilt, regret. [➡FEELINGS ABOUT THE PAST; 533] *Opposite:* self-congratulation.

self-respect *n* **self-esteem**, self-confidence, confidence, dignity, pride, self-worth, sense of worth. [➡CONFIDENCE AND COMPOSURE; 500] *Opposite:* self-hatred.

self-restraint *n* **self-control**, self-discipline, discipline, willpower, moderation, restraint. [➡STRENGTH OF WILL; 502] *Opposite:* abandon.

self-righteous (*disapproving*) *adj* **sanctimonious**, smug, self-satisfied, complacent, pious, haughty, supercilious, hoity-toity (*informal*), pompous, hypocritical, pretentious, holier-than-thou (*informal*). [➡AFFECTATION, SELF-SATISFACTION, AND SNOBBISHNESS; 508] *Opposite:* humble.

self-righteousness *n* **sanctimoniousness**, smugness, complacency, piety, superciliousness, haughtiness, pomposity, conceit, self-satisfaction, pretentiousness, hypocrisy. [➡AFFECTATION, SELF-SATISFACTION, AND SNOBBISHNESS; 508] *Opposite:* humility.

self-rule *n* **self-government**, independence, self-determination, autonomy, self-governance, sovereignty. [➡STYLES AND SYSTEMS OF GOVERNMENT; 806] *Opposite:* dependence.

self-sacrifice *n* **altruism**, unselfishness, selflessness, self-denial, martyrdom. [➡GENEROSITY AND KINDNESS; 496] *Opposite:* selfishness.

self-sacrificing *adj* **altruistic**, unselfish, selfless, noble, self-denying. [➡GENEROSITY AND KINDNESS; 496] *Opposite:* selfish.

selfsame *adj* **very same**, identical, very, exact, same. [➡SAMENESS; 151] *Opposite:* different.

self-satisfaction *n* **smugness**, complacency, self-righteousness (*disapproving*), conceit, arrogance, pride, self-assurance, narcissism. [➡AFFECTATION, SELF-SATISFACTION, AND SNOBBISHNESS; 508] *Opposite:* self-doubt.

self-satisfied *adj* **smug**, pleased with yourself, self-righteous (*disapproving*), conceited, arrogant, proud, self-assured, narcissistic, complacent. [➡AFFECTATION, SELF-SATISFACTION, AND SNOBBISHNESS; 508]

self-seeker *n* [➡SELF-IMPORTANT AND SELF-SEEKING PEOPLE; 949]

self-seeking *adj* **selfish**, self-centred, self-regarding, egocentric, egoistic, egotistic, egotistical, self-absorbed, self-interested. [➡SELFISH AND UNKIND; 506] *Opposite:* selfless.

self-service restaurant *type of* **eating place.** [➡HOTELS, RESTAURANTS, AND CLUBS; 1081]

self-serving *adj* **selfish**, egotistic, egotistical, self-centred, narcissistic, egocentric, self-absorbed, self-interested. [➡SELFISH AND UNKIND; 506] *Opposite:* altruistic.

self-starter *n* [➡PEOPLE WHO ARE APPROVED OF; 955]

self-starting *adj* [➡HARD-WORKING AND COMMITTED; 501]

self-styled *adj* **self-appointed**, self-proclaimed, so-called, professed, soi-disant (*literary*), would-be. [➡NAME AND DESCRIBE; 666] *Opposite:* elected.

self-sufficiency *n* **independence**, autonomy, self-reliance, self-support. [➡RELATIONSHIP TO ANOTHER; 973] *Opposite:* dependence.

self-sufficient *adj* **independent**, autonomous, self-reliant, self-supporting, self-financing, self-contained. [➡RELATIONSHIP TO ANOTHER; 973] *Opposite:* dependent.

self-supporting *adj* **self-sufficient**, self-financing, profitable, healthy, successful, self-sustaining, economically viable. [➡ECONOMICAL AND RESOURCEFUL; 208] *Opposite:* struggling.

self-sustaining *adj* [➡PERMANENCE: WITHOUT END; 94]

self-will *n* **determination**, obstinacy, stubbornness, pigheadedness, wilfulness, intransigence, inflexibility. [➡UNWILLINGNESS AND STUBBORNNESS; 565] *Opposite:* weakness.

self-willed *adj* **headstrong**, obstinate, determined, stubborn, pigheaded, wilful. [➡UNWILLINGNESS AND STUBBORNNESS; 565] *Opposite:* weak-willed.

self-worth *n* **self-esteem**, self-respect, self-confidence, pride, dignity, positive self-image, amour-propre (*formal*). [➡PSYCHOLOGY AND THE MIND; 770] *Opposite:* worthlessness.

sell **1** *v* **vend**, flog (*informal*), get rid of, shift (*informal*), wholesale, trade, peddle, retail, hawk, dump, unload. [➡SELL; 442] *Opposite:* buy. **2** *v* **put up for sale**, market, offer, deal in, have, push (*slang*), put on sale, handle. [➡SELL; 442] *Opposite:* buy. **3** *v* **be bought**, go, be snapped up, be popular, be in demand, sell like hotcakes (*US*). [➡SELL; 442] **4** *v* **persuade people to buy**, market, promote, advertise, plug (*informal*), shift (*informal*), turn over. [➡SELL; 442]

seller *n* **vendor**, retailer, wholesaler, supplier, merchant, trader, broker, purveyor (*formal*), dealer, hawker, pedlar. [➡SELLER; 443] *Opposite:* buyer.

selling *n* **vending**, sales, marketing, trade, retailing, export, hawking, peddling. [➡BUSINESS ACTIVITIES AND PHENOMENA; 795] *Opposite:* buying.

sell out **1** *v* **run out**, be out of stock, be snapped up, go, be unavailable. [➡USE UP AND WASTE; 475] *Opposite:* stock up. **2** *v* **give in**, give up, sell your soul, betray your principles, cave in, surrender, deliver up. [➡FAIL OR BE UNSUCCESSFUL; 75]

sellout **1** *n* **box-office hit**, hit, smash hit, smash, best-seller, success, triumph. *Opposite:* flop. (*informal*). [➡SUCCESS; 82] **2** *n* (*informal*) **betrayal**, treachery, disloyalty, apostasy, stab in the back (*informal*), co-option, co-optation. [➡UNKIND ACTION OR BEHAVIOUR; 297] *Opposite:* loyalty. **3** *n*

(*US informal*) **traitor**, opportunist, turncoat, renegade, apostate. [➡ LAZY OR UNSUCCESSFUL PEOPLE; 948] *Opposite:* loyalist.

semantic *adj* [➡ ASPECTS OF LANGUAGE; 683]

semantics *n* [➡ ASPECTS OF LANGUAGE; 683]

semblance **1** *n* **trace**, shred, fragment, measure, modicum, hint. [➡ FEW, LITTLE, SMALL AMOUNT; 119] **2** *n* **appearance**, impression, air, resemblance, façade, veneer, aspect, likeness, look. [➡ APPEARANCE AND ATMOSPHERE; 1236]

semen *n* [➡ EGGS AND SPAWN; 728]

semester *type of* **time period.** [➡ TIMES OF YEAR; 88]

semi *see* **semitrailer.**

semiautomatic *type of* **gun.** [➡ WEAPONS FOR SHOOTING; 1155]

semicircle *type of* **rounded shape.** [➡ ROUNDED SHAPE; 1217]

semicircular *adj* [➡ ROUNDED SHAPE; 1217]

semiconscious *adj* **half-conscious**, half-awake, half-asleep, surfacing, dazed, stunned, knocked out, insensible. [➡ TIRED, ASLEEP AND UNCONSCIOUS; 739]

semidarkness *n* **twilight**, half-light, dusk, dimness, gloom, gloaming (*literary*), shadow, shade, dark. [➡ DESCRIBING LIGHT; 1227]

semidesert *n* [➡ DESERTS AND PLAINS; 1045]

semidetached *type of* **house.** [➡ RESIDENTIAL BUILDINGS; 1077]

semifinal *n* **round**, heat, leg, match, game. [➡ NON-AGGRESSIVE/SPORTING EVENT; 40]

seminal *adj* **influential**, important, formative, pivotal, inspiring, inspirational, groundbreaking, epoch-making, original, germinal (*formal*), creative. [➡ IMPORTANT; 195] *Opposite:* unimportant.

seminal moment *n* [➡ DECISIVE MOMENTS; 44]

seminar **1** *n* **meeting**, session, round table, discussion, conference, assembly, talk, colloquium, forum. [➡ MEETINGS AND ASSEMBLIES; 43] **2** *n* **discussion group**, tutorial, class, evening class, talk, colloquium. [➡ LESSONS, COURSE WORK, AND EXAMINATIONS; 842]

seminary *n* **theological college**, college, training college, academy, institute, school. [➡ EDUCATIONAL INSTITUTIONS; 813]

semiprecious stone *n* [➡ PRECIOUS STONES; 1277]

semitrailer (*US*) *type of* **commercial or industrial vehicle.** [➡ VEHICLES; 1144]

senate *n* **governing body**, legislature, congress, assembly, ruling body, committee, board, council. [➡ LEGISLATIVE BODIES AND LEGISLATION; 809]

senator *n* **senate member**, politician, representative, legislator, congresswoman, congressman, stateswoman, statesman, governor, political figure. [➡ POLITICAL OFFICES AND POLITICIANS; 808]

send **1** *v* **direct**, refer, guide, show, lead, conduct. [➡ ACCOMPANY AND FOLLOW; 338] **2** *v* **post**, transmit, dispatch, forward, convey, remit, send off, send out, relay, mail (*US*). [➡ DESPATCH AND SEND; 334] *Opposite:* receive. **3** *v* **transmit**, project, broadcast, disseminate, give off, emit. [➡ EMIT AND EMANATE; 362] **4** *v* **propel**, hurl, fling, throw, fire, launch, drive, deliver, shoot, cast. [➡ THROW SOMETHING; 335] *Opposite:* bring.

send down **1** *v* **expel**, rusticate, banish, dismiss, send away. [➡ REVOKE STATUS; 460] *Opposite:* enrol. **2** *v* (*slang*) **imprison**, jail, incarcerate (*formal*), put inside (*informal*), lock up, lock away, put away (*informal*), detain, confine. [➡ THE POLICE, ARREST, AND PRE-TRIAL PROCEEDINGS; 818] *Opposite:* release.

send for *v* **request**, summon, call for, order, assemble, gather. [➡ INITIATE AND ESTABLISH COMMUNICATION; 681] *Opposite:* dismiss.

send forth (*archaic or literary*) *v* **produce**, give out, emit, spout, put out, sprout, issue. [➡ EMIT AND EMANATE; 362] *Opposite:* retract.

send off *v* **dispatch**, send, post, send away, transmit, forward, convey, remit, mail (*US*). [➡ DESPATCH AND SEND; 334] *Opposite:* receive.

sendoff *n* **goodbye**, farewell, leave-taking (*literary*), valediction (*formal*), leaving party, leaving do. [➡ END; 54] *Opposite:* welcome.

send on *v* **forward**, redirect, readdress, transfer, pass on, relay. [➡ DESPATCH AND SEND; 334] *Opposite:* return.

send over the edge *v* [➡ UPSET, DISTRESS, AND HUMILIATE; 568]

send packing (*informal*) *v* **dismiss**, discharge (*formal*), expel, evict, turn out, throw out, drive out, send home, send away, banish. [➡ EJECT AND EXCLUDE; 341] *Opposite:* welcome.

send to Coventry *v* **ostracize**, ignore, freeze out, exclude, boycott, blackball. [➡ REFUSING OR REJECTING RELATIONS; 975]

sendup (*informal*) *n* **parody**, lampoon, takeoff, skit, imitation, impersonation, caricature, mockery, satire, spoof, burlesque. [➡ JOKES AND TEASING; 675]

send up **1** *v* **raise**, elevate, heighten, boost, augment (*formal*), bump up (*informal*). [➡ MOVE SOMETHING: UPWARDS; 329] *Opposite:* lower. **2** *v* (*informal*) **lampoon**, satirize, mock, parody, mimic, take off (*informal*), impersonate, ape, make fun of, burlesque, caricature, ridicule. [➡ JOKES AND TEASING; 675]

See Compare and Contrast at **ridicule.**

send your apologies *v* [➡ APOLOGIZE AND RETRACT; 684]

senile *adj* **confused**, disorientated, forgetful, failing, absent-minded, doddering, senescent. [➡ ECCENTRICITY AND IRRATIONALITY; 563]

senior **1** *adj* **older**, elder, oldest, eldest, first-born. [➡ OLD, OLD-FASHIONED; 168] *Opposite:* junior. **2** *n* **elder**, first-born, elder sibling, big brother, big sister. [➡ SAME GENERATION RELATIVES; 957] *Opposite:* junior. **3** *adj* **high-ranking**, high-grade, superior, higher, leading, chief, major, primary, above, over. [➡ CLASS STATUS; 889] *Opposite:* junior. **4** *n* (*US*) **senior citizen**, pensioner, OAP, golden ager (*US*), retired person. [➡ OLD PERSON; 920] **5** *n* **boss**, superior, chief, manager, leader, director, higher-up (*informal*), high-up (*informal*), head. [➡ BOSSES AND MANAGEMENT; 965] *Opposite:* junior.

senior citizen *n* **pensioner**, OAP, retired person, senior, golden ager (*US*). [➡ OLD PERSON; 920]

seniority *n* **superiority**, supremacy, precedence, priority, position, tenure, rank. [➡ SUPERIORITY; 153]

sensation 1 *n* **feeling**, sense, impression, awareness, consciousness, perception, responsiveness. [➡ THE SENSES; 697] *Opposite:* numbness. 2 *n* **commotion**, stir, fuss, uproar, rumpus, ruckus, to-do (*informal*), thrill, buzz (*informal*). [➡ CHAOS AND UPROAR; 51] *Opposite:* lull. 3 *n* **phenomenon**, miracle, wonder, marvel, spectacle, runaway success. [➡ AMAZING THING; 212]

sensational 1 *adj* **extraordinary**, dramatic, astonishing, unbelievable, historic, memorable. [➡ EXTRAORDINARY: UNCOMMON; 206] *Opposite:* predictable. 2 *adj* (*informal*) **amazing**, astounding, marvellous, exciting, thrilling, breathtaking, out of this world, magnificent, incredible, striking, spectacular, remarkable. [➡ EXTRAORDINARY: AMAZING; 205] *Opposite:* boring. 3 *adj* **startling**, shocking, scandalous, melodramatic, lurid, sensationalist, exaggerated. [➡ IN POOR TASTE; 230] *Opposite:* understated.

sensationalism *n* **exaggeration**, overstatement, luridness, scandal, melodrama, shock tactics. [➡ IN POOR TASTE; 230] *Opposite:* understatement.

sensationalist *adj* **startling**, shocking, scandalous, melodramatic, lurid, sensational. [➡ IN POOR TASTE; 230] *Opposite:* understated.

sense 1 *n* **feeling**, sensation, awareness, perception. [➡ THE SENSES; 697] 2 *n* **appreciation**, impression, consciousness, awareness, feeling, perception. [➡ FEELINGS; 532] 3 *n* **intelligence**, brains, intellect, wisdom, sagacity, common sense, nous (*informal*), logic, good judgment. [➡ DESCRIBING SOMEBODY'S INTELLECT; 524] *Opposite:* folly. 4 *n* **purpose**, point, reason, function, end, advantage. [➡ INTENTION AND PURPOSE; 773] 5 *n* **opinion**, view, viewpoint, consensus, mood, feeling. [➡ POINT OF VIEW; 768] 6 *n* **gist**, substance, drift, nub, idea, essence. [➡ MEANING; 691] 7 *n* **meaning**, denotation, significance, signification, implication, connotation. [➡ MEANING; 691] 8 *v* **perceive**, feel, have a feeling, get the impression, discern, be aware of. [➡ USING THE SENSES; 698] *Opposite:* observe. 9 *v* **intuit**, guess, suspect, pick up, feel, feel in your bones, infer. [➡ UNDERSTAND AND GRASP; 760] 10 *v* **detect**, identify, distinguish, recognize, know, pick up. [➡ DEVELOP THEORIES AND REASON; 745]

senseless 1 *adj* **stupid**, silly, foolish, mindless, idiotic, inane, mad. [➡ BIZARRE AND PECULIAR; 258] *Opposite:* sensible. 2 *adj* **unconscious**, comatose, numb, deadened, knocked out, passed out, insensible. [➡ TIRED, ASLEEP AND UNCONSCIOUS; 739] *Opposite:* conscious. 3 *adj* **pointless**, ridiculous, absurd, meaningless, futile, vain, nonsensical, useless, irrational. [➡ REDUNDANT AND USELESS; 241] *Opposite:* worthwhile.

senselessness 1 *n* **stupidity**, silliness, foolishness, madness, idiocy, inanity, mindlessness. [➡ BIZARRE AND PECULIAR; 258] *Opposite:* sense. 2 *n* **pointlessness**, ridiculousness, absurdity, irrationality, meaninglessness, futility, uselessness. [➡ REDUNDANT AND USELESS; 241]

sense of humour *n* [➡ CHEERFULNESS OF OUTLOOK; 504]

sense of taste *n* [➡ TASTE; 704]

senses *n* [➡ THE SENSES; 697]

sensibility *n* **responsiveness**, deep feeling, emotional response, receptivity, susceptibility, feeling, awareness. [➡ FEELINGS; 532] *Opposite:* insensitivity.

sensible 1 *adj* **level-headed**, sane, rational, reasonable, shrewd, wise, sagacious (*formal*), prudent, judicious. [➡ POSITIVE INTELLECTUAL CHARACTERISTICS; 525] *Opposite:* foolish. 2 *adj* **practical**, serviceable, workable, functional, utilitarian, no-nonsense. [➡ USEFULNESS; 200] *Opposite:* impractical. 3 *adj* (*formal*) **aware**, conscious, cognizant (*formal*), mindful. [➡ WIDE AWAKE AND CONSCIOUS; 736]

See Compare and Contrast at **aware**.

sensibleness *n* **rationality**, level-headedness, reasonableness, shrewdness, wisdom, sagacity, prudence, judiciousness. [➡ POSITIVE INTELLECTUAL CHARACTERISTICS; 525] *Opposite:* foolishness.

sensibly *adv* **level-headedly**, rationally, reasonably, wisely, shrewdly, sagaciously (*formal*), sagely (*literary*), prudently, judiciously. [➡ POSITIVE INTELLECTUAL CHARACTERISTICS; 525] *Opposite:* foolishly.

sensitive 1 *adj* **responsive**, receptive, susceptible, aware, perceptive, impressionable. [➡ POSITIVE INTELLECTUAL CHARACTERISTICS; 525] *Opposite:* indifferent. 2 *adj* **delicate**, irritable, susceptible, allergic, difficult, problematic. [➡ WEAKNESS; 242] *Opposite:* robust. 3 *adj* **subtle**, delicate, complex, searching, penetrating, profound. [➡ THE NATURE OF IDEAS; 772] *Opposite:* superficial. 4 *adj* **thoughtful**, sympathetic, understanding, perceptive, considerate, caring. [➡ GENEROSITY AND KINDNESS; 496] *Opposite:* unsympathetic. 5 *adj* **thin-skinned**, easily upset, easily hurt, hypersensitive, vulnerable, touchy. [➡ EXCESSIVE SENSITIVITY; 512] *Opposite:* impervious. 6 *adj* **awkward**, tricky, difficult, sticky, delicate, embarrassing. [➡ EMOTIONALLY UNPLEASANT AND UPSETTING; 228] *Opposite:* straightforward. 7 *adj* **secret**, confidential, classified, top secret, hush-hush (*informal*), restricted. [➡ SECRET AND UNKNOWN; 180] *Opposite:* public. 8 *adj* **precise**, exact, delicate, finely tuned, responsive. [➡ EXACT; 204] *Opposite:* imprecise.

sensitively *adv* **thoughtfully**, sympathetically, delicately, perceptively, considerately, caringly, with sensitivity. [➡ POSITIVE INTELLECTUAL CHARACTERISTICS; 525] *Opposite:* unsympathetically.

sensitivity *n* **compassion**, sympathy, understanding, kindliness, warmth, feeling, thoughtfulness. [➡ GENEROSITY AND KINDNESS; 496] *Opposite:* indifference.

sensitize 1 *v* **alert**, make aware, inform, explain, brief, warn, prepare. [➡ INFORM AND ANNOUNCE; 612] *Opposite:* desensitize. 2 *v* **expose**, make sensitive, trigger, induce, provoke, set off. [➡ CAUSE TO HAPPEN; 31] *Opposite:* desensitize.

sensor *n* **device**, measuring device, instrument, radar, beam, feeler, antenna. [➡ DEVICES; 1114]

sensual 1 *adj* **sexual**, erotic, voluptuous, fleshly, carnal, sexy. [➡ PHYSICALLY PLEASANT; 187] *Opposite:* ascetic. 2 *adj* **sensory**, carnal, bodily, physical, corporeal, fleshly, animal. [➡ LIVING THINGS AND LIVING; 976] *Opposite:* intellectual.

sensualist *n* [➡ PLEASURE-SEEKERS AND HEDONISTS; 886]

sensuous *adj* **sumptuous**, opulent, rich, deep, intense, voluptuous, lush, luxurious. [➡PHYSICALLY PLEASANT; 187] *Opposite:* ascetic.

sentence 1 *n* **judgment**, verdict, ruling, decree, condemnation, punishment, prison term, stretch. [➡TRIAL, PUNISHMENT, AND LEGAL OUTCOMES; 819] 2 *v* **pass judgment**, condemn, punish, send to prison, pronounce judgment on, penalize. [➡TRIAL, PUNISHMENT, AND LEGAL OUTCOMES; 819] *Opposite:* acquit. 3 *type of* **grammatical term**. [➡ASPECTS OF LANGUAGE; 683]

sentence structure *n* [➡ASPECTS OF LANGUAGE; 683]

sententious *adj* **moralizing**, moralistic, judgmental, critical, censorious, disapproving. [➡ACCUSATORY AND DISAPPROVING; 635] *Opposite:* approving.

sentience *n* [➡KNOWLEDGE AND WISDOM; 559]

sentient 1 *adj* **conscious**, animate, flesh-and-blood, alive, living, live, breathing, aware, alert. [➡LIVING THINGS AND LIVING; 976] *Opposite:* inanimate. 2 *adj* **emotional**, responsive, sensitive, perceptive, feeling, sentimental. [➡POSITIVE INTELLECTUAL CHARACTERISTICS; 525] *Opposite:* intellectual.

sentiment 1 *n* **feeling**, emotion, response, reaction, attitude, opinion, outlook. [➡FEELINGS; 532] 2 *n* **sentimentality**, mawkishness, gush, corn (*informal*), soppiness (*informal*), romanticism. [➡IN POOR TASTE; 230]

sentimental *adj* **mawkish**, romantic, soppy (*informal*), slushy, gushy, maudlin, syrupy, emotional, corny, sloppy (*informal*), schmaltzy (*informal*). [➡IN POOR TASTE; 230] *Opposite:* cynical.

sentimentality *n* **mawkishness**, soppiness (*informal*), sloppiness (*informal*), corniness, slushiness, romanticism, schmaltziness (*informal*). [➡IN POOR TASTE; 230] *Opposite:* cynicism.

sentimentalize *v* **gush**, emotionalize, romanticize, wax lyrical (*literary*). [➡DREAM, IMAGINE, AND FANTASIZE; 750]

sentinel *n* **sentry**, lookout, guard, watch, watchman, custodian, patrol. [➡PEOPLE WHO GUARD AND PROTECT; 846]

sentry *n* **guard**, sentinel, patrol, lookout, watch, watchman, custodian. [➡PEOPLE WHO GUARD AND PROTECT; 846]

sentry box *type of* **outbuilding**. [➡ANCILLARY BUILDINGS; 1079]

separable *adj* **divisible**, distinguishable, detachable, discrete, separate, independent. [➡UNRELATEDNESS AND SEPARATENESS; 147] *Opposite:* inseparable.

separate 1 *adj* **unconnected**, individual, independent, unattached, autonomous, solitary. [➡RELATIONSHIP TO ANOTHER; 973] *Opposite:* connected. 2 *adj* **distinct**, discrete, detached, dispersed, isolated, single. [➡UNRELATEDNESS AND SEPARATENESS; 147] *Opposite:* attached. 3 *v* **split up**, split, divorce, part, part company, become estranged. [➡REFUSING OR REJECTING RELATIONS; 975] *Opposite:* marry. 4 *v* **divide**, part, disconnect, undo, split, split up, break up, take apart, detach. [➡SEPARATE AND DIVIDE; 402] *Opposite:* unite. 5 *v* **break away**, secede, branch out, break free, break, split up, withdraw, pull out. [➡ABSENT ONESELF; 8] *Opposite:* join.

separately 1 *adv* **unconnectedly**, independently, alone, individually, singly, one by one, on their own. [➡ACTING INDEPENDENTLY; 285] *Opposite:* together. 2 *adv* **distinctly**, unconnectedly, disjointedly, discretely. [➡UNRELATEDNESS AND SEPARATENESS; 147] *Opposite:* together.

separateness *n* **distinction**, disconnectedness, separation, distinctiveness, difference, discreteness. [➡DIFFERENCE; 150]

separate off *v* **divide**, divide off, split off, detach, sever, set apart, set aside, keep apart, isolate, segregate. [➡SEPARATE AND DIVIDE; 402]

separate out *v* **strain**, filter, pass through a filter, sieve, extract. *Opposite:* cohere. (*formal*). [➡SEPARATE AND DIVIDE; 402]

separation 1 *n* **parting**, departure, leave-taking (*literary*), goodbye, farewell. [➡END; 54] *Opposite:* meeting. 2 *n* **division**, severance, taking apart, partition, disjunction, disconnection. [➡SEPARATE AND DIVIDE; 402] *Opposite:* unification. 3 *n* **split-up**, split, divorce, estrangement, rift, parting. [➡END; 54] *Opposite:* marriage.

separatist *n* **dissenter**, secessionist, protester, rebel, freedom fighter, separationist. [➡UNCOOPERATIVE OR REBELLIOUS PERSON; 567]

separator 1 *n* **divider**, barrier, partition, dividing wall, screen, wedge. [➡WALLS AND PARTITIONS; 1103] 2 *n* **sieve**, strainer, filter, extractor, centrifuge. [➡PARTS OF MACHINES AND TOOLS; 1117] *Opposite:* blender.

septet *type of* **band**. [➡MUSICIANS AND SINGERS; 908]

septic *adj* **poisoned**, infected, festering, gangrenous, diseased, putrefying. [➡SICKNESS; 730] *Opposite:* healthy.

septic tank *n* [➡CONTAINERS, RECEPTACLES, AND PACKAGING; 1244]

sepulchral *adj* **funereal**, sombre, sad, dismal, melancholy, gloomy. [➡EMOTIONALLY UNPLEASANT AND UPSETTING; 228] *Opposite:* cheery.

sepulchre *n* **vault**, tomb, grave, crypt, burial chamber, mausoleum, resting place. [➡BURIAL PLACES AND ACCESSORIES; 930]

sequel 1 *n* **consequence**, development, result, outcome, upshot, effect. [➡RESULTS AND OUTCOMES; 83] *Opposite:* prelude. 2 *n* **follow-on**, continuation, conclusion, follow-up. [➡AFTER, LAST, AND FOLLOWING; 166] *Opposite:* prequel.

sequence 1 *n* **series**, succession, run, progression, chain, string, cycle. [➡CHAIN OF EVENTS; 163] 2 *n* **order**, arrangement, classification, categorization, system, structure. [➡COLLECTIONS AND MIXTURES OF THINGS; 1243] *Opposite:* disarray.

sequence of events *n* [➡EVENTS AND OCCURRENCES; 35]

sequential 1 *adj* **in sequence**, consecutive, in order, successive, chronological, serial, progressive. [➡CHAIN OF EVENTS; 163] *Opposite:* jumbled. 2 *adj* **consequent**, resulting, resultant, ensuing, following, subsequent. [➡AFTER, LAST, AND FOLLOWING; 166] *Opposite:* previous.

sequentially *adv* **in sequence**, in succession, successively, in order, consecutively, one after another, serially, chronologically, one after the other. [➡AFTER, LAST, AND FOLLOWING; 166] *Opposite:* out of order.

sequester 1 *v* (*formal*) **isolate**, separate, segregate, cut off, set apart, keep apart, insulate, quarantine. [➡SEPARATE AND DIVIDE; 402] 2 *v* **confiscate**, requisition, appropriate, impound, seize, repossess. [➡TAKE SOMETHING AWAY; 426] *Opposite:* restore.

sequestered (*formal*) *adj* [➡SECRET AND UNKNOWN; 180]

sequestrate *v* **confiscate**, seize, appropriate, repossess, impound, take, requisition. [➡TAKE SOMETHING AWAY; 426] *Opposite:* release.

sequestration *n* **confiscation**, appropriation, impounding, seizure, requisitioning, repossession. [➡TAKE SOMETHING AWAY; 426] *Opposite:* restoration.

sequin *n* **spangle**, bead, bauble, star, decoration, trimming. [➡ORNAMENTS AND DECORATIONS; 1247]

sequoia *type of* **evergreen tree**. [➡EVERGREEN AND CONIFEROUS TREES; 1029]

seraph *n* [➡RELIGIOUS CONCEPTS; 777]

serenade *v* **sing**, croon, court, entertain, divert, regale. [➡MUSIC, SONGS, AND SINGING; 907]

serendipity *n* **fate**, destiny, karma, providence, luck, fortune, coincidence, accident, kismet, chance. [➡LUCK; 784] *Opposite:* design.

serene 1 *adj* **tranquil**, calm, peaceful, still, quiet, placid. [➡PEACEFULNESS AND GENTLENESS; 215] *Opposite:* bustling. 2 *adj* **calm**, composed, unruffled, cool, unflustered, laid-back (*informal*). [➡CALMNESS, CONFIDENCE, AND COMPOSURE; 537] *Opposite:* agitated.

serenely *adv* **calmly**, placidly, peacefully, coolly, quietly, tranquilly. [➡CALMNESS, CONFIDENCE, AND COMPOSURE; 537] *Opposite:* agitatedly.

serenity 1 *n* **tranquillity**, calmness, peacefulness, quietude, quietness, stillness. [➡PEACEFULNESS AND GENTLENESS; 215] *Opposite:* bustle. 2 *n* **composure**, coolness, poise, equanimity, contentment, repose, mellowness. [➡CALMNESS, CONFIDENCE, AND COMPOSURE; 537] *Opposite:* panic.

serial *adj* **sequential**, successive, consecutive, ongoing, in order, in sequence. [➡AFTER, LAST, AND FOLLOWING; 166] *Opposite:* out of order.

series *n* **sequence**, succession, run, chain, string, cycle, progression. [➡CHAIN OF EVENTS; 163]

series of events *n* [➡EVENTS AND OCCURRENCES; 35]

serious 1 *adj* **dangerous**, acute, life-threatening, critical, severe, worrying. [➡DANGEROUS; 237] *Opposite:* minor. 2 *adj* **important**, momentous, significant, crucial, vital, critical, considerable, major, fundamental. [➡IMPORTANT; 195] *Opposite:* trivial. 3 *adj* **thought-provoking**, meaningful, intense, deep, profound, powerful. [➡THE NATURE OF IDEAS; 772] *Opposite:* lightweight. 4 *adj* **thoughtful**, grave, solemn, sombre, stern, grim, severe, staid, sober, unsmiling, quiet, serious-minded, humourless. [➡NEGATIVE OF OUTLOOK; 515] *Opposite:* lighthearted. 5 *adj* **earnest**, sincere, genuine, honest, resolute, decided, determined. [➡HONEST AND OPEN; 631] *Opposite:* flippant.

seriously 1 *adv* **badly**, dangerously, critically, fatally, acutely, gravely. [➡CRITICALLY AND SERIOUSLY; 132] *Opposite:* slightly. 2 *adv* **earnestly**, truly, sincerely, genuinely, honestly, really. [➡HONEST AND RELIABLE; 503] *Opposite:* jokingly. 3 *adv* (*informal*) **extremely**, very, really, totally, utterly, completely. [➡TO A GREAT EXTENT; 130]

serious-minded *adj* **earnest**, sensible, sedate, steady, determined, resolute, serious. [➡POSITIVE INTELLECTUAL CHARACTERISTICS; 525] *Opposite:* frivolous.

seriousness 1 *n* **importance**, significance, gravity, weightiness, momentousness, solemnity, urgency. [➡IMPORTANCE AND SIGNIFICANCE; 193] *Opposite:* triviality. 2 *n* **earnestness**, sincerity, genuineness, honesty, resoluteness, determination. [➡HONEST AND RELIABLE; 503] *Opposite:* flippancy.

sermon 1 *n* **talk**, address, homily, discourse, oration, lecture. [➡RELIGIONS AND RELIGIOUS PRACTICES; 778] *Opposite:* conversation. 2 *n* **talking-to** (*informal*), homily, harangue, telling-off (*informal*), ticking-off (*informal*), lecture. [➡CRITICISMS AND ANGRY OUTBURSTS; 50] *Opposite:* praise.

sermonize *v* **preach**, pontificate, moralize, hold forth, lecture, harangue. [➡INSTRUCT AND TEACH; 610] *Opposite:* flatter.

serpent 1 *n* **traitor**, liar, cheat, sneak, troublemaker, snake in the grass, schemer. [➡PEOPLE WHO DECEIVE; 662] *Opposite:* friend. 2 *n* (*literary*) **snake**, sea serpent, sea snake. [➡SNAKE; 995]

serpentine *adj* **winding**, meandering, twisting, bending, roundabout, circuitous, indirect. [➡DIRECTION OF MOTION; 346] *Opposite:* straight.

serrated *adj* **jagged**, toothed, notched, ragged, saw-toothed. [➡ANGULAR SHAPE; 1216] *Opposite:* smooth.

servant *n* **domestic**, retainer, help. [➡WORKER; 836] *Opposite:* employer.

servant

◆ *types of servant*
butler, chambermaid, cleaner, cook, factotum, flunky, footman, lackey, maid, maidservant, major-domo, valet

serve 1 *v* **supply**, dish up, serve up, hand out, hand round, give out, dole out (*informal*), provide, distribute. [➡DISPENSE, RATION, AND DISTRIBUTE; 435] 2 *v* **wait on**, wait at table, wait, attend, tend, minister. [➡WORK-RELATED ACTIVITIES; 834] 3 *v* **function**, work, operate, act, perform, behave. [➡FUNCTION SUCCESSFULLY; 470] 4 *v* **work for**, help, aid, attend, assist, oblige. [➡HELP; 294]

server *type of* **hardware**. [➡COMPUTERS AND COMPUTING; 1126]

service 1 *n* **help**, assistance, use, benefit, advantage, good turn. [➡KIND ACTION OR BEHAVIOUR; 296] *Opposite:* disservice. 2 *n* **facility**, provision, package, deal, amenity. [➡USEFULNESS; 200] 3 *n* **ceremony**, ritual, rite, sacrament, mass, observance. [➡RELIGIONS AND RELIGIOUS PRACTICES; 778] 4 *n* **overhaul**, examination, check, once-over (*informal*), tune-up, maintenance. [➡REPAIR AND MEND; 377] 5 *v* **repair**, overhaul, examine, tune, check, retune. [➡REPAIR AND MEND; 377]

serviceable 1 *adj* **durable**, hard-wearing, strong, stout, tough, sturdy. [➡STRENGTH; 202] *Opposite:* flimsy. 2 *adj* **working**, operative, functional, in working order, usable, workable. [➡IN GOOD REPAIR; 1231] *Opposite:* broken. 3 *adj* **effect-**

ive, helpful, practical, useful, utilitarian, convenient, efficient. [➡USEFULNESS; 200] *Opposite:* impractical.

service for the dead *n* [➡BURIAL AND PREPARATION FOR BURIAL; 929]

service provider *n* [➡THE INTERNET; 1127]

services 1 *n* **service station**, motorway facilities, motorway service station, service area, filling station, facilities, amenities, rest area, gas station (*US*), rest stop (*US*). [➡RETAIL OUTLETS; 1082] **2** *n* **service industries**, service sector, service jobs, customer services. [➡BUSINESS PRODUCTS; 796] *Opposite:* manufacturing. **3** *n* **public amenities**, civic amenities, amenities, public services, council services, essential services, local services. [➡SOCIAL WELFARE; 812] **4** *n* **armed forces**, forces, military, armed services, security forces, defence. [➡THE ARMED FORCES; 827]

service station *type of* **retail outlet.** [➡RETAIL OUTLETS; 1082]

servile *adj* **submissive**, fawning, subservient, sycophantic, obsequious, grovelling, toadying. [➡INGRATIATING; 639] *Opposite:* proud.

servility *n* [➡INGRATIATING; 639]

serving *n* **portion**, helping, plateful, ration, quota, allocation. [➡AMOUNT AND QUANTITY; 112]

serving dish *n* **platter**, salver, plate, tray, dish. [➡TABLEWARE, CUTLERY, AND KITCHENWARE; 861]

serving spoon *type of* **cutlery.** [➡TABLEWARE, CUTLERY, AND KITCHENWARE; 861]

servitude 1 *n* **slavery**, bondage, serfdom, enslavement, vassalage, thraldom. [➡CAPTIVITY AND LOSS OF FREEDOM; 249] *Opposite:* freedom. **2** *n* **subjection**, subjugation, subordination, dependence, dependency, subservience. [➡RELATIONSHIP TO ANOTHER; 973] *Opposite:* liberty.

sesame oil *type of* **cooking fat and oil.** [➡FATS AND OILS; 1172]

session 1 *n* **meeting**, sitting, assembly, conference, gathering, hearing. [➡MEETINGS AND ASSEMBLIES; 43] **2** *n* **term**, period, semester, trimester, year, academic year. [➡LESSONS, COURSE WORK, AND EXAMINATIONS; 842] **3** *n* **shift**, stint, go, spell, phase, turn. [➡PERIOD OF TIME; 90]

set 1 *v* **put**, place, locate, position, situate (*formal*), deposit, lay down, rest, plonk, plunk, park (*slang*). [➡POSITION SOMETHING; 326] *Opposite:* pick up. **2** *v* **establish**, fix, agree, appoint, decide, settle on, arrange. [➡MAKE DECISIONS AND CHOICES; 753] *Opposite:* change. **3** *v* **adjust**, regulate, synchronize, align, programme, calibrate, tune. [➡CHANGE; 373] **4** *v* **become hard**, harden, go hard, solidify, congeal, coagulate, gel. [➡HARDEN, CONGEAL, DRY; 388] *Opposite:* liquefy. **5** *adj* **established**, usual, customary, traditional, conventional, agreed, fixed, regular, arranged, prearranged, normal. [➡ORDER AND ORGANISATION; 207] *Opposite:* changing. **6** *adj* **inflexible**, obstinate, determined, resolute, resolved, rigid, stubborn, unbending, hardheaded, unyielding, set in your ways. [➡UNWILLINGNESS AND STUBBORNNESS; 565] *Opposite:* flexible. **7** *adj* **ready**, prepared, fit, primed, organized, geared up. [➡ORDER AND ORGANISATION; 207] *Opposite:* unprepared. **8** *adj* **firm**, congealed, solid, hard, frozen. [➡DENSITY AND CONSISTENCY; 1206] *Opposite:* liquid. **9** *n* **scenery**, stage set, film set, setting, location, backdrop. [➡IN THE THEATRE; 906] **10** *n* **collection**, group, arrangement, array, series, suite. [➡COLLECTIONS AND MIXTURES OF THINGS; 1243] *Opposite:* individual. **11** *n* **circle**, group, clique, gang, crowd. [➡FRIENDS AND ACQUAINTANCES; 936] **12** *see* **sett.**

set about *v* **begin**, tackle, start, launch into, get down to, make a start. [➡START AN ACTION; 261]

set against 1 *v* **compare**, contrast, consider, set side by side, oppose, juxtapose. [➡EXAMINE AND ASSESS; 754] **2** *v* **pit against**, turn against, set as rivals, set in opposition, alienate, disaffect, make unfriendly, estrange. [➡ACCUSE, BLAME, AND CRITICIZE; 642] *Opposite:* bring together.

set alight *v* **kindle**, light, ignite, set light to, set fire to, set on fire, put a match to, burn. [➡FIRE, FLAMMABILITY, AND BURNING; 1164] *Opposite:* put out.

set apart 1 *v* **reserve**, put aside, keep on one side, set aside, separate, keep apart, isolate, sequester (*formal*). [➡STORE AND KEEP; 454] **2** *v* **distinguish**, differentiate, single out, make something stand out, mark out, isolate, identify, characterize, typify, pinpoint. [➡DIFFERENCE; 150]

set aside 1 *v* **reserve**, save, keep back, put to one side, lay by, leave behind. [➡STORE AND KEEP; 454] *Opposite:* use up. **2** *v* **forget**, break free from, shake off, reject, dismiss, put on the back burner. [➡FORGET, FORGIVE, AND ACCEPT; 749]

set back *v* **delay**, hinder, hold up, impede, slow down, retard, arrest. [➡DELAY ACTION OR OCCURRENCE; 279] *Opposite:* facilitate.

setback *n* **hindrance**, holdup, delay, impediment, stumbling block, obstruction, obstacle. [➡PROBLEM; 257] *Opposite:* boost.

set down 1 *v* **put down**, lay down, place, deposit, put, plonk, plunk. [➡MOVE SOMETHING: DOWNWARDS; 330] **2** *v* **write down**, report, record, chronicle, write out, transcribe, draft, set forth (*formal*). [➡RECORD SOMETHING; 372]

set eyes on *v* [➡SEE; 700]

set fire to *v* **kindle**, light, ignite, set light to, set alight, set on fire, put a match to, burn. [➡FIRE, FLAMMABILITY, AND BURNING; 1164] *Opposite:* put out.

set foot in *v* **enter**, go in, come into, show your face, turn up, show up (*informal*). [➡ARRIVE; 12]

set forth 1 *v* (*formal*) **state**, describe, express, lay down, present, submit, propose, lay out, set down. [➡EXPLAIN AND CLARIFY; 611] **2** *v* (*literary*) **leave**, depart, set out, set off, start out, head off, go. [➡ABSENT ONESELF; 8]

set free 1 *v* **liberate**, free, release, discharge, deliver (*literary*), let go, let out, emancipate. [➡FREEDOM AND LIBERTY; 209] *Opposite:* imprison. **2** *v* **untie**, unloose, unshackle, unleash, let loose, unfetter. [➡UNFASTEN AND UNDO; 410] *Opposite:* tie up.

set in *v* **come to stay**, be here to stay, take root, become established, become entrenched, continue. [➡CONTINUE TO EXIST; 17] *Opposite:* pass.

set in motion *v* **start**, initiate, begin, kick-start, set off, trigger, activate, set up, cause, start off. [➡CAUSE TO START; 266] *Opposite:* set in motion.

set in train *v* [➡CAUSE TO HAPPEN; 31]

set light to *v* [➡FIRE, FLAMMABILITY, AND BURNING; 1164]

set of circumstances *n* [➡SITUATIONS; 71]

set off 1 *v* **start out**, set out, begin, leave, get going, hit the road, head out. [➡ABSENT ONESELF; 8] *Opposite:* finish. 2 *v* **detonate**, explode, light, ignite, trigger, let off, arm, blow up, fire. [➡CAUSE TO START; 266] *Opposite:* defuse. 3 *v* **start**, begin, commence (*formal*), start off, burst out, break into, embark on. [➡START AN ACTION; 261] 4 *v* **initiate**, instigate, launch, inaugurate, begin, start, introduce. [➡CAUSE TO START; 266] 5 *v* **draw attention to**, display, bring out, highlight, enhance, show to advantage, emphasize. [➡CAUSE TO APPEAR; 5]

set on *v* **attack**, set upon, assault, lay into, terrorize, beat up (*informal*). [➡PHYSICAL ATTACK AND PUNISHMENT; 416]

set on fire *v* [➡FIRE, FLAMMABILITY, AND BURNING; 1164]

set out 1 *v* **leave**, set off, depart, go, move off, start out, head off, set forth (*literary*). [➡ABSENT ONESELF; 8] 2 *v* **embark on**, start, begin, commence (*formal*), set off, start off. [➡START AN ACTION; 261] 3 *v* **plan**, aim, intend, determine, design. [➡ATTEMPT AN ACTION; 262] 4 *v* **display**, lay out, arrange, present, show, exhibit. [➡CAUSE TO APPEAR; 5] 5 *v* **explain**, specify, define, describe, detail, give particulars of, give an account of, outline, elaborate, illustrate. [➡EXPLAIN AND CLARIFY; 611]

set phrase *n* **expression**, phrase, idiom, turn of phrase, saying, stock phrase, formula, cliché, term. [➡FIGURES OF SPEECH; 674]

set right *v* **correct**, rectify, right, put right, put to rights, sort out, put on the right track. [➡EXPLAIN AND CLARIFY; 611] *Opposite:* mislead.

set rolling *v* [➡CAUSE TO HAPPEN; 31]

set sail *v* [➡ABSENT ONESELF; 8]

set store by *v* **deem important**, value, esteem, prize, regard highly, put a premium on, rate, appreciate. [➡LIKE, LOVE, VALUE AND ENJOY; 579]

sett 1 *n* **paving stone**, paving slab, paver, stone, slab, flag, flagstone, cobble, cobblestone, tile. [➡BUILDING MATERIALS; 1076] 2 *type of* **den or nest**. [➡ANIMAL OR BIRD ACCOMMODATION; 1078]

settee *n* **sofa**, couch, chaise longue, divan, futon, davenport (*US*), day bed. [➡FURNITURE; 858]

setter *type of* **large dog**. [➡DOG; 980]

set the ball rolling *v* [➡CAUSE TO HAPPEN; 31]

setting *n* **location**, surroundings, scenery, situation, background, set, locale, site, venue, backdrop. [➡PLACE; 1064]

settle 1 *v* **resolve**, reconcile, clear up, straighten out, mend, patch up. [➡CORRECT AND PUT RIGHT; 378] 2 *v* **stay**, inhabit, put down roots, set up house, establish yourself, colonize, stay on, remain. [➡INHABIT; 20] *Opposite:* take off. 3 *v* **land**, perch, alight, roost, come to rest. [➡GO DOWNWARDS; 308] *Opposite:* take off. 4 *v* **become peaceful**, become calm, settle down, calm down, relax, slow down. [➡CHANGE OF MOOD AND COMPOSURE; 581] *Opposite:* fluster. 5 *v* **pay**, defray (*formal*), discharge, clear, foot, settle up. [➡GIVE MONEY; 434] *Opposite:* owe. 6 *v* **sink**, drop, descend, fall, go to the bottom, lie. [➡GO DOWNWARDS; 308] *Opposite:* rise.

settled *adj* **established**, stable, solid, firm, steady, mature. [➡CERTAIN; 175] *Opposite:* unsettled.

settle down 1 *v* **become less restless**, quieten down, relax, calm down, snuggle down, slow down, take it easy. [➡CHANGE OF MOOD AND COMPOSURE; 581] *Opposite:* agitate. 2 *v* **sink**, drop, descend, fall, stabilize, settle. [➡GO DOWNWARDS; 308] *Opposite:* rise.

settle for *v* **agree to**, accept, make do with, take, be happy with, compromise on. [➡ACCEPT POSSESSION; 451] *Opposite:* refuse.

settle in 1 *v* **adapt**, acclimatize, adjust, get used to it, find your feet, fit in. [➡CHANGE; 373] 2 *v* **get comfortable**, get comfy, snuggle down, park yourself (*informal*), ensconce yourself, remain. [➡CHANGE OF MOOD AND COMPOSURE; 581]

settlement 1 *n* **resolution**, conclusion, completion, decision, agreement, arrangement. [➡SOLUTION; 216] 2 *n* **payment**, defrayal, clearance, clearing, reimbursement, disbursement, expenditure. [➡MONEY, PAYMENTS, AND CHARGES; 800] *Opposite:* receipt. 3 *n* **community**, village, town, township, colony, commune, hamlet, neighbourhood, suburb. [➡HUMAN SETTLEMENTS; 1069]

settle on *v* **choose**, pick, select, go for (*informal*), decide on, agree on. [➡MAKE DECISIONS AND CHOICES; 753] *Opposite:* reject.

settler *n* **colonizer**, colonist, pioneer, pilgrim, immigrant, incomer, early settler. [➡PEOPLE LIVING AWAY FROM HOME; 887]

settle up *v* **pay the bill**, pay, cough up (*informal*), pay up, ante up (*US informal*), shell out (*informal*), settle the debt, fork out (*informal*). [➡GIVE MONEY; 434] *Opposite:* quibble.

settling of scores *n* [➡VENGEANCE AND REVENGE; 686]

set-to (*informal*) *n* **confrontation**, quarrel, altercation, disagreement, difference of opinion, row, war of words, flare-up (*informal*), debate, squabble, argument. [➡ARGUMENT; 47] *Opposite:* reconciliation.

set to 1 *v* **buckle down** (*informal*), knuckle down (*informal*), get on with it, put your shoulder to the wheel, make a start, get started, start work, start. [➡START AN ACTION; 261] 2 *v* **come to blows**, start fighting, lay into, grapple, tussle, wrestle, go for, raise your fists. [➡COMPETE, CONTEND, AND COMBAT; 304]

set up 1 *v* **establish**, inaugurate, found, institute, launch, organize, prepare. [➡INSTITUTE AND INAUGURATE; 349] 2 *v* **erect**, raise, build, construct, put up, assemble. [➡BUILD; 353] 3 *v* (*informal*) **frame**, trap, fix (*informal*), entrap, trick, entice, fit up (*slang*), stitch up (*slang*). [➡DECEPTION AND LIES; 661]

setup 1 *n* **system**, arrangement, format, situation, structure, circumstance, operation, way things work, outfit (*informal*), framework, organization. [➡WAYS OF DOING THINGS; 295] 2 *n* (*informal*) **frame**, trap, trick, deception, con trick (*informal*), con, confidence trick, fraud, swindle, confidence game (*US*), con game (*US informal*), sting (*US slang*). [➡DECEPTION AND LIES; 661]

set upon *v* **attack**, assault, lay into, assail, pounce on, ambush. [➡PHYSICAL ATTACK AND PUNISHMENT; 416] *Opposite:* defend.

seventh heaven *n* **bliss**, ecstasy, heaven, nirvana,

cloud nine, rapture, delight, elation, joy, happiness. [➡ PLEASANT SITUATIONS; 74] *Opposite:* despair.

sever 1 *v* **cut**, split, separate, undo, disunite, dissolve, break. [➡ SEPARATE AND DIVIDE; 402] *Opposite:* unite. 2 *v* **cut off**, chop off, lop off, shear off, slice off, amputate, remove. [➡ EXTRACT AND SEVER; 342] *Opposite:* attach.

several *adj* **some**, quite a few (*informal*), quite a lot of, a number of, numerous, more than a few. [➡ AMOUNT AND QUANTITY; 112]

severally *adv* **separately**, individually, one at a time, one by one, in turn, respectively. [➡ UNRELATEDNESS AND SEPARATENESS; 147] *Opposite:* together.

severance 1 *n* **separation**, detachment, disconnection, division, taking apart, partition (*formal*), cutting off, uncoupling. [➡ SEPARATE AND DIVIDE; 402] *Opposite:* joining. 2 *n* **compensation**, redundancy pay, redundancy money, severance pay, golden handshake (*informal*), golden parachute (*informal*), termination pay. [➡ MONEY, PAYMENTS, AND CHARGES; 800]

severe 1 *adj* **harsh**, stern, strict, cruel, brutal, ruthless, relentless, rigorous, difficult. [➡ EMOTIONALLY UNPLEASANT AND UPSETTING; 228] *Opposite:* gentle. 2 *adj* **acute**, grave, critical, serious, dangerous, awful, terrible. [➡ DANGEROUS; 237] *Opposite:* slight. 3 *adj* **plain**, simple, Spartan, unadorned, unembellished, undecorated, stark, austere. [➡ PLAIN; 233] *Opposite:* ornate.

severely *adv* **harshly**, sternly, strictly, cruelly, brutally, ruthlessly, relentlessly, rigorously. [➡ EMOTIONALLY UNPLEASANT AND UPSETTING; 228] *Opposite:* gently.

severity 1 *n* **harshness**, sternness, strictness, cruelty, brutality, ruthlessness, relentlessness, rigorousness, difficulty. [➡ EMOTIONALLY UNPLEASANT AND UPSETTING; 228] *Opposite:* gentleness. 2 *n* **gravity**, seriousness, acuteness, dangerousness, awfulness. [➡ DANGER; 236] *Opposite:* insignificance. 3 *n* **plainness**, simplicity, starkness, bareness, austerity. [➡ PLAIN; 233] *Opposite:* warmth.

Sèvres *type of* **pottery**. [➡ POTTERY; 1134]

sew *v* **stitch**, seam, baste, hem, embroider, darn. [➡ CRAFTS AND CARVING; 356] *Opposite:* unpick.

sewage *n* [➡ UNPLEASANT AND DIRTY SUBSTANCES; 1267]

sewer *n* **drain**, septic tank, cesspit, cesspool, open drain, gutter, culvert, sink, sump. [➡ WATERCOURSES; 1110]

sewing *n* **stitching**, hemming, embroidery, darning, tapestry, needlepoint, needlework, basting. [➡ CRAFTS AND CARVING; 356]

sew up 1 *v* **stitch up**, sew, stitch, darn, repair, mend. [➡ REPAIR AND MEND; 377] *Opposite:* unpick. 2 *v* **settle**, clinch, tie up, finalize, finish, complete. [➡ COMPLETE AN ACTION; 264]

sex *n* **gender**, sexual category, masculinity, femininity. [➡ GENDER IDENTITY AND SEXUALITY; 932]

sexism *n* [➡ PREJUDICE; 551]

sexless *adj* [➡ GENDER IDENTITY AND SEXUALITY; 932]

sextet *type of* **band**. [➡ MUSICIANS AND SINGERS; 908]

sexual *adj* [➡ REPRODUCTION AND HEREDITY; 726]

sexual category *n* [➡ GENDER IDENTITY AND SEXUALITY; 932]

sexual characteristics *n* [➡ GENDER IDENTITY AND SEXUALITY; 932]

sexual maturity *n* [➡ REPRODUCTION AND HEREDITY; 726]

sexy *adj* [➡ PEOPLE'S PHYSICAL APPEARANCE; 476]

shabbiness 1 *n* **scruffiness**, untidiness, dilapidation, seediness, raggedness, grunginess (*informal*). [➡ BADLY GROOMED; 484] *Opposite:* elegance. 2 *n* **nastiness**, cruelty, meanness, disrespect, negligence. [➡ UNKIND ACTION OR BEHAVIOUR; 297] *Opposite:* decency.

shabby 1 *adj* **scruffy**, untidy, ragged, tattered, worn out, threadbare, dilapidated, grungy (*informal*), unkempt, poorly maintained. [➡ BADLY GROOMED; 484] *Opposite:* elegant. 2 *adj* **nasty**, cruel, mean, dishonourable, contemptible, despicable, unfair, rotten, disrespectful. [➡ SELFISH AND UNKIND; 506] *Opposite:* respectful.

shack *type of* **house**. [➡ RESIDENTIAL BUILDINGS; 1077]

shackle 1 *v* **fetter**, manacle, handcuff, chain, put in irons, bind. [➡ CAPTIVITY AND LOSS OF FREEDOM; 249] *Opposite:* free. 2 *v* **constrain**, restrict, impede, hamper, hinder, obstruct, thwart. [➡ AVOID, PREVENT, LIMIT, AND CONTROL; 278] *Opposite:* encourage.

shackles *n* **fetters**, manacles, chains, restraints, irons. [➡ FASTENERS, LINKS, AND NETWORKS; 1246]

shade 1 *n* **shadow**, dark, darkness, gloom, gloominess, dimness. [➡ DESCRIBING LIGHT; 1227] *Opposite:* light. 2 *n* **blind**, screen, awning, canopy, cover, shield. [➡ COVERS AND COATINGS; 1245] 3 *n* **hue**, tint, tinge, colour, tone. [➡ DESCRIBING COLOURS; 1225] 4 *n* **hint**, trace, suggestion, touch, dash, little bit, shadow. [➡ FEW, LITTLE, SMALL AMOUNT; 119] 5 *v* **cover**, shield, protect, screen, veil, mask, shelter, hide, conceal. [➡ CAUSE TO DISAPPEAR; 6] *Opposite:* expose. 6 *v* **darken**, eclipse, blot out, shadow, block out. [➡ CHANGE OF COLOUR; 392] *Opposite:* brighten. 7 *v* **fill in**, hatch, colour, colour in, block in. [➡ CHANGE OF COLOUR; 392]

shades (*informal*) *n* **sunglasses**, sunspecs (*informal*), dark glasses, tinted lenses. [➡ GLASSES AND SPECTACLES; 1124]

shadiness 1 *n* **dishonesty**, crookedness, underhandedness, shiftiness, suspiciousness, deviousness, dubiousness. [➡ MORALLY BAD; 776] *Opposite:* honesty. 2 *n* **dimness**, dark, darkness, shadowiness, obscurity, shade. [➡ DESCRIBING LIGHT; 1227] *Opposite:* brightness.

shadow 1 *n* **shade**, silhouette, outline, dark, darkness, gloom, gloominess, dusk, dimness. [➡ SHAPE; 1215] *Opposite:* light. 2 *n* **ghost**, spectre, spirit, wraith, apparition, phantom. [➡ THE SUPERNATURAL; 788] 3 *n* **constant companion**, alter ego, other self, double, doppelgänger. [➡ SUPPORTERS, PROTECTORS, AND COMPATRIOTS; 970] 4 *n* **private investigator**, private eye (*informal*), private detective, sleuth (*informal*), tail (*informal*), tracker, gumshoe (*US informal*). [➡ ENEMIES AND TORMENTORS; 969] 5 *n* **follower**, stalker, tail (*informal*), pursuer, tracker. [➡ ENEMIES AND TORMENTORS; 969] 6 *n* **hint**, trace, suggestion, touch, shade, flicker. [➡ FEW, LITTLE, SMALL AMOUNT; 119] 7 *v* **follow**, tail (*informal*), trail, track, stalk, observe, pursue, go after, chase. [➡ ACCOMPANY AND FOLLOW; 338] 8 *v* **darken**, eclipse, blot out, shade. [➡ CAUSE TO DISAPPEAR; 6] *Opposite:* brighten.

See Compare and Contrast at **follow.**

shadows *n* **shade**, dark, darkness, obscurity, dimness, gloom. [➡DESCRIBING LIGHT; 1227] *Opposite:* light.

shadowy 1 *adj* **indistinct**, obscure, vague, indistinguishable, unclear, dim, faint. [➡IMPERCEPTIBLE; 26] *Opposite:* distinct. 2 *adj* **dim**, dark, murky, gloomy, poorly lit, shady. [➡DESCRIBING LIGHT; 1227] *Opposite:* bright. 3 *adj* **ghostly**, spectral, ethereal, sinister, mysterious, shrouded in mystery, eerie. [➡SECRET AND UNKNOWN; 180] *Opposite:* material.

shady 1 *adj* **out of the sun**, in the shade, shaded, under the trees, cool, dappled, sheltered. [➡DESCRIBING LIGHT; 1227] *Opposite:* sunny. 2 *adj* **dishonest**, crooked (*informal*), underhand, shifty, suspicious, devious, dubious, doubtful, fishy (*informal*), disreputable, suspect. [➡MORALLY BAD; 776] *Opposite:* aboveboard.

shaft *part of* **engine**. [➡PARTS OF AN ENGINE; 1143]

shag *type of* **seabird**. [➡SEABIRD; 1002]

shagginess *n* **hairiness**, unkemptness, dishevelment, untidiness, bushiness. [➡HAIR; 485] *Opposite:* tidiness.

shaggy *adj* **hairy**, unkempt, dishevelled, bushy, unshorn, hirsute. [➡DESCRIBING HAIR; 487] *Opposite:* tidy.

shaggy dog story *n* [➡DECEPTION AND LIES; 661]

shake 1 *v* **tremble**, quiver, quake, shudder, shiver, judder, wobble, vibrate, quaver. [➡PHYSICAL REACTIONS; 317] 2 *v* **agitate**, stir, blend, move up and down, jiggle, waggle, mix. [➡COMBINE AND MIX; 401] *Opposite:* steady. 3 *v* **unsettle**, unnerve, disturb, distress, upset, alarm. [➡UPSET, DISTRESS, AND HUMILIATE; 568] *Opposite:* reassure. 4 *v* **brandish**, flourish, flaunt, wave, wield. [➡MOVE SOMETHING ON THE SPOT; 337] 5 *n* **jiggle**, wobble, agitation, vibration, quiver, tremor. [➡MOVE SOMETHING ON THE SPOT; 337] *Opposite:* stillness.

shakedown (*US slang*) *n* [➡CRIMES; 817]

shaken *adj* [➡CONFUSION, ANXIETY, AND WORRY; 541]

shake off 1 *v* **get rid of**, get away from, lose, elude, leave behind, give somebody the slip. [➡AVOID OR ESCAPE CONTACT; 419] 2 *v* **recover from**, recuperate from, get over, get rid of. [➡FALL ILL, TREAT, AND RECOVER; 729] *Opposite:* succumb.

shake-out *n* **transformation**, radical change, upheaval, overhaul, reorganization, reform, revamp, rethink, rearrangement, reshuffle, restructuring, shake-up. [➡CHANGE; 373]

shake-up *n* **transformation**, radical change, upheaval, overhaul, reorganization, reform, revamp, rethink, rearrangement, reshuffle, restructuring, shake-out. [➡CHANGE; 373]

shake up 1 *v* **transform**, overhaul, change drastically, revamp, rethink, modify, alter, rejig (*informal*), improve. [➡CHANGE; 373] *Opposite:* leave alone. 2 *v* **upset**, disturb, distress, shock, alarm, knock for six (*informal*), traumatize, devastate, stun, perturb, unsettle, worry. [➡FRIGHTEN AND SHOCK; 569] *Opposite:* calm down. 3 *v* **mix**, blend, combine, agitate, shake, stir. [➡COMBINE AND MIX; 401]

shakiness 1 *n* **tremor**, shaking, trembling, shake, jerkiness, unsteadiness. [➡DESCRIBING BODY MOVEMENTS; 289] *Opposite:* control. 2 *n* **wobbliness**, instability, flimsiness, fragility, insubstantiality. [➡WEAKNESS; 242] *Opposite:* sturdiness. 3 *n* **uncertainty**, precariousness, instability, unreliability, weakness, fragility, tenuousness. [➡UNCERTAIN; 176] *Opposite:* reliability.

shaking *n* **vibration**, jolting, juddering, rocking, rattling, shuddering, wobbling, bumping, quivering. [➡DESCRIBING BODY MOVEMENTS; 289]

shaky 1 *adj* **wobbly**, unstable, unsteady, insecure, rickety, precarious. [➡DANGEROUS; 237] *Opposite:* steady. 2 *adj* **trembling**, shaking, quivering, quaking, shuddering, shivering. [➡ILL AND SICK; 741] *Opposite:* composed. 3 *adj* **unsupported**, unsound, questionable, dubious, doubtful, uncertain, unreliable. [➡UNCERTAIN; 176] *Opposite:* dependable.

shale *type of* **stone**. [➡STONES, ROCKS, AND BOULDERS; 1057]

shallow 1 *adj* **low**, thin, light, narrow, surface. [➡DEPTH: SHALLOW; 1201] *Opposite:* deep. 2 *adj* **superficial**, trivial, slight, insubstantial, petty, one-dimensional, silly. [➡THE NATURE OF IDEAS; 772] *Opposite:* profound.

shallowly *adv* **superficially**, trivially, frivolously, pettily, triflingly, foolishly. [➡THE NATURE OF IDEAS; 772] *Opposite:* deeply.

shallowness 1 *n* [➡AFFECTATION, SELF-SATISFACTION, AND SNOBBISHNESS; 508] 2 *n* [➡DEPTH: SHALLOW; 1201]

sham 1 *n* **pretence**, deception, charade, con, fraud, act. [➡DECEPTION AND LIES; 661] 2 *n* **impostor**, charlatan, con, fake, fraud, cheat. [➡PEOPLE WHO DECEIVE; 662] 3 *n* (*US*) [➡SOFT FURNISHINGS, LINEN, AND DRAPERY; 860] 4 *adj* **fake**, mock, bogus, imitation, pretended, pretend. [➡FALSE AND UNREAL; 174] *Opposite:* bona fide. 5 *v* **pretend**, fake, put it on, act, play, imitate. [➡PRETEND AND MIMIC; 60] *Opposite:* real.

shaman *n* [➡RELIGIOUS PEOPLE; 779]

shamanism *n* [➡RELIGIOUS PEOPLE; 779]

shamble *v* **shuffle**, amble, waddle, drag your feet, walk. [➡MOVE SLOWLY; 315] *Opposite:* stride.

shambles 1 *n* **fiasco**, disaster, failure, mess, hash (*informal*). [➡DISASTERS; 253] *Opposite:* success. 2 *n* **mess**, muddle, tip, dump. [➡DISORDER AND CHAOS; 246]

shambling *adj* **awkward**, ungainly, clumsy, uncoordinated, lumbering. [➡DESCRIBING BODY MOVEMENTS; 289] *Opposite:* graceful.

shambolic (*informal*) *adj* **disorganized**, chaotic, messy, chaotic, haphazard, confused, muddled. [➡DISORDER AND CHAOS; 246] *Opposite:* orderly.

shame 1 *n* **disgrace**, embarrassment, dishonour, humiliation, indignity, ignominy, infamy. [➡EMBARRASSMENT AND HUMILIATION; 543] *Opposite:* pride. 2 *v* **embarrass**, discredit, disgrace, humiliate, mortify, dishonour, degrade, make uncomfortable, bring into disrepute, bring shame on, defame. [➡UPSET, DISTRESS, AND HUMILIATE; 568] *Opposite:* honour.

shamefaced *adj* **ashamed**, embarrassed, sheepish, hangdog, awkward, humiliated, guilty, mortified. [➡EMBARRASSMENT AND HUMILIATION; 543] *Opposite:* proud.

shameful *adj* **disgraceful**, reprehensible, dishonourable, discreditable, shocking, appalling. [➡DISGUSTING AND REPULSIVE; 231] *Opposite:* honourable.

shameless *adj* **brazen**, barefaced, unabashed, blatant, unashamed. [➡BAD MANNERS AND SOCIAL SKILLS; 522] *Opposite:* ashamed.

shamelessness *n* **lack of remorse**, brazenness, hard-heartedness, boldness, impudence, impenitence. [➡BAD MANNERS AND SOCIAL SKILLS; 522] *Opposite:* repentance.

shampoo *n* [➡PERSONAL HYGIENE; 492]

shanghai *v* [➡CAUSE OR COMPEL TO ACT; 272]

Shangri-la *n* [➡NON-EXISTENT PLACE; 1065]

shank 1 *n* **stem**, shaft, trunk, rod, bar, pole. [➡STICKS, POLES, AND WEDGES; 1253] 2 *part of* **horse**. [➡HORSE; 985]

shanty *n* [➡UNDESIRABLE ACCOMMODATION; 856]

shanty town *n* [➡UNDESIRABLE ACCOMMODATION; 856]

shape 1 *n* **form**, figure, outline, silhouette, profile, contour. [➡SHAPE; 1215] 2 *n* **character**, nature, form, identity, structure, appearance. [➡STATE; 1207] 3 *v* **influence**, affect, model, mould, whittle, manipulate, smooth, sculpt, form. [➡CHANGE; 373]

shape

◆ *types of angular shape*
box, cross, cube, diamond, dodecahedron, dogleg, lozenge, oblong, parallelogram, pentagon, polygon, pyramid, quadrangle, quadrilateral, rectangle, rhomboid, rhombus, square, star, tetragon, tetrahedron, trapezium, trapezoid, triangle

◆ *types of rounded shape*
arc, arch, ball, bend, bow, bulb, circle, circlet, coil, cone, crescent, curl, curve, cylinder, dome, figure of eight, globe, heart, hemisphere, helix, hoop, horseshoe, kidney, loop, orb, oval, ring, round, semicircle, sphere, spheroid, spiral, teardrop

shapeless *adj* **baggy**, loose-fitting, formless, ill-defined, amorphous, fluid. [➡SHAPELESSNESS; 1218] *Opposite:* defined.

shapelessness *n* **amorphousness**, formlessness, bagginess, fluidity. [➡SHAPELESSNESS; 1218] *Opposite:* symmetry.

shapely *adj* **well-formed**, attractive, well-rounded, pleasing, regular, curvaceous, statuesque. [➡BUILD; 478] *Opposite:* straight.

shape up 1 *v* **develop**, progress, improve, come along, come together, fall into place, advance. [➡GET BETTER; 376] 2 *v* **improve**, pull your socks up (*informal*), get it together, reform, mend your ways, turn over a new leaf. [➡GET BETTER; 376]

shard *n* **sliver**, splinter, spike, shaving, chip, piece, fragment, potsherd. [➡SMALL PIECE; 127]

share 1 *v* **split**, go halves, divvy (*informal*), divide, divide up, carve up (*informal*). [➡SEPARATE AND DIVIDE; 402] 2 *v* **distribute**, allocate, assign, apportion, allot, dole out (*informal*), give out. [➡DISPENSE, RATION, AND DISTRIBUTE; 435] 3 *v* **communicate**, let somebody in on, impart, reveal, disclose. [➡INFORM AND ANNOUNCE; 612] 4 *n* **part**, portion, segment, cut, stake, bit, piece. [➡AMOUNT AND QUANTITY; 112] *Opposite:* whole.

shared *adj* **common**, communal, joint, mutual, collective, combined. [➡BELONGING OR RELATING TO PEOPLE; 943]

shareholder *n* [➡PEOPLE INVOLVED IN FINANCE; 804]

share out *v* **divide up**, dole out (*informal*), give out, carve up (*informal*), distribute, allot, split, allocate, divide. [➡DISPENSE, RATION, AND DISTRIBUTE; 435]

shark 1 *n* (*informal*) [➡SUPERFICIAL OR INSINCERE PEOPLE; 951] 2 *type of* **sea fish**. [➡SEA FISH; 1009]

sharp 1 *adj* **pointed**, razor-sharp, jagged, prickly, spiky. [➡PHYSICAL TEXTURE; 1221] *Opposite:* blunt. 2 *adj* **quick**, intelligent, razor-sharp, incisive, astute, clever, on the ball (*informal*), quick-witted, sharp-witted. [➡POSITIVE INTELLECTUAL CHARACTERISTICS; 525] *Opposite:* dull. 3 *adj* **abrupt**, sudden, quick, brusque, urgent. [➡HAPPENING QUICKLY; 104] *Opposite:* gentle. 4 *adj* **shrill**, piercing, loud, high-pitched, strident. [➡LOUD OR UNPLEASANT SOUNDS; 1265] *Opposite:* soft. 5 *adj* **harsh**, severe, snappy, sarcastic, snappish, angry, critical, biting, accusatory (*formal*). [➡BAD-TEMPERED AND HUMOURLESS; 627] *Opposite:* gentle. 6 *adj* **severe**, acute, strong, hard, intense. [➡PHYSICALLY UNPLEASANT; 227] *Opposite:* mild. 7 *adj* **sour**, tangy, acid, pungent, tart, bitter. [➡TASTE; 704] *Opposite:* sweet. 8 *adj* **clear**, well-defined, definite, clear-cut, distinct, precise, in focus. [➡CONCISE AND CLEAR; 203] *Opposite:* imprecise. 9 *adv* **exactly**, precisely, on the dot, promptly, punctually. [➡PROMPTNESS: ON TIME; 99]

sharpen 1 *v* **hone**, whet, grind, file. [➡REPAIR AND MEND; 377] *Opposite:* blunt. 2 *v* **improve**, hone, perfect, brush up, refine, polish. [➡IMPROVE SOMETHING; 375] *Opposite:* worsen.

sharp-eyed 1 *adj* **observant**, watchful, alert, vigilant, attentive, perceptive, wide-awake (*informal*), on the ball (*informal*), sharp-sighted. [➡POSITIVE INTELLECTUAL CHARACTERISTICS; 525] *Opposite:* unobservant. 2 *adj* **eagle-eyed**, with good eyesight, with good vision, with eyes like a hawk, hawk-eyed, sharp-sighted. [➡SEE; 700] *Opposite:* short-sighted.

sharpish (*informal*) *adv* **quickly**, fast, straightaway, right away, immediately, without delay, with no messing about. [➡HAPPENING QUICKLY; 104] *Opposite:* eventually.

sharply 1 *adv* **abruptly**, suddenly, hard, tight. [➡HAPPENING QUICKLY; 104] *Opposite:* gradually. 2 *adv* **harshly**, severely, cuttingly, unkindly, snappishly, tersely, tartly, caustically, crossly, angrily. [➡BAD-TEMPERED AND HUMOURLESS; 627] *Opposite:* gently. 3 *adv* **alarmingly**, steeply, greatly, dramatically, suddenly, precipitously, out of control. [➡HAPPENING QUICKLY; 104] *Opposite:* gradually. 4 *adv* **briskly**, abruptly, suddenly, smartly, swiftly, quickly. [➡HAPPENING QUICKLY; 104] *Opposite:* slowly. 5 *adv* **extremely**, clearly, acutely, distinctly, deeply, intensely. [➡STRENGTH; 202] *Opposite:* subtly. 6 *adv* **clearly**, distinctly, strikingly, obviously, eye-catchingly, in sharp contrast. [➡CONCISE AND CLEAR; 203] *Opposite:* hazily.

sharpness 1 *n* **acuity**, perceptiveness, intelligence, quickness, keenness, alertness, astuteness, perspicacity, quick-wittedness. [➡POSITIVE INTELLECTUAL CHARACTERISTICS; 525] *Opposite:* slowness. 2 *n* **harshness**, severity, unkindness, snappishness, terseness, tartness, crossness, anger. [➡BAD-

TEMPERED AND HUMOURLESS; 627] *Opposite:* gentleness. **3** *n* **clarity**, definition, distinctness, contrast, intensity. [➡CONCISE AND CLEAR; 203] *Opposite:* haziness. **4** *n* **acidity**, sourness, bitterness, zing (*informal*), zest, bite. [➡TASTE; 704] *Opposite:* sweetness.

sharp-sighted **1** *adj* **eagle-eyed**, with good eyesight, with good vision, with eyes like a hawk, hawk-eyed, sharp-eyed. [➡SEE; 700] *Opposite:* myopic. **2** *adj* **observant**, watchful, alert, vigilant, attentive, perceptive, wide-awake (*informal*), on the ball (*informal*), sharp-eyed. [➡POSITIVE INTELLECTUAL CHARACTERISTICS; 525] *Opposite:* unobservant.

sharp-tasting *adj* [➡TASTE; 704]

sharp-tongued *adj* **sarcastic**, harsh, mean, brusque, critical, hurtful, cruel, unsympathetic. [➡RUDE AND HOSTILE; 626] *Opposite:* gentle.

sharp-witted *adj* **quick**, sharp, quick-witted, quick-thinking, quick on the uptake (*informal*), on the ball (*informal*), bright, intelligent, smart, clever. [➡POSITIVE INTELLECTUAL CHARACTERISTICS; 525]

shatter **1** *v* **smash**, break, smash to smithereens, splinter, destroy, blow apart, fragment, explode, ruin. [➡TEAR, BREAK, AND CUT; 361] **2** *v* **destroy**, wreck, crush, demolish. [➡DESTRUCTION AND DEMOLITION; 360] *Opposite:* build up.

shattered **1** *adj* **devastated**, crushed, traumatized, horrified, suffering. [➡SADNESS, DISTRESS, AND DESPAIR; 540] **2** *adj* **tired**, exhausted, whacked (*informal*), all in, wiped out (*slang*), spent, dead beat (*informal*), prostrate, beat (*informal*), worn out. [➡TIRED, ASLEEP AND UNCONSCIOUS; 739] *Opposite:* lively.

shattering *adj* **devastating**, crushing, shocking, earth-shattering, cataclysmic, catastrophic. [➡EMOTIONALLY UNPLEASANT AND UPSETTING; 228] *Opposite:* wonderful.

shatterproof *adj* **indestructible**, unbreakable, non-breaking, resistant, strengthened, toughened, reinforced, durable, safety. [➡DURABLE; 1209]

shave *v* **cut off**, shear, cut, trim. [➡EXTRACT AND SEVER; 342]

shaved *adj* [➡FACIAL HAIR; 490]

shaven *adj* [➡FACIAL HAIR; 490]

shaving *n* **chip**, splinter, flake, shred, sliver. [➡SMALL PIECE; 127] *Opposite:* chunk.

shaving brush *type of* **cosmetic tool.** [➡HAND TOOLS; 1118]

shaving cream *n* [➡PERSONAL HYGIENE; 492]

shavings *n* [➡REMAINDER AND REMAINDERS; 123]

shawl *n* **wrap**, stole, scarf, cloak. [➡HABERDASHERY, MILLINERY, AND LINGERIE; 867]

sheaf *n* **bundle**, cluster, clump, wad, stack, pile, bunch. [➡AMOUNT OF SOLID OR SEMI-SOLID; 115]

shear *v* **cut off**, shave, clip, trim, crop, cut. [➡EXTRACT AND SEVER; 342]

shears *type of* **cutting tool.** [➡CUTTING TOOLS; 1119]

sheath **1** *n* **cover**, case, casing, covering, scabbard. [➡COVERS AND COATINGS; 1245] **2** *type of* **dress.** [➡GARMENTS AND OUTFITS; 865]

sheathe **1** *v* **put away**, replace, stash (*informal*), retract. [➡POSITION SOMETHING: BETWEEN, BESIDE, OR INSIDE SOMETHING; 327] *Opposite:* take out. **2** *v* **envelop**, swathe, cloak, wrap, drape, cover, shroud, swaddle, sheath, enclose. [➡DECORATE, ADORN, AND APPLY COATINGS; 406]

sheathing *n* **casing**, covering, outer layer, jacket, shield, cover, shell. [➡COVERS AND COATINGS; 1245]

shebeen *type of* **bar or club.** [➡HOTELS, RESTAURANTS, AND CLUBS; 1081]

shed **1** *type of* **outbuilding.** [➡ANCILLARY BUILDINGS; 1079] **2** *type of* **storage space.** [➡STORES AND STORAGE BUILDINGS; 1087]

shed light on *v* **clarify**, explain, illuminate, elucidate (*formal*), clear up, resolve. [➡EXPLAIN AND CLARIFY; 611]

shedload *n* [➡MANY, MUCH, LARGE AMOUNT; 117]

shed tears *v* [➡CRYING; 651]

sheen *n* **shine**, polish, lustre, gloss, gleam, patina. [➡VISUAL TEXTURE; 1220]

sheep **1** *n* **ewe**, ram, lamb. [➡FARM ANIMAL; 982] **2** *n* **conformist**, follower, traditionalist, copycat (*informal*), lemming, yes man. [➡LAZY OR UNSUCCESSFUL PEOPLE; 948] *Opposite:* individualist.

sheepdog *type of* **large dog.** [➡DOG; 980]

sheepish *adj* **ashamed**, shamefaced, embarrassed, hangdog, guilty, awkward, uncomfortable. [➡EMBARRASSMENT AND HUMILIATION; 543] *Opposite:* unashamed.

sheepishness *n* **shame**, embarrassment, guilt, awkwardness, self-consciousness, humiliation. [➡EMBARRASSMENT AND HUMILIATION; 543]

sheepskin *type of* **leather.** [➡FABRICS; 1131]

sheer **1** *adj* **pure**, complete, absolute, utter, unalloyed, total. [➡ABSOLUTE AND ABSOLUTELY; 131] **2** *adj* **steep**, vertical, perpendicular, precipitous, sharp. [➡ORIENTATION AND ALIGNMENT; 1222] *Opposite:* gentle. **3** *adj* **fine**, translucent, thin, diaphanous, filmy, gossamer. [➡VISUAL TEXTURE; 1220] *Opposite:* thick. **4** *adv* **vertically**, straight up, plumb, precipitously, steeply. [➡ORIENTATION AND ALIGNMENT; 1222]

sheerness *n* **fineness**, thinness, translucence, filminess. [➡VISUAL TEXTURE; 1220] *Opposite:* thickness.

sheet **1** *n* **piece**, page, leaf, slip, pane. [➡AMOUNT OF SOLID OR SEMI-SOLID; 115] **2** *n* **expanse**, mass, area, layer. [➡COVERS AND COATINGS; 1245] **3** *part of* **sailing vessel.** [➡PARTS OF A SHIP OR BOAT; 1150]

sheet down *v* **pour**, rain cats and dogs (*informal*), tip down (*informal*), rain heavily, chuck it down (*informal*). [➡CLOUDY AND RAINY WEATHER; 1052]

sheeting down *adj* [➡CLOUDY AND RAINY WEATHER; 1052]

sheet lightning *n* [➡WINDY AND STORMY WEATHER; 1053]

sheik *n* **leader**, ruler, chief, chieftain, head. [➡IMPORTANT OR FAMOUS PEOPLE; 893]

shelf **1** *n* **ledge**, sill, projection, bookshelf, mantelpiece, mantelshelf. [➡SUPPORTS AND BASES; 1254] 2 *n* **layer**, ridge, step, rock shelf. [➡GEOLOGICAL FEATURES; 1056]

shell 1 *n* **case**, casing, covering, shield, crust, skin, armour, defence. [➡COVERS AND COATINGS; 1245] 2 *n* **husk**, skeleton, carcass, remains. [➡REMAINDER AND REMAINDERS; 123] 3 *n* **bomb**, explosive, missile, mortar, projectile. [➡PROJECTILES; 1158] 4 *v* **bombard**, shoot at, fire at, open fire on, shoot down, bomb. [➡DESTRUCTION AND DEMOLITION; 360]

shellfish 1 *n* **prawn**, shrimp, oyster, mussel, cockle, whelk, clam. [➡SEA FOOD; 1189] 2 *type of* **crustacean**. [➡AQUATIC INVERTEBRATE; 1022]

shelling *n* [➡WARFARE AND WAR; 830]

shell-like (*informal humorous*) *n* [➡THE EAR; 707]

shell out (*informal*) *v* **pay out**, pay up, cough up (*informal*), fork out (*informal*), pay, spend, give. [➡GIVE MONEY; 434]

shell pink *type of* **pink**. [➡COLOURS; 1223]

shell suit *type of* **sportswear**. [➡GARMENTS AND OUTFITS; 865]

shelter 1 *n* **protection**, cover, refuge, haven, sanctuary, asylum, safe haven. [➡SAFE BUILDINGS OR PLACES; 1092] 2 *n* **housing**, accommodation, living quarters, lodging, somewhere to stay, somewhere to live, a roof over your head, accommodations (*US*). [➡ACCOMMODATION; 855] 3 *v* **protect**, shield, cover, defend, harbour, take in, give refuge. [➡PREVENT CONTACT OR ATTACK; 420] 4 *v* **take shelter**, take refuge, take cover, hide. [➡AVOID OR ESCAPE CONTACT; 419]

sheltered 1 *adj* **protected**, cosy, cushy (*informal*), privileged, comfortable, wrapped in cotton wool, shielded. [➡SAFE AND SAFETY; 192] *Opposite:* harsh. 2 *adj* **secluded**, protected, shielded, isolated, insulated, shaded. [➡SAFE AND SAFETY; 192] *Opposite:* exposed.

shelve *v* **put on hold**, put on ice, defer, abandon, cancel, drop, postpone, set aside, table (*US*). [➡DELAY ACTION OR OCCURRENCE; 279]

shemozzle (*dated informal*) *n* [➡CHAOS AND UPROAR; 51]

shenanigans (*informal*) 1 *n* **carry-on** (*informal*), to-do (*informal*), monkey business (*informal*), mischief, trickery, trouble, monkeyshines (*US*). [➡CHAOS AND UPROAR; 51] 2 *n* **pranks**, tricks, tomfoolery (*informal*), high jinks (*informal*), messing about, larking about, mischief, playfulness, joking around. [➡JOKES AND TEASING; 675]

shepherd *v* **marshal**, drive, guide, steer, propel, direct. [➡ACCOMPANY AND FOLLOW; 338]

sherd *see* **shard**.

sheriff (*US*) *n* [➡PEOPLE IN LAW COURTS; 820]

sheriff's officer (*US*) *n* [➡PEOPLE IN LAW COURTS; 820]

Shetland pony *type of* **horse**. [➡HORSE; 985]

shield 1 *n* **protection**, armour, defence, safeguard, buffer. [➡COVERS AND COATINGS; 1245] 2 *v* **protect**, guard, defend, shelter, screen, safeguard. [➡PREVENT CONTACT OR ATTACK; 420] *Opposite:* expose.

See Compare and Contrast at **safeguard**.

shielded *adj* **protected**, safeguarded, isolated, defended, sheltered, spared. [➡SAFE AND SAFETY; 192] *Opposite:* exposed.

shift 1 *v* **move**, budge, vary, transfer, change, alter, swing, modify. [➡POSITION SOMETHING; 326] 2 *v* **remove**, get rid of, loosen, lift, clean, erase. [➡REMOVE SOMETHING; 339] 3 *v* (*informal*) **hurry up**, get a move on (*informal*), buck up (*informal dated*), get moving, hurry. [➡MOVE FAST; 314] *Opposite:* slow down. 4 *n* **move**, swing, modification, alteration, change, transference. [➡CHANGE; 373] 5 *n* **stint**, spell, scheduled time, period, turn. [➡PERIOD OF TIME; 90] 6 *type of* **dress**. [➡GARMENTS AND OUTFITS; 865]

See Compare and Contrast at **change**.

shiftiness *n* [➡DECEITFUL; 514]

shifting *adj* **unstable**, ever-changing, fluctuating, fluid, flowing, kaleidoscopic. [➡FINITENESS, VARIABILITY, AND TRANSIENCE; 96] *Opposite:* fixed.

shiftless *adj* **lazy**, suspicious, dubious, idle, dishonest, good-for-nothing, untrustworthy, indolent, deceitful, slothful (*formal*), workshy, devious, inefficient. [➡LIFELESS, LAZY, AND UNENTHUSIASTIC; 507] *Opposite:* industrious.

shift the blame *v* [➡ACCUSE, BLAME, AND CRITICIZE; 642]

shifty *adj* **suspicious**, dubious, dishonest, untrustworthy, deceitful, devious. [➡DECEITFUL; 514] *Opposite:* trustworthy.

shillelagh *type of* **club**. [➡BLUNT INSTRUMENTS AND WHIPS; 1157]

shilly-shallier *n* [➡LAZY OR UNSUCCESSFUL PEOPLE; 948]

shilly-shally 1 *v* **waver**, dilly-dally, dither, hesitate, vacillate, hang back, falter, hem and haw, um and ah. [➡HESITATE; 273] *Opposite:* decide. 2 *v* **waste time**, mess about (*informal*), hang around, hang about, dawdle, delay, dally, mess around (*informal*). [➡MOVE SLOWLY; 315] *Opposite:* forge ahead.

shilly-shallying *n* [➡LIFELESS, LAZY, AND UNENTHUSIASTIC; 507]

shimmer *v* **sparkle**, glisten, shine, glitter, gleam, flicker, twinkle. [➡LIGHT EMISSION; 369]

shimmering *adj* **iridescent**, sparkling, shining, gleaming, glistening, glittering, flickering. [➡DESCRIBING LIGHT; 1227]

shimmery *adj* [➡VISUAL TEXTURE; 1220]

shimmy *v* [➡MOVE FAST; 314]

shin *part of* **leg or foot**. [➡LEG AND FOOT; 695]

shindig (*informal*) *n* **party**, bash, jamboree, do (*informal*), get-together (*informal*). [➡PARTIES, DANCES, AND CELEBRATIONS; 37]

shine 1 *v* **excel**, be good at, stand out, have a gift for, be skilled at, do well. *Opposite:* bomb. (*informal*). [➡SUCCEED AND WIN; 79] 2 *v* **glow**, gleam, glimmer, sparkle, glitter, shimmer, glisten, twinkle, flicker, flash. [➡LIGHT EMISSION; 369] 3 *v* **polish**, burnish, buff, buff up, put a shine on. [➡CLEAN AND

POLISH; 404] **4** *n* **sheen**, polish, lustre, gloss, gleam, patina, sparkle, twinkle. [➡VISUAL TEXTURE; 1220]

shingle *n* [➡BUILDING MATERIALS; 1076]

shininess *n* [➡VISUAL TEXTURE; 1220]

shining *adj* **outstanding**, excellent, admirable, brilliant, superb, exceptional, magnificent, wonderful, splendid. [➡EXTRAORDINARY: AMAZING; 205] *Opposite:* poor.

shining example *n* [➡PERFECT EXAMPLES AND EMBODIMENTS; 67]

shinty *type of* **ball game.** [➡HOBBIES, GAMES, AND SPORTS; 875]

shiny *adj* **glossy**, gleaming, sparkly, glittery, polished, shimmering, glistening, burnished, reflective. [➡DESCRIBING LIGHT; 1227] *Opposite:* dull.

ship **1** *n* **vessel**, craft, boat. [➡SHIPS AND BOATS; 1149] **2** *v* **send**, transport, distribute, dispatch, convey. [➡DESPATCH AND SEND; 334] **3** [➡PARTS OF A SHIP OR BOAT; 1150]

ship

◆ *types of motor vessel*
barge, cabin cruiser, canal boat, coaster, dredger, factory ship, ferry, ferryboat, freighter, houseboat, hovercraft, hydrofoil, launch, lifeboat, lighter, lightship, motorboat, powerboat, speedboat, steamboat, steamer, tanker, trawler, tug, tugboat (*US*)

◆ *types of sailing vessel*
barque, brig, brigantine, catamaran, catboat, dhow, felucca, junk, ketch, sailboat (*US*), sailing boat, schooner, sloop, smack, trimaran, yacht

◆ *types of military vessel*
aircraft carrier, battle cruiser, battleship, cruiser, cutter, destroyer, frigate, gunboat, minesweeper, PT boat (*US*), submarine, warship

◆ *types of small vessel*
canoe, dinghy, dory, gondola, kayak, life raft, narrow boat, pedalo, pirogue, punt, raft, rowboat (*US*), rowing boat, sampan, scull, skiff

◆ *types of historical vessel*
clipper, flagship, galleon, galley, Indiaman, longboat, longship, man-of-war, tall ship, windjammer

◆ *parts of a ship or boat*
bilge, bow, bridge, cabin, capstan, crow's nest, deck, engine room, fo'c's'le, galley, gunwale, helm, hold, hull, keel, oarlock (*US*), outboard motor, outrigger, poop, prow, rowlock, rudder, stateroom, stern, superstructure, tiller

◆ *parts of a sailing vessel*
boom, bowsprit, fore-and-aft sail (*US*), gaff, gaffsail, jib, mainsail, mainstay, mast, mizzen, pennant, sheet, shroud, spanker, spinnaker, topsail

shipment *n* **consignment**, delivery, batch, load, cargo, freight. [➡TRANSPORTATION, TRANSPORTERS, AND CARGOS; 323]

shipping *n* **delivery**, transport, distribution, carriage, freight, shipment, conveyance. [➡TRANSPORTATION, TRANSPORTERS, AND CARGOS; 323]

shipping canal *n* [➡WATERWAYS AND SEAWAYS; 1107]

shipping lane *n* [➡WATERWAYS AND SEAWAYS; 1107]

shipshape *adj* **in order**, neat, tidy, organized, spick-and-span, in apple-pie order. [➡ORDER AND ORGANISATION; 207] *Opposite:* untidy.

shipyard *type of* **industrial site.** [➡INDUSTRIAL BUILDINGS; 1086]

shire *n* [➡COUNTRIES AND REGIONS; 1066]

shire horse *type of* **horse.** [➡HORSE; 985]

shirk *v* **evade**, avoid, dodge, duck, get out of, wriggle out of, shun. [➡NOT DO AND REFUSE TO DO; 275] *Opposite:* accept.

shirker *n* **lazy person**, skiver (*informal*), slacker, lazybones (*informal*), idler, loafer, slouch (*informal*), clock-watcher. [➡LAZY OR UNSUCCESSFUL PEOPLE; 948] *Opposite:* worker.

shirt *type of* **top.** [➡GARMENTS AND OUTFITS; 865]

shirtdress *type of* **dress.** [➡GARMENTS AND OUTFITS; 865]

shish kebab *n* [➡PREPARED DISHES; 1169]

shiver **1** *v* **shake**, tremble, quiver, quake, shudder. [➡PHYSICAL REACTIONS; 317] **2** *n* **quiver**, shudder, tremor, tremble, quake (*informal*), frisson. [➡PHYSICAL REACTIONS; 317]

shoal *type of* **herd.** [➡GROUP OF ANIMALS; 993]

shock **1** *n* **surprise**, jolt, blow, kick in the teeth, bolt from the blue, upset, fright. [➡SUDDEN EVENT; 52] **2** *n* **distress**, numbness, devastation, disbelief, astonishment, amazement. [➡SURPRISE, SHOCK, AND AMAZEMENT; 546] **3** *v* **stun**, alarm, surprise, fright, astonish, astound, take aback, amaze, stagger, flabbergast (*informal*), take the wind out of your sails, knock for six (*informal*). [➡FRIGHTEN AND SHOCK; 569] *Opposite:* calm. **4** *v* **traumatize**, upset, devastate, knock for six (*informal*), shake up, alarm, disturb. [➡UPSET, DISTRESS, AND HUMILIATE; 568] *Opposite:* reassure. **5** *v* **scandalize**, outrage, appal, offend, provoke. [➡FRIGHTEN AND SHOCK; 569]

shockability *n* [➡NEGATIVE INTELLECTUAL CHARACTERISTICS; 526]

shock absorber *n* [➡PARTS OF MACHINES AND TOOLS; 1117]

shocked **1** *adj* **surprised**, stunned, dazed, upset, shaken, traumatized, knocked for six (*informal*), taken aback. [➡SURPRISE, SHOCK, AND AMAZEMENT; 546] *Opposite:* indifferent. **2** *adj* **scandalized**, outraged, appalled, offended. [➡SURPRISE, SHOCK, AND AMAZEMENT; 546] *Opposite:* indifferent.

shocking *adj* **appalling**, dreadful, scandalous, outrageous, awful, disgusting, deplorable, wicked. [➡EMOTIONALLY UNPLEASANT AND UPSETTING; 228]

shockingly **1** *adv* **outrageously**, astonishingly, disgracefully, unpardonably, appallingly, amazingly. [➡UNACCEPTABLE AND UNFORGIVEABLE; 226] *Opposite:* understandably. **2** *adv* **startlingly**, horrifically, distressingly, upsettingly, disturbingly, grotesquely, gruesomely. [➡EMOTIONALLY UNPLEASANT AND UPSETTING; 228] *Opposite:* tastefully. **3** *adv* **atrociously**, lamentably, appallingly, frightfully, dreadfully, unspeakably. [➡TO A GREAT EXTENT; 130]

shocking pink *type of* **pink.** [➡COLOURS; 1223]

shock wave **1** *n* **repercussion**, reaction, shock, effect. [➡RESULTS AND OUTCOMES; 83] **2** *n* **tremor**, shudder, shock, trembling, agitation, start. [➡SUDDEN EVENT; 52]

shoddily 1 *adv* **carelessly**, poorly, badly, sloppily (*informal*), cheaply. [➡BAD AND BADLY; 224] *Opposite:* carefully. 2 *adv* **inconsiderately**, meanly, badly, unkindly, disgracefully. [➡SELFISH AND UNKIND; 506] *Opposite:* considerately.

shoddy 1 *adj* **careless**, slapdash, sloppy, low, inferior, low-down, cheap, substandard, poor, trashy, lousy (*informal*). [➡BAD AND BADLY; 224] *Opposite:* fine. 2 *adj* **inconsiderate**, mean, unkind, rotten, lousy (*informal*), disgraceful. [➡SELFISH AND UNKIND; 506] *Opposite:* considerate.

shoe *type of* **shoe**. [➡FOOTWEAR; 871]

shoelace *n* **cord**, lace, bootlace, tie, fastener. [➡FASTENERS, LINKS, AND NETWORKS; 1246]

shoo away *v* **chase off**, drive away, frighten away, scare off. [➡EJECT AND EXCLUDE; 341] *Opposite:* invite.

shoot 1 *v* **fire**, discharge (*formal*), let off, open fire, fire off, fire at, bombard, snipe. [➡USE TOOLS AND MACHINERY; 469] 2 *v* **gun down** (*informal*), kill, injure, wound, maim, blow away (*slang*), shoot down. [➡KILL; 923] 3 *v* **spurt**, squirt, burst, jet, gush, force. [➡LIQUID EMISSION; 371] 4 *v* (*informal*) **dart**, dash, run, race, zip (*informal*), speed, spurt, zoom, whiz. [➡MOVE FAST; 314] 5 *v* **film**, photograph, take. [➡RECORD SOMETHING; 372] 6 *v* **aim**, point, direct, cast, score, net. [➡THROW SOMETHING; 335] 7 *v* **start to grow**, produce buds, develop, appear, sprout. [➡GROW AND CULTIVATE; 352]

shoot down 1 *v* **bring down**, gun down (*informal*), kill, slaughter, destroy, murder, fell. [➡KILL; 923] 2 *v* **attack**, tear to shreds, rubbish, pick holes in, pillory, criticize, pan, trash (*US informal*). [➡ACCUSE, BLAME, AND CRITICIZE; 642]

shooter (*informal*) *n* [➡WEAPONS FOR SHOOTING; 1155]

shooting 1 *n* **gunfire**, shelling, bombardment, fire, firing. [➡AGGRESSIVE EVENT; 39] 2 *n* **killing**, murder, assassination, execution, slaying, homicide. [➡CAUSES OF DEATH; 921]

shooting star *type of* **heavenly body**. [➡CELESTIAL BODIES; 1060]

shoot the breeze (*US slang*) *v* **chat**, gas (*informal*), natter (*informal*), yap (*informal*), gossip, chinwag (*US*), schmooze (*US slang*), chew the fat (*slang*). [➡TWO-WAY COMMUNICATION; 608]

shoot up *v* **appear**, soar, rocket, spring up, mushroom, rise, increase, develop, grow, go sky-high, go through the ceiling, skyrocket (*informal*). [➡CHANGE OF SIZE: BIGGER; 393] *Opposite:* plummet.

shop 1 *n* **store**, outlet, emporium (*formal or humorous*), showroom. [➡RETAIL OUTLETS; 1082] 2 *n* **spree**, shopping spree, shopping expedition, walk round the shops, retail therapy (*humorous*), binge. [➡SALES AND SHOWS; 444] 3 *n* **workshop**, plant, factory, garage, yard, works. [➡PLACE OF EMPLOYMENT; 832] 4 *v* **go shopping**, buy groceries, go window-shopping, go on a spree, go to the shops, window-shop, do the marketing (*US*). [➡PURCHASE; 423] 5 *v* (*slang*) **betray**, inform, sneak, grass (*slang*), snitch (*slang*), tell, squeal (*slang disapproving*). [➡BETRAY CONFIDENCES AND GOSSIP; 619]

shop

◆ *types of retail outlet*
bazaar, beauty parlour, bookshop, boutique, chain store, chemist, chemist's, convenience store (*US*), corner shop, covered market, department store, dime store (*US*), dispensary, druggist (*US*), drugstore (*US*), duty-free, filling station, flea market, garden centre, gas station (*US*), general store (*US*), hair salon, hairdresser's, hypermarket, kiosk, mall, mart, mom-and-pop store (*US*), newsstand, nursery, petrol station, pharmacy, post office, saleroom, service station, supercenter (*US*), superstore, thrift shop (*US*), undertaker's, warehouse

◆ *types of food outlet*
bakery, bodega (*US*), butcher's, candy store (*US*), chip shop, deli, delicatessen, drive-through, farmers' market, fishmonger's, greengrocer's, grocer's, grocery store, refreshment stand, supermarket, sweetshop, takeaway, takeout (*US*)

shop assistant *n* [➡SELLER; 443]

shopkeeper *n* **retailer**, storekeeper (*US*), seller, salesperson, merchant, trader. [➡BUSINESS PEOPLE; 794]

shoplift *v* **steal**, rob, pilfer, filch (*informal*), thieve, pinch (*informal*), knock off (*slang*), pocket, nick (*slang*). [➡STEAL AND ROB; 427]

shoplifting *n* **stealing**, theft, thieving, pilfering, larceny (*dated*), nicking (*slang*), pinching (*informal*). [➡CRIMES; 817]

shopper *n* **customer**, consumer, buyer, purchaser, bargain hunter, punter (*informal*). [➡PURCHASER; 425]

shopping *n* **errands**, spending, shop, weekly shop, clothes shopping, grocery shopping, supermarket run, bargain hunting. [➡HOBBIES, GAMES, AND SPORTS; 875]

shopping arcade *n* [➡RETAIL OUTLETS; 1082]

shopping bag *type of* **bag**. [➡CONTAINERS, RECEPTACLES, AND PACKAGING; 1244]

shopping basket *type of* **bag**. [➡CONTAINERS, RECEPTACLES, AND PACKAGING; 1244]

shopping centre *n* **shopping precinct**, arcade, pedestrian precinct, shopping complex, mall (*US*), shopping plaza (*US*), strip mall (*US*), outlet mall (*US*). [➡RETAIL OUTLETS; 1082]

shopping complex *n* [➡RETAIL OUTLETS; 1082]

shopping mall (*US*) *n* **shopping precinct**, arcade, pedestrian precinct, shopping complex, arcade, mall (*US*), strip mall (*US*), shoppipng plaza (*US*), outlet mall (*US*). [➡RETAIL OUTLETS; 1082]

shore *n* **coast**, beach, seashore, coastline, seaboard, oceanfront, shoreline. [➡THE SEAS, OCEANS, AND SHORES; 1041]

shoreline *n* **beach**, shore, seashore, water's edge, coastline, oceanfront. [➡THE SEAS, OCEANS, AND SHORES; 1041]

shore up *v* **prop up**, support, hold up, buttress, bolster, reinforce. [➡IMPROVE STRENGTH AND DURABILITY; 379]

shorn of *adj* **deprived of**, stripped of, minus, less, lacking. [➡LACK OF POSSESSION; 446]

short 1 *adj* **small**, little, petite, tiny, diminutive, squat, undersized, stunted. [➡LENGTH: SHORT; 1197] *Opposite:* tall. 2 *adj* **brief**, quick, rapid, fleeting, passing. [➡HAPPENING QUICKLY; 104] *Opposite:* lengthy. 3 *adj* **concise**, succinct, condensed, brief, to the point, terse. [➡CONCISE AND CLEAR; 203] *Opposite:* long. 4 *adj* **curt**, brusque, snappy, abrupt, unfriendly, terse, brisk, sharp. [➡BAD-TEMPERED AND HUMOURLESS; 627] *Opposite:* friendly. 5 *adv* **midstream**, abruptly, suddenly, sharply. [➡HAPPENING QUICKLY; 104] *Opposite:* gradually. 6 *n* (*informal*) **shot** (*informal*), tot, drink, measure, snifter (*informal*), nip. [➡DRINKS; 1186]

shortage *n* **lack**, scarcity, deficiency, dearth, famine, absence, unavailability. [➡TOO FEW, TOO LITTLE; 120] *Opposite:* excess.

See Compare and Contrast at **lack**.

short and sweet *adj* [➡FINITENESS, VARIABILITY, AND TRANSIENCE; 96]

short break *n* **break**, rest, holiday, weekend away, midweek break, a few days away, weekend break, vacation. [➡PERIOD OF REST; 91]

shortcoming *n* **inadequacy**, failing, fault, deficiency, limitation, weakness, defect, flaw. [➡FAULTS, FLAWS, AND WEAKNESSES; 252] *Opposite:* virtue.

short course *n* **crash course**, intensive course, introductory course, refresher course. [➡LESSONS, COURSE WORK, AND EXAMINATIONS; 842]

shortcrust pastry *n* [➡BREAD, FLOUR, AND BREAD PRODUCTS; 1178]

short-eared owl *type of* **owl**. [➡OWL; 1001]

shorten *v* **cut down**, cut, cut back, curtail, abbreviate, abridge, condense, contract, truncate, reduce, compress, telescope, take up, diminish. [➡CHANGE OF SIZE: SMALLER; 394] *Opposite:* lengthen.

shortening (*US*) *n* **fat**, lard, margarine, butter, suet. [➡FATS AND OILS; 1172]

shortfall *n* **deficit**, loss, underperformance, gap, lack, shortage. [➡TOO FEW, TOO LITTLE; 120] *Opposite:* excess.

short form *n* **abbreviation**, shortening, contraction, acronym, ellipsis. [➡ASPECTS OF LANGUAGE; 683]

short-handed *adj* **short-staffed**, understaffed, short. [➡TOO FEW, TOO LITTLE; 120]

short-list *v* **select**, choose, pick out, cream off, narrow down, sift. [➡MAKE DECISIONS AND CHOICES; 753]

short-lived *adj* **brief**, fleeting, transitory, passing, short, ephemeral, short-term, momentary, transient. [➡FINITENESS, VARIABILITY, AND TRANSIENCE; 96] *Opposite:* long-lasting.

shortly 1 *adv* **soon**, before long, in a while, in a minute, in a moment, in a bit, presently, just, right away. [➡FUTURE; 86] *Opposite:* later. 2 *adv* **curtly**, brusquely, abruptly, briskly, tersely, sharply, gruffly, rudely, discourteously. [➡BAD-TEMPERED AND HUMOURLESS; 627] *Opposite:* pleasantly.

shortness 1 *n* **smallness**, tininess, squatness, dumpiness. [➡LENGTH: SHORT; 1197] *Opposite:* tallness. 2 *n* **quickness**, rapidity, speed, transience. [➡FINITENESS, VARIABILITY, AND TRANSIENCE; 96] *Opposite:* length. 3 *n* **briefness**, brevity, terseness, conciseness, concision, succinctness. [➡CONCISE AND CLEAR; 203] *Opposite:* length. 4 *n* **curtness**, brusqueness, abruptness, briskness, terseness, sharpness, gruffness, rudeness, discourtesy. [➡BAD-TEMPERED AND HUMOURLESS; 627] *Opposite:* pleasantness.

short of *prep* **apart from**, other than, without, bar. [➡NOT; 135] *Opposite:* including.

short of money *adj* [➡POVERTY AND POOR; 892]

short-range *adj* [➡CLOSENESS; 160]

shorts *type of* **trousers**. [➡GARMENTS AND OUTFITS; 865]

short-sighted 1 *adj* **myopic**, nearsighted (*US*). [➡SEE; 700] *Opposite:* farsighted. 2 *adj* **ill-considered**, thoughtless, unthinking, imprudent (*formal*), ill-advised, ill-judged, unwise, rash, hasty, short-term, short-range, limited, restricted. [➡THE NATURE OF IDEAS; 772] *Opposite:* farsighted.

short-sightedness 1 *n* **myopia**, nearsightedness (*US*). [➡SEE; 700] 2 *n* **thoughtlessness**, imprudence, rashness, hastiness. [➡NEGATIVE INTELLECTUAL CHARACTERISTICS; 526] *Opposite:* farsightedness.

short-staffed *adj* **short-handed**, understaffed, understrength. [➡TOO FEW, TOO LITTLE; 120]

short story *n* **novella**, tale, story, fable, parable. [➡FICTION AND DRAMA; 913] *Opposite:* epic.

short-tempered *adj* **quick-tempered**, irritable, impatient, irascible, touchy, tetchy (*informal*), crotchety (*informal*), cranky (*US informal*), grouchy (*informal*). [➡IRRITATION AND ANGER; 542]

short-term *adj* **temporary**, immediate, instant, short-range, interim, stopgap, makeshift. [➡FINITENESS, VARIABILITY, AND TRANSIENCE; 96] *Opposite:* long-term.

shortwave radio *n* [➡TELEVISION AND RADIO; 607]

shot 1 *n* **gunshot**, potshot, round, volley, report, bang, blast, explosion. [➡IMPACT SOUNDS; 1259] 2 *n* **bullet**, cannonball, slug, gunshot, buckshot, ammunition, pellets, shells. [➡PROJECTILES; 1158] 3 *n* **picture**, photo, photograph, snapshot, snap, frame, view, scene, sequence, composition. [➡PHOTOGRAPHY AND PHOTOGRAPHIC EQUIPMENT; 1121] 4 *n* **try**, go, attempt, turn, crack (*informal*), bash (*informal*), stab (*informal*). [➡ATTEMPT AN ACTION; 262] 5 *n* (*informal*) **injection**, jab (*informal*), inoculation, vaccination. [➡REMEDIES, TREATMENTS AND OPERATIONS; 732] 6 *n* (*informal*) **measure**, drink, glass, tot, slug (*informal*), jigger (*informal*). [➡AMOUNT AND QUANTITY; 112] 7 *type of* **sports equipment**. [➡SPORTS EQUIPMENT; 879]

shotgun *type of* **gun**. [➡WEAPONS FOR SHOOTING; 1155]

shot in the arm *n* **boost**, fillip, spur, kick-start, stimulus, lift, tonic, push. [➡TREAT; 211]

shot in the dark *n* **guess**, conjecture, speculation, potshot, shot (*informal*), attempt. [➡ATTEMPT AN ACTION; 262]

shot put *type of* **track and field**. [➡HOBBIES, GAMES, AND SPORTS; 875]

should *v* **ought to**, had better, have a duty to, be duty-bound to, must, have to, would. [➡NEED AND REQUIRE; 465]

shoulder 1 *v* **bear**, take on, accept, assume, carry, take up. [➡ACCEPT POSSESSION; 451] *Opposite:* refuse. 2 *type of* **cut**, *part of* **torso**. [➡TORSO; 694]

shoulder bag *type of* **handbag**. [➡CONTAINERS, RECEPTACLES, AND PACKAGING; 1244]

shoulder blade *type of* **bone**. [➡THE BONES AND JOINTS; 720]

shoulder to shoulder *adv* [➡CLOSENESS; 160]

shout 1 *v* **yell**, cry, scream, bellow, screech, bark, bawl, roar, holler (*informal*), call, call out. [➡SOUND EMISSION BY PEOPLE; 364] *Opposite:* whisper. 2 *n* **cry**, yell, scream, bellow, screech, bark, roar, holler (*informal*), call. [➡SOUNDS MADE BY PEOPLE; 1261] *Opposite:* whisper.

shout at *v* **tell off** (*informal*), tick off (*informal*), yell at, scold, reprimand, haul over the coals, berate, criticize, chew out (*US informal*). [➡ACCUSE, BLAME, AND CRITICIZE; 642] *Opposite:* praise.

shouting match *n* [➡ARGUMENT; 47]

shove 1 *v* **push**, thrust, heave, propel, jostle, shunt, move, elbow, ram, jolt. [➡PUSH, PULL, SLIDE; 336] *Opposite:* pull. 2 *v* **put**, throw, toss, chuck (*informal*), slap, bung (*informal*), sling, fling. [➡POSITION SOMETHING; 326] 3 *n* **thrust**, push, heave, jolt, pull. [➡PUSH, PULL, SLIDE; 336]

shovel 1 *n* **spade**, scoop, trowel, tool. [➡SPOONS, SCOOPS, AND SHOVELS; 1120] 2 *v* **scoop**, move, dig, spoon, heap, ladle. [➡USE TOOLS AND MACHINERY; 469]

shove off (*informal*) *v* [➡RUN AWAY AND AVOID; 10]

show 1 *v* **present**, display, exhibit, expose, disclose, indicate, reveal, bare, parade, show off, flaunt, flash, flourish, put under somebody's nose, put on view. [➡CAUSE TO APPEAR; 5] *Opposite:* hide. 2 *v* **stand out**, stick out, show up, appear, surface, catch the eye. [➡ARRIVE; 12] 3 *v* **accompany**, take, guide, direct, point, steer. [➡ACCOMPANY AND FOLLOW; 338] 4 *v* **prove**, illustrate, demonstrate, confirm, indicate, establish. [➡MEAN SOMETHING; 61] *Opposite:* disprove. 5 *v* **demonstrate**, illustrate, explain, teach, point out, indicate, spell out. [➡EXPLAIN AND CLARIFY; 611] 6 *n* **demonstration**, display, expression, illustration, confirmation, appearance, indication, spectacle. [➡PERFORMANCES AND SHOWS; 42] 7 *n* **performance**, musical, cabaret, play, film, programme, TV show, radio show, act, entertainment, showing, presentation, viewing, screening, movie (*US*). [➡PERFORMANCES AND SHOWS; 42] 8 *n* **fair**, fête, exhibition, trade show, county show, agricultural show, fashion show, flower show, event, extravaganza, display. [➡SALES AND SHOWS; 444]

show a clean pair of heels *v* [➡RUN AWAY AND AVOID; 10]

show appreciation *v* [➡PRAISE AND ENCOURAGE; 648]

show biz (*informal*) *n* [➡ENTERTAINMENT; 872]

showboat (*informal*) *v* [➡BOAST; 617]

show business *n* **the stage**, theatre, the boards, films (*informal*), film, movies, television, show biz (*informal*). [➡THE PERFORMING ARTS; 904]

showcase 1 *n* **glass case**, cabinet, display case, display cabinet, vitrine. [➡FURNITURE; 858] 2 *n* **platform**, vehicle, setting, stage. [➡ADVERTISING AND PUBLICITY; 605]

showdown *n* **confrontation**, head-to-head, face-off, row, fight, argument, quarrel, conflict, shoot-out. [➡ARGUMENT; 47]

shower 1 *n* **wash**, dip, rinse, spray. [➡CLEAN AND POLISH; 404] 2 *n* **cascade**, burst, deluge, hail, spray, sprinkling, flood, splatter. [➡MANY, MUCH, LARGE AMOUNT; 117] 3 *n* **cloudburst**, downpour, storm, rainstorm, flurry, drizzle, rainfall. [➡CLOUDY AND RAINY WEATHER; 1052] 4 *v* **wash**, clean up, freshen up, rinse. [➡CLEAN AND POLISH; 404] 5 *v* **rain**, rain down, pour, pour down, spit, sprinkle (*US*), fall, drop, spill. [➡CLOUDY AND RAINY WEATHER; 1052] 6 *v* **overwhelm**, inundate, flood, deluge, bombard, cover. [➡GIVE TOO MUCH; 438] 7 *type of* **plumbing fittings**. [➡FITTINGS; 859]

showery *adj* **rainy**, wet, changeable, damp, spitting, drizzly. [➡CLOUDY AND RAINY WEATHER; 1052] *Opposite:* dry.

showground *n* **arena**, ring, enclosure, field, ground, fairground. [➡URBAN OUTDOOR SPACES; 1071]

show in *v* [➡ACCOMPANY AND FOLLOW; 338]

showiness 1 *n* **impressiveness**, attractiveness, splendour, magnificence, drama. [➡BEAUTY AND ATTRACTIVENESS; 190] *Opposite:* modesty. 2 *n* **ostentation**, flashiness, show, gaudiness, garishness, tastelessness, brashness, vulgarity, glitz, jazziness, brassiness, pretension. [➡IN POOR TASTE; 230] *Opposite:* discretion.

showing *n* **presentation**, performance, viewing, screening, display, show. [➡PERFORMANCES AND SHOWS; 42]

showing off *n* **bravado**, boastfulness, boasting, bragging, posturing, bluster, swagger, exhibitionism. [➡BOAST; 617]

show jumping *n* [➡HOBBIES, GAMES, AND SPORTS; 875]

show-off (*informal*) *n* **boaster**, braggart, poser (*informal disapproving*), bragger, know-all (*informal*), bighead (*informal*), exhibitionist. [➡SELF-IMPORTANT AND SELF-SEEKING PEOPLE; 949]

show off 1 *v* **boast**, brag, shoot your mouth off, fly your own kite, blow your own trumpet (*informal*), sing your own praises, pose, swank (*informal*), swagger, blow your own horn (*US*). [➡BOAST; 617] 2 *v* **display**, flaunt, flash (*informal*), parade, flourish. [➡CAUSE TO APPEAR; 5] *Opposite:* hide.

show of hands *n* [➡GESTURES AND GESTICULATION; 654]

show out *v* [➡ACCOMPANY AND FOLLOW; 338]

showpiece *n* **centrepiece**, pride and joy, focus, attraction, pièce de résistance, masterpiece. [➡PERFECT EXAMPLES AND EMBODIMENTS; 67]

showroom *n* **shop**, outlet, store. [➡RETAIL OUTLETS; 1082]

show the way *v* [➡ACCOMPANY AND FOLLOW; 338]

show to the door *v* [➡ACCOMPANY AND FOLLOW; 338]

show up 1 *v* (*informal*) **come**, turn up, arrive, put in an appearance, appear, show your face, roll up, attend, crop up (*informal*). [➡ARRIVE; 12] 2 *v* **highlight**, emphasize, point up, bring to light, reveal, disclose, expose, indicate. [➡CAUSE TO APPEAR; 5] *Opposite:* hide. **3** *v* **stand out**, stick out, show, catch your eye, come to light, emerge. [➡APPEAR AND EMERGE; 3] **4** *v* **embarrass**, humiliate, put somebody to shame, mortify, shame, make a fool of, score off. [➡UPSET, DISTRESS, AND HUMILIATE; 568]

showy 1 *adj* **impressive**, attractive, eye-catching, splendid, magnificent, spectacular, dramatic. [➡BEAUTY AND ATTRACTIVENESS; 190] *Opposite:* modest. **2** *adj* **ostentatious**, flashy, gaudy, garish, tasteless, brash, vulgar, glitzy, jazzy (*slang*), pretentious. [➡IN POOR TASTE; 230] *Opposite:* restrained.

show your face *v* **turn up**, appear, show up (*informal*), put in an appearance, come, arrive, roll up, attend, emerge, surface. [➡ARRIVE; 12] *Opposite:* hide.

shred 1 *n* **scrap**, strip, bit, piece, sliver, tatter, shaving, paring, crumb, fragment. [➡SMALL PIECE; 127] *Opposite:* whole. **2** *v* **slice**, cut up, tear up, rip up, grate, mince, chop, destroy, grind. [➡TEAR, BREAK, AND CUT; 361]

shrew *type of* **rodent**. [➡RODENT; 989]

shrewd *adj* **astute**, sharp, on the ball (*informal*), smart, perceptive, discerning, insightful, wise, clever, intelligent, cunning, crafty, sharp-witted, canny, sensible, accurate, judicious. [➡POSITIVE INTELLECTUAL CHARACTERISTICS; 525] *Opposite:* naive.

shrewdness *n* **astuteness**, sharpness, smartness, perceptiveness, discernment, insight, judgment, wisdom, cleverness, intelligence, cunning, craftiness, guile, canniness, accuracy, judiciousness. [➡POSITIVE INTELLECTUAL CHARACTERISTICS; 525] *Opposite:* naivety.

shrewish *adj* [➡DIFFICULT TO PLEASE; 516]

shrewishness *n* [➡DIFFICULT TO PLEASE; 516]

shriek *n* **screech**, scream, yell, cry, yelp, shout, call. [➡SOUNDS MADE BY PEOPLE; 1261] *Opposite:* whisper.

shrill *adj* **piercing**, high-pitched, strident, penetrating, harsh, sharp, jarring. [➡LOUD OR UNPLEASANT SOUNDS; 1265] *Opposite:* low.

shrillness *n* [➡LOUD OR UNPLEASANT SOUNDS; 1265]

shrilly *adv* **piercingly**, stridently, penetratingly, harshly, sharply, jarringly. [➡LOUD OR UNPLEASANT SOUNDS; 1265] *Opposite:* soothingly.

shrimp *type of* **crustacean**. [➡AQUATIC INVERTEBRATE; 1022]

shrine 1 *n* **memorial**, monument, tomb, grave, sanctuary, tabernacle, reliquary, stupa. [➡RELIGIOUS OBJECTS; 780] **2** *type of* **place of worship**. [➡RELIGIOUS BUILDINGS; 1084]

shrink 1 *v* **contract**, shrivel, wither, telescope, shorten, dry up, waste away, disappear. [➡CHANGE OF SIZE: SMALLER; 394] *Opposite:* grow. **2** *v* **fall**, drop, decrease, decline, diminish, lessen, dwindle, minimize. [➡CHANGE OF SIZE: SMALLER; 394] *Opposite:* rise. **3** *v* **cower**, cringe, flinch, recoil, draw back, back away, pull back, back off, fall back, grovel, shy away, withdraw, shrink away, shrink back. [➡PHYSICAL REACTIONS; 317] *Opposite:* stand your ground. **4** *n* (*slang*) **psychiatrist**, psychoanalyst, therapist, counsellor, analyst. [➡PEOPLE WHO WORK IN MEDICINE; 848]

See Compare and Contrast at **recoil**.

shrinkage *n* **reduction**, decrease, decline, contraction, fall, drop, disappearance. [➡CHANGE OF SIZE: SMALLER; 394] *Opposite:* growth.

shrink back *v* **recoil**, cringe, shrink away, shy away, flinch, draw back, withdraw, retreat, cower, back away, pull back, back off, fall back, grovel. [➡GO BACKWARDS; 310] *Opposite:* advance.

shrink from *v* **recoil from**, baulk at, avoid, shirk, shun, turn away from, spurn, reject, eschew. [➡NOT DO AND REFUSE TO DO; 275] *Opposite:* welcome.

shrivel *v* **shrink**, wither, dry up, contract, curl up, waste away, telescope, shorten. [➡CHANGE OF SIZE: SMALLER; 394] *Opposite:* expand.

shrivelled *adj* [➡SMALL; 1194]

See Compare and Contrast at **dry**.

shrivel up *v* [➡CHANGE OF SHAPE; 386]

shroud 1 *n* **covering**, cover, blanket, layer, cloak, mantle (*literary*). [➡COVERS AND COATINGS; 1245] **2** *part of* **spacecraft**. [➡SPACE VEHICLES; 1062] **3** *part of* **sailing vessel**. [➡PARTS OF A SHIP OR BOAT; 1150]

shrouded in mystery *adj* [➡SECRET AND UNKNOWN; 180]

shrub *n* **bush**, plant, tree, flowering shrub. [➡BUSHES AND SHRUBS; 1027]

shrub

◆ *types of shrub or bush*
azalea, bramble, briar, broom, camellia, elder, forsythia, gardenia, gorse, hawthorn, heather, hydrangea, laurel, lavender, lilac, magnolia, privet, pussy willow, rhododendron, rose, sagebrush, witch hazel

shrubbery *n* **bushes**, undergrowth, border, herbaceous border, hedging. [➡BUSHES AND SHRUBS; 1027]

shrug *n* [➡GESTURES AND GESTICULATION; 654]

shrug off *v* **dismiss**, pooh-pooh, ignore, treat lightly, make light of, pay no heed to, disregard, reject. [➡NOT PAY ATTENTION; 765]

shrunken *adj* **wasted**, emaciated, dried up, withered, shrivelled, contracted. [➡CHANGE OF SIZE: SMALLER; 394] *Opposite:* bloated.

shudder 1 *v* **shake**, tremble, shiver, wince, quake, judder, quiver, jolt, wobble, vibrate, convulse. [➡PHYSICAL REACTIONS; 317] **2** *n* **tremble**, shake, shiver, tremor, judder, jolt, wince, quake (*informal*), convulsion, agitation. [➡PHYSICAL REACTIONS; 317]

shuffle 1 *v* **scuffle**, hobble, trundle, shamble, lumber, slouch, waddle. [➡WALK UNSTEADILY; 316] **2** *v* **mix up**, jumble up, muddle up, rearrange, reorder, transpose. [➡COMBINE AND MIX; 401]

shufti (*informal*) *n* [➡LOOKING AND LOOKS; 701]

shun *v* **avoid**, turn away from, spurn, reject, eschew, ignore, shirk, recoil from, baulk at, shrink from. [➡REFUSING OR REJECTING RELATIONS; 975] *Opposite:* court.

shunt 1 *v* **push**, shove, move, shift, propel, force, thrust, jolt. [➡PUSH, PULL, SLIDE; 336] 2 *n* (*informal*) **collision**, crash, smash, accident, prang (*informal*). [➡TRAFFIC ACCIDENTS; 256] 3 *v* (*informal*) **hit**, collide with, smash into, bump into. [➡CONTACT: IMPACT; 414] 4 *n* **shove**, thrust, jolt, push, diversion, bypass. [➡PUSH, PULL, SLIDE; 336]

shush 1 *interj* [➡UNFAVOURABLE NON-VERBAL RESPONSES; 655] 2 *v* (*informal*) **silence**, shut up, quieten, quieten down, hush, belt up (*slang*), pipe down (*informal*). [➡WITHHOLD INFORMATION; 688]

shut 1 *v* **close**, close up, push to, fasten, secure, bolt, lock, lock up, shut up, slam to, snap to. [➡FASTEN, LINK, AND JOIN; 409] *Opposite:* open. 2 *v* **close down**, close, shut up shop, shut down, go out of business, go bankrupt, go bust (*informal*), go into liquidation, go to the wall, fold, fail, collapse, go under, liquidate, wind up. [➡FAIL OR BE UNSUCCESSFUL; 75] *Opposite:* start up.

shutdown *n* **closure**, cessation, stoppage, halt, end, blackout. [➡WORK-RELATED ACTIVITIES; 834]

shut down *v* [➡STOP ACTING; 265]

shuteye (*informal*) *n* [➡SLEEP AND DREAM; 724]

shut in 1 *v* **confine**, cage, restrain, imprison, lock in, close in, enclose, shut up. [➡CAPTIVITY AND LOSS OF FREEDOM; 249] *Opposite:* let loose. 2 *adj* **captive**, imprisoned, locked in, confined, caged, restrained, closed in, shut up. [➡CAPTIVITY AND LOSS OF FREEDOM; 249] *Opposite:* free.

shut off 1 *v* **switch off**, turn off, close off, close down, shut down, stop, cut out, block, impede. [➡CAUSE TO STOP; 267] *Opposite:* turn on. 2 *v* **isolate**, cut off, separate, seclude, set apart, sequester (*formal*). [➡SEPARATE AND DIVIDE; 402]

shut out *v* **lock out**, keep out, exclude, keep off, debar, keep at arm's length. [➡EJECT AND EXCLUDE; 341] *Opposite:* let in.

shutter *part of* **photographic equipment**. [➡PHOTOGRAPHY AND PHOTOGRAPHIC EQUIPMENT; 1121]

shuttle 1 *v* **travel**, go, ferry, transport, transfer, carry, take. [➡TRAVEL: WAYS OF TRAVELLING; 321] 2 *type of* **public service vehicle**. [➡VEHICLES; 1144]

shuttlecock *type of* **sport equipment**. [➡SPORTS EQUIPMENT; 879]

shut up 1 *v* (*informal*) **be quiet**, fall silent, clam up (*informal*), quieten down, pipe down (*informal*). [➡WITHHOLD INFORMATION; 688] 2 *v* **confine**, imprison, cage, shut in, lock in, close in, enclose, restrain. [➡CAPTIVITY AND LOSS OF FREEDOM; 249] *Opposite:* let loose. 3 *v* (*informal*) **silence**, hush, gag, muzzle, cut off, stifle. [➡AVOID, PREVENT, LIMIT, AND CONTROL; 278] 4 *v* **close**, close up, lock, lock up, secure, fasten, bolt. [➡FASTEN, LINK, AND JOIN; 409] *Opposite:* open up.

shut up shop 1 *v* **stop**, call it a day, turn in, pack in (*informal*), close, shut. [➡STOP ACTING; 265] *Opposite:* start up. 2 *v* **close**, shut, close down, shut down, go out of business, go bankrupt, go bust (*informal*), go to the wall, go into liquidation, fold, collapse, fail, go under. [➡BUSINESS ACTIVITIES AND PHENOMENA; 795] *Opposite:* start up.

shy 1 *adj* **introverted**, retiring, withdrawn, timid, bashful, diffident, inhibited, reticent, reserved, quiet, coy. [➡RETICENT AND UNFORTHCOMING; 632] *Opposite:* outgoing. 2 *adj* **cautious**, wary, nervous, afraid, fearful, reluctant. [➡INSECURITY AND LOSS OF COMPOSURE; 545] *Opposite:* confident.

shy away *v* **retreat**, shrink, recoil, flinch, back off, back away, draw back, cringe, cower. [➡GO BACKWARDS; 310]

shyly 1 *adv* **timidly**, bashfully, reticently, reservedly, diffidently, quietly, warily, coyly. [➡RETICENT AND UNFORTHCOMING; 632] *Opposite:* boldly. 2 *adv* **cautiously**, warily, nervously, fearfully, reluctantly. [➡INSECURITY AND LOSS OF COMPOSURE; 545] *Opposite:* confidently.

shyness *n* **introversion**, timidity, bashfulness, inhibition, reticence, reserve, diffidence, quietness, coyness, caution, wariness, nervousness. [➡RETICENT AND UNFORTHCOMING; 632] *Opposite:* boldness.

Siamese cat *type of* **cat**. [➡FELINE; 983]

sibling *type of* **same generation relative**. [➡SAME GENERATION RELATIVES; 957]

sibyl *n* [➡PEOPLE WITH SUPERNATURAL POWERS; 789]

sick 1 *adj* **ill**, unwell, poorly (*informal*), off-colour, below par (*informal*), bad, under the weather, ailing (*dated*), out of sorts, pale. [➡ILL AND SICK; 741] *Opposite:* well. 2 *adj* **nauseous**, queasy, bilious, green around the gills (*informal*), dizzy. [➡ILL AND SICK; 741] 3 *adj* (*informal*) **tasteless**, in bad taste, gruesome, bizarre, sickening, revolting, vile, nauseating. [➡IN POOR TASTE; 230] 4 *adj* **fed up** (*informal*), bored, up to here, had it (*informal*), sick and tired, sick to the back teeth, sick to death. [➡SADNESS, DISTRESS, AND DESPAIR; 540] 5 *n* (*informal*) **vomit**, spew, puke (*informal*), barf (*US informal*), chunder (*informal*), vomitus (*technical*), bile (*literary*). [➡VOMIT AND BELCH; 713]

sick and tired *adj* **fed up** (*informal*), sick, sick to the back teeth, up to here, sick to death, bored. [➡SADNESS, DISTRESS, AND DESPAIR; 540]

sickbay *n* **infirmary**, sanatorium, sickroom, hospital. [➡HOSPITALS AND CLINICS; 826]

sicken *v* **nauseate**, turn your stomach, repel, disgust, make sick, appal, shock, revolt, repulse. [➡UPSET, DISTRESS, AND HUMILIATE; 568]

sickened *adj* [➡SADNESS, DISTRESS, AND DESPAIR; 540]

sickening 1 *adj* **disgusting**, nauseating, stomach-churning, shocking, appalling, revolting, repulsive, repellent, terrible, horrible, vile, stomach-turning (*US*). [➡DISGUSTING AND REPULSIVE; 231] *Opposite:* appealing. 2 *adj* (*informal*) **annoying**, maddening, irritating, infuriating, disappointing, galling, trying. [➡IRRITATING; 229] *Opposite:* pleasing.

sickle *type of* **cutting tool**. [➡CUTTING TOOLS; 1119]

sickly 1 *adj* **unhealthy**, weak, ill, poorly (*informal*), unwell, ailing (*dated*), pale, wan. [➡UNFIT AND WEAK; 740] *Opposite:* healthy. 2 *adj* **cloying**, overpowering, disgusting, suffocating, nauseating, sickening. [➡DISGUSTING AND REPULSIVE; 231] *Opposite:* appealing. 3 *adj* **saccharine**, sentimental, cloying, sickly-sweet, mawkish, sugary, soppy (*informal*). [➡IN POOR TASTE; 230] *Opposite:* tough.

sickly-sweet *adj* **saccharine**, cloying, mawkish, soppy (*informal*), sentimental, nauseating, sickening. [➡ IN POOR TASTE; 230]

sickness 1 *n* **illness**, disease, virus, bug (*informal*), condition, bad health, ill health, infection. [➡ SICKNESS; 730] *Opposite:* health. 2 *n* **nausea**, vomiting, queasiness, biliousness, throwing up (*informal*). [➡ DISORDERS OF THE DIGESTIVE SYSTEM; 714]

sick to death *adj* [➡ IRRITATION AND ANGER; 542]

sick to the back teeth *adj* [➡ IRRITATION AND ANGER; 542]

sick up (*informal*) *v* **vomit**, spew, throw up (*informal*), puke (*slang*), hurl (*slang*), barf (*US informal*). [➡ VOMIT AND BELCH; 713]

side 1 *n* **surface**, face, elevation, wall, plane. [➡ EXTREMITIES OF PHYSICAL OBJECTS; 1249] 2 *n* **part**, area, region, section, segment, zone, quarter. [➡ AREA AND RANGE; 111] 3 *n* **edge**, boundary, flank, bank, periphery, margin, fringe, border. [➡ EXTREMITIES OF PHYSICAL OBJECTS; 1249] 4 *n* **aspect**, facet, feature, quality, characteristic, trait. [➡ QUALITIES AND CHARACTERISTICS; 1190] 5 *n* **team**, squad, line-up, group, gang, camp. [➡ GROUPS WITH A COMMON INTEREST; 938] 6 *type of* **cut**. [➡ TYPES AND CUTS OF MEAT; 1176]

sideboard *type of* **cabinet**. [➡ FURNITURE; 858]

sideburns *n* [➡ FACIAL HAIR; 490]

side by side *adj* [➡ CLOSENESS; 160]

side dish *part of* **meal**. [➡ MEALS AND PARTS OF MEALS; 1168]

side effect *n* **unexpected result**, secondary effect, byproduct, consequence, knock-on effect, result. [➡ RESULTS AND OUTCOMES; 83]

sidekick (*informal*) *n* **assistant**, helper, associate, subordinate, partner, colleague. [➡ COLLEAGUES AND EQUALS; 967] *Opposite:* boss.

sidelight *type of* **external feature**. [➡ VEHICLES; 1144]

sideline 1 *n* **hobby**, pastime, offshoot, secondary activity, second job, spin-off, byproduct, second string to your bow. [➡ LEISURE AND RECREATION; 874] *Opposite:* career. 2 *v* **put aside**, shelve, put off, slow pedal, put on the back burner, suspend. [➡ NOT PAY ATTENTION; 765] *Opposite:* promote. 3 *v* **relegate**, demote, exclude, downgrade, lay off, dismiss. [➡ REVOKE STATUS; 460] *Opposite:* promote.

sidelong *adj* **sideways**, oblique, slanting, indirect, askew, aslant. [➡ DIRECTION OF MOTION; 346] *Opposite:* direct.

side mirror (*US*) *type of* **external feature**. [➡ VEHICLES; 1144]

sidereal *adj* [➡ THE SUPERNATURAL; 788]

sidesplitting *adj* **hilarious**, hysterical (*informal*), riotous, uproarious, rollicking, rib-tickling (*informal*), funny, comic, comical. [➡ FUNNY AND AMUSING; 217] *Opposite:* dull.

See Compare and Contrast at **funny**.

sidestep *v* **avoid**, evade, dodge, duck, bypass, skirt. [➡ NOT DO AND REFUSE TO DO; 275]

side street *n* **alley**, back street, lane, side road. [➡ ROADS; 1105]

sidetrack *v* **distract**, deflect, divert, change the subject, get off the point, lose the thread. [➡ CONFUSE AND BEWILDER; 572]

sidetracked *adj* [➡ PENSIVENESS AND INTEREST; 539]

side view *n* **cross section**, profile, section, side, aspect. [➡ DRAWINGS, CHARTS AND TABLES; 595]

sidewalk (*US*) *n* **path**, footway, walkway, footpath, pavement. [➡ PATHWAYS; 1109]

sideways 1 *adj* **oblique**, slanting, indirect, sidelong, slanted, sideward. [➡ DIRECTION OF MOTION; 346] *Opposite:* straight. 2 *adv* **to one side**, to the left, to the right, askew, askance, aslant. [➡ DIRECTION OF MOTION; 346] *Opposite:* straight.

sidewinder *type of* **poisonous snake**. [➡ SNAKE; 995]

side with *v* **back**, support, take somebody's side, be in somebody's camp, take somebody's part, be on somebody's side. [➡ APPROVE AND CONFIRM; 647] *Opposite:* oppose.

sidle *v* **edge**, creep, slither, snake, inch, slink. [➡ MOVE SLOWLY; 315]

siege *n* **blockade**, cordon, barrier, barricade, obstruction, restriction. [➡ AGGRESSIVE EVENT; 39]

siesta *n* **rest**, nap, sleep, snooze (*informal*), forty winks (*informal*), catnap. [➡ SLEEP AND DREAM; 724]

sieve *type of* **utensil**. [➡ TABLEWARE, CUTLERY, AND KITCHENWARE; 861]

sift 1 *v* **sieve**, filter, separate, put through a sieve, strain. [➡ SEPARATE AND DIVIDE; 402] 2 *v* **sort through**, go through, go through with a fine-tooth comb, examine, select, scrutinize. [➡ SEEK POSSESSION AND SEARCH; 457]

sigh 1 *v* **exhale**, heave a sigh, moan, groan, breathe. [➡ SOUND EMISSION BY PEOPLE; 364] *Opposite:* inhale. 2 *v* **yearn**, long, hanker, pine, want, desire. [➡ DESIRE AND WANT; 580] *Opposite:* dislike. 3 *n* **exhalation**, moan, groan, complaint, lament. [➡ SOUNDS MADE BY PEOPLE; 1261]

sight 1 *n* **vision**, eyesight, ability to see. [➡ SEE; 700] 2 *n* **view**, spectacle, prospect, picture, scene, vista, vision, display. [➡ VIEWS AND OUTLOOKS; 1072] 3 *v* **notice**, catch sight of, spot, espy (*formal*), see, glimpse, observe, view. [➡ SEE; 700] *Opposite:* miss.

sighted *adj* **seeing**, keen-sighted, partially sighted, long-sighted, eagle-eyed, short-sighted, nearsighted (*US*), far-sighted (*US*). [➡ SEE; 700] *Opposite:* blind.

sightless *adj* [➡ SEE; 700]

sightlessness *n* [➡ SEE; 700]

sights *n* **tourist attractions**, places of interest, highlights, wonders, marvels. [➡ TRAVEL: SIGHT-SEEING AND TOURISM; 322]

sightsee *v* [➡ TRAVEL: WAYS OF TRAVELLING; 321]

sightseeing *n* **tourism**, visiting the attractions, going to places of interest, seeing the sights, exploration. [➡ TRAVEL: SIGHT-SEEING AND TOURISM; 322]

sightseer *n* **tourist**, visitor, holidaymaker, day tripper,

tripper (*informal*), vacationer (*US*). [➡TRAVEL: TRAVELLERS AND WALKERS; 320] *Opposite:* resident.

sign 1 *n* **symbol**, mark, emblem, insignia, logo, badge. [➡SYMBOLS, SIGNS, AND NUMBERS; 597] 2 *n* **signal**, indication, symptom, warning, clue, hint. [➡INDICATIONS, SIGNS, AND WARNINGS; 68] 3 *n* **notice**, poster, road sign, hoarding, placard, billboard. [➡SIGNPOSTS, SIGNALS AND BILLBOARDS; 596] 4 *n* **trace**, track, trail, footprint, mark, scent. [➡REPRESENTATIONS AND GENERAL EXAMPLES; 65] 5 *n* **omen**, warning, portent, premonition, indication, prediction. [➡FATE, DESTINY, AND ASTROLOGY; 783] 6 *v* **autograph**, sign your name, initial, authorize, endorse. [➡NAME AND DESCRIBE; 666] 7 *v* **employ**, contract, hire, engage, take on, retain, sign up. [➡CONFER STATUS; 459] *Opposite:* dismiss. 8 *v* **make signs**, signal, gesture, motion, indicate, gesticulate. [➡GESTURES AND GESTICULATION; 654]

Compare and Contrast: ***sign, indication, symptom***

CORE MEANING: SOMETHING THAT SUGGESTS THE PRESENCE OR OCCURRENCE OF SOMETHING ELSE

sign something that suggests the presence or occurrence of another thing, whether concrete or abstract, that is not immediately apparent; ***indication*** used in a similar way to *sign*, but most commonly of abstract things; ***symptom*** a physical sign that suggests the presence of a particular problem, or of a medical condition.

signal 1 *n* **sign**, indication, gesture, indicator, motion, warning sign, hint, pointer. [➡GESTURES AND GESTICULATION; 654] 2 *v* **communicate**, indicate, suggest, intimate, hint, imply. [➡SUGGEST, HINT, AND COMMENT; 613] 3 *v* **gesture**, gesticulate, motion, sign, beckon, wave, nod. [➡GESTURES AND GESTICULATION; 654] 4 *v* **indicate**, mark, herald, portend, announce, usher in. [➡MEAN SOMETHING; 61]

signally *adv* **completely**, notably, totally, absolutely, one hundred per cent, unmistakably, conspicuously, obviously. [➡ABSOLUTE AND ABSOLUTELY; 131]

signatory *n* **party**, participant, guarantor, countersigner, the undersigned, cosigner. [➡PEOPLE INVOLVED IN FINANCE; 804]

signature *n* **name**, autograph, cross, moniker (*slang*), monogram, mark, sign, initials, John Hancock (*US informal*). [➡SYMBOLS, SIGNS, AND NUMBERS; 597]

signboard *n* **sign**, signpost, notice, hoarding, road sign, billboard. [➡SIGNPOSTS, SIGNALS AND BILLBOARDS; 596]

significance 1 *n* **importance**, impact, substance, consequence (*formal*), weight, moment (*formal*), magnitude. [➡IMPORTANCE AND SIGNIFICANCE; 193] *Opposite:* meaninglessness. 2 *n* **meaning**, implication, import, consequence (*formal*), worth, connotation. [➡MEANING; 691]

significant 1 *adj* **meaningful**, knowing, meaning, suggestive, expressive, pointed. [➡ENTHUSIASTIC AND INQUISITIVE; 629] *Opposite:* blank. 2 *adj* **important**, major, noteworthy, momentous, substantial, weighty. [➡IMPORTANT; 195] *Opposite:* insignificant. 3 *adj* **considerable**, large, major, big, sizable, hefty, substantial. [➡LARGE; 1192] *Opposite:* paltry.

significantly 1 *adv* **considerably**, appreciably, drastically, notably, radically, extensively, substantially, a lot. [➡TO A GREAT EXTENT; 130] 2 *adv* **meaningfully**, knowingly, suggestively, pointedly, expressively. [➡INTERESTING AND MEANINGFUL; 191] *Opposite:* innocently.

significant other *n* **partner**, lover, spouse, other half, better half. [➡SEXUAL AND ROMANTIC RELATIONSHIPS; 964]

signification *n* **meaning**, sense, gist, significance, denotation, connotation. [➡MEANING; 691]

signify *v* **mean**, indicate, show, imply, suggest, be a sign of, denote, connote. [➡MEAN SOMETHING; 61]

signing 1 *n* **ratification**, validation, adoption, passing, authorization, formal acceptance. [➡PERMIT AND ALLOW; 670] *Opposite:* rejection. 2 *n* **new employee**, new player, new arrival, recruit, acquisition. [➡WORKER; 836]

sign on *v* **enlist**, sign up, enrol, put your name down for, register, join. [➡PARTICIPATE; 293]

signpost 1 *n* **signboard**, sign, notice, marker, road sign, finger post. [➡SIGNPOSTS, SIGNALS AND BILLBOARDS; 596] 2 *n* **indication**, suggestion, pointer, marker, sign, signal. [➡INDICATIONS, SIGNS, AND WARNINGS; 68] 3 *v* **flag**, mark, indicate, label, designate, point out. [➡MEAN SOMETHING; 61] *Opposite:* conceal.

sign up 1 *v* **recruit**, employ, sign, take somebody on, contract, hire. [➡CONFER STATUS; 459] *Opposite:* fire. 2 *v* **enlist**, join, enrol, become a member, put your name down, register, sign on, draft (*US*). [➡PARTICIPATE; 293] *Opposite:* quit.

silage *n* **fodder**, feed, grass, forage. [➡ANIMAL FEED; 1167]

silence 1 *n* **quietness**, quiet, hush, stillness, peace, calm. [➡ABSENCE OF SOUND; 1256] *Opposite:* noise. 2 *n* **muteness**, taciturnity, reticence, reserve, uncommunicativeness, dumbness. [➡RETICENT AND UNFORTHCOMING; 632] *Opposite:* chatter. 3 *v* **make quiet**, quieten, shut up (*informal*), hush, shush (*informal*), muzzle. [➡AVOID, PREVENT, LIMIT, AND CONTROL; 278] 4 *v* **stop**, put an end to, gag, stifle, suppress, quash, smother, curb. [➡CAUSE TO STOP; 267] *Opposite:* encourage.

silencer *type of* **external feature**. [➡VEHICLES; 1144]

silent 1 *adj* **still**, hushed, soundless, noiseless, quiet, inaudible. [➡ABSENCE OF SOUND; 1256] *Opposite:* noisy. 2 *adj* **mute**, tongue-tied, uncommunicative, taciturn, reticent, reserved, quiet. [➡RETICENT AND UNFORTHCOMING; 632] *Opposite:* talkative. 3 *adj* **unspoken**, unvoiced, voiceless, tacit, wordless, understood. [➡SECRET AND UNKNOWN; 180] *Opposite:* spoken.

Compare and Contrast: ***silent, quiet, reticent, taciturn, uncommunicative***

CORE MEANING: NOT SPEAKING OR NOT SAYING MUCH

silent not speaking or communicating at any particular time, especially through choice, or not inclined to speak much; ***quiet*** not inclined to speak much, often because of shyness; ***reticent*** unwilling to communicate very much, talk a lot, or reveal all the facts; ***taciturn*** habitually reserved in speech and manner; ***uncommunicative*** not willing to say much, especially not to reveal information, or tending not to say much.

silently *adv* **noiselessly**, without a sound, soundlessly, wordlessly, mutely, inaudibly. [➡ABSENCE OF SOUND; 1256] *Opposite:* noisily.

silhouette *n* **outline**, shape, shadow, profile, line, figure. [➡SHAPE; 1215]

silicate *type of* **mineral**. [➡MINERALS; 1276]

silk *type of* **fabric from animals**. [➡FABRICS; 1131]

silken *adj* **smooth**, soft, silky, silky-smooth, glossy, shiny, sleek. [➡PHYSICAL TEXTURE; 1221] *Opposite:* coarse.

silkiness *n* [➡PHYSICAL TEXTURE; 1221]

silkworm *type of* **insect stages of development**. [➡INSECT STAGES; 1020]

silky 1 *adj* **glossy**, smooth, soft, silken, silky-smooth, shiny, sleek. [➡PHYSICAL TEXTURE; 1221] *Opposite:* rough. 2 *adj* **smooth**, honeyed, mellifluous, sweet, unctuous, refined. [➡SOFT OR PLEASANT SOUNDS; 1264] *Opposite:* harsh.

silky-smooth *adj* [➡PHYSICAL TEXTURE; 1221]

sill *n* **ledge**, shelf, ridge, projection, windowsill. [➡WINDOWS; 1099]

silliness 1 *n* **stupidity**, ridiculousness, daftness (*informal*), childishness, madness, idiocy, absurdity, inanity, folly. [➡BIZARRE AND PECULIAR; 258] *Opposite:* sense. 2 *n* **triviality**, meaninglessness, mindlessness, puerility, inanity, senselessness, pointlessness. [➡UNIMPORTANT AND UNNECESSARY; 239] *Opposite:* importance.

silly 1 *adj* **stupid**, ridiculous, daft (*informal*), impractical, childish, asinine, juvenile. [➡FUNNY AND AMUSING; 217] *Opposite:* sensible. 2 *adj* **trivial**, meaningless, mindless, puerile, senseless, pointless, inane. [➡UNIMPORTANT AND UNNECESSARY; 239] *Opposite:* important.

silo *type of* **storage space**. [➡STORES AND STORAGE BUILDINGS; 1087]

silt *n* **deposit**, mud, sediment, sludge, residue. [➡EROSION PRODUCTS AND SOIL; 1058]

silver 1 *type of* **metal**. [➡METALS; 1275] 2 *type of* **white**. [➡COLOURS; 1223]

silver birch *type of* **deciduous tree**. [➡DECIDUOUS TREES; 1028]

silver grey *type of* **grey**. [➡COLOURS; 1223]

silver jubilee *n* [➡CEREMONIES AND ANNIVERSARIES; 38]

silver-plated *adj* [➡METALS; 1275]

silverside *type of* **cut**. [➡TYPES AND CUTS OF MEAT; 1176]

silver-tongued *adj* **eloquent**, smooth-talking, grandiloquent, fluent, flattering, persuasive. [➡ELOQUENT, TALKATIVE AND LONG-WINDED; 633] *Opposite:* tongue-tied.

silverware *n* [➡TABLEWARE, CUTLERY, AND KITCHENWARE; 861]

silvery *adj* **silver**, grey, hoary, shiny. [➡DESCRIBING COLOURS; 1225]

similar *adj* **alike**, like, comparable, parallel, analogous, related, akin. [➡SIMILARITY; 149] *Opposite:* dissimilar.

similarity *n* **resemblance**, comparison, likeness, parallel, correspondence, connection, match, relationship. [➡SIMILARITY; 149] *Opposite:* difference.

similarly 1 *adv* **alike**, in the same way, comparably, analogously, relatedly. [➡SIMILARITY; 149] *Opposite:* differently. 2 *adv* **likewise**, also, in the same way, correspondingly, equally, by the same token. [➡ALSO; 136] *Opposite:* on the contrary.

simile *n* [➡FIGURES OF SPEECH; 674]

similitude (*formal*) *n* **similarity**, resemblance, likeness, sameness, semblance, identicalness. [➡SIMILARITY; 149] *Opposite:* difference.

simmer 1 *v* **boil**, bubble, cook. [➡COOKING AND FOOD PREPARATION; 354] 2 *v* **seethe**, rumble, bubble, boil, fester, smoulder. [➡FROTH AND EFFERVESCE; 390]

simmer down *v* **cool down**, calm down, cool off (*informal*), settle down, cool it (*informal*), chill out (*slang*), regain your self-control, compose yourself, back off. [➡CHANGE OF MOOD AND COMPOSURE; 581] *Opposite:* blow your top (*informal*).

simoom *type of* **wind**. [➡WINDY AND STORMY WEATHER; 1053]

simper 1 *v* **smirk**, grimace, sneer, look smug, look coy, grin, smile. [➡FACIAL EXPRESSION; 652] *Opposite:* frown. 2 *n* **grimace**, smirk, sneer, smug look, coy look. [➡FACIAL EXPRESSION; 652] *Opposite:* frown.

simple 1 *adj* **easy**, straightforward, uncomplicated, trouble-free, effortless, undemanding. [➡EASE AND SIMPLICITY; 201] *Opposite:* difficult. 2 *adj* **plain**, minimal, unadorned, unfussy, down-to-earth, clean, clear-cut, regular, unpretentious, austere. [➡PLAIN; 233] *Opposite:* fancy. 3 *adj* **humble**, modest, unassuming, unpretentious, meek, artless. [➡NATURALNESS; 498] *Opposite:* pretentious. 4 *adj* **guileless**, ingenuous, naive, unsophisticated, green, unworldly. [➡NEGATIVE INTELLECTUAL CHARACTERISTICS; 526] *Opposite:* sophisticated.

simple-minded 1 *adj* **simplistic**, crude, basic, one-dimensional, unsophisticated. [➡THE NATURE OF IDEAS; 772] *Opposite:* subtle. 2 *adj* **naive**, childlike, unsophisticated, artless, guileless, ingenuous, innocent, candid. [➡NEGATIVE INTELLECTUAL CHARACTERISTICS; 526] *Opposite:* sophisticated.

simplicity 1 *n* **ease**, straightforwardness, effortlessness, easiness, uncomplicatedness. [➡EASE AND SIMPLICITY; 201] *Opposite:* difficulty. 2 *n* **plainness**, minimalism, unfussiness, cleanness, lack of adornment, austerity. [➡PLAIN; 233] 3 *n* **humility**, modesty, unpretentiousness, meekness, artlessness, unassumingness. [➡NATURALNESS; 498] *Opposite:* pride. 4 *n* **guilelessness**, naivety, ingenuousness, lack of sophistication, artlessness, candour, innocence. [➡LEVEL OF EDUCATION AND SOPHISTICATION; 894] *Opposite:* sophistication.

simplified *adj* **cut down**, basic, easy, abridged, shortened. [➡EASE AND SIMPLICITY; 201] *Opposite:* complex.

simplify *v* **make simpler**, make easier, make straightforward, abridge, shorten, streamline, reduce to the bare bones. [➡CHANGE; 373] *Opposite:* complicate.

simplistic *adj* **naive**, unsophisticated, crude, basic, one-dimensional, simple-minded. [➡THE NATURE OF IDEAS; 772] *Opposite:* sophisticated.

simply 1 *adv* **just**, only, merely, purely, basically, solely. [➡ABSOLUTE AND ABSOLUTELY; 131] 2 *adv* **easily**, straightforwardly, in basic terms, in simple terms, in words of one syllable, crudely. [➡EASE AND SIMPLICITY; 201] *Opposite:* elaborately. 3 *adv* **plainly**, minimally, cleanly, austerely, unpretentiously. [➡PLAIN; 233] *Opposite:* elaborately. 4 *adv* **frankly**, absolutely, obviously, undeniably, unquestionably, easily. [➡CERTAIN; 175] 5 *adv* **modestly**, humbly, unassumingly, meekly, unpretentiously, artlessly. [➡NATURALNESS; 498] *Opposite:* proudly. 6 *adv* **naively**, guilelessly, ingenuously, candidly, innocently, naturally. [➡NEGATIVE INTELLECTUAL CHARACTERISTICS; 526] *Opposite:* knowingly.

simulate 1 *v* **replicate**, reproduce, imitate, suggest, copy, create, conjure up, mock up. [➡PRETEND AND MIMIC; 60] 2 *v* **fake**, pretend, feign, put on, sham, act out. [➡PRETEND AND MIMIC; 60] 3 *v* **mimic**, ape, copy, take off (*informal*), imitate, parrot. [➡PRETEND AND MIMIC; 60]

simulated 1 *adj* **virtual**, cyber-, computer-generated. [➡FALSE AND UNREAL; 174] 2 *adj* **fake**, imitation, pretend, counterfeit, sham, fabricated. [➡FALSE AND UNREAL; 174] *Opposite:* genuine.

simulation *n* **imitation**, reproduction, replication, recreation, mock-up, model. [➡FALSE AND UNREAL; 174]

simulator *n* **simulant**, emulator, trainer. [➡COMPUTERS AND COMPUTING; 1126]

simulcast *v* [➡TELEVISION AND RADIO; 607]

simultaneity *n* [➡CONCURRENT AND CONTEMPORANEOUS; 165]

simultaneous *adj* **concurrent**, immediate, instantaneous, real-time, synchronized, coinciding, coincident. [➡CONCURRENT AND CONTEMPORANEOUS; 165] *Opposite:* separate.

sin 1 *n* **crime**, misdemeanour, transgression, misdeed (*formal*), wrongdoing, lapse. [➡MORALLY BAD; 776] *Opposite:* good deed. 2 *n* **wickedness**, iniquity, depravity, turpitude (*formal or literary*), immorality, debauchery, evil. [➡RELIGIOUS CONCEPTS; 777] *Opposite:* goodness. 3 *v* **transgress**, do wrong, commit a crime, err, lapse, be led astray, succumb to temptation. [➡RELIGIONS AND RELIGIOUS PRACTICES; 778]

since 1 *conj* **as**, because, given that, seeing as, in view of the fact that, while. [➡CAUSATION; 169] 2 *adv* **meanwhile**, in the meantime, subsequently, later, then. [➡AFTER, LAST, AND FOLLOWING; 166]

sincere 1 *adj* **honest**, open, frank, natural, straight, unaffected, candid. [➡NATURALNESS; 498] *Opposite:* disingenuous. 2 *adj* **heartfelt**, genuine, truthful, earnest, serious, authentic. [➡HONEST AND RELIABLE; 503] *Opposite:* insincere.

sincerely 1 *adv* **honestly**, openly, frankly, naturally, unaffectedly, candidly. [➡NATURALNESS; 498] *Opposite:* disingenuously. 2 *adv* **genuinely**, truthfully, earnestly, seriously, authentically, really, truly. [➡HONEST AND RELIABLE; 503] *Opposite:* insincerely.

sincerity *n* **genuineness**, honesty, earnestness, naturalness, unaffectedness, authenticity, candour. [➡HONEST AND OPEN; 631] *Opposite:* insincerity.

since time began *adv* [➡PERMANENCE: WITHOUT END; 94]

since time immemorial *adv* **since time began**, always, for all time, for as long as anyone can remember, for donkey's years. [➡PERMANENCE: WITHOUT END; 94]

sinecure *n* **cushy number**, easy ride, plum job, plum (*informal*), soft option, doddle (*informal*). [➡EASY WORK; 300]

sine qua non *n* **prerequisite**, essential, condition, precondition, requirement, necessity, must, must-have. [➡MOST IMPORTANT THING; 198]

sinew 1 *n* (*literary*) **strength**, vigour, muscularity, brawn, power, stamina. [➡MUSCLES AND MUSCULATURE; 480] *Opposite:* frailty. 2 *type of* **muscle or tendon**. [➡THE MUSCLES; 719]

sinewy *adj* **wiry**, lean, strong, muscly, brawny, powerful. [➡BUILD; 478] *Opposite:* frail.

sinfonia *type of* **instrumental music**. [➡MUSIC, SONGS, AND SINGING; 907]

sinfonietta *type of* **band**. [➡MUSICIANS AND SINGERS; 908]

sinful *adj* **wicked**, bad, evil, corrupt, errant, sinning, aberrant, immoral, iniquitous. [➡RELIGIOUS CONCEPTS; 777] *Opposite:* virtuous.

sinfulness *n* [➡RELIGIOUS CONCEPTS; 777]

sing 1 *v* **croon**, chant, intone (*formal*), hum, warble, carol. [➡MUSIC, SONGS, AND SINGING; 907] 2 *v* **resonate**, buzz, hum, purr, vibrate, reverberate. [➡EMIT CONTINUOUS SOUNDS; 367] 3 *v* (*slang*) **confess**, talk, own up, spill the beans (*informal*), come clean (*informal*), implicate, grass (*slang*), give the game away, let on, blow cover, let the cat out of the bag. [➡BETRAY CONFIDENCES AND GOSSIP; 619]

singe *v* **scorch**, burn, char, sear. [➡FIRE, FLAMMABILITY, AND BURNING; 1164]

singed *adj* [➡FIRE, FLAMMABILITY, AND BURNING; 1164]

singer 1 *n* **vocalist**, songster, lead singer, soloist. [➡MUSICIANS AND SINGERS; 908] 2 *type of* **entertainer**. [➡WORKERS IN ENTERTAINMENT AND MEDIA; 873]

singing 1 *n* **vocals**, songs, vocal music, chanting, warbling, crooning. [➡MUSIC, SONGS, AND SINGING; 907] 2 *adj* **vocal**, choral, melodic, whistling, humming, ringing. [➡MUSICAL TERMS; 912] *Opposite:* instrumental.

single 1 *adj* **solitary**, on its own, lone, sole, solo, only. [➡SOLITARINESS; 941] 2 *adj* **particular**, distinct, separate, specific, definite. [➡UNRELATEDNESS AND SEPARATENESS; 147] *Opposite:* general. 3 *adj* **unmarried**, unattached, lone, free. [➡MARITAL STATUS; 890] *Opposite:* attached. 4 *n* **record**, song, track, release. [➡RECORDINGS AND PLAYERS; 911]

single bed *type of* **bed**. [➡FURNITURE; 858]

single-handed 1 *adj* **unassisted**, unaided, lone, solo, unaccompanied, single-handedly. [➡ACTING INDEPENDENTLY; 285] *Opposite:* assisted. 2 *adv* **by yourself**, on your own, alone, without help, without assistance, solo. [➡ACTING INDEPENDENTLY; 285]

single-lens reflex *type of* **photographic equipment**. [➡PHOTOGRAPHY AND PHOTOGRAPHIC EQUIPMENT; 1121]

single-minded *adj* **focused**, dedicated, steadfast, resolute, dogged, driven, persistent, tenacious, obsessed, unswerving, unwavering. [➡STRENGTH OF WILL; 502] *Opposite:* unfocused.

single-mindedness *n* **sense of purpose**, concentration, application, attention, focus, vision, dedication, determination, drive, perseverance. [➡HARD-WORKING AND COMMITTED; 501] *Opposite:* aimlessness.

single out *v* **pick out**, choose, select, identify, pull out, pluck out, pick on, set apart, differentiate, distinguish, isolate. [➡MAKE DECISIONS AND CHOICES; 753]

single parent *type of* **older relative.** [➡OLDER GENERATION RELATIVES; 959]

singleton *type of* **offspring.** [➡YOUNGER GENERATION RELATIVES; 958]

singly *adv* **individually**, alone, one by one, one at a time, piecemeal, separately. [➡UNRELATEDNESS AND SEPARATENESS; 147] *Opposite:* together.

sing out *v* **call out**, pipe up, speak up, speak out, shout, yell, let everybody know. [➡UTTER AND PRONOUNCE; 609]

sing the praises of *v* **eulogize** (*formal*), acclaim, praise, lionize, extol, rave. [➡PRAISE AND ENCOURAGE; 648] *Opposite:* criticize.

singular *adj* **remarkable**, extraordinary, particular, outstanding, curious, odd, unusual. [➡EXTRAORDINARY: UNCOMMON; 206]

singularity *n* **distinctiveness**, individuality, originality, uniqueness, peculiarity. [➡EXTRAORDINARY: UNCOMMON; 206]

sing your own praises *v* **blow your own trumpet** (*informal*), fly your own kite, swagger, try to make an impression, brag, boast, blow your own horn (*US*). [➡BOAST; 617]

sinister *adj* **menacing**, ominous, threatening, evil, disturbing, creepy (*informal*), baleful. [➡DANGEROUS; 237]

sink 1 *v* **go under**, go down, go under the surface, be submerged, go downwards, descend, drop. [➡GO DOWNWARDS; 308] *Opposite:* float. 2 *v* **fall**, descend, drop, decline, go down, lapse, worsen, deteriorate. [➡GET WORSE; 382] *Opposite:* rise. 3 *v* **dig**, drill, mine, bore. [➡BUILD; 353] 4 *n* **basin**, bowl, hand basin, wash-hand basin. [➡FITTINGS; 859]

sink in *v* **go in**, enter, penetrate, diffuse, permeate, be absorbed. [➡UNDERSTAND AND GRASP; 760]

sink without trace *v* [➡DISAPPEAR; 4]

sinless *adj* [➡RELIGIOUS CONCEPTS; 777]

sinner *n* [➡RELIGIOUS CONCEPTS; 777]

sinuous *adj* **lithe**, supple, twisting, winding, graceful, flowing. [➡DESCRIBING BODY MOVEMENTS; 289]

sip 1 *v* **taste**, drink, swallow, sup. [➡DRINK; 712] 2 *n* **drink**, swallow, taste, drop, mouthful, nip. [➡DRINK; 712]

siphon *v* **draw off**, tap, drain off. [➡EMPTY AND UNLOAD; 408]

siren *n* **alarm**, alert, warning, alarm bell, danger signal, distress signal. [➡SIGNALLING; 1139]

sirloin *type of* **steak.** [➡TYPES AND CUTS OF MEAT; 1176]

sirocco *type of* **wind.** [➡WINDY AND STORMY WEATHER; 1053]

sisal *type of* **fibre.** [➡PLANT MATERIALS; 1132]

sister 1 *adj* **fellow**, parallel, associated, corresponding, equivalent, related. [➡RELATED; 143] 2 *n* **nun**, holy sister, religious, vestal (*literary*). [➡RELIGIOUS PEOPLE; 779] 3 *n* **friend**, supporter, ally, associate. [➡FRIENDS; 963] 4 *type of* **same generation relative.** [➡SAME GENERATION RELATIVES; 957]

sisterhood *n* [➡GROUPS WITH A COMMON INTEREST; 938]

sister-in-law *type of* **in-law.** [➡RELATIVES BY MARRIAGE; 960]

sit 1 *v* **be seated**, sit down, take a seat, take the weight off your feet, take a pew, park yourself. [➡ASSUME A POSITION; 318] *Opposite:* stand. 2 *v* **assemble**, meet, convene, be in session. [➡GET CLOSER TOGETHER; 311] *Opposite:* disperse. 3 *v* **be placed**, be positioned, lie, rest, be on top of, be situated. [➡EXIST IN A PLACE; 19]

sit about *v* [➡LACK OF ACTIVITY; 343]

sitar *type of* **stringed instrument.** [➡MUSICAL INSTRUMENTS; 910]

sit around *v* **kill time**, do nothing, lounge around, hang about, hang around, hang out (*informal*), sit about. [➡LACK OF ACTIVITY; 343]

sitcom (*informal*) *type of* **broadcast.** [➡TELEVISION AND RADIO; 607]

sit down *v* **be seated**, take a seat, take the weight off your feet, park yourself, take a pew. [➡ASSUME A POSITION; 318] *Opposite:* stand up.

sit-down (*informal*) *n* **rest**, break, breather (*informal*), respite. [➡PERIOD OF REST; 91]

site 1 *n* **place**, location, spot, position. [➡PLACE; 1064] 2 *v* **put**, position, place, situate (*formal*), locate, establish, set. [➡POSITION SOMETHING; 326]

sit-in *n* **protest**, demonstration, demo (*informal*), rally, march, vigil. [➡MEETINGS AND ASSEMBLIES; 43]

sit on your heels *v* [➡LACK OF ACTIVITY; 343]

sitting *n* **session**, meeting, hearing. [➡MEETINGS AND ASSEMBLIES; 43]

sitting room *type of* **room in the home.** [➡TYPES OF ROOM; 1096]

situate (*formal*) *v* **place**, set, put, locate, position, station, site, establish. [➡POSITION SOMETHING; 326]

situated (*formal*) *adj* **located**, positioned, set, placed, sited, found. [➡GENERAL LOCATIONS; 159]

situation 1 *n* **state of affairs**, circumstances, state, condition, status quo. [➡SITUATIONS; 71] 2 *n* **location**, position, site, place, setting, spot. [➡PLACE; 1064] 3 *n* (*formal*) **job**, post, position. [➡JOB; 833]

sitz bath *type of* **plumbing fittings.** [➡FITTINGS; 859]

sixth sense *n* **intuition**, feeling, hunch, ESP. [➡THE SUPERNATURAL; 788]

sizable *adj* **substantial**, generous, good-sized, ample, large, comfortable, spacious. [➡LARGE; 1192]

size *n* **dimension**, mass, bulk, amount, extent, volume, range, magnitude. [➡SIZE AND DIMENSIONS; 1191]

sizeable *see* **sizable.**

size up *v* **assess**, look somebody up and down, take stock of, evaluate, appraise. [➡ASSESS QUALITY; 756]

sizzle 1 *v* **crackle**, spit, hiss, sputter. [➡EMIT CONTINUOUS SOUNDS; 367] 2 *type of* **continuous sound.** [➡CONTINUOUS SOUNDS; 1257]

sizzling (*informal*) *adj* **boiling**, red-hot, scorching (*informal*), baking, roasting (*informal*), stifling, steamy, blistering, sweltering, blazing. [➡TEMPERATURE: HOT; 1228] *Opposite:* freezing.

ska *type of* **popular music.** [➡MUSIC, SONGS, AND SINGING; 907]

skate *type of* **flatfish.** [➡SEA FISH; 1009]

skate over (*informal*) *v* **skim over**, dismiss, pass over, skirt around, fail to deal with, avoid, evade, bypass. [➡NOT PAY ATTENTION; 765] *Opposite:* dwell on.

skean *type of* **sword or knife.** [➡SWORDS AND KNIVES; 1156]

skedaddle (*slang*) *v* [➡RUN AWAY AND AVOID; 10]

skein 1 *n* **hank**, ball, bundle, length, coil, reel. [➡AMOUNT OF SOLID OR SEMI-SOLID; 115] 2 *type of* **flock.** [➡GROUP OF BIRDS; 1007]

skeletal *adj* **thin**, emaciated, skinny, gaunt, wasted, undernourished. [➡BUILD; 478] *Opposite:* obese.

skeleton 1 *n* **frame**, bones, carcass. [➡THE BONES AND JOINTS; 720] 2 *n* **plan**, outline, framework, bare bones (*informal*), sketch. [➡REPRESENTATIONS AND GENERAL EXAMPLES; 65] 3 *adj* **minimum**, basic, essential, minimal. [➡FUNDAMENTAL; 196] *Opposite:* full.

sketch 1 *n* **draft**, plan, drawing, rough copy, rough, rough draft, first attempt, outline. [➡DRAWINGS, CHARTS AND TABLES; 595] 2 *v* **draw**, outline, draft, delineate, block in, rough out. [➡CREATE IMAGES; 357]

sketchbook *n* [➡WRITING AND DRAWING IMPLEMENTS, AND MEDIA; 602]

sketchiness *n* [➡VAGUENESS; 244]

sketchpad *n* [➡WRITING AND DRAWING IMPLEMENTS, AND MEDIA; 602]

sketchy *adj* **vague**, unclear, hazy, imprecise, woolly, rough, superficial. [➡VAGUENESS; 244] *Opposite:* detailed.

skew 1 *v* **tilt**, slant, twist, angle, slope, tip. [➡MOVE SOMETHING: INTO A NEW POSITION OR OVERTURN; 331] *Opposite:* straighten. 2 *v* **distort**, bias, slant, twist, spin, weight, colour. [➡FALSIFY AND CHEAT; 177]

skewbald *adj* [➡DESCRIBING PATTERNS; 1226]

skewed 1 *adj* **tilted**, slanted, twisted, crooked, askew, lopsided, skewwhiff, cockeyed, wonky (*informal*), at an angle, off-centre, out of true. [➡ORIENTATION AND ALIGNMENT; 1222] *Opposite:* straight. 2 *adj* **distorted**, biased, slanted, prejudiced, partial, coloured, one-sided. [➡INCORRECT AND ERRONEOUS; 223] *Opposite:* objective.

skewer 1 *n* **spit**, brochette, spike, spear, needle, pin, point, rod, stick. [➡STICKS, POLES, AND WEDGES; 1253] 2 *v* **impale**, spear, spike, run through (*literary*), pierce, stab, bayonet. [➡TEAR, BREAK, AND CUT; 361]

skewwhiff (*informal*) *adj* **crooked**, lopsided, tilted, cockeyed, slanted, skewed, askew, out of true, wonky (*informal*), off-centre. [➡ORIENTATION AND ALIGNMENT; 1222] *Opposite:* straight.

skid *v* **slip**, slide, slew, lither, spin out. [➡CHANGE DIRECTION OF MOTION; 345]

skiff *type of* **small vessel.** [➡SHIPS AND BOATS; 1149]

skiing *type of* **winter sport.** [➡HOBBIES, GAMES, AND SPORTS; 875]

ski jump *type of* **winter sport.** [➡HOBBIES, GAMES, AND SPORTS; 875]

skilful *adj* **clever**, adroit, dexterous, skilled, expert, practised, adept, competent, proficient. [➡TALENTED AND SKILFUL; 528] *Opposite:* incompetent.

skilfulness *n* [➡SKILLS, TALENTS, AND ABILITIES; 527]

skill *n* **ability**, talent, cleverness, dexterity, expertise, proficiency, skilfulness, handiness, knack, aptitude, competence, flair. [➡SKILLS, TALENTS, AND ABILITIES; 527]

See Compare and Contrast at **ability.**

skilled *adj* **accomplished**, expert, capable, able, trained, skilful, experienced, practised, proficient, competent, consummate. [➡TALENTED AND SKILFUL; 528] *Opposite:* untrained.

skillet *n* [➡TABLEWARE, CUTLERY, AND KITCHENWARE; 861]

skim 1 *v* **glide**, fly, float, soar. [➡MOVE FAST; 314] 2 *v* **scan**, speed-read, browse, glance at, flick through. [➡READ; 759] *Opposite:* peruse.

skim off *v* **cull**, cream off, hive off, handpick, cherry-pick (*disapproving*), choose, select, opt for, go for (*informal*), plump for. [➡MAKE DECISIONS AND CHOICES; 753]

skimp *v* **stint**, withhold, hold back on, be sparing with, pinch, spare. [➡FOREGO AND DENY ONESELF; 450] *Opposite:* lavish.

skimpy *adj* **meagre**, insufficient, scanty, inadequate, sparse, scant. [➡TOO FEW, TOO LITTLE; 120] *Opposite:* generous.

skin 1 *n* **hide**, pelt, fur, coat. [➡THE SKIN; 721] 2 *n* **casing**, covering, membrane, crust, coating, rind, peel, film. [➡COVERS AND COATINGS; 1245] 3 *v* **peel**, pare, excoriate, desquamate. [➡COOKING AND FOOD PREPARATION; 354] 4 *v* **graze**, scrape, flay, scuff. [➡WOUND A PERSON OR ANIMAL; 384] 5 *part of* **fruit.** [➡FRUIT AND VEGETABLES; 1175]

skin-and-bone *adj* [➡BUILD; 478]

skin and bones *adj* [➡BUILD; 478]

skincare product *n* [➡PERSONAL HYGIENE; 492]

skin colour *n* [➡COMPLEXION; 481]

skin-deep *adj* **superficial**, on the surface, on the outside, shallow, artificial, external, surface. [➡UNIMPORTANT AND UNNECESSARY; 239]

skinflint *n* **miser**, cheapskate (*informal*), niggard, penny pincher (*informal*), pinchpenny, scrooge (*informal*), meanie (*informal*). [➡FINANCIALLY MEAN PEOPLE; 952]

skink *type of* **reptile.** [➡REPTILES; 994]

skinniness *n* **gauntness**, scrawniness, thinness, boniness, leanness, emaciation. [➡BUILD; 478] *Opposite:* plumpness.

skinny *adj* **thin**, lean, undernourished, emaciated, scrawny, scraggy, skeletal. [➡BUILD; 478] *Opposite:* fat.

See Compare and Contrast at **thin**.

skint (*informal*) *adj* [➡POVERTY AND POOR; 892]

skintight *adj* [➡DESCRIBING CLOTHES; 869]

skin tone *n* **skin colour**, complexion, skin, facial appearance, flesh colour. [➡COMPLEXION; 481]

skip 1 *v* **hop**, bounce, prance, gambol, caper, frisk. [➡BOUNCE, UNDULATE, AND VIBRATE; 309] 2 *v* **omit**, leave out, miss out, miss, pass over, give a miss (*informal*). [➡NOT PAY ATTENTION; 765] 3 *v* (*informal*) **avoid**, miss, cut (*informal*), bunk off (*informal*). [➡RUN AWAY AND AVOID; 10] *Opposite:* attend.

skiplane *type of* **civil aircraft**. [➡AIRCRAFT; 1147]

skip off (*informal*) *v* **make yourself scarce** (*informal*), beat it (*informal*), make a sharp exit, do a runner, do a moonlight flit, duck out, abscond, run away, leave. [➡RUN AWAY AND AVOID; 10] *Opposite:* stay put.

skipper (*informal*) *n* **captain**, boss, chief, head, person in charge. [➡BOSSES AND MANAGEMENT; 965]

skirmish 1 *n* **battle**, fight, engagement, scuffle, clash, conflict, brawl, encounter, tussle. [➡AGGRESSIVE EVENT; 39] 2 *v* **clash**, fight, scuffle, tussle, scrap. [➡COMPETE, CONTEND, AND COMBAT; 304]

See Compare and Contrast at **fight**.

skirt 1 *v* **border**, edge, adjoin, abut, neighbour, hug, line. [➡EXIST IN CLOSE PROXIMITY; 21] 2 *v* **go around**, avoid, evade, bypass, edge past, circle. [➡MOVE PAST, INTO OR THROUGH SOMETHING; 332] 3 *v* **skim over**, skate over (*informal*), pass over, avoid, evade, bypass, duck. [➡NOT PAY ATTENTION; 765] *Opposite:* tackle. 4 *n* [➡GARMENTS AND OUTFITS; 865]

skirt

◆ *types of skirt*
dirndl, hobble skirt, kilt, miniskirt, sarong, tutu

skit *n* **parody**, satire, spoof, sketch, burlesque, sendup (*informal*). [➡JOKES AND TEASING; 675]

skittish 1 *adj* **wary**, jumpy, edgy, nervous, uneasy, panicky, flappable. [➡INSECURITY AND LOSS OF COMPOSURE; 545] 2 *adj* **playful**, lively, frisky, excited, restless, animated. [➡POSITIVE IMPATIENCE, ENTHUSIASM, AND ALERTNESS; 538]

skiver (*informal*) *n* **shirker**, layabout, lazybones (*informal*), idler, freeloader (*informal*). *Opposite:* go-getter. (*informal*). [➡LAZY OR UNSUCCESSFUL PEOPLE; 948]

skua *type of* **seabird**. [➡SEABIRD; 1002]

skulduggery (*humorous*) *n* **trickery**, tricks, shenanigans (*informal*), monkey business (*informal*), dishonesty, cheating, mischief. [➡BAD BEHAVIOUR OR ACTION; 255] *Opposite:* honesty.

skulk 1 *v* **lurk**, loiter, creep, prowl, lie in wait. [➡LACK OF ACTIVITY; 343] 2 *type of* **herd**. [➡GROUP OF ANIMALS; 993]

skull 1 *n* (*informal*) **mind**, brain, head, noddle (*dated informal*), noggin, pate (*archaic or humorous*). [➡HEAD; 693] 2 *type of* **bone**. [➡THE BONES AND JOINTS; 720]

skullcap *type of* **headgear**. [➡HABERDASHERY, MILLINERY, AND LINGERIE; 867]

skunk 1 *n* (*slang*) [➡SUPERFICIAL OR INSINCERE PEOPLE; 951] 2 *type of* **small mammal**. [➡SMALL MAMMAL; 990]

sky *n* **heaven**, firmament (*literary*), blue, atmosphere. [➡THE EARTH'S ATMOSPHERE; 1040]

sky blue *type of* **blue**. [➡COLOURS; 1223]

skydive *v* [➡HOBBIES, GAMES, AND SPORTS; 875]

sky-high *adj* **excessive**, very high, elevated, exorbitant, over-the-top. [➡EXPENSIVE AND OVERPRICED; 248]

skyjack *v* **hijack**, seize, take over, take control of, capture, commandeer. [➡STEAL AND ROB; 427]

skylark *type of* **songbird**. [➡SONGBIRD; 1003]

skylight *type of* **window**. [➡WINDOWS; 1099]

skyline *n* **horizon**, distant, prospect, vista. [➡VIEWS AND OUTLOOKS; 1072]

skyrocket (*informal*) *v* **rise steeply**, hit the roof, go through the ceiling, climb sharply, shoot up, increase rapidly. [➡CHANGE OF SIZE: BIGGER; 393] *Opposite:* plummet.

skyscraper *n* **multistorey building**, tower, high-rise building. [➡RESIDENTIAL BUILDINGS; 1077]

skyward 1 *adv* **heavenward**, upward, up, above, aloft, into the sky, into the clouds. [➡DIRECTION OF MOTION; 346] 2 *adj* **upward**, heavenward, aloft. [➡DIRECTION OF MOTION; 346]

skywards *see* **skyward**.

slab *n* **lump**, chunk, block, hunk, piece, portion, wedge. [➡LARGE PIECE; 128]

slack 1 *adj* **loose**, limp, relaxed, baggy, floppy, drooping, sagging. [➡MALLEABLE AND ELASTIC; 1211] *Opposite:* taut. 2 *adj* **careless**, inattentive, idle, inefficient, unprofessional, lazy, workshy, inactive, negligent, remiss, sloppy, slovenly. [➡LIFELESS, LAZY, AND UNENTHUSIASTIC; 507] *Opposite:* diligent. 3 *adj* **slow-moving**, slow, dull, quiet, sluggish. [➡BORING AND UNINTERESTING; 235] *Opposite:* brisk.

slacken *v* **loosen**, relax, release, slacken off. [➡CHANGE OF INTENSITY: LESS; 396] *Opposite:* tighten.

slacker *n* **idler**, lazybones (*informal*), loafer, shirker, skiver (*informal*), freeloader (*informal*). [➡LAZY OR UNSUCCESSFUL PEOPLE; 948]

slackly *adv* **loosely**, limply, floppily, droopily. [➡MALLEABLE AND ELASTIC; 1211] *Opposite:* tightly.

slackness 1 *n* **looseness**, limpness, bagginess, floppiness, droopiness. [➡SHAPELESSNESS; 1218] *Opposite:* tautness. 2 *n* **sloppiness** (*informal*), carelessness, negligence, laxity, inattention, laziness. [➡LIFELESS, LAZY, AND UNENTHUSIASTIC; 507] *Opposite:* meticulousness.

slacks *type of* **trousers**. [➡GARMENTS AND OUTFITS; 865]

slag *n* [➡UNPLEASANT AND DIRTY SUBSTANCES; 1267]

slake *v* **quench**, satisfy, satiate, sate, extinguish. [➡CAUSE TO STOP; 267] *Opposite:* exacerbate.

slalom *type of* **winter sport.** [➡HOBBIES, GAMES, AND SPORTS; 875]

slam 1 *v* (*informal*) **criticize**, slate, pan (*informal*), roast (*informal*), berate, disparage, deride. [➡ACCUSE, BLAME, AND CRITICIZE; 642] *Opposite:* praise. 2 *type of* **impact sound.** [➡IMPACT SOUNDS; 1259]

slam-dunk *n* [➡SPORTS TERMS; 877]

slam into *v* [➡CONTACT: IMPACT; 414]

slammer (*slang*) *n* [➡BUILDINGS FOR CONFINING PEOPLE; 1093]

slander 1 *n* **defamation**, calumny (*formal*), character assasination, disparagement, vilification. [➡INSULTS, ABUSE, AND SWEARING; 659] 2 *n* **slur**, smear, slight, calumny (*formal*), insult. [➡INSULTS, ABUSE, AND SWEARING; 659] 3 *v* **insult**, malign, slur, smear, disparage, vilify, slight, defame. [➡INSULTS, ABUSE, AND SWEARING; 659] *Opposite:* compliment.

See Compare and Contrast at **malign.**

slanderer *n* [➡PEOPLE WHO DECEIVE; 662]

slanderous *adj* **libellous**, defamatory, insulting, malicious, disparaging. [➡INSULTS, ABUSE, AND SWEARING; 659]

slang *n* **jargon**, vernacular, colloquial speech, dialect, argot. [➡THE SPOKEN WORD; 672]

slanging match *n* **argument**, shouting match, spat, quarrel, row, fight. [➡ARGUMENT; 47]

slant 1 *v* **incline**, lean, skew, slope, tilt, list. [➡MOVE SOMETHING: INTO A NEW POSITION OR OVERTURN; 331] 2 *n* **angle**, incline, diagonal, pitch, gradient, slope. [➡ORIENTATION AND ALIGNMENT; 1222] 3 *n* **viewpoint**, angle, attitude, point of view, perspective. [➡POINT OF VIEW; 768]

slanted *adj* **biased**, prejudiced, one-sided, partial, unfair, distorted, imbalanced, skewed, coloured. [➡THE NATURE OF IDEAS; 772] *Opposite:* balanced.

slanting *adj* **angled**, at an angle, sloping, on a slope, oblique, diagonal, inclined, aslant, leaning, sideways. [➡ORIENTATION AND ALIGNMENT; 1222] *Opposite:* level.

slantways *adv* **diagonally**, crossways, crosswise, at an angle, obliquely, transversely, aslant, askew, on the slant, slantwise. [➡ORIENTATION AND ALIGNMENT; 1222] *Opposite:* straight.

slantwise *adv* **diagonally**, crosswise, crossways, at an angle, obliquely, transversely, aslant, askew, on the slant. [➡ORIENTATION AND ALIGNMENT; 1222] *Opposite:* straight.

slap 1 *n* **smack**, blow, spank, cuff, clout, whack. [➡PHYSICAL ATTACK AND PUNISHMENT; 416] 2 *v* **hit**, smack, spank, cuff, swipe, clout, whack. [➡PHYSICAL ATTACK AND PUNISHMENT; 416]

slapdash *adj* **sloppy** (*informal*), messy, clumsy, careless, hasty, hurried, haphazard, shoddy. [➡INCAUTIOUS AND CARELESS; 284] *Opposite:* meticulous.

slaphappy *adj* **slapdash**, careless, haphazard, hit-and-miss, irresponsible, casual, chaotic, hasty. [➡INCAUTIOUS AND CARELESS; 284] *Opposite:* meticulous.

slapstick *n* **knockabout**, farce, clowning, burlesque, comedy, humour. [➡JOKES AND TEASING; 675]

slash 1 *v* **cut**, hack, slice, gash, slit, rip, lacerate. [➡TEAR, BREAK, AND CUT; 361] 2 *v* **reduce**, cut, lower, drop, decrease. [➡CHANGE OF SIZE: SMALLER; 394] *Opposite:* increase. 3 *n* **laceration**, gash, slit, tear, rip, cut. [➡HOLES, GAPS, AND FORKS; 1251]

slat *n* **plank**, board, lath. [➡BUILDING MATERIALS; 1076]

slate 1 *n* [➡BUILDING MATERIALS; 1076] 2 *v* (*informal*) **criticize**, censure, disparage, pan (*informal*), find fault with, pick holes in, condemn, lash, nitpick. [➡ACCUSE, BLAME, AND CRITICIZE; 642] 3 *type of* **grey.** [➡COLOURS; 1223] 4 *type of* **stone.** [➡STONES, ROCKS, AND BOULDERS; 1057]

slate blue *type of* **blue.** [➡COLOURS; 1223]

slatternly *adj* [➡BADLY GROOMED; 484]

slaughter 1 *v* (*slang*) **defeat**, thrash, hammer (*informal*), overwhelm, rout, crush, trounce, beat. [➡BEAT AND DEFEAT; 80] 2 *v* **kill**, murder, massacre, slay (*formal or literary*), butcher. [➡KILL; 923] 3 *n* **killing**, murder, massacre, carnage, butchery. [➡CAUSES OF DEATH; 921]

See Compare and Contrast at **kill.**

slaughterhouse *type of* **industrial site.** [➡INDUSTRIAL BUILDINGS; 1086]

slave ant *type of* **ant.** [➡ANTS; 1014]

slave-making ant *type of* **ant.** [➡ANTS; 1014]

slaver *v* **drool**, slobber, dribble, salivate. [➡EXCRETION AND EXCRETA; 723]

slay (*formal or literary*) *v* **kill**, murder, assassinate, massacre, eliminate, slaughter, butcher, exterminate. [➡KILL; 923]

See Compare and Contrast at **kill.**

slayer (*formal or literary*) *n* **killer**, butcher, homicide, murderer, cause of death, executioner, parricide, exterminator, assassin, slaughterer, contract killer, eradicator, demolisher, destroyer. [➡PEOPLE WHO KILL; 924]

slaying *n* [➡CAUSES OF DEATH; 921]

sleaze *n* **corruption**, dishonesty, malpractice, scandal, foul play, sharp practice, skulduggery (*humorous*), shenanigans (*informal*). *Opposite:* probity. (*formal*). [➡MORALLY BAD; 776]

sleaziness *n* [➡MORALLY BAD; 776]

sleazy 1 *adj* **seedy**, sordid, squalid, grubby, grotty. [➡DISGUSTING AND REPULSIVE; 231] 2 *adj* **corrupt**, immoral, dishonest, crooked (*informal*), dodgy (*informal*), shady, slimy, untrustworthy. [➡MORALLY BAD; 776] *Opposite:* honest.

sled (*US*) *type of* **leisure vehicle.** [➡VEHICLES; 1144]

sledge *type of* **leisure vehicle.** [➡VEHICLES; 1144]

sleek *adj* **smooth**, shiny, glossy, silky, lustrous. [➡PHYSICAL TEXTURE; 1221]

sleep 1 *n* **slumber**, nap, snooze (*informal*), doze, siesta, forty winks (*informal*), kip (*informal*), catnap. [➡SLEEP AND DREAM; 724] 2 *v* **be asleep**, have forty winks (*informal*), slumber, be dead to the world, nap, snooze (*informal*), kip (*informal*), doze, catnap, have a siesta, take a nap, have a lie-down. [➡SLEEP AND DREAM; 724]

sleeper *part of* **train**. [➡RAILWAYS; 1106]

sleepers (*US*) *type of* **sleepwear**. [➡GARMENTS AND OUTFITS; 865]

sleepily *adv* **drowsily**, dozily, woozily, wearily, blearily, groggily. [➡TIRED, ASLEEP AND UNCONSCIOUS; 739] *Opposite:* alertly.

sleep in *v* **oversleep**, lie in (*informal*), sleep late, stay in bed, snooze on, ignore the alarm, sleep too long. [➡SLEEP AND DREAM; 724]

sleepiness *n* **drowsiness**, tiredness, lethargy, somnolence, lassitude, torpor. [➡TIRED, ASLEEP AND UNCONSCIOUS; 739] *Opposite:* alertness.

sleeping car *part of* **train**. [➡RAILWAYS; 1106]

sleeping quarters *type of* **room in the home**. [➡TYPES OF ROOM; 1096]

sleepless 1 *adj* **wakeful**, restless, disturbed, unsleeping, awake. [➡WIDE AWAKE AND CONSCIOUS; 736] 2 *adj* **alert**, active, vigilant, attentive, ready, lively. [➡POSITIVE IMPATIENCE, ENTHUSIASM, AND ALERTNESS; 538]

sleeplessness 1 *n* **insomnia**, wakefulness, restlessness. [➡SLEEP AND DREAM; 724] 2 *n* **alertness**, vigilance, readiness, liveliness. [➡POSITIVE IMPATIENCE, ENTHUSIASM, AND ALERTNESS; 538]

sleepsuit *type of* **sleepwear**. [➡GARMENTS AND OUTFITS; 865]

sleepwear (*US*) *n* [➡GARMENTS AND OUTFITS; 865]

sleepwear

◆ *types of sleepwear*
bathrobe (*US*), dressing gown, housecoat, negligée, nightcap, nightclothes, nightdress, nightgown, nightie, nightshirt, nightwear, peignoir, pyjamas, sleepers (*US*), sleepsuit

sleepy 1 *adj* **drowsy**, tired, lethargic, heavy-eyed, sluggish, somnolent. [➡TIRED, ASLEEP AND UNCONSCIOUS; 739] *Opposite:* alert. 2 *adj* **quiet**, dull, slow, inactive, peaceful, boring. [➡BORING AND UNINTERESTING; 235] *Opposite:* lively.

sleet *n* **slush**, snow, frozen rain. [➡COLD WEATHER; 1051]

sleeve 1 *n* **cover**, jacket, protective cover, envelope, dust jacket, outer cover, sheath, wrapper. [➡CONTAINERS, RECEPTACLES, AND PACKAGING; 1244] 2 *part of* **garment**. [➡PARTS OF A GARMENT; 870]

sleigh *type of* **leisure vehicle**. [➡VEHICLES; 1144]

sleight of hand *n* **dexterity**, skill, adroitness, cunning, trickery, surreptitiousness. [➡SKILLS, TALENTS, AND ABILITIES; 527]

slender 1 *adj* **slim**, slight, lean, trim, willowy. [➡BUILD; 478] *Opposite:* fat. 2 *adj* **small**, slim, meagre, slight, little. [➡SMALL; 1194] *Opposite:* considerable.

See Compare and Contrast at **thin**.

slenderness *n* **thinness**, slimness, skinniness, fineness, narrowness. [➡BUILD; 478] *Opposite:* stoutness.

sleuth 1 *v* **investigate**, look for clues, spy, snoop (*informal*), look into things, check things out, conduct an inquiry. [➡EXAMINE AND ASSESS; 754] 2 *v* **track**, tail, follow, pursue, stalk, shadow, dog, hunt down, track down. [➡ACCOMPANY AND FOLLOW; 338] 3 *n* (*informal*) **detective**, private eye (*informal*), gumshoe (*US informal*), Sherlock Holmes, investigator. [➡THE POLICE, ARREST, AND PRE-TRIAL PROCEEDINGS; 818]

slew *v* **veer**, swing, slide, skid, swerve, slither. [➡CHANGE DIRECTION OF MOTION; 345]

slice 1 *n* **piece**, sliver, wedge, portion, segment, serving. [➡AMOUNT OF SOLID OR SEMI-SOLID; 115] 2 *n* **share**, cut, portion, part, percentage. [➡AMOUNT OF SOLID OR SEMI-SOLID; 115] 3 *v* **cut**, share, carve, divide, cut up. [➡TEAR, BREAK, AND CUT; 361]

slick 1 *adj* **polished**, professional, efficient, glossy, smooth. [➡ORDER AND ORGANISATION; 207] *Opposite:* shoddy. 2 *adj* **glib**, superficial, untrustworthy, shallow, facile. [➡LACK OF COMMITMENT AND UNRELIABILITY; 510] 3 *adj* **slippery**, smooth, glossy, shiny, glassy, slimy, greasy. [➡PHYSICAL TEXTURE; 1221]

slide 1 *v* **glide**, slither, slip, skim, skate, skid. [➡PUSH, PULL, SLIDE; 336] 2 *v* **go down**, fall, decrease, diminish, drop. [➡CHANGE OF INTENSITY: LESS; 396] *Opposite:* rise.

sliding doors *n* [➡DOORS AND ACCESS POINTS; 1100]

slight 1 *adj* **small**, minor, unimportant, trivial, insignificant, slender, slim. [➡FEW, LITTLE, SMALL AMOUNT; 119] *Opposite:* considerable. 2 *adj* **slim**, delicate, thin, feeble, slender. [➡BUILD; 478] *Opposite:* stocky. 3 *n* **snub**, insult, slur, smear, rebuff, affront. [➡UNKIND ACTION OR BEHAVIOUR; 297] 4 *v* **insult**, offend, snub, scorn, affront. [➡INSULTS, ABUSE, AND SWEARING; 659]

slightly 1 *adv* **somewhat**, to some extent, a little, a touch, a tad (*informal*). [➡TO A CERTAIN EXTENT; 134] *Opposite:* considerably. 2 *adv* **marginally**, faintly, vaguely. [➡FEW, LITTLE, SMALL AMOUNT; 119] *Opposite:* considerably.

slim 1 *adj* **thin**, trim, slender, slight, lean, wiry, svelte. [➡BUILD; 478] *Opposite:* fat. 2 *adj* **faint**, slender, remote, poor, slight, unlikely. [➡IMPOSSIBLE AND IMPROBABLE; 179] *Opposite:* considerable. 3 *v* **diet**, go on a diet, lose weight, watch your weight, reduce (*US*). [➡EAT AND NOT EAT; 711]

See Compare and Contrast at **thin**.

slim down *v* **reduce**, streamline, rationalize, cut, scale back (*US*), cut back. [➡CHANGE OF SIZE: SMALLER; 394] *Opposite:* expand.

slime *n* **paste**, mucus, gunge (*informal*), goo (*informal*), gunk (*informal*), glop (*US informal*), goop (*US informal*). [➡UNPLEASANT AND DIRTY SUBSTANCES; 1267]

sliminess *n* [➡PHYSICAL TEXTURE; 1221]

slimming *adj* **low-fat**, light, diet, low-calorie, healthy. [➡FOOD; 1166] *Opposite:* fattening.

slimness 1 *n* **narrowness**, fineness, slightness, thinness, flatness, shallowness. [➡WIDTH: NARROW AND THIN; 1199] *Opposite:* bulkiness. 2 *n* **slenderness**, leanness, svelteness, trimness, thinness, fineness, elegance. [➡BUILD; 478] *Opposite:* plumpness.

slimy 1 *adj* **greasy**, oily, slippery, slick. [➡PHYSICAL TEXTURE; 1221] 2 *adj* **smarmy**, oily, creepy (*informal*), grovelling, sycophantic, unctuous, ingratiating. [➡INGRATIATING; 639]

sling 1 *v* **throw**, toss, lob, fling, hurl, chuck (*informal*). [➡THROW SOMETHING; 335] 2 *v* **hang**, suspend, dangle, drape, hook up. [➡MOVE SOMETHING ON THE SPOT; 337]

slingback *type of* **shoe**. [➡FOOTWEAR; 871]

slink *v* **creep**, sneak, tiptoe, slope off (*informal*), steal, skulk. [➡MOVE SLOWLY; 315]

slip 1 *v* **trip**, fall, lose your balance, lose your footing, tumble, stumble. [➡GO DOWNWARDS; 308] 2 *v* **slide**, glide, slither, skid, skate. [➡PROCEED AND GO; 306] 3 *v* **sneak**, steal, creep, flit, slope (*informal*), slink. [➡PROCEED AND GO; 306] 4 *n* **blunder**, slip-up (*informal*), mistake, error, omission, gaffe. [➡MISTAKES; 251] 5 *type of* **lower body underwear**. [➡HABERDASHERY, MILLINERY, AND LINGERIE; 867]

See Compare and Contrast at **mistake**.

slip back *v* **revert**, relapse, lapse, slide back, return, slip. [➡GO BACKWARDS; 310]

slipcase *n* [➡SOFT FURNISHINGS, LINEN, AND DRAPERY; 860]

slipcover *n* [➡SOFT FURNISHINGS, LINEN, AND DRAPERY; 860]

slip of the tongue *n* [➡MISTAKES; 251]

slipper *type of* **shoe**. [➡FOOTWEAR; 871]

slipperiness *n* [➡DECEITFUL; 514]

slippery 1 *adj* **greasy**, oily, slick, icy, slimy, glassy, smooth. [➡PHYSICAL TEXTURE; 1221] *Opposite:* dry. 2 *adj* **sneaky**, shifty, crafty, devious, dodgy (*informal*), dishonest, untrustworthy. [➡DECEITFUL; 514] *Opposite:* trustworthy.

slippery customer *n* [➡PEOPLE WHO DECEIVE; 662]

slip road *type of* **minor road**. [➡ROADS; 1105]

slipshod *adj* **careless**, shoddy, slapdash, sloppy, slack. [➡INCAUTIOUS AND CARELESS; 284] *Opposite:* thorough.

slip-up (*informal*) *n* **blunder**, slip, mistake, error, omission, gaffe. [➡MISTAKES; 251]

slip up (*informal*) *v* **make a mistake**, go wrong, get it wrong, blunder, err, trip up, goof, foul up (*informal*), mess up (*informal*). [➡FAIL OR BE UNSUCCESSFUL; 75]

slit 1 *v* **cut**, slash, gash, slice, nick. [➡TEAR, BREAK, AND CUT; 361] 2 *n* **opening**, cut, slash, gash, slot, hole, gap. [➡HOLES, GAPS, AND FORKS; 1251]

See Compare and Contrast at **tear**.

slither *v* **slide**, glide, slink, slip, skid. [➡PROCEED AND GO; 306]

sliver *n* **slice**, shaving, splinter, flake, shard. [➡SMALL PIECE; 127]

slob around (*informal*) *v* [➡LACK OF ACTIVITY; 343]

slobber *v* **drool**, dribble, salivate, slaver. [➡EXCRETION AND EXCRETA; 723]

slog 1 *v* **plod**, trudge, tramp, trek, hike, trail, schlep (*US informal*). [➡MOVE SLOWLY; 315] 2 *v* **work**, labour, toil, graft (*informal*), grind, struggle. [➡HARD WORK OR EFFORT; 299] 3 *n* **trek**, hike, tramp, trail, marathon, schlep (*US informal*). [➡PROCEED AND GO; 306] 4 *n* **drag**, effort, strain, graft (*informal*), grind, struggle. [➡HARD WORK OR EFFORT; 299]

slogan *n* **motto**, saying, jingle, catch phrase, watchword, refrain, mantra. [➡THE SPOKEN WORD; 672]

sloop *type of* **sailing vessel**. [➡SHIPS AND BOATS; 1149]

slop *v* **spill**, slosh, splatter, splash, swill, wash. [➡SPREAD AND SCATTER; 333]

slope 1 *n* **gradient**, incline, hill, rise, angle, slant, grade (*US*), drop, ramp. [➡ORIENTATION AND ALIGNMENT; 1222] 2 *v* **incline**, slant, tilt, lean, rise, fall, drop, angle. [➡MOVE SOMETHING: INTO A NEW POSITION OR OVERTURN; 331]

slope off (*informal*) *v* **slink**, creep, sneak, skulk, steal away, escape, disappear, vanish. [➡ABSENT ONESELF; 8]

sloping *adj* [➡ORIENTATION AND ALIGNMENT; 1222]

sloppiness 1 *n* **messiness**, untidiness, disorder, chaos, slovenliness. [➡DISORDER AND CHAOS; 246] *Opposite:* tidiness. 2 *n* (*informal*) **slackness**, shoddiness, carelessness, negligence, laxity, laziness, inaccuracy, ineptness, incompetence, amateurishness. [➡LIFELESS, LAZY, AND UNENTHUSIASTIC; 507] *Opposite:* meticulousness. 3 *n* (*informal*) **soppiness** (*informal*), slushiness, sentimentality, sentiment, schmaltz (*informal*). [➡IN POOR TASTE; 230]

sloppy 1 *adj* **messy**, untidy, disordered, chaotic, slovenly. [➡DISORDER AND CHAOS; 246] *Opposite:* tidy. 2 *adj* (*informal*) **slack**, shoddy, careless, poor, slipshod, casual, slapdash, inept, incompetent, amateurish, lax, negligent, lazy, inaccurate. [➡INCAUTIOUS AND CARELESS; 284] *Opposite:* meticulous. 3 *adj* (*informal*) **soppy**, slushy, sentimental, romantic, schmaltzy (*informal*), corny, gushing, mushy, syrupy, mawkish, tacky. [➡IN POOR TASTE; 230]

slops *n* [➡UNPLEASANT AND DIRTY SUBSTANCES; 1267]

slosh *v* **spill**, slop, splatter, splash, swill, wash. [➡SPREAD AND SCATTER; 333]

slot 1 *n* **slit**, hole, opening, niche, space, aperture. [➡HOLES, GAPS, AND FORKS; 1251] 2 *n* **time**, window, opening, space, period, gap. [➡PAUSES AND PHASES; 56] 3 *v* **position**, locate, fit, insert, slip, slide, drop in, lower. [➡Position Something: Between, Beside or Inside Something; 327]

sloth 1 *n* **laziness**, idleness, indolence, apathy, sluggishness, languor, lethargy. [➡LIFELESS, LAZY, AND UNENTHUSIASTIC; 507] *Opposite:* liveliness. 2 *type of* **small mammal**. [➡SMALL MAMMAL; 990]

slothful (*formal*) *adj* **lazy**, idle, sluggish, inactive, indolent, apathetic, languid, lethargic. [➡LIFELESS, LAZY, AND UNENTHUSIASTIC; 507] *Opposite:* energetic.

slothfulness (*formal*) *n* **laziness**, indolence, idleness, sluggishness, languor, lethargy. [➡LIFELESS, LAZY, AND UNENTHUSIASTIC; 507] *Opposite:* liveliness.

slot in *v* **fit in**, squeeze in, accommodate, accept, see, schedule. [➡ARRANGE AND CREATE ORDER; 358]

slouch 1 *v* **slump**, droop, stoop, sprawl, lounge, sag, hunch. [➡ASSUME A POSITION; 318] 2 *n* (*informal*) **idler**, lazybones (*informal*), loafer, slacker, shirker, skiver (*informal*), freeloader (*informal*). [➡LAZY OR UNSUCCESSFUL PEOPLE; 948]

slovenliness *n* [➡BADLY GROOMED; 484]

slovenly *adj* **careless**, dishevelled, untidy, messy, unkempt, sloppy. [➡BADLY GROOMED; 484]

slow 1 *adj* **sluggish**, unhurried, measured, deliberate, dawdling, leisurely, relaxed, gentle, gradual. [➡MOVING SLOWLY; 105] *Opposite:* fast. 2 *adj* **time-consuming**, drawn-out, protracted, lengthy, lingering, gradual, long-winded, laborious, painful. [➡HAPPENING SLOWLY; 106] *Opposite:* quick. 3 *v* **slow down**, decelerate, brake, reduce, slacken. [➡CHANGE OF SPEED: LESS; 398]

slow as molasses (*US*) *adj* [➡HAPPENING SLOWLY; 106]

slow but sure *adj* [➡MOVING SLOWLY; 105]

slow cook *v* [➡COOKING AND FOOD PREPARATION; 354]

slow down 1 *v* **decelerate**, slow up, slow, brake, reduce speed. [➡CHANGE OF SPEED: LESS; 398] *Opposite:* speed up. 2 *v* **hold up**, hold back, delay, slow, retard, hinder, set back, impede. [➡DELAY ACTION OR OCCURRENCE; 279] *Opposite:* speed up.

slow-going *adj* [➡HAPPENING SLOWLY; 106]

slow handclap *n* [➡APPLAUSE; 653]

slow lane *n* [➡ROADS; 1105]

slowly *adv* **gradually**, unhurriedly, bit by bit, little by little, at a snail's pace, leisurely, sluggishly, deliberately, gently. [➡HAPPENING SLOWLY; 106] *Opposite:* quickly.

slowly but surely *adv* [➡MOVING SLOWLY; 105]

slow-moving *adj* [➡MOVING SLOWLY; 105]

slowness *n* **leisureliness**, sluggishness, deliberateness, gradualness. [➡SPEED; 102] *Opposite:* fastness.

slow-paced *adj* [➡HAPPENING SLOWLY; 106]

slow up 1 *v* **hold up**, hold back, delay, slow, retard, hinder, set back, impede. [➡SHIRK AND DELAY; 274] *Opposite:* speed up. 2 *v* [➡CHANGE OF SPEED: LESS; 398]

slow-witted *adj* [➡NEGATIVE INTELLECTUAL CHARACTERISTICS; 526]

slowworm *type of* **reptile**. [➡REPTILES; 994]

sludge *n* **mud**, slush, mire, muck, slop, slurry. [➡UNPLEASANT AND DIRTY SUBSTANCES; 1267]

sludgy *adj* [➡FLUID AND NON-SOLID; 1212]

slug 1 *n* **bullet**, shot, shell, cartridge, pellet, ball, projectile, round. [➡PROJECTILES; 1158] 2 *n* (*informal*) **swig** (*informal*), shot, gulp, glug (*informal*), swallow, mouthful, glassful, drink, hit. [➡DRINK; 712] *Opposite:* sip. 3 *n* **blow**, belt (*informal*), hit, thump, punch, whack, wallop (*informal*), clout. [➡PHYSICAL ATTACK AND PUNISHMENT; 416] 4 *v* **hit**, belt (*informal*), thump, strike, punch, whack, wallop (*informal*), clout. [➡PHYSICAL ATTACK AND PUNISHMENT; 416] 5 *v* (*informal*) **swallow**, swig (*informal*), gulp, down, knock back (*informal*), drink, quaff (*literary or humorous*), swill. [➡DRINK; 712] *Opposite:* sip. 6 *type of* **land invertebrate**. [➡LAND INVERTEBRATE; 1021]

sluggish *adj* **inactive**, lethargic, slow, listless, slothful (*formal*), lazy. [➡MOVING SLOWLY; 105] *Opposite:* energetic.

sluggishness *n* **lethargy**, slowness, listlessness, sloth, laziness. [➡SPEED; 102] *Opposite:* alertness.

sluice 1 *n* **channel**, conduit, race, drain, gutter, stream. [➡WATERCOURSES; 1110] 2 *v* **clean**, flush, rinse, hose, wash, flood. [➡CLEAN AND POLISH; 404]

sluicegate *n* [➡BARRIERS; 1112]

slum *n* **shanty town**, favela, purlieu (*formal*). [➡UNDESIRABLE ACCOMMODATION; 856]

slumber 1 *v* **sleep**, snooze (*informal*), drowse, doze, be dead to the world, catnap, snooze. [➡SLEEP AND DREAM; 724] 2 *n* **sleep**, snooze (*informal*), doze, nap, forty winks (*informal*), catnap, siesta, lie-down (*informal*), rest. [➡SLEEP AND DREAM; 724] 3 *n* **rest**, inactivity, inertia, torpor, laziness, stagnation. [➡PERIOD OF REST; 91]

slumbering *adj* [➡TIRED, ASLEEP AND UNCONSCIOUS; 739]

slump 1 *v* **collapse**, fall, sink, tumble, sag, lurch. [➡ASSUME A POSITION; 318] 2 *v* **slouch**, bend, hunch, droop, sprawl, sag. [➡TAKE UP A NEW POSITION; 313] 3 *n* **recession**, crash, collapse, decline, plummet, drop, depression, plunge, fall, nose dive. [➡MARKET FORCES; 803] *Opposite:* rise. 4 *n* **decrease**, decline, collapse, crash, plummet, drop, plunge, fall, nose-dive. [➡FAILURE; 77] *Opposite:* rise.

slumped *adj* [➡ORIENTATION AND ALIGNMENT; 1222]

slur 1 *v* **speak**, run together, blend, overlap, overrun, elide. [➡WITTER AND BABBLE; 618] 2 *v* **demean**, smear, insult, slight, besmirch, denigrate. [➡ACCUSE, BLAME, AND CRITICIZE; 642] 3 *n* **smear**, disgrace, insult, slight, stain, affront. [➡INSULTS, ABUSE, AND SWEARING; 659]

slurp 1 *v* **gulp**, glug (*informal*), suck, drink, swallow, swig (*informal*), down, knock back (*informal*). [➡DRINK; 712] 2 *n* **smack**, suck, glug (*informal*), gulp. [➡SOUNDS MADE BY PEOPLE; 1261] 3 *n* **mouthful**, glug (*informal*), swig (*informal*), swallow, drink, sip, gulp, taste. [➡DRINK; 712]

slurred *adj* **indistinct**, inaudible, unclear, garbled, incoherent. [➡INARTICULATE, RAMBLING, AND AWKWARD; 634] *Opposite:* distinct.

slurry *n* [➡UNPLEASANT AND DIRTY SUBSTANCES; 1267]

slush *n* **sludge**, mud, mire, muck, slurry. [➡UNPLEASANT AND DIRTY SUBSTANCES; 1267]

slushy 1 *adj* **snowy**, icy, wet, mushy, sloppy, sludgy. [➡WET; 1239] *Opposite:* dry. 2 *adj* **sentimental**, mushy, corny, schmaltzy (*informal*), syrupy, mawkish, tacky, soppy, gushing. [➡IN POOR TASTE; 230] *Opposite:* unsentimental.

sly 1 *adj* **crafty**, cunning, clever, skilful, knowing, nifty (*informal*), artful, shrewd, ingenious, astute. [➡TALENTED AND

SKILFUL; 528] 2 *adj* **evasive**, wily, devious, furtive, underhand, tricky, deceitful, surreptitious, sneaky, dishonest. [➡DECEITFUL; 514] *Opposite:* honest.

slyness 1 *n* **craftiness**, cunning, skill, artfulness, cleverness, shrewdness, ingenuity, astuteness. [➡SKILLS, TALENTS, AND ABILITIES; 527] *Opposite:* clumsiness. 2 *n* **sneakiness**, evasiveness, furtiveness, dishonesty, underhandedness, deviousness, deceit, deceitfulness, shiftiness. [➡DECEITFUL; 514] *Opposite:* openness.

smack 1 *v* **hit**, slap, hit, clout, slap, cuff, spank, spank, whack, whack. [➡PHYSICAL ATTACK AND PUNISHMENT; 416] 2 *v* **suggest**, imply, hint at, look like, sound like, be reminiscent of, remind of. [➡SEEM TO BE SOMETHING; 58] 3 *n* **slap**, blow, clout, cuff, spank, whack. [➡PHYSICAL ATTACK AND PUNISHMENT; 416] 4 *n* **taste**, flavour, tang, bite, savour. [➡TASTE; 704] 5 *type of* **sailing vessel**. [➡SHIPS AND BOATS; 1149]

smacker (*informal*) *n* [➡PHYSICAL CONTACT AS COMMUNICATION; 656]

smack of *v* [➡SEEM TO BE SOMETHING; 58]

small 1 *adj* **little**, minute, tiny, diminutive, miniature, petite, undersized. [➡SMALL; 1194] *Opposite:* big. 2 *adj* **unimportant**, trivial, slight, lesser, minor, insignificant, trifling. [➡UNIMPORTANT AND UNNECESSARY; 239] *Opposite:* major.

small amount *n* [➡FEW, LITTLE, SMALL AMOUNT; 119]

small arms *n* **weapons**, guns, firearms, side arms, pistols, handguns, rifles, weaponry, arms, firepower. [➡WEAPONS; 1153]

small beer (*informal*) *n* [➡UNIMPORTANT AND UNNECESSARY; 239]

small-boned *adj* [➡BUILD; 478]

smallholding *n* **farm**, croft, plot, allotment. [➡AGRICULTURE AND FARMING; 1074]

small intestine *part of* **digestive tract**. [➡THE DIGESTIVE TRACT; 710]

smallness *n* **tininess**, littleness, minuteness, compactness. [➡SMALL; 1194] *Opposite:* largeness.

small potatoes (*informal*) *n* [➡UNIMPORTANT AND UNNECESSARY; 239]

smalls (*informal or humorous*) *n* **undies** (*informal*), underwear, underclothes, underclothing. [➡HABERDASHERY, MILLINERY, AND LINGERIE; 867]

small-scale 1 *adj* **limited**, modest, moderate, minor, unimportant, minimal. [➡UNIMPORTANT AND UNNECESSARY; 239] *Opposite:* large-scale. 2 *adj* **little**, small, miniature, minuscule, tiny, reduced. [➡SMALL; 1194] *Opposite:* large-scale.

small screen (*informal*) *n* **television**, TV (*informal*), tube (*US*), telly, box (*slang*), goggle-box (*dated informal*), boob tube (*US informal*). [➡TELEVISION AND RADIO; 607]

small talk *n* **chat**, chitchat (*informal*), conversation, pleasantries, gossip, chatter. [➡INFORMAL COMMUNICATION; 45]

small-time (*informal*) *adj* **petty**, unimportant, local, minor, insignificant. [➡UNIMPORTANT AND UNNECESSARY; 239] *Opposite:* major.

smarminess *n* [➡INGRATIATING; 639]

smarmy *adj* **sycophantic**, oily, slimy, grovelling, creepy (*informal*), unctuous, ingratiating. [➡INGRATIATING; 639]

smart 1 *adj* **elegant**, tidy, stylish, chic, well-dressed, well-turned-out, well-groomed, neat, dapper, dashing. [➡WELL GROOMED; 483] *Opposite:* shabby. 2 *adj* **clever**, intelligent, bright, brainy (*informal*), sharp, quick. [➡POSITIVE INTELLECTUAL CHARACTERISTICS; 525] *Opposite:* stupid. 3 *adj* **insolent**, rude, facetious, clever, disrespectful, impertinent (*formal*), sarcastic. [➡RUDE AND HOSTILE; 626] 4 *adj* **fashionable**, trendy (*informal*), chic, glamorous, hip (*slang*), stylish, voguish, glitzy, ritzy (*informal*), swanky (*informal*), elegant. [➡WELL GROOMED; 483] 5 *adj* **lively**, brisk, vigorous, energetic, quick, rapid, speedy. [➡MOVING QUICKLY; 103] 6 *v* **sting**, burn, hurt, chafe, tingle, prickle. [➡PAIN AND OTHER PHYSICAL SENSATIONS; 734]

See Compare and Contrast at **intelligent**.

smart aleck (*informal*) *n* **know-all** (*informal*), clever Dick (*informal*), clever clogs (*informal*), smarty-pants (*informal*), wag (*dated*), wiseacre (*informal*), wise guy (*US informal*). [➡SELF-IMPORTANT AND SELF-SEEKING PEOPLE; 949]

smart-alecky (*informal*) *adj* [➡POMPOUS, LOUD, AND OVER-CONFIDENT; 636]

smart bomb *type of* **explosive weapon**. [➡EXPLOSIVES; 1154]

smart card *n* [➡E-COMMERCE; 1128]

smarten 1 *v* **spruce up**, clean up, revamp, do up, doll up (*informal*), redecorate, tidy up, neaten, improve, jazz up. [➡IMPROVE APPEARANCE; 380] *Opposite:* let go. 2 *v* **speed up**, accelerate, quicken, increase, pick up. [➡CHANGE OF SPEED: MORE; 397] *Opposite:* slow.

smarten up 1 *v* **spruce up**, clean up, revamp, do up, doll up (*informal*), redecorate, tidy up, improve, jazz up. [➡IMPROVE APPEARANCE; 380] *Opposite:* let go. 2 *v* **brighten up**, liven up, cheer up, pep up (*informal*), enliven, energize, stimulate, boost, get your act together (*informal*). [➡IMPROVE SOMETHING; 375] *Opposite:* stagnate.

smartly 1 *adv* **stylishly**, nattily, neatly, tidily, elegantly. [➡WELL GROOMED; 483] *Opposite:* untidily. 2 *adv* **vigorously**, briskly, energetically, quickly, rapidly, speedily. [➡MOVING QUICKLY; 103]

smartly dressed *adj* [➡WELL GROOMED; 483]

smartness *n* **neatness**, tidiness, elegance, stylishness, chicness. [➡WELL GROOMED; 483] *Opposite:* untidiness.

smarts (*US informal*) *n* [➡GARMENTS AND OUTFITS; 865]

smarty-pants (*informal*) *n* **know-all** (*informal*), clever clogs (*informal*), clever Dick (*informal*), wise guy (*US informal*), smart aleck (*informal*), wag (*dated*), wiseacre (*informal*). [➡SELF-IMPORTANT AND SELF-SEEKING PEOPLE; 949]

smash 1 *v* **shatter**, break, crash, demolish, destroy, crush. [➡DESTRUCTION AND DEMOLITION; 360] *Opposite:* repair. 2 *n* **crash**, bang, crunch. [➡IMPACT SOUNDS; 1259] 3 *n* **blow**, chop, punch, kick, volley, slam, slam-dunk. [➡SPORTS TERMS; 877] 4 *n* **accident**, crash, collision, pile-up (*informal*), wreck (*US*), fender-bender (*US informal*). [➡TRAFFIC ACCIDENTS; 256]

smasher (*informal*) *n* **cracker** (*informal*), corker (*dated* *informal*), ace (*informal*), knockout (*informal*), beauty, looker (*informal*), gem (*informal*). [➡AMAZING THING; 212]

smash hit *n* [➡SUCCESS; 82]

smashing 1 *interj* [➡COMPLIMENTS; 658] 2 *adj* (*informal*) **great** (*informal*), wonderful, marvellous, brilliant (*informal*), terrific (*informal*), fabulous, splendid, superb, excellent, lovely, super (*informal*). [➡EXTRAORDINARY: AMAZING; 205] *Opposite:* dreadful.

smash into *v* [➡CONTACT: IMPACT; 414]

smash to smithereens *v* [➡DESTRUCTION AND DEMOLITION; 360]

smash-up *n* **crash**, collision, accident, prang (*informal*), pile-up (*informal*), wreck (*US*), fender-bender (*US informal*). [➡TRAFFIC ACCIDENTS; 256]

smash up *v* **wreck**, write off, damage, ruin, trash (*informal*), total (*US slang*). [➡DESTRUCTION AND DEMOLITION; 360]

smattering *n* **bit**, modicum, dash, smidgen (*informal*), iota, little. [➡FEW, LITTLE, SMALL AMOUNT; 119] *Opposite:* lot.

smear 1 *v* **spread**, coat, daub, cover, wipe, rub. [➡DECORATE, ADORN, AND APPLY COATINGS; 406] 2 *v* **sully**, discredit, disgrace, besmirch, tarnish, bring into disrepute, ruin, badmouth (*slang*), do down (*informal*), slander, denigrate, slur. [➡INSULTS, ABUSE, AND SWEARING; 659] *Opposite:* praise. 3 *n* **mark**, smudge, blotch, stain, blot, splodge, splotch (*US*). [➡FAULTS, FLAWS, AND WEAKNESSES; 252] 4 *n* **slur**, insult, slight, affront, slander, libel. [➡INSULTS, ABUSE, AND SWEARING; 659]

smear campaign *n* **mudslinging**, whispering campaign, muckraking, defamation, slander, libel, vilification, talk, gossip, rumour. [➡GOSSIP; 679]

smell 1 *v* **stink**, pong (*informal*), whiff (*informal*), reek. [➡SMELL EMISSION; 370] 2 *v* **sniff**, sense, get a whiff of, suspect, taste, feel. [➡SMELL AND SMELLING; 706] 3 *n* **odour**, aroma, scent, pong (*informal*), perfume, whiff, fragrance, bouquet, stink, stench, reek. [➡SMELL AND SMELLING; 706]

Compare and Contrast: ***smell, odour, aroma, bouquet, scent, perfume, fragrance, stink, stench, reek***

CORE MEANING: THE WAY SOMETHING SMELLS

smell a neutral, pleasant, or unpleasant quality detected by the nerves of the nose; ***odour*** a neutral or unpleasant smell; ***aroma*** a distinctive pleasant smell, especially one related to cooking or food; ***bouquet*** a characteristic pleasant smell, usually associated with fine wines; ***scent*** a pleasant, sweet smell, for example the smell of flowers, or the characteristic smell given off by a particular animal; ***perfume*** a sweet, pleasant, and heady smell, especially the smell of flowers or plants; ***fragrance*** a sweet pleasant smell, especially a delicate or subtle one; ***stink*** a strong unpleasant smell; ***stench*** a strong unpleasant smell, especially one associated with burning or decay; ***reek*** a strong unpleasant smell.

smelliness *n* [➡SMELL AND SMELLING; 706]

smelly *adj* **stinking**, reeking, foul, pongy (*informal*), whiffy (*informal*), malodorous, putrid, fetid. [➡SMELL AND SMELLING; 706] *Opposite:* fragrant.

smelt 1 *v* **melt**, melt down. [➡SOFTEN, LIQUEFY, DAMPEN; 389] 2 *v* **found**, cast, produce, manufacture. [➡MANUFACTURE; 350]

smidge (*informal*) *n* [➡FEW, LITTLE, SMALL AMOUNT; 119]

smidgen (*informal*) *n* **dash**, drop, bit, splash, morsel, soupçon, taste, hint. [➡FEW, LITTLE, SMALL AMOUNT; 119]

smidgeon (*informal*) *see* **smidgen**.

smidgin (*informal*) *see* **smidgen**.

smile 1 *v* **grin**, beam, smirk, leer, sneer. [➡FACIAL EXPRESSION; 652] *Opposite:* frown. 2 *n* **beam**, grin, smirk, leer. [➡FACIAL EXPRESSION; 652] *Opposite:* frown.

smiley 1 *adj* **smiling**, happy, cheery, sunny, cheerful. [➡FACIAL EXPRESSION; 652] *Opposite:* miserable. 2 *n* **emoticon**, smiley face, symbol, sign-off (*US*). [➡COMPUTERS AND COMPUTING; 1126]

smiling *adj* [➡FACIAL EXPRESSION; 652]

smirk 1 *n* **grin**, leer, sneer, simper. [➡FACIAL EXPRESSION; 652] 2 *v* **sneer**, leer, grin, simper. [➡FACIAL EXPRESSION; 652]

smite (*archaic or literary*) *v* **hit**, strike, beat, punch, thrash, thump, cuff, smack, slug. [➡PHYSICAL ATTACK AND PUNISHMENT; 416]

smithereens (*informal*) *n* **pieces**, bits, fragments, shards. [➡SMALL PIECE; 127]

smithy *type of* **factory**. [➡INDUSTRIAL BUILDINGS; 1086]

smitten (*humorous or archaic or literary*) *adj* **in love**, besotted, enamoured, head over heels in love, infatuated, taken, hooked (*slang*), lovesick. [➡APPRECIATION AND GRATITUDE; 536] *Opposite:* indifferent.

smock *type of* **top**. [➡GARMENTS AND OUTFITS; 865]

smocking *type of* **handicraft**. [➡CRAFTS AND CARVING; 356]

smog *n* **pollution**, smoke, fog, haze. [➡CLOUDY AND RAINY WEATHER; 1052]

smogginess *n* [➡CLOUDY AND RAINY WEATHER; 1052]

smoggy *adj* [➡CLOUDY AND RAINY WEATHER; 1052]

smoke 1 *n* **fumes**, smog, poisonous gas, firedamp, chokedamp, biogas. [➡PRODUCTS OF FIRE; 1165] 2 *v* **burn**, be on fire, smoulder. [➡FIRE, FLAMMABILITY, AND BURNING; 1164]

smoke alarm *n* **device**, smoke detector, fire alarm, sensor. [➡HOUSEHOLD APPLIANCES; 1116]

smoke and mirrors (*US*) *n* [➡DECEPTION AND LIES; 661]

smoke bomb *type of* **explosive weapon**. [➡EXPLOSIVES; 1154]

smoked *adj* [➡STATE OF PREPARED FOOD; 1170]

smoke detector *n* **smoke alarm**, fire alarm, sensor. [➡HOUSEHOLD APPLIANCES; 1116]

smoke out 1 *v* **drive out**, force out, turn out, eject, expel. [➡EJECT AND EXCLUDE; 341] *Opposite:* bring in. 2 *v* **bring to light**, reveal, expose, unearth, discover, disclose. [➡CAUSE TO APPEAR; 5] *Opposite:* conceal.

smoker 1 *n* **cigarette smoker**, pipe smoker, cigar smoker, chain-smoker, heavy smoker, light smoker. [➡DEVOTEES AND ADDICTED PEOPLE; 557] 2 *n* **smoking compartment**, smoking car, smoking carriage. [➡RAILWAYS; 1106]

smoke screen 1 *n* **cloud of smoke**, wall of smoke, camouflage, cover. [➡PRODUCTS OF FIRE; 1165] 2 *n* **cover-up**, cover, camouflage, screen, mask, blind, decoy, diversion, red herring. [➡DECEPTION AND LIES; 661]

smokestack *part of* **building**. [➡PARTS OF A BUILDING; 1094]

smoking car *part of* **train**. [➡RAILWAYS; 1106]

smoking carriage *part of* **train**. [➡RAILWAYS; 1106]

smoking compartment *part of* **train**. [➡RAILWAYS; 1106]

smoking jacket *type of* **jacket**. [➡GARMENTS AND OUTFITS; 865]

smoky *adj* **misty**, murky, cloudy, foggy, hazy, opaque, grey, smoke-filled. [➡VISUAL TEXTURE; 1220] *Opposite:* clear.

smooch (*informal*) 1 *v* **kiss**, cuddle, hug, hold each other close, caress, embrace, canoodle (*informal*), neck (*dated*), snog (*slang*). [➡PHYSICAL CONTACT AS COMMUNICATION; 656] 2 *n* **cuddle**, kiss, hug, caress, embrace, snog (*slang*). [➡PHYSICAL CONTACT AS COMMUNICATION; 656]

smooth 1 *adj* **flat**, even, level, horizontal, plane. [➡PHYSICAL TEXTURE; 1221] *Opposite:* uneven. 2 *adj* **easy**, flowing, effortless, efficient. [➡EASE AND SIMPLICITY; 201] 3 *adj* **charming**, suave, persuasive, glib, silver-tongued, slick. [➡ELOQUENT, TALKATIVE AND LONG-WINDED; 633] *Opposite:* gauche. 4 *adj* **soft**, silky, downy, velvety, shiny, glossy. [➡PHYSICAL TEXTURE; 1221] *Opposite:* rough. 5 *v* **flatten**, smooth out, level, iron, press. [➡CHANGE OF SHAPE; 386] *Opposite:* crumple.

smooth down *v* **flatten**, iron out, paste down, smooth out, even out, uncrease, level, tidy, adjust, arrange. [➡CHANGE OF SHAPE; 386] *Opposite:* scrunch.

smoothie 1 *n* (*informal*) **charmer**, poser (*informal disapproving*), smooth talker, smooth character, fast talker. [➡SUPERFICIAL OR INSINCERE PEOPLE; 951] 2 *n* **drink**, fruit juice, milk shake, yogurt drink. [➡DRINKS; 1186]

smoothly *adv* **easily**, effortlessly, efficiently, well, slickly. [➡EASE AND SIMPLICITY; 201] *Opposite:* awkwardly.

smooth muscle *type of* **muscle or tendon**. [➡THE MUSCLES; 719]

smoothness 1 *n* **flatness**, evenness, levelness. [➡PHYSICAL TEXTURE; 1221] *Opposite:* unevenness. 2 *n* **ease**, effortlessness, efficiency. [➡EASE AND SIMPLICITY; 201] *Opposite:* awkwardness. 3 *n* **charm**, suaveness, persuasiveness, glibness, slickness. [➡ELOQUENT, TALKATIVE AND LONG-WINDED; 633] *Opposite:* gaucheness. 4 *n* **softness**, silkiness, velvetiness, sleekness. [➡PHYSICAL TEXTURE; 1221] *Opposite:* roughness.

smooth out 1 *v* **flatten**, iron out, paste down, smooth down, even out, uncrease, level, tidy, adjust, arrange. [➡CHANGE OF SHAPE; 386] *Opposite:* crease. 2 *v* **ease**, calm, defuse, soothe, smooth over, iron out, sort out, resolve, clear up. [➡CORRECT AND PUT RIGHT; 378] *Opposite:* stir up.

smooth over *v* **ease**, calm, defuse, soothe, smooth out, iron out, sort out, resolve, clear up. [➡CORRECT AND PUT RIGHT; 378] *Opposite:* stir up.

smooth-shaven *adj* [➡FACIAL HAIR; 490]

smooth talk *n* **sweet talk** (*informal*), soft soap (*informal*), flattery, blarney (*informal*), flannel (*informal*), guff (*informal*), nonsense, rubbish, garbage, claptrap (*informal*). [➡MEANINGLESS SPEECH OR WRITING; 677] *Opposite:* sincerity.

smooth-tongued *adj* **smooth-talking**, silver-tongued, eloquent, persuasive, convincing, hard to resist, fast-talking. [➡ELOQUENT, TALKATIVE AND LONG-WINDED; 633]

smoothy *see* **smoothie**.

smother 1 *v* **suffocate**, stifle, choke, asphyxiate. [➡KILL; 923] 2 *v* **overwhelm**, overpower, oppress, suffocate, stifle, restrict. [➡GIVE TOO MUCH; 438] 3 *v* **suppress**, repress, stifle, hold back, restrain, conceal, hide, check. [➡AVOID, PREVENT, LIMIT, AND CONTROL; 278] *Opposite:* express.

smoulder 1 *v* **burn**, smoke, glow. [➡FIRE, FLAMMABILITY, AND BURNING; 1164] 2 *v* **fume**, seethe, glower, burn, boil, be angry, bristle. [➡GIVING VENT TO EMOTIONS; 680] 3 *v* **lurk**, fester, rumble, linger, persist, endure, grow, increase. [➡CONTINUE TO EXIST; 17]

smouldering *adj* [➡FIRE, FLAMMABILITY, AND BURNING; 1164]

smudge 1 *n* **blotch**, smear, stain, mark, splodge, blemish, splotch (*US*). [➡FAULTS, FLAWS, AND WEAKNESSES; 252] 2 *v* **smear**, blur, distort, blot, smirch. [➡DECORATE, ADORN, AND APPLY COATINGS; 406]

smudged *adj* [➡DIRTY; 1234]

smug *adj* **self-satisfied**, superior, self-righteous (*disapproving*), arrogant, conceited, full of yourself, haughty, complacent, self-assured. [➡AFFECTATION, SELF-SATISFACTION, AND SNOBBISHNESS; 508] *Opposite:* humble.

smuggle *v* **handle contraband**, traffic, run, sneak in, bring in, rustle. [➡STEAL AND ROB; 427]

smug look *n* [➡FACIAL EXPRESSION; 652]

smugness *n* **complacency**, arrogance, self-satisfaction, conceit, self-righteousness (*disapproving*), haughtiness, self-assuredness, self-sufficiency. [➡AFFECTATION, SELF-SATISFACTION, AND SNOBBISHNESS; 508] *Opposite:* humility.

smut 1 *n* **obscenity**, dirt, filth, pornography, erotica. [➡MORALLY BAD; 776] 2 *n* **soot**, smudge, ash, grime, dirt, dust, muck (*informal*), filth, speck. [➡PRODUCTS OF FIRE; 1165]

smuttiness (*informal*) *n* [➡MORALLY BAD; 776]

smutty 1 *adj* (*informal*) **obscene**, dirty, pornographic, filthy, naughty (*humorous*), explicit, blue (*informal*), mucky. [➡MORALLY BAD; 776] 2 *adj* **sooty**, smudged, grimy, dirty, grubby, soiled, dusty, mucky (*informal*), filthy, black. [➡DIRTY; 1234] *Opposite:* pristine.

snack *type of* **meal**. [➡MEALS AND PARTS OF MEALS; 1168]

snack bar *type of* **eating place**. [➡HOTELS, RESTAURANTS, AND CLUBS; 1081]

snaffle (*informal*) *v* **steal**, pinch (*informal*), rob, pilfer, filch (*informal*), swipe (*informal*), lift (*informal*), pocket, knock off (*slang*), nick (*slang*), take. [➡STEAL AND ROB; 427]

snafu (*informal*) *n* [➡PROBLEM; 257]

snag 1 *n* **problem**, hitch, difficulty, obstacle, hurdle, catch (*informal*), holdup. [➡PROBLEM; 257] 2 *v* **catch**, rip, tear. [➡TEAR, BREAK, AND CUT; 361]

snail *type of* **land invertebrate.** [➡LAND INVERTEBRATE; 1021]

snail mail (*informal*) *n* **postal service**, post, surface mail, airmail, mail. [➡LETTERS AND WRITTEN MESSAGES; 585]

snail-paced *adj* [➡HAPPENING SLOWLY; 106]

snake 1 *n* **serpent** (*literary*), sea snake, water snake. [➡SNAKE; 995] 2 *v* **wind**, bend, twist, meander, turn. [➡PROCEED AND GO; 306]

snake

◆ *types of non-poisonous snake*
anaconda, blacksnake, boa, boa constrictor, garter snake, grass snake, king snake, python, rat snake, water snake, whip snake

◆ *types of poisonous snake*
adder, asp, cobra, copperhead, coral snake, diamondback, fer-de-lance, horned viper, mamba, pit viper, puff adder, rattler, rattlesnake, ringhals, sea snake, sidewinder, taipan, viper, water moccasin

snake in the grass *n* [➡INTERFERING PEOPLE AND TELLTALES; 950]

snake oil (*US*) *n* [➡DECEPTION AND LIES; 661]

snakeskin *type of* **leather.** [➡FABRICS; 1131]

snaky *adj* **winding**, windy, bendy, twisting, meandering, zigzag, coiling. [➡DIRECTION OF MOTION; 346] *Opposite:* straight.

snap 1 *v* **break**, crack, shatter, give way, come apart. [➡TEAR, BREAK, AND CUT; 361] 2 *v* **retort**, bark, shout, yell, speak sharply, jump down someone's throat. [➡GIVING VENT TO EMOTIONS; 680] 3 *v* **bite**, nip, bite at. [➡EAT AND NOT EAT; 711] 4 *n* (*US*) **piece of cake** (*informal*), breeze (*informal*), walk in the park (*informal*), cinch (*informal*), doddle (*informal*), child's play, nothing, gift (*informal*). [➡EASY WORK; 300] 5 *n* (*US*) **press stud**, popper, press fastener, stud, fastening, fastener. [➡FASTENERS, LINKS, AND NETWORKS; 1246] 6 *adj* **sudden**, spur-of-the-moment, impulsive, spontaneous, instant, quick. [➡HAPPENING QUICKLY; 104] *Opposite:* considered.

snapdragon *type of* **perennial flower.** [➡FLOWERS; 1032]

snapper *type of* **tropical sea fish.** [➡SEA FISH; 1009]

snappiness *n* [➡BAD-TEMPERED AND HUMOURLESS; 627]

snapping point *n* [➡DECISIVE MOMENTS; 44]

snappish *adj* **irritable**, tetchy (*informal*), snappy, snippy (*informal*), bad-tempered, short-tempered, ratty (*informal*), sharp, curt, brusque, ill-humoured. [➡BAD-TEMPERED AND HUMOURLESS; 627] *Opposite:* good-natured.

snappishness *n* [➡BAD-TEMPERED AND HUMOURLESS; 627]

snappy 1 *adj* **irritable**, tetchy (*informal*), snippy (*informal*), bad-tempered, short-tempered, ratty (*informal*), sharp, curt, brusque, impatient, abrupt, terse, ill-humoured. [➡BAD-TEMPERED AND HUMOURLESS; 627] *Opposite:* good-natured. 2 *adj* (*informal*) **lively**, brisk, interesting, stimulating, to the point, relevant, pertinent, tight. [➡INTERESTING AND MEANINGFUL; 191] *Opposite:* dull. 3 *adj* **hasty**, quick, fast, speedy, rapid, swift. [➡HAPPENING QUICKLY; 104] *Opposite:* slow. 4 *adj* (*informal*) **stylish**, chic, fashionable, trendy (*informal*), snazzy (*informal*), classy (*informal*), smart, elegant. [➡WELL GROOMED; 483] *Opposite:* dowdy.

snapshot 1 *n* **photo**, photograph, picture, snap, Polaroid, portrait, print, shot. [➡PHOTOGRAPHY AND PHOTOGRAPHIC EQUIPMENT; 1121] 2 *n* **view**, glimpse, outline, idea, thumbnail sketch, record, description. [➡RECORDS; 586]

snap up *v* **grab**, seize, pounce on, take up. [➡GET; 421]

snare 1 *n* **trap**, noose, gin, lasso. [➡CAPTIVITY AND LOSS OF FREEDOM; 249] 2 *v* **catch**, trap, capture, ensnare, entrap. [➡CAPTIVITY AND LOSS OF FREEDOM; 249]

snare drum *type of* **percussion instrument.** [➡MUSICAL INSTRUMENTS; 910]

snarl 1 *v* **growl**, roar, bellow. [➡SOUND EMISSION BY ANIMALS OR BIRDS; 365] 2 *v* **speak angrily**, bark, growl, snap, rasp, grumble. [➡SOUND EMISSION BY PEOPLE; 364] 3 *type of* **animal sound.** [➡SOUNDS MADE BY ANIMALS; 1260]

snarl-up *n* **blockage**, holdup, jam, traffic jam, logjam, tangle, gridlock. [➡PROBLEM; 257]

snarl up *v* **jam up**, back up, grind to a halt, come to a standstill, reach gridlock, get held up, get blocked up, get tangled up. [➡FAIL OR CEASE TO FUNCTION; 471] *Opposite:* free up.

snatch 1 *v* **grab**, grasp, seize, take. [➡CONTACT: HOLD; 412] 2 *v* **steal**, pinch (*informal*), nick (*slang*), filch (*informal*), run off with. [➡STEAL AND ROB; 427] 3 *v* (*US informal*) **kidnap**, abduct, seize, shanghai, capture, hijack, take prisoner, take hostage. [➡CAPTIVITY AND LOSS OF FREEDOM; 249] *Opposite:* release.

snazziness (*informal*) *n* [➡WELL GROOMED; 483]

snazzy (*informal*) *adj* **flashy**, bright, colourful, loud, ostentatious, flamboyant, fashionable. [➡WELL GROOMED; 483] *Opposite:* drab.

sneak 1 *v* **tell tales**, inform, tell, grass (*slang*), snitch (*slang*). [➡BETRAY CONFIDENCES AND GOSSIP; 619] 2 *v* **slip**, steal, creep, slink, tiptoe. [➡MOVE SLOWLY; 315] 3 *n* **telltale**, informer, tattletale (*US informal*), grass (*slang*), snitch (*slang*). [➡INTERFERING PEOPLE AND TELLTALES; 950]

sneak a look *v* [➡LOOKING AND LOOKS; 701]

sneaker (*US*) *type of* **shoe.** [➡FOOTWEAR; 871]

sneakiness *n* **slyness**, furtiveness, stealth, deviousness, cunning, underhandedness, guile, wiles, artfulness, shiftiness, unfairness. [➡DECEITFUL; 514] *Opposite:* openness.

sneaking *adj* **niggling**, uneasy, nagging, uncomfortable, worrying. [➡IRRITATING; 229]

sneak preview *n* **advance showing**, premiere, preview, screening, advance screening, viewing. [➡PERFORMANCES AND SHOWS; 42]

sneak thief *n* **pickpocket**, shoplifter, burglar, thief, robber. [➡CRIMINALS; 821]

sneak up on 1 *v* **creep up on**, steal up on, come up on, come up behind, surprise, take by surprise, catch unawares, approach unnoticed. [➡ACCOMPANY AND FOLLOW; 338] **2** *v* **catch out** (*informal*), catch napping, catch unawares, take by surprise, surprise, creep up on, steal up on. [➡SURPRISE AND IMPRESS; 575]

sneaky *adj* **sly**, devious, shifty, underhand, mean, tricky, duplicitous, guileful. [➡DECEITFUL; 514] *Opposite:* honest.

sneer *v* **scorn**, scoff, turn your nose up at, mock, deride, laugh at, snigger, jeer, smirk, disparage, snicker (*US*). [➡PROTEST AND EXPRESS DISAPPROVAL; 643]

sneering *adj* **scornful**, contemptuous, disdainful, sarcastic, arrogant, condescending, derisive, mocking, disparaging, critical. [➡MOCKING AND DISMISSIVE; 637] *Opposite:* admiring.

sneeze **1** *n* **sniff**, sniffle, snuffle, splutter, snort, snivel. [➡BREATHE AND NOT BREATHE; 717] **2** *v* **sniffle**, sniff, snuffle, splutter, snort, snivel. [➡BREATHE AND NOT BREATHE; 717]

snicker **1** *v* **whinny**, neigh, snort, snuffle, bray. [➡SOUND EMISSION BY PEOPLE; 364] **2** *v* (*US*) **snigger**, laugh, smirk, mock, deride, sneer. [➡LAUGHTER; 650] **3** *n* **neigh**, whinny, snort, snuffle, bray. [➡SOUNDS MADE BY PEOPLE; 1261] **4** *n* (*US*) **snigger**, laugh, sneer, snort. [➡LAUGHTER; 650]

snickering *n* [➡LAUGHTER; 650]

snide *adj* **sarcastic**, mean, nasty (*informal*), unpleasant, malicious, spiteful, unkind, hurtful, cutting. [➡RUDE AND HOSTILE; 626] *Opposite:* pleasant.

sniff **1** *v* **snuffle**, breathe, inhale. [➡BREATHE AND NOT BREATHE; 717] *Opposite:* exhale. **2** *v* **smell**, scent, get a whiff of, catch the scent of. [➡SMELL AND SMELLING; 706] **3** *n* **breath**, snort, snuffle, lungful, inhalation. [➡BREATHE AND NOT BREATHE; 717]

sniff at *v* **turn your nose up at**, sneer at, hold in contempt, look down on, scorn, disdain, refuse, reject, turn down. [➡FOREGO AND DENY ONESELF; 450] *Opposite:* accept.

sniffle **1** *v* **sniff**, snuffle, snivel, snort, splutter. [➡BREATHE AND NOT BREATHE; 717] **2** *v* **whimper**, snivel, grizzle (*informal*), cry, weep, sob, blubber (*informal*), whinge (*informal*), blub (*informal*), whine. [➡CRYING; 651] **3** *n* **snuffle**, sniff, snivel, snort, splutter. [➡SOUNDS MADE BY PEOPLE; 1261]

sniff out (*informal*) *v* **discover**, find, unearth, track down, detect, bring to light, reveal, expose, nose out. [➡FIND; 464]

sniffy (*informal*) *adj* **contemptuous**, haughty, disdainful, scornful, snooty (*informal*), superior, stuck-up (*informal*), proud, arrogant, supercilious. [➡AFFECTATION, SELF-SATISFACTION, AND SNOBBISHNESS; 508] *Opposite:* humble.

snifter (*informal*) *n* **drink**, tipple (*informal*), nightcap, tot, shot (*informal*), wee dram, splash, nip, jigger (*informal*), short (*informal*), dram. [➡DRINKS; 1186]

snigger **1** *v* **laugh**, smirk, mock, deride, sneer, snicker (*US*). [➡LAUGHTER; 650] **2** *n* **laugh**, sneer, snort, snicker (*US*). [➡LAUGHTER; 650] **3** *type of* **human sound**. [➡SOUNDS MADE BY PEOPLE; 1261]

sniggering *n* [➡LAUGHTER; 650]

snip **1** *v* **cut**, shear, slice, nick, trim, clip. [➡TEAR, BREAK, AND CUT; 361] **2** *n* (*informal*) **bargain**, good deal, good buy, steal (*informal*), giveaway (*informal*). [➡ECONOMICAL AND RESOURCEFUL; 208]

snipe *type of* **freshwater bird**. [➡FRESHWATER BIRD; 1000]

sniper *n* **gunman**, marksman, assassin, rifleman, shooter. [➡PEOPLE WHO KILL; 924]

snippet *n* **extract**, piece, bit, scrap. [➡SMALL PIECE; 127]

snippy (*informal*) *adj* **irritable**, tetchy (*informal*), snappy, grumpy, crabby, grouchy (*informal*), ratty (*informal*), sharp, short, out of sorts, curt, abrupt, blunt. [➡BAD-TEMPERED AND HUMOURLESS; 627] *Opposite:* good-tempered.

snitch (*slang*) **1** *v* **pilfer**, steal, rob, pinch (*informal*), swipe (*informal*), filch (*informal*), lift (*informal*), take, rip off (*informal*), knock off (*slang*), cop (*slang*), purloin (*formal*). [➡STEAL AND ROB; 427] **2** *v* **talk**, tell, tell tales, blab (*informal*), inform on, grass (*slang*), spill the beans (*informal*), let the cat out of the bag, split (*informal*), tattle (*slang disapproving*), squeal (*slang disapproving*), stool (*US slang*). [➡BETRAY CONFIDENCES AND GOSSIP; 619] **3** *n* **informer**, telltale, sneak, tattler, tattletale (*US*), grass (*slang*), stool pigeon (*slang*), blabbermouth (*informal*), snout (*slang*), stoolie (*US slang*), mole, squealer (*slang disapproving*), plant (*informal*), betrayer, tipster. [➡INTERFERING PEOPLE AND TELLTALES; 950]

snivel *v* **sob**, sniff, cry, weep, blub (*informal*), whinge (*informal*), whimper, moan, sniffle, boohoo, blubber (*informal*). [➡CRYING; 651]

snivelling *adj* [➡CRYING; 651]

snob *n* **social climber** (*disapproving*), name-dropper, elitist. [➡SUPERFICIAL OR INSINCERE PEOPLE; 951]

snobbery *n* **arrogance**, superciliousness, condescension, snobbishness, snootiness (*informal*), pretentiousness, conceit, pomposity, affectedness. [➡AFFECTATION, SELF-SATISFACTION, AND SNOBBISHNESS; 508] *Opposite:* humility.

snobbish *adj* **snooty** (*informal*), high and mighty, toffee-nosed (*informal*), superior, stuck-up (*informal*), snobby, arrogant, conceited, condescending, supercilious, patronizing, pretentious. [➡AFFECTATION, SELF-SATISFACTION, AND SNOBBISHNESS; 508] *Opposite:* humble.

snobbishness *n* **snootiness** (*informal*), snobbery, condescension, superciliousness, pretentiousness, haughtiness, arrogance, disdain, pomposity, affectedness. [➡AFFECTATION, SELF-SATISFACTION, AND SNOBBISHNESS; 508] *Opposite:* humility.

snobby (*informal*) *adj* **high and mighty**, stuck-up (*informal*), snooty (*informal*), superior, snobbish, toffee-nosed (*informal*), arrogant, conceited, condescending, supercilious, pretentious. [➡AFFECTATION, SELF-SATISFACTION, AND SNOBBISHNESS; 508] *Opposite:* humble.

snog (*slang*) **1** *v* **kiss**, neck (*dated*), cuddle, hug, smooch (*informal*), embrace, canoodle (*informal*). [➡PHYSICAL CONTACT AS COMMUNICATION; 656] **2** *n* **cuddle**, kiss, hug, smooch (*informal*), embrace, canoodle (*informal*). [➡PHYSICAL CONTACT AS COMMUNICATION; 656]

snooker **1** *v* (*informal*) **thwart**, stymie, put paid to (*informal*), obstruct, hinder, stop, frustrate, foil, dash, circumvent. [➡MAKE IMPOSSIBLE; 277] *Opposite:* assist. 2 *type of* **target ball game.** [➡HOBBIES, GAMES, AND SPORTS; 875]

snoop (*informal*) 1 *v* **spy**, poke around, watch, nose around (*informal*), sneak, pry, interfere, meddle, poke your nose in. [➡LOOKING AND LOOKS; 701] *Opposite:* mind your own business. 2 *n* **spy**, sneak, meddler, intruder, eavesdropper. [➡INTERFERING PEOPLE AND TELLTALES; 950]

snootily (*informal*) *adv* **snobbishly**, condescendingly, superciliously, patronizingly, pretentiously, haughtily, arrogantly, disdainfully, pompously, affectedly. [➡POMPOUS, LOUD, AND OVER-CONFIDENT; 636] *Opposite:* humbly.

snootiness (*informal*) 1 *n* **snobbishness**, snobbery, condescension, superciliousness, pretentiousness, haughtiness, arrogance, disdain, pomposity, affectedness. [➡AFFECTATION, SELF-SATISFACTION, AND SNOBBISHNESS; 508] *Opposite:* humility. 2 *n* **exclusivity**, exclusiveness, poshness (*informal*), selectness. [➡EXPENSIVE AND LUXURIOUS; 219]

snooty (*informal*) *adj* **high and mighty**, stuck-up (*informal*), condescending, patronizing, supercilious, snobby (*informal*), snobbish, toffee-nosed (*informal*), superior, pretentious. [➡AFFECTATION, SELF-SATISFACTION, AND SNOBBISHNESS; 508] *Opposite:* humble.

snooze (*informal*) 1 *v* **doze**, sleep, doze off, nap, nod off, catnap, kip (*informal*), siesta. [➡SLEEP AND DREAM; 724] *Opposite:* wake up. 2 *n* **sleep**, doze, nap, kip (*informal*), catnap, forty winks (*informal*), siesta. [➡SLEEP AND DREAM; 724]

snore *v* **snort**, breathe heavily, snuffle, wheeze. [➡BREATHE AND NOT BREATHE; 717]

snorkel *v* **swim**, dive, scuba dive. [➡HOBBIES, GAMES, AND SPORTS; 875]

snorkeller *n* [➡PEOPLE IN SPORTS AND LEISURE; 876]

snort *v* **grunt**, exhale, breathe out, inhale, draw in, breathe in, sniff, expire. [➡BREATHE AND NOT BREATHE; 717]

snout 1 *n* **nose**, muzzle, proboscis, schnozzle (*US slang*). [➡THE NOSE; 705] 2 *n* (*slang*) **informer**, informant, sneak, mole, snitch (*slang*), stool pigeon (*slang*), grass (*slang*), squealer (*slang disapproving*), stoolie (*US slang*). [➡INTERFERING PEOPLE AND TELLTALES; 950]

snow *n* **sleet**, snowflake, slush, hail, ice, snowfall, snowstorm, blizzard, flurry. [➡COLD WEATHER; 1051]

snowball *v* **increase**, mount, soar, balloon, swell, grow quickly, escalate, magnify, burgeon (*literary*), expand, multiply. [➡CHANGE OF SIZE: BIGGER; 393] *Opposite:* decrease.

snowboarding *type of* **winter sport.** [➡HOBBIES, GAMES, AND SPORTS; 875]

snowbound *adj* **snowed in**, snowed up, cut off, isolated, shut in, blockaded. [➡COLD WEATHER; 1051]

snowdrop *type of* **flower grown from bulb.** [➡FLOWERS FROM BULBS; 1030]

snowfall *n* **snowstorm**, snow, flurry, blizzard, whiteout. [➡COLD WEATHER; 1051]

snow flurry *n* [➡COLD WEATHER; 1051]

snow job (*US slang*) *n* [➡DECEPTION AND LIES; 661]

snowmobile *type of* **leisure vehicle.** [➡VEHICLES; 1144]

snow pea (*US*) *type of* **pulse.** [➡BEANS AND PULSES; 1188]

snowplough *type of* **commercial or industrial vehicle.** [➡VEHICLES; 1144]

snowshoe *type of* **shoe.** [➡FOOTWEAR; 871]

snowsquall *n* [➡COLD WEATHER; 1051]

snowstorm *n* **blizzard**, hail, snowfall, flurry, snow flurry, whiteout, sleet. [➡COLD WEATHER; 1051]

snow under 1 *v* **inundate**, swamp, bury, overwhelm, overload, bog down (*informal*), drown, flood, deluge, submerge, engulf. [➡GIVE TOO MUCH; 438] 2 *v* (*US*) **defeat**, bear, overcome, crush, rout, trounce, thrash, cream (*US informal*). [➡BEAT AND DEFEAT; 80]

snow-white *n type of* **white.** [➡COLOURS; 1223]

snowy *adj* **snow-white**, hoary, white. [➡DESCRIBING COLOURS; 1225]

snowy owl *type of* **owl.** [➡OWL; 1001]

snub 1 *v* **ignore**, coldshoulder, slight, look right through, cut, rebuff, rebuke, shame, humiliate, give the brushoff, ostracize. [➡REFUSING OR REJECTING RELATIONS; 975] *Opposite:* acknowledge. 2 *n* **rebuff**, slight, rejection, rebuke, brushoff (*informal*), insult, humiliation. [➡DENY AND REJECT; 645]

snub-nosed *adj* **button-nosed**, pug-nosed, retroussé. [➡FACIAL CHARACTERISTICS; 482]

snuff 1 *v* **extinguish**, put out, douse, snuff out, blow out, smother, quench. [➡CAUSE TO STOP; 267] *Opposite:* light. 2 *v* (*informal*) **destroy**, put out, kill, eliminate, abolish, eradicate, annihilate. [➡KILL; 923] *Opposite:* save.

snuffle 1 *v* **sniff**, sniffle, snort, snivel, splutter, breathe noisily, inhale, exhale, pant. [➡BREATHE AND NOT BREATHE; 717] 2 *n* **snort**, sniff, sniffle, snivel, splutter, breath, inhalation, exhalation, pant. [➡BREATHE AND NOT BREATHE; 717]

snug 1 *adj* **cosy**, warm, comfortable, comfy (*informal*), homely, inviting, homey, sheltered. [➡PHYSICALLY PLEASANT; 187] *Opposite:* uncomfortable. 2 *adj* **close**, well-fitting, neat, close-fitting, tight, secure. [➡DESCRIBING CLOTHES; 869] *Opposite:* loose.

snuggle *v* **nestle**, nuzzle, cuddle, burrow, huddle, snug. [➡GET CLOSER TOGETHER; 311]

so *adv* **consequently** (*formal*), as a result, thus (*formal*), therefore, subsequently, accordingly, hence (*formal*). [➡CAUSATION; 169]

soak 1 *v* **immerse**, steep, marinate, infuse, saturate, bathe, penetrate, pervade. [➡SOFTEN, LIQUEFY, DAMPEN; 389] 2 *v* **drench**, douse, saturate, wet, drown, sop. [➡SOFTEN, LIQUEFY, DAMPEN; 389] *Opposite:* dry out.

soaked *adj* **wet through**, saturated, sodden, waterlogged, drenched, dripping, dripping wet, sopping, sopping wet, soaking, soaking wet, wringing wet. [➡WET; 1239] *Opposite:* dry.

soaked to the skin *adj* [➡WET; 1239]

soaking *adj* **drenched**, soaked, soaking wet, sopping wet, sopping, saturated, sodden, wet through, soaked to the skin, like a drowned rat, wringing, wringing wet, waterlogged. [➡WET; 1239] *Opposite:* dry.

See Compare and Contrast at **wet.**

soaking wet *adj* [➡WET; 1239]

so-and-so (*informal*) *n* **thingamajig** (*informal*), thingummy (*informal*), thingamabob (*informal*), whatshisname (*informal*), whatshername (*informal*), whatchamacallit. [➡NAME AND DESCRIBE; 666]

soap 1 *n* **cleanser**, detergent, shampoo, soap powder, washing powder, lather, bubbles, soapsuds, suds. [➡CLEANING AGENTS; 863] 2 *n* (*informal*) **serial**, soap opera, series, programme. [➡TELEVISION AND RADIO; 607] 3 *v* **cleanse**, lather, wash, wash down, shampoo, sanitize, sterilize, disinfect. [➡CLEAN AND POLISH; 404]

soap opera *n* **serial**, soap, series. [➡TELEVISION AND RADIO; 607]

soap powder *n* **detergent**, washing powder, soap, soapsuds, cleanser, suds. [➡CLEANING AGENTS; 863]

soapstone *type of* **stone.** [➡STONES, ROCKS, AND BOULDERS; 1057]

soapsuds *n* **foam**, lather, suds, froth, bubbles. [➡FROTH; 1272]

soapy *adj* [➡VISUAL TEXTURE; 1220]

soar 1 *v* **fly**, ascend, climb, wheel, circle, rise, mount. [➡GO UPWARDS; 307] *Opposite:* plummet. 2 *v* **rise**, rocket, climb, mount, increase, go through the roof, go sky-high, escalate, arise (*archaic or literary*), shoot up, skyrocket (*informal*). [➡CHANGE OF INTENSITY: MORE; 395] *Opposite:* decrease.

soaring *adj* **rising**, mounting, climbing, spiralling, increasing, elevated, high, sky-high. [➡CHANGE OF INTENSITY: MORE; 395] *Opposite:* plummeting.

sob *v* **moan**, cry, weep, snivel, sniffle, sniff, snuffle, shed tears, tears, blub (*informal*), bawl (*informal*), howl, blubber (*informal*). [➡CRYING; 651]

sobbing *n* **crying**, weeping, bawling (*informal*), howling, blubbing (*informal*), snivelling. [➡CRYING; 651]

sober 1 *adj* **abstemious**, clear-headed, temperate, teetotal, moderate, restrained. [➡ABSTEMIOUSNESS AND SELF-DENIAL; 882] 2 *adj* **serious**, sombre, solemn, thoughtful, calm, grave, unexcited, unruffled, subdued, restrained, severe, sedate, staid. [➡CONFIDENCE AND COMPOSURE; 500] *Opposite:* frivolous. 3 *adj* **dull**, sombre, drab, dreary, staid, plain, subdued. [➡DESCRIBING COLOURS; 1225] *Opposite:* bright.

soberly 1 *adv* **seriously**, solemnly, sombrely, gravely, glumly, mournfully, dolefully, thoughtfully, pensively, sadly. [➡BAD-TEMPERED AND HUMOURLESS; 627] *Opposite:* frivolously. 2 *adv* **dully**, sombrely, drably, plainly, simply, severely, seriously, ascetically, quietly, moderately. [➡BORING AND UNINTERESTING; 235] *Opposite:* brightly. 3 *adv* **rationally**, judiciously, level-headedly, clear-headedly, lucidly, sensibly, cautiously, coherently, rigorously, strictly. [➡POSITIVE INTELLECTUAL CHARACTERISTICS; 525] *Opposite:* fancifully.

soberness 1 *n* **seriousness**, solemnity, sombreness, gravity, glumness, mournfulness, dolefulness, thoughtfulness, pensiveness, sadness. [➡BAD-TEMPERED AND HUMOURLESS; 627] *Opposite:* frivolity. 2 *n* **dullness**, sombreness, drabness, plainness, simplicity, severity, seriousness, asceticism, moderation, sobriety. [➡BORING AND UNINTERESTING; 235] *Opposite:* brightness. 3 *n* **rationality**, judiciousness, level-headedness, clear-headedness, lucidity, sense, caution, coherence, rigour, strictness. [➡POSITIVE INTELLECTUAL CHARACTERISTICS; 525]

sobriety 1 *n* **abstemiousness**, abstinence, temperance, moderation, soberness, clear-headedness. [➡ABSTEMIOUSNESS AND SELF-DENIAL; 882] 2 *n* **seriousness**, sombreness, solemnity, thoughtfulness, calm, gravity, sedateness, staidness. [➡CONFIDENCE AND COMPOSURE; 500] *Opposite:* flippancy.

sobriquet *n* **nickname**, pet name, moniker (*slang*), term of endearment, alias, assumed name, name, label, handle (*slang*), tag, epithet, code name, appellation (*formal*). [➡NAME AND DESCRIBE; 666]

sob story (*informal*) *n* **tale of woe**, hard-luck story, sorry tale, sad story. [➡THE ORAL TRADITION; 678]

so-called *adj* **supposed**, alleged, ostensible, purported (*formal*), self-styled, professed, pretended. [➡FALSE AND UNREAL; 174]

soccer (*US*) *type of* **ball game.** [➡HOBBIES, GAMES, AND SPORTS; 875]

sociability 1 *n* **gregariousness**, companionability, conviviality, hospitability. [➡FRIENDLINESS AND SOCIABILITY; 495] 2 *n* **friendliness**, pleasantness, amiability, affability, geniality, cordiality, openness, civility. [➡FRIENDLINESS AND SOCIABILITY; 495]

sociable 1 *adj* **gregarious**, companionable, convivial, good company, hospitable. [➡FRIENDLINESS AND SOCIABILITY; 495] *Opposite:* retiring. 2 *adj* **friendly**, outgoing, amiable, warm, affable, genial, cordial, jovial. [➡FRIENDLINESS AND SOCIABILITY; 495] *Opposite:* unsociable.

social 1 *adj* **communal**, community, common, societal, public, shared, collective, group. [➡BELONGING OR RELATING TO PEOPLE; 943] 2 *n* **party**, get-together (*informal*), do (*informal*), gathering. [➡PARTIES, DANCES, AND CELEBRATIONS; 37]

social call *n* [➡INFORMAL COMMUNICATION; 45]

social circle *n* [➡FRIENDS AND ACQUAINTANCES; 936]

social class *n* [➡STATUS; 888]

social climber (*disapproving*) *n* **hanger-on**, sycophant, toady, creep (*informal*), snob, bootlicker (*informal disapproving*), socialite. [➡SUPERFICIAL OR INSINCERE PEOPLE; 951]

social conscience *n* [➡MORALLY GOOD; 775]

social democracy *n* [➡STYLES AND SYSTEMS OF GOVERNMENT; 806]

social democrat *n* [➡PHILOSOPHICAL AND POLITICAL THINKERS; 782]

social event *n* [➡PARTIES, DANCES, AND CELEBRATIONS; 37]

socialism *n* **collectivism**, social democracy, public ownership, communism, communalism, classless society. [➡STYLES AND SYSTEMS OF GOVERNMENT; 806]

socialist *n* **collectivist**, social democrat, communist, communalist. [➡PHILOSOPHICAL AND POLITICAL THINKERS; 782]

socialist realism *type of* **20th-century art movement.** [➡ARTISTIC MOVEMENTS AND STYLES; 899]

socialite *n* **person about town** (*dated*), jet-setter (*informal*), trendsetter, one of the in-crowd (*informal*), one of the beautiful people, member of café society, one of the glitterati, social climber (*disapproving*). [➡IMPORTANT OR FAMOUS PEOPLE; 893]

socialize *v* **meet people**, go out, get out, mix, mingle, entertain, hang out (*informal*), party (*informal*). [➡ESTABLISHING RELATIONSHIPS WITH OTHERS; 974]

socially 1 *adv* **communally**, publicly, within society, generally, collectively. [➡BELONGING OR RELATING TO PEOPLE; 943] 2 *adv* **in public**, in a social context, with other people, in a crowd. [➡ACTING WITH OTHERS; 286] 3 *adv* **as a friend**, outside of work, informally, on a social basis. [➡RELATIONSHIP TO ANOTHER; 973]

social responsibility *n* [➡MORALLY GOOD; 775]

social standing *n* [➡STATUS; 888]

societal *adj* **social**, group, shared, general, common, communal, collective, public. [➡BELONGING OR RELATING TO PEOPLE; 943]

society 1 *n* **civilization**, culture, humanity, the social order, the world. [➡PERSON; 931] 2 *n* **people**, the public, the general public, the populace, the population. [➡GROUPS IN SOCIETY; 940] 3 *n* **association**, union, group, guild, league, organization, club, institute, circle. [➡CLUBS AND SOCIETIES; 939] 4 *n* **high society**, the upper classes, polite society, the upper crust (*informal*). [➡CLASS STATUS; 889]

sock 1 *v* (*informal*) **hit**, punch, thump, whack, thwack, wallop (*informal*), smack, strike. [➡PHYSICAL ATTACK AND PUNISHMENT; 416] 2 *n* (*informal*) **hit**, punch, thump, whack, thwack, wallop (*informal*), smack. [➡PHYSICAL ATTACK AND PUNISHMENT; 416] 3 *type of* **lower body underwear.** [➡HABERDASHERY, MILLINERY, AND LINGERIE; 867]

socket 1 *n* **hole**, opening, hollow. [➡FASTENERS, LINKS, AND NETWORKS; 1246] 2 *n* **power point**, plug (*informal*), outlet. [➡FITTINGS; 859]

socket spanner *type of* **general tool.** [➡HAND TOOLS; 1118]

socket wrench *type of* **general tool.** [➡HAND TOOLS; 1118]

sod *n* **turf**, clod, grass, earth. [➡EROSION PRODUCTS AND SOIL; 1058]

soda bread *type of* **bread.** [➡BREAD, FLOUR, AND BREAD PRODUCTS; 1178]

sodden *adj* **saturated**, soaking, soaked, soaking wet, sopping wet, sopping, wet, wet through, drenched, wringing wet, wringing. [➡WET; 1239] *Opposite:* dry.

See Compare and Contrast at **wet.**

sofa *n* **settee**, couch, chaise longue, day bed, futon, lounger. [➡FURNITURE; 858]

sofa bed *type of* **bed.** [➡FURNITURE; 858]

so far *adv* **up to now**, thus far, hitherto (*formal*), until now, to date. [➡PAST; 84]

soft 1 *adj* **yielding**, squashy, spongy, supple, pliable, elastic, malleable, flexible, bendable, ductile, limp. [➡MALLEABLE AND ELASTIC; 1211] *Opposite:* hard. 2 *adj* **smooth**, silky, supple, velvety. [➡PHYSICAL TEXTURE; 1221] *Opposite:* rough. 3 *adj* **low**, mellifluous, melodious, faint, muted, quiet. [➡SOFT OR PLEASANT SOUNDS; 1264] *Opposite:* loud. 4 *adj* **gentle**, flowing, delicate, subtle, understated, muted. [➡PHYSICALLY PLEASANT; 187] *Opposite:* harsh. 5 *adj* **dim**, diffused, mellow, subtle, gentle. [➡DESCRIBING LIGHT; 1227] *Opposite:* bright. 6 *adj* **lenient**, lax, easy, forgiving, indulgent, easygoing, spineless, weak, undemanding. [➡GENEROSITY AND KINDNESS; 496] *Opposite:* strict. 7 *adj* **tender**, sensitive, gentle, kind, sympathetic, soft-hearted, pleasant, sentimental. [➡GENEROSITY AND KINDNESS; 496] *Opposite:* hardhearted. 8 *adj* **pathetic** (*informal*), wet, drippy (*slang*), weak, soppy (*informal*), overindulgent. [➡COWARDICE AND WEAKNESS OF WILL; 509]

softball *type of* **ball game.** [➡HOBBIES, GAMES, AND SPORTS; 875]

soft-boiled *adj* **soft-hearted**, soft, sympathetic, sentimental, indulgent, lenient. *Opposite:* hard-boiled. (*informal*). [➡GENEROSITY AND KINDNESS; 496]

soften 1 *v* **unstiffen**, relax, make softer, make pliable. [➡SOFTEN, LIQUEFY, DAMPEN; 389] *Opposite:* harden. 2 *v* **alleviate**, lessen, reduce, diminish, mitigate, allay. [➡CHANGE OF INTENSITY: LESS; 396] *Opposite:* exacerbate. 3 *v* **moderate**, relax, temper, tone down, assuage, allay, mollify. [➡CHANGE OF INTENSITY: LESS; 396]

soft furnishings *n* **upholstery**, curtains, rugs, cushions, fabrics, throws, drapes (*US*). [➡SOFT FURNISHINGS, LINEN, AND DRAPERY; 860]

soft-hearted *adj* **sympathetic**, kind, caring, warm, good-natured, considerate, affectionate, loving, soft. [➡GENEROSITY AND KINDNESS; 496] *Opposite:* hardhearted.

soft-heartedness *n* [➡GENEROSITY AND KINDNESS; 496]

softie *see* **softy.**

softly 1 *adv* **tenderly**, delicately, gently, kindly, sympathetically, sensitively, quietly. [➡GENEROSITY AND KINDNESS; 496] *Opposite:* severely. 2 *adv* **quietly**, gently, mellifluously, melodiously, faintly. [➡SOFT OR PLEASANT SOUNDS; 1264] *Opposite:* harshly. 3 *adv* **dimly**, gently, faintly, lightly, subtly. [➡DESCRIBING LIGHT; 1227] *Opposite:* brightly.

softly lit *adj* [➡DESCRIBING LIGHT; 1227]

softly-softly *adj* **cautious**, discreet, tentative, cagey (*informal*), vigilant, mindful. [➡PEACEFULNESS AND GENTLENESS; 215] *Opposite:* heavy-handed.

softness 1 *n* **gentleness**, smoothness, quietness, faintness. [➡PEACEFULNESS AND GENTLENESS; 215] *Opposite:* harshness. 2 *n* **pliability**, suppleness, flexibility, elasticity, malleability. [➡MALLEABLE AND ELASTIC; 1211]

soft on *adj* [➡APPRECIATION AND GRATITUDE; 536]

soft option *n* [➡EASY WORK; 300]

soft palate *part of* **mouth.** [➡THE MOUTH; 703]

soft-pedal (*informal*) *v* **play down**, downplay, make light of, underplay, minimize, make little of. [➡CHANGE OF INTENSITY: LESS; 396] *Opposite:* emphasize.

soft sell *(informal)* *n* **persuasion**, persuasiveness, coercion, sweet-talking *(informal)*, soft-soaping *(informal)*, subtlety. [➡BUSINESS ACTIVITIES AND PHENOMENA; 795]

soft-soap *(informal)* *v* **flatter**, sweet-talk *(informal)*, butter up *(informal)*, suck up to *(informal)*, play up to, lay it on thick, lay it on with a trowel *(informal)*. [➡FLATTER AND FAWN; 622]

soft-spoken *adj* **quiet**, gentle, calm, tranquil, serene. [➡RETICENT AND UNFORTHCOMING; 632] *Opposite:* loud.

soft spot *n* **weakness**, predilection *(formal)*, partiality, affection, weak spot, liking, fondness, penchant, inclination, preference, fancy. [➡APPRECIATION AND GRATITUDE; 536]

soft touch *n* **pushover** *(informal)*, easy prey, sucker *(informal)*, softy *(informal)*, easy target, easy mark *(US)*. [➡VICTIMS OF DECEIT; 663]

software *n* [➡COMPUTERS AND COMPUTING; 1126]

software design *n* [➡COMPUTERS AND COMPUTING; 1126]

software development *n* [➡COMPUTERS AND COMPUTING; 1126]

softy *(informal)* *n* **soft touch**, easy target, easy prey, sucker *(informal)*. [➡VICTIMS OF DECEIT; 663]

sogginess *n* [➡MOIST; 1240]

soggy *adj* **damp**, wet, moist, mushy, squelchy, sodden, waterlogged. [➡MOIST; 1240] *Opposite:* dry.

soi-disant *(literary)* *adj* **self-styled**, so-called, self-proclaimed, self-confessed, self-appointed, professed. [➡FALSE AND UNREAL; 174]

soigné *adj* **well-groomed**, well turned-out, neat, elegant, chic, stylish. [➡WELL GROOMED; 483] *Opposite:* dowdy.

soil 1 *n* **earth**, dirt, topsoil, mud, dust, loam. [➡EROSION PRODUCTS AND SOIL; 1058] 2 *n* **territory**, land, country, ground. [➡COUNTRIES AND REGIONS; 1066] 3 *v* **dirty**, get dirty, foul, sully *(literary)*, muddy, stain. [➡DIRTY AND CONTAMINATE; 405] *Opposite:* cleanse.

See Compare and Contrast at **dirty**.

soiled *adj* **dirty**, grubby, mucky *(informal)*, muddy, stained, filthy. [➡DIRTY; 1234] *Opposite:* clean.

See Compare and Contrast at **dirty**.

soiree *(formal)* *n* **party**, celebration, dinner party, evening, cocktail party, function, get-together *(informal)*, gathering, event, evening party *(US)*, do *(informal)*, drinks party. [➡PARTIES, DANCES, AND CELEBRATIONS; 37]

soirée *(formal)* *see* **soiree**.

sojourn *(literary)* 1 *n* **visit**, stay, stop, stopover. [➡TRAVEL: JOURNEYS AND TRIPS; 319] 2 *v* **stay**, stop, remain, dwell *(literary)*, abide *(archaic)*. [➡INHABIT; 20]

solace *n* **comfort**, consolation, support, relief, succour *(literary)*, help. [➡KIND ACTION OR BEHAVIOUR; 296] *Opposite:* aggravation.

solar cell *part of* **spacecraft**. [➡SPACE VEHICLES; 1062]

solar heating *n* [➡HEATING, REFRIGERATION, AND VENTILATION; 1141]

solarium *n* **conservatory**, sun lounge, suntrap, greenhouse, sun parlor *(US)*. [➡BUILDINGS FOR PUBLIC ENTERTAINMENT; 1083]

solar plexus *part of* **torso**. [➡TORSO; 694]

solar system *n* [➡THE SOLAR SYSTEM AND ASTRONOMY; 1059]

solder *v* **join**, fuse, weld, bond, connect, repair. [➡USE TOOLS AND MACHINERY; 469]

soldering iron *type of* **general tool**. [➡HAND TOOLS; 1118]

soldier 1 *n* **fighter**, combatant, warrior, regular, legionnaire, GI, squaddie *(slang)*. [➡MILITARY PERSONNEL; 828] 2 *n* **private**, sapper, gunner, corporal, sergeant, trooper, squaddie *(slang)*, guardsman. [➡MILITARY PERSONNEL; 828] 3 *n* **worker**, supporter, campaigner, crusader, workhorse. [➡WORKER; 836]

soldier of fortune *n* **mercenary**, adventurer, hired gun *(slang)*. [➡PEOPLE WHO KILL; 924] *Opposite:* regular.

soldier on *v* **persevere**, continue, carry on, keep on, keep going, persist. [➡CONTINUE AN ACTION; 263] *Opposite:* give up.

sold on *adj* [➡APPRECIATION AND GRATITUDE; 536]

sole 1 *adj* **only**, solitary, single, individual, singular, lone, one and only. [➡EXTRAORDINARY: UNCOMMON; 206] 2 *adj* **exclusive**, private, unique, special, individual. [➡UNRELATEDNESS AND SEPARATENESS; 147] 3 *type of* **flatfish**. [➡SEA FISH; 1009] 4 *part of* **leg or foot**. [➡LEG AND FOOT; 695]

solecism *n* **error**, mistake, blunder, faux pas *(literary)*, gaffe, bloomer *(informal humorous)*, slip, blooper *(US informal humorous)*. [➡MISTAKES; 251]

solely *adv* **exclusively**, only, merely, just, uniquely, specially. [➡MAINLY AND PRIMARILY; 138]

solemn 1 *adj* **earnest**, sincere, serious, firm, grave, intense. [➡PENSIVENESS AND INTEREST; 539] *Opposite:* flippant. 2 *adj* **sombre**, grave, serious, sober, sad, glum, humourless, lugubrious. [➡BAD-TEMPERED AND HUMOURLESS; 627] *Opposite:* cheerful. 3 *adj* **formal**, official, ceremonial, ritual, sacred, holy. [➡RELIGIOUS CONCEPTS; 777]

solemnity *n* **sombreness**, gravity, seriousness, soberness, sadness, glumness. [➡BAD-TEMPERED AND HUMOURLESS; 627]

solemnize *v* **celebrate**, honour, make official, formalize, sanctify, observe. [➡RELIGIONS AND RELIGIOUS PRACTICES; 778]

solicit 1 *v* **ask for**, beg, importune *(formal)*, seek, petition for, plead for, request, crave. [➡REQUEST AND DEMAND; 664] *Opposite:* grant. 2 *v* **ask**, petition, implore *(formal)*, beseech *(literary)*, lobby, plead with. [➡REQUEST AND DEMAND; 664]

solicitor *n* **lawyer**, advocate, legal representative, attorney *(US)*. [➡PEOPLE IN LAW COURTS; 820]

solicitous *adj* **considerate**, caring, attentive, concerned, kind. [➡GENEROSITY AND KINDNESS; 496] *Opposite:* uncaring.

solicitousness *n* **concern**, attentiveness, consideration, care, kindness, solicitude. [➡GENEROSITY AND KINDNESS; 496]

solicitude 1 *n* **concern**, attentiveness, consideration, care, kindness, solicitousness. [➡GENEROSITY AND KINDNESS; 496] *Opposite:* negligence. 2 *n* **anxiety**, concern, worry, unease, apprehension, apprehensiveness. [➡FEELINGS ABOUT THE FUTURE; 534] *Opposite:* serenity.

solid 1 *adj* **hard**, rock-hard, rock-solid, concrete, firm, unyielding, frozen, dense, compact, compacted. [➡RIGID AND HARD; 1210] *Opposite:* soft. 2 *adj* **dense**, unbroken, continuous, closed, blocked, sealed. [➡DENSITY AND CONSISTENCY; 1206] *Opposite:* hollow. 3 *adj* **pure**, genuine, unadulterated, one hundred per cent, unmixed, real. [➡TRUE AND REAL; 172] 4 *adj* **sturdy**, strong, secure, fixed, firm, safe, stable, sound, substantial, robust, rugged. [➡DENSITY AND CONSISTENCY; 1206] *Opposite:* weak. 5 *adj* **unanimous**, universal, widespread, popular, general, total, consistent. [➡HARMONY; 156] *Opposite:* patchy. 6 *adj* **reliable**, dependable, sound, trustworthy, level-headed. [➡HONEST AND RELIABLE; 503] *Opposite:* unreliable. 7 *n* **object**, thing, artefact, item, entity, article. [➡SOLIDS; 1273] 8 *n* **figure**, pyramid, tetrahedron, sphere, icosahedron, dodecahedron, cube. [➡ANGULAR SHAPE; 1216]

solidarity *n* **unity**, harmony, cohesion, commonality, camaraderie, team spirit, esprit de corps, unanimity. [➡HARMONY; 156] *Opposite:* discord.

solidify *v* **harden**, go hard, coagulate, congeal, set, freeze. [➡HARDEN, CONGEAL, DRY; 388] *Opposite:* dissolve.

solidity *n* **hardness**, firmness, solidness, sturdiness, strength, toughness. [➡DENSITY AND CONSISTENCY; 1206] *Opposite:* softness.

solidly 1 *adv* **firmly**, sturdily, stably, steadily, soundly, dependably. [➡SAFE AND SAFETY; 192] *Opposite:* weakly. 2 *adv* **unanimously**, universally, totally, consistently, one hundred per cent, to the hilt, all the way. [➡WHOLENESS AND COMPLETENESS; 199] *Opposite:* sporadically.

solidness *n* **hardness**, firmness, sturdiness, solidity, strength, toughness. [➡DENSITY AND CONSISTENCY; 1206]

soliloquy *n* **monologue**, speech, declamation, oration, dramatic monologue. [➡THE ORAL TRADITION; 678]

solipsism *n* [➡PSYCHOLOGY AND THE MIND; 770]

solipsistic *adj* [➡PSYCHOLOGY AND THE MIND; 770]

solitaire *n* **single stone**, gemstone, jewel, diamond, precious stone, sparkler (*informal*). [➡JEWELLERY; 866]

solitariness *n* [➡SOLITARINESS; 941]

solitary 1 *adj* **lone**, single, sole, individual, solo, unaccompanied. [➡SOLITARINESS; 941] *Opposite:* accompanied. 2 *adj* **private**, unsociable, unsocial, self-contained, self-sufficient, independent, lonely, retiring, friendless, introverted. [➡UNFRIENDLINESS AND UNSOCIABILITY; 505] *Opposite:* sociable. 3 *adj* **isolated**, desolate, out-of-the-way, secluded, unfrequented, remote. [➡DISTANCE; 161]

solitary confinement *n* **isolation**, imprisonment, confinement, incarceration (*formal*), detention, custody, solitary. [➡CAPTIVITY AND LOSS OF FREEDOM; 249]

solitude *n* **loneliness**, privacy, isolation, seclusion, separateness, aloneness. [➡SOLITARINESS; 941]

solo 1 *adj* **single**, unaccompanied, lone. [➡ACTING INDEPENDENTLY; 285] 2 *adv* **alone**, on your own, singly, by yourself. [➡ACTING INDEPENDENTLY; 285]

soloist *n* **artist**, artiste, musician, singer, vocalist, star, virtuoso. [➡MUSICIANS AND SINGERS; 908] *Opposite:* accompanist.

solon (*literary*) *n* **sage** (*literary*), statesman, adviser, mentor, elder statesman. [➡TALENTED OR INTELLIGENT PERSON; 529]

so long (*informal*) *interj* **goodbye**, ciao (*informal*), see you later (*informal*), farewell (*literary*), bye (*informal*), bye-bye (*informal*), adieu. [➡GREETINGS, FAREWELLS, AND SALUTATIONS; 660]

so long as *conj* [➡CAUSATION; 169]

solstice *n* [➡TIMES OF YEAR; 88]

solubility *n* **dissolvability**, deliquescence. [➡DENSITY AND CONSISTENCY; 1206] *Opposite:* insolubility.

soluble 1 *adj* **dissolvable**, deliquescent. [➡DENSITY AND CONSISTENCY; 1206] *Opposite:* insoluble. 2 *adj* **solvable**, answerable, fathomable, resolvable, decipherable, doable. [➡EASE AND SIMPLICITY; 201] *Opposite:* insoluble.

solution 1 *n* **answer**, key, explanation, resolution, way out, result. [➡SOLUTION; 216] *Opposite:* problem. 2 *n* **mix**, mixture, liquid, blend, cocktail. [➡LIQUIDS; 1268]

solvable *adj* **soluble**, resolvable, fathomable, answerable, decipherable, doable. [➡EASE AND SIMPLICITY; 201] *Opposite:* insoluble.

solve *v* **resolve**, crack, answer, explain, get to the bottom of, unravel, decipher, work out, disentangle, unscramble, elucidate (*formal*). [➡SOLVE AND INTERPRET; 761]

solvency *n* **creditworthiness**, affluence, wealth, soundness, comfort. [➡WEALTH AND WEALTHY; 891]

solvent 1 *adj* **in the black**, in credit, in funds, in the money, in clover, flush (*informal*), in the chips (*US*). [➡WEALTH AND WEALTHY; 891] *Opposite:* insolvent. 2 *n* [➡LIQUIDS; 1268]

soma *n* [➡BODY; 692]

sombre 1 *adj* **dull**, gloomy, drab, dingy, melancholy. [➡SADNESS, DISTRESS, AND DESPAIR; 540] *Opposite:* bright. 2 *adj* **muted**, dark, dull, solemn, funereal, drab, subdued. [➡DESCRIBING COLOURS; 1225] *Opposite:* bright. 3 *adj* **gloomy**, sad, depressed, melancholy, funereal, sepulchral, dismal, lugubrious. [➡EMOTIONALLY UNPLEASANT AND UPSETTING; 228] *Opposite:* cheerful.

sombrely 1 *adv* **dully**, dismally, gloomily, darkly, drably, dingily. [➡DESCRIBING COLOURS; 1225] *Opposite:* brightly. 2 *adv* **solemnly**, seriously, gravely, soberly, sadly, lugubriously. [➡SADNESS, DISTRESS, AND DESPAIR; 540] *Opposite:* cheerfully.

sombreness *n* [➡SADNESS, DISTRESS, AND DESPAIR; 540]

sombrero *type of* **hat**. [➡HABERDASHERY, MILLINERY, AND LINGERIE; 867]

some 1 *adv* **approximately**, about, around, roughly, more or less, nearly, round about. [➡APPROXIMATELY; 133] *Opposite:* exactly. 2 *adj* **a number of**, a quantity of, a little, a few, several, various. [➡AMOUNT AND QUANTITY; 112] *Opposite:* all. 3 *adj* **certain**, particular, selected, specific. [➡AMOUNT AND QUANTITY; 112]

somebody 1 *pron* **some person**, someone. [➡PERSON; 931]

Opposite: nobody. **2** *n* **big shot** (*informal*), celebrity, someone, big cheese (*slang*), bigwig (*informal*), name, superstar. [➡ IMPORTANT OR FAMOUS PEOPLE; 893] *Opposite:* nobody.

someday *adv* **one day**, sooner or later, sometime, soon, in the future, one of these days. [➡ FUTURE; 86] *Opposite:* never.

somehow *adv* **one way or another**, someway, by hook or by crook, come what may, come hell or high water. [➡ WAYS OF DOING THINGS; 295]

someone **1** *pron* **somebody**, some person. [➡ PERSON; 931] *Opposite:* no one. **2** *n* **big shot** (*informal*), celebrity, somebody, big name, star, superstar, name. [➡ IMPORTANT OR FAMOUS PEOPLE; 893] *Opposite:* nobody.

someplace (*US informal*) *adv* **somewhere**, wherever, anywhere, anyplace (*US informal*). [➡ GENERAL LOCATIONS; 159]

somersault **1** *n* **tumble**, forward roll, flip-flop, cartwheel, flip. [➡ FIDGET AND FROLIC; 312] **2** *v* **turn over**, tumble, flip over, cartwheel, flip. [➡ BOUNCE, UNDULATE, AND VIBRATE; 309]

something *adv* **a little**, somewhat, a bit (*informal*), to some degree, rather, approximately, roughly. [➡ TO A CERTAIN EXTENT; 134] *Opposite:* exactly.

something else entirely *n* [➡ DIFFERENCE; 150]

sometime **1** *adv* **at some point**, someday, at some time, in the future, one day, one of these days. [➡ FUTURE; 86] *Opposite:* never. **2** *adj* (*formal*) **former**, onetime, erstwhile (*formal*), ex (*informal*), previous, earlier. [➡ PAST; 84] *Opposite:* current.

some time ago *adv* [➡ PAST; 84]

sometimes *adv* **occasionally**, now and then, every now and then, every so often, now and again, from time to time, at times, on occasion. [➡ NEVER AND INFREQUENCY; 97] *Opposite:* always.

someway *adv* **somehow**, one way or another, in some way, by some means, by hook or by crook, come what may, come hell or high water. [➡ WAYS OF DOING THINGS; 295]

somewhat *adv* **rather**, fairly, slightly, to some extent, to a certain degree, a bit (*informal*), to a certain extent, to some degree. [➡ TO A CERTAIN EXTENT; 134]

somewhere *adv* **wherever**, anywhere, anyplace (*US informal*), someplace (*US informal*). [➡ GENERAL LOCATIONS; 159]

somnolence *n* [➡ SLEEP AND DREAM; 724]

somnolent *adj* **sleepy**, drowsy, dozy, half asleep, half awake, lethargic, torpid. [➡ TIRED, ASLEEP AND UNCONSCIOUS; 739]

son **1** *n* **child**, kid (*informal*), lad, boy. [➡ CHILD OR YOUTH; 945] **2** *type of* **younger relative**. [➡ YOUNGER GENERATION RELATIVES; 958]

sonata *type of* **instrumental music**. [➡ MUSIC, SONGS, AND SINGING; 907]

son et lumière *n* **entertainment**, spectacle, light show, tableau, spectacular. [➡ ENTERTAINMENT; 872]

song **1** *n* **tune**, melody, air, refrain, jingle, ditty, nursery rhyme, chorus, solo, carol, hymn, chant, ballad, folk song, piece, number, composition. [➡ MUSIC, SONGS, AND SINGING; 907] **2** *n* **birdsong**, call, warble, warbling, cry, chirrup, coo, cooing, mating song, mating call. [➡ SOUNDS MADE BY BIRDS; 1262]

song and dance (*informal*) *n* **fuss**, drama, commotion, palaver, hysterics, to-do (*informal*), histrionics, scene. [➡ CHAOS AND UPROAR; 51]

songbird

◆ *types of songbird*
warbler, woodlark, meadowlark, skylark, blackbird, bluebird, flycatcher, hedge sparrow, lark, linnet, nightingale, nightjar, oriole, pied wagtail, pipit, thrush, titmouse, wagtail, weaverbird, yellowhammer

songbook *n* **anthology**, collection, hymn book, book, hymnal, psalter. [➡ BOOKS AND BOOKLETS; 591]

songsmith *n* [➡ MUSICIANS AND SINGERS; 908]

songster *n* **singer**, vocalist, lead singer, soloist, chanteuse, diva. [➡ MUSICIANS AND SINGERS; 908]

songwriter *n* **composer**, lyricist, songsmith, poet, librettist, writer, artist. [➡ MUSICIANS AND SINGERS; 908]

sonic *adj* **auditory**, aural, audible, sound. [➡ ACOUSTICS; 1137]

sonic boom *n* **boom**, shock wave, noise, rumble, roar, echo, vibration. [➡ CONTINUOUS SOUNDS; 1257]

son-in-law *type of* **in-law**. [➡ RELATIVES BY MARRIAGE; 960]

sonnet *n* **poem**, verse, rhyme, Petrarchan sonnet, Shakespearian sonnet. [➡ POETRY AND VERSE; 915]

sonny (*informal*) *n* **lad**, boyo (*informal*), kid (*informal*), young man, kiddo (*informal*), my boy, my lad, sunshine (*informal*). [➡ MALE PERSON; 934]

sonny boy *see* **sonny**.

sonority *n* **resonance**, fullness, roundness, richness, reverberation, vibration. [➡ SOUNDS; 1255] *Opposite:* reediness.

sonorous *adj* **loud**, deep, resonant, echoing, booming, resounding, plangent. [➡ SOFT OR PLEASANT SOUNDS; 1264] *Opposite:* thin.

soon *adv* **almost immediately**, quickly, rapidly, shortly, presently, before long, in a little while, in next to no time, momentarily (*US*). [➡ FUTURE; 86]

sooner **1** *adv* **earlier**, faster, more quickly, more rapidly, nearer, closer. [➡ PROMPTNESS: EARLY; 98] *Opposite:* later. **2** *adv* **rather**, more readily, more willingly, preferably, as soon. [➡ THE WILL AND WILLINGNESS; 564]

sooner or later *adv* **eventually**, one day, someday, in time, in due course, sometime. [➡ FUTURE; 86] *Opposite:* never.

soon-to-be *adj* [➡ FUTURE; 86]

soot *n* **dust**, powder, grime, ashes, dirt, coal, smoke, smut, ash, clinker. [➡ PRODUCTS OF FIRE; 1165]

soothe **1** *v* **ease**, relieve, alleviate, reduce, palliate, lessen. [➡ CORRECT AND PUT RIGHT; 378] *Opposite:* aggravate. **2** *v* **calm**, pacify, quieten, appease, mollify, lull, relax. [➡ SOOTHE AND CALM; 574] *Opposite:* excite.

soothing *adj* **calming**, comforting, restful, gentle, peaceful, relaxing. [➡CALMING; 189] *Opposite:* irritating.

soothsayer *n* **fortune-teller**, oracle, seer, astrologer, clairvoyant, mystic. [➡PEOPLE WITH SUPERNATURAL POWERS; 789]

sooty *adj* **dirty**, grimy, black, filthy, dusty, smutty, smoky, mucky (*informal*), grungy (*informal*). [➡DIRTY; 1234] *Opposite:* clean.

sop *n* **concession**, offering, bribe, pacifier, backhander (*informal*), gesture. [➡GIFTS; 439]

sophism *n* [➡DECEPTION AND LIES; 661]

sophist *n* [➡PEOPLE WHO DECEIVE; 662]

sophistic *adj* [➡FALSE AND UNREAL; 174]

sophisticate 1 *v* **educate**, school, mould, acculturate, tutor. [➡INSTRUCT AND TEACH; 610] 2 *n* **socialite**, trendsetter, connoisseur, aesthete, jet-setter (*informal*), trendy (*informal*), cognoscente. [➡PLEASURE-SEEKERS AND HEDONISTS; 886] *Opposite:* hoi polloi.

sophisticated 1 *adj* **urbane**, classy (*informal*), cultured, chic, erudite, refined, stylish. [➡LEVEL OF EDUCATION AND SOPHISTICATION; 894] *Opposite:* gauche. 2 *adj* **clever**, advanced, high-level, complex, erudite, high-tech, state-of-the-art, cutting-edge, leading-edge, modern. [➡DESCRIBING TECHNOLOGY; 1159] *Opposite:* crude.

sophistication 1 *n* **refinement**, classiness (*informal*), style, chic, urbanity, elegance. [➡LEVEL OF EDUCATION AND SOPHISTICATION; 894] *Opposite:* naivety. 2 *n* **complexity**, cleverness, erudition, difficulty, intricacy. [➡POSITIVELY COMPLEX OR COMPLICATED; 218] *Opposite:* crudeness.

sophistry *n* **casuistry**, fallaciousness, illogicality, sophism, dishonesty, fraudulence. [➡DECEPTION AND LIES; 661] *Opposite:* logic.

soporific 1 *adj* **sleep-inducing**, calming, tranquillizing, hypnotic (*informal*), narcotic. [➡TIRED, ASLEEP AND UNCONSCIOUS; 739] 2 *adj* **tedious**, boring, interminable, turgid, endless, monotonous, dull. [➡BORING AND UNINTERESTING; 235] *Opposite:* stimulating.

sopping *adj* **drenched**, soaked, dripping, sodden, saturated, sopping wet, waterlogged, wringing wet, soaking, wet. [➡WET; 1239] *Opposite:* dry.

See Compare and Contrast at **wet**.

sopping wet *adj* [➡WET; 1239]

soppy 1 *adj* (*informal*) **sentimental**, mawkish, soft, slushy, schmaltzy (*informal*), corny, mushy, wet. [➡IN POOR TASTE; 230] *Opposite:* unsentimental. 2 *adj* **soaked**, wet, sopping wet, sopping, dripping, drenched, waterlogged, saturated, sodden, wringing wet, soaking, dripping wet. [➡WET; 1239] *Opposite:* dry.

soprano 1 *n* **singer**, vocalist, soloist, chanteuse, diva. [➡MUSICIANS AND SINGERS; 908] 2 *adj* **high**, high-pitched, shrill, piercing, soaring. [➡MUSICAL TERMS; 912] *Opposite:* bass. 3 *type of* **musical register**. [➡MUSICAL TERMS; 912]

sop up *v* **soak up**, mop up, sponge, absorb, wipe, take in. [➡GET RID OF SOMETHING; 452]

sorbet *n* **water ice**, fruit ice, ice, dessert, pudding, sherbet (*US*), sweet. [➡CAKES, BISCUITS, AND DESSERTS; 1180]

sorcerer *n* **wizard**, magician, enchanter, magus, witch, necromancer (*literary*). [➡PEOPLE WITH SUPERNATURAL POWERS; 789]

sorceress *n* **witch**, enchantress, sibyl, magician, necromancer (*literary*). [➡PEOPLE WITH SUPERNATURAL POWERS; 789]

sorcery *n* **witchcraft**, wizardry, magic, black magic, enchantment, witchery, necromancy (*literary*), bewitchment, conjuring. [➡THE SUPERNATURAL; 788]

sordid 1 *adj* **base**, disreputable, sleazy, repugnant, disgusting, despicable, ignoble, wretched, nasty (*informal*), degenerate, decadent. [➡DISGUSTING AND REPULSIVE; 231] *Opposite:* uplifting. 2 *adj* **squalid**, distasteful, disgusting, low, dirty, grimy, grubby, foul, filthy, grungy (*informal*), rundown. [➡DIRTY; 1234] *Opposite:* pleasant.

sordidness 1 *n* **baseness**, sleaze, unpleasantness, repugnance, wretchedness, nastiness, decadence. [➡MORALLY BAD; 776] *Opposite:* pleasantness. 2 *n* **squalor**, grime, filth, squalidness, grubbiness, filthiness, foulness. [➡DIRTY; 1234] *Opposite:* cleanliness.

sore 1 *adj* **painful**, tender, uncomfortable, stinging, aching, raw. [➡PAIN AND OTHER PHYSICAL SENSATIONS; 734] *Opposite:* comfortable. 2 *adj* **annoying**, sensitive, embarrassing, controversial, difficult, awkward, contentious. [➡EMOTIONALLY UNPLEASANT AND UPSETTING; 228] *Opposite:* uncontroversial. 3 *adj* (*informal*) **angry**, cross, mad, annoyed, upset, resentful, bitter, offended. [➡IRRITATION AND ANGER; 542] *Opposite:* pleased. 4 *n* **wound**, abscess, lesion, eruption, blister, boil, spot, infection. [➡CONDITIONS AFFECTING THE SKIN; 722]

sorely (*formal*) *adv* **deeply**, truly, greatly, very much, really, profoundly. [➡TO A GREAT EXTENT; 130] *Opposite:* not at all.

soreness *n* **tenderness**, pain, discomfort, distress, agony, ache, aching, hurt, redness. [➡PAIN AND OTHER PHYSICAL SENSATIONS; 734]

sorghum *type of* **cereal**. [➡CEREAL FOODS; 1177]

sorority (*US*) *n* [➡GROUPS WITH A COMMON INTEREST; 938]

sorrel 1 *type of* **salad vegetable**. [➡FRUIT AND VEGETABLES; 1175] 2 *type of* **brown**. [➡COLOURS; 1223]

sorrow 1 *n* **grief**, mourning, sadness, distress, sorrowfulness, unhappiness, disappointment, regret. [➡SADNESS, DISTRESS, AND DESPAIR; 540] *Opposite:* joy. 2 *v* (*literary*) **grieve**, mourn, wail, lament, weep, cry. *Opposite:* rejoice. (*literary*). [➡BE CONCERNED AND CARE; 582]

sorrowful 1 *adj* **sad**, mournful, grief-stricken, distressed, unhappy, regretful, sorrowing, troubled. [➡SADNESS, DISTRESS, AND DESPAIR; 540] *Opposite:* joyful. 2 *adj* **tragic**, sad, solemn, unhappy, distressing, troubling. [➡EMOTIONALLY UNPLEASANT AND UPSETTING; 228] *Opposite:* happy.

sorrowfully *adv* **sadly**, mournfully, regretfully, with regret, unhappily, miserably. [➡SADNESS, DISTRESS, AND DESPAIR; 540] *Opposite:* joyfully.

sorrowfulness *n* [➡SADNESS, DISTRESS, AND DESPAIR; 540]

sorrowing *adj* **sad**, mournful, grief-stricken, distressed, unhappy, regretful, sorrowful, troubled. [➡SADNESS, DISTRESS, AND DESPAIR; 540] *Opposite:* joyful.

sorry 1 *adj* **apologetic**, regretful, remorseful, repentant, sad, unhappy. [➡EMBARRASSMENT AND HUMILIATION; 543] *Opposite:* glad. 2 *adj* **pitiful**, miserable, wretched, forlorn, pathetic, poor. [➡BAD AND BADLY; 224] *Opposite:* fine.

sort 1 *n* **category**, kind, class, type, genus, species, variety, nature, ilk, order. [➡VARIETY, TYPE, KIND; 146] 2 *n* (*informal*) **personality type**, person, character, type, individual, soul. [➡PERSON; 931] 3 *v* **arrange**, classify, rank, place, sort out, separate, categorize, group, assort, organize, order. [➡ARRANGE AND CREATE ORDER; 358] *Opposite:* mix up.

See Compare and Contrast at **type**.

sorted (*informal*) *adj* **organized**, arranged, in hand, under control, dealt with, fixed, in the bag (*informal*), fixed up. [➡ORDER AND ORGANISATION; 207]

sortie 1 *n* **attack**, manoeuvre, foray, incursion, inroad, raid. [➡AGGRESSIVE EVENT; 39] *Opposite:* retreat. 2 *n* (*humorous*) **excursion**, trip, outing, journey, jaunt, trek. [➡TRAVEL: JOURNEYS AND TRIPS; 319]

sort of (*informal*) *adv* [➡TO A CERTAIN EXTENT; 134]

sort out 1 *v* **resolve**, deal with, solve, iron out, fix, settle, see to, work out. [➡CARRY OUT AN ACTION; 270] 2 *v* **put in order**, arrange, file, disentangle, tidy up, order, organize. [➡ARRANGE AND CREATE ORDER; 358] *Opposite:* mix up. 3 *v* **separate**, distinguish, segregate, sort, divide. [➡SEPARATE AND DIVIDE; 402] 4 *v* (*informal*) **punish**, reprimand, tell off (*informal*), tick off (*informal*), scold, deal with, rebuke, admonish, chide, reprove, take to task. [➡ACCUSE, BLAME, AND CRITICIZE; 642] *Opposite:* reward.

SOS *n* **distress signal**, cry for help, call for help, alarm, flare, alert, signal. [➡SIGNPOSTS, SIGNALS AND BILLBOARDS; 596]

so-so (*informal*) *adj* **average**, fair, mediocre, unremarkable, indifferent, passable, okay (*informal*), all right, run-of-the-mill, medium, middling, ordinary. [➡ACCEPTABLE AND PASSABLE; 220] *Opposite:* exceptional.

sotto voce 1 *adv* **quietly**, softly, inaudibly, gently, faintly, indistinctly, in a murmur. [➡SOFT OR PLEASANT SOUNDS; 1264] *Opposite:* loudly. 2 *adj* **soft**, quiet, gentle, inaudible, hushed, whispered, muted, low, murmured. [➡SOFT OR PLEASANT SOUNDS; 1264] *Opposite:* loud. 3 *type of* **musical term**. [➡MUSIC, SONGS, AND SINGING; 907]

soufflé *type of* **dessert**. [➡CAKES, BISCUITS, AND DESSERTS; 1180]

sought-after *adj* **desirable**, coveted, in demand, exclusive, fashionable, popular, preferred, trendy (*informal*). [➡POPULAR AND WANTED; 221] *Opposite:* unpopular.

souk *n* **bazaar**, market, marketplace, flea market, emporium (*formal or humorous*). [➡SALES AND SHOWS; 444]

soul 1 *n* **spirit**, consciousness, psyche, will, essence, being. [➡RELIGIOUS CONCEPTS; 777] 2 *n* **depth**, personality, atmosphere, emotion, passion, ambience, feeling, humanity, compassion, empathy. [➡APPEARANCE AND ATMOSPHERE; 1236] 3 *n* **individual**, person, anyone, someone, example, human being. [➡PERSON; 931] 4 *n* **soul music**, gospel, R & B, rhythm and blues, blues, funk. [➡MUSIC, SONGS, AND SINGING; 907]

soul-destroying *adj* **demoralizing**, depressing, disheartening, unfulfilling, boring, tedious, unsatisfying, monotonous. [➡EMOTIONALLY UNPLEASANT AND UPSETTING; 228] *Opposite:* satisfying.

soulful *adj* **expressive**, affecting, sad, moving, poignant, touching, mournful, emotional. [➡EMOTIONALLY PLEASANT; 188] *Opposite:* emotionless.

soulfulness *n* **expressiveness**, sadness, poignancy, emotion, mournfulness, feeling. [➡SADNESS, DISTRESS, AND DESPAIR; 540]

soulless *adj* **bleak**, utilitarian, characterless, inexpressive, insensitive, unfeeling, faceless, grey. [➡BORING AND UNINTERESTING; 235] *Opposite:* soulful.

soul mate *n* **friend**, mate, buddy (*US informal*), bosom friend, boon companion, crony (*US*), confidant, confidante, pal (*informal*), chum (*informal*), partner, companion, bosom buddy (*US*). [➡FRIENDS; 963]

soul music *n* [➡MUSIC, SONGS, AND SINGING; 907]

soul-searching *n* **thought**, deliberation (*formal*), consideration, contemplation, introspection, assessment, judgment, examination. [➡THINK AND REFLECT; 744]

sound 1 *n* **noise**, resonance, hum, echo, thud, reverberation, crash, jingle, swish, clatter, vibration, crunch, tinkle, jangle, clank, splash. [➡SOUNDS; 1255] *Opposite:* silence. 2 *v* **seem**, appear, look. [➡SEEM TO BE SOMETHING; 58] 3 *v* **go off**, ring out, explode, ring, wail, clang. [➡EMIT CONTINUOUS SOUNDS; 367] 4 *v* **announce**, ring out, declare, signal, express, call, advertise, broadcast, proclaim. [➡INFORM AND ANNOUNCE; 612] 5 *adj* **whole**, healthy, unblemished, perfect, normal, fit, sturdy, intact, undamaged. [➡FINE; 738] *Opposite:* infirm. 6 *adj* **sensible**, good, firm, unassailable, reliable, watertight, secure. [➡SAFE AND SAFETY; 192] *Opposite:* unsound. 7 *adj* **complete**, comprehensive, wide-ranging, all-encompassing, thorough, rigorous, encyclopedic. [➡WHOLENESS AND COMPLETENESS; 199] *Opposite:* superficial. 8 *adj* **thorough**, firm, rigorous, good, hard, severe, thoroughgoing. [➡WHOLENESS AND COMPLETENESS; 199] *Opposite:* half-hearted. 9 *n* **strait**, channel, inlet, fjord. [➡THE SEAS, OCEANS, AND SHORES; 1041]

sound

◆ *types of animal sound*
baa, bark, bays, bray, caterwaul, croak, growl, grunt, hiss, howl, mews, miaows, moos, neighs, oinks, purr, roar, snarl, squeak, squeal, whinny, woofs, yap, yelp

◆ *types of ringing sound*
beep, bleep, chime, chink, clang, clank, clink, ding, ding-a-ling, ding-dongs, honks, hoot, jangle, jingle, knell, peal, ping, pip, ring, ting, tinkle, toll, tootle (*informal*)

◆ *types of continuous sound*
beep, bleep, boom, burble, buzz, chug, crackle, creak, drone, gurgle, hiss, honk, hoot, hum, purl (*literary*), purr, rasp, rattle, roar, rumble, rustle, sizzle, sonic boom, swish, swoosh, throb, thunder, toot, whirr, whiz, whoosh

◆ *types of impact sound*
bang, beat, bong, bonk (*informal*), boom, bump, clang, clank, clap, clash, clatter, click, clip-clop, clop, clunk, crack, crash, patter, pitter-patter, plop, plunk, pop, ratatat-tat, slam, smash, splash, splat, squelch, squish, tap, thud, thump, thwack, ticks, ticktock, wham

◆ *types of human sound*
babble, bawl, bellow, boo, catcall, chatter, chortle, chuckle, cry, gasp, giggle, groan, grunt, holler, howl, hum, moan, murmur, mutter, peep, screak (*US*), scream, screech, shout, shriek, sigh, slurp, snicker (*US*), sniffle, snigger, splutter, squeal, titter, wail, wheeze, whimper, whine, whisper, whistle, whoop, yell

◆ *types of bird sound*
caw, cheep, chirp, chirrup, cluck, cock-a-doodle-doo, coo, hoot, peep, quack, screak (*US*), screech, squawk, trill, tweet, twitter, warble

See Compare and Contrast at **valid.**

sound asleep *adj* **sleeping**, slumbering, out, fast asleep, dead to the world, sleeping like a baby, sleeping like a log. [➡TIRED, ASLEEP AND UNCONSCIOUS; 739] *Opposite:* awake.

sound bite *n* **comment**, announcement, statement, declaration, response, remark, observation, quote. [➡INFORM AND ANNOUNCE; 612]

sound card *type of* **hardware.** [➡COMPUTERS AND COMPUTING; 1126]

sound effect *n* **sound**, recording, effect, special effect. [➡SOUNDS; 1255]

sounding board *n* **confidant**, confidante, close friend, best friend, intimate, best mate, friend. [➡FRIENDS; 963]

soundings *n* **enquiries**, investigations, research, surveys, market research, polls. [➡ASK PEOPLE QUESTIONS; 667]

soundless *adj* **silent**, noiseless, still, quiet, mute, speechless. [➡ABSENCE OF SOUND; 1256] *Opposite:* noisy.

soundlessness *n* [➡ABSENCE OF SOUND; 1256]

soundly 1 *adv* **deeply**, well, like a log, peacefully, fast. [➡TO A GREAT EXTENT; 130] *Opposite:* fitfully. 2 *adv* **thoroughly**, roundly, severely, firmly, decisively, completely. [➡WHOLENESS AND COMPLETENESS; 199]

soundness 1 *n* **wholeness**, completeness, health, healthiness, fitness, intactness, sturdiness, robustness, strength. [➡FIT AND STRONG; 737] *Opposite:* infirmity. 2 *n* **reliability**, unassailability, security, accuracy, dependability, trustworthiness, safety. [➡SAFE AND SAFETY; 192] *Opposite:* unreliability. 3 *n* **completeness**, comprehensiveness, thoroughness, depth, range, breadth. [➡WHOLENESS AND COMPLETENESS; 199] *Opposite:* superficiality.

sound off (*informal*) *v* **mouth off** (*informal*), hold forth, go on, have your say, speak up, speak out, rant and rave, fulminate, rage. [➡GIVING VENT TO EMOTIONS; 680]

sound out *v* **investigate**, test, explore, survey, look into, probe, feel out, check out. [➡EXAMINE AND ASSESS; 754]

soundproof 1 *adj* **impenetrable**, insulated, lined, padded, sealed, protected. [➡ACOUSTICS; 1137] 2 *v* **insulate**, line, seal, pad, protect, mask. [➡DECORATE, ADORN, AND APPLY COATINGS; 406]

soundproofing *n* [➡ACOUSTICS; 1137]

sound quality *n* [➡QUALITY OF SOUNDS; 1263]

sound system 1 *n* **hi-fi**, stereo, music centre, stereo system, audio system, boom box (*US*), CD player, record player, cassette recorder, tape deck, cassette deck. [➡RECORDINGS AND PLAYERS; 911] 2 *type of* **audio equipment.** [➡AUDIO EQUIPMENT; 1138]

soundtrack 1 *n* **recording**, music, dialogue, sound, sound effects, background music, incidental music. [➡RECORDINGS AND PLAYERS; 911] 2 *n* **music**, album, LP, tape, CD, DVD. [➡RECORDINGS AND PLAYERS; 911]

soup

◆ *types of soup*
bisque, borscht, bouillabaisse, bouillon, broth, chowder, cock-a-leekie, consommé, gazpacho, gumbo, julienne, minestrone, mulligatawny, pea soup, potage, Scotch broth, vichyssoise

soupçon *n* **hint**, touch, speck, morsel, modicum, dash, smidgen (*informal*), drop, bit, trace, splash, tad (*informal*). [➡FEW, LITTLE, SMALL AMOUNT; 119] *Opposite:* surfeit.

soup ladle *type of* **utensil.** [➡TABLEWARE, CUTLERY, AND KITCHENWARE; 861]

soupspoon *type of* **cutlery.** [➡TABLEWARE, CUTLERY, AND KITCHENWARE; 861]

soup up (*informal*) *v* **boost**, beef up (*informal*), enhance, tune up, modify, upgrade, tweak (*informal*). [➡IMPROVE STRENGTH AND DURABILITY; 379]

sour 1 *adj* **acid**, tart, bitter, acerbic, vinegary, dry, tangy, acrid. [➡TASTE; 704] *Opposite:* sweet. 2 *adj* **bad**, rancid, off, curdled, rank (*literary*), fetid. [➡DECAYING OR INFESTED; 1235] *Opposite:* fresh. 3 *adj* **bitter**, disagreeable, unpleasant, bad-tempered, resentful, hostile, unfriendly. [➡BAD-TEMPERED AND HUMOURLESS; 627] *Opposite:* agreeable. 4 *v* **curdle**, go sour, go off, ferment, turn, go bad. [➡GET WORSE; 382] 5 *v* **taint**, ruin, harm, spoil, embitter, damage. [➡WORSEN SOMETHING; 381] *Opposite:* improve.

source 1 *n* **basis**, foundation, starting place, cause, font, spring, birthplace, cradle, home. [➡BEGINNING; 53] 2 *n* **informant**, spokesperson, informer, supplier, grass (*slang*), nark (*slang*), squealer (*slang disapproving*), stool pigeon (*slang*), snout (*slang*), snitch (*slang*), rat (*slang*), stoolie (*US slang*). [➡INTERFERING PEOPLE AND TELLTALES; 950] 3 *n* **resource**, supply, fund, mine, well. [➡COLLECTIONS AND MIXTURES OF THINGS; 1243] 4 *n* **natural spring**, upwelling, fount, fountain. [➡RIVERS, LAKES, AND STREAMS; 1042] 5 *v* **obtain**, find, track down, trace, track, locate. [➡FIND; 464]

See Compare and Contrast at **origin.**

sour grapes *n* **resentment**, jealousy, bitterness, ill feeling, envy, ill will, scorn. [➡ANTAGONISM; 553]

sourly 1 *adv* **tartly**, bitterly, drily, acridly, acidly, sharply. [➡TASTE; 704] *Opposite:* sweetly. 2 *adv* **disagreeably**, unpleasantly, bitterly, resentfully, spitefully, nastily. [➡BAD-TEMPERED AND HUMOURLESS; 627] *Opposite:* agreeably.

sourness 1 *n* **acidity**, tartness, bitterness, tang, acridness, dryness. [➡TASTE; 704] *Opposite:* sweetness. 2 *n* **bitterness**, resentment, acrimony, unpleasantness, hostility, unfriendliness, spite. [➡ANTAGONISM; 553] *Opposite:* pleasantness.

sourpuss (*informal*) *n* **grouch** (*informal*), moaner (*informal*), complainer, grumbler, grump (*informal*), whiner, misery (*informal*). [➡GRUMPY AND NEGATIVE PEOPLE; 953]

sousaphone *type of* **brass instrument**. [➡MUSICAL INSTRUMENTS; 910]

sous-chef *n* [➡DOMESTIC AND KITCHEN WORKERS; 850]

souse 1 *v* **pickle**, marinade, soak, steep, preserve, infuse. [➡COOKING AND FOOD PREPARATION; 354] 2 *v* **soak**, steep, douse, saturate, immerse, plunge, bathe, drench, dunk, submerge, sink. [➡SOFTEN, LIQUEFY, DAMPEN; 389]

soused (*slang*) *adj* [➡UNDER THE INFLUENCE OF DRUGS OR ALCOHOL; 742]

southeaster *type of* **wind**. [➡WINDY AND STORMY WEATHER; 1053]

southwester *type of* **wind**. [➡WINDY AND STORMY WEATHER; 1053]

souvenir *n* **memento**, reminder, keepsake, knick-knack, remembrance, relic, token. [➡ORNAMENTS AND DECORATIONS; 1247]

sou'wester *type of* **hat**. [➡HABERDASHERY, MILLINERY, AND LINGERIE; 867]

sovereign 1 *n* **monarch**, ruler, potentate, king, queen, emperor, empress, sultan, rajah. [➡RULERS AND ARISTOCRACY; 823] 2 *adj* **independent**, autonomous, self-governing, free, self-determining. [➡STYLES AND SYSTEMS OF GOVERNMENT; 806] 3 *adj* **supreme**, dominant, ascendant, predominant, absolute. [➡MOST IMPORTANT AND MAIN; 194] 4 *adj* **outstanding**, superior, supreme, excellent, matchless, peerless. [➡SUPERIORITY; 153]

sovereign state *n* [➡STYLES AND SYSTEMS OF GOVERNMENT; 806]

sovereignty 1 *n* **dominion**, control, rule, power, authority, dominance. [➡ROYALNESS; 825] 2 *n* **independence**, autonomy, self-government, freedom, self-determination. [➡RELATIONSHIP TO ANOTHER; 973]

sow 1 *v* **spread**, propagate, disseminate, scatter, strew, fling, seed, plant. [➡SPREAD AND SCATTER; 333] 2 *type of* **female animal**. [➡MALE OR FEMALE ANIMAL; 978]

soya bean *type of* **pulse**. [➡BEANS AND PULSES; 1188]

soy sauce *type of* **seasonings, sauces, and dips**. [➡SEASONINGS AND SAUCES; 1173]

sozzled (*informal*) *adj* [➡UNDER THE INFLUENCE OF DRUGS OR ALCOHOL; 742]

spa 1 *n* **health resort**, thalassotherapy centre, sanatorium, health spa, health farm. [➡BUILDINGS FOR PUBLIC ENTERTAINMENT; 1083] 2 *n* **whirlpool bath**, plunge pool, Turkish bath, sauna, hot tub, bath. [➡FITTINGS; 859]

space 1 *n* **solar system**, galaxy, outer space, deep space, universe, cosmos. [➡THE SOLAR SYSTEM AND ASTRONOMY; 1059] 2 *n* (*informal*) **leeway**, freedom, autonomy, liberty, latitude, room, room for manoeuvre, scope, opportunity, breathing space, elbowroom. [➡FREEDOM AND LIBERTY; 209] 3 *n* **interval**, time, period, pause, window, break, gap. [➡PAUSES AND PHASES; 56] 4 *n* **area**, place, seat, bay, plot, gap. [➡PLACE; 1064] 5 *v* **spread out**, move apart, space out, set apart. [➡POSITION SOMETHING; 326]

space-age *adj* **hi-tech**, automated, up-to-the-minute, state-of-the-art, new, modern, ultramodern, futuristic. [➡DESCRIBING TECHNOLOGY; 1159]

space-bar *type of* **hardware**. [➡COMPUTERS AND COMPUTING; 1126]

space cadet (*slang*) *n* **dreamer**, idealist, daydreamer, fantasist. [➡LAZY OR UNSUCCESSFUL PEOPLE; 948]

space capsule *n* **spacecraft**, spaceship, rocket, capsule, vehicle, pod, cabin. [➡SPACE VEHICLES; 1062]

spacecraft *n* **rocket**, rocket ship (*US*), ship, space capsule, space rocket, space shuttle, space station, spacelab, spaceship. [➡SPACE VEHICLES; 1062]

spacecraft

◆ *types of spacecraft*
biosatellite, lander, launch vehicle, lunar module, multistage rocket, orbital space station, orbiter, rocket, rocket ship (*US*), rover, satellite, space capsule, space probe, space rocket, space shuttle, space station, spacelab

◆ *parts of a spacecraft*
booster rocket, bus, cabin, command module, drogue parachute, footpad, grain, life-support system, nose cone, plasma engine, pod, retropack, rocket engine, shroud, solar cell, stage, thruster

spaced-out (*slang*) *adj* **dreamy**, lightheaded, inattentive, dazed, woozy, confused. [➡CONFUSION, ANXIETY, AND WORRY; 541] *Opposite:* alert.

spaceflight *n* **flight**, rocket flight, shuttle flight, space travel, orbiting. [➡SPACE TRAVEL AND EXPLORATION; 1061]

space heater *type of* **heating appliance**. [➡HEATING, REFRIGERATION, AND VENTILATION; 1141]

space heating *n* [➡HEATING, REFRIGERATION, AND VENTILATION; 1141]

spacelab *type of* **spacecraft**. [➡SPACE VEHICLES; 1062]

spaceman *n* [➡SPACE TRAVEL AND EXPLORATION; 1061]

space mission *n* [➡SPACE TRAVEL AND EXPLORATION; 1061]

space pilot *n* [➡SPACE TRAVEL AND EXPLORATION; 1061]

space platform *see* **space station**.

space probe *n* **rover**, lander, spacecraft, satellite, probe, vehicle, explorer, pod, spaceship. [➡SPACE VEHICLES; 1062]

spacer *n* **insertion**, insert, piece, part, bar. [➡PARTS OF MACHINES AND TOOLS; 1117]

space rocket *n* [➡SPACE VEHICLES; 1062]

spaceship 1 *n* **space capsule**, space shuttle, lunar module, ship, capsule, spacecraft, space rocket, mother ship, rocket ship (*US*). [➡SPACE VEHICLES; 1062] 2 *n* **flying saucer**, alien craft, UFO, unidentified flying object. [➡SCIENCE FICTION; 1063]

space shuttle *n* **space capsule**, launch vehicle, spacecraft, vehicle, spaceship, rocket, space shot, shuttle, transport. [➡SPACE VEHICLES; 1062]

space station *n* **spacecraft**, space platform, orbital space station, spacelab, satellite, spaceship, ship, base, artificial satellite. [➡SPACE VEHICLES; 1062]

space travel *n* [➡SPACE TRAVEL AND EXPLORATION; 1061]

space traveller *n* [➡SPACE TRAVEL AND EXPLORATION; 1061]

spacewalk *n* **excursion**, extravehicular activity, EVA, moonwalk, mission, task. [➡SPACE TRAVEL AND EXPLORATION; 1061]

spacewoman *n* [➡SPACE TRAVEL AND EXPLORATION; 1061]

spacing 1 *n* **space**, arrangement, layout, spaces, gaps, design, typography, graphics, positioning. [➡PLACE; 1064] 2 *n* **arranging**, positioning, placing, ordering, spacing out, spreading out. [➡MOVE SOMETHING TO ANOTHER LOCATION; 325]

spacious *adj* **roomy**, airy, large, open, expansive, commodious, capacious, voluminous. [➡LARGE; 1192] *Opposite:* cramped.

spaciousness *n* [➡SIZE AND DIMENSIONS; 1191]

spacy (*slang*) *adj* **dazed**, woozy, dreamy, spaced-out (*slang*), confused, out of it, lightheaded, inattentive, stoned (*informal*), trippy (*slang*). [➡CONFUSION, ANXIETY, AND WORRY; 541] *Opposite:* alert.

spade 1 *n* **garden spade**, shovel, scoop, snow shovel. [➡SPOONS, SCOOPS, AND SHOVELS; 1120] 2 *v* **dig**, shovel, scoop, excavate, fill in, pile up, heap up, dig out, dig in. [➡USE TOOLS AND MACHINERY; 469] 3 *type of* **general tool**. [➡HAND TOOLS; 1118]

spadework *n* **groundwork**, legwork (*informal*), research, drudgery, preliminaries, preparatory work. [➡WORK IN GENERAL; 298]

spaghetti *type of* **pasta**. [➡PASTA; 1179]

spaghetti western *n* [➡FILM; 901]

spam 1 *n* **junk mail**, unsolicited mail, junk (*informal*), mail, direct mail, garbage (*US*). [➡LETTERS AND WRITTEN MESSAGES; 585] 2 *v* **e-mail**, post, block, send, distribute, clog, copy, duplicate. [➡THE INTERNET; 1127]

span 1 *n* **distance**, width, length, extent, area. [➡WIDTH: WIDE; 1198] 2 *n* **time**, duration, period, limit. [➡PERIOD OF TIME; 90] 3 *v* **cross**, cover, reach over, extend over, bridge, traverse. [➡EXIST IN CLOSE PROXIMITY; 21]

spangle 1 *n* **sequin**, bead, bauble, star. [➡ORNAMENTS AND DECORATIONS; 1247] 2 *v* **sprinkle**, stud, pepper, dot, spot, dot with, speckle. [➡DECORATE, ADORN, AND APPLY COATINGS; 406] 3 *v* **sparkle**, glitter, shine, glisten, twinkle, wink. [➡LIGHT EMISSION; 369]

spaniel *type of* **small dog**. [➡DOG; 980]

Spanish guitar *type of* **stringed instrument**. [➡MUSICAL INSTRUMENTS; 910]

spank *v* **whack**, smack, slap, hit, strike, tan (*informal*), give somebody a hiding (*informal*), thrash, paddle (*US*). [➡PHYSICAL ATTACK AND PUNISHMENT; 416]

spanker *part of* **sailing vessel**. [➡SHIPS AND BOATS; 1149]

spanking 1 *n* **smacking**, smack, slap, thrashing, beating, hiding (*informal*). [➡PHYSICAL ATTACK AND PUNISHMENT; 416] 2 *adj* **remarkable**, excellent, outstanding, wonderful, marvellous, exceptional, whopping, magnificent. [➡EXTRAORDINARY: UNCOMMON; 206] *Opposite:* ordinary. 3 *adj* **vigorous**, brisk, rapid, fast, lively, energetic. [➡MOVING QUICKLY; 103] *Opposite:* weak.

spanking new *adj* **pristine**, brand-new, new, unused, fresh, mint. [➡NEW, MODERN; 167] *Opposite:* old.

spanner *type of* **general tool**. [➡HAND TOOLS; 1118]

spar 1 *n* **pole**, arm, boom, mast, rod. [➡STICKS, POLES, AND WEDGES; 1253] 2 *v* **scuffle**, fight, box, exchange blows, scrap, brawl. [➡COMPETE, CONTEND, AND COMBAT; 304] 3 *v* **argue**, fence, dispute, squabble, bicker, wrangle. [➡ARGUE AND FIGHT – TWO-WAY; 644] *Opposite:* agree.

spare 1 *v* **show mercy to**, free, release, save, pardon, forgive. [➡FREEDOM AND LIBERTY; 209] *Opposite:* condemn. 2 *v* **afford**, do without, get by without, manage without, give up, release. [➡FOREGO AND DENY ONESELF; 450] *Opposite:* need. 3 *adj* **replacement**, extra, auxiliary, additional, emergency, stand-by, unused. [➡MORE AND EXCESS; 122] *Opposite:* main. 4 *adj* **sparse**, thin, mean, insubstantial, frugal, stark. [➡TOO FEW, TOO LITTLE; 120] *Opposite:* abundant.

spare part *n* **reserve**, extra, stand-by, part, replacement, spare, backup, new part. [➡PARTS OF MACHINES AND TOOLS; 1117]

sparerib *type of* **cut**. [➡TYPES AND CUTS OF MEAT; 1176]

spare room *type of* **room in the home**. [➡TYPES OF ROOM; 1096]

spare time *n* **free time**, leisure time, time off, downtime (*US*). [➡PERIOD OF REST; 91]

spare tyre (*informal humorous*) *n* [➡EXTRA WEIGHT; 479]

sparing 1 *adj* **frugal**, parsimonious, economical, careful, thrifty, cautious, scant, mean. [➡FINANCIALLY MEAN AND GRASPING; 520] *Opposite:* generous. 2 *adj* **meagre**, sparse, limited, restricted, insufficient, scanty. [➡TOO FEW, TOO LITTLE; 120] *Opposite:* plentiful.

spark 1 *n* **flash**, flicker, sparkle, arc, glint, fire. [➡PRODUCTS OF FIRE; 1165] 2 *n* **stimulus**, catalyst, incentive, spur, trigger, inspiration. [➡BEGINNING; 53] 3 *v* **sparkle**, flicker, glimmer, glint, glow, ignite, flash. [➡LIGHT EMISSION; 369] 4 *v* **generate**, produce, inspire, initiate, set off, create, incite, kindle, trigger. [➡CAUSE TO START; 266]

sparkle 1 *v* **shine**, glitter, glisten, flash, flicker, twinkle, glint, spark, shimmer. [➡LIGHT EMISSION; 369] 2 *v* **fizzle**, bubble, fizz, ferment, effervesce. [➡FROTH AND EFFERVESCE; 390] 3 *v* **excel**, scintillate, shine, come into your own, come to life, stand out. [➡SUCCEED AND WIN; 79] 4 *v* **effervesce**, bubble, froth, fizz. [➡FROTH AND EFFERVESCE; 390] 5 *n* **life**, vivacity, energy, enthusiasm, go (*informal*), oomph, brio (*literary*), gusto. [➡ENERGY AND ENTHUSIASM; 497] *Opposite:* apathy. 6 *n* **effervescence**, carbonation, bubbles, aeration, gassiness, fizz. [➡FROTH; 1272]

sparkler (*informal*) 1 *n* **gem**, diamond, gemstone, jewel, rock (*informal*), precious stone. [➡ PRECIOUS STONES; 1277] **2** *type of* **firework.** [➡ EXPLOSIVES; 1154]

sparkling 1 *adj* **glittering**, glistening, twinkling, sparkly, iridescent, spangled, glittery, shimmering, shiny, flashing. [➡ VISUAL TEXTURE; 1220] *Opposite:* dull. **2** *adj* **vivacious**, witty, brilliant, scintillating, vibrant, animated, lively, dynamic, full of life, entertaining. [➡ EMOTIONALLY PLEASANT; 188] *Opposite:* dull. **3** *adj* **fizzy**, effervescent, carbonated, bubbly, aerated, gassy (*informal*), bubbling, fizzing, gaseous. [➡ DRINKS; 1186] *Opposite:* still.

sparkly *adj* **glittering**, glistening, twinkling, sparkling, iridescent, spangled, glittery, shimmering, shiny, flashing. [➡ VISUAL TEXTURE; 1220] *Opposite:* dull.

spark off *v* **generate**, produce, inspire, initiate, set off, create, incite, kindle, trigger. [➡ CAUSE TO START; 266]

spark plug *part of* **engine.** [➡ PARTS OF AN ENGINE; 1143]

sparky *adj* **lively**, spirited, enthusiastic, bubbly, feisty (*informal*), zippy, spunky (*informal*). [➡ ENERGY AND ENTHUSIASM; 497] *Opposite:* lifeless.

sparring partner *n* **opponent**, adversary, sworn enemy, foe (*literary*), counterpart, opposite number. [➡ COLLEAGUES AND EQUALS; 967]

sparrow *type of* **common bird.** [➡ BIRD; 997]

sparrowhawk *type of* **bird of prey.** [➡ BIRD OF PREY; 998]

sparse *adj* **thin**, spare, scant, light, scarce, bare, meagre, scrubby. [➡ TOO FEW, TOO LITTLE; 120] *Opposite:* dense.

sparseness *n* **thinness**, scarceness, scarcity, meagreness, bareness, scantiness. [➡ TOO FEW, TOO LITTLE; 120]

spartan *adj* **frugal**, simple, basic, bare, severe, plain, austere. [➡ ABSTEMIOUSNESS AND SELF-DENIAL; 882] *Opposite:* luxurious.

spasm *n* **shudder**, contraction, seizure, ripple, paroxysm, twinge, tremor. [➡ PHYSICAL REACTIONS; 317]

spasmodic *adj* **fitful**, irregular, intermittent, occasional, sporadic, discontinuous. [➡ NEVER AND INFREQUENCY; 97] *Opposite:* continuous.

spat *n* **quarrel**, fight, row, argument, barney (*informal*), tiff, squabble. [➡ ARGUMENT; 47]

spate *n* **flood**, rash, epidemic, wave, sequence, series, outbreak, welter, flurry, run. [➡ SUDDEN EVENT; 52]

spatial *adj* **three-dimensional**, 3-D, longitudinal, latitudinal, altitudinal, four-dimensional, 4-D. [➡ GENERAL LOCATIONS; 159]

spatter 1 *v* **shower**, spray, sprinkle, scatter, splash, disperse. [➡ SPREAD AND SCATTER; 333] **2** *v* **spray**, splatter, shower, mark, splash, cover, emit. [➡ DECORATE, ADORN, AND APPLY COATINGS; 406]

spatula *type of* **utensil.** [➡ TABLEWARE, CUTLERY, AND KITCHENWARE; 861]

spawn 1 *n* **roe**, frogspawn, fish eggs, eggs, seed. [➡ EGGS AND SPAWN; 728] **2** *n* **brood**, issue, offspring, progeny, young. [➡ YOUNGER GENERATION RELATIVES; 958] **3** *v* **lay**, deposit, produce. [➡ REPRODUCTION AND HEREDITY; 726] **4** *v* **reproduce**, give birth, procreate, breed, hatch, germinate. [➡ REPRODUCTION AND HEREDITY; 726] **5** *v* **create**, generate, produce, initiate, set off. [➡ ENGENDER; 351]

spay *v* **neuter**, sterilize, emasculate (*formal or literary*), castrate, operate on, geld, make sterile. [➡ STERILIZE; 727]

speak 1 *v* **chatter**, talk, verbalize, articulate, chat, natter (*informal*), yak (*informal*). *Opposite:* shut up. (*informal*). [➡ WITTER AND BABBLE; 618] **2** *v* **say**, tell, express, state, voice, declare, communicate. [➡ UTTER AND PRONOUNCE; 609] **3** *v* **be fluent in**, converse in, speak a language. [➡ UTTER AND PRONOUNCE; 609] **4** *v* **address**, lecture, preach, give a talk, give a lecture, talk. [➡ INSTRUCT AND TEACH; 610]

speakeasy (*slang*) *type of* **bar or club.** [➡ HOTELS, RESTAURANTS, AND CLUBS; 1081]

speaker 1 *n* **utterer**, chatterer, reciter, talker. [➡ SPEAKERS AND ORATORS; 604] **2** *n* **orator**, lecturer, narrator, spokesman, spokeswoman, spokesperson. [➡ WORKERS IN ENTERTAINMENT AND MEDIA; 873] **3** *part of* **audio equipment.** [➡ AUDIO EQUIPMENT; 1138]

speak for *v* **speak on behalf of**, represent, act on behalf of, stand for, argue for, appear for, speak up for, sit for, answer for. [➡ APPROVE AND CONFIRM; 647]

speak ill of *v* [➡ ACCUSE, BLAME, AND CRITICIZE; 642]

speaking *n* **speech**, language, communication, discourse, talking, dialogue, spoken language, spoken communication, oral communication, verbal communication. [➡ COMMUNICATION; 603]

speak out 1 *v* **be frank**, speak your mind, say your piece, have your say, speak up, protest. [➡ PROTEST AND EXPRESS DISAPPROVAL; 643] *Opposite:* equivocate. **2** *v* **talk loudly**, raise your voice, exclaim, shout, speak up. [➡ UTTER AND PRONOUNCE; 609] *Opposite:* mutter.

speak sharply *v* [➡ ACCUSE, BLAME, AND CRITICIZE; 642]

speak to 1 *v* **get in touch with**, contact, approach, talk to, address, talk with. [➡ INITIATE AND ESTABLISH COMMUNICATION; 681] **2** *v* (*formal*) **discuss**, consider, go into, deal with, address, mention, examine. [➡ ATTEMPT AN ACTION; 262] **3** *v* **reprimand**, discipline, reprove, tell off (*informal*), tick off (*informal*), talk to, have a word with, scold, lecture, talk with. [➡ PROTEST AND EXPRESS DISAPPROVAL; 643]

speak up 1 *v* **speak out**, exclaim, talk loudly, raise your voice, shout. [➡ UTTER AND PRONOUNCE; 609] *Opposite:* mutter. **2** *v* **be frank**, speak your mind, say your piece, have your say, protest, speak out. [➡ PROTEST AND EXPRESS DISAPPROVAL; 643] *Opposite:* equivocate.

speak up for *v* **support**, back, argue for, defend, approve, advocate, champion. [➡ APPROVE AND CONFIRM; 647] *Opposite:* attack.

speak well of *v* [➡ APPROVE AND CONFIRM; 647]

speak your mind *v* **be frank**, not beat about the bush, speak up, speak out, make yourself be heard, sound off, share your feelings, spit it out (*informal*). [➡ PROTEST AND EXPRESS DISAPPROVAL; 643] *Opposite:* equivocate.

spear 1 *n* **lance**, spike, javelin, assegai, harpoon, gaff. [➡ PROJECTILES; 1158] **2** *v* **impale**, spike, stab, pierce, run through (*literary*), gouge, stick. [➡ STAB; 417]

spearhead 1 *n* **driving force**, forefront, head, lead, leader, leading light, commander. [➡ IMPORTANT OR FAMOUS PEOPLE; 893] 2 *v* **lead**, front, head, organize, direct, command. [➡ BE IN CHARGE; 271]

spearmint *type of* **herb.** [➡ HERBS AND SPICES; 1174]

special 1 *adj* **superior**, distinct, different, exceptional, distinctive, singular, unusual, extraordinary, out of the ordinary, unique. [➡ SUPERIORITY; 153] *Opposite:* ordinary. 2 *adj* **individual**, specific, particular, distinct, one, separate, unique. [➡ EXTRAORDINARY: UNCOMMON; 206] *Opposite:* general.

special consideration *n* **dispensation**, concession, allowance, indulgence, preference. [➡ PERMIT AND ALLOW; 670]

special delivery *n* **express**, courier, premium rate, overnight delivery, registered post, registered mail. [➡ LETTERS AND WRITTEN MESSAGES; 585]

special education *n* **special needs education**, literacy tuition, numeracy tuition, specialist tuition, specialist support, remedial education, compensatory education. [➡ TEACHING; 839]

special effects *n* **effects**, FX, computer graphics, lighting, morphing, camerawork, pyrotechnics, post-production. [➡ TELEVISION AND RADIO; 607]

special interest group *n* [➡ GROUPS WITH A COMMON INTEREST; 938]

specialism *n* **specialization**, narrowing down, detail, in-depth study, concentration, narrowness, expert knowledge. [➡ SUBJECT AREA; 769]

specialist *n* **authority**, expert, boffin (*informal*), maven, whiz (*informal*), consultant, doyen. [➡ TALENTED OR INTELLIGENT PERSON; 529]

speciality *n* **specialism**, area of expertise, subject, sphere, forte, area, field, line, domain, department. [➡ SUBJECT AREA; 769]

specialization 1 *n* **specialism**, narrowing down, concentration, focusing in, gaining expertise, gaining in-depth knowledge, knowledge, expert knowledge, special study. [➡ SUBJECT AREA; 769] 2 *n* **adaptation**, change, mutation, selection, evolution, transmutation. [➡ CHANGE; 373]

specialize *v* **concentrate**, focus, dedicate yourself to, major in. [➡ STUDYING; 844]

specialized *adj* **particular**, dedicated, focused, specific, expert. [➡ EXTRAORDINARY: UNCOMMON; 206] *Opposite:* generalized.

specially 1 *adv* **particularly**, in particular, especially, specifically, expressly. [➡ EXTRAORDINARY: AMAZING; 205] *Opposite:* generally. 2 *adv* **personally**, individually, to order. [➡ ACTING INDEPENDENTLY; 285]

specially made *adj* **custom-built**, custom-made, made to measure, made to order, tailor-made, bespoke. [➡ EXTRAORDINARY: UNCOMMON; 206] *Opposite:* off-the-shelf.

special needs education *n* [➡ TEACHING; 839]

special occasion *n* [➡ PARTIES, DANCES, AND CELEBRATIONS; 37]

species *n* **class**, type, kind, sort, genus, variety, order, group. [➡ VARIETY, TYPE, KIND; 146]

See Compare and Contrast at **type**.

specific 1 *adj* **exact**, precise, detailed, explicit, definite, unambiguous. [➡ EXACT; 204] *Opposite:* vague. 2 *adj* **particular**, peculiar, exclusive, special, restricted, limited. [➡ UNRELATEDNESS AND SEPARATENESS; 147] *Opposite:* general. 3 *adj* **distinctive**, particular, express, identifiable, certain, given. [➡ EXTRAORDINARY: UNCOMMON; 206] *Opposite:* indefinite. 4 *n* **detail**, particular, aspect, feature, fact, point. [➡ BASIC DETAILS; 689] *Opposite:* generality.

specification *n* **requirement**, condition, plan, order, arrangement, measurement, design, pattern, description. [➡ BASIC DETAILS; 689]

specifics *n* [➡ BASIC DETAILS; 689]

specified 1 *adj* **stated**, quantified, definite, spelt out, detailed, itemized, identified, indicated, listed. [➡ EXACT; 204] *Opposite:* unstated. 2 *adj* **stipulated**, required, postulated, restricted, insisted on, agreed. [➡ EXACT; 204] *Opposite:* optional.

specify 1 *v* **state**, identify, spell out, detail, give, indicate, list, enumerate, itemize. [➡ UTTER AND PRONOUNCE; 609] *Opposite:* suggest. 2 *v* **stipulate**, agree, lay down, postulate, require, insist on. [➡ CLAIM, INSIST, AND EMPHASIZE; 615]

specimen *n* [➡ REPRESENTATIONS AND GENERAL EXAMPLES; 65]

specious *adj* **false**, hollow, erroneous, baseless, inaccurate, unfounded, fallacious, phoney, sham, bogus, incorrect, untrue, unsound, wrong, spurious, misleading, deceptive. [➡ FALSE AND UNREAL; 174] *Opposite:* valid.

speciousness *n* **falsity**, hollowness, inaccuracy, falseness, deceptiveness, erroneousness, spuriousness, phoniness, bogusness. [➡ FALSE AND UNREAL; 174] *Opposite:* validity.

speck 1 *n* **dot**, fleck, spot, dab, blob. [➡ SMALL PIECE; 127] 2 *n* **particle**, fragment, crumb, iota, scrap, smidgen (*informal*). [➡ SMALL PIECE; 127] 3 *v* **dot**, fleck, spot, speckle, stipple, spatter, dust, dapple. [➡ DECORATE, ADORN, AND APPLY COATINGS; 406]

specked *adj* [➡ DESCRIBING PATTERNS; 1226]

speckle 1 *n* **fleck**, mark, speck, spot, dot. [➡ SMALL PIECE; 127] 2 *v* **mark**, fleck, dust, stipple, dot, spatter, speck, spot, dapple. [➡ DECORATE, ADORN, AND APPLY COATINGS; 406]

speckled *adj* **spotted**, freckled, dotted, stippled, dappled, spattered, specked. [➡ DESCRIBING PATTERNS; 1226]

specs (*informal*) *n* **spectacles**, glasses, goggles, eyeglasses (*US formal*), pince-nez, monocle. [➡ GLASSES AND SPECTACLES; 1124]

spectacle 1 *n* **sight**, scene, vision, marvel, phenomenon, wonder. [➡ AMAZING THING; 212] 2 *n* **display**, show, demonstration, exhibition, event, pageant, parade, performance. [➡ PERFORMANCES AND SHOWS; 42]

spectacles *n* **glasses**, specs (*informal*), goggles, eyeglasses (*US formal*), pince-nez, monocle. [➡ GLASSES AND SPECTACLES; 1124]

spectacular 1 *adj* **stunning**, impressive, amazing, fantastic, fabulous, magnificent, brilliant, dramatic, dazzling, breathtaking, astonishing, marvellous, wonderful, exciting, incredible, extravagant. [➡ EXTRAORDINARY: AMAZING; 205] *Opposite:* humdrum. 2 *adj* **remarkable**, huge, great, enormous, mighty, almighty (*informal*), outstanding. [➡ LARGE; 1192] *Opposite:* unimpressive. 3 *n* **show**, display, performance, extravaganza, special, gala, pageant. [➡ PERFORMANCES AND SHOWS; 42]

spectacularly *adv* **enormously**, hugely, outstandingly, fabulously, stunningly, amazingly, dramatically, marvellously, astonishingly, wonderfully. [➡ EXTRAORDINARY: AMAZING; 205] *Opposite:* mildly.

spectate *v* **watch**, look on, observe, take in, look, watch from a distance, witness, view. [➡ LOOKING AND LOOKS; 701] *Opposite:* participate.

spectator *n* **viewer**, watcher, observer, onlooker, bystander, witness, eyewitness. [➡ LOOKERS AND SPECTATORS; 702] *Opposite:* participant.

spectral *adj* **ghostly**, phantom, ethereal, supernatural, ghostlike, shadowlike, shadowy, unearthly. [➡ THE SUPERNATURAL; 788] *Opposite:* real.

spectre 1 *n* **ghost**, apparition, phantom, spirit, spook, wraith, vision. [➡ THE SUPERNATURAL; 788] 2 *n* **threat**, menace, shadow, danger, possibility, anticipation, worry, Sword of Damocles. [➡ DANGER; 236]

spectrum *n* **range**, band, field, gamut, variety, continuum, scale. [➡ DEGREE AND EXTENT; 110]

speculate 1 *v* **wonder**, guess, conjecture, hypothesize, reason, suppose, surmise. [➡ QUESTION THINGS; 752] *Opposite:* know. 2 *v* **consider**, contemplate, cogitate (*formal*), reflect on, ponder, deliberate. [➡ THINK AND REFLECT; 744] *Opposite:* decide. 3 *v* **gamble**, take risks, hazard, risk, venture, take a chance. [➡ GAMBLE AND TAKE RISKS; 467]

speculation *n* **conjecture**, rumour, opinion, gossip, assumption, theory, guesswork, supposition, hearsay. [➡ GOSSIP; 679] *Opposite:* fact.

speculative 1 *adj* **tentative**, approximate, rough, exploratory, provisional. [➡ UNCERTAIN; 176] *Opposite:* definite. 2 *adj* **hypothetical**, notional, theoretical, academic, abstract, projected. [➡ UNCERTAIN; 176] *Opposite:* proven. 3 *adj* **dicey** (*informal*), dangerous, risky, unpredictable, uncertain. [➡ DANGEROUS; 237] *Opposite:* safe.

speculator *n* **risk-taker**, investor, entrepreneur, opportunist, adventurer, wheeler-dealer (*informal*), fortune hunter. [➡ PEOPLE INVOLVED IN FINANCE; 804]

speculum *type of* **medical instrument**. [➡ HAND TOOLS; 1118]

speech 1 *n* **language**, talking, verbal communication, dialogue, words, communication, discourse, speaking, spoken language, oral communication, spoken communication. [➡ THE SPOKEN WORD; 672] 2 *n* **tongue**, idiom, dialect, vernacular, native tongue. [➡ COMMUNICATION; 603] 3 *n* **lecture**, oration, sermon, talk, homily, discourse, address. [➡ NEUTRAL ONE-WAY COMMUNICATION; 49]

speech disorder *n* [➡ ASPECTS OF LANGUAGE; 683]

speechify (*informal*) *v* **pontificate**, lecture, pronounce, preach, hold forth, spout. [➡ INSTRUCT AND TEACH; 610]

speech impediment *n* [➡ ASPECTS OF LANGUAGE; 683]

speechless *adj* **astonished**, astounded, amazed, dumbstruck, wordless, thunderstruck, gobsmacked (*slang*), flabbergasted (*informal*). [➡ SURPRISE, SHOCK, AND AMAZEMENT; 546] *Opposite:* garrulous.

speechlessness *n* [➡ SURPRISE, SHOCK, AND AMAZEMENT; 546]

speechmaker *n* **speaker**, orator, raconteur, preacher, lecturer, communicator. [➡ SPEAKERS AND ORATORS; 604]

speed 1 *n* **pace**, rate, velocity, momentum, tempo. [➡ SPEED; 102] 2 *n* **haste**, hurry, swiftness, speediness, hustle, rapidity, quickness, promptness. [➡ SPEED; 102] *Opposite:* slowness. 3 *v* **race**, fly, zip (*informal*), zoom, break the speed limit, drive too fast, hurry, hustle, run, burn rubber, rush. [➡ MOVE FAST; 314] *Opposite:* crawl.

speedboat *type of* **motor vessel**. [➡ SHIPS AND BOATS; 1149]

speed camera *type of* **photographic equipment**. [➡ PHOTOGRAPHY AND PHOTOGRAPHIC EQUIPMENT; 1121]

speedily *adv* **quickly**, promptly, soon, hastily, hurriedly, rapidly, swiftly, fast, without delay, against the clock, immediately, with alacrity. [➡ MOVING QUICKLY; 103] *Opposite:* slowly.

speediness 1 *n* **quickness**, promptness, hastiness, rapidity, speed, pace, haste, hustle. [➡ SPEED; 102] *Opposite:* slowness. 2 *n* **fastness**, swiftness, nimbleness, rapidness, fleetness (*literary*). [➡ SPEED; 102] *Opposite:* sluggishness.

speeding *adj* **fast-moving**, hurtling, flying, moving, fast, rapid, speedy. [➡ MOVING QUICKLY; 103] *Opposite:* slow.

speed limit *n* **maximum speed**, top speed, permitted speed, limit, restriction. [➡ TRANSPORTATION, TRANSPORTERS, AND CARGOS; 323]

speedo *type of* **measuring device**. [➡ MEASURING DEVICES; 1122]

speedometer 1 *n* **speedo**, clock, gauge. [➡ VEHICLES; 1144] 2 *type of* **measuring device**. [➡ MEASURING DEVICES; 1122]

speed-read *v* **skim**, scan, read. [➡ READ; 759]

speed skating *type of* **winter sport**. [➡ HOBBIES, GAMES, AND SPORTS; 875]

speed trap *n* **radar trap**, police trap, traffic control. [➡ TRAVEL: TRAFFIC PROBLEMS AND HOLDUPS; 324]

speed up *v* **accelerate**, get faster, get a move on (*informal*), get moving, get going, hurry up, expedite. [➡ CHANGE OF SPEED: MORE; 397] *Opposite:* slow down.

speedway 1 *n* **track**, course, circuit, racetrack. [➡ URBAN OUTDOOR SPACES; 1071] 2 (*US*) *type of* **major road**. [➡ ROADS; 1105]

speedy 1 *adj* **quick**, immediate, prompt, early, fast, swift, rapid, hasty, hurried, breakneck. [➡ MOVING QUICKLY; 103] *Opposite:* slow. 2 *adj* **fast-moving**, speeding, fast, swift, nimble, rapid, fleet (*literary*). [➡ MOVING QUICKLY; 103] *Opposite:* slow.

speleologist *n* [➡ PEOPLE IN SPORTS AND LEISURE; 876]

spell 1 *v* **signify**, mean, bring, predict, imply, presage, suggest, indicate, denote, bring about, lead to, result in, end in, connote, add up to. [➡MEAN SOMETHING; 61] **2** *n* **incantation**, curse, enchantment, hex, evil eye, invocation. [➡THE SUPERNATURAL; 788] **3** *n* **influence**, fascination, thrall, glamour, enchantment, charm, bewitchment. [➡THE SUPERNATURAL; 788] **4** *n* (*informal*) **bout**, interlude, stretch, session, time period, time, stretch of time, period, turn. [➡SHORT PERIOD OF TIME; 93]

spellbind *v* [➡APPEAL TO AND AROUSE INTEREST; 576]

spellbinding *adj* **mesmerizing**, hypnotic (*informal*), enthralling, riveting (*informal*), entrancing, fascinating, captivating, absorbing, engrossing, gripping. [➡INTERESTING AND MEANINGFUL; 191] *Opposite:* boring.

spellbound *adj* **enthralled**, fascinated, awestruck, rapt, captivated, mesmerized. [➡PENSIVENESS AND INTEREST; 539] *Opposite:* distracted.

spell-check *v* **check**, check over, check through, correct, proofread. [➡EXAMINE AND ASSESS; 754]

spell checker *type of* **software**. [➡COMPUTERS AND COMPUTING; 1126]

spell out *v* **make obvious**, explain in simple terms, make clear, explain, interpret, explicate, clarify, elucidate (*formal*). [➡EXPLAIN AND CLARIFY; 611] *Opposite:* obfuscate.

spelunker *n* [➡PEOPLE IN SPORTS AND LEISURE; 876]

spend **1** *v* **use**, use up, waste, fritter, squander, consume, finish, exhaust, throw away, run through. [➡USE UP AND WASTE; 475] *Opposite:* save. **2** *v* **devote**, apply, employ, fill, occupy, pass, use. [➡GIVE AND PROVIDE; 431] **3** *v* **pay**, expend, pay out, splurge, lay out. [➡GIVE MONEY; 434]

spending *n* **expenditure**, expenses, costs, payments, outgoings, outlay, disbursements. [➡ACCOUNTING, BANKING, AND BUDGETING; 799] *Opposite:* earnings.

spending money *n* **cash**, money, ready cash, readies (*informal*), pin money, pocket money, mad money (*US informal*). [➡MONEY; 140] *Opposite:* savings.

spendthrift **1** *n* **wastrel**, squanderer, waster, prodigal, profligate. [➡PLEASURE-SEEKERS AND HEDONISTS; 886] *Opposite:* miser. **2** *adj* **wasteful**, extravagant, improvident (*formal*), prodigal, reckless, profligate. [➡PLEASURE-SEEKING AND EXCESS; 885] *Opposite:* miserly.

spent **1** *adj* **exhausted**, tired, bushed (*informal*), whacked (*informal*), washed-out, worn-out. [➡TIRED, ASLEEP AND UNCONSCIOUS; 739] *Opposite:* fresh. **2** *adj* **consumed**, used up, expended, paid, paid out, disbursed. [➡ABSENT AND UNAVAILABLE; 7] *Opposite:* saved. **3** *adj* **finished**, over, done, completed, over and done with, at an end. [➡ABSENT AND UNAVAILABLE; 7] *Opposite:* new.

sperm **1** *n* **semen**, seed, ejaculate, spermatozoa. [➡EGGS AND SPAWN; 728] **2** *n* **cell**, gamete, spermatozoon. [➡EGGS AND SPAWN; 728]

spermatozoon *n* **sperm**, cell, gamete. [➡EGGS AND SPAWN; 728]

sperm whale *type of* **whale**. [➡WHALE; 991]

spew **1** *v* **disgorge**, discharge, vomit, send out, churn out, spew out, eject, emit. [➡LIQUID EMISSION; 371] **2** *v* **pour out**, pour forth, gush, flow, stream, spill. [➡LIQUID EMISSION; 371] *Opposite:* dribble. **3** *n* **vomit**, sick (*informal*), puke (*slang*). [➡VOMIT AND BELCH; 713]

sphere **1** *n* **ball**, globe, orb, bubble. [➡ROUNDED SHAPE; 1217] **2** *n* **area**, speciality, subject, field, area of interest, forte, department, realm. [➡SUBJECT AREA; 769] **3** *n* **sphere of influence**, compass, scope, range, domain, province, circle. [➡SUBJECT AREA; 769]

sphere of activity *n* [➡SUBJECT AREA; 769]

sphere of influence *n* [➡SUBJECT AREA; 769]

spherical *adj* **sphere-shaped**, globular, rotund, circular, round, orbicular (*formal*). [➡ROUNDED SHAPE; 1217] *Opposite:* flat.

sphericalness *n* [➡ROUNDED SHAPE; 1217]

spheroid *type of* **rounded shape**. [➡ROUNDED SHAPE; 1217]

sphincter *type of* **muscle or tendon**. [➡THE MUSCLES; 719]

sphinx *type of* **mythological creature**. [➡MYTHICAL CREATURES; 1036]

sphinxlike *adj* **enigmatic**, mysterious, cryptic, bemusing, baffling, impenetrable, inscrutable. [➡DIFFICULTY AND COMPLEXITY; 243] *Opposite:* transparent.

spice **1** *n* **interest**, excitement, flavour, zing (*informal*), go (*informal*), colour, a little something, zest, seasoning, pizzazz (*informal*). [➡INTERESTING AND MEANINGFUL; 191] *Opposite:* blandness. **2** *v* **season**, flavour, enhance, lace. [➡COOKING AND FOOD PREPARATION; 354] **3** *v* **enliven**, liven up, ginger up, pep up (*informal*), lace, add zest to, add a little something to, jazz up (*informal*), season. [➡IMPROVE SOMETHING; 375] *Opposite:* tone down.

spice

◆ *types of spice*
allspice, aniseed, black pepper, caraway seed, cardamom, cayenne pepper, chilli, cinnamon, clove, coriander, cumin, fenugreek, ginger, ginseng, mace, mustard, nutmeg, paprika, pepper, peppercorn, saffron, turmeric, white pepper

spiced *adj* [➡TASTE; 704]

spicey *adj* [➡TASTE; 704]

spick-and-span **1** *adj* **tidy**, clean, neat, immaculate, spotless, neat and tidy, perfect. [➡ORDER AND ORGANISATION; 207] *Opposite:* untidy. **2** *adj* **in perfect condition**, immaculate, as new, in tiptop condition, in mint condition, perfect, mint. [➡CLEAN; 1232] *Opposite:* used.

spicy *adj* **hot**, spiced, curried, piquant, peppery, fiery, zesty. [➡TASTE; 704] *Opposite:* mild.

spider *type of* **arachnid**. [➡ARACHNIDS; 1018]

spider monkey *type of* **primate**. [➡PRIMATE; 988]

spider plant *type of* **foliage plant**. [➡FOLIAGE PLANTS; 1035]

spidery **1** *adj* **thin**, spindly, angular, squiggly, jerky, irregular. [➡WIDTH: NARROW AND THIN; 1199] *Opposite:* bold. **2** *adj* **gangling**, spindly, lanky, skinny, thin, ungainly. [➡BUILD; 478] *Opposite:* plump.

spiel (*informal*) 1 *n* **patter**, speech, lecture, pitch (*informal*), talk, waffle (*informal*), guff (*informal*). [➡MEANINGLESS SPEECH OR WRITING; 677] 2 *v* **waffle** (*informal*), prattle, pitch, go on, burble (*informal*), hold forth, jabber, witter (*informal*). [➡WITTER AND BABBLE; 618]

spigot 1 *n* **stopper**, plug, bung, cork, peg. [➡PARTS OF MACHINES AND TOOLS; 1117] 2 *n* (*US*) **tap**, valve, standpipe, spout, faucet (*US*). [➡FITTINGS; 859] 3 *n* **projection**, end, tip, point, spike. [➡STICKS, POLES, AND WEDGES; 1253]

spike 1 *n* **point**, barb, spear, thorn, spine, prickle. [➡ANGULAR SHAPE; 1216] 2 *v* (*informal*) **thwart**, confound, frustrate, dash, quash, mess up (*informal*), scotch. [➡MAKE IMPOSSIBLE; 277] *Opposite:* foster. 3 *v* **spear**, impale, pierce, run through (*literary*), skewer. [➡STAB; 417]

spiked *adj* **spiky**, sharp, pointed, hobnailed, jagged, spiny. [➡PHYSICAL TEXTURE; 1221] *Opposite:* smooth.

spikes *type of* **sports equipment**. [➡SPORTS EQUIPMENT; 879]

spikiness *n* [➡PHYSICAL TEXTURE; 1221]

spiky *adj* **prickly**, thorny, sharp, bristly, spiny, pointed. [➡PHYSICAL TEXTURE; 1221] *Opposite:* smooth.

spill 1 *v* **slop**, drip, leak, trickle, dribble, spill out, fall, drop, tip out, spatter. [➡SPREAD AND SCATTER; 333] *Opposite:* absorb. 2 *n* (*informal*) **tumble**, fall, roll, trip, stumble. [➡DISASTERS; 253] 3 *n* **leak**, spillage, escape, discharge, overflow, overspill, slick. [➡EMIT AND EMANATE; 362]

spillage 1 *n* **spilling**, spill, discharge, emission, leak, leakage, overflow, release. [➡EMIT AND EMANATE; 362] 2 *n* **wastage**, waste, loss, spill, slick, puddle. [➡MORE AND EXCESS; 122]

spill over 1 *v* **overflow**, brim over, leak out, run over, spill out, pour out, overspill. [➡LIQUID EMISSION; 371] 2 *v* **spread**, extend, overflow, advance, creep, radiate, sprawl. [➡TAKE UP A NEW POSITION; 313]

spill the beans (*informal*) *v* **let the cat out of the bag**, give the game away, tell, let on, blow somebody's cover, grass (*slang*), confess. [➡BETRAY CONFIDENCES AND GOSSIP; 619] *Opposite:* keep secret.

spin 1 *v* **turn**, rotate, revolve, gyrate, whirl, swirl, twist, twirl. [➡MOVE SOMETHING ON THE SPOT; 337] 2 *n* **gyration**, rotation, turn, whirl, swirl, twist, twirl, revolution. [➡MOVE SOMETHING ON THE SPOT; 337] 3 *n* **drive**, outing, run, trip, jaunt, turn. [➡TRAVEL: JOURNEYS AND TRIPS; 319] 4 *n* (*informal*) **point of view**, viewpoint, slant, angle, bias, perspective, complexion. [➡POINT OF VIEW; 768]

spinach *type of* **vegetable**. [➡FRUIT AND VEGETABLES; 1175]

spinal *adj* **back**, backbone, vertebral. [➡THE BONES AND JOINTS; 720]

spinal column *n* **spine**, back, backbone, vertebrae, vertebral column. [➡THE BONES AND JOINTS; 720]

spin a yarn (*informal*) *v* [➡DECEPTION AND LIES; 661]

spindle 1 *n* **rod**, bar, shaft, axle, pole. [➡STICKS, POLES, AND WEDGES; 1253] 2 *n* **leg**, baluster, support, pole, vertical, upright, shaft. [➡STICKS, POLES, AND WEDGES; 1253]

spindly *adj* **skinny**, gangly, lanky, thin, frail, gangling. [➡BUILD; 478] *Opposite:* sturdy.

spin doctor (*informal*) *n* **PR expert**, propagandist, publicist, representative, marketing expert, adviser, public relations expert, spokesperson, commentator. [➡POLITICAL OFFICES AND POLITICIANS; 808]

spin doctoring (*slang*) *n* [➡GOVERNMENT POLICIES; 810]

spin-drier *see* **spin-dryer**.

spindrift *n* **spray**, sea spray, foam, mist, vapour, haze, moisture. [➡THE SEAS, OCEANS, AND SHORES; 1041]

spin-dryer *type of* **appliance**. [➡HOUSEHOLD APPLIANCES; 1116]

spine *n* **spinal column**, vertebral column, backbone, back, vertebrae. [➡THE BONES AND JOINTS; 720]

spine-chilling *adj* **bloodcurdling**, chilling, terrifying, petrifying, scary (*informal*), frightening, spine-tingling, macabre. [➡FRIGHTENING; 232] *Opposite:* comforting.

spineless *adj* **pathetic** (*informal*), gutless, cowardly, weak, timid, spiritless, weak-willed, faint-hearted, craven. [➡COWARDICE AND WEAKNESS OF WILL; 509] *Opposite:* strong-willed.

> *See Compare and Contrast at* **cowardly**.

spinelessness *n* **weakness**, gutlessness, cowardice, feebleness, faint-heartedness, fear, fearfulness, ineffectiveness, uselessness. [➡COWARDICE AND WEAKNESS OF WILL; 509] *Opposite:* determination.

spinet *type of* **keyboard**. [➡MUSICAL INSTRUMENTS; 910]

spine-tingling *adj* **hair-raising**, thrilling, frightening, scary (*informal*), gripping, exciting, chilling, spine-chilling, bloodcurdling, macabre. [➡FRIGHTENING; 232] *Opposite:* soothing.

spinifex *type of* **grass**. [➡GRASS; 1031]

spinnaker *part of* **sailing vessel**. [➡PARTS OF A SHIP OR BOAT; 1150]

spinner *n* **rotator**, whirler, whirligig, turner, gyrator. [➡DEVICES; 1114]

spinney *n* **wood**, thicket, copse, coppice, grove. [➡WOODS, FORESTS, AND JUNGLES; 1047]

spin-off 1 *v* **derive**, result, develop, grow, follow on, produce. [➡CAUSE TO HAPPEN; 31] 2 *n* **byproduct**, derivative, offshoot, extra, bonus, incidental, supplement, sequel, follow-on, follow-up. [➡RESULTS AND OUTCOMES; 83]

spin out *v* **drag out**, prolong, keep going, draw out, eke out, extend, lengthen. [➡CAUSE TO CONTINUE; 268] *Opposite:* cut.

spinster *n* [➡MARITAL STATUS; 890]

spiny *adj* **barbed**, prickly, jaggy (*informal*), spiky, bristly, thorny, scratchy, sharp. [➡PHYSICAL TEXTURE; 1221] *Opposite:* smooth.

spiral 1 *v* **escalate**, increase, get worse, run away, rise, mushroom, climb, shoot up, rocket. [➡GET WORSE; 382] *Opposite:* plummet. 2 *v* **fly**, rise, ascend, descend, soar, eddy, swirl, curl, twist. [➡GO UPWARDS; 307] **3** *type of* **rounded shape.** [➡ROUNDED SHAPE; 1217]

spire *n* **tip**, spike, pinnacle, point, top, peak, summit. [➡PARTS OF RELIGIOUS BUILDINGS; 1085] *Opposite:* base.

spirillum *type of* **microorganism.** [➡MICROORGANISMS, FUNGI, AND ALGAE; 1023]

spirit **1** *n* **soul**, inner self, life force, chi, essence, life. [➡RELIGIOUS CONCEPTS; 777] *Opposite:* body. **2** *n* **will**, strength, courage, character, guts (*slang*), strength of mind, fortitude, moral fibre, determination, chutzpah (*informal*), heart, mettle. [➡STRENGTH OF WILL; 502] **3** *n* **disposition**, temperament, attitude, nature, temper, personality, character, outlook. [➡TEMPERAMENT AND BEHAVIOUR; 493] **4** *n* **feeling**, attitude, mood, tendency, atmosphere, air. [➡FEELINGS; 532] **5** *n* **ghost**, soul, ghoul, phantom, apparition, spectre, spook. [➡THE SUPERNATURAL; 788] **6** *v* **remove**, take away, whisk off, steal, abduct, kidnap. [➡TAKE SOMETHING AWAY; 426]

spirited *adj* **forceful**, feisty (*informal*), determined, strong-willed, vigorous, energetic, lively, animated, ardent, high-spirited. [➡STRENGTH OF WILL; 502] *Opposite:* lacklustre.

spiritedness *n* [➡ENERGY AND ENTHUSIASM; 497]

spiritless *adj* **spineless**, pathetic (*informal*), gutless, cowardly, sad, dejected, downcast, downhearted, depressed, dispirited, apathetic. [➡COWARDICE AND WEAKNESS OF WILL; 509] *Opposite:* energetic.

spiritlessly *adv* [➡WITHOUT ENTHUSIASM; 288]

spirit level *type of* **measuring device.** [➡MEASURING DEVICES; 1122]

spirits *n* **emotional state**, frame of mind, state of mind, mental state, feelings, mood. [➡FEELINGS; 532]

spiritual **1** *adj* **religious**, holy, sacred, divine, heavenly, saintly, mystical. [➡RELIGIOUS CONCEPTS; 777] *Opposite:* secular. **2** *adj* **mental**, emotional, psychological, temperamental, internal. [➡PSYCHOLOGY AND THE MIND; 770] *Opposite:* physical. **3** *type of* **vocal music.** [➡MUSIC, SONGS, AND SINGING; 907]

spiritual enlightenment *n* [➡RELIGIOUS CONCEPTS; 777]

spiritual guide *n* [➡RELIGIOUS PEOPLE; 779]

spiritualist *n* **medium**, clairvoyant, seer, psychic, mystic, shaman, diviner. [➡PEOPLE WITH SUPERNATURAL POWERS; 789]

spirituality *n* **holiness**, sanctity, religiousness, otherworldliness, unworldliness, piety, devoutness, mysticism. [➡RELIGIOUS CONCEPTS; 777]

spiritual leader *n* [➡RELIGIOUS PEOPLE; 779]

spirit world *n* [➡THE SUPERNATURAL; 788]

spirochaete *type of* **microorganism.** [➡MICROORGANISMS, FUNGI, AND ALGAE; 1023]

spit **1** *v* **expectorate**, splutter, hawk, expel, gob (*slang*). [➡EXCRETION AND EXCRETA; 723] *Opposite:* swallow. **2** *v* **sputter**, sizzle, pop, spatter, spurt, splatter. [➡EMIT CONTINUOUS SOUNDS; 367] **3** *v* **utter**, splutter, hiss, mutter, say, express. [➡BETRAY CONFIDENCES AND GOSSIP; 619] **4** *v* **rain**, shower, drizzle, mizzle (*regional*), sprinkle (*US*). [➡CLOUDY AND RAINY WEATHER; 1052] **5** *n* **saliva**, spittle, sputum, dribble. [➡EXCRETION AND EXCRETA; 723] **6** *n* **skewer**, rotisserie, brochette, rod, broach. [➡TABLEWARE, CUTLERY, AND KITCHENWARE; 861] **7** *v* **impale**, skewer, spear, spike, run through. [➡TEAR, BREAK, AND CUT; 361]

spit and polish (*informal*) *n* **meticulousness**, tidiness, cleanliness, orderliness, neatness, smartness, care. [➡CLEAN AND POLISH; 404]

spite *n* **malice**, ill will, ill feeling, vindictiveness, meanness, nastiness, unkindness, spitefulness, malevolence, viciousness. [➡ANTAGONISM; 553] *Opposite:* goodwill.

spiteful *adj* **malicious**, vindictive, mean, nasty, vicious, malevolent, unpleasant, unkind, hurtful, horrid. [➡SELFISH AND UNKIND; 506] *Opposite:* kind.

spitefulness *n* **malice**, ill will, ill feeling, vindictiveness, meanness, nastiness, unkindness, spite, malevolence, viciousness. [➡ANTAGONISM; 553] *Opposite:* goodwill.

spitting distance (*informal*) *n* [➡CLOSENESS; 160]

spitting image (*informal*) *n* **double**, dead ringer (*informal*), twin, clone, chip off the old block (*informal*), image, spit, doppelgänger. [➡COPIES AND REPLICAS; 152]

spittle *n* **saliva**, spit, sputum, dribble. [➡EXCRETION AND EXCRETA; 723]

spit up *v* [➡VOMIT AND BELCH; 713]

splash **1** *v* **plop**, slop, spatter, spray, slap, smack, splat. [➡SPREAD AND SCATTER; 333] **2** *v* **splatter**, get water on, wet, dash, spray, spatter. [➡SPREAD AND SCATTER; 333] *Opposite:* dab. **3** *v* **wallow**, wade, plop, flap, flop, stamp, jump. [➡FIDGET AND FROLIC; 312] *Opposite:* glide. **4** *type of* **impact sound.** [➡IMPACT SOUNDS; 1259]

splashguard (*US*) *type of* **external feature.** [➡VEHICLES; 1144]

splash out *v* [➡GIVE MONEY; 434]

splashy **1** *adj* **gaudy**, garish, bright, bold, colourful, multicoloured. [➡DESCRIBING COLOURS; 1225] *Opposite:* drab. **2** *adj* (*informal*) **showy**, ostentatious, flamboyant, flashy, bold, sensational. [➡IN POOR TASTE; 230] *Opposite:* restrained.

splat *n* **smack**, splash, plop, slop, slap. [➡IMPACT SOUNDS; 1259]

splatter *v* **splash**, spatter, bespatter, dash, spray, wet. [➡SPREAD AND SCATTER; 333]

splay **1** *v* **spread**, spread out, spread wide, open, open out, open up, expand, separate, widen, divide. [➡CHANGE OF SIZE: BIGGER; 393] *Opposite:* close up. **2** *v* **turn out**, turn outwards, twist, bend, distort. [➡CHANGE OF SHAPE; 386] **3** *adj* **outspread**, splayed, splayed-out, spread, spread-out, open, separated. [➡ORIENTATION AND ALIGNMENT; 1222] **4** *n* **slope**, bevel, slant, angle, incline. [➡ORIENTATION AND ALIGNMENT; 1222]

spleen **1** *n* **ill temper**, anger, irritation, annoyance, grumpiness, temper, pique, malice, malevolence, spite. [➡SADNESS, DISTRESS, AND DESPAIR; 540] *Opposite:* contentment. **2** *part of* **digestive tract.** [➡THE DIGESTIVE TRACT; 710]

splendid **1** *adj* **magnificent**, grand, superb, impressive, fine, glorious. [➡ADMIRABLE AND COMMENDABLE; 186] *Opposite:* unimpressive. **2** *adj* **excellent**, marvellous, wonderful, fabulous, super (*informal*), great (*informal*). [➡EXTRAORDINARY: AMAZING; 205]

splendiferous (*humorous*) *adj* **magnificent**, splendid, superlative, wonderful, superb, excellent, outstanding, marvellous, glorious. [➡EXTRAORDINARY: AMAZING; 205] *Opposite:* abysmal.

splendiferousness (*humorous*) *n* **magnificence**, splendidness, superlativeness, wonderfulness, superbness, excellence, marvellousness, glory. [➡EXTRAORDINARY: AMAZING; 205] *Opposite:* inadequacy.

splendour 1 *n* **magnificence**, glory, grandeur, brilliance, impressiveness, majesty, splendidness, luxury, excellence, finery. [➡EXTRAORDINARY: AMAZING; 205] *Opposite:* drabness. 2 *n* **wonder**, marvel, glory, triumph, miracle, sensation, sight, spectacle. [➡AMAZING THING; 212]

splenetic *adj* **bad-tempered**, spiteful, irritable, peevish, waspish, fractious. [➡NEGATIVE OF OUTLOOK; 515] *Opposite:* good-tempered.

splenetically *adv* **bad-temperedly**, spitefully, irritably, peevishly, waspishly, fractiously. [➡NEGATIVE OF OUTLOOK; 515] *Opposite:* good-temperedly.

splice 1 *v* **join**, intertwine, interweave, merge, fix together, unite, link, tie together, join together. [➡FASTEN, LINK, AND JOIN; 409] *Opposite:* split. 2 *v* (*slang*) **marry**, join in matrimony, join together, wed, hitch, unite. [➡ESTABLISHING RELATIONSHIPS WITH OTHERS; 974] *Opposite:* divorce. 3 *n* **seam**, join, connection, link, joint. [➡EXTREMITIES OF PHYSICAL OBJECTS; 1249]

spline 1 *n* **key**, tooth, blade, fin, projection. [➡PARTS OF MACHINES AND TOOLS; 1117] 2 *n* **connecting strip**, connector, connection, joining strip, link. [➡FASTENERS, LINKS, AND NETWORKS; 1246]

splint *v* **immobilize**, strap, bind, bandage, secure, support. [➡FASTEN, LINK, AND JOIN; 409]

splinter 1 *n* **fragment**, particle, piece, shard, sliver, chip. [➡SMALL PIECE; 127] 2 *v* **fall apart**, crack, disintegrate, come apart, break up, fragment, shatter. [➡TEAR, BREAK, AND CUT; 361] *Opposite:* mend.

splintered *adj* [➡IN BAD REPAIR; 1233]

splinter group *n* **faction**, sect, offshoot, subset, minority, branch. [➡GROUPS WITH A COMMON INTEREST; 938]

split 1 *v* **divide**, rip, tear, crack, come apart, break, rend, cleave, separate. [➡TEAR, BREAK, AND CUT; 361] *Opposite:* join. 2 *v* (*slang*) **go**, leave, depart, make yourself scarce (*informal*), head off, blow (*slang*). [➡ABSENT ONESELF; 8] *Opposite:* stay. 3 *n* **tear**, hole, rip, crack, fissure, opening. [➡HOLES, GAPS, AND FORKS; 1251] 4 *n* **difference**, breach, breakup, divergence, rift. [➡DISHARMONY; 157] *Opposite:* reconciliation. 5 *n* **splitting**, ripping, tearing, cracking, rupture, separation. [➡TEAR, BREAK, AND CUT; 361] 6 *n* **crack**, division, rift, rent, break. [➡DISHARMONY; 157]

split hairs *v* **quibble**, equivocate, be pedantic, argue, mince matters, nitpick, cavil. [➡PROTEST AND EXPRESS DISAPPROVAL; 643]

split-level *adj* **two-tier**, twin-tier, twin-level, two-level. [➡ORIENTATION AND ALIGNMENT; 1222]

split on (*informal*) *v* **inform**, tell on, grass up (*slang*), give away, blow the whistle, betray. [➡BETRAY CONFIDENCES AND GOSSIP; 619] *Opposite:* protect.

split-second *adj* **instant**, instantaneous, immediate, prompt, high-speed, lightning. [➡HAPPENING QUICKLY; 104] *Opposite:* tardy.

split second *n* **instant**, moment, flash, the twinkling of an eye, jiffy (*informal*), second, minute, tick (*informal*), twinkling. [➡SHORT PERIOD OF TIME; 93]

splitting *adj* **excruciating**, unbearable, piercing, intense, severe, terrible, awful, dreadful, frightful. [➡PHYSICALLY UNPLEASANT; 227] *Opposite:* slight.

split-up *n* **breakup**, separation, dissolution, ending, divorce, annulment. [➡END; 54] *Opposite:* marriage.

split up *v* **part**, break up, split, go your separate ways, end things, separate. [➡REFUSING OR REJECTING RELATIONS; 975]

splodge 1 *n* **spot**, stain, mark, blot, blotch, daub, blemish, splotch. [➡FAULTS, FLAWS, AND WEAKNESSES; 252] 2 *v* **mark**, stain, spot, blemish, blot, blotch, daub, splotch. [➡DECORATE, ADORN, AND APPLY COATINGS; 406]

splotch 1 *n* **spot**, stain, mark, blot, blotch, daub, blemish, splodge. [➡AMOUNT OF SOLID OR SEMI-SOLID; 115] 2 *v* **mark**, stain, spot, blemish, blot, blotch, daub, splodge. [➡DECORATE, ADORN, AND APPLY COATINGS; 406]

splurge 1 *v* **spend**, fritter, waste, waste, squander, run through, shell out, splash out, lay out, blow (*slang*). [➡GIVE MONEY; 434] *Opposite:* save. 2 *v* (*informal*) **indulge**, binge, wallow, spoil, treat, luxuriate. [➡OVERDO SOMETHING; 291] 3 *n* (*informal*) **bout**, spree, binge, orgy, bender (*slang*), session. [➡PERIOD OF TIME; 90] 4 *n* (*informal*) **display**, exhibition, show, parade, demonstration, spectacle. [➡PERFORMANCES AND SHOWS; 42]

splutter 1 *v* **choke**, gasp, cough, spit, stutter. [➡BREATHE AND NOT BREATHE; 717] 2 *type of* **human sound**. [➡SOUNDS MADE BY PEOPLE; 1261]

spoil 1 *v* **ruin**, mess up (*informal*), blemish, blot, blight, impair. [➡WORSEN SOMETHING; 381] *Opposite:* improve. 2 *v* **indulge**, pander to, be soft on, pamper, cosset, make a fuss of, treat, make a fuss over, make much of. [➡TAKE CARE OF AND SPOIL; 301] *Opposite:* neglect. 3 *v* **decay**, go rotten, rot, go bad, go off, putrefy, decompose. [➡GO BAD AND CORRODE; 391]

spoilage 1 *n* **decay**, rot, decomposition, degeneration, putrefaction, damage. [➡WORSEN SOMETHING; 381] 2 *n* **waste**, wastage, loss, leakage, spillage, damage. [➡NUISANCES; 254]

spoiled 1 *adj* **ruined**, damaged, decayed, rotted, rotten, tainted, wasted, sour, rancid. [➡DECAYING OR INFESTED; 1235] *Opposite:* fresh. 2 *adj* **overindulged**, ruined, wilful, self-centred, precocious, brattish. [➡DIFFICULT TO PLEASE; 516] *Opposite:* neglected.

spoiled brat *n* [➡MISCHIEVOUS OR BADLY-BEHAVED CHILD; 946]

spoiler *type of* **external feature**. [➡VEHICLES; 1144]

spoiling for a fight *adj* [➡IRRITATION AND ANGER; 542]

spoils 1 *n* **plunder**, loot, booty, swag (*slang*), haul, pickings. [➡PROCEEDS OF CRIME; 428] 2 *n* **reward**, prize, gain, profit, earnings, winnings. [➡REWARDS AND AWARDS; 440]

spoilsport *n* **killjoy**, stuffed shirt, wet blanket (*informal*), curmudgeon, misery (*informal*), dog in the manger. [➡GRUMPY AND NEGATIVE PEOPLE; 953]

spoilt *see* **spoiled**.

spoke 1 *n* **rod**, bar, rib, strut, shaft, spar, stay, spindle. [➡STICKS, POLES, AND WEDGES; 1253] 2 *n* **rung**, step, foothold, strut, bar, rod. [➡STICKS, POLES, AND WEDGES; 1253] 3 *part of* **bike** (*informal*). [➡BIKES, CARS, AND CARRIAGES; 1148]

spoken *adj* **verbal**, vocal, oral, articulated, vocalized, pronounced, enunciated. [➡THE SPOKEN WORD; 672] *Opposite:* written.

See Compare and Contrast at **verbal**.

spoken for *adj* **reserved**, kept back, taken, booked, earmarked, set aside. [➡ABSENT AND UNAVAILABLE; 7] *Opposite:* available.

spokesperson *n* **representative**, speaker, voice, spokesman, spokeswoman, proxy, envoy. [➡WORKERS IN ENTERTAINMENT AND MEDIA; 873]

sponge 1 *n* (*informal*) [➡LAZY OR UNSUCCESSFUL PEOPLE; 948] 2 *v* **clean**, wipe, wash, rub, mop, swab. [➡CLEAN AND POLISH; 404] 3 *type of* **aquatic invertebrate**. [➡AQUATIC INVERTEBRATE; 1022]

sponge cake *type of* **cake**. [➡CAKES, BISCUITS, AND DESSERTS; 1180]

sponger (*informal*) *n* **parasite**, hanger-on, scrounger (*informal*), freeloader (*informal*), idler, cadger (*informal*), user. [➡LAZY OR UNSUCCESSFUL PEOPLE; 948] *Opposite:* donor.

sponginess *n* [➡PHYSICAL TEXTURE; 1221]

spongy 1 *adj* **soft**, springy, malleable, elastic, flexible, cushioned. [➡MALLEABLE AND ELASTIC; 1211] *Opposite:* firm. 2 *adj* **absorbent**, porous, osmotic, permeable, penetrable, absorptive. [➡DENSITY AND CONSISTENCY; 1206] *Opposite:* impermeable. 3 *adj* **soggy**, squishy, moist, sodden, waterlogged, boggy. [➡WET; 1239] *Opposite:* dry.

sponsor 1 *n* **backer**, guarantor, patron, promoter, champion, benefactor, supporter, underwriter, angel. [➡REPRESENTATIVES AND PATRONS; 968] 2 *v* **back**, support, pay for, subsidize, fund, underwrite. [➡GIVE MONEY; 434]

See Compare and Contrast at **backer**.

sponsorship *n* **backing**, support, protection, patronage, funding, aid, finance. [➡BUSINESS ACTIVITIES AND PHENOMENA; 795]

spontaneity *n* **impulsiveness**, naturalness, artlessness, extemporaneity, freedom, impulse. [➡NATURALNESS; 498] *Opposite:* constraint.

spontaneous *adj* **impulsive**, unprompted, spur-of-the-moment, natural, artless, unstructured, unplanned, extemporaneous, free, instinctive, unrehearsed, unconstrained. [➡AUTOMATIC AND INSTINCTIVE; 281] *Opposite:* planned.

spoof 1 *n* **hoax**, prank, leg-pull (*informal*), deception, trick, bluff. [➡DECEPTION AND LIES; 661] 2 *n* **sendup** (*informal*), parody, takeoff (*informal*), satire, skit, burlesque, caricature. [➡JOKES AND TEASING; 675] 3 *v* **deceive**, fool, pull somebody's leg (*informal*), trick, bluff, hoax. [➡DECEPTION AND LIES; 661] 4 *v* **satirize**, send up (*informal*), take off (*informal*), burlesque, parody, caricature. [➡JOKES AND TEASING; 675]

spook 1 *n* (*informal*) **ghost**, wraith, phantom, spectre, apparition, spirit, vision. [➡THE SUPERNATURAL; 788] 2 *n* **spy**, sleuth (*informal*), snoop (*informal*), mole, double agent, snooper (*informal*). [➡INTERFERING PEOPLE AND TELLTALES; 950] 3 *v* **startle**, surprise, shock, alarm, agitate, disturb, frighten. [➡FRIGHTEN AND SHOCK; 569] *Opposite:* soothe.

spookiness (*informal*) *n* [➡FRIGHTENING; 232]

spooky 1 *adj* (*informal*) **scary** (*informal*), frightening, ghostly, unnerving, mysterious, eerie, uncanny, disturbing. [➡FRIGHTENING; 232] *Opposite:* reassuring. 2 *adj* **strange**, amazing, odd, unnerving, extraordinary, unusual, bizarre. [➡BIZARRE AND PECULIAR; 258] *Opposite:* normal.

spool 1 *n* **reel**, coil, pin, bobbin. [➡CONTAINERS, RECEPTACLES, AND PACKAGING; 1244] 2 *v* **wind**, reel, coil, roll. [➡POSITION SOMETHING: AROUND SOMETHING; 328]

spoon 1 *v* **serve**, ladle, spoon over, spoon out, dollop (*informal*), serve up. [➡COOKING AND FOOD PREPARATION; 354] 2 *type of* **cutlery**. [➡TABLEWARE, CUTLERY, AND KITCHENWARE; 861]

spoonbill *type of* **freshwater bird**. [➡FRESHWATER BIRD; 1000]

spoonerism 1 *n* **slip of the tongue**, mistake, error, Freudian slip, tongue twister, gaffe. [➡MISTAKES; 251] 2 *type of* **wordplay**. [➡JOKES AND TEASING; 675]

spoon-feed 1 *v* **feed**, nourish, take care of, look after, care for, nurture. [➡TAKE CARE OF AND SPOIL; 301] *Opposite:* neglect. 2 *v* **mollycoddle**, overindulge, wait on hand and foot, do everything for, run around after, wrap in cotton wool, spoil, ruin. [➡TAKE CARE OF AND SPOIL; 301] *Opposite:* neglect.

spoonful *n* **dollop** (*informal*), spoon, portion, serving, teaspoonful, dessertspoonful, tablespoonful. [➡AMOUNT AND QUANTITY; 112]

spoor 1 *n* **trail**, track, paw prints, hoof marks, footmarks, footprints. [➡EVIDENCE AND PROOF; 69] 2 *v* **track**, stalk, follow, trail, hunt, pursue, tail. [➡ACCOMPANY AND FOLLOW; 338]

sporadic *adj* **irregular**, intermittent, infrequent, periodic, erratic, patchy, random. [➡NEVER AND INFREQUENCY; 97] *Opposite:* regular.

See Compare and Contrast at **periodic**.

spore *n* **reproductive structure**, dormant bacterium, bacterium, microorganism. [➡PARTS OF TREES AND PLANTS; 1026]

sporran *n* **pouch**, purse, bag. [➡CONTAINERS, RECEPTACLES, AND PACKAGING; 1244]

sport 1 *n* (*formal*) [➡JOKES AND TEASING; 675] 2 *n* **diversion**, game, amusement, hobby, pastime, entertainment. [➡HOBBIES, GAMES, AND SPORTS; 875] *Opposite:* work. 3 *v* (*informal*) **wear**, don (*formal*), display, exhibit, show off, model. [➡DRESS, WEAR, AND UNDRESS; 868] 4 *type of* **broadcast**. [➡TELEVISION AND RADIO; 607]

sport

◆ *types of sports equipment*
ball, bat, bowl, club, discus, football, glove, helmet, hockey stick, javelin, lacrosse stick, mitt, pad, pigskin (*US*), puck, racket, shot, shuttlecock, spikes, tee, wicket

◆ *types of ball game*
American football, Australian Rules, baseball, basketball, cricket, field hockey (*US*), football, hockey, hurling, lacrosse, netball, rounders, rugby, Rugby League, Rugby Union, shinty, softball

◆ *types of court game*
badminton, jai alai, rackets, squash, table tennis, tennis, volleyball

◆ *types of combat sport*
aikido, boxing, fencing, judo, karate, kendo, kickboxing, kung fu, sumo, tae kwon do, wrestling

◆ *types of target ball game*
billiards, boules, bowling, bowls, croquet, golf, lawn bowling (*US*), pool, snooker

◆ *types of track and field*
cross-country, decathlon, discus, hammer throw, heptathlon, high jump, javelin, long jump, marathon, modern pentathlon, pole vault, relay race, shot put, sprint, steeplechase, triathlon, triple jump

◆ *types of winter sport*
biathlon, bobsled (*US*), bobsleigh, cross-country skiing, curling, downhill, figure skating, hockey (*US*), ice dancing, ice hockey, ski jump, skiing, slalom, snowboarding, speed skating, toboggan

sporting *adj* **fair**, generous, honourable, decent, honest, evenhanded. [➡MORALLY GOOD; 775] *Opposite:* dishonest.

sporting chance *n* **fair chance**, good chance, decent chance, fair shot, reasonable chance, sporting shot, even chance. [➡POSSIBLE AND PROBABLE; 178]

sporting event *n* [➡NON-AGGRESSIVE/SPORTING EVENT; 40]

sports 1 *adj* **sporting**, games, athletic. [➡HOBBIES, GAMES, AND SPORTS; 875] 2 *adj* **casual**, informal, leisure, outdoor, leisurewear. [➡DESCRIBING CLOTHES; 869]

sports activities *n* [➡LEISURE AND RECREATION; 874]

sports car *type of* **car**. [➡BIKES, CARS, AND CARRIAGES; 1148]

sportscast *n* **sports broadcast**, sports update, sports programme, televised sports event, televised match, televised tournament, televised final. [➡TELEVISION AND RADIO; 607]

sportscaster *n* **sports broadcaster**, sports presenter, sports commentator, sports reporter, sports correspondent, sports journalist. [➡WORKERS IN ENTERTAINMENT AND MEDIA; 873]

sports centre *n* [➡BUILDINGS FOR PUBLIC ENTERTAINMENT; 1083]

sports event *n* [➡NON-AGGRESSIVE/SPORTING EVENT; 40]

sports field *n* [➡URBAN OUTDOOR SPACES; 1071]

sports ground *n* **stadium**, arena, pitch, field, ground, track. [➡URBAN OUTDOOR SPACES; 1071]

sports hall *n* [➡BUILDINGS FOR PUBLIC ENTERTAINMENT; 1083]

sports jacket *type of* **jacket**. [➡GARMENTS AND OUTFITS; 865]

sportsperson *n* **competitor**, player, contestant, athlete. [➡PEOPLE IN SPORTS AND LEISURE; 876]

sports stadium *n* [➡BUILDINGS FOR PUBLIC ENTERTAINMENT; 1083]

sportswear

◆ *types of sportswear*
bathing costume (*dated*), bathing suit (*US*), bathing trunks, beachwear, bikini, leotard, shell suit, sweat suit (*US*), sweatpants, swimming costume, swimming trunks, swimsuit, swimwear, tracksuit, trunks, two-piece, wet suit

sporty 1 *adj* **athletic**, active, good at sport, fit, muscular, energetic. [➡HOBBIES, GAMES, AND SPORTS; 875] *Opposite:* lazy. 2 *adj* **flashy**, stylish, jaunty, natty, snazzy (*informal*), jazzy (*slang*), nifty (*informal*). [➡DESCRIBING CLOTHES; 869] *Opposite:* formal.

spot 1 *n* **mark**, blemish, stain, smudge, speck, dot. [➡SMALL PIECE; 127] 2 *n* (*informal*) **predicament**, mess, difficulty, awkward situation, quandary, plight. [➡DIFFICULT SITUATIONS; 72] 3 *n* **pimple**, pustule, boil, blackhead, whitehead, blocked pore, zit (*slang*). [➡CONDITIONS AFFECTING THE SKIN; 722] 4 *n* **place**, location, site, setting, corner, situation, position, point. [➡PLACE; 1064] 5 *n* **bit**, soupçon, tad (*informal*), touch, smidgen (*informal*), dash. [➡FEW, LITTLE, SMALL AMOUNT; 119] 6 *n* **advertisement**, advert (*informal*), ad, commercial, plug (*informal*), promotion. [➡ADVERTISING AND PUBLICITY; 605] 7 *v* **notice**, spy, recognize, catch a glimpse of, catch sight of, see, perceive, discern, identify. [➡SEE; 700] *Opposite:* miss. 8 *v* **stain**, dirty, blemish, smudge, speck, sully (*literary*). [➡DIRTY AND CONTAMINATE; 405] *Opposite:* clean.

spot check *n* **inspection**, check, search, examination, visit, inquiry. [➡EXAMINE AND ASSESS; 754]

spot-check *v* **inspect**, check, search, examine, double-check, monitor. [➡EXAMINE AND ASSESS; 754]

spotless 1 *adj* **immaculate**, spick and span, clean, clean as a new pin, pristine, gleaming, squeaky-clean. [➡CLEAN; 1232] *Opposite:* dirty. 2 *adj* **unblemished**, flawless, perfect, faultless, impeccable, untarnished, wholesome, innocent, stainless, irreproachable. [➡MORALLY GOOD; 775] *Opposite:* flawed.

spotlessly *adv* **immaculately**, impeccably, perfectly, flawlessly, faultlessly, absolutely. [➡ABSOLUTE AND ABSOLUTELY; 131]

spotlessly clean *adj* [➡CLEAN; 1232]

spotlessness 1 *n* **cleanliness**, cleanness, pristineness, immaculateness, neatness, hygiene. [➡CLEAN; 1232] *Opposite:* dirtiness. 2 *n* **flawlessness**, wholesomeness, innocence, stainlessness, irreproachability, perfection. [➡MORALLY GOOD; 775] *Opposite:* imperfection.

spotlight 1 *n* **attention**, limelight, fuss, focus, interest, public eye. [➡ATTENTION AND ATTENTIVENESS; 764] *Opposite:* anonymity. 2 *v* **highlight**, point up, draw attention to, underline, focus on, underscore, illuminate. [➡CLAIM, INSIST, AND EMPHASIZE; 615] *Opposite:* obscure. **3** *type of* **light.** [➡LIGHT; 1163]

spot-on (*informal*) **1** *adj* **exactly right**, dead right, bang on (*informal*), accurate, correct, perfect. [➡EXACT; 204] *Opposite:* wrong. **2** *adj* **ideal**, just right, perfect, hunky-dory (*informal*), just what we need, just what the doctor ordered. [➡CORRECT; 183] *Opposite:* disastrous.

spotted *adj* **dotted**, marked, speckled, dappled, mottled, stippled, specked, flecked, patterned. [➡DESCRIBING PATTERNS; 1226] *Opposite:* plain.

spotty **1** *adj* **mottled**, patterned, blotchy, spotted, dotted, marked, speckled, dappled, stippled, specked, flecked. [➡DESCRIBING PATTERNS; 1226] **2** *adj* **blemished**, pockmarked, covered with spots, pimpled, pimply, blotchy. [➡COMPLEXION; 481] *Opposite:* unblemished.

spouse *n* **other half**, wife, husband, next of kin, partner, significant other. [➡RELATIVES BY MARRIAGE; 960]

spout **1** *v* **spew out**, shoot out, send forth (*archaic or literary*), discharge, spurt, emit, gush, issue. [➡LIQUID EMISSION; 371] *Opposite:* retain. **2** *v* **talk**, utter, pontificate, rabbit on (*informal*), ramble on, sermonize. [➡WITTER AND BABBLE; 618] **3** *n* **jet**, fountain, stream, column, spurt, spray, geyser. [➡AMOUNT OF LIQUID; 114] **4** *n* **tube**, pipe, nozzle, outlet, spray, rose. [➡FITTINGS; 859]

sprain *v* **twist**, pull, injure, rick, strain, crick, wrench, turn. [➡FALL ILL, TREAT, AND RECOVER; 729]

sprat *type of* **sea fish.** [➡SEA FISH; 1009]

sprawl **1** *v* **slump**, spread out, collapse, lounge, loll, slouch, lie. [➡ASSUME A POSITION; 318] *Opposite:* curl up. **2** *v* **spread out**, cover, extend over, stretch over, trail, ramble, straggle. [➡EXIST IN A PLACE; 19] *Opposite:* shrink. **3** *n* **stretch**, mass, extension, spread, straggle, trail. [➡HUMAN SETTLEMENTS; 1069]

sprawled *adj* [➡ORIENTATION AND ALIGNMENT; 1222]

sprawling *adj* **extensive**, rambling, expansive, straggling, straggly, spreading. [➡WIDTH: WIDE; 1198] *Opposite:* contained.

spray **1** *n* **gush**, squirt, mist, jet, fountain, shower. [➡AMOUNT OF LIQUID; 114] **2** *n* **atomizer**, aerosol, spray can, pump dispenser, sprayer, can. [➡CONTAINERS, RECEPTACLES, AND PACKAGING; 1244] **3** *v* **scatter**, squirt, send out, spew, spurt, gush. [➡SPREAD AND SCATTER; 333] **4** *v* **cover**, drench, squirt, mist, dose, apply. [➡DECORATE, ADORN, AND APPLY COATINGS; 406] **5** *n* **sprig**, bouquet, stem, posy, buttonhole, bunch, nosegay. [➡COLLECTIONS AND MIXTURES OF THINGS; 1243]

spray can *n* **aerosol**, atomizer, spray, pump dispenser, sprayer, can. [➡CONTAINERS, RECEPTACLES, AND PACKAGING; 1244]

spray gun *n* **spray**, atomizer, airbrush, sprayer, diffuser. [➡CONTAINERS, RECEPTACLES, AND PACKAGING; 1244]

spread **1** *v* **open out**, unfold, place, lay out, put out, smooth out, unfurl, unroll. [➡SPREAD AND SCATTER; 333] *Opposite:* furl. **2** *v* **increase**, extend, multiply, reach, stretch, broaden, widen, swell, proliferate, expand, mushroom. [➡CHANGE OF SIZE: BIGGER; 393] *Opposite:* shrink. **3** *v* **last**, continue, go on, carry on, persist. [➡CONTINUE TO EXIST; 17] **4** *v* **broadcast**, disseminate, circulate, promulgate (*formal*), publish, propagate. [➡INFORM AND ANNOUNCE; 612] **5** *v* **apply**, put on, smear, daub, butter, paste. [➡DECORATE, ADORN, AND APPLY COATINGS; 406] *Opposite:* remove. **6** *v* **disperse**, distribute, share out, allot, divide, give out, scatter, strew. [➡DISPENSE, RATION, AND DISTRIBUTE; 435] **7** *n* **range**, extent, increase, coverage, span, sweep, compass, expanse, distribution, allotment, division, diffusion. [➡DEGREE AND EXTENT; 110] **8** *n* **variety**, range, selection, array, assortment, choice. [➡COLLECTIONS AND MIXTURES OF THINGS; 1243] **9** *n* **ranch**, estate, farm, plantation, station, holding. [➡AGRICULTURE AND FARMING; 1074] **10** *n* (*informal*) **feast**, banquet, blowout (*slang*), binge, meal, supper. [➡MEALS AND PARTS OF MEALS; 1168]

spread about *v* [➡INFORM AND ANNOUNCE; 612]

spread abroad *v* [➡INFORM AND ANNOUNCE; 612]

spread-eagled *adj* **sprawled**, sprawling, prone, prostrate, face down, lying down. [➡ORIENTATION AND ALIGNMENT; 1222] *Opposite:* erect.

spread out **1** *v* **move apart**, divide up, split up. [➡SEPARATE AND DIVIDE; 402] *Opposite:* amass. **2** *v* **extend**, cover, spread, go as far as, stretch. [➡EXIST IN A PLACE; 19] **3** *v* **share out**, share, divide up, split up. [➡DISPENSE, RATION, AND DISTRIBUTE; 435]

spread rumours *v* [➡GOSSIP; 679]

spreadsheet **1** *n* **worksheet**, database, table. [➡DRAWINGS, CHARTS AND TABLES; 595] **2** *type of* **software.** [➡COMPUTERS AND COMPUTING; 1126]

spread the word *v* [➡INFORM AND ANNOUNCE; 612]

spread your wings *v* [➡PREPARE FOR ACTION; 290]

spree **1** *n* **binge**, extravaganza, bender (*slang*), fling, splurge (*informal*), orgy. [➡EVENTS AND OCCURRENCES; 35] **2** *n* **jaunt**, outing, trip, excursion, break, day out, away day. [➡TRAVEL: JOURNEYS AND TRIPS; 319]

sprig *n* **spray**, twig, stem, branch, twiglet, shoot. [➡PARTS OF TREES AND PLANTS; 1026]

sprightliness *n* [➡FIT AND STRONG; 737]

sprightly *adj* **energetic**, active, spry, full of beans (*informal*), lively, agile, nimble, vigorous. [➡FIT AND STRONG; 737] *Opposite:* lethargic.

spring **1** *v* **jump**, leap, bounce, pounce, launch yourself, bound, skip. [➡BOUNCE, UNDULATE, AND VIBRATE; 309] **2** *n* **coil**, spiral, helix, mainspring, hairspring. [➡PARTS OF MACHINES AND TOOLS; 1117] **3** *n* **elasticity**, springiness, bounce, give, flexibility, movement. [➡MALLEABLE AND ELASTIC; 1211] *Opposite:* rigidity. **4** *n* **leap**, bound, jump, bounce, vault. [➡BOUNCE, UNDULATE, AND VIBRATE; 309] **5** *n* **springtime**, Easter, Eastertide, Eastertime, seedtime, springtide (*literary*). [➡TIMES OF YEAR; 88] **6** *n* **source**, upwelling, fount, fountain, water source. [➡BEGINNING; 53]

spring back *v* **ricochet**, recoil, shrink. [➡GO BACKWARDS; 310]

springboard *n* **catalyst**, facilitator, spur, trigger, launch pad, foundation. [➡BEGINNING; 53] *Opposite:* brake.

springbok *type of* **deer or antelope.** [➡DEER AND ANTELOPE; 981]

spring clean *n* [➡CLEAN AND POLISH; 404]

spring-clean *v* **scour**, scrub, blitz (*informal*), wash down, dust down, clean out, spruce up. [➡CLEAN AND POLISH; 404] *Opposite:* dirty.

spring-cleaning *n* [➡CLEAN AND POLISH; 404]

springiness *n* [➡MALLEABLE AND ELASTIC; 1211]

spring onion *type of* **salad vegetable.** [➡FRUIT AND VEGETABLES; 1175]

springtide (*literary*) *n* [➡TIMES OF YEAR; 88]

springtime *n* **season**, spring, springtide (*literary*), Eastertime, Eastertide, Easter, seedtime. [➡TIMES OF YEAR; 88] *Opposite:* autumn.

spring up *v* **appear**, emerge, pop up, come into existence, mushroom, develop, burst forth, crop up (*informal*), arrive, arise. [➡SUDDENLY COME INTO EXISTENCE; 2] *Opposite:* disappear.

springy *adj* **bouncy**, elastic, supple, pliable, soft, yielding. [➡MALLEABLE AND ELASTIC; 1211] *Opposite:* unyielding.

sprinkle 1 *v* **shake over**, dust, scatter, cover. [➡DECORATE, ADORN, AND APPLY COATINGS; 406] 2 *v* **intersperse**, pepper, strew, scatter, litter. [➡SPREAD AND SCATTER; 333] 3 *v* (*US*) **rain**, drizzle, shower. [➡CLOUDY AND RAINY WEATHER; 1052] 4 *n* **sprinkling**, shake, dusting, scattering, scatter, peppering, dash, smidgen (*informal*). [➡FEW, LITTLE, SMALL AMOUNT; 119]

sprinkler 1 *n* **sprayer**, irrigator, waterer, spray, hose. [➡FITTINGS; 859] 2 *n* **nozzle**, rose, showerhead, spray, diffuser, filter. [➡FITTINGS; 859]

sprinkling *n* **smidgen** (*informal*), scattering, dash, shake, pinch, bit, touch, smattering, sprinkle. [➡FEW, LITTLE, SMALL AMOUNT; 119] *Opposite:* heap.

sprint 1 *n* **dash**, race, run, 100 metres, cycle race. [➡NON-AGGRESSIVE/SPORTING EVENT; 40] *Opposite:* marathon. 2 *v* **hurry**, run, dash, race, gallop, tear. [➡MOVE FAST; 314] *Opposite:* dawdle. 3 *type of* **track and field.** [➡HOBBIES, GAMES, AND SPORTS; 875]

sprinter *n* **runner**, athlete, sportsperson, racer, cyclist, competitor. [➡PEOPLE IN SPORTS AND LEISURE; 876]

sprite *n* **fairy**, nymph, elf, goblin, dryad, leprechaun, brownie, gnome. [➡MYTHICAL BEINGS; 790]

sprocket *n* **tooth**, cog, notch, projection, sprocket wheel. [➡PARTS OF MACHINES AND TOOLS; 1117]

sprocket wheel *n* [➡PARTS OF MACHINES AND TOOLS; 1117]

sprog (*slang*) *n* **kid** (*informal*), nipper (*informal*), youngster, brat, little one, tot (*informal*), child, baby, toddler. [➡CHILD OR YOUTH; 945]

sprout 1 *v* **grow**, shoot, develop, bud, spring, germinate, push up, vegetate, burgeon (*literary*). [➡GROW AND CULTIVATE; 352] *Opposite:* wither. 2 *v* **spring up**, spring, emerge, appear, pop up, grow, bud, develop. [➡GROW AND CULTIVATE; 352] 3 *n* **shoot**, bud, leaf, young branch, new growth. [➡PARTS OF TREES AND PLANTS; 1026]

spruce 1 *type of* **evergreen tree.** [➡EVERGREEN AND CONIFEROUS TREES; 1029] 2 *adj* **smart**, neat, dapper, trim, elegant, well-groomed, natty. [➡WELL GROOMED; 483] *Opposite:* scruffy.

spruce up *v* **smarten**, smarten up, tidy, neaten, improve, put in order, clean up. *Opposite:* mess up. (*informal*). [➡IMPROVE APPEARANCE; 380]

spry *adj* **sprightly**, lively, active, agile, energetic, alert, nimble, supple, quick, brisk. [➡FIT AND STRONG; 737] *Opposite:* slow.

spryness *n* [➡FIT AND STRONG; 737]

spud (*informal*) *n* **potato**, tater (*regional*), murphy (*dated informal*). [➡FRUIT AND VEGETABLES; 1175]

spume (*literary*) *n* **foam**, surf, spray, froth, bubbles. [➡THE SEAS, OCEANS, AND SHORES; 1041]

spunk (*informal*) *n* **pluck**, spirit, toughness, determination, nerve, guts (*slang*), courage, bravery, boldness, bottle (*informal*). [➡COURAGE; 499] *Opposite:* cowardice.

spunky (*informal*) *adj* **plucky**, spirited, tough, determined, energetic, gutsy (*informal*), courageous, brave, bold, lively. [➡COURAGE; 499] *Opposite:* cowardly.

spun-out *adj* [➡HAPPENING SLOWLY; 106]

spur 1 *n* **incentive**, stimulus, incitement, provocation, motive, fillip, goad, impulse, inducement, catalyst. [➡CAUSATION; 169] *Opposite:* disincentive. 2 *n* **ridge**, mountainside, projection, edge, saddle, outcrop. [➡MOUNTAINS AND HILLS; 1044] 3 *n* **branch**, limb, shoot, offshoot, outgrowth. [➡SUBDIVISIONS AND OFFSHOOTS; 1252] 4 *n* **spike**, point, barb, spine. [➡ANGULAR SHAPE; 1216] 5 *v* (*literary*) **hurry up**, hasten, speed up, speed, rush, drive on, press forward. [➡CHANGE OF SPEED: MORE; 397] *Opposite:* delay. 6 *v* **urge**, encourage, incite, prompt, stimulate, goad, impel, drive, prod, provoke, spur on. [➡CAUSE OR COMPEL TO ACT; 272] *Opposite:* discourage.

See Compare and Contrast at **motive.**

spurious *adj* **false**, bogus, fake, forged, counterfeit, imitation, specious, inauthentic, sham, phoney. [➡FALSE AND UNREAL; 174] *Opposite:* genuine.

spurn *v* **reject**, snub, slight, rebuff, repulse, scorn, despise, disdain, look down on, hold in contempt. [➡REFUSING OR REJECTING RELATIONS; 975] *Opposite:* accept.

spur-of-the-moment *adj* **spontaneous**, impulsive, unplanned, impromptu, unpremeditated. [➡AUTOMATIC AND INSTINCTIVE; 281] *Opposite:* planned.

spurt 1 *n* **jet**, spray, squirt, gush, spout, emission. [➡AMOUNT OF LIQUID; 114] *Opposite:* trickle. 2 *n* **increase**, burst, surge, rush, swell, wave. [➡MORE AND EXCESS; 122] 3 *v* **gush**, spray, burst, jet, erupt, squirt, surge, shoot, rush, spout, emit, issue. [➡LIQUID EMISSION; 371] *Opposite:* trickle.

spur to action *v* [➡CAUSE OR COMPEL TO ACT; 272]

sputter 1 *v* **pop**, splutter, spit, sizzle, crackle. [➡EMIT CONTINUOUS SOUNDS; 367] 2 *v* **splutter**, gasp, spit, stammer, snort. [➡BREATHE AND NOT BREATHE; 717]

sputum *n* **mucus**, phlegm, saliva, spit, spittle. [➡EXCRETION AND EXCRETA; 723]

spy 1 *n* **secret agent**, undercover agent, double agent, mole, infiltrator, plant. [➡INTERFERING PEOPLE AND TELLTALES; 950] 2 *v* watch, eavesdrop, listen in, observe, scrutinize. [➡LOOKING AND LOOKS; 701] 3 *v* **work undercover**, snoop (*informal*), nose around (*informal*), pry, reconnoitre. [➡EXAMINE AND ASSESS; 754] 4 *v* **spot**, glimpse, notice, observe, see, behold (*archaic or literary*), discern, espy (*formal*). [➡SEE; 700] 5 *v* **discover**, search out, detect, find out, observe, notice. [➡LEARN AND DISCOVER; 763] *Opposite:* overlook. 6 *v* **investigate**, poke around, explore, search, research, examine. [➡LOOKING AND LOOKS; 701]

spyglass *type of* **optical instrument**. [➡OPTICAL INSTRUMENTS; 1123]

spyhole *n* **peephole**, slot, chink, opening, window, hole. [➡HOLES, GAPS, AND FORKS; 1251]

spying *n* **undercover work**, intelligence work, espionage, eavesdropping, snooping (*informal*), infiltration. [➡EXAMINE AND ASSESS; 754]

spy out *v* **discover**, uncover, seek out, sniff out, nose out, find. [➡FIND; 464] *Opposite:* overlook.

squab *type of* **young bird**. [➡YOUNG BIRD; 1004]

squabble 1 *n* **quarrel**, row, tiff, dispute, argument, fight, disagreement, spat. [➡ARGUMENT; 47] *Opposite:* reconciliation. 2 *v* **argue**, bicker, quarrel, disagree, have words, row, fight, wrangle. [➡ARGUE AND FIGHT – TWO-WAY; 644] *Opposite:* make up.

squad *n* **group**, team, crew, company, gang, troop, bevy, posse (*informal*), squadron, set, force. [➡GROUPS OF PEOPLE; 935]

squad car *n* **police car**, patrol car, panda car, cruiser (*US*), prowl car (*US dated*). [➡VEHICLES; 1144]

squaddie (*slang*) *n* **soldier**, private, regular. [➡MILITARY PERSONNEL; 828]

squadron *n* **regiment**, troop, team, squad, company, unit, group. [➡MILITARY PERSONNEL; 828]

squalid 1 *adj* **filthy**, dirty, foul, nasty, fetid, unclean, neglected, grimy, grubby. [➡DIRTY; 1234] *Opposite:* clean. 2 *adj* **seedy**, repulsive, sordid, sleazy, low, immoral, dishonest, disreputable. [➡MORALLY BAD; 776] *Opposite:* charming.

See Compare and Contrast at **dirty**.

squalidness *n* [➡IN BAD REPAIR; 1233]

squall *n* **storm**, gust of wind, windstorm, gust, tempest (*literary*), shower. [➡WINDY AND STORMY WEATHER; 1053]

squally *adj* **stormy**, gusty, blustery, wild, inclement. [➡WINDY AND STORMY WEATHER; 1053] *Opposite:* fine.

squalor 1 *n* **filth**, dirt, dirtiness, foulness, grime, uncleanliness, shabbiness, uncleanness. [➡DIRTY; 1234] *Opposite:* cleanliness. 2 *n* **nastiness**, sordidness, unpleasantness, degradation, immorality, sleaziness, seediness, meanness. [➡MORALLY BAD; 776] *Opposite:* charm.

squander *v* **waste**, spend, throw away, fritter away, dissipate, misuse, lavish, consume. [➡USE UP AND WASTE; 475] *Opposite:* save.

square 1 *n* **four-sided figure**, quadrangle, tetragon, rectangle, parallelogram. [➡ANGULAR SHAPE; 1216] 2 *n* (*slang dated*) **fogy**, stick-in-the-mud (*informal*), fuddy-duddy (*informal*), stuffed shirt (*informal*), reactionary, diehard. [➡UNCOOPERATIVE OR REBELLIOUS PERSON; 567] 3 *n* **plaza**, open area, marketplace, place, parade, piazza. [➡URBAN OUTDOOR SPACES; 1071] 4 *adj* (*slang dated*) **intransigent**, reactionary, conservative, traditionalist, dyed-in-the-wool, fogyish, conformist, stick-in-the-mud (*informal*). [➡CONSERVATIVE AND UNADVENTUROUS; 518] 5 *adj* **four-sided**, right-angled, rectangular, quadrangular, tetragonal. [➡ANGULAR SHAPE; 1216] 6 *adj* **fair**, honest, genuine, just, straight, upright, ethical. [➡MORALLY GOOD; 775] *Opposite:* dishonest. 7 *v* **shape**, form, file down, sharpen, even up, square off. [➡CRAFTS AND CARVING; 356] 8 *v* **adjust**, align, realign, set straight, straighten, even up, level. [➡ARRANGE AND CREATE ORDER; 358] *Opposite:* unbalance. 9 *v* **pay off**, settle, clear, pay, discharge (*formal*), balance. [➡GIVE MONEY; 434] 10 *v* **agree**, harmonize, accord, fit, tally, concur, check. [➡TWO-WAY COMMUNICATION; 608] *Opposite:* conflict. 11 *adv* **at right angles**, directly, straight. [➡ORIENTATION AND ALIGNMENT; 1222] 12 *adv* (*informal*) **fairly**, honestly, openly, straightforwardly, straight, justly. [➡MORALLY GOOD; 775]

square bracket *type of* **punctuation mark**. [➡ASPECTS OF LANGUAGE; 683]

square dance *type of* **dance**. [➡DANCE; 903]

squarely *adv* **directly**, exactly, evenly, head-on, straight. [➡EXACT; 204] *Opposite:* indirectly.

square meal *n* **nourishment**, hot meal, proper meal, food, sustenance. [➡MEALS AND PARTS OF MEALS; 1168] *Opposite:* snack.

square up 1 *v* **settle up**, even up, be quits (*informal*), settle your debts, settle the bill, pay up, cough up (*informal*). [➡GIVE MONEY; 434] 2 *v* **work out**, turn out fine, sort itself out, be arranged, be organized, be set out, sort out, arrange, organize. [➡ARRANGE AND CREATE ORDER; 358] *Opposite:* go wrong. 3 *v* **face up to**, confront, look something in the eye, tackle, take on, deal with, get to grips with. [➡COMPETE, CONTEND, AND COMBAT; 304] *Opposite:* evade. 4 *v* **put up your fists**, make a stand, put up a fight, stand your ground, take up the gauntlet, take up the challenge. [➡ASSUME A POSITION; 318] *Opposite:* run away.

squash 1 *v* **crush**, flatten, compress, pulp, mash, pound, squeeze, press. [➡CHANGE OF SHAPE; 386] *Opposite:* reshape. 2 *v* **cram**, squeeze, wedge, force, jam, pack, crowd, ram. [➡FILL; 407] *Opposite:* coax. 3 *v* **overcome**, stop, conquer, suppress, quash, quell, annihilate (*informal*). [➡BEAT AND DEFEAT; 80] *Opposite:* encourage. 4 *n* **squeeze**, crush, congestion, crowd, jam. [➡FULL; 1238] 5 *type of* **court game**. [➡HOBBIES, GAMES, AND SPORTS; 875] 6 *type of* **vegetable**. [➡FRUIT AND VEGETABLES; 1175] 7 *n* [➡DRINKS; 1186]

squash up *v* [➡GET CLOSER TOGETHER; 311]

squashy *adj* **soft**, yielding, spongy, springy, mushy, pliable, pulpy. [➡MALLEABLE AND ELASTIC; 1211] *Opposite:* firm.

squat 1 *v* **crouch**, sit on your heels, hunker down, bend. [➡ASSUME A POSITION; 318] *Opposite:* stand. 2 *adj* **short**, thickset, thick, stubby, stocky, pudgy (*informal*). [➡BUILD; 478] *Opposite:* tall.

squatness *n* [➡BUILD; 478]

squatter *n* **unlawful tenant**, unlawful resident, resident, trespasser. [➡INHABITANT; 857]

squawk 1 *v* **screech**, call, cry, squeal, shriek, scream.

[➡SOUND EMISSION BY ANIMALS OR BIRDS; 365] **2** *v* (*informal*) **complain**, protest, whine, wail, moan (*informal*), grumble. [➡COMPLAIN AND NAG; 687] **3** *n* **harsh call**, cry, screech, shriek, squeal, scream. [➡SOUNDS MADE BY BIRDS; 1262] **4** *n* **protest**, complaint, whine, wail, moan (*informal*), grumble. [➡CRITICISMS AND ANGRY OUTBURSTS; 50]

squeak **1** *v* **squeal**, whine, yelp, shrill, pipe, peep, screech. [➡SOUND EMISSION BY ANIMALS OR BIRDS; 365] **2** *type of* **animal sound**. [➡SOUNDS MADE BY ANIMALS; 1260]

squeak through (*informal*) *v* **scrape through**, scrape by, manage, achieve, do. [➡SUCCEED AND WIN; 79]

squeaky *adj* **high-pitched**, shrill, whiny, noisy, creaky, rusty. [➡LOUD OR UNPLEASANT SOUNDS; 1265]

squeaky-clean **1** *adj* **virtuous**, righteous, pure, honourable, unimpeachable, unassailable, untouchable, impeccable, flawless, perfect. [➡MORALLY GOOD; 775] *Opposite:* corrupt. **2** *adj* [➡CLEAN; 1232]

squeal **1** *n* **screech**, yelp, shriek, yell, cry, howl, wail, scream, squeak. [➡SOUNDS MADE BY PEOPLE; 1261] **2** *v* (*slang*) **inform**, betray, sneak on, denounce, tell on, tattle, blow the whistle on, grass (*slang*), grass up (*slang*), snitch (*slang*). [➡BETRAY CONFIDENCES AND GOSSIP; 619] **3** *v* **yell**, cry, shriek, yelp, howl, wail, scream, squawk, screech, squeak. [➡SOUND EMISSION BY ANIMALS OR BIRDS; 365] **4** *type of* **animal sound**. [➡SOUNDS MADE BY ANIMALS; 1260]

squealer (*slang disapproving*) *n* [➡INTERFERING PEOPLE AND TELLTALES; 950]

squeal on (*US slang disapproving*) *v* [➡BETRAY CONFIDENCES AND GOSSIP; 619]

squeamish **1** *adj* **nauseous**, queasy, sick, woozy. [➡ILL AND SICK; 741] **2** *adj* **delicate**, easily upset, easily offended, prudish, puritanical, prim, strait-laced. [➡EXCESSIVE SENSITIVITY; 512] *Opposite:* strong. **3** *adj* **fastidious**, particular, scrupulous, fussy, uncompromising. [➡DIFFICULT TO PLEASE; 516] *Opposite:* easygoing.

squeamishness **1** *n* **queasiness**, nauseousness, sickness, seediness (*informal*), qualmishness. [➡ILL AND SICK; 741] **2** *n* **delicacy**, prudishness, prudery, shockability, puritanism, primness. [➡EXCESSIVE SENSITIVITY; 512] *Opposite:* toughness.

squeeze **1** *v* **press**, squash, compress, constrict, pinch, mould. [➡CONTACT: EXERT PRESSURE; 415] **2** *v* **find time for**, make time for, make room for, fit in, slot in. [➡CARRY OUT AN ACTION; 270] **3** *v* **grip**, hold on, grasp, hug, clutch, clasp. [➡CONTACT: HOLD; 412] *Opposite:* release. **4** *v* **hug**, embrace, cuddle, enfold, clasp, clutch, hold, press. [➡CONTACT: EXERT PRESSURE; 415] *Opposite:* release. **5** *v* **crush**, squash, cram, crowd, jam, pack, stuff, wedge, force, ram. [➡FILL; 407] *Opposite:* coax. **6** *v* **extract**, wring, expel, drive out, mangle. [➡CHANGE OF SHAPE; 386] **7** *v* **pressurize**, put pressure on, lean on (*informal*), harass, hassle (*informal*), oppress. [➡CAUSE OR COMPEL TO ACT; 272]

squeeze out *v* **exclude**, express, force out, freeze out, ostracize, gouge out, shut out, press out. [➡REFUSING OR REJECTING RELATIONS; 975]

squeeze up *v* [➡GET CLOSER TOGETHER; 311]

squelch **1** *v* **squish**, splash, splosh, suck, gurgle, splish-splash (*US*). [➡EMIT SOUNDS THROUGH IMPACT AND ABRASION; 366] **2** *v* (*slang*) **suppress**, silence, scotch, squash, quash, crush, stifle, check, repress. [➡MAKE IMPOSSIBLE; 277] *Opposite:* broadcast. **3** *v* **crush**, squash, flatten, trample, squish, tread on, stamp on. [➡CHANGE OF SHAPE; 386] **4** *n* (*slang*) [➡CRITICISMS AND ANGRY OUTBURSTS; 50] **5** *n* **splash**, squish, splish-splash (*US*), splosh, suck, gurgle. [➡IMPACT SOUNDS; 1259]

squelchy *adj* **soggy**, squishy, wet, squidgy, watery, damp, squashy. [➡WET; 1239] *Opposite:* dry.

squib *type of* **firework**. [➡EXPLOSIVES; 1154]

squid *type of* **aquatic invertebrate**. [➡AQUATIC INVERTEBRATE; 1022]

squidgy **1** *adj* **soggy**, squelchy, slimy, mushy, marshy, wet, damp, moist, gooey, sloppy. [➡WET; 1239] *Opposite:* dry. **2** *adj* **squashy**, spongy, springy, pliable, soft, yielding. [➡MALLEABLE AND ELASTIC; 1211] *Opposite:* firm.

squiffy (*informal*) *adj* [➡UNDER THE INFLUENCE OF DRUGS OR ALCOHOL; 742]

squiggle *n* **scribble**, wavy line, doodle, ornamentation, flourish, scrawl, curlicue, mark. [➡WRITING; 584]

squiggly *adj* **wavy**, curvy, wobbly, bumpy, scribbly, meandering, snaky. [➡ROUNDED SHAPE; 1217] *Opposite:* straight.

squillion *n* [➡MANY, MUCH, LARGE AMOUNT; 117]

squint **1** *v* **narrow your eyes**, peer, peek, look, glance. [➡LOOKING AND LOOKS; 701] **2** *n* **peep**, peer, quick look, glance, glimpse, peek. [➡LOOKING AND LOOKS; 701] **3** *adj* (*informal*) **crooked**, lopsided, cross-eyed, off balance, uneven, tilted, askew. [➡ORIENTATION AND ALIGNMENT; 1222] *Opposite:* straight. **4** *adv* (*informal*) **lopsidedly**, askew, crookedly, unevenly. [➡ORIENTATION AND ALIGNMENT; 1222] *Opposite:* straight.

squire **1** *n* **landowner**, lord, landlord, owner, proprietor, landholder, laird. [➡RICH PEOPLE; 895] *Opposite:* tenant. **2** *n* **attendant**, retainer, steward, man, servant, page. [➡DOMESTIC AND KITCHEN WORKERS; 850]

squirm **1** *v* **wriggle**, writhe, twist, turn, fidget, struggle. [➡FIDGET AND FROLIC; 312] **2** *v* **feel shame**, feel embarrassment, feel remorse, feel guilty, feel awkward, feel humiliated. [➡CHANGE OF MOOD AND COMPOSURE; 581]

squirmy *adj* [➡INSECURITY AND LOSS OF COMPOSURE; 545]

squirrel **1** *n* (*informal*) **hoarder**, magpie (*informal*), collector, accumulator, saver, pack rat (*US informal*). [➡PEOPLE WHO COLLECT THINGS; 455] **2** *v* **hoard**, collect, accumulate, stash (*informal*), store, put aside, save, salt away, squirrel away, stockpile. [➡STORE AND KEEP; 454] *Opposite:* throw out. **3** *type of* **rodent**. [➡RODENT; 989]

squirrel away *v* [➡STORE AND KEEP; 454]

squirt **1** *v* **spurt**, shoot, jet, gush, spray, spew, spout, squeeze. [➡LIQUID EMISSION; 371] **2** *n* **spurt**, jet, fountain, stream, spray, shot (*informal*), squeeze. [➡AMOUNT OF LIQUID; 114]

squirt gun (*US*) *type of* **toy**. [➡TOYS; 880]

squish **1** *v* **squeeze**, crush, squash, squelch, pinch, squirt. [➡CHANGE OF SHAPE; 386] **2** *v* **splash**, squelch, splosh, suck, gurgle, splish-splash (*US*). [➡EMIT SOUNDS THROUGH IMPACT AND ABRA-

SION; 366] **3** *n* **squelch**, splash, splish-splash (*US*), splosh, suck, gurgle. [➡IMPACT SOUNDS; 1259]

squishy *adj* **squelchy**, soggy, soft, mushy, squidgy, spongy, slimy, wet, damp, moist, gooey, marshy, sloppy. [➡WET; 1239] *Opposite:* firm.

stab **1** *v* **knife**, wound, pierce, cut, spear, run through (*literary*), stick, gouge, gore. [➡STAB; 417] **2** *n* **pang**, twinge, ache, pain, prick, feeling, sensation. [➡PAIN AND OTHER PHYSICAL SENSATIONS; 734] **3** *n* (*informal*) **attempt**, go, try, bash (*informal*), crack (*informal*), shot, guess. [➡ATTEMPT AN ACTION; 262]

stabbing **1** *n* **knife attack**, assault, wounding, attack. [➡AGGRESSIVE EVENT; 39] **2** *adj* **sharp**, acute, piercing, shooting, intense, severe. [➡PAIN AND OTHER PHYSICAL SENSATIONS; 734]

stability *n* **constancy**, steadiness, firmness, solidity, permanence, immovability, strength. [➡PERMANENCE: WITHOUT CHANGE; 95] *Opposite:* instability.

stabilization *n* **steadying**, steadiness, maintenance, balance, equilibrium, evening out, calming. [➡PROGRESS AND ADVANCEMENT; 214] *Opposite:* change.

stabilize *v* **become stable**, even out, become constant, calm, calm down, soothe, alleviate, steady. [➡IMPROVE SOMETHING; 375] *Opposite:* change.

stab in the back (*informal*) **1** *v* **betray**, let down, be disloyal to, sell out, wound, attack. [➡BETRAY CONFIDENCES AND GOSSIP; 619] **2** *n* **betrayal**, wound, attack, act of disloyalty, act of treachery. [➡UNKIND ACTION OR BEHAVIOUR; 297]

stable **1** *adj* **steady**, unchanging, even, constant, firm, unwavering, sure, established, secure, committed, longstanding. [➡STRENGTH; 202] *Opposite:* changeable. **2** *adj* **secure**, fixed, firm, permanent, rigid, durable, sure, fast. [➡PERMANENCE: WITHOUT CHANGE; 95] *Opposite:* unstable. **3** *adj* **calm**, steady, even, settled, level-headed, collected. [➡CALMNESS, CONFIDENCE, AND COMPOSURE; 537] *Opposite:* erratic. **4** *n* **stall**, shed, stabling. [➡ANIMAL OR BIRD ACCOMMODATION; 1078] **5** *n* **team**, gang, string, group, lineup, set. [➡GROUPS OF PEOPLE; 935]

staccato **1** *adj* **clipped**, disjointed, disconnected, faltering, monosyllabic. [➡INARTICULATE, RAMBLING, AND AWKWARD; 634] **2** *type of* **musical term.** [➡MUSICAL TERMS; 912]

stack **1** *n* **pile**, heap, mass, mound, mountain, load. [➡MANY, MUCH, LARGE AMOUNT; 117] **2** *n* **chimney**, smokestack, flue. [➡ROOFS, ROOF PARTS, AND CEILINGS; 1102] **3** *v* **pile**, load, heap, mound, amass, assemble. [➡MOVE SOMETHING: INTO A NEW POSITION OR OVERTURN; 331]

stacked *adj* **loaded**, weighted, set, slanted, fixed, arranged. [➡FULL; 1238]

stacks (*informal*) *n* **masses**, loads (*informal*), heaps (*informal*), lots, piles (*informal*), tons (*informal*). [➡MANY, MUCH, LARGE AMOUNT; 117]

stack up (*US*) **1** *v* **measure up**, stand up, compare, line up, stand comparison. [➡ASSESS QUALITY; 756] **2** *v* **add up**, accumulate, come to, total, make, amount to, make a total of. [➡AMOUNT TO AND EQUAL; 70]

stadium *n* **sports ground**, arena, pitch, ground, field, ring, bowl (*US*). [➡URBAN OUTDOOR SPACES; 1071]

staff **1** *n* **employees**, personnel, workers, workforce, team, body, force, human resources, organization. [➡THE WORK FORCE; 837] **2** *n* **rod**, cane, pole, wand, stick, baton. [➡STICKS, POLES, AND WEDGES; 1253] **3** *v* **operate**, run, work, control, supervise, man. [➡BE IN CHARGE; 271]

stag *type of* **male animal.** [➡MALE OR FEMALE ANIMAL; 978]

stag beetle *type of* **beetle.** [➡BEETLES AND WEEVILS; 1016]

stage **1** *n* **phase**, period, step, point, leg, juncture, time. [➡PERIOD OF TIME; 90] **2** *n* **platform**, rostrum, stand, scaffold, podium, dais. [➡STAGES, PLATFORMS, AND RAISED AREAS; 1097] **3** *n* **theatre**, arena, playhouse, the boards. [➡IN THE THEATRE; 906] **4** *v* **put on**, perform, present, show, play, act, do. [➡INSTITUTE AND INAUGURATE; 349] **5** *part of* **spacecraft.** [➡SPACE VEHICLES; 1062]

stagecoach **1** *n* **carriage**, horse-drawn carriage, cart. [➡BIKES, CARS, AND CARRIAGES; 1148] **2** *type of* **wagon or carriage.** [➡VEHICLES; 1144]

stage door *n* **back door**, side door, entrance, way in, exit, way out. [➡IN THE THEATRE; 906]

stage fright *n* **first-night nerves**, fear, panic, nerves (*informal*). [➡FEELINGS ABOUT THE FUTURE; 534]

stage-manage *v* **engineer**, contrive, manipulate, devise, set up, control, direct, manoeuvre. [➡CAUSE TO HAPPEN; 31]

stage name *n* **pseudonym**, alias, assumed name, professional name. [➡NAME AND DESCRIBE; 666]

stage whisper *n* **aside**, mutter, murmur. [➡IN THE THEATRE; 906] *Opposite:* shout.

stagey *see* **stagy.**

stagflation *n* **slump**, recession, downturn, stagnation, inflation, standstill. [➡MARKET FORCES; 803] *Opposite:* growth.

stagger **1** *v* **reel**, lurch, sway, totter, wobble, teeter, stumble, walk unsteadily. [➡WALK UNSTEADILY; 316] **2** *v* **astound**, amaze, shock, stun, surprise, astonish, confound, shake, take by surprise. [➡SURPRISE AND IMPRESS; 575] **3** *v* **alternate**, vary, zigzag, rotate, space out, spread out, step. [➡ARRANGE AND CREATE ORDER; 358] *Opposite:* overlap.

staggered **1** *adj* **stunned**, shocked, amazed, gobsmacked (*slang*), flabbergasted (*informal*), astounded, taken aback, surprised, nonplussed. [➡SURPRISE, SHOCK, AND AMAZEMENT; 546] *Opposite:* unaffected. **2** *adj* **alternated**, spread out, spaced out, zigzagged. [➡ORIENTATION AND ALIGNMENT; 1222]

staggering *adj* **astounding**, amazing, confounding, overwhelming, stunning, shocking, surprising, incredible, astonishing, unbelievable, hard to believe. [➡EXTRAORDINARY: AMAZING; 205]

staging *n* **performance**, dramatization, production, enactment, presentation. [➡PERFORMANCES AND SHOWS; 42]

staging post *n* **stopover**, halt, stop, break, half-way house, port of call. [➡TRANSPORTATION, TRANSPORTERS, AND CARGOS; 323]

stagnant **1** *adj* **still**, motionless, stationary, standing, immobile, quiet. [➡LACK OF ACTIVITY; 343] *Opposite:* moving. **2** *adj* **sluggish**, inactive, inert, torpid, dull, dormant, moribund, heavy. [➡BORING AND UNINTERESTING; 235] *Opposite:* active.

stagnate **1** *v* **stand still**, come to a halt, grind to a halt, be idle, languish, idle, decline. [➡GET WORSE; 382] *Opposite:* progress. **2** *v* **fester**, rot, deteriorate, go off, decay, go rancid, go stale, go bad. [➡GO BAD AND CORRODE; 391] **3** *v* **vegetate**, be inactive, idle, be idle, sit around, do nothing. [➡LACK OF ACTIVITY; 343]

stagnation *n* **inactivity**, inaction, inertia, torpor, sluggishness, immobility, lack of progress, unproductivity. [➡LACK OF ACTIVITY; 343] *Opposite:* movement.

stagy (*disapproving*) *adj* **theatrical**, dramatic, histrionic, exaggerated, artificial, melodramatic, studied, affected. [➡AFFECTATION, SELF-SATISFACTION, AND SNOBBISHNESS; 508] *Opposite:* unaffected.

staid *adj* **sedate**, serious, grave, sober, dull, calm, settled, demure, stolid, solid, unadventurous, steady. [➡CONSERVATIVE AND UNADVENTUROUS; 518] *Opposite:* exciting.

staidness *n* [➡CONSERVATIVE AND UNADVENTUROUS; 518]

stain **1** *n* **mark**, blemish, spot, blot, imperfection, discoloration, tarnish. [➡FAULTS, FLAWS, AND WEAKNESSES; 252] **2** *n* **tint**, dye, colour, tinge, pigment, colourwash. [➡DYES AND COLOURANTS; 1269] **3** *n* **stigma**, slur, disgrace, dishonour, blemish, reproach, contamination, shame, infamy. [➡NUISANCES; 254] **4** *v* **blemish**, tarnish, soil, discolour, mark, tinge, dirty, blot, spot, dye. [➡DIRTY AND CONTAMINATE; 405] **5** *v* **disgrace**, sully, taint, defile (*formal*), debase, dishonour, pollute, contaminate, corrupt, deprave. [➡WORSEN SOMETHING; 381] *Opposite:* honour.

stained *adj* **discoloured**, marked, blemished, tainted, tarnished, damaged. [➡DIRTY; 1234]

stained glass *type of* **glass**. [➡GLASS; 1135]

stainless steel *type of* **metal**. [➡METALS; 1275]

stair **1** *n* **step**, tread, rung. [➡SUPPORTS AND BASES; 1254] **2** *n* **staircase**, stairway, flight of steps, set of steps, flight of stairs, stairs. [➡STAIRS AND STOREYS; 1101]

staircase **1** *n* **stairway**, stair, stairs, flight of steps, set of steps, flight of stairs. [➡STAIRS AND STOREYS; 1101] **2** *part of* **building**. [➡PARTS OF A BUILDING; 1094]

stairs **1** *n* **staircase**, stair, stairway, flight of steps, set of steps, flight of stairs. [➡STAIRS AND STOREYS; 1101] **2** *part of* **building**. [➡PARTS OF A BUILDING; 1094]

stairway **1** *n* **staircase**, stair, stairs, flight of steps, set of steps, flight of stairs. [➡STAIRS AND STOREYS; 1101] **2** *part of* **building**. [➡PARTS OF A BUILDING; 1094]

stairwell **1** *n* **hall**, entrance hall, vestibule, staircase, stairs, steps, shaft. [➡STAIRS AND STOREYS; 1101] **2** *part of* **building**. [➡PARTS OF A BUILDING; 1094]

stake **1** *n* **bet**, wager, ante, risk, venture, hazard, pledge, chance. [➡GAMBLE AND TAKE RISKS; 467] **2** *n* **post**, pale, pole, palisade, picket, stick, rod. [➡STICKS, POLES, AND WEDGES; 1253] **3** *n* **investment**, claim, share, involvement, concern, interest. [➡MONEY, PAYMENTS, AND CHARGES; 800] **4** *n* **prize**, winnings, purse, stakes. [➡GAMBLE AND TAKE RISKS; 467] **5** *v* **risk**, gamble, bet, venture, hazard, wager. [➡GAMBLE AND TAKE RISKS; 467]

stakeholder *n* **investor**, shareholder, backer, sponsor, participant, patron, interested party. [➡PEOPLE INVOLVED IN FINANCE; 804]

stakeout (*informal*) *n* **close watch**, watch, observation, investigation, examination, surveillance, supervision, vigil, guard. [➡LOOKING AND LOOKS; 701]

stake out **1** *v* (*informal*) **spy on**, watch, keep under surveillance, keep watch on, keep an eye on, keep under watch. [➡LOOKING AND LOOKS; 701] **2** *v* **mark out**, demarcate, delimit (*formal*), chalk out, measure out, fence off. [➡SEPARATE AND DIVIDE; 402] **3** *v* **establish**, clarify, define, limit, restrict, delimit (*formal*), describe. [➡NAME AND DESCRIBE; 666]

stake race (*US*) *n* [➡NON-AGGRESSIVE/SPORTING EVENT; 40]

stakes **1** *n* **risk**, risk factor, danger, element of danger. [➡GAMBLE AND TAKE RISKS; 467] **2** *n* **reward**, prize, recompense, incentive, winnings. [➡GAMBLE AND TAKE RISKS; 467]

stale **1** *adj* **decayed**, sour, old, musty, hard, fusty, out-of-date, past its sell-by date, gone off, flat, past its best. [➡DECAYING OR INFESTED; 1235] *Opposite:* fresh. **2** *adj* **hackneyed**, worn-out, tired, overused, boring, clichéd, unoriginal, insipid, vapid, humdrum, pedestrian, ho-hum (*informal*). [➡BORING AND UNINTERESTING; 235] *Opposite:* original.

stalemate *n* **impasse**, deadlock, standoff, logjam, standstill. [➡DIFFICULT SITUATIONS; 72]

staleness *n* **mustiness**, mouldiness, decay, flatness, sourness, fustiness. [➡DECAYING OR INFESTED; 1235] *Opposite:* freshness.

stalk **1** *n* **stem**, shoot, twig, branch, trunk. [➡STICKS, POLES, AND WEDGES; 1253] **2** *v* **follow**, trail, track, pursue, shadow, hunt, haunt, tail, hound, lurk, prowl, menace, chase. [➡ACCOMPANY AND FOLLOW; 338]

See Compare and Contrast at **follow**.

stalker *n* **prowler**, pursuer, shadow, tracker, follower, Peeping Tom, lurker. [➡CRIMINALS; 821]

stall **1** *n* **booth**, stand, arcade, shop, kiosk, boutique. [➡ANCILLARY BUILDINGS; 1079] **2** *n* **compartment**, pen, coop, shed, cubicle, box, loosebox, box stall (*US*). [➡ALCOVES, CUBICLES, AND COMPARTMENTS; 1095] **3** *v* **stop**, cut out, freeze, pause, halt, come to a standstill, peter out, shut down. [➡FAIL OR CEASE TO FUNCTION; 471] *Opposite:* keep going. **4** *type of* **seating**. [➡FURNITURE; 858] **5** *type of* **pen or cage**. [➡ANIMAL OR BIRD ACCOMMODATION; 1078] **6** *v* **delay**, put off, defer, postpone, suspend, shelve, hold over, arrest, impede, check. [➡DELAY ACTION OR OCCURRENCE; 279] *Opposite:* advance. **7** *v* **play for time**, prevaricate, equivocate, hedge, hesitate, dither, delay, put off, temporize. [➡SHIRK AND DELAY; 274]

stallion *type of* **male animal**. [➡MALE OR FEMALE ANIMAL; 978]

stalwart **1** *adj* **strong**, muscular, athletic, brawny, sturdy, robust, rugged, hefty, well-built, strapping (*informal*), burly, powerfully built. [➡BUILD; 478] *Opposite:* feeble. **2** *adj* **resolute**, vigorous, determined, committed, unfaltering, steadfast, unwavering, staunch, firm, unshakable. [➡HARD-WORKING AND COMMITTED; 501] *Opposite:* uncommitted. **3** *adj* **brave**, courageous, daring, fearless, bold, valiant, audacious, intrepid (*literary or humorous*), stouthearted, indomitable. [➡COURAGE; 499] *Opposite:* cowardly.

stalwartly *adv* **dependably**, loyally, faithfully, steadfastly, unfalteringly, unwaveringly, staunchly, constantly, dedicatedly, reliably, firmly, unshakably. [➡ HARD-WORKING AND COMMITTED; 501] *Opposite:* unreliably.

stamina *n* **staying power**, endurance, energy, resilience, resistance, determination, doggedness, strength, fortitude, sturdiness, grit, hardiness, vigour, perseverance. [➡ STRENGTH OF WILL; 502] *Opposite:* frailty.

stammer 1 *v* **stumble**, stutter, falter, hesitate, pause, splutter, hem and haw, hum and haw, mumble. [➡ WITTER AND BABBLE; 618] 2 *n* **stutter**, hesitant speech, speech impediment. [➡ INARTICULATE, RAMBLING, AND AWKWARD; 634]

stamp 1 *n* **mark**, imprint, mould, cast, hallmark, earmark, print, impression, endorsement, seal, signature, identification, trademark, label, brand. [➡ SYMBOLS, SIGNS, AND NUMBERS; 597] 2 *n* **character**, kind, make, sort, type, quality, form, variety, characteristic. [➡ VARIETY, TYPE, KIND; 146] 3 *v* **trample**, stomp, crush, squash, plod, trudge, pound, beat. [➡ CONTACT: EXERT PRESSURE; 415] 4 *v* **imprint**, engrave, inscribe, fix, impress, mark, earmark, hallmark, brand, print, seal. [➡ CREATE IMAGES; 357]

stampede 1 *n* **rush**, mad dash, flight, rout, pandemonium, retreat, panic, charge. [➡ CHAOS AND UPROAR; 51] 2 *v* **rush**, hurry, run, dash, sprint, take flight, flee, scatter, charge. [➡ MOVE FAST; 314]

stamping ground (*informal*) *n* **patch**, haunt, hangout (*informal*), place, home, territory, familiar territory. [➡ PLACE; 1064]

stamp out *v* **eradicate**, banish, destroy, remove, extinguish, wipe out (*informal*), eliminate, abolish, put an end to, get rid of, crush, put down, squelch (*slang*), suppress. [➡ GET RID OF SOMETHING; 452] *Opposite:* cultivate.

stance 1 *n* **posture**, carriage (*formal*), deportment (*formal*), bearing, attitude. [➡ TEMPERAMENT AND BEHAVIOUR; 493] 2 *n* **attitude**, position, stand, standpoint, view, viewpoint, point of view, opinion, perspective, outlook. [➡ POINT OF VIEW; 768]

stanch *see* **staunch**.

stanchion *n* [➡ SUPPORTS AND BASES; 1254]

stand 1 *v* **rise**, get up, stand up, arise (*archaic or literary*), get to your feet, be on your feet. [➡ ASSUME A POSITION; 318] *Opposite:* sit. 2 *v* **place**, situate (*formal*), position, set, put, locate, rest, plonk (*informal*), park (*slang*), deposit. [➡ POSITION SOMETHING; 326] 3 *v* **erect**, mount, hoist, put up, stick up, rear, raise, set upright. [➡ POSITION SOMETHING; 326] 4 *v* **remain**, halt, stop, continue, exist, pause, stay, remain motionless, remain standing, endure, survive, last, hold, prevail, persist. [➡ CONTINUE TO EXIST; 17] 5 *v* **tolerate**, endure, put up with, abide, bear, withstand, stand for, brook (*formal*), stomach, cope with, sustain, survive, take, suffer. [➡ TOLERATE AND ENDURE; 767] 6 *n* **attitude**, opinion, stance, position, viewpoint, standpoint, point of view, view, outlook, policy. [➡ POINT OF VIEW; 768] 7 *n* **stop**, standstill, stay, rest, halt. [➡ LACK OF ACTIVITY; 343] 8 *n* **stall**, counter, booth, kiosk, tent. [➡ ANCILLARY BUILDINGS; 1079] 9 *n* **platform**, rostrum, stage, place, post, position, dais, podium. [➡ SUPPORTS AND BASES; 1254] 10 *n* **rack**, frame, support, holder, shelf, bracket. [➡ SUPPORTS AND BASES; 1254]

standard 1 *n* **criterion**, benchmark, touchstone, paradigm, yardstick, model, pattern, measure, requirement, guideline, specification. [➡ PERFECT EXAMPLES AND EMBODIMENTS; 67] 2 *n* **norm**, average, mean, par, level, degree, rank. [➡ SCORES AND EVALUATIONS; 599] *Opposite:* aberration. 3 *n* **flag**, banner, ensign, pennant, streamer, colours, emblem, jack. [➡ SYMBOLS, SIGNS, AND NUMBERS; 597] 4 *adj* **normal**, typical, average, usual, ordinary, set, customary, orthodox, prevailing, accepted, traditional, basic, everyday, universal, regular, stock. [➡ ACCEPTABLE AND PASSABLE; 220] *Opposite:* unusual.

standard-bearer *n* **leader**, ringleader, prime mover, spearhead, director, chief, commander, captain. [➡ IMPORTANT OR FAMOUS PEOPLE; 893]

standardize *v* **regulate**, homogenize, normalize, even out, regiment, stereotype, order, systematize. [➡ ARRANGE AND CREATE ORDER; 358]

standard lamp *type of* **light**. [➡ LIGHT; 1163]

standard-length *adj* [➡ LENGTH: LONG; 1196]

standard of living *n* **level of comfort**, means, level of affluence, wealth, lifestyle, way of life. [➡ LIFESTYLE; 881]

standards *n* **principles**, values, morals, ethics, ideals, canon. [➡ MORAL CONCEPTS; 774]

standard-size *adj* [➡ MEDIUM; 1195]

stand by *v* **support**, stick by, back, stick up for, side with, defend, uphold, be there for, maintain, back up. [➡ APPROVE AND CONFIRM; 647] *Opposite:* abandon.

stand-by 1 *n* **reserve**, deputy, supply (*formal*), stand-in, double, understudy. [➡ COLLEAGUES AND EQUALS; 967] 2 *n* **substitute**, replacement, spare, backup, reserve. [➡ MORE AND EXCESS; 122] 3 *adj* **reserve**, fallback, replacement, stand-in, deputy, understudy. [➡ MORE AND EXCESS; 122] 4 *adj* **last-minute**, late. [➡ PROMPTNESS: LATE; 100] *Opposite:* reserved.

stand down *v* **resign**, step down, quit, bow out, give up, call it a day. [➡ STOP ACTING; 265]

stand firm *v* **persevere**, stand your ground, hold on, hold out, dig in your heels, persist. [➡ CONTINUE AN ACTION; 263] *Opposite:* yield.

stand for 1 *v* **put up with**, tolerate, abide, brook (*formal*), withstand, stand, accept, bear, endure, suffer, take. [➡ TOLERATE AND ENDURE; 767] 2 *v* **mean**, signify, represent, denote, symbolize, emblematize (*formal*), indicate. [➡ MEAN SOMETHING; 61] 3 *v* **advocate**, promote, support, champion, endorse, sponsor. [➡ APPROVE AND CONFIRM; 647]

stand in *v* **fill in**, substitute, deputize, take somebody's place, do somebody's work, cover, temp, understudy, double, alternate. [➡ REPRESENT SOMETHING OR SOMEBODY; 59]

stand-in *n* **replacement**, understudy, deputy, substitute, reserve, double, lieutenant, stand-by. [➡ SUBSTITUTES AND STAND-INS; 400]

stand in for *v* **take the place of**, deputize for, substitute for, cover for, do the work of, understudy. [➡ REPRESENT SOMETHING OR SOMEBODY; 59]

standing 1 *n* **rank**, status, position, reputation, station, repute (*formal*), eminence, footing, place, ranking, order, grade. [➡ STATUS; 888] 2 *n* **duration**, existence, continuance, age, tenure, term, life. [➡PERIOD OF TIME; 90] **3** *adj* **established**, settled, fixed, immovable, durable, lasting, permanent. [➡PERMANENCE: WITHOUT END; 94] *Opposite:* temporary. **4** *adj* **stand-up**, vertical, upright, upended, perpendicular, erect. [➡ORIENTATION AND ALIGNMENT; 1222] *Opposite:* horizontal.

standing order *n* **rule**, order, instruction, protocol, procedure, guideline. [➡WAYS OF DOING THINGS; 295]

standing ovation *n* [➡APPLAUSE; 653]

standing stone *n* **obelisk**, menhir, dolmen, megalith, column, stone circle. [➡ANCIENT MANMADE STRUCTURES; 1088]

standoff **1** *n* **stalemate**, impasse, deadlock, logjam, standstill. [➡DIFFICULT SITUATIONS; 72] **2** *n* (*US*) **tie**, draw, dead heat, photo finish. [➡RESULTS AND OUTCOMES; 83]

standoffish *adj* **distant**, aloof, superior, unapproachable, cold, unfriendly, reticent, unforthcoming, reserved, unsociable, supercilious, detached, snobbish, withdrawn, snooty (*informal*), remote. [➡UNFRIENDLINESS AND UNSOCIABILITY; 505] *Opposite:* affable.

standoffishness *n* [➡UNFRIENDLINESS AND UNSOCIABILITY; 505]

stand out **1** *v* **be obvious**, be prominent, show up, be conspicuous, stick out, be clear, be noticeable, be notable. [➡APPEAR AND EMERGE; 3] **2** *v* **project**, jut, protrude, jut out, stick out, poke out, overhang. [➡ARRIVE; 12]

standpipe *n* **water pipe**, tap, emergency pipe, water supply, hydrant, fire hydrant, faucet (*US*), fireplug (*US*). [➡WATERCOURSES; 1110]

standpoint *n* **point of view**, position, stance, angle, viewpoint, perspective, opinion, outlook, view. [➡POINT OF VIEW; 768]

standstill *n* **halt**, stop, stoppage, full stop, cessation, end, dead end. [➡LACK OF ACTIVITY; 343]

stand the pace *v* [➡TOLERATE AND ENDURE; 767]

stand-up *n* [➡JOKES AND TEASING; 675]

standup **1** *adj* **intense**, fierce, furious, blazing, violent, noisy, aggressive. [➡EMOTIONALLY UNPLEASANT AND UPSETTING; 228] *Opposite:* mild. **2** *adj* **erect**, upright, standing, upstanding, vertical. [➡ORIENTATION AND ALIGNMENT; 1222] *Opposite:* flat. **3** *adj* **solo**, improvised, off-the-cuff. [➡ACTING INDEPENDENTLY; 285] *Opposite:* rehearsed.

stand up **1** *v* **rise**, stand, get to your feet, get up, arise (*archaic or literary*). [➡ASSUME A POSITION; 318] *Opposite:* sit down. **2** *v* **endure**, last, survive, continue, hold out. [➡CONTINUE TO EXIST; 17]

standup comedian *n* [➡WORKERS IN ENTERTAINMENT AND MEDIA; 873]

stand up to *v* **face**, brave, take on, meet head-on, confront, challenge, resist, defy. [➡ACCUSE, BLAME, AND CRITICIZE; 642] *Opposite:* avoid.

stand your ground *v* **stand firm**, persist, persevere, reserve, hold out, hold on, dig in your heels. [➡CLAIM, INSIST, AND EMPHASIZE; 615] *Opposite:* give in.

stanza *n* **verse**, section, stave, couplet, triplet, canto. [➡POETRY AND VERSE; 915]

staphylococcus *type of* **microorganism**. [➡MICROORGANISMS, FUNGI, AND ALGAE; 1023]

staple **1** *n* **clip**, fastener, nail, tack, pin. [➡FASTENERS, LINKS, AND NETWORKS; 1246] **2** *v* **fasten**, affix, clip, attach, secure, fix, nail, pin, tack. [➡FASTEN, LINK, AND JOIN; 409] **3** *adj* **main**, chief, principal, essential, primary, indispensable, basic, fundamental, core, key, prime, vital. [➡FUNDAMENTAL; 196] *Opposite:* minor.

star **1** *v* **feature**, showcase, head the cast, top the bill, play the lead, take the lead. [➡PARTICIPATE; 293] **2** *v* **do well**, excel, shine, succeed, stand out, steal the show. [➡SUCCEED AND WIN; 79] **3** *type of* **angular shape**. [➡ANGULAR SHAPE; 1216]

star

◆ *types of star or star system*
black hole, brown dwarf, constellation, dark star, dwarf star, galaxy, giant star, nebula, nova, pulsar, quasar, red giant, sun, supernova, white dwarf

star attraction *n* [➡AMAZING THING; 212]

star billing *n* **top billing**, star status, top of the bill, main attraction, star turn, big name. [➡THE PERFORMING ARTS; 904]

starboard *adj* **right-hand**, right, right-side. [➡DIRECTION OF MOTION; 346] *Opposite:* port.

starch *type of* **nutrient**. [➡FOOD COMPONENTS; 1187]

starched *adj* [➡UNFRIENDLINESS AND UNSOCIABILITY; 505]

starchiness *n* [➡UNFRIENDLINESS AND UNSOCIABILITY; 505]

starchy *adj* **stiff**, solemn, prudish, prim, austere, stuffy, staid. [➡UNFRIENDLINESS AND UNSOCIABILITY; 505] *Opposite:* relaxed.

star-crossed *adj* **ill-fated**, unlucky, ill-starred (*formal*), doomed, unfortunate. [➡BAD LUCK AND UNLUCKY; 785] *Opposite:* lucky.

stardom *n* **fame**, celebrity, prominence, renown, glory, recognition, eminence. [➡KNOWN AND FAMOUS; 182] *Opposite:* anonymity.

stardust *n* **romance**, dreaminess, sentiment, emotion, feeling, fantasy. [➡NONEXISTENT THINGS; 23]

stare **1** *v* **gaze**, gape, gawk (*informal*), look intently, ogle, rubberneck (*informal*), glare, glower, watch. [➡LOOKING AND LOOKS; 701] *Opposite:* ignore. **2** *n* **intent look**, gaze, gape, gawp (*informal*), glare, glower. [➡FACIAL EXPRESSION; 652]

See Compare and Contrast at **gaze**.

stare down (*US*) *v* [➡LOOKING AND LOOKS; 701]

stare into space *v* [➡LOOKING AND LOOKS; 701]

stare out *v* **outstare**, stare at, look at, gaze at, stare down (*US*). [➡LOOKING AND LOOKS; 701]

starfish *type of* **aquatic invertebrate**. [➡AQUATIC INVERTEBRATE; 1022]

star in *v* **play the lead in**, feature in, act in, play in, head the cast, top the bill. [➡PARTICIPATE; 293]

stark 1 *adj* **bleak**, bare, barren, desolate, austere, severe, harsh. [➡PLAIN; 233] *Opposite:* opulent. 2 *adj* **complete**, utter, absolute, sheer, downright, pure, out-and-out, total. [➡ABSOLUTE AND ABSOLUTELY; 131] *Opposite:* partial. 3 *adj* **plain**, unambiguous, simple, blunt, unadulterated, unadorned, unembellished, blatant, glaring. [➡HONEST AND OPEN; 631] *Opposite:* ambiguous. 4 *adv* **completely**, utterly, entirely, wholly, fully, absolutely, altogether. [➡ABSOLUTE AND ABSOLUTELY; 131] *Opposite:* partially.

starkers (*informal*) *adj* [➡DRESS, WEAR, AND UNDRESS; 868]

stark-naked *adj* [➡DRESS, WEAR, AND UNDRESS; 868]

starkness 1 *n* **austerity**, bleakness, harshness, severity, sparseness, asceticism, abstemiousness, simplicity, bareness. [➡PLAIN; 233] *Opposite:* opulence. 2 *n* **unambiguity**, blatancy, harshness, bluntness, frankness, baldness, plainness, outspokenness. [➡HONEST AND OPEN; 631] *Opposite:* ambiguity.

starlet *n* **actor**, rising young star, new talent, star of tomorrow, star in the making, wannabe (*informal disapproving*), minor actor, unknown, ingénue. [➡PERFORMERS; 905]

starlight *n* **glow**, gleam, sheen, twinkle, sparkle, glint, glitter, flicker, moonlight, light. [➡LIGHT; 1163]

starling *type of* **common bird.** [➡BIRD; 997]

starlit *adj* **starry**, bright, glowing, gleaming, twinkling, sparkling, glinting, glittering, flickering, moonlit. [➡DESCRIBING LIGHT; 1227] *Opposite:* dark.

starry *adj* **glittery**, shiny, bright, sparkly, brilliant, shining, sparkling, twinkling, lustrous, spangled. [➡DESCRIBING LIGHT; 1227] *Opposite:* dull.

starry-eyed *adj* **dreamy**, optimistic, idealistic, head-in-the-clouds, happy. [➡PLEASURE, EXCITEMENT, AND ELATION; 535] *Opposite:* cynical.

starship *n* **spaceship**, space shuttle, space station, flying saucer. [➡SCIENCE FICTION; 1063]

star sign *n* **sign of the zodiac**, birth sign, sun sign, sign, constellation, house. [➡FATE, DESTINY, AND ASTROLOGY; 783]

star sign

◆ *types of star sign*
Aquarius, Aries, Cancer, Capricorn, Gemini, Leo, Libra, Pisces, Sagittarius, Scorpio, Taurus, Virgo

star-spangled *adj* [➡DESCRIBING PATTERNS; 1226]

star-studded *adj* **star-spangled**, starry, all-star, stellar, celebrity, big-name, glittering, glamorous, glitzy. [➡THE PERFORMING ARTS; 904] *Opposite:* unknown.

star system *n* **constellation**, galaxy, Milky Way, solar system. [➡THE SOLAR SYSTEM AND ASTRONOMY; 1059]

start 1 *v* **begin**, commence (*formal*), start off, get going, set off, open, kick off (*informal*), get under way, switch on, fire up. [➡START AN ACTION; 261] *Opposite:* finish. 2 *v* **create**, found, begin, establish, set up, initiate, institute, launch, pioneer, inaugurate, father. [➡INSTITUTE AND INAUGURATE; 349] 3 *v* **set out**, leave, set off, depart, get going, be on your way, be off, start off, take off, start out. [➡ABSENT ONESELF; 8] *Opposite:* arrive. 4 *v* **jump**, recoil, flinch, shrink, twitch, jerk. [➡PHYSICAL REACTIONS; 317] 5 *n* **beginning**, birth, foundation, onset, dawn, opening, outset, inception (*formal*), initiation, commencement (*formal*). [➡BEGINNING; 53] 6 *n* **lead**, advantage, edge, boon, plus (*informal*), gain, head start. [➡ADVANTAGE; 213] 7 *n* **twitch**, jump, jerk, flinch, jolt. [➡PHYSICAL REACTIONS; 317] 8 *n* **shock**, fright, surprise, turn. [➡SURPRISE, SHOCK, AND AMAZEMENT; 546]

start afresh *v* [➡RECOMMENCE AND RESUME; 269]

start again *v* [➡RECOMMENCE AND RESUME; 269]

start anew *v* [➡RECOMMENCE AND RESUME; 269]

starter 1 *n* **hors d'oeuvre**, first course, appetizer, meze, tapas, antipasto. [➡MEALS AND PARTS OF MEALS; 1168] 2 *part of* **engine.** [➡PARTS OF AN ENGINE; 1143]

starting point 1 *n* **basis**, base, foundation, point of departure, beginning, start, origin, kickoff (*informal*), square one. [➡BEGINNING; 53] 2 *n* **starting line**, starting block, starting grid, starting post, starting gate. [➡SPORTS TERMS; 877] *Opposite:* finishing line.

startle *v* **surprise**, disconcert, shock, alarm, frighten, amaze, astound, scare, astonish, disturb, disquiet (*archaic or literary*). [➡SURPRISE AND IMPRESS; 575]

startled *adj* **surprised**, disconcerted, alarmed, astonished, amazed, frightened, shocked, stunned, scared. [➡SURPRISE, SHOCK, AND AMAZEMENT; 546]

startling *adj* **surprising**, astonishing, amazing, astounding, staggering, shocking, upsetting, disquieting. [➡EXTRAORDINARY: AMAZING; 205] *Opposite:* comforting.

start off 1 *v* **begin**, commence (*formal*), get going, start out, start, make a start, kick off (*informal*). [➡START AN ACTION; 261] *Opposite:* finish. 2 *v* **set off**, set in motion, start out, be off, get going, start, take off, be on your way. [➡ABSENT ONESELF; 8] *Opposite:* arrive.

start on 1 *v* **begin**, tackle, deal with, embark on, get going on, get underway, make a start on, attack. [➡START AN ACTION; 261] *Opposite:* finish. 2 *v* (*informal*) **scold**, tell off (*informal*), tick off (*informal*), harass, pester, nag, annoy. [➡ACCUSE, BLAME, AND CRITICIZE; 642]

start out 1 *v* **start off**, start, begin, set off, set forth (*literary*), get going, set out, take off, be on your way, be off. [➡ABSENT ONESELF; 8] *Opposite:* arrive. 2 *v* **intend**, mean, plan, propose, expect, undertake. [➡START AN ACTION; 261]

start over (*US*) *v* [➡RECOMMENCE AND RESUME; 269]

start the ball rolling *v* [➡CAUSE TO START; 266]

start up 1 *v* **switch on**, turn on, fire up, power up, ignite, activate, get going, wind up (*informal*). [➡USE TOOLS AND MACHINERY; 469] *Opposite:* turn off. 2 *v* **set up**, open, begin, launch, create, initiate, inaugurate, bring into being, install, introduce. [➡INSTITUTE AND INAUGURATE; 349] *Opposite:* close down. 3 *v* **pipe up**, resound, be heard, begin, start, commence (*formal*). [➡INTERRUPT AND BUTT IN; 620] *Opposite:* quieten down.

4 *v* **leap up**, jump up, stand up, get up, rise, arise (*archaic or literary*), stir, start. [➡GO UPWARDS; 307] *Opposite:* sit down.

startup 1 *n* [➡BEGINNING; 53] **2** *n* [➡E-COMMERCE; 1128]

start up again *v* [➡HAPPEN AGAIN; 28]

star turn *n* **main attraction**, star attraction, big name, top of the bill, top act, headliner (*US*). [➡PERFORMERS; 905]

starvation *n* **hunger**, malnourishment, undernourishment, famishment, famine, food shortage. [➡EAT AND NOT EAT; 711]

starve *v* **have nothing to eat**, go hungry, famish, be malnourished, go short of food, waste away, be hungry, waste with hunger. [➡EAT AND NOT EAT; 711] *Opposite:* eat.

starved 1 *adj* (*informal*) **ravenous**, hungry, famished, starving (*informal*). [➡EAT AND NOT EAT; 711] *Opposite:* replete. **2** *adj* **deprived**, bereft, devoid, lacking, without. [➡LACK OF POSSESSION; 446]

starved of *adj* [➡LACK OF POSSESSION; 446]

starving (*informal*) *adj* **ravenous**, hungry, famished, starved (*informal*). [➡EAT AND NOT EAT; 711] *Opposite:* replete.

stash 1 *n* **supply**, hideaway, hoard, mass, pile, stockpile, stack, reserve, heap, store. [➡MANY, MUCH, LARGE AMOUNT; 117] **2** *v* (*informal*) **hide**, hoard, put away, put by, stockpile, salt away, secrete, squirrel, store. [➡STORE AND KEEP; 454]

stash away *v* [➡STORE AND KEEP; 454]

stasis *n* **stability**, motionlessness, status quo, continuity, inertia, stillness, immobility, lack of change, balance, equilibrium. [➡LACK OF ACTIVITY; 343] *Opposite:* change.

state 1 *n* **condition**, situation, position, status, circumstances, shape. [➡STATE; 1207] **2** *n* (*informal*) **confusion**, turmoil, disarray, disorder, chaos, mess. [➡DIFFICULT SITUATIONS; 72] **3** *n* **federation**, kingdom, nation, land, territory, country. [➡COUNTRIES AND REGIONS; 1066] **4** *n* **grandeur**, ceremony, pomp, splendour, glory, dignity, majesty, magnificence. [➡ROYALNESS; 825] **5** *adj* **public**, government, municipal, state-run, state-owned, national. [➡GOVERNMENT AND POLITICS; 805] **6** *adj* **formal**, official, stately, imperial, royal, majestic, ceremonial. [➡ROYALNESS; 825] **7** *v* **utter**, affirm, declare, assert, aver (*formal*), express, maintain, say, testify, avow (*formal*). [➡INFORM AND ANNOUNCE; 612]

statecraft *n* **government**, management, governance, administration, direction, control, statesmanship, diplomacy. [➡GOVERNMENT AND POLITICS; 805]

stateless *adj* **homeless**, nationless, displaced, refugee, outlawed, exiled, deported, asylum-seeking, expatriate. [➡NOMADIC AND ROOTLESS LIFESTYLES; 884]

state line (*US*) *n* **border**, border line, frontier, boundary. [➡GEOGRAPHICAL BORDERS AND BOUNDARIES; 1068]

stateliness *n* **grandeur**, pomp, glory, dignity, majesty, splendour, formality, magnificence. [➡ROYALNESS; 825]

stately *adj* **grand**, splendid, dignified, imperial, majestic, noble, regal, gracious, august (*formal*), distinguished, imposing. [➡ROYALNESS; 825] *Opposite:* modest.

stately home *n* **mansion**, manor, hall, country house, great house, pile, family seat, palace, castle, chateau. [➡RESIDENTIAL BUILDINGS; 1077]

statement 1 *n* **declaration**, announcement, report, account, speech, proclamation, assertion, avowal (*formal*), testimony, testimonial. [➡INFORM AND ANNOUNCE; 612] **2** *n* **record**, account, report, receipt, invoice. [➡RECORDS; 586]

state of affairs *n* **situation**, set of circumstances, condition, setup, position, state of play, setting, picture. [➡SITUATIONS; 71]

state of emergency *n* [➡DIFFICULT SITUATIONS; 72]

state of grace *n* [➡PLEASANT SITUATIONS; 74]

state of mind *n* **mood**, temper, attitude, feelings, spirits, disposition, mentality. [➡PSYCHOLOGY AND THE MIND; 770]

state of play *n* [➡SITUATIONS; 71]

state-of-the-art *adj* **advanced**, high-tech, up-to-the-minute, up-to-date, contemporary, modern, ultramodern. [➡DESCRIBING TECHNOLOGY; 1159] *Opposite:* antiquated.

state of things *n* [➡SITUATIONS; 71]

state of undress *n* [➡DRESS, WEAR, AND UNDRESS; 868]

state-owned *adj* **public**, public-sector, state, state-run, nationalized, government, publicly owned, national, municipal. [➡BELONGING OR RELATING TO PEOPLE; 943] *Opposite:* private.

stateroom 1 *n* **first-class compartment**, first-class cabin, sleeping compartment, berth, sleeper. [➡TYPES OF ROOM; 1096] **2** *part of* **ship or boat.** [➡PARTS OF A SHIP OR BOAT; 1150]

state school 1 *n* (*US informal*) **reformatory**, juvenile institution, penal institution, prison. [➡BUILDINGS FOR CONFINING PEOPLE; 1093] **2** *type of* **school.** [➡EDUCATIONAL INSTITUTIONS; 813]

state secret *n* **confidential matter**, affair of state, top-secret matter, confidential information, classified material. [➡SECRETS AND MYSTERIES; 181]

static 1 *adj* **still**, motionless, stationary, inert, standing, stagnant, immobile, inactive, fixed, unmoving. [➡LACK OF ACTIVITY; 343] *Opposite:* moving. **2** *adj* **unchanging**, constant, invariable, unvarying. [➡PERMANENCE: WITHOUT CHANGE; 95] *Opposite:* dynamic.

station 1 *n* **position**, place, post, location, situation. [➡PLACE; 1064] **2** *n* **rank**, class, status, position, level, standing. [➡STATUS; 888] **3** *v* **post**, base, position, place, situate (*formal*), locate. [➡POSITION SOMETHING; 326]

stationary *adj* **motionless**, still, immobile, inactive, fixed, at a stop, at a standstill, at a halt, standing, unmoving, static, inert. [➡LACK OF ACTIVITY; 343] *Opposite:* moving.

stationery *n* **writing materials**, writing implements, pen and paper, writing paper, notepaper, notebook, notepad, envelopes, pencils. [➡WRITING AND DRAWING IMPLEMENTS, AND MEDIA; 602]

station wagon (*US*) *type of* **car.** [➡BIKES, CARS, AND CARRIAGES; 1148]

statistic *n* **number**, figure, digit, piece of data, measurement, indicator, fact, value. [➡MATHS; 598]

statistics *n* **figures**, data, numbers, information. [➡BASIC DETAILS; 689]

statoscope *type of* **measuring device**. [➡MEASURING DEVICES; 1122]

statuary *n* **sculptures**, statues, figures, monuments, busts, effigies, statuettes, figurines, heads, bronzes. [➡SCULPTURE; 902]

statue *n* **figurine**, figure, sculpture, statuette, effigy, bust, head, bronze, image, model, icon. [➡SCULPTURE; 902]

statuesque *adj* **stately**, elegant, graceful, majestic, dignified, poised, grand, well-proportioned. [➡BUILD; 478] *Opposite:* ungainly.

statuette *n* **figurine**, sculpture, statue, figure, model, bust, head, bronze, carving. [➡SCULPTURE; 902]

stature 1 *n* **build**, height, physique, figure, tallness, size. [➡BUILD; 478] 2 *n* **standing**, importance, prominence, status, rank, reputation, distinction, eminence. [➡STATUS; 888]

status 1 *n* **rank**, position, standing, grade, station. [➡STATUS; 888] 2 *n* **eminence**, prestige, prominence, importance, significance, repute (*formal*), reputation. [➡IMPORTANCE AND SIGNIFICANCE; 193] 3 *n* **category**, condition, class, type, stage, level. [➡VARIETY, TYPE, KIND; 146]

status quo *n* **current situation**, existing state of affairs, present circumstances, how things stand. [➡SITUATIONS; 71]

status symbol *n* **asset**, must-have, prize possession. [➡POSSESSIONS; 462]

statute *n* **decree**, act, ruling, edict, order, law, bill. [➡THE LAW AND LEGAL AUTHORITY; 814]

statute book *n* **body of law**, record, legislation, legal code, law book. [➡THE LAW AND LEGAL AUTHORITY; 814]

statute law *n* **written law**, law, constitution, legislation, acts of Congress (*US*). [➡THE LAW AND LEGAL AUTHORITY; 814]

statutory *adj* **constitutional**, legislative, legal. [➡LEGAL; 815]

staunch 1 *v* **stop**, stem, halt, hold back, curb, curtail, hinder, restrict, lessen, decrease, slow, cut off, check, reduce. [➡CAUSE TO STOP; 267] 2 *adj* **loyal**, faithful, steadfast, reliable, dependable, constant, firm, devoted, unfaltering, unwavering, resolute, committed, stalwart. [➡HARD-WORKING AND COMMITTED; 501] *Opposite:* wavering.

stave 1 *n* **plank**, slat, board, lath, band, strip, piece, wood. [➡BUILDING MATERIALS; 1076] 2 *n* **bar**, rung, tread, step, crosspiece, crossbar, foothold. [➡SUPPORTS AND BASES; 1254] 3 *n* **stanza**, verse, section, couplet, triplet, canto. [➡POETRY AND VERSE; 915]

stave in *v* [➡CHANGE OF SHAPE; 386]

stave off *v* **fend off**, keep at bay, hold off, delay, deflect, hinder, avoid, repel, hold back, ward off. [➡DELAY ACTION OR OCCURRENCE; 279]

stay 1 *v* **remain**, wait, hang about, continue, keep on, hang around. [➡CONTINUE TO EXIST; 17] *Opposite:* go. 2 *v* **reside**, live, dwell (*literary*), inhabit, settle, lodge (*dated*). [➡INHABIT; 20] 3 *v* **stop**, halt, delay, defer, put off, postpone, adjourn. [➡DELAY ACTION OR OCCURRENCE; 279] 4 *n* **visit**, break, holiday, sojourn (*literary*), stopover, vacation. [➡PERIOD OF REST; 91] 5 *n* **halt**, stop, delay, deferment, adjournment, postponement. [➡PAUSES AND PHASES; 56]

stayer *n* [➡PEOPLE WHO ARE APPROVED OF; 955]

staying power *n* **stamina**, endurance, determination, doggedness, vigour, energy, resilience, resistance, strength, fortitude, grit. [➡STRENGTH OF WILL; 502] *Opposite:* frailty.

stay on *v* **remain**, stay, stay put, stay behind, stay out, wait, linger, settle, settle down. [➡CONTINUE AN ACTION; 263] *Opposite:* leave.

stay out *v* **stop out** (*informal*), stay on, keep out, be out, stay behind, stay put, stay, remain, make a night of it. [➡CONTINUE AN ACTION; 263]

stay put *v* **remain**, stay, sit tight (*informal*), abide (*archaic*), stay still, tarry, hang on, wait. [➡LACK OF ACTIVITY; 343] *Opposite:* move.

stay still *v* [➡LACK OF ACTIVITY; 343]

stay the course *v* [➡TOLERATE AND ENDURE; 767]

stay up *v* **stop up**, burn the candle at both ends, stay up till all hours, burn the midnight oil, maintain a vigil, make a night of it. [➡CONTINUE AN ACTION; 263]

steadfast 1 *adj* **unwavering**, unfaltering, resolute, committed, dedicated, unswerving, persistent, firm. [➡HARD-WORKING AND COMMITTED; 501] *Opposite:* wavering. 2 *adj* **loyal**, trusty, dependable, faithful, trustworthy, devoted, stalwart, reliable, constant. *Opposite:* inconstant. (*literary*). [➡HONEST AND RELIABLE; 503]

steadfastness 1 *n* **resoluteness**, commitment, dedication, persistence, determination. [➡HARD-WORKING AND COMMITTED; 501] *Opposite:* wavering. 2 *n* **loyalty**, faithfulness, trustworthiness, devotion, dependability. [➡HONEST AND RELIABLE; 503] *Opposite:* disloyalty.

steadily *adv* **progressively**, gradually, increasingly, little by little, bit by bit, inch by inch. [➡HAPPENING SLOWLY; 106] *Opposite:* suddenly.

steadiness 1 *n* **control**, stability, firmness, balance, equilibrium. [➡HARMONY; 156] *Opposite:* unsteadiness. 2 *n* **calmness**, composure, equanimity, serenity, reliability, dependability, self-possession, control. [➡CONFIDENCE AND COMPOSURE; 500] *Opposite:* excitability.

steady 1 *adj* **stable**, firm, fixed, solid, sturdy, sound, secure, balanced. [➡SAFE AND SAFETY; 192] *Opposite:* rickety. 2 *adj* **continual**, constant, perpetual, never-ending, ceaseless, relentless, unbroken, continuous, unremitting. [➡PERMANENCE: WITHOUT END; 94] *Opposite:* intermittent. 3 *adj* **even**, regular, uniform, unchanging, unvarying, constant. [➡PERMANENCE: WITHOUT CHANGE; 95] *Opposite:* irregular. 4 *adj* **calm**, cool, collected, composed, unruffled, unexcitable. [➡CONFIDENCE AND COMPOSURE; 500] *Opposite:* excitable. 5 *v* **stabilize**, secure, fix, support, strengthen. [➡IMPROVE STRENGTH AND DURABILITY; 379] *Opposite:* undermine.

steak *type of* **cut**. [➡TYPES AND CUTS OF MEAT; 1176]

steakhouse *type of* **eating place**. [➡HOTELS, RESTAURANTS, AND CLUBS; 1081]

steak knife *type of* **cutlery.** [➡ TABLEWARE, CUTLERY, AND KITCHENWARE; 861]

steak pie *n* [➡ PREPARED DISHES; 1169]

steal 1 *v* **pinch** (*informal*), nick (*slang*), whip (*informal*), pilfer, filch (*informal*), misappropriate, appropriate, embezzle, pocket, purloin (*formal*), thieve, rob, take, lift (*informal*). [➡ STEAL AND ROB; 427] *Opposite:* return. 2 *v* **creep**, sneak, slip, slink, tiptoe, slope. [➡ MOVE SLOWLY; 315] 3 *n* (*informal*) **bargain**, snip (*informal*), giveaway (*informal*), good deal, good buy. *Opposite:* rip-off. (*informal*). [➡ ECONOMICAL AND RESOURCEFUL; 208]

Compare and Contrast: ***steal, pinch, nick, filch, purloin, pilfer, embezzle, misappropriate***

CORE MEANING: THE TAKING OF PROPERTY UNLAWFULLY

steal to take something that belongs to somebody else, illegally or without the owner's permission; ***pinch*** (*informal*) to steal something; ***nick*** (*slang*) to steal something; ***filch*** (*informal*) to steal something furtively and opportunistically, usually a small item or something of little value; ***purloin*** (*formal*) to steal something, sometimes used humorously or euphemistically; ***pilfer*** to steal small items of little value, especially habitually; ***embezzle*** to take for personal use money or property that has been given on trust by others, without their knowledge; ***misappropriate*** to take something, especially money, dishonestly or in order to use it for an improper or illegal purpose.

steal a look *v* [➡ LOOKING AND LOOKS; 701]

steal away *v* [➡ RUN AWAY AND AVOID; 10]

stealing *n* **theft**, robbery, burglary, larceny (*dated*), thieving, pilfering, shoplifting, pinching (*informal*), nicking (*slang*), pocketing, embezzlement, appropriation. [➡ CRIMES; 817]

stealth *n* **furtiveness**, surreptitiousness, sneakiness, slyness, craftiness, secrecy, covertness. [➡ SECRET AND UNKNOWN; 180] *Opposite:* openness.

stealth bomber *type of* **military aircraft.** [➡ AIRCRAFT; 1147]

stealthy *adj* **furtive**, surreptitious, sly, silent, cautious, sneaky, crafty, secret, covert, clandestine, quiet. [➡ SECRET AND UNKNOWN; 180] *Opposite:* blatant.

See Compare and Contrast at **secret**.

steam *n* **vapour**, condensation, haze, mist, fog. [➡ GASES; 1274]

steamboat *type of* **motor vessel.** [➡ SHIPS AND BOATS; 1149]

steam engine 1 *part of* **train.** [➡ RAILWAYS; 1106] 2 *type of* **rail vehicle.** [➡ RAILWAYS; 1106]

steamer *type of* **motor vessel.** [➡ SHIPS AND BOATS; 1149]

steamroll *see* **steamroller.**

steamroller 1 *v* **compress**, bulldoze, flatten, crush, squash, trample, demolish, roll over, drive over. [➡ CHANGE OF SHAPE; 386] 2 *v* **crush**, squash, demolish, destroy, overwhelm, dismiss, smash. [➡ DENY AND REJECT; 645] 3 *v* **force**, compel, coerce, bludgeon, bully, intimidate, drive. [➡ CAUSE OR COMPEL TO ACT; 272] 4 *type of* **commercial or industrial vehicle.** [➡ VEHICLES; 1144]

steam up *v* **mist up**, fog up, cloud, cloud over, mist over. [➡ SOFTEN, LIQUEFY, DAMPEN; 389]

steamy 1 *adj* **humid**, muggy, damp, sticky, hot and sticky, clammy, stifling, moist. [➡ HOT WEATHER; 1050] 2 *adj* **misted up**, misty, fogged up, foggy, steamed up, cloudy, clouded. [➡ VISUAL TEXTURE; 1220] *Opposite:* clear.

steed (*literary*) *n* **horse**, pony, mount, charger. [➡ HORSE; 985]

steel 1 *v* **strengthen**, toughen, harden, fortify, brace. [➡ PREPARE FOR ACTION; 290] 2 *type of* **metal.** [➡ METALS; 1275]

steel band *type of* **band.** [➡ MUSICIANS AND SINGERS; 908]

steel blue *type of* **blue.** [➡ COLOURS; 1223]

steel drum *type of* **percussion instrument.** [➡ MUSICAL INSTRUMENTS; 910]

steel grey *type of* **grey.** [➡ COLOURS; 1223]

steel guitar *type of* **stringed instrument.** [➡ MUSICAL INSTRUMENTS; 910]

steelworks *type of* **industrial site.** [➡ INDUSTRIAL BUILDINGS; 1086]

steely 1 *adj* **hard**, strong, tough, sturdy, rugged. [➡ STRENGTH; 202] *Opposite:* soft. 2 *adj* **determined**, resolute, unyielding, unbending, rigid, firm, unwavering. [➡ STRENGTH OF WILL; 502] *Opposite:* irresolute.

steel yourself *v* **brace yourself**, harden your heart, pluck up your courage, prepare yourself, compose yourself, get ready. [➡ PREPARE FOR ACTION; 290]

steep 1 *adj* (*informal*) **unreasonable**, extreme, excessive, expensive, dear, exorbitant, extortionate. [➡ EXPENSIVE AND OVERPRICED; 248] *Opposite:* reasonable. 2 *adj* **sheer**, vertical, sharp, precipitous, abrupt, sudden. [➡ ORIENTATION AND ALIGNMENT; 1222] *Opposite:* gentle. 3 *v* **soak**, immerse, drench, submerge, suffuse, saturate, marinate, stand. [➡ SOFTEN, LIQUEFY, DAMPEN; 389] 4 *v* **imbue**, permeate, infuse. [➡ FILL; 407]

steeped *adj* [➡ WET; 1239]

steeple *n* **tower**, spire, turret, bell tower, belfry, campanile. [➡ PARTS OF RELIGIOUS BUILDINGS; 1085]

steeplechase 1 *n* **point-to-point**, horse race, stake race (*US*). [➡ NON-AGGRESSIVE/SPORTING EVENT; 40] 2 *n* **hurdles**, footrace, flat race, track race, track event, sprint. [➡ NON-AGGRESSIVE/SPORTING EVENT; 40] 3 *type of* **track and field.** [➡ HOBBIES, GAMES, AND SPORTS; 875]

steeplechaser *n* [➡ PEOPLE IN SPORTS AND LEISURE; 876]

steeply *adv* **sharply**, precipitously, abruptly, suddenly. [➡ ORIENTATION AND ALIGNMENT; 1222] *Opposite:* gently.

steepness *n* **sharpness**, abruptness, gradient, sheerness. [➡ ORIENTATION AND ALIGNMENT; 1222] *Opposite:* gentleness.

steer 1 *v* **control**, drive, pilot, navigate, manoeuvre. [➡ TRAVEL: WAYS OF TRAVELLING; 321] 2 *v* **direct**, guide, point, conduct, lead. [➡ACCOMPANY AND FOLLOW; 338] **3** *type of* **male animal.** [➡MALE OR FEMALE ANIMAL; 978]

See Compare and Contrast at **guide.**

steerage *n* **third class**, bottom deck, tourist class, lower deck. [➡TRANSPORTATION, TRANSPORTERS, AND CARGOS; 323]

steering committee *n* **steering group**, board, panel, team, commission, council, committee. [➡INSTITUTIONS; 791]

steering wheel *type of* **controls.** [➡VEHICLES; 1144]

stegosaur *type of* **dinosaur.** [➡DINOSAUR; 996]

stein *n* [➡CONTAINERS, RECEPTACLES, AND PACKAGING; 1244]

stellar 1 *adj* **astral**, astronomical, astrophysical, solar, planetary, cosmological. [➡THE SOLAR SYSTEM AND ASTRONOMY; 1059] *Opposite:* earthly. **2** *adj* **all-star**, star-studded, star-spangled, starry, celebrity, big-name, glittering, glamorous, glitzy. [➡THE PERFORMING ARTS; 904] *Opposite:* unknown.

stem 1 *n* **stalk**, shoot, trunk, twig, branch. [➡STICKS, POLES, AND WEDGES; 1253] **2** *v* **stop**, staunch, halt, curtail, restrict, slow, lessen, decrease, cut off, curb, hinder, hold back, stanch, reduce, check. [➡AVOID, PREVENT, LIMIT, AND CONTROL; 278] *Opposite:* accelerate.

stem from *v* **arise from**, originate from, come from, derive from, develop from, spring from, be a result of, be caused by. [➡CAUSATION; 169]

stench *n* **stink**, reek, pong (*informal*), unpleasant smell, disgusting odour. [➡SMELL AND SMELLING; 706] *Opposite:* perfume.

See Compare and Contrast at **smell.**

stencil 1 *n* **template**, cutout, guide, plate, pattern, model, shape, outline. [➡ARTWORKS; 898] **2** *n* **pattern**, design, lettering, motif, border, frieze, decoration, ornament. [➡ORNAMENTS AND DECORATIONS; 1247] **3** *v* **decorate**, adorn, paint, ornament. [➡DECORATE, ADORN, AND APPLY COATINGS; 406] **4** *v* **apply**, paint, work, draw, trace. [➡CREATE IMAGES; 357]

stentor *type of* **microorganism.** [➡MICROORGANISMS, FUNGI, AND ALGAE; 1023]

stentorian *adj* **loud**, powerful, booming, thunderous, deafening, earsplitting, roaring. [➡LOUD OR UNPLEASANT SOUNDS; 1265] *Opposite:* quiet.

step 1 *n* **pace**, footstep, stride. [➡PROCEED AND GO; 306] **2** *n* **move**, movement, action, measure. [➡ACTIONS OR UNDERTAKINGS; 260] **3** *n* **stage**, phase, period. [➡PAUSES AND PHASES; 56] **4** *n* **stair**, rung, tread. [➡STAIRS AND STOREYS; 1101] **5** *v* **walk**, tread, march, pace, move, stride. [➡PROCEED AND GO; 306]

step aerobics *n* **leisure**, exercise, keep fit, workout, training, gymnastics, aerobics. [➡HOBBIES, GAMES, AND SPORTS; 875]

stepbrother *type of* **same generation relative.** [➡SAME GENERATION RELATIVES; 957]

step by step *adv* **gradually**, bit by bit, little by little, piece by piece, a bit at a time, a step at a time, inch by inch, stage by stage, slowly but surely, progressively. [➡HAPPENING SLOWLY; 106] *Opposite:* all at once.

stepchild *type of* **younger relative.** [➡YOUNGER GENERATION RELATIVES; 958]

stepdaughter *type of* **younger relative//younger relative.** [➡YOUNGER GENERATION RELATIVES; 958]

step down 1 *v* **stand down**, resign, retire, bow out, withdraw, quit, call it a day, give up, go, stand aside. [➡STOP ACTING; 265] *Opposite:* stay on. **2** *v* **decrease**, reduce, lower, lessen, restrict, drop, phase out, tail off, whittle down, shorten. [➡CHANGE OF INTENSITY: LESS; 396] *Opposite:* step up.

stepfather *type of* **older relative.** [➡OLDER GENERATION RELATIVES; 959]

step in *v* **intervene**, intercede, interpose, interrupt, get involved, mediate. [➡INTERRUPT AND BUTT IN; 620]

stepladder *n* **ladder**, steps, portable ladder, folding ladder, stairs. [➡SUPPORTS AND BASES; 1254]

stepmother *type of* **older relative.** [➡OLDER GENERATION RELATIVES; 959]

step on it (*slang*) *v* **drive fast**, put your foot down, accelerate, hurry, hit the gas (*US*), floor it (*US slang*). [➡CHANGE OF SPEED: MORE; 397]

step on the gas (*US*) *v* [➡CHANGE OF SPEED: MORE; 397]

step out 1 *v* **go out**, step outside, pop out (*informal*), nip out, leave, absent yourself. [➡ABSENT ONESELF; 8] *Opposite:* stay put. **2** *v* **march**, tear along, rush, stride, dash, zoom, speed up, jog, leg it (*informal*), stomp, hightail it (*slang*). [➡MOVE FAST; 314] *Opposite:* crawl.

stepparent *type of* **older relative.** [➡OLDER GENERATION RELATIVES; 959]

steppe *n* **prairie**, grassland, plain, savanna, pampas. [➡DESERTS AND PLAINS; 1045]

stepping stone 1 *n* **stone**, boulder, rock, foothold, bridge. [➡SUPPORTS AND BASES; 1254] **2** *n* **stage**, step, means of access, stage of progress, stage of advancement, springboard, contact, way in. [➡ADVANTAGE; 213]

stepsister *type of* **same generation relative.** [➡SAME GENERATION RELATIVES; 957]

stepson *type of* **younger relative.** [➡YOUNGER GENERATION RELATIVES; 958]

step up *v* **increase**, intensify, improve, maximize, accelerate, boost. [➡CHANGE OF INTENSITY: MORE; 395] *Opposite:* lower.

stereo 1 *n* [➡ACOUSTICS; 1137] **2** *type of* **audio equipment.** [➡AUDIO EQUIPMENT; 1138]

stereophonic *adj* **stereo**, audio, binaural, hi-fi, high-fidelity. [➡ACOUSTICS; 1137]

stereo system *type of* **audio equipment.** [➡AUDIO EQUIPMENT; 1138]

stereotype *v* **typecast**, label, pigeonhole, categorize, cast, fix. [➡NAME AND DESCRIBE; 666]

stereotypical *adj* **conventional**, orthodox, formulaic, banal, hackneyed, clichéd, trite. [➡SAMENESS; 151] *Opposite:* original.

sterile 1 *adj* **germ-free**, disinfected, antiseptic, sterilized, spotlessly clean, hygienic, sanitary. [➡CLEAN; 1232] *Opposite:* dirty. 2 *adj* **barren**, childless, unfruitful, fruitless, unproductive, infertile, bare. [➡REPRODUCTION AND HEREDITY; 726]

sterility 1 *n* **barrenness**, unfruitfulness, unproductiveness, desolation, bareness. [➡REDUNDANT AND USELESS; 241] *Opposite:* fruitfulness. 2 *n* **infertility**, barrenness, childlessness, subfertility, unproductiveness, impotence. [➡REPRODUCTION AND HEREDITY; 726] *Opposite:* fertility. 3 *n* **cleanness**, antisepsis, disinfection, decontamination, purity. [➡CLEAN; 1232] *Opposite:* contamination. 4 *n* **dullness**, uncreativeness, unimaginativeness, lack of imagination, lack of creativity, banality. [➡BORING AND UNINTERESTING; 235] *Opposite:* imaginativeness.

sterilization 1 *n* **purification**, cleansing, disinfection, fumigation, decontamination, pasteurization. [➡CLEAN AND POLISH; 404] 2 *n* **neutering**, vasectomy, hysterectomy, castration, gelding, spaying. [➡STERILIZE; 727]

sterilize 1 *v* **disinfect**, bleach, make germ-free, fumigate, sanitize, purify, clean thoroughly. [➡CLEAN AND POLISH; 404] 2 *v* **neuter**, spay, geld, castrate. [➡STERILIZE; 727]

sterilized *adj* [➡CLEAN; 1232]

sterilizer *n* **disinfectant**, germicide, antiseptic, bactericide, sanitizer, purifier, cleaning agent. [➡CLEANING AGENTS; 863]

sterling 1 *adj* **genuine**, authentic, true, pure, real. [➡TRUE AND REAL; 172] *Opposite:* spurious. 2 *adj* **excellent**, exceptional, matchless, incomparable, worthy, first-rate. [➡GOOD, WELL, BETTER; 184] *Opposite:* mediocre.

stern 1 *adj* **strict**, harsh, severe, austere, unsympathetic, unyielding, uncompromising, hardhearted, firm. [➡DIFFICULT TO PLEASE; 516] *Opposite:* easygoing. 2 *adj* **grim**, forbidding, formidable, dour, serious, sombre, grave, unsmiling, humourless. [➡BAD-TEMPERED AND HUMOURLESS; 627] *Opposite:* cheerful. 3 *part of* **ship or boat.** [➡PARTS OF A SHIP OR BOAT; 1150]

sternness 1 *n* **severity**, strictness, harshness, firmness, austerity. [➡DIFFICULT TO PLEASE; 516] *Opposite:* leniency. 2 *n* **grimness**, seriousness, sombreness, gravity, humourlessness. [➡BAD-TEMPERED AND HUMOURLESS; 627] *Opposite:* cheerfulness.

sternum *type of* **bone.** [➡THE BONES AND JOINTS; 720]

stet *v* **let it stand**, restore, retain, undo, ignore, undelete, override. [➡FOREIGN WORDS AND PHRASES; 673] *Opposite:* delete.

stethoscope *type of* **medical instrument.** [➡HAND TOOLS; 1118]

stew 1 *n* (*informal*) **difficult situation**, state (*informal*), flap (*informal*), tizzy (*informal*), lather (*informal*), fix (*informal*). [➡DIFFICULT SITUATIONS; 72] 2 *v* **simmer**, boil slowly, braise, casserole, parboil, poach, cook slowly. [➡COOKING AND FOOD PREPARATION; 354] 3 *v* **be upset**, be troubled, be agitated, worry, trouble, fret, fuss. [➡GIVING VENT TO EMOTIONS; 680]

stewed 1 *adj* [➡STATE OF PREPARED FOOD; 1170] 2 *adj* (*slang*) **drunk**, plastered (*informal*), smashed (*informal*), under the influence (*informal*), inebriated (*formal*), intoxicated (*formal*). [➡UNDER THE INFLUENCE OF DRUGS OR ALCOHOL; 742]

stick 1 *n* **twig**, cane, baton, rod, staff, switch, pole, branch. [➡STICKS, POLES, AND WEDGES; 1253] 2 *v* **attach**, glue, fix, fasten, join, fuse, gum, paste, affix, weld, bond. [➡FASTEN, LINK, AND JOIN; 409] *Opposite:* detach. 3 *v* (*informal*) **put**, lay, place, set, deposit, plonk, plunk. [➡POSITION SOMETHING; 326] 4 *v* (*informal*) **push**, put, thrust, shove, poke. [➡POSITION SOMETHING; 326] *Opposite:* withdraw. 5 *v* **spear**, stab, penetrate, pierce, spike, gore, run through (*literary*), jab (*informal*). [➡STAB; 417]

stick around (*informal*) 1 *v* **linger**, wait, stay, remain, hang about, hang around, hang out (*informal*). [➡EXIST IN A PLACE; 19] *Opposite:* leave. 2 *v* **stay with**, hang around, hang around with, hang out with (*informal*), remain with, be associated with. [➡ESTABLISHING RELATIONSHIPS WITH OTHERS; 974] *Opposite:* leave.

stick at *v* **persist at**, continue with, persist, persevere with, see through, stay with, continue, stick with, persevere. [➡CONTINUE AN ACTION; 263] *Opposite:* give up.

stick by *v* **remain loyal to**, stay loyal to, remain faithful to, support, adhere to, stand by, be there for. [➡TAKE CARE OF AND SPOIL; 301] *Opposite:* let down.

sticker *n* **label**, sticky label, sign, marker, bumper sticker, transfer, decal (*US*). [➡SYMBOLS, SIGNS, AND NUMBERS; 597]

stickiness *n* **tackiness**, gluiness, gumminess, adhesiveness, pastiness. [➡PHYSICAL TEXTURE; 1221]

sticking plaster (*formal*) *n* **plaster**, dressing, bandage, pad, corn plaster, lint, adhesive, adhesive bandage (*US*). [➡COVERS AND COATINGS; 1245]

sticking point *n* **stumbling block**, bone of contention, impasse, obstacle, deadlock. [➡PROBLEM; 257]

stick-in-the-mud (*informal*) *n* **fuddy-duddy** (*informal*), reactionary, stuffed shirt (*informal*), diehard, fogy. [➡UNCOOPERATIVE OR REBELLIOUS PERSON; 567]

stick it out *v* [➡TOLERATE AND ENDURE; 767]

stickleback *type of* **freshwater fish.** [➡FRESHWATER FISH; 1010]

stickler *n* **pedant**, nitpicker, perfectionist, martinet, hard taskmaster, strict disciplinarian. [➡GRUMPY AND NEGATIVE PEOPLE; 953]

stick out 1 *v* **extend**, poke out, jut out, push out, thrust out, hold out. [➡CAUSE TO APPEAR; 5] 2 *v* **put up with**, endure, bear, weather, see through, withstand, bear with, persevere, persist. [➡TOLERATE AND ENDURE; 767] *Opposite:* give up.

stick out like a sore thumb *v* [➡APPEAR AND EMERGE; 3]

sticks (*informal*) *n* [➡REMOTE PLACES; 1046]

stick to 1 *v* **follow**, obey, abide by, stand by, remain faithful to. [➡OBEY AND ABIDE BY; 302] *Opposite:* abandon. 2 *v* **adhere**, cling, follow, cling to, hold, keep to. [➡CONTINUE AN ACTION; 263]

stick together *v* **stay close**, remain unified, remain loyal, remain friendly, concur, cooperate, cohere (*formal*). [➡ESTABLISHING RELATIONSHIPS WITH OTHERS; 974] *Opposite:* split up.

stick up 1 *v* **protrude**, point upwards, point up, stand up, bristle, stand on end. [➡GO UPWARDS; 307] 2 *v* **point up**, cock, prick up, make vertical, raise up, raise. [➡GO UPWARDS; 307] 3 *v* (*US informal*) **rob**, hold up, mug, steal from, pull a gun on, attack. [➡STEAL AND ROB; 427]

stickup (*US informal*) *n* **armed robbery**, mugging, robbery, attack, assault, burglary, holdup. [➡CRIMES; 817]

stick up for *v* **support**, defend, stand up for, stand by, argue for, insist. [➡APPROVE AND CONFIRM; 647]

stick with 1 *v* **persist with**, continue with, persevere with, see through, stay with, stick out. [➡CONTINUE AN ACTION; 263] *Opposite:* give up. 2 *v* **stay loyal to**, remain loyal to, remain faithful to, stay close to, stay with, stick by. [➡ESTABLISHING RELATIONSHIPS WITH OTHERS; 974] *Opposite:* abandon.

sticky 1 *adj* **tacky**, gluey, gummy, adhesive, pasty. [➡PHYSICAL TEXTURE; 1221] 2 *adj* (*informal*) **difficult**, tricky, delicate, awkward, sensitive, complicated. [➡DIFFICULTY AND COMPLEXITY; 243] 3 *adj* **muggy**, humid, close, clammy, sultry, oppressive, steamy, hot. [➡HOT WEATHER; 1050] *Opposite:* dry.

stick your nose in *v* [➡INTERRUPT AND BUTT IN; 620]

stick your oar in *v* [➡INTERRUPT AND BUTT IN; 620]

sticky situation *n* [➡DIFFICULT SITUATIONS; 72]

sticky wicket (*informal*) *n* **tricky situation**, awkward situation, difficult situation, difficult problem, embarrassing problem, embarrassing situation, predicament, plight, fix (*informal*), hole (*informal*). [➡DIFFICULT SITUATIONS; 72]

stiff 1 *adj* **rigid**, firm, inflexible, unbending, unbendable, taut, hard, solid, unyielding. [➡RIGID AND HARD; 1210] *Opposite:* limp. 2 *adj* **severe**, harsh, drastic, stringent, excessive, extreme, steep (*informal*). [➡ABSOLUTE AND ABSOLUTELY; 131] *Opposite:* lenient. 3 *adj* **formal**, stuffy, standoffish, aloof, pompous, stilted, wooden. [➡LEVELS OF FORMALITY; 523] *Opposite:* relaxed. 4 *adj* **strong**, vigorous, powerful, robust, intense. [➡STRENGTH; 202] *Opposite:* weak. 5 *adj* **demanding**, exacting, arduous, testing, tough, laborious, rigorous, difficult, taxing. [➡PHYSICALLY UNPLEASANT; 227] *Opposite:* easy. 6 *adj* **aching**, painful, arthritic, tender, sore. [➡INJURED; 743] 7 *n* (*slang*) **dead body**, body, corpse, cadaver, goner (*slang*), carcass. [➡DEAD PERSON; 926] 8 *n* (*US slang*) **person**, body (*informal*), soul, individual, guy (*informal*), bod (*slang*). [➡PERSON; 931]

stiffen 1 *v* **harden**, thicken, solidify, congeal, become rigid. [➡HARDEN, CONGEAL, DRY; 388] *Opposite:* soften. 2 *v* **strengthen**, make stronger, reinforce, toughen, brace. [➡IMPROVE STRENGTH AND DURABILITY; 379] *Opposite:* weaken.

stiffly 1 *adv* **rigidly**, firmly, inflexibly, unbendingly, tautly, straight, bolt upright. [➡RIGID AND HARD; 1210] 2 *adv* **painfully**, awkwardly, laboriously, arthritically, uncomfortably, with difficulty. [➡PHYSICALLY UNPLEASANT; 227] *Opposite:* easily. 3 *adv* **formally**, distantly, crisply, unbendingly, correctly, punctiliously. [➡LEVELS OF FORMALITY; 523] *Opposite:* easily.

stiff-necked *adj* **obstinate**, arrogant, stubborn, proud, haughty, refractory, aloof, unyielding, unbending. [➡REBELLIOUSNESS AND DISOBEDIENCE; 566] *Opposite:* yielding.

stiffness 1 *n* **rigidity**, firmness, inflexibility, tautness, hardness, solidity. [➡RIGID AND HARD; 1210] *Opposite:* limpness. 2 *n* **severity**, harshness, stringency, excessiveness, extremity, steepness (*informal*). [➡TOO MUCH; 118] *Opposite:* leniency. 3 *n* **formality**, stuffiness, standoffishness, aloofness, pomposity, woodenness. [➡LEVELS OF FORMALITY; 523] *Opposite:* informality. 4 *n* **strength**, vigour, power, robustness, intensity. [➡STRENGTH; 202] *Opposite:* weakness. 5 *n* **difficulty**, arduousness, laboriousness, rigorousness, toughness, painfulness. [➡PHYSICALLY UNPLEASANT; 227] *Opposite:* ease.

stifle 1 *v* **smother**, asphyxiate, throttle, suffocate, choke, strangle. [➡KILL; 923] 2 *v* **suppress**, repress, restrain, curb, hold back, keep in check, check. [➡WITHHOLD INFORMATION; 688] *Opposite:* let out.

stifling 1 *adj* **hot**, boiling, airless, muggy, close, stuffy, roasting (*informal*). [➡HOT WEATHER; 1050] *Opposite:* cool. 2 *adj* **oppressive**, repressive, overpowering, restrictive, inhibiting, domineering. [➡EMOTIONALLY UNPLEASANT AND UPSETTING; 228] *Opposite:* liberating.

stigma *n* **shame**, disgrace, dishonour, humiliation. [➡NUISANCES; 254]

stigmatize *v* **brand**, slur, defame, mark out, pillory, denounce. [➡INSULTS, ABUSE, AND SWEARING; 659]

stile *n* **step**, steps, rung, rungs, fence, access. [➡STAIRS AND STOREYS; 1101]

stiletto *type of* **sword or knife**. [➡SWORDS AND KNIVES; 1156]

stiletto heel *type of* **shoe**. [➡FOOTWEAR; 871]

still 1 *adj* **motionless**, immobile, unmoving, at rest, at a standstill, at a halt, tranquil, silent, stagnant, static, quiet, stationary. [➡LACK OF ACTIVITY; 343] *Opposite:* moving. 2 *adj* **flat**, nonsparkling, nonfizzy. [➡DRINKS; 1186] 3 *v* **calm**, allay, dispel, banish, quieten, subdue, calm down. [➡CHANGE OF INTENSITY: LESS; 396] *Opposite:* stir up. 4 *adv* **even now**, in spite of everything, even so, nevertheless, nonetheless, be that as it may, however, notwithstanding (*formal*), yet, even. [➡ALTHOUGH, NEVERTHELESS, AND DESPITE; 170]

stillborn 1 *adj* **born dead**, dead at birth, deceased (*formal*), miscarried, aborted, dead. [➡DEAD AND DYING; 925] 2 *adj* **ineffectual**, useless, ineffective, unsuccessful, abortive, fruitless. [➡REDUNDANT AND USELESS; 241] *Opposite:* successful.

still life *n* [➡ARTWORKS; 898]

stillness *n* **motionlessness**, immobility, silence, quietness, tranquillity, calm. [➡LACK OF ACTIVITY; 343] *Opposite:* movement.

stilt 1 *n* **post**, column, support, pillar, pole, prop. [➡STICKS, POLES, AND WEDGES; 1253] 2 *type of* **toy**. [➡TOYS; 880]

stilted *adj* **affected**, stiff, wooden, mannered, unnatural, pretentious, artificial, pompous, bombastic. [➡INARTICULATE, RAMBLING, AND AWKWARD; 634] *Opposite:* natural.

stiltedness *n* [➡INARTICULATE, RAMBLING, AND AWKWARD; 634]

Stilton *type of* **hard cheese**. [➡DAIRY PRODUCTS AND CHEESES; 1182]

stimulant 1 *n* **stimulating substance**, tonic, pep pill (*dated*), pick-me-up (*informal*), upper (*slang*). [➡REMEDIES, TREATMENTS AND OPERATIONS; 732] *Opposite:* sedative. 2 *adj* **stimulating**, intoxicating (*formal*), tonic, restorative, intoxicant, energizing. [➡REMEDIES, TREATMENTS AND OPERATIONS; 732] *Opposite:* sedative.

stimulate 1 *v* **rouse**, arouse, kindle, excite, inspire, motivate, encourage, fuel, incite, fire up. [➡ENCOURAGE; 577] *Opposite:* dampen. 2 *v* **quicken**, accelerate, increase, invigorate, promote, speed, speed up, intensify. [➡CHANGE OF INTENSITY: MORE; 395] *Opposite:* slow down.

stimulating 1 *adj* **inspiring**, encouraging, motivating, interesting, thought-provoking, exciting. [➡INTERESTING AND MEANINGFUL; 191] *Opposite:* boring. 2 *adj* **invigorating**, refreshing, energizing, rousing. [➡PHYSICALLY PLEASANT; 187] *Opposite:* relaxing.

stimulation *n* **inspiration**, motivation, encouragement, stimulus, incentive, spur, prompt. [➡CAUSATION; 169]

stimulus *n* **incentive**, spur, inducement, impetus, provocation, motivation, incitement. [➡CAUSATION; 169]

sting 1 *v* **smart**, prick, tingle, throb, hurt. [➡PAIN AND OTHER PHYSICAL SENSATIONS; 734] 2 *n* (*US slang*) **swindle**, hoax, fraud, racket, rip-off (*informal*), confidence trick, scam (*slang*), con. [➡DECEPTION AND LIES; 661]

stinger *type of* **parts of insects**. [➡PARTS OF AN INSECT; 1019]

stingily *adv* **grudgingly**, ungenerously, parsimoniously, tightfistedly, meanly. [➡FINANCIALLY MEAN AND GRASPING; 520] *Opposite:* generously.

stinginess *n* **miserliness**, ungenerousness, parsimony, meanness, tightfistedness. [➡FINANCIALLY MEAN AND GRASPING; 520]

stinging *adj* **hurtful**, cutting, harsh, hard, cruel, callous, vicious. [➡RUDE AND HOSTILE; 626]

stinging nettle *type of* **weed**. [➡WEEDS AND THISTLES; 1034]

stingray *type of* **flatfish**. [➡SEA FISH; 1009]

stingy (*informal*) *adj* **miserly**, ungenerous, parsimonious, sparing, grudging, mean, tightfisted, penny-pinching (*informal*). [➡FINANCIALLY MEAN AND GRASPING; 520] *Opposite:* generous.

stink 1 *v* **smell horrible**, reek, smell, hum (*informal*), pong (*informal*), whiff (*informal*), niff (*slang*). [➡SMELL EMISSION; 370] 2 *n* **stench**, smell, horrible smell, pong (*informal*), reek, unpleasant odour, whiff (*informal*). [➡SMELL AND SMELLING; 706] *Opposite:* perfume. 3 *n* (*informal*) **fuss**, scandal, uproar, rumpus, commotion, brouhaha (*formal*). [➡CHAOS AND UPROAR; 51]

See Compare and Contrast at **smell**.

stinker *n* **shocker** (*informal*), problem, horror (*informal*), nightmare, poser (*informal disapproving*), bastard (*slang*). [➡NUISANCES; 254] *Opposite:* delight.

stinkhorn *type of* **fungus**. [➡MICROORGANISMS, FUNGI, AND ALGAE; 1023]

stinking *adj* **foul-smelling**, reeking, smelly, humming (*informal*), stinky, rotten, putrid, rank (*literary*), malodorous, fetid, foul (*informal*). [➡SMELL AND SMELLING; 706]

stink out *v* **make smelly**, permeate, pervade, overpower, fill with a smell, make stinky. [➡SMELL EMISSION; 370] *Opposite:* deodorize.

stinky 1 *adj* **smelly**, stinking, foul-smelling, putrid, rotten, malodorous, foul, fetid. [➡SMELL AND SMELLING; 706] *Opposite:* fragrant. 2 *adj* **nasty**, unfair, dishonest, devious, mean-spirited, unpleasant. [➡SELFISH AND UNKIND; 506] *Opposite:* pleasant.

stint *n* **spell**, stretch, time, shift, period, turn. [➡SHORT PERIOD OF TIME; 93]

stint on *v* **be sparing with**, be mean with, be parsimonious with, be frugal with, ration, skimp on. [➡FOREGO AND DENY ONESELF; 450]

stipend *n* **allowance**, salary, payment, pay, wage, reward, scholarship, fellowship. [➡INCOME; 461]

See Compare and Contrast at **wage**.

stipendiary 1 *adj* **paid**, salaried, earning, remunerated, breadwinning, wage-earning. [➡TYPES OF WORK; 835] 2 *n* **earner**, wage earner, breadwinner, payee, employee, recipient. [➡WORKER; 836]

stipple *v* **dab**, paint, dot, speckle, fleck, mottle, draw. [➡DECORATE, ADORN, AND APPLY COATINGS; 406]

stippled *adj* **mottled**, dappled, speckled, spotted, flecked, dotted. [➡DESCRIBING PATTERNS; 1226]

stipulate *v* **specify**, lay down, instruct, order, require, demand, insist on. [➡CLAIM, INSIST, AND EMPHASIZE; 615]

stipulation *n* **condition**, requirement, proviso, demand, specification, prerequisite, provision, clause. [➡NECESSARY AND ESSENTIAL; 197]

stir 1 *v* **mix**, blend, swirl, fold, whip, whisk, beat. [➡COOKING AND FOOD PREPARATION; 354] 2 *v* **rouse**, wake up, move, budge, shift, get up, get going. [➡GO UPWARDS; 307] 3 *v* **awaken**, arouse, revive, call to mind, bring back, stir up. [➡REMIND; 748] 4 *v* **motivate**, incite, provoke, excite, inspire, stimulate, fire up, stir up. [➡APPEAL TO AND AROUSE INTEREST; 576] 5 *v* **agitate**, cause feeling, disturb, trouble, upset. [➡UPSET, DISTRESS, AND HUMILIATE; 568] 6 *n* **commotion**, disturbance, fuss, to-do (*informal*), uproar, hue and cry, hullabaloo, hubbub. [➡CHAOS AND UPROAR; 51]

stir-crazy (*informal or humorous*) *adj* **mentally unsettled**, restless, frantic, distraught, agitated, fidgety, jumpy, antsy (*US informal*). [➡IRRITATION AND ANGER; 542]

stir-fried *adj* [➡STATE OF PREPARED FOOD; 1170]

stir-fry 1 *v* **fry**, pan-fry, sauté. [➡COOKING AND FOOD PREPARATION; 354] 2 *type of* **cooked dish**. [➡PREPARED DISHES; 1169]

stirred up *adj* [➡POSITIVE IMPATIENCE, ENTHUSIASM, AND ALERTNESS; 538]

stirrer (*informal*) *n* **troublemaker**, agitator, agent provocateur, firebrand, mischief-maker, rabble-rouser (*disapproving*). [➡INTERFERING PEOPLE AND TELLTALES; 950] *Opposite:* peacemaker.

stirring *adj* **rousing**, inspiring, moving, emotive, exciting, thrilling, magnificent. [➡EMOTIONALLY PLEASANT; 188] *Opposite:* uninspiring.

stirrup *n* **foot support**, strap, loop, ring. [➡FASTENERS, LINKS, AND NETWORKS; 1246]

stir up *v* **awaken**, reawaken, bring back, kindle, inflame, inspire, provoke, incite, instigate, agitate. [➡REMIND; 748] *Opposite:* calm.

stitch 1 *v* **sew**, sew up, stitch up, darn, baste, tack. [➡CRAFTS AND CARVING; 356] 2 *v* **suture**, sew up, close. [➡FASTEN, LINK, AND JOIN; 409]

stitching *n* **sewing**, stitches, seam, needlework, embroidery, edging, edge, hemming. [➡CRAFTS AND CARVING; 356]

stitch up (*slang*) *v* **frame** (*slang*), fit up (*slang*), set up (*informal*), implicate, incriminate. [➡FALSIFY AND CHEAT; 177]

stoat *type of* **small mammal**. [➡SMALL MAMMAL; 990]

stock 1 *n* **supply**, stockpile, hoard, stash (*informal*), reserve, accumulation, collection, store. [➡STORES AND STORAGE BUILDINGS; 1087] 2 *n* **livestock**, farm animals, domestic animals, cattle, sheep, pigs, horses. [➡FARM ANIMAL; 982] 3 *adj* **standard**, typical, routine, run-of-the-mill, ordinary, normal. [➡ORDINARINESS; 245] 4 *v* **keep**, have a supply of, have available, carry, supply, sell, deal in, provide. [➡STORE AND KEEP; 454]

stockade 1 *n* **barrier**, fence, enclosure, palisade, paling. [➡BARRIERS; 1112] 2 *n* **enclosure**, fort, pen, fenced area, enclosed area, corral (*US*), yard. [➡FORTRESSES AND FORTIFICATIONS; 1089]

stockbroker *n* **securities broker**, broker, investment analyst, financial adviser, investment banker, trader. [➡PEOPLE INVOLVED IN FINANCE; 804]

stock car *n* **racing car**, hot rod (*slang*), dragster. [➡BIKES, CARS, AND CARRIAGES; 1148]

stock cube *n* **concentrate**, vegetable extract, meat extract, dried food, broth, seasoning, flavouring, bouillon cube (*US*). [➡SEASONINGS AND SAUCES; 1173]

stock exchange *n* **stock market**, trading, bourse, exchange, money market, market. [➡ACCOUNTING, BANKING, AND BUDGETING; 799]

stockholder *n* **shareholder**, bondholder, owner, stakeholder, investor. [➡BUSINESS PEOPLE; 794]

stockiness *n* [➡BUILD; 478]

stocking filler *n* **Christmas present**, Christmas gift, small present, small gift, extra, stocking stuffer (*US*). [➡GIFTS; 439]

stockings *n* **leg coverings**, nylons, hose, tights, leggings, thigh-highs, knee-highs, pantyhose (*US*). [➡HABERDASHERY, MILLINERY, AND LINGERIE; 867]

stocking stuffer (*US*) *n* **stocking filler**, Christmas present, Christmas gift, small present, small gift, trinket, token. [➡GIFTS; 439]

stock-in-trade 1 *n* **basic resource**, staple, commodity. [➡BUSINESS PRODUCTS; 796] 2 *n* **goods**, equipment, stock, merchandise, wares, range. [➡BUSINESS PRODUCTS; 796]

stockist *n* **seller**, shop, store, wholesaler, retailer, dealer, vendor. [➡SELLER; 443]

stock market *n* **financial market**, stock exchange, exchange, market, bourse, money market. [➡ACCOUNTING, BANKING, AND BUDGETING; 799]

stock phrase *n* [➡THE ORAL TRADITION; 678]

stockpile 1 *n* **supply**, hoard, accumulation, stash (*informal*), store, stock. [➡STORES AND STORAGE BUILDINGS; 1087] 2 *v* **build up stocks**, stock up on, store up, store, squirrel away, hoard, amass, salt away, accumulate, collect. [➡STORE AND KEEP; 454]

See Compare and Contrast at **collect**.

stockroom *n* **storeroom**, storehouse, store, warehouse. [➡STORES AND STORAGE BUILDINGS; 1087]

stocks 1 *n* **instrument of punishment**, punishment device, framework, pillory, ducking stool, cucking stool. [➡ANCIENT MANMADE STRUCTURES; 1088] 2 *n* **shares**, bonds, dividends. [➡MONEY, PAYMENTS, AND CHARGES; 800]

stock-still *adv* **motionless**, completely still, absolutely still, immobile, without moving, unmoving, stationary. [➡LACK OF ACTIVITY; 343] *Opposite:* moving.

stocktaking 1 *n* **evaluation**, assessment, appraisal, reassessment, reappraisal, taking stock. [➡EXAMINE AND ASSESS; 754] 2 *n* **inventory**, listing, itemizing, counting, checking, examination, valuing. [➡BUSINESS ACTIVITIES AND PHENOMENA; 795]

stock up *v* **stockpile**, hoard, save up, collect, lay in, store up, accumulate, amass, gather, squirrel away. [➡STORE AND KEEP; 454]

stock up on *v* [➡STORE AND KEEP; 454]

stocky *adj* **thickset**, sturdy, solid, stout, chunky (*informal*), squat, burly, hefty. [➡BUILD; 478] *Opposite:* slight.

stockyard *n* **yard**, enclosure, farmyard, farm, enclosed yard, pen. [➡THE COUNTRYSIDE AND OUTDOOR SPACES; 1070]

stodge (*informal*) 1 *n* **heavy food**, solid food, filling food, starchy food, substantial food. [➡FOOD; 1166] 2 *n* **something dull**, something stuffy, something boring, dull subject, turgidity, unreadability. [➡BORING AND UNINTERESTING; 235]

stodgy (*informal*) 1 *adj* **heavy**, filling, starchy, indigestible, hard to digest. [➡FOOD; 1166] *Opposite:* light. 2 *adj* **dull**, turgid, uninteresting, unexciting, stuffy, boring, tedious, dreary, stilted. [➡BORING AND UNINTERESTING; 235] *Opposite:* lively.

stoic 1 *n* **impassive person**, patient person, fatalist, ascetic, unfeeling person. [➡PHILOSOPHICAL AND POLITICAL THINKERS; 782] 2 *see* **stoical**.

See Compare and Contrast at **impassive**.

stoical *adj* **long-suffering**, uncomplaining, impassive, forbearing (*formal*), enduring, tolerant, patient, resigned, indifferent, apathetic, passive, stoic. [➡STRENGTH OF WILL; 502] *Opposite:* excitable.

stoicism *n* **impassiveness**, endurance, patience, indifference, fortitude, resignation. [➡STRENGTH OF WILL; 502] *Opposite:* excitability.

stoke *v* **put fuel on**, stoke up, add fuel to, fuel. [➡FIRE, FLAMMABILITY, AND BURNING; 1164]

stoke up 1 *v* **stoke**, put fuel on, add fuel to. [➡FIRE,

FLAMMABILITY, AND BURNING; 1164] **2** *v* **strengthen**, intensify, stir up, stoke, fuel, encourage, add to. [➡CHANGE OF INTENSITY: MORE; 395]

STOL *type of* **civil aircraft**. [➡AIRCRAFT; 1147]

stole *n* **garment**, shawl, wrap, scarf, pashmina, tippet, boa. [➡HABERDASHERY, MILLINERY, AND LINGERIE; 867]

stolid *adj* **impassive**, unresponsive, dull, emotionless, insensitive, indifferent, slow-witted. [➡NEGATIVE INTELLECTUAL CHARACTERISTICS; 526] *Opposite:* emotional.

See Compare and Contrast at **impassive**.

stomach *part of* **digestive tract**. [➡THE DIGESTIVE TRACT; 710]

stomachache *n* **stomach pain**, bellyache (*informal*), tummy ache (*informal*), tummy pain (*informal*), colic, indigestion, cramp, stitch, heartburn, upset stomach. [➡DISORDERS OF THE DIGESTIVE SYSTEM; 714]

stomach-churning *adj* **sickening**, nauseating, disgusting, revolting, repulsive, stomach-turning, repellant, gross (*slang*), vile, foul (*informal*). [➡DISGUSTING AND REPULSIVE; 231] *Opposite:* appealing.

stomach pain *n* [➡DISORDERS OF THE DIGESTIVE SYSTEM; 714]

stomach pump (*informal*) *n* **suction pump**, suction device, aspirator, siphon, syringe, drain. [➡REMEDIES, TREATMENTS AND OPERATIONS; 732]

stomach-turning *adj* **sickening**, nauseating, stomach-churning, revolting, disgusting, repulsive, repellent, gross (*slang*), vile, foul (*informal*). [➡DISGUSTING AND REPULSIVE; 231] *Opposite:* appealing.

stomp *v* **tread heavily**, stamp, tramp, clump, plod, trudge, clomp. [➡PROCEED AND GO; 306]

stone *part of* **fruit**. [➡FRUIT AND VEGETABLES; 1175]

stone

◆ *types of stone*
alabaster, basalt, chalk, conglomerate, flint, gneiss, granite, hornblende, lava, limestone, malachite, marble, pumice, quartzite, sandstone, schist, shale, slate, soapstone, tuff

stone circle *n* [➡ANCIENT MANMADE STRUCTURES; 1088]

stone-cold **1** *adj* **very cold**, chilly, icy, frozen, freezing, frigid. [➡TEMPERATURE: COLD; 1230] *Opposite:* boiling. **2** *adv* (*informal*) **completely**, absolutely, utterly, totally, dead, extremely, fully. [➡ABSOLUTE AND ABSOLUTELY; 131]

stone-dead *adj* **lifeless**, deceased (*formal*), departed (*formal or literary*), cold, dead as a dodo, dead as a doornail. *Opposite:* alive and kicking. (*informal*). [➡DEAD AND DYING; 925]

stoneground *adj* **ground**, milled, crushed, powdered. [➡NOT IN A NATURAL STATE; 1214]

stone's throw *n* **short distance**, stonecast, spitting distance (*informal*), no distance, short way, hop, skip and jump, striking distance, short walk. [➡CLOSENESS; 160]

stonewall (*informal*) **1** *v* **evade**, obstruct, avoid, refuse, rebuff, resist, put off. [➡DELAY ACTION OR OCCURRENCE; 279] *Opposite:* cooperate. **2** *v* **delay**, hold off, hold back, stall. [➡SHIRK AND DELAY; 274]

stoneware *type of* **pottery**. [➡POTTERY; 1134]

stonewashed *adj* **faded**, worn, distressed, washed-out, bleached, pale. [➡DESCRIBING CLOTHES; 869]

stonework *n* **masonry**, brickwork, walls. [➡BUILDING MATERIALS; 1076]

stonewort *type of* **alga**. [➡MICROORGANISMS, FUNGI, AND ALGAE; 1023]

stonker (*slang*) *n* [➡BIG THINGS; 1193]

stonking (*slang*) **1** *adj* **excellent**, brilliant, wonderful, fabulous, great (*informal*), terrific (*informal*), wicked (*slang*). [➡EXTRAORDINARY: AMAZING; 205] *Opposite:* awful. **2** *adv* **extremely**, brilliantly, wonderfully, marvellously, fabulously. [➡EXTRAORDINARY: AMAZING; 205]

stony **1** *adj* (*informal*) **penniless**, impoverished, impecunious (*formal*), broke (*informal*), poor, bankrupt, stone-broke (*US*). [➡POVERTY AND POOR; 892] *Opposite:* well-off. **2** *adj* **rocky**, flinty, pebbly, rock-strewn, shingly, gritty, gravelly, rough. [➡PHYSICAL TEXTURE; 1221] **3** *adj* **pitiless**, unfeeling, unsympathetic, unyielding, flinty, compassionless, unfriendly, cruel, hard, cold. [➡SELFISH AND UNKIND; 506] *Opposite:* compassionate.

stony-broke (*informal*) *adj* **penniless**, impoverished, impecunious (*formal*), broke (*informal*), stony (*informal*), poor, bankrupt, stone-broke (*US*). [➡POVERTY AND POOR; 892] *Opposite:* well-off.

stony-faced *adj* **expressionless**, unemotional, unfriendly, blank, cold, grave. [➡FACIAL EXPRESSION; 652] *Opposite:* smiling.

stony-hearted *adj* **hardhearted**, unfeeling, pitiless, unsympathetic, hard, cruel. [➡SELFISH AND UNKIND; 506] *Opposite:* soft-hearted.

stooge *n* **straight partner**, comic actor, comedian, butt, foil, straight man, feed, entertainer. [➡WORKERS IN ENTERTAINMENT AND MEDIA; 873]

stool *n* **seat**, chair, footrest, bench, couch, pew. [➡FURNITURE; 858]

stoolie (*US slang*) *n* [➡INTERFERING PEOPLE AND TELLTALES; 950]

stool pigeon (*slang*) *n* [➡INTERFERING PEOPLE AND TELLTALES; 950]

stoop **1** *v* **bend down**, bend forwards, bend over, bend, lean forwards, crouch, crouch down. [➡ASSUME A POSITION; 318] *Opposite:* straighten up. **2** *v* **lower yourself**, condescend, deign, debase yourself, patronize. [➡CHANGE OF MOOD AND COMPOSURE; 581] **3** *see* **stoup**.

stooped *adj* [➡BUILD; 478]

stooping *adj* [➡BUILD; 478]

stop **1** *v* **discontinue**, end, bring to an end, bring to a close, bring to a standstill, bring to a halt. [➡CAUSE TO STOP; 267] *Opposite:* begin. **2** *v* **prevent**, impede, hinder, prohibit, obstruct, bar, ban. [➡MAKE IMPOSSIBLE; 277] *Opposite:* permit. **3** *v* **end**, finish, come to an end, be over, break off, cease, peter out. [➡CEASE TO EXIST; 22] *Opposite:* begin. 4 *v* **pause**, interrupt, break off, stop off, take a break, adjourn, halt, rest. [➡STOP ACTING; 265] 5 *v* **block**, block up, block off, obstruct, plug, plug up, stop up. [➡FILL; 407] 6 *n* **halt**, break, rest, sojourn (*literary*), stopover, stay. [➡PERIOD OF REST; 91]

stop by *v* **drop in**, call by, pop in (*informal*), call, call in, visit, stop off, come by. [➡INITIATE AND ESTABLISH COMMUNICATION; 681]

stopcock *n* **valve**, tap, cock, spigot, stopper, switch, faucet (*US*). [➡PARTS OF MACHINES AND TOOLS; 1117]

stop dead *v* [➡FAIL OR CEASE TO FUNCTION; 471]

stopgap *n* **temporary solution**, substitute, makeshift, expedient, temporary measure, contrivance. [➡SOLUTION; 216]

stoplight (*US*) *type of* **external feature**. [➡VEHICLES; 1144]

stop off *n* **call**, call in, stop by, stop, drop in, visit. [➡ARRIVAL; 13]

stop out (*informal*) *v* **stay out**, stay out late, come home late, stay away, sleep over. [➡CONTINUE AN ACTION; 263]

stopover *n* **break in your journey**, stop, halt, pause, stop-off, layover (*US*). [➡PERIOD OF REST; 91]

stoppage 1 *n* **strike**, work stoppage, industrial action, wildcat strike, go-slow, work to rule, walkout, slowdown (*US*). [➡WORK-RELATED ACTIVITIES; 834] 2 *n* **blockage**, obstruction, obstacle, barrier. [➡PROBLEM; 257]

stoppage time *n* **injury time**, timeout, extra time, overtime, extension, additional playing time. [➡SPORTS TERMS; 877]

stopped 1 *adj* **stationary**, still, at a standstill, immobile, motionless, not moving. [➡LACK OF ACTIVITY; 343] *Opposite:* moving. 2 *adj* **clogged**, blocked, congested, backed up, stopped up, bunged, closed. [➡IN BAD REPAIR; 1233] *Opposite:* open. 3 *adj* **not working**, out of order, out of commission, packed up (*informal*), worn-out, crashed, given up the ghost (*informal*). [➡IN BAD REPAIR; 1233] *Opposite:* working.

stopper *n* **plug**, bung, cork, top, lid, closure, cover. [➡COVERS AND COATINGS; 1245]

stop press *n* **late news**, recent news, last-minute news, news flash, postscript, addendum. [➡NEWSPAPERS; 606]

stop up *v* **plug**, plug up, block, block up, block off, bung, bung up (*informal*). [➡FILL; 407]

stopwatch *type of* **clock**. [➡CLOCKS AND TIMERS; 1125]

stop working *v* **break down**, break, fail, pack up (*informal*), seize up. [➡FAIL OR CEASE TO FUNCTION; 471] *Opposite:* function.

storage 1 *n* **storing**, stowage, stowing, packing, loading, putting away, tidying away. [➡STORE AND KEEP; 454] 2 *n* **storage space**, storage capacity, storage area, stowage, room, space, accommodation. [➡STORES AND STORAGE BUILDINGS; 1087]

storage

◆ *types of storage space*
armoury, arms depot, arsenal, barn, bunker, cellar, depository, depot, dump, elevator (*US*), garage, gasometer, grain elevator (*US*), granary, hangar, hayloft, hold, landfill, larder, loft, luggage compartment, magazine, morgue, mortuary, pantry, rubbish dump, shed, silo, strongroom, treasury, warehouse, water tower, weapon store, woodshed

storage bin *type of* **container**. [➡CONTAINERS, RECEPTACLES, AND PACKAGING; 1244]

storage heater *type of* **heating appliance**. [➡HEATING, REFRIGERATION, AND VENTILATION; 1141]

storage tank *type of* **container**. [➡CONTAINERS, RECEPTACLES, AND PACKAGING; 1244]

store 1 *v* **put away**, stow, keep, deposit, put in storage, warehouse, stockpile. [➡STORE AND KEEP; 454] 2 *n* **supply**, stockpile, hoard, accumulation, collection, mass, pile, stock. [➡COLLECTIONS AND MIXTURES OF THINGS; 1243] 3 *n* **shop**, outlet, emporium (*formal or humorous*), showroom. [➡RETAIL OUTLETS; 1082] 4 *n* **warehouse**, depository, depot, stockroom, repository, storeroom. [➡STORES AND STORAGE BUILDINGS; 1087]

storehouse *n* [➡STORES AND STORAGE BUILDINGS; 1087]

storeroom *n* [➡STORES AND STORAGE BUILDINGS; 1087]

stores *n* **supplies**, provisions, equipment, goods, food, rations, vittles (*archaic*). [➡POSSESSIONS; 462]

store up *v* **amass**, hoard, save, accumulate, stockpile, squirrel away, collect, salt away. [➡STORE AND KEEP; 454]

storey *n* **floor**, level, section, division, landing, tier, layer. [➡STAIRS AND STOREYS; 1101]

stork *type of* **freshwater bird**. [➡FRESHWATER BIRD; 1000]

storm 1 *n* **tempest**, squall, gale, hurricane, tornado, rainstorm, snowstorm, blizzard, thunderstorm, typhoon, cyclone, downpour. [➡WINDY AND STORMY WEATHER; 1053] 2 *n* **outburst**, outbreak, explosion, eruption, flare-up (*informal*), wave. [➡SUDDEN EVENT; 52] 3 *v* **capture**, carry, take by storm, overmaster, take. [➡BEAT AND DEFEAT; 80] 4 *v* **rage**, fume, rant and rave, thunder, bluster. [➡GIVING VENT TO EMOTIONS; 680] 5 *v* **stamp**, stomp, stalk, flounce, march. [➡MOVE FAST; 314]

stormbound *adj* **housebound**, confined, isolated, cut off, snowed in, snowbound, detained. [➡CAPTIVITY AND LOSS OF FREEDOM; 249]

storm cloud 1 *n* **sign of violence**, omen, herald, harbinger, danger signal, gathering storm. [➡INDICATIONS, SIGNS, AND WARNINGS; 68] 2 *type of* **cloud**. [➡CLOUDY AND RAINY WEATHER; 1052]

storm drain *n* **drain**, storm-water sewer, gutter, channel, drainage system. [➡WATERCOURSES; 1110]

stormily 1 *adv* **tempestuously**, violently, turbulently, vehemently, furiously, passionately. [➡BAD-TEMPERED AND HUMOURLESS; 627] *Opposite:* placidly. 2 *adv* **thunderily**, windily. [➡WINDY AND STORMY WEATHER; 1053] *Opposite:* calmly.

storm in *v* [➡ARRIVE; 12]

storm in a teacup *n* [➡DIFFICULT SITUATIONS; 72]

storminess 1 *n* **tempestuousness**, violence, turbulence, fieriness, passion, frenzy. [➡EMOTIONALLY UNPLEASANT AND UPSETTING; 228] *Opposite:* placidity. 2 *n* **wildness**, windiness, blusteriness. [➡WINDY AND STORMY WEATHER; 1053] *Opposite:* calmness.

storm out *v* [➡ABSENT ONESELF; 8]

storm petrel *type of* **seabird.** [➡SEABIRD; 1002]

stormproof *adj* **storm-resistant**, protected, strong, tough, waterproof, windproof. [➡IN GOOD REPAIR; 1231]

storm-tossed *adj* **choppy**, stormy, rough, battered, wild, weather-beaten. [➡WINDY AND STORMY WEATHER; 1053] *Opposite:* calm.

stormy 1 *adj* **squally**, rainy, thundery, blustery, windy, wild. [➡WINDY AND STORMY WEATHER; 1053] *Opposite:* calm. 2 *adj* **tempestuous**, violent, turbulent, unsettled, volatile, fiery, passionate, vehement, frenzied. [➡EMOTIONALLY UNPLEASANT AND UPSETTING; 228] *Opposite:* placid.

story 1 *n* **tale**, narrative, account, legend, yarn (*informal*), chronicle, anecdote, fairy tale. [➡THE ORAL TRADITION; 678] 2 *n* **account**, report, version, statement, description. [➡BASIC DETAILS; 689] 3 *n* (*informal*) **lie**, fib (*informal*), untruth, falsehood, whopper (*informal*), barefaced lie, porky (*slang*). [➡DECEPTION AND LIES; 661] 4 *n* **article**, piece, feature, report, item, scoop. [➡NEWSPAPERS; 606]

story book *n* [➡BOOKS AND BOOKLETS; 591]

storybook *adj* **fairy-tale**, fictional, make-believe, mythical, fanciful, imaginary. [➡FALSE AND UNREAL; 174] *Opposite:* real.

storyland *n* [➡NON-EXISTENT PLACE; 1065]

story line *n* **plot**, narrative, story, theme, scenario, subplot. [➡THE ORAL TRADITION; 678]

storyteller 1 *n* **narrator**, teller of tales, teller, relater, raconteur, bard (*literary or humorous*), minstrel. [➡SPEAKERS AND ORATORS; 604] 2 *n* (*informal*) **liar**, fibber (*informal*), prevaricator, deceiver, fabricator. [➡PEOPLE WHO DECEIVE; 662]

stoup *n* **basin**, vessel, bowl, receptacle, chalice, font. [➡CONTAINERS, RECEPTACLES, AND PACKAGING; 1244]

stout 1 *adj* **thickset**, heavy, solid, plump, chubby, corpulent (*formal or literary*), fat, fleshy, overweight, hefty, portly, round. [➡BUILD; 478] *Opposite:* slender. 2 *adj* **brave**, firm, stalwart, determined, resolute, doughty (*literary*), plucky, bold, valiant, courageous, heroic. [➡COURAGE; 499] *Opposite:* faint-hearted. 3 *adj* **sturdy**, strong, solid, substantial, tough, well-built, robust, heavy-duty. [➡STRENGTH; 202] *Opposite:* flimsy.

stouthearted *adj* **courageous**, brave, resolute, bold, dauntless (*literary*), valiant, heroic. [➡COURAGE; 499] *Opposite:* cowardly.

stoutheartedness *n* [➡COURAGE; 499]

stoutness 1 *n* **fatness**, heaviness, solidity, plumpness, chubbiness, fleshiness, squatness. [➡BUILD; 478] *Opposite:* slenderness. 2 *n* **sturdiness**, solidity, strength, heftiness, toughness. [➡STRENGTH; 202] *Opposite:* flimsiness. 3 *n* **bravery**, firmness, stalwartness, determination, resoluteness, doughtiness, stoutheartedness, pluckiness, boldness, fearlessness. [➡COURAGE; 499]

stove 1 *n* **cooker**, hob, hot plate, oven, range, cooktop (*US*). [➡TABLEWARE, CUTLERY, AND KITCHENWARE; 861] 2 *type of* **appliance.** [➡HOUSEHOLD APPLIANCES; 1116]

stovepipe hat *type of* **hat.** [➡HABERDASHERY, MILLINERY, AND LINGERIE; 867]

stow *v* **put away**, tidy away, put, pack, store, deposit, put in storage. [➡STORE AND KEEP; 454]

stowage *n* **stowing**, storage, packing, loading, putting away, tidying away. [➡STORE AND KEEP; 454]

stowaway *n* **fare-dodger**, runaway, escapee, escaper, fugitive, refugee. [➡RUNAWAYS AND ABSENTEES; 9]

straddle 1 *v* **be astride**, bestride, sit astride, stand astride. [➡EXIST IN CLOSE PROXIMITY; 21] 2 *v* **span**, include, bestride, overlap, link, connect, be on both sides of. [➡CREATING CONNECTIONS; 145]

strafe 1 *v* **bombard**, attack, fire at, shell, blitz, pepper, barrage, cannonade. [➡PHYSICAL ATTACK AND PUNISHMENT; 416] 2 *v* (*slang*) **punish**, reprimand, rebuke, tear a strip off, penalize, admonish, chastise (*formal*). [➡ACCUSE, BLAME, AND CRITICIZE; 642] *Opposite:* commend. 3 *n* **aerial attack**, bombardment, air attack, blitz, shelling, barrage, cannonade, bombing, attack. [➡WARFARE AND WAR; 830]

straggle 1 *v* **lag**, lag behind, trail, trail behind, fall behind, drop behind, drop back. [➡MOVE SLOWLY; 315] 2 *v* **spread untidily**, spread out, sprawl, extend, spread. [➡EXIST IN A PLACE; 19] 3 *v* **stray**, err, ramble, maunder, meander, rove, drift, wander. [➡AIMLESS AND ERRANT MOTION; 344] *Opposite:* keep up.

straggler *n* **dawdler**, laggard, slowcoach (*informal*), loiterer, lingerer, foot-dragger (*informal*), slowpoke (*US informal*). [➡LAZY OR UNSUCCESSFUL PEOPLE; 948] *Opposite:* leader.

straggly *adj* **untidy**, unkempt, messy, dishevelled, sprawling, higgledy-piggledy. [➡DESCRIBING HAIR; 487] *Opposite:* tidy.

straight 1 *adj* **candid**, frank, direct, open, honest, truthful, forthright, up-front (*informal*), blunt, straight-talking. [➡HONEST AND OPEN; 631] *Opposite:* devious. 2 *adj* **level**, upright, horizontal, vertical, perpendicular, erect, even, in line. [➡ORIENTATION AND ALIGNMENT; 1222] *Opposite:* askew. 3 *adj* **honest**, straightforward, fair, law-abiding, aboveboard, respectable, upright, trustworthy. [➡HONEST AND RELIABLE; 503] *Opposite:* dishonest. 4 *adj* **consecutive**, successive, uninterrupted, in a row, running. [➡AFTER, LAST, AND FOLLOWING; 166] 5 *adj* **undiluted**, neat, plain, unmixed, unadulterated, pure, as it comes. [➡RAW AND NATURAL; 1213] *Opposite:* diluted. 6 *adj* **tidy**, neat, in order, orderly, organized, arranged, sorted out, shipshape. [➡ORDER AND ORGANISATION; 207] *Opposite:* untidy. 7 *adj* (*slang*) **conventional**, traditional, conservative, orthodox, square (*slang dated*). [➡CONSERVATIVE AND UNADVENTUROUS; 518] *Opposite:* unconventional. 8 *adv* **as the crow flies**, in a straight line, directly, from A to B, by the shortest possible route. [➡DIRECTION OF MOTION; 346] *Opposite:* indirectly. 9 *adv* **directly**, without delay, immediately, at once, instantly, without stopping, right away, straightaway. [➡PRESENT; 85] *Opposite:* later.

straightaway *adv* **immediately**, at once, without delay, right away, promptly, directly, straight, without further ado, straight off (*informal*), now, without hesitation. [➡PRESENT; 85] *Opposite:* later.

straighten 1 *v* **make straight**, straighten out, unbend, uncurl, flatten, smooth down. [➡CHANGE OF SHAPE; 386] *Opposite:* bend. 2 *v* **make level**, level, set straight, straighten up, adjust, align. [➡ARRANGE AND CREATE ORDER; 358] 3 *v* **tidy**, tidy up, order, arrange, organize. [➡ARRANGE AND CREATE ORDER; 358]

straighten out 1 *v* **make straight**, straighten, unbend, uncurl, flatten, smooth down. [➡CHANGE OF SHAPE; 386] *Opposite:* bend. 2 *v* **put right**, sort out, set right, settle, rectify, correct. [➡CORRECT AND PUT RIGHT; 378] *Opposite:* confuse.

straighten up *v* **align**, justify, straighten, level, make flush, adjust. [➡ARRANGE AND CREATE ORDER; 358]

straight-faced *adj* **deadpan**, poker-faced, expressionless, blank, serious, impassive, solemn, grave, unsmiling, stony-faced. [➡FACIAL EXPRESSION; 652] *Opposite:* smiling.

straightforward 1 *adj* **frank**, forthright, candid, upfront (*informal*), direct, honest, open, straight, sincere. [➡HONEST AND OPEN; 631] *Opposite:* devious. 2 *adj* **easy**, simple, facile, uncomplicated, clear-cut, basic, undemanding. [➡EASE AND SIMPLICITY; 201] *Opposite:* complicated.

straightforwardness 1 *n* **frankness**, candour, honesty, truthfulness, openness, sincerity, forthrightness, directness. [➡HONEST AND OPEN; 631] *Opposite:* deviousness. 2 *n* **ease**, facility, simplicity, clarity, easiness. [➡EASE AND SIMPLICITY; 201] *Opposite:* difficulty.

straight off (*informal*) *adv* **at once**, right away, straightaway, immediately, without delay, then and there, directly, promptly. [➡PRESENT; 85] *Opposite:* later.

straight out *adv* **unhesitatingly**, without hesitation, directly, straight, without beating about the bush, getting straight to the point, straight from the shoulder. [➡HONEST AND OPEN; 631]

straight-out 1 *adj* (*informal*) **blunt**, unrestrained, direct, frank, honest, straightforward. [➡HONEST AND OPEN; 631] *Opposite:* restrained. 2 *adj* (*US informal*) **total**, complete, utter, out-and-out, thorough, consummate. [➡ABSOLUTE AND ABSOLUTELY; 131]

straight-talking *adj* **blunt**, direct, frank, candid, upfront (*informal*), forthright, plain-spoken. [➡HONEST AND OPEN; 631] *Opposite:* evasive.

straight-thinking *adj* [➡POSITIVE INTELLECTUAL CHARACTERISTICS; 525]

straight up (*slang*) *interj* **honestly**, truly, really, exactly, indeed, absolutely. [➡WORDS AND PHRASES EMPHASIZING THE TRUTH OF A MATTER; 173]

straightway (*archaic*) *adv* [➡PRESENT; 85]

strain 1 *v* **make a great effort**, try hard, struggle, labour, endeavour, strive, exert yourself. [➡HARD WORK OR EFFORT; 299] 2 *v* **damage**, injure, hurt, pull, sprain, twist, stretch, crick, wrench. [➡WOUND A PERSON OR ANIMAL; 384] 3 *v* **drain**, sieve, filter, sift, separate. [➡SEPARATE AND DIVIDE; 402] 4 *v* **tax**, overburden, overload, burden, overtax. [➡GIVE TOO MUCH; 438] 5 *n* **nervous tension**, tension, stress, worry, anxiety, pressure, trauma, burden. [➡CONFUSION, ANXIETY, AND WORRY; 541] 6 *n* **exertion**, effort, tension, struggle, force, wrench. [➡HARD WORK OR EFFORT; 299] 7 *n* **injury**, sprain, wrench, crick. [➡PAIN AND OTHER PHYSICAL SENSATIONS; 734] 8 *n* **breed**, species, type, form, sort, variety, kind, subspecies. [➡VARIETY, TYPE, KIND; 146]

strained 1 *adj* **tense**, forced, artificial, awkward, laboured, false, unnatural. [➡EMOTIONALLY UNPLEASANT AND UPSETTING; 228] *Opposite:* natural. 2 *adj* **stressed**, tense, worried, nervous, nervy (*informal*), anxious, edgy, overwrought. [➡CONFUSION, ANXIETY, AND WORRY; 541] *Opposite:* calm.

strainer *type of* **utensil**. [➡TABLEWARE, CUTLERY, AND KITCHENWARE; 861]

straining at the leash *adj* **raring to go**, keen, eager, enthusiastic, impatient, zealous, champing at the bit. [➡POSITIVE IMPATIENCE, ENTHUSIASM, AND ALERTNESS; 538] *Opposite:* indifferent.

strait *n* **passage**, channel, canal, sound. [➡THE SEAS, OCEANS, AND SHORES; 1041]

straitened *adj* **impoverished**, severe, distressed, difficult, pinched, reduced. [➡POVERTY AND POOR; 892] *Opposite:* comfortable.

straitjacket *n* **restriction**, limitation, restraint, shackles, constraint, repression. [➡CAPTIVITY AND LOSS OF FREEDOM; 249] *Opposite:* freedom.

strait-laced *adj* **prudish**, puritanical, prim, moralistic, strict, severe, narrow-minded, goody-goody (*informal*), proper. [➡CONSERVATIVE AND UNADVENTUROUS; 518] *Opposite:* broad-minded.

strait-lacedness *n* [➡CONSERVATIVE AND UNADVENTUROUS; 518]

strand 1 *v* **cut off**, maroon, trap, leave high and dry, abandon, leave. [➡REFUSING OR REJECTING RELATIONS; 975] *Opposite:* rescue. 2 *n* **thread**, filament, fibre, string, wire. [➡AMOUNT OF SOLID OR SEMI-SOLID; 115] 3 *n* **lock**, tress, wisp, curl. [➡AMOUNT OF SOLID OR SEMI-SOLID; 115] 4 *n* **element**, component, constituent, aspect, feature, part, thread. [➡PHYSICAL OBJECTS; 1242]

strange 1 *adj* **odd**, bizarre, outlandish, eccentric, weird, weird and wonderful, extraordinary, out of the ordinary, peculiar, abnormal, unexpected. [➡BIZARRE AND PECULIAR; 258] *Opposite:* normal. 2 *adj* **unfamiliar**, foreign, alien, unknown, mysterious, different, exotic, new, novel. [➡EXTRAORDINARY: UNCOMMON; 206] *Opposite:* familiar. 3 *adj* **inexplicable**, surprising, funny, astonishing, perplexing, incomprehensible, puzzling, enigmatic, unexpected, remarkable. [➡BIZARRE AND PECULIAR; 258] *Opposite:* unsurprising.

strangely 1 *adv* **oddly**, bizarrely, outlandishly, eccentrically, weirdly, extraordinarily, peculiarly, abnormally. [➡BIZARRE AND PECULIAR; 258] *Opposite:* normally. 2 *adv* **inexplicably**, surprisingly, funnily, astonishingly, perplexingly, incomprehensibly, puzzlingly, enigmatically, unexpectedly, remarkably. [➡EXTRAORDINARY: AMAZING; 205] *Opposite:* unsurprisingly.

strangeness *n* **weirdness**, peculiarity, eccentricity, abnormality, crankiness (*informal*), incongruity, oddity, bizarreness, oddness, outlandishness. [➡BIZARRE AND PECULIAR; 258] *Opposite:* normality.

stranger *n* **foreigner**, alien, outsider, visitor, guest, new arrival. [➡STRANGERS; 972]

strangle 1 *v* **choke**, strangulate, throttle, garrotte, asphyxiate, smother, suffocate, crush. [➡KILL; 923] 2 *v* **stifle**, repress, suppress, inhibit, smother. [➡AVOID, PREVENT, LIMIT, AND CONTROL; 278] *Opposite:* express.

stranglehold 1 *n* **strong hold**, throttlehold, iron grip, grip, lock, headlock, clinch, clamp. [➡CAPTIVITY AND LOSS OF FREEDOM; 249] 2 *n* **power**, dominion, control, sway, domination, monopoly. [➡CAPTIVITY AND LOSS OF FREEDOM; 249]

strangulate *v* **strangle**, throttle, choke, smother, asphyxiate, suffocate, crush. [➡KILL; 923]

strangulation *n* **strangling**, throttling, choking, smothering, asphyxiation, suffocation, crushing. [➡CAUSES OF DEATH; 921]

strap 1 *n* **band**, fastening, belt, strip, leash, tie. [➡FASTENERS, LINKS, AND NETWORKS; 1246] 2 *v* **fasten**, belt, secure, lash, buckle, tie, bind. [➡FASTEN, LINK, AND JOIN; 409] 3 *part of* **garment**. [➡PARTS OF A GARMENT; 870]

straphanger (*informal*) *n* **passenger**, traveller, commuter, rider. [➡TRAVEL: TRAVELLERS AND WALKERS; 320]

strapline *n* **subheading**, subhead, heading, head, title, byline. [➡NEWSPAPERS; 606]

strapped (*informal*) *adj* **needy**, wanting, short of money, strapped for cash (*informal*), skint (*informal*), impecunious (*formal*), impoverished, broke (*informal*), poor, short. *Opposite:* flush. (*informal*). [➡POVERTY AND POOR; 892]

strapped for cash (*informal*) *adj* [➡POVERTY AND POOR; 892]

strapping (*informal*) *adj* **robust**, broad-shouldered, burly, well-built, sturdy, brawny, stalwart, muscular, beefy. [➡BUILD; 478] *Opposite:* delicate.

strass *n* [➡ORNAMENTS AND DECORATIONS; 1247]

stratagem *n* **trick**, ruse, ploy, wile, subterfuge, feint, dodge, device, scheme, plot, tactic, manoeuvre. [➡WAYS OF DOING THINGS; 295]

strategic *adj* **planned**, tactical, calculated, deliberate, premeditated, considered, intentional. [➡INTENTIONAL AND DELIBERATE; 280] *Opposite:* unplanned.

strategist *n* **tactician**, planner, policymaker, plotter, schemer. [➡POLITICAL OFFICES AND POLITICIANS; 808]

strategy *n* **plan**, scheme, policy, approach, tactic, line of attack, stratagem. [➡WAYS OF DOING THINGS; 295]

stratocumulus *type of* **cloud**. [➡CLOUDY AND RAINY WEATHER; 1052]

stratosphere *n* [➡THE EARTH'S ATMOSPHERE; 1040]

stratum (*formal*) *n* **layer**, band, level, division, section, branch, echelon, vein. [➡COVERS AND COATINGS; 1245]

stratus *type of* **cloud**. [➡CLOUDY AND RAINY WEATHER; 1052]

straw 1 *n* **grass**, hay, stubble, chaff. [➡ANIMAL FEED; 1167] 2 *type of* **fibre**. [➡PLANT MATERIALS; 1132]

strawberry *type of* **fruit**. [➡FRUIT AND VEGETABLES; 1175]

straw-hat (*US*) *adj* **summer**, seasonal, temporary, travelling, summer stock (*US*). [➡FINITENESS, VARIABILITY, AND TRANSIENCE; 96]

straw poll *n* **poll**, opinion poll, show of hands, referendum, questionnaire, consultation, survey. [➡ELECTIONS AND SUFFRAGE; 807]

stray 1 *v* **wander away**, wander off, go astray, get lost, drift, lose your way, lose one's way. [➡AIMLESS AND ERRANT MOTION; 344] 2 *adj* **lost**, wandering, abandoned, homeless, vagrant. [➡AIMLESS AND ERRANT MOTION; 344]

streak 1 *n* **line**, band, strip, stripe, vein, smudge, splash, flash. [➡PATTERNS; 1224] 2 *n* **element**, side, trait, characteristic, quality, aspect, trace. [➡TEMPERAMENT AND BEHAVIOUR; 493] 3 *n* **run**, stretch, roll. [➡PERIOD OF TIME; 90] 4 *v* **mark**, stripe, stain, line, fleck, daub, smudge. [➡DECORATE, ADORN, AND APPLY COATINGS; 406] 5 *v* **move fast**, fly, flash, zoom, whiz, rush, shoot (*informal*), dart, zip (*informal*), speed, sprint. [➡MOVE FAST; 314]

streaky *adj* **stripy**, striped, striated, banded, lined, barred. [➡DESCRIBING PATTERNS; 1226]

stream 1 *n* **watercourse**, brook, river, beck, torrent, rivulet, tributary, creek (*US*), crick (*US regional*). [➡RIVERS, LAKES, AND STREAMS; 1042] 2 *n* **jet**, spurt, torrent, cascade. [➡AMOUNT OF LIQUID; 114] 3 *n* **flood**, torrent, barrage, onslaught. [➡SUDDEN EVENT; 52] 4 *v* **flow**, pour out, flood, gush, spill, run, issue, course. [➡LIQUID EMISSION; 371]

streamer *n* **flag**, banner, bunting, ribbon, decoration. [➡ORNAMENTS AND DECORATIONS; 1247]

streamline *v* **rationalize**, modernize, update, reorganize, restructure, simplify. [➡ARRANGE AND CREATE ORDER; 358]

streamlined 1 *adj* **sleek**, smooth, slick, aerodynamic. [➡ROUNDED SHAPE; 1217] 2 *adj* **efficient**, rationalized, modernized, updated, reorganized, restructured, simplified, well-run. [➡ECONOMICAL AND RESOURCEFUL; 208] *Opposite:* cumbersome.

street *type of* **minor road**. [➡ROADS; 1105]

streetcar (*US*) *type of* **rail vehicle**. [➡RAILWAYS; 1106]

streetcar line (*US*) *type of* **railway**. [➡RAILWAYS; 1106]

street credibility *n* **coolness**, credibility, cred (*informal*), hipness (*slang*), sophistication, fashionableness, trendiness (*informal*). [➡LEVEL OF EDUCATION AND SOPHISTICATION; 894]

street entertainer *n* [➡WORKERS IN ENTERTAINMENT AND MEDIA; 873]

streetlamp *type of* **light**. [➡LIGHT; 1163]

streetlight *type of* **light**. [➡LIGHT; 1163]

street musician *n* [➡WORKERS IN ENTERTAINMENT AND MEDIA; 873]

street party *n* [➡PARTIES, DANCES, AND CELEBRATIONS; 37]

street performer *n* [➡WORKERS IN ENTERTAINMENT AND MEDIA; 873]

street trader *n* [➡SELLER; 443]

streetwise (*informal*) *adj* **astute**, quick-witted, sharp-witted, smart, on the ball (*informal*), sharp, experienced, shrewd, hardened, tough. [➡POSITIVE INTELLECTUAL CHARACTERISTICS; 525] *Opposite:* inexperienced.

strength 1 *n* **power**, force, might, potency, muscle, vigour. [➡STRENGTH; 202] *Opposite:* weakness. 2 *n* **strong point**, strong suit, forte, asset, métier, gift. [➡SOURCE OF HAPPINESS, PLEASURE, OR IMPROVEMENT; 210] *Opposite:* weakness. 3 *n* **intensity**, concentration, dilution, depth, potency, power. [➡STRENGTH; 202]

strengthen *v* **make stronger**, reinforce, fortify, brace, toughen, build up. [➡IMPROVE STRENGTH AND DURABILITY; 379] *Opposite:* weaken.

strength of character *n* [➡STRENGTH OF WILL; 502]

strength of mind *n* **resolve**, determination, strength, fortitude, willpower, moral fibre, heart, courage, grit, firmness. [➡STRENGTH OF WILL; 502] *Opposite:* weakness.

strength of will *n* [➡STRENGTH OF WILL; 502]

strenuous 1 *adj* **taxing**, tiring, arduous, exhausting, demanding, backbreaking, laborious, tough, hard. [➡PHYSICALLY UNPLEASANT; 227] *Opposite:* light. 2 *adj* **active**, energetic, determined, spirited, tireless, persistent, vigorous, dogged. [➡STRENGTH OF WILL; 502] *Opposite:* half-hearted.

See Compare and Contrast at **hard.**

strenuously *adv* **actively**, energetically, spiritedly, tirelessly, persistently, vigorously, doggedly. [➡STRENGTH OF WILL; 502] *Opposite:* half-heartedly.

streptococcus *type of* **microorganism**. [➡MICROORGANISMS, FUNGI, AND ALGAE; 1023]

stress 1 *n* **strain**, anxiety, worry, tension, trauma, hassle (*informal*), pressure. [➡CONFUSION, ANXIETY, AND WORRY; 541] 2 *n* **emphasis**, importance, weight, accent, urgency. [➡MOST IMPORTANT THING; 198] 3 *v* **emphasize**, lay emphasis on, underline, underscore, accentuate, point up, highlight. [➡CLAIM, INSIST, AND EMPHASIZE; 615]

See Compare and Contrast at **worry.**

stressed *adj* **harassed**, worried, strained, stressed out (*informal*), tense, hassled (*informal*), anxious, frazzled (*informal*), jittery. [➡CONFUSION, ANXIETY, AND WORRY; 541] *Opposite:* relaxed.

stressed out (*informal*) *adj* **harassed**, worried, strained, stressed, tense, hassled (*informal*), anxious, frazzled (*informal*), jittery. [➡CONFUSION, ANXIETY, AND WORRY; 541] *Opposite:* relaxed.

stress-free *adj* [➡CALMING; 189]

stressful *adj* **demanding**, taxing, worrying, traumatic, tense, nerve-racking, hectic. [➡EMOTIONALLY UNPLEASANT AND UPSETTING; 228] *Opposite:* relaxing.

stress out (*informal*) *v* **worry**, bother, get to, hassle (*informal*), harass, perturb. [➡UPSET, DISTRESS, AND HUMILIATE; 568] *Opposite:* relax.

stretch 1 *v* **extend**, elongate, enlarge, widen, broaden, distend, draw out. [➡CHANGE OF SIZE: BIGGER; 393] *Opposite:* shrink. 2 *v* **spread out**, extend, unfold, spread, unroll. [➡EXIST IN A PLACE; 19] 3 *v* **be elastic**, give, expand, yield. [➡CHANGE OF SIZE: BIGGER; 393] 4 *n* **give**, bounce, spring, elasticity. [➡MALLEABLE AND ELASTIC; 1211] *Opposite:* rigidity. 5 *n* **section**, expanse, bit, area, sweep, tract. [➡AREA AND RANGE; 111] 6 *n* **spell**, period, stint, time, run, term. [➡PERIOD OF TIME; 90]

stretchable *adj* [➡MALLEABLE AND ELASTIC; 1211]

stretch a point 1 *v* **make an allowance**, bend the rules, turn a blind eye, make an exception. [➡NOT PAY ATTENTION; 765] 2 *v* **exaggerate**, overstate, inflate, amplify, embroider, embellish. [➡CLAIM, INSIST, AND EMPHASIZE; 615] *Opposite:* understate.

stretched 1 *adj* **extended**, outstretched, elongated, expanded, lengthened, outspread. [➡LENGTH: LONG; 1196] *Opposite:* contracted. 2 *adj* **strained**, overextended, pushed, fraught, busy, hard-pressed, stressed, under pressure, struggling. [➡IN TROUBLE AND DISADVANTAGED; 73] *Opposite:* relaxed.

stretch out *v* **recline**, lie back, bask, lounge, sprawl, repose. [➡ASSUME A POSITION; 318]

stretch the truth *v* [➡DECEPTION AND LIES; 661]

stretchy *adj* **elastic**, flexible, springy, pliable. [➡MALLEABLE AND ELASTIC; 1211] *Opposite:* rigid.

strew 1 *v* **scatter**, throw, disperse, distribute, spread, cast. [➡SPREAD AND SCATTER; 333] *Opposite:* gather. 2 *v* **litter**, cover, fill, sprinkle, dot, clutter, pepper. [➡DECORATE, ADORN, AND APPLY COATINGS; 406]

striated muscle *type of* **muscle or tendon**. [➡THE MUSCLES; 719]

striation *n* **pattern**, marking, corrugation, incision, ridge, groove. [➡PATTERNS; 1224]

stricken 1 *adj* **troubled**, tormented, wracked, disturbed, traumatized, distracted. [➡CONFUSION, ANXIETY, AND WORRY; 541] 2 *adj* **laid low**, afflicted, suffering, affected, wracked, infected. [➡ILL AND SICK; 741] *Opposite:* well. 3 *adj* **injured**, damaged, wounded, hurt, struck. [➡INJURED; 743]

strict 1 *adj* **severe**, firm, stern, harsh, stringent, austere, authoritarian, exacting, rigorous. [➡DIFFICULT TO PLEASE; 516] *Opposite:* lenient. 2 *adj* **exact**, precise, accurate, narrow, meticulous, close, true, faithful. [➡EXACT; 204] *Opposite:* inaccurate.

strictness 1 *n* **severity**, firmness, sternness, harshness, stringency, austerity, rigorousness. [➡DIFFICULT TO PLEASE; 516] *Opposite:* leniency. 2 *n* **exactitude**, precision, accuracy, narrowness, meticulousness, closeness, faithfulness. [➡EXACT; 204] *Opposite:* inaccuracy.

stricture (*formal*) 1 *n* **criticism**, attack, rebuke, telling off, censure, dressing-down. [➡CRITICISMS AND ANGRY OUTBURSTS; 50] 2 *n* **restriction**, restraint, limit, constraint, limitation, boundary. [➡CAPTIVITY AND LOSS OF FREEDOM; 249]

stride 1 *v* **step**, walk, pace, tread, march, tramp, stomp, step out. [➡MOVE FAST; 314] 2 *n* **pace**, step, tread, gait, walk. [➡PROCEED AND GO; 306] 3 *n* **advance**, progress, development, improvement, headway. [➡PROGRESS AND ADVANCEMENT; 214]

strident 1 *adj* **loud**, harsh, grating, shrill, raucous, piercing, discordant. [➡LOUD OR UNPLEASANT SOUNDS; 1265] *Opposite:* soft. 2 *adj* **vociferous**, forceful, persuasive, clamorous, baying, vocal, noisy. [➡POMPOUS, LOUD, AND OVER-CONFIDENT; 636] *Opposite:* gentle.

strife *n* **trouble**, conflict, discord, contention, fighting, dissension, friction, rivalry. [➡DISHARMONY; 157] *Opposite:* harmony.

strike 1 *v* **hit**, beat, smack, sock (*informal*), belt (*informal*), thump, wallop (*informal*), clout, clobber (*informal*), punch. [➡PHYSICAL ATTACK AND PUNISHMENT; 416] 2 *v* **collide with**, hit, crash into, smash into, bump into, run into, come into contact with. [➡CONTACT: IMPACT; 414] *Opposite:* miss. 3 *v* **occur to**, come to mind, dawn on, hit, come to, register, cross your mind. [➡APPEAR AND EMERGE; 3] 4 *v* **attack**, launch an attack, fall on, set on, hit, assail, assault, raid. [➡DESTRUCTION AND DEMOLITION; 360] 5 *v* **discover**, hit upon, light on, stumble across, chance upon, happen upon, uncover, unearth, turn up. [➡FIND; 464] 6 *v* **take industrial action**, stop work, come out, down tools, walk out, go on a go-slow, work to rule. [➡WORK-RELATED ACTIVITIES; 834] 7 *v* **reach**, arrive at, attain, achieve, effect (*formal*), arrange. [➡INSTITUTE AND INAUGURATE; 349] 8 *n* **raid**, attack, assault, foray, air strike, incursion. [➡AGGRESSIVE EVENT; 39] 9 *n* **industrial action**, go-slow, walkout, work-to-rule, work stoppage, slowdown (*US*). [➡WORK-RELATED ACTIVITIES; 834]

strike back *v* [➡VENGEANCE AND REVENGE; 686]

strike down 1 *v* **knock down**, floor, fell, bring down, knock out, lay out (*informal*), KO (*informal*). [➡PHYSICAL ATTACK AND PUNISHMENT; 416] 2 *v* **afflict**, lay low, infect, affect, make ill. [➡ILL AND SICK; 741] 3 *v* **kill**, bring down, wipe out (*slang*), murder, assassinate, slay (*formal or literary*), slaughter. [➡KILL; 923]

strike it rich *v* **hit the jackpot**, come into money, rake it in (*informal*), make your fortune, make a pile (*informal*), make a bundle (*slang*), laugh all the way to the bank, clean up (*slang*). [➡GET MONEY OR REWARD; 422]

strike off *v* **delete**, cross off, remove, withdraw. [➡GET RID OF SOMETHING; 452] *Opposite:* include.

strike out 1 *v* **cross out**, delete, score out, strike through, cancel, erase, remove. [➡DELETE AND ERASE; 340] 2 *v* **set out**, leave, depart, go, move off, start out, head off, set forth (*literary*). [➡ABSENT ONESELF; 8] *Opposite:* arrive. 3 *v* **attack**, lash out, set on, assail. [➡PHYSICAL ATTACK AND PUNISHMENT; 416] 4 *v* (*US informal*) **fail**, fall short, miss the boat, bomb (*informal*), flop (*informal*), mismanage. [➡FAIL OR BE UNSUCCESSFUL; 75]

striker 1 *n* **picket**, picketer, demonstrator, protester. [➡WORKER; 836] 2 *n* **football player**, forward, attacker, winger. [➡PEOPLE IN SPORTS AND LEISURE; 876]

strike up *v* **start**, begin, commence (*formal*), initiate, make a start. [➡CAUSE TO START; 266] *Opposite:* stop.

strike up a friendship *v* [➡ESTABLISHING RELATIONSHIPS WITH OTHERS; 974]

strike while the iron's hot *v* **take the opportunity**, make hay while the sun shines (*informal*), grab the chance, make the most of it. [➡START AN ACTION; 261]

striking 1 *adj* **conspicuous**, noticeable, marked, remarkable, salient, outstanding, prominent, unusual, arresting, out of the ordinary. [➡EXTRAORDINARY: AMAZING; 205] *Opposite:* inconspicuous. 2 *adj* **good-looking**, handsome, attractive, eye-catching, beautiful, stunning. [➡PEOPLE'S PHYSICAL APPEARANCE; 476]

striking distance *n* **spitting distance** (*informal*), stone's throw, short distance, a hairsbreadth, hop, skip, and jump. [➡CLOSENESS; 160]

strikingly *adv* **noticeably**, markedly, conspicuously, outstandingly, prominently, unusually, remarkably, stunningly. [➡EXTRAORDINARY: AMAZING; 205]

string 1 *n* **cord**, thread, filament, twine, rope. [➡FASTENERS, LINKS, AND NETWORKS; 1246] 2 *n* **sequence**, series, run, chain, succession, row, line. [➡COLLECTIONS AND MIXTURES OF THINGS; 1243]

string along (*informal*) 1 *v* **deceive**, mislead, lead on, give the runaround (*informal*), lead up the garden path, send on a wild-goose chase. [➡DECEPTION AND LIES; 661] 2 *v* **tag along**, hang around, go along, go along for the ride, stick around (*informal*), join in, take part. [➡ACCOMPANY AND FOLLOW; 338] 3 *v* **agree**, go along with, be of one mind, concur, approve, support. [➡AGREE; 646] *Opposite:* disagree.

string band *type of* **band**. [➡MUSICIANS AND SINGERS; 908]

string bean *type of* **pulse**. [➡BEANS AND PULSES; 1188]

stringency *n* **severity**, strictness, rigour, harshness, inflexibility, rigidity, toughness. [➡EMOTIONALLY UNPLEASANT AND UPSETTING; 228] *Opposite:* flexibility.

stringent *adj* **severe**, strict, rigorous, stern, harsh, tough, inflexible, rigid. [➡EMOTIONALLY UNPLEASANT AND UPSETTING; 228] *Opposite:* lax.

stringer *n* **journalist**, reporter, correspondent, columnist, writer. [➡WORKERS IN ENTERTAINMENT AND MEDIA; 873]

string quartet *type of* **band**. [➡MUSICIANS AND SINGERS; 908]

string vest *type of* **upper body underwear**. [➡HABERDASHERY, MILLINERY, AND LINGERIE; 867]

stringy *adj* **tough**, chewy, sinewy, gristly, fibrous. [➡STATE OF PREPARED FOOD; 1170] *Opposite:* tender.

strip 1 *v* **undress**, strip off, disrobe (*formal*), doff, shed, peel off. [➡DRESS, WEAR, AND UNDRESS; 868] *Opposite:* dress. 2 *v* **deprive**, take away, divest, deny, rid. *Opposite:* furnish. (*formal*). [➡TAKE SOMETHING AWAY; 426] 3 *n* **band**, sliver, shred, ribbon, slip, bit, stripe, belt. [➡AREA AND RANGE; 111]

stripe *n* **band of colour**, strip, band, line, streak, bar. [➡PATTERNS; 1224]

striped *adj* [➡DESCRIBING PATTERNS; 1226]

striplight *type of* **light**. [➡LIGHT; 1163]

strip off *v* [➡DRESS, WEAR, AND UNDRESS; 868]

stripped *adj* **bare**, exposed, unprotected, uncovered, unvarnished, unpainted. [➡LESS; 124] *Opposite:* coated.

stripped-down *adj* **lean**, spare, sparse, minimalist, utilitarian, Spartan, functional, basic. [➡LESS; 124]

stripped of *adj* [➡LACK OF POSSESSION; 446]

stripy *adj* [➡DESCRIBING PATTERNS; 1226]

strive *v* **struggle**, endeavour, go all out, do your best, do your utmost, make every effort, try hard, attempt, try, do all you can, pull out all the stops. [➡HARD WORK OR EFFORT; 299]

stroke 1 *n* **hit**, blow, knock, rap, lash, thump, whack. [➡CONTACT: IMPACT; 414] 2 *n* **rub**, caress, fondle, pat. [➡CONTACT: TOUCH; 413] 3 *v* **caress**, fondle, pat, rub. [➡CONTACT: TOUCH; 413]

stroke of luck *n* [➡LUCK; 784]

stroll 1 *v* **walk**, amble, saunter, promenade (*formal*), ramble, go for a constitutional, wander. [➡MOVE SLOWLY; 315] 2 *n* **saunter**, walk, amble, promenade (*formal*), turn, wander, meander, ramble, constitutional. [➡PROCEED AND GO; 306]

stroller (*US*) *n* **buggy**, pushchair, baby carriage (*US*), baby buggy (*US regional*). [➡BIKES, CARS, AND CARRIAGES; 1148]

strong 1 *adj* **powerful**, burly, brawny, muscular, strapping (*informal*), sturdy, well-built, tough, beefy, stalwart. [➡BUILD; 478] *Opposite:* weak. 2 *adj* **robust**, sturdy, stout, solid, durable, hard-wearing, resilient, tough, heavy-duty. [➡DURABLE; 1209] *Opposite:* fragile. 3 *adj* **glaring**, dazzling, bright, stark, brilliant, intense. [➡DESCRIBING LIGHT; 1227] *Opposite:* dim. 4 *adj* **keen**, staunch, dedicated, firm, fanatical, zealous, eager. [➡ENERGY AND ENTHUSIASM; 497] *Opposite:* indifferent. 5 *adj* **convincing**, sound, clear, clear-cut, persuasive, compelling, effective, formidable. [➡SAFE AND SAFETY; 192] *Opposite:* weak. 6 *adj* **fervent**, great, intense, deep, deep-seated, fierce, powerful, potent, passionate, ardent. [➡STRENGTH; 202] *Opposite:* weak. 7 *adj* **intense**, concentrated, pungent, piquant, spicy, hot, sharp, biting. [➡TASTE; 704] *Opposite:* insipid.

strong-arm (*informal*) 1 *adj* **coercive**, forcible, violent, physical, forceful, bullying, aggressive. [➡FRIGHTENING; 232] *Opposite:* peaceable. 2 *v* **coerce**, compel, force, frighten, bully, threaten. [➡CAUSE OR COMPEL TO ACT; 272]

strongbox *n* **safe-deposit box**, cash box, safe, coffer, vault. [➡CONTAINERS, RECEPTACLES, AND PACKAGING; 1244]

stronghold *n* **fortress**, refuge, bastion, citadel, sanctuary, fastness (*archaic or literary*), fort, castle. [➡FORTRESSES AND FORTIFICATIONS; 1089]

strong-minded 1 *adj* **determined**, dogged, persevering, persistent, resolute, unyielding, single-minded, tenacious, unwavering, strong-willed, indomitable, firm, uncompromising. [➡STRENGTH OF WILL; 502] *Opposite:* weak-willed. 2 *adj* **confident**, clear-thinking, certain, intelligent, decisive, independent. [➡POSITIVE INTELLECTUAL CHARACTERISTICS; 525]

strong-mindedness 1 *n* **determination**, doggedness, perseverance, persistence, resoluteness, unyieldingness, single-mindedness, tenacity, indomitability, firmness. [➡STRENGTH OF WILL; 502] *Opposite:* vacillation. 2 *n* **confidence**, strength, strength of character, character, clarity, certainty, intelligence, decisiveness, independence. [➡POSITIVE INTELLECTUAL CHARACTERISTICS; 525] *Opposite:* weakness.

strong point *n* **strength**, strong suit, forte, asset, métier. [➡SOURCE OF HAPPINESS, PLEASURE, OR IMPROVEMENT; 210] *Opposite:* weakness.

strongroom *type of* **storage space**. [➡STORES AND STORAGE BUILDINGS; 1087]

strong suit *n* **forte**, strength, strong point, métier, asset. [➡SOURCE OF HAPPINESS, PLEASURE, OR IMPROVEMENT; 210] *Opposite:* weakness.

strong-willed *adj* **resolute**, determined, strong-minded, iron-willed, unbending, inflexible, uncompromising, forceful, decisive. [➡STRENGTH OF WILL; 502] *Opposite:* weak.

strop (*informal*) *n* **bad mood**, bad temper, huff, pet, rage, sulk. [➡IRRITATION AND ANGER; 542]

strophe *n* [➡ASPECTS OF LANGUAGE; 683]

stroppiness (*informal*) *n* **awkwardness**, uncooperativeness, obstreperousness, difficultness, unhelpfulness, obstructiveness, bolshiness (*informal*), perverseness, bloody-mindedness (*informal*), ill temper. [➡IRRITATION AND ANGER; 542]

stroppy (*informal*) *adj* **awkward**, uncooperative, obstreperous, difficult, unhelpful, obstructive, bolshie (*informal*), perverse, bloody-minded (*informal*), bad-tempered. [➡DIFFICULT TO PLEASE; 516] *Opposite:* amiable.

structural 1 *adj* **physical**, mechanical, organizational, operational. [➡BUILDING AND ARCHITECTURE; 1075] 2 *adj* **basic**, important, essential, fundamental, underlying. [➡IMPORTANT; 195]

structure 1 *n* **construction**, assembly, building, edifice, erection (*formal*). [➡BUILDING AND ARCHITECTURE; 1075] 2 *n* **arrangement**, organization, construction, configuration, makeup, constitution, formation, composition. [➡QUALITIES AND CHARACTERISTICS; 1190] 3 *v* **arrange**, construct, configure, put together, make up, shape, constitute (*formal*), form, organize, build up. [➡ARRANGE AND CREATE ORDER; 358]

structured 1 *adj* **organized**, planned, controlled, designed, arranged, tight, well-thought-out, regulated, systematized, coordinated. [➡ORDER AND ORGANISATION; 207] *Opposite:* unstructured. 2 *adj* **defined**, coordinated, well-defined, designed, formal, fitted, shaped. [➡DESCRIBING CLOTHES; 869] *Opposite:* amorphous.

struggle 1 *v* **strive**, try, strain, fight, work hard, labour, toil. [➡HARD WORK OR EFFORT; 299] 2 *v* **fight**, grapple, tussle, wrestle, brawl, scuffle, battle. [➡COMPETE, CONTEND, AND COMBAT; 304] 3 *v* **writhe**, wriggle, thrash about, thrash, resist, fight back, fight, kick. [➡FIDGET AND FROLIC; 312] 4 *n* **tussle**, fight, brawl, scrap (*informal*), scuffle, skirmish, melee, free-for-all (*informal*), battle. [➡AGGRESSIVE EVENT; 39] 5 *n* **effort**, exertion, labour, toil, work. [➡HARD WORK OR EFFORT; 299]

struggle on *v* [➡TOLERATE AND ENDURE; 767]

struggle through *v* [➡TOLERATE AND ENDURE; 767]

strum *v* **play**, thrum, improvise, jam, noodle (*slang*), twang. [➡MUSIC, SONGS, AND SINGING; 907]

strung out (*informal*) *adj* **overwrought**, tense, tired, nervous, worked up (*informal*), irritable, fractious. [➡IRRITATION AND ANGER; 542] *Opposite:* relaxed.

strung up (*informal*) *adj* [➡IRRITATION AND ANGER; 542]

strut 1 *v* **swagger**, march, parade, prance, sashay (*humorous*), walk. [➡MOVE FAST; 314] 2 *n* **support**, rod, brace, crosspiece, girder, bar, beam. [➡BUILDING MATERIALS; 1076]

stub 1 *n* **stump**, end, remains, remnant, counterfoil. [➡RUBBISH AND USELESS OBJECTS; 1248] 2 *v* **hit**, bump, bang, bash (*informal*), knock. [➡CONTACT: IMPACT; 414]

stubble 1 *n* **stalks**, stems, rubbish, debris, refuse, leavings, straw. [➡RUBBISH AND USELESS OBJECTS; 1248] 2 *n* **whiskers**, five o'clock shadow, growth, beard, moustache. [➡FACIAL HAIR; 490]

stubbly *adj* [➡FACIAL HAIR; 490]

stubborn 1 *adj* **persistent**, dogged, tenacious, persevering, determined, stalwart. [➡STRENGTH OF WILL; 502] *Opposite:* half-hearted. 2 *adj* **obstinate**, immovable, inflexible, wilful, mulish, bolshie (*informal*), obdurate, intractable (*formal*), pigheaded. [➡UNWILLINGNESS AND STUBBORNNESS; 565] *Opposite:* flexible.

stubbornness 1 *n* **persistence**, tenacity, perseverance, doggedness, stalwartness, determination. [➡STRENGTH OF WILL; 502] 2 *n* **obstinacy**, inflexibility, obduracy, pigheadedness, mulishness, intractability (*formal*), bolshiness (*informal*), wilfulness. [➡UNWILLINGNESS AND STUBBORNNESS; 565] *Opposite:* flexibility.

stubby *adj* **short**, broad, thick, stumpy, squat, stout. [➡BUILD; 478] *Opposite:* slender.

stub out *v* **extinguish**, put out, snuff. [➡CAUSE TO STOP; 267]

stucco *n* [➡BUILDING MATERIALS; 1076]

stuccowork *n* [➡BUILDING MATERIALS; 1076]

stuck 1 *adj* **wedged**, fixed, trapped, caught, jammed, immovable, held. [➡LACK OF ACTIVITY; 343] *Opposite:* loose. 2 *adj* **baffled**, mystified, puzzled, without an answer, at a complete loss, stumped. [➡CONFUSION, ANXIETY, AND WORRY; 541]

stuck on (*informal*) *adj* [➡APPRECIATION AND GRATITUDE; 536]

stuck-up (*informal*) *adj* **snobbish**, arrogant, conceited, superior, self-important, condescending, toffee-nosed (*informal*), haughty, snooty. [➡AFFECTATION, SELF-SATISFACTION, AND SNOBBISHNESS; 508] *Opposite:* unassuming.

stud 1 *n* **knob**, boss, rivet, nail, screw, protrusion, button, bump. [➡FASTENERS, LINKS, AND NETWORKS; 1246] 2 *v* **boss**, fit with studs, decorate, fasten, rivet, secure, emboss. [➡FASTEN, LINK, AND JOIN; 409] 3 *v* **dot**, pepper, sprinkle, scatter, speckle, cover. [➡DECORATE, ADORN, AND APPLY COATINGS; 406] 4 *type of* **jewellery**. [➡JEWELLERY; 866]

student *n* **scholar**, pupil, schoolboy, schoolgirl, schoolchild, undergraduate, apprentice, learner. [➡STUDENTS AND PUPILS; 841]

student loan *n* **loan**, bank loan, government loan, educational loan, subsidized loan. [➡MONEY, PAYMENTS, AND CHARGES; 800]

studied *adj* **deliberate**, intentional, calculated, considered, premeditated, planned, wilful. [➡INTENTIONAL AND DELIBERATE; 280] *Opposite:* spontaneous.

studio 1 *n* **workplace**, workshop, workroom, atelier, pottery, workspace. [➡PLACE OF EMPLOYMENT; 832] 2 *n* **academy**, conservatory, dance school, ballet school, dance academy. [➡EDUCATIONAL INSTITUTIONS; 813] 3 (*US*) *type of* **apartment**. [➡RESIDENTIAL BUILDINGS; 1077]

studio couch *type of* **bed**. [➡FURNITURE; 858]

studio flat *type of* **apartment**. [➡RESIDENTIAL BUILDINGS; 1077]

studious 1 *adj* **thoughtful**, serious, reflective, bookish, scholarly, academic, intellectual, erudite, brainy (*informal*). [➡LEVEL OF EDUCATION AND SOPHISTICATION; 894] *Opposite:* frivolous. 2 *adj* **diligent**, painstaking, careful, assiduous, industrious, meticulous, hard-working, earnest, purposeful, determined. [➡HARD-WORKING AND COMMITTED; 501] *Opposite:* careless.

studiously 1 *adv* **thoughtfully**, seriously, reflectively, deeply, intensely, profoundly. [➡ENTHUSIASTIC AND INQUISITIVE; 629] *Opposite:* frivolously. 2 *adv* **diligently**, painstakingly, carefully, assiduously, industriously, meticulously, earnestly, purposefully, determinedly. [➡HARD-WORKING AND COMMITTED; 501] *Opposite:* carelessly.

studiousness 1 *n* **thoughtfulness**, application, seriousness, concentration, focus, inattention. [➡POSITIVE INTELLECTUAL CHARACTERISTICS; 525] 2 *n* **diligence**, care, assiduousness, industry, meticulousness, conscientiousness. [➡HARD-WORKING AND COMMITTED; 501] *Opposite:* carelessness.

study 1 *v* **learn**, take in, bone up (*informal*), revise, grind, swot (*informal*), swot up (*informal*), cram (*informal*), read, hit the books (*US informal*), review (*US*). [➡STUDYING; 844] *Opposite:* forget. 2 *v* **investigate**, research, experiment, examine, consider, scrutinize, look into, explore, probe, delve into, analyse. [➡EXAMINE AND ASSESS; 754] 3 *n* **learning**, education, training, revision, schoolwork, lessons, homework, scholarship. [➡LESSONS, COURSE WORK, AND EXAMINATIONS; 842] 4 *n* **investigation**, survey, experiment, review, inquiry, research, analysis, examination, search, scrutiny, consideration. [➡EXAMINE AND ASSESS; 754] 5 *n* **report**, findings, conclusions, research paper, analysis, paper, feedback. [➡ANALYTICAL NONFICTION WRITING; 593] 6 *type of* **room in the home**. [➡TYPES OF ROOM; 1096]

study leave *n* [➡PERIOD OF REST; 91]

stuff 1 *v* **fill**, pack, cram, ram, jam, stow, load, squeeze. [➡FILL; 407] 2 *n* **material**, substance, matter, raw material. [➡SUBSTANCES; 1266] 3 *n* **things**, objects, bits and pieces (*informal*), paraphernalia, junk (*informal*), articles, mess, packages, gear. [➡PHYSICAL OBJECTS; 1242] 4 *n* **possessions**, belongings, things, kit, gear (*informal*), tackle, personal effects, property, equipment, effects (*formal*). [➡POSSESSIONS; 462]

stuff and nonsense *n* [➡MEANINGLESS SPEECH OR WRITING; 677]

stuffed 1 *adj* **filled**, lined, packed, jammed, crammed, jam-packed (*informal*), bursting. [➡FULL; 1238] 2 *adj* (*informal*) **full**, fit to burst, replete, sated, satiated, bloated, satisfied. [➡EAT AND NOT EAT; 711] *Opposite:* hungry.

stuffed shirt (*informal*) *n* **fogy**, old fogy, fuddy-duddy (*informal*), stick-in-the-mud (*informal*), wet blanket (*informal*), killjoy, spoilsport. [➡SELF-IMPORTANT AND SELF-SEEKING PEOPLE; 949]

stuffily *adv* **staidly**, strait-lacedly, standoffishly, conventionally, strictly, pompously, formally. [➡UNFRIENDLINESS AND UNSOCIABILITY; 505] *Opposite:* informally.

stuffiness 1 *n* **airlessness**, staleness, closeness, mugginess, fug. [➡HOT WEATHER; 1050] *Opposite:* freshness. 2 *n* **formality**, conventionality, staidness, standoffishness, pomposity, aloofness, strictness. [➡UNFRIENDLINESS AND UNSOCIABILITY; 505] *Opposite:* informality.

stuffing *n* [➡CENTRAL PARTS OF PHYSICAL OBJECTS; 1250]

stuff up (*informal*) *v* **mess up** (*informal*), blow it (*slang*), botch, make a mess of, foul up (*informal*). [➡ MESS UP AND MAKE MISTAKES; 473] *Opposite:* sort out.

stuffy 1 *adj* **airless**, stale, smelly, hot, warm, dry, smoky, suffocating, fusty, unventilated, stifling. [➡ HOT WEATHER; 1050] *Opposite:* fresh. 2 *adj* **strait-laced**, old-fashioned, conventional, formal, pompous, strict, dry, narrow, smug, supercilious, stodgy. [➡ UNFRIENDLINESS AND UNSOCIABILITY; 505] *Opposite:* informal. 3 *adj* **congested**, blocked up, bunged up (*informal*), rheumy, stopped up, clogged up. [➡ FULL; 1238] *Opposite:* clear.

stultify 1 *v* **bore**, dull, numb, deaden, put off, put to sleep. [➡ BORE AND FAIL TO INTEREST; 571] *Opposite:* stimulate. 2 *v* **make a fool of**, belittle, set up (*informal*), ridicule, humiliate. [➡ JOKES AND TEASING; 675] 3 *v* **negate** (*formal*), cancel out, block, render useless, pre-empt, vitiate, cripple, hamstring, queer somebody's pitch. [➡ MAKE IMPOSSIBLE; 277] *Opposite:* advance.

stultifying *adj* [➡ PHYSICALLY UNPLEASANT; 227]

stumble 1 *v* **trip**, trip up, lose your footing, lose your balance, falter, fall, sprawl, lurch, topple. [➡ GO DOWNWARDS; 308] 2 *v* **stagger**, lurch, sway, blunder, roll, totter, teeter, reel, flounder, hobble, pitch. [➡ WALK UNSTEADILY; 316] 3 *v* **hesitate**, stop and start, hem and haw, falter, stammer, stutter, blunder, pause, waver. [➡ HESITATE; 273] 4 *v* **come across**, find, discover, happen on, chance on, turn up, hit on, fall upon, blunder across. [➡ FIND; 464] 5 *n* **blunder**, trip, stagger, false step, mishap, upset, accident, misstep, spill, fall. [➡ DISASTERS; 253] 6 *n* **mistake**, hesitation, slip, slip-up (*informal*), blunder, bungle (*informal*). [➡ MISTAKES; 251]

See Compare and Contrast at **hesitate**.

stumble across *v* [➡ FIND; 464]

stumble on *v* [➡ FIND; 464]

stumble upon *v* [➡ FIND; 464]

stumbling block *n* **obstacle**, problem, difficulty, sticking point, obstruction, barrier, snag, hindrance, impediment, hurdle. [➡ PROBLEM; 257] *Opposite:* aid.

stump 1 *n* **base**, stub, butt, end, remains, remnant, nubbin. [➡ RUBBISH AND USELESS OBJECTS; 1248] 2 *v* **baffle**, puzzle, perplex, mystify, nonplus, bewilder, flummox (*informal*), confound, confuse, bamboozle (*informal*), dumbfound, stymie. [➡ CONFUSE AND BEWILDER; 572] *Opposite:* enlighten.

stumped *adj* [➡ CONFUSION, ANXIETY, AND WORRY; 541]

stump up (*informal*) *v* **come up with**, cough up (*informal*), pay, provide, put in, contribute. [➡ GIVE MONEY; 434] *Opposite:* withhold.

stumpy *adj* **squat**, stubby, short, thickset, broad, stocky, diminutive. [➡ BUILD; 478] *Opposite:* lanky.

stun 1 *v* **knock out**, lay out (*informal*), paralyse, numb, daze, put out of action, stupefy. [➡ FALL ILL, TREAT, AND RECOVER; 729] *Opposite:* bring round. 2 *v* **shock**, upset, dumbfound, daze, amaze, astonish, astound, stagger, confound, bewilder, flabbergast, startle. [➡ CONFUSE AND BEWILDER; 572]

stung *adj* [➡ SADNESS, DISTRESS, AND DESPAIR; 540]

stunned *adj* [➡ SURPRISE, SHOCK, AND AMAZEMENT; 546]

stunner (*informal*) *n* **knockout** (*informal*), star, smash, sensation, wow (*informal*), hit, triumph, blockbuster (*informal*), lulu (*slang*), humdinger (*slang*), doozy (*US slang*). [➡ AMAZING THING; 212]

stunning *adj* **spectacular**, striking, fabulous, splendid, superb, magnificent, gorgeous, exquisite, impressive. [➡ EXTRAORDINARY: AMAZING; 205] *Opposite:* unimpressive.

stunningly *adv* **spectacularly**, strikingly, fabulously, splendidly, superbly, magnificently, gorgeously, exquisitely, impressively, astoundingly, astonishingly. [➡ EXTRAORDINARY: UNCOMMON; 206] *Opposite:* unimpressively.

stunt 1 *v* **inhibit**, restrict, arrest, hold back, impede, slow up, slow down, check, curtail, curb, cramp. [➡ DELAY ACTION OR OCCURRENCE; 279] *Opposite:* assist. 2 *n* **feat**, exploit, act, deed, show, tour de force, trick, number. [➡ ACTIONS OR UNDERTAKINGS; 260]

stunted *adj* **underdeveloped**, undersized, small, short, little, diminutive. [➡ LENGTH: SHORT; 1197]

stupefaction 1 *n* (*literary*) **amazement**, astonishment, wonder, surprise, awe, wonderment. [➡ SURPRISE, SHOCK, AND AMAZEMENT; 546] 2 *n* **confusion**, befuddlement, bemusement, perplexity, bewilderment, wooziness, doziness. [➡ CONFUSION, ANXIETY, AND WORRY; 541]

stupefied 1 *adj* **confused**, fuddled, punch-drunk, stunned, befuddled, bemused, muddled, dazed, staggered. [➡ CONFUSION, ANXIETY, AND WORRY; 541] *Opposite:* clear-headed. 2 *adj* **amazed**, astonished, astounded, stunned, dazed, confounded, shocked, baffled, mystified, surprised. [➡ SURPRISE, SHOCK, AND AMAZEMENT; 546]

stupefy 1 *v* **amaze**, astonish, astound, surprise, stagger, overwhelm, shock, flabbergast, nonplus. [➡ SURPRISE AND IMPRESS; 575] 2 *v* **confuse**, befuddle, bewilder, stun, perplex, bemuse, daze, dumbfound, stagger. [➡ CONFUSE AND BEWILDER; 572] *Opposite:* enlighten.

stupendous 1 *adj* **astonishing**, astounding, amazing, surprising, stunning, awesome, breathtaking, remarkable. [➡ EXTRAORDINARY: AMAZING; 205] *Opposite:* unremarkable. 2 *adj* **fantastic**, wonderful, terrific (*informal*), out of this world, marvellous, great, fabulous, splendid. [➡ EXTRAORDINARY: AMAZING; 205] *Opposite:* awful. 3 *adj* **huge**, vast, large, colossal, enormous, gigantic, considerable, mammoth, prodigious, tremendous. [➡ LARGE; 1192] *Opposite:* tiny.

stupendously *adv* **tremendously**, impressively, amazingly, exceptionally, remarkably, strikingly, spectacularly, terrifically, massively (*informal*), extremely, astoundingly. [➡ TO A GREAT EXTENT; 130] *Opposite:* slightly.

stupid 1 *adj* **unintelligent**, dull, brainless, obtuse, witless. [➡ NEGATIVE INTELLECTUAL CHARACTERISTICS; 526] *Opposite:* intelligent. 2 *adj* **foolish**, fatuous, inane, nonsensical, silly, daft (*informal*), futile, ludicrous, ridiculous, laughable, senseless, absurd, asinine. [➡ BIZARRE AND PECULIAR; 258] *Opposite:* sensible. 3 *adj* **unwise**, senseless, ill-advised, imprudent (*formal*), injudicious, thoughtless, rash, irresponsible, reckless, heedless. [➡ THE NATURE OF IDEAS; 772] *Opposite:* wise.

stupidity *n* **foolishness**, foolhardiness, silliness, inanity, folly, futility, senselessness, absurdity. [➡NEGATIVE INTELLECTUAL CHARACTERISTICS; 526] *Opposite:* sense.

stupidly *adv* **foolishly**, unwisely, naively, unthinkingly, inanely, senselessly, nonsensically. [➡NEGATIVE INTELLECTUAL CHARACTERISTICS; 526] *Opposite:* sensibly.

stupor 1 *n* **torpor**, lethargy, inertness, limpness, blankness, vacancy, apathy, inertia. [➡PAIN AND OTHER PHYSICAL SENSATIONS; 734] *Opposite:* activeness. 2 *n* **daze**, dream, trance, shock, stupefaction (*literary*), numbness, paralysis. [➡SURPRISE, SHOCK, AND AMAZEMENT; 546] *Opposite:* consciousness.

sturdily *adv* **strongly**, solidly, firmly, securely, robustly, vigorously, durably. [➡STRENGTH; 202] *Opposite:* weakly.

sturdiness *n* **strength**, solidity, durability, toughness, hardiness, robustness, vigour. [➡DURABLE; 1209] *Opposite:* weakness.

sturdy 1 *adj* **well-built**, strong, robust, powerful, strapping (*informal*), muscular, brawny, mighty, burly. [➡BUILD; 478] *Opposite:* frail. 2 *adj* **well-made**, durable, robust, tough, hard-wearing, strong, solid, secure, substantial, rugged. [➡DURABLE; 1209] *Opposite:* rickety. 3 *adj* **resolute**, decisive, determined, strenuous, enthusiastic, energetic, forceful, steadfast. [➡STRENGTH OF WILL; 502] *Opposite:* feeble.

sturgeon *type of* **sea fish**. [➡SEA FISH; 1009]

stutter 1 *v* **stammer**, trip over your tongue, falter, stumble, hesitate, mumble, sputter, splutter. [➡WITTER AND BABBLE; 618] *Opposite:* enunciate. 2 *n* **stammer**, speech disorder, impediment, impairment, speech impediment. [➡INARTICULATE, RAMBLING, AND AWKWARD; 634]

sty 1 *n* **cyst**, swelling, lump, boil, sore, spot. [➡CONDITIONS AFFECTING THE SKIN; 722] 2 *type of* **pen or cage**. [➡ANIMAL OR BIRD ACCOMMODATION; 1078]

style 1 *n* **design**, type, sort, form, variety, quality, character, kind, pattern, mould. [➡VARIETY, TYPE, KIND; 146] 2 *n* **method**, approach, way, manner, fashion, technique, mode. [➡WAYS OF DOING THINGS; 295] 3 *n* **flair**, panache, chic, bravura, stylishness, smartness, good taste, elegance, grace, polish, class, charm. [➡WELL GROOMED; 483] *Opposite:* gracelessness. 4 *n* **luxury**, luxuriousness, extravagance, lavishness, opulence, grandeur, elegance, comfort, wealth. [➡EXPENSIVE AND LUXURIOUS; 219] 5 *v* (*formal*) **name**, call, nickname, label, term, dub, entitle. [➡NAME AND DESCRIBE; 666] 6 *v* **fashion**, design, shape, cut, adapt, tailor. [➡CHANGE OF SHAPE; 386]

styling gel *n* [➡PERSONAL HYGIENE; 492]

styling spray *n* [➡PERSONAL HYGIENE; 492]

stylish *adj* **fashionable**, sophisticated, chic, modish, trendy (*informal*), smart, elegant, tasteful, classy (*informal*), voguish, polished. [➡WELL GROOMED; 483] *Opposite:* unfashionable.

stylishness *n* **style**, flair, chic, panache, smartness, good taste, elegance, grace. [➡WELL GROOMED; 483] *Opposite:* dowdiness.

stylistic *adj* **formal**, technical, literary, musical, artistic, aesthetic. [➡ARTISTIC MOVEMENTS AND STYLES; 899] *Opposite:* spontaneous.

stylize *v* **formalize**, abstract, schematize, systematize, outline, reduce, portray, render (*formal*). [➡CREATE IMAGES; 357]

stylized *adj* **conventional**, artificial, formalized, formal, unnatural, flat, schematic. [➡FALSE AND UNREAL; 174] *Opposite:* natural.

stylus *part of* **audio equipment**. [➡AUDIO EQUIPMENT; 1138]

stymie 1 *v* **hinder**, prevent, block, thwart, confound, frustrate, upset, stump, mystify, baffle. [➡MAKE IMPOSSIBLE; 277] *Opposite:* enable. 2 *n* **impasse**, dead end, stalemate, standstill, deadlock, standoff. [➡PROBLEM; 257] *Opposite:* breakthrough.

stymied *adj* [➡CONFUSION, ANXIETY, AND WORRY; 541]

suave *adj* **urbane**, smooth, polished, polite, sophisticated, formal, impeccable, gracious, charming, mannerly. [➡LEVEL OF EDUCATION AND SOPHISTICATION; 894] *Opposite:* awkward.

sub (*informal*) *v* [➡CHANGE ONE THING FOR ANOTHER; 399]

subatomic particle *see* **elementary particle**.

subcategory *n* **subsection**, subclass, subgroup, subdivision. [➡VARIETY, TYPE, KIND; 146]

subcompact (*US*) *type of* **car**. [➡BIKES, CARS, AND CARRIAGES; 1148]

subconscious *adj* **unconscious**, intuitive, hidden, unintentional, involuntary, subliminal. [➡PSYCHOLOGY AND THE MIND; 770] *Opposite:* deliberate.

subcontract *v* **delegate**, farm out, contract out, commission, mandate, authorize. [➡BUSINESS ACTIVITIES AND PHENOMENA; 795] *Opposite:* contract.

subcultural *adj* **cultural**, social, ethnic, religious, sociological, socioanthropological, sociocultural, anthropological. [➡BELONGING OR RELATING TO PEOPLE; 943]

subculture *n* **subgroup**, culture, grouping, group, subdivision, division. [➡GROUPS IN SOCIETY; 940]

subcutaneous *adj* **hypodermic**, hypodermal, intravenous, internal, dermatological, dermal, medical. [➡THE SKIN; 721]

subdirectory 1 *n* **division**, subdivision, directory, file, storage, space. [➡SUBDIVISIONS AND OFFSHOOTS; 1252] 2 *type of* **software**. [➡COMPUTERS AND COMPUTING; 1126]

subdivide *v* **divide**, section, segment, split, cut, partition, divide up, split up, cut up. [➡SEPARATE AND DIVIDE; 402] *Opposite:* unify.

subdivision 1 *n* **section**, part, division, sector, tract, development, portion, slice, unit. [➡AREA AND RANGE; 111] 2 *n* **division**, sectioning, segmenting, separation, splitting up, partitioning. [➡SEPARATE AND DIVIDE; 402] *Opposite:* unification.

subdue 1 *v* **restrain**, suppress, hold back, control, discipline, tame, check. [➡AVOID, PREVENT, LIMIT, AND CONTROL; 278] 2 *v* **pacify**, calm, calm down, soothe, mollify, placate, reduce, soften, moderate. [➡SOOTHE AND CALM; 574] 3 *v* **subjugate**, conquer, vanquish, defeat, overpower, overcome, crush, quell, overwhelm. [➡BEAT AND DEFEAT; 80]

subdued 1 *adj* **passive**, cowed, submissive, quiet, unresponsive, restrained, serious, downcast. [➡NEUTRALITY AND INDIFFERENCE; 554] *Opposite:* uplifted. 2 *adj* **gentle**, low, restrained, muted, subtle, soft, hushed, quiet. [➡DESCRIBING LIGHT; 1227] *Opposite:* loud.

subeditor *n* **assistant editor**, editorial assistant, assistant, deputy editor, deputy, second in command, copy editor, sub (*informal*), editor, proofreader, checker. [➡WORKERS IN ENTERTAINMENT AND MEDIA; 873]

subgroup *n* **subcategory**, subsection, subclass, subdivision, smaller group, minor group. [➡VARIETY, TYPE, KIND; 146]

subhuman *adj* **bestial**, animal, inhuman, inhumane, wicked, less than human. [➡BEASTLY AND BRUTISH; 511]

subject 1 *n* **topic**, theme, focus, subject matter, area under discussion, question, issue, matter, business, substance, text. [➡SUBJECT AREA; 769] 2 *n* **subordinate**, vassal, liege, dependent, citizen. [➡SUBORDINATES AND ASSISTANTS; 966] *Opposite:* sovereign. 3 *n* **field**, speciality, study, discipline, area. [➡SUBJECT AREA; 769] 4 *type of* **grammatical term**. [➡ASPECTS OF LANGUAGE; 683]

Compare and Contrast: ***subject, topic, subject, matter, matter, theme, burden***

CORE MEANING: WHAT IS UNDER DISCUSSION

subject a matter that is under discussion or investigation; ***topic*** a matter dealt with in a text or discussion; ***subject matter*** the material dealt with in a film, discussion, or other pursuit; ***matter*** the material that is dealt with in speech or writing, as opposed to its presentation; ***theme*** a distinct, recurring, and unifying idea in music, literature, art, or film; ***burden*** (*literary*) the main argument or recurrent theme in music or literature.

subjection *n* **domination**, subjugation, overpowering, enslavement, oppression. [➡FAILURE; 77]

subjective 1 *adj* **slanted**, biased, prejudiced, skewed, one-sided. [➡THE NATURE OF IDEAS; 772] *Opposite:* objective. 2 *adj* **individual**, particular, idiosyncratic, independent, personal. [➡BELONGING OR RELATING TO INDIVIDUALS; 944] *Opposite:* general.

subjectively *adv* **personally**, individually, one-sidedly, instinctively, intuitively, emotionally. [➡THE NATURE OF IDEAS; 772] *Opposite:* objectively.

subjectivity *n* **bias**, prejudice, partisanship, partiality. [➡THE NATURE OF IDEAS; 772] *Opposite:* objectivity.

subject matter *n* **topic**, theme, subject, focus, question, issue, matter, business, substance, text. [➡SUBJECT AREA; 769]

See Compare and Contrast at **subject**.

subject to 1 *v* **cause to experience**, cause to undergo, expose to, put through, make susceptible, make liable, make prone. [➡CAUSE OR COMPEL TO ACT; 272] 2 *adj* **conditional on**, dependent on, depending on, bound by, answerable to. [➡RECIPROCITY AND INTERDEPENDENCE; 148] *Opposite:* unrelated.

subjugate *v* **conquer**, vanquish, subdue, defeat, overpower, overcome, crush, suppress, quell, overwhelm. [➡BEAT AND DEFEAT; 80] *Opposite:* liberate.

subjunctive *type of* **grammatical term**. [➡ASPECTS OF LANGUAGE; 683]

sublease *v* [➡LEND, LEASE, AND BORROW; 429]

sublet *v* [➡LEND, LEASE, AND BORROW; 429]

sublimate *v* **channel**, redirect, transfer, direct, reroute. [➡DESPATCH AND SEND; 334]

sublimation *n* **redirection**, transferral, direction, rerouting, division. [➡PSYCHOLOGY AND THE MIND; 770]

sublime 1 *adj* **inspiring**, inspirational, uplifting, awe-inspiring, moving, transcendent, magnificent, heavenly, exalted (*formal*), beautiful. [➡EMOTIONALLY PLEASANT; 188] *Opposite:* ridiculous. 2 *adj* (*informal*) **excellent**, superb, splendid, marvellous, wonderful, great, terrific. [➡EXTRAORDINARY: UNCOMMON; 206]

subliminal *adj* **subconscious**, unconscious, hidden, concealed, unintentional. [➡PSYCHOLOGY AND THE MIND; 770] *Opposite:* conscious.

submachine gun *type of* **gun**. [➡WEAPONS FOR SHOOTING; 1155]

submarine *type of* **military vessel**. [➡SHIPS AND BOATS; 1149]

submerge 1 *v* **plunge**, immerse, dip, sink, duck, lower. [➡MOVE SOMETHING: DOWNWARDS; 330] 2 *v* **suppress**, conceal, hide, stifle. [➡WITHHOLD INFORMATION; 688] *Opposite:* reveal.

submerged *adj* **underwater**, flooded, inundated, waterlogged, sunken. [➡WET; 1239]

submicroscopic *adj* [➡SMALL; 1194]

submission 1 *n* **obedience**, compliance, capitulation, surrender, acquiescence, deference, assent. [➡THE WILL AND WILLINGNESS; 564] *Opposite:* resistance. 2 *n* **proposal**, suggestion, plan, tender, offer, idea. [➡OFFICIAL DOCUMENTS; 587]

submissive *adj* **obedient**, passive, compliant, acquiescent, subservient, docile, meek, dutiful, tractable, deferential, accommodating. [➡THE WILL AND WILLINGNESS; 564] *Opposite:* assertive.

submit 1 *v* **present**, propose, tender, offer, suggest. [➡SUGGEST, HINT, AND COMMENT; 613] *Opposite:* withdraw. 2 *v* **give in**, yield, agree to, acquiesce, resign yourself to, defer to, bow to, surrender, capitulate. [➡FORGET, FORGIVE, AND ACCEPT; 749] *Opposite:* resist.

See Compare and Contrast at **yield**.

subnormal *adj* **substandard**, second-rate, poor, inferior, below average, deficient, insufficient. [➡INFERIORITY; 154] *Opposite:* superior.

subordinate 1 *adj* **secondary**, lesser, subsidiary, inferior, lower, outranked, subservient, minor. [➡RELATIONSHIP TO ANOTHER; 973] *Opposite:* main. 2 *n* **assistant**, junior, underling, minion, aide, dependent, attendant. [➡SUBORDINATES AND ASSISTANTS; 966] *Opposite:* boss.

subordination *n* **relegation**, demotion, reduction, subservience. [➡INFERIORITY; 154]

suborn *v* **incite**, bribe, induce, entice, corrupt, pay off (*informal*). [➡CAUSE OR COMPEL TO ACT; 272]

subpoena 1 *n* **summons**, order, call. [➡TRIAL, PUNISHMENT, AND LEGAL OUTCOMES; 819] 2 *v* **summon**, compel, require, order, command. [➡TRIAL, PUNISHMENT, AND LEGAL OUTCOMES; 819]

subscribe 1 *v* **donate to**, give to, pledge, promise, contribute, kick in (*US informal*), pitch in, chip in (*informal*). [➡GIVE MONEY; 434] 2 *v* **agree with**, approve of, support, condone, hold with, advocate, endorse, assent, go along with. [➡AGREE; 646] *Opposite:* disagree.

subscription *n* **payment**, donation, contribution. [➡EXPENDITURE; 424]

subsequent *adj* **following**, succeeding, ensuing, successive, consequent, later. [➡AFTER, LAST, AND FOLLOWING; 166] *Opposite:* preceding.

subservient *adj* **obedient**, compliant, acquiescent, docile, deferential, passive, meek, servile, submissive. [➡RELATIONSHIP TO ANOTHER; 973] *Opposite:* assertive.

subset *n* **subsection**, subdivision, subgroup, subcategory, subclass. [➡VARIETY, TYPE, KIND; 146]

subside 1 *v* **collapse**, cave in, fall down, drop, sink, slip, settle, descend, sag. [➡GO DOWNWARDS; 308] *Opposite:* rise. 2 *v* **diminish**, lessen, decrease, dwindle, wane, recede, abate (*formal or literary*), quieten down, settle down, moderate. [➡CHANGE OF INTENSITY: LESS; 396] *Opposite:* build up.

subsidence *n* **subsiding**, sinking, settling, dropping, collapsing, falling, descending, sagging. [➡EROSION AND WEATHERING; 1055]

subsidiary 1 *adj* **supplementary**, auxiliary, ancillary, additional, contributory, secondary, extra. [➡MORE AND EXCESS; 122] *Opposite:* main. 2 *adj* **subordinate**, lesser, secondary, junior, lower, minor. [➡INFERIORITY; 154] *Opposite:* major. 3 *n* **company**, firm, holding, business, affiliate, division, branch. [➡BUSINESS ENTERPRISES AND RELATED BODIES; 793]

subsidize *v* **finance**, fund, sponsor, back, support, promote, bankroll (*informal*), endow, stake, underwrite. [➡GIVE MONEY; 434]

subsidy *n* **funding**, financial backing, grant, support, subvention (*formal*), aid, appropriation, backing, sponsorship, subsidization. [➡EXPENDITURE; 424]

subsist *v* **exist**, survive, live, make ends meet, keep going, eke out a living, keep your head above water. [➡CONTINUE TO EXIST; 17]

subsistence *n* **survival**, existence, maintenance, sustenance. [➡PERMANENCE: WITHOUT END; 94] *Opposite:* affluence.

subspecies *n* **category**, strain, genus, sort, class. [➡VARIETY, TYPE, KIND; 146]

substance 1 *n* **material**, matter, stuff, ingredient, body, constituent, element. [➡SUBSTANCES; 1266] 2 *n* **core**, essence, import, gist, nub, basis, crux, theme, soul. [➡MOST IMPORTANT THING; 198] 3 *n* **affluence**, property, money, means, wealth, riches. [➡POSSESSIONS; 462] *Opposite:* poverty.

substandard *adj* **inferior**, second-rate, poor, subnormal, below average, deficient, insufficient. [➡INFERIORITY; 154] *Opposite:* superior.

substantial *adj* **considerable**, large, extensive, significant, important, generous, ample, sizable, plentiful, big, abundant. [➡LARGE; 1192] *Opposite:* small.

substantially *adv* **considerably**, significantly, noticeably, markedly, greatly, substantively, extensively. [➡TO A GREAT EXTENT; 130] *Opposite:* insignificantly.

substantiate *v* **validate**, authenticate, verify, corroborate, prove, confirm, demonstrate, bear out, support. [➡APPROVE AND CONFIRM; 647] *Opposite:* disprove.

substantiated *adj* [➡TRUE AND REAL; 172]

substantiation *n* **corroboration**, confirmation, validation, authentication, support, evidence, demonstration, verification, proof. [➡EVIDENCE AND PROOF; 69]

substantive 1 *adj* **practical**, applicable, functional, utilitarian. [➡USEFULNESS; 200] *Opposite:* impractical. 2 *adj* **essential**, fundamental, basic, central, elementary, principal, primary. [➡IMPORTANT; 195] 3 *adj* **independent**, autonomous, separate, individual. [➡FREEDOM AND LIBERTY; 209] 4 *adj* **substantial**, decent, considerable, respectable, significant, sizable, plentiful, big, large, abundant. [➡LARGE; 1192] 5 *type of* **word class**. [➡ASPECTS OF LANGUAGE; 683]

substantively 1 *adv* **practically**, functionally, applicably. [➡USEFULNESS; 200] 2 *adv* **essentially**, fundamentally, basically, centrally, elementarily, principally, primarily. [➡IMPORTANT; 195] 3 *adv* **independently**, autonomously, individually, separately. [➡FREEDOM AND LIBERTY; 209] 4 *adv* **substantially**, considerably, significantly, noticeably, markedly, greatly, extensively. [➡TO A GREAT EXTENT; 130] *Opposite:* insignificantly.

substitute 1 *v* **replace with**, exchange, use instead, switch, swap (*informal*). [➡CHANGE ONE THING FOR ANOTHER; 399] 2 *v* **stand in for**, fill in for, take the place of, relieve, deputize for, replace. [➡REPRESENT SOMETHING OR SOMEBODY; 59] 3 *n* **alternative**, replacement, stand-in, locum, surrogate, proxy, deputy, reserve, alternate (*US*). [➡SUBSTITUTES AND STAND-INS; 400]

substitution *n* **replacement**, switch, exchange, changeover, swap (*informal*), change. [➡CHANGE ONE THING FOR ANOTHER; 399]

substratum *n* [➡COVERS AND COATINGS; 1245]

subsume *v* **include**, incorporate, count, list, consider. [➡CREATING CONNECTIONS; 145]

subterfuge *n* **trick**, ploy, ruse, stratagem, manoeuvre, dodge, deception, artifice (*formal*), machination, duplicity, con. [➡DECEPTION AND LIES; 661]

subterranean 1 *adj* **underground**, deep, below ground, buried, hidden, concealed. [➡IMPERCEPTIBLE; 26] 2 *adj* **secret**, clandestine, underground, covert, arcane, hidden, surreptitious. [➡SECRET AND UNKNOWN; 180] *Opposite:* open.

subtext *n* **implication**, hidden agenda, suggestion, connotation, intimation, insinuation, hint. [➡MEANING; 691]

subtitle *n* **caption**, legend, surtitle, supertitle. [➡FILM; 901]

subtle 1 *adj* **slight**, faint, fine, thin, imperceptible, negligible. [➡IMPERCEPTIBLE; 26] *Opposite:* obvious. 2 *adj* **understated**, delicate, indirect, elusive, refined, restrained. [➡POSITIVELY COMPLEX OR COMPLICATED; 218] *Opposite:* blatant. 3 *adj* **intelligent**, experienced, sensitive, shrewd, perceptive, clever. [➡POSITIVE INTELLECTUAL CHARACTERISTICS; 525] *Opposite:* obtuse. 4 *adj* **cunning**, sly, crafty, devious, tricky, artful. [➡DECEITFUL; 514]

subtleness 1 *n* **delicacy**, subtlety, refinement, intricacy, elusiveness, restraint. [➡POSITIVELY COMPLEX OR COMPLICATED; 218] 2 *n* **intelligence**, experience, sensitivity, shrewdness, perceptiveness, cleverness. [➡POSITIVE INTELLECTUAL CHARACTERISTICS; 525] 3 *n* **cunning**, deviousness, slyness, craftiness, trickiness, artfulness. [➡DECEITFUL; 514]

subtlety 1 *n* **delicacy**, subtleness, refinement, intricacy, elusiveness, restraint. [➡POSITIVELY COMPLEX OR COMPLICATED; 218] 2 *n* **detail**, nicety, fine point, nuance. [➡FEW, LITTLE, SMALL AMOUNT; 119] 3 *n* **sensitivity**, delicacy, tact, discernment, finesse. [➡GOOD MANNERS AND SOCIAL SKILLS; 521]

subtly 1 *adv* **faintly**, delicately, finely, thinly, slightly, imperceptibly, negligibly. [➡TO A CERTAIN EXTENT; 134] *Opposite:* obviously. 2 *adv* **intelligently**, sensitively, shrewdly, perceptively, cleverly. [➡POSITIVE INTELLECTUAL CHARACTERISTICS; 525] 3 *adv* **cunningly**, slyly, ingeniously, deviously, craftily, trickily, artfully. [➡DECEITFUL; 514]

subtract *v* **take away**, take from, take off, deduct, withdraw, detract. [➡REMOVE SOMETHING; 339] *Opposite:* add.

subtraction *n* **deduction**, removal, withdrawal, debit, deletion, detraction. [➡MATHS; 598]

suburb *n* **conurbation**, district, environs, development, area, exurbia (*US*), green belt, outskirts. [➡HUMAN SETTLEMENTS; 1069] *Opposite:* centre.

suburban *adj* **outlying**, peripheral, out-of-town, outer, residential. [➡HUMAN SETTLEMENTS; 1069] *Opposite:* central.

suburbia *n* **suburbs**, commuter belt, conurbation, environs, exurbia (*US*), outskirts, green belt. [➡HUMAN SETTLEMENTS; 1069] *Opposite:* centre.

subvention (*formal*) 1 *n* **grant**, subsidy, payment, donation, endowment, allocation. [➡MONEY, PAYMENTS, AND CHARGES; 800] 2 *n* **aid**, support, backing, sponsorship, funding, assistance. [➡MONEY, PAYMENTS, AND CHARGES; 800]

subversion *n* **rebellion**, sedition, treason, mutiny, insurrection, sabotage, agitation, destabilization. [➡UNWILLINGNESS AND STUBBORNNESS; 565] *Opposite:* compliance.

subversive 1 *adj* **dissident**, rebellious, revolutionary, insubordinate, seditious, insurrectionary, destabilizing, treasonous, traitorous. [➡REBELLIOUSNESS AND DISOBEDIENCE; 566] *Opposite:* law-abiding. 2 *n* **traitor**, quisling (*dated*), collaborator, mutineer, revolutionary, insubordinate, rebel. [➡UNCOOPERATIVE OR REBELLIOUS PERSON; 567] *Opposite:* patriot.

subvert *v* **undermine**, overthrow, destabilize, sabotage, disrupt, bring down, topple. [➡AVOID, PREVENT, LIMIT, AND CONTROL; 278] *Opposite:* support.

subway 1 *n* **underpass**, tunnel, passageway. [➡BRIDGES, TUNNELS, CROSSINGS, AND JUNCTIONS; 1111] 2 (*US*) *type of* **railway**. [➡RAILWAYS; 1106]

subzero *adj* **freezing**, arctic (*informal*), bitter, icy, ice-cold, glacial, polar. [➡COLD WEATHER; 1051] *Opposite:* tropical.

succeed 1 *v* **achieve**, accomplish, hit the target, turn out well, be successful, win, triumph, go well, work, come off (*informal*), bear fruit. [➡SUCCEED AND WIN; 79] *Opposite:* fail. 2 *v* **make it** (*informal*), do well, get ahead, prosper, be successful, thrive, flourish, get to the top, climb the ladder, make good. [➡SUCCEED AND WIN; 79] *Opposite:* fail. 3 *v* **follow**, come after, replace, supersede, supplant. [➡HAPPEN; 27] *Opposite:* precede.

succeeding *adj* **following**, subsequent, ensuing, next, successive, later, consequent, future, impending. [➡AFTER, LAST, AND FOLLOWING; 166] *Opposite:* preceding.

success 1 *n* **achievement**, accomplishment, victory, triumph, feat, realization, attainment. [➡SUCCESS; 82] *Opposite:* failure. 2 *n* **hit**, winner, sensation, star, triumph, success story. [➡ADVANTAGE; 213] *Opposite:* failure.

successful 1 *adj* **fruitful**, positive, effective, efficacious (*formal*). [➡SUCCESSFUL AND PROMISING; 81] *Opposite:* unsuccessful. 2 *adj* **popular**, prosperous, up-and-coming, well-off, wealthy, rich. [➡WEALTH AND WEALTHY; 891] 3 *adj* **flourishing**, thriving, booming, profitable, lucrative, productive. [➡SUCCESSFUL AND PROMISING; 81] *Opposite:* ailing.

successfully 1 *adv* **positively**, effectively, efficaciously, fruitfully, magnificently, well. [➡SUCCESSFUL AND PROMISING; 81] *Opposite:* unsuccessfully. 2 *adv* **productively**, fruitfully, profitably, lucratively, well. [➡SUCCESSFUL AND PROMISING; 81] *Opposite:* badly.

successfulness *n* **success**, utility, worth, effectiveness, value, merit. [➡SUCCESS; 82] *Opposite:* uselessness.

succession *n* **series**, sequence, chain, run, string, train, progression. [➡CHAIN OF EVENTS; 163] *Opposite:* individual.

successive *adj* **consecutive**, succeeding, following, sequential, uninterrupted, continual, continuous, straight, in a row. [➡AFTER, LAST, AND FOLLOWING; 166] *Opposite:* single.

successor *n* **heir**, inheritor, replacement, beneficiary. [➡SUBORDINATES AND ASSISTANTS; 966] *Opposite:* predecessor.

success story *n* **success**, winner, sensation, hit, triumph, fairy tale. [➡SUCCESS; 82]

succinct *adj* **concise**, pithy, brief, to the point, laconic, neat, crisp. [➡SUCCINCT AND TO-THE-POINT; 641] *Opposite:* long-winded.

succinctness *n* **concision**, pithiness, conciseness, brevity, briefness, economy, terseness, shortness, clarity, crispness, neatness. [➡SUCCINCT AND TO-THE-POINT; 641] *Opposite:* long-windedness.

succour (*literary*) 1 *n* **help**, relief, aid, support, assistance, rescue, comfort. [➡KIND ACTION OR BEHAVIOUR; 296] 2 *n* **benefactor**, help, support, rescuer, provider, helpmate. [➡SUBORDINATES AND ASSISTANTS; 966] *Opposite:* enemy. 3 *v* **comfort**, aid, relieve, rescue, support, assist, help. [➡TAKE CARE OF AND SPOIL; 301] *Opposite:* abandon.

succulence *n* **juiciness**, lusciousness, tenderness, moistness, tastiness, deliciousness, lushness. [➡TASTE; 704] *Opposite:* dryness.

succulent *adj* **juicy**, moist, tender, luscious, delicious, tasty, mouthwatering. [➡TASTE; 704] *Opposite:* dry.

succumb 1 *v* **give way**, yield, give in, submit, surrender, capitulate, accede. [➡FAIL OR BE UNSUCCESSFUL; 75] *Opposite:* withstand. 2 *v* **die**, pass away, expire, perish (*literary*), depart. [➡DIE; 922]

See Compare and Contrast at **yield**.

such as *adv* **for example**, like, namely, viz. [➡EXPRESSIONS INTRODUCING EXAMPLES; 64]

suck 1 *v* **draw**, pull on, lap, slurp, drink, imbibe (*formal or humorous*). [➡DRINK; 712] 2 *v* **extract**, draw, pull, force, take out, withdraw. [➡GET; 421] 3 *v* **pull**, draw, force, sweep, bear, carry. [➡MOVE SOMETHING TO ANOTHER LOCATION; 325] 4 *n* **slurp**, draw, pull, drink, taste, mouthful. [➡DRINK; 712]

suck dry *v* [➡USE UP AND WASTE; 475]

sucker 1 *n* (*informal*) **mug** (*slang*), pushover (*informal*), gull, mark (*slang*), fall guy (*slang*), dupe, chump (*dated informal*). [➡VICTIMS OF DECEIT; 663] 2 *n* (*US slang*) **thing**, contraption, so-and-so (*informal*), blighter, critter (*US*). [➡PHYSICAL OBJECTS; 1242] 3 *v* (*informal*) **trick**, con, fool, gull, dupe, take in, deceive, cheat, swindle, hoodwink (*slang*), bamboozle (*informal*). [➡DECEPTION AND LIES; 661]

suck in 1 *v* **involve**, implicate, entangle, embroil, draw in, drag in, pull in. [➡CAUSE OR COMPEL TO ACT; 272] *Opposite:* exclude. 2 *v* **breathe in**, inhale, draw in, take in, pull in, gasp. [➡BREATHE AND NOT BREATHE; 717]

suck the life out of *v* [➡USE UP AND WASTE; 475]

suck up 1 *v* **absorb**, soak up, take up, sop up. [➡GET; 421] 2 *v* (*informal*) **ingratiate yourself**, flatter, crawl (*informal*), butter up (*informal*), grovel, creep (*informal*), toady. [➡FLATTER AND FAWN; 622]

sucrose *type of* **nutrient**. [➡FOOD COMPONENTS; 1187]

suction *n* **force**, pressure, pull, draw, drag. [➡ENERGY GENERAL; 1160]

sudden *adj* **unexpected**, abrupt, rapid, swift, hasty, impulsive, quick, speedy, precipitous. [➡HAPPENING QUICKLY; 104] *Opposite:* gradual.

suddenness *n* **unexpectedness**, quickness, abruptness, rapidity, swiftness, speed, precipitousness. [➡SPEED; 102]

suds *n* **lather**, bubbles, foam, froth, spume (*literary*). [➡FROTH; 1272]

sudsy *adj* [➡PHYSICAL TEXTURE; 1221]

sue 1 *v* (*formal*) **petition**, beg, implore (*formal*), plead, appeal. [➡REQUEST AND DEMAND; 664] 2 *v* **litigate**, prosecute, indict, file a suit, charge. [➡TRIAL, PUNISHMENT, AND LEGAL OUTCOMES; 819]

suede *type of* **leather**. [➡FABRICS; 1131]

suet *type of* **cooking fat and oil**. [➡FATS AND OILS; 1172]

suffer 1 *v* **feel pain**, hurt, agonize, ache, smart, grieve, writhe. [➡PAIN AND OTHER PHYSICAL SENSATIONS; 734] 2 *v* **undergo**, experience, bear, endure, go through, live through, feel. [➡EXPERIENCE AND ENCOUNTER; 583] 3 *v* **tolerate**, endure, bear, put up with, stand, stomach. [➡TOLERATE AND ENDURE; 767] 4 *v* **deteriorate**, fall off, be impaired, drop off (*informal*). [➡GET WORSE; 382]

sufferance 1 *n* **tolerance**, toleration, acquiescence, allowance, permission, leniency. [➡NEUTRALITY AND INDIFFERENCE; 554] *Opposite:* prohibition. 2 *n* **endurance**, stamina, staying power, stoicism, fortitude. [➡STRENGTH OF WILL; 502]

sufferer *n* **invalid**, victim, patient, case, martyr, casualty. [➡UNFIT AND WEAK; 740]

suffering 1 *n* **pain**, distress, agony, torment, affliction. [➡PAIN AND OTHER PHYSICAL SENSATIONS; 734] 2 *n* **sorrow**, grief, misery, woe, anguish, travail. [➡SADNESS, DISTRESS, AND DESPAIR; 540]

suffice (*formal*) *v* **be sufficient**, do, serve, suit. [➡ENOUGH AND SUFFICIENT; 129]

sufficiency *n* **modicum**, right amount, adequacy, abundance, plenty. [➡ENOUGH AND SUFFICIENT; 129] *Opposite:* insufficiency.

sufficient *adj* **adequate**, enough, satisfactory, necessary, appropriate, ample, plenty, abundant. [➡ENOUGH AND SUFFICIENT; 129] *Opposite:* inadequate.

See Compare and Contrast at **enough**.

suffix *type of* **grammatical term**. [➡ASPECTS OF LANGUAGE; 683]

suffocate *v* **smother**, choke, stifle, throttle, asphyxiate, gag, quash, snuff out. [➡KILL; 923]

suffocation *n* [➡CAUSES OF DEATH; 921]

suffrage *n* [➡ELECTIONS AND SUFFRAGE; 807]

suffragette *n* [➡ELECTIONS AND SUFFRAGE; 807]

suffuse *v* **spread through**, pervade, fill, saturate, flood, permeate, imbue, steep, cover, diffuse. [➡FILL; 407]

sugar 1 *n* (*informal*) **honey**, sweetie (*informal*), sweetheart, love (*informal*), darling, dearest, pet, baby (*slang*), precious. [➡ENDEARMENTS; 657] 2 *v* **sweeten**, dress up, disguise, titivate, improve, make over. [➡IMPROVE APPEARANCE; 380] 3 *type of* **nutrient**. [➡FOOD COMPONENTS; 1187]

sugar beet *type of* **root vegetable**. [➡FRUIT AND VEGETABLES; 1175]

sugar cane *type of* **grass**. [➡GRASS; 1031]

sugary 1 *adj* **sweet**, syrupy, sickly, sugared, sweetened. [➡TASTE; 704] *Opposite:* bitter. 2 *adj* **sentimental**, mawkish, soppy (*informal*), gushy, mushy, syrupy, sickly, gooey (*informal*), saccharine. [➡IN POOR TASTE; 230] *Opposite:* dry.

suggest 1 *v* **propose**, put forward, advise, recommend, advocate, submit. [➡SUGGEST, HINT, AND COMMENT; 613] *Opposite:* veto. 2 *v* **imply**, insinuate, intimate, indicate, hint, allude. [➡MEAN SOMETHING; 61] *Opposite:* state. 3 *v* **remind**, bring to mind, call to mind, evoke, conjure up, be redolent of, smack of. [➡REMIND; 748]

See Compare and Contrast at **recommend**.

suggestibility *n* **susceptibility**, openness, vulnerability, credulousness, credulity, gullibility, malleability. [➡NEGATIVE INTELLECTUAL CHARACTERISTICS; 526] *Opposite:* strong-mindedness.

suggestible *adj* **susceptible**, impressionable, gullible, credulous, malleable. [➡NEGATIVE INTELLECTUAL CHARACTERISTICS; 526] *Opposite:* strong-minded.

suggestion 1 *n* **proposal**, proposition, submission, recommendation, idea, offer, plan, counsel (*formal or literary*), prompting, advice. [➡ADVICE; 690] *Opposite:* order. 2 *n* **implication**, hint, insinuation, intimation, indication, innuendo. [➡SUGGEST, HINT, AND COMMENT; 613] *Opposite:* statement. 3 *n* **evocation**, air, aura, hint, trace, tinge, sign, shade, touch, taste. [➡APPEARANCE AND ATMOSPHERE; 1236]

suggestive 1 *adj* **evocative**, redolent, reminiscent, indicative, expressive, recalling, allusive. [➡REPRESENTATIVE; 66] 2 *adj* **improper**, indelicate, off-colour (*informal*), indecent, lewd, risqué. [➡MORALLY BAD; 776]

suicidal 1 *adj* (*informal*) **desperate**, cheerless, hopeless, unhappy, miserable, morbid, forlorn. [➡SADNESS, DISTRESS, AND DESPAIR; 540] 2 *adj* **dangerous**, treacherous, perilous, reckless, madcap. [➡DANGEROUS; 237] *Opposite:* sensible.

suicide 1 *n* **death**, self-destruction, self-immolation (*formal*). [➡CAUSES OF DEATH; 921] 2 *n* **recklessness**, rashness, perversity, irresponsibility, madness. [➡ECCENTRICITY AND IRRATIONALITY; 563]

suit 1 *n* **costume**, ensemble, dress suit, trouser suit, uniform, outfit, getup (*informal*), garb. [➡CLOTHES AND ACCESSORIES; 864] 2 *v* **go with**, match, fit, be fitting, agree with, conform to, befit, harmonize. [➡APPROPRIATE, SUITABLE, ADVISABLE; 185] *Opposite:* clash. 3 *v* **flatter**, become, show up, enhance. [➡DRESS, WEAR, AND UNDRESS; 868]

suit

◆ *types of suit*
boiler suit, business suit, catsuit, dress suit, jump suit, overalls, pantsuit (*US*), trouser suit, zoot suit

suitability *n* **appropriateness**, aptness, fittingness, fitness, correctness, rightness. [➡APPROPRIATE, SUITABLE, ADVISABLE; 185] *Opposite:* unsuitability.

suitable *adj* **appropriate**, apposite, fit, apt, right, proper, meet (*archaic*), seemly. [➡APPROPRIATE, SUITABLE, ADVISABLE; 185] *Opposite:* inappropriate.

suitcase *n* **case**, luggage, baggage, bag, valise, overnight case, grip, portmanteau. [➡CONTAINERS, RECEPTACLES, AND PACKAGING; 1244]

suite 1 *n* **set**, collection, group, complement. [➡COLLECTIONS AND MIXTURES OF THINGS; 1243] 2 *type of* **instrumental music**. [➡MUSIC, SONGS, AND SINGING; 907]

suited *adj* **right**, matched, well-matched, appropriate, apposite, apt, fit, befitting, suitable. [➡APPROPRIATE, SUITABLE, ADVISABLE; 185] *Opposite:* wrong.

suit of armour *n* [➡GARMENTS AND OUTFITS; 865]

suitor (*formal*) *n* [➡SEXUAL AND ROMANTIC RELATIONSHIPS; 964]

sulk 1 *v* **mope**, be in a mood, feel sorry for yourself, be in a huff, be in a strop (*informal*), pout, grumble, fret, be in a funk (*US informal*). *Opposite:* rejoice. (*literary*). [➡GIVING VENT TO EMOTIONS; 680] 2 *n* **bad temper**, mood, temper, huff, strop (*informal*), bad mood, funk (*US dated informal*). [➡IRRITATION AND ANGER; 542]

sulkiness *n* **moodiness**, resentfulness, temper, bad temper, moroseness, sullenness, huffiness, stroppiness (*informal*), bad mood, crankiness (*US informal*). [➡IRRITATION AND ANGER; 542] *Opposite:* joviality.

sulky *adj* **morose**, angry, resentful, sullen, unsociable, bad-tempered, uncooperative, cross, petulant, brooding, grouchy (*informal*), in a mood, in a huff (*informal*), in a strop (*informal*), in a funk (*US informal*). [➡IRRITATION AND ANGER; 542] *Opposite:* jovial.

sullen 1 *adj* **surly**, morose, hostile, bad-tempered, dour, brooding, glowering, angry, grim, gloomy, ill-humoured. [➡BAD-TEMPERED AND HUMOURLESS; 627] *Opposite:* friendly. 2 *adj* (*literary*) **leaden**, cloudy, dull, grey, brooding, gloomy, dark, sombre, overcast, glowering. [➡WINDY AND STORMY WEATHER; 1053] *Opposite:* bright.

sullenly *adv* **morosely**, hostilely, bad-temperedly, grimly, angrily, dourly, gloomily, resentfully, crossly, sourly, grumpily. [➡BAD-TEMPERED AND HUMOURLESS; 627] *Opposite:* cheerfully.

sullenness *n* **surliness**, hostility, bad temper, moodiness, moroseness, glumness, grumpiness, grouchiness (*informal*), petulance, resentment. [➡BAD-TEMPERED AND HUMOURLESS; 627] *Opposite:* friendliness.

sullied 1 *adj* [➡MORALLY BAD; 776] 2 *adj* (*literary*) [➡DIRTY; 1234]

sully 1 *v* **tarnish**, taint, smear, denigrate, spoil, defile (*formal*), vilify, dishonour, discredit, corrupt, disgrace, defame. [➡PROTEST AND EXPRESS DISAPPROVAL; 643] *Opposite:* praise. 2 *v* (*literary*) **pollute**, contaminate, dirty, soil, befoul (*archaic or literary*), foul, stain, adulterate. [➡DIRTY AND CONTAMINATE; 405] *Opposite:* clean.

sulphur *type of* **mineral**. [➡MINERALS; 1276]

sulphurous *adj* **acrid**, reeking, stinking, foul, bitter, harsh. [➡SMELL AND SMELLING; 706]

sultan *n* [➡RULERS AND ARISTOCRACY; 823]

sultana *type of* **berry**. [➡FRUIT AND VEGETABLES; 1175]

sultriness *n* [➡HOT WEATHER; 1050]

sultry *adj* **hot**, humid, muggy, stifling, oppressive, close, sticky, airless, sweltering, baking, scorching (*informal*), boiling, roasting (*informal*). [➡HOT WEATHER; 1050] *Opposite:* fresh.

sum 1 *n* **figure**, amount, quantity, entirety, totality, summation. [➡ALL; 126] 2 *n* **calculation**, addition, computation, summation. [➡MATHS; 598]

summarily *adv* **instantly**, immediately, instantaneously, abruptly, suddenly, swiftly, rapidly, without delay, at once, straightaway, right away, precipitously. [➡HAPPENING QUICKLY; 104] *Opposite:* eventually.

summarize *v* **sum up**, précis, abridge, recap, recapitulate (*formal*), go over, run through, condense, encapsulate, digest, synopsize, review. [➡EXPLAIN AND CLARIFY; 611] *Opposite:* elaborate.

summary 1 *n* **précis**, synopsis, digest, sum-up, outline, rundown, abstract, extraction, abridgment, résumé, summation, brief, condensation, review. [➡SUMMARIES, OUTLINES, AND EXCERPTS; 589] *Opposite:* exposition. 2 *adj* **swift**, rapid, instant, immediate, instantaneous, hasty, sudden, precipitate, rushed, abrupt, peremptory. [➡HAPPENING QUICKLY; 104] *Opposite:* considered. 3 *adj* **short**, brief, concise, abridged, succinct, condensed, terse. [➡CONCISE AND CLEAR; 203]

summation 1 *n* **addition**, calculation, computation, sum. [➡ASSESS QUANTITY; 758] 2 *n* **sum total**, total, sum, final total, grand total, aggregate, final amount, whole, tally. [➡ALL; 126] 3 *n* **summary**, summing up, synopsis, outline, précis, rundown, abstract, digest, brief, résumé, condensation, sum-up. [➡SUMMARIES, OUTLINES, AND EXCERPTS; 589]

summer 1 *n* **summertime**, dog days, midsummer, solstice. [➡TIMES OF YEAR; 88] *Opposite:* winter. 2 *n* **warm weather**, sun, sunshine, warmth, heat, summertime. [➡TIMES OF YEAR; 88] 3 *n* **prime**, best time, summertime, best years, golden age, halcyon days (*literary*). [➡PLEASANT SITUATIONS; 74]

summer clothes *n* [➡GARMENTS AND OUTFITS; 865]

summerhouse *n* **gazebo**, pagoda, hut, shed, shelter. [➡ANCILLARY BUILDINGS; 1079]

summer solstice *n* [➡TIMES OF YEAR; 88]

summertime *n* **summer**, dog days, midsummer, solstice, season. [➡TIMES OF YEAR; 88]

summery *adj* **warm**, balmy, sunny, hot. [➡HOT WEATHER; 1050] *Opposite:* wintry.

summit 1 *n* **peak**, top, pinnacle, apex, acme, zenith, brow, crown, hilltop, tip, crest. [➡EXTREMITIES OF PHYSICAL OBJECTS; 1249] *Opposite:* base. 2 *n* **conference**, meeting, summit meeting, talks. [➡MEETINGS AND ASSEMBLIES; 43]

summit meeting *n* [➡MEETINGS AND ASSEMBLIES; 43]

summon 1 *v* **call**, send for, call for, call upon, bid (*archaic*), beckon, subpoena. [➡CAUSE OR COMPEL TO ACT; 272] *Opposite:* dismiss. 2 *v* **convene**, call together, get together, gather, assemble. [➡INITIATE AND ESTABLISH COMMUNICATION; 681] *Opposite:* dismiss. 3 *v* **muster**, rouse, find, activate, rally, mobilize. [➡CAUSE OR COMPEL TO ACT; 272]

summons *n* **order**, writ, directive, command, subpoena. [➡TRIAL, PUNISHMENT, AND LEGAL OUTCOMES; 819]

sumo *type of* **combat sport**. [➡HOBBIES, GAMES, AND SPORTS; 875]

sump *part of* **engine**. [➡PARTS OF AN ENGINE; 1143]

sumptuous *adj* **costly**, lavish, splendid, opulent, plush (*informal*), spectacular, superb, magnificent, grand, elaborate, luxurious, extravagant. [➡EXPENSIVE AND LUXURIOUS; 219] *Opposite:* meagre.

sumptuousness *n* **luxuriousness**, luxury, lavishness, splendour, opulence, magnificence, grandness, extravagance. [➡EXPENSIVE AND LUXURIOUS; 219]

sums (*informal*) *n* **mathematics**, arithmetic, maths, calculation. [➡MATHS; 598]

sum total *n* **whole**, totality, entirety, aggregate, summation, sum, grand total. [➡ALL; 126]

sum up *v* **summarize**, recap, recapitulate (*formal*), synopsize, encapsulate, abridge, condense, review. [➡EXPLAIN AND CLARIFY; 611] *Opposite:* elaborate.

sun *type of* **star or star system**. [➡CELESTIAL BODIES; 1060]

sunbaked *adj* **hardened**, dried, sun-dried, heated, cracked, baked. [➡DRY; 1241]

sunbathe *v* **sun yourself**, bask, tan, catch some rays (*slang*). [➡LEISURE AND RECREATION; 874]

sunbeam *n* **ray**, beam, shaft, sunlight, sunshine. [➡LIGHT; 1163]

sunblock *n* [➡PERSONAL HYGIENE; 492]

sunburn *n* [➡CONDITIONS AFFECTING THE SKIN; 722]

sunburnt *adj* [➡CONDITIONS AFFECTING THE SKIN; 722]

sundae *type of* **dessert**. [➡CAKES, BISCUITS, AND DESSERTS; 1180]

Sunday best *n* **best clothes**, finery, formal wear, best bib and tucker (*informal*). [➡GARMENTS AND OUTFITS; 865]

sun deck *n* [➡STAGES, PLATFORMS, AND RAISED AREAS; 1097]

sunder (*literary*) *v* **separate**, divide, split, sever, cut, break, cleave. [➡TEAR, BREAK, AND CUT; 361]

sundial *type of* **clock**. [➡CLOCKS AND TIMERS; 1125]

sundown *n* **sunset**, nightfall, twilight, dusk, evening, night, eventide (*literary*). [➡TIMES OF DAY; 87] *Opposite:* sunrise.

sundress *type of* **dress**. [➡GARMENTS AND OUTFITS; 865]

sun-dried *adj* **dried**, preserved, dried up, dehydrated, jerked, desiccated. [➡STATE OF PREPARED FOOD; 1170] *Opposite:* fresh.

sundries *n* **miscellany**, miscellanea, hotchpotch, assortment, odds and ends, variety, mixture. [➡COLLECTIONS AND MIXTURES OF THINGS; 1243]

sundry *adj* **various**, miscellaneous, assorted, varied, different, diverse, heterogeneous, divers (*formal*), several, manifold, motley, multifarious. [➡DIFFERENCE; 150] *Opposite:* uniform.

sunflower *type of* **annual flower**. [➡FLOWERS; 1032]

sunflower oil *type of* **cooking fat and oil**. [➡FATS AND OILS; 1172]

sunglasses *type of* **glasses**. [➡GLASSES AND SPECTACLES; 1124]

sunhat *type of* **hat**. [➡HABERDASHERY, MILLINERY, AND LINGERIE; 867]

sunk 1 *adj* **ruined**, dashed, in trouble, done for (*informal*), defeated, destroyed. [➡UNSUCCESSFUL AND UNPROMISING; 76] *Opposite:* successful. 2 *adj* **depressed**, downcast, downhearted, dejected, in the dumps, despondent, feeling low. [➡SADNESS, DISTRESS, AND DESPAIR; 540] *Opposite:* happy.

sunken 1 *adj* **submerged**, underwater, immersed. [➡GENERAL LOCATIONS; 159] 2 *adj* **hollow**, gaunt, deep-set, cadaverous, pinched, drawn. [➡FACIAL CHARACTERISTICS; 482] 3 *adj* **recessed**, lower, settled, dipped, depressed. [➡ORIENTATION AND ALIGNMENT; 1222] *Opposite:* raised.

sunlamp *type of* **light**. [➡LIGHT; 1163]

sunless *adj* **dark**, cloudy, overcast, murky, gloomy, grey, shady, bleak, dim. [➡CLOUDY AND RAINY WEATHER; 1052] *Opposite:* sunny.

sunlight *n* **sunshine**, daylight, light, rays, sunbeams. [➡LIGHT; 1163]

sunlit *adj* **sunny**, bright, light, sundrenched, bathed in light. [➡DESCRIBING LIGHT; 1227] *Opposite:* dark.

sun lotion *n* [➡PERSONAL HYGIENE; 492]

sun lounge *type of* **room in the home.** [➡TYPES OF ROOM; 1096]

sunlounger *type of* **seating.** [➡FURNITURE; 858]

sunnily *adv* **cheerfully**, cheerily, happily, genially, gaily, brightly, affably, smilingly, lightheartedly. [➡CHEERFULNESS OF OUTLOOK; 504] *Opposite:* gloomily.

sunny 1 *adj* **sunlit**, bright, luminous, brilliant, unclouded, fine, sunshiny, clear, fair, light. [➡HOT WEATHER; 1050] *Opposite:* dark. 2 *adj* **cheerful**, cheery, bright, bright and breezy, positive, optimistic, happy, smiling, beaming, genial, cordial, jolly, affable, warm, lighthearted, good-natured. [➡CHEERFULNESS OF OUTLOOK; 504] *Opposite:* gloomy.

sunrise *n* **dawn**, daybreak, break of day, first light, daylight, morning, crack of dawn, sunup (*US*). [➡TIMES OF DAY; 87] *Opposite:* sunset.

sunroof *part of* **external structure.** [➡EXTERNAL PARTS OF A VEHICLE; 1146]

sunroom (*US*) *type of* **room in the home.** [➡TYPES OF ROOM; 1096]

sunscreen *n* **sun cream**, suntan lotion, sunblock. [➡PERSONAL HYGIENE; 492]

sunset *n* **sundown**, dusk, evening, night, nightfall, twilight, the end of the day, day's end. [➡TIMES OF DAY; 87] *Opposite:* sunrise.

sunshade *n* **parasol**, umbrella, garden umbrella, beach umbrella, awning. [➡COVERS AND COATINGS; 1245]

sunshine *n* **sunlight**, light, rays, sunbeams, brightness, glare, daylight. [➡LIGHT; 1163]

sunshiny *adj* [➡HOT WEATHER; 1050]

sunspecs (*informal*) *n* **dark glasses**, shades (*informal*), sunglasses. [➡GLASSES AND SPECTACLES; 1124]

sunspot (*informal*) *n* **resort**, tourist spot, holiday resort, beach resort, vacationland (*US*). [➡URBAN OUTDOOR SPACES; 1071]

suntan *n* [➡CONDITIONS AFFECTING THE SKIN; 722]

suntan cream *n* [➡PERSONAL HYGIENE; 492]

suntan lotion *n* **sun lotion**, sun cream, suntan cream, sunscreen, sunblock, tanning lotion, suntan oil, sun protection, tanning oil. [➡PERSONAL HYGIENE; 492]

suntanned *adj* **brown**, tanned, bronzed, sunburnt. [➡COMPLEXION; 481] *Opposite:* pale.

suntan oil *n* [➡PERSONAL HYGIENE; 492]

sunup (*US*) *n* **dawn**, sunrise, daybreak, break of day, morning, daylight, first light, crack of dawn. [➡TIMES OF DAY; 87] *Opposite:* nightfall.

sup 1 *v* **spoon**, sip, drink, partake of, lap, suck, swallow. [➡DRINK; 712] *Opposite:* gulp. 2 *n* **mouthful**, sip, swallow, drink, draught, nip, drop, taste. [➡DRINK; 712] *Opposite:* gulp.

super 1 *adj* (*informal*) **wonderful**, fantastic, great, marvellous, fabulous, tremendous, excellent, splendid, terrific (*informal*), superb, brilliant, ace (*informal*), outstanding, cracking (*informal*). [➡EXTRAORDINARY: AMAZING; 205] *Opposite:* awful. 2 *adj* **superior**, better, enhanced, improved, outstanding, high-quality, best quality, first class, high-class, topnotch. [➡SUPERIORITY; 153] *Opposite:* inferior.

superabundant *adj* **overabundant**, in excess, excessive, extra, abounding, profuse, surplus. [➡TOO MUCH; 118] *Opposite:* insufficient.

superannuated 1 *adj* **retired**, pensioned off, discharged, elderly, aged, old. [➡OLD AGE; 919] *Opposite:* working. 2 *adj* **out-of-date**, antiquated, out of fashion, outmoded, passé, old, obsolete. [➡OLD, OLD-FASHIONED; 168] *Opposite:* fashionable. 3 *adj* **worn out**, worn, unusable, used up, useless, dilapidated, old, aged, decrepit. [➡OLD, OLD-FASHIONED; 168] *Opposite:* new.

superb *adj* **excellent**, outstanding, wonderful, terrific (*informal*), splendid, fabulous, fantastic, marvellous, magnificent, superlative, tremendous, brilliant, inspired, first-class, first-rate. [➡EXTRAORDINARY: AMAZING; 205] *Opposite:* abysmal.

superbug *n* **supergerm**, bug (*informal*), germ, microorganism, pathogen. [➡MICROORGANISMS, FUNGI, AND ALGAE; 1023]

supercenter (*US*) *type of* **retail outlet.** [➡RETAIL OUTLETS; 1082]

supercharge 1 *v* **boost**, soup up (*informal*), modify, charge, power up, amplify. [➡IMPROVE STRENGTH AND DURABILITY; 379] *Opposite:* downgrade. 2 *v* **charge**, overdo, load, overload, hype, colour. [➡OVERDO SOMETHING; 291] *Opposite:* understate.

supercilious *adj* **arrogant**, contemptuous, disdainful, pompous, superior, scornful, stuck-up (*informal*), snooty (*informal*), condescending, haughty, patronizing, snobbish. [➡AFFECTATION, SELF-SATISFACTION, AND SNOBBISHNESS; 508] *Opposite:* humble.

superciliousness *n* **arrogance**, contemptuousness, contempt, condescension, haughtiness, disdain, pomposity, scorn, snootiness (*informal*), snobbishness. [➡AFFECTATION, SELF-SATISFACTION, AND SNOBBISHNESS; 508] *Opposite:* humility.

supercomputer *type of* **computer.** [➡COMPUTERS AND COMPUTING; 1126]

supercool (*informal*) *adj* **cool**, modern, contemporary, wicked (*slang*), hip (*slang*), trendy (*informal*), fashionable, funky (*informal*). [➡NEW, MODERN; 167] *Opposite:* passé.

super-duper (*informal*) *adj* **excellent**, super (*informal*), wicked (*informal*), marvellous, colossal, impressive, pleasing, great (*informal*), wonderful, fantastic, fabulous, tremendous, splendid, terrific (*informal*). [➡EXTRAORDINARY: AMAZING; 205] *Opposite:* inferior.

superego *n* **conscience**, integrity, scruples, sense of propriety, sense of judgment, sense of right and wrong, morality. [➡PSYCHOLOGY AND THE MIND; 770]

superficial 1 *adj* **shallow**, trivial, trifling, unimportant, paltry, frivolous, insignificant, meaningless, lightweight, inconsequential, passing, light, hollow, trite. [➡UNIMPORTANT AND UNNECESSARY; 239] *Opposite:* profound. 2 *adj* **surface**, shallow, external, exterior, on the surface, outward, skin-deep, outer. [➡FALSE AND UNREAL; 174] *Opposite:* deep. 3 *adj* **insincere**, shallow, artificial, phoney, apparent, seeming, posturing, feigning, glib. [➡AFFECTATION, SELF-SATISFACTION, AND SNOBBISHNESS; 508] *Opposite:* sincere. 4 *adj* **cursory**, sketchy, rapid, hasty, quick, casual. [➡HAPPENING QUICKLY; 104] *Opposite:* thorough.

superficiality *n* **shallowness**, triviality, frivolity, levity, paltriness, insignificance, hollowness, triteness. [➡BORING AND UNINTERESTING; 235] *Opposite:* profundity.

superficially 1 *adv* **apparently**, seemingly, supposedly, outwardly, ostensibly, externally, to all appearances, on the face of it, at first glance. [➡FALSE AND UNREAL; 174] *Opposite:* wholly. 2 *adv* **cursorily**, sketchily, rapidly, hastily, casually, quickly, lightly. [➡HAPPENING QUICKLY; 104] *Opposite:* thoroughly.

superfine 1 *adj* **delicate**, fine, light, sheer, fragile, flimsy, wispy, thin, translucent. [➡FRAGILE; 1208] *Opposite:* coarse. 2 *adj* **superior**, first-class, first-rate, high-quality, best, excellent. [➡SUPERIORITY; 153] *Opposite:* inferior.

superfluity 1 *n* **oversupply**, excess, overabundance, surfeit, surplus, plethora, glut, flood. [➡TOO MUCH; 118] *Opposite:* insufficiency. 2 *n* **luxury**, extra, frill, trifle, indulgence. [➡AMAZING THING; 212] *Opposite:* necessity.

superfluous *adj* **extra**, surplus, redundant, unnecessary, unessential, excessive, unneeded, needless, gratuitous, spare. [➡TOO MUCH; 118] *Opposite:* basic.

superglue *n* [➡ADHESIVES; 1270]

supergrass (*informal*) *n* **informer**, grass (*slang*), informant, squealer (*slang disapproving*), rat (*slang*). [➡INTERFERING PEOPLE AND TELLTALES; 950]

superhero *n* **champion**, crusader, rescuer, fighter, protector, hero. [➡PEOPLE WHO ARE APPROVED OF; 955]

superhighway 1 *n* [➡THE INTERNET; 1127] 2 (*US*) *type of* **major road.** [➡ROADS; 1105]

superhuman *adj* **phenomenal**, prodigious, staggering, heroic, exceptional, formidable, herculean, extraordinary, godlike, omnipotent, supreme. [➡EXTRAORDINARY: AMAZING; 205] *Opposite:* normal.

superimpose *v* **place over**, overlay, lay over, apply to, cover. [➡Position Something: Between, Beside or Inside Something; 327]

superintend *v* **supervise**, manage, oversee, administer, control, run, be in charge of, direct, watch, mind. [➡BE IN CHARGE; 271] *Opposite:* ignore.

superintendent *n* **manager**, supervisor, administrator, officer, controller, overseer, inspector, examiner, director, head, chief, leader. [➡BOSSES AND MANAGEMENT; 965] *Opposite:* underling.

superior 1 *adj* **better**, better-quality, advanced, improved, enhanced, a cut above, finer. [➡SUPERIORITY; 153] *Opposite:* inferior. 2 *adj* **excellent**, high-class, top-quality, exclusive, first-class, best quality, untouchable, choice, exceptional, outstanding, expert, fine, notable, nonpareil. [➡EXTRAORDINARY: AMAZING; 205] *Opposite:* second-rate. 3 *adj* **higher**, upper, over, above. [➡RELATIVE LOCATION; 162] *Opposite:* lower. 4 *adj* **condescending**, arrogant, disdainful, supercilious, stuck-up (*informal*), aloof, aristocratic, pompous, snooty (*informal*), self-important, haughty, patronizing, imperious, high and mighty, snobbish. [➡AFFECTATION, SELF-SATISFACTION, AND SNOBBISHNESS; 508] *Opposite:* humble. 5 *adj* **larger**, greater, bigger, higher, more, grander, loftier, longer. [➡SUPERIORITY; 153] *Opposite:* smaller. 6 *n* **boss**, manager, chief, elder, better, director, supervisor, leader, senior, higher-up (*informal*), commander. [➡BOSSES AND MANAGEMENT; 965] *Opposite:* inferior.

superiority 1 *n* **advantage**, dominance, lead, pre-eminence, power, control, authority, supremacy, ascendancy, predominance, upper hand. [➡SUPERIORITY; 153] *Opposite:* inferiority. 2 *n* **condescension**, arrogance, haughtiness, disdain, aloofness, pomposity, snootiness (*informal*), self-importance, superciliousness, snobbishness. [➡AFFECTATION, SELF-SATISFACTION, AND SNOBBISHNESS; 508] *Opposite:* humility.

superiority complex *n* **superiority**, inflated ego, self-importance, disdain, superciliousness, haughtiness. [➡PSYCHOLOGY AND THE MIND; 770] *Opposite:* inferiority complex.

superlative *adj* **excellent**, unmatched, unbeatable, untouchable, best, matchless, outstanding, exceptional, incomparable, without equal, unparalleled, beyond compare, top, consummate, unrivalled, supreme, unique, peerless. [➡EXTRAORDINARY: AMAZING; 205] *Opposite:* unremarkable.

supermarket *type of* **food outlet.** [➡RETAIL OUTLETS; 1082]

supernatural *adj* **paranormal**, mystic, mystical, ghostly, ghostlike, uncanny, weird, bizarre, eerie, magic, unnatural, preternatural, psychic, unearthly. [➡THE SUPERNATURAL; 788] *Opposite:* natural.

supernova *type of* **star or star system.** [➡CELESTIAL BODIES; 1060]

supernumerary 1 *adj* **extra**, excessive, superfluous, spare, surplus, unrequired. [➡MORE AND EXCESS; 122] *Opposite:* necessary. 2 *adj* **substitute**, extra, auxiliary, ancillary, stand-by, additional, temporary. [➡MORE AND EXCESS; 122] *Opposite:* permanent.

superpower *n* **world power**, giant, power bloc, global force, global influence. [➡TERRITORIES AND GROUPS OF NATIONS; 1067]

supersaver *n* **discount**, special offer, concession. [➡TRANSPORTATION, TRANSPORTERS, AND CARGOS; 323]

supersede *v* **succeed**, take over, overtake, supplant, replace, surpass, displace. [➡CHANGE ONE THING FOR ANOTHER; 399] *Opposite:* precede.

superstar *n* **star**, megastar, celebrity, icon, luminary, big name, idol. [➡TALENTED OR INTELLIGENT PERSON; 529] *Opposite:* nobody.

superstition *n* **fallacy**, false notion, delusion, misconception, fantasy, falsehood, falsity, irrational belief. [➡THE SUPERNATURAL; 788]

superstitious *adj* **credulous**, gullible, illogical, irrational, delusory, illusory. [➡NEGATIVE INTELLECTUAL CHARACTERISTICS; 526] *Opposite:* rational.

superstore *type of* **retail outlet**. [➡RETAIL OUTLETS; 1082]

superstructure 1 *n* **structure**, construction, elevation, frame, framework. [➡QUALITIES AND CHARACTERISTICS; 1190] *Opposite:* foundation. 2 *n* **idea**, concept, system, structure, argument, theory, deduction, model, elaboration. [➡IDEA AND THOUGHT; 771] *Opposite:* premise. 3 *part of* **ship or boat**. [➡PARTS OF A SHIP OR BOAT; 1150]

supertitle *n* **surtitle**, caption, legend, subtitle. [➡NEWSPAPERS; 606]

supervene (*formal*) 1 *v* **interrupt**, impinge (*formal*), charge in, butt in, appear, turn up, crop up (*informal*). [➡HAPPEN; 27] 2 *v* **ensue**, follow, supersede, succeed, pursue, follow on, chase after. [➡HAPPEN; 27]

supervise *v* **oversee**, manage, administer, control, run, direct, take charge of, handle, superintend, observe, organize, watch, preside over, regulate, conduct. [➡BE IN CHARGE; 271] *Opposite:* neglect.

supervision 1 *n* **management**, direction, administration, regulation, command, control, observation, organization, guidance. [➡BUSINESS ACTIVITIES AND PHENOMENA; 795] *Opposite:* neglect. 2 *n* **care**, custody, guardianship, protection, guidance, charge. [➡RESPONSIBILITY; 171]

supervision order *n* **charge**, order, authorization, mandate, appointment, nomination. [➡SOCIAL WELFARE; 812]

supervisor *n* **manager**, administrator, superintendent, controller, overseer, director, boss, superior, head, chief. [➡BOSSES AND MANAGEMENT; 965] *Opposite:* underling.

supervisory *adj* **managerial**, administrative, superintendent, managing, controlling, directorial, guiding, regulatory, conducting. [➡EXAMINE AND ASSESS; 754] *Opposite:* subordinate.

supine 1 *adj* **recumbent** (*literary*), flat, horizontal, flat on one's back, prostrate, prone. [➡ORIENTATION AND ALIGNMENT; 1222] *Opposite:* standing. 2 *adj* **lethargic**, passive, inactive, apathetic, listless, enervated, inert. [➡TIRED, ASLEEP AND UNCONSCIOUS; 739] *Opposite:* vigorous.

supper *type of* **meal**. [➡MEALS AND PARTS OF MEALS; 1168]

suppertime *n* [➡TIMES OF DAY; 87]

supplant *v* **oust**, displace, succeed, replace, unseat, supersede, usurp, depose. [➡CHANGE ONE THING FOR ANOTHER; 399] *Opposite:* install.

supple 1 *adj* **lithe**, agile, mobile, double-jointed, sinuous, limber, flexible, elastic, coordinated, graceful. [➡AGILITY OF THE BODY; 477] *Opposite:* stiff. 2 *adj* **flexible**, elastic, plastic, pliant, pliable, malleable, bendable. [➡MALLEABLE AND ELASTIC; 1211] *Opposite:* rigid.

supplement 1 *n* **addition**, extra, complement, enhancement, increase, increment, add-on, appendage, adjunct, extension, insertion. [➡MORE AND EXCESS; 122] *Opposite:* deduction. 2 *n* **section**, insert, appendix, attachment, rider, codicil (*formal*), postscript, addendum, annex. [➡PARTS OF BOOKS AND DOCUMENTS; 594] 3 *v* **add**, complement, accompany, enhance, augment (*formal*), improve, increase, fill out, append, insert, extend. [➡CHANGE OF SIZE: BIGGER; 393] *Opposite:* deduct.

supplemental *adj* **additional**, extra, added, top-up, supplementary, complementary, incremental, add-on, auxiliary, ancillary, accompanying. [➡MORE AND EXCESS; 122] *Opposite:* deducted.

supplementary *adj* **extra**, additional, added, add-on, top-up, supplemental, accompanying, complementary, auxiliary, ancillary. [➡MORE AND EXCESS; 122] *Opposite:* deducted.

suppleness *n* **litheness**, agility, mobility, flexibility, limberness, elasticity, sinuousness, double-jointedness, coordination, grace. [➡AGILITY OF THE BODY; 477] *Opposite:* stiffness.

suppliant (*formal*) 1 *adj* **supplicant** (*formal*), supplicatory (*formal*), prayerful, petitionary, begging, pleading. [➡REQUEST AND DEMAND; 664] *Opposite:* beneficent. 2 *n* **supplicant** (*formal*), petitioner, applicant, aspirant, suitor, beggar, appellant, mendicant. [➡PEOPLE WHO MAKE REQUESTS; 665] *Opposite:* benefactor.

supplicant (*formal*) *n* **petitioner**, suppliant (*formal*), applicant, suitor, aspirant, beggar, appellant, mendicant. [➡PEOPLE WHO MAKE REQUESTS; 665] *Opposite:* donor.

supplicate (*formal*) *v* **appeal**, petition, request, beg, plead, beseech (*literary*), implore (*formal*), entreat (*formal*), pray, sue (*formal*), solicit. [➡REQUEST AND DEMAND; 664] *Opposite:* grant.

supplication (*formal*) *n* **appeal**, request, entreaty, petition, plea, prayer, suit (*formal*), application, solicitation. [➡REQUEST AND DEMAND; 664] *Opposite:* concession.

supplicatory (*formal*) *adj* [➡REQUEST AND DEMAND; 664]

supplier *n* **provider**, trader, seller, dealer, contractor, purveyor (*formal*), merchant. [➡SELLER; 443] *Opposite:* consumer.

supplies *n* **provisions**, materials, goods, food, stores, purchases, articles, equipment, deliveries, necessities, stock. [➡PHYSICAL OBJECTS; 1242]

supply 1 *v* **provide**, give, make available, sell, bring, deliver, contribute, furnish (*formal*), equip, distribute, deal, trade, outfit, stock, present. [➡EQUIP AND SUPPLY; 436] *Opposite:* receive. 2 *n* **amount**, quantity, fund, reserve, stock, hoard, resource, source, stream, allocation, store, provision. [➡AMOUNT AND QUANTITY; 112] *Opposite:* dearth.

supply teacher *n* [➡EDUCATORS; 840]

support 1 *v* **hold up**, reinforce, prop up, maintain, shore up, keep up, buoy, buttress, brace, stay, sustain. [➡CAUSE TO CONTINUE; 268] *Opposite:* weaken. 2 *v* **sustain**, provide for, keep, take care of, look after, care for, fend for, maintain, subsidize, underwrite. [➡TAKE CARE OF AND SPOIL; 301] *Opposite:* neglect. 3 *v* **help**, encourage, back up, aid, be there for, assist, sponsor, comfort, carry, strengthen. [➡APPROVE AND CONFIRM; 647] *Opposite:* abandon. 4 *v* **favour**, champion, back, follow, espouse, adopt, cheer on, be in favour of, defend, uphold, stand up for, advocate, speak up for. [➡APPROVE AND CONFIRM; 647] *Opposite:* oppose. **5** *v* **corroborate**, confirm, verify, bear witness, prove, bear out, strengthen, authenticate, substantiate, uphold, bolster, endorse, make good, establish, vouch for, warrant, ratify, validate. [➡APPROVE AND CONFIRM; 647] *Opposite:* deny. **6** *v* (*literary*) **bear**, hold, carry, sustain, take, stand, tolerate. [➡TOLERATE AND ENDURE; 767] **7** *n* **prop**, foundation, scaffold, brace, stanchion, buttress, reinforcement, base, pillar, column, joist, bracket, underpinning. [➡SUPPORTS AND BASES; 1254] *Opposite:* weakness. **8** *n* **sustenance**, provision, care, funding, funds, backing, financial assistance, maintenance, upkeep, livelihood. [➡MONEY, PAYMENTS, AND CHARGES; 800] *Opposite:* abandonment. **9** *n* **corroboration**, confirmation, verification, authentication, substantiation, endorsement, proof, validation, warrant, ratification. [➡EVIDENCE AND PROOF; 69] *Opposite:* denial. **10** *n* **assistance**, encouragement, backing, help, aid, sponsorship, finance, defence, patronage, boost, furtherance, promotion. [➡KIND ACTION OR BEHAVIOUR; 296] *Opposite:* opposition.

supportable (*literary*) *adj* **tolerable**, bearable, acceptable, manageable, sustainable, maintainable, viable, workable, justifiable, defensible. [➡ACCEPTABLE AND PASSABLE; 220] *Opposite:* insupportable.

supporter *n* **follower**, fan, enthusiast, devotee, ally, backer, adherent, sponsor, advocate, exponent, helper, defender, champion, patron, benefactor, guardian. [➡SUPPORTERS, PROTECTORS, AND COMPATRIOTS; 970] *Opposite:* detractor.

support group *n* **encounter group**, forum, self-help group, therapy group, circle, group. [➡GROUPS WITH A COMMON INTEREST; 938]

support hose (*US*) *n* **stockings**, nylons, tights, support tights, legwear, hosiery, pantyhose (*US*). [➡HABERDASHERY, MILLINERY, AND LINGERIE; 867]

supporting *adj* **secondary**, backup, subsidiary, supportive, auxiliary, ancillary, associate, assistant, accompanying, supplementary. [➡MORE AND EXCESS; 122] *Opposite:* primary.

supportive *adj* **helpful**, caring, sympathetic, compassionate, reassuring, understanding, encouraging, kind, loyal, empathetic. [➡GENEROSITY AND KINDNESS; 496] *Opposite:* unhelpful.

support stockings *n* **support tights**, nylons, legwear, tights, stockings, pantyhose (*US*). [➡HABERDASHERY, MILLINERY, AND LINGERIE; 867]

support system *n* **friends**, network, helpers, group, support, family, contacts. [➡GROUPS WITH A COMMON INTEREST; 938]

suppose **1** *v* **presume**, assume, understand, believe, expect, reason, infer, think, consider, guess, reckon. [➡DREAM, IMAGINE, AND FANTASIZE; 750] **2** *v* **imagine**, pretend, consider, theorize, hypothesize, postulate, predicate (*formal*), posit (*formal*). [➡DEVELOP THEORIES AND REASON; 745]

supposed **1** *adj* **hypothetical**, theoretical, imaginary, fictional, made-up, invented. [➡FALSE AND UNREAL; 174] *Opposite:* actual. **2** *adj* **thought**, believed, assumed, alleged, understood, rumoured, said, held. [➡UNCERTAIN; 176] *Opposite:* known.

supposedly *adv* **allegedly**, evidently, apparently, purportedly (*formal*), theoretically, hypothetically, by all accounts, so they say, so it is said, it would seem. [➡UNCERTAIN; 176] *Opposite:* actually.

supposing *conj* **assuming**, suppose, let's say, let's assume, say, if, imagine, what if. [➡SUGGEST, HINT, AND COMMENT; 613]

supposition **1** *n* **belief**, guess, idea, theory, possibility, hypothesis, assumption, deduction, conclusion, presumption, opinion, surmise, thesis. [➡IDEA AND THOUGHT; 771] *Opposite:* fact. **2** *n* **guesswork**, inference, hypothesis, speculation, conjecture. [➡DREAM, IMAGINE, AND FANTASIZE; 750] *Opposite:* knowledge.

suppress **1** *v* **hold back**, repress, stifle, restrain, contain, curb, stem, smother, keep in check, control, cover up, hide, conceal, keep inside, bottle up, check, block out. [➡NOT PAY ATTENTION; 765] *Opposite:* express. **2** *v* **overpower**, overwhelm, overturn, conquer, defeat, destroy, subdue, quash, quell, crush, put down, clamp down on, control, dominate, squash, overcome, snuff out. [➡BEAT AND DEFEAT; 80] *Opposite:* submit. **3** *v* **hush up** (*informal*), muffle, withhold, censor, squelch (*slang*), smother, quash, stifle, kill, sit on, put the lid on, cover up, bury, silence. [➡WITHHOLD INFORMATION; 688] *Opposite:* publicize.

suppression **1** *n* **repression**, containment, control, restraint, inhibition. [➡CAPTIVITY AND LOSS OF FREEDOM; 249] *Opposite:* expression. **2** *n* **conquest**, defeat, destruction, overthrow, subdual, clampdown, overpowering, snuffing out (*informal*), dominance. [➡BEAT AND DEFEAT; 80] **3** *n* **withholding**, cover-up, concealment, censorship, veil of secrecy, wraps, conspiracy of silence, squashing, silencing. [➡WITHHOLD INFORMATION; 688] *Opposite:* revelation.

suppurate *v* **discharge pus**, fester, weep, ooze, seep, exude. [➡EXCRETION AND EXCRETA; 723]

supranational *adj* **multinational**, international, cosmopolitan, worldwide, universal, global, supernational. [➡COUNTRIES AND REGIONS; 1066] *Opposite:* local.

supremacist *n* **chauvinist**, racist, white supremacist, xenophobe, bigot, sexist. [➡PHILOSOPHICAL AND POLITICAL THINKERS; 782]

supremacy **1** *n* **pre-eminence**, ascendancy, primacy, superiority, domination, incomparability, dominance. [➡SUPERIORITY; 153] *Opposite:* inferiority. **2** *n* **reign**, sovereignty, rule, authority, power, hegemony (*formal*), control, omnipotence. [➡STYLES AND SYSTEMS OF GOVERNMENT; 806]

supreme **1** *adj* **highest**, best, ultimate, superlative, utmost, absolute, extreme, top, great, greatest, matchless, untouchable, unbeatable, unmatched, nonpareil, consummate, incomparable. [➡SUPERIORITY; 153] *Opposite:* worst. **2** *adj* **sovereign**, dominant, uppermost, first, highest, chief, topmost. [➡MOST IMPORTANT AND MAIN; 194]

supremely *adv* **extremely**, completely, enormously, absolutely, superlatively, tremendously, utterly, totally, really, particularly, very. [➡TO A GREAT EXTENT; 130]

supremo (*informal*) *n* **leader**, head, chief, authority, expert, guru. [➡BOSSES AND MANAGEMENT; 965]

surcharge **1** *v* **charge extra**, charge again, charge more, tack on, levy again, add, tax again. [➡MONEY, PAYMENTS, AND CHARGES; 800] 2 *n* **extra charge**, supplement, extra, price, hidden extra, extra payment, additional charge, addition, padding. [➡MONEY, PAYMENTS, AND CHARGES; 800]

sure 1 *adj* **unquestionable**, undisputable, certain, definite, guaranteed, assured, sure-fire (*informal*), inevitable, indubitable (*formal*), bound to be, unerring, conclusive, infallible, accurate. [➡CERTAIN; 175] *Opposite:* uncertain. 2 *adj* **certain**, in no doubt, convinced, positive, confident, definite, clear in your mind, persuaded. [➡CERTAINTY; 562] *Opposite:* uncertain. 3 *adj* **dependable**, reliable, effective, trustworthy, trusty, loyal, solid, constant, firm, true, steady. [➡HONEST AND RELIABLE; 503] *Opposite:* unreliable. 4 *adv* (*US informal*) **really**, certainly, surely, definitely, positively, absolutely, for sure (*informal*), for certain, clearly, indeed. [➡EXPRESSIONS OF AGREEMENT; 649] *Opposite:* doubtfully. 5 *adv* (*US informal*) **of course**, yes, certainly, all right, by all means, yes indeed, surely, OK (*informal*), positively, absolutely, you bet (*US informal*), sure thing (*US informal*). [➡EXPRESSIONS OF AGREEMENT; 649]

sure bet *n* [➡CERTAIN; 175]

sure enough *adv* [➡EXPRESSIONS OF AGREEMENT; 649]

sure-fire (*informal*) *adj* **guaranteed**, dependable, safe, assured, foolproof, never-failing, sure, certain. [➡CERTAIN; 175] *Opposite:* doubtful.

sure-footed 1 *adj* **agile**, skilled, confident, skilful, nimble, adroit. [➡TALENTED AND SKILFUL; 528] *Opposite:* clumsy. 2 *adj* **confident**, competent, unerring, capable, infallible, certain. [➡CERTAIN; 175]

surely 1 *adv* **certainly**, definitely, of course, for sure (*informal*), without doubt, unquestionably, indisputably, indubitably (*formal*), incontestably, indeed, absolutely, clearly. [➡CERTAIN; 175] *Opposite:* doubtfully. 2 *adv* **confidently**, assuredly, with conviction, with confidence, with assurance. [➡CONFIDENCE AND COMPOSURE; 500] *Opposite:* insecurely.

sureness *n* **certainty**, certitude, confidence, assurance, firm belief. [➡CERTAINTY; 562] *Opposite:* uncertainty.

sure of yourself *adj* **confident**, self-confident, assured, self-assured, poised, secure. [➡CONFIDENCE AND COMPOSURE; 500] *Opposite:* insecure.

sure thing 1 *n* (*informal*) **certainty**, cert (*informal*), cinch (*informal*), safe bet, piece of cake (*informal*), doddle (*informal*), odds-on chance, winner. [➡CERTAIN; 175] 2 *adv* (*US informal*) **yes**, certainly, of course, sure (*informal*), surely, for sure (*informal*), OK (*informal*), absolutely, all right, yes indeed, by all means, you bet (*US informal*). [➡EXPRESSIONS OF AGREEMENT; 649]

surety *n* **security**, indemnity, guarantee, warranty, bond, deposit, collateral, down payment. [➡INSURANCE; 801]

surf *n* **waves**, breakers, rollers, whitecaps, spray, sea. [➡THE SEAS, OCEANS, AND SHORES; 1041]

surface 1 *n* **outside**, top, exterior, façade, side, shell, plane, face. [➡EXTREMITIES OF PHYSICAL OBJECTS; 1249] *Opposite:* inside. 2 *adj* **superficial**, shallow, external, exterior, outward, apparent, seeming. [➡FALSE AND UNREAL; 174] *Opposite:* inner. 3 *v* **rise**, float up, come up, go up, emerge, ascend, break the surface, appear. [➡GO UPWARDS; 307] *Opposite:* sink. 4 *v* **appear**, reappear, turn up, show up, pop up. [➡APPEAR AND EMERGE; 3] 5 *v* **become known**, come to light, come out, come out in the open, emerge, get out. [➡APPEAR AND EMERGE; 3] 6 *v* **coat**, cover, skim, overlay, resurface. [➡DECORATE, ADORN, AND APPLY COATINGS; 406]

surface mail *n* **overland mail**, snail mail (*informal*), regular mail, first-class mail, second-class mail, registered mail, special delivery. [➡LETTERS AND WRITTEN MESSAGES; 585] *Opposite:* airmail.

surfeit *n* **excess**, surplus, glut, flood, oversupply, overabundance, plethora, profusion. [➡TOO MUCH; 118] *Opposite:* deficit.

surge 1 *v* **rush**, rush forward, flow, pour, gush, course, heave, pitch, swell, rise, well up, flood, stream, spill over, spill out. [➡MOVE FAST; 314] 2 *n* **flow**, outpouring, gush, rush, heave, pitch, swell, upwelling, flood, stream, spill, wave. [➡AMOUNT OF LIQUID; 114]

surgeon *n* **doctor**, physician, medical practitioner, specialist, neurosurgeon, plastic surgeon. [➡PEOPLE WHO WORK IN MEDICINE; 848]

surgery *type of* **room in public buildings.** [➡TYPES OF ROOM; 1096]

surgical 1 *adj* **medical**, clinical, operating, invasive. [➡REMEDIES, TREATMENTS AND OPERATIONS; 732] 2 *adj* **precise**, exact, accurate, definite, meticulous, punctilious. [➡EXACT; 204] *Opposite:* imprecise.

surliness *n* [➡BAD MANNERS AND SOCIAL SKILLS; 522]

surly *adj* **gruff**, brusque, abrupt, short, curt, churlish, rude, impolite, discourteous, disagreeable, bad-tempered, truculent, grumpy, short-tempered, tetchy (*informal*), irritable, sullen, boorish, grouchy (*informal*), unfriendly, crabby, unhelpful. [➡BAD-TEMPERED AND HUMOURLESS; 627] *Opposite:* friendly.

surmise 1 *v* **guess**, deduce, infer, construe, gather, work out, conclude, assume, presume, suppose, conjecture, imagine, suspect, postulate, hypothesize, theorize, speculate. [➡GUESS; 755] *Opposite:* know. 2 *n* **guesswork**, deduction, inference, conclusion, assumption, presumption, supposition, conjecture, suspicion, postulation, hypothesis, theory, speculation. [➡GUESS; 755] *Opposite:* knowledge.

surmount 1 *v* **overcome**, prevail, conquer, triumph, get through, vanquish, defeat, transcend. [➡BEAT AND DEFEAT; 80] *Opposite:* fail. 2 *v* (*formal*) **scale**, climb, top, clear, ascend, mount. [➡GO UPWARDS; 307]

surmountable *adj* **manageable**, conquerable, resolvable, controllable, winnable, attainable, possible, soluble, doable. [➡POSSIBLE AND PROBABLE; 178] *Opposite:* intractable.

surname *n* **last name**, family name, cognomen (*formal*). [➡NAME AND DESCRIBE; 666] *Opposite:* first name.

surpass *v* **exceed**, better, outdo, outshine, improve on, go beyond, outstrip, do better than, go one better than, top, transcend, beat. [➡BEAT AND DEFEAT; 80] *Opposite:* follow.

surpassing (*literary*) *adj* **outstanding**, superior, exceptional, greater, better. [➡EXTRAORDINARY: AMAZING; 205]

surplice *type of* **top.** [➡GARMENTS AND OUTFITS; 865]

surplus 1 *n* **excess**, extra, spare, leftovers, remainder, superfluity, overage, surfeit, oversupply, overflow, plethora, glut. [➡TOO MUCH; 118] *Opposite:* shortfall. 2 *adj* **extra**, excess, spare, remaining, additional, over, superfluous, not needed, excessive, unnecessary, redundant, residual, leftover. [➡MORE AND EXCESS; 122] *Opposite:* essential.

surplus to requirements *adj* [➡UNIMPORTANT AND UNNECESSARY; 239]

surprise 1 *v* **astonish**, startle, alarm, astound, amaze, flabbergast (*informal*), stagger, stun, shock, take the wind out of your sails, take aback, bowl over, knock for six (*informal*), take by surprise, render speechless, daze, dumbfound. [➡SURPRISE AND IMPRESS; 575] 2 *v* **catch unawares**, catch napping, take by surprise, burst in on, intrude on, come upon, interrupt, disturb, disrupt. [➡ARRIVE; 12] 3 *n* **shock**, revelation, bolt from the blue, disclosure, bombshell (*informal*), shocker (*informal*). [➡SUDDEN EVENT; 52] 4 *n* **astonishment**, amazement, wonder, disbelief, shock. [➡SURPRISE, SHOCK, AND AMAZEMENT; 546]

surprised *adj* **astonished**, astounded, amazed, taken aback, flabbergasted (*informal*), staggered, stunned, shocked, knocked for six (*informal*), bowled over, startled, stupefied. [➡SURPRISE, SHOCK, AND AMAZEMENT; 546]

surprising *adj* **astonishing**, astounding, amazing, shocking, startling, unexpected, unanticipated, unforeseen, unpredicted, extraordinary, remarkable, overwhelming. [➡EXTRAORDINARY: AMAZING; 205] *Opposite:* expected.

surprisingly 1 *adv* **astonishingly**, astoundingly, amazingly, unexpectedly, unpredictably, shockingly, startlingly, remarkably. [➡EXTRAORDINARY: AMAZING; 205] 2 *adv* **to my surprise**, to my amazement, out of the blue, without warning, without prior notice. [➡EXPRESSIONS OF SURPRISE; 547]

surreal *adj* **strange**, weird, odd, unreal, dreamlike, fantastic, bizarre. [➡BIZARRE AND PECULIAR; 258] *Opposite:* ordinary.

surrealism *type of* **20th-century art movement**. [➡ARTISTIC MOVEMENTS AND STYLES; 899]

surrender 1 *v* **give in**, give up, admit defeat, lay down your arms, submit, yield, capitulate, throw in the towel (*informal*). [➡FAIL OR BE UNSUCCESSFUL; 75] *Opposite:* hold out. 2 *v* **relinquish**, give up, hand over, part with, cede (*formal*), forfeit, abandon, concede, renounce, waive. [➡FOREGO AND DENY ONESELF; 450] *Opposite:* retain. 3 *n* **admission of defeat**, submission, laying down of arms, capitulation, renunciation. [➡FAILURE; 77]

See Compare and Contrast at **yield**.

surreptitious *adj* **furtive**, secret, sneaky, sly, covert, clandestine, stealthy, secretive, underhand, hush-hush (*informal*). [➡SECRET AND UNKNOWN; 180] *Opposite:* open.

See Compare and Contrast at **secret**.

surreptitiousness *n* **secrecy**, covertness, discretion, concealment, stealth, sneakiness, furtiveness, cunning, slyness, craftiness. [➡SECRET AND UNKNOWN; 180] *Opposite:* openness.

surrogacy *n* **substitution**, surrogate motherhood, proxy, standing in, surrogateship, replacement. [➡CHANGE ONE THING FOR ANOTHER; 399]

surrogate *n* **substitute**, replacement, proxy, stand-in, deputy, alternate (*US*), backup, understudy. [➡SUBSTITUTES AND STAND-INS; 400]

surround 1 *v* **enclose**, encircle, encase, enfold, envelop, border, contain, bound, circumscribe, encompass, ring, girdle (*literary*). [➡EXIST IN CLOSE PROXIMITY; 21] 2 *v* **besiege**, lay siege to, encircle, hem in. [➡EXIST IN CLOSE PROXIMITY; 21] 3 *n* **border**, mantle (*literary*), mount, edge, edging, frame, setting, rim. [➡EXTREMITIES OF PHYSICAL OBJECTS; 1249]

surrounding *adj* **nearby**, close, adjacent, neighbouring, immediate, adjoining, contiguous (*formal*), near, proximate. [➡CLOSENESS; 160] *Opposite:* distant.

surroundings *n* **environs**, surrounds, setting, environment, background, backdrop, milieu (*formal*), context, situation, habitat. [➡PLACE; 1064]

surtax *n* **surcharge**, tax, levy, extra, supplement. [➡TAX AND TAXATION; 802] *Opposite:* relief.

surtitle *n* **supertitle**, translation, libretto, dialogue, caption, title, text. [➡FILM; 901] *Opposite:* subtitle.

surveillance *n* **observation**, investigation, scrutiny, reconnaissance, stakeout (*informal*), shadowing, following, tailing (*informal*). [➡LOOKING AND LOOKS; 701]

survey 1 *n* **analysis**, appraisal, scrutiny, evaluation, assessment, consideration. [➡EXAMINE AND ASSESS; 754] 2 *n* **inspection**, examination, investigation, review, inquiry, study, canvass, probe. [➡EXAMINE AND ASSESS; 754] 3 *v* **look at**, consider, peruse, regard, think about, look over. [➡LOOKING AND LOOKS; 701] 4 *v* **examine**, study, inspect, assess, analyse, appraise, evaluate, look over, consider, scan, review. [➡EXAMINE AND ASSESS; 754] 5 *v* **plot**, chart, map out, measure, graph, gauge, fathom, plumb. [➡ASSESS QUANTITY; 758] *Opposite:* sketch.

surveyor *n* **inspector**, assessor, examiner, reviewer, evaluator, chartered surveyor. [➡SURVEYORS, EXAMINERS, AND JUDGES; 853]

survival *n* **existence**, endurance, being, subsistence, persistence, continued existence. [➡PERMANENCE: WITHOUT END; 94] *Opposite:* death.

survive 1 *v* **live**, live on, endure, carry on, go on, persist, continue, last, subsist, stay alive. *Opposite:* perish. (*literary*). [➡CONTINUE TO EXIST; 17] 2 *v* **outlive**, outlast, live through. [➡CONTINUE TO EXIST; 17] *Opposite:* die.

surviving *adj* **living**, alive, enduring, persisting, remaining, ongoing, extant, current, existing, lasting. [➡PERMANENCE: WITHOUT END; 94] *Opposite:* gone.

survivor *n* **fighter**, stayer, sticker, toughie (*informal*). [➡PEOPLE WHO ARE APPROVED OF; 955]

susceptibility 1 *n* **vulnerability**, defencelessness, weakness, exposure, predisposition, proneness, liability. [➡WEAKNESS; 242] *Opposite:* imperviousness. 2 *n* **sensitivity**, receptiveness, openness, touchiness, impressionableness, responsiveness, sensibility, impressionability. [➡EXCESSIVE SENSITIVITY; 512] *Opposite:* hardness.

susceptible 1 *adj* **sensitive**, receptive, open, impressionable, swayable, amenable, suggestible. [➡NEGATIVE INTELLECTUAL CHARACTERISTICS; 526] *Opposite:* impervious. 2 *adj* **vulnerable**, at risk, liable, prone, disposed, inclined, subject, predisposed. [➡IN DANGER; 238] *Opposite:* invulnerable.

suspect 1 *v* **think**, believe, suppose, imagine, guess, deduce, infer, presume, assume, speculate. [➡UNCERTAINTY; 560] 2 *v* **doubt**, distrust, mistrust, have doubts, disbelieve, be suspicious, be wary, question. [➡QUESTION THINGS; 752] *Opposite:* trust. 3 *n* **accused**, defendant, respondent. [➡TRIAL, PUNISHMENT, AND LEGAL OUTCOMES; 819] 4 *adj* **suspicious**, doubtful, dubious, unsure, questionable, odd, shady, uncertain. [➡UNCERTAIN; 176] *Opposite:* trustworthy.

suspend 1 *v* **hang**, hang up, dangle, swing, string up, overhang, append. [➡MOVE SOMETHING ON THE SPOT; 337] 2 *v* **interrupt**, check, break off, adjourn, hold, stop, quit, halt. [➡CAUSE TO STOP; 267] *Opposite:* resume. 3 *v* **postpone**, put on hold, defer, table (*US*), delay, stay, shelve, put on ice, put back, put off, push back. [➡DELAY ACTION OR OCCURRENCE; 279] *Opposite:* bring forward.

suspended 1 *adj* **hanging**, pendent (*formal or literary*), floating, hovering, dangling, strung up, in the air, overhanging. [➡ORIENTATION AND ALIGNMENT; 1222] 2 *adj* **postponed**, put off, deferred, adjourned, held over, on hold, on ice, on the back burner, up in the air. [➡NOT HAPPENING; 34] *Opposite:* advanced. 3 *adj* **barred**, banned, proscribed, excluded. [➡REFUSE PERMISSION AND NOT ALLOW; 671]

suspended sentence *n* **deferred sentence**, deferment, sentence, punishment, judgment, penalty, ruling. [➡TRIAL, PUNISHMENT, AND LEGAL OUTCOMES; 819]

suspenders (*US*) *type of* **accessory**. [➡HABERDASHERY, MILLINERY, AND LINGERIE; 867]

suspense 1 *n* **anticipation**, expectation, expectancy, excitement, tension, thrill. [➡FEELINGS ABOUT THE FUTURE; 534] *Opposite:* flatness. 2 *n* **uncertainty**, unsureness, doubt, insecurity, confusion, doubtfulness, indecision. [➡UNCERTAINTY; 560] *Opposite:* knowledge. 3 *n* **anxiety**, apprehension, tension, fear, nervousness, trepidation, edginess, uneasiness. [➡FEELINGS ABOUT THE FUTURE; 534] *Opposite:* calm.

suspenseful *adj* [➡INTERESTING AND MEANINGFUL; 191]

suspension *n* **interruption**, holdup, check, postponement, delay, deferment, deferral, pause. [➡DELAY ACTION OR OCCURRENCE; 279] *Opposite:* resumption.

suspension bridge *type of* **bridge**. [➡BRIDGES, TUNNELS, CROSSINGS, AND JUNCTIONS; 1111]

suspicion 1 *n* **doubt**, question, inkling, misgiving, feeling, notion, thought, idea, hunch. [➡FEELINGS; 532] *Opposite:* certainty. 2 *n* **mistrust**, apprehension, distrust, disbelief, wariness, scepticism. [➡UNCERTAINTY; 560] *Opposite:* trust. 3 *n* **hint**, suggestion, trace, smidgen (*informal*), touch, tinge, soupçon. [➡FEW, LITTLE, SMALL AMOUNT; 119]

suspicious 1 *adj* **suspect**, dubious, dodgy (*informal*), shady, shifty, untrustworthy, questionable, unreliable. [➡UNCERTAIN; 176] *Opposite:* trustworthy. 2 *adj* **doubtful**, distrustful, mistrustful, apprehensive, wary, guarded, chary, sceptical, dubious, leery (*informal*). [➡UNCERTAINTY; 560] *Opposite:* sure.

suss (*informal*) *v* **solve**, figure out, work out, crack, decipher, puzzle out, resolve. [➡SOLVE AND INTERPRET; 761]

sustain 1 *v* **withstand**, bear, tolerate, endure, weather, put up with, brook, stand. [➡TOLERATE AND ENDURE; 767] *Opposite:* buckle. 2 *v* **experience**, undergo, suffer, incur, contract, meet with, encounter. [➡EXPERIENCE AND ENCOUNTER; 583] 3 *v* **maintain**, continue, carry on, keep up, keep going, uphold, prolong, protract. [➡CAUSE TO CONTINUE; 268] *Opposite:* quit. 4 *v* **nourish**, keep you going, feed, nurture. [➡TAKE CARE OF AND SPOIL; 301] *Opposite:* deplete. 5 *v* **support**, hold up, prop up, keep up, maintain, take. [➡AGREE; 646]

sustainability *n* [➡PERMANENCE: WITHOUT END; 94]

sustainable 1 *adj* **maintainable**, bearable, supportable (*literary*), justifiable, workable, defensible, viable. [➡PERMANENCE: WITHOUT END; 94] 2 *adj* **ecological**, environmental, green, natural, balanced, organic. [➡ECONOMICAL AND RESOURCEFUL; 208] *Opposite:* unsustainable.

sustained *adj* **continued**, constant, continual, continuous, nonstop, unrelenting, unremitting, persistent, unceasing, prolonged, chronic, lasting, perpetual, unbroken, uninterrupted, never-ending, endless. [➡PERMANENCE: WITHOUT END; 94] *Opposite:* temporary.

sustenance *n* **nourishment**, food, nutrition, provisions, rations, victuals, edibles, fuel, wherewithal. [➡FOOD; 1166] *Opposite:* deprivation.

susurrate *v* **rustle**, whisper, murmur, breathe. [➡EMIT CONTINUOUS SOUNDS; 367]

suture 1 *n* **seam**, join, junction, joint, closure, seal. [➡FASTENERS, LINKS, AND NETWORKS; 1246] 2 *v* **sew**, sew up, stitch, stitch up, close, seal. [➡FASTEN, LINK, AND JOIN; 409] *Opposite:* cut.

SUV *type of* **leisure vehicle**. [➡VEHICLES; 1144]

suzerain *n* **superpower**, colonial power, ruling nation. [➡RULERS AND ARISTOCRACY; 823]

svelte *adj* **lithe**, graceful, slender, willowy, sylphlike, slim, lissome. [➡BUILD; 478] *Opposite:* stocky.

svelteness *n* [➡BUILD; 478]

Svengali *n* **manipulator**, controller, guru, charmer, guide, manager, influence. [➡BOSSES AND MANAGEMENT; 965]

swab 1 *n* **gauze**, lint, cloth, wipe, pad, wad. [➡COVERS AND COATINGS; 1245] 2 *v* **wipe**, clean, cleanse, moisten, wash, sponge, dab, mop, wash out. [➡CLEAN AND POLISH; 404]

swaddle *v* **wrap**, bandage, wrap up, swathe, envelop, enfold, shroud. [➡DECORATE, ADORN, AND APPLY COATINGS; 406] *Opposite:* unwrap.

swag 1 *n* **curtain**, drape, hanging, drapery. [➡SOFT FURNISHINGS, LINEN, AND DRAPERY; 860] 2 *n* **festoon**, garland, chain. [➡ORNAMENTS AND DECORATIONS; 1247] 3 *n* (*slang*) **loot**, booty, plunder, spoils, haul, contraband. [➡PROCEEDS OF CRIME; 428]

swagger 1 *v* **strut**, parade, flounce, prance, sweep, sway, show off, sashay (*humorous*), saunter. [➡PROCEED AND GO; 306] *Opposite:* creep. 2 *n* **boastfulness**, arrogance, bluster, conceit, boasting, bragging, showing-off. [➡BOAST; 617] *Opposite:* timidity.

swaggering 1 *adj* **boastful**, boasting, blustering, bragging, vaunting, bombastic. [➡POMPOUS, LOUD, AND OVER-CONFIDENT; 636] *Opposite:* modest. 2 *adj* **self-important**, self-satisfied, strutting, smug, arrogant, conceited, hubristic. [➡AFFECTATION, SELF-SATISFACTION, AND SNOBBISHNESS; 508] *Opposite:* self-effacing.

swags *n* [➡SOFT FURNISHINGS, LINEN, AND DRAPERY; 860]

swain (*literary*) *n* **admirer**, beau (*dated*), boyfriend, young man, lover, suitor (*formal*). [➡SEXUAL AND ROMANTIC RELATIONSHIPS; 964]

swallow 1 *v* **ingest**, consume, take in, down, eat, drink, imbibe (*formal or humorous*). [➡EAT AND NOT EAT; 711] *Opposite:* vomit. 2 *v* **gulp**, sip, gulp down, swig (*informal*), gobble up, scarf down (*US slang*), guzzle (*informal*), swill. [➡DRINK; 712] *Opposite:* regurgitate. 3 *v* **destroy**, engulf, swallow up, take over, gobble up, consume, absorb. [➡CAUSE TO DISAPPEAR; 6] 4 *v* **suppress**, repress, choke back, hold back, hide, conceal, withhold. [➡WITHHOLD INFORMATION; 688] *Opposite:* express. 5 *v* (*informal*) **believe**, accept, fall for, buy (*US informal*), credit, allow (*formal*). [➡FORGET, FORGIVE, AND ACCEPT; 749] *Opposite:* reject. 6 *v* **retract**, take back, back down, recant, eat your words. [➡APOLOGIZE AND RETRACT; 684] 7 *n* **gulp**, sip, nip, swig (*informal*), mouthful, bite. [➡DRINK; 712] 8 *type of* **common bird.** [➡BIRD; 997]

swallowtail *type of* **butterfly.** [➡MOTHS AND BUTTERFLIES; 1015]

swami *n* [➡RELIGIOUS PEOPLE; 779]

swamp 1 *n* **wetland**, marsh, bog, mire, fen, quagmire, slough, bayou (*US*), everglade (*US*). [➡WETLANDS; 1043] 2 *v* **flood**, inundate, deluge, engulf, drown, drench, sink. [➡FILL; 407] *Opposite:* drain. 3 *v* **overwhelm**, snow under, overload, bog down (*informal*), inundate, flood, drown, submerge, engulf, besiege. [➡GIVE TOO MUCH; 438]

swampland *n* **swamps**, marshes, marshland, bog, wetland, bayou (*US*), everglade (*US*). [➡WETLANDS; 1043]

swampy *adj* **marshy**, boggy, muddy, slushy, squelchy, wet. [➡WET; 1239] *Opposite:* dry.

swan 1 *v* (*informal*) **wander**, drift, float, laze, idle, loaf. [➡AIMLESS AND ERRANT MOTION; 344] 2 *type of* **freshwater bird.** [➡FRESHWATER BIRD; 1000]

swank 1 *n* (*informal*) **show-off** (*informal*), bragger, swaggerer, exhibitionist, boaster. [➡BOAST; 617] 2 *v* (*informal*) **show off**, swagger, strut, parade, boast, brag. [➡BOAST; 617] 3 *adj* (*US informal*) **swanky** (*informal*), posh (*informal*), ritzy (*informal*), upmarket, swish (*informal*), classy (*informal*), glamorous, smart, high-class. [➡EXPENSIVE AND LUXURIOUS; 219] *Opposite:* downmarket.

swanky (*informal*) *adj* **posh** (*informal*), ritzy (*informal*), swish (*informal*), classy (*informal*), upmarket, glamorous, high-class, stylish, elegant, swank (*US informal*). [➡EXPENSIVE AND LUXURIOUS; 219] *Opposite:* second-rate.

swan song *n* **farewell**, final act, last act, curtain, finale, leave-taking (*literary*), valediction (*formal*). [➡END; 54] *Opposite:* debut.

swap (*informal*) 1 *v* **exchange**, trade, barter, do a deal, change, transact, negotiate, dicker (*informal*), give and take. [➡EXCHANGE AND INTERCHANGE; 449] 2 *n* **changeover**, substitution, exchange, switch, interchange, change. [➡EXCHANGE AND INTERCHANGE; 449]

swap over *v* **switch**, change over, change round, interchange, change places, exchange. [➡CHANGE ONE THING FOR ANOTHER; 399]

sward *n* **turf**, grass, grassland, green, lawn, meadow. [➡THE COUNTRYSIDE AND OUTDOOR SPACES; 1070]

swarm 1 *n* **group**, cloud, flight. [➡MANY, MUCH, LARGE AMOUNT; 117] 2 *n* **horde**, crowd, throng, flock, bevy, multitude, pack, mass, mob, drove, herd. [➡GROUPS OF PEOPLE; 935] 3 *v* **crowd**, throng, mass, flock, pile, flood. [➡GET CLOSER TOGETHER; 311] 4 *v* **teem**, be overrun, bristle, be alive with, be full, be packed, abound, surge. [➡PROSPER AND ABOUND; 16] 5 *v* **group**, hover, circle, fly, rise, migrate. [➡GET CLOSER TOGETHER; 311] 6 *type of* **flock.** [➡GROUP OF BIRDS; 1007]

swarming *adj* **crawling**, teeming, brimming, overrun, crowded, swamped, flooded, packed. [➡FULL; 1238] *Opposite:* empty.

swarthy *adj* **dark**, weather-beaten, dark-complexioned, leathery, tanned, tawny, olive-skinned. [➡COMPLEXION; 481] *Opposite:* pale.

swashbuckler 1 *n* **adventurer**, daredevil, swash, buccaneer, pirate, swaggerer, fortune hunter. [➡PLEASURE-SEEKERS AND HEDONISTS; 886] 2 *n* **action movie**, pirate film, period film, action film, actioner (*informal*), adventure movie. [➡FILM; 901]

swashbuckling 1 *adj* **daring**, adventurous, heroic, exciting, cavalier, rumbustious. [➡COURAGE; 499] *Opposite:* timid. 2 *adj* **strutting**, swaggering, boasting, blustery, blustering, posturing. [➡AFFECTATION, SELF-SATISFACTION, AND SNOBBISHNESS; 508] *Opposite:* modest.

swat *v* **swipe**, zap (*informal*), slap, hit, smack, belt (*informal*), thwack, bash (*informal*), clobber (*informal*), whack, knock, strike, wallop (*informal*), punch, deck (*informal*). [➡PHYSICAL ATTACK AND PUNISHMENT; 416]

swatch *n* **sample**, batch, strip, snip, piece, tester, length. [➡REPRESENTATIONS AND GENERAL EXAMPLES; 65]

swathe 1 *v* **wrap**, cover, bandage, bind, entwine, sheathe. [➡DECORATE, ADORN, AND APPLY COATINGS; 406] *Opposite:* unwrap. 2 *v* **enfold**, envelop, drape, cloak, shroud, surround, swaddle. [➡DECORATE, ADORN, AND APPLY COATINGS; 406] *Opposite:* expose. 3 *n* **strip**, ribbon, band, wrapping, bandage, binding. [➡FASTENERS, LINKS, AND NETWORKS; 1246]

sway 1 *v* **swing**, waver, oscillate, move to and fro, rock, wave, fluctuate, vacillate, shift, vary. [➡BOUNCE, UNDULATE, AND VIBRATE; 309] 2 *v* **bend**, lean, veer, slant, tilt, tip over, reel, totter, wobble, stagger, rock. [➡MOVE SOMETHING ON THE SPOT; 337] 3 *v* **influence**, bias, affect, control, persuade, convince, manipulate, win over, move, prompt, motivate. [➡ENCOURAGE; 577] 4 *n* **power**, influence, control, authority, command, mastery, rule, dominance, grip. [➡RELATIONSHIP TO ANOTHER; 973] *Opposite:* subjection.

swear 1 *v* **affirm**, assert, declare, claim, maintain, insist, avow (*formal*). [➡CLAIM, INSIST, AND EMPHASIZE; 615] 2 *v* **vow**, pledge, promise, give your word, attest, aver, guarantee, undertake. [➡PROMISE AND ASSURE; 685] 3 *v* **curse**, blaspheme, execrate (*literary or formal*), damn, utter profanities, cuss (*informal*). [➡INSULTS, ABUSE, AND SWEARING; 659] *Opposite:* bless.

swear an oath *v* [➡PROMISE AND ASSURE; 685]

swear by *v* **trust**, rely on, depend on, have faith in, put your faith in, count on, believe in. [➡LIKE, LOVE, VALUE AND ENJOY; 579] *Opposite:* doubt.

swear in *v* **inaugurate**, install, initiate, invest (*formal*), induct, administer an oath to. [➡CONFER STATUS; 459] *Opposite:* discharge.

swear off *v* **give up**, renounce, abstain from, desist from, stop, come off, eschew. [➡FOREGO AND DENY ONESELF; 450]

swearword *n* **expletive**, four-letter word, curse, oath, bad language, profanity, obscenity, cussword (*US informal*). [➡INSULTS, ABUSE, AND SWEARING; 659]

sweat 1 *v* (*informal*) **worry**, fret, panic, be anxious, be concerned, be agitated, be on pins and needles, be afraid, dread. [➡BE CONCERNED AND CARE; 582] *Opposite:* relax. 2 *v* **perspire**, swelter, wilt, drip. [➡EXCRETION AND EXCRETA; 723]

sweat blood *v* [➡HARD WORK OR EFFORT; 299]

sweater *type of* **sweater or cardigan.** [➡GARMENTS AND OUTFITS; 865]

sweat out *v* **wait out**, see through, endure, see out, stick out, see through to the bitter end, sit out. [➡TOLERATE AND ENDURE; 767] *Opposite:* give up on.

sweatpants *type of* **sportswear.** [➡GARMENTS AND OUTFITS; 865]

sweatshirt *type of* **top.** [➡GARMENTS AND OUTFITS; 865]

sweatshop 1 *n* **factory**, shop, workshop, place of work, works, plant. [➡PLACE OF EMPLOYMENT; 832] 2 *type of* **factory.** [➡INDUSTRIAL BUILDINGS; 1086]

sweat suit (*US*) *type of* **sportswear.** [➡GARMENTS AND OUTFITS; 865]

sweaty 1 *adj* **perspiring**, covered with sweat, clammy, damp, sticky, moist, drenched, dripping, soaked, wet. [➡WET; 1239] *Opposite:* dry. 2 *adj* **hot**, boiling, warm, sticky, sultry, humid. [➡HOT WEATHER; 1050] *Opposite:* cool.

swede *type of* **root vegetable.** [➡FRUIT AND VEGETABLES; 1175]

sweep 1 *v* **brush**, clean up, tidy up, pick up, clear away, brush off, brush away, scoop up, clear, remove, clear up, sweep up, clean. [➡CLEAN AND POLISH; 404] 2 *v* **speed**, zoom, race, fly, zip (*informal*), dash, whiz, dart, rush, hurry. [➡MOVE FAST; 314] *Opposite:* creep. 3 *v* **carry**, move, seize, grab, take. [➡GET; 421] 4 *v* **arc**, arch, bend, bow, curve, swoop, swing, swish. [➡CHANGE DIRECTION OF MOTION; 345] 5 *n* (*informal*) **sweepstake**, lottery, draw, raffle, game of chance, prize draw. [➡GAMBLE AND TAKE RISKS; 467] 6 *n* **arc**, arch, bend, bow, swing, stroke, swish, swoop, curve. [➡ROUNDED SHAPE; 1217] 7 *n* **scope**, range, extent, stretch, span, distance. [➡DEGREE AND EXTENT; 110]

sweep aside *v* **dismiss**, ignore, brush aside, have done with, reject. [➡NOT PAY ATTENTION; 765] *Opposite:* consider.

sweep away 1 *v* **bowl over**, astonish, carry away, astound, overwhelm, amaze, impress, stagger, flabbergast (*informal*), dumbfound. [➡SURPRISE AND IMPRESS; 575] 2 *v* **brush**, sweep up, clean up, clear up, remove, sweep, clear, scoop up, brush away, clean, pick up, whisk, gather, tidy up. [➡CLEAN AND POLISH; 404]

sweeping 1 *adj* **far-reaching**, comprehensive, all-encompassing, extensive, across-the-board, wide, widespread, broad, wide-ranging, full, wholesale, inclusive. [➡LARGE; 1192] *Opposite:* restricted. 2 *adj* **indiscriminate**, generalized, general, broad, blanket, unselective. [➡VAGUENESS; 244] *Opposite:* specific.

sweeps (*US informal*) *n* [➡GAMBLE AND TAKE RISKS; 467]

sweep somebody off his/her feet *v* **attract**, enchant, charm, allure, beguile, fascinate, bewitch, dazzle, carry away, bowl over [➡SURPRISE AND IMPRESS; 575]. *Opposite:* turn off (*informal*).

sweepstake *n* **lottery**, sweep (*informal*), draw, raffle, game of chance, prize draw, sweepstakes (*US*), sweeps (*US informal*). [➡GAMBLE AND TAKE RISKS; 467]

sweep under the carpet *v* [➡NOT PAY ATTENTION; 765]

sweep up *v* **brush**, tidy up, clean, pick up, clean up, clear up, remove, sweep, clear, scoop up, brush away, clear away. [➡CLEAN AND POLISH; 404]

sweet 1 *adj* **sugary**, syrupy, saccharine, sweetened, honeyed. [➡TASTE; 704] *Opposite:* bitter. 2 *adj* **fresh**, pure, wholesome. [➡CLEAN; 1232] *Opposite:* foul. 3 *adj* **sweet-smelling**, fragrant, perfumed, scented, odorous. [➡SMELL AND SMELLING; 706] *Opposite:* smelly. 4 *adj* **melodious**, melodic, harmonious, musical, tuneful, dulcet, easy on the ear, pleasant, mellifluous. [➡SOFT OR PLEASANT SOUNDS; 1264] *Opposite:* harsh. 5 *adj* **satisfying**, gratifying, enjoyable, rewarding, pleasing, agreeable, pleasurable. [➡EMOTIONALLY PLEASANT; 188] *Opposite:* unrewarding. 6 *adj* **kind**, thoughtful, considerate, pleasant, amiable, friendly, caring, gentle, good-natured, soft-hearted, agreeable, sweet-tempered, accommodating, obliging, sympathetic. [➡GENEROSITY AND KINDNESS; 496] 7 *adj* **lovable**, charming, engaging, appealing, attractive, delightful, adorable, cute. [➡BEAUTY AND ATTRACTIVENESS; 190] *Opposite:* unappealing. 8 *n* **bonbon**, sweetie (*informal*), chew, mint, confection, confectionery, sweetmeat (*archaic*), candy (*US*). [➡CONFECTIONERY; 1181] 9 *n* **pudding**, afters (*informal*), dessert. [➡MEALS AND PARTS OF MEALS; 1168]

sweetcorn *type of* **vegetable.** [➡FRUIT AND VEGETABLES; 1175]

sweet course *part of* **meal.** [➡MEALS AND PARTS OF MEALS; 1168]

sweeten 1 *v* **make sweeter**, add sugar to, sugar-coat, candy-coat (*US*), sugar, honey, crystallize. [➡COOKING AND FOOD PREPARATION; 354] 2 *v* **enhance**, improve, better, augment (*formal*), intensify, heighten. [➡IMPROVE SOMETHING; 375] 3 *v* **pacify**, mollify, appease, soothe, soften up. [➡SOOTHE AND CALM; 574] *Opposite:* aggravate.

sweetener 1 *n* (*informal*) **bribe**, backhander (*informal*), inducement, carrot. [➡BRIBES; 441] 2 *n* **sweet substance**, sugar, saccharine, aspartame. [➡ADDITIVES; 1171]

sweetening *n* **sweet substance**, sweetener, sugar, saccharine, aspartame, honey, molasses, treacle, syrup, corn syrup (*US*). [➡ADDITIVES; 1171]

sweetheart *n* **darling**, dear, love (*informal*), dearest, beloved, sweetie (*informal*), sugar (*informal*), pet, babe (*slang*), honey (*US informal*), precious. [➡ENDEARMENTS; 657]

sweetie (*informal*) 1 *n* **darling**, dear, love (*informal*), dearest, beloved, sweetheart, sugar (*informal*), pet, babe (*slang*), precious, honey (*US informal*). [➡ENDEARMENTS; 657] 2 *type of* **confectionery**. [➡CONFECTIONERY; 1181]

sweetie pie (*informal*) *n* **sweetheart**, dear, sweetie (*informal*), darling, honey (*US informal*), pet. [➡ENDEARMENTS; 657]

sweetly 1 *adv* **pleasantly**, kindly, thoughtfully, considerately, amiably. [➡GENEROSITY AND KINDNESS; 496] *Opposite:* unkindly. 2 *adv* **harmoniously**, beautifully, melodiously, melodically, musically, tunefully, pleasantly, pleasingly, agreeably. [➡SOFT OR PLEASANT SOUNDS; 1264] *Opposite:* harshly.

sweetmeat (*archaic*) *type of* **confectionery**. [➡CONFECTIONERY; 1181]

sweetness 1 *n* **sugariness**, syrupiness, saccharinity. [➡TASTE; 704] *Opposite:* sourness. 2 *n* **charm**, cuteness, appeal, attractiveness, delightfulness, adorability. [➡BEAUTY AND ATTRACTIVENESS; 190] 3 *n* **kindness**, thoughtfulness, consideration, pleasantness, amiability, friendliness, agreeableness. [➡GENEROSITY AND KINDNESS; 496] *Opposite:* unkindness. 4 *n* **freshness**, pureness, purity, wholesomeness. [➡CLEAN; 1232] 5 *n* **melodiousness**, harmony, pleasantness, mellifluousness. [➡SOFT OR PLEASANT SOUNDS; 1264] *Opposite:* harshness.

sweetness and light *n* **pleasantness**, harmony, peace, friendliness, concord, amiability. [➡HARMONY; 156] *Opposite:* unpleasantness.

sweet nothings *n* **romantic words**, romantic phrases, loving words, endearments, pillow talk, honeyed words. [➡ENDEARMENTS; 657]

sweet pea *type of* **annual flower**. [➡FLOWERS; 1032]

sweet pepper *type of* **salad vegetable**. [➡FRUIT AND VEGETABLES; 1175]

sweet potato *type of* **root vegetable**. [➡FRUIT AND VEGETABLES; 1175]

sweetshop *type of* **food outlet**. [➡RETAIL OUTLETS; 1082]

sweet-smelling *adj* **aromatic**, perfumed, fragrant, sweet-scented, fresh. [➡SMELL AND SMELLING; 706] *Opposite:* smelly.

sweet-talk (*informal*) *v* **charm**, flatter, butter up (*informal*), smooth-talk, persuade, cajole, coax, blandish (*formal*). [➡FLATTER AND FAWN; 622]

sweet talk (*informal*) *n* **flattery**, smooth talk, flannel (*informal*), blarney (*informal*), blandishment (*formal*), cajolery, soft soap (*informal*). [➡INGRATIATING; 639]

sweet-tempered *adj* [➡CHEERFULNESS OF OUTLOOK; 504]

sweet tooth *n* **craving**, taste, fondness, liking, relish, weakness, chocolate addiction, sugar craving. [➡TASTE; 704]

swell 1 *v* **puff up**, puff out, swell up, bulge, bloat, distend, engorge, inflate, balloon. [➡CHANGE OF SIZE: BIGGER; 393] *Opposite:* deflate. 2 *v* **increase**, grow, enlarge, inflate, expand, mushroom, proliferate. [➡CHANGE OF SIZE: BIGGER; 393] *Opposite:* decrease. 3 *v* **add to**, augment (*formal*), increase, enhance, improve, expand, amplify, enlarge, supplement, heighten, intensify, raise. [➡CHANGE OF SIZE: BIGGER; 393] *Opposite:* diminish. 4 *n* **wave**, undulation, billow, breaker, surge, roller. [➡THE SEAS, OCEANS, AND SHORES; 1041] 5 *n* (*dated informal*) **fop**, dandy (*dated*), clotheshorse, beau (*archaic*), coxcomb (*archaic*), fashion plate, dude (*US slang*). [➡MALE PERSON; 934] 6 *adj* (*US dated informal*) **great** (*informal*), brilliant (*informal*), really nice, super (*informal*), fantastic, wonderful, marvellous, fabulous, tremendous, good, excellent, terrific (*informal*). [➡EXTRAORDINARY: AMAZING; 205] *Opposite:* awful.

swelled head (*US*) *n* [➡SELF-IMPORTANT AND SELF-SEEKING PEOPLE; 949]

swellheaded (*US informal*) *adj* **conceited**, full of yourself, vain, cocky (*informal*), self-important, too big for your boots (*informal*), stuck-up (*informal*), puffed up, self-satisfied, swollen-headed. [➡POMPOUS, LOUD, AND OVER-CONFIDENT; 636] *Opposite:* modest.

swelling *n* **bulge**, bump, puffiness, inflammation, distension, enlargement, engorgement, growth, blister, bunion, boil, abscess, protuberance. [➡ILL AND SICK; 741]

swelter *v* **feel hot**, sweat, perspire, boil (*informal*), overheat, roast (*informal*), bake (*informal*), burn. [➡EXCRETION AND EXCRETA; 723] *Opposite:* shiver.

sweltering *adj* **boiling**, scorching (*informal*), baking, burning up, red-hot, sizzling (*informal*), blistering, oppressive, roasting (*informal*). [➡HOT WEATHER; 1050] *Opposite:* freezing.

swerve *v* **veer**, veer off, turn sharply, swing over, change direction, diverge, deviate. [➡CHANGE DIRECTION OF MOTION; 345]

swift 1 *n* **quick**, speedy, fast, rapid, prompt, sudden. [➡MOVING QUICKLY; 103] 2 *type of* **common bird**. [➡BIRD; 997]

swiftly *adv* **quickly**, speedily, fast, summarily, rapidly, at the double, promptly, suddenly, in the blink of an eye, like greased lightning, like a shot, expeditiously, precipitously, instantly, immediately, in a flash. [➡MOVING QUICKLY; 103] *Opposite:* slowly.

swiftness *n* **rapidity**, quickness, fleetness (*literary*), fastness, pace, speed, speediness, velocity, dispatch, alacrity, precipitousness, expeditiousness. [➡SPEED; 102] *Opposite:* slowness.

swig (*informal*) 1 *v* **quaff** (*literary or humorous*), guzzle (*informal*), drink, swill, imbibe (*formal or humorous*), toss off, take a drop. [➡DRINK; 712] 2 *n* **mouthful**, draught, nip, drink. [➡DRINK; 712]

swill 1 *v* **rinse**, sluice, wash out, wash down, swab, clean, wash. [➡CLEAN AND POLISH; 404] 2 *v* **gulp down**, swig (*informal*), guzzle (*informal*), quaff (*literary or humorous*), knock back (*informal*). [➡DRINK; 712] 3 *n* **pig food**, slops, pigswill, mash, scraps. [➡ANIMAL FEED; 1167]

swim 1 *v* **bathe**, go for a dip, go swimming. [➡HOBBIES, GAMES, AND SPORTS; 875] 2 *v* **spin**, whirl, reel, sway. [➡MOVE SOMETHING ON THE SPOT; 337]

swimming baths (*dated*) *n* **pool**, swimming pool, baths. [➡BUILDINGS FOR PUBLIC ENTERTAINMENT; 1083]

swimming costume *type of* **sportswear**. [➡GARMENTS AND OUTFITS; 865]

swimmingly *adv* **successfully**, well, smoothly, easily, like a house on fire, satisfactorily, like clockwork, effortlessly. [➡GOOD, WELL, BETTER; 184] *Opposite:* laboriously.

swimming pool *n* **pool**, swimming baths, lido, baths. [➡BUILDINGS FOR PUBLIC ENTERTAINMENT; 1083]

swimming trunks *type of* **sportswear**. [➡GARMENTS AND OUTFITS; 865]

swimsuit *type of* **sportswear**. [➡GARMENTS AND OUTFITS; 865]

swimwear *type of* **sportswear**. [➡GARMENTS AND OUTFITS; 865]

swindle 1 *v* **cheat**, con, dupe, trick, scam (*slang*), fiddle (*informal*), double-cross, deceive, defraud, rip off (*informal*), sting (*informal*), fleece (*informal*), do out of (*informal*), bilk (*informal*). [➡STEAL AND ROB; 427] 2 *n* **fraud**, hoax, embezzlement, racket (*informal*), rip-off (*informal*), confidence trick, scam (*slang*), con. [➡DECEPTION AND LIES; 661]

swindler *n* **cheat**, con artist (*slang*), trickster, shark (*informal*), charlatan, fraud, bilker (*informal*), embezzler, faker, con man (*informal*). [➡PEOPLE WHO DECEIVE; 662]

swine *n* **hog**, boar, pig. [➡FARM ANIMAL; 982]

swing 1 *v* **dangle**, hang, hang down, be suspended, sway, suspend, droop, depend (*archaic*). [➡MOVE SOMETHING ON THE SPOT; 337] 2 *v* **swerve**, veer, reel, pivot, rotate, turn. [➡CHANGE DIRECTION OF MOTION; 345] 3 *v* **rock**, fluctuate, move back and forth, sway, move backwards and forwards, roll, turn round, spin round, spin around, swivel round, veer, move to and fro, oscillate, shift, alter, change, vacillate, alternate, swivel around, whirl around. [➡BOUNCE, UNDULATE, AND VIBRATE; 309] 4 *v* (*informal*) **manage**, succeed in, accomplish, arrange, bring off, pull off (*informal*). [➡CARRY OUT AN ACTION; 270] 5 *n* **swipe**, smack, slap, thump, blow, strike, punch. [➡PHYSICAL ATTACK AND PUNISHMENT; 416] 6 *type of* **popular music**. [➡MUSIC, SONGS, AND SINGING; 907]

swing at *v* **hit**, hit out at, lash out, strike, thump, smack, slap, swipe, punch. [➡PHYSICAL ATTACK AND PUNISHMENT; 416]

swing bridge *type of* **bridge**. [➡BRIDGES, TUNNELS, CROSSINGS, AND JUNCTIONS; 1111]

swing by (*US*) *v* [➡ARRIVE; 12]

swingeing *adj* **severe**, harmful, punishing, harsh, draconian, stringent. [➡PHYSICALLY UNPLEASANT; 227] *Opposite:* mild.

swing round *v* **wheel round**, spin round, wheel around, turn round, swivel round, swerve, veer round, swerve round, twirl round, whirl round. [➡CHANGE DIRECTION OF MOTION; 345]

swipe 1 *v* (*informal*) **steal**, pinch (*informal*), nick (*slang*), pilfer, make off with, walk off with, whip (*informal*), run off with, filch (*informal*), snatch, take, lift (*informal*), cop (*slang*). [➡STEAL AND ROB; 427] 2 *v* **hit**, swing at, lash out, hit out at, strike, slap, smack, thump, whack, bash (*informal*), punch. [➡PHYSICAL ATTACK AND PUNISHMENT; 416] 3 *n* **blow**, hit, swing, slap, smack, thump, bash (*informal*), punch. [➡PHYSICAL ATTACK AND PUNISHMENT; 416] 4 *n* (*informal*) **critical remark**, cutting remark, dig, putdown (*informal*). [➡CRITICISMS AND ANGRY OUTBURSTS; 50] *Opposite:* compliment.

swipe card *n* **plastic card**, magnetic card, smart card, key card, credit card, bank card, debit card. [➡ACCOUNTING, BANKING, AND BUDGETING; 799]

swirl 1 *v* **whirl**, twirl, spin, eddy, churn. [➡MOVE SOMETHING ON THE SPOT; 337] 2 *n* **twirl**, whirl, spin, eddy. [➡MOVE SOMETHING ON THE SPOT; 337]

swish 1 *v* **hiss**, whoosh, whistle, whisper, rustle. [➡EMIT CONTINUOUS SOUNDS; 367] 2 *n* **rustle**, hiss, whoosh, whisper, whistle. [➡CONTINUOUS SOUNDS; 1257] 3 *adj* (*informal*) **posh** (*informal*), smart, upmarket, classy (*informal*), ritzy (*informal*), swanky (*informal*), fashionable, trendy (*informal*), high-class, chic, stylish. [➡EXPENSIVE AND LUXURIOUS; 219] *Opposite:* downmarket.

Swiss chard *type of* **vegetable**. [➡FRUIT AND VEGETABLES; 1175]

Swiss roll *type of* **cake**. [➡CAKES, BISCUITS, AND DESSERTS; 1180]

switch 1 *n* **control**, lever, button, knob, key, regulator. [➡PARTS OF MACHINES AND TOOLS; 1117] 2 *n* **change**, shift, adjustment, difference, modification, alteration. [➡CHANGE; 373] 3 *n* **exchange**, substitution, swap (*informal*), changeover, replacement, trade. [➡EXCHANGE AND INTERCHANGE; 449] 4 *n* **whip**, lash, crop, cat-o'-nine-tails. [➡BLUNT INSTRUMENTS AND WHIPS; 1157]

switchback *n* **bend**, twist, zigzag, hairpin, turn, corner. [➡ROADS; 1105]

switchblade (*US*) *type of* **knife**. [➡CUTTING TOOLS; 1119]

switchboard *type of* **telecommunications equipment**. [➡TELECOMMUNICATIONS; 1129]

switch off 1 *v* **shut down**, stop, deactivate, disconnect, cut, kill (*informal*), turn off. [➡CAUSE TO STOP; 267] *Opposite:* switch on. 2 *v* (*informal*) **relax**, unwind, stop worrying, stop paying attention, chill out (*slang*). [➡CHANGE OF MOOD AND COMPOSURE; 581]

switch on *v* **turn on**, start, start up, activate, connect, begin, commence (*formal*). [➡CAUSE TO START; 266] *Opposite:* switch off.

swivel *v* **spin**, rotate, revolve, pivot, turn round, twist, twirl, wheel. [➡MOVE SOMETHING ON THE SPOT; 337]

swivel chair *type of* **seating**. [➡FURNITURE; 858]

swivel round *v* [➡MOVE SOMETHING ON THE SPOT; 337]

swizz *n* [➡NUISANCES; 254]

swollen *adj* **distended**, inflamed, engorged, puffy, puffed-up, enlarged, inflated, bloated, blown up. [➡CHANGE OF SIZE: BIGGER; 393]

swollen head *n* **conceit**, self-conceit, pride, vanity, arrogance, self-satisfaction, self-importance, swelled head (*US*). [➡AFFECTATION, SELF-SATISFACTION, AND SNOBBISHNESS; 508] *Opposite:* modesty.

swollen-headed *adj* **conceited**, full of yourself, vain, cocky (*informal*), self-important, too big for your boots (*informal*), stuck-up (*informal*), puffed up, self-satisfied, swellheaded (*US*). [➡POMPOUS, LOUD, AND OVER-CONFIDENT; 636] *Opposite:* modest.

swoon 1 *v* **pass out**, faint, black out, lose consciousness, faint away, collapse, keel over (*informal*). [➡TIRED, ASLEEP AND UNCONSCIOUS; 739] 2 *n* **faint**, blackout, loss of consciousness, unconsciousness. [➡ILLNESSES AND DISORDERS; 733]

swoop *v* **pounce**, jump, leap, dive, fly down, lunge, plunge. [➡GO DOWNWARDS; 308]

swoosh 1 *n* **rustle**, swish, rush, swirl, whiz, whirl. [➡CONTINUOUS SOUNDS; 1257] 2 *v* **rustle**, swish, rush, swirl, whiz, whirl. [➡MOVE FAST; 314]

sword

◆ *types of sword or knife*
battleaxe, bayonet, bowie knife, broadsword, claymore, cutlass, dagger, dirk, foil, lance, machete, poleaxe, rapier, sabre, scimitar, skean, stiletto, swordstick, tomahawk

sword fighter *n* [➡PEOPLE IN SPORTS AND LEISURE; 876]

sword fighting *n* [➡HOBBIES, GAMES, AND SPORTS; 875]

swordfish *type of* **tropical sea fish.** [➡SEA FISH; 1009]

sword grass *type of* **grass.** [➡GRASS; 1031]

swordplay *n* **sword fighting**, fencing, duelling, foil fencing, combat. [➡NON-AGGRESSIVE/SPORTING EVENT; 40]

swordstick *type of* **sword or knife.** [➡SWORDS AND KNIVES; 1156]

sworn *adj* **avowed** (*formal*), confirmed, affirmed. [➡CERTAINTY; 562]

sworn enemy *n* [➡ENEMIES AND TORMENTORS; 969]

swot (*informal*) *v* **study**, cram (*informal*), revise, mug up (*informal*), bone up (*informal*), review (*US*). [➡STUDYING; 844]

swung dash *type of* **punctuation mark.** [➡ASPECTS OF LANGUAGE; 683]

sybarite *n* **voluptuary**, sensualist, hedonist, epicurean, pleasure-lover. [➡PLEASURE-SEEKERS AND HEDONISTS; 886] *Opposite:* Spartan.

sybaritic *adj* [➡PLEASURE-SEEKING AND EXCESS; 885]

sycamore *type of* **deciduous tree.** [➡DECIDUOUS TREES; 1028]

sycophancy *n* **servility**, obsequiousness, flattery, fawning, toadying, sucking up (*informal*), brownnosing (*slang*). [➡INGRATIATING; 639]

sycophant *n* **toady**, flatterer, bootlicker (*informal disapproving*), minion, yes man. [➡SUPERFICIAL OR INSINCERE PEOPLE; 951]

sycophantic *adj* **ingratiating**, flattering, kowtowing, obsequious, apple-polishing (*US slang*). [➡INGRATIATING; 639]

syllable *n* [➡ASPECTS OF LANGUAGE; 683]

syllabub *type of* **dessert.** [➡CAKES, BISCUITS, AND DESSERTS; 1180]

syllabus *n* **course outline**, curriculum, programme, programme of study, prospectus. [➡LISTS AND SCHEDULES; 588]

syllaweb *n* [➡THE INTERNET; 1127]

sylph *n* **nymph**, sprite, fairy, dryad, naiad. [➡MYTHICAL BEINGS; 790]

sylphlike *adj* **slender**, willowy, lithe, slim, graceful, svelte, slight. [➡BUILD; 478] *Opposite:* hefty.

symbiosis *n* **cooperation**, interdependence, relationship, association, synergy, interaction. [➡RECIPROCITY AND INTERDEPENDENCE; 148] *Opposite:* independence.

symbiotic *adj* **mutually beneficial**, interdependent, synergetic, cooperative, reciprocal, mutual, related, associated. [➡RECIPROCITY AND INTERDEPENDENCE; 148] *Opposite:* independent.

symbol 1 *n* **sign**, representation, character, figure, mark, icon, pictogram. [➡SYMBOLS, SIGNS, AND NUMBERS; 597] 2 *n* **emblem**, image, badge, logo. [➡SYMBOLS, SIGNS, AND NUMBERS; 597]

symbolic *adj* **representative**, figurative, emblematic, representational. [➡REPRESENTATIVE; 66]

symbolism 1 *n* **imagery**, allegory, representation. [➡REPRESENTATIONS AND GENERAL EXAMPLES; 65] 2 *type of* **pre-20th-century art movement.** [➡ARTISTIC MOVEMENTS AND STYLES; 899]

symbolize *v* **represent**, be a symbol of, be a sign of, signify, stand for, denote, indicate, mean, imply, suggest, embody, epitomize. [➡REPRESENT SOMETHING OR SOMEBODY; 59]

symmetrical *adj* **balanced**, even, equal, proportioned, regular. [➡EQUALITY; 155] *Opposite:* asymmetrical.

symmetry *n* **regularity**, balance, equilibrium, evenness, proportion. [➡EQUALITY; 155] *Opposite:* asymmetry.

sympathetic 1 *adj* **understanding**, concerned, kind, kindly, compassionate, caring, considerate, sensitive, kind-hearted, supportive, benevolent. [➡GENEROSITY AND KINDNESS; 496] *Opposite:* unfeeling. 2 *adj* **approving**, in agreement, in accord, supportive, well-disposed, in favour. [➡HARMONY; 156] *Opposite:* against. 3 *adj* **agreeable**, congenial, likable, friendly, amiable, affable, genial, pleasant. [➡FRIENDLINESS AND SOCIABILITY; 495] *Opposite:* disagreeable.

sympathize *v* **empathize**, feel sorry for, commiserate, express sympathy, understand, identify, feel for, be supportive, pity. [➡BE CONCERNED AND CARE; 582]

sympathizer *n* **partisan**, backer, follower, adherent, well-wisher, champion, supporter. [➡SUPPORTERS, PROTECTORS, AND COMPATRIOTS; 970] *Opposite:* opponent.

sympathy 1 *n* **understanding**, compassion, kindness, consideration, empathy, fellow feeling. [➡COMPASSION AND FORGIVENESS; 552] *Opposite:* incomprehension. 2 *n* **pity**, commiseration, condolences. [➡COMPASSION AND FORGIVENESS; 552] 3 *n* **approval**, agreement, support, backing. [➡HARMONY; 156]

symphonic *adj* **musical**, orchestral, instrumental, classical, philharmonic, ensemble. [➡MUSICAL TERMS; 912]

symphony *type of* **instrumental music.** [➡MUSIC, SONGS, AND SINGING; 907]

symphony orchestra *type of* **band.** [➡MUSICIANS AND SINGERS; 908]

symposium *n* **conference**, seminar, meeting, convention. [➡MEETINGS AND ASSEMBLIES; 43]

symptom *n* **indication**, sign, warning sign, indicator. [➡INDICATIONS, SIGNS, AND WARNINGS; 68]

symptomatic *adj* **indicative**, suggestive, characteristic. [➡REPRESENTATIVE; 66]

synagogue *type of* **place of worship.** [➡RELIGIOUS BUILDINGS; 1084]

synchronicity *n* [➡CONCURRENT AND CONTEMPORANEOUS; 165]

synchronism *n* [➡CONCURRENT AND CONTEMPORANEOUS; 165]

synchronize *v* **harmonize**, coordinate, orchestrate, bring into line, match. [➡ARRANGE AND CREATE ORDER; 358]

synchronized *adj* **coordinated**, harmonized, corresponding, matched, in time, in step, in line. [➡CONCURRENT AND CONTEMPORANEOUS; 165]

synchronous *adj* [➡CONCURRENT AND CONTEMPORANEOUS; 165]

syncopate *v* **modify**, play, shift, swing, stress, accent. [➡CHANGE; 373]

syncopation *n* **shift of accent**, modification, accent, stress, rhythm. [➡MUSICAL TERMS; 912]

syndicate *n* **association**, collective, consortium, organization, group. [➡GROUPS WITH A COMMON INTEREST; 938]

syndrome *n* **condition**, disease, pattern, set of symptoms, disorder. [➡SICKNESS; 730]

synergetic *adj* [➡RECIPROCITY AND INTERDEPENDENCE; 148]

synergy *n* **working together**, interaction, cooperation, combined effect, collaboration, concerted effort. [➡RECIPROCITY AND INTERDEPENDENCE; 148]

synonym *n* **alternative word**, alternative expression, other word, substitute, replacement. [➡ASPECTS OF LANGUAGE; 683]

synonymous *adj* **identical**, the same, one and the same, equal, tantamount. [➡SAMENESS; 151] *Opposite:* different.

synopsis *n* **outline**, rundown, précis, summing up, summary, summation, abridgment, abstract. [➡SUMMARIES, OUTLINES, AND EXCERPTS; 589]

syntax *n* **grammar**, sentence structure, language rules, composition, word order, arrangement. [➡ASPECTS OF LANGUAGE; 683]

synthesis **1** *n* **mixture**, amalgamation, combination, blend, fusion. [➡COLLECTIONS AND MIXTURES OF THINGS; 1243] *Opposite:* separation. **2** *n* **production**, creation, making, manufacture. [➡CREATION; 347]

synthesize **1** *v* **manufacture**, create, make, produce. [➡MANUFACTURE; 350] **2** *v* **fuse**, blend, combine, amalgamate, integrate, join. [➡COMBINE AND MIX; 401] *Opposite:* separate.

synthesizer *type of* **keyboard.** [➡MUSICAL INSTRUMENTS; 910]

synthetic **1** *adj* **artificial**, fake, mock, imitation, faux. [➡FALSE AND UNREAL; 174] *Opposite:* real. **2** *adj* **insincere**, sham, bogus, put on, phoney. [➡AFFECTATION, SELF-SATISFACTION, AND SNOBBISHNESS; 508] *Opposite:* genuine.

syringe *type of* **medical instrument.** [➡HAND TOOLS; 1118]

syrup *n* **sweet liquid**, molasses, sauce, golden syrup, treacle, maple syrup, corn syrup (*US*). [➡SUGAR AND PRESERVES; 1183]

syrupy *adj* **sugary**, thick, treacly, sweet. [➡TASTE; 704]

system **1** *n* **scheme**, arrangement, classification, structure, organism, organization, coordination. [➡ORDER AND ORGANIZATION; 207] **2** *n* **method**, technique, procedure, routine, approach, practice. [➡WAYS OF DOING THINGS; 295] **3** *n* **orderliness**, regularity, method, logic. [➡ORDER AND ORGANIZATION; 207] *Opposite:* disorder.

systematic *adj* **methodical**, orderly, organized, efficient, logical, regular. [➡ORDER AND ORGANIZATION; 207] *Opposite:* disorganized.

systematically *adv* **methodically**, thoroughly, steadily, analytically, scientifically. [➡ORDER AND ORGANIZATION; 207] *Opposite:* haphazardly.

systematization *n* [➡ARRANGE AND CREATE ORDER; 358]

systematize *v* **arrange**, order, regulate, sort, classify, standardize, put in order, organize. [➡ARRANGE AND CREATE ORDER; 358]

systemic *adj* **universal**, complete, general. [➡ALL; 126]

systemize *v* [➡ARRANGE AND CREATE ORDER; 358]

system of government *n* [➡STYLES AND SYSTEMS OF GOVERNMENT; 806]

systems analyst *n* [➡COMPUTERS AND COMPUTING; 1126]

T

ta (*informal*) *interj* **thank you**, thanks, cheers. [➡GREETINGS, FAREWELLS, AND SALUTATIONS; 660]

tab 1 *n* **tag**, flap, label, ticket, stub, strip. [➡NAME AND DESCRIBE; 666] 2 *n* (*US informal*) **bill**, check, account, running total. [➡RECEIPTS AND INVOICES; 592]

tabard *type of* **top.** [➡GARMENTS AND OUTFITS; 865]

tabby *type of* **cat.** [➡FELINE; 983]

tabby cat *see* **tabby.**

tabernacle 1 *n* **chest**, cabinet, container, case, box, coffer. [➡CONTAINERS, RECEPTACLES, AND PACKAGING; 1244] 2 *type of* **church.** [➡RELIGIOUS BUILDINGS; 1084]

tabla *type of* **percussion instrument.** [➡MUSICAL INSTRUMENTS; 910]

table 1 *n* **bench**, board, desk, counter, stand, stall, slab, tabletop. [➡FURNITURE; 858] 2 *n* **food**, fare, diet, provision, menu, board. [➡FOOD; 1166] 3 *n* **chart**, graph, diagram, spreadsheet, record, register, index, list, catalogue, schedule. [➡DRAWINGS, CHARTS AND TABLES; 595] 4 *v* **propose**, put forward, submit, suggest, enter, move. [➡SUGGEST, HINT, AND COMMENT; 613] *Opposite:* withdraw. 5 *v* (*US*) **postpone**, shelve, defer, put on the back burner, put on ice, hold over, put off. [➡DELAY ACTION OR OCCURRENCE; 279] *Opposite:* bring forward.

table

◆ *types of table*
writing desk, bedside table, card table, coffee table, console, davenport, desk, dining table, dressing table, end table, escritoire, gateleg table, night table (*US*), occasional table, Pembroke table, roll-top desk, tea table, trestle table, vanity table, worktable

tableau *n* **display**, picture, montage, scene, representation, image, description. [➡ARTWORKS; 898]

tablecloth *n* **cover**, cloth, covering. [➡SOFT FURNISHINGS, LINEN, AND DRAPERY; 860]

table knife *type of* **knife.** [➡CUTTING TOOLS; 1119]

table lamp *n* [➡LIGHTING; 862]

tableland *n* **plain**, flatland, prairie, plateau, upland, mesa. [➡DESERTS AND PLAINS; 1045] *Opposite:* lowland.

table linen *n* [➡SOFT FURNISHINGS, LINEN, AND DRAPERY; 860]

table mat *n* **place mat**, coaster, mat, pad, trivet. [➡TABLEWARE, CUTLERY, AND KITCHENWARE; 861]

tablespoon *type of* **cutlery.** [➡TABLEWARE, CUTLERY, AND KITCHENWARE; 861]

tablespoonful *n* [➡AMOUNT AND QUANTITY; 112]

tablet 1 *n* **pill**, capsule, lozenge. [➡REMEDIES, TREATMENTS AND OPERATIONS; 732] 2 *n* **slab**, block, bar, cake, lump. [➡AMOUNT OF SOLID OR SEMI-SOLID; 115]

tablet computer *type of* **computer.** [➡COMPUTERS AND COMPUTING; 1126]

table tennis *type of* **court game.** [➡HOBBIES, GAMES, AND SPORTS; 875]

tableware *n* **crockery**, plates, dishes, dinner service, tea service, cutlery, glassware, glasses, bowls. [➡TABLEWARE, CUTLERY, AND KITCHENWARE; 861]

tabloid 1 *n* [➡NEWSPAPERS; 606] 2 *adj* **sensationalist**, shocking, lurid, scandalous, yellow, florid. [➡NEWSPAPERS; 606]

taboo 1 *adj* **offensive**, unmentionable, unthinkable, distasteful, off-limits, out of bounds. [➡MORALLY BAD; 776] 2 *adj* **forbidden**, banned, prohibited, barred, proscribed, outlawed. [➡REFUSE PERMISSION AND NOT ALLOW; 671] *Opposite:* acceptable. 3 *n* **ban**, prohibition, bar, restriction, proscription (*formal*), interdict. [➡CAPTIVITY AND LOSS OF FREEDOM; 249] 4 *v* **forbid**, ban, prohibit, bar, proscribe, outlaw. [➡REFUSE PERMISSION AND NOT ALLOW; 671] *Opposite:* allow.

tabor *type of* **percussion instrument.** [➡MUSICAL INSTRUMENTS; 910]

tabular *adj* **flat**, level, smooth, even, horizontal, plane. [➡ORIENTATION AND ALIGNMENT; 1222]

tabulate *v* **tabularize**, chart, arrange, organize, present, set out, formulate, lay out. [➡ARRANGE AND CREATE ORDER; 358]

tabulation *n* **tabularization**, arrangement, organization, presentation, formulation, layout. [➡DRAWINGS, CHARTS AND TABLES; 595]

tachometer *type of* **measuring device.** [➡MEASURING DEVICES; 1122]

tacit *adj* **unspoken**, implicit, inferred, implied, understood, unstated, silent, wordless. [➡KNOWN AND FAMOUS; 182] *Opposite:* explicit.

taciturn *adj* **reserved**, uncommunicative, reticent, silent, quiet, introverted, shy, distant, aloof. [➡RETICENT AND UNFORTHCOMING; 632] *Opposite:* garrulous.

See Compare and Contrast at **silent.**

taciturnity *n* **reserve**, uncommunicativeness, reticence, silence, quietness, introversion, shyness, distance, aloofness. [➡RETICENT AND UNFORTHCOMING; 632] *Opposite:* garrulousness.

tack 1 *n* **nail**, pin, screw, staple, clip, fastener. [➡FASTENERS, LINKS, AND NETWORKS; 1246] 2 *n* **approach**, tactic, line, method, policy, scheme, ploy. [➡WAYS OF DOING THINGS; 295] 3 *n* **direction**, path, bearing, course, way, line, route. [➡DIRECTION OF MOTION; 346] 4 *v* **pin**, nail, fasten, attach, affix, fix, staple, clip. [➡FASTEN, LINK, AND JOIN; 409] *Opposite:* unfasten. 5 *v* **append**, add on, tag on, stick on, attach, throw in. [➡ FASTEN, LINK, AND JOIN; 409] *Opposite:* remove.

tackiness (*informal*) *n* **tastelessness**, bad taste, vulgarity, cheapness, nastiness, tawdriness, crudeness, crudity, showiness, ostentation. [➡ IN POOR TASTE; 230] *Opposite:* taste.

tackle 1 *n* **challenge**, attack, block, confrontation, throw, grab, hold. [➡ NON-AGGRESSIVE/SPORTING EVENT; 40] 2 *n* **equipment**, gear (*informal*), apparatus, kit, outfit, tools, trappings, implements, rigging. [➡ DEVICES; 1114] 3 *v* **undertake**, begin, embark upon, attempt, engage in, deal with, attack. [➡ ATTEMPT AN ACTION; 262] 4 *v* **confront**, challenge, face, speak to, collar, bend somebody's ear. [➡ INITIATE AND ESTABLISH COMMUNICATION; 681] 5 *v* **block**, stop, throw, seize, grab, bring down, halt, attack, grasp, wrestle. [➡ PHYSICAL ATTACK AND PUNISHMENT; 416]

tacky 1 *adj* **sticky**, messy, gluey, gummy, adhesive, wet, viscous, waxy. [➡ PHYSICAL TEXTURE; 1221] *Opposite:* dry. 2 *adj* (*informal*) **tasteless**, in bad taste, vulgar, cheap, nasty, tawdry, low, crude, showy, ostentatious. [➡ IN POOR TASTE; 230] *Opposite:* tasteful.

tact *n* **diplomacy**, discretion, sensitivity, delicacy, thoughtfulness, consideration, perception, insight, discernment, skill, dexterity, subtlety, judgment, care, politeness. [➡ GOOD MANNERS AND SOCIAL SKILLS; 521] *Opposite:* tactlessness.

tactful *adj* **diplomatic**, discreet, sensitive, delicate, thoughtful, considerate, perceptive, insightful, discerning, skilful, dexterous, subtle, judicious, careful, polite, kind. [➡ GOOD MANNERS AND SOCIAL SKILLS; 521] *Opposite:* tactless.

tactfulness *n* [➡ GOOD MANNERS AND SOCIAL SKILLS; 521]

tactic *n* **method**, approach, course, ploy, policy, scheme, way, line, tack, device, trick, manoeuvre. [➡ WAYS OF DOING THINGS; 295]

tactical *adj* **strategic**, planned, premeditated, pre-emptive, psychological, considered, calculated, deliberate, intentional, purposeful, defensive. [➡ INTENTIONAL AND DELIBERATE; 280] *Opposite:* accidental.

tactician *n* **strategist**, negotiator, planner, schemer, diplomat, spin doctor (*informal*). [➡ POLITICAL OFFICES AND POLITICIANS; 808]

tactics *n* **strategy**, planning, campaign, manoeuvres, devices, diplomacy, policy, procedure, scheme. [➡ WAYS OF DOING THINGS; 295]

tactile 1 *adj* **tangible**, palpable, perceptible, physical, concrete, solid. [➡ PERCEPTIBLE; 25] *Opposite:* intangible. 2 *adj* **demonstrative**, touchy-feely (*informal*), physical, affectionate. [➡ HONEST AND OPEN; 631] *Opposite:* reserved.

tactless *adj* **insensitive**, undiplomatic, indiscreet, indelicate, thoughtless, inconsiderate, unfeeling, injudicious, careless, impolite, unthinking, rude, unkind, clumsy, gauche, crass. [➡ BAD MANNERS AND SOCIAL SKILLS; 522] *Opposite:* tactful.

tactlessness *n* **insensitivity**, indiscretion, indelicacy, thoughtlessness, inconsiderateness, injudiciousness, carelessness, impoliteness, rudeness, unkindness, clumsiness, gaucheness, crassness. [➡ BAD MANNERS AND SOCIAL SKILLS; 522] *Opposite:* tact.

tad (*informal*) *n* **bit**, little, touch, mite, dash, soupçon, smidgen (*informal*). [➡ FEW, LITTLE, SMALL AMOUNT; 119] *Opposite:* lot.

tae kwon do *type of* **combat sport**. [➡ HOBBIES, GAMES, AND SPORTS; 875]

taffeta *type of* **fabric from animals**. [➡ FABRICS; 1131]

taffy (*US*) *type of* **confectionery**. [➡ CONFECTIONERY; 1181]

tag 1 *n* **label**, ticket, tab, docket, identifier, code, chip, device. [➡ NAME AND DESCRIBE; 666] 2 *v* **mark**, label, ticket, docket, identify. [➡ NAME AND DESCRIBE; 666] 3 *v* **append**, tack on, add on, attach, stick on, throw in. [➡ FASTEN, LINK, AND JOIN; 409] *Opposite:* remove.

tag along *v* **link up**, join in, follow, accompany, go with, come with, associate with. [➡ ACCOMPANY AND FOLLOW; 338]

tagliatelle *type of* **pasta**. [➡ PASTA; 1179]

tail 1 *n* (*informal*) **follower**, shadow, stalker, pursuer, tracker. [➡ ENEMIES AND TORMENTORS; 969] 2 *v* (*informal*) **follow**, trail, track, shadow, stalk, pursue, go after, chase. [➡ ACCOMPANY AND FOLLOW; 338] 3 *part of* **aircraft**, *part of* **bird**, *part of* **fish**. [➡ AIRCRAFT; 1147]

See Compare and Contrast at **follow**.

tailback *n* **traffic jam**, queue, line, gridlock, logjam. [➡ TRAVEL: TRAFFIC PROBLEMS AND HOLDUPS; 324]

tailboard *see* **tailgate**.

tail coat *type of* **jacket**. [➡ GARMENTS AND OUTFITS; 865]

tail end *n* **end**, close, ending, conclusion, finish, remainder, residue, remnant. [➡ END; 54] *Opposite:* start.

tailgate 1 *v* **dog**, hound, be hard on the heels of, follow, pursue, tail. [➡ ACCOMPANY AND FOLLOW; 338] 2 *part of* **external structure**. [➡ EXTERNAL PARTS OF A VEHICLE; 1146]

tail light *n* **rear light**, tail lamp, brake light, stoplight (*US*). [➡ EXTERNAL PARTS OF A VEHICLE; 1146] *Opposite:* headlight.

tail off *v* **fade**, peter out, dwindle, decrease, fall away, wane, drop, tail away. [➡ DISAPPEAR; 4] *Opposite:* increase.

tailor 1 *v* **make**, make to measure, cut, fashion, mould, style, shape. [➡ CREATION; 347] 2 *v* **adapt**, customize, custom-build, modify, fit, alter, convert, personalize, design, style. [➡ CHANGE; 373]

tailored 1 *adj* **custom-made**, bespoke, made-to-measure, tailor-made, handmade, designer, couturier, personalized, made-to-order (*US*). [➡ DESCRIBING CLOTHES; 869] *Opposite:* off-the-peg. 2 *adj* **fitted**, shaped, well-cut, figure-hugging, close-fitting, trim, formal. [➡ DESCRIBING CLOTHES; 869] *Opposite:* casual. 3 *adj* **adapted**, customized, custom-built, modified, altered, converted, personalized, designed, styled. [➡ CHANGE; 373]

tailor-made 1 *adj* **perfect**, ideal, right, spot-on (*informal*), suitable, appropriate. [➡ CORRECT; 183] *Opposite:* wrong. 2 *adj* **made-to-measure**, bespoke, custom-made, tailored, handmade, designer, couturier, personalized, made-to-order (*US*). [➡ DESCRIBING CLOTHES; 869] *Opposite:* off-the-peg.

tailpiece *n* **end**, end piece, finale, finial, coda, postscript, appendix. [➡ EXTREMITIES OF PHYSICAL OBJECTS; 1249]

tailplane *part of* **aircraft**. [➡ AIRCRAFT; 1147]

tail rotor *part of* **aircraft**. [➡ AIRCRAFT; 1147]

tails *type of* **jacket**. [➡ GARMENTS AND OUTFITS; 865]

tailspin 1 *n* **nose dive**, dive, spin, spiral, descent, fall, plunge. [➡ GO DOWNWARDS; 308] 2 *n* (*informal*) **panic**, flap, tizzy (*informal*), turmoil, flat spin, whirl, funk (*dated informal*). [➡ DIFFICULT SITUATIONS; 72]

taint 1 *v* **contaminate**, pollute, stain, spoil, infect, soil, dirty, foul, ruin, corrupt, defile (*formal*), poison, blemish. [➡ DIRTY AND CONTAMINATE; 405] *Opposite:* enhance. 2 *n* **stain**, blemish, blot, defect, fault, flaw, smear, spot, stigma, disgrace. [➡ FAULTS, FLAWS, AND WEAKNESSES; 252]

tainted *adj* **contaminated**, polluted, stained, spoiled, soiled, infected, dirtied, fouled, ruined, corrupted, defiled (*formal*), poisoned, blemished. [➡ DIRTY; 1234] *Opposite:* pure.

taipan *type of* **poisonous snake**. [➡ SNAKE; 995]

take 1 *v* **remove**, appropriate, acquire, grab, seize, procure, steal, rob, filch (*informal*), pocket, purloin (*formal*), pilfer. [➡ STEAL AND ROB; 427] *Opposite:* give. 2 *v* **carry**, transfer, fetch, bring, transport, convey, haul, ferry, cart. [➡ MOVE SOMETHING TO ANOTHER LOCATION; 325] 3 *v* **conquer**, capture, win, seize, secure, overcome, occupy, gain, appropriate, hijack, take over, annex. [➡ BEAT AND DEFEAT; 80] *Opposite:* lose. 4 *v* **grasp**, grab, seize, catch, catch on to, catch hold of, grab hold of, receive. [➡ CONTACT: HOLD; 412] *Opposite:* drop. 5 *v* **choose**, select, procure, receive, buy, purchase, pay for, hire, rent, lease, reserve, book, engage. [➡ PURCHASE; 423] 6 *v* **accompany**, bring, escort, guide, lead, usher, conduct, convey, show. [➡ ACCOMPANY AND FOLLOW; 338] 7 *v* **undertake**, adopt, accept, take on, assume, shoulder. [➡ CARRY OUT AN ACTION; 270] *Opposite:* refuse. 8 *v* **bear**, stand, endure, tolerate, suffer, accept, withstand, abide, brook, swallow, undergo. [➡ TOLERATE AND ENDURE; 767] *Opposite:* reject. 9 *v* **support**, hold up, hold, bear, manage. [➡ TOLERATE AND ENDURE; 767] 10 *v* **contain**, hold, accept, accommodate, house, support, hold up. [➡ HOLD AND CONTAIN; 456] 11 *v* **study**, learn, read, do, take up. [➡ STUDYING; 844] *Opposite:* teach. 12 *v* **consider**, look at, discuss, examine, think about, ponder. [➡ PAY ATTENTION; 766] 13 *v* **require**, need, demand, use, accept, expend, call on, consume, swallow. [➡ NEED AND REQUIRE; 465] *Opposite:* reject. 14 *v* **derive**, draw, experience, feel, extract, obtain, get. [➡ UNDERSTAND AND GRASP; 760] 15 *v* **presume**, assume, believe, consider, perceive, hold, regard, understand, deem (*formal*), interpret, deduce. [➡ UNDERSTAND AND GRASP; 760] 16 *v* **succeed**, work, stick, root, come off (*informal*). [➡ FUNCTION SUCCESSFULLY; 470] *Opposite:* fail. 17 *v* **subtract**, deduct, take away, take off, remove, eliminate. [➡ REMOVE SOMETHING; 339] *Opposite:* add. 18 *n* **receipts**, takings, earnings, income, revenue, gross, proceeds, profits, returns, yield. [➡ INCOME; 461] *Opposite:* expenditure. 19 *n* **shot**, sequence, scene. [➡ FILM; 901] 20 *n* **impression**, interpretation, opinion, view, point of view, angle. [➡ POINT OF VIEW; 768]

take aback *v* **surprise**, stun, shock, nonplus, knock for six (*informal*), bowl over, disconcert, startle. [➡ SURPRISE AND IMPRESS; 575]

take a break *v* **rest**, relax, take a breather (*informal*), take time out, take five (*informal*), come up for air, pause, put your feet up, take a rest, ease off, stop, break off. [➡ LACK OF ACTIVITY; 343] *Opposite:* press on.

take a breather (*informal*) *v* **rest**, relax, take a break, take time out, take five (*informal*), come up for air, pause, put your feet up, take a rest, ease off, stop, break off. [➡ LACK OF ACTIVITY; 343] *Opposite:* press on.

take account of *v* **allow for**, take into consideration, bear in mind, make allowances for, keep in mind, take on board, consider, think about. [➡ PAY ATTENTION; 766] *Opposite:* ignore.

take a chance *v* **gamble**, venture, risk it, chance it, stick your neck out, play with fire, ask for trouble, ask for it, skate on thin ice, tread on dangerous ground. [➡ GAMBLE AND TAKE RISKS; 467] *Opposite:* play safe.

take action *v* **act**, do something, take the plunge, take the bull by the horns, get stuck in, take steps, make a start, go for it (*slang*), proceed, start. [➡ CARRY OUT AN ACTION; 270]

take a deep breath *v* [➡ PREPARE FOR ACTION; 290]

take a dim view of *v* **disapprove of**, not think much of, frown on, object to, dislike, deplore. [➡ DISLIKE AND HATE; 578] *Opposite:* approve.

take advantage of somebody *v* **exploit**, use, mistreat, abuse, rip off (*informal*), take for a ride, manipulate. [➡ CAUSE OR COMPEL TO ACT; 272]

take advantage of something *v* **make the most of**, cash in on, profit from, exploit, make use of, manipulate, capitalize on. [➡ MAKE GOOD USE OF SOMETHING; 474]

take a fancy to *v* **like**, approve of, take a shine to (*informal*), take a liking to, be fond of, love, be keen on. [➡ LIKE, LOVE, VALUE AND ENJOY; 579] *Opposite:* dislike.

take after *v* **resemble**, act like, imitate, look like, bear a resemblance to, be like. [➡ SEEM TO BE SOMETHING; 58] *Opposite:* differ.

take a gamble *v* **gamble**, venture, risk it, chance it, stick your neck out, play with fire, ask for trouble, ask for it, skate on thin ice, tread on dangerous ground. [➡ GAMBLE AND TAKE RISKS; 467] *Opposite:* play safe.

take a liking to *v* [➡ LIKE, LOVE, VALUE AND ENJOY; 579]

take a look at *v* [➡ LOOKING AND LOOKS; 701]

take amiss *v* **take the wrong way**, take exception, take umbrage, take offence, be put out, get the wrong end of the stick, get the wrong impression, misconstrue, get the wrong idea, misunderstand, misinterpret. [➡ MISUNDERSTAND AND FAIL TO GRASP; 762] *Opposite:* understand.

take a nap *v* [➡ SLEEP AND DREAM; 724]

take an oath *v* **promise**, swear, pledge, vow, give your word. [➡ PROMISE AND ASSURE; 685]

take apart 1 *v* **dismantle**, take to bits, take to pieces, break up, pull apart, undo, strip down, disassemble. [➡UNFASTEN AND UNDO; 410] *Opposite:* assemble. 2 *v* (*informal*) **criticize**, censure, pan (*informal*), condemn, lash. [➡ACCUSE, BLAME, AND CRITICIZE; 642]

take a rain check (*US informal*) *v* [➡SHIRK AND DELAY; 274]

take a rest *v* [➡LACK OF ACTIVITY; 343]

take a shine to (*informal*) *v* [➡LIKE, LOVE, VALUE AND ENJOY; 579]

take a shot at *v* [➡ATTEMPT AN ACTION; 262]

take as read *v* **accept**, believe, take at face value, take for granted, assume, presume. [➡FORGET, FORGIVE, AND ACCEPT; 749] *Opposite:* challenge.

take a stab at (*informal*) *v* [➡ATTEMPT AN ACTION; 262]

take at face value *v* **believe**, swallow (*informal*), accept, take as read, take for granted, rely on, not read the small print. [➡FORGET, FORGIVE, AND ACCEPT; 749] *Opposite:* question.

take a turn for the worse *v* **go from bad to worse**, deteriorate, decline, slip, relapse, go downhill. [➡GET WORSE; 382] *Opposite:* improve.

take away 1 *v* **remove**, cart off, carry off, carry away, take off, withdraw. [➡REMOVE SOMETHING; 339] *Opposite:* bring. 2 *v* **subtract**, deduct, take, take off. [➡REMOVE SOMETHING; 339] *Opposite:* add.

takeaway 1 *adj* **ready-made**, precooked, prepared, to go, carryout, takeout (*US*). [➡STATE OF PREPARED FOOD; 1170] 2 *n* **ready-made meal**, fast food, carryout, takeout (*US*), ready meal. [➡MEALS AND PARTS OF MEALS; 1168] 3 *type of* **food outlet**. [➡RETAIL OUTLETS; 1082]

take back 1 *v* **withdraw**, retract, recant, renounce, disclaim, revoke, disavow (*formal*), recall, backpedal, eat your words (*informal*), backtrack, apologize, eat humble pie, eat crow (*US informal*). [➡APOLOGIZE AND RETRACT; 684] *Opposite:* stick to. 2 *v* **regain**, recapture, retake, recover, retrieve, restore, repossess. [➡REGAIN POSSESSION; 430] *Opposite:* give back. 3 *v* **return**, exchange, swap (*informal*), refund, redeem, trade in. [➡EXCHANGE AND INTERCHANGE; 449] *Opposite:* keep. 4 *v* **reinstate**, reaccept, bring back, welcome back, have back, reassume. [➡ACCEPT POSSESSION; 451] 5 *v* **remind**, transport, jog your memory, ring a bell (*informal*), put you in mind of, make you think of. [➡REMIND; 748]

take by storm 1 *v* **capture**, overwhelm, storm, seize, conquer, overrun, win, attack. [➡CAPTIVITY AND LOSS OF FREEDOM; 249] 2 *v* **captivate**, enthral, bowl over, knock out (*informal*), impress, charm. [➡SURPRISE AND IMPRESS; 575]

take by surprise *v* **surprise**, burst in on, catch napping, take unawares, catch unawares, ambush, catch on the hop, startle, creep up on. [➡SURPRISE AND IMPRESS; 575]

take care 1 *v* **be careful**, pay attention, mind out, look out, watch out, watch your step, go easy (*informal*). [➡PAY ATTENTION; 766] 2 *v* **make sure**, ensure, make certain, ascertain (*formal*), confirm, check, assure yourself. [➡PREDICT AND ANTICIPATE; 751]

take care of 1 *v* **look after**, care for, nurse, tend, support, watch over. [➡TAKE CARE OF AND SPOIL; 301] *Opposite:* neglect. 2 *v* **deal with**, see to, handle, manage, do, undertake, look after, sort out. [➡BE IN CHARGE; 271]

take charge *v* **take control**, take over, assume responsibility, hold the fort, take the reins, take up the baton, step in, come to power. [➡BE IN CHARGE; 271] *Opposite:* step down.

take control *v* **take charge**, take over, assume responsibility, hold the fort, take the reins, take up the baton, step in, come to power. [➡BE IN CHARGE; 271] *Opposite:* step down.

take cover *v* **hide**, take shelter, shelter, take refuge, conceal yourself, vanish, disappear. [➡RUN AWAY AND AVOID; 10] *Opposite:* emerge.

take down 1 *v* **note**, jot down, write down, make a note of, record, minute, transcribe. [➡RECORD SOMETHING; 372] 2 *v* **dismantle**, demolish, knock down, pull down, take apart, take to bits, take to pieces. [➡UNFASTEN AND UNDO; 410] *Opposite:* put up. 3 *v* **humiliate**, humble, deflate, embarrass, mortify, abash, crush. [➡UPSET, DISTRESS, AND HUMILIATE; 568] *Opposite:* puff up.

take effect *v* **come into force**, come into operation, come into effect, start up, start, begin, commence (*formal*), succeed, happen. [➡HAPPEN; 27]

take exception *v* **take offence**, take umbrage, be put out, object, disapprove, take a dim view, protest, come out against. [➡DISLIKE AND HATE; 578] *Opposite:* welcome.

take five (*informal*) *v* **take a break**, take time out, take a rest, take a breather (*informal*), rest, relax, put your feet up, come up for air, ease off, break off, stop, pause. [➡STOP ACTING; 265] *Opposite:* keep on.

take flight *v* **run away**, run off, flee, take off, decamp, scatter, make yourself scarce (*informal*), skedaddle (*slang*), scarper (*slang*), abscond, vamoose (*US slang*). [➡RUN AWAY AND AVOID; 10] *Opposite:* stay put.

take for a ride *v* **cheat**, deceive, swindle, trick, con, dupe, fool, mislead, defraud, hoodwink, lead somebody up the garden path, have, have on (*informal*). [➡DECEPTION AND LIES; 661]

take for granted 1 *v* **assume**, presume, take as read, expect, count on, presuppose. [➡PREDICT AND ANTICIPATE; 751] 2 *v* **undervalue**, underrate, hold cheap, hold in contempt, disregard. [➡DISLIKE AND HATE; 578] *Opposite:* appreciate.

take for granted *v* **undervalue**, underrate, hold cheap, hold in contempt, disregard. [➡DISLIKE AND HATE; 578] *Opposite:* appreciate.

take form *v* [➡GRADUALLY COME INTO EXISTENCE; 1]

take great delight in *v* [➡LIKE, LOVE, VALUE AND ENJOY; 579]

take heart *v* **cheer up**, perk up, brighten up, buck up (*informal*), take comfort, snap out of it. [➡CHANGE OF MOOD AND COMPOSURE; 581] *Opposite:* lose heart.

take heed *v* [➡PAY ATTENTION; 766]

take home *v* **make**, be paid, net, clear (*informal*), earn, get, pull down (*US slang*). [➡GET MONEY OR REWARD; 422]

take-home pay *n* **net income**, net salary, net wages, net pay, net income after deductions, pay packet, after-tax income (*US*), pay envelope (*US*). [➡ INCOME; 461]

take in 1 *v* **absorb**, understand, comprehend, grasp, assimilate, learn, discern, realize, accept, take on board, remember. [➡ UNDERSTAND AND GRASP; 760] *Opposite:* ignore. 2 *v* **include**, contain, comprise, encompass, cover, enclose, embrace. [➡ POSSESS; 445] *Opposite:* exclude. 3 *v* **deceive**, dupe, fool, mislead, trick, swindle, defraud, cheat, con, hoodwink, take for a ride, lead up the garden path, have, have on (*informal*). [➡ DECEPTION AND LIES; 661] 4 *v* **let in**, receive, admit, entertain, accommodate, welcome. [➡ ACCEPT POSSESSION; 451] *Opposite:* bar. 5 *v* **reduce**, alter, shrink, shorten, draw in, narrow, gather. [➡ CHANGE OF SIZE: SMALLER; 394] *Opposite:* let out.

take in hand *v* **deal with**, cope with, tackle, get to grips with, take on, take control of, take charge of. [➡ BE IN CHARGE; 271]

take into consideration *v* **allow for**, take into account, bear in mind, make allowances for, keep in mind, take on board, consider, think about. [➡ PAY ATTENTION; 766] *Opposite:* ignore.

take into custody *v* **arrest**, detain, pick up (*informal*), pull in (*slang*), imprison, confine, hold. [➡ THE POLICE, ARREST, AND PRE-TRIAL PROCEEDINGS; 818] *Opposite:* release.

take in your stride *v* **deal with**, cope with, accept, take on board, manage, handle, shrug off, swallow. [➡ FORGET, FORGIVE, AND ACCEPT; 749]

take issue with *v* **disagree**, differ, beg to differ, oppose, challenge, take up on, be at odds with somebody. [➡ DENY AND REJECT; 645] *Opposite:* agree.

take it easy 1 *v* **relax**, unwind, chill out (*slang*), put your feet up, laze about, laze around, lounge about, lounge around, loaf, take a break, take a breather (*informal*), take five (*informal*), hang loose (*informal*). [➡ STOP ACTING; 265] 2 *v* **calm down**, lighten up (*informal*), relax, chill out (*slang*), simmer down, keep your shirt on. [➡ CHANGE OF MOOD AND COMPOSURE; 581] *Opposite:* explode.

take leave *v* [➡ ABSENT ONESELF; 8]

take legal action *v* **go to court**, sue, press charges, prosecute, litigate, file a suit, bring a claim. [➡ TRIAL, PUNISHMENT, AND LEGAL OUTCOMES; 819]

taken *adj* **occupied**, in use, engaged, spoken for, busy, reserved, booked. [➡ ABSENT AND UNAVAILABLE; 7] *Opposite:* free.

taken aback *adj* **stunned**, shocked, dumbfounded, knocked for six (*informal*), speechless, bowled over, astonished, astounded, amazed, gobsmacked (*slang*), surprised, dazed, bemused, stupefied. [➡ SURPRISE, SHOCK, AND AMAZEMENT; 546]

take no heed of *v* [➡ NOT PAY ATTENTION; 765]

take no notice of *v* **ignore**, disregard, pay no attention, pay no heed, close your eyes, pass by, brush aside, be oblivious, forget. [➡ NOT PAY ATTENTION; 765]

take note *v* [➡ PAY ATTENTION; 766]

take notice *v* [➡ PAY ATTENTION; 766]

taken with *adj* [➡ APPRECIATION AND GRATITUDE; 536]

take off 1 *v* **remove**, discard, strip off, slip out of, peel off, doff, divest yourself of (*formal or humorous*). [➡ DRESS, WEAR, AND UNDRESS; 868] *Opposite:* put on. 2 *v* **deduct**, subtract, take away, take, remove, eliminate. [➡ REMOVE SOMETHING; 339] *Opposite:* add. 3 *v* (*informal*) **parody**, imitate, mimic, impersonate, satirize, send up (*informal*), caricature, copy. [➡ PRETEND AND MIMIC; 60] 4 *v* **cancel**, suspend, discontinue, scrub (*informal*), abolish, do away with. [➡ CAUSE TO STOP; 267] *Opposite:* reinstate. 5 *v* **launch**, depart, leave, lift off, fly off, take to the air, ascend. [➡ GO UPWARDS; 307] 6 *v* (*informal*) **leave**, go, depart, disappear, scoot (*informal*), scarper (*slang*), skedaddle (*slang*), set out, strike out, set off. [➡ ABSENT ONESELF; 8] *Opposite:* stay. 7 *v* (*informal*) **succeed**, catch on (*informal*), flourish, bloom, boom, prosper, thrive. *Opposite:* flop. (*informal*). [➡ SUCCEED AND WIN; 79]

See Compare and Contrast at **imitate**.

takeoff 1 *n* **departure**, ascent, launch, lift off, start, beginning. [➡ BEGINNING; 53] *Opposite:* touchdown. 2 *n* (*informal*) **imitation**, impersonation, impression, sendup (*informal*), parody, skit, caricature, burlesque, copy, simulation. [➡ REPRESENTATIONS AND GENERAL EXAMPLES; 65]

take offence *v* **take exception**, take umbrage, take amiss, take the wrong way, be put out, go off in a huff, smart, mind, object. [➡ DISLIKE AND HATE; 578]

take on 1 *v* **undertake**, assume, deal with, accept, adopt, tackle, handle, shoulder, take. [➡ CARRY OUT AN ACTION; 270] *Opposite:* refuse. 2 *v* **employ**, hire, engage, sign, bring on board, recruit, appoint, enlist, retain. [➡ CONFER STATUS; 459] *Opposite:* fire. 3 *v* **adopt**, acquire, gain, display, show, exhibit. [➡ GET; 421] *Opposite:* lose. 4 *v* **face**, confront, oppose, fight, vie with, stand up to, brave. [➡ ACCUSE, BLAME, AND CRITICIZE; 642]

take on board 1 *v* **understand**, grasp, comprehend, realize, absorb, assimilate. [➡ UNDERSTAND AND GRASP; 760] *Opposite:* deny. 2 *v* **accept**, include, accommodate, implement, allow for, take into account, take into consideration, bear in mind, acknowledge, swallow (*informal*). [➡ FORGET, FORGIVE, AND ACCEPT; 749] *Opposite:* reject.

take out 1 *v* **remove**, extract, pull out, bring out, fish out, cut out, filter out. [➡ EXTRACT AND SEVER; 342] *Opposite:* insert. 2 *v* **arrange**, organize, set up, obtain, acquire, get. [➡ GET; 421] *Opposite:* cancel. 3 *v* **ask out**, invite out, accompany, treat, take, entertain, date. [➡ ESTABLISHING RELATIONSHIPS WITH OTHERS; 974] 4 *v* **vent**, direct, aim, express, relieve. [➡ GIVING VENT TO EMOTIONS; 680] 5 *v* (*slang*) **destroy**, kill, blast, neutralize, wipe out (*slang*), get rid of, take care of, shoot, gun down (*informal*), bomb. [➡ KILL; 923]

takeout (*US*) 1 *adj* **ready-made**, precooked, prepared, to go, takeaway, carryout. [➡ STATE OF PREPARED FOOD; 1170] 2 *n* **ready-made meal**, ready meal, fast food, takeaway, carryout. [➡ MEALS AND PARTS OF MEALS; 1168] 3 *type of* **meal**, *type of* **food outlet**. [➡ RETAIL OUTLETS; 1082]

take over 1 *v* **take possession of**, annex, capture, hijack, seize, occupy, appropriate, take, conquer, secure, gain, overcome. *Opposite:* cede. (*formal*). [➡ TAKE SOMETHING AWAY; 426] 2 *v* **take control**, take charge, take the reins, step in, assume responsibility, take up the baton, come to power, hold the fort. [➡ BE IN CHARGE; 271] *Opposite:* step down.

takeover *n* **coup**, overthrow, seizure, appropriation, occupation, annexation, coup d'état, buyout, purchase. [➡SUDDEN EVENT; 52]

take part *v* **join in**, participate, play, play a part, cooperate, have a hand in, opt in. *Opposite:* opt out. (*informal*). [➡PARTICIPATE; 293]

take place *v* **happen**, occur, come to pass (*archaic or literary*), have effect, go on, come about, come off (*informal*), transpire. [➡HAPPEN; 27]

take pleasure in *v* **delight in**, enjoy, be taken with, love, take great delight in, adore, like. [➡LIKE, LOVE, VALUE AND ENJOY; 579] *Opposite:* hate.

take possession of *v* **take over**, take control of, sequester, impound, occupy, appropriate, annex, seize, commandeer, hijack, capture. [➡TAKE SOMETHING AWAY; 426] *Opposite:* abandon.

take precedence *v* **have priority**, outweigh, come first, come before, predominate, lead, have the advantage. [➡MOST IMPORTANT AND MAIN; 194]

take prisoner *v* **capture**, take captive, take hostage, seize, imprison, kidnap, snatch (*US informal*). [➡CAPTIVITY AND LOSS OF FREEDOM; 249] *Opposite:* release.

taker *n* **customer**, client, patron, punter (*informal*), purchaser, buyer, player, participant, user. [➡PURCHASER; 425]

take root *v* **set in**, develop, start, grow, settle in, bed in, take hold. [➡GRADUALLY COME INTO EXISTENCE; 1]

take shape *v* **form**, develop, crystallize, gel (*informal*), take form, shape up, solidify, come together. [➡GRADUALLY COME INTO EXISTENCE; 1] *Opposite:* dissolve.

take steps *v* **make a start**, proceed, start, take action, do something, act, take the plunge, take the bull by the horns, go for it (*slang*), get stuck in. [➡CARRY OUT AN ACTION; 270]

take stock *v* **reflect**, weigh up, sum up, think over, count your blessings, contemplate, examine, consider, assess. [➡EXAMINE AND ASSESS; 754]

take the blame *v* **take the rap** (*slang*), carry the can (*informal*), take responsibility, face the music, own up, get it in the neck (*informal*). [➡ADMIT AND CONFESS; 616] *Opposite:* get away with.

take the bull by the horns *v* **take the plunge**, bite the bullet, grasp the nettle, take the initiative, go for it (*slang*), jump in, plunge in, dive in, show your mettle, face the music. [➡START AN ACTION; 261] *Opposite:* hold back.

take the edge off *v* **dampen**, blunt, dilute, relieve, mitigate, tone down, lessen, alleviate, reduce, defuse, detract from. [➡CHANGE OF INTENSITY: LESS; 396] *Opposite:* heighten.

take the floor *v* [➡BE IN CHARGE; 271]

take the lead *v* **blaze a trail**, set a trend, originate, break new ground, break through, show the way, take the initiative, get ahead, forge ahead. [➡SUCCEED AND WIN; 79] *Opposite:* fall behind.

take the mickey (*informal*) *v* **tease**, make fun of, pull somebody's leg (*informal*), laugh at, bait, kid, goad, have on (*informal*), provoke. [➡JOKES AND TEASING; 675]

take the place of *v* **replace**, succeed, displace, supersede, take over from, substitute, relieve, fill in, cover for, deputize, stand in. [➡REPRESENT SOMETHING OR SOMEBODY; 59]

take the plunge *v* **dive in**, go for it (*slang*), jump in, throw caution to the wind, take the bull by the horns, bite the bullet, plunge in, commit. [➡START AN ACTION; 261] *Opposite:* hold back.

take the rap (*slang*) *v* **take the blame**, carry the can (*informal*), take responsibility, face the music, own up, get it in the neck (*informal*). [➡ADMIT AND CONFESS; 616] *Opposite:* get off.

take the rough with the smooth *v* **take the bad with the good**, make the best of things, make the best of a bad job, look on the bright side, grin and bear it (*informal*), keep your chin up, go with the flow, keep smiling. [➡TOLERATE AND ENDURE; 767]

take the wrong way *v* [➡MISUNDERSTAND AND FAIL TO GRASP; 762]

take to 1 *v* **warm to**, take a fancy to, take a shine to (*informal*), take a liking to, hit it off (*informal*), fall for, get on with, befriend. [➡LIKE, LOVE, VALUE AND ENJOY; 579] *Opposite:* dislike. **2** *v* **begin**, start, commence (*formal*), take up, go in for. [➡START AN ACTION; 261] *Opposite:* stop.

take to court *v* **prosecute**, sue, take legal action, press charges, file a suit, bring a claim. [➡TRIAL, PUNISHMENT, AND LEGAL OUTCOMES; 819]

take to flight *v* [➡RUN AWAY AND AVOID; 10]

take to pieces *v* **take apart**, take to bits, dismantle, disassemble, strip down, break up, pull apart, undo, assemble. [➡UNFASTEN AND UNDO; 410] *Opposite:* put together.

take to task *v* **reprimand**, scold, rebuke, reprove, tick off (*informal*), tell off (*informal*), give a talking-to (*informal*), haul over the coals, slap on the wrist (*informal*), rap on/over the knuckles (*informal*), give a wigging (*dated informal*), criticize. [➡ACCUSE, BLAME, AND CRITICIZE; 642] *Opposite:* praise.

take to your heels *v* **run away**, run off, flee, run, show a clean pair of heels, fly, take flight, beat it (*informal*), scarper (*slang*), skedaddle (*slang*), vamoose (*US slang*). [➡RUN AWAY AND AVOID; 10] *Opposite:* stay put.

take umbrage *v* [➡CHANGE OF MOOD AND COMPOSURE; 581]

take unawares *v* **surprise**, catch on the hop, catch out, catch off guard, take by surprise, startle, wrong-foot, burst in on, creep up on. [➡SURPRISE AND IMPRESS; 575]

take-up *n* **acceptance**, reception, use, participation, response. [➡ACCEPT POSSESSION; 451]

take up 1 *v* **start**, go in for, adopt, engage in, assume, begin, take to, commence (*formal*), accept. [➡START AN ACTION; 261] *Opposite:* give up. **2** *v* **continue**, resume, go on, pick up, carry on, recommence (*formal*), restart. [➡CONTINUE AN ACTION; 263] *Opposite:* leave off. **3** *v* **raise**, lift, pick up, gather up, hoist, winch, elevate. [➡MOVE SOMETHING: UPWARDS; 329] *Opposite:* put down. **4** *v* **shorten**, raise, lift, pin up, gather up, hem. [➡CHANGE OF SIZE: SMALLER; 394] *Opposite:* let down. **5** *v*

occupy, fill, cover, absorb, consume, monopolize, use up. [➡USE UP AND WASTE; 475]

take up the baton *v* **take control**, take charge, take over, take the reins, step in, come to power, hold the fort. [➡BE IN CHARGE; 271] *Opposite:* step down.

take up the gauntlet *v* **accept a challenge**, take on, confront, stand up to. [➡COMPETE, CONTEND, AND COMBAT; 304]

taking *adj* **captivating**, attractive, enchanting, pleasing, winning, charming, delightful, compelling, fascinating, intriguing. [➡BEAUTY AND ATTRACTIVENESS; 190] *Opposite:* unattractive.

taking place *adj* [➡HAPPENING AND IN PROGRESS; 32]

takings *n* **earnings**, income, proceeds, profits, receipts, returns, revenue, gross, take, yield. [➡INCOME; 461] *Opposite:* expenditure.

tale 1 *n* **account**, fiction, romance, anecdote, legend, saga, relation, fable, parable, narrative, story, yarn (*informal*). [➡THE ORAL TRADITION; 678] **2** *n* **lie**, fib (*informal*), untruth, rumour, falsehood, story, fabrication, gossip. [➡DECEPTION AND LIES; 661] *Opposite:* truth.

talent *n* **aptitude**, flair, gift, bent, capacity, faculty, ability, knack, endowment, genius, skill. [➡SKILLS, TALENTS, AND ABILITIES; 527]

Compare and Contrast: ***talent, gift, aptitude, flair, bent, knack, genius***

CORE MEANING: THE NATURAL ABILITY TO DO SOMETHING WELL

talent a natural ability to do something well that can be developed by training; ***gift*** a natural ability, especially an artistic ability, or a social skill; ***aptitude*** a natural ability to do or learn something, especially one that is not yet fully developed; ***flair*** a natural ability to do something well, especially creative or artistic ability; ***bent*** a natural ability, inclination, or liking for something; ***knack*** an intuitive ability to do something well, especially one that might not be developed by training; ***genius*** exceptional intellectual or creative ability.

talented *adj* **gifted**, able, brilliant, artistic, endowed, capable, clever. [➡TALENTED AND SKILFUL; 528]

talentless *adj* [➡UNSKILLED; 530]

taleteller *n* **squealer** (*slang disapproving*), informer, snitch (*slang*), stool pigeon (*slang*), rat (*slang*), turncoat, stooge (*US slang*). [➡INTERFERING PEOPLE AND TELLTALES; 950]

talisman *n* **stone**, jewel, amulet, charm, trinket, object, mascot. [➡LUCKY CHARMS; 786]

talk 1 *v* **communicate**, speak, chat, gossip, chatter, natter (*informal*), gab (*informal*), yak (*informal*), express, utter. [➡TWO-WAY COMMUNICATION; 608] **2** *v* **converse**, debate, compare notes, have a word, have a discussion, discuss, negotiate, confer, reason, deliberate, consult, parley. [➡TWO-WAY COMMUNICATION; 608] **3** *v* **confess**, betray, rat (*informal*), turn over, inform, crack, tell, break, give up, squeal (*slang disapproving*), sing (*slang*). [➡BETRAY CONFIDENCES AND GOSSIP; 619] **4** *n* **gossip**, conversation, rumour, chatter, speculation, whispers. [➡GOSSIP; 679] **5** *n* **conversation**, exchange, dialogue, tête-à-tête, heart-to-heart, discourse, chat, gossip, natter (*informal*), chatter, chitchat (*informal*), gab (*informal*), yak (*informal*). [➡INFORMAL COMMUNICATION; 45] **6** *n* **lecture**, speech, address, discourse, oration, sermon. [➡NEUTRAL ONE-WAY COMMUNICATION; 49] **7** *n* **language**, words, vocabulary, jargon, speech, dialect, slang. [➡THE SPOKEN WORD; 672]

talk a mile a minute (*US*) *v* [➡WITTER AND BABBLE; 618]

talkative *adj* **chatty**, loquacious (*formal*), verbose, garrulous, voluble, fluent, glib, gossipy. [➡ELOQUENT, TALKATIVE AND LONG-WINDED; 633] *Opposite:* reticent.

Compare and Contrast: ***talkative, chatty, gossipy, garrulous, loquacious***

CORE MEANING: TALKING A LOT

talkative willing to talk readily and at length; ***chatty*** talking a lot, about unimportant things, in a friendly way; ***gossipy*** talking a lot about other people and their lives, often unkindly or maliciously; ***garrulous*** excessively or pointlessly talkative; ***loquacious*** (*formal*) tending to talk a great deal.

talkativeness *n* **chattiness**, loquaciousness (*formal*), loquacity (*formal*), verbosity, garrulousness, volubility, fluency, glibness, wordiness. [➡ELOQUENT, TALKATIVE AND LONG-WINDED; 633] *Opposite:* reticence.

talk back *v* **argue**, answer back, defy, retort, quibble, be cheeky, sass (*US informal*), come back (*US*). [➡REPLY AND ANSWER; 669]

talker *n* **communicator**, conversationalist, speaker, chatterbox (*informal*), gabber (*informal*), schmoozer (*slang*), gossip, chatterer, orator, public speaker, raconteur. [➡SPEAKERS AND ORATORS; 604]

talk gibberish *v* [➡WITTER AND BABBLE; 618]

talkie (*dated*) *n* **feature**, film, movie, flick (*informal*), picture, newsreel, motion picture (*US formal or technical*). [➡FILM; 901] *Opposite:* silent.

talking 1 *n* **speaking**, conversation, chat, chatting, chitchat (*informal*), gossip, chatter, schmooze (*slang*), yak (*informal*), gabbing (*informal*). [➡INFORMAL COMMUNICATION; 45] **2** *n* **debate**, words, discussion, negotiation, conference, deliberation, consultation, exchange, dialogue. [➡COMMUNICATION; 603]

talking point *n* **topic of conversation**, debating point, issue, question, hot topic, controversial subject, subject of debate. [➡SUBJECT AREA; 769]

talking-to (*informal*) *n* **telling-off** (*informal*), ticking-off (*informal*), dressing-down, reprimand, lecture, tongue-lashing, scolding, telling off, bawling out (*informal*). [➡CRITICISMS AND ANGRY OUTBURSTS; 50]

talk into *v* **persuade**, coax, induce, convince, move, prevail on, cajole, talk over, twist somebody's arm (*informal*). [➡CAUSE OR COMPEL TO ACT; 272] *Opposite:* talk out of.

talk nineteen to the dozen *v* [➡WITTER AND BABBLE; 618]

talk out of *v* **dissuade**, sway, put off, discourage, deter, advise against, turn against, change somebody's mind. [➡AVOID, PREVENT, LIMIT, AND CONTROL; 278] *Opposite:* talk into.

talk over *v* **discuss**, negotiate, debate, review, go into, deliberate. [➡TWO-WAY COMMUNICATION; 608]

talk rubbish *v* [➡WITTER AND BABBLE; 618]

talks *n* **negotiations**, discussions, summit, dialogue, conference, discussion, panel, parley. [➡NEGOTIATION AND DEBATE; 46]

talk show *type of* **broadcast**. [➡TELEVISION AND RADIO; 607]

talk ten to the dozen (*US*) *v* [➡WITTER AND BABBLE; 618]

talk the hind legs off a donkey *v* [➡WITTER AND BABBLE; 618]

talk turkey (*informal*) *v* **open up**, put your cards on the table, get down to brass tacks, get to the point, get to the nitty-gritty, tell the truth, get down to business, not beat about the bush, not pull your punches. [➡INFORM AND ANNOUNCE; 612] *Opposite:* equivocate.

talky (*US*) *n* [➡FILM; 901]

tall 1 *adj* **high**, big, giant, lofty, lanky, elevated, soaring, towering, monumental, colossal, large. [➡HEIGHT: HIGH; 1202] *Opposite:* short. 2 *adj* **difficult**, hard, complicated, demanding, trying, substantial. [➡DIFFICULTY AND COMPLEXITY; 243] *Opposite:* easy. 3 *adj* **incredible**, unbelievable, unlikely, far-fetched, exaggerated, untrue. [➡FALSE AND UNREAL; 174] *Opposite:* likely.

tallboy *type of* **cabinet**. [➡FURNITURE; 858]

tallness *n* **height**, loftiness, size, lankiness, stature, elevation. [➡HEIGHT: HIGH; 1202] *Opposite:* shortness.

tall ship *type of* **historical vessel**. [➡SHIPS AND BOATS; 1149]

tall story *n* **cock-and-bull story**, unlikely story, tale, yarn (*informal*), tall tale, fairy tale, fairy story, lie, fib (*informal*), untruth. [➡DECEPTION AND LIES; 661]

tall tale *n* **cock-and-bull story**, unlikely story, tale, yarn (*informal*), tall story, fairy tale, fairy story, lie, fib (*informal*), untruth. [➡DECEPTION AND LIES; 661]

tally 1 *v* **match**, correspond, agree, check, equate, square, coincide, accord, fit, harmonize. [➡EQUALITY; 155] *Opposite:* clash. 2 *v* **compute**, count, reckon, score, total, register, record, note, calculate, mark. [➡ASSESS QUANTITY; 758] 3 *n* **score**, count, total, reckoning, calculation, record, register, note, account, mark. [➡SCORES AND EVALUATIONS; 599]

talon *n* **claw**, nail, fingernail, hook, spur, pincer. [➡PARTS OF A BIRD; 1006]

tambourine *type of* **percussion instrument**. [➡MUSICAL INSTRUMENTS; 910]

tame 1 *adj* **domestic**, domesticated, broken, trained, disciplined, pacified, cultivated, friendly, approachable. [➡SAFE AND SAFETY; 192] *Opposite:* wild. 2 *adj* **docile**, meek, compliant, subdued, unresisting, submissive, obedient, gentle, peaceful. [➡THE WILL AND WILLINGNESS; 564] *Opposite:* rebellious. 3 *adj* **bland**, dull, insipid, boring, unexciting, flat, uninspired, tedious. [➡BORING AND UNINTERESTING; 235] *Opposite:* exciting. 4 *v* **domesticate**, break in, train, discipline, pacify, cultivate, reclaim. [➡INSTRUCT AND TEACH; 610] 5 *v* **repress**, suppress, overcome, subjugate, subdue, conquer, humble, curb, control, moderate. [➡AVOID, PREVENT, LIMIT, AND CONTROL; 278]

tamely 1 *adv* **docilely**, meekly, compliantly, submissively, obediently, gently, peacefully. [➡THE WILL AND WILLINGNESS; 564] *Opposite:* rebelliously. 2 *adv* **blandly**, dully, insipidly, boringly, unexcitingly, flatly, tediously, languidly. [➡BORING AND UNINTERESTING; 235] *Opposite:* excitingly.

tameness 1 *n* **docility**, meekness, compliance, submissiveness, obedience, gentleness, peacefulness, acceptance. [➡PEACEFULNESS AND GENTLENESS; 215] *Opposite:* rebelliousness. 2 *n* **blandness**, dullness, insipidness, flatness, tedium. [➡BORING AND UNINTERESTING; 235] *Opposite:* excitement.

tam-o'-shanter *type of* **headgear**. [➡HABERDASHERY, MILLINERY, AND LINGERIE; 867]

tamp *v* **fill**, pack, stuff, cram, compress, push, tap, force. [➡FILL; 407]

tamper 1 *v* **interfere**, meddle, fiddle (*informal*), mess about (*informal*), monkey with, fool with, tinker, alter, damage, mess around (*informal*). [➡WORSEN SOMETHING; 381] 2 *v* **corrupt**, rig, influence, fix (*informal*), manipulate, bribe. [➡FALSIFY AND CHEAT; 177]

tampon *n* **plug**, pad, wad, swab, compress, dressing, bung. [➡REMEDIES, TREATMENTS AND OPERATIONS; 732]

tan 1 *n* **suntan**, sunburn, colour, bronze, brownness. [➡COMPLEXION; 481] 2 *v* **bronze**, go brown, brown, toast, burn. [➡CHANGE OF COLOUR; 392] 3 *v* **treat**, preserve, process, dye, wash. [➡CLEAN AND POLISH; 404] 4 *adj* (*US*) **tanned**, suntanned, sunburnt, bronzed, dark, brown. [➡COMPLEXION; 481] 5 *type of* **brown**. [➡COLOURS; 1223]

tandem *type of* **bike** (*informal*). [➡BIKES, CARS, AND CARRIAGES; 1148]

tandem bicycle (*US*) *type of* **bike** (*informal*). [➡BIKES, CARS, AND CARRIAGES; 1148]

tandoor *n* [➡TABLEWARE, CUTLERY, AND KITCHENWARE; 861]

tang *n* **trace**, hint, smack, suggestion, flavour, aftertaste, savour, smell, whiff, odour. [➡FEW, LITTLE, SMALL AMOUNT; 119]

tangent *n* **line**, curve, angle, refraction, curvature. [➡ORIENTATION AND ALIGNMENT; 1222]

tangential *adj* **peripheral**, lateral, oblique, divergent, indirect, loose, vague. [➡VAGUENESS; 244] *Opposite:* central.

tangerine 1 *type of* **orange**. [➡COLOURS; 1223] 2 *type of* **citrus**. [➡FRUIT AND VEGETABLES; 1175]

tangibility 1 *n* **palpability**, perceptibility, physicality, reality, solidity, concreteness, corporeality, presence, visibility. [➡PERCEPTIBLE; 25] *Opposite:* intangibility. 2 *n* **actuality**, reality, clarity, plainness, obviousness. [➡TRUE AND REAL; 172] *Opposite:* intangibility.

tangible 1 *adj* **palpable**, touchable, perceptible, concrete, physical, noticeable, real, solid, definite, substantial, material, corporeal, visible. [➡PERCEPTIBLE; 25] *Opposite:* intangible. 2 *adj* **actual**, substantial, real, certain, evident, definite, plain, clear, demonstrable, quantifiable, obvious, hard, solid. [➡TRUE AND REAL; 172] *Opposite:* intangible.

tanginess *n* [➡TASTE; 704]

tangle 1 *v* **knot**, twist, snarl, interweave, intertwine, entangle, entwine, jumble, mat, tousle, wind. [➡COMBINE AND MIX; 401] *Opposite:* untangle. 2 *v* **snag**, catch, snarl, snare, hook. [➡FASTEN, LINK, AND JOIN; 409] *Opposite:* undo. 3 *v* **trap**, catch, ensnare, entangle, enmesh, mix up, confuse. [➡CAPTIVITY AND LOSS OF FREEDOM; 249] *Opposite:* release. 4 *v* **come up against**, confront, mess with, square up, oppose, face. [➡INTERRUPT AND BUTT IN; 620] *Opposite:* avoid. 5 *n* **mass**, jumble, knot, mesh, web, twist, welter. [➡COLLECTIONS AND MIXTURES OF THINGS; 1243] 6 *n* **mess**, jam, difficulty, mix-up, complication, maze, jumble, disorder. [➡DISORDER AND CHAOS; 246] 7 *type of* **alga**. [➡MICROORGANISMS, FUNGI, AND ALGAE; 1023]

tangled 1 *adj* **knotted**, twisted, snarled, interwoven, intertwined, entangled, entwined, jumbled, matted, tousled, scrambled. [➡IN BAD REPAIR; 1233] *Opposite:* straight. 2 *adj* **complicated**, confused, knotty, complex, messy, mixed-up (*informal*), intricate, disordered. [➡DIFFICULTY AND COMPLEXITY; 243] *Opposite:* straightforward.

tango *type of* **dance**. [➡DANCE; 903]

tangy *adj* **pungent**, sharp, strong, piquant, tasty, spicy, flavourful. [➡TASTE; 704] *Opposite:* bland.

tank 1 *n* **cistern**, boiler, reservoir, container, chamber, vat. [➡CONTAINERS, RECEPTACLES, AND PACKAGING; 1244] 2 *type of* **military vehicle**. [➡VEHICLES; 1144]

tankard *n* **mug**, beer mug, jug, stein, toby jug, cup. [➡TABLEWARE, CUTLERY, AND KITCHENWARE; 861]

tanked-up (*slang*) *adj* [➡UNDER THE INFLUENCE OF DRUGS OR ALCOHOL; 742]

tank engine *part of* **train**. [➡RAILWAYS; 1106]

tanker 1 *n* **transporter**, freighter, lorry, truck. [➡BIKES, CARS, AND CARRIAGES; 1148] 2 *type of* **motor vessel**. [➡SHIPS AND BOATS; 1149] 3 *type of* **commercial or industrial vehicle**. [➡VEHICLES; 1144]

tank top *type of* **top**. [➡GARMENTS AND OUTFITS; 865]

tanned *adj* **brown**, bronzed, suntanned, dark, sunburnt, tan (*US*). [➡COMPLEXION; 481] *Opposite:* pale.

tannery *type of* **industrial site**. [➡INDUSTRIAL BUILDINGS; 1086]

tantalize *v* **tease**, entice, torment, torture, tempt, provoke, wind up (*informal*), frustrate. *Opposite:* turn off. (*informal*). [➡APPEAL TO AND AROUSE INTEREST; 576]

tantalizing *adj* **enticing**, teasing, tormenting, tempting, provocative, provoking, frustrating, alluring, exciting. [➡INTERESTING AND MEANINGFUL; 191] *Opposite:* boring.

tantamount *adj* **equal**, equivalent, the same as, synonymous, as good as, identical, indistinguishable, close. [➡SAMENESS; 151] *Opposite:* different.

tantrum *n* **outburst**, fit of temper, fit, frenzy, paddy (*informal*), fret, pet, sulk, rage, paroxysm. [➡CRITICISMS AND ANGRY OUTBURSTS; 50]

tap 1 *n* **blow**, rap, knock, bang, beat, hit, pat. [➡CONTACT: IMPACT; 414] 2 *type of* **impact sound**. [➡IMPACT SOUNDS; 1259] 3 *n* **stopper**, plug, bung, cork. [➡COVERS AND COATINGS; 1245] 4 *n* **valve**, stopcock, spout, spigot, faucet (*US*). [➡FITTINGS; 859] 5 *v* **rap**, knock, bang, beat, strike, hit, pat, drum. [➡CONTACT: IMPACT; 414] 6 *v* **draw off**, draw out, extract, run off, release, collect. [➡GET; 421] *Opposite:* block up. 7 *v* **bug**, listen in on, record, monitor, intercept, eavesdrop on, overhear. [➡LISTEN AND LISTENERS; 709] 8 *v* (*informal*) **use**, utilize, draw on, draw off, exploit, milk (*informal*), mine, take advantage of. [➡MAKE GOOD USE OF SOMETHING; 474] 9 *v* (*US*) **appoint**, select, nominate, commission, recruit, employ, detail. [➡CONFER STATUS; 459] *Opposite:* pass over.

tapas *part of* **meal**. [➡MEALS AND PARTS OF MEALS; 1168]

tap dance *type of* **dance**. [➡DANCE; 903]

tape 1 *n* **ribbon**, strip, string, tie, band, binding. [➡FASTENERS, LINKS, AND NETWORKS; 1246] 2 *n* **adhesive tape**, sticky tape, insulating tape, masking tape, packing tape, parcel tape, duct tape (*US*), friction tape (*US*). [➡FASTENERS, LINKS, AND NETWORKS; 1246] 3 *n* **cassette**, cassette tape, video, video tape, video cassette, audiotape, audiocassette, cartridge, magnetic tape, recording, tape recording, copy. [➡RECORDINGS AND PLAYERS; 911] 4 *n* **tape measure**, measuring tape, measure, tapeline. [➡MEASURING DEVICES; 1122] 5 *v* **record**, tape-record, copy, save, video, videotape. [➡RECORD SOMETHING; 372] 6 *v* **stick**, fasten, attach, secure, bind, fix. [➡FASTEN, LINK, AND JOIN; 409]

tape deck *type of* **audio equipment**. [➡AUDIO EQUIPMENT; 1138]

tape measure *n* **tape**, measuring tape, measure, rule, ruler, steel rule, tapeline. [➡MEASURING DEVICES; 1122]

tape player *type of* **audio equipment**. [➡AUDIO EQUIPMENT; 1138]

taper 1 *v* **narrow**, come to a point, thin down, dwindle, elongate, attenuate, shape. [➡CHANGE OF SIZE: SMALLER; 394] *Opposite:* widen. 2 *v* **reduce**, phase out, taper off, tail off, diminish, decrease, lessen, shrink, peter out, contract. [➡CHANGE OF INTENSITY: LESS; 396] *Opposite:* increase. 3 *n* **candle**, spill, match, torch, light, flame. [➡LIGHTING; 862] 4 *n* **narrowing**, point, thinning down, dwindling, elongation. [➡CHANGE OF SIZE: SMALLER; 394]

tape-record *v* **tape**, record, copy, save, video, videotape. [➡RECORD SOMETHING; 372]

tape recorder *type of* **audio equipment**. [➡AUDIO EQUIPMENT; 1138]

tapered 1 *adj* **tapering**, narrowing, pointed, elongated, shaped, conical, thinning, thin, dwindling, attenuated. [➡ANGULAR SHAPE; 1216] *Opposite:* flared. 2 *adj* **gradually reduced**, phased out, tailed off, diminished, decreased, lessened, petered out. [➡CHANGE OF SIZE: SMALLER; 394]

tapering *adj* **tapered**, narrowing, pointed, elongated, shaped, conical, thinning, thin, dwindling, attenuating. [➡ANGULAR SHAPE; 1216] *Opposite:* widening.

tapestry 1 *n* **wall hanging**, drapery, arras. [➡SOFT FURNISHINGS, LINEN, AND DRAPERY; 860] 2 *type of* **handicraft**. [➡CRAFTS AND CARVING; 356]

tapeworm *type of* **parasitic insect**. [➡PARASITES; 1017]

tappet *part of* **engine**. [➡PARTS OF AN ENGINE; 1143]

taps *n* [➡TIMES OF DAY; 87]

tar *n* **asphalt**, pitch, macadam, blacktop (*US*). [➡BUILDING MATERIALS; 1076]

tarantula *type of* **arachnid.** [➡ARACHNIDS; 1018]

tardiness *n* **lateness**, delay, belatedness, unpunctuality. [➡PROMPTNESS: LATE; 100] *Opposite:* punctuality.

tardy *adj* **late**, delayed, overdue, belated, unpunctual. [➡PROMPTNESS: LATE; 100] *Opposite:* punctual.

target 1 *n* **board**, mark, bull's eye, bull, goal. [➡SYMBOLS, SIGNS, AND NUMBERS; 597] 2 *n* **aim**, goal, objective, object, focus, end, intention. [➡INTENTION AND PURPOSE; 773] 3 *n* **butt**, focus, object, recipient, foil, scapegoat, victim. [➡PERSON; 931] 4 *v* **aim at**, aim for, focus on, home in on, seek out, go for (*informal*), go after, pursue. [➡PAY ATTENTION; 766] 5 *v* **direct**, aim, point, level, train, steer. [➡POSITION SOMETHING; 326]

tariff 1 *n* **tax**, duty, due, excise, levy, toll, import tax, export tax. [➡TAX AND TAXATION; 802] 2 *n* **price**, price list, rate, charge, cost, fare, bill, menu, bill of fare. [➡MONEY, PAYMENTS, AND CHARGES; 800]

Tarmac (*US*) *n* **tar**, asphalt, pitch, macadam, blacktop (*US*). [➡BUILDING MATERIALS; 1076]

tarn *n* **lake**, pool, pond, loch, mere (*archaic or literary*), lagoon, water. [➡RIVERS, LAKES, AND STREAMS; 1042]

tarnish 1 *v* **dull**, discolour, stain, smear, smudge, blot, blemish, taint, dirty, blacken, mark, oxidize, corrode, rust. [➡DIRTY AND CONTAMINATE; 405] *Opposite:* clean. 2 *v* **sully**, damage, stain, taint, blot, harm, destroy, blacken, blemish, spoil, ruin. [➡WORSEN SOMETHING; 381] *Opposite:* enhance.

tarnished 1 *adj* **dull**, discoloured, stained, smeared, smudged, blotted, blemished, tainted, dirty, blackened, marked, oxidized, corroded, rusty. [➡IN BAD REPAIR; 1233] *Opposite:* shiny. 2 *adj* **sullied**, damaged, stained, tainted, blotted, harmed, destroyed, blackened, blemished, spoiled, ruined. [➡MORALLY BAD; 776] *Opposite:* enhanced.

tarp (*informal*) *n* [➡COVERS AND COATINGS; 1245]

tarpaulin 1 *n* **canvas**, tarp (*informal*), cover, sheet, sheeting. [➡COVERS AND COATINGS; 1245] 2 *type of* **fabric from plants.** [➡FABRICS; 1131]

tarragon *type of* **herb.** [➡HERBS AND SPICES; 1174]

tarry 1 *v* **remain**, stay, stay put, visit, sojourn (*literary*). [➡CONTINUE TO EXIST; 17] 2 *v* **linger**, loiter, dawdle, hang around, hesitate, delay, wait. [➡SHIRK AND DELAY; 274]

tart 1 *adj* **sharp**, acid, acidic, sour, bitter. [➡TASTE; 704] *Opposite:* sweet. 2 *adj* **acerbic**, biting, sharp, sour, acid, bitter, critical, cutting, unkind, unpleasant, sarcastic, disapproving, cruel. [➡BAD-TEMPERED AND HUMOURLESS; 627] *Opposite:* kind. 3 *n* **pie**, tartlet, pastry, quiche, flan. [➡CAKES, BISCUITS, AND DESSERTS; 1180]

tartan *n* **pattern**, plaid, check. [➡PATTERNS; 1224]

tartar *n* **plaque**, deposit, residue, coating, scale, film, calculus. [➡COVERS AND COATINGS; 1245]

tartare sauce *type of* **seasonings, sauces, and dips.** [➡SEASONINGS AND SAUCES; 1173]

tartar sauce *see* **tartare sauce.**

tartly *adv* **acerbically**, bitingly, sharply, sourly, acidly, bitterly, critically, cuttingly, unkindly, unpleasantly, sarcastically, disapprovingly, cruelly. [➡BAD-TEMPERED AND HUMOURLESS; 627] *Opposite:* kindly.

tartness 1 *n* **sharpness**, acidity, sourness, bitterness. [➡TASTE; 704] *Opposite:* sweetness. 2 *n* **acerbity**, sharpness, sourness, acidity, bitterness, unkindness, unpleasantness, sarcasm, disapproval, cruelty. [➡BAD-TEMPERED AND HUMOURLESS; 627] *Opposite:* kindness.

tart up (*informal*) *v* **smarten up**, tidy up, decorate, do up, doll up (*informal*), make up, prettify, clean up. [➡IMPROVE APPEARANCE; 380]

tarty *adj* [➡MORALLY BAD; 776]

task *n* **job**, chore, duty, mission, commission, assignment, undertaking, brief, errand, charge. [➡WORK IN GENERAL; 298]

task force *n* **team**, unit, squad, detail, crew, cadre, group, working party, hit squad (*slang*). [➡GROUPS WITH A COMMON INTEREST; 938]

Tasmanian devil *type of* **marsupial.** [➡MARSUPIAL; 992]

tassel *n* **bobble**, tuft, fringe, braid, edging, trimming. [➡ORNAMENTS AND DECORATIONS; 1247]

taste 1 *n* **sense of taste**, palate, discrimination, sensitivity, perception, taste buds. [➡TASTE; 704] 2 *n* **flavour**, tang, savour, hint, smack, aftertaste. [➡TASTE; 704] 3 *n* **try**, sample, test, bite, nibble, drink, sip, bit, taster. [➡REPRESENTATIONS AND GENERAL EXAMPLES; 65] 4 *n* **liking**, preference, predilection (*formal*), leaning, penchant, fondness. [➡LIKE, LOVE, VALUE AND ENJOY; 579] *Opposite:* dislike. 5 *n* **discrimination**, discernment, judgment, tastefulness, good taste, sophistication, refinement, style, class (*informal*). [➡LEVEL OF EDUCATION AND SOPHISTICATION; 894] 6 *v* **discern**, pick up, recognize, get, feel, notice, savour. [➡USING THE SENSES; 698] 7 *v* **sample**, try, test, eat, bite, nibble, drink, sip. [➡DRINK; 712] *Opposite:* devour. 8 *v* **experience**, sample, preview, get a taste of, get a hint of, be exposed to. [➡EXPERIENCE AND ENCOUNTER; 583]

taste bud *part of* **mouth.** [➡THE MOUTH; 703]

tasteful *adj* **discerning**, discriminating, sophisticated, refined, stylish, classy (*informal*), aesthetic, attractive, elegant, chic, beautiful. [➡LEVEL OF EDUCATION AND SOPHISTICATION; 894] *Opposite:* tasteless.

tastefulness *n* **discernment**, discrimination, judgment, taste, sophistication, refinement, style, good taste, class (*informal*), aestheticism, attractiveness, elegance, chic, beauty. [➡LEVEL OF EDUCATION AND SOPHISTICATION; 894] *Opposite:* tastelessness.

tasteless 1 *adj* **bland**, flavourless, flat, insipid, weak, dull, unsavoury. [➡TASTE; 704] *Opposite:* tasty. 2 *adj* **in bad taste**, in poor taste, cheap, flash (*informal*), flashy, loud, garish, vulgar, offensive, crude, distasteful, tactless, indelicate. [➡IN POOR TASTE; 230] *Opposite:* tasteful.

tastelessness 1 *n* **blandness**, flavourlessness, flatness, insipidness, weakness, dullness, unsavouriness. [➡TASTE; 704] *Opposite:* tastiness. 2 *n* **bad taste**, poor taste, cheapness, flashiness, loudness, garishness, vulgarity, offensiveness, crudeness, distastefulness, tactlessness, indelicacy. [➡ IN POOR TASTE; 230] *Opposite:* tastefulness.

taster 1 *n* **analyst**, sampler, buyer, specialist, connoisseur, blender. [➡ SURVEYORS, EXAMINERS, AND JUDGES; 853] 2 *n* **preview**, foretaste, appetizer, sample, excerpt. [➡ INDICATIONS, SIGNS, AND WARNINGS; 68]

tastiness *n* **deliciousness**, flavour, scrumptiousness (*informal*), yumminess, juiciness, succulence. [➡ TASTE; 704] *Opposite:* tastelessness.

tasty *adj* **delicious**, flavoursome, mouthwatering, appetizing, scrumptious (*informal*), yummy, juicy, succulent. [➡ TASTE; 704] *Opposite:* tasteless.

tat (*informal*) *n* **rubbish**, junk (*informal*), jumble, scrap, seconds, bric-a-brac. [➡ RUBBISH AND USELESS OBJECTS; 1248]

tatami *n* [➡ SOFT FURNISHINGS, LINEN, AND DRAPERY; 860]

tater (*regional*) *type of* **root vegetable**. [➡ FRUIT AND VEGETABLES; 1175]

tattered *adj* **torn**, ragged, tatty, dilapidated, frayed, threadbare, scruffy, shabby, unkempt. [➡ IN BAD REPAIR; 1233] *Opposite:* smart.

tatters *n* **rags**, shreds, bits, pieces, strips, ruins. [➡ RUBBISH AND USELESS OBJECTS; 1248]

tattiness *n* **shabbiness**, scruffiness, raggedness, dilapidation, untidiness, seediness, disrepair. [➡ IN BAD REPAIR; 1233] *Opposite:* smartness.

tatting *type of* **handicraft**. [➡ CRAFTS AND CARVING; 356]

tattle 1 *v* **gossip**, tittle-tattle, dish the dirt (*informal*), snitch (*slang*), sneak, grass (*slang*), prattle, chat, chatter, talk. *Opposite:* keep secret. (*informal*). [➡ BETRAY CONFIDENCES AND GOSSIP; 619] 2 *n* **gossip**, tattler, snitch (*slang*), sneak, grass (*slang*), telltale, informer, informant, rat (*slang*), talebearer, squealer (*slang disapproving*), stool pigeon (*slang*), tattletale (*US informal*). [➡ INTERFERING PEOPLE AND TELLTALES; 950] 3 *n* **tittle-tattle**, gossip, prattle, chat, chatter, hearsay. [➡ GOSSIP; 679] *Opposite:* fact.

tattler *n* **gossip**, tattle, snitch (*slang*), sneak, grass (*slang*), telltale, informer, informant, talebearer, rat (*slang*), squealer (*slang disapproving*), stool pigeon (*slang*), tattletale (*US informal*). [➡ INTERFERING PEOPLE AND TELLTALES; 950]

tattletale (*US*) *n* **talebearer**, telltale, tattler, informer, snitch (*slang*), rat (*slang*), squealer (*slang disapproving*). [➡ INTERFERING PEOPLE AND TELLTALES; 950]

tattoo 1 *n* **design**, pattern, picture, decoration, mark. [➡ DRAWINGS, CHARTS AND TABLES; 595] 2 *n* **signal**, summons, call, recall, order, command. [➡ SIGNALLING; 1139] 3 *n* **parade**, display, tournament, show, pageant, cavalcade, march-past. [➡ PERFORMANCES AND SHOWS; 42]

tatty *adj* **shabby**, worn, scruffy, dog-eared, down-at-heel, run-down, ragged, frayed, dilapidated, seedy. [➡ IN BAD REPAIR; 1233] *Opposite:* smart.

taunt 1 *v* **mock**, tease, jeer, sneer, goad, insult, criticize, ridicule, deride, provoke. [➡ JOKES AND TEASING; 675] *Opposite:* compliment. 2 *n* **insult**, gibe, sneer, affront, criticism, verbal abuse, derision. [➡ INSULTS, ABUSE, AND SWEARING; 659] *Opposite:* compliment.

taunting *adj* **mocking**, provocative, provoking, teasing, spiteful, hurtful, derisive, jeering. [➡ MOCKING AND DISMISSIVE; 637] *Opposite:* kind.

tauon *type of* **elementary particle**. [➡ ELEMENTARY PARTICLES; 1278]

taupe *type of* **grey**. [➡ COLOURS; 1223]

Taurus *type of* **star sign**. [➡ FATE, DESTINY, AND ASTROLOGY; 783]

taut 1 *adj* **tight**, stretched, rigid, stiff, tense, extended, strained, firm, inflexible, hard. [➡ RIGID AND HARD; 1210] *Opposite:* slack. 2 *adj* **tense**, worried, anxious, stressed, nervous, wired, edgy, on edge, strung out. [➡ CONFUSION, ANXIETY, AND WORRY; 541] *Opposite:* calm.

tauten *v* **tighten**, stretch, stiffen, pull tight, tense, extend, strain, firm up, constrict, squeeze, contract. [➡ CHANGE OF SIZE: SMALLER; 394] *Opposite:* slacken.

tautness *n* **tightness**, tension, pull, stretch, rigidity, stiffness, firmness, strain, inflexibility, hardness. [➡ RIGID AND HARD; 1210] *Opposite:* slackness.

tautological *adj* **repetitious**, repetitive, inelegant, reiterative, redundant, superfluous, unneeded, unnecessary, uncalled-for. [➡ UNIMPORTANT AND UNNECESSARY; 239]

tautology *n* **repetition**, reiteration, duplication, redundancy, superfluity. [➡ UNIMPORTANT AND UNNECESSARY; 239]

tavern (*dated*) *n* **inn**, pub, hostelry (*archaic or humorous*), local, watering hole (*informal*), bar. [➡ HOTELS, RESTAURANTS, AND CLUBS; 1081]

tawdriness *n* **cheapness**, gaudiness, flashiness, showiness, tastelessness, crudeness, flamboyance. [➡ IN POOR TASTE; 230] *Opposite:* tastefulness.

tawdry *adj* **cheap**, gaudy, flashy, showy, tasteless, crude, flamboyant. [➡ IN POOR TASTE; 230] *Opposite:* tasteful.

tawny *type of* **brown**. [➡ COLOURS; 1223]

tawny owl *type of* **owl**. [➡ OWL; 1001]

tax 1 *n* **duty**, levy, toll, excise, tariff. [➡ TAX AND TAXATION; 802] 2 *v* **charge**, assess, hit, burden, cream off, deduct. [➡ TAX AND TAXATION; 802] *Opposite:* exempt. 3 *v* **strain**, overtax, overstretch, stretch, overload, burden, challenge, ask too much of, drain, exhaust, test. [➡ GIVE TOO MUCH; 438] *Opposite:* relieve. 4 *v* **accuse**, reproach, blame, confront, present, charge. [➡ ACCUSE, BLAME, AND CRITICIZE; 642]

taxable *adj* **chargeable**, assessable, dutiable, rateable, payable. [➡ TAX AND TAXATION; 802] *Opposite:* tax-exempt.

taxation 1 *n* **fiscal policy**, tax policy, tax system, revenue system, taxes, assessment. [➡ TAX AND TAXATION; 802] 2 *n* **duty**, levy, toll, dues, excise, monies (*formal*), taxes. [➡ TAX AND TAXATION; 802]

tax-exempt *adj* **exempt from taxation**, exempt, untaxed, tax-free, duty-free, non-VAT, toll-free (*US*). [➡ TAX AND TAXATION; 802] *Opposite:* taxable.

tax free *adj* [➡ TAX AND TAXATION; 802]

taxi *type of* **commercial or industrial vehicle.** [➡VEHICLES; 1144]

taxing *adj* **demanding**, tough, difficult, strenuous, challenging, wearing, tiring, exhausting, draining. [➡DIFFICULTY AND COMPLEXITY; 243] *Opposite:* effortless.

taxonomy *n* **classification**, nomenclature, taxonomic system, catalogue, categorization, grouping, arrangement, organization. [➡NAME AND DESCRIBE; 666]

taxpayer *n* [➡TAX AND TAXATION; 802]

tax policy *n* [➡TAX AND TAXATION; 802]

tax system *n* [➡TAX AND TAXATION; 802]

T-bone steak *type of* **steak.** [➡TYPES AND CUTS OF MEAT; 1176]

tchotchke (*US*) *n* [➡ORNAMENTS AND DECORATIONS; 1247]

tea 1 *n* **drink**, infusion, tisane, brew, decoction. [➡DRINKS; 1186] 2 *type of* **meal.** [➡MEALS AND PARTS OF MEALS; 1168]

tea break *n* **break**, coffee break, rest, breather (*informal*), refreshment break, elevenses. [➡PERIOD OF REST; 91]

tea caddy *type of* **container.** [➡CONTAINERS, RECEPTACLES, AND PACKAGING; 1244]

teach 1 *v* **impart**, communicate, show, explain, clarify, instil, give a grounding in, equip with, inculcate with. [➡INSTRUCT AND TEACH; 610] *Opposite:* learn. 2 *v* **educate**, tutor, lecture, instruct, coach, train, school, drill, edify. [➡INSTRUCT AND TEACH; 610] *Opposite:* learn.

> **Compare and Contrast:** ***teach, educate, train, instruct, coach, tutor, school, drill***
>
> CORE MEANING: TO CAUSE TO ACQUIRE KNOWLEDGE OR SKILL IN SOMETHING
>
> ***teach*** to impart knowledge or skill to somebody by instruction or example; ***educate*** to increase the knowledge or develop the abilities of somebody by formal teaching or training, especially in a school or college context; ***train*** to teach the skills necessary for a particular task or job by means of instruction, observation, and practice; ***instruct*** to teach somebody a subject or how to do something, not necessarily in a school or college context; ***coach*** to give special tuition to one person or a small group of people, especially in preparation for an exam, or to teach sports or artistic skills; ***tutor*** to give somebody individual tuition on a particular subject or in a particular skill; ***school*** to train somebody in a particular skill or area of expertise in a thorough and detailed way; ***drill*** to teach something by means of repeated exercises and practice.

teacher *n* **educator**, tutor, instructor, coach, trainer, lecturer, professor, governess, schoolteacher. [➡EDUCATORS; 840] *Opposite:* student.

teacher's pet *n* [➡STUDENTS AND PUPILS; 841]

teaching 1 *n* **education**, lessons, instruction, coaching, training, schooling. [➡TEACHING; 839] *Opposite:* learning. 2 *n* **philosophy**, ideas, principles, beliefs, thinking, credo, doctrine. [➡IDEA AND THOUGHT; 771]

teaching body *n* [➡EDUCATORS; 840]

teaching staff *n* [➡EDUCATORS; 840]

teak *type of* **deciduous tree.** [➡DECIDUOUS TREES; 1028]

teal *type of* **freshwater bird.** [➡FRESHWATER BIRD; 1000]

team 1 *n* **side**, squad, players, lineup, crew, club. [➡GROUPS WITH A COMMON INTEREST; 938] 2 *n* **group**, band, crew, gang, panel, party, unit, squad. [➡GROUPS OF PEOPLE; 935]

team-mate *n* **colleague**, co-player, partner, captain, fellow player. [➡COLLEAGUES AND EQUALS; 967]

teamster 1 *n* **driver**, carter, charioteer, handler, trainer. [➡DRIVERS; 1152] 2 *n* (*US*) **lorry driver**, haulier, truck driver, trucker, driver. [➡DRIVERS; 1152]

team up *v* **join forces**, collaborate, cooperate, work together, get together, come together, unite. [➡PARTICIPATE; 293] *Opposite:* split up.

teamwork *n* **cooperation**, collaboration, joint effort, solidarity, communication, coordination. [➡RECIPROCITY AND INTERDEPENDENCE; 148]

teapot *n* [➡TABLEWARE, CUTLERY, AND KITCHENWARE; 861]

tear 1 *v* **rip**, slash, gash, scratch, slit, shred, rend, split, destroy. [➡TEAR, BREAK, AND CUT; 361] *Opposite:* join. 2 *v* **sprain**, rip, pull, injure, damage, hurt, wrench. [➡WORSEN SOMETHING; 381] 3 *v* **snatch**, rip, grab, wrench, pluck, force, pull, remove. [➡EXTRACT AND SEVER; 342] *Opposite:* coax. 4 *v* **dash**, rush, hurry, rip, streak, charge, speed, pelt, zip (*informal*), run. [➡MOVE FAST; 314] *Opposite:* saunter. 5 *n* **slit**, rip, split, slash, gash, hole, rent, scratch. [➡HOLES, GAPS, AND FORKS; 1251] *Opposite:* join.

> **Compare and Contrast:** ***tear, rend, rip, slit***
>
> CORE MEANING: TO PULL APART FORCIBLY
>
> ***tear*** to pull something apart, either by accident or on purpose, leaving jagged edges; ***rend*** to pull something apart violently; ***rip*** to tear something with a sudden rough splitting action, especially accidentally, accompanied by a distinctive noise; ***split*** to divide something into two parts with a single movement usually by force.

tear apart 1 *v* **destroy**, fragment, wreck, separate, dismantle, demolish, break. [➡TEAR, BREAK, AND CUT; 361] *Opposite:* reunite. 2 *v* **distress**, disturb, devastate, pain, hurt, upset, trouble. [➡UPSET, DISTRESS, AND HUMILIATE; 568] *Opposite:* reassure.

tear a strip off *v* [➡ACCUSE, BLAME, AND CRITICIZE; 642]

tearaway *n* **hooligan** (*informal*), delinquent, yob (*informal*), yobbo (*informal*), troublemaker, hoodlum, rascal (*humorous*). [➡MISCHIEVOUS OR BADLY-BEHAVED CHILD; 946]

tear away *v* **drag away**, pull away, haul away, depart, leave, make tracks (*informal*), be off. [➡ABSENT ONESELF; 8] *Opposite:* linger.

tear down *v* **demolish**, rip down, pull down, destroy, remove, break up, flatten, dismantle, raze to the ground. [➡DESTRUCTION AND DEMOLITION; 360] *Opposite:* construct.

teardrop 1 *n* **tear**, drop, droplet, drip, bead, blob, spot.

[➡ EXCRETION AND EXCRETA; 723] **2** *type of* **rounded shape.** [➡ ROUNDED SHAPE; 1217]

tearful 1 *adj* **in tears**, crying, weepy (*informal*), weeping, sobbing, howling, bawling (*informal*), snivelling, wailing, rueful. [➡ SADNESS, DISTRESS, AND DESPAIR; 540] **2** *adj* **sad**, emotional, unhappy, mournful, melancholy, sorrowful, upsetting. [➡ EMOTIONALLY UNPLEASANT AND UPSETTING; 228] *Opposite:* cheerful.

tearfully *adv* **sadly**, with a tear in the eye, weepily (*informal*), unhappily, miserably, disconsolately, mournfully, sorrowfully, ruefully. [➡ SADNESS, DISTRESS, AND DESPAIR; 540] *Opposite:* cheerfully.

tear gas *type of* **gas.** [➡ GASES; 1274]

tear into *v* **lay into**, attack, go for, round on, set on, pitch into (*informal*), fly into, criticize. [➡ ACCUSE, BLAME, AND CRITICIZE; 642] *Opposite:* praise.

tear-jerker (*informal*) *n* **sentimental story**, weepie (*informal*), sob story (*informal*), drama, tragedy, sad story. [➡ FILM; 901] *Opposite:* comedy.

tear limb from limb *v* [➡ WOUND A PERSON OR ANIMAL; 384]

tearoom *type of* **eating place.** [➡ HOTELS, RESTAURANTS, AND CLUBS; 1081]

tear to pieces *v* [➡ ACCUSE, BLAME, AND CRITICIZE; 642]

tear to shreds *v* [➡ ACCUSE, BLAME, AND CRITICIZE; 642]

tear up *v* **rip up**, shred, destroy, rip to pieces, rip to shreds, trash (*informal*). [➡ DESTRUCTION AND DEMOLITION; 360]

teary *adj* [➡ FACIAL EXPRESSION; 652]

teary-eyed *adj* [➡ FACIAL EXPRESSION; 652]

tease 1 *v* **joke**, laugh, mock, kid, mess about (*informal*), taunt, laugh at, rib (*informal*), make fun of, pull somebody's leg (*informal*), rag (*dated*), mess around (*informal*), josh (*informal*). [➡ JOKES AND TEASING; 675] **2** *v* **torment**, harass, pester, bother, annoy, provoke, badger, irritate, goad, bait. [➡ ANGER AND ANNOY; 570] *Opposite:* pet. **3** *v* **tantalize**, arouse, lead somebody on, encourage, excite, manipulate. [➡ APPEAL TO AND AROUSE INTEREST; 576] *Opposite:* satisfy. **4** *n* **joker**, clown, mocker, leg-puller (*informal*), teaser, tormenter, josher (*US informal*). [➡ JOKERS AND TEASES; 676]

teaser 1 *n* **puzzle**, puzzler, brainteaser, tough one, mystery, conundrum, riddle. [➡ JOKES AND TEASING; 675] **2** *n* **tease**, joker, clown, mocker, leg-puller (*informal*), josher (*US informal*). [➡ JOKERS AND TEASES; 676]

tea service *n* **tea set**, cups and saucers, china, porcelain, crockery. [➡ TABLEWARE, CUTLERY, AND KITCHENWARE; 861]

tea set *n* **tea service**, cups and saucers, china, crockery, porcelain. [➡ TABLEWARE, CUTLERY, AND KITCHENWARE; 861]

teasing 1 *adj* **playful**, mocking, tongue-in-cheek, mischievous, jokey, bantering, joshing (*informal*). [➡ JOKES AND TEASING; 675] *Opposite:* serious. **2** *adj* **provocative**, coy, flirtatious, coquettish (*literary*), suggestive, tempting, tantalizing, enigmatic. [➡ UNINTERESTED AND DETACHED; 630] *Opposite:* straightforward. **3** *n* **playfulness**, banter, leg-pulling (*informal*), ribbing (*informal*), repartee, raillery. [➡ JOKES AND TEASING; 675] *Opposite:* seriousness.

teaspoon *type of* **cutlery.** [➡ TABLEWARE, CUTLERY, AND KITCHENWARE; 861]

teaspoonful *n* [➡ AMOUNT AND QUANTITY; 112]

tea table *type of* **table.** [➡ FURNITURE; 858]

tea-time *n* **dinnertime**, suppertime, mealtime, time for tea, time for dinner, chowtime (*US slang*). [➡ TIMES OF DAY; 87]

tea towel *n* [➡ TABLEWARE, CUTLERY, AND KITCHENWARE; 861]

tea urn *n* [➡ TABLEWARE, CUTLERY, AND KITCHENWARE; 861]

tech (*informal*) *n* [➡ EDUCATIONAL INSTITUTIONS; 813]

technical 1 *adj* **technological**, scientific, industrial, mechanical. [➡ DESCRIBING TECHNOLOGY; 1159] **2** *adj* **practical**, mechanical, procedural, methodological, methodical. [➡ POSITIVE INTELLECTUAL CHARACTERISTICS; 525] **3** *adj* **nominal**, official, strict, narrow, literal, pedantic. [➡ EXACT; 204] *Opposite:* loose. **4** *adj* **specialized**, precise, official, professional, specialist, expert. [➡ EXACT; 204] *Opposite:* general.

technical college *n* [➡ EDUCATIONAL INSTITUTIONS; 813]

technicalities *n* [➡ BASIC DETAILS; 689]

technicality *n* **detail**, small point, trifle. [➡ UNIMPORTANT AND UNNECESSARY; 239]

technician *n* **specialist**, expert, operator, mechanic, engineer, skilled worker. [➡ WORKER; 836]

technique *n* **method**, system, practice, modus operandi, procedure, skill. [➡ WAYS OF DOING THINGS; 295]

technobabble *n* [➡ MEANINGLESS SPEECH OR WRITING; 677]

technological *adj* **technical**, scientific, industrial, high-tech. [➡ DESCRIBING TECHNOLOGY; 1159]

technologist *n* **scientist**, engineer, technician, boffin (*informal*), maven. [➡ WORKER; 836]

technology 1 *n* **equipment**, machinery, tools. [➡ MACHINERY; 1113] **2** *n* **skill**, knowledge, expertise, know-how (*informal*). [➡ SKILLS, TALENTS, AND ABILITIES; 527]

technophobia *type of* **phobia.** [➡ FEARS AND PHOBIAS; 555]

teddy 1 *type of* **upper body underwear.** [➡ HABERDASHERY, MILLINERY, AND LINGERIE; 867] **2** *see* **teddy bear.**

teddy bear *type of* **toy.** [➡ TOYS; 880]

teddy boy *n* [➡ DEVOTEES AND ADDICTED PEOPLE; 557]

tedious *adj* **boring**, dull, deadly (*informal*), dreary, monotonous, mind-numbing, tiresome, wearisome, wearying, uninteresting. [➡ BORING AND UNINTERESTING; 235] *Opposite:* interesting.

See Compare and Contrast at **boring.**

tediousness *n* **tedium**, boredom, dullness, deadliness (*informal*), dreariness, monotony, tiresomeness. [➡ BORING AND UNINTERESTING; 235] *Opposite:* excitement.

tedium *n* **tediousness**, boredom, dullness, deadliness (*informal*), dreariness, monotony, tiresomeness. [➡BORING AND UNINTERESTING; 235] *Opposite:* excitement.

tee 1 *type of* **sports equipment**. [➡SPORTS EQUIPMENT; 879] 2 (*US informal*) *type of* **top**. [➡GARMENTS AND OUTFITS; 865]

teed off (*US informal*) *adj* **angry**, annoyed, irritated, furious, fuming, peeved (*informal*), hacked off (*informal*), ticked off (*US informal*), fed up (*informal*). [➡IRRITATION AND ANGER; 542] *Opposite:* calm.

teem 1 *v* **swarm**, crowd, abound, be full, be stuffed, be loaded, be crammed. [➡PROSPER AND ABOUND; 16] 2 *v* **pour**, pelt, rain cats and dogs (*informal*), stream, rain, bucket (*informal*). [➡CLOUDY AND RAINY WEATHER; 1052] *Opposite:* drizzle.

teeming *adj* **swarming**, packed, crowded, heaving, crawling, seething, jam-packed (*informal*). [➡FULL; 1238] *Opposite:* empty.

teen (*informal*) 1 *adj* **teenage**, adolescent, youth, young, juvenile. [➡BABYHOOD, CHILDHOOD AND ADOLESCENCE; 917] 2 *n* **teenager**, adolescent, young person, youth, youngster, young adult, juvenile, minor. [➡CHILD OR YOUTH; 945]

teenage *adj* **adolescent**, teen (*informal*), young, youth, juvenile. [➡BABYHOOD, CHILDHOOD AND ADOLESCENCE; 917]

teenager *n* **adolescent**, young person, youth, youngster, young adult, juvenile, teen (*informal*), minor. [➡CHILD OR YOUTH; 945]

See Compare and Contrast at **youth**.

teens *n* **adolescence**, youth, young adulthood. [➡BABYHOOD, CHILDHOOD AND ADOLESCENCE; 917]

teensy (*informal*) *adj* [➡SMALL; 1194]

teensy-weensy (*informal*) *adj* [➡SMALL; 1194]

teeny (*informal*) *adj* **tiny**, teensy (*informal*), teeny-weeny (*informal*), teensy-weensy (*informal*), small, little, minute, wee, minuscule, microscopic, miniature. [➡SMALL; 1194] *Opposite:* enormous.

teeny-weeny (*informal*) *adj* **tiny**, teensy (*informal*), teeny (*informal*), teensy-weensy (*informal*), small, little, minute, wee, minuscule, microscopic, miniature. [➡SMALL; 1194] *Opposite:* enormous.

tee off *v* **drive off**, start, begin, commence (*formal*), kick off (*informal*), initiate. [➡START AN ACTION; 261]

tee shirt *see* **T-shirt**.

teeter *v* **totter**, stagger, wobble, shake, dodder, waver, hover, reel, rock, sway, lurch, weave. [➡WALK UNSTEADILY; 316]

teething troubles *n* **problems**, glitches, difficulties, snags, hitches, complications. [➡PROBLEM; 257]

teetotal *adj* **dry**, nondrinking, abstemious, abstinent, sober, on the wagon. [➡ABSTEMIOUSNESS AND SELF-DENIAL; 882]

teetotalism *n* [➡ABSTEMIOUSNESS AND SELF-DENIAL; 882]

teetotaller *n* [➡ASCETIC PEOPLE; 883]

telecast *v* [➡TELEVISION AND RADIO; 607]

telecaster *n* **broadcaster**, presenter, announcer, commentator, newsreader, anchor. [➡WORKERS IN ENTERTAINMENT AND MEDIA; 873]

telecommunication

◆ *types of telecommunications equipment*
aerial, answering machine, antenna (*US*), beeper (*informal*), bleeper, blower (*dated informal*), bug, cable, cellphone, cellular phone, e-mail, fax, intercom, landline, mast, mobile phone, modem, pager, payphone, phone, phonecard, receiver, satellite, satellite dish, switchboard, telephone, telex, transmitter, videophone, voice mail, walkie-talkie, wiretap

telecommunications *n* [➡COMMUNICATION; 603]

telecommuter *n* **homeworker**, teleworker, freelancer, outworker. [➡WORKER; 836]

telecommuting *n* **working from home**, freelancing, outworking. [➡TYPES OF WORK; 835]

telegram *n* **wire**, cable, message, telegraph, telex, cablegram. [➡LETTERS AND WRITTEN MESSAGES; 585]

telegraph *v* **send by wire**, send a message, cable, wire, transmit, telex. [➡DESPATCH AND SEND; 334]

telegraphic *adj* **concise**, abbreviated, condensed, truncated, succinct, compressed, elliptical, brief, pithy, curt. [➡SUCCINCT AND TO-THE-POINT; 641] *Opposite:* verbose.

telekinetic *adj* [➡THE SUPERNATURAL; 788]

telemarketing *n* **telephone selling**, telesales, marketing, sales. [➡BUSINESS ACTIVITIES AND PHENOMENA; 795]

telepathic *adj* **clairvoyant**, psychic, telekinetic, extrasensory, subconscious, parapsychological, intuitive. [➡THE SUPERNATURAL; 788]

telepathist *n* [➡PEOPLE WITH SUPERNATURAL POWERS; 789]

telepathy *n* **thought transference**, ESP, extrasensory perception, mind-reading, sixth sense, intuition. [➡THE SUPERNATURAL; 788]

telephone 1 *v* **phone**, call, ring, give somebody a ring (*informal*), give somebody a bell (*informal*), buzz (*informal*), give somebody a call, give somebody a tinkle (*informal*). [➡TELEPHONE AND PAGE; 682] 2 *type of* **telecommunications equipment**. [➡TELECOMMUNICATIONS; 1129]

telephone call *n* **call**, ring, bell (*informal*), phone call, buzz (*informal*), tinkle. [➡TELEPHONE COMMUNICATION; 48]

telephonist *n* [➡OFFICE WORKERS; 847]

telephoto lens *part of* **photographic equipment**. [➡PHOTOGRAPHY AND PHOTOGRAPHIC EQUIPMENT; 1121]

telesales *n* **telemarketing**, telephone sales, marketing, sales. [➡BUSINESS ACTIVITIES AND PHENOMENA; 795]

telescope *type of* **optical instrument**. [➡OPTICAL INSTRUMENTS; 1123]

telescopic 1 *adj* **magnifying**, enlarging, telephoto, zoom.

[➡CHANGE OF SIZE: BIGGER; 393] **2** *adj* **collapsible**, retractable, foldaway, foldup, compactible. [➡CHANGE OF SHAPE; 386]

telestich *type of* **wordplay**. [➡JOKES AND TEASING; 675]

telethon *n* **fundraiser**, phone-in, charity appeal, broadcast, appeal, solicitation, benefit. [➡TELEVISION AND RADIO; 607]

televise *v* **broadcast**, emit, relay, put out, put on, show, telecast, simulcast, air. [➡TELEVISION AND RADIO; 607]

television *n* **TV** (*informal*), small screen (*informal*), box (*slang*), boob tube (*US informal*), telly, goggle-box (*dated informal*), tube (*US*). [➡HOUSEHOLD APPLIANCES; 1116]

teleworker *n* **telecommuter**, homeworker, freelancer, outworker. [➡WORKER; 836]

teleworking *n* **telecommuting**, freelancing, outworking, homeworking. [➡TYPES OF WORK; 835]

telex *type of* **telecommunications equipment**. [➡TELECOMMUNICATIONS; 1129]

tell **1** *v* **inform**, let know, say, advise, notify, put in the picture, enlighten, acquaint with. [➡INFORM AND ANNOUNCE; 612] **2** *v* **relate**, narrate, recount, describe, report, impart. [➡RECITE, REPEAT, AND NARRATE; 621] **3** *v* **express**, say, voice, communicate, state, articulate, speak, convey. [➡UTTER AND PRONOUNCE; 609] **4** *v* **instruct**, order, direct, command, charge, ask, request. [➡REQUEST AND DEMAND; 664] **5** *v* **distinguish**, recognize, differentiate, identify, discriminate, know, judge. [➡LEARN AND DISCOVER; 763] *Opposite:* confuse. **6** *v* **divulge**, disclose, expose, reveal, inform, snitch (*slang*), blab (*informal*), tell on, tattle, grass (*slang*), gossip, spill the beans (*informal*), split on (*informal*), let the cat out of the bag (*informal*), sneak. [➡BETRAY CONFIDENCES AND GOSSIP; 619]

tell against *v* **count against**, go against, work against, weigh against. [➡DELAY ACTION OR OCCURRENCE; 279]

tell apart *v* **distinguish**, differentiate, tell one from another, identify, tell the difference between, discriminate. [➡MAKE DECISIONS AND CHOICES; 753]

teller *n* **cashier**, banker, bank clerk. [➡PEOPLE INVOLVED IN FINANCE; 804]

telling **1** *adj* **revealing**, informative, significant, telltale, indicative, illuminating. [➡INTERESTING AND MEANINGFUL; 191] *Opposite:* uninformative. **2** *adj* **effective**, expressive, important, significant, influential, powerful, forceful, impressive, decisive, potent. [➡STRENGTH; 202] *Opposite:* ineffective.

telling-off (*informal*) *n* **reprimand**, talking-to (*informal*), scolding, dressing-down, lecture, tongue-lashing, bawling-out (*US informal*), ticking-off (*informal*). [➡CRITICISMS AND ANGRY OUTBURSTS; 50]

tell it how it is (*informal*) *v* [➡ADMIT AND CONFESS; 616]

tell lies *v* [➡DECEPTION AND LIES; 661]

tell off (*informal*) *v* **reprimand**, scold, rebuke, tick off (*informal*), give a talking-to, haul over the coals, rake over the coals (*US*), take to task, reproach. [➡ACCUSE, BLAME, AND CRITICIZE; 642] *Opposite:* commend.

tell on *v* [➡BETRAY CONFIDENCES AND GOSSIP; 619]

tell stories *v* **tell lies**, lie, fib (*informal*), tell untruths, prevaricate, fabricate, spin a yarn (*informal*). [➡DECEPTION AND LIES; 661]

telltale **1** *adj* **revealing**, informative, betraying, significant, divulging, telling, indicative, illuminating. [➡INTERESTING AND MEANINGFUL; 191] *Opposite:* uninformative. **2** *n* (*informal*) **snitch** (*slang*), sneak, blabbermouth (*informal*), grass (*slang*), gossip, informer, rat (*slang*), squealer (*slang disapproving*), tattletale (*US informal*), stool pigeon (*slang*). [➡INTERFERING PEOPLE AND TELLTALES; 950]

tell tales *v* [➡BETRAY CONFIDENCES AND GOSSIP; 619]

telltale sign *n* [➡EVIDENCE AND PROOF; 69]

tell the truth *v* **be honest**, give your word, be straight with, be open, be truthful, speak the truth, stick to the facts, give the true story. [➡ADMIT AND CONFESS; 616]

tell untruths *v* [➡DECEPTION AND LIES; 661]

telly *n* [➡TELEVISION AND RADIO; 607]

temerity *n* **nerve**, audacity, gall, cheek (*informal*), boldness, impudence, impertinence, chutzpah (*informal*). [➡BAD MANNERS AND SOCIAL SKILLS; 522] *Opposite:* reticence.

temp **1** *n* **temporary worker**, office temporary, fill-in, stand-in, temporary secretary. [➡OFFICE WORKERS; 847] **2** *v* **do temporary work**, fill in, stand in. [➡WORK-RELATED ACTIVITIES; 834]

temper **1** *n* **anger**, rage, bad mood, bad humour, mood, sulk, strop (*informal*), tantrum, fit of pique. [➡IRRITATION AND ANGER; 542] **2** *n* **disposition**, temperament, attitude (*informal*), state of mind, frame of mind, humour, mood, spirit, nature, character. [➡TEMPERAMENT AND BEHAVIOUR; 493] **3** *v* **moderate**, mitigate, alleviate, soften, lighten, assuage, lessen, tone down, soothe, calm, palliate. [➡CHANGE OF INTENSITY: LESS; 396] *Opposite:* intensify.

temperament *n* **nature**, character, personality, disposition, temper, spirit, outlook, makeup, humour. [➡TEMPERAMENT AND BEHAVIOUR; 493]

temperamental *adj* **unpredictable**, erratic, unreliable, undependable, up and down, volatile, changeable, variable. [➡LACK OF COMMITMENT AND UNRELIABILITY; 510] *Opposite:* consistent.

temperance **1** *n* **teetotalism**, sobriety, abstinence, abstemiousness, soberness. [➡ABSTEMIOUSNESS AND SELF-DENIAL; 882] *Opposite:* intemperance. **2** *n* **self-control**, restraint, self-restraint, moderation, self-denial, self-discipline. [➡STRENGTH OF WILL; 502] *Opposite:* indulgence.

temperate **1** *adj* **restrained**, self-controlled, controlled, moderate, reasonable, mild, measured, reserved, muted. [➡CONFIDENCE AND COMPOSURE; 500] *Opposite:* intemperate. **2** *adj* **moderate**, mild, clement, pleasant, comfortable. [➡COLD WEATHER; 1051] *Opposite:* extreme.

temperately *adv* **mildly**, moderately, quietly, with restraint, calmly, smoothly, equably. [➡CONFIDENCE AND COMPOSURE; 500] *Opposite:* intemperately.

temperateness *n* [➡CONFIDENCE AND COMPOSURE; 500]

temperature *n* [➡TEMPERATURE: HOT; 1228]

tempered *adj* **hardened**, toughened, hard, annealed, strengthened. [➡RIGID AND HARD; 1210]

tempest 1 *n* (*literary*) **storm**, gale, thunderstorm, hurricane, cyclone, rainstorm, snowstorm, blizzard, whirlwind, high winds. [➡WINDY AND STORMY WEATHER; 1053] *Opposite:* calm. 2 *n* **uproar**, commotion, tumult, upheaval, disturbance, riot, brouhaha (*formal*). [➡CHAOS AND UPROAR; 51]

tempestuous 1 *adj* **stormy**, rough, turbulent, intemperate, inclement, windy, blustery. [➡WINDY AND STORMY WEATHER; 1053] *Opposite:* calm. 2 *adj* **emotional**, stormy, passionate, turbulent, uncontrolled, violent, hysterical, intense, wild, changeable. [➡EMOTIONALLY UNPLEASANT AND UPSETTING; 228] *Opposite:* relaxed.

tempestuously *adv* **emotionally**, passionately, turbulently, wildly, furiously, stormily, violently, hysterically, intensely, changeably. [➡EMOTIONALLY UNPLEASANT AND UPSETTING; 228] *Opposite:* calmly.

tempestuousness *n* **violence**, passion, turbulence, fury, storminess, wildness, intensity, changeability, drama. [➡EMOTIONALLY UNPLEASANT AND UPSETTING; 228] *Opposite:* calm.

template *n* **pattern**, master, stencil, model, prototype, original, outline, shape. [➡ARTWORKS; 898]

temple 1 *type of* **place of worship**. [➡RELIGIOUS BUILDINGS; 1084] 2 *part of* **head**. [➡HEAD; 693]

tempo *n* **beat**, speed, pulse, rhythm, measure, time, pace. [➡MUSICAL TERMS; 912]

temporal 1 *adj* **chronological**, time-based, sequential, progressive, historical. [➡CHAIN OF EVENTS; 163] *Opposite:* spatial. 2 *adj* **worldly**, earthly, secular, lay, profane, mundane, terrestrial, mortal. [➡RELIGIOUS CONCEPTS; 777] *Opposite:* spiritual.

temporariness *n* [➡FINITENESS, VARIABILITY, AND TRANSIENCE; 96]

temporary *adj* **provisional**, transitory, short-term, short-lived, fleeting, passing, ephemeral, evanescent (*literary*), transient, acting, interim, pro tem. [➡FINITENESS, VARIABILITY, AND TRANSIENCE; 96] *Opposite:* permanent.

> **Compare and Contrast:** ***temporary, fleeting, passing, transitory, ephemeral, evanescent, short-lived***
>
> CORE MEANING: LASTING ONLY A SHORT TIME
>
> ***temporary*** lasting or designed to last for a short time; ***fleeting*** brief or rapid; ***passing*** superficial and not long-lasting; ***transitory*** existing only for a short time; ***ephemeral*** lasting for a short time and leaving no permanent trace; ***evanescent*** (*literary*) disappearing after a short time and soon forgotten; ***short-lived*** lasting for a short time.

temporize *v* **delay**, defer, procrastinate, take your time, hesitate, tarry, put off. [➡HESITATE; 273] *Opposite:* set to.

tempt 1 *v* **lure**, allure, entice, attract, excite, arouse, seduce, make your mouth water, tantalize, turn on (*informal*). [➡APPEAL TO AND AROUSE INTEREST; 576] *Opposite:* repel. 2 *v* **invite**, attract, appeal, draw, move. [➡APPEAL TO AND AROUSE INTEREST; 576] *Opposite:* put off.

temptation 1 *n* **desire**, craving, urge, impulse, compulsion, appetite, wish, longing. [➡DESIRE AND WANT; 580] *Opposite:* repulsion. 2 *n* **persuasion**, coaxing, inducement, enticement, invitation, attraction. [➡DESIRE AND WANT; 580] *Opposite:* repulsion. 3 *n* **lure**, enticement, attraction, offer, invitation, pull (*informal*), inducement, turn-on (*informal*). [➡APPRECIATION AND GRATITUDE; 536]

tempted *adj* **of a mind to**, desirous (*formal*), attracted, interested, curious, drawn. [➡DESIRE AND WANT; 580] *Opposite:* uninterested.

tempting *adj* **alluring**, enticing, attractive, appealing, inviting, seductive, mouthwatering, tantalizing, irresistible, persuasive. [➡INTERESTING AND MEANINGFUL; 191] *Opposite:* unappealing.

tenable *adj* **reasonable**, acceptable, defensible, plausible, rational, sound, justifiable. [➡POSSIBLE AND PROBABLE; 178] *Opposite:* untenable.

tenacious *adj* **stubborn**, obstinate, resolute, firm, persistent, insistent, dogged, determined, steadfast, inflexible. [➡STRENGTH OF WILL; 502] *Opposite:* irresolute.

tenaciousness *n* [➡STRENGTH OF WILL; 502]

tenacity *n* **stubbornness**, obstinacy, resolve, firmness, persistence, insistence, doggedness, determination, steadfastness, tenaciousness. [➡UNWILLINGNESS AND STUBBORNNESS; 565] *Opposite:* irresolution.

tenancy *n* **occupancy**, rental, contract, lease, tenure, occupation. [➡ACCOMMODATION; 855] *Opposite:* ownership.

tenant *n* **renter**, occupier, occupant, resident, lodger, boarder, paying guest, leaseholder, lessee. [➡INHABITANT; 857] *Opposite:* landlord.

ten a penny *adj* **commonplace**, ordinary, run-of-the-mill, common, a dime a dozen (*US*). [➡ORDINARINESS; 245] *Opposite:* rare.

tench *type of* **freshwater fish**. [➡FRESHWATER FISH; 1010]

tend 1 *v* **have a habit of**, have a tendency to, incline, lean towards, be disposed, be likely to, be apt to, be wont to. [➡LIKE, LOVE, VALUE AND ENJOY; 579] 2 *v* **incline**, veer, lean, bend, verge. [➡CHANGE DIRECTION OF MOTION; 345] 3 *v* **look after**, care for, take care of, cultivate, attend to, minister to. [➡TAKE CARE OF AND SPOIL; 301] *Opposite:* neglect. 4 *v* **be in charge of**, manage, keep an eye on, watch over, watch, supervise, mind. [➡BE IN CHARGE; 271]

tendency 1 *n* **propensity** (*formal*), bent, leaning, inclination, predisposition, penchant, affinity. [➡TEMPERAMENT AND BEHAVIOUR; 493] 2 *n* **trend**, drift, movement, bias, current, shift. [➡DIRECTION OF MOTION; 346]

tendentious *adj* **provocative**, opinionated, biased, partisan, subjective, argumentative, prejudiced, one-sided, questionable, doubtful, partial. [➡THE NATURE OF IDEAS; 772] *Opposite:* impartial.

tender 1 *adj* **sensitive**, delicate, sore, raw, painful, inflamed, bruised, aching. [➡PAIN AND OTHER PHYSICAL SENSATIONS; 734] 2 *adj* **loving**, caring, affectionate, fond, kind, kind-hearted, gentle, warm, compassionate. [➡GENEROSITY AND KINDNESS; 496] *Opposite:* rough. 3 *adj* **young**, youthful, immature, inexperienced, impressionable, green, unsophisticated.

[➡UNSKILLED; 530] *Opposite:* seasoned. 4 *v* **offer**, proffer, present, give, hand in, put forward, suggest, submit, propose. [➡SUGGEST, HINT, AND COMMENT; 613] *Opposite:* withdraw. 5 *n* **proposal**, proposition, bid, offer, submission, estimate. [➡REQUEST AND DEMAND; 664]

tenderfoot (*informal*) *n* **novice**, recruit, raw recruit, newcomer, beginner, tyro, greenhorn, neophyte, rookie (*US informal*). [➡UNSKILLED PERSON; 531] *Opposite:* old hand.

tenderhearted *adj* **soft-hearted**, compassionate, sympathetic, kind, soft, tender, benevolent, sensitive, indulgent, gentle. [➡GENEROSITY AND KINDNESS; 496] *Opposite:* hardhearted.

tenderheartedness *n* **soft-heartedness**, compassion, sympathy, tenderness, kindness, benevolence, sensitivity, gentleness, indulgence, softness. [➡GENEROSITY AND KINDNESS; 496] *Opposite:* hardheartedness.

tenderize *v* **beat**, smash, hit, soak, steep, marinate. [➡COOKING AND FOOD PREPARATION; 354]

tenderloin *type of* **steak**. [➡TYPES AND CUTS OF MEAT; 1176]

tenderly *adv* **sympathetically**, lovingly, caringly, affectionately, fondly, kindly, kind-heartedly, gently, warmly, compassionately. [➡GENEROSITY AND KINDNESS; 496] *Opposite:* unkindly.

tenderness 1 *n* **sympathy**, gentleness, kindness, kind-heartedness, fondness, love, caring, affection, warmth, compassion, softness. [➡GENEROSITY AND KINDNESS; 496] *Opposite:* unkindness. 2 *n* **sensitivity**, soreness, rawness, painfulness, inflammation, ache, bruising. [➡SICKNESS; 730]

tendon *type of* **muscle or tendon**. [➡THE MUSCLES; 719]

tendril 1 *n* **stem**, vine, shoot, frond, branch. [➡PARTS OF TREES AND PLANTS; 1026] 2 *n* (*literary*) **twist**, coil, wisp, lock, curl, ringlet, strand. [➡AMOUNT OF SOLID OR SEMI-SOLID; 115]

tenebrous (*literary*) *adj* [➡DESCRIBING LIGHT; 1227]

tenement *n* **block of flats**, apartment block, high-rise, apartment building (*US*), housing project (*US*), apartment house (*US*). [➡RESIDENTIAL BUILDINGS; 1077]

tenet (*formal*) *n* **principle**, theory, idea, assumption, belief, doctrine, dogma, precept (*formal*). [➡IDEA AND THOUGHT; 771]

ten-gallon hat *type of* **hat**. [➡HABERDASHERY, MILLINERY, AND LINGERIE; 867]

tenner (*informal*) *n* [➡CURRENCIES; 798]

tennis *type of* **court game**. [➡HOBBIES, GAMES, AND SPORTS; 875]

tenor 1 *n* **mood**, tone, gist, drift, meaning, sense, theme, intention, tendency, purpose, nature. [➡MEANING; 691] 2 *type of* **musical register**. [➡MUSICAL TERMS; 912]

tense 1 *adj* **anxious**, nervous, stressed, worried, edgy, jumpy, overwrought, uptight (*informal*), on edge, apprehensive, jittery, twitchy (*informal*). [➡CONFUSION, ANXIETY, AND WORRY; 541] *Opposite:* relaxed. 2 *adj* **taut**, tight, rigid, stiff, strained, tensed. [➡RIGID AND HARD; 1210] *Opposite:* loose.

tensely *adv* **anxiously**, nervously, edgily, jumpily, apprehensively, worriedly. [➡CONFUSION, ANXIETY, AND WORRY; 541] *Opposite:* calmly.

tensile *adj* **ductile**, stretchy, stretchable, workable, malleable, flexible. [➡MALLEABLE AND ELASTIC; 1211] *Opposite:* rigid.

tension 1 *n* **worry**, nervousness, anxiety, stress, strain, pressure, apprehension. [➡FEELINGS ABOUT THE FUTURE; 534] *Opposite:* relaxation. 2 *n* **conflict**, ill feeling, friction, hostility, mistrust, unease, strain, stress. [➡DISHARMONY; 157] *Opposite:* ease. 3 *n* **tautness**, tightness, stiffness, strain, pressure, pull. [➡RIGID AND HARD; 1210] *Opposite:* relaxation.

ten-speed *type of* **bike** (*informal*). [➡BIKES, CARS, AND CARRIAGES; 1148]

tent *n* **shelter**, marquee, bivouac, camp, pavilion. [➡RESIDENTIAL BUILDINGS; 1077]

tentacle *n* **limb**, organ, appendage, feeler, antenna, member, arm. [➡ARM AND HAND; 696]

tentative 1 *adj* **hesitant**, cautious, faltering, unsure, timid, shy, uncertain. [➡INSECURITY AND LOSS OF COMPOSURE; 545] *Opposite:* sure. 2 *adj* **provisional**, exploratory, speculative, unconfirmed, indefinite, unsettled, not final, rough, open to consideration. [➡UNCERTAIN; 176] *Opposite:* definite.

tentatively *adv* **hesitantly**, cautiously, falteringly, uncertainly, timidly, shyly. [➡INSECURITY AND LOSS OF COMPOSURE; 545] *Opposite:* boldly.

tenuous *adj* **weak**, shaky, unsubstantiated, questionable, feeble, vague, unconvincing, half-hearted. [➡VAGUENESS; 244] *Opposite:* convincing.

tenuousness *n* [➡VAGUENESS; 244]

tenure 1 *n* **tenancy**, freehold, occupancy, occupation, lease, contract. [➡ACCOMMODATION; 855] *Opposite:* ownership. 2 *n* (*formal*) **term**, duration, span, period, time, stretch, stint. [➡PERIOD OF TIME; 90]

tepid 1 *adj* **lukewarm**, hand hot, blood hot, warmish, warm, barely warm. [➡TEMPERATURE: MEDIUM; 1229] *Opposite:* icy. 2 *adj* **unenthusiastic**, half-hearted, lukewarm, indifferent, apathetic, moderate, lackadaisical. [➡NEUTRALITY AND INDIFFERENCE; 554] *Opposite:* enthusiastic.

tercentenary *n* **300th anniversary**, anniversary, commemoration, celebration, festival, 300th year. [➡CEREMONIES AND ANNIVERSARIES; 38]

term 1 *n* **word**, expression, phrase, name, idiom. [➡ASPECTS OF LANGUAGE; 683] 2 *n* (*formal*) **period**, time, stretch, tenure, span, duration, stint. [➡PERIOD OF TIME; 90] 3 *v* **call**, name, label, dub, designate, characterize. [➡NAME AND DESCRIBE; 666]

terminal 1 *adj* **fatal**, incurable, deadly, mortal, lethal, life-threatening. [➡DEADLY; 928] *Opposite:* curable. 2 *n* **station**, airport, rail terminal, passenger terminal, terminus, depot. [➡PUBLIC BUILDINGS AND MEETING PLACES; 1080] 3 *n* **workstation**, visual display unit, VDU, computer, monitor. [➡COMPUTERS AND COMPUTING; 1126]

See Compare and Contrast at **deadly**.

terminally *adv* **fatally**, incurably, mortally, lethally, critically. [➡CRITICALLY AND SERIOUSLY; 132]

terminal moraine *n* [➡EROSION PRODUCTS AND SOIL; 1058]

terminate 1 *v* (*formal*) **end**, finish, come to an end, conclude, stop, cease, expire, lapse. [➡CAUSE TO STOP; 267] *Opposite:* start. 2 *v* (*US*) **dismiss**, fire (*informal*), sack (*informal*), let go, lay off, axe (*informal*). [➡REVOKE STATUS; 460] *Opposite:* hire.

termination (*formal*) *n* **end**, finish, close, expiry, conclusion, closure, dissolution, cessation. [➡END; 54] *Opposite:* start.

terminology *n* **terms**, language, expressions, vocabulary, jargon, lingo (*informal*), lexicon, lexis. [➡ASPECTS OF LANGUAGE; 683]

terminus *n* **last stop**, station, end of the line, depot, garage, terminal. [➡PUBLIC BUILDINGS AND MEETING PLACES; 1080]

termite *type of* **ant**. [➡ANTS; 1014]

term of endearment *n* [➡ENDEARMENTS; 657]

term paper (*US*) *n* [➡LESSONS, COURSE WORK, AND EXAMINATIONS; 842]

terms 1 *n* **footing**, rapport, relations, relationship, standing, position. [➡RELATIONSHIP TO ANOTHER; 973] 2 *n* **conditions**, stipulations, provisos, provisions, requisites. [➡NECESSARY AND ESSENTIAL; 197] 3 *n* **language**, expressions, vocabulary, terminology, jargon, nomenclature, lexis. [➡ASPECTS OF LANGUAGE; 683]

tern *type of* **seabird**. [➡SEABIRD; 1002]

terrace *n* **walkway**, promenade, patio, veranda, porch (*US*). [➡URBAN OUTDOOR SPACES; 1071]

terraced 1 *adj* **in terraces**, stepped, ridged, tiered, split-level, on different levels. [➡MOUNTAINS AND HILLS; 1044] *Opposite:* smooth. 2 *adj* **adjoining**, attached, joined. [➡BUILDING AND ARCHITECTURE; 1075] *Opposite:* detached.

terraced house *type of* **house**. [➡RESIDENTIAL BUILDINGS; 1077]

terracotta *type of* **pottery**. [➡POTTERY; 1134]

terra firma *n* [➡THE SEAS, OCEANS, AND SHORES; 1041]

terrain *n* **land**, topography, territory, ground, landscape, environment. [➡THE COUNTRYSIDE AND OUTDOOR SPACES; 1070]

terrapin *type of* **reptile**. [➡REPTILES; 994]

terrazzo *n* [➡BUILDING MATERIALS; 1076]

terrestrial 1 *adj* **earthly**, worldly, global, telluric. [➡THE EARTH; 1039] *Opposite:* extraterrestrial. 2 *adj* **land-dwelling**, surface-dwelling, land, earthbound. [➡THE EARTH; 1039]

terrible 1 *adj* **extreme**, severe, serious, grave, intense, excessive. [➡BAD AND BADLY; 224] *Opposite:* mild. 2 *adj* **horrible**, horrifying, horrific, horrendous, frightful, shocking, terrifying. [➡EMOTIONALLY UNPLEASANT AND UPSETTING; 228] *Opposite:* pleasant. 3 *adj* **awful**, dreadful, rotten, appalling, poor, abysmal. [➡BAD AND BADLY; 224] *Opposite:* wonderful.

terribly 1 *adv* **very**, extremely, tremendously, exceedingly, incredibly, inordinately, enormously. [➡TO A GREAT EXTENT; 130] *Opposite:* slightly. 2 *adv* **awfully**, appallingly, offensively, intolerably, horribly, dreadfully. [➡BAD AND BADLY; 224] *Opposite:* pleasantly.

terrier *type of* **small dog**. [➡DOG; 980]

terrific 1 *adj* (*informal*) **wonderful**, super (*informal*), marvellous, excellent, remarkable, superb, great, tremendous. [➡EXTRAORDINARY: UNCOMMON; 206] *Opposite:* dreadful. 2 *adj* **enormous**, great, huge, massive, tremendous, awesome, extreme, excessive. [➡LARGE; 1192] *Opposite:* insignificant.

terrifically *adv* **very**, extremely, tremendously, exceedingly, incredibly, excessively, greatly. [➡TO A GREAT EXTENT; 130] *Opposite:* slightly.

terrified *adj* **frightened**, horrified, scared, scared stiff, petrified, shocked, alarmed. [➡FEAR AND PANIC; 544] *Opposite:* unafraid.

terrify *v* **frighten**, horrify, scare, petrify, shock, alarm, panic. [➡FRIGHTEN AND SHOCK; 569] *Opposite:* comfort.

terrifying *adj* **frightening**, petrifying, scary (*informal*), chilling, startling, alarming, disturbing, distressing, worrying, horrifying, shocking, dreadful, terrible, dangerous. [➡FRIGHTENING; 232] *Opposite:* reassuring.

territorial 1 *adj* **regional**, local, land, provincial, national, international, state. [➡COUNTRIES AND REGIONS; 1066] 2 *adj* **defensive**, protective, possessive, assertive, jealous. [➡ENVY AND JEALOUSY; 549]

territorial army *n* [➡THE ARMED FORCES; 827]

territory 1 *n* **land**, terrain, ground, area, region, zone, place, space. [➡PLACE; 1064] 2 *n* **country**, land, state, province, region, domain, area, zone, district. [➡TERRITORIES AND GROUPS OF NATIONS; 1067] 3 *n* **field**, subject, speciality, area, terrain, sphere, arena, zone, compass. [➡SUBJECT AREA; 769] 4 *n* **patch**, beat, domain, pitch, property, home, range, land, ground. [➡GEOGRAPHICAL BORDERS AND BOUNDARIES; 1068]

terror 1 *n* **fear**, horror, dread, fright, alarm, trepidation, shock, panic. [➡FEAR AND PANIC; 544] *Opposite:* security. 2 *n* (*informal*) **pest** (*informal*), nuisance, horror (*informal*), troublemaker, ruffian (*dated*), imp. [➡MISCHIEVOUS OR BADLY-BEHAVED CHILD; 946]

terrorism *n* **violence**, intimidation, radicalism, extremism, bombing, kidnapping, assassination, sabotage. [➡CRIMES; 817]

terrorist *n* **guerrilla**, radical, extremist, fanatic, bomber, kidnapper, assassin, saboteur. [➡CRIMINALS; 821]

terrorization *n* [➡UNKIND ACTION OR BEHAVIOUR; 297]

terrorize *v* **terrify**, frighten, scare, threaten, intimidate, bully, coerce. [➡FRIGHTEN AND SHOCK; 569] *Opposite:* reassure.

terrorized *adj* [➡FEAR AND PANIC; 544]

terror-stricken *adj* **terrified**, petrified, scared to death, scared stiff, frightened out of your wits, panic-stricken, horror-struck, terrorized, afraid, alarmed, horrified. [➡FEAR AND PANIC; 544] *Opposite:* calm.

terry (*US*) *type of* **fabric from plants**. [➡FABRICS; 1131]

terry cloth (*US*) *type of* **fabric from plants**. [➡FABRICS; 1131]

terry towelling *type of* **fabric from plants**. [➡FABRICS; 1131]

terse 1 *adj* **abrupt**, curt, short, brusque, clipped, snappy, snappish. [➡ BAD-TEMPERED AND HUMOURLESS; 627] *Opposite:* expansive. 2 *adj* **concise**, brief, succinct, pithy, short and sweet. [➡ SUCCINCT AND TO-THE-POINT; 641] *Opposite:* wordy.

terseness 1 *n* **abruptness**, curtness, shortness, brusqueness, snappishness. [➡ BAD-TEMPERED AND HUMOURLESS; 627] *Opposite:* expansiveness. 2 *n* **concision**, brevity, succinctness, pithiness, economy. [➡ SUCCINCT AND TO-THE-POINT; 641] *Opposite:* verbosity.

test 1 *n* **examination**, exam, quiz, trial, assessment, check, experiment, investigation, analysis, assay, scan. [➡ EXAMINE AND ASSESS; 754] 2 *n* **trial run**, trial, test drive, run-through, practice, review, tryout. [➡ PREPARATORY EVENT; 57] 3 *n* **proof**, evidence, sign, criterion, yardstick, acid test, litmus test. [➡ INDICATIONS, SIGNS, AND WARNINGS; 68] 4 *n* **trial**, ordeal, hardship, tribulation, torment, difficulty. [➡ NUISANCES; 254] 5 *v* **try**, try out, put to the test, examine, quiz, assess, check, put something through its paces, experiment with, investigate, analyse, scan. [➡ EXAMINE AND ASSESS; 754] 6 *see* **test match**.

testament *n* **evidence**, witness, testimony, proof, demonstration, verification, authentication, indication. [➡ EVIDENCE AND PROOF; 69]

test drive *n* **trial run**, trial, drive, run, spin, test, tryout. [➡ PREPARATORY EVENT; 57]

test-drive *v* **try out**, try, take for a spin, put something through its paces, drive, test. [➡ USE TOOLS AND MACHINERY; 469]

tested *adj* **verified**, tried, confirmed, established, experienced, seasoned. [➡ OLD, OLD-FASHIONED; 168] *Opposite:* untried.

tester *n* **sample**, trial size, free sample, free gift. [➡ REPRESENTATIONS AND GENERAL EXAMPLES; 65]

testify 1 *v* **give evidence**, bear witness, appear, swear, state, attest, affirm. [➡ CLAIM, INSIST, AND EMPHASIZE; 615] 2 *v* (*formal*) **prove**, show, confirm, bear out, indicate, demonstrate, bear witness, attest. [➡ APPROVE AND CONFIRM; 647] *Opposite:* disprove.

testily (*informal*) *adv* **irritably**, grumpily, impatiently, touchily, tetchily (*informal*), grouchily (*informal*), crabbily, crossly, temperamentally, snappily, crankily (*informal*), petulantly, peevishly, cantankerously, bad-temperedly. [➡ BAD-TEMPERED AND HUMOURLESS; 627]

testimonial 1 *n* **recommendation**, reference, endorsement, confirmation, statement, declaration. [➡ LETTERS AND WRITTEN MESSAGES; 585] 2 *n* **tribute**, honour, reward, celebration, acknowledgment, recognition, monument. [➡ NAME AND DESCRIBE; 666]

testimony 1 *n* **evidence**, statement, declaration, deposition, affidavit. [➡ OFFICIAL DOCUMENTS; 587] 2 *n* **testament**, evidence, witness, proof, demonstration, verification, authentication, indication. [➡ EVIDENCE AND PROOF; 69]

testiness (*informal*) *n* **irritability**, temper, grumpiness, impatience, touchiness, tetchiness (*informal*), grouchiness (*informal*), crabbiness, crossness, snappiness, crankiness (*US informal*), petulance, peevishness, cantankerousness, bad temper. [➡ EXCESSIVE SENSITIVITY; 512]

testing *adj* **challenging**, difficult, taxing, tough, trying, hard. [➡ DIFFICULTY AND COMPLEXITY; 243] *Opposite:* easy.

test match *n* **international**, test, match, game, cricket match, rugby match. [➡ NON-AGGRESSIVE/SPORTING EVENT; 40]

test run *n* [➡ PREPARATORY EVENT; 57]

testy (*informal*) *adj* **bad-tempered**, irritable, grumpy, impatient, touchy, tetchy (*informal*), grouchy (*informal*), crabby, crotchety (*informal*), cross, temperamental, snappy, cranky (*US informal*), petulant, peevish, cantankerous. [➡ IRRITATION AND ANGER; 542] *Opposite:* even-tempered.

tetchily (*informal*) *adv* **irritably**, grumpily, impatiently, touchily, testily (*informal*), grouchily (*informal*), crabbily, crossly, temperamentally, snappily, crankily (*informal*), petulantly, peevishly, cantankerously, bad-temperedly. [➡ BAD-TEMPERED AND HUMOURLESS; 627]

tetchiness (*informal*) *n* **temper**, irritability, grumpiness, impatience, touchiness, testiness (*informal*), grouchiness (*informal*), crabbiness, crossness, snappiness, crankiness (*US informal*), petulance, peevishness, cantankerousness, bad temper. [➡ EXCESSIVE SENSITIVITY; 512]

tetchy (*informal*) *adj* **bad-tempered**, irritable, grumpy, impatient, touchy, testy (*informal*), grouchy (*informal*), crabby, crotchety (*informal*), cross, temperamental, snappy, cranky (*US informal*), petulant, peevish. [➡ IRRITATION AND ANGER; 542] *Opposite:* even-tempered.

tête-à-tête *n* [➡ INFORMAL COMMUNICATION; 45]

tether 1 *n* **rope**, chain, lead, rein, tie, fetter, truss, leash. [➡ FASTENERS, LINKS, AND NETWORKS; 1246] 2 *v* **tie up**, tie, hitch, fasten, secure, rope, chain, bind, truss. [➡ FASTEN, LINK, AND JOIN; 409] *Opposite:* release.

tetragon *type of* **angular shape**. [➡ ANGULAR SHAPE; 1216]

tetrahedron *type of* **angular shape**. [➡ ANGULAR SHAPE; 1216]

text 1 *n* **manuscript**, transcript, typescript, writing, script, copy, edition, version. [➡ WRITING; 584] 2 *n* **passage**, piece, article, extract, content, wording. [➡ WRITING; 584] 3 *n* **textbook**, set book, schoolbook, course book, reader, primer, manual, workbook. [➡ BOOKS AND BOOKLETS; 591]

textbook 1 *n* **text**, set book, schoolbook, course book, reader, primer, manual, workbook. [➡ BOOKS AND BOOKLETS; 591] 2 *adj* **model**, classic, typical, prime, definitive, exemplary, stock, paradigmatic. [➡ REPRESENTATIVE; 66] *Opposite:* atypical.

textile *n* **fabric**, cloth, material, piece goods, yard goods, knit, weave. [➡ TEXTILES AND THREADS; 1130]

textual *adj* **written**, word-based, documented, documentary, stylistic, recorded, literal, verbatim. [➡ WRITING; 584]

texture *n* **feel**, touch, surface, consistency, quality, grain, roughness, smoothness, coarseness, fineness. [➡ TEXTURE; 1219]

textured *adj* **surfaced**, raised, rough, coarse, bumpy. [➡ PHYSICAL TEXTURE; 1221] *Opposite:* smooth.

TGV [➡ BIKES, CARS, AND CARRIAGES; 1148]

thank *v* **express thanks**, show gratitude, express gratitude, show appreciation, be grateful, acknowledge, recognize. [➡ PRAISE AND ENCOURAGE; 648]

thankful 1 *adj* **grateful**, appreciative, gratified, obliged, beholden. [➡APPRECIATION AND GRATITUDE; 536] *Opposite:* ungrateful. 2 *adj* **pleased**, glad, relieved, happy, satisfied, content. [➡PLEASURE, EXCITEMENT, AND ELATION; 535] *Opposite:* dissatisfied.

thankfully 1 *adv* (*informal*) **luckily**, happily, mercifully, fortunately, as luck would have it. [➡LUCK; 784] 2 *adv* **gratefully**, appreciatively, with gratitude, with thanks. [➡APPRECIATION AND GRATITUDE; 536] *Opposite:* ungratefully.

thankfulness *n* **gratitude**, thanks, appreciation, appreciativeness, recognition, acknowledgment. [➡APPRECIATION AND GRATITUDE; 536] *Opposite:* ingratitude.

thank goodness *adv* [➡EXPRESSIONS OF AGREEMENT; 649]

thank heavens *adv* [➡EXPRESSIONS OF AGREEMENT; 649]

thankless *adj* **unappreciated**, unrewarding, unacknowledged, taken for granted, difficult, trying. [➡EMOTIONALLY UNPLEASANT AND UPSETTING; 228] *Opposite:* rewarding.

thanks *n* **gratitude**, appreciation, thankfulness, appreciativeness, recognition, obligation, acknowledgment. [➡APPRECIATION AND GRATITUDE; 536] *Opposite:* ingratitude.

thanks a lot *interj* [➡EXPRESSIONS OF AGREEMENT; 649]

thanks to *prep* **because of**, on account of, due to, owing to, as a result of, through. [➡CAUSATION; 169]

thank you *interj* [➡EXPRESSIONS OF AGREEMENT; 649]

thatch 1 *n* **roofing**, roof, straw, rushes, reeds, hay, covering. [➡BUILDING MATERIALS; 1076] 2 *n* **thick hair**, hair, shock, mop, mane (*literary or informal*), locks (*literary*), tresses, mass, pelt. [➡HAIR; 485]

thaw *v* **melt**, defrost, soften, liquefy, warm up. [➡SOFTEN, LIQUEFY, DAMPEN; 389] *Opposite:* freeze.

theatre 1 *n* **playhouse**, auditorium, theatre-in-the-round, cinema, hall, lecture theatre, moviehouse (*US*). [➡BUILDINGS FOR PUBLIC ENTERTAINMENT; 1083] 2 *n* **drama**, plays, dramatic art, the stage, acting, show business, thespianism, dramaturgy, dramatics, role-playing. [➡THE PERFORMING ARTS; 904] 3 *n* **sphere**, focus, realm, scene, site, field, place of action, area, place. [➡PLACE; 1064]

theatre company *n* [➡PERFORMERS; 905]

theatregoer *n* **playgoer**, drama-lover, thespian, spectator, literati (*formal*), culture vulture (*informal*). [➡IN THE THEATRE; 906]

theatre group *n* [➡PERFORMERS; 905]

theatre-in-the-round *n* [➡THE PERFORMING ARTS; 904]

theatrical 1 *adj* **dramatic**, acting, stage, dramaturgical, histrionic, melodramatic. [➡THE PERFORMING ARTS; 904] 2 *adj* **melodramatic**, dramatic, hammy (*informal*), histrionic, exaggerated, over-the-top (*informal*), affected, artificial, mannered, pretentious, emotional, ostentatious, showy, flamboyant, stagy (*disapproving*). [➡AFFECTATION, SELF-SATISFACTION, AND SNOBBISHNESS; 508] *Opposite:* restrained.

the back of beyond *n* [➡REMOTE PLACES; 1046]

the boards *n* [➡IN THE THEATRE; 906]

theft *n* **robbery**, stealing, burglary, shoplifting, holdup, mugging, larceny (*dated*), embezzlement, pilfering, thievery. [➡CRIMES; 817]

Compare and Contrast: ***theft, robbery, burglary, holdup, mugging, shoplifting, embezzlement, larceny***

CORE MEANING: TAKING PROPERTY UNLAWFULLY

theft the unlawful taking of somebody else's property or money; ***robbery*** the act of illegally taking something that belongs to somebody else, especially by using force, threats, or violence; ***burglary*** the act of illegally entering a building, usually in order to steal; ***holdup*** a robbery involving the threat or use of guns; ***mugging*** an attack on somebody with the motive of robbery; ***shoplifting*** stealing goods from shops while pretending to shop; ***embezzlement*** the unlawful taking of money by somebody who has been placed in a position of trust, especially taking money from an employer; ***larceny*** the former crime of unlawful taking and removal of another person's property.

the gods (*informal*) *n* [➡IN THE THEATRE; 906]

the here and now *n* [➡PRESENT; 85]

theism *n* **faith**, belief, religion, piety. [➡RELIGIOUS CONCEPTS; 777] *Opposite:* atheism.

theme 1 *n* **subject**, topic, idea, subject matter, matter, argument, premise, thesis. [➡SUBJECT AREA; 769] 2 *n* **melody**, music, refrain, leitmotif, theme tune, theme song, signature tune. [➡MUSIC, SONGS, AND SINGING; 907]

See Compare and Contrast at **subject**.

theme park *n* [➡URBAN OUTDOOR SPACES; 1071]

theme song *n* [➡MUSIC, SONGS, AND SINGING; 907]

theme tune *n* [➡MUSIC, SONGS, AND SINGING; 907]

then 1 *adv* **at that time**, at that moment, at that point, at that juncture, then and there, formerly, before. [➡PAST; 84] *Opposite:* now. 2 *adv* **next**, afterwards, subsequently, later, and, after that, thenceforth, thenceforward. [➡AFTER, LAST, AND FOLLOWING; 166] 3 *adv* **in that case**, so, therefore. [➡CAUSATION; 169] 4 *adv* **on the other hand**, but then, then again, but then again, nonetheless, nevertheless. [➡EXPRESSIONS INTRODUCING EXTRA INFORMATION; 137] 5 *adv* **and**, in addition, too, also, besides. [➡EXPRESSIONS INTRODUCING EXTRA INFORMATION; 137]

thence (*formal or literary*) 1 *adv* **on**, onward, forward, thereafter, then, thenceforward, thenceforth. [➡CAUSATION; 169] 2 *adv* **therefore**, so, thus (*formal*), then. [➡CAUSATION; 169] 3 *adv* **thereafter**, thenceforth, then, from then on, from that time on, subsequently, afterwards. *Opposite:* hitherto. (*formal*). [➡AFTER, LAST, AND FOLLOWING; 166]

thenceforth *adv* **from then on**, from that time on, thence (*formal or literary*), thereafter, subsequently, then, afterwards. *Opposite:* hitherto. (*formal*). [➡AFTER, LAST, AND FOLLOWING; 166]

thenceforward *adv* **then**, on, onward, forward, thereafter, thence (*formal or literary*), thenceforth, subsequently, from then on, from that time on, afterwards. *Opposite:* hitherto. (*formal*). [➡AFTER, LAST, AND FOLLOWING; 166]

the Net (*informal*) *n* [➡THE INTERNET; 1127]

theodolite *type of* **measuring device.** [➡MEASURING DEVICES; 1122]

theological *adj* **religious**, scriptural, doctrinal, dogmatic, spiritual, mystical. [➡RELIGIOUS CONCEPTS; 777]

theological college *n* [➡EDUCATIONAL INSTITUTIONS; 813]

theology *n* **divinity**, religion, religious studies, doctrine, dogmatics, spirituality, mysticism. [➡RELIGIOUS CONCEPTS; 777]

theophobia *type of* **phobia.** [➡FEARS AND PHOBIAS; 555]

theorem *n* **proposition**, formula, deduction, statement, proposal, hypothesis. [➡MATHS; 598]

theoretical *adj* **theoretic**, hypothetical, academic, notional, imaginary, conjectural, speculative, abstract. [➡FALSE AND UNREAL; 174] *Opposite:* concrete.

theorist *n* **philosopher**, thinker, theoretician, theorizer, academic, planner. [➡PHILOSOPHICAL AND POLITICAL THINKERS; 782]

theorize *v* **hypothesize**, conjecture, imagine, conceive, posit (*formal*), put forward, speculate. [➡DEVELOP THEORIES AND REASON; 745]

theory 1 *n* **philosophy**, model, concept, system, scheme, idea, notion, principle, belief, rule, technique. [➡WAYS OF DOING THINGS; 295] 2 *n* **hypothesis**, premise, presumption, conjecture, supposition, speculation, assumption, guess. [➡IDEA AND THOUGHT; 771]

therapeutic 1 *adj* **curative**, remedial, corrective, restorative, medicinal, beneficial. [➡REMEDIES, TREATMENTS AND OPERATIONS; 732] *Opposite:* preventive. 2 *adj* **healing**, relaxing, calming, satisfying, helpful, salutary, beneficial, tonic. [➡CALMING; 189] *Opposite:* stressful.

therapist *n* **psychoanalyst**, psychotherapist, analyst, psychiatrist, counsellor. [➡PEOPLE WHO WORK IN MEDICINE; 848]

therapy *n* **treatment**, rehabilitation, healing, help, remedy, cure. [➡REMEDIES, TREATMENTS AND OPERATIONS; 732]

thereabouts *adv* **around there**, around then, near there, in that area, or so. [➡APPROXIMATELY; 133]

thereafter *adv* **after that**, from that time on, afterwards, subsequently, then, next, from then on, later. [➡AFTER, LAST, AND FOLLOWING; 166] *Opposite:* previously.

the real McCoy (*informal*) *n* **the real thing**, the genuine article, the very thing. [➡TRUE AND REAL; 172]

the real thing *n* [➡TRUE AND REAL; 172]

thereby *adv* **thus** (*formal*), so, in that way, by this means, in so doing, in this manner. [➡WAYS OF DOING THINGS; 295]

therefore *adv* **consequently** (*formal*), so, and so, then, as a result, thus (*formal*), for that reason, hence (*formal*). [➡CAUSATION; 169]

there or thereabouts (*informal*) *adv* **about**, approximately, roughly, more or less, near enough. [➡APPROXIMATELY; 133] *Opposite:* exactly.

thereupon (*formal*) *adv* **immediately**, directly, consequently (*formal*), thus (*formal*), subsequently, accordingly, forthwith (*formal*), straightaway, instantly. [➡AFTER, LAST, AND FOLLOWING; 166]

thermal 1 *adj* **warm**, hot, tepid, volcanic. [➡TEMPERATURE: HOT; 1228] *Opposite:* cool. 2 *n* **warm air**, current, updraught. [➡WINDY AND STORMY WEATHER; 1053]

thermometer *type of* **measuring device.** [➡MEASURING DEVICES; 1122]

thermos *n* [➡CONTAINERS, RECEPTACLES, AND PACKAGING; 1244]

thermosphere *n* [➡THE EARTH'S ATMOSPHERE; 1040]

thermostat *n* **regulator**, control, device, bimetallic strip, sensor. [➡PARTS OF MACHINES AND TOOLS; 1117]

thesaurus *n* **dictionary**, vocabulary list, word list, lexicon, glossary. [➡LISTS AND SCHEDULES; 588]

these days *n* [➡PRESENT; 85]

thesis 1 *n* **dissertation**, paper, essay, composition, treatise. [➡ANALYTICAL NONFICTION WRITING; 593] 2 *n* **proposition**, theory, notion, hypothesis, idea, opinion, view, proposal, argument. [➡IDEA AND THOUGHT; 771] *Opposite:* antithesis.

thespian 1 *n* **actor**, actress, player, artiste, personality, entertainer. [➡PERFORMERS; 905] 2 *adj* (*literary*) **theatrical**, dramatic, melodramatic, stagy (*disapproving*), histrionic. [➡THE PERFORMING ARTS; 904]

thew (*literary*) *n* [➡THE MUSCLES; 719]

the Web (*informal*) *n* [➡THE INTERNET; 1127]

the whole *pron* [➡ALL; 126]

the whole ball of wax (*US informal*) *n* [➡ALL; 126]

the whole enchilada (*US slang*) *n* [➡ALL; 126]

the whole kit and caboodle (*informal*) *n* [➡ALL; 126]

the whole lot *n* [➡ALL; 126]

the whole shebang (*informal*) *n* [➡ALL; 126]

the worse for wear 1 *adj* **dilapidated**, tatty, beat-up (*informal*), shabby, battered, decrepit, worn, scruffy, rundown. [➡IN BAD REPAIR; 1233] *Opposite:* pristine. 2 *adj* **unwell**, tired, off-colour, poorly (*informal*), pale, peaky, sickly, wan, drawn, peaked (*US*). [➡UNFIT AND WEAK; 740] *Opposite:* well.

thick 1 *adj* **deep**, broad, fat, wide, chunky, bulky, substantial, swollen. [➡WIDTH: WIDE; 1198] *Opposite:* thin. 2 *adj* **viscous**, syrupy, gooey, glutinous, heavy, stodgy, stiff, gelatinous, coagulated, clotted. [➡PHYSICAL TEXTURE; 1221] *Opposite:* runny. 3 *adj* **dense**, profuse, bushy, impenetrable, copious, abundant, heavy, generous, concentrated. [➡DENSITY AND CONSISTENCY; 1206] *Opposite:* thin. 4 *adj* **filled**, full, covered, crowded, teeming, bursting, overflowing, packed. [➡FULL; 1238] *Opposite:* empty. 5 *adj* **pronounced**, impenetrable, distinct, extreme, marked, broad. [➡DIFFICULTY AND COMPLEXITY; 243] *Opposite:* slight. 6 *adj* **indistinct**, slurred, muffled, hoarse, gruff, throaty. [➡LOUD OR UNPLEASANT SOUNDS; 1265] *Opposite:* clear.

thick as thieves *adj* [➡RELATIONSHIP TO ANOTHER; 973]

thicken *v* **congeal**, stiffen, set, solidify, clot, coagulate, condense. [➡HARDEN, CONGEAL, DRY; 388] *Opposite:* thin.

thicket *n* **copse**, coppice, grove, covert, undergrowth, brush, wood. [➡WOODS, FORESTS, AND JUNGLES; 1047] *Opposite:* clearing.

thickly 1 *adv* **densely**, heavily, profusely, abundantly, copiously, generously. [➡MANY, MUCH, LARGE AMOUNT; 117] *Opposite:* thinly. 2 *adv* **throatily**, in a slurred voice, indistinctly, hoarsely, gruffly. [➡LOUD OR UNPLEASANT SOUNDS; 1265] *Opposite:* clearly.

thickness 1 *n* **viscosity**, stiffness, body, texture, stodginess. [➡DENSITY AND CONSISTENCY; 1206] *Opposite:* fluidity. 2 *n* **width**, breadth, depth, wideness, chunkiness, fatness. [➡WIDTH: WIDE; 1198] *Opposite:* thinness.

thickset *adj* **stocky**, heavy, hefty, bulky, chunky (*informal*), solid, strapping (*informal*), husky (*US*). [➡BUILD; 478] *Opposite:* slight.

thick-skinned 1 *adj* **unsympathetic**, insensitive, callous, unfeeling, tactless, obtuse. [➡BAD MANNERS AND SOCIAL SKILLS; 522] *Opposite:* sensitive. 2 *adj* **impervious**, unconcerned, unmoved, tough, hardened, hard-boiled (*informal*). [➡NEUTRALITY AND INDIFFERENCE; 554] *Opposite:* thin-skinned.

thief *n* **robber**, burglar, shoplifter, pickpocket, bandit, crook (*informal*). [➡CRIMINALS; 821]

thieve *v* **steal**, rob, shoplift, raid, burgle, pinch (*informal*), nick (*slang*), pilfer, filch (*informal*). [➡STEAL AND ROB; 427] *Opposite:* return.

thieving *n* [➡CRIMES; 817]

thigh *part of* **leg or foot**. [➡LEG AND FOOT; 695]

thigh-highs *type of* **lower body underwear**. [➡HABERDASHERY, MILLINERY, AND LINGERIE; 867]

thimble *n* **cover**, cap, protector. [➡COVERS AND COATINGS; 1245]

thimbleful *n* [➡FEW, LITTLE, SMALL AMOUNT; 119]

thin 1 *adj* **narrow**, fine, slim, threadlike, slender, delicate, shallow, wafer-thin. [➡FRAGILE; 1208] *Opposite:* thick. 2 *adj* **skinny**, slim, slender, bony, lean, emaciated, skeletal, slight, scraggy, scrawny. [➡BUILD; 478] *Opposite:* fat. 3 *adj* **watery**, weak, dilute, diluted, runny, insipid. [➡FLUID AND NONSOLID; 1212] *Opposite:* thick. 4 *adj* **sheer**, gauzy, diaphanous, light, fine, lightweight. [➡VISUAL TEXTURE; 1220] *Opposite:* thick. 5 *adj* **reedy**, high, tinny, shrill, squeaky, cracked. [➡LOUD OR UNPLEASANT SOUNDS; 1265] *Opposite:* resonant. 6 *v* **water down**, dilute, thin out, weaken, disperse, rarefy. [➡CHANGE OF INTENSITY: LESS; 396] *Opposite:* condense.

Compare and Contrast: *thin, lean, slim, slender, emaciated, scraggy, scrawny, skinny*

CORE MEANING: WITHOUT MUCH FLESH, THE OPPOSITE OF FAT

thin having little body fat; ***lean*** muscular and fit-looking without excess fat; ***slim*** pleasingly thin and well-proportioned; ***slender*** gracefully and attractively thin; ***emaciated*** unhealthily thin, usually because of illness or starvation; ***scraggy or scrawny*** unpleasantly or unhealthily thin and bony; ***skinny*** extremely thin.

thing 1 *n* **object**, article, item, entity, gadget, device, mechanism, machine, contraption, thingamajig (*informal*). [➡PHYSICAL OBJECTS; 1242] 2 *n* **occurrence**, event, incident, phenomenon, matter, affair, business. [➡EVENTS AND OCCURRENCES; 35] 3 *n* **detail**, point, idea, issue, feature, factor. [➡SUBJECT AREA; 769] 4 *n* (*informal*) **obsession**, fixation, mania, craze, preoccupation, fascination. [➡FADS, FETISHES, AND IDOLATRY; 556]

thingamabob (*informal*) *n* **whatsit** (*informal*), thingamajig (*informal*), thingummy (*informal*), thingy (*informal*), doodah (*informal*), gizmo (*informal*), thing, widget (*humorous*), doohickey (*US informal*), doodad (*US informal*). [➡PHYSICAL OBJECTS; 1242]

thingamajig (*informal*) *n* [➡PHYSICAL OBJECTS; 1242]

things *n* **belongings**, clothes, gear (*informal*), possessions, equipment, effects (*formal*), stuff, kit. [➡POSSESSIONS; 462]

thingumabob (*informal*) *n* [➡PHYSICAL OBJECTS; 1242]

thingumajig (*informal*) *n* [➡PHYSICAL OBJECTS; 1242]

thingummy (*informal*) *n* [➡PHYSICAL OBJECTS; 1242]

thingy (*informal*) *n* **thingummy** (*informal*), whatsit (*informal*), thingamabob (*informal*), thingamajig (*informal*), thingumajig (*informal*), doodah (*informal*), gizmo (*informal*), thing, widget (*humorous*), doodad (*US informal*), doohickey (*US informal*). [➡PHYSICAL OBJECTS; 1242]

think 1 *v* **reason**, contemplate, reflect, ponder, deliberate, consider, meditate, mull over, weigh up, ruminate, cogitate (*formal*). [➡DEVELOP THEORIES AND REASON; 745] *Opposite:* act. 2 *v* **believe**, feel, consider, deem (*formal*), judge, agree, suppose, assume, imagine, sense. [➡HAVE AN OPINION OF SOMETHING; 757] *Opposite:* doubt.

think a lot of *v* [➡LIKE, LOVE, VALUE AND ENJOY; 579]

think badly of *v* [➡DISLIKE AND HATE; 578]

thinker *n* **philosopher**, theorist, intellectual, academic, scholar, sage (*literary*). [➡PHILOSOPHICAL AND POLITICAL THINKERS; 782] *Opposite:* doer.

think highly of *v* [➡LIKE, LOVE, VALUE AND ENJOY; 579]

thinking 1 *adj* **rational**, thoughtful, intelligent, discerning, intellectual, sophisticated. [➡POSITIVE INTELLECTUAL CHARACTERISTICS; 525] *Opposite:* unthinking. 2 *n* **thoughts**, philosophy, idea, theory, accepted wisdom, opinion, view, assessment, belief. [➡IDEA AND THOUGHT; 771]

think little of *v* [➡DISLIKE AND HATE; 578]

think over *v* **reflect**, deliberate, ponder, weigh up, chew over, contemplate, mull over, consider, chew on. [➡THINK AND REFLECT; 744] *Opposite:* forget.

think-tank *n* **committee**, body, advisory board, group pf experts, commission, panel. [➡LEGISLATIVE BODIES AND LEGISLATION; 809]

think the world of *v* **have a high regard for**, think highly of, like, have a high opinion of, look up to, admire. [➡LIKE, LOVE, VALUE AND ENJOY; 579]

think through *v* **consider**, contemplate, ponder, mull over, weigh up. [➡THINK AND REFLECT; 744]

think twice *v* **think carefully**, be careful, be wary, take heed, consider, step back, weigh up. [➡THINK AND REFLECT; 744]

think up *v* **invent**, devise, come up with, create, cook up (*informal*), dream up, mastermind, plan. [➡DEVELOP THEORIES AND REASON; 745]

thinly *adv* **finely**, lightly, delicately, sparsely, sparingly. [➡TO A CERTAIN EXTENT; 134] *Opposite:* thickly.

thinner *n* **solvent**, diluent, diluter, stripper, cleaner, turpentine. [➡LIQUIDS; 1268]

thinness 1 *n* **narrowness**, fineness, slenderness, slimness, shallowness, delicacy. [➡WIDTH: NARROW AND THIN; 1199] *Opposite:* thickness. 2 *n* **skinniness**, emaciation, leanness, boniness, lankiness, slimness, slenderness, slightness. [➡BUILD; 478] *Opposite:* fatness.

thin on the ground *adj* [➡TOO FEW, TOO LITTLE; 120]

thin on top *adj* [➡BALDNESS AND BALDING; 488]

thin-skinned *adj* **sensitive**, hypersensitive, easily upset, emotional, touchy, prickly (*informal*), tetchy (*informal*). [➡EXCESSIVE SENSITIVITY; 512] *Opposite:* thick-skinned.

third *n* [➡MEASUREABLE PORTION; 125]

third party *n* **intermediary**, go-between, arbitrator. [➡REPRESENTATIVES AND PATRONS; 968]

third-rate *adj* **poor quality**, inferior, mediocre, poor, shoddy, substandard. [➡INFERIORITY; 154] *Opposite:* first-class.

thirst 1 *n* **dehydration**, dryness, thirstiness, thirsting. [➡ILL AND SICK; 741] 2 *n* **craving**, desire, longing, hunger, eagerness, yearning, appetite. [➡DESIRE AND WANT; 580] *Opposite:* apathy. 3 *v* **desire**, crave, want, ache, pine. [➡DESIRE AND WANT; 580]

thirstily *adv* **deeply**, eagerly, gratefully, desperately, greedily. [➡DESIRE AND WANT; 580]

thirst-quencher *n* [➡DRINKS; 1186]

thirsty 1 *adj* **dehydrated**, dry, parched, thirsting, gasping. [➡DRINK; 712] 2 *adj* **desiring**, craving, eager, keen, hungry, desirous (*formal*), yearning, longing, voracious, avid. [➡DESIRE AND WANT; 580] *Opposite:* apathetic.

this day and age *n* [➡PRESENT; 85]

this instant *adv* [➡PRESENT; 85]

thistle *type of* **weed.** [➡WEEDS AND THISTLES; 1034]

Thomson's gazelle *type of* **deer or antelope.** [➡DEER AND ANTELOPE; 981]

thong 1 *n* **string**, cord, band, strap, belt, tie. [➡FASTENERS, LINKS, AND NETWORKS; 1246] 2 *type of* **shoe.** [➡FOOTWEAR; 871] 3 *type of* **lower body underwear.** [➡HABERDASHERY, MILLINERY, AND LINGERIE; 867]

thorax 1 *part of* **torso.** [➡TORSO; 694] 2 *part of* **insect.** [➡PARTS OF AN INSECT; 1019]

thorn *n* **prickle**, barb, spike, spine, point, bristle. [➡PARTS OF TREES AND PLANTS; 1026]

thorn apple *type of* **weed.** [➡WEEDS AND THISTLES; 1034]

thorn in somebody's flesh *n* [➡NUISANCES; 254]

thorn in somebody's side *n* [➡NUISANCES; 254]

thorny 1 *adj* **tricky**, problematic, awkward, controversial, knotty, tough, hard, difficult. [➡DIFFICULTY AND COMPLEXITY; 243] *Opposite:* uncontroversial. 2 *adj* **prickly**, barbed, spiky, spiny, pointed, bristly. [➡PHYSICAL TEXTURE; 1221]

thorough 1 *adj* **methodical**, careful, systematic, painstaking, meticulous, scrupulous, punctilious, assiduous. [➡POSITIVE INTELLECTUAL CHARACTERISTICS; 525] *Opposite:* careless. 2 *adj* **full**, detailed, systematic, exhaustive, in-depth, comprehensive, thoroughgoing, methodical, careful, painstaking, meticulous, scrupulous. [➡WHOLENESS AND COMPLETENESS; 199] *Opposite:* careless. 3 *adj* **absolute**, complete, total, out-and-out, utter, thoroughgoing, straight-out (*US informal*). [➡ABSOLUTE AND ABSOLUTELY; 131] *Opposite:* partial.

See Compare and Contrast at **careful**.

thoroughbred *adj* **pedigree**, purebred, pure. [➡CLASS STATUS; 889]

thoroughfare *n* **main road**, through road, street, road, way, access road, through street (*US*). [➡ROADS; 1105]

thoroughgoing 1 *adj* **full**, detailed, systematic, exhaustive, in-depth, comprehensive, thorough, methodical, careful, painstaking, meticulous, scrupulous. [➡WHOLENESS AND COMPLETENESS; 199] *Opposite:* careless. 2 *adj* **complete**, thorough, absolute, total, out-and-out, utter. [➡ABSOLUTE AND ABSOLUTELY; 131] *Opposite:* partial.

thoroughly 1 *adv* **methodically**, carefully, systematically, painstakingly, meticulously, scrupulously, in detail, comprehensively, exhaustively, fully. [➡WHOLENESS AND COMPLETENESS; 199] *Opposite:* carelessly. 2 *adv* **completely**, absolutely, totally, utterly, from top to bottom. [➡ABSOLUTE AND ABSOLUTELY; 131] *Opposite:* partially.

thoroughness *n* **care**, attention to detail, meticulousness, scrupulousness, diligence, carefulness. [➡HARDWORKING AND COMMITTED; 501] *Opposite:* carelessness.

though 1 *conj* **although**, while, even if, even though, despite the fact that. [➡ALTHOUGH, NEVERTHELESS, AND DESPITE; 170] 2 *adv* **however**, and yet, yet, nevertheless, nonetheless, still, all the same. [➡ALTHOUGH, NEVERTHELESS, AND DESPITE; 170]

thought 1 *n* **consideration**, contemplation, thinking, deliberation (*formal*), attention, reflection, meditation. [➡IDEA AND THOUGHT; 771] 2 *n* **idea**, notion, brain wave, inspiration, concept, belief, theory, opinion, plan, conception. [➡IDEA AND THOUGHT; 771] 3 *n* **ideas**, philosophy, thinking, notions, accepted wisdom, planning, concept, design. [➡IDEA AND THOUGHT; 771]

thoughtful 1 *adj* **considerate**, kind, caring, unselfish, selfless, attentive, sympathetic, solicitous, helpful, kind-hearted. [➡GENEROSITY AND KINDNESS; 496] *Opposite:* thoughtless. 2 *adj* **pensive**, meditative, contemplative, brooding, reflective, deep in thought, absorbed, introspective, wistful. [➡PENSIVENESS AND INTEREST; 539] 3 *adj* **careful**, meticulous, painstaking, thorough, deep, accurate, precise. [➡POSITIVE INTELLECTUAL CHARACTERISTICS; 525] *Opposite:* superficial.

thoughtfulness 1 *n* **consideration**, kindness, care, unselfishness, selflessness, attentiveness, attention, sympathy, solicitude, kind-heartedness. [➡GENEROSITY AND KINDNESS; 496] *Opposite:* thoughtlessness. 2 *n* **pensiveness**, meditation, contemplation, reflection, thought, introspection, wistfulness. [➡ATTENTION AND ATTENTIVENESS; 764] 3 *n* **care**, attention to detail, attention, thought, carefulness, meticulousness, thoroughness, accuracy, precision. [➡POSITIVE INTELLECTUAL CHARACTERISTICS; 525] *Opposite:* superficiality.

thoughtless 1 *adj* **inconsiderate**, unkind, uncaring, selfish, insensitive, tactless, rude, impolite. [➡SELFISH AND UNKIND; 506] *Opposite:* thoughtful. 2 *adj* **careless**, heedless, reckless, negligent, unthinking, inattentive, foolish, stupid, absent-minded. [➡INCAUTIOUS AND CARELESS; 284] *Opposite:* prudent.

thoughtlessness 1 *n* **inconsideration**, unkindness, selfishness, insensitivity, tactlessness, rudeness, impoliteness. [➡SELFISH AND UNKIND; 506] *Opposite:* thoughtfulness. 2 *n* **carelessness**, heedlessness, recklessness, negligence, inattention, inattentiveness, foolishness, stupidity, absent-mindedness. [➡LACK OF COMMITMENT AND UNRELIABILITY; 510] *Opposite:* prudence.

thought processes *n* [➡PSYCHOLOGY AND THE MIND; 770]

thought-provoking *adj* **stimulating**, challenging, provocative, interesting, inspiring. [➡INTERESTING AND MEANINGFUL; 191] *Opposite:* dull.

thoughts *n* **opinion**, view, point of view, feelings, judgment, belief. [➡POINT OF VIEW; 768]

thought transference *n* [➡THE SUPERNATURAL; 788]

thought up *adj* [➡FALSE AND UNREAL; 174]

Thousand Island dressing *type of* **seasonings, sauces, and dips.** [➡SEASONINGS AND SAUCES; 1173]

thrash 1 *v* **beat**, whip, give a hiding, spank, smack, batter, lash, flog, flay. [➡PHYSICAL ATTACK AND PUNISHMENT; 416] 2 *v* **defeat**, beat, hammer (*informal*), trounce, slaughter, walk over (*informal*), whip, paste, cream (*US informal*). [➡BEAT AND DEFEAT; 80] *Opposite:* lose. 3 *v* **toss**, writhe, flail, squirm, roll, wriggle, wiggle, toss and turn. [➡FIDGET AND FROLIC; 312]

See Compare and Contrast at **defeat.**

thrash about *v* [➡FIDGET AND FROLIC; 312]

thrashing 1 *n* **beating**, whipping, hiding (*informal*), spanking, battering, lashing, flogging, flaying. [➡PHYSICAL ATTACK AND PUNISHMENT; 416] 2 *n* **defeat**, rout, downfall, conquest, beating, hammering (*informal*), trouncing, whipping (*informal*), pasting (*informal*). [➡BEAT AND DEFEAT; 80] *Opposite:* victory.

thrash out *v* **hammer out**, resolve, solve, discuss, debate, go into, look into, settle, arrive at, hash out (*US*). [➡TWO-WAY COMMUNICATION; 608]

thread 1 *n* **cotton**, cord, yarn, strand, fibre, filament, line. [➡TEXTILES AND THREADS; 1130] 2 *n* **idea**, drift, gist, sequence, story line, theme, plot, train of thought. [➡IDEA AND THOUGHT; 771] 3 *v* **string**, wind, loop, lace, pass through, pass into, ease. [➡FASTEN, LINK, AND JOIN; 409] 4 *v* **make your way**, pick your way, edge through, squeeze through, negotiate, ease. [➡PROCEED AND GO; 306]

threadbare 1 *adj* **worn**, worn-out, shabby, ragged, thin, frayed, tatty, scruffy, tattered. [➡IN BAD REPAIR; 1233] *Opposite:* new. 2 *adj* **well-worn**, trite, hackneyed, clichéd, banal, stale, boring, ineffective, corny. [➡REDUNDANT AND USELESS; 241] *Opposite:* original.

threat 1 *n* **warning**, menace, intimidation. [➡ADVISE AND WARN; 614] 2 *n* **danger**, risk, hazard, menace, peril. [➡DANGER; 236] *Opposite:* promise.

threaten 1 *v* **intimidate**, bully, menace, warn, terrorize, pressurize, pressure, frighten. [➡UPSET, DISTRESS, AND HUMILIATE; 568] *Opposite:* reassure. 2 *v* **endanger**, jeopardize, imperil (*formal*), menace, compromise, cloud. [➡PUT AT RISK; 385] *Opposite:* guard. 3 *v* **loom**, lurk, hover, impend (*literary*), portend, creep up. [➡ABOUT TO HAPPEN; 33]

threatened *adj* **endangered**, at risk, in peril, vulnerable, dying out, disappearing. [➡IN DANGER; 238] *Opposite:* safe.

threatening 1 *adj* **intimidating**, bullying, menacing, hostile, aggressive, frightening, nasty. [➡RUDE AND HOSTILE; 626] *Opposite:* reassuring. 2 *adj* **ominous**, menacing, foreboding, inauspicious, sinister, dark, portentous. [➡DANGEROUS; 237] *Opposite:* reassuring.

three-dimensional 1 *adj* **three-D**, solid, deep. [➡ORIENTATION AND ALIGNMENT; 1222] *Opposite:* two-dimensional. 2 *adj* **believable**, realistic, convincing, lifelike, true-to-life, real, credible, vivid. [➡TRUE AND REAL; 172] *Opposite:* two-dimensional.

three sheets to the wind (*informal*) *adj* [➡UNDER THE INFLUENCE OF DRUGS OR ALCOHOL; 742]

threesome *n* [➡GROUPS OF PEOPLE; 935]

three-wheeler 1 *type of* **car.** [➡BIKES, CARS, AND CARRIAGES; 1148] 2 *type of* **bike** (*informal*). [➡BIKES, CARS, AND CARRIAGES; 1148]

thresh *v* **winnow**, flail, separate, beat, rub. [➡SEPARATE AND DIVIDE; 402]

threshold 1 *n* **doorway**, door, doorstep, entrance, entry. [➡DOORS AND ACCESS POINTS; 1100] 2 *n* **starting point**, verge, brink, edge, dawn, beginning, onset, inception (*formal*). [➡BEGINNING; 53] *Opposite:* end. 3 *n* **level**, limit, maximum, ceiling, outside, divide, line, base, tolerance. [➡MAJORITY; 139]

thrift *n* **frugality**, economy, carefulness, caution, prudence, parsimony. [➡ECONOMICAL AND RESOURCEFUL; 208] *Opposite:* extravagance.

thrift shop (*US*) *type of* **retail outlet.** [➡RETAIL OUTLETS; 1082]

thrifty *adj* **frugal**, economical, careful, cautious, prudent, sparing, parsimonious. [➡ECONOMICAL AND RESOURCEFUL; 208] *Opposite:* extravagant.

thrill 1 *v* **excite**, electrify, exhilarate, delight, inspire, stimulate, stir, rouse, elate, overjoy, grip. [➡PLEASE AND AMUSE; 573] *Opposite:* bore. 2 *n* **kick** (*informal*), buzz (*informal*), adventure, delight, joy, pleasure, quiver, tremble. [➡AMAZING THING; 212] *Opposite:* bore.

thrilled *adj* **excited**, electrified, exhilarated, ecstatic, elated, delighted, overjoyed, over the moon, on cloud nine (*informal*), pleased, tickled. [➡PLEASURE, EXCITEMENT, AND ELATION; 535] *Opposite:* disappointed.

thrilled to bits (*informal*) *adj* [➡PLEASURE, EXCITEMENT, AND ELATION; 535]

thrilled to pieces (*US informal*) *adj* [➡PLEASURE, EXCITEMENT, AND ELATION; 535]

thriller *n* **whodunit**, murder mystery, crime novel, detective story, page-turner, actioner (*informal*), adventure movie. [➡FILM; 901]

thrilling *adj* **exciting**, electrifying, exhilarating, delightful, inspiring, stimulating, stirring, rousing, gripping, awe-inspiring, awesome, spine-tingling, breathtaking. [➡EMOTIONALLY PLEASANT; 188] *Opposite:* boring.

thrive 1 *v* **grow well**, be healthy, flourish, bloom, blossom. [➡PROSPER AND ABOUND; 16] *Opposite:* deteriorate. 2 *v* **flourish**, prosper, boom, bloom, blossom, succeed, increase. [➡SUCCEED AND WIN; 79] *Opposite:* fail.

thriving *adj* **flourishing**, prosperous, booming, blooming, blossoming, successful. [➡SUCCESSFUL AND PROMISING; 81] *Opposite:* failing.

throat 1 *part of* **digestive tract.** [➡THE DIGESTIVE TRACT; 710] 2 *part of* **respiratory system.** [➡RESPIRATORY ORGANS; 716]

throaty *adj* **husky**, hoarse, croaky, gruff, guttural, deep, low, thick, harsh. [➡LOUD OR UNPLEASANT SOUNDS; 1265] *Opposite:* piping.

throb 1 *v* **pound**, thump, pulsate, pulse, thud, beat, vibrate, ache. [➡PHYSICAL REACTIONS; 317] 2 *n* **pounding**, thump, pulsation, pulse, rhythm, thud, beat, vibration, ache, pain. [➡CONTINUOUS SOUNDS; 1257]

thrombosis *n* **coagulation**, clotting, blockage, occlusion. [➡THE BLOOD AND CIRCULATION; 718]

throne 1 *n* **seat**, chair, cathedra. [➡SUPPORTS AND BASES; 1254] 2 *n* **power**, authority, sovereignty, command, rule, dominion. [➡REALMS AND RULES; 824]

throng 1 *n* **multitude**, mass, crowd, horde, swarm, mob, host. [➡GROUPS OF PEOPLE; 935] *Opposite:* few. 2 *v* **crowd**, pack, jam, cram, inundate, swamp, flood, flock, fill. [➡GET CLOSER TOGETHER; 311] *Opposite:* disperse.

throng together *v* [➡GET CLOSER TOGETHER; 311]

throttle 1 *v* **regulate**, control, adjust, correct, check, curb. [➡AVOID, PREVENT, LIMIT, AND CONTROL; 278] 2 *v* **strangle**, choke, garrotte, strangulate, suffocate, stifle, smother, asphyxiate. [➡KILL; 923] 3 *v* **silence**, gag, muzzle, stifle, shut up (*informal*), subdue, check, curb, restrain, repress, suppress, hold back, inhibit. [➡WITHHOLD INFORMATION; 688]

through 1 *prep* **across**, past, throughout, within, round, around, about, beyond, amid, amidst, among, amongst. [➡RELATIVE LOCATION; 162] 2 *prep* **during**, throughout, during the course of, in. [➡CONCURRENT AND CONTEMPORANEOUS; 165] 3 *prep* **via**, out of, by way of, by means of. [➡CAUSATION; 169] 4 *prep* **because of**, owing to, due to, as a result of. [➡CAUSATION; 169]

through and through *adv* **completely**, totally, entirely, utterly, at heart, to the core. [➡ABSOLUTE AND ABSOLUTELY; 131] *Opposite:* partially.

throughout *prep* **through**, during, all over, during the course of, in. [➡CONCURRENT AND CONTEMPORANEOUS; 165]

throughput *n* **amount**, quantity, data, material, output, input. [➡AMOUNT AND QUANTITY; 112]

through road *n* [➡ROADS; 1105]

through street (*US*) *n* [➡ROADS; 1105]

throughway (*US*) *type of* **major road.** [➡ROADS; 1105]

throw 1 *v* **fling**, toss, hurl, chuck (*informal*), pitch, heave (*informal*), lob, propel, cast, bowl. [➡THROW SOMETHING; 335] *Opposite:* catch. 2 *v* **drop**, leave, put, cast, toss, fling. [➡THROW SOMETHING; 335] 3 *v* **project**, cast, direct, send out, beam, shine, emit. [➡LIGHT EMISSION; 369] 4 *v* (*informal*) **confuse**, puzzle, bewilder, perplex, baffle, bamboozle (*informal*), nonplus, flummox (*informal*), disconcert, surprise, catch somebody off balance, catch somebody unawares. [➡CONFUSE AND BEWILDER; 572] 5 *v* **move**, flick, switch, connect, disconnect, put on, put off. [➡CAUSE TO START; 266] 6 *v* **organize**, arrange, host, give, hold, have. [➡CAUSE TO HAPPEN; 31] 7 *n* **toss**, lob, heave, pitch, fling, chuck (*informal*), shy. [➡THROW SOMETHING; 335] 8 *n* **rug**, cover, blanket, shawl, coverlet, loose cover, slip cover (*US*). [➡SOFT FURNISHINGS, LINEN, AND DRAPERY; 860]

Compare and Contrast: ***throw, chuck, fling, heave, hurl, toss, cast***

CORE MEANING: TO SEND SOMETHING THROUGH THE AIR

throw to cause something to go through the air using a physical movement; ***chuck*** (*informal*) to throw something in a reckless or aimless way; ***fling*** to throw something fast using a lot of force; ***heave*** (*informal*) to throw something large or heavy with effort in a particular direction; ***hurl*** to throw something with great force; ***toss*** to throw something small or light in a casual or careless way; ***cast*** to throw something to a particular place or into a particular thing, or to throw a fishing line or net.

throw a fit (*informal*) *v* [➡GIVING VENT TO EMOTIONS; 680]

throw a monkey wrench in the works (*US informal*) *v* [➡MAKE IMPOSSIBLE; 277]

throw a spanner in the works *v* [➡MAKE IMPOSSIBLE; 277]

throw a tantrum *v* [➡GIVING VENT TO EMOTIONS; 680]

throw away 1 *v* **discard**, throw out, get rid of, dispose of, ditch (*informal*), dump, scrap, bin, jettison, reject. [➡GET RID OF SOMETHING; 452] *Opposite:* keep. 2 *v* **waste**, squander, fritter away, blow (*slang*), ruin, spoil. [➡USE UP AND WASTE; 475] *Opposite:* make the most of.

throwaway 1 *adj* **disposable**, paper, plastic. [➡FINITENESS, VARIABILITY, AND TRANSIENCE; 96] 2 *adj* **wasteful**, profligate, extravagant, careless, improvident (*formal*), uneconomical. [➡WASTEFUL AND UNECONOMICAL; 247] *Opposite:* frugal. 3 *adj* **off-the-cuff**, casual, offhand, passing, spontaneous, incidental. [➡UNINTERESTED AND DETACHED; 630] *Opposite:* intended.

throw a wobbly (*informal*) *v* [➡GIVING VENT TO EMOTIONS; 680]

throwback *n* **reversion**, regression, resemblance, relic, retrogression, recession, return. [➡PAST; 84]

throw caution to the wind *v* [➡CHANGE OF MOOD AND COMPOSURE; 581]

throw cushion *n* [➡SOFT FURNISHINGS, LINEN, AND DRAPERY; 860]

throw in 1 *v* **add**, drop in, include, mention, refer to, contribute. [➡SUGGEST, HINT, AND COMMENT; 613] 2 *v* **include**, add, give, tack on, add on, give away. [➡GIVE AND PROVIDE; 431]

throw in the sponge (*informal*) *v* [➡FAIL OR BE UNSUCCESSFUL; 75]

throw in the towel (*informal*) *v* **give in**, surrender, give up, admit defeat, concede, throw in your hand (*informal*). [➡FAIL OR BE UNSUCCESSFUL; 75] *Opposite:* stand firm.

throw light on *v* [➡EXPLAIN AND CLARIFY; 611]

thrown off balance *adj* [➡INSECURITY AND LOSS OF COMPOSURE; 545]

throw off 1 *v* **shake off**, shed, shrug off, get rid of, discard, drop. [➡GET RID OF SOMETHING; 452] *Opposite:* keep. 2 *v* **elude**, evade, escape, give somebody the slip, shake off, lose. [➡AVOID OR ESCAPE CONTACT; 419]

throw out 1 *v* **discard**, throw away, get rid of, dispose of, ditch (*informal*), dump, scrap, bin, jettison, reject. [➡GET RID OF SOMETHING; 452] *Opposite:* keep. 2 *v* **expel**, kick out (*informal*), eject, chuck out (*informal*), show the door, fire (*informal*), dismiss. [➡EJECT AND EXCLUDE; 341] *Opposite:* welcome. 3 *v* **dismiss**, reject, disallow, turn down, refuse, kick out (*informal*). [➡FOREGO AND DENY ONESELF; 450] *Opposite:* pass.

throw pillow *n* [➡SOFT FURNISHINGS, LINEN, AND DRAPERY; 860]

throw up 1 *v* (*informal*) **abandon**, give up, relinquish, resign, throw away, drop. [➡FOREGO AND DENY ONESELF; 450] *Opposite:* keep. 2 *v* **cause**, create, produce, bring to light, pose, turn up, reveal, unearth. [➡CAUSE TO APPEAR; 5] *Opposite:* conceal. 3 *v* (*informal*) **vomit**, be sick, heave (*informal*), gag, retch, spew, puke (*slang*), hurl (*slang*). [➡VOMIT AND BELCH; 713]

throw yourself into *v* **engross yourself in**, immerse yourself in, bury yourself in, devote yourself to, commit to, pitch into (*informal*). [➡PARTICIPATE; 293]

thrum *v* **strum**, pluck, twang, play, brush, tap, drum. [➡EMIT CONTINUOUS SOUNDS; 367]

thrush *type of* **songbird**. [➡SONGBIRD; 1003]

thrust 1 *v* **push**, shove, force, propel, prod, plunge, drive, insert. [➡PUSH, PULL, SLIDE; 336] 2 *v* **stretch**, extend, stretch out, reach, reach out, jut, stab, soar. [➡MOVE SOMETHING TO ANOTHER LOCATION; 325] 3 *n* **shove**, push, prod, lunge, drive, plunge, insertion, stab. [➡PUSH, PULL, SLIDE; 336] 4 *n* **attack**, assault, offensive, push, drive, onslaught. [➡SUDDEN EVENT; 52] 5 *n* **point**, gist, meaning, focus, direction, aim, purpose. [➡MEANING; 691] 6 *n* **power**, force, propulsion, momentum, impetus, drive. [➡ENERGY GENERAL; 1160]

thruster *part of* **spacecraft**. [➡SPACE VEHICLES; 1062]

thruway (*US*) *type of* **major road**. [➡ROADS; 1105]

thud *type of* **impact sound**. [➡IMPACT SOUNDS; 1259]

thug *n* **brute**, hooligan (*informal*), heavy (*slang*), yob (*informal*), ruffian (*dated*), criminal, mugger, hoodlum, gangster, goon (*US*), hood (*US slang*). [➡VILLAINS AND THUGS; 947]

thumb 1 *v* **flick through**, flip through, leaf through, skim, browse through, scan, glance at, look at, turn over, skip through. [➡LOOKING AND LOOKS; 701] *Opposite:* pore over. 2 *part of* **arm or hand**. [➡ARM AND HAND; 696]

thumb a lift *v* [➡TRAVEL: WAYS OF TRAVELLING; 321]

thumbnail *part of* **arm or hand**. [➡ARM AND HAND; 696]

thumbs-down (*informal*) *n* **disapproval**, rejection, denial, red light (*informal*), no, veto, rebuff, negation. *Opposite:* thumbs-up. (*informal*). [➡REFUSE PERMISSION AND NOT ALLOW; 671]

thumbs-up (*informal*) *n* **okay** (*informal*), approval, acceptance, agreement, endorsement, ratification, green light, yes. *Opposite:* thumbs-down. (*informal*). [➡PERMIT AND ALLOW; 670]

thump 1 *v* **punch**, hit, whack, pummel. [➡PHYSICAL ATTACK AND PUNISHMENT; 416] 2 *type of* **impact sound**. [➡IMPACT SOUNDS; 1259]

thumping (*informal*) 1 *adj* **large**, huge, enormous, impressive. [➡LARGE; 1192] 2 *adv* **very**, exceptionally, extremely, inordinately, really. [➡TO A GREAT EXTENT; 130]

thunder 1 *n* **din**, boom, rumble, roar, clap, crack, rumbling. [➡CONTINUOUS SOUNDS; 1257] 2 *v* **boom**, roar, resound, rumble, clap, crack. [➡EMIT CONTINUOUS SOUNDS; 367] 3 *v* **shout**, bellow, boom, roar, yell, bark. [➡SOUND EMISSION BY PEOPLE; 364] *Opposite:* whisper.

thunderbolt 1 *n* **thunderclap**, clap of thunder, thunder, crash of thunder, flash of lightning. [➡WINDY AND STORMY WEATHER; 1053] 2 *n* **shock**, turn-up for the book (*informal*), bolt from the blue, eye opener, kick in the face, surprise. [➡SUDDEN EVENT; 52]

thunderclap 1 *n* **thunderbolt**, crash of thunder, clap of thunder, thunder, flash of lightning. [➡WINDY AND STORMY WEATHER; 1053] 2 *n* **shock**, thunderbolt, turn-up for the book (*informal*), bolt from the blue, eye opener, kick in the face, surprise. [➡SUDDEN EVENT; 52]

thundercloud *type of* **cloud**. [➡CLOUDY AND RAINY WEATHER; 1052]

thunderhead (*US*) *type of* **cloud**. [➡CLOUDY AND RAINY WEATHER; 1052]

thundering (*dated informal*) 1 *adj* **great**, impressive, large, extreme, big, enormous. [➡LARGE; 1192] 2 *adv* **very**, extremely, enormously, hugely, inordinately, impressively, exceptionally. [➡TO A GREAT EXTENT; 130]

thunderous *adj* **deafening**, loud, roaring, booming, crashing, rolling. [➡LOUD OR UNPLEASANT SOUNDS; 1265]

thunderstorm *n* **storm**, downpour, deluge, rainstorm, cloudburst, tempest (*literary*). [➡WINDY AND STORMY WEATHER; 1053]

thunderstruck *adj* **incredulous**, amazed, taken aback, flabbergasted (*informal*), stunned, shocked, astonished, astounded, bowled over, staggered, dumbfounded, gobsmacked (*slang*). [➡SURPRISE, SHOCK, AND AMAZEMENT; 546]

thundery *adj* [➡WINDY AND STORMY WEATHER; 1053]

thus (*formal*) 1 *adv* **therefore**, consequently (*formal*), as a result, so, accordingly, hence (*formal*), in consequence (*formal*), as a consequence. [➡RESULTS AND OUTCOMES; 83] **2** *adv* **like this**, in this way, in this manner, as follows, like so, in this fashion, along these lines. [➡WAYS OF DOING THINGS; 295]

thus far *adv* **up till now**, up to now, yet, so far, hitherto (*formal*), to date, up until now. [➡PAST; 84]

thwack **1** *n* **smack**, clap, knock, rap, whack, sock (*informal*), wallop (*informal*). [➡PHYSICAL ATTACK AND PUNISHMENT; 416] **2** *v* **hit**, strike, whack, wallop (*informal*), smack, slap. [➡PHYSICAL ATTACK AND PUNISHMENT; 416] **3** *type of* **impact sound.** [➡IMPACT SOUNDS; 1259]

thwart *v* **frustrate**, spoil, prevent, foil, ruin, put paid to (*informal*), put a stop to, stop, impede, hinder, obstruct. [➡MAKE IMPOSSIBLE; 277]

thylacine *type of* **marsupial.** [➡MARSUPIAL; 992]

thyme *type of* **herb.** [➡HERBS AND SPICES; 1174]

tiara *type of* **jewellery.** [➡JEWELLERY; 866]

tibia *type of* **bone.** [➡THE BONES AND JOINTS; 720]

tic *n* **twitch**, spasm, convulsion, fit, paroxysm. [➡PHYSICAL REACTIONS; 317]

tick **1** *n* (*informal*) **moment**, second, minute, instant, jiffy (*informal*), trice, flash. [➡SHORT PERIOD OF TIME; 93] **2** *type of* **impact sound.** [➡IMPACT SOUNDS; 1259] **3** *type of* **parasitic insect.** [➡PARASITES; 1017]

ticked off (*US informal*) *adj* [➡IRRITATION AND ANGER; 542]

ticket **1** *n* **permit**, travel document, voucher, receipt, coupon. [➡OFFICIAL DOCUMENTS; 587] **2** *n* **label**, tag, tab, marker, sticker, docket. [➡NAME AND DESCRIBE; 666]

ticking *type of* **fabric from plants.** [➡FABRICS; 1131]

ticking-off (*informal*) *n* **telling-off** (*informal*), reprimand, rebuke, scolding, talking-to (*informal*), dressing-down, carpeting (*informal*). [➡CRITICISMS AND ANGRY OUTBURSTS; 50] *Opposite:* commendation.

tickle **1** *v* **prickle**, irritate, scratch, itch. [➡PAIN AND OTHER PHYSICAL SENSATIONS; 734] **2** *v* **amuse**, entertain, delight, please, make somebody laugh. [➡PLEASE AND AMUSE; 573]

tickled *adj* [➡PLEASURE, EXCITEMENT, AND ELATION; 535]

tickled pink (*informal*) *adj* **delighted**, thrilled, overjoyed, over the moon, pleased, thrilled to bits (*informal*), thrilled to pieces (*US informal*). [➡PLEASURE, EXCITEMENT, AND ELATION; 535] *Opposite:* horrified.

tickle pink *v* [➡PLEASE AND AMUSE; 573]

tickler **1** *n* (*informal*) **puzzle**, riddle, problem, enigma, poser, conundrum. [➡PROBLEM; 257] **2** *n* (*US*) **reminder**, prompt, follow-up, chaser. [➡MEMORY; 746]

ticklish *adj* **tricky**, delicate, thorny, awkward, problematic, difficult, hard, sensitive. [➡DIFFICULTY AND COMPLEXITY; 243] *Opposite:* straightforward.

tickly *adj* **prickly**, itchy, irritating, scratchy. [➡PHYSICAL TEXTURE; 1221]

tick off **1** *v* (*informal*) **tell off** (*informal*), rebuke, scold, give a talking-to (*informal*), reprimand, reprove, haul over the coals, take to task. [➡ACCUSE, BLAME, AND CRITICIZE; 642] **2** *v* (*US informal*) **annoy**, irritate, bug (*informal*), bother, get on your nerves. [➡ANGER AND ANNOY; 570]

ticktock *type of* **impact sound.** [➡IMPACT SOUNDS; 1259]

tidal *adj* [➡THE SEAS, OCEANS, AND SHORES; 1041]

tidal wave **1** *n* **tsunami**, bore, eagre. [➡THE SEAS, OCEANS, AND SHORES; 1041] **2** *n* **surge**, wave, swell, deluge. [➡SUDDEN EVENT; 52]

tiddler (*informal*) *n* [➡CHILD OR YOUTH; 945]

tiddly (*informal*) *adj* **teeny** (*informal*), weeny (*informal*), minute, titchy (*informal*), teeny-weeny (*informal*), teensy (*informal*), teensy-weensy (*informal*), small. *Opposite:* ginormous. (*informal*). [➡SMALL; 1194]

tiddlywink *type of* **game piece.** [➡GAMES PIECES; 878]

tide *n* **current**, flow, surge, wave, drift, stream. [➡THE SEAS, OCEANS, AND SHORES; 1041]

tidily *adv* **neatly**, in an orderly way, methodically, well-orderedly, meticulously, trimly, precisely. [➡ORDER AND ORGANISATION; 207] *Opposite:* untidily.

tidiness *n* **neatness**, trimness, orderliness, well-orderedness, order, regulation, organization, arrangement. [➡ORDER AND ORGANISATION; 207]

tidings (*literary*) *n* **news**, notification, intelligence, information, word, reports, communication, lowdown (*informal*). [➡BASIC DETAILS; 689]

tidy **1** *adj* **neat**, orderly, shipshape, in order, organized, spick and span, uncluttered. [➡ORDER AND ORGANISATION; 207] *Opposite:* untidy. **2** *adj* **smart**, immaculate, well-groomed, well-turned-out, dapper, spruce, trim, neat. [➡WELL GROOMED; 483] *Opposite:* untidy. **3** *adj* **large**, fair, considerable, sizable, reasonable, ample. [➡LARGE; 1192] *Opposite:* small. **4** *v* **neaten**, tidy up, clear up, straighten, arrange, organize. [➡ARRANGE AND CREATE ORDER; 358]

tidy sum (*informal*) *n* [➡LARGE AMOUNT OF MONEY; 141]

tidy up *v* **tidy**, clear up, neaten, straighten, arrange, organize, sort out, make spick and span, spruce up. *Opposite:* mess up. (*informal*). [➡ARRANGE AND CREATE ORDER; 358]

tie **1** *v* **bind**, fasten, secure, attach, lash, knot, strap, fix, join, bring together. [➡FASTEN, LINK, AND JOIN; 409] *Opposite:* untie. **2** *v* **be equal**, draw, be neck and neck (*informal*), finish equal, finish even. [➡EQUALITY; 155] **3** *n* **bond**, link, connection, relation, join. [➡CONNECTION; 144] **4** *n* **draw**, dead heat, equal finish, stalemate. [➡DIFFICULT SITUATIONS; 72] **5** *type of* **accessory.** [➡HABERDASHERY, MILLINERY, AND LINGERIE; 867]

tie-break *n* [➡SPORTS TERMS; 877]

tiebreaker *n* **deciding game**, tie-break, decider. [➡SPORTS TERMS; 877]

tie clasp (*US*) *type of* **jewellery.** [➡JEWELLERY; 866]

tie clip *type of* **jewellery.** [➡JEWELLERY; 866]

tied up *adj* **unavailable**, engaged, occupied, busy, otherwise engaged. [➡ABSENT AND UNAVAILABLE; 7] *Opposite:* available.

tie in *v* **connect**, associate, relate, link, join, coordinate, affiliate. [➡CREATING CONNECTIONS; 145] *Opposite:* disconnect.

tie-in *n* **link**, relationship, connection, linkup, association, affiliation, tie-up. [➡CONNECTION; 144]

tie in knots *v* **confuse**, muddle, mix up, baffle, bewilder, perplex, puzzle. [➡CONFUSE AND BEWILDER; 572]

tiepin *type of* **jewellery**. [➡JEWELLERY; 866]

tier *n* **row**, level, layer, stage, rank, step, storey. [➡STAIRS AND STOREYS; 1101]

tie tack (*US*) *type of* **jewellery**. [➡JEWELLERY; 866]

tie the knot (*informal*) *v* **get married**, marry, wed, get hitched (*informal*), walk down the aisle, get spliced (*slang*). [➡ESTABLISHING RELATIONSHIPS WITH OTHERS; 974]

tie-up **1** *n* **link**, connection, linkup, association, relationship, affiliation, tie-in. [➡CONNECTION; 144] **2** *n* (*US*) **delay**, holdup, stoppage, obstruction, hitch, snafu (*informal*). [➡PROBLEM; 257]

tie up **1** *v* **lash**, truss, fasten, lace, tie, bind, fix together, join. [➡FASTEN, LINK, AND JOIN; 409] **2** *v* **complete**, clinch, finalize, resolve, end, wrap up (*informal*), finish off. [➡COMPLETE AN ACTION; 264]

tiff *n* **quarrel**, argument, row, falling-out, squabble, disagreement, spat, contretemps (*formal*), dispute. [➡ARGUMENT; 47]

tiger *type of* **cat**. [➡FELINE; 983]

tiger moth *type of* **moth**. [➡MOTHS AND BUTTERFLIES; 1015]

tiger swallowtail *type of* **butterfly**. [➡MOTHS AND BUTTERFLIES; 1015]

tight **1** *adj* (*slang*) [➡UNDER THE INFLUENCE OF DRUGS OR ALCOHOL; 742] **2** *adj* **taut**, stretched, tense, firm, stiff, rigid, constricted. [➡RIGID AND HARD; 1210] *Opposite:* loose. **3** *adj* **close-fitting**, body-hugging, skintight, snug, constricted, fitted. [➡DESCRIBING CLOTHES; 869] *Opposite:* baggy. **4** *adj* **firm**, fixed, strong, unyielding, tough. [➡STRENGTH; 202] *Opposite:* weak. **5** *adj* **strict**, stringent, harsh, firm, tough, severe, stern. [➡ORDER AND ORGANISATION; 207] *Opposite:* lax. **6** *adj* **stingy** (*informal*), mean, miserly, tightfisted, parsimonious, niggardly. [➡FINANCIALLY MEAN AND GRASPING; 520] *Opposite:* generous. **7** *adj* **difficult**, problematic, awkward, tricky, tough, troublesome, sticky (*informal*). [➡DIFFICULTY AND COMPLEXITY; 243] *Opposite:* easy.

tight corner *n* [➡DIFFICULT SITUATIONS; 72]

tighten *v* **make tighter**, tauten, constrict, stiffen, squeeze, tighten up, tense. [➡CONTACT: EXERT PRESSURE; 415] *Opposite:* loosen.

tighten your belt *v* **cut back**, economize, retrench, draw in your horns, pull in your horns (*US*). [➡FOREGO AND DENY ONESELF; 450]

tightfisted *adj* **mean**, stingy (*informal*), tight, grasping, miserly, parsimonious, niggardly. [➡FINANCIALLY MEAN AND GRASPING; 520] *Opposite:* generous.

tightfistedness *n* **scrimping**, meanness, stinginess, tightness, miserliness, parsimony, niggardliness. [➡FINANCIALLY MEAN AND GRASPING; 520] *Opposite:* generosity.

tight-fitting *adj* **tight**, close-fitting, snug, figure-hugging, skintight, fitted. [➡DESCRIBING CLOTHES; 869] *Opposite:* baggy.

tightknit *adj* **closely connected**, integrated, united, interwoven, intertwined. [➡CLOSENESS; 160]

tight-lipped *adj* **silent**, uncommunicative, reticent, withdrawn, taciturn, reserved, quiet, mute, unforthcoming. *Opposite:* loquacious. (*formal*). [➡RETICENT AND UNFORTHCOMING; 632]

tightly **1** *adv* **firmly**, strongly, forcefully, closely, securely. [➡STRENGTH; 202] *Opposite:* loosely. **2** *adv* **closely**, compactly, snugly, cosily. [➡CLOSENESS; 160] *Opposite:* loosely.

tightness *n* **tension**, tautness, stiffness, rigidity. [➡RIGID AND HARD; 1210] *Opposite:* looseness.

tights *type of* **lower body underwear**. [➡HABERDASHERY, MILLINERY, AND LINGERIE; 867]

tight situation *n* [➡DIFFICULT SITUATIONS; 72]

tight spot *n* **fix** (*informal*), tight corner, scrape (*informal*), difficult position, tricky situation, predicament, quandary. [➡DIFFICULT SITUATIONS; 72]

tigress *type of* **female animal**. [➡MALE OR FEMALE ANIMAL; 978]

tilapia *type of* **freshwater fish**. [➡FRESHWATER FISH; 1010]

tilde *type of* **diacritic**. [➡ASPECTS OF LANGUAGE; 683]

tile *n* [➡BUILDING MATERIALS; 1076]

till **1** *n* **cash register**, cash box, box, drawer, tray. [➡CONTAINERS, RECEPTACLES, AND PACKAGING; 1244] **2** *v* **plough**, dig, cultivate, turn over, rake, hoe, prepare. [➡USE TOOLS AND MACHINERY; 469]

tiller *part of* **ship or boat**. [➡PARTS OF A SHIP OR BOAT; 1150]

tilt **1** *v* **tip**, slope, slant, lean, list, angle, roll, incline, bend. [➡TAKE UP A NEW POSITION; 313] *Opposite:* straighten up. **2** *n* **slope**, slant, angle, gradient, incline, list. [➡ORIENTATION AND ALIGNMENT; 1222]

tilt back *v* [➡TAKE UP A NEW POSITION; 313]

tilted *adj* **slanted**, slanting, sloping, sloped, lopsided, skewed, skewwhiff (*informal*), crooked, angled, leaning, listing. [➡ORIENTATION AND ALIGNMENT; 1222] *Opposite:* flat.

tilting *adj* [➡ORIENTATION AND ALIGNMENT; 1222]

timber *n* **wood**, logs, planks, kindling, lumber (*US*). [➡BUILDING MATERIALS; 1076]

timbre *n* **tone**, pitch, resonance, sound, quality, tenor, lowness, highness. [➡QUALITY OF SOUNDS; 1263]

time **1** *n* **period**, while, spell, stretch, stint, interval, phase, stage. [➡PERIOD OF TIME; 90] **2** *n* **occasion**, instance, moment, point, instant, minute, hour, point in time, moment in time. [➡SHORT PERIOD OF TIME; 93] **3** *n* **era**, age, epoch, period, season, generation. [➡EPOCHS AND ERAS; 89] **4** *n* **tempo**, measure, rhythm, beat, speed, pace. [➡MUSICAL TERMS; 912] **5** *v* **count**, measure, clock, calculate, record. [➡ASSESS QUANTITY; 758] **6** *v* **schedule**, programme, timetable, plan, arrange, organize, book, set up. [➡CAUSE TO HAPPEN; 31]

time

◆ *types of time period*
calendar month, fortnight, leap year, lunar month, month, quarter, semester, trimester, week, weekend, year

time after time *adv* **again and again**, time and again, time and time again, over and over again, over and over, repeatedly. [➡FREQUENT AND OFTEN; 107] *Opposite:* rarely.

time ahead *n* [➡FUTURE; 86]

time and again *adv* **time after time**, again and again, time and time again, over and over again, over and over, repeatedly. [➡AGAIN; 109] *Opposite:* rarely.

time and time again *adv* [➡AGAIN; 109]

time bomb 1 *n* **tinderbox**, volcano, accident waiting to happen, flashpoint. [➡PROBLEM; 257] 2 *type of* **explosive weapon**. [➡EXPLOSIVES; 1154]

time-consuming *adj* **laborious**, slow, inefficient, long, onerous, arduous, timewasting. [➡BORING AND UNINTERESTING; 235] *Opposite:* timesaving.

time-honoured *adj* **traditional**, customary, habitual, age-old, respected, long-standing, historic, ancient, usual, conventional. [➡OLD, OLD-FASHIONED; 168] *Opposite:* recent.

time immemorial *n* [➡PERMANENCE: WITHOUT END; 94]

time lag *n* **lapse**, interlude, gap, interval, pause, delay. [➡PAUSES AND PHASES; 56]

timeless *adj* **eternal**, ageless, enduring, undying, everlasting, unending, abiding, endless, changeless, unchanging, immutable. [➡PERMANENCE: WITHOUT END; 94] *Opposite:* ephemeral.

timelessness *n* **agelessness**, endurance, endlessness, changelessness, immutability, constancy, invariability, persistence. [➡PERMANENCE: WITHOUT END; 94] *Opposite:* ephemeralness.

timely *adj* **opportune**, well-timed, appropriate, apt, judicious, sensible, suitable. [➡APPROPRIATE, SUITABLE, ADVISABLE; 185] *Opposite:* untimely.

time off *n* **leisure**, free time, spare time, leave, holiday, vacation, time out (*US*). [➡PERIOD OF REST; 91]

time out (*US*) *n* **time off**, leave, breathing space, respite, break, rest. [➡PERIOD OF REST; 91]

timepiece *n* **chronometer**, timer, clock. [➡CLOCKS AND TIMERS; 1125]

timer *n* [➡CLOCKS AND TIMERS; 1125]

timesaving *adj* **quick**, streamlined, efficient, effective, improved, better. [➡ECONOMICAL AND RESOURCEFUL; 208] *Opposite:* time-consuming.

timescale *n* **timetable**, schedule, programme, time, period, span. [➡PERIOD OF TIME; 90]

timeserver *n* **opportunist**, weathercock, waverer, equivocator, vacillator, don't know (*informal*), turncoat. [➡LAZY OR UNSUCCESSFUL PEOPLE; 948] *Opposite:* stalwart.

times gone by *n* [➡PAST; 84]

times of yore *n* [➡PAST; 84]

time span *n* **duration**, period, extent, length, span, stretch. [➡PERIOD OF TIME; 90]

times past *n* [➡PAST; 84]

timetable 1 *n* **schedule**, agenda, plan, programme, calendar, diary, rota. [➡LISTS AND SCHEDULES; 588] 2 *v* **schedule**, arrange, plan, organize, programme, book, set up, time. [➡PREPARE FOR ACTION; 290]

time to come *n* [➡FUTURE; 86]

timewaster *n* [➡LAZY OR UNSUCCESSFUL PEOPLE; 948]

time without end *n* [➡PERMANENCE: WITHOUT END; 94]

timeworn 1 *adj* **shabby**, tattered, threadbare, worn, well-worn, worn-out, tatty, frayed, used. [➡IN BAD REPAIR; 1233] *Opposite:* brand-new. 2 *adj* **hackneyed**, overworked, stale, trite, stock, cliché-ridden, unoriginal, clichéd, well-worn, corny, banal, old hat (*informal*). [➡REDUNDANT AND USELESS; 241] *Opposite:* original.

timid *adj* **nervous**, shy, fearful, timorous, diffident, coy, bashful, reticent, retiring, faint-hearted, cowardly, frightened, tentative, apprehensive, hesitant. [➡RETICENT AND UNFORTHCOMING; 632] *Opposite:* bold.

timidity *n* **nervousness**, shyness, fearfulness, timorousness, diffidence, coyness, bashfulness, reticence, faint-heartedness, cowardice, tentativeness, apprehension, apprehensiveness, hesitancy. [➡RETICENT AND UNFORTHCOMING; 632] *Opposite:* boldness.

timing *n* **judgment**, technique, skill, effectiveness, control, mastery. [➡SKILLS, TALENTS, AND ABILITIES; 527]

timorous *adj* **nervous**, fearful, timid, frightened, scared, afraid, shy, apprehensive, bashful, diffident, coy, retiring, reticent, cowardly, faint-hearted, hesitant. [➡RETICENT AND UNFORTHCOMING; 632] *Opposite:* brave.

timorousness *n* **nervousness**, fearfulness, timidity, shyness, fear, apprehensiveness, apprehension, bashfulness, diffidence, coyness, hesitancy, cowardice, faint-heartedness, reticence. [➡RETICENT AND UNFORTHCOMING; 632] *Opposite:* bravery.

timothy *type of* **grass**. [➡GRASS; 1031]

timpani *type of* **percussion instrument**. [➡MUSICAL INSTRUMENTS; 910]

timpanist *n* [➡MUSICIANS AND SINGERS; 908]

tin 1 *n* **can**, tin can, canister, container, cylinder. [➡CONTAINERS, RECEPTACLES, AND PACKAGING; 1244] 2 *n* **box**, container, caddy, biscuit tin, cake tin, baking tray, cookie tin (*US*), baking sheet (*US*). [➡CONTAINERS, RECEPTACLES, AND PACKAGING; 1244] 3 *type of* **metal**. [➡METALS; 1275]

tincture 1 *n* **solution**, essence, distillate, extract, distillation, mixture. [➡LIQUIDS; 1268] 2 *n* **tinge**, tint, hint, nuance, tone, cast, shade, colour, colouring, coloration. [➡ FEW, LITTLE, SMALL AMOUNT; 119]

tinder *n* **kindling**, firewood, brushwood, sticks, twigs. [➡ ENERGY SOURCES; 1161]

tinderbox *n* **flashpoint**, crucible, volcano, no-go area, accident waiting to happen, time bomb. [➡ PROBLEM; 257]

ting 1 *n type of* **ringing sound**. [➡ RINGING AND TOOTING SOUNDS; 1258] 2 *v* **ding**, ting-a-ling, ring, ping, tinkle, jingle, trill. [➡ EMIT RINGING AND TOOTING SOUNDS; 368] *Opposite:* thud.

ting-a-ling *v* [➡ EMIT RINGING AND TOOTING SOUNDS; 368]

tinge 1 *n* **hint**, touch, dash, drop, trace, bit, shade, suggestion, tint, nuance, element. [➡ FEW, LITTLE, SMALL AMOUNT; 119] 2 *v* **tint**, colour, stain, shade, mix, combine, mingle. [➡ CHANGE OF COLOUR; 392]

tingle 1 *v* **prickle**, sting, itch, tickle, prick, burn. [➡ PAIN AND OTHER PHYSICAL SENSATIONS; 734] 2 *n* **sting**, prickle, itch, tickle, prick, burn, pins and needles, irritation. [➡ PAIN AND OTHER PHYSICAL SENSATIONS; 734]

tingling *adj* **prickly**, itchy, scratchy, burning, stinging, tickling. [➡ PAIN AND OTHER PHYSICAL SENSATIONS; 734]

tininess *n* [➡ SMALL; 1194]

tinker *v* **fiddle**, tamper, interfere, mess around (*informal*), fool around, play, monkey around, toy, mend, repair, fix, put right. [➡ REPAIR AND MEND; 377]

tinkle 1 *v* **ring**, jingle, clink, chink, ding, ping, chime. [➡ EMIT RINGING AND TOOTING SOUNDS; 368] 2 *n* **jingle**, ring, clink, chink, ding, ping, chime. [➡ RINGING AND TOOTING SOUNDS; 1258] 3 *n* (*informal*) **call**, ring, buzz (*informal*), bell (*informal*), phone, phone call, telephone call. [➡ TELEPHONE COMMUNICATION; 48] 4 *type of* **ringing sound**. [➡ CONTINUOUS SOUNDS; 1257]

tinned *adj* [➡ STATE OF PREPARED FOOD; 1170]

tinny 1 *adj* **thin**, high, metallic, shrill, ringing, harsh, reedy. [➡ LOUD OR UNPLEASANT SOUNDS; 1265] *Opposite:* resonant. 2 *adj* **shoddy**, cheap, tacky (*informal*), worthless, inferior, poor. [➡ IN POOR TASTE; 230]

tin-opener *type of* **utensil**. [➡ TABLEWARE, CUTLERY, AND KITCHENWARE; 861]

tinsel 1 *n* **metallic thread**, glitter, streamer, spangle, decoration, chain, banner. [➡ ORNAMENTS AND DECORATIONS; 1247] 2 *n* **showiness**, glitz, flashiness, pretentiousness, glitter, dazzle, splendour, glamour, glitziness. [➡ IN POOR TASTE; 230]

tint 1 *n* **shade**, colour, hue, touch, trace, tone, tinge, hint, dash, drop. [➡ DESCRIBING COLOURS; 1225] 2 *n* **rinse**, dye, colourant, streak, highlight, lowlight. [➡ DYES AND COLOURANTS; 1269] 3 *v* **dye**, colour, shade, streak, rinse, highlight, lowlight. [➡ CHANGE OF COLOUR; 392]

tinted *adj* [➡ DESCRIBING COLOURS; 1225]

tiny *adj* **minute**, miniature, minuscule, small, little, petite, infinitesimal, teeny (*informal*), diminutive, microscopic, insignificant. [➡ SMALL; 1194] *Opposite:* enormous.

tip 1 *v* **tilt**, slope, slant, lean, list, angle, roll, incline, bend. [➡ TAKE UP A NEW POSITION; 313] *Opposite:* straighten. 2 *v* **knock over**, pour, empty, spill, knock, overturn, upturn, upend, upset, tip up, tip over, turn turtle, capsize. [➡ MOVE SOMETHING: INTO A NEW POSITION OR OVERTURN; 331] 3 *n* **slope**, slant, angle, gradient, incline, tilt, lean, list, roll, bend. [➡ ORIENTATION AND ALIGNMENT; 1222] 4 *n* **rubbish dump**, civic amenity point, landfill, garbage dump (*US*). [➡ URBAN OUTDOOR SPACES; 1071] 5 *n* (*informal*) **dump** (*informal*), hole (*informal*), hovel, pigsty, pigpen (*US*). [➡ UNDESIRABLE ACCOMMODATION; 856] 6 *n* **gratuity**, gift, reward, bonus, extra, bribe, backhander (*informal*). [➡ GIFTS; 439] 7 *n* **warning**, tip-off (*informal*), clue, pointer, prompt, hint, forewarning, nod. [➡ ADVICE; 690] 8 *n* **hint**, suggestion, idea, pointer. [➡ ADVICE; 690] 9 *v* **give**, slip, reward, pay, bribe. [➡ GIVE MONEY; 434]

tip-off (*informal*) *n* **warning**, clue, hint, pointer, prompt, tip, forewarning, nod. [➡ ADVICE; 690]

tip off *v* **warn**, inform, advise, forewarn, tip the wink (*informal*), tell. [➡ ADVISE AND WARN; 614]

tippet *type of* **headgear**. [➡ HABERDASHERY, MILLINERY, AND LINGERIE; 867]

tipple (*informal*) *n* [➡ DRINKS; 1186]

tipster *n* **adviser**, consultant, analyst, informant, informer, speculator. [➡ PEOPLE INVOLVED IN FINANCE; 804]

tipsy *adj* [➡ UNDER THE INFLUENCE OF DRUGS OR ALCOHOL; 742]

tip the wink (*informal*) *v* [➡ ADVISE AND WARN; 614]

tiptoe *v* **creep**, sneak, steal, skulk, glide, slink, tread. [➡ MOVE SLOWLY; 315] *Opposite:* stamp.

tiptop (*informal*) *adj* **first-rate**, excellent, superb, first-class, superlative, topnotch (*informal*), best. [➡ SUPERIORITY; 153] *Opposite:* dreadful.

tirade *n* **outburst**, invective (*formal*), rant, diatribe, harangue, lecture. [➡ CRITICISMS AND ANGRY OUTBURSTS; 50]

tire *v* **exhaust**, wear out, drain, fatigue, enervate, weary. [➡ USE UP AND WASTE; 475]

tired 1 *adj* **weary**, sleepy, drowsy, fatigued, exhausted, worn-out, drained, bushed (*informal*), all in, beat (*informal*), shattered, wiped out (*slang*), dog-tired (*informal*), done in (*informal*), whacked (*informal*), tired out, spent. [➡ TIRED, ASLEEP AND UNCONSCIOUS; 739] *Opposite:* energetic. 2 *adj* **bored**, weary, fed up (*informal*), sick, jaded, dissatisfied. [➡ SADNESS, DISTRESS, AND DESPAIR; 540] 3 *adj* **overused**, trite, hackneyed, clichéd, old, worn-out, jaded, stale, corny. [➡ BORING AND UNINTERESTING; 235] *Opposite:* fresh.

tiredly *adv* **wearily**, sleepily, drowsily, blearily, groggily, woozily. [➡ TIRED, ASLEEP AND UNCONSCIOUS; 739] *Opposite:* energetically.

tiredness *n* **weariness**, sleepiness, fatigue, drowsiness, exhaustion, grogginess, wooziness. [➡ TIRED, ASLEEP AND UNCONSCIOUS; 739] *Opposite:* energy.

tired out *adj* **exhausted**, shattered, worn-out, wiped out (*slang*), dog-tired (*informal*), fit to drop (*informal*), whacked (*informal*), beat (*informal*), bushed (*informal*), done in (*informal*), spent, weary, all in. [➡ TIRED, ASLEEP AND UNCONSCIOUS; 739] *Opposite:* energetic.

tireless *adj* **untiring**, diligent, determined, unstinting, assiduous, indefatigable, industrious, vigorous, unflagging. [➡ENERGY AND ENTHUSIASM; 497] *Opposite:* weary.

tirelessness *n* **diligence**, determination, assiduousness, indefatigability, industriousness, vigour. [➡ENERGY AND ENTHUSIASM; 497] *Opposite:* weariness.

tiresome *adj* **annoying**, irritating, tedious, wearisome, dull, boring, exasperating, irksome. [➡IRRITATING; 229]

tiring *adj* **exhausting**, strenuous, arduous, wearing, demanding, laborious. [➡PHYSICALLY UNPLEASANT; 227]

tisane *n* [➡DRINKS; 1186]

tissue 1 *n* **soft tissue**, fleshy tissue, flesh, matter, material, skin, muscle, nerve. [➡THE SKIN; 721] 2 *n* **web**, net, network, mass, series, chain. [➡FASTENERS, LINKS, AND NETWORKS; 1246]

tissue of lies *n* [➡DECEPTION AND LIES; 661]

tit *type of* **common bird**. [➡BIRD; 997]

titan *n* **giant**, superman, superwoman, genius. [➡PEOPLE WHO ARE APPROVED OF; 955] *Opposite:* nobody.

titanic *adj* **colossal**, monumental, immense, gigantic, massive, enormous, huge, giant. [➡LARGE; 1192] *Opposite:* insignificant.

titanium *type of* **metal**. [➡METALS; 1275]

titanosaur *type of* **dinosaur**. [➡DINOSAUR; 996]

titbit 1 *n* **morsel**, taste, bite, dainty, delicacy, goody, treat, bonne bouche. [➡MEALS AND PARTS OF MEALS; 1168] 2 *n* **gossip**, snippet, scrap, scandal, news, rumour. [➡GOSSIP; 679]

titch (*informal*) *n* **little person**, pip squeak (*informal*), shorty (*informal*), tiddler (*informal*). *Opposite:* bruiser. (*informal*). [➡CHILD OR YOUTH; 945]

titchy (*informal*) *adj* **tiny**, teeny (*informal*), weeny (*informal*), teeny-weeny (*informal*), teensy (*informal*), teensy-weensy (*informal*), tiddly (*informal*), minute, miniature. [➡SMALL; 1194] *Opposite:* massive.

tit for tat *n* **retaliation**, blow for blow, revenge, reprisal, vengeance, retribution, an eye for an eye, a tooth for a tooth, a taste of your own medicine, a game at which two can play. [➡VENGEANCE AND REVENGE; 686]

tit-for-tat *adj* [➡VENGEANCE AND REVENGE; 686]

tithe *n* **church tax**, tax, duty, contribution, portion, charity. [➡RELIGIONS AND RELIGIOUS PRACTICES; 778]

titian *type of* **orange**. [➡COLOURS; 1223]

titillate *v* [➡APPEAL TO AND AROUSE INTEREST; 576]

titillating *adj* [➡INTERESTING AND MEANINGFUL; 191]

titivate *v* **do up**, tart up (*informal*), dress up, adorn, decorate, beautify. [➡IMPROVE APPEARANCE; 380]

titivation *n* **adornment**, embellishment, beautification, prettification, enhancement, sprucing up, ornamentation, trimming, gilding. [➡IMPROVE APPEARANCE; 380]

title 1 *n* **name**, heading, label, designation. [➡NAME AND DESCRIBE; 666] 2 *n* **championship**, trophy, cup, award. [➡NON-AGGRESSIVE/SPORTING EVENT; 40] 3 *n* **ownership**, entitlement, deed, right, claim. [➡POSSESS; 445] 4 *v* **call**, name, label, designate, refer to, identify. [➡NAME AND DESCRIBE; 666]

titled *adj* **noble**, aristocratic, patrician, highborn (*literary*), blue-blooded, upper-class, well-bred. [➡CLASS STATUS; 889]

title deed *n* **title**, deed, document, proof of ownership, ownership, legal paper. [➡OFFICIAL DOCUMENTS; 587]

titleholder 1 *n* **champion**, winner, reigning champion, cupholder. [➡PEOPLE IN SPORTS AND LEISURE; 876] 2 *n* **owner**, proprietor, possessor, vendor, holder, landlord. [➡OWNERS; 447]

title page *n* **front page**, title, opening page, frontispiece. [➡PARTS OF BOOKS AND DOCUMENTS; 594]

titmouse *type of* **songbird**. [➡SONGBIRD; 1003]

titter *type of* **human sound**. [➡SOUNDS MADE BY PEOPLE; 1261]

tittle *n* [➡SMALL PIECE; 127]

tittle-tattle 1 *n* **gossip**, scandal, rumour, hearsay, chit-chat (*informal*), tale, word of mouth, idle talk, word, report, talk. [➡GOSSIP; 679] 2 *v* **gossip**, chatter, prattle, yak (*informal*), chinwag, blather (*informal*). [➡BETRAY CONFIDENCES AND GOSSIP; 619]

titular *adj* **nominal**, in name only, supposed, ostensible, so-called. [➡FALSE AND UNREAL; 174] *Opposite:* actual.

tizzy (*informal*) *n* **flap** (*informal*), lather (*informal*), state (*informal*), panic, dither. [➡INSECURITY AND LOSS OF COMPOSURE; 545]

T-junction *n* **junction**, intersection, fork, road junction. [➡BRIDGES, TUNNELS, CROSSINGS, AND JUNCTIONS; 1111]

TNT *type of* **explosive material**. [➡EXPLOSIVES; 1154]

toad *type of* **amphibian**. [➡AMPHIBIANS; 1008]

toadstool *type of* **fungus**. [➡MICROORGANISMS, FUNGI, AND ALGAE; 1023]

toady 1 *n* **flatterer**, sycophant, creep (*informal*), crawler (*informal*), groveller. [➡SUPERFICIAL OR INSINCERE PEOPLE; 951] 2 *v* **grovel**, fawn, creep (*informal*), crawl (*informal*), flatter, kowtow. [➡FLATTER AND FAWN; 622]

toadying 1 *n* **obsequiousness**, sycophancy, servility, flattery, fawning, grovelling, bowing and scraping, creeping (*informal*), crawling (*informal*). [➡INGRATIATING; 639] 2 *adj* **obsequious**, sycophantic, servile, flattering, fawning, smarmy, grovelling. [➡INGRATIATING; 639]

to all intents and purposes *adv* **practically**, in practice, virtually, pretty much (*informal*), as good as, pretty well (*informal*). [➡TO A CERTAIN EXTENT; 134]

to and fro *adv* **back and forth**, hither and yon, backwards and forwards, up and down, hither and thither, here and there. [➡DIRECTION OF MOTION; 346]

toast 1 *n* **toasted bread**, grilled bread, browned bread, heated bread, bread. [➡BREAD, FLOUR, AND BREAD PRODUCTS; 1178] 2 *n* **salute**, tribute, pledge, health. [➡GREETINGS, FAREWELLS, AND SALUTATIONS; 660] 3 *n* **darling**, favourite, delight, sweetheart. [➡PEOPLE WHO ARE APPROVED OF; 955] 4 *v* **grill**, brown, crisp, heat, cook, colour. [➡COOKING AND FOOD PREPARATION; 354] 5 *v* **warm**, warm up, heat, heat up, roast, bake, cook. [➡COOKING AND FOOD PREPARATION; 354] *Opposite:* freeze. **6** *v* **drink to**, pledge, salute, drink the health of. [➡PRAISE AND ENCOURAGE; 648]

toaster *type of* **appliance**. [➡HOUSEHOLD APPLIANCES; 1116]

toasty *adj* **warm**, snug, cosy, pleasant. [➡HOT WEATHER; 1050] *Opposite:* chilly.

to be brief *adv* [➡SUMMARIZING EXPRESSIONS; 623]

to be fair *adv* [➡EXPRESSIONS OF OPINION; 624]

to be frank *adv* [➡EXPRESSIONS OF OPINION; 624]

to be honest *adv* [➡EXPRESSIONS OF OPINION; 624]

to blame *adj* **responsible**, guilty, culpable, at fault, liable. [➡MORALLY BAD; 776] *Opposite:* innocent.

toboggan **1** *n* **sleigh**, sledge, bobsleigh, luge, sled (*US*), bobsled (*US*). [➡VEHICLES; 1144] **2** *v* **sleigh**, sledge, sled (*US*), luge. [➡TRAVEL: WAYS OF TRAVELLING; 321] **3** *v* **slip**, slide, hurtle, tumble. [➡GO DOWNWARDS; 308] **4** *type of* **winter sport**. [➡HOBBIES, GAMES, AND SPORTS; 875]

to boot *adv* [➡EXPRESSIONS INTRODUCING EXTRA INFORMATION; 137]

to cap it all *adv* **on top of everything else**, to make matters worse, to top it all off, in addition, additionally. [➡EXPRESSIONS INTRODUCING EXTRA INFORMATION; 137]

tocsin *n* **alarm**, warning, bell, siren, signal. [➡SIGNALLING; 1139]

to cut a long story short *adv* **in short**, in a word, in a nutshell, to put it briefly, in brief, to come to the point. [➡SUMMARIZING EXPRESSIONS; 623]

to date *adv* **up to the present time**, so far, up to now, as yet, up till now, thus far. [➡PAST; 84]

today *adv* **nowadays**, these days, currently, now, at the moment, at present. [➡PRESENT; 85]

toddle **1** *v* **totter**, patter, pad, waddle. [➡WALK UNSTEADILY; 316] **2** *v* (*informal*) **walk**, stroll, amble. [➡MOVE SLOWLY; 315]

toddler *n* **tot** (*informal*), child, kid (*informal*), baby. [➡CHILD OR YOUTH; 945]

to die for *adj* [➡POPULAR AND WANTED; 221]

to-do (*informal*) *n* **fuss**, commotion, bother, scene, kerfuffle (*informal*). [➡CHAOS AND UPROAR; 51]

toe *part of* **leg or foot**. [➡LEG AND FOOT; 695]

toe-curling (*informal*) *adj* [➡EMOTIONALLY UNPLEASANT AND UPSETTING; 228]

toehold *n* **start**, advantage, jumping-off point, beginning, entry, way in. [➡BEGINNING; 53]

toenail *part of* **leg or foot**. [➡LEG AND FOOT; 695]

toe the line *v* [➡OBEY AND ABIDE BY; 302]

to excess *adv* **in large amounts**, excessively, too much, profligately, lavishly, wastefully, extravagantly. [➡TOO MUCH; 118] *Opposite:* in moderation.

toff (*informal*) *n* **swell** (*dated informal*), dandy (*dated*), smart person, posh person, rich person, upper-class person. [➡RICH PEOPLE; 895]

toffee *type of* **confectionery**. [➡CONFECTIONERY; 1181]

toffee apple *type of* **confectionery on a stick**. [➡CONFECTIONERY; 1181]

toffee-nosed (*informal*) *adj* [➡AFFECTATION, SELF-SATISFACTION, AND SNOBBISHNESS; 508]

together **1** *adv* **jointly**, as one, mutually, in concert, collectively. [➡ACTING WITH OTHERS; 286] *Opposite:* alone. **2** *adv* **simultaneously**, at once, at the same time, concurrently, all together, in sync (*informal*). [➡CONCURRENT AND CONTEMPORANEOUS; 165] *Opposite:* separately. **3** *adj* (*informal*) **composed**, calm, collected, organized, cool, unruffled, self-possessed, laid-back (*informal*). [➡CALMNESS, CONFIDENCE, AND COMPOSURE; 537] *Opposite:* flustered.

togetherness *n* **closeness**, intimacy, devotedness, friendship, inseparability, inseparableness, attachment. [➡RELATIONSHIP TO ANOTHER; 973] *Opposite:* estrangement.

together with *prep* **as well as**, plus (*informal*), accompanied by, with, alongside, in addition to, beside. [➡ALSO; 136]

toggle **1** *n* **fastener**, peg, button, buckle, clasp, catch, fastening, closure. [➡FASTENERS, LINKS, AND NETWORKS; 1246] **2** *n* **switch**, key, command, button, lever. [➡PARTS OF MACHINES AND TOOLS; 1117] **3** *v* **change**, change over, switch, move, transfer, move on, swap (*informal*). [➡COMPUTERS AND COMPUTING; 1126]

togs (*informal*) *n* **clothes**, rig out (*informal*), outfit, dress, clothing, getup (*informal*), gear (*informal*), kit, attire (*formal*). [➡CLOTHES AND ACCESSORIES; 864]

to hand *adv* [➡PRESENT AND AVAILABLE; 11]

toil **1** *n* **work**, labour, drudgery, slog, sweat (*informal*), hard work, donkeywork (*informal*), grind (*informal*). [➡HARD WORK OR EFFORT; 299] *Opposite:* relaxation. **2** *v* **labour**, strive, work, slog, slave, knuckle down (*informal*), beaver (*informal*), plug away (*informal*), keep your head down, sweat (*informal*). [➡HARD WORK OR EFFORT; 299] *Opposite:* laze around.

See Compare and Contrast at **work**.

toiler *n* [➡WORKER; 836]

toilet **1** *n* **lavatory**, chamber pot, urinal, latrine, privy (*informal*), commode. [➡FITTINGS; 859] **2** *n* (*formal*) **toilette** (*literary*), washing, dressing, grooming, bathing, ablutions (*formal or humorous*), getting dressed, preparations, getting ready. [➡PERSONAL HYGIENE; 492] **3** *n* **WC**, ladies, gents, lavatory, powder room, water closet, bathroom, public convenience, restroom (*US*), washroom (*US*), john (*US informal*). [➡TYPES OF ROOM; 1096]

toiletry *n* **soap**, shampoo, shaving cream, toothpaste, deodorant, beauty product, skincare product, cosmetic product. [➡PERSONAL HYGIENE; 492]

toilette (*literary*) *n* **toilet** (*formal*), dressing, grooming, bathing, ablutions (*formal or humorous*), getting dressed, preparations, getting ready, washing. [➡PERSONAL HYGIENE; 492]

toilet water *n* **cologne**, eau de cologne, eau de toilette, scent, aftershave, perfume. [➡PERSONAL HYGIENE; 492]

toilsome *adj* [➡EMOTIONALLY UNPLEASANT AND UPSETTING; 228]

to-ing and fro-ing *n* [➡FIDGET AND FROLIC; 312]

token 1 *n* **mark**, demonstration, sign, symbol, indication, gesture, proof. [➡REPRESENTATIONS AND GENERAL EXAMPLES; 65] 2 *n* **voucher**, coupon, slip, coin. [➡RECEIPTS AND INVOICES; 592] 3 *n* **keepsake**, remembrance, souvenir, reminder, memento. [➡ORNAMENTS AND DECORATIONS; 1247] 4 *adj* **symbolic**, nominal, perfunctory, empty. [➡REPRESENTATIVE; 66]

tolerable 1 *adj* **bearable**, acceptable, supportable (*literary*), endurable. [➡ACCEPTABLE AND PASSABLE; 220] *Opposite:* unbearable. 2 *adj* **reasonable**, average, okay (*informal*), passable, fair, adequate, all right, satisfactory, not bad, pretty good. [➡ACCEPTABLE AND PASSABLE; 220] *Opposite:* intolerable.

tolerance *n* **broad-mindedness**, acceptance, open-mindedness, lenience, forbearance (*formal*), charity, patience. [➡POSITIVE INTELLECTUAL CHARACTERISTICS; 525] *Opposite:* intolerance.

tolerant *adj* **accepting**, easygoing, lenient, broad-minded, open-minded, liberal, forbearing (*formal*), understanding, charitable. [➡POSITIVE INTELLECTUAL CHARACTERISTICS; 525] *Opposite:* intolerant.

tolerate *v* **stand**, bear, abide, put up with, endure, accept, stomach, stand for, allow. [➡TOLERATE AND ENDURE; 767] *Opposite:* forbid.

toleration *n* **allowance**, acceptance, open-mindedness, broad-mindedness, liberality, understanding, consideration. [➡POSITIVE INTELLECTUAL CHARACTERISTICS; 525] *Opposite:* prejudice.

toll 1 *n* **fee**, tax, levy, payment, duty, excise, charge. [➡EXPENDITURE; 424] 2 *v* **ring**, peal, ding, ding-dong. [➡EMIT RINGING AND TOOTING SOUNDS; 368] 3 *n* **peal**, ring, ding-dong, clang, ding-a-ling. [➡RINGING AND TOOTING SOUNDS; 1258]

tollbooth *n* **barrier**, gate, kiosk, booth, ticket office. [➡DOORS AND ACCESS POINTS; 1100]

toll-free (*US*) *adj* **free**, complimentary, gratis, cost-free, costless. [➡GIFTS; 439]

tollgate *n* **barrier**, gate, entrance, exit. [➡DOORS AND ACCESS POINTS; 1100]

toll road *type of* **major road**. [➡ROADS; 1105]

tom *type of* **male animal**. [➡MALE OR FEMALE ANIMAL; 978]

tomahawk *type of* **sword or knife**. [➡SWORDS AND KNIVES; 1156]

tomato *type of* **salad vegetable**. [➡FRUIT AND VEGETABLES; 1175]

tomb *n* **burial chamber**, catacomb, ossuary (*formal*), grave, burial place, crypt, vault, last resting place, sepulchre. [➡BURIAL PLACES AND ACCESSORIES; 930]

tombola *n* **lottery**, draw, raffle, game of chance. [➡GAMBLE AND TAKE RISKS; 467]

tomboyish *adj* **boyish**, unladylike, mannish, boisterous, unruly. [➡GENDER IDENTITY AND SEXUALITY; 932]

tombstone *n* **headstone**, gravestone, monument. [➡MONUMENTS; 1091]

tomcat *type of* **male animal**. [➡MALE OR FEMALE ANIMAL; 978]

tome *n* **book**, volume, digest, work. [➡BOOKS AND BOOKLETS; 591]

tomfoolery (*informal*) *n* **silliness**, horseplay, mischief, clowning, monkey business (*informal*), larking around, fooling around, playing around, joking, high jinks (*informal*), shenanigans (*informal*), pranks, monkeyshines (*US*). [➡JOKES AND TEASING; 675] *Opposite:* sensibleness.

Tommy gun (*informal*) *type of* **gun**. [➡WEAPONS FOR SHOOTING; 1155]

tom-tom *type of* **percussion instrument**. [➡MUSICAL INSTRUMENTS; 910]

to my amazement *adv* [➡EXPRESSIONS OF SURPRISE; 547]

to my mind *adv* [➡EXPRESSIONS OF OPINION; 624]

to my surprise *adv* [➡EXPRESSIONS OF SURPRISE; 547]

ton (*informal*) *n* **mass**, mountain, stack (*informal*), lot, heap (*informal*), ocean. [➡MANY, MUCH, LARGE AMOUNT; 117]

tonality *n* **tone**, timbre, pitch, sound, sound quality. [➡QUALITY OF SOUNDS; 1263]

tone 1 *n* **sound**, pitch, quality, timbre. [➡QUALITY OF SOUNDS; 1263] 2 *n* **quality**, manner, character, attitude, tendency, nature, air. [➡APPEARANCE AND ATMOSPHERE; 1236] 3 *n* **character**, atmosphere, feel, ambience. [➡APPEARANCE AND ATMOSPHERE; 1236] 4 *n* **colour**, hue, tint, tinge, shade. [➡DESCRIBING COLOURS; 1225]

tone arm *part of* **audio equipment**. [➡AUDIO EQUIPMENT; 1138]

tone down *v* **dilute**, moderate, soften, restrain, modulate, diminish, weaken, reduce. [➡CHANGE OF INTENSITY: LESS; 396] *Opposite:* intensify.

toneless *adj* **colourless**, expressionless, monotonous, neutral, monochrome, dull. [➡UNINTERESTED AND DETACHED; 630] *Opposite:* vibrant.

toner 1 *n* **cleanser**, cleansing milk, skin preparation, astringent, cosmetic. [➡PERSONAL HYGIENE; 492] 2 *n* **ink**, liquid ink, powdered ink. [➡PRINTING; 601]

tone up *v* **firm up**, strengthen, get in shape, exercise. [➡IMPROVE APPEARANCE; 380]

tongs *type of* **general tool**. [➡HAND TOOLS; 1118]

tongue 1 *n* **language**, patois, dialect, speech, idiom. [➡THE SPOKEN WORD; 672] 2 *part of* **mouth**. [➡THE MOUTH; 703]

> *See Compare and Contrast at* **language**.

tongue-in-cheek *adj* **lighthearted**, ironic, insincere, flippant, whimsical, joking, funny, sardonic, humorous. [➡MOCKING AND DISMISSIVE; 637] *Opposite:* serious.

tongue-lashing *n* [➡CRITICISMS AND ANGRY OUTBURSTS; 50]

tongue-tied *adj* **speechless**, shy, awkward, silent, inarticulate, embarrassed, timid. [➡RETICENT AND UNFORTHCOMING; 632] *Opposite:* talkative.

tongue twister *n* [➡FIGURES OF SPEECH; 674]

tonic *n* **boost**, fillip, stimulant, pick-me-up (*informal*), shot in the arm, livener, energizer, refresher. [➡TREAT; 211]

tonnage *n* **weight**, heaviness, capacity, size. [➡WEIGHT: HEAVY; 1204]

tons 1 *adv* **a lot**, a great deal, loads (*informal*), heaps (*informal*), lots. [➡MANY, MUCH, LARGE AMOUNT; 117] 2 *n* (*informal*) **masses** (*informal*), lots, oodles (*informal*), plenty, loads (*informal*), piles (*informal*). [➡MANY, MUCH, LARGE AMOUNT; 117]

tonsils *part of* **mouth**. [➡THE MOUTH; 703]

tonsured *adj* [➡BALDNESS AND BALDING; 488]

tony (*US informal*) *adj* **elegant**, posh (*informal*), expensive, stylish, fashionable, well-heeled (*informal*). [➡EXPENSIVE AND LUXURIOUS; 219]

too 1 *adv* **also**, as well, in addition, besides, moreover, else, to boot. [➡ALSO; 136] 2 *adv* **excessively**, overly, extremely, exceedingly, overmuch. [➡TOO MUCH; 118] *Opposite:* insufficiently.

too few *adj* [➡TOO FEW, TOO LITTLE; 120]

tool *n* **instrument**, implement, device, means, utensil, apparatus, contrivance, gizmo (*informal*). [➡DEVICES; 1114]

tool

◆ *types of carpentry tool*
awl, bradawl, drill, hammer, jigsaw, mallet, plane, sander, saw, vice

◆ *types of medical instrument*
forceps, lancet, probe, scalpel, speculum, stethoscope, syringe

◆ *types of general tool*
bellows, blowtorch, crowbar, file, grease gun, jack, jemmy, lathe, machine tool, pincers, pliers, plumb line, plunger, poker, pump, punch, rasp, screwdriver, socket spanner, socket wrench, soldering iron, spade, spanner, tongs, trowel, wrench (*US*)

◆ *types of cosmetic tool*
comb, emery board, hairbrush, nail clippers, nail file, nail scissors, nailbrush, razor, shaving brush, tweezers

too little *adj* [➡TOO FEW, TOO LITTLE; 120]

too much *adj* [➡MORE AND EXCESS; 122]

toot *type of* **continuous sound**. [➡RINGING AND TOOTING SOUNDS; 1258]

tooth 1 *n* **fang**, tusk, chopper (*slang*). [➡THE MOUTH; 703] 2 *n* **indentation**, projection, tine, cog, prong. [➡PARTS OF MACHINES AND TOOLS; 1117]

tooth

◆ *types of tooth*
baby tooth, bucktooth (*informal*), canine, chopper, cuspid, denture, eyetooth, fang, incisor, milk tooth, molar, premolar, wisdom tooth

toothless *adj* **powerless**, useless, impotent, ineffective, ineffectual, incapable. [➡WEAKNESS; 242] *Opposite:* effective.

toothpaste *n* [➡PERSONAL HYGIENE; 492]

toothsome *adj* **delicious**, palatable, tasty, appetizing, mouthwatering, scrumptious (*informal*). [➡TASTE; 704] *Opposite:* unappetizing.

tootle (*informal*) 1 *v* **drive slowly**, go slowly, pootle, meander, wend your way, crawl, creep. [➡MOVE SLOWLY; 315] *Opposite:* dash. 2 *v* **hoot**, toot, sound, honk, beep, sound the horn. [➡EMIT RINGING AND TOOTING SOUNDS; 368] 3 *n* **drive**, pootle, meander, crawl. [➡TRAVEL: JOURNEYS AND TRIPS; 319] *Opposite:* dash. 4 *n* **toot**, honk, beep, hoot. [➡RINGING AND TOOTING SOUNDS; 1258]

top 1 *n* **pinnacle**, summit, peak, apex, crown, crest, acme, zenith. [➡EXTREMITIES OF PHYSICAL OBJECTS; 1249] *Opposite:* bottom. 2 *n* **cork**, lid, cap, cover, stopper. [➡COVERS AND COATINGS; 1245] 3 *adj* **highest**, topmost, maximum, uppermost. [➡RELATIVE LOCATION; 162] *Opposite:* bottom. 4 *adj* **best**, first, chief, principal, important, leading, eminent. [➡SUPERIORITY; 153] 5 *v* **outdo**, surpass, better, improve on, cap, crown, exceed, excel, beat. [➡BEAT AND DEFEAT; 80] 6 *v* (*slang*) **kill**, murder, slaughter, execute, slay (*formal or literary*). [➡KILL; 923]

top

◆ *types of top*
basque, blouse, bodice, body warmer, bolero, boob tube (*slang*), gilet, halter, jerkin, polo shirt, shirt, smock, surplice, sweatshirt, T-shirt, tabard, tank top, tee, tube top (*US*), tunic, vest (*US*), vestment, waistcoat

◆ *types of sweater or cardigan*
twinset, cardigan, crew neck, jersey, jumper, polo neck, pullover, sweater, V neck

topaz *type of* **gemstone**. [➡PRECIOUS STONES; 1277]

top brass (*informal*) *n* [➡IMPORTANT OR FAMOUS PEOPLE; 893]

top-class *adj* **best**, world-class, first-class, first-rate, top-flight, premier, premium, unrivalled, topnotch (*informal*), outstanding, exceptional. [➡SUPERIORITY; 153]

topcoat (*dated*) *type of* **overcoat**. [➡GARMENTS AND OUTFITS; 865]

top dog (*informal*) *n* [➡IMPORTANT OR FAMOUS PEOPLE; 893]

top drawer 1 *n* **cream**, crème de la crème, elite, pick, best. [➡SUPERIORITY; 153] 2 *n* **aristocracy**, nobility, high society, gentry, upper class, upper crust (*informal*). [➡CLASS STATUS; 889]

top-drawer 1 *adj* **top-flight**, best, topnotch (*informal*), first-rate, first-class, premium, premier. [➡SUPERIORITY; 153] 2 *adj* **upper class**, high class, noble, titled, aristocratic. [➡CLASS STATUS; 889]

topee *type of* **headgear**. [➡HABERDASHERY, MILLINERY, AND LINGERIE; 867]

top-flight *adj* **top-drawer**, best, first-rate, first-class, premium, topnotch (*informal*), premier, top-class. [➡SUPERIORITY; 153]

top gun (*US informal*) *n* [➡IMPORTANT OR FAMOUS PEOPLE; 893]

top hat *type of* **hat**. [➡HABERDASHERY, MILLINERY, AND LINGERIE; 867]

top-heavy *adj* **unbalanced**, unstable, uneven, disproportionate, lopsided. [➡ORIENTATION AND ALIGNMENT; 1222]

topic *n* **theme**, subject, matter, issue, subject matter, focus. [➡SUBJECT AREA; 769]

See Compare and Contrast at **subject**.

topical *adj* **up-to-date**, interesting, current, newsworthy, contemporary, relevant. [➡PRESENT; 85]

topicality *n* **interest**, relevance, newsworthiness, current interest, contemporaneity, contemporaneousness. [➡PRESENT; 85]

topknot *type of* **hairstyle**. [➡HAIR STYLES AND HAIR PIECES; 489]

top-level *adj* **highest**, most senior, most important, most powerful. [➡MOST IMPORTANT AND MAIN; 194]

topmost *adj* **highest**, uppermost, top, peak. [➡SUPERIORITY; 153]

top name *n* [➡IMPORTANT OR FAMOUS PEOPLE; 893]

topnotch (*informal*) *adj* **top-class**, first-rate, superior, first-class, excellent, top-quality, superlative, exclusive, premium, best, top, premier. [➡SUPERIORITY; 153] *Opposite:* inferior.

top-of-the-range *adj* **best**, most expensive, exclusive, premium, premier, excellent. [➡SUPERIORITY; 153] *Opposite:* basic.

topographical *adj* **geographical**, structural, natural, landscape, environmental. [➡THE EARTH; 1039]

topography *n* **features**, landscape, geography, structure, countryside. [➡THE COUNTRYSIDE AND OUTDOOR SPACES; 1070]

topper *type of* **hat**. [➡HABERDASHERY, MILLINERY, AND LINGERIE; 867]

topping *n* **top layer**, coating, glaze, garnish, frosting, icing, covering, decoration. [➡COVERS AND COATINGS; 1245] *Opposite:* filling.

topple 1 *v* **fall over**, tip over, collapse, fall, tumble, knock down, upset, knock over. [➡GO DOWNWARDS; 308] 2 *v* **bring down**, overthrow, depose, oust, remove, unseat. [➡GET RID OF SOMETHING; 452]

top-quality *adj* **choice**, select, fine, rare. [➡SUPERIORITY; 153]

top-ranking *adj* **high-ranking**, senior, important, powerful, high-level. [➡IMPORTANT; 195]

top-rated *adj* **favourite**, popular, well-liked, top, top ten, number one. [➡POPULAR AND WANTED; 221] *Opposite:* unpopular.

top round *type of* **cut**. [➡TYPES AND CUTS OF MEAT; 1176]

tops (*informal*) *adv* **at most**, as a maximum, max (*slang*), at the most. [➡MAJORITY; 139]

topsail *part of* **sailing vessel**. [➡SHIPS AND BOATS; 1149]

top-secret *adj* **undercover**, covert, secret, clandestine, restricted, privileged, classified, confidential, hush-hush (*informal*). [➡SECRET AND UNKNOWN; 180]

topside *type of* **cut**. [➡TYPES AND CUTS OF MEAT; 1176]

topsoil *n* **soil**, earth, loam, dirt, peat. [➡EROSION PRODUCTS AND SOIL; 1058]

topspin *n* **forward spin**, spin, momentum, force, impetus, energy. [➡SPORTS TERMS; 877]

topsy-turvy *adj* **confused**, disordered, chaotic, in disarray, upside down, in a mess, all over the place (*informal*), mixed up, disorganized. [➡DISORDER AND CHAOS; 246] *Opposite:* orderly.

top-up 1 *n* **refill**, fill-up, replenishment, extra serving, extra measure, more. [➡DRINK; 712] 2 *n* **supplement**, increase, increment, extra, addition, add-on. [➡MORE AND EXCESS; 122]

top up 1 *v* **refill**, replenish, refuel, freshen. [➡FILL; 407] 2 *v* **make up**, augment, complete, chip in (*informal*). [➡FILL; 407]

to put it briefly *adv* [➡SUMMARIZING EXPRESSIONS; 623]

top yourself (*slang*) *v* [➡DIE; 922]

toque *type of* **hat**. [➡HABERDASHERY, MILLINERY, AND LINGERIE; 867]

tor *n* **peak**, crag, outcrop, rock face. [➡MOUNTAINS AND HILLS; 1044]

torch 1 *n* **penlight**, light, lamp, lantern, flash (*US informal*), flashlight (*US*). [➡LIGHT; 1163] 2 *v* (*informal*) **burn down**, set on fire, set light to, put a match to, set fire to, incinerate. [➡FIRE, FLAMMABILITY, AND BURNING; 1164]

torchlight 1 *n* **beam**, light, illumination, lamplight. [➡DESCRIBING LIGHT; 1227] 2 *type of* **light**. [➡LIGHT; 1163]

torment 1 *v* **annoy**, tease, plague, persecute, taunt, pester, bother, harass, trouble, torture. [➡ANGER AND ANNOY; 570] *Opposite:* comfort. 2 *n* **anguish**, suffering, agony, distress, pain, torture, stress. [➡SADNESS, DISTRESS, AND DESPAIR; 540] *Opposite:* pleasure. 3 *n* **nuisance**, bane, plague, pest (*informal*), pain in the neck (*informal*), annoyance, irritation. [➡NUISANCES; 254] *Opposite:* delight.

tormented *adj* **anguished**, tortured, distressed, grief-stricken, plagued, persecuted, haunted. [➡SADNESS, DISTRESS, AND DESPAIR; 540]

tormenter *see* **tormentor**.

tormenting *adj* [➡EMOTIONALLY UNPLEASANT AND UPSETTING; 228]

tormentor *n* **oppressor**, tyrant, persecutor, bully, teaser. [➡ENEMIES AND TORMENTORS; 969]

torn 1 *adj* **ripped**, frayed, ragged, tattered, shabby, shredded, in rags, in tatters, in shreds. [➡IN BAD REPAIR; 1233] 2 *adj* **undecided**, uncertain, in a quandary, in a dilemma, unable to decide, in two minds, dithering, wavering. [➡UNCERTAINTY; 560] *Opposite:* decided.

tornado *n* **hurricane**, whirlwind, cyclone, storm, windstorm, twister (*US informal*). [➡WINDY AND STORMY WEATHER; 1053]

torpedo 1 *v* (*informal*) **ruin**, destroy, wreck, spoil, thwart, sink, scupper. [➡MAKE IMPOSSIBLE; 277] 2 *type of* **explosive weapon**. [➡EXPLOSIVES; 1154] 3 (*US*) *type of* **firework**. [➡EXPLOSIVES; 1154]

torpid *adj* **lazy**, languorous, listless, sluggish, apathetic, sleepy, dreamy, slow, unhurried, indolent, stagnant, lethargic. [➡LIFELESS, LAZY, AND UNENTHUSIASTIC; 507] *Opposite:* energetic.

torpor *n* **inactivity**, inertia, indolence, languor, lethargy, listlessness, apathy. [➡LIFELESS, LAZY, AND UNENTHUSIASTIC; 507] *Opposite:* excitement.

torque 1 *n* **rotating force**, rotation, twisting, turning, turning force, spin, force. [➡ENERGY GENERAL; 1160] 2 *type of* **necklace**. [➡JEWELLERY; 866]

torrent 1 *n* **rush**, flood, flow, deluge, gush, inundation (*formal*), stream, surge, downpour, rainstorm, cloudburst, driving rain, soaker, shower. [➡CLOUDY AND RAINY WEATHER; 1052] *Opposite:* trickle. 2 *n* **outburst**, flood, flow, tide, stream, deluge, outpouring. [➡SUDDEN EVENT; 52]

torrential *adj* **heavy**, pouring, driving, lashing, drenching, severe. [➡CLOUDY AND RAINY WEATHER; 1052] *Opposite:* light.

torrid *adj* **hot**, stifling, sweltering, scorching (*informal*), boiling, burning, baking, sizzling (*informal*). [➡HOT WEATHER; 1050] *Opposite:* cool.

torridness *n* [➡MORALLY BAD; 776]

torsion *n* **twisting**, turning, turning force, rotation, spin, force. [➡ENERGY GENERAL; 1160]

torso

◆ *parts of a torso*
abdomen, armpit, back, belly, bellybutton (*informal*), bosom, bottom, breast, bust, buttock, chest, groin, hip, midriff, navel, neck, nipple, rib cage, shoulder, solar plexus, thorax, waist, waistline

tort *n* **wrongful act**, unlawful act, illegal act, offence, misdemeanour, wrongdoing, misdeed (*formal*). [➡CRIMES; 817]

tortellini *type of* **pasta**. [➡PASTA; 1179]

tortilla *type of* **bread**. [➡BREAD, FLOUR, AND BREAD PRODUCTS; 1178]

tortoise *type of* **reptile**. [➡REPTILES; 994]

tortoiseshell 1 *type of* **cat**. [➡FELINE; 983] 2 *type of* **butterfly**. [➡MOTHS AND BUTTERFLIES; 1015]

tortuous 1 *adj* **twisting**, winding, convoluted, circuitous, indirect, roundabout, meandering. [➡DIRECTION OF MOTION; 346] *Opposite:* direct. 2 *adj* **complex**, complicated, intricate, difficult, involved, byzantine, labyrinthine. [➡DIFFICULTY AND COMPLEXITY; 243] *Opposite:* simple. 3 *adj* **devious**, deceitful, crafty, sly, artful, dishonest, false. [➡FALSE AND UNREAL; 174] *Opposite:* straightforward.

torture 1 *v* **torment**, afflict, persecute, brutalize, punish, mistreat. [➡UPSET, DISTRESS, AND HUMILIATE; 568] 2 *n* **agony**, torment, anguish, pain, suffering, distress, cruelty. [➡SADNESS, DISTRESS, AND DESPAIR; 540]

torturer *n* **intimidator**, bully, pesterer, harasser, teaser, tormentor, persecutor, oppressor. [➡ENEMIES AND TORMENTORS; 969]

tosh (*dated informal*) *n* **rubbish**, nonsense, twaddle (*informal*), bunkum (*informal*), tripe (*informal*), claptrap (*informal*), stuff and nonsense. [➡MEANINGLESS SPEECH OR WRITING; 677]

toss 1 *v* **throw**, pitch, fling, lob, chuck (*informal*), hurl, let fly, flip. [➡THROW SOMETHING; 335] 2 *v* **mix**, stir, blend, mix up. [➡COMBINE AND MIX; 401] 3 *n* **lob**, throw, pitch, chuck (*informal*), heave, fling, shy. [➡THROW SOMETHING; 335]

See Compare and Contrast at **throw**.

toss and turn *v* [➡FIDGET AND FROLIC; 312]

toss off *v* [➡DRINK; 712]

toss-up *n* **even chance**, chance, risk, fifty-fifty, luck of the draw, hit or miss. [➡CHANCE, COINCIDENCE, AND ACCIDENT; 787]

to sum up *adv* [➡SUMMARIZING EXPRESSIONS; 623]

tot 1 *n* **dram**, snifter (*informal*), finger, thimbleful. [➡DRINK; 712] 2 *n* (*informal*) **toddler**, child, kid (*informal*), baby, small child. [➡CHILD OR YOUTH; 945]

total 1 *n* **sum**, whole, entirety, full amount, totality. [➡ALL; 126] 2 *adj* **entire**, whole, full, complete, aggregate. [➡WHOLENESS AND COMPLETENESS; 199] *Opposite:* partial. 3 *adj* **complete**, absolute, unmitigated, unreserved, out-and-out, full-blown, utter. [➡ABSOLUTE AND ABSOLUTELY; 131] 4 *v* **add up**, count up, tot up, calculate, sum, compute, totalize. [➡ASSESS QUANTITY; 758] 5 *v* **amount to**, add up to, come to, equal, make. [➡AMOUNT TO AND EQUAL; 70] 6 *v* (*US slang*) **write off**, wreck, destroy, smash, ruin. [➡DESTRUCTION AND DEMOLITION; 360]

totalitarian *adj* **authoritarian**, tyrannous, one-party, oppressive, autocratic, despotic, tyrannical, dictatorial. [➡STYLES AND SYSTEMS OF GOVERNMENT; 806] *Opposite:* democratic.

totalitarianism *n* **despotism**, absolutism, tyranny, autocracy, authoritarianism, dictatorship. [➡STYLES AND SYSTEMS OF GOVERNMENT; 806]

totality *n* **entirety**, whole, total, sum, full amount. [➡ALL; 126] *Opposite:* part.

totally *adv* **completely**, entirely, absolutely, wholly, fully, thoroughly, utterly, perfectly. [➡ABSOLUTE AND ABSOLUTELY; 131] *Opposite:* partly.

tote (*informal*) 1 *v* **carry**, cart, lug, haul, heave, drag, transport. [➡MOVE SOMETHING TO ANOTHER LOCATION; 325] 2 *v* **bear**, carry, hold, wield, brandish. [➡CONTACT: HOLD; 412]

tote bag *type of* **bag**. [➡CONTAINERS, RECEPTACLES, AND PACKAGING; 1244]

to tell the truth *adv* [➡EXPRESSIONS OF OPINION; 624]

totem 1 *n* **ritual object**, sacred symbol, icon, charm, talisman, amulet. [➡LUCKY CHARMS; 786] 2 *n* **symbol**, representation, emblem, image, icon. [➡REPRESENTATIONS AND GENERAL EXAMPLES; 65]

totemic *adj* **symbolic**, emblematic, iconic, representative. [➡REPRESENTATIVE; 66]

to the fore *adv* [➡RELATIVE LOCATION; 162]

to the left *adv* [➡RELATIVE LOCATION; 162]

to the letter *adv* **exactly**, precisely, literally, word for word, accurately, strictly. [➡EXACT; 204]

to the point *adj* **relevant**, apt, apposite, pertinent, germane (*formal*). [➡FUNDAMENTAL; 196] *Opposite:* irrelevant.

to the rear *adj* [➡GENERAL LOCATIONS; 159]

to the right *adv* [➡RELATIVE LOCATION; 162]

totter *v* **walk unsteadily**, stagger, wobble, teeter, stumble, reel, flounder, falter. [➡WALK UNSTEADILY; 316]

tot up *v* **add up**, add together, count up, total, calculate, compute. [➡ASSESS QUANTITY; 758]

touch 1 *n* **pat**, tap, stroke, fondle, feel, pressure. [➡CONTACT: TOUCH; 413] 2 *n* **trace**, bit, dash, drop, hint, soupçon, tad (*informal*), little. [➡FEW, LITTLE, SMALL AMOUNT; 119] 3 *n* **style**, facility, gift, knack, ability, talent, flair. [➡SKILLS, TALENTS, AND ABILITIES; 527] 4 *v* **handle**, feel, finger, tap, stroke, contact, pat, fondle, caress. [➡CONTACT: TOUCH; 413] 5 *v* **converge**, meet, come into contact, join, contact, link. [➡CREATING CONNECTIONS; 145] *Opposite:* separate. 6 *v* **move**, affect, upset, stir, touch a chord, impress. [➡SURPRISE AND IMPRESS; 575] 7 *v* **match**, come close to, meet, rival, equal, compete with. [➡COMPETE, CONTEND, AND COMBAT; 304]

touch-and-go *adj* **uncertain**, unpredictable, doubtful, dicey (*informal*), unknown, risky, in the balance, shaky. [➡CERTAIN; 175] *Opposite:* certain.

touchdown 1 *n* **landing**, descent, arrival. [➡ARRIVAL; 13] 2 *n* **score**, try, point. [➡SPORTS TERMS; 877]

touched 1 *adj* **affected**, moved, warmed, heartened, impressed, gladdened, gratified. [➡PLEASURE, EXCITEMENT, AND ELATION; 535] *Opposite:* unmoved. 2 *adj* (*literary*) **tinged**, tinted, shaded, marked, streaked, spattered. [➡DECORATE, ADORN, AND APPLY COATINGS; 406]

touchily *adv* **irritably**, crossly, impatiently, petulantly, cantankerously, grumpily, tetchily (*informal*), moodily, sulkily, indignantly, huffily, crankily (*informal*). [➡BAD-TEMPERED AND HUMOURLESS; 627] *Opposite:* calmly.

touchiness *n* **tetchiness** (*informal*), irritability, impatience, grumpiness, cantankerousness, moodiness, crossness, bad temper, petulance, sulkiness, huffiness, sensitivity, crankiness (*US informal*). [➡EXCESSIVE SENSITIVITY; 512] *Opposite:* composure.

touching *adj* **moving**, poignant, stirring, tender, pitiful, emotive, sad, heartbreaking, heartrending, affecting. [➡EMOTIONALLY PLEASANT; 188]

touch on *v* **deal with**, refer to, mention, treat, allude to, talk about, go into, discuss, touch upon, be concerned with. [➡SUGGEST, HINT, AND COMMENT; 613]

touch screen *type of* **hardware**. [➡COMPUTERS AND COMPUTING; 1126]

touchstone *n* **criterion**, standard, benchmark, yardstick, hallmark. [➡SCORES AND EVALUATIONS; 599]

touch up *v* **retouch**, restore, freshen, freshen up, refurbish, repaint, smarten up, improve. [➡DECORATE, ADORN, AND APPLY COATINGS; 406]

touchy 1 *adj* **sensitive**, quick-tempered, prickly (*informal*), impatient, petulant, cantankerous, grumpy, tetchy (*informal*), moody, sulky, huffy, cranky (*US informal*). [➡EXCESSIVE SENSITIVITY; 512] *Opposite:* even-tempered. 2 *adj* **delicate**, sensitive, tricky, awkward, ticklish, precarious. [➡DIFFICULTY AND COMPLEXITY; 243]

touchy-feely (*informal*) *adj* **demonstrative**, expressive, effusive, unreserved, emotional, gushing, unrestrained, sentimental. [➡HONEST AND OPEN; 631] *Opposite:* undemonstrative.

tough 1 *adj* **durable**, strong, sturdy, robust, hardy, resilient, independent. [➡STRENGTH; 202] *Opposite:* weak. 2 *adj* **hard**, chewy, stringy, stiff, leathery, gristly. [➡STATE OF PREPARED FOOD; 1170] *Opposite:* tender. 3 *adj* **threatening**, rough, hard, harsh, dangerous, hard-hitting. [➡DANGEROUS; 237] *Opposite:* pleasant. 4 *adj* **difficult**, hard, demanding, exacting, arduous, strenuous, daunting, taxing, challenging, tricky, testing. [➡DIFFICULTY AND COMPLEXITY; 243] *Opposite:* easy. 5 *adj* **severe**, strict, rigid, inflexible, stern, harsh, stringent, firm, uncompromising, unbending, hardheaded. [➡DIFFICULT TO PLEASE; 516] *Opposite:* lenient.

See Compare and Contrast at **hard**.

tough as old boots *adj* [➡STATE OF PREPARED FOOD; 1170]

toughen *v* **strengthen**, harden, build up, reinforce, fortify, shore up, beef up (*informal*), firm up. [➡IMPROVE STRENGTH AND DURABILITY; 379] *Opposite:* weaken.

toughened *adj* **hardened**, reinforced, strengthened, fortified, unbreakable, galvanized, tempered. [➡DURABLE; 1209]

tough it out (*informal*) *v* [➡TOLERATE AND ENDURE; 767]

toughly 1 *adv* **durably**, strongly, sturdily, solidly, resiliently, soundly. [➡STRENGTH; 202] *Opposite:* flimsily. 2 *adv* **determinedly**, firmly, resolutely, doggedly, decisively, strongly. [➡STRENGTH OF WILL; 502] *Opposite:* weakly. 3 *adv* **severely**, strictly, rigidly, inflexibly, sternly, harshly, stringently, firmly, uncompromisingly, unbendingly. [➡DIFFICULT TO PLEASE; 516] *Opposite:* leniently.

tough-minded *adj* **realistic**, determined, tough, single-minded, resilient, strong, gutsy (*informal*), unsentimental. [➡STRENGTH OF WILL; 502] *Opposite:* weak-willed.

toughness 1 *n* **durability**, hardiness, robustness, roughness, stoutness, stiffness, sturdiness, strength, resilience. [➡STRENGTH; 202] *Opposite:* flimsiness. 2 *n* **hardness**, chewiness, stringiness, stiffness. [➡PHYSICAL TEXTURE; 1221] *Opposite:* tenderness. 3 *n* **roughness**, harshness, hardness, danger. [➡PHYSICALLY UNPLEASANT; 227] *Opposite:* pleasantness. 4 *n* **difficulty**, arduousness, strenuousness, challenge, trickiness. [➡DIFFICULTY AND COMPLEXITY; 243] *Opposite:* ease. 5 *n* **severity**, strictness, rigidity, inflexibility, firmness, sternness. [➡DIFFICULT TO PLEASE; 516] *Opposite:* leniency.

toupee *n* **wig**, hairpiece, hair extension. [➡HAIR STYLES AND HAIR PIECES; 489]

tour 1 *n* **trip**, excursion, expedition, outing, journey, visit, circuit. [➡TRAVEL: JOURNEYS AND TRIPS; 319] 2 *v* **sightsee**, explore, visit, travel around, go around. [➡TRAVEL: WAYS OF TRAVELLING; 321]

tour guide *n* [➡TRAVEL: SIGHT-SEEING AND TOURISM; 322]

touring company *n* [➡PERFORMERS; 905]

tourism *n* **travel**, holiday business, leisure industry, service sector, vacation industry (*US*). [➡TRAVEL: SIGHT-SEEING AND TOURISM; 322]

tourist *n* **traveller**, sightseer, visitor, holidaymaker, day tripper, vacationer (*US*). [➡TRAVEL: TRAVELLERS AND WALKERS; 320]

tourist attractions *n* [➡TRAVEL: SIGHT-SEEING AND TOURISM; 322]

tourist centre *n* [➡TRAVEL: SIGHT-SEEING AND TOURISM; 322]

tourist class *n* [➡TRAVEL: SIGHT-SEEING AND TOURISM; 322]

tourist spot *n* [➡TRAVEL: SIGHT-SEEING AND TOURISM; 322]

touristy *adj* **crowded**, busy, much-frequented, popular, overvisited, spoiled. [➡POPULAR AND WANTED; 221] *Opposite:* quiet.

tourmaline *type of* **gemstone**. [➡PRECIOUS STONES; 1277]

tournament *n* **contest**, competition, event, tourney, game, play-offs, match. [➡NON-AGGRESSIVE/SPORTING EVENT; 40]

tourney *n* [➡NON-AGGRESSIVE/SPORTING EVENT; 40]

tourniquet *n* **band**, strap, bandage. [➡FASTENERS, LINKS, AND NETWORKS; 1246]

tousle *v* **tangle**, ruffle, rumple, dishevel, mess up (*informal*), disorder, disarrange. [➡CREATE DISORDER AND CAUSE CHAOS; 359] *Opposite:* tidy.

tousled *adj* **dishevelled**, messy, tangled, ruffled, windswept, rumpled, disarranged. [➡DESCRIBING HAIR; 487] *Opposite:* tidy.

tout 1 *v* **advertise**, hype, flaunt, push, plug (*informal*), publicize, peddle, flog (*informal*), puff, ballyhoo, pile it on (*informal*), lay it on thick. [➡SELL; 442] *Opposite:* understate. 2 *n* **seller**, hawker, peddler, vendor. [➡SELLER; 443]

tow *v* **pull**, drag, draw, haul, lug, tug. [➡PUSH, PULL, SLIDE; 336]

See Compare and Contrast at **pull**.

towards 1 *prep* **in the direction of**, to, near, just before. [➡DIRECTION OF MOTION; 346] 2 *prep* **regarding**, concerning, for, about, on, with regard to, with respect to, on the subject of, in relation to. [➡EXPRESSIONS OF REFERENCE; 63]

towel 1 *n* **cloth**, bath towel, bath sheet, hand towel, guest towel, tea towel, dishtowel (*US*). [➡SOFT FURNISHINGS, LINEN, AND DRAPERY; 860] 2 *v* **dry**, rub down, rub, wipe, dab, blot. [➡CLEAN AND POLISH; 404]

towelling *type of* **fabric from plants**. [➡FABRICS; 1131]

tower 1 *v* **loom**, overlook, be head and shoulders above, soar, rise. [➡EXIST IN A PLACE; 19] 2 *v* **surpass**, exceed, excel, top, transcend, outstrip, outdo, outclass. [➡BEAT AND DEFEAT; 80]

tower block *n* [➡RESIDENTIAL BUILDINGS; 1077]

towering *adj* **high**, tall, soaring, lofty, immense, gigantic. [➡HEIGHT: HIGH; 1202] *Opposite:* short.

tower of strength (*informal*) *n* **rock**, mainstay, anchor, helper, advocate, support, pillar. [➡PEOPLE WHO ARE APPROVED OF; 955]

tow-headed *adj* [➡HAIR COLOUR; 486]

town *n* **municipality**, city, settlement, township, metropolis. [➡HUMAN SETTLEMENTS; 1069]

See Compare and Contrast at **city**.

town centre *n* [➡HUMAN SETTLEMENTS; 1069]

town house *type of* **house**. [➡RESIDENTIAL BUILDINGS; 1077]

townie (*informal*) *n* **town dweller**, city dweller, urbanite, city slicker. [➡INHABITANT; 857]

townsfolk *n* **townspeople**, populace, residents, inhabitants. [➡INHABITANT; 857]

township *n* **small town**, urban area, settlement, town, hamlet, community, parish, village, municipality. [➡HUMAN SETTLEMENTS; 1069]

townspeople *n* **townsfolk**, populace, residents, inhabitants. [➡GROUPS IN SOCIETY; 940]

town square *n* [➡URBAN OUTDOOR SPACES; 1071]

towpath *n* **path**, footpath, bridleway, canal path, track, pathway. [➡PATHWAYS; 1109]

towrope *n* **towline**, rope, line, cable, cord. [➡FASTENERS, LINKS, AND NETWORKS; 1246]

tow truck (*US*) *type of* **commercial or industrial vehicle**. [➡VEHICLES; 1144]

toxic *adj* **poisonous**, deadly, lethal, noxious, contaminated. [➡DANGEROUS; 237] *Opposite:* harmless.

toxicity *n* **poisonousness**, venomousness, deadliness, noxiousness, harmfulness, injuriousness. [➡DANGER; 236] *Opposite:* harmlessness.

toxic waste *n* [➡UNPLEASANT AND DIRTY SUBSTANCES; 1267]

toxin *n* **poison**, pollutant, contaminant, venom. [➡UNPLEASANT AND DIRTY SUBSTANCES; 1267]

toy

◆ *types of toy*
beach ball, building blocks, doll, doll's house, dolly (*babytalk*), glove puppet, hand puppet (*US*), jack-in-the-box, jigsaw, jigsaw puzzle, kaleidoscope, kite, marble, playhouse, popgun, puppet, rag doll, rocking horse, squirt gun (*US*), stilt, teddy bear, water pistol, Wendy house, yo-yo

toy with 1 *v* **flirt with**, tease, philander (*disapproving*). [➡APPEAL TO AND AROUSE INTEREST; 576] 2 *v* **play with**, fiddle with, fidget with, handle, finger. [➡CONTACT: TOUCH; 413] 3 *v* **think about**, consider, ponder, contemplate, entertain, speculate, play around with. [➡THINK AND REFLECT; 744] *Opposite:* dismiss.

trace 1 *n* **sign**, indication, evidence, remnant, residue, mark, vestige. [➡EVIDENCE AND PROOF; 69] 2 *n* **suggestion**, hint, dash, drop, touch, bit, smidgen (*informal*), tinge, smattering. [➡FEW, LITTLE, SMALL AMOUNT; 119] 3 *v* **find**, locate, discover, hunt down, track down, pin down, track, follow, trail. [➡FIND; 464] 4 *v* **draw**, outline, copy, mark out, sketch, map out. [➡CREATE IMAGES; 357]

traceable *adj* [➡PERCEPTIBLE; 25]

tracery *n* **decoration**, pattern, design, interlacing, ornamentation, motif. [➡ORNAMENTS AND DECORATIONS; 1247]

trachea *part of* **respiratory system**. [➡RESPIRATORY ORGANS; 716]

track 1 *n* **trail**, footprints, footsteps, path, trace, marks, paw marks, hoof marks, imprints, spoor. [➡EVIDENCE AND PROOF; 69] 2 *n* **path**, pathway, road, way, trail, roadway, footpath, trajectory. [➡PATHWAYS; 1109] 3 *v* **follow**, hunt down, chase, pursue, stalk, trace, trail. [➡ACCOMPANY AND FOLLOW; 338] 4 *type of* **minor road**. [➡ROADS; 1105]

track down *v* **find**, hunt down, catch, capture, discover, unearth, locate, trace. [➡FIND; 464]

tracker *n* **trailer**, follower, chaser, hunter, shadow, tail, pursuer, private investigator, private eye (*informal*), private detective, bounty hunter. [➡ENEMIES AND TORMENTORS; 969]

tracksuit *type of* **sportswear**. [➡GARMENTS AND OUTFITS; 865]

tract 1 *n* **area**, territory, zone, region, expanse, swathe, band, strip. [➡AREA AND RANGE; 111] 2 *n* **pamphlet**, article, treatise, leaflet. [➡BOOKS AND BOOKLETS; 591]

tractability 1 *n* **docility**, controllability, manageability, obedience, manipulability, submissiveness, compliance, amenableness. [➡THE WILL AND WILLINGNESS; 564] *Opposite:* intractability. 2 *n* **malleability**, pliability, workability, ductility, elasticity, plasticity, flexibility, pliancy, bendiness. [➡MALLEABLE AND ELASTIC; 1211] *Opposite:* intractability.

tractable 1 *adj* **docile**, controllable, manageable, obedient, manipulable, submissive, amenable, biddable, compliant, pliant, yielding, easily swayed, impressionable, suggestible. [➡THE WILL AND WILLINGNESS; 564] *Opposite:* intractable. 2 *adj* **malleable**, pliable, workable, ductile, elastic, plastic, flexible, bendable, pliant. [➡MALLEABLE AND ELASTIC; 1211] *Opposite:* intractable.

traction 1 *n* **adhesive friction**, grip, purchase, adhesion. [➡ENERGY GENERAL; 1160] 2 *n* **power**, tractive force, pull, tow, tug. [➡ENERGY GENERAL; 1160]

tractor *type of* **commercial or industrial vehicle**. [➡VEHICLES; 1144]

trade 1 *n* **commerce**, business, industry, market, dealings, transactions. [➡BUSINESS ENTERPRISES AND RELATED BODIES; 793] 2 *n* **occupation**, job, employment, line of work, profession, craft, vocation, skill. [➡PROFESSIONS; 845] 3 *n* **customers**, public, patrons, custom, clientele. [➡PURCHASER; 425] 4 *v* **deal**, buy and sell, do business, operate, traffic, import, export, merchandize, transact. [➡SELL; 442] 5 *v* **exchange**, swap (*informal*), barter, dicker (*informal*), negotiate. [➡EXCHANGE AND INTERCHANGE; 449]

trade event *n* [➡SALES AND SHOWS; 444]

trade fair *n* **exhibition**, exposition, fair, display, show. [➡SALES AND SHOWS; 444]

trade in *v* **exchange**, merchandize, redeem, give in part payment, swap (*informal*), barter. [➡EXCHANGE AND INTERCHANGE; 449]

trade-in *n* **part exchange**, exchange, swap (*informal*), deal, transaction. [➡EXCHANGE AND INTERCHANGE; 449]

trademark 1 *n* **symbol**, logo, emblem, brand. [➡SYMBOLS, SIGNS, AND NUMBERS; 597] 2 *n* **characteristic**, feature, trait, attribute, facet, quality, hallmark. [➡PERSONAL ECCENTRICITIES; 494]

trade name *n* **brand name**, brand, trademark, name, registered trademark, label, product name. [➡NAME AND DESCRIBE; 666]

trade-off *n* **compromise**, balance, adjustment, interchange, transaction, quid pro quo. [➡EXCHANGE AND INTERCHANGE; 449]

trader *n* **dealer**, buyer, seller, broker, agent, merchant. [➡SELLER; 443]

trade school [➡EDUCATIONAL INSTITUTIONS; 813]

trade show *n* [➡SALES AND SHOWS; 444]

tradesperson *n* [➡BUSINESS PEOPLE; 794]

trade union *n* [➡BUSINESS ENTERPRISES AND RELATED BODIES; 793]

trade wind *type of* **wind**. [➡WINDY AND STORMY WEATHER; 1053]

tradition *n* **custom**, institution, ritual, habit, convention, belief, folklore, practice. [➡WAYS OF DOING THINGS; 295] *Opposite:* innovation.

See Compare and Contrast at **habit**.

traditional *adj* **usual**, conventional, customary, established, fixed, long-established, time-honoured, habitual, accepted, old-fashioned. [➡OLD, OLD-FASHIONED; 168] *Opposite:* progressive.

traditionalism *n* **conventionalism**, conservatism, conformity, orthodoxy, fundamentalism. [➡PHILOSOPHIES AND BELIEFS; 781] *Opposite:* progressivism.

traditionalist 1 *n* **conservative**, purist, fundamentalist, conformist. [➡PHILOSOPHICAL AND POLITICAL THINKERS; 782] *Opposite:* progressive. 2 *adj* **traditional**, conservative, purist, old-school, orthodox, conventional, fundamentalist. [➡CONSERVATIVE AND UNADVENTUROUS; 518] *Opposite:* progressive.

traditionalistic *see* **traditionalist**.

traditionally *adv* **usually**, conventionally, customarily, habitually, by tradition. [➡USUALLY; 108] *Opposite:* occasionally.

traduce *v* **criticize**, disparage, malign, run down, defame, denigrate, vilify. [➡ACCUSE, BLAME, AND CRITICIZE; 642] *Opposite:* praise.

traffic 1 *n* **road traffic**, traffic flow, circulation, stream of traffic, rush-hour traffic, commuter traffic. [➡VEHICLES; 1144] 2 *n* **transportation**, movement, passage, to-ing and fro-ing, travel, transport, transfer. [➡TRAVEL: SIGHT-SEEING AND TOURISM; 322] 3 *n* **trade**, commerce, business, dealings, transactions, negotiations. [➡EXCHANGE AND INTERCHANGE; 449] 4 *v* **have dealings**, deal in, trade, trade in, transfer, do business, operate, handle, market, buy and sell. [➡EXCHANGE AND INTERCHANGE; 449] 5 *v* **smuggle**, run, handle. [➡BUSINESS ACTIVITIES AND PHENOMENA; 795]

traffic circle (*US*) *n* [➡ BRIDGES, TUNNELS, CROSSINGS, AND JUNCTIONS; 1111]

traffic-free *adj* [➡ PATHWAYS; 1109]

traffic island *n* [➡ BRIDGES, TUNNELS, CROSSINGS, AND JUNCTIONS; 1111]

traffic jam *n* **tailback**, bottleneck, gridlock, holdup, tie-up (*US*). [➡ TRAVEL: TRAFFIC PROBLEMS AND HOLDUPS; 324]

traffic junction *n* [➡ BRIDGES, TUNNELS, CROSSINGS, AND JUNCTIONS; 1111]

traffic lane *n* [➡ ROADS; 1105]

traffic light *type of* **light**. [➡ LIGHT; 1163]

tragedian *n* [➡ WRITERS AND STYLES; 914]

tragedy *n* **disaster**, calamity, catastrophe, misfortune, heartbreak. [➡ DISASTERS; 253] *Opposite:* joy.

tragic *adj* **sad**, disastrous, catastrophic, heartbreaking, heartrending, awful, terrible, dreadful, appalling, unfortunate, wretched. [➡ EMOTIONALLY UNPLEASANT AND UPSETTING; 228] *Opposite:* joyous.

tragicomic *adj* **bittersweet**, poignant, affecting, moving. [➡ EMOTIONALLY UNPLEASANT AND UPSETTING; 228]

trail 1 *v* **tug**, drag, pull, draw, tow, haul. [➡ PUSH, PULL, SLIDE; 336] *Opposite:* push. 2 *v* **follow**, track, tail, shadow, trace, stalk, pursue, chase. [➡ ACCOMPANY AND FOLLOW; 338] 3 *v* **drop back**, lag behind, fall behind, straggle, follow on, lag, linger behind, dawdle, hang back. [➡ MOVE SLOWLY; 315] *Opposite:* lead. 4 *n* **path**, track, way, road, footpath, route, trajectory. [➡ PATHWAYS; 1109] 5 *n* **track**, footprints, footsteps, paw marks, paw prints, hoof marks, trace, imprints, marks. [➡ EVIDENCE AND PROOF; 69]

See Compare and Contrast at **follow**.

trail away *v* **fade**, disappear, grow faint, die away, diminish, tail off. [➡ DISAPPEAR; 4] *Opposite:* intensify.

trailblazer *n* **pioneer**, leader, innovator, entrepreneur, architect, creator, originator, initiator, catalyst, torchbearer. [➡ DESIGNERS, CREATORS AND INSTIGATORS; 348]

trailer *n* **clip**, preview, promo (*informal*), advert (*informal*), ad. [➡ ADVERTISING AND PUBLICITY; 605]

trail off *v* [➡ DISAPPEAR; 4]

train 1 *n* **procession**, file, convoy, line. [➡ GROUPS OF PEOPLE; 935] 2 *n* **sequence**, chain, succession, string, series, progression. [➡ CHAIN OF EVENTS; 163] 3 *v* **teach**, coach, educate, instruct, tutor, school, prepare, guide. [➡ INSTRUCT AND TEACH; 610] 4 *v* **exercise**, work out, keep fit, keep in shape. [➡ HOBBIES, GAMES, AND SPORTS; 875] 5 *v* **aim**, direct, focus, point, line up. [➡ PREPARE FOR ACTION; 290] 6 *type of* **rail vehicle**. [➡ RAILWAYS; 1106]

See Compare and Contrast at **teach**.

trained *adj* **skilled**, qualified, proficient, accomplished, competent, expert. [➡ TALENTED AND SKILFUL; 528]

trainee *n* **apprentice**, learner, novice, beginner. [➡ UNSKILLED PERSON; 531] *Opposite:* trainer.

See Compare and Contrast at **beginner**.

trainer 1 *n* **coach**, teacher, guide, instructor, mentor. [➡ EDUCATORS; 840] 2 *type of* **shoe**. [➡ FOOTWEAR; 871]

training 1 *n* **tuition**, education, schooling, teaching, guidance, preparation, instruction. [➡ TEACHING; 839] 2 *n* **exercise**, working out, keep fit, physical activity, drill. [➡ HOBBIES, GAMES, AND SPORTS; 875]

training college *n* [➡ EDUCATIONAL INSTITUTIONS; 813]

train of thought *n* [➡ IDEA AND THOUGHT; 771]

traipse (*informal*) *v* **trudge**, tramp, plod, slog, trek, trail. [➡ PROCEED AND GO; 306]

trait *n* **mannerism**, peculiarity, attribute, characteristic, feature, quality. [➡ QUALITIES AND CHARACTERISTICS; 1190]

traitor *n* **conspirator**, collaborator, turncoat, defector, deserter, spy, double agent, quisling (*dated*). [➡ PEOPLE WHO DECEIVE; 662] *Opposite:* loyalist.

traitorous *adj* **disloyal**, perfidious (*literary*), faithless, duplicitous, deceitful, treacherous. [➡ LACK OF COMMITMENT AND UNRELIABILITY; 510]

trajectory *n* **route**, course, flight, path, line, arc, trail, trace, track, curve. [➡ DIRECTION OF MOTION; 346]

tram *type of* **rail vehicle**. [➡ RAILWAYS; 1106]

trammel 1 *n* **restriction**, limitation, hindrance, curb, constraint, impediment, handicap. [➡ CAPTIVITY AND LOSS OF FREEDOM; 249] 2 *v* **confine**, limit, restrain, restrict, hinder, hamper. [➡ AVOID, PREVENT, LIMIT, AND CONTROL; 278] 3 *v* **ensnare**, snare, catch, net, entangle, trap. [➡ CAPTIVITY AND LOSS OF FREEDOM; 249]

tramontana *type of* **wind**. [➡ WINDY AND STORMY WEATHER; 1053]

tramp 1 *n* **vagrant**, homeless person, beggar, vagabond, hobo. [➡ POOR PEOPLE; 896] 2 *n* **traipse**, march, trek, hike, trudge, walk, plod, trail, slog, roam, ramble, schlep (*informal*). [➡ PROCEED AND GO; 306] 3 *v* **trudge**, trek, hike, traipse, march, plod, walk, trail, slog, roam, ramble, schlep (*informal*). [➡ PROCEED AND GO; 306]

trample *v* **crush**, flatten, walk on, stamp on, step on, tread on, walk over (*informal*), squash. [➡ CHANGE OF SHAPE; 386]

tramway *type of* **railway**. [➡ RAILWAYS; 1106]

trance *n* **dream**, daze, spell, stupor, reverie, daydream, sleep, abstraction. [➡ DREAM, IMAGINE, AND FANTASIZE; 750] *Opposite:* alertness.

tranquil 1 *adj* **calm**, serene, peaceful, still, relaxing, restful, soothing, quiet. [➡ PEACEFULNESS AND GENTLENESS; 215] *Opposite:* noisy. 2 *adj* **composed**, calm, cool, unruffled, unperturbed, self-possessed, unflustered, relaxed, laid-back (*informal*), unworried, placid, serene. [➡ CALMNESS, CONFIDENCE, AND COMPOSURE; 537] *Opposite:* agitated.

tranquillity 1 *n* **calm**, serenity, stillness, peacefulness, hush, quietness, calmness, peace and quiet. [➡ PEACEFULNESS AND GENTLENESS; 215] *Opposite:* turmoil. 2 *n* **composure**, equanimity, calmness, coolness, self-possession, serenity, peace of mind, level-headedness. [➡CONFIDENCE AND COMPOSURE; 500] *Opposite:* panic.

tranquillize *v* **sedate**, calm, put out, put under, knock out, anaesthetize. [➡FALL ILL, TREAT, AND RECOVER; 729]

tranquillizing *adj* [➡CALMING; 189]

tranquilly *adv* **serenely**, calmly, quietly, coolly, unperturbedly, unworriedly. [➡CALMNESS, CONFIDENCE, AND COMPOSURE; 537] *Opposite:* anxiously.

transact *v* **carry out**, conduct, manage, handle, perform, do, execute, conclude, discharge (*formal*), take care of, deal with, implement. [➡CARRY OUT AN ACTION; 270]

transaction *n* **deal**, business, contract, matter, operation, business deal. [➡PURCHASE; 423]

transatlantic *adj* **transoceanic**, intercontinental, long-haul. [➡DISTANCE; 161]

transcend *v* **rise above**, go beyond, exceed, go above, excel, surpass, outdo. [➡BEAT AND DEFEAT; 80]

transcendence 1 *n* **divine existence**, otherworldliness, state of grace, perfection, wholeness. [➡RELIGIOUS CONCEPTS; 777] *Opposite:* mundaneness. 2 *n* **superiority**, greatness, excellence, pre-eminence, loftiness, supremacy. [➡SUPERIORITY; 153] *Opposite:* inferiority.

transcendent 1 *adj* **superior**, excellent, supreme, great, unequalled, unmatched. [➡SUPERIORITY; 153] *Opposite:* inferior. 2 *adj* **divine**, perfect, heavenly, supernatural, otherworldly, unlimited, unconfined. [➡RELIGIOUS CONCEPTS; 777] 3 *adj* **mystical**, awe-inspiring, uplifting, inspirational, inspiring, moving, sublime, transcendental. [➡EMOTIONALLY PLEASANT; 188]

transcendental 1 *adj* **mystical**, awe-inspiring, uplifting, inspirational, inspiring, moving, sublime, transcendent. [➡EMOTIONALLY PLEASANT; 188] 2 *adj* **divine**, perfect, heavenly, supernatural, otherworldly, unlimited, unconfined, spiritual. [➡RELIGIOUS CONCEPTS; 777]

transcontinental *adj* **pancontinental**, coast-to-coast, continent-wide. [➡GEOGRAPHICAL BORDERS AND BOUNDARIES; 1068]

transcribe *v* **copy out**, write out, copy, set down, write down, record. [➡RECORD SOMETHING; 372]

transcript *n* **record**, transcription, copy, text. [➡RECORDS; 586]

transcription *n* **record**, transcript, copy, text. [➡RECORDS; 586]

transect *v* **divide**, bisect, cut, split, cut across. [➡SEPARATE AND DIVIDE; 402]

transept *n* [➡PARTS OF RELIGIOUS BUILDINGS; 1085]

transfer 1 *v* **move**, transport, relocate, remove, shift, convey, reassign. [➡MOVE SOMETHING TO ANOTHER LOCATION; 325] 2 *v* **transmit**, convey, hand on, hand over, turn over, assign, sign over, pass on. [➡DESPATCH AND SEND; 334] 3 *n* **transmission**, handover, assignment, allocation, transference, transferral. [➡EXCHANGE AND INTERCHANGE; 449] 4 *n* **relocation**, removal, move, resettlement, displacement. [➡MOVE SOMETHING TO ANOTHER LOCATION; 325]

transference *n* **transfer**, conversion, devolution, conveyance, transmission, transferral. [➡EXCHANGE AND INTERCHANGE; 449]

transferral *n* [➡EXCHANGE AND INTERCHANGE; 449]

transfiguration *n* **metamorphosis**, transformation, makeover, change, conversion, transmutation, alteration. [➡CHANGE; 373]

transfigure *v* **change**, metamorphose, transform, convert, transmute, alter. [➡CHANGE; 373]

transfix 1 *v* **fascinate**, mesmerize, engross, spellbind, hypnotize, grip, hold, rivet (*informal*), root to the spot. [➡APPEAL TO AND AROUSE INTEREST; 576] 2 *v* **stab**, spike, gore, run through, pierce. [➡STAB; 417]

transfixed *adj* [➡PENSIVENESS AND INTEREST; 539]

transform *v* **alter**, convert, make over, transmute, renovate, change. [➡CHANGE; 373]

See Compare and Contrast at **change**.

transformation *n* **alteration**, conversion, revolution, renovation, makeover, change. [➡CHANGE; 373]

transgress *v* **misbehave**, disobey, go astray, lapse, sin, contravene, break the rules, do wrong, violate the law. [➡DISOBEY; 303] *Opposite:* behave.

transgression *n* **wrongdoing**, misbehaviour, disobedience, lapse, sin, contravention, misdemeanour, indiscretion, offence, crime, misdemeanor (*US*). [➡BAD BEHAVIOUR OR ACTION; 255]

transgressor *n* **wrongdoer**, lawbreaker, sinner, offender, criminal, malefactor (*formal*), evildoer. [➡CRIMINALS; 821]

transience *n* **briefness**, brevity, impermanence, transitoriness, shortness, fleetingness, ephemerality, evanescence. [➡FINITENESS, VARIABILITY, AND TRANSIENCE; 96] *Opposite:* permanence.

transient *adj* **fleeting**, brief, passing, transitory, temporary, momentary, short-lived, ephemeral, evanescent. [➡FINITENESS, VARIABILITY, AND TRANSIENCE; 96] *Opposite:* permanent.

transistor *type of* **audio equipment**. [➡AUDIO EQUIPMENT; 1138]

transit *n* **transportation**, transfer, transport, travel, shipment, passage, journey. [➡TRANSPORTATION, TRANSPORTERS, AND CARGOS; 323]

transition *n* **changeover**, shift, change, alteration, move, switch, evolution, conversion. [➡CHANGE; 373]

transitional *adj* **intermediate**, in-between, interim, provisional, temporary, impermanent, makeshift. [➡FINITENESS, VARIABILITY, AND TRANSIENCE; 96] *Opposite:* permanent.

transitive *type of* **grammatical term**. [➡ASPECTS OF LANGUAGE; 683]

transitory *adj* **fleeting**, passing, brief, temporary, momentary, short-lived, ephemeral, evanescent, transient. [➡FINITENESS, VARIABILITY, AND TRANSIENCE; 96] *Opposite:* permanent.

translate 1 *v* **interpret**, decode, decipher, render (*formal*), explain. [➡SOLVE AND INTERPRET; 761] 2 *v* **convert**, transform, transmute, turn, change. [➡CHANGE; 373]

translation *n* **conversion**, paraphrase, version, rendition, interpretation. [➡SUMMARIES, OUTLINES, AND EXCERPTS; 589]

translator *n* **interpreter**, decoder, decipherer, converter. [➡PEOPLE WHO WORK WITH LANGUAGE AND CODE; 854]

transliterate *v* **transcribe**, convert, translate, render (*formal*), transmute, transform. [➡CHANGE; 373]

transliteration *n* **transcription**, conversion, translation, transformation, rendering, transmutation. [➡CHANGE; 373]

translucence 1 *n* **semitransparency**, sheerness, filminess, limpidity, pellucidity (*literary*), transparency, translucency. [➡VISUAL TEXTURE; 1220] *Opposite:* opacity. 2 *n* **glow**, luminosity, brightness, luminescence, luminousness, lucidity, translucency. [➡DESCRIBING LIGHT; 1227] *Opposite:* dullness.

translucency *n* [➡VISUAL TEXTURE; 1220]

translucent 1 *adj* **transparent**, semitransparent, see-through, lucid, clear, lucent. [➡VISUAL TEXTURE; 1220] *Opposite:* opaque. 2 *adj* **glowing**, luminous, radiant, shining, lustrous, gleaming. [➡DESCRIBING LIGHT; 1227] *Opposite:* dull.

transmigrate *v* **wander**, migrate, travel, shift, drift, move. [➡TRAVEL: WAYS OF TRAVELLING; 321] *Opposite:* settle.

transmigration *n* **migration**, wandering, travelling, movement, shifting, drifting. [➡SELF-PROPULSION; 305]

transmissible *adj* **communicable**, infectious, contagious, catching. [➡SICKNESS; 730]

transmission 1 *n* **spread**, communication, diffusion, conduction. [➡DISPENSE, RATION, AND DISTRIBUTE; 435] 2 *n* **programme**, show, broadcast. [➡TELEVISION AND RADIO; 607]

transmit 1 *v* **convey**, hand on, spread, communicate, diffuse, conduct, pass on, transfer. [➡DESPATCH AND SEND; 334] 2 *v* **put on the air**, send out, put out, broadcast. [➡EMIT AND EMANATE; 362]

transmittable *adj* **communicable**, infectious, catching, contagious. [➡SICKNESS; 730]

transmittal *n* [➡EXCHANGE AND INTERCHANGE; 449]

transmittance *n* **transmission**, diffusion, conduction, transfer, transferral, transference, spread. [➡EXCHANGE AND INTERCHANGE; 449]

transmitter *type of* **telecommunications equipment**. [➡TELECOMMUNICATIONS; 1129]

transmogrification *n* [➡CHANGE; 373]

transmogrify *v* [➡CHANGE; 373]

transmutation *n* **transfiguration**, transmogrification, change, transformation, alteration, metamorphosis, mutation, conversion. [➡CHANGE; 373]

transmute *v* **transfigure**, transmogrify, transform, alter, change, turn, convert, metamorphose. [➡CHANGE; 373]

See Compare and Contrast at **change**.

transnational 1 *adj* **international**, multinational, transcontinental, intercontinental, global, worldwide, large-scale. [➡GEOGRAPHICAL BORDERS AND BOUNDARIES; 1068] 2 *n* **multinational**, conglomerate, corporation. [➡BUSINESS ENTERPRISES AND RELATED BODIES; 793]

transom (*US*) *type of* **window**. [➡WINDOWS; 1099]

transparency 1 *n* **clearness**, limpidity, pellucidity (*literary*), translucence, filminess, sheerness. [➡VISUAL TEXTURE; 1220] *Opposite:* opacity. 2 *n* **slide**, photograph, photo, shot. [➡PHOTOGRAPHY AND PHOTOGRAPHIC EQUIPMENT; 1121] *Opposite:* print. 3 *n* **clarity**, plainness, obviousness, directness, unambiguousness, unmistakability, intelligibility, comprehensibility, simplicity, lucidity, openness, candidness. [➡CONCISE AND CLEAR; 203] *Opposite:* ambiguousness.

transparent 1 *adj* **see-through**, clear, translucent, crystal clear. [➡VISUAL TEXTURE; 1220] *Opposite:* opaque. 2 *adj* **obvious**, clear, apparent, plain, evident, visible, patent, blatant, understandable. [➡PERCEPTIBLE; 25] *Opposite:* unclear.

transparently *adv* **clearly**, plainly, visibly, obviously, patently, blatantly, evidently. [➡PERCEPTIBLE; 25]

transpire *v* **happen**, occur, take place, come about, come to pass (*archaic or literary*), go on, go down (*slang*). [➡HAPPEN; 27]

transplant *v* **remove**, relocate, move, transfer, shift, resettle, uproot, displace. [➡MOVE SOMETHING TO ANOTHER LOCATION; 325]

transplantation *n* **relocation**, movement, transfer, replacement, uprooting, removal, displacement. [➡MOVE SOMETHING TO ANOTHER LOCATION; 325]

transport 1 *v* **convey**, move, bring, carry, transfer, ship. [➡DESPATCH AND SEND; 334] 2 *n* **conveyance**, carriage, transportation, transference, passage. [➡TRANSPORTATION, TRANSPORTERS, AND CARGOS; 323] 3 *n* **vehicle**, transportation, conveyance, means of transport. [➡VEHICLES; 1144] 4 *type of* **military aircraft**. [➡AIRCRAFT; 1147]

transportable *adj* **mobile**, portable, movable, travel, transferable, lightweight. [➡TRANSPORTATION, TRANSPORTERS, AND CARGOS; 323]

transportation *n* **transport**, conveyance, carriage, transference, passage. [➡TRANSPORTATION, TRANSPORTERS, AND CARGOS; 323]

transport café *type of* **eating place**. [➡HOTELS, RESTAURANTS, AND CLUBS; 1081]

transported *adj* [➡PLEASURE, EXCITEMENT, AND ELATION; 535]

transporter 1 *n* **carrier**, haulier, courier, shipper, delivery service. [➡TRANSPORTATION, TRANSPORTERS, AND CARGOS; 323] 2 *type of* **commercial or industrial vehicle**. [➡BIKES, CARS, AND CARRIAGES; 1148]

transposal *n* [➡EXCHANGE AND INTERCHANGE; 449]

transpose 1 *v* **invert**, switch, swap (*informal*), reverse, exchange. [➡EXCHANGE AND INTERCHANGE; 449] 2 *v* **move**, transfer, rearrange, alter, reorder, move around. [➡ MOVE SOMETHING TO ANOTHER LOCATION; 325]

transposition 1 *n* **reversal**, inversion, switch, swap (*informal*), exchange, substitution. [➡ EXCHANGE AND INTERCHANGE; 449] 2 *n* **rearrangement**, reordering, recasting, relocation, shuffle. [➡ MOVE SOMETHING TO ANOTHER LOCATION; 325]

transubstantiation (*formal*) *n* **conversion**, transformation, metamorphosis, mutation, alteration, change. [➡ CHANGE; 373]

transverse *adj* **crosswise**, at right angles, sloping, oblique, slanting, crossways, diagonal, corner to corner. [➡ ORIENTATION AND ALIGNMENT; 1222]

trap 1 *n* **ruse**, trick, snare, deception, con, ploy, setup (*informal*). [➡ DECEPTION AND LIES; 661] 2 *n* **mouth**, trap (*informal*), gob (*slang*), cakehole (*slang*). [➡ THE MOUTH; 703] 3 *v* **trick**, deceive, dupe, con, ensnare, take in, set up (*informal*). [➡ DECEPTION AND LIES; 661] 4 *v* **catch**, ensnare, entrap, ambush, corner, shut in, fence in, lock in, confine, block. [➡ CAPTIVITY AND LOSS OF FREEDOM; 249] *Opposite:* release. 5 *type of* **wagon or carriage**. [➡ VEHICLES; 1144]

trap door *n* **hatch**, flap, small door, entrance, doorway, access. [➡ DOORS AND ACCESS POINTS; 1100]

trapdoor spider *type of* **arachnid**. [➡ ARACHNIDS; 1018]

trapeze artist *n* [➡ WORKERS IN ENTERTAINMENT AND MEDIA; 873]

trapezium *type of* **angular shape**. [➡ ANGULAR SHAPE; 1216]

trapezoid *type of* **angular shape**. [➡ ANGULAR SHAPE; 1216]

trapezoidal *adj* [➡ ANGULAR SHAPE; 1216]

trapped 1 *adj* **shut in**, locked in, stuck, surrounded, hemmed in, cut off, imprisoned, entombed, ensnared, confined. [➡ CAPTIVITY AND LOSS OF FREEDOM; 249] *Opposite:* released. 2 *adj* **stuck**, caught, jammed, stuck fast, wedged, fixed. [➡ LACK OF ACTIVITY; 343] *Opposite:* free.

trappings *n* **accessories**, accoutrements, paraphernalia, trimmings, frills, symbols. [➡ PHYSICAL OBJECTS; 1242]

trash 1 *n* **nonsense**, rubbish, drivel, gibberish, hogwash (*informal*), hot air (*informal*), double talk, bunk (*slang*), bunkum (*informal*), malarkey (*informal*). [➡ MEANINGLESS SPEECH OR WRITING; 677] 2 *n* (*US*) **rubbish**, waste, refuse, litter, junk (*informal*), debris, scrap, garbage (*US*). [➡ RUBBISH AND USELESS OBJECTS; 1248] 3 *v* (*informal*) **wreck**, destroy, ruin, damage, smash, spoil, demolish, ravage, vandalize. [➡ DESTRUCTION AND DEMOLITION; 360] 4 *v* (*US informal*) **condemn**, rubbish, slate, criticize, pan (*informal*), knock (*slang*), censure. [➡ ACCUSE, BLAME, AND CRITICIZE; 642] *Opposite:* praise.

trash can (*US*) *n* [➡ CONTAINERS, RECEPTACLES, AND PACKAGING; 1244]

trashy *adj* **cheap**, tacky (*informal*), worthless, tasteless, shabby, rubbishy, poor quality, shoddy, crummy (*informal*). [➡ IN BAD REPAIR; 1233] *Opposite:* quality.

trattoria *type of* **eating place**. [➡ HOTELS, RESTAURANTS, AND CLUBS; 1081]

trauma *n* **shock**, upset, disturbance, ordeal, suffering, strain, distress, damage, pain. [➡ DIFFICULT SITUATIONS; 72]

traumatic *adj* **shocking**, disturbing, upsetting, distressing, harrowing, stressful, painful. [➡ EMOTIONALLY UNPLEASANT AND UPSETTING; 228]

traumatize 1 *v* **shock**, upset, distress, devastate, disturb, stress, torment. [➡ UPSET, DISTRESS, AND HUMILIATE; 568] 2 *v* **injure**, hurt, wound, fracture, break, cut, lacerate, gash. [➡ WOUND A PERSON OR ANIMAL; 384]

traumatized *adj* **disturbed**, shocked, upset, troubled, distressed, in shock, devastated. [➡ SADNESS, DISTRESS, AND DESPAIR; 540] *Opposite:* unaffected.

travail *n* **hard work**, toil, effort, exertion, labour, struggle, graft (*informal*). [➡ HARD WORK OR EFFORT; 299]

travel 1 *v* **journey**, tour, take a trip, voyage, trek, go, pass through, move, cover. [➡ TRAVEL: WAYS OF TRAVELLING; 321] 2 *adj* **portable**, lightweight, foldaway, collapsible, transportable, mobile. [➡ SMALL; 1194]

travel bug *n* [➡ HOBBIES, GAMES, AND SPORTS; 875]

travel case *type of* **baggage**. [➡ CONTAINERS, RECEPTACLES, AND PACKAGING; 1244]

travel guide *n* [➡ TRAVEL: SIGHT-SEEING AND TOURISM; 322]

traveller 1 *n* **itinerant**, New Age traveller, nomad, rover, wanderer, travelling worker (*US*). [➡ NOMADIC AND ROOTLESS LIFESTYLES; 884] 2 *n* **explorer**, voyager, tourist, holidaymaker, trekker, tripper (*informal*), sightseer, visitor, vacationer (*US*). [➡ TRAVEL: TRAVELLERS AND WALKERS; 320]

travelogue *n* **travel piece**, talk, lecture, travel programme. [➡ TELEVISION AND RADIO; 607]

travels *n* **voyage**, journey, trip, exploration, trekking, touring. [➡ TRAVEL: JOURNEYS AND TRIPS; 319]

travel-sick *adj* **queasy**, nauseous, unwell, ill, seasick, carsick, airsick. [➡ ILL AND SICK; 741]

traverse *v* **cross**, pass through, negotiate, navigate, go across, go over, crisscross. [➡ MOVE PAST, INTO OR THROUGH SOMETHING; 332]

travesty *n* **charade**, caricature, sham, parody, mockery, pretence, farce. [➡ DECEPTION AND LIES; 661]

trawl 1 *n* **search**, investigation, hunt, rummage, scan, look. [➡ SEEK POSSESSION AND SEARCH; 457] 2 *v* **hunt**, search, rummage around, sift, look through, scan, check. [➡ SEEK POSSESSION AND SEARCH; 457]

trawler *type of* **motor vessel**. [➡ SHIPS AND BOATS; 1149]

tray 1 *n* **salver**, platter, serving dish, plate, baking tray, oven tray. [➡ TABLEWARE, CUTLERY, AND KITCHENWARE; 861] 2 *n* **receptacle**, container, in-tray, out-tray. [➡ CONTAINERS, RECEPTACLES, AND PACKAGING; 1244]

treacherous 1 *adj* **unfaithful**, traitorous, disloyal, deceitful, false, double-crossing, perfidious (*literary*), underhand, two-faced, untrustworthy, shifty, duplicitous. [➡ DECEITFUL; 514] *Opposite:* loyal. 2 *adj* **dangerous**, hazardous, precarious, unsafe, perilous, risky, dodgy (*informal*), unstable, unsound. [➡ DANGEROUS; 237] *Opposite:* safe.

treacherousness *n* [➡ LACK OF COMMITMENT AND UNRELIABILITY; 510]

treachery *n* **deceit**, treason, deceitfulness, perfidy (*literary*), sedition, disloyalty, duplicity, betrayal. [➡LACK OF COMMITMENT AND UNRELIABILITY; 510] *Opposite:* loyalty.

treacle *n* [➡SUGAR AND PRESERVES; 1183]

treacly 1 *adj* **sticky**, glutinous, gooey, gluey, syrupy, gummy, cloying, tacky, glue-like. [➡PHYSICAL TEXTURE; 1221] 2 *adj* **sentimental**, mawkish, romanticized, romantic, soppy (*informal*), slushy, corny, cloying, syrupy. [➡IN POOR TASTE; 230]

tread 1 *v* **trample**, crush, squash, flatten, stomp, press. [➡CHANGE OF SHAPE; 386] 2 *v* **walk**, step, stride, tramp, pace, plod. [➡PROCEED AND GO; 306] 3 *n* **step**, footstep, footfall, tramp, stamp, plod. [➡IMPACT SOUNDS; 1259]

treadle *n* **foot pedal**, lever, control. [➡PARTS OF MACHINES AND TOOLS; 1117]

treadmill *n* **daily grind**, routine, drudgery, toil, slog, grindstone. [➡HARD WORK OR EFFORT; 299]

treason *n* **sedition**, treachery, disloyalty, subversion, betrayal, duplicity, high treason. [➡MORALLY BAD; 776] *Opposite:* allegiance.

treasonable *adj* **traitorous**, treacherous, subversive, disloyal, rebellious, seditious, mutinous. [➡MORALLY BAD; 776]

treasure 1 *n* **wealth**, riches, money, valuables, cache, hoard, booty, plunder. [➡FINANCIAL ASSETS; 463] 2 *n* **gem** (*informal*), star, paragon, pearl, peach (*informal*), prize. [➡AMAZING THING; 212] 3 *v* **cherish**, value, prize, adore, hold dear, appreciate. [➡LIKE, LOVE, VALUE AND ENJOY; 579] *Opposite:* neglect.

treasured *adj* **dear**, precious, loved, cherished, beloved, valued, adored, prized. [➡POPULAR AND WANTED; 221]

treasurer *n* **banker**, bursar, bookkeeper, accountant, financial officer. [➡BUSINESS PEOPLE; 794]

treasury *type of* **storage space**. [➡STORES AND STORAGE BUILDINGS; 1087]

treat 1 *v* **regard**, consider, think of, behave towards, act towards, deal with, handle. [➡CARRY OUT AN ACTION; 270] 2 *v* **care for**, take care of, doctor, cure, nurse, heal, minister to, remedy. [➡TAKE CARE OF AND SPOIL; 301] 3 *v* **pay for**, pick up the check, pick up the tab, pay the bill, give. [➡GIVE MONEY; 434] 4 *v* **indulge**, spoil, pamper, make a fuss of. [➡TAKE CARE OF AND SPOIL; 301] 5 *v* **deal with**, go into, discuss, handle, touch on, talk about, talk over, talk of, consider, take up, be concerned with. [➡BE ABOUT SOMETHING; 62] 6 *n* **luxury**, extravagance, indulgence, delight, pleasure. [➡AMAZING THING; 212] *Opposite:* necessity.

treatise *n* **dissertation**, discourse, essay, thesis, paper, exposition, article, piece, tract. [➡ANALYTICAL NONFICTION WRITING; 593]

treat like royalty *v* [➡TAKE CARE OF AND SPOIL; 301]

treatment 1 *n* **cure**, healing, care, therapy, medicine, medication, remedy. [➡REMEDIES, TREATMENTS AND OPERATIONS; 732] 2 *n* **handling**, behaviour, conduct, dealing, management, usage. [➡WAYS OF DOING THINGS; 295]

treaty *n* **agreement**, accord, contract, pact, truce, settlement. [➡OFFICIAL DOCUMENTS; 587]

treble 1 *adj* **triple**, three times, thrice, threefold. [➡APPORTIONMENT; 113] 2 *adj* **high-pitched**, high, shrill, piping. [➡SOFT OR PLEASANT SOUNDS; 1264] 3 *v* **increase**, triple, increase threefold, increase by three, multiply, swell. [➡CHANGE OF INTENSITY: MORE; 395]

tree 1 *n* **sapling**, bush, shrub. [➡PLANTS AND TREES; 1024] 2 *n* **diagram**, tree diagram, family tree, hierarchy, pyramid, graphic. [➡DRAWINGS, CHARTS AND TABLES; 595]

tree frog *type of* **amphibian**. [➡AMPHIBIANS; 1008]

treetop *n* **crown**, canopy, foliage. [➡PARTS OF TREES AND PLANTS; 1026]

trek 1 *v* **hike**, walk, ramble, march, tramp, trudge, trail, slog, wander, journey, travel. [➡TRAVEL: WAYS OF TRAVELLING; 321] 2 *n* **walk**, hike, ramble, journey, march, tramp, slog, trudge, trail, wander. [➡TRAVEL: JOURNEYS AND TRIPS; 319]

trekker *n* [➡TRAVEL: TRAVELLERS AND WALKERS; 320]

trekking *n* [➡HOBBIES, GAMES, AND SPORTS; 875]

trellis *n* **lattice**, grille, fence, fencing, frame, framework. [➡BARRIERS; 1112]

tremble 1 *v* **shiver**, shake, shudder, quake (*informal*), quiver, judder, quaver. [➡PHYSICAL REACTIONS; 317] 2 *n* **shake**, shiver, shudder, quake, quiver, tremor, vibration, wobble, judder, quaver. [➡PHYSICAL REACTIONS; 317]

trembling 1 *n* **shaking**, vibrating, quivering, shuddering, wobbling, quaking. [➡DESCRIBING BODY MOVEMENTS; 289] 2 *adj* **unsteady**, vibrating, quivering, shuddering, quaking, wobbly, shaky, rocky, juddering. [➡DESCRIBING BODY MOVEMENTS; 289] *Opposite:* still. 3 *adj* **timorous**, tremulous, nervous, terrified, fearful, apprehensive. [➡FEAR AND PANIC; 544] *Opposite:* confident.

tremblingly *adv* **fearfully**, nervously, apprehensively, timorously, tremulously, hesitantly. [➡FEAR AND PANIC; 544] *Opposite:* confidently.

tremendous 1 *adj* **great**, incredible, fabulous, terrific, marvellous, wonderful, fantastic, remarkable, awesome, magnificent, sensational, out of this world, super (*informal*), superb. [➡EXTRAORDINARY: AMAZING; 205] *Opposite:* awful. 2 *adj* **huge**, great, enormous, vast, immense, monstrous, awe-inspiring, terrific, colossal, massive, impressive, humongous (*informal*). [➡LARGE; 1192] *Opposite:* tiny.

tremendously *adv* **very**, extremely, greatly, enormously, vastly, immensely, terrifically, massively (*informal*), remarkably, exceptionally, extraordinarily, exceedingly, impressively. [➡TO A GREAT EXTENT; 130] *Opposite:* slightly.

tremor 1 *n* **shake**, tremble, vibration, quiver, shiver, shudder, judder, quaver. [➡PHYSICAL REACTIONS; 317] 2 *n* **earthquake**, quake (*informal*), shock. [➡VOLCANOES AND EARTHQUAKES; 1054]

tremulous 1 *adj* **unsteady**, quivering, trembling, quavering, shaky, wobbly. [➡DESCRIBING BODY MOVEMENTS; 289] *Opposite:* steady. 2 *adj* **timid**, timorous, trembling, shy, fearful, bashful, shrinking, nervous. [➡FEAR AND PANIC; 544] *Opposite:* confident.

tremulously *adv* **tremblingly**, quaveringly, unsteadily, shakily. [➡DESCRIBING BODY MOVEMENTS; 289] *Opposite:* confidently.

trench *n* **ditch**, channel, drain, dugout, trough, gutter, furrow. [➡WATERCOURSES; 1110]

trenchancy *n* **incisiveness**, forcefulness, acerbity, brutality, directness, outspokenness. [➡RUDE AND HOSTILE; 626] *Opposite:* gentleness.

trenchant *adj* **incisive**, cutting, sharp, biting, acerbic, severe, scathing, forceful, direct, forthright, caustic, penetrating. [➡RUDE AND HOSTILE; 626] *Opposite:* mild.

trend 1 *n* **tendency**, drift, leaning, inclination, movement, development. [➡DIRECTION OF MOTION; 346] 2 *n* **fashion**, style, look, craze, vogue, thing (*informal*), fad. [➡FADS, FETISHES, AND IDOLATRY; 556]

trendsetter *n* **innovator**, pacesetter, modernizer, leader, leading light, guru. [➡DESIGNERS, CREATORS AND INSTIGATORS; 348] *Opposite:* imitator.

trendsetting *adj* **influential**, innovative, cutting-edge, leading, new, inventive. [➡EXTRAORDINARY: AMAZING; 205] *Opposite:* conventional.

trendy (*informal*) *adj* **fashionable**, in, up-to-the-minute, hip (*slang*), cool, stylish, chic, all the rage, popular, up-to-date. [➡POPULAR AND WANTED; 221] *Opposite:* unfashionable.

trepidation *n* **fear**, anxiety, unease, nervousness, apprehension, consternation, foreboding, concern, misgivings, disquiet. [➡FEELINGS ABOUT THE FUTURE; 534] *Opposite:* equanimity.

trespass *v* **intrude**, infringe, encroach, invade, interlope. [➡ARRIVE; 12]

trespasser *n* **intruder**, squatter, snooper (*informal*), interloper. [➡CRIMINALS; 821] *Opposite:* guest.

tress *n* **lock**, strand, curl, tuft, wisp. [➡AMOUNT OF SOLID OR SEMI-SOLID; 115]

tresses *n* **locks** (*literary*), hair, curls, ringlets. [➡HAIR; 485]

trestle *n* **support**, bracket, stand, frame, framework, base. [➡SUPPORTS AND BASES; 1254]

trestle table *type of* **table**. [➡FURNITURE; 858]

trews *type of* **trousers**. [➡GARMENTS AND OUTFITS; 865]

triad *n* **trio**, threesome, triangle, troika, triumvirate, triplet. [➡GROUPS OF PEOPLE; 935]

trial 1 *n* **test**, examination, experiment, tryout, audition, assessment. [➡PREPARATORY EVENT; 57] 2 *n* **hearing**, court case, court-martial, prosecution, legal proceedings, legal action. [➡TRIAL, PUNISHMENT, AND LEGAL OUTCOMES; 819] 3 *n* **ordeal**, hardship, suffering, trouble, misery, distress, burden, worry, difficulty, anxiety, tribulation, pain. [➡NUISANCES; 254] 4 *adj* **experimental**, probationary, pilot, provisional, test, sample. [➡EXAMINE AND ASSESS; 754]

trial lawyer *n* [➡PEOPLE IN LAW COURTS; 820]

trial run *n* [➡PREPARATORY EVENT; 57]

trial size *adj* [➡SMALL; 1194]

triangle 1 *n* **threesome**, trio, three-way relationship. [➡GROUPS OF PEOPLE; 935] 2 *type of* **angular shape**. [➡ANGULAR SHAPE; 1216] 3 *type of* **percussion instrument**. [➡MUSICAL INSTRUMENTS; 910]

triangular *adj* **three-sided**, trilateral, three-cornered, wedge-shaped, deltoid. [➡ANGULAR SHAPE; 1216]

triathlon *type of* **track and field**. [➡HOBBIES, GAMES, AND SPORTS; 875]

tribal *adj* **ethnic**, family, ancestral, familial, group. [➡THE FAMILY; 956]

tribe 1 *n* **people**, ethnic group, community, society, population. [➡GROUPS OF PEOPLE; 935] 2 *n* (*informal*) **family**, clan, people (*informal*), kinfolk. [➡THE FAMILY; 956]

tribulation *n* **misfortune**, trial, suffering, ordeal, distress, difficulty, trouble, problem, hardship, misery, pain. [➡NUISANCES; 254]

tribunal 1 *n* **court**, court of law, law court. [➡TRIAL, PUNISHMENT, AND LEGAL OUTCOMES; 819] 2 *n* **board**, panel, committee, body. [➡BUSINESS ENTERPRISES AND RELATED BODIES; 793]

tributary *n* **branch**, arm, offshoot, river, stream. [➡RIVERS, LAKES, AND STREAMS; 1042]

tribute 1 *n* **compliment**, mark of respect, honour, praise, acknowledgment, esteem, accolade, homage. [➡PRAISE AND ENCOURAGE; 648] 2 *n* **tax**, duty, excise, toll, payment, fee, levy. [➡TAX AND TAXATION; 802]

trice *n* **instant**, flash, jiffy (*informal*), moment, twinkling, no time, blink of an eye. [➡SHORT PERIOD OF TIME; 93]

triceps *type of* **muscle or tendon**. [➡THE MUSCLES; 719]

triceratops *type of* **dinosaur**. [➡DINOSAUR; 996]

trick 1 *n* **deception**, ploy, ruse, hoax, dodge, swindle, trap, scam (*slang*). [➡DECEPTION AND LIES; 661] 2 *n* **joke**, prank, stunt, caper. [➡JOKES AND TEASING; 675] 3 *n* **knack**, technique, skill, secret. [➡SKILLS, TALENTS, AND ABILITIES; 527] 4 *n* **habit**, mannerism, trait, characteristic, way, quirk. [➡PERSONAL ECCENTRICITIES; 494] 5 *v* **deceive**, cheat, mislead, trap, fool, dupe, hoodwink, con. [➡DECEPTION AND LIES; 661] 6 *adj* **fake**, false, artificial, bogus, hoax, pretend. [➡FALSE AND UNREAL; 174] *Opposite:* real.

trickery 1 *n* **deception**, deceit, fraud, scam (*slang*), sting (*US slang*). [➡DECEPTION AND LIES; 661] 2 *n* **dishonesty**, deception, deceit, fraudulence, chicanery, hocus-pocus. [➡DECEPTION AND LIES; 661]

trickily *adv* **craftily**, sneakily, guilefully, cunningly, slyly, deviously, cleverly. [➡DECEITFUL; 514] *Opposite:* straightforwardly.

trickiness 1 *n* **difficulty**, complication, delicacy, awkwardness, intricacy, complexity. [➡DIFFICULTY AND COMPLEXITY; 243] *Opposite:* simplicity. 2 *n* **craftiness**, slipperiness, deviousness, slyness, duplicity, deceitfulness, wiliness, sneakiness, cleverness, cunning. [➡DECEITFUL; 514] *Opposite:* honesty.

trickle 1 *v* **drip**, drop, seep, dribble, ooze, filter. [➡LIQUID EMISSION; 371] *Opposite:* flood. 2 *n* **dribble**, drop, drip. [➡AMOUNT OF LIQUID; 114] *Opposite:* flood.

trickster *n* **cheat**, swindler, con artist (*slang*), charlatan, fraud, slippery customer. [➡PEOPLE WHO DECEIVE; 662]

tricky 1 *adj* **complicated**, delicate, awkward, fiddly (*informal*), thorny, problematic, complex, difficult, risky. [➡DIFFICULTY AND COMPLEXITY; 243] *Opposite:* simple. 2 *adj* **devious**, sly, deceitful, crafty, cunning, scheming, wily, artful, slippery. [➡DECEITFUL; 514] *Opposite:* straight.

tricky situation *n* [➡DIFFICULT SITUATIONS; 72]

tricycle *type of* **bike** (*informal*). [➡BIKES, CARS, AND CARRIAGES; 1148]

trier 1 *n* **tester**, experimenter, taster, volunteer, guinea pig, user. [➡WORKER; 836] 2 *n* **sticker**, fighter, striver, struggler, stayer, go-getter (*informal*). [➡PEOPLE WHO ARE APPROVED OF; 955] *Opposite:* defeatist.

trifle 1 *n* **nothing**, frippery, triviality. [➡UNIMPORTANT AND UNNECESSARY; 239] 2 *n* **tad** (*informal*), smidgen, bit, little, drop, touch. [➡FEW, LITTLE, SMALL AMOUNT; 119]

trifling *adj* **trivial**, petty, small, tiny, silly, slight, unimportant, negligible, inconsequential, minor, marginal, frivolous, insignificant. [➡UNIMPORTANT AND UNNECESSARY; 239] *Opposite:* significant.

trigger *v* **activate**, set off, cause, generate, start, prompt, elicit, produce, initiate, spark. [➡CAUSE TO START; 266] *Opposite:* halt.

trigger-happy (*informal*) *adj* **rash**, violent, dangerous, wild, unpredictable. [➡AGGRESSIVE AND BELLIGERENT; 519]

trigger off *v* **activate**, set off, cause, generate, start, prompt, elicit, produce, initiate, spark off. [➡CAUSE TO START; 266] *Opposite:* halt.

trigonometry *n* [➡MATHS; 598]

trilateral *adj* [➡ANGULAR SHAPE; 1216]

trilby *type of* **hat**. [➡HABERDASHERY, MILLINERY, AND LINGERIE; 867]

trill 1 *v* **warble**, quaver, shrill, tweet, vibration. [➡SOUND EMISSION BY ANIMALS OR BIRDS; 365] 2 *type of* **bird sound**. [➡SOUNDS MADE BY BIRDS; 1262]

trillion (*informal*) *n* **tons** (*informal*), loads (*informal*), stacks (*informal*), masses (*informal*), lots, heaps (*informal*). [➡MANY, MUCH, LARGE AMOUNT; 117]

trilogy *n* **series**, sequence, set, cycle, trio. [➡BOOKS AND BOOKLETS; 591]

trim 1 *v* **clip**, cut, shear, pare, prune, shave, lop off. [➡EXTRACT AND SEVER; 342] *Opposite:* lengthen. 2 *v* **cut back**, prune, decrease, lower, shave, lop off, edit, truncate, reduce. *Opposite:* augment. (*formal*). [➡CHANGE OF SIZE: SMALLER; 394] 3 *v* **decorate**, adorn, embroider, embellish, edge, border, deck (*literary*). [➡DECORATE, ADORN, AND APPLY COATINGS; 406] 4 *adj* **tidy**, orderly, smart, spruce, dapper, spick and span, neat, natty. [➡ORDER AND ORGANISATION; 207] *Opposite:* messy. 5 *adj* **slim**, fit, shapely, sleek, slender, lean, neat, in shape. [➡BUILD; 478] *Opposite:* bulky. 6 *n* **decoration**, adornment, frill, edge, border. [➡ORNAMENTS AND DECORATIONS; 1247]

trimaran *type of* **sailing vessel**. [➡SHIPS AND BOATS; 1149]

trimester *type of* **time period**. [➡TIMES OF YEAR; 88]

trimly *adv* **neatly**, sleekly, compactly, tidily. [➡ORDER AND ORGANISATION; 207]

trimming *n* **decoration**, adornment, frill, garnish, extra, edge, border. [➡ORNAMENTS AND DECORATIONS; 1247]

trimmings 1 *n* **side dishes**, extras, accompaniments, fixings (*US informal*). [➡PREPARED DISHES; 1169] 2 *n* **extras**, bits and pieces (*informal*), appurtenances (*formal*), accompaniments, add-ons, accessories, embellishments. [➡ORNAMENTS AND DECORATIONS; 1247] 3 *n* **clippings**, parings, bits, pieces, nail clippings, nail parings. [➡REMAINDER AND REMAINDERS; 123]

trimness *n* **neatness**, compactness, tidiness, sleekness, thinness, leanness, slenderness. [➡SMALL; 1194]

trinity *n* **threesome**, trio, triad, troika. [➡GROUPS OF PEOPLE; 935]

trinket *n* **ornament**, charm, knick-knack, bauble, gewgaw. [➡ORNAMENTS AND DECORATIONS; 1247]

trio 1 *n* **threesome**, triad, troika, trinity, triangle. [➡GROUPS OF PEOPLE; 935] 2 *type of* **band**. [➡MUSICIANS AND SINGERS; 908]

trip 1 *n* **journey**, tour, excursion, expedition, outing, voyage, jaunt, spree, visit. [➡TRAVEL: JOURNEYS AND TRIPS; 319] 2 *n* **slip**, stumble, tumble, fall. [➡GO DOWNWARDS; 308] 3 *v* **stumble**, trip up, slip, tumble, falter, fall, lose your footing. [➡GO DOWNWARDS; 308] 4 *v* **skip**, hop, prance, caper, dance. [➡FIDGET AND FROLIC; 312]

tripartite *adj* **three-way**, three-party, multilateral, triple. [➡APPORTIONMENT; 113]

tripe (*informal*) *n* **rubbish**, nonsense, garbage, drivel, rot (*informal*), claptrap (*informal*), twaddle (*informal*), trash. [➡MEANINGLESS SPEECH OR WRITING; 677] *Opposite:* fact.

triple 1 *adj* **tripartite**, three-way, three-layered, triple-decker. [➡APPORTIONMENT; 113] *Opposite:* single. 2 *adj* **treble**, threefold, multiple. [➡APPORTIONMENT; 113] *Opposite:* single. 3 *v* **treble**, triplicate, multiply by three, increase, augment (*formal*), boost. [➡CHANGE OF SIZE: BIGGER; 393] *Opposite:* reduce.

triple jump *type of* **track and field**. [➡HOBBIES, GAMES, AND SPORTS; 875]

triplet 1 *n* **trio**, triad, threesome, troika. [➡GROUPS OF PEOPLE; 935] 2 *type of* **offspring**. [➡YOUNGER GENERATION RELATIVES; 958]

tripod *type of* **photographic equipment**. [➡PHOTOGRAPHY AND PHOTOGRAPHIC EQUIPMENT; 1121]

tripper (*informal*) *n* **tourist**, day tripper, holidaymaker, visitor, excursionist (*dated*). [➡TRAVEL: TRAVELLERS AND WALKERS; 320]

trip up 1 *v* **stumble**, trip, slip, tumble, fall, lose your footing. [➡GO DOWNWARDS; 308] 2 *v* **trap**, catch out (*informal*), trick, confuse, disconcert, unsettle, wrong-foot. [➡CONFUSE AND BEWILDER; 572]

trite *adj* **commonplace**, stale, tired, pedestrian, worn, hackneyed, clichéd, banal, unoriginal, stock, corny. [➡ORDINARINESS; 245] *Opposite:* original.

triteness *n* **dullness**, tiredness, staleness, corniness, banality, unoriginality. [➡ORDINARINESS; 245] *Opposite:* originality.

triumph 1 *n* **victory**, achievement, conquest, accomplishment, coup, feat, success. [➡SUCCESS; 82] *Opposite:* failure. **2** *n* **rejoicing**, pride, elation, delight, satisfaction, jubilation, exultation, glee, joy. [➡PLEASURE, EXCITEMENT, AND ELATION; 535] *Opposite:* sorrow. **3** *v* **succeed**, prevail, win, overcome, be victorious, win out, win through, carry the day. [➡SUCCEED AND WIN; 79] *Opposite:* lose.

triumphal *adj* **ceremonial**, commemorative, victory, heroic, celebratory, great, grand. [➡SUCCESSFUL AND PROMISING; 81]

triumphant **1** *adj* **winning**, victorious, glorious, dominant, proud, conquering. [➡SUCCESSFUL AND PROMISING; 81] **2** *adj* **exultant**, celebratory, jubilant, elated, delighted, gleeful. [➡PLEASURE, EXCITEMENT, AND ELATION; 535] *Opposite:* sorrowful.

triumphantly *adv* **exultantly**, jubilantly, elatedly, delightedly, gleefully. [➡SUCCESSFUL AND PROMISING; 81] *Opposite:* sorrowfully.

triumph over *v* **overcome**, defeat, beat, prevail over, get the better of, humiliate, vanquish, conquer. [➡BEAT AND DEFEAT; 80]

triumvirate *n* **trio**, threesome, triad, troika. [➡GROUPS OF PEOPLE; 935]

trivet *n* **stand**, support, rest, tripod. [➡SUPPORTS AND BASES; 1254]

trivia *n* **minutiae**, trivialities, froth, nonsense, small beer (*informal*), small potatoes (*informal*), trifles. [➡UNIMPORTANT AND UNNECESSARY; 239] *Opposite:* essentials.

trivial *adj* **unimportant**, small, inconsequential, slight, trifling, petty, marginal, frivolous, negligible, minor, insignificant. [➡UNIMPORTANT AND UNNECESSARY; 239] *Opposite:* crucial.

triviality **1** *n* **unimportance**, inconsequence, worthlessness, insignificance, pettiness, inconsequentiality, frivolity. [➡UNIMPORTANT AND UNNECESSARY; 239] *Opposite:* importance. **2** *n* **trifle**, nothing, frippery. [➡UNIMPORTANT AND UNNECESSARY; 239]

trivialize *v* **play down**, belittle, underestimate, make light of, tone down. [➡UNDERDO SOMETHING; 292] *Opposite:* highlight.

trivialness *n* [➡ORDINARINESS; 245]

troika **1** *n* **trio**, triumvirate, threesome, triad. [➡GROUPS OF PEOPLE; 935] **2** *type of* **wagon or carriage**. [➡VEHICLES; 1144]

troll **1** *v* **fish**, angle, trail, spin, lure. [➡SEEK POSSESSION AND SEARCH; 457] **2** *v* **amble**, wander, saunter, drift, walk, stroll. [➡MOVE SLOWLY; 315] **3** *n* **giant**, ogre, hobgoblin, goblin, monster. [➡MYTHICAL BEINGS; 790]

trolley *n* [➡BIKES, CARS, AND CARRIAGES; 1148]

trombone *type of* **brass instrument**. [➡MUSICAL INSTRUMENTS; 910]

troop **1** *n* **crowd**, horde, throng, multitude, herd, flock, drove, company, pack, group. [➡GROUPS OF PEOPLE; 935] **2** *v* **move**, gather, rally, come together, get together, congregate. [➡GET CLOSER TOGETHER; 311] **3** *v* **march**, parade, stream, trudge, traipse, file. [➡PROCEED AND GO; 306] **4** *type of* **herd**. [➡GROUP OF ANIMALS; 993]

trooper *n* [➡PEOPLE WHO ARE APPROVED OF; 955]

troops *n* [➡THE ARMED FORCES; 827]

trophy *n* **cup**, award, medal, crown, title, plaque, plate, shield, prize. [➡REWARDS AND AWARDS; 440]

tropical *adj* **hot**, steamy, humid, sultry, stifling. [➡HOT WEATHER; 1050] *Opposite:* temperate.

tropical forest *n* [➡WOODS, FORESTS, AND JUNGLES; 1047]

tropical storm *n* [➡WINDY AND STORMY WEATHER; 1053]

troposphere *n* [➡THE EARTH'S ATMOSPHERE; 1040]

trot *v* **jog**, run, hurry, scurry, scamper. [➡MOVE FAST; 314] *Opposite:* saunter.

Trotskyism *n* [➡PHILOSOPHIES AND BELIEFS; 781]

trotter *type of* **horse**. [➡HORSE; 985]

troubadour *n* **minstrel**, musician, bard (*literary or humorous*), poet, wandering minstrel. [➡MUSICIANS AND SINGERS; 908]

trouble **1** *n* **problem**, difficulty, dilemma, nuisance, snag, danger, hitch, fault, hassle (*informal*), trial, tribulation, mess. [➡DANGER; 236] *Opposite:* ease. **2** *n* **worry**, concern, distress, anxiety, care, misfortune, suffering, woe. [➡CONFUSION, ANXIETY, AND WORRY; 541] **3** *n* **complaint**, ailment, disease, illness, malady, upset, disorder, condition. [➡SICKNESS; 730] *Opposite:* good health. **4** *n* **effort**, bother, inconvenience, work, thought, attention, care. [➡HARD WORK OR EFFORT; 299] **5** *n* **strife**, unrest, disorder, disturbance, discontent, disruption, turmoil, conflict, discord, bother. [➡DISHARMONY; 157] *Opposite:* accord. **6** *v* **concern**, worry, distress, agitate, bother, harass, perturb, vex, hassle (*informal*), bug (*informal*), upset, disturb. [➡UPSET, DISTRESS, AND HUMILIATE; 568] **7** *v* **bother**, put out, inconvenience, disturb, burden, weigh down, interrupt. [➡UPSET, DISTRESS, AND HUMILIATE; 568] **8** *v* **make an effort**, take pains, exert yourself, bother. [➡ATTEMPT AN ACTION; 262] *Opposite:* hang back.

See Compare and Contrast at **bother**.

troubled **1** *adj* **anxious**, concerned, bothered, worried, disturbed, distressed, uneasy, upset, unsettled. [➡CONFUSION, ANXIETY, AND WORRY; 541] *Opposite:* calm. **2** *adj* **problematic**, tricky, awkward, difficult. [➡DIFFICULTY AND COMPLEXITY; 243] *Opposite:* easy.

trouble-free *adj* **easy**, simple, painless, straightforward, uncomplicated. [➡EASE AND SIMPLICITY; 201] *Opposite:* troublesome.

troublemaker *n* **pest** (*informal*), mischief-maker, menace, scallywag (*dated informal*), agitator, firebrand, rabble-rouser (*disapproving*). [➡UNCOOPERATIVE OR REBELLIOUS PERSON; 567]

troubleshooter **1** *n* **technician**, engineer, mechanic, problem solver, expert, genius, whiz (*informal*). [➡TALENTED OR INTELLIGENT PERSON; 529] **2** *n* **mediator**, consultant, ombudsman, adviser, counsellor, problem solver. [➡OFFICE WORKERS; 847]

troublesome **1** *adj* **worrying**, upsetting, bothersome, wearisome, difficult, hard, niggling, problematic, taxing, trying. [➡IRRITATING; 229] *Opposite:* trouble-free. **2** *adj* **dis-**

orderly, rowdy, unruly, uncooperative, undisciplined, disruptive, unmanageable, badly behaved, difficult, naughty. [➡REBELLIOUSNESS AND DISOBEDIENCE; 566] *Opposite:* well-behaved.

troubling *adj* [➡EMOTIONALLY UNPLEASANT AND UPSETTING; 228]

trough 1 *n* **manger**, crib, rack, holder. [➡CONTAINERS, RECEPTACLES, AND PACKAGING; 1244] 2 *n* **channel**, furrow, trench, gutter, ditch, drain. [➡HOLES, GAPS, AND FORKS; 1251] 3 *n* **depression**, low, low pressure area. [➡WINDY AND STORMY WEATHER; 1053] *Opposite:* ridge.

trounce *v* **beat**, thrash, rout, crush, overwhelm, slaughter (*slang*), hammer (*informal*), defeat, stuff, cream (*US informal*). [➡BEAT AND DEFEAT; 80]

See Compare and Contrast at **defeat**.

trounced *adj* [➡BEATEN AND DEFEATED; 78]

trouncing *n* **pasting** (*informal*), hiding (*informal*), routing, hammering (*informal*), thrashing, crushing, drubbing, beating. [➡BEAT AND DEFEAT; 80]

troupe *n* **company**, cast, band, ensemble, group. [➡GROUPS OF PEOPLE; 935]

trousers

◆ *types of trousers*
bell-bottom trousers, Bermuda shorts, breeches, capri pants, chinos, cords, culottes, dungarees, fatigues, hiphuggers (*US*), hipsters, hot pants, jeans, jodhpurs, khakis, knickerbockers, lederhosen, leggings, pedal pushers, plus fours, salopettes, shorts, slacks, trews

trouser suit *type of* **suit**. [➡GARMENTS AND OUTFITS; 865]

trousseau *n* **bridal goods**, bottom drawer, hope chest (*US*). [➡SOFT FURNISHINGS, LINEN, AND DRAPERY; 860]

trout *type of* **freshwater fish**. [➡FRESHWATER FISH; 1010]

trowel *type of* **general tool**. [➡HAND TOOLS; 1118]

truancy *n* **absence**, nonattendance, absenteeism, malingering (*disapproving*), skiving (*informal*), bunking off (*informal*). [➡ABSENT AND UNAVAILABLE; 7] *Opposite:* attendance.

truant 1 *n* **absentee**, malingerer (*disapproving*), shirker, skiver (*informal*). [➡RUNAWAYS AND ABSENTEES; 9] 2 *v* **shirk**, skive (*informal*), malinger (*disapproving*), bunk off (*informal*), go AWOL, play hooky (*informal*). [➡RUN AWAY AND AVOID; 10]

truce *n* **ceasefire**, armistice, treaty, peace, respite, break, lull. [➡PEACEFULNESS AND GENTLENESS; 215]

truck *type of* **commercial or industrial vehicle**. [➡VEHICLES; 1144]

truck driver *n* [➡DRIVERS; 1152]

trucker *n* [➡DRIVERS; 1152]

truck farm (*US*) *n* [➡AGRICULTURE AND FARMING; 1074]

truckload *n* [➡MANY, MUCH, LARGE AMOUNT; 117]

truck stop (*US*) *type of* **eating place**. [➡HOTELS, RESTAURANTS, AND CLUBS; 1081]

truculence *n* **defiance**, belligerence, sullenness, cussedness (*informal*), insolence, impertinence. [➡AGGRESSIVE AND BELLIGERENT; 519] *Opposite:* enthusiasm.

truculent *adj* **hostile**, belligerent, defiant, quarrelsome, argumentative, aggressive, fractious, confrontational, obstreperous, sullen, surly, cussed (*informal*), insolent. [➡AGGRESSIVE AND BELLIGERENT; 519] *Opposite:* easygoing.

trudge 1 *v* **tramp**, traipse, slog, plod, trek, hike, march, lumber, trail. [➡MOVE SLOWLY; 315] 2 *n* **slog**, trek, hike, march, haul, trail. [➡PROCEED AND GO; 306]

true 1 *adj* **factual**, accurate, right, spot-on (*informal*), correct, proper, real, exact. [➡TRUE AND REAL; 172] *Opposite:* false. 2 *adj* **real**, genuine, actual, valid, authentic, veritable, bona fide, rightful, sincere. [➡TRUE AND REAL; 172] *Opposite:* fake. 3 *adj* **faithful**, dedicated, constant, loyal, sincere, firm, staunch, confirmed, dutiful, devoted. [➡HONEST AND RELIABLE; 503] *Opposite:* unfaithful.

true-blue 1 *adj* **right-wing**, traditional, conservative, diehard, old-school. [➡STYLES AND SYSTEMS OF GOVERNMENT; 806] 2 *adj* (*US*) **loyal**, incorruptible, faithful, honest, staunch, orthodox. [➡HONEST AND RELIABLE; 503] *Opposite:* disloyal.

true-life *adj* **genuine**, realistic, real-life, real, true, factual. [➡TRUE AND REAL; 172]

true to life *adj* **realistic**, convincing, accurate, authentic, lifelike. [➡TRUE AND REAL; 172] *Opposite:* unrealistic.

truffle 1 *type of* **confectionery**. [➡CONFECTIONERY; 1181] 2 *type of* **fungus**. [➡MICROORGANISMS, FUNGI, AND ALGAE; 1023]

truism *n* **axiom**, cliché, maxim, platitude, saying. [➡FIGURES OF SPEECH; 674]

truly 1 *adv* **really**, in fact, beyond doubt, actually, indeed, in reality. [➡TRUE AND REAL; 172] 2 *adv* **sincerely**, faithfully, honestly, in all honesty, genuinely, really. [➡TRUE AND REAL; 172] *Opposite:* insincerely. 3 *adv* **very**, greatly, really, indeed, exceptionally, enormously, extremely. [➡TO A GREAT EXTENT; 130]

trump *v* **outdo**, go one better, call somebody's bluff, undermine, outmanoeuvre, steal a march on somebody, catch somebody napping, outplay. [➡BEAT AND DEFEAT; 80]

trumped-up *adj* **false**, fake, invented, made-up, fabricated, falsified, phoney. [➡FALSE AND UNREAL; 174] *Opposite:* genuine.

trumpet *type of* **brass trumpet**. [➡MUSICAL INSTRUMENTS; 910]

truncate *v* **shorten**, abbreviate, trim, cut, prune, pare. [➡CHANGE OF SIZE: SMALLER; 394] *Opposite:* lengthen.

truncated *adj* [➡UNFINISHEDNESS; 240]

truncheon *type of* **club**. [➡BLUNT INSTRUMENTS AND WHIPS; 1157]

trundle 1 *v* **roll**, roll along, rattle, labour, wheel, push, lumber, drive. [➡PUSH, PULL, SLIDE; 336] 2 *v* **traipse**, trail, saunter, toddle (*informal*), lumber, wander. [➡MOVE SLOWLY; 315]

trundle bed *type of* **bed**. [➡FURNITURE; 858]

trunk 1 *n* **stem**, bole, stalk. [➡PARTS OF TREES AND PLANTS; 1026] 2 *type of* **container**. [➡CONTAINERS, RECEPTACLES, AND PACKAGING; 1244] 3 (*US*) *part of* **external structure**. [➡EXTERNAL PARTS OF A VEHICLE; 1146]

trunk road *type of* **major road**. [➡ROADS; 1105]

trunk route (*US*) *type of* **major road**. [➡ROADS; 1105]

trunks *n* **swimming trunks**, bathing trunks, shorts. [➡GARMENTS AND OUTFITS; 865]

truss *v* **bind**, tie up, tie, tether, string. [➡FASTEN, LINK, AND JOIN; 409]

trust 1 *n* **faith**, belief, hope, conviction, confidence, expectation, reliance, dependence. [➡CERTAINTY; 562] *Opposite:* distrust. 2 *n* **custody**, care, protection, responsibility, guard, charge. [➡RESPONSIBILITY; 171] 3 *n* (*US*) **consortium**, cartel, syndicate, group, organization. [➡GROUPS WITH A COMMON INTEREST; 938] 4 *v* **have faith in**, believe, rely on, depend on, confide in, have confidence in, count on, bank on, be sure about. [➡CERTAINTY; 562] *Opposite:* distrust. 5 *v* **hope**, believe, expect, assume, suppose, presume. [➡PREDICT AND ANTICIPATE; 751] *Opposite:* despair. 6 *v* **entrust**, confide, assign, consign, commit. [➡GIVE AND PROVIDE; 431]

trustee 1 *n* **fund manager**, fund administrator, director. [➡BUSINESS PEOPLE; 794] 2 *n* **representative**, deputy, agent, executor, executrix, guardian. [➡SUPPORTERS, PROTECTORS, AND COMPATRIOTS; 970]

trustfulness *n* **unwariness**, credulity, innocence, lack of caution, trustingness, naivety. [➡NEGATIVE INTELLECTUAL CHARACTERISTICS; 526] *Opposite:* wariness.

trusting *adj* **gullible**, credulous, unquestioning, believing, naive, innocent. [➡NEGATIVE INTELLECTUAL CHARACTERISTICS; 526] *Opposite:* suspicious.

trustworthiness *n* **honesty**, dependability, reliability, fidelity, constancy, responsibility, credibility. [➡HONEST AND RELIABLE; 503] *Opposite:* dishonesty.

trustworthy *adj* **dependable**, reliable, responsible, truthful, honest, constant, honourable, upright, faithful, trusty. [➡HONEST AND RELIABLE; 503] *Opposite:* corrupt.

trusty *adj* **faithful**, dependable, reliable, constant, loyal, predictable, trustworthy. [➡HONEST AND RELIABLE; 503] *Opposite:* unreliable.

truth 1 *n* **fact**, certainty, reality, actuality, veracity, verity (*formal*). [➡TRUE AND REAL; 172] *Opposite:* untruth. 2 *n* **honesty**, integrity, fidelity, sincerity. [➡HONEST AND RELIABLE; 503]

truthful 1 *adj* **honest**, straight, frank, open, straightforward, ingenuous, candid. [➡HONEST AND RELIABLE; 503] *Opposite:* dishonest. 2 *adj* **correct**, true, reliable, accurate, exact, literal, factual, faithful, proper, right. [➡EXACT; 204] *Opposite:* false.

truthfully *adv* **honestly**, candidly, frankly, openly, straightforwardly, straight, truly. [➡HONEST AND RELIABLE; 503] *Opposite:* dishonestly.

truthfulness 1 *n* **honesty**, truth, candour, frankness, openness, straightforwardness, directness. [➡HONEST AND RELIABLE; 503] *Opposite:* dishonesty. 2 *n* **accuracy**, reliability, correctness, exactitude, faithfulness, truth. [➡EXACT; 204] *Opposite:* inaccuracy.

try 1 *v* **attempt**, endeavour, strive, aim, seek, undertake, make an effort, take a crack at (*informal*), have a go (*informal*), struggle. [➡ATTEMPT AN ACTION; 262] 2 *v* **test**, sample, taste, appraise, evaluate, experiment with, check out, give it a go. [➡EXAMINE AND ASSESS; 754] 3 *v* **strain**, vex, tax, exasperate, annoy, irritate, frustrate. [➡ANGER AND ANNOY; 570] *Opposite:* soothe. 4 *v* **judge**, put on trial, hear, take to court. [➡TRIAL, PUNISHMENT, AND LEGAL OUTCOMES; 819] 5 *n* **attempt**, effort, go, crack (*informal*), bash (*informal*), stab (*informal*), shot (*informal*). [➡ATTEMPT AN ACTION; 262]

Compare and Contrast: ***try, attempt, endeavour, strive***

CORE MEANING: TO MAKE AN EFFORT TO DO SOMETHING

try to make an effort or an attempt to do or achieve something; ***attempt*** to make an effort to do something, especially without much expectation of success; ***endeavour*** to make a serious and sincere effort to do or achieve something; ***strive*** to make persistent efforts to achieve something.

trying *adj* **annoying**, tiresome, irritating, wearisome, frustrating, demanding, vexing, exasperating, taxing, difficult. [➡EMOTIONALLY UNPLEASANT AND UPSETTING; 228] *Opposite:* soothing.

try out *v* **test**, sample, check out, experiment with, give it a go, appraise, evaluate, audition, rehearse. [➡EXAMINE AND ASSESS; 754]

tryout *n* **trial**, test, evaluation, audition, assessment, rehearsal, run-through, practice. [➡PREPARATORY EVENT; 57]

tryst *n* **assignation**, rendezvous, meeting, date, encounter, tête-à-tête. [➡MEETINGS AND ASSEMBLIES; 43]

try your hand *v* **have a go** (*informal*), have a bash (*informal*), experiment, try out, have a stab (*informal*), have a crack (*informal*), have a shot, make an attempt. [➡ATTEMPT AN ACTION; 262]

tsar *n* [➡RULERS AND ARISTOCRACY; 823]

tsarina *n* [➡RULERS AND ARISTOCRACY; 823]

tsarism *n* [➡STYLES AND SYSTEMS OF GOVERNMENT; 806]

tsaritsa *n* [➡RULERS AND ARISTOCRACY; 823]

tsetse fly *type of* **flying insect**. [➡FLYING INSECTS; 1013]

T-shirt *type of* **top**. [➡GARMENTS AND OUTFITS; 865]

tsunami *n* [➡THE SEAS, OCEANS, AND SHORES; 1041]

tub 1 *n* **container**, carton, pot, drum, barrel, cask, butt. [➡CONTAINERS, RECEPTACLES, AND PACKAGING; 1244] 2 *n* **bath**, hip bath, hot tub, plunge bath, bathtub. [➡FITTINGS; 859]

tuba *type of* **brass instrument**. [➡MUSICAL INSTRUMENTS; 910]

tubbiness (*informal*) *n* [➡BUILD; 478]

tubby (*informal*) *adj* **plump**, podgy, chubby, portly, overweight, flabby (*informal*), heavy, pudgy (*US informal*). [➡BUILD; 478] *Opposite:* skinny.

tube 1 *n* **pipe**, cylinder, hose, conduit, duct, spout. [➡ WATERCOURSES; 1110] 2 *type of* **railway.** [➡ RAILWAYS; 1106] 3 *n* (*US*) [➡ TELEVISION AND RADIO; 607]

tuber *n* **storage organ**, rhizome, root, underground stem. [➡ PARTS OF TREES AND PLANTS; 1026]

tube top (*US*) *type of* **top.** [➡ GARMENTS AND OUTFITS; 865]

tubing *n* **tubes**, pipes, plumbing. [➡ WATERCOURSES; 1110]

tubular *adj* **tube-shaped**, cylindrical, tube-like, hollow. [➡ ROUNDED SHAPE; 1217]

tubular bells *type of* **percussion instrument.** [➡ MUSICAL INSTRUMENTS; 910]

tuck 1 *v* **insert**, put, push, slip, place, stick (*informal*), pop (*informal*). [➡ POSITION SOMETHING; 326] *Opposite:* remove. 2 *v* **pleat**, fold, dart, gather, pucker, ruche. [➡ CHANGE OF SHAPE; 386] 3 *n* **pleat**, fold, dart, gather, pucker, ruche. [➡ CHANGE OF SHAPE; 386] 4 *n* **food**, nosh (*informal*), grub (*informal*), tucker (*informal*). [➡ FOOD; 1166]

tucker (*informal*) *n* **food**, nosh (*informal*), grub (*informal*), tuck, chow (*slang*). [➡ FOOD; 1166]

tuck in (*informal*) *v* [➡ EAT AND NOT EAT; 711]

Tudor *type of* **pre-20th-century architecture.** [➡ BUILDING AND ARCHITECTURE; 1075]

tuff *type of* **stone.** [➡ STONES, ROCKS, AND BOULDERS; 1057]

tuft *n* **clump**, tussock, cluster, bunch, truss, tassel. [➡ AMOUNT OF SOLID OR SEMI-SOLID; 115]

tug 1 *v* **pull**, tow, haul, heave, jerk, yank, wrench. [➡ PUSH, PULL, SLIDE; 336] *Opposite:* push. 2 *n* **yank**, heave, pull, jerk, haul, wrench. [➡ PUSH, PULL, SLIDE; 336] *Opposite:* push. 3 *type of* **motor vessel.** [➡ SHIPS AND BOATS; 1149]

See Compare and Contrast at **pull.**

tug of war *n* **tussle**, power struggle, struggle, battle, wrangle, scrimmage. [➡ AGGRESSIVE EVENT; 39] *Opposite:* agreement.

tuition *n* **instruction**, teaching, schooling, training, education, guidance, coaching. [➡ TEACHING; 839]

tulip *type of* **flower grown from bulb.** [➡ FLOWERS FROM BULBS; 1030]

tulle *type of* **synthetic fabric.** [➡ FABRICS; 1131]

tum (*informal*) *n* [➡ THE DIGESTIVE TRACT; 710]

tumble 1 *v* **fall over**, fall down, stumble, trip up, topple, lurch. [➡ GO DOWNWARDS; 308] *Opposite:* stand up. 2 *v* **plummet**, drop, nose-dive, plunge, dive, fall. [➡ CHANGE OF INTENSITY: LESS; 396] *Opposite:* rise.

tumbledown *adj* **ramshackle**, rickety, run-down, derelict, dilapidated, ruined, crumbling. [➡ IN BAD REPAIR; 1233]

tumble dryer *type of* **appliance.** [➡ HOUSEHOLD APPLIANCES; 1116]

tumbler 1 *n* **glass**, tall glass, beaker, whisky glass, highball glass (*US*). [➡ TABLEWARE, CUTLERY, AND KITCHENWARE; 861] 2 *n* **acrobat**, gymnast, aerialist, trapeze artist, entertainer. [➡ PEOPLE IN SPORTS AND LEISURE; 876]

tumbleweed *type of* **weed.** [➡ WEEDS AND THISTLES; 1034]

tumbril *type of* **wagon or carriage.** [➡ BIKES, CARS, AND CARRIAGES; 1148]

tummy (*informal*) *n* **stomach**, belly (*informal*), abdomen, paunch, pot, gut. [➡ THE DIGESTIVE TRACT; 710]

tummy ache (*informal*) *n* [➡ DISORDERS OF THE DIGESTIVE SYSTEM; 714]

tummy pain (*informal*) *n* [➡ DISORDERS OF THE DIGESTIVE SYSTEM; 714]

tumour *n* **growth**, lump, malignant tumour, benign tumour, cancer, polyp. [➡ ILLNESSES AND DISORDERS; 733]

tumult *n* **uproar**, commotion, clamour, hubbub, hullabaloo, din, turmoil, furore, mayhem (*informal*), confusion, chaos, disorder, turbulence. [➡ CHAOS AND UPROAR; 51] *Opposite:* peace.

tumultuous 1 *adj* **unrestrained**, unbridled, riotous, boisterous, rowdy, wild, joyous, festive, noisy. [➡ LOUD OR UNPLEASANT SOUNDS; 1265] 2 *adj* **turbulent**, confused, chaotic, agitated. [➡ DISORDER AND CHAOS; 246]

tumulus *n* [➡ BURIAL PLACES AND ACCESSORIES; 930]

tuna *type of* **tropical sea fish.** [➡ SEA FISH; 1009]

tundra *n* [➡ DESERTS AND PLAINS; 1045]

tune 1 *n* **melody**, song, air, jingle, harmony, refrain. [➡ MUSIC, SONGS, AND SINGING; 907] 2 *v* **adjust**, fine-tune, change, alter, modify, tweak (*informal*), regulate, pitch. [➡ CORRECT AND PUT RIGHT; 378]

tuneful *adj* **melodic**, melodious, harmonious, musical, pleasant, sweet. [➡ SOFT OR PLEASANT SOUNDS; 1264] *Opposite:* discordant.

tunefulness *n* [➡ SOFT OR PLEASANT SOUNDS; 1264]

tuneless *adj* **unmusical**, droning, monotone, atonal, monotonous, discordant. [➡ LOUD OR UNPLEASANT SOUNDS; 1265] *Opposite:* tuneful.

tuner *type of* **audio equipment.** [➡ AUDIO EQUIPMENT; 1138]

tune-up *n* **service**, overhaul, fine-tune, once-over (*informal*), check, maintenance. [➡ EXAMINE AND ASSESS; 754]

tungsten *type of* **metal.** [➡ METALS; 1275]

tunic *type of* **top.** [➡ GARMENTS AND OUTFITS; 865]

tunnel 1 *n* **channel**, passageway, subway, shaft, underpass. [➡ BRIDGES, TUNNELS, CROSSINGS, AND JUNCTIONS; 1111] *Opposite:* bridge. 2 *n* **burrow**, hole, warren, earth, sett, den, lair. [➡ ANIMAL OR BIRD ACCOMMODATION; 1078] 3 *v* **excavate**, burrow, dig, mine, channel, sap. [➡ USE TOOLS AND MACHINERY; 469]

turban *type of* **headgear.** [➡ HABERDASHERY, MILLINERY, AND LINGERIE; 867]

turbid 1 *adj* **muddy**, cloudy, opaque, dirty, murky, thick. [➡ DENSITY AND CONSISTENCY; 1206] *Opposite:* clear. 2 *adj* **confused**, muddled, disorganized, scrambled, chaotic, unclear. [➡ DISORDER AND CHAOS; 246] *Opposite:* clear.

turbine *n* [➡ ENGINES AND HYDRAULICS; 1142]

turbofan *part of* **aircraft.** [➡AIRCRAFT; 1147]

turbojet *part of* **aircraft.** [➡AIRCRAFT; 1147]

turboprop *part of* **aircraft.** [➡AIRCRAFT; 1147]

turbot *type of* **flatfish.** [➡SEA FISH; 1009]

turbulence *n* **commotion**, confusion, turmoil, disorder, unrest, instability, hurly-burly, uproar, tumult, furore, chaos, mayhem (*informal*), havoc. [➡CHAOS AND UPROAR; 51] *Opposite:* calm.

turbulent 1 *adj* **confused**, unstable, chaotic, tumultuous, in turmoil, disorderly. [➡DISORDER AND CHAOS; 246] *Opposite:* orderly. 2 *adj* **violent**, rowdy, unruly, riotous, quarrelsome, restless. [➡REBELLIOUSNESS AND DISOBEDIENCE; 566] *Opposite:* peaceful. 3 *adj* **stormy**, tempestuous, raging, choppy, blustery, wild, windy, unsettled. [➡WINDY AND STORMY WEATHER; 1053] *Opposite:* settled.

turbulently *adv* **tempestuously**, stormily, passionately, violently, restlessly. [➡REBELLIOUSNESS AND DISOBEDIENCE; 566] *Opposite:* smoothly.

tureen *n* **bowl**, serving dish, dish, casserole. [➡TABLEWARE, CUTLERY, AND KITCHENWARE; 861]

turf 1 *n* **lawn**, grass, pasture, meadow, verdure, grazing. [➡THE COUNTRYSIDE AND OUTDOOR SPACES; 1070] 2 *n* (*informal*) **area of expertise**, sphere of influence, field, territory, orbit, ambit. [➡SUBJECT AREA; 769] 3 *n* (*informal*) **territory**, patch, beat, neighbourhood, home turf, haunt, neck of the woods. [➡PLACE; 1064]

turf out (*slang*) *v* **oust**, throw out, turn out, eject, expel, evict, kick out (*informal*), force out, get rid of, chuck out (*informal*). [➡EJECT AND EXCLUDE; 341] *Opposite:* welcome.

turgid *adj* **pompous**, boring, dull, hard going, stilted, pretentious, affected, solemn, self-important, ponderous, stuffy. [➡BORING AND UNINTERESTING; 235] *Opposite:* amusing.

turkey 1 *n* (*US slang*) **failure**, flop, washout (*informal*), dud (*informal*), fiasco, lemon (*informal*). [➡FAILURE; 77] *Opposite:* success. 2 *type of* **fowl.** [➡FOOD BIRD; 999] 3 *type of* **meat.** [➡TYPES AND CUTS OF MEAT; 1176]

Turkish coffee *n type of* **coffee.** [➡DRINKS; 1186]

turmeric *type of* **spice.** [➡HERBS AND SPICES; 1174]

turmoil *n* **chaos**, disorder, confusion, uproar, mayhem (*informal*), tumult, commotion, havoc, turbulence, unrest, upheaval, instability. [➡CHAOS AND UPROAR; 51] *Opposite:* order.

turn 1 *v* **twist**, revolve, rotate, go around, spin, roll, twirl, gyrate, circle. [➡MOVE SOMETHING ON THE SPOT; 337] 2 *v* **direct**, aim, point, focus, set, set sights on, concentrate. [➡POSITION SOMETHING; 326] 3 *v* **bend**, change direction, bear, veer, meander, curve. [➡CHANGE DIRECTION OF MOTION; 345] 4 *v* **go**, become, alter, convert, transform, metamorphose, change. [➡CHANGE; 373] 5 *v* **curdle**, go sour, sour, spoil, go off, go bad. [➡GET WORSE; 382] 6 *n* **bend**, corner, junction, fork, curve. [➡ROUNDED SHAPE; 1217] 7 *n* **rotation**, revolution, twist, spin, twirl, roll, circle. [➡MOVE SOMETHING ON THE SPOT; 337] 8 *n* **fright**, scare, shock, start, jolt, surprise. [➡SUDDEN EVENT; 52] 9 *n* **fit**, seizure, attack, funny turn, spasm, bout. [➡PAIN AND OTHER PHYSICAL SENSATIONS; 734] 10 *n* **ride**, spin, jaunt, trip, outing, excursion, drive. [➡TRAVEL: JOURNEYS AND TRIPS; 319] 11 *n* **errand**, favour, good turn, service, good deed. [➡KIND ACTION OR BEHAVIOUR; 296] 12 *n* **performance**, act, skit, sketch, party piece, recitation. [➡PERFORMANCES AND SHOWS; 42] 13 *n* **go**, try, shot (*informal*), chance, crack (*informal*), opportunity. [➡ACTIONS OR UNDERTAKINGS; 260]

turn a blind eye to *v* **overlook**, ignore, take no notice of, disregard, excuse, let pass, let ride, condone. [➡NOT PAY ATTENTION; 765] *Opposite:* condemn.

turnabout *n* **reversal**, sea change, U-turn, turnaround, turnround, change, shift. [➡DECISIVE MOMENTS; 44]

turn against *v* **turn on**, reject, rebuff, spurn, exclude, coldshoulder. [➡REFUSING OR REJECTING RELATIONS; 975]

turnaround *see* **turnround.**

turn away *v* **dismiss**, reject, repel, rebuff, refuse, spurn. [➡REFUSING OR REJECTING RELATIONS; 975] *Opposite:* welcome.

turn away from *v* **reject**, give up, abandon, abjure, forswear (*archaic or literary*), relinquish. [➡FOREGO AND DENY ONESELF; 450] *Opposite:* take up.

turn back 1 *v* **go back**, retrace your steps, return. [➡GO BACKWARDS; 310] *Opposite:* continue. 2 *v* **fold back**, fold down, fold over, turn down, turn over. [➡CHANGE OF SHAPE; 386]

turncoat *n* **traitor**, deserter, defector, collaborator, double agent, spy. [➡PEOPLE WHO DECEIVE; 662]

turn down 1 *v* **refuse**, decline, reject, disallow, veto, rebuff. [➡FOREGO AND DENY ONESELF; 450] *Opposite:* accept. 2 *v* **lessen**, lower, decrease, reduce, muffle, mute. [➡CHANGE OF INTENSITY: LESS; 396] *Opposite:* turn up.

turned-out *adj* **groomed**, dressed, presented, got up (*informal*), clad. [➡DRESS, WEAR, AND UNDRESS; 868]

turn in 1 *v* **hand in**, hand over, give in, remit, submit, give back, deliver, surrender. [➡PROFFER AND HAND OVER; 432] 2 *v* **inform on**, grass on (*slang*), blow the whistle on, betray, report, hand over, shop (*slang*), snitch on (*slang*), turn over. [➡BETRAY CONFIDENCES AND GOSSIP; 619] 3 *v* (*informal*) **go to bed**, hit the sack (*informal*), go to sleep. [➡SLEEP AND DREAM; 724] *Opposite:* rise.

turning 1 *n* **turn-off**, junction, exit, minor road, ramp, off-ramp, turn. [➡BRIDGES, TUNNELS, CROSSINGS, AND JUNCTIONS; 1111] *Opposite:* entrance. 2 *n* **joinery**, carpentry, woodwork, carving, cabinetmaking. [➡CRAFTS AND CARVING; 356]

turning point *n* **crossroads**, defining moment, decisive moment, crisis, watershed, milestone. [➡DECISIVE MOMENTS; 44]

turnip *type of* **root vegetable.** [➡FRUIT AND VEGETABLES; 1175]

turn-off *n* **turning**, exit, junction, minor road, turn. [➡BRIDGES, TUNNELS, CROSSINGS, AND JUNCTIONS; 1111]

turn off 1 *v* **switch off**, deactivate, shut down, disable, stop, turn out. [➡CAUSE TO STOP; 267] *Opposite:* turn on. 2 *v* (*informal*) **disgust**, irritate, bore, deter, displease, repel, discourage. [➡BORE AND FAIL TO INTEREST; 571] *Opposite:* attract. 3 *v* **relax**, unwind, switch off, wind down, take it easy. [➡CHANGE OF MOOD AND COMPOSURE; 581] *Opposite:* gear up.

turn of phrase *n* **way with words**, way of putting things, way of speaking, style, manner, choice of words. [➡ASPECTS OF LANGUAGE; 683]

turn on 1 *v* **switch on**, start, activate, get going, set in motion, trigger, initiate, put on. [➡CAUSE TO START; 266] *Opposite:* turn off. 2 *v* **depend on**, rest on, hinge on, centre on, hang on. [➡RECIPROCITY AND INTERDEPENDENCE; 148] 3 *v* **attack**, go for, round on, lay into, set upon, fall on. [➡PHYSICAL ATTACK AND PUNISHMENT; 416] *Opposite:* defend. 4 *v* (*informal*) **arouse**, excite, interest, enthuse, stimulate, please. [➡APPEAL TO AND AROUSE INTEREST; 576] *Opposite:* turn off.

turn out 1 *v* **switch off**, deactivate, shut down, disable, stop, turn off. [➡CAUSE TO STOP; 267] *Opposite:* turn on. 2 *v* **attend**, turn up, show up, appear, put in an appearance, come. [➡ARRIVE; 12] 3 *v* **evict**, throw out, turf out (*slang*), empty, eject, expel, kick out (*informal*), force out, get rid of, chuck out (*informal*), send away. [➡EJECT AND EXCLUDE; 341] *Opposite:* welcome. 4 *v* **end up**, work out, come out, transpire, result, come about, finish up, happen, become, come to pass (*archaic or literary*). [➡HAPPEN; 27] 5 *v* **produce**, make, manufacture, churn out, assemble, fabricate. [➡MANUFACTURE; 350]

turnout *n* **crowd**, audience, attendance, gathering. [➡AUDIENCES AND ATTENDEES; 937]

turn over 1 *v* **capsize**, flip over, overturn, upturn, turn turtle, keel over. [➡MOVE SOMETHING: INTO A NEW POSITION OR OVERTURN; 331] 2 *v* **mull over**, think about, go over, consider, reflect on, brood over. [➡THINK AND REFLECT; 744] 3 *v* **hand over**, hand in, give in, remit, submit, deliver. [➡PROFFER AND HAND OVER; 432] *Opposite:* hold onto. 4 *v* (*slang*) **rob**, burgle, steal, clean out (*informal*), plunder, loot. [➡STEAL AND ROB; 427]

turnover 1 *n* **incomings**, income, gross revenue, business, revenue, takings. [➡ACCOUNTING, BANKING, AND BUDGETING; 799] *Opposite:* costs. 2 *n* **throughput**, sales, trade, business, buying and selling. [➡BUSINESS PRODUCTS; 796] 3 *n* **staff renewal rate**, hiring and firing rate, staff resignation rate, staff resignations, staff turnover. [➡EXCHANGE AND INTERCHANGE; 449] 4 *type of* **cake**. [➡CAKES, BISCUITS, AND DESSERTS; 1180]

turnpike *type of* **major road**. [➡ROADS; 1105]

turn round 1 *v* **complete**, finish, accomplish, process. [➡COMPLETE AN ACTION; 264] 2 *v* **improve**, boost, increase, bump up (*informal*). [➡IMPROVE SOMETHING; 375]

turnround 1 *n* **dispatch**, processing, completion. [➡END; 54] 2 *n* **reversal**, sea change, U-turn, turnabout, change, shift. [➡DECISIVE MOMENTS; 44]

turnstile *n* **gate**, barrier, entrance, park entrance, kissing gate. [➡DOORS AND ACCESS POINTS; 1100]

turntable *part of* **audio equipment**. [➡AUDIO EQUIPMENT; 1138]

turn the corner *v* **get better**, start to improve, be on the up (*informal*), look up, be on the turn, be out of danger. [➡GET BETTER; 376]

turn to *v* **consult**, refer to, fall back on, resort to, rely on, talk to, ask for help. [➡INITIATE AND ESTABLISH COMMUNICATION; 681]

turn turtle *v* **capsize**, flip over, turn over, overturn, upturn, keel over. [➡MOVE SOMETHING: INTO A NEW POSITION OR OVERTURN; 331]

turn up 1 *v* **increase**, amplify, intensify, boost, step up, raise. [➡CHANGE OF INTENSITY: MORE; 395] *Opposite:* turn down. 2 *v* **come to light**, crop up (*informal*), surface, appear, reappear, materialize. [➡APPEAR AND EMERGE; 3] *Opposite:* disappear. 3 *v* **find**, uncover, unearth, dig up, discover, reveal. [➡FIND; 464] *Opposite:* conceal. 4 *v* **arrive**, appear, show up (*informal*), attend, put in an appearance, come. [➡ARRIVE; 12]

turn-up *part of* **garment**. [➡PARTS OF A GARMENT; 870]

turn your back *v* [➡ABSENT ONESELF; 8]

turn your back on *v* **ignore**, abandon, leave behind, put behind you, forsake, disregard, snub, desert. [➡NOT PAY ATTENTION; 765] *Opposite:* take care of.

turn your nose up at *v* **scorn**, disdain, sneer at, sniff at, reject, turn down, refuse. [➡FOREGO AND DENY ONESELF; 450] *Opposite:* accept.

turn your stomach *v* **sicken**, disgust, repel, revolt, nauseate, make you heave (*informal*), turn off (*informal*). [➡UPSET, DISTRESS, AND HUMILIATE; 568] *Opposite:* attract.

turpitude (*formal or literary*) *n* **immorality**, wickedness, depravity, baseness, improbity (*formal*). [➡MORALLY BAD; 776]

turquoise 1 *type of* **gemstone**. [➡PRECIOUS STONES; 1277] 2 *type of* **blue**. [➡COLOURS; 1223]

turret *n* **tower**, battlement, steeple, bartizan. [➡TOWERS; 1098]

turtle *type of* **reptile**. [➡REPTILES; 994]

turtledove *type of* **common bird**. [➡BIRD; 997]

tussle 1 *v* **fight**, brawl, scrap (*informal*), scuffle, clash, struggle. [➡COMPETE, CONTEND, AND COMBAT; 304] 2 *n* **brawl**, fight, scrap (*informal*), struggle, scuffle, clash, mêlée, dust-up. [➡AGGRESSIVE EVENT; 39]

tussock moth *type of* **moth**. [➡MOTHS AND BUTTERFLIES; 1015]

tut *v* [➡UNFAVOURABLE NON-VERBAL RESPONSES; 655]

tutelage *n* **instruction**, guidance, teaching, coaching, expert hand, wing. [➡TEACHING; 839]

tutor 1 *n* **teacher**, instructor, don, professor, lecturer, trainer, coach. [➡EDUCATORS; 840] 2 *v* **teach**, educate, instruct, school, coach, train, lecture. [➡INSTRUCT AND TEACH; 610]

See Compare and Contrast at **teach**.

tutorial *n* **class**, lesson, seminar, lecture, discussion group. [➡LESSONS, COURSE WORK, AND EXAMINATIONS; 842]

tutu *type of* **skirt**. [➡GARMENTS AND OUTFITS; 865]

tux (*US informal*) *type of* **jacket**. [➡GARMENTS AND OUTFITS; 865]

tuxedo (*US*) *type of* **jacket**. [➡GARMENTS AND OUTFITS; 865]

TV (*informal*) *n* **television**, small screen (*informal*), box (*slang*), tube (*US*), telly, boob tube (*US informal*), goggle-box (*dated informal*). [➡TELEVISION AND RADIO; 607]

TV dinner *type of* **meal**. [➡MEALS AND PARTS OF MEALS; 1168]

TV set *n* [➡TELEVISION AND RADIO; 607]

twaddle (*informal*) *n* **nonsense**, balderdash, rubbish, drivel, claptrap (*informal*), garbage, tripe (*informal*), baloney (*informal*). [➡MEANINGLESS SPEECH OR WRITING; 677] *Opposite:* sense.

twang 1 *n* **accent**, drawl, intonation, inflection, resonance. [➡THE SPOKEN WORD; 672] 2 *v* **reverberate**, vibrate, ping, plunk. [➡MUSIC, SONGS, AND SINGING; 907]

tweak 1 *v* **pinch**, nip, jerk, twist, tug, pull, yank. [➡CONTACT: TOUCH; 413] 2 *v* (*informal*) **fine-tune**, correct, adjust, modify, regulate. [➡CHANGE; 373] 3 *n* **nip**, pinch, twist, jerk, tug, pull, yank. [➡CONTACT: TOUCH; 413]

twee *adj* **pretty-pretty** (*informal*), bijou (*humorous*), dainty, cutesy, sweet, chocolate-box. [➡BEAUTY AND ATTRACTIVENESS; 190]

tweed *type of* **fabric from animals.** [➡FABRICS; 1131]

tweedy *adj* **casual**, informal, sporty, horsey, outdoor. [➡DESCRIBING CLOTHES; 869]

tweet 1 *v* **chirp**, peep, chirrup, twitter, cheep. [➡SOUND EMISSION BY ANIMALS OR BIRDS; 365] 2 *type of* **bird sound.** [➡SOUNDS MADE BY BIRDS; 1262]

tweezers *type of* **cosmetic tool.** [➡HAND TOOLS; 1118]

twelve-tone *type of* **classical music.** [➡MUSIC, SONGS, AND SINGING; 907]

twenty-four-hour-a-day *adj* [➡PERMANENCE: WITHOUT END; 94]

twenty-four/seven *adv* **around the clock**, all the time, constantly, always. [➡PERMANENCE: WITHOUT END; 94]

twice *adv* **two times**, double, twofold. [➡APPORTIONMENT; 113]

twiddle *v* **fidget**, fiddle, play, toy, handle, wiggle. [➡MOVE SOMETHING ON THE SPOT; 337]

twiddle your thumbs *v* [➡LACK OF ACTIVITY; 343]

twig 1 *n* **branch**, shoot, stem, stick. [➡PARTS OF TREES AND PLANTS; 1026] 2 *v* (*informal*) **understand**, grasp, comprehend, get (*informal*), cotton on (*informal*), catch on (*informal*), realize, discern. [➡UNDERSTAND AND GRASP; 760]

twilight *n* **dusk**, nightfall, evening, sunset, sundown. [➡TIMES OF DAY; 87] *Opposite:* dawn.

twilit *adj* **dusky**, shady, shadowy, crepuscular (*literary*), tenebrous (*literary*), moonlit. [➡DESCRIBING LIGHT; 1227] *Opposite:* sunlit.

twill *type of* **fabric from animals.** [➡FABRICS; 1131]

twin 1 *n* **double**, lookalike (*informal*), doppelgänger, clone, identical twin, Siamese twin, mirror image. [➡COPIES AND REPLICAS; 152] 2 *type of* **offspring.** [➡YOUNGER GENERATION RELATIVES; 958] 3 *adj* **identical**, matching, alike, indistinguishable, like. [➡SAMENESS; 151] *Opposite:* different. 4 *adj* **dual**, double, twofold, paired. [➡APPORTIONMENT; 113] *Opposite:* single. 5 *v* **pair**, link, join, match, associate, connect, relate. [➡CREATING CONNECTIONS; 145]

twin bed *type of* **bed.** [➡FURNITURE; 858]

twine 1 *n* **string**, thread, cord, yarn. [➡FASTENERS, LINKS, AND NETWORKS; 1246] 2 *v* **coil**, twist, wind, loop, snake, twirl, weave, curl, bend, wrap around. [➡POSITION SOMETHING: AROUND SOMETHING; 328]

twinge *n* **pang**, pain, stitch, ache, wrench, cramp, stab, spasm. [➡PAIN AND OTHER PHYSICAL SENSATIONS; 734]

twinkle 1 *v* **shine**, sparkle, glimmer, gleam, flicker, glow, glitter. [➡LIGHT EMISSION; 369] 2 *n* **sparkle**, shine, gleam, glimmer, flicker, glow, glitter. [➡LIGHT; 1163]

twinkling *n* **flash**, second, moment, split second, instant, blink. [➡SHORT PERIOD OF TIME; 93]

twin-lens reflex *type of* **photographic equipment.** [➡PHOTOGRAPHY AND PHOTOGRAPHIC EQUIPMENT; 1121]

twinset *type of* **sweater or cardigan.** [➡GARMENTS AND OUTFITS; 865]

twirl 1 *v* **wind**, coil, twist, curl, bend, loop, snake, weave, twine. [➡POSITION SOMETHING: AROUND SOMETHING; 328] 2 *v* **spin**, rotate, whirl, turn, revolve, pirouette. [➡MOVE SOMETHING ON THE SPOT; 337] 3 *n* **coil**, spiral, twist, loop. [➡ROUNDED SHAPE; 1217] 4 *n* **whirl**, spin, revolution, rotation, turn, pirouette. [➡MOVE SOMETHING ON THE SPOT; 337]

twist 1 *v* **wind**, coil, curl, bend, twirl, entwine, interweave, weave, loop, snake. [➡POSITION SOMETHING: AROUND SOMETHING; 328] 2 *v* **rotate**, turn, screw, unscrew, wind, wring. [➡MOVE SOMETHING ON THE SPOT; 337] 3 *v* **sprain**, pull, hurt, injure, turn, wrench. [➡WOUND A PERSON OR ANIMAL; 384] 4 *v* **distort**, misrepresent, alter, manipulate, warp, change. [➡FALSIFY AND CHEAT; 177] *Opposite:* clarify. 5 *v* **meander**, snake, wind, curve, bend, twist and turn, zigzag, loop. [➡CHANGE DIRECTION OF MOTION; 345] 6 *v* **contort**, screw up, grimace, crumple, writhe. [➡CHANGE OF SHAPE; 386] 7 *n* **rotation**, screw, wind, turn. [➡MOVE SOMETHING ON THE SPOT; 337] 8 *n* **spiral**, coil, kink, curl, bend, curve, turn. [➡ROUNDED SHAPE; 1217] 9 *n* **development**, change, turn, incident, event, variation, surprise. [➡DECISIVE MOMENTS; 44]

twist and turn *v* [➡CHANGE DIRECTION OF MOTION; 345]

twisted 1 *adj* **warped**, perverse, sick, perverted, abnormal. [➡ECCENTRICITY AND IRRATIONALITY; 563] *Opposite:* wholesome. 2 *adj* **misshapen**, distorted, warped, bent, deformed, out of shape, awry. [➡ORIENTATION AND ALIGNMENT; 1222] *Opposite:* straight.

twister (*US informal*) *n* [➡WINDY AND STORMY WEATHER; 1053]

twisting *adj* **winding**, meandering, bendy, twisty, windy, snaking. [➡DIRECTION OF MOTION; 346]

twist of fate *n* [➡DECISIVE MOMENTS; 44]

twist somebody's arm *v* **compel**, force, pressure, coerce, persuade, bring pressure upon, pressurize, convince, press. [➡CAUSE OR COMPEL TO ACT; 272]

twisty *adj* **winding**, tortuous, meandering, bendy, snaking, twisting. [➡DIRECTION OF MOTION; 346] *Opposite:* straight.

twit (*dated*) *n* [➡LAZY OR UNSUCCESSFUL PEOPLE; 948]

twitch 1 *v* **jerk**, jolt, shudder, yank, convulse, tremble, contract. [➡PHYSICAL REACTIONS; 317] 2 *n* **tic**, spasm, jerk, jolt, convulsion, shudder, tremor, contraction. [➡PHYSICAL REACTIONS; 317]

twitcher (*informal*) *n* [➡PEOPLE IN SPORTS AND LEISURE; 876]

twitchily *adv* **nervously**, anxiously, uneasily, edgily, agitatedly, restlessly, jumpily. [➡INSECURITY AND LOSS OF COMPOSURE; 545]

twitchiness *n* **jitteriness**, jumpiness, restlessness, uneasiness, nervousness, agitation. [➡INSECURITY AND LOSS OF COMPOSURE; 545]

twitchy (*informal*) *adj* **nervous**, fidgety, on edge, agitated, jumpy, edgy, jittery, restless, nervy (*informal*). [➡CONFUSION, ANXIETY, AND WORRY; 541] *Opposite:* still.

twitter *type of* **bird sound.** [➡SOUNDS MADE BY BIRDS; 1262]

two a penny *adj* [➡ORDINARINESS; 245]

twoc (*slang*) *n* [➡CRIMES; 817]

twoccer (*slang*) *n* [➡CRIMINALS; 821]

two-dimensional 1 *adj* **flat**, flattened, plane, smooth, level, surface. [➡ORIENTATION AND ALIGNMENT; 1222] *Opposite:* three-dimensional. 2 *adj* **superficial**, shallow, oversimplified, formulaic, cardboard, weak. [➡BORING AND UNINTERESTING; 235] *Opposite:* complex.

two-faced *adj* **hypocritical**, false, insincere, deceitful, double dealing, disingenuous, duplicitous, treacherous. [➡DECEITFUL; 514] *Opposite:* genuine.

two-facedness *n* [➡DECEITFUL; 514]

twofold *adj* **double**, dual, twin. [➡APPORTIONMENT; 113]

two-piece *type of* **sportswear.** [➡GARMENTS AND OUTFITS; 865]

twosome *n* **pair**, duo, couple, two of a kind. [➡GROUPS OF PEOPLE; 935]

two-time 1 *v* **betray**, mislead, stab in the back (*informal*), deceive, double-cross, take in, swindle, trick. [➡DECEPTION AND LIES; 661] 2 *v* **be unfaithful**, cheat, cuckold (*archaic*), deceive, step out (*informal*), play away (*informal*). [➡DECEPTION AND LIES; 661]

two-tone *adj* **stripy**, striped, light-and-dark, two-hued, two-toned. [➡DESCRIBING COLOURS; 1225]

two-way *adj* **reciprocal**, cooperative, shared, mutual, collaborative, give-and-take (*informal*). [➡RECIPROCITY AND INTERDEPENDENCE; 148]

tycoon *n* **magnate**, mogul, business person, industrialist. [➡BUSINESS PEOPLE; 794]

tyke *n* **monkey** (*informal*), scamp (*informal*), rascal (*humorous*), child, imp, tearaway, urchin. [➡MISCHIEVOUS OR BADLY-BEHAVED CHILD; 946]

tympanic membrane (*technical*) *n* [➡THE EAR; 707]

tympanum (*technical*) *n* [➡THE EAR; 707]

type 1 *n* (*informal*) **character**, individual, person, sort. [➡PERSON; 931] 2 *n* **kind**, sort, category, form, nature, brand, style, variety, manner, mode, class. [➡VARIETY, TYPE, KIND; 146] 3 *n* **font**, typeface, lettering, print, style, typography. [➡PRINTING; 601] 4 *v* **key**, input, enter, key in. [➡RECORD SOMETHING; 372]

Compare and Contrast: *type, kind, sort, category, class, species, genre*

CORE MEANING: A GROUP HAVING A COMMON QUALITY OR QUALITIES

type a group of individuals or items with strongly marked and readily defined similarities; ***kind*** a group of individuals or items connected by shared characteristics; ***sort*** a general word used in the same way as *kind*; ***category*** a set of things that are classified together because of common characteristics; ***class*** used in the same way as *category*; ***species*** a specific group of animals, plants, insects, or other organisms, used in formal taxonomic classification; ***genre*** a particular style of painting, writing, dance, or other art form.

typecast *v* **stereotype**, pigeonhole, categorize, limit, restrict, label. [➡NAME AND DESCRIBE; 666]

typeface *n* **script**, type, font, lettering, print, typography, style. [➡PRINTING; 601]

typescript *n* [➡PRINTING; 601]

typesetter *n* [➡PRINTING; 601]

typesetting *n* [➡PRINTING; 601]

typhoon *n* **storm**, cyclone, tornado, hurricane, tropical storm. [➡WINDY AND STORMY WEATHER; 1053]

typical 1 *adj* **characteristic**, archetypal, distinctive, representative, emblematic, classic. [➡REPRESENTATIVE; 66] *Opposite:* uncharacteristic. 2 *adj* **usual**, normal, standard, mainstream, average, conventional, regular, predictable. [➡ORDINARINESS; 245] *Opposite:* unusual.

typically 1 *adv* **characteristically**, classically, naturally, stereotypically, archetypally. [➡REPRESENTATIVE; 66] *Opposite:* uncharacteristically. 2 *adv* **normally**, usually, on average, in general, by and large, more often than not, as a rule, habitually, predictably. [➡USUALLY; 108] *Opposite:* unusually.

typify *v* **characterize**, epitomize, symbolize, exemplify, personify, illustrate, demonstrate, represent. [➡REPRESENT SOMETHING OR SOMEBODY; 59]

typo (*informal*) *n* **misprint**, typographical error, keyboarding error, error, mistake. [➡PRINTING; 601] *Opposite:* correction.

typography 1 *n* **design**, typesetting, formatting, layout, composition. [➡PRINTING; 601] 2 *n* **print style**, font, type, lettering, script. [➡PRINTING; 601]

tyrannical *adj* **oppressive**, dictatorial, autocratic, despotic, authoritarian, totalitarian, cruel, harsh, domineering, overbearing. [➡BOSSY AND OVERBEARING; 517]

tyrannize *v* **oppress**, dictate, bully, domineer, intimidate, terrorize, torment, browbeat, persecute. [➡UPSET, DISTRESS, AND HUMILIATE; 568]

tyrannosaur *type of* **dinosaur.** [➡DINOSAUR; 996]

tyrannous *adj* [➡SELFISH AND UNKIND; 506]

tyranny *n* **oppression**, dictatorship, autocracy, domination, despotism, totalitarianism, cruelty, oppressiveness, bullying. [➡UNKIND ACTION OR BEHAVIOUR; 297]

tyrant *n* **oppressor**, dictator, bully, autocrat, despot, tormenter, persecutor, martinet. [➡VILLAINS AND THUGS; 947]

tyre 1 *type of* **external feature.** [➡VEHICLES; 1144] 2 *part of* **bike** (*informal*). [➡BIKES, CARS, AND CARRIAGES; 1148]

tyro *n* **novice**, beginner, learner, newcomer, trainee, apprentice, neophyte, greenhorn. [➡UNSKILLED PERSON; 531] *Opposite:* veteran.

See Compare and Contrast at **beginner.**

U

ubiquitous *adj* **omnipresent**, universal, pervasive, global, abundant, permeating. [➡ PRESENT AND AVAILABLE; 11]

ubiquitousness *n* [➡ PRESENT AND AVAILABLE; 11]

ubiquity *n* [➡ PRESENT AND AVAILABLE; 11]

UFO *n* **flying saucer**, spaceship, spacecraft. [➡ SCIENCE FICTION; 1063]

ugliness 1 *n* **unattractiveness**, unsightliness, hideousness, repulsiveness. [➡ PEOPLE'S PHYSICAL APPEARANCE; 476] *Opposite:* attractiveness. 2 *n* **violence**, hostility, cruelty, viciousness, malice, spitefulness, evil. [➡ UNKIND ACTION OR BEHAVIOUR; 297] *Opposite:* friendliness. 3 *n* **unpleasantness**, dreadfulness, horridness, obnoxiousness, foulness, disagreeableness. [➡ UGLINESS AND UNATTRACTIVENESS; 234]

ugly 1 *adj* **unattractive**, hideous, unsightly, revolting, repulsive. [➡ UGLINESS AND UNATTRACTIVENESS; 234] *Opposite:* attractive. 2 *adj* **nasty**, threatening, dangerous, intimidating, menacing, hostile, aggressive, bad-tempered, sour, violent. [➡ RUDE AND HOSTILE; 626] *Opposite:* friendly. 3 *adj* **unpleasant**, horrible, dreadful, horrid, obnoxious, foul, disagreeable. [➡ EMOTIONALLY UNPLEASANT AND UPSETTING; 228] *Opposite:* nice.

ukulele *type of* **stringed instrument**. [➡ MUSICAL INSTRUMENTS; 910]

ulcer *n* **boil**, abscess, pustule, carbuncle, sore. [➡ DISORDERS OF THE DIGESTIVE SYSTEM; 714]

ulna *type of* **bone**. [➡ THE BONES AND JOINTS; 720]

ulterior *adj* **hidden**, concealed, secret, underhand, unknown, mysterious, clandestine, underlying. [➡ SECRET AND UNKNOWN; 180] *Opposite:* transparent.

ulterior motive *n* **hidden agenda**, arrière-pensée (*formal*), mental reservation. [➡ CAUSATION; 169]

ultimate 1 *adj* **final**, last, eventual, decisive, definitive, vital, crucial, critical. [➡ IMPORTANT; 195] *Opposite:* first. 2 *adj* **fundamental**, basic, essential, supreme, extreme, greatest, best. [➡ FUNDAMENTAL; 196] *Opposite:* superficial.

ultimately *adv* **in the end**, eventually, in due course, finally, at last, at the end of the day, in the long run. [➡ AFTER, LAST, AND FOLLOWING; 166] *Opposite:* initially.

ultimatum *n* **challenge**, demand, requirement, petition, stipulation, proposition, proviso, last word. [➡ REQUEST AND DEMAND; 664]

ultra *adj* **extreme**, radical, revolutionary, excessive, extremist, over-the-top (*informal*), outré. [➡ TOO MUCH; 118] *Opposite:* mainstream.

ultramarine *type of* **blue**. [➡ COLOURS; 1223]

ultramodern *adj* **avant-garde**, progressive, modernistic, radical, futuristic, forward-looking, ahead of its time, high-tech. [➡ NEW, MODERN; 167] *Opposite:* old-fashioned.

umber *type of* **brown**. [➡ COLOURS; 1223]

umbilicus (*technical*) *n* [➡ REPRODUCTION AND HEREDITY; 726]

umbrage *n* **offence**, exception, resentment, affront, slight, annoyance, aggravation, irritation, exasperation. [➡ FEELINGS ABOUT THE PAST; 533]

umbrella 1 *n* **parasol**, brolly (*informal*), sunshade, canopy, gamp (*archaic informal*). [➡ COVERS AND COATINGS; 1245] 2 *n* **aegis**, auspices, authority, protection, support, sponsorship, backing, patronage, supervision. [➡ RESPONSIBILITY; 171]

umlaut *type of* **diacritic**. [➡ ASPECTS OF LANGUAGE; 683]

umpire 1 *n* **referee**, adjudicator, arbitrator, arbiter, mediator, moderator, official. [➡ PEOPLE IN SPORTS AND LEISURE; 876] 2 *v* **adjudicate**, referee, arbitrate, judge, mediate, officiate, supervise. [➡ ASSESS QUALITY; 756]

umpteen (*informal*) *adj* **countless**, numerous, innumerable, millions of, loads of (*informal*), myriad, scads of (*informal*), tons of (*informal*), lots of. [➡ MANY, MUCH, LARGE AMOUNT; 117]

unabashed *adj* **unashamed**, unembarrassed, shameless, bold, brazen, forward, blatant, brash, forthright. [➡ CALMNESS, CONFIDENCE, AND COMPOSURE; 537] *Opposite:* abashed.

unabated *adj* **persistent**, undiminished, relentless, unrelieved, unrelenting, unrestricted, unceasing, unchanged, constant. [➡ PERMANENCE: WITHOUT END; 94] *Opposite:* reduced.

unable *adj* **powerless**, incapable, impotent, inept, incompetent. [➡ UNSKILLED; 530] *Opposite:* able.

unabridged *adj* **full-length**, complete, whole, entire, uncut, unexpurgated, unedited. [➡ WHOLENESS AND COMPLETENESS; 199] *Opposite:* abridged.

unacceptable *adj* **intolerable**, insupportable, undesirable, objectionable, deplorable, offensive, improper, obnoxious, distasteful. [➡ UNACCEPTABLE AND UNFORGIVEABLE; 226] *Opposite:* acceptable.

unaccommodating *adj* **unhelpful**, awkward, uncooperative, difficult, disobliging, troublesome. [➡ UNWILLINGNESS AND STUBBORNNESS; 565] *Opposite:* helpful.

unaccompanied *adj* **alone**, by yourself, on your own, lone, solitary, solo, single-handed. [➡ ACTING INDEPENDENTLY; 285]

unaccomplished 1 *adj* **unfinished**, incomplete, uncompleted, unexecuted, unfulfilled, unconsummated, undone, unresolved. [➡ UNFINISHEDNESS; 240] *Opposite:* accomplished. 2 *adj* **unskilful**, amateurish, unpolished, inexpert, untalented, talentless, inept, undeveloped. [➡UNSKILLED; 530] *Opposite:* accomplished.

unaccountable *adj* **inexplicable**, puzzling, strange, unfathomable, baffling, peculiar, unexplainable, incomprehensible, extraordinary. [➡BIZARRE AND PECULIAR; 258] *Opposite:* explicable.

unaccounted-for *adj* **missing**, lost, absent, gone, disappeared, vanished. [➡ABSENT AND UNAVAILABLE; 7]

unaccustomed 1 *adj* **unused**, not used, inexperienced, unfamiliar, unacquainted. [➡UNSKILLED; 530] *Opposite:* accustomed. 2 *adj* **unfamiliar**, unusual, different, new, strange, alien, untried, uncommon. [➡DIFFERENCE; 150] *Opposite:* accustomed.

unachievable *adj* **unattainable**, impracticable, impossible, unfeasible, inaccessible. [➡IMPOSSIBLE AND IMPROBABLE; 179] *Opposite:* achievable.

unacquainted *adj* **ignorant**, unaccustomed, unaware, uninformed, unknowledgeable. [➡KNOWLEDGE AND WISDOM; 559] *Opposite:* knowledgeable.

unadorned *adj* **plain**, bare, austere, simple, unembellished, bald. [➡PLAIN; 233] *Opposite:* ornate.

unadulterated *adj* **pure**, untouched, untainted, complete, unmodified, unsullied, unalloyed, undiluted, neat. [➡WHOLENESS AND COMPLETENESS; 199] *Opposite:* tainted.

unadventurous *adj* **cautious**, conservative, careful, safe, timid, shy, hesitant, stay-at-home. [➡CONSERVATIVE AND UNADVENTUROUS; 518] *Opposite:* daredevil.

unaffected 1 *adj* **unchanged**, unaltered, unmoved, impervious, impassive, untouched. [➡NEUTRALITY AND INDIFFERENCE; 554] *Opposite:* different. 2 *adj* **genuine**, natural, unpretentious, sincere, modest, artless, guileless. [➡NATURALNESS; 498] *Opposite:* pretentious.

unaffectedly *adv* **genuinely**, modestly, naturally, unpretentiously, sincerely, simply, ingenuously, artlessly, guilelessly. [➡NATURALNESS; 498] *Opposite:* pretentiously.

unaffectedness *n* **genuineness**, modesty, naturalness, unpretentiousness, sincerity, simplicity, ingenuousness, guilelessness, artlessness. [➡NATURALNESS; 498] *Opposite:* pretentiousness.

unaffordable *adj* [➡EXPENSIVE AND OVERPRICED; 248]

unafraid *adj* **fearless**, bold, confident, brave, courageous, undaunted, stouthearted. [➡CALMNESS, CONFIDENCE, AND COMPOSURE; 537] *Opposite:* afraid.

unaided *adv* **unassisted**, independently, by yourself, of your own accord, on your own, single-handedly, solo. [➡ACTING INDEPENDENTLY; 285] *Opposite:* jointly.

unalike *adj* [➡DIFFERENCE; 150]

unalleviated *adj* **constant**, unrelieved, unremitting, unmitigated, inexorable, unbearable. [➡PERMANENCE: WITHOUT END; 94] *Opposite:* intermittent.

unalloyed *adj* **pure**, sheer, absolute, total, utter, complete, unadulterated, undiminished, undiluted. [➡WHOLENESS AND COMPLETENESS; 199] *Opposite:* partial.

unalterable *adj* **unchangeable**, fixed, irreversible, final, set, permanent. [➡PERMANENCE: WITHOUT CHANGE; 95] *Opposite:* impermanent.

unambiguous *adj* **unmistakable**, clear-cut, explicit, definite, decided, unequivocal, instantly recognizable, clear. [➡EXACT; 204] *Opposite:* vague.

unambiguously *adv* **unmistakably**, decidedly, definitely, explicitly, clearly, unequivocally, recognizably. [➡CONCISE AND CLEAR; 203] *Opposite:* vaguely.

unambitious *adj* **unaspiring**, unenterprising, unthrusting, unassertive, lazy, passive, apathetic. [➡LIFELESS, LAZY, AND UNENTHUSIASTIC; 507] *Opposite:* ambitious.

unanimity *n* [➡HARMONY; 156]

unanimous *adj* **common**, agreed, undisputed, undivided, united. [➡HARMONY; 156] *Opposite:* undecided.

unannounced *adj* **unexpected**, impromptu, spontaneous, surprise. [➡UNINTENTIONAL AND ACCIDENTAL; 282] *Opposite:* arranged.

unanswerable *adj* **unfathomable**, insoluble, unresolvable, unsolvable, inexplicable, incomprehensible, insuperable. [➡DIFFICULTY AND COMPLEXITY; 243]

unanticipated *adj* **surprising**, unexpected, unlooked-for, unforeseen, unsuspected, unimagined. [➡SECRET AND UNKNOWN; 180] *Opposite:* expected.

unapologetic *adj* **impenitent**, unrepentant, unreformed, unremorseful, unregretful. [➡SELFISH AND UNKIND; 506] *Opposite:* penitent.

unappealing *adj* **unattractive**, unpleasant, disagreeable, uninviting, unlikable, unappetizing, ugly. [➡UGLINESS AND UNATTRACTIVENESS; 234] *Opposite:* appealing.

unappetizing *adj* **unattractive**, unpleasant, unenticing, uninviting, unpalatable, unsavoury. [➡UGLINESS AND UNATTRACTIVENESS; 234] *Opposite:* appetizing.

unappreciated *adj* [➡UNPOPULAR AND UNWANTED; 259]

unapprised *adj* [➡IGNORANCE; 558]

unapproachability *n* [➡UNFRIENDLINESS AND UNSOCIABILITY; 505]

unapproachable *adj* **distant**, unfriendly, aloof, cold, standoffish, remote, withdrawn, unsociable. [➡UNFRIENDLINESS AND UNSOCIABILITY; 505] *Opposite:* approachable.

unarguable *adj* **beyond doubt**, incontestable, incontrovertible, indisputable, beyond question, unquestionable, unanswerable. [➡NECESSARY AND ESSENTIAL; 197] *Opposite:* arguable.

unarmed *adj* **unprotected**, defenceless, exposed, vulnerable, weaponless. [➡IN DANGER; 238] *Opposite:* armed.

unashamed *adj* **unembarrassed**, unapologetic, blatant, brazen, barefaced, insolent, bold, shameless, flagrant, immodest, unabashed. [➡CALMNESS, CONFIDENCE, AND COMPOSURE; 537] *Opposite:* ashamed.

unashamedly *adv* **unapologetically**, flagrantly, blatantly, brazenly, boldly, defiantly, shamelessly, insolently, immodestly, openly. [➡HONEST AND OPEN; 631] *Opposite:* discreetly.

unasked 1 *adj* **unsolicited**, uninvited, unsought, unexpected, uncanvassed, undreamed-of, unimaginable. [➡UNPOPULAR AND UNWANTED; 259] *Opposite:* expected. 2 *adj* **uninvited**, unwelcome, excluded, unexpected, left out, unbidden, unsummoned. [➡UNPOPULAR AND UNWANTED; 259]

unasked-for *adj* [➡UNPOPULAR AND UNWANTED; 259]

unassailable 1 *adj* **incontrovertible**, unquestionable, impregnable, irrefutable, indisputable, undeniable, incontestable, conclusive, sound, watertight. [➡CERTAIN; 175] *Opposite:* tenuous. 2 *adj* **invincible**, unbeatable, impregnable, indomitable, invulnerable. [➡STRENGTH; 202] *Opposite:* vulnerable.

unassertive *adj* [➡COWARDICE AND WEAKNESS OF WILL; 509]

unassisted *adj* **unaided**, single-handed, solo, lone. [➡ACTING INDEPENDENTLY; 285] *Opposite:* assisted.

unassuming *adj* **modest**, humble, self-effacing, unassertive, meek, inconspicuous, ordinary, unpretentious, down-to-earth. [➡NATURALNESS; 498] *Opposite:* arrogant.

unassumingness *n* [➡NATURALNESS; 498]

unattached *adj* **free**, uncommitted, single, unmarried, separated. [➡MARITAL STATUS; 890] *Opposite:* attached.

unattainable *adj* **unachievable**, impossible, unfeasible, inaccessible, unreachable. [➡IMPOSSIBLE AND IMPROBABLE; 179] *Opposite:* attainable.

unattractive *adj* **unappealing**, ugly, nasty, unpleasant, distasteful, repellent, uninviting, unsightly. [➡UGLINESS AND UNATTRACTIVENESS; 234] *Opposite:* attractive.

unattractiveness *n* **ugliness**, unpleasantness, unsightliness, distastefulness, repulsiveness, nastiness. [➡UGLINESS AND UNATTRACTIVENESS; 234] *Opposite:* attractiveness.

unauthorized *adj* **illegal**, unlawful, unofficial, unsanctioned, unlicensed, unapproved, unconstitutional, illicit. [➡ILLEGAL; 816] *Opposite:* legitimate.

unavailability *n* **unobtainability**, inaccessibility, unattainability, unreachability, absence, unapproachability. [➡ABSENT AND UNAVAILABLE; 7] *Opposite:* availability.

unavailable 1 *adj* **unobtainable**, inaccessible, unattainable, unreachable, absent, unapproachable. [➡ABSENT AND UNAVAILABLE; 7] *Opposite:* available. 2 *adj* **engaged**, busy, occupied, unobtainable. [➡ABSENT AND UNAVAILABLE; 7] *Opposite:* available.

unavailing *adj* **vain**, unsuccessful, futile, failed, ineffective, fruitless, abortive, pointless. [➡REDUNDANT AND USELESS; 241] *Opposite:* successful.

unavoidability *n* **inevitability**, inescapability, certainty, necessity, obligation, requirement, inexorability (*formal*). [➡CERTAIN; 175]

unavoidable *adj* **inevitable**, inescapable, obvious, manifest, obligatory, necessary, mandatory, compulsory, required, inexorable (*formal*). [➡CERTAIN; 175] *Opposite:* avoidable.

unavoidably *adv* **inevitably**, inescapably, manifestly, necessarily, compulsorily. [➡NECESSARY AND ESSENTIAL; 197]

unaware *adj* **ignorant**, uninformed, oblivious, unconscious, unmindful, heedless, unacquainted, naive, innocent. [➡IGNORANCE; 558] *Opposite:* conscious.

unawares *adv* **by surprise**, off guard, unexpectedly, on the hop (*informal*). [➡UNINTENTIONAL AND ACCIDENTAL; 282]

unbalance *v* **disturb**, unhinge, derange, distort, destabilize, confuse. [➡CONFUSE AND BEWILDER; 572] *Opposite:* stabilize.

unbalanced 1 *adj* **uneven**, lopsided, unequal, crooked, top-heavy. [➡ORIENTATION AND ALIGNMENT; 1222] *Opposite:* even. 2 *adj* **unstable**, disturbed, unhinged, deranged. [➡PSYCHOLOGY AND THE MIND; 770] *Opposite:* well-balanced. 3 *adj* **biased**, one-sided, inequitable, prejudiced, unfair, misleading, partial. [➡THE NATURE OF IDEAS; 772] *Opposite:* impartial.

unbearable *adj* **intolerable**, agonizing, excruciating, awful, insufferable, horrendous, insupportable, unendurable. [➡EMOTIONALLY UNPLEASANT AND UPSETTING; 228] *Opposite:* tolerable.

unbeatable *adj* **invincible**, supreme, unassailable, unconquerable, peerless, matchless, indomitable. [➡STRENGTH; 202] *Opposite:* vulnerable.

unbeaten *adj* **undefeated**, unsurpassed, successful, triumphant, victorious, unbowed, winning, champion, number one (*informal*), the best, top-ranking. [➡EXTRAORDINARY: AMAZING; 205]

unbecoming *adj* **improper**, inappropriate, incorrect, unsuitable, unflattering, unfitting, indelicate, indecorous. [➡INAPPROPRIATE AND UNSUITABLE; 225] *Opposite:* fitting.

unbecomingness *n* [➡INAPPROPRIATE AND UNSUITABLE; 225]

unbelief *n* **nonbelief**, scepticism, incredulity, agnosticism, atheism. [➡RELIGIOUS CONCEPTS; 777] *Opposite:* faith.

unbelievable 1 *adj* **implausible**, incredible, far-fetched, fantastic, unlikely, fanciful, preposterous, improbable, unreal. [➡IMPOSSIBLE AND IMPROBABLE; 179] *Opposite:* plausible. 2 *adj* **incredible**, amazing, extraordinary, astonishing, great, enormous, mind-boggling. [➡EXTRAORDINARY: AMAZING; 205] *Opposite:* ordinary.

unbelievably *adv* **extraordinarily**, incredibly, extremely, very, exceptionally, amazingly, astonishingly. [➡EXTRAORDINARY: AMAZING; 205] *Opposite:* unremarkably.

unbeliever *n* **nonbeliever**, sceptic, atheist, agnostic, freethinker, doubter. [➡RELIGIOUS PEOPLE; 779] *Opposite:* believer.

unbelieving *adj* **incredulous**, sceptical, doubting, suspicious, questioning. [➡UNCERTAINTY; 560] *Opposite:* credulous.

unbend *v* **straighten**, release, free, relax, loosen, flatten. [➡CHANGE OF SHAPE; 386] *Opposite:* bend.

unbending *adj* **inflexible**, fixed, rigid, adamant, obdurate, dogmatic, doctrinaire, formal, pitiless. [➡UNWILLINGNESS AND STUBBORNNESS; 565] *Opposite:* flexible.

unbiased *adj* **impartial**, balanced, dispassionate, neutral, unprejudiced, fair, evenhanded, equitable (*formal*), disinterested, fair-minded, detached. [➡THE NATURE OF IDEAS; 772] *Opposite:* partial.

unbind *v* **untie**, release, free, undo, liberate, unfetter, unchain, set free. [➡UNFASTEN AND UNDO; 410] *Opposite:* bind.

unblemished *adj* **flawless**, perfect, untarnished, pure, blameless, clear, immaculate. [➡MORALLY GOOD; 775] *Opposite:* flawed.

unblinking *adj* [➡FACIAL EXPRESSION; 652]

unblock *v* **clear**, unclog, free, clear out, clean out, free up (*informal*). [➡EMPTY AND UNLOAD; 408] *Opposite:* block.

unbolt *v* **unfasten**, unlock, open, unscrew, release, unhook, undo. [➡UNFASTEN AND UNDO; 410] *Opposite:* lock.

unbothered *adj* [➡CALMNESS, CONFIDENCE, AND COMPOSURE; 537]

unbounded *adj* **limitless**, unrestrained, abundant, boundless, uncontrolled, absolute, infinite, immeasurable. [➡FREEDOM AND LIBERTY; 209] *Opposite:* limited.

unbowed *adj* **undefeated**, defiant, stubborn, determined, relentless, unyielding, resolved. [➡UNWILLINGNESS AND STUBBORNNESS; 565] *Opposite:* defeated.

unbreakable *adj* **indestructible**, strong, permanent, indissoluble, firm, hard, resilient, shatterproof. [➡STRENGTH; 202] *Opposite:* fragile.

unbridled *adj* **unrestrained**, uncontrolled, uninhibited, unconcealed, unchecked, intemperate, rampant. [➡FREEDOM AND LIBERTY; 209] *Opposite:* contained.

unbroken *adj* **continuous**, constant, uninterrupted, steady, complete, endless, perpetual. [➡PERMANENCE: WITHOUT END; 94] *Opposite:* intermittent.

unbuckle *v* [➡UNFASTEN AND UNDO; 410]

unburden (*formal*) *v* **relieve**, divest, free, release, let go, confess. [➡ADMIT AND CONFESS; 616] *Opposite:* brood.

unbutton *v* **undo**, open, unfasten. [➡UNFASTEN AND UNDO; 410] *Opposite:* fasten.

uncalled-for *adj* **unjustified**, unwarranted, undeserved, unprovoked, gratuitous, indefensible, unnecessary, needless, inexcusable, unforgivable, rude, unjustifiable, undue, wanton, unfair. [➡UNIMPORTANT AND UNNECESSARY; 239] *Opposite:* justifiable.

uncanniness *n* [➡BIZARRE AND PECULIAR; 258]

uncanny *adj* **eerie**, weird, strange, mysterious, creepy (*informal*), supernatural. [➡BIZARRE AND PECULIAR; 258]

uncap *v* [➡UNFASTEN AND UNDO; 410]

uncared-for *adj* **neglected**, unloved, untended, unkempt, unattended, dilapidated, dishevelled, forgotten, abandoned. [➡IN BAD REPAIR; 1233] *Opposite:* cherished.

uncaring *adj* **hardhearted**, unfeeling, heartless, indifferent, cold, callous, selfish, insensible. [➡NEUTRALITY AND INDIFFERENCE; 554] *Opposite:* caring.

unceasing *adj* **constant**, continuous, interminable, never-ending, perpetual, unending, nonstop, endless. [➡PERMANENCE: WITHOUT END; 94] *Opposite:* sporadic.

unceremonious *adj* **abrupt**, hasty, rushed, terse, rude, brusque, curt, callous. [➡INCAUTIOUS AND CARELESS; 284] *Opposite:* gracious.

uncertain 1 *adj* **unsure**, vague, doubtful, hesitant, undecided, indecisive, tentative, in doubt, dubious. [➡UNCERTAINTY; 560] *Opposite:* sure. 2 *adj* **indeterminate**, inexact, undefined, indefinite, ambiguous, unclear, tentative, unreliable, changeable. [➡UNCERTAIN; 176] *Opposite:* exact.

See Compare and Contrast at **doubtful**.

uncertainly *adv* **hesitantly**, indecisively, tentatively, nervously, anxiously, apprehensively, timidly, doubtfully. [➡UNCERTAINTY; 560] *Opposite:* confidently.

uncertainness *n* [➡UNCERTAIN; 176]

uncertainty *n* **doubt**, indecision, hesitation, vagueness, ambiguity, insecurity. [➡UNCERTAINTY; 560] *Opposite:* confidence.

unchain *v* **release**, unlock, unfetter, unshackle, liberate, free. [➡FREEDOM AND LIBERTY; 209] *Opposite:* chain.

unchangeable *adj* **fixed**, unalterable, unvarying, constant, unchanged, consistent, inflexible, unmovable. [➡PERMANENCE: WITHOUT CHANGE; 95] *Opposite:* changeable.

unchanged *adj* **unaffected**, unmoved, untouched, unbothered. [➡PERMANENCE: WITHOUT CHANGE; 95] *Opposite:* affected.

unchanging *adj* **static**, fixed, invariable, unchangeable, rigid, inflexible, set, ageless. [➡PERMANENCE: WITHOUT CHANGE; 95] *Opposite:* flexible.

uncharacteristic *adj* **unusual**, atypical, abnormal, out of character, unexpected, aberrant, strange. [➡BIZARRE AND PECULIAR; 258] *Opposite:* typical.

uncharitable *adj* **mean**, unkind, hurtful, spiteful, cruel, mean-spirited, harsh, unmerciful, heartless. [➡SELFISH AND UNKIND; 506] *Opposite:* generous.

uncharted *adj* **unexplored**, new, unfamiliar, unmapped, unknown, alien, strange, uncultivated. [➡SECRET AND UNKNOWN; 180] *Opposite:* familiar.

unchaste *adj* [➡MORALLY BAD; 776]

unchasteness *n* [➡MORALLY BAD; 776]

unchecked *adj* **unimpeded**, unrestrained, unhindered, unrestricted, unconstrained, unbridled, abandoned, free. [➡FREEDOM AND LIBERTY; 209] *Opposite:* restricted.

uncivil *adj* **rude**, discourteous, impolite, insulting, bad-mannered, unfriendly. [➡BAD MANNERS AND SOCIAL SKILLS; 522] *Opposite:* courteous.

uncivilized 1 *adj* **primitive**, barbaric, uncultured, unsophisticated, crude. [➡IGNORANCE; 558] *Opposite:* civilized. 2 *adj* **remote**, distant, far-off, isolated, unreachable, uninhabitable. [➡LEVEL OF EDUCATION AND SOPHISTICATION; 894] *Opposite:* reachable. **3** *adj* **coarse**, impolite, discourteous, unrefined, vulgar, uncouth, uncultured, rude. [➡BAD MANNERS AND SOCIAL SKILLS; 522] *Opposite:* polite.

unclasp *v* **unfasten**, undo, open, unbuckle, untie, unpin, unlock. [➡UNFASTEN AND UNDO; 410] *Opposite:* fasten.

unclassified **1** *adj* **random**, unsystematic, disorganized, unorganized, uncategorized, confused, haphazard, higgledy-piggledy, unarranged, disordered. [➡DISORDER AND CHAOS; 246] *Opposite:* organized. **2** *adj* **open**, public, released, unconcealed, accessible, public domain. [➡KNOWN AND FAMOUS; 182] *Opposite:* secret.

uncle *type of* **older relative.** [➡OLDER GENERATION RELATIVES; 959]

unclean **1** *adj* **impure**, dirty, contaminated, polluted, infected, tainted, unhygienic, grimy, filthy, squalid, unsanitary, soiled. [➡DIRTY; 1234] *Opposite:* clean. **2** *adj* **unchaste**, sinful, impure, unworthy, immoral. [➡MORALLY BAD; 776] *Opposite:* chaste.

See Compare and Contrast at **dirty.**

uncleanliness *n* [➡DIRTY; 1234]

uncleanness **1** *n* **dirtiness**, filthiness, impurity, griminess, squalor, unsanitariness. [➡DIRTY; 1234] *Opposite:* cleanness. **2** *n* **unchasteness**, sinfulness, impurity, unworthiness, immorality. [➡MORALLY BAD; 776] *Opposite:* chasteness.

unclear **1** *adj* **indistinct**, hazy, indeterminate, blurred, indistinguishable, vague, imprecise, ambiguous. [➡VAGUENESS; 244] *Opposite:* clear. **2** *adj* **uncertain**, doubtful, undecided, unsure, in doubt, vague. [➡UNCERTAIN; 176] *Opposite:* definite.

unclearly *adv* **indistinctly**, vaguely, imprecisely, ambiguously, indecisively, indistinguishably, indeterminately. [➡VAGUENESS; 244] *Opposite:* precisely.

unclearness *n* [➡VAGUENESS; 244]

unclench *v* **relax**, release, open, untighten, let go, slacken, loosen. [➡PHYSICAL REACTIONS; 317] *Opposite:* tighten.

unclog *v* **unblock**, clear, free, release, clean out, sluice. [➡EMPTY AND UNLOAD; 408] *Opposite:* block.

unclothe *v* **undress**, strip, unrobe, uncover, disrobe (*formal*). [➡DRESS, WEAR, AND UNDRESS; 868] *Opposite:* dress.

unclothed *adj* **bare**, naked, uncovered, undressed, nude, stripped. [➡DRESS, WEAR, AND UNDRESS; 868] *Opposite:* dressed.

See Compare and Contrast at **naked.**

uncoil *v* **unravel**, unwind, undo, untwist, release, straighten, straighten out. [➡TAKE UP A NEW POSITION; 313] *Opposite:* twist.

uncomfortable **1** *adj* **painful**, tight, rough, scratchy, itchy, bumpy, prickly, sore. [➡PAIN AND OTHER PHYSICAL SENSATIONS; 734] *Opposite:* comfortable. **2** *adj* **awkward**, uneasy, embarrassing, difficult, tricky, unpleasant, unnerving, distressing, ill at ease. [➡EMOTIONALLY UNPLEASANT AND UPSETTING; 228] *Opposite:* comfortable.

uncomfortably *adv* **awkwardly**, uneasily, anxiously, unnervingly, dangerously, trickily, unpleasantly, disturbingly, worryingly, painfully. [➡EMOTIONALLY UNPLEASANT AND UPSETTING; 228] *Opposite:* comfortably.

uncommitted *adj* **casual**, uninterested, indifferent, unattached, free, apathetic. [➡NEUTRALITY AND INDIFFERENCE; 554] *Opposite:* committed.

uncommon *adj* **rare**, unusual, infrequent, scarce, special, exceptional, singular, surprising. [➡EXTRAORDINARY: UNCOMMON; 206] *Opposite:* common.

uncommunicative *adj* **reserved**, reticent, taciturn, silent, withdrawn, unforthcoming, tight-lipped. [➡RETICENT AND UNFORTHCOMING; 632] *Opposite:* talkative.

See Compare and Contrast at **silent.**

uncommunicativeness *n* [➡RETICENT AND UNFORTHCOMING; 632]

uncomplaining *adj* **accepting**, tolerant, long-suffering, patient, accommodating, forgiving. [➡CHEERFULNESS OF OUTLOOK; 504] *Opposite:* intolerant.

uncompleted *adj* [➡UNFINISHEDNESS; 240]

uncomplicated *adj* **simple**, straightforward, unfussy, basic, unsophisticated, easy, down-to-earth. [➡EASE AND SIMPLICITY; 201] *Opposite:* complex.

uncomplicatedness *n* [➡EASE AND SIMPLICITY; 201]

uncomplimentary *adj* **disparaging**, derogatory, unflattering, negative, pejorative (*formal*), rude, damning. [➡RUDE AND HOSTILE; 626] *Opposite:* complimentary.

uncompromising *adj* **inflexible**, rigid, adamant, unbending, obdurate, stubborn, categorical, hard-nosed (*informal*). [➡UNWILLINGNESS AND STUBBORNNESS; 565] *Opposite:* flexible.

unconcealed *adj* **obvious**, open, evident, apparent, blatant, unrestrained. [➡PERCEPTIBLE; 25] *Opposite:* hidden.

unconcern *n* **indifference**, apathy, disregard, nonchalance, disinterest, detachment. [➡NEUTRALITY AND INDIFFERENCE; 554] *Opposite:* anxiety.

unconcerned *adj* **indifferent**, unworried, nonchalant, undaunted, undisturbed, blasé, apathetic, carefree, blithe (*literary*). [➡NEUTRALITY AND INDIFFERENCE; 554] *Opposite:* anxious.

unconditional *adj* **unqualified**, total, categorical, absolute, unrestricted, unreserved. [➡WHOLENESS AND COMPLETENESS; 199] *Opposite:* qualified.

unconditioned *adj* **unrestricted**, limitless, undefined, unlimited, open-ended, with no strings. [➡FREEDOM AND LIBERTY; 209] *Opposite:* restricted.

unconfident *adj* **insecure**, unsure, nervous, apprehensive, self-doubting, uncertain, anxious. [➡INSECURITY AND LOSS OF COMPOSURE; 545] *Opposite:* self-assured.

unconfined *adj* **free**, liberated, released, loose, at large, free-range, unconstrained. [➡FREEDOM AND LIBERTY; 209] *Opposite:* restricted.

unconfirmed *adj* **unverified**, unsubstantiated, unproven, unofficial, hearsay, unendorsed, unsupported, unsupervised, invalid, uncorroborated. [➡UNCERTAIN; 176] *Opposite:* verified.

unconformity *n* **originality**, uniqueness, unconventionality, eccentricity, abnormality, individualism, rebelliousness, freethinking. [➡UNRELATEDNESS AND SEPARATENESS; 147] *Opposite:* conformity.

uncongenial *adj* **disagreeable**, unfriendly, unwelcoming, unpleasant, inhospitable, cool, incompatible. [➡BAD-TEMPERED AND HUMOURLESS; 627] *Opposite:* friendly.

unconnected *adj* **separate**, unrelated, independent, distinct, isolated, disparate. [➡UNRELATEDNESS AND SEPARATENESS; 147] *Opposite:* linked.

unconquerable *adj* **unbeatable**, unassailable, unattainable, insurmountable, indomitable, undefeated, impregnable, invincible. [➡STRENGTH; 202] *Opposite:* vulnerable.

unconquered *adj* [➡SUCCESSFUL AND PROMISING; 81]

unconscionable 1 *adj* **unacceptable**, shocking, horrifying, immoral, reprehensible, inconceivable, outrageous, unthinkable, appalling. [➡EMOTIONALLY UNPLEASANT AND UPSETTING; 228] *Opposite:* acceptable. 2 *adj* **unreasonable**, beyond the pale, over-the-top (*informal*), irrational, ridiculous, illogical, extreme. [➡BIZARRE AND PECULIAR; 258] *Opposite:* reasonable.

unconscious 1 *adj* **comatose**, insentient, insensible, out cold, cataleptic, out for the count (*informal*), lifeless, knocked out, down for the count (*US*). [➡TIRED, ASLEEP AND UNCONSCIOUS; 739] *Opposite:* awake. 2 *adj* **unaware**, oblivious, ignorant, unwitting, insensible, uninformed. [➡IGNORANCE; 558] *Opposite:* aware. 3 *adj* **unintentional**, automatic, mechanical, instinctive, involuntary, reflex, intuitive. [➡UNINTENTIONAL AND ACCIDENTAL; 282] *Opposite:* deliberate. 4 *n* **ID**, superego, ego, self, psyche, mind. [➡PSYCHOLOGY AND THE MIND; 770]

unconsciously *adv* **unintentionally**, automatically, mechanically, instinctively, involuntarily, reflexively, intuitively. [➡UNINTENTIONAL AND ACCIDENTAL; 282] *Opposite:* deliberately.

unconsciousness *n* **oblivion**, sleep, nothingness, insentience, catalepsy, coma, blackout, swoon. [➡TIRED, ASLEEP AND UNCONSCIOUS; 739] *Opposite:* consciousness.

unconsecrated *adj* [➡MORALLY BAD; 776]

unconsidered *adj* **hasty**, unthinking, impulsive, knee-jerk (*informal*), reactive, imprudent (*formal*), rash, immediate. [➡INCAUTIOUS AND CARELESS; 284] *Opposite:* considered.

unconstitutional *adj* **illegal**, unauthorized, unlawful, undemocratic, unofficial, illegitimate. [➡LEGAL; 815] *Opposite:* lawful.

unconstrained *adj* **unimpeded**, free, unrestrained, unrestricted, unhindered, untrammelled, unconfined. [➡FREEDOM AND LIBERTY; 209] *Opposite:* restricted.

unconstructive *adj* **unhelpful**, negative, unenthusiastic, uncooperative, ineffectual. [➡REDUNDANT AND USELESS; 241] *Opposite:* constructive.

uncontaminated *adj* **pure**, clean, unadulterated, antiseptic, sterilized, unpolluted, germ-free, untainted, uncorrupted, undamaged. [➡CLEAN; 1232] *Opposite:* contaminated.

uncontrollable 1 *adj* **irrepressible**, uncontainable, overpowering, wild, overwhelming, strong, intense, abandoned, hysterical, frenzied, violent. [➡STRENGTH; 202] 2 *adj* **unruly**, disobedient, out of control, unmanageable, disorderly, wild, badly-behaved. [➡UNWILLINGNESS AND STUBBORNNESS; 565] *Opposite:* well-behaved.

uncontrollably *adv* **irrepressibly**, overpoweringly, hysterically, nonstop, wildly, frenziedly, violently, overwhelmingly, strongly, intensely. [➡STRENGTH; 202] *Opposite:* calmly.

uncontrolled *adj* **unrestrained**, abandoned, wild, hysterical, uninhibited, frenzied. [➡ECCENTRICITY AND IRRATIONALITY; 563] *Opposite:* restrained.

uncontroversial *adj* **undisputed**, uncontentious, uncontended, unquestionable, indisputable, undebatable, definitive, authoritative, accepted, self-evident. [➡CERTAIN; 175] *Opposite:* controversial.

unconventional *adj* **eccentric**, unusual, alternative, avant-garde, strange, original, progressive, exceptional, irregular, odd, quirky. [➡EXTRAORDINARY: UNCOMMON; 206] *Opposite:* conventional.

unconventionality *n* **eccentricity**, originality, nonconformity, oddness, quirkiness, unusualness, irregularity, strangeness. [➡EXTRAORDINARY: UNCOMMON; 206] *Opposite:* conventionality.

unconvinced *adj* **sceptical**, incredulous, disbelieving, unimpressed, unmoved, dubious, unsure, uncertain. [➡UNCERTAINTY; 560] *Opposite:* convinced.

unconvincing *adj* **unpersuasive**, unimpressive, weak, feeble, unsuccessful, vain, implausible. [➡UNCERTAIN; 176] *Opposite:* persuasive.

uncooked *adj* **raw**, rare, fresh, unprepared. [➡STATE OF PREPARED FOOD; 1170] *Opposite:* cooked.

uncool (*slang*) *adj* **old-fashioned**, conservative, strait-laced, unrelaxed, uptight (*informal*), unhip (*informal*), straight (*slang*). [➡CONSERVATIVE AND UNADVENTUROUS; 518] *Opposite:* trendy (*informal*).

uncooperative *adj* **unhelpful**, disobliging, awkward, obstinate, contrary, stubborn, truculent, difficult, perverse. [➡UNWILLINGNESS AND STUBBORNNESS; 565] *Opposite:* amenable.

uncoordinated *adj* **clumsy**, ungainly, awkward, ungraceful, inept, all fingers and thumbs, all thumbs (*US*). [➡AGILITY OF THE BODY; 477] *Opposite:* graceful.

uncork 1 *v* **open**, break open, unplug, break into, pop open, prise open, pry open (*US*). [➡UNFASTEN AND UNDO; 410] *Opposite:* plug. 2 *v* **unleash**, release, give vent to, pour out, set free, express. [➡GIVING VENT TO EMOTIONS; 680] *Opposite:* hold in.

uncorrupted *adj* **unadulterated**, unspoiled, uncontaminated, chaste, pure, innocent, virtuous, untouched, unaffected. [➡CLEAN; 1232] *Opposite:* corrupted.

uncountable *adj* [➡MANY, MUCH, LARGE AMOUNT; 117]

uncounted *adj* **innumerable**, countless, numerous, myriad, incalculable. [➡MANY, MUCH, LARGE AMOUNT; 117] *Opposite:* few.

uncouple *v* **undo**, disengage, separate, detach, unyoke, unfasten, disjoin. [➡UNFASTEN AND UNDO; 410] *Opposite:* join.

uncouth *adj* **rude**, uncivilized, bad-mannered, ill-mannered, foul-mouthed, coarse, vulgar, improper, impolite, crude. [➡BAD MANNERS AND SOCIAL SKILLS; 522] *Opposite:* polite.

uncouthness *n* **rudeness**, vulgarity, bad manners, crudeness, coarseness, impropriety. [➡BAD MANNERS AND SOCIAL SKILLS; 522] *Opposite:* politeness.

uncover *v* **expose**, discover, reveal, unearth, find out, come across, bare, find, disclose. [➡FIND; 464] *Opposite:* conceal.

uncovered *adj* **exposed**, bare, open, naked, revealed, discovered, disclosed. [➡PERCEPTIBLE; 25] *Opposite:* concealed.

uncovering *n* **exposure**, discovery, disclosure, revelation, light. [➡FIND; 464] *Opposite:* concealment.

uncritical *adj* **indiscriminating**, accepting, credulous, naive, gullible, trusting, unsuspecting, impressionable. [➡NEGATIVE INTELLECTUAL CHARACTERISTICS; 526] *Opposite:* discriminating.

unction 1 *n* **balm**, ointment, salve, oil, lotion, cream, unguent. [➡LOTIONS, PASTES, AND GELS; 1271] 2 *n* **earnestness**, fervour, zeal, passion, enthusiasm, faith, ardour. [➡POSITIVE IMPATIENCE, ENTHUSIASM, AND ALERTNESS; 538]

unctuous 1 *adj* **ingratiating**, sycophantic, slimy, smarmy, obsequious, grovelling, creepy (*informal*), smug, oily (*disapproving*), phoney. [➡INGRATIATING; 639] *Opposite:* arrogant. 2 *adj* **oily**, greasy, fatty, slippery, slimy, well-coated. [➡PHYSICAL TEXTURE; 1221]

unctuousness *n* [➡INGRATIATING; 639]

uncultivated 1 *adj* **unrefined**, unsophisticated, coarse, uncultured, unpolished, uncivilized. [➡LEVEL OF EDUCATION AND SOPHISTICATION; 894] *Opposite:* refined. 2 *adj* **fallow**, untilled, unplanted, unfarmed. [➡REDUNDANT AND USELESS; 241] *Opposite:* cultivated.

uncultured *adj* **unrefined**, philistine, boorish, unsophisticated, uncultivated, uncivilized, uncouth, coarse. [➡LEVEL OF EDUCATION AND SOPHISTICATION; 894] *Opposite:* refined.

uncurl *v* **straighten**, straighten out, uncoil, flatten, unwind. [➡TAKE UP A NEW POSITION; 313] *Opposite:* curl.

uncut *adj* **unabridged**, complete, full-length, unedited, uncensored, unexpurgated. [➡WHOLENESS AND COMPLETENESS; 199] *Opposite:* abridged.

undamaged *adj* **unspoiled**, untouched, unharmed, unhurt, intact, safe, pure, uncontaminated. [➡IN GOOD REPAIR; 1231] *Opposite:* spoiled.

undaunted *adj* **fearless**, unconcerned, unworried, carefree, undisturbed, impervious, unafraid, undeterred. [➡CALMNESS, CONFIDENCE, AND COMPOSURE; 537] *Opposite:* scared.

undeceive *v* **inform**, tell, apprise (*formal*), notify, enlighten, disabuse, put in the picture. [➡INFORM AND ANNOUNCE; 612] *Opposite:* deceive.

undecided 1 *adj* **in two minds**, in doubt, dithering, vacillating, uncertain, irresolute, hesitant, indecisive, unsure. [➡UNCERTAINTY; 560] *Opposite:* decided. 2 *adj* **in doubt**, unresolved, open, unclear, vague, ambivalent, doubtful, ambiguous, uncertain. [➡UNCERTAIN; 176] *Opposite:* certain.

undecipherable *adj* **illegible**, unreadable, inexplicable, mysterious, unfathomable, unexplained. [➡SECRET AND UNKNOWN; 180] *Opposite:* legible.

undecorated *adj* **plain**, simple, unornamented, austere, Spartan, bare, understated. [➡PLAIN; 233] *Opposite:* ornate.

undefeatable *adj* [➡SUCCESSFUL AND PROMISING; 81]

undefeated *adj* **unbeaten**, reigning, unvanquished, unconquered, unsubdued, unbowed. [➡SUCCESSFUL AND PROMISING; 81] *Opposite:* defeated.

undefended *adj* **unguarded**, unprotected, unfortified, unpatrolled, deserted, defenceless, exposed, vulnerable. [➡IN DANGER; 238] *Opposite:* defended.

undefiled *adj* **unsullied**, pure, unpolluted, unblemished, unstained, unsoiled, clean, clear, whole, spotless. [➡MORALLY GOOD; 775] *Opposite:* defiled (*formal*).

undefined *adj* **indeterminate**, vague, approximate, open-ended, indefinite, undecided, unclear. [➡VAGUENESS; 244] *Opposite:* defined.

undemanding *adj* **easy**, straightforward, light, simple, unchallenging, cushy (*informal*). [➡BORING AND UNINTERESTING; 235] *Opposite:* demanding.

undemocratic *adj* **inequitable**, unfair, autocratic, high-handed, dictatorial, unconstitutional, unjust. [➡STYLES AND SYSTEMS OF GOVERNMENT; 806] *Opposite:* democratic.

undemonstrative *adj* **unemotional**, restrained, phlegmatic, stoical, impassive, apathetic, reticent. [➡LIFELESS, LAZY, AND UNENTHUSIASTIC; 507] *Opposite:* demonstrative.

undemonstratively *adv* **unemotionally**, restrainedly, phlegmatically, stoically, impassively, apathetically, reticently. [➡RETICENT AND UNFORTHCOMING; 632] *Opposite:* demonstratively.

undemonstrativeness *n* **restraint**, passivity, apathy, reticence, phlegm, stoicism, impassiveness. [➡RETICENT AND UNFORTHCOMING; 632]

undeniable *adj* **irrefutable**, indisputable, incontestable, incontrovertible, unquestionable, patent, indubitable (*formal*), definite. [➡CERTAIN; 175] *Opposite:* questionable.

undependability *n* **unreliability**, untrustworthiness, unpredictability, capriciousness, fickleness. [➡LACK OF COMMITMENT AND UNRELIABILITY; 510] *Opposite:* dependability.

undependable *adj* **unreliable**, unpredictable, variable, erratic, fickle, capricious, untrustworthy. [➡LACK OF COMMITMENT AND UNRELIABILITY; 510] *Opposite:* dependable.

under 1 *prep* **beneath** (*formal*), below, in, underneath. [➡RELATIVE LOCATION; 162] *Opposite:* above. 2 *prep* **below**, less than. [➡LESS; 124] *Opposite:* over.

underachieve *v* **disappoint**, flounder, drift, drop out, underperform. [➡UNDERDO SOMETHING; 292] *Opposite:* excel.

under a cloud *adj* [➡IN TROUBLE AND DISADVANTAGED; 73]

under a curse *adj* [➡IN TROUBLE AND DISADVANTAGED; 73]

underage *adj* **juvenile**, immature, youthful, young, callow. [➡BABYHOOD, CHILDHOOD AND ADOLESCENCE; 917]

under arrest *adj* **detained**, held, in custody, imprisoned, jailed, apprehended, seized. [➡CAPTIVITY AND LOSS OF FREEDOM; 249] *Opposite:* released.

under attack *adj* **embattled**, besieged, beleaguered, beset, battered, under fire. [➡IN TROUBLE AND DISADVANTAGED; 73]

undercarriage *part of* **aircraft**. [➡AIRCRAFT; 1147]

underclothes *n* **underwear**, underclothing, underthings, undies (*informal*). [➡HABERDASHERY, MILLINERY, AND LINGERIE; 867]

underclothing *n* **underwear**, underclothes, underthings, undies (*informal*). [➡HABERDASHERY, MILLINERY, AND LINGERIE; 867]

undercoat *n* [➡COVERS AND COATINGS; 1245]

undercook *v* **underdo**, parboil, half-bake, prebake, precook. [➡COOKING AND FOOD PREPARATION; 354] *Opposite:* overcook.

undercooked *adj* [➡STATE OF PREPARED FOOD; 1170]

undercover *adj* **secret**, hidden, covert, disguised, clandestine, buried, concealed, obscured. [➡SECRET AND UNKNOWN; 180] *Opposite:* open.

undercurrent 1 *n* **current**, tide, undertow, pull, stream, flow. [➡RIVERS, LAKES, AND STREAMS; 1042] 2 *n* **feeling**, hint, undertow, suggestion, connotation, trace, tinge, nuance. [➡MEANING; 691]

undercut *v* **undermine**, destabilize, detract, weaken, damage, demean, belittle. [➡WORSEN SOMETHING; 381] *Opposite:* strengthen.

underdeveloped *adj* **immature**, small, undersized, weak, unused, unfledged, infantile. [➡SMALL; 1194]

underdo *v* **undercook**, parboil, half-bake, prebake, precook. [➡COOKING AND FOOD PREPARATION; 354] *Opposite:* overdo.

underdog *n* **loser**, small fry, runner up, second best, little guy. [➡LAZY OR UNSUCCESSFUL PEOPLE; 948]

underdone *adj* **rare**, bloody, pink, undercooked. [➡STATE OF PREPARED FOOD; 1170] *Opposite:* overdone.

under duress *adv* [➡WITHOUT ENTHUSIASM; 288]

underemphasize *v* **play down**, understate, underplay, minimize, underrate, undervalue. [➡UNDERDO SOMETHING; 292] *Opposite:* overemphasize.

underestimate *v* **undervalue**, underrate, misjudge, miscalculate. [➡UNDERDO SOMETHING; 292] *Opposite:* overestimate.

underestimated *adj* [➡UNPOPULAR AND UNWANTED; 259]

underfed *adj* **malnourished**, starving, frail, weak, undernourished, hungry, thin, famished. [➡BUILD; 478] *Opposite:* well-fed.

under fire *adj* **targeted**, beleaguered, embattled, besieged, beset, battered. [➡IN TROUBLE AND DISADVANTAGED; 73]

undergarments *n* [➡HABERDASHERY, MILLINERY, AND LINGERIE; 867]

undergo *v* **experience**, feel, suffer, endure, undertake, go through, submit to. [➡EXPERIENCE AND ENCOUNTER; 583] *Opposite:* avoid.

undergraduate *n* [➡STUDENTS AND PUPILS; 841]

underground 1 *adj* **subterranean**, below ground, covered, buried, deep, hidden. [➡IMPERCEPTIBLE; 26] 2 *adj* **subversive**, secretive, dissident, alternative, covert, concealed. [➡SECRET AND UNKNOWN; 180] *Opposite:* open. 3 *type of* **railway**. [➡RAILWAYS; 1106]

undergrowth *n* **bushes**, scrub, brushwood, vegetation, understorey. [➡VEGETATION; 1025]

underhand 1 *adj* **deceitful**, dishonest, sneaky, mean, sly, low, secretive, secret, crafty, underhanded, below the belt. [➡SECRET AND UNKNOWN; 180] *Opposite:* open. 2 *adv* **deceitfully**, dishonestly, sneakily, slyly, craftily, secretively, meanly. [➡DECEITFUL; 514] *Opposite:* openly.

underhanded *see* **underhand**.

underhandedly *adv* **deceitfully**, dishonestly, sneakily, slyly, secretively, craftily, meanly. [➡DECEITFUL; 514] *Opposite:* openly.

underlie *v* **lie beneath**, lie behind, motivate, cause, inspire, trigger, bring about. [➡CAUSE TO HAPPEN; 31]

underline *v* **underscore**, emphasize, highlight, feature, stress, point out, accentuate. [➡CLAIM, INSIST, AND EMPHASIZE; 615] *Opposite:* ignore.

underling *n* **minion**, inferior, subject, junior, subordinate, assistant. [➡SUBORDINATES AND ASSISTANTS; 966] *Opposite:* superior.

underlying *adj* **fundamental**, original, causal, primary, basic, core, essential, principal, main. [➡CAUSATION; 169]

undermine *v* **weaken**, dent, chip away at, challenge, destabilize, demoralize, undercut, damage, emasculate (*formal*). [➡WORSEN SOMETHING; 381] *Opposite:* bolster.

underneath 1 *prep* **under**, beneath (*formal*), below. [➡RELATIVE LOCATION; 162] *Opposite:* on top of. 2 *n* **base**, bottom, underside, footing, foundation, substructure. [➡SUPPORTS AND BASES; 1254] *Opposite:* top.

under negotiation *adj* **under discussion**, on the agenda, on the table, under debate. [➡HAPPENING AND IN PROGRESS; 32]

under no circumstances *adv* **by no means**, on no account, not at all, in no way, never. [➡NOT; 135]

undernourished *adj* **malnourished**, underfed, starved, hungry, famished. [➡BUILD; 478] *Opposite:* well-fed.

undernourishment *n* **malnutrition**, starvation, hunger, famine. [➡DISORDERS OF THE DIGESTIVE SYSTEM; 714]

underpants *type of* **lower body underwear.** [➡HABERDASHERY, MILLINERY, AND LINGERIE; 867]

under par (*informal*) *adj* [➡UNFIT AND WEAK; 740]

underpass *n* [➡BRIDGES, TUNNELS, CROSSINGS, AND JUNCTIONS; 1111]

underperform *v* **fail**, underachieve, disappoint, flounder, drift. [➡UNDERDO SOMETHING; 292] *Opposite:* excel.

underpin 1 *v* **shore up**, prop up, reinforce, support, buttress, fortify, underprop, jack up, strengthen, hold up. [➡IMPROVE STRENGTH AND DURABILITY; 379] *Opposite:* undermine. **2** *v* **support**, lie beneath, underlie, give support to, bolster, fortify. [➡IMPROVE STRENGTH AND DURABILITY; 379] *Opposite:* weaken.

underpinning *n* **foundation**, reinforcement, groundwork, keystone, bedrock, footing, substructure. [➡SUPPORTS AND BASES; 1254]

underplay *v* **make light of**, minimize, understate, play down, talk down, dismiss, underemphasize. [➡UNDERDO SOMETHING; 292] *Opposite:* overplay.

under pressure *adj* **stressed**, under duress, harried, on the spot, beleaguered, harassed, hassled (*informal*). [➡IN TROUBLE AND DISADVANTAGED; 73] *Opposite:* unstressed.

underprice *v* **cheapen**, undersell, underrepresent, understate. [➡SELL; 442] *Opposite:* overprice.

underprivileged *adj* **disadvantaged**, deprived, poor, needy, hard up (*informal*), neglected, unfortunate. [➡POVERTY AND POOR; 892] *Opposite:* well-off.

underprop *v* **underpin**, shore up, prop up, jack up, reinforce, support, buttress, fortify, hold up. [➡IMPROVE STRENGTH AND DURABILITY; 379] *Opposite:* undermine.

under protest *adv* [➡WITHOUT ENTHUSIASM; 288]

underrate *v* **undervalue**, underestimate, think little of, devalue, misjudge, play down. [➡UNDERDO SOMETHING; 292] *Opposite:* overrate.

underrated *adj* **undervalued**, underestimated, unappreciated, unrecognized, misunderstood, belittled. [➡UNPOPULAR AND UNWANTED; 259] *Opposite:* overrated.

underrepresent *v* **understate**, undersell, lessen, play down, make light of, diminish. [➡UNDERDO SOMETHING; 292] *Opposite:* overemphasize.

underscore *v* **underline**, highlight, emphasize, accentuate, call attention to, draw attention to, stress, feature, point out. [➡CLAIM, INSIST, AND EMPHASIZE; 615] *Opposite:* ignore.

undersea *adj* **submarine**, underwater, bathyal, bathypelagic. [➡THE SEAS, OCEANS, AND SHORES; 1041]

undersell *v* **understate**, play down, make light of, denigrate, cheapen, underrepresent, underprice. [➡SELL; 442] *Opposite:* oversell.

undershirt (*US*) *type of* **upper body underwear.** [➡HABERDASHERY, MILLINERY, AND LINGERIE; 867]

undershrub *n* **subshrub**, bush, plant. [➡BUSHES AND SHRUBS; 1027]

underside *n* **base**, bottom, underneath, basement, foundation, footing. [➡SUPPORTS AND BASES; 1254]

undersize *adj* [➡SMALL; 1194]

undersized *adj* **puny**, underdeveloped, small, short, stunted, feeble, measly (*informal*). [➡SMALL; 1194]

underskirt *type of* **lower body underwear.** [➡HABERDASHERY, MILLINERY, AND LINGERIE; 867]

understand 1 *v* **comprehend**, appreciate, know, recognize, realize, be aware of, be familiar with, be au fait with, apprehend, cognize (*formal*), fathom, grasp, take in, figure out, work out, twig (*informal*), get it, get the picture (*informal*), see, be with you, cotton on (*informal*), absorb. [➡UNDERSTAND AND GRASP; 760] **2** *v* **sympathize**, empathize, identify, appreciate. [➡BE CONCERNED AND CARE; 582]

understandable *adj* **comprehensible**, clear, logical, reasonable, fathomable, plausible. [➡CONCISE AND CLEAR; 203] *Opposite:* incomprehensible.

understanding 1 *adj* **sympathetic**, empathetic, considerate, thoughtful, kind, accepting, indulgent, appreciative, supportive, tolerant, aware. [➡GENEROSITY AND KINDNESS; 496] *Opposite:* unsympathetic. **2** *n* **agreement**, arrangement, deal, contract, settlement, accord, pact, bond, harmony. [➡HARMONY; 156] **3** *n* **sympathy**, empathy, identification, consideration, kindness, compassion, indulgence, tolerance, support. [➡COMPASSION AND FORGIVENESS; 552] *Opposite:* indifference. **4** *n* **grasp**, perception, intellect, mind, wit, intelligence, cleverness, ability, sense, insight, knowledge, comprehension, awareness, appreciation, discernment, conception. [➡POSITIVE INTELLECTUAL CHARACTERISTICS; 525] *Opposite:* ignorance. **5** *n* **interpretation**, construction, personal feeling, estimation, perception, belief, opinion. [➡POINT OF VIEW; 768]

understate *v* **play down**, minimize, devalue, belittle, make little of. [➡UNDERDO SOMETHING; 292] *Opposite:* exaggerate.

understated *adj* **modest**, inconspicuous, discreet, unfussy, minimalist, simple, low-key, unassuming, unobtrusive, unpretentious, restrained. [➡ACCEPTABLE AND PASSABLE; 220] *Opposite:* exaggerated.

understatement *n* **irony**, dryness, sarcasm, underestimation. [➡JOKES AND TEASING; 675] *Opposite:* exaggeration.

understood *adj* **unspoken**, tacit, silent, unstated, unwritten, implicit, assumed, agreed, implied. [➡KNOWN AND FAMOUS; 182] *Opposite:* explicit.

understorey *n* **forest floor**, bushes, underwood, brush, scrub, undergrowth. [➡VEGETATION; 1025]

understrength 1 *adj* **understaffed**, short-handed, short-staffed, short, down, below par, reduced. [➡TOO FEW, TOO LITTLE; 120] **2** *adj* **dilute**, weak, thin, diluted, watered down, watery. [➡DIFFICULTY AND COMPLEXITY; 243]

understudy *n* **substitute**, cover, stand-by, stand-in, replacement, double, deputy. [➡COLLEAGUES AND EQUALS; 967]

undertake *v* **take on**, assume, start, commence (*formal*), embark on, carry out, agree to, accept, take upon yourself. [➡ATTEMPT AN ACTION; 262] *Opposite:* relinquish.

undertaker *n* **funeral director**, embalmer, mortician (*US*). [➡BURIAL AND PREPARATION FOR BURIAL; 929]

undertaker's *type of* **retail outlet**. [➡RETAIL OUTLETS; 1082]

undertaking *n* **responsibility**, task, job, enterprise, commission, mission, duty, activity. [➡ACTIONS OR UNDERTAKINGS; 260]

under-the-counter *adj* **illegal**, unofficial, secret, illicit, wrongful, on the side, criminal, under-the-table. [➡ILLEGAL; 816] *Opposite:* aboveboard.

under-the-table *adj* **underhand**, unofficial, secret, surreptitious, sneaky, on the side, furtive, under-the-counter, hush-hush (*informal*), clandestine, unreported, undisclosed. [➡SECRET AND UNKNOWN; 180] *Opposite:* aboveboard.

under the weather *adj* **poorly** (*informal*), off-colour, ill, unwell, sick, below par (*informal*), run-down. [➡ILL AND SICK; 741] *Opposite:* well.

underthings *n* **underwear**, underclothes, underclothing, undies (*informal*). [➡HABERDASHERY, MILLINERY, AND LINGERIE; 867]

undertone *n* **hint**, suggestion, trace, tinge, undercurrent, air, feeling, connotation, nuance. [➡FEW, LITTLE, SMALL AMOUNT; 119] *Opposite:* overtone.

undertow *n* **current**, undercurrent, tide, pull, stream, flow. [➡THE SEAS, OCEANS, AND SHORES; 1041]

undervalue *v* **underrate**, underestimate, play down, devalue, belittle. [➡UNDERDO SOMETHING; 292] *Opposite:* overrate.

undervalued *adj* [➡UNPOPULAR AND UNWANTED; 259]

underwater **1** *adj* **submerged**, sunken, flooded, subaquatic, subsurface, immersed, inundated. [➡ORIENTATION AND ALIGNMENT; 1222] *Opposite:* dry. **2** *adj* **undersea**, submarine, sunken, submerged, marine. [➡GENERAL LOCATIONS; 159]

underway *adj* **happening**, in progress, ongoing, on the go, proceeding, in motion. [➡HAPPENING AND IN PROGRESS; 32]

underwear *n* **underclothes**, underclothing, underthings, undies (*informal*). [➡HABERDASHERY, MILLINERY, AND LINGERIE; 867]

underwear

◆ *types of lower body underwear*
bloomers (*dated*), boxer shorts, briefs, camiknickers, corset, crinoline, drawers, foundation garment, G-string, garter, girdle, jockstrap, knee-highs, knickers, legwarmer, long johns, nylons, panties, pants, pantyhose (*US*), petticoat, slip, sock, stockings, support hose (*US*), support stockings, thigh-highs, thong, tights, underpants, underskirt

◆ *types of upper body underwear*
basque, body, body stocking, bodysuit, bra, camisole, chemise, string vest, teddy, undershirt, union suit (*US*), vest

underweight *adj* **skinny**, skin-and-bone, scrawny, half-starved, underfed, malnourished, emaciated. [➡BUILD; 478] *Opposite:* overweight.

underwing *type of* **moth**. [➡FLYING INSECTS; 1013]

underwired *adj* [➡DESCRIBING CLOTHES; 869]

underworld **1** *n* **gangland**, criminal world, nether world. [➡CRIMINALS; 821] **2** *adj* **criminal**, gangland, illicit, illegal, unlawful, felonious. [➡ILLEGAL; 816] *Opposite:* legal.

under wraps (*informal*) *adj* **hidden**, secret, confidential, private, buried, covert, concealed, obscured. [➡SECRET AND UNKNOWN; 180] *Opposite:* open.

underwrite *v* **guarantee**, countersign, back, endorse, fund, finance, support, bankroll (*informal*), subsidize. [➡BUSINESS PRODUCTS; 796]

underwriter *n* **sponsor**, backer, supporter, guarantor, financier, benefactor, bankroller (*informal*). [➡REPRESENTATIVES AND PATRONS; 968]

undeserved *adj* **unwarranted**, unmerited, unearned, unfair, unjustifiable, unjustified. [➡UNPOPULAR AND UNWANTED; 259] *Opposite:* deserved.

undesirable *adj* **unwanted**, unwelcome, uninvited, objectionable, disagreeable, adverse, detrimental, unattractive, disadvantageous. [➡UNPOPULAR AND UNWANTED; 259] *Opposite:* desirable.

undetectable *adj* **untraceable**, indiscernible, unnoticeable, imperceptible, invisible, inaudible, faint. [➡IMPERCEPTIBLE; 26] *Opposite:* obvious.

undetected *adj* [➡SECRET AND UNKNOWN; 180]

undetermined **1** *adj* **hesitating**, undecided, irresolute, unsettled, vacillating, sitting on the fence, uncertain, wavering, hesitant, unsure, faltering. [➡UNCERTAINTY; 560] *Opposite:* decided. **2** *adj* **unresolved**, indeterminate, indefinite, undecided, incalculable, uncertain, undefined, unsettled, unspecified. [➡UNCERTAIN; 176] *Opposite:* definite. **3** *adj* **unknown**, undiscovered, unidentified, unheard of, unfamiliar, unspecified. [➡SECRET AND UNKNOWN; 180] *Opposite:* known.

undeterred *adj* [➡CALMNESS, CONFIDENCE, AND COMPOSURE; 537]

undeveloped *adj* **immature**, young, embryonic, unripe, emergent, new, untrained. [➡NEW, MODERN; 167] *Opposite:* mature.

undeviating *adj* **unswerving**, firm, solid, absolute, total, unshakable, loyal, undying, unequivocal. [➡HARD-WORKING AND COMMITTED; 501] *Opposite:* shaky.

undies (*informal*) *n* **underwear**, underclothes, underclothing, underthings. [➡HABERDASHERY, MILLINERY, AND LINGERIE; 867]

undifferentiated *adj* [➡SAMENESS; 151]

undignified *adj* **unseemly**, unbecoming, indecorous, improper, humiliating, degrading, shameful, inappropriate. [➡INAPPROPRIATE AND UNSUITABLE; 225] *Opposite:* dignified.

undiluted *adj* **straight**, neat, unadulterated, unmixed, full-strength, pure. [➡RAW AND NATURAL; 1213] *Opposite:* diluted.

undiplomatic *adj* **tactless**, crass, thoughtless, indiscreet, inconsiderate, blunt, unthinking, unsubtle, insensitive, indelicate. [➡BAD MANNERS AND SOCIAL SKILLS; 522] *Opposite:* diplomatic.

undirected *adj* **purposeless**, aimless, objectiveless, directionless, pointless, wandering. [➡DIRECTION OF MOTION; 346] *Opposite:* purposeful.

undiscerning *adj* [➡NEGATIVE INTELLECTUAL CHARACTERISTICS; 526]

undisciplined *adj* **unmanageable**, out of control, wild, unruly, disobedient, disorderly, disruptive, riotous. [➡UNWILLINGNESS AND STUBBORNNESS; 565] *Opposite:* well-behaved.

undisclosed *adj* **secret**, unnamed, hidden, unrevealed, unidentified, private, anonymous, nameless. [➡SECRET AND UNKNOWN; 180] *Opposite:* known.

undiscovered *adj* [➡SECRET AND UNKNOWN; 180]

undisguised *adj* **unconcealed**, unchallenged, open, uncontested, overt, accepted, obvious, recognized, evident, plain, blatant. [➡PERCEPTIBLE; 25] *Opposite:* concealed.

undisposed *adj* **unwilling**, loath, reluctant, unprepared, hesitant, wary, uninclined. [➡UNWILLINGNESS AND STUBBORNNESS; 565] *Opposite:* disposed.

undisputable *adj* [➡CERTAIN; 175]

undisputed *adj* **acknowledged**, undoubted, certain, undeniable, unquestionable, definite. [➡CERTAIN; 175] *Opposite:* questionable.

undistinctive *adj* [➡ORDINARINESS; 245]

undistinguished *adj* **ordinary**, everyday, run-of-the-mill, commonplace, nothing special, unremarkable, unexceptional, mediocre, indifferent. [➡ORDINARINESS; 245] *Opposite:* unusual.

undistorted *adj* **factual**, truthful, exact, accurate, unembroidered, unvarnished, matter-of-fact, plain, faithful, unembellished. [➡TRUE AND REAL; 172] *Opposite:* inaccurate.

undisturbed 1 *adj* **uninterrupted**, in peace, unbroken, unobstructed. [➡WHOLENESS AND COMPLETENESS; 199] *Opposite:* interrupted. 2 *adj* **untouched**, intact, whole, flawless, undamaged, in situ, unmoved. [➡IN GOOD REPAIR; 1231] *Opposite:* damaged. 3 *adj* **peaceful**, serene, composed, at peace, at ease, unflustered, unworried. [➡CALMNESS, CONFIDENCE, AND COMPOSURE; 537] *Opposite:* anxious.

undivided *adj* **complete**, entire, whole, total, full, exclusive, unbroken. [➡WHOLENESS AND COMPLETENESS; 199] *Opposite:* partial.

undo 1 *v* **unfasten**, untie, unbutton, loosen, disengage, unwrap, open, unknot, unravel. [➡UNFASTEN AND UNDO; 410] *Opposite:* fasten. 2 *v* **cancel out**, negate (*formal*), cancel, nullify, invalidate, render null and void, reverse, work against. [➡MAKE IMPOSSIBLE; 277]

undoing *n* **downfall**, ruin, ruination, collapse, destruction, humiliation, shame, defeat. [➡FAILURE; 77] *Opposite:* making.

undone 1 *adj* **uncompleted**, unfinished, incomplete, half-done, unconcluded, half-finished. [➡DIFFICULTY AND COMPLEXITY; 243] *Opposite:* done. 2 *adj* **unfastened**, open, gaping, unzipped, unbuttoned, unlocked, untied. [➡UNFASTEN AND UNDO; 410] 3 *adj* **ruined**, in trouble, lost, done for (*informal*), for the high jump (*informal*), in deep water, destroyed, for it (*informal*). [➡IN TROUBLE AND DISADVANTAGED; 73] *Opposite:* fine.

undoubted *adj* **certain**, sure, absolute, definite, indubitable (*formal*), undisputed, unquestionable, indisputable. [➡CERTAIN; 175] *Opposite:* doubtful.

undreamed-of *adj* **unexpected**, unhoped-for, unimaginable, unanticipated, unlooked-for, surprising. [➡EXTRAORDINARY: AMAZING; 205] *Opposite:* doubtfully.

undress *v* **strip off**, strip, unclothe, uncloak, bare, disrobe (*formal*). [➡DRESS, WEAR, AND UNDRESS; 868] *Opposite:* dress.

undressed *adj* **naked**, bare, nude, stripped, in your birthday suit (*slang humorous*), with nothing on, in the buff (*informal*), unclothed. [➡DRESS, WEAR, AND UNDRESS; 868] *Opposite:* dressed.

See Compare and Contrast at **naked.**

undue *adj* **unwarranted**, excessive, unnecessary, unjustified, unjustifiable, gratuitous, uncalled-for. [➡UNIMPORTANT AND UNNECESSARY; 239] *Opposite:* justified.

undulant (*literary*) *adj* **undulating**, rolling, rising and falling, swelling, heaving, surging, rippling. [➡ROUNDED SHAPE; 1217]

undulate *v* **roll**, ripple, rise and fall, swell, heave, surge. [➡BOUNCE, UNDULATE, AND VIBRATE; 309]

undulating *adj* **rolling**, rising and falling, swelling, heaving, surging, rippling, undulant (*literary*). [➡ROUNDED SHAPE; 1217]

undulation *n* **wave**, ripple, furrow, crinkle, wrinkle, fold. [➡BOUNCE, UNDULATE, AND VIBRATE; 309]

unduly *adv* **excessively**, overly, disproportionately, unjustifiably, undeservedly, improperly. [➡TO A GREAT EXTENT; 130] *Opposite:* justifiably.

undying *adj* **unending**, never-ending, endless, perpetual, eternal, everlasting, abiding, enduring, constant, ceaseless. [➡PERMANENCE: WITHOUT END; 94] *Opposite:* inconstant.

unearned *adj* **undeserved**, unwarranted, unmerited, unjustified, uncalled-for, inappropriate. [➡INCORRECT AND ERRONEOUS; 223]

unearth 1 *v* **dig up**, exhume, disinter, excavate, extract. [➡BURIAL AND PREPARATION FOR BURIAL; 929] *Opposite:* bury. 2 *v* **disclose**, uncover, discover, find, expose, reveal, bring to light, come across, happen upon. [➡FIND; 464] *Opposite:* cover up.

unearthly 1 *adj* **eerie**, weird, bizarre, strange, macabre, creepy (*informal*), ghostly, mysterious, supernatural, unnatural. [➡BIZARRE AND PECULIAR; 258] *Opposite:* normal. 2 *adj* **unreasonable**, inappropriate, outrageous, ridiculous, absurd. [➡UNACCEPTABLE AND UNFORGIVEABLE; 226] *Opposite:* acceptable.

unease *n* **anxiety**, nervousness, restlessness, awkwardness, uneasiness, disquiet, discomfort, agitation, apprehension, worry. [➡FEELINGS ABOUT THE FUTURE; 534] *Opposite:* calm.

uneasiness *n* **anxiety**, nervousness, restlessness, awkwardness, unease, disquiet, discomfort, agitation, apprehension, worry. [➡FEELINGS ABOUT THE FUTURE; 534] *Opposite:* calmness.

uneasy *adj* **anxious**, nervous, troubled, uncomfortable, ill at ease, perturbed, edgy, on edge, apprehensive, tense. [➡CONFUSION, ANXIETY, AND WORRY; 541] *Opposite:* calm.

uneconomic 1 *adj* **unprofitable**, unviable, lossmaking, profitless. [➡UNSUCCESSFUL AND UNPROMISING; 76] *Opposite:* profitable. 2 *adj* **inefficient**, wasteful, uneconomical, improvident (*formal*), extravagant, profligate. [➡WASTEFUL AND UNECONOMICAL; 247] *Opposite:* efficient.

uneconomical *adj* **inefficient**, wasteful, extravagant, uneconomic, profligate, improvident (*formal*). [➡WASTEFUL AND UNECONOMICAL; 247] *Opposite:* efficient.

unedited *adj* **complete**, unabridged, unexpurgated, uncut, full-length, whole, unrevised, full. [➡WHOLENESS AND COMPLETENESS; 199] *Opposite:* edited.

uneducated *adj* **unschooled**, untaught, ignorant, illiterate, uninformed, untutored, unqualified. [➡UNSKILLED; 530] *Opposite:* educated.

unembarrassed *adj* [➡CALMNESS, CONFIDENCE, AND COMPOSURE; 537]

unembellished 1 *adj* **unadorned**, plain, without ornamentation, simple, straightforward. [➡ORDINARINESS; 245] *Opposite:* fancy. 2 *adj* **factual**, unembroidered, undistorted, truthful, straightforward, unvarnished, exact, accurate, literal, faithful. [➡TRUE AND REAL; 172] *Opposite:* fictional.

unembroidered *adj* **factual**, unembellished, undistorted, truthful, unvarnished, exact, straightforward, accurate, literal, matter-of-fact, florid. [➡TRUE AND REAL; 172]

unemotional *adj* **impassive**, dispassionate, undemonstrative, unresponsive, detached, inexpressive, poker-faced, composed, objective, cold. [➡NEUTRALITY AND INDIFFERENCE; 554] *Opposite:* emotional.

unemployed *adj* **jobless**, out of work, out of a job, unwaged, laid off, made redundant, on the dole (*informal*), receiving benefit, idle, not working, on unemployment (*US*). [➡EMPLOYMENT STATUS; 831] *Opposite:* employed.

unemployment *n* **joblessness**, job loss, redundancy, idleness. [➡WORK-RELATED ACTIVITIES; 834] *Opposite:* employment.

unending *adj* **endless**, never-ending, eternal, everlasting, interminable, unrelenting, continuous, incessant, relentless, unremitting. [➡PERMANENCE: WITHOUT END; 94] *Opposite:* finite.

unendurable *adj* **insufferable**, unbearable, intolerable, insupportable, excruciating, agonizing, painful. [➡EMOTIONALLY UNPLEASANT AND UPSETTING; 228] *Opposite:* bearable.

unenlightened 1 *adj* **superstitious**, prejudiced, ignorant, uncivilized, benighted, unaware. [➡NEGATIVE INTELLECTUAL CHARACTERISTICS; 526] *Opposite:* rational. 2 *adj* **ignorant**, benighted, uneducated, uninformed, unsophisticated, uncivilized. [➡IGNORANCE; 558] *Opposite:* informed.

unenthusiastic *adj* **apathetic**, indifferent, unresponsive, lukewarm, half-hearted, subdued, cool, unimpressed, unexcited, uninterested. [➡NEUTRALITY AND INDIFFERENCE; 554] *Opposite:* enthusiastic.

unenticing *adj* [➡UGLINESS AND UNATTRACTIVENESS; 234]

unenviable *adj* **undesirable**, disagreeable, unpleasant, uninviting, objectionable, unpopular, unwelcome, unattractive, unappealing, distasteful. [➡UNPOPULAR AND UNWANTED; 259] *Opposite:* enviable.

unenviably *adv* **undesirably**, unpleasantly, thanklessly, disagreeably, painfully, uncomfortably. [➡EMOTIONALLY UNPLEASANT AND UPSETTING; 228] *Opposite:* enviably.

unequal 1 *adj* **uneven**, unbalanced, lopsided, asymmetrical, disproportionate, disparate, irregular, dissimilar. [➡DIFFERENCE; 150] *Opposite:* equal. 2 *adj* **unfair**, inequitable, one-sided, mismatched, unbalanced. [➡MORALLY BAD; 776] *Opposite:* fair. 3 *adj* **unsatisfactory**, unfit, unable, incapable, inadequate, wanting. [➡UNSKILLED; 530]

unequalled *adj* **unrivalled**, matchless, unsurpassed, incomparable, unique, unmatched, unparalleled, unchallenged, superior. [➡SUPERIORITY; 153] *Opposite:* ordinary.

unequally 1 *adv* **unevenly**, lopsidedly, inequitably, asymmetrically, irregularly, disproportionately. [➡DIFFERENCE; 150] *Opposite:* evenly. 2 *adv* **unfairly**, inequitably, one-sidedly, unjustly. [➡MORALLY BAD; 776] *Opposite:* fairly.

unequivocal *adj* **clear**, plain, unambiguous, unmistakable, explicit, indisputable, undeniable, obvious, definite. [➡CONCISE AND CLEAR; 203]

unerring *adj* **certain**, sure, absolute, positive, definite, unmistaken, correct, spot-on (*informal*), infallible, faultless. [➡CERTAINTY; 562] *Opposite:* faulty.

unessential *adj* **dispensable**, superfluous, unnecessary, replaceable, expendable, nonessential. [➡UNIMPORTANT AND UNNECESSARY; 239] *Opposite:* essential.

unethical *adj* **unprincipled**, immoral, wrong, bad, unscrupulous, dishonourable, disreputable, corrupt, depraved. [➡MORALLY BAD; 776] *Opposite:* ethical.

uneven 1 *adj* **rough**, jagged, bumpy, patchy, irregular, potholed, rutted. [➡PHYSICAL TEXTURE; 1221] *Opposite:* level. 2 *adj* **unequal**, unbalanced, lopsided, asymmetrical, disproportionate, irregular, unsymmetrical, top-heavy. [➡DIFFERENCE; 150] *Opposite:* equal. 3 *adj* **mismatched**, one-sided, unfair, unbalanced, disproportionate. [➡DISHARMONY; 157] *Opposite:* fair.

unevenly *adv* **unequally**, asymmetrically, irregularly, unsymmetrically, disproportionately. [➡DIFFERENCE; 150] *Opposite:* equally.

unevenness 1 *n* **roughness**, jaggedness, bumpiness, patchiness. [➡PHYSICAL TEXTURE; 1221] *Opposite:* evenness. 2 *n* **inequality**, disproportion, irregularity, one-sidedness, disparity, asymmetry. [➡DISHARMONY; 157] *Opposite:* equality.

uneventful *adj* **boring**, monotonous, ordinary, humdrum, dull, run of the mill, everyday, nothing to write home about, unexciting. [➡ORDINARINESS; 245] *Opposite:* exciting.

unexceptionable *adj* **inoffensive**, unobjectionable, faultless, irreproachable, acceptable, beyond reproach, satisfactory. [➡ACCEPTABLE AND PASSABLE; 220]. *Opposite:* exceptionable (*formal*).

unexceptional *adj* **undistinguished**, nondescript, anonymous, modest, indifferent, unremarkable, inconspicuous, run-of-the-mill, typical, normal. [➡ORDINARINESS; 245] *Opposite:* extraordinary.

unexcited *adj* **calm**, restrained, subdued, unresponsive, impassive, unimpressed, unenthusiastic, indifferent, tepid, lukewarm. [➡NEUTRALITY AND INDIFFERENCE; 554] *Opposite:* excited.

unexciting *adj* **dull**, boring, tedious, monotonous, humdrum, dreary, insipid, uninteresting, tame, lacklustre. [➡BORING AND UNINTERESTING; 235] *Opposite:* exciting.

unexpected *adj* **unforeseen**, unanticipated, unpredicted, surprising, startling, astonishing, sudden, out of the blue. [➡UNINTENTIONAL AND ACCIDENTAL; 282] *Opposite:* expected.

unexplainable *adj* [➡BIZARRE AND PECULIAR; 258]

unexplained *adj* **mysterious**, unsolved, inexplicable, impenetrable, arcane, secret, baffling. [➡SECRET AND UNKNOWN; 180] *Opposite:* apparent.

unexplored *adj* [➡SECRET AND UNKNOWN; 180]

unexpressed *adj* **unstated**, unspoken, unsaid, unknown. [➡SECRET AND UNKNOWN; 180] *Opposite:* articulated.

unexpurgated *adj* [➡WHOLENESS AND COMPLETENESS; 199]

unfading *adj* [➡PERMANENCE: WITHOUT END; 94]

unfailing *adj* **reliable**, certain, dependable, trustworthy, constant, consistent, abiding, lasting, unshakable, enduring. [➡PERMANENCE: WITHOUT END; 94] *Opposite:* erratic.

unfair 1 *adj* **unjust**, inequitable, iniquitous, unwarranted, unmerited, undue, unreasonable, excessive, wrong, undeserved. [➡MORALLY BAD; 776] *Opposite:* fair. 2 *adj* **unethical**, dishonest, dishonourable, deceitful, underhand, unscrupulous, crooked (*informal*), devious, fraudulent, false. [➡MORALLY BAD; 776] *Opposite:* honest. 3 *adj* **partial**, one-sided, biased, prejudicial, discriminating, bigoted. [➡MORALLY BAD; 776] *Opposite:* fair.

unfairness 1 *n* **injustice**, wrongness, wrong, iniquitousness, unreasonableness, inequitableness, inequity, excess, inequality. [➡MORALLY BAD; 776] *Opposite:* fairness. 2 *n* **unethicalness**, unethicality, dishonesty, dishonourableness, deceitfulness, fraudulence, falseness, underhandedness, crookedness. [➡MORALLY BAD; 776] *Opposite:* honesty. 3 *n* **partiality**, one-sidedness, bias, prejudice, discrimination, inequity, favouritism, bigotry. [➡PREJUDICE; 551] *Opposite:* fairness.

unfaithful *adj* **disloyal**, false, untrue, adulterous, two-timing (*informal*), treacherous, traitorous, faithless, double-crossing. [➡DECEITFUL; 514] *Opposite:* faithful.

unfaithfulness *n* **disloyalty**, infidelity, falseness, adultery, treachery, betrayal, deceitfulness, faithlessness. [➡BAD BEHAVIOUR OR ACTION; 255] *Opposite:* faithfulness.

unfaltering *adj* **untiring**, indefatigable, tireless, unflagging, persistent, tenacious, resolute, determined, constant, steadfast, dogged. [➡HARD-WORKING AND COMMITTED; 501] *Opposite:* faltering.

unfamiliar 1 *adj* **unknown**, new, untried, strange, alien, different, unusual, foreign, exotic. [➡SECRET AND UNKNOWN; 180] *Opposite:* familiar. 2 *adj* **unacquainted**, unaccustomed, unaware, unversed, unskilled, inexperienced, ignorant, unused. [➡UNSKILLED; 530] *Opposite:* familiar.

unfamiliarity 1 *n* **newness**, strangeness, unusualness, foreignness, exoticism, exoticness. [➡BIZARRE AND PECULIAR; 258] *Opposite:* familiarity. 2 *n* **unaccustomedness**, unacquaintedness, inexperience, ignorance, unawareness. [➡IGNORANCE; 558] *Opposite:* familiarity.

unfashionable *adj* **out-of-date**, outmoded, dated, old-fashioned, behind the times, obsolete, defunct, passé, outdated. [➡OLD, OLD-FASHIONED; 168] *Opposite:* trendy (*informal*).

unfasten *v* **undo**, unhook, unlock, disengage, detach, untie, unbutton, release, uncouple, unbolt. [➡UNFASTEN AND UNDO; 410] *Opposite:* fasten.

unfastened *adj* **undone**, loosened, untied, unbuttoned, unzipped, unlaced, open, unsecured, loose, unattached, unhooked, unstuck. [➡UNFASTEN AND UNDO; 410] *Opposite:* fastened.

unfathomability *n* [➡DIFFICULTY AND COMPLEXITY; 243]

unfathomable 1 *adj* **deep**, profound, bottomless, unsounded, unplumbed, immeasurable, vast. [➡DEPTH: DEEP; 1200] *Opposite:* shallow. 2 *adj* **incomprehensible**, impenetrable, inscrutable, unknowable, indecipherable, arcane, enigmatic, mysterious, inexplicable. [➡SECRET AND UNKNOWN; 180] *Opposite:* straightforward.

unfathomableness *n* [➡DIFFICULTY AND COMPLEXITY; 243]

unfavourable 1 *adj* **disapproving**, negative, uncomplimentary, opposed, hostile, critical, harsh, disparaging. [➡ACCUSATORY AND DISAPPROVING; 635] *Opposite:* approving. 2 *adj* **harmful**, adverse, bad, detrimental, disadvantageous, damaging. [➡BAD AND BADLY; 224] *Opposite:* beneficial.

unfeasibility *n* [➡IMPOSSIBLE AND IMPROBABLE; 179]

unfeasible *adj* **impracticable**, impractical, unworkable, unachievable, out of the question, impossible, unrealistic, unattainable. [➡IMPOSSIBLE AND IMPROBABLE; 179] *Opposite:* feasible.

unfeeling *adj* **unsympathetic**, hardhearted, callous, cruel, heartless, pitiless, cold, insensitive, uncaring, inhuman. [➡SELFISH AND UNKIND; 506] *Opposite:* sympathetic.

unfeigned *adj* [➡TRUE AND REAL; 172]

unfetter *v* **release**, liberate, free, unchain, unshackle, unbind, untie, set free, let loose. [➡FREEDOM AND LIBERTY; 209] *Opposite:* fetter.

unfettered *adj* **freed**, unencumbered, unconstrained, unregulated, autonomous, unrestrained, unrestricted, unbound, unchained. [➡FREEDOM AND LIBERTY; 209] *Opposite:* constrained.

unfilled *adj* **empty**, vacant, void, unoccupied, untaken. [➡EMPTY; 1237] *Opposite:* full.

See Compare and Contrast at **vacant.**

unfinished *adj* **incomplete**, uncompleted, fragmentary, partial, ongoing, in progress. [➡UNFINISHEDNESS; 240] *Opposite:* finished.

unfit 1 *adj* **unsuitable**, inappropriate, unsuited, inapt, unacceptable. [➡INAPPROPRIATE AND UNSUITABLE; 225] *Opposite:* suitable. 2 *adj* **unqualified**, incompetent, inept, useless, incapable, inadequate, ineligible, inexpert, hopeless, untrained. [➡UNSKILLED; 530] *Opposite:* competent. 3 *adj* **out of shape**, flabby (*informal*), out of condition, unhealthy, ailing (*dated*), weak, puny, frail. [➡UNFIT AND WEAK; 740] *Opposite:* fit.

unfitted *adj* **unsuited**, unequipped, unprepared, unsuitable, unqualified, incompatible. [➡INAPPROPRIATE AND UNSUITABLE; 225] *Opposite:* fitted.

unfitting *adj* **unsuitable**, inappropriate, unbecoming, out of place, unseemly, unacceptable, improper, unfortunate, incorrect. [➡INAPPROPRIATE AND UNSUITABLE; 225] *Opposite:* fitting.

unfix *v* **detach**, loosen, disengage, separate, undo, free. [➡UNFASTEN AND UNDO; 410] *Opposite:* attach.

unfixed *adj* [➡IN BAD REPAIR; 1233]

unflagging *adj* **untiring**, indefatigable, tireless, unfaltering, persistent, tenacious, resolute, determined, steadfast, constant, loyal. [➡HARD-WORKING AND COMMITTED; 501] *Opposite:* weak.

unflappability *n* **calmness**, coolness, patience, composure, control, imperturbability, phlegm. [➡CONFIDENCE AND COMPOSURE; 500] *Opposite:* excitability.

unflappable *adj* **composed**, calm, unflustered, collected, imperturbable, unexcitable, level-headed, cool as a cucumber, cool, serene, self-possessed. [➡CONFIDENCE AND COMPOSURE; 500] *Opposite:* anxious.

unflattering *adj* **unbecoming**, unattractive, unappealing, ugly, critical, uncomplimentary, faultfinding, unfavourable. [➡UGLINESS AND UNATTRACTIVENESS; 234] *Opposite:* becoming.

unfledged *adj* **inexperienced**, naive, innocent, fresh, immature, ignorant. [➡IGNORANCE; 558] *Opposite:* experienced.

unflinching *adj* **unwavering**, constant, steady, undaunted, persistent, resolute, dogged, steadfast, staunch, fearless. [➡CERTAINTY; 562] *Opposite:* wavering.

unflustered *adj* **composed**, calm, unflappable, collected, imperturbable, unruffled, level-headed, cool, in control, serene. [➡CALMNESS, CONFIDENCE, AND COMPOSURE; 537] *Opposite:* agitated.

unfocused 1 *adj* **blurred**, unclear, fuzzy, indistinct, bleary, out-of-focus. [➡VISUAL TEXTURE; 1220] *Opposite:* clear. 2 *adj* **ill-defined**, nonspecific, imprecise, woolly, vague. [➡VAGUENESS; 244] *Opposite:* focused.

unfold 1 *v* **open out**, open up, unfurl, spread out, display, unroll, unwrap. [➡CAUSE TO APPEAR; 5] *Opposite:* fold up. 2 *v* **explain**, clarify, make known, disclose, reveal, describe. [➡EXPLAIN AND CLARIFY; 611] *Opposite:* conceal. 3 *v* **develop**, evolve, grow, progress, advance, expand. [➡GRADUALLY COME INTO EXISTENCE; 1] *Opposite:* deteriorate.

unforced *adj* **voluntary**, natural, spontaneous, unwitting, unprompted, effortless, artless, genuine. [➡THE WILL AND WILLINGNESS; 564] *Opposite:* forced.

unforeseeable *adj* **unexpected**, unanticipated, undreamed-of, unpredictable, surprise. [➡SECRET AND UNKNOWN; 180] *Opposite:* predictable.

unforeseen *adj* **unexpected**, unanticipated, unpredicted, surprising, startling, astonishing, sudden. [➡UNINTENTIONAL AND ACCIDENTAL; 282] *Opposite:* expected.

unforgettable *adj* **memorable**, remarkable, treasured, cherished, haunting, extraordinary, impressive, notable, exceptional. [➡EXTRAORDINARY: AMAZING; 205] *Opposite:* unremarkable.

unforgettably *adv* **memorably**, remarkably, hauntingly, notably, exceptionally, extraordinarily. [➡INTERESTING AND MEANINGFUL; 191] *Opposite:* unremarkably.

unforgivable *adj* **unpardonable**, inexcusable, indefensible, unjustifiable, intolerable, deplorable, reprehensible, beyond the pale. [➡UNACCEPTABLE AND UNFORGIVABLE; 226] *Opposite:* understandable.

unforgiving 1 *adj* **intolerant**, merciless, pitiless, remorseless, vindictive, ruthless, callous, unmoved. [➡SELFISH AND UNKIND; 506] *Opposite:* tolerant. 2 *adj* **demanding**, exacting, taxing, challenging, hard, difficult. [➡PHYSICALLY UNPLEASANT; 227] *Opposite:* easy.

unformed 1 *adj* **shapeless**, formless, indistinct, imprecise, amorphous, embryonic. [➡SHAPELESSNESS; 1218] *Opposite:* distinct. 2 *adj* **undeveloped**, immature, green, callow, underdeveloped, inexperienced. [➡IGNORANCE; 558] *Opposite:* mature.

unformulated *adj* **vague**, indistinct, unclear, hazy, nebulous, imprecise. [➡THE NATURE OF IDEAS; 772] *Opposite:* clear.

unforthcoming *adj* **uncommunicative**, reticent, taciturn, standoffish, distant, terse, laconic. [➡RETICENT AND UNFORTHCOMING; 632] *Opposite:* voluble.

unfortified *adj* [➡RAW AND NATURAL; 1213]

unfortunate 1 *adj* **unlucky**, luckless, unsuccessful, unhappy, ill-fated, ill-starred (*formal*). [➡BAD LUCK AND UNLUCKY; 785] *Opposite:* lucky. 2 *adj* **disastrous**, calamitous, doomed, hopeless, fateful, ruinous. [➡EMOTIONALLY UNPLEASANT AND UPSETTING; 228] *Opposite:* fortunate. 3 *adj* **inappropriate**, inopportune, ill-timed, tactless, untimely, ill-advised, regrettable, awkward. [➡INAPPROPRIATE AND UNSUITABLE; 225] *Opposite:* timely. 4 *n* **wretch**, underdog, loser, lame duck, weakling. [➡BAD LUCK AND UNLUCKY; 785]

unfortunately 1 *adv* **unluckily**, unhappily, regrettably, sadly, alas. [➡EXPRESSIONS OF REGRET; 548] *Opposite:* fortunately. 2 *adv* **inappropriately**, inopportunely, tactlessly, ill-advisedly, regrettably, awkwardly. [➡INAPPROPRIATE AND UNSUITABLE; 225] *Opposite:* appropriately.

unfounded *adj* **groundless**, unsupported, baseless,

unsubstantiated, speculative, tenuous, unproven. [➡FALSE AND UNREAL; 174] *Opposite:* proven.

unfreeze *v* **relax**, rescind, repeal, release, liberate, undo. [➡FREEDOM AND LIBERTY; 209] *Opposite:* freeze.

unfrequented *adj* **lonely**, neglected, isolated, quiet, desolate, lone, solitary. [➡UNPOPULAR AND UNWANTED; 259] *Opposite:* busy.

unfriendliness *n* **aloofness**, surliness, coldness, coolness, frostiness, unsociability, inhospitality, hostility, antagonism, animosity. [➡ANTAGONISM; 553] *Opposite:* friendliness.

unfriendly 1 *adj* **aloof**, distant, surly, cold, frosty, cool, unsociable, inhospitable, hostile, antagonistic. [➡UNFRIENDLINESS AND UNSOCIABILITY; 505] *Opposite:* friendly. 2 *adj* **unfavourable**, ill-disposed, inimical, hostile, inauspicious, unpromising. [➡RUDE AND HOSTILE; 626] *Opposite:* well-disposed.

unfruitful 1 *adj* **unsuccessful**, unprofitable, unproductive, unrewarding, fruitless, vain. [➡REDUNDANT AND USELESS; 241] *Opposite:* profitable. 2 *adj* **infertile**, sterile, barren, bare, fruitless, childless. [➡REPRODUCTION AND HEREDITY; 726] *Opposite:* fertile.

unfunny *adj* [➡BIZARRE AND PECULIAR; 258]

unfurl *v* **open out**, open up, unfold, spread out, expand, develop. [➡CAUSE TO APPEAR; 5] *Opposite:* fold up.

unfurnished *adj* **bare**, empty, unequipped, unfitted. [➡EMPTY; 1237] *Opposite:* furnished.

unfussy *adj* **understated**, simple, uncomplicated, modest, plain, economical, austere. [➡PLAIN; 233] *Opposite:* fussy.

ungainliness 1 *n* **gracelessness**, awkwardness, clumsiness, inelegance, gaucheness, maladroitness (*formal*). [➡AGILITY OF THE BODY; 477] *Opposite:* gracefulness. 2 *n* **awkwardness**, unwieldiness, cumbersomeness, heaviness, clumsiness, inconvenience, bulkiness. [➡WEIGHT: HEAVY; 1204] *Opposite:* convenience.

ungainly 1 *adj* **graceless**, awkward, clumsy, inelegant, ungraceful, uncoordinated, maladroit (*formal*), gauche, shambling. [➡AGILITY OF THE BODY; 477] *Opposite:* graceful. 2 *adj* **awkward**, unwieldy, cumbersome, inconvenient, heavy, clumsy, bulky, unmanageable. [➡WEIGHT: HEAVY; 1204] *Opposite:* convenient.

ungallant *adj* [➡BAD MANNERS AND SOCIAL SKILLS; 522]

ungenerous 1 *adj* **stingy** (*informal*), miserly, tightfisted, penny-pinching (*informal*), mean, parsimonious, grudging, measly (*informal*), niggardly. [➡FINANCIALLY MEAN AND GRASPING; 520] *Opposite:* generous. 2 *adj* **mean-spirited**, nasty, mean, unkind, cruel, callous, uncaring, heartless, selfish, ignoble. [➡SELFISH AND UNKIND; 506] *Opposite:* kind.

ungentlemanly *adj* [➡BAD MANNERS AND SOCIAL SKILLS; 522]

unglamorous *adj* [➡UGLINESS AND UNATTRACTIVENESS; 234]

unglued 1 *adj* **separated**, detached, parted, disconnected, divided, disjointed. [➡UNFASTEN AND UNDO; 410] *Opposite:* whole. 2 *adj* (*informal*) **upset**, angry, disconcerted, hysterical, unnerved, uncontrolled. [➡INSECURITY AND LOSS OF COMPOSURE; 545] *Opposite:* calm.

ungodliness *n* [➡RELIGIOUS CONCEPTS; 777]

ungodly 1 *adj* **impious**, irreligious, irreverent, blasphemous, profane, disrespectful. [➡RELIGIOUS CONCEPTS; 777] *Opposite:* pious. 2 *adj* **wicked**, sinful, immoral, corrupt, depraved, vile. [➡MORALLY BAD; 776] *Opposite:* virtuous. 3 *adj* (*informal*) **unreasonable**, unearthly, late, unsocial, ridiculous, absurd. [➡BIZARRE AND PECULIAR; 258] *Opposite:* reasonable.

ungovernable *adj* **intractable** (*formal*), uncontrollable, out of control, unmanageable, unruly, anarchic, undisciplined, headstrong, unrestrained, wild. [➡REBELLIOUSNESS AND DISOBEDIENCE; 566] *Opposite:* controllable.

ungraceful 1 *adj* **clumsy**, ungainly, graceless, uncoordinated, lumbering, awkward, inelegant, gawky (*informal*), gauche, maladroit (*formal*). [➡AGILITY OF THE BODY; 477] *Opposite:* elegant. 2 *adj* **rude**, impolite, discourteous, gruff, brusque, ill-bred, churlish. [➡BAD MANNERS AND SOCIAL SKILLS; 522] *Opposite:* polite.

ungracious *adj* **ill-mannered**, discourteous, rude, impolite, bad-mannered, uncivil, disrespectful, insolent, churlish, brusque. [➡BAD MANNERS AND SOCIAL SKILLS; 522] *Opposite:* gracious.

ungraciously *adv* **ill-manneredly**, discourteously, rudely, impolitely, uncivilly, disrespectfully, insolently, churlishly, brusquely. [➡RUDE AND HOSTILE; 626] *Opposite:* graciously.

ungraciousness *n* [➡BAD MANNERS AND SOCIAL SKILLS; 522]

ungrateful 1 *adj* **unappreciative**, thankless, churlish, unmindful, ungracious. [➡BAD MANNERS AND SOCIAL SKILLS; 522] *Opposite:* grateful. 2 *adj* **unpleasant**, unrewarding, thankless, unsatisfying. [➡EMOTIONALLY UNPLEASANT AND UPSETTING; 228] *Opposite:* rewarding.

ungratefully *adv* **unappreciatively**, churlishly, thanklessly, ungraciously. [➡BAD MANNERS AND SOCIAL SKILLS; 522] *Opposite:* gratefully.

ungratefulness *n* **unappreciativeness**, ingratitude, churlishness, thanklessness, ungraciousness. [➡BAD MANNERS AND SOCIAL SKILLS; 522] *Opposite:* gratitude.

unguarded 1 *adj* **unprotected**, undefended, unshielded, unfortified, defenceless, exposed, vulnerable, weak. [➡IN DANGER; 238] *Opposite:* guarded. 2 *adj* **unwary**, careless, indiscreet, thoughtless, imprudent (*formal*), rash, unthinking, reckless. [➡INCAUTIOUS AND CARELESS; 284] *Opposite:* guarded.

unguent *n* **ointment**, salve, balm, lotion, oil, liniment, cream. [➡LOTIONS, PASTES, AND GELS; 1271]

unhampered *adj* **unrestricted**, unimpeded, unhindered, unconstrained, free. [➡FREEDOM AND LIBERTY; 209] *Opposite:* restricted.

unhappily 1 *adv* **sadly**, miserably, discontentedly, despondently, dejectedly, gloomily, forlornly, sorrowfully, glumly, mournfully. [➡SADNESS, DISTRESS, AND DESPAIR; 540] *Opposite:* happily. 2 *adv* **unfortunately**, unluckily, regrettably, alas, sadly. [➡EXPRESSIONS OF REGRET; 548] *Opposite:* luckily.

unhappiness *n* **sadness**, sorrow, grief, misery, discontent, despondency, gloom, melancholy, depression, despair. [➡SADNESS, DISTRESS, AND DESPAIR; 540] *Opposite:* happiness.

unhappy 1 *adj* **sad**, miserable, discontented, despondent, dejected, gloomy, forlorn, sorrowful, melancholic, depressed, down. [➡SADNESS, DISTRESS, AND DESPAIR; 540] *Opposite:* happy. 2 *adj* **unfortunate**, ill-fated, hopeless, doomed, fateful, calamitous. [➡BAD LUCK AND UNLUCKY; 785] *Opposite:* fortunate. 3 *adj* **inappropriate**, ill-chosen, infelicitous, tactless, unfortunate, unsuitable. [➡INAPPROPRIATE AND UNSUITABLE; 225] *Opposite:* well-chosen. 4 *adj* **displeased**, annoyed, upset, angry, disappointed, put out. [➡SADNESS, DISTRESS, AND DESPAIR; 540] *Opposite:* pleased.

unharmed *adj* **uninjured**, unhurt, unscathed, undamaged, unscratched, without a scratch, safe and sound, in one piece, untouched, intact. [➡FINE; 738] *Opposite:* harmed.

unharmonious *adj* [➡DISHARMONY; 157]

unhazardous *adj* [➡SAFE AND SAFETY; 192]

unhealthy 1 *adj* **sick**, unfit, out of condition, out of shape, sickly, anaemic, pallid, frail, weak, ill, unwell. [➡UNFIT AND WEAK; 740] *Opposite:* well. 2 *adj* **harmful**, detrimental, injurious, damaging, unwholesome, insanitary, noxious, unhygienic, insalubrious (*formal*). [➡DANGEROUS; 237] *Opposite:* healthy. 3 *adj* **corrupt**, unwholesome, morbid, unnatural, insalubrious (*formal*), ghoulish. [➡MORALLY BAD; 776] *Opposite:* wholesome.

unheard *adj* **unheeded**, disregarded, ignored, overlooked, unnoticed, unremarked. [➡IMPERCEPTIBLE; 26]

unheard-of 1 *adj* **unknown**, unfamiliar, new, obscure, undiscovered, unsung. [➡EXTRAORDINARY: UNCOMMON; 206] *Opposite:* well-known. 2 *adj* **unprecedented**, exceptional, extraordinary, novel, unusual, original, unimaginable, undreamed-of, rare. [➡SECRET AND UNKNOWN; 180] *Opposite:* ordinary. 3 *adj* **offensive**, rude, disgusting, repulsive, shocking, repugnant, outrageous. [➡DISGUSTING AND REPULSIVE; 231] *Opposite:* inoffensive.

unhelpful 1 *adj* **uncooperative**, contrary, awkward, unaccommodating, obstructive, unsupportive, disobliging. [➡UNWILLINGNESS AND STUBBORNNESS; 565] *Opposite:* helpful. 2 *adj* **useless**, unconstructive, impractical, unnecessary, negative, adverse, of no use. [➡REDUNDANT AND USELESS; 241] *Opposite:* useful.

unhelpfulness 1 *n* **uncooperativeness**, unsupportiveness, contrariness, impractically. [➡UNWILLINGNESS AND STUBBORNNESS; 565] *Opposite:* helpfulness. 2 *n* **uselessness**, negativity, pointlessness, needlessness, worthlessness. [➡REDUNDANT AND USELESS; 241] *Opposite:* usefulness.

unhesitating *adj* **prompt**, unreserved, wholehearted, confident, forthright, rapid, swift, certain, unwavering. [➡CONFIDENCE AND COMPOSURE; 500] *Opposite:* tentative.

unhidden *adj* [➡KNOWN AND FAMOUS; 182]

unhindered *adj* **unimpeded**, unconstrained, unrestricted, unobstructed, unchecked, unopposed. [➡FREEDOM AND LIBERTY; 209]

unhinge *v* **unbalance**, derange, madden, drive insane, disturb, confuse, send over the edge. [➡UPSET, DISTRESS, AND HUMILIATE; 568]

unhinged *adj* **unbalanced**, deranged, disturbed, irrational, crackers (*informal*). [➡ECCENTRICITY AND IRRATIONALITY; 563] *Opposite:* sane.

unhip (*informal*) *adj* [➡OLD, OLD-FASHIONED; 168]

unhitch *v* **unfasten**, untie, undo, uncouple, detach, release. [➡UNFASTEN AND UNDO; 410] *Opposite:* fasten.

unholy 1 *adj* **unconsecrated**, unhallowed, unblessed, profane, secular. [➡RELIGIOUS CONCEPTS; 777] *Opposite:* consecrated. 2 *adj* **ungodly**, blasphemous, secular, immoral, unconsecrated, evil. [➡MORALLY BAD; 776] *Opposite:* holy. 3 *adj* **outrageous**, ungodly, disgraceful, scandalous, shocking, atrocious. [➡DISGUSTING AND REPULSIVE; 231]

unhook *v* **undo**, release, uncouple, detach, disengage, free. [➡UNFASTEN AND UNDO; 410] *Opposite:* hook.

unhoped-for *adj* **unexpected**, unanticipated, surprising, undreamed-of, unforeseen, unimaginable. [➡EXTRAORDINARY: UNCOMMON; 206] *Opposite:* expected.

unhopeful *adj* **doubtful**, despondent, gloomy, dejected, pessimistic, downbeat, discouraged, downhearted, negative, uncertain. [➡SADNESS, DISTRESS, AND DESPAIR; 540] *Opposite:* hopeful.

unhurried *adj* **slow**, easygoing, dawdling, calm, deliberate, measured, thorough, painstaking, precise, leisurely, methodical. [➡CAUTIOUS AND CAREFUL; 283] *Opposite:* hurried.

unhurt *adj* **uninjured**, unharmed, undamaged, unscathed, safe, safe and sound, without a scratch, unscratched, unscarred. [➡FINE; 738] *Opposite:* hurt.

unhygienic *adj* **insanitary**, unclean, polluted, unhealthy, foul, dirty. [➡DIRTY; 1234] *Opposite:* hygienic.

unicorn *type of* **mythological creature**. [➡MYTHICAL CREATURES; 1036]

unicycle *type of* **bike** (*informal*). [➡BIKES, CARS, AND CARRIAGES; 1148]

unidentified *adj* **nameless**, anonymous, faceless, unnamed, unknown, undisclosed, unrevealed, mysterious. [➡SECRET AND UNKNOWN; 180] *Opposite:* known.

unidentified flying object *see* **UFO**.

unification *n* **amalgamation**, union, merger, alliance, association, confederation, integration, confederacy, fusion. [➡SOCIAL, POLITICAL, AND ECONOMIC CHANGE; 374] *Opposite:* split.

unified *adj* **united**, combined, amalgamated, incorporated, integrated, joined, fused, cohesive. [➡RELATED; 143] *Opposite:* disjointed.

uniform 1 *n* **livery**, dress, costume, garb, attire (*formal*), outfit, regalia. [➡GARMENTS AND OUTFITS; 865] 2 *adj* **unchanging**, unvarying, even, unbroken, undeviating, constant. [➡PHYSICAL TEXTURE; 1221] *Opposite:* uneven. 3 *adj* **consistent**, standardized, homogeneous, harmonized, regular, monotonous. [➡PERMANENCE: WITHOUT CHANGE; 95] *Opposite:* inconsistent. 4 *adj* **identical**, like, alike, similar, equal, equivalent, same. [➡SAMENESS; 151] *Opposite:* different.

uniformity *n* **consistency**, regularity, standardization, homogeneousness, homogeneity, evenness, equality, equivalence, sameness. [➡SAMENESS; 151] *Opposite:* inconsistency.

uniformly *adv* **consistently**, homogeneously, unvaryingly, evenly, equally, equivalently, regularly. [➡SAMENESS; 151] *Opposite:* inconsistently.

unify *v* **unite**, join, amalgamate, merge, combine, coalesce, fuse, bring together. [➡CREATING CONNECTIONS; 145] *Opposite:* separate.

unilateral *adj* **one-sided**, independent, autonomous, autarchic, individual. [➡ACTING INDEPENDENTLY; 285] *Opposite:* joint.

unimaginable *adj* **inconceivable**, unbelievable, incredible, unthinkable, indescribable, beyond belief, mind-boggling, undreamed-of. [➡IMPOSSIBLE AND IMPROBABLE; 179] *Opposite:* conceivable.

unimaginative *adj* **dull**, boring, insipid, bland, uninspired, unoriginal, derivative, lacklustre, unexciting, mundane, ordinary, routine. [➡BORING AND UNINTERESTING; 235] *Opposite:* imaginative.

unimaginativeness *n* **dullness**, insipidness, blandness, unoriginality, mundaneness, ordinariness. [➡BORING AND UNINTERESTING; 235] *Opposite:* imaginativeness.

unimpaired *adj* **undamaged**, unaffected, unhindered, perfect, operational, working. [➡WHOLENESS AND COMPLETENESS; 199] *Opposite:* impaired.

unimpassioned *adj* **unemotional**, cool, detached, sober, calm, dispassionate. [➡BORING AND UNINTERESTING; 235] *Opposite:* impassioned.

unimpeachable *adj* **faultless**, flawless, impeccable, irreproachable, blameless, unassailable, spotless, perfect. [➡MORALLY GOOD; 775] *Opposite:* blameworthy.

unimpeded *adj* **without hindrance**, unhindered, unhampered, unchecked, unconstrained, unobstructed, unrestrained, unrestricted. [➡FREEDOM AND LIBERTY; 209] *Opposite:* hindered.

unimportance *n* **insignificance**, inconsequentiality, irrelevance, slightness, triviality, pettiness. [➡UNIMPORTANT AND UNNECESSARY; 239] *Opposite:* importance.

unimportant *adj* **inconsequential**, slight, insignificant, trivial, trifling, petty, minor, irrelevant, immaterial, negligible, no great shakes, of no great concern. [➡UNIMPORTANT AND UNNECESSARY; 239] *Opposite:* important.

unimposing *adj* [➡ORDINARINESS; 245]

unimpressed *adj* **unenthusiastic**, uninspired, unconvinced, unmoved, indifferent, apathetic, uninterested, blasé. [➡NEUTRALITY AND INDIFFERENCE; 554] *Opposite:* enthusiastic.

unimpressive *adj* **uninspiring**, indifferent, mediocre, unimposing, insignificant, average, insipid, ordinary, nothing special. [➡ORDINARINESS; 245] *Opposite:* impressive.

unimproved *adj* **unchanged**, unaltered, unrestored, authentic, original, unworked, virgin. [➡UNFINISHEDNESS; 240] *Opposite:* improved.

unincorporated *adj* **independent**, separate, distinct, stand-alone, autonomous, self-governing. [➡UNRELATEDNESS AND SEPARATENESS; 147] *Opposite:* incorporated.

unindustrialized *adj* **undeveloped**, farming, agricultural, rural. [➡THE COUNTRYSIDE AND OUTDOOR SPACES; 1070] *Opposite:* industrialized.

uninformative *adj* **unhelpful**, vague, uncommunicative, unproductive, useless. [➡VAGUENESS; 244] *Opposite:* informative.

uninformed *adj* **ignorant**, uneducated, unapprised, unaware, unacquainted, unfamiliar, in the dark. [➡IGNORANCE; 558] *Opposite:* informed.

uninhabitable *adj* **derelict**, dilapidated, ramshackle, tumbledown, run-down, ruined. [➡IN BAD REPAIR; 1233] *Opposite:* habitable.

uninhabited *adj* **unoccupied**, unpopulated, deserted, abandoned, unpeopled, vacant, desolate, empty, forsaken, isolated. [➡EMPTY; 1237] *Opposite:* inhabited.

uninhibited **1** *adj* **unrestrained**, outgoing, unconstrained, candid, open, natural, unreserved, spontaneous, frank, overt. [➡HONEST AND OPEN; 631] *Opposite:* shy. **2** *adj* **wanton**, abandoned, dissolute, licentious (*formal*), immodest, immoral. [➡MORALLY BAD; 776] *Opposite:* restrained.

uninhibitedly *adv* **overtly**, candidly, openly, naturally, frankly, unreservedly, spontaneously. [➡HONEST AND OPEN; 631] *Opposite:* shyly.

uninitiated *adj* **inexperienced**, unskilled, unversed, unqualified, untrained, inexpert, green. [➡UNSKILLED; 530] *Opposite:* experienced.

uninjured *adj* **unhurt**, unharmed, undamaged, intact, safe, safe and sound, unscathed. [➡FINE; 738] *Opposite:* hurt.

uninspired *adj* **bland**, insipid, boring, dull, unimaginative, unoriginal, featureless, characterless. [➡ORDINARINESS; 245] *Opposite:* inspired.

uninspiring *adj* **dull**, lacklustre, lifeless, boring, tame, bland, uneventful, undistinguished. [➡BORING AND UNINTERESTING; 235] *Opposite:* inspiring.

uninstructed *adj* **untaught**, unschooled, uneducated, uninformed, untutored, ignorant, unversed, in the dark. [➡IGNORANCE; 558] *Opposite:* educated.

unintelligence *n* [➡NEGATIVE INTELLECTUAL CHARACTERISTICS; 526]

unintelligent *adj* **stupid**, foolish, silly, inane, daft (*informal*). [➡NEGATIVE INTELLECTUAL CHARACTERISTICS; 526] *Opposite:* clever.

unintelligibility *n* [➡DIFFICULTY AND COMPLEXITY; 243]

unintelligible *adj* **incomprehensible**, inarticulate, incoherent, garbled, jumbled, indecipherable, meaningless, inaudible, indistinct. [➡DIFFICULTY AND COMPLEXITY; 243] *Opposite:* intelligible.

unintelligibly *adv* **incomprehensibly**, gibberingly, incoherently, inarticulately, ramblingly, impenetrably, indistinctly, inaudibly, unclearly. [➡INARTICULATE, RAMBLING, AND AWKWARD; 634] *Opposite:* intelligibly.

unintended *adj* **unintentional**, accidental, inadvertent, unplanned, chance, involuntary, unpremeditated. [➡UNINTENTIONAL AND ACCIDENTAL; 282] *Opposite:* intentional.

unintentional *adj* **accidental**, inadvertent, unintended, unplanned, chance, involuntary, unpremeditated. [➡UNINTENTIONAL AND ACCIDENTAL; 282] *Opposite:* intentional.

uninterested *adj* **indifferent**, apathetic, blasé, impassive, unconcerned, unresponsive, dispassionate, aloof, remote, casual, distant. [➡NEUTRALITY AND INDIFFERENCE; 554] *Opposite:* concerned.

uninteresting *adj* **boring**, dull, unexciting, tedious, monotonous, dreary, dry, arid, insipid, characterless. [➡BORING AND UNINTERESTING; 235] *Opposite:* interesting.

See Compare and Contrast at **boring**.

uninterrupted *adj* **continuous**, continual, nonstop, incessant, never-ending, endless, constant, unremitting, ceaseless, unbroken. [➡PERMANENCE: WITHOUT END; 94] *Opposite:* sporadic.

uninvited *adj* **unwelcome**, unwanted, undesirable, unsought, unsolicited, unasked-for. [➡UNPOPULAR AND UNWANTED; 259] *Opposite:* welcome.

uninviting *adj* **unappealing**, unattractive, bleak, unpalatable, disgusting, nasty, unpleasant, repellent, unenticing, distasteful. [➡UGLINESS AND UNATTRACTIVENESS; 234] *Opposite:* attractive.

uninvolved 1 *adj* **detached**, removed, aloof, unconcerned, indifferent, impassive, disinterested, distant. [➡NEUTRALITY AND INDIFFERENCE; 554] *Opposite:* involved. 2 *adj* **uncomplicated**, straightforward, easy, simple, plain. [➡EASE AND SIMPLICITY; 201] *Opposite:* convoluted. 3 *adj* **single**, footloose and fancy free, unmarried, unattached, free, solo. [➡MARITAL STATUS; 890] *Opposite:* attached (*informal*).

union 1 *n* **amalgamation**, combination, blending, coming together, joining together, unification, merger. [➡CONNECTION; 144] *Opposite:* separation. 2 *n* **coalition**, alliance, association, confederacy, confederation, federation, league, society, guild, club. [➡CLUBS AND SOCIETIES; 939] 3 *n* **agreement**, harmony, accord, unity, unison, concord. [➡HARMONY; 156] *Opposite:* discord. 4 *n* **marriage**, matrimony, wedlock, bond, wedding, tie. [➡MARRIED STATE; 961] *Opposite:* divorce.

union suit (*US*) *type of* **upper body underwear**. [➡HABERDASHERY, MILLINERY, AND LINGERIE; 867]

unique *adj* **sole**, single, one-off, exclusive, exceptional, inimitable, distinctive, matchless, irreplaceable, rare. [➡EXTRAORDINARY: UNCOMMON; 206] *Opposite:* common.

uniqueness *n* **individuality**, exclusivity, exceptionality, inimitability, distinctiveness, matchlessness, rareness. [➡EXTRAORDINARY: UNCOMMON; 206] *Opposite:* commonness.

unison *n* **agreement**, harmony, accord, unity, union, unanimity. [➡HARMONY; 156] *Opposite:* discord.

unit 1 *n* **component**, element, part, piece, item, thing, entity, division, building block, constituent. [➡PHYSICAL OBJECTS; 1242] 2 *n* **corps**, detachment, group, company, troop, organization, section. [➡GROUPS OF PEOPLE; 935]

unite 1 *v* **join**, fuse, mix, bond, come together, bring together, connect, amalgamate, merge, blend, combine, unify. [➡COMBINE AND MIX; 401] *Opposite:* separate. 2 *v* **marry**, wed, hitch, bond, tie, yoke, join in matrimony, join in wedlock. [➡ESTABLISHING RELATIONSHIPS WITH OTHERS; 974]

united *adj* **joint**, combined, amalgamated, unified, cohesive, integrated, aggregate. [➡RELATED; 143] *Opposite:* separated.

unitize 1 *v* **bring together**, unite, combine, centralize, condense, focus. [➡COMBINE AND MIX; 401] *Opposite:* separate. 2 *v* **separate**, take apart, break up, divide up, disassemble, split up. [➡SEPARATE AND DIVIDE; 402] *Opposite:* join.

unity *n* **agreement**, harmony, accord, unison, union, concord, unanimity. [➡HARMONY; 156] *Opposite:* disarray.

universal *adj* **worldwide**, widespread, general, common, collective, total, entire, complete, unanimous, comprehensive. [➡WHOLENESS AND COMPLETENESS; 199] *Opposite:* local.

See Compare and Contrast at **widespread**.

universalism *n* **breadth**, amplitude, diversity, gamut, spectrum. [➡WHOLENESS AND COMPLETENESS; 199]

universe *n* **cosmos**, world, creation, life, space, earth. [➡THE SOLAR SYSTEM AND ASTRONOMY; 1059]

university *n* **institution of higher education**, further education college, college, academia, academy, academe (*formal*), school (*US*). [➡EDUCATIONAL INSTITUTIONS; 813]

unjam *v* [➡UNFASTEN AND UNDO; 410]

unjust *adj* **unfair**, undue, undeserved, unmerited, unwarranted, unreasonable, partial, biased, prejudiced, discriminatory. [➡UNACCEPTABLE AND UNFORGIVABLE; 226] *Opposite:* just.

unjustifiable *adj* **indefensible**, unwarrantable, inexcusable, unforgivable, unpardonable, uncalled-for, untenable, beyond the pale. [➡UNACCEPTABLE AND UNFORGIVABLE; 226] *Opposite:* justifiable.

unjustified *adj* **unfounded**, baseless, unfair, unwarranted, unpardonable, groundless, inexcusable. [➡UNACCEPTABLE AND UNFORGIVABLE; 226] *Opposite:* justified.

unjustly *adv* **unfairly**, unreasonably, partially, one-sidedly, discriminatorily, prejudicially, irrationally. [➡NEGATIVE INTELLECTUAL CHARACTERISTICS; 526] *Opposite:* fairly.

unkempt *adj* **dishevelled**, untidy, rumpled, tousled, messy, scruffy, down-at-heel. [➡DESCRIBING HAIR; 487] *Opposite:* tidy.

unkind *adj* **nasty**, mean, cruel, callous, heartless, harsh. [➡SELFISH AND UNKIND; 506] *Opposite:* kind.

unkindness *n* **nastiness**, meanness, cruelty, callousness, heartlessness, harshness. [➡SELFISH AND UNKIND; 506] *Opposite:* kindness.

unknot *v* **untie**, undo, unpick, disentangle, unstitch, unlace, disengage. [➡UNFASTEN AND UNDO; 410] *Opposite:* knot.

unknowable *adj* **incomprehensible**, enigmatic, mysterious, indecipherable, arcane, inexplicable, impenetrable, inscrutable. [➡SECRET AND UNKNOWN; 180] *Opposite:* comprehensible.

unknowing 1 *adj* **unwitting**, ingenuous, naive, innocent, ignorant, unaware. [➡IGNORANCE; 558] *Opposite:* knowing. 2 *adj* **unintentional**, accidental, inadvertent, unintended, unplanned, unforeseen. [➡UNINTENTIONAL AND ACCIDENTAL; 282] *Opposite:* deliberate.

unknowingly *adv* **naively**, innocently, mistakenly, unwittingly, accidentally, unintentionally, unsuspectingly, inadvertently. [➡UNINTENTIONAL AND ACCIDENTAL; 282] *Opposite:* deliberately.

unknowledgeable *adj* [➡IGNORANCE; 558]

unknown 1 *adj* **unidentified**, indefinite, mysterious, strange, unfamiliar, unheard of, nameless, anonymous, new, unspecified, undetermined. [➡SECRET AND UNKNOWN; 180] *Opposite:* known. 2 *adj* **unfamiliar**, strange, foreign, alien, undiscovered, new, virgin. [➡NEW, MODERN; 167] *Opposite:* familiar. 3 *n* **nonentity**, nobody, newcomer, beginner, stranger, mystery. [➡STRANGERS; 972] *Opposite:* celebrity.

unlaboured *adj* **effortless**, easy, painless, trouble-free, carefree, smooth, natural, casual. [➡EASE AND SIMPLICITY; 201] *Opposite:* laboured.

unlace *v* **undo**, unfasten, unthread, unknot, untie, loosen. [➡UNFASTEN AND UNDO; 410] *Opposite:* lace.

unladylike *adj* [➡BAD MANNERS AND SOCIAL SKILLS; 522]

unlatch *v* **open**, undo, unfasten, unlock, unbolt. [➡UNFASTEN AND UNDO; 410] *Opposite:* latch.

unlawful *adj* **illegal**, illicit, against the law, illegitimate, criminal, dishonest, unauthorized, prohibited, improper. [➡ILLEGAL; 816] *Opposite:* lawful.

unlawful act *n* [➡CRIMES; 817]

unlawful activity *n* [➡CRIMES; 817]

unlawfulness *n* [➡ILLEGAL; 816]

unlearned *adj* **uneducated**, illiterate, unschooled, unlettered, untutored, untaught, untrained. [➡IGNORANCE; 558] *Opposite:* educated.

unleash *v* **set free**, give a free rein to, allow to run free, allow to run riot, uncheck, unbridle, let loose, release. [➡FREEDOM AND LIBERTY; 209] *Opposite:* control.

unless *conj* **if not**, if, except, save, but for, without, lest. [➡CAUSATION; 169]

unlettered *adj* **uneducated**, illiterate, unschooled, untaught, untutored, unlearned. [➡UNSKILLED; 530] *Opposite:* educated.

unlicensed *adj* **uninhibited**, unrestricted, unrestrained, abandoned, immoral, unconstrained, carefree. [➡UNSKILLED; 530] *Opposite:* inhibited.

unlikable *adj* [➡UNPOPULAR AND UNWANTED; 259]

unlike *adj* **different**, dissimilar, nothing like, distinct, contrasting, disparate. [➡DIFFERENCE; 150] *Opposite:* like.

unlikelihood *n* **improbability**, doubtfulness, implausibility, dubiousness, questionability, incongruousness. [➡IMPOSSIBLE AND IMPROBABLE; 179] *Opposite:* likelihood.

unlikeliness *n* [➡IMPOSSIBLE AND IMPROBABLE; 179]

unlikely 1 *adj* **improbable**, doubtful, dubious, questionable. [➡IMPOSSIBLE AND IMPROBABLE; 179] *Opposite:* likely. 2 *adj* **implausible**, dubious, doubtful, suspect, incongruous, unbelievable. [➡UNCERTAIN; 176] *Opposite:* credible.

unlimited *adj* **limitless**, infinite, unrestricted, unrestrained, boundless, unconstrained, on tap, indefinite, ad lib, ad nauseam, bottomless. [➡FREEDOM AND LIBERTY; 209] *Opposite:* limited.

unlisted *adj* **private**, ex-directory, unpublished, confidential, secret, unpublicized. [➡SECRET AND UNKNOWN; 180] *Opposite:* listed.

unlit *adj* **dark**, darkened, dim, pitch-black, murky, gloomy. [➡DESCRIBING LIGHT; 1227] *Opposite:* bright.

unload *v* **unpack**, drop off, drop, deliver, take down, discharge, unburden. [➡EMPTY AND UNLOAD; 408] *Opposite:* load.

unlock 1 *v* **undo**, release, unchain, open, unbolt, disengage, unfasten. [➡UNFASTEN AND UNDO; 410] *Opposite:* lock. 2 *v* **solve**, reveal, answer, crack (*informal*), expose, get to the bottom of, unravel, work out, explain. [➡SOLVE AND INTERPRET; 761]

unlooked-for *adj* **unexpected**, undreamed-of, unanticipated, uninvited, unsolicited, spontaneous, unprompted. [➡UNPOPULAR AND UNWANTED; 259] *Opposite:* expected.

unloose *v* **set free**, release, let out, unleash, let off the lead, loose. [➡FREEDOM AND LIBERTY; 209] *Opposite:* tie up.

unloved *adj* [➡UNPOPULAR AND UNWANTED; 259]

unlovely *adj* **unattractive**, objectionable, obnoxious, nasty, ugly. [➡UGLINESS AND UNATTRACTIVENESS; 234] *Opposite:* attractive.

unluckily *adv* **unfortunately**, fatefully, unhappily, inauspiciously, ominously, tragically, haplessly. [➡BAD LUCK AND UNLUCKY; 785] *Opposite:* luckily.

unluckiness *n* **bad luck**, misfortune, ill luck, mishap. [➡BAD LUCK AND UNLUCKY; 785] *Opposite:* luck.

unlucky 1 *adj* **unsuccessful**, wretched, hapless, unfortunate, tragic, luckless. [➡BAD LUCK AND UNLUCKY; 785] *Opposite:* lucky. 2 *adj* **inauspicious**, fateful, ill-fated, doomed, star-crossed, ill-starred (*formal*), ill-omened, ominous, baleful. [➡FATE, DESTINY, AND ASTROLOGY; 783] *Opposite:* fortunate.

unmake 1 *v* **undo**, take apart, reverse, deconstruct, dismantle, reorganize. [➡DESTRUCTION AND DEMOLITION; 360] *Opposite:* put back. 2 *v* **demote**, fire, sack, replace, expel, vote out, impeach. [➡REVOKE STATUS; 460]

unmanageable *adj* **uncontrollable**, unruly, riotous, out of control, out of hand, wild, impossible, insurmountable. [➡DISORDER AND CHAOS; 246] *Opposite:* manageable.

unmanliness *n* **weakness**, cowardliness, timidity, fearfulness, apprehension, shyness. [➡COWARDICE AND WEAKNESS OF WILL; 509] *Opposite:* manliness.

unmanly *adj* **weak**, cowardly, timid, fearful, apprehensive, cringing. [➡COWARDICE AND WEAKNESS OF WILL; 509] *Opposite:* manly.

unmannered 1 *adj* **rude**, boorish, impolite, crude, coarse, loutish. [➡BAD MANNERS AND SOCIAL SKILLS; 522] *Opposite:* well-mannered. 2 *adj* **unaffected**, easy, natural, genuine, simple, sincere, unpretentious. [➡NATURALNESS; 498] *Opposite:* affected.

unmannerly *adj* **rude**, impolite, ill-mannered, bad-mannered, disrespectful, insolent, brusque, uncivil. [➡BAD MANNERS AND SOCIAL SKILLS; 522] *Opposite:* polite.

unmapped *adj* [➡SECRET AND UNKNOWN; 180]

unmarked *adj* **spotless**, unblemished, pristine, immaculate, perfect, without a scratch, intact, undamaged. [➡CLEAN; 1232] *Opposite:* marked.

unmarried *adj* **single**, unattached, bachelor, spinster, free. [➡MARITAL STATUS; 890] *Opposite:* married.

unmask *v* **expose**, blow the whistle on, reveal, unveil, debunk, uncover, make public, bare, make known, lay bare. [➡CAUSE TO APPEAR; 5] *Opposite:* conceal.

unmatched *adj* **supreme**, matchless, unrivalled, consummate, unparalleled, unsurpassed, unequalled, beyond compare, incomparable, unique. [➡SUPERIORITY; 153]

unmeant *adj* **unintended**, accidental, inadvertent, unplanned, unintentional. [➡UNINTENTIONAL AND ACCIDENTAL; 282] *Opposite:* deliberate.

unmelodic *adj* [➡LOUD OR UNPLEASANT SOUNDS; 1265]

unmelodious *adj* [➡LOUD OR UNPLEASANT SOUNDS; 1265]

unmemorable *adj* [➡ORDINARINESS; 245]

unmentionable 1 *adj* **taboo**, offensive, prohibited, forbidden, restricted, proscribed, out of bounds, off-limits. [➡UNACCEPTABLE AND UNFORGIVABLE; 226] *Opposite:* respectable. 2 *n* **taboo**, no-go area, anathema, no-no (*informal*). [➡CAPTIVITY AND LOSS OF FREEDOM; 249]

unmerciful 1 *adj* **cruel**, severe, harsh, hard, unsparing, unforgiving, unkind, merciless, punitive. [➡SELFISH AND UNKIND; 506] *Opposite:* merciful. 2 *adj* **excessive**, unrelenting, extreme, remorseless, unremitting, constant, merciless. [➡EMOTIONALLY UNPLEASANT AND UPSETTING; 228]

unmerited *adj* **undeserved**, unwarranted, unjustified, unearned, unjust, unfair. [➡MORALLY BAD; 776] *Opposite:* fair.

unmindful *adj* **unaware**, oblivious, unconscious, careless, heedless, forgetful, neglectful. [➡NEUTRALITY AND INDIFFERENCE; 554] *Opposite:* mindful.

unmistakable *adj* **obvious**, definite, distinctive, unambiguous, unique, evident, inimitable, particular. [➡CONCISE AND CLEAR; 203] *Opposite:* ambiguous.

unmistakably *adv* **obviously**, clearly, distinctly, unambiguously, definitely, unquestionably. [➡PERCEPTIBLE; 25] *Opposite:* ambiguously.

unmitigated *adj* **sheer**, pure, absolute, unadulterated, unalloyed, utter, complete, total. [➡ABSOLUTE AND ABSOLUTELY; 131]

unmodified *adj* **original**, unchanged, basic, untouched. [➡PERMANENCE: WITHOUT CHANGE; 95] *Opposite:* modified.

unmotivated *adj* **apathetic**, unenthusiastic, indifferent, shiftless, uninterested, lazy. [➡NEUTRALITY AND INDIFFERENCE; 554] *Opposite:* keen.

unmovable *adj* **inflexible**, rigid, stubborn, obstinate, obdurate, unbending, unwavering, adamant, unyielding, unrelenting, firm. [➡UNWILLINGNESS AND STUBBORNNESS; 565] *Opposite:* flexible.

unmoved *adj* **indifferent**, unaffected, cold, unresponsive, insensitive, unyielding, impassive, unfeeling, oblivious, firm, adamant. [➡NEUTRALITY AND INDIFFERENCE; 554] *Opposite:* touched.

See Compare and Contrast at **impassive**.

unmoving *adj* **still**, motionless, inactive, lifeless, inert, frozen. [➡LACK OF ACTIVITY; 343] *Opposite:* moving.

unmusical *adj* **unmelodic**, dissonant, discordant, jarring, harsh, cacophonous, inharmonious. [➡LOUD OR UNPLEASANT SOUNDS; 1265] *Opposite:* musical.

unnamed *adj* **unidentified**, anonymous, unspecified, nameless, unknown, undisclosed. [➡SECRET AND UNKNOWN; 180] *Opposite:* named.

unnatural 1 *adj* **abnormal**, aberrant, atypical, unusual, perverted, deviant, anomalous. [➡BIZARRE AND PECULIAR; 258] *Opposite:* normal. 2 *adj* **unusual**, abnormal, strange, odd, peculiar, atypical, irregular, uncommon, surprising. [➡BIZARRE AND PECULIAR; 258] *Opposite:* typical. 3 *adj* **supernatural**, weird, bizarre, paranormal, uncanny, inexplicable, eerie, strange, extraordinary. [➡BIZARRE AND PECULIAR; 258] *Opposite:* ordinary. 4 *adj* **artificial**, contrived, affected, insincere, pretend, feigned, false, manufactured, put-on, pretentious. [➡FALSE AND UNREAL; 174] *Opposite:* natural.

unnaturally 1 *adv* **abnormally**, unusually, extraordinarily, inexplicably, oddly, strangely, uncharacteristically. [➡BIZARRE AND PECULIAR; 258] *Opposite:* normally. 2 *adv* **artificially**, insincerely, stiffly, affectedly, falsely, pretentiously. [➡FALSE AND UNREAL; 174] *Opposite:* naturally.

unnaturalness *n* **strangeness**, oddness, weirdness, abnormality, irregularity, bizarreness. [➡BIZARRE AND PECULIAR; 258] *Opposite:* normality.

unnecessary *adj* **needless**, pointless, redundant, superfluous, gratuitous, unwarranted, uncalled-for, excessive, avoidable, preventable. [➡UNIMPORTANT AND UNNECESSARY; 239] *Opposite:* necessary.

unneeded *adj* **extra**, superfluous, unnecessary, surplus, unwanted. [➡UNIMPORTANT AND UNNECESSARY; 239] *Opposite:* necessary.

unnerve *v* **alarm**, frighten, scare, upset, nonplus, surprise, demoralize, discourage, worry, set back. [➡UPSET, DISTRESS, AND HUMILIATE; 568] *Opposite:* calm.

unnerved *adj* **frightened**, scared, alarmed, unsettled, anxious, panic-stricken, panicky, intimidated, demoralized, upset. [➡FEAR AND PANIC; 544] *Opposite:* calm.

unnerving *adj* **frightening**, scary (*informal*), unsettling, discomforting (*formal*), demoralizing, intimidating, upsetting, alarming. [➡EMOTIONALLY UNPLEASANT AND UPSETTING; 228] *Opposite:* comforting.

unnoticeable *adj* **invisible**, imperceptible, unremarkable, inconspicuous, hidden, camouflaged, unobtrusive, discreet. [➡ IMPERCEPTIBLE; 26] *Opposite:* conspicuous.

unnoticed *adj* **unobserved**, overlooked, ignored, unseen, disregarded, undetected. [➡ SECRET AND UNKNOWN; 180]

unnumbered 1 *adj* **numberless**, numerous, myriad, countless, many, untold. [➡ SECRET AND UNKNOWN; 180] *Opposite:* few. 2 *adj* **unidentified**, unmarked, untagged. [➡ NAME AND DESCRIBE; 666]

unobjectionable *adj* **inoffensive**, agreeable, pleasant, innocuous, harmless. [➡ ACCEPTABLE AND PASSABLE; 220] *Opposite:* unpleasant.

unobservant *adj* **inattentive**, unperceptive, incurious, negligent, careless. [➡ NEGATIVE INTELLECTUAL CHARACTERISTICS; 526] *Opposite:* observant.

unobserved *adj* **unnoticed**, ignored, overlooked, unseen, disregarded, undetected. [➡ SECRET AND UNKNOWN; 180] *Opposite:* evident.

unobstructed *adj* **clear**, free, unhindered, passable, open, unbarred. [➡ FREEDOM AND LIBERTY; 209] *Opposite:* barred.

unobtainable *adj* **unavailable**, unattainable, inaccessible, out of stock. [➡ ABSENT AND UNAVAILABLE; 7] *Opposite:* available.

unobtrusive *adj* **inconspicuous**, unremarkable, modest, bland, discreet, understated, unassuming, self-effacing, shy, low-profile. [➡ RETICENT AND UNFORTHCOMING; 632] *Opposite:* conspicuous.

unoccupied 1 *adj* **inactive**, at a loose end, idle, unemployed, out of work. [➡ LACK OF ACTIVITY; 343] *Opposite:* busy. 2 *adj* **vacant**, untenanted, empty, disused, unused, uninhabited, unlived in, unpopulated, deserted, unfilled. [➡ EMPTY; 1237] *Opposite:* occupied.

See Compare and Contrast at **vacant**.

unoffending *adj* [➡ ACCEPTABLE AND PASSABLE; 220]

unofficial *adj* **unauthorized**, unsanctioned, informal, unendorsed, private, off-the-record. [➡ ILLEGAL; 816] *Opposite:* official.

unopposed *adj* **unchallenged**, unobstructed, unrestricted, unhampered, unimpeded, unrestrained. [➡ FREEDOM AND LIBERTY; 209] *Opposite:* challenged.

unorganized 1 *adj* **chaotic**, disorganized, muddled, messy, shambolic (*informal*), disorderly. [➡ DISORDER AND CHAOS; 246] *Opposite:* well-organized. 2 *adj* **careless**, disorganized, unprepared, sloppy, slapdash, messy. [➡ INCAUTIOUS AND CARELESS; 284] *Opposite:* methodical.

unoriginal *adj* **derivative**, copied, imitative, clichéd, banal, trite, hackneyed, uninspired, commonplace, corny, plagiarized. [➡ OLD, OLD-FASHIONED; 168] *Opposite:* original.

unoriginality *n* **derivativeness**, triteness, staleness, imitativeness, banality, uninventiveness, unimaginativeness. [➡ BORING AND UNINTERESTING; 235] *Opposite:* originality.

unorthodox *adj* **unconventional**, nonconformist, untraditional, unusual, eccentric, heretical, anarchic, revolutionary. [➡ BIZARRE AND PECULIAR; 258] *Opposite:* orthodox.

unpack *v* **unload**, take out, empty, undo, empty out, discharge. [➡ EMPTY AND UNLOAD; 408] *Opposite:* pack up.

unpaid 1 *adj* **unsettled**, outstanding, overdue, due, owing, in arrears. [➡ OWE AND DESERVE; 466] *Opposite:* paid. 2 *adj* **voluntary**, amateur, honorary, free. [➡ EMPLOYMENT STATUS; 831] *Opposite:* paid.

unpalatable 1 *adj* **inedible**, indigestible, disgusting, revolting, foul-tasting, unpleasant, nasty, bad. [➡ TASTE; 704] *Opposite:* tasty. 2 *adj* **unacceptable**, unpleasant, painful, disagreeable, harsh, distasteful. [➡ EMOTIONALLY UNPLEASANT AND UPSETTING; 228] *Opposite:* acceptable.

unparalleled *adj* **unmatched**, supreme, matchless, beyond compare, unequalled, incomparable, consummate. [➡ SUPERIORITY; 153] *Opposite:* mediocre.

unpardonable *adj* **unforgivable**, indefensible, inexcusable, deplorable, reprehensible, intolerable, awful. [➡ UNACCEPTABLE AND UNFORGIVABLE; 226] *Opposite:* understandable.

unpeg *v* **undo**, unfasten, untie, detach, release, uncouple. [➡ UNFASTEN AND UNDO; 410] *Opposite:* fasten.

unperceptive *adj* **undiscerning**, unobservant, insensitive, obtuse, indiscriminating, inattentive. [➡ NEGATIVE INTELLECTUAL CHARACTERISTICS; 526] *Opposite:* perceptive.

unperturbed *adj* **calm**, at peace, tranquil, collected, composed, cool, at ease, untroubled, unruffled, unworried. [➡ CALMNESS, CONFIDENCE, AND COMPOSURE; 537] *Opposite:* anxious.

unpick *v* **unravel**, untangle, untie, undo, disentangle, unstitch. [➡ UNFASTEN AND UNDO; 410]

unpin *v* [➡ UNFASTEN AND UNDO; 410]

unpitying *adj* [➡ SELFISH AND UNKIND; 506]

unplanned 1 *adj* **unintended**, accidental, unintentional, unexpected, inadvertent, unforeseen. [➡ UNINTENTIONAL AND ACCIDENTAL; 282] *Opposite:* planned. 2 *adj* **spontaneous**, impromptu, ad hoc, unprepared, spur-of-the-moment, impulsive, unscheduled, out of the blue. [➡ HAPPENING QUICKLY; 104] *Opposite:* planned.

unpleasant 1 *adj* **disagreeable**, nasty, unlikable, horrible, horrid, distasteful, objectionable, obnoxious, repulsive, foul, bad. [➡ DISGUSTING AND REPULSIVE; 231] *Opposite:* pleasant. 2 *adj* **unfriendly**, disagreeable, hostile, cold, unkind, spiteful, nasty. [➡ SELFISH AND UNKIND; 506] *Opposite:* friendly.

unpleasantly 1 *adv* **disagreeably**, nastily, horribly, distastefully, objectionably, obnoxiously, repulsively, unattractively. [➡ DISGUSTING AND REPULSIVE; 231] *Opposite:* pleasantly. 2 *adv* **nastily**, hostilely, coldly, unkindly, offensively, spitefully. [➡ SELFISH AND UNKIND; 506] *Opposite:* nicely.

unpleasantness 1 *n* **disagreeableness**, unlikableness, nastiness, horribleness, horridness, distastefulness, objectionableness, obnoxiousness, repulsiveness, foulness, badness. [➡ EMOTIONALLY UNPLEASANT AND UPSETTING; 228] *Opposite:* pleasantness. 2 *n* **ill feeling**, trouble, fuss, bother, upset, scandal. [➡ DISHARMONY; 157] *Opposite:* harmony. 3 *n* **unfriendliness**, spitefulness, nastiness, unkindness, offensiveness, hostility, coldness. [➡ SELFISH AND UNKIND; 506] *Opposite:* friendliness. 4 *n* **disagreement**, conflict, argument, quarrel, dispute, difference of opinion. [➡ ARGUMENT; 47] *Opposite:* agreement.

unplug 1 *v* **unblock**, clear, free, clean, release, open up. [➡ CLEAN AND POLISH; 404] 2 *v* **undo**, switch off, disconnect, take out, remove, disengage. [➡ CAUSE TO STOP; 267] *Opposite:* plug in.

unplumbed *adj* **unsounded**, mysterious, unfathomable, enigmatic, unexplored, unknowable, incomprehensible. [➡ DEPTH: DEEP; 1200] *Opposite:* known.

unpolluted *adj* **clean**, pure, uncontaminated, untainted, fresh, clear, sterilized. [➡ CLEAN; 1232] *Opposite:* contaminated.

unpopular *adj* **disliked**, hated, out of favour, shunned, detested, ostracized. [➡ UNPOPULAR AND UNWANTED; 259] *Opposite:* popular.

unpopulated *adj* **abandoned**, deserted, depopulated, uninhabited, empty, desolate, unoccupied. [➡ EMPTY; 1237] *Opposite:* overcrowded.

unpractised *adj* **inexperienced**, unrehearsed, unschooled, untrained, unfamiliar, green. [➡ UNSKILLED; 530] *Opposite:* practised.

unprecedented *adj* **unparalleled**, extraordinary, record, first-time, unique, exceptional, unmatched. [➡ EXTRAORDINARY: UNCOMMON; 206] *Opposite:* ordinary.

unpredictability *n* **randomness**, impulsiveness, volatility, fickleness, changeableness, changeability, irregularity, capriciousness, instability. [➡ FINITENESS, VARIABILITY, AND TRANSIENCE; 96] *Opposite:* predictability.

unpredictable *adj* **random**, erratic, changeable, impulsive, volatile, fickle, irregular, capricious, variable, arbitrary, unstable. [➡ FINITENESS, VARIABILITY, AND TRANSIENCE; 96] *Opposite:* predictable.

unpredicted *adj* **surprising**, unexpected, shock, astonishing, unforeseen, sudden. [➡ EXTRAORDINARY: AMAZING; 205] *Opposite:* predicted.

unprejudiced *adj* **fair**, neutral, tolerant, unbiased, evenhanded, impartial, balanced, objective, rational, open-minded. [➡ MORALLY GOOD; 775] *Opposite:* biased.

unpremeditated *adj* **unplanned**, unintended, impulsive, spur-of-the-moment, sudden, accidental, chance, inadvertent. [➡ UNINTENTIONAL AND ACCIDENTAL; 282] *Opposite:* premeditated.

unprepared 1 *adj* **unready**, unsuspecting, ill-equipped, unqualified, untrained, cold, unwary. [➡ UNSKILLED; 530] *Opposite:* prepared. 2 *adj* **improvised**, unrehearsed, ad hoc, impromptu, spontaneous, spur-of-the-moment, ad lib, ad libitum, off the cuff. [➡ HAPPENING QUICKLY; 104] *Opposite:* rehearsed.

unprepossessing *adj* **ugly**, unattractive, plain, unpleasant, uninviting, ill-favoured, homely. [➡ PEOPLE'S PHYSICAL APPEARANCE; 476] *Opposite:* attractive.

unpretentious *adj* **modest**, unassuming, unaffected, natural, self-effacing, humble, plain, without airs, down-to-earth, simple. [➡ NATURALNESS; 498] *Opposite:* pretentious.

unpretentiousness *n* **modesty**, humility, humbleness, simplicity, artlessness, ingenuousness, unaffectedness, naturalness. [➡ NATURALNESS; 498] *Opposite:* grandiosity.

unprincipled *adj* **dishonest**, corrupt, amoral, immoral, devious, cheating, deceitful, wrong, unethical, dishonourable. [➡ MORALLY BAD; 776] *Opposite:* honest.

unprintable *adj* **rude**, foul, offensive, shocking, coarse, vulgar, crass, obscene, scandalous, libellous. [➡ MORALLY BAD; 776] *Opposite:* inoffensive.

unproblematic *adj* **easy**, smooth, without a hitch, straightforward, trouble-free, simple, uncomplicated. [➡ EASE AND SIMPLICITY; 201] *Opposite:* tricky.

unprocessed *adj* **natural**, whole, unrefined, untreated, crude, organic, macrobiotic. [➡ RAW AND NATURAL; 1213]

unproductive 1 *adj* **fruitless**, infertile, barren, sterile, blocked, uncreative. [➡ REDUNDANT AND USELESS; 241] *Opposite:* fertile. 2 *adj* **idle**, lazy, slow, wasteful, inefficient, ineffective, useless. [➡ WASTEFUL AND UNECONOMICAL; 247] *Opposite:* productive.

unproductiveness 1 *n* **fruitlessness**, unfruitfulness, barrenness, sterility, infertility, uncreativeness. [➡ REDUNDANT AND USELESS; 241] *Opposite:* fertility. 2 *n* **idleness**, laziness, slowness, inefficiency, wastefulness, ineffectiveness, uselessness. [➡ WASTEFUL AND UNECONOMICAL; 247] *Opposite:* productiveness.

unprofessed *adj* [➡ SECRET AND UNKNOWN; 180]

unprofessional 1 *adj* **unethical**, unprincipled, immoral, dishonourable, wrong, improper. [➡ MORALLY BAD; 776] *Opposite:* ethical. 2 *adj* **amateurish**, amateur, slack, inexpert, shoddy, incompetent, sloppy (*informal*), slapdash. [➡ UNSKILLED; 530] *Opposite:* expert.

unprofitable 1 *adj* **lossmaking**, unsuccessful, running at a loss, nonpaying, insolvent, nonprofitmaking, unbeneficial. [➡ UNSUCCESSFUL AND UNPROMISING; 76] *Opposite:* profitable. 2 *adj* **unhelpful**, useless, pointless, futile, fruitless, wasteful, vain. [➡ REDUNDANT AND USELESS; 241] *Opposite:* helpful.

unpromising *adj* **gloomy**, bleak, discouraging, doubtful, off-putting, unhopeful, dubious. [➡ UNSUCCESSFUL AND UNPROMISING; 76] *Opposite:* encouraging.

unprompted *adj* **spontaneous**, unforced, impulsive, off your own bat (*informal*), willing, voluntary. [➡ THE WILL AND WILLINGNESS; 564] *Opposite:* forced.

unpronounceable *adj* **unsayable**, difficult, impossible, inarticulate. [➡ THE SPOKEN WORD; 672]

unpronounced *adj* **silent**, mute, unvoiced, unspoken, unsaid, unarticulated. [➡ IMPERCEPTIBLE; 26] *Opposite:* voiced.

unpropitious *adj* [➡ INAPPROPRIATE AND UNSUITABLE; 225]

unprotected *adj* **defenceless**, undefended, open to attack, insecure, vulnerable, unguarded, isolated, exposed, unshielded, at risk. [➡ IN DANGER; 238] *Opposite:* secure.

unproven *adj* **unverified**, unconfirmed, untried, untested, undocumented. [➡ UNCERTAIN; 176] *Opposite:* proven.

unprovoked *adj* **gratuitous**, wanton, senseless, motiveless, uncalled-for, meaningless, malicious. [➡REDUNDANT AND USELESS; 241] *Opposite:* provoked.

unpunctual *adj* [➡PROMPTNESS: LATE; 100]

unpunctuality *n* [➡PROMPTNESS: LATE; 100]

unqualified 1 *adj* **untrained**, unprofessional, ill-equipped, inexpert, untaught, unskilled, incompetent. [➡UNSKILLED; 530] *Opposite:* trained. 2 *adj* **definite**, unreserved, absolute, complete, utter, outright, categorical, out-and-out, total. [➡ABSOLUTE AND ABSOLUTELY; 131] *Opposite:* qualified.

unquantifiable *adj* **immeasurable**, uncountable, unidentifiable, indefinable, indeterminate, unspecifiable, countless, incalculable. [➡SECRET AND UNKNOWN; 180] *Opposite:* quantifiable.

unquenchable *adj* [➡PERMANENCE: WITHOUT END; 94]

unquestionable *adj* **indisputable**, incontestable, absolute, undeniable, categorical, conclusive, without doubt, indubitable (*formal*), incontrovertible. [➡CERTAIN; 175] *Opposite:* arguable.

unquestioned *adj* **undisputed**, accepted, unchallenged, automatic, logical, obvious. [➡CERTAIN; 175] *Opposite:* questionable.

unquestioning *adj* **unthinking**, wholehearted, obedient, absolute, automatic, unhesitating. [➡AUTOMATIC AND INSTINCTIVE; 281] *Opposite:* reluctant.

unquiet 1 *adj* **noisy**, turbulent, loud, rowdy, rackety (*dated*), boisterous, uproarious. [➡LOUD OR UNPLEASANT SOUNDS; 1265] *Opposite:* quiet. 2 *adj* **anxious**, unsettled, restless, agitated, fidgety, turbulent, jumpy. [➡CONFUSION, ANXIETY, AND WORRY; 541] *Opposite:* calm. 3 *n* **noise**, noisiness, loudness, rowdiness, boisterousness, uproariousness. [➡SOUNDS; 1255] *Opposite:* quietness. 4 *n* **anxiety**, concern, agitation, restlessness, disquiet, turbulence, fidgetiness. [➡CONFUSION, ANXIETY, AND WORRY; 541] *Opposite:* calmness.

unravel 1 *v* **undo**, untie, unknot, loosen, disentangle, untangle, unpick, unstitch, work loose, come undone. [➡UNFASTEN AND UNDO; 410] *Opposite:* tie. 2 *v* **solve**, clear up, resolve, sort out, get to the bottom of, work out. [➡SOLVE AND INTERPRET; 761] 3 *v* **fail**, go wrong, fall apart, collapse, crumble, break down, fall to pieces. [➡FAIL OR BE UNSUCCESSFUL; 75] *Opposite:* come together.

unreachable *adj* [➡ABSENT AND UNAVAILABLE; 7]

unreadable 1 *adj* **illegible**, incomprehensible, indecipherable, scrawled, scribbled, untidy. [➡DIFFICULTY AND COMPLEXITY; 243] *Opposite:* legible. 2 *adj* **impenetrable**, dense, tedious, turgid, boring, difficult, heavy. [➡BORING AND UNINTERESTING; 235] *Opposite:* readable. 3 *adj* **blank**, expressionless, impassive, poker-faced, inscrutable. [➡FACIAL EXPRESSION; 652]

unreal 1 *adj* **false**, artificial, imitation, fake, pretend, faux, replica, mock, reproduction, unnatural. [➡FALSE AND UNREAL; 174] *Opposite:* genuine. 2 *adj* **imaginary**, dreamlike, illusory, fantastic, out of this world (*informal*), weird, incredible. [➡BIZARRE AND PECULIAR; 258] *Opposite:* real.

unrealistic *adj* **impractical**, idealistic, impracticable, improbable, unlikely, unworkable, naive. [➡IMPOSSIBLE AND IMPROBABLE; 179] *Opposite:* practical.

unreality 1 *n* **illusoriness**, strangeness, incongruity, oddness, weirdness, fantasy, abnormality. [➡FALSE AND UNREAL; 174] *Opposite:* reality. 2 *n* **fantasy**, delusion, fancy, self-delusion, illusion, fiction. [➡DREAM, IMAGINE, AND FANTASIZE; 750] *Opposite:* reality.

unreasonable 1 *adj* **irrational**, perverse, arbitrary, unreasoning, awkward, stroppy (*informal*), bad-tempered, difficult. [➡DIFFICULT TO PLEASE; 516] *Opposite:* rational. 2 *adj* **excessive**, exorbitant, immoderate (*formal*), extravagant, extreme, unwarranted, unnecessary, unprovoked, uncalled-for, imbalanced, out of all proportion, unjust, unfair. [➡MORALLY BAD; 776] *Opposite:* reasonable.

unreasonableness 1 *n* **irrationality**, arbitrariness, awkwardness, stroppiness (*informal*), perverseness, difficultness. [➡DIFFICULT TO PLEASE; 516] *Opposite:* rationality. 2 *n* **excessiveness**, injustice, exorbitantness, extravagance, immoderation (*formal*), immoderateness (*formal*), unfairness. [➡TOO MUCH; 118] *Opposite:* reasonableness.

unreasonably 1 *adv* **irrationally**, arbitrarily, unreasoningly, awkwardly, perversely, difficulty, stroppily (*informal*). [➡DIFFICULT TO PLEASE; 516] *Opposite:* rationally. 2 *adv* **excessively**, unjustly, unduly, unfairly, immoderately (*formal*). [➡THE NATURE OF IDEAS; 772] *Opposite:* reasonably.

unreceptive *adj* **disinclined**, ill-disposed, unwilling, unteachable, defensive, intolerant, adamant, impervious, rigid. [➡UNWILLINGNESS AND STUBBORNNESS; 565] *Opposite:* receptive.

unreceptiveness *n* [➡NEGATIVE INTELLECTUAL CHARACTERISTICS; 526]

unreconstructed 1 *adj* **old-fashioned**, unchanging, unrepentant, dyed-in-the-wool, traditional, unreformed, inveterate, diehard, unapologetic. [➡CONSERVATIVE AND UNADVENTUROUS; 518] 2 *adj* **unrestored**, untransformed, unaltered, unchanged, unvaried. [➡PERMANENCE: WITHOUT CHANGE; 95]

unrefined 1 *adj* **unprocessed**, untreated, raw, crude, untouched, whole, organic, natural, coarse. [➡RAW AND NATURAL; 1213] *Opposite:* refined. 2 *adj* **vulgar**, unsophisticated, uncultured, crude, coarse, uncivilized, rough, loutish. [➡BAD MANNERS AND SOCIAL SKILLS; 522] *Opposite:* sophisticated.

unreformed *adj* **unapologetic**, unrepentant, dyed-in-the-wool, inveterate, diehard, traditional, unreconstructed. [➡CONSERVATIVE AND UNADVENTUROUS; 518] *Opposite:* reformed.

unrehearsed *adj* **unprepared**, impromptu, off-the-cuff, spontaneous, impulsive, cold, improvised, unplanned, ad lib, ad libitum, spur-of-the-moment. [➡HAPPENING QUICKLY; 104] *Opposite:* prepared.

unrelated 1 *adj* **unconnected**, separate, distinct, dissimilar, disparate, discrete, isolated. [➡UNRELATEDNESS AND SEPARATENESS; 147] *Opposite:* linked. 2 *adj* **irrelevant**, beside the point, extraneous, unconnected, impertinent (*formal*). [➡UNRELATEDNESS AND SEPARATENESS; 147] *Opposite:* relevant.

unrelenting *adj* **remorseless**, relentless, insistent, merciless, pitiless, pounding, unremitting, implacable (*formal*), indefatigable, unyielding, persistent, unmovable, inexorable. [➡PERMANENCE: WITHOUT END; 94] *Opposite:* yielding.

unreliability 1 *n* **undependability**, untrustworthiness, unpredictability, changeableness, irregularity, capriciousness, fickleness. [➡LACK OF COMMITMENT AND UNRELIABILITY; 510] *Opposite:* dependability. 2 *n* **inaccuracy**, fallibility, untrustworthiness, flimsiness, dubiousness, erroneousness. [➡FAULTS, FLAWS, AND WEAKNESSES; 252] *Opposite:* reliability.

unreliable 1 *adj* **undependable**, fly-by-night, variable, unpredictable, changeable, erratic, fickle, capricious, untrustworthy. [➡LACK OF COMMITMENT AND UNRELIABILITY; 510] *Opposite:* dependable. 2 *adj* **inaccurate**, fallacious, flimsy, threadbare, untrue, falsified, anecdotal, erroneous, doubtful, untrustworthy. [➡FALSE AND UNREAL; 174] *Opposite:* reliable.

unreliableness *n* [➡LACK OF COMMITMENT AND UNRELIABILITY; 510]

unrelieved *adj* **constant**, unbroken, chronic, unmitigated, unalleviated, unremitting, unrelenting, continuous, incessant. [➡PERMANENCE: WITHOUT END; 94] *Opposite:* intermittent.

unremarkable *adj* **ordinary**, everyday, commonplace, average, typical, discreet, inconspicuous, unexceptional, routine, normal. [➡ORDINARINESS; 245] *Opposite:* remarkable.

unremarkably *adv* **ordinarily**, inconspicuously, discreetly, unexceptionally, routinely, typically, normally. [➡IMPERCEPTIBLE; 26] *Opposite:* remarkably.

unremitting *adj* **constant**, incessant, continuous, chronic, unrelenting, unrelieved, assiduous, unalleviated, interminable, relentless, endless. [➡PERMANENCE: WITHOUT END; 94] *Opposite:* intermittent.

unremorseful *adj* **unrepentant**, unapologetic, impenitent, unashamed, shameless, unabashed. [➡IRRITATION AND ANGER; 542] *Opposite:* apologetic.

unrepentant *adj* **impenitent**, unapologetic, unashamed, shameless, unremorseful, unabashed. [➡RUDE AND HOSTILE; 626] *Opposite:* remorseful.

unrequired *adj* [➡UNPOPULAR AND UNWANTED; 259]

unreserved 1 *adj* **unqualified**, total, complete, utter, absolute, wholehearted, unconditional. [➡WHOLENESS AND COMPLETENESS; 199] *Opposite:* qualified. 2 *adj* **open**, demonstrative, candid, frank, extrovert, extroverted, uninhibited, outgoing, talkative, chatty, outspoken. [➡HONEST AND OPEN; 631] *Opposite:* reserved.

unresisting *adj* [➡THE WILL AND WILLINGNESS; 564]

unresolved *adj* **unsettled**, unanswered, uncertain, vague, up in the air, unsolved, fluid, in doubt, unclear. [➡UNCERTAIN; 176] *Opposite:* settled.

unresponsive *adj* **unfeeling**, insensitive, indifferent, impassive, uncaring, cold, unsympathetic, poker-faced, expressionless, unemotional. [➡NEUTRALITY AND INDIFFERENCE; 554] *Opposite:* responsive.

unresponsiveness *n* **unfeelingness**, insensitivity, indifference, impassiveness, coldness, unconcern. [➡NEUTRALITY AND INDIFFERENCE; 554] *Opposite:* responsiveness.

unrest 1 *n* **discontent**, turbulence, strife, conflict, disturbance, fighting, turmoil, disorder, instability, trouble. [➡CHAOS AND UPROAR; 51] *Opposite:* calm. 2 *n* **anxiousness**, anxiety, disquiet, worry, uneasiness, unease, apprehension, restlessness, nervousness, agitation, fear. [➡FEELINGS ABOUT THE FUTURE; 534] *Opposite:* peace.

unrestrained *adj* **uncontrolled**, wild, unrestricted, abandoned, uninhibited, unreserved, unrepressed. [➡FREEDOM AND LIBERTY; 209] *Opposite:* restrained.

unrestricted *adj* **open**, unobstructed, unhindered, unlimited, unhampered, at liberty, free, limitless. [➡FREEDOM AND LIBERTY; 209] *Opposite:* restricted.

unrevealed *adj* **secret**, hidden, unknown, mysterious, clandestine, private, undisclosed, concealed, unidentified. [➡SECRET AND UNKNOWN; 180] *Opposite:* known.

unrewarding *adj* **thankless**, fruitless, unfulfilling, unsatisfactory, difficult. [➡EMOTIONALLY UNPLEASANT AND UPSETTING; 228] *Opposite:* satisfying.

unrighteous 1 *adj* **sinful**, wicked, evil, irreligious, unholy, bad, impure. [➡MORALLY BAD; 776] *Opposite:* righteous. 2 *adj* **unjust**, unfair, ill-deserved, unkind, wrong, mean. [➡MORALLY BAD; 776] *Opposite:* just.

unripe *adj* **immature**, green, young, fresh, undeveloped. [➡NEW, MODERN; 167] *Opposite:* ripe.

unrivalled *adj* **unequalled**, unique, singular, unsurpassed, extraordinary, unparalleled, unmatched, incomparable, matchless, unbeatable, unchallenged. [➡EXTRAORDINARY: UNCOMMON; 206] *Opposite:* ordinary.

unroll *v* **open**, unfurl, stretch out, spread out, unfold, undo, open out. [➡CAUSE TO APPEAR; 5] *Opposite:* roll up.

unruffled *adj* **calm**, tranquil, unmoved, in control, at ease, relaxed, unflustered, composed, cool, unperturbed. [➡CALMNESS, CONFIDENCE, AND COMPOSURE; 537] *Opposite:* flustered.

unruliness *n* **boisterousness**, disruptiveness, disorderliness, rowdiness, intractability (*formal*), recalcitrance, obstreperousness, wilfulness, waywardness, disobedience, wildness. [➡CHAOS AND UPROAR; 51] *Opposite:* orderliness.

unruly *adj* **boisterous**, disruptive, disorderly, rowdy, disobedient, wild, uncontrollable, unmanageable, intractable (*formal*), recalcitrant, obstreperous, wilful, wayward. [➡REBELLIOUSNESS AND DISOBEDIENCE; 566] *Opposite:* orderly.

Compare and Contrast: ***unruly, intractable, recalcitrant, obstreperous, wilful, wild, wayward***

CORE MEANING: NOT SUBMITTING TO CONTROL

unruly boisterous, disruptive, and difficult to control or discipline; ***intractable*** (*formal*) strong-willed and rebellious, refusing to be controlled or to submit to discipline; ***recalcitrant*** obstinate and defiant in refusing to submit to discipline or control; ***obstreperous*** noisy, difficult to control, and uncooperative; ***wilful*** stubbornly disobedient and disregarding the opinions or advice of others; ***wild*** showing a general lack of control or restraint; ***wayward*** disobedient and uncontrollable.

unrushed *adj* **unhurried**, slow, in your own time, at your own pace, leisurely, calm. [➡ MOVING SLOWLY; 105] *Opposite:* hurried.

unsafe *adj* **dangerous**, insecure, hazardous, risky, perilous, precarious, treacherous. [➡ DANGEROUS; 237] *Opposite:* secure.

unsaid *adj* **tacit**, unspoken, implicit, silent, unstated, unarticulated, unexpressed. [➡ SECRET AND UNKNOWN; 180] *Opposite:* spoken.

unsalaried *adj* [➡ EMPLOYMENT STATUS; 831]

unsalvageable *adj* [➡ IN BAD REPAIR; 1233]

unsanitariness *n* [➡ DIRTY; 1234]

unsanitary *adj* [➡ DIRTY; 1234]

unsatisfactorily *adv* **inadequately**, unacceptably, insufficiently, disappointingly, poorly. [➡ INAPPROPRIATE AND UNSUITABLE; 225] *Opposite:* satisfactorily.

unsatisfactory *adj* **inadequate**, unacceptable, substandard, disappointing, insufficient, poor. [➡ UNACCEPTABLE AND UNFORGIVABLE; 226] *Opposite:* acceptable.

unsatisfied *adj* **displeased**, discontented, unhappy, unfulfilled, disgruntled, disappointed, unconvinced. [➡ SADNESS, DISTRESS, AND DESPAIR; 540] *Opposite:* pleased.

unsatisfying *adj* [➡ UNACCEPTABLE AND UNFORGIVABLE; 226]

unsavouriness *n* [➡ MORALLY BAD; 776]

unsavoury 1 *adj* **unpleasant**, disagreeable, revolting, disgusting, repellent, nasty, grubby, sleazy, seedy, unwelcome, distasteful. [➡ DISGUSTING AND REPULSIVE; 231] *Opposite:* pleasant. 2 *adj* **immoral**, unpleasant, villainous, shady, unacceptable, dodgy (*informal*), suspect, dishonest, untrustworthy, disreputable. [➡ MORALLY BAD; 776] *Opposite:* wholesome.

unscathed *adj* **unharmed**, intact, unhurt, untouched, safe, safe and sound, without a scratch, unmarked. [➡ FINE; 738] *Opposite:* injured.

unschooled *adj* **uneducated**, untaught, untutored, untrained, illiterate. [➡ IGNORANCE; 558] *Opposite:* educated.

unscientific *adj* **intuitive**, instinctive, irrational, unempirical, seat-of-the-pants, half-baked (*informal*). [➡ THE NATURE OF IDEAS; 772] *Opposite:* systematic.

unscramble *v* **decode**, sort out, decipher, work out, make out, order, decrypt, crack. [➡ SOLVE AND INTERPRET; 761] *Opposite:* encode.

unscrew *v* **take off**, remove, detach, loosen, undo. [➡ UNFASTEN AND UNDO; 410] *Opposite:* tighten.

unscripted *adj* **unplanned**, unexpected, impromptu, impulsive, unscheduled, off-the-cuff, ad lib, ad libitum. [➡ UNINTENTIONAL AND ACCIDENTAL; 282]

unscrupulous *adj* **dishonest**, unprincipled, corrupt, crooked (*informal*), dodgy (*informal*), immoral, deceitful, devious, ruthless. [➡ DECEITFUL; 514] *Opposite:* honest.

unscrupulously *adv* **dishonestly**, immorally, corruptly, crookedly (*informal*), deceitfully, deviously, ruthlessly. [➡ MORALLY BAD; 776] *Opposite:* honestly.

unscrupulousness *n* **dishonesty**, corruptness, crookedness, immorality, deviousness, ruthlessness, deceit. [➡ MORALLY BAD; 776] *Opposite:* honesty.

unseal *v* **open**, uncap, unstop, break open, unscrew. [➡ UNFASTEN AND UNDO; 410] *Opposite:* seal.

unseasonable 1 *adj* **unusual**, abnormal, unexpected, odd, strange, uncommon. [➡ BIZARRE AND PECULIAR; 258] *Opposite:* seasonable. 2 *adj* **untimely**, inopportune, ill-timed, inconvenient, unwelcome, obtrusive, unexpected. [➡ PROMPTNESS: BADLY TIMED; 101] *Opposite:* seasonable.

unseasonably 1 *adv* **unusually**, abnormally, unexpectedly, oddly, strangely, uncommonly. [➡ BIZARRE AND PECULIAR; 258] 2 *adv* **inopportunely**, inconveniently, unwelcomely, obtrusively, unexpectedly. [➡ PROMPTNESS: BADLY TIMED; 101]

unseasoned *adj* [➡ STATE OF PREPARED FOOD; 1170]

unseat *v* **depose**, oust, overthrow, dethrone, remove. [➡ REVOKE STATUS; 460] *Opposite:* enthrone (*formal*).

unseemliness *n* **impropriety**, tastelessness, uncouthness, loutishness, rudeness, indecorousness, inappropriateness. [➡ MORALLY BAD; 776] *Opposite:* propriety.

unseemly *adj* **inappropriate**, rude, uncouth, improper, indecorous, unsuitable, unbecoming, tasteless. [➡ INAPPROPRIATE AND UNSUITABLE; 225] *Opposite:* proper.

unseen *adj* **hidden**, unnoticed, unobserved, invisible, concealed, undetected. [➡ IMPERCEPTIBLE; 26] *Opposite:* noticeable.

unselective *adj* **indiscriminating**, undiscerning, blanket, haphazard, random, indiscriminate. [➡ DISORDER AND CHAOS; 246] *Opposite:* discerning.

unselfish *adj* **selfless**, generous, noble, magnanimous, liberal, kind, thoughtful, considerate, altruistic. [➡ GENEROSITY AND KINDNESS; 496] *Opposite:* selfish.

unselfishness *n* **selflessness**, generosity, magnanimity, kindness, consideration, thoughtfulness, altruism. [➡ GENEROSITY AND KINDNESS; 496] *Opposite:* selfishness.

unsentimental *adj* **unemotional**, impassive, unfeeling, hard-bitten, hard-boiled (*informal*), tough, cynical. [➡ POSITIVE INTELLECTUAL CHARACTERISTICS; 525] *Opposite:* sentimental.

unsettle *v* **worry**, disturb, upset, disconcert, unnerve, perturb, disquiet (*archaic or literary*), bother, fluster. [➡ UPSET, DISTRESS, AND HUMILIATE; 568] *Opposite:* soothe.

unsettled 1 *adj* **anxious**, worried, disturbed, upset, disconcerted, ill at ease, uneasy, troubled, uncomfortable, tense, flustered. [➡ CONFUSION, ANXIETY, AND WORRY; 541] *Opposite:* at ease. 2 *adj* **changeable**, variable, unpredictable, uncertain, changing. [➡ FINITENESS, VARIABILITY, AND TRANSIENCE; 96] *Opposite:* settled. 3 *adj* **undecided**, unresolved, undetermined, open-ended, arguable, debatable, moot. [➡ UNCERTAIN; 176] *Opposite:* decided.

unsettling *adj* **upsetting**, worrying, disturbing, disconcerting, disquieting, troubling. [➡ EMOTIONALLY UNPLEASANT AND UPSETTING; 228] *Opposite:* soothing.

unshackle *v* **release**, unchain, let loose, set free, liberate, unleash. [➡FREEDOM AND LIBERTY; 209] *Opposite:* chain.

unshakable *adj* **steadfast**, resolute, constant, unwavering, entrenched, staunch, immovable, unflinching, sure, firm, unswerving. [➡CERTAINTY; 562] *Opposite:* wavering.

unshaped *adj* **unformed**, formless, shapeless, amorphous, indistinct, unstructured. [➡SHAPELESSNESS; 1218] *Opposite:* shaped.

unshaven *adj* [➡FACIAL HAIR; 490]

unsheathe *v* **draw**, pull, remove, extract, rake out, uncover. [➡REMOVE SOMETHING; 339]

unshorn *adj* [➡DESCRIBING HAIR; 487]

unsightliness *n* **ugliness**, hideousness, horridness, unpleasantness, nastiness, unattractiveness. [➡UGLINESS AND UNATTRACTIVENESS; 234] *Opposite:* attractiveness.

unsightly *adj* **unattractive**, ugly, hideous, unpleasant, unprepossessing, nasty, horrid, unappealing. [➡UGLINESS AND UNATTRACTIVENESS; 234] *Opposite:* attractive.

unskilful *adj* **inept**, unskilled, untrained, untalented, incompetent, ham-handed (*informal*), ham-fisted (*informal*), gawky (*informal*), awkward, amateurish, clumsy. [➡UNSKILLED; 530] *Opposite:* skilful.

unskilfulness *n* [➡UNSKILLED; 530]

unskilled *adj* **inexpert**, amateurish, untrained, uneducated, unqualified, inexperienced, unskilful. [➡UNSKILLED; 530] *Opposite:* trained.

unsmiling *adj* **stern**, severe, serious, dour, grim-faced, disapproving. [➡BAD-TEMPERED AND HUMOURLESS; 627] *Opposite:* cordial.

unsnag *v* **disentangle**, clear, free, untangle, release. [➡UNFASTEN AND UNDO; 410] *Opposite:* snag.

unsnarl *v* **disentangle**, clear, free, untangle, unblock. [➡UNFASTEN AND UNDO; 410] *Opposite:* tangle.

unsociable *adj* **unfriendly**, antisocial, aloof, shy, standoffish, distant, hostile, cold. [➡UNFRIENDLINESS AND UNSOCIABILITY; 505] *Opposite:* friendly.

unsoiled *adj* [➡CLEAN; 1232]

unsolicited *adj* **unwelcome**, unwanted, uninvited, unsought, spontaneous, voluntary, uncalled-for. [➡UNPOPULAR AND UNWANTED; 259] *Opposite:* requested.

unsolvable *adj* **impenetrable**, unknowable, impossible, unfathomable, insoluble. [➡DIFFICULTY AND COMPLEXITY; 243] *Opposite:* soluble.

unsolved *adj* **unexplained**, unresolved, mysterious, baffling. [➡DIFFICULTY AND COMPLEXITY; 243] *Opposite:* resolved.

unsophisticated 1 *adj* **unworldly**, naive, inexperienced, ingenuous, simple, artless, innocent, childlike, natural. [➡NATURALNESS; 498] *Opposite:* sophisticated. 2 *adj* **crude**, simple, unrefined, basic, primitive, straightforward. [➡ORDINARINESS; 245] *Opposite:* advanced.

unsophisticatedly *adv* **naively**, artlessly, ingenuously, innocently, naturally, simply, plainly. [➡NATURALNESS; 498]

unsought *adj* **unsolicited**, spontaneous, uninvited, uncalled-for, unwanted, unlooked-for. [➡UNPOPULAR AND UNWANTED; 259]

unsound 1 *adj* **ill**, frail, unwell, unhealthy, poorly (*informal*), sick. [➡UNFIT AND WEAK; 740] *Opposite:* well. 2 *adj* **unsafe**, unstable, rickety, in poor condition, ramshackle, unsteady, shaky, wobbly. [➡DANGEROUS; 237] *Opposite:* secure. 3 *adj* **illogical**, specious, flawed, fallacious, erroneous, faulty, unreliable. [➡THE NATURE OF IDEAS; 772] *Opposite:* reliable.

unsound reasoning *n* [➡NEGATIVE INTELLECTUAL CHARACTERISTICS; 526]

unsparing 1 *adj* **merciless**, harsh, cruel, unforgiving, severe, hard, unkind, excessive, unrelenting. [➡SELFISH AND UNKIND; 506] *Opposite:* merciful. 2 *adj* **generous**, munificent, openhanded, liberal, charitable, unstinting, bountiful (*literary*). [➡GENEROSITY AND KINDNESS; 496] *Opposite:* sparing.

unspeakable 1 *adj* **awful**, disgusting, appalling, foul, revolting, horrifying, terrifying, terrible, horrendous. [➡DISGUSTING AND REPULSIVE; 231] 2 *adj* **indescribable**, inexpressible, unutterable, undefinable, ineffable (*formal*). [➡EXTRAORDINARY: AMAZING; 205]

unspeakably 1 *adv* **indescribably**, inexpressibly, unutterably, undefinably, ineffably (*formal*), unbelievably. [➡TO A GREAT EXTENT; 130] 2 *adv* **terribly**, awfully, disgustingly, appallingly, horribly, horrendously, dreadfully. [➡DISGUSTING AND REPULSIVE; 231]

unspeaking *adj* **silent**, mute, wordless, still, speechless, dumbstruck. [➡COMMUNICATIVE STYLE; 625] *Opposite:* verbose.

unspecified *adj* **unnamed**, indefinite, vague, indeterminate, undetermined, unstipulated. [➡VAGUENESS; 244] *Opposite:* specific.

unspectacular *adj* [➡ORDINARINESS; 245]

unspiritual *adj* **earthly**, worldly, mundane, irreligious. [➡RELIGIOUS CONCEPTS; 777] *Opposite:* spiritual.

unspoiled 1 *adj* **pristine**, pure, perfect, untouched, unharmed, unblemished, undamaged, intact, well-preserved, unchanged. [➡IN GOOD REPAIR; 1231] *Opposite:* marred. 2 *adj* **uncorrupted**, natural, innocent, pure, wholesome, artless. [➡NATURALNESS; 498] *Opposite:* spoiled.

unspoilt *see* **unspoiled**.

unspoken *adj* **tacit**, understood, silent, implicit, undeclared, assumed, unsaid, unexpressed. [➡SECRET AND UNKNOWN; 180] *Opposite:* explicit.

unsporting *adj* **dishonest**, unfair, dishonourable, disreputable, mean-spirited. [➡SELFISH AND UNKIND; 506] *Opposite:* sporting.

unsportsmanlike *adj* **dirty**, dishonest, nasty, foul, unethical, bad. [➡DECEITFUL; 514] *Opposite:* exemplary.

unspotted 1 *adj* **unstained**, clean, spotless, unblemished, pristine, stainless, immaculate. [➡CLEAN; 1232] *Opposite:* spotted. 2 *adj* **pure**, moral, unblemished, faultless, righteous, good. [➡MORALLY GOOD; 775] *Opposite:* impure. 3 *adj* **unob-**

served, unseen, unnoticed, unperceived, undiscovered, invisible. [➡IMPERCEPTIBLE; 26] *Opposite:* seen.

unstable 1 *adj* **unbalanced**, uneven, unhinged, wobbly, rickety, unsound, unsteady, insecure. [➡DANGEROUS; 237] *Opposite:* steady. 2 *adj* **volatile**, unpredictable, unsteady, erratic, variable, changeable. [➡LACK OF COMMITMENT AND UNRELIABILITY; 510] *Opposite:* stable.

unstated *adj* **unspecified**, unspoken, tacit, understood, implicit, assumed, unsaid, unexpressed. [➡THE NATURE OF IDEAS; 772] *Opposite:* specified.

unsteadily 1 *adv* **wobblingly**, tremblingly, tremulously, waveringly, unstably, shakily, unevenly, precariously, treacherously, totteringly. [➡DANGEROUS; 237] *Opposite:* securely. 2 *adv* **changeably**, erratically, variably, unreliably, unregularly, inconstantly, waveringly. [➡FINITENESS, VARIABILITY, AND TRANSIENCE; 96] *Opposite:* constantly.

unsteadiness 1 *n* **tremulousness**, instability, shakiness, unevenness, precariousness, treacherousness, wobbliness. [➡DANGER; 236] *Opposite:* stability. 2 *n* **changeability**, erraticism, variability, unreliability, irregularity, inconstancy. [➡FINITENESS, VARIABILITY, AND TRANSIENCE; 96] *Opposite:* constancy.

unsteady 1 *adj* **wobbly**, shaky, unstable, uneven, rickety, trembling, tremulous, wavering, vacillating, precarious, treacherous, tottering. [➡DANGEROUS; 237] *Opposite:* stable. 2 *adj* **changeable**, erratic, variable, unreliable, irregular, inconstant, wavering. [➡LACK OF COMMITMENT AND UNRELIABILITY; 510] *Opposite:* constant.

unstick *v* **release**, free, take off, take down, take apart, prise, pry (*US*). [➡UNFASTEN AND UNDO; 410] *Opposite:* stick.

unstinting *adj* **generous**, charitable, openhanded, liberal, unsparing, bountiful (*literary*), magnanimous. [➡GENEROSITY AND KINDNESS; 496] *Opposite:* stingy (*informal*).

unstipulated *adj* **unspecified**, unstated, unmentioned, understood, undeclared. [➡VAGUENESS; 244] *Opposite:* specified.

unstop *v* **unblock**, free, clear, unplug, open up, release. [➡UNFASTEN AND UNDO; 410] *Opposite:* stop.

unstoppable *adj* **irresistible**, overwhelming, overpowering, persistent, unrelenting, persisting, persevering, inexorable (*formal*), relentless, inevitable, inescapable. [➡PERMANENCE: WITHOUT END; 94] *Opposite:* avoidable.

unstrained *adj* **cloudy**, milky, opaque, murky. [➡VISUAL TEXTURE; 1220] *Opposite:* clear.

unstrap *v* **undo**, remove, unbuckle, unshackle, unleash, free. [➡UNFASTEN AND UNDO; 410] *Opposite:* tie up.

unstressed *adj* **relaxed**, laid-back (*informal*), carefree, at ease, cool, calm, tranquil, serene. [➡CHEERFULNESS OF OUTLOOK; 504] *Opposite:* stressed.

unstructured *adj* **formless**, shapeless, amorphous, free. [➡SHAPELESSNESS; 1218] *Opposite:* structured.

unstudied *adj* **unaffected**, natural, genuine, sincere, relaxed, open. [➡NATURALNESS; 498] *Opposite:* affected.

unsubstantiated *adj* **unconfirmed**, unproven, unsupported, uncorroborated. [➡UNCERTAIN; 176] *Opposite:* proven.

unsubtle *adj* [➡PERCEPTIBLE; 25]

unsuccessful *adj* **ineffective**, failed, vain, unproductive, abortive, futile, fruitless, disastrous. [➡UNSUCCESSFUL AND UNPROMISING; 76] *Opposite:* successful.

unsuitability *n* **inappropriateness**, inaptness, unbecomingness, incongruity, incompatibility, unacceptability, improperness, unseemliness. [➡INAPPROPRIATE AND UNSUITABLE; 225] *Opposite:* appropriateness.

unsuitable *adj* **inappropriate**, unbecoming, unfitting, inapt, unbefitting, incongruous, incompatible, out of place, improper, unacceptable, unseemly. [➡INAPPROPRIATE AND UNSUITABLE; 225] *Opposite:* appropriate.

unsullied *adj* **pure**, clean, unblemished, faultless, untarnished, immaculate. [➡CLEAN; 1232] *Opposite:* tarnished.

unsung *adj* **unacknowledged**, silent, unrecognized, anonymous, backroom, nameless, unrewarded. [➡SECRET AND UNKNOWN; 180] *Opposite:* renowned.

unsupported *adj* **uncorroborated**, unconfirmed, unsubstantiated, unverified, unfounded, unproven. [➡UNCERTAIN; 176] *Opposite:* supported.

unsure 1 *adj* **uncertain**, doubtful, unconvinced, dubious, suspicious, undecided, sceptical. [➡UNCERTAINTY; 560] *Opposite:* certain. 2 *adj* **unconfident**, hesitant, shy, insecure, irresolute, uncertain. [➡INSECURITY AND LOSS OF COMPOSURE; 545] *Opposite:* confident.

See Compare and Contrast at **doubtful**.

unsurpassed *adj* **unrivalled**, unmatched, supreme, incomparable, unequalled, unparalleled, matchless, consummate. [➡SUPERIORITY; 153] *Opposite:* ordinary.

unsurprising *adj* **predictable**, foreseeable, expected, anticipated, foreseen. [➡BORING AND UNINTERESTING; 235] *Opposite:* surprising.

unsurprisingly *adv* **of course**, naturally, obviously, expectedly, predictably. [➡WORDS AND PHRASES EMPHASIZING THE TRUTH OF A MATTER; 173] *Opposite:* surprisingly.

unsuspected *adj* **unanticipated**, unpredicted, unknown, unimagined, surprise, hidden. [➡SECRET AND UNKNOWN; 180] *Opposite:* known.

unsuspecting *adj* **unwary**, gullible, credulous, innocent, unsuspicious, naive. [➡CALMNESS, CONFIDENCE, AND COMPOSURE; 537] *Opposite:* wary.

unsustainable *adj* **unjustifiable**, unmaintainable, unverifiable, untenable, indefensible, unmanageable, unsanctionable. [➡UNACCEPTABLE AND UNFORGIVABLE; 226] *Opposite:* sustainable.

unswerving *adj* **unwavering**, staunch, reliable, trusty, solid, constant, steadfast, unshakable. [➡CERTAINTY; 562] *Opposite:* wavering.

unsymmetrical *adj* **asymmetrical**, uneven, irregular, lopsided. [➡ORIENTATION AND ALIGNMENT; 1222] *Opposite:* symmetrical.

unsympathetic *adj* **unfeeling**, uncaring, insensitive, cold, indifferent, heartless, hard, cruel, unconcerned. [➡SELFISH AND UNKIND; 506] *Opposite:* caring.

unsystematic *adj* **haphazard**, random, chaotic, disorganized, disorderly, muddled, slapdash, unmethodical. [➡DISORDER AND CHAOS; 246] *Opposite:* organized.

untainted *adj* **unpolluted**, undamaged, unblemished, unspoiled, pure, uncorrupted. [➡CLEAN; 1232] *Opposite:* tainted.

untaken *adj* **available**, unclaimed, unoccupied, free, spare. [➡PRESENT AND AVAILABLE; 11] *Opposite:* taken.

untalented *adj* [➡UNSKILLED; 530]

untangle *v* **unravel**, disentangle, untie, unpick, straighten out. [➡UNFASTEN AND UNDO; 410] *Opposite:* tangle.

untapped *adj* **unused**, unexploited, untouched, available, intact. [➡PRESENT AND AVAILABLE; 11] *Opposite:* used.

untarnished *adj* **unblemished**, clean, spotless, shining, unsullied, faultless, immaculate. [➡CLEAN; 1232] *Opposite:* blemished.

untaught *adj* **untutored**, uneducated, untrained, natural, born, instinctive, innate, inherent. [➡IGNORANCE; 558] *Opposite:* trained.

untenable *adj* **indefensible**, unsustainable, weak, unsound, shaky, invalid, flawed. [➡IMPOSSIBLE AND IMPROBABLE; 179] *Opposite:* watertight.

untested 1 *adj* **untried**, unproven, inexperienced, inexpert, new, raw. [➡NEW, MODERN; 167] *Opposite:* experienced. 2 *adj* **experimental**, untried, unapproved, unverified, unproven, uncertified, unconfirmed, unproved. [➡UNCERTAIN; 176] *Opposite:* safe.

untether *v* **release**, untie, unstrap, unchain, free, unleash. [➡UNFASTEN AND UNDO; 410] *Opposite:* tie up.

unthinkable 1 *adj* **absurd**, ridiculous, unlikely, impossible, improbable, extraordinary. [➡BIZARRE AND PECULIAR; 258] *Opposite:* likely. 2 *adj* **unimaginable**, impossible, fantastic, unbelievable, incredible, inconceivable. [➡IMPOSSIBLE AND IMPROBABLE; 179] *Opposite:* conceivable.

unthinking 1 *adj* **careless**, thoughtless, tactless, undiplomatic, inconsiderate, indiscreet, blunt. [➡INCAUTIOUS AND CARELESS; 284] *Opposite:* thoughtful. 2 *adj* **instinctive**, automatic, mechanical, intuitive, impulsive. [➡AUTOMATIC AND INSTINCTIVE; 281] *Opposite:* calculated.

unthinkingness *n* [➡NEGATIVE INTELLECTUAL CHARACTERISTICS; 526]

unthreatened *adj* **secure**, safe, safe and sound, protected, impregnable. [➡SAFE AND SAFETY; 192] *Opposite:* threatened.

untidily *adv* **messily**, shabbily, scruffily, sloppily. [➡DISORDER AND CHAOS; 246] *Opposite:* neatly.

untidiness *n* **mess**, disorder, muddle, disarray, jumble, clutter, chaos. [➡DISORDER AND CHAOS; 246] *Opposite:* order.

untidy 1 *adj* **messy**, in a mess, in a state (*informal*), disorderly, muddled, jumbled, cluttered, chaotic. [➡DISORDER AND CHAOS; 246] *Opposite:* neat. 2 *adj* **unkempt**, ragged, shabby, scruffy, bedraggled, dishevelled, rumpled. [➡BADLY GROOMED; 484] *Opposite:* smart.

untie 1 *v* **unknot**, unfasten, loosen, undo, unravel, unpick, disentangle, untangle. [➡UNFASTEN AND UNDO; 410] *Opposite:* fasten. 2 *v* **release**, free, set free, unleash, let loose. [➡FREEDOM AND LIBERTY; 209] *Opposite:* tie up.

until *prep* **up until**, while waiting for, pending, till, up to. [➡FUTURE; 86]

until further notice *adv* [➡FUTURE; 86]

until now *adv* **up till now**, so far, thus far, as yet, up to now, hitherto (*formal*), to date. [➡PAST; 84]

until recently *adv* [➡PAST; 84]

until the end of time *adv* [➡PERMANENCE: WITHOUT END; 94]

untimely 1 *adj* **ill-timed**, inconvenient, inappropriate, unfortunate, inopportune, unseasonable. [➡PROMPTNESS: BADLY TIMED; 101] *Opposite:* timely. 2 *adj* **premature**, early, precocious, advance. [➡PROMPTNESS: EARLY; 98] *Opposite:* late.

untiring *adj* **tireless**, determined, dogged, indefatigable, constant, steady, persistent, patient. [➡STRENGTH OF WILL; 502] *Opposite:* faltering.

untold 1 *adj* **indescribable**, ineffable (*formal*), inexpressible, indefinable. [➡EXTRAORDINARY: UNCOMMON; 206] 2 *adj* **uncountable**, countless, innumerable, myriad, numberless, incalculable, unnumbered. [➡MANY, MUCH, LARGE AMOUNT; 117] *Opposite:* few.

untouchable *adj* **unattainable**, matchless, superlative, superior, unrivalled, unchallenged, unbeatable, unparalleled, unassailable. [➡EXTRAORDINARY: AMAZING; 205] *Opposite:* ordinary.

untouched 1 *adj* **unhurt**, intact, unharmed, undamaged, safe and sound, unscathed, uninjured. [➡FINE; 738] *Opposite:* injured. 2 *adj* **unaffected**, indifferent, unmoved, unimpressed, unconcerned. [➡NEUTRALITY AND INDIFFERENCE; 554] *Opposite:* affected.

untoward 1 *adj* **annoying**, unpleasant, inconvenient, troublesome, awkward, problematic, unfortunate. [➡IRRITATING; 229] *Opposite:* pleasant. 2 *adj* **inappropriate**, unfitting, unseemly, improper, unbecoming, indecent. [➡INAPPROPRIATE AND UNSUITABLE; 225] *Opposite:* appropriate.

untraceable *adj* [➡IMPERCEPTIBLE; 26]

untrained *adj* **untaught**, inexpert, untutored, unqualified, inexperienced, amateur. [➡IGNORANCE; 558] *Opposite:* trained.

untrammelled *adj* **unrestricted**, free, unhindered, unimpeded, liberated, unrestrained. [➡FREEDOM AND LIBERTY; 209] *Opposite:* restrained.

untreated *adj* **unprocessed**, unrefined, natural, raw, crude, basic. [➡RAW AND NATURAL; 1213] *Opposite:* treated.

untried *adj* **untested**, inexperienced, unproven, new, novel, experimental. [➡NEW, MODERN; 167] *Opposite:* tested.

untroubled *adj* **peaceful**, calm, tranquil, undisturbed, unflustered, serene, unruffled, unworried, placid. [➡CALMNESS, CONFIDENCE, AND COMPOSURE; 537] *Opposite:* troubled.

untrue 1 *adj* **false**, incorrect, wrong, fallacious, untruthful, fictitious, fictional, imaginary. [➡FALSE AND UNREAL; 174] *Opposite:* true. 2 *adj* **cheating**, unfaithful, disloyal, treacherous, two-faced, faithless, deceitful, untrustworthy. [➡DECEITFUL; 514] *Opposite:* faithful.

untrustworthiness *n* **unreliability**, undependability, dishonesty, deceitfulness, disloyalty, treachery, deviousness. [➡DECEITFUL; 514] *Opposite:* dependability.

untrustworthy *adj* **unreliable**, undependable, dishonest, deceitful, disloyal, treacherous, devious. [➡DECEITFUL; 514] *Opposite:* dependable.

untruth *n* **lie**, falsehood, fiction, fabrication, deceit, story (*informal*), tale, fib (*informal*). [➡DECEPTION AND LIES; 661] *Opposite:* truth.

See Compare and Contrast at **lie**.

untruthful *adj* **lying**, mendacious, fibbing (*informal*), dishonest, deceitful, false, deceptive, misleading, fabricated, fictitious. [➡FALSE AND UNREAL; 174] *Opposite:* truthful.

untruthfulness *n* **dishonesty**, deceit, lies, falsehood, fabrication, mendacity, deception. [➡DECEPTION AND LIES; 661] *Opposite:* truthfulness.

untutored *adj* **untaught**, uneducated, untrained, unschooled, unqualified, inexperienced, illiterate. [➡UNSKILLED; 530] *Opposite:* educated.

unusable *adj* **useless**, out of commission, unworkable, inoperative, broken. [➡IN BAD REPAIR; 1233] *Opposite:* usable.

unused 1 *adj* **new**, brand-new, fresh, pristine. [➡NEW, MODERN; 167] *Opposite:* used. 2 *adj* **idle**, vacant, unemployed, unexploited, fallow. [➡LACK OF ACTIVITY; 343] 3 *adj* **unaccustomed**, unfamiliar, unacquainted, inexperienced. [➡UNSKILLED; 530] *Opposite:* familiar.

unusual 1 *adj* **uncommon**, rare, infrequent, scarce, few and far between (*informal*), unfamiliar. [➡EXTRAORDINARY: UNCOMMON; 206] *Opposite:* common. 2 *adj* **strange**, odd, curious, extraordinary, abnormal, remarkable, bizarre, atypical. [➡BIZARRE AND PECULIAR; 258] *Opposite:* ordinary.

unusualness *n* [➡EXTRAORDINARY: UNCOMMON; 206]

unutterable *adj* **unspeakable**, indescribable, inexpressible, ineffable (*formal*), indefinable. [➡UNACCEPTABLE AND UNFORGIVABLE; 226]

unvalued *adj* [➡UNPOPULAR AND UNWANTED; 259]

unvanquished *adj* [➡SUCCESSFUL AND PROMISING; 81]

unvaried *adj* [➡PERMANENCE: WITHOUT CHANGE; 95]

unvarnished *adj* **plain**, straight, honest, unembellished, literal, exact, unadulterated, naked, unembroidered, unadorned, simple, straightforward. [➡TRUE AND REAL; 172] *Opposite:* embellished.

unvarying *adj* **unwavering**, constant, unchanging, consistent, inflexible, regular, habitual, stable, steady. [➡PERMANENCE: WITHOUT CHANGE; 95] *Opposite:* varying.

unveil 1 *v* **uncover**, unwrap, bare, expose. [➡CAUSE TO APPEAR; 5] *Opposite:* cover. 2 *v* **reveal**, expose, make public, divulge, show, disclose, uncover. [➡INFORM AND ANNOUNCE; 612] *Opposite:* conceal.

unveiling 1 *n* **opening**, launch, presentation, inauguration, debut, entrance. [➡CEREMONIES AND ANNIVERSARIES; 38] *Opposite:* closure. 2 *n* **revelation**, disclosure, exposure, uncovering, release, announcement. [➡INFORM AND ANNOUNCE; 612] *Opposite:* cover-up.

unventilated *adj* **airless**, stuffy, unaired, close, stale. [➡DIRTY; 1234] *Opposite:* airy.

unverified *adj* **unconfirmed**, unsupported, unsubstantiated, uncorroborated, unproven, unendorsed. [➡UNCERTAIN; 176] *Opposite:* verified.

unversed *adj* [➡IGNORANCE; 558]

unviability *n* [➡IMPOSSIBLE AND IMPROBABLE; 179]

unviable *adj* [➡IMPOSSIBLE AND IMPROBABLE; 179]

unvoiced *adj* **unspoken**, silent, secret, hidden, mute, tacit, unexpressed. [➡SECRET AND UNKNOWN; 180] *Opposite:* spoken.

unwaged *adj* **unemployed**, jobless, on the dole (*informal*), out of work, redundant, on welfare (*US*). [➡EMPLOYMENT STATUS; 831] *Opposite:* employed.

unwanted 1 *adj* **surplus**, superfluous, unnecessary, discarded, redundant, useless. [➡MORE AND EXCESS; 122] *Opposite:* necessary. 2 *adj* **unwelcome**, unsolicited, annoying, undesirable, uninvited. [➡UNPOPULAR AND UNWANTED; 259] *Opposite:* welcome.

unwariness *n* **incautiousness**, unguardedness, rashness, carelessness, gullibility, credulity, naivety, imprudence. [➡NEGATIVE INTELLECTUAL CHARACTERISTICS; 526] *Opposite:* wariness.

unwarrantable *adj* **uncalled-for**, indefensible, unjustifiable, unforgivable, inexcusable, unpardonable, deplorable. [➡UNIMPORTANT AND UNNECESSARY; 239]

unwarranted *adj* **unjustified**, undeserved, unnecessary, gratuitous, needless, uncalled-for, unprovoked, superfluous. [➡UNIMPORTANT AND UNNECESSARY; 239] *Opposite:* justified.

unwary *adj* **imprudent** (*formal*), unguarded, rash, careless, unsuspecting, innocent, gullible, credulous, reckless, naive, trusting, incautious. [➡NEGATIVE INTELLECTUAL CHARACTERISTICS; 526] *Opposite:* wary.

unwashed *adj* **dirty**, grubby, grimy, sordid, squalid. [➡DIRTY; 1234] *Opposite:* clean.

unwavering *adj* **firm**, staunch, solid, steadfast, untiring, dogged, resolute, steady, unswerving. [➡CERTAINTY; 562] *Opposite:* irresolute.

unwearied *adj* **unflagging**, tireless, indefatigable, uncomplaining, unceasing, long-suffering, persistent. [➡STRENGTH OF WILL; 502]

unwelcome *adj* **unwanted**, undesirable, annoying,

unsolicited, uninvited. [➡ UNPOPULAR AND UNWANTED; 259] *Opposite:* welcome.

unwelcoming *adj* **hostile**, unfriendly, standoffish, unreceptive, inhospitable, cold, frosty. [➡ UNFRIENDLINESS AND UNSOCIABILITY; 505] *Opposite:* friendly.

unwell *adj* **ill**, indisposed (*formal*), poorly (*informal*), sick, under the weather, ailing (*dated*), out of sorts, below par (*informal*), off-colour. [➡ ILL AND SICK; 741] *Opposite:* well.

unwholesome *adj* **unpleasant**, distasteful, objectionable, nasty, disagreeable, noxious, harmful, insalubrious (*formal*). [➡ DISGUSTING AND REPULSIVE; 231] *Opposite:* pleasant.

unwholesomeness 1 *n* **foulness**, insalubriousness, noxiousness, unhealthiness, harmfulness. [➡ DISGUSTING AND REPULSIVE; 231] *Opposite:* wholesomeness. 2 *n* **coarseness**, indecency, vulgarity, foulness, profanity, obscenity, immorality. [➡ MORALLY BAD; 776] *Opposite:* wholesomeness.

unwieldiness *n* [➡ LARGE; 1192]

unwieldy *adj* **awkward**, heavy, bulky, cumbersome, clumsy, ungainly, unmanageable. [➡ WEIGHT: HEAVY; 1204] *Opposite:* manageable.

unwilling *adj* **reluctant**, disinclined, averse (*formal*), grudging, loath, indisposed (*formal*), unenthusiastic, hesitant. [➡ UNWILLINGNESS AND STUBBORNNESS; 565] *Opposite:* willing.

Compare and Contrast: ***unwilling, reluctant, disinclined, averse, hesitant, loath***

CORE MEANING: LACKING THE DESIRE TO DO SOMETHING

unwilling not prepared to do something; ***reluctant*** showing no enthusiasm for doing something and only doing it if forced; ***disinclined*** showing a lack of enthusiasm for something rather than a strong objection to it; ***averse*** (*formal*) strongly opposed to or disliking something; ***hesitant*** not keen to do something because of uncertainty or lack of confidence; ***loath*** having reservations about doing something.

unwillingness *n* **reluctance**, disinclination, refusal, indisposition, aversion, opposition. [➡ UNWILLINGNESS AND STUBBORNNESS; 565] *Opposite:* willingness.

unwind 1 *v* **undo**, loosen, unravel, untwist, disentangle, uncoil. [➡ UNFASTEN AND UNDO; 410] *Opposite:* wind. 2 *v* **relax**, wind down, slow down, calm down, chill out (*slang*). [➡ CHANGE OF MOOD AND COMPOSURE; 581] *Opposite:* work up.

unwise *adj* **foolish**, imprudent (*formal*), rash, ill-advised, injudicious, reckless, hasty, irresponsible, stupid, risky. [➡ DANGEROUS; 237] *Opposite:* prudent.

unwisely *adv* **foolishly**, imprudently (*formal*), rashly, ill-advisedly, injudiciously, recklessly, hastily, irresponsibly, stupidly, riskily. [➡ INCAUTIOUS AND CARELESS; 284] *Opposite:* prudently.

unwitting 1 *adj* **unaware**, unsuspecting, ignorant, innocent, unconscious, unknowing. [➡ IGNORANCE; 558] *Opposite:* knowing. 2 *adj* **accidental**, involuntary, unintentional, coincidental, inadvertent, chance. [➡ UNINTENTIONAL AND ACCIDENTAL; 282] *Opposite:* deliberate.

unwonted *adj* **unusual**, atypical, uncharacteristic, singular, unexpected, uncommon. [➡ EXTRAORDINARY: AMAZING; 205] *Opposite:* customary.

unworkable *adj* **impracticable**, unusable, unfeasible, ineffectual, impractical. [➡ REDUNDANT AND USELESS; 241] *Opposite:* viable.

unworldliness *n* **innocence**, naivety, simplicity, ingenuousness, callowness, greenness, artlessness, unsophisticatedness, inexperience. [➡ NEGATIVE INTELLECTUAL CHARACTERISTICS; 526] *Opposite:* worldliness.

unworldly *adj* **inexperienced**, callow, green, ingenuous, artless, unsophisticated, naive, innocent. [➡ IGNORANCE; 558] *Opposite:* experienced.

unworried *adj* **calm**, untroubled, at ease, unruffled, unflustered, tranquil, unconcerned, unperturbed, relaxed. [➡ CALMNESS, CONFIDENCE, AND COMPOSURE; 537] *Opposite:* perturbed.

unworthiness 1 *n* **worthlessness**, contemptibility, pitifulness, unfitness. [➡ REDUNDANT AND USELESS; 241] 2 *n* **shamefulness**, dishonour, discredit, shame, disgrace, disrepute. [➡ MORALLY BAD; 776]

unworthy 1 *adj* **undeserving**, worthless, contemptible, pitiful, unfit. [➡ REDUNDANT AND USELESS; 241] *Opposite:* deserving. 2 *adj* **shameful**, degrading, dishonourable, disgraceful, disreputable. [➡ MORALLY BAD; 776] *Opposite:* reputable.

unwrap *v* **undo**, unpack, remove, open, tear open. [➡ UNFASTEN AND UNDO; 410] *Opposite:* wrap.

unwritten 1 *adj* **spoken**, oral, unrecorded, vocal, unprinted. [➡ COMMUNICATIVE STYLE; 625] *Opposite:* written. 2 *adj* **understood**, accepted, traditional, tacit, known. [➡ KNOWN AND FAMOUS; 182]

unyielding 1 *adj* **firm**, unbending, obstinate, steadfast, obdurate, immovable, tough, uncompromising, adamant, staunch, stubborn. [➡ UNWILLINGNESS AND STUBBORNNESS; 565] *Opposite:* acquiescent. 2 *adj* **inflexible**, rigid, stiff, unbending, solid, durable. [➡ RIGID AND HARD; 1210] *Opposite:* flexible.

unyoke *v* **untie**, separate, disjoin, unhook, loose, untether, unstrap. [➡ UNFASTEN AND UNDO; 410] *Opposite:* join.

unzip 1 *v* **undo**, unfasten, open, disengage, free. [➡ UNFASTEN AND UNDO; 410] 2 *v* **open**, expand, access, decompress. [➡ COMPUTERS AND COMPUTING; 1126] *Opposite:* compress.

up 1 *adj* **awake**, out of bed, up and about, active, up and doing, up and around (*US*). [➡ WIDE AWAKE AND CONSCIOUS; 736] *Opposite:* asleep. 2 *adj* **happy**, upbeat (*informal*), positive, optimistic, hopeful, cheerful, cheery. [➡ PLEASURE, EXCITEMENT, AND ELATION; 535] *Opposite:* down. 3 *adj* **winning**, in the lead, ahead, leading. [➡ SUCCESSFUL AND PROMISING; 81] *Opposite:* behind.

up and about *adj* **awake**, up, out of bed, active, up and doing, up and around (*US*). [➡ WIDE AWAKE AND CONSCIOUS; 736] *Opposite:* asleep.

up-and-coming *adj* **emerging**, rising, budding, promising, talented. [➡ FUTURE; 86] *Opposite:* over-the-hill.

up and down 1 *adj* **moody**, temperamental, changeable, tempestuous, turbulent, highly-strung. [➡SADNESS, DISTRESS, AND DESPAIR; 540] *Opposite:* equable. 2 *adj* **rising and falling**, bobbing, bouncing. [➡DIRECTION OF MOTION; 346]

up and running *adj* [➡HAPPENING AND IN PROGRESS; 32]

upbeat (*informal*) *adj* **optimistic**, cheerful, positive, buoyant, bubbly, up, happy, cheery. [➡PLEASURE, EXCITEMENT, AND ELATION; 535] *Opposite:* downbeat.

upbraid *v* **scold**, tell off (*informal*), tick off (*informal*), reproach, tear a strip off, chastise (*formal*), reprimand, rebuke, censure. [➡ACCUSE, BLAME, AND CRITICIZE; 642] *Opposite:* praise.

upbringing *n* **education**, childhood, background, rearing, nurture, past. [➡BABYHOOD, CHILDHOOD AND ADOLESCENCE; 917]

upchuck (*informal*) *v* [➡VOMIT AND BELCH; 713]

upcoming (*US*) *adj* **future**, imminent, forthcoming, impending, approaching, coming. [➡ABOUT TO HAPPEN; 33] *Opposite:* past.

update 1 *v* **inform**, bring up-to-date, keep informed, keep posted, fill in, apprise (*formal*). [➡INFORM AND ANNOUNCE; 612] 2 *v* **modernize**, revise, renew, bring up-to-date, renovate. [➡IMPROVE SOMETHING; 375]

upend *v* **turn over**, tip up, tip over, upset, topple, flip over, overturn, turn turtle. [➡MOVE SOMETHING: INTO A NEW POSITION OR OVERTURN; 331] *Opposite:* right.

upended *adj* [➡ORIENTATION AND ALIGNMENT; 1222]

up for grabs (*informal*) *adj* **available**, free, going begging, for the taking. [➡PRESENT AND AVAILABLE; 11] *Opposite:* unavailable.

up-front (*informal*) *adj* **straightforward**, honest, frank, plain-spoken, open, forthright, candid, direct, blunt. [➡HONEST AND OPEN; 631] *Opposite:* coy.

upgrade 1 *v* **promote**, advance, elevate, raise, move up, progress, exalt. [➡CONFER STATUS; 459] *Opposite:* demote. 2 *v* **improve**, update, renew, modernize, renovate, enhance, transform, convert, develop, reconstruct, advance. [➡IMPROVE SOMETHING; 375] *Opposite:* downgrade. 3 *n* **promotion**, advancement, elevation, exaltation. [➡CONFER STATUS; 459] *Opposite:* demotion. 4 *n* **improvement**, upgrading, renovation, modernization, enhancement, transformation, conversion, development, reconstruction. [➡PROGRESS AND ADVANCEMENT; 214]

upgrading 1 *n* **promotion**, advancement, step up, advance, progression, progress, elevation. [➡CONFER STATUS; 459] *Opposite:* demotion. 2 *n* **improvement**, renovation, modernization, transformation, enhancement, conversion, development, reconstruction. [➡IMPROVE SOMETHING; 375]

upheaval *n* **disturbance**, turmoil, disorder, confusion, cataclysm, commotion, disruption, mayhem (*informal*). [➡CHAOS AND UPROAR; 51] *Opposite:* peace.

upheave *v* **lift up**, raise, thrust up, elevate, lift, rouse up. [➡MOVE SOMETHING: UPWARDS; 329] *Opposite:* drop.

uphill 1 *adj* **climbing**, ascending, rising, mounting. [➡ORIENTATION AND ALIGNMENT; 1222] *Opposite:* downhill. 2 *adj* **difficult**, hard, arduous, demanding, tough, trying, taxing. [➡PHYSICALLY UNPLEASANT; 227] *Opposite:* easy.

uphill battle *n* [➡HARD WORK OR EFFORT; 299]

uphold *v* **support**, sustain, maintain, defend, endorse, advocate, espouse, encourage. [➡APPROVE AND CONFIRM; 647]

upholster *v* **furnish** (*formal*), cover, pad, stuff, fill, decorate. [➡DECORATE, ADORN, AND APPLY COATINGS; 406]

upholstery *n* **fabric**, furnishings, covers, furniture, material, padding, stuffing. [➡SOFT FURNISHINGS, LINEN, AND DRAPERY; 860]

up in arms *adj* **angry**, indignant, offended, resentful, exasperated, furious, enraged, incensed, infuriated. [➡IRRITATION AND ANGER; 542] *Opposite:* unconcerned.

up in the air *adj* **uncertain**, undecided, vague, in the balance, unsettled. [➡VAGUENESS; 244] *Opposite:* decided.

upkeep *n* **maintenance**, repairs, keep, conservation, preservation, running. [➡PERMANENCE: WITHOUT END; 94]

upland *n* **moorland**, high ground, highland, plateau, tableland. [➡DESERTS AND PLAINS; 1045] *Opposite:* lowland.

uplift 1 *v* **elevate**, raise, hoist, lift. [➡MOVE SOMETHING: UPWARDS; 329] *Opposite:* drop. 2 *v* **inspire**, enrich, improve, move, hearten, raise, stir. [➡ENCOURAGE; 577] *Opposite:* depress.

See Compare and Contrast at **raise**.

uplifted *adj* [➡PLEASURE, EXCITEMENT, AND ELATION; 535]

uplifting *adj* **inspiring**, elevating, improving, enriching, heartening, moving, inspirational, stirring. [➡EMOTIONALLY PLEASANT; 188] *Opposite:* depressing.

uplighter 1 *n* **standard lamp**, spotlight, spot, table lamp, bedside lamp, desk lamp, lamp, floor lamp (*US*). [➡LIGHTING; 862] 2 *type of* **light**. [➡LIGHT; 1163]

upmarket *adj* **expensive**, high-class, smart, chic, posh (*informal*), exclusive, glamorous, classy (*informal*), swanky (*informal*), upscale (*US*). [➡EXPENSIVE AND LUXURIOUS; 219] *Opposite:* downmarket.

up on *adj* [➡KNOWLEDGE AND WISDOM; 559]

upper *adj* **higher**, greater, better, superior. [➡SUPERIORITY; 153] *Opposite:* lower.

upper atmosphere *n* [➡THE EARTH'S ATMOSPHERE; 1040]

upper circle *n* **gallery**, loggia, balcony, circle, dress circle, gods (*informal*). [➡IN THE THEATRE; 906]

upper class *n* **aristocracy**, nobility, noblesse, gentry, upper crust (*informal*), elite. [➡CLASS STATUS; 889] *Opposite:* lower class.

upper-class *adj* **aristocratic**, noble, highborn (*literary*), blue-blooded. [➡CLASS STATUS; 889] *Opposite:* lower-class.

upper crust (*informal*) *n* **upper class**, aristocracy, nobility, gentry, noblesse, elite. [➡CLASS STATUS; 889] *Opposite:* proletariat.

uppercut *n* **blow**, punch, hit, haymaker (*slang*). [➡ PHYSICAL ATTACK AND PUNISHMENT; 416]

upper hand *n* **advantage**, initiative, ascendancy, edge, control, superiority, dominance. [➡ SOURCE OF HAPPINESS, PLEASURE, OR IMPROVEMENT; 210] *Opposite:* disadvantage.

uppermost 1 *adj* **highest**, top, topmost, upmost. [➡ RELATIVE LOCATION; 162] *Opposite:* bottom. 2 *adj* **primary**, main, principal, chief, greatest, dominant. [➡ MOST IMPORTANT AND MAIN; 194] *Opposite:* last.

uppity 1 *adj* (*informal*) **presumptuous**, pretentious, snobbish, haughty, bumptious, superior, arrogant. [➡ AFFECTATION, SELF-SATISFACTION, AND SNOBBISHNESS; 508] *Opposite:* humble. 2 *adj* (*dated informal*) **stubborn**, difficult, cantankerous, irritable, tetchy (*informal*), crotchety (*informal*). [➡ DIFFICULT TO PLEASE; 516] *Opposite:* flexible.

uprate *v* **increase**, raise, upgrade, augment (*formal*), up, adjust, enhance, improve. [➡ IMPROVE SOMETHING; 375] *Opposite:* decrease.

upright 1 *adj* **standing**, straight, vertical, erect. [➡ ORIENTATION AND ALIGNMENT; 1222] *Opposite:* horizontal. 2 *adj* **righteous**, moral, honourable, decent, honest, respectable, conscientious, upstanding, principled. [➡ MORALLY GOOD; 775] *Opposite:* immoral.

uprightness *n* **righteousness**, morality, honourableness, decency, honesty, respectability, honour, worthiness. [➡ MORALLY GOOD; 775] *Opposite:* immorality.

upright piano *type of* **keyboard**. [➡ MUSICAL INSTRUMENTS; 910]

uprising *n* **rebellion**, revolution, revolt, rising, unrest, mutiny, disturbance, civil disobedience, insurrection. [➡ AGGRESSIVE EVENT; 39]

uproar *n* **disturbance**, noise, chaos, pandemonium, upheaval, tumult, din, racket (*informal*), hue and cry, hullabaloo, turbulence, hubbub. [➡ CHAOS AND UPROAR; 51] *Opposite:* quiet.

uproarious *adj* **hilarious**, hysterical (*informal*), funny, riotous, raucous, boisterous. [➡ FUNNY AND AMUSING; 217]

uproariousness *n* [➡ CHAOS AND UPROAR; 51]

uproot 1 *v* **pull up**, deracinate, dig up, rip up. [➡ MOVE SOMETHING: UPWARDS; 329] *Opposite:* plant. 2 *v* **displace**, evacuate, move on, relocate. [➡ MOVE SOMETHING TO ANOTHER LOCATION; 325] *Opposite:* settle.

uprush *n* **rush**, surge, updraught, draught, blast, current. [➡ SUDDEN EVENT; 52]

ups and downs *n* [➡ EVENTS AND OCCURRENCES; 35]

upscale (*US*) *adj* **upmarket**, smart, exclusive, expensive, posh (*informal*), high-class, glamorous, classy (*informal*), chic, swanky (*informal*), ritzy (*informal*), prestigious. [➡ EXPENSIVE AND LUXURIOUS; 219] *Opposite:* downmarket.

upset 1 *v* **spill**, knock over, tip over, overturn, upend. [➡ MOVE SOMETHING: INTO A NEW POSITION OR OVERTURN; 331] *Opposite:* right. 2 *v* **disturb**, disrupt, reorder, reverse, mix up, disorganize, spoil, unbalance, change. [➡ CREATE DISORDER AND CAUSE CHAOS; 359] *Opposite:* order. 3 *v* **distress**, hurt, disturb, sadden, trouble, wound, offend, disappoint, disconcert, displease, grieve. [➡ UPSET, DISTRESS, AND HUMILIATE; 568] *Opposite:* please. 4 *n* **defeat**, disappointment, affront, letdown, shock, setback, distress. [➡ SADNESS, DISTRESS, AND DESPAIR; 540] 5 *n* **surprise**, shock, confusion, disarray, turn-up (*informal*), disruption, disturbance, turmoil, commotion, shake-up. [➡ CHAOS AND UPROAR; 51] 6 *adj* **sad**, disturbed, unhappy, hurt, disappointed, saddened, dismayed, wounded, offended, distressed, troubled, distraught. [➡ SADNESS, DISTRESS, AND DESPAIR; 540] *Opposite:* composed.

upset stomach *n* **indigestion**, stomachache, heartburn, bellyache (*informal*), tummy ache (*informal*). [➡ DISORDERS OF THE DIGESTIVE SYSTEM; 714]

upsetting *adj* **distressing**, disturbing, hurtful, offensive, disappointing, disconcerting, displeasing, shocking, harrowing. [➡ EMOTIONALLY UNPLEASANT AND UPSETTING; 228] *Opposite:* pleasing.

upshift (*US*) *v* **change up**, change gear, gear up (*US*). [➡ USE TOOLS AND MACHINERY; 469]

upshot *n* **result**, outcome, consequence, effect, end, end result, conclusion. [➡ RESULTS AND OUTCOMES; 83]

upside *n* **advantage**, benefit, plus (*informal*), positive (*informal*). [➡ SOURCE OF HAPPINESS, PLEASURE, OR IMPROVEMENT; 210] *Opposite:* disadvantage.

upside down *adv* [➡ ORIENTATION AND ALIGNMENT; 1222]

upside-down 1 *adj* **upturned**, wrong way up, wrong side up, overturned, on its head, inverted, reversed. [➡ ORIENTATION AND ALIGNMENT; 1222] *Opposite:* upright. 2 *adj* **in a mess**, in a state (*informal*), messy, untidy, topsy-turvy, in disorder, in disarray, chaotic, disorganized. [➡ DISORDER AND CHAOS; 246] *Opposite:* orderly.

upstage *v* **outdo**, outmanoeuvre, put somebody's nose out of joint, outshine, surpass, put in the shade, leave standing, go one better than. [➡ BEAT AND DEFEAT; 80]

upstanding *adj* **virtuous**, honest, decent, respectable, honourable, trustworthy, good, moral. [➡ MORALLY GOOD; 775] *Opposite:* degenerate.

upstart *n* **nobody**, unknown, parvenu, arriviste (*disapproving*), nonentity, newcomer, social climber (*disapproving*), nouveau riche. [➡ SELF-IMPORTANT AND SELF-SEEKING PEOPLE; 949] *Opposite:* grandee.

upstretched *adj* **raised**, upraised, upturned, outstretched, extended, upthrust. [➡ ORIENTATION AND ALIGNMENT; 1222] *Opposite:* hanging down.

upsurge *n* **increase**, rise, surge, gain, expansion, improvement. [➡ CHANGE OF INTENSITY: MORE; 395] *Opposite:* decrease.

upswing *n* **increase**, improvement, upturn, pick-up (*informal*), turnround, upsurge. [➡ CHANGE OF SIZE: BIGGER; 393] *Opposite:* downswing.

uptake 1 *n* **acceptance**, approval, interest, commitment, agreement, application, endorsement, curiosity. [➡ APPROVE AND CONFIRM; 647] *Opposite:* refusal. 2 *n* **understanding**, comprehension, perception, appreciation, apprehension, realization. [➡ UNDERSTAND AND GRASP; 760] *Opposite:* incomprehension.

up-tempo *adj* **exciting**, lively, fast, frenetic, upbeat (*informal*), rapid. [➡HAPPENING QUICKLY; 104] *Opposite:* dull.

up the creek (*informal*) *adj* **in trouble**, in dire straits, in difficulty, in hot water (*informal*), in a predicament, in a fix (*informal*). [➡IN TROUBLE AND DISADVANTAGED; 73]

up the creek without a paddle (*informal*) *adj* [➡IN TROUBLE AND DISADVANTAGED; 73]

uptight (*informal*) *adj* **tense**, worked up (*informal*), bothered, in a state (*informal*), anxious, neurotic (*informal*), edgy, uneasy. [➡POSITIVE IMPATIENCE, ENTHUSIASM, AND ALERTNESS; 538] *Opposite:* calm.

up till now *adv* **so far**, thus far, hitherto (*formal*), until now, to date, up to now, as yet. [➡PAST; 84]

up-to-date 1 *adj* **informed**, in touch, conversant, in the know, au fait. [➡KNOWLEDGE AND WISDOM; 559] 2 *adj* **current**, latest, new, brand-new, modern, innovative, up-to-the-minute, fresh, state-of-the-art, newfangled, novel, contemporary, advanced. [➡DESCRIBING TECHNOLOGY; 1159] *Opposite:* old-fashioned. 3 *adj* **fashionable**, trendy (*informal*), with-it (*dated informal*), à la mode (*dated*), cool, chic, upscale (*US*). [➡NEW, MODERN; 167] *Opposite:* passé.

up to now *adv* **until now**, so far, thus far, hitherto (*formal*), to date, up till now, as yet. [➡PAST; 84]

up to scratch (*informal*) *adj* [➡ACCEPTABLE AND PASSABLE; 220]

up to speed *adj* **in control**, on top of things, au fait, at home, informed. [➡HAPPENING AND IN PROGRESS; 32] *Opposite:* ignorant.

up to standard *adj* [➡ACCEPTABLE AND PASSABLE; 220]

up-to-the-minute *adj* **latest**, current, contemporary, state-of-the-art, contemporaneous, modern, up-to-date. [➡NEW, MODERN; 167] *Opposite:* out-of-date.

up to the present moment *adv* [➡PAST; 84]

up to the present time *adv* [➡PAST; 84]

up to your ears *adj* **busy**, snowed under, swamped, flooded, rushed off your feet, inundated. [➡IN TROUBLE AND DISADVANTAGED; 73] *Opposite:* idle.

upturn 1 *v* **overturn**, capsize, tip over, upset, turn turtle, turn over, upend. [➡MOVE SOMETHING: INTO A NEW POSITION OR OVERTURN; 331] *Opposite:* right. 2 *n* **improvement**, recovery, revival, growth, expansion, rise, increase, upsurge. [➡PROGRESS AND ADVANCEMENT; 214] *Opposite:* slump.

upturned *adj* [➡ORIENTATION AND ALIGNMENT; 1222]

up until now *adv* [➡PAST; 84]

upward 1 *adj* **ascendant**, mounting, skyward, uphill, ascending, rising. [➡ORIENTATION AND ALIGNMENT; 1222] *Opposite:* downward. 2 *adj* **rising**, improving, increasing, growing, expanding, surging. [➡DIRECTION OF MOTION; 346] *Opposite:* downward.

upwardly mobile *adj* [➡CLASS STATUS; 889]

upwards *adv* **up**, uphill, higher, skyward, in the air, aloft. [➡DIRECTION OF MOTION; 346]

upwelling *n* **upsurge**, surge, burst, outburst, outpouring, gush, emergence, flood, swell, spring. [➡SUDDEN EVENT; 52]

upwind *adj* **windward**, exposed, open, bare, windy. [➡GENERAL LOCATIONS; 159] *Opposite:* leeward.

up with *adj* **abreast**, up-to-date, familiar, conversant, au fait, au courant. [➡KNOWLEDGE AND WISDOM; 559]

uranium *type of* **metal**. [➡METALS; 1275]

Uranus *type of* **planet**. [➡CELESTIAL BODIES; 1060]

urban *adj* **city**, town, built-up, municipal, inner-city, metropolitan, borough. [➡HUMAN SETTLEMENTS; 1069] *Opposite:* rural.

urbane *adj* **sophisticated**, refined, courteous, suave, polished, stylish, smooth, genteel, elegant, cultured. [➡GOOD MANNERS AND SOCIAL SKILLS; 521] *Opposite:* unsophisticated.

urbanite *n* **metropolitan**, cosmopolitan, citizen, resident, townie (*informal*). [➡INHABITANT; 857] *Opposite:* rustic.

urbanity *n* **sophistication**, refinement, courteousness, courtesy, suaveness, polish, genteelness, gentility, culture, civility. [➡GOOD MANNERS AND SOCIAL SKILLS; 521] *Opposite:* uncouthness.

urbanization *n* **development**, suburbanization, expansion, sprawl, spread, growth. [➡HUMAN SETTLEMENTS; 1069]

urban myth *n* **myth**, story (*informal*), folk tale, tale, tall story, fable, legend, tall tale (*US*). [➡THE ORAL TRADITION; 678]

urban sprawl *n* **urbanization**, development, suburbia, sprawl, expansion, overspill. [➡HUMAN SETTLEMENTS; 1069]

urchin *n* **ragamuffin** (*dated*), imp, rascal (*humorous*), tyke, hooligan (*informal*), tearaway, kid (*informal*), brat. [➡CHILD OR YOUTH; 945]

urge 1 *v* **advise**, commend, admonish, counsel (*formal or literary*), prevail on, insist, press. [➡ADVISE AND WARN; 614] *Opposite:* dissuade. 2 *v* **advocate**, beg, recommend, advise, plead, implore (*formal*), exhort, beseech (*literary*), appeal. [➡REQUEST AND DEMAND; 664] 3 *v* **encourage**, drive, push, force, impel, incite, goad, egg on, compel. [➡CAUSE OR COMPEL TO ACT; 272] *Opposite:* discourage. 4 *n* **need**, wish, impulse, desire, inclination, longing, itch, compulsion, craving, yearning. [➡DESIRE AND WANT; 580] *Opposite:* disinclination.

urgency 1 *n* **need**, exigency, importance, necessity, hurry, rush, pressure. [➡IMPORTANCE AND SIGNIFICANCE; 193] *Opposite:* unimportance. 2 *n* **earnestness**, insistence, perseverance, firmness, resolve, determination, resolution. [➡POSITIVE IMPATIENCE, ENTHUSIASM, AND ALERTNESS; 538] *Opposite:* vacillation.

urgent 1 *adj* **vital**, crucial, pressing, imperative, burning, critical, serious, exigent (*formal*), important. [➡IMPORTANT; 195] *Opposite:* trivial. 2 *adj* **earnest**, insistent, importunate (*formal*), persuasive, pleading, beseeching (*literary*), demanding. [➡ENTHUSIASTIC AND INQUISITIVE; 629] *Opposite:* half-hearted.

urgently *adv* **immediately**, straightaway, instantly, at once, directly, right away, now. [➡PRESENT; 85] *Opposite:* whenever.

urinate *v* [➡EXCRETION AND EXCRETA; 723]

urine *n* [➡EXCRETION AND EXCRETA; 723]

URL *n* [➡THE INTERNET; 1127]

urn *n* **vase**, container, vessel, pot, jug, pitcher. [➡CONTAINERS, RECEPTACLES, AND PACKAGING; 1244]

usable *adj* **functional**, practical, serviceable, working, functioning, operational, operating, in working order. [➡IN GOOD REPAIR; 1231] *Opposite:* unusable.

usage 1 *n* **treatment**, handling, control, management, running, use, manipulation. [➡USE; 468] 2 *n* **practice**, procedure, custom, norm, tradition, habit. [➡WAYS OF DOING THINGS; 295]

use 1 *v* **employ**, make use of, utilize, exercise, bring into play, apply, exploit, draw on. [➡USE; 468] *Opposite:* forgo. 2 *v* **consume**, expend, spend, exhaust, use up, deplete, exploit, get through, wear out, waste. [➡USE UP AND WASTE; 475] *Opposite:* conserve. 3 *v* **manipulate**, exploit, take advantage of, mistreat, abuse. [➡MISUSE AND ABUSE; 472] 4 *v* **behave**, handle, treat, manipulate, manage, operate, work. [➡USE TOOLS AND MACHINERY; 469] 5 *v* **benefit**, make use of, enjoy, avail yourself of, tap, source, luxuriate, take pleasure in. [➡MAKE GOOD USE OF SOMETHING; 474] 6 *n* **expenditure**, consumption, wear and tear, wastage, depletion, exhaustion. [➡USE UP AND WASTE; 475] *Opposite:* saving. 7 *n* **treatment**, handling, manipulation, exploitation, management, operation. [➡USE; 468] 8 *n* **employment**, application, utilization, exploitation, consumption, exercise. [➡USE; 468] *Opposite:* disuse. 9 *n* (*literary or archaic*) **usage**, custom, habit, practice, routine, procedure. [➡WAYS OF DOING THINGS; 295] 10 *n* **purpose**, function, application, service, role, utility. [➡INTENTION AND PURPOSE; 773] 11 *n* **usefulness**, help, assistance, benefit, aid, worth, advantage, value. [➡USEFULNESS; 200] *Opposite:* harm.

Compare and Contrast: ***use, employ, make use of, utilize***

CORE MEANING: TO PUT SOMETHING TO USE

use to put something into action or service; ***employ*** to make use of something such as a tool or a resource in a particular way; ***make use of*** to use what is readily available, especially in a sensible or economical way; ***utilize*** to find a practical or unintended use for something.

used 1 *adj* **second-hand**, castoff, hand-me-down, charity, recycled, jumble-sale, rummage-sale (*US*). [➡OLD, OLD-FASHIONED; 168] *Opposite:* new. 2 *adj* **expended**, old, worn, worn out, consumed, run down, exhausted, depleted, spent, finished. [➡IN BAD REPAIR; 1233] *Opposite:* remaining.

used to 1 *adj* **accustomed**, hardened, inured, schooled, conditioned, in the habit of. [➡KNOWLEDGE AND WISDOM; 559] *Opposite:* unaccustomed. 2 *adj* **familiar**, at home, au fait, at ease, easy, comfortable, accustomed. [➡KNOWLEDGE AND WISDOM; 559] *Opposite:* unfamiliar.

used up *adj* [➡ABSENT AND UNAVAILABLE; 7]

useful 1 *adj* **practical**, helpful, serviceable, of use, constructive, positive, handy, nifty (*informal*), effective, informative, functional. [➡USEFULNESS; 200] *Opposite:* useless. 2 *adj* **convenient**, valuable, beneficial, advantageous, expedient, suitable, worthwhile. [➡GOOD, WELL, BETTER; 184] *Opposite:* disadvantageous.

usefulness 1 *n* **practicality**, helpfulness, worth, utility, convenience, expediency, efficacy, effectiveness, niftiness (*informal*), handiness. [➡USEFULNESS; 200] *Opposite:* uselessness. 2 *n* **valuableness**, convenience, advantageousness, expediency, suitability, worthwhileness. [➡GOOD, WELL, BETTER; 184]

useless 1 *adj* **unusable**, impractical, unserviceable, inoperable, unworkable, inadequate, of no use, hopeless. [➡REDUNDANT AND USELESS; 241] *Opposite:* useful. 2 *adj* **unsuccessful**, futile, ineffectual, unavailing, worthless, ineffective. [➡UNSUCCESSFUL AND UNPROMISING; 76] *Opposite:* successful. 3 *adj* (*informal*) **inept**, hopeless, pathetic (*informal*), incompetent, inefficient, ineffectual, ineffective. [➡UNSKILLED; 530] *Opposite:* effective.

uselessness 1 *n* **impracticality**, unusableness, unserviceableness, inoperability, unworkability, inadequacy, hopelessness. [➡REDUNDANT AND USELESS; 241] *Opposite:* usefulness. 2 *n* **unsuccessfulness**, pointlessness, futility, ineffectualness, ineffectiveness, worthlessness. [➡UNSUCCESSFUL AND UNPROMISING; 76] *Opposite:* successfulness. 3 *n* (*informal*) **ineptness**, hopelessness, pointlessness, futility, ineffectiveness, incompetence, inefficiency, ineffectualness. [➡UNSKILLED; 530] *Opposite:* effectiveness.

user *n* **operator**, worker, employer, manipulator, handler, manager. [➡BOSSES AND MANAGEMENT; 965]

user-friendliness *n* **accessibility**, manageability, easiness, handiness, manipulability, convenience, availability. [➡USEFULNESS; 200] *Opposite:* inaccessibility.

user-friendly *adj* **accessible**, comprehensible, intelligible, manipulable, manageable, easy. [➡USEFULNESS; 200] *Opposite:* inaccessible.

use up *v* **expend**, consume, exhaust, wear out, deplete, exploit, go through, get through. [➡USE UP AND WASTE; 475] *Opposite:* conserve.

usher 1 *n* **attendant**, escort, guide, leader, conductor, marshal, helper. [➡BOSSES AND MANAGEMENT; 965] 2 *v* **escort**, conduct, guide, steer, pilot, help, lead, accompany, marshal, shepherd. [➡ACCOMPANY AND FOLLOW; 338]

usher in *v* **herald**, introduce, lead to, announce, signal, bring in, open up, inaugurate, launch. [➡CAUSE TO HAPPEN; 31] *Opposite:* see out.

usual 1 *adj* **normal**, typical, common, standard, natural, traditional. [➡ORDINARINESS; 245] *Opposite:* exceptional. 2 *adj* **habitual**, routine, everyday, familiar, predictable, regular, customary, wonted (*formal*). [➡ORDINARINESS; 245] *Opposite:* irregular.

Compare and Contrast: ***usual, customary, habitual, routine, wonted***

CORE MEANING: OFTEN DONE, USED, BOUGHT OR CONSUMED

usual normal, common, or typical; ***customary*** conforming to regular or typical practice; ***habitual*** done so often or repeatedly that the behaviour or practice has become ingrained; ***routine*** normal, regular, and not unusual in any way, even predictable, repetitive, and monotonous; ***wonted*** (*formal*) usual or typical.

usually *adv* **normally**, typically, customarily, generally, by and large, commonly, habitually, ordinarily, as a rule, frequently, mostly, regularly. [➡ USUALLY; 108] *Opposite:* exceptionally.

usurer *n* [➡ CRIMINALS; 821]

usurious *adj* [➡ ILLEGAL; 816]

usurp *v* **seize**, appropriate, take over, arrogate (*formal*), assume, commandeer, grab, take. [➡ TAKE SOMETHING AWAY; 426] *Opposite:* surrender.

usury *n* **moneylending**, lending, loaning, interest, overcharging, extortion, daylight robbery (*informal*), highway robbery (*US informal*). [➡ CRIMES; 817]

utensil *n* **tool**, instrument, implement, appliance, device, gadget. [➡ DEVICES; 1114]

utensil

◆ *types of utensil*
beater, blender, bottle opener, can opener, corkscrew, drainer, food processor, grater, grinder, juice extractor, juicer, lemon squeezer, liquidizer, mill, mincer, mixer, mortar, nutcracker, opener, peeler, pestle, reamer (*US*), sieve, soup ladle, spatula, strainer, tin-opener, whisk

utilitarian *adj* **practical**, useful, serviceable, no-frills (*informal*), functional, down-to-earth, effective. [➡ USEFULNESS; 200] *Opposite:* useless.

utility 1 *n* **usefulness**, practicality, efficiency, handiness, niftiness (*informal*), helpfulness, efficacy, effectiveness, functionality. [➡ USEFULNESS; 200] *Opposite:* uselessness. 2 *n* **convenience**, service, benefit, worth, advantage, value. [➡ SOURCE OF HAPPINESS, PLEASURE, OR IMPROVEMENT; 210] *Opposite:* worthlessness.

utility room *type of* **room in the home.** [➡ TYPES OF ROOM; 1096]

utilization *n* **use**, application, employment, deployment, operation, consumption, exploitation. [➡ USE; 468]

utilize *v* **use**, apply, employ, operate, develop, exploit, consume, make use of, make the most of. [➡ USE; 468] *Opposite:* forgo.

See Compare and Contrast at **use.**

utmost 1 *adj* **greatest**, highest, extreme, chief, supreme, maximum, paramount, ultimate. [➡ SUPERIORITY; 153] *Opposite:* least. 2 *adj* **farthest**, extreme, most distant, farthermost, remotest, outside, uttermost. [➡ DISTANCE; 161]

utopia *n* **ideal**, paradise, never-never land, heaven, Shangri-la, dreamland, seventh heaven. [➡ NON-EXISTENT PLACE; 1065]

utopian 1 *adj* **ideal**, perfect, ultimate, best, model, supreme. [➡ ADMIRABLE AND COMMENDABLE; 186] 2 *adj* **idealistic**, naive, impracticable, impractical, unworkable, unrealistic, quixotic, romantic. [➡ PHILOSOPHIES AND BELIEFS; 781] *Opposite:* pragmatic. 3 *n* **idealist**, romantic, visionary, dreamer, purist, Don Quixote, reformer. [➡ PHILOSOPHICAL AND POLITICAL THINKERS; 782] *Opposite:* pragmatist.

utter 1 *v* **say**, pronounce, express, state, voice, speak, articulate, emit. [➡ UTTER AND PRONOUNCE; 609] 2 *adj* **absolute**, total, complete, sheer, downright, unreserved, unqualified, thorough, out-and-out. [➡ ABSOLUTE AND ABSOLUTELY; 131] *Opposite:* partial.

utterance 1 *n* **word**, sound, note, noise, exclamation. [➡ THE SPOKEN WORD; 672] *Opposite:* silence. 2 *n* **statement**, speech, remark, declaration, announcement, communication, thesis, expression. [➡ COMMUNICATION; 603]

U-turn 1 *n* **turn**, rotation, revolution, about-turn, volte-face, about-face (*US*). [➡ CHANGE DIRECTION OF MOTION; 345] 2 *n* **change**, reversal, climb-down, volte face, about-turn, about-face (*US*). [➡ DECISIVE MOMENTS; 44]

uvula *part of* **mouth.** [➡ THE MOUTH; 703]

vacancy *n* **job**, post, situation (*formal*), position, opening, opportunity. [➡JOB; 833]

vacant 1 *adj* **empty**, available, unoccupied, not in use, unfilled, untaken, void, unused, free, clear. [➡PRESENT AND AVAILABLE; 11] *Opposite:* occupied. 2 *adj* **blank**, empty, expressionless, indifferent, vacuous, inane, uncomprehending. [➡NEUTRALITY AND INDIFFERENCE; 554] *Opposite:* alert.

Compare and Contrast: ***vacant, unoccupied, empty, void***

CORE MEANING: LACKING CONTENTS OR OCCUPANTS

vacant without occupants or contents, often temporarily; ***unoccupied*** not lived in by anybody, or currently without occupants; ***empty*** not containing or holding anything, or without occupants; ***void*** having no contents, or having no incumbent, occupant, or holder.

vacantly *adv* **blankly**, emptily, expressionlessly, vacuously, inanely, indifferently. [➡NEUTRALITY AND INDIFFERENCE; 554] *Opposite:* alertly.

vacate 1 *v* **empty**, evacuate, clear out, free, divest, eject, remove. [➡EMPTY AND UNLOAD; 408] *Opposite:* fill. 2 *v* **leave**, relinquish, check out, give up, depart, quit, evacuate. [➡ABSENT ONESELF; 8] *Opposite:* occupy.

vacation *n* **holiday**, break, trip, rest, retreat, leave, escape. [➡PERIOD OF REST; 91]

vacationer (*US*) *n* **holidaymaker**, tripper (*informal*), traveller, vacationist (*US*). [➡TRAVEL: TRAVELLERS AND WALKERS; 320]

vacation industry (*US*) *n* [➡TRAVEL: SIGHT-SEEING AND TOURISM; 322]

vacationland (*US*) *n* [➡TRAVEL: SIGHT-SEEING AND TOURISM; 322]

vaccinate *v* **inoculate**, immunize, protect, jab (*informal*). [➡FALL ILL, TREAT, AND RECOVER; 729] *Opposite:* expose.

vaccination *n* **inoculation**, injection, jab (*informal*), immunization, shot (*informal*). [➡HEALING; 731]

vaccine *n* **inoculation**, injection, serum, preparation, shot (*informal*). [➡REMEDIES, TREATMENTS AND OPERATIONS; 732]

vacillate *v* **waver**, hesitate, chop and change, dither, think twice, equivocate, sit on the fence, shilly-shally. [➡HESITATE; 273] *Opposite:* decide.

See Compare and Contrast at **hesitate**.

vacillating *adj* **irresolute**, indecisive, hesitant, dithering, fickle, wavering, equivocal, ambivalent, in two minds. [➡UNCERTAINTY; 560] *Opposite:* resolute.

vacillation *n* **indecisiveness**, irresoluteness, indecision, irresolution, hesitancy, uncertainty, equivocation, ambivalence. [➡UNCERTAINTY; 560] *Opposite:* resolution.

vacuity (*formal*) *n* **emptiness**, space, void, nothingness, vacuum, blankness, vacantness. [➡HOLES, GAPS, AND FORKS; 1251]

vacuous 1 *adj* **empty**, blank, vacant, void, hollow, unfilled. [➡EMPTY; 1237] *Opposite:* full. 2 *adj* **stupid**, unintelligent, gormless (*informal*), inane, vacant. [➡NEGATIVE INTELLECTUAL CHARACTERISTICS; 526] *Opposite:* bright.

vacuously *adv* **stupidly**, unintelligently, blankly, gormlessly (*informal*), inanely, dimly, vacantly. [➡NEGATIVE INTELLECTUAL CHARACTERISTICS; 526] *Opposite:* brightly.

vacuousness *n* [➡NEGATIVE INTELLECTUAL CHARACTERISTICS; 526]

vacuum *n* **void**, space, emptiness, nothingness, blankness, vacuity (*formal*). [➡HOLES, GAPS, AND FORKS; 1251]

vade mecum *n* [➡TRAVEL: SIGHT-SEEING AND TOURISM; 322]

vagabond *n* **vagrant**, tramp, beggar, drifter, traveller, wanderer, gypsy, nomad, hobo. [➡POOR PEOPLE; 896] *Opposite:* resident.

vagaries *n* [➡EVENTS AND OCCURRENCES; 35]

vagary *n* **whim**, fancy, notion, mood, quirk, whimsy, caprice. [➡CHANCE EVENT; 36] *Opposite:* choice.

vagrancy *n* **homelessness**, penury, destitution, rootlessness, begging, pennilessness, panhandling. [➡POVERTY AND POOR; 892] *Opposite:* residence.

vagrant 1 *n* **vagabond**, tramp, beggar, drifter, hobo, street person, wanderer, nomad. [➡POOR PEOPLE; 896] *Opposite:* resident. 2 *adj* **nomadic**, itinerant, wandering, roaming, roving, travelling. [➡NOMADIC AND ROOTLESS LIFESTYLES; 884] *Opposite:* settled.

vague 1 *adj* **unclear**, imprecise, indefinite, ambiguous, equivocal, nebulous, elusive, inexplicit, indefinable. [➡VAGUENESS; 244] *Opposite:* definite. 2 *adj* **indistinct**, unclear, indistinguishable, hazy, fuzzy, formless, blurred. [➡VAGUENESS; 244] *Opposite:* clear. 3 *adj* **absent-minded**, abstracted, distracted, distant, unclear, dreamy, pensive, scatterbrained. [➡NEGATIVE INTELLECTUAL CHARACTERISTICS; 526] *Opposite:* alert.

vaguely 1 *adv* **unclearly**, imprecisely, indefinitely, ambiguously, nebulously, elusively, indefinably, loosely. [➡VAGUENESS; 244] *Opposite:* definitely. 2 *adv* **indistinctly**, unclearly, dimly, hazily, fuzzily, formlessly, imprecisely. [➡VAGUENESS; 244] *Opposite:* clearly.

vagueness 1 *n* **nebulousness**, imprecision, indistinctness, ambiguity, elusiveness. [➡VAGUENESS; 244] *Opposite:* precision. 2 *n* **abstraction**, absent-mindedness, pensiveness, dreaminess. [➡NEGATIVE INTELLECTUAL CHARACTERISTICS; 526] *Opposite:* attentiveness. 3 *n* **haziness**, fuzziness, formlessness, imprecision, blurredness, indistinctness. [➡VAGUENESS; 244] *Opposite:* clarity.

vain 1 *adj* **proud**, conceited, narcissistic, vainglorious, arrogant, self-important, bigheaded (*informal*). [➡POMPOUS, LOUD, AND OVER-CONFIDENT; 636] *Opposite:* humble. 2 *adj* **otiose**, unsuccessful, hopeless, unproductive, futile, useless, abortive, worthless, ineffective. [➡UNSUCCESSFUL AND UNPROMISING; 76] *Opposite:* successful. 3 *adj* **empty**, hollow, idle, pointless, futile. [➡REDUNDANT AND USELESS; 241] *Opposite:* reliable.

Compare and Contrast: ***vain, empty, hollow, idle***

CORE MEANING: WITHOUT VALUE OR WORTH

vain failing to have or unlikely to have the intended or desired result; ***empty*** lacking substance, sincerity or truthfulness; ***hollow*** not sincere or genuine; ***idle*** unlikely to be carried out or impossible to put into effect.

vainglorious (*literary*) *adj* **proud**, boastful, self-important, conceited, puffed up, pompous, bigheaded (*informal*), arrogant. [➡POMPOUS, LOUD, AND OVER-CONFIDENT; 636]

vainly *adv* **unsuccessfully**, ineffectively, in vain, unproductively, hopelessly, futilely, uselessly, worthlessly. [➡UNSUCCESSFUL AND UNPROMISING; 76] *Opposite:* successfully.

valance *n* [➡SOFT FURNISHINGS, LINEN, AND DRAPERY; 860]

vale (*literary*) *n* **valley**, dale, gorge, dell (*literary*). [➡GEOLOGICAL FEATURES; 1056] *Opposite:* hill.

valediction (*formal*) *n* **farewell**, goodbye, sendoff, adieu, leave-taking (*literary*). [➡GREETINGS, FAREWELLS, AND SALUTATIONS; 660]

valedictory (*formal*) 1 *n* **farewell**, leave-taking (*literary*), goodbye, parting. [➡END; 54] *Opposite:* welcome. 2 *adj* **parting**, farewell, goodbye, final, last. [➡AFTER, LAST, AND FOLLOWING; 166] *Opposite:* welcoming.

valentine *n* [➡SEXUAL AND ROMANTIC RELATIONSHIPS; 964]

valet 1 *v* **clean**, clean out, vacuum, tidy, polish. [➡CLEAN AND POLISH; 404] 2 *type of* **servant**. [➡DOMESTIC AND KITCHEN WORKERS; 850]

valetudinarian 1 *n* **convalescent**, patient, invalid, valetudinary. [➡UNFIT AND WEAK; 740] 2 *n* **hypochondriac**, neurotic (*informal*), valetudinary. [➡GRUMPY AND NEGATIVE PEOPLE; 953] 3 *adj* **sickly**, feeble, unhealthy, frail, poorly (*informal*), weak, valetudinary. [➡UNFIT AND WEAK; 740] *Opposite:* healthy.

valiant *adj* **brave**, courageous, heroic, fearless, noble, gallant (*literary*), intrepid (*literary or humorous*), bold. [➡COURAGE; 499] *Opposite:* cowardly.

valiantness *n* [➡COURAGE; 499]

valid 1 *adj* **reasonable**, sound, rational, justifiable, legitimate, well-founded, defensible, bona fide. [➡TRUE AND REAL; 172] *Opposite:* unjustifiable. 2 *adj* **lawful**, legal, binding, effective, in force. [➡LEGAL; 815] *Opposite:* illegal. 3 *adj* **usable**, acceptable, authorized, endorsed, official, unexpired. [➡USEFULNESS; 200] *Opposite:* unusable. 4 *adj* **convincing**, compelling, sound, persuasive, rational, cogent, logical. [➡ACCEPTABLE AND PASSABLE; 220] *Opposite:* unconvincing.

Compare and Contrast: ***valid, cogent, convincing, reasonable, sound***

CORE MEANING: BEING WORTHY OF ACCEPTANCE OR CREDENCE

valid having a solid foundation or justification; ***cogent*** forceful and convincing to the intellect and reason; ***convincing*** likely to overcome doubts and win the support of those who hear it; ***reasonable*** acceptable and according to common sense; ***sound*** based on good sense and acceptable reasoning and worthy of approval.

validate 1 *v* **prove**, substantiate, confirm, authenticate, corroborate, bear out, endorse, justify, support. [➡PERMIT AND ALLOW; 670] *Opposite:* disprove. 2 *v* **authorize**, certify, endorse, ratify, legalize. [➡TRIAL, PUNISHMENT, AND LEGAL OUTCOMES; 819] *Opposite:* invalidate.

validation 1 *n* **authentication**, proof, endorsement, confirmation, corroboration, justification, substantiation, support. [➡EVIDENCE AND PROOF; 69] 2 *n* **authorization**, endorsement, ratification, certification, legalization. [➡LEGAL; 815] *Opposite:* invalidation.

validity 1 *n* **legality**, authority, legitimacy, authenticity, lawfulness. [➡TRUE AND REAL; 172] 2 *n* **cogency** (*formal*), rationality, legitimacy, soundness, strength, force, weight, power, authority. [➡USEFULNESS; 200] *Opposite:* weakness.

valise *type of* **baggage**. [➡CONTAINERS, RECEPTACLES, AND PACKAGING; 1244]

valley *n* **vale** (*literary*), gorge, dale, dell (*literary*), basin. [➡GEOLOGICAL FEATURES; 1056] *Opposite:* hill.

valorous *adj* **noble**, intrepid (*literary or humorous*), brave, courageous, heroic, gallant (*literary*), fearless, bold, valiant, lionhearted, plucky. [➡COURAGE; 499] *Opposite:* cowardly.

valour *n* **boldness**, courage, bravery, heroism, fearlessness, gallantry, pluck, spirit. [➡COURAGE; 499] *Opposite:* cowardice.

valuable 1 *adj* **costly**, expensive, priceless, dear, important, precious. [➡EXPENSIVE AND LUXURIOUS; 219] *Opposite:* inexpensive. 2 *adj* **invaluable**, valued, helpful, important, useful, constructive, beneficial, indispensable, effective, worthwhile, advantageous. [➡USEFULNESS; 200] *Opposite:* worthless. 3 *adj* **valued**, appreciated, respected, treasured, dear, cherished, prized, loved, esteemed. [➡POPULAR AND WANTED; 221]

valuate *v* [➡ASSESS QUALITY; 756]

valuation *n* **estimate**, assessment, evaluation, appraisal, survey, judgment, estimation. [➡SCORES AND EVALUATIONS; 599]

value 1 *n* **worth**, price, cost, rate, charge. [➡EXPENDITURE; 424] 2 *n* **benefit**, importance, worth, significance, usefulness, use, consequence (*formal*), merit, help, profit. [➡USEFULNESS; 200] *Opposite:* insignificance. 3 *v* **rate**, assess, estimate, evaluate, appraise, price, survey. [➡ASSESS QUALITY; 756] 4 *v* **prize**, appreciate, respect, esteem, treasure, cherish, set store by, regard highly. [➡LIKE, LOVE, VALUE AND ENJOY; 579] *Opposite:* scorn.

valued *adj* **appreciated**, respected, esteemed, treasured, cherished, dear, loved, prized. [➡ USEFULNESS; 200]

valueless *adj* **inconsequential**, worthless, insignificant, paltry, miserable, useless. [➡ REDUNDANT AND USELESS; 241] *Opposite:* valuable.

values *n* **principles**, standards, morals, ethics, ideals, tenets (*formal*), beliefs. [➡ MORALLY GOOD; 775]

valve 1 *n* **regulator**, controller, stopcock, tap, spigot, faucet (*US*). [➡ PARTS OF MACHINES AND TOOLS; 1117] 2 *part of* **engine**. [➡ PARTS OF AN ENGINE; 1143]

vamoose (*US slang*) *v* [➡ ABSENT ONESELF; 8]

vampire 1 *n* **parasite**, freeloader (*informal*), sponger (*informal*), scrounger (*informal*), hanger-on, predator, sponge. [➡ LAZY OR UNSUCCESSFUL PEOPLE; 948] 2 *type of* **mythological creature**. [➡ MYTHICAL CREATURES; 1036]

vampire bat *type of* **flying mammal**. [➡ FLYING MAMMAL; 984]

vamp up *v* **repair**, rework, revamp, do up, modernize, refurbish, renovate. [➡ IMPROVE APPEARANCE; 380]

van 1 *type of* **commercial or industrial vehicle**. [➡ VEHICLES; 1144] 2 *n* **forefront**, front, lead, head, vanguard, pole position, cutting edge. [➡ MOST IMPORTANT THING; 198]

vandal *n* **miscreant** (*literary*), criminal, trespasser, hooligan (*informal*), delinquent, thug, ruffian (*dated*). [➡ VILLAINS AND THUGS; 947]

vandalism *n* **damage**, destruction, defacement, wreckage, sabotage, harm. [➡ BAD BEHAVIOUR OR ACTION; 255]

vandalize *v* **destroy**, damage, deface, wreck, break, smash up, sabotage, spoil. [➡ WORSEN APPEARANCE; 383]

vane *n* **blade**, slat, fin, plate, strip, sheet. [➡ EXTREMITIES OF PHYSICAL OBJECTS; 1249]

vang *n* [➡ FASTENERS, LINKS, AND NETWORKS; 1246]

vanguard 1 *n* **front line**, front, advance guard. [➡ THE ARMED FORCES; 827] *Opposite:* rearguard. 2 *n* **forefront**, front, lead, head, cutting edge, van, precursor, forerunner. [➡ MOST IMPORTANT THING; 198]

vanilla (*slang*) *adj* **plain**, ordinary, boring, unexciting, bland, insipid, dull. [➡ BORING AND UNINTERESTING; 235] *Opposite:* interesting.

vanish 1 *v* **disappear**, evaporate, go missing, fade away, peter out, go. [➡ DISAPPEAR; 4] *Opposite:* appear. 2 *v* **become extinct**, die out, disappear, cease to exist, be exterminated, be wiped out (*slang*). [➡ CEASE TO EXIST; 22]

vanished *adj* **disappeared**, missing, died out, wiped out (*informal*), gone, extinct. [➡ ABSENT AND UNAVAILABLE; 7] *Opposite:* present.

vanity 1 *n* **pride**, narcissism, self-importance, conceit, arrogance, egotism, airs, bigheadedness (*informal*). [➡ MORALLY BAD; 776] *Opposite:* humility. 2 *n* **futility**, emptiness, uselessness, pointlessness, worthlessness, ineffectuality, insignificance, ineffectiveness, hollowness, unreality. [➡ REDUNDANT AND USELESS; 241] *Opposite:* value. 3 (*US*) *type of* **plumbing fittings**. [➡ FITTINGS; 859]

vanity case *type of* **baggage**. [➡ CONTAINERS, RECEPTACLES, AND PACKAGING; 1244]

vanity table (*US*) *type of* **table**. [➡ FURNITURE; 858]

vanity unit *type of* **plumbing fittings**. [➡ FITTINGS; 859]

vanquish *v* **defeat**, conquer, subjugate, crush, annihilate (*informal*), subdue, overcome, rout, overpower, triumph over. [➡ BEAT AND DEFEAT; 80] *Opposite:* surrender.

See Compare and Contrast at **defeat**.

vanquished *adj* [➡ BEATEN AND DEFEATED; 78]

vantage point 1 *n* **viewpoint**, viewing platform, belvedere, lookout, crow's nest. [➡ TOWERS; 1098] 2 *n* **standpoint**, viewpoint, angle, point of view, perspective, position. [➡ POINT OF VIEW; 768]

vapid 1 *adj* **lifeless**, uninteresting, unexciting, vacuous, tame, uninspiring, flat, dull. [➡ BORING AND UNINTERESTING; 235] *Opposite:* lively. 2 *adj* **flavourless**, insipid, tasteless, weak, tame, bland, watery. [➡ TASTE; 704] *Opposite:* tasty.

vapidity *n* [➡ ORDINARINESS; 245]

vapidness *n* [➡ ORDINARINESS; 245]

vaporize 1 *v* **turn to vapour**, evaporate, boil away, boil, heat. [➡ FROTH AND EFFERVESCE; 390] *Opposite:* condense. 2 *v* **vanish**, disappear, evaporate, fade away, go away, dispel, drive away. [➡ DISAPPEAR; 4] 3 *v* **destroy**, annihilate, burn, incinerate, burn away, decimate, obliterate. [➡ KILL; 923] *Opposite:* preserve.

vaporizer *n* **nebulizer**, atomizer, aerosol, spray, inhaler, spray can, steamer. [➡ CONTAINERS, RECEPTACLES, AND PACKAGING; 1244]

vaporous 1 *adj* **gaseous**, smoky, misty, steamy, foggy, cloudy, clouded, hazy, murky. [➡ FLUID AND NON-SOLID; 1212] 2 *adj* **volatile**, unstable, unpredictable, explosive, flammable. [➡ FIRE, FLAMMABILITY, AND BURNING; 1164] *Opposite:* stable. 3 *adj* **insubstantial**, ephemeral, impermanent, evanescent, nebulous, wraithlike, ethereal, unsubstantial. [➡ FINITENESS, VARIABILITY, AND TRANSIENCE; 96] *Opposite:* solid. 4 *adj* **fanciful**, ridiculous, implausible, fantastic, unreal, insubstantial. [➡ BIZARRE AND PECULIAR; 258] *Opposite:* real. 5 *adj* **murky**, hazy, cloudy, obscure, dim, clouded. [➡ VAGUENESS; 244] *Opposite:* clear.

vapour 1 *n* **gas**, air, ether. [➡ GASES; 1274] 2 *n* **clouds**, fumes, smoke, water vapour, miasma, mist, steam, fog, haze. [➡ GASES; 1274] 3 *n* **aerosol**, spray, mist. [➡ GASES; 1274]

variability 1 *n* **erraticism**, inconsistency, capriciousness, changeability, unpredictability. [➡ UNCERTAIN; 176] *Opposite:* predictability. 2 *n* **unevenness**, patchiness, irregularity, inconsistency. [➡ FINITENESS, VARIABILITY, AND TRANSIENCE; 96] *Opposite:* consistency. 3 *n* **flexibility**, adaptability, alterability, fickleness, inconstancy, mutability. [➡ FINITENESS, VARIABILITY, AND TRANSIENCE; 96] *Opposite:* fixedness.

variable 1 *adj* **varying**, changing, fluctuating, changeable, erratic, unpredictable, capricious, wavering. [➡ UNCERTAIN; 176] *Opposite:* constant. 2 *adj* **uneven**, patchy, up-and-down, irregular, inconsistent. [➡ FINITENESS, VARIABILITY, AND TRANSIENCE; 96] *Opposite:* consistent. 3 *adj* **mutable**, adjustable, flexible, capricious, inconstant, fickle, adaptable, movable, alterable. [➡FINITENESS, VARIABILITY, AND TRANSIENCE; 96] *Opposite:* fixed.

variableness *n* [➡FINITENESS, VARIABILITY, AND TRANSIENCE; 96]

variance 1 *n* **alteration**, modification, adjustment, change. [➡CHANGE; 373] 2 *n* **divergence**, disparity, difference, discrepancy, inconsistency, variation. [➡DIFFERENCE; 150] *Opposite:* consistency. 3 *n* **conflict**, clash, dissent, dispute, difference of opinion, disagreement. [➡DISHARMONY; 157] *Opposite:* agreement.

variant 1 *adj* **irregular**, different, optional, modified, abnormal, alternative. [➡DIFFERENCE; 150] 2 *n* **variation**, alternative, deviation, modification, departure, option, alternate (*US*). [➡DIFFERENCE; 150]

variation 1 *n* **variant**, adaptation, reworking, departure, alteration, deviation, modification, change. [➡CHANGE; 373] 2 *n* **difference**, disparity, dissimilarity, distinction, discrepancy, deviation. [➡DIFFERENCE; 150] *Opposite:* similarity.

varicoloured *adj* [➡DESCRIBING COLOURS; 1225]

varied *adj* **heterogeneous**, diverse, wide-ranging, mixed, different, various, assorted, miscellaneous, sundry. [➡DIFFERENCE; 150] *Opposite:* homogeneous.

variegated *adj* **spotted**, pied, dappled, speckled, flecked, patchy, mottled, multicoloured. [➡DESCRIBING PATTERNS; 1226] *Opposite:* uniform.

variety 1 *n* **diversity**, change, variability, variation. [➡CHANGE; 373] 2 *n* **type**, kind, form, sort, category, strain, class, make, brand. [➡VARIETY, TYPE, KIND; 146] 3 *n* **collection**, diversity, assortment, selection, multiplicity, range, mixture, array. [➡COLLECTIONS AND MIXTURES OF THINGS; 1243]

variety meats (*US*) *n* [➡TYPES AND CUTS OF MEAT; 1176]

variety show *n* **show**, revue, cabaret, entertainment, performance, spectacular, floor show. [➡THE PERFORMING ARTS; 904]

various 1 *adj* **numerous**, many, a number of, several, countless, innumerable. [➡MANY, MUCH, LARGE AMOUNT; 117] *Opposite:* few. 2 *adj* **a variety of**, a range of, an assortment of, a mixture of, different, a choice of, diverse, assorted. [➡DIFFERENCE; 150] *Opposite:* same.

varnish 1 *n* **lacquer**, paint, finish, glaze, polish, shiny surface, patina, gloss, resin. [➡COVERS AND COATINGS; 1245] 2 *v* **paint**, glaze, finish, polish, lacquer, stain. [➡DECORATE, ADORN, AND APPLY COATINGS; 406]

vary 1 *v* **change**, alter, fluctuate, adjust, adapt, modify. [➡CHANGE; 373] *Opposite:* standardize. 2 *v* **diverge**, differ, be different, contrast, fluctuate, disagree. [➡DIFFERENCE; 150] *Opposite:* conform.

See Compare and Contrast at **change**.

varying *adj* [➡DIFFERENCE; 150]

vascular *adj* [➡THE BLOOD AND CIRCULATION; 718]

vase *n* **rose bowl**, urn, jug, pot, container, bud vase. [➡CONTAINERS, RECEPTACLES, AND PACKAGING; 1244]

vasectomize *v* [➡STERILIZE; 727]

vasectomy *n* [➡STERILIZE; 727]

vassal *n* [➡SUBORDINATES AND ASSISTANTS; 966]

vast *adj* **massive**, huge, enormous, gigantic, immense, cosmic, infinite, titanic, immeasurable, measureless (*literary*), incalculable, limitless. [➡LARGE; 1192] *Opposite:* small.

vastly *adv* **massively** (*informal*), much, greatly, infinitely, immensely, immeasurably, hugely, enormously, very, extremely. [➡TO A GREAT EXTENT; 130] *Opposite:* slightly.

vastness *n* **massiveness**, incalculability, limitlessness, immensity, hugeness, enormity. [➡LARGE; 1192]

vat *n* **container**, cask, barrel, tank, drum, tub, bin, silo. [➡CONTAINERS, RECEPTACLES, AND PACKAGING; 1244]

VAT *n* [➡TAX AND TAXATION; 802]

vatic *adj* [➡THE SUPERNATURAL; 788]

vaudeville (*US*) *n* **show**, entertainment, variety show, music hall, revue, floor show, cabaret, burlesque (*US*). [➡THE PERFORMING ARTS; 904]

vault 1 *n* **arch**, dome, cupola. [➡ROOFS, ROOF PARTS, AND CEILINGS; 1102] 2 *n* **strongroom**, treasury, treasure house. [➡TYPES OF ROOM; 1096] 3 *n* **crypt**, cellar, undercroft, burial chamber, tomb, catacomb, mausoleum, ossuary (*formal*). [➡PARTS OF RELIGIOUS BUILDINGS; 1085] 4 *v* **jump**, leap, spring, hurdle, bound. [➡BOUNCE, UNDULATE, AND VIBRATE; 309]

vaulted *adj* **curved**, domed, arched. [➡ROUNDED SHAPE; 1217]

vaunt *v* **puff**, boast, brag, show off, hype, flaunt, exult in, promote, push, make much of, crow. [➡BOAST; 617] *Opposite:* play down.

vaunted *adj* **overhyped** (*informal*), hyped, praised, promoted, advertised, flaunted, made much of, publicized. [➡POPULAR AND WANTED; 221] *Opposite:* downplayed.

VCR (*US*) *type of* **video equipment**. [➡PHOTOGRAPHY AND PHOTOGRAPHIC EQUIPMENT; 1121]

VDT *type of* **hardware**. [➡COMPUTERS AND COMPUTING; 1126]

VDU *type of* **hardware**. [➡COMPUTERS AND COMPUTING; 1126]

veal *type of* **meat**. [➡TYPES AND CUTS OF MEAT; 1176]

vector *n* **course**, trajectory, path, flight path, route, direction. [➡DIRECTION OF MOTION; 346]

veer *v* **change course**, turn, swing, swerve, bend, change direction, deviate, go around. [➡CHANGE DIRECTION OF MOTION; 345]

vegan *n* **fruitarian**, vegetarian, veggie (*informal*). [➡EATERS, GOURMETS, AND DIETARY CHOICES; 715]

vegetable *adj* **plant**, herbal, vegetal. [➡VEGETATION; 1025]

vegetable

◆ *types of vegetable*
artichoke, asparagus, aubergine, brassica, broccoli, Brussels sprout, cabbage, cauliflower, collard greens (*US*), courgette, eggplant (*US*), fennel, garlic, greens, kale, leek, legume, marrow, marrow squash (*US*), okra, onion, pumpkin, spinach, squash, sweetcorn, Swiss chard, zucchini (*US*)

◆ *types of root vegetable*
beet, beetroot, carrot, cassava, mangel-wurzel, new potato, parsnip, potato, rutabaga, spud (*informal*), sugar beet, swede, sweet potato, tater (*regional*), turnip, yam

vegetable garden *n* [➡GARDENS; 1073]

vegetable oil *type of* **cooking fat and oil.** [➡FATS AND OILS; 1172]

vegetable patch *n* [➡GARDENS; 1073]

vegetarian 1 *n* **fruitarian**, vegan, lactovegetarian, veggie (*informal*). [➡EATERS, GOURMETS, AND DIETARY CHOICES; 715] 2 *adj* **fruitarian**, vegan, lactovegetarian, veggie (*informal*), veg (*informal*). [➡EATERS, GOURMETS, AND DIETARY CHOICES; 715]

vegetate *v* **veg out** (*informal*), sit around, stagnate, twiddle your thumbs, kill time, loaf. [➡LACK OF ACTIVITY; 343]

vegetation *n* **plants**, plant life, flora, undergrowth, foliage, shrubbery. [➡VEGETATION; 1025]

veggie (*informal*) *n* **lactovegetarian**, fruitarian, vegetarian, vegan. [➡EATERS, GOURMETS, AND DIETARY CHOICES; 715]

veg out (*informal*) *v* [➡LACK OF ACTIVITY; 343]

vehemence *n* **forcefulness**, intensity, fervour, passion, violence, strength, vigour, enthusiasm. [➡ENERGY AND ENTHUSIASM; 497] *Opposite:* indifference.

vehement *adj* **fervent**, passionate, heated, violent, intense, vigorous. [➡ENTHUSIASTIC AND INQUISITIVE; 629] *Opposite:* apathetic.

vehemently *adv* **fervently**, fervidly, passionately, hotly, heatedly, strongly, violently, intensely, vigorously. [➡ELOQUENT, TALKATIVE AND LONG-WINDED; 633] *Opposite:* impassively.

vehicle *n* **medium**, means of expression, channel, means, mouthpiece, instrument, agent, conduit, tool, intermediary. [➡WAYS OF DOING THINGS; 295]

vehicle

◆ *types of commercial or industrial vehicle*
articulated lorry, black cab, breakdown lorry, bulldozer, cab, combine harvester, digger, dump truck (*US*), dumper truck, earthmover, hackney cab, hackney carriage, hearse, juggernaut, lorry, minicab, pick-up, removal van, roadroller, semitrailer (*US*), snowplough, steamroller, tanker, taxi, tow truck (*US*), tractor, transporter, truck, van, wrecker (*US*), yellow cab (*US*)

◆ *types of leisure vehicle*
bobsled (*US*), bobsleigh, camper, camper van, caravan, chair lift, dogsled, dune buggy, go-cart, land yacht, luge, mobile home, motor home, RV (*US*), sled (*US*), sledge, sleigh, snowmobile, SUV (*US*), toboggan

◆ *types of public service vehicle*
ambulance, bus, charabanc, coach, dustcart, fire engine, firetruck (*US*), garbage truck (*US*), minibus, panda car (*informal*), police car, prowl car (*US*), shuttle, squad car

◆ *types of military vehicle*
amphibian, armoured car, jeep, tank

◆ *types of external feature*
blinker, brake light, bumper, exhaust pipe, fog light, headlight, hubcap, indicator, license plate (*US*), luggage rack (*US*), mud flap, muffler (*US*), number plate, parking light (*US*), roof rack, side mirror (*US*), sidelight, silencer, splashguard (*US*), spoiler, stoplight (*US*), tail light, tyre, wheel, windscreen wiper, windshield wiper (*US*), wing mirror

◆ *parts of an external structure*
aerofoil, axle, bodywork, bonnet, boot, chassis, coachwork, fender (*US*), fin, grille, hood (*US*), hull, mud flap, mudguard, sunroof, tail light, tailgate, trunk (*US*), wheel, windscreen, windshield (*US*), wing

◆ *types of controls*
accelerator, brake, choke, clutch, gear lever, gearshift (*US*), horn, pedal, rev counter, speedometer, steering wheel, wheel

◆ *types of internal feature*
back seat, booster seat, cab, child seat, dashboard, driver's seat (*US*), driving seat, glove compartment, headrest, passenger seat, rearview mirror, seat belt

veil 1 *n* **mask**, blanket, shroud, covering, curtain, pall, cloak. [➡COVERS AND COATINGS; 1245] 2 *v* **cover**, conceal, hide, mask, cloak, shroud, envelop, obscure. [➡CAUSE TO DISAPPEAR; 6] *Opposite:* reveal. 3 *type of* **accessory.** [➡HABERDASHERY, MILLINERY, AND LINGERIE; 867]

veiled 1 *adj* **indirect**, oblique, obscure, covert, roundabout, implied, disguised. [➡SECRET AND UNKNOWN; 180] *Opposite:* overt. 2 *adj* **masked**, cloaked, shrouded, covered, hooded. [➡DRESS, WEAR, AND UNDRESS; 868] *Opposite:* uncovered.

vein 1 *n* **layer**, seam, lode, stratum, deposit. [➡COVERS AND COATINGS; 1245] 2 *n* **mood**, frame of mind, manner, strain, attitude, disposition, tone, hint, trace. [➡APPEARANCE AND ATMOSPHERE; 1236] 3 *n* **streak**, strip, stripe, line. [➡FEW, LITTLE, SMALL AMOUNT; 119] 4 *type of* **blood vessel.** [➡THE BLOOD AND CIRCULATION; 718]

veined *adj* **patterned**, marbled, lined, streaked. [➡DESCRIBING PATTERNS; 1226]

veld *n* **grassland**, savanna, prairie, plain. [➡DESERTS AND PLAINS; 1045]

veldt *see* **veld.**

velocity *n* **speed**, rate, rapidity, swiftness, pace, haste, quickness. [➡SPEED; 102]

velvet *type of* **fabric from plants.** [➡FABRICS; 1131]

velvetiness *n* [➡PHYSICAL TEXTURE; 1221]

velvety *adj* **soft**, smooth, silky, downy, furry. [➡PHYSICAL TEXTURE; 1221] *Opposite:* rough.

venal 1 *adj* **corruptible**, mercenary, bribable, bent, unprincipled. [➡MORALLY BAD; 776] *Opposite:* honest. 2 *adj* **corrupt**, degenerate, decadent, lawless, amoral, crooked (*informal*). [➡MORALLY BAD; 776] *Opposite:* aboveboard.

venality *n* [➡MORALLY BAD; 776]

vend *v* **sell**, trade, deal in, hawk, flog (*informal*), supply. [➡SELL; 442]

vendetta 1 *n* **feud**, blood feud, quarrel, dispute, grudge. [➡ARGUMENT; 47] 2 *n* **campaign**, crusade, war, battle, hate campaign. [➡BAD BEHAVIOUR OR ACTION; 255]

vending machine *n* **slot machine**, dispenser, coin-operated machine. [➡MACHINES AND MACHINE PARTS; 1115]

vendor *n* **seller**, retailer, dealer, supplier, merchant, hawker. [➡SELLER; 443]

veneer 1 *n* **covering**, facing, finish, surface, layer, coating. [➡COVERS AND COATINGS; 1245] 2 *n* **appearance**, semblance, pretence, guise, show, mask, façade. [➡FALSE AND UNREAL; 174] 3 *v* **cover**, finish, conceal, plate. [➡DECORATE, ADORN, AND APPLY COATINGS; 406]

venerable *adj* **respected**, august (*formal*), esteemed, honoured, revered, admired. [➡POPULAR AND WANTED; 221] *Opposite:* disreputable.

venerate *v* **revere**, worship, adore, idolize, esteem, honour, respect, look up to, admire. [➡LIKE, LOVE, VALUE AND ENJOY; 579] *Opposite:* disrespect.

venerated *adj* [➡POPULAR AND WANTED; 221]

veneration *n* **worship**, adoration, reverence, honour, respect, admiration, regard. [➡LOVE, RESPECT, AND GOODWILL; 550] *Opposite:* disdain.

See Compare and Contrast at **regard**.

venetian blind *n* [➡SOFT FURNISHINGS, LINEN, AND DRAPERY; 860]

Venetian glass *type of* **glass**. [➡GLASS; 1135]

vengeance *n* **revenge**, retribution, reprisal, retaliation, punishment. [➡VENGEANCE AND REVENGE; 686]

vengeful *adj* **vindictive**, implacable (*formal*), unforgiving, revengeful, resentful, rancorous. [➡IRRITATION AND ANGER; 542] *Opposite:* merciful.

venial *adj* **forgivable**, excusable, pardonable, understandable, minor, mild, allowable. [➡ACCEPTABLE AND PASSABLE; 220] *Opposite:* unforgivable.

venison *type of* **meat**. [➡TYPES AND CUTS OF MEAT; 1176]

venom 1 *n* **poison**, toxin, bane. [➡UNPLEASANT AND DIRTY SUBSTANCES; 1267] *Opposite:* antidote. 2 *n* **malice**, spite, rancour, spleen, acrimony, hatred, bitterness, virulence, vituperation, malevolence. [➡ANTAGONISM; 553] *Opposite:* affection.

venomous 1 *adj* **poisonous**, deadly, toxic, noxious, lethal. [➡DEADLY; 928] *Opposite:* harmless. 2 *adj* **malicious**, spiteful, virulent, bitter, rancorous, vituperative, malevolent, cruel, full of spleen, dripping venom, full of gall. [➡RUDE AND HOSTILE; 626]

venomously *adv* **spitefully**, maliciously, rancorously, malevolently, vituperatively, cruelly, bitterly. [➡RUDE AND HOSTILE; 626]

vent 1 *n* **opening**, outlet, aperture, escape, exhaust, chimney, flue, hole, gap. [➡HOLES, GAPS, AND FORKS; 1251] 2 *v* **express**, give vent to, find expression for, voice, expel, emit, utter, escape, declare. [➡INFORM AND ANNOUNCE; 612] *Opposite:* suppress.

ventilate 1 *v* **air**, aerate, air out, freshen. [➡CLEAN AND POLISH; 404] 2 *v* **publicize**, make public, make known, air, express, discuss, examine. [➡INFORM AND ANNOUNCE; 612]

ventilation *n* **air circulation**, airing, aeration. [➡HEATING, REFRIGERATION, AND VENTILATION; 1141]

ventilation system *n* [➡HEATING, REFRIGERATION, AND VENTILATION; 1141]

ventilator 1 *n* **fan**, vent, opening, flue, aperture, duct, air duct. [➡HEATING, REFRIGERATION, AND VENTILATION; 1141] 2 *n* **life support machine**, respirator, breathing apparatus, iron lung. [➡BREATHE AND NOT BREATHE; 717]

ventriloquist *type of* **entertainer**. [➡WORKERS IN ENTERTAINMENT AND MEDIA; 873]

venture 1 *n* **undertaking**, course, endeavour, project, mission, enterprise. [➡ACTIONS OR UNDERTAKINGS; 260] 2 *n* **business enterprise**, undertaking, scheme, project, endeavour, gamble, risk, speculation. [➡BUSINESS ENTERPRISES AND RELATED BODIES; 793] 3 *v* **hazard**, dare, undertake, brave, try, take on, risk, embark on. [➡ATTEMPT AN ACTION; 262] 4 *v* **offer**, put forward, volunteer, express, say, submit. [➡SUGGEST, HINT, AND COMMENT; 613] 5 *v* **presume**, dare, be so bold, take the liberty, have the audacity, have the nerve, have the cheek. [➡SUGGEST, HINT, AND COMMENT; 613]

venture capitalist *n* [➡PEOPLE INVOLVED IN FINANCE; 804]

venture forth *v* [➡ABSENT ONESELF; 8]

venturesome (*formal*) 1 *adj* **daring**, adventurous, enterprising, intrepid (*literary or humorous*), bold, brave, audacious. [➡COURAGE; 499] *Opposite:* cautious. 2 *adj* **hazardous**, chancy, dicey (*informal*), dangerous, risky, perilous. [➡DANGEROUS; 237] *Opposite:* safe.

venue *n* **site**, place, location, scene, setting, spot. [➡PLACE; 1064]

venule *type of* **blood vessel**. [➡THE BLOOD AND CIRCULATION; 718]

Venus *type of* **planet**. [➡CELESTIAL BODIES; 1060]

veracious *adj* **honest**, truthful, genuine, principled, dependable, ethical, reliable. [➡TRUE AND REAL; 172] *Opposite:* dishonest.

veracity 1 *n* **truth**, accuracy, reliability, genuineness, authenticity, legitimacy, exactness, validity. [➡TRUE AND REAL; 172] *Opposite:* falsity. 2 *n* **truthfulness**, honesty, integrity, uprightness, reliability, candour. [➡HONEST AND RELIABLE; 503] *Opposite:* dishonesty.

veranda 1 *n* **terrace**, balcony, loggia, gallery, portico, porch. [➡STAGES, PLATFORMS, AND RAISED AREAS; 1097] 2 *part of* **building**. [➡PARTS OF A BUILDING; 1094]

verb *type of* **word class**. [➡ASPECTS OF LANGUAGE; 683]

verbal *adj* **spoken**, oral, vocal, unwritten, voiced, speaking, uttered, stated. [➡THE SPOKEN WORD; 672] *Opposite:* unspoken.

Compare and Contrast: ***verbal, spoken, oral***

CORE MEANING: EXPRESSED IN WORDS

verbal using words, especially spoken words, rather than pictures or physical action; ***spoken*** expressed with the voice; ***oral*** expressed in spoken words rather than in writing.

verbal abuse *n* [➡INSULTS, ABUSE, AND SWEARING; 659]

verbal assault *n* [➡INSULTS, ABUSE, AND SWEARING; 659]

verbal communication *n* [➡COMMUNICATION; 603]

verbalization *n* **articulation**, expression, speech, voicing. [➡THE SPOKEN WORD; 672]

verbalize *v* **express**, articulate, voice, put into words, speak. [➡UTTER AND PRONOUNCE; 609]

verbatim 1 *adj* **exact**, word for word, precise, literal, word-perfect, strict, letter-perfect (*US*). [➡EXACT; 204] *Opposite:* imprecise. 2 *adv* **word for word**, exactly, precisely, to the letter, literally, accurately, faithfully. [➡EXACT; 204] *Opposite:* approximately.

verbiage *n* **verbosity**, waffle (*informal*), gobbledegook (*informal disapproving*), circumlocution, redundancy, pleonasm, nonsense. [➡MEANINGLESS SPEECH OR WRITING; 677]

verbose *adj* **wordy**, prolix, long-winded, talkative, bombastic, effusive, pompous, garrulous, pretentious, loquacious (*formal*), rambling. [➡INARTICULATE, RAMBLING, AND AWKWARD; 634] *Opposite:* taciturn.

See Compare and Contrast at **wordy**.

verboseness *n* [➡MEANINGLESS SPEECH OR WRITING; 677]

verbosity *n* **long-windedness**, verboseness, loquaciousness (*formal*), garrulity, wordiness, prolixity, turgidity. [➡MEANINGLESS SPEECH OR WRITING; 677] *Opposite:* succinctness.

verdant *adj* **green**, lush, luxuriant, fertile, leafy, grassy. [➡VEGETATION; 1025]

verdict *n* **decision**, judgment, finding, result, outcome, ruling, decree, conclusion. [➡TRIAL, PUNISHMENT, AND LEGAL OUTCOMES; 819]

verdigris *n* **patina**, tarnish, corrosion, greenness, coloration, rust. [➡COVERS AND COATINGS; 1245]

verdure *n* **greenery**, lushness, vegetation, flora, plant life, plants. [➡VEGETATION; 1025]

verge 1 *n* **edge**, border, threshold, approach, limit, brink, margin, boundary. [➡EXTREMITIES OF PHYSICAL OBJECTS; 1249] 2 *v* **be near to**, approach, border on, come close to, near, be close to, be similar to. [➡EXIST IN CLOSE PROXIMITY; 21]

verge on *see* **verge**.

verging on *adj* **almost**, bordering on, close to, tantamount to. [➡SIMILARITY; 149]

verifiable *adj* **demonstrable**, provable, confirmable, supportable (*literary*), certifiable, showable. [➡CERTAIN; 175] *Opposite:* moot.

verification *n* **confirmation**, corroboration, proof, substantiation, authentication, certification. [➡EVIDENCE AND PROOF; 69] *Opposite:* contradiction.

verified *adj* **confirmed**, proved, shown, tested, substantiated, corroborated, certified. [➡CERTAIN; 175] *Opposite:* unconfirmed.

verify *v* **confirm**, bear out, prove, authenticate, validate, substantiate, corroborate, make sure, attest. [➡APPROVE AND CONFIRM; 647] *Opposite:* disprove.

verisimilitude (*formal*) *n* **truth**, credibility, authenticity, reliability, plausibility, likelihood. [➡TRUE AND REAL; 172] *Opposite:* falsity.

veritable *adj* **absolute**, real, genuine, out-and-out, authentic, actual, proper, true. [➡TRUE AND REAL; 172] *Opposite:* false.

verity (*formal*) *n* **truth**, fact, principle, reality, sincerity, factualness. [➡TRUE AND REAL; 172]

vermicelli *type of* **pasta**. [➡PASTA; 1179]

vermilion *type of* **red**. [➡COLOURS; 1223]

vermin *n* [➡LAZY OR UNSUCCESSFUL PEOPLE; 948]

verminous *adj* **infested**, pest-ridden, louse-ridden, rat-infested, crawling, alive. [➡DECAYING OR INFESTED; 1235]

vernacular *n* **dialect**, language, lingo (*informal*), patois, argot, colloquial speech, lingua franca. [➡THE SPOKEN WORD; 672]

verruca *n* [➡CONDITIONS AFFECTING THE SKIN; 722]

versatile 1 *adj* **adaptable**, flexible, resourceful, multitalented, all-round, all-around (*US*). [➡TALENTED AND SKILFUL; 528] *Opposite:* limited. 2 *adj* **multipurpose**, adaptable, handy, useful, nifty (*informal*). [➡USEFULNESS; 200] *Opposite:* inflexible.

versatility *n* **adaptability**, flexibility, resourcefulness, usefulness, changeability. [➡USEFULNESS; 200] *Opposite:* inflexibility.

verse 1 *n* **stanza**, canto, section, unit. [➡POETRY AND VERSE; 915] 2 *n* **poetry**, rhyme, blank verse, free verse, doggerel. [➡POETRY AND VERSE; 915] *Opposite:* prose.

versed *adj* **experienced**, competent, conversant, proficient, knowledgeable, familiar, skilled. [➡KNOWLEDGE AND WISDOM; 559] *Opposite:* inexperienced.

versed in *adj* [➡KNOWLEDGE AND WISDOM; 559]

versifier *n* [➡WRITERS AND STYLES; 914]

version 1 *n* **account**, description, report, side, story. [➡POINT OF VIEW; 768] 2 *n* **form**, type, variety, kind, sort, style. [➡VARIETY, TYPE, KIND; 146] 3 *n* **adaptation**, edition, translation, rendering. [➡SUMMARIES, OUTLINES, AND EXCERPTS; 589]

versus 1 *prep* **against**, contra, in competition with. [➡OPPOSITE; 158] 2 *prep* **as opposed to**, contrasted with, set against, against, as against. [➡FOREIGN WORDS AND PHRASES; 673]

vertebra *type of* **bone**. [➡THE BONES AND JOINTS; 720]

vertebral *adj* [➡THE BONES AND JOINTS; 720]

vertebral column *n* [➡THE BONES AND JOINTS; 720]

vertebrate *n* **animal**, mammal, bird, reptile, amphibian, fish. [➡LIVING THINGS AND LIVING; 976] *Opposite:* invertebrate.

vertex *n* **apex**, summit, height, pinnacle, apogee, acme, zenith, peak, top. [➡EXTREMITIES OF PHYSICAL OBJECTS; 1249] *Opposite:* base.

vertical *adj* **perpendicular**, upright, erect, straight up, straight down, plumb. [➡ORIENTATION AND ALIGNMENT; 1222] *Opposite:* horizontal.

vertiginous *adj* **high**, dizzying, tall, lofty, exposed, open. [➡HEIGHT: HIGH; 1202]

vertigo *n* **dizziness**, giddiness, unsteadiness, faintness, lightheadedness. [➡ILL AND SICK; 741]

verve *n* **vitality**, energy, dynamism, vigour, vim (*informal*), dash, spirit, life, animation, get-up-and-go (*informal*), enthusiasm. [➡POSITIVE IMPATIENCE, ENTHUSIASM, AND ALERTNESS; 538] *Opposite:* lethargy.

very 1 *adv* **extremely**, incredibly, awfully, exceptionally, exceedingly, especially, dreadfully, extraordinarily, enormously, fantastically, vastly. [➡TO A GREAT EXTENT; 130] 2 *adj* **actual**, self-same, same, identical, exact, precise, right, appropriate. [➡SAMENESS; 151]

vessel 1 *n* **container**, pot, bowl, jug, pitcher, receptacle, ewer, basin, bottle. [➡CONTAINERS, RECEPTACLES, AND PACKAGING; 1244] 2 *n* **boat**, ship, craft. [➡SHIPS AND BOATS; 1149]

vest 1 *v* **confer** (*formal*), bestow (*formal*), devolve, consign, entrust, assign, lodge. [➡GIVE AND PROVIDE; 431] 2 *type of* **upper body underwear**. [➡HABERDASHERY, MILLINERY, AND LINGERIE; 867] 3 (*US*) *type of* **top**. [➡GARMENTS AND OUTFITS; 865]

vestal (*literary*) *n* [➡RELIGIOUS PEOPLE; 779]

vested interest 1 *n* **special interest**, interest, concern, stake, investment, agenda. [➡ATTENTION AND ATTENTIVENESS; 764] 2 *n* **stakeholder**, supporter, shareholder. [➡BUSINESS PEOPLE; 794]

vestibule 1 *n* **entrance hall**, foyer, lobby, antechamber, atrium, hallway, porch, reception area. [➡DOORS AND ACCESS POINTS; 1100] 2 *part of* **building**. [➡PARTS OF A BUILDING; 1094]

vestige *n* **trace**, sign, mark, indication, hint, suggestion, remnant, evidence. [➡SMALL PIECE; 127]

vestigial 1 *adj* **residual**, remaining, imperceptible, token. [➡IMPERCEPTIBLE; 26] 2 *adj* **nonfunctioning**, functionless, stunted, degenerate, atrophic, shrunken, undeveloped, useless. [➡REDUNDANT AND USELESS; 241] *Opposite:* functional.

vestment 1 *n* **robe**, garment, dress, habit, uniform, apparel. [➡CLOTHES AND ACCESSORIES; 864] 2 *n* **surplice**, chasuble, cope, vesture. [➡GARMENTS AND OUTFITS; 865]

vet *v* **examine**, check, scrutinize, inspect, assess, investigate, evaluate, look over, give the once-over (*informal*). [➡EXAMINE AND ASSESS; 754]

veteran *n* **expert**, old hand, past master, trouper, old-timer. [➡TALENTED OR INTELLIGENT PERSON; 529] *Opposite:* novice.

veto 1 *n* **rejection**, refusal, bar, proscription (*formal*), disallowance, prevention, quashing. [➡REFUSE PERMISSION AND NOT ALLOW; 671] *Opposite:* approval. 2 *n* **prohibition**, ban, sanction, embargo, order, notice, censure. [➡REFUSE PERMISSION AND NOT ALLOW; 671] *Opposite:* release. 3 *v* **reject**, turn down, bar, disallow, refuse, dissent, disapprove. [➡REFUSE PERMISSION AND NOT ALLOW; 671] *Opposite:* approve. 4 *v* **prohibit**, ban, forbid, outlaw, proscribe, censure, disallow. [➡REFUSE PERMISSION AND NOT ALLOW; 671] *Opposite:* sanction.

vex 1 *v* **annoy**, upset, displease, irk, irritate, anger, aggravate (*informal*), exasperate, rile (*informal*), incense, bug (*informal*). [➡ANGER AND ANNOY; 570] *Opposite:* pacify. 2 *v* **agitate**, distress, trouble, bother, torment, worry, upset. [➡UPSET, DISTRESS, AND HUMILIATE; 568] *Opposite:* placate. 3 *v* **confound**, confuse, perplex, puzzle, tease, mix up, muddle. [➡CONFUSE AND BEWILDER; 572] *Opposite:* enlighten.

See Compare and Contrast at **annoy**.

vexation *n* **annoyance**, upset, displeasure, bother, irritation, aggravation (*informal*), exasperation, anger. [➡IRRITATION AND ANGER; 542] *Opposite:* satisfaction.

vexatious *adj* **annoying**, upsetting, irritating, troublesome, bothersome, exasperating, distressing, aggravating (*informal*), irksome. [➡IRRITATING; 229] *Opposite:* placatory.

vexed 1 *adj* **irritated**, provoked, annoyed, upset, angry, displeased, cross, aggravated (*informal*), exasperated, irked. [➡IRRITATION AND ANGER; 542] *Opposite:* calm. 2 *adj* **debated**, controversial, contentious, fractious, problematic, troublesome, tricky, awkward, difficult. [➡DIFFICULTY AND COMPLEXITY; 243] *Opposite:* uncomplicated.

vexing *adj* **annoying**, puzzling, frustrating, worrying, worrisome, disturbing, troublesome, difficult. [➡IRRITATING; 229] *Opposite:* easy.

via *prep* **by way of**, through, by. [➡DIRECTION OF MOTION; 346]

viability *n* **practicability**, feasibility, practicality, capability, sustainability, possibility. [➡POSSIBLE AND PROBABLE; 178] *Opposite:* impracticality.

viable *adj* **practicable**, worthwhile, feasible, practical, sustainable, workable, possible, doable. [➡POSSIBLE AND PROBABLE; 178] *Opposite:* impossible.

viaduct *type of* **bridge**. [➡BRIDGES, TUNNELS, CROSSINGS, AND JUNCTIONS; 1111]

vial *n* **ampoule**, vessel, container, flask, bottle, phial. [➡CONTAINERS, RECEPTACLES, AND PACKAGING; 1244]

vibe (*slang*) *n* **feeling**, atmosphere, ambience, feel, sense, air. [➡APPEARANCE AND ATMOSPHERE; 1236]

vibrancy *n* **vitality**, vivacity, animation, enthusiasm, effervescence, liveliness, joie de vivre. [➡POSITIVE IMPATIENCE, ENTHUSIASM, AND ALERTNESS; 538] *Opposite:* lethargy.

vibrant 1 *adj* **pulsating**, energetic, vibrating, effervescent, alive, bubbly, lively, exciting. [➡EMOTIONALLY PLEASANT; 188] *Opposite:* listless. 2 *adj* **bright**, dazzling, vivid, brilliant, flamboyant, colourful, luminous, radiant, garish, lurid. [➡DESCRIBING COLOURS; 1225] *Opposite:* dull.

vibrantly *adv* **brightly**, dazzlingly, vividly, brilliantly, flamboyantly, colourfully, luminously, garishly, luridly. [➡DESCRIBING COLOURS; 1225] *Opposite:* dully.

vibraphone *type of* **percussion instrument**. [➡MUSICAL INSTRUMENTS; 910]

vibrate *v* **shake**, quiver, tremble, shudder, judder, beat, pulsate, oscillate. [➡BOUNCE, UNDULATE, AND VIBRATE; 309]

vibration *n* **shaking**, quivering, trembling, shuddering, juddering, pulsation, tremor. [➡PHYSICAL REACTIONS; 317] *Opposite:* stillness.

vicar *n* [➡RELIGIOUS PEOPLE; 779]

vicarage *n* [➡RELIGIOUS BUILDINGS; 1084]

vicarious 1 *adj* **displaced**, indirect, remote, removed, distanced, relayed, second-hand, mediated. [➡DISTANCE; 161] *Opposite:* direct. 2 *adj* **empathetic**, sympathetic, assumed, imagined, adopted. [➡RELATED; 143] 3 *adj* **delegated**, surrogate, substitute, proxy, deputized, passed on. [➡RELATED; 143]

vice 1 *n* **depravity**, iniquity, evil, wickedness, immorality, corruption, badness, sin. [➡MORALLY BAD; 776] *Opposite:* goodness. 2 *n* **defect**, failing, flaw, imperfection, fault, weakness, foible, shortcoming. [➡FAULTS, FLAWS, AND WEAKNESSES; 252] *Opposite:* strength. 3 *type of* **carpentry tool**. [➡HAND TOOLS; 1118]

vice squad *n* [➡THE POLICE, ARREST, AND PRE-TRIAL PROCEEDINGS; 818]

vichyssoise *type of* **soup**. [➡SOUP; 1185]

vicinal 1 *adj* **neighbouring**, adjacent, nearby, close, proximate, local. [➡CLOSENESS; 160] *Opposite:* distant. 2 *adj* **local**, district, municipal, regional, provincial, parochial, borough, neighbourhood. [➡HUMAN SETTLEMENTS; 1069] *Opposite:* international.

vicinity *n* **neighbourhood**, environs, locality, district, area, locale, purlieu. [➡PLACE; 1064]

vicious 1 *adj* **ferocious**, savage, wild, brutish, fierce, inhuman, violent, sadistic. [➡MORALLY BAD; 776] *Opposite:* gentle. 2 *adj* **spiteful**, malicious, mean, rancorous, backbiting, venomous, nasty, cruel, brutal, hurtful. [➡RUDE AND HOSTILE; 626] *Opposite:* kind.

vicious circle *n* **catch-22**, no-win situation, impasse, stalemate. [➡DIFFICULT SITUATIONS; 72]

viciously 1 *adv* **ferociously**, fiercely, savagely, wildly, brutishly, inhumanly, violently, sadistically, cruelly. [➡MORALLY BAD; 776] *Opposite:* gently. 2 *adv* **maliciously**, spitefully, meanly, hurtfully, rancorously, venomously, brutally, nastily, cruelly. [➡RUDE AND HOSTILE; 626] *Opposite:* kindly.

viciousness 1 *n* **ferociousness**, savagery, wildness, brutishness, ferocity, fierceness, violence, sadism, inhumanity. [➡UNKIND ACTION OR BEHAVIOUR; 297] *Opposite:* gentleness. 2 *n* **maliciousness**, meanness, spitefulness, rancorousness, venomousness, hurtfulness, cruelty, brutality, unkindness, nastiness, malice. [➡SELFISH AND UNKIND; 506] *Opposite:* kindness.

vicissitudes *n* **changes**, variations, vagaries, ups and downs, fluctuations, deviations. [➡CHANGE; 373]

victim 1 *n* **fatality**, casualty, sufferer, injured party. [➡DEAD PERSON; 926] 2 *n* **dupe**, butt, target, object, prey, quarry. [➡VICTIMS OF DECEIT; 663]

victimization *n* **persecution**, discrimination, oppression, ill-treatment, harassment, abuse. [➡UNKIND ACTION OR BEHAVIOUR; 297] *Opposite:* favouritism.

victimize *v* **persecute**, discriminate against, harass, oppress, pick on, ill-treat, abuse, have it in for. [➡WOUND A PERSON OR ANIMAL; 384] *Opposite:* favour.

victor *n* **winner**, champion, champ (*informal*), conqueror, medallist, prizewinner. [➡TALENTED OR INTELLIGENT PERSON; 529] *Opposite:* loser.

Victorian *type of* **pre-20th-century architecture**. [➡BUILDING AND ARCHITECTURE; 1075]

victorious *adj* **winning**, triumphant, champion, prizewinning, successful, conquering. [➡SUCCESSFUL AND PROMISING; 81] *Opposite:* losing.

victory *n* **conquest**, triumph, win, success. [➡SUCCESS; 82] *Opposite:* defeat.

victuals *n* **food**, provisions, supplies, provender (*literary or humorous*), foodstuffs, food and drink, comestibles (*formal*), eats (*slang*). [➡FOOD; 1166]

video *v* **videotape**, record, tape, film, capture. [➡RECORD SOMETHING; 372]

> **video**
>
> ◆ *types of video equipment*
> camcorder, DVD, palmcorder, VCR (*US*), video camera, video cassette, video cassette recorder, video recorder, video tape recorder, videodisk, videotape

video camera *type of* **video equipment**. [➡PHOTOGRAPHY AND PHOTOGRAPHIC EQUIPMENT; 1121]

video cassette *type of* **video equipment**. [➡PHOTOGRAPHY AND PHOTOGRAPHIC EQUIPMENT; 1121]

video cassette recorder *type of* **video equipment**. [➡PHOTOGRAPHY AND PHOTOGRAPHIC EQUIPMENT; 1121]

videoconference *n* [➡MEETINGS AND ASSEMBLIES; 43]

videodisk *type of* **video equipment**. [➡PHOTOGRAPHY AND PHOTOGRAPHIC EQUIPMENT; 1121]

video display terminal *n* **screen**, monitor, interface, terminal, viewer, display. [➡COMPUTERS AND COMPUTING; 1126]

videophone *type of* **telecommunications equipment**. [➡TELECOMMUNICATIONS; 1129]

video recorder *type of* **video equipment.** [➡PHOTOGRAPHY AND PHOTOGRAPHIC EQUIPMENT; 1121]

videotape 1 *v* **record**, video, tape, film, capture. [➡RECORD SOMETHING; 372] 2 *type of* **video equipment.** [➡PHOTOGRAPHY AND PHOTOGRAPHIC EQUIPMENT; 1121]

video tape recorder *type of* **video equipment.** [➡PHOTOGRAPHY AND PHOTOGRAPHIC EQUIPMENT; 1121]

vie *v* **compete**, contend, contest, strive, fight, rival, oppose, struggle. [➡COMPETE, CONTEND, AND COMBAT; 304] *Opposite:* collaborate.

view 1 *n* **sight**, vision, observation, examination, scrutiny, analysis, inspection. [➡SEE; 700] 2 *n* **scene**, picture, spectacle, prospect, vista, aspect, outlook, landscape, panorama. [➡VIEWS AND OUTLOOKS; 1072] 3 *n* **opinion**, interpretation, assessment, understanding. [➡POINT OF VIEW; 768] 4 *v* **look at**, see, regard, behold (*archaic or literary*), observe, notice, watch. [➡LOOKING AND LOOKS; 701] 5 *v* **inspect**, examine, look over, look at, observe, scrutinize, check over, survey. [➡EXAMINE AND ASSESS; 754] 6 *v* **consider**, regard, think of, perceive, look on, deem (*formal*), assess. [➡HAVE AN OPINION OF SOMETHING; 757]

viewable 1 *adj* **available**, on view, on display, accessible. [➡PRESENT AND AVAILABLE; 11] 2 *adj* **fit**, presentable, acceptable, all right, appropriate, decent, suitable. [➡ACCEPTABLE AND PASSABLE; 220] *Opposite:* inappropriate.

viewer *n* **watcher**, spectator, onlooker, ogler, observer, eyewitness, witness. [➡LOOKERS AND SPECTATORS; 702]

viewfinder *part of* **photographic equipment.** [➡PHOTOGRAPHY AND PHOTOGRAPHIC EQUIPMENT; 1121]

viewing 1 *n* **watching**, inspecting, seeing, observing, looking. [➡LOOKING AND LOOKS; 701] 2 *n* **programming**, broadcasts, programmes, broadcasting, showing, screening, presentation, transmission. [➡TELEVISION AND RADIO; 607]

viewing platform *n* [➡STAGES, PLATFORMS, AND RAISED AREAS; 1097]

viewpoint 1 *n* **point of view**, view, perspective, standpoint, position, stance, opinion. [➡POINT OF VIEW; 768] 2 *n* **vantage point**, viewing platform, belvedere, lookout, crow's nest. [➡TOWERS; 1098]

vigil *n* **night watch**, watch, wake. [➡BURIAL AND PREPARATION FOR BURIAL; 929]

vigilance *n* **watchfulness**, attentiveness, observance, care, caution, alertness, awareness. [➡POSITIVE IMPATIENCE, ENTHUSIASM, AND ALERTNESS; 538] *Opposite:* slackness.

vigilant *adj* **watchful**, alert, attentive, on your guard, wary, cautious, observant, heedful, on the alert, aware. [➡POSITIVE IMPATIENCE, ENTHUSIASM, AND ALERTNESS; 538] *Opposite:* slack.

See Compare and Contrast at **cautious.**

vignette 1 *n* **design**, decoration, illustration, frontispiece, picture, print. [➡ORNAMENTS AND DECORATIONS; 1247] 2 *n* **essay**, article, piece, monograph. [➡ANALYTICAL NONFICTION WRITING; 593] 3 *n* **picture**, painting, drawing, photograph, print, illustration. [➡DRAWINGS, CHARTS AND TABLES; 595] 4 *n* **scene**, extract, clip, fragment, snippet, snatch. [➡SUMMARIES, OUTLINES, AND EXCERPTS; 589]

vigorous *adj* **robust**, active, strong, energetic, dynamic, vital, hearty, forceful, exuberant, spirited. [➡ENERGY AND ENTHUSIASM; 497] *Opposite:* feeble.

vigour 1 *n* **vitality**, energy, robustness, strength, heartiness, potency, exuberance, dynamism, drive, power, vim (*informal*), brio (*literary*). [➡POSITIVE IMPATIENCE, ENTHUSIASM, AND ALERTNESS; 538] *Opposite:* lethargy. 2 *n* **intensity**, forcefulness, force, ferocity, vim (*informal*), gusto, spirit, punch. [➡ENERGY AND ENTHUSIASM; 497] *Opposite:* feebleness. 3 *n* **potency**, strength, life, robustness, stamina, staying power. [➡STRENGTH OF WILL; 502] *Opposite:* weakness.

vile 1 *adj* **disgusting**, abhorrent (*formal*), loathsome, revolting, dreadful, awful, abominable, hateful, despicable, contemptible. [➡UNACCEPTABLE AND UNFORGIVABLE; 226] *Opposite:* admirable. 2 *adj* **evil**, wicked, shameful, depraved, base, degraded, low, abominable. [➡MORALLY BAD; 776] *Opposite:* good. 3 *adj* **unpleasant**, horrid, horrible, repulsive, nasty, foul, repellent, terrible. [➡DISGUSTING AND REPULSIVE; 231] *Opposite:* pleasant.

See Compare and Contrast at **mean.**

vileness 1 *n* **evil**, depravity, wickedness, lowness, degradation, baseness, turpitude (*formal or literary*), abomination, contemptibility, despicability. [➡MORALLY BAD; 776] *Opposite:* goodness. 2 *n* **unpleasantness**, dreadfulness, awfulness, horridness, horribleness, terribleness, loathsomeness, nastiness, repulsiveness, repellence, foulness. [➡DISGUSTING AND REPULSIVE; 231] *Opposite:* pleasantness.

vilification *n* **maliciousness**, abuse, disparagement, criticism, backbiting, denigration, abasement (*literary*), slander, libel, defamation. [➡CRITICISMS AND ANGRY OUTBURSTS; 50] *Opposite:* acclaim.

vilified *adj* [➡UNPOPULAR AND UNWANTED; 259]

vilify *v* **malign**, abuse, denigrate, belittle, disparage, libel, slander, criticize, pillory, run down. [➡ACCUSE, BLAME, AND CRITICIZE; 642] *Opposite:* compliment.

See Compare and Contrast at **malign.**

villa *type of* **house.** [➡RESIDENTIAL BUILDINGS; 1077]

village *n* **hamlet**, rural community, settlement. [➡HUMAN SETTLEMENTS; 1069]

villager *n* **country dweller**, rustic, country cousin (*dated*). [➡INHABITANT; 857]

village square *n* [➡URBAN OUTDOOR SPACES; 1071]

villain 1 *n* **baddie** (*informal*), scoundrel, rogue, desperado (*literary*), heavy, nasty (*informal*). [➡VILLAINS AND THUGS; 947] *Opposite:* hero. 2 *n* (*slang*) **criminal**, felon, gangster, thug, outlaw, lawbreaker, hood (*US slang*). [➡CRIMINALS; 821]

villainous 1 *adj* **wicked**, criminal, heinous, depraved, iniquitous, base, evil, infamous, bad, maleficent, debased. [➡MORALLY BAD; 776] *Opposite:* good. 2 *adj* **unpleasant**, undesirable, obnoxious, offensive, unreliable, vile, hateful, disgusting, detestable, loathsome. [➡DISGUSTING AND REPULSIVE; 231] *Opposite:* pleasant.

villainy *n* **wickedness**, wrongdoing, evil, foul play, badness, treachery, crime. [➡MORALLY BAD; 776] *Opposite:* goodness.

vim (*informal*) *n* **vitality**, energy, exuberance, verve, vigour, zest, dash, spirit, enthusiasm, punch, panache. [➡POSITIVE IMPATIENCE, ENTHUSIASM, AND ALERTNESS; 538] *Opposite:* lethargy.

vindicate 1 *v* **clear**, exonerate, exculpate (*formal*), absolve, acquit. [➡FORGET, FORGIVE, AND ACCEPT; 749] *Opposite:* implicate. 2 *v* **justify**, maintain, claim, support, defend, assert, prove, uphold. [➡APPROVE AND CONFIRM; 647]

vindication 1 *n* **exculpation** (*formal*), exoneration, absolution, acquittal. [➡FORGET, FORGIVE, AND ACCEPT; 749] *Opposite:* implication. 2 *n* **justification**, evidence, proof, assertion. [➡EVIDENCE AND PROOF; 69]

vindictive 1 *adj* **vengeful**, unforgiving, revengeful, rancorous, implacable (*formal*), resentful, bitter, ruthless, merciless, pitiless. [➡IRRITATION AND ANGER; 542] *Opposite:* forgiving. 2 *adj* **spiteful**, malicious, mean, cruel, hurtful, nasty, unkind, malevolent. [➡SELFISH AND UNKIND; 506] *Opposite:* kind.

vindictively *adv* **spitefully**, maliciously, hurtfully, cruelly, nastily, unkindly, meanly, malevolently. [➡SELFISH AND UNKIND; 506] *Opposite:* kindly.

vindictiveness *n* **spite**, malice, cruelty, nastiness, unkindness, meanness, maliciousness, malevolence. [➡ANTAGONISM; 553] *Opposite:* kindness.

vine *n* **climber**, creeper, liana. [➡CLIMBERS; 1033]

vinegar *type of* **seasonings, sauces, and dips.** [➡SEASONINGS AND SAUCES; 1173]

vinegary 1 *adj* **sour**, astringent, acidic, acid, tart, sharp, acrid, acerbic. [➡TASTE; 704] *Opposite:* sweet. 2 *adj* **irritable**, sour, bitter, embittered, unpleasant, resentful, acerbic, tart. [➡DIFFICULT TO PLEASE; 516] *Opposite:* pleasant.

vino (*informal*) *n* [➡DRINKS; 1186]

vintage 1 *n* **era**, time, age, epoch, period. [➡EPOCHS AND ERAS; 89] 2 *adj* **classic**, typical, traditional, essential, prime, pure, first-class, archetypal, first-rate. [➡SUPERIORITY; 153] *Opposite:* atypical. 3 *adj* **out-of-date**, dated, antique, old, outmoded, antiquated, old-fashioned. [➡OLD, OLD-FASHIONED; 168] *Opposite:* new.

vinyl 1 *n* **LPs**, records, discs, singles, albums. [➡RECORDINGS AND PLAYERS; 911] 2 *type of* **plastic.** [➡PLASTICS; 1133]

viol *type of* **stringed instrument.** [➡MUSICAL INSTRUMENTS; 910]

viola *type of* **stringed instrument.** [➡MUSICAL INSTRUMENTS; 910]

viola da gamba *type of* **stringed instrument.** [➡MUSICAL INSTRUMENTS; 910]

violate 1 *v* **disregard**, infringe, defy, breach, disobey, flout, break, contravene. [➡DISOBEY; 303] *Opposite:* obey. 2 *v* **disrupt**, disturb, interrupt, encroach upon, intrude upon, break up. [➡INTERRUPT AND BUTT IN; 620] *Opposite:* respect. 3 *v* **defile**, desecrate, spoil, destroy, ruin, abuse, despoil, damage, harm. [➡WORSEN SOMETHING; 381] *Opposite:* respect.

violation 1 *n* **infringement**, breach, contravention, defiance, disobedience. [➡BAD BEHAVIOUR OR ACTION; 255] *Opposite:* obedience. 2 *n* **disruption**, intrusion, encroachment, disturbance, interruption. [➡BAD MANNERS AND SOCIAL SKILLS; 522] *Opposite:* respect. 3 *n* **defilement**, desecration, destruction, ruin, abuse, damage, harm. [➡DESTRUCTION AND DEMOLITION; 360] *Opposite:* respect.

violence 1 *n* **physical force**, pugnaciousness, pugnacity, aggression, fighting, savagery, brutality, cruelty, sadism, bloodshed, carnage. [➡UNKIND ACTION OR BEHAVIOUR; 297] *Opposite:* peacefulness. 2 *n* **ferocity**, strength, force, fierceness, viciousness, vehemence, forcefulness, passion, might, intensity, power. [➡DIFFICULTY AND COMPLEXITY; 243] *Opposite:* gentleness.

violent 1 *adj* **pugnacious**, aggressive, brutal, cruel, sadistic, vicious. [➡MORALLY BAD; 776] *Opposite:* peaceful. 2 *adj* **fierce**, ferocious, vehement, vicious, forceful, passionate, intense, powerful, furious, strong. [➡ENTHUSIASTIC AND INQUISITIVE; 629] *Opposite:* gentle.

violently 1 *adv* **pugnaciously**, aggressively, brutally, cruelly, sadistically, viciously. [➡SELFISH AND UNKIND; 506] *Opposite:* peacefully. 2 *adv* **fiercely**, ferociously, vehemently, viciously, forcefully, passionately, intensely, hard, powerfully, strongly. [➡DIFFICULTY AND COMPLEXITY; 243] *Opposite:* gently.

violet 1 *type of* **perennial flower.** [➡FLOWERS; 1032] 2 *type of* **purple.** [➡COLOURS; 1223]

violin *type of* **stringed instrument.** [➡MUSICAL INSTRUMENTS; 910]

violoncello (*formal*) *type of* **stringed instrument.** [➡MUSICAL INSTRUMENTS; 910]

VIP *n* **dignitary**, big shot (*informal*), name, luminary, star, celebrity, public figure, bigwig (*informal*). [➡IMPORTANT OR FAMOUS PEOPLE; 893]

viper *type of* **poisonous snake.** [➡SNAKE; 995]

viperish *adj* **malicious**, spiteful, nasty, unkind, malevolent, unpleasant. [➡SELFISH AND UNKIND; 506] *Opposite:* kind.

viral *adj* [➡MICROORGANISMS, FUNGI, AND ALGAE; 1023]

Virginia creeper *type of* **climber.** [➡CLIMBERS; 1033]

Virgo *type of* **star sign.** [➡FATE, DESTINY, AND ASTROLOGY; 783]

viridian *type of* **green.** [➡COLOURS; 1223]

virtual 1 *adj* **near**, practical, effective, fundamental, essential, implicit. [➡APPROXIMATELY; 133] *Opposite:* actual. 2 *adj* **computer-generated**, simulated, cybernetic. [➡COMPUTERS AND COMPUTING; 1126]

virtually 1 *adv* **in effect**, effectively, essentially, fundamentally, to all intents and purposes, practically. [➡SUMMARIZING EXPRESSIONS; 623] 2 *adv* **almost**, nearly, near, nigh on, close to, next to. [➡TO A CERTAIN EXTENT; 134]

virtual reality *n* **computer modelling**, simulated reality, computer simulation, simulation, VR, cyberspace, computer graphics. [➡COMPUTERS AND COMPUTING; 1126]

virtue 1 *n* **goodness**, righteousness, integrity, honesty, morality, uprightness. [➡MORALLY GOOD; 775] *Opposite:* wickedness. 2 *n* **asset**, feature, quality, advantage, benefit, plus, pro. [➡SOURCE OF HAPPINESS, PLEASURE, OR IMPROVEMENT; 210] *Opposite:* disadvantage.

virtuosity *n* **skill**, technique, brilliance, flair, talent, ability, expertise. [➡SKILLS, TALENTS, AND ABILITIES; 527]

virtuoso 1 *n* **musician**, bravura player, artist, maestro. [➡MUSICIANS AND SINGERS; 908] 2 *n* **wunderkind**, genius, wizard (*informal*), prodigy, ace (*informal*), maven. [➡TALENTED OR INTELLIGENT PERSON; 529]

virtuous *adj* **good**, righteous, worthy, honourable, moral, upright, honest. [➡MORALLY GOOD; 775] *Opposite:* bad.

virtuousness *n* [➡MORALLY GOOD; 775]

virulent 1 *adj* **infectious**, contagious, poisonous, lethal, strong, dangerous, active, powerful, potent. [➡STRENGTH; 202] *Opposite:* weak. 2 *adj* **malicious**, bitter, vituperative, venomous, fierce, harsh, spiteful, hostile. [➡RUDE AND HOSTILE; 626] *Opposite:* kind.

virus 1 *n* **illness**, infection, sickness, disease. [➡ILLNESSES AND DISORDERS; 733] 2 *n* **computer program**, Trojan horse, worm. [➡COMPUTERS AND COMPUTING; 1126] 3 *type of* **microorganism**. [➡MICROORGANISMS, FUNGI, AND ALGAE; 1023]

visa *n* **endorsement**, pass, entry permit, documents, papers. [➡OFFICIAL DOCUMENTS; 587]

visage 1 *n* (*literary*) **face**, expression, countenance, features, mug (*informal*), phizog (*slang*). [➡HEAD; 693] 2 *n* **look**, appearance, aspect, mien (*literary*), form. [➡APPEARANCE AND ATMOSPHERE; 1236]

vis-à-vis 1 *prep* **regarding**, in relation to, in respect of, re, with reference to, concerning, about, with regard to, apropos (*formal*). [➡FOREIGN WORDS AND PHRASES; 673] 2 *prep* **versus**, compared with, contrasted with, in comparison with, opposite to, face to face with. [➡FOREIGN WORDS AND PHRASES; 673]

viscera *n* **internal organs**, intestines, entrails, innards (*informal*), insides (*informal*), guts, bowels. [➡THE DIGESTIVE TRACT; 710]

visceral *adj* **instinctual**, instinctive, intuitive, gut, primitive, animal, primeval. [➡AUTOMATIC AND INSTINCTIVE; 281] *Opposite:* reasoned.

viscid *adj* **thick**, sticky, gooey, gluey, treacly, gummy, viscous, tacky. [➡PHYSICAL TEXTURE; 1221] *Opposite:* runny.

viscose *type of* **synthetic fabric**. [➡FABRICS; 1131]

viscosity *n* **viscidness**, thickness, stickiness, gluiness, gooeyness, tackiness, gumminess. [➡DENSITY AND CONSISTENCY; 1206] *Opposite:* fluidity.

viscount *type of* **aristocrat**. [➡RULERS AND ARISTOCRACY; 823]

viscountess *type of* **aristocrat**. [➡RULERS AND ARISTOCRACY; 823]

viscous *adj* **viscid**, thick, sticky, glutinous, gelatinous, gluey, tacky, gooey, gummy, treacly. [➡PHYSICAL TEXTURE; 1221] *Opposite:* runny.

visibility 1 *n* **discernibility**, perceptibility, conspicuousness, distinguishability, prominence, reflectiveness, reflectivity, brightness, luminosity. [➡PERCEPTIBLE; 25] *Opposite:* invisibility. 2 *n* **prominence**, familiarity, profile, image, high profile. [➡KNOWN AND FAMOUS; 182]

visible *adj* **noticeable**, observable, perceptible, evident, in evidence, discernible, detectable, obvious. [➡PERCEPTIBLE; 25] *Opposite:* invisible.

vision 1 *n* **eyesight**, sight, ability to see. [➡SEE; 700] 2 *n* **concept**, mental picture, idea, image, visualization. [➡IDEA AND THOUGHT; 771] 3 *n* **revelation**, prophecy, dream, hallucination, apparition. [➡DREAM, IMAGINE, AND FANTASIZE; 750] 4 *n* **foresight**, imagination, forethought, prescience, farsightedness. [➡PREDICT AND ANTICIPATE; 751]

visionary 1 *adj* **inventive**, creative, farsighted, prescient, original, prophetic, imaginative. [➡POSITIVE INTELLECTUAL CHARACTERISTICS; 525] *Opposite:* short-sighted. 2 *adj* **unrealistic**, impracticable, quixotic, fanciful, unworkable, idealistic, unrealizable. [➡IMPOSSIBLE AND IMPROBABLE; 179] *Opposite:* practicable. 3 *n* **prophet**, dreamer, thinker, seer. [➡RELIGIOUS PEOPLE; 779]

visit 1 *v* **call on**, call in on, drop in on, go to see, pop in (*informal*), pay a visit. [➡INITIATE AND ESTABLISH COMMUNICATION; 681] 2 *v* **go to**, go to see, stay in, stay at, stop with, stop at, holiday at, stay. [➡HOBBIES, GAMES, AND SPORTS; 875] 3 *n* **social call**, official visit, call, duty call. [➡ARRIVAL; 13] 4 *n* **stay**, stopover, holiday, break, trip, outing, vacation. [➡TRAVEL: JOURNEYS AND TRIPS; 319]

visitation 1 *n* **visit**, examination, inspection, check, checkup. [➡EXAMINE AND ASSESS; 754] 2 *n* **punishment**, curse, calamity, blight, catastrophe, disaster. [➡DISASTERS; 253]

visitor *n* **caller**, guest, tourist, sightseer. [➡TRAVEL: TRAVELLERS AND WALKERS; 320]

visitor centre *n* **tourist centre**, information office, inquiry office, information point, help point. [➡TRAVEL: SIGHTSEEING AND TOURISM; 322]

visor *n* **screen**, blind, eyeshade. [➡COVERS AND COATINGS; 1245]

vista *n* **view**, panorama, outlook, scene, landscape, seascape. [➡VIEWS AND OUTLOOKS; 1072]

visual 1 *adj* **graphic**, pictorial, filmic, painterly, photographic, graphical. [➡ARTISTIC MOVEMENTS AND STYLES; 899] 2 *adj* **pictorial**, imagistic, graphic, concrete, graphical, visible. [➡PERCEPTIBLE; 25] 3 *adj* **optical**, chromatic, ophthalmic, ocular. [➡SEE; 700] 4 *n* **graphic**, visual aid, illustration, picture, photograph, chart, graph. [➡DRAWINGS, CHARTS AND TABLES; 595]

visual aid *n* **model**, film, video, chart, illustration, diagram, image, visual. [➡DRAWINGS, CHARTS AND TABLES; 595]

visual art *n* [➡THE PICTORIAL ARTS; 897]

visual display unit *type of* **hardware**. [➡COMPUTERS AND COMPUTING; 1126]

visualization 1 *n* **imagining**, conjuring up, picturing, conception. [➡DREAM, IMAGINE, AND FANTASIZE; 750] 2 *n* **mental image**, mental picture, vision, hallucination, image, picture. [➡NONEXISTENT THINGS; 23] 3 *n* **positive thinking**, therapy, cognitive therapy, meditation, image creation. [➡PSYCHOLOGY AND THE MIND; 770]

visualize *v* **imagine**, envisage, picture, see in your mind's eye, dream of, think about, envision. [➡DREAM, IMAGINE, AND FANTASIZE; 750]

vital 1 *adj* **important**, crucial, fundamental, imperative, essential, critical, central, necessary. [➡ IMPORTANT; 195] *Opposite:* unimportant. **2** *adj* **energetic**, vigorous, vivacious, dynamic, vibrant, bubbly, spirited, animated, lively. [➡ ENERGY AND ENTHUSIASM; 497] *Opposite:* lifeless.

See Compare and Contrast at **necessary**.

vitality *n* **liveliness**, energy, vivacity, vigour, life, animation, buoyance, verve, get-up-and-go (*informal*), joie de vivre, strength. [➡ ENERGY AND ENTHUSIASM; 497] *Opposite:* lethargy.

vitalize *v* **animate**, energize, buoy up, bolster, hearten, enliven, embolden, invigorate. [➡ IMPROVE STRENGTH AND DURABILITY; 379] *Opposite:* deaden.

vitally *adv* **extremely**, indispensably, enormously, absolutely, really, very, crucially, critically, fundamentally, essentially. [➡ IMPORTANT; 195]

vitamin *type of* **nutrient**. [➡ FOOD COMPONENTS; 1187]

vitreous *adj* **enamel**, vitric, vitriform, glasslike, glassy, clear, transparent, translucent, vitrified, fused, crystal. [➡ VISUAL TEXTURE; 1220]

vitriol *n* **hatred**, bitterness, venom, bile (*literary*), spleen, sarcasm, contempt, scorn, hurtfulness, cruelty, maliciousness, viciousness. [➡ RUDE AND HOSTILE; 626] *Opposite:* love.

vitriolic *adj* **spiteful**, venomous, hurtful, acerbic, bitter, cruel, rancorous, malicious, hateful, sarcastic, vicious, caustic. [➡ RUDE AND HOSTILE; 626] *Opposite:* kind.

vittles (*archaic*) *n* [➡ FOOD; 1166]

vituperate *v* [➡ ACCUSE, BLAME, AND CRITICIZE; 642]

vituperation **1** *n* **outburst**, attack, criticism, censuring, condemnation, dressing down. [➡ CRITICISMS AND ANGRY OUTBURSTS; 50] **2** *n* **abuse**, venom, vitriol, savaging, mauling, criticism, censure, reproach, reprimand. [➡ CRITICISMS AND ANGRY OUTBURSTS; 50]

vituperative *adj* **insulting**, abusive, offensive, malicious, slanderous, scathing, critical, censorious. [➡ ACCUSATORY AND DISAPPROVING; 635]

vivacious *adj* **vibrant**, lively, bubbly, cheerful, spirited, full of life, energetic, chirpy (*informal*), effervescent, animated. [➡ ENERGY AND ENTHUSIASM; 497] *Opposite:* languid.

vivaciousness *n* [➡ ENERGY AND ENTHUSIASM; 497]

vivacity *n* **high-spiritedness**, liveliness, animation, verve, vivaciousness, exuberance, cheerfulness, energy, life, chirpiness (*informal*), sparkle, vitality. [➡ ENERGY AND ENTHUSIASM; 497] *Opposite:* lethargy.

viva voce *adj* [➡ LESSONS, COURSE WORK, AND EXAMINATIONS; 842]

vivid **1** *adj* **intense**, rich, gaudy, bright, glowing, vibrant, brilliant, colourful, flamboyant. [➡ DESCRIBING COLOURS; 1225] *Opposite:* dull. **2** *adj* **fresh**, distinct, clear, crystal clear, lucid, plain. [➡ CONCISE AND CLEAR; 203] *Opposite:* vague. **3** *adj* **striking**, powerful, strong, clear, intense, graphic. [➡ STRENGTH; 202] *Opposite:* understated. **4** *adj* **active**, lively, creative, ingenious, original, inventive. [➡ INTERESTING AND MEANINGFUL; 191] *Opposite:* prosaic.

vividly **1** *adv* **intensely**, richly, gaudily, brightly, vibrantly, brilliantly, colourfully. [➡ DESCRIBING COLOURS; 1225] *Opposite:* dully. **2** *adv* **distinctly**, clearly, lucidly, freshly, plainly, keenly, acutely. [➡ CONCISE AND CLEAR; 203] *Opposite:* vaguely. **3** *adv* **strikingly**, powerfully, strongly, clearly, intensely, graphically. [➡ STRENGTH; 202]

vividness **1** *n* **richness**, gaudiness, colourfulness, brightness, vibrancy, brilliance, intensity, radiance. [➡ DESCRIBING COLOURS; 1225] *Opposite:* dullness. **2** *n* **freshness**, distinctness, clarity, lucidity, clearness, plainness. [➡ CONCISE AND CLEAR; 203] *Opposite:* vagueness. **3** *n* **power**, strength, clarity, intensity. [➡ STRENGTH; 202] **4** *n* **liveliness**, creativity, ingeniousness, flamboyance, intensity, richness, originality, inventiveness. [➡ ENERGY AND ENTHUSIASM; 497] *Opposite:* prosaicness.

vixen *type of* **female animal**. [➡ MALE OR FEMALE ANIMAL; 978]

viz *adv* [➡ EXPRESSIONS INTRODUCING EXAMPLES; 64]

V neck *type of* **sweater or cardigan**. [➡ GARMENTS AND OUTFITS; 865]

vocabulary **1** *n* **language**, words, terms, expressions, terminology, lexis, jargon. [➡ ASPECTS OF LANGUAGE; 683] **2** *n* **dictionary**, glossary, lexicon, word list. [➡ LISTS AND SCHEDULES; 588]

See Compare and Contrast at **language**.

vocal **1** *adj* **uttered**, verbal, voiced, spoken, unwritten, speaking, singing, choral, oral. [➡ THE SPOKEN WORD; 672] *Opposite:* silent. **2** *adj* **outspoken**, frank, insistent, vociferous, voluble, forceful, strident, raucous, noisy, loud, forthright. [➡ ENTHUSIASTIC AND INQUISITIVE; 629] *Opposite:* quiet.

vocal cords *part of* **respiratory system**. [➡ RESPIRATORY ORGANS; 716]

vocalist *n* **singer**, lead vocalist, backing vocalist, lead singer, backing singer, songster, backup singer (*US*), backup vocalist (*US*). [➡ MUSICIANS AND SINGERS; 908]

vocalize *v* **express**, voice, articulate, give voice to, put into words, state, enunciate, spell out, talk about, put forward, utter, intone, chant. [➡ UTTER AND PRONOUNCE; 609]

vocally *adv* **outspokenly**, frankly, insistently, vociferously, volubly, forcefully, raucously, noisily, stridently, loudly. [➡ ENTHUSIASTIC AND INQUISITIVE; 629] *Opposite:* quietly.

vocals *n* **lyrics**, words, singing, chorus. [➡ MUSIC, SONGS, AND SINGING; 907]

vocation **1** *n* **career**, profession, job, occupation, work, trade, craft, art. [➡ PROFESSIONS; 845] **2** *n* **calling**, aptitude, inclination, talent, bent, urge, natural ability. [➡ SKILLS, TALENTS, AND ABILITIES; 527]

vocational *adj* **occupational**, professional, job-related, career, work, employment. [➡ EMPLOYMENT STATUS; 831]

vocational school (*US*) *type of* **school**. [➡ EDUCATIONAL INSTITUTIONS; 813]

vociferate *v* [➡ PROTEST AND EXPRESS DISAPPROVAL; 643]

vociferous *adj* **clamorous**, vocal, loud, voluble, raucous, strident, noisy, enthusiastic. [➡ENTHUSIASTIC AND INQUISITIVE; 629] *Opposite:* quiet.

vogue *n* **fashion**, trend, craze, rage, mode, fad, style. [➡FADS, FETISHES, AND IDOLATRY; 556]

voguish 1 *adj* **fashionable**, elegant, chic, stylish, classy (*informal*), modish, à la mode (*dated*). [➡WELL GROOMED; 483] *Opposite:* unfashionable. 2 *adj* **passing**, in vogue, in, hip (*slang*), up-to-the-minute, popular, trendy (*informal*), now, happening (*informal*), all the rage, faddish (*US*). [➡POPULAR AND WANTED; 221] *Opposite:* unpopular.

voice 1 *n* **speech**, singing, vocal sound, power of speech. [➡COMMUNICATION; 603] 2 *n* **opinion**, say, right of speech, expression, declaration. [➡POINT OF VIEW; 768] 3 *v* **express**, opine (*formal*), assert, declare, proclaim. [➡CLAIM, INSIST, AND EMPHASIZE; 615] 4 *v* **pronounce**, articulate, utter, intone. [➡UTTER AND PRONOUNCE; 609]

voice box *type of* **respiratory system**. [➡RESPIRATORY ORGANS; 716]

voiced *adj* **stated**, enunciated, spoken, uttered, expressed, articulated, pronounced. [➡KNOWN AND FAMOUS; 182]

voiceless 1 *adj* **silent**, unspeaking, mute, taciturn, wordless, uncommunicative. [➡RETICENT AND UNFORTHCOMING; 632] *Opposite:* speaking. 2 *adj* **unrepresented**, disenfranchised, invisible, ignored, forgotten, abandoned, overlooked, disadvantaged. [➡CLASS STATUS; 889] *Opposite:* represented.

voice mail *type of* **telecommunications equipment**. [➡TELECOMMUNICATIONS; 1129]

voiceover *n* **narration**, commentary, narrative. [➡TELEVISION AND RADIO; 607]

void 1 *adj* **annulled**, cancelled, invalid, null and void, negated (*formal*). [➡REDUNDANT AND USELESS; 241] *Opposite:* valid. 2 *n* **empty space**, emptiness, vacuum, hollowness, abyss, space, nothingness, cavity, hole. [➡HOLES, GAPS, AND FORKS; 1251] 3 *v* **cancel**, annul, render null and void, vacate, reject, throw out, empty. [➡GET RID OF SOMETHING; 452]

See Compare and Contrast at **vacant**.

voilà *interj* [➡FOREIGN WORDS AND PHRASES; 673]

volatile 1 *adj* **unpredictable**, explosive, hot-blooded, impulsive, fickle, capricious, hot-tempered. [➡EXCESSIVE SENSITIVITY; 512] *Opposite:* placid. 2 *adj* **precarious**, dangerous, hazardous, unstable, explosive, changeable. [➡DANGEROUS; 237] *Opposite:* stable.

volatility *n* **instability**, unpredictability, precariousness, hot-bloodedness, explosiveness, impulsiveness, capriciousness. [➡DANGER; 236] *Opposite:* stability.

volcanic *adj* [➡VOLCANOES AND EARTHQUAKES; 1054]

volcanic activity *n* [➡VOLCANOES AND EARTHQUAKES; 1054]

volcano *n* [➡VOLCANOES AND EARTHQUAKES; 1054]

vole *type of* **rodent**. [➡RODENT; 989]

volition *n* **wish**, will, decision, choice, desire, preference, option. [➡THE WILL AND WILLINGNESS; 564] *Opposite:* coercion.

volley 1 *n* **torrent**, shower, stream, cascade, barrage, hail, broadside. [➡SUDDEN EVENT; 52] 2 *v* **lob**, hit, strike, kick. [➡THROW SOMETHING; 335]

volleyball *type of* **court game**. [➡HOBBIES, GAMES, AND SPORTS; 875]

volte-face *n* **about-turn**, U-turn, reversal, change of direction, change of heart, turn, about-face (*US*). [➡DECISIVE MOMENTS; 44]

voluble *adj* **vociferous**, fluent, articulate, verbose, talkative, garrulous. [➡ELOQUENT, TALKATIVE AND LONG-WINDED; 633] *Opposite:* taciturn.

volume 1 *n* **quantity**, amount, degree, size, level, number. [➡AMOUNT AND QUANTITY; 112] 2 *n* **capacity**, size, dimensions, measurements, bulk. [➡SIZE AND DIMENSIONS; 1191] 3 *n* **book**, tome, work. [➡BOOKS AND BOOKLETS; 591] 4 *n* **part**, section, edition. [➡BOOKS AND BOOKLETS; 591]

voluminous *adj* **big**, huge, large, capacious, roomy, ample, baggy. [➡LARGE; 1192] *Opposite:* small.

voluminousness *n* [➡LARGE; 1192]

voluntarily *adv* **willingly**, of your own accord, happily, gladly, freely. [➡THE WILL AND WILLINGNESS; 564] *Opposite:* reluctantly.

voluntary 1 *adj* **unpaid**, charitable, volunteer. [➡EMPLOYMENT STATUS; 831] *Opposite:* professional. 2 *adj* **intended**, intentional, controlled, deliberate, chosen, with intent. [➡INTENTIONAL AND DELIBERATE; 280] *Opposite:* involuntary.

volunteer 1 *n* **helper**, unpaid worker, candy striper (*US*). [➡WORKER; 836] 2 *v* **offer**, come forward, agree, step up, undertake. [➡AGREE; 646] 3 *v* **give**, offer, tell, advise, inform, notify, acquaint. [➡INFORM AND ANNOUNCE; 612]

voluptuary *n* [➡PLEASURE-SEEKERS AND HEDONISTS; 886]

voluptuous *adj* [➡BUILD; 478]

vomit 1 *v* **be sick**, throw up (*informal*), heave (*informal*), be nauseous, be nauseated, gag, retch, spew, puke (*slang*), hurl (*slang*), barf (*US informal*). [➡VOMIT AND BELCH; 713] 2 *v* **expel**, spew out, spew forth, eject, ejaculate, send forth (*archaic or literary*), send out, throw out, emit. [➡LIQUID EMISSION; 371] 3 *n* **sick**, puke (*slang*), barf (*informal*), chunder (*informal*), vomitus (*technical*), bile (*literary*). [➡VOMIT AND BELCH; 713]

vomitus (*technical*) *n* [➡VOMIT AND BELCH; 713]

voodoo *n* [➡THE SUPERNATURAL; 788]

voracious *adj* **insatiable**, avid, hungry, ravenous, gluttonous, greedy, rapacious. [➡FINANCIALLY MEAN AND GRASPING; 520] *Opposite:* sated.

voraciousness *n* **greed**, greediness, gluttony, hunger, rapaciousness, avidity. [➡FINANCIALLY MEAN AND GRASPING; 520]

vortex 1 *n* **whirlpool**, whirlwind, waterspout, tornado, cyclone, maelstrom, twister (*US informal*). [➡WINDY AND STORMY WEATHER; 1053] 2 *n* **quagmire**, morass, maelstrom, turbulence, whirlwind, blizzard, storm, flood, tidal wave. [➡DIFFICULT SITUATIONS; 72]

vorticism *type of* **20th-century art movement**. [➡ARTISTIC MOVEMENTS AND STYLES; 899]

votary *n* [➡DEVOTEES AND ADDICTED PEOPLE; 557]

vote 1 *n* **ballot**, election, division, secret ballot, show of hands, poll. [➡ELECTIONS AND SUFFRAGE; 807] 2 *v* **choose**, cast your vote, elect, opt for, support, back, return. [➡MAKE DECISIONS AND CHOICES; 753]

voter *n* **elector**, constituent, supporter, backer. [➡ELECTIONS AND SUFFRAGE; 807]

votive 1 *adj* **supplicatory** (*formal*), ritual, prayerful, precatory (*formal*). [➡REQUEST AND DEMAND; 664] 2 *adj* **promised**, pledged, vowed, contractual, agreed. [➡RELIGIOUS CONCEPTS; 777]

voucher *n* **coupon**, chit (*dated*), ticket, receipt, check (*US*). [➡RECEIPTS AND INVOICES; 592]

vouch for *v* **speak for**, support, guarantee, back up, stand up for, endorse, certify. [➡APPROVE AND CONFIRM; 647]

vouchsafe 1 *v* **give**, grant, offer, bestow (*formal*). [➡GIVE AND PROVIDE; 431] 2 *v* (*formal*) **promise**, agree, allow, permit, consent, approve. [➡PROMISE AND ASSURE; 685]

vow 1 *n* **promise**, oath, pledge, guarantee, declaration, undertaking. [➡PROMISE AND ASSURE; 685] 2 *v* **swear**, promise, guarantee, undertake, declare, assert, pledge. [➡PROMISE AND ASSURE; 685]

voyage 1 *n* **journey**, trip, expedition, passage, crossing, cruise, flight, tour. [➡TRAVEL: JOURNEYS AND TRIPS; 319] 2 *v* **journey**, sail, cruise, travel. [➡TRAVEL: WAYS OF TRAVELLING; 321]

voyager *n* **traveller**, explorer, adventurer, tourist, vacationer (*US*). [➡TRAVEL: TRAVELLERS AND WALKERS; 320]

voyeur *n* **nosy parker** (*informal*), busybody (*informal*), rubberneck (*informal*), ghoul, observer, onlooker, spy, watcher, viewer. [➡SUPERFICIAL OR INSINCERE PEOPLE; 951]

voyeurism *n* **prurience**, ghoulishness, nosiness (*informal*), rubbernecking (*informal*). [➡LOOKING AND LOOKS; 701]

voyeuristic *adj* **prurient**, morbid, ghoulish, nosy, unhealthy. [➡NOSY AND INTERFERING; 513]

VR *n* [➡COMPUTERS AND COMPUTING; 1126]

VTOL *type of* **military aircraft.** [➡AIRCRAFT; 1147]

vulgar 1 *adj* **rude**, offensive, crude, bad, earthy, blue (*informal*), improper, naughty (*humorous*), coarse. [➡MORALLY BAD; 776] *Opposite:* decent. 2 *adj* **tasteless**, brash, common, kitsch, ostentatious, outlandish. [➡IN POOR TASTE; 230] *Opposite:* tasteful. 3 *adj* **bad-mannered**, uncouth, discourteous, unrefined, rude, ill-mannered, rough, loutish, boorish. [➡BAD MANNERS AND SOCIAL SKILLS; 522] *Opposite:* polite.

vulgarian *n* [➡LEVEL OF EDUCATION AND SOPHISTICATION; 894]

vulgarism 1 *n* **obscenity**, swear word, four-letter word, expletive, rude word, bad word, vulgarity, profanity, oath. [➡INSULTS, ABUSE, AND SWEARING; 659] 2 *n* **colloquialism**, popular expression, idiom, common term. [➡FIGURES OF SPEECH; 674]

vulgarity 1 *n* **rudeness**, offensiveness, crudeness, crudity, earthiness, impropriety. [➡MORALLY BAD; 776] *Opposite:* decency. 2 *n* **bad manners**, uncouthness, rudeness, loutishness, boorishness. [➡BAD MANNERS AND SOCIAL SKILLS; 522] *Opposite:* politeness. 3 *n* **tastelessness**, brashness, ostentatiousness, commonness, kitsch. [➡IN POOR TASTE; 230] *Opposite:* tastefulness. 4 *n* **swear word**, bad language, four-letter word, rude word, expletive, vulgarism, oath. [➡INSULTS, ABUSE, AND SWEARING; 659]

vulgar language *n* **swear word**, bad language, four-letter word, rude word, vulgarity, expletive, vulgarism. [➡INSULTS, ABUSE, AND SWEARING; 659]

vulnerability *n* **susceptibility**, weakness, defencelessness, helplessness, exposure, liability. [➡DANGER; 236] *Opposite:* invincibility.

vulnerable *adj* **susceptible**, weak, defenceless, helpless, exposed, in danger, at risk. [➡IN DANGER; 238] *Opposite:* invincible.

vulpine *adj* [➡BEASTLY AND BRUTISH; 511]

vulture *type of* **scavenger.** [➡BIRD; 997]

vulturine *adj* **opportunistic**, exploitative, greedy, avaricious, grasping. [➡BEASTLY AND BRUTISH; 511]

wackiness (*informal*) *n* **zaniness**, silliness, craziness (*informal*), wildness, eccentricity, oddness, strangeness. [➡ BIZARRE AND PECULIAR; 258] *Opposite:* conventionality.

wacky (*informal*) *adj* **silly**, crazy (*informal*), zany, madcap, way out, off the wall, wild (*informal*). [➡ BIZARRE AND PECULIAR; 258] *Opposite:* conventional.

wad 1 *n* **bundle**, roll, sheaf, stack, pile. [➡ COLLECTIONS AND MIXTURES OF THINGS; 1243] 2 *n* **lump**, mass, cushion, clump, chunk. [➡ LARGE PIECE; 128] 3 *n* **twist**, chew, portion, gob (*slang*). [➡ MANY, MUCH, LARGE AMOUNT; 117] 4 *n* (*US informal*) [➡ LARGE AMOUNT OF MONEY; 141] 5 *v* **plug**, lag, stuff, fill, pad. [➡ FILL; 407] 6 *v* **compress**, scrunch, squeeze, compact, screw, crumple. [➡ CHANGE OF SHAPE; 386]

wadding *n* **padding**, lining, insulation, lagging, filling, stuffing. [➡ CENTRAL PARTS OF PHYSICAL OBJECTS; 1250]

waddle *v* **toddle**, sway, shuffle, wobble. [➡ WALK UNSTEADILY; 316]

wade *v* **paddle**, stride, walk, splash. [➡ PROCEED AND GO; 306]

wader *type of* **seabird**. [➡ SEABIRD; 1002]

waders *type of* **boot**. [➡ FOOTWEAR; 871]

wade through *v* **plough through**, struggle through, battle through, tackle, deal with, buckle down and do (*informal*), plug away (*informal*). [➡ CONTINUE AN ACTION; 263]

wafer-thin *adj* **thin**, paper-thin, slim. [➡ WIDTH: NARROW AND THIN; 1199]

waffle 1 *v* (*informal*) **go on**, rabbit on (*informal*), ramble, make small talk, blether (*informal*), blabber, babble, blather (*informal*). [➡ WITTER AND BABBLE; 618] 2 *v* (*US informal*) **equivocate**, prevaricate, vacillate, beat about the bush, dither, waver, shilly-shally. [➡ HESITATE; 273] 3 *n* (*informal*) **gobbledegook** (*informal disapproving*), flannel (*informal*), nonsense, rubbish, flimflam (*slang*), guff (*informal*), blether (*informal*), drivel, blather (*informal*), hooey (*informal*), balderdash. [➡ MEANINGLESS SPEECH OR WRITING; 677] 4 *type of* **pancake**. [➡ CAKES, BISCUITS, AND DESSERTS; 1180]

waft 1 *v* **drift**, float, glide, sail, fan, blow. [➡ MOVE FAST; 314] 2 *n* **puff**, breath, gust, breeze, draught. [➡ AMOUNT OF GAS; 116]

wag 1 *v* **wave to and fro**, move from side to side, flap, wiggle, waggle, shake, twitch. [➡ MOVE SOMETHING ON THE SPOT; 337] 2 *n* **wiggle**, waggle, shake, twitch, wave. [➡ MOVE SOMETHING ON THE SPOT; 337] 3 *n* (*dated*) **wit**, humorist, comedian, comic, joker, satirist. [➡ JOKERS AND TEASES; 676]

wage 1 *n* **salary**, pay, earnings, income, take-home pay, remuneration, fee, honorarium, stipend, emolument (*formal*). [➡ INCOME; 461] 2 *v* **carry on**, conduct, pursue, engage in, fight, instigate. [➡ CARRY OUT AN ACTION; 270]

Compare and Contrast: ***wage, salary, pay, fee, remuneration, emolument, honorarium, stipend***

CORE MEANING: MONEY GIVEN FOR WORK DONE

wage a fixed regular payment made on an hourly, weekly, or daily basis, especially to manual workers; ***salary*** a fixed regular annual sum, usually paid on a monthly basis, especially to clerical or professional workers; ***pay*** a *wage* or *salary*; ***fee*** a payment made to a professional person by a client; ***remuneration*** payment for work, goods, or services; ***emolument*** (*formal*) any payment for work; ***honorarium*** money given in exchange for services for which there is normally no fixed charge; ***stipend*** a regular payment or allowance for living expenses, especially one made to a member of the clergy.

waged *adj* [➡ EMPLOYMENT STATUS; 831]

wage earner *n* **breadwinner**, provider, earner, worker, supporter, wage slave (*informal*). [➡ WORKER; 836]

wage packet *n* **wage**, salary, pay packet, wages, earnings, income. [➡ INCOME; 461]

wager 1 *n* **bet**, gamble, flutter (*informal*), stake, ante. [➡ GAMBLE AND TAKE RISKS; 467] 2 *v* **bet**, gamble, stake, risk, venture, lay a wager, have a flutter (*informal*). [➡ GAMBLE AND TAKE RISKS; 467]

wages *n* **salary**, pay, earnings, income, take-home pay, remuneration, gross, net. [➡ INCOME; 461]

wage war on *v* **oppose**, combat, resist, fight, do battle, battle. [➡ COMPETE, CONTEND, AND COMBAT; 304]

waggish (*dated*) *adj* **humorous**, witty, mischievous, droll, jocular, facetious, amusing. [➡ GOOD-TEMPERED AND HUMOROUS; 628]

waggishness (*dated*) *n* **humorousness**, wit, mischievousness, mischief, drollness, jocularity, facetiousness. [➡ GOOD-TEMPERED AND HUMOROUS; 628]

waggle *v* **wiggle**, wag, shake, wave to and fro, move from side to side, jiggle, joggle, flap. [➡ MOVE SOMETHING ON THE SPOT; 337]

wagon 1 *n* **railway wagon**, carriage, car, coach. [➡ BIKES, CARS, AND CARRIAGES; 1148] 2 *part of* **train**. [➡ RAILWAYS; 1106]

wagon

◆ *types of wagon or carriage*

barouche, brougham, buggy, carriage, cart, chariot, coach, Conestoga wagon, covered wagon, dray, landau, landaulet, phaeton, prairie schooner, stagecoach, trap, troika, tumbril

wagtail *type of* **songbird.** [➡SONGBIRD; 1003]

waif *n* **stray**, soul, urchin, orphan, ragamuffin (*dated*). [➡CHILD OR YOUTH; 945]

waiflike *adj* [➡BUILD; 478]

wail 1 *v* **howl**, moan, weep, yowl, keen, scream, cry, screech. [➡SOUND EMISSION BY PEOPLE; 364] 2 *v* **complain**, fuss, kick up a storm, whine, raise a ruckus (*US*). [➡COMPLAIN AND NAG; 687] 3 *n* **howl**, moan, yowl, scream, cry, screech, yelp, whine. [➡SOUNDS MADE BY PEOPLE; 1261] 4 *n* **complaint**, protest, whine, fuss, scream, howling. [➡COMPLAIN AND NAG; 687]

wainscot 1 *n* **panelling**, wainscoting, cladding, lining. [➡BUILDING MATERIALS; 1076] 2 *type of* **general fittings.** [➡FITTINGS; 859]

waist *part of* **torso.** [➡TORSO; 694]

waistband *part of* **garment.** [➡PARTS OF A GARMENT; 870]

waistcoat *type of* **top.** [➡GARMENTS AND OUTFITS; 865]

waistline *n* **waist**, middle, midriff. [➡TORSO; 694]

wait 1 *v* **stay**, remain, hang around, linger, stop, kill time, pass the time. [➡CONTINUE TO EXIST; 17] 2 *v* **delay**, pause, hold your fire, postpone, hang on, hold your horses (*informal*), put off. [➡SHIRK AND DELAY; 274] *Opposite:* begin. 3 *v* **expect**, anticipate, await, wait on. [➡PREDICT AND ANTICIPATE; 751] 4 *n* **delay**, pause, interval, postponement, gap, time lag. [➡PERIOD OF TIME; 90]

waiter *n* **server**, attendant, maître d'hôtel, maître d', head waiter, waitperson (*US*), waitron (*US slang*). [➡DOMESTIC AND KITCHEN WORKERS; 850]

waiting area *n* **concourse**, foyer, meeting point, waiting room, reception. [➡PUBLIC BUILDINGS AND MEETING PLACES; 1080]

waiting room *type of* **room in public buildings.** [➡TYPES OF ROOM; 1096]

wait on 1 *v* **care for**, serve, mother, nurse, take care of, minister to. [➡TAKE CARE OF AND SPOIL; 301] 2 *v* (*informal*) **expect**, anticipate, await, wait for. [➡PREDICT AND ANTICIPATE; 751]

waive *v* **surrender**, give up, relinquish, put aside, ignore, abandon, renounce. [➡FORGET, FORGIVE, AND ACCEPT; 749] *Opposite:* retain.

waiver 1 *n* **disclaimer**, relinquishment, renunciation, abdication, abandonment, sacrifice, loss. [➡FORGO AND DENY ONESELF; 450] 2 *n* **contract**, agreement, bond. [➡OFFICIAL DOCUMENTS; 587]

wake 1 *v* **wake up**, awaken, stir, come round, come to, get up, rouse, waken (*formal*), come around (*US*). [➡WAKE AND REGAIN CONSCIOUSNESS; 725] 2 *v* **arouse**, stir, awaken, rouse, kindle, challenge. [➡APPEAL TO AND AROUSE INTEREST; 576] *Opposite:* stifle.

wakeful 1 *adj* **restless**, disturbed, sleepless, unable to sleep, insomniac, tossing and turning, awake, restive. [➡WIDE AWAKE AND CONSCIOUS; 736] *Opposite:* drowsy. 2 *adj* **alert**, vigilant, on guard, attentive, aware, on the lookout, watchful. [➡POSITIVE IMPATIENCE, ENTHUSIASM, AND ALERTNESS; 538] *Opposite:* inattentive.

wakefulness 1 *n* **restlessness**, sleeplessness, insomnia, tossing and turning, restiveness. [➡WAKE AND REGAIN CONSCIOUSNESS; 725] *Opposite:* drowsiness. 2 *n* **alertness**, vigilance, attentiveness, awareness, watchfulness. [➡POSITIVE IMPATIENCE, ENTHUSIASM, AND ALERTNESS; 538] *Opposite:* inattentiveness.

waken (*formal*) 1 *v* **awaken**, wake up, wake, arouse, get up. [➡WAKE AND REGAIN CONSCIOUSNESS; 725] 2 *v* **arouse**, stir, awaken, kindle, rouse, challenge. [➡APPEAL TO AND AROUSE INTEREST; 576] *Opposite:* suppress.

wakening *n* [➡WAKE AND REGAIN CONSCIOUSNESS; 725]

wake up 1 *v* **wake**, awaken, stir, come round, come to, get up, rouse, come around (*US*). [➡WAKE AND REGAIN CONSCIOUSNESS; 725] 2 *v* **liven up**, come to life, come alive, revive, animate, galvanize, perk up, get going. [➡CHANGE OF MOOD AND COMPOSURE; 581]

waking *n* [➡WAKE AND REGAIN CONSCIOUSNESS; 725]

walk 1 *v* **go on foot**, stroll, amble, saunter, promenade (*formal*), march, hike, stride, toddle, perambulate (*formal*). [➡PROCEED AND GO; 306] 2 *n* **stroll**, saunter, march, amble, promenade (*formal*). [➡PROCEED AND GO; 306] 3 *n* **gait**, pace, tread, stride, way of walking. [➡TEMPERAMENT AND BEHAVIOUR; 493]

walkabout (*informal*) *n* **walk**, stroll, saunter, amble, tour, wander, trip. [➡TRAVEL: JOURNEYS AND TRIPS; 319]

walk a tightrope *v* **tread dangerously**, invite trouble, ask for trouble, ask for it, skate on thin ice, take a chance, walk a thin line. [➡GAMBLE AND TAKE RISKS; 467]

walkaway (*US informal*) *n* **cinch** (*informal*), piece of cake (*informal*), breeze (*informal*), pushover (*informal*), walkover (*informal*). [➡EASY WORK; 300] *Opposite:* challenge.

walk away 1 *v* **abandon**, leave, withdraw, abdicate, back down from, run away. [➡RUN AWAY AND AVOID; 10] 2 *v* **defeat**, beat, annihilate (*informal*), overpower, trounce, thrash, cream (*US informal*). [➡SUCCEED AND WIN; 79]

walk down the aisle *v* **get married**, marry, tie the knot (*informal*), get hitched (*informal*), wed (*formal or literary*), get spliced (*slang*). [➡ESTABLISHING RELATIONSHIPS WITH OTHERS; 974]

walker *n* **hiker**, rambler, stroller, mall walker (*US*). [➡TRAVEL: TRAVELLERS AND WALKERS; 320]

walkie-talkie *type of* **telecommunications equipment.** [➡TELECOMMUNICATIONS; 1129]

walking *adj* **outdoor**, hiking, rambling, cross-country, heavy-duty, tough, hard-wearing. [➡DESCRIBING CLOTHES; 869]

walking boot *type of* **boot.** [➡FOOTWEAR; 871]

walking stick *n* **cane**, stick, bamboo, staff. [➡STICKS, POLES, AND WEDGES; 1253]

walk in on *v* **barge in**, march in, interrupt, intrude, butt in, blunder in. [➡ARRIVE; 12]

walk in the park (*informal*) *n* [➡EASY WORK; 300]

walk it (*informal*) *v* [➡SUCCEED AND WIN; 79]

walk off *v* **turn your back**, walk away, leave, go, quit, abandon ship, desert, walk out. [➡ABSENT ONESELF; 8] *Opposite:* remain.

walk off with *v* **steal**, pinch (*informal*), filch (*informal*), embezzle, pocket, appropriate, knock off (*slang*), take, lift (*informal*), shoplift, cop (*slang*), nick (*slang*), purloin (*formal*), swipe (*informal*). [➡STEAL AND ROB; 427]

walk-on *n* **bit part**, cameo, minor part, minor role, nonspeaking part. [➡PERFORMERS; 905]

walk out 1 *v* **leave**, storm out, go off in a huff, flounce out, take yourself off (*informal*). [➡RUN AWAY AND AVOID; 10] 2 *v* **go on strike**, down tools, take industrial action, stop work. [➡WORK-RELATED ACTIVITIES; 834]

walkout *n* **strike**, stoppage, protest, industrial action. [➡WORK-RELATED ACTIVITIES; 834]

walk out on (*informal*) *v* **leave**, abandon, leave in the lurch, ditch (*informal*), go, throw over (*informal*), desert, dump (*informal*). [➡REFUSING OR REJECTING RELATIONS; 975]

walk over (*informal*) *v* **defeat**, beat, annihilate (*informal*), overpower, trounce, thrash, cream (*US informal*). [➡BEAT AND DEFEAT; 80]

walkover (*informal*) *n* **pushover** (*informal*), easy victory, child's play, doddle (*informal*), runaway, runaway victory, cakewalk (*informal*), cinch (*informal*), piece of cake (*informal*). [➡EASY WORK; 300] *Opposite:* challenge.

walk through *v* **rehearse**, practise, run through. [➡PREPARE FOR ACTION; 290]

walkway 1 *n* **path**, footpath, pathway, pavement, alley, causeway, catwalk, boardwalk, sidewalk (*US*). [➡PATHWAYS; 1109] 2 *n* **aisle**, corridor, passage, passageway. [➡PATHWAYS; 1109] 3 *type of* **bridge**. [➡BRIDGES, TUNNELS, CROSSINGS, AND JUNCTIONS; 1111]

wall *n* **partition**, divider, screen, panel, bulkhead. [➡WALLS AND PARTITIONS; 1103]

wallaby *type of* **marsupial**. [➡MARSUPIAL; 992]

wallet *n* **folder**, file, case, holder. [➡CONTAINERS, RECEPTACLES, AND PACKAGING; 1244]

wallop (*informal*) 1 *v* **thump**, bash (*informal*), biff (*informal*), smack, thwack, strike, hit, punch, whack, bang, bump, crack. [➡PHYSICAL ATTACK AND PUNISHMENT; 416] 2 *v* **defeat**, beat, trounce, whip, destroy, cream (*US informal*), shut out (*US*). [➡BEAT AND DEFEAT; 80] 3 *n* **blow**, thump, bash, biff (*informal*), smack, thwack, punch, whack, bang, bump, crack, hit. [➡CONTACT: IMPACT; 414] 4 *n* **pizazz** (*informal*), fizz, buzz (*informal*), punch, clout, bang (*informal*). [➡TREAT; 211]

walloping (*informal*) 1 *n* **beating**, thrashing, hiding (*informal*). [➡PHYSICAL ATTACK AND PUNISHMENT; 416] 2 *n* **defeat**, drubbing, hiding (*informal*). [➡BEAT AND DEFEAT; 80] 3 *adj* **whopping** (*informal*), huge, enormous, gigantic, stupendous, massive, mammoth. [➡LARGE; 1192] 4 *adv* **extremely**, very, tremendously, inordinately, massively (*informal*), stupendously, breathtakingly, outrageously. [➡TO A GREAT EXTENT; 130]

wallow *v* **flounder**, stumble, lurch, stagger, welter, reel. [➡AIMLESS AND ERRANT MOTION; 344]

wallow in *v* **enjoy**, bask in, revel in, relish, make the most of, take pleasure in, luxuriate in, glory in, exult in, roll about in, immerse yourself in, indulge in, delight in. [➡LIKE, LOVE, VALUE AND ENJOY; 579]

wallpaper 1 *n* **wall covering**, paper, lining paper. [➡COVERS AND COATINGS; 1245] 2 *type of* **software**. [➡COMPUTERS AND COMPUTING; 1126]

wall-to-wall (*informal*) *adj* **omnipresent**, all-pervasive, nonstop, ceaseless, never-ending, unending, endless, continuous. [➡GENERAL LOCATIONS; 159]

walnut 1 *type of* **nut**. [➡NUTS; 1184] 2 *type of* **brown**. [➡COLOURS; 1223]

walrus *type of* **marine mammal**. [➡MARINE MAMMAL; 987]

walrus moustache *n* [➡FACIAL HAIR; 490]

waltz 1 *n* (*informal*) **cinch** (*informal*), piece of cake (*informal*), breeze (*informal*), pushover (*informal*), walkover (*informal*), snap (*US*), walkaway (*US informal*). [➡EASY WORK; 300] 2 *v* **walk**, stroll, swan, breeze, saunter. [➡PROCEED AND GO; 306] 3 *v* **romp**, sail, steam, zip (*informal*), whizz, cruise, zap (*informal*). [➡MOVE FAST; 314] 4 *type of* **dance**. [➡DANCE; 903]

wan 1 *adj* **pallid**, ashen, ashy, drawn, washed-out, white, grey, waxen, pale. [➡COMPLEXION; 481] 2 *adj* **listless**, feeble, weak, down, depressed, low. [➡UNFIT AND WEAK; 740] *Opposite:* strong.

wand *n* **baton**, stick, rod, pointer. [➡STICKS, POLES, AND WEDGES; 1253]

wander 1 *v* **stroll**, meander, walk, mosey (*informal*), mooch (*slang*), ramble, roam, amble. [➡MOVE SLOWLY; 315] 2 *v* **drift**, stray, digress, lose the point, lose the thread, lose concentration, go off at a tangent, deviate. [➡NOT PAY ATTENTION; 765] 3 *n* **walk**, stroll, mosey (*informal*), mooch (*slang*), ramble. [➡PROCEED AND GO; 306]

wander away *v* [➡ABSENT ONESELF; 8]

wanderer *n* **nomad**, vagrant, itinerant, traveller, rover, rambler, drifter, rolling stone, tramp, hobo. [➡TRAVEL: TRAVELLERS AND WALKERS; 320]

wandering *adj* **itinerant**, nomadic, peripatetic, travelling, drifting, rootless, roving. [➡AIMLESS AND ERRANT MOTION; 344] *Opposite:* settled.

wanderlust *n* **desire to travel**, itchy feet, travel bug. [➡DESIRE AND WANT; 580]

wander off *v* [➡ABSENT ONESELF; 8]

wane *v* **diminish**, decrease, decline, get smaller, fade, disappear, vanish. [➡DISAPPEAR; 4] *Opposite:* wax.

wangle (*informal*) *v* **engineer**, contrive, get (*informal*), obtain, fix (*informal*), swing (*informal*), finagle (*informal*). [➡OBTAIN POSSESSION BY PERSUASION; 458]

waning *adj* **fading**, declining, weakening, diminishing, disappearing, vanishing. [➡CEASE TO EXIST; 22] *Opposite:* increasing.

wannabe (*informal*) 1 *n* **hopeful**, aspirant, imitator, clone, copycat (*informal*), camp follower, fellow traveller, would-be (*informal*). [➡SUPPORTERS, PROTECTORS, AND COMPATRIOTS; 970]

2 *adj* **aspiring**, would-be, hopeful, budding, potential, embryonic. [➡POSITIVE IMPATIENCE, ENTHUSIASM, AND ALERTNESS; 538]

wanness *n* [➡COMPLEXION; 481]

want **1** *v* **desire**, wish for, fancy (*informal*), long for, crave, covet, yearn for, hanker after, be after, be looking for, hope for, aspire. [➡DESIRE AND WANT; 580] **2** *v* **need**, require, lack, be short of, miss. [➡REQUEST AND DEMAND; 664] **3** *n* **lack**, absence, shortage, scarcity, dearth, deficiency. [➡NON-EXISTENCE; 24] **4** *n* **poverty**, famine, hunger, need, neediness. [➡POVERTY AND POOR; 892]

Compare and Contrast: ***want, desire, wish, long, yearn, covet, crave***

CORE MEANING: TO SEEK TO HAVE, DO, OR ACHIEVE SOMETHING

want to feel a need or desire for something; ***desire*** to want something very strongly; ***wish*** to have a strong, sometimes unrealistic, desire for something or to do something; ***long*** to have a strong desire for somebody or something, especially something difficult to achieve; ***yearn*** to want something very much, especially with a feeling of sadness when it seems unlikely that it can ever be obtained; ***covet*** to have a strong desire to possess something that belongs to somebody else, or (*formal*) to want something very much; ***crave*** to want something very much, especially when this desire is physical.

want ad (*US informal*) *n* [➡ADVERTISING AND PUBLICITY; 605]

wanted *adj* **required**, sought, sought after, hunted, desired, needed. [➡POPULAR AND WANTED; 221]

wanting **1** *adj* **deficient**, inadequate, imperfect, not good enough, not up to standard, not up to scratch (*informal*), defective, below par. [➡INAPPROPRIATE AND UNSUITABLE; 225] *Opposite:* adequate. **2** *prep* **without**, lacking, in need of, short of, sans (*literary or humorous*), minus. [➡LACK OF POSSESSION; 446]

wanton **1** *adj* **gratuitous**, motiveless, meaningless, reckless, needless, unjustifiable, wilful, uncalled-for, unprovoked. [➡UNIMPORTANT AND UNNECESSARY; 239] *Opposite:* justifiable. **2** *adj* **immoral**, immodest, abandoned, licentious (*formal*), lustful, impious, dissipated, dissolute, shameless. [➡MORALLY BAD; 776] *Opposite:* restrained. **3** *adj* **malevolent**, malicious, cruel, vicious, nasty, maleficent. [➡SELFISH AND UNKIND; 506] *Opposite:* benign. **4** *adj* **excessive**, extravagant, unrestrained, heedless, unreasonable, restrained. [➡BAD MANNERS AND SOCIAL SKILLS; 522]

wantonness *n* **depravity**, debauchery, immorality, shamelessness, licentiousness (*formal*), impiety, dissipation, dissoluteness. [➡MORALLY BAD; 776] *Opposite:* restraint.

wants *n* **needs**, requirements, desires, requests, wishes. [➡DESIRE AND WANT; 580]

wap *n* [➡THE INTERNET; 1127]

war **1** *n* **conflict**, warfare, hostilities, fighting, confrontation, combat, action. [➡WARFARE AND WAR; 830] *Opposite:* peace. **2** *n* **campaign**, battle, struggle, crusade. [➡AGGRESSIVE EVENT; 39] **3** *n* **competition**, rivalry, feud, battle, struggle. [➡DISHARMONY; 157]

See Compare and Contrast at **fight**.

warble **1** *v* **sing**, trill, pipe up, chirrup, sing out. [➡SOUND EMISSION BY ANIMALS OR BIRDS; 365] **2** *type of* **bird sound**. [➡SOUNDS MADE BY BIRDS; 1262]

warbler *type of* **songbird**. [➡SONGBIRD; 1003]

war cry *n* **battle cry**, rallying call, call to arms. [➡THE SPOKEN WORD; 672]

ward *type of* **room in public buildings**. [➡TYPES OF ROOM; 1096]

warden *n* **custodian**, curator, keeper, steward, superintendent, supervisor, guardian. [➡PEOPLE WHO GUARD AND PROTECT; 846]

warder **1** *n* **prison officer**, jailer, custodian, guard, turnkey (*archaic*), warden (*US*). [➡PEOPLE WHO GUARD AND PROTECT; 846] **2** *n* **guard**, custodian, keeper, monitor, sentry, sentinel. [➡PEOPLE WHO GUARD AND PROTECT; 846]

ward off *v* **defend against**, protect against, deflect, hold off, keep at bay, fend off, fight off, discourage. [➡AVOID OR ESCAPE CONTACT; 419]

wardrobe **1** *n* **clothes**, clothing, attire (*formal*), apparel, gear (*informal*). [➡CLOTHES AND ACCESSORIES; 864] **2** *type of* **cabinet**. [➡FURNITURE; 858]

warehouse **1** *type of* **retail outlet**. [➡RETAIL OUTLETS; 1082] **2** *type of* **storage space**. [➡STORES AND STORAGE BUILDINGS; 1087]

wares *n* **goods**, merchandise, produce, products, commodities, stuff. [➡BUSINESS PRODUCTS; 796]

warfare **1** *n* **fighting**, conflict, combat, war. [➡WARFARE AND WAR; 830] **2** *n* **rivalry**, feud, competition, contest, struggle. [➡RELATIONSHIP TO ANOTHER; 973]

warhead *type of* **explosive material**. [➡EXPLOSIVES; 1154]

warhorse **1** *n* **veteran**, campaigner, warrior, stalwart, old hand, master. [➡MILITARY PERSONNEL; 828] **2** *type of* **horse**. [➡HORSE; 985]

wariness *n* **caution**, suspicion, care, circumspection, guardedness, caginess (*informal*). [➡FEELINGS ABOUT THE FUTURE; 534] *Opposite:* recklessness.

warlike **1** *adj* **belligerent**, aggressive, bellicose, confrontational, hostile, pugnacious. [➡AGGRESSIVE AND BELLIGERENT; 519] *Opposite:* friendly. **2** *adj* **martial**, military, militaristic, warring, war. [➡MILITARY; 829]

warlock *n* **sorcerer**, wizard, necromancer (*literary*), enchanter, witch. [➡PEOPLE WITH SUPERNATURAL POWERS; 789]

warlord *n* **military leader**, general, chieftain, guerrilla leader, commander. [➡MILITARY PERSONNEL; 828]

warm **1** *adj* **temperate**, tepid, balmy, hot, lukewarm. [➡HOT WEATHER; 1050] *Opposite:* cool. **2** *adj* **kind**, kindly, warm-hearted, kind-hearted, friendly, cordial, convivial, genial, hospitable, welcoming, congenial, amiable, affectionate, loving, tender. [➡FRIENDLINESS AND SOCIABILITY; 495] *Opposite:* unfriendly. **3** *adj* **cosy**, inviting, restful, cheerful, cheery, snug, welcoming. [➡PHYSICALLY PLEASANT; 187] *Opposite:* unwelcoming. **4** *adj* **lively**, passionate, ardent, fiery, enthusiastic, zealous. [➡APPRECIATION AND GRATITUDE; 536] *Opposite:* cool. **5** *adj* **sincere**, heartfelt, deep, earnest, wholehearted. [➡HONEST AND RELIABLE; 503] **6** *v* **heat**, heat up, reheat, warm up, melt, thaw, thaw out. [➡CHANGE OF TEMPERATURE; 387] *Opposite:* cool. **7** *v* **take to**, become fond of, take a liking to, take a fancy to, take a shine to (*informal*), hit it off (*informal*), get on with, get along with (*US*). [➡LIKE, LOVE, VALUE AND ENJOY; 579] *Opposite:* cool off. **8** *v* **become enthusiastic about**, get going on, get fired up about, get excited, become enthused, get stirred up. [➡CHANGE OF MOOD AND COMPOSURE; 581] **9** *n* **warmth**, warmness, heat. [➡TEMPERATURE: MEDIUM; 1229] *Opposite:* cold.

warm-blooded *adj* **passionate**, impetuous, enthusiastic, ardent, emotional, excitable, spirited. [➡ENERGY AND ENTHUSIASM; 497] *Opposite:* cold-blooded.

war memorial *n* [➡MONUMENTS; 1091]

warm front *n* [➡HOT WEATHER; 1050]

warm-hearted *adj* **kindly**, tender, kind, sympathetic, affectionate, loving, compassionate, kind-hearted. [➡GENEROSITY AND KINDNESS; 496] *Opposite:* cold-hearted.

warm-heartedness *n* **tenderness**, kindness, sympathy, affection, love, compassion, kind-heartedness. [➡GENEROSITY AND KINDNESS; 496] *Opposite:* cold-heartedness.

warmly **1** *adv* **lovingly**, tenderly, kindly, sincerely, affectionately. [➡GENEROSITY AND KINDNESS; 496] **2** *adv* **ardently**, enthusiastically, passionately, eagerly, with enthusiasm, with eagerness, with fervour. [➡ENTHUSIASTIC AND INQUISITIVE; 629] *Opposite:* apathetically. **3** *adv* **cordially**, genially, in a friendly way, amiably. [➡FRIENDLINESS AND SOCIABILITY; 495]

warmness **1** *n* **balminess**, temperateness, high temperature. [➡HOT WEATHER; 1050] *Opposite:* coldness. **2** *n* **warmth**, heat, hotness. [➡TEMPERATURE: MEDIUM; 1229] *Opposite:* coldness. **3** *n* **warm-heartedness**, kind-heartedness, kindness, friendliness, affection, cordiality, hospitableness, tenderness. [➡GENEROSITY AND KINDNESS; 496] *Opposite:* unkindness. **4** *n* **eagerness**, passion, enthusiasm, ardour, fervour. [➡POSITIVE IMPATIENCE, ENTHUSIASM, AND ALERTNESS; 538] *Opposite:* apathy.

warmonger *n* **hawk**, belligerent, jingo, jingoist, aggressor, sabre-rattler. [➡UNCOOPERATIVE OR REBELLIOUS PERSON; 567] *Opposite:* peacemaker.

warmongering *n* **sabre rattling**, belligerence, aggression, jingoism, hawkishness. [➡REBELLIOUSNESS AND DISOBEDIENCE; 566] *Opposite:* peacemaking.

warmth **1** *n* **balminess**, temperateness, heat, warmness. [➡TEMPERATURE: MEDIUM; 1229] *Opposite:* cold. **2** *n* **friendliness**, cordiality, warm-heartedness, kind-heartedness, warmness, affection, tenderness, love, kindness, kindliness. [➡LOVE, RESPECT, AND GOODWILL; 550] *Opposite:* cold-heartedness. **3** *n* **friendliness**, hospitality, cordiality, conviviality, geniality, amiability. [➡GENEROSITY AND KINDNESS; 496] *Opposite:* unfriendliness. **4** *n* **enthusiasm**, eagerness, earnestness, ardour, fervour, warmness, passion. [➡POSITIVE IMPATIENCE, ENTHUSIASM, AND ALERTNESS; 538] *Opposite:* apathy.

warm through *v* [➡MEAL PREPARATION; 355]

warm to *v* [➡LIKE, LOVE, VALUE AND ENJOY; 579]

warm-up *n* **exercises**, limbering up, loosening up, preparation. [➡PREPARATORY EVENT; 57]

warm up **1** *v* **limber up**, loosen up, get loose, stretch. [➡PREPARE FOR ACTION; 290] *Opposite:* cool off. **2** *v* **warm**, heat, heat up, reheat, warm through, melt, thaw, thaw out, warm over (*US*). [➡CHANGE OF TEMPERATURE; 387] *Opposite:* cool off.

warm weather *n* [➡HOT WEATHER; 1050]

warn **1** *v* **caution**, advise, counsel (*formal or literary*), inform, notify, tell, tip off. [➡ADVISE AND WARN; 614] **2** *v* **alert**, forewarn, advise, tell, notify, give notice. [➡ADVISE AND WARN; 614]

warning **1** *n* **threat**, indication, portent, forewarning, sign, omen. [➡INDICATIONS, SIGNS, AND WARNINGS; 68] **2** *n* **notice**, caution, caveat, word of warning, advice, counsel (*formal or literary*), admonition, forewarning. [➡ADVICE; 690] **3** *adj* **cautionary**, threatening, cautioning. [➡ADVISE AND WARN; 614]

warn off *v* **deter**, discourage, dissuade, put off, scare off, frighten off. [➡ADVISE AND WARN; 614]

war of words *n* **argument**, row, slanging match, disagreement, fight, slinging match (*US*). [➡ARGUMENT; 47]

warp **1** *v* **distort**, twist, deform, bend, buckle, go out of shape. [➡CHANGE OF SHAPE; 386] *Opposite:* straighten. **2** *v* **change**, pervert, damage, distort, misrepresent, confuse, bend, twist. [➡FALSIFY AND CHEAT; 177] **3** *n* **twist**, bend, distortion, deviation, alteration, change. [➡CHANGE OF SHAPE; 386]

warped **1** *adj* **misshapen**, distorted, deformed, twisted, bent, out of shape. [➡IN BAD REPAIR; 1233] **2** *adj* **changed**, damaged, distorted, misrepresented, confused, bent, perverted, twisted. [➡BIZARRE AND PECULIAR; 258] **3** *adj* **partial**, biased, one-sided, prejudiced, skewed. [➡INCORRECT AND ERRONEOUS; 223] *Opposite:* impartial.

warrant **1** *n* **authorization**, permit, licence, authority, certification. [➡OFFICIAL DOCUMENTS; 587] **2** *v* **merit**, deserve, necessitate, call for, demand, justify. [➡NEED AND REQUIRE; 465] **3** *v* **guarantee**, affirm, certify, secure, assure, insure. [➡PROMISE AND ASSURE; 685]

warranty *n* **guarantee**, contract, pledge, assurance. [➡OFFICIAL DOCUMENTS; 587]

war-ravaged *adj* [➡IN BAD REPAIR; 1233]

warren **1** *n* **hole**, earth, habitat, burrow, lair, den. [➡ANIMAL OR BIRD ACCOMMODATION; 1078] **2** *n* **maze**, labyrinth, catacomb. [➡DISORDER AND CHAOS; 246]

warring *adj* **belligerent**, combatant, fighting, sparring, opposing, contending, aggressive. [➡REBELLIOUSNESS AND DISOBEDIENCE; 566] *Opposite:* friendly.

warrior *n* **soldier**, fighter, combatant, trooper. [➡MILITARY PERSONNEL; 828]

war-scarred *adj* [➡IN BAD REPAIR; 1233]

warship *type of* **military vessel**. [➡SHIPS AND BOATS; 1149]

wart *n* **lump**, growth, verruca. [➡CONDITIONS AFFECTING THE SKIN; 722]

wart hog *type of* **large mammal**. [➡LARGE MAMMAL; 986]

war-torn *adj* **war-ravaged**, frontline, battle-weary, war-scarred, battle-scarred, battle-damaged, bomb-damaged, devastated, disrupted. [➡ IN BAD REPAIR; 1233] *Opposite:* peaceful.

warts and all *adv* [➡ ALL; 126]

wary *adj* **watchful**, cautious, suspicious, distrustful, mistrustful, chary, guarded, circumspect, careful. [➡ INSECURITY AND LOSS OF COMPOSURE; 545] *Opposite:* careless.

See Compare and Contrast at **cautious**.

wash 1 *v* **clean**, bathe, rinse, sponge down, wash down, cleanse, sluice, swab, shampoo, launder. [➡ CLEAN AND POLISH; 404] 2 *v* **bathe**, bath, clean up, wash up (*US*). [➡ CLEAN AND POLISH; 404] 3 *v* **flow over**, splash, lap, swish, pound, slap, lave (*archaic*). [➡ TAKE UP A NEW POSITION; 313] 4 *v* **erode**, wash away, carry away, bear away, sweep away. [➡ DELETE AND ERASE; 340] 5 *n* **shower**, shampoo, sponge, rinse, wash-down, launder, swab, bath. [➡ CLEAN AND POLISH; 404] 6 *n* **washing**, layer, film, coat, overlay, coating. [➡ COVERS AND COATINGS; 1245] 7 *n* **stain**, tint, rinse, suffusion, colouring. [➡ DYES AND COLOURANTS; 1269]

washable *adj* **colourfast**, easy-care, noniron, preshrunk, launderable, unfading, wash-and-wear, permanent-press. [➡ DESCRIBING CLOTHES; 869]

wash-and-wear *adj* [➡ DESCRIBING CLOTHES; 869]

washbasin *n* **hand basin**, basin, bowl, sink, washbowl. [➡ FITTINGS; 859]

washbowl *n* **washbasin**, basin, sink, hand basin. [➡ FITTINGS; 859]

wash down *v* **clean**, rinse, sluice, sponge down, hose down, wash. [➡ CLEAN AND POLISH; 404]

washed-out 1 *adj* **wan**, pallid, ashen, ashy, drawn, white, grey, pale. [➡ COMPLEXION; 481] 2 *adj* **exhausted**, done in (*informal*), tired out, used up, drained, all in, beat (*informal*), wasted (*slang*). [➡ TIRED, ASLEEP AND UNCONSCIOUS; 739] *Opposite:* energetic.

washed-up (*informal*) *adj* **unsuccessful**, finished, defeated, through, done for (*informal*), failed, has been, manqué. [➡ IN TROUBLE AND DISADVANTAGED; 73] *Opposite:* successful.

washer *n* **seal**, gasket, liner, ring, lining. [➡ FASTENERS, LINKS, AND NETWORKS; 1246]

wash-hand basin *type of* **plumbing fittings**. [➡ FITTINGS; 859]

washing 1 *n* **laundry**, dirty linen, dirty clothes. [➡ CLOTHES AND ACCESSORIES; 864] 2 *n* **wash**, weekly wash, clothes wash. [➡ CLOTHES AND ACCESSORIES; 864] 3 *n* **coat**, coating, film, layer, overlay, wash. [➡ COVERS AND COATINGS; 1245]

washing machine *type of* **appliance**. [➡ HOUSEHOLD APPLIANCES; 1116]

wash out *v* **wash**, rinse, flush, swill, hose. [➡ CLEAN AND POLISH; 404]

washout (*informal*) *n* **failure**, dead loss, disaster, disappointment, flop (*informal*), bomb (*US informal*). [➡ FAILURE; 77] *Opposite:* success.

wash over *v* **flow over**, engulf, sweep over, overwhelm, come over, swamp, overflow. [➡ HAPPEN TO SOMEBODY; 30]

washroom (*US*) *n* **toilet**, lavatory, bathroom, gents, ladies, powder room, men's room (*US*), ladies' room (*US*), restroom (*US*). [➡ TYPES OF ROOM; 1096]

wash your hands of *v* **disown**, abandon, refuse to have anything to do with, absolve yourself, ignore, reject. [➡ NOT PAY ATTENTION; 765]

wasp *type of* **flying insect**. [➡ FLYING INSECTS; 1013]

waspish 1 *adj* **irritable**, touchy, irascible, cantankerous, peevish, tetchy (*informal*), waspy. [➡ IRRITATION AND ANGER; 542] *Opposite:* affable. 2 *adj* **malignant**, spiteful, malicious, nasty, vindictive, venomous, waspy. [➡ RUDE AND HOSTILE; 626] *Opposite:* friendly.

waspishness 1 *n* **irritability**, touchiness, irascibility, cantankerousness, peevishness, bad temper, tetchiness (*informal*). [➡ SELFISH AND UNKIND; 506] *Opposite:* affability. 2 *n* **spitefulness**, spite, malice, maliciousness, nastiness, vindictiveness, venomousness, venom. [➡ RUDE AND HOSTILE; 626] *Opposite:* friendliness.

waspy *adj* [➡ RUDE AND HOSTILE; 626]

wastage *n* **waste**, surplus, excess, leftovers. [➡ REMAINDER AND REMAINDERS; 123]

waste 1 *v* **squander**, fritter away, misuse, dissipate, throw away, blow (*slang*). [➡ USE UP AND WASTE; 475] *Opposite:* save. 2 *v* **atrophy**, wither, become emaciated, waste away, weaken. [➡ GET WORSE; 382] *Opposite:* strengthen. 3 *v* **ravage**, devastate, ruin, spoil, despoil, destroy. [➡ DESTRUCTION AND DEMOLITION; 360] 4 *v* (*slang*) **kill**, murder, assassinate, execute, dispatch, bump off (*slang*). [➡ KILL; 923] 5 *n* **litter**, rubbish, garbage (*US*), trash (*US*). [➡ RUBBISH AND USELESS OBJECTS; 1248] 6 *adj* **excess**, surplus, unwanted, discarded, remaining, spare, leftover, unused. [➡ MORE AND EXCESS; 122] 7 *adj* **uncultivated**, barren, bare, fallow. [➡ EMPTY; 1237] *Opposite:* cultivated.

waste away *v* **wither**, waste, atrophy, become emaciated, weaken. [➡ GET WORSE; 382] *Opposite:* strengthen.

wastebasket (*US*) *n* [➡ CONTAINERS, RECEPTACLES, AND PACKAGING; 1244]

waste bin *n* [➡ CONTAINERS, RECEPTACLES, AND PACKAGING; 1244]

wasted 1 *adj* (*slang*) **exhausted**, tired, worn out, done in (*informal*), shattered, tired out, whacked (*informal*), washed out, dead beat (*informal*). [➡ UNDER THE INFLUENCE OF DRUGS OR ALCOHOL; 742] *Opposite:* fresh. 2 *adj* **missed**, misused, lost, unexploited, unused, squandered. [➡ IN BAD REPAIR; 1233] 3 *adj* **futile**, fruitless, unproductive, worthless, useless, pointless, needless. [➡ UNIMPORTANT AND UNNECESSARY; 239] *Opposite:* worthwhile. 4 *adj* **ravaged**, withered, shrunken, atrophied, emaciated, thin, cadaverous. [➡ BUILD; 478] *Opposite:* healthy.

waste disposal unit *type of* **appliance**. [➡ HOUSEHOLD APPLIANCES; 1116]

wasteful *adj* **extravagant**, careless, uneconomical, profligate, lavish, inefficient, spendthrift, improvident (*formal*). [➡ WASTEFUL AND UNECONOMICAL; 247] *Opposite:* frugal.

wastefulness *n* **extravagance**, carelessness, profligacy, improvidence, lavishness, squandering. [➡WASTEFUL AND UNECONOMICAL; 247] *Opposite:* frugality.

wasteland *n* **wilds**, wilderness, desert, badlands. [➡URBAN OUTDOOR SPACES; 1071]

wastepaper basket *n* [➡CONTAINERS, RECEPTACLES, AND PACKAGING; 1244]

wastepaper bin *n* [➡CONTAINERS, RECEPTACLES, AND PACKAGING; 1244]

waste pipe *n* [➡WATERCOURSES; 1110]

waste product *n* [➡UNPLEASANT AND DIRTY SUBSTANCES; 1267]

waster *n* [➡LAZY OR UNSUCCESSFUL PEOPLE; 948]

wastes *n* **wilds**, wilderness, wastelands. [➡DESERTS AND PLAINS; 1045]

wasting away *adj* [➡UNFIT AND WEAK; 740]

wastrel *n* [➡LAZY OR UNSUCCESSFUL PEOPLE; 948]

watch 1 *n* **guard**, lookout, sentry, sentinel, watchdog. [➡PEOPLE WHO GUARD AND PROTECT; 846] 2 *v* **observe**, look at, stare at, gaze at, survey, view, examine, scrutinize, inspect. [➡LOOKING AND LOOKS; 701] *Opposite:* ignore. 3 *v* **pay attention to**, beware, mind, be cautious about, consider, keep an eye on, attend to. [➡PAY ATTENTION; 766] 4 *v* **look after**, keep an eye on, mind, guard, watch over, take care of. [➡TAKE CARE OF AND SPOIL; 301] *Opposite:* neglect. 5 *v* **spy on**, stalk, keep under observation, keep an eye on, keep under surveillance. [➡ACCOMPANY AND FOLLOW; 338] 6 *type of* **clock**. [➡CLOCKS AND TIMERS; 1125]

watchdog *n* **ombudsman**, supervisory body, regulator, overseer. [➡BUSINESS ENTERPRISES AND RELATED BODIES; 793]

watcher *n* **observer**, onlooker, spectator, viewer, witness. [➡LOOKERS AND SPECTATORS; 702]

watchful *adj* **observant**, attentive, alert, vigilant, on the alert, on the lookout. [➡POSITIVE IMPATIENCE, ENTHUSIASM, AND ALERTNESS; 538] *Opposite:* inattentive.

watchfulness *n* **alertness**, attention, vigilance, caution, care. [➡POSITIVE INTELLECTUAL CHARACTERISTICS; 525] *Opposite:* inattentiveness.

watchman *n* **night watchman**, guard, security guard, custodian, caretaker. [➡PEOPLE WHO GUARD AND PROTECT; 846]

watch out 1 *v* **be careful**, look out, be alert, be wary, take care, be cautious, take heed, be watchful, pay attention, mind out. [➡PAY ATTENTION; 766] 2 *v* **look out**, look, wait, watch, be on the lookout, keep your eyes open, be vigilant, keep a sharp lookout. [➡LOOKING AND LOOKS; 701]

watch over *v* **supervise**, look after, keep an eye on, guard, mind, watch. [➡TAKE CARE OF AND SPOIL; 301] *Opposite:* neglect.

watchtower *n* **lookout tower**, lookout post, observation tower, crow's nest. [➡TOWERS; 1098]

watchword *n* **motto**, slogan, maxim, byword, catch phrase, saying. [➡THE SPOKEN WORD; 672]

watch your step *v* **be careful**, take care, watch out, look out, pay attention, mind out, be cautious, mind your Ps and Qs. [➡PAY ATTENTION; 766]

watch your weight *v* **be on a diet**, diet, slim, watch what you eat, cut down, count calories, cut back, watch your waistline, reduce (*US*). [➡EAT AND NOT EAT; 711]

water 1 *n* **liquid**, rainwater, seawater, mineral water, tap water, bath water, H_2O. [➡LIQUIDS; 1268] 2 *v* **soak**, spray, irrigate, drench, sprinkle, hose, hose down, wet, dampen. [➡SOFTEN, LIQUEFY, DAMPEN; 389] 3 *v* **fill with tears**, stream, run, fill up, well. [➡LIQUID EMISSION; 371]

water bed *type of* **bed**. [➡FURNITURE; 858]

water beetle *type of* **beetle**. [➡BEETLES AND WEEVILS; 1016]

water bird *n* **waterfowl**, freshwater bird, duck. [➡FRESHWATER BIRD; 1000]

waterborne *adj* **aquatic**, floating, marine, riverine. [➡SICKNESS; 730]

watercolourist *n* [➡ARTISTS; 900]

watercourse 1 *n* **ditch**, conduit, drain, culvert. [➡WATERCOURSES; 1110] 2 *n* **waterway**, channel, stream, river, rivulet, brook, canal. [➡RIVERS, LAKES, AND STREAMS; 1042]

watercress *type of* **salad vegetable**. [➡FRUIT AND VEGETABLES; 1175]

water down 1 *v* **dilute**, thin down, weaken, attenuate. [➡CHANGE OF INTENSITY: LESS; 396] *Opposite:* thicken. 2 *v* **soften**, reduce, moderate, mitigate, regulate, tone down, temper. [➡CHANGE OF INTENSITY: LESS; 396] *Opposite:* beef up (*informal*).

watered-down 1 *adj* **diluted**, dilute, thin, weak, insipid, bland, watery, wishy-washy (*informal*). [➡WEAKNESS; 242] *Opposite:* concentrated. 2 *adj* **moderated**, weakened, vapid, qualified, toned-down, diluted. [➡WEAKNESS; 242] *Opposite:* unqualified.

waterfall *n* **cascade**, cataract, falls, weir, force. [➡RIVERS, LAKES, AND STREAMS; 1042]

water flea *type of* **crustacean**. [➡AQUATIC INVERTEBRATE; 1022]

waterfowl 1 *n* **water bird**, freshwater bird, duck. [➡FRESHWATER BIRD; 1000] 2 *type of* **fowl**. [➡FOOD BIRD; 999]

waterfront *n* **harbour**, lakefront, seafront, oceanfront, water's edge, riverside. [➡THE SEAS, OCEANS, AND SHORES; 1041]

water hole *n* **oasis**, pool, pond, water source, spring, watering hole, wallow. [➡RIVERS, LAKES, AND STREAMS; 1042]

watering hole *n* **oasis**, pool, pond, water hole, wallow, water source, spring. [➡RIVERS, LAKES, AND STREAMS; 1042]

waterless *adj* **dry**, arid, parched, dehydrated. [➡DRY; 1241]

waterlessness *n* [➡DRY; 1241]

water line 1 *n* **load line**, Plimsoll line, Plimsoll mark, watermark. [➡THE SEAS, OCEANS, AND SHORES; 1041] 2 *n* **tideline**, tidemark, watermark, high watermark, floodmark. [➡THE SEAS, OCEANS, AND SHORES; 1041]

waterlogged *adj* **sodden**, sopping, drenched, wet, soaking, saturated, soaked. [➡WET; 1239] *Opposite:* dry.

watermark 1 *n* **mark**, imprint, logo, emblem. [➡DRAWINGS, CHARTS AND TABLES; 595] 2 *n* **water line**, load line, Plimsoll line, Plimsoll mark. [➡SYMBOLS, SIGNS, AND NUMBERS; 597] 3 *n* **tideline**, tidemark, water line, high watermark, floodmark. [➡THE SEAS, OCEANS, AND SHORES; 1041]

watermelon *type of* **fruit.** [➡FRUIT AND VEGETABLES; 1175]

water mill *type of* **factory.** [➡INDUSTRIAL BUILDINGS; 1086]

water moccasin *type of* **poisonous snake.** [➡SNAKE; 995]

water pipe *n* [➡WATERCOURSES; 1110]

water pistol *type of* **toy.** [➡TOYS; 880]

waterproof *adj* **water-resistant**, rainproof, watertight, impermeable. [➡IN GOOD REPAIR; 1231] *Opposite:* permeable.

waterproofed *adj* [➡IN GOOD REPAIR; 1231]

waterproof jacket *type of* **jacket.** [➡GARMENTS AND OUTFITS; 865]

water-resistant *adj* [➡IN GOOD REPAIR; 1231]

watershed *n* **turning point**, defining moment, breaking point, seminal moment, crisis, crunch. [➡DECISIVE MOMENTS; 44]

waterside 1 *n* **riverbank**, shore, bank, water's edge, waterfront, seafront, oceanfront, seaside, beach, sea shore, shoreline, lakeside, riverside, quayside, lakefront. [➡THE SEAS, OCEANS, AND SHORES; 1041] 2 *adj* **waterfront**, beachfront, seaside, lakeside, riverside, littoral. [➡THE SEAS, OCEANS, AND SHORES; 1041]

water snake *type of* **non-poisonous snake.** [➡SNAKE; 995]

watertight 1 *adj* **sealed**, waterproof, impermeable, rainproof. [➡IN GOOD REPAIR; 1231] *Opposite:* permeable. 2 *adj* **incontrovertible**, unassailable, sound, firm, irrefutable, indisputable. [➡CERTAIN; 175] *Opposite:* weak.

water tower *type of* **storage space.** [➡STORES AND STORAGE BUILDINGS; 1087]

water vapour *n* [➡GASES; 1274]

waterway *n* **watercourse**, canal, river, channel, stream, shipping canal. [➡RIVERS, LAKES, AND STREAMS; 1042]

waterworks *n* **tears**, crying, weeping, blubbering (*informal*), blubbing (*informal*), sobbing. [➡CRYING; 651]

watery 1 *adj* **wet**, soggy, squelchy, boggy, moist, waterlogged. [➡WET; 1239] *Opposite:* dry. 2 *adj* **watered-down**, thin, weak, runny, dilute, diluted. [➡FLUID AND NON-SOLID; 1212] *Opposite:* thick. 3 *adj* **feeble**, weak, faint, wan, hazy, dim, pale. [➡WEAKNESS; 242] *Opposite:* forceful. 4 *adj* **bland**, tasteless, insipid, weak, diluted, dilute, watered-down. [➡TASTE; 704] *Opposite:* strong.

wave 1 *v* **gesticulate**, gesture, signal, beckon. [➡GESTURES AND GESTICULATION; 654] 2 *v* **brandish**, flourish, wield, wag, shake, flail. [➡MOVE SOMETHING ON THE SPOT; 337] 3 *v* **flutter**, flap, sway, undulate, move to and fro. [➡BOUNCE, UNDULATE, AND VIBRATE; 309] 4 *n* **breaker**, roller, dumper, ripple, surge, surf, swell. [➡THE SEAS, OCEANS, AND SHORES; 1041] 5 *n* **upsurge**, groundswell, tendency, trend, movement, surge, flood, surf, swell. [➡SUDDEN EVENT; 52] 6 *n* **gesture**, signal, sign. [➡GESTURES AND GESTICULATION; 654] 7 *n* **rash**, spate, outbreak, epidemic, series, flood, eruption. [➡SUDDEN EVENT; 52] 8 *n* **current**, surge, impulse, oscillation, undulation. [➡ENERGY GENERAL; 1160] 9 *n* **curl**, kink, undulation, ringlet. [➡HAIR; 485]

waver 1 *v* **dither**, hesitate, be indecisive, be irresolute, vacillate, falter, shilly-shally, hem and haw, whiffle waffle (*US*). [➡HESITATE; 273] 2 *v* **tremble**, shake, flutter, flicker, shudder, quiver. [➡PHYSICAL REACTIONS; 317]

See Compare and Contrast at **hesitate**.

wavering 1 *n* **fluctuation**, vacillation, indecisiveness, irresolution, uncertainty, indecision, hesitation, hesitancy. [➡UNCERTAINTY; 560] *Opposite:* resolution. 2 *adj* **indecisive**, uncertain, undecided, vacillating, uncommitted, irresolute. [➡UNCERTAINTY; 560] *Opposite:* decisive. 3 *adj* **flickering**, shaky, trembling, quivering, unsteady, shaking, wobbling. [➡DESCRIBING BODY MOVEMENTS; 289]

waveringly *adv* **indecisively**, uncertainly, irresolutely, vacillatingly, hesitantly, ditheringly, undecidedly. [➡UNCERTAINTY; 560] *Opposite:* decisively.

waviness *n* **curliness**, twistiness, crinkliness, unevenness, undulation, corrugation, sinuosity. [➡ROUNDED SHAPE; 1217]

wavy *adj* **curly**, curvy, crimped, undulating. [➡DESCRIBING HAIR; 487] *Opposite:* straight.

wax 1 *n* **beeswax**, candlewax, tallow. [➡SOLIDS; 1273] 2 *v* **polish**, shine, buff, put a shine on, buff up. [➡CLEAN AND POLISH; 404] 3 *v* (*literary*) **expand**, increase, enlarge, get bigger, grow, swell. [➡CHANGE OF SIZE: BIGGER; 393] *Opposite:* wane. 4 *v* (*literary*) **become**, turn, grow, start to be. [➡GRADUALLY COME INTO EXISTENCE; 1]

waxen *adj* **pale**, pallid, ashen, ashy, wan, white, washed-out, grey, pasty, sickly, colourless. [➡COMPLEXION; 481]

waxiness *n* **greasiness**, fattiness, slipperiness, shininess, slickness. [➡PHYSICAL TEXTURE; 1221]

waxwork *n* **figure**, manikin, model, effigy, replica, representation. [➡SCULPTURE; 902]

way 1 *n* **method**, means, technique, mode, system, approach, manner, line of attack, tactic, fashion, style. [➡WAYS OF DOING THINGS; 295] 2 *n* **custom**, style, practice, tradition, discipline. [➡WAYS OF DOING THINGS; 295] 3 *n* **route**, road, direction, path. [➡ROADS; 1105] 4 *n* **street**, avenue, lane, path, pathway, track. [➡ROADS; 1105]

wayfarer (*literary*) *n* **traveller**, wanderer, walker, rover, roamer, journeyer, voyager. [➡TRAVEL: TRAVELLERS AND WALKERS; 320]

waylay *v* **accost**, intercept, buttonhole (*informal*), surprise, ambush, lie in wait for, approach, stop, nail, bushwhack (*US informal*). [➡INITIATE AND ESTABLISH COMMUNICATION; 681]

way of life *n* **lifestyle**, customs, habits, traditions. [➡LIFESTYLE; 881]

way of thinking *n* **ideas**, beliefs, opinion, philosophy, position, mindset, point of view, viewpoint. [➡POINT OF VIEW; 768]

way-out 1 *adj* (*informal*) **unusual**, peculiar, odd, strange, weird, far-out, eccentric, unconventional, avant-garde. [➡BIZARRE AND PECULIAR; 258] *Opposite:* conventional. 2 *adj* (*dated informal*) **excellent**, wonderful, terrific, great (*informal*), super (*informal*), fantastic. [➡EXTRAORDINARY: AMAZING; 205]

ways *n* **habits**, conduct, customs, behaviour, traditions. [➡TEMPERAMENT AND BEHAVIOUR; 493]

ways and means *n* **methods**, approaches, means, devices, systems, procedures. [➡WAYS OF DOING THINGS; 295]

wayside *n* **roadside**, verge, kerb, edge, hard shoulder, shoulder (*US*). [➡PATHWAYS; 1109]

way to go (*US informal*) *interj* [➡COMPLIMENTS; 658]

wayward *adj* **wilful**, naughty, unruly, errant, disobedient, badly behaved, strong-willed, rebellious, insubordinate, defiant, contrary, ornery (*US informal*). [➡REBELLIOUSNESS AND DISOBEDIENCE; 566] *Opposite:* well-behaved.

See Compare and Contrast at **unruly**.

waywardness *n* **wilfulness**, naughtiness, disobedience, unruliness, rebelliousness, defiance, contrariness. [➡REBELLIOUSNESS AND DISOBEDIENCE; 566] *Opposite:* obedience.

weak 1 *adj* **feeble**, frail, infirm, debilitated, decrepit (*archaic or humorous*), puny, scrawny, enervated. [➡BUILD; 478] *Opposite:* robust. 2 *adj* **tired**, faint, anaemic, exhausted, drained, enervated, limp, floppy, shaky. [➡UNFIT AND WEAK; 740] *Opposite:* strong. 3 *adj* **delicate**, insubstantial, flimsy, wispy, fragile. [➡FRAGILE; 1208] *Opposite:* sturdy. 4 *adj* **vulnerable**, defenceless, helpless, unprotected, unguarded, exposed. [➡IN DANGER; 238] *Opposite:* invulnerable. 5 *adj* **powerless**, ineffectual, toothless, inadequate, feeble, ineffective. [➡WEAKNESS; 242] *Opposite:* powerful. 6 *adj* **cowardly**, spineless, faint-hearted, timid, weak-willed, irresolute, easily led, corruptible, vacillating. [➡COWARDICE AND WEAKNESS OF WILL; 509] *Opposite:* bold. 7 *adj* **faint**, feeble, low, dim, soft, imperceptible. [➡IMPERCEPTIBLE; 26] *Opposite:* strong. 8 *adj* **watery**, diluted, insipid, bland, tasteless, flavourless, watered-down, dilute. [➡FLUID AND NON-SOLID; 1212] *Opposite:* strong. 9 *adj* **unconvincing**, half-hearted, ineffectual, feeble, implausible, flimsy, uncertain. [➡UNCERTAIN; 176] *Opposite:* convincing.

Compare and Contrast: ***weak, feeble, frail, infirm, debilitated, decrepit, enervated***

CORE MEANING: LACKING PHYSICAL STRENGTH OR ENERGY

weak not physically fit or mentally strong; ***feeble*** lacking physical or mental strength or health; ***frail*** in a physically weak state as a result of illness or advanced years; ***infirm*** lacking strength as a result of advanced years or long illness; ***debilitated*** with strength and energy temporarily diminished, as a result of illness or physical exertion; ***decrepit*** (*archaic or humorous*) made weak by advanced years; ***enervated*** made weak and tired by physical or mental exertion.

weaken 1 *v* **grow weaker**, deteriorate, fail, decline, wane, fade, flag, abate (*formal or literary*), dwindle, wear off, subside, reduce, lessen, diminish, fall off. [➡DISAPPEAR; 4] *Opposite:* strengthen. 2 *v* **give in**, cave in, give way, yield, vacillate, hesitate, falter, waver. [➡FORGET, FORGIVE, AND ACCEPT; 749] *Opposite:* stand firm. 3 *v* **damage**, destabilize, detract from, shake, undermine. [➡CHANGE OF INTENSITY: LESS; 396] *Opposite:* bolster. 4 *v* **dilute**, water down, thin, adulterate. [➡CHANGE OF INTENSITY: LESS; 396] *Opposite:* strengthen. 5 *v* **enfeeble**, exhaust, enervate, debilitate, sap, impair. [➡WOUND A PERSON OR ANIMAL; 384] *Opposite:* fortify.

weakened *adj* **debilitated**, enfeebled, deteriorated, declining, faded, sapped. [➡IN BAD REPAIR; 1233]

weakening *n* **deterioration**, decline, damage, destabilization, undermining, decay. [➡CHANGE OF INTENSITY: LESS; 396] *Opposite:* strengthening.

weak-kneed *adj* **spineless**, cowardly, weak, feeble, submissive, weak-willed, cowed, pusillanimous (*formal*). [➡COWARDICE AND WEAKNESS OF WILL; 509] *Opposite:* courageous.

weakly *adv* **feebly**, faintly, dimly, softly, inadequately, half-heartedly, uncertainly, insipidly, blandly, indecisively, unconvincingly, ineffectually. [➡IMPERCEPTIBLE; 26] *Opposite:* strongly.

weakness 1 *n* **flaw**, fault, Achilles' heel, weak spot, weak point, failing, limitation, disadvantage, drawback, difficulty, chink in somebody's armour. [➡FAULTS, FLAWS, AND WEAKNESSES; 252] *Opposite:* strength. 2 *n* **frailty**, feebleness, flimsiness, fragility, debility, infirmity. [➡UNFIT AND WEAK; 740] *Opposite:* robustness. 3 *n* **powerlessness**, vulnerability, defencelessness, helplessness, impotence. [➡WEAKNESS; 242] *Opposite:* strength. 4 *n* **fondness**, liking, taste, soft spot, penchant, partiality, predilection (*formal*), appetite. [➡LIKE, LOVE, VALUE AND ENJOY; 579] *Opposite:* dislike. 5 *n* **faintness**, softness, dimness, paleness, feebleness. [➡IMPERCEPTIBLE; 26] *Opposite:* strength.

weak point *n* **weakness**, Achilles' heel, failing, fault, weak spot, limitation, drawback, flaw, chink in somebody's armour. [➡FAULTS, FLAWS, AND WEAKNESSES; 252] *Opposite:* strong point.

weak spot *n* **weakness**, Achilles' heel, failing, fault, weak point, chink in somebody's armour, flaw, drawback, limitation. [➡FAULTS, FLAWS, AND WEAKNESSES; 252]

weak-willed *adj* **irresolute**, spineless, vacillating, easily led, spiritless, lily-livered (*literary*), weak, biddable. [➡COWARDICE AND WEAKNESS OF WILL; 509] *Opposite:* resolute.

weal *n* **swelling**, welt, wound, contusion (*technical*), mark. [➡CONDITIONS AFFECTING THE SKIN; 722]

wealth 1 *n* **riches**, prosperity, affluence, means, assets, capital, mammon (*disapproving*), possessions, material goods, worldly goods, funds, treasure, fortune, resources, holdings. [➡FINANCIAL ASSETS; 463] *Opposite:* poverty. 2 *n* **large quantity**, abundance, cornucopia, variety, choice, store, multiplicity, profusion, multitude, plethora, array. [➡MANY, MUCH, LARGE AMOUNT; 117] *Opposite:* dearth.

wealthy *adj* **rich**, well-off, well-to-do, affluent, prosperous, moneyed, well-heeled (*informal*), rolling in it (*informal*), flush (*informal*), loaded (*slang*). [➡WEALTH AND WEALTHY; 891] *Opposite:* poor.

weapon 1 *n* **armament**, firearm, missile, gun. [➡WEAPONS; 1153] 2 *n* **defence**, deterrent, big stick. [➡WEAPONS; 1153]

weaponry *n* **arms**, armaments, arsenal, weapons, ordnance, munitions. [➡WEAPONS; 1153]

weapon store *n* **arsenal**, armoury, storeroom, store, cache, stash (*informal*), stockpile, munitions store. [➡STORES AND STORAGE BUILDINGS; 1087]

wear 1 *v* **be dressed in**, dress in, sport (*informal*), show off, have on, put on. [➡DRESS, WEAR, AND UNDRESS; 868] 2 *v* **display**, bear, carry, hold, show. [➡CAUSE TO APPEAR; 5] 3 *v* **rub**, fray, scuff, grind, wear out, wear through, wear down, wear away, erode. [➡DELETE AND ERASE; 340] 4 *n* **deterioration**, wear and tear, friction, abrasion, scuffing, attrition, erosion, corrosion. [➡IN BAD REPAIR; 1233] 5 *n* **attire** (*formal*), dress, clothing, clothes, garments, uniform, costume, apparel, garb. [➡CLOTHES AND ACCESSORIES; 864]

wear and tear *n* **deterioration**, wear, attrition, abrasion, erosion, corrosion, wearing away. [➡IN BAD REPAIR; 1233]

wear away *v* **erode**, wear down, wear out, eat at, eat away at. [➡DELETE AND ERASE; 340]

wear down *v* **overcome**, weaken, erode, wear away, wear out, eat away, break down. [➡DELETE AND ERASE; 340]

wearily *adv* **resignedly**, jadedly, with a sigh, despairingly, unenthusiastically, tiredly. [➡WITHOUT ENTHUSIASM; 288] *Opposite:* energetically.

weariness *n* **tiredness**, exhaustion, fatigue, lethargy, inertia, apathy, disillusionment, lassitude. [➡NEUTRALITY AND INDIFFERENCE; 554] *Opposite:* energy.

wearing *adj* **tiring**, exhausting, trying, tiresome, wearisome, irksome, taxing, draining. [➡IRRITATING; 229] *Opposite:* refreshing.

wearisome *adj* **tiresome**, boring, tedious, trying, thankless, frustrating, wearying, uninteresting, dreary. [➡EMOTIONALLY UNPLEASANT AND UPSETTING; 228] *Opposite:* stimulating.

wear off *v* **abate** (*formal or literary*), weaken, fade, lessen, diminish, disappear, subside, wane. [➡CHANGE OF INTENSITY: LESS; 396] *Opposite:* increase.

wear out 1 *v* **exhaust**, tire out, fatigue, sap, drain, wear down. [➡TIRED, ASLEEP AND UNCONSCIOUS; 739] *Opposite:* invigorate. 2 *v* **use up**, run down, fray, deplete, trash (*informal*). [➡USE UP AND WASTE; 475] *Opposite:* renovate.

weary 1 *adj* **tired**, tired out, all in, exhausted, worn out, fatigued, done in (*informal*), whacked (*informal*), shattered, drained, beat (*informal*), wiped out (*slang*), sleepy, somnolent, drowsy. [➡TIRED, ASLEEP AND UNCONSCIOUS; 739] *Opposite:* fresh. 2 *adj* **disillusioned**, disenchanted, jaded, worn down, fed up (*informal*). [➡NEUTRALITY AND INDIFFERENCE; 554] 3 *v* **drain**, sap, exhaust, tire, lose patience. [➡BORE AND FAIL TO INTEREST; 571]

wearying *adj* **tiresome**, wearisome, tiring, exhausting, wearing, taxing, trying, draining. [➡PHYSICALLY UNPLEASANT; 227]

wear yourself out *v* **tire yourself out**, exhaust yourself, run yourself into the ground, overdo it, burn the candle at both ends. [➡OVERDO SOMETHING; 291]

weasel *type of* **small mammal**. [➡SMALL MAMMAL; 990]

weasel word (*informal*) *n* [➡FIGURES OF SPEECH; 674]

weather 1 *n* **climate**, meteorological conditions, elements. [➡WEATHER AND CLIMATE; 1049] 2 *v* **endure**, withstand, sit out, ride out, last out, stick out, survive, live through, get through, come through. [➡CONTINUE TO EXIST; 17] *Opposite:* succumb. 3 *v* **erode**, season, toughen, harden, coarsen, wear away. [➡WORSEN APPEARANCE; 383]

weather-beaten *adj* **worn**, battered, windswept, weathered, gnarled, wrinkled, craggy, eroded, lined. [➡IN BAD REPAIR; 1233]

weather-bound *adj* **delayed**, held up, fogbound, snowbound, postponed, icebound, stormbound. [➡WINDY AND STORMY WEATHER; 1053]

weathercock *n* **weather vane**, wind indicator, wind gauge, anemometer, windsock. [➡MEASURING DEVICES; 1122]

weathered *adj* **worn**, battered, windswept, weather-beaten, gnarled, wrinkled, craggy, eroded. [➡IN BAD REPAIR; 1233]

weatherproof *adj* **watertight**, waterproof, rainproof, stormproof, windproof, galeproof, impermeable. [➡IN GOOD REPAIR; 1231]

weather vane *n* **wind indicator**, wind gauge, weathercock, anemometer, windsock. [➡MEASURING DEVICES; 1122]

weave 1 *v* **interlace**, lace, intertwine, plait, knit, entwine, merge, unite, interweave. [➡CRAFTS AND CARVING; 356] *Opposite:* unpick. 2 *v* **invent**, create, compose, construct, fabricate, contrive, put together, concoct, make up, spin, tell. [➡CREATION; 347] 3 *n* **pile**, texture, nap. [➡TEXTURE; 1219] 4 *v* **zigzag**, stagger, wind, twist, crisscross, snake, meander, lurch, careen. [➡CHANGE DIRECTION OF MOTION; 345]

weaverbird *type of* **songbird**. [➡SONGBIRD; 1003]

weaving *type of* **handicraft**. [➡CRAFTS AND CARVING; 356]

web 1 *n* **network**, mesh, net, tissue, grid. [➡FASTENERS, LINKS, AND NETWORKS; 1246] 2 *part of* **bird**. [➡BIRD; 997]

webbing *n* **lattice**, trellis, netting, network, strap work. [➡FASTENERS, LINKS, AND NETWORKS; 1246]

web conferencing *n* [➡THE INTERNET; 1127]

web folio *n* [➡THE INTERNET; 1127]

webpage *n* [➡THE INTERNET; 1127]

website *n* [➡THE INTERNET; 1127]

wed 1 *v* (*formal or literary*) **marry**, espouse (*archaic*), take in marriage. [➡ESTABLISHING RELATIONSHIPS WITH OTHERS; 974] *Opposite:* divorce. 2 *v* **get married**, get hitched (*informal*), walk down the aisle, tie the knot (*informal*), say "I do", get spliced (*slang*). [➡ESTABLISHING RELATIONSHIPS WITH OTHERS; 974] *Opposite:* split up. 3 *v* **join in matrimony**, marry, join in wedlock, unite. [➡ESTABLISHING RELATIONSHIPS WITH OTHERS; 974] 4 *v* **unite**, join, link, marry, merge, fuse, ally, yoke. [➡FASTEN, LINK, AND JOIN; 409] *Opposite:* separate.

wedded 1 *adj* **marital**, conjugal, married, connubial (*formal*), matrimonial. [➡MARRIED STATE; 961] 2 *adj* **committed**, devoted, linked, connected, attached, married. [➡RELATED; 143] *Opposite:* unattached.

wedding *n* **marriage**, nuptials (*literary*), wedding ceremony, marriage ceremony. [➡CEREMONIES AND ANNIVERSARIES; 38] *Opposite:* divorce.

wedding cake *type of* **cake.** [➡CAKES, BISCUITS, AND DESSERTS; 1180]

wedding ceremony *n* [➡CEREMONIES AND ANNIVERSARIES; 38]

wedding dress *type of* **dress.** [➡GARMENTS AND OUTFITS; 865]

wedge 1 *n* **segment**, block, chock, sliver, hunk, piece, slice. [➡AMOUNT OF SOLID OR SEMI-SOLID; 115] 2 *v* **lodge**, hold, fix, jam, block, chock. [➡POSITION SOMETHING: BETWEEN, BESIDE, OR INSIDE SOMETHING; 327] *Opposite:* dislodge. 3 *v* **cram**, pack, jam, ram, stuff, push, thrust, force, squeeze. [➡POSITION SOMETHING: BETWEEN, BESIDE, OR INSIDE SOMETHING; 327]

wedge heel *type of* **shoe.** [➡FOOTWEAR; 871]

wedge-shaped *adj* [➡ANGULAR SHAPE; 1216]

wedlock *n* **matrimony**, marriage, married state. [➡MARRIED STATE; 961]

wee *adj* **small**, minute, petite, little, tiny, diminutive, miniature. [➡SMALL; 1194] *Opposite:* big.

weed *v* **hoe**, tidy, pick over, clear. [➡EXTRACT AND SEVER; 342]

weed

◆ *types of weed*
bindweed, burdock, chickweed, dandelion, dock, goldenrod, jimsonweed (*US*), nettle, poison ivy, poison oak, ragweed, stinging nettle, thistle, thorn apple, tumbleweed

weed out *v* **remove**, extract, discard, get rid of, eliminate, reject, set aside. [➡EXTRACT AND SEVER; 342] *Opposite:* select.

weeds (*archaic or literary*) *n* [➡CLOTHES AND ACCESSORIES; 864]

weedy *adj* **weak**, puny, thin, scraggy, feeble, frail. [➡UNFIT AND WEAK; 740] *Opposite:* strong.

week *type of* **time period.** [➡TIMES OF YEAR; 88]

weekend 1 *n type of* **time period.** [➡TIMES OF YEAR; 88] 2 *v* **stay**, holiday, take a break, visit, vacation (*US*). [➡TRAVEL: WAYS OF TRAVELLING; 321]

weekend bag *type of* **baggage.** [➡CONTAINERS, RECEPTACLES, AND PACKAGING; 1244]

weekender *n* **tourist**, holidaymaker, visitor, sightseer, vacationer (*US*). [➡TRAVEL: TRAVELLERS AND WALKERS; 320]

weensy (*informal*) *adj* [➡SMALL; 1194]

weeny (*informal*) *adj* **tiny**, little, small, wee, minute, weensy, teeny (*informal*), teensy (*informal*), teeny-weeny (*informal*), teensy-weensy (*informal*). [➡SMALL; 1194] *Opposite:* huge.

weep 1 *v* **cry**, sob, blubber (*informal*), wail, bawl (*informal*), snivel, boohoo, blub (*informal*), shed tears. [➡CRYING; 651] 2 *v* **leak**, suppurate, seep, exude, ooze, discharge, drip. [➡LIQUID EMISSION; 371]

weepie (*informal*) *n* **tear-jerker** (*informal*), movie, film, melodrama. [➡FILM; 901]

weepy 1 *adj* (*informal*) **tearful**, emotional, sad, miserable, sensitive, maudlin, mawkish. [➡SADNESS, DISTRESS, AND DESPAIR; 540] 2 *adj* **oversentimental**, slushy, mushy, syrupy, overemotional, mawkish. [➡IN POOR TASTE; 230]

weevil *type of* **beetle.** [➡BEETLES AND WEEVILS; 1016]

weigh *v* **consider**, ponder, weigh up, think about, evaluate, meditate on, reflect on, mull over, chew over, assess, think over, contemplate, deliberate. [➡ASSESS QUALITY; 756]

weigh against *v* **count against**, tell against, militate against, countervail. [➡AVOID, PREVENT, LIMIT, AND CONTROL; 278]

weighbridge *type of* **measuring device.** [➡MEASURING DEVICES; 1122]

weigh down 1 *v* **worry**, depress, get down, trouble, burden, afflict. [➡UPSET, DISTRESS, AND HUMILIATE; 568] *Opposite:* hearten. 2 *v* **burden**, load down, overload, charge, encumber. [➡GIVE TOO MUCH; 438]

weighed down *adj* **oppressed**, burdened, worried, troubled, overloaded, fraught, beset, beleaguered, plagued. [➡SADNESS, DISTRESS, AND DESPAIR; 540] *Opposite:* untroubled.

weighing machine *type of* **measuring device.** [➡MEASURING DEVICES; 1122]

weighing scale (*US*) *type of* **measuring device.** [➡MEASURING DEVICES; 1122]

weighing scales *type of* **measuring device.** [➡MEASURING DEVICES; 1122]

weigh into (*informal*) *v* [➡PHYSICAL ATTACK AND PUNISHMENT; 416]

weight 1 *n* **heaviness**, mass, bulk, weightiness, heft (*US*). [➡WEIGHT: HEAVY; 1204] 2 *n* **burden**, load, encumbrance. [➡PROBLEM; 257] 3 *n* **influence**, power, clout (*informal*), substance, significance, import, importance, consequence (*formal*), authority. [➡IMPORTANCE AND SIGNIFICANCE; 193]

weighted *adj* **biased**, prejudiced, slanted, subjective, one-sided, partisan. [➡FALSE AND UNREAL; 174] *Opposite:* impartial.

weightiness 1 *n* **weight**, heaviness, mass, bulk, heft (*US*). [➡WEIGHT: HEAVY; 1204] 2 *n* **gravity**, seriousness, importance, heaviness, import, significance, consequence (*formal*). [➡IMPORTANCE AND SIGNIFICANCE; 193]

weighting *n* **allowance**, premium, increment. [➡WORK-RELATED ACTIVITIES; 834]

weightless *adj* **light**, feathery, insubstantial, ethereal, airy, floaty. [➡WEIGHT: LIGHT; 1205] *Opposite:* heavy.

weightlessness *n* [➡WEIGHT: LIGHT; 1205]

weighty 1 *adj* **heavy**, big, substantial, hefty, bulky, cumbersome. [➡WEIGHT: HEAVY; 1204] *Opposite:* insubstantial. 2 *adj* **important**, serious, grave, solemn, momentous, influential, significant. [➡IMPORTANT; 195] *Opposite:* frivolous.

weigh up *v* **assess**, evaluate, consider, examine, size up, balance, ponder, think about, take stock of, contemplate, deliberate, reflect on, chew over, mull over. [➡ASSESS QUALITY; 756]

weir *n* **dam**, barrage, dike, barrier, wall, levee. [➡RIVERS, LAKES, AND STREAMS; 1042]

weird *adj* **strange**, odd, bizarre, peculiar, uncanny, eerie, creepy (*informal*), unusual, curious, improbable. [➡BIZARRE AND PECULIAR; 258] *Opposite:* normal.

weird and wonderful *adj* [➡EXTRAORDINARY: AMAZING; 205]

weirdness *n* **strangeness**, oddness, eeriness, creepiness (*informal*), eccentricity, improbability. [➡BIZARRE AND PECULIAR; 258] *Opposite:* normality.

welcome 1 *adj* **at home**, comfortable, at ease, relaxed, comfy (*informal*). [➡CALMNESS, CONFIDENCE, AND COMPOSURE; 537] *Opposite:* unwelcome. 2 *adj* **appreciated**, pleasurable, delightful, pleasing, pleasant, acceptable. [➡ACCEPTABLE AND PASSABLE; 220] *Opposite:* unwelcome. 3 *adj* **longed-for**, long-awaited, timely, opportune, heaven-sent. [➡POPULAR AND WANTED; 221] *Opposite:* untimely. 4 *n* **greeting**, reception, salutation, salute, hospitality, red carpet treatment. [➡GREETINGS, FAREWELLS, AND SALUTATIONS; 660] *Opposite:* farewell. 5 *v* **greet**, receive, hail, meet, salute, cheer, applaud. [➡INITIATE AND ESTABLISH COMMUNICATION; 681] *Opposite:* snub. 6 *v* **accept**, appreciate, approve, jump at, be grateful for, embrace, applaud. [➡ACCEPT POSSESSION; 451] *Opposite:* reject.

welcoming *adj* **friendly**, warm, hospitable, convivial, openhearted. [➡EMOTIONALLY PLEASANT; 188] *Opposite:* unwelcoming.

weld 1 *v* **fuse**, join, repair, solder, link, connect, bond. [➡FASTEN, LINK, AND JOIN; 409] *Opposite:* separate. 2 *n* **repair**, join, link, joint, bond, seal, seam. [➡FASTENERS, LINKS, AND NETWORKS; 1246]

welfare 1 *n* **wellbeing**, interests, happiness, good, safety, health, prosperity. [➡SAFE AND SAFETY; 192] *Opposite:* harm. 2 *n* (*US*) **benefits**, aid, assistance, dole (*informal*). [➡SOCIAL WELFARE; 812]

well 1 *n* **shaft**, bore, borehole, pit. [➡HOLES, GAPS, AND FORKS; 1251] 2 *n* **spring**, fountain, fount (*literary*), source, water supply, fountainhead, wellspring. [➡RIVERS, LAKES, AND STREAMS; 1042] 3 *v* **spring up**, brim, surge, rise, gush, flood. [➡LIQUID EMISSION; 371] *Opposite:* subside. 4 *v* **grow**, rise, swell, intensify, increase, grow stronger. [➡CHANGE OF INTENSITY: MORE; 395] *Opposite:* subside. 5 *adv* **pleasingly**, splendidly, perfectly, pleasantly, nicely, desirably. [➡EMOTIONALLY PLEASANT; 188] *Opposite:* badly. 6 *adv* **properly**, ethically, acceptably, correctly, suitably, agreeably. [➡CORRECT; 183] *Opposite:* improperly. 7 *adv* **competently**, ably, skilfully, capably, satisfactorily, expertly. [➡GOOD, WELL, BETTER; 184] *Opposite:* badly. 8 *adv* **justly**, appropriately, fairly, fittingly, justifiably. [➡GOOD, WELL, BETTER; 184] *Opposite:* unfairly. 9 *adv* **comfortably**, easily, agreeably. [➡PHYSICALLY PLEASANT; 187] 10 *adv* **favourably**, highly, admiringly, kindly, positively, fondly, benevolently. [➡GOOD, WELL, BETTER; 184] *Opposite:* unfavourably. 11 *adv* **thoroughly**, fully, carefully, completely, meticulously. [➡WHOLENESS AND COMPLETENESS; 199] *Opposite:* partially. 12 *adv* **clearly**, precisely, in detail, distinctly, perfectly, efficiently, effectively. [➡CONCISE AND CLEAR; 203] *Opposite:* poorly. 13 *adv* **familiarly**, intimately, closely, personally, deeply. [➡WHOLENESS AND COMPLETENESS; 199] *Opposite:* slightly. 14 *adv* **good-naturedly**, good-humouredly, cheerfully, jovially, genially, jestingly (*literary*). [➡GOOD-TEMPERED AND HUMOROUS; 628] 15 *adv* (*slang*) **very**, extremely, completely, utterly, totally, thoroughly. [➡ABSOLUTE AND ABSOLUTELY; 131] 16 *adj* **healthy**, fine (*informal*), glowing, fit, fighting fit, on form, in good health, able-bodied, sound, thriving, in good form (*US*). [➡FIT AND STRONG; 737] *Opposite:* unwell. 17 *adj* **satisfactory**, fine (*informal*), all right, good, lucky, fortunate, okay (*informal*). [➡GOOD, WELL, BETTER; 184] *Opposite:* unsatisfactory. 18 *interj* **anyway**, anyhow, in any case, to cut a long story short, now then, so. [➡SUMMARIZING EXPRESSIONS; 623]

well-acquainted *adj* [➡RELATIONSHIP TO ANOTHER; 973]

well-adjusted *adj* **stable**, normal, level-headed, well-balanced, sane, steady, secure. [➡CONFIDENCE AND COMPOSURE; 500] *Opposite:* maladjusted.

well-advised *adj* **sensible**, prudent, wise, judicious, shrewd, astute. [➡THE NATURE OF IDEAS; 772] *Opposite:* ill-advised.

well-appointed *adj* **well-equipped**, well-resourced, fully furnished, well-furnished, luxurious. [➡USEFULNESS; 200]

well-argued *adj* **clear**, clearly stated, cogent, sensible, lucid, rational, logical. [➡CONCISE AND CLEAR; 203] *Opposite:* illogical.

well-balanced 1 *adj* **sensible**, rational, stable, judicious, well-adjusted, level-headed, steady. [➡POSITIVE INTELLECTUAL CHARACTERISTICS; 525] *Opposite:* unstable. 2 *adj* **harmonious**, balanced, well-proportioned, proportionate, coordinated. [➡HARMONY; 156] *Opposite:* unbalanced.

well-behaved *adj* **good**, obedient, dutiful, well-mannered, polite, biddable. [➡GOOD MANNERS AND SOCIAL SKILLS; 521] *Opposite:* disobedient.

wellbeing *n* **happiness**, comfort, security, good, welfare, safety, health, good fortune. [➡PLEASANT SITUATIONS; 74]

well-beloved 1 *adj* **loved**, cherished, desired, beloved, adored, treasured. [➡POPULAR AND WANTED; 221] *Opposite:* hated. 2 *adj* **respected**, honoured, venerated, revered, esteemed. [➡POPULAR AND WANTED; 221] *Opposite:* disgraced.

wellborn *adj* **aristocratic**, blue-blooded, highborn (*literary*), noble, patrician, genteel (*dated*). [➡CLASS STATUS; 889] *Opposite:* lowly.

well-bred *adj* **polite**, well-mannered, mannerly, courteous, refined. [➡GOOD MANNERS AND SOCIAL SKILLS; 521] *Opposite:* common.

well-built *adj* **sturdy**, strong, muscular, muscly, burly, solid, powerful. [➡BUILD; 478] *Opposite:* puny.

well-chosen *adj* **choice**, appropriate, apposite, apt, relevant, pertinent, suitable. [➡APPROPRIATE, SUITABLE, ADVISABLE; 185] *Opposite:* inappropriate.

well-defined *adj* **distinct**, sharp, definite, clear, precise, exact. [➡CONCISE AND CLEAR; 203] *Opposite:* vague.

well-designed *adj* **elegant**, stylish, well-made, chic, classy (*informal*), ingenious, clever, handy. [➡BEAUTY AND ATTRACTIVENESS; 190] *Opposite:* clumsy.

well-developed 1 *adj* **well-built**, strong, toned, finely honed, muscular, powerful, strapping (*informal*). [➡BUILD; 478] *Opposite:* puny. 2 *adj* **sophisticated**, well-rounded, strong, mature, acute, keen, sharp. [➡STRENGTH; 202] *Opposite:* underdeveloped.

well-disposed *adj* **approving**, friendly, kindly, sympathetic, benevolent, supportive. [➡APPRECIATION AND GRATITUDE; 536] *Opposite:* hostile.

well done *interj* **bravo**, congratulations, hurrah, good for you, good on you, hooray, way to go (*US informal*), good job (*US*). [➡COMPLIMENTS; 658]

well-dressed *adj* **smart**, chic, stylish, elegant, well turned-out, dapper, spruce, neat, well-groomed, well-presented. [➡WELL GROOMED; 483] *Opposite:* scruffy.

well-educated *adj* **cultured**, erudite, knowledgeable, well-read, learned. [➡KNOWLEDGE AND WISDOM; 559] *Opposite:* ignorant.

well-endowed 1 *adj* **affluent**, wealthy, well-to-do, rich, moneyed, prosperous, well-off, well-heeled (*informal*), loaded (*slang*), well-fixed (*US informal*). [➡WEALTH AND WEALTHY; 891] *Opposite:* poor. 2 *adj* **gifted**, skilled, talented, able, skilful, accomplished. [➡TALENTED AND SKILFUL; 528]

well-equipped *adj* **well-appointed**, well-resourced, well-furnished, luxurious, lavish. [➡IN GOOD REPAIR; 1231] *Opposite:* Spartan.

well-established *adj* **firm**, deep-rooted, unshakable, fixed, ingrained, entrenched. [➡PERMANENCE: WITHOUT END; 94] *Opposite:* shaky.

well-expressed *adj* **eloquent**, persuasive, fluent, expressive, articulate, telling. [➡ELOQUENT, TALKATIVE AND LONG-WINDED; 633] *Opposite:* inarticulate.

well-fed 1 *adj* **healthy**, well-nourished, thriving, flourishing. [➡EAT AND NOT EAT; 711] 2 *adj* **overweight**, fat, obese, bulky, stout, portly, matronly. [➡BUILD; 478] *Opposite:* thin.

well-fixed (*US informal*) *adj* **well-to-do**, wealthy, prosperous, well-off, moneyed, well-endowed, rich, well-heeled (*informal*), loaded (*slang*). [➡WEALTH AND WEALTHY; 891] *Opposite:* poor.

well-founded *adj* **logical**, understandable, justifiable, substantiated, sound, rational, well-grounded. [➡THE NATURE OF IDEAS; 772] *Opposite:* illogical.

well-groomed *adj* **well-turned-out**, well-dressed, smart, dapper, spruce, neat, well-presented. [➡WELL GROOMED; 483] *Opposite:* unkempt.

well-grounded 1 *adj* **knowledgeable**, well-informed, au fait, conversant, well-acquainted, in the know. [➡THE NATURE OF IDEAS; 772] *Opposite:* ignorant. 2 *adj* **well-founded**, logical, understandable, justifiable, substantiated, sound, rational. [➡CONCISE AND CLEAR; 203] *Opposite:* illogical.

well-heeled (*informal*) *adj* **wealthy**, well-off, comfortable, rich, affluent, well-to-do, moneyed, prosperous, loaded (*slang*), well-fixed (*US informal*). [➡WEALTH AND WEALTHY; 891] *Opposite:* poor.

well-informed *adj* **knowledgeable**, informed, in the know, up-to-date, educated, well-read. [➡KNOWLEDGE AND WISDOM; 559] *Opposite:* uneducated.

wellington *see* **wellington boot**.

wellington boot *type of* **boot**. [➡FOOTWEAR; 871]

well-intentioned *adj* **well-meant**, well-meaning, kindly, goodhearted, benevolent, benign. [➡GENEROSITY AND KINDNESS; 496] *Opposite:* malicious.

well-kept 1 *adj* **neat**, tidy, well-maintained, orderly, ordered, spick-and-span. [➡ORDER AND ORGANISATION; 207] *Opposite:* untidy. 2 *adj* **preserved**, safe, cherished, treasured, confidential, hidden. [➡SECRET AND UNKNOWN; 180]

well-known *adj* **famous**, renowned, eminent, familiar, recognized, celebrated, distinguished, illustrious, notorious, infamous. [➡KNOWN AND FAMOUS; 182] *Opposite:* unknown.

well-mannered *adj* **polite**, mannerly, decent, decorous, courteous, refined, well-bred. [➡GOOD MANNERS AND SOCIAL SKILLS; 521] *Opposite:* impolite.

well-matched *adj* **compatible**, suited, complementary, well-suited, suitable, like-minded. [➡HARMONY; 156] *Opposite:* incompatible.

well-meaning *adj* **well-intentioned**, kind, kindly, goodhearted, benevolent, benign, kind-hearted. [➡GENEROSITY AND KINDNESS; 496] *Opposite:* malicious.

well-meant *adj* **well-intentioned**, kind, kindly, good-hearted, goodhearted, benevolent, benign. [➡GENEROSITY AND KINDNESS; 496] *Opposite:* malicious.

well-nigh *adv* **nearly**, almost, nigh on, practically, just about, virtually. [➡TO A CERTAIN EXTENT; 134] *Opposite:* totally.

well-off 1 *adj* **wealthy**, rich, well-heeled (*informal*), comfortable, affluent, prosperous, well-to-do, moneyed, loaded (*slang*). [➡WEALTH AND WEALTHY; 891] *Opposite:* poor. 2 *adj* **lucky**, fortunate, in luck, privileged, blessed, favoured. [➡LUCK; 784] *Opposite:* unfortunate.

well-oiled *adj* **efficient**, smooth-running, well-organized, effective, well-ordered, disciplined. [➡ORDER AND ORGANISATION; 207] *Opposite:* inefficient.

well-ordered *adj* **tidy**, regimented, disciplined, efficient, well-organized, ordered, effective, regular, neat. [➡ORDER AND ORGANISATION; 207] *Opposite:* inefficient.

well-organized *adj* **efficient**, disciplined, well-ordered, regimented, ordered, effective. [➡ORDER AND ORGANISATION; 207] *Opposite:* inefficient.

well-paid *adj* **lucrative**, money-spinning (*informal*), profitable, productive, rewarding, remunerative, gainful. [➡ECONOMICAL AND RESOURCEFUL; 208]

well-presented *adj* [➡BEAUTY AND ATTRACTIVENESS; 190]

well-preserved *adj* **youthful**, fresh-looking, young-looking, girlish, boyish, young. [➡PEOPLE'S PHYSICAL APPEARANCE; 476] *Opposite:* wizened.

well-read *adj* **knowledgeable**, educated, cultured, erudite, well-educated, well-informed, well-versed. [➡KNOWLEDGE AND WISDOM; 559] *Opposite:* uninformed.

well-regarded *adj* [➡POPULAR AND WANTED; 221]

well-respected *adj* [➡POPULAR AND WANTED; 221]

well-rounded 1 *adj* **experienced**, seasoned, accomplished, well-versed, mature. [➡LEVEL OF EDUCATION AND SOPHISTICATION; 894] *Opposite:* inexperienced. 2 *adj* **comprehensive**, varied, wide, balanced, broad, extensive. [➡WHOLENESS AND COMPLETENESS; 199] *Opposite:* narrow. 3 *adj* **shapely**, pleasing, well-formed, attractive, curvaceous, comely (*archaic or literary*). [➡BUILD; 478] *Opposite:* unattractive.

well-spoken *adj* **articulate**, eloquent, refined, fluent, coherent, clear. [➡ELOQUENT, TALKATIVE AND LONG-WINDED; 633] *Opposite:* inarticulate.

well-suited *adj* **compatible**, well-matched, complementary, of a kind, suited, suitable, like-minded. [➡HARMONY; 156] *Opposite:* incompatible.

well-thought-of *adj* **respected**, esteemed, highly regarded, reputable, admired, revered. [➡POPULAR AND WANTED; 221] *Opposite:* despised.

well-thought-out *adj* **well-planned**, well-organized, clever, ingenious, elegant, neat, considered. [➡THE NATURE OF IDEAS; 772] *Opposite:* disorganized.

well-timed *adj* **timely**, opportune, propitious, felicitous, appropriate, convenient. [➡GOOD, WELL, BETTER; 184] *Opposite:* untimely.

well-to-do *adj* **wealthy**, rich, well-off, well-heeled (*informal*), affluent, prosperous, comfortable, moneyed, loaded (*slang*), well-fixed (*US informal*). [➡WEALTH AND WEALTHY; 891] *Opposite:* poor.

well-tried *adj* **tried and tested**, established, certified, well-founded, well-grounded, tried and true (*US*). [➡PERMANENCE: WITHOUT END; 94] *Opposite:* untried.

well-turned 1 *adj* **shapely**, graceful, comely (*archaic or literary*), elegant, well-formed, pretty. [➡BEAUTY AND ATTRACTIVENESS; 190] *Opposite:* inelegant. 2 *adj* **eloquent**, well-crafted, well-expressed, articulate, witty. [➡ELOQUENT, TALKATIVE AND LONG-WINDED; 633] *Opposite:* clumsy.

well-turned-out *adj* **neat**, smart, spruce, dapper, well-dressed, stylish, chic, well-groomed, well-presented. [➡WELL GROOMED; 483] *Opposite:* unkempt.

well under way *adj* [➡HAPPENING AND IN PROGRESS; 32]

well up *v* **surge**, gush forth, spring up, arise (*archaic or literary*), spill over, emanate, flow, issue, swell. [➡LIQUID EMISSION; 371] *Opposite:* subside.

well-versed *adj* **knowledgeable**, familiar, experienced, informed, well-read, well-informed. [➡KNOWLEDGE AND WISDOM; 559] *Opposite:* ignorant.

well-wisher *n* **supporter**, guardian angel (*informal*), sympathizer, friend. [➡SUPPORTERS, PROTECTORS, AND COMPATRIOTS; 970] *Opposite:* detractor.

well-worn 1 *adj* **worn**, worn out, ragged, threadbare, frayed, shabby, tattered. [➡IN BAD REPAIR; 1233] *Opposite:* brand-new. 2 *adj* **hackneyed**, timeworn, unoriginal, banal, overworked, clichéd, stale, trite, corny. [➡BORING AND UNINTERESTING; 235] *Opposite:* original.

welt *n* **weal**, swelling, ridge, wound, mark, stripe, bump. [➡CONDITIONS AFFECTING THE SKIN; 722]

welter 1 *n* **flurry**, jumble, mass, confusion, muddle. [➡DISORDER AND CHAOS; 246] 2 *v* **wallow**, roll, pitch and toss. [➡MOVE SOMETHING ON THE SPOT; 337]

wend *v* **proceed**, go, travel, move, journey, progress. [➡PROCEED AND GO; 306] *Opposite:* stay put.

Wendy house *type of* **toy**. [➡TOYS; 880]

Wensleydale *type of* **hard cheese**. [➡DAIRY PRODUCTS AND CHEESES; 1182]

werewolf *type of* **mythological creature**. [➡MYTHICAL CREATURES; 1036]

westerly *type of* **wind**. [➡WINDY AND STORMY WEATHER; 1053]

western *n* **cowboy film**, spaghetti western, horse opera. [➡FILM; 901]

wet 1 *adj* **damp**, soaked, soaking, drenched, sodden, soggy, sopping, dripping, moist, dank, humid, watery, wet through. [➡WET; 1239] *Opposite:* dry. 2 *adj* **rainy**, showery, drizzly, damp, misty, foggy, raining, pouring, drizzling, bucketing (*informal*). [➡CLOUDY AND RAINY WEATHER; 1052] *Opposite:* dry. 3 *n* **moisture**, wetness, liquid, damp, dampness, water. [➡WET; 1239] *Opposite:* dry. 4 *n* **wet weather**, rain, drizzle, damp, dampness. [➡CLOUDY AND RAINY WEATHER; 1052] *Opposite:* dry. 5 *v* **make wet**, dampen, moisten, soak, saturate, drench, douse, spray, splash, sprinkle. [➡SOFTEN, LIQUEFY, DAMPEN; 389] *Opposite:* dry.

> **Compare and Contrast:** ***wet, damp, moist, dank, humid, sodden, soaking, sopping***
>
> CORE MEANING: NOT DRY
>
> ***wet*** a general word used to cover everything from paint that is not yet quite dry to something that is completely covered in water; ***damp*** slightly wet, especially undesirably so; ***moist*** slightly wet, especially desirably so; ***dank*** unpleasantly damp and cold; ***humid*** with a relatively high moisture content in the air; ***sodden*** saturated with moisture; ***soaking*** (*informal*) extremely and undesirably wet, especially because of being rained on; ***sopping*** thoroughly and undesirably wet.

wet behind the ears *adj* [➡UNSKILLED; 530]

wet blanket (*informal*) *n* **spoilsport**, killjoy, party pooper (*informal*), stick-in-the-mud (*informal*), stuffed shirt (*informal*), misery (*informal*). [➡GRUMPY AND NEGATIVE PEOPLE; 953]

wether *type of* **male animal**. [➡MALE OR FEMALE ANIMAL; 978]

wetland *n* **marsh**, swamp, fen, bog, marshes, fens, fenland, marshland, peat bog, wetlands. [➡WETLANDS; 1043] *Opposite:* desert.

wetness *n* **dampness**, damp, humidity, condensation, moisture, liquid, water. [➡WET; 1239] *Opposite:* dryness.

wet suit *type of* **sportswear**. [➡GARMENTS AND OUTFITS; 865]

wet weather *n* [➡CLOUDY AND RAINY WEATHER; 1052]

whack 1 *v* **hit**, wallop (*informal*), thump, slap, strike, clout, thwack, belt (*informal*), smack. [➡PHYSICAL ATTACK AND PUNISHMENT; 416] 2 *n* **thump**, blow, wallop (*informal*), slap, thwack, clout, smack. [➡PHYSICAL ATTACK AND PUNISHMENT; 416]

whacked (*informal*) *adj* **tired out**, shattered, exhausted, worn-out, beat (*informal*), fit to drop (*informal*), dog-tired (*informal*), tired, all in, done in (*informal*), wiped out (*slang*), done for (*informal*), bushed (*informal*), spent. [➡ TIRED, ASLEEP AND UNCONSCIOUS; 739] *Opposite:* fresh.

whacking (*informal*) *adj* **huge**, enormous, massive, gigantic, mammoth, whopping (*informal*), colossal, gargantuan. [➡ LARGE; 1192] *Opposite:* piddling (*informal*).

whale *type of* **marine mammal.** [➡ MARINE MAMMAL; 987]

whale

◆ *types of whale*
blue whale, grey whale, humpback whale, killer whale, minke whale, narwhal, pilot whale, right whale, sperm whale, white whale

wham (*informal*) *type of* **impact sound.** [➡ IMPACT SOUNDS; 1259]

whammy (*informal*) *n* [➡ PROBLEM; 257]

wharf *n* **quay**, quayside, jetty, pier, dock, dockside, waterfront, landing stage. [➡ WATERWAYS AND SEAWAYS; 1107]

whatchamacallit *n* **thingy** (*informal*), thingummy (*informal*), thingumabob (*informal*), thingamajig (*informal*), whatsit (*informal*), whatnot, doodah (*informal*), thingamabob, thingumajig, doodad (*US informal*), doohickey (*US informal*). [➡ PHYSICAL OBJECTS; 1242]

whatever 1 *pron* **anything**, everything, all, no matter what, whatsoever. [➡ ALL; 126] 2 *adv* **at all**, whatsoever, of any kind. [➡ ALL; 126]

what is more *adv* [➡ EXPRESSIONS INTRODUCING EXTRA INFORMATION; 137]

whatnot *type of* **cabinet.** [➡ FURNITURE; 858]

whatsit (*informal*) *n* [➡ PHYSICAL OBJECTS; 1242]

what's more *adv* **besides**, moreover, in addition, also, plus (*informal*), furthermore. [➡ EXPRESSIONS INTRODUCING EXTRA INFORMATION; 137]

whatsoever *adj* **at all**, whatever, of any kind. [➡ ALL; 126]

wheat *type of* **cereal.** [➡ CEREAL FOODS; 1177]

wheatmeal *type of* **flour.** [➡ BREAD, FLOUR, AND BREAD PRODUCTS; 1178]

wheedle 1 *v* **coax**, cajole, inveigle, charm, persuade, talk. [➡ CAUSE OR COMPEL TO ACT; 272] *Opposite:* bully. 2 *v* **coax out**, winkle out, get out, draw out, obtain, extract, finagle (*informal*). [➡ OBTAIN POSSESSION BY PERSUASION; 458]

wheel 1 *v* **roll**, trundle, manoeuvre, move. [➡ MOVE SOMETHING ON THE SPOT; 337] 2 *v* **turn**, veer, swing, circle, swivel, rotate. [➡ CHANGE DIRECTION OF MOTION; 345] 3 *part of* **external feature.** [➡ VEHICLES; 1144] 4 (*informal*) *type of* **controls.** [➡ VEHICLES; 1144] 5 *part of* **external structure.** [➡ BIKES, CARS, AND CARRIAGES; 1148] 6 *part of* **bike** (*informal*). [➡ BIKES, CARS, AND CARRIAGES; 1148]

wheel about *v* [➡ CHANGE DIRECTION OF MOTION; 345]

wheel around *v* **swivel around**, swing around, turn round, spin around, turn full circle, veer. [➡ CHANGE DIRECTION OF MOTION; 345]

wheel clamp *n* **clamp**, lock, immobilizer, Denver boot (*US*). [➡ FASTENERS, LINKS, AND NETWORKS; 1246]

wheel-clamp *v* **clamp**, immobilize, secure, lock. [➡ FASTEN, LINK, AND JOIN; 409]

wheeler-dealer (*informal*) *n* **fixer**, negotiator, dealer, trader. [➡ BUSINESS PEOPLE; 794]

wheelie bin *n* [➡ CONTAINERS, RECEPTACLES, AND PACKAGING; 1244]

wheel round *v* [➡ CHANGE DIRECTION OF MOTION; 345]

wheels (*slang*) *n* **car**, automobile, motor (*informal*). [➡ BIKES, CARS, AND CARRIAGES; 1148]

wheeze 1 *v* **breathe heavily**, gasp, rasp, pant, rattle, cough, whistle, puff. [➡ BREATHE AND NOT BREATHE; 717] 2 *v* **speak hoarsely**, whisper, hiss, rasp, pant, gasp. [➡ SOUND EMISSION BY PEOPLE; 364] 3 *n* **rattle**, rasp, gasp, whistle. [➡ SOUNDS MADE BY PEOPLE; 1261]

wheeziness *n* **breathlessness**, hoarseness, gasping, puffing, panting, huskiness, breathiness, chestiness, frog in the throat. [➡ BREATHE AND NOT BREATHE; 717]

wheezy *adj* **breathless**, hoarse, short of breath, out of breath, husky, breathy, chesty, rasping, puffing, panting, gasping. [➡ BREATHE AND NOT BREATHE; 717]

whelk *type of* **aquatic invertebrate.** [➡ AQUATIC INVERTEBRATE; 1022]

whelp 1 *n* **cub**, pup, puppy, baby, offspring, runt. [➡ YOUNG ANIMAL; 977] 2 *v* **give birth**, bear young, pup, cub, litter. [➡ REPRODUCTION AND HEREDITY; 726]

when all's said and done *adv* **all things considered**, at the end of the day, basically, all in all, altogether, the long and short of it. [➡ SUMMARIZING EXPRESSIONS; 623]

whenever *conj* **every time**, each time, each and every time, on every occasion, when, whensoever. [➡ AFTER, LAST, AND FOLLOWING; 166]

whereabouts *n* **location**, situation, position, site, place, locus. [➡ PLACE; 1064]

whereas *conj* **while**, where, but, however, although, though. [➡ ALTHOUGH, NEVERTHELESS, AND DESPITE; 170]

whereupon (*formal*) *conj* **at which point**, at which, as a result of which, so, and so. [➡ AFTER, LAST, AND FOLLOWING; 166]

wherewithal *n* **means**, ability, resources, money, finances, funds, assets. [➡ POSSESSIONS; 462]

whet 1 *v* **sharpen**, hone, grind, file. [➡ CLEAN AND POLISH; 404] *Opposite:* blunt. 2 *v* **stimulate**, arouse, augment, rouse, kindle, increase, awaken. [➡ CHANGE OF INTENSITY: MORE; 395] *Opposite:* quell.

whiff 1 *n* **smell**, aroma, scent, odour, reek, pong (*informal*). [➡ SMELL AND SMELLING; 706] 2 *n* **trace**, vestige, sign, hint, soupçon, suggestion, whisper. [➡ FEW, LITTLE, SMALL AMOUNT; 119] 3 *v* (*informal*) **reek**, pong (*informal*), smell, stink, hum (*informal*). [➡ SMELL EMISSION; 370]

whiffle waffle (*US*) *n* [➡ MEANINGLESS SPEECH OR WRITING; 677]

whiffy (*informal*) *adj* **smelly**, niffy (*slang*), stinking, foul-smelling, pongy (*informal*), stinky (*informal*), rank (*literary*), fetid, humming (*informal*), malodorous. [➡SMELL AND SMELLING; 706] *Opposite:* fragrant.

while 1 *conj* **as**, at the same time as, even as, during which. [➡CONCURRENT AND CONTEMPORANEOUS; 165] 2 *conj* **but**, however, in contrast, whereas. [➡ALTHOUGH, NEVERTHELESS, AND DESPITE; 170] 3 *conj* **even though**, though, although, despite the fact, whereas. [➡ALTHOUGH, NEVERTHELESS, AND DESPITE; 170] 4 *n* **time**, period, interval, little, bit. [➡PERIOD OF TIME; 90]

while away *v* **pass**, spend, idle, fritter away, kill. [➡USE UP AND WASTE; 475]

whim *n* **impulse**, urge, notion, quirk, caprice, fancy. [➡FEELINGS ABOUT THE FUTURE; 534]

whimper 1 *v* **cry**, whine, sob, snivel, whinge (*informal*), moan, gripe (*informal*), grumble. [➡CRYING; 651] 2 *type of* **human sound.** [➡SOUNDS MADE BY PEOPLE; 1261]

whimsical 1 *adj* **fanciful**, quirky, unusual, imaginative, original, creative, impulsive. [➡EXTRAORDINARY: UNCOMMON; 206] *Opposite:* practical. 2 *adj* **amusing**, playful, humorous, witty, quaint, old-fashioned, off-the-wall, quirky. [➡FUNNY AND AMUSING; 217] *Opposite:* serious. 3 *adj* **erratic**, unpredictable, random, impulsive, capricious, flighty, fickle, wayward. [➡LACK OF COMMITMENT AND UNRELIABILITY; 510] *Opposite:* dependable.

whimsicality 1 *n* **fancifulness**, quirkiness, imaginativeness, originality, creativity, impulsiveness. [➡EXTRAORDINARY: AMAZING; 205] *Opposite:* practicality. 2 *n* **playfulness**, humorousness, whimsy, wit, quaintness, quirkiness. [➡PERSONAL ECCENTRICITIES; 494] *Opposite:* seriousness. 3 *n* **unpredictability**, impulsiveness, randomness, capriciousness, flightiness, fickleness, waywardness. [➡LACK OF COMMITMENT AND UNRELIABILITY; 510] *Opposite:* dependability.

whimsically 1 *adv* **fancifully**, quirkily, imaginatively, creatively, impulsively, originally, unusually. [➡EXTRAORDINARY: UNCOMMON; 206] *Opposite:* practically. 2 *adv* **playfully**, amusingly, humorously, wittily, quaintly, endearingly, quirkily. [➡FUNNY AND AMUSING; 217] *Opposite:* seriously. 3 *adv* **unpredictably**, erratically, randomly, impulsively, capriciously, flightily, waywardly. [➡LACK OF COMMITMENT AND UNRELIABILITY; 510] *Opposite:* dependably.

whimsy 1 *n* **quaintness**, oddity, oddness, eccentricity, quirkiness, humorousness, whimsicality. [➡PERSONAL ECCENTRICITIES; 494] *Opposite:* seriousness. 2 *n* **fancy**, flight of fancy, whim, caprice, fantasy, notion, quirk. [➡IDEA AND THOUGHT; 771]

whine 1 *v* **whimper**, cry, whinge (*informal*), moan, wail, bleat, plead. [➡SOUND EMISSION BY PEOPLE; 364] 2 *v* **grumble**, gripe (*informal*), complain, moan (*informal*), bellyache (*informal*), kvetch (*informal*), grouse (*informal*). [➡COMPLAIN AND NAG; 687] *Opposite:* accept. 3 *v* **wail**, moan, howl, drone, hum, screech, squeal, scream. [➡SOUND EMISSION BY ANIMALS OR BIRDS; 365] 4 *n* **complaint**, moan (*informal*), whinge (*informal*), wail, whimper, cry. [➡COMPLAIN AND NAG; 687] 5 *type of* **human sound.** [➡SOUNDS MADE BY PEOPLE; 1261]

See Compare and Contrast at **complain.**

whiner *n* **whinger** (*informal*), moaner (*informal*), misery (*informal*), grumbler, complainer, grouch (*informal*). [➡GRUMPY AND NEGATIVE PEOPLE; 953]

whinge (*informal*) *v* **whine**, moan (*informal*), complain, whimper, bleat, bellyache (*informal*), kvetch (*informal*), gripe (*informal*). [➡COMPLAIN AND NAG; 687] *Opposite:* accept.

whingeing (*informal*) *n* [➡BAD-TEMPERED AND HUMOURLESS; 627]

whinger (*informal*) *n* **whiner**, moaner (*informal*), misery (*informal*), grumbler, complainer, grouch (*informal*), malcontent, kvetch (*informal*). [➡GRUMPY AND NEGATIVE PEOPLE; 953]

whingey (*informal*) *adj* [➡BAD-TEMPERED AND HUMOURLESS; 627]

whinny 1 *v* **neigh**, whicker, nicker. [➡SOUND EMISSION BY ANIMALS OR BIRDS; 365] 2 *type of* **animal sound.** [➡SOUNDS MADE BY ANIMALS; 1260]

whiny *adj* [➡BAD-TEMPERED AND HUMOURLESS; 627]

whip 1 *v* (*informal*) **steal**, take, rob, thieve, nick (*slang*), pinch (*informal*). [➡STEAL AND ROB; 427] 2 *v* **flog**, thrash, beat, belt (*informal*), lash, flagellate. [➡WHIP AND CLUB; 418] 3 *v* **whisk**, beat, cream, aerate, stir. [➡COOKING AND FOOD PREPARATION; 354] 4 *n* **lash**, crop, cat-o'-nine-tails, switch. [➡BLUNT INSTRUMENTS AND WHIPS; 1157]

whiplash *n* **blow**, stroke, lash, hit, impact. [➡CONTACT: IMPACT; 414]

whippersnapper (*dated*) *n* [➡MISCHIEVOUS OR BADLY-BEHAVED CHILD; 946]

whippet *type of* **small dog.** [➡DOG; 980]

whipping (*informal*) *n* [➡BEAT AND DEFEAT; 80]

whipping boy *n* [➡SUBORDINATES AND ASSISTANTS; 966]

whip-round (*informal*) *n* **collection**, appeal, kitty, fund. [➡MONEY; 140]

whip snake *type of* **non-poisonous snake.** [➡SNAKE; 995]

whip up 1 *v* **stir up**, drum up, incite, provoke, arouse. [➡CAUSE TO HAPPEN; 31] *Opposite:* pacify. 2 *v* (*informal*) **throw together** (*informal*), rustle up (*informal*), rattle off, prepare, concoct, cook, produce. [➡MEAL PREPARATION; 355]

whirl 1 *v* **spin**, twirl, reel, rotate, turn, swivel. [➡MOVE SOMETHING ON THE SPOT; 337] 2 *n* **rotation**, spin, twirl, turn, twizzle (*informal*), flick. [➡MOVE SOMETHING ON THE SPOT; 337] 3 *n* **flurry**, bustle, hustle, commotion, tumult. [➡DISORDER AND CHAOS; 246]

whirlpool 1 *n* **eddy**, vortex, swirl, current, waterspout. [➡THE SEAS, OCEANS, AND SHORES; 1041] 2 (*US*) *type of* **plumbing fittings.** [➡FITTINGS; 859]

whirlpool bath *type of* **plumbing fittings.** [➡FITTINGS; 859]

whirlwind 1 *n* **tornado**, hurricane, cyclone, waterspout, vortex, dust devil, twister (*US informal*). [➡WINDY AND STORMY WEATHER; 1053] 2 *adj* **rapid**, short-lived, tumultuous, brief, swift, hasty, lightning. [➡HAPPENING QUICKLY; 104] *Opposite:* leisurely.

whirr 1 *v* **hum**, purr, buzz, whine, drone. [➡EMIT CONTINUOUS SOUNDS; 367] 2 *type of* **continuous sound.** [➡CONTINUOUS SOUNDS; 1257]

whisk 1 *v* **beat**, whip, cream, aerate, stir. [➡COOKING AND FOOD PREPARATION; 354] 2 *v* **take**, bundle, bustle, hustle, whip, zip (*informal*). [➡MOVE FAST; 314] *Opposite:* drag. 3 *type of* **utensil.** [➡TABLEWARE, CUTLERY, AND KITCHENWARE; 861]

whisker *n* **fraction**, inch, millimetre, hair's-breadth. [➡FEW, LITTLE, SMALL AMOUNT; 119]

whiskers *n* **facial hair**, sideburns, moustache, muttonchops, stubble, growth, beard, goatee. [➡FACIAL HAIR; 490]

whiskery *adj* [➡FACIAL HAIR; 490]

whisper 1 *v* **murmur**, sigh, mutter, breathe, utter, hiss, mouth. [➡SOUND EMISSION BY PEOPLE; 364] *Opposite:* shout. 2 *n* **rumour**, word, gossip, tale, hint. [➡GOSSIP; 679] 3 *type of* **human sound**. [➡SOUNDS MADE BY PEOPLE; 1261]

whispered *adj* [➡SOFT OR PLEASANT SOUNDS; 1264]

whistle 1 *v* **screech**, shrill, shriek, hoot, toot. [➡EMIT RINGING AND TOOTING SOUNDS; 368] 2 *n* **toot**, shriek, signal, screech, hoot. [➡SOUNDS MADE BY PEOPLE; 1261]

whistle-blower *n* **informer**, mole, telltale, snitch (*slang*), grass (*slang*), stool pigeon (*slang*), tattletale (*US informal*). [➡INTERFERING PEOPLE AND TELLTALES; 950]

whistle-stop *adj* **barnstorming**, whirlwind, lightning, rapid, speedy. [➡HAPPENING QUICKLY; 104] *Opposite:* relaxed.

whit (*informal*) *n* **iota**, bit, jot, grain, speck, fig. [➡SMALL PIECE; 127]

white 1 *adj* **snowy**, silver, silvery, bleached, grey, greying, hoary. [➡HAIR COLOUR; 486] *Opposite:* black. 2 *adj* **pale**, pallid, ashen, wan, washed-out, anaemic, waxen, drawn, pasty, grey. [➡COMPLEXION; 481] *Opposite:* flushed. 3 *adj* **frosty**, snowy, hoary, icy, frozen, freezing. [➡COLD WEATHER; 1051] 4 *type of* **colour**. [➡COLOURS; 1223]

> **white**
>
> ◆ *types of white*
> cream, eggshell, ivory, magnolia, off-white, oyster, pearl, platinum, silver, snow white

white ant *type of* **ant**. [➡ANTS; 1014]

white as a sheet *adj* [➡COMPLEXION; 481]

whitebait *type of* **sea fish**. [➡SEA FISH; 1009]

white blood cells *n* [➡THE BLOOD AND CIRCULATION; 718]

white bread *type of* **bread**. [➡BREAD, FLOUR, AND BREAD PRODUCTS; 1178]

whitecap *n* **crest**, surf, breaker, white horses, wave. [➡THE SEAS, OCEANS, AND SHORES; 1041]

white-collar *adj* **professional**, managerial, management, salaried, office, executive, administrative. [➡TYPES OF WORK; 835] *Opposite:* blue-collar.

white corpuscle *n* [➡THE BLOOD AND CIRCULATION; 718]

white dwarf *type of* **star or star system**. [➡CELESTIAL BODIES; 1060]

whitefly *type of* **flying insect**. [➡FLYING INSECTS; 1013]

whitehead *n* [➡CONDITIONS AFFECTING THE SKIN; 722]

white-hot 1 *adj* **incandescent**, glowing, white, luminescent, hot, molten. [➡TEMPERATURE: HOT; 1228] *Opposite:* ice-cold. 2 *adj* **intense**, fevered, frenetic, frenzied, excited. [➡PLEASURE, EXCITEMENT, AND ELATION; 535] *Opposite:* lethargic.

white-knuckle *adj* **exhilarating**, frightening, terrifying, exciting, roller-coaster, adrenalin-charged, nerve-racking. [➡FRIGHTENING; 232] *Opposite:* safe.

white lie *n* [➡DECEPTION AND LIES; 661]

> *See Compare and Contrast at* **lie**.

white lightning (*US*) *n* [➡DRINKS; 1186]

whiten *v* **blanch**, whitewash, bleach, fade, pale. [➡CHANGE OF COLOUR; 392] *Opposite:* darken.

whiteness *n* **paleness**, milkiness, lightness, pallor, wanness, anaemia, sallowness, pastiness. [➡COMPLEXION; 481] *Opposite:* ruddiness.

whiteout *n* **blizzard**, snowstorm, storm, snowfall, snow-squall. [➡WINDY AND STORMY WEATHER; 1053]

white pepper *type of* **spice**. [➡HERBS AND SPICES; 1174]

whitewash 1 *n* **distemper**, lime, whitening, paint. [➡DYES AND COLOURANTS; 1269] 2 *n* **cover-up**, deception, conspiracy, plot, concealment, misrepresentation. [➡DECEPTION AND LIES; 661] *Opposite:* exposure. 3 *n* (*informal*) **defeat**, rout, one-horse race, wipeout (*informal*), trouncing, beating, setback, shutout (*US*). [➡BEAT AND DEFEAT; 80] *Opposite:* triumph. 4 *v* **paint**, decorate, distemper, cover, smear, daub. [➡DECORATE, ADORN, AND APPLY COATINGS; 406] 5 *v* **misrepresent**, cover up, conceal, explain away, gloss over, sweep under the carpet, suppress. [➡CAUSE TO DISAPPEAR; 6] *Opposite:* expose. 6 *v* **trounce**, defeat, beat, rout, outclass, crush, see off, shut out (*US*), cream (*US informal*). [➡BEAT AND DEFEAT; 80] *Opposite:* succumb.

white water 1 *n* **rapids**, torrents, foam, spray, current. [➡THE SEAS, OCEANS, AND SHORES; 1041] 2 *n* **shallows**, shoals, sandbanks, sandbar. [➡THE SEAS, OCEANS, AND SHORES; 1041]

white whale *type of* **whale**. [➡WHALE; 991]

whiting *type of* **sea fish**. [➡SEA FISH; 1009]

whittle *v* **carve**, shape, fashion, shave, sculpt, cut. [➡CRAFTS AND CARVING; 356]

whittle away *v* **eat into**, erode, eat away at, reduce, consume, corrode. [➡USE UP AND WASTE; 475] *Opposite:* build up.

whittle down *v* **cut down**, trim, pare down, reduce, diminish, lessen. [➡CHANGE OF SIZE: SMALLER; 394] *Opposite:* increase.

whiz 1 *v* **whirr**, hum, hiss, buzz, rattle, whoosh. [➡EMIT CONTINUOUS SOUNDS; 367] 2 *v* **dash**, nip (*informal*), pop (*informal*), zip (*informal*), go, zap (*informal*), shoot (*informal*). [➡MOVE FAST; 314] *Opposite:* dawdle. 3 *n* **whirring**, humming, hissing, buzzing, rattling, whoosh. [➡CONTINUOUS SOUNDS; 1257] 4 *n* (*informal*) **expert**, prodigy, whiz kid (*informal*), bright spark (*informal*), genius, boffin (*informal*), wizard (*informal*). [➡TALENTED OR INTELLIGENT PERSON; 529]

whiz kid (*informal*) *n* **prodigy**, wizard (*informal*), expert, whiz (*informal*), bright spark (*informal*), genius, boffin (*informal*). [➡TALENTED OR INTELLIGENT PERSON; 529]

whizz *v* [➡MOVE FAST; 314]

whodunit *n* **mystery**, thriller, cliffhanger. [➡FICTION AND DRAMA; 913]

whole 1 *adj* **entire**, complete, full, in one piece, total, unabridged, uncut. [➡WHOLENESS AND COMPLETENESS; 199] *Opposite:* partial. 2 *adj* **intact**, in one piece, unbroken, undivided, undented, unspoiled. [➡IN GOOD REPAIR; 1231] *Opposite:* broken. 3 *adj* **unimpaired**, healthy, sound, fit, well, sturdy. [➡FINE; 738] *Opposite:* unhealthy. 4 *adj* **healed**, cured, healthy, restored, rehabilitated, mended. [➡FIT AND STRONG; 737] *Opposite:* ill. 5 *n* **sum total**, aggregate, total, unit, entity, ensemble. [➡MEASUREABLE PORTION; 125] 6 *n* **entirety**, totality, unity, everything, all. [➡ALL; 126] *Opposite:* part.

wholehearted *adj* **enthusiastic**, passionate, unreserved, total, unstinting, unequivocal, hundred per cent, unswerving, committed. [➡POSITIVE IMPATIENCE, ENTHUSIASM, AND ALERTNESS; 538] *Opposite:* grudging.

whole lot *n* [➡ALL; 126]

wholemeal *type of* **flour**. [➡BREAD, FLOUR, AND BREAD PRODUCTS; 1178]

wholeness *n* **completeness**, entirety, totality, unity, fullness, comprehensiveness. [➡WHOLENESS AND COMPLETENESS; 199]

wholesale 1 *adj* **extensive**, comprehensive, across-the-board, indiscriminate, blanket, general. [➡WHOLENESS AND COMPLETENESS; 199] *Opposite:* partial. 2 *adv* **indiscriminately**, extensively, comprehensively, generally, broadly, universally. [➡WHOLENESS AND COMPLETENESS; 199] *Opposite:* partially.

wholesaler *n* **trader**, retailer, supplier, dealer, vendor, broker, merchant, importer, exporter. [➡BUSINESS PEOPLE; 794]

wholesome 1 *adj* **healthy**, healthful, nutritious, good, nourishing, hearty, health-giving. [➡FOOD; 1166] *Opposite:* unwholesome. 2 *adj* **decent**, moral, clean, honest, clean-living, open-faced, upright. [➡MORALLY GOOD; 775] *Opposite:* unwholesome. 3 *adj* **sensible**, open, honest, commonsensical, practical, helpful. [➡POSITIVE INTELLECTUAL CHARACTERISTICS; 525] *Opposite:* unhelpful. 4 *adj* **fit**, healthy, fresh-faced, clean-cut, ruddy, blooming, hale and hearty. [➡COMPLEXION; 481] *Opposite:* unhealthy.

wholesomeness 1 *n* **freshness**, healthiness, healthfulness, naturalness, goodness, nutritiousness, purity. [➡FOOD; 1166] *Opposite:* unwholesomeness. 2 *n* **morality**, uprightness, decency, integrity, virtuousness, righteousness, respectability, virtue. [➡MORALLY GOOD; 775] *Opposite:* immorality. 3 *n* **common sense**, sense, practicality, good sense, openness, helpfulness. [➡POSITIVE INTELLECTUAL CHARACTERISTICS; 525] *Opposite:* impracticality. 4 *n* **healthiness**, fitness, glow, ruddiness, haleness. [➡COMPLEXION; 481] *Opposite:* unwholesomeness.

whole-wheat (*US*) *type of* **flour**. [➡BREAD, FLOUR, AND BREAD PRODUCTS; 1178]

wholly 1 *adv* **completely**, entirely, totally, altogether, utterly, in every respect. [➡WHOLENESS AND COMPLETENESS; 199] *Opposite:* partially. 2 *adv* **solely**, exclusively, only, just, absolutely, entirely. [➡ABSOLUTE AND ABSOLUTELY; 131] *Opposite:* generally.

whoop 1 *v* **cry out**, shout, scream, howl, hoot, yell, roar, holler (*informal*). [➡GIVING VENT TO EMOTIONS; 680] 2 *n* **shout**, cry, howl, scream, hoot, yell, roar, holler (*informal*). [➡SOUNDS MADE BY PEOPLE; 1261]

whoosh 1 *n* **rushing**, hiss, swish, whistle, roar, whisper, rustle. [➡CONTINUOUS SOUNDS; 1257] 2 *n* **dash**, zoom, rush, spurt, surge, burst, spate. [➡SUDDEN EVENT; 52] 3 *v* **zoom**, whistle, swish, hiss, roar, whisper, rustle. [➡EMIT CONTINUOUS SOUNDS; 367] 4 *v* **rush**, shoot (*informal*), zoom, burst, whistle, whiz, zap (*informal*), zip (*informal*). [➡MOVE FAST; 314] *Opposite:* dawdle.

whopper (*informal*) 1 *n* **monster**, giant, whale (*informal*), elephant, Goliath, leviathan, mammoth. [➡BIG THINGS; 1193] 2 *n* **lie**, fib (*informal*), untruth, story (*informal*), tale, fabrication, falsehood. [➡DECEPTION AND LIES; 661] *Opposite:* truth.

whopping 1 *n* [➡BEAT AND DEFEAT; 80] 2 *adj* (*informal*) **enormous**, gigantic, monstrous, huge, big, massive, mammoth. [➡LARGE; 1192] *Opposite:* tiny.

whorl *n* **spiral**, coil, curl, twist, swirl, vortex. [➡ROUNDED SHAPE; 1217]

whortleberry *type of* **berry**. [➡FRUIT AND VEGETABLES; 1175]

whys and wherefores *n* **reasons**, ins and outs, details, the full picture, motives, explanations. [➡BASIC DETAILS; 689]

wicked 1 *adj* **evil**, bad, wrong, depraved, immoral, iniquitous, sinful, impious, heinous, nefarious, fiendish. [➡MORALLY BAD; 776] *Opposite:* good. 2 *adj* (*informal*) **distressing**, dreadful, awful, atrocious, severe, appalling, terrible. [➡EMOTIONALLY UNPLEASANT AND UPSETTING; 228] *Opposite:* excellent. 3 *adj* **mischievous**, naughty, cheeky, roguish, impish, teasing. [➡JOKES AND TEASING; 675] *Opposite:* respectful. 4 *adj* **mean**, cutting, acerbic, sharp, malicious, sarcastic. [➡RUDE AND HOSTILE; 626] *Opposite:* gentle. 5 *adj* (*slang*) **good**, great, terrific, cool (*slang*), fabulous, fab (*dated informal*), fantastic, impressive. [➡EXTRAORDINARY: AMAZING; 205] *Opposite:* unimpressive.

wickedly 1 *adv* **mischievously**, impishly, roguishly, teasingly, naughtily, cheekily (*informal*). [➡JOKES AND TEASING; 675] *Opposite:* respectfully. 2 *adv* **meanly**, acerbically, sharply, maliciously, sarcastically, hurtfully. [➡RUDE AND HOSTILE; 626] *Opposite:* gently.

wickedness 1 *n* **evil**, badness, iniquity, sin, impiety, malice, evilness. [➡MORALLY BAD; 776] *Opposite:* goodness. 2 *n* **impishness**, cheekiness (*informal*), naughtiness, mischievousness. [➡JOKES AND TEASING; 675]

wicker *n* **cane**, rattan, wickerwork, bamboo. [➡PLANT MATERIALS; 1132]

wicket 1 *n* **gate**, door, opening, aperture, entrance, exit. [➡DOORS AND ACCESS POINTS; 1100] 2 *type of* **sports equipment**. [➡SPORTS EQUIPMENT; 879]

wide 1 *adj* **broad**, ample, large, thick, spacious, expansive, open. [➡WIDTH: WIDE; 1198] *Opposite:* narrow. 2 *adj* **extensive**, varied, widespread, inclusive, eclectic, catholic, comprehensive, wide-ranging. [➡WHOLENESS AND COMPLETENESS; 199] *Opposite:* narrow. 3 *adj* **baggy**, roomy, loose, loose-fitting, capacious, comfortable. [➡DESCRIBING CLOTHES; 869] *Opposite:* tight. 4 *adv* **off course**, off target, off the mark, wide of the mark, out. [➡ORIENTATION AND ALIGNMENT; 1222]

wide-awake (*informal*) *adj* **fully awake**, alert, on the ball (*informal*), bright-eyed and bushy-tailed, perky, watchful, vigilant. [➡POSITIVE IMPATIENCE, ENTHUSIASM, AND ALERTNESS; 538] *Opposite:* asleep.

wide-eyed 1 *adj* **amazed**, astonished, open-mouthed, dumbfounded, gobsmacked (*slang*), flabbergasted (*informal*). [➡SURPRISE, SHOCK, AND AMAZEMENT; 546] *Opposite:* impassive. 2 *adj* **naive**, innocent, inexperienced, green, credulous, gullible. [➡NEGATIVE INTELLECTUAL CHARACTERISTICS; 526] *Opposite:* knowing.

widely *adv* **extensively**, broadly, generally, far and wide, commonly, usually. [➡GENERAL LOCATIONS; 159] *Opposite:* narrowly.

widen *v* **broaden**, extend, expand, enlarge, make wider, amplify. [➡CHANGE OF SIZE: BIGGER; 393] *Opposite:* narrow.

wide of the mark *adj* [➡INCORRECT AND ERRONEOUS; 223]

wide-open 1 *adj* **open wide**, gaping, agape (*literary*), yawning, cavernous. [➡WIDTH: WIDE; 1198] 2 *adj* **unpredictable**, undecided, anybody's guess, up for grabs (*informal*), unsettled, in the balance, indeterminate, up in the air. [➡UNCERTAIN; 176] *Opposite:* settled. 3 *adj* **vulnerable**, unprotected, exposed, unguarded, at risk, in danger, defenceless. [➡IN DANGER; 238] *Opposite:* protected.

wide-ranging *adj* **extensive**, widespread, comprehensive, across-the-board, inclusive, thorough, sweeping, all-embracing. [➡WHOLENESS AND COMPLETENESS; 199] *Opposite:* narrow.

widespread *adj* **extensive**, prevalent, general, common, rife, pervasive, epidemic. [➡PRESENT AND AVAILABLE; 11] *Opposite:* limited.

Compare and Contrast: *widespread, prevalent, rife, epidemic, universal*

CORE MEANING: OCCURRING OVER A WIDE AREA

widespread existing or happening in many places, or affecting many people; ***prevalent*** occurring commonly or widely as a dominant feature; ***rife*** full of or severely affected by something undesirable that occurs frequently or in great numbers over a wide area, especially when it appears to be uncontrollable; ***epidemic*** spreading more quickly and more extensively than expected; ***universal*** affecting the whole world, or present everywhere.

widget (*humorous*) *n* [➡PHYSICAL OBJECTS; 1242]

widow *n* [➡MARITAL STATUS; 890]

widowed *adj* [➡MARITAL STATUS; 890]

widower *n* [➡MARITAL STATUS; 890]

width *n* **breadth**, thickness, girth, size, measurement. [➡WIDTH: WIDE; 1198]

wield 1 *v* **exercise**, exert, use, have, employ, apply. [➡USE; 468] 2 *v* **brandish**, manipulate, handle, ply, carry, sport (*informal*), wave around. [➡MOVE SOMETHING ON THE SPOT; 337] *Opposite:* conceal.

wiener (*US*) *type of* **processed meat**. [➡TYPES AND CUTS OF MEAT; 1176]

wienerwurst (*US*) *type of* **processed meat**. [➡TYPES AND CUTS OF MEAT; 1176]

wife *n* **spouse**, partner, mate, consort, helpmeet (*archaic*). [➡RELATIVES BY MARRIAGE; 960]

wife-to-be *n* [➡RELATIVES BY MARRIAGE; 960]

wig 1 *v* (*dated informal*) [➡ACCUSE, BLAME, AND CRITICIZE; 642] 2 *n* **toupee**, hairpiece, periwig, rug (*informal*), extension. [➡HAIR STYLES AND HAIR PIECES; 489]

wiggle 1 *v* **wriggle**, waggle, twist, jiggle, squirm, worm. [➡MOVE SOMETHING ON THE SPOT; 337] 2 *n* **jiggle**, shake, wriggle, twist, waggle. [➡MOVE SOMETHING ON THE SPOT; 337]

wiggly *adj* **undulating**, wavy, curved, curvy, curving, meandering, sinuous. [➡DIRECTION OF MOTION; 346] *Opposite:* straight.

wigwam *n* **dwelling** (*formal*), tepee, tent, yurt, hut, lodge. [➡RESIDENTIAL BUILDINGS; 1077]

wild 1 *adj* **untamed**, undomesticated, uncultivated, natural, feral. [➡DANGEROUS; 237] *Opposite:* tame. 2 *adj* (*informal*) **outrageous**, madcap, crazy (*informal*), foolish, unconventional, irrational, reckless. [➡BIZARRE AND PECULIAR; 258] *Opposite:* sensible. 3 *adj* **rough**, desolate, barren, remote, uninhabited, bare, harsh. [➡PHYSICALLY UNPLEASANT; 227] *Opposite:* gentle. 4 *adj* **stormy**, blustery, squally, tempestuous, windswept, turbulent, rough. [➡WINDY AND STORMY WEATHER; 1053] *Opposite:* calm. 5 *adj* **enthusiastic**, eager, crazy (*informal*), mad, excited, thrilled. [➡PLEASURE, EXCITEMENT, AND ELATION; 535] *Opposite:* unenthusiastic. 6 *adj* **rowdy**, undisciplined, riotous, unruly, rough, unmanageable, uncontrollable, disorderly. [➡REBELLIOUSNESS AND DISOBEDIENCE; 566] *Opposite:* orderly. 7 *adj* **overwhelmed**, overcome, overpowered, devastated, destroyed. [➡IN BAD REPAIR; 1233] 8 *adj* **untidy**, dishevelled, unkempt, tousled, messy, scruffy. [➡BADLY GROOMED; 484] *Opposite:* tidy.

See Compare and Contrast at **unruly**.

wild boar *type of* **meat**. [➡TYPES AND CUTS OF MEAT; 1176]

wildcat *type of* **cat**. [➡FELINE; 983]

wilderness *n* **wilds**, rough country, wasteland, desert, outback. [➡DESERTS AND PLAINS; 1045]

wildfowl *type of* **fowl**. [➡FOOD BIRD; 999]

wildlife *n* **flora and fauna**, nature, natural world, environment, biota. [➡LIVING THINGS AND LIVING; 976]

wildlife park *n* [➡THE COUNTRYSIDE AND OUTDOOR SPACES; 1070]

wildlife refuge *n* [➡THE COUNTRYSIDE AND OUTDOOR SPACES; 1070]

wildlife sanctuary *n* [➡THE COUNTRYSIDE AND OUTDOOR SPACES; 1070]

wildly 1 *adv* **enthusiastically**, madly, passionately, excitedly, eagerly, violently. [➡PLEASURE, EXCITEMENT, AND ELATION; 535] *Opposite:* indifferently. 2 *adv* **rowdily**, riotously, uncontrollably, noisily, outrageously, roughly. [➡REBELLIOUSNESS AND DISOBEDIENCE; 566] *Opposite:* calmly.

wildness 1 *n* **roughness**, remoteness, desolation, barrenness, harshness. [➡DIFFICULTY AND COMPLEXITY; 243] 2 *n* (*informal*) **recklessness**, craziness (*informal*), madness, foolishness, passion, waywardness, zaniness. [➡ECCENTRICITY AND

IRRATIONALITY; 563] 3 *n* **rowdiness**, lack of control, lack of discipline, unruliness, roughness, violence. [➡REBELLIOUSNESS AND DISOBEDIENCE; 566] *Opposite:* orderliness.

wilds *n* [➡THE COUNTRYSIDE AND OUTDOOR SPACES; 1070]

wiles *n* **tricks**, trickery, guile, deceit, artifice (*formal*). [➡DECEPTION AND LIES; 661]

wilful 1 *adj* **deliberate**, determined, intentional, conscious, malicious, purposive, malevolent, malign, maleficent. [➡INTENTIONAL AND DELIBERATE; 280] *Opposite:* unwitting. 2 *adj* **stubborn**, obstinate, headstrong, perverse, obstreperous, awkward, unruly, self-willed, difficult. [➡UNWILLINGNESS AND STUBBORNNESS; 565] *Opposite:* compliant.

See Compare and Contrast at **unruly**.

wilfulness 1 *n* **premeditation**, consciousness, deliberateness, maliciousness, purposiveness, malevolence, malice. [➡ANTAGONISM; 553] 2 *n* **stubbornness**, obstinacy, perverseness, perversity, obstreperousness, awkwardness, unruliness. [➡UNWILLINGNESS AND STUBBORNNESS; 565] *Opposite:* compliance.

wiliness *n* **cunning**, wiles, craftiness, guile, craft, slyness, deviousness, sneakiness, shrewdness, astuteness, scheming, cleverness. [➡POSITIVE INTELLECTUAL CHARACTERISTICS; 525] *Opposite:* ingenuousness.

will 1 *n* **mind**, brain, consciousness, thoughts, thought processes, self-determination. [➡PSYCHOLOGY AND THE MIND; 770] 2 *n* **determination**, resolve, willpower, motivation, spirit, strength of character, self-control, backbone, drive, guts (*slang*). [➡THE WILL AND WILLINGNESS; 564] 3 *n* **desire**, inclination, wish, longing, determination, ambition. [➡DESIRE AND WANT; 580] 4 *n* (*formal*) **bidding**, command, dictate, wish, desire, instructions. [➡DESIRE AND WANT; 580] 5 *v* **want**, wish, yearn, desire, long, pray, hope against hope. [➡DESIRE AND WANT; 580]

willies (*informal*) *n* **jitters** (*informal*), creeps (*informal*), shakes, heebie-jeebies (*slang*), shivers (*informal*), goose pimples, butterflies (*informal*). [➡FEAR AND PANIC; 544]

willing 1 *adj* **prepared**, ready, set, agreeable, disposed, happy, inclined. [➡THE WILL AND WILLINGNESS; 564] *Opposite:* unwilling. 2 *adj* **eager**, keen, enthusiastic, game, helpful, cooperative, alacritous. [➡POSITIVE IMPATIENCE, ENTHUSIASM, AND ALERTNESS; 538] *Opposite:* reluctant.

willingly 1 *adv* **freely**, readily, gladly, happily, cheerfully, voluntarily, of your own accord, without a fight. [➡THE WILL AND WILLINGNESS; 564] *Opposite:* unwillingly. 2 *adv* **eagerly**, enthusiastically, keenly, cooperatively, readily, happily, gamely, with a will. [➡WITH ENTHUSIASM; 287] *Opposite:* reluctantly.

willingness 1 *n* **readiness**, inclination, will, preparedness, disposition. [➡THE WILL AND WILLINGNESS; 564] *Opposite:* unwillingness. 2 *n* **enthusiasm**, alacrity, motivation, eagerness, keenness, cooperation, commitment. [➡POSITIVE IMPATIENCE, ENTHUSIASM, AND ALERTNESS; 538] *Opposite:* reluctance.

willing to please *adj* [➡THE WILL AND WILLINGNESS; 564]

will-o'-the-wisp *n* [➡NONEXISTENT THINGS; 23]

willow *type of* **deciduous tree.** [➡DECIDUOUS TREES; 1028]

willowy 1 *adj* **graceful**, slim, elegant, lissom, svelte, lithe. [➡BUILD; 478] *Opposite:* stocky. 2 *adj* **flexible**, bendable, malleable, springy, supple. [➡MALLEABLE AND ELASTIC; 1211] *Opposite:* stiff.

willpower *n* **determination**, resolve, resolution, iron will, strength of will, strength of mind, self-control, self-discipline. [➡STRENGTH OF WILL; 502] *Opposite:* weakness.

willy-nilly 1 *adv* **regardless**, anyway, in any case, like it or not, unceremoniously. [➡UNINTENTIONAL AND ACCIDENTAL; 282] 2 *adj* **haphazard**, random, unsystematic, arbitrary, unselective. [➡DISORDER AND CHAOS; 246] *Opposite:* methodical.

wilt *v* **droop**, shrivel, wither, fade, wane, sag. [➡CEASE TO EXIST; 22] *Opposite:* flourish.

wilted *adj* [➡IN BAD REPAIR; 1233]

wily *adj* **crafty**, cunning, guileful, sly, devious, sneaky, shrewd, astute, scheming, clever. [➡DECEITFUL; 514] *Opposite:* ingenuous.

win 1 *v* **come first**, succeed, triumph, be victorious, be successful, prevail. [➡SUCCEED AND WIN; 79] *Opposite:* lose. 2 *v* **gain**, earn, secure, attain, collect, accomplish, acquire, obtain, achieve. [➡GET; 421] *Opposite:* lose. 3 *n* **victory**, success, triumph, landslide, conquest. [➡SUCCESS; 82] *Opposite:* defeat.

wince 1 *n* **grimace**, scowl, flinch, gasp, cringe, shudder. [➡FACIAL EXPRESSION; 652] *Opposite:* smile. 2 *n* **cringe**, recoil, flinch, jump, start. [➡PHYSICAL REACTIONS; 317] 3 *v* **grimace**, scowl, shudder, flinch, gasp, blench. [➡FACIAL EXPRESSION; 652] *Opposite:* smile. 4 *v* **recoil**, flinch, jump, cringe, shrink, start, shy, blench. [➡PHYSICAL REACTIONS; 317]

See Compare and Contrast at **recoil**.

winceyette *type of* **fabric from plants.** [➡FABRICS; 1131]

winch 1 *n* **hoist**, windlass, pulley, crane, capstan, crank, lifter, block and tackle. [➡MACHINES AND MACHINE PARTS; 1115] 2 *v* **raise**, hoist, lift, lift up, pull, haul, wind. [➡MOVE SOMETHING: UPWARDS; 329]

wind 1 *n* **current of air**, breeze, gale, squall, gust, airstream. [➡WINDY AND STORMY WEATHER; 1053] 2 *v* **snake**, meander, bend, curve, twist, twist and turn. [➡CHANGE DIRECTION OF MOTION; 345] 3 *v* **coil**, twist, encircle, roll, wrap around, curl, twine. [➡POSITION SOMETHING: AROUND SOMETHING; 328] *Opposite:* unwind.

wind

◆ *types of wind*
antitrade, bise, chinook, cyclone, foehn, harmattan, hurricane, khamsin, levanter, mistral, monsoon, northeaster, northwester, Santa Ana, simoom, sirocco, southeaster, southwester, tornado, trade wind, tramontana, typhoon, westerly

windbag (*informal*) *n* **bore**, bigmouth (*informal*), blabbermouth (*informal*), chatterbox (*informal*), smart aleck (*informal*), wiseacre (*informal*). [➡INTERFERING PEOPLE AND TELLTALES; 950]

windbreak *n* **shelter**, panel, barrier, screen, fence, wall, hedge, hedgerow, windscreen (*US*). [➡BARRIERS; 1112]

windcheater *type of* **jacket**. [➡GARMENTS AND OUTFITS; 865]

wind down *v* **relax**, unwind, rest, chill out (*slang*), loosen up, hang loose (*informal*). [➡CHANGE OF MOOD AND COMPOSURE; 581]

winded *adj* **breathless**, out of breath, short of breath, panting, gasping, puffing. [➡INJURED; 743]

windfall *n* **bonus**, handout, bonanza, payout, dividend, win. [➡TREAT; 211]

wind gauge *type of* **measuring device**. [➡MEASURING DEVICES; 1122]

winding *adj* **zigzagging**, snaky, snaking, twisting, curving, windy, meandering. [➡ROUNDED SHAPE; 1217] *Opposite:* straight.

windjammer *type of* **historical vessel**. [➡SHIPS AND BOATS; 1149]

windlass *n* **winch**, hoist, crane, capstan, pulley, lifter, crank. [➡MACHINES AND MACHINE PARTS; 1115]

window 1 *n* **pane**, windowpane, glass, glazing. [➡WINDOWS; 1099] 2 *n* **gap**, space, opening, hole. [➡HOLES, GAPS, AND FORKS; 1251] 3 *n* **opportunity**, period, chance, slot, window of opportunity. [➡SHORT PERIOD OF TIME; 93] 4 *n* **dialogue box**, box, frame, display, interface, graphic. [➡COMPUTERS AND COMPUTING; 1126] 5 *part of* **building**. [➡PARTS OF A BUILDING; 1094]

window

◆ *parts of a window*
ledge, pane, sill, window ledge, windowpane, windowsill

◆ *types of window*
bay window, casement, dormer window, fanlight, French window, lancet window, picture window, porthole, rose window, sash window, skylight, transom (*US*)

window ledge *part of* **window**. [➡WINDOWS; 1099]

windowpane *n* **pane**, window, glass, glazing. [➡WINDOWS; 1099]

windowsill *n* **ledge**, window ledge, sill, shelf. [➡WINDOWS; 1099]

windpipe *part of* **respiratory system**. [➡RESPIRATORY ORGANS; 716]

windscreen 1 *part of* **external structure**. [➡EXTERNAL PARTS OF A VEHICLE; 1146] 2 *n* (*US*) **windbreak**, screen, shelter, barrier. [➡BARRIERS; 1112]

windscreen wiper *type of* **external feature**. [➡VEHICLES; 1144]

windshield (*US*) *part of* **external structure**. [➡EXTERNAL PARTS OF A VEHICLE; 1146]

windshield wiper (*US*) *type of* **external feature**. [➡VEHICLES; 1144]

windsock *type of* **measuring device**. [➡MEASURING DEVICES; 1122]

Windsor chair *type of* **seating**. [➡FURNITURE; 858]

windstorm *n* **storm**, wind, gale, hurricane, cyclone, tornado, whirlwind, twister (*US informal*), dust devil. [➡WINDY AND STORMY WEATHER; 1053]

windswept *adj* **desolate**, windy, barren, inhospitable, exposed, bleak, unsheltered, bare. [➡EMPTY; 1237] *Opposite:* sheltered.

wind-up 1 *n* (*informal*) **joke**, trick, prank, practical joke, tease, April fool. [➡JOKES AND TEASING; 675] 2 *adj* **clockwork**, mechanical, spring-operated, manual. [➡MACHINERY; 1113]

wind up 1 *v* **liquidate**, terminate (*formal*), close down, close, shut down. [➡BUSINESS ACTIVITIES AND PHENOMENA; 795] 2 *v* **end**, conclude, bring to an end, complete, finish, wrap up (*informal*), close, shut down. [➡COMPLETE AN ACTION; 264] *Opposite:* start off. 3 *v* (*informal*) **infuriate**, enrage, madden, annoy, irritate, put your back up. [➡ANGER AND ANNOY; 570] *Opposite:* amuse. 4 *v* (*informal*) **tease**, have somebody on, kid, fool, pull somebody's leg (*informal*), tell somebody stories, make fun of. [➡JOKES AND TEASING; 675] 5 *v* (*US*) **prepare**, get ready, take aim, pitch. [➡PREPARE FOR ACTION; 290]

windy 1 *adj* **blustery**, breezy, stormy, blowy (*informal*), gusty, squally, bracing, turbulent. [➡WINDY AND STORMY WEATHER; 1053] *Opposite:* still. 2 *adj* (*informal*) **wordy**, voluble, verbose, pompous, bombastic, boastful. [➡POMPOUS, LOUD, AND OVER-CONFIDENT; 636] *Opposite:* meek.

wine *type of* **red**. [➡COLOURS; 1223]

wine bar *type of* **bar or club**. [➡HOTELS, RESTAURANTS, AND CLUBS; 1081]

winery (*US*) *n* **vineyard**, wine producer, wine grower, estate, chateau, vinery. [➡INDUSTRIAL BUILDINGS; 1086]

wing 1 *n* **annexe**, extension, part, arm, section. [➡PARTS OF A BUILDING; 1094] 2 *n* **division**, subdivision, arm, section, department, branch. [➡SUBDIVISIONS AND OFFSHOOTS; 1252] 3 *part of* **aircraft**. [➡AIRCRAFT; 1147] 4 *part of* **bird**. [➡PARTS OF A BIRD; 1006] 5 *type of* **cut**. [➡TYPES AND CUTS OF MEAT; 1176] 6 *part of* **insect**. [➡PARTS OF AN INSECT; 1019] 7 *part of* **external structure**. [➡EXTERNAL PARTS OF A VEHICLE; 1146] 8 *v* **fly**, head, speed, race, whiz, dash, hurry. [➡MOVE FAST; 314] 9 *v* **injure**, wound, hurt, maim, shoot, damage. [➡WOUND A PERSON OR ANIMAL; 384]

wing chair *type of* **seating**. [➡FURNITURE; 858]

winged *adj* **flying**, aerial, airborne, alar, feathered, avian. [➡GENERAL LOCATIONS; 159]

wing mirror *type of* **external feature**. [➡VEHICLES; 1144]

wingtip 1 *part of* **bird**. [➡PARTS OF A BIRD; 1006] 2 (*US*) *type of* **shoe**. [➡FOOTWEAR; 871]

wink *v* **flash**, twinkle, sparkle, glitter, glint, shine. [➡LIGHT EMISSION; 369]

winkle *type of* **aquatic invertebrate**. [➡AQUATIC INVERTEBRATE; 1022]

winkle out *v* **extract**, worm, draw out, prise, wheedle, coax. [➡OBTAIN POSSESSION BY PERSUASION; 458]

winner 1 *n* **victor**, champion, champ (*informal*), conqueror, leader, frontrunner (*informal*). [➡IMPORTANT OR FAMOUS PEOPLE; 893] *Opposite:* loser. 2 *n* **success**, hit, cert (*informal*), sure thing (*informal*), sensation, triumph. [➡SUCCESS; 82] *Opposite:* failure.

winning 1 *adj* **successful**, triumphant, victorious, best, champion, star. [➡SUCCESSFUL AND PROMISING; 81] 2 *adj* **charming**, captivating, endearing, persuasive, engaging, disarming, appealing, prepossessing, attractive. [➡PEOPLE'S PHYSICAL APPEARANCE; 476] *Opposite:* unprepossessing.

winningly *adv* **charmingly**, captivatingly, endearingly, persuasively, disarmingly, winsomely, convincingly, believably, credibly. [➡BEAUTY AND ATTRACTIVENESS; 190]

winnings *n* **prize money**, prize, money, earnings, loot (*informal*), receipts, takings, kitty, jackpot. [➡INCOME; 461]

winnow *v* **examine**, go through, sort through, pick over, inspect, sort. [➡EXAMINE AND ASSESS; 754]

win over *v* **convince**, persuade, convert, win round, bring round, gain somebody's support, get somebody on your side, charm. [➡ENCOURAGE; 577]

winsome *adj* **charming**, fetching, sweet, lovely, attractive, engaging, endearing, appealing, pleasant. [➡PEOPLE'S PHYSICAL APPEARANCE; 476]

winter 1 *n* **wintertime**, midwinter, depth of winter. [➡TIMES OF YEAR; 88] *Opposite:* summer. 2 *n* **end**, twilight, close, closing, ending, conclusion, decline. [➡END; 54]

winter solstice *n* [➡TIMES OF YEAR; 88]

wintertime *n* [➡TIMES OF YEAR; 88]

wintriness *n* **chilliness**, coldness, bitterness, iciness, bleakness, frostiness. [➡COLD WEATHER; 1051] *Opposite:* warmth.

wintry *adj* **chilly**, cold, bracing, freezing, nippy, bitter, icy, bleak, frosty. [➡COLD WEATHER; 1051] *Opposite:* summery.

wipe 1 *v* **rub**, polish, mop, swab, clean, dry. [➡CLEAN AND POLISH; 404] 2 *v* **erase**, remove, delete, obliterate, destroy, record over. [➡DELETE AND ERASE; 340] 3 *v* **smear**, spread, rub, distribute, streak, apply, sponge, dab. [➡DECORATE, ADORN, AND APPLY COATINGS; 406]

wiped out (*slang*) *adj* **beat** (*informal*), exhausted, tired, shattered, bushed (*informal*), worn-out, done for (*informal*), dead (*informal*), all in, whacked (*informal*), drained, knackered (*slang*), wiped (*US*). [➡TIRED, ASLEEP, AND UNCONSCIOUS; 739] *Opposite:* full of beans (*informal*).

wipe out 1 *v* (*informal*) **annihilate**, destroy, eradicate, obliterate, exterminate, eliminate, remove. [➡DELETE AND ERASE; 340] *Opposite:* protect. 2 *v* (*slang*) **kill**, murder, assassinate, do in (*informal*), do away with (*informal*), take out, finish off (*informal*). [➡KILL; 923]

wipe the floor with (*informal*) *v* **defeat**, beat hollow, thrash, trounce, walk over (*informal*), outclass, crush, annihilate (*informal*), slaughter (*slang*), cream (*US informal*). [➡BEAT AND DEFEAT; 80]

wipe the slate clean (*informal*) *v* **make a fresh start**, start afresh, forgive and forget, bury the hatchet, let bygones be bygones, turn over a new leaf, start over (*US*). [➡FORGET, FORGIVE, AND ACCEPT; 749]

wire 1 *n* **flex**, cable, lead, line, filament, cord. [➡ELECTRONICS AND ELECTRICS; 1136] 2 *v* **connect**, hook up, install, equip. [➡FASTEN, LINK, AND JOIN; 409]

wired 1 *adj* **strengthened**, supported, reinforced, held together, bound, underwired. [➡DESCRIBING CLOTHES; 869] 2 *adj* (*informal*) **online**, on the Net, on the Web, connected, kitted out, equipped. [➡COMPUTERS AND COMPUTING; 1126] 3 *adj* (*slang*) **nervous**, on edge, hyper (*informal*), edgy, strung out (*informal*), taut, tense, restless, manic (*informal*). [➡CONFUSION, ANXIETY, AND WORRY; 541] 4 *adj* (*US slang*) **bugged**, tapped, miked (*informal*), miked up (*informal*), wired up, under surveillance. [➡ACOUSTICS; 1137]

wireless (*dated*) *type of* **audio equipment**. [➡AUDIO EQUIPMENT; 1138]

wiretap 1 *v* **tap**, bug, monitor, listen in on, eavesdrop, spy. [➡LISTEN AND LISTENERS; 709] 2 *n* **bug** (*informal*), tap, monitor. [➡TELECOMMUNICATIONS; 1129]

wiriness 1 *n* **leanness**, slimness, thinness, muscularity, sinewiness, strength, toughness. [➡MUSCLES AND MUSCULATURE; 480] *Opposite:* fatness. 2 *n* **coarseness**, stiffness, bristliness, roughness, scratchiness, toughness. [➡PHYSICAL TEXTURE; 1221] *Opposite:* softness.

wiry 1 *adj* **lean**, slim, thin, muscular, sinewy, strong, tough. [➡MUSCLES AND MUSCULATURE; 480] *Opposite:* fat. 2 *adj* **coarse**, stiff, bristly, rough, scratchy, tough, thick. [➡PHYSICAL TEXTURE; 1221] *Opposite:* soft.

wisdom *n* **understanding**, sense, knowledge, insight, perception, astuteness, acumen, intelligence, prudence, sagacity. [➡KNOWLEDGE AND WISDOM; 559] *Opposite:* foolishness.

wisdom tooth *type of* **tooth**. [➡THE MOUTH; 703]

wise 1 *adj* **astute**, intelligent, clever, prudent, sage (*literary*), sensible, judicious, sagacious (*formal*). [➡POSITIVE INTELLECTUAL CHARACTERISTICS; 525] *Opposite:* foolish. 2 *adj* **knowledgeable**, learned, informed, erudite, aware, clued-up, in the know, au fait. [➡KNOWLEDGE AND WISDOM; 559] *Opposite:* ignorant. 3 *adj* **shrewd**, cunning, crafty, devious, wily, sly, artful. [➡POSITIVE INTELLECTUAL CHARACTERISTICS; 525]

wiseacre (*informal*) *n* [➡JOKERS AND TEASES; 676]

wisecrack (*informal*) 1 *n* **witticism**, quip, riposte, gibe, retort, joke, gag, jest (*literary*), one-liner, epigram, bon mot. [➡JOKES AND TEASING; 675] 2 *v* **joke**, quip, jest (*literary*), gibe, retort, gag. [➡JOKES AND TEASING; 675]

wisecracker (*informal*) *n* [➡JOKERS AND TEASES; 676]

wise guy (*US informal*) *n* [➡SELF-IMPORTANT AND SELF-SEEKING PEOPLE; 949]

wish 1 *v* **want**, desire, crave, require, covet, need. [➡DESIRE AND WANT; 580] 2 *v* **demand**, ask, request, ask for, bid, command. [➡REQUEST AND DEMAND; 664] 3 *n* **desire**, aspiration, hope, yearning, longing, craving, fancy, inclination. [➡DESIRE AND WANT; 580] *Opposite:* disinclination. 4 *n* **request**, demand, bidding, command, requirement. [➡REQUEST AND DEMAND; 664]

See Compare and Contrast at **want**.

wishbone *part of* **bird**. [➡PARTS OF A BIRD; 1006]

wished-for *adj* [➡POPULAR AND WANTED; 221]

wishful thinking *n* **delusion**, fantasy, self-delusion, self-deception, idealism. [➡NONEXISTENT THINGS; 23] *Opposite:* reality.

wishy-washy (*informal*) 1 *adj* **indecisive**, irresolute, namby-pamby (*informal*), weak, feeble, spineless, spiritless, ineffectual, pathetic (*informal*), ineffective. [➡COWARDICE AND WEAKNESS OF WILL; 509] *Opposite:* decisive. 2 *adj* **watery**, insipid, bland, tasteless, weak, watered-down, flavourless. [➡TASTE; 704] *Opposite:* strong.

wisp *n* **strand**, scrap, tendril, thread, lock, curl, tuft. [➡SMALL PIECE; 127]

wispy *adj* **flimsy**, fine, thin, light, slight, delicate. [➡FRAGILE; 1208] *Opposite:* substantial.

wisteria *type of* **climber**. [➡CLIMBERS; 1033]

wistful *adj* **pensive**, melancholy, thoughtful, reflective, contemplative, regretful, sad, longing. [➡PENSIVENESS AND INTEREST; 539] *Opposite:* satisfied.

wistfulness *n* **melancholy**, pensiveness, reminiscence, nostalgia, dreaminess, absent-mindedness. [➡FEELINGS ABOUT THE PAST; 533] *Opposite:* contentment.

wit 1 *n* **wittiness**, waggishness (*dated*), jocularity, facetiousness, fun, humour. [➡JOKES AND TEASING; 675] *Opposite:* seriousness. 2 *n* **comedian**, humorist, comic, joker, satirist, clown, wag (*dated*). [➡JOKERS AND TEASES; 676] 3 *n* **intelligence**, smartness, cleverness, intellect, keenness, incisiveness, sharpness. [➡DESCRIBING SOMEBODY'S INTELLECT; 524] *Opposite:* stupidity.

witch *n* **enchantress**, sorceress, magician, necromancer (*literary*), occultist. [➡PEOPLE WITH SUPERNATURAL POWERS; 789]

witchcraft *n* [➡THE SUPERNATURAL; 788]

witch doctor *n* **shaman**, healer, soothsayer, medium, druid, magician. [➡PEOPLE WITH SUPERNATURAL POWERS; 789]

witchery *n* [➡THE SUPERNATURAL; 788]

witch hazel *type of* **shrub or bush**. [➡BUSHES AND SHRUBS; 1027]

with 1 *prep* **together with**, along with, in conjunction with, beside, alongside, next to. [➡RELATIVE LOCATION; 162] *Opposite:* without. 2 *prep* **in addition to**, plus, including, as well as, and. [➡ALSO; 136] *Opposite:* without.

with alacrity *adv* [➡HAPPENING QUICKLY; 104]

with all mod cons (*informal*) *adj* **well-appointed**, modern, comfortable, luxurious, modernized, well-equipped. [➡USEFULNESS; 200]

with bated breath *adv* **expectantly**, in anticipation, on the edge of your seat, anxiously, hopefully, eagerly, on edge. [➡APPRECIATION AND GRATITUDE; 536]

with care *adv* [➡CAUTIOUS AND CAREFUL; 283]

with child (*archaic or literary*) *adj* [➡REPRODUCTION AND HEREDITY; 726]

withdraw 1 *v* **remove**, take out, extract, pull out, draw, take away. [➡EXTRACT AND SEVER; 342] *Opposite:* insert. 2 *v* **retract**, renounce, disavow (*formal*), revoke, take back, unsay. [➡APOLOGIZE AND RETRACT; 684] *Opposite:* confirm. 3 *v* **leave**, depart, retire, pull out, retreat, go away. [➡ABSENT ONESELF; 8] *Opposite:* remain.

withdrawal 1 *n* **removal**, extraction, drawing, taking out, taking away. [➡REMOVE SOMETHING; 339] *Opposite:* insertion. 2 *n* **retraction**, renunciation, disavowal (*formal*), revocation, disclaimer, abjuration. [➡APOLOGIZE AND RETRACT; 684] *Opposite:* confirmation. 3 *n* **retreat**, departure, leaving, abandonment, retirement, secession. [➡END; 54] *Opposite:* arrival. 4 *n* **alienation**, depression, isolation, detachment. [➡SOLITARINESS; 941]

withdraw from the world *v* [➡RUN AWAY AND AVOID; 10]

withdrawn *adj* **reserved**, inhibited, solitary, introverted, introvert, quiet, thoughtful. [➡NEUTRALITY AND INDIFFERENCE; 554] *Opposite:* outgoing.

with ease *adv* **easily**, effortlessly, confidently, efficiently, smoothly. [➡EASE AND SIMPLICITY; 201]

with enthusiasm *adv* [➡WITH ENTHUSIASM; 287]

wither 1 *v* **shrivel**, wilt, dry up, shrink, droop, fade. [➡HARDEN, CONGEAL, DRY; 388] *Opposite:* bloom. 2 *v* **weaken**, waste away, decline, fade, wane, wilt. [➡CEASE TO EXIST; 22] *Opposite:* strengthen. 3 *v* **crush**, mortify, humiliate, abash, put down, discomfit (*formal*). [➡UPSET, DISTRESS, AND HUMILIATE; 568]

withered *adj* [➡DECAYING OR INFESTED; 1235]

withering *adj* **contemptuous**, scornful, sarcastic, sneering, arrogant, crushing, dismissive, disdainful. [➡MOCKING AND DISMISSIVE; 637] *Opposite:* complimentary.

withers *part of* **horse**. [➡HORSE; 985]

with fervour *adv* [➡WITH ENTHUSIASM; 287]

with good cheer *adv* [➡WITH ENTHUSIASM; 287]

with gusto *adv* [➡WITH ENTHUSIASM; 287]

withheld *adj* [➡ABSENT AND UNAVAILABLE; 7]

with hindsight *adv* **in retrospect**, retrospectively, looking back, from experience. [➡SUMMARIZING EXPRESSIONS; 623]

withhold *v* **hold back**, keep back, refuse, deny, suppress, reserve. [➡STORE AND KEEP; 454] *Opposite:* give.

withhold information *v* [➡WITHHOLD INFORMATION; 688]

within *adv* **inside**, in, indoors, in the interior. [➡GENERAL LOCATIONS; 159] *Opposite:* outside.

within an ace of *prep* **within reach of**, a hair's-breadth from, a stone's throw from, on the verge of. [➡CLOSENESS; 160]

within grasp *adj* [➡PRESENT AND AVAILABLE; 11]

within reach *adj* **within your grasp**, reachable, accessible, at hand, at your fingertips, attainable. [➡CLOSENESS; 160]

within reach of *prep* [➡CLOSENESS; 160]

within spitting distance (*informal*) *adj* [➡CLOSENESS; 160]

within walking distance *adj* [➡CLOSENESS; 160]

within your rights *adj* **justified**, correct, right, vindicable, vindicated, innocent. [➡MORALLY GOOD; 775] *Opposite:* unjustified.

with it (*informal*) *adj* [➡POSITIVE INTELLECTUAL CHARACTERISTICS; 525]

with-it (*dated informal*) *adj* **trendy** (*informal*), cool, fashionable, up-to-date, hip (*slang*), modern, modish, happening (*informal*). [➡NEW, MODERN; 167]

with no holds barred *adv* [➡WITH ENTHUSIASM; 287]

with one accord (*formal*) *adv* **simultaneously**, as one, in unison, together, unanimously, all together, with one heart (*US*). [➡ACTING WITH OTHERS; 286]

with one heart (*US*) *adv* [➡ACTING WITH OTHERS; 286]

with one voice *adv* **unanimously**, simultaneously, as one, all together, in unison, with one accord (*formal*), with one heart (*US*). [➡ACTING WITH OTHERS; 286]

without *prep* **devoid of**, lacking, minus, sans (*literary or humorous*), in default of. [➡LESS; 124] *Opposite:* with.

without a doubt *adv* **undoubtedly**, without doubt, without question, certainly, no doubt, indubitably (*formal*), doubtless, beyond doubt, definitely, unquestionably. [➡EXPRESSIONS OF AGREEMENT; 649] *Opposite:* possibly.

without a second thought *adv* **without hesitation**, unhesitatingly, straightaway, without question, readily, confidently, surely. [➡HAPPENING QUICKLY; 104] *Opposite:* hesitantly.

without a shadow of a doubt *adv* [➡CERTAIN; 175]

without a sound *adv* [➡ABSENCE OF SOUND; 1256]

without demur *adv* [➡HAPPENING QUICKLY; 104]

without doubt *adv* [➡CERTAIN; 175]

without due care and attention *adv* [➡INCAUTIOUS AND CARELESS; 284]

without due consideration *adv* [➡INCAUTIOUS AND CARELESS; 284]

without end *adv* [➡PERMANENCE: WITHOUT END; 94]

without equal *adj* [➡EXTRAORDINARY: UNCOMMON; 206]

without fail *adv* **for certain**, reliably, like clockwork, unfailingly, dependably, religiously. [➡UNCERTAIN; 176]

without fear *adv* [➡COURAGE; 499]

without foundation *adj* [➡FALSE AND UNREAL; 174]

without further ado *adv* **immediately**, at once, straightaway, forthwith (*formal*), without delay, at the double, right away, straightway (*archaic*). [➡HAPPENING QUICKLY; 104]

without help *adv* [➡ACTING INDEPENDENTLY; 285]

without hesitation *adv* [➡HAPPENING QUICKLY; 104]

without precedent *adj* **unprecedented**, unheard-of, unique, unparalleled, groundbreaking, original. [➡EXTRAORDINARY: UNCOMMON; 206] *Opposite:* unoriginal.

without question *adv* [➡CERTAIN; 175]

with passion *adv* [➡WITH ENTHUSIASM; 287]

with reason *adv* **rightly**, with good cause, justifiably, justly, properly, correctly. [➡CORRECT; 183] *Opposite:* unjustifiably.

with reference to *prep* **regarding**, with regard to, in regard to, as regards, relating to, pertaining to, in connection with, concerning, about, apropos (*formal*), vis-à-vis, re, respecting. [➡EXPRESSIONS OF REFERENCE; 63]

with regard to *prep* **regarding**, as regards, with reference to, relating to, pertaining to, in connection with, concerning, about, apropos (*formal*), vis-à-vis, in regard to, re, respecting. [➡EXPRESSIONS OF REFERENCE; 63]

with respect to *prep* **regarding**, respecting, with regard to, in regard to, relating to, as regards, pertaining to, about, concerning, apropos (*formal*), in connection with, re, vis-à-vis. [➡EXPRESSIONS OF REFERENCE; 63]

withstand *v* **endure**, survive, resist, bear, weather, tolerate. [➡CONTINUE TO EXIST; 17]

with your back to the wall *adj* **in trouble**, in difficulties, in a tight corner, in a tight spot, in dire straits, in hot water (*informal*), in a jam (*informal*), in a fix (*informal*), up the creek (*informal*), up the creek without a paddle (*informal*), between a rock and a hard place. [➡IN TROUBLE AND DISADVANTAGED; 73]

witless *adj* **foolish**, stupid, mindless, unintelligent, silly, clueless (*informal*). [➡NEGATIVE INTELLECTUAL CHARACTERISTICS; 526] *Opposite:* sensible.

witlessness *n* [➡NEGATIVE INTELLECTUAL CHARACTERISTICS; 526]

witness 1 *n* **observer**, spectator, bystander, onlooker, watcher, eyewitness. [➡LOOKERS AND SPECTATORS; 702] 2 *v* **see**, observe, view, perceive, behold (*archaic or literary*), watch. [➡SEE; 700] 3 *v* **countersign**, endorse, sign, attest, authenticate, corroborate, certify, notarize. [➡NAME AND DESCRIBE; 666]

wits *n* **reason**, shrewdness, acumen, faculties, mind, intelligence, brains, intellect, common sense, understanding. [➡DESCRIBING SOMEBODY'S INTELLECT; 524]

witter (*informal*) *v* **prattle**, gabble, go on, rattle on, chatter, babble, prate. [➡WITTER AND BABBLE; 618]

wittering (*informal*) *n* **chatter**, babble, prattle, blather (*informal*), gabble, waffle (*informal*). [➡MEANINGLESS SPEECH OR WRITING; 677]

witticism *n* **quip**, joke, riposte, gibe, one-liner, retort, gag, jest (*literary*), wisecrack (*informal*), bon mot. [➡JOKES AND TEASING; 675]

wittiness *n* **cleverness**, sharpness, keenness, comedy, sense of humour, drollness, humour, funniness. [➡POSITIVE INTELLECTUAL CHARACTERISTICS; 525] *Opposite:* dullness.

wittingly *adv* **knowingly**, consciously, purposely, on purpose, intentionally, deliberately. [➡INTENTIONAL AND DELIBERATE; 280] *Opposite:* unwittingly.

witty *adj* **amusing**, droll, humorous, funny, entertaining, clever, sharp, inventive. [➡FUNNY AND AMUSING; 217] *Opposite:* dull.

See Compare and Contrast at **funny.**

wiz (*informal*) *n* [➡TALENTED OR INTELLIGENT PERSON; 529]

wizard 1 *n* **sorcerer**, warlock, magician, shaman, witch doctor, conjurer. [➡PEOPLE WITH SUPERNATURAL POWERS; 789] 2 *n* (*informal*) **expert**, prodigy, genius, virtuoso, boffin (*informal*), ace (*informal*), whiz (*informal*), whiz kid (*informal*), wiz (*informal*), dab hand (*informal*). [➡TALENTED OR INTELLIGENT PERSON; 529]

wizardry 1 *n* **sorcery**, magic, divination, shamanism, spells, witchcraft. [➡THE SUPERNATURAL; 788] 2 *n* **skill**, expertise, genius, brilliance, know-how (*informal*), accomplishment. [➡SKILLS, TALENTS, AND ABILITIES; 527]

wizened *adj* **wrinkled**, lined, wrinkly, withered, crinkly, shrivelled. [➡FACIAL CHARACTERISTICS; 482] *Opposite:* smooth.

wobble 1 *v* **shake**, vibrate, tremble, bob, quiver, sway. [➡PHYSICAL REACTIONS; 317] 2 *v* **quaver**, wave, shake, vary, oscillate, fluctuate. [➡MOVE SOMETHING ON THE SPOT; 337] 3 *v* **dither**, waver, vacillate, shilly-shally, hesitate, dilly-dally, falter. [➡HESITATE; 273]

wobbliness 1 *n* **shakiness**, unsteadiness, instability, ricketiness, wonkiness (*informal*), rockiness. [➡WEAKNESS; 242] *Opposite:* steadiness. 2 *n* (*informal*) **weakness**, unsteadiness, shakiness, trembling, reeling, vertigo. [➡DESCRIBING BODY MOVEMENTS; 289] *Opposite:* steadiness.

wobbly 1 *adj* **shaky**, unsteady, unstable, rickety, wonky (*informal*), rocky. [➡WEAKNESS; 242] *Opposite:* steady. 2 *adj* (*informal*) **weak**, shaky, trembling, woozy, dizzy, unsteady, faint, unwell. [➡UNFIT AND WEAK; 740] *Opposite:* fit.

wodge (*informal*) *n* **lump**, chunk, pile, heap, handful, fistful, wad. [➡LARGE PIECE; 128] *Opposite:* fragment.

woe 1 *n* **affliction**, misfortune, calamity, disaster, trouble, trial. [➡DISASTERS; 253] *Opposite:* joy. 2 *n* **grief**, distress, anguish, affliction, sadness, despair, misery, wretchedness. [➡SADNESS, DISTRESS, AND DESPAIR; 540] *Opposite:* happiness.

woebegone *adj* **miserable**, anguished, despairing, sad, wretched, distressed, sorrowful. [➡SADNESS, DISTRESS, AND DESPAIR; 540] *Opposite:* cheerful.

woeful 1 *adj* **unhappy**, doleful, sad, sorrowful, mournful, miserable. [➡SADNESS, DISTRESS, AND DESPAIR; 540] *Opposite:* cheerful. 2 *adj* **distressing**, traumatic, harrowing, tragic, unpleasant, depressing, upsetting. [➡EMOTIONALLY UNPLEASANT AND UPSETTING; 228] 3 *adj* **pathetic**, pitiful, regrettable, bad, inadequate, deplorable. [➡BAD AND BADLY; 224] *Opposite:* wonderful.

wok *n* **pan**, frying pan, skillet. [➡TABLEWARE, CUTLERY, AND KITCHENWARE; 861]

wolf 1 *v* **gobble**, bolt, gulp down, devour, scoff (*informal*), guzzle (*informal*), gorge, put away (*informal*). [➡EAT AND NOT EAT; 711] *Opposite:* nibble. 2 *n* (*informal*) **Casanova**, Don Juan, Romeo, Lothario (*literary*), womanizer (*disapproving*), philanderer (*dated disapproving*). [➡PLEASURE-SEEKERS AND HEDONISTS; 886] 3 *type of* **canine.** [➡CANINE; 979]

wolfhound *type of* **large dog.** [➡DOG; 980]

wolf spider *type of* **arachnid.** [➡ARACHNIDS; 1018]

wolverine *type of* **small mammal.** [➡SMALL MAMMAL; 990]

woman *n* **female**, lady, matron. [➡FEMALE PERSON; 933] *Opposite:* man.

womanhood 1 *n* **adulthood**, maturity, independence. [➡ADULTHOOD; 918] *Opposite:* manhood. 2 *n* **women**, womankind, females, womenfolk. [➡FEMALE PERSON; 933] *Opposite:* mankind.

womanizer (*disapproving*) *n* [➡PLEASURE-SEEKERS AND HEDONISTS; 886]

womankind *n* **women**, womanhood, females, womenfolk. [➡FEMALE PERSON; 933] *Opposite:* mankind.

womanlike *adj* [➡GENDER IDENTITY AND SEXUALITY; 932]

womanliness *n* [➡GENDER IDENTITY AND SEXUALITY; 932]

womanly *adj* **female**, feminine. [➡GENDER IDENTITY AND SEXUALITY; 932] *Opposite:* manly.

wombat *type of* **marsupial.** [➡MARSUPIAL; 992]

wonder 1 *n* **surprise**, astonishment, awe, amazement, admiration, incredulity. [➡SURPRISE, SHOCK, AND AMAZEMENT; 546] 2 *n* **miracle**, phenomenon, marvel, sensation, curiosity, spectacle. [➡AMAZING THING; 212] 3 *v* **speculate**, doubt, question, conjecture, ponder, deliberate. [➡QUESTION THINGS; 752] 4 *v* **marvel**, admire, gaze at, be amazed. [➡PRAISE AND ENCOURAGE; 648]

wonderful 1 *adj* **magnificent**, superb, amazing, astonishing, fantastic, breathtaking, marvellous. [➡EXTRAORDINARY: AMAZING; 205] *Opposite:* awful. 2 *adj* **delightful**, pleasing, great, brilliant, perfect, ideal. [➡EXTRAORDINARY: AMAZING; 205]

wonderland *n* **utopia**, paradise, heaven, never-never land, nirvana, seventh heaven, fairyland. [➡NON-EXISTENT PLACE; 1065]

wonderment *n* **amazement**, astonishment, stupefaction (*literary*), awe, surprise, bewilderment, admiration. [➡SURPRISE, SHOCK, AND AMAZEMENT; 546]

wondrous (*literary*) *adj* **wonderful**, astounding, incredible, astonishing, extraordinary, miraculous, phenomenal, amazing, marvellous. [➡EXTRAORDINARY: AMAZING; 205] *Opposite:* mediocre.

wonky (*informal*) 1 *adj* **unreliable**, unsteady, insecure, wobbly, dodgy (*informal*), shaky. [➡WEAKNESS; 242] *Opposite:* steady. 2 *adj* **askew**, skewwhiff (*informal*), wrong, uneven, bent, off-centre. [➡ORIENTATION AND ALIGNMENT; 1222] *Opposite:* level.

wont (*formal*) 1 *adj* **accustomed**, used, in the habit of, inclined, liable, habituated (*formal*). [➡THE WILL AND WILLINGNESS; 564] *Opposite:* unaccustomed. 2 *n* **habit**, custom, tendency, preference, practice, predilection (*formal*). [➡WAYS OF DOING THINGS; 295]

See Compare and Contrast at **habit.**

wonted (*formal*) *adj* **usual**, typical, customary, preferred, chosen, of choice, habitual. [➡ORDINARINESS; 245] *Opposite:* unaccustomed.

See Compare and Contrast at **usual**.

woo (*literary*) *v* **court**, persuade, encourage, entice, pursue, flatter. [➡ESTABLISHING RELATIONSHIPS WITH OTHERS; 974] *Opposite:* discourage.

wood 1 *n* **timber**, firewood, logs, planks, kindling, lumber (*US*). [➡BUILDING MATERIALS; 1076] 2 *n* **forest**, woodland, copse, covert, coppice, thicket. [➡WOODS, FORESTS, AND JUNGLES; 1047]

woodbine *type of* **climber**. [➡CLIMBERS; 1033]

woodcarving 1 *n* **carving**, sculpture, woodwork, art, craft. [➡CRAFTS AND CARVING; 356] 2 *n* **sculpture**, figure, embellishment, adornment, feature, design, pattern. [➡SCULPTURE; 902]

woodchuck *type of* **rodent**. [➡RODENT; 989]

woodcock *type of* **fowl**. [➡FOOD BIRD; 999]

woodcut 1 *n* **block**, carving, design, matrix. [➡ARTWORKS; 898] 2 *n* **print**, engraving, picture, illustration, portrait, diagram, map. [➡ARTWORKS; 898]

wooded *adj* **forested**, woody, timbered, arboreal, sylvan (*literary*). [➡VEGETATION; 1025]

wooden 1 *adj* **wood**, timber, woody, ligneous. [➡RIGID AND HARD; 1210] 2 *adj* **stilted**, inexpressive, stiff, emotionless, deadpan, impassive. [➡FACIAL EXPRESSION; 652] *Opposite:* expressive. 3 *adj* **dull**, toneless, flat. [➡UNINTERESTED AND DETACHED; 630] *Opposite:* resonant.

woodenly 1 *adv* **awkwardly**, clumsily, gracelessly, stiffly, uncomfortably, inelegantly. [➡INARTICULATE, RAMBLING, AND AWKWARD; 634] *Opposite:* gracefully. 2 *adv* **inexpressively**, stiltedly, ineptly, unconvincingly, mechanically. [➡FACIAL EXPRESSION; 652] *Opposite:* expressively. 3 *adv* **dully**, tonelessly, flatly. [➡UNINTERESTED AND DETACHED; 630] *Opposite:* resonantly.

woodenness 1 *n* **awkwardness**, clumsiness, gracelessness, stiffness, discomfort, inelegance. [➡INARTICULATE, RAMBLING, AND AWKWARD; 634] *Opposite:* gracefulness. 2 *n* **inexpressiveness**, stiltedness, ineptness, unconvincingness, mechanicalness, artificiality. [➡FACIAL EXPRESSION; 652] *Opposite:* expressivity. 3 *n* **dullness**, tonelessness, flatness. [➡UNINTERESTED AND DETACHED; 630] *Opposite:* resonance.

woodland *n* **forest**, wood, woods. [➡WOODS, FORESTS, AND JUNGLES; 1047]

woodlark *type of* **songbird**. [➡SONGBIRD; 1003]

woodlouse *type of* **land invertebrate**. [➡LAND INVERTEBRATE; 1021]

wood nymph *n* [➡MYTHICAL BEINGS; 790]

woodpecker *type of* **common bird**. [➡BIRD; 997]

woods *n* **wood**, forest, woodland, copse, covert, coppice, thicket. [➡WOODS, FORESTS, AND JUNGLES; 1047]

woodshed *n* **shed**, outbuilding, outhouse, garden shed, potting shed, lean-to, hut. [➡STORES AND STORAGE BUILDINGS; 1087]

woodwork 1 *n* **carpentry**, joinery, cabinetmaking, turning. [➡CRAFTS AND CARVING; 356] 2 *n* **fittings**, fixtures, doors, window frames, skirting boards, skirting, wainscot, panelling. [➡FITTINGS; 859] 3 *n* (*informal*) **goalpost**, crossbar, upright, goal, post, bar. [➡SPORTS TERMS; 877]

woodwork

◆ *types of woodwork*
cabinetmaking, carpentry, carving, joinery, marquetry, woodcarving

woodworm *type of* **insect stages of development**. [➡INSECT STAGES; 1020]

woody *adj* **forested**, wooded, timbered, woodland, arboreal, sylvan (*literary*). [➡VEGETATION; 1025]

woof 1 *v* [➡SOUND EMISSION BY ANIMALS OR BIRDS; 365] 2 *n* **bark**, yap, yelp. [➡SOUNDS MADE BY ANIMALS; 1260]

wool *type of* **fabric from animals**. [➡FABRICS; 1131]

woolgather *v* [➡DREAM, IMAGINE, AND FANTASIZE; 750]

woolgatherer *n* [➡LAZY OR UNSUCCESSFUL PEOPLE; 948]

woolgathering *n* [➡DREAM, IMAGINE, AND FANTASIZE; 750]

woollen *adj* **knitted**, woven, wool, woolly, crocheted, spun. [➡PHYSICAL TEXTURE; 1221]

woollens *n* **clothing**, sweaters, jumpers, cardigans. [➡GARMENTS AND OUTFITS; 865]

woolliness *n* **vagueness**, haziness, obscurity, confusion. [➡VAGUENESS; 244]

woolly 1 *adj* **woollen**, knitted, woven, wool, crocheted. [➡PHYSICAL TEXTURE; 1221] 2 *adj* **vague**, confused, unfocused, unclear, ill-defined, woolly-headed, woolly-minded. [➡VAGUENESS; 244] *Opposite:* clear.

woolly-headed *adj* [➡NEGATIVE INTELLECTUAL CHARACTERISTICS; 526]

woolly-minded *adj* [➡NEGATIVE INTELLECTUAL CHARACTERISTICS; 526]

wooziness *n* [➡ILL AND SICK; 741]

woozy *adj* **dizzy**, faint, lightheaded, unsteady, nauseous. [➡ILL AND SICK; 741] *Opposite:* clear-headed.

Worcester sauce *type of* **seasonings, sauces, and dips**. [➡SEASONINGS AND SAUCES; 1173]

word 1 *n* **term**, expression, name. [➡ASPECTS OF LANGUAGE; 683] 2 *n* **chat**, conversation, talk, discussion, announcement, comment, declaration, statement. [➡INFORMAL COMMUNICATION; 45] 3 *n* **information**, news, tidings (*literary*), gen (*informal*), info (*informal*), communication, skinny (*US slang*). [➡BASIC DETAILS; 689] 4 *n* **rumour**, buzz (*informal*), report, whisper, gossip, tittle-tattle, hearsay. [➡GOSSIP; 679] 5 *n* **promise**, assurance, guarantee, oath, pledge, declaration, undertaking, assertion. [➡PROMISE AND ASSURE; 685] 6 *n* **command**, order, authorization, say-so (*informal*), go-ahead (*informal*), okay (*informal*). [➡REQUEST AND DEMAND; 664] 7 *n* **password**, code word, magic word, key word. [➡COMMUNICATION; 603] 8 *v* **express**, phrase, couch, utter, articulate, verbalize, formulate. [➡UTTER AND PRONOUNCE; 609]

word for word *adv* **verbatim**, in the same words, faithfully, exactly, precisely, accurately, to the letter. [➡EXACT; 204] *Opposite:* loosely.

word-for-word *adj* **verbatim**, faithful, exact, precise, accurate, strict. [➡EXACT; 204] *Opposite:* loose.

wordiness *n* **long-windedness**, verbosity, loquaciousness (*formal*), prolixity. [➡MEANINGLESS SPEECH OR WRITING; 677] *Opposite:* conciseness.

wording *n* **phrasing**, words, language, phraseology, diction, expression. [➡ASPECTS OF LANGUAGE; 683]

wordless *adj* **silent**, mute, nonverbal, mimed, gestured, telepathic. [➡ABSENCE OF SOUND; 1256]

word list *n* **vocabulary**, glossary, dictionary, thesaurus, lexicon. [➡LISTS AND SCHEDULES; 588]

word of honour *n* [➡PROMISE AND ASSURE; 685]

word-perfect 1 *adj* **verbatim**, word for word, perfect, impeccable, consummate, prepared, letter-perfect (*US*). [➡EXACT; 204] *Opposite:* unprepared. 2 *adj* **correct**, accurate, exact, precise, literal. [➡EXACT; 204]

wordplay *n* **punning**, puns, repartee, wit, banter, badinage. [➡JOKES AND TEASING; 675]

wordplay

◆ *types of wordplay*
acrostic, anagram, logogram, malapropism, palindrome, pun, spoonerism, telestich

word processor *type of* **software**. [➡COMPUTERS AND COMPUTING; 1126]

words 1 *n* **argument**, disagreement, difference of opinion, dispute, confrontation, falling out. [➡ARGUMENT; 47] 2 *n* **lyrics**, verses, chorus, libretto, text. [➡MUSIC, SONGS, AND SINGING; 907]

wordy *adj* **verbose**, long-winded, rambling, loquacious (*formal*), prolix, diffuse. [➡INARTICULATE, RAMBLING, AND AWKWARD; 634] *Opposite:* concise.

Compare and Contrast: *wordy, verbose, long-winded, rambling, prolix, diffuse*

CORE MEANING: TOO LONG OR NOT CONCISELY EXPRESSED

wordy using an excessive number of words in writing or speech; ***verbose*** expressed in language that is not precise; ***long-winded*** tediously wordy in speech or writing; ***rambling*** excessively long with many changes of subject, making it difficult to follow; ***prolix*** tiresomely wordy; ***diffuse*** lacking organization and conciseness.

work 1 *n* **labour**, employment, job, vocation, occupation. [➡JOB; 833] 2 *n* **effort**, exertion, labour, toil, slog, drudgery, graft (*informal*), grind (*informal*). [➡HARD WORK OR EFFORT; 299] 3 *n* **composition**, design, creation, opus, masterpiece, piece, product, production, handiwork, oeuvre (*formal*). [➡ARTWORKS; 898] 4 *v* **toil**, labour, slog, drudge. [➡WORK-RELATED ACTIVITIES; 834] 5 *v* **perform**, effect (*formal*), bring about, produce. [➡CARRY OUT AN ACTION; 270] 6 *v* **succeed**, be successful, work out, come off (*informal*), thrive. [➡SUCCEED AND WIN; 79] 7 *v* **operate**, control, drive, run, function. [➡FUNCTION SUCCESSFULLY; 470]

Compare and Contrast: *work, labour, toil, drudgery*

CORE MEANING: SUSTAINED EFFORT REQUIRED TO DO OR PRODUCE SOMETHING

work the physical and mental effort employed to do or achieve something; ***labour*** strenuous work, usually physical; ***toil*** tiring, often tedious, physical work; ***drudgery*** work that is strenuous and not at all rewarding, sustained over a long period.

workable *adj* **practical**, practicable, feasible, doable. [➡POSSIBLE AND PROBABLE; 178] *Opposite:* impracticable.

workaday *adj* **everyday**, ordinary, plain, homespun, commonplace, mundane, routine. [➡ORDINARINESS; 245] *Opposite:* extraordinary.

work against *v* **counteract**, negate (*formal*), cancel out, oppose, run counter to, interfere with. [➡AVOID, PREVENT, LIMIT, AND CONTROL; 278] *Opposite:* support.

workaholic *n* **overachiever**, type A, workhorse (*informal*). [➡WORKER; 836]

workbench *n* **bench**, worktop, work surface, worktable. [➡FITTINGS; 859]

workbook *n* **exercise book**, schoolbook, notebook, jotter, notepad, book, legal pad (*US*), scratchpad (*US*). [➡WRITING AND DRAWING IMPLEMENTS, AND MEDIA; 602]

work day and night *v* [➡HARD WORK OR EFFORT; 299]

worked up (*informal*) *adj* **agitated**, upset, excited, worried, hot and bothered, in a state (*informal*). [➡CONFUSION, ANXIETY, AND WORRY; 541] *Opposite:* calm.

worker *n* **employee**, member of staff, hand, operative, wage earner. [➡WORKER; 836]

work flat out *v* [➡HARD WORK OR EFFORT; 299]

workforce *n* **personnel**, staff, employees, workers, human resources, labour force. [➡THE WORK FORCE; 837]

work hard *v* [➡HARD WORK OR EFFORT; 299]

workhorse 1 *n* (*informal*) **hard worker**, good worker, rock, mainstay, pillar, doer, toiler, slogger. [➡PEOPLE WHO ARE APPROVED OF; 955] 2 *type of* **horse**. [➡HORSE; 985]

working 1 *adj* **operational**, functioning, effective, running. [➡HAPPENING AND IN PROGRESS; 32] 2 *adj* **employed**, occupied, at work, in work, salaried, waged. [➡EMPLOYMENT STATUS; 831]

working class *n* **manual workers**, hoi polloi, the masses, proletariat, wage-earners. [➡CLASS STATUS; 889]

working-class *adj* [➡CLASS STATUS; 889]

working example *n* [➡REPRESENTATIONS AND GENERAL EXAMPLES; 65]

working from home *adj* [➡EMPLOYMENT STATUS; 831]

working group *n* **task force**, team, ad hoc group, working party, committee, unit. [➡WORKER; 836]

working out *n* **exercising**, physical exercise, exercise, training, physical training, gymnastics, aerobics, keep fit. [➡HOBBIES, GAMES, AND SPORTS; 875]

working party *n* **task force**, team, ad hoc group, working group, committee, unit. [➡WORKER; 836]

workings *n* **mechanism**, machinery, works, moving parts. [➡CENTRAL PARTS OF PHYSICAL OBJECTS; 1250]

work like a dog *v* [➡HARD WORK OR EFFORT; 299]

workload *n* **amount of work**, assignment, job, load, capacity, capability. [➡WORK IN GENERAL; 298]

workmate *n* **colleague**, coworker, fellow worker. [➡COLLEAGUES AND EQUALS; 967]

work of art 1 *n* **objet d'art**, oeuvre (*formal*), creation, painting, sculpture, picture, piece, masterpiece, opus, magnum opus. [➡ARTWORKS; 898] 2 *n* **masterpiece**, beauty, tour de force, pièce de résistance, work of genius. [➡AMAZING THING; 212] *Opposite:* disaster (*informal*).

work on 1 *v* **develop**, hone, build up, work up, perfect, improve, practise. [➡IMPROVE SOMETHING; 375] 2 *v* **influence**, sway, persuade, pressurize, pressure. [➡CAUSE OR COMPEL TO ACT; 272]

work out 1 *v* **exercise**, train, drill. [➡HOBBIES, GAMES, AND SPORTS; 875] 2 *v* **solve**, figure out, crack, decipher, resolve, puzzle out, deduce, infer, conclude. [➡SOLVE AND INTERPRET; 761] 3 *v* **understand**, comprehend, make sense of, fathom, conceive. [➡UNDERSTAND AND GRASP; 760] 4 *v* **plan**, devise, outline, sketch, arrange, set up, develop. [➡DEVELOP THEORIES AND REASON; 745]

See Compare and Contrast at **deduce**.

workout 1 *n* **exercise session**, exercises, training, aerobics, callisthenics, weightlifting, keep fit. [➡HOBBIES, GAMES, AND SPORTS; 875] 2 *n* **test**, road test, trial, run. [➡PREPARATORY EVENT; 57]

work overtime *v* [➡HARD WORK OR EFFORT; 299]

workplace *n* **place of work**, workshop, workstation, work, office, factory, shop floor, factory floor, workroom. [➡PLACE OF EMPLOYMENT; 832]

workroom *n* **room**, workshop, study, office, studio, workplace. [➡PLACE OF EMPLOYMENT; 832]

works 1 *n* (*informal*) **everything**, the whole thing, the lot, all of it, the whole kit and caboodle (*informal*). [➡PHYSICAL OBJECTS; 1242] 2 *n* **mechanism**, workings, machinery, moving parts. [➡CENTRAL PARTS OF PHYSICAL OBJECTS; 1250] 3 *type of* **factory**. [➡INDUSTRIAL BUILDINGS; 1086]

worksheet 1 *n* **homework sheet**, questionnaire, test, quiz, question sheet. [➡LISTS AND SCHEDULES; 588] 2 *n* **schedule**, job sheet, log, record. [➡RECORDS; 586]

workshop *type of* **factory**. [➡INDUSTRIAL BUILDINGS; 1086]

workshy *adj* **lazy**, idle, indolent, slothful (*formal*), apathetic, shirking. [➡LIFELESS, LAZY, AND UNENTHUSIASTIC; 507]

workspace *n* **working area**, workstation, workplace, booth, cubicle, desk, office. [➡PLACE OF EMPLOYMENT; 832]

workstation 1 *n* **workplace**, workspace, computer terminal. [➡PLACE OF EMPLOYMENT; 832] 2 *type of* **computer**. [➡COMPUTERS AND COMPUTING; 1126]

work surface *n* **surface**, worktop, workbench, workspace, work unit, countertop, table top, counter. [➡FITTINGS; 859]

worktable *type of* **table**. [➡FURNITURE; 858]

worktop *n* **counter**, bench, work surface. [➡FITTINGS; 859]

work to rule *v* **go slow**, take industrial action, slow down. [➡WORK-RELATED ACTIVITIES; 834]

work-to-rule *n* **go-slow**, industrial action, slowdown (*US*). [➡WORK-RELATED ACTIVITIES; 834]

work up 1 *v* **develop**, work on, hone, improve, refine, cultivate. [➡IMPROVE SOMETHING; 375] 2 *v* **agitate**, upset, disturb, provoke, irritate, nettle (*informal*), stress out (*informal*). [➡ANGER AND ANNOY; 570] *Opposite:* calm.

workup *n* **diagnosis**, examination, checkup, medical. [➡EXAMINE AND ASSESS; 754]

work up a sweat *v* [➡HARD WORK OR EFFORT; 299]

world 1 *n* **Earth**, planet, globe. [➡THE EARTH; 1039] 2 *n* **biosphere**, ecosphere, creation, all God's creatures, flora and fauna, natural world. [➡NATURE AND THE ENVIRONMENT; 1038] 3 *n* **humankind**, humanity, the human race. [➡GROUPS IN SOCIETY; 940] 4 *n* **domain**, realm, sphere, circle, area. [➡SUBJECT AREA; 769]

world-beater *n* **champion**, superstar, number one (*informal*), one in a million, one-off, star, classic. [➡AMAZING THING; 212]

world-class *adj* **first-rate**, first-class, superlative, top-notch (*informal*), outstanding. [➡SUPERIORITY; 153]

world-famous *adj* **famous**, renowned, popular, acclaimed, notorious, well-loved, celebrated. [➡KNOWN AND FAMOUS; 182] *Opposite:* unknown.

worldliness 1 *n* **materialism**, consumerism, acquisitiveness, greed, secularism. [➡MORALLY BAD; 776] 2 *n* **experience**, knowledge, sophistication, worldly wisdom. [➡KNOWLEDGE AND WISDOM; 559]

worldly *adj* **sophisticated**, experienced, mature, knowing, worldly wise. [➡KNOWLEDGE AND WISDOM; 559] *Opposite:* naive.

worldly goods *n* **possessions**, belongings, assets, property. [➡POSSESSIONS; 462]

worldly-wise *adj* **sophisticated**, experienced, mature, knowing, worldly. [➡KNOWLEDGE AND WISDOM; 559] *Opposite:* naive.

world-shattering *adj* [➡EXTRAORDINARY: UNCOMMON; 206]

world-weariness *n* **discontent**, melancholy, boredom, ennui. [➡SADNESS, DISTRESS, AND DESPAIR; 540]

world-weary *adj* **jaded**, discontented, bored, melancholic. [➡NEUTRALITY AND INDIFFERENCE; 554]

worldwide *adj* **universal**, international, all-inclusive, wide-reaching, global. [➡GENERAL LOCATIONS; 159] *Opposite:* local.

World Wide Web *n* [➡THE INTERNET; 1127]

worm *type of* **land invertebrate.** [➡LAND INVERTEBRATE; 1021]

worm-eaten 1 *adj* **wormy**, worm-infested, holey, rotten, decaying, putrid, flyblown, maggoty, putrescent. [➡DECAYING OR INFESTED; 1235] 2 *adj* **dilapidated**, ramshackle, tumbledown, rickety. [➡IN BAD REPAIR; 1233]

worm-infested *adj* [➡DECAYING OR INFESTED; 1235]

worm out *v* **elicit**, find out, coax out, ferret out, sniff out (*informal*), inveigle. [➡SEEK POSSESSION AND SEARCH; 457]

wormy *adj* [➡DECAYING OR INFESTED; 1235]

worn *adj* **damaged**, shabby, tatty, dog-eared, dilapidated, tattered, worn out, threadbare. [➡IN BAD REPAIR; 1233]

worn down *adj* **overcome**, weakened, browbeaten, downtrodden, oppressed. [➡NEUTRALITY AND INDIFFERENCE; 554]

worn out 1 *adj* **exhausted**, tired, done in (*informal*), done for (*informal*), dead beat (*informal*), beat (*informal*), wiped out (*informal*), whacked (*informal*), dog-tired (*informal*). [➡TIRED, ASLEEP, AND UNCONSCIOUS; 739] 2 *adj* **tatty**, tattered, shabby, dilapidated, battered, the worse for wear, beat up (*informal*), threadbare. [➡IN BAD REPAIR; 1233]

worn to shreds *adj* [➡IN BAD REPAIR; 1233]

worried *adj* **concerned**, anxious, apprehensive, nervous, bothered, troubled, vexed, upset, agitated. [➡CONFUSION, ANXIETY, AND WORRY; 541] *Opposite:* unconcerned.

worried sick *adj* [➡CONFUSION, ANXIETY, AND WORRY; 541]

worrier *n* **pessimist**, neurotic (*informal*), worryguts (*informal*), fidget, fusspot (*informal*), worrywart (*US informal*), fussbudget (*US informal*). [➡GRUMPY AND NEGATIVE PEOPLE; 953]

worrisome *adj* **troublesome**, worrying, annoying, irritating, bothersome. [➡IRRITATING; 229]

worry 1 *v* **be anxious**, fret, be troubled, be concerned, be bothered, agonize, lose sleep, stew, fuss. [➡BE CONCERNED AND CARE; 582] 2 *v* **annoy**, pester, bother, trouble, disturb, irk, bug (*informal*). [➡ANGER AND ANNOY; 570] 3 *v* **touch**, pick, interfere with, claw at, tear at, fiddle with. [➡CONTACT: TOUCH; 413] 4 *n* **anxiety**, unease, uneasiness, disquiet, discomfort, apprehension, nervousness, stress, angst, care. [➡FEELINGS ABOUT THE FUTURE; 534]

Compare and Contrast: ***worry, unease, care, anxiety, angst, stress***

CORE MEANING: LACK OF PEACE OF MIND

worry a troubled state of mind resulting from concern about current or potential difficulties; ***unease*** a feeling of anxiousness or lack of satisfaction with a situation; ***care*** a state of troubled anxiety; ***anxiety*** nervous apprehension about a future event or a general fear of possible misfortune; ***angst*** nonspecific chronic anxiety about the human condition or the state of the world; ***stress*** the worry and nervous apprehension related to a particular situation or event, for example a job or the process of moving house.

worryguts (*informal*) *n* [➡GRUMPY AND NEGATIVE PEOPLE; 953]

worrying *adj* **perturbing**, disturbing, upsetting, disquieting, nerve-racking, distressing, tormenting. [➡IRRITATING; 229] *Opposite:* reassuring.

worrywart (*US informal*) *n* [➡GRUMPY AND NEGATIVE PEOPLE; 953]

worse *adj* **not as good as**, inferior, of inferior quality, poorer, of poorer quality, shoddier. [➡BAD AND BADLY; 224] *Opposite:* better.

worsen 1 *v* **get worse**, deteriorate, degenerate, go downhill, degrade. [➡GET WORSE; 382] *Opposite:* improve. 2 *v* **make something worse**, exacerbate, aggravate, impair, inflame. [➡WORSEN SOMETHING; 381] *Opposite:* improve.

worsening *n* **deterioration**, aggravation, degeneration, decline. [➡WORSEN SOMETHING; 381] *Opposite:* improvement.

worship 1 *v* **adore**, love, revere, adulate, deify, pray to, venerate. [➡RELIGIONS AND RELIGIOUS PRACTICES; 778] 2 *n* **adoration**, love, reverence, respect, devotion, adulation, veneration. [➡LOVE, RESPECT, AND GOODWILL; 550]

worshipful *adj* **reverential**, respectful, reverent, deferential, adoring. [➡APPRECIATION AND GRATITUDE; 536]

worshipper *n* **celebrant**, adorer, venerator, participant, believer. [➡RELIGIOUS PEOPLE; 779]

worst *adj* **nastiest**, vilest, poorest, wickedest, foulest. [➡BAD AND BADLY; 224] *Opposite:* best.

worsted *type of* **fabric from animals.** [➡FABRICS; 1131]

worth 1 *n* **value**, price, cost, rate. [➡MONEY, PAYMENTS, AND CHARGES; 800] 2 *n* **merit**, appeal, significance, attraction, importance, value, meaning. [➡IMPORTANCE AND SIGNIFICANCE; 193] 3 *n* **wealth**, means, assets, value, substance. [➡POSSESSIONS; 462]

worthiness 1 *n* **merit**, value, worth, praiseworthiness. [➡SOURCE OF HAPPINESS, PLEASURE, OR IMPROVEMENT; 210] 2 *n* **dullness**, earnestness, boringness, routineness. [➡BORING AND UNINTERESTING; 235]

worthless 1 *adj* **valueless**, of no value, of little worth, insignificant, useless, without value, no use, rubbish. [➡REDUNDANT AND USELESS; 241] *Opposite:* valuable. 2 *adj* **empty**, hollow, meaningless, futile, pointless. [➡REDUNDANT AND USELESS; 241]

worthlessness *n* **insignificance**, unimportance, irrelevance, triviality. [➡REDUNDANT AND USELESS; 241] *Opposite:* value.

worth mentioning *adj* [➡INTERESTING AND MEANINGFUL; 191]

worthwhile *adj* **valuable**, useful, meaningful, sensible, advisable, worthy. [➡USEFULNESS; 200] *Opposite:* worthless.

worthy 1 *adj* **commendable**, praiseworthy, laudable, admirable, valuable, worthwhile, creditable. [➡ADMIRABLE AND COMMENDABLE; 186] 2 *adj* **well-intentioned**, well-meaning, earnest, pedestrian, dull, routine. [➡BORING AND UNINTERESTING; 235]

worthy of note *adj* [➡INTERESTING AND MEANINGFUL; 191]

would-be *adj* **hopeful**, aspiring, prospective, wannabe (*informal disapproving*), budding, potential, embryonic, possible. [➡POSSIBLE AND PROBABLE; 178]

wound 1 *n* **injury**, lesion, cut, gash, sore, abrasion, laceration. [➡PAIN AND OTHER PHYSICAL SENSATIONS; 734] **2** *v* **injure**, hurt, harm, damage, mutilate, maim, lacerate. [➡WOUND A PERSON OR ANIMAL; 384] **3** *v* **offend**, upset, hurt, injure, distress. [➡UPSET, DISTRESS, AND HUMILIATE; 568]

See Compare and Contrast at **harm**.

wounded **1** *adj* **injured**, hurt, suffering. [➡INJURED; 743] **2** *adj* **offended**, hurt, upset, distressed, aggrieved, stung, anguished, pained. [➡SADNESS, DISTRESS, AND DESPAIR; 540]

wounding *adj* **hurtful**, cutting, acerbic, sharp. [➡RUDE AND HOSTILE; 626] *Opposite:* kind.

wound up (*informal*) *adj* **stressed**, stressed out (*informal*), upset, tense, infuriated, exasperated, annoyed, irritated. [➡IRRITATION AND ANGER; 542] *Opposite:* relaxed.

wow (*informal*) *n* **winner**, smash, triumph, sensation, knockout (*informal*). [➡AMAZING THING; 212] *Opposite:* flop (*informal*).

wraith *n* **ghost**, phantom, apparition, spirit, spectre, shade (*literary*). [➡THE SUPERNATURAL; 788]

wraithlike *adj* [➡BUILD; 478]

wrangle **1** *v* **argue**, dispute, quarrel, bicker, squabble, fight, battle, disagree. [➡ARGUE AND FIGHT – TWO-WAY; 644] **2** *n* **dispute**, argument, quarrel, squabble, disagreement, altercation, tussle, spat, row. [➡ARGUMENT; 47]

wrangler (*US*) *n* **farm hand**, cowboy, cowpoke (*informal*), cowgirl, ranch hand (*US*). [➡FARMERS, GARDENERS, AND MANUAL WORKERS; 849]

wrap **1** *v* **enfold**, drape, swathe, cover, envelop, bind, enclose. [➡DECORATE, ADORN, AND APPLY COATINGS; 406] **2** *v* **wrap up**, gift wrap, package. [➡DECORATE, ADORN, AND APPLY COATINGS; 406] *Opposite:* unwrap. **3** *n* **shawl**, cloak, stole, cape. [➡HABERDASHERY, MILLINERY, AND LINGERIE; 867] **4** *n* **wrapping**, packaging, casing, covering. [➡COVERS AND COATINGS; 1245]

wrap in cotton wool *v* [➡TAKE CARE OF AND SPOIL; 301]

wrapped up in *adj* **engrossed**, absorbed, preoccupied, obsessed, fascinated, gripped, hooked (*slang*). [➡PENSIVENESS AND INTEREST; 539]

wrapper *n* **covering**, wrapping, wrap, cover, packaging, package. [➡COVERS AND COATINGS; 1245]

wrapping *n* **packaging**, covering, casing, wrap, cover. [➡COVERS AND COATINGS; 1245]

wrap up **1** *v* **wrap**, gift wrap, parcel, package. [➡DECORATE, ADORN, AND APPLY COATINGS; 406] *Opposite:* unwrap. **2** *v* (*informal*) **conclude**, complete, finish, finish off, end, bring to a close. [➡COMPLETE AN ACTION; 264] **3** *v* **dress warmly**, bundle up (*informal*), muffle up. [➡DRESS, WEAR, AND UNDRESS; 868]

wrath *n* **anger**, rage, fury, ire (*literary*), madness. [➡IRRITATION AND ANGER; 542]

See Compare and Contrast at **anger**.

wrathful *adj* **furious**, angry, irate, enraged, fuming, steaming (*informal*). [➡IRRITATION AND ANGER; 542]

wreak *v* **cause**, do, inflict, create, bring about. [➡CAUSE TO HAPPEN; 31]

wreath *n* **garland**, circlet, headdress, laurel. [➡ORNAMENTS AND DECORATIONS; 1247]

wreathe **1** *v* **adorn**, cover, garland, swathe, festoon. [➡DECORATE, ADORN, AND APPLY COATINGS; 406] **2** *v* **twist**, writhe, coil, wind. [➡POSITION SOMETHING: AROUND SOMETHING; 328]

wreck **1** *v* **destroy**, ruin, demolish, break, shatter, smash, spoil, reduce to rubble. [➡DESTRUCTION AND DEMOLITION; 360] **2** *n* **ruin**, remains, wreckage, shell, hulk, shipwreck. [➡RUBBISH AND USELESS OBJECTS; 1248] **3** *n* (*US*) **crash**, collision, accident, smash-up, fender bender (*US informal*). [➡TRAFFIC ACCIDENTS; 256]

wreckage *n* **ruins**, remains, debris, wreck, rubble, shards. [➡RUBBISH AND USELESS OBJECTS; 1248]

wrecked **1** *adj* (*informal*) **exhausted**, worn-out, bushed (*informal*), done in (*informal*). [➡TIRED, ASLEEP, AND UNCONSCIOUS; 739] **2** *adj* **broken**, smashed, damaged, ruined, cracked, destroyed. [➡IN BAD REPAIR; 1233]

wrecker (*US*) *type of* **commercial or industrial vehicle**. [➡VEHICLES; 1144]

wren *type of* **common bird**. [➡BIRD; 997]

wrench **1** *v* **strain**, injure, hurt, pull, sprain, twist, stretch, crick, damage. [➡WOUND A PERSON OR ANIMAL; 384] **2** *v* **pull**, tug, haul, heave, jerk, yank. [➡PUSH, PULL, SLIDE; 336] **3** *n* **injury**, sprain, strain, crick. [➡PAIN AND OTHER PHYSICAL SENSATIONS; 734] **4** *n* **pull**, tug, haul, heave, jerk, yank. [➡PUSH, PULL, SLIDE; 336] **5** (*US*) *type of* **general tool**. [➡HAND TOOLS; 1118]

wrest **1** *v* **gain**, take, seize, grasp. [➡GET; 421] **2** *v* **grab**, snatch, tug, pull. [➡CONTACT: HOLD; 412]

wrestle *v* **struggle**, fight, grapple, tussle, brawl. [➡COMPETE, CONTEND, AND COMBAT; 304]

wrestler *n* [➡PEOPLE IN SPORTS AND LEISURE; 876]

wrestling *type of* **combat sport**. [➡HOBBIES, GAMES, AND SPORTS; 875]

wretch **1** *n* **unfortunate**, victim, languisher, sufferer, poor thing. [➡BAD LUCK AND UNLUCKY; 785] **2** *n* (*formal*) **scoundrel**, rascal, rogue, villain, blackguard, rotter (*informal dated*), cad (*dated*). [➡VILLAINS AND THUGS; 947] **3** *n* (*humorous*) **rogue**, rascal, imp, horror (*informal*), scallywag (*dated informal*). [➡LAZY OR UNSUCCESSFUL PEOPLE; 948]

wretched **1** *adj* **miserable**, desolate, heartbroken, pitiful, dejected, abject. [➡SADNESS, DISTRESS, AND DESPAIR; 540] *Opposite:* happy. **2** *adj* **worthless**, base, despicable, inadequate, inferior, shameful, vile. [➡INAPPROPRIATE AND UNSUITABLE; 225] *Opposite:* noble.

wretchedly **1** *adv* **miserably**, desolately, pitifully, dejectedly, piteously. [➡SADNESS, DISTRESS, AND DESPAIR; 540] *Opposite:* happily. **2** *adv* **dreadfully**, terribly, shamefully, hopelessly, woefully, extremely. [➡CRITICALLY AND SERIOUSLY; 132]

wretchedness *n* **misery**, woe, unhappiness, dejection, desolation. [➡SADNESS, DISTRESS, AND DESPAIR; 540] *Opposite:* happiness.

wriggle *v* **wiggle**, writhe, turn, squirm, twist, fidget. [➡FIDGET AND FROLIC; 312]

wriggle out of *v* [➡NOT DO AND REFUSE TO DO; 275]

wring *v* **squeeze**, twist, mangle, press, compress. [➡CONTACT: EXERT PRESSURE; 415]

wringing *adj* [➡WET; 1239]

wringing wet *adj* [➡WET; 1239]

wrinkle 1 *n* **crease**, crinkle, line, fold, furrow. [➡CHANGE OF SHAPE; 386] 2 *v* **screw**, crumple, crinkle, crease, fold, rumple. [➡CHANGE OF SHAPE; 386] *Opposite:* smooth.

wrinkled 1 *adj* **crumpled**, creased, crinkly, rucked, rumpled. [➡IN BAD REPAIR; 1233] *Opposite:* smooth. 2 *adj* **wrinkly**, wizened, weathered, lined, furrowed, craggy. [➡FACIAL CHARACTERISTICS; 482] *Opposite:* smooth.

wrinkly *adj* **lined**, creased, furrowed, wrinkled, wizened, weathered. [➡FACIAL CHARACTERISTICS; 482] *Opposite:* smooth.

wrist *part of* **arm or hand.** [➡ARM AND HAND; 696]

wristlet *type of* **jewellery.** [➡JEWELLERY; 866]

wristwatch *type of* **clock.** [➡CLOCKS AND TIMERS; 1125]

writ *n* **summons**, court order, injunction, TRO (*US*), temporary restraining order (*US*). [➡TRIAL, PUNISHMENT, AND LEGAL OUTCOMES; 819]

write 1 *v* **inscribe**, put pen to paper, transcribe, engrave, carve, pen. [➡CREATE IMAGES; 357] 2 *v* **write down**, put in writing, note down, enter, record, jot down. [➡RECORD SOMETHING; 372] 3 *v* **compose**, create, script, author, devise. [➡CREATION; 347] 4 *v* **send a letter to**, drop a line to, correspond with, contact, get in touch with. [➡INITIATE AND ESTABLISH COMMUNICATION; 681]

write down *v* **record**, note down, jot down, set down, put in writing, minute. [➡RECORD SOMETHING; 372]

write off 1 *v* (*informal*) **cancel**, forget, disregard, set aside, abandon, dismiss, reject. [➡FORGET, FORGIVE, AND ACCEPT; 749] 2 *v* **wreck**, ruin, destroy, demolish, total (*US slang*), trash (*US informal*). [➡DESTRUCTION AND DEMOLITION; 360]

writer *n* **author**, novelist, playwright, poet, journalist, essayist, critic. [➡WRITERS AND STYLES; 914]

write-up *n* **report**, article, piece, review, critique. [➡ANALYTICAL NONFICTION WRITING; 593]

writhe *v* **squirm**, wriggle, twist, struggle, thrash, thrash about. [➡FIDGET AND FROLIC; 312]

writing 1 *n* **script**, symbols, inscription, marks, characters, letters, lettering. [➡WRITING; 584] 2 *n* **text**, literature, prose, journalism, copy. [➡FICTION AND DRAMA; 913]

writing board *n* [➡WRITING AND DRAWING IMPLEMENTS, AND MEDIA; 602]

writing desk *type of* **table.** [➡FURNITURE; 858]

writing pad *n* [➡WRITING AND DRAWING IMPLEMENTS, AND MEDIA; 602]

writing paper *n* [➡WRITING AND DRAWING IMPLEMENTS, AND MEDIA; 602]

written *adj* **on paper**, printed, in black and white, in print. [➡WRITING; 584]

written off (*informal*) *adj* [➡IN BAD REPAIR; 1233]

wrong 1 *adj* **incorrect**, mistaken, erroneous, off beam, wide of the mark. [➡INCORRECT AND ERRONEOUS; 223] *Opposite:* right. 2 *adj* **immoral**, wicked, dishonest, illegal, sinful, iniquitous, criminal, unethical. [➡MORALLY BAD; 776] *Opposite:* right. 3 *adj* **amiss**, not right, unsuitable, improper, inappropriate, incorrect. [➡MORALLY BAD; 776] *Opposite:* suitable. 4 *n* **sin**, crime, injury, harm, damage, insult, injustice, offence. [➡MORALLY BAD; 776] 5 *v* **insult**, injure, wound, harm, ill-treat, abuse, sin against, offend, trespass (*archaic*). [➡INSULTS, ABUSE, AND SWEARING; 659]

wrongdoer *n* **criminal**, offender, sinner, reprobate, outlaw, malefactor (*formal*), evildoer, transgressor. [➡VILLAINS AND THUGS; 947]

wrongdoing *n* **bad behaviour**, unlawful activity, crime, offence, misconduct. [➡CRIMES; 817]

wrong-foot *v* **catch out**, surprise, take unawares, take by surprise, throw (*informal*), trip up, outmanoeuvre. [➡SURPRISE AND IMPRESS; 575]

wrongful *adj* **illegal**, unlawful, unfair, unjust, criminal, wicked, evil. [➡ILLEGAL; 816] *Opposite:* rightful.

wrongful act *n* [➡CRIMES; 817]

wrongfully 1 *adv* **unlawfully**, illegally, wrongly, improperly. [➡ILLEGAL; 816] 2 *adv* **unfairly**, unjustly, inequitably. [➡MORALLY BAD; 776]

wrong-headed 1 *adj* **unreasonable**, obstinate, stubborn, perverse. [➡NEGATIVE INTELLECTUAL CHARACTERISTICS; 526] 2 *adj* **irrational**, unreasoning, unthinking, ill-considered, ill-conceived, misguided, mistaken. [➡THE NATURE OF IDEAS; 772]

wrong-headedness *n* [➡NEGATIVE INTELLECTUAL CHARACTERISTICS; 526]

wrongly 1 *adv* **incorrectly**, mistakenly, erroneously, imperfectly, faultily, accidentally, by mistake. [➡INCORRECT AND ERRONEOUS; 223] *Opposite:* correctly. 2 *adv* **immorally**, wickedly, dishonestly, illegally, sinfully, criminally, unlawfully. [➡MORALLY BAD; 776] *Opposite:* rightly. 3 *adv* **unsuitably**, improperly, inappropriately, incorrectly. [➡INAPPROPRIATE AND UNSUITABLE; 225] *Opposite:* suitably.

wrong side up *adj* [➡ORIENTATION AND ALIGNMENT; 1222]

wrong way up *adj* [➡ORIENTATION AND ALIGNMENT; 1222]

wrought-up *adj* **tense**, nervous, agitated, excited, worked up (*informal*), on edge, edgy, twitchy (*informal*), jumpy. [➡CONFUSION, ANXIETY, AND WORRY; 541]

wry *adj* **ironic**, cynical, sardonic, dry, droll. [➡MOCKING AND DISMISSIVE; 637]

wryness *n* **humour**, irony, satire, dryness, drollness. [➡JOKES AND TEASING; 675]

wunderkind *n* [➡TALENTED OR INTELLIGENT PERSON; 529]

XYZ

xenophobia *n* **chauvinism**, racial intolerance, dislike of foreigners, nationalism, prejudice, racism. [➡ PREJUDICE; 551] *Opposite:* tolerance.

xenophobic *adj* **chauvinistic**, intolerant, nationalistic, prejudiced, racist. [➡ NEGATIVE INTELLECTUAL CHARACTERISTICS; 526] *Opposite:* tolerant.

xenopus *type of* **amphibian**. [➡ AMPHIBIANS; 1008]

xylophone *type of* **percussion instrument**. [➡ MUSICAL INSTRUMENTS; 910]

yacht *type of* **sailing vessel**. [➡ SHIPS AND BOATS; 1149]

yak (*informal*) **1** *v* **chatter**, chat, natter (*informal*), talk, gossip, chew the fat (*slang*), rap (*slang*), gab (*informal*), schmooze (*slang*), shoot the breeze (*US slang*). [➡ TWO-WAY COMMUNICATION; 608] **2** *n* **chat**, chinwag (*informal*), natter (*informal*), heart-to-heart, talk, gossip, rap (*slang*), gab (*informal*), schmooze (*slang*). [➡ INFORMAL COMMUNICATION; 45]

yam *type of* **root vegetable**. [➡ FRUIT AND VEGETABLES; 1175]

yammer (*informal*) **1** *v* **chatter**, chat, talk, blab (*informal*), gossip, yatter (*informal*), burble (*informal*), yap (*informal*). [➡ GOSSIP; 679] **2** *n* **chatter**, chat, talk, blab (*informal*), gossip, yatter (*informal*), yap (*informal*). [➡ INFORMAL COMMUNICATION; 45]

yank **1** *v* **pull**, tug, jerk, wrench, snatch, heave, haul. [➡ PUSH, PULL, SLIDE; 336] **2** *n* **tug**, pull, jerk, wrench, heave. [➡ PUSH, PULL, SLIDE; 336]

See Compare and Contrast at **pull**.

yank somebody's chain (*US informal*) *v* [➡ JOKES AND TEASING; 675]

yap **1** *v* **bark**, yelp, bay, woof. [➡ SOUND EMISSION BY ANIMALS OR BIRDS; 365] **2** *v* (*informal*) **yammer** (*informal*), chatter, chat, talk, blab (*informal*), gossip, yatter (*informal*). [➡ GOSSIP; 679] **3** *n* **yelp**, bark, woof, baying. [➡ SOUNDS MADE BY ANIMALS; 1260] **4** *n* (*informal*) **yammer** (*informal*), chatter, chat, talk, blab (*informal*), gossip, yatter (*informal*), burble (*informal*). [➡ INFORMAL COMMUNICATION; 45]

yard **1** *n* **patio**, courtyard, terrace, back yard. [➡ THE COUNTRYSIDE AND OUTDOOR SPACES; 1070] **2** *n* **enclosure**, work area, storage area. [➡ URBAN OUTDOOR SPACES; 1071] **3** *n* (*US*) **plot**, patch, grass, lawn. [➡ THE COUNTRYSIDE AND OUTDOOR SPACES; 1070]

yard sale (*US*) *n* [➡ SALES AND SHOWS; 444]

yardstick *n* **measure**, index, gauge, benchmark, standard, touchstone. [➡ SCORES AND EVALUATIONS; 599]

yarmulke *type of* **headgear**. [➡ HABERDASHERY, MILLINERY, AND LINGERIE; 867]

yarn **1** *n* **thread**, fibre, wool. [➡ TEXTILES AND THREADS; 1130] **2** *n* (*informal*) **story**, tale, tall story, shaggy dog story, anecdote, joke, tall tale (*US*), fish story (*US*). [➡ THE ORAL TRADITION; 678]

yashmak *type of* **headgear**. [➡ HABERDASHERY, MILLINERY, AND LINGERIE; 867]

yaw *v* [➡ TAKE UP A NEW POSITION; 313]

yawn **1** *v* **stretch**, stretch yourself, rub your eyes, sigh, nod, drowse. [➡ SLEEP AND DREAM; 724] **2** *v* **gape**, split, fly open, gap, crack. [➡ SEPARATE AND DIVIDE; 402] *Opposite:* close up. **3** *n* **bore**, drag (*informal*), nonevent, waste of time, mind-numbing experience. [➡ NUISANCES; 254] *Opposite:* laugh.

yawning *adj* **deep**, cavernous, gaping, wide, open, vast. [➡ DEPTH: DEEP; 1200] *Opposite:* narrow.

yea (*archaic*) *interj* [➡ EXPRESSIONS OF AGREEMENT; 649]

yeah (*informal*) *interj* [➡ EXPRESSIONS OF AGREEMENT; 649]

year *type of* **time period**. [➡ TIMES OF YEAR; 88]

yearbook *n* **annual**, annual report, almanac. [➡ RECORDS; 586]

yearling *type of* **young animal**. [➡ YOUNG ANIMAL; 977]

yearly **1** *adj* **annual**, twelve-monthly, year on year. [➡ TIMES OF YEAR; 88] **2** *adv* **annually**, every year, once a year. [➡ TIMES OF YEAR; 88]

yearn *v* **desire**, long, crave, ache, hanker, want, covet, hunger, thirst. [➡ DESIRE AND WANT; 580]

See Compare and Contrast at **want**.

yearning *n* **desire**, longing, yen, hunger, thirst, ache, craving, nostalgia, urge, hankering. [➡ DESIRE AND WANT; 580]

yearningly *adv* **longingly**, desirously (*formal*), wistfully, unrequitedly, achingly, nostalgically. [➡ DESIRE AND WANT; 580]

year-round *adj* **constant**, continual, continuous, perennial. [➡ PERMANENCE: WITHOUT END; 94]

years *n* **ages** (*informal*), centuries (*informal*), donkey's years (*informal*), a month of Sundays (*informal*), an age, aeons, an inordinate length of time, yonks (*slang*). [➡ LONG PERIOD OF TIME; 92]

years to come *n* [➡ FUTURE; 86]

yeast *type of* **fungus**. [➡ MICROORGANISMS, FUNGI, AND ALGAE; 1023]

yell **1** *v* **shout**, scream, shriek, roar, bellow, bawl, screech, howl, holler (*informal*). [➡ SOUND EMISSION BY PEOPLE; 364] **2** *n* **shriek**, shout, scream, roar, bellow, screech, howl, holler (*informal*). [➡ SOUNDS MADE BY PEOPLE; 1261]

yell at *v* **scold**, shout at, tell off (*informal*), bawl out (*informal*), tear off a strip, rebuke, lash, chew out (*US informal*). [➡ACCUSE, BLAME, AND CRITICIZE; 642]

yellow *type of* **colour.** [➡COLOURS; 1223]

yellow

◆ *types of yellow*
canary yellow, champagne, chrome yellow, citrine, citron, flaxen, lemon, lemon yellow, mustard, saffron

See Compare and Contrast at **cowardly.**

yellow cab (*US*) *type of* **commercial or industrial vehicle.** [➡VEHICLES; 1144]

yellowed *adj* [➡IN BAD REPAIR; 1233]

yellowhammer *type of* **songbird.** [➡SONGBIRD; 1003]

yelp 1 *v* **bark**, yap, cry, squeal, squeak. [➡SOUND EMISSION BY ANIMALS OR BIRDS; 365] 2 *n* **yap**, bark, cry, squeal, squeak. [➡SOUNDS MADE BY ANIMALS; 1260]

yen *n* **urge**, desire, wish, longing, yearning, craving, hankering. [➡DESIRE AND WANT; 580]

yep (*informal*) *interj* [➡EXPRESSIONS OF AGREEMENT; 649]

yes 1 *adv* **affirmative**, sure, certainly, absolutely, of course, indeed, naturally, surely, sure thing (*US informal*). [➡EXPRESSIONS OF AGREEMENT; 649] *Opposite:* no. 2 *n* **thumbs-up** (*informal*), affirmative, positive response, aye (*regional*), okay (*informal*), nod. [➡AGREE; 646] *Opposite:* no.

yes indeed *adv* [➡EXPRESSIONS OF AGREEMENT; 649]

yesterday *n* [➡PAST; 84]

yesteryear *n* **past**, long ago, former times, days gone by, olden days. [➡PAST; 84] *Opposite:* today.

yet 1 *adv* **up till now**, so far, thus far, hitherto (*formal*), until now. [➡PAST; 84] 2 *adv* **however**, nevertheless, nonetheless, still, in spite of that, but. [➡ALTHOUGH, NEVERTHELESS, AND DESPITE; 170]

yet again *adv* **once more**, again, once again, over again. [➡EXPRESSIONS INTRODUCING EXTRA INFORMATION; 137]

yeti *n* [➡MYTHICAL BEINGS; 790]

yet to be *adv* [➡FUTURE; 86]

yet to come *adj* [➡FUTURE; 86]

yew *type of* **evergreen tree.** [➡EVERGREEN AND CONIFEROUS TREES; 1029]

yield 1 *v* **produce**, bear, generate, bring in, return, bring forth. [➡ENGENDER; 351] 2 *v* **give way**, submit, acquiesce, capitulate, accede, defer, surrender, succumb, give in. [➡FAIL OR BE UNSUCCESSFUL; 75] *Opposite:* resist. 3 *v* **give up**, concede, grant, relinquish, resign, surrender. [➡GIVE AND PROVIDE; 431] *Opposite:* keep. 4 *n* **harvest**, crop, produce, vintage. [➡AMOUNT AND QUANTITY; 112] 5 *n* **profit**, earnings, income, revenue, return. [➡INCOME; 461]

Compare and Contrast: ***yield, capitulate, submit, succumb, surrender***

CORE MEANING: TO GIVE WAY

yield to give way to something such as force, pressure, entreaty, or persuasion; ***capitulate*** to cease to resist a superior force, especially one that seems invincible, sometimes without having offered much active opposition; ***submit*** to accept somebody else's authority or will, especially reluctantly or under pressure; ***succumb*** to give in to something due to weakness or a failure to offer much active opposition; ***surrender*** to give way to the power of another and stop offering resistance, usually after active opposition.

yielding 1 *adj* **soft**, elastic, springy, squashy, resilient. [➡MALLEABLE AND ELASTIC; 1211] *Opposite:* firm. 2 *adj* **compliant**, acquiescent, docile, accommodating, tractable, malleable. [➡GENEROSITY AND KINDNESS; 496] *Opposite:* stubborn.

yob (*informal*) *n* **thug**, yobbo (*informal*), hooligan (*informal*), hoodlum, ruffian (*dated*), vandal. [➡VILLAINS AND THUGS; 947]

yobbo (*informal*) *n* [➡VILLAINS AND THUGS; 947]

yodel *type of* **vocal music.** [➡MUSIC, SONGS, AND SINGING; 907]

yoke *n* **repression**, oppression, burden, bondage, encumbrance, drag, load, annoyance. [➡NUISANCES; 254]

yomp (*informal*) *v* **trudge**, march, clump, stomp, clomp, galumph (*informal*). [➡PROCEED AND GO; 306]

yonder (*regional*) *adv* [➡GENERAL LOCATIONS; 159]

yonks (*slang*) *n* [➡LONG PERIOD OF TIME; 92]

you bet! (*informal*) *interj* [➡EXPRESSIONS OF AGREEMENT; 649]

young 1 *adj* **youthful**, little, juvenile, adolescent, immature, childish, babyish, infantile. [➡BABYHOOD, CHILDHOOD, AND ADOLESCENCE; 917] *Opposite:* old. 2 *adj* **new**, early, undeveloped, fledgling, beginning, fresh. [➡NEW, MODERN; 167] *Opposite:* established. 3 *n* **offspring**, children, babies, litter, brood, issue, progeny. [➡YOUNGER GENERATION RELATIVES; 958]

young

◆ *types of young animal*
bullock, calf, colt, cub, fawn, foal, heifer, joey, kid, kitten, lamb, leveret, piglet, pup, puppy, whelp, yearling

◆ *types of young bird*
chick, cygnet, duckling, eaglet, eyas, fledgling, gosling, nestling, owlet, pullet, squab

young child *n* [➡CHILD OR YOUTH; 945]

younger generation *n* **young people**, youth, teenagers, adolescents, youngsters, kids (*informal*). [➡CHILD OR YOUTH; 945]

young lady *n* [➡FEMALE PERSON; 933]

young-looking *adj* [➡PEOPLE'S PHYSICAL APPEARANCE; 476]

young man *n* [➡MALE PERSON; 934]

young offenders' institution *n* [➡ BUILDINGS FOR CONFINING PEOPLE; 1093]

young people *n* [➡ CHILD OR YOUTH; 945]

young person *n* **teenager**, adolescent, youngster, juvenile, child, minor, teen (*informal*), kid (*informal*). [➡ CHILD OR YOUTH; 945] *Opposite:* adult.

youngster *n* **child**, kid (*informal*), young person, teenager, youth, adolescent, minor, teen (*informal*). [➡ CHILD OR YOUTH; 945] *Opposite:* adult.

See Compare and Contrast at **youth**.

young'un (*informal*) *n* [➡ CHILD OR YOUTH; 945]

you said it! *interj* [➡ EXPRESSIONS OF AGREEMENT; 649]

youth 1 *n* **childhood**, adolescence, formative years, infancy, early life, early stages, minority. [➡ BABYHOOD, CHILDHOOD, AND ADOLESCENCE; 917] 2 *n* **child**, teenager, youngster, minor, young person, kid (*informal*). [➡ CHILD OR YOUTH; 945]

Compare and Contrast: ***youth, child, kid, teenager, youngster***

CORE MEANING: SOMEBODY WHO IS YOUNG

youth a man or boy who is in his teens or early twenties; ***child*** a young person between birth and the onset of puberty; ***kid*** (*informal*) a child or young person; ***teenager*** somebody between the ages of thirteen and nineteen; ***youngster*** somebody who is young, or (*humorous*) somebody younger than others mentioned or present.

youth club *type of* **bar or club**. [➡ HOTELS, RESTAURANTS, AND CLUBS; 1081]

youth custody centre *n* [➡ BUILDINGS FOR CONFINING PEOPLE; 1093]

youthful 1 *adj* **young**, childlike, childish, boyish, girlish, young at heart, young-looking. [➡ PEOPLE'S PHYSICAL APPEARANCE; 476] *Opposite:* old. 2 *adj* **vigorous**, energetic, lively, enthusiastic, active, sprightly. [➡ ENERGY AND ENTHUSIASM; 497] *Opposite:* sluggish.

youthfulness 1 *n* **youth**, freshness, newness, childishness, first flush of youth, boyish charm. [➡ PEOPLE'S PHYSICAL APPEARANCE; 476] *Opposite:* age. 2 *n* **enthusiasm**, energy, radiance, vigour, liveliness, vivacity, bloom. [➡ ENERGY AND ENTHUSIASM; 497] *Opposite:* sluggishness.

youth hostel *type of* **hotel**. [➡ HOTELS, RESTAURANTS, AND CLUBS; 1081]

yowl *v* **howl**, squall, squeal, wail, caterwaul. [➡ SOUND EMISSION BY ANIMALS OR BIRDS; 365]

yo-yo *type of* **toy**. [➡ TOYS; 880]

yucca *type of* **foliage plant**. [➡ FOLIAGE PLANTS; 1035]

yucky (*informal*) *adj* **nasty**, revolting, horrid, unpleasant, disgusting, repugnant. [➡ TASTE; 704] *Opposite:* yummy.

yumminess *n* [➡ TASTE; 704]

yummy *adj* **delicious**, tasty, mouthwatering, scrumptious (*informal*), delectable, luscious, scrummy (*informal*). [➡ TASTE; 704] *Opposite:* yucky (*informal*).

yurt *n* [➡ RESIDENTIAL BUILDINGS; 1077]

zany *adj* **crazy** (*informal*), madcap, wacky (*informal*), unconventional. [➡ FUNNY AND AMUSING; 217]

zap (*informal*) 1 *v* **destroy**, kill, annihilate, exterminate, delete, obliterate. [➡ DESTRUCTION AND DEMOLITION; 360] 2 *v* **change channels**, switch channels, flick through, cruise, surf. [➡ TELEVISION AND RADIO; 607] 3 *v* **whiz**, zip (*informal*), zoom, tear, rip, shoot, dash. [➡ MOVE FAST; 314] *Opposite:* dawdle.

zappy (*informal*) *adj* **lively**, forceful, striking, eye-catching, energetic. [➡ INTERESTING AND MEANINGFUL; 191]

zeal *n* **enthusiasm**, passion, fanaticism, fervour, ardour, keenness, eagerness, vehemence, intensity. [➡ POSITIVE IMPATIENCE, ENTHUSIASM, AND ALERTNESS; 538] *Opposite:* apathy.

zealot *n* **extremist**, fanatic, bigot, evangelist, dogmatist, enthusiast. [➡ DEVOTEES AND ADDICTED PEOPLE; 557] *Opposite:* moderate.

zealotry *n* [➡ FADS, FETISHES, AND IDOLATRY; 556]

zealous *adj* **enthusiastic**, keen, passionate, fervent, ardent, fanatical, obsessive, eager, extreme, vehement, intense. [➡ ENERGY AND ENTHUSIASM; 497] *Opposite:* apathetic.

zebra *type of* **large mammal**. [➡ LARGE MAMMAL; 986]

zebra crossing *n* [➡ BRIDGES, TUNNELS, CROSSINGS, AND JUNCTIONS; 1111]

zenith *n* **peak**, summit, pinnacle, top, acme, high point, apex. [➡ EXTREMITIES OF PHYSICAL OBJECTS; 1249] *Opposite:* nadir.

zeppelin *n* **airship**, dirigible, blimp, aircraft, balloon. [➡ AIRCRAFT; 1147]

zero *n* **nothing**, nil, nought, zilch (*informal*), zip (*US informal*), zippo (*US informal*). [➡ NONE; 121]

zest 1 *n* **enthusiasm**, keenness, gusto, relish, appetite, passion. [➡ POSITIVE IMPATIENCE, ENTHUSIASM, AND ALERTNESS; 538] *Opposite:* apathy. 2 *n* **taste**, tang, piquancy, bite, spice. [➡ TASTE; 704]

zestful *adj* **enthusiastic**, keen, passionate, dynamic, energetic. [➡ PENSIVENESS AND INTEREST; 539] *Opposite:* apathetic.

zesty *adj* [➡ TASTE; 704]

zigzag *v* **wind**, meander, crisscross, weave, snake, twist and turn, corkscrew. [➡ CHANGE DIRECTION OF MOTION; 345]

zilch (*informal*) *n* **nothing**, zero, nil, nought, zip (*US informal*), zippo (*US informal*). [➡ NONE; 121]

zillion (*informal*) *n* **squillion**, million, billion, gazillion (*slang*), shedload, truckload, mountain. [➡ MANY, MUCH, LARGE AMOUNT; 117]

zinc *type of* **metal**. [➡ METALS; 1275]

zing (*informal*) *n* **vitality**, dynamism, energy, punch, vigour. [➡ POSITIVE IMPATIENCE, ENTHUSIASM, AND ALERTNESS; 538] *Opposite:* lifelessness.

zip 1 *n* (*informal*) **energy**, vigour, vitality, dynamism, punch, go (*informal*), pep (*informal*), spunk (*informal*). [➡ POSITIVE IMPATIENCE, ENTHUSIASM, AND ALERTNESS; 538] *Opposite:* apathy. 2 *part of* **garment**. [➡ PARTS OF A GARMENT; 870] 3 *n* (*US informal*) **nothing**, zilch (*informal*), nil, zero, zippo (*US informal*). [➡ NONE; 121] 4 *v* (*informal*) **go fast**, whiz, zoom, rocket, burn (*informal*), whoosh, go like a bullet. [➡ MOVE FAST; 314] *Opposite:* dawdle. 5 *v* (*informal*) [➡ COMPUTERS AND COMPUTING; 1126]

zippy (*informal*) 1 *adj* **energetic**, lively, peppy (*informal*), spunky (*informal*), vigorous, dynamic. [➡ ENERGY AND ENTHUSIASM; 497] *Opposite:* sluggish. 2 *adj* **fast**, nippy, swift, rapid, nifty (*informal*), peppy (*informal*). [➡ MOVING QUICKLY; 103] *Opposite:* sluggish.

zit (*slang*) *n* **pimple**, spot, boil. [➡ CONDITIONS AFFECTING THE SKIN; 722]

zither *type of* **stringed instrument**. [➡ MUSICAL INSTRUMENTS; 910]

zizz (*informal*) *n* [➡ SLEEP AND DREAM; 724]

zodiac *n* **astrologer's chart**, astrological diagram, astrological calendar. [➡ FATE, DESTINY, AND ASTROLOGY; 783]

zodiacal *adj* **astrological**, horoscopic, celestial. [➡ FATE, DESTINY, AND ASTROLOGY; 783]

zombie (*informal*) *n* **automaton**, robot, machine, sleepwalker (*informal*). [➡ LAZY OR UNSUCCESSFUL PEOPLE; 948]

zonal *adj* **regional**, territorial, area, district, zone-specific, region-specific. [➡ COUNTRIES AND REGIONS; 1066]

zone *n* **area**, region, district, sector, neighbourhood, precinct. [➡ PLACE; 1064]

zoo *n* **zoological gardens**, menagerie, safari park, wildlife park, wildlife refuge, game reserve, city farm, children's zoo, park reserve, petting zoo (*US*). [➡ URBAN OUTDOOR SPACES; 1071]

zoological *adj* [➡ BIOLOGICAL SCIENCES; 1037]

zoological gardens *n* [➡ URBAN OUTDOOR SPACES; 1071]

zoology *type of* **bioscience**. [➡ BIOLOGICAL SCIENCES; 1037]

zoom 1 *v* **go fast**, whiz, whoosh, zip (*informal*), rocket, go like a bullet, burn (*informal*). [➡ MOVE FAST; 314] *Opposite:* dawdle. 2 *v* **increase**, skyrocket (*informal*), shoot up, rise, rocket, take off. [➡ GO UPWARDS; 307] *Opposite:* plummet.

zoom in *v* **home in**, pinpoint, focus, narrow down, concentrate, zero in. [➡ FIND; 464]

zoom lens *part of* **photographic equipment**. [➡ PHOTOGRAPHY AND PHOTOGRAPHIC EQUIPMENT; 1121]

zoophobia *type of* **phobia**. [➡ FEARS AND PHOBIAS; 555]

zoot suit *type of* **suit**. [➡ GARMENTS AND OUTFITS; 865]

zori *type of* **shoe**. [➡ FOOTWEAR; 871]

zucchini (*US*) *type of* **vegetable**. [➡ FRUIT AND VEGETABLES; 1175]

THEMATIC SECTION

The Way Things Are or Seem to Be

Becoming, Appearing, and Disappearing

1 Gradually Come into Existence

Great oaks from little acorns grow. **Proverb**

(*v*) appear, arise, become, come, come into being, come out of, crystallize, derive, descend, develop, emanate, emerge, ensue, evolve, flow, form, gel (*informal*), grow up, issue, jell, make, materialize, originate, prove, rise, rise up, *take form*, take root, take shape, unfold, wax (*literary*)

2 Suddenly Come into Existence

The one and only basis of the moral life must be spontaneity, that is, the immediate, the unreflective. **Jean-Paul Sartre**

(*v*) break into, break out, burst out, come on, come up, crop up (*informal*), dawn, erupt, flare up, kick in (*informal*), spring up

3 Appear and Emerge

At a given moment I open my eyes and exist. And before that, during all eternity, what was there? Nothing. **Ugo Betti**

(*v*) appear, break, come into sight, come out, come to light, emerge, fall into place, get round, glare, leak out, leap out at, loom, make inroads, materialize, obtrude, occur, rear its head, *rematerialize*, rise, show up, stand out, *stick out like a sore thumb*, strike, surface, turn up

4 Disappear

In the night reason disappears, only the lives of things remaining. **Antoine de Saint-Exupéry**

(*v*) clear, decline, decrease, disappear, dry up, dwindle, ebb, evaporate, fade, fade away, fail, *fall away*, fizzle, give out, go away, let up, melt, *melt away*, peter out, run down, run out, *sink without trace*, tail off, trail away, *trail off*, vanish, vaporize, wane, weaken

5 Cause to Appear

For words, like Nature, half reveal/And half conceal the Soul within. **Alfred Tennyson**

(*v*) bare, bring out, bring to light, call attention to, conjure, conjure up, demonstrate, dig up, disinter (*formal*), display, disport (*archaic or humorous*), draw, dredge up, evidence, evince, exhibit, expose, feature, flash (*informal*), flaunt, invoke, lay bare, manifest, mine, model, open up, parade, present, preview, register, render (*formal*), reveal, revive, set off, set out, show, show off, show up, smoke out, stick out, throw up, unfold, unfurl, unmask, unroll, unveil, wear

6 Cause to Disappear

There is a theory which states that if ever anyone discovers exactly what the Universe is for and why it is here, it will instantly disappear. **Douglas Adams**

(*v*) blanket, block off, blot out, blur, bury, camouflage, cloak, cloister, closet, cloud, conceal, cover, cover up, disguise, dissimulate (*formal*), drown, eclipse, encase, encode, enshroud, extinguish, heel in, hide, mask, mist over, obscure, paper over, plough under, screen, secrete, shade, shadow, swallow, veil, whitewash

See also REMOVE SOMETHING (339)

7 Absent and Unavailable

It's when the thing itself is missing that you have to supply the word. **Henri de Montherlant**

(*adj*) absent, *absent without leave*, away, AWOL, busy, discontinued, engaged, forgotten, gone, irrecoverable, irretrievable, lacking, *long-gone*, long-lost (*humorous*), lost, mislaid, misplaced, missing, occupied, *omitted*, on loan, *out of stock*, over, reserved, spent, spoken for, taken, tied up, unaccounted-for, unavailable, unobtainable, *unreachable*, *used up*, vanished, *withheld*

(*adv*) out

(*n*) absence, exception, exile, nonattendance, no-show, omission, truancy, unavailability

See also NONEXISTENCE (24)

8 Absent Oneself

Absence makes the heart grow fonder,/Isle of Beauty, Fare thee well! **Thomas Haynes Bayly**

(*v*) absent yourself, check out, clear out, depart, disperse, *excuse yourself*, exit, *flounce out*, get off, go, go away, go off, *go off in a huff*, head off, *hit the road*, leave, make off, make tracks (*informal*), *make yourself scarce* (*informal*), move on, move out, *pull away*, pull out, push off, put forth (*formal*), quit, retire, run along, sally, separate, set forth (*literary*), set off, set out, *set sail*, slope off (*informal*), split (*slang*), start, start off, start out, step out, *storm out*, strike out, *take leave*, take off (*informal*), tear away, *turn your back*, vacate, *vamoose* (*US slang*), *venture forth*, walk off, *wander away*, *wander off*, withdraw

9 Runaways and Absentees

I fled Him, down the labyrinthine ways/Of my own mind; and in the mist of tears. **Francis Thompson**

(*n*) absconder, absentee, deserter, escapee, fugitive, outlaw, runaway, stowaway, truant

10 Run Away and Avoid

Stop the World, I Want to Get Off **Anthony Newley**

(*v*) abandon, *abandon ship*, abscond, bail out, *beat a hasty retreat*, beat it (*informal*), bolt, break out, *bunk off* (*informal*), *buzz off* (*informal*), clear off (*informal*), cut loose (*informal*), decamp, defect, desert, do a bunk (*informal*), *do a moonlight flit, do a runner*, elope, escape, evacuate, flee, fly, fly the coop (*informal*), forsake, get away, get out, *go AWOL*, go missing, *go underground*, hide, *hightail it* (*slang*), hole up (*slang*), *jump ship, leg it* (*informal*), light out (*informal*), *make a break for it, make a dash for it, make a run for it, make a sharp exit*, play hooky (*informal*), *play truant*, run away, *run for it*, run off, scarper (*slang*), *scat* (*informal*), scoot (*informal*), scram (*informal*), *shove off* (*informal*), *show a clean pair of heels, skedaddle* (*slang*), skip (*informal*), skip off (*informal*), *steal away*, take cover, take flight, *take to flight*, take to your heels, truant, walk away, walk out, *withdraw from the world*

11 Present and Available

Sometime they'll give a war and nobody will come. **Carl Sandburg**

(*adj*) attached, at the ready, available, down, endemic, epidemic, ever-present, existent (*formal*), forthcoming, going, *going begging*, immanent (*formal*), *in attendance*, included, *in evidence, in existence*, in hand, *in situ*, listed, obtainable, omnipresent, on board, on tap, open, out, participatory, pervasive, present, prevalent, *procurable*, public, reachable, rife, ubiquitous, untaken, untapped, up for grabs (*informal*), vacant, viewable, widespread, *within grasp*

(*adv*) aboard (*informal*), about, around, *in the area*, on hand, on stand-by, *to hand*

(*n*) attendance, availability, currency, pervasiveness, presence, prevalence, *ubiquitousness, ubiquity*

12 Arrive

The hero appears only when the tiger is dead. **Burmese proverb**

(*v*) appear, arrive, attend, barge in, *blunder in*, book in, *breeze in*, burst in on, butt in, call in, catch napping, check in, close in, come, come along, come back, come round, descend, draw near, drop in, enter, gain access, gatecrash, get in, get into, get to, go in, go into, *heave into view* (*literary*), hit (*slang*), *hove into view* (*literary*), invade, make, poke, *pop by*, pop in (*informal*), *pop round* (*informal*), present, project, put in an appearance, raid, reach, re-enter, report, resurface, return, roll in, roll up, set foot in, show, show up (*informal*), show your face, stand out, *storm in*, surprise, *swing by* (*US*), trespass, turn out, turn up, walk in on

13 Arrival

The story of my life is about back entrances and side doors and secret elevators and other ways of getting in and out of places so that people won't bother you. **Greta Garbo**

(*n*) appearance, arrival, call, coming, debarkation, disembarkation, entrance, entry, homecoming, immigration, incursion (*formal*), infestation, inflow, influx, infringement, landfall, landing, penetration, re-entry, return, stop off, touchdown, visit

14 Arrive by Transport

When a train pulls into a great city I am reminded of the closing moments of an overture. **Graham Greene**

(*v*) alight, berth, come in, debark, disembark, dock, land, pull up

Being and Not Being

15 Exist

There are two senses, and two only, of the word "exist": one exists as a thing or else one exists as a consciousness. **Maurice Merleau-Ponty**

(*v*) be, be alive, exist, live

16 Prosper and Abound

Earth's crammed with heaven,/And every common bush afire with God. **Elizabeth Barrett Browning**

(*v*) abound, be alive with, bloom (*literary*), blossom, blossom out, boom, bristle, burgeon (*literary*), flourish, flower, infest, overflow with, predominate, prevail (*formal*), proliferate, prosper, seethe, swarm, teem, thrive

17 Continue to Exist

We always find something, eh, Didi, to give us the impression that we exist? **Samuel Beckett**

(*v*) abide (*archaic*), bear up, come through, continue, cope, endure, exist, extend, fare, fend for yourself, get along, get by, get over, get through, hold, hold up, keep, last, last out, lie, live on, make do, make ends meet, manage, outlast, outlive, outride, outstay, overwinter, persist, remain, run, scrape by, see out, set in, smoulder, spread, stand, stand up, stay, subsist, survive, tarry, wait, weather, withstand

18 Exist with Others

Until knowledge is understood in human and political terms as something to be won to the service of coexistence and community, not of particular races, nations, or religions, the future augurs badly. **Edward W. Said**

(*v*) coexist, cohabit (*formal*), colonize, concur, *co-occur*

19 Exist in a Place

There is only one home to the life of a tortoise; there is only one shell to the soul of man. **Wole Soyinka**

(*v*) be, be there, cling, come, come from, extend, frequent, haunt, hover, jut, lie, lie about, look out, overhang, overlook, patronize (*formal*), perch, protrude, remain, reside, roost, run through, sit, sprawl, spread out, stick around (*informal*), straggle, stretch, tower

20 Inhabit

I believe that if God had wanted us to share our homes with insects, He would not have made them so unattractive. **Dave Barry**

(*v*) abide (*archaic*), board, dwell (*literary*), encamp,

inhabit, live, lodge, occupy, people, populate, reside, settle, sojourn (*literary*), stay

21 Exist in Close Proximity

Do not love your neighbour as yourself. If you are on good terms with yourself it is an impertinence; if on bad, an injury. **George Bernard Shaw**

(*v*) abut, adjoin, be adjoining, beleaguer, besiege, border, border on, bound, box in, circle, communicate, dominate, edge, encircle, enclose, enfold, engulf, envelop, face, flank, frame, hedge, lie off, mould, *neighbour*, overlap, *overlie*, ring, skirt, span, straddle, surround, verge

See also POSITION SOMETHING: AROUND SOMETHING (328)

22 Cease to Exist

Fish die belly-upward and rise to the surface; it is their way of falling. **André Gide**

(*adj*) declining, diminishing, dwindling, dying, fading, falling, flagging, waning

(*v*) be no more, *cease to exist*, collapse, decay, *dematerialize*, *die a death*, die away, die off, die out, diminish, disappear, disintegrate, dissolve, end, expire, fade, falter, flag, gutter, implode, languish, lapse, pass away, stop, vanish, wilt, wither

See also CAUSES OF DEATH (921), DEAD AND DYING (925)

23 Nonexistent Things

A robust sense of reality is very necessary in framing a correct analysis of propositions about unicorns, golden mountains, round squares, and other such pseudo-objects. **Bertrand Russell**

(*n*) *castles in Spain*, castles in the air, *castles in the sky* (*US*), chimera, concoction, delusion, dream, fancy, fantasy, *fata morgana* (*literary*), figment, *figment of the imagination*, flight of fancy, hallucination, illusion, mirage, myth, optical illusion, phantasmagoria, pipe dream, pretence, stardust, visualization, *will-o'-the-wisp*, wishful thinking

See also NON-EXISTENT PLACE (1065), MYTHICAL CREATURES (1036), MYTHICAL BEINGS (790)

24 Nonexistence

What's past, and what's to come is strew'd with husks/And formless ruin of oblivion. **William Shakespeare**

(*n*) lack, nonexistence, nothingness, oblivion, want

See also ABSENT AND UNAVAILABLE (7)

25 Perceptible

In a dark time, the eye begins to see. **Theodore Roethke**

(*adj*) apparent, attention-grabbing, audible, broad, clear, conspicuous, cut-and-dried, demonstrable, detectable, discernible, distinct, distinguishable, glaring, identifiable, *in plain sight*, knowable, manifest, marked, measurable, naked, noticeable, observable, obtrusive, obvious, *on display*, *on show*, *on view*, outright, outward, overt, palpable, patent, *perceivable*, perceptible, physical, plain, prominent, pronounced, *protruding*, protrusive, proud, tactile, tangible, *traceable*, transparent, unconcealed, uncovered, undisguised, *unsubtle*, visible, visual

(*adv*) aloud, conspicuously, demonstrably, distinctly, evidently, externally, glaringly, *in full view*, *in sight*, in the open, on the surface, plainly, prominently, transparently, unmistakably

(*n*) audibility, blatancy, *conspicuousness*, *distinctness*, *distinguishability*, nakedness, obviousness, *overtness*, *palpability*, *perceptibility*, plainness, tangibility, visibility

See also THE SENSES (697)

26 Imperceptible

We never knows wot's hidden in each other's hearts; and if we had glass winders there, we'd need keep the shutters up. **Charles Dickens**

(*adj*) *cloaked*, concealed, delicate, discreet, disembodied, disguised, fine, hidden, ignored, impalpable (*formal*), imperceptible, inappreciable, inarticulate, inaudible, inconspicuous, indiscernible, indistinct, indistinguishable, insensible, intangible, invisible, latent, light, masked, obscure, *out of focus*, out of sight, *out of view*, quiet, recessive, *secreted*, shadowy, subterranean, subtle, underground, undetectable, unheard, unnoticeable, unpronounced, unseen, unspotted, *untraceable*, vestigial, weak

(*adv*) delicately, *indistinguishably*, intangibly, invisibly, lightly, obscurely, unremarkably, weakly

(*n*) *impalpability* (*formal*), *imperceptibility*, inarticulacy, inaudibility, *inconspicuousness*, *indiscernibility*, indistinctness, intangibility, invisibility, latency, weakness

See also THE SENSES (697), ABSENCE OF SOUND (1256)

Happen

27 Happen

But the universe exists, things must happen in it, all equally improbable, and man is one of these things. **Jacques Lucien Monod**

(*v*) arise, be, come, come about, come to pass (*archaic or literary*), elapse, ensue, follow, *get under way*, go by, go down (*slang*), go on, happen, intervene, occur, pan out (*informal*), pass, result, run, succeed, supervene (*formal*), take effect, take place, transpire, turn out

28 Happen Again

Anything that, in happening, causes itself to happen, happens again. **Douglas Adams**

(*v*) reappear, recur, *re-emerge*, resurface, *start up again*

See also AGAIN (109)

29 Repetition

Experience isn't interesting till it begins to repeat itself—in fact, till it does that, it hardly is experience. **Elizabeth Bowen**

(*n*) encore, reappearance, rebirth, *recommencement*, recrudescence, recurrence, rediscovery, reinstatement, *rekindling*, renaissance, *reoccurrence*, repeat, repetition, *repetitiousness*, *repetitiveness*, replay, resumption, resurgence, resurrection, resuscitation

See also AGAIN (109), RECOMMENCE AND RESUME (269)

30 Happen to Somebody

Every man meets his Waterloo at last. **Wendell Phillips**

(*v*) attack, become of, befall (*archaic or literary*), beset, come over, curse, descend, grip, hit, wash over

See also EXPERIENCE AND ENCOUNTER (583)

31 Cause to Happen

We have no other notion of cause and effect, but that of certain objects, which have always conjoin'd *together, and which in all past instances have always been found inseparable.* **David Hume**

(*v*) *actualize*, arrange, beget, *blaze a trail*, bring, bring about, bring forward, *bring to fruition*, *bring to pass*, call, call down, *call forth*, cause, connive, contrive, convene, determine, dictate, effect (*formal*), elicit, engineer, ensure, entail, excite, ferment, fix, foment (*formal*), forward, *give rise to*, have, hold, ignite, incur, induce, inflict, instigate, jump-start, kindle, lead, lead to, leave, make, make certain, make for, make happen, mean, motivate, occasion, orchestrate, organize, plan, plot, prearrange, precipitate, predestine, predetermine, present, programme, promote, prompt, provoke, push through, put on, raise, rekindle, restart, result, see, see to it, sensitize, *set in train*, *set rolling*, *set the ball rolling*, spin-off, stage-manage, throw, time, underlie, usher in, whip up, wreak

32 Happening and In Progress

Going to trial with a lawyer who considers your life-style a Crime in Progress is not a happy prospect. **Hunter S. Thompson**

(*adj*) active, afoot, astir, developmental, effective, functional, *going on*, in commission, in force, in full swing, in hand, *in progress*, *in the wind*, *in the works*, on the go, on the move, *on track*, operating, operational, operative, progressive, rolling, *taking place*, under negotiation, underway, *up and running*, up to speed, *well under way*, working

(*adv*) in flagrante delicto, in the throes of, midstream, midway, on, progressively

33 About to Happen

You can only predict things after they've happened. **Eugène Ionesco**

(*adj*) awakening, bordering on, developing, imminent, impending, in for, *in store*, in the air, in the offing, in the pipeline, *in the stars*, looming, oncoming, onrushing, *on the agenda*, *on the horizon*, pendant, pendent (*formal or literary*), pending, poised, primed, projected, renascent, resurgent, upcoming (*US*)

(*adv*) *about to happen*, on the point of, on the verge of, on the way

(*v*) await, be on course, brew, impend, lie in wait, loom, threaten

See also FUTURE (86)

34 Not Happening

Sometimes virtual crimes lie dormant, and operas are stored away in a maestro's head, only to await the creative influence of genius to inspire their opening bars. **Joaquim Maria Machado de Assis**

(*adj*) *cancelled*, in abeyance, in limbo, *on hold*, *on ice*, *on the back burner*, *postponed*, suspended

Events and Occurrences

35 Events and Occurrences

You put up with the bloody and botched events in the hope of the one occasion when it becomes beautiful. **Peter Brook**

(*n*) adventure, binge, business, caper, chain reaction, circumstance (*formal*), *comings and goings*, development, episode, escapade, event, experience, fact, goings-on (*informal*), go-round (*US informal*), happening, incident, instalment, merry-go-round, occasion, occurrence, phenomenon, proceedings, *sequence of events*, *series of events*, spree, thing, *ups and downs*, *vagaries*

See also CHAIN OF EVENTS (163)

36 Chance Event

Not only does God play dice. He does not tell us where they fall. **Stephen Hawking**

(*n*) *chance meeting*, *chance occurrence*, coincidence, contingency, encounter, eventuality (*formal*), fluke (*informal*), freak, happenstance, quirk, vagary

See also LUCK (784)

37 Parties, Dances, and Celebrations

If an earthquake were to engulf England to-morrow, the English would manage to meet and dine somewhere among the rubbish, just to celebrate the event. **Douglas Jerrold**

(*adj*) celebratory, festive

(*n*) banquet, bash, *beanfeast* (*dated informal*), benefit, bop (*informal*), carnival, carousal (*literary*), carousing (*literary*), ceilidh, celebration, *cocktail party*, dance, do (*informal*), *drinks party*, *fayre*, feast, festival, festivities, festivity, fête, fiesta, function, gala, *garden party*, *hoedown* (*US*), holiday, hop (*dated informal*), jamboree, jollification, knees-up (*informal*), levee, masque, merrymaking, *orgy*, pageant, pageantry, parade, party, prom (*US*), rave, rave-up (*dated slang*), reception, revel, revelry, *revels*, saturnalia, shindig (*informal*), social, *social event*, soiree (*formal*), *special occasion*, *street party*

38 Ceremonies and Anniversaries

The punctuation of anniversaries is...like the closing of doors, one after another between you and what you want to hold on to. **Anne Morrow Lindbergh**

(*adj*) bridal, ceremonial, commemorative, nuptial, processional, ritual, ritualistic

(*adv*) ritually

(*n*) anniversary, betrothal (*formal*), bicentenary, bicentennial (*US*), celebration, centenary, centennial (*US*), ceremonial, ceremony, commemoration, commemorative (*US*), graduation, inauguration, induction, jubilee, marriage, memory, nuptials (*literary or humorous*), observance, pomp, *silver jubilee*, tercentenary, unveiling, wedding, *wedding ceremony*

39 Aggressive Event

Detested sport,/That owes its pleasures to another's pain. **William Cowper**

(*n*) action, affray, aggression, air raid, air strike, assault, battle, beating, bloodbath, bombardment, brawl, broil (*US archaic*), combat, conflict, confrontation, counterattack, coup, coup d'état, dogfight, duel, fight, fighting, *fist fight*, foray, fray, gunfight, *holocaust*, hostilities, incursion, insurgence, insurgency, insurrection, invasion, march, melee, mutiny, offence, onslaught, ouster, pitched battle, punch-up (*informal*), rebellion, revolt, revolution, riot, rising, scrap (*informal*), scrape (*informal*), scrimmage, scuffle, shooting, siege, skirmish, sortie, stabbing, strike, struggle, tug of war, tussle, uprising, war

40 Non-Aggressive/Sporting Event

Play the game, but don't believe in it. **Ralph Ellison**

(*n*) challenge, championship, competition, contest, crusade, dare, derby, drive, fight, final, fixture, game, games, gymkhana, knockabout (*informal*), match, photo finish, play-off, point-to-point, premiership, quarterfinal, quiz, race, regatta, rematch, rodeo, semifinal, *sporting event*, *sports event*, sprint, *stake race* (*US*), steeplechase, swordplay, tackle, test match, title, tournament, *tourney*

41 Competitors

One has to be a fox in order to recognize traps, and a lion to frighten off wolves. **Niccolò Machiavelli**

(*n*) candidate, challenger, champ (*informal*), champion, competitor, contender, contestant, duellist, entrant, fighter, finalist, gladiator, hopeful, medallist, nominee, participant, pretender, runner

See also PEOPLE IN SPORTS AND LEISURE (876), COMPETE, CONTEND, AND COMBAT (304)

42 Performances and Shows

The only true performance is the one which attains madness. **Mick Jagger**

(*n*) act, airshow, cabaret, cavalcade, *charity appeal*, *charity event*, *charity performance*, circus (*informal*), concert, *county show*, demonstration, display, enactment, entertainment, exhibit, exhibition, exposition, extravaganza, fair, *fashion show*, *flower show*, *gig* (*informal*), *horse show*, marchpast, masque, matinée, performance, play, premiere, preview, reading, recital, recitation, recitative, repertory, retrospective, revue, road show, screening, show, showing, sneak preview, spectacle, spectacular, splurge (*informal*), staging, tattoo, turn

See also ENTERTAINMENT (872), MUSIC, SONGS, AND SINGING (907), THE PERFORMING ARTS (904)

43 Meetings and Assemblies

Oh, if only I could be President and Congress, too, just for ten minutes. **Theodore Roosevelt**

(*n*) AGM, *annual general meeting*, appointment, assembly, assignation, audience, blind date, briefing, *business meeting*, caucus, clinic, colloquium, colloquy (*formal*), conclave, concourse, conference, congress, convention, date, *deliberations* (*formal*), demo (*informal*), demonstration, engagement, forum, fundraiser, gathering, get-together (*informal*), interview, meeting, muster, plenary, *plenary meeting*, *plenary session*, plenum, press conference, procession, protest, protest march, protest rally, rally, rendezvous, reunion, round table, salon, seminar, session, sit-in, sitting, summit, *summit meeting*, symposium, tryst, *videoconference*

See also AUDIENCES AND ATTENDEES (937)

44 Decisive Moments

The good things in history are usually of very short duration, but afterwards have a decisive influence over what happens over long periods of time. **Hannah Arendt**

(*n*) about-face (*US*), about-turn, boiling point, breaking point, cave-in, change of heart, *cliffhanger*, climax, climb-down, crisis, *crisis point*, crossroads, crunch, decider, defining moment, eye opener, flashpoint, highlight, high point, high spot, knife-edge, landmark, milestone, *point of no return*, red-letter day, reversal, reversion, *seminal moment*, *snapping point*, turnabout, turning point, turnround, twist, *twist of fate*, U-turn, volte-face, watershed

45 Informal Communication

It usually takes more than three weeks to prepare a good impromptu speech. **Mark Twain**

(*n*) *badinage*, chat, chatter, chinwag (*informal*), chitchat (*informal*), *confab* (*informal*), conversation, dialogue (*formal*), discourse, discussion, exchange, gab (*informal*), *gabbing* (*informal*), gossip, heart-to-heart, natter (*informal*), one-to-one, palaver, pleasantries, *powwow* (*informal*), schmooze (*slang*), small talk, *social call*, talk, talking, *tête-à-tête*, word, yak (*informal*), yammer (*informal*), yap (*informal*)

See also MEANINGLESS SPEECH OR WRITING (677), GOSSIP (679), TWO-WAY COMMUNICATION (608)

46 Negotiation and Debate

It's a well-known proposition that you know who's going to win a negotiation: it's he who pauses the longest. **Robert Holmes à Court**

(*n*) airing, arbitration, consultation, debate, deliberation, dialogue, head-to-head, intercession, mediation, negotiation, negotiations, parley, talks

47 Argument

The quarrels of lovers are the renewal of love. **Terence**

(*n*) altercation, argument, barney (*informal*), brush, bust-up (*informal*), clash, collision, conflict, confrontation, *contretemps* (*formal*), controversy, crossfire, dialectic, difference, *difference of opinion*, ding-dong (*informal*), disagreement, disputation (*formal*), dispute, face-off, falling-out, feud, fight, flare-up (*informal*), go-around (*US informal*), go-round (*US informal*), incident, infighting, misunderstanding, *power struggle*, quarrel, rhubarb (*US*), rift, row, run-in (*informal*), rupture, set-to (*informal*), *shouting match*, showdown, slanging match, spat, squabble, tiff, unpleasantness, vendetta, war of words, words, wrangle

See also CHAOS AND UPROAR (51), ARGUE AND FIGHT – TWO-WAY (644)

48 Telephone Communication

Speaking to astronauts on the moon *And this certainly has to be the most historic phone call ever made.* **Richard Nixon**

(*n*) bell (*informal*), buzz (*informal*), call, *phone call*, ring, telephone call, tinkle (*informal*)

See also TELEPHONE AND PAGE (682)

49 Neutral One-Way Communication

A professor is one who talks in someone else's sleep. **W. H. Auden**

(*n*) address, aside, declaration, discourse, disquisition (*formal*), excursion (*formal*), exposition, homily, ice-breaker, improvisation, interjection, lecture, monologue, narration, oration, *panegyric* (*formal*), *passing comment*, patter, pep talk (*informal*), peroration (*formal*), pleasantry, presentation, regurgitation, rendition, report, speech, talk

50 Criticisms and Angry Outbursts

The secret of our tragedy is/that our screams are louder than our voices/and our swords taller than ourselves. **Nizar Qabbani**

(*n*) accusation, admonishment, admonition, attack, broadside, castigation (*formal*), chastisement (*formal*), condemnation, contention, *contumely* (*archaic or literary*), criticism, denigration, denunciation, deprecation, diatribe, disparagement, earful (*informal*), eulogy, explosion, flak (*informal*), going-over (*informal*), harangue, imputation, intimidation, invective (*formal*), *jeremiad* (*literary*), knock (*informal*), lecture, mauling, moralizing, mouthful, objection, obloquy (*formal or literary*), outcry, outpouring, *paddy* (*informal*), paroxysm, *Parthian shot*, parting shot, philippic, polemic, protestation, public disgrace, putdown (*informal*), rant, rebuke, recrimination, remonstrance, reprimand, reproach, reproof, rollicking (*informal*), sabre rattling, scolding, sermon, squawk, *squelch* (*slang*), stricture (*formal*), swipe (*informal*), talking-to (*informal*), tantrum, telling-off (*informal*), ticking-off (*informal*), tirade, *tongue-lashing*, vilification, vituperation

See also ACCUSE, BLAME, AND CRITICIZE (642)

51 Chaos and Uproar

There is nothing stable in the world; uproar's your only music. **John Keats**

(*n*) ado, anarchy, ballyhoo, bedlam, bloodletting, boisterousness, brouhaha (*formal*), bustle, cacophony, carry-on (*informal*), clamour, commotion, din, disturbance, *donnybrook*, ferment, *foofaraw*, fracas, free-for-all (*informal*), furore, fuss, high jinks (*informal*), hijinks (*informal*), histrionics, hoo-hah (*slang*), hubbub, hue and cry, hullabaloo, hurly-burly, hustle and bustle, kerfuffle (*informal*), lawlessness, melodrama, outcry, palaver, pandemonium, racket (*informal*), raucousness, rough-and-tumble, roughhouse (*informal*), rout, row, rowdiness, ruckus, ruction, ructions, rumpus, scene, scrimmage, scrum, sensation, *shemozzle* (*dated informal*), shenanigans (*informal*), song and dance (*informal*), stampede, stink (*informal*), stir, tempest, to-do (*informal*), tumult, turbulence, turmoil, unrest, unruliness, upheaval, uproar, *uproariousness*, upset

See also ARGUMENT (47)

52 Sudden Event

ACCIDENT, *n. An inevitable occurrence due to the action of immutable natural laws.* **Ambrose Bierce**

(*n*) ambush, attack, barrage, blackout, blast, blitz (*informal*), bolt from the blue, bombardment, bombshell (*informal*), boom, burst, cannonade, detonation, epidemic, eruption, explosion, flurry, fright, gallop, gust, hail, implosion, jailbreak, jolt, onrush, outbreak, outburst, raid, rain, rash, rush, sally, salvo, scramble, shock, shock wave, spate, storm, stream, surprise, takeover, thrust, thunderbolt, thunderclap, tidal wave, torrent, turn, uprush, upwelling, volley, wave, whoosh

53 Beginning

With the possible exception of the equator, everything begins somewhere. **Peter Fleming**

(*n*) accession, activation, advent, appearance, authorship, awakening, baptism, base, baseline, basis, beginning, birth, birthplace, blastoff, breeding ground, bridgehead, brink, catalyst, christening, commencement (*formal*), conception, constitution, creation, dawn, debut, derivation, embryo, emergence, entrée, establishment, font (*literary*), forefront, fountain, fountainhead, genesis, germ, germination, get-go (*US informal*), goad, head, hotbed, ignition, impulsion, inauguration, inception (*formal*), incitement, induction, infancy, initiation, installation, instigation, institution, *intro* (*informal*), introduction, investiture, jump-start, kickoff (*informal*), kick-start (*informal*), launch, launching pad, lead-in, leading edge, *liftoff*, materialization, mobilization, *naissance*, nativity, occasion, onset, opener (*informal*), opening, orientation, origin, *origination*, outset, passport, planning, *point of departure*, preliminary, prelude, preparation, preproduction, principle, progenitor, prologue, prompt, prompting, provenance, *push-start*, rebirth, registration, reintroduction, reissue, repository, root, roots, run-up, seed, source, spark, spring, springboard, start, starting point, *startup*, takeoff, threshold, toehold

54 End

We sometimes congratulate ourselves at the moment of waking from a troubled dream; it may be so the moment after death. **Nathaniel Hawthorne**

(*n*) abolition, abrogation (*formal*), adieu, annulment, autumn, breakaway, breakout, breakup, cessation, clampdown, cleanup, close, closedown, closing stages, closure, coda, completion, conclusion, *coup de grâce*, crack-up (*informal*), culmination, curfew, cutoff, deadline, death, deathblow, death knell, death warrant, decay, demerger, demise (*formal*), denouement (*formal*), departing, departure, desertion, destination, disappearance, disconnection, discontinuation, disengagement, disintegration, dissolution, divorce, elopement, end, ending, eradication, escape, evaporation, exit, exodus, *expiration*, expiry, extinction, farewell, finale, finalization, finish, flight, freeze, fruition, getaway, going, goodbye, halt, invalidation, *last leg*, *last nail in the coffin*, last resort, last straw, leave-taking (*literary*), neutralization, occlusion, parting, passing, perfection, pullout, retirement, retreat, ruination, secession, sendoff, separation, split-up, swan song, tail end, termination (*formal*), turnround, valedictory (*formal*), winter, withdrawal

See also DEATH AND BEREAVEMENT (927)

55 Intermediate Stages

There is no cure for birth and death save to enjoy the interval. **George Santayana**

(*n*) acme, *apogee*, flowering, golden age, high, low, low point, prime

See also PERIOD OF TIME (90), PERIOD OF REST (91)

56 Pauses and Phases

It is not enough/to be pause, to be hole/to be void, to be silent. **Edward Kamau Brathwaite**

(*n*) break, breakoff, breathing space, ceasefire, deferral, gap, grace period, hiatus, interception, interim, interlude, intermission, interregnum, interruption, interval, juncture, lag, layover (*US*), leg, let-up (*informal*), lull, meantime, moratorium, pause, phase, pit stop, plateau, respite, slot, space, stay, step, time lag

See also PERIOD OF TIME (90), PERIOD OF REST (91), LACK OF ACTIVITY (343)

57 Preparatory Event

When we mean to build,/We first survey the plot, then draw the model. **William Shakespeare**

(*n*) audition, casting, dress rehearsal, drill, dry run, dummy run, field test, fire drill, knock-up, practice, *practice session*, probation, rehearsal, road test, run-through, test, test drive, *test run*, trial, *trial run*, tryout, warm-up, workout

See also PREPARE FOR ACTION (290)

Seeming, Appearing to Be, and Representing

58 Seem to Be Something

All that we see or seem/Is but a dream within a dream. **Edgar Allan Poe**

(*v*) appear, approach, be close to, come across, feel like, look, reek, resemble, seem, smack, *smack of*, sound, take after

59 Represent Something or Somebody

How can we be sure that we are not impostors? **Jacques Lacan**

(*v*) act, *act for*, *act on behalf of*, be a symbol of, *betoken* (*literary*), capture, characterize, depict, deputize, embody, epitomize, exemplify, herald, illustrate, immortalize, mime, mirror, objectify, *personate*, personify, portray, present, reflect, represent, stand in, stand in for, substitute, symbolize, take the place of, typify

60 Pretend and Mimic

Those who do not want to imitate anything, produce nothing. **Salvador Dalí**

(*v*) act, affect, ape, assume, copy, emulate, fake, feign, imitate, impersonate, let on, look like, masquerade, mime, mimic, mirror, mock, parody, parrot, pass for, personify, play, play-act (*informal*), pose, pretend, pretend to be, put on, put on an act, reflect, role-play, sham, simulate, take off (*informal*)

See also JOKES AND TEASING (675)

61 Mean Something

The use...of words is to be sensible marks of ideas, and the ideas they stand for are their proper and immediate signification. **John Locke**

(*v*) add up, augur, be a sign of, bespeak, bode, connote, convey, count, denote, foreshadow, hang together, imply, indicate, make a statement, make out, make sense, mark, matter, mean, portend, presage, prognosticate, promise, refer, show, signal, signify, signpost, spell, stand for, suggest

See also MEANING (691)

62 Be About Something

Any general statement is like a check drawn on a bank. Its value depends on what is there to meet it. **Ezra Pound**

(*v*) appertain (*formal*), apply, be anchored in, centre, concern, cover, have to do with, involve, pertain to, refer, regard, rest on, treat

63 Expressions of Reference

A spade is never so merely a spade as the word/Spade would imply. **Christopher Fry**

(*adj*) abovementioned, aforementioned (*formal*), aforesaid (*formal*), said

(*conj*) as far as, seeing, *seeing as*, *seeing that*

(*prep*) about, according to, apropos (*formal*), as per, as regards, as to, concerning, considering, due to, on the subject of, re, regarding, relating to, relative to, respecting, towards, with reference to, with regard to, with respect to

64 Expressions Introducing Examples

A precedent embalms a principle. **William Scott**

(*adv*) for a kickoff (*informal*), *for a start*, *for example*, *for instance*, namely, such as, *viz*

65 Representations and General Examples

Modern art can only be born where signs become symbols. **Wassily Kandinsky**

(*n*) carbon copy, casting, characterization, copy, counterfeit, cross section, decoy, demo (*informal*), depiction, draft, dummy, effigy, emulation, example, *exemplification*, expression, fabrication, *graven image*, guise, guy, illustration, image, imagery, imitation, imitator, impersonation, impression, imprint, incarnation, instance, likeness, macrocosm, manifestation, mannequin, mask, microcosm, mimicry, misrepresentation, mock-up, model, mouthpiece, parody, parrot, pattern, persona, *personation*, personification, picture, piece, plug, portrait, portrayal, precedent, proxy, redolence, reflection, rendering, replication, representation, sample, sampler, sampling, scarecrow, sign, skeleton, *specimen*, swatch, symbolism, takeoff (*informal*), taste, tester, token, totem, *working example*

66 Representative

Imaginative consciousness represents a certain type of thought; a thought which is constituted in and by its object. **Jean-Paul Sartre**

(*adj*) acting, archetypal, archetypical, characteristic, classic, classical, diagrammatic, distinctive, emblematic, emblematical, exemplary (*formal*), expressive, figurative, illustrative, implicit, incarnate, indicative, *prototypical*, quintessential, redolent, representational, representative, suggestive, symbolic, symptomatic, textbook, token, totemic, typical

(*adv*) by way of, *redolently*, typically

67 Perfect Examples and Embodiments

So excellent a king, that was to this/Hyperion to a satyr. **William Shakespeare**

(*n*) archetype, baseline, bastion, beacon (*literary*), benchmark, byword, *case in point*, classic, core, *crème de la crème*, crystallization, distillation, embodiment, epitome, example, exemplar (*literary*), guide, ideal, index, litmus test, model, norm, original, paradigm, paragon, prototype, quintessence, role model, *shining example*, showpiece, standard

68 Indications, Signs, and Warnings

Signatures of all things I am here to read,/seaspawn and seawrack, the nearing tide, that rusty/boot. Snot-green, bluesilver, rust: coloured signs. **James Joyce**

(*n*) appetizer, augury, auspice, cue, forerunner, foretaste, harbinger, herald (*literary*), idea, indication, lead, mark, marker, omen, portent, precursor, prognostication, reminder, sign, signpost, storm cloud, symptom, taster, test, warning

69 Evidence and Proof

What is now proved was once, only imagin'd. **William Blake**

(*n*) a case in point, acid test, authority, case, confirmation, demonstration, evidence, facts, fingerprint, follow-on, footprint, giveaway, indictment, lead, proof, *proof of identity*, *proof of ownership*, *proof positive*, scent, spoor, substantiation, support, *telltale sign*, testament, testimony, trace, track, trail, validation, verification, vindication

70 Amount to and Equal

Enough is equal to a feast. **Henry Fielding**

(*v*) account for, add up to, amount to, average, boil down to (*informal*), come down to, come to, consist, constitute, equal, make up, number, *run to*, stack up (*US*), total

Situations and Outcomes

71 Situations

In some situations the right answer is the best answer, the wrong answer is the second best answer, and no answer is the worst answer. **Scott McNealy**

(*n*) affair, backdrop, background, *best-case scenario*, canvas, case, circumstance, climate, conditions, context, environment, forum, *how the land lies*, *how things stand*, landscape, lie of the land (*informal*), *present circumstances*, scenario, *set of circumstances*, situation, state of affairs, *state of play*, *state of things*, status quo

72 Difficult Situations

Comin' in on a Wing and a Prayer **Harold Adamson**

(*n*) adversity, bind, catch-22, close shave, crucible, crucifixion, deadlock, disfavour, disgrace, dishonour, disrepute, distress, emergency, entanglement, firing line, fix (*informal*), flashpoint, front line, *hard times*, *harsh conditions*, hell, *hornet's nest*, hot water (*informal*), hurry, imbroglio (*formal or literary*), impasse, indignity, jam (*informal*), kettle of fish, mess, minefield, nadir, *no-win situation*, obloquy (*formal or literary*), ordeal, pass, pickle (*informal*), plight, predicament, pressure, purgatory, quagmire, quandary, rock bottom, ruin, ruination, scrape (*informal*), spot (*informal*), stalemate, standoff, state (*informal*), *state of emergency*, stew (*informal*), *sticky situation*, sticky wicket (*informal*), *storm in a teacup*, tailspin (*informal*), tie, *tight corner*, *tight situation*, tight spot, trauma, *tricky situation*, vicious circle, vortex

See also UNCERTAINTY (560), PROBLEM (257)

73 In Trouble and Disadvantaged

Like a dull actor now/I have forgot my part and I am out,/Even to a full disgrace. **William Shakespeare**

(*adj*) abused, aggrieved, at a disadvantage, *between a rock and a hard place*, disgraced, disregarded, done for (*informal*), doomed, down, hamstrung, *hard-pressed*, high and dry, ill-used, *in a bind*, in a fix (*informal*), in a jam (*informal*), *in a predicament*, in a rush, *in a spot of bother* (*informal*), *in a tight corner*, *in a tight spot*, *in bad odour*, *in deep trouble*, *in deep water*, *in difficulty*, in dire straits, *in disgrace*, in hot water, *in serious trouble*, in the doghouse (*informal*), *in the lurch*, in the soup (*informal*), in the wrong, in trouble, losing, lost, mistreated, misunderstood, neglected, on the horns of a dilemma, on the spot, *oppressed*, *ostracized*, *ousted*, *out of favour*, *overburdened*, *overlooked*, *overstretched*, *overworked*, *persecuted*, pressed, *pressed for time*, pushed (*informal*), put-upon, stretched, *under a cloud*, *under a curse*, under attack, under fire, under pressure, undone, up the creek (*informal*), *up the creek without a paddle* (*informal*), up to your ears, washed-up (*informal*), with your back to the wall

See also BEATEN AND DEFEATED (78), IN DANGER (238)

74 Pleasant Situations

Bliss was it in that dawn to be alive,/But to be young was very heaven! **William Wordsworth**

(*adj*) *in the ascendant*, *in the lap of luxury*, *in the lead*, *in your prime*

(*n*) *bed of roses*, *cloud nine*, *clover*, domesticity, ease, *easy street*, *glory days*, good life, *halcyon days* (*literary*), *heaven on earth*, heyday, high life, *honeymoon period*, idyll, *lap of luxury*, *life of ease*, *life of Riley*, nirvana, pinnacle, *primrose path* (*literary*), *salad days* (*literary*), seventh heaven, *state of grace*, summer, wellbeing

See also SUCCESSFUL AND PROMISING (81)

75 Fail or Be Unsuccessful

My reputation grew with every failure. **George Bernard Shaw**

(*v*) backfire, bite the dust (*informal*), bomb (*informal*), cease trading, collapse, come down, come to grief, *come to naught* (*archaic or literary*), come to nothing, fail, fall by the wayside, fall down, fall flat, fall short, fall through, flop (*informal*), flunk (*informal*), fold, founder, free-fall, go bankrupt, *go belly up*, go down (*informal*), go down like a lead balloon (*slang*), *go down the drain*, *go down the tube* (*informal*), *go into liquidation*, *go off the rails*, *go pear-shaped* (*informal*), *go to seed*, go under, go up in smoke, go wrong, knuckle under, leave much to be desired, lose, lose out (*informal*), miscarry (*formal*), misfire, nose-dive, regress, sell out, shut, slip up (*informal*), strike out (*US informal*), succumb, surrender, *throw in the sponge* (*informal*), throw in the towel (*informal*), unravel, yield

76 Unsuccessful and Unpromising

Many go out for wool, and come home shorn themselves. **Miguel de Cervantes**

(*adj*) abortive, ailing, botched, disastrous, failed, failing, fruitless, frustrated, ill-omened, inauspicious, manqué, ruined, sunk, uneconomic, unprofitable, unpromising, unsuccessful, useless, vain

(*adv*) in vain, vainly

(*n*) uselessness

77 Failure

Failure is inevitable. Success is elusive. **Steven Spielberg**

(*n*) also-ran, anticlimax, ashes, bathos, breakdown, capitulation, collapse, comedown (*informal*), crash, decline, descent, disaster (*informal*), downfall, dud (*informal*), failure, fiasco, flop (*informal*), free fall, goner (*slang*), lemon (*informal*), letdown, loss, malfunction, meltdown (*informal*), nonstarter (*informal*), rout, ruin, slump, subjection, surrender, turkey (*US slang*), undoing, washout (*informal*)

78 Beaten and Defeated

A man is not finished when he is defeated. He is finished when he quits. **Richard Nixon**

(*adj*) beaten, *conquered*, defeated, finished, *overpowered*, overwhelmed, *trounced*, *vanquished*

See also IN TROUBLE AND DISADVANTAGED (73)

79 Succeed and Win

It is not enough to succeed. Others must fail. **Gore Vidal**

(*v*) ace (*US slang*), achieve, arrive, attain, bear fruit, be a success, blossom, bring home the bacon (*informal*), burgeon (*literary*), carry off, catch on (*informal*), come first, come off (*informal*), *come out on top*, compare, compete, excel, forge ahead, fulfil, gain ground, get ahead, get away with, get in, get somewhere, *go well*, *hit the big time* (*slang*), *hit the jackpot*, land on your feet, lead, live up to, make, make a name for yourself, make a splash, make good, make headway, make inroads, make it (*informal*), make out, make progress, make the grade, make your mark, manage, *max* (*US slang*), motor (*slang*), pass, *pass with flying colours*, pay off, peak, prevail, prosper, pull off (*informal*), qualify, romp (*informal*), sail through, shine, sparkle, squeak through (*informal*), star, succeed, take off (*informal*), take the lead, thrive, triumph, walk away, *walk it* (*informal*), win, work

80 Beat and Defeat

As always, victory finds a hundred fathers, but defeat is an orphan. **Galeazzo Ciano**

(*n*) annihilation, beating, conquest, defeat, drubbing, hammering (*informal*), *licking* (*informal*), pasting (*informal*), pounding, pulverization (*informal*), rout, suppression, thrashing, trouncing, walloping (*informal*), *whipping* (*informal*), whitewash (*informal*), *whopping*

(*v*) annihilate (*informal*), beat, beggar, best, better (*formal*), blow away (*US slang*), break, break down, bring down, cap, conquer, cream (*US informal*), crush, defeat, demolish (*informal*), destroy, down, drub, eclipse, emulate, finish (*informal*), get the better of, go one better, hammer (*informal*), improve on, knock out, leave behind, lick (*informal*), make mincemeat of, master, outclass, outdistance, outdo, outface, outflank, outfox, outgrow, outjockey, outmanoeuvre, outnumber, outpace, outperform, outride, outrun, outshine, outsmart, outstrip, outwit, overcome, overhaul, overpower, overshadow, overthrow, overwhelm, pip (*informal*), *pip to the post* (*informal*), pulverize (*informal*), put in the shade, quash, rise above, rise to (*informal*), rival, rout, run rings around, see off, slaughter (*slang*), snow under (*US*), squash, storm, subdue, subjugate, suppress, surmount, surpass, take, thrash, top, tower, transcend, triumph over, trounce, trump, upstage, vanquish, walk over (*informal*), wallop (*informal*), whitewash, wipe the floor with (*informal*)

81 Successful and Promising

Success is counted sweetest/By those who ne'er succeed. **Emily Dickinson**

(*adj*) alive, auspicious, bestselling, blockbusting, blooming, blossoming, boom, booming, budding, burgeoning, flourishing, fruitful, going, *going strong*, mobile, money-making, money-spinning (*informal*), prizewinning, prolific, promising, *propitious*, *prospering*, prosperous, rampant, rank, roaring, rosy, runaway (*informal*), successful, thriving, triumphal, triumphant, *unconquered*, *undefeatable*, undefeated, *unvanquished*, up, victorious, winning

(*adv*) famously, in front, on the move, on the up and up (*informal*), on top, promisingly, rampantly, successfully, triumphantly

See also PLEASANT SITUATIONS (74)

82 Success

Eighty percent of success is showing up. **Woody Allen**

(*n*) accomplishment, achievement, attainment, blockbuster (*informal*), checkmate, close call, conquest, coup, fruitfulness, fulfilment, glory, good name, headway, landslide, laurels, life's work, lifework (*US*), mobility, passage, progress, *propitiousness*, realization, runaway success, *runaway victory*, sellout, *smash hit*, success, successfulness, success story, triumph, victory, win, winner

83 Results and Outcomes

Our greatest glory is not in never falling, but in rising every time we fall. **Confucius**

(*adj*) ensuing, secondary

(*adv*) as a result, duly, in consequence (*formal*), in the event, thus (*formal*)

(*n*) aftereffect, aftermath, *aftershock*, avail, backlash, bottom line, brunt, byproduct, child, close thing, comeuppance (*informal*), consequence, corollary, dead heat, derivative, draw, effect, end product, end result, fallout, fate, finding, fruit, hangover, impact, impression, judgment, *just deserts*, *just reward*, knock-on effect, narrow escape, narrow squeak, near miss, near thing (*informal*), offshoot, outcome, outgrowth, penalty, price, product, punishment, ramification, ravages, reflex, repercussion, result, reverberations, scar, sequel, shock wave, side effect, spin-off, standoff (*US*), upshot

Concepts and Ideas

Time, Duration, and Speed

84 Past

The past is never dead, it is not even past. **William Faulkner**

(*adj*) all over, ancient, *ancient history*, antebellum, antediluvian, bygone, defunct, erstwhile, ex, former, in retrospect, lapsed, long-ago, old, onetime, outgoing, over and done with, past, prehistoric, primal, primeval, primitive, primordial, retroactive, retrospective, sometime (*formal*)

(*adv*) ago, at one time, *heretofore* (*formal*), historically, hitherto (*formal*), in retrospect, *in the past*, lately, latterly, of late, once, *once upon a time*, originally, recently, retrospectively, so far, *some time ago*, then, thus far, to date, until now, *until recently*, up till now, up to now, *up to the present moment, up to the present time, up until now*, yet

(*n*) antecedents, antiquity, *bygone days*, days gone by, *former times*, history, *long ago*, past, *past history*, prehistory, run-up, throwback, *times gone by, times of yore, times past, yesterday*, yesteryear

See also BEFORE, FIRST, AND PRECEDING (164), OLD, OLD-FASHIONED (168)

85 Present

PRESENT, *n. That part of eternity dividing the domain of disappointment from the realm of hope.* **Ambrose Bierce**

(*adj*) contemporary, current, existing, extant, firsthand, latter-day, modern-day, present, present-day, prevailing, topical

(*adv*) already, at once, at present, at the moment, at the present time, *at this moment*, at this moment in time, *at this point, at this point in time*, at this time, for now, for the meantime, for the time being, forthwith (*formal*), here, *in this day and age*, just, just now, meanwhile, newly, now, nowadays, presently, *right now*, straight, straightaway, straight off (*informal*), *straightway* (*archaic*), *this instant*, today, urgently

(*n*) actuality, present, present day, *the here and now, these days, this day and age*, topicality

86 Future

Time present and time past/Are both perhaps present in time future,/And time future contained in time past. **T. S. Eliot**

(*adj*) advanced, anticipated, approaching, at hand, awaited, coming, coming up, designate, due, elect, embryonic, emergent, expected, foreseeable, forthcoming, future, incipient, intended, in the making, *in the near future*, long-range, nascent, prospective, ready, *soon-to-be*, up-and-coming, *yet to come*

(*adv*) ahead, anon (*archaic or literary*), awhile (*literary*), before long, by and by (*literary*), hence (*formal*), henceforth (*formal*), *henceforward* (*formal*), hereafter (*formal*), *in a bit*, in a jiffy (*informal*), *in a little while, in a minute, in a second, in a short time, in a tick* (*informal*), *in a trice*, in a while, in due course, *in future, in half a shake*, in store, *in the fullness of time, in the future, in the long run, in the short term*, in time, momentarily (*US*), *one of these days*, presently, shortly, someday, sometime, soon, sooner or later, *until further notice, yet to be*

(*n*) future, *imminence*, lead time, outlook, posterity, *time ahead, time to come, years to come*

(*prep*) about to, ahead of, close to, on the threshold of, pending, until

See also ABOUT TO HAPPEN (33)

87 Times of Day

And wisely tell what hour o' the day/The clock does strike, by algebra. **Samuel Butler**

(*adj*) a.m., circadian, daily, diurnal, late, nightly, nocturnal, *off-peak*, per diem, p.m., *quotidian* (*formal*)

(*adv*) late, nightly

(*n*) afternoon, bedtime, break of day, cockcrow (*archaic or literary*), crack of dawn, darkness, date, dawn, day, daybreak, daylight, daytime, dinnertime, dusk, even (*literary*), evening, *eventide* (*literary*), first light, hour, lights out, *lunchtime*, mealtime, midday, midnight, morning, night, nightfall, nighttime, noon, noonday (*literary*), reveille, roll call, sundown, sunrise, sunset, sunup (*US*), *suppertime, taps*, tea-time, twilight

See also CLOCKS AND TIMERS (1125)

88 Times of Year

Four seasons fill the measure of the year;/There are four seasons in the mind of man. **John Keats**

(*adj*) annual, autumnal, biannual, biennial, monthly, quarterly, seasonal, yearly

(*adv*) biweekly, *fortnightly*, monthly, per annum, yearly

(*n*) autumn, birthdate, birthday, date, day, *dog days, Eastertide* (*literary*), *Eastertime, equinox*, eve, fall (*US*), midsummer, midweek, midwinter, season, *solstice*, spring, *springtide* (*literary*), springtime, summer, *summer solstice*, summertime, winter, *winter solstice, wintertime*

types of time period calendar month, fortnight, leap year, lunar month, month, quarter, semester, trimester, week, weekend, year

89 Epochs and Eras

History is a clock that people use to tell their political and cultural time of day. **John Henrik Clarke**

(*n*) age, century, decade, epoch, era, generation, lifetime, millennium, period, time, vintage

90 Period of Time

Art is long, life short; judgment difficult, opportunity transient. **Johann Wolfgang von Goethe**

(*n*) chapter, duration, extension, hour, lapse, length, life, period, run, session, shift, span, splurge (*informal*), stage, standing, streak, stretch, tenure (*formal*), term (*formal*), time, timescale, time span, wait, while

See also PAUSES AND PHASES (56), CHAIN OF EVENTS (163), INTERMEDIATE STAGES (55)

91 Period of Rest

It is well to lie fallow for a while. **Martin Farquhar Tupper**

(*n*) break, breather (*informal*), coffee break, *day off*, downtime, free time, furlough, holiday, *hols* (*informal*), leave, *leave of absence*, *leisure time*, lie-in (*informal*), *lunch break*, minibreak (*informal*), pause, playtime, *public holiday*, recess, *refreshment break*, repose, respite, rest, retirement, sabbatical, short break, sit-down (*informal*), slumber, spare time, stay, stop, stopover, *study leave*, tea break, time off, time out (*US*), vacation

See also LACK OF ACTIVITY (343), PAUSES AND PHASES (56)

92 Long Period of Time

Hold Infinity in the palm of your hand/And Eternity in an hour. **William Blake**

(*n*) aeon, *aeons*, ages (*informal*), donkey's years (*informal*), eternity, lifetime (*informal*), years, *yonks* (*slang*)

93 Short Period of Time

Thought is only a flash between two long nights, but this flash is everything. **Jules Henri Poincaré**

(*n*) bit, *blink of an eye*, bout, dose (*informal*), flash, instant, *jiff*, jiffy (*informal*), minute, mo (*informal*), moment, nanosecond, point, second, spell (*informal*), split second, stint, tick (*informal*), time, trice, twinkling, window

94 Permanence: Without End

History never stops. It progresses ceaselessly day and night. Trying to stop it is like trying to stop Geography. **Augusto Monterroso**

(*adj*) abiding, ageless, all-weather, *around-the-clock*, boundless, ceaseless, chronic, classic, constant, continual, continuing, continuous, customary, deathless, endless, enduring, eternal, evergreen, everlasting, full-time, habitual, haunting, immemorial, immortal, imperishable (*literary*), incessant, indelible, indestructible, indissoluble, ineradicable, *inextinguishable*, infinite, ingrained, insistent, interminable, lasting, lifelong, limitless, lingering, long-lasting, long-lived, long-standing, long-term, never-ending, nonstop, ongoing, perennial, permanent, perpetual, persistent, prolonged, relentless, remaining, remorseless, rooted, round-the-clock, *self-sustaining*, standing, steady, surviving, sustainable, sustained, timeless, *twenty-four-hour-a-day*, unabated, unalleviated, unbroken, unceasing, undying, unending, *unfading*, unfailing, uninterrupted, *unquenchable*, unrelenting, unrelieved, unremitting, unstoppable, well-established, well-tried, year-round

(*adv*) ad infinitum, ad nauseam, all along, all the time, always, around the clock, at every turn, consistently, constantly, day after day, *day in day out*, ever, evermore (*literary*), forever, forevermore (*literary*), for life, *immortally*, imperishably (*literary*), indefinitely, indelibly, indestructibly, *in perpetuity*, irrevocably, on, on end, *since time began*, since time immemorial, twenty-four/seven, *until the end of time*, *without end*

(*n*) *ceaselessness*, continuance, continuation, *continuousness*, *continuum*, endurance, *immortality*, imperishability (*literary*), *indestructibility*, *infinitude*, infinity, *limitlessness*, longevity, maintenance, permanence, perpetuation, perpetuity, persistence, preservation, prolongation, protraction, relentlessness, *remorselessness*, subsistence, survival, *sustainability*, *time immemorial*, timelessness, *time without end*, upkeep

95 Permanence: Without Change

Who can speak of eternity without a solecism, or think thereof without an ecstasy? Time we may comprehend, 'tis but five days elder than ourselves. **Thomas Browne**

(*adj*) changeless, consistent, constant, even, fixed, flat, immutable, incorruptible, inexorable (*formal*), invariable, irreparable, irreversible, irrevocable, non-negotiable, same, stable, static, steady, unalterable, unchangeable, unchanged, unchanging, uniform, unmodified, unreconstructed, *unvaried*, unvarying

(*adv*) consistently, fixedly, inexorably (*formal*)

(*n*) *changelessness*, consistency, constancy, continuity, fixedness, *immutability*, *invariability*, stability

96 Finiteness, Variability, and Transience

All finite things reveal infinitude. **Theodore Roethke**

(*adj*) alternate, changeable, changing, chequered, closed, discontinuous, disposable, episodic, erratic, evanescent, finite, fitful, floating, fluctuating, fluid, freakish, here today and gone tomorrow, impermanent, inconsistent, inconstant, interim, intermittent, irregular, movable, mutable, patchy, periodic, protean, provisional, provisory, reversible, seasonal, shifting, *short and sweet*, short-lived, short-term, straw-hat (*US*), temporary, throwaway, transient, transitional, transitory, unpredictable, unsettled, vaporous, variable

(*adv*) alternately, ephemerally, irregularly, off and on, quickly, unsteadily

(*n*) brevity, changeability, discontinuity, ephemeralness, *evanescence*, fluctuation, fluidity, impermanence, *mutability*, patchiness, shortness, *temporariness*, transience, unpredictability, unsteadiness, variability, *variableness*

97 Never and Infrequency

You may as well expect pears from an elm. **Miguel de Cervantes**

(*adj*) casual, episodic, few and far between (*informal*), infrequent, occasional, *once-in-a-lifetime*, rare, scattered, spasmodic, sporadic

(*adv*) at times, *every now and again*, every now and then, *every so often*, from time to time, *hardly ever*, never, now and again, now and then, *once in a blue moon* (*informal*), once in a while, rarely, seldom, sometimes

(*n*) exceptionality, infrequency

98 Promptness: Early

Three o'clock is always too late or too early for anything you want to do. **Jean-Paul Sartre**

(*adj*) early, premature, untimely

(*adv*) ahead, *ahead of schedule*, ahead of time, beforehand, early, *in plenty of time*, in time, sooner

99 Promptness: On Time

The only way to be sure of catching a train is to miss the one before it. **G. K. Chesterton**

(*adj*) on time, prompt, punctual

(*adv*) at the appointed time, *in good time*, *in the nick of time*, on the dot, on time, sharp

(*n*) promptness, punctuality

100 Promptness: Late

I've been on a calendar, but never on time. **Marilyn Monroe**

(*adj*) behind, behindhand, behind schedule, belated, delayed, eleventh-hour, last-minute, late, overdue, standby, tardy, *unpunctual*

(*adv*) late

(*n*) *belatedness*, *eleventh hour*, last minute, lateness, tardiness, *unpunctuality*

101 Promptness: Badly Timed

Vain favour! coming, like most other favours long deferred and often wished for, too late! **Charlotte Brontë**

(*adj*) badly timed, ill-timed, inconvenient, inexpedient, inopportune, *mistimed*, *out of sync*, unseasonable, untimely

(*adv*) unseasonably

102 Speed

Or like a poet woo the moon,/Riding an armchair for my steed,/And with a flashing pen harpoon/Terrific metaphors of speed. **Roy Campbell**

(*n*) abruptness, acceleration, alacrity, briskness, cadence, celerity (*formal*), differential, fastness, *fleetness* (*literary*), haste, *momentariness*, pace, *precipitateness*, *precipitousness*, promptness, quickness, rapidity, *rapidness*, rate, readiness, rush, slowness, sluggishness, speed, speediness, suddenness, swiftness, velocity

See also CHANGE OF SPEED: MORE (397), CHANGE OF SPEED: LESS (398)

103 Moving Quickly

Celerity is never more admir'd/Than by the negligent. **William Shakespeare**

(*adj*) accelerated, agile, brisk, fast, gushing, hasty, *hurtling*, nippy, plunging, precipitate, quick, rapid, rattling, smart, spanking, speeding, speedy, zippy (*informal*)

(*adv*) agilely, at a lick (*informal*), at a rate of knots, at the double, briskly, cleanly, fast, *full speed ahead*, *full steam ahead*, hotfoot, in a flash, in a hurry, *like a bat out of hell* (*informal*), *like the wind*, quickly, smartly, speedily, swiftly

(*n*) swift

See also MOVE FAST (314)

104 Happening Quickly

The dawn speeds a man on his journey, and speeds him too in his work. **Hesiod**

(*adj*) abrupt, *alacritous*, breakneck, brief, cracking (*informal*), cursory, double-quick (*informal*), ephemeral, expeditious, express, extemporaneous, extempore, extraordinaire, fast, fleeting, flying, fugitive, headlong, hurried, immediate, in a hurry, instant, instantaneous, lightning, machine-gun, meteoric, momentary, overnight, passing, precipitate, prompt, quick, quick-fire, *rapid-fire*, ready, rushed, sharp, short, snap, snappy, split-second, sudden, summary, superficial, unplanned, unprepared, unrehearsed, up-tempo, whirlwind, whistle-stop

(*adv*) all at once, all of a sudden, apace, at speed, directly (*formal*), double-quick (*informal*), extempore, furiously, hastily, headlong, hurriedly, immediately, in a flash, in a rush, *in haste*, in less than no time, *in next to no time*, *in no time*, *in one fell swoop*, instantly, *in the blink of an eye*, *in the twinkling of an eye*, *in two shakes of a lamb's tail*, lickety-split (*informal*), *like a bolt from the blue*, like a shot, like greased lightning, momentarily, now, on the spot, out of the blue, outright, overnight, pdq (*informal*), pell-mell, posthaste, pronto (*informal*), *quick as a flash*, quickly, readily, responsively, right away, sharpish (*informal*), sharply, short, summarily, superficially, *with alacrity*, without a second thought, *without demur*, without further ado, *without hesitation*

(*interj*) chop-chop (*informal*)

105 Moving Slowly

How slow the Wind—/how slow the sea—/how late their feathers be! **Emily Dickinson**

(*adj*) dawdling, dilatory, inert, languid, languorous, leaden, leisurely, measured, plodding, poky (*US*), sedate, slow, *slow but sure*, *slow-moving*, sluggish, unrushed

(*adv*) painfully, *slowly but surely*

See also MOVE SLOWLY (315)

106 Happening Slowly

To live is to be slowly born. **Antoine de Saint-Exupéry**

(*adj*) draggy (*informal*), drawn-out, extended, gradual, lengthy, lingering, long, long-drawn-out, marathon, organic, protracted, retarded, slow, *slow as molasses* (*US*), *slow-going*, *slow-paced*, *snail-paced*, *spun-out* (*adv*) at your leisure, at your own pace, bit by bit, by degrees, day by day, little by little, slowly, steadily, step by step

107 Frequent and Often

Man is frequently overwhelmed by the immense and alien power of the universe. **Wilson Harris**

(*adj*) congenital, constant, cyclical, frequent, monthly, periodic, recurrent, recurring, regular, repeated, rhythmic

(*adv*) daily, much, often, on and off, regularly, repetitively, time after time

(*n*) frequency, incidence, occurrence, rhythm

108 Usually

It's deadly commonplace, but, after all, the commonplaces are the great poetic truths. **Robert Louis Stevenson**

(*adv*) as a rule, averagely, broadly, by and large, characteristically, commonly, conventionally, customarily, generally, generically, globally, habitually, historically, in general, *in most cases*, mainly, more often than not, mostly, normally, on the whole, ordinarily, overall, popularly, routinely, traditionally, typically, usually

109 Again

Once more unto the breach, dear friends, once more. **William Shakespeare**

(*adv*) afresh, again, again and again, *all over again*, anew, *de novo*, newly, *once again*, *once more*, *over again*, *over and over*, *over and over again*, time and again, *time and time again*

See also REPETITION (29), HAPPEN AGAIN (28), RECOMMENCE AND RESUME (269)

Quantity, Portion, Extent, and Degree

110 Degree and Extent

Measure what is measurable, and make measurable what is not so. **Galileo**

(*n*) ambit, breadth, degree, dilution, extent, gamut, gradation, grasp, layer, level, margin, measure, notch, orbit, parameter, percentage, perspective, portion, proportion, radius, rate, reach, room, scale, scope, spectrum, spread, sweep

111 Area and Range

The wonder is, not that the field of the stars is so vast, but that man has measured it. **Anatole France**

(*n*) area, band, column, corridor, cross section, elbowroom, file, lap, line, mileage, module, panel, parcel, part, patch, piece, plot, queue, range, row, scale, section, sector, segment, side, stretch, strip, subdivision, tract

112 Amount and Quantity

I must have a prodigious quantity of mind; it takes me as much as a week, sometimes, to make it up. **Mark Twain**

(*adj*) any, certain, selected, several, some

(*n*) allocation, amount, buildup, burden, complement, count, *dessertspoonful*, diet, dosage, dose, element, figure, finger, fix (*humorous*), fund, helping, intake, lot, number, pair, part, payload, portion, quantity, ration, serving, share, shot (*informal*), spoonful, supply, *tablespoonful*, *teaspoonful*, throughput, volume, yield

113 Apportionment

All who joy would win/Must share it,—Happiness was born a twin. **Lord Byron**

(*adj*) bipartite, double, dual, *duple*, per capita, *per head*, *per person*, treble, tripartite, triple, twin, twofold

(*adv*) apiece, double, piecemeal, twice

(*prep*) per

114 Amount of Liquid

You don't water a camel with a spoon. **U.S. proverb**

(*n*) bead, dab, dash, dewdrop, dot, drip, drop, droplet, gush, jet, puddle, spout, spray, spurt, squirt, stream, surge, trickle

See also DRINK (712)

115 Amount of Solid or Semi-Solid

When the aggregate amount of solid matter transported by rivers...shall be reduced to arithmetical computation, the result will appear most astonishing. **Charles Lyell**

(*n*) bale, bar, blob, brick, briquette, cake, chew (*US*), chuck, clod, clot, clove, coagulation, daub, divot, dollop (*informal*), fist, fistful, glob (*informal*), gob (*slang*), *gobbet*, hank, ingot, length, lump, nugget, part, piece, *plateful*, plug, rasher, ream, ribbon, ruck, sheaf, sheet, skein, slice, splotch, strand, tablet, tendril (*literary*), tress, tuft, wedge

116 Amount of Gas

It was a giant column that soon took the shape of a supramundane mushroom. Referring to the explosion of an atomic bomb. **William L. Laurence**

(*n*) billow, breath, pall, plume, puff, waft

117 Many, Much, Large Amount

My bounty is as boundless as the sea,/My love as deep; the more I give to thee,/The more I have, for both are infinite. **William Shakespeare**

(*adj*) abounding, abundant, *aplenty*, appreciable, bounteous (*literary*), bountiful (*literary*), bumper, copious, countless, galore, generous, goodly, great, handsome, incalculable, incredible (*informal*), inexhaustible, innumerable, large, lavish, liberal, lush, luxuriant, manifold, many, much, multiple, *multitudinous*, myriad, numberless, numerous, opulent, plenteous (*literary*), plentiful, princely, profuse, prolific (*formal*), rich, umpteen (*informal*), *uncountable*, uncounted, untold, various

(*adv*) a good deal, a great deal, a lot, appreciably, hand

over fist, handsomely, heaps (*informal*), *in a big way*, in abundance, in bulk, in force, in strength, *in throngs*, lavishly, liberally, miles (*informal*), much, thickly, tons

(*n*) abundance, accretion, acres (*informal*), avalanche, bags of (*informal*), bank, bounty (*literary*), buckets (*informal*), *busload*, coachload, cornucopia, deluge, dozens (*informal*), droves, flood, flood tide, gallons, *gazillion* (*slang*), heap, heaps (*informal*), *hordes*, horn of plenty, host, inundation (*formal*), *large amount*, lashings, lavishness, loads (*informal*), lots, lushness, luxuriance, masses (*informal*), maximum, millions, mine, mound, mountain, *multifariousness*, multiplicity, multitude, myriad, *numerousness*, oodles (*informal*), pile, plenty, plurality, pots (*informal*), predominance, preponderance (*formal*), profusion, raft (*informal*), scads (*informal*), *scores*, *shedload*, shower, *squillion*, stack, stacks (*informal*), stash, swarm, ton (*informal*), tons (*informal*), trillion (*informal*), *truckload*, wad, wealth, zillion (*informal*)

(*pron*) a lot, no end of (*informal*)

118 Too Much

'Tis not the drinking that is to be blamed, but the excess. **Edward Dyer**

(*adj*) astronomical (*informal*), *de trop*, excessive, inordinate, inundated, lavish, *OTT* (*informal*), *overabundant*, overmuch, over-the-top (*informal*), superabundant, superfluous, ultra

(*adv*) disproportionately, lavishly, overmuch, to excess, too

(*n*) excess, excessiveness, *exorbitance*, glut, *immoderateness* (*formal*), inundation (*formal*), overabundance, overcrowding, overkill, overload, overmuch, overspill, oversupply, plethora, stiffness, superfluity, surfeit, surplus, unreasonableness

119 Few, Little, Small Amount

There are no intrinsic reasons for the scarcity of capital. **John Maynard Keynes**

(*adj*) endangered, few, least, marginal, minimal, minor, *not many*, one or two, piddling (*informal*), slight

(*adv*) gently, remotely, slightly

(*n*) *a drop in the bucket* (*US*), *a drop in the ocean*, billionth, element, flavour, flicker, glimpse, handful, hint, iota, jot, minimum, mite (*dated*), modicum, note, *not much*, nuance, ounce, pin (*dated informal*), pinch, scattering, scent, scintilla, semblance, shade, shadow, *small amount*, smattering, *smidge* (*informal*), smidgen (*informal*), soupçon, spot, sprinkle, sprinkling, subtlety, suspicion, tad (*informal*), tang, *thimbleful*, tincture, tinge, touch, trace, trifle, undertone, vein, whiff, whisker

(*pron*) a few, little

120 Too Few, Too Little

Just one being is lacking, and the whole world is empty of people. **Alphonse de Lamartine**

(*adj*) bare, inadequate, incommensurate, inquorate, in short supply, insufficient, lacking in, low, meagre, mean, measly (*informal*), mere, mingy (*informal*), niggardly, nugatory, paltry, scant, scanty, scarce, short-handed, short-staffed, skimpy, spare, sparing, sparse, *thin on the ground*, *too few*, *too little*, understrength

(*n*) austerity, dearth, deficiency, deficit, dispossession, drought, inadequacy, insufficiency, loss, meagreness, nonexistence, *paltriness*, paucity, poverty, rareness, rarity, *scantiness*, *scantness*, scarceness, scarcity, shortage, shortfall, sparseness

(*pron*) *hardly any*

121 None

None but himself can be his parallel. **Lewis Theobald**

(*adj*) no

(*n*) cipher, *goose egg* (*slang*), nil, nix (*US dated slang*), nought, zero, zilch (*informal*), zip (*US informal*)

(*pron*) nobody, none, no one, nothing

122 More and Excess

To seek the beauteous eye of heaven to garnish,/Is wasteful and ridiculous excess. **William Shakespeare**

(*adj*) accompanying, added, additional, add-on, another, auxiliary, emergency, excess, extra, further, last, more, new, other, residual, spare, stand-by, subsidiary, supernumerary, supplemental, supplementary, supporting, surplus, *too much*, unwanted, waste

(*adv*) else, extra

(*n*) *added extras*, addition, add-on, alloy, *appurtenance* (*formal*), backlog, backup, bonus, extra, frills, inclusion, makeweight, overflow, permeation, proliferation, *reinforcements*, replenishment, spillage, spurt, stand-by, supplement, top-up

(*prep*) above, in excess of, over

123 Remainder and Remainders

The poem is not made up of these letters that I plant like nails, but of the white that remains on the paper. **Paul Claudel**

(*n*) balance, carryover, clippings, deposition, dinosaur, dregs (*literary*), end, fossil, leavings, *lees*, leftover, leftovers, legacy, oddments, *ort* (*US*), *parings*, peelings, relic, remainder, *remainders*, remains, remnant, *remnants*, rest, ruin, scraps, *shavings*, shell, trimmings, wastage

See also RUBBISH AND USELESS OBJECTS (1248), UNPLEASANT AND DIRTY SUBSTANCES (1267)

124 Less

Less is more. **Ludwig Mies van der Rohe**

(*adj*) expurgated, fewer, less, stripped, stripped-down

(*n*) abatement, cutback, dip, drop, falloff, haemorrhage, minus, relaxation

(*prep*) below, less, under, without

125 Measureable Portion

I have measured out my life with coffee spoons. **T. S. Eliot**

(*n*) cut (*informal*), fourth, fraction, golden mean, *half*, mean, per cent, percentage (*informal*), *percentile*, proportion, quarter, *quartile*, quota, quotient, ratio, *third*, whole

126 All

All is for the best in the best of all possible worlds. **Voltaire**

(*adj*) across-the-board, aggregate (*formal*), all in, all-or-nothing, any, at large, each, every, gross, *hundred per cent*, systemic, whatsoever

(*adv*) all told, altogether, bag and baggage, en bloc, en masse, globally, in all, *in its entirety, in total*, lock, stock, and barrel, *warts and all*, whatever

(*n*) all-comers, caboodle (*informal*), everybody, everyone, everything, *grand total*, sum, summation, sum total, *the whole ball of wax* (*US informal*), *the whole enchilada* (*US slang*), *the whole kit and caboodle* (*informal*), *the whole lot, the whole shebang* (*informal*), total, totality, whole, *whole lot*

(*pron*) all, all and sundry, each, one and all, *the whole*, whatever

See also WHOLENESS AND COMPLETENESS (199)

127 Small Piece

It is a small thing that is taken to measure a big thing. **African (Ashanti) proverb**

(*n*) atom, bit, bite, chip, chipping, chippings, crumb, filing, flake, fleck, fraction, fragment, globule, granule, molecule, morsel, mote, nibble, nip, particle, pip, scale, scrap, shard, shaving, shred, sliver, smithereens (*informal*), snippet, speck, speckle, splinter, spot, *tittle*, vestige, whit (*informal*), wisp

128 Large Piece

There is always something larger than what is large. **Anaxagoras**

(*n*) block, chunk, hunk, slab, wad, wodge (*informal*)

129 Enough and Sufficient

The greatest thing in the world is to know how to be self-sufficient. **Michel de Montaigne**

(*adj*) adequate, ample, enough, moderate, plenty (*informal*), satisfying, sufficient

(*adv*) amply, plenty (*US informal*)

(*n*) adequacy, average, quorum, sufficiency

(*v*) suffice (*formal*)

130 To a Great Extent

What we think and feel and are is to a great extent determined by the state of our ductless glands and our viscera. **Aldous Huxley**

(*adv*) acutely, agonizingly, altogether, astronomically (*informal*), awfully, big time (*slang*), by far, considerably, cracking (*informal*), crushingly, dearly, deeply, desperately, devoutly (*formal*), dreadfully, eminently, enormously, especially, ever so, excessively, extensively, extra, extraordinarily, extremely, fairly, famously, far, far and away, fearfully (*informal*), fiendishly, fiercely, gigantically, greatly, grossly, heartily, heavily, highly, hopelessly, horribly, hugely, immaculately, immeasurably, immensely, implicitly, impossibly, incalculably, incredibly (*informal*), indescribably, inestimably, infinitely, *inordinately*, in particular, intensely, jolly (*dated informal*), madly, massively (*informal*), measurably, mightily, monstrously, monumentally, mortally, most, notoriously, overly, overpoweringly, overwhelmingly, particularly, peculiarly, plumb (*US informal*), powerfully, pre-eminently, prodigiously, profoundly, rather, real (*US informal*), really, richly, right, savagely, seriously (*informal*), shockingly, significantly, sorely (*formal*), soundly, stupendously, substantially, substantively, supremely, terribly, terrifically, thumping (*informal*), thundering (*dated informal*), tremendously, truly, unduly, unspeakably, vastly, very, walloping (*informal*)

131 Absolute and Absolutely

To die for a religion is easier than to live it absolutely. **Jorge Luis Borges**

(*adj*) abject, absolute, arrant, blank, blithering (*informal*), complete, consummate, definitive, drastic, entire, flat, great, mortal, out-and-out, outright, pure, rank, sheer, stark, stiff, straight-out (*US informal*), thorough, thoroughgoing, total, unmitigated, unqualified, utter

(*adv*) decidedly, definitively, diametrically, directly, downright, dramatically, exclusively, just, outright, purely, quite, radically, roundly, signally, simply, spotlessly, stark, stone-cold (*informal*), thoroughly, through and through, totally, well (*slang*), wholly

132 Critically and Seriously

Everything must be taken seriously, nothing tragically. **Adolphe Thiers**

(*adv*) badly, bitterly, critically, dangerously, deadly, deathly, fatally, frightfully, gravely, grievously, lethally, mortally, seriously, terminally, wretchedly

133 Approximately

None of us can estimate what we do when we do it from instinct. **Luigi Pirandello**

(*adj*) approximate, ballpark (*US informal*), broad, crude, inexact, pushing, rough, virtual

(*adv*) about, crudely, *give or take*, going on for, *in the region of*, just about, more or less, *near enough*, nigh on, *of the order of, or so*, roughly, *roughly speaking*, say, some, thereabouts, there or thereabouts (*informal*)

(*prep*) around, circa, round about

See also VAGUENESS (244)

134 To a Certain Extent

Partial nuclear disarmament...is...like talking about partial circumcision. **Robin Williams**

(*adj*) comparative, relative

(*adv*) a bit (*informal*), almost, any, as good as, barely, by a hair's-breadth, close on, close to, fairly, fractionally, hardly, ill, imperceptibly, in moderation, in part, just, kind of (*informal*), little, marginally, merely, mildly, minimally, moderately, modestly, narrowly, near, nearly, negligibly, not quite, only, partially, partly, partway, practically, pretty, quite, rather, reasonably, remotely, scarcely, slightly, something, somewhat, *sort of* (*informal*), subtly, thinly, to all intents and purposes, virtually, well-nigh

135 Not

Outside the huge negations pass/Like whirlwinds writing on the grass. **George Barker**

(*adv*) by no means, even less, negatively, never, no, on no account, on the contrary, under no circumstances

(*prep*) apart from, aside from, bar, barring, but, except, *except for*, excepting (*formal*), excluding, irrespective of, minus, not counting, notwithstanding (*formal*), regardless, *sans* (*literary or humorous*), save, *save for*, short of

136 Also

Every spark adds to the fire. **U.S. proverb**

(*adj*) either, plus

(*adv*) also, as well, besides, equally, similarly, too

(*conj*) and, and/or, as well as

(*prep*) along with, among, apart from, aside from, coupled with, cum (*informal*), including, in conjunction with, in cooperation with, over and above, plus, together with, with

137 Expressions Introducing Extra Information

I knew one that when he wrote a letter, he would put that which was most material in the postscript, as if it had been a by-matter. **Francis Bacon**

(*adv*) additionally, alternatively, besides, by the way, furthermore, in addition, in addition to, in any case, in any event, incidentally, inter alia (*formal*), *into the bargain*, likewise, moreover, nay (*archaic or literary*), secondly, then, *to boot*, to cap it all, *what is more*, what's more, yet again

138 Mainly and Primarily

Be careful still of the main chance. **John Dryden**

(*adv*) above all, chiefly, especially, essentially, even more, first and foremost, in essence, largely, *most of all*, mostly, on balance, particularly, predominantly, preponderantly, primarily, principally, purely, solely

See also MOST IMPORTANT AND MAIN (194)

139 Majority

Fools are in a terrible, overwhelming majority, all the wide world over. **Henrik Ibsen**

(*adv*) tops (*informal*)

(*n*) bulk, ceiling, greatest, limit, lion's share, majority, maximum, plurality (*US*), threshold

(*pron*) most

140 Money

If you borrow $2000 dollars from a bank and can't pay it back, you have a problem, but if you borrow a million and can't repay, they have a problem. **Anonymous**

(*n*) bread (*dated slang*), cash, change, coin, *dosh* (*slang*), dough (*slang*), kitty, lolly (*informal*), loot (*informal*), money, nest egg, pool, *readies* (*informal*), *ready cash*, *ready money*, spending money, whip-round (*informal*)

See also EXPENDITURE (424), FINANCIAL ASSETS (463), MONEY, PAYMENTS, AND CHARGES (800)

141 Large Amount of Money

Where large sums of money are concerned, it is advisable to trust nobody. **Agatha Christie**

(*n*) an arm and a leg (*informal*), bomb (*informal*), *boodle* (*slang*), bundle (*slang*), fortune, mint (*informal*), pile (*informal*), *tidy sum* (*informal*), *wad* (*US informal*)

142 Small Amount of Money

Lack of money is the root of all evil. **George Bernard Shaw**

(*n*) bagatelle (*formal*), chicken feed (*informal*), peanuts (*informal*), pin money, pittance, pocket money

Relatedness and Connection

143 Related

It is the attainment of a new kind of relationship with others and with himself which ultimately heals the patient. **Anthony Storr**

(*adj*) *affiliated*, aligned, allied, amalgamated, associate, associated, attendant, caught up, causative, cognate, coincidental, concomitant, confederate, connected, contextual, cumulative, imitative, in-built, incidental, incorporated, indivisible, inherent, instrumental, integral, integrated, interactive, involved, joined, kindred, linked, piggyback, related, sister, unified, united, vicarious, wedded

(*adv*) accompanied by

(*prep*) after, by

144 Connections

A hidden connection is stronger than an obvious one. **Heraclitus**

(*n*) adhesion, affiliation, alignment, allegiance, alliance, amalgamation, attribution, axis, bond, bonding, bridge, causality, coincidence (*formal*), common denominator, communion, comparison, concomitance, confluence, conjunction, connection, consolidation, convergence, correlation, correspondence, coupling, hierarchy, interplay, intersection, involvement, junction, juxtaposition, kinship, ladder, liaison, ligature (*formal*), link, linkage, linkup, membership, nexus, order, overlap, pecking order, pertinence, rapport, *relatedness*, relationship, relativity, rubric, tie, tie-in, tie-up, union

See also FASTEN, LINK, AND JOIN (409)

145 Creating Connection

The word connects the visible trace with the invisible thing. . .like a frail emergency bridge flung over an abyss. **Italo Calvino**

(*v*) affiliate, ascribe (*formal*), associate, blame, bracket, bring together, compare, confederate, connect, correlate, correspond, equate, federate, identify, implicate, impute, interact, interconnect, interrelate, intersect, involve, join, join together, liken, link, meet, overlap, pair, relate, straddle, subsume, tie in, touch, twin, unify

See also COMBINE AND MIX (401)

146 Variety, Type, Kind

Variety is the soul of pleasure. **Aphra Behn**

(*n*) bracket, brand, breed, category, class, classification, description, division, family, fashion, form, genre, genus, grade, grouping, hue, ilk, isotope, kind, make, mode, model, mould, nature, pigeonhole, sort, species, stamp, status, strain, style, subcategory, subgroup, subset, subspecies, type, variety, version

147 Unrelatedness and Separateness

I never found the companion that was so companionable as solitude. **Henry David Thoreau**

(*adj*) breakaway, detachable, detached, discrete, divisible, exclusive, foreign, freestanding, heterogeneous, individual, isolated, lone, removable, separable, separate, single, sole, specific, unconnected, unincorporated, unrelated

(*adv*) aside, distinctively, independently, in isolation, separately, severally, singly

(*n*) disjointedness, distinctiveness, independence, individuality, otherness, randomness, unconformity

See also EXTRAORDINARY: UNCOMMON (206), SAMENESS (151)

148 Reciprocity and Interdependence

Action and counteraction...in the natural and in the political world...draws out the harmony of the universe. **Edmund Burke**

(*adj*) conditional, contingent, dependent, ensemble, inseparable, interdependent, interracial, modular, multilateral, mutual, reciprocal, subject to, symbiotic, *synergetic*, two-way

(*adv*) communally, inextricably

(*n*) arrangement, collaboration, complicity, cooperation, dependence, give-and-take (*informal*), reciprocation, reciprocity, reliance, symbiosis, synergy, teamwork

(*v*) accompany, depend, depend on, hang on, hinge on, live off, rely, ride, turn on

See also ACTING WITH OTHERS (286)

149 Similarity

As lyke as one pease is to another. **John Lyly**

(*adj*) akin, alike, analogous, close, comparable, derivative, like, mimetic, *not unlike*, *of a kind*, *on a par*, reminiscent, resembling, similar, verging on

(*adv*) similarly

(*n*) affinity, *alikeness*, analogue, community, likeness, resemblance, similarity, similitude (*formal*)

(*prep*) after, close to, like, near

150 Difference

There is more difference within the sexes than between them. **Ivy Compton-Burnett**

(*adj*) alternate, alternative, assorted, catholic, clashing, composite, contrasting, deviant, different, disparate, disproportionate, dissimilar, distinct, distinguishable, divergent, divers (*formal*), diverse, eclectic, else, loose, miscellaneous, mixed, motley, multicultural, multifarious, multipartite, multiracial, *nothing like*, pluralistic, poles apart, ragtag, sundry, unaccustomed, *unalike*, unequal, uneven, unlike, variant, varied, various, *varying*

(*adv*) differently, diversely, else, in lieu, *in sharp contrast*, instead, rather, unequally, unevenly

(*n*) a whole new ball game (*slang*), contrast, deviance, deviation, dichotomy, difference, differentiation, digression, disagreement, discrepancy, discrimination, disparity, disproportion, dissimilarity, distinction, divergence, dualism, duality, eclecticism, gap, *heterogeneity*, imbalance, inconsistency, inequality, irregularity, nonconformity, *odd one out*, particularity, pluralism, separateness, *something else entirely*, variance, variant, variation

(*prep*) far from, instead of

(*v*) contrast, differ, disagree, *run counter to*, set apart, vary

See also OPPOSITE (158)

151 Sameness

The man who views the world at 50 the same as he did at 20 has wasted 30 years of his life. **Muhammad Ali**

(*adj*) duplicate, equal, exchangeable, homogeneous, identical, indistinguishable, interchangeable, *like two peas in a pod*, matching, no different, one and the same, one-to-one, portmanteau, same, selfsame, stereotypical, synonymous, tantamount, twin, *undifferentiated*, uniform, very

(*adv*) *homogeneously*, uniformly

(*n*) duplication, homogeneity, homogeneousness, *identicalness*, monotony, oneness, reduplication, regularity, sameness, uniformity

See also UNRELATEDNESS AND SEPARATENESS (147)

152 Copies and Replicas

Man, as he is, is not a genuine article. He is an imitation of something, and a very bad imitation. **Peter Ouspensky**

(*n*) backup, chip off the old block (*informal*), clone, copy, dead ringer (*informal*), doppelgänger, double, dummy, duplicate, duplication, facsimile, knockoff (*informal*), lookalike (*informal*), mirror image, reflection, replica, reprint, reproduction, spitting image (*informal*), twin

See also COPY AND DUPLICATE (403)

153 Superiority

Sometimes I feel so unutterably superior to the people surrounding me that I marvel at my ability to live among them. **Kenneth Williams**

(*adj*) a cut above, advanced, choice, chosen, exalted (*formal*), finest, foremost, greater, highest, high-grade, in charge, lofty, noble, optimum, peak, peerless, picked, preferential, premier, premium, prime, red-carpet, select, sovereign, special, super, superfine, superior, supreme, tiptop (*informal*), top, top-class, top-drawer, top-flight, topmost, topnotch (*informal*), top-of-the-range, top-quality, transcendent, unequalled, unmatched, unparalleled, unsurpassed, upper, utmost, vintage, world-class

(*n*) ascendancy, cream, edge, flower, precedence, predominance, pre-eminence, seniority, superiority, supremacy, top drawer, transcendence

See also EXTRAORDINARY: AMAZING (205)

154 Inferiority

No one can make you feel inferior without your consent. **Eleanor Roosevelt**

(*adj*) ancillary, assistant, buck (*US*), inferior, junior, lesser, lower, minor, second-rate, subnormal, subsidiary, substandard, third-rate

(*adv*) below

(*n*) inferiority, subordination

See also ORDINARINESS (245)

155 Equality

EQUALITY*...is the thing. It is the only true and central premise from which constructive ideas can radiate freely and be operated without prejudice.* **Mervyn Peake**

(*adj*) commensurate (*formal*), democratic, egalitarian, equal, equitable (*formal*), equivalent, even, evenhanded, fair, level, nondiscriminatory, on a par with, parallel, proportional, proportionate, quits (*informal*), symmetrical

(*adv*) equally, evenhandedly, fairly, fifty-fifty, neck and neck (*informal*)

(*n*) analogy, equal, equality, equity (*formal*), equivalence, equivalent, evenhandedness, fairness, level pegging, match, offset, parallel, parity, rival, symmetry

(*prep*) as good as

(*v*) balance out, be consistent with, come up to, draw, equal, equalize, even out, fit, match, rival, tally, tie

See also MORALLY GOOD (775)

156 Harmony

I have cherished the ideal of a democratic and free society in which all persons live together in harmony and with equal opportunites. **Nelson Mandela**

(*adj*) *at one with*, cohesive, compatible, complementary, compliant, congruent (*formal*), consistent, consonant (*formal*), corresponding, harmonious, harmonized, harmonizing, integrated, *in tune*, like-minded, matching, *of one mind*, on the same wavelength, solid, sympathetic, unanimous, well-balanced, well-matched, well-suited

(*adv*) *in agreement*, *in harmony*, in line, in step, *in sync* (*informal*), in time

(*n*) accord, agreement, armistice, balance, bargain, coexistence, cohesion, complement, compliance, conciliation, concord, concurrence, conformity, *congeniality*, consensus, détente, *entente*, equilibrium, harmony, indenture, oneness, peace, peace agreement, peacemaking, quid pro quo, rapprochement (*formal*), reunion, solidarity, steadiness, sweetness and light, sympathy, *unanimity*, understanding, union, unison, unity

(*prep*) according to, in line with

(*v*) accord, agree, be compatible, belong, chime in, coexist, cohere (*formal*), coincide, complement, compromise, conform, fulfil, harmonize, match, mix, satisfy

157 Disharmony

Out of the tension of duality life always produces a "third" that seems somehow incommensurable or paradoxical. **Carl Gustav Jung**

(*adj*) adverse, at loggerheads, at odds, at variance, conflicting, contradictory, contrary, differing, discordant, disharmonious, divisive, factious, ill-assorted, incompatible, *incongruent*, inconsistent, inharmonious, *in opposition*, irreconcilable, mismatched, schismatic, uneven, *unharmonious*

(*n*) agitation, breach, contradiction, discord, disharmony, dissension, dissent, dissonance, disunity, division, divisiveness, faction, friction, incompatibility, *incongruence*, *incongruousness*, irony, misalliance, mismatch, quibble, schism, split, strife, tension, trouble, unevenness, unpleasantness, variance, war

(*v*) be at odds, be at variance, belie, clash, conflict, contradict, counter, fall foul of

See also DISORDER AND CHAOS (246)

158 Opposite

The comic is the perception of the opposite; humor is the feeling of it. **Umberto Eco**

(*adj*) converse, inverse, obverse, opposed, opposing, opposite, reverse

(*adv*) conversely, on the other hand

(*n*) antithesis, contrary, converse, inverse, negation, obverse, opposite, polarity, pole, reverse

(*prep*) against, counter to, versus

See also DIFFERENCE (150)

159 General Locations

My centre is giving way, my right is retreating; situation excellent. I shall attack. **Ferdinand Foch**

(*adj*) aerial, airborne, alfresco, all-around (*US*), all-round, dotted, extensive, far-flung, flying, general, indoor, inland, inside, interior, inward, leeward, left-hand, midair, national, nationwide, open-air, outboard, outdoor, outside, right-hand, scattered, situated (*formal*), spatial, sunken, *to the rear*, underwater, upwind, wall-to-wall (*informal*), winged, worldwide

(*adv*) alfresco, all over the place (*informal*), aloft, anyplace (*US informal*), anywhere, around, downstairs, everywhere, far and wide, herewith, high and low, in, *in back* (*US*), in-between, indoors, in front, inside, *in the background*, in the midst of, *in the rear* (*US*), midway, out, outdoors, out-of-doors, outside, overhead, someplace (*US informal*), somewhere, widely, within, *yonder* (*regional*)

See also PLACE (1064)

160 Closeness

Once the realization is accepted that even between the closest *human beings infinite distances continue to exist, a wonderful living side by side can grow up.* **Rainer Maria Rilke**

(*adj*) abutting, adjacent, adjoining, bonded, bordering, close, close at hand, close by, close-run, connected, *contiguous* (*formal*), *face-to-face*, hand-to-hand, handy, head-on, head-to-head, immediate, local, near, nearby, neighbouring, next-door, nigh, *proximate*, *short-range*, *side by side*, surrounding, tightknit, vicinal, within reach, *within spitting distance* (*informal*), *within walking distance*

(*adv*) around, at hand, cheek by jowl, cheek-to-cheek, closely, face to face, handily, head-to-head, hereabouts, immediately, *in close proximity*, *in easy reach*, *in the vicinity*, intimately, locally, near, nearby, next door, point-blank, *round here*, *shoulder to shoulder*, tightly

(*n*) closeness, *contiguity* (*formal*), earshot, handiness, hearing, nearness, propinquity (*formal*), proximity, *spitting distance* (*informal*), stone's throw, striking distance

(*prep*) against, along, alongside, around, at the side of, near, outside, within an ace of, *within reach of*

161 Distance

Man is slightly nearer to the atom than the stars. From his central position he can survey the grandest works of Nature with the astronomer, or the minutest works with the physicist. **Arthur Eddington**

(*adj*) distant, extreme, far, *far away*, faraway, far-flung, far-off, *farthermost*, farthest, foreign, furthermost, furthest, inaccessible, isolated, lonely, lonesome (*US*), *off the beaten path* (*US*), off the beaten track (*informal*), opposite, outermost, outlying, outmost, out-of-the-way, private, remote, solitary, transatlantic, utmost, vicarious

(*adv*) afar (*literary*), apart, far, far afield, *far off*, *in the distance*

(*n*) distance, isolation, miles (*informal*), remoteness

162 Relative Location

That white horse you see in the park could be a zebra synchronized with the railings. **Ann Jellicoe**

(*adj*) bottom, bottommost, built-in, equidistant, fitted, frontal, halfway, hind, hindmost (*literary*), in-between, inside, intermediary, intermediate, *intertwined*, *interwoven*, lowermost, mid, middle, nearside (*US*), nether (*formal*), peripheral, rearmost, rearward, superior, top, uppermost

(*adv*) abreast, ahead, astern, at the rear, behind, below, beneath (*formal*), halfway, *to the fore*, *to the left*, *to the right*

(*prep*) aboard, above, after, amid, amidst, among, around, astride, atop (*literary*), before, behind, beneath (*formal*), beside, between, beyond, by, facing, in, in between, in front of, inside, on, on top of, opposite, over, round, through, under, underneath, with

163 Chain of Events

The hour of their crime does not strike simultaneously for all nations. This explains the permanence of history. **E. M. Cioran**

(*adj*) chronological, sequential, temporal

(*n*) chain, chronology, cycle, kaleidoscope, progression, sequence, series, succession, train

See also PERIOD OF TIME (90), EVENTS AND OCCURRENCES (35)

164 Before, First, and Preceding

The original is unfaithful to the translation. **Jorge Luis Borges**

(*adj*) appointed, earlier, earliest, early, eldest, fast, first, foregoing, inaugural, initial, introductory, last, maiden, original, past, preceding, predetermined, pre-existing, preliminary, preparatory, prescribed, preset, previous, primary, prior

(*adv*) as yet, at first, at the outset, at the start, before, before now, earlier, first, firstly, in advance, prior to

(*n*) *antecedence*, antecedent, predecessor

(*prep*) ahead of, before, by

(*v*) *antecede*, antedate, anticipate, precede, predate, pre-exist, prefigure

See also PAST (84)

165 Concurrent and Contemporaneous

Contemporary man has rationalized the myths, but he has not been able to destroy them. **Octavio Paz**

(*adj*) coexistent, coextensive, concomitant, concurrent, contemporaneous, simultaneous, synchronized, *synchronous*

(*adv*) all at once, all together, at once, at one fell swoop, at one go, at that moment, at the same time, *contemporarily*, together

(*conj*) as, immediately, while

(*n*) coexistence, concurrence, *contemporaneity*, *contemporaneousness*, *contemporaries*, *simultaneity*, *synchronicity*, *synchronism*

(*prep*) amid, amidst, during, *in the course of*, pending, through, throughout

166 After, Last, and Following

For all at last return to the sea—to Oceanus, the ocean river, like the ever-flowing stream of time, the beginning and the end. **Rachel Carson**

(*adj*) back-to-back, closing, concluding, consecutive, consequent, consequential, dying, eventual, final, following, follow-on, last, last-ditch, latter, *next to last*, penultimate, posterior (*formal*), resultant, resulting, second, sequential, serial, straight, subsequent, succeeding, successive, valedictory (*formal*)

(*adv*) after, after that, afterwards, at last, at length, at long last, finally, in a row, in order, *in sequence*, *in succession*, in the end, just, just now, late, later, latterly, next, once, one after another, one after the other, one by one, on the trot, running, sequentially, since, then, thence (*formal or literary*), thenceforth, thenceforward, thereafter, thereupon (*formal*), ultimately

(*conj*) after, as soon as, whenever, whereupon (*formal*)

(*n*) follow-up, sequel

(*prep*) after, as of (*formal*)

167 New, Modern

Fashion is made to become unfashionable. **Coco Chanel**

(*adj*) ageless, ahead of its time, avant-garde, brand-new, cool, cutting-edge, fashionable, fresh, funky (*informal*), futuristic, happening (*informal*), hip (*slang*), in, incoming, innovative, latest, modern, new, newborn, newfangled, pop (*informal*), reborn, recent, spanking new, supercool (*informal*), ultramodern, undeveloped, unknown, unripe, untested, untried, unused, up-to-date, up-to-the-minute, with-it (*dated informal*), young

(*adv*) freshly

(*n*) cutting edge, *hipness* (*slang*), innovation, modernity

168 Old, Old-Fashioned

For an idea ever to be fashionable is ominous, since it must afterwards be always old-fashioned. **George Santayana**

(*adj*) age-old, anachronistic, ancient, antediluvian (*informal*), antiquated, antique, archaic, atavistic, behind the times, *centuries old*, dated, folk, hand-me-down, historic, historical, hoary, institutionalized, long-established, medieval, obsolescent, obsolete, old, olden (*archaic or literary*), old-fashioned, old hat (*informal*), old-style, old-time, old-world, out, outdated, outmoded, out-of-date, *out of fashion*, outworn, passé, poky (*US*), prehistoric, primitive, primordial, retro, roman, second-hand, senior, superannuated, tested, time-honoured, traditional, unfashionable, *unhip* (*informal*), unoriginal, used, vintage

(*n*) anachronism, maturity, obsolescence, *outmodedness*, primitiveness, ripeness

See also PAST (84), IN BAD REPAIR (1233)

169 Causation

The final cause of the World at large, we allege to be the consciousness of its own freedom on the part of Spirit, and ipso facto, the reality of that freedom. **G. W. F. Hegel**

(*adj*) causal, contributory, extenuating, underlying

(*adv*) accordingly, consequently (*formal*), hence (*formal*), ipso facto, so, then, thence (*formal or literary*), therefore

(*conj*) and, as, as long as, because, forasmuch as (*formal*), given that, in order to, inasmuch as, insofar as (*formal*), insomuch as, in that, provided, provided that, providing, since, *so long as*, unless

(*n*) agency, agent, case, causation, cause, enticement, excuse, explanation, factor, grounds, hidden agenda, impetus, incentive, inspiration, mitigation, motivation, motivator, motive, occasion, pretext, push, reason, spur, stimulation, stimulus, ulterior motive

(*prep*) as a result of, because of, given, in the light of, in the name of, in view of, on account of, on the strength of, owing to, thanks to, through

(*v*) be caused by, come from, stem from

170 Although, Nevertheless, and Despite

I have always found that the man whose second thoughts are good is worth watching. **J. M. Barrie**

(*adv*) after all, all the same, anyhow, anyway, aside, at least, be that as it may, but then again, come what may, even so, however, in any case, just the same, leastways (*informal*), leastwise (*US regional informal*), nevertheless, nonetheless, notwithstanding (*formal*), otherwise, still, though, yet

(*conj*) albeit, although, even if, though, whereas, while

(*prep*) despite, for all, in spite of, in the face of

171 Responsibility

Alas, after a certain age every man is responsible for his face. **Albert Camus**

(*adj*) accountable, answerable, bound, duty-bound, liable, responsible

(*n*) accountability, aegis, *answerability*, auspices, buck (*informal*), care, charge, control, custody, debt, duty, incumbency (*formal*), mantle (*formal*), onus, responsibility, supervision, trust, umbrella

See also MORALLY BAD (776)

Truth, Reality, Certainty, and Possibility

172 True and Real

The life of an honest man must be a perpetual infidelity. **Charles Pierre Péguy**

(*adj*) actual, authentic, autobiographical, biographical, bona fide, canonical, card-carrying, *certifiable*, concrete, convincing, credible, de facto, devout (*formal*), earnest, effective, empirical, *fact-based*, factional, factual, faithful, fully-fledged, genuine, heartfelt, kosher (*informal*), legitimate, lifelike, literal, material, matter-of-fact, native, natural, naturalistic, nonfiction, objective, official, practical, pukka (*informal*), pure, real, realistic, real-life, real-world, self-confessed, solid, sterling, *substantiated*, tangible, three-dimensional, true, true-life, true to life, undistorted, unembellished, unembroidered, *unfeigned*, unvarnished, valid, veracious, veritable

(*adv*) by nature, convincingly, effectively, factually, honestly, indeed, in effect, in fact, in reality, legitimately, literally, naturally, physically, truly

(*n*) absolute, actuality, authenticity, believability, credence, credibility, fact, fact of life, faithfulness, genuineness, justice, legitimacy, reality, *real life*, realness, real world, tangibility, the real McCoy (*informal*), *the real thing*, truth, validity, veracity, verisimilitude (*formal*), verity (*formal*)

173 Words and Phrases Emphasizing the Truth of a Matter

If the truth were self-evident, eloquence would be unnecessary. **Cicero**

(*adv*) actually, as a matter of fact, from the horse's mouth, if truth be told, in actual fact, in fact, in point of fact, *in truth*, really, unsurprisingly

(*interj*) straight up (*slang*)

174 False and Unreal

If there were a verb meaning "to believe falsely", it would not have any significant first person, present indicative. **Ludwig Wittgenstein**

(*adj*) abstract, academic, allegorical, *all in the mind*, apocryphal, artificial, assumed, bogus, canned, cardboard, *chimerical*, *conjectural*, contrived, copied, counterfeit, *counterfeited*, deceptive, delusive, distorted, diversionary, dreamlike, dummy, ersatz (*disapproving*), fabled, fabricated, factitious, fairy-tale, fake, *faked*, fallacious, false, falsified, *fantastical*, faux, feigned, fictional, fictitious, forged, fraudulent, hypothetical, illusive, illusory, imaginary, imagined, imitation, inauthentic, incorporeal (*formal*), incredible, invalid, invented, invisible, legendary, literary, loaded, made-up, magic, magical, make-believe, man-made, mendacious, meretricious, *metaphoric*, metaphorical, misleading, mock, mythical, mythological, nominal, nonexistent, notional, perverted, phoney, plastic, pretend, *pretended*, professed, propagandist, *pseudo*, purported (*formal*), put-on, quasi, reproduction, seeming, sham, simulated, so-called, soi-disant (*literary*), *sophistic*, specious, spurious, storybook, stylized, superficial, supposed, surface, synthetic, tall, theoretical, *thought up*, titular, tortuous, trick, trumped-up, unfounded, unnatural, unreal, unreliable, untrue, untruthful, weighted, *without foundation*

(*adv*) deceitfully, falsely, incredibly, in name only, nominally, on paper, professedly, superficially, unnaturally

(*n*) deceptiveness, fiction, *illusoriness*, *imaginariness*, *immateriality*, *immaterialness*, magic, *phoniness*, simulation, speciousness, unreality, veneer

See also NONEXISTENT THINGS (23), DECEPTION AND LIES (661), AFFECTATION, SELF-SATISFACTION, AND SNOBBISHNESS (508)

175 Certain

Science has proof without any certainty. **Ashley Montagu**

(*adj*) absolute, agreed, airtight, arranged, assured, axiomatic, bound, carried, cast-iron, categorical, certain, clear, conclusive, decided, definite, demonstrable, evident, final, foregone, guaranteed, inalienable (*formal*), incontestable, incontrovertible, indisputable, indubitable (*formal*), ineluctable (*literary*), inescapable, inevitable, infallible, in the bag (*informal*), irrefutable, positive, preordained, provable, proven, resounding, self-evident, settled, sure, sure-fire (*informal*), surefooted, touch-and-go, unassailable, unavoidable, uncontroversial, undeniable, *undisputable*, undisputed, undoubted, unquestionable, unquestioned, verifiable, verified, watertight

(*adv*) admittedly, *beyond a doubt*, *beyond a shadow of a doubt*, *beyond doubt*, *beyond question*, certainly, clearly, definitely, doubtless, easily, finally, for sure (*informal*), hands down, indeed, infallibly, manifestly, no doubt, of course, positively, rightly (*informal*), simply, surely, *without a shadow of a doubt*, *without doubt*, *without question*

(*n*) authentication, cert (*informal*), certainty, cinch (*informal*), definiteness, finality, guarantee, *indisputability*, inevitability, inexorability (*formal*), inexorableness (*formal*), infallibility, predictability, predictableness, *safe bet*, *sure bet*, sure thing (*informal*), unavoidability

See also CERTAINTY (562)

176 Uncertain

When nothing is sure, everything is possible. **Margaret Drabble**

(*adj*) alleged, anecdotal, apparent, arguable, assumed, baseless, borderline, circumstantial, contentious, controversial, debatable, disputable, dodgy (*informal*), doubtful, dubious, flimsy, fuzzy, iffy (*informal*), incalculable, inconclusive, indecisive, indefinite, indeterminable, indeterminate, in doubt, *in question*, moot, negotiable, notional, *open to question*, ostensible, *ostensive* (*formal*), presumptive (*formal*), problematical, putative, questionable, reputed, rumoured, shaky, speculative, supposed, suspect, suspicious, tentative, uncertain, unclear, unconfirmed, unconvincing, undecided, undetermined, unlikely, unproven, unresolved, unsettled, unsubstantiated, unsupported, untested, unverified, variable, weak, wide-open

(*adv*) abstractly, apparently, at first glance, at first sight, evidently, incalculably, *indeterminately*, notionally, problematically (*US*), questionably, reportedly, seemingly, supposedly, without fail

(*conj*) in case, lest

(*n*) disequilibrium, dubiety (*formal*), dubiousness, if, *inconstancy*, indecisiveness, *indeterminacy*, shakiness, *uncertainness*, variability

See also UNCERTAINTY (560)

177 Falsify and Cheat

A man is to be cheated into passion, but to be reasoned into truth. **John Dryden**

(*v*) cheat, cook the books (*slang*), counterfeit, crib (*informal*), fake, falsify, fiddle (*informal*), fit up (*slang*), fix (*informal*), forge, frame (*slang*), fudge (*informal*), juggle, manoeuvre, massage, misrepresent, pervert, rig, skew, stitch up (*slang*), tamper, twist, warp

See also DECEPTION AND LIES (661), COPY AND DUPLICATE (403)

178 Possible and Probable

Probable impossibilities are to be preferred to improbable possibilities. **Aristotle**

(*adj*) achievable, attainable, believable, calculable, conceivable, credible, discretionary, doable, earthly, feasible, foreseeable, hopeful, imaginable, in the running, likely, logical, on the cards (*informal*), operable, optional, plausible, possible, potential, practicable, predictable, probable, realizable, surmountable, tenable, viable, workable, would-be (*adv*) arguably, credibly, debatably, hopefully, humanly, ideally, in principle, in theory, maybe, *most likely*, *most probably*, odds-on (*informal*), perchance (*archaic or literary*), perhaps, possibly, presumably

(*n*) chance, danger, feasibility, hope, horizon, likelihood, off chance, plausibility, possibility, practicability, probability, prospect, risk, room, scope, sporting chance, viability

179 Impossible and Improbable

How next to impossible is the exercise of virtue! It requires a constant watchfulness, constant guard. **William Golding**

(*adj*) doubtful, fairy-tale, fanciful, fantastic, far-fetched, *highly unlikely*, implausible, impossible, impracticable, improbable, inconceivable, inoperable, out, out of the question, outside, remote, slim, unachievable, unattainable, unbelievable, unfeasible, unimaginable, unlikely, unrealistic, untenable, unthinkable, *unviable*, visionary

(*adv*) indefensibly

(*n*) doubtfulness, hopelessness, implausibility, impossibility, impracticability, impracticality, improbability, inaccessibility, *unfeasibility*, unlikelihood, *unlikeliness*, *unviability*

180 Secret and Unknown

I know that's a secret, for it's whispered everywhere. **William Congreve**

(*adj*) alien, anonymous, arcane, backroom, between ourselves, buried, censored, clandestine, classified, cloak-and-dagger, closet, concealed, confidential, cosmetic, covert, cryptic, deep, elusive, enigmatic, faceless, furtive, hidden, hole-and-corner, hush-hush (*informal*), imponderable, informal, inmost, inner, innermost, inside, intimate, invisible, inward, latent, *little-known*, mystery, nameless, obscure, off the record, outside, pent-up, private, privileged, quiet, recondite, repressed, restricted, secluded, secret, sensitive, *sequestered* (*formal*), shadowy, *shrouded in mystery*, silent, stealthy, subterranean, surreptitious, top-secret, ulterior, unanticipated, uncharted, undecipherable, undercover, underground, underhand, under-the-table, under wraps (*informal*), *undetected*, undetermined, undisclosed, *undiscovered*, unexplained, *unexplored*, unexpressed, unfamiliar, unfathomable, unforeseeable, unheard-of, unidentified, unknowable, unknown, unlisted, *unmapped*, unnamed, unnoticed, unnumbered, unobserved, *unprofessed*, unquantifiable, unrevealed, unsaid, unspoken, unsung, unsuspected, unvoiced, veiled, well-kept

(*adv*) abstrusely, anonymously, backstage, behind closed doors, behind the scenes, behind your back, confidentially, implicitly, in camera, incognito, in confidence, informally, *in secrecy*, in secret, inwardly, on the sly, privately, secretly

(*n*) anonymity, concealment, covertness, furtiveness, mystery, mystique, obscurity, privacy, seclusion, secrecy, *secretiveness*, stealth, surreptitiousness

181 Secrets and Mysteries

I cannot forecast to you the action of Russia. It is a riddle wrapped in a mystery inside an enigma. **Winston Churchill**

(*n*) closed book, confidence, conundrum, enigma, imponderable, mystery, paradox, poser, problem, puzzle, puzzler, secret, state secret

See also DIFFICULTY AND COMPLEXITY (243)

182 Known and Famous

For famous men have the whole earth as their memorial. **Pericles**

(*adj*) acknowledged, all-star, avowed (*formal*), celebrated, eminent, established, exposed, fabled, famed, familiar, famous, given, grand, great, ill-disguised, illustrious, immortal, important, infamous, institutional, *in the limelight*, in the open, *in the public domain*, known, legendary, noted, notorious (*archaic*), out, *out in the open*, popular, pre-eminent, prestigious, professed, prominent, proverbial, putative, recognizable, recognized, rehearsed, renowned, tacit, unclassified, understood, *unhidden*, unwritten, voiced, well-known, world-famous

(*adv*) publicly

(*n*) celebrity, fame, high profile, infamy, limelight, name, notoriety, popularity, prestige, prominence, renown, stardom, visibility

See also IMPORTANT OR FAMOUS PEOPLE (893)

Positive Qualities of things

183 Correct

I know I'm not clever but I'm always right. **J. M. Barrie**

(*adj*) applicable, correct, explicable, faultless, flawless, impeccable, infallible, maximal, right, spot-on (*informal*), tailor-made

(*adv*) according to plan, A-OK (*informal*), beautifully, correctly, nicely, right, rightly, well, with reason

(*n*) faultlessness, infallibility, perfection, rectitude (*formal*), rightness

See also MORALLY GOOD (775), EXACT (204)

184 Good, Well, Better

It is better to die on your feet than to live on your knees. **Dolores Ibárruri**

(*adj*) *above average*, best, better, blue-chip, dandy (*US informal*), enhanced, favourable, fine, golden, good, *Grade A*, grand, *high-quality*, ideal, improved, *just right*, optimal, peachy (*informal*), perfect, preferable, redeeming, regenerative, seamless, sterling, useful, well, well-timed

(*adv*) favourably, finely, flawlessly, perfectly, swimmingly, well

(*n*) flawlessness, *impeccability*, *ne plus ultra* (*formal*), optimum, quality, usefulness

185 Appropriate, Suitable, Advisable

The thing to remember is that each time of life has its appropriate rewards, whereas when you're dead it's hard to find the light switch. **Woody Allen**

(*adj*) accredited, advisable, apposite, appropriate, approved, apropos (*formal*), apt, becoming, befitting, convenient, cut out for, decent, due, eligible, expedient, favourable, felicitous, fit, fitting, *hunky-dory* (*informal*), in accordance, in keeping, kosher (*informal*), *meet* (*archaic*), model, opportune, proper, qualified, right, ringside, savoury, seasonable, seemly, suitable, suited, timely, well-chosen

(*adv*) accordingly, aptly, correctly, *in good taste*, properly, relevantly, right

(*n*) advisability, *appositeness*, appropriateness, conventionality, correctness, desirability, eligibility, felicity, fitness, fittingness, *opportuneness*, rightness, suitability

(*v*) be appropriate, befit, behove (*formal*), suit

186 Admirable and Commendable

Always do right. This will gratify some people, and astonish the rest. **Mark Twain**

(*adj*) admirable, commendable, creditable, deserving, estimable, exemplary, golden, invaluable, laudable, meritorious (*formal*), number one (*informal*), plum (*informal*), plus, praiseworthy, pukka, reputable, respectable, splendid, utopian, worthy

187 Physically Pleasant

A thing of beauty is a joy for ever:/Its loveliness increases; it will never/Pass into nothingness. **John Keats**

(*adj*) bracing, brisk, comfortable, comfy (*informal*), cosy, easy, energizing, erotic, *exhilarating*, invigorating, livable, painkilling, palliative, *paradisiac*, refreshing, *rejuvenating*, revitalizing, sensual, sensuous, snug, soft, stimulating, warm

(*adv*) attractively, cosily, *fulsomely*, graciously, well

(*n*) amenity

188 Emotionally Pleasant

Wrapt in a pleasing fit of melancholy. **John Milton**

(*adj*) action-packed, agreeable, atmospheric, blessed, blissful, bustling, calmative, cathartic, cheering, comforting, conducive, cosy, delicious, delightful, disarming, divine (*informal or humorous*), easy, electrifying, elegiac (*formal*), emotional, emotive, encouraging, enjoyable, entertaining, eventful, exciting, familiar, feel-good, flattering, fulfilling, fun (*informal*), good, grateful (*archaic or literary*), gratifying, groovy (*dated slang*), heady, heartwarming, heavenly, hopeful, intoxicating, joyful, lovely, lyric, melting, nice, pacific, pacifist, pleasant, pleasing, pleasurable, poetic, proud, quiet, recreational, relaxed, rewarding, rose-coloured, rose-tinted, rosy, rousing, satisfying, soulful, sparkling, stirring, sublime, sweet, thrilling, touching, transcendent, transcendental, uplifting, vibrant, welcoming

(*adv*) agreeably, cosily, divinely (*informal*), enchantingly, endearingly, familiarly, favourably, headily, quietly, well

(*n*) deliciousness, *delightfulness*

189 Calming

Music that gentlier on the spirit lies,/Than tir'd eyelids upon tir'd eyes. **Alfred Tennyson**

(*adj*) calming, cathartic, conciliatory, *consolatory*, downbeat (*informal*), emollient, escapist, halcyon (*literary*), heartening, honeyed, idyllic, mitigating, palliative, placatory, propitiatory (*formal*), reassuring, relaxing, restful, restorative, sedative, soothing, *stress-free*, therapeutic, *tranquillizing*

(*n*) *restfulness*

190 Beauty and Attractiveness

Only stay quiet while my mind remembers/The beauty of fire from the beauty of embers. **John Masefield**

(*adj*) adorable, appealing, arresting, attractive, beauteous (*literary*), beautiful, becoming, beguiling, *bewitching*, captivating, charming, darling, decorative, delectable, delicate, diamanté, enchanting, endearing, engaging, enticing, exquisite, eye-catching, flattering, frilly, gorgeous, graceful, idyllic, lovable, lovely, nice, nifty, ornamental, *picture-perfect*, picture-postcard, picturesque, *pleasing to the eye*, prepossessing (*formal*), quaint, resplendent, scenic, showy, sweet, taking, twee, well-designed, *well-presented*, well-turned

(*adv*) beautifully, delectably, delicately, exquisitely, picturesquely, winningly

(*n*) appeal, attractiveness, beauty, character, charm, cuteness, delicacy, desirability, dreaminess, exquisiteness, glamour, glitter, good taste, gorgeousness, gracefulness, lure, magic, magnificence, *picturesqueness*, quaintness, showiness, sweetness

See also PEOPLE'S PHYSICAL APPEARANCE (476)

191 Interesting and Meaningful

It is more important that a proposition be interesting than that it be true. **A. N. Whitehead**

(*adj*) absorbing, alluring, appetizing, catchy, challenging, charged, charismatic, colourful, compelling, compulsive, cultural, deep, didactic, edifying, educational, electric, engrossing, enlightening, enthralling, entrancing, evocative, fascinating, gripping, hypnotic (*informal*), *hypnotizing*, illuminating, informative, ingenious, inspirational, inspiring, instructive, interesting, intriguing, inviting, irresistible, juicy (*informal*), magnetic, meaningful, meaty, mesmeric, mesmerizing, motivating, newsworthy, newsy, *of interest*, piquant, pregnant, provocative, revealing, riveting (*informal*), scintillating, snappy (*informal*), spellbinding, stimulating, *suspenseful*, tantalizing, telling, telltale, tempting, thought-provoking, *titillating*, vivid, *worth mentioning*, *worthy of note*, zappy (*informal*)

(*adv*) electrifyingly, enticingly, expressively, refreshingly, revealingly, significantly, unforgettably

(*n*) allure, charisma, magnetism, pizzazz (*informal*), pull (*informal*), punchiness, *razzle-dazzle*, razzmatazz, spice

192 Safe and Safety

It's often safer to be in chains than to be free. **Franz Kafka**

(*adj*) airworthy, bulletproof (*informal*), childproof, custodial, fail-safe, firm, flameproof, foolproof, fortified, *goofproof* (*US informal*), guarded, harmless, innocent, innocuous, inoffensive, *in safe hands*, inviolate, *nonfatal*, *nonhazardous*, nontoxic, onside, *out of harm's way*, precautionary, preservative, protected, protective, repellent, *risk-free*, roadworthy, rock-solid, safe, *safe as houses*, secure, sheltered, shielded, sound, steady, strong, tame, *unhazardous*, unthreatened

(*adv*) innocently, onside, safely, securely, solidly

(*n*) airworthiness, asylum, bulwark, defence, firmness, harmlessness, impunity, indemnity, *invulnerability*, lifeline, preventive, protection, protectiveness, roadworthiness, safeguard, safekeeping, safety, safety net, safety valve, sanctuary, security, self-defence, soundness, welfare

193 Importance and Significance

I find no hint throughout the universe/Of good or ill, of blessing or of curse;/I find alone Necessity Supreme. **James Thomson**

(*n*) accentuation, bearing, centrality, consequence (*formal*), consideration, emphasis, gravitas (*formal*), gravity, greatness, hold, *imperativeness*, import, importance, interest, invaluableness, magnitude, meaning, meaningfulness, merit, moment (*formal*), *momentousness*, necessitude, notability, pregnancy, preponderance (*formal*), primacy, purport, relevance, seriousness, significance, status, urgency, weight, weightiness, worth

194 Most Important and Main

It has long been an axiom of mine that the little things are infinitely the most important. **Arthur Conan Doyle**

(*adj*) *all-important*, ascendant, chief, core, deciding, determining, dominant, first, flagship, landmark, lead, leading, magic, main, major, master, number one, overarching, overriding, paramount, predominant, preponderant, primary, prime, principal, quantum, ruling, salient, sovereign, supreme, top-level, uppermost

(*v*) bulk large, come first, outweigh, take precedence

See also MAINLY AND PRIMARILY (138)

195 Important

The essential thing in life is not conquering but fighting well. **Pierre de Coubertin**

(*adj*) acute, at issue, big, burning, cardinal, central, consequential, critical, crucial, decisive, definite, earth-shaking, earthshattering, elevated, epoch-making, exigent (*formal*), fatal, fateful, fundamental, grave, great, heavy-duty (*informal*), high, high-profile, historic, immediate, important, key, keynote, large-scale, life-and-death, major, material, meaningful, momentous, monumental, of note, pertinent, ponderable, portentous, pressing, relevant, resonant, seminal, serious, significant, structural, substantive, top-ranking, ultimate, urgent, vital, weighty

(*adv*) critically, decisively, importantly, indispensably, materially, portentously, substantively, vitally

196 Fundamental

The core reductive mistake is...the idea of a single fundamental explanation. **Mary Midgley**

(*adj*) alpha, basic, bread-and-butter, constituent, elemental, essential, first, focal, formative, fundamental, germane (*formal*), instant, integral, intrinsic, pivotal, primary, radical, skeleton, staple, to the point, ultimate

(*adv*) at heart, at the heart of, centre stage, fundamentally

197 Necessary and Essential

We have to believe in free will. We've got no choice. **Isaac Bashevis Singer**

(*adj*) binding, compulsory, *de rigueur* (*formal*), essential, imperative, indispensable, mandatory, necessary, *necessitous* (*formal*), *needed*, needful (*formal or archaic*), obligatory, of the essence, required, requisite (*formal*), unarguable

(*adv*) if need be, of necessity, perforce (*literary*), unavoidably

(*n*) condition, demand, disclaimer, exigency (*formal*), if, necessity, precondition, prerequisite, provision, proviso, qualification, requirement, reservation, stipulation, terms

198 Most Important Thing

Winning isn't everything. It's the only thing. **Vince Lombardi**

(*n*) accent, bedrock, big deal (*informal*), bread and butter, centrepiece, core, crux, determinant, essence, essentials, flagship, imperative, influence, keynote, keystone, lifeblood, linchpin, mainspring, mainstay, marrow (*literary*), meat, must, necessity, need, nub, pith, priority, sine qua non, stress, substance, van, vanguard

See also NEED AND REQUIRE (465)

199 Wholeness and Completeness

Now a whole is that which has a beginning, a middle, and an end. **Aristotle**

(*adj*) absolute, all-around (*US*), all-embracing, all-encompassing, all-inclusive, all-out, all-round, blanket, blow-by-blow, broad, broadly-based, catchall, coast-to-coast, complete, completed, comprehensive, concluded, convincing, cut-and-dried, detailed, done, *done and dusted*, encyclopedic, entire, exhaustive, far-reaching, finished, full, full-blown, full-length, full-scale, fully-fledged, fully-grown, general, generalized, global, implicit, in-depth, inclusive, intact, integral, intercontinental, intimate, mass, overall, perfect, plenary (*formal*), radical, sound, thorough, thoroughgoing, total, unabridged, unadulterated, unalloyed, unconditional, uncut, undisturbed, undivided, unedited, *unexpurgated*, unimpaired, universal, unreserved, well-rounded, whole, wholesale, wide, wide-ranging

(*adv*) all (*informal*), back to front, completely, extensively, flatly, fully, in depth, in detail, in full, inside out, intimately, perfectly, solidly, soundly, thoroughly, well, wholesale, wholly (*n*) broadness, completeness, comprehensiveness, entirety, *fait accompli*, soundness, universalism, wholeness

See also ALL (126)

200 Usefulness

Have nothing in your houses that you do not know to be useful, or believe to be beautiful. **William Morris**

(*adj*) accessible, adaptable, adjustable, advantageous, all-purpose, applied, approachable, beneficent, beneficial, character-building, clever, convenient, convertible, effective, effectual (*formal*), efficacious (*formal*), elastic, expedient, exploitable, fecund, fertile, functional, gainful, good, hands-on, handy, helpful, lucrative, manageable, multipurpose, nifty (*informal*), *of use*, practical, productive, profitable, redeemable, remedial, salutary, sensible, serviceable, substantive, useful, user-friendly, utilitarian, valid, valuable, valued, versatile, well-appointed, with all mod cons (*informal*), worthwhile

(*adv*) accessibly, constructively, conveniently, effectively, expediently, handily, ideally, substantively

(*n*) accessibility, adaptability, approachability, convenience, effectiveness, efficacy, expediency, fertility, helpfulness, *niftiness* (*informal*), practicality, productiveness, profitability, richness, service, use, usefulness, user-friendliness, utility, validity, value, versatility

201 Ease and Simplicity

Everything should be made as simple as possible, but not simpler. **Albert Einstein**

(*adj*) accessible, austere, bare, basic, black-and-white, classic, cushy (*informal*), downhill, easy, easy-peasy (*informal*), effortless, elementary, fathomable, *hassle-free* (*informal*), introductory, *labour-saving*, light, minimalist, open-and-shut, painless, *plain sailing*, quiet, rudimentary, simple, simplified, smooth, soluble, solvable, straightforward, trouble-free, uncomplicated, uninvolved, unlaboured, unproblematic

(*adv*) accessibly, easily, readily, simply, smoothly, with ease

(*n*) ease, effortlessness, fluency, fluidity, minimalism, neatness, plainness, simplicity, smoothness, straightforwardness, *uncomplicatedness*

202 Strength

I count life just a stuff/To try the soul's strength on. **Robert Browning**

(*adj*) acute, aggressive, *all-consuming*, all-powerful, almighty, armoured, armour-plated, at an advantage, authoritative, blazing, buoyant, burning, clear, commanding, compelling, concentrated, concerted, deep, deep-rooted, defensible, defensive, draconian, driving, emphatic, exquisite, ferocious, fierce, fiery, forceful, forcible, fortified, *hard-hitting*, hard-wearing, heavy-duty, impregnable, indestructible, infectious, influential, intense, intensive, intoxicating (*formal*), invincible, inviolable, irresistible, keen, masterful, mighty, omnipotent, overpowering, overwhelming, penetrating, penetrative, physical, plenipotentiary, potent, powerful, profound, proof, *puissant* (*literary*), rabid, raging, raw, resistant, rich, rugged, serviceable, stable, steely, stiff, stout, strong, telling, tight, tough, unassailable, unbeatable, unbreakable, unconquerable, uncontrollable, virulent, vivid, well-developed

(*adv*) authoritatively, fiercely, firmly, forcibly, headily, heavily, irresistibly, keenly, powerfully, sharply, sturdily, tightly, toughly, uncontrollably, vividly

(*n*) authoritativeness, authority, command, defences, depth, dominance, domination, dominion, ferocity, force, forcefulness, grip, hegemony (*formal*), intensity, invincibility, keenness, leverage, mastery, might, muscle (*informal*), omnipotence, potency, power, profoundness, profundity, rawness, richness, ruggedness, stiffness, stoutness, strength, toughness, vividness

See also DURABLE (1209), HARD-WORKING AND COMMITTED (501), FIT AND STRONG (737)

203 Concise and Clear

As clear and as manifest as the nose in a man's face. **Robert Burton**

(*adj*) clear, clear-cut, comprehensible, concrete, crystal clear, decipherable, defined, explicit, fine, graphic, in focus, intelligible, legible, limpid, nice, picturesque, *plain as a pikestaff*, prima facie, readable, self-explanatory, sharp, short, summary, understandable, unequivocal, unmistakable, vivid, well-argued, well-defined, well-grounded

(*adv*) cogently, finely, nicely, sharply, unambiguously, vividly, well

(*n*) clarity, clearness, lucidity, lucidness, nicety, *preciseness*, sharpness, shortness, transparency, vividness

204 Exact

Ramp up my genius, be not retrograde;/But boldly nominate a spade a spade. **Ben Jonson**

(*adj*) accurate, bang on (*informal*), certain, close, correct, definite, delicate, direct, exact, explicit, express, fingertip, letter-perfect (*US*), literal, mathematical, minute, particular, perfect, photographic, precise, rigorous, scientific, sensitive, specific, specified, spot-on (*informal*), strict, surgical, technical, truthful, unambiguous, verbatim, word-for-word, word-perfect

(*adv*) closely, delicately, exactly, just, on the button (*informal*), *on the nail*, on the nose (*US informal*), pat, plumb (*informal*), squarely, to the letter, verbatim, word for word

(*n*) accuracy, attention to detail, care, clockwork, correctness, definition, delicacy, exactitude, exactness, precision, rigorousness, strictness, truthfulness

See also CORRECT (183), MORALLY GOOD (775)

205 Extraordinary: Amazing

I have had a dream, past the wit of man to say what dream it was. **William Shakespeare**

(*adj*) A1 (*informal*), acclaimed, ace (*informal*), all-time, amazing, ambitious, astonishing, astounding, awe-inspiring, awesome, blinding (*informal*), breathtaking, brilliant (*informal*), consummate, cool (*slang*), cracking (*informal*), dazzling, definitive, dreamy, elite, epic, especial, excellent, exceptional, executive, exquisite, extraordinaire, extraordinary, fabulous, fairy-tale, fantastic, far-out (*slang*), fearsome, first-class, first-rate, flamboyant, formidable, glittering, glorious, godlike, golden, grand, grandiose, great, groundbreaking, honorary, *huge* (*informal*), humbling, impressive, incomparable, incredible, indescribable, ineffable (*formal*), inexpressible, inimitable, inspired, leonine, magic, magical, magisterial, magnificent, majestic, marvellous, matchless, memorable, mind-blowing (*informal*), miraculous, notable, noteworthy, out of this world (*informal*), outstanding, phenomenal, powerful, prodigious, redoubtable, remarkable, sensational (*informal*), shining, smashing (*informal*), spectacular, splendid, splendiferous (*humorous*), staggering, startling, stonking (*slang*), striking, stunning, stupendous, super (*informal*), superb, super-duper (*informal*), superhuman, superior, superlative, surpassing (*literary*), surprising, swell (*US dated informal*), tremendous, trendsetting, unbeaten, unbelievable, undreamed-of, unforgettable, unpredicted, unspeakable, untouchable, unwonted, way-out (*dated informal*), *weird and wonderful*, wicked (*slang*), wonderful, wondrous (*literary*)

(*adv*) awesomely, brilliantly, devastatingly, exceedingly, exquisitely, formidably, grandly, greatly, indescribably, marvellously, outstandingly, powerfully, prodigiously, specially, spectacularly, stonking (*slang*), strangely, strikingly, surprisingly, unbelievably

(*n*) excellence, fineness, flamboyance, grandeur, grandiosity, grandness, greatness, impressiveness, majesty, originality, prodigiousness, *remarkability*, *remarkableness*, splendiferousness (*humorous*), splendour, whimsicality

See also SUPERIORITY (153)

206 Extraordinary: Uncommon

When you can do the common things of life in an uncommon way you'll command the attention of the world. **George Washington Carver**

(*adj*) all-round, alternative, banner (*US*), bravura, custom-built, customized, custom-made, different, distinguishing, exotic, experimental, extraordinary, foreign, fresh, fringe, iconoclastic, idealized, idiosyncratic, imposing, individual, irreplaceable, made-to-measure, made-to-order (*US*), millennial, *never-to-be-repeated*, new, nonpareil, nonstandard, novel, one, one and only, one of a kind, one-off, original, out of the ordinary, out-of-the-way, particular, peculiar, proper, proud, rare, rarefied, recherché, revolutionary, *ripping* (*dated informal*), rip-roaring (*informal*), rollicking, scarce, sensational, singular, sole, spanking, special, specialized, specially made, specific, strange, sublime (*informal*), terrific (*informal*), uncommon, unconventional, unheard-of, unhoped-for, unique, unprecedented, unrivalled, untold, unusual, whimsical, *without equal*, without precedent, *world-shattering*

(*adv*) extraordinarily, stunningly, whimsically

(*n*) curiosity, freshness, memorability, newness, novelty, one-off, peculiarity, rareness, rarity, scarceness, scarcity, singularity, unconventionality, uniqueness, *unusualness*

See also UNRELATEDNESS AND SEPARATENESS (147)

207 Order and Organization

How could things have been as they are, were there not an original, inherent principle or order somewhere? **David Hume**

(*adj*) clean, controlled, disciplined, geared up, geometric, hierarchical, methodological, neat, on an even keel, ordered, orderly, organized, prim, procedural, regimental, regimented, regular, regulatory, ripe, set, shipshape, slick, sorted (*informal*), spick-and-span, straight, structured, systematic, tidy, tight, trim, well-kept, well-oiled, well-ordered, well-organized

(*adv*) like clockwork, neatly, regularly, systematically, tidily, trimly

(*n*) coherence, compactness, discipline, neatness, normality, order, orderliness, organization, scheme, system, tidiness

208 Economical and Resourceful

Heaven has its seasons; Earth has its resources; Man has his government. This means that man is capable of forming a trinity with the other two. **Xunzi**

(*adj*) biodegradable, conservative, cost-effective, eco-friendly, economic, economical, efficient, environmental, fertile, productive, profitable, profitmaking, provident, *recyclable*, *recycled*, reusable, rich, self-supporting, streamlined, sustainable, thrifty, time-saving, well-paid

(*adv*) on a shoestring

(*n*) bargain, *cost-effectiveness*, economy, keenness, profitability, snip (*informal*), steal (*informal*), thrift

See also CHEAP AND INEXPENSIVE (222), MAKE GOOD USE OF SOMETHING (474)

209 Freedom and Liberty

Freedom is always and exclusively the freedom for the one who thinks differently. **Rosa Luxemburg**

(*adj*) at large, at leisure, at liberty, classless, elective, *emancipated*, excused, exempt, free, free-range, freewheeling (*US*), immune, independent, in the clear, loose, on the run, redemptive, substantive, unbounded, unbridled, unchecked, unconditioned, unconfined, unconstrained, unfettered, unhampered, unhindered, unimpeded, unlimited, unobstructed, unopposed, unrestrained, unrestricted, untrammelled

(*adv*) freely, independently, on the loose, scot-free, substantively

(*n*) breadth, carte blanche, catharsis, deliverance (*formal*), delivery, demob (*informal*), demobilization, discharge, dispensation, elbowroom, emancipation, empowerment, exemption, exoneration, freedom, freeing, immunity, independence, latitude, leeway, legroom, liberation, liberty, licence, *manumission* (*formal*), privilege, redemption, release, relief, remittance, rescue, salvation, space (*informal*)

(*v*) clear, decontrol, deliver (*literary*), demob (*informal*), demobilize, deregulate, discharge, dislodge, emancipate, excuse, free, let go, let loose, let out, liberate, ransom, redeem, release, rescue, save, set free, spare, unchain, unfetter, unfreeze, unleash, unloose, unshackle, untie

210 Source of Happiness, Pleasure, or Improvement

Happiness: a good bank account, a good cook, a good digestion. **Jean-Jacques Rousseau**

(*n*) advantage, asset, backing, beauty, benediction, benefit, blessing, boon, break (*informal*), change for the better, encouragement, favour, favourite, godsend, golden opportunity, good, good thing, good word, initiative, interest, jump-start, kudos, lead, manna, merit, mileage (*informal*), pick, *pick of the bunch*, *pick of the litter*, *pièce de résistance*, plus (*informal*), plus point, pole position, prerogative, *redeeming feature*, *redeeming quality*, saving grace, strength, strong point, strong suit, upper hand, upside, utility, virtue, worthiness

211 Treat

The great consolation in life is to say what one thinks. **Voltaire**

(*n*) amends, bait, balm, bonanza, boost, comfort, comforter, compensation, consolation, crutch, draw, feast, festiveness, festivity, fillip, gas (*informal*), *giggle* (*informal*), glory, gold mine, high (*informal*), joy, kick (*informal*), *lifesaver* (*informal*), lift, magnet, mercy, pick-me-up (*informal*), pleasantness, pride and joy, privilege, satisfaction, shot in the arm, tonic, wallop (*informal*), windfall

212 Amazing Thing

I wonder if we could contrive...some magnificent myth that would in itself carry conviction to our whole community. **Plato**

(*n*) beaut (*US informal*), buzz (*informal*), *corker* (*dated informal*), *cracker* (*informal*), *dilly* (*US slang*), *doozy* (*US slang*), dream, gem (*informal*), goody, hit, *humdinger* (*slang*), *icing on the cake*, indulgence, *jewel in the crown*, *jim-dandy* (*US informal*), knockout (*informal*), luxury, marvel, miracle, nonessential, peach (*informal*), pearl, phenomenon, plum (*informal*), portent (*formal*), sensation, smasher (*informal*), spectacle, splendour, *star attraction*, stunner (*informal*), superfluity, thrill, treasure, treat, wonder, work of art, world-beater, wow (*informal*)

213 Advantage

Success is man's god. **Aeschylus**

(*n*) beachhead, bestseller, foothold, footing, gateway, gold (*informal*), head start, jackpot, let-out, moneymaker, money-spinner (*informal*), record, start, stepping stone, success

214 Progress and Advancement

We have stopped believing in progress. What progress that is! **Jorge Luis Borges**

(*n*) advance, advancement, betterment (*formal*), breakthrough, comeback, cultivation, development, enhancement, evolution, fast track, growth, improvement, movement, opening, opportunity, progression, recovery, reform, reformation, regeneration, rehabilitation, stabilization, stride, upgrade, upturn

215 Peacefulness and Gentleness

That sweet, deep sleep, so close to tranquil death. **Virgil**

(*adj*) bloodless, gentle, nonviolent, pacific, peaceable, peaceful, quiet, relaxed, serene, softly-softly, tranquil

(*adv*) gently, peaceably, peacefully

(*n*) gentleness, law and order, mildness, nonaggression, nonviolence, order, peace, *peace and quiet*, peacefulness, peacekeeping, peace offering, *peace of mind*, peacetime, quietness, serenity, softness, tameness, tranquillity, truce

216 Solution

What destroys one man preserves another. **Corneille**

(*n*) answer, antidote, compromise, cure-all, fallback, fix (*informal*), key, panacea, reconciliation, recourse, remedy, resolution, result, settlement, solution, stopgap

217 Funny and Amusing

Everything is funny, as long as it's happening to somebody else. **Will Rogers**

(*adj*) amusing, comic, comical, daft (*informal*), droll, farcical, foolhardy, foolish, funny, hilarious, humorous, hysterical (*informal*), ironic, ironical, light, lighthearted, madcap, priceless (*informal*), *rib-tickling* (*informal*), side-splitting, silly, uproarious, whimsical, witty, zany

(*adv*) drolly, entertainingly, foolishly, funnily, riotously, whimsically

(*n*) a bundle of laughs, *comicality*, *comicalness*, *drollness*, funniness, hilariousness, hoot (*slang*), humour, riot (*informal*)

See also BIZARRE AND PECULIAR (258)

218 Positively Complex or Complicated

An object the sum of its complications, seen/And unseen. This is everybody's world. **Wallace Stevens**

(*adj*) advanced, challenging, complex, compound, cosmopolitan, elaborate, esoteric, fancy, flowery, high-level, irreducible, many-sided, multifaceted, subtle

(*adv*) elaborately

(*n*) intricacy, *ornateness*, sophistication, subtleness, subtlety

219 Expensive and Luxurious

Every tooth in a man's head is more valuable than a diamond. **Miguel de Cervantes**

(*adj*) baronial, costly, deluxe, exclusive, expensive, fancy, high-class, lush, luxurious, opulent, ornate, palatial, plush (*informal*), posh (*informal*), precious, priceless, rich, royal, sumptuous, swank (*US informal*), swanky (*informal*), swish (*informal*), tony (*US informal*), upmarket, upscale (*US*), valuable

(*adv*) expensively, ornately, richly

(*n*) exclusiveness, lushness, luxuriousness, luxury, opulence, preciousness, richness, snootiness (*informal*), style, sumptuousness

See also EXPENSIVE AND OVERPRICED (248)

220 Acceptable and Passable

Only the mediocre are always at their best. **Jean Giraudoux**

(*adj*) acceptable, adequate, admissible, allowable, all right, bearable, decent, defensible, endurable, excusable, fair, fair enough, *fair to middling*, fine (*informal*), forgivable, good enough, homely, in order, legitimate, livable, medium, middle, middling, moderate, normal, not bad, okay (*informal*), orthodox, palatable, passable, potable, presentable, reasonable, regular, respectable, satisfactory, so-so (*informal*), standard, supportable (*literary*), tolerable, understated, unexceptionable, unobjectionable, *unoffending*, *up to scratch* (*informal*), *up to standard*, valid, venial, viewable, welcome

(*adv*) acceptably, adequately, all right, averagely, defensibly, inoffensively, normally, passably

(*n*) acceptability, adequacy, admissibility, legitimacy

(*v*) measure up, pass muster

221 Popular and Wanted

All wars are popular for the first thirty days. **Arthur Schlesinger, Jr.**

(*adj*) admired, adored, *all the rage*, beloved, cherished, coveted, dear, desirable, desired, enviable, esteemed, exquisite, favourite, handpicked, *in demand*, justified, *longed-for*, looked-for, loved, marketable, *much-admired*, much-loved, pet, popular, precious, preferred, prized, recognized, respected, revered, reverend (*formal*), sought-after, *to die for*, top-rated, touristy, treasured, trendy (*informal*), valuable, vaunted, venerable, *venerated*, voguish, wanted, welcome, well-beloved, *well-regarded*, *well-respected*, well-thought-of, *wished-for*

(*adv*) desirably

See also LIKE, LOVE, VALUE, AND ENJOY (579)

222 Cheap and Inexpensive

If we cannot be free, at least we can be cheap! **Frank Zappa**

(*adj*) affordable, bargain, bargain basement, buckshee (*informal*), budget, cheap, *cheap and nasty*, *cheapo* (*informal*), competitive, cut-price, *cut-rate* (*US*), dirt-cheap (*informal*), discounted, economy, giveaway (*informal*), inexpensive, keen, knockdown, reasonable, reduced

(*adv*) buckshee (*informal*), cheaply, dirt-cheap (*informal*), on the cheap (*informal*)

See also ECONOMICAL AND RESOURCEFUL (208)

Negative Qualities of Things

223 Incorrect and Erroneous

No amount of experimentation can ever prove me right; a single experiment can prove me wrong. **Albert Einstein**

(*adj*) amiss, at fault, awry, erroneous, false, faulty, inaccurate, incorrect, in the wrong, mistaken, off beam, skewed, unearned, warped, *wide of the mark*, wrong

(*adv*) amiss, falsely, faultily, wrongly

(*n*) falseness, inaccuracy, incorrectness, invalidity, *mindlessness*

See also MORALLY BAD (776)

224 Bad and Badly

I never resist temptation because I have found that things that are bad for me never tempt me. **George Bernard Shaw**

(*adj*) abysmal, aggravated, appalling, atrocious, awful, bad, catastrophic, confounded (*informal*), deplorable, despicable, disappointing, execrable, fearful (*informal*), frightful, grievous, grim (*informal*), ill, irrecoverable, irremediable, lamentable, lousy (*informal*), mindless, painful, pitiful, rotten (*informal*), seedy, shoddy, sorry, terrible, unfavourable, woeful, worse, worst

(*adv*) atrociously, awfully, badly, deplorably, grimly (*informal*), ill, mindlessly, negatively, painfully, pitifully, rotten (*informal*), rottenly (*informal*), shoddily, terribly

225 Inappropriate and Unsuitable

A puritan's a person who pours righteous indignation into the wrong things. **G. K. Chesterton**

(*adj*) *below average*, below par (*informal*), *below standard*, deficient, *displeasing*, inapplicable, inapposite (*formal*), inappropriate, *inapt*, incorrect, inexpedient (*formal*), infra dig (*informal*), inglorious, irregular, laughable, misplaced, out of order (*regional informal*), pathetic (*informal*), unbecoming, undignified, unfit, unfitted, unfitting, unfortunate, unhappy, *unpropitious*, unseemly, unsuitable, untoward, wanting, wretched

(*adv*) deficiently, improperly (*formal*), indefensibly, unfortunately, unsatisfactorily, wrongly

(*n*) inapplicability, inappositeness (*formal*), inappropriateness, *inaptness*, insufficiency, *unbecomingness*, unsuitability

226 Unacceptable and Unforgivable

Laws can be unjust because they are contrary to the divine good...in no way is it permissible to observe them. **Thomas Aquinas**

(*adj*) beyond the pale, contemptible, cursed (*informal*), dire, discreditable, disgraceful, exceptionable (*formal*), forbidden, improper, indefensible, inexcusable, monstrous, *not on*, outrageous, outré, paltry, punishable, reprehensible, scabby (*slang*), second class, unacceptable, unearthly, unforgivable, unjust, unjustifiable, unjustified, unmentionable, unpardonable, unsatisfactory, *unsatisfying*, unsustainable, unutterable, vile

(*adv*) improperly, *reprehensively*, shockingly

(*n*) *contemptibility*, *contemptibleness*

227 Physically Unpleasant

I'm sure if everyone knew how physically cruel dancing really is, nobody would watch. **Margot Fonteyn**

(*adj*) airless, backbreaking, bumpy, claustrophobic, coercive, *crippling*, debilitating, difficult, draining, energetic, enervating, excruciating, exhausting, exigent (*formal*), *fatiguing*, forcible, foul, gory, grinding, harsh, high-pressure, hostile, *incapacitating*, incommodious (*formal*), inhospitable, invasive, murderous (*informal*), operose (*formal*), punishing, *racking*, rough, rugged, searing, sharp, splitting, stiff, strenuous, *stultifying*, swingeing, tiring, unforgiving, uphill, wearying, wild

(*adv*) arduously, painfully, roughly, stiffly

(*n*) harshness, roughness, ruggedness, stiffness, toughness

See also PAIN AND OTHER PHYSICAL SENSATIONS (734)

228 Emotionally Unpleasant and Upsetting

The superior man is satisfied and composed; the mean man is always full of distress. **Confucius**

(*adj*) accursed (*archaic or literary*), affecting, affective, agonizing, alarmist, appalling, bittersweet, calamitous, cheerless, cloying, cruel, crushing, crying, dark, deathly, degrading, demoralizing, deplorable, depressing, depressive, desolate, detestable, devastating, disagreeable, discomfiting (*formal*), disconcerting, discouraging, disheartening, dismal, dispiriting, disquieting, distressing, disturbing, embarrassing, excruciating, forbidding, foul (*informal*), funereal, grievous, grim, gritty, gruelling, harrowing, heartbreaking, heartrending, hopeless, horrendous, horrible, horrid, horrifying, humiliating, hurtful, ignominious, impossible, intolerable, invidious, jarring, joyless, lachrymose (*literary*), lamentable (*literary*), lugubrious, messy, miserable, mortifying, moving, nameless, nerve-racking, numbing, off-putting, oppressive, opprobrious, painful, pathetic, personal, *perturbing*, piteous, poignant, regrettable, rotten (*informal*), sad, *saddening*, sensitive, sepulchral, severe, shattering, shocking, sombre, sore, sorrowful, soul-destroying, standup, stifling, stormy, strained, stressful, stringent, tearful, tempestuous, terrible, thankless, *toe-curling* (*informal*), *toilsome*, *tormenting*, tragic, tragicomic, traumatic, *troubling*, trying, ugly, unbearable, uncomfortable, unconscionable, unendurable, unfortunate, ungrateful, unmerciful, unnerving, unpalatable, unrewarding, unsettling, upsetting, wearisome, wicked (*informal*), woeful

(*adv*) grievously, grimly, horribly, painfully, severely, shockingly, tempestuously, uncomfortably, unenviably

(*n*) aggro (*slang*), cheerlessness, dreariness, grimness, messiness, relentlessness, severity, storminess, stringency, tempestuousness, unpleasantness

229 Irritating

Being misunderstood by someone is vexation. Being misunderstood by everyone is tragedy. **Liu Shahe**

(*adj*) aggravating, annoying, bothersome, burdensome, cursed, disruptive, distracting, exasperating, frustrating, galling, grating, infuriating, insufferable, insupportable, irksome, irritating, maddening, nagging, niggling, pesky (*US informal*), pestilent (*literary or humorous*), provoking, sickening (*informal*), sneaking, tiresome, troublesome, untoward, vexatious, vexing, wearing, worrisome, worrying

(*adv*) grindingly, inconveniently, inopportunely

230 In Poor Taste

The aristocratic pleasure of displeasing is not the only delight that bad taste can yield. One can love a certain kind of vulgarity for its own sake. **Aldous Huxley**

(*adj*) arty-crafty (*informal disapproving*), baroque, brash, cheap, cheesy (*informal*), chintzy (*informal disapproving*), chocolate-box, *cringe-making* (*informal*), cutesy, extravagant, flash (*informal*), flashy, florid, fussy, garish, gaudy, glitzy, gooey (*informal*), icky (*informal*), in bad taste, inelegant, *in poor taste*, kiss-and-tell (*informal*), kitsch, kitschy, loud, lurid, maudlin, mawkish, meretricious (*formal*), mushy, naff (*informal*), ostentatious, overstated, pompous, punk (*informal*), purple, raffish, *ritzy* (*informal*), saccharine, schlocky (*US slang*), schmaltzy (*informal*), sensational, sensationalist, sentimental, showy, sick (*informal*), sickly, sickly-sweet, sloppy (*informal*), slushy, soppy (*informal*), splashy (*informal*), sugary, tacky (*informal*), tasteless, tawdry, tinny, treacly, vulgar, weepy

(*adv*) fussily, inelegantly

(*n*) bad taste, cheapness, flashiness, fussiness, garishness, gaudiness, glitziness, goo (*informal*), inelegance, kitsch, mawkishness, mush, ostentation, *ostentatiousness*, pompousness, schmaltz (*informal*), *schmaltziness* (*informal*), sensationalism, sentiment, sentimentality, showiness, sloppiness (*informal*), tackiness (*informal*), tastelessness, tawdriness, tinsel, vulgarity

231 Disgusting and Repulsive

Something nasty in the woodshed. **Stella Gibbons**

(*adj*) abhorrent (*formal*), abominable, disgusting, dislikable, distasteful, dreadful, evil, foul, ghastly, gory, gross (*informal*), hateful, horrendous (*informal*), horrid, horrific, icky (*informal*), loathsome, nasty, nauseating, nauseous, noisome, noxious, objectionable, obnoxious, obscene, odious, offensive, off-putting, rebarbative (*formal*), *repellant*, repellent, repugnant, repulsive, revolting, *revulsive*, sanguinary (*formal*), seamy, shameful, sickening, sickly, sleazy, sordid, stomach-churning, stomach-turning, unheard-of, unholy, unpleasant, unsavoury, unspeakable, unwholesome, vile, villainous

(*adv*) appallingly, atrociously, foully, grossly (*informal*), unpleasantly, unspeakably

(*n*) atrociousness, distastefulness, dreadfulness, fearfulness (*informal*), frightfulness, *grossness*, horridness, *obnoxiousness*, obscenity, repulsiveness, rottenness (*informal*), unwholesomeness, vileness

232 Frightening

It is a terrible thing for a man to find out suddenly that all his life he has been speaking nothing but the truth. **Oscar Wilde**

(*adj*) alarming, bloodcurdling, bullyboy, chilling, creepy (*informal*), daunting, doomy (*informal*), fearful, fearsome, formidable, frightening, ghastly, ghoulish, Gothic, grim, grisly, gruesome, haunted, horrible, horrid, horrifying, intimidating, macabre, morbid, nail-biting, nightmare, nightmarish, petrifying, scary (*informal*), spine-chilling, spine-tingling, spooky (*informal*), strong-arm (*informal*), terrifying, white-knuckle

(*adv*) fearfully, formidably, grimly

(*n*) creepiness (*informal*), *eeriness*, fearfulness, grimness, grisliness, gruesomeness, horridness, *scariness*, *spookiness* (*informal*)

233 Plain

An honest tale speeds best being plainly told. **William Shakespeare**

(*adj*) austere, bare, bleak, drab, featureless, homely, homespun, low-key, mere, no-frills (*informal*), nondescript, plain, severe, simple, stark, unadorned, undecorated, unfussy

(*adv*) plainly, simply

(*n*) austerity, bareness, bleakness, severity, simplicity, starkness

See also ORDINARINESS (245)

234 Ugliness and Unattractiveness

A good heart will help you to a bonny face, my lad...and a bad one will turn the bonniest into something worse than ugly. **Emily Brontë**

(*adj*) distorted, grim, grotesque, hideous, monstrous, ugly, unappealing, unappetizing, unattractive, *unenticing*, unflattering, *unglamorous*, uninviting, unlovely, unsightly

(*adv*) grotesquely

(*n*) blot on the landscape, grimness, hideousness, ugliness, unattractiveness, unsightliness

See also PEOPLE'S PHYSICAL APPEARANCE (476)

235 Boring and Uninteresting

A universe in which everything is known would be static and dull, as boring as the heaven of some weak-minded theologians. **Carl Sagan**

(*adj*) anodyne, antiseptic, arid, banal, bland, boring, characterless, clichéd, *cliché-ridden*, colourless, commonplace, corny, dead, deadly (*informal*), drab, dragging, draggy (*informal*), dreary, dry, dull, facile, flat, formulaic, fusty, hackneyed, humdrum, humourless, impersonal, indistinctive, insipid, institutional, jejune, lacklustre, lifeless, menial, mindless, mind-numbing, monochromatic, monochrome, monotonous, mouldy, mundane, overused, platitudinous, ponderous, predictable, prosaic, repetitious, repetitive, routine, samey (*informal*), slack, sleepy, soporific, soulless, stagnant, stale, stodgy (*informal*), tame, tedious, time-consuming, tired, turgid, two-dimensional, undemanding, unexciting, unimaginative, unimpassioned, uninspiring, uninteresting, unreadable, unsurprising, vanilla (*slang*), vapid, well-worn, worthy

(*adv*) drably, drearily, dully, flatly, heavily, insipidly, ponderously, soberly, tamely

(*n*) blandness, boredom, *characterlessness*, drabness, dreariness, dullness, flatness, insipidness, monotony, mundaneness, ordinariness, platitude, predictability, predictableness, prosaicness, sameness, soberness, sterility, stodge (*informal*), superficiality, tameness, tediousness, tedium, unimaginativeness, unoriginality, worthiness

See also BORE AND FAIL TO INTEREST (571)

236 Danger

Diseases of the soul are more dangerous and more numerous than those of the body. **Cicero**

(*n*) danger, *dangerousness*, defencelessness, destructiveness, firetrap, hazard, *hazardousness*, *insidiousness*, instability, jeopardy, menace, nakedness, *noxiousness*, peril, *perilousness*, perniciousness, powder keg, *precariousness*, rapaciousness, *recipe for disaster*, risk, *risk factor*, riskiness, rockiness, severity, spectre, threat, toxicity, trouble, unsteadiness, volatility, vulnerability

See also PUT AT RISK (385)

237 Dangerous

A desperate disease requires a dangerous remedy. **Guy Fawkes**

(*adj*) adverse, bad, baleful, bleak, brooding, cancerous, carcinogenic, cataclysmic, chancy, costly, critical, damaging, dangerous, daring, dark, deadly, deleterious (*formal*), desperate, destructive, detrimental, devastating, dicey (*informal*), disadvantageous, dodgy (*informal*), explosive, extreme, fatal, feral, ferocious, forbidding, foreboding, grave, hair-raising, hairy (*informal*), harmful, hazardous, iffy (*informal*), ill, inadvisable, inimical, injurious, insecure, insidious, internecine, leaky (*informal*), lethal, major, malign, man-eating, menacing, *mephitic* (*literary*), nasty, negative, noxious, ominous, parlous (*archaic or humorous*), perilous, pernicious, pestilent, precarious, prejudicial, rapacious, risky, rocky, ruinous, savage, serious, severe, shaky, sinister, speculative, suicidal, threatening, tough, toxic, treacherous, unhealthy, unsafe, unsound, unstable, unsteady, unwise, venturesome (*formal*), volatile, wild

(*adv*) adversely, dangerously, disadvantageously, ferociously, ill, unsteadily

See also DEADLY (928)

238 In Danger

Look back, and smile at perils past. **Sir Walter Scott**

(*adj*) at risk, at stake, defenceless, disappearing, *imperilled* (*formal*), *in danger*, *in jeopardy*, *in peril*, on the rocks (*informal*), open, *open to attack*, protected, susceptible, threatened, unarmed, undefended, unguarded, unprotected, vulnerable, weak, wide-open

(*adv*) at risk

See also IN TROUBLE AND DISADVANTAGED (73)

239 Unimportant and Unnecessary

To a mind of sufficient intellectual power, the whole of mathematics would appear trivial, as trivial as the statement that a four-footed animal is an animal. **Bertrand Russell**

(*adj*) avoidable, beside the point, derisory, expendable, extraneous, fiddling, footling (*informal*), frivolous, frothy, idle, immaterial, inconsequential, inconsiderable, inessential, insignificant, irrelevant, lightweight, little, marginal, meaningless, mild, negligible, neither here nor there, niggling, nonessential, null, of no account, of no consequence, *of no importance*, peripheral, pettifogging, petty, piffling (*informal*), preventable, secondary, silly, skin-deep, small, small-scale, small-time (*informal*), superficial, *surplus to requirements*, tautological, trifling, trivial, uncalled-for, undue, unessential, unimportant, unnecessary, unneeded, unwarrantable, unwarranted, wanton, wasted

(*adv*) inappreciably, indirectly, peripherally

(*n*) anonymity, frivolity, frothiness, inconsequence, inconsequentiality, indifference, insignificance, irrelevance, meaninglessness, pettiness, silliness, *small beer* (*informal*), *small potatoes* (*informal*), tautology, technicality, trifle, trivia, triviality, unimportance

See also REDUNDANT AND USELESS (241)

240 Unfinishedness

Think nothing done while aught remains to do. **Samuel Rogers**

(*adj*) bitty, crude, fragmentary, fragmented, incomplete, limited, partial, patchy, piecemeal, scrappy, *truncated*, unaccomplished, *uncompleted*, unfinished, unimproved

(*adv*) crudely, piecemeal

(*n*) crudeness, patchiness

241 Redundant and Useless

'Tis not necessary to light a candle to the sun. **Algernon Sidney**

(*adj*) absurd, bootless, dead, dispensable, dud (*informal*), empty, extraneous, fallow, fatuous, *functionless*, futile, *garbagy*, *good-for-nothing*, gratuitous, groundless, hollow, idle, impractical, inadmissible, ineffective, invalid, meaningless, needless, *no good*, *no great shakes*, *no use*, *of no use*, *of no value*, otiose, outmoded, pointless, puny, purposeless, redundant, senseless, stillborn, threadbare, timeworn, unavailing, unconstructive, uncultivated, unfruitful, unhelpful, unproductive, unprofitable, unprovoked, unworkable, unworthy, useless, vain, valueless, vestigial, void, worthless

(*adv*) gratuitously, idly, *purposelessly*, redundantly

(*n*) absurdness, defectiveness, emptiness, fruitlessness, futility, gratuitousness, hollowness, ineffectiveness, invalidity, needlessness, pointlessness, *purposelessness*, senselessness, sterility, unhelpfulness, unproductiveness, unworthiness, uselessness, vanity, worthlessness

See also UNIMPORTANT AND UNNECESSARY (239)

242 Weakness

Never support two weaknesses at the same time. **Thornton Wilder**

(*adj*) anaemic, delicate, feeble, flimsy, fragile, frail, indefensible, insubstantial, pitiable, pitiful, poor, powerless, sensitive, toothless, watered-down, watery, weak, wobbly, wonky (*informal*)

(*adv*) feebly, flimsily, pitifully, poorly

(*n*) delicacy, delicateness, faintness, feebleness, flimsiness, insubstantiality, powerlessness, shakiness, susceptibility, weakness, wobbliness

See also COWARDICE AND WEAKNESS OF WILL (509), UNFIT AND WEAK (740)

243 Difficulty and Complexity

It is as easy to count atomies as to resolve the propositions of a lover. **William Shakespeare**

(*adj*) abstruse, arduous, awkward, *bemusing*, bewildering, bureaucratic, busy, byzantine, complex, complicated, confusing, convoluted, crenellated, delicate, demanding, dense, difficult, elaborate, exacting, extreme, fathomless, fiddly (*informal*), fiendish, flaming, formidable, grandiose, hard, *hard to follow*, heavy, *heavy-going*, *horny*, illegible, impenetrable, inaccessible, incomprehensible, indecipherable, indescribable, indigestible, inextricable, insoluble, insuperable, insurmountable, intractable, intricate, involved, knotty, laborious, laboured, *labour-intensive*, labyrinthine, leaden, mind-bending (*informal*), mind-boggling (*informal*), nasty (*informal*), nice, no joke, obscure, onerous, opaque, ornate, painful, pernickety (*informal*), perplexing, problem, problematic, puzzling, rigorous, rocky, sphinxlike, sticky (*informal*), tall, tangled, taxing, testing, thick, thorny, ticklish, tight, tortuous, touchy, tough, tricky, troubled, unanswerable, understrength, undone, unintelligible, unreadable, unsolvable, unsolved, vexed

(*adv*) formidably, hard, obscurely, overtime, problematically, violently

(*n*) abstruseness, acuteness, arduousness, complexity, denseness, depth, difficulty, *elaborateness*, ferocity, fierceness, fragility, grandiosity, impenetrability, inaccessibility, *incomprehensibility*, insolubility, *insuperability*, intractability, laboriousness, nitpicking, *obtuseness*, *onerousness*, opacity, profundity, rigorousness, rigour, toughness, trickiness, *unfathomability*, *unfathomableness*, *unintelligibility*, violence, wildness

See also SECRETS AND MYSTERIES (181)

244 Vagueness

It is easy to be certain. One has only to be sufficiently vague. **C. S. Peirce**

(*adj*) airy-fairy (*informal*), ambiguous, blurred, blurry, cloudy, dim, distant, double-edged, ethereal, euphemistic, foggy, fuzzy, general, ghostlike, ghostly, hazy, ill-defined, imprecise, impressionistic, inchoate (*formal*), indefinable, indefinite, indeterminable, indeterminate, indistinct, indistinguishable, inexplicit, intangible, misty, muzzy, nebulous, nonspecific, open-ended, sketchy, sweeping, tangential, tenuous, unclear, undefined, unfocused, uninformative, unspecified, unstipulated, up in the air, vague, vaporous, woolly

(*adv*) dimly, distantly, fuzzily, hazily, unclearly, vaguely

(*n*) ambiguity, ambiguousness, blur, carelessness, cloudiness, dimness, fuzziness, haziness, *impreciseness*, imprecision, incoherence, indistinctness, inexactness, intangibility, mistiness, *nebulousness*, obliqueness, obscurity, penumbra, roughness, *sketchiness*, *tenuousness*, *unclearness*, vagueness, woolliness

See also APPROXIMATELY (133)

245 **Ordinariness**

Some men are born mediocre, some men achieve mediocrity, and some men have mediocrity thrust upon them. **Joseph Heller**

(*adj*) accepted, accustomed, a dime a dozen (*US*), anonymous, average, below par, bog-standard (*informal*), cheap, common, *common or garden*, commonplace, conventional, customary, day-to-day, *downhome* (*US informal*), downmarket, downscale (*US*), everyday, familiar, forgettable, formulaic, *garden-variety* (*US*), general, generic, habitual, indifferent, low-grade, lowly, mainstream, mass-produced, mediocre, middle-of-the-road, middling, modest, natural, *nothing special*, *nothing to write home about*, off-the-shelf, one-dimensional, ordinary, overrated, pedestrian, prevailing, prosaic, proverbial, ritual, routine, run-of-the-mill, second best, stock, ten a penny, trite, *two a penny*, typical, *undistinctive*, undistinguished, unembellished, uneventful, unexceptional, *unimposing*, unimpressive, uninspired, *unmemorable*, unremarkable, unsophisticated, *unspectacular*, usual, wonted (*formal*), workaday

(*adv*) conventionally

(*n*) banality, commonness, *commonplaceness*, conformity, mediocrity, ordinariness, poorness, primitiveness, *routineness*, triteness, *trivialness*, *vapidity*, *vapidness*

See also INFERIORITY (154), PLAIN (233)

246 **Disorder and Chaos**

Things fall apart; the centre cannot hold;/Mere anarchy is loosed upon the world. **W. B. Yeats**

(*adj*) all over the place (*informal*), anarchic, chaotic, cluttered, confused, desultory, disarranged, disordered, disorderly, disorganized, frantic, frenetic, furious, haphazard, haywire (*informal*), hectic, helter-skelter, higgledy-piggledy, hit-and-miss, *in a jumble*, in a mess, *in a muddle*, in disarray, indiscriminate, jumbled, knockabout, lawless, messy, muddled, rampant, random, riotous, rough, scattershot, scrappy, self-contradictory, shambolic (*informal*), sloppy, topsy-turvy, tumultuous, turbid, turbulent, unclassified, unmanageable, unorganized, unselective, unsystematic, untidy, upside-down, willy-nilly

(*adv*) at random, desultorily, helter-skelter, pell-mell, riotously, untidily

(*n*) chaos, clutter, confusion, derangement, disarray, dislocation, disorder, disorderliness, distraction, farce, frenzy, furiousness, *haphazardness*, havoc, *hugger-mugger*, hurry, jumble, jungle, labyrinth, litter, maelstrom, mayhem (*informal*), maze, mess, messiness, misrule, morass, muddle, *riotousness*, roughness, shambles, sloppiness, tangle, untidiness, warren, welter, whirl

See also DISHARMONY (157)

247 **Wasteful and Uneconomical**

Men deal with life as children with their play,/Who first misuse, then cast their toys away. **William Cowper**

(*adj*) extravagant, inefficient, misspent, profligate, throwaway, uneconomic, uneconomical, unproductive, wasteful

(*adv*) profligately

(*n*) extravagance, inefficiency, unproductiveness, wastefulness

See also USE UP AND WASTE (475)

248 **Expensive and Overpriced**

Computers are big, expensive, fast, dumb adding-machine-typewriters. **Robert Townsend**

(*adj*) costly, dear, exorbitant, expensive, extortionate, high, overpriced, pricey (*informal*), prohibitive, sky-high, steep (*informal*), *unaffordable*

See also EXPENSIVE AND LUXURIOUS (219)

249 **Captivity and Loss of Freedom**

Caged birds accept each other but flight is what they long for. **Tennessee Williams**

(*adj*) bounded, caged, captive, confined, constrained, constricted, contained, covered, custodial, detained, encased, enclosed, enforced, forced, *hemmed in*, imprisoned, *incarcerated* (*formal*), *in prison*, inside (*informal*), involuntary, *jailed*, localized, *locked up*, occupied, on a tight rein, out of bounds, repressed, repressive, restricted, restrictive, shut in, stormbound, trapped, under arrest

(*n*) bondage, captivity, capture, compulsion, confinement, constraint, constriction, control, curb, custody, detention, duress, entrapment, imprisonment, incarceration, in custody, internment, prison, repression, restraint, restriction, ring-fence, round-up, seizure, servitude, snare, solitary confinement, straitjacket, stranglehold, stricture (*formal*), suppression, taboo, trammel, unmentionable

(*v*) cage, capture, catch, confine, constrict, contain, coop up, enmesh, enslave, ensnare, entangle, fetter, foul, gag, handcuff, hem in, *hold captive*, hold in, *hold prisoner*, immure (*literary*), keep down, kidnap, localize, lock away, manacle, occupy, oppress, pen, pen up, pin, pin down, *pull in* (*slang*), quarantine, repress, restrain, round up, seize, shackle, shut in, shut up, snare, snatch (*US informal*), take by storm, take prisoner, tangle, trammel, trap

See also THE POLICE, ARREST, AND PRE-TRIAL PROCEEDINGS (818), BUILDINGS FOR CONFINING PEOPLE (1093)

250 **Captives and Prisoners**

It is not the world that confines you, you yourself are the World, which holds you so fast a prisoner with yourself in yourself. **Angelus Silesius**

(*n*) captive, con (*slang*), convict, detainee, hostage, inmate, internee, jailbird (*slang*), prisoner

See also CRIMINALS (821)

251 **Mistakes**

To conduct great matters and never commit a fault is above the force of human nature. **Plutarch**

(*n*) aberration, anomaly, bloomer (*informal humorous*),

blooper (*US informal humorous*), blunder, *boner* (*informal*), boob (*informal*), boo-boo (*informal*), botch (*informal*), clanger (*informal*), cockup (*informal*), confusion, error, false impression, fault, faux pas (*literary*), foul-up (*informal*), freak, fumble, gaffe, goof (*informal*), howler (*informal*), inaccuracy, inadvertence, lapse, mess-up (*informal*), miscalculation, miscarriage (*formal*), misconception, mishit, misjudgment, misprint, miss, misspelling, misstep, mistake, mix-up, omission, oversight, own goal, slip, *slip of the tongue*, slip-up (*informal*), solecism, spoonerism, stumble

See also MESS UP AND MAKE MISTAKES (473), MISUNDERSTAND AND FAIL TO GRASP (762)

252 Faults, Flaws, and Weaknesses

The deficits in the eyelashes are not apparent to the eye. **Tamil proverb**

(*n*) abnormality, Achilles heel, apology (*humorous*), awfulness, bad habit, blemish, blight, blind spot, blip, blot, blotch, blur, bug (*informal*), chink in somebody's armour, chip, crack, damage, debility, defect, deficiency, demerit, disadvantage, failing, fault, flaw, frailty, *handicap*, hole, impairment, imperfection, inadequacy, inferiority, limitation, loophole, mark, scuff, shortcoming, smear, smudge, splodge, stain, taint, unreliability, vice, weakness, weak point, weak spot

253 Disasters

When disasters come at the same time, they compete with each other. **Naguib Mahfouz**

(*n*) accident, belly flop, blow, body blow, bomb (*US informal*), calamity, cataclysm, catastrophe, cave-in, crisis, *damp squib* (*informal*), debacle, destroyer, disaster, doom, drama, killer, misadventure, misfortune, mishap, nonevent, nose dive, pity, shambles, spill (*informal*), stumble, tragedy, visitation, woe

254 Nuisances

Roses have thorns, and silver fountains mud;/Clouds and eclipses stain both moon and sun. **William Shakespeare**

(*n*) abomination, affliction, aggro (*slang*), anathema, bane, bind, bone of contention, bother, bummer (*slang*), burden, cancer, canker, chill, chore, cost, curse, disappointment, disservice, disturbance, downer (*informal*), downside, *drag* (*informal*), drawback, encumbrance, excrescence, expense, eyesore, forfeit, grievance, hassle (*informal*), headache (*informal*), ill, imposition, inconvenience, *incubus*, irritant, irritation, let (*archaic*), loss, menace (*informal*), minus, mischief, monstrosity, nuisance, pain (*informal*), *pain in the neck* (*informal*), pall, peeve (*informal*), pest (*informal*), plague, provocation, rigmarole, scandal, scourge, spoilage, stain, stigma, stinker, *swizz*, test, *thorn in somebody's flesh*, *thorn in somebody's side*, torment, trial, tribulation, yawn, yoke

255 Bad Behaviour or Action

For every inch that is not fool is rogue. **John Dryden**

(*n*) breach, carrying-on (*informal*), conspiracy, contravention, defacement, delinquency, dereliction, desecration, encroachment, enormity, impishness, indecency, indiscretion, infamy, interference, intrusion, irregularity, irresponsibility, mischief, mischievousness, misdemeanour, monkey business (*informal*), outrage, perverseness, rabble-rousing, roguery, roguishness, rottenness (*informal*), skulduggery (*humorous*), transgression, unfaithfulness, vandalism, vendetta, violation

256 Traffic Accidents

The crash of the whole solar and stellar systems could only kill you once. **Thomas Carlyle**

(*n*) accident, blowout (*slang*), collision, crack-up (*informal*), crash, *fender-bender* (*US informal*), pile-up (*informal*), *rear-ender* (*US*), shunt (*informal*), smash, smash-up, wreck (*US*)

See also TRAVEL: TRAFFIC PROBLEMS AND HOLDUPS (324), PROBLEM (257)

257 Problem

The best way to solve any problem is to remove its cause. **Martin Luther King, Jr.**

(*n*) albatross, bar, barrier, *bete noir* (*literary*), blockage, brake, bugbear, but (*informal*), catch (*informal*), complication, con, congestion, damper, dead end, deathtrap (*informal*), delay, demon, dent (*informal*), deterrence, detriment, difficulty, dilemma, discouragement, disincentive, disruption, fly in the ointment, football, frustration, fuss, glitch, gremlin (*informal*), handful (*informal*), hiccup (*informal*), hindrance, hitch, holdup, hot potato, hurdle, impediment, interference, jinx, kick in the teeth, liability, matter, millstone, no-no (*informal*), objection, obstacle, obstruction, pitfall, prevention, problem, relapse, retardation, reversal, reverse, setback, *snafu* (*informal*), snag, snarl-up, sticking point, stoppage, stumbling block, stymie, teething troubles, tickler (*informal*), tie-up (*US*), time bomb, tinderbox, weight, *whammy* (*informal*)

See also DIFFICULT SITUATIONS (72), TRAVEL: TRAFFIC PROBLEMS AND HOLDUPS (324)

258 Bizarre and Peculiar

They were a tense and peculiar family, the Oedipuses, weren't they? **Max Beerbohm**

(*adj*) aberrant, abnormal, absurd, anomalous, atypical, baffling, *bathetic*, bizarre, blown-up, cockeyed (*informal*), crackbrained, cranky (*informal*), cuckoo (*informal*), cult, curious, dotty, eccentric, eerie, exaggerated, fishy (*informal*), freaky, funny, gonzo (*US slang*), grotesque, *idiotic*, inane, incongruous, inexplicable, inflated, inhuman, insane, irrational, kinky (*informal*), ludicrous, mysterious, mystifying, nonsensical, odd, *oddball* (*informal*), offbeat, off-centre, off-the-wall (*informal*), *otherworldly*, *out in left field* (*US*), outlandish, *out to lunch* (*slang*), overblown, paradoxical, peculiar, phantasmagoric, preposterous, quaint, queer (*dated*), quirky, rich (*informal*), ridiculous, risible, rum (*dated informal*), senseless, spooky, strange, stupid, surreal, unaccountable, uncanny, uncharacteristic, unconscionable, unearthly, *unexplainable*, *unfunny*, ungodly (*informal*), unnatural, unorthodox, unreal, unseasonable, unthinkable, unusual, vaporous, wacky (*informal*), warped, way-out (*informal*), weird, wild (*informal*) (*adv*) absurdly, eerily, funnily, grotesquely, improbably, paradoxically, peculiarly, queerly (*dated*), *risibly*, strangely, unnaturally, unseasonably

(*n*) absurdity, absurdness, *bizarreness*, crankiness (*informal*), *curiousness*, *inaneness*, inanity, incongruity, irrationality, ludicrousness, mysteriousness, oddity, oddness, *otherworldliness*, *outlandishness*, peculiarity, preposterousness, quaintness, queerness (*dated*), quirkiness, ridiculousness, risibility, senselessness, silliness, strangeness, *uncanniness*, unfamiliarity, unnaturalness, wackiness (*informal*), weirdness

See also FUNNY AND AMUSING (217)

259 Unpopular and Unwanted

My definition of a free society is a society where it is safe to be unpopular. **Adlai Stevenson**

(*adj*) abandoned, castoff, despised, *detested*, discarded, disregarded, expendable, hated, ineligible, *loathed*, *reviled*, *ridiculed*, scorned, *unappreciated*, unasked, *unasked-for*, *underestimated*, underrated, *undervalued*, undeserved, undesirable, unenviable, unfrequented, uninvited, *unlikable*, unlooked-for, *unloved*, unpopular, *unrequired*, unsolicited, unsought, *unvalued*, unwanted, unwelcome, *vilified*

See also DISLIKE AND HATE (578)

Move and Function

Action: Start, Continue, and Finish

260 Actions or Undertakings

Great actions are not always true sons/Of great and mighty resolutions. **Samuel Butler**

(*n*) act, action, activity, affairs, antics, contribution, deed, departure, doings (*informal*), endeavour, enterprise, exploit, feat, handiwork, manoeuvre, move, movements, performance, precaution, project, step, stunt, turn, undertaking, venture

261 Start an Action

The origin of action—its efficient, not its final cause—is choice, and that of choice is desire and reasoning with a view to an end. **Aristotle**

(*v*) act on, approach, attack, begin, bestir yourself (*formal*), blaze, break new ground, buckle down (*informal*), buck up (*informal dated*), commence (*formal*), embark on, enter on, enter upon, get cracking (*informal*), get down to, get down to business, *get down to it*, get going, get on, *get stuck in*, *get to work*, get underway, initiate, jump in, kick off (*informal*), lapse into, launch, launch into, launch out, lead off, lead the way, lead up to, make a start, move into, open, pioneer, preface, prefix, set about, set off, set out, set to, start, start off, start on, start out, strike while the iron's hot, take the bull by the horns, take the plunge, take to, take up, tee off

262 Attempt an Action

Accustom yourself continually to make many acts of love, for they enkindle and melt the soul. **Saint Teresa of Ávila**

(*n*) attempt, bash (*informal*), bid, effort, endeavour, go, long shot, potshot, shot, shot in the dark, stab (*informal*), try

(*v*) address, aim, assay (*literary*), attempt, bid, bother, dare, do, endeavour, essay (*formal*), field-test, *give a shot* (*informal*), *give it a try*, go after, go for (*informal*), *go for it* (*slang*), *grapple with*, *grasp the nettle*, *have a bash* (*informal*), *have a crack* (*informal*), *have a go* (*informal*), *have a shot*, *have a stab* (*informal*), make a stab at (*informal*), seek, seek to, set out, speak to (*formal*), tackle, *take a shot at*, *take a stab at* (*informal*), trouble, try, try your hand, undertake, venture

263 Continue an Action

There must be a beginning of any great matter, but the continuing unto the end until it be thoroughly finished yields the true glory. **Francis Drake**

(*v*) beaver (*informal*), brazen out, carry on, chug (*informal*), continue, drag out, get on, go on, hang on, hold your own, keep, keep at, *keep at it*, keep going, keep on, keep up, persevere, persist, pick up, plough on, plough through, plug (*informal*), *plug away* (*informal*), *press ahead*, press on, proceed, run on, see through, soldier on, stand firm, stay on, stay out, stay up, stick at, stick to, stick with, stop out (*informal*), take up, wade through

264 Complete an Action

Time is a traitor, millimeter by millimeter it betrays/the hope of uniting discontinuity,/of securing the incomplete. **Antonio Martínez-Sarrión**

(*v*) be through with, *bring to completion*, close, come in, complete, conclude, consummate, crown, end up, finalize, finish, finish off, follow through, fulfil, get done, go the distance, make, mop up (*informal*), perfect, seal, sew up, tie up, turn round, wind up, wrap up (*informal*)

265 Stop Acting

But it stopped short—never to go again—/When the old man died. Referring to a clock. **Henry Clay Work**

(*v*) adjourn (*informal*), break, break off, call it a day, *call it quits* (*informal*), cease, chill (*slang*), chuck (*informal*), chuck in (*informal*), close, close down, come to a close, come to a halt, come to an end, come to a standstill, come to rest, come up for air, culminate, desist, drop, drop out, freeze, give over (*informal*), give up, give up on, jack in (*informal*), kick, knock off (*informal*), lay off (*informal*), leave off, log off, pack in (*informal*), pack up, pause, put your feet up, quit, refrain, *shut down*, shut up shop, stand down, step down, stop, take five (*informal*), take it easy

266 Cause to Start

Liberty does not consist in mere declarations of the rights of man. It consists in the translation of those declarations into definite action. **Woodrow Wilson**

(*v*) activate, actuate (*formal*), awaken, begin, bring in, bring on, christen (*informal*), crank up, detonate, galvanize, get going, implement, inaugurate, jump-start, kick-start, *phase in*, set in motion, set off, spark, spark off, *start the ball rolling*, strike up, switch on, throw, trigger, trigger off, turn on

See also INSTITUTE AND INAUGURATE (349)

267 Cause to Stop

Life in itself is short enough, but the physicians with their art, know to their amusement, how to make it still shorter. **Petrarch**

(*v*) abandon, abort, arrest (*formal*), blow out, break, bring to a close, *bring to a halt*, bring to an end, *bring to a standstill*, call a halt, call off, cancel, close down, cut, cut off, cut short, deactivate, destroy, disable, discontinue, dissolve, end, extinguish, freeze, halt, hush, immobilize, inactivate, intercept, interrupt, kill off, mothball, nip in the bud (*informal*), nix (*US slang*), *phase out*, pull the plug, put an end to, put a stop to, put down, put out, *put paid to* (*informal*), *put the lid on*, quell, quench, raise, scratch, shut off, silence, slake, snuff, staunch, stop, stub out, suspend, switch off, take off, terminate (*formal*), turn off, turn out, unplug

See also MAKE IMPOSSIBLE (277)

268 Cause to Continue

To preserve a man alive in the midst of so many chances and hostilities, is as great a miracle as to create him. **Jeremy Taylor**

(*v*) buoy, continue, draw out, eke out, extend, further, keep the ball rolling, maintain, nurse, nurture, perpetuate, prolong, protract, spin out, support, sustain

269 Recommence and Resume

The chain of memory is resurrection. **Charles Olson**

(*v*) reactivate, reawaken, recommence, reconvene, redo, rehash, renew, repeat, replay, reprise, resit, restart, resume, retake, *start afresh*, *start again*, *start anew*, *start over* (*US*)

See also REPETITION (29), AGAIN (109)

270 Carry Out an Action

The greatest pleasure I know, is to do a good action by stealth, and to have it found out by accident. **Charles Lamb**

(*n*) accomplishment, enforcement, execution, implementation, manipulation, performance, perpetration, pursuance (*formal*), running

(*v*) accomplish, acquit yourself, act, attend to, behave, blitz (*informal*), bring off, carry out, come to grips with, commit, conduct yourself, dare, deal with, dispose of (*formal*), do, enforce, execute, field, fit in, get into your stride, give, go about, handle, have, juggle, make short work of, manage, manipulate, operate, perform, perpetrate, ply, practise, process, pursue, put into action, put into effect, put into operation, put into practice, realize, respond, run through, see to, sort out, squeeze, swing (*informal*), take, take action, take on, take steps, transact, treat, wage, work

271 Be In Charge

You don't lead by pointing a finger and telling people some place to go. You lead by going to that place and making a case. **Ken Kesey**

(*v*) administer, administrate, be in charge of, captain, chair, conduct, control, direct, edit, govern, head, hold sway, manage, officiate, overlook, oversee, pace, preside, reign, rule, rule the roost, run, spearhead, staff, superintend, supervise, take care of, take charge, take control, take in hand, take over, *take the floor*, take up the baton, tend

272 Cause or Compel to Act

The people may be made to follow a course of action, but they may not be made to understand it. **Confucius**

(*v*) bind, blackmail, bludgeon, boss, boss about, boss around, bribe, buffalo (*informal*), bulldoze (*informal*), buy off, cajole, call in, chivvy, coax, coerce, command, compel, constrain, detail, dominate, dragoon, drive, egg, egg on, enforce, enjoin (*formal*), exhort, force, get, goad, impel, incite, induce, influence, instruct, inveigle, involve, jockey, lean on (*informal*), let in for (*informal*), make, manipulate, motivate, move, nobble (*informal*), obligate, oblige, order about, order around, persuade, press, press-gang, pressure, pressurize, prevail on, *prevail upon*, prod, prompt, push, *push into*, *put pressure on*, *put the arm on* (*US informal*), put up to, railroad (*informal*), require, *rope in*, rouse, *seduce*, *shanghai*, spur, *spur to action*, squeeze, steamroller, strong-arm (*informal*), subject to, suborn, suck in, summon, take advantage of somebody, talk into, twist somebody's arm, urge, wheedle, work on

See also APPEAL TO AND AROUSE INTEREST (576)

273 Hesitate

Thus conscience does make cowards of us all;/And thus the native hue of resolution/Is sicklied o'er with the pale cast of thought. **William Shakespeare**

(*v*) baulk, blench, buck, dither, dry up (*informal*), faff about (*informal*), faff around (*informal*), falter, flounder, *hem and haw*, hesitate, *hum and haw*, lose the thread, oscillate, pause, pussyfoot (*informal*), shilly-shally, stumble, temporize, vacillate, waffle (*US informal*), waver, wobble

274 Shirk and Delay

Delay is the deadliest form of denial. **Cyril Northcote Parkinson**

(*v*) bide your time, dally, dilly-dally, drag your feet, fudge (*informal*), *hang fire*, hang on, hold off, hold on, leave, procrastinate, slow up, stall, stonewall (*informal*), *take a rain check* (*US informal*), tarry, wait

See also DELAY ACTION OR OCCURRENCE (279)

275 Not Do and Refuse to Do

No task is a long one but the task on which one dare not start. It becomes a nightmare. **Charles Baudelaire**

(*v*) abstain, back out, baulk, *beg off*, bottle out (*informal*), *bow out*, capitulate, chicken out (*slang*), *cry off* (*informal*), dig in your heels, duck, duck out, eschew, *fight shy of*, *fink out* (*US slang*), forbear (*formal*), forgo, get out of, get round, jib, keep off, malinger (*disapproving*), neglect, omit, opt out (*informal*), rat on (*informal*), rebel, renege, resist, shirk, shrink from, sidestep, *wriggle out of*

276 Make Possible

There is radiance in the darkness...all you need do is to cultivate the courage to look. **Obafemi Awolowo**

(*v*) abet, assure, choreograph, cultivate, ease, emcee (*informal*), enable, encourage, expedite (*formal*), facilitate, fast-track, favour, foster, let through

277 Make Impossible

I am the spirit that always denies. **Johann Wolfgang von Goethe**

(*v*) bar, block, blockade, cancel out, combat, count against, counter, counteract, damp, dash, derail, disarm, discourage, embargo, exclude, foil, foreclose (*formal*), forestall, frustrate, gag, inhibit, keep from, keep out, muzzle, overrule, overturn, *paralyse*, preclude (*formal*), prevent, *put a spanner in the works*, put a spoke in somebody's wheel, put a wrench in the works (*US*), put off, rain off, rain out (*US*), sabotage, scotch, scupper, scuttle, snooker (*informal*), spike (*informal*), squelch (*slang*), stop, stultify, stymie, *throw a monkey wrench in the works* (*US informal*), *throw a spanner in the works*, thwart, torpedo (*informal*), undo

See also CAUSE TO STOP (267)

278 Avoid, Prevent, Limit, and Control

A speculator is a man who observes the future, and acts before it occurs. **Bernard Mannes Baruch**

(*adj*) deterrent, obstructionist, pre-emptive, preventive

(*n*) avoidance, check, curtailment, delimitation (*formal*), deterrent, nonproliferation, obstructionism, preclusion (*formal*), pre-emption, prevention, sabotage

(*v*) avert, avoid, boycott, bridle, check, circumscribe (*formal*), clamp down, constrain, contain, control, cramp, crimp, curb, curtail, dam, debilitate, encumber, get in the way, hamper, help, hinder, hold back, impede, inhibit, interfere, keep, keep back, keep down, keep in check, keep the lid on, keep under control, limit, manage, micromanage, moderate, obstruct, obviate, organize, peg, police, pre-empt, regiment, *rein back*, rein in, restrain, restrict, ring-fence, save, shackle, shut up (*informal*), silence, smother, stem, strangle, subdue, subvert, talk out of, tame, throttle, trammel, weigh against, work against

279 Delay Action or Occurrence

Delay always breeds danger. **Miguel de Cervantes**

(*n*) adjournment, dawdling, deferment, delay, *dilly-dallying*, postponement, procrastination, *rain check* (*US informal*), rearrangement, rescheduling, suspension

(*v*) adjourn, carry over, dawdle, defer, delay, detain, hold over, hold up, mothball, postpone, put back, put off, put on hold, put on ice, put on the back burner, rearrange, reschedule, retard, set back, shelve, slow down, stall, stave off, stay, stonewall (*informal*), stunt, suspend, table (*US*), tell against

See also SHIRK AND DELAY (274)

280 Intentional and Deliberate

We know what a person thinks not when he tells us what he thinks, but by his actions. **Isaac Bashevis Singer**

(*adj*) blatant, calculated, conscious, controlled, deliberate, face-saving, flagrant, gross, intended, intentional, knowing, meant, planned, prearranged, premeditated, programmed, scheduled, self-imposed, strategic, studied, tactical, voluntary, wilful

(*adv*) advisedly, by design, calculatingly, consciously, decisively, deliberately, designedly, enterprisingly, expressly, in broad daylight, in cold blood, nakedly, on purpose, purposely, wittingly

281 Automatic and Instinctive

Mistrust first impulses; they are nearly always good. **Charles Maurice de Talleyrand**

(*adj*) automatic, instinctive, involuntary, knee-jerk (*informal*), mechanical, mechanistic, perfunctory, reflexive, spontaneous, spur-of-the-moment, unquestioning, unthinking, visceral

(*adv*) by itself, impulsively, inevitably, instinctively, involuntarily, of its own accord, on the spur of the moment

282 Unintentional and Accidental

Improvisation is the touchstone of wit. **Molière**

(*adj*) ad hoc, ad-lib, arbitrary, impromptu, improvised, inadvertent, indirect, irrespective, motiveless, offhand, off-the-cuff, unannounced, unconscious, unexpected, unforeseen, unintended, unintentional, unknowing, unmeant, unplanned, unpremeditated, unscripted, unwitting

(*adv*) accidentally, by accident, by mistake, capriciously, offhandedly, *on a whim*, *on impulse*, unawares, unconsciously, unknowingly, willy-nilly

See also CHANCE, COINCIDENCE, AND ACCIDENT (787)

283 Cautious and Careful

Some craven scruple/Of thinking too precisely on th' event. **William Shakespeare**

(*adj*) careful, cautious, deliberate, fastidious, measured, methodical, unhurried

(*adv*) deliberately, gingerly, meticulously, microscopically, minutely, narrowly, *with care*

284 Incautious and Careless

To lose one parent, Mr. Worthing, may be regarded as a misfortune; to lose both looks like carelessness. **Oscar Wilde**

(*adj*) brash (*US*), careless, desperate, improvident (*formal*), imprudent (*formal*), inattentive, incautious, perfunctory, precipitate, precipitous, rash, remiss, slapdash, slaphappy, slipshod, sloppy (*informal*), thoughtless, unceremonious, unconsidered, unguarded, unorganized, unthinking

(*adv*) carelessly, distractedly, frenziedly, gracelessly, headily, lightly, like mad, loosely (*dated*), mindlessly, no holds barred, unwisely, *without due care and attention*, *without due consideration*

285 Acting Independently

Deliberation is the work of many men. Action, of one alone. **Charles De Gaulle**

(*adj*) lone, single-handed, solo, standup, unaccompanied, unassisted, unilateral

(*adv*) all by yourself, alone, by yourself, independently, individually, in person, in the flesh, in your own right, on your own, separately, single-handed, solo, specially, unaided, *without help*

See also SOLITARINESS (941)

286 Acting with Others

Every sin is the result of a collaboration. **Stephen Crane**

(*adj*) assisted, bilateral, collaborative, combined, concerted, joint

(*adv*) all together, as one, collectively, cooperatively, in chorus, in concert, in step, in tandem, *in unison*, socially, together, with one accord (*formal*), *with one heart* (*US*), with one voice

See also RECIPROCITY AND INTERDEPENDENCE (148)

287 With Enthusiasm

Man is only truly great when he acts from the passions. **Benjamin Disraeli**

(*adv*) actively, avidly, busily, eagerly, energetically, enthusiastically, *feistily* (*informal*), friskily, greedily, heartily, hungrily, intently, madly, perkily, purposefully, ravenously, willingly, *with enthusiasm*, *with fervour*, *with good cheer*, *with gusto*, *with no holds barred*, *with passion*

See also THE WILL AND WILLINGNESS (564)

288 Without Enthusiasm

If you want to know where the apathy is, you're probably sitting on it. **Florynce R. Kennedy**

(*adv*) forcibly, half-heartedly, lazily, lethargically, reluctantly, resignedly, *spiritlessly*, *under duress*, *under protest*, wearily

See also UNWILLINGNESS AND STUBBORNNESS (565), NEUTRALITY AND INDIFFERENCE (554)

289 Describing Body Movements

A dance is a measured pace, as a verse is a measured speech. **Francis Bacon**

(*adj*) blundering, bumbling (*informal*), clumsy, convulsive, dainty, doddering, jerky, jumpy, neat, nifty, quick, quivering, shambling, sinuous, trembling, tremulous, wavering

(*adv*) jumpily, neatly, tremulously

(*n*) jerkiness, jumpiness, neatness, quivering, shakiness, shaking, trembling, wobbliness (*informal*)

See also AGILITY OF THE BODY (477)

290 Prepare for Action

A cause is like champagne and high heels—one must be prepared to suffer for it. **Arnold Bennett**

(*v*) bite the bullet, brace yourself, gear up, get ready, gird your loins, grit your teeth, intend, lead up to, limber up, line up, *make preparations*, mean, *pave the way*, pluck up courage, polish up on, practise, prepare, *prepare the ground*, *prepare the way*, prepare yourself, *preplan*, propose, psych (*US*), psych up (*informal*), purport (*formal*), ready, *ready yourself*, rehearse, schedule, scheme, *spread your wings*, steel, steel yourself, *take a deep breath*, timetable, train, walk through, warm up, wind up (*US*)

See also PREPARATORY EVENT (57)

291 Overdo Something

A man's reach should exceed his grasp,/Or what's a heaven for? **Robert Browning**

(*v*) binge, *bite off more than you can chew*, burn out (*informal*), double-book, dramatize, exceed, *get carried away*, gild the lily, go beyond, go over the top, *go too far*, ham, *ham it up*, make a point of, make much of, overact, overcompensate, overdo, *overdo it*, overdo things, *overdramatize*, overeat, *over-egg the pudding*, overestimate, overextend, overindulge, overpitch, overprotect, overreach, overreact, oversimplify, overstay, overstep, overstrain, overstretch, overuse, overvalue, play to the gallery, play up, *push the boat out* (*informal*), rush, splurge (*informal*), supercharge, wear yourself out

292 Underdo Something

Anything worth doing is worth doing poorly at first. **Robert Downey, Jr.**

(*v*) go easy on (*informal*), make light of, minimize, play down, trivialize, underachieve, underemphasize, underestimate, underperform, underplay, underrate, underrepresent, understate, undervalue

293 Participate

A life is not important except in the impact it has on other lives. **Jackie Robinson**

(*v*) appear, contribute, dabble, enlist, enrol, enter, enter into, feature, figure, get in on the act (*informal*), get involved, go in for, have a hand in, hold the fort, impose, infringe, integrate, intercede, intervene, join, join in, matriculate, observe, partake, participate, play, *play a part*, register, sign on, sign up, star, star in, take part, team up, throw yourself into

294 Help

Everybody wants to do something to help, but nobody wants to be the first. **Pearl Bailey**

(*v*) abet, accommodate, aid, aid and abet, assist, bail out, collaborate, cooperate, *give a hand*, help, help out, lend a hand, make yourself useful, *pitch in*, pull together, *rally round*, serve

See also KIND ACTION OR BEHAVIOUR (296), TAKE CARE OF AND SPOIL (301)

295 Ways of Doing Things

Suit the action to the word, the word to the action; with this special observance, that you o'erstep not the modesty of nature. **William Shakespeare**

(*adv*) by dint of, by means of, how, like so, somehow, someway, thereby, thus (*formal*)

(*n*) algorithm, alternative, apparatus, approach, arrangement, avenue, bureaucracy, channel, choreography, code, *code of behaviour*, code of conduct, code of practice, conduct, contrivance, convention, course, course of action, criterion, custom, departure, design, device, doctrine, expedient, form, formality, formula, framework, gambit, game plan, gimmick, going, golden rule, gold standard, ground rule, *guidelines, guiding principle*, habit, improvisation, institution, instrument, intrigue, law, *line of attack*, machine, machinery, manner, manoeuvre, means, mechanics, mechanism, medium, method, methodology, *modus*, modus operandi, modus vivendi, mores, movement, operation, organ (*formal*), outlet, plan, plot, ploy, policy, practice, *praxis* (*formal*), predetermination, principle, procedure, process, programme, protocol, recipe, red tape (*informal*), regime, regimen, regulation, rite, ritual, route, routine, rubric, *rules and regulations*, scheme, setup, standing order, stratagem, strategy, style, system, tack, tactic, tactics, technique, theory, tradition, treatment, usage, use (*literary or archaic*), vehicle, way, ways and means, wont (*formal*)

296 Kind Action or Behaviour

Evil has encircled man from all sides, so man has devised good in all courses of action. **Naguib Mahfouz**

(*n*) aid, assist (*US*), assistance, attention, backup, benevolence, care, charity, concession, facilitation, favour, gesture, good deed, good offices, good turn, hand, help, helping hand, indulgence, intervention, ministration (*formal*), participation, philanthropy, relief, service, solace, succour (*literary*), support, turn

See also HELP (294)

297 Unkind Action or Behaviour

Malice is of a low stature, but it hath very long arms. **Sir George Savile**

(*n*) abuse, abusiveness, aggression, aggressiveness, assault, atrocity, attack, barbarity, betrayal, blood lust, brushoff (*informal*), brutality, bullying, cold shoulder, cruelty, fierceness, footwork, foul play, harassment, horridness, ill-treatment, maltreatment, mistreatment, nastiness, oppression, ostracism, persecution, punishment, *sadism*, savagery, sellout (*informal*), shabbiness, slight, stab in the back (*informal*), *terrorization*, tyranny, ugliness, viciousness, victimization, violence

298 Work in General

That state is a state of slavery in which a man does what he likes to do in his spare time and in his working time that which is required of him. **Eric Gill**

(*n*) brief, case, chore, commission, commitment, errand, groundwork, housekeeping, job, maintenance, mission, obligation, occupation, responsibility, spadework, task, workload

See also JOB (833)

299 Hard Work or Effort

If hard work were such a wonderful thing, surely the rich would have kept it all to themselves. **Lane Kirkland**

(*n*) *blood, sweat, and tears*, campaign, *concerted effort*, difficulty, donkeywork (*informal*), drudgery, effort, exertion, graft (*informal*), grind (*informal*), *hard graft, hard labour, hard work, heavy labour*, industry (*formal or literary*), labour, legwork (*informal*), long haul (*informal*), pains, schlep (*informal*), slog, strain, struggle, toil, travail, treadmill, trouble, *uphill battle*, work

(*v*) bend over backwards, burn the candle at both ends, burn the midnight oil, drudge, exert yourself, graft (*informal*), knuckle down (*informal*), labour, leave no stone unturned, make an effort, move heaven and earth, *move mountains*, overwork, pull out all the stops, put your back into, slog, strain, strive, struggle, *sweat blood*, toil, *work day and night, work flat out, work hard, work like a dog, work overtime, work up a sweat*

300 Easy Work

Our work is sometimes less difficult than our amusements. **Louis XIV**

(*n*) blowout (*slang*), breeze (*informal*), cakewalk (*informal*), child's play, cinch (*informal*), *cushy number*, doddle (*informal*), doss (*slang*), *easy ride, kid's stuff*, picnic (*informal*), piece of cake (*informal*), romp (*informal*), sinecure, snap (*US*), *soft option*, walkaway (*US informal*), *walk in the park* (*informal*), walkover (*informal*), waltz (*informal*)

301 Take Care of and Spoil

We are unimportant. We are here to serve, to heal the wounds and give love. **Marike de Klerk**

(*v*) accommodate, baby, babysit, be there for, billet, bring up, care, *care for*, chaperone, cocoon, coddle, cosset, doctor, dose, father, feed, fend for, foster, *fuss over, give refuge, give shelter to*, go easy on (*informal*), heal, humour, indulge, keep, let up on, lodge, look after, make a fuss of, mean well, mind, minister (*formal*), mollycoddle, mother, nurse, nurture, pamper, pet, *provide for*, put up, quarter, raise, roll out the red carpet, *run around after*, spoil, spoon-feed, stick by, succour (*literary*), support, sustain, take care of, tend, treat, *treat like royalty*, wait on, watch, watch over, *wrap in cotton wool*

See also HELP (294), KIND ACTION OR BEHAVIOUR (296)

302 Obey and Abide by

The man who obeys is nearly always better than the man who commands. **Ernest Renan**

(*v*) abide by, adhere, behave, comply, conform, follow, fulfil, honour, jump (*informal*), keep, keep to, obey, observe, play the game, respect, stick to, *toe the line*

303 Disobey

I have within me an impossibility of obeying. **René Chateaubriand**

(*v*) breach, break, contravene, defy, disobey, flout, fly in the face of, go against, infringe, misbehave, offend, overstep, transgress, violate

304 Compete, Contend, and Combat

Mad as the sea and wind when both contend/Which is the mightier. **William Shakespeare**

(*v*) battle, brawl, broil (*US archaic*), bushwhack (*US informal*), campaign, combat, come to blows, compete, confront, contend, crusade, *do battle*, duel, engage, enter, fence, feud, fight, grapple, hit back, jockey, labour, oppose, outbrave (*archaic*), outface, pit, play off, race, rebel, resist, rival, run, scrap, scuffle, set to, skirmish, spar, square up, struggle, take up the gauntlet, touch, tussle, vie, wage war on, wrestle

See also PEOPLE IN SPORTS AND LEISURE (876), COMPETITORS (41)

Movement and Locomotion

305 Self-Propulsion

Motion being eternal, the first mover, if there is but one, will be eternal also. **Aristotle**

(*n*) circulation, locomotion, mobility, motion, movement, transmigration

306 Proceed and Go

Not to go back, is somewhat to advance,/And men must walk at least before they dance. **Alexander Pope**

(*n*) canter, dash, escape, hobble, hop, *lope*, pace, promenade (*formal*), ramble, run, saunter, slog, step, stride, stroll, tramp, trudge, walk, wander

(*v*) advance, approach, circle, circulate, clomp, come, course, file, filter, float, flow, fly, freewheel, get, glide, go, go forward, goose step, graduate, gravitate, head, hike, hover, jaywalk, lollop, make for, make your way, march, move, move ahead, move along, move forward, move in on, move over, overshoot, pace, parade, patrol, *perambulate* (*formal*), progress, promenade (*formal*), prowl, puddle, ramble, ride, round, slip, slither, snake, step, stomp, swagger, thread, traipse (*informal*), tramp, tread, troop, wade, walk, waltz, wend, yomp (*informal*)

307 Go Upwards

He who ascends to mountain-tops shall find/The loftiest peaks most wrapt in clouds and snow. **Lord Byron**

(*n*) ascension (*formal*), ascent, climb, levitation, rise, scramble

(*v*) arise (*archaic or literary*), ascend, billow, bristle, clamber, climb, get to your feet, levitate, mount, move up, perk up, pole-vault, pounce, ride up, rise, scramble, soar, spiral, start up, stick up, stir, surface, surmount (*formal*), take off, zoom

See also MOVE SOMETHING: UPWARDS (329)

308 Go Downwards

Reckon the climb before reckoning the descent. **Lebanese proverb**

(*n*) descent, dive, drop, free fall, nose dive, plunge, tailspin, trip

(*v*) alight, bite the dust (*informal*), cascade, climb down, come down, crash-land, dangle, descend, dip, dismount, dive, drop, fall, fall down, fall over, free-fall, get down, go down, gravitate, lapse, nose-dive, pitch, plummet, plunge, settle, settle down, sink, slip, stumble, subside, swoop, toboggan, topple, trip, trip up, tumble

See also MOVE SOMETHING: DOWNWARDS (330)

309 Bounce, Undulate, and Vibrate

The way up and the way down are one and the same. **Heraclitus**

(*n*) bound, jump, leap, oscillation, pounce, ripple, rise and fall, spring, undulation

(*v*) bob, bobble, bounce, buck, heave, hop, hurdle, jump, kangaroo (*informal*), leap, leapfrog, oscillate, pitch, *pitch and toss*, *pogo*, quake, ripple, seesaw, skip, somersault, spring, sway, swing, undulate, vault, vibrate, wave

310 Go Backwards

The people who live in the past must yield to the people who live in the future. Otherwise the world would begin to turn the other way round. **Arnold Bennett**

(*n*) regression

(*v*) back, back away, back off, backtrack, back up, draw back, ebb, fall back, fall behind, go back, go backwards, jump back, move away, move back, pull back, recede, recoil, retrace, retreat, retrogress, return, reverse, revert, shrink back, shy away, slip back, spring back, turn back

311 Get Closer Together

Let's meet, and either do, or die. **Beaumont & Fletcher**

(*v*) assemble, band together, bear down on, bunch, burrow, close, close up, cluster, come together, concentrate, congregate, crowd, *cuddle up*, encroach, flock, gather, *gather together*, group, *group together*, huddle, *huddle together*, *huddle up*, mass, meet, mobilize, move towards, muster, nestle, press (*literary*), press together, queue, rally, reassemble, sit, snuggle, *squash up*, *squeeze up*, swarm, throng, *throng together*, troop

312 Fidget and Frolic

VLADIMIR *Well, shall we go?*/ESTRAGON *Yes, let's go.*/They do not move. **Samuel Beckett**

(*n*) boogie, cartwheel, flip-flop, handspring, romp, somersault, *to-ing and fro-ing*

(*v*) boogie (*informal*), bop (*informal*), caper, cartwheel, cavort, dabble, dance, exercise, fidget, flail about, flounder, frisk, frolic, gambol, go around, groove (*slang*), horse around, jig, *kick up your heels*, loosen up, prance, reel, romp, splash, squirm, struggle, thrash, *thrash about*, *toss and turn*, trip, wriggle, writhe

313 Take Up a New Position

Whatever is in motion must be moved by something else. **Thomas Aquinas**

(*v*) bank, droop, founder, hang, keel over (*informal*), list, loll, lose your footing, lurch, move along, open out, open up, pitch, roll, slump, spill over, tilt, *tilt back*, tip, uncoil, uncurl, wash, *yaw*

314 Move Fast

In skating over thin ice, our safety is in our speed. **Ralph Waldo Emerson**

(*v*) beetle (*informal*), belt (*informal*), bowl, bundle (*informal*), burn (*informal*), burst, bustle, canter, career, charge, chase, come at, cruise, dart, dash, flash, flit, *floor it* (*US slang*), flounce, fly, gallop, *go full tilt*, hasten, *hit the gas* (*US*), hurry, hurtle, hustle (*informal*), jog, lunge, make a beeline for, motor (*informal*), move fast, nip (*informal*), plunge, pop (*informal*), pour, prance, race, rattle through, rip, rocket, romp, run, rush, sail, sashay (*humorous*), scamper, scoot (*informal*), scramble, screech, scud, scurry, scuttle, shift (*informal*), *shimmy*, shoot (*informal*), skim, speed, sprint, stampede, step out, storm, streak, stride, strut, surge, sweep, swoosh, tear, trot, waft, waltz, whisk, whiz, *whizz*, whoosh, wing, zap (*informal*), zip (*informal*), zoom

See also MOVING QUICKLY (103)

315 Move Slowly

Well it is known that ambition can creep as well as soar. **Edmund Burke**

(*v*) amble, coast, crawl, creep, dawdle, delay, drag, drift, drop back, drop behind, edge, fall behind, *galumph* (*informal*), hang about, hang around, hang back, inch, lag, linger, loiter, *maunder*, mooch (*slang*), moon, mosey (*informal*), pad, percolate, plod, potter, pussyfoot (*informal*), saunter, schlep (*informal*), shamble, shilly-shally, sidle, slink, slog, sneak, steal, straggle, stroll, tiptoe, toddle (*informal*), tootle (*informal*), trail, troll, trudge, trundle, wander

See also MOVING SLOWLY (105)

316 Walk Unsteadily

It is charming to totter into vogue. **Horace Walpole**

(*v*) bumble, dodder, falter, hobble, labour, limp, lumber, reel, shuffle, stagger, stumble, teeter, toddle, totter, waddle

317 Physical Reactions

Something bent down and took hold of me and shook me like the end of the world...with each flash a great jolt drubbed me. **Sylvia Plath**

(*n*) jerk, jump, kick, pounding, pulsation, pulse, quiver, recoil, seizure, shiver, shudder, spasm, start, tic, tremble, tremor, twitch, vibration, wince

(*v*) convulse, cower, cringe, dodder, flinch, jerk, jump, kick, lock, palpitate, pound, pulsate, pulse, quail, quake, quaver, quiver, shake, shiver, shrink, shudder, start, throb, tremble, twitch, unclench, waver, wince, wobble

318 Assume a Position

Squat like a toad, close at the ear of Eve. **John Milton**

(*v*) bend, bestride, crouch, curl up, duck, grovel, huddle, hunch, hunker, hunker down, kneel, lean, lie, lie back, lie down, mount, plop down, plump, plunk down, poise, pose, recline, retire, sit, sit down, slouch, slump, sprawl, square up, squat, stand, stand up, stoop, stretch out

319 Travel: Journeys and Trips

A journey is a person in itself, no two are alike. **John Steinbeck**

(*n*) airing, *away day*, circuit, crossing, cruise, day out, day trip, detour, emigration, excursion, expedition, exploration, flight, *hajj*, hike, hop (*informal*), jaunt, journey, junket, long haul (*informal*), march, migration, odyssey, outing, passage, peregrination (*literary*), ride, round trip, run, safari, sojourn (*literary*), sortie (*humorous*), spin, spree, tootle (*informal*), tour, travels, trek, trip, turn, visit, voyage, walkabout (*informal*)

See also VEHICLES (1144)

320 Travel: Travellers and Walkers

I took my mind a walk/or my mind took me a walk—/whichever was the truth of it. **Norman McCaig**

(*n*) adventurer, backpacker, biker, day tripper, deck hand, explorer, fare, globetrotter, *hajji*, *hitchhiker*, holidaymaker, jaywalker, *jet-setter* (*informal*), mariner, *New Age traveller*, passenger, pathfinder, pedestrian, pilgrim, rambler, ranger, roamer, rover, *sailor*, sightseer, strap-hanger (*informal*), tourist, traveller, *trekker*, tripper (*informal*), vacationer (*US*), visitor, voyager, walker, wanderer, wayfarer (*literary*), weekender

See also PEOPLE IN SPORTS AND LEISURE (876)

321 Travel: Ways of Travelling

No other form of transport in the rest of my life has ever come up to the bliss of my pram. **Osbert Lancaster**

(*adj*) mounted, onboard, on the road

(*adv*) en route, on foot, on the move, on tour

(*v*) *backpack*, board, bus, circumnavigate (*formal*), commute, cover, cox, coxswain, cruise, drive, embark, emigrate, explore, ferry, gallivant (*informal*), get off, get on, globetrot, go, go around, guide, hitch, hitchhike, immigrate, island-hop, journey, migrate, motor, navigate, orbit, paddle, pass through, pedal, pilot, remount, revisit, ride, row, sail, scull, shuttle, *sightsee*, steer, *thumb a lift*, toboggan, tour, transmigrate, travel, trek, voyage, weekend

See also COMMUNICATION NETWORKS (1104)

322 Travel: Sight-Seeing and Tourism

Tourism is the march of stupidity. **Don DeLillo**

(*n*) courier, guide, sights, sightseeing, *tour guide*, tourism, *tourist attractions*, *tourist centre*, *tourist class*, *tourist spot*, traffic, *travel guide*, *vacation industry* (*US*), *vacationland* (*US*), *vade mecum*, visitor centre

323 Transportation, Transporters, and Cargos

Rowing home to haven in sunny Palestine,/With a cargo of ivory,/. . .Sandalwood, cedarwood, and sweet white wine. **John Masefield**

(*adj*) mobile, movable, oceangoing, seafaring, seagoing, transportable

(*n*) cargo, carriage, carrier, consignment, conveyance, delivery, freight, load, shipment, shipping, speed limit, staging post, steerage, supersaver, transit, transport, transportation, transporter

See also COMMUNICATION NETWORKS (1104)

324 Travel: Traffic Problems and Holdups

Rush hour*: that hour when traffic is almost at a standstill.* **J. C. Morton**

(*n*) backup (*US*), bottleneck, gridlock, jam, logjam, queue, roadworks, speed trap, tailback, traffic jam

See also PROBLEM (257), TRAFFIC ACCIDENTS (256)

325 Move Something to Another Location

A poem is energy transferred from where the poet got it. . .by way of the poem itself to, all the way over to, the reader. **Charles Olson**

(*n*) conduction, deployment, dislocation, dispersal, dispersion, displacement, distribution, move, placement, redeployment, redirection, relocation, repatriation, repositioning, resettlement, spacing, transfer, transplantation, transposition

(*v*) bear, bring, bring back, budge, canalize (*formal*), carry, cart, channel, deliver, displace, disturb, funnel, hustle, move, offload, put aside, put back, rehouse, relocate, resettle, run, suck, take, thrust, tote (*informal*), transfer, transplant, transpose, uproot

326 Position Something

(*v*) arrange, centre, change round, deploy, deposit, direct, dispose (*formal*), ensconce (*archaic or literary*), hang, hang out, hang up, install, lay out, leave, line up, load, locate, move, park (*informal*), pile, place, plant, plonk, plop (*informal*), *plump down*, point, pop (*informal*), position, put, rack, replace, reposition, seat, set, shift, shove, site, situate (*formal*), space, stand, station, stick (*informal*), target, tuck, turn

327 Position Something: Between, Beside, or Inside Something

(*v*) embed, implant, incorporate, inject, insert, intercalate, intercut, interlace, interlard, interleave, interlock, interpose, intertwine, interweave, juxtapose, sandwich, sheathe, slot, superimpose, wedge

328 Position Something: Around Something

(*v*) coil, curl, furl, loop, spool, twine, twirl, twist, wind, wreathe

See also EXIST IN CLOSE PROXIMITY (21)

329 Move Something: Upwards

(*v*) elevate, grub, heft (*US*), hoist, jack up, level, lift, pick up, raise, send up, take up, upheave, uplift, uproot, winch

See also GO UPWARDS (307)

330 Move Something: Downwards

(*v*) depress, down, drop, dunk, immerse, lay, lay down, let down, lower, plunge, put down, set down, submerge

See also GO DOWNWARDS (308)

331 Move Something: Into a New Position or Overturn

(*v*) aim, angle, bowl over, bring down, capsize, cock, fell, flatten, flip, flip over, invert, keel, keel over (*informal*), knock down, knock over, lean, mow down, orient, orientate, overturn, prop up, rest, retract, skew, slant, slope, stack, tip, turn over, turn turtle, upend, upset, upturn

332 Move Past, Into, or Through Something

(*v*) breach, break into, break through, crisscross, cross, drive, entrench, ford, get ahead of, get through, infiltrate, inset, instil, interpolate, leapfrog, near, negotiate, pass, pass by, penetrate, percolate, permeate, pervade, push in, queue-jump, run through, skirt, traverse

333 Spread and Scatter

Money is like muck, not good except it be spread. **Francis Bacon**

(*v*) broadcast, diffract, dissipate, pepper, punctuate, rake, scatter, slop, slosh, sow, spatter, spill, splash, splatter, spray, spread, sprinkle, strew

334 Despatch and Send

Sir, more than kisses, letters mingle souls. **John Donne**

(*v*) address, airdrop, airlift, airmail, catapult, consign, convey, dispatch, e-mail, extradite, fax, forward, launch, mail (*US*), misdirect, post, redeploy, redirect, refer, remit, return, route, second, send, send off, send on, ship, sublimate, telegraph, transfer, transmit, transport

335 Throw Something

It is a mathematical fact that the casting of this pebble from my hand alters the centre of gravity of the universe. **Thomas Carlyle**

(*n*) lob, pass, throw, toss

(*v*) blast off, blow, blow away, bowl, bung (*informal*), cast, chuck (*informal*), dash (*formal*), flick, fling, flirt, heave (*informal*), hurl, launch, let fly, lob, pass, pelt, pitch, pitchfork, project, propel, punt, send, shoot, sling, throw, toss, volley

336 Push, Pull, Slide

The man who pulls the plow gets the plunder in politics. **Huey Long**

(*n*) putt, shove, shunt, thrust, tug, wrench, yank

(*v*) caddie, drag, draw, drive, ease, float, haul, heave, hydroplane, impel (*formal*), jerk, lug, pole, pull, push, putt, roll, shove, shunt, slide, thrust, tow, trail, trundle, tug, wrench, yank

337 Move Something on the Spot

Midnight shakes the memory/As a madman shakes a dead geranium. **T. S. Eliot**

(*n*) flap, gyration, jerk, jolt, judder, rev, revolution, rotation, shake, spin, swirl, turn, twirl, twist, wag, whirl, wiggle

(*v*) agitate, bat, brandish, crank, dandle, fan, flail, flourish, flutter, gyrate, jar, jerk, jiggle, joggle, jolt, judder, lash, nod, pirouette, pivot, revolve, rewind, rock, rotate, screw, shake, sling, spin, suspend, sway, swim, swing, swirl, swivel, *swivel round*, turn, twiddle, twirl, twist, wag, waggle, wave, welter, wheel, whirl, wield, wiggle, wobble

338 Accompany and Follow

She is so conjunctive to my life and soul/That, as the star moves not but in his sphere,/I could not but by her. **William Shakespeare**

(*v*) accompany, catch up, chase, come along, conduct, creep up on, direct, dog, drive, escort, follow, frogmarch, gain on, give chase (*formal*), go around (*informal*), go round, guide, head, herd, home in, hound, hunt, keep up, lead, lock on, mob, overtake, partner, pick up, pursue, run after, see, see off, see out, send, shadow, shepherd, show, *show in*, *show out*, *show the way*, *show to the door*, sleuth, sneak up on, spoor, stalk, steer, string along (*informal*), tag along, tail (*informal*), tailgate, take, track, trail, usher, watch

339 Remove Something

Do not remove a fly from your friend's forehead with a hatchet. **Proverb**

(*n*) abstraction, deduction, deletion, disposal, elimination, erasure, excision, expression, extraction, extrication, purge, removal, withdrawal

(*v*) carry off, cart off, deduct, denude, extricate, lop, pluck, remove, shift, subtract, take, take away, take off, unsheathe

See also CAUSE TO DISAPPEAR (6), GET RID OF SOMETHING (452), TAKE SOMETHING AWAY (426)

340 Delete and Erase

Every sentence...that appears in the public press is perused and revised and deleted in the interests of advertisers and bondholders. **John Dos Passos**

(*v*) burn, cross out, cut, delete, edit out, efface, erase, expunge, remove, rub out, strike out, wash, wear, wear away, wear down, wipe, wipe out (*informal*)

341 Eject and Exclude

It is an old maxim of mine that when you have excluded the impossible, whatever remains, however improbable, must be the truth. **Arthur Conan Doyle**

(*n*) banishment, deportation, evacuation, eviction, exclusion, expulsion, extradition, segregation

(*v*) banish, boot out (*informal*), count out, deport, draw off, eject, evacuate, evict, exile, expel, express, fire (*informal*), force out, keep off, kick out (*informal*), lay off, omit, oust, pump, repatriate, repel, segregate, send packing (*informal*), shoo away, shut out, smoke out, throw out, turf out (*slang*), turn out

See also REVOKE STATUS (460)

342 Extract and Sever

Time will not be ours for ever,/He, at length, our good will sever. **Ben Jonson**

(*v*) abstract, amputate, aspirate, crop, cut off, cut out, deadhead, excise, extract, fish out (*informal*), gouge, gouge out, lop, mow, pare, pluck, prune, pull, pull out, pull to pieces, quarry, scythe, sever, shave, shear, take out, tear, trim, weed, weed out, withdraw

343 Lack of Activity

Nothing in progression can rest on its original plan. We may as well think of rocking a grown man in the cradle of an infant. **Edmund Burke**

(*adj*) aground, at rest, beached, becalmed, dead, dormant, frozen, idle, immobile, impacted, inactive, inert, jammed, motionless, poised, quiescent (*formal*), *run aground*, stagnant, static, stationary, still, stopped, stuck, trapped, unmoving, unoccupied, unused

(*adv*) aboard, at a standstill, quiescently (*formal*), stockstill

(*n*) gridlock, idleness, immobility, inaction, inactivity, inertia, languor, lassitude, logjam, motionlessness, quiescence (*formal*), repose, stagnation, stand, standstill, stasis, stillness

(*v*) balance, bask, *flop about*, *flop around*, fool about, fool around, footle (*informal*), freewheel, goldbrick (*informal*), *hang loose* (*informal*), hang out (*informal*), idle, *kick back* (*informal*), kill time, knock about (*informal*), laze, laze about, laze around, lie about (*informal*), lie around (*informal*), loaf, *loaf about*, *loaf around*, loiter, *loll around*, lollop, lounge, *lounge about*, *lounge around*, lurk, mess about (*informal*), mess around (*informal*), mooch (*US slang*), potter, relax, repose (*formal*), rest, *rest up*, *sit about*, sit around, *sit on your heels*, skulk, *slob around* (*informal*), stagnate, stay put, *stay still*, take a break, take a breather (*informal*), *take a rest*, *twiddle your thumbs*, vegetate, *veg out* (*informal*)

See also PERIOD OF REST (91), PAUSES AND PHASES (56)

344 Aimless and Errant Motion

Wandering between two worlds, one dead,/The other powerless to be born. **Matthew Arnold**

(*adj*) adrift, lost, off course, stray, wandering

(*adv*) adrift, astray

(*v*) blunder, *careen*, *flail around*, get lost, go adrift, go astray, lose your bearings, lose your way, lurch, meander, puddle, roam, rove, straggle, stray, swan (*informal*), wallow

345 Change Direction of Motion

Digressions, incontestably, are...the life, the soul of reading; take them out of this book for instance, you might as well take the book along with them. **Laurence Sterne**

(*n*) about-face (*US*), about-turn, deflection, deviation, diffraction, refraction, U-turn

(*v*) avert, boomerang, *change course*, change direction, deflect, depart, deviate, divert, *do a U-turn*, dogleg, *double back*, glance off, head off, jackknife, meander, radiate, rebound, refract, ricochet, skid, slew, sweep, swerve, swing, swing round, tend, turn, twist, *twist and turn*, veer, weave, wheel, *wheel about*, wheel around, *wheel round*, wind, zigzag

346 Direction of Motion

Truly there is a tide in the affairs of men; but there is no gulf-stream setting forever in one direction. **James Russell Lowell**

(*adj*) *anticlockwise*, ascendant (*literary*), *back-and-forth*, backward, ballistic, *clockwise*, *counterclockwise* (*US*), descendent, devious, direct, directional, downward, forward, gyratory, inbound, incoming, indirect, ingoing, inward, landward, left-handed, one-way, onward, *outbound*, outgoing, *outward-bound*, pitching, rearwards, receding, recessive, retrograde, retrogressive, revolving, right-handed, *rightward*, rotary, serpentine, sidelong, sideways, skyward, snaky, starboard, tortuous, twisting, twisty, undirected, up and down, upward, wiggly

(*adv*) ashore, aside, astern, *as the crow flies*, asunder (*formal*), back, back and forth, backwards, backwards and forwards, by way of, circuitously, direct, directly, *downriver*, *downwards*, due, earthwards, forth (*formal*), forwards, frontwards, headfirst, headlong, head-on, head over heels, heavenwards, hither and thither, *hither and yon*, home, inland, inshore, inwards, landwards, onward, outwards, rearward, rearwards, round, *seawards*, sideways, skyward, straight, to and fro, upwards

(*n*) course, direction, orbit, path, tack, tendency, trajectory, trend, vector

(*prep*) down, towards, via

Creation, Production, and Emission

347 Creation

We live at a time when man believes himself fabulously capable of creation, but he does not know what to create. **José Ortega y Gasset**

(*n*) authorship, casting, construction, creation, discovery, erection, fabrication, formation, formulation, generation, invention, making, manufacture, manufacturing, output, production, publishing, reconstitution, reconstruction, recreation, redevelopment, synthesis

(*v*) breed, bring forth, build, cobble together, construct, create, design, determine, fashion, form, invent, knock together (*informal*), knock up (*informal*), make, make up, map out, pose, produce, put together, *recreate*, re-create, *redesign*, re-establish, remake, remix, rig up, tailor, weave, write

348 Designers, Creators, and Instigators

Every animal leaves traces of what it was; man alone leaves traces of what he created. **Jacob Bronowski**

(*n*) architect, author, creator, designer, developer, discoverer, executor, facilitator, father, founder, generator, *graphic designer*, initiator, instigator, inventor, maker, manufacturer, originator, pioneer, planner, producer, propagator, trailblazer, trendsetter

349 Institute and Inaugurate

In analyzing history do not be too profound, for often the causes are quite superficial. **Ralph Waldo Emerson**

(*v*) base, bring into being, carve out, coin, compose, conceive, constitute (*formal*), create, devise, erect, establish, form, formulate, found, generate, ground, improvise, inaugurate, install, instate, institute, introduce, launch, mastermind, mount, orchestrate, originate, predicate (*formal*), *redevise*, reintroduce, reissue, restore, set up, stage, start, start up, strike

See also CAUSE TO START (266)

350 Manufacture

Nothing should be made by man's labour which is not worth making or which must be made by labour degrading to the makers. **William Morris**

(*v*) cast, churn out, craft, create, develop, fabricate, forge, knock off (*informal*), make, manufacture, mass-produce, mechanize, mint, mould, prefabricate, smelt, synthesize, turn out

351 Engender

Eminence engenders enemies. **C. L. R. James**

(*v*) bear, breed, bring forth, cast, engender, hatch, have, spawn, yield

352 Grow and Cultivate

I have a garden of my own,/But so with roses overgrown,/And lilies, that you would it guess/To be a little wilderness. **Andrew Marvell**

(*n*) cultivation, fertilization, pollination, propagation

(*v*) afforest, bloom, blossom, bud, come into bud, come into flower, crop, cultivate, farm, fertilize, flower, fruit, germinate, grow, irrigate, mulch, pick, plant, pollinate, propagate, rear, repot, seed, shoot, sprout

353 Build

When we build let us think that we build for ever. **John Ruskin**

(*v*) assemble, build, construct, erect, jerry-build, make, piece together, pitch, put together, put up, raise, reassemble, reconstitute, reconstruct, redevelop, rig, set up, sink

354 Cooking and Food Preparation

Cookery. . .a form of pandering which corresponds to medicine. **Plato**

(*n*) *cookery*, cooking, heating

(*v*) barbecue, beat, boil, braise, brew, broil (*US*), brown, caramelize, casserole, *chargrill*, cook, cream, cure, deseed, fillet, flavour, flour, frizzle, fry, garnish, grate, griddle, grill, gut, hash, heat, homogenize, kipper, liquidize, make, marinate, microwave, overcook, overdo, *pan-fry*, *parboil*, pare, pasteurize, peel, pickle, poach, pot, *prebake*, precook, preheat, purée, *recook*, *refry*, reheat, roast, sauté, scald, season, simmer, skin, *slow cook*, souse, spice, spoon, stew, stir, stir-fry, sweeten, tenderize, toast, undercook, underdo, whip, whisk

See also STATE OF PREPARED FOOD (1170)

355 Meal Preparation

The vulgar boil, the learned roast an egg. **Alexander Pope**

(*v*) concoct, cook up, fix (*informal*), prepare, rustle up (*informal*), *scare up* (*US informal*), *warm through*, whip up (*informal*)

356 Crafts and Carving

That lyf so short, the craft so long to lerne,/Th' assay so hard, so sharp the conquerynge. **Geoffrey Chaucer**

(*n*) handicraft, handwork, *needlecraft*, sampler, turning, woodwork

(*v*) baste, braid, carve, darn, embroider, fit, hem, hew, model, run up, sculpt, sew, square, stitch, weave, whittle

types of handicraft appliqué, crochet, dressmaking, embroidery, knitting, lacemaking, macramé, needlepoint, needlework, sewing, smocking, stitching, tapestry, tatting, weaving

types of woodwork cabinetmaking, carpentry, carving, joinery, marquetry, woodcarving

See also HOBBIES, GAMES, AND SPORTS (875)

357 Create Images

The painting is finished when it has blotted out the idea. **Georges Braque**

(*v*) airbrush, brand, chalk, doodle, draft, draw, draw up, emboss, engrave, etch, hatch, inscribe, map, monogram, outline, photograph, postmark, print, sketch, stamp, stencil, stylize, trace, write

358 Arrange and Create Order

Oh! Blessed rage for order, pale Ramon/The maker's rage to order words of the sea. **Wallace Stevens**

(*n*) cataloguing, categorization, clear-out, codification, collation, compilation, coordination, formalization, orchestration, oversight, prioritization, rationalization, realignment, rearrangement, regimentation, reorganization, reshuffle, restructuring, *systematization*

(*v*) align, array (*formal*), assort, average out, blitz (*informal*), bring into line, bring together, catalogue, categorize, choreograph, class, classify, clear, clear up, codify, collate, comb, compose, configure, coordinate, counterbalance, disentangle, even out, even up, filter, fix up, formalize, format, grade, graduate, group, harmonize, homogenize, justify, line up, marshal, neaten, order, organize, pack, plan, prioritize, programme, pull together, put away, rationalize, readjust, realign, reallocate, rearrange, redistribute, regiment, regroup, regulate, rejig (*informal*), reorder, reorganize, reshuffle, restructure, rig, schematize, slot in, sort, sort out, square, square up, stagger, standardize, straighten, straighten up, streamline, structure, synchronize, systematize, *systemize*, tabulate, tidy, tidy up

See also IMPROVE SOMETHING (375)

359 Create Disorder and Cause Chaos

Where eldest Night/And Chaos, ancestors of Nature, hold/Eternal anarchy, amidst the noise/Of endless wars, and by confusion stand. **John Milton**

(*v*) *clutter up*, complicate, confuse, derange, disarrange, dislocate, disorganize, disrupt, disturb, garble, jumble, mess up (*informal*), mistime, muddle, muddle up, obfuscate, obscure, riffle, scramble, tousle, upset

See also WORSEN SOMETHING (381), MESS UP AND MAKE MISTAKES (473)

360 Destruction and Demolition

The body politic, like the human body, begins to die from the moment of its birth, and bears in itself the causes of its destruction. **Jean-Jacques Rousseau**

(*n*) demolition, depredation, despoilment, destruction, devastation, harm, mutilation, obliteration, pulverization, violation

(*v*) annihilate, blast, blow up, bombard, bulldoze, burst, chew up, consume, damage, decimate, deforest, degrade, demolish, destroy, devastate, dynamite, explode, extinguish, go off, knock down, *lay waste*, level, machine-gun, mutilate, nuke (*slang*), obliterate, pull down, puncture, rack, ravage, raze, *raze to the ground*, *reduce to ashes*, *reduce to rubble*, ruin, sack, shatter, shell, smash, *smash to smithereens*, smash up, strike, tear down, tear up, total

(*US slang*), trash (*informal*), unmake, waste, wreck, write off, zap (*informal*)

See also WORSEN SOMETHING (381), CONTACT: IMPACT (414), FIRE, FLAMMABILITY, AND BURNING (1164)

361 Tear, Break, and Cut

Smashing things, tearing them up, using the tongs as a sword—these represent the...weapons of the child's primary sadism. **Melanie Klein**

(*n*) breakage, breakup, dissection, fragmentation, split

(*v*) bisect, bore, break, break up, bust (*informal*), carve, chip, chop, chop up, cleave, clip, come apart, crack, crumble, cut, cut down, cut up, dash (*formal*), dice, dig, dint, dissect, drill, fall apart, fall to bits, flake, fracture, fragment, fray, gash, give, grind, grind down, hack, halve, hew, incise, indent, lacerate, ladder, lance, mince, nick, nip, open up, perforate, pierce, pound, prick, pull apart, pulverize, punch, puncture, razor, rend, riddle, rip, *rip apart*, *rip open*, *rip to pieces*, *rip to shreds*, rip up, *rive* (*literary*), rupture, scarify, score, scrape, shatter, shred, skewer, slash, slice, slit, snag, snap, snip, spit, splinter, split, sunder (*literary*), tear, tear apart

362 Emit and Emanate

Women are not the moon. Emit your own light. **Bai Fengxi**

(*n*) discharge, emission, leak, leakage, outflow, secretion, seepage, spill, spillage

(*v*) debouch, emanate (*formal*), emit, escape, exude, foam, froth, give off, give out, go out, issue, let out, ooze, produce, pump out, radiate, send, send forth (*archaic or literary*), transmit

363 Sound Emission

Be not afeard. The isle is full of noises,/Sounds, and sweet airs, that give delight, and hurt not. **William Shakespeare**

(*v*) *make a racket*, pipe down (*informal*), quieten down, *re-echo*, resound, reverberate, ring

See also SOUNDS (1255)

364 Sound Emission by People

A human being...is a whispering in the steam pipes on a cold night. **Christopher Darlington Morley**

(*v*) bawl, bray, clamour, croak, croon, cry, exclaim, groan, gurgle, holler (*informal*), hoot, keen, moan, screak (*US*), scream, screech, shout, sigh, snarl, snicker, thunder, wail, wheeze, whine, whisper, yell

See also SOUNDS MADE BY PEOPLE (1261)

365 Sound Emission by Animals or Birds

The forms take shape in the dark air:/Puss-purr of leopard, footfall of padding bear. **T. S. Eliot**

(*v*) bark, bay, bray, caterwaul, caw, cheep, cluck, croak, crow, growl, grunt, howl, mew, miaow, peep, purr, screak (*US*), snarl, squawk, squeak, squeal, trill, tweet, warble, whine, whinny, *woof*, yap, yelp, yowl

See also SOUNDS MADE BY ANIMALS (1260), SOUNDS MADE BY BIRDS (1262)

366 Emit Sounds Through Impact and Abrasion

(*v*) beat, clack, clang, clash, clatter, click, clink, clonk, clump, crackle, crash, creak, drum, grind, groan, jangle, jingle, patter, plunk, pop, rasp, rattle, squelch, squish

367 Emit Continuous Sounds

(*v*) beep, blare, blare out, blast (*informal*), blast out, boom, burble, buzz, drone, echo, fizzle, gargle, gurgle, hiss, hum, purl (*literary*), rumble, sing, sizzle, sound, spit, sputter, susurrate, swish, thrum, thunder, whirr, whiz, whoosh

368 Emit Ringing and Tooting Sounds

(*v*) chime, ding, honk, hoot, knell, *parp*, peal, ping, quaver, resonate, ring, ring out, ting, *ting-a-ling*, tinkle, toll, tootle (*informal*), whistle

369 Light Emission

Be thou the rainbow to the storms of life!/The evening beam that smiles the clouds away,/And tints to-morrow with prophetic ray! **Lord Byron**

(*v*) beam, blink, burn, flash, flicker, floodlight, *fluoresce*, glance, glare, gleam, glimmer, glint, glisten, glitter, illuminate, *illumine* (*literary*), incandesce, indicate, irradiate, light up, *luminesce*, scintillate, shimmer, shine, spangle, spark, sparkle, throw, twinkle, wink

See also DESCRIBING LIGHT (1227)

370 Smell Emission

Precious odours—most fragrant when they are incensed or crushed. **Francis Bacon**

(*v*) hum (*informal*), niff (*slang*), pong (*informal*), reek, smell, stink, stink out, whiff (*informal*)

See also SMELL AND SMELLING (706)

371 Liquid Emission

Spilled water is not picked up again. **African (Bemba) proverb**

(*v*) discharge, disgorge, dribble, drip, drop, exude, gush, leach, leak, ooze, pour, secrete, seep, shoot, spew, spill over, spout, spurt, squirt, stream, trickle, vomit, water, weep, well, well up

372 Record Something

What is not recorded is not remembered. **Benazir Bhutto**

(*v*) annotate, catalogue, chart, chronicle, compile, document, enter, fictionalize, file, fill in, fill out, film, ghostwrite, input, inscribe, itemize, jot down, key, keyboard, key in, list, log, make a note of, make out, minute, note, *note down*, pen, pencil, plot, prerecord, punctuate, put down, put in writing, record, register, rough out, scrawl, scribble, set down, shoot, take down, tape, tape-record, transcribe, type, video, videotape, write, write down

See also WRITING (584), COPY AND DUPLICATE (403)

Change and Transformation

373 Change

All conservatism is based upon the idea that if you leave things alone you leave them as they are. But you do not. If you leave a thing alone you leave it to a torrent of change. **G. K. Chesterton**

(*adj*) changed, edited, modified, reconstructed, tailored

(*n*) acclimatization, accommodation, adaptation, adjustment, alchemy, alteration, alternation, amendment, assimilation, biorhythm, calibration, change, conversion, diversification, diversion, dynamics, ebb and flow, *expurgation*, flux, graduation, habituation (*formal*), inurement, inversion, maturation, metamorphosis, modification, modulation, move, mutation, normalization, orientation, permutation, readjustment, reconstitution, redistribution, redraft, regulation, revival, revocation, revolution, rewrite, sea change, shake-out, shake-up, shift, specialization, switch, transfiguration, transformation, transition, transliteration, *transmogrification*, transmutation, transubstantiation (*formal*), variance, variation, variety, vicissitudes

(*v*) acclimate, acclimatize, accommodate, act on, adapt, adjust, affect, age, alter, alternate, change, change round, colour, condition, convert, customize, develop, distort, diversify, doctor, ebb and flow, elaborate, fiddle, flavour, fluctuate, gear to, get used to, get your bearings, go, grow up, impinge (*formal*), individualize, inflect, influence, level off, level out, make a difference, mature, metamorphose, militate, modify, modulate, morph, mould, mutate, naturalize, objectify, personalize, range, react, readjust, recast, reconstitute, re-form, *reformat*, *reinvent*, reset, reshape, revolutionize, ripen, set, settle in, shake up, shape, simplify, syncopate, tailor, transfigure, transform, translate, transliterate, *transmogrify*, transmute, turn, tweak (*informal*), vary

374 Social, Political, and Economic Change

Revolution is...as natural as natural selection, as devastating as natural selection, and as horrible. **William Golding**

(*n*) *denationalization*, depopulation, gentrification, industrialization, modernization, perestroika, politicization, *regionalization*, unification

(*v*) *denationalize*, depoliticize, disestablish, gentrify, industrialize, modernize, nationalize, politicize, *regionalize*, reunify

See also GOVERNMENT AND POLITICS (805)

375 Improve Something

Let a king recall that to improve his realm is better than to increase his territory. **Desiderius Erasmus**

(*n*) amelioration, correction, enrichment, fine-tuning, overhaul, *palliation*, rectification, redemption, refinement, refining, rejuvenation, renewal, renovation, revision, revitalization, upgrading

(*v*) add, advance, ameliorate (*formal*), animate, become, benefit, better (*formal*), brighten, bring alive, bring to life, brush up, change for the better, civilize, correct, defuse, enhance, enliven, enrich, grace, groom, heal, help, hone, humanize, improve, innovate, lighten, liven up, make better, mellow, normalize, optimize, *palliate*, pep up (*informal*), perfect, polish, polish up, profit, raise, refine, reform, regularize, rehabilitate, remodel, renew, sharpen, smarten up, spice, stabilize, sweeten, turn round, update, upgrade, uprate, work on, work up

See also ARRANGE AND CREATE ORDER (358)

376 Get Better

If I had my way I'd make health catching instead of disease. **Robert G. Ingersoll**

(*v*) bounce back, buck up, come alive, come along, get better, improve, look up, make progress, mend, move on, outgrow, pick up (*informal*), progress, pull through, revive, shape up, turn the corner

377 Repair and Mend

Many men on the point of an edifying death would be furious if they were suddenly restored to life. **Cesare Pavese**

(*n*) mend, mending, refit, refurbishment, repair, restoration, service

(*v*) cobble, debug, fix, fix up, heel, knit, maintain, mend, overhaul, patch, patch up, piece, put back together, rebuild, recondition, refit, renew, renovate, repair, restore, rewire, service, sew up, sharpen, tinker

378 Correct and Put Right

As if religion was intended/For nothing else but to be mended. **Samuel Butler**

(*v*) amend, calibrate, compensate, correct, ease, edit, emend, *expurgate*, fine-tune, iron out, make up, mend, neutralize, offset, put right, rationalize, reconcile, rectify, redraft, redress, regenerate, remedy, revise, reword, rework, rewrite, right, settle, smooth out, smooth over, soothe, straighten out, tune

379 Improve Strength and Durability

He is a man of brick. As if he was born as a baby literally of clay and decades of exposure have baked him to the colour and hardness of brick. **John Updike**

(*n*) consolidation, fortification, rearmament, reinforcement

(*v*) barricade, beef up (*informal*), boost, boost up, breathe new life into, buffer, buttress, cement, confirm (*formal*), consolidate, empower, energize, feed, firm up, fortify, give a boost, *give a new lease of life*, harden, invigorate, nourish, pad, reanimate, rearm, rebuild, recharge, refresh, reincarnate, reinforce, rejuvenate, resurrect, resuscitate, revitalize, revive, revivify, shore up, soup up (*informal*), steady, stiffen, strengthen, supercharge, toughen, underpin, underprop, vitalize

380 Improve Appearance

It is proportion that beautifies everything, this whole Universe consists of it, and Musicke is measured by it. **Orlando Gibbons**

(*n*) adornment, beautification, decoration, facelift, makeover, ornamentation, revamp, titivation

(*v*) beautify, coiffure (*formal*), decorate, embellish, glamorize, *glam up* (*slang*), *gussy up* (*US informal*), jazz up (*informal*), landscape, manicure, preen, prettify, *pretty up*, primp, retouch, revamp, smarten, smarten up, spruce up, sugar, tart up (*informal*), titivate, tone up, vamp up

See also DECORATE, ADORN, AND APPLY COATINGS (406)

381 Worsen Something

For sweetest things turn sourest by their deeds:/Lilies that fester smell far worse than weeds. **William Shakespeare**

(*adj*) degenerative, deteriorating, regressive, retrograde, retrogressive

(*n*) debasement, decay, degeneration, destabilization, deterioration, impoverishment, regression, retrogression, reversion, spoilage, worsening

(*v*) aggravate, break down, cast a shadow over, cheapen, chip away at, debase, defile (*formal*), deprave, desecrate, destabilize, detract, eat into, exacerbate, fan the flames, impair, inflame, mar, pervert, put a damper on, reduce, sour, spoil, stain, tamper, tarnish, tear, undercut, undermine, violate, worsen

See also DESTRUCTION AND DEMOLITION (360)

382 Get Worse

Everything is perfect coming from the hands of the Creator; everything degenerates in the hands of man. **Jean-Jacques Rousseau**

(*v*) atrophy, backslide, degenerate, descend, deteriorate, droop, fester, *get worse*, go down, go downhill, go from bad to worse, go to pot (*informal*), go to rack and ruin (*informal*), go to the dogs (*informal*), languish, lapse, lapse into, pall, regress, relapse, retrogress, revert, sink, sour, spiral, stagnate, suffer, take a turn for the worse, turn, waste, waste away, worsen

383 Worsen Appearance

What deep wounds ever closed without a scar? **Lord Byron**

(*v*) abrade, blast, blemish, blight, blot, bruise, chafe, chip, deface, dent, litter, roughen, ruffle, scar, scrape, scratch, scuff, vandalize, weather

See also DESTRUCTION AND DEMOLITION (360), FIRE, FLAMMABILITY, AND BURNING (1164)

384 Wound a Person or Animal

Would you hurt a man keenest, strike at his self-love. **Lew Wallace**

(*n*) disfigurement, dismemberment

(*v*) abuse, batter, brutalize, dehumanize, disembowel, disfigure, dismember, enfeeble, *eviscerate*, excoriate, graze, harm, hurt, ill-treat, ill-use, incapacitate, infect, injure, *interfere with*, knife, knock out, maim, maltreat, mangle, mess about (*informal*), mess around (*informal*), misuse, overcome, pull, rick, rough up (*informal*), rub, skin, strain, *tear limb from limb*, traumatize, twist, victimize, weaken, wing, wound, wrench

See also PHYSICAL ATTACK AND PUNISHMENT (416), KILL (923), ILL AND SICK (741)

385 Put at Risk

Those who mill around at the crossroads of history do so at their own peril. **David L. Boren**

(*v*) endanger, expose, hurt, imperil (*formal*), jeopardize, menace, put at risk, put in danger, risk, threaten

See also DANGER (236)

386 Change of Shape

Spirits when they please/Can either sex assume, or both. . ./Not tied or manacled with joint or limb,/Nor founded on the brittle strength of bones,/Like cumbrous flesh. **John Milton**

(*adj*) collapsible, foldaway, folding, foldup, inflatable, pop-up, retractable, telescopic

(*n*) crease, crinkle, deformation, distortion, fold, pleat, pucker, ruck, tuck, warp, wrinkle

(*v*) arch, backcomb, bend, blur, bow, buckle, bulge, cave in, collapse, contort, crease, crimp, crinkle, crumple, crush, curve, deform, distort, double, double up, flatten, flex, flop, fluff, fold, fold up, frizz, frizzle, furrow, gather, hammer out, hang down, indent, kilt, level, macerate, mash, open out, perm, pleat, powder, press, pucker, pulp, purse, ridge, riffle, roll up, ruck, rumple, sag, screw, scrunch, *shrivel up*, smooth, smooth down, smooth out, splay, squash, squeeze, squelch, squish, *stave in*, steamroller, straighten, straighten out, style, trample, tread, tuck, turn back, twist, unbend, wad, warp, wrinkle

387 Change of Temperature

As Freezing persons, recollect the Snow/First—Chill—then Stupor—then the letting go. **Emily Dickinson**

(*v*) bake (*informal*), boil over, chill, cool, cool down, cool off, ice, refrigerate, warm, warm up

388 Harden, Congeal, Dry

Beauty halts and freezes the melting flux of nature. **Camille Paglia**

(*n*) coagulation, fossilization, icing, *ossification*, *petrification*

(*v*) anneal, bake, calcify, clot, coagulate, coarsen, *comminute*, concentrate, congeal, curdle, dehydrate, desiccate, dry, dry out, dry up, firm, fossilize, freeze, freeze up, gel, go hard, harden, ice, ice over, ice up, jell, jellify, jelly, mummify, ossify, parch, petrify, set, solidify, stiffen, thicken, wither

389 Soften, Liquefy, Dampen

For pity melts the mind to love. **John Dryden**

(*v*) bathe, damp, dampen, defrost, de-ice, *deliquesce*, deluge, dip, dissolve, douse, drench, drown, film over, humidify, infuse, liquefy, macerate, melt, moisten, moisturize, penetrate, render, saturate, smelt, soak, soften, souse, steam up, steep, thaw, water, wet

390 Froth and Effervesce

What is fame? an empty bubble;/Gold? a transient, shining trouble. **James Grainger**

(*v*) bubble, effervesce, fizz, froth, lather, seethe, simmer, sparkle, vaporize

391 Go Bad and Corrode

When I die I want to decompose in a barrel of porter and have it served in all the pubs in Dublin. **J. P. Donleavy**

(*n*) corrosion, decomposition, *oxidation*, oxidization, rot, rust

(*v*) corrode, curdle (*informal*), decay, decompose, degrade, gangrene, go bad, *go mouldy*, go off, *go rancid*, *go rotten*, *go sour*, *go stale*, moulder, oxidize, putrefy, rot, rust, spoil, stagnate

392 Change of Colour

'Tis the last rose of summer/Left blooming alone;/All her lovely companions/Are faded and gone. **Thomas Moore**

(*v*) blacken, blanch, bleach, blench, brighten, burn, colour, darken, discolour, dye, flush, pale, peroxide, redden, rouge (*dated*), shade, tan, tinge, tint, whiten

393 Change of Size: Bigger

The mind, once expanded to the dimensions of larger ideas, never returns to its original size. **Oliver Wendell Holmes**

(*adj*) accumulative, burgeoning, distended, flaring, growing, swollen, telescopic

(*n*) accretion, accrual, accumulation, aggrandizement, amplification, appreciation, distension, enlargement, expansion, explosion, extension, groundswell, growth, magnification, maximization, upswing

(*v*) accrue, aggrandize, average up, balloon, billow, bloat, blow up, boost, boost up, broaden, build up, bulk up (*informal*), bump up (*informal*), climb, complement, develop, dilate, distend, elongate, engorge, enlarge, expand, extend, fatten, fatten up, fill out, flesh out, flex, gain, get bigger, get longer, go through the roof, grow, increase, inflate, leap, lengthen, let down, let out, magnify, make up, maximize, multiply, mushroom, open out, outspread, pad, plump up, puff out, puff up, pump up, put on, quadruple, raise, rocket (*informal*), shoot up, skyrocket (*informal*), snowball, splay, spread, stretch, supplement, swell, triple, wax (*literary*), widen

394 Change of Size: Smaller

Learning which does not advance each day will daily decrease. **Chinese proverb**

(*adj*) abbreviated, abridged, condensed, decreasing, edited, potted (*informal*), shrunken, tapered

(*n*) constriction, contraction, cut, decrease, dent (*informal*), depletion, detraction, fall, miniaturization, narrowing, reduction, remission, shrinkage, taper

(*v*) abbreviate, abridge, abstract, average down, cap, chop down, compact, compress, condense, contract, cut, cut back, cut down, decrease, deflate, dent, erode, fall, fall off, get less, get smaller, get thinner, halve, let down, macerate, miniaturize, narrow, narrow down, pare down, prune, shorten, shrink, shrivel, slash, slim down, take in, take up, taper, tauten, trim, truncate, whittle down

395 Change of Intensity: More

The intensity of an idea depends upon the somatic excitation with which it is connected. **Wilhelm Reich**

(*adj*) escalating, mounting, rising, soaring

(*n*) aggravation, augmentation, climb, crescendo, escalation, gain, increase, increment, intensification, leap, multiplication, rise, upsurge

(*v*) amplify, augment (*formal*), bolster, deepen, double, eke out, enlarge, escalate, exalt (*formal*), fan, fortify, fuel, *go sky-high*, heighten, hot up (*informal*), inflate, intensify, jack up, mount, ramify, ratchet, redouble, scale up, soar, step up, stimulate, stoke up, treble, turn up, well, whet

396 Change of Intensity: Less

Moderation is a fatal thing. **Oscar Wilde**

(*n*) alleviation, attenuation, de-escalation, depreciation, dilution, diminution, dive, mitigation, qualification, sag, weakening

(*v*) abate (*formal or literary*), allay, alleviate, assuage, attenuate, blunt, cool, cushion, damp down, dampen, deaden, deepen, de-escalate, depreciate, devalue, die down, dilute, dim, diminish, dive, douse, downplay, dull, eat away, enervate, fade, grow less, lessen, liberalize, lighten, lower, minimize, mitigate, moderate, modify, modulate, muffle, pale, qualify, quell, quieten, recede, reduce, relax, relieve, remit, sap, satiate, satisfy, scale down, slacken, slide, soften, soft-pedal (*informal*), step down, still, subside, take the edge off, taper, temper, thin, tone down, tumble, turn down, water down, weaken, wear off

397 Change of Speed: More

In my time, the follies of the town crept slowly among us, but now they travel faster than a stagecoach. **Oliver Goldsmith**

(*n*) acceleration

(*v*) accelerate, get a move on (*informal*), get moving, hurry, hurry up, open up (*informal*), pick up, *pick up speed*, *pick up the pace*, quicken, rev, smarten, speed up, spur (*literary*), step on it (*slang*), *step on the gas* (*US*)

See also SPEED (102)

398 Change of Speed: Less

Ah! the clock is always slow;/It is later than you think. **Robert W. Service**

(*n*) deceleration

(*v*) brake, decelerate, *reduce speed*, slow, slow down, *slow up*

See also SPEED (102)

399 Change One Thing for Another

Love, in the form in which it exists in society, is nothing but the exchange of two fantasies. **Nicolas Chamfort**

(*n*) changeover, conversion, inversion, substitution, surrogacy

(*v*) alternate, change over, commute, convert, depute,

fill in, override, relieve, replace, reverse, rotate, *sub* (*informal*), substitute, supersede, supplant, swap over

See also EXCHANGE AND INTERCHANGE (449)

400 Substitutes and Stand-Ins

A vacuum is a hell of a lot better than some of the stuff that nature replaces it with. **Tennessee Williams**

(*n*) alternate (*US*), fill-in, replacement, stand-in, substitute, surrogate

401 Combine and Mix

Mix a little foolishness with your serious plans: it's lovely to be silly at the right moment. **Horace**

(*n*) absorption, agglutination, assimilation, coalescence, cross-fertilization, desegregation, fusion, graft, hybrid, incorporation, injection, insertion, integration

(*v*) agglutinate, aggregate, amalgamate, assemble, assimilate, blend, bring together, build in, call together, centralize, churn, coalesce, cohere (*formal*), collect, combine, *commingle* (*literary*), compose, *conflate*, confuse, consolidate, crossbreed, desegregate, embroil, emulsify, engage, federate, fit in, focus, fuse, gather, heap, heap up, *hybridize*, include, integrate, intermingle, intermix, intersperse, lace, lump, *lump together*, marshal, mat, meld, merge, mingle, mix, mix up, pile up, pool, ravel, reunite, shake, shake up, shuffle, synthesize, tangle, toss, unite, unitize

See also CREATING CONNECTIONS (145)

402 Separate and Divide

True Love in this differs from gold and clay,/That to divide is not to take away. **Percy Bysshe Shelley**

(*n*) bisection, demarcation, detachment, diaspora, dissociation, division, filtration, fission, graduation, insulation, marginalization, partition, polarization, segmentation, separation, severance, subdivision

(*v*) bifurcate, branch, branch off, branch out, break away, break down, break off, break open, break up, come between, cordon off, decentralize, delimit (*formal*), demarcate, disassociate, disband, disjoint, *dissever* (*formal*), dissociate, distinguish, diverge, divide, divorce, *divvy up* (*informal*), fan out, filter, gape, *go separate ways*, graduate, halve, hive off, insulate, isolate, marginalize, part, partition, polarize, quarter, ramify, riddle, scatter, screen, secede, seclude, section, segment, separate, separate off, separate out, sequester (*formal*), sever, share, shut off, sift, sort out, spread out, stake out, strain, subdivide, thresh, transect, unitize, yawn

See also UNFASTEN AND UNDO (410)

403 Copy and Duplicate

All art is but imitation of nature. **Seneca the Elder**

(*v*) back up, clone, copy, download, duplicate, photocopy, plagiarize, reduplicate, replicate, reprint, reproduce

See also FALSIFY AND CHEAT (177), COPIES AND REPLICAS (152), RECORD SOMETHING (372)

404 Clean and Polish

What separates two people most profoundly is a different sense and degree of cleanliness. **Friedrich Wilhelm Nietzsche**

(*n*) ablutions (*formal or humorous*), bath, cleaning, cleansing, desalination, detoxification, distillation, fumigation, going-over (*informal*), irradiation, pasteurization, purification, refining, rinse, scrub, shower, spit and polish (*informal*), *spring clean*, *spring-cleaning*, sterilization, wash

(*v*) aerate, air, bath, brush, buff, burnish, clarify, clean, cleanse, clean up, decontaminate, deodorize, desalinate, descale, detoxify, disinfect, distil, dry-clean, dust, finish, flush, freshen, freshen up, fumigate, gargle, grind, groom, hone, hose, hose down, iron, launder, moisturize, mop, mop up, polish, polish up, purge, purify, refine, rub, rub down, sand, sandpaper, sanitize, scald, scour, scrub, shine, shower, sluice, soap, sponge, spring-clean, sterilize, swab, sweep, sweep away, sweep up, swill, tan, towel, unplug, valet, ventilate, wash, wash down, wash out, wax, whet, wipe

See also CLEAN (1232)

405 Dirty and Contaminate

Reactors breed plutonium/bloodcells pay their dues/radiation keeps leaking & seeping/and i've got the Chernobyl Three Mile Island Blues. **Jayne Cortez**

(*n*) adulteration, contamination, infection, *pollution*

(*v*) adulterate, *begrime* (*literary*), *besmear*, *bespatter*, contaminate, dirty, foul, infect, mark, poison, pollute, soil, spot, stain, sully (*literary*), taint, tarnish

See also DIRTY (1234)

406 Decorate, Adorn, and Apply Coatings

PAINTING, n. The art of protecting flat surfaces from the weather and exposing them to the critic. **Ambrose Bierce**

(*adj*) beaded, beady, bedecked (*literary*), coated, crusted, decorated, festooned, nonstick, paved, sealed, touched (*literary*)

(*v*) adorn, anoint, apply, array (*literary*), bandage, baste, bedeck (*literary*), blazon, blob, braid, cake, cap, carpet (*literary*), caulk, coat, cover, dab, daub, decorate, drape, dress, dress up, dust, emblazon, enamel, festoon, gift-wrap, *gild*, *gird* (*literary*), glamorize, glaze, grace, grease, grout, ice, insulate, lag, laminate, line, lubricate, *mottle*, oil, ornament, overlay, pack, package, paint, paper over, parcel, parcel up, pave, perfume, personalize, plaster, plate, redecorate, refurbish, repaint, *repaper*, resurface, rustproof, scent, sheathe, smear, smudge, soundproof, spangle, spatter, speck, speckle, splodge, splotch, spray, spread, sprinkle, stencil, stipple, streak, strew, stud, surface, swaddle, swathe, touch up, trim, upholster, varnish, veneer, whitewash, wipe, wrap, wrap up, wreathe

See also IMPROVE APPEARANCE (380), ORNAMENTS AND DECORATIONS (1247)

407 Fill

One of the few remaining freedoms we have is the blank page. No one can prescribe how we should fill it. **James Kelman**

(*v*) absorb, block up, bung up (*informal*), choke, clog, clog up, clutter, congest, cram, crowd, fill, fill in, fill up, imbue, impregnate, infuse, jam, *jam-pack* (*informal*), load, load up, overflow, pack, *pad out*, permeate, plug, refill, refuel, reload, replenish, restock, sate, satiate, squash, squeeze, steep, stop, stop up, stuff, suffuse, swamp, tamp, top up, wad

See also FULL (1238)

408 Empty and Unload

It is not good to unpack in an open place. **Tamil proverb**

(*v*) clean out, clear, clear out, decant, deflate, depopulate, empty, free up, gut, hollow, overspill, pour, scrape out, siphon, unblock, unclog, unload, unpack, vacate

See also EMPTY (1237)

409 Fasten, Link, and Join

If two lives join, there is oft a scar./They are one and one, with a shadowy third;/One near one is too far. **Robert Browning**

(*adj*) articulated, barred, clip-on, closed, joined, mounted, sealed

(*n*) connection, implantation, installation, ligature, occlusion, reconnection

(*v*) add, affix, anchor, append, attach, belt, belt up, bind, bolt, bond, bridge, buckle, bundle up, button, catch, cauterize, cement, chain, chock, cinch, clamp, clip, close, close up, *conjoin* (*formal*), connect, converge, couple, dovetail, entwine, fasten, fix, glue, graft, gum, harness, hitch, hold, hook, hook up, interlink, intermesh, join, knit, knot, lace, lash, lock, lodge, mesh, moor, mount, nail, paste, peg, pin, plait, plug in, reconnect, *recouple*, rivet, rope, screw, seal, secure, shut, shut up, splice, splint, staple, stick, stitch, strap, stud, suture, tack, tag, tangle, tape, tether, thread, tie, tie up, truss, wed, weld, wheel-clamp, wire

See also CONNECTION (144), FASTENERS, LINKS, AND NETWORKS (1246)

410 Unfasten and Undo

Unaccommodated man is no more but such a poor, bare, forked animal as thou art. Off, off, you lendings! Come; unbutton here. **William Shakespeare**

(*adj*) disconnected, open, undone, unfastened, unglued

(*v*) cut off, detach, disassemble, disconnect, disengage, disjoint, dislocate, *dismantle*, disunite, divide, free up (*informal*), jemmy, loosen, open, prise, *prise open*, pry (*US*), *pry open* (*US*), set free, take apart, take down, take to pieces, unbind, unbolt, *unbuckle*, unbutton, *uncap*, unclasp, uncork, uncouple, undo, unfasten, unfix, unhitch, unhook, *unjam*, unknot, unlace, unlatch, unlock, unpeg, unpick, *unpin*, unravel, unscrew, unseal, unsnag, unsnarl, unstick, unstop, unstrap, untangle, untether, untie, unwind, unwrap, unyoke, unzip

See also FASTENERS, LINKS, AND NETWORKS (1246), SEPARATE AND DIVIDE (402)

411 Bar and Obstruct Access

I'll put a spoke among your wheels. **Francis Beaumont**

(*v*) bar, batten, block off, board up, enclose, fence, lock, occlude, picket, seal off, secure

Contact and Impact

412 Contact: Hold

I have embraced the summer dawn. **Arthur Rimbaud**

(*n*) *clutch*, grasp, grip, hold, lunge, purchase

(*v*) adhere, capture, catch, *catch hold of*, clasp, cleave (*literary*), clinch, cling, clutch, cradle, gather up, get a hold of (*US*), grab, grab hold of, grapple, grasp, grip, hang on, hold, hold close, hold on, hold onto, lunge, prop, reach, seize, snatch, squeeze, take, tote (*informal*), wrest

See also PHYSICAL CONTACT AS COMMUNICATION (656)

413 Contact: Touch

Whatever you touch and believe in. . .today, is going to be—like the reality of yesterday—an illusion tomorrow. **Luigi Pirandello**

(*n*) brush, dig, jab, jerk, nip, nudge, pat, peck, poke, prod, stroke, touch, tweak

(*v*) brush, *brush against*, caress, claw, come into contact, dig, dig into, fiddle, fidget, finger, fondle, graze, grope (*informal*), handle, jab, kiss, mess about (*informal*), mess around (*informal*), monkey with, nip, nudge, nuzzle, pat, paw, peck, pet, poke, prod, scrabble, scratch, stroke, touch, toy with, tweak, worry

414 Contact: Impact

When he goes hunting/he aims at a bird and/brings a landscape down. **Norman McCaig**

(*n*) bash (*informal*), beat, blow, bump, hit, impact, stroke, tap, wallop (*informal*), whiplash

(*v*) bang, bang into, barge, barge into, batter, beat, bonk (*informal*), buffet, bump, bump into, butt, *career into*, catch, collide, crack, crash, elbow, hit, jog, jostle, kick, lash, lob, plough into, pound, prang (*informal*), rear-end (*US*), run into, run over, shunt (*informal*), *slam into*, *smash into*, strike, stub, tap

See also DESTRUCTION AND DEMOLITION (360), IMPACT SOUNDS (1259)

415 Contact: Exert Pressure

The force of mind is only as great as its expression; its depth only as deep as its power to expand and lose itself. **G. W. F. Hegel**

(*n*) massage, pull

(*v*) bear down on, clench, constrict, force, grit, jam, knead, massage, pack, pat, pinch, pinion, press, pull, rub, rub down, squeeze, stamp, tighten, wring

416 Physical Attack and Punishment

I'm all for bringing back the birch, but only between consenting adults. **Gore Vidal**

(*n*) bang, bash (*informal*), battering, buffeting, clout, flagellation, hammering, head-butt, hiding (*informal*), knock, lash, *pummelling*, punch, rap, slap, slug, smack, sock (*informal*), spanking, swing, swipe, thrashing, thwack, uppercut, walloping (*informal*), whack

(*v*) assail, assault, attack, bash (*informal*), baste, beat up (*informal*), belabour (*literary or humorous*), belt (*informal*), biff (*informal*), bite, bop (*informal*), box, clobber (*informal*), clock (*slang*), clout, cuff, deck (*informal*), exchange blows, flail, give a beating, go for, hammer (*informal*), head-butt, hit, hit out, kick, kick in, knock, knock about (*informal*), *KO* (*informal*), lash, lash out, lay about, lay into, light into (*informal*), manhandle, maul, mishandle, mob, molest, mug, nobble (*informal*), overrun, pounce, pummel, punch, *put the boot in*, rap, sally, savage, set on, set upon, slap, slug, smack, smite (*archaic or literary*), sock (*informal*), spank, strafe, strike, strike down, strike out, swat, swing at, swipe, tackle, thrash, thump, thwack, turn on, wallop (*informal*), *weigh into* (*informal*), whack

See also WOUND A PERSON OR ANIMAL (384)

417 Stab

We are more sensible of one little touch of a surgeon's lancet than of twenty wounds with a sword in the heat of fight. **Michel de Montaigne**

(*v*) bayonet, gore, impale, run through (*literary*), spear, spike, stab, stick, transfix

See also KILL (923), USE TOOLS AND MACHINERY (469), WOUND A PERSON OR ANIMAL (384)

418 Whip and Club

A whipping never hurts so much as the thought that you are being whipped. **Edgar Watson Howe**

(*v*) birch, bludgeon, cane, club, cosh, cudgel, flagellate, flay, flog, whip

See also KILL (923), BLUNT INSTRUMENTS AND WHIPS (1157)

419 Avoid or Escape Contact

The apostles of the martial virtues...tend not to die fighting when the time comes. History is full of ignominious getaways by the great and famous. **George Orwell**

(*v*) avoid, break free, bypass, dodge, elude, escape, fend off, get away from, give a wide berth, give somebody the slip, head off, hold off, keep at bay, keep away, nestle, outrun, parry, repulse, shake off, shelter, throw off, ward off

420 Prevent Contact or Attack

The ultimate result of shielding men from the effects of folly, is to fill the world with fools. **Herbert Spencer**

(*n*) conservation, preservation, safeguarding

(*v*) cover, cushion, defend, deflect, fight off, fortify, guard, harbour, keep from, pillow, protect, safeguard, shelter, shield

Obtaining, Losing, and Exchanging Possession

421 Get

The knowledge of the world is only to be acquired in the world, and not in a closet. **Lord Chesterfield**

(*v*) accede, accumulate, acquire, amass, attract, bag, benefit from, capture, catch, clock up, collar (*slang*), come by, cull, derive, develop, distil, draw, drum up, enlist, fetch, field, find, gain, garner, gather, get, get hold of, *glean*, harvest, have, help yourself, land, lay in, net (*informal*), obtain, pluck, pot, procure, purchase, reach, reap, retake, *run to ground*, run up, scare up (*US informal*), scoop, scrape together, scratch together, screw up, secure, seize, snap up, suck, suck up, sweep, take on, take out, tap, win, wrest

422 Get Money or Reward

Not all that tempts your wand'ring eyes/And heedless hearts, is lawful prize;/Nor all that glisters, gold. **Thomas Gray**

(*v*) bring, bring home the bacon (*informal*), bring in, chalk up, claim, clean up (*slang*), clear (*informal*), come into, debit, earn, gross, inherit, make, net, profit, rack up (*informal*), *rake it in* (*informal*), reap, score, strike it rich, take home

423 Purchase

When I want a peerage, I shall buy one like an honest man. **Lord Northcliffe**

(*n*) acquisition, buy, mail order, purchase, transaction

(*v*) afford, barter, book, buy, buy out, charter, import, order, purchase, shop, take

See also GIVE MONEY (434)

424 Expenditure

Superfluous wealth can buy superfluities only. **Henry David Thoreau**

(*n*) admission, asking price, bill, charge, concession, cost, costs, damage (*informal*), disbursement, expenditure, expense, fare, investment, outgoings, outlay, payout, postage, prepayment, price, rate, subscription, subsidy, toll, value

See also MONEY (140), MONEY, PAYMENTS, AND CHARGES (800)

425 Purchaser

In a consumer society there are inevitably two kinds of slaves: the prisoners of addiction and the prisoners of envy. **Ivan Illich**

(*n*) buyer, consumer, customer, patron, procurer, punter (*informal*), purchaser, shopper, taker, trade

See also SELLER (443)

426 Take Something Away

Property is organised robbery. **George Bernard Shaw**

(*n*) annexation, apprehension, appropriation, arrogation (*formal*), commandeering, confiscation, monopolization, seizure, sequestration (*v*) annex, appropriate, arrogate (*formal*), bankrupt, capture, clean out (*informal*), commandeer, confiscate, deprive, dispossess (*archaic or formal*), divest, *do out of* (*informal*), dock, embargo, expropriate, extract, freeload (*informal*), gouge (*US*), grab, hijack, hog (*informal*), impound, impoverish, leap at, monopolize, overcharge, requisition, rip, seize, sequester, sequestrate, spirit, strip, take over, take possession of, usurp

See also REMOVE SOMETHING (339), CAUSE TO DISAPPEAR (6)

427 Steal and Rob

A man who will steal for *me will steal* from *me.* **Theodore Roosevelt**

(*v*) abduct, borrow, break in, burglarize (*US*), burgle, *carjack*, con, defraud, despoil, embezzle, extort, fiddle (*informal*), filch (*informal*), fleece (*informal*), hijack (*informal*), hold up, joyride, knock off (*slang*), launder, lift (*informal*), loot, make off with, maraud, misappropriate, mooch (*US slang*), nab, nick (*slang*), nip (*US*), *peculate* (*formal*), pilfer, pillage, pinch (*informal*), plunder, poach, pocket, purloin (*formal*), *purse-snatch* (*US*), raid, ram-raid, ransack, rip off (*informal*), rob, shoplift, skyjack, smuggle, snaffle (*informal*), snatch, snitch (*slang*), steal, stick up (*US informal*), swindle, swipe (*informal*), take, thieve, turn over (*slang*), walk off with, whip (*informal*)

See also CRIMES (817), CRIMINALS (821)

428 Proceeds of Crime

Stolen sweets are always sweeter,/Stolen kisses much completer. **Leigh Hunt**

(*n*) booty, *contraband*, hush money (*informal*), *ill-gotten gains*, loot, pickings, pillage, plunder, ransom, spoils, swag (*slang*)

429 Lend, Lease, and Borrow

Your borrowers of books*—those mutilators of collections, spoilers of the symmetry of shelves, and creators of odd volumes.* **Charles Lamb**

(*v*) borrow, hire, hire out, lease, *lease out*, lend, let, loan, rent, *rent out*, reserve, *sublease*, *sublet*

430 Regain Possession

Yet beauty, though injurious, hath strange power,/After offence returning, to regain/Love once possessed. **John Milton**

(*n*) reclamation, recovery, recuperation, refund, reimbursement, repossession, restitution, retrieval

(*v*) call in, claw back, get back, recapture, reclaim, recoup, recover, recuperate, regain, repossess, retrieve, salvage, take back

431 Give and Provide

The manner of giving is worth more than the gift. **Corneille**

(*v*) accord, afford (*formal*), ascribe (*formal*), attach, bestow (*formal*), come up with, commend, commit, contribute, dedicate, deliver, devolve, devote, donate, entrust, fulfil, give, give back, give up, grant, lend, make up, provide, raffle, reciprocate, return, spend, throw in, trust, vest, vouchsafe, yield

432 Proffer and Hand Over

Liberality lies less in giving liberally than in the timeliness of the gift. **Jean de La Bruyère**

(*v*) extend, give in, give over to, give up, hand, hand in, hand over, hold out, lay before, present, proffer, turn in, turn over

433 Bequeath and Bequests

Behold, I do not give lectures or a little charity,/When I give I give myself. **Walt Whitman**

(*n*) bequest, birthright, endowment, heirloom, heritage, inheritance, legacy

(*v*) bequeath, hand down, *hand on*, leave, *pass down*

434 Give Money

The man who leaves money to charity in his will is only giving away what no longer belongs to him. **Voltaire**

(*v*) amortize, bank, bankroll (*informal*), chip in (*informal*), cough up (*informal*), defray (*formal*), deposit, dissipate, expend (*formal*), finance, *fork out* (*informal*), *fork over* (*US informal*), *fork up* (*informal*), indemnify, invest, lash out (*informal*), launch out (*informal*), outlay, pay, put back, put in, put into, put up, refund, reimburse, remit, remunerate, settle, settle up, shell out (*informal*), spend, *splash out*, splurge, sponsor, square, square up, stump up (*informal*), subscribe, subsidize, tip, treat

See also PURCHASE (423)

435 Dispense, Ration, and Distribute

There is only a certain sized cake to be divided up, and if a lot of people want a larger slice they can only take it from others. **Stafford Cripps**

(*n*) administration, allocation, allotment, assignment, carve-up, delegation, diffusion, distribution, division, issue, penetration, presentation, provision, transmission

(*v*) administer, allocate, allot, allow, apportion, assign, budget, carve up (*informal*), consign, contract out, deal, deal out, delegate, diffuse, disburse, dish out (*informal*), dispense, distribute, divide, divvy (*informal*), dole out (*informal*), dot, drop off (*informal*), earmark, export, farm out, give, give away, give out, hand out, *hand round*, issue, make available, mete out, offer, parcel out, pass, pass out, piece out, portion, ration, ration out, serve, share, share out, spread, spread out

436 Equip and Supply

Once we are destined to live out our lives in the prison of our mind, our one duty is to furnish it well. **Peter Ustinov**

(*v*) arm, cater, deliver, equip, feed into, fill, fit, fit out, fit up, furnish (*formal*), house, install, kit out, lay on, outfit, pipe, ply, provide, rearm, render (*formal*), rig out (*informal*), supply

437 Reward

Vice is its own reward. **Quentin Crisp**

(*v*) award, compensate, confer (*formal*), endow, liquidate, pay back, pay off, recompense, redeem, repay, reward

See also REWARDS AND AWARDS (440)

438 Give Too Much

The only man who wasn't spoilt by being lionized was Daniel. **Herbert Beerbohm Tree**

(*v*) *bog down* (*informal*), bombard, burden, cloy, deluge, *dump on*, flood, fob off, foist, force-feed, impose, inundate, land with (*informal*), lavish, load, lumber (*informal*), overburden, overload, overstress, oversupply, overtax, *palm off*, rain, saddle with, saturate, shower, smother, snow under, strain, swamp, tax, weigh down

439 Gifts

If one receives a plum one must return a peach. **Vietnamese proverb**

(*adj*) at no cost, complimentary, for nothing, free, free of charge, gratis, gratuitous, on the house, toll-free (*US*)

(*n*) alms, concession, contribution, donation, dowry, favour, freebie (*informal*), free gift, fringe benefit, gift, giveaway (*informal*), grant, gratuity, handout, honorarium, largesse, offering, patronage, pledge, present, sop, stocking filler, stocking stuffer (*US*), tip

440 Rewards and Awards

He who never ventures beyond actuality will never win the prize of truth. **Friedrich von Schiller**

(*n*) accolade, award, bonus, bounty, commendation, compensation, crown, cup, decoration, desert, distinction, gong (*slang*), honour, indemnity, perk, perquisite (*formal*), prize, profit, recompense, redress, restitution, reward, spoils, trophy

See also REWARD (437)

441 Bribes

Richer than doing nothing for a bribe,/Prouder than rustling in unpaid-for silk. **William Shakespeare**

(*n*) backhander (*informal*), baksheesh, bribe, bung (*slang*), carrot, inducement, kickback, payoff (*informal*), payola (*US informal*), sweetener (*informal*)

442 Sell

Money demands that you sell, not your weakness to men's stupidity, but your talent to their reason. **Ayn Rand**

(*adj*) for sale, on sale, saleable

(*adv*) on the market

(*v*) bill, bring out, cash in, deal, export, flog (*informal*), handle, hawk, hustle (*US slang*), invoice, knock down, market, merchandise, outsell, pawn, peddle, purvey (*formal*), push (*slang*), put on the market, retail, sell, tout, trade, underprice, undersell, vend

443 Seller

Every one lives by selling something. **Robert Louis Stevenson**

(*n*) hawker, merchant, pedlar, purveyor (*formal*), pusher (*slang*), retailer, sales assistant, *salesclerk* (*US*), *sales manager*, salesperson, *sales rep* (*informal*), sales representative, seller, *shop assistant*, stockist, *street trader*, supplier, tout, trader, vendor

See also PURCHASER (425)

444 Sales and Shows

Pile it high, sell it cheap. **Jack Cohen**

(*n*) auction, *car boot sale*, demo (*informal*), fair, fête, *garage sale*, *jumble sale*, presentation, raffle, rummage sale (*US*), sale, shop, show, souk, *trade event*, trade fair, *trade show*, *yard sale* (*US*)

445 Possess

The metaphor is probably the most fertile power possessed by man. **José Ortega y Gasset**

(*n*) claim, entitlement, occupancy, ownership, possession, title

(*v*) bear, boast, comprise, consist, constitute, corner the market, encompass, enjoy, have, *have possession of*, hold, include, incorporate, keep, make, own, possess, take in

446 Lack of Possession

The great curse of our modern society is not so much the lack of money as the fact that the lack of money condemns a man to a squalid and incomplete existence. **Christopher Dawson**

(*adj*) bereft, deficient, deprived of, devoid, empty-handed, exclusive of, intestate, needful (*formal*), shorn of, starved, *starved of*, *stripped of*

(*prep*) failing, minus, wanting

447 Owners

When I buy pictures/...I look at that of which I may regard myself as the imaginary possessor. **Marianne Moore**

(*n*) bearer, beneficiary, freeholder, holder, landholder, landlady, landlord, landowner, licentiate, mistress, owner, possessor, proprietor, recipient, titleholder

448 Lose and Forfeit

There are occasions when it is undoubtedly better to incur loss than to make gain. **Plautus**

(*v*) forfeit, let slip, lose, lose track of, mislay, misplace, miss out, miss the boat, moult

See also GET RID OF SOMETHING (452)

449 Exchange and Interchange

It is best not to swap horses in mid-stream. **Abraham Lincoln**

(*n*) cross-fertilization, deal, exchange, handover, interchange, redemption, referral, rotation, swap (*informal*), switch, trade-in, trade-off, traffic, transfer, transference, *transferral*, *transmittal*, transmittance, *transposal*, transposition, turnover

(*v*) change, change round, cross-fertilize, exchange, hock (*slang*), interchange, redeem, rotate, swap (*informal*), take back, trade, trade in, traffic, transpose

See also CHANGE ONE THING FOR ANOTHER (399)

450 Forgo and Deny Oneself

Easy for nuns to talk about giving up things. That's what they do for a living. **Garrison Keillor**

(*n*) abdication, abjuration, abnegation (*formal*), avoidance, renunciation, waiver

(*v*) abdicate, abjure (*literary*), abnegate (*formal*), cut out, decline, deny, disown, do without, economize, forego, forfeit, forsake, forswear (*archaic or literary*), give up, go without, immolate (*literary*), miss, *pass up*, refuse, reject, relinquish, renounce, sacrifice, scrimp, skimp, sniff at, spare, stint on, surrender, swear off, throw out, throw up (*informal*), tighten your belt, turn away from, turn down, turn your nose up at

See also ABSTEMIOUSNESS AND SELF-DENIAL (882)

451 Accept Possession

Words are the tokens current and accepted for conceits, as moneys are for values. **Francis Bacon**

(*n*) acceptance, receipt, reception, take-up

(*v*) accept, adopt, assume, bear, embrace, receive, settle for, shoulder, take back, take in, welcome

452 Get Rid of Something

You've got the brain of a four-year-old boy, and I bet he was glad to get rid of it. **Groucho Marx**

(*v*) abandon, act out, banish, bin, cast aside, cast away, cast off, cast out (*formal*), chuck (*informal*), *chuck out* (*informal*), clean up, consign, cull, demolish (*informal*), deselect, discard, dispel, *dispense with*, dispose of, dump, eject, eliminate, eradicate, exorcize, get free of, get rid of, *get shot of* (*informal*), jettison, junk (*informal*), leave behind, lose, offload, plunk, purge, rid, root out, see off (*informal*), sop up, stamp out, strike off, throw away, throw off, throw out, topple, void

See also REMOVE SOMETHING (339), LOSE AND FORFEIT (448)

453 Abolish and Annul

We all know that books burn—yet. . .no force can abolish memory. **Franklin D. Roosevelt**

(*v*) abolish, abrogate (*formal*), annul, cancel, do away with, invalidate, nullify, quash, repeal, rescind, reverse, revoke, scrap, scratch, scrub (*informal*)

454 Store and Keep

To expect a man to retain everything that he has ever read is like expecting him to carry about in his body everything that he has ever eaten. **Arthur Schopenhauer**

(*n*) keeping, retention, storage, stowage

(*v*) bank, cache, carry, cling, collect, compile, conserve, heap up, hive, hoard, hold back, hold down (*informal*), hold onto, keep, keep back, keep in, lock away, preserve, put aside, put away, put by, reserve, retain, salt away, save, set apart, set aside, squirrel, *squirrel away*, stash (*informal*), *stash away*, stock, stock up, *stock up on*, stockpile, store, store up, stow, withhold

See also STORES AND STORAGE BUILDINGS (1087)

455 People Who Collect Things

I am a sort of collector of religions: and the curious thing is that I find I can believe in them all. **George Bernard Shaw**

(*n*) accumulator, beachcomber, collector, hoarder, magpie (*informal*), miser, saver, squirrel (*informal*)

456 Hold and Contain

The valuable part of words is the thought therein contained. **Zhuangzi**

(*v*) accommodate, bear, carry, comprehend (*formal*), contain, embrace, enclose, hold, house, kennel, seat, take

457 Seek Possession and Search

He who seeking asses found a kingdom. **John Milton**

(*n*) chase, delve, dragnet, forage, hunt, pursuit, quest, search, trawl

(*v*) burrow, *cast about*, *cast around*, comb, delve (*archaic*), dredge, ferret, *ferret about*, ferret around, ferret out, fish, forage, frisk, fumble, *go in search of*, grope, grub, hunt, hunt down, look for, nose (*informal*), *nose about* (*informal*), *nose around* (*informal*), poke, *poke around*, prospect, quest, rake, ransack, rifle, root, *rootle*, root out, rummage, sap, scavenge, scour, scout, *scout around*, scrabble, scrounge (*informal*), search, search through, seek, seek out, sift, trawl, troll, worm out

458 Obtain Possession by Persuasion

You can stroke people with words. **F. Scott Fitzgerald**

(*v*) angle for, bargain, *cadge* (*informal*), elicit, finagle (*informal*), fish for, mooch (*informal*), prise, raise, scrounge (*informal*), wangle (*informal*), wheedle, winkle out

459 Confer Status

Titles distinguish the mediocre, embarrass the superior, and are disgraced by the inferior. **George Bernard Shaw**

(*n*) elevation, *investment* (*formal*), nomination, preferment (*formal*), promotion, re-election, restoration, upgrade, upgrading

(*v*) appoint, assign, beatify, canonize, commission, contract, co-opt, decorate, designate, dignify, elect, elevate, enthrone (*formal*), hire, inaugurate, induct, invest (*formal*), king, make, name, nominate, *ordain*, place, promote, reinstate, sign, sign up, swear in, take on, tap (*US*), upgrade

460 Revoke Status

Modern heretics are not burned at the stake. They are relegated to backwaters or pressured to resign. **Art Kleiner**

(*n*) demotion, deposition, disenfranchisement, dismissal, relegation, sacking (*informal*)

(*v*) axe (*informal*), blacklist, can (*US slang*), cashier, decommission, defrock, demote, depose, dethrone, discharge, disenfranchise, disinherit, dismiss, displace, downgrade, expel, *give notice*, *give somebody their cards*, *give the boot* (*informal*), *give the elbow* (*informal*), *give the heave-ho* (*informal*), *give the push* (*informal*), *give the sack* (*informal*), idle, *make redundant*, *reduce to the ranks*, relegate, relieve, sack (*informal*), send down, sideline, terminate (*US*), unmake, unseat

See also EJECT AND EXCLUDE (341)

461 Income

There are few sorrows, however poignant, in which a good income is of no avail. **Logan Pearsall Smith**

(*n*) allowance, annuity, bread and butter, bursary, commission, earnings, emolument (*formal or humorous*), fee, gain, gate, *gross revenue*, harvest, income, livelihood, living, means, *net income*, pay, payback, pay cheque, payment, payoff (*informal*), payout, pay packet, paystub (*US*), proceeds, profit, purse, remuneration, rent, rental, return, returns, revenue, royalty, salary, stipend, take, take-home pay, takings, wage, wage packet, wages, winnings, yield

See also MONEY (140), FINANCIAL ASSETS (463)

462 Possessions

Why grab possessions like thieves, or divide them like socialists, when you can ignore them like wise men? **Natalie Clifford Barney**

(*n*) acres, asset, baggage, bags, belongings, bits and bobs (*informal*), bits and pieces (*informal*), chattels, clobber (*informal*), effects (*formal*), freehold, gear (*informal*), goods, *goods and chattels*, holding, kit, paraphernalia, *personal belongings*, personal effects, *personal possessions*, *personal property*, possessions, property, real estate (*US*), realty, status symbol, stores, stuff, substance, things, wherewithal, worldly goods, worth

463 Financial Assets

And, as their wealth increaseth, so enclose/Infinite riches in a little room. **Christopher Marlowe**

(*n*) assets, bullion, capital, coffers, estate, fortune, gold, *liquid assets*, liquidity, mammon (*disapproving*), reserves, resources, riches, richness, savings, treasure, wealth

See also MONEY (140), INCOME (461)

464 Find

What the superior man seeks is in himself. What the mean man seeks is in others. **Confucius**

(*n*) acquisition, detection, discovery, find, procurement, uncovering

(*v*) catch, chance on, come across, come upon, dig out (*informal*), dig out, dig up (*informal*), discover, excavate, ferret out, find, find out, *happen on*, *happen upon*, localize, locate, look up, pin down, pinpoint, search out, sniff out (*informal*), source, spy out, strike, stumble, *stumble across*, *stumble on*, *stumble upon*, trace, track down, turn up, uncover, unearth, zoom in

465 Need and Require

It is necessary to assume something which is necessary of itself, and has no cause of its necessity outside itself...is rather the cause of necessity in other things. **Thomas Aquinas**

(*v*) demand, have, *have need of*, involve, lack, must, necessitate, need, require, should, take, warrant

See also MOST IMPORTANT THING (198)

466 Owe and Deserve

I owe a duty, where I cannot love. **Aphra Behn**

(*adj*) due, in line for, outstanding, owed, owing, payable, unpaid

(*n*) amortization, arrears, debt, default

(*v*) default, deserve, earn, merit, owe

467 Gamble and Take Risks

Life is a gamble, at terrible odds—if it was a bet, you wouldn't take it. **Tom Stoppard**

(*n*) accumulator, ante, bet, cardsharping, chance, flutter (*informal*), gamble, gambling, lottery, odds, punt, stake, stakes, sweep (*informal*), *sweeps* (*US informal*), sweepstake, tombola, wager

(*v*) bet, challenge, chance, dare, dice, dice with death, gamble, gamble away, *have a flutter* (*informal*), hazard, *lay a wager*, *lay bets*, outbid, *put money on*, risk, run a risk, speculate, stake, take a chance, take a gamble, wager, walk a tightrope

Using and Functioning

468 Use

O, it is excellent/To have a giant's strength! But it is tyrannous/To use it like a giant. **William Shakespeare**

(*n*) appliance, application, deployment, exercise (*formal*), exploitation, handling, manipulation, operating, operation, usage, use, utilization

(*v*) apply, control, deploy, draw on, employ, exercise, exert, handle, harness, make use of, manipulate, ply, *put to use*, resort to, run, use, utilize, wield

469 Use Tools and Machinery

If you are an anvil, bear the strokes; if you become a hammer, strike. **Lebanese proverb**

(*v*) dig, drive, file, fire, fire up, fuel, hammer, hoe, log in, log on, log out, man, open up, pitchfork, plough, rake, rasp, saw, scoop, shoot, shovel, solder, spade, start up, test-drive, till, tunnel, upshift (*US*), use

See also STAB (417), WHIP AND CLUB (418)

470 Function Successfully

Get on with it, keep moving, keep in/speed, the nerves, their speed, the perceptions,/...keep it moving as fast as you/can. **Charles Olson**

(*v*) act, function, go, idle, operate, serve, take, work

471 Fail or Cease to Function

Honorable errors do not count as failures in science, but as seeds for progress. **Stephen Jay Gould**

(*v*) act up, break, break down, conk out (*informal*), crack, crack up (*informal*), crash, die, fail, give out, *go awry*, *go dead*, *go haywire* (*informal*), *go on the blink* (*informal*), go to waste, *grind to a halt*, jam, labour, malfunction, pack up (*informal*), seize up, snarl up, stall, *stop dead*, stop working

472 Misuse and Abuse

The greater the power, the more dangerous the abuse. **Edmund Burke**

(*n*) abuse, exploitation, malpractice, manipulation, misapplication, mismanagement, misuse, perversion (*disapproving*)

(*v*) abuse, corrupt, exploit, *meddle with*, misapply, misdirect, *misemploy*, mishit, mismanage, misspend, mistreat, misuse, pollute, prey on, use

473 Mess Up and Make Mistakes

Great men too make mistakes, and many among them do it so often that one is almost tempted to call them little men. **Georg Christoph Lichtenberg**

(*v*) blunder, bodge (*informal*), boob (*informal*), botch, *botch up*, bungle (*informal*), butcher (*informal*), err (*formal*), *flub* (*US slang*), fluff (*informal*), *fluff up*, *foul up* (*informal*), fumble, goof (*informal*), go wrong, *hash up* (*informal*), make a dog's breakfast/dinner of, make a hash of (*informal*), make a mess of, *make a mistake*, *make a pig's ear of*, mess up (*informal*), mishandle, muck up (*informal*), muff, stuff up (*informal*)

See also MISTAKES (251)

474 Make Good Use of Something

The ass will carry his load, but not a double load; ride not a free horse to death. **Miguel de Cervantes**

(*v*) avail yourself, capitalize, capitalize on, cash in on, develop, exploit, get the most out of, make the most of, maximize, milk (*informal*), profiteer, put to good use, recycle, reprocess, reuse, take advantage of something, tap (*informal*), use

See also ECONOMICAL AND RESOURCEFUL (208)

475 Use Up and Waste

Time waste differs from material waste in that there can be no salvage. **Henry Ford**

(*n*) consumption, overuse, use

(*v*) bleed (*informal*), bleed dry (*informal*), blow (*slang*), burn, consume, deplete, dispose of (*formal*), drain, eat into, eat up, exhaust, expend, finish, finish off, fritter away, get through, gobble (*informal humorous*), gobble up, go through, guzzle (*informal*), idle away, knacker (*slang*), lose, run through, sell out, spend, squander, *suck dry*, *suck the life out of*, take up, throw away, tire, use, use up, waste, wear out, while away, whittle away

See also WASTEFUL AND UNECONOMICAL (247)

People and their Way of Life

Qualities and Characteristics

476 People's Physical Appearance

A man who looks a part has the soul of that part. **Guy de Maupassant**

(*adj*) attractive, beautiful, bonny, boyish, cherubic, *comely* (*archaic or literary*), cute, dishy (*informal*), fair, fetching, good-looking, handsome, hunky (*informal*), ill-favoured, nice-looking, photogenic, plain, pretty, ravishing, *sexy*, striking, unprepossessing, well-preserved, winning, winsome, *young-looking*, youthful

(*n*) attractiveness, *comeliness* (*archaic or literary*), good looks, loveliness, prettiness, ugliness, youthfulness

See also BEAUTY AND ATTRACTIVENESS (190), UGLINESS AND UNATTRACTIVENESS (234)

477 Agility of the Body

I have the body of a man half my age. Unfortunately, he's in terrible shape. **George Foreman**

(*adj*) acrobatic, *all fingers and thumbs*, *all thumbs*, athletic, awkward, *butterfingered* (*informal*), double-jointed, elephantine, feline, gawky (*informal*), graceful, graceless, gymnastic, inelegant, light, light-footed, limber, lissom, lithe, lithesome (*archaic or literary*), loose-limbed, lumbering, lumpy, mincing, nimble, supple, uncoordinated, ungainly, ungraceful

(*adv*) awkwardly, lightly

(*n*) agility, athleticism, awkwardness, clumsiness, *gaucherie*, gawkiness (*informal*), heavy-handedness, lightness, *litheness*, nimbleness, suppleness, ungainliness

See also DESCRIBING BODY MOVEMENTS (289)

478 Build

Of physiology from top to toe I sing. **Walt Whitman**

(*adj*) *androgynous*, angular, bandy-legged, *barrel-chested*, birdlike, bony, bowlegged, burly, butch, buxom (*humorous*), cadaverous, chubby, chunky (*informal*), corpulent (*formal or literary*), curvaceous, elfin, emaciated, fat, fleshy, full, gangling, gangly, gaunt, gross, heavyset, hefty, husky (*US*), lanky, large, lean, *leggy*, matronly, obese, overweight, paunchy, pear-shaped, petite, pigeon-breasted, plump, podgy, portly, *potbellied*, pudgy (*informal*), puny, rangy, *rawboned*, reedy, rotund, round-shouldered, rugged, scraggy, scrawny, shapely, sinewy, skeletal, *skin-and-bone*, *skin and bones*, skinny, slender, slight, slim, *small-boned*, spidery, spindly, squat, stalwart, statuesque, stocky, *stooped*, *stooping*, stout, strapping (*informal*), strong, stubby, stumpy, sturdy, svelte, sylphlike, thickset, thin, trim, tubby (*informal*), underfed, undernourished, underweight, *voluptuous*, *waiflike*, wasted, weak, well-built, well-developed, well-fed, well-rounded, willowy, *wraithlike*

(*n*) angularity, *boniness*, *brawniness*, burliness, chubbiness, *chunkiness* (*informal*), *corpulence* (*formal or literary*), *dumpiness*, emaciation, fatness, fleshiness, fullness, gauntness, *lankiness*, obesity, physique, plumpness, *podginess*, portliness, *pudginess* (*informal*), *ranginess*, rotundity, *rotundness*, roundness, ruggedness, *scrawniness*, skinniness, slenderness, slimness, *squatness*, stature, *stockiness*, stoutness, *svelteness*, thinness, *tubbiness* (*informal*)

See also HEIGHT: HIGH (1202), WEIGHT: HEAVY (1204)

479 Extra Weight

I have tried to remove weight, sometimes from people, sometimes from heavenly bodies, sometimes from cities. **Italo Calvino**

(*n*) *beer belly* (*slang*), *beer gut* (*slang*), flab, *love handles* (*informal*), paunch, *pot* (*informal*), *potbelly*, *spare tyre* (*informal humorous*)

480 Muscles and Musculature

The brain has muscles for thinking as the legs have muscles for walking. **Julien Offroy de La Mettrie**

(*adj*) beefy, brawny, bullish, bullnecked, meaty, *muscly*, muscular, powerful, wiry

(*n*) beefiness, brawn, flabbiness (*informal*), *muscularity*, sinew (*literary*), wiriness

See also THE MUSCLES (719)

481 Complexion

His complexion was the sort you find in those who suffer from piles. . .but there's nothing anyone can do about that: the Petersburg climate is to blame. **Nikolay Gogol**

(*adj*) *acned*, ashen, ashy, bloodless, blotchy, blowzy (*disapproving*), bronzed, brown, cadaverous (*literary*), chalky, clear, deathlike, florid, flushed, *freckly*, ghastly (*literary*), glowing, hardy, *olive-skinned*, pale, pallid, pasty, pasty-faced, *pimpled*, pimply, pink, red-faced, rosy, rubicund (*literary*), ruddy, rugged, sallow, spotty, suntanned, swarthy, tan (*US*), tanned, wan, washed-out, waxen, white, *white as a sheet*, wholesome

(*n*) colouring, complexion, freckle, pallor, *pastiness*, redness, rosiness, ruddiness, *sallowness*, *skin colour*, skin tone, tan, *wanness*, whiteness, wholesomeness

See also THE SKIN (721)

482 Facial Characteristics

My face looks like a wedding cake left out in the rain. **W. H. Auden**

(*adj*) baby-faced, beady (*informal*), *button-nosed*, craggy, dimpled, fresh-faced, haggard, lined, lived-in, owlish, *owl-like*, pinched, popeyed, *pug-nosed*, snub-nosed, sunken, wizened, wrinkled, wrinkly

(*n*) crease, *crow's foot*, dimple, feature, lineament (*literary*)

See also HEAD (693), FACIAL HAIR (490)

483 Well Groomed

A man who's active and incisive/can yet keep nail-care much in mind. **Alexander Pushkin**

(*adj*) chic, chipper (*informal*), clean-cut, dandified, *dandyish* (*dated*), dapper, dashing, debonair, elegant, fashion-conscious, foppish, glamorous, modish, natty, presentable, rakish, sartorial, smart, *smartly dressed*, snappy (*informal*), snazzy (*informal*), soigné, spruce, stylish, tidy, voguish, well-dressed, well-groomed, well-turned-out

(*adv*) fashionably, gracefully, smartly

(*n*) chic, daintiness, dress sense, elegance, glamour, glitz, glitziness, grace, smartness, *snazziness* (*informal*), style, stylishness

See also DRESS, WEAR, AND UNDRESS (868), DESCRIBING CLOTHES (869)

484 Badly Groomed

The elect, the elected...they come here bright as dimes,/and die dishevelled and soft. **Robert Lowell**

(*adj*) blowzy, dishevelled, dowdy, frowzy, *frumpy*, raddled, ragged, raggedy, ragtag, ratty (*informal*), scraggly, scruffy, shabby, *slatternly*, slovenly, untidy, wild

(*adv*) dowdily, inelegantly, raggedly, rattily (*informal*)

(*n*) dowdiness, *frumpiness*, inelegance, raggedness, shabbiness, *slovenliness*

See also DRESS, WEAR, AND UNDRESS (868), DESCRIBING CLOTHES (869)

485 Hair

When a woman isn't beautiful, people always say, "You have lovely eyes, you have lovely hair." **Anton Chekhov**

(*n*) curl, fuzz, hair, hairiness, *hirsuteness*, lock, mane (*literary or informal*), ringlet, *ringlets*, shagginess, thatch, tresses, wave

486 Hair Colour

Only God, my dear,/Could love you for yourself alone/And not your yellow hair. **W. B. Yeats**

(*adj*) blond, brunette, carroty, *chestnut-haired*, dark, fair, fair-haired, flaxen, *golden-haired*, hoary, redheaded, *tow-headed*, white

487 Describing Hair

'Tis the voice of the lobster; I heard him declare,/"You have baked me too brown, I must sugar my hair." **Lewis Carroll**

(*adj*) *backcombed*, bouffant, bushy, clipped, close-cropped, *crimped*, *cropped*, flyaway, *frizzed*, frizzy, fuzzy, hairy, hirsute, lank, shaggy, straggly, tousled, unkempt, *unshorn*, wavy

488 Baldness and Balding

According to the doctors, I'm only suffering from a light form of premature baldness. **Federico Fellini**

(*adj*) bald, *bald as a coot*, baldheaded, balding, hairless, *thin on top*, *tonsured*

(*n*) baldness

489 Hair Styles and Hair Pieces

Very hard for a man with a wig to keep order. **Evelyn Waugh**

(*n*) coiffure (*formal*), haircut, hairdo (*informal*), hairdressing, *hairpiece*, hairstyle, periwig, rug (*informal*), toupee, wig

types of hairstyle Afro, bangs (*US*), beehive, big hair (*informal*), bob, bouffant, braids, bun, bunches, buzz cut (*US*), chignon, cornrow, cowlick, crew cut, crop, dreadlocks, flat top, French pleat, fringe, mohawk (*US*), mohican, mullet, pageboy, pigtail, plait, pompadour, ponytail, quiff, ringlet, topknot

490 Facial Hair

Old men and comets have been reverenced for the same reason; their long beards, and pretences to foretell events. **Jonathan Swift**

(*adj*) bearded, *beardless*, *bewhiskered*, clean-shaven, *shaved*, *shaven*, *smooth-shaven*, *stubbly*, *unshaven*, *whiskery*

(*n*) beard, bristle, *facial hair*, *five o'clock shadow*, *goatee*, *handlebar moustache*, *moustache*, *muttonchops*, *pencil moustache*, *sideburns*, stubble, *walrus moustache*, whiskers

See also FACIAL CHARACTERISTICS (482)

491 Makeup and Beauty Products

You can now see the Female Eunuch the world over...Wherever you see nail varnish, lipstick, brassieres, and high heels, the Eunuch has set up her camp. **Germaine Greer**

(*n*) *beauty product*, blush (*US*), blusher, cleanser, cosmetic, *eyeliner*, *eye pencil*, *eye shadow*, face pack, *face powder*, facial, *greasepaint*, kohl, *lipstick*, makeup, *makeup remover*, *maquillage*, *mascara*, moisturizer, mouthwash, mudpack, *nail polish*, rouge (*dated*)

492 Personal Hygiene

Every Englishman's home is his hospital, particularly the bathroom. **Oliver St. John Gogarty**

(*n*) *aftershave*, attar, *body mist*, *body spray*, *breath freshener*, cologne, deodorant, eau de cologne, *eau de toilette*, essence, fragrance, loofah, patchouli, pedicure, perfume, *personal hygiene*, scent, *shampoo*, *shaving cream*, *skincare product*, *styling gel*, *styling spray*, *sunblock*, *sun lotion*, sunscreen, *suntan cream*, suntan lotion, *suntan oil*, toilet (*formal*), toiletry, toilette (*literary*), toilet water, toner, *toothpaste*

493 Temperament and Behaviour

He who lacks temperament must look for ornament. **Karl Kraus**

(*n*) affectation, animus, antics, attitude, bearing, bedside manner, behaviour, carriage (*formal*), character, comportment (*formal*), conduct, delivery, demeanour, deportment (*formal*), disposition, eccentricity, gait, habit, heart, identity, instinct, line, makeup, manner, manners, mien (*literary*), nature, personality, poise, pose, position, posture, predisposition, presence, propensity (*formal*), public image, spirit, stance, streak, temper, temperament, tendency, walk, ways

494 Personal Eccentricities

Cultivate only the habits that you are willing should master you. **Elbert Hubbard**

(*n*) distinction, eccentricity, foible, idiosyncrasy, oddity, particularity, quirk, trademark, trick, whimsicality, whimsy

495 Friendliness and Sociability

Society is no comfort/To one not sociable. **William Shakespeare**

(*adj*) accessible, affable, affectionate, agreeable, amiable, approachable, brotherly, charitable, chummy (*informal*), close, companionable, *comradely*, congenial, convivial, cordial, demonstrative, easygoing, extrovert, friendly, genial, good-natured, gregarious, hospitable, likable, loving, neighbourly, open, outgoing, peaceable, personable, pleasant, receptive, responsive, sociable, sympathetic, warm

(*adv*) peaceably, receptively, warmly

(*n*) affability, amiability, approachability, bonhomie, *companionability*, conviviality, cordiality, extroversion, familiarity, friendliness, geniality, *good-naturedness*, gregariousness, hospitality, *matiness*, neighbourliness, pleasantness, receptiveness, receptivity, responsiveness, sociability

496 Generosity and Kindness

I must be cruel only to be kind. **William Shakespeare**

(*adj*) altruistic, attentive, beneficent, benevolent, benign, big-hearted, bounteous (*literary*), bountiful (*literary*), careful, caring, charitable, compassionate, considerate, *consoling*, devoted, fatherly, fond, forgiving, freehanded (*US*), generous, gentle, goodhearted, humane, indulgent, kind, kind-hearted, kindly, large-hearted, lenient, long-suffering, magnanimous, maternal, merciful, mild, motherly, munificent, nice, open-handed, openhearted, *peace-loving*, philanthropic, pitying, public-spirited, remissive, selfless, self-sacrificing, sensitive, soft, soft-boiled, soft-hearted, solicitous, supportive, sweet, sympathetic, tender, tenderhearted, thoughtful, understanding, unselfish, unsparing, unstinting, warm-hearted, well-intentioned, well-meaning, well-meant, yielding

(*adv*) devotedly, generously, kindly, maternally, mildly, softly, sweetly, tenderly, warmly

(*n*) altruism, beneficence, benignity, consideration, fatherliness, forbearance (*formal*), generosity, gentleness, helpfulness, humanity, kind-heartedness, kindliness, kindness, largesse, lenience, leniency, magnanimity, mellowness, *mercifulness*, munificence, open-handedness, openheartedness, selflessness, self-sacrifice, sensitivity, *soft-heartedness*, solicitousness, solicitude, sweetness, tenderheartedness, tenderness, thoughtfulness, unselfishness, warm-heartedness, warmness, warmth

497 Energy and Enthusiasm

Nothing is so contagious as enthusiasm...It is the genius of sincerity and truth accomplishes no victories without it. **Bulwer Lytton**

(*adj*) abuzz, active, alive, ardent, boisterous, bouncy, devoted, dynamic, ebullient, effervescent, energetic, exuberant, fanatic, feisty (*informal*), frisky, frolicsome, full of beans (*informal*), full of life, go-getting (*informal*), gung ho (*informal*), hearty, high-spirited, irrepressible, jaunty, keen, kittenish, lively, mettlesome, motivated, peppy (*informal*), playful, proactive, sassy (*US*), self-motivated, sparky, strong, tireless, vigorous, vital, vivacious, warm-blooded, youthful, zealous, zippy (*informal*)

(*adv*) keenly, playfully

(*n*) activeness, alertness, animation, bounciness, dash, dedication, devotion, drive, dynamism, ebullience, effervescence, élan (*literary*), energy, expansiveness, *feistiness* (*informal*), get-up-and-go (*informal*), go, heartiness, jazz (*slang*), keenness, life, liveliness, oomph, panache, pep (*informal*), perkiness, playfulness, punch, sap, sassiness (*US*), sparkle, *spiritedness*, tirelessness, vehemence, vigour, vitality, *vivaciousness*, vivacity, vividness, youthfulness

See also ENTHUSIASTIC AND INQUISITIVE (629), POSITIVE IMPATIENCE, ENTHUSIASM, AND ALERTNESS (538)

498 Naturalness

First feelings are always the most natural. **Louis XIV**

(*adj*) artless, folksy (*US*), guileless, ingenuous, just-folks (*US informal*), modest, naive, natural, rough-and-ready, self-effacing, simple, sincere, unaffected, unassuming, unmannered, unpretentious, unsophisticated, unspoiled, unstudied

(*adv*) naturally, simply, sincerely, unaffectedly, unsophisticatedly

(*n*) artlessness, *guilelessness*, ingenuousness, naivety, naturalness, simplicity, spontaneity, unaffectedness, *unassumingness*, unpretentiousness

See also HONEST AND OPEN (631)

499 Courage

Real nobility is based on scorn, courage, and profound indifference. **Albert Camus**

(*adj*) adventuresome, adventurous, audacious, bold, brave, courageous, daredevil, daring, dashing (*dated*), dauntless (*literary*), doughty (*literary*), fearless, gallant (*literary*), game, gritty, gutsy (*informal*), heroic, intrepid (*literary or humorous*), lionhearted, manful, nervy (*US informal*), plucky, scrappy, spunky (*informal*), stalwart, stout, stouthearted, swashbuckling, valiant, valorous, venturesome (*formal*)

(*adv*) audaciously, boldly, daringly, dashingly, gamely, *without fear*

(*n*) audaciousness, audacity, backbone, boldness, bottle (*informal*), bravery, bravura, *courageousness*, daring, *dauntlessness* (*literary*), derring-do (*literary*), fearlessness, fibre, fortitude, gallantry (*literary*), grit, gumption (*informal*), guts (*slang*), heart, heroics, heroism, *intrepidity*, *lionheartedness*, manhood, mettle, nerve, pluck, pluckiness, prowess, spunk (*informal*), *stoutheartedness*, stoutness, *valiantness*, valour

500 Confidence and Composure

Confidence and hope do more good than physic. **Galen**

(*adj*) assertive, assured, balanced, bold, *bold as brass*, can-do (*informal*), confident, controlled, crisp, dignified, equable, even-tempered, imperturbable, *laid back*, level-headed, mellow, patient, permissive, placid, poised, presidential, secure, sedate, self-assertive, self-assured, self-confident, self-possessed, sober, steady, sure of yourself, temperate, unflappable, unhesitating, well-adjusted

(*adv*) boldly, patiently, presidentially, sedately, surely, temperately

(*n*) aplomb, assertiveness, assurance, authoritativeness, boldness, confidence, dignity, discretion, flair, *imperturbability*, level-headedness, lucidness, patience, phlegm, poise, pride, restraint, sang-froid (*formal*), security, *sedateness*, self-assurance, *self-assuredness*, self-confidence, self-possession, self-regard, self-respect, sobriety, steadiness, *temperateness*, tranquillity, unflappability

See also CALMNESS, CONFIDENCE, AND COMPOSURE (537), SOOTHE AND CALM (574)

501 Hard-Working and Committed

I have nothing to offer but blood, toil, tears and sweat. **Winston Churchill**

(*adj*) ambitious, aspirational, assiduous, businesslike, busy, careerist, committed, conscientious, constant, dedicated, devoted, diligent, driven, dutiful, efficient, faithful, *hard-working*, idealistic, industrious, loyal, meticulous, organized, painstaking, precise, punctilious, scrupulous, sedulous (*literary*), *self-starting*, stalwart, staunch, steadfast, studious, undeviating, unfaltering, unflagging

(*adv*) ambitiously, dedicatedly, devotedly, faithfully, stalwartly, studiously

(*n*) application, assiduity, assiduousness, careerism, carefulness, commitment, constancy, diligence, efficiency, fastidiousness, firmness, idealism, industriousness, insistence, loyalty, meticulousness, perfectionism, punctiliousness, purposefulness, *sedulity* (*literary*), *sedulousness* (*literary*), single-mindedness, steadfastness, studiousness, thoroughness

See also STRENGTH OF WILL (502)

502 Strength of Will

There is no such thing as a great talent without great will-power. **Honoré de Balzac**

(*adj*) determined, forbearing (*formal*), indefatigable, indomitable, invulnerable, iron, patient, persevering, persistent, resilient, *self-controlled*, *self-disciplined*, single-minded, spirited, steely, stoical, strenuous, strong-minded, strong-willed, stubborn, sturdy, tenacious, tough-minded, untiring, unwearied

(*adv*) resiliently, strenuously, toughly

(*n*) determination, discipline, endurance, hardiness, *indomitability*, patience, perseverance, persistence, resilience, resoluteness, resolution, resolve, ruggedness, self-control, self-discipline, self-restraint, spirit, stamina, staying power, stoicism, *strength of character*, strength of mind, *strength of will*, strong-mindedness, stubbornness, sufferance, temperance, *tenaciousness*, vigour, willpower

See also HARD-WORKING AND COMMITTED (501), STRENGTH (202)

503 Honest and Reliable

An honest God's the noblest work of man. **Samuel Butler**

(*adj*) above reproach, above suspicion, authoritative, confidential, conscientious, dependable, fast, genuine, high-minded, honest, incorruptible, irreproachable, just, on the level (*informal*), orderly, principled, real, reliable, religious, responsible, safe, scrupulous, sincere, solid, steadfast, straight, sure, true, true-blue (*US*), trustworthy, trusty, truthful, warm

(*adv*) religiously, responsibly, seriously, sincerely, truthfully

(*n*) conscientiousness, dependability, faithfulness, frankness, honesty, reliability, *scrupulousness*, seriousness, steadfastness, trustworthiness, truth, truthfulness, veracity

See also HONEST AND OPEN (631), MORALLY GOOD (775)

504 Cheerfulness of Outlook

An optimist, in the atomic age, thinks the future is uncertain. **Russell M. Crouse**

(*adj*) blithe (*literary*), breezy, bright, *bright-eyed and bushy-tailed*, bubbly, constructive, freewheeling (*US*), fun-loving, giggly, good-humoured, good-tempered, happy-go-lucky, jolly, jovial, optimistic, perky, pert, playful, positive, puckish, rambunctious, risible (*formal*), sunny, *sweet-tempered*, uncomplaining, unstressed

(*adv*) sunnily

(*n*) *blitheness* (*literary*), breeziness, *bubbliness*, buoyancy, *chirpiness* (*informal*), exuberance, frivolity, humour, pertness, playfulness, rambunctiousness, risibility (*formal*), *sense of humour*

See also ENTHUSIASTIC AND INQUISITIVE (629)

505 Unfriendliness and Unsociability

A little disdain is not amiss; a little scorn is alluring. **William Congreve**

(*adj*) aloof, antisocial, chilly, clannish, cliquey, closed, cold, *compassionless*, elitist, frigid, frosty, haughty, icy, inhospitable, remote, reserved, sanguinary (*formal*), solitary, standoffish, *starched*, starchy, stuffy, unapproachable, unfriendly, unsociable, unwelcoming

(*adv*) stuffily

(*n*) aloofness, austerity, dourness, frigidity, frostiness, iciness, mischievousness (*formal*), remoteness, reservation, *standoffishness*, *starchiness*, stuffiness, *unapproachability*

See also RUDE AND HOSTILE (626), BAD MANNERS AND SOCIAL SKILLS (522)

506 Selfish and Unkind

The cruelty of most people is lack of imagination, their brutality is ignorance. **Kurt Tucholsky**

(*adj*) antisocial, brutal, brutish, callous, charmless, cold-blooded, cold-hearted, cruel, cutthroat, egocentric, egoistic, *egoistical*, *egotistic*, *egotistical*, flinty, ghoulish, hard, *hard as nails*, hard-bitten, hard-boiled (*informal*), hardened, hardhearted, *hard-nosed* (*informal*), harsh, heartless, inconsiderate, inhuman, insensate (*literary*), insensitive, intolerant, judgmental, loveless, malicious, malignant, mean, *mean-minded*, mean-spirited, mercenary, merciless, mischievous (*formal*), nasty, obdurate, parasitic, petty, picaresque, piggish, pitiless, possessive, predatory, proprietary, ruthless, savage, self-absorbed, self-centred, self-indulgent, self-interested, selfish, self-obsessed, self-regarding, self-seeking, self-serving, shabby, shoddy, spiteful, stinky, stony, stony-hearted, thoughtless, *tyrannous*, unapologetic, uncharitable, unfeeling, unforgiving, ungenerous, unkind, unmerciful, *unpitying*, unpleasant, unsparing, unsporting, unsympathetic, vindictive, viperish, wanton

(*adv*) brutishly, cruelly, fiendishly, inhumanly, insensitively, malignantly, malignly, meanly, nastily, savagely, shoddily, unpleasantly, vindictively, violently

(*n*) brutishness, callousness, *egocentricity*, *egocentrism*, egoism, egotism, ferociousness, hardheartedness, harshness, heartlessness, implacability (*formal*), *inconsiderateness*, inhumanity, insensitivity, *maliciousness*, malignancy, *mean-mindedness*, *mean-spiritedness*, meanness, mercilessness, pettiness, pitilessness, possessiveness, ruthlessness, self-absorption, self-centredness, self-indulgence, self-interest, selfishness, self-love, self-regard, thoughtlessness, unkindness, unpleasantness, viciousness, waspishness

See also BEASTLY AND BRUTISH (511)

507 Lifeless, Lazy, and Unenthusiastic

I make no secret of the fact that I would rather lie on a sofa than sweep beneath it. **Shirley Conran**

(*adj*) bone idle, idle, inactive, inanimate, indolent, lazy, passive, phlegmatic, shiftless, slack, slothful (*formal*), torpid, unambitious, undemonstrative, workshy

(*adv*) idly, phlegmatically

(*n*) inactivity, indolence, laziness, passiveness, passivity, *shilly-shallying*, slackness, sloppiness (*informal*), sloth, slothfulness (*formal*), torpor

508 Affectation, Self-Satisfaction, and Snobbishness

It is impossible, in our condition of society, not to be sometimes a Snob. **William Makepeace Thackeray**

(*adj*) affected, chichi (*disapproving*), dramatic, genteel, goody-goody (*informal*), gracious, *hammy* (*informal*), hifalutin (*informal*), high and mighty, highfalutin (*informal*), histrionic, hoity-toity (*informal*), holier-than-thou (*informal*), immodest, la-di-da (*informal*), larger-than-life, mannered, melodramatic, moralistic, narcissistic, pious, plummy, pompous, pontifical, portentous, precious, pretentious, proud, sanctimonious (*disapproving*), self-righteous (*disapproving*), self-satisfied, smug, sniffy (*informal*), snobbish, snobby (*informal*), snooty (*informal*), stagy (*disapproving*), stuck-up (*informal*), supercilious, superficial, superior, swaggering, swashbuckling, synthetic, theatrical, *toffee-nosed* (*informal*), uppity (*informal*)

(*adv*) dramatically, portentously (*disapproving*), preciously, proudly

(*n*) affectation, affectedness, artificiality, conceit, *conceitedness*, dramatics, haughtiness, narcissism, piety, piousness, pomposity, pompousness, *portentousness*, posturing, preciousness, pretension, pretentiousness, *sanctimoniousness*, self-conceit, self-righteousness, self-satisfaction, *shallowness*, smugness, snobbery, snobbishness, snootiness (*informal*), superciliousness, superiority, swollen head

See also FALSE AND UNREAL (174)

509 Cowardice and Weakness of Will

None but a coward dares to boast that he has never known fear. **Ferdinand Foch**

(*adj*) chicken (*informal*), cowardly, craven (*literary*), emasculated, faint-hearted, fallible, gutless, helpless, inhibited, *lily-livered* (*literary*), namby-pamby (*informal*), pusillanimous (*formal*), soft, spineless, spiritless, *unassertive*, unmanly, weak, weak-kneed, weak-willed, wishy-washy (*informal*)

(*n*) cowardice, *cowardliness*, *cravenness* (*literary*), *faint-heartedness*, feebleness, *gutlessness*, helplessness, pliability, pusillanimity (*formal*), spinelessness, unmanliness

See also WEAKNESS (242)

510 Lack of Commitment and Unreliability

I am a feather for each wind that blows. **William Shakespeare**

(*adj*) aimless, capricious, cavalier, delinquent (*formal*), disloyal, ditsy (*US informal*), dizzy (*informal*), faithless, feckless, fey, fickle, flighty, fly-by-night, giddy (*dated*), heady, hotheaded, impetuous, impish, impulsive, irresponsible, loose (*dated*), mercurial, neglectful, negligent, reckless, roving, slick, temperamental, traitorous, undependable, unreliable, unstable, unsteady, whimsical

(*adv*) giddily (*dated*), whimsically

(*n*) aimlessness, capriciousness, casualness, changeability, disloyalty, excitability, expediency, faddiness, fecklessness, fickleness, flightiness, hastiness, impetuosity, impetuousness, impulsiveness, laxity, laxness, looseness (*dated*), moodiness, rashness, recklessness, thoughtlessness, *treacherousness*, treachery, undependability, unreliability, *unreliableness*, whimsicality

511 Beastly and Brutish

A belief in a supernatural source of evil is not necessary; men alone are quite capable of every wickedness. **Joseph Conrad**

(*adj*) beastly (*dated informal*), bitchy (*slang*), brutish, *hoggish*, *hoglike*, inhuman, inhumane, piggish, piggy, porcine, reptilian, subhuman, *vulpine*, vulturine

(*adv*) inhumanly

See also SELFISH AND UNKIND (506), PLEASURE-SEEKERS AND HEDONISTS (886)

512 Excessive Sensitivity

Some people are so sensitive they feel snubbed if an epidemic overlooks them. **Frank McKinney Hubbard**

(*adj*) demure, excitable, explosive, highly-strung, hot-tempered, hyper (*informal*), hyperactive, overemotional, oversensitive, oversentimental, passionate, prickly (*informal*), prim, prudish, quicksilver, quick-tempered, reactive, sensitive, squeamish, thin-skinned, touchy, volatile

(*n*) *hotheadedness*, *hypersensitivity*, *oversensitivity*, primness, prudery, prudishness, squeamishness, susceptibility, testiness (*informal*), tetchiness (*informal*), touchiness

See also BAD-TEMPERED AND HUMOURLESS (627)

513 Nosy and Interfering

The people who are regarded as moral luminaries are those who forego ordinary pleasures themselves and find compensation in interfering with the pleasures of others. **Bertrand Russell**

(*adj*) inquisitive, interfering, intrusive, invasive, meddlesome, meddling, nosy (*informal*), obtrusive, prying, rubbernecked (*informal*), voyeuristic

(*n*) indiscretion, inquisitiveness, intrusiveness, meddling, *nosiness* (*informal*)

514 Deceitful

Force and fraud are in war the two cardinal virtues. **Thomas Hobbes**

(*adj*) arch, artful, bent (*slang*), byzantine, calculating, captious, cheating, conniving, crafty, crooked (*informal*), cunning, deceitful, deceiving, designing, devious, dishonest, disingenuous, double-dealing, double-faced, duplicitous, foxy, guileful, hypocritical, inconstant (*literary*), insincere, lying, Machiavellian, manipulative, mealy-mouthed (*disapproving*), mendacious, perfidious (*literary*), phoney, roguish, scheming, shifty, slippery, sly, sneaky, subtle, treacherous, tricky, two-faced, unfaithful, unscrupulous, unsportsmanlike, untrue, untrustworthy, wily

(*adv*) archly, crookedly (*informal*), deviously, mendaciously, subtly, trickily, underhand, underhandedly

(*n*) archness, artfulness, craft, craftiness, crookedness, cunning, deceitfulness, deviousness, disingenuousness, *duplicitousness*, furtiveness, guile, hypocrisy, insincerity, mendacity, *perfidiousness* (*literary*), roguery, roguishness, *shiftiness*, *slipperiness*, slyness, sneakiness, subtleness, trickiness, *two-facedness*, untrustworthiness

See also DECEPTION AND LIES (661), MORALLY BAD (776), FALSE AND UNREAL (174)

515 Negative of Outlook

The pessimist is the man who believes things couldn't possibly be worse, to which the optimist replies "Oh yes they could." **Vladimir Bukovsky**

(*adj*) case-hardened, curmudgeonly, cynical, defeatist, humourless, *ill-humoured*, jaded, jaundiced, mirthless, pessimistic, self-critical, serious, splenetic

(*adv*) splenetically

See also GRUMPY AND NEGATIVE PEOPLE (953)

516 Difficult to Please

A cat loves fish, but hates to get his fur wet. **Anonymous**

(*adj*) argumentative, blimpish, bolshie (*informal*), *cantankerous*, captious, choosy (*informal*), demanding, disputatious (*formal*), disputative (*formal*), faddy, fastidious, faultfinding, finicky, fussy, *hard to please*, hypercritical, moody, nitpicking, overcritical, particular, pernickety (*informal*), perverse, picky, quarrelsome, rigid, *shrewish*, spoiled, squeamish, stern, strict, stroppy (*informal*), tough, unreasonable, uppity (*dated informal*), vinegary

(*adv*) fussily, moodily, rigidly, toughly, unreasonably

(*n*) *argumentativeness*, *bad-temperedness*, *cantankerousness*, *choosiness*, *churlishness*, *crotchetiness* (*informal*), disputatiousness (*formal*), faddishness (*US*), faithlessness, fussiness, grouchiness (*informal*), *huffiness*, importunity (*formal*), particularity, *pernicketiness* (*informal*), *pickiness*, primness, rigidity, rigour, *shrewishness*, sternness, strictness, toughness, unreasonableness

517 Bossy and Overbearing

Where a system of oppression has become institutionalized it is unnecessary for individuals to be oppressive. **Florynce R. Kennedy**

(*adj*) authoritarian, autocratic, bossy, competitive, despotic, dictatorial, dominant, domineering, heavy-handed, high-handed, imperative (*formal*), imperious, importunate (*formal*), magisterial, megalomaniac, officious, overbearing, overconfident, overweening, possessive, proprietorial, pushy (*informal*), self-opinionated, tyrannical

(*adv*) bossily, imperiously, magisterially

(*n*) bossiness, brass (*informal*), heavy-handedness, high-handedness, imperiousness, megalomania, *officiousness*, *overbearingness*, overconfidence, pushiness

See also POMPOUS, LOUD, AND OVER-CONFIDENT (636)

518 Conservative and Unadventurous

The most awful thing about power is not that it corrupts absolutely but that it makes people so utterly boring, so predictable. **Chinua Achebe**

(*adj*) conformist, conservative, conventional, dyed-in-the-wool, hidebound, square (*slang dated*), staid, straight (*slang*), strait-laced, traditionalist, unadventurous, uncool (*slang*), unreconstructed, unreformed

(*n*) *staidness, strait-lacedness*

See also BORING AND UNINTERESTING (235)

519 Aggressive and Belligerent

The great questions of our day cannot be solved by speeches and majority votes. . .but by iron and blood. **Prince Otto von Bismarck**

(*adj*) adversarial, bellicose, belligerent, *brattish*, bratty, contentious, disagreeable, fierce, fighting, homicidal, hostile, hot-blooded, ill-natured, ill-tempered, irascible, liverish, martial, poisonous, pugnacious, sadistic, scrappy, trigger-happy (*informal*), truculent, warlike

(*adv*) fiercely, poisonously

(*n*) aggressiveness, *bellicosity*, belligerence, bitchiness (*slang*), destructiveness, *irascibility*, pugnaciousness, truculence

See also RUDE AND HOSTILE (626)

520 Financially Mean and Grasping

Everybody wants to do something to help, but nobody wants to be the first. **Pearl Bailey**

(*adj*) accumulative, acquisitive, bloodsucking, cheap, cheeseparing, chintzy (*US*), close, close-fisted (*informal*), economical, frugal, gluttonous, grasping, greedy, illiberal (*formal*), insatiable, materialistic, mean, miserly, *moneygrubbing*, niggardly, parsimonious, penny-pinching (*informal*), *penny-wise*, penurious (*literary*), pinchpenny, rapacious, ravening, ravenous, sparing, stingy (*informal*), tight, tightfisted, ungenerous, voracious

(*adv*) greedily, meanly, stingily

(*n*) acquisitiveness, cheapness, cheeseparing, economy, frugality, *graspingness*, greed, greediness, insatiability, meanness, miserliness, *niggardliness*, parsimoniousness, parsimony, rapaciousness, stinginess, tightfistedness, voraciousness

See also FINANCIALLY MEAN PEOPLE (952)

521 Good Manners and Social Skills

Friends and good manners will carry you where money won't go. **Margaret Walker**

(*adj*) chivalrous, civil, civilized, courteous, courtly, decent, decorous, delicate, demure, diplomatic, discreet, domesticated, gallant, genteel, gentlemanly, good, *good-mannered*, graceful, gracious, mannerly, mild-mannered, nice, polished, polite, politically correct, proper, proud, punctilious, refined, respectful, tactful, urbane, well-behaved, well-bred, well-mannered

(*adv*) civilly, decently, delicately, demurely, graciously, nicely, nobly, politely

(*n*) attentiveness, chivalry, civility, class, classiness (*informal*), courteousness, courtesy, decency, *decorousness*, decorum, delicacy, *demureness*, dignity, diplomacy, etiquette, finesse, gallantry, *genteelness*, gentility, good manners, gracefulness, graciousness, honour, manners, moderation, modesty, polish, politeness, *politesse*, political correctness, propriety, punctiliousness, refinement, subtlety, tact, *tactfulness*, urbanity

522 Bad Manners and Social Skills

I don't mind if you don't like my manners. I don't like 'em myself. They're pretty bad. I grieve over 'em on long winter evenings. **Humphrey Bogart**

(*adj*) badly behaved, bad-mannered, caddish, cheeky, childish, churlish, crass, discourteous, disrespectful, forward, gauche, graceless, ill-bred, ill-mannered, immature, impolite, impudent, indecorous, indelicate, indiscreet, infantile, juvenile, loutish, low-minded, misanthropic, mischievous, offensive, politically incorrect, presumptuous, primitive, raffish, rascally (*humorous*), roguish, rough, rough-hewn, rude, sassy (*US*), saucy, shameless, tactless, thick-skinned, uncivil, uncivilized, uncouth, undiplomatic, *ungallant*, *ungentlemanly*, ungraceful, ungracious, ungrateful, *unladylike*, unmannered, unmannerly, unrefined, vulgar, wanton

(*adv*) badly, brazenly, *churlishly*, gracelessly, immaturely, impertinently (*formal*), insolently, mischievously, offensively, ungratefully

(*n*) abrasiveness, attitude (*informal*), audacity, backchat (*informal*), back talk (*US*), bad manners, boorishness, cattiness, cheek (*informal*), cheekiness, childishness, chutzpah (*informal*), coarseness, cold-bloodedness, cold-heartedness, contemptuousness, coolness, crassness, crudeness, crudity, discourteousness, discourtesy, effrontery, face (*informal*), front, gall, gaucheness, gracelessness, grimness, hutzpah (*informal*), immaturity, immodesty, impertinence, impoliteness, impropriety, impudence, incivility, *indecorousness*, indecorum, indelicacy, *indelicateness*, ingratitude, insolence, irreverence, lip (*slang*), loutishness, mouth (*informal*), nerve, offensiveness, presumption, presumptuousness, pugnacity, roughness, rudeness, sassiness (*US*), sauce (*informal*), shamelessness, *surliness*, tactlessness, temerity, uncouthness, *ungraciousness*, ungratefulness, violation, vulgarity

See also RUDE AND HOSTILE (626), UNFRIENDLINESS AND UNSOCIABILITY (505)

523 Levels of Formality

It is not everyone who has the right to be plainly dressed. **Napoleon I**

(*adj*) abject, ceremonious, chatty, formal, humble, informal, intimate, majestic, prim, prissy, stiff

(*adv*) abjectly, humbly, informally, intimately, stiffly

(*n*) abjection, formality, informality, intimacy, primness, prissiness, stiffness

524 Describing Somebody's Intellect

The more intelligence one has the more people one finds original. Commonplace people see no difference between men. **Blaise Pascal**

(*n*) brain, brainpower, brains, intellect, invention, judgment, mind, reason, sense, wit, wits

See also THE NATURE OF IDEAS (772)

525 Positive Intellectual Characteristics

Sublime moments, heroic acts, are rather the deeds of an exalted intelligence than of the will. **Pío Baroja**

(*adj*) able, acute, agile, astute, brainy (*informal*), bright, broad-minded, canny, clear-headed, clear-sighted, *clear-thinking*, clever, *compos mentis*, creative, cunning, cute, dexterous, discerning, discriminating, disinterested, down-to-earth, eagle-eyed, enlightened, enterprising, exact, fair-minded, fiendish, focused, forward-thinking, freethinking, hardheaded, imaginative, incisive, independent, inquiring, inquisitive, insightful, intellectual, intelligent, intuitive, inventive, judicious, keen, lambent, liberated, logical, mature, nonjudgmental, observant, on the ball (*informal*), open-minded, penetrating, penetrative, perceptive, percipient, perspicacious, *perspicuous*, pervious, philosophic, philosophical, piercing, politic, practical, pragmatic, progressive, provident, prudent, prudential, purposeful, quick, *quick off the mark*, quick on the uptake (*informal*), *quick-thinking*, quick-witted, rational, ready, realistic, reasonable, receptive, resourceful, retentive, right-minded, *right-thinking*, sagacious (*formal*), sane, selective, sensible, sensitive, sentient, serious-minded, sharp, sharp-eyed, sharp-sighted, sharp-witted, shrewd, smart, *straight-thinking*, streetwise (*informal*), strong-minded, subtle, technical, thinking, thorough, thoughtful, tolerant, unsentimental, visionary, well-balanced, wholesome, wise, *with it* (*informal*)

(*adv*) cleverly, critically, independently, maturely, permissively, piercingly, practically, reasonably, sagely (*literary*), sensibly, sensitively, soberly, subtly

(*n*) acuity, acuteness, astuteness, brilliance, broad-mindedness, *canniness*, carefulness, caution, cautiousness, cleverness, common sense, creativeness, creativity, cuteness, detachment, dexterity, discernment, discrimination, disinterestedness, enterprise, far-sightedness, foresight, genius, gumption (*informal*), head, horse sense (*informal*), imagination, imaginativeness, *incisiveness*, individualism, ingenuity, initiative, inquisitiveness, insight, insightfulness, inspiration, intelligence, intuitiveness, inventiveness, judiciousness, keenness, lucidity, *moxie* (*US slang*), nous, open-mindedness, penetration, perceptiveness, percipience, permissiveness, perspicacity, *perspicuity*, practicality, pragmatism, presence of mind, progressiveness, providence, provision, prudence, quickness, quick-wittedness, rationality, realism, reasonableness, receptiveness, resourcefulness, rigour, *saneness*, sanity, selectivity, sensibleness, sharpness, shrewdness, soberness, strong-mindedness, studiousness, subtleness, thoughtfulness, tolerance, toleration, understanding, watchfulness, wholesomeness, wiliness, wittiness

See also KNOWLEDGE AND WISDOM (559), THE NATURE OF IDEAS (772), LEVEL OF EDUCATION AND SOPHISTICATION (894)

526 Negative Intellectual Characteristics

No one ever went broke underestimating the intelligence of the American people. **H. L. Mencken**

(*adj*) absent-minded, asinine, babyish, benighted, bigoted, birdbrained (*informal*), blinkered, bovine (*literary*), brainless, chauvinistic, childish, childlike, class-conscious, closed, closed-minded (*US*), credulous, daffy (*informal*), deluded, dewy-eyed, doctrinaire, dogmatic, *dopey*, dotty, dozy, dull, *dull-witted*, empty-headed, exploitable, extreme, feeble-minded (*archaic*), foolish, forgetful, frivolous, gormless (*informal*), gullible, *homophobic*, hysterical, idealistic, illiberal, *imperceptive*, impractical, impressionable, indecisive, indiscreet, indiscriminate, ineffectual, ingenuous, insular, jejune, jingoistic, juvenile, light-minded, malleable, middlebrow (*informal*), muddleheaded, myopic, naive, narrow-minded, *obsessional*, obsessive, obtuse, opinionated, overactive, overenthusiastic, parochial, partisan, pedantic, petty, *petty-minded*, *picayune* (*US informal*), prejudiced, puerile, quixotic, racist, reactionary, romantic, scatterbrained, scatty (*informal*), sectarian, simple, simple-minded, *slow-witted*, stolid, stupid, suggestible, superstitious, susceptible, trusting, uncritical, *undiscerning*, unenlightened, unintelligent, unobservant, unperceptive, unwary, vacuous, vague, wide-eyed, witless, *woolly-headed*, *woolly-minded*, wrong-headed, xenophobic

(*adv*) ambitiously, blindly, dully, fatuously, fixatedly, ill-advisedly, indecisively, ingenuously, innocently, intolerantly, simply, stupidly, unjustly, vacuously

(*n*) absent-mindedness, blindness, blinkeredness, *callowness*, *closed-mindedness*, credulity, *credulousness*, daftness (*informal*), dogmatism, fallibility, fatuity (*formal*), feeble-mindedness, folly, foolhardiness, foolishness, forgetfulness, gullibility, idealism, *idiocy*, immaturity, *impressionability*, *impressionableness*, imprudence, inadvertence, inanity, indiscretion, ineffectuality, *ineffectualness*, innocence, insularity, madness, myopia, narrow-mindedness, parochialism, pedantry, *pettifoggery*, pettiness, *petty-mindedness*, provincialism (*disapproving*), puerility, *scattiness* (*informal*), *shockability*, short-sightedness, stupidity, suggestibility, trustfulness, *unintelligence*, *unreceptiveness*, *unsound reasoning*, *unthinkingness*, unwariness, unworldliness, *vacuousness*, vagueness, *witlessness*, *wrong-headedness*

See also PREJUDICE (551), IGNORANCE (558), THE NATURE OF IDEAS (772)

527 Skills, Talents, and Abilities

Talent develops in quiet places, character in the full current of human life. **Johann Wolfgang von Goethe**

(*n*) ability, accomplishment, acrobatics, acumen, adeptness, adroitness, aptitude, art, artistry, attainment, calibre, capability, capacity, clout (*informal*), competence, control, coordination, craft, craftsmanship, cunning, deftness, dexterity, *dexterousness*, ear, endowment, expertness, eye, facility, faculty, finesse, flair, forte, gift, handiness, handiwork, instinct, knack, know-how (*informal*), *legerdemain*, makings, mastery, merit, *natural ability*, *natural gift*, potential, power, precociousness, precocity, professionalism, proficiency, promise, prowess, qualification, *skilfulness*, skill, sleight of hand, slyness, talent, technology, timing, touch, trick, virtuosity, vocation, wizardry

528 Talented and Skilful

If a man has talent and cannot use it, he has failed...If he has a talent and learns somehow to use the whole of it, he has...won a satisfaction and a triumph few men ever know. **Thomas Wolfe**

(*adj*) able, accomplished, adept, adroit, all-around (*US*), apt, bilingual, born, brilliant, capable, clever, competent, consummate, deft, dexterous, equal to, expert, finished, gifted, good, handy, high-powered, ingenious, magisterial, masterful, masterly, *multitalented*, polished, practised, precocious, proficient, promising, seasoned, skilful, skilled, sly, sure-footed, talented, trained, versatile, well-endowed

(*adv*) ably, brilliantly, capably, ingeniously, magisterially, professionally

529 Talented or Intelligent Person

Whom the gods wish to destroy they first call promising. **Cyril Connolly**

(*n*) ace, achiever, authority, boffin (*informal*), *boy wonder*, brain (*informal*), *brainbox*, *bright spark* (*informal*), buff, *clever clogs* (*informal*), *clever Dick* (*informal*), connoisseur, dab hand (*informal*), demon (*informal*), expert, genius, guru, maestro, magician, marvel, master, mastermind, maven, mind, mistress, old hand, phenomenon, polymath, powerhouse (*informal*), pro, prodigy, professional, pundit, sage (*literary*), savant, scholar, solon (*literary*), specialist, superstar, troubleshooter, veteran, victor, virtuoso, whiz (*informal*), whiz kid (*informal*), *wiz* (*informal*), wizard (*informal*), *wunderkind*

See also PEOPLE WHO ARE APPROVED OF (955)

530 Unskilled

To be conscious that you are ignorant is a great step to knowledge. **Benjamin Disraeli**

(*adj*) amateur, amateurish, bungling (*informal*), cack-handed (*informal*), callow, fledgling, ham-fisted (*informal*), ham-handed (*informal*), heavy-handed, hopeless, illiterate, impotent, inadequate, incapable, incompetent, inept, inexperienced, inexpert, lay, maladroit (*formal*), new, raw, rusty, *talentless*, tender, unable, unaccomplished, unaccustomed, uneducated, unequal, unfamiliar, unfit, uninitiated, unlettered, unlicensed, unpractised, unprepared, unprofessional, unqualified, unskilful, unskilled, *untalented*, untutored, unused, useless (*informal*), *wet behind the ears*

(*n*) amateurishness, disorganization, gracelessness, *ham-fistedness* (*informal*), *ham-handedness* (*informal*), hopelessness, impotence, inability, incompetence, ineptitude, ineptness, inexperience, maladroitness (*formal*), rawness, *unskilfulness*, uselessness (*informal*)

531 Unskilled Person

Man arrives as a novice at each age of his life. **Nicolas Chamfort**

(*n*) amateur, apprentice, beginner, bungler (*informal*), cub, dilettante, fledgling, greenhorn, junior, laity, learner, neophyte, newcomer, novice, pledge (*US*), *raw recruit*, rookie (*US informal*), tenderfoot (*informal*), trainee, tyro

Emotions and States of Mind

532 Feelings

Few people realize that they are looking at the world of their own thoughts and the world of their own feelings. **Wallace Stevens**

(*n*) emotion, feeling, gut feeling, gut reaction, hunch, instinct, intuition, mood, morale, notion, sense, sensibility, sentiment, spirit, spirits, suspicion

533 Feelings About the Past

The urban man is an uprooted tree, he can put out leaves, flowers and grow fruit but what a nostalgia his leaf, flower, and fruit will always have for mother earth. **Juan Ramón Jiménez**

(*n*) bitterness, compunction, contrition, guilt, guiltiness, guilty conscience, nostalgia, qualm, regret, remorse, repentance, resentment, resignation, romance, self-reproach, umbrage, wistfulness

534 Feelings About the Future

The future is like heaven—everyone exalts it but no one wants to go there now. **James Baldwin**

(*n*) ambition, angst, anticipation, apprehension, aspiration, bleakness, bullishness (*informal*), compulsion, defeatism, expectancy, expectation, fearfulness, foreboding, foreknowledge (*formal*), fright, gloom, gloominess, hope, hopefulness, hopelessness, impatience, misgiving, motivation, negativity, nerves (*informal*), nerviness, nervousness, optimism, oracle, pessimism, premonition, presentiment, qualm, reluctance, second thoughts, solicitude, stage fright, suspense, tension, trepidation, unease, uneasiness, unrest, wariness, whim, worry

See also DESIRE AND WANT (580), PREDICT AND ANTICIPATE (751)

535 Pleasure, Excitement, and Elation

Fine pictures, fine statues, beautiful music; pleasure for the senses, and let the devil take the soul! **Benito Pérez Galdós**

(*adj*) abandoned, afire, aflame, agape (*literary*), *all of a flutter*, amused, *aroused*, buoyant, *carried away*, cheerful, cheery, chipper (*informal*), chirpy (*informal*), cock-a-hoop, content, contented, delighted, delirious, ecstatic, elated, *enraptured* (*formal*), *enthused*, euphoric, excited, exhilarated, expectant, exultant, feverish, fired up, glad, *gladdened*, gleeful, *gloating*, *gratified*, happy, honoured, hot, infected, *in good spirits, in high spirits, in raptures, in seventh heaven*, joyful, joyous, jubilant, keyed up (*informal*), light, lighthearted, manic (*informal*), merry, mirthful, on cloud nine (*informal*), on fire, overexcited, overjoyed, over the moon, pleased, proud, radiant, rapt, rapturous, satiated, satisfied, starry-eyed, thankful, thrilled, *thrilled to bits* (*informal*), *thrilled to pieces* (*US informal*), *tickled*, tickled pink (*informal*), touched, *transported*, triumphant, up, upbeat (*informal*), *uplifted*, white-hot, wild

(*adv*) aflutter, blissfully, buoyantly, cheerfully, excitedly, expectantly, gaily, happily, jauntily, joyfully, lightheartedly, wildly

(*n*) afterglow, arousal, bliss, brightness, cheer, cheerfulness, cheeriness, delectation (*formal*), delight, delirium, ecstasy, elation, enchantment, enjoyment, euphoria, exaltation (*formal*), exhilaration, exultation, fascination, felicity, fervour, gaiety, gladness, glee, *gleefulness, good humour*, gusto, happiness, high spirits, jauntiness, joie de vivre, jolliness, jollity, joviality, joy, joyfulness, joyousness, jubilation, merriment, pleasure, radiance, rapture, relish, rhapsody, romance, satisfaction, triumph

See also PLEASE AND AMUSE (573)

536 Appreciation and Gratitude

I want to thank you for stopping the applause. It is impossible for me to look humble for any period of time. **Henry Kissinger**

(*adj*) admiring, adoring, amorous, appreciative, approving, bedazzled (*literary*), besotted, *bewitched*, born-again, broody, captivated, charmed, chuffed (*informal*), crazy (*informal*), doting, dotty (*informal*), enamoured, enchanted, enthusiastic, fanatical, fervent, *fervid*, fulfilled, grateful, *head over heels in love*, hung up (*informal*), inclined, indebted, infatuated, *in favour, in love*, into, keen on, lovesick, *love-struck*, mad, misty-eyed, *obligated*, obliged, partial to, rabid, romantic, smitten (*humorous or archaic or literary*), *soft on, sold on, stuck on* (*informal*), *taken with*, thankful, warm, well-disposed, worshipful

(*adv*) devotedly, gratefully, head over heels, in earnest, rabidly, thankfully, with bated breath

(*n*) appreciation, contentment, devotion, druthers (*informal*), gratefulness, gratification, gratitude, liking, penchant, predilection (*formal*), preference, pride, proclivity, recognition, satisfaction, soft spot, temptation, thankfulness, thanks

537 Calmness, Confidence, and Composure

Calmness is great advantage; he that lets another chafe may warm him at his fire, mark all his wand'rings and enjoy his frets, as cunning fencers suffer heat to tire. **George Herbert**

(*adj*) accustomed, adamant, all set, at ease, at home, at peace, at rest, bullish (*informal*), calm, carefree, chilled (*slang*), *chilled out* (*slang*), collected, comfortable, comforted, composed, convinced, cool, fluent, fluid, fortified, *heartened*, hopeful, laid-back (*informal*), lucid, philosophic, philosophical, ready, *ready and waiting, ready for action, ready for anything, reassured*, relieved, sanguine, serene, stable, together (*informal*), tranquil, unabashed, unafraid, unashamed, *unbothered*, undaunted, *undeterred*, undisturbed, *unembarrassed*, unflustered, unperturbed, unruffled, unsuspecting, untroubled, unworried, welcome

(*adv*) bullishly (*informal*), comfortably, coolly, fluently, hopefully, quietly, serenely, tranquilly

(*n*) *amour-propre* (*formal*), bravado, calm, calmness, carefreeness, complacency, composure, confidence, coolness, courage, credit, cynicism, equanimity, faith, fulfilment, placidity, reassurance, *sanguinity*, serenity

See also CONFIDENCE AND COMPOSURE (500), SOOTHE AND CALM (574)

538 Positive Impatience, Enthusiasm, and Alertness

One's prime is elusive. . .be on the alert to recognize your prime at whatever time of your life it may occur. You must then live it to the full. **Muriel Spark**

(*adj*) agog, alert, alive, animated, anxious, bursting (*informal*), desirous (*formal*), desperate, edgy, fevered, heedful, hungry, impatient, *in a tizzy* (*informal*), inspired, *in suspense*, itching, *like a cat on a hot tin roof, like a cat on hot bricks*, mindful, on the alert, passionate, prepared, *psyched up* (*informal*), restive, restless, skittish, sleepless, *stirred up*, straining at the leash, uptight (*informal*), vigilant, wakeful, wannabe (*informal*), watchful, wholehearted, wide-awake (*informal*), willing

(*adv*) breathlessly, *desirously* (*formal*), edgily, jumpily, on your mettle, passionately

(*n*) ambition, buoyancy, drive, eagerness, enthusiasm, excitement, friskiness, go (*informal*), immersion, impulse, *itchy feet, mindfulness*, passion, preparedness, purpose, restiveness, restlessness, sleeplessness, unction, urgency, verve, vibrancy, vigilance, vigour, vim (*informal*), wakefulness, warmness, warmth, willingness, zeal, zest, zing (*informal*), zip (*informal*)

See also ENERGY AND ENTHUSIASM (497)

539 Pensiveness and Interest

Philosophy, as we use the word, is a fight against the fascination which forms of expression exert upon us. **Ludwig Wittgenstein**

(*adj*) absorbed, *all ears* (*informal*), attentive, *beguiled*, captive, caught up, contemplative, curious, daydreaming, deep in thought, engrossed, enthralled, *entranced*, fascinated, fixated, grave, gripped, hooked (*slang*), immersed, intent, interested, introspective, knee-deep, lost, lost in thought, meditative, *mesmerized*, musing, nostalgic, obsessed, pensive, profound, rapt, reflective, *riveted* (*informal*), ruminant, ruminative, *sidetracked*, solemn, spellbound, thoughtful, *transfixed*, wistful, wrapped up in, zestful

(*adv*) broodingly

See also APPEAL TO AND AROUSE INTEREST (576), ATTENTION AND ATTENTIVENESS (764)

540 Sadness, Distress, and Despair

My only hope lies in my despair. **Racine**

(*adj*) afflicted, affronted, aggrieved, agonized, angst-ridden, anguished, bad, beleaguered, beside yourself, besieged, bleak, blue (*informal*), broken, brokenhearted, broody, browned-off (*dated slang*), bruised, burdened, careworn, *chagrined*, cheesed off (*informal*), choked (*informal*), *choked up* (*US informal*), *close to tears*, *conscience-stricken*, crestfallen, crying, cut up (*informal*), deflated, dejected, demoralized, depressed, desolate, despairing, desperate, despondent, devastated, disappointed, disconsolate, discontented, discouraged, disenchanted, disgusted, disheartened, disillusioned, dismayed, dispirited, distressed, doleful, doom-laden, down, downcast, downhearted, down in the dumps, *down in the mouth* (*informal*), downtrodden, dreary, fatalistic, fed up (*informal*), forlorn, gloomy, glum, grief-stricken, gutted (*informal*), harassed, harried, heartbroken, heavy-hearted (*literary*), heavy-laden (*literary*), homesick, hopeless, horrified, huffy, hurried, hurt, hurting, *in a funk* (*US informal*), in a huff (*informal*), *in a mood*, in a state (*informal*), *in a strop* (*informal*), inconsolable, *in despair*, *in distress*, *in low spirits*, *insulted*, *in the doldrums*, *in the dumps*, *in turmoil*, lachrymose (*literary*), lousy (*informal*), low, malcontent, melancholic, melancholy, miffed (*informal*), miserable, morbid, morose, mournful, negative, offended, overwhelmed, pained, plaintive, pressured, prostrate, rotten (*informal*), sad, *saddened*, saturnine, self-pitying, shattered, sick, sick and tired, *sickened*, sombre, sorrowful, sorrowing, *stung*, suicidal (*informal*), sunk, tearful, tired, tormented, traumatized, unhappy, unhopeful, unsatisfied, up and down, upset, weepy (*informal*), weighed down, woebegone, woeful, wounded, wretched

(*adv*) abjectly, bleakly, broodily, desolately, desperately, forlornly, gloomily, hopelessly, miserably, negatively, regretfully, sadly, sombrely, sorrowfully, tearfully, unhappily, wretchedly

(*n*) abjection, agony, anguish, blackness, blues (*informal*), broodiness, consternation, *contriteness*, dejection, demoralization, depression, desolation, despair, desperation, despondency, disappointment, discontent, discontentment, discouragement, disenchantment, disillusionment, dismay, distress, doldrums, dolefulness, glumness, gravity, grief, heartache, heartbreak, *homesickness*, horror, hurt, joylessness, lugubriousness, malaise, martyrdom, melancholy, misery, *moroseness*, mournfulness, pain, pathos, perturbation, poignance, poignancy, regret, sadness, self-pity, *sombreness*, sorrow, *sorrowfulness*, soulfulness, spleen, suffering, torment, torture, unhappiness, upset, woe, world-weariness, wretchedness

See also UPSET, DISTRESS, AND HUMILIATE (568)

541 Confusion, Anxiety, and Worry

Confusion is a word we have invented for an order which is not understood. **Henry Miller**

(*adj*) addled, addlepated (*archaic*), agitated, alarmed, anxious, apprehensive, at sea, baffled, *bamboozled* (*informal*), befuddled, bemused, beset, bewildered, bogged down (*informal*), bothered, browbeaten, clouded, concerned, confounded, confused, dazed, desperate, disconcerted, *disorientated*, distracted, distraught, disturbed, excited, fearful, flummoxed (*informal*), flustered, frantic, fraught, fretful, *fuddled*, *hassled* (*informal*), haunted, het up (*informal*), hot and bothered, hung up (*informal*), *in a flap* (*informal*), *in a frenzy*, *in a lather* (*informal*), *in high dudgeon*, jittery, jumpy, lost, *mired*, mixed-up (*informal*), moonstruck (*informal humorous*), muddled, mystified, nervous, nervy (*informal*), nonplussed, on edge, on tenterhooks, overstrung, overwrought, perplexed, perturbed, preoccupied, punch-drunk (*informal*), punchy, puzzled, *shaken*, spaced-out (*slang*), spacy (*slang*), strained, stressed, stressed out (*informal*), stricken, stuck, *stumped*, stupefied, *stymied*, taut, tense, troubled, twitchy (*informal*), uneasy, unquiet, unsettled, wired (*slang*), worked up (*informal*), worried, *worried sick*, wrought-up

(*adv*) distractedly, fearfully, tensely

(*n*) agitation, anxiety, *anxiousness*, bafflement, befuddlement, bewilderment, blankness, care, concern, confusion, daze, desperation, disorientation, distraction, fear, fogginess, fretfulness, fuddle, *jitteriness*, jitters (*informal*), jumpiness, mystification, niggle, perplexity, preoccupation, puzzlement, strain, stress, stupefaction, trouble, unquiet

See also CONFUSE AND BEWILDER (572)

542 Irritation and Anger

Anger is a momentary madness, so control your passion or it will control you. **Horace**

(*adj*) aggravated (*informal*), angry, annoyed, antagonistic, antipathetic, *antsy* (*US informal*), *apoplectic*, bad-tempered, beside yourself, bitter, *choleric* (*literary*), combative, confrontational, crabbed, crabby, cranky (*US informal*), crazed, cross, crotchety (*informal*), disgruntled, displeased, dissatisfied, embittered, enraged, exasperated, fractious, frenzied, frustrated, fuming, furious, glowering, grizzly, grouchy (*informal*), grumpy, *hacked off* (*informal*), hopping mad (*informal*), hot under the collar (*informal*), hypersensitive, ill-disposed, impatient, impenitent, *in a bad mood*, incensed, indignant, infuriated, inimical, irate, *ireful* (*literary*), *irked*, irritable, irritated, livid, mad, maddened, *narked* (*informal*), *nettled* (*informal*), offensive, on the warpath (*informal*), out of sorts, outraged, overheated, peeved (*informal*), peevish, pettish, petulant, piqued, provoked, rancorous, ratty (*informal*), remorseless, *repelled*, repulsed, resentful, *revengeful*, revolted, *riled* (*informal*), seething, short-tempered, *sick to death*, *sick to the back teeth*, sore (*informal*), *spoiling for a fight*, stir-crazy (*informal or humorous*), strung out (*informal*), *strung up* (*informal*), sulky, teed off (*US informal*), testy (*informal*), tetchy (*informal*), *ticked off* (*US informal*), unremorseful, up in arms, vengeful, vexed, vindictive, waspish, wound up (*informal*), wrathful

(*adv*) furiously, lividly, *rattily* (*informal*)

(*n*) abhorrence, aggravation (*informal*), anger, annoyance, aversion, bad mood, bad temper, bile (*literary*), blackness, *choler* (*archaic or literary*), crabbiness, crankiness (*US informal*), detestation, disapproval, displeasure, dissatisfaction, exasperation, *excoriation* (*formal*), frustration, furiousness, fury, fuse, grumpiness, hate, hatred, huff, ill humour, impatience, indignation, ire (*literary*), irritability, irritation, mood, offence, opprobriousness, opprobrium, outrage, passion, peevishness, pet, petulance, pique, rage, reprehension, strop (*informal*), stroppiness (*informal*), sulk, sulkiness, temper, vexation, wrath

See also ANGER AND ANNOY (570)

543 Embarrassment and Humiliation

Speak the truth and shame the Devil. **François Rabelais**

(*adj*) abashed, apologetic, ashamed, contrite, deprecatory, embarrassed, guilt-ridden, guilty, hangdog, humbled, humiliated, mortified, penitent, penitential, red-faced, regretful, remorseful, repentant, rueful, shamefaced, sheepish, sorry

(*adv*) regretfully

(*n*) abasement (*literary*), chagrin, confusion, debasement, degradation, discomfiture (*formal*), discomfort, discomposure, embarrassment, humiliation, ignominy, inhibition, mortification, opprobriousness, opprobrium, self-abasement, shame, sheepishness

544 Fear and Panic

He who has been bitten by a snake fears a piece of string. **Persian proverb**

(*adj*) afraid, cowed, frightened, horror-stricken, hunted, *hysteric*, hysterical, *in a panic*, in awe of, intimidated, *panicked*, panicky, panic-stricken, petrified, phobic, scared, *scared rigid*, *scared stiff*, *scared to death*, terrified, *terrorized*, terror-stricken, trembling, tremulous, unnerved

(*n*) alarm, awe, butterflies (*informal*), chill, dread, fear, heebie-jeebies (*slang*), hysterics, lather (*informal*), panic, scare, terror, willies (*informal*)

See also FEARS AND PHOBIAS (555), FRIGHTEN AND SHOCK (569)

545 Insecurity and Loss of Composure

Life is our reaction to the basic insecurity which constitutes its substance. **José Ortega y Gasset**

(*adj*) *all at sea*, *aquiver*, *at a complete loss*, *at a loose end*, awkward, cagey (*informal*), chary, circumspect, *daunted*, defensive, *discomfited* (*formal*), *disquieted* (*archaic or literary*), doomy (*informal*), downbeat, fidgety, guarded, halting, hesitant, hyper (*informal*), ill at ease, jealous, mistrustful, paranoid, queasy, self-conscious, shy, skittish, *squirmy*, tentative, *thrown off balance*, unconfident, unglued (*informal*), unsure, wary

(*adv*) awkwardly, cagily (*informal*), defensively, falteringly, insecurely, shyly, tentatively, twitchily

(*n*) abandon, apprehensiveness, awkwardness, caginess (*informal*), *chariness*, circumspection, disquiet, *edginess*, excitement, fever, fidgetiness, fire, flap (*informal*), flutter, frenzy, giddiness (*dated*), heat, hesitancy, hysteria, insecurity, jealousy, *self-consciousness*, *self-contempt*, *self-disgust*, *self-dislike*, self-doubt, self-hatred, *self-loathing*, tizzy (*informal*), twitchiness

546 Surprise, Shock, and Amazement

Between ourselves the best thing of all is a combination of the surprising and the beautiful. **Ludwig van Beethoven**

(*adj*) aghast, amazed, appalled, astonished, astounded, awestricken, awestruck, bowled over, dumbfounded, *dumbstruck*, electrified, flabbergasted (*informal*), *gobsmacked* (*slang*), horrified, horror-struck, *impressed*, *in a daze*, *in a state of shock*, incredulous, in disbelief, *in shock*, knocked for six (*informal*), knocked out (*informal*), open-mouthed, *overawed*, overwhelmed, *scandalized*, shocked, speechless, staggered, startled, *stunned*, stupefied, surprised, taken aback, thunderstruck, wide-eyed

(*adv*) *in awe*

(*n*) amazement, astonishment, awe, *bemusement*, incomprehension, incredulity, shock, *speechlessness*, start, stupefaction (*literary*), stupor, surprise, wonder, wonderment

See also SURPRISE AND IMPRESS (575)

547 Expressions of Surprise

Perhaps one has to be very old before one learns how to be amused rather than shocked. **Pearl Buck**

(*adv*) fortunately, paradoxically, surprisingly, *to my amazement*, *to my surprise*

(*interj*) *gee* (*US informal*), *gee whiz* (*US informal*), golly (*dated informal*), *goodness gracious*, goody (*informal*), gosh (*informal*), *heavens* (*informal*), *heavens to Betsy* (*US informal*), *hey presto* (*informal*), ho hum (*informal*), *hooray*, *hurrah*, *jeepers* (*dated informal*), *my*, *my goodness*, *my word* (*dated*), *oh my* (*US informal*)

548 Expressions of Regret

But with the morning cool repentance came. **Sir Walter Scott**

(*adv*) alas, sadly, unfortunately, unhappily

(*interj*) commiserations

549 Envy and Jealousy

Envy will merit as its shade pursue,/But like a shadow proves the substance true. **Alexander Pope**

(*adj*) covetous, envious, *green-eyed*, *green with envy*, jealous, territorial

(*n*) avidity, *enviousness*, envy, jealousy, possessiveness, protectiveness, *resentfulness*

550 Love, Respect, and Goodwill

Be warm, but pure: be amorous, but be chaste. **Lord Byron**

(*n*) admiration, adoration, adulation, affection, affinity, ardour, attachment, crush (*informal*), deference, devotion, esteem, fondness, goodwill, homage, honour, infatuation, love, lust, obeisance, regard, respect, respectfulness, reverence, veneration, warmth, worship

551 Prejudice

Prejudice is planted in childhood, learnt like table manners and cadences of speech, nurtured through fictions like Uncle Tom's Cabin *and* Gone With the Wind. **Beryl Bainbridge**

(*n*) bias, chauvinism, discrimination, elitism, exclusiveness, favouritism, flag-waving, intolerance, jingoism, misanthropy, nepotism, partisanship, prejudice, racism, *sexism*, unfairness, xenophobia

See also NEGATIVE INTELLECTUAL CHARACTERISTICS (526)

552 Compassion and Forgiveness

It is the enemy who can truly teach us to practice the virtues of compassion and tolerance. **Dalai Lama**

(*n*) *commiseration*, compassion, condolence, empathy, feeling, fellow feeling, forgiveness, heart, identification, mercy, pity, sympathy, understanding

553 Antagonism

Antagonism is a form of struggle within a contradiction, but not the universal form. **Mao Zedong**

(*n*) acrimony, animosity, animus, antagonism, antipathy, bad blood, bad feeling, *censoriousness*, censure, chill, chilliness, condescension, contempt, disapprobation (*formal*), disrespect, enmity, grudge, *hard feelings*, hostility, ill feeling, ill will, lese majesty, malice, rancorousness, rancour, *reproachfulness*, scorn, *scornfulness*, sour grapes, sourness, spite, spitefulness, unfriendliness, venom, vindictiveness, wilfulness

See also RUDE AND HOSTILE (626)

554 Neutrality and Indifference

It is not the neutrals or the lukewarm who make history. **Adolf Hitler**

(*adj*) absent, abstracted, alienated, apathetic, blasé, blithe, bored, *bored rigid*, *bored stiff*, *bored to death*, *bored to tears*, businesslike, careless, casual, catatonic, chill, clinical, complacent, damp, deaf, detached, disaffected, dispassionate, distracted, distrait (*literary*), dreamy, dry-eyed, emotionless, faraway, half-hearted, hands-off, heedless, immune, impartial, impassive, impervious, in a rut, in a world of your own, incurious, indifferent, insensitive, *insouciant*, inured to, lackadaisical, lax, lukewarm, *miles away*, negligent (*literary*), neutral, nonchalant, nonpartisan, numb, off-guard, passionless, robotic, subdued, tepid, thick-skinned, unaffected, uncaring, uncommitted, unconcerned, unemotional, unenthusiastic, unexcited, unimpressed, uninterested, uninvolved, unmindful, unmotivated, unmoved, unresponsive, untouched, vacant, weary, withdrawn, world-weary, worn down

(*adv*) absently, blithely, carelessly, casually, damply, dreamily, *lukewarmly*, neutrally, numbly, vacantly

(*n*) apathy, casualness, coldness, demotivation, detachment, disaffection, disinterest, dispassion, disregard, ennui, glibness, heedlessness, immunity, impartiality, *impassiveness*, *impassivity*, imperviousness, indifference, insouciance, laissez-faire, laxity, laxness, neutrality, nonchalance, numbness, sufferance, unconcern, unresponsiveness, weariness

See also UNWILLINGNESS AND STUBBORNNESS (565), WITHOUT ENTHUSIASM (288), UNINTERESTED AND DETACHED (630)

555 Fears and Phobias

The taxonomy of fear has long been a subject of interest to psychiatrists, who have delighted in compiling lists of phobias and calling them by Greek names. **Anthony Stevens**

(*adj*) phobic

(*n*) paranoia, phobia

(*v*) be afraid, fear, have a horror of

types of phobia acrophobia, agoraphobia, ailurophobia, arachnophobia, claustrophobia, hydrophobia, necrophobia, nyctophobia, photophobia, pyrophobia, technophobia, theophobia, zoophobia

See also FEAR AND PANIC (544)

556 Fads, Fetishes, and Idolatry

Fashions, after all, are only induced epidemics. **George Bernard Shaw**

(*n*) addiction, bandwagon, canonization, craze, cult, enthusiasm, extremism, fad, fanaticism, fashion, fetish, fixation, hero worship, hobbyhorse, icon, idolatry, idolization, mania, obsession, *obsessiveness*, overenthusiasm, overexcitement, partisanship, *pyromania*, *religious fervour*, *religious zeal*, thing (*informal*), trend, vogue, *zealotry*

557 Devotees and Addicted People

One week he's in polka dots, the next week he's in stripes./'Cos he's a dedicated follower of fashion. **Ray Davies**

(*n*) acolyte, addict, adherent, advocate, aficionada, aficionado, arbiter, *bibliophile*, *book lover*, booster (*US*), campaigner, canvasser, champion, crusader, defender, devotee, enthusiast, exponent, fan, fanatic, freak (*informal*), gladiator, groupie (*informal*), hanger-on, *hero-worshipper*, idealist, idolater, loyalist, maniac, monarchist, nut (*informal*), partisan, patriot, proponent, proposer, pyromaniac, reader, rocker (*informal*), royalist, smoker, *teddy boy*, *votary*, zealot

558 Ignorance

Ignorance is the mother of devotion. **Jeremy Taylor**

(*adj*) at a loss, clueless (*informal*), ignorant, insensible, insensitive, oblivious, *unapprised*, unaware, uncivilized, unconscious, unenlightened, unfledged, unformed, uninformed, uninstructed, unknowing, *unknowledgeable*, unlearned, unschooled, untaught, untrained, *unversed*, unwitting, unworldly

(*n*) amnesia, *cluelessness* (*informal*), ignorance, oblivion, unfamiliarity

See also NEGATIVE INTELLECTUAL CHARACTERISTICS (526), UNCERTAINTY (560)

559 Knowledge and Wisdom

A study of history shows that civilizations that abandon the quest for knowledge are doomed to disintegration. **Bernard Lovell**

(*adj*) abreast, academic, accustomed to, *all-knowing*, *all-seeing*, at home, *au courant*, *au fait*, aware, bookish, *clued in* (*US*), clued-up (*informal*), cognizant (*formal*), conditioned, conscious, conversant, experienced, familiar, informed, in the know, *in the picture*, knowing, knowledgeable, learned, numerate, omniscient, on top of, plugged-in (*informal*), primed, privy, sapient, unacquainted, *up on*, up-to-date, up with, used to, versed, *versed in*, well-educated, well-informed, well-read, well-versed, wise, worldly, worldly-wise

(*adv*) by heart, by rote, like the back of your hand

(*n*) acquaintance, acquaintanceship, awakening, awareness, cognizance (*formal*), command, comprehension, consciousness, *conversance*, enlightenment, erudition, experience, expertise, exposure, familiarity, familiarization, *gen* (*informal*), good judgment, good sense, grasp, grounding, ken, knowledge, learning, literacy, maturity, nous (*informal*), numeracy, omniscience, precognition, recognition, *sagaciousness* (*formal*), sagacity, *sapience*, savoir-faire, savvy (*informal*), scholarship, *sentience*, wisdom, worldliness

(*v*) be acquainted with, discern, *have down pat* (*US*), *have knowledge of*, *have off pat*, know, know back to front, know backward and forward (*US*), know backwards

See also POSITIVE INTELLECTUAL CHARACTERISTICS (525), CERTAINTY (562)

560 Uncertainty

Negative Capability, *that is, when a man is capable of being in uncertainties, mysteries, doubts, without any irritable reaching after fact and reason.* **John Keats**

(*adj*) agnostic, ambivalent, clingy, disbelieving, distrustful, doubtful, doubting, dubious, faltering, *in a cleft stick*, *in a dilemma*, *in a quandary*, insecure, *in two minds*, irresolute, leery (*informal*), on the fence, pendulous, sceptical, suspicious, torn, unbelieving, uncertain, unconvinced, undecided, undetermined, unsure, vacillating, wavering

(*adv*) askance, doubtfully, dubiously, uncertainly, waveringly

(*n*) agnosticism, ambivalence, disbelief, disbeliever, distrust, dithering, doubt, doubter, doubtfulness, dubiousness, hesitation, *incertitude*, indecision, indecisiveness, *irresoluteness*, irresolution, mistrust, query, question, question mark, reservations, sceptic, scepticism, scruple, suspense, suspicion, uncertainty, vacillation, wavering

(*v*) disbelieve, doubt, expect, feel, suspect

See also DIFFICULT SITUATIONS (72), UNCERTAIN (176), IGNORANCE (558)

561 Expressions of Uncertainty

Doubt is a necessary precondition to meaningful action. **Donald Barthelme**

(*adv*) apparently, by all accounts, *on the face of it*, *rumour has it that*, seemingly

562 Certainty

Faith is a risk and a gamble. Absolute certainty can never be faith. **Adam Clayton Powell, Jr.**

(*adj*) certain, confident, convinced, decided, decisive, definite, firm, *in no doubt*, peremptory, *persuaded*, positive, resolute, resolved, sure, sworn, unerring, unflinching, unshakable, unswerving, unwavering

(*adv*) certainly, firmly

(*n*) authority, belief, certainty, certitude, conviction, decision, decisiveness, sureness, trust

(*v*) believe, lean on, put your faith in, trust

See also CERTAIN (175), KNOWLEDGE AND WISDOM (559)

563 Eccentricity and Irrationality

The irregular side of nature, the discontinuous and erratic side—these have been puzzles to science, or worse, monstrosities. **James Gleick**

(*adj*) barmy (*informal*), batty (*informal*), berserk, bonkers (*informal*), cracked (*informal*), *crackers* (*informal*), crazy (*informal*), demented (*informal*), *deranged*, *dippy*, disturbed, *nuts* (*slang*), pathological, possessed, potty (*informal*), raving, round the bend (*informal*), round the twist (*slang*), senile, twisted, uncontrolled, unhinged

(*adv*) crazily (*informal*)

(*n*) character, craziness (*informal*), derangement, eccentric, insanity, suicide, wildness (*informal*)

564 The Will and Willingness

Will power is the only tensile strength of one's own disposition. One cannot increase it by a single ounce. **Cesare Pavese**

(*adj*) accepting, accommodating, acquiescent, agreeable, amenable, *amendable*, apt to, biddable, *complaisant*, compliant, controllable, cooperative, disposed, docile, flexible, forthcoming, game, glad, helpful, liable, likely, meek, minded (*formal*), obliging, pliable, pliant, predisposed (*formal*), pressing, prone, raring, ready, resigned, submissive, tame, tractable, unforced, unprompted, *unresisting*, willing, *willing to please*, wont (*formal*)

(*adv*) by choice, cheerfully, compliantly, cooperatively, flexibly, happily, helpfully, of your own accord, readily, sooner, tamely, voluntarily, willingly

(*n*) adherence, amenability, compliance, conformism, *cooperativeness*, docility, malleability, meekness, obedience, observance, pliancy, readiness, submission, tractability, volition, will, willingness

See also WITH ENTHUSIASM (287)

565 Unwillingness and Stubbornness

He who is reluctant to recognize me opposes me. **Frantz Fanon**

(*adj*) anarchic, anti (*informal*), averse (*formal*), bloody-minded (*informal*), bullheaded (*informal*), confirmed, contrary, cussed (*informal*), diehard, difficult, disinclined, dogged, dour, factional, grudging, hard-core, hardline, headstrong, immovable, implacable (*formal*), incorrigible, incurable, indisposed (*formal*), inexorable, inflexible, intractable (*formal*), intransigent, inveterate, *iron-willed*, irredeemable, loath, mulish, obdurate, obstinate, opposed to, opposing, pertinacious, perverse, pigheaded, rebellious, reluctant, seditious, self-willed, set, stubborn, unaccommodating, unbending, unbowed, uncompromising, uncontrollable, uncooperative, undisciplined, undisposed, unhelpful, unmovable, unreceptive, unwilling, unyielding, wilful

(*adv*) contrarily, dourly, inflexibly, obdurately

(*n*) bloody-mindedness (*informal*), *bolshiness* (*informal*), contrariness, disinclination, doggedness, dourness, hesitation, indisposition, inflexibility, intractability (*formal*), intransigence, mulishness, noncooperation, obduracy, *obdurateness*, obstinacy, opposition, perverseness, perversity, pigheadedness, rebelliousness, resistance, sedition, *seditiousness*, self-will, stubbornness, subversion, tenacity, unhelpfulness, unwillingness, wilfulness

(*prep*) against

See also NEUTRALITY AND INDIFFERENCE (554), WITHOUT ENTHUSIASM (288)

566 Rebelliousness and Disobedience

Acts of disobedience are the postal service of disbelief. **Muhyid-Din Abu Zakariyya ibn Sharaf al-Nawawi**

(*adj*) anarchistic, awkward, bad, *begrudging*, blocking, challenging, defiant, disobedient, disobliging, disorderly, dissident, extremist, *fogyish*, hawkish, insubordinate, insurgent, mad, militant, mutinous, naughty, noncompliant, nonconformist, obstreperous, obstructive, ornery (*US informal*), rabble-rousing, radical, raucous, rebellious, recalcitrant, refractory, resistant, revolutionary, riotous, rowdy, stiff-necked, subversive, troublesome, turbulent, ungovernable, unruly, warring, wayward, wild

(*adv*) rowdily, turbulently, wildly

(*n*) bullheadedness (*informal*), cussedness (*informal*), defiance, disobedience, disruptiveness, dissidence, freedom, indiscipline, insubordination, militancy, naughtiness, noncompliance, nonconformity, *obstreperousness*, *obstructiveness*, rebelliousness, recalcitrance, resistance, warmongering, waywardness, wildness

567 Uncooperative or Rebellious Person

What is a rebel? A man who says no: but whose refusal does not imply a renunciation. **Albert Camus**

(*n*) abolitionist, activist, agitator, apostate, attacker, combatant, conservative, counter-revolutionary, defector, demagogue, demonstrator, diehard, dissenter, dissident, firebrand, *fogy*, fuddy-duddy (*informal*), guerrilla, heckler, hothead, iconoclast, incendiary (*formal*), insurgent, intransigent (*formal*), malcontent, marcher, militant, mischief-maker, mutineer, nonconformist, obscurantist, picket, protester, rabble-rouser (*disapproving*), radical, reactionary, rebel, revolutionary, rioter, saboteur, *sabre-rattler*, separatist, square (*slang dated*), stick-in-the-mud (*informal*), subversive, troublemaker, warmonger

568 Upset, Distress, and Humiliate

When you have a great cause to fight for, the moment of greatest humiliation is the moment when the spirit is proudest. **Christabel Pankhurst**

(*v*) abase (*literary*), affect, afflict, aggrieve (*formal*), ail (*archaic or literary*), appal, beleaguer, belittle, beset (*formal*), bother, *bring down a peg*, *bring down to earth*, *bring into disrepute*, *bring shame on*, brutalize, burn up (*US informal*), cast down, cause offence, chasten, chill, concern, crucify, crush, debase, deflate, degrade, demean, demoralize, demotivate, depress, derange, deter, devastate, devour (*literary*), disaffect, disappoint, discourage, *disenchant*, disgrace, dishearten, dishonour, disillusion, dismay, dispirit, disquiet (*archaic or literary*), distress, disturb, eat (*slang*), emasculate (*formal*), embarrass, embitter, fail, faze, flurry, gnaw, grieve, grind down, gross out (*slang*), horrify, humble, humiliate, hurt, incommode (*formal*), let down, *make a monkey of* (*informal*), mortify, nauseate, offend, oppress, overcome, overexcite, overpower, overtake, pain, persecute, perturb, pierce, plague, preoccupy, prey on, psych (*US*), put off, rattle, *reduce to tears*, repel, revolt, sadden, scar, *send over the edge*, shake, shame, shock, show up, sicken, stir, stress out (*informal*), take down, tear apart, threaten, torture, traumatize, trouble, turn your stomach, tyrannize, unhinge, unnerve, unsettle, upset, vex, weigh down, wither, wound

See also SADNESS, DISTRESS, AND DESPAIR (540)

569 Frighten and Shock

You can discover what your enemy fears most by observing the means he uses to frighten you. **Eric Hoffer**

(*v*) alarm, bully, cow, daunt, disgust, frighten, horrify, intimidate, menace, overawe, panic, petrify, *root to the spot*, scandalize, scare, scare off, scarify (*informal*), scourge, shake up, shock, spook, terrify, terrorize

See also FEAR AND PANIC (544)

570 Anger and Annoy

Anger is one of the sinews of the soul. **Thomas Fuller**

(*v*) aggravate (*informal*), anger, annoy, antagonize, bother, bug (*informal*), chafe, *cheese off* (*informal*), cross, disgruntle, displease, dissatisfy, disturb, drive up the wall (*informal*), enrage, exasperate, frustrate, gall, get at, get on your nerves, get to, grate, gravel (*US informal*), *hack off* (*informal*), harass, haunt, incense, inconvenience, inflame, infuriate, irk, irritate, jar, madden, make somebody's blood boil, make somebody's hackles rise, miff (*informal*), molest, nag, nark (*informal*), needle (*informal*), nettle (*informal*), niggle, outrage, peeve (*informal*), pester, pique, plague, provoke, put out, put somebody's back up (*informal*), rankle, rile (*informal*), rub up the wrong way, ruffle, tease, tick off (*US informal*), torment, try, vex, wind up (*informal*), work up, worry

See also IRRITATION AND ANGER (542)

571 Bore and Fail to Interest

I have ten commandments. The first nine are, thou shalt not bore. The tenth is, thou shalt have right of final cut. **Billy Wilder**

(*v*) bore, *bore rigid*, *bore stiff*, *bore to death*, *bore to tears*, disincline, stultify, turn off (*informal*), weary

See also BORING AND UNINTERESTING (235)

572 Confuse and Bewilder

By the glare of false science betray'd,/That leads to bewilder, and dazzles to blind. **James Beattie**

(*v*) *abash*, agitate, baffle, bamboozle (*informal*), *bedazzle*, *bedevil*, befuddle, bemuse, bewilder, boggle (*informal*), buffalo (*US informal*), confound, confuse, daze, dazzle, defeat, *discombobulate* (*informal*), discomfit (*formal*), disconcert, disorient, disorientate, distract, *drive insane*, *drive mad* (*informal*), *drive round the bend*, dumbfound, elude, flabbergast (*informal*), floor, flummox (*informal*), fluster, fog, fox, fuddle, gravel, mess up (*informal*), muddle, mystify, nonplus, perplex, poleaxe, *psych out* (*informal*), put off, puzzle, *render speechless*, sidetrack, stump, stun, stupefy, throw (*informal*), tie in knots, trip up, unbalance, vex

See also CONFUSION, ANXIETY, AND WORRY (541)

573 Please and Amuse

The beautiful *is that which pleases universally without a concept.* **Immanuel Kant**

(*v*) amuse, cheer up, content, crack up (*informal*), crease up (*informal*), delight, disarm, distract, divert, elate, entertain, gladden, gratify, oblige, please, regale, satisfy, thrill, tickle, *tickle pink*

See also PLEASURE, EXCITEMENT, AND ELATION (535)

574 Soothe and Calm

Isn't everyone consoled when faced with a trouble or fact he does not understand, by a word? **Luigi Pirandello**

(*v*) appease, bring round, calm, comfort, console, desensitize, inure, lull, mollify, pacify, placate, propitiate (*formal*), reassure, salve, satisfy, soothe, subdue, sweeten

See also CALMNESS, CONFIDENCE, AND COMPOSURE (537), CONFIDENCE AND COMPOSURE (500)

575 Surprise and Impress

Stars open among the lilies./Are you not blinded by such expressionless sirens?/This is the silence of astounded souls. **Sylvia Plath**

(*v*) amaze, astonish, astound, blow away (*US slang*), bowl over, catch unawares, dazzle, enrapture (*formal*), enthral, entrance, exhilarate, impress, *knock for six* (*informal*), knock over (*informal*), knock your socks off, rock (*informal*), sneak up on, stagger, startle, stupefy, surprise, sweep away, sweep sombody off his/her feet, take aback, take by storm, take by surprise, take unawares, touch, wrong-foot

See also SURPRISE, SHOCK, AND AMAZEMENT (546)

576 Appeal to and Arouse Interest

You do not get a man's most effective criticism until you provoke him. **Henry David Thoreau**

(*v*) absorb, amuse, appeal, arouse, arrest (*formal*), attract, bait, beguile, *bewitch*, captivate, capture your imagination, charm, divert, draw, draw in, eat up, electrify, enchant, engage, engross, enthuse, entice, excite, fascinate, grab (*informal*), grip, hypnotize, infect, inspire, interest, intrigue, invite, involve, lead on, lure, magnetize, mesmerize, nobble (*informal*), obsess, occupy, pack in, pique, prejudice, pull, pull in, ravish, reach, rivet (*informal*), rouse, scintillate, *spellbind*, stir, tantalize, tease, tempt, *titillate*, toy with, transfix, turn on (*informal*), wake, waken (*formal*)

See also CAUSE OR COMPEL TO ACT (272), PENSIVENESS AND INTEREST (539)

577 Encourage

In this country it is good to kill an admiral from time to time, to encourage the others. **Voltaire**

(*v*) brighten up, build up, buoy up, dispose, embolden, encourage, fire, fire up, fortify, give a lift, hearten, incline, lift, liven, perk up, persuade, predispose (*formal*), raise your spirits, stimulate, sway, uplift, win over

See also CAUSE OR COMPEL TO ACT (272)

578 Dislike and Hate

We have just enough religion to make us hate, but not enough to make us love one another. **Jonathan Swift**

(*n*) abomination (*literary*), allergy (*informal*), disdain, disfavour, disgust, dislike, distaste, loathing, nausea (*literary*), odium, repugnance, repulsion, revulsion

(*v*) abhor (*formal*), abominate (*formal*), *bear a grudge*, begrudge, despise, detest, disapprove, disdain, dislike, dread, frown on, frown upon, hate, have it in for, *hold in contempt*, loathe, look down on, mistrust, resent, take a dim view of, take exception, take for granted, take offence, *think badly of*, *think little of*

See also UNPOPULAR AND UNWANTED (259)

579 Like, Love, Value, and Enjoy

They that love beyond the world cannot be separated by it. **William Penn**

(*n*) approval, inclination, keenness, leaning, orientation, partiality, taste, weakness

(*prep*) all for, for, in favour of

(*v*) admire, adore, appreciate, bank on, bask, be attracted, be crazy about (*informal*), be partial to, be sure of, canonize, care, cherish, count on, deify, delight, depend on, enjoy, enshrine, esteem, fall for, fancy (*informal*), *fetishize*, follow, glory in, go for (*informal*), go in for, *have a crush on* (*informal*), *have a high opinion of*, *have a high regard for*, *have a soft spot for*, *have a weakness for*, *hero-worship*, *hold dear*, hold in high regard, *hold in the highest regard*, honour, idealize, idolize, incline, lap up, latch onto, lean, like, look up to, love, luxuriate, prefer, pride yourself on, privilege, prize, put a premium on, *regard highly*, relish, respect, revel, revere, romance, romanticize, savour, set store by, swear by, take a fancy to, *take a liking to*, *take a shine to* (*informal*), *take great delight in*, take pleasure in, take to, tend, *think a lot of*, *think highly of*, think the world of, treasure, value, venerate, wallow in, warm, *warm to*

See also POPULAR AND WANTED (221)

580 Desire and Want

The desire of the moth for the star. **James Joyce**

(*adj*) aspiring, avid, bent, *champing at the bit*, dependent, dying to, eager, gasping, hungry (*informal*), intent, tempted, thirsty

(*adv*) thirstily, yearningly

(*n*) aching (*formal*), appetite, craving, dependence, desire, *desirousness* (*formal*), dream, hankering, hope, hunger, impulse, impulsion, itch, longing, passion, temptation, thirst, urge, wanderlust, wants, will, wish, yearning, yen

(*prep*) after

(*v*) ache (*formal*), aspire, be after, be burning to, be spoiling for, cling, covet, crave, desire, envy, feel like, hanker, *hanker after*, *have a yen for*, have your eye on, hunger, *hunger after*, itch, languish, long for, lust, miss, pine, pray, sigh, thirst, want, will, wish, yearn

See also FEELINGS ABOUT THE FUTURE (534)

581 Change of Mood and Composure

Before the cherry orchard was sold everybody was worried and upset, but as soon as it was all settled finally and once for all, everybody calmed down, and felt quite cheerful. **Anton Chekhov**

(*v*) *acclimatize yourself*, *accustom yourself*, adapt, attune, be carried away, brighten, buck up (*informal*), calm down, chill out (*slang*), compose yourself, cool down, cool off (*informal*), demean yourself, despair, ease up, flap (*informal*), get a grip (*informal*), give up, give up on, habituate, immerse, keep your cool, *let yourself go*, lighten up (*informal*), light up, look on the bright side, loosen up, lose heart, lose your nerve, lower yourself, make a fool of yourself, make an exhibition of yourself, mellow, mope, *nerve yourself*, pull yourself together (*informal*), rally, regret, relax, rise to the bait, rue, settle, settle down, settle in, simmer down, squirm, stoop, switch off (*informal*), take heart, take it easy, *take umbrage*, *throw caution to the wind*, turn off, unwind, wake up, warm, wind down

582 Be Concerned and Care

Nothing is more fatal to Health, *than an* over Care *of it.* **Benjamin Franklin**

(*v*) be a bundle of nerves (*informal*), be bothered, be concerned, care, eat your heart out (*informal*), empathize, feel for, feel sorry for, fret, fuss, grudge, identify with, mind, pity, sorrow (*literary*), sweat (*informal*), sympathize, understand, worry

583 Experience and Encounter

History is the record of an encounter between character and circumstance. **Donald Creighton**

(*v*) bump into, come into contact, *come up against*, *contend with*, encounter, experience, *fall prey to*, *fall victim to*, go through, have, *have a brush with*, incur, know, labour under, live through, meet, plumb, rack, run into, run the gauntlet, suffer, sustain, taste, undergo

See also HAPPEN TO SOMEBODY (30)

The Written Word

584 Writing

A good book is a piece of writing that implies that things don't exist, a kind of absence, or death...it is futile to look outside the book for a realm that is located beyond the words. **Orhan Pamuk**

(*adj*) annotated, printed, scrawled, scribbled, textual, written

(*adv*) in print

(*n*) calligraphy, copy, dictation, document, graffiti, hand, handwriting, lettering, printing, scrawl, scribble, script, squiggle, text, writing

See also RECORD SOMETHING (372)

585 Letters and Written Messages

When an actor has money he doesn't send letters, he sends telegrams. **Anton Chekhov**

(*n*) aerogram, aide-mémoire (*formal*), billet-doux (*literary*), *cablegram*, card, communiqué, dispatch, e-mail, epistle (*formal*), fax, inscription, letter, letter card, mail, mailbag, memo, memorandum, message, missive, note, notelet, postbag, postcard, reference, resignation, snail mail (*informal*), spam, special delivery, surface mail, telegram, testimonial

586 Records

The critic is the historian who records the order of creation. **Margaret Fuller**

(*n*) almanac, annals, archive, books, chronicle, diary, docket, dossier, entry, file, journal, ledger, library, log, logbook, memoir, minutes, proceedings, readout, scorecard, scoresheet, snapshot, statement, transcript, transcription, worksheet, yearbook

587 Official Documents

Remove the document—and you remove the man. **Mikhail Bulgakov**

(*n*) accord, affidavit, agreement, blueprint, card, certificate, certification, charter, concord, contract, convention, covenant, credentials, deed, documentation, edict, form, guarantee, ID, identification, identity card, insurance policy, licence, manifesto, ordinance, pass, passport, patent, permit, policy, scroll, submission, testimony, ticket, title deed, treaty, visa, waiver, warrant, warranty

588 Lists and Schedules

Hungry Joe collected lists of fatal diseases and arranged them in alphabetical order so that he could put his finger without delay on any one he wanted to worry about. **Joseph Heller**

(*n*) agenda, bibliography, calendar, catalogue, checklist, chronology, diary, dictionary, glossary, index, inventory, lexicon, *lexis*, list, listing, listings, mailing list, menu, organizer, personal organizer, petition, planner, programme, register, roll call, roster, rota, schedule, syllabus, thesaurus, timetable, vocabulary, word list, worksheet

589 Summaries, Outlines, and Excerpts

Good things, when short, are twice as good. **Baltasar Gracián**

(*n*) abridgment, abstract, aide-mémoire (*formal*), article, blurb (*slang*), brief, citation, clause, clip, clipping, condensation, *curriculum vitae*, CV, digest, excerpt, extract, generality, generalization, itinerary, listing, outline, paraphrase, précis, profile, quotation, quote, recap, recapitulation (*formal*), refresher, résumé, rough copy, round-up, rundown, run-through, schema, summary, summation, synopsis, translation, version, vignette

590 Manuals and Instructions

The most important thing about Spaceship Earth—an instruction book didn't come with it. **R. Buckminster Fuller**

(*n*) cheque, fact sheet, guide, guidebook, handbook, information sheet, manual, primer, prospectus, rubric, rulebook

591 Books and Booklets

The good of a book lies in being read. **Umberto Eco**

(*n*) album, atlas, book, booklet, brochure, bumf (*informal*), casebook, codex, digest, edition, encyclopedia, limited edition, literature, manuscript, memoirs, monograph, novel, *palimpsest*, pamphlet, paperback, phrase book, picture book, publication, songbook, *story book*, text, textbook, tome, tract, trilogy, volume

See also FICTION AND DRAMA (913)

592 Receipts and Invoices

We are all gratified by advancing the frontiers of scientific knowledge, but the only thing that ever gets invoiced is the product. **Richard J. Mahoney**

(*n*) account, bill, check (*US*), chit (*dated*), coupon, docket, invoice, payslip, postmark, *proof of posting*, *proof of purchase*, receipt, tab (*US informal*), token, voucher

593 Analytical Nonfiction Writing

It requires a very unusual mind to undertake the analysis of the obvious. **A. N. Whitehead**

(*n*) article, commentary, critique, dissertation, essay, memoir, paper, piece of writing, study, thesis, treatise, vignette, write-up

See also NEWSPAPERS (606)

594 Parts of Books and Documents

A page of history is worth a volume of logic. **Oliver Wendell Holmes, Jr.**

(*n*) addendum, annotation, appendix, caption, chapter, coda, codicil (*formal*), cross-reference, dateline, enclosure, epilogue, episode, flyleaf, footer, footnote, foreword, frontispiece, gloss, header, heading, insert, insertion, inset, introduction, leaf, notation, note, paragraph, passage, postscript, preamble, preface, pullout, rider, supplement, title page

595 Drawings, Charts, and Tables

Just as the painters seek to imitate objects exactly. . .geometricians and astronomers delineate on a flat plane solid objects, such as octahedrons and cubes and all spherical bodies, like the stars, the heavens, and the earth. **Nicephorus Gregoras**

(*n*) chart, design, diagram, drawing, figure, floor plan, graph, ground plan, illustration, *illustrations*, layout, *lithograph*, map, milestone, *pictogram*, piechart, protraction, rough, scheme, scribble, side view, sketch, spreadsheet, table, tabulation, tattoo, tree, vignette, visual, visual aid, watermark

See also THE PICTORIAL ARTS (897)

596 Signposts, Signals, and Billboards

I think that I shall never see/A billboard lovely as a tree. **Ogden Nash**

(*n*) alarm, alert, banner, beacon, billboard, buoy, cairn, hoarding, mayday, nameplate, notice, noticeboard, placard, plaque, poster, road sign, scoreboard, sign, signboard, signpost, SOS

597 Symbols, Signs, and Numbers

Numbers constitute the only universal language. **Nathanael West**

(*adj*) alphabetic, alphabetical

(*n*) ABC, alphabet, ampersand, arrow, asterisk, badge, brand, chevron, cipher, coat of arms, code, colours, combination, crest, cross, decimal, device, digit, emblem, *emoticon*, ensign, figure, flag, *glyph*, gonfalon, hallmark, hieroglyph, *ideogram*, imprint, insignia, letter, logo, *mimeograph*, notation, number, patch, pennant, pennon, pictograph, rubric, rune, sign, signature, stamp, standard, sticker, symbol, target, trademark, watermark

types of alphabet Arabic, Braille, Cyrillic, Greek, Hebrew, hieroglyphics, phonetic alphabet, Roman alphabet, runic

598 Maths

(*adj*) *arithmetical*, binary, digital, mathematical, mean, numerical, quantifiable, quantitative

(*adv*) per cent

(*n*) *algebra*, *arithmetic*, *arithmetic mean*, calculation, *calculus*, coefficient, computation, equation, *geometry*, integer, mathematics, median, numeral, par, reckoning, statistic, subtraction, sum, sums (*informal*), theorem, *trigonometry*

599 Scores and Evaluations

Read not to contradict and confute, nor to believe and take for granted, nor to find talk and discourse, but to weigh and consider. **Francis Bacon**

(*n*) appraisal, calibration, count, estimate, evaluation, grade, mark, quotation, quote, rating, reappraisal, reassessment, record, re-count, result, score, standard, tally, touchstone, valuation, yardstick

600 Written Conventions

All styles are good except the tiresome sort. **Voltaire**

(*adv*) a.k.a., e.g., et al., etc., idem, i.e., *NB*, passim (*formal*), PS, *PTO*

601 Printing

I, according to my copy, have done set it in imprint, to the intent that noble men may see and learn the noble acts of chivalry. **William Caxton**

(*adj*) bold, italic, lightface, roman

(*n*) font, printing, toner, type, typeface, *typescript*, *typesetter*, *typesetting*, typo (*informal*), typography

602 Writing and Drawing Implements, and Media

(*n*) blackboard, blotter (*US*), *chalkboard* (*US*), easel, *gouache*, jotter, notepad, notepaper, pad, page, *papyrus*, *parchment*, pastel, rubber stamp, *scratchpad* (*US*), *scribbler*, *scribbling pad*, seal, *sketchbook*, *sketchpad*, stationery, workbook, *writing board*, *writing pad*, *writing paper*

types of pen ballpoint, crayon, felt-tipped pen, fountain pen, highlighter, marker, quill, rollerball

Communication and Interaction

603 Communication

The present century, in proclaiming the advent of a new age of communication and information...forgot to deal with the great problem of talk, which is how to find someone to listen. **Theodore Zeldin**

(*n*) chemistry, communication, communications, contact, correspondence, dealings, fraternization, interaction, intercourse, *nonverbal communication*, oratory, self-expression, speaking, speech, talking, *telecommunications*, utterance, *verbal communication*, voice, word

604 Speakers and Orators

The arrow belongs not to the archer when it has once left the bow; the word no longer belongs to the speaker when it has once passed his lips. **Heinrich Heine**

(*n*) conversationalist, debater, interlocutor, orator, polemicist, propagandist, proselytizer, purveyor (*formal*), raconteur, rhetorician, schmoozer (*slang*), speaker, speechmaker, storyteller, talker

605 Advertising and Publicity

Advertising may be described as the science of arresting human intelligence long enough to get money from it. **Stephen Leacock**

(*adj*) promotional

(*n*) ad, advert (*informal*), advertisement, advertising, bill (*US*), buildup, *bulk mail* (*US*), circular, commercial, direct mail, flier, flysheet, handbill, handout, hype, infomercial, junk mail, leaflet, mailer (*US*), mailshot, media, newsletter, personal (*US*), personal ad, plug (*informal*), press release, preview, promo (*informal*), promotion, propaganda, publicity, public relations, road show, showcase, spot, trailer, *want ad* (*US informal*)

(*v*) advertise, bill (*US*), hype, plug (*informal*), promote

606 Newspapers

A good newspaper is never nearly good enough but a lousy newspaper is a joy forever. **Garrison Keillor**

(*adj*) front-page, journalistic, tabloid

(*n*) broadsheet, bulletin, byline, circulation, column, comic, comics, coverage, editorial, exposé, exposure, feature, gazette, *glossy magazine*, headline, issue, journal, journalism, leading article, *mag* (*informal*), magazine, masthead, monthly, newspaper, newsprint, newssheet, organ (*formal*), paper, periodical, photojournalism, quarterly, *rag* (*informal*), reportage, review, scoop (*informal*), stop press, story, strapline, supertitle, *tabloid*

See also ANALYTICAL NONFICTION WRITING (593), WORKERS IN ENTERTAINMENT AND MEDIA (873)

607 Television and Radio

Why should people go out and pay money to see bad movies when they can stay at home and see bad television for nothing? **Samuel Goldwyn**

(*adj*) on-screen, on the air

(*n*) airplay, airwaves, boob tube (*US informal*), box (*slang*), broadcast, bulletin, CB, channel, flash, footage, *goggle-box* (*dated informal*), miniseries, newsroom, photo opportunity, programme, reception, rerun, *satellite television*, *shortwave radio*, small screen (*informal*), special effects, *telly*, transmission, *tube* (*US*), TV (*informal*), *TV set*, viewing, voiceover

(*v*) broadcast, rerun, screen, *simulcast*, *telecast*, televise, zap (*informal*)

types of broadcast call-in (*US*), chat show, commercial, concert, current affairs, distance learning, docudrama, documentary, drama, game show, infomercial, infotainment, news, newscast, news flash, newsreel, phone-in, play, sitcom (*informal*), soap (*informal*), soap opera, sport, sportscast, talk show (*US*), telethon, travelogue

See also WORKERS IN ENTERTAINMENT AND MEDIA (873)

608 Two-way Communication

Online conversation is...talking by writing. **John Coate**

(*v*) bandy, brainstorm, chat, chew the fat (*slang*), chinwag (*US*), chitchat (*informal*), chorus, communicate, compare notes, confer, converse, cross-fertilize, debate, discourse (*formal*), discuss, gab (*informal*), hammer out, intercommunicate, *jaw* (*slang*), *make small talk*, mediate, natter (*informal*), negotiate, parley, rap (*US slang*), schmooze (*slang*), shoot the breeze (*US slang*), square, talk, talk over, thrash out, yak (*informal*)

See also INFORMAL COMMUNICATION (45), GOSSIP (679), MEANINGLESS SPEECH OR WRITING (677)

609 Utter and Pronounce

I always start too soon and arrive too late and eventually come back in the middle—stuttering. **Jean-Luc Godard**

(*v*) ad-lib, articulate, aspirate, call, call out, enunciate, express, extemporize, externalize, formulate, improvise, intone, mouth, observe, orate (*formal*), phrase, pontificate, presume, print, pronounce, rap out, say, sing out, speak, speak out, speak up, specify, tell, utter, verbalize, vocalize, voice, word

610 Instruct and Teach

It is the supreme art of the teacher to awaken joy in creative expression and knowledge. **Albert Einstein**

(*v*) address, brainwash, break in, coach, convert, convince, declaim, discipline, domesticate, drill, drum in, edify, educate, equip, *expatiate*, familiarize, force-feed, ground, imprint, inculcate, indoctrinate, induct, infuse, ingrain, initiate, instil, instruct, introduce, lecture, orate, *perorate* (*formal*), potty-train (*informal*), preach, prepare, prime, proselytize, re-educate, rehabilitate, school, sermonize, sophisticate, speak, speechify (*informal*), tame, teach, train, tutor

See also TEACHING (839), EDUCATORS (840)

611 Explain and Clarify

Never explain: your friends don't need it and your enemies won't believe it. **Victor Grayson**

(*adj*) descriptive, explanatory, interpretative, interpretive

(*n*) account, alibi (*informal*), amplification, clarification, delineation (*formal*), demystification, dilation, elaboration, elucidation, explanation, *explication*, formulation, illumination, interpretation, justification, plea, popularization, rationalization

(*v*) account for, amplify, be blunt, bring home, clarify, clear up, demonstrate, demystify, describe, detail, develop, dilate, elaborate, elucidate (*formal*), encapsulate, enlighten, enunciate, expand upon, explain, explicate, expound, fill in, generalize, get across, *give a rough idea*, give instructions, go into detail, illuminate, interpret, irradiate, justify, lay it on the line (*informal*), lay out, make clear, nail down, outline, popularize, précis, put across, put into words, recap, recapitulate (*formal*), run by, run over, set forth (*formal*), set out, set right, shed light on, show, spell out, summarize, sum up, *throw light on*, unfold

612 Inform and Announce

A drama critic is a person who surprises the playwright by informing him what he meant. **Wilson Mizner**

(*n*) affirmation, announcement, declassification, disinterment (*formal*), dissemination, enunciation, leak, notification, popularization, proclamation, promulgation (*formal*), pronouncement, propagation, revelation, sound bite, statement, unveiling

(*v*) acquaint, advertise, advise, air, announce, *apprise* (*formal*), brief, bring up-to-date, broadcast, bugle, circulate, communicate, declare, declassify, disabuse, disclose, disseminate, editorialize, get over, give out, herald, impart, inform, introduce, issue, let in on, let into, let know, make known, make public, notify, pass on, point out, popularize, post, present, proclaim, promulgate (*formal*), pronounce, propagate, publicize, publish, put about, put forward, put out, relay, release, remind, sensitize, share, sound, spread, *spread about*, *spread abroad*, *spread the word*, state, talk turkey (*informal*), tell, undeceive, unveil, update, vent, ventilate, volunteer

613 Suggest, Hint, and Comment

Had I been present at the Creation, I would have given some useful hints for the better ordering of the universe. **Alfonso X**

(*conj*) supposing

(*n*) allusion, comment, commentary, evocation, hint, inference, innuendo, insinuation, intimation, mention, motion, mover, observation, offer, overtone, proposal, proposition, reference, remark, rumbling (*informal*), suggestion

(*v*) adduce (*formal*), allude, bid, bring forward, bring up, broach, comment, commentate, drag in, drag up, enter, float, hazard, hint, imply, infer, insinuate, intimate, mention, moot, note, offer, pitch, present (*formal*), propose, propound, put forth (*formal*), put forward, put in, raise, rake up (*informal*), refer, remark, signal, submit, suggest, table, tender, throw in, touch on, venture

614 Advise and Warn

Advice is seldom welcome; and those who want it the most always like it the least. **Lord Chesterfield**

(*adj*) admonitory, advisory, cautionary, dissuasive, warning

(*n*) dissuasion, notice, threat

(*v*) advise, alert, caution, counsel, dissuade, forearm, forewarn, preach, prescribe, recommend, tip off, *tip the wink* (*informal*), urge, warn, warn off

See also ADVICE (690)

615 Claim, Insist, and Emphasize

For what is *passes so swiftly and irrevocably into what* was, *no human claim can be of the least significance.* **Joyce Carol Oates**

(*n*) allegation, assertion, claim, exaggeration, iteration, overstatement, overstress, reaffirmation, reassertion, reinforcement, reiteration, representation

(*v*) accent, accentuate, affirm, allege, argue, assert, aver (*formal*), avow (*formal*), bang on (*informal*), belabour, blow up (*informal*), claim, contend, din, embroider, emphasize, exaggerate, highlight, impress, insist, labour, *labour the point*, *lay it on thick*, *lay it on with a trowel* (*informal*), maintain, make a big thing of, make a mountain out of a molehill, opine (*formal*), overemphasize, overplay, overrate, oversell, overstate, overstress, play up, plead, point out, point up, protest, purport, put your foot down, ram home, reaffirm, reason, reassert, reinforce, specify, spotlight, stand your ground, stipulate, stress, stretch a point, swear, testify, underline, underscore, voice

616 Admit and Confess

It is not the criminal things which are hardest to confess, but the ridiculous and shameful. **Jean-Jacques Rousseau**

(*n*) admission, avowal (*formal*), confession, disclosure, revelation, self-incrimination

(*v*) admit, allow (*formal*), come clean (*informal*), come out with, confess, *disburden* (*archaic*), *fess up* (*US informal*), get it off your chest, let on, make a clean breast of things, own (*formal*), own up, profess, take the blame, take the rap (*slang*), *tell it how it is* (*informal*), tell the truth, unburden (*formal*)

617 Boast

I'm so fast I could hit you before God gets the news. **Muhammad Ali**

(*n*) aggrandizement (*formal*), boast, boasting, *braggadocio*, bragging, embellishment, flatulence, grandiloquence, grandiosity, rhetoric, self-aggrandizement, self-congratulation, self-flattery, self-glorification, self-promotion, showing off, swagger, swank (*informal*)

(*v*) aggrandize (*formal*), blow your own trumpet (*informal*), boast, brag, crow, embellish, gloat, grandstand (*US*), lay it on, *mouth off* (*informal*), roister, *showboat* (*informal*), show off, sing your own praises, swank (*informal*), vaunt

See also POMPOUS, LOUD, AND OVER-CONFIDENT (636)

618 Witter and Babble

The arts babblative and scribblative. **Robert Southey**

(*v*) babble, blabber, blather (*informal*), blether (*informal*), *blither* (*informal*), bumble, burble (*informal*), chatter, digress, diverge, *drone on*, footle (*informal*), gabble, gibber, *gibbering*, go on, gush, hold forth, jabber, mispronounce, mumble, murmur, mutter, patter, prate, prattle, rabbit (*informal*), *rabbit on* (*informal*), ramble, ramble on, rattle on, rave, slur, speak, spiel (*informal*), spout, stammer, stutter, *talk a mile a minute* (*US*), *talk gibberish, talk nineteen to the dozen, talk rubbish, talk ten to the dozen* (*US*), *talk the hind legs off a donkey*, waffle (*informal*), witter (*informal*)

See also MEANINGLESS SPEECH OR WRITING (677)

619 Betray Confidences and Gossip

I delight in sinning and hate to compose a mask for gossip. **Sulpicia**

(*v*) betray, blab (*informal*), *blow somebody's cover, blow the gaff* (*slang*), blow the whistle, blurt, burst out, confide, *dish the dirt* (*informal*), divulge, ejaculate (*literary*), expose, give away, give up, gossip, grass (*slang*), *grass on* (*slang*), grass up (*slang*), inform, leak, *let drop*, let out, let slip, let the cat out of the bag, pour out, put your foot in it (*informal*), put your foot in your mouth (*informal*), rat on (*informal*), reveal, say, shop (*slang*), sing (*slang*), sneak, snitch (*slang*), spill the beans (*informal*), spit, split on (*informal*), squeal (*slang*), *squeal on* (*US slang disapproving*), stab in the back (*informal*), talk, tattle, tell, *tell on, tell tales*, tittle-tattle, turn in

See also INTERFERING PEOPLE AND TELLTALES (950), GOSSIP (679)

620 Interrupt and Butt In

Writing is a way of talking without being interrupted. **Jules Renard**

(*v*) barge in, break in, burst in on, butt in, chime in, chip in (*informal*), contribute, cut in, cut off, get a word in edgeways, *horn in* (*informal*), interfere, interject, interpolate, interpose, interrupt, intrude, meddle, muscle in (*informal*), obtrude, pipe up, put in, put your oar in, start up, step in, *stick your nose in, stick your oar in*, tangle, violate

621 Recite, Repeat, and Narrate

It's better to be quotable than to be honest. **Tom Stoppard**

(*v*) cite (*formal*), dictate, echo, iterate, misquote, narrate, paraphrase, quote, rattle off, read, read out, recite, recount, reel off, regurgitate, reiterate, relate, repeat, rephrase, report, restate, retell, tell

622 Flatter and Fawn

Be advised that all flatterers live at the expense of those who listen to them. **Jean de La Fontaine**

(*v*) abase yourself (*literary*), *blandish* (*formal*), butter up (*informal*), court, crawl (*informal*), creep (*informal*), fawn, flannel (*informal*), flatter, grovel, soft-soap (*informal*), suck up (*informal*), sweet-talk (*informal*), toady

See also PRAISE AND ENCOURAGE (648), INGRATIATING (639)

623 Summarizing Expressions

An aphorism is something which spares the writer an essay by way of commentary, but in consequence is deeply shocking to the reader. **Peter Altenberg**

(*adv*) all in all, all things considered, altogether, as it were (*formal*), at any rate, at least, at the end of the day, essentially, generally speaking, in a nutshell, in brief, *in other words*, in short, *in sum, in summary*, in the main, lastly, *to be brief*, to cut a long story short, *to put it briefly, to sum up*, virtually, when all's said and done, with hindsight

(*interj*) Bob's your uncle (*informal*), well

624 Expressions of Opinion

A man's opinion on tramcars matters; his opinion on Botticelli matters; his opinion on all things does not matter. **G. K. Chesterton**

(*adv*) *as far as I'm concerned*, between ourselves, *between you and me, between you, me, and the bedpost* (*US*), *between you, me, and the gatepost, if you ask me, in all fairness, in all honesty, in all likelihood, in all probability*, in my book, *in my opinion, in my view*, personally, *to be fair, to be frank, to be honest, to my mind, to tell the truth*

625 Communicative Style

Proper words in proper places, make the true definition of a style. **Jonathan Swift**

(*adj*) colloquial, conversational, idiomatic, unspeaking, unwritten

626 Rude and Hostile

The right people are rude. They can afford to be. **Somerset Maugham**

(*adj*) abrasive, abusive, acerbic, acid, acrid, acrimonious, astringent, audacious, austere, backhanded, barbed, biting, bitter, boorish, brutish, catty, caustic, coarse, cool, corrosive, crude, cutting, destructive, forbidding, foul-mouthed, glacial, grim, impertinent (*formal*), incendiary, insolent, irreverent, mordant, piquant, pointed, provocative, rude, scurrilous, sharp-tongued, smart, snide, stinging, threatening, trenchant, ugly, uncomplimentary, unfriendly, unrepentant, venomous, vicious, virulent, vitriolic, waspish, *waspy*, wicked, wounding

(*adv*) abrasively, acidly, belligerently, bitchily (*slang*), bitingly, bitterly, blackly, cheekily, coarsely, cold-bloodedly, condescendingly, contemptuously, critically, crudely, cuttingly, cynically, derisively, disputatiously (*formal*), frigidly, frostily, ghoulishly, grimly, haughtily, head-on, icily, pointedly, ungraciously, venomously, viciously, wickedly

(*n*) acerbity, trenchancy, vitriol, waspishness

See also BAD MANNERS AND SOCIAL SKILLS (522), AGGRESSIVE AND BELLIGERENT (519), RUDE AND HOSTILE (626)

627 Bad-Tempered and Humourless

The sort of eye that can open an oyster at sixty paces. **P. G. Wodehouse**

(*adj*) abrupt, brisk, brusque, churlish, crusty, curt, earnest, gruff, po-faced, querulous, sharp, short, snappish, snappy, snippy (*informal*), solemn, sour, stern, sullen, surly, tart, terse, uncongenial, unsmiling, *whingey* (*informal*), *whiny*

(*adv*) angrily, blackly, crossly, darkly, dourly, earnestly, ghoulishly, gravely, grimly, *grouchily* (*informal*), heavily, huffily, indignantly, sharply, shortly, soberly, sourly, stormily, sullenly, tartly, testily (*informal*), tetchily (*informal*), touchily

(*n*) asperity (*formal*), briskness, earnestness, gruffness, querulousness, sharpness, shortness, *snappiness*, *snappishness*, soberness, solemnity, sternness, sullenness, tartness, terseness, *whingeing* (*informal*)

628 Good-Tempered and Humorous

Good humour is the seasoning of truth. **Johann Heinrich Pestalozzi**

(*adj*) airy, avuncular, hearty, jesting (*literary*), *jocose* (*literary*), jocular, *jocund* (*literary*), jokey, joking, waggish (*dated*)

(*adv*) airily, blithely (*literary*), breezily, brightly, *convivially*, drily, equably, frivolously, giddily, good-humouredly, good-temperedly, heartily, humorously, jokily, jovially, levelly, mirthfully, pertly, playfully, puckishly, well

(*n*) airiness, facetiousness, flippancy, *jocundity* (*literary*), *jokiness*, *jovialness*, levity, waggishness (*dated*)

629 Enthusiastic and Inquisitive

Only connect the prose and the passion, and both will be exalted. **E. M. Forster**

(*adj*) appreciative, emphatic, forceful, fulsome, gutsy (*informal*), heated, impassioned, inquisitorial, interrogative, questioning, quizzical, rhapsodic, searching, significant, urgent, vehement, violent, vocal, vociferous

(*adv*) ardently, assertively, boisterously, *ebulliently*, effusively, emotionally, expansively, ferociously, gushingly, highly, hotly, positively, studiously, vocally, warmly

See also CHEERFULNESS OF OUTLOOK (504), ENERGY AND ENTHUSIASM (497)

630 Uninterested and Detached

Perfect behavior is born of complete indifference. **Cesare Pavese**

(*adj*) casual, clever, crisp, distant, flippant, glib, impersonal, inexpressive, offhand, teasing, throwaway, toneless, wooden

(*adv*) aloofly, casually, coldly, coolly, dispassionately, distantly, dully, impassively, offhandedly, parrot-fashion (*informal*), woodenly

(*n*) abruptness, blankness, brusqueness, distance, *offhandness*, woodenness

See also NEUTRALITY AND INDIFFERENCE (554), WITHOUT ENTHUSIASM (288)

631 Honest and Open

He that resolves to deal with none but honest men must leave off dealing. **Thomas Fuller**

(*adj*) bald, bald-faced (*US*), barefaced, bluff, blunt, candid, direct, explicit, expressive, forthright, frank, free, full-frontal (*informal*), heart-to-heart, hearty, matter-of-fact, no-nonsense, open, outspoken, plain, *plain-speaking*, plain-spoken, polemic, punchy, serious, stark, straight, straightforward, straight-out (*informal*), straight-talking, tactile, touchy-feely (*informal*), uninhibited, unreserved, up-front (*informal*)

(*adv*) avowedly (*formal*), baldly, bluntly, demonstratively, directly, expansively, explicitly, face to face, from the bottom of your heart, honestly, ingenuously, openly, outright, plainly, point-blank, straight out, unashamedly, uninhibitedly

(*n*) astringency, baldness, bluffness, bluntness, candidness, candour, directness, forthrightness, forwardness, freedom, *matter-of-factness*, openness, outspokenness, plainness, *plain-spokenness*, sincerity, starkness, straightforwardness

See also HONEST AND RELIABLE (503)

632 Reticent and Unforthcoming

The cruellest lies are often told in silence. **Robert Louis Stevenson**

(*adj*) allusive, backward, bashful, blushing, buttoned-down (*US informal*), camera-shy, close, close-lipped, closemouthed, coy, diffident, equivocal, evasive, humble, impersonal, implied, indirect, inscrutable, introvert, introverted, ironic, ironical, modest, monosyllabic, mum (*informal*), mysterious, noncommittal, private, restrained, reticent, retiring, secretive, self-deprecating, shy, silent, soft-spoken, taciturn, tight-lipped, timid, timorous, tongue-tied, uncommunicative, unforthcoming, unobtrusive, voiceless

(*adv*) darkly, demurely, guardedly, humbly, modestly, reservedly, shyly, undemonstratively

(*n*) bashfulness, diffidence, elusiveness, evasiveness, humbleness, humility, inscrutability, reticence, self-deprecation, shyness, silence, taciturnity, timidity, timorousness, *uncommunicativeness*, undemonstrativeness

633 Eloquent, Talkative, and Long-Winded

Revolutions are always verbose. **Leon Trotsky**

(*adj*) articulate, chatty, communicative, conversational, declamatory, demagogic, descriptive, discursive, effusive, eloquent, emotional, expansive, fluent, gabby (*informal*), garrulous, gaseous (*informal*), gassy (*informal*), glib, grandiose, high-flown, inflammatory, insistent, laconic, loquacious (*formal*), lucid, lyrical, oratorical, persuasive, poetic, pungent, silver-tongued, smooth, smooth-tongued, talkative, voluble, well-expressed, well-spoken, well-turned

(*adv*) *chattily*, commandingly, evocatively, feelingly, long-windedly, vehemently

(*n*) articulacy, articulateness, *chattiness*, discursiveness, eloquence, expressivity, garrulousness, *gift of the gab* (*informal*), glibness, *laconicism*, long-windedness, *loquaciousness* (*formal*), oratory, persuasion, persuasiveness, pungency, smoothness, talkativeness

634 Inarticulate, Rambling, and Awkward

If I reprehend any thing in this world, it is the use of my oracular tongue, and a nice derangement of epitaphs! **Richard Brinsley Sheridan**

(*adj*) circuitous, circumlocutory, diffuse, disjointed, disquisitional (*formal*), elliptical, flatulent, forced, garbled, inarticulate, incoherent, long-winded, mumbled, oblique, *prattling*, prolix, rambling, roundabout, slurred, staccato, stilted, verbose, wordy

(*adv*) at length (*formal*), circuitously, diffusely, *gibberingly*, hollowly, in a roundabout way, indirectly, *ramblingly*, unintelligibly, woodenly

(*n*) circularity, circumlocution, inarticulacy, *inarticulateness*, stammer, *stiltedness*, stutter, woodenness

635 Accusatory and Disapproving

Go out and speak for the inarticulate and the submerged. **Lord Beaverbrook**

(*adj*) accusatorial (*formal*), *accusatory* (*formal*), accusing, admonitory, carping, *castigatory* (*formal*), censorious, condemnatory, critical, damning, defamatory, deprecating, deprecatory, depreciatory, derogatory, disapproving, disparaging, moralizing, pejorative (*formal*), querulous, reprehensive, reproachful, reproving, scalding, scathing, sententious, unfavourable, vituperative

(*adv*) *accusatorially* (*formal*), querulously

636 Pompous, Loud, and Over-Confident

The louder he talked of his honour, the faster we counted our spoons. **Ralph Waldo Emerson**

(*adj*) arrogant, assuming, bigheaded (*informal*), boastful, boasting, bold-faced, bombastic, bragging, brash, brassy, brazen, bumptious, cocksure, cocky (*informal*), conceited, condescending, contemptuous, full of yourself, grandiloquent, gushing, high-sounding, in-your-face (*slang*), lofty, loud, loudmouthed (*informal*), *magniloquent*, *mouthy* (*informal*), orotund (*formal*), overblown, peremptory, perky, protrusive, puffed-up, pushing, rhetorical, rumbustious, *self-admiring*, *self-aggrandizing*, self-important, self-opinionated, *smart-alecky* (*informal*), strident, swaggering, swellheaded (*US informal*), swollen-headed, vain, vainglorious (*literary*), windy (*informal*)

(*adv*) brashly, disruptively, grandly, immodestly, loftily, loudly, magisterially, *orotundly* (*formal*), peremptorily, perkily, *sanctimoniously*, snootily (*informal*)

(*n*) boastfulness, brashness, brazenness, bumptiousness, *cockiness*, *cocksureness*, hauteur (*formal*), loftiness, *magniloquence*, *mouthiness* (*informal*), *orotundity*, perkiness, puffiness, self-importance

See also BOAST (617), BOSSY AND OVERBEARING (517)

637 Mocking and Dismissive

Mock on, Mock on, Voltaire, Rousseau:/Mock on, Mock on: 'tis all in vain! **William Blake**

(*adj*) belittling, cynical, derisive, disdainful, dismissive, dry, facetious, flip (*informal*), jeering, mocking, opprobrious, patronizing, sarcastic, sardonic, satirical, *scoffing*, scornful, sneering, taunting, tongue-in-cheek, withering, wry

(*adv*) cynically, frivolously

(*n*) dryness, sarcasm, *sardonicism*

638 Expressing Respect and Approval

Self-respect—the secure feeling that no one, as yet, is suspicious. **H. L. Mencken**

(*adj*) adulatory, affirmative, *approbatory*, complimentary, deferential, favourable, glowing, laudatory, obedient, oriented, reverent, reverential

(*adv*) appreciatively, approvingly, cap in hand, favourably

(*prep*) pro

See also APPROVE AND CONFIRM (647)

639 Ingratiating

Good intentions can be evil,/Both hands can be full of grease./You know that sometimes Satan comes as a man of peace. **Bob Dylan**

(*adj*) fawning, flattering, ingratiating, obsequious, servile, slimy, smarmy, sycophantic, toadying, unctuous

(*n*) blandishment, blarney (*informal*), *cajolery*, flannel (*informal*), flattery, jive (*US slang*), obsequiousness, *ser-*

vility, *smarminess*, sweet talk (*informal*), sycophancy, toadying, *unctuousness*

See also FLATTER AND FAWN (622)

640 Flirtatious

Merely innocent flirtation,/Not quite adultery, but adulteration. **Lord Byron**

(*adj*) *coquettish* (*literary*), coy, *flirtatious*, kittenish

641 Succinct and To-The-Point

I strive to be brief, and I become obscure. **Horace**

(*adj*) brief, clipped, concise, pithy, succinct, telegraphic, terse

(*n*) brevity, conciseness, concision, curtness, pithiness, succinctness, terseness

See also RUDE AND HOSTILE (626)

642 Accuse, Blame, and Criticize

The worst libel is the truth. **Proverb**

(*v*) accuse, admonish, *anathematize*, assail, attack, barrack (*informal*), bash (*informal*), bawl out (*informal*), beard, berate, besmirch, bitch (*slang*), blame, blast (*informal*), call down (*US*), carpet (*informal*), castigate (*formal*), challenge, charge, chasten, chastise (*formal*), chew out (*US informal*), chide (*literary*), come down on, *come down on like a ton of bricks* (*informal*), condemn, conflict, confront, corner, criticize, denigrate, denounce, depreciate, dis (*slang*), disparage, dress down, excoriate (*formal*), fault, *find fault with*, flay, gang up on, hammer (*informal*), harangue, haul over the coals, have a go at (*informal*), have up (*informal*), heckle, hector, *hold accountable*, *hold responsible*, *hurl abuse*, *hurl insults*, impute, incriminate, judge, knock (*informal*), lambaste, lash, lash out, lay into (*informal*), lecture, maul, moralize, nag, pan (*informal*), pass the buck (*informal*), penalize, pick holes in, pillory, *point the finger*, pull to pieces, pull up, punish, put down (*informal*), *rake over the coals* (*US*), rap on/over the knuckles (*informal*), *read the riot act*, rebuke, *reprehend*, reprimand, reproach, reprove, resist, rubbish (*informal*), run down, savage, scapegoat, scold, set against, *shift the blame*, shoot down, shout at, slam (*informal*), slate (*informal*), slur, sort out (*informal*), *speak ill of*, *speak sharply*, stand up to, start on (*informal*), strafe (*slang*), take apart (*informal*), take on, take to task, tax, *tear a strip off*, tear into, *tear to pieces*, *tear to shreds*, tell off (*informal*), tick off (*informal*), traduce, trash (*US informal*), upbraid, vilify, *vituperate*, *wig* (*dated informal*), yell at

See also CRITICISMS AND ANGRY OUTBURSTS (50)

643 Protest and Express Disapproval

I disapprove of what you say, but I will defend to the death your right to say it. **Voltaire**

(*v*) agitate, be against, blacken, bluster, censure, condemn, decry (*formal*), demonstrate, demur, denounce, denunciate (*formal*), deplore, deprecate, deride, disagree, disapprove (*formal*), disrespect, dissent, diverge, do down (*informal*), expostulate, fight, fight back, fulminate, gibe, hit out, inveigh (*formal*), *kick up a rumpus*, *kick up a storm*, make waves, object, pass judgment, picket, *pour scorn on*, protest, quibble, rail, *raise a fuss*, *raise a ruckus* (*US*), raise objections, remonstrate, revolt, ridicule, riot, rise, rise up, rock the boat (*informal*), say your piece, scoff, scorn, sneer, speak out, speak to, speak up, speak your mind, split hairs, sully, *vociferate*

See also UNFAVOURABLE NON-VERBAL RESPONSES (655)

644 Argue and Fight – Two-Way

The daughter of debate, that eke discord doth sow. **Elizabeth I**

(*v*) altercate, argue, bandy words with, bicker, cavil, clash, cross swords, dicker (*informal*), differ, disagree, dispute, fall out, haggle, joust, lock horns, quarrel, row, spar, squabble, wrangle

See also ARGUMENT (47)

645 Deny and Reject

We have been taught to hate or deny our differences rather than to welcome them. **Nancy Kline**

(*n*) contradiction, denial, disavowal (*formal*), disclaimer, negation, rebuff, rebuttal, refusal, refutation, rejection, renunciation, repudiation, snub

(*v*) abjure, *beg to differ*, challenge, contest, contradict, debunk, deny, disavow (*formal*), disclaim, disprove, explode, forswear (*archaic or literary*), gainsay (*formal*), give the lie to, howl down, *naysay* (*US*), negate (*formal*), pass by, pooh-pooh, rebut, refute, repudiate, scorn, steamroller, take issue with

646 Agree

He is indeed one of the very greatest masters of painting. . .And I may add that in this opinion Mr. Whistler himself entirely concurs. **Oscar Wilde**

(*n*) acceptance, accession, acknowledgment, acquiescence, assent, espousal, green light, yes

(*v*) accede, accept, acknowledge, acquiesce, agree, assent, come forward, concur, consent, defer, deign, fall in with, grant, *panegyrize* (*formal*), say yes, see eye to eye, string along (*informal*), subscribe, sustain, volunteer

647 Approve and Confirm

Let age approve of youth, and death complete the same! **Robert Browning**

(*n*) accreditation, adoption, advocacy, approval, blessing, commendation, enactment, endorsement, nomination, okay (*informal*), promotion, proselytization, ratification, recommendation, sanction, uptake

(*v*) accept, accredit, advocate, affirm, answer for, approve, attest, authenticate, back up, bear out, bless, buy (*US informal*), carry, certify, champion, check, cinch (*dated informal*), clinch, *come down in favour of*, conclude, confirm, corroborate, credit, defend, enact, endorse, espouse, excuse, explain, favour, get behind, go with, hail, hold up, hold with, make sure, okay (*informal*), pass, plead, promote, prove, push, ratify, recommend, rubber-stamp, second, side with, speak for, speak up for, *speak well of*, stand by, stand for, stick up for, substantiate, support, testify (*formal*), uphold, verify, vindicate, vouch for

See also EXPRESSING RESPECT AND APPROVAL (638)

648 Praise and Encourage

Flow gently, sweet Afton, among thy green braes;/Flow gently, I'll sing thee a song in thy praise. **Robert Burns**

(*n*) acclaim, acclamation, applause, approbation, compliment, credit, deification (*formal*), *encomium* (*formal*), exaltation (*formal*), glorification, plaudit, praise, puff, respects, tribute

(*v*) acclaim, adulate, applaud, celebrate, cheer, cheer on, commend, compliment, congratulate, credit, eat up (*informal*), emblazon (*literary*), encourage, enthuse, eulogize (*formal*), exalt (*formal*), extol (*formal or literary*), fête, glorify, hymn, laud, lionize, magnify (*formal*), mark, marvel, *pay homage to*, *pay tribute*, play up to, praise, *praise to the skies*, put on a pedestal, rave, recognize, rhapsodize, root, *root for*, *show appreciation*, sing the praises of, thank, toast, wonder

See also FLATTER AND FAWN (622), APPLAUSE (653)

649 Expressions of Agreement

When you say that you agree to a thing in principle you mean that you have not the slightest intention of carrying it out in practice. **Prince Otto von Bismarck**

(*adv*) all right, by all means, by hook or by crook, for sure, naturally, no matter what, of course, *OK* (*informal*), *okeydokey* (*informal humorous*), righto (*dated informal*), sure (*US informal*), *sure enough*, sure thing (*US informal*), *thank goodness*, *thank heavens*, without a doubt, yes, *yes indeed*

(*interj*) all right, amen (*informal*), aye (*regional*), fair enough (*informal*), no problem (*informal*), okay (*informal*), roger (*informal*), *thanks a lot*, *thank you*, *yea* (*archaic*), *yeah* (*informal*), *yep* (*informal*), *you bet!* (*informal*), *you said it!*

650 Laughter

Laughter is as ridiculous as it is deceptive. **Paul Verlaine**

(*n*) belly laugh, giggle, guffaw, hysterics (*informal*), laughter, mirth, *mirthfulness*, snicker (*US*), *snickering*, snigger, *sniggering*

(*v*) cackle, chortle, chuckle, fall about (*informal*), giggle, grin, guffaw, *have hysterics* (*informal*), kill yourself laughing, laugh, *laugh your head off*, *roll in the aisles*, *scream with laughter*, snicker (*US*), snigger

651 Crying

It's not whether you really cry. It's whether the audience thinks you are crying. **Ingrid Bergman**

(*adj*) *in floods*, *in floods of tears*, *in tears*, misty-eyed, *snivelling*

(*n*) *blubbering* (*informal*), sobbing, waterworks

(*v*) bawl (*informal*), blub (*informal*), blubber (*informal*), burst into tears, cry, *cry your eyes out*, grizzle (*informal*), *shed tears*, sniffle, snivel, sob, weep, whimper

652 Facial Expression

A smile that snapped back after using, like a stretched rubber band. **Sinclair Lewis**

(*adj*) beaming, beatific (*literary*), blank, bug-eyed (*informal*), deadpan, dour, drawn, expressionless, glassy, glazed, *goggle-eyed*, *grim-faced*, *grinning*, impassive, mobile, penetrating, poker-faced, round-eyed, smiley, *smiling*, stony-faced, straight-faced, *teary*, *teary-eyed*, *unblinking*, unreadable, wooden

(*adv*) blankly, woodenly

(*n*) beam, *black look*, *dirty look*, expression, face, *facial expression*, frown, glare, grimace, grin, leer, *long face*, rictus, scowl, simper, smile, smirk, *smug look*, stare, wince, woodenness

(*v*) beam, blush, colour, frown, glare, *glare at*, glow, glower, gnash, *go pale*, *go red*, *go white*, grimace, keep a straight face, *knit your brow*, leer, look daggers, pout, *pull a face*, *purse your lips*, scowl, simper, smile, smirk, wince

653 Applause

Applause is a receipt, not a note of demand. **Artur Schnabel**

(*n*) acclamation, applause, clapping, hand, ovation, *round of applause*, *slow handclap*, *standing ovation*

(*v*) applaud, clap

See also PRAISE AND ENCOURAGE (648)

654 Gestures and Gesticulation

All the dancer's gestures are signs of things, and the dance...signifies and displays something over and above the pleasure of the senses. **Saint Augustine of Hippo**

(*n*) body language, bow, *bowing and scraping*, curtsy, flourish, genuflection, gesticulation, gesture, kowtow, mannerism, motion, nod, obeisance (*formal*), pat on the back (*informal*), prostration, salute, *show of hands*, *shrug*, signal, wave

(*v*) acknowledge, beckon, bob, bow, *bow and scrape*, cue, curtsy, genuflect, gesticulate, gesture, greet, hail, indicate, kowtow, motion, nod to, prostrate yourself, salaam, salute, sign, signal, wave

655 Unfavourable Non-Verbal Responses

Her very frowns are fairer far,/Than smiles of other maidens are. **Samuel Taylor Coleridge**

(*interj*) hush, *shush*

(*n*) boo, *Bronx cheer* (*US informal*), heckling, *hiss*, *raspberry* (*slang*)

(*v*) boo, catcall, hiss, jeer, *tut*

See also PROTEST AND EXPRESS DISAPPROVAL (643)

656 Physical Contact as Communication

You cannot shake hands with a clenched fist. **Indira Gandhi**

(*n*) bear hug, caress, cuddle, embrace, handshake, hug, kiss, *osculation* (*formal or humorous*), peck (*informal*), *smacker* (*informal*), smooch (*informal*), snog (*slang*) (*v*) canoodle (*informal*), chuck, cuddle, dandle, embrace, *French kiss*, hug, kiss, neck (*dated*), osculate (*formal or humorous*), peck, smooch (*informal*), snog (*slang*)

See also CONTACT: HOLD (412)

657 Endearments

Come live with me, and be my love,/And we will some new pleasures prove. **John Donne**

(*n*) babe (*slang*), baby (*slang*), darling, dear, dearest, dearie (*informal*), ducks (*regional informal*), *ducky* (*dated informal*), endearment, honey (*US informal*), *honeybun* (*US informal*), *honeybunch* (*US informal*), *honey-pie* (*US informal*), *kiddo* (*informal*), love, *lovey* (*informal*), pet, poppet (*informal*), sugar (*informal*), sweetheart, sweetie (*informal*), sweetie pie (*informal*), sweet nothings, *term of endearment*

658 Compliments

If God made us in His image, we have certainly returned the compliment. **Voltaire**

(*interj*) *bravo*, congratulations, *good job* (*US*), *good on you*, *smashing*, *way to go* (*US informal*), well done

659 Insults, Abuse, and Swearing

One does not insult the river god while crossing the river. **Proverb**

(*adj*) dysphemistic, insulting, slanderous

(*n*) abuse, affront, aspersion, backbiting, bad language, belittlement, blasphemy, brickbat, calumny (*formal*), character assassination, curse, defamation, denigration, detraction (*formal*), dirty word, dysphemism, *execration* (*literary or formal*), expletive, four-letter word, imprecation (*formal*), insult, jeer, jeering, jibe, name-calling, oath, obscenity, offence, profanity, slander, slur, smear, swearword, taunt, *verbal abuse*, *verbal assault*, vulgarism, vulgarity, vulgar language

(*v*) abuse, affront, attack somebody's dignity, badmouth (*slang*), blaspheme, call names, condescend, curse, cuss (*informal*), defame, denigrate, dis (*slang*), discredit, *eff and blind* (*slang*), *execrate* (*literary or formal*), humble, imprecate (*formal*), insult, jeer at, malign, patronize, revile, slander, slight, smear, stigmatize, swear, wrong

660 Greetings, Farewells, and Salutations

Faithless is he that says farewell when the road darkens. **J. R. R. Tolkien**

(*interj*) adieu, adios (*informal*), *auf Wiedersehen*, *au revoir*, *bon voyage*, bye (*informal*), bye-bye (*informal*), *bye for now* (*informal*), cheerio (*informal*), cheers, ciao (*informal*), *good afternoon*, goodbye, *good day*, *good luck*, *good morning*, goodnight, *hasta la vista* (*informal*), hello, *hi* (*informal*), *howdy* (*US informal*), night (*informal*), sayonara, *see you* (*informal*), *see you later* (*informal*), so long (*informal*), ta (*informal*)

(*n*) acknowledgment, *condolences*, farewell (*literary*), felicitations (*formal*), greeting, reception, salaam, salutation, *salutations* (*formal*), toast, valediction (*formal*), welcome

661 Deception and Lies

Cunning and deceit will every time serve a man better than force. **Niccolò Machiavelli**

(*n*) act, artifice (*formal*), *barefaced lie*, bluff, booby trap, brinkmanship, cabal, cant, charade, *charlatanism*, cheating, *cock-and-bull story*, con, *confidence game* (*US*), *confidence trick*, *con game* (*US informal*), *con trick* (*informal*), deceit, deception, dirty tricks, dishonesty, disinformation, dissimulation (*formal*), distortion, double-cross, double-dealing, *doublespeak*, double talk, duplicity, fabrication, fairy story, fairy tale, fake, *fallaciousness*, falsehood, falseness, falsification, falsity, feint, fib (*informal*), *fibbing* (*informal*), fiction, fix (*informal*), *flimflam* (*slang*), frame-up (*slang*), fraud, fraudulence, gold brick, *half-truth*, hoax, humbug, illusion, imposture (*formal*), intrigue, invention, *jiggery-pokery* (*informal*), lese majesty, lie, lying, machination, mannerism, masquerade, *mendaciousness*, misinformation, mockery, noose, obfuscation, perfidy (*literary*), perjury, *porky* (*slang*), pose (*disapproving*), pretence, prevarication, propaganda, put-on (*informal*), quackery, red herring, rip-off (*informal*), romance, ruse, scam (*slang*), setup (*informal*), *shaggy dog story*, sham, *smoke and mirrors* (*US*), smoke screen, *snake oil* (*US*), *snow job* (*US slang*), *sophism*, sophistry, spoof, sting (*US slang*), story (*informal*), subterfuge, swindle, tale, tall story, tall tale, *tissue of lies*, trap, travesty, trick, trickery, untruth, untruthfulness, *white lie*, whitewash, whopper (*informal*), wiles

(*v*) bamboozle (*informal*), *bear false witness*, bilk (*informal*), bluff, con (*informal*), deceive, decoy, delude, dissemble, do (*informal*), double-cross, dupe, entrap, fabricate, fib (*informal*), flirt, fob off, fool, fox, hoax, hoodwink, inflate, kid (*informal*), lead astray, *lead up the garden path*, libel, lie, make a fool of, misinform, mislead, overreach, pass off, perjure, play games with, prevaricate, pull a fast one (*slang*), pull the wool over somebody's eyes, scam (*slang*), set up (*informal*), *spin a yarn* (*informal*), spoof, *stretch the truth*, string along (*informal*), sucker (*informal*), take for a ride, take in, *tell lies*, tell stories, *tell untruths*, trap, trick, two-time

See also FALSE AND UNREAL (174), FALSIFY AND CHEAT (177), DECEITFUL (514)

662 People who Deceive

He led a double life. Did that make him a liar? He did not feel a liar. He was a man of two truths. **Iris Murdoch**

(*n*) cardsharp, charlatan, cheat, collaborator, con artist (*slang*), *confidence trickster*, *con man* (*informal*), conniver, conspirator, deceiver, *dissembler* (*formal*), double-crosser, double-dealer, faker, *fast talker*, fibber (*informal*), flatterer, fraud, fraudster, hoaxer, *huckster*, *hustler*, hypocrite, impostor, *intriguer*, *liar*, mountebank (*literary*), *perjurer*, phoney, plant (*informal*), plotter, *prevaricator*, profiteer, quack, *scammer* (*slang*), schemer, serpent, sham, *slanderer*, *slippery customer*, *sophist*, storyteller (*informal*), swindler, traitor, trickster, turncoat

See also SUPERFICIAL OR INSINCERE PEOPLE (951)

663 Victims of Deceit

The intellect is always fooled by the heart. **François La Rochefoucauld**

(*n*) dupe, fall guy (*informal*), monkey (*informal*), mug (*slang*), pigeon (*informal*), pushover (*informal*), scapegoat, soft touch, softy (*informal*), sucker (*informal*), victim

664 Request and Demand

Ask no one's view but your own. **Persius**

(*adj*) beseeching (*literary*), imploring (*formal*), pleading, suppliant (*formal*), *supplicatory* (*formal*), votive

(*n*) appeal, application, behest (*formal*), bid, bidding, call, charge, claim, clamour, command, commission, decree, demand, dictate, diktat, directive, entreaty, entry, fiat, importunity (*formal*), instruction, invitation, invite (*informal*), mandate, order, plea, prayer, prescript (*formal*), request, requisition, supplication (*formal*), tender, ultimatum, wish, word

(*v*) adjure, appeal, apply, ask, ask for, bay for, beg, beseech (*literary*), bid (*archaic*), call, call down, call for, call on, call out for, call upon, claim, clamour, command, crave (*archaic*), cry out, decree, demand, desire (*formal*), dictate, direct (*formal*), entreat (*formal*), exact, expect, implore (*formal*), insist, invite, invoke, lay claim to, lay down, lay down the law, lobby, ordain (*formal*), order, petition, plead, pray, prescribe, press, press for, provide, *push for*, request, requisition, seek, solicit, sue (*formal*), supplicate (*formal*), tell, urge, want, wish

665 People Who Make Requests

Not everybody can be a leader, but everybody can be an intermediary. **Theodore Zeldin**

(*n*) claimant, petitioner, suppliant (*formal*), supplicant (*formal*)

666 Name and Describe

The act of naming is the great and solemn consolation of mankind. **Elias Canetti**

(*adj*) alias, code-named, entitled, named, née, qualified, self-styled, unnumbered

(*n*) alias, appellation (*formal*), assumed name, autograph, brand, brand name, Christian name, *cognomen* (*formal*), definition, delineation, description, designation, epithet, family name, first name, forename, given name, handle (*slang*), honour, identification, inscription, *John Hancock* (*US informal*), label, last name, marque, *matronymic*, *middle name*, misnomer, mnemonic, moniker (*slang*), name, naming, nickname, *nom de guerre*, nom de plume, nomenclature, *paternal name*, *patronymic*, pen name, pet name, *praenomen*, pseudonym, *second name*, so-and-so (*informal*), sobriquet, stage name, surname, tab, tag, taxonomy, testimonial, ticket, title, trade name

(*v*) anthropomorphize, asterisk, backdate, brand, call, call a spade a spade, characterize, christen, couch, define, delineate, describe, designate, docket, dub, entitle, enumerate, finger (*slang*), flag, humanize, identify, inscribe, invoke, issue, label, mark out, name, name-drop, nickname, paint, particularize, pick out, picture, pigeonhole, preview, profile, rename, sign, stake out, stereotype, style (*formal*), tag, term, title, typecast, witness

667 Ask People Questions

The world is but a school of inquiry. **Michel de Montaigne**

(*n*) catechism, debriefing, inquiry, inquisition, interrogation, opinion poll, query, question, questionnaire, soundings

(*v*) ballot, consult, cross-examine, debrief, enquire, *give the third degree* (*informal*), grill (*informal*), inquire, interrogate, interview, make inquiries, poll, pose, pry, pump, query, question, quiz

See also QUESTION THINGS (752)

668 Questioners

The historian is...the skilled detective who asks questions, locates and follows clues. **John Clive**

(*n*) canvasser, inquisitor, questioner

669 Reply and Answer

Today we no longer seek...Our thinking is a thought in retreat or in reply. **Maurice Merleau-Ponty**

(*n*) acknowledgment, answer, comeback, feedback, reaction, rejoinder (*formal*), reply, response, retort, riposte

(*v*) acknowledge, answer, answer back, come back (*US*), greet, react, rejoin (*formal*), reply, respond, retort, riposte, talk back

670 Permit and Allow

Finding language that will allow people to act together while cherishing each other's individuality is probably the...truly revolutionary function of writers. **Gloria Steinem**

(*adj*) entitled, free-and-easy, laissez-faire, lax, licensed, permissible, permitted

(*n*) access, admission, admittance, all clear, authorization, clearance, confirmation, consent, empowerment, entrance, fiat, franchise, go-ahead (*informal*), leave (*formal*), mandate, power, sanction, say-so (*informal*), signing, special consideration, thumbs-up (*informal*)

(*v*) admit, agree, allow, approve, authorize, concur, condescend, consent, decriminalize, empower, entitle, franchise, *give leave* (*formal*), give permission, *give the go-ahead*, invest, leave, let, let in, let into, let pass, license, mandate, permit, sanction, validate

671 Refuse Permission and Not Allow

Forbidden fruit is sweet. **Proverb**

(*adj*) banned, barred, disallowed, disqualified, not allowed, off-limits, out, proscribed, *proscriptive* (*formal*), suspended, taboo

(*n*) blackout, circumscription (*formal*), denial, disbarment, disqualification, exclusion, gag, interdict, negative, no, permission, proscription (*formal*), red light (*informal*), renunciation, sanction, thumbs-down (*informal*), veto

(*v*) ban, bar, confine, crack down (*informal*), criminalize, debar, deny, disallow, disbar, disqualify, estop (*archaic*), forbid, ground, hold, interdict, outlaw, overrule, prohibit, proscribe, rule out, taboo, veto

672 The Spoken Word

And the whole earth was of one language, and of one speech. **Bible**

(*adj*) articulated, broad, oral, spoken, unpronounceable, verbal, vocal

(*n*) accent, argot, articulation, cadence, catch phrase, catchword, effusion, expression, intonation, language, mispronunciation, modulation, monologue, parlance, patois, pidgin, pronunciation, rhetoric, slang, slogan, speech, talk, tongue, twang, utterance, verbalization, vernacular, war cry, watchword

673 Foreign Words and Phrases

Hebrew and Arabic,/which are like stones on the tongue and sand on the throat,/have softened for tourists like oil. **Yehuda Amichai**

(*adj*) *pro bono*, pro tem

(*adv*) de facto, entre nous (*formal*), et cetera, per se (*formal*), prima facie, *pro rata*, pro tem

(*interj*) *voilà*

(*n*) *je ne sais quoi*, *pro forma*

(*prep*) *contra*, in memoriam, versus, vis-à-vis

(*v*) stet

674 Figures of Speech

Through metaphor to reconcile/the people and the stones./Compose. (No ideas but in things.) Invent! **William Carlos Williams**

(*n*) aphorism, axiom, buzzword (*informal*), byword, cliché, colloquialism, epigram, euphemism, figure of speech, formula, generality, hyperbole, idiom, maxim, metaphor, motto, parenthesis, platitude, proverb, refrain, saw, saying, set phrase, *simile*, *tongue twister*, truism, vulgarism, *weasel word* (*informal*)

675 Jokes and Teasing

Forgive, O Lord, my little jokes on Thee/And I'll forgive Thy great big one on me. **Robert Frost**

(*adj*) facetious, *punning*, teasing, wicked

(*adv*) at somebody's expense, *in jest*, wickedly

(*n*) banter, barb, boisterousness, bon mot, brainteaser, buffoonery, burlesque, *canard* (*literary*), caricature, chaff, chestnut (*informal*), clowning, crack (*informal*), derision, dig, facetiousness, fencing, *fun and games*, funny (*informal*), gag (*informal*), gibe, humour, in-joke, irony, jape (*archaic*), jest (*literary*), jesting (*literary*), jocularity, joke, joking, *joshing* (*informal*), knockabout, lampoon, lark, laugh (*informal*), laughing stock, leg-pull (*informal*), *leg-pulling* (*informal*), mockery, one-liner, pantomime (*informal*), parody, pastiche, practical joke, prank, *private joke*, quip, raillery, repartee, *ribbing* (*informal*), riddle, ridicule, *running joke*, satire, sendup (*informal*), shenanigans (*informal*), skit, slapstick, spoof, *sport* (*formal*), *stand-up*, teaser, teasing, tomfoolery (*informal*), trick, understatement, wickedness, wind-up (*informal*), wisecrack (*informal*), wit, witticism, wordplay, wryness

(*v*) bait, banter, burlesque, chaff, clown, *clown around*, crack a joke, *goof around* (*US informal*), *goof off* (*US informal*), guy (*regional informal*), *have a joke with*, *have a lark*, *have a laugh*, have on (*informal*), *horse about*, jape (*archaic*), jest (*literary*), jibe, joke, josh (*informal*), kid, lampoon, lark about, lark around, laugh at, laugh out of court, *lollygag* (*dated*), make fun of, mess about (*informal*), mess around (*informal*), mimic, mock, monkey around, parody, pick on, play, poke fun at, pull somebody's leg (*informal*), quip, rag (*dated*), razz (*US informal*), rib (*informal*), ride (*US informal*), satirize, send up (*informal*), spoof, stultify, take the mickey (*informal*), taunt, tease, wind up (*informal*), wisecrack (*informal*), *yank somebody's chain* (*US informal*)

types of wordplay acrostic, anagram, logogram, malapropism, palindrome, pun, spoonerism, telestich

See also PRETEND AND MIMIC (60), ENTERTAINMENT (872)

676 Jokers and Teases

He who endeavours to ridicule other people, especially in things of a serious nature, becomes himself a jest. **Giovanni Boccaccio**

(*n*) *clown* (*informal*), cutup (*US informal*), humorist, jester, joker, *josher* (*US informal*), kidder, mimic, mocker, prankster, *punster*, rascal (*humorous*), scream (*informal*), tease, teaser, wag (*dated*), *wiseacre* (*informal*), *wisecracker* (*informal*), wit

See also WORKERS IN ENTERTAINMENT AND MEDIA (873)

677 Meaningless Speech or Writing

Whenever a poet or preacher, chief or wizard spouts gibberish, the human race spends centuries deciphering the message. **Umberto Eco**

(*n*) aside, balderdash, baloney (*informal*), bilge (*informal*), blather (*informal*), blether (*informal*), bombast, bunk (*slang*), bunkum (*informal*), cant, chicanery, claptrap (*informal*), codswallop (*informal*), crud (*informal*), doggerel, double Dutch (*informal*), double talk, drivel, footle (*informal*), froth, fudge (*informal*), gabble, garbage, gas (*informal*), gibberish, gobbledegook (*informal disapproving*), guff (*informal*), hogwash (*informal*), hokum (*US informal disapproving*), hooey (*informal*), *hoopla* (*US informal*), hot air (*informal*), humbug, jargon, jazz (*US slang*), legalese, *malarkey* (*informal*), moonshine, mumbo jumbo (*informal*), *nattering* (*informal*), nonsense, oratory, padding, pap, piffle (*informal*), *pleonasm*, poppycock (*dated informal*), prattle, *prolixity*, rigmarole, rot (*informal*), rubbish, smooth talk, spiel (*informal*), *stuff and nonsense*, *technobabble*, tosh (*dated informal*), trash, tripe (*informal*), twaddle (*informal*), verbiage, *verboseness*, verbosity, waffle (*informal*), *whiffle waffle* (*US*), wittering (*informal*), wordiness

See also WITTER AND BABBLE (618), INFORMAL COMMUNICATION (45)

678 The Oral Tradition

Old man history tells us that it's better to be a little more noisy. A silent era cannot be a little more noisy. **Liu Binyan**

(*n*) adage, allegory, anecdote, dictum (*formal*), fable, fairy story, folklore, *folk story*, folk tale, *folk tales*, legend, lore, myth, mythology, narration, narrative, narrator, *oral tradition*, parable, plot, rumour, saga, scene, sob story (*informal*), soliloquy, *stock phrase*, story, story line, tale, urban myth, yarn (*informal*)

679 Gossip

History a distillation of rumour. **Thomas Carlyle**

(*adv*) second-hand

(*n*) buzz (*informal*), dirt, fallacy, gossip, grapevine, hearsay, muckraking, mudslinging, *rumourmongering*, scandal, *scandalmongering*, *scuttlebutt* (*US slang*), smear campaign, speculation, talk, tattle, titbit, tittle-tattle, whisper, word

(*v*) gas (*informal*), purvey, rumour, *spread rumours*, yammer (*informal*), yap (*informal*)

See also INTERFERING PEOPLE AND TELLTALES (950), BETRAY CONFIDENCES AND GOSSIP (619), INFORMAL COMMUNICATION (45)

680 Giving Vent to Emotions

Where can you scream? It's a serious question: where can you go in society and scream? **R. D. Laing**

(*v*) be angry, bellow, *blow a fuse* (*informal*), *blow a gasket* (*informal*), blow up (*informal*), blow your top (*informal*), boil, *boil with rage*, break down, *break down and cry*, bridle, bristle, *burst out crying*, choke, cluck, commiserate, create (*informal*), cry out, erupt, explode, exult, flip (*slang*), flip your lid (*slang*), fly into a rage, fly off the handle (*informal*), foam at the mouth, *freak out* (*informal*), fume, get angry, *get in a lather* (*informal*), *get in a state*, get on your high horse, *get stirred up*, gnash your teeth, *go ballistic* (*slang*), *go bananas* (*informal*), go berserk, *go beserk*, go mad, go off the deep end, *go on the rampage*, *go postal* (*US informal*), go to pieces, go wild, grieve, *have a fit* (*informal*), *have kittens* (*informal*), hit the roof, lament, let fly, *let off steam*, *let rip* (*informal*), lose control, lose it (*informal*), lose your cool (*informal*), lose your patience, lose your rag (*slang*), lose your temper, make a scene, mourn, open up, panic, rage, rampage, rant, rant and rave, rejoice (*literary*), run amok, run riot, see red (*informal*), seethe, smoulder, snap, sound off (*informal*), stew, storm, sulk, take out, *throw a fit* (*informal*), *throw a tantrum*, *throw a wobbly* (*informal*), uncork, whoop

681 Initiate and Establish Communication

The word, even the most contradictory word, preserves contact—it is silence which isolates. **Thomas Mann**

(*v*) accost, ambush, approach, *ask out*, be in contact with, break the ice, buttonhole (*informal*), call, call by, call on, call out, come over, commune, contact, correspond, court, drop a line, encounter, face, get at, hear from, hook up (*informal*), keep up with, liaise, look up, make contact, make yourself known, nobble (*informal*), reach, rendezvous, see, send for, speak to, stop by, summon, tackle, turn to, visit, waylay, welcome, write

See also ESTABLISHING RELATIONSHIPS WITH OTHERS (974)

682 Telephone and Page

You cannot settle the problems of Europe by long-distance telephone calls and telegrams. **Ernest Bevin**

(*v*) bleep, call, call in, call up, dial, get hold of, get in touch with, *give a bell* (*informal*), *give a buzz* (*informal*), *give a call*, *give a ring*, *give a tinkle*, hang up, page, phone, *phone up*, ring, ring off, ring up, telephone

See also TELEPHONE COMMUNICATION (48), TELECOMMUNICATIONS (1129)

683 Aspects of Language

I master the language of others. Mine does what it wants with me. **Karl Kraus**

(*adj*) alliterative, grammatical, informal, lexical, linguistic, multilingual, phrasal, polysyllabic, rhetorical, *semantic*

(*n*) abbreviation, accentuation, acronym, alliteration, assonance, brogue, burr, *coinage*, *collocation*, contraction, diacritic, dialect, diction, drawl, *elision*, ellipsis, elocution, enunciation, *etymology*, grammar, idiolect, idiom, jargon, language, lexicon, *lilt*, lingo (*informal*), *lingua franca*, linguistics, *locution*, monosyllable, neologism, nomenclature, *oxymoron*, paragraph, password, patois, patter, phrase, phraseology, phrasing, polysyllable, *Received Pronunciation*, regionalism, rhetoric, RP, *semantics*, *sentence structure*, short form, *speech disorder*, *speech impediment*, *strophe*, *syllable*, synonym, syntax, term, terminology, terms, turn of phrase, vocabulary, word, wording

types of grammatical term adjunct, affix, attributive, clause, conditional, conjugation, diphthong, indicative, infinitive, inflection, intransitive, modal, nominative, object, participle, plural, predicate, prefix, prenominal, preterite, sentence, subject, subjunctive, suffix, transitive

types of word class adjective, adverb, article, conjunction, definite article, determiner, indefinite article, interjection, modifier, noun, particle, phrasal verb, preposition, pronoun, proper noun, qualifier, quantifier, substantive, verb

types of diacritic accent, acute, angstrom, apostrophe, cedilla, circumflex, diaeresis, grave, hácek, tilde, umlaut

types of punctuation mark asterisk, backslash, bracket, colon, comma, dash, exclamation mark, full stop, hyphen, inverted comma, parenthesis, period (*US*), point, question mark, quotation mark, square bracket, swung dash

684 Apologize and Retract

Apologies only account for that which they do not alter. **Benjamin Disraeli**

(*n*) apology, appeasement, atonement, attestation, *expiation*, olive branch, penance, penitence, placation, propitiation (*formal*), recantation, retraction, withdrawal

(*v*) apologize, atone (*formal*), back down, back off, backpedal, backtrack, *beg forgiveness*, climb down, conciliate, countermand, crawl, eat crow (*US informal*), *eat humble pie*, eat your words (*informal*), go back on, lift, make amends, *make reparations*, recall, recant, regret (*formal*), repent, retract, say sorry, *send your apologies*, swallow, take back, withdraw

685 Promise and Assure

Promises are the uniquely human way of ordering the future, making it predictable and reliable. **Hannah Arendt**

(*n*) assurance, binder (*US*), bond, commitment, compact, oath, obligation, pact, pledge, promise, resolution, vow, word, *word of honour*

(*v*) assure, commit, give your word, guarantee, keep your word, pledge, promise, swear, *swear an oath*, take an oath, vouchsafe (*formal*), vow, warrant

686 Vengeance and Revenge

A man that studieth revenge keeps his own wounds green. **Francis Bacon**

(*adj*) punitive, recriminatory, retaliatory, retributive, *tit-for-tat*

(*n*) reprisal, retaliation, retribution, revenge, *settling of scores*, tit for tat, vengeance

(*v*) answer for, avenge, get back at, get even, get your own back, pay back, retaliate, revenge, *strike back*

687 Complain and Nag

Who complains without cause, let a cause be made for him. **Welsh proverb**

(*n*) beef (*slang*), bellyache (*informal*), carping, *chunter* (*informal*), complaint, faultfinding, grievance, gripe (*informal*), grouch (*informal*), grouse (*informal*), grumble, hairsplitting, moan (*informal*), niggle, persecution, protest, wail, whine

(*v*) badger, beef (*slang*), bellyache (*informal*), bemoan, bewail (*formal*), bitch (*US slang*), bleat, browbeat, carp, carry on, complain, croak (*informal*), deplore, dog, find fault, go on at (*informal*), gripe (*informal*), grizzle (*informal*), groan (*informal*), grouch (*informal*), grouse (*informal*), grumble, harp on, harry, hassle (*informal*), huff, importune (*formal*), keep on at (*informal*), kick up a fuss, *kvetch* (*informal*), make a fuss, moan (*informal*), murmur, mutter, nag, nark (*informal*), niggle, nitpick, persecute, ply, squawk (*informal*), wail, whine, whinge (*informal*)

688 Withhold Information

The most difficult secret for a man to keep is his own opinion of himself. **Marcel Pagnol**

(*n*) censorship, cover-up, equivocation, evasion, suppression

(*v*) belt up (*slang*), bottle up, bowdlerize, button up (*informal*), censor, choke back, clam up (*informal*), conceal, cover up, dissemble (*formal*), draw a veil over, equivocate, evade, gulp back, hide, hold out on, hush up (*informal*), internalize, keep, keep a secret, keep back, keep from, keep in the dark, keep mum (*informal*), *keep quiet*, keep secret, *keep to yourself*, keep under wraps, *keep under your hat*, parry, play your cards close to your chest, repress, shush (*informal*), shut up (*informal*), stifle, submerge, suppress, swallow, throttle, *withhold information*

689 Basic Details

All my novels are an accumulation of detail. I'm a bit of a bower-bird. **Patrick White**

(*n*) ABC, advice, baseline, basics, brass tacks, brief, *building blocks*, bulletin, content, data, *datum*, details, dynamics, elements, fact, facts, *fine points*, *first principles*, flesh, fundamentals, *generalities*, info (*informal*), information, input, ins and outs, intelligence, intricacies, knowledge, *lowdown* (*informal*), material, minutiae, news, nicety, nitty-gritty (*informal*), nuts and bolts (*informal*), particulars, release, rudiments, specific, specification, *specifics*, statistics, story, *technicalities*, tidings (*literary*), whys and wherefores, word

690 Advice

One gives nothing so freely as advice. **François La Rochefoucauld**

(*n*) advice, caution, caveat, clue, counsel (*formal or literary*), directions, discouragement, exhortation (*formal*), forewarning, guidance, guideline, hint, home truth, invitation, pointer, recommendation, suggestion, tip, tip-off (*informal*), warning

See also ADVISE AND WARN (614)

691 Meaning

The least of things with a meaning is worth more in life than the greatest of things without it. **Carl Gustav Jung**

(*n*) association, connotation, denotation, drift, effect, gist, implication, lesson, meaning, message, moral, point, resonance, sense, significance, signification, subtext, tenor, thrust, undercurrent

See also MEAN SOMETHING (61)

The Human Body and Bodily Functions

692 Body

If anything is sacred the human body is sacred. **Walt Whitman**

(*n*) body, flesh, organ, person, *soma*

693 Head

Uneasy lies the head that wears a crown. **William Shakespeare**

(*n*) bonce (*informal*), countenance, head, *maxilla*, mug (*informal*), noddle (*dated informal*), noggin (*dated informal*), *noodle* (*slang*), nut (*informal*), pate (*archaic or humorous*), phiz (*slang*), *phizog* (*slang*), physiognomy, *puss* (*slang*), skull (*informal*), visage (*literary*)

parts of a head crown, ear, earlobe, face, forehead, hair, nape, scalp, temple

parts of a face brow, cheek, chin, chops (*informal*), eye, jaw, jawline, jowl, mandible, mouth, nose

See also FACIAL CHARACTERISTICS (482)

694 Torso

DIAPHRAGM, n. A muscular partition separating disorders of the chest from disorders of the bowels. **Ambrose Bierce**

(*n*) appendage, backside (*informal*), extremity, haunch, limb, member, rump

parts of a torso abdomen, armpit, back, belly, bellybutton (*informal*), bosom, bottom, breast, bust, buttock, chest, groin, hip, midriff, navel, neck, nipple, rib cage, shoulder, solar plexus, thorax, waist, waistline

695 Leg and Foot

You cannot make a man by standing a sheep on its hind legs. But by standing a flock of sheep in that position you can make a crowd of men. **Max Beerbohm**

(*n*) foreleg, *hindleg*, leg, *peg* (*informal*), *pins* (*informal*)

parts of a leg or foot ankle, big toe, calf, foot, haunch, heel, instep, knee, lap, little toe, shin, sole, thigh, toe, toenail

696 Arm and Hand

An arm/Rose up from out the bosom of the lake,/Clothed in white samite, mystic, wonderful. **Alfred Tennyson**

(*n*) arm, claw, mitt (*slang*), nipper, paw (*informal*), tentacle

parts of an arm or hand ball, cuticle, elbow, finger, fingernail, fingerprint, fingertip, fist, forearm, forefinger, hand, hangnail, heel, index finger, knuckle, little finger, middle finger, palm, pinkie (*informal*), ring finger, thumb, thumbnail, wrist

697 The Senses

But perhaps it is this distrust of our senses that prevents us from feeling comfortable in the universe. **Italo Calvino**

(*n*) ear, faculty, feeling, perception, sensation, sense, *senses*

See also PERCEPTIBLE (25), IMPERCEPTIBLE (26)

698 Using the Senses

The five senses are as spies. Each one of them has been entrusted with making one of the arts, so the eye has been entrusted with the world of colours, hearing with the world of voices, and so on. **Muhammad**

(*v*) detect, feel, sense, taste

See also CONTACT: HOLD (412)

699 The Eye

Explore thyself. Herein are demanded the eye and the nerve. **Henry David Thoreau**

(*n*) *cornea*, *eyeball*, *eyebrow*, *eyelash*, *eyelid*, *iris*, *lens*, *orbit*, *pupil*, *retina*

700 See

We should not ask ourselves if we perceive the world truly; on the contrary: the world is that which we perceive. **Maurice Merleau-Ponty**

(*adj*) bleary, blind, bloodshot, hawk-eyed, *keen-sighted*, *long-sighted*, myopic, nearsighted (*US*), ocular, *ophthalmic*, optical, *partially sighted*, photosensitive, sharp-eyed, sharp-sighted, short-sighted, sighted, *sightless*, visual

(*adv*) blindly

(*n*) blindness, eyesight, line of sight, lookover (*informal*), look-see (*informal*), myopia, *nearsightedness* (*US*), observation, regard (*formal*), short-sightedness, sight, *sightlessness*, view, vision

(*v*) catch a glimpse of, catch sight of, *descry* (*literary*), espy (*formal*), glimpse, perceive, see, *set eyes on*, sight, spot, spy, witness

See also READ (759)

701 Looking and Looks

Look round this universe. . .The whole presents nothing but the idea of blind nature, impregnated by a great vivifying principle. **David Hume**

(*n*) contemplation, dekko (*informal*), eyeful (*informal*), gander (*informal*), gaze, glance, glimpse, peek, peep, recce (*slang*), reconnoitre, riffle, *rubbernecking* (*informal*), *shufti* (*informal*), squint, stakeout (*informal*), surveillance, viewing, voyeurism

(*v*) behold (*archaic or literary*), blink, browse, *cast an eye over*, contemplate, discern, distinguish, examine, eye, eyeball (*informal*), *eye up*, flip through, follow, gape, gawk (*informal*), gawp (*informal*), gaze, glance, goggle, *have a look at*, *have a look-see* (*US*), invigilate, keep an eye on, leaf through, look, look back, make out, observe, ogle, overlook, peek, peep, peer, read, recce (*slang*), regard, riffle, rubberneck (*informal*), scan, scout, see, *sneak a look*, snoop (*informal*), spectate, spy, squint, stake out (*informal*), stare, *stare down* (*US*), *stare into space*, stare out, *steal a look*, survey, *take a look at*, thumb, view, watch, watch out

702 Lookers and Spectators

All in all the creative act is not performed by the artist alone; the spectator brings the work in contact with the external world by deciphering and interpreting its inner qualifications and thus adds his contribution to the creative act. **Marcel Duchamp**

(*n*) bystander, eyewitness, invigilator, looker, observer, onlooker, spectator, viewer, watcher, witness

703 The Mouth

A portrait is a picture in which there is something wrong with the mouth. **Eugene Speicher**

(*n*) *cakehole* (*slang*), *gob* (*slang*), *maw*, mouth, trap

parts of a mouth adenoids, denture, gum, lip, palate, roof, soft palate, taste bud, tongue, tonsils, tooth, uvula

types of tooth baby tooth, bucktooth (*informal*), canine, chopper, cuspid, denture, eyetooth, fang, incisor, milk tooth, molar, premolar, wisdom tooth

704 Taste

I hate a man who swallows it, affecting not to know what he is eating. I suspect his taste in higher matters. **Charles Lamb**

(*adj*) acid, acidic, acrid, appetizing, bitter, bland, brackish, briny, cloying, delectable, delicious, *delish* (*slang*), flavourful, flavourless, *flavoursome*, foul-tasting, fresh, fruity, full-bodied, hot, insipid, lemony, limy, *lip-smacking*, luscious, mature, mellow, mild, moreish (*informal*), mouthwatering, palatable, peppery, piquant, pungent, rancid, rich, saccharine, saline, salty, *savourless*, savoury, scrummy (*informal*), scrumptious (*informal*), sharp, *sharp-tasting*, sour, *spiced*, *spicey*, spicy, strong, succulent, sugary, sweet, syrupy, tangy, tart, tasteless, tasty, toothsome, unpalatable, vapid, vinegary, watery, wishy-washy (*informal*), yucky (*informal*), yummy, *zesty*

(*adv*) acridly, delectably, sourly

(*n*) acidity, *aftertaste*, bite, bitterness, blandness, deliciousness, flavour, *flavourlessness*, freshness, fullness, hotness, insipidness, juiciness, lusciousness, mellowness, *pepperiness*, piquancy, pungency, rancidness, savour, *savourlessness*, *scrumptiousness* (*informal*), *sense of taste*, sharpness, smack, sourness, succulence, sweetness, sweet tooth, *tanginess*, tartness, taste, tastelessness, tastiness, *yumminess*, zest

705 The Nose

Any nose/May ravage with impunity a rose. **Robert Browning**

(*adj*) *nasal*

(*n*) *conk* (*slang*), nose, *nostril*, *schnozzle* (*US slang*), snout

706 Smell and Smelling

No matter how well you clean a goat it will still smell like a goat. **Philippine proverb**

(*adj*) aromatic, *cheesy*, foul-smelling, foxy, fragranced, fragrant, funky (*US slang*), heady, humming (*informal*), malodorous, musky, niffy (*slang*), *odoriferous* (*formal or technical*), odorous (*literary*), odourless, perfumed, pongy (*informal*), rank (*literary*), redolent, ripe (*informal*), scented, smelly, stinking, stinky, sulphurous, sweet, sweet-smelling, whiffy (*informal*)

(*n*) aroma, BO (*informal*), *body odour*, bouquet, fragrance, fume, funk (*US slang*), hum (*informal*), musk, niff (*slang*), odour, perfume, pong (*informal*), *rankness*, redolence (*literary*), reek, scent, smell, *smelliness*, stench, stink, whiff

(*v*) scent, smell, sniff

See also SMELL EMISSION (370)

707 The Ear

A knavish speech sleeps in a foolish ear. **William Shakespeare**

(*n*) *auricle*, ear, eardrum, *earlobe*, *outer ear*, *shell-like* (*informal humorous*), *tympanic membrane* (*technical*), *tympanum* (*technical*)

708 Hear

There is no worse lie than a truth misunderstood by those who hear it. **William James**

(*adj*) audio, auditory, aural, deaf, *hearing-impaired*

(*v*) catch, hear, receive

709 Listen and Listeners

But I did not remove my glasses, for I had not asked for her company in the first place, and there is a limit to what one can listen to with the naked eye. **Muriel Spark**

(*n*) auditor (*formal*), eavesdropper, listener

(*v*) bug, *earwig* (*humorous*), eavesdrop, hear, *hearken* (*archaic*), *lend an ear*, listen, listen in, listen up (*informal*), overhear, *pin your ears back* (*informal*), tap, wiretap

710 The Digestive Tract

The abdomen is the reason why man does not easily take himself for a god. **Friedrich Wilhelm Nietzsche**

(*adj*) abdominal, gastric, gastrointestinal, intestinal, *peptic*

(*n*) bowels, guts, innards (*informal*), insides (*informal*), *tum* (*informal*), tummy (*informal*), viscera

parts of a digestive tract alimentary canal, anus, appendix, bile duct, bladder, bowel, caecum, colon, duodenum, gallbladder, gullet, gut, intestine, kidney, large intestine, liver, oesophagus, pancreas, rectum, small intestine, spleen, stomach, throat

711 Eat and Not Eat

Appetite comes with eating. **François Rabelais**

(*adj*) digestive, famished, full, full up, hungry, malnourished, peckish (*informal*), ravenous, replete, sated, satiated, starved (*informal*), starving (*informal*), stuffed (*informal*), well-fed

(*n*) appetite, consumption, digestion, fast, *gourmandise*, *gourmandizing*, hunger, mastication, metabolism, ravenousness, rumination, starvation

(*v*) bite, bolt, champ, chew, chew up, chomp (*informal*), chow down (*US informal*), chug (*US slang*), consume, crunch, demolish (*informal*), devour, diet, digest, dine, down, eat, *famish*, fast, feast, feed, finish up, gobble, gobble down, gorge, graze, gulp, gulp down, guzzle (*informal*), have, ingest, lose weight, masticate, metabolize, munch, nibble, nosh (*informal*), nourish, partake (*formal*), peck, pig out (*informal*), polish off, put away (*informal*), raven (*literary*), ruminate, scarf (*US slang*), scarf down (*US slang*), scoff (*informal*), slim, snap, starve, swallow, *tuck in* (*informal*), watch your weight, wolf

See also FOOD (1166)

712 Drink

Drinking when we are not thirsty and making love all year round, madam; that is all there is to distinguish us from other animals. **Pierre-Augustin Caron de Beaumarchais**

(*adj*) dry, gasping, parched (*informal*), thirsty

(*n*) draught (*dated*), drink, *glassful*, gulp, mouthful, sip, slug (*informal*), slurp, suck, sup, swallow, swig (*informal*), top-up, tot

(*v*) *chugalug* (*US informal*), drink, *glug* (*informal*), imbibe (*formal or humorous*), knock back (*informal*), lap, lap up, put back, quaff (*literary or humorous*), quench, sip, slug (*informal*), slurp, suck, sup, swallow, swig (*informal*), swill, taste, *toss off*

See also AMOUNT OF LIQUID (114)

713 Vomit and Belch

There's not a sea the passenger e'er pukes in,/Turns up more dangerous breakers than the Euxine. **Lord Byron**

(*n*) *barf* (*US informal*), belch, *burp*, puke (*slang*), regurgitation, sick (*informal*), spew, vomit, *vomitus* (*technical*)

(*v*) barf (*US informal*), belch, bring up, *burp*, gag, *hiccup* (*informal*), hurl (*slang*), puke (*slang*), regurgitate, retch, sick up (*informal*), *spit up*, throw up (*informal*), *upchuck* (*informal*), vomit

714 Disorders of the Digestive System

An indigestion is an excellent common-place for two people that never met before. **William Hazlitt**

(*n*) *acid stomach*, bellyache (*informal*), colic, dyspepsia (*technical*), heartburn, indigestion, *malnourishment*, malnutrition, sickness, stomachache, *stomach pain*, *tummy ache* (*informal*), *tummy pain* (*informal*), ulcer, undernourishment, upset stomach

715 Eaters, Gourmets, and Dietary Choices

Tell me what you eat and I will tell you what you are. **Anthelme Brillat-Savarin**

(*adj*) carnivorous, vegetarian

(*n*) carnivore, dieter, diner, eater, epicure, foodie (*informal*), food lover, gastronome, gourmand, gourmet, vegan, vegetarian, veggie (*informal*)

See also PLEASURE-SEEKERS AND HEDONISTS (886)

716 Respiratory Organs

Cough. *A convulsion of the lungs, vellicated by some sharp serosity.* **Samuel Johnson**

(*adj*) bronchial, pulmonary

parts of a respiratory system air sac, airway, alveolus, bronchial tube, bronchiole, bronchus, larynx, lung, pharynx, throat, trachea, vocal cords, voice box, windpipe

717 Breathe and Not Breathe

No life that breathes with human breath/Has ever truly long'd for death. **Alfred Tennyson**

(*adj*) breathy, puffing, respiratory, *rheumy*, wheezy

(*n*) asphyxia, breath, breathing, breathlessness, *chestiness*, gasp, inhalation, mouth-to-mouth, puffing, respiration, respirator, *rheum*, sneeze, sniff, snuffle, ventilator, wheeziness

(*v*) breathe, exhale, huff, *hyperventilate*, inhale, pant, puff, respire, sneeze, sniff, sniffle, snore, snort, snuffle, splutter, sputter, suck in, wheeze

718 The Blood and Circulation

Nothing like blood, sir, in hosses, dawgs, and men. **William Makepeace Thackeray**

(*adj*) *cardiac*, cardiovascular, intravenous, *vascular*

(*n*) *anaemia*, bleed, bleeding, blood, bloodstream, lifeblood (*literary*), nosebleed, *plasma*, *red corpuscle*, thrombosis, *white blood cells*, *white corpuscle*

(*v*) bleed, haemorrhage

types of blood vessel aorta, artery, capillary, jugular vein, vein, venule

719 The Muscles

The human body...indeed is like a ship; its bones being the stiff standing-rigging, and the sinews the small running ropes, that manage all the motions. **Herman Melville**

(*n*) *brawn*, muscle, *thew* (*literary*)

types of muscle or tendon abdominals, Achilles tendon, biceps, diaphragm, hamstring, pectoral, quadriceps, sinew, smooth muscle, sphincter, striated muscle, tendon, triceps

See also MUSCLES AND MUSCULATURE (480)

720 The Bones and Joints

Parents are the bones on which children sharpen their teeth. **Peter Ustinov**

(*adj*) arthritic, pelvic, rheumatic, spinal, *vertebral*

(*n*) arthritis, back, carcass, *cartilage*, frame, gristle, *repetitive strain injury*, skeleton, *vertebral column*

types of bone backbone, breastbone, cheekbone, coccyx, collarbone, cranium, femur, fibula, humerus, jawbone, kneecap, long bone, patella (*technical*), pelvis, radius, rib, shoulder blade, skull, spinal column, spine, sternum, tibia, ulna, vertebra

721 The Skin

Skin is like wax paper that holds everything in without dripping. **Art Linkletter**

(*adj*) *dermal*, *dermatological*, subcutaneous

(*n*) *dermis*, epidermis, flesh, follicle, fur, hair, *integument*, membrane, pelt, skin, tissue

See also COMPLEXION (481)

722 Conditions Affecting the Skin

Style, like sheer silk, too often hides eczema. **Albert Camus**

(*adj*) calloused, pocked, pockmarked, prickly, purulent, scabrous, *sunburnt*

(*n*) abrasion, abscess, bedsore, birthmark, bite, blackhead, blister, *blood blister*, boil, bruise, bump, bunion, burn, callus, carbuncle, cellulite, chilblain, dandruff, *furuncle* (*technical*), *goose pimples*, *heat rash*, *hives*, itchiness, *melanoma*, *naevus*, *oedema*, pimple, pockmark, *pressure sore*, prickle, prickling, *prickly heat*, pustule, rash, rawness, redness, rubbing, scab, scar, scurf, sore, spot, sty, *sunburn*, *suntan*, *verruca*, wart, weal, welt, *whitehead*, zit (*slang*)

723 Excretion and Excreta

People will swim through shit if you put a few bob in it. **Peter Sellers**

(*adj*) *excretory*, purgative (*formal*)

(*n*) body fluid, catarrh, defecation, droppings, *excrement*, *excreta* (*technical*), *excretion*, *faeces*, *lymph*, manure, mucus, perspiration, phlegm, purgative (*formal*), pus, saliva, spit, spittle, sputum, teardrop, *urine*

(*v*) blister, defecate (*formal or technical*), dribble, drool, eliminate (*technical*), *excrete*, gob (*slang*), perspire, salivate, slaver, slobber, spit, suppurate, sweat, swelter, *urinate*

See also UNPLEASANT AND DIRTY SUBSTANCES (1267)

724 Sleep and Dream

He used to sleep like a glass of water/held up in the hand of a very young girl. **Rita Dove**

(*n*) bye-byes (*babytalk*), catnap, doss, doze, forty winks (*informal*), insomnia, kip (*informal*), lie-down (*informal*), nap, nightmare, *shuteye* (*informal*), siesta, sleep, sleeplessness, slumber, snooze (*informal*), *somnolence*, *zizz* (*informal*)

(*v*) *catch some z's* (*US informal*), catnap, conk out (*informal*), doss (*slang*), doze, doze off, drop off (*informal*), drowse, fall asleep, flake out (*slang*), go to bed, go to sleep, *have forty winks* (*informal*), hibernate, hit the hay (*informal*), hit the sack (*informal*), lie in (*informal*), nap, nod off, oversleep, sleep, sleep in, slumber, snooze (*informal*), *take a nap*, turn in (*informal*), yawn

See also TIRED, ASLEEP, AND UNCONSCIOUS (739)

725 Wake and Regain Consciousness

Was it a vision, or a waking dream?/Fled is that music:—Do I wake or sleep? **John Keats**

(*n*) wakefulness, *wakening*, *waking*

(*v*) awaken, bring round, bring to, come round, come to, come to life, *regain consciousness*, wake, waken (*formal*), wake up

See also WIDE AWAKE AND CONSCIOUS (736)

726 Reproduction and Heredity

Every baby born into the world is a finer one than the last. **Charles Dickens**

(*adj*) antenatal, asexual, barren, birth, congenital, developmental, expectant, expecting, fecund (*formal*), genetic, *gravid* (*technical*), *heavy with child* (*archaic or literary*), hereditary, heritable, inborn, inbred, infertile, innate, instinctive, *in the club* (*slang*), *in the family way* (*dated informal*), *perinatal*, postnatal, *postpartum*, pregnant, *prenatal*, *procreative*, reproductive, *sexual*, sterile, unfruitful, *with child* (*archaic or literary*)

(*adv*) hereditarily

(*n*) *artificial insemination*, *autogamy*, barrenness, birth, childbearing, childbirth, chromosome, confinement (*dated*), fecundity, fertilization, gene, gestation, *gravidity* (*technical*), *gravidness* (*technical*), infertility, *insemination*, labour, *miscarriage*, motherhood, *ovary*, *parturition* (*formal*), pregnancy, *procreation*, reproduction, RNA, self-fertilization, *sexual maturity*, sterility, *umbilicus* (*technical*)

(*v*) calve, engender (*formal*), father, fertilize, foal, incubate, *inseminate*, interbreed, mate, *procreate*, proliferate, pup, reproduce, spawn, whelp

727 Sterilize

Vasectomy means not ever having to say you're sorry. **Larry Adler**

(*n*) *castration*, *hysterectomy*, sterilization, *vasectomy*

(*v*) *castrate*, geld, neuter, spay, sterilize, *vasectomize*

728 Eggs and Spawn

A hen is only an egg's way of making another egg. **Samuel Butler**

(*n*) egg, frogspawn, *ova*, *ovule*, *ovum*, *reproductive cell*, *semen*, spawn, sperm, spermatozoon

729 Fall Ill, Treat, and Recover

A person often falls very ill in order to become someone else and then returns to health much disappointed. **Elias Canetti**

(*v*) black out, catch, come down with, contract, convalesce, cure, faint, get, go under, immunize, inject, inoculate, lose consciousness, pass out, quarantine, rebound, recover, recuperate, resurrect, resuscitate, revive, sedate, shake off, sprain, stun, tranquillize, vaccinate

See also ILL AND SICK (741)

730 Sickness

No man needs curing of his individual sickness; his universal malady is what he should look to. **Djuna Barnes**

(*adj*) allergic, cancerous, *carcinomatous*, catching, communicable, contagious, gangrenous, incurable, infectious, infective, inoperable, pathological, septic, transmissible, transmittable, waterborne

(*n*) complaint, condition, disease, disorder, epidemic, incubation, malady, malaise, malignancy, pandemic, pestilence (*archaic*), plague, puffiness, sickness, syndrome, tenderness, trouble

731 Healing

Earth hath no sorrow that heaven cannot heal. **Thomas Moore**

(*adj*) better, convalescent, curable, curative, healing, holistic, immune, on the mend, operable, recuperative

(*n*) *acupressure*, aftercare, *alternative therapy*, convalescence, cure, first aid, healing, immune system, immunity, immunization, recuperation, resuscitation, revival, vaccination

732 Remedies, Treatments, and Operations

Well, now, there's a remedy for everything except death. **Miguel de Cervantes**

(*adj*) anaesthetic, analgesic, anodyne (*literary*), depressant, medical, medicated, medicinal, pharmaceutical, stimulant, surgical, therapeutic (*n*) anaesthetic, analgesia, analgesic, biopsy, booster, capsule, checkup, depressant, drug, elixir, emollient, expectorant, facelift, ice pack, inhaler, injection, inoculation, jab (*informal*), lozenge, manipulation, medical, medicament, medication, medicine, nostrum, operation, painkiller, pharmaceutical, physical therapy (*US*), physiotherapy, pill, placebo, plastic surgery, prescription, purge, quarantine, reflexology, remedy, sedation, sedative, shot (*informal*), stimulant, stomach pump (*informal*), tablet, tampon, therapy, treatment, vaccine

(*v*) anaesthetize, put to sleep, put under

733 Illnesses and Disorders

Most of those evils we poor mortals know/From doctors and imagination flow. **Charles Churchill**

(*adj*) ingrowing

(*n*) affliction, ailment, allergy, back pain, blackout, cancer, cold, collapse, cyst, disability, disablement, fever, fit, *flu*, gall, ganglion, gangrene, growth, heart attack (*informal*), infection, influenza, lesion, polyp, RSI, *sarcoma*, *sciatica*, swoon, tumour, virus

734 Pain and other Physical Sensations

Remember that pain has this most excellent quality: if prolonged it cannot be severe, and if severe it cannot be prolonged. **Seneca the Younger**

(*adj*) aching, achy, burning, *dyspeptic*, *in pain*, itchy, numb, numbing, painful, paroxysmal, psychedelic, raw, sore, stabbing, tender, tingling, uncomfortable

(*n*) ache, aching, backache, contraction, convulsion, cramp, crick, discomfort, flush, fog, hurt, injury, irritation, itch, lumbago, numbness, pain, pang, paroxysm, pins and needles, soreness, stab, strain, stupor, suffering, tingle, turn, twinge, wound, wrench

(*v*) ache, bite, boil, burn, crick, hurt, irritate, itch, numb, prickle, smart, sting, suffer, tickle, tingle

See also PHYSICALLY UNPLEASANT (227)

735 Physical States

To animate, in the precise sense of the word: to give life to. **Federico García Lorca**

(*n*) constitution, fitness, health, healthiness

736 Wide Awake and Conscious

Music, Beauty, are within us...great works are those that awaken our spirit. **Louis-Ferdinand Céline**

(*adj*) astir, awake, aware, conscious, fresh, invigorated, *refreshed*, *reinvigorated*, *rejuvenated*, *revitalized*, *revived*, sensible (*formal*), sleepless, up, up and about, wakeful

(*n*) awareness

See also WAKE AND REGAIN CONSCIOUSNESS (725)

737 Fit and Strong

Nutritional research, like a modern star of Bethlehem, brings hope that sickness need not be a part of life. **Adelle Davis**

(*adj*) able-bodied, alive and kicking (*informal*), buff (*US informal*), *fighting fit*, fit, full-blooded, hale, *hale and hearty*, healthy, *in fine fettle*, *in good condition*, *in good form* (*US*), *in good health*, in good shape, *in peak condition*, *in shape*, lusty, mobile, red-blooded, rested, robust, sprightly, spry, well, whole

(*n*) good health, robustness, soundness, *sprightliness*, *spryness*

See also STRENGTH (202)

738 Fine

Health is the first of all liberties, and happiness gives us the energy which is the basis of health. **Henri Frédéric Amiel**

(*adj*) alive and well, all right, *in the pink* (*dated*), *on form*, *on top form*, right, safe, safe and sound, sound, unharmed, unhurt, uninjured, unscathed, untouched, whole

739 Tired, Asleep, and Unconscious

A drowsy numbness pains/My sense. **John Keats**

(*adj*) all in, anaesthetized, asleep, beat (*informal*), bleary-eyed, burned-out, bushed (*informal*), *cataleptic*, catatonic (*informal*), comatose, *conked-out* (*informal*), dead, dead beat (*informal*), deadened, dead to the world, dog-tired (*informal*), done for (*informal*), *done in* (*informal*), dormant, dozy, drained, droopy, drowsy, *enervated*, exhausted, *fast asleep*, fatigued, *fit to drop* (*informal*), footsore, frazzled (*informal*), fried (*US slang*), groggy, had it (*informal*), insensate, insensible, insentient, jaded, knackered (*slang*), knocked out, *languishing*, lethargic, lifeless, listless, logy (*US*), out, *out cold*, out for the count (*informal*), pooped (*informal*), puffed, *puffed out*, *ready to drop*, run-down, semiconscious, senseless, shattered, sleepy, *slumbering*, somnolent, soporific, sound asleep, spent, supine, tired, tired out, unconscious, washed-out, weary, whacked (*informal*), wiped out (*slang*), worn out, wrecked (*informal*)

(*adv*) blearily, dozily, groggily, lifelessly, sleepily, tiredly

(*n*) analgesia, *catalepsy*, coma, doziness, droopiness, drowsiness, *enervation*, exhaustion, fatigue, fugue, grogginess, lethargy, lifelessness, *listlessness*, loss of consciousness, morbidity, prostration, sleepiness, tiredness, unconsciousness

(*v*) exhaust, swoon, wear out

See also SLEEP AND DREAM (724)

740 Unfit and Weak

Minds like bodies, will often fall into a pimpled, ill-conditioned state from mere excess of comfort. **Charles Dickens**

(*adj*) at death's door, bedridden, below par (*informal*), burnt-out, cadaverous (*formal or literary*), crummy (*informal*), debilitated, decrepit (*archaic or humorous*), dizzy, doddery, feeble, flabby (*informal*), fragile, frail, funny, in bad shape, incapable, incapacitated, *in poor condition*, invalid, *out of condition*, *out of shape*, peaked (*US*), peaky, ropy (*informal*), run-down, sickly, the worse for wear, *under par* (*informal*), unfit, unhealthy, unsound, valetudinarian, wan, *wasting away*, weak, weedy, wobbly (*informal*)

(*adv*) dizzily, feebly

(*n*) decrepitude, dizziness, fragility, frailty, invalid, martyr, sufferer, valetudinarian, weakness

See also WEAKNESS (242)

741 Ill and Sick

To preserve one's health by too strict a regime is in itself a tedious malady. **François La Rochefoucauld**

(*adj*) ailing (*dated*), airsick, bilious, bloated, breathless, burning, burning up, carsick, delirious, diseased, *disease-ridden*, faint, febrile, gammy (*informal*), gasping, ghastly (*informal*), giddy, *green around the gills* (*informal*), grim (*informal*), ill, indisposed (*formal*), infected, infirm, inflamed, *in poor health*, laid up, light-headed, muzzy, *nauseated*, nauseous, off-colour, out of breath, out of sorts, poorly (*informal*), queasy, queer (*dated*), rabid, rotten (*informal*), rough (*informal*), seasick, seedy (*informal*), shaky, sick, squeamish, stricken, travel-sick, under the weather, unwell, woozy

(*adv*) muzzily, queasily

(*n*) airsickness, burnout, dehydration, delirium, faintness, giddiness, hotness, ill health, illness, incapacity, indisposition, infirmity, inflammation, nausea, queasiness, roughness (*informal*), *seediness* (*informal*), squeamishness, swelling, thirst, vertigo, *wooziness*

(*v*) ail (*archaic or literary*), go down with (*informal*), have, strike down

See also INJURED (743), FALL ILL, TREAT, AND RECOVER (729)

742 Under the Influence of Drugs or Alcohol

I've a head like a concertina, I've a tongue like a button-stick,/I've a mouth like an old potato, and I'm more than a little sick. **Rudyard Kipling**

(*adj*) *addicted*, *blitzed* (*informal*), *bombed* (*slang*), drunk, *happy* (*informal*), inebriated (*formal*), *intoxicated* (*formal*), *liquored up* (*US informal*), *one over the eight* (*informal*), *out of it*, *paralytic* (*informal*), *plastered* (*informal*), *rat-arsed* (*slang*), *sedated*, *soused* (*slang*), *sozzled* (*informal*), *squiffy* (*informal*), stewed (*slang*), *tanked-up* (*slang*), *three sheets to the wind* (*informal*), *tight* (*slang*), *tipsy*, wasted (*slang*)

(*n*) dependence, habit, *inebriation*, intoxication

743 Injured

This land absorbs the skins of martyrs./. . .We are its wound, but a wound that fights. **Mahmoud Darwish**

(*adj*) battered, black-and-blue, bloody, bruised, harmed, hors de combat, ill-treated, injured, livid, stiff, stricken, winded, wounded

See also ILL AND SICK (741), WOUND A PERSON OR ANIMAL (384)

The Mind and Mental Processes

744 Think and Reflect

Thinking is the most unhealthy thing in the world, and people die of it just as they die of any other disease. **Oscar Wilde**

(*n*) cogitation (*formal*), contemplation, deliberation (*formal*), heart-searching, introspection, meditation, premeditation, reflection, rethink, rumination, soul-searching

(*v*) agonize, brood, *chew on*, chew over, *chew the cud*, cogitate (*formal*), concentrate, consider, contemplate, deliberate, dwell on, entertain, flirt with, go back over, harbour, *intellectualize*, meditate, mull, mull over, muse, *perpend* (*archaic*), ponder, rack your brains, reflect, ruminate, see, speculate, think over, think through, think twice, toy with, turn over

See also ATTENTION AND ATTENTIVENESS (764)

745 Develop Theories and Reason

Nothing is so practical as a good theory. **Kurt Levin**

(*v*) abstract, assume, collude, conceive, conspire, cook up (*informal*), count, deduce, do, figure, hatch, have, hold, hypothesize, imagine, machinate, philosophize, piece out (*US*), piece together, posit (*formal*), postulate, rationalize, reason, reckon, sense, suppose, theorize, think, think up, work out

See also IDEA AND THOUGHT (771), ATTENTION AND ATTENTIVENESS (764)

746 Memory

It has memory's ear/that can hear without/having to hear. **Marianne Moore**

(*n*) flashback, hindsight, memory, recall, recognition, recollection, remembrance, reminiscence, retention, retrospect, rote, tickler (*US*)

747 Remember

Memory believes before knowing remembers. Believes longer than recollects, longer than knowing even wonders. **William Faulkner**

(*v*) bear in mind, celebrate, commemorate, *commit to memory*, keep count, keep in mind, look back, make a note of, make a point of, memorize, recall, recapture, recollect, rediscover, relive, remember, reminisce, retain

748 Remind

When you sleep you remind me of the dead. **Siegfried Sassoon**

(*v*) bring back, bring to mind, call to mind, conjure up, evoke, hark back, remind, ring a bell (*informal*), stir, stir up, suggest, take back

749 Forget, Forgive, and Accept

If there's anyone listening to whom I owe money, I'm prepared to forget it if you are. **Errol Flynn**

(*n*) acceptance, exoneration, forgiveness, vindication

(*v*) absolve, admit defeat, bow to, bury the hatchet, carry the can (*informal*), cave in, cede (*formal*), come round, come to terms with, concede, exculpate (*formal*), excuse, exempt, exonerate, face, face the music, face up to, fall for, forget, forgive, get over, give in, go along with, lap up, laugh off, leave behind, *let bygones be bygones*, let off, live down, miss, overlook, pardon, purge (*formal*), put behind you, relent, reprieve, resign yourself, set aside, submit, swallow (*informal*), take as read, take at face value, take in your stride, take on board, vindicate, waive, weaken, wipe the slate clean (*informal*), write off (*informal*)

750 Dream, Imagine, and Fantasize

The power of dreams...is tied to the multiformity of animals: with their disappearance one may soon expect the dreams to dry up as well. **Elias Canetti**

(*n*) daydream, daydreaming, imagination, make-believe, reverie, romanticism, supposition, trance, unreality, vision, visualization, *woolgathering*

(*v*) conceive, concoct, contemplate, daydream, dream, dream up, fancy, fantasize, hallucinate, have in mind, imagine, invent, make believe, make up, moon (*literary or humorous*), picture, pretend, romance, romanticize, see, see in your mind's eye, sentimentalize, suppose, visualize, *woolgather*

See also NONEXISTENT THINGS (23)

751 Predict and Anticipate

My doctor has advised me to cut back on predictions. **Conor Cruise O'Brien**

(*adj*) predicted, predictive, premonitory, prescient, prophetic

(*n*) divination, ESP, forecast, foresight, forethought, prediction, prescience, prognosis, prognostication, projection, prophecy, vision

(*v*) anticipate, await, bargain for, bargain on, bet (*informal*), conspire, contemplate, design, envisage (*formal*), envision, expect, forecast, foresee, forestall (*archaic*), foretell (*literary*), hope, lick your lips, look ahead, look forward to, predict, prejudge, presume, presuppose, prognosticate, project, prophesy, reckon on (*informal*), reckon with, scent, second-guess, take care, take for granted, trust, wait, wait on (*informal*)

See also FEELINGS ABOUT THE FUTURE (534)

752 Question Things

I am too much of a sceptic to deny the possibility of anything. **T. H. Huxley**

(*v*) call into question, canvass, daresay, debate, discredit, dispute, distrust, impugn (*formal*), inquire into, look into, query, question, speculate, suspect, wonder

See also ASK PEOPLE QUESTIONS (667)

753 Make Decisions and Choices

He had decided to live for ever or die in the attempt. **Joseph Heller**

(*n*) alternative, choice, decision, discretion, option, pleasure (*formal or literary*), resolution, resort

(*v*) agree, appoint (*formal*), arrive, burn your boats, burn your bridges, change direction, change your mind, cherry-pick, choose, choose up (*US*), come down on the side of, come to a decision, conclude, cream off, decide, designate, determine, diagnose, dispose, elect, fall back on, firm up, go for (*informal*), have second thoughts, make up your mind, mean business, mean it, opt, pick, *pick and choose*, pick out, please, plump for, postulate (*formal*), predetermine, prioritize, render (*formal*), resolve, rethink, select, set, settle on, short-list, single out, skim off, tell apart, vote

754 Examine and Assess

The examined life has always been pretty well confined to a privileged class. **Edgar Z. Friedenberg**

(*adj*) diagnostic, estimated, exploratory, investigative, probing, retrospective, supervisory, trial

(*n*) analysis, anatomy, audit, breakdown, check, comparison, criticism, crosscheck, dialectic, dissection, double check, estimate, examination, experiment, experimentation, exploration, going-over (*informal*), inquiry, inspection, investigation, once-over (*informal*), perusal, postmortem, probe, reading, reconnaissance, reconsideration, re-examination, research, revaluation, review, road test, scan, screening, scrutiny, spot check, spying, stocktaking, study, survey, test, tune-up, visitation, workup

(*v*) analyse, appraise, assay, assess, audit, audition, balance, break down, check, check out, check over, check up on, compare, consult, contrast, control, criticize, critique, crosscheck, deconstruct, delve, differentiate, dig into, dissect, distinguish, double-check, do your homework (*informal*), examine, experiment, explore, gauge, give the once-over (*informal*), go into, go over, go through, guess, inspect, investigate, judge, keep track of, look, look over, monitor, parse, pore over, probe, reappraise, reassess, reconnoitre, reconsider, re-examine, refer, referee, research, revalue, revert, review, revisit, road-test, sample, scan, screen, scrutinize, see about, set against, sleuth, sound out, spell-check, spot-check, spy, study, survey, take stock, test, try, try out, vet, view, winnow

755 Guess

What I have learned I no longer know. The little that I do know, I guessed. **Nicolas Chamfort**

(*n*) *ballpark figure* (*informal*), conjecture, educated guess, guess, guesstimate (*informal*), guesswork, surmise

(*v*) conjecture, guess, guesstimate (*informal*), surmise

756 Assess Quality

The quality of moral behaviour varies in inverse ratio to the number of human beings involved. **Aldous Huxley**

(*v*) adjudge, adjudicate, arbitrate, evaluate, examine, judge, mark, overestimate, peg, price, rank, rate, size up, stack up (*US*), umpire, *valuate*, value, weigh, weigh up

757 Have an Opinion of Something

The English think of an opinion as something which a decent person, if he has the misfortune to have one, does all he can to hide. **Margaret Halsey**

(*v*) believe, consider, deduce, deem (*formal*), judge, regard, think, view

758 Assess Quantity

Size determines an object, but scale determines art. **Robert Smithson**

(*n*) addition, approximation, estimation, summation

(*v*) add, add up, assess, balance, calculate, compute, count, count up, enumerate, estimate, fathom, judge, measure, miscount, quantify, quote, reckon, re-count, score, survey, tally, time, tot up, total

759 Read

The simpler the alphabet, the easier it is to read. **Joan Miró**

(*v*) dip into, flick through, peruse, proofread, read, reread, run through, skim, speed-read

See also SEE (700)

760 Understand and Grasp

The apprehension that one is someone else is all that one needs to believe that the world has changed from top to bottom. **Orhan Pamuk**

(*n*) appreciation, conception, grip, inference, realization, uptake

(*v*) absorb, accept, appreciate, catch on (*informal*), click (*informal*), comprehend, construe, cotton on (*informal*), dawn, digest, discern, discriminate, divine, fathom, figure out, follow, gather, get (*informal*), get it, get the drift, get the hang of, get the message (*informal*), get the picture (*informal*), *get to grips with*, *get up to speed*, grasp, intuit, latch on (*informal*), penetrate, perceive, pick up, pick up on (*informal*), plumb, realize, recognize, see, see into, see through, sense, sink in, take, take in, take on board, twig (*informal*), understand, work out

761 Solve and Interpret

Interpretation is the revenge of the intellectual upon art. **Susan Sontag**

(*v*) answer, break, crack (*informal*), decipher, decode, extrapolate, infer, interpret, make out, make sense of, penetrate, puzzle out, read, *read between the lines*, resolve, solve, suss (*informal*), translate, unlock, unravel, unscramble, work out

762 Misunderstand and Fail to Grasp

Is an intelligent human being likely to be much more than a large-scale manufacturer of misunderstanding? **Philip Roth**

(*n*) cross-purposes, delusion, misapprehension, misconstruction, misinterpretation, misjudgment, misunderstanding

(*v*) *get hold of the wrong end of the stick*, get it wrong, get the wrong end of the stick, get the wrong idea, *get the wrong impression*, misapprehend (*formal*), miscalculate, *miscomprehend*, misconceive, misconstrue, mishear, misinterpret, misjudge, *misperceive*, misread, miss, miss the point, mistake, misunderstand, mix up, take amiss, *take the wrong way*

See also MISTAKES (251)

763 Learn and Discover

The man of reflection discovers Truth; but the one who enjoys it and makes use of its heavenly gifts is the man of action. **Benito Pérez Galdós**

(*v*) accustom, acquire, ascertain (*formal*), assimilate, become aware of, catch out (*informal*), determine, discover, establish, familiarize yourself, find out, *get wind of*, hear, hit on, hit upon, internalize, learn, note, notice, observe, orient, orientate, recognize, see, spy, tell

764 Attention and Attentiveness

It's easy to get people's attention, what counts is getting their interest. **A. Philip Randolph**

(*n*) absorption, attention, attentiveness, *beguilement*, concentration, curiosity, focus, heed, intentness, interest, involvement, mind, pensiveness, spotlight, thoughtfulness, vested interest

See also THINK AND REFLECT (744), DEVELOP THEORIES AND REASON (745), PENSIVENESS AND INTEREST (539)

765 Not Pay Attention

My thoughts ran a wool-gathering; and I did like the countryman who looked for his ass while he was mounted on his back. **Miguel de Cervantes**

(*n*) abstractedness, abstraction, avoidance, circumvention, cop-out (*slang*), dreaminess, evasion, inattention, inattentiveness, neglect, negligence

(*v*) avoid, blank out, block out, blot out, blow off (*US slang*), circumvent, close your eyes to, condone, cop out (*slang*), cut out, discount, dismiss, disregard, distance, dodge, evade, exclude, fight back, forget, give a miss (*informal*), gloss over, hedge, hold in, ignore, leapfrog, leave out, let pass, let ride, mind your own business, miss out, neglect, overlook, override, pardon, pass by, pass over, *pay no attention*, *pay no heed*, put aside, rule out, shrug off, sideline, skate over (*informal*), skip, skirt, stretch a point, suppress, sweep aside, *sweep under the carpet*, *take no heed of*, take no notice of, turn a blind eye to, turn your back on, wander, wash your hands of

766 Pay Attention

The quality of your attention determines the quality of other people's thinking. **Nancy Kline**

(*v*) allow for, apply yourself, attend, be aware of, beware, consider, engage, *give heed*, hark (*literary or humorous*), heed, look out, mind, *pay attention*, *pay heed*, play safe, respect, take, take account of, take care, *take heed*, take into consideration, *take note*, *take notice*, target, watch, watch out, watch your step

767 Tolerate and Endure

We tolerate shapes in human beings that would horrify us if we saw them in a horse. **William Ralph Inge**

(*v*) abide, accept, bear, bear the brunt, bear with, brave, brave out, brook (*formal*), come out of, countenance (*formal*), endure, get a raw deal, get it in the neck (*informal*), grin and bear it (*informal*), hack (*informal*), have, hear of, hold on, hold out, hold your own, keep your chin up, live with, lump (*informal*), make allowances, make the best of a bad job, make the best of things, put on a brave front, put up with, resist, ride out, stand, stand for, *stand the pace, stay the course, stick it out*, stick out, *struggle on, struggle through*, suffer, support (*literary*), sustain, sweat out, take, take the rough with the smooth, tolerate, *tough it out* (*informal*)

768 Point of View

The worth of a man is certain only if he is prepared to sacrifice his own life for his convictions. **Henning von Tresckow**

(*n*) angle, argument, aspect, assessment, attitude, belief, *belief system*, contention, conviction, diagnosis, estimation, feeling, frame of reference, gloss, judgment, mentality, mind, mindset, opinion, orthodoxy, outlook, perception, perspective, persuasion, point, point of view, politics, position, preconception, premise, presumption, presupposition, reckoning, remonstrance, say, school of thought, sense, slant, spin (*informal*), stance, stand, standpoint, take, thoughts, understanding, vantage point, version, view, viewpoint, voice, way of thinking

769 Subject Area

There is no such thing on earth as an uninteresting subject; the only thing that can exist is an uninterested person. **G. K. Chesterton**

(*n*) area, *area of expertise, bailiwick*, branch, business, concern, consideration, department (*informal*), field, issue, jurisdiction, line, matter, motif, point, preserve, province, question, realm, remit, respect, science, specialism, speciality, specialization, sphere, *sphere of activity, sphere of influence*, subject, subject matter, talking point, territory, theme, thing, topic, turf (*informal*), world

770 Psychology and the Mind

Psychology has a long past, but only a short history. **Hermann Ebbinghaus**

(*adj*) behavioural, cognitive, compulsive, maladjusted, mental, mixed-up (*informal*), neurological, neurotic (*informal*), primeval, psychic, psychological, psychosomatic, *solipsistic*, spiritual, subconscious, subliminal, unbalanced

(*adv*) intellectually

(*n*) analysis, autosuggestion, being, cognition, complex (*informal*), conditioning, counselling, daemon, ego, frame of mind, *guilt complex*, hang-up (*informal*), inferiority complex, influence, intelligence quotient, introversion, IQ, *lateral thinking*, maladjustment, marbles (*slang*), *nervous breakdown, nervous tension*, neurosis (*dated*), person (*formal*), psyche, *psychiatry, psychoanalysis*, psychology, *psychosis, psychotherapy*, reason, self, self-esteem, self-help, self-image, self-preservation, self-worth, *solipsism*, state of mind, sublimation, superego, superiority complex, *thought processes*, unconscious, visualization, will

771 Idea and Thought

Ideas do not show themselves productive with those who suggest them. . .but with those persevering workers who feel them strongly and put all their faith and love in their efficacy. **Santiago Ramón y Cajal**

(*n*) abstraction, afterthought, *arrière-pensée* (*formal*), assumption, brainchild, brainstorm, brain wave (*informal*), caprice, concept, conception, conclusion, consideration, construct, construction, deduction, dictate, dogma, ethic, feeling, *fixed idea*, hypothesis, idea, idée fixe, illusion, image, initiative, inkling, inspiration, ism (*informal*), logic, maxim, *mental image, mental picture*, musing, notion, overview, precept (*formal*), premeditation, premise, principle, *ratiocination* (*formal*), rationale, reasoning, rhyme or reason, superstructure, supposition, teaching, tenet (*formal*), theory, thesis, thinking, thought, thread, *train of thought*, vision, whimsy

See also DEVELOP THEORIES AND REASON (745)

772 The Nature of Ideas

Many ideas grow better when transplanted into another mind than in the one where they sprang up. **Oliver Wendell Holmes, Jr.**

(*adj*) analytic, analytical, backward-looking, biased, careful, cerebral, clinical, cogent, coherent, *commonsense, commonsensical*, considered, crackpot (*informal*), critical, deductive, deep, deep-seated, deliberative (*formal*), farsighted, forward-looking, gut, half-baked (*informal*), heuristic, highbrow, idle, ill-advised, ill-conceived, ill-considered, ill-founded, ill-judged, illogical, impolitic (*formal*), in-built, injudicious, intuitive, just, knee-jerk (*informal*), liberal, lowbrow (*disapproving*), misbegotten, misconceived, misguided, modern, muddleheaded, neat, objective, obscurantist, one-sided, partial, philosophical, political, preconceived, prescriptive, pure, rational, reasoned, retrospective, sane, sensitive, serious, shallow, short-sighted, simple-minded, simplistic, slanted, stupid, subjective, tendentious, unbalanced, unbiased, unformulated, unscientific, unsound, unstated, well-advised, well-founded, well-grounded, well-thought-out, wrong-headed

(*adv*) comprehensibly, intuitively, neatly, shallowly, subjectively, unreasonably

(*n*) cogency (*formal*), fatuousness, illogicality, injudiciousness, liberalism, navel-gazing, neatness, objectivity, one-sidedness, partiality, prejudice, prescriptiveness, profoundness, profundity, sanity, subjectivity

See also DESCRIBING SOMEBODY'S INTELLECT (524)

773 Intention and Purpose

Intention is the measure for rendering actions true, so that where intention is sound action is sound, and where it is corrupt then action is corrupt. **Muhyid-Din Abu Zakariyya ibn Sharaf al-Nawawi**

(*n*) aim, butt, calculation, casuistry, design, destination, destiny, direction, end, function, goal, idea, intent (*formal*), intention, object, objective, point, pretence, purport, purpose, raison d'être, reason, scheme, sense, target, use

(*prep*) for

Philosophies, Beliefs, and Morality

774 Moral Concepts

Morality which is based on ideas, or on an ideal, is an unmitigated evil. **D. H. Lawrence**

(*n*) conscience, ethics, ethos, honesty, ideal, morality, morals, standards

See also DECEPTION AND LIES (661)

775 Morally Good

Man's goodness is a flame that can be hidden but never extinguished. **Nelson Mandela**

(*adj*) *above criticism*, aboveboard, angelic, balanced, blameless, characterful, chaste, civilizing, clean, decent, ethical, good, gracious, guiltless, harmless, honourable, humanitarian, humanizing, innocent, in the right, just, justifiable, law-abiding, meek, moral, noble, pure (*literary*), refining, reformed, right, *right and proper*, righteous, sporting, spotless, square, squeaky-clean, unblemished, undefiled, unimpeachable, unprejudiced, unspotted, upright, upstanding, virtuous, wholesome, within your rights

(*adv*) by rights, decently, deservedly, formally, *irreproachably*, justly, purely, square (*informal*)

(*n*) character, chasteness, *chastity*, citizenship, clemency, decency, devotion (*formal*), dignity, good faith, goodness, grace, *guiltlessness*, harmlessness, honour, *incorruptibility*, innocence, integrity, *irreproachability*, justice, meekness, morality, nobility, nobleness, piety, piousness, probity (*formal*), propriety, purity, rectitude, respectability, right, righteousness, *seemliness*, *social conscience*, *social responsibility*, spotlessness, uprightness, values, virtue, *virtuousness*, wholesomeness

See also EQUALITY (155), CORRECT (183), HONEST AND RELIABLE (503)

776 Morally Bad

A bad cause will ever be supported by bad means and bad men. **Thomas Paine**

(*adj*) abusive, *adulterous*, aggressive, amoral, avaricious, bad, barbaric, barbarous, base, *bawdy*, bestial, blameworthy, bloodthirsty, brutal, brutish, *carnal* (*formal*), cat-and-mouse, corrupt, criminal, culpable, dastardly, debauched, defiled (*formal*), degenerate, delinquent, depraved, dirty, discriminatory, dishonourable, disreputable, disrespectable, dubious, earthy, errant, evil, exploitative, extracurricular (*informal*), extramarital, fast, fiendish, filthy, fleshly, foul, greedy, gross, grubby, guilty, heinous, heretical, honest, ignoble, ill, immoral, impious, improper (*formal*), improper, indecent, indefensible, inequitable, infamous, iniquitous, *lascivious*, lecherous, *lewd*, *libidinous* (*formal*), *licentious* (*formal*), light-fingered, louche, *lustful*, *maleficent*, malevolent, nasty (*informal*), nefarious, notorious, obscene, off-colour (*informal*), oppressive, overindulgent, pernicious, perverted, profane, profligate, promiscuous (*disapproving*), prurient, racy, rakish, rascally, *raunchy* (*informal*), responsible, ribald, risqué, salacious, scandalous, shady, sleazy, smutty (*informal*), squalid, suggestive, *sullied*, taboo, tarnished, *tarty*, to blame, treasonable, *unchaste*, unclean, *unconsecrated*, unequal, unethical, unfair, ungodly, unhealthy, unholy, uninhibited, unmerited, unprincipled, unprintable, unprofessional, unreasonable, unrighteous, unsavoury, unworthy, venal, vicious, vile, villainous, violent, vulgar, wanton, wicked, wrong

(*adv*) contemptibly, discreditably, faithlessly, grossly, improperly, oppressively, *profanely* (*formal*), *rakishly*, unequally, unscrupulously, viciously, wrongfully, wrongly

(*n*) *adultery*, amorality, arrogance, avarice, avariciousness, badness, barbarism, barbarity, baseness, bestiality, bigotry, blame, bloodthirstiness, *carnality* (*formal*), coercion, corruption, *corruptness*, covetousness, crime, culpability, cupidity (*formal*), debauchery, decadence, degeneracy, delinquency (*formal*), depravity, despotism, evil, evilness, excess, excesses, fault, filth, filthiness, foulness, foul play, gluttony, greed, greediness, grubbiness, guilt, guiltiness, heresy, immorality, impiety, impiousness, *improbity* (*formal*), incorrectness, indecency, inequity (*formal*), infection, infidelity, iniquity, injustice, intemperance, *lewdness*, licence, *licentiousness* (*formal*), *maleficence*, malevolence, *malfeasance*, misbehaviour, misconduct, misdeed (*formal*), *nefariousness*, obscenity, opportunism, opportunistic, overindulgence, peccadillo, perniciousness, pride, *profanation* (*formal*), *prurience*, shadiness, sin, sleaze, *sleaziness*, smut, *smuttiness* (*informal*), sordidness, squalor, *torridness*, treason, turpitude (*formal or literary*), *unchasteness*, uncleanness, unfairness, *unsavouriness*, unscrupulousness, unseemliness, unwholesomeness, unworthiness, vanity, *venality*, vice, vileness, villainy, vulgarity, wantonness, wickedness, worldliness, wrong

See also INCORRECT AND ERRONEOUS (223), ILLEGAL (816), DECEITFUL (514)

777 Religious Concepts

Things divine are believed in/But by those who themselves are so. **Friedrich Hölderlin**

(*adj*) baptismal, biblical, blasphemous, blessed, celestial, cherubic, clerical, consecrated, devout, divine, fleshly, *godless*, godly (*formal*), hallowed, heavenly, holy, irreligious, mortal, pious, *precatory* (*formal*), religious, revered, sacred, sacrilegious, sacrosanct, saintly, sanctified, secular, sinful, *sinless*, solemn, spiritual, temporal, theological, transcendent, transcendental, ungodly, unholy, unspiritual, votive

(*adv*) devoutly

(*n*) *act of contrition*, afterlife, angel, apocalypse, *archangel*, Armageddon, blasphemer, blasphemy, bull, catechism, cherub, consecration, credo, *Day of Judgment*, deity, devoutness, *divine intervention*, doomsday, *eternal life*, *evil spirit*, faith, *fire and brimstone*, *fundamentalism*, god, goddess, *godlessness*, godliness, grace, heaven, hell (*formal*), *heretic*, holiness, *holy day*, *holy of holies*, *holy rites*, inferno, *Judgment Day*, karma, libation, *limbo*, monotheism, nether world (*formal*), *next world*, nirvana, paradise, pardon, perdition, polytheism, *promised land*, reincarnation, religiousness, *sacredness*, sacrilege, saintliness, *saint's day*, *sanctification*, sanctity, *seraph*, sin, *sinfulness*, *sinner*, soul, spirit, *spiritual enlightenment*, spirituality, theism, theology, transcendence, unbelief, *ungodliness*

778 Religions and Religious Practices

The mystical and the ethical...There is no holiness and therefore no living religion without both elements. **Paul Tillich**

(*adj*) devotional, ecclesiastical, evangelical, interdenominational, pontifical, priestly (*formal or literary*), reverend, sacerdotal, sectarian

(*n*) absolution, adoration, beatification, blessing, canonization, catechism, christening, creed, devotions, dirge, excommunication, incantation, invocation, litany, liturgy, mantra, ordination, pilgrimage, praise, prayer, purdah, religion, requiem, rite, ritual, sacrament, sermon, service, tithe

(*v*) adore, baptize, bless, *catechize*, christen, consecrate, defile (*formal*), *evangelize*, excommunicate, expiate, hallow, praise, pray, sanctify, sin, solemnize, worship

See also INSTITUTIONS (791)

779 Religious People

Religions, which condemn the pleasures of sense, drive men to seek the pleasures of power. **Bertrand Russell**

(*n*) *abbot*, apostle, *archbishop*, *archbishopric*, *army chaplain*, believer, *bishop*, *bishopric*, *catechesis*, chaplain, churchgoer, clergy, *clergyman*, *clergywoman*, cleric, *communicant*, congregation, cult, *druid*, ecclesiastic, *evangelist*, father, *friar*, *fundamentalist*, guru, *Holy Father*, *holy man*, *holy sister*, laity, lama, maharishi, martyr, minister, missionary, monk, nonbeliever, *nun*, *padre*, *parish priest*, parson, pastor, patriarch, pontiff, pope, preacher, prelate, *presbyter*, priest, priesthood, primacy, primate, *prison chaplain*, pulpit, rabbi, rector, reverend, *saint*, *shaman*, *shamanism*, sister, *spiritual guide*, *spiritual leader*, *swami*, unbeliever, *vestal* (*literary*), *vicar*, visionary, worshipper

780 Religious Objects

Holy images...perfect our understanding, move our will, refresh our memory of divine things. **Francisco Pacheco**

(*n*) breviary, crèche, cross, idol, missal, *paten*, *prayer book*, psalm, psalter, pulpit, reliquary, shrine

See also PARTS OF RELIGIOUS BUILDINGS (1085)

781 Philosophies and Beliefs

Philosophy is the childhood of the intellect, and a culture that tries to skip it will never grow up. **Thomas Nagel**

(*adj*) atheistic, ideological, *Leninist*, *Maoist*, *Marxist*, metaphysical, militarist, militaristic, nationalistic, nihilistic, patriotic, philosophic, relativist, utopian

(*n*) atheism, communism, culture, empiricism, fatalism, feminism, free will, ideology, *leftism*, *Leninism*, liberty, *Maoism*, *Marxism*, materialism, militarism, nationalism, nihilism, *pantheism*, patriotism, philosophy, progressivism, radicalism, relativism, traditionalism, *Trotskyism*

782 Philosophical and Political Thinkers

The philosophers have only interpreted the world in various ways; the point is to change it. **Karl Marx**

(*n*) agnostic, anarchist, atheist, bolshevik (*informal*), bolshie (*informal dated*), communist, ecologist, empiricist, environmentalist, *existentialist*, extremist, feminist, freethinker, *leftie* (*informal*), *leftist*, left-winger, missionary, modernizer, moralist, nihilist, pacifist, philosopher, realist, reformer, reformist, relativist, revisionist, right-winger, *social democrat*, socialist, stoic, supremacist, theorist, thinker, traditionalist, utopian

783 Fate, Destiny, and Astrology

There's a divinity that shapes our ends,/Rough-hew them how we will. **William Shakespeare**

(*adj*) astral, astrological, destined, doomed, fated, meant, predestined, predetermined, providential, unlucky, zodiacal

(*n*) astrologer, *astrologist*, astrology, *birth sign*, destiny, doom, fate, fortune, kismet, lot, luck, nemesis (*literary*), portion (*literary*), predestination, predetermination, providence, sign, star sign, zodiac

types of star sign Aquarius, Aries, Cancer, Capricorn, Gemini, Leo, Libra, Pisces, Sagittarius, Scorpio, Taurus, Virgo

784 Luck

Fortune is for all; judgment is theirs who have won it for themselves. **Aeschylus**

(*adj*) charmed, felicitous, *fluky* (*informal*), fortunate, happy, *in luck*, jammy (*informal*), lucky, merciful, providential, well-off

(*adv*) fortunately, happily, providentially, thankfully (*informal*)

(*n*) fortune, good fortune, *happenchance*, lottery, luck, *luck of the draw*, *lucky break*, lucky dip, potluck, serendipity, *stroke of luck*

See also CHANCE EVENT (36)

785 Bad Luck and Unlucky

We are all strong enough to bear the misfortunes of others. **François La Rochefoucauld**

(*adj*) accident-prone, accursed (*archaic or literary*), fateful, hapless, ill-fated, ill-starred (*formal*), luckless, star-crossed, unfortunate, unhappy, unlucky

(*adv*) unluckily

(*n*) bad luck, haplessness, hex, malediction (*formal*), mischance, unfortunate, unluckiness, wretch

786 Lucky Charms

It is the customary fate of new truths to begin as heresies and to end as superstitions. **T. H. Huxley**

(*n*) fetish, *good luck charm*, horseshoe, *juju*, lucky charm, mascot, philtre (*literary*), talisman, totem

787 Chance, Coincidence, and Accident

Time/moves about/dressed/in fortune/or misfortune. **Johannes Bobrowski**

(*adj*) accidental, casual, chance, coincidental, fortuitous

(*adv*) by chance, by coincidence, coincidentally

(*n*) accident, chance, toss-up

See also UNINTENTIONAL AND ACCIDENTAL (282)

788 The Supernatural

Religion/Has made an honest woman of the supernatural,/And we won't have it kicking over the traces again. **Christopher Fry**

(*adj*) clairvoyant, extrasensory, magic, magical, mystic, mystical, *occult*, *oracular*, *paranormal*, *parapsychological*, premonitory, preternatural (*literary*), psychic, psychical, *second-sighted*, *sidereal*, spectral, supernatural, *telekinetic*, telepathic, *vatic*

(*interj*) abracadabra

(*n*) apparition, augury, banshee, *black magic*, clairvoyance, demon, *extrasensory perception*, *fortune telling*, *ghost*, *ghoul*, *ghoulishness*, intuition, magic, phantasm, phantom, poltergeist, premonition, presage, presence, second sight, shadow, sixth sense, sorcery, spectre, spell, spirit, *spirit world*, spook (*informal*), superstition, telepathy, *thought transference*, *voodoo*, *witchcraft*, *witchery*, wizardry, wraith

789 People with Supernatural Powers

Mystics always hope that science will some day overtake them. **Booth Tarkington**

(*n*) clairvoyant, *faith healer*, fortune-teller, magician, *magus*, mystic, *occultist*, oracle, *parapsychologist*, prognosticator, prophet, psychic, seer, *sibyl*, soothsayer, sorcerer, sorceress, spiritualist, *telepathist*, warlock, witch, witch doctor, wizard

790 Mythical Beings

There is precious little in civilization to appeal to a Yeti. **Edmund Hillary**

(*n*) Abominable Snowman, *Bigfoot*, bogey, bugaboo, daemon, dryad, elf, fairy, *fay* (*literary*), genie, *giant*, gnome, goblin, hobgoblin, imp, leprechaun, little people, *naiad*, nymph, ogre, pixie, sasquatch, sprite, sylph, troll, *wood nymph*, *yeti*

See also MYTHICAL CREATURES (1036), NONEXISTENT THINGS (23)

Social Structures and Institutions

791 Institutions

Any institution which does not suppose the people good, and the magistrate corruptible, is evil. **Maximilien Robespierre**

(*n*) agency, authority, body, brotherhood, establishment, federation, fellowship, guild, infrastructure, institute, institution, polity, steering committee

See also RELIGIONS AND RELIGIOUS PRACTICES (778)

792 Business

What good is the moon if you cannot buy it or sell it? **Ivan Boesky**

(*adj*) business, commercial, corporate, entrepreneurial, industrial, mercantile

(*n*) big business, business, commerce, direction, industry, marketplace

See also PROFESSIONS (845)

793 Business Enterprises and Related Bodies

CORPORATION, *n. An ingenious device for securing individual profit without individual responsibility.* **Ambrose Bierce**

(*n*) business, chain, combine, company, concern, concession (*US*), conglomerate, consortium, co-op (*informal*), corporation, dealership, enterprise, firm, house, *joint-stock company*, *joint venture*, labor union (*US*), limited company, *limited liability company*, multinational, operation, outlet, partnership, *PLC*, presidium, *public limited company*, subsidiary, trade, *trade union*, transnational, tribunal, venture, watchdog

See also GROUPS WITH A COMMON INTEREST (938)

794 Business People

If you drag an executive away from business, he goes on running on the spot, pawing the ground, talking business. **Jean Baudrillard**

(*n*) adventurer, advertiser, bidder, businessperson, capitalist, *captain of industry*, CEO, chair, chairperson, chief executive, C in C, contractor, developer, director, directorate, director-general, directorship, distributor, entrepreneur, *exec* (*informal*), executive, hotelier, importer, industrialist, landlady, landlord, manager, *MD*, member, merchant, middleman, officer, official, payer, promoter, secretary-general, shopkeeper, stockholder, *tradesperson*, treasurer, trustee, tycoon, vested interest, wheeler-dealer (*informal*), wholesaler

795 Business Activities and Phenomena

Commerce is the art of exploiting the need or desire someone has for something. **Edmond de Goncourt**

(*n*) aftercare, asset-stripping, booking, business, buyout, client, clientele, custom, end user, flotation, import, importation, industrial espionage, liquidation, management, marketing, merger, monopoly, privatization, procurement, protectiveness, purchase, receivership, reservation, retail, retrenchment, sale, salesperson, selling, soft sell (*informal*), sponsorship, stocktaking, supervision, telemarketing, telesales

(*v*) axe, downsize, go bust (*informal*), go out of business, go to the wall, knock off (*informal*), liquidate, open up, package, privatize, retrench, revalue, shut up shop, subcontract, traffic, wind up

796 Business Products

Creation comes before distribution—or there will be nothing to distribute. **Ayn Rand**

(*n*) commodity, goods, merchandise, productivity, services, stock-in-trade, turnover, wares

(*v*) underwrite

797 Finance and Economics

Economics is as much a study in fantasy and aspiration as in hard numbers—maybe more so. **Theodore Roszak**

(*adj*) *accounting*, budgetary, economic, financial, in debit, inflationary, lossmaking, monetary, negotiable, nonnegotiable, pecuniary, proprietary, recessionary

798 Currencies

Finance is the art of passing currency from hand to hand until it finally disappears. **Robert W. Sarnoff**

(*n*) banknote, buck (*US informal*), currency, dollar, *fiver*, pound, *quid* (*informal*), *tenner* (*informal*)

See also MONEY (140)

799 Accounting, Banking, and Budgeting

Capital accounting in its formally most rational shape...presupposes the battle of man with man. **Max Weber**

(*n*) account, *account holder*, accounts, advance, assessment, ATM (*US*), bank account, banking, bankruptcy, budget, *building society*, cashpoint, cost-cutting, crash, debit, expenses, fund, funding, futures, insolvency, loan, mortgage, nonpayment, payroll, *profit and loss*, *profit margin*, spending, stock exchange, stock market, swipe card, turnover

(*v*) appreciate, bank, crash, fund, mortgage, negotiate, pay in, reflate

800 Money, Payments, and Charges

Money differs from an automobile, a mistress, or cancer in being equally important to those who have it and those who do not. **J. K. Galbraith**

(*n*) abatement, airfare, alimony, blood money, capitation, damages, deposit, discount, dividend, down payment, fee, finance, finances, going rate, *golden handshake* (*informal*), *golden parachute* (*informal*), maintenance, markdown, mark-up, money, nonperformance (*US*), outflow, overheads, pension, petty cash, premium, rake-off (*informal*), rebate, remittance, rental, reparation, repayment, reserves, retainer, saving, scholarship, security, seed capital, seed money, settlement, severance, stake, stocks, student loan, subvention (*formal*), support, surcharge, tariff, worth

(*v*) discharge (*formal*), discount, impose, levy, overprice, surcharge

See also MONEY (140), EXPENDITURE (424)

801 Insurance

INSURANCE, n. An ingenious modern game of chance in which the player is permitted to enjoy the comfortable conviction that he is beating the man who keeps the table. **Ambrose Bierce**

(*n*) collateral, deposit, insurance, insurance policy, insurer, reinsurance, surety

(*v*) indemnify, insure, reinsure, secure

802 Tax and Taxation

He's spending a year dead for tax reasons. **Douglas Adams**

(*adj*) chargeable, duty-free (*informal*), net, taxable, tax-exempt, *tax free*

(*n*) capitation, dues, duty, income tax, levy, *pay-as-you-earn*, PAYE, *revenue system*, surtax, tariff, tax, taxation, *taxpayer*, *tax policy*, *tax system*, tribute, *VAT*

(*v*) tax

803 Market Forces

It doesn't take much to derail a market that has gone to the moon. **Stephen S. Roach**

(*n*) deflation, depression, devaluation, downswing, downturn, inflation, recession, reflation, slump, stagflation

804 People Involved in Finance

A baited banker thus desponds...They have his soul, who have his bonds. **Jonathan Swift**

(*n*) accountant, *accounts clerk*, *actuary*, analyst, auditor, banker, *bookkeeper*, broker, cashier, *chartered accountant*, dealer, debtor, defaulter, depositor, financier, guarantor, investor, lender, liquidator, *market analyst*, moneylender, payee, *securities broker*, *shareholder*, signatory, speculator, stakeholder, stockbroker, teller, tipster, *venture capitalist*

See also OFFICE WORKERS (847)

805 Government and Politics

Governments need to have both shepherds and butchers. **Voltaire**

(*adj*) governmental, home, interstate, legislative, ministerial, political, state

(*n*) establishment, government, politics, regime, statecraft

See also SOCIAL, POLITICAL, AND ECONOMIC CHANGE (374)

806 Styles and Systems of Government

The voice of the people is the voice of God. **Kemal Ataturk**

(*adj*) autocratic, autonomous, bicameral, bipartisan, bureaucratic, capitalist, centrist, collectivist, colonial, colonialist, counter-revolutionary, democratic, diplomatic, *expansionist*, federal, feudal, industrialized, internationalist, left-wing, monopolistic, nonaligned, noninterventionist, parliamentary, patriarchal, populist, presidential, protectionist, republican, revisionist, rightist, right-wing, self-governing, sovereign, totalitarian, true-blue, undemocratic

(*n*) absolutism, autarchy, authoritarianism, autocracy, autonomy, bureaucracy, centralism, centre, collectivism, colonial, colonialism, colonization, decentralization, democracy, devolution, dictatorship, *expansionism*, home rule, imperialism, isolationism, junta, martial law, *military government*, *military rule*, misrule, monarchism, nationalism, nonalignment, nonintervention, obscurantism, *ochlocracy*, *parliamentary government*, protectionism, protectionist, raison d'état, *realpolitik*, regionalism, republicanism, reunification, revisionism, self-determination, self-government, self-rule, *social democracy*, socialism, *sovereign state*, supremacy, *system of government*, totalitarianism, *tsarism*

See also SOCIAL, POLITICAL, AND ECONOMIC CHANGE (374)

807 Elections and Suffrage

The vote is the most powerful instrument ever devised by man for breaking down injustice. **Lyndon Baines Johnson**

(*adj*) elected, elective, electoral

(*n*) abstainer, abstention, ballot, by-election, candidacy, census, election, elector, electorate, enfranchisement, *general election*, plebiscite, poll, polling, polling booth, putsch, referendum, *secret ballot*, straw poll, *suffrage*, *suffragette*, vote, voter

(*v*) abstain, campaign, canvass, electioneer, enfranchise, naturalize, re-elect

808 Political Offices and Politicians

The politician is an acrobat. He keeps his balance by saying the opposite of what he does. **Maurice Barrès**

(*n*) administrator, attaché, bureaucrat, chancellor, commissioner, congressperson, consul, democrat, diplomat, *frontbencher*, governorship, head of government, head of state, incumbent, lawmaker, mandarin, mandate, *member of parliament*, *MP*, nationalist, office holder, parliamentarian, *PM*, politician, premier, premiership, presidency, president, prime minister, republican, senator, spin doctor (*informal*), strategist, tactician

See also OFFICE WORKERS (847)

809 Legislative Bodies and Legislation

A parliament can do any thing but make a man a woman, and a woman a man. **Earl of Pembroke**

(*n*) administration, assembly, bureau, CIA, constitution, diet, embargo, injunction, junta, legislature, parliament, ruling body, senate, think-tank

810 Government Policies

Our policy is directed not against any country or doctrine but against hunger, poverty, desperation, and chaos. **George Marshall**

(*n*) activism, centralization, diplomacy, infiltration, party line, platform, politicking, *spin doctoring* (*slang*)

811 Administrative Officers

A civil servant doesn't make jokes. **Eugène Ionesco**

(*n*) chamberlain, civil servant, council, customs, diplomat, embassy, mission, officialdom (*informal*), registrar, registration, registry

812 Social Welfare

In place of the conception of the Power-State we are led to that of the Welfare-State. **William Temple**

(*n*) benefit, *public amenities*, *public services*, *public transport*, sanitation, services, supervision order, welfare (*US*)

813 Educational Institutions

Education is a leading out of what is already there in the pupil's soul. **Muriel Spark**

(*n*) *academe* (*formal*), academia, *academic circles*, *academic world*, alma mater, classroom, college, *college of further education*, *conservatoire*, conservatory, crèche, ivory tower, *medical school*, nursery, playschool, *poly* (*informal*), polytechnic, school, *school of dance*, *school of the arts*, seminary, studio, *tech* (*informal*), *technical college*, *theological college*, *training college*, university

types of school academy, boarding school, comprehensive, elementary school (*US*), grade school (*US*), grammar school, high school, infant school, junior high (*US*), junior school, kindergarten (*US*), middle school, nursery school, prep school, preschool, primary school, private school, public school, state school, vocational school (*US*)

See also EDUCATION (838)

814 The Law and Legal Authority

The big print giveth and the fine print taketh away. **Fulton J. Sheen**

(*n*) act, ban, bylaw, civil liberties, civil rights, criminalization, human rights, judiciary, jurisdiction, law, law and order, legislation, liability, penalization, probate, prohibition, right, rule, statute, statute book, statute law

815 Legal

When the President does it, that means it is not illegal. **Richard Nixon**

(*adj*) allowed, authorized, constitutional, endorsed, judicial, lawful, legal, *legit* (*slang*), legitimate, licit, rightful, statutory, unconstitutional, valid

(*adv*) aboveboard, legitimately, rightly

(*n*) legality, legitimacy, rightfulness, validation

See also MORALLY GOOD (775)

816 Illegal

People got so used to staying indoors/that curfews were declared illegal. **Can Yücel**

(*adj*) actionable, *against the law*, banned, bigamous, *bookable*, bootleg, chargeable, criminal, *felonious*, illegal, illegitimate, ill-gotten, illicit, indictable, *larcenous*, libellous, litigable, null, null and void, piratic, prohibited, unauthorized, under-the-counter, underworld, unlawful, unofficial, *usurious*, wrongful

(*adv*) criminally, wrongfully

(*n*) illegality, *illicitness*, *unlawfulness*

See also MORALLY BAD (776)

817 Crimes

How many crimes committed merely because their authors could not endure being wrong! **Albert Camus**

(*n*) abduction, *aggravated burglary*, *armed robbery*, arson, banditry, bigamy, blackmail, breach of the peace, break-in, breaking, *breaking and entering*, bribery, burglary, *carjacking*, *car theft*, corruption, crime, criminality, despoliation, *disorderly conduct*, embezzlement, extortion, felony, fiddle (*informal*), fiddling (*informal*), forgery, fraud, gangland, heist (*US slang*), *highway robbery* (*US informal*), hijack, holdup, illegality, infraction, infringement, joyride, joyriding, larceny (*dated*), libel, misappropriation, misdemeanour, mugging, offence, *organized crime*, *petty larceny*, *pilfering*, plagiarism, *public disturbance*, *public nuisance*, racket (*informal*), *racketeering*, robbery, *shakedown* (*US slang*), shoplifting, stealing, stickup (*US informal*), terrorism, theft, *thieving*, tort, *twoc* (*slang*), *unlawful act*, *unlawful activity*, usury, wrongdoing, *wrongful act*

See also STEAL AND ROB (427)

818 The Police, Arrest, and Pre-Trial Proceedings

Police and government officials have contempt for innocence; they are, in some way, offended by an innocent man. **Walter Mosley**

(*n*) *agent provocateur*, arrest, bobby (*dated informal*), bust (*slang*), charge, *constable*, *constabulary*, detective, *drug squad*, *fraud squad*, *judicial proceedings*, *law enforcement agency* (*US*), *law enforcement officer*, *legislator*, *litigant*, marshal, officer, *PC*, police, *police cadet*, *police constable*, *police department* (*US*), police force, police officer, policeman, policewoman, polygraph, private detective, private eye (*informal*), private investigator, *riot police*, sleuth (*informal*), *vice squad*

(*v*) apprehend, arrest, bust, detain, imprison, incarcerate (*formal*), intern, jail, lock up, nab (*informal*), put away (*informal*), *put behind bars*, *put in jail*, *put in prison*, send down (*slang*), take into custody

See also CAPTIVITY AND LOSS OF FREEDOM (249), BUILDINGS FOR CONFINING PEOPLE (1093)

819 Trial, Punishment, and Legal Outcomes

Punishment has passed from being an art of unsupportable sensations to an economy of suspended rights. **Michel Foucault**

(*adj*) disciplinary, penal

(*n*) acquittal, action, adjudication, amnesty, *appellant*, arraignment, assize (*US*), assizes, award, bail, bill, call, *capital punishment*, case, condemnation, conviction, court, court case, courthouse, court order, criminalization, cross-examination, cross-questioning, decriminalization, defence, deposition, discipline, exculpation (*formal*), finding, fine, forfeiture, gagging order, hearing, high court, indictment, industrial tribunal, jury, lawsuit, legal eagle (*slang*), legalization, litigation, miscarriage of justice, mistrial, parole, penalty, plaint, plaintiff, plea, prosecution, recidivism, *release on bail*, remand, reprieve, restraining order, ruling, sentence, subpoena, summons, suspect, suspended sentence, trial, tribunal, verdict, writ

(*v*) acquit, adjudge, arraign, bail out, condemn, convict, criminalize, cross-question, discipline, fine, hear, impeach, indict, legalize, legislate, litigate, notarize, parole, plea-bargain, prosecute, *release on parole*, remand, sentence, subpoena, sue, take legal action, take to court, try, validate

820 People in Law Courts

If there were no bad people there would be no good lawyers. **Charles Dickens**

(*n*) accuser, attorney (*US*), *attorney at law* (*US*), bailiff, barrister, brief (*informal*), *criminal lawyer* (*US*), defendant, *district attorney* (*US*), investigator, JP, judge, juror, justice, *Justice of the Peace*, lawgiver, lawyer, magistrate, notary, *prosecuting attorney*, prosecutor (*US*), *public defender* (*US*), *public prosecutor*, QC, *Queen's Counsel*, respondent, *sheriff* (*US*), *sheriff's officer* (*US*), solicitor, *trial lawyer*

See also SURVEYORS, EXAMINERS, AND JUDGES (853)

821 Criminals

What man have you ever seen who was content with one crime only? **Juvenal**

(*n*) abductor, accessory, accomplice, arsonist, assassin, *bag-snatcher*, bandit, bigamist, blackmailer, brigand (*literary*), burglar, captor, *carjacker*, *car thief*, *cat burglar*, *cattle thief*, counterfeiter, criminal, *criminal world*, crook (*informal*), culprit, delinquent, embezzler, felon, forger, gangster, *guilty party*, *hardened criminal*, hit squad (*slang*), *horse thief*, *housebreaker* (*US*), incendiary (*formal*), joyrider, *kidnapper*, *larcenist*, lawbreaker, looter, mafia, *Mafioso*, malefactor (*formal*), mugger, *nether world* (*literary*), offender, *old lag* (*slang*), partner in crime, *Peeping Tom*, *perp* (*US slang*), perpetrator, *petty thief*, pickpocket, pilferer, pillager, plagiarist, poacher, *purse snatcher* (*US*), racketeer, raider, ram-raider, recidivist, *reoffender*, *repeat offender*, ring, robber, rustler, sneak thief, stalker, terrorist, thief, transgressor, trespasser, *twoccer* (*slang*), underworld, *usurer*, villain (*slang*)

See also STEAL AND ROB (427), VILLAINS AND THUGS (947), CAPTIVES AND PRISONERS (250)

822 Charity and Charitable Institutions

In charity there is no excess. **Francis Bacon**

(*adj*) nonprofitmaking

(*n*) *aid agency*, *aid organization*, *charitable foundation*, *charitable organization*, *charitable trust*, charity, foundation, fundraiser, good cause, orphanage

823 Rulers and Aristocracy

A monarchy is a merchantman which sails well, but will sometimes strike a rock, and go to the bottom; whilst a republic is a raft which would never sink, but then your feet are always in the water. **Fisher Ames**

(*n*) emir, emperor, empress, monarch, noble, nobleman, noblewoman, patrician, peer, peerage, peer of the realm, Pharaoh, potentate, rajah, rani, regent, *royal family*, royals, royalty, ruler, sovereign, *sultan*, suzerain, *tsar*, *tsarina*, *tsaritsa*

types of aristocrat baron, baroness, baronet, count, countess, crown prince, duchess, duke, earl, king, knight, maharajah, maharani, marchioness, marquess, prince, princess, queen, viscount, viscountess

824 Realms and Rules

The king, and his faithful subjects, the lords and commons of this realm, the triple cord, which no man can break. **Edmund Burke**

(*n*) *demesne* (*formal*), duchy, dynasty, kingdom, monarchy, reign, rule, throne

825 Royalness

That perfect bliss and sole felicity,/The sweet fruition of an earthly crown. **Christopher Marlowe**

(*adj*) imperial, kingly, queenly, regal, royal, state, stately

(*adv*) royally

(*n*) kingship, sovereignty, state, stateliness

826 Hospitals and Clinics

There they stand, isolated, majestic, imperious...the asylums which our forefathers built with such immense solidity to express the notions of their day. **Enoch Powell**

(*n*) clinic, hospice, hospital, infirmary, intensive care, intensive care unit, *nursing home*, *residential care*, *residential home*, *rest home*, sanatorium, sickbay

See also PEOPLE WHO WORK IN MEDICINE (848)

827 The Armed Forces

If you don't want to use the army, I should like to borrow it for a while. Yours respectfully, A. Lincoln. **Abraham Lincoln**

(*n*) *airborne army*, *air force*, airpower, armed forces, *armed services*, army, cavalry, corps, defence force, forces, *ground forces*, *infantry*, *land army*, land forces, *merchant navy*, military, *military establishment*, *military unit*, militia, *national guard*, navy, services, *territorial army*, *troops*, vanguard

828 Military Personnel

The soldier's body becomes a stock of accessories that are not his property. **Antoine de Saint-Exupéry**

(*n*) adjutant, aide-de-camp, *army cadet*, *artilleryman*, *bombardier*, *brigadier*, *colonel*, *combat officer*, commandant, commander, *commando*, conscript, detachment, detail, *dog of war*, *field marshal*, *fusilier*, GI, gunner, *legionnaire*, line officer, mercenary, *military attaché*, noncombatant, officer, paramilitary, patrol, platoon, rating, regiment, regular, reservist, *rifleman*, soldier, squaddie (*slang*), squadron, warhorse, warlord, warrior

See also PROFESSIONS (845)

829 Military

When I was in the military, they gave me a medal for killing two men, and a discharge for loving one. **Leonard Matlovich**

(*adj*) armed, gung ho (*informal*), martial, militarized, military, paramilitary, warlike

830 Warfare and War

What they could do with round here is a good war. **Bertolt Brecht**

(*n*) *airborne operation*, *air offensive*, armament, *arms reduction*, *army camp*, battlefield, battleground, blitz, *blitzkrieg*, call-up, charge, combat zone, conscription, disarmament, engagement, exercises, firing line, operation, rearmament, *saturation bombing*, *shelling*, strafe, war, warfare

(*v*) battle, blitz, bomb, conscript, fight, join up, outflank

Work and Leisure: Lifestyles and the Home

831 Employment Status

The test of a vocation is the love of the drudgery it involves. **Logan Pearsall Smith**

(*adj*) active, amateur, employed, freelance, honorary, incumbent (*formal*), *in employment*, *in work*, jobbing, jobless, *laid off*, off duty, *on benefit*, on call, *on the dole* (*informal*), *on unemployment* (*US*), *on welfare* (*US*), part-time, peripatetic, probationary, professional, *receiving benefit*, redundant, retired, salaried, self-employed, unemployed, unpaid, *unsalaried*, unwaged, vocational, voluntary, *waged*, working, *working from home*

(*adv*) professionally

832 Place of Employment

Stick close to your desks and never go to sea,/And you all may be Rulers of the Queen's Navee! **W. S. Gilbert**

(*n*) base, branch, cooperative, dealership, head office, headquarters, kibbutz, ministry, office, shop, studio, sweatshop, workplace, workroom, workspace, workstation

833 Job

It's a recession when your neighbour loses his job; it's a depression when you lose yours. **Harry S. Truman**

(*n*) appointment, assignment, capacity, commission, duty, engagement, incumbency (*formal*), internship (*US*), job, labour, livelihood, part, placement, post, posting, presidency, residency, role, situation (*formal*), vacancy, work

See also WORK IN GENERAL (298)

834 Work-Related Activities

There is dignity in work only when it is work freely accepted. **Albert Camus**

(*n*) absenteeism, *admin*, administration, appointment, employ, employment, fire practice, furlough (*US*), go-slow, incumbency (*formal*), industrial action, *joblessness*, job-sharing, layoff, overtime, paperwork, patrol, picket, recruitment, redundancy, shutdown, stoppage, strike, unemployment, walkout, weighting, work-to-rule

(*v*) employ, engage, moonlight (*informal*), recruit, resign, retire, serve, strike, temp, walk out, work, work to rule

835 Types of Work

The price one pays for pursuing any profession or calling is an intimate knowledge of its ugly side. **James Baldwin**

(*adj*) administrative, blue-collar, clerical, executive, in-service, managerial, manual, nonprofessional, occupational, organizational, paid, sedentary, stipendiary, white-collar

(*adv*) cash-in-hand

(*n*) *casual work*, *freelancing*, *homeworking*, *manual labour*, *outworking*, *part-time work*, piecework, telecommuting, teleworking

836 Worker

The worker becomes an ever cheaper commodity the more commodities he creates. **Karl Marx**

(*n*) applicant, aspirant, breadwinner, *casual worker*, *commuter*, *dogsbody* (*informal*), drudge, *factory worker*, *freelancer*, full-timer, gofer (*informal*), hack (*informal*), *homeworker*, *job-sharer*, labourer, labour force, *manual labourer*, *manual worker*, *office worker*, operative, operator, *outworker*, *paper-pusher* (*informal*), part-timer, *part-time worker*, *pencil pusher* (*US*), penpusher (*informal*), performer, *portfolio worker*, *seasonal worker*, servant, signing, soldier, stipendiary, striker, technician, technologist, telecommuter, teleworker, *toiler*, trier, volunteer, wage earner, workaholic, worker, working group, working party

See also SUBORDINATES AND ASSISTANTS (966), COLLEAGUES AND EQUALS (967), BOSSES AND MANAGEMENT (965)

837 The Work Force

The only irreplaceable capital an organization possesses is the knowledge and ability of its people. **Andrew Carnegie**

(*n*) crew, labour, personnel, staff, workforce

838 Education

Education is simply the soul of a society as it passes from one generation to another. **G. K. Chesterton**

(*adj*) academic, collegial, extramural, intramural, pedagogical, professorial, scholastic

See also EDUCATIONAL INSTITUTIONS (813)

839 Teaching

Education is an admirable thing, but it is well to remember from time to time that nothing that is worth knowing can be taught. **Oscar Wilde**

(*n*) coaching, development, edification, education, enrolment, induction, initiation, instruction, parenting, *pedagogics* (*formal*), pedagogy, potty-training (*informal*), preparation, re-education, schooling, special education, *special needs education*, teaching, training, tuition, tutelage

See also INSTRUCT AND TEACH (610)

840 Educators

A schoolmaster should have an atmosphere of awe, and walk wonderingly, as if he was amazed at being himself. **Walter Bagehot**

(*n*) academic, coach, demonstrator, domestication, don, *educationalist*, educator, faculty, governess, *head*, *headmaster*, *headmistress*, head teacher, indoctrination, instructor, lecturer, mistress, pedagogue, professor, provost, rector, *schoolteacher*, *supply teacher*, teacher, *teaching body*, *teaching staff*, trainer, tutor

See also INSTRUCT AND TEACH (610), PROFESSIONS (845)

841 Students and Pupils

Time is a great teacher, but unfortunately it kills all its pupils. **Hector Berlioz**

(*n*) *abecedarian*, alumna, alumnus, boarder, cadet, class, classmate, fraternity (*US*), fresher (*informal*), *graduate student*, intake, intern, *medical student*, *plebe* (*US*), *postgrad* (*informal*), postgraduate, prefect, preschooler (*US*), pupil, researcher, *schoolboy*, schoolchild, *schoolgirl*, *schoolkid* (*informal*), student, *teacher's pet*, *undergraduate*

842 Lessons, Course Work, and Examinations

Examinations are formidable even to the best prepared, for the greatest fool may ask more than the wisest man can answer. **Charles Colton**

(*adj*) extracurricular, intercollegiate, *viva voce*

(*n*) apprenticeship, articles, class, commencement (*US formal*), course, coursework, crash course, curriculum, discipline, discussion group, divinity, exam, examination, fieldwork, graduation, homework, *humanities*, lesson, matriculation, *medical training*, *PE*, physical education, *prep* (*informal*), *pupillage* (*formal*), *religious education*, *religious instruction*, *religious studies*, resit, retake, *revision*, *schoolwork*, seminar, session, short course, study, *term paper* (*US*), tutorial

843 Qualifications

People at the top of the tree are those without qualifications to detain them at the bottom. **Peter Ustinov**

(*adj*) certified

(*n*) credential, diploma, doctor, doctorate, headship, *qualification*

844 Studying

You taught me language; and my profit on't/Is, I know how to curse: the red plague rid you/For learning me your language! **William Shakespeare**

(*v*) bone up (*informal*), cram (*informal*), gen up (*informal*), keep abreast of, learn, master, matriculate, mug up (*informal*), read, read up, review (*US*), revise, specialize, study, swot (*informal*), take

845 Professions

Writing is the only profession where no one considers you ridiculous if you earn no money. **Jules Renard**

(*n*) avocation (*formal*), calling, career, craft, job, *line of work*, métier, mission, niche, occupation, profession, trade, vocation

See also MILITARY PERSONNEL (828), EDUCATORS (840), WORKERS IN ENTERTAINMENT AND MEDIA (873)

846 People who Guard and Protect

(*n*) babysitter, bailiff, bodyguard, caretaker, concierge, curator, custodian, defender, guard, handler, jailer, *janitor*, keeper, lifeguard, lookout, minder, nanny, *night watchman*, porter, scout, *security guard*, *security officer*, sentinel, sentry, warden, warder, watch, watchman

847 Office Workers

(*n*) *clerical worker*, clerk, *office assistant*, receptionist, secretary, *telephonist*, temp, troubleshooter

See also PEOPLE INVOLVED IN FINANCE (804), POLITICAL OFFICES AND POLITICIANS (808)

848 People who Work in Medicine

(*n*) analyst, *clinician*, doctor, GP, healer, medic (*informal*), *medical practitioner*, *naturopath*, *neurosurgeon*, *nurse*, pharmacist, *pharmacologist*, physician, *plastic surgeon*, practitioner, *psychiatrist*, *psychoanalyst*, *psychotherapist*, registrar, shrink (*slang*), surgeon, therapist

See also HOSPITALS AND CLINICS (826)

849 Farmers, Gardeners, and Manual Workers

(*n*) *blue-collar worker*, cowboy, cultivator, digger, farmer, farm hand, gamekeeper, gardener, machinist, *mechanic*, miner, navvy (*dated*), peasant, rancher, *ranch hand* (*US*), reaper, wrangler (*US*)

850 Domestic and Kitchen Workers

(*n*) *barista*, char, *chef*, *commis chef*, home help, *housekeeper*, *sous-chef*, squire, waiter

types of servant butler, chambermaid, cleaner, cook, factotum, flunky, footman, lackey, maid, maidservant, major-domo, valet

851 Hair Stylists

(*n*) barber, *coiffeur* (*formal*), *coiffeuse* (*formal*), hairdresser, *hair stylist*

852 Messengers and Couriers

(*n*) bearer, courier, dispatch rider, herald, messenger, runner

See also DRIVERS (1152)

853 Surveyors, Examiners, and Judges

(*n*) *chartered surveyor*, checker, critic, examiner, inspector, judge, *ombudsman*, sampler, selector, surveyor, taster

See also PEOPLE IN LAW COURTS (820)

854 People who Work with Language and Code

(*n*) decoder, interpreter, *linguist*, polyglot, translator

855 Accommodation

A house is a machine for living in. **Le Corbusier**

(*adj*) domestic, *domiciliary*, home, household

(*n*) abode (*literary*), accommodation, *accommodation address*, accommodations (*US*), *bed and board*, billet, board, digs (*dated informal*), domicile (*formal*), dwelling (*formal*), freehold, habitation, home, housing, let, *living quarters*, lodging, lodgings (*dated*), pad (*slang dated*), place, *private residence*, quarters, residence, rooms, shelter, tenancy, tenure

See also RESIDENTIAL BUILDINGS (1077)

856 Undesirable Accommodation

Born in a cellar, and living in a garret. **Samuel Foote**

(*n*) dump (*informal*), *favela*, *fleabag* (*US informal*), *flophouse* (*US informal*), garrison, *ghetto*, hole (*informal*), hovel, lair (*informal*), pigpen (*US*), pigsty, purlieu (*formal*), *shanty*, *shanty town*, slum, tip (*informal*)

857 Inhabitant

What's the good of a home, if you are never in it? **George Grossmith**

(*n*) burgher, citizen, *city dweller*, constituent, *crofter*, denizen, dweller, inhabitant, islander, local, lodger, national, native, occupant, occupier, *paying guest*, people, resident, roomer (*US*), squatter, tenant, townie (*informal*), townsfolk, urbanite, villager

See also GROUPS IN SOCIETY (940)

858 Furniture

No furniture so charming as books. **Sydney Smith**

(*n*) arm, armrest, bedhead, bedstead, bookshelf, coatrack, coat stand, footrest, footstool, furniture, *hassock*, *hat stand*, *headboard*, lectern, ottoman, pouf, *reading desk*, *reading stand*, seat, seating, showcase, table

types of bed bassinet, berth, bunk, bunk bed, camp bed,

carrycot, cot, couchette, cradle, crib (*US*), day bed, divan, double bed, four-poster, futon, hammock, king-size bed, Moses basket, Murphy bed (*US*), queen-size bed, single bed, sofa bed, studio couch, trundle bed, twin bed, water bed

types of cabinet armoire, bookcase, breakfront, bureau, cassone, chest of drawers, china closet, closet, cocktail cabinet, commode, credenza, cupboard, display cabinet, display case, dresser, drinks cabinet, highboy (*US*), lowboy, press, secretary, sideboard, tallboy, wardrobe, whatnot

types of seating Adirondack chair (*US*), armchair, bench, bleachers (*US*), Boston rocker, bucket seat, carver, chair, chaise longue, chesterfield, couch, davenport (*US*), deck chair, easy chair, highchair, ladder-back, lounger, love seat, pew, recliner, rocking chair, settee, sofa, stall, stool, sunlounger, swivel chair, Windsor chair, wing chair

types of table bedside table, card table, coffee table, console, davenport, desk, dining table, dressing table, end table, escritoire, gateleg table, night table (*US*), occasional table, Pembroke table, roll-top desk, tea table, trestle table, vanity table, worktable, writing desk

859 Fittings

(*n*) fittings, fixture, interior decoration, woodwork, work surface

types of plumbing fittings ball cock, basin, bath, bathtub, bidet, drinking fountain, faucet (*US*), hand basin, hot tub, nozzle, plumbing, rose, sauna, shower, sink, sitz bath, spa, spigot (*US*), spout, sprinkler, tap, toilet, tub, vanity (*US*), vanity unit, washbasin, washbowl, wash-hand basin, whirlpool (*US*), whirlpool bath

types of general fittings ceiling rose, chimneypiece, dado, fender, fireplace, looking glass, mantel, mantelpiece, mirror, picture molding (*US*), picture rail, radiator, socket, wainscot, workbench, worktop

860 Soft Furnishings, Linen, and Drapery

(*n*) *arras*, beanbag, bedclothes, bedcovers, bedding, bed linen, bedspread, carpet, carpeting, cloth, comforter (*US*), *continental quilt*, coverlet, curtain, cushion, dish-cloth, drapery, dust cloth (*US*), duster, duvet, eiderdown, *electric blanket*, *fitted carpet*, *floorcovering*, *floor cushion*, furnishings, hanging, *hearth rug*, lampshade, layette, mat, mattress, napkin, pad (*US*), *pallet*, *palliasse*, pelmet, pillow, pillowcase, *pillow sham* (*US*), *pillowslip*, quilt, rug, *sham* (*US*), *slipcase*, *slipcover*, soft furnishings, swag, *swags*, tablecloth, *table linen*, tapestry, *tatami*, throw, *throw cushion*, *throw pillow*, towel, trousseau, upholstery, *valance*, *venetian blind*

861 Tableware, Cutlery, and Kitchenware

(*n*) *baking dish*, *baking sheet* (*US*), *baking tray*, bowl, carafe, china, *cocotte*, crockery, cup, cutlery, decanter, *dinner service*, dish, ewer, filter, flagon, flask, frying pan, glass, *glassware*, goblet, jug, kettle, oven, *oven dish*, *oven tray*, *ovenware*, pan, pitcher, place mat, place setting, plate, platter, *pressure cooker*, ramekin, salver, samovar, saucepan, saucer, serving dish, *silverware*, *skillet*, spit, stove, table mat, tableware, *tandoor*, tankard, *teapot*, tea service, tea set, *tea towel*, *tea urn*, tray, tumbler, tureen, wok

types of cutlery butter knife, cake slice, carving knife, chopstick, dessertspoon, fish knife, fork, knife, pastry fork, pastry slice, serving spoon, soupspoon, spoon, steak knife, tablespoon, teaspoon

types of utensil beater, blender, bottle opener, can opener, corkscrew, drainer, food processor, grater, grinder, juice extractor, juicer, lemon squeezer, liquidizer, mill, mincer, mixer, mortar, nutcracker, opener, peeler, pestle, reamer (*US*), sieve, soup ladle, spatula, strainer, tin-opener, whisk

See also HOUSEHOLD APPLIANCES (1116)

862 Lighting

(*n*) *bedside lamp*, candelabrum, candle, candlestick, *desk lamp*, *fairy lights*, *floor lamp* (*US*), sconce, *table lamp*, taper, uplighter

See also LIGHT (1163)

863 Cleaning Agents

(*n*) cleaner, cleanser, detergent, disinfectant, purifier, soap, soap powder, sterilizer

864 Clothes and Accessories

Beware of all enterprises that require new clothes. **Henry David Thoreau**

(*n*) apparel, array, attire (*formal*), clobber (*informal*), clothes, clothing, costume, disguise, dress, *duds* (*informal*), ensemble, finery, full dress, garb, garment, gear (*informal*), *get-out*, getup (*informal*), glad rags (*informal*), guise, habit, kit, laundry, outfit, raiment (*formal*), rig (*informal*), *rigout*, suit, togs (*informal*), vestment, wardrobe, washing, wear, *weeds* (*archaic or literary*)

865 Garments and Outfits

None of the Emperor's clothes had ever had such a success before. "But, Daddy, he's got nothing on!" piped up a small child. **Hans Christian Andersen**

(*n*) apron, armour, *babywear*, battledress, *best bib and tucker* (*informal*), *best clothes*, *best togs* (*informal*), *black tie*, *castoffs*, *casual clothes*, *casuals*, *casual wear*, *ceremonial dress*, *civilian clothes*, *civvies*, *coordinates*, *coveralls*, *dress uniform*, *formal attire*, *formal wear*, *haberdashery* (*US*), leisurewear, livery, *men's clothing*, menswear, mufti, *one-piece*, *outerwear*, *protective clothing*, *sleepwear* (*US*), *smarts* (*US informal*), *suit of armour*, *summer clothes*, Sunday best, uniform, woollens

types of jacket anorak, blazer, blouson, bomber jacket, dinner jacket, DJ, flak jacket, fleece, jacket, Nehru jacket, reefer (*US*), reefer jacket, smoking jacket, sports jacket, tail coat, tails, tux (*US informal*), tuxedo (*US*), waterproof jacket, windcheater

types of overcoat cagoule, cape, cloak, duffel coat, frock coat, gabardine, greatcoat, mac (*informal*), mackintosh (*dated*), overcoat, parka, poncho, raincoat, topcoat

types of skirt dirndl, hobble skirt, kilt, miniskirt, sarong, tutu

types of sleepwear bathrobe (*US*), dressing gown, housecoat, negligée, nightcap, nightclothes, nightdress, nightgown, nightie, nightshirt, nightwear, peignoir, pyjamas, sleepers (*US*), sleepsuit

types of sportswear bathing costume (*dated*), bathing suit (*US*), bathing trunks, beachwear, bikini, leotard, shell suit, sweatpants, sweat suit (*US*), swimming costume, swimming trunks, swimsuit, swimwear, tracksuit, trunks, two-piece, wet suit

types of suit boiler suit, business suit, catsuit, dress suit, jump suit, overalls, pantsuit (*US*), trouser suit, zoot suit

types of top basque, blouse, bodice, body warmer, bolero, boob tube (*slang*), gilet, halter, jerkin, polo shirt, shirt, smock, surplice, sweatshirt, tabard, tank top, tee, T-shirt, tube top (*US*), tunic, vest (*US*), vestment, waistcoat

types of trousers bell-bottom trousers, Bermuda shorts, breeches, capri pants, chinos, cords, culottes, dungarees, fatigues, hip-huggers (*US*), hipsters, hot pants, jeans, jodhpurs, khakis, knickerbockers, lederhosen, leggings, pedal pushers, plus fours, salopettes, shorts, slacks, trews

types of dress ballgown, cheongsam, evening dress, evening gown (*US*), frock, gown, gymslip, jumper (*US*), kaftan, kimono, muumuu, pinafore, robe, sari, sheath, shift, shirtdress, sundress, wedding dress

types of sweater or cardigan cardigan, crew neck, jersey, jumper, polo neck, pullover, sweater, twinset, V neck

866 Jewellery

Kissing your hand may make you feel very very good but a diamond and sapphire bracelet lasts forever. **Anita Loos**

(*n*) coronet, crown, diadem, solitaire

types of jewellery anklet, armlet, badge, bangle, bracelet, brooch, cameo, charm, cuff link, eardrop, earring, necklace, nose ring, nose stud, pin, ring, stud, tiara, tie clasp (*US*), tie clip, tiepin, tie tack (*US*), wristlet

types of necklace beads, chain, choker, collar, locket, medallion, necklet, pendant, torque

See also ORNAMENTS AND DECORATIONS (1247)

867 Haberdashery, Millinery, and Lingerie

Hats divide generally into three classes: offensive hats, defensive hats, and shrapnel. **Katharine Whitehorn**

(*n*) *hosiery*, lingerie, smalls (*informal or humorous*), underclothes, underclothing, *undergarments*, underthings, underwear, undies (*informal*)

types of headgear Alice band, balaclava, bandeau, baseball cap, bearskin, beret, biretta, bobble hat, busby, cap, chaplet, cloth cap, cowl, crash helmet, fez, glengarry, hairband, hard hat, hat, headband, headdress, headscarf, headsquare, helmet, hood, mantilla, mobcap, nightcap, skullcap, tam-o'-shanter, tippet, topee, turban, yarmulke, yashmak

types of lower body underwear bloomers (*dated*), boxer shorts, briefs, camiknickers, corset, crinoline, drawers, foundation garment, garter, girdle, G-string, jockstrap, knee-highs, knickers, legwarmer, long johns, nylons, panties, pants, pantyhose (*US*), petticoat, slip, sock, stockings, support hose (*US*), support stockings, thigh-highs, thong, tights, underpants, underskirt

types of hat boater, bonnet, bowler hat, cloche, cowboy hat, deerstalker, derby (*US*), fedora, homburg, Panama hat, picture hat, pillbox, porkpie hat, rain hat, sailor hat, sombrero, sou'wester, stovepipe hat, sunhat, ten-gallon hat, top hat, topper, toque, trilby

types of upper body underwear basque, body, body stocking, bodysuit, bra, camisole, chemise, string vest, teddy, undershirt, union suit (*US*), vest

types of accessory bandanna, belt, bootlace, bow tie, braces, cravat, cummerbund, dicky (*informal*), dicky bow (*informal*), earmuffs, glove, handkerchief, hat, jewellery, mitt, mitten, muff, muffler, neckerchief (*US*), necktie (*US*), pashmina, sash, scarf, shawl, stole, suspenders (*US*), tie, veil, wrap

868 Dress, Wear, and Undress

Woe to him who doesn't know how to wear his mask, be he king or pope! **Luigi Pirandello**

(*adj*) *attired* (*formal*), bare, barefoot, clad, decent (*informal*), dressed, *garbed*, *got up* (*informal*), *in the altogether* (*informal*), *in the buff* (*informal*), *in the nude*, in the raw (*informal*), liveried, naked, nude, *starkers* (*informal*), *stark-naked*, turned-out, unclothed, undressed, veiled

(*n*) nakedness, nudity, *state of undress*

(*v*) accessorize, bundle up (*informal*), clothe, deck (*literary*), disrobe (*formal*), doff, doll up (*informal*), don (*formal*), dress, garb, get into, have on, put on, rig out (*informal*), sport (*informal*), strip, *strip off*, suit, take off, unclothe, undress, wear, wrap up

See also WELL GROOMED (483)

869 Describing Clothes

(*adj*) *ankle-length*, bespoke, *bias-cut*, black-tie, *body-hugging*, clingy (*informal*), close-fitting, décolleté, designer, dressy, drip-dry, *figure-hugging*, fitted, flared, full-fashioned (*US*), *in vogue*, knockabout, loose, loose-fitting, *low-cut*, *low-necked*, noniron, off-the-peg, *permanent-press*, plain-clothes, plunging, preppy (*US informal*), *preshrunk*, prêt-à-porter, ready-made, ready-to-wear, revealing, reversible, scanty, *skintight*, snug, sports, sporty, stonewashed, structured, tailored, tailor-made, tight, tight-fitting, tweedy, *underwired*, walking, washable, *wash-and-wear*, wide, wired

(*adv*) scantily

See also WELL GROOMED (483), BADLY GROOMED (484)

870 Parts of a Garment

parts of a garment brim, buckle, button, buttonhole, coat-tail, collar, cuff, décolletage, drawstring, gusset, hem, lace, lapel, leg, lining, neck, neckband, neckline, pocket, sash, sleeve, strap, turn-up, waistband, zip

See also FASTENERS, LINKS, AND NETWORKS (1246)

871 Footwear

Can you take your country with you on the soles of your shoes? **Georg Büchner**

types of boot boot, bootee, cowboy boot, galoshes, gum boot, hiking boot, jackboot, mukluk, rubber (*US*), waders, walking boot, wellington boot

types of shoe ballet shoe, brogue, clog, court shoe, espadrille, flip-flop (*informal*), jelly, moccasin, mule, oxford, platform, plimsoll, pump, sandal, sandshoe, slingback, slipper, sneaker (*US*), snowshoe, stiletto heel, thong, trainer, wedge heel, wingtip (*US*), zori

872 Entertainment

I have noticed that what cats most appreciate in a human being is not the ability to produce food which they take for granted—but his or her entertainment value. **Geoffrey Household**

(*n*) amusement, carousel, comedy, entertainment, escapism, fun, hilarity, karaoke, nightlife, *party piece*, pleasure, roundabout, *show biz* (*informal*), son et lumière

(*v*) busk, entertain, headline (*US*), host, introduce

See also PERFORMANCES AND SHOWS (42), FILM (901), THE PERFORMING ARTS (904)

873 Workers in Entertainment and Media

Journalists say a thing that they know isn't true, in the hope that if they keep on saying it long enough it will be true. **Arnold Bennett**

(*n*) anchor, anchorperson, announcer, broadcaster, columnist, commentator, correspondent, critic, double act, editor, emcee (*informal*), entertainer, floor manager, forecaster, hack (*informal*), host, hostess, humorist, imitator, interpreter, interviewer, journalist, *journo* (*informal*), lineup, MC, newshawk (*US informal*), newshound (*informal*), newsman, newspaperman, newspaperwoman, newsreader, newswoman, *paparazzo*, presenter, press, press officer, proofreader, publisher, question master, *radio presenter*, reporter, reviewer, ringmaster, satirist, speaker, spokesperson, sportscaster, *standup comedian*, stooge, *street entertainer*, *street musician*, *street performer*, stringer, subeditor, telecaster, *trapeze artist*

types of entertainer actor, busker, clown, comedian, comic, conjurer, co-star, dancer, DJ, film star, impressionist, juggler, magician, mime, movie star (*US*), musician, singer, ventriloquist

See also JOKERS AND TEASES (676), NEWSPAPERS (606), TELEVISION AND RADIO (607)

874 Leisure and Recreation

We are closer to the ants than to the butterflies. Very few people can endure much leisure. **Gerald Brenan**

(*n*) activity, avocation (*formal*), distraction, diversion, escape, game, hobby, horseplay, interest, leisure, *leisure pursuit*, pastime, play, pursuit, recreation, relaxation, sideline, *sports activities*

(*v*) carouse (*literary*), celebrate, enjoy yourself, fool about, fool around, gad (*humorous*), go out, *large it* (*informal*), let your hair down, live it up (*slang*), *make merry*, muck about (*informal*), paint the town red (*informal*), party (*informal*), play, *raise the spirits*, revel, roister, sunbathe

875 Hobbies, Games, and Sports

Serious sport...is war minus the shooting. **George Orwell**

(*adj*) sports, sporty

(*n*) acrobatics, aerobatics, aerobics, *alpinism*, *amateur dramatics*, *amateur photographer*, *angling*, athletics, ball game, *bingo*, callisthenics, climbing, crossword, dip, exercise, fishing, gymnastics, *horseback riding* (*US*), hunting, isometrics, keep fit, motocross, *mountain climbing*, *mountaineering*, *orienteering*, pony-trekking, PT, pugilism, riding, *rock climbing*, rugger (*informal*), *sailing*, shopping, *show jumping*, sport, step aerobics, *sword fighting*, training, *travel bug*, *trekking*, working out, workout

(*v*) bathe, bivouac, camp, conjure, fish, garden, holiday, jockey, keep fit, picnic, roller-skate, *scuba dive*, *skydive*, snorkel, swim, train, visit, work out

types of ball game American football, Australian Rules, baseball, basketball, cricket, field hockey (*US*), football, hockey, hurling, lacrosse, netball, rounders, rugby, shinty, softball

types of court game badminton, jai alai, rackets, squash, table tennis, tennis, volleyball

types of combat sport aikido, boxing, fencing, judo, karate, kendo, kickboxing, kung fu, sumo, tae kwon do, wrestling

types of target ball game billiards, boules, bowling, bowls, croquet, golf, lawn bowling (*US*), pool, snooker

types of track and field cross-country, decathlon, discus, hammer throw, heptathlon, high jump, javelin, long jump, marathon, modern pentathlon, pole vault, relay race, shot put, sprint, steeplechase, triathlon, triple jump

types of winter sport biathlon, bobsled (*US*), bobsleigh, cross-country skiing, curling, downhill, figure skating, hockey (*US*), ice dancing, ice hockey, skiing, ski jump, slalom, snowboarding, speed skating, toboggan

876 People in Sports and Leisure

How vainly men themselves amaze/To win the palm, the oak, or bays. **Andrew Marvell**

(*n*) acrobat, *alpinist*, arbitrator, athlete, *baseball player*, bather, batsman, beachcomber, birdwatcher, body builder, bookworm (*informal*), boxer, caddie, camper, *caver*, cheerleader, climber, *cricketer*, diver, *fencer*, fielder, flier (*US informal*), *funambulist*, gambler, *gymnast*, *high roller* (*slang*), hiker, horseman, horsewoman, hunter, jockey, jogger, jumper, mountaineer, *ornithologist*, photographer, player, potholer, pug (*informal*), pugilist, racer, ref (*informal*), *rock climber*, rocker, rower, runner, runner-up, *scuba diver*, *snorkeller*, *speleologist*, *spelunker*, sportsperson, sprinter, *steeplechaser*, striker, *sword fighter*, titleholder, tumbler, *twitcher* (*informal*), umpire, *wrestler*

See also TRAVEL: TRAVELLERS AND WALKERS (320), COMPETITORS (41), COMPETE, CONTEND, AND COMBAT (304)

877 Sports Terms

(*n*) bully-off, deuce, goal, goalmouth, header, injury time, innings, lap, no ball, *slam-dunk*, smash, starting point, stoppage time, *tie-break*, tiebreaker, topspin, touchdown, woodwork (*informal*)

878 Games Pieces

types of game piece checker (*US*), chessman (*US*), chesspiece, chip, counter, domino, draught, jack, tiddlywink

879 Sports Equipment

types of sports equipment ball, bat, bowl, club, discus, football, glove, helmet, hockey stick, javelin, lacrosse stick, mitt, pad, pigskin (*US*), puck, racket, shot, shuttlecock, spikes, tee, wicket

880 Toys

Deceive boys with toys, but men with oaths. **Lysander**

(*n*) plaything

types of toy beach ball, building blocks, doll, doll's house, dolly (*babytalk*), glove puppet, hand puppet (*US*), jack-in-the-box, jigsaw, jigsaw puzzle, kaleidoscope, kite, marble, playhouse, popgun, puppet, rag doll, rocking horse, squirt gun (*US*), stilt, teddy bear, water pistol, Wendy house, yo-yo

881 Lifestyle

I've been trying for some time now to develop a lifestyle that doesn't require my presence. **Garry Trudeau**

(*n*) ethnicity, lifestyle, modus vivendi, standard of living, way of life

882 Abstemiousness and Self-Denial

Self-denial is not a virtue; it is only the effect of prudence on rascality. **George Bernard Shaw**

(*adj*) abstemious, abstinent, ascetic, *clean-living*, dry, monastic, *on the wagon*, *puritanical*, *self-denying*, sober, spartan, teetotal

(*n*) abstemiousness, abstinence, asceticism, *puritanism*, self-denial, sobriety, *teetotalism*, temperance

See also FOREGO AND DENY ONESELF (450)

883 Ascetic People

Throughout history power has been the vice of the ascetic. **Bertrand Russell**

(*n*) abstainer, ascetic, *celibate*, moralist, *puritan*, *teetotaller*

See also FOREGO AND DENY ONESELF (450)

884 Nomadic and Rootless Lifestyles

Over all the world/Men move unhoming, and eternally/Concerned: a swarm of bees who have lost their queen. **Christopher Fry**

(*adj*) dispossessed, drifting, itinerant, migrant, migratory, nomadic, nonresident, roaming, rootless, roving, stateless, vagrant

(*n*) dosser (*slang*), drifter, gadabout (*humorous*), gypsy, hobo, knight, migrant, nomad, runabout, traveller

See also SOLITARINESS (941)

885 Pleasure-Seeking and Excess

Nothing succeeds like excess. **Oscar Wilde**

(*adj*) bohemian, decadent, dissipated, dissolute, epicurean, fancy-free, footloose, gutsy (*informal*), hedonistic, immoderate (*formal*), intemperate, luxurious, *philandering* (*disapproving*), *pleasure-loving*, prodigal, self-indulgent, spendthrift, *sybaritic*

(*adv*) decadently, intemperately

(*n*) dissipation, dissoluteness, *epicureanism*, hedonism, immoderation (*formal*), *pleasure-seeking*, *prodigality*, profligacy, self-gratification, self-indulgence

See also MORALLY BAD (776)

886 Pleasure-Seekers and Hedonists

DEBAUCHEE, *n. One who has so earnestly pursued pleasure that he has had the misfortune to overtake it.* **Ambrose Bierce**

(*n*) aesthete, bohemian, bon vivant (*literary*), *bon viveur* (*literary*), *carouser* (*literary*), Casanova, *debauchee* (*formal*), *Don Juan*, *Don Quixote*, *drunkard*, extrovert, gannet (*informal*), *gigolo*, glutton, guts (*informal*), hedonist, *libertine*, *Lothario* (*literary*), merrymaker, *party animal* (*informal*), partygoer, philanderer (*disapproving*), pig (*informal*), *pleasure-lover*, *pleasure-seeker*, raver (*informal*), reveller, roisterer, Romeo, *roué* (*literary*), *satyr*, *sensualist*, sophisticate, spendthrift, swashbuckler, sybarite, *voluptuary*, wolf (*informal*), *womanizer* (*disapproving*)

See also EATERS, GOURMETS, AND DIETARY CHOICES (715), MORALLY BAD (776), BEASTLY AND BRUTISH (511)

887 People Living Away From Home

Soaring falcon, noble Poet, come to my aid...help me to live without roots: ever on the move: my only sustenance your nourishing language. **Juan Goytisolo**

(*n*) colonist, colonizer, deportee, emigrant, *émigré*, evacuee, exile, expat (*informal*), expatriate, immigrant, migrant, refugee, settler

888 Status

Status is an influence at every level...all part of what I call plutography: depicting the acts of the rich. **Tom Wolfe**

(*n*) background, blood, bloodline, breeding, cachet, chieftainship, citizenship, credit, echelon, importance, place, position, rank, ranking, reputation, repute (*formal*), *social class*, *social standing*, standing, station, stature, status

889 Class Status

There are two classes in good society in England. The equestrian classes and the neurotic classes. **George Bernard Shaw**

(*adj*) aristocratic, august (*formal*), blue-blooded, bourgeois, cut-glass, *highborn* (*literary*), *high-ranking*, humble, landed, lower-class, *middle-class*, noble, patrician, pedigree, poor, posh (*informal*), pukka (*informal*), purebred, senior, thoroughbred, titled, top-drawer, upper-class, *upwardly mobile*, voiceless, wellborn, *working-class*

(*n*) aristocracy, aristocrat, bourgeois, caste, *chattering classes*, *commoner*, eminence, gentleman, gentry, grass-roots, high society, high-up (*informal*), hoi polloi, *landed gentry*, lower class, lowliness, masses, mob (*informal*), nob (*informal*), nobility, parvenu, peasant, peerage, proletariat, society, top drawer, upper class, upper crust (*informal*), working class

890 Marital Status

Married life requires shared mystery even when all the facts are known. **Richard Ford**

(*adj*) divorced, eligible, engaged, *footloose and fancy free*, marriageable, on your own, single, unattached, uninvolved, unmarried, *widowed*

(*n*) bachelor, cohabitation (*formal*), marriageability, *spinster*, *widow*, *widower*

See also MARRIED STATE (961)

891 Wealth and Wealthy

Wealth has never been a sufficient source of honour in itself. It must be advertised, and the normal medium is obtrusively expensive goods. **J. K. Galbraith**

(*adj*) affluent, better-off, *born with a silver spoon in your mouth*, comfortable, developed, fat, *flush* (*informal*), fortunate, gracious, in clover, in credit, *in funds*, in the black, *in the chips* (*US*), in the money, leisured, loaded (*slang*), moneyed, *nouveau riche*, privileged, propertied, prosperous, rich, rolling in it (*informal*), solvent, successful, wealthy, well-endowed, well-fixed (*US informal*), well-heeled (*informal*), well-off, well-to-do

(*adv*) prosperously

(*n*) affluence, opulence, prosperity, *rich and famous*, solvency

892 Poverty and Poor

Money is better than poverty, if only for financial reasons. **Woody Allen**

(*adj*) badly off, bankrupt, broke (*informal*), cleaned out (*informal*), dependent, depressed, deprived, destitute, disadvantaged, down-and-out, *down-at-heel*, *flat broke* (*informal*), hard up (*informal*), homeless, impecunious (*formal*), impoverished, in arrears, in debt, indigent (*formal*), *in need*, insolvent, in the red, landless, mean (*archaic*), mendicant, needy, *on the breadline*, *on the skids* (*slang*), *on the streets*, *out of cash*, overdrawn, penniless, penurious (*literary*), poor, poverty-stricken, pushed (*informal*), *short of money*, *skint* (*informal*), stony (*informal*), stony-broke (*informal*), straitened, strapped (*informal*), *strapped for cash* (*informal*), underprivileged

(*adv*) from hand to mouth, meanly

(*n*) deprivation, destitution, hardship, *homelessness*, *impecuniousness* (*formal*), impoverishment, indigence (*formal*), misery, need, neediness, *pennilessness*, penury, poorness, poverty, privation, vagrancy, want

893 Important or Famous People

A celebrity is a person who works hard all his life to become known, then wears dark glasses to avoid being recognized. **Fred Allen**

(*n*) authority figure, baron, big cheese (*slang*), biggie (*informal*), big name, big shot (*informal*), bigwig (*informal*), captain, *celeb* (*informal*), *czar*, dignitary, doyen, doyenne, *figurehead*, frontrunner (*informal*), *glitterati*, grandee, haut monde, *head honcho* (*US slang*), heavyweight (*informal*), high achiever, high-flier, *honcho* (*US slang*), hotshot (*informal*), household name, *important person*, impresario, *kahuna* (*US informal*), *key player*, king, kingpin (*informal*), lead, leader, leading light, legend, luminary, *megastar*, mover, *mover and shaker*, name, notability, notable, number one (*informal*), pacemaker, personage (*formal*), personality, prince, principal, public figure, queen, sheik, socialite, somebody, someone, spearhead, standard-bearer, *top brass* (*informal*), *top dog* (*informal*), *top gun* (*US informal*), *top name*, VIP, winner

See also KNOWN AND FAMOUS (182)

894 Level of Education and Sophistication

Hip is the sophistication of the wise primitive in a giant jungle. **Norman Mailer**

(*adj*) art-house, citified (*disapproving*), classy (*informal*), collegiate, common, countrified, cross-cultural, cultivated, cultured, distinguished, donnish, earthy, educated, erudite, folksy, gross, innocent, lettered, literary, literate, philistine (*disapproving*), polite, provincial (*disapproving*), scholarly, sophisticated, studious, suave, tasteful, uncivilized, uncultivated, uncultured, well-rounded

(*adv*) culturally

(*n*) bookishness, *bumpkin* (*informal*), civilization, *cognoscente*, cognoscenti, crudity, cultivation, culture, egghead (*informal*), elite, highbrow, ingenuousness, intellectual, intelligentsia, letters, literati (*formal*), philistinism (*disapproving*), simplicity, sophistication, street credibility, taste, tastefulness, *vulgarian*

See also POSITIVE INTELLECTUAL CHARACTERISTICS (525)

895 Rich People

We may see the small value God has for riches, by the people he gives them to. **Alexander Pope**

(*n*) *beau monde*, *beautiful people*, billionaire, *café society*, celebrity, *fat cat* (*slang*), *idle rich*, jet set (*informal*), laird, magnate, millionaire, mogul, moneybags (*informal*), moneymaker, multimillionaire, plutocrat, property owner, squire, toff (*informal*)

896 Poor People

I owe much; I have nothing; the rest I leave to the poor. **François Rabelais**

(*n*) beggar, have-nots, mendicant (*formal*), *panhandler* (*US*), pauper, *poor person*, tramp, vagabond, vagrant

897 The Pictorial Arts

Paint becomes painting when color establishes surface. **Jules Olitski**

(*n*) animation, art, *fine art*, *graphic arts*, painting, photography, portraiture, *visual art*

See also DRAWINGS, CHARTS, AND TABLES (595)

898 Artworks

A great work of art bears its meaning on its face. **C. L. R. James**

(*n*) adaptation, artwork, blowup, CAD, canvas, caricature, cartoon, carving, close-up, composition, doodle, engraving, etching, fresco, frieze, icon, image, *magnum opus*, masterpiece, masterwork, motif, mural, objet d'art, oeuvre (*formal*), *oil painting*, *old master*, opus, painting, picture, print, remake, rubbing, stencil, *still life*, tableau, template, woodcut, work, work of art

899 Artistic Movements and Styles

We cannot use Impressionism when we paint a huge street in New York, nor can we use Futurism when we paint a beautiful woman...May our brush keep time with our vibrations. **Joan Miró**

(*adj*) abstract, aesthetic, artistic, arty-crafty (*informal*), baroque, cubist, freehand, graphic, modernistic, photographic, pictographic, pictorial, stylistic, visual

types of 20th-century art movement abstract expressionism, art deco, conceptual art, constructivism, cubism, Dada, expressionism, Fauvism, futurism, minimalism, modernism, op art, photorealism, pop art, postmodernism, socialist realism, surrealism, vorticism

types of pre-20th-century art movement art nouveau, Arts and Crafts, Baroque, classicism, impressionism, Mannerism, pointillism, postimpressionism, Pre-Raphaelitism, realism, Renaissance, Romanticism, symbolism

900 Artists

There is no neutral naturalism. The artist, no less than the writer, needs a vocabulary before he can embark on a "copy" of reality. **E. H. Gombrich**

(*n*) artisan, artist, caricaturist, cartoonist, *miniaturist*, painter, *sculptor*, *watercolourist*

901 Film

A film is a petrified fountain of thought. **Jean Cocteau**

(*n*) *actioner* (*informal*), *action movie*, *adventure movie*, *animated film*, *animatronics*, *B film*, biopic, B movie, *B picture*, cartoon, cinema, cinematography, *cowboy film*, *feature film*, film, flick (*informal*), motion picture (*formal or technical*), movie (*US*), movies, *moving picture*, picture, rushes, screening, screenplay, *screen test*, *spaghetti western*, subtitle, surtitle, swashbuckler, take, talkie (*dated*), *talky* (*US*), tear-jerker (*informal*), thriller, weepie (*informal*), western

See also ENTERTAINMENT (872)

902 Sculpture

You can't make a sculpture, in my opinion, without involving your body. You move and you feel and you breathe and you touch. **Barbara Hepworth**

(*n*) bas-relief, bronze, bust, death mask, figurine, gargoyle, sculpture, statuary, statue, statuette, waxwork, woodcarving

903 Dance

Lighter than a cork I danced on the waves. **Arthur Rimbaud**

(*n*) choreography, *lambada*, *lindy hop*, *merengue*, pirouette

types of dance ballet, belly dance, bop (*informal*), bossa nova, cancan, cha-cha, Charleston, fandango, flamenco, foxtrot, jig, jitterbug, jive, line dancing, mambo, minuet, polka, quadrille, quickstep, rumba, salsa, samba, square dance, tango, tap dance, waltz

See also PERFORMANCES AND SHOWS (42)

904 The Performing Arts

Art cannot be described. It proves itself only in its performance. **Gerhard Richter**

(*adj*) audiovisual, cinematic, star-studded, stellar, theatrical, thespian (*literary*)

(*n*) acting, costume drama, *dramaturgy*, *performance art*, *performing arts*, repertory, *repertory theatre*, role-playing, show business, star billing, theatre, *theatre-in-the-round*, variety show, vaudeville (*US*)

(*v*) act, act out, co-star, enact, feature, headline (*US*), perform, recast

See also PERFORMANCES AND SHOWS (42), ENTERTAINMENT (872)

905 Performers

An actor is never so great as when he reminds you of an animal—falling like a cat, lying like a dog, moving like a fox. **François Truffaut**

(*n*) actor, actress, cast, company, co-star, *dramatis personae*, performer, player, *repertory company*, role, starlet, star turn, *theatre company*, *theatre group*, thespian, *touring company*, walk-on

906 In the Theatre

We respond to a drama to that extent to which it corresponds to our dreamlife. **David Mamet**

(*n*) backcloth, backdrop, cameo, *dress circle*, footlights, *front of house*, *gods* (*informal*), playgoer, scenery, set, stage, stage door, stage whisper, theatregoer, *the boards*, *the gods* (*informal*), upper circle

907 Music, Songs, and Singing

One composes because of an interior impulse; music has no other sources of improvisation any longer, apart from our own spirit. **Karlheinz Stockhausen**

(*n*) air, carol, chant, *chanting*, chorus, descant, ditty, elegy, intonation, jingle, lullaby, lyrics, melody, music, orchestration, piece of music, romance, singing, *soul music*, theme, *theme song*, *theme tune*, tune, vocals, words (*v*) chant, intone (*formal*), pipe, pluck, riff, serenade, sing, strum, twang

types of instrumental music capriccio, concerto, fantasia, fugue, intermezzo, nocturne, overture, prelude, rondo, scherzo, sinfonia, sonata, suite, symphony

types of vocal music anthem, aria, ballad, cantata, canticle, chorale, coloratura, folk song, hymn, madrigal, mass, oratorio, pop song, requiem, song, spiritual, yodel

types of popular music bebop, bhangra, blues, calypso, country, drum and bass, dub, folk, funk, garage, gospel, jazz, mambo, pop, punk, rap, reggae, rhythm and blues, rock, rock and roll, salsa, samba, ska, soul, swing

types of classical music Baroque, chamber music, comic opera, early music, opera, operetta, Romantic, twelve-tone

See also PERFORMANCES AND SHOWS (42)

908 Musicians and Singers

A musician, if he's a messenger, is like a child who hasn't been handled too many times by man, hasn't had too many fingerprints across his brain. **Jimi Hendrix**

(*n*) accompanist, artist, artiste, band, cellist, *chanteuse*, chorister, composer, consort, diva, drummer, folk singer, group, *guitarist*, instrumentalist, keyboarder, *lyricist*, minstrel, musician, *percussionist*, *pianist*, rapper, rocker (*informal*), *rock musician*, *rock singer*, *rock star*, singer, soloist, *songsmith*, songster, songwriter, soprano, *timpanist*, troubadour, virtuoso, vocalist

types of band big band, brass band, chamber orchestra, choir, chorale, chorus, dance band, duo, ensemble, jazz band, octet, orchestra, pipe band, pop group, quartet, quintet, septet, sextet, sinfonietta, steel band, string band, string quartet, symphony orchestra, trio

909 Notes and Chords

The heart of the melody can never be put down on paper. **Pablo Casals**

(*n*) chord, fanfare, instrumentation, key, leitmotif, meter, reprise, rhythm, riff

910 Musical Instruments

Knowing how to play an instrument is the barest superficiality if one is thinking of becoming a musician. It is the ideas that one utilizes instinctively *that determine the degree of profundity any artist reaches.* **Imamu Amiri Baraka**

types of keyboard accordion, baby grand, celesta, clavichord, concertina, grand piano, harpsichord, organ, piano, pianoforte, spinet, synthesizer, upright piano

types of percussion instrument bass drum, bongo drums, castanet, chimes, conga drum, cymbal, drum, gamelan, glockenspiel, gong, kettledrum, maraca, marimba, metallophone, snare drum, steel drum, tabla, tabor, tambourine, timpani, tom-tom, triangle, tubular bells, vibraphone, xylophone

types of stringed instrument balalaika, banjo, bass guitar, bouzouki, cello, double bass, electric guitar, fiddle, guitar, harp, Hawaiian guitar, lute, lyre, mandolin, sitar, Spanish guitar, steel guitar, ukulele, viol, viola, viola da gamba, violin, violoncello, zither

types of wind instrument bagpipes, bassoon, clarinet, cor anglais, crumhorn, didgeridoo, English horn (*US*), fife, flute, harmonica, nose flute, oboe, ocarina, panpipes, penny whistle, piccolo, recorder

types of brass instrument bugle, cornet, euphonium, flugelhorn, French horn, horn, post horn, saxhorn, saxophone, sousaphone, trombone, trumpet, tuba

911 Recordings and Players

People don't understand the sort of fight it takes to record what you want, to record the way you want to record it. **Billie Holiday**

(*n*) album, cassette, CD player, hi-fi, *LP*, playback, recording, remix, single, sound system, soundtrack, tape, vinyl

See also AUDIO EQUIPMENT (1138)

912 Musical Terms

I tried to resist his overtures, but he plied me with symphonies, quartettes, chamber music, and cantatas. **S. J. Perelman**

(*adj*) choral, funky (*slang*), orchestral, *philharmonic*, rhythmic, singing, symphonic

(*adv*) in concert

(*n*) cadenza, *libretto*, *ostinato*, syncopation, tempo, time

types of musical register alto, baritone, bass, countertenor, falsetto, mezzo-soprano, soprano, tenor

types of musical term a cappella, adagio, allegro, andante, appassionato, arpeggio, capriccioso, con brio, crescendo, decrescendo (*US*), diminuendo, forte, fortissimo, grave, larghetto, largo, legato, lentissimo, lento, moderato, pianissimo, piano, pizzicato, sotto voce, staccato

913 Fiction and Drama

A novel is a static thing that one moves through; a play is a dynamic thing that moves past one. **Kenneth Tynan**

(*n*) autobiography, biography, burlesque (*US*), *crime novel*, *detective novel*, *detective story*, doggerel, drama, dramatization, epic, fairy tale, fiction, fictionalization, *graphic novel*, history, instalment, literature, melodrama, mystery, novelette, novella, prequel, prose, romance, romp (*informal*), *science fiction*, script, short story, whodunit, writing

See also BOOKS AND BOOKLETS (591), SCIENCE FICTION (1063)

914 Writers and Styles

An author arrives at a good style when his language performs what is required of it without shyness. **Cyril Connolly**

(*n*) author, *autobiographer*, bard (*literary or humorous*), biographer, diarist, dramatist, exponent, ghostwriter, librettist, literati (*formal*), *memoirist*, novelist, parodist, playwright, poet, *poetaster*, *portraitist*, *potboiler*, propagandist, screenwriter, scribe, scriptwriter, *tragedian*, *versifier*, writer

915 Poetry and Verse

Poetry is the supreme fiction. **Wallace Stevens**

(*n*) canto, couplet, *free verse*, *limerick*, ode, poem, *poesy* (*archaic or literary*), poetry, quatrain, rhyme, sonnet, stanza, stave, verse

916 The Stages of Life

The four stages of man are infancy, childhood, adolescence, and obsolescence. **Art Linkletter**

(*n*) age, being, existence, life, life cycle, life expectancy, life span, lifetime, mortality

917 Babyhood, Childhood, and Adolescence

I have all that I lost/and I go carrying my childhood/like a favorite flower/that perfumes my hand. **Gabriela Mistral**

(*adj*) adolescent, immature, infantile, neonatal, newborn, *preadolescent*, prepubescent, preschool, *pubertal*, pubescent, teen (*informal*), teenage, underage, young

(*n*) adolescence, babyhood, boyhood, childhood, early years, formative years, girlhood, immaturity, infancy, puberty, teens, upbringing, youth

See also CHILD OR YOUTH (945)

918 Adulthood

Adults are obsolete children. **Dr. Seuss**

(*adj*) adult, big, grown, grown-up, mature

(*n*) adulthood, majority, manhood, maturity, *prime of life*, womanhood

919 Old Age

Self-parody is the first portent of age. **Larry McMurtry**

(*adj*) aged, elderly, geriatric, old, over-the-hill, superannuated

920 Old Person

If I'd known I was gonna live this long, I'd have taken better care of myself. **Eubie Blake**

(*n*) *golden ager* (*US*), *OAP*, *old fogy*, *old person*, *old-timer*, pensioner, senior (*US*), senior citizen

921 Causes of Death

I feel nothing, apart from a certain difficulty in continuing to exist. **Bernard le Bovier Fontenelle**

(*n*) asphyxiation, assassination, bloodshed, butchery, carnage, crucifixion, decapitation, decimation, execution, extermination, genocide, gore, hanging, *hara-kiri*, homicide, *immolation* (*formal*), killing, manslaughter, martyrdom, massacre, murder, *parricide*, patricide, pogrom, self-immolation (*formal*), shooting, slaughter, *slaying*, strangulation, *suffocation*, suicide

See also CEASE TO EXIST (22)

922 Die

He who would teach men to die would at the same time teach them to live. **Michel de Montaigne**

(*v*) bite the dust (*informal*), breathe your last (*literary*), *commit hara-kiri*, *commit suicide*, *commit suttee*, *croak* (*slang*), depart (*formal*), *depart this life* (*formal*), die, die of, drown, end it all, expire (*formal or literary*), *give up the ghost* (*literary*), go, *go to meet your maker*, kick the bucket (*slang*), kill yourself, pass away, perish (*literary*), *pop your clogs* (*informal*), succumb, *top yourself* (*slang*)

923 Kill

The man who murdered his parents, then pleaded for mercy on the grounds that he was an orphan. **Abraham Lincoln**

(*v*) asphyxiate, assassinate, behead, blow away (*slang*), bump off (*slang*), butcher, choke, crucify, cut down (*informal*), decapitate, dispatch, dispose of, do away with (*informal*), do in (*informal*), eliminate, execute, exterminate, finish off (*informal*), *garrotte*, guillotine, gun down (*informal*), hang, immolate (*formal*), kill, knock off (*slang*), liquidate, lynch, massacre, mow down, murder, poison, prey on, put to death, shoot, shoot down, slaughter, slay (*formal or literary*), smother, snuff (*informal*), stifle, strangle, strangulate, strike down, suffocate, take out (*slang*), throttle, top (*slang*), vaporize, waste (*slang*), wipe out (*slang*)

See also WOUND A PERSON OR ANIMAL (384), STAB (417), WHIP AND CLUB (418)

924 People who Kill

Kill a man, and you are a murderer. Kill millions of men, and you are a conqueror. Kill everyone, and you are a god. **Jean Rostand**

(*n*) butcher, gunman, *hired gun* (*slang*), hit man (*slang*), hunter, killer, murderer, patricide, poisoner, slayer (*formal or literary*), sniper, soldier of fortune

925 Dead and Dying

If I must die,/I will encounter darkness as a bride,/And hug it in mine arms. **William Shakespeare**

(*adj*) at peace, at rest, dead, *dead as a dodo*, *dead as a doornail*, deceased (*formal*), defunct, departed (*formal or literary*), extinct, gone (*informal*), inanimate, in extremis, late, moribund, *no longer with us*, *passed on*, stillborn, stone-dead

See also CEASE TO EXIST (22)

926 Dead Person

He'd make a lovely corpse. **Charles Dickens**

(*n*) body, cadaver, carrion, casualty, corpse, death, death toll, deceased (*formal*), fatality, martyr, prey, quarry, remains, stiff (*slang*), victim

927 Death and Bereavement

Happiness is beneficial for the body, but it is grief that develops the powers of the mind. **Marcel Proust**

(*adj*) bereaved, bereft, *in mourning*

(*n*) bereavement, death, decease (*formal*), demise (*formal*), end, expiry (*formal or literary*), fatality, *grieving*, loss, mourner, mourning, passing, *rigor mortis*

See also END (54)

928 Deadly

There is no trap so deadly as the trap you set for yourself. **Raymond Chandler**

(*adj*) deadly, fatal, life-threatening, malignant, mortal, murderous, poisonous, terminal, venomous

See also DANGEROUS (237)

929 Burial and Preparation for Burial

When we attend the funerals of our friends we grieve for them, but when we go to those of other people it is chiefly our own deaths that we mourn for. **Gerald Brenan**

(*adj*) *funerary*, obituary, posthumous, *post-obit* (*formal*)

(*n*) autopsy, burial, cemetery, cremation, disinterment, epitaph, funeral, *funeral director*, *funeral home* (*US*), *funeral Mass*, *funeral rites*, *gravedigger*, *grave mound*, inquest, interment (*formal*), monument, *mortician* (*US*), mummy (*informal*), obituary, *pallbearer*, postmortem, *postmortem examination*, *service for the dead*, undertaker, vigil

(*v*) bury, disinter, embalm, exhume, inter (*formal*), *lay to rest*, mummify, unearth

930 Burial Places and Accessories

The grave is either like a ditch from the ditches of Hell, or like a luxuriant garden from the luxuriant gardens of Paradise. **Al-Tirmidhi**

(*n*) barrow, burial ground, burial place, casket (*US*), catacomb, *charnel house*, churchyard, coffin, *God's Acre* (*literary*), grave, gravestone, graveyard, headstone, necropolis, ossuary (*formal*), *resting place*, sarcophagus, sepulchre, tomb, *tumulus*

See also MONUMENTS (1091)

People

931 Person

The liberty of the individual must be thus far limited; he must not make himself a nuisance to other people. **John Stuart Mill**

(*n*) adult, bod (*slang*), character, civilian, cookie (*informal*), creature, figure, hominid, hominoid, *homo sapiens*, human, human being, humanity, humankind, *humanoid*, human race, individual, machine, mankind, *mensch* (*informal*), mortal, party, person, persona, society, sort (*informal*), soul, stiff (*US slang*), target, type (*informal*)

(*pron*) anybody, anyone, somebody, someone

932 Gender Identity and Sexuality

There is no essential sexuality. Maleness and femaleness are something we are dressed in. **Naomi Wallace**

(*adj*) asexual, *epicene*, female, feminine, *genderless*, *girlish*, hermaphrodite, laddish (*informal*), macho, male, manly, masculine, *sexless*, tomboyish, *womanlike*, womanly

(*n*) femininity, gender, *girlishness*, *hermaphroditism*, machismo, manliness, masculinity, sex, *sexual category*, *sexual characteristics*, *womanliness*

933 Female Person

Man is defined as a human being and woman as a female—whenever she behaves as a human being she is said to imitate the male. **Simone de Beauvoir**

(*n*) *damsel* (*archaic or literary*), female, *girl*, lady, lass, lassie (*informal*), *mademoiselle*, maiden, matron, woman, womanhood, womankind, *young lady*

934 Male Person

The male ego with few exceptions is elephantine to start with. **Bette Davis**

(*n*) beau (*archaic*), bloke (*informal*), boy, cat (*US dated slang*), chap (*informal*), codger (*informal*), dandy (*dated*), dude (*US slang*), *fella* (*informal*), fellow (*dated*), fop, *geezer* (*informal*), gent (*dated informal*), gentleman, guv (*informal*), guvnor (*dated informal*), guy (*informal*), *hipster* (*dated informal*), lad (*informal*), laddie (*informal*), male, man, manhood, mankind (*dated*), prince (*US informal*), sonny (*informal*), swell (*dated informal*), *young man*

935 Groups of People

A crowd is not company, and faces are but a gallery of pictures, and talk but a tinkling cymbal, where there is no love. **Francis Bacon**

(*n*) age group, army, band, bunch (*informal*), cadre, cohort, colony, committee, contingent, convoy, corps, couple, crew (*informal*), crowd, crush, double, drove, duet, duo, foursome, gaggle, gang, generation, group, grouping, herd, horde, huddle, junta, knot, legion, lineup, mob, multitude, organization, outfit (*informal*), pack, panel, party, phalanx, pool, press, rabble, school, squad, stable, swarm, team, *threesome*, throng, train, triad, triangle, tribe, trinity, trio, triplet, triumvirate, troika, troop, troupe, twosome, unit

See also THE FAMILY (956)

936 Friends and Acquaintances

The good person is related to his friend as to himself (for his friend is another self). **Aristotle**

(*n*) acquaintanceship, circle, clan (*informal*), clique, company, *coterie*, entourage, gang, guys (*informal*), in-crowd (*informal*), in-group, posse (*informal*), retinue, set, *social circle*

See also FRIENDS (963)

937 Audiences and Attendees

Audiences? No, the plural is impossible. Whether it be in Butte, Montana, or Broadway, it's an audience. The same great hulking monster with four thousand eyes and forty thousand teeth. **John Barrymore**

(*n*) assemblage, attendance, audience, concourse, conference, congregation, gate, turnout

See also MEETINGS AND ASSEMBLIES (43)

938 Groups with a Common Interest

There is apt to be a lunatic fringe among the votaries of any forward movement. **Theodore Roosevelt**

(*n*) alliance, brigade, cabal, cadre, camp, cartel, caucus, cell, coalition, collective, commission, confederacy, confederation, crowd, delegation, deputation, enclave, expedition, faction, fraternity, *ginger group*, group, interest group, league, lineup, lobby, lobby group, membership, minority, movement, party, readership, search party, sect, *self-help group*, side, *sisterhood*, *sorority* (*US*), *special interest group*, splinter group, support group, support system, syndicate, task force, team, trust (*US*)

See also BUSINESS ENTERPRISES AND RELATED BODIES (793)

939 Clubs and Societies

Please accept my resignation. I don't want to belong to any club that will accept me as a member. **Groucho Marx**

(*n*) association, club, interest group, order, society, union

940 Groups in Society

(*n*) citizenry (*formal*), civilization, community, constituency, country, culture, edifice, folk, folks (*informal*), general public, nation, people, populace, population, public, race, *rank and file*, society, subculture, townspeople, world

See also INHABITANT (857)

941 Solitariness

You find in solitude only what you take to it. **Juan Ramón Jiménez**

(*adj*) *all alone*, alone, aloof, cloistered, deserted, forlorn, forsaken, *friendless*, incommunicado, isolated, lone, lonely, lonesome (*US*), marooned, monkish, only, reclusive, single, solitary

(*adv*) aloofly

(*n*) alienation, aloofness, inaccessibility, loneliness, *lonesomeness* (*US*), privacy, *reclusiveness*, *solitariness*, solitude, withdrawal

See also ACTING INDEPENDENTLY (285), NOMADIC AND ROOTLESS LIFESTYLES (884)

942 Solitary People

But there comes a moment in everybody's life when he must decide whether he'll live among human beings or not—a fool among fools or a fool alone. **Thornton Wilder**

(*n*) anchorite, castaway, *eremite* (*literary*), foundling (*dated*), free spirit, hermit, individualist, introvert, *leper*, loner, *lone wolf*, maverick, misfit, oddity, outcast, outsider, recluse

943 Belonging or Relating to People

Individuals pass like shadows; but the commonwealth is fixed and stable. **Edmund Burke**

(*adj*) civil, collective, collegial, common, communal, cooperative, corporate, cultural, ethnic, grassroots, majority, national, nationalized, proletarian, public, racial, shared, social, societal, state-owned, subcultural

(*adv*) culturally, socially

944 Belonging or Relating to Individuals

A man may be in as just possession of truth as of a city, and yet be forced to surrender. **Thomas Browne**

(*adj*) individual, internal, internecine, minority, one-to-one, own, personal, private, proprietary, respective, subjective

(*adv*) firsthand, one-to-one, personally

945 Child or Youth

A child is a guest in the house, to be loved and respected—never possessed, since he belongs to God. **J. D. Salinger**

(*n*) adolescent, babe (*literary or archaic*), *babe in arms*, baby, child, infant, juvenile, kid (*informal*), kiddy (*informal*), lad, minor, moppet (*informal*), *neonate*, newborn, nipper (*informal*), orphan, prepubescent, *preteen*, *preteenager*, ragamuffin (*dated*), *rug rat* (*informal humorous*), sapling (*literary*), son, sprog (*slang*), teen (*informal*), teenager, *tiddler* (*informal*), titch (*informal*), toddler, tot (*informal*), urchin, waif, *young child*, younger generation, *young people*, young person, youngster, *young'un* (*informal*), youth

See also BABYHOOD, CHILDHOOD, AND ADOLESCENCE (917)

946 Mischievous or Badly-Behaved Child

It was no wonder that people were so horrible when they started life as children. **Kingsley Amis**

(*n*) brat, imp, mischief, monkey (*informal*), pup, puppy, *rapscallion* (*archaic or humorous*), rascal, scallywag (*dated informal*), scamp (*informal*), *spoiled brat*, tearaway, terror (*informal*), tyke, *whippersnapper* (*dated*)

947 Villains and Thugs

One murder makes a villain. Millions a hero. Numbers sanctify. **Charlie Chaplin**

(*n*) *adulterer*, animal, *antihero*, autocrat, baddie (*informal*), *bad guy*, beast, blackguard, boor, bruiser (*informal*), brute, buccaneer, bully, bullyboy, cad (*dated*), caveman (*informal*), cowboy (*informal*), desperado (*literary*), despot, *devil*, dictator, disciplinarian, evildoer, fiend, goon (*US*), gorilla (*informal*), *hatchet man* (*slang*), heavy (*slang*), heavyweight, hood, hoodlum, hooligan (*informal*), manipulator, marauder, miscreant (*literary*), mobster (*US informal*), monster, moocher (*informal*), oppressor, pig (*informal*), predator, prowler, rake, rat (*slang*), renegade, reprobate, rogue, rotter (*informal dated*), roughneck (*informal*), ruffian (*dated*), savage, scoundrel, thug, tyrant, vandal, villain, wretch (*formal*), wrongdoer, yob (*informal*), *yobbo* (*informal*)

See also CRIMINALS (821)

948 Lazy or Unsuccessful People

That indolent but agreeable condition of doing nothing. **Pliny the Younger**

(*n*) backslider, boob (*informal*), buffoon, *bumbler*, cadger (*informal*), conformist, coward, creep (*informal*), dawdler, daydreamer, deadbeat (*slang*), defeatist, ditherer, dreamer, *fraidy-cat* (*US informal*), freeloader (*informal*), goldbricker (*US informal*), idealist, idler, joke, laggard, *lame duck*, latecomer, layabout, lazybones (*informal*), lemming, lightweight, loafer, loser, lotus-eater, *lowlife* (*informal*), *malingerer* (*disapproving*), minnow, ne'er-do-well (*dated*), nobody, nonentity, nothing, parasite, *pariah*, *persona non grata*, plodder, quitter (*informal*), runt, *scaredy-cat* (*informal*), scrounger (*informal*), sellout (*US informal*), sheep, *shilly-shallier*, shirker, skiver (*informal*), slacker, slouch (*informal*), space cadet (*slang*), *sponge* (*informal*), sponger (*informal*), straggler, timeserver, *timewaster*, *twit* (*dated*), underdog, vampire, *vermin*, *waster*, *wastrel*, *woolgatherer*, wretch (*humorous*), zombie (*informal*)

949 Self-Important and Self-Seeking People

EGOIST, *n. A person of low taste, more interested in himself than in me.* **Ambrose Bierce**

(*n*) *arriviste* (*disapproving*), *attention-seeker*, bighead (*informal*), bigmouth (*informal*), blower (*US informal*), *blowhard* (*US*), *boaster*, braggart, *bragger*, chauvinist, daredevil, egoist, egomaniac, egotist, exhibitionist, *fashion victim*, *jingoist*, know-all (*informal*), *loudmouth* (*informal*), megalomaniac, name-dropper, *narcissist*, peacock, pseud, roisterer, *self-seeker*, show-off (*informal*), smart aleck (*informal*), smarty-pants (*informal*), stuffed shirt (*informal*), *swelled head* (*US*), upstart, *wise guy* (*US informal*)

950 Interfering People and Telltales

No one gossips about other people's secret virtues. **Bertrand Russell**

(*n*) accuser, bigmouth (*informal*), blabbermouth (*informal*), busybody (*informal*), chatterbox (*informal*), chatterer, *do-gooder* (*informal*), double agent, fusspot (*informal*), gossip, gossipmonger, grass (*slang*), infiltrator, informant, informer, interloper, magpie (*informal*), meddler, mole, muckraker, mudslinger, nark (*slang*), nitpicker, *nosy parker* (*informal*), obstructionist, ringleader, rumour mill, rumourmonger, scandalmonger, secret agent, *snake in the grass*, sneak, snitch (*slang*), snoop (*informal*), snout (*slang*), source, spook, spy, *squealer* (*slang*), stirrer (*informal*), *stool pigeon* (*slang*), *stoolie* (*US slang*), supergrass (*informal*), taleteller, tattle, tattler, tattletale (*US*), telltale (*informal*), whistle-blower, windbag (*informal*)

See also BETRAY CONFIDENCES AND GOSSIP (619)

951 Superficial or Insincere People

In our way we were both snobs, and no snob welcomes another who has risen with him. **Cecil Beaton**

(*n*) *bootlicker* (*informal*), chameleon, charmer, courtier, gold brick (*informal*), *gold digger*, goody-goody (*informal*), *goody two-shoes* (*informal*), lapdog, *leech*, *ligger* (*informal*), opportunist, *poser* (*informal*), poseur, *shark* (*informal*), *skunk* (*slang*), smoothie (*informal*), snob, social climber, sycophant, toady, voyeur

See also PEOPLE WHO DECEIVE (662)

952 Financially Mean People

Who lendeth nothing is an ugly and wicked creature. **François Rabelais**

(*n*) cheapskate (*informal*), curmudgeon, meanie (*informal*), miser, niggard, penny pincher (*informal*), pinchpenny, scrooge (*informal*), skinflint

See also FINANCIALLY MEAN AND GRASPING (520)

953 Grumpy and Negative People

Petulance is not sarcasm, and...insolence is not invective. **Benjamin Disraeli**

(*n*) alarmist, *backbiter*, bigot, *carper*, *Cassandra*, complainer, crank (*informal*), crosspatch (*dated informal*), cynic, detractor, *dog in the manger*, faultfinder, fussbudget (*US informal*), gadfly (*dated*), *gloomy Gus* (*US*), grouch (*informal*), grumbler, *hardliner*, *hard taskmaster*, *homophobe*, *hypochondriac*, killjoy, knocker (*informal*), martinet, misanthrope, misanthropist, misery (*informal*), moaner (*informal*), party pooper (*informal*), pedant, perfectionist, pessimist, philistine (*disapproving*), purist, scaremonger, sourpuss (*informal*), spoilsport, stickler, valetudinarian, wet blanket (*informal*), whiner, whinger (*informal*), worrier, *worryguts* (*informal*), *worrywart* (*US informal*)

See also NEGATIVE OF OUTLOOK (515)

954 Dirty and Slovenly People

She wears her clothes, as if they were thrown on her with a pitchfork. **Jonathan Swift**

(*n*) dumper, litterbug (*informal*), litter lout (*informal*), polluter

955 People who are Approved Of

Today's hero, the urban animal...can no longer be exclusively national, or even European, but instead must be...fertilized by the contributions of any number of different civilizations. **Juan Goytisolo**

(*n*) *altruist*, *battler*, *blue-eyed boy* (*informal*), careerist, darling, doer, dynamo (*informal*), go-getter (*informal*), good guy (*US informal*), goody, *guardian angel* (*informal*), hero, heroine, idol, *knight in shining armour*, liberator, *life and soul of the party*, live wire (*informal*), messiah, optimist, pet, philanthropist, pillar, pragmatist, protagonist, pussycat (*informal*), rainmaker (*US informal*), *rationalist*, *ray of sunshine*, rock, saviour, *self-starter*, *stayer*, superhero, survivor, titan, toast, tower of strength (*informal*), trier, *trooper*, workhorse (*informal*)

See also TALENTED OR INTELLIGENT PERSON (529), MORALLY GOOD (775)

Relationships with Others

956 The Family

The family is strongest where objective reality is most likely to be misinterpreted. **Don DeLillo**

(*adj*) ancestral, biological, dynastic, familial, family, filial, fraternal, genealogical, hereditary, parental, tribal

(*n*) ancestor, ancestry, blood, *blood relation*, *blood relative*, clan, *close relative*, connections, descendant, descent, dynasty, extraction, family, family circle, *family member*, family tree, family unit, flesh, *flesh and blood*, folks, forebear, genealogy, hearth, home, house, household, kin, kindred, kinfolk, kinsfolk, *kinsman* (*formal*), *kinswoman* (*formal*), kith and kin, line, lineage, loved ones, menfolk, *nearest and dearest*, next of kin, *nuclear family*, parentage, pedigree, people (*informal*), relations, relative, tribe (*informal*)

See also GROUPS OF PEOPLE (935)

957 Same Generation Relatives

Too many cousins ruin the shopkeeper. **Proverb**

types of same generation relative brother, cousin, second cousin, senior, sibling, sister, stepbrother, stepsister

958 Younger Generation Relatives

Every generation revolts against its fathers and makes friends with its grandfathers. **Lewis Mumford**

(*n*) brood, *first-born*, heir, issue, offspring, progeny, scion, spawn, young

types of offspring only child, quadruplet, quintuplet, singleton, triplet, twin

types of younger relative child, daughter, dependant, grandchild, granddaughter, grandson, great-grandchild, great-granddaughter, great-grandson, great-nephew, great-niece, nephew, niece, son, stepchild, stepdaughter, stepson

959 Older Generation Relatives

Parents are sometimes a bit of a disappointment to their children. They don't fulfil the promise of their early years. **Anthony Powell**

(*n*) *adoptive parent*, ancestor, *forebear*, *forefather*, forerunner, *gramps* (*informal*), guvnor (*dated informal*), ma (*informal*), *mam* (*regional informal*), mama (*informal*), *mammy* (*informal*), *mater* (*dated informal or humorous*), *materfamilias* (*literary*), matriarch, *momma* (*US informal*), *mommy* (*US informal*), mummy (*informal*), *nan* (*informal*), *nana* (*informal*), nanny (*informal*), *papa* (*informal dated*), pater (*dated slang or humorous*), paterfamilias, patriarch, *poppa* (*US*), progenitor

types of older relative aunt, biological parent, dad (*informal*), daddy (*informal*), father, gran, granddad (*informal*), grandfather, grandma, grandmother, grandpa, grandparent, granny, great-aunt, great-grandfather, great-grandmother, great-grandparent, great-uncle, lone parent, mom (*US*), mother, mum (*informal*), parent, single parent, stepfather, stepmother, stepparent, uncle

960 Relatives by Marriage

A husband is what is left of the lover after the nerve has been extracted. **Helen Rowland**

(*n*) betrothed (*formal*), bride, *bride and groom*, bridegroom, consort (*formal*), fiancé, fiancée, *groomsman*, *hubby* (*informal*), husband, *husband-to-be*, intended (*dated or humorous*), newlywed, partner, spouse, wife, *wife-to-be*

types of in-law brother-in-law, daughter-in-law, father-in-law, mother-in-law, sister-in-law, son-in-law

961 Married State

Every marriage tends to consist of an aristocrat and a peasant. Of a teacher and a learner. **John Updike**

(*adj*) conjugal, connubial (*formal*), marital, married, matrimonial, wedded

(*n*) matrimony, union, wedlock

See also MARITAL STATUS (890)

962 Adoption, Fostering, and Extended Family

I had cherished a profound conviction that her bringing me up by hand, gave her no right to bring me up by jerks. **Charles Dickens**

(*n*) *carer*, caretaker (*US*), foster child, *foster father*, *foster mother*, foster parent, *godparent*, guardian, guardianship, protégé

963 Friends

Love is rarer than genius itself. And friendship is rarer than love. **Charles Pierre Péguy**

(*n*) acquaintance, ally, *amigo*, associate, *best friend*, *best mate*, blood brother, *boon companion*, *bosom buddy* (*US*), *bosom friend*, brother, buddy (*US informal*), caller, chum (*informal*), *close friend*, cohort (*US disapproving*), companion, company, comrade, confidant, *confidante*, *confrère* (*formal*), friend, guest, house guest, mate, pal (*informal*), pen friend, pen pal (*informal*), playfellow (*dated*), playmate, *schoolmate*, sister, soul mate, sounding board

See also FRIENDS AND ACQUAINTANCES (936)

964 Sexual and Romantic Relationships

A lover without indiscretion is no lover at all. **Thomas Hardy**

(*n*) beau (*dated*), boyfriend, *cohabitee*, *concubine*, courtship, dalliance (*literary*), *ex* (*informal*), flirtation, girlfriend, *inamorata* (*literary*), item (*informal*), *ladyfriend* (*informal humorous*), matchmaker, mistress, *old flame* (*informal*), *other half*, *paramour* (*literary*), past love, romance, significant other, *suitor* (*formal*), swain (*literary*), *valentine*

965 Bosses and Management

The first responsibility of a leader is to define reality. **Max de Pree**

(*n*) acolyte, boss, chief, chieftain, consultant, controller, elder, employee, employer, gaffer (*informal*), governor, guv (*informal*), guvnor (*dated informal*), head, interviewer, leader, line manager, management, master, mistress, organizer, overseer, principal, ranger, senior, skipper (*informal*), superintendent, superior, supervisor, supremo (*informal*), Svengali, user, usher

See also WORKER (836)

966 Subordinates and Assistants

The crow does not roost with the phoenix. **Chinese proverb**

(*n*) adjunct, affiliate, aide, amanuensis, assistant, attendant, concierge (*US*), deputy, flunky (*informal*), functionary, helper, helpmate, *helpmeet* (*archaic*), inferior, interviewee, *lieutenant*, *locum*, minion, personal assistant, puppet, recruit, representative, right hand, subject, subordinate, successor, succour (*literary*), underling, *vassal*, *whipping boy*

See also WORKER (836)

967 Colleagues and Equals

When we ask advice, we are usually looking for an accomplice. **Joseph Louis Lagrange**

(*n*) associate, collaborator, colleague, contemporary, counterpart, coworker, fellow, mate, opposite number, partner, peer, peer group, reserve, roomie (*US informal*), roommate, sidekick (*informal*), sparring partner, standby, team-mate, understudy, workmate

See also WORKER (836)

968 Representatives and Patrons

Patron. *Commonly a wretch who supports with insolence, and is paid with flattery.* **Samuel Johnson**

(*n*) agent, ambassador, angel, backer, benefactor, delegate, donor, emissary, envoy, intermediary, legate, middleman, negotiator, patron, plenipotentiary, provider, proxy, rep (*informal*), representative, sponsor, third party, underwriter

969 Enemies and Tormentors

There's a snake hidden in the grass. **Virgil**

(*n*) accuser, adversary, aggressor, antagonist, archenemy, assailant, avenger, chaser, conqueror, critic, enemy, foe (*literary*), invader, nemesis, opponent, opposition, persecutor, pursuer, rival, shadow, *sworn enemy*, tail (*informal*), tormentor, torturer, tracker

970 Supporters, Protectors, and Compatriots

Comrades, leave me here a little, while as yet 'tis early morn:/Leave me here, and when you want me, sound upon the bugle-horn. **Alfred Tennyson**

(*n*) admirer, alter ego, apologist, apostle, best man, bridesmaid, *caregiver* (*US*), *chaperon*, chaperone, *co-author*, co-conspirator, compatriot, confederate, connections, contact, contributor, correspondent, countryman, countrywoman, cousin, crony (*disapproving*), custodian, disciple, escort, favourite, flatmate, follower, guardian, outrider, party, preserver, *proselyte*, protector, provider, rescuer, seconder, shadow, supporter, sympathizer, trustee, wannabe (*informal*), well-wisher

971 Advisers, Judges, and Arbiters

A judge is a law student who marks his own examination papers. **H. L. Mencken**

(*n*) adjudicator, adviser, appeaser, arbiter, assessor, conciliator, counsellor, evaluator, go-between, guidance counsellor, guide, master, mediator, mentor, moderator, monitor, peacekeeper, peacemaker, piggy in the middle, referee, regulator

972 Strangers

Be not forgetful to entertain strangers: for thereby some have entertained angels unawares. **Bible**

(*n*) alien, foreigner, gatecrasher, incomer, interloper, intruder, newcomer, nonmember, nonresident, passer-by, stranger, unknown

973 Relationship to Another

Hunger is my native place in the land of the passions. Hunger for. . .a fellowship founded on righteousness, and a righteousness attained in fellowship. **Dag Hammarskjöld**

(*adj*) *acquainted*, adoptive, amicable, attached (*informal*), beholden, bosom (*informal*), close-knit, *codependent*, confidential, estranged, fond of, foster, fraternal, harmonious, indebtedness, independent, inferior, inseparable, interpersonal, intimate, maternal, matey, monogamous, *pally* (*informal*), paternal, paternalistic, platonic, reliant, right-hand, rival, self-contained, self-reliant, self-sufficient, separate, subordinate, subservient, *thick as thieves*, *well-acquainted*

(*adv*) amicably, harmoniously, socially

(*n*) acquaintance, amity (*formal*), antagonism, association, brotherhood, camaraderie, chumminess (*informal*), closeness, collusion, companionship, company, *comradeship*, dependency, estrangement, fatherhood, fellowship, fidelity, fling (*informal*), fraternity, friendship, guidance, independence, intimacy, kinship, leadership, maternity, monogamy, parentage, parenthood, partnership, paternalism, paternity, *peaceful coexistence*, power, relations, rivalry, romance, self-reliance, self-sufficiency, servitude, sovereignty, sway, terms, togetherness, warfare

974 Establishing Relationships with Others

Ye gods! annihilate but space and time./And make two lovers happy. **Alexander Pope**

(*v*) align, ally, ask, associate, assort with, be accepted, become acquainted, befriend, bond, chat up (*informal*), circulate (*informal*), click (*informal*), connect, consort with (*formal*), cooperate, cosy up, court (*dated*), curry favour, endear, espouse (*archaic*), fall in with, fraternize, gel (*informal*), *get acquainted*, get along (*US*), get hitched (*informal*), *get in good with* (*US*), get in with, get married, get on, get to know, *go around with* (*informal*), go in with, go with (*informal*), greet, hang about, hang around, hang out (*informal*), hit it off (*informal*), hit on (*US slang*), hobnob (*disapproving*), ingratiate, insinuate, integrate, jell, join forces, join up, latch onto, make contacts, make friends, *make overtures*, make points with (*US*), make somebody's acquaintance, make up, marry, meet, merge, mess about (*informal*), mess around (*informal*), mingle, mix, pander to, *pay court to* (*dated*), receive, relate, remarry, romance, run around, socialize, splice (*slang*), stick around (*informal*), stick together, stick with, *strike up a friendship*, take out, tie the knot (*informal*), unite, walk down the aisle, wed, woo (*literary*)

See also INITIATE AND ESTABLISH COMMUNICATION (681)

975 Refusing or Rejecting Relations

Learn to reject friendship, or rather the dream of friendship...friendship ought to be a gratuitous joy, like the joys afforded by art. **Simone Weil**

(*v*) alienate, blackball, break up, break with, brush off, bust up (*informal*), *cut dead*, desert, ditch (*informal*), dump (*informal*), freeze out, *give the brushoff, give the bum's rush* (*slang*), give the cold shoulder to, jilt, leave, leave alone, leave be, leave in peace, let alone, let be, look through, maroon, orphan, ostracize, rebuff, repulse, send to Coventry, separate, shun, snub, split up, spurn, squeeze out, strand, turn against, turn away, walk out on (*informal*)

The World Around Us

Living Things

976 Living Things and Living

The generations of living things pass in a short time, and like runners hand on the torch of life. **Lucretius**

(*adj*) alive, animal, animate, bodily, breathing, *flesh-and-blood*, fleshly, human, live, living, organic, physical, sensual, sentient

(*n*) animal, beast, being, biped, brute (*literary*), creature, fauna, *flora and fauna*, *life form*, *living being*, living thing, mammal, organism, pet, quadruped, vertebrate, wildlife

977 Young Animal

types of young animal bullock, calf, colt, cub, fawn, foal, heifer, joey, kid, kitten, lamb, leveret, piglet, pup, puppy, whelp, yearling

978 Male or Female Animal

types of male animal billy goat, boar, buck, bull, bullock, colt, hart, jackass, ram, stag, stallion, steer, tom, tomcat, wether

types of female animal bitch, cow, dam, doe, ewe, filly, heifer, hind, jenny, lioness, mare, nanny goat, sow, tigress, vixen

979 Canine

types of canine aardwolf, coyote, dingo, dog, fox, hyena, jackal, wolf

980 Dog

(*adj*) canine, *doggy*

(*n*) canine (*humorous*), cur, dog, hound, mongrel, *mutt* (*slang*), pooch (*informal*), *pye-dog*

types of small dog affenpinscher, basenji, basset, beagle, bull terrier, chihuahua, chow, corgi, dachshund, fox-hound, Pekingese, poodle, pug, spaniel, terrier, whippet

types of large dog Afghan hound, Alsatian, bloodhound, borzoi, boxer, bulldog, collie, dalmatian, Doberman pinscher, German shepherd (*US*), greyhound, guide dog, husky, Labrador, mastiff, retriever, Rottweiler, Saint Bernard, setter, sheepdog, wolfhound

981 Deer and Antelope

types of deer or antelope antelope, caribou, chamois, chevrotain, dik-dik, elk, gazelle, gnu, impala, moose, okapi, reindeer, springbok, Thomson's gazelle

982 Farm Animal

(*n*) cattle, *livestock*, stock, swine

types of farm animal cow, donkey, goat, hog, horse, mule, ox, pig, sheep

983 Feline

(*n*) cat, kitty (*informal*), moggy (*slang*), puss (*informal*), pussy (*informal*), pussycat

types of cat big cat, bobcat, Burmese cat, cheetah, jaguar, leopard, lion, lynx, Manx cat, mountain lion (*US*), ocelot, panther, Persian cat, puma, Siamese cat, tabby, tiger, tortoiseshell, wildcat

984 Flying Mammal

types of flying mammal flying fox, flying squirrel, fruit bat, pipistrelle, vampire bat

985 Horse

(*adj*) equestrian, *equine*, horsey

(*n*) horse, mount, steed (*literary*)

parts of a horse croup, fetlock, flank, foreleg, hind-quarters, hock, hoof, mane, pastern, shank, withers

types of horse Arabian horse, ass, bronco, brood mare, carthorse, charger, cob, hack, hunter, mustang, pack-horse, pony, racehorse, saddle horse, Shetland pony, shire horse, thoroughbred, trotter, warhorse, work-horse, zebra

986 Large Mammal

types of large mammal alpaca, bactrian camel, bear, bison, boar, buffalo, camel, dromedary, elephant, giraffe, hippo-potamus, llama, panda, polar bear, rhinoceros, wart hog

987 Marine Mammal

types of marine mammal dolphin, dugong, grampus, manatee, porpoise, seal, sea lion, walrus, whale

988 Primate

types of primate ape, aye-aye, baboon, Barbary ape, bonnet monkey, capuchin, chimp, chimpanzee, colobus, gibbon, gorilla, human, lemur, macaque, mandrill, marmoset, monkey, orang-utan, proboscis monkey, rhesus monkey, spider monkey

989 Rodent

types of rodent beaver, capybara, chinchilla, chipmunk, coypu, dormouse, gerbil, gopher, groundhog, guinea pig, hamster, jerboa, lemming, marmot, mole, mouse, muskrat, prairie dog, rat, shrew, squirrel, vole, wood-chuck

990 Small Mammal

types of small mammal anteater, armadillo, badger, ferret, hare, hedgehog, hyrax, marten, mink, mongoose, otter, pine marten, polecat, porcupine, rabbit, raccoon, skunk, sloth, stoat, weasel, wolverine

991 Whale

types of whale blue whale, grey whale, humpback whale, killer whale, minke whale, narwhal, pilot whale, right whale, sperm whale, white whale

992 Marsupial

types of marsupial bandicoot, bettong, bilby, kangaroo, koala, opossum, phalanger, potoroo, Tasmanian devil, thylacine, wallaby, wombat

993 Group of Animals

types of herd bevy, colony, drove, flock, gam, kennel, litter, pack, pod, pride, school, shoal, skulk, troop

994 Reptile

types of reptile alligator, basilisk, bearded dragon, cayman, chameleon, crocodile, gecko, gila monster, glass snake, goanna, horned lizard, iguana, Komodo dragon, lizard, moloch, monitor lizard, mugger, skink, slow-worm, terrapin, tortoise, turtle

995 Snake

(*n*) *sea serpent*, serpent (*literary*), snake

types of non-poisonous snake anaconda, blacksnake, boa, boa constrictor, garter snake, grass snake, king snake, python, rat snake, water snake, whip snake

types of poisonous snake adder, asp, cobra, copperhead, coral snake, diamondback, fer-de-lance, horned viper, mamba, pit viper, puff adder, rattler, rattlesnake, ring-hals, sea snake, sidewinder, taipan, viper, water moc-casin

996 Dinosaur

types of dinosaur allosaurus, ankylosaur, brachiosaurus, brontosaurus, cotylosaur, dicynodont, diplodocus, had-rosaur, ichthyosaur, iguanodon, megalosaur, mosasaur, pelycosaur, plesiosaur, pteranodon, pterodactyl, ptero-saur, stegosaur, titanosaur, triceratops, tyrannosaur

997 Bird

types of common bird blue jay, bluetit, camp robber (*US regional*), cardinal, chaffinch, chickadee, cuckoo, dove, finch, house martin, jay, martin, nuthatch, pigeon, robin, sparrow, starling, swallow, swift, tit, turtledove, wood-pecker, wren

types of pet bird budgerigar, canary, cockatoo, homing pigeon, lovebird, macaw, parakeet, parrot

types of flightless bird dodo, emu, kiwi, ostrich, peacock, penguin

types of scavenger buzzard (*US*), condor, crow, jackdaw, lammergeier, magpie, marabou, raven, rook, vulture

998 Bird of Prey

types of bird of prey bald eagle, buteo (*US*), buzzard, eagle, falcon, golden eagle, hawk, kestrel, kite, osprey, peregrine falcon, sea eagle, sparrowhawk

999 Food Bird

types of fowl bantam, broiler (*US*), chicken, duck, goose, grouse, guinea fowl, partridge, pheasant, pigeon, quail, turkey, waterfowl, wildfowl, woodcock

1000 Freshwater Bird

(*n*) water bird, waterfowl

types of freshwater bird barnacle goose, bittern, Canada goose, canvasback, coot, crane, diver, duck, egret, fla-mingo, grebe, heron, ibis, kingfisher, loon (*US*), mallard, merganser, moorhen, snipe, spoonbill, stork, swan, teal

1001 Owl

types of owl barn owl, fish owl, hoot owl, little owl, long-eared owl, screech owl, short-eared owl, snowy owl, tawny owl

1002 Seabird

types of seabird albatross, auk, avocet, cormorant, fulmar, gannet, guillemot, gull, kittiwake, oystercatcher, pelican, plover, puffin, seagull, shag, skua, storm petrel, tern, wader

1003 Songbird

types of songbird blackbird, bluebird, flycatcher, hedge sparrow, lark, linnet, meadowlark, nightingale, nightjar, oriole, pied wagtail, pipit, skylark, thrush, titmouse, wagtail, warbler, weaverbird, woodlark, yellowhammer

1004 Young Bird

types of young bird chick, cygnet, duckling, eaglet, eyas, fledgling, gosling, nestling, owlet, pullet, squab

1005 Male or Female Bird

types of male or female bird capon, cob, cock, cockerel, drake, duck, gander, goose, hen, pen, rooster

1006 Parts of a Bird

parts of a bird beak, bill, carina, cockscomb, comb, crest, crop, down, feather, gizzard, gorge, plumage, plume, quill, ruff, tail, talon, web, wing, wingtip, wishbone

1007 Group of Birds

types of flock bevy, brood, clutch, covey, flight, gaggle, skein, swarm

1008 Amphibian

types of amphibian axolotl, bullfrog, cane toad, frog, horned toad, midwife toad, natterjack toad, newt, sala-mander, toad, tree frog, xenopus

1009 Sea Fish

types of tropical sea fish barracuda, flying fish, kingfish, mahi-mahi, marlin, pomfret, sailfish, sawfish, snapper, stingray, swordfish, tuna

types of flatfish angelfish, flounder, halibut, lemon sole, manta (*US*), manta ray, plaice, pompano, ray, skate, sole, stingray, turbot

types of sea fish anchovy, anglerfish, cod, coley, dogfish, eel, haddock, hake, herring, John Dory, ling, mackerel, monkfish, pilchard, salmon, sardine, sea bream, shark, sprat, sturgeon, whitebait, whiting

1010 Freshwater Fish

types of freshwater fish bass, bream, carp, catfish, crappie, goldfish, grayling, guppy, loach, minnow, mullet, Nile perch, perch, pike, piranha, roach, stickleback, tench, tilapia, trout

1011 Parts of a Fish

parts of a fish air bladder, anal fin, dorsal fin, fin, gill, pectoral fin, pelvic fin, roe, scale, tail

1012 Insect

(*n*) bug, creepy-crawly (*informal*), gnat, insect, pest

1013 Flying Insect

types of flying insect aphid, bee, black fly, bluebottle, bumblebee, cicada, crane fly, daddy longlegs, deer fly, dragonfly, firefly, fruit fly, gnat, grasshopper, greenfly, hornet, horsefly, locust, mayfly, midge, mosquito, no-see-um (*US*), punkie (*US*), tsetse fly, wasp, whitefly

1014 Ant

types of ant army ant, leafcutter ant, Pharaoh ant, red ant, slave ant, slave-making ant, termite, white ant

1015 Moths and Butterflies

types of moth cinnabar moth, clearwing, clothes moth, death's head moth, emperor moth, goat moth, gypsy moth, hawk moth, luna moth, peppered moth, pyralid, tiger moth, tussock moth, underwing

types of butterfly cabbage butterfly (*US*), cabbage white, Camberwell beauty, emperor butterfly, monarch butterfly, mourning cloak (*US*), painted lady, peacock butterfly, red admiral, swallowtail, tiger swallowtail, tortoiseshell

1016 Beetles and Weevils

types of beetle cockroach, Colorado beetle, Colorado potato beetle (*US*), deathwatch beetle, dung beetle, flea beetle, Japanese beetle, ladybird, ladybug (*US*), rhinoceros beetle, roach (*informal*), scarab, stag beetle, water beetle, weevil

1017 Parasites

(*adj*) parasitic

(*n*) bloodsucker, parasite

types of parasitic insect bedbug, botfly, chigoe, crab louse, deer tick, flea, gadfly, harvest mite, head louse, horsefly, louse, mite, sand flea (*US*), sandfly, tapeworm, tick

1018 Arachnids

types of arachnid black widow, daddy longlegs (*US*), funnel-web spider, mite, money spider, scorpion, spider, tarantula, trapdoor spider, wolf spider

1019 Parts of an Insect

parts of an insect abdomen, antenna, feeler, proboscis, thorax, wing

1020 Insect Stages

types of insect stages of development caterpillar, chrysalis, glowworm, grub, imago, larva, maggot, nit, pupa, silkworm, woodworm

1021 Land Invertebrate

types of land invertebrate centipede, earthworm, millipede, mollusc, slug, snail, woodlouse, worm

1022 Aquatic Invertebrate

types of aquatic invertebrate abalone, barnacle, clam, cockle, conch, coral, crustacean, cuttlefish, jellyfish, limpet, mollusc, mussel, octopus, oyster, Portuguese man-of-war, quahog, scallop, sea anemone, sea urchin, sponge, squid, starfish, whelk, winkle

types of crustacean bivalve, crab, crayfish, hermit crab, horseshoe crab, langoustine, lobster, prawn, sand flea (*US*), sand hopper, shellfish, shrimp, water flea

See also SEA FOOD (1189)

1023 Microorganisms, Fungi, and Algae

The Microbe is so very small/You cannot make him out at all.
Hilaire Belloc

(*adj*) *amoebic*, bacterial, fungal, *microbial*, *viral*

(*n*) bug (*informal*), germ, microbe, microorganism, superbug

types of microorganism amoeba, bacteriophage, bacterium, botulinum, candida, ciliate, coccus, E. coli, flagellate, listeria, mycoplasma, protozoan, rhizopod, salmonella, spirillum, spirochaete, staphylococcus, stentor, streptococcus, virus

types of fungus beefsteak fungus, boletus, bracket fungus, cep, chanterelle, death cap, destroying angel, fairy ring champignon, field mushroom, fly agaric, horn of plenty, ink-cap, lichen, mildew, morel, mould, mushroom, orange-peel fungus, oyster mushroom, puffball, stinkhorn, toadstool, truffle, yeast

types of alga bladder wrack, brown alga, fucus, green alga, gulfweed, Irish moss, kelp, laminaria, phytoplankton, pond scum, red alga, rockweed, sea lettuce, seaweed, sea wrack, stonewort, tangle

1024 Plants and Trees

Trees are poems that the earth writes upon the sky. **Kahlil Gibran**

(*n*) plant, sapling, seedling, tree

See also WOODS, FORESTS, AND JUNGLES (1047)

1025 Vegetation

(*adj*) blooming, grassy, leafy, mossy, vegetable, verdant, wooded, woody

(*n*) brushwood, bushes, flora, greenery, greens (*US*), scrub, undergrowth, understorey, vegetation, verdure

1026 Parts of Trees and Plants

(*n*) *achene*, bloom (*literary*), blossom, bole, bough, branch, bud, bulb, burr, canopy, catkin, cutting, *fir cone*, floret, flower, foliage, frond, fruit, gum, husk, latex, leaf, nectar, needle, offshoot, pine cone, pod, resin, rhizome, root, rosebud, sap, scion, *seed case*, *seed husk*, *seed pod*, spore, sprig, sprout, tendril, thorn, treetop, trunk, tuber, twig

1027 Bushes and Shrubs

(*n*) bush, hedge, hedgerow, shrub, shrubbery, undershrub

types of shrub or bush azalea, bramble, briar, broom, camellia, elder, forsythia, gardenia, gorse, hawthorn, heather, hydrangea, laurel, lavender, lilac, magnolia, privet, pussy willow, rhododendron, rose, sagebrush, witch hazel

1028 Deciduous Trees

types of deciduous tree acacia, alder, ash, aspen, baobab, beech, birch, chestnut, elm, ginkgo, hickory, horse chestnut, laburnum, lime, maple, mesquite, mimosa, oak, plane tree, poplar, rowan, sassafras, silver birch, sycamore, teak, willow

1029 Evergreen and Coniferous Trees

(*n*) *evergreen*

types of evergreen tree bo tree, bunya, carob, cedar, cola, cypress, eucalyptus, fir, fir tree, gum tree, holly, juniper, kahikatea, kauri, larch, mahogany, mangrove, monkey puzzle, pine, redwood, sandalwood, sequoia, spruce, yew

1030 Flowers from Bulbs

types of flowers grown from bulbs anemone, bluebell, crocus, cyclamen, daffodil, dahlia, freesia, gladiolus, hyacinth, iris, jonquil, lily, narcissus, snowdrop, tulip

1031 Grass

types of grass bamboo, beach grass, bluegrass, bulrush, couch grass, crab grass, esparto, fescue, Kentucky bluegrass, lyme grass, marram, meadow fescue, pampas grass, reed, rye-grass, spinifex, sugar cane, sword grass, timothy

1032 Flowers

types of annual flower aster, forget-me-not, lobelia, love-in-a-mist, marigold, nasturtium, pansy, petunia, poppy, sunflower, sweet pea

types of perennial flower African violet, aquilegia, begonia, buttercup, carnation, chrysanthemum, columbine (*US*), cowslip, daisy, delphinium, foxglove, fuchsia, geranium, lily of the valley, lotus, love-lies-bleeding, lupin, orchid, pelargonium, peony, pink, primrose, rose, snapdragon, violet

1033 Climbers

(*n*) climber, creeper, vine

types of climber bougainvillea, bryony, clematis, convolvulus, grapevine, honeysuckle, ivy, jasmine, kudzu, liana, morning glory, passionflower, poison ivy, rattan, sarsaparilla, Virginia creeper, wisteria, woodbine

1034 Weeds and Thistles

types of weed bindweed, burdock, chickweed, dandelion, dock, goldenrod, jimsonweed (*US*), nettle, poison ivy, poison oak, ragweed, stinging nettle, thistle, thorn apple, tumbleweed

1035 Foliage Plants

(*n*) *bonsai*, houseplant, *pot plant*, *potted plant* (*US*)

types of foliage plant aspidistra, coleus, fern, moss, poinsettia, rubber plant, sansevieria, spider plant, yucca

1036 Mythical Creatures

A dragon stranded in shallow water furnishes amusement for the shrimps. **Chinese proverb**

types of mythological creature centaur, Chimera, dragon, griffin, mermaid, sphinx, unicorn, vampire, werewolf

See also MYTHICAL BEINGS (790), NONEXISTENT THINGS (23)

1037 Biological Sciences

No species. . .possesses a purpose beyond the imperatives created by genetic history. **Edward O. Wilson**

(*adj*) anatomical, bacteriological, biochemical, biological, botanical, ecological, microbiological, natural, physiological, *zoological*

types of bioscience anatomy, bacteriology, biochemistry, biology, botany, ecology, genetics, microbiology, molecular biology, physiology, zoology

The Natural Environment and The Forces of Nature

1038 Nature and the Environment

Nature contains the elements, in colour and form, of all pictures, as the keyboard contains the notes of all music. **James Abbott McNeill Whistler**

(*n*) biosphere, creation, ecosystem, environment, natural world, nature, world

1039 The Earth

The earth is blue like an orange. **Paul Éluard**

(*adj*) earthly, geographic, geographical, terrestrial, topographical

(*n*) earth, globe, planet, world

1040 The Earth's Atmosphere

Man has in him the silence of the sea, the noise of the earth and the music of the air. **Rabindranath Tagore**

(*n*) aerospace, air, atmosphere, ether (*literary*), *exosphere*, firmament (*literary*), heaven, *ionosphere*, *mesosphere*, *ozonosphere*, sky, *stratosphere*, *thermosphere*, *troposphere*, *upper atmosphere*

1041 The Seas, Oceans, and Shores

The voice of the sea speaks to the soul. **Kate Chopin**

(*adj*) aquatic, coastal, deep-sea, landlocked, littoral, marine, maritime, nautical, naval, ocean, oceanic, sea, *tidal*, undersea, waterside

(*n*) bay, beach, *bight*, breaker, briny, cape, coast, coastline, cove, creek, delta, dry land, dune, ebb, firth, fjord, flood tide, foreshore, groundswell, gulf, harbour, haven (*literary*), headland, hinterland, inlet, isthmus, lagoon, lakeside, landfall, lido, littoral, mouth, ocean, point, port, promontory, reef, roller, sand, sandbank, sandbar, sea, seaboard, seacoast, seafront, seaport, seashore, seaside, shore, shoreline, sound, spindrift, spume (*literary*), strait, surf, swell, *terra firma*, tidal wave, tide, *tsunami*, undertow, waterfront, water line, watermark, waterside, wave, whirlpool, whitecap, white water

1042 Rivers, Lakes, and Streams

You can't step twice into the same river. **Heraclitus**

(*n*) bayou (*US*), beck, broad, brook, burn, cascade, cataract, chute, creek (*US*), current, eddy, estuary, fall, flow, font (*literary*), fount (*literary*), fountain, fountainhead, geyser, lagoon, lake, loch, lough, mere (*archaic or literary*), pond, pool, rapids, reservoir, river, *riverbank*, riverside, rivulet, sault (*US*), source, stream, tarn, tributary, undercurrent, watercourse, waterfall, water hole, watering hole, waterway, weir, well

1043 Wetlands

My ghost town—/A place of interminable afternoons.../Of so many hesitant surrenders to/Enfolding bog. **Michael Longley**

(*n*) bog, *everglade* (*US*), fen, fenland, floodplain, marsh, marshland, mire, morass, *mudflat*, quagmire, quicksand, *salt flat*, swamp, swampland, wetland

1044 Mountains and Hills

Mountains are the beginning and the end of all natural scenery. **John Ruskin**

(*adj*) alpine, hilly, mountainous, terraced

(*n*) *alp*, ascent, bluff, butte, cliff, crag, foothill, glacier, grade (*US*), gradient, high ground, highland, hill, hillock, hilltop, hummock, incline, knoll, massif, mesa, mound, mountain, mountainside, mountaintop, pass, peak, rise, rock face, scarp, spur, tor

1045 Deserts and Plains

The mesa plain had an appearance of great antiquity, and of incompleteness...the country was still waiting to be made into a landscape. **Willa Cather**

(*n*) bush, desert, dust bowl, grassland, *heath*, *heathland*, lowland, moonscape, moor, moorland, *pampas*, plain, plateau, prairie, savanna, *scrubland*, *semidesert*, steppe, tableland, *tundra*, upland, veld, wastes, wilderness

1046 Remote Places

Space isn't remote at all. It's only an hour's drive away if your car could go straight upwards. **Fred Hoyle**

(*n*) back country (*US*), backwater, backwoods, *badlands*, boondocks (*US informal*), outback, *sticks* (*informal*), *the back of beyond*

1047 Woods, Forests, and Jungles

Are not these woods/More free from peril than the envious court? **William Shakespeare**

(*n*) coppice, copse, covert, forest, grove, jungle, orchard, *rain forest*, spinney, thicket, *tropical forest*, wood, woodland, woods

See also PLANTS AND TREES (1024)

1048 The Continents and Islands

It is not easy to shake off the spell of island life. **Joseph Conrad**

(*n*) *archipelago*, atoll, continent, island, isle, islet, landmass, mainland, peninsula

1049 Weather and Climate

The climate and the chemical properties of the Earth now and throughout its history seem always to have been optimal for life. **James Lovelock**

(*adj*) barometric, *climatic*, meteorological

(*n*) climate, *climatology*, clime (*literary*), isobar, isotherm, meteorology, weather

1050 Hot Weather

"Heat, ma'am!" I said; "it was so dreadful here that I found there was nothing left for it but to take off my flesh and sit in my bones." **Sydney Smith**

(*adj*) baking, balmy, blistering, boiling, *boiling hot*, clammy, clear, clement, close, cloudless, fair, fine, fuggy, good, hot, mild, muggy, oppressive, roasting (*informal*), scorching (*informal*), searing, steamy, sticky, stifling, stuffy, sultry, summery, sunny, *sunshiny*, sweaty, sweltering, toasty, torrid, tropical, warm

(*n*) *balminess*, closeness, fug, heat wave, *Indian summer*, mugginess, stuffiness, *sultriness*, *warm front*, warmness, *warm weather*

See also TEMPERATURE: HOT (1228)

1051 Cold Weather

The ways deep and the weather sharp,/The very dead of winter. **T. S. Eliot**

(*adj*) arctic (*informal*), biting, bitter, bleak, chill, chilly, cool, crisp, cutting, freezing, frosted, frosty, frozen, glacial, ice-cold, icy, inclement, keen, miserable, nippy, *parky* (*informal*), perishing, piercing, polar, raw, snowbound, subzero, temperate, white, wintry

(*n*) blizzard, chill, chilliness, *cold front*, cold snap, *cold spell*, coolness, frost, frostiness, hoar frost, ice, keenness, rawness, rime, sleet, snow, snowfall, *snow flurry*, *snowsquall*, snowstorm, wintriness

See also TEMPERATURE: COLD (1230)

1052 Cloudy and Rainy Weather

Rain is grace; rain is the sky condescending to the earth; without rain there would be no life. **John Updike**

(*adj*) *bucketing* (*informal*), cloudy, driving, *drizzling*, drizzly, dull, foggy, hazy, leaden, misty, murky, overcast, pouring, rainy, *sheeting down*, showery, *smoggy*, sunless, torrential, wet

(*n*) *brume* (*literary*), clamminess, cloud, cloudburst, cloudiness, deluge, downpour, *driving rain*, drizzle, dullness, flash flood, flood, fog, fogginess, haze, haziness, *heavy shower*, mist, mistiness, *mizzle* (*regional*), monsoon, murkiness, *peasouper*, precipitation, rain, rainbow, *raindrops*, rainfall, rainstorm, rainwater, *rainy season*, shower, smog, *smogginess*, torrent, wet, *wet weather*

(*v*) bucket (*informal*), *bucket down* (*informal*), chuck down (*informal*), *cloud over*, *come down in sheets* (*informal*), *come down in torrents*, drizzle, haze, pelt, *pelt down*, pour, *pour with rain*, rain, rain cats and dogs (*informal*), sheet down, shower, spit, sprinkle (*US*), teem

types of cloud altocumulus, altostratus, cirrocumulus, cirrus, cumulonimbus, cumulus, funnel cloud, mare's-tail, nimbus, rain cloud, storm cloud, stratocumulus, stratus, thundercloud, thunderhead (*US*)

1053 Windy and Stormy Weather

Hoist up saile while gale doth last,/Tide and wind stay no man's pleasure. **Robert Southwell**

(*adj*) blowy (*informal*), blustery, breezy, choppy, *gale-force*, gusty, howling, rough, squally, storm-tossed, stormy, sullen (*literary*), tempestuous, *thundery*, turbulent, weather-bound, wild, windy

(*n*) boisterousness, breeze, draught, flurry, *forked lightning*, *fulguration* (*formal*), gale, gust, headwind, lightning, puff, roughness, *sheet lightning*, squall, storm, storminess, tempest (*literary*), thermal, thunderbolt, thunderclap, thunderstorm, *tropical storm*, trough, *twister* (*US informal*), vortex, whirlwind, whiteout, wind, windstorm

(*v*) blow, bluster, gust

types of wind antitrade, bise, chinook, cyclone, foehn, harmattan, hurricane, khamsin, levanter, mistral, monsoon, northeaster, northwester, Santa Ana, simoom, sirocco, southeaster, southwester, tornado, trade wind, tramontana, typhoon, westerly

1054 Volcanoes and Earthquakes

You no more win a war than you can win an earthquake. **Jeannette Rankin**

(*adj*) *seismic*, *volcanic*

(*n*) earthquake, fault line, *natural disaster*, quake (*informal*), *seismic activity*, *seismic wave*, tremor, *volcanic activity*, *volcano*

1055 Erosion and Weathering

For water continually dropping will wear hard rocks hollow. **Plutarch**

(*n*) attrition, avalanche, erosion, landslide, *landslip*, *mudslide*, subsidence

1056 Geological Features

It was a miracle of rare device,/A sunny pleasure-dome with caves of ice! **Samuel Taylor Coleridge**

(*n*) bowl, canyon, cave, cavern, cirque, col, *corrie*, crater, crevasse, *cwm*, dale, defile, escarpment, floe, gap, *glaciated valley*, glen, gorge, grotto, gulch (*US*), gully, *iceberg*, *icecap*, outcrop, overhang, pothole, precipice, ravine, shelf, vale (*literary*), valley

1057 Stones, Rocks, and Boulders

When the torrent sweeps a man against a boulder, you must expect him to scream, and you need not be surprised if the scream is sometimes a theory. **Robert Louis Stevenson**

(*n*) boulder, cobble, cobblestone, gravel, magma, ore, pebble, rock, sarsen

types of stone alabaster, basalt, chalk, conglomerate, flint, gneiss, granite, hornblende, lava, limestone, malachite, marble, pumice, quartzite, sandstone, schist, shale, slate, soapstone, tuff

1058 Erosion Products and Soil

An inch of soil is an inch of gold. **Vietnamese proverb**

(*adj*) alluvial, *sedimentary*

(*n*) clay, dirt, *glacial deposit*, grit, *loam*, moraine, mud, peat, *permafrost*, sand, scree, silt, sod, soil, *terminal moraine*, topsoil

Space and the Universe

1059 The Solar System and Astronomy

Astronomy teaches the correct use of the sun and the planets. **Stephen Leacock**

(*adj*) astral, astronomical, celestial, cosmic, extraterrestrial, galactic, intergalactic, interplanetary, interstellar, lunar, planetary, stellar

(*n*) astronomer, astronomy, cosmos, *Milky Way*, outer space, *solar system*, space, star system, universe

1060 Celestial Bodies

In my studies of astronomy and philosophy I hold this opinion about the universe, that the Sun remains fixed in the centre of the circle of heavenly bodies, without changing its place. **Galileo**

types of heavenly body asteroid, bolide, comet, falling star, fireball, meteor, meteorite, moon, planet, shooting star

types of planet Earth, Jupiter, Mars, Mercury, Neptune, Pluto, Saturn, Uranus, Venus

types of star or star system black hole, brown dwarf, constellation, dark star, dwarf star, galaxy, giant star, nebula, nova, pulsar, quasar, red giant, sun, supernova, white dwarf

1061 Space Travel and Exploration

Outer space is no place for a person of breeding. **Lady Violet Bonham-Carter**

(*n*) astronaut, *cosmonaut*, moonshot, spaceflight, *spaceman, space mission, space pilot, space travel, space traveller*, spacewalk, *spacewoman*

1062 Space Vehicles

I am a passenger on the spaceship, Earth. **R. Buckminster Fuller**

(*n*) spacecraft, spaceship

types of spacecraft biosatellite, lander, launch vehicle, lunar module, multistage rocket, orbital space station, orbiter, rocket, rocket ship (*US*), rover, satellite, space capsule, spacelab, space probe, space rocket, space shuttle, space station

parts of a spacecraft booster rocket, bus, cabin, command module, drogue parachute, footpad, grain, life-support system, nose cone, plasma engine, pod, retropack, rocket engine, shroud, solar cell, stage, thruster

See also VEHICLES (1144)

1063 Science Fiction

Science fiction is the search for a definition of mankind and his status in the universe which will stand in our advanced but confused state of knowledge. **Brian Aldiss**

(*n*) alien, *alien craft*, android, earthling, extraterrestrial, flying saucer, little green man (*humorous*), Martian, spaceship, starship, UFO

See also FICTION AND DRAMA (913)

Places and Human Geography

1064 Place

If time imposes on us its evolution, place also imposes upon us its reality. **Gamal Abdel Nasser**

(*n*) area, corner, domain, dominion, element, environment, environs, habitat, hood (*US slang*), landmark, locale, locality, location, *locus*, matrix, milieu (*formal*), *neck of the woods*, neighbourhood, place, point, position, power base, precinct, premises, property, purlieu, scene, seat, setting, site, situation, space, spacing, spot, stamping ground (*informal*), station, surroundings, territory, theatre, turf (*informal*), venue, vicinity, whereabouts, zone

See also GENERAL LOCATIONS (159)

1065 Non-Existent Place

The unrest which keeps the never stopping clock of metaphysics going is the thought that the non-existence of the world is just as possible as its existence. **William James**

(*n*) *arcadia*, cloud-cuckoo-land, dreamland, dream world, *El Dorado*, fairyland, *fantasy world, land of make-believe, never-never land*, paradise (*informal*), *Shangri-la, storyland*, utopia, wonderland

See also NONEXISTENT THINGS (23)

1066 Countries and Regions

If people behaved in the way nations do they would all be put in straitjackets. **Tennessee Williams**

(*adj*) aboriginal, domestic, indigenous, intergovernmental, international, local, multinational, native, overseas, regional, supranational, territorial, zonal

(*adv*) abroad, nationally, nationwide, overseas

(*n*) canton, country, county, dependency, district, emirate, fatherland, heartland, home, homeland, land, motherland, nation, nationality, nation-state, native land, principality, province, provinces, region, republic, sector, *shire*, soil, state

1067 Territories and Groups of Nations

Colonies are made to be lost. **Henri de Montherlant**

(*n*) bloc, colony, commonwealth, empire, enclave, power, protectorate, realm, satellite, superpower, territory

1068 Geographical Borders and Boundaries

The love of one's country is a natural thing. But why should love stop at the border? **Pablo Casals**

(*adj*) transcontinental, transnational

(*n*) border, borderland, borderline, dividing line, division, frontier, front line, iron curtain, state line (*US*), territory

1069 Human Settlements

If cities were built by the sound of music, then some edifices would appear to be constructed by grave, solemn tones; others to have danced forth to light, fantastic airs. **Nathaniel Hawthorne**

(*adj*) built-in, built-up, city, civic, inner-city, metropolitan, municipal, provincial, residential, suburban, urban, vicinal

(*n*) bivouac, borough, camp, capital, centre, city, commune, community, constituency, conurbation, encampment, estate, hamlet, homestead, home town, *housing development* (*US*), housing estate, *housing project* (*US*), inner city, laager, land, metropolis, municipality, outpost, outskirts, parish, quarter, *residential area*, settlement, sprawl, suburb, suburbia, town, *town centre*, township, urbanization, urban sprawl, village

1070 The Countryside and Outdoor Spaces

Fortunate too is the man who has come to know the gods of the countryside. **Virgil**

(*adj*) bucolic, countrified, cross-country, greenfield, open, pastoral, rural, rustic, unindustrialized

(*n*) barnyard, campground (*US*), *camping area*, campsite, clearing, common, country, *countryside*, dell (*literary*), enclosure, estate, farmyard, field, firebreak, fireguard, geography, glade, grass, *green belt*, greenfield site, ground, grounds, holding, land, landscape, lea (*literary*), ley, meadow, *meadowland*, *millpond*, *national park*, *nature preserve* (*US*), *nature reserve*, *paddock*, parkland, *pasturage*, pasture, *pastureland*, plantation, preserve (*US*), reservation, reserve, *safari park*, sanctuary, stockyard, sward, terrain, topography, turf, *wildlife park*, *wildlife refuge*, *wildlife sanctuary*, *wilds*, yard

1071 Urban Outdoor Spaces

The Park throughout is a single work of art, and as such subject to the primary law of every work of art, namely, that it shall be framed upon a single, noble motive. **Frederick Law Olmsted**

(*n*) *adventure playground*, amusement park, arena, ballpark (*US*), bazaar, bomb site, brownfield site, campus, carnival (*US*), concourse, court, courtyard, fairground, field, forecourt, funfair, *goods yard*, ground, industrial estate, lido, market, marketplace, *market square*, menagerie, park, parking, piazza, pitch, playground, playing field, plaza, precincts, quad (*informal*), quadrangle, racecourse, racetrack, raceway, *recreation area*, *recreation ground*, *school yard*, *science park*, scrapheap, *scrapyard*, showground, speedway, *sports field*, sports ground, square, stadium, sunspot (*informal*), terrace, *theme park*, tip, *town square*, *village square*, wasteland, yard, zoo, *zoological gardens*

1072 Views and Outlooks

'Tis distance lends enchantment to the view,/And robes the mountain in its azure hue. **Thomas Campbell**

(*n*) outlook, panorama, perspective, prospect, scene, scenery, sight, skyline, view, vista

1073 Gardens

You may drive out nature with a pitchfork, yet she'll be constantly running back. **Horace**

(*n*) allotment, arbour, back yard, bed, border, *botanical garden*, bower, flowerbed, garden, *kitchen garden*, *lawn*, *patio*, rockery, rock garden, *rose garden*, *vegetable garden*, *vegetable patch*

1074 Agriculture and Farming

Man...must fit his actions into the rhythm of the seasons and the often mysterious requirements of organic life. **E. F. Schumacher**

(*adj*) agrarian, agricultural, *agronomic*, horticultural

(*n*) agribusiness, *agricultural science*, *agricultural show*, agriculture, *agroindustry*, *agronomy*, *croft*, farm, farming, *farmland*, farmstead, horticulture, *market garden*, ranch, smallholding, spread, *truck farm* (*US*)

Buildings and Structures

1075 Building and Architecture

Architecture is inhabited sculpture. **Constantin Brancusi**

(*adj*) *architectural*, purpose-built, roofed, structural, terraced

(*n*) architecture, assembly, building, complex, construction, edifice, erection (*formal*), fabric, habitation, structure

types of 20th-century architecture art deco, Bauhaus, brutalist, Federation, moderne, modernist, postmodern

types of pre-20th-century architecture art nouveau, Baroque, Byzantine, cinquecento, classical, colonial, Corinthian, Decorated, Doric, Elizabethan, Empire, Georgian, Gothic, Gothic revival, Ionic, Moorish, neoclassical, Norman, Palladian, perpendicular, Renaissance, rococo, Romanesque, Tudor, Victorian

1076 Building Materials

(*n*) *adobe*, beam, bitumen, block, board, *breeze block*, *brick*, *bricks and mortar*, brickwork, cantilever, *cement*, *chipboard*, *cinder block* (*US*), *clapboard*, *concrete*, cornerstone, *fibreboard*, filler, flagstone, *floorboards*, flooring, *floor tiles*, girder, grout, insulator, joist, lumber (*US*), masonry, *mortar*, moulding, *parget*, *pargeting*, parquet, *parquetry*, paving, *paving slab*, *paving stone*, pebbledash, piping, *plank*, *planking*, *plaster*, *plasterboard*, plasterwork, *plywood*, pointing, *putty*, rafter, rib, roofing, roughcast, *sand*, *sealant*, sett, *shingle*, slat, *slate*, stave, stonework, strut, *stucco*, *stuccowork*, tar, Tarmac (*US*), *terrazzo*, thatch, *tile*, timber, wainscot, wood

1077 Residential Buildings

(*n*) *apartment block*, *apartment building* (*US*), *apartment house* (*US*), barracks, block, *block of flats*, *casern*, *condo* (*US informal*), co-op (*US informal*), dorm (*informal*), dormitory, dosshouse (*slang*), hall, hall of residence, high-rise, house, lodge, *palace*, skyscraper, tenement, tent, *tower block*, wigwam, *yurt*

types of house bothy, brownstone (*US*), bungalow, cabana (*US*), cabin, Cape Cod (*US*), chalet, chateau, cottage, country house, detached house, farmhouse, grange, hacienda, homestead, igloo, manor, manor house, mansion, pied-à-terre, ranch, ranch house (*US*), row house (*US*), semidetached, shack, stately home, terraced house, town house, villa

types of apartment apartment (*US*), bedsit, bedsitter, bedsitting room, condominium (*US*), duplex (*US*), efficiency apartment (*US*), flat, garden apartment (*US*), garden flat, loft, maisonette, penthouse, studio (*US*), studio flat

See also ACCOMMODATION (855)

1078 Animal or Bird Accommodation

(*n*) cage, pen, run

types of den or nest burrow, drey, earth, eyrie, form, hole, lair, lodge, nest, sett, tunnel, warren

types of pen or cage apiary, aquarium, aviary, beehive, birdcage, chicken coop, chicken run, coop, corral (*US*), cowshed, doghouse (*US*), dovecote, henhouse, hutch, kennel, piggery, pigsty, pound, stable, stall, sty

1079 Ancillary Buildings

(*n*) *ancillary building*, annexe, arcade, colonnade, extension, gallery, outbuilding

types of outbuilding barn, booth, byre (*regional*), carport, conservatory, cowshed, garage, garden shed, gatehouse, gazebo, glasshouse, greenhouse, guardhouse, hothouse, hut, kiosk, lean-to, lodge, orangery, outhouse, pavilion, pergola, potting shed, privy (*informal*), sentry box, shed, stall, stand, summerhouse

1080 Public Buildings and Meeting Places

(*n*) assembly point, centre, depot (*US*), gathering place, hangout (*informal*), haunt, home, rendezvous, terminal, terminus, waiting area

1081 Hotels, Restaurants, and Clubs

(*n*) bar

types of eating place bistro, brasserie, café, cafeteria, canteen, coffee bar, coffee shop, commons, diner, dining hall, eatery, greasy spoon, hole-in-the-wall (*informal*), hostelry (*archaic or humorous*), luncheonette (*US*), lunchroom (*US*), mess, mess hall, pizzeria, roadside café, self-service restaurant, snack bar, steakhouse, tearoom, transport café, trattoria, truck stop (*US*)

types of hotel B & B (*informal*), bed and breakfast, boarding house, boutique hotel, guesthouse, hostel, inn, lodge, lodging house (*dated*), motel, pension, rooming house (*US*), youth hostel

types of bar or club bodega, casino, club, country club, joint (*slang*), local (*informal*), nightclub, nightspot, pub, roadhouse, saloon, shebeen, speakeasy, tavern (*archaic*), wine bar

1082 Retail Outlets

(*n*) arcade, emporium (*formal or humorous*), parlour, plaza (*US*), retailer, *retail outlet*, *retail store*, salon, services, shop, *shopping arcade*, shopping centre, *shopping complex*, shopping mall (*US*), showroom, store

types of retail outlet bazaar, beauty parlour, bookshop, boutique, chain store, chemist, chemist's, convenience store (*US*), corner shop, covered market, department store, dime store (*US*), dispensary, druggist (*US*), drugstore (*US*), duty-free, filling station, flea market, garden centre, gas station (*US*), general store (*US*), hairdresser's, hair salon, hypermarket, kiosk, mall, mart, mom-and-pop store (*US*), newsstand, nursery, petrol station, pharmacy, post office, saleroom, service station, supercenter (*US*), superstore, thrift shop (*US*), undertaker's, warehouse

types of food outlet bakery, bodega (*US*), butcher's, candy store (*US*), chip shop, deli, delicatessen, drive-through, farmers' market, fishmonger's, greengrocer's, grocer's, grocery store, refreshment stand, supermarket, sweetshop, takeaway, takeout (*US*)

1083 Buildings for Public Entertainment

(*n*) amphitheatre, *amusement arcade*, amusements, *assembly hall*, *assembly room*, auditorium, bandstand, baths, bowl (*US*), bullring, cabaret, casino, *cinema*, *circus*, *concert hall*, dive (*informal*), *exhibition hall*, *fitness centre*, fleapit, gym (*informal*), gymnasium, *honky-tonk* (*US slang*), *lecture hall*, *lecture room*, *lecture theatre*, leisure centre, marquee, multiplex, museum, *music hall*, *opera house*, *picture house* (*dated*), *planetarium*, playhouse, rink, solarium, spa, *sports centre*, *sports hall*, *sports stadium*, swimming baths (*dated*), swimming pool, theatre

1084 Religious Buildings

(*n*) cloister, *convent*, friary, *hermitage*, *house of God*, house of worship, manse, monastery, nunnery, parsonage, priory, rectory, sanctum, *vicarage*

types of place of worship church, gurdwara, mosque, shrine, synagogue, temple

types of church abbey, basilica, cathedral, chapel, meeting house, minster, tabernacle

1085 Parts of Religious Buildings

(*n*) abbey, altar, *apse*, *chancel*, *chantry*, cloister, crypt, *nave*, spire, steeple, *transept*, vault

See also RELIGIOUS OBJECTS (780)

1086 Industrial Buildings

types of factory assembly plant, brewery, cannery, distillery, forge, foundry, machine shop, maquiladora, mill, mint, plant, pottery, sawmill, smithy, steelworks, sweatshop, water mill, works, workshop

types of industrial site abattoir, business park, coalfield, colliery, depot, dock, dockyard, enterprise zone, garage, gasworks, industrial estate, industrial park, industrial zone, lab (*informal*), laboratory, mine, nuclear power plant (*US*), nuclear power station, nuclear reprocessing plant, office block, oil rig, pit, pithead, power plant, power station, quarry, refinery, rig, shipyard, slaughterhouse, tannery, winery (*US*)

See also ENERGY STORAGE AND GENERATION (1162)

1087 Stores and Storage Buildings

(*n*) repository, stock, stockpile, stockroom, storage, store, *storehouse*, *storeroom*

types of storage space armoury, arms depot, arsenal, barn, bunker, cellar, depository, depot, dump, elevator (*US*), garage, gasometer, grain elevator (*US*), granary, hangar, hayloft, hold, landfill, larder, loft, luggage compartment, magazine, morgue, mortuary, pantry, rubbish dump, shed, silo, strongroom, treasury, warehouse, water tower, weapon store, woodshed

See also STORE AND KEEP (454)

1088 Ancient Manmade Structures

(*n*) dolmen, gallows, megalith, milepost, monolith, scaffold, standing stone, stocks, *stone circle*

1089 Fortresses and Fortifications

(*n*) bastion, castle, citadel, defences, earthwork, fastness (*archaic or literary*), fort, fortification, fortress, pillbox, redoubt (*literary*), stockade, stronghold

1090 Parts of Fortresses

(*n*) barbican, battlements, *parapet*, portcullis, rampart

1091 Monuments

(*n*) burial chamber, cairn, cenotaph, mausoleum, memorial, *memorial stone*, monument, obelisk, tombstone, *war memorial*

See also BURIAL PLACES AND ACCESSORIES (930)

1092 Safe Buildings or Places

(*n*) asylum, bolthole, bunker, haven, hideaway, hideout, hidey-hole (*informal*), hiding place, hostel, lee, oasis, *place of safety*, refuge, retreat, safe haven, safe house, safe place, sanctuary, sanctum, shelter

1093 Buildings for Confining People

(*n*) borstal, cell, *clink* (*dated slang*), dungeon, *gaol*, guardhouse, *house of correction*, jail, lockup, nick (*slang*), oubliette, *pen* (*US slang*), *penal colony*, *penal complex* (*US*), *penal institution*, penitentiary (*US*), *pokey* (*US dated slang*), prison, *prison cell*, reformatory, *remand home*, *secure unit*, *slammer* (*slang*), state school (*US informal*), *young offenders' institution*, *youth custody centre*

See also CAPTIVITY AND LOSS OF FREEDOM (249), THE POLICE, ARREST, AND PRE-TRIAL PROCEEDINGS (818)

1094 Parts of a Building

parts of a building balcony, buttress, ceiling, chimney, colonnade, doorway, elevator (*US*), escalator, exterior, façade, fire escape, frame, frontage, gable, guttering, landing, lift, paternoster, porch, roof, smokestack, staircase, stairs, stairway, stairwell, veranda, vestibule, wall, window, wing

1095 Alcoves, Cubicles, and Compartments

(*n*) alcove, bay, booth, box, cabin, cockpit, compartment, cubbyhole, cubicle, fireplace, fireside, hearth, inglenook, loge, niche, nook, recess, stall

1096 Types of Room

(*n*) airlock, chamber, facilities, room

types of room in public buildings antechamber, anteroom, ballroom, boardroom, cell, changing room, classroom, cloakroom, dining hall, dormitory, dressing room, entrance hall, foyer, gallery, games room, hall, lavatory, library, lobby, lounge, meeting room, men's room (*US*), office, operating room (*US*), powder room, reception room, refectory, rest room, schoolroom, stateroom, surgery, vault, waiting room, ward, washroom (*US*)

types of room in the home atelier, attic, bathroom, bedchamber (*archaic or literary*), bedroom, boudoir, boxroom, closet (*US*), day room, den, dining room, drawing room, family room, garret, guestroom, kitchen, kitchenette, living room, loft, parlour, playroom, recreation room, rec room (*US*), salon, scullery, sitting room, sleeping quarters, spare room, study, sun lounge, sunroom (*US*), toilet, utility room

1097 Stages, Platforms, and Raised Areas

(*n*) balcony, catwalk, dais, *lanai*, *loggia*, platform, podium, rostrum, stage, *sun deck*, veranda, *viewing platform*

1098 Towers

(*n*) belfry, *bell tower*, *campanile*, listening post, lookout, *lookout tower*, minaret, *observation tower*, observatory, pylon, rotunda, turret, vantage point, viewpoint, watchtower

1099 Windows

(*n*) window

parts of a window ledge, pane, sill, window ledge, windowpane, windowsill

types of window bay window, casement, dormer window, fanlight, French window, lancet window, picture window, porthole, rose window, sash window, skylight, transom (*US*), windows

1100 Doors and Access Points

(*n*) access, aisle, arch, archway, atrium, check-in, corridor, door, doorplate, doorstep, doorway, entrance, entrance hall, entry, exit, foyer, front door, gate, gateway, hallway, ingress (*formal*), lobby, portal (*literary*), portico, *sliding doors*, threshold, tollbooth, tollgate, trap door, turnstile, vestibule, wicket

1101 Stairs and Storeys

(*n*) balcony, banister, basement, *elevator* (*US*), *entresol*, escalator, fire escape, floor, gallery, ladder, *landing*, *lift*, *lower ground floor*, mezzanine, *mezzanine floor*, paternoster, stair, staircase, stairs, stairway, stairwell, step, stile, storey, tier

1102 Roofs, Roof Parts, and Ceilings

(*n*) *ceiling*, *cornice*, *coving*, cupola, dado, *dado rail*, dome, *eaves*, flue, funnel, guttering, mansard, *roof space*, rooftop, rose, stack, vault

1103 Walls and Partitions

(*n*) bulkhead, divider, partition, purdah, screen, separator, wall

See also BARRIERS (1112)

1104 Communication Networks

Civilization is a movement, not a condition; it is a voyage, not a harbour. **Arnold Toynbee**

(*adj*) arterial, intercity, mainline

(*n*) communications, infrastructure

See also TRAVEL: WAYS OF TRAVELLING (321), TRANSPORTATION, TRANSPORTERS, AND CARGOS (323)

1105 Roads

(*n*) carriageway, circuit, *fast lane*, pavement (*US*), pull-in (*dated*), ramp, road, roadway, route, *slow lane*, switchback, thoroughfare, *through road*, *through street* (*US*), *traffic lane*, way

types of major road A-road, artery, avenue, beltway (*US*), boulevard, bypass, clearway, divided highway (*US*), dual carriageway, expressway (*US*), flyover, freeway (*US*), highway, interstate (*US*), limited-access highway (*US*), main road, motorway, parkway, ring road, speedway (*US*), superhighway (*US*), throughway (*US*), thru-way (*US*), toll road, trunk road, trunk route (*US*), turn-pike

types of minor road access road, access strip, alley, alleyway, backstreet, blind alley, B-road, byroad, byway, cart track, cul-de-sac, dead end, dirt track, esplanade, lane, mews, parade, path, promenade, ramp (*US*), side road, side street, slip road, street, track

1106 Railways

(*n*) line, main line, *rail line*, *rail network*, *rail route*, *rail terminal*, *rail transportation system* (*US*), *rail transport system*, railhead, *railroad station*, railway

parts of a train cabin, caboose (*US*), car, carriage, coach, compartment, dining car (*US*), freight car, locomotive, luggage compartment, Pullman, restaurant car, sleeper, sleeping car, smoker, smoking car, smoking carriage, smoking compartment, steam engine, tank engine, wagon

types of rail vehicle cable car, funicular, locomotive, steam engine, streetcar (*US*), train, tram

types of railway cable railroad (*US*), cable railway, funicular railway, light railway, metro, monorail, streetcar line (*US*), subway (*US*), tramway, tube, underground

1107 Waterways and Seaways

(*n*) anchorage, berth, breakwater, canal, channel, dock, dockside, dockyard, floodgate, jetty, landing, landing stage, marina, mooring, pier, quay, quayside, sea lane, seaway, *shipping canal*, *shipping lane*, wharf

1108 Airways

(*n*) aerodrome, airfield, airport, airspace, airstrip, airway, aviation, helideck, helipad, heliport, helistop, landing field, landing strip, runway

1109 Pathways

(*adj*) pedestrianized, *traffic-free*

(*n*) boardwalk, bridle path, *bridleway*, duckboard, footpath, footway, gangway, ley, passage, passageway, path, pathway, pavement, *pedestrian precinct*, prom, promenade, ramp, run, sidewalk (*US*), towpath, track, trail, walkway, wayside

1110 Watercourses

(*n*) aqueduct, canal, catheter, cesspit, channel, chute, conduit, culvert, ditch, drain, duct, dyke, *fosse*, furrow, gutter, hose, hosepipe, intake, moat, outfall, pipe, pipeline, raceway, *runnel*, sewer, sluice, standpipe, storm drain, trench, tube, tubing, *waste pipe*, watercourse, *water pipe*

1111 Bridges, Tunnels, Crossings, and Junctions

(*n*) catacomb, catwalk, causeway, cloverleaf, corner, crossing, crossroads, ford, interchange, intersection, level crossing, pedestrian crossing, pelican crossing, *railway crossing*, roundabout, subway, T-junction, *traffic circle* (*US*), *traffic island*, *traffic junction*, tunnel, turn-off, turning, *underpass*, *zebra crossing*

types of bridge aqueduct, arch bridge, Bailey bridge, bascule bridge, beam bridge, cable-stayed bridge, cantilever bridge, drawbridge, flyover, footbridge, gangplank, humpback bridge, overpass, pontoon bridge, suspension bridge, swing bridge, viaduct, walkway

1112 Barriers

(*n*) bank, barrage, barricade, barrier, blockade, bulwark, checkpoint, cordon, dam, dyke, embankment, fence, fencing, groyne, jump, levee, *paling*, *palisade*, railing, ring-fence, roadblock, sea wall, *sluicegate*, stockade, trellis, windbreak, windscreen (*US*)

See also WALLS AND PARTITIONS (1103)

Technology

1113 Machinery

Technology is the knack of so arranging the world that we don't have to experience it. **Max Frisch**

(*adj*) automated, automatic, bionic, mechanized, push-button, robotic, wind-up

(*n*) automation, instrumentation, machinery, mechanization, robotics, technology

1114 Devices

(*n*) apparatus, contraption, contrivance, device, equipment, gadget, gizmo (*informal*), hardware, implement, installation, instrument, invention, kit, machine, mechanism, robot, sensor, spinner, tackle, tool, utensil

1115 Machines and Machine Parts

(*n*) automaton, crane, derrick, dispenser, gantry, hoist, vending machine, winch, windlass

1116 Household Appliances

(*n*) appliance

types of appliance blender, coffeemaker, cooker, dishwasher, dryer, furnace, grill, hob, iron, microwave, microwave oven, minibar, percolator, range, rotisserie, smoke alarm, smoke detector, spin-dryer, stove, television, toaster, tumble dryer, washing machine

See also TABLEWARE, CUTLERY, AND KITCHENWARE (861)

1117 Parts of Machines and Tools

(*n*) adapter, *armature*, attachment, button, circuitry, clock, clockwork, cog, cogwheel, control panel, controls, cutout, damper, detector, dial, dimmer, fulcrum, gasket, *gearwheel*, hand, handle, indicator, *instrument panel*, key, keyboard, knob, lever, machinery, moving parts, needle, *pawl*, pendulum, pivot, pointer, pulley, ratchet, regulator, safety valve, separator, *shock absorber*, spacer, spare part, spigot, spline, spring, sprocket, *sprocket wheel*, stopcock, switch, thermostat, toggle, tooth, treadle, valve

1118 Hand Tools

(*n*) broom, brush, *mop*

types of carpentry tool awl, bradawl, drill, hammer, jigsaw, mallet, plane, sander, saw, vice

types of medical instrument forceps, lancet, probe, scalpel, speculum, stethoscope, syringe

types of general tool bellows, blowtorch, crowbar, file, grease gun, jack, jemmy, lathe, machine tool, pincers, pliers, plumb line, plunger, poker, pump, punch, rasp, screwdriver, socket spanner, socket wrench, soldering iron, spade, spanner, tongs, trowel, wrench (*US*)

types of cosmetic tool comb, emery board, hairbrush, nailbrush, nail clippers, nail file, nail scissors, razor, shaving brush, tweezers

1119 Cutting Tools

types of knife bread knife, butcher's knife, carving knife, cleaver, flick knife, jackknife, paperknife, penknife, pocketknife (*US*), switchblade (*US*), table knife

types of cutting tool axe, billhook, chisel, chopper, clippers, cutter, hatchet, hoe, knife, machete, pickaxe, plough, razor blade, scissors, scythe, secateurs, shears, sickle

1120 Spoons, Scoops, and Shovels

(*n*) dipper, *ladle*, scoop, shovel, spade

1121 Photography and Photographic Equipment

(*n*) mug shot, photo, photocopy, photograph, print, scan, shot, snapshot, transparency

types of video equipment camcorder, DVD, palmcorder, VCR (*US*), video camera, video cassette, video cassette recorder, videodisk, video recorder, videotape, video tape recorder

parts of photographic equipment autofocus, diaphragm, exposure meter, film, filter, fisheye lens, flash, lens, lens cap, rangefinder, shutter, telephoto lens, viewfinder, zoom lens

types of photographic equipment box camera, camera, cine camera, darkroom, developer, disc camera, enlarger, microfiche, microfilm, movie camera (*US*), pinhole camera, printer, projector, reflex camera, single-lens reflex, speed camera, tripod, twin-lens reflex

1122 Measuring Devices

(*n*) *counter*, gauge, measure, measuring device, meter

types of measuring device altimeter, anemometer, aneroid barometer, balance, barograph, barometer, callipers, clock, compass, dipstick, dividers, dropper, Geiger counter, level (*US*), measuring tape, micrometer, mileometer, odometer (*US*), pipette, protractor, quadrant, rule, scale, speedo, speedometer, spirit level, statoscope, tachometer, tape, tape measure, theodolite, thermometer, weathercock, weather vane, weighbridge, weighing machine, weighing scale (*US*), weighing scales, wind gauge, windsock

1123 Optical Instruments

types of optical instrument astronomical telescope, binoculars, electron microscope, laser, magnifying glass, microscope, optometer, periscope, spyglass, telescope

1124 Glasses and Spectacles

types of glasses bifocals, dark glasses, eyeglasses (*US formal*), goggles, monocle, pince-nez, shades (*informal*), specs (*informal*), spectacles, sunglasses, sunspecs (*informal*)

1125 Clocks and Timers

(*n*) *chronometer*, clock, *metronome*, timepiece, *timer*

types of clock alarm, alarm clock, clock radio, cuckoo clock, grandfather clock, hourglass, longcase clock, pocket watch, stopwatch, sundial, watch, wristwatch

See also TIMES OF DAY (87)

1126 Computers and Computing

(*adj*) electronic, off-line, online, *real-time*, virtual, wired (*informal*)

(*n*) *computer graphics*, *computer modelling*, *computer processing*, *computer program*, *computer programmer*, *computer science*, *computer scientist*, *computer technology*, cybernetics, data processing, information processing, information retrieval, information technology, IT, multimedia, programmer, programming, *software*, *software design*, *software development*, *systems analyst*, virtual reality, *VR*

(*v*) access, initialize, reboot, toggle, unzip, *zip* (*informal*)

types of computer adder, calculator, hand-held computer, laptop, mainframe, microcomputer, minicomputer, notebook, palmtop, PC, personal computer, personal organizer, supercomputer, tablet computer, workstation

types of software accumulator, application, bit map, browser, buffer, bus, cache, computer-aided design, cursor, database, directory, emoticon, firmware, interface, macro, memory, pixel, program, RAM, readout,

ROM, simulator, smiley, spell checker, spreadsheet, subdirectory, virus, wallpaper, window, word processor

types of hardware accelerator card, backspace, CD-ROM, central processing unit, chip, console, disk, disk drive, diskette, DVD, floppy disk, hard disk, integrated circuit, joystick, keyboard, microchip, microprocessor, modem, monitor, motherboard, mouse, numeric keypad, port, printed circuit, printer, processor, scanner, screen, server, sound card, space-bar, terminal, touch screen, VDT, VDU, video display terminal, visual display unit

1127 The Internet

(*n*) bandwidth, *click rate*, *cookie*, cyberspace, *encryption*, home page, information superhighway, *Internet*, *service provider*, *superhighway*, *syllaweb*, *the Net* (*informal*), *the Web* (*informal*), *URL*, *wap*, *web conferencing*, *web folio*, *webpage*, *website*, *World Wide Web*

(*v*) encrypt, *flame*, spam

1128 E-Commerce

(*adj*) *bricks-and-mortar*, *clicks-and-mortar*

(*adv*) *B2B*, *B2C*, *BtoB*, *P2P*

(*n*) *access profile*, *cybermall*, *cybermarketing*, *cybermediary*, *digital cash*, *digital signature*, *e-business*, *e-commerce*, *electronic cash*, *electronic signature*, *e-mall*, *e-tailing*, *infomediary*, *m-commerce*, *online banking*, *payment gateway*, *point and click agreement*, *secure electronic transaction*, *smart card*, *startup*

1129 Telecommunications

types of telecommunications equipment aerial, answering machine, antenna (*US*), beeper (*informal*), bleeper, blower (*dated informal*), bug, cable, cellphone, cellular phone, e-mail, fax, intercom, landline, mast, mobile phone, modem, pager, payphone, phone, phonecard, receiver, satellite, satellite dish, switchboard, telephone, telex, transmitter, videophone, voice mail, walkie-talkie, wiretap

See also TELEPHONE AND PAGE (682), TELEPHONE COMMUNICATION (48)

1130 Textiles and Threads

(*n*) catgut, cloth, fabric, fibre, filament, material, *natural fibre*, purl, textile, thread, yarn

1131 Fabrics

types of fabric from animals alpaca, angora, astrakhan, baize, bearskin, brocade, camel hair, cashmere, chenille, crepe de Chine, felt, flannel, fur, gabardine, horsehair, jersey, lambswool, leather, loden, mohair, sheepskin, silk, snakeskin, taffeta, tweed, twill, wool, worsted

types of fabric from plants burlap, calico, canvas, cheesecloth, chintz, corduroy, cotton, denim, drill, flannelette, gauze, gingham, hessian, linen, moleskin, muslin, organdy, poplin, sacking, tarpaulin, terry, terry cloth (*US*), terry towelling, ticking, towelling, velvet, winceyette

types of leather buckskin, calf, calfskin, chamois, hide, kid, morocco, patent leather, pigskin, rawhide, sheepskin, snakeskin, suede

types of synthetic fabric acrylic, chiffon, crêpe, fishnet, fleece, lamé, moquette, nylon, percale, polyester, PVC, rayon, sateen, satin, tulle, viscose

1132 Plant Materials

types of fibre cane, coconut matting, coir, fibreglass, jute, kapok, matting, raffia, ramie, rattan, sisal, straw, wicker

1133 Plastics

types of plastic acetate, celluloid, epoxide, latex, melamine, neoprene, polyethylene (*US*), polystyrene, polythene, polyurethane, vinyl

1134 Pottery

types of pottery bone china, ceramic, china, delft, Dresden china, earthenware, enamel, faience, Limoges, Meissen (*US*), porcelain, Sèvres, stoneware, terracotta

1135 Glass

types of glass bulletproof glass, crystal, cut glass, ground glass, lead glass, optical glass, plate glass, quartz glass, safety glass, stained glass, Venetian glass

1136 Electronics and Electrics

(*adj*) electrified, electronic

(*n*) anode, control, controller, electrode, electronics, limiter, plug (*informal*), point, power line, power point, resistor, rheostat, wire

1137 Acoustics

(*adj*) acoustic, *high-fidelity*, mono, sonic, soundproof, stereophonic, wired (*US slang*)

(*n*) acoustics, atmospherics, damper, mono, *soundproofing*, *stereo*

1138 Audio Equipment

types of audio equipment amp, amplifier, boom box (*US*), cassette recorder, CD player, compact disc player, gramophone (*dated*), hi-fi, horn, jukebox, megaphone, PA, personal stereo, phonograph (*US*), preamplifier, radio, radio set, record player, sound system, stereo, stereo system, tape deck, tape player, tape recorder, transistor, tuner, wireless (*dated*)

parts of audio equipment audiotape, cartridge, cassette, CD, compact disc, DVD, earphone, earphones, earpiece, handset, headphones, headpiece, headset, loudspeaker, microphone, record, speaker, stylus, tone arm, turntable

See also RECORDINGS AND PLAYERS (911)

1139 Signalling

(*n*) *alarm bell*, *all-clear signal*, bell, buzzer, fire alarm, foghorn, klaxon, red light, reveille, siren, tattoo, tocsin

1140 Navigation

(*adj*) navigational

(*n*) bearing, heading, latitude, longitude, map reading, navigation, navigator, orientation, radar, reference

1141 Heating, Refrigeration, and Ventilation

(*adj*) air-conditioned

(*n*) aeration, *air-circulation system*, air conditioning, *air-cooling system, air duct, air exchange system*, airing, *central heating*, cooler, heating, refrigeration, *solar heating, space heating*, ventilation, *ventilation system*, ventilator

types of cooling appliance air conditioner, air cooler, air exchanger, deepfreeze, freezer, fridge, fridge-freezer, icebox (*US*), refrigerator

types of heating appliance boiler, electric fire, heater, immersion heater, quartz heater, radiator, space heater, storage heater

1142 Engines and Hydraulics

(*adj*) mechanical, motor, motorized

(*n*) engine, motor, *turbine*

1143 Parts of an Engine

parts of an engine ball bearing, cam, camshaft, cog, cogwheel, coil, crank, crankshaft, cylinder, gasket, gear, gearbox, gearing, lever, oil pan (*US*), piston, pump, radiator, seal, shaft, spark plug, starter, sump, tappet, valve

1144 Vehicles

The car has become the carapace, the protective and aggressive shell, of urban and suburban man. **Marshall McLuhan**

(*n*) pedal, speedometer, traffic, transport

types of commercial or industrial vehicle articulated lorry, black cab, breakdown lorry, bulldozer, cab, combine harvester, digger, dumper truck, dump truck (*US*), earthmover, hackney cab, hackney carriage, hearse, juggernaut, lorry, minicab, pick-up, removal van, roadroller, semitrailer (*US*), snowplough, steamroller, tanker, taxi, tow truck (*US*), tractor, transporter, truck, van, wrecker (*US*), yellow cab (*US*)

types of leisure vehicle bobsled (*US*), bobsleigh, camper, camper van, caravan, chair lift, dogsled, dune buggy, go-cart, land yacht, luge, mobile home, motor home, RV (*US*), sled (*US*), sledge, sleigh, snowmobile, SUV (*US*), toboggan

types of public service vehicle ambulance, bus, charabanc, coach, dustcart, fire engine, firetruck (*US*), garbage truck (*US*), minibus, panda car (*informal*), police car, prowl car (*US*), shuttle, squad car

types of military vehicle amphibian, armoured car, jeep, tank

See also TRAVEL: JOURNEYS AND TRIPS (319), COMMUNICATION NETWORKS (1104), SPACE VEHICLES (1062)

1145 Internal Parts of a Vehicle

types of controls accelerator, brake, choke, clutch, gear lever, gearshift (*US*), horn, pedal, rev counter, speedometer, steering wheel, wheel

types of internal feature back seat, booster seat, cab, child seat, dashboard, driver's seat (*US*), driving seat, glove compartment, headrest, passenger seat, rearview mirror, seat belt

1146 External Parts of a Vehicle

(*n*) kick-start, plate

types of external feature blinker, brake light, bumper, exhaust pipe, fog light, headlight, hubcap, indicator, license plate (*US*), luggage rack (*US*), mud flap, muffler (*US*), number plate, parking light (*US*), roof rack, sidelight, side mirror (*US*), silencer, splashguard (*US*), spoiler, stoplight (*US*), tail light, tyre, wheel, windscreen wiper, windshield wiper (*US*), wing mirror

parts of an external structure aerofoil, axle, bodywork, bonnet, boot, chassis, coachwork, fender (*US*), fin, grille, hood (*US*), hull, mud flap, mudguard, sunroof, tailgate, tail light, trunk (*US*), wheel, windscreen, windshield (*US*), wing

1147 Aircraft

(*n*) aeroplane, aircraft, airline, airplane (*US*), balloon, plane

types of military aircraft bomber, convertiplane, fighter, fighter-bomber, helicopter gunship, stealth bomber, transport, VTOL

types of civil aircraft airliner, airship, autogiro, biplane, blimp, dirigible, executive jet, glider, hang glider, helicopter, jet, light aircraft, light plane (*US*), microlight, monoplane, paraglider, seaplane, skiplane, STOL, zeppelin

parts of an aircraft aileron, air brake, autopilot, cabin, cockpit, ejection seat (*US*), ejector seat, fin, flight deck, flight recorder, fuselage, jet engine, joystick, landing gear, nose cone, nose wheel, propeller, rotor, rudder, tail, tailplane, tail rotor, turbofan, turbojet, turboprop, undercarriage, wing

1148 Bikes, Cars, and Carriages

(*n*) *auto* (*informal*), *automobile*, barrow, caboose (*US*), car, combine, digger, earthmover, jalopy (*dated informal*), motor (*dated or informal*), *old banger* (*informal*), perambulator (*formal*), pram, pushcart, pushchair, rattletrap (*informal*), *rust bucket* (*informal humorous*), RV, stock car, stroller (*US*), tanker, *trolley*, wagon, wheels (*slang*)

parts of a bike brake, chain, crossbar, derailleur, fender (*US*), handlebars, mudguard, pedal, reflector, seat, spoke, tyre, wheel

types of bike bicycle, boneshaker, cycle, dirt bike, exercise bike, moped, motorbike, motorcycle, motor scooter, mountain bike, penny-farthing, push-bike (*dated informal*), racing bike, rickshaw, scooter, scrambler, tandem, tandem bicycle (*US*), ten-speed, three-wheeler, trail bike, tricycle, unicycle

types of car all-terrain vehicle, banger (*informal*), beater (*US informal*), compact, convertible, coupé, dragster, estate car, four-by-four, hatchback, hot rod (*slang*), limo, limousine, minivan, people carrier, racing car, runabout, saloon, sedan (*US*), sports car, station wagon (*US*), stock car, subcompact (*US*), three-wheeler

types of wagon or carriage barouche, brougham, buggy, carriage, cart, chariot, coach, Conestoga wagon, covered wagon, dray, landau, landaulet, phaeton, prairie schooner, stagecoach, trap, troika, tumbril

1149 Ships and Boats

(*n*) boat, craft, ship, vessel

types of motor vessel barge, cabin cruiser, canal boat, coaster, dredger, factory ship, ferry, ferryboat, freighter, houseboat, hovercraft, hydrofoil, launch, lifeboat, lighter, lightship, motorboat, powerboat, speedboat, steamboat, steamer, tanker, trawler, tug, tugboat (*US*)

types of sailing vessel barque, brig, brigantine, catamaran, catboat, dhow, felucca, junk, ketch, sailboat (*US*), sailing boat, schooner, sloop, smack, trimaran, yacht

types of military vessel aircraft carrier, battle cruiser, battleship, cruiser, cutter, destroyer, frigate, gunboat, minesweeper, PT boat (*US*), submarine, warship

types of small vessel canoe, dinghy, dory, gondola, kayak, life raft, narrow boat, pedalo, pirogue, punt, raft, rowboat (*US*), rowing boat, sampan, scull, skiff

types of historical vessel clipper, flagship, galleon, galley, Indiaman, longboat, longship, man-of-war, tall ship, windjammer

1150 Parts of a Ship or Boat

(*n*) blade, *boat hook*, oar, paddle, scull

parts of a sailing vessel boom, bowsprit, fore-and-aft sail (*US*), gaff, gaffsail, jib, mainsail, mainstay, mast, mizzen, pennant, sheet, shroud, spanker, spinnaker, topsail

parts of a ship or boat bilge, bow, bridge, cabin, capstan, crow's nest, deck, engine room, fo'c's'le, galley, gunwale, helm, hold, hull, keel, oarlock (*US*), outboard motor, outrigger, poop, prow, rowlock, rudder, stateroom, stern, superstructure, tiller

1151 Groups of Vehicles

(*n*) armada, caravan, convoy, fleet, flotilla, motorcade

1152 Drivers

(*n*) *aeronaut*, aviator, chauffeur, driver, motorist, *pilot*, teamster, *truck driver*, *trucker*

See also PROFESSIONS (845)

1153 Weapons

Every gun that is made, every warship launched, every rocket fired signifies, in the final sense, a theft from those who hunger and are not fed, those who are cold and are not clothed. **Dwight D. Eisenhower**

(*n*) ammo (*informal*), ammunition, armaments, arms, artillery, firepower, guns, munitions, ordnance, small arms, weapon, weaponry

1154 Explosives

types of explosive material dynamite, gelignite, gunpowder, napalm, nitroglycerine, plastic explosive, propellant, TNT, warhead

types of firework banger, Catherine wheel, cherry bomb (*US*), firecracker, fizgig, girandole, pinwheel (*US*), rocket, Roman candle, sparkler, squib, torpedo (*US*)

types of explosive weapon A-bomb, antiballistic missile, atom bomb, atomic bomb (*US*), ballistic missile, bomb, booby trap, depth charge, firebomb, guided missile, hand grenade, hydrogen bomb, mine, missile, Molotov cocktail, nail bomb, neutron bomb, nuclear missile, nuclear warhead, nuclear weapon, petrol bomb, smart bomb, smoke bomb, time bomb, torpedo, warhead

1155 Weapons for Shooting

(*n*) firearm, gun, *shooter* (*informal*)

types of gun air pistol, air rifle, antiaircraft gun, automatic, bazooka, blunderbuss, cannon, carbine, flamethrower, handgun, howitzer, machine gun, magnum, mortar, musket, pistol, revolver, rifle, sawed-off shotgun (*US*), sawn-off shotgun, semiautomatic, shotgun, submachine gun, Tommy gun (*informal*)

types of bow crossbow, Cupid's bow, longbow

1156 Swords and Knives

types of sword or knife battleaxe, bayonet, bowie knife, broadsword, claymore, cutlass, dagger, dirk, foil, lance, machete, poleaxe, rapier, sabre, scimitar, skean, stiletto, swordstick, tomahawk

1157 Blunt Instruments and Whips

(*n*) birch, cat-o'-nine-tails, club, lash, switch, whip

types of club baton, billy club (*US*), blackjack, bludgeon, cosh, cudgel, mace, nightstick (*US*), shillelagh, truncheon

See also WHIP AND CLUB (418)

1158 Projectiles

types of projectile arrow, arrowhead, assegai, bolt, boomerang, brickbat, buckshot, bullet, cannonball, dart, dumdum bullet, grenade, harpoon, javelin, lance, pellet, plastic bullet, rubber bullet, shell, shot, slug, spear

1159 Describing Technology

(*adj*) cordless, high-tech, *hi-tech*, industrial, pilot, pioneering, pneumatic, radio-controlled, self-acting, sophisticated, space-age, state-of-the-art, technical, technological, up-to-date

Energy, Fuels, and Foods

1160 Energy General

Energy is Eternal Delight. **William Blake**

(*n*) attraction, combustion, energy, force, friction, gravitation, gravity, impetus, impulse, magnet, magnetism, momentum, pressure, propulsion, rubbing, suction, thrust, torque, torsion, traction, wave

1161 Energy Sources

(*adj*) atomic, electric, nuclear, radioactive

(*n*) electricity, firewood, fuel, *gasoline* (*US*), kerosene (*US*), *paraffin*, *paraffin oil*, *petrol*, *petroleum*, radiation, radioactivity, tinder

1162 Energy Storage and Generation

(*n*) *battery*, dynamo, *generator*, reactor

See also INDUSTRIAL BUILDINGS (1086)

1163 Light

(*n*) beam, candlelight, daylight, firelight, flare, flash, glare, glitter, glow, illumination, illuminations, incandescence, irradiation, lighting, moonbeam, nimbus, radiance, ray, scintillation, starlight, sunbeam, sunlight, sunshine, twinkle

types of light arc lamp, chandelier, flashlight (*US*), floodlight, fluorescent lamp, footlights, hurricane lamp, lamp, lamppost, lantern, LED, light bulb, neon light, nightlight, penlight, searchlight, spotlight, standard lamp, streetlamp, streetlight, striplight, sunlamp, torch, torchlight, traffic light, uplighter

See also LIGHTING (862), LIGHT EMISSION (369), DESCRIBING LIGHT (1227)

1164 Fire, Flammability, and Burning

Look not for fire in Hell, each man brings his own fire. **Yasar Kemal**

(*adj*) ablaze, afire, aflame, aglow, alight, blazing, burning, combustible, fireproof, flame-retardant, flaming, flammable, incendiary, incombustible, in flames, inflammable, nonflammable, on fire, *singed*, *smouldering*, vaporous

(*n*) beacon, blaze, bonfire, brazier, *brush fire*, burner, conflagration, fire, fireball, flame, *forest fire*, forge, furnace, *incineration*, incinerator, inferno, kiln, pyre, *pyrotechnics*

(*v*) blaze, burn, burn down, burn up, *burst into flames*, *catch fire*, *catch light*, char, cremate, fire up, flame, flare, frizzle, go up, go up in smoke, gut, ignite, incinerate, kindle, let off, light, put a match to, scald, scorch, sear, set alight, set fire to, *set light to*, *set on fire*, singe, smoke, smoulder, stoke, stoke up, torch (*informal*)

See also DESTRUCTION AND DEMOLITION (360), WORSEN APPEARANCE (383)

1165 Products of Fire

I am ashes where once I was fire. **Lord Byron**

(*n*) ash, cinders, *clinker*, ember, smoke, smoke screen, smut, soot, spark

1166 Food

Food is the beginning of wisdom. The first condition of putting any thing into your head and heart, is to put something into your stomach. **Ludwig Andreas Feuerbach**

(*adj*) *comestible* (*formal*), culinary, dietary, digestible, edible, fattening, filling, gastronomic, hearty, indigestible, inedible, nourishing, nutritional, nutritious, nutritive, organic, slimming, stodgy (*informal*), wholesome

(*n*) bread, chow (*slang*), chuck (*US regional*), *comestibles* (*formal*), cuisine, diet, eats (*slang*), famine, fare, food, foodstuff, gastronomy, groceries, grub (*informal*), junk food, manna, meal, nosh (*informal*), nourishment, nutrition, produce, provender (*literary or humorous*), provisions, rations, refreshment, refreshments, stodge (*informal*), sustenance, table, tuck, tucker (*informal*), victuals, *vittles* (*archaic*), wholesomeness

See also EAT AND NOT EAT (711)

1167 Animal Feed

(*n*) birdseed, feed, *feedstuff*, fodder, forage, hay, pigswill, provender (*archaic*), silage, straw, swill

1168 Meals and Parts of Meals

(*n*) blowout (*slang*), *bonne bouche*, carryout, collation, feast, nosh-up (*informal*), repast (*literary*), spread (*informal*), square meal

parts of a meal afters (*informal*), antipasto, aperitif, appetizer, canapé, delicacy, dessert, entrée, hors d'oeuvre, main course, meze, nibbles, pud (*informal*), pudding, side dish, starter, sweet, sweet course, tapas

types of meal banquet, barbecue, breakfast, brunch, buffet, clambake, cookout (*US*), dinner, elevenses, English breakfast, high tea, lunch, picnic, ready-made meal, snack, supper, takeaway, takeout (*US*), tea, titbit, TV dinner

1169 Prepared Dishes

(*n*) butty (*informal*), *club sandwich*, *cocktail snacks*, dish, *fast food*, *finger food*, fixings (*US*), *hoagie* (*US*), mash, *meat pie*, sandwich, *sarnie* (*informal*), *shish kebab*, *steak pie*, trimmings

types of cooked dish casserole, cassoulet, chop suey, chow mein, couscous, curry, fish cake, fondue, fricassee, fry-up, goulash, gruel, Irish stew, kedgeree, mixed grill, nasi goreng, paella, pilaf (*US*), pilau, pizza, ragout, ratatouille, risotto, stir-fry

1170 State of Prepared Food

(*adj*) *al dente*, *barbecued*, *braised*, *broiled* (*US*), burnt, *burnt to a crisp*, candied, canned, *charbroiled* (*US*), chewy, cooked, *curried*, *fried*, *glacé*, gristly, gutted, instant, jellied, long-life, *marinated*, *microwaved*, mulled, overcooked, overdone, pickled, pink, *poached*, potted, *precooked*, preserved, rare, raw, rubbery, *sautéed*, *smoked*, *stewed*, *stir-fried*, stringy, sun-dried, takeaway, takeout (*US*), *tinned*, tough, *tough as old boots*, uncooked, *undercooked*, underdone, *unseasoned*

See also COOKING AND FOOD PREPARATION (354)

1171 Additives

(*n*) additive, flavour, flavouring, preservative, sweetener, sweetening

1172 Fats and Oils

(*n*) fat, grease, oil

types of cooking fat and oil butter, canola oil, corn oil, dripping, ghee, lard, margarine, olive oil, peanut oil, rape oil, sesame oil, shortening (*US*), suet, sunflower oil, vegetable oil

1173 Seasonings and Sauces

(*n*) arrowroot, aspic, *condiment*, garnish, seasoning

types of pickle chutney, cornichon, gherkin, piccalilli, pickled cucumber

types of seasonings, sauces, and dips apple sauce, barbecue sauce, béchamel sauce, brown sauce, chilli sauce, coulis, dressing, French dressing, gravy, guacamole, ketchup, marinade, mayonnaise, mint sauce, salad cream, satay, soy sauce, stock cube, tartare sauce, Thousand Island dressing, vinegar, Worcester sauce

1174 Herbs and Spices

types of herb angelica, basil, bay leaf, camomile, caraway, chervil, chive, cilantro (*US*), coriander, dill, fennel, hyssop, lemon grass, lovage, marjoram, mint, oregano, parsley, rosemary, sage, savory, spearmint, tarragon, thyme

types of spice allspice, aniseed, black pepper, caraway seed, cardamom, cayenne pepper, chilli, cinnamon, clove, coriander, cumin, fenugreek, ginger, ginseng, mace, mustard, nutmeg, paprika, pepper, peppercorn, saffron, turmeric, white pepper

1175 Fruit and Vegetables

types of processed potato chip, crisp, croquette, French fries, fries, hash browns (*US*), home fries (*US*), jacket potato, knish, latke, mash, potato cake, potato chip, potato pancake, rösti

types of berry bilberry, blackberry, blackcurrant, blueberry, boysenberry, cranberry, currant, elderberry, gooseberry, huckleberry, juniper, loganberry, mulberry, raisin, raspberry, redcurrant, rowan, sultana, whortleberry

types of citrus clementine, grapefruit, lemon, lime, mandarin, orange, pomelo, satsuma, tangerine

types of fruit apple, apricot, avocado, banana, cherry, damson, date, fig, grape, guava, kiwi fruit, mango, melon, nectarine, olive, papaya, passion fruit, peach, pear, pineapple, plum, pomegranate, quince, strawberry, watermelon

types of salad vegetable alfalfa, bean sprout, capsicum, celery, chicory, coleslaw, cress, cucumber, endive, green onion (*US*), lettuce, pepper, radicchio, radish, scallion, sorrel, spring onion, sweet pepper, tomato, watercress

types of vegetable artichoke, asparagus, aubergine, brassica, broccoli, Brussels sprout, cabbage, cauliflower, collard greens (*US*), courgette, eggplant (*US*), fennel, garlic, greens, kale, leek, legume, marrow, marrow squash (*US*), okra, onion, pumpkin, spinach, squash, sweetcorn, Swiss chard, zucchini (*US*)

parts of a fruit flesh, juice, kernel, peel, pip, pit (*US*), pith, pulp, rind, seed, skin, stone

types of root vegetable beet, beetroot, carrot, cassava, mangel-wurzel, new potato, parsnip, potato, rutabaga, spud (*informal*), sugar beet, swede, sweet potato, tater (*regional*), turnip, yam

1176 Types and Cuts of Meat

(*n*) flesh, game, giblets, kebab, meat, *offal*, *variety meats* (*US*)

types of meat beef, chicken, duck, gammon, goat, goose, grouse, hare, lamb, mutton, partridge, pheasant, pork, rabbit, turkey, veal, venison, wild boar

types of processed meat bacon, bologna (*US*), burger, frankfurter, ground beef, ground meat, ham, hamburger, liver sausage, liverwurst (*US*), meatball, meat loaf, mince, minced beef, minced meat, mincemeat, mortadella, pâté, patty, pepperoni, rissole, salami, sausage, saveloy, wiener (*US*), wienerwurst (*US*)

types of steak Chateaubriand, fillet, porterhouse steak, rump, sirloin, T-bone steak, tenderloin

types of cut best end, breast, brisket, chop, chuck, chump, cutlet, drumstick, flank, foreshank, hock, joint, leg, loin, neck, rasher, rib, round, scrag end, shoulder, side, silverside, sparerib, steak, top round (*US*), topside, wing

1177 Cereal Foods

(*n*) *breakfast cereal*, cereal, *grits* (*US*), porridge

types of cereal barley, corn (*US*), maize, millet, oat, rice, rye, sorghum, wheat

1178 Bread, Flour, and Bread Products

(*n*) *choux pastry*, *Cornish pasty*, *filo pastry*, *flaky pastry*, flan, pastry, pasty, patty, *puff pastry*, quiche, *shortcrust pastry*

types of bread baguette, black bread, brown bread, chapati, ciabatta, corn bread (*US*), cottage loaf, crouton, focaccia, matzo, nan, pitta, poppadom, pumpernickel, puri, roti, rye bread, soda bread, toast, tortilla, white bread

types of flour cornflour, cornmeal, cornstarch (*US*), meal, plain flour, self-raising flour, self-rising flour (*US*), wheatmeal, wholemeal, whole-wheat (*US*)

types of roll or bun bagel, bap, bun, croissant, crumpet, English muffin (*US*), muffin, roll

1179 Pasta

types of pasta cannelloni, capellini, cappelletti, conchiglie, fettuccine, fusilli, lasagne, linguine, macaroni, penne, ravioli, rigatoni, spaghetti, tagliatelle, tortellini, vermicelli

1180 Cakes, Biscuits, and Desserts

(*n*) *biscuit*, cake, *cookie*, pastry

types of dessert blancmange, cobbler, crème brûlée, crème caramel, crisp (*US*), crumble, custard, flan, fruit salad, ice cream, jelly, junket, meringue, mousse, pie, pudding, sorbet, soufflé, sundae, syllabub, tart

types of pancake battercake (*US*), blini, blintz, crêpe, drop scone, flapjack (*US*), griddlecake, hotcake (*US*), johnnycake (*US*), waffle

types of cake brownie, carrot cake, cheesecake, Christmas cake, coffee cake, cupcake, Danish pastry, devil's food cake, doughnut, éclair, flapjack, fruitcake, gateau, gingerbread, jelly roll (*US*), macaroon, Madeira cake, madeleine, mince pie, muffin, seedcake, sponge cake, Swiss roll, turnover, wedding cake

1181 Confectionery

(*n*) goody

types of confectionery bubblegum, bonbon, butterscotch, candy (*US*), caramel, chewing gum, chocolate, fondant, fudge, gobstopper, gum, gumdrop, jawbreaker (*US*), jellybean, liquorice, marshmallow, marzipan, nougat, peppermint, praline, sweet, sweetie (*informal*), sweetmeat (*archaic*), taffy (*US*), toffee, truffle

types of confectionery on a stick candy apple (*US*), candyfloss, cotton candy (*US*), lollipop, lolly (*informal*), toffee apple

1182 Dairy Products and Cheeses

types of soft cheese Brie, Camembert, chèvre, cottage cheese, cream cheese, curd, Danish blue, Dolcelatte, feta, Gorgonzola, mascarpone, mozzarella, ricotta, Roquefort

types of hard cheese caerphilly, cheddar, Cheshire, Edam, Emmental, Emmenthaler (*US*), Gouda, Gruyère, haloumi, Monterey Jack, Parmesan, pecorino, Stilton, Wensleydale

1183 Sugar and Preserves

(*n*) *corn syrup* (*US*), frosting, *golden syrup*, *maple syrup*, molasses, syrup, *treacle*

types of preserve compote, conserve, honey, jam, jelly, lekvar, lemon curd, marmalade, mincemeat, peanut butter

1184 Nuts

types of nut acorn, almond, brazil nut, cashew, chestnut, cob, cobnut, coconut, cola nut, groundnut, hazelnut, hickory nut, horse chestnut, macadamia nut, monkey nut, peanut, pecan, pine nut, pistachio, walnut

1185 Soup

types of soup bisque, borscht, bouillabaisse, bouillon, broth, chowder, cock-a-leekie, consommé, gazpacho, gumbo, julienne, minestrone, mulligatawny, pea soup, potage, Scotch broth, vichyssoise

1186 Drinks

(*adj*) alcoholic, nonalcoholic, sparkling, still

(*n*) beverage (*formal*), *bevvy* (*slang*), brew (*informal*), *cordial*, *dram*, drink, elixir, *fruit juice*, *home-brew*, *hooch* (*US slang*), *hot toddy*, lemon, *lemonade*, libation (*humorous*), liquor, moonshine (*informal*), nightcap, nip, plonk (*informal*), *potation* (*literary*), poteen, short (*informal*), smoothie, snifter (*informal*), *squash*, tea, *thirst-quencher*, *tipple* (*informal*), *tisane*, *vino* (*informal*), *white lightning* (*US*)

types of coffee café au lait, café noir, caffè latte, cappuccino, decaf, espresso, Greek coffee, Irish coffee, latte, mocha, Turkish coffee

1187 Food Components

(*n*) albumen, bran, cholesterol, roughage, *saturated fat*, *saturated fatty acid*

types of nutrient amino acid, carbohydrate, dextrose, fat, fibre, fructose, glucose, lactose, mineral, protein, salt, starch, sucrose, sugar, vitamin

1188 Beans and Pulses

types of pulse bean, black bean, black-eyed bean, black-eyed pea (*US*), broad bean, butter bean, chickpea, fava bean (*US*), French bean, garbanzo, haricot, kidney bean, lentil, lima bean, mangetout, mung bean, navy bean (*US*), pea, petits pois, pinto bean, runner bean, snow pea (*US*), soya bean, string bean

1189 Sea Food

(*n*) caviar, *scampi*, shellfish

See also AQUATIC INVERTEBRATE (1022)

Physical Qualities of Objects

1190 Qualities and Characteristics

Things are entirely what they appear to be and behind them...there is nothing. **Jean-Paul Sartre**

(*n*) anatomy, aspect, attribute, characteristic, component, composition, constitution, detail, dimension, element, fabric, facet, feature, fibre, formation, framework, hallmark, makeup, organization, physics, quality, side, structure, superstructure, trait

1191 Size and Dimensions

There is a right physical size for every idea. **Henry Moore**

(*n*) acreage, acres, bulk, calibre, capacity, compass, dimension, dimensions, expanse, extent, greatness, mass, measurement, *proportions*, size, *spaciousness*, volume

1192 Large

(*adj*) airy, almighty (*informal*), awkward, big, bulging, bulky, capacious, cavernous, colossal, commodious, considerable, cosmic, *cumbrous* (*archaic or literary*), elephantine, enormous, expansive, extensive, extra-large, fantastic, fat, full-size, galactic (*informal*), gargantuan, giant, *giant-sized*, gigantic, ginormous (*informal*), global, good-sized, grand, great, herculean, huge, hulking, humongous (*informal*), immeasurable, immense, inestimable, infinite, jumbo, king-size, large, life-size, mammoth, massive, maxi, measurable, measureless (*literary*), *mega*, mighty, monolithic, monster, monstrous, monumental, mountainous, outsize, oversize, prodigious, queen-size, rambling, roomy, significant, sizable, spacious, spectacular, stupendous, substantial, substantive, sweeping, terrific, thumping (*informal*), thundering (*dated informal*), tidy, titanic, tremendous, vast, voluminous, walloping (*informal*), whacking (*informal*), whopping (*informal*)

(*n*) airiness, amplitude, bulkiness, *capaciousness*, *chunkiness*, *cumbersomeness*, enormity, expansiveness, extensiveness, *immenseness*, immensity, largeness, magnitude, *ponderousness*, prodigiousness, roominess, *unwieldiness*, vastness, *voluminousness*

1193 Big Things

(*n*) *behemoth*, biggie (*informal*), colossus, *giant*, *leviathan*, monster, *stonker* (*slang*), whopper (*informal*)

1194 Small

(*adj*) atomic, beady, bijou (*humorous*), bitty (*US informal*), compact, confined, cramped, diminutive, dinky (*informal*), fractional, incommodious (*formal*), infinitesimal, itsy-bitsy (*informal*), *itty-bitty* (*informal*), little, microscopic, mini, miniature, minimal, minimum, minuscule, minute, miserable, miserly, modest, neat, nominal, peewee, pint-size (*informal*), *pint-sized* (*informal*), pitiful, pocket, pocket-sized, poky (*informal*), pygmy, *shrivelled*, slender, small, small-scale, *submicroscopic*, *teensy* (*informal*), *teensy-weensy* (*informal*), teeny (*informal*), teeny-weeny (*informal*), tiddly (*informal*), tiny, titchy (*informal*), travel, *trial size*, underdeveloped, *undersize*, undersized, wee, *weensy* (*informal*), weeny (*informal*)

(*n*) minuteness, smallness, *tininess*, trimness

1195 Medium

(*adj*) *medium-large*, *medium-sized*, *standard-size*

1196 Length: Long

The only thing I regret about my past life is the length of it. If I had my past life over again I'd make all the same mistakes—only sooner. **Tallulah Bankhead**

(*adj*) elongated, full-length, long, *standard-length*, stretched

(*n*) length, *lengthiness*

1197 Length: Short

(*adj*) short, stunted

(*n*) shortness

1198 Width: Wide

A wide screen just makes a bad film twice as bad. **Samuel Goldwyn**

(*adj*) big, broad, gaping, sprawling, thick, wide, wide-open

(*n*) breadth, broadness, diameter, girth, radius, span, thickness, width

1199 Width: Narrow and Thin

(*adj*) fine, gauzy, narrow, *paper-thin*, spidery, wafer-thin

(*n*) fineness, narrowness, slimness, thinness

1200 Depth: Deep

The gods approve/The depth, and not the tumult, of the soul. **William Wordsworth**

(*adj*) bottomless, deep, fathomless, unfathomable, unplumbed, yawning

(*n*) deepness, depth, *fathomlessness*, profoundness, profundity

1201 Depth: Shallow

(*adj*) shallow

(*n*) *shallowness*

1202 Height: High

Never measure the height of a mountain, until you have reached the top. Then you will see how low it was. **Dag Hammarskjöld**

(*adj*) big, elevated, high, high-rise, lofty, multistorey, tall, towering, vertiginous

(*n*) altitude, elevation, height, tallness

See also BUILD (478)

1203 Height: Low

(*adj*) low, low-lying, low-rise

See also BUILD (478)

1204 Weight: Heavy

The weight of the world/is love./Under the burden/of solitude. **Allen Ginsberg**

(*adj*) chunky, clumpy, clunky, cumbersome, heavy, hefty, leaden, massive, ponderous, ungainly, unwieldy, weighty

(*n*) ballast, heaviness, heft (*US*), heftiness, makeweight, tonnage, ungainliness, weight, weightiness

See also BUILD (478)

1205 Weight: Light

You often lighten your troubles by telling of them. **Corneille**

(*adj*) buoyant, light, portable, weightless

(*n*) buoyancy, lightness, portability, *weightlessness*

See also BUILD (478)

1206 Density and Consistency

Matter. . .a convenient formula for describing what happens where it isn't. **Bertrand Russell**

(*adj*) beaten, close, *coagulated*, compact, *congealed*, dense, impenetrable, impervious, *penetrable*, permeable, pervious, porous, set, solid, soluble, spongy, thick, turbid

(*adv*) compactly

(*n*) compactness, concentration, condensation, consistency, denseness, density, impenetrability, impermeability, imperviousness, *penetrability*, permeability, permeation, *perviousness*, *porosity*, *porousness*, solidity, solidness, solubility, thickness, viscosity

1207 State

(*n*) condition, form, shape, state

1208 Fragile

(*adj*) breakable, brittle, crumbly, ethereal, fine, fragile, frangible, friable, papery, superfine, thin, weak, wispy

(*n*) brittleness, fragility, *friability*

1209 Durable

(*adj*) durable, imperishable, impermeable, resilient, rock-solid, rustproof, shatterproof, strong, sturdy, toughened

(*n*) durability, imperishability, resilience, sturdiness

See also STRENGTH (202)

1210 Rigid and Hard

(*adj*) blown-up, bulletproof, *calcified*, firm, hard, immobile, immovable, inelastic, inflexible, knotted, *ligneous*, *ossified*, petrified, rigid, rock-hard, solid, stiff, taut, tempered, tense, tight, unyielding, wooden

(*adv*) fast, stiffly

(*n*) firmness, hardness, inflexibility, rigidity, rigour, stiffness, tautness, tension, tightness

1211 Malleable and Elastic

(*adj*) bendable, bendy, bouncy, droopy, ductile, elastic, elasticated, expandable, flaccid, flexible, floppy, *jellylike*, lax, limp, loose, malleable, mushy, plastic, pliable, pliant, slack, soft, spongy, springy, squashy, squidgy, *stretchable*, stretchy, supple, tensile, tractable, willowy, yielding

(*adv*) flexibly, loosely, slackly

(*n*) *bendability*, *bendiness*, bounciness, droopiness, flexibility, floppiness, limpness, malleability, plasticity, pliability, pliancy, softness, spring, *springiness*, stretch, tractability

1212 Fluid and Non-solid

The terrible fluidity of self-revelation. **Henry James**

(*adj*) absorbent, *absorptive*, dilute, diluted, fluid, gaseous, gassy, *gloopy* (*informal*), *glue-like*, *goopy* (*US informal*), *liquefied*, *liquescent*, liquid, molten, runny, seething, *sludgy*, thin, vaporous, watery, weak

(*n*) absorbency, *absorptivity*, *gluiness*, *gooeyness*, *gumminess*, *liquescence*, liquidity, *mushiness*, *runniness*

1213 Raw and Natural

(*adj*) coarse, crude, macrobiotic, natural, neat, perishable, raw, rough-hewn, straight, undiluted, *unfortified*, unprocessed, unrefined, untreated

(*adv*) naturally

1214 Not in a Natural State

(*adj*) concentrated, condensed, ground, manufactured, pasteurized, *processed*, *purified*, stoneground

1215 Shape

If a fish is the movement of water embodied, given shape, then a cat is a diagram and pattern of subtle air. **Doris Lessing**

(*n*) build, bulk, configuration, contour, cutout, figure, form, format, hulk, mass, morphology, outline, profile, shadow, shape, silhouette

1216 Angular Shape

(*adj*) *aquiline*, beaked, *deltoid*, equilateral, forked, *hexagonal*, irregular, *octagonal*, peaked, *pentagonal*, pointed, *pointy*, polygonal, ragged, rectangular, rectilinear, right-angled, serrated, tapered, tapering, *trapezoidal*, triangular, *trilateral*, *wedge-shaped*

(*adv*) raggedly

(*n*) barb, corner, *pointiness*, raggedness, solid, spike, spur

types of angular shape box, cross, cube, diamond, dodecahedron, dogleg, lozenge, oblong, parallelogram, pentagon, polygon, pyramid, quadrangle, quadrilateral, rectangle, rhomboid, rhombus, square, star, tetragon, tetrahedron, trapezium, trapezoid, triangle

1217 Rounded Shape

(*adj*) aerodynamic, arched, bandy, *bell-shaped*, bent, blunt, bowed, bulbous, camelback (*US*), circular, coiled, concave, convex, curly, curved, *curvilinear*, curving, curvy, cylindrical, domed, elliptical, flowing, globular, *helical*, *hemispherical*, hollow, hooked, lumpy, meandering, *orbicular* (*formal*), ovate, *ovoid*, prominent, protuberant, puffy, recurvate, rolling, rounded, *semicircular*, spherical, squiggly, streamlined, tubular, undulant (*literary*), undulating, vaulted, winding

(*n*) curvature, *curviness*, halo, hump, kink, knob, knot, knuckle, lump, node, nodule, prominence, protuberance, radius, *rondure* (*literary*), *sphericalness*, sweep, turn, twirl, twist, waviness, whorl

types of rounded shape arc, arch, ball, bend, bow, bulb, circle, circlet, coil, cone, crescent, curl, curve, cylinder, dome, figure of eight, globe, heart, helix, hemisphere, hoop, horseshoe, kidney, loop, orb, oval, ring, round, semicircle, sphere, spheroid, spiral, teardrop

1218 Shapelessness

Twice or thrice had I loved thee,/Before I knew thy face or name/So in a voice, so in a shapelesse flame,/Angels affect us oft, and worshipped be. **John Donne**

(*adj*) amorphous, baggy, formless, loose, sagging, *saggy*, shapeless, unformed, unshaped, unstructured

(*adv*) loosely

(*n*) *amorphousness*, bagginess, *formlessness*, looseness, *misshapenness*, *sagginess*, shapelessness, slackness

1219 Texture

He gave the impression that very many cities had rubbed him smooth. **Graham Greene**

(*n*) feel, finish, nap, pile, roughness, texture, weave

1220 Visual Texture

(*adj*) clear, cloudy, crystalline, diaphanous, effervescent, filmy, fizzy, frothy, glassy, glazed, gleaming, glossy, gossamer, *grainy*, heavy, iridescent, lacy, limpid, matte, metallic, milky, muddy, *opalescent*, opaque, pearly, *pellucid* (*literary*), polished, satiny, see-through, sheer, *shimmery*, smoky, *soapy*, sparkling, sparkly, steamy, thin, translucent, transparent, unfocused, unstrained, vitreous (*n*) clearness, cloudiness, frosting, frothiness, fuzziness, glossiness, *graininess*, lustre, muddiness, opacity, *opaqueness*, patina, *pellucidity* (*literary*), polish, sheen, sheerness, shine, *shininess*, translucence, *translucency*, transparency

1221 Physical Texture

(*adj*) abrasive, bald, barbed, bobbly, bristly, brushed, bubbly, bumpy, caustic, chalky, chunky, coarse, cobbled, corrosive, corrugated, crinkled, crisp, crispy, crunchy, crusty, cuddly, downy, even, fat, fatty, feathery, fibrous, fleecy, floury, fluffy, fluted, furred, furry, gelatinous, gluey, glutinous, gooey, granular, granulated, gravelly, greasy, gritty, gummy, icky (*informal*), jagged, keen (*literary*), knobbly, laminated, level, mucous, oily, *oleaginous*, peachy, pitted, plated, potholed, powdered, powdery, prickly, resinous, ribbed, rock-strewn, rocky, rough, rough-hewn, ruched, rugged, rutted, scaly, scratchy, sharp, silken, silky, *silky-smooth*, sleek, slick, slimy, slippery, smooth, soft, spiked, spiky, spiny, sticky, stony, *sudsy*, tacky, textured, thick, thorny, tickly, treacly, unctuous, uneven, uniform, velvety, viscid, viscous, wiry, woollen, woolly

(*adv*) coarsely, evenly, levelly, roughly

(*n*) bumpiness, clamminess, coarseness, downiness, evenness, flatness, fleeciness, fluffiness, furriness, fuzziness, greasiness, jaggedness, keenness (*literary*), *oleaginousness*, roughness, ruggedness, *silkiness*, *sliminess*, smoothness, *spikiness*, *sponginess*, stickiness, toughness, unevenness, *velvetiness*, waxiness, wiriness

1222 Orientation and Alignment

Where there is matter, there is geometry. **Johannes Kepler**

(*adj*) agape (*literary*), ajar, aslant, asymmetric, awry, bevelled, breadthways, breadthwise (*US*), buried, cock-eyed, craggy, crooked, *dangling*, deformed, diagonal, diffuse, end on, erect, flat, flush, folded, glancing, horizontal, inclined, inside out, lateral, level, linear, lopsided, malformed, misaligned, misshapen, multilateral, mutant, oblique, off-centre, *off the beam* (*US*), *on a slope*, *out of kilter*, *out of true*, outspread, outstretched, *overturned*, pendent, pendulous, perpendicular, plumb, precipitous, prone, prostrate, radial, recumbent (*literary*), sheer, skewed, skewwhiff (*informal*), slanting, *sloping*, *slumped*, splay, split-level, *sprawled*, spread-eagled, squint (*informal*), staggered, standing, standup, steep, straight, sunken, supine, suspended, tabular, three-dimensional, tilted, *tilting*, top-heavy, transverse, twisted, two-dimensional, unbalanced, underwater, unsymmetrical, *upended*, uphill, upright, upside-down, upstretched, *upturned*, upward, vertical, wonky (*informal*), *wrong side up*, *wrong way up*

(*adv*) across, askew, aslant, *at an angle*, *athwart*, *at right angles*, back to front, backwards, *bolt upright*, breadthways, breadthwise (*US*), *cater-cornered* (*US*), *catty-cornered* (*US*), crookedly, *crossways*, crosswise, edgeways, endways, endwise, in line, *kitty-cornered* (*US*), lengthways, lengthwise, *off balance*, *on the cross*, *on the slant*, sheer, slantways, slantwise, square, squint (*informal*), steeply, *upside down*, wide

(*n*) alignment, asymmetry, deformity, inclination, list, lopsidedness, malformation, obliqueness, orientation, slant, slope, splay, steepness, tangent, tilt, tip

1223 Colours

Color is sensibility turned into matter, matter in its primordial state. **Yves Klein**

types of yellow canary yellow, champagne, chrome yellow, citrine, citron, flaxen, lemon, lemon yellow, mustard, saffron

types of black blue-black, coal black, ebony, inky, jet black, pitch-black, raven, sable

types of green apple green, aquamarine, avocado, bottle green, chartreuse, emerald green, forest green, grass green, jade, jade green, lime green, Lincoln green, lovat, Nile green, olive green, pea green, sage green, sea green, viridian

types of grey ash, battleship grey, charcoal grey, dove grey, grizzled, gunmetal, pearl grey, pewter, putty, silver grey, slate, steel grey, taupe

types of orange amber, apricot, flame, ginger, gold, golden, ochre, old gold, peach, tangerine, titian

types of pink cerise, coral, fuchsia, raspberry, rose, salmon pink, shell pink, shocking pink

types of purple amethyst, aubergine, heliotrope, lavender, lilac, mauve, plum, violet

types of red blood red, brick red, burgundy, carmine, carnation, cherry red, claret, crimson, damask, garnet, magenta, maroon, oxblood, pillar-box red, puce, ruby, scarlet, vermilion, wine

types of white cream, eggshell, ivory, magnolia, off-white, oyster, pearl, platinum, silver, snow white

types of blue azure, cobalt blue, cornflower blue, cyan, electric blue, ice blue, indigo, lapis lazuli, midnight blue, navy blue, peacock blue, powder blue, Prussian blue, royal blue, sapphire, saxe blue, sky blue, slate blue, steel blue, turquoise, ultramarine

types of brown auburn, bay, bronze, burnt sienna, burnt umber, caramel, chestnut, chocolate, copper, hazel, henna, khaki, liver, mahogany, mocha, mousy, nut-brown, roan, russet, sorrel, tan, tawny, umber, walnut

types of colour beige, black, blue, brown, green, grey, orange, pink, purple, red, white, yellow

types of beige buff, butterscotch, café au lait, camel, coffee, dun, ecru, fawn, flesh colour, honey, oatmeal

1224 Patterns

Art is the imposing of a pattern on experience, and our aesthetic enjoyment is recognition of the pattern. **A. N. Whitehead**

(*n*) design, line, livery (*literary*), marking, *paisley*, pattern, pigmentation, streak, striation, stripe, tartan

1225 Describing Colours

Colours seen by candle-light/Will not look the same by day. **Elizabeth Barrett Browning**

(*adj*) bleached, brilliant, coloured, colourful, colourless, dirty, discoloured, dull, dusky, faint, *homochromatic*, *homochromous*, jazzy (*slang*), kaleidoscopic, light, light-coloured, lurid, *many-coloured*, *many-hued*, monochromatic, monochrome, multicolour, neutral, pale, parti-coloured, pastel, *polychromatic*, *polychrome*, *prismatic*, psychedelic, rainbow, roseate, rosy, silvery, snowy, sober, sombre, splashy, *tinted*, two-tone, *varicoloured*, vibrant, vivid

(*adv*) dully, faintly, sombrely, vibrantly, vividly

(*n*) bloom, coloration, discoloration, dullness, dye, hue, luridness, patina, shade, tint, tone, vividness

1226 Describing Patterns

(*adj*) barred, candy-striped, checked, chequered, dappled, flecked, floral, *floral-patterned*, flowered, *flower-patterned*, flowery, freckled, inlaid, lined, marbled, mottled, patterned, pepper-and-salt, piebald, pied, plaid, self-coloured, *skewbald*, *specked*, speckled, spotted, spotty, *star-spangled*, stippled, streaky, *striped*, *stripy*, variegated, veined

1227 Describing Light

But yet the light that led astray/Was light from Heaven. **Robert Burns**

(*adj*) black, *black as night*, blinding, bright, brilliant, candlelit, clouded, *crepuscular* (*literary*), dark, dazzling, dim, *flickering*, floodlit, fluorescent, glaring, *glimmering*, *glinting*, glistening, glittery, gloomy, glowing, gold, incandescent, lambent, light, lucid, *luminescent*, luminous, lustreless, lustrous, pale, pitch-dark, radiant, refulgent (*literary*), shadowy, shady, shimmering, shiny, soft, *softly lit*, starlit, starry, strong, subdued, sunlit, *tenebrous* (*literary*), translucent, twilit, unlit

(*adv*) brightly, brilliantly, dimly, softly

(*n*) blackness, blaze, brightness, brilliance, dark, dazzle, dimness, *fluorescence*, gleam, glimmer, glint, glisten, gloom, gloominess, light, lucidity, *luminescence*, luminosity, murk, penumbra, refulgence (*literary*), semi-darkness, shade, shadiness, shadows, torchlight, translucence

See also LIGHT EMISSION (369)

1228 Temperature: Hot

The bourgeois prefers comfort to pleasure, convenience to liberty, and a pleasant temperature to the deathly inner consuming fire. **Hermann Hesse**

(*adj*) burning, *burning hot*, fiery, hot, *piping hot*, red-hot, scalding, sizzling (*informal*), thermal, white-hot

(*n*) heat, hotness, *temperature*

See also HOT WEATHER (1050)

1229 Temperature: Medium

(*adj*) *hand-hot*, lukewarm, tepid

(*n*) warm, warmness, warmth

See also WEATHER AND CLIMATE (1049)

1230 Temperature: Cold

(*adj*) chilled, cold, frigid, iced, perished (*informal*), stone-cold

(*n*) cold, coldness

See also COLD WEATHER (1051)

1231 In Good Repair

The body must be repaired and supported, if we would preserve the mind in all its vigour. **Pliny the Younger**

(*adj*) airtight, finished, fresh, habitable, hermetic, inhabitable, *in tiptop condition*, inviolate, *in working order*, leakproof, lived-in, mature, matured, navigable, *neat and tidy*, negotiable, new, passable, perfect, preserved, protected, rainproof, *renovated*, ripe, *rust-free*, seamless, secure, serviceable, stormproof, undamaged, undisturbed, unspoiled, usable, waterproof, *waterproofed*, *water-resistant*, watertight, weatherproof, well-equipped, whole

1232 Clean

(*adj*) antiseptic, aseptic, clean, *clean as a new pin*, crystal clear, *dirt-free*, *disinfected*, drinkable, fresh, germ-free, healthful, healthy, hygienic, immaculate, pristine, pure, salubrious (*formal*), sanitary, *sanitized*, spick-and-span, spotless, *spotlessly clean*, *squeaky-clean*, sterile, *sterilized*, sweet, uncontaminated, uncorrupted, unmarked, unpolluted, *unsoiled*, unspotted, unsullied, untainted, untarnished

(*n*) cleanliness, cleanness, freshness, hygiene, pureness, purity, *sanitariness*, spotlessness, sterility, sweetness

See also CLEAN AND POLISH (404)

1233 In Bad Repair

Every life is, more or less, a ruin among whose debris we have to discover what the person ought to have been. **José Ortega y Gasset**

(*adj*) addled, barren, battered, beaten-up, beat-up (*informal*), bedraggled, *beyond repair*, blemished, blown-up, broken, broken-down, burned-out, burnt-out, bust (*informal*), busted (*US informal*), *chipped*, clapped-out (*informal*), corrupted, cracked, creaky (*informal*), creased, crinkly, crummy (*informal*), crumpled, crushed, damaged, decrepit, defective, deflated, deformed, *demolished*, derelict, desolate, destroyed, dilapidated, dingy, *disfigured*, distorted, disused, dog-eared, down, duff (*informal*), eroded, *falling apart*, *falling down*, falling to pieces, faulty, flaky, flawed, *fractured*, frayed, furrowed, gnarled, gory, grotty (*informal*), grungy (*informal*), had it (*informal*), holey, impaired, impassable, imperfect, in a state (*informal*), *in bad repair*, *in bits*, inoperative, *in pieces*, *in rags*, *in ruins*, insecure, *in shreds*, *in tatters*, jerry-built, *jerry-rigged*, *junky*, kaput (*informal*), kinky, leaky, makeshift, *mangled*, mangy (*informal*), marred, matted, mean, *messed up* (*informal*), moribund, moth-eaten, *mutilated*, on its last legs, on the blink (*informal*), out of commission, out of order, overgrown, patchwork (*US*), peeling, *poorly maintained*, poor-quality, *punctured*, ragged, raggedy, ramshackle, ratty (*US informal*), rickety, *ripped*, riven (*literary*), ropy (*informal*), rough-and-ready, rubbishy, ruined, rumpled, run-down, rusty, scabby, *scarred*, scorched, *scratched*, *scrubby*, *seen better days*, *splintered*, stopped, tangled, tarnished, tattered, tatty, the worse for wear, threadbare, timeworn, torn, trashy, tumbledown, uncared-for, *unfixed*, uninhabitable, *unsalvageable*, unusable, used, warped, *war-ravaged*, *war-scarred*, war-torn, wasted, weakened, weather-beaten, weathered, well-worn, wild, *wilted*, worm-eaten, worn, worn out, *worn to shreds*, wrecked, wrinkled, *written off* (*informal*), *yellowed*

(*n*) barrenness, decrepitude, degradation, dereliction, dilapidation, dinginess, disrepair, disuse, *grunginess* (*informal*), poor quality, *ricketiness*, *ropiness* (*informal*), *scragginess*, *squalidness*, tattiness, wear, wear and tear

See also OLD, OLD-FASHIONED (168)

1234 Dirty

(*adj*) *begrimed* (*literary*), *besmirched*, contaminated, cruddy (*slang*), defiled (*formal*), dingy, *dirtied*, dirty, dusty, filthy, flyblown, foul, fusty, grimy, grubby, gungy (*informal*), gunky (*informal*), impure, insalubrious (*formal*), insanitary, mouldy, mucky (*informal*), muddy, *mud-spattered*, musty, pestilent, polluted, *scummy*, *scuzzy* (*US slang*), *smudged*, smutty, soiled, sooty, sordid, squalid, stained, *sullied* (*literary*), tainted, unclean, unhygienic, *unsanitary*, unventilated, unwashed

(*n*) dinginess, dirtiness, filthiness, foulness, griminess, grubbiness, muckiness (*informal*), muddiness, mustiness, sordidness, squalor, *uncleanliness*, uncleanness, *unsanitariness*

See also DIRTY AND CONTAMINATE (405)

1235 Decaying or Infested

(*adj*) bad, corroded, crumbling, decayed, decaying, decomposed, decomposing, *deteriorated*, fetid, flyblown, infected, *infested*, *louse-ridden*, *maggoty*, *mildewed*, *mildewy*, *mouldering*, mouldy, off, *pestilential*, *pest-ridden*, *plague-ridden*, *pus-filled*, pussy, *putrefied*, *putrescent*, putrid, *rat-infested*, rotten, rotting, sour, spoiled, stale, verminous, *withered*, worm-eaten, *worm-infested*, *wormy*

(*n*) mouldiness, putrefaction, rottenness, staleness

1236 Appearance and Atmosphere

The environment can act on the subject only to the exact extent that he comprehends it; that is, transforms it into a situation. Hence no objective description of this environment could be of any use to us. **Jean-Paul Sartre**

(*n*) air, ambience, appearance, aspect, atmosphere, aura, complexion, composition, effect, exterior, façade, feel, feeling, guise, image, impression, imprint, karma (*informal*), look, mood, odour, ring, semblance, soul, suggestion, tone, vein, vibe (*slang*), visage

1237 Empty

There is nothing in the world except empty curved space. Matter, charge, electromagnetism, and other fields are only manifestations of the curvature of space. **John Archibald Wheeler**

(*adj*) abandoned, bare, blank, cavernous, clear, deserted, empty, fallow, hollow, unfilled, unfurnished, uninhabited, unoccupied, unpopulated, vacuous, waste, windswept

(*n*) abandonment, blankness, clearness, desolation, emptiness

See also EMPTY AND UNLOAD (408)

1238 Full

A full bottle won't shake; a half-empty one will. **Chinese proverb**

(*adj*) alive, awash, blocked, blown-up, brimful, brimming, bulging (*informal*), bursting, bursting at the seams, buzzing, caked, chock-a-block (*informal*), chock-full (*informal*), *choked*, *choked up*, *clogged*, *clogged up*, congested, crammed, crowded, dense, encrusted, *engorged*, fraught, full, full of, *full to bursting*, *full to capacity*, *full to overflowing*, full up, furnished, heaving, inhabited, jammed, jam-packed (*informal*), laden, loaded, overcrowded, overflowing, overladen, overloaded, overrun, overstuffed, packed, populous, replete, rife, saturated, seething, stacked, stuffed, stuffy, swarming, teeming, thick

(*n*) congestion, *engorgement*, saturation, squash

See also FILL (407)

1239 Wet

Much water goeth by the mill/That the miller knoweth not of. **John Heywood**

(*adj*) afloat, awash, boggy, drenched, dripping, *dripping wet*, flooded, inundated, juicy, marshy, saturated, slushy, soaked, *soaked to the skin*, soaking, *soaking wet*, sodden, sopping, *sopping wet*, soppy, spongy, squelchy, squidgy, squishy, *steeped*, submerged, swampy, sweaty, waterlogged, watery, wet, *wringing*, *wringing wet*

(*n*) immersion, saturation, wet, wetness

1240 Moist

I see a lily on thy brow,/With anguish moist and fever dew. **John Keats**

(*adj*) beaded, clammy, damp, dank, dewy, humid, moist, soggy

(*n*) condensation, damp, dampness, dankness, dew, humidity, moistness, moisture, *sogginess*

1241 Dry

The fountains are dry and the roses over. **Sylvia Plath**

(*adj*) arid, bone dry, dehydrated, desiccated, dried, dry, *dry as a bone*, parched, scorched, sunbaked, waterless

(*n*) aridity, aridness, desiccation, dryness, *waterlessness*

Physical Objects

1242 Physical Objects

An object in possession seldom retains the same charm that it had in pursuit. **Pliny the Younger**

(*n*) accompaniment, accoutrement, adjunct, amenity, appendage, artefact, article, constituent, *doodad* (*US informal*), *doodah* (*informal*), *doofer* (*slang*), doohickey (*US informal*), entity, facility, gadget, *hoojamaflip* (*informal*), ingredient, item, jazz (*slang*), makings, materials, member, object, product, strand, stuff, sucker (*US slang*), supplies, thing, thingamabob (*informal*), *thingamajig* (*informal*), *thingumabob* (*informal*), *thingumajig* (*informal*), *thingummy* (*informal*), thingy (*informal*), trappings, unit, whatchamacallit, *whatsit* (*informal*), *widget* (*humorous*), works (*informal*)

1243 Collections and Mixtures of Things

The true University of these days is a collection of books. **Thomas Carlyle**

(*n*) accumulation, *admixture*, agglomeration, aggregate (*formal*), aggregation, alloy, amalgam, amalgamation, anthology, armoury, arrangement, array, arsenal, assemblage, assortment, bank, batch, battery, bits and bobs (*informal*), bits and pieces (*informal*), blend, body, bouquet, brew, bunch, bundle, cache, catalogue, categorization, choice, classification, clump, cluster, cocktail, collage, collection, combination, *compendium*, compilation, composite, compound, concoction, *conflation*, conglomeration, constellation, crop, diversity, emulsion, ensemble, farrago, galaxy, *grab bag* (*US*), group, hoard, hotchpotch, infusion, inventory, kaleidoscope, litany, lot, marriage, medley, melange (*literary or formal*), meld, *melding*, melee, melting pot, memorabilia, merger, *miscellanea*, miscellany, mishmash, mix, mixed bag, mixture, montage, mosaic, multimedia, nosegay, omnibus, pack, package, panoply, patchwork, portfolio (*formal*), posy, potion, potpourri, procession, ragbag (*informal*), range, repertoire, repertory, reserve, resource, selection, sequence, set, source, spray, spread, store, string, suite, sundries, synthesis, tangle, variety, wad

1244 Containers, Receptacles, and Packaging

I might give my life for my friend, but he had better not ask me to do up a parcel. **Logan Pearsall Smith**

(*n*) aerosol, ampoule, atomizer, basin, basket, bath, beaker, bedpan, billfold (*US*), bin, binder, birdbath, bobbin, bottle, bucket, *bud vase*, bunker, butt, canister, capsule, carousel, cassette, cauldron, chalice (*literary*), *chamber pot*, cistern, coffer, cool bag, cool box, cradle, crucible, demijohn, dragnet, dustbin, dustpan, file, *firkin*, flowerpot, garbage can (*US*), hayrack, *hip flask*, inkwell, in-tray, letterbox, magnum, mailbox (*US*), *maildrop* (*US*), mailer, manger, money box, mould, package, packaging, packet, *pail*, parcel, phial, piggy bank, pillar box, planter, pocket, portfolio, postbox, propagator, *rain barrel* (*US*), receptacle, reel, *rehoboam*, roll, rubbish bin, sac, sachet, saddlebag, scabbard, *septic tank*, sleeve, spool, spray, spray can, spray gun, *stein*, stoup, strongbox, tabernacle, tank, *thermos*, till, tin, *trash can* (*US*), tray, trough, tub, urn, vaporizer, vase, vat, vessel, vial, wallet, *wastebasket* (*US*), *waste bin*, *wastepaper basket*, *wastepaper bin*, *wheelie bin*

types of container barrel, billycan, biscuit tin, box, caddy, can, cardboard box, carton, cartridge, case, cask, casket, chest, cover, crate, creel, cylinder, drawer, drum, hamper, holder, jam jar, jar, jerry can, keg, pencil case, pigeonhole, pillbox, pot, punnet, storage bin, storage tank, tea caddy, trunk

types of bag bum bag, carrier, carrier bag, clutch bag, fanny pack (*US*), handbag, mailbag, nosebag, pocketbook, postbag, pouch, purse, reticule, satchel, shopping bag, shopping basket, shoulder bag, sporran, tote bag

types of baggage attaché case, backpack, briefcase, carryall (*US*), carrycase, case, duffel bag, haversack, holdall, kitbag, knapsack, luggage, overnight bag, pack, portmanteau, rucksack, travel case, suitcase, valise, vanity case, weekend bag

1245 Covers and Coatings

Never judge a cover by its book. **Fran Lebowitz**

(*n*) armour, asphalt, awning, bandage, bed, beermat, blacktop (*US*), blanket, blind, blindfold, *brolly* (*informal*), buffer, bung, camouflage, canopy, cap, carapace, cardboard, carpet, casing, cladding, cloak (*literary*), cloche, coat, coating, cocoon, compress, cover, covering, crust, dressing, dubbin, dust jacket, dustsheet, eggshell, enamel, envelope, film, fireguard, fixative, gilt, glaze, gloss, glossiness (*informal*), grate, grating, gridiron, grille, ground cloth (*US*), groundsheet, guard, housing, icing, incrustation, insulation, jacket, lacquer, lagging, layer, leaf, lid, liner, lining, macadam, mantle (*literary*), mulch, nutshell, parasol, patch, patina, plaster, plating, plug, ply, poultice, protective covering, protector, rendering, scale, screen, scurf, seal, seam, shade, sheath, sheathing, sheet, shell, shield, shroud, skin, sticking plaster (*formal*), stopper, stratum (*formal*), *substratum*, sunshade, swab, tap, *tarp* (*informal*), tarpaulin, tartar, thimble, top, topping, umbrella, *undercoat*, varnish, veil, vein, veneer, verdigris, visor, wallpaper, wash, washing, wrap, wrapper, wrapping

1246 Fasteners, Links, and Networks

Our buttons operate in synchronization with ourselves; they form a sort of cheap and comfortable senate, which always votes in favor of our motions. **Joaquim Maria Machado de Assis**

(*n*) belt, binding, bolt, buckle, catch, chain, cinch, clasp, clip, cord, coupling, crisscross, cuff (*slang*), *Denver boot* (*US*), dowel, drawstring, fastener, fastening, fetter, *flange*, gag, gossamer, grid, guyrope, halter, handcuff, *hasp*, hawser, hook, hook and eye, join, joint, juncture (*formal*), key, knot, lace, lanyard, lariat (*US*), lasso, latch, lattice, lead, leash, ligature, line, lock, manacle, maze, mesh, nail, net, netting, network, node, noose, *padlock*, *paperclip*, peg, *popper*, press stud, rein, restraint, rigging, ripcord, rivet, rope, safety belt, shackles, shoelace, snap (*US*), socket, spline, staple, stirrup, strap, string, stud, suture, swathe, tack, tape, tether, thong, tissue, toggle, tourniquet, towrope, twine, *vang*, washer, web, webbing, weld, wheel clamp

See also FASTEN, LINK, AND JOIN (409), UNFASTEN AND UNDO (410), PARTS OF A GARMENT (870)

1247 Ornaments and Decorations

Ornament should consist of enrichment of the essential construction of the building. **Augustus Pugin**

(*n*) accessory, *accoutrements*, amulet, antiquity, bauble, beading, belt, bobble, bunting, button (*US*), buttonhole, charm, corsage, curio, decor, decoration, *doily*, embellishment, epaulette, festoon, filigree, fixings (*US informal*), flourish, frill, fringe, garland, garnish, gather, *gewgaw*, glitter, headpiece, inlay, ironwork, jewel, keepsake, knick-knack, knocker, *lei*, marquetry, medal, medallion, memento, monogram, mould, oddments, ornament, piping, pompom, pottery, purl, *refrigerator magnet* (*US*), regalia, reminder, rhinestone, ribbon, rose, rosette, scallop, sequin, souvenir, spangle, stencil, *strass*, streamer, swag, tassel, *tchotchke* (*US*), tinsel, token, tracery, trim, trimming, trimmings, trinket, vignette, wreath

See also DECORATE, ADORN, AND APPLY COATINGS (406), JEWELLERY (866)

1248 Rubbish and Useless Objects

An Aristotle was but the rubbish of an Adam, and Athens but the rudiments of Paradise. **Robert South**

(*n*) bric-a-brac, castoff, cull, debris, detritus, driftwood, dross, flotsam, *flotsam and jetsam*, *frippery*, garbage (*US*), jetsam, jumble, junk (*informal*), kitsch, litter, odds and ends, *odds and sods*, rag, refuse, rubbish, rubble, schlock (*US slang*), stub, stubble, stump, tat (*informal*), tatters, trash (*US*), waste, wreck, wreckage

See also UNPLEASANT AND DIRTY SUBSTANCES (1267), REMAINDER AND REMAINDERS (123)

1249 Extremities of Physical Objects

Think of it, soldiers; from the summit of these pyramids, forty centuries look down upon you. **Napoleon I**

(*adj*) exterior, external, fringe, outer

(*n*) apex, baseline, bed, blade, border, bottom, boundary, bounds, brim, brink, brow, bulge, butt, cap, circumference, confines, crest, crown, cusp, cutting edge, dead end, edge, edging, end, extreme, extremity, face, facet, flank, flap, flat, floor, foot, fore (*literary*), forefront, frame, fringe, front, head, height, horn, hulk, interface, leaf, ledge, limit, limits, line, lip, lobe, margin, matrix, meridian (*literary*), mould, mouth, neck, nib, *nubbin*, *nub end*, obverse, outside, overlap, peak, perimeter, periphery, pinnacle, pit, plating, point, prickle, projection, prong, protrusion, rear, rearguard, reverse, ridge, rim, seam, side, splice, summit, surface, surround, tailpiece, top, vane, verge, vertex, zenith

1250 Central Parts of Physical Objects

I live in peace with men and at war with my innards. **Antonio Machado**

(*adj*) central, inner, internal

(*n*) backbone, body, bosom (*literary*), bull's eye, centre, core, entrails, *epicentre*, filler, filling, flesh, focal point, focus, foreground, guts, hinge, hub, inside, interior, kernel, mass, mecca, middle, midpoint, midst, nerve centre, nucleus, packing, pad, padding, pulp, *stuffing*, wadding, workings, works

1251 Holes, Gaps, and Forks

(*n*) abyss, airlock, aperture, armhole, bifurcation, blank, borehole, branch, breach, cavity, chamber, chasm, chink, cleft, coalmine, crack, cranny, crevice, cut, dent, depression, diggings, ding (*US informal*), dint, dip, divide, dugout, eyelet, fissure, flute, fracture, gap, gash, gouge, graze, groove, gulf, gully, hole, hollow, hollowness, impression, imprint, incision, indentation, interstice, interval, keyhole, laceration, lacuna (*literary*), *mail slot* (*US*), nick, notch, opening, orifice (*literary*), outlet, peephole, perforation, pinprick, pit, plughole, pore, pothole, prick, puncture, rent, rift, rip, rupture, rut, score, scrape, scratch, slash, slit, slot, split, spyhole, tear, trough, vacuity (*formal*), vacuum, vent, void, well, window

1252 Subdivisions and Offshoots

(*n*) arm, branch, department, division, fork, limb, spur, subdirectory, wing

1253 Sticks, Poles, and Wedges

(*n*) baluster, balustrade, bar, baton, beanpole, bollard, boom, broomstick, caber, cane, chock, column, crook, crosier, crutch, drumstick, flagpole, flagstaff, gatepost, goad, guardrail, handrail, maypole, picket, pile, pillar, pointer, pole, post, rail, rod, sceptre, shank, skewer, spar, spigot, spindle, spoke, staff, stake, stalk, stem, stick, stilt, walking stick, wand

1254 Supports and Bases

(*n*) abutment, base, bedrock, bier, brace, bracket, derrick, footing, foundation, grassroots, hanger, jamb, leg, mount, pedestal, *pilaster*, plinth, podium (*US*), pontoon, prop, rack, rest, rung, scaffold, scaffolding, shelf, stair, *stanchion*, stand, stave, stepladder, stepping stone, support, throne, trestle, trivet, underneath, underpinning, underside

Sounds

1255 Sounds

When it sounds good, it is *good.* **Duke Ellington**

(*n*) echo, noise, reverberation, sonority, sound, sound effect, unquiet

See also SOUND EMISSION (363)

1256 Absence of Sound

All artists dream of a silence which they must enter, as some creatures return to the sea to spawn. **Iris Murdoch**

(*adj*) *dumb*, mute, noiseless, quiet, silent, soundless, wordless

(*adv*) quietly, silently, *without a sound*

(*n*) hush, *noiselessness*, quiet, quietness, silence, *soundlessness*

See also IMPERCEPTIBLE (26)

1257 Continuous Sounds

The most persistent sound which reverberates through men's history is the beating of war drums. **Arthur Koestler**

types of continuous sound beep, bleep, boom, burble, buzz, chug, crackle, creak, drone, gurgle, hiss, honk, hoot, hum, purl (*literary*), purr, rasp, rattle, roar, r rustle, sizzle, sonic boom, swish, swoosh, throb, th toot, whirr, whiz, whoosh

1258 Ringing and Tooting Sounds

types of ringing and tooting sound beep, bleep, chime, chink, clang, clank, clink, ding, ding-a-ling, ding-dong, honk, hoot, jangle, jingle, knell, peal, ping, pip, ring, ting, tinkle, toll, tootle (*informal*)

1259 Impact Sounds

(*n*) drumming, drum roll, firing, footfall, footstep, gunfire, gunshot, *paradiddle*, percussion (*formal*), report, ricochet, shot, tread

types of impact sound bang, beat, bong, bonk (*informal*), boom, bump, clang, clank, clap, clash, clatter, click, clip-clop, clop, clunk, crack, crash, patter, pitter-patter, plop, plunk, pop, ratatat-tat, slam, smash, splash, splat, squelch, squish, tap, thud, thump, thwack, tick, ticktock, wham

See also CONTACT: IMPACT (414)

1260 Sounds Made by Animals

One dog barks at something and a hundred bark at the sound. **Chinese proverb**

types of animal sound baa, bark, bay, bray, caterwaul, croak, growl, grunt, howl, mew, miaow, moo, neigh, oink, purr, roar, snarl, squeak, squeal, whinny, woof, yap, yelp

See also SOUND EMISSION BY ANIMALS OR BIRDS (365)

1261 Sounds Made by People

All the live murmur of a summer's day. **Matthew Arnold**

(*n*) battle cry, call, death rattle, distress signal, exclamation, lament, lamentation

types of human sound babble, bawl, bellow, boo, catcall, chatter, chortle, chuckle, cry, gasp, giggle, groan, grunt, holler, howl, hum, moan, murmur, mutter, peep, screak (*US*), scream, screech, shout, shriek, sigh, slurp, snicker (*US*), sniffle, snigger, splutter, squeal, titter, wail, wheeze, whimper, whine, whisper, whistle, whoop, yell

See also SOUND EMISSION BY PEOPLE (364)

1262 Sounds Made by Birds

A nightingale dies for shame if another bird sings better. **Robert Burton**

(*n*) birdsong, call, cheeping, song

types of bird sound caw, cheep, chirp, chirrup, cluck, cock-a-doodle-doo, coo, hoot, peep, quack, screak (*US*), screech, squawk, trill, tweet, twitter, warble

See also SOUND EMISSION BY ANIMALS OR BIRDS (365)

1263 Quality of Sounds

Heard melodies are sweet, but those unheard/Are sweeter; therefore, ye soft pipes, play on. **John Keats**

(*n*) *sound quality*, timbre, tonality, tone

1264 Soft or Pleasant Sounds

(*adj*) *assonant*, bass, clear, deep, dulcet, *easy on the ear*, *euphonious*, faint, fruity, *harmonic*, harmonious, hollow, honeyed, humming, hushed, low, low-pitched, lyric, mellifluous, mellow, melodic, melodious, muffled, *murmured*, musical, muted, orotund (*formal*), *plangent*, plummy, pure, *quavering*, silky, soft, sonorous, sotto voce, sweet, treble, tuneful, *whispered*

(*adv*) faintly, harmoniously, hollowly, softly, sotto voce, sweetly

(*n*) deepness, *euphoniousness*, *euphony*, faintness, *harmoniousness*, *mellifluousness*, mellowness, melodiousness, pureness, reediness, resonance, sweetness, *tunefulness*

1265 Loud or Unpleasant Sounds

(*adj*) adenoidal, atonal, blaring, booming, brassy, braying, cacophonous, carrying, chesty, clamorous, *clanging*, creaky, *croaky*, deafening, discordant, dissonant, earsplitting, echoing, full, grating, gravelly, grinding, gruff, guttural, harsh, high, high-pitched, hoarse, husky, inharmonious, jarring, loud, metallic, *monophonic*, noisy, off-key, penetrating, piercing, piping, rasping, reedy, resonant, *resonating*, resounding, *reverberant*, reverberating, roaring, rough, sharp, shrill, squeaky, stentorian, strident, thick, thin, throaty, thunderous, tinny, tumultuous, tuneless, *unmelodic*, *unmelodious*, unmusical, unquiet

(*adv*) aloud, grindingly, huskily, loudly, off-key, out loud, piercingly, shrilly, thickly

(*n*) atonality, discord, edge, gruffness, hoarseness, huskiness, loudness, monotone, *noisiness*, pitch, roughness, *shrillness*

Substances

1266 Substances

Beware that you do not lose the substance by grasping at the shadow. **Aesop**

(*n*) chemical, material, matrix, matter, natural resource, *raw material*, reagent, sediment, stuff, substance

1267 Unpleasant and Dirty Substances

(*n*) bilge, cobwebs, crud (*slang*), dinge, dirt, dregs, dung, dust, *effluence*, effluent, fat, fertilizer, filth, fluff, *gloop* (*informal*), *glop* (*US informal*), goo (*informal*), *gook* (*US informal*), goop (*US informal*), grime, grounds, grouts, grunge (*informal*), *guano*, gunge (*informal*), gunk (*informal*), impurity, mould, muck, ordure (*formal*), pesticide, poison, pollutant, pollution, residue, scum, *sewage*, *slag*, slime, *slops*, sludge, *slurry*, slush, *toxic waste*, toxin, venom, *waste product*

See also REMAINDER AND REMAINDERS (123), RUBBISH AND USELESS OBJECTS (1248), EXCRETION AND EXCRETA (723)

1268 Liquids

(*n*) brine, distillate, distillation, fluid, juice, liquid, liquor, oil, salt water, solution, *solvent*, thinner, tincture, water

1269 Dyes and Colourants

(*n*) cochineal, colour, colourant, dye, peroxide, pigment, rinse, stain, tint, wash, whitewash

1270 Adhesives

(*n*) adhesive, cement, fixative, glue, gum, paste, *superglue*

1271 Lotions, Pastes, and Gels

(*n*) balm, cream, gel, jelly, liniment, lotion, mush, ointment, paste, pulp, purée, salve, unction, unguent

1272 Froth

(*n*) effervescence, fizz, foam, froth, lather, soapsuds, sparkle, suds

1273 Solids

O! that this too too solid flesh would melt,/Thaw, and resolve itself into a dew. **William Shakespeare**

(*n*) concentrate, deposit, powder, rubber, solid, wax

1274 Gases

There can no great smoke arise, but there must be some fire. **John Lyly**

(*n*) *biogas*, fume, *fumes*, gas, miasma, steam, vapour, *water vapour*

types of gas acetylene, argon, butane, chlorine, coal gas, greenhouse gas, helium, hydrogen, inert gas, marsh gas, methane, mustard gas, natural gas, neon, nerve gas, nitrogen, nitrous oxide, noble gas, oxygen, poison gas, propellant, tear gas

1275 Metals

(*adj*) gilded, gilt, golden, gold-plated, metallic, *silver-plated*

types of metal aluminium, aluminum (*US*), brass, bronze, chromium, copper, gold, iron, lead, magnesium, mercury, molybdenum, nickel, pewter, platinum, radium, silver, stainless steel, steel, tin, titanium, tungsten, uranium, zinc

1276 Minerals

types of mineral arsenic, asbestos, asphalt, bauxite, carbon, clay, coal, coke, feldspar, fluorite, graphite, gypsum, jet, kaolin, lime, mica, pyrite, quartz, silicate, sulphur

1277 Precious Stones

Sweet are the uses of adversity,/Which like the toad, ugly and venomous,/Wears yet a precious jewel in his head. **William Shakespeare**

(*n*) crystal, diamanté, gem, gemstone, jewel, precious stone, *semiprecious stone*, sparkler (*informal*)

types of gemstone agate, amethyst, aquamarine, beryl, bloodstone, carnelian, chalcedony, chrysoprase, diamond, emerald, garnet, jade, lapis lazuli, moonstone, mother-of-pearl, onyx, opal, pearl, ruby, sapphire, sard, topaz, tourmaline, turquoise

1278 Elementary Particles

MASTER *They split the atom by firing particles at it, at 5,500 miles a second./*BOY *Good heavens. And they only split it?* **Will Hay**

types of elementary particle antineutron, antiproton, antiquark, baryon, boson, electron, fermion, hadron, kaon, lepton, meson, muon, neutrino, neutron, photon, pion, positron, proton, quark, tauon